M000168658

COMPREHENSIVE CONCORDANCE *of the* Holy Bible

COMPREHENSIVE

CONCORDANCE

of the

Holy Bible

A Complete Concordance of Terms Providing
Fast Access to the Entire Bible

David K. Stabnow, Editor

Nashville, Tennessee

The Holman CSB Comprehensive Concordance

ISBN 10: 0-8054-9459-6
ISBN 13: 978-08054-9459-4

Printed in China
1 2 3 4 5 6 09 08 07 06 05
RRD

Contents

Introduction to
The Holman CSB Comprehensive Concordance

A concordance is a list of the words that appear in a written work, giving the reference for the places each word occurs. Concordances have been made for many books, but the book that has most often been the subject of a concordance is the Bible. A Bible concordance is used when you want to find a familiar passage or when you want to study what the Bible says on a particular subject. There are many concordances available for the King James Version and other translations of the Bible, but since every translation is a little bit different, it is best to use a concordance that has been prepared for the version of the Bible you are studying. This concordance has been prepared for the Holman Christian Standard Bible.

Types of Concordances

There are three types of Bible concordances: abridged, comprehensive, and exhaustive. An "abridged" or "abbreviated" concordance contains a selection of key words and a partial list of their occurrences. The intention is to index all the words that a student of the Bible might be expected to need in order to find key passages in the Bible. For example, an abridged concordance would include the word **SHEPHERD** and a reference to Psalm 23:1, "The Lord is my **s**." An abridged concordance might also include biblical phrases such as "Son of Man" or "faithful love," or it could have descriptions of people and places and a partial listing of where they are mentioned in the Bible. The *Holman Pocket Bible Concordance* is an abridged concordance. Any concordance found in the back of a Bible is also an abridged concordance.

A "comprehensive" or "complete" concordance includes all the words in the Bible with the exception of certain common words such as "the" and "and." Of the words that are included, all occurrences are listed. That is, in this *Holman CSB Comprehensive Concordance* under **SHEPHERD** all 73 occurrences are listed. There are also separate entries for **SHEPHERD'S**, **SHEPHERDED**, **SHEPHERDESS**, **SHEPHERDING**, **SHEPHERDS**, and **SHEPHERDS'**.

An "exhaustive" concordance is like a comprehensive concordance, except that it will connect each indexed word to the Hebrew, Aramaic, or Greek word from which it is translated. For example, in many exhaustive concordances the word "world" in John 3:16 is indexed to Greek word number 2889 in Strong's lexicon. The lexicon is included in the back of the concordance. Exhaustive concordances will often have a shorter list of excluded words, and some even include a listing for each excluded word of all the verses where that word is found.

How to Read the Keywords and Entries

In this *Holman CSB Comprehensive Concordance*, all of the 15,214 different words ("keywords") that make up the vocabulary of the Holman CSB are listed in bold letters. After each keyword there is a number giving the frequency of that word in the Holman CSB. In the example below, **ACACIAS** *(2)* means that the plural noun "acacias" occurs twice in the Bible. Concordance entries are listed under each keyword showing the phrases in which the word occurs. In each entry, the position of the keyword in the phrase is indicated by the first letter in boldface. If the word is capitalized in the Bible, the letter is capitalized in the concordance. In the example, the word "acacias" is capitalized in Joel 3:18 but not in Isaiah 41:19.

ACACIAS	*(2)*
in the desert, **a**, myrtles, and	Is 41:19
house, watering the Valley of **A**.	Jl 3:18

Alphabetization

This concordance is alphabetized according to the rules of computer databases. In this system, apostrophes and hyphens are counted as characters and are listed before other characters. Therefore, the words related to "father" are found in the following order: **FATHER, FATHER'S, FATHER-IN-LAW, FATHERED, FATHERING, FATHERLESS, FATHERS, FATHERS'**.

Cross References

There are several people and places in the Bible that are known by more than one name. For example, Abraham was formerly known as Abram, and Jerusalem was also known as (a.k.a.) Ariel, Jebus, Salem, and Zion. For this reason, under **ABRAHAM** it reads "AKA ABRAM" and under **JERUSALEM** it reads "AKA ARIEL, JEBUS, SALEM, ZION."

The alternate names indicated with "AKA" mean that at least one person or place known by one name is also known by the other name. For example, there are four people in the Bible named Levi. One of them, the Apostle, was also known as Matthew. So there is a note at the entry **LEVI** saying "AKA MATTHEW." This does not mean that all four persons named Levi were also known as Matthew, only that at least one of them was.

Excluded Words

Common words are not the memorable, key words that would be useful for looking up a familiar passage. That is, if someone were looking for the verse that says, "I am the good shepherd," he would not look under **I** or **AM** or **THE.** If he were to try to do so, he would be overwhelmed. He would have to look through 8,514 entries for **I**, 1,141 for **AM**, or 54,495 for **THE**! Rather, he should look under **SHEPHERD** or maybe **GOOD**. **SHEPHERD** only occurs 73 times, and **GOOD** 636 times.

Because the purpose of a concordance is to make it easy for a person to find a familiar verse, and because the easiest way to look for a familiar verse is by looking through the entries for the exceptional or less frequent words, some of the most frequent and unexceptional words in the Bible are excluded from this concordance. In all, there are 263 keywords excluded from this concordance. Most articles, conjunctions, prepositions, and pronouns are excluded. There are also some other common words omitted. A complete list of the excluded words is on pages xi-xii.

Listings Divided between Words and Proper Nouns

The word "mark" appears in the Bible as a noun and a verb, but "Mark" is also a proper noun—a man's name. The following words are listed both as words and as proper nouns: **BEER, CHERUB, EPHAH, EPHOD, HEN, IRON, LOT, MARK, PUT, RAM,** and **SIN**. The two usages are listed separately, with the proper noun second. **ON** and **SO** are only listed as proper nouns; as words they are excluded.

How to Use a Concordance

One way that you might use a concordance is to find a passage when you know some of the words in it, but you can't quote it exactly and you don't know where it's found. Say, for example, that you are thinking of the passage that says something about how Christians, as representatives of Christ to the world, appeal to people to be reconciled to God.

You can't look for this verse under common words like "we," "to," and "the" because those words aren't listed in this concordance. You could look for it under **CHRIST, WORLD, PEOPLE**, or **GOD**, but those words are quite frequent, and it would take a long time to look through the many entries. For example, "God" occurs 4,054 times in the Holman CSB. Even so, if you remembered that this is something that Paul said, you could restrict your search to the use of those words in the writings of Paul. Still, "God" occurs 423 times in Paul's letters.

It would be better to look for this passage under the significant but less frequent words: **REPRESENTATIVES, APPEAL**, or **RECONCILED**. Note that you might have to look under all the related words. That is, when you look for **APPEAL**, you should also look under **APPEALED, APPEALING**, and **APPEALS**.

As it turns out, you wouldn't find the passage you're looking for under **REPRESENTATIVES**, but under **APPEALING** you would find the phrase "that God is **a** through us" in 2 Corinthians 5:20, where it says,

"Therefore, we are ambassadors for Christ; certain that God is appealing through us, we plead on Christ's behalf, 'Be reconciled to God.' "

The other way you might use this concordance is to do a word study. For example, after reading 2 Corinthians 5:20, you might want to know more about how the Bible uses the word "reconcile." You would find three entries under **RECONCILE**, seven under **RECONCILED**, four under **RECONCILIATION**, and one under **RECONCILING**. If you were to read all of those passages in context, you would learn a lot about reconciliation in the Bible.

Our Prayer

A tool is not generally the object of attention. Rather, the product a worker creates using the tool rightly receives the honor. Take, for example, a carpenter's hammer. Certainly there is a considerable difference between one hammer and another with regard to quality, beauty, and the way it feels in the carpenter's hand, but the more appropriate target of attention and praise is the house built by the person who wields the hammer. This concordance is but a tool. We at Holman Bible Publishers have made every effort to assure that it is of good quality, esthetically pleasing, and a joy to use. However, most of all we hope that it is an effective tool in the hand of the person who is conducting private devotions, developing a personal theology, writing a sermon, or constructing a lesson. We pray that the product of your labor will be worthy of honor—that when you have used this tool to create something, your Master will say, "Well done, good and faithful slave!"

David K. Stabnow
May 2005

List of Excluded Words

The Holman CSB contains a total of 717,939 words, with a vocabulary of 15,214 different words ("keywords"). In this *Holman CSB Comprehensive Concordance*, articles, conjunctions, prepositions, and pronouns (except "mine") are excluded. There are also some other common words omitted. The following list represents the exclusion of 263 keywords and 420,455 concordance entries. This number takes into account a partial inclusion of 124 entries for 8 of these keywords. Therefore, this concordance includes a total of 297,484 concordance entries, with a complete listing for 14,951 keywords and a partial listing for 8 keywords.

A
ABOUT
ABOVE
ACCORDING
ACROSS
AFTER
AFTERWARDS
AGAIN
AGAINST
AHEAD
ALL
ALMOST
ALONG
ALREADY
ALSO
ALTHOUGH
AM *
AMONG
AN
AND
ANSWERED
ANSWERING
ANY
ANYONE
ANYONE'S
ANYTHING
ANYWHERE
ARE
AREN'T
AROUND
AS
ASIDE
ASK
ASKED
ASKING
ASKS
AT
AWAY
BE
BECAUSE
BEEN
BEFORE
BEHIND
BELOW
BENEATH
BESIDE
BESIDES
BETWEEN
BEYOND
BOTH
BUT
BY
CAREFULLY
CERTAINLY
CLEARLY
COMPLETELY
CONCERNING
CONTINUALLY
COULD
COULDN'T
DID
DIDN'T
DO
DOES *
DOESN'T
DOING
DON'T
DONE
DOWN
DURING
EACH
EITHER
ESPECIALLY
EVEN
EVER
EVERYBODY
EVERYONE
EVERYONE'S
EVERYTHING
EVERYTHING'S
EVERYWHERE
EXCEPT
EXTREMELY
FAR
FOR
FORTH
FORWARD
FROM
FURTHER
FURTHERMORE
GO
GOES
GOING
GONE
GREATLY
HAD
HADN'T
HAS
HASN'T
HAVE
HAVEN'T
HAVING
HE
HE'LL
HE'S
HER
HERE
HERE'S
HERS
HERSELF
HIM
HIMSELF
HIS
HOW
HOWEVER
I *
I'D
I'LL
I'M
I'VE
IF
IN
INCLUDING
INDEED
INSIDE
INSTEAD
INTO
IS
ISN'T
IT
IT'S
ITS
ITSELF
LET
LET'S
LETS
LETTING
LIKE
LIKEWISE
ME
MEANWHILE
MY
MYSELF
NEAR
NEVER
NEVERTHELESS
NO
NOBODY
NONE
NOR
NOT
NOW
OF

OFF
OFTEN
ON *
ONE'S
ONES
ONESELF
OPPOSITE *
OR
OTHERWISE
OUR
OURS
OURSELVES
OUT
OVER
PERHAPS
RATHER
REALLY
REGARDING
SAID
SAY
SAYING *
SAYS
SHALL
SHE
SHE'LL
SHE'S
SHOULD
SHOULDN'T
SINCE
SO *
SOMEBODY
SOMEONE
SOMEONE'S
SOMETHING
SOON
SURELY
THAN
THAT
THAT'S
THE
THEIR
THEIRS
THEM
THEMSELVES
THEN
THERE
THERE'S
THEREFORE
THESE
THEY
THEY'LL
THEY'RE
THEY'VE
THIS
THOSE
THOUGH
THROUGH
THROUGHOUT
TO
TOO
TOWARD
UNDER
UNDERNEATH
UNLESS
UNTIL
UP
UPON
US
VERY
WAS
WASN'T
WE
WE'LL
WE'RE
WE'VE
WENT
WERE
WEREN'T
WHAT
WHAT'S
WHATEVER
WHEN
WHENEVER
WHERE
WHEREVER
WHETHER
WHICH
WHILE
WHO
WHOEVER
WHOM
WHOMEVER
WHOSE
WHY
WILL *
WITH
WITHIN
WITHOUT
WON'T
WOULD
WOULDN'T
YET
YOU
YOU'LL
YOU'RE
YOU'VE
YOUR
YOURS
YOURSELF
YOURSELVES

* **AM** and **I** are listed six times under **I AM**, as the name of God and as Jesus' affirmation of His own deity. **DOES** is listed twice as the plural of *doe*. **ON** is listed five times as a proper noun. **OPPOSITE** is listed three times as a noun meaning *contrary.* **SAYING** is listed twelve times as a noun meaning *proverb.* **SO** is listed once as a proper noun. **WILL** is listed 95 times as a noun or verb of volition.

Bible Book Abbreviations

Genesis	Gn
Exodus	Ex
Leviticus	Lv
Numbers	Nm
Deuteronomy	Dt
Joshua	Jos
Judges	Jdg
Ruth	Ru
1 Samuel	1Sm
2 Samuel	2Sm
1 Kings	1Kg
2 Kings	2Kg
1 Chronicles	1Ch
2 Chronicles	2Ch
Ezra	Ezr
Nehemiah	Neh
Esther	Est
Job	Jb
Psalms	Ps
Proverbs	Pr
Ecclesiastes	Ec
Song of Songs	Sg
Isaiah	Is
Jeremiah	Jr
Lamentations	Lm
Ezekiel	Ezk
Daniel	Dn
Hosea	Hs
Joel	Jl
Amos	Am
Obadiah	Ob
Jonah	Jnh
Micah	Mc
Nahum	Nah
Habakkuk	Hab
Zephaniah	Zph
Haggai	Hg
Zechariah	Zch
Malachi	Mal

Matthew	Mt
Mark	Mk
Luke	Lk
John	Jn
Acts	Ac
Romans	Rm
1 Corinthians	1Co
2 Corinthians	2Co
Galatians	Gl
Ephesians	Eph
Philippians	Php
Colossians	Col
1 Thessalonians	1Th
2 Thessalonians	2Th
1 Timothy	1Tm
2 Timothy	2Tm
Titus	Ti
Philemon	Phm
Hebrews	Heb
James	Jms
1 Peter	1Pt
2 Peter	2Pt
1 John	1Jn
2 John	2Jn
3 John	3Jn
Jude	Jd
Revelation	Rv

A

A (9495)
(See pp. xi-xii.)

AARON (303)

Isn't A the Levite your brother? Ex 4:14
Now the LORD had said to A, Ex 4:27
Moses told A everything the LORD Ex 4:28
Then Moses and A went and Ex 4:29
A repeated everything the LORD Ex 4:30
Moses and A went in and said to Ex 5:1
them, "Moses and A, why are you Ex 5:4
they confronted Moses and A, Ex 5:20
to Moses and A and gave them Ex 6:13
and she bore him A and Moses. Ex 6:20
A married Elisheba, daughter of Ex 6:23
It was this A and Moses whom the Ex 6:26
Moses and A were the ones who Ex 6:27
and A your brother will be your Ex 7:1
then A your brother must declare Ex 7:2
So Moses and A did ⌊this⌋; Ex 7:6
80 years old and A 83 when they Ex 7:7
The LORD said to Moses and A, Ex 7:8
Perform a miracle, tell A: Ex 7:9
Moses and A went in to Pharaoh Ex 7:10
A threw down his staff before Ex 7:10
the LORD said to Moses, "Tell A: Ex 7:19
Moses and A did just as the LORD Ex 7:20
then said to Moses, "Tell A: Ex 8:5
When A stretched out his hand Ex 8:6
summoned Moses and A and said, Ex 8:8
After Moses and A went out from Ex 8:12
the LORD said to Moses, "Tell A: Ex 8:16
A stretched out his hand with Ex 8:17
summoned Moses and A and said, Ex 8:25
the LORD said to Moses and A, Ex 9:8
Pharaoh sent for Moses and A. Ex 9:27
Moses and A went in to Pharaoh Ex 10:3
So Moses and A were brought back Ex 10:8
sent for Moses and A and said, Ex 10:16
and A did all these wonders Ex 11:10
said to Moses and A in the land Ex 12:1
had commanded Moses and A. Ex 12:28
Moses and A during the night Ex 12:31
The LORD said to Moses and A, Ex 12:43
had commanded Moses and A. Ex 12:50
Moses and A in the wilderness Ex 16:2
So Moses and A said to all the Ex 16:6
Then Moses told A, "Say to the Ex 16:9
As A was speaking to the entire Ex 16:10
Moses told A, "Take a container Ex 16:33
A placed it before the testimony Ex 16:34
while Moses, A, and Hur went up Ex 17:10
Then A and Hur supported his Ex 17:12
and A came with all the elders Ex 18:12
Go down and come back with A. Ex 19:24
LORD, you and A, Nadab, and Ex 24:1
Then Moses went up with A, Ex 24:9
A and Hur are here with you. Ex 24:14
A and his sons are to tend the Ex 27:21
your brother A, with his sons, Ex 28:1
Me as priest—A, his sons Nadab Ex 28:1
garments for your brother A, Ex 28:2
your brother A and his sons so Ex 28:4
A will carry their names on his Ex 28:12
A is to carry the names of Ex 28:29
A will continually carry the Ex 28:30
must be ⌊worn by⌋ A whenever he Ex 28:35
forehead so that A may bear the Ex 28:38
on your brother A and his sons; Ex 28:41
must be ⌊worn by⌋ A and his sons Ex 28:43
statute for A and for his Ex 28:43
Bring A and his sons to the Ex 29:4
and clothe A with the tunic, Ex 29:5
around both A and his sons. Ex 29:9
you will ordain A and his sons. Ex 29:9
A and his sons must lay their Ex 29:10
and A and his sons are to lay Ex 29:15
A and his sons must lay their Ex 29:19
them⌋ on A and his garments, Ex 29:21
in the hands of A and his sons Ex 29:24
Consecrate for A and his sons Ex 29:27
will belong to A and his sons as Ex 29:28
that belong to A are to belong Ex 29:29
A and his sons are to eat the Ex 29:32
you are to do for A and his sons Ex 29:35
also consecrate A and his sons Ex 29:44
A must burn fragrant incense on Ex 30:7
When A sets up the lamps at Ex 30:8
Once a year A is to perform the Ex 30:10
A and his sons must wash their Ex 30:19
for A and his descendants Ex 30:21
Anoint A and his sons and Ex 30:30
holy garments for A the priest Ex 31:10
around A and said to him Ex 32:1
Then A replied to them, "Take Ex 32:2
ears and brought ⌊them⌋ to A. Ex 32:3
When A saw ⌊this⌋, he built an Ex 32:5
Moses asked A, "What did this Ex 32:21
be enraged, my lord," A replied. Ex 32:22
for A had let them get out of Ex 32:25
did with the calf A had made. Ex 32:35
When A and all the Israelites Ex 34:30
so A and all the leaders of the Ex 34:31
holy garments for A the priest Ex 35:19
of Ithamar son of A the priest. Ex 38:21
garments for A from the blue, Ex 39:1
woven linen for A and his sons. Ex 39:27
holy garments for A the priest Ex 39:41
Then bring A and his sons to the Ex 40:12
Clothe A with the holy garments, Ex 40:13
Moses, A, and his sons washed Ex 40:31
The sons of A the priest will Lv 1:7
will belong to A and his sons, Lv 2:3
will belong to A and his sons, Lv 2:10
Command A and his sons: Lv 6:9
A and his sons may eat the rest Lv 6:16
offering that A and his sons Lv 6:20
Tell A and his sons: This is the Lv 6:25
belongs to A and his sons. Lv 7:31
The son of A who presents the Lv 7:33
assigned them to A the priest Lv 7:34
to the LORD for A and his sons Lv 7:35
Take A, his sons with him, the Lv 8:2
Moses presented A and his sons Lv 8:6
put the tunic on A, wrapped the Lv 8:7
and A and his sons laid their Lv 8:14
and A and his sons laid their Lv 8:18
and A and his sons laid their Lv 8:22
in the hands of A and his sons Lv 8:27
them⌋ on A and his garments, Lv 8:30
he consecrated A and his Lv 8:30
Moses said to A and his sons, Lv 8:31
A and his sons are to eat it. Lv 8:31
So A and his sons did everything Lv 8:36
the eighth day Moses summoned A, Lv 9:1
He said to A, "Take a young bull Lv 9:2
Then Moses said to A, "Approach Lv 9:7
So A approached the altar and Lv 9:8
A presented the people's Lv 9:15
A burned the fat portions on the Lv 9:20
A lifted up his hands toward the Lv 9:22
Moses and A then entered the Lv 9:23
Moses said to A, "This is what Lv 10:3
But A remained silent. Lv 10:3
Moses said to A and his sons Lv 10:6
The LORD spoke to A: Lv 10:8
Moses spoke to A and his Lv 10:12
But A replied to Moses, "See, Lv 10:19
The LORD spoke to Moses and A: Lv 11:1
The LORD spoke to Moses and A: Lv 13:1
be brought to A the priest or to Lv 13:2
The LORD spoke to Moses and A: Lv 14:33
The LORD spoke to Moses and A: Lv 15:1
your brother A that he may not Lv 16:2
A is to enter the ⌊most⌋ holy Lv 16:3
A will present the bull for his Lv 16:6
After A casts lots for the two Lv 16:8
When A presents the bull for his Lv 16:11
A will lay both his hands on the Lv 16:21
Then A is to enter the tent of Lv 16:23
Speak to A, his sons, and all Lv 17:2
Tell A: None of your descendants Lv 21:17
descendant of A the priest who Lv 21:21
said ⌊this⌋ to A and his sons Lv 21:24
Tell A and his sons to deal Lv 22:2
Speak to A, his sons, and all Lv 22:18
A is to tend it regularly from Lv 24:3
It belongs to A and his sons, Lv 24:9
You and A are to register those Nm 1:3
Moses and A took these men who Nm 1:17
the men Moses and A registered, Nm 1:44
The LORD spoke to Moses and A: Nm 2:1
family records of A and Moses at Nm 3:1
the direction of A their father. Nm 3:4
present them to A the priest to Nm 3:6
the Levites to A and his sons; Nm 3:9
are to appoint A and his sons to Nm 3:10
was Eleazar son of A the priest; Nm 3:32
Moses, A, and his sons, who Nm 3:38
that Moses and A registered by Nm 3:39
the money to A and his sons as Nm 3:48
money to A and his sons Nm 3:51
The LORD spoke to Moses and A: Nm 4:1
A and his sons are to go in, Nm 4:5
A and his sons are to finish Nm 4:15
son of A the priest, has Nm 4:16
the LORD spoke to Moses and A: Nm 4:17
A and his sons are to go in and Nm 4:19
the command of A and his sons; Nm 4:27
of Ithamar son of A the priest. Nm 4:28
of Ithamar son of A the priest." Nm 4:33
So Moses, A, and the leaders of Nm 4:34
Moses and A registered them at Nm 4:37
command Moses and A registered Nm 4:41
Moses and A registered them at Nm 4:45
Moses, A, and the leaders of Nm 4:46
Tell A and his sons how you are Nm 6:23
of Ithamar son of A the priest. Nm 7:8
Speak to A and tell him: Nm 8:2
So A did this; he set up its Nm 8:3
A is to present the Levites Nm 8:11
stand before A and his sons, Nm 8:13
exclusively to A and his sons to Nm 8:19
Moses, A, and the entire Nm 8:20
then A presented them before the Nm 8:21
A also made atonement for them Nm 8:21
the presence of A and his sons. Nm 8:22
before Moses and A the same day Nm 9:6
The sons of A, the priests, are Nm 10:8
Miriam and A criticized Moses Nm 12:1
said to Moses, A, and Miriam, Nm 12:4
and summoned A and Miriam. Nm 12:5
When A turned toward her, he saw Nm 12:10
back to Moses, A, and the entire Nm 13:26
complained about Moses and A, Nm 14:2
Then Moses and A fell down with Nm 14:5
the LORD spoke to Moses and A: Nm 14:26
him to Moses, A, and the entire Nm 15:33
Moses and A and told them, Nm 16:3
As for A, who is he that you Nm 16:11
tomorrow—you, they, and A. Nm 16:16
and A ⌊are⌋ each ⌊to present⌋ Nm 16:17
meeting along with Moses and A. Nm 16:18
The LORD spoke to Moses and A, Nm 16:20
Moses and A fell facedown and Nm 16:22
Eleazar son of A the priest to Nm 16:37
the lineage of A should approach Nm 16:40
complained about Moses and A, Nm 16:41
Moses and A turned toward the Nm 16:42
Moses and A went to the front of Nm 16:43
Then Moses told A, "Take your Nm 16:46
So A took his firepan as Moses Nm 16:47
A then returned to Moses at the Nm 16:50
LORD said to A, "You, your sons Nm 18:1
Then the LORD spoke to A, Nm 18:8
The LORD told A, "You will not Nm 18:20
some of it to A the priest as Nm 18:28
The LORD spoke to Moses and A, Nm 19:1
assembled against Moses and A. Nm 20:2
Then Moses and A went from the Nm 20:6
your brother A are to speak to Nm 20:8
and A summoned the assembly Nm 20:10
the LORD said to Moses and A, Nm 20:12
said to Moses and A at Mount Hor Nm 20:23
A will be gathered to his Nm 20:24
Take A and his son Eleazar and Nm 20:25
A will be gathered ⌊to his Nm 20:26
A died there on top of the Nm 20:28
saw that A had passed away, Nm 20:29
Eleazar, son of A the priest, Nm 25:7
Eleazar, son of A the priest, Nm 25:11
and Eleazar son of A the priest, Nm 26:1
who fought against Moses and A; Nm 26:9
A, Moses, and their sister Nm 26:59
and Ithamar were born to A, Nm 26:60
by Moses and A the priest when Nm 26:64
your people, as A your brother Nm 27:13
the leadership of Moses and A. Nm 33:1
A the priest climbed Mount Hor Nm 33:38
A was 123 years old when he died Nm 33:39
enough with A to destroy him. Dt 9:20
But I prayed for A at that time Dt 9:20
A died and was buried there, Dt 10:6

as your brother A died on Mount	Dt 32:50
the descendants of A the priest	Jos 21:4
descendants of A from the	Jos 21:10
the descendants of A the priest:	Jos 21:13
priests, the descendants of A.	Jos 21:19
Then I sent Moses and A,	Jos 24:5
And Eleazar son of A died,	Jos 24:33
Eleazar, son of A, was serving	Jdg 20:28
Moses and A and who brought	1Sm 12:6
and He sent them Moses and A,	1Sm 12:8
Amram's children: A, Moses, and	1Ch 6:3
But A and his sons did all the	1Ch 6:49
the house of A, with 3,700 men	1Ch 12:27
of A and the Levites:	1Ch 15:4
sons: A and Moses. Aaron,	1Ch 23:13
A, along with his descendants,	1Ch 23:13
the sons of A with the service	1Ch 23:28
the sons of A, in the service	1Ch 23:32
of A were as follows:	1Ch 24:1
received from their ancestor A,	1Ch 24:19
sons of A did in the presence	1Ch 24:31
son of Kemuel; for A, Zadok;	1Ch 27:17
of A and the Levites,	2Ch 13:9
the LORD are descendants of A,	2Ch 13:10
descendants of A, have the right	2Ch 26:18
he told the descendants of A,	2Ch 29:21
and to the descendants of A,	2Ch 31:19
the descendants of A, were busy	2Ch 35:14
priests, the descendants of A.	2Ch 35:14
Eleazar's son, A the chief	Ezr 7:5
for the descendants of A.	Neh 12:47
by the hand of Moses and A.	Ps 77:20
Moses and A were among His	Ps 99:6
His servant, and A, whom He had	Ps 105:26
were envious of Moses and of A,	Ps 106:16
House of A, trust in the LORD!	Ps 115:10
He will bless the house of A;	Ps 115:12
Let the house of A say, "His	Ps 118:3
House of A, praise the LORD!	Ps 135:19
sent Moses, A, and Miriam ahead	Mc 6:4
was from the daughters of A,	Lk 1:5
They told A: Make us gods who	Ac 7:40
is called by God, just as A was.	Heb 5:4
as being in the order of A?	Heb 7:11

AARON'S (49)

A son Eleazar married one of the	Ex 6:25
But A staff swallowed their	Ex 7:12
the prophetess, A sister, took	Ex 15:20
to make A garments for	Ex 28:3
also be over A heart whenever he	Ex 28:30
It will be on A forehead so that	Ex 28:38
headbands for A sons to ⌊give	Ex 28:40
and put it on A right earlobe,	Ex 29:20
from the ram of A ordination and	Ex 29:26
A sons the priests are to	Lv 1:5
A sons the priests are to	Lv 1:8
A sons the priests will sprinkle	Lv 1:11
and bring it to A sons the	Lv 2:2
Then A sons the priests will	Lv 3:2
A sons will burn it on the altar	Lv 3:5
A sons will sprinkle its blood	Lv 3:8
A sons will sprinkle its blood	Lv 3:13
A sons will present it before	Lv 6:14
Any male among A descendants may	Lv 6:18
who is of A sons and will be	Lv 6:22
equally to all of A sons.	Lv 7:10
anointing oil on A head and	Lv 8:12
Then Moses presented A sons,	Lv 8:13
and put ⌊it⌋ on A right earlobe,	Lv 8:23
also presented A sons and put	Lv 8:24
A sons brought the blood to him,	Lv 9:9
A sons brought him the blood,	Lv 9:12
A sons brought him the blood,	Lv 9:18
A sons Nadab and Abihu each took	Lv 10:1
sons of A uncle Uzziel,	Lv 10:4
and Ithamar, A surviving sons,	Lv 10:16
death of two of A sons when they	Lv 16:1
Speak to A sons, the priests,	Lv 21:1
No man of A descendants who has	Lv 22:4
These are the names of A sons:	Nm 3:2
These are the names of A sons,	Nm 3:3
Write A name on Levi's staff,	Nm 17:3
A staff was among them.	Nm 17:6
testimony and saw that A staff,	Nm 17:8
Put A rod back in front of the	Nm 17:10
Remove A garments and put them	Nm 20:26
Moses removed A garments and	Nm 20:28
and Miriam. A sons: Nadab, Abihu	1Ch 6:3
These are A sons: his son	1Ch 6:50
the places assigned to A sons	1Ch 6:54
A sons were given: Hebron (a	1Ch 6:57
A sons were Nadab, Abihu,	1Ch 24:1
running down A beard, on his	Ps 133:2
the manna, A rod that budded,	Heb 9:4

AARONIC (1)

A priest of A descent must	Neh 10:38

ABADDON (7)

God, and A has no covering	Jb 26:6
A and Death say, "We have heard	Jb 28:22
a fire that consumes down to A;	Jb 31:12
grave, Your faithfulness in A?	Ps 88:11
Sheol and A lie open before the	Pr 15:11
Sheol and A are never satisfied,	Pr 27:20
in Hebrew is A, and in Greek he	Rv 9:11

ABAGTHA (1)

Harbona, Bigtha, A, Zethar, and	Est 1:10

ABANA (1)

Aren't A and Pharpar, the rivers	2Kg 5:12

ABANDON (48)

They will a Me and break the	Dt 31:16
I will a them and hide My face	Dt 31:17
Don't a your servants.	Jos 10:6
will certainly not a the LORD to	Jos 24:16
If you a the LORD and worship	Jos 24:20
The LORD will not a His people,	1Sm 12:22
and not a My people Israel.	1Kg 6:13
May He not a us or leave us.	1Kg 8:57
I will a the remnant of My	2Kg 21:14
you turn away and a My statutes	2Ch 7:19
you, but if you a Him, He will	2Ch 15:2
you abandon Him, He will a you.	2Ch 15:2
anger is against all who a Him."	Ezr 8:22
love, and You did not a them.	Neh 9:17
You did not a them in the	Neh 9:19
did not destroy them or a them,	Neh 9:31
For You will not a me to Sheol;	Ps 16:10
not leave me or a me, God of my	Ps 27:9
if my father and mother a me,	Ps 27:10
will not a His faithful ones.	Ps 37:28
LORD, do not a me; my God, do	Ps 38:21
my strength fails, do not a me.	Ps 71:9
old and gray, God, do not a me.	Ps 71:18
and a Your displeasure with us.	Ps 85:4
His people or a His heritage,	Ps 94:14
keep Your statutes; never a me.	Ps 119:8
but I did not a Your precepts.	Ps 119:87
David, a promise He will not a:	Ps 132:11
do not a the work of Your hands.	Ps 138:8
those who a the right paths	Pr 2:13
Don't a my teaching.	Pr 4:2
Don't a wisdom, and she will	Pr 4:6
Don't a your friend or your	Pr 27:10
and those who a the LORD will	Is 1:28
Let the wicked one a his way,	Is 55:7
right and does not a the justice	Is 58:2
But you who a the LORD, who	Is 65:11
it is for you to a the LORD your	Jr 2:19
I would a my people and depart	Jr 9:2
days ⌊his riches⌋ will a him,	Jr 17:11
all who a You will be put to	Jr 17:13
A the towns! Live in the cliffs,	Jr 48:28
A your orphans; I will preserve	Jr 49:11
not be healed. A her! Let each	Jr 51:9
will a you on the land and hurl	Ezk 32:4
favor those who a the holy	Dn 11:30
He will a them until the time	Mc 5:3
among the Gentiles to a Moses,	Ac 21:21

ABANDONED (88)

For the land a by them will make	Lv 26:43
is because they a the covenant	Dt 29:25
He a the God who made him and	Dt 32:15
and a the LORD, the God of their	Jdg 2:12
they a Him and worshiped Baal	Jdg 2:13
the LORD has a us and handed us	Jdg 6:13
They a the LORD and did not	Jdg 10:6
We have a our God and worshiped	Jdg 10:10
But you have a Me and worshiped	Jdg 10:13
for we a the LORD and worshiped	1Sm 12:10
My master a me when I got sick	1Sm 30:13
they a the cities and fled.	1Sm 31:7
The Philistines a their idols	2Sm 5:21
the king—you would have a me."	2Sm 18:13
Because they a the LORD their	1Kg 9:9
For they have a Me;	1Kg 11:33
because you have a the LORD's	1Kg 18:18
Israelites have a Your covenant,	1Kg 19:10
Israelites have a Your covenant,	1Kg 19:14
They a all the commandments of	2Kg 17:16
He a the LORD God of his	2Kg 21:22
because they have a Me and	2Kg 22:17
they a their cities and fled.	1Ch 10:7
The Philistines a their idols	1Ch 14:12
Because they a the LORD God of	2Ch 7:22
he a the law of the LORD—	2Ch 12:1
says: 'You have a Me; therefore,	2Ch 12:5
I have a you into the hand of	2Ch 12:5
We have not a Him;	2Ch 13:10
our God, while you have a Him.	2Ch 13:11
because he had a the LORD God	2Ch 21:10
they a the temple of the LORD	2Ch 24:18
Because you have a the LORD,	2Ch 24:20
the LORD, He has a you.' "	2Ch 24:20
of Judah had a the LORD God	2Ch 24:24
because they had a the LORD God	2Ch 28:6
They a Him, turned their faces	2Ch 29:6
because they have a Me and	2Ch 34:25
our God has not a us in our	Ezr 9:9
For we have a the commandments	Ezr 9:10
So You a them to the power of	Neh 9:28
in a houses destined to become	Jb 15:28
the earth be a on your account,	Jb 18:4
my acquaintances have a me.	Jb 19:13
For he oppressed and a the poor;	Jb 20:19
You have not a those who seek	Ps 9:10
the righteous a or his children	Ps 37:25
saying, "God has a him;	Ps 71:11
He a the tabernacle at Shiloh,	Ps 78:60
a among the dead. I am like the	Ps 88:5
They have a the LORD;	Is 1:4
Daughter Zion is a like a	Is 1:8
For You have a Your people,	Is 2:6
two kings you dread will be a.	Is 7:16
Like one gathering a eggs,	Is 10:14
will be like the a woods and	Is 17:9
mountaintops that were a because	Is 17:9
pastures a and forsaken like a	Is 27:10
be forsaken, the busy city a.	Is 32:14
Zion says, "The LORD has a me;	Is 49:14
did when they a Me to burn	Jr 1:16
They have a Me, the fountain of	Jr 2:13
Every city is a; no inhabitant	Jr 4:29
children have a Me and sworn	Jr 5:7
Just as you a Me and served	Jr 5:19
rejected and a the generation	Jr 7:29
is because they a My law I set	Jr 9:13
ashamed, for we have a the land;	Jr 9:19
I have a My house;	Jr 12:7
Because your fathers a Me"—	Jr 16:11
they a Me and did not keep My	Jr 16:11
for they have a the fountain of	Jr 17:13
they have a Me and made this	Jr 19:4
Because they a the covenant of	Jr 22:9
can the city of praise not be a,	Jr 49:25
has a His footstool in the day	Lm 2:1
a us for ⌊our⌋ entire lives?	Lm 5:20
The LORD has a the land."	Ezk 8:12
The LORD has a the land;	Ezk 9:9
earth left its shade and a it.	Ezk 31:12
the desolate ruins and a cities,	Ezk 36:4
for they have a their devotion	Hs 4:10
She lies a on her land, with no	Am 5:2
For Gaza will be a, and Ashkelon	Zph 2:4
See, your house is a to you.	Lk 13:35
we are persecuted but not a;	2Co 4:9
have a themselves to the error	Jd 11
you have a the love ⌊you had⌋ at	Rv 2:4

ABANDONING (6)

of your actions in a Me.	Dt 28:20
a Me and worshiping other gods.	1Sm 8:8
fled at twilight a their tents,	2Kg 7:7
on yourself by a the LORD your	Jr 2:17
been promiscuous by a the LORD.	Hs 1:2
a the straight path, they have	2Pt 2:15

ABANDONS (4)

even if he a the fear of the	Jb 6:14
She a her eggs on the ground and	Jb 39:14
who a the companion of her youth	Pr 2:17
gives birth and a ⌊her fawn⌋	Jr 14:5

ABARIM (5)

mountain of the A ⌊range⌋ and	Nm 27:12
camped in the A ⌊range⌋ facing	Nm 33:47
departed from the A ⌊range⌋ and	Nm 33:48

Mount Nebo in the A ⌊range⌋ in Dt 32:49
cry out from A, for all your Jr 22:20

ABATE *(1)*
and my gnawing pains never a. Jb 30:17

ABBA *(3)*
And He said, "A, Father! Mk 14:36
by whom we cry out, "A, Father!" Rm 8:15
hearts, crying, "A , Father!" Gl 4:6

ABDA *(2)*
(AKA OBADIAH)
and Adoniram son of A, in charge 1Kg 4:6
and A son of Shammua, son of Neh 11:17

ABDEEL *(1)*
son of A to seize Baruch Jr 36:26

ABDI *(3)*
Kishi, son of A, son of Malluch 1Ch 6:44
Kish son of A and Azariah son of 2Ch 29:12
Zechariah, Jehiel, A, Jeremoth, Ezr 10:26

ABDIEL *(1)*
Ahi son of A, son of Guni, 1Ch 5:15

ABDON *(8)*
(AKA EBRON)
its pasturelands, A with its Jos 21:30
After Elon, A son of Hillel, who Jdg 12:13
A judged Israel eight years, Jdg 12:14
its pasturelands, A and its 1Ch 6:74
A, Zichri, Hanan, 1Ch 8:23
A was his firstborn son, then 1Ch 8:30
A was his firstborn son, then 1Ch 9:36
son of Shaphan, A son of Micah, 2Ch 34:20

ABEDNEGO *(15)*
(AKA AZARIAH)
Meshach; and to Azariah, A. Dn 1:7
and A to manage the province of Dn 2:49
Shadrach, Meshach, and A. Dn 3:12
in Shadrach, Meshach, and A. Dn 3:13
Meshach, and A, is it true that Dn 3:14
and A replied to the king, Dn 3:16
toward Shadrach, Meshach, and A. Dn 3:19
and A and throw them into the Dn 3:20
Shadrach, Meshach, and A up. Dn 3:22
Meshach, and A fell, bound, Dn 3:23
Meshach, and A, you servants Dn 3:26
and A came out of the fire. Dn 3:26
God of Shadrach, Meshach, and A! Dn 3:28
A will be torn limb from limb Dn 3:29
A in the province of Babylon. Dn 3:30

ABEL *(15)*
gave birth to his brother A. Gn 4:2
Now A became a shepherd of a Gn 4:2
And A also presented ⌊an Gn 4:4
had regard for A and his Gn 4:4
Cain said to his brother A, Gn 4:8
his brother A and killed him. Gn 4:8
"Where is your brother A?" Gn 4:9
me another child in place of A, Gn 4:25
of Israel to A of Beth-maacah. 2Sm 20:14
Sheba in A of Beth-maacah. 2Sm 20:15
'Seek counsel in A,' and that's 2Sm 20:18
of righteous A to the blood Mt 23:35
from the blood of A to the blood Lk 11:51
By faith A offered to God a Heb 11:4
things than the ⌊blood⌋ of A. Heb 12:24

ABEL-BETH-MAACAH *(2)*
(AKA ABEL-MAIM)
Ijon, Dan, A, all Chinneroth, 1Kg 15:20
Ijon, A, Janoah, Kedesh, 2Kg 15:29

ABEL-KERAMIM *(1)*
entrance of Minnith and to A. Jdg 11:33

ABEL-MAIM *(1)*
(AKA ABEL-BETH-MAACAH)
attacked Ijon, Dan, A, and all 2Ch 16:4

ABEL-MEHOLAH *(3)*
as the border of A near Tabbath. Jdg 7:22
from Beth-shean to A, as far as 1Kg 4:12
of Shaphat from A as prophet in 1Kg 19:16

ABEL-MIZRAIM *(1)*
Therefore the place is named A. Gn 50:11

ABHOR *(4)*
not reject or a them so as to Lv 26:44
are to utterly detest and a it, Dt 7:26
I hate and a falsehood, ⌊but⌋ I Ps 119:163
who a justice and pervert Mc 3:9

ABHORRED *(4)*
all these things, and I a them. Lv 20:23
My ordinances and a My statutes. Lv 26:43
and He a His own inheritance. Ps 106:40
despised, to one a by people, to Is 49:7

ABHORRENT *(6)*
since that is a to them. Gn 43:32
shepherds are a to Egyptians." Gn 46:34
it is a to the LORD your God. Dt 7:25
not bring any a thing into your Dt 7:26
their detestable and a idols." Jr 16:18
they made their a images from Ezk 7:20

ABHORRENTLY *(3)*
ashamed when they acted so a? Jr 6:15
ashamed when they acted so a? Jr 8:12
more a than they ⌊did⌋. Ezk 16:52

ABHORS *(1)*
LORD a a man of bloodshed and Ps 5:6

ABI *(1)*
(AKA ABIJAH)
mother's name was A daughter of 2Kg 18:2

ABI-ALBON *(1)*
(AKA ABIEL)
A the Arbathite, Azmaveth the 2Sm 23:31

ABIASAPH *(1)*
Assir, Elkanah, and A. Ex 6:24

ABIATHAR *(28)*
His name was A, and he fled to 1Sm 22:20
A told David that Saul had 1Sm 22:21
David said to A, "I knew that 1Sm 22:22
A son of Ahimelech fled to David 1Sm 23:6
him, he said to A the priest, 1Sm 23:9
David said to A the priest, 1Sm 30:7
So A brought it to him, 1Sm 30:7
Ahimelech son of A were priests; 2Sm 8:17
and A offered ⌊sacrifices⌋ until 2Sm 15:24
So Zadok and A returned the ark 2Sm 15:29
Won't Zadok and A the priests be 2Sm 15:35
to Zadok and A the priests. 2Sm 15:35
told the priests Zadok and A, 2Sm 17:15
to the priests, Zadok and A: 2Sm 19:11
Zadok and A were priests; 2Sm 20:25
Zeruiah and with A the priest. 1Kg 1:7
the king's sons, A the priest, 1Kg 1:19
of the army, and A the priest. 1Kg 1:25
Jonathan son of A the priest, 1Kg 1:42
for him, for A the priest, and 1Kg 2:22
The king said to A the priest, 1Kg 2:26
So Solomon banished A from being 1Kg 2:27
Zadok and A, priests; 1Kg 4:4
Zadok and A and the Levites 1Ch 15:11
Ahimelech son of A were priests; 1Ch 18:16
Ahimelech son of A, and the 1Ch 24:6
Jehoiada son of Benaiah, then A. 1Ch 27:34
in the time of A the high priest Mk 2:26

ABIATHAR'S *(3)*
son Ahimaaz and A son Jonathan. 2Sm 15:27
son Ahimaaz and A son Jonathan, 2Sm 15:36
Zadok the priest in A place. 1Kg 2:35

ABIB *(6)*
(AKA NISAN)
in the month of A, you are Ex 13:4
time in the month of A, Ex 23:15
in the month of A as I commanded Ex 34:18
out of Egypt in the month of A. Ex 34:18
the month of A and celebrate Dt 16:1
by night in the month of A. Dt 16:1

ABIDA *(2)*
Epher, Hanoch, A, and Eldaah. Gn 25:4
Epher, Hanoch, A, and Eldaah. 1Ch 1:33

ABIDAN *(5)*
A son of Gideoni from Benjamin; Nm 1:11
is A son of Gideoni. Nm 2:22
the ninth day A son of Gideoni, Nm 7:60
offering of A son of Gideoni. Nm 7:65
A son of Gideoni was over the Nm 10:24

ABIDE *(2)*
You must a by the verdict they Dt 17:10
You must a by the instruction Dt 17:11

ABIDES *(1)*
for anger a in the heart of Ec 7:9

ABIEL *(3)*
(AKA ABI-ALBON)
of Benjamin named Kish son of A, 1Sm 9:1
Abner's father was Ner son of A. 1Sm 14:51
wadis of Gaash, A the Arbathite, 1Ch 11:32

ABIEZER *(6)*
the sons of A, Helek, Asriel, Jos 17:2
better than the vintage of A? Jdg 8:2
A the Anathothite, Mebunnai the 2Sm 23:27
birth to Ishhod, A, and Mahlah. 1Ch 7:18
the Tekoite, A the Anathothite, 1Ch 11:28
month, was A the Anathothite 1Ch 27:12

ABIEZRITE *(1)*
which belonged to Joash, the A. Jdg 6:11

ABIEZRITES *(3)*
in Ophrah of the A until today. Jdg 6:24
horn and the A rallied behind Jdg 6:34
father Joash in Ophrah of the A. Jdg 8:32

ABIGAIL *(18)*
Nabal, and his wife's name, A. 1Sm 25:3
of Nabal's young men informed A 1Sm 25:14
A hurried, taking 200 loaves of 1Sm 25:18
When A saw David, she quickly 1Sm 25:23
Then David said to A, "Praise to 1Sm 25:32
Then A went to Nabal, and there 1Sm 25:36
speak to A about marrying him. 1Sm 25:39
servants came to A at Carmel, 1Sm 25:40
Then A got up quickly, and with 1Sm 25:42
of Jezreel and A of Carmel, 1Sm 27:3
Jezreelite and A the widow of 1Sm 30:5
Ahinoam the Jezreelite and A, 2Sm 2:2
was Chileab, by A, the widow of 2Sm 3:3
Ithra had married A daughter of 2Sm 17:25
A was a sister to Zeruiah, 2Sm 17:25
sisters were Zeruiah and A. 1Ch 2:16
mother was A, and his father 1Ch 2:17
born⌋ second, by A of Carmel; 1Ch 3:1

ABIHAIL *(6)*
clans was Zuriel son of A; Nm 3:35
Abishur's wife was named A, 1Ch 2:29
were the sons of A son of Huri, 1Ch 5:14
Jerimoth and of A daughter of 2Ch 11:18
Esther was the daughter of A, Est 2:15
Queen Esther daughter of A, Est 9:29

ABIHU *(12)*
bore him Nadab and A, Eleazar Ex 6:23
Aaron, Nadab, and A, and 70 of Ex 24:1
Aaron, Nadab, and A, and 70 of Ex 24:9
sons Nadab and A, Eleazar and Ex 28:1
sons Nadab and A each took his Lv 10:1
the firstborn, and A, Eleazar, Nm 3:2
But Nadab and A died in the Nm 3:4
Nadab, A, Eleazar, and Ithamar Nm 26:60
but Nadab and A died when they Nm 26:61
Nadab, A, Eleazar, and Ithamar. 1Ch 6:3
sons were Nadab, A, Eleazar, and 1Ch 24:1
Nadab and A died before their 1Ch 24:2

ABIHUD *(1)*
Bela's sons: Addar, Gera, A, 1Ch 8:3

ABIJAH *(25)*
(AKA ABIJAM)
was Joel and his second was A. 1Sm 8:2
At that time A son of Jeroboam 1Kg 14:1
his wife A bore him Ashhur the 1Ch 2:24
his son was A, his son Asa, his 1Ch 3:10
Joel, and his second son A. 1Ch 6:28
Omri, Jeremoth, A, Anathoth, and 1Ch 7:8
to Hakkoz, the eighth to A, 1Ch 24:10
She bore him A, Attai, Ziza, and 2Ch 11:20
appointed A son of Maacah as 2Ch 11:22
His son A became king in his 2Ch 12:16
Jeroboam, A became king over 2Ch 13:1
was war between A and Jeroboam. 2Ch 13:2
A set his army of warriors in 2Ch 13:3
Then A stood on Mount Zemaraim, 2Ch 13:4
all Israel before A and Judah. 2Ch 13:15
A and his people struck them 2Ch 13:17
A pursued Jeroboam and captured 2Ch 13:19
However, A grew strong, acquired 2Ch 13:21
A rested with his fathers and 2Ch 14:1
mother's name was A daughter of 2Ch 29:1
Meshullam, A, Mijamin, Neh 10:7
Iddo, Ginnethoi, A, Neh 12:4
Zichri of A, Piltai of Moadiah, Neh 12:17
fathered A, Abijah fathered Mt 1:7
fathered Abijah, A fathered Asa, Mt 1:7

ABIJAH'S *(3)*
his power during A reign; 2Ch 13:20

rest of the events of **A** ⌊reign⌋, 2Ch 13:22
was a priest of **A** division named Lk 1:5

ABIJAM *(5)*
(AKA ABIJAH)
His son **A** became king in his 1Kg 14:31
son of Nebat, **A** became king over 1Kg 15:1
A walked in all the sins his 1Kg 15:3
also war between **A** and Jeroboam. 1Kg 15:7
A rested with his fathers and 1Kg 15:8

ABIJAM'S *(1)*
rest of the events of **A** ⌊reign⌋, 1Kg 15:7

ABILENE *(1)*
and Lysanias tetrarch of **A**, Lk 3:1

ABILITY *(13)*
and **a** in every craft Ex 31:3
and **a** in every kind of craft Ex 35:31
⌊the **a**⌋ to teach ⌊others⌋. Ex 35:34
and my own **a** have gained this Dt 8:17
to the best of my **a** I've made 1Ch 29:2
I lack man's **a** to understand. Pr 30:2
and the **a** to interpret dreams, Dn 5:12
to each according to his own **a**. Mt 25:15
Spirit gave them **a** for speech. Ac 2:4
according to his **a**, determined Ac 11:29
but there is no **a** to do it. Rm 7:18
to their **a** and beyond their 2Co 8:3
ability and beyond their **a**, 2Co 8:3

ABIMAEL *(2)*
Obal, **A**, Sheba, Gn 10:28
Ebal, **A**, Sheba, 1Ch 1:22

ABIMELECH *(64)*
So **A** king of Gerar had Sarah Gn 20:2
But God came to **A** in a dream by Gn 20:3
Now **A** had not approached her, Gn 20:4
Early in the morning **A** got up, Gn 20:8
A called Abraham in and said Gn 20:9
A also said to Abraham, "What Gn 20:10
Then **A** took sheep and cattle and Gn 20:14
A said, "Look, my land is before Gn 20:15
and God healed **A**, his wife, and Gn 20:17
At that time **A**, with Phicol the Gn 21:22
complained to **A** because of the Gn 21:25
A replied, "I don't know who did Gn 21:26
and cattle and gave them to **A**, Gn 21:27
A said to Abraham, "Why have Gn 21:29
at Beer-sheba, **A** and Phicol, Gn 21:32
And Isaac went to **A**, king of the Gn 26:1
A king of the Philistines looked Gn 26:8
A sent for Isaac and said, Gn 26:9
A said, "What is this you've Gn 26:10
So **A** warned all the people with Gn 26:11
And **A** said to Isaac, "Leave us, Gn 26:16
Then **A** came to him from Gerar Gn 26:26
him a son, and he named him **A**. Jdg 8:31
A son of Jerubbaal went to his Jdg 9:1
and they were favorable to **A**, Jdg 9:3
A hired worthless and reckless Jdg 9:4
to make **A** king at the oak Jdg 9:6
and honestly in making **A** king, Jdg 9:16
stone, and made **A**, the son of Jdg 9:18
rejoice in **A** and may he also Jdg 9:19
may fire come from **A** and consume Jdg 9:20
and Beth-millo and consume **A**." Jdg 9:20
there because of his brother **A**. Jdg 9:21
When **A** had ruled over Israel Jdg 9:22
spirit between **A** and the lords Jdg 9:23
They treated **A** deceitfully, Jdg 9:23
be avenged on their brother **A**, Jdg 9:24
So this was reported to **A**. Jdg 9:25
ate and drank, they cursed **A**. Jdg 9:27
Who is **A** and who is Shechem that Jdg 9:28
Why should we serve **A**? Jdg 9:28
in my power, I would remove **A**." Jdg 9:29
So he said to **A**, "Gather your Jdg 9:29
sent messengers secretly to **A**, Jdg 9:31
So **A** and all the people with him Jdg 9:34
Then **A** and the people who were Jdg 9:35
is **A** that we should serve him? Jdg 9:38
of Shechem and fought against **A**, Jdg 9:39
but **A** pursued him, and Gaal fled Jdg 9:40
A stayed in Arumah, and Zebul Jdg 9:41
this was reported to **A**. Jdg 9:42
Then **A** and the units that were Jdg 9:44
A fought against the city that Jdg 9:45
was reported to **A** that all the Jdg 9:47
So **A** and all the people who were Jdg 9:48
A took his ax in his hand and Jdg 9:48
his own branch and followed **A**. Jdg 9:49
A went to Thebez, camped against Jdg 9:50
When **A** came to attack the tower, Jdg 9:52
Israelites saw that **A** was dead, Jdg 9:55
the evil that **A** had done against Jdg 9:56
After **A**, Tola son of Puah, son Jdg 10:1
struck **A** son of Jerubbesheth? 2Sm 11:21
be insane in the presence of **A**, Ps 34:1

ABIMELECH'S *(3)*
all the wombs in **A** household on Gn 20:18
water well that **A** servants had Gn 21:25
of a millstone on **A** head and Jdg 9:53

ABINADAB *(8)*
Jesse called **A** and presented him 1Sm 16:8
the firstborn, **A**, the next, 1Sm 17:13
Jonathan, **A**, and Malchishua 1Sm 31:2
Ahio, sons of **A**, were guiding 2Sm 6:3
A was ⌊born⌋ second, Shimea 1Ch 2:13
Malchishua, **A**, and Esh-baal. 1Ch 8:33
Malchishua, **A**, and Esh-baal. 1Ch 9:39
Jonathan, **A**, and Malchishua. 1Ch 10:2

ABINADAB'S *(4)*
and took it to **A** house on the 1Sm 7:1
and transported it from **A** house, 2Sm 6:3
ark of God from **A** house on the 2Sm 6:4
At **A** house, they set the ark of 1Ch 13:7

ABINOAM *(4)*
Barak son of **A** from Kedesh Jdg 4:6
Barak son of **A** had gone up Mount Jdg 4:12
Deborah and Barak son of **A** sang: Jdg 5:1
of your captives, son of **A**!" Jdg 5:12

ABIRAM *(11)*
Dathan and **A**, sons of Eliab, Nm 16:1
Moses sent for Dathan and **A**, Nm 16:12
of Korah, Dathan, and **A**." Nm 16:24
got up and went to Dathan and **A**, Nm 16:25
of Korah, Dathan, and **A**. Nm 16:27
Dathan and **A** came out and stood Nm 16:27
were Nemuel, Dathan, and **A**. Nm 26:9
It was Dathan and **A**, chosen by Nm 26:9
and what He did to Dathan and **A**, Dt 11:6
At the cost of **A** his firstborn, 1Kg 16:34
it covered the assembly of **A**. Ps 106:17

ABISHAG *(5)*
they found **A** the Shunammite and 1Kg 1:3
A the Shunammite was serving him 1Kg 1:15
Let him give me **A** the Shunammite 1Kg 2:17
Let **A** the Shunammite be given to 1Kg 2:21
you requesting **A** the Shunammite 1Kg 2:22

ABISHAI *(25)*
Joab's brother **A** son of Zeruiah, 1Sm 26:6
"I'll go with you," answered **A**. 1Sm 26:6
David and **A** came to the troops, 1Sm 26:7
Then **A** said to David, "Today God 1Sm 26:8
David said to **A**, "Don't destroy 1Sm 26:9
Joab, **A**, and Asahel. 2Sm 2:18
but Joab and **A** pursued Abner. 2Sm 2:24
and his brother **A** killed Abner 2Sm 3:30
of his brother **A** who lined up in 2Sm 10:10
fled before **A** and entered the 2Sm 10:14
Then **A** son of Zeruiah said to 2Sm 16:9
Then David said to **A** and all his 2Sm 16:11
Joab's brother **A** son of Zeruiah, 2Sm 18:2
commanded Joab, **A**, and Ittai, 2Sm 18:5
command you, **A**, and Ittai, 2Sm 18:12
A son of Zeruiah asked, 2Sm 19:21
David said to **A**, "Sheba son of 2Sm 20:6
and his brother **A** pursued Sheba 2Sm 20:10
But **A** son of Zeruiah came to his 2Sm 21:17
A, Joab's brother and son of 2Sm 23:18
A, Joab, and Asahel. 1Ch 2:16
A, Joab's brother, was the 1Ch 11:20
A son of Zeruiah struck down 1Ch 18:12
the command of his brother **A**, 1Ch 19:11
Joab's brother **A** and entered the 1Ch 19:15

ABISHAI'S *(1)*
marched out under **A** command; 2Sm 20:7

ABISHALOM *(2)*
name was Maacah daughter of **A**. 1Kg 15:2
name was Maacah daughter of **A**. 1Kg 15:10

ABISHUA *(4)*
Phinehas fathered **A**; 1Ch 6:4
A fathered Bukki; Bukki fathered 1Ch 6:5
his son Phinehas, his son **A**, 1Ch 6:50
A, Naaman, Ahoah, 1Ch 8:4

ABISHUA'S *(1)*
A son, Phinehas's son, Eleazar's Ezr 7:5

ABISHUR *(1)*
Shammai's sons: Nadab and **A**. 1Ch 2:28

ABISHUR'S *(1)*
A wife was named Abihail, who 1Ch 2:29

ABITAL *(2)*
fifth was Shephatiah, son of **A**; 2Sm 3:4
Shephatiah, by **A**, was fifth; 1Ch 3:3

ABITUB *(1)*
sons by Hushim: **A** and Elpaal. 1Ch 8:11

ABIUD *(2)*
fathered **A**, Abiud fathered Mt 1:13
fathered Abiud, **A** fathered Mt 1:13

ABLAZE *(8)*
coals were set **a** by it. 2Sm 22:9
sets coals **a**, and flames pour Jb 41:21
coals were set **a** by it. Ps 18:8
Babylon's homes have been set **a**, Jr 51:30
I wish it were already set **a**! Lk 12:49
our hearts **a** within us while He Lk 24:32
you to keep **a** the gift of God 2Tm 1:6
a great mountain **a** with fire was Rv 8:8

ABLE *(146)*
if you are **a** to count them." Gn 15:5
"I am not **a** to," Joseph answered Gn 41:16
no one will be **a** to raise his Gn 41:44
one will be **a** to see the land. Ex 10:5
from all the people **a** men, Ex 18:21
you, you will be **a** to endure, Ex 18:23
people will be **a** to go home Ex 18:23
So Moses chose **a** men from all Ex 18:25
I will be **a** to pay for your Ex 32:30
You will not be **a** to stand Lv 26:37
and will be **a** to conceive Nm 5:28
the LORD wasn't **a** to bring this Nm 14:16
I may be **a** to defeat them and Nm 22:6
I may be **a** to fight against them Nm 22:11
I really not **a** to reward you?" Nm 22:37
will not be **a** to destroy them Dt 7:22
one will be **a** to stand against Dt 7:24
the LORD wasn't **a** to bring them Dt 9:28
one will be **a** to stand against Dt 11:25
one will be **a** to stand against Jos 1:5
You will not be **a** to stand Jos 7:13
of them will be **a** to stand Jos 10:8
enemies were **a** to stand against Jos 21:44
will not be **a** to say to our Jos 22:27
no one has been **a** to stand Jos 23:9
You will not be **a** to worship the Jos 24:19
was I **a** to do compared to you? Jdg 8:3
Am I **a** to have any more sons who Ru 1:11
Who is **a** to stand in the 1Sm 6:20
lord the king is **a** to discern 2Sm 14:17
For who is **a** to judge this great 1Kg 3:9
was not **a** to build a temple 1Kg 5:3
priests were not **a** to continue 1Kg 8:11
that no one will ⌊be **a**⌋ to say: 2Kg 9:37
but were not **a** to conquer him. 2Kg 16:5
if you're **a** to supply riders 2Kg 18:23
that we should be **a** to give as 1Ch 29:14
But who is **a** to build a temple 2Ch 2:6
priests were not **a** to continue 2Ch 5:14
priests were not **a** to enter the 2Ch 7:2
were not **a** to go to Tarshish. 2Ch 20:37
The LORD is **a** to give you much 2Ch 25:9
they weren't **a** to skin all the 2Ch 29:34
they were not **a** to observe it at 2Ch 30:3
the lands been **a** to deliver 2Ch 32:13
destroyed was **a** to deliver his 2Ch 32:14
God should be **a** to do the same 2Ch 32:14
kingdom has been **a** to deliver 2Ch 32:15
will never be **a** to rebuild the Neh 4:10
everyone who is **a** to understand Neh 10:28
warriors was **a** to lift a hand. Ps 76:5
Is God **a** to provide food in the Ps 78:19
But he is not **a** to contend with Ec 6:10
will be **a** to do anything for Is 19:15
they are not **a** to rescue the Is 46:2
you will be **a** to succeed; Is 47:12
you might be **a** to do what is Jr 13:23
who are **a** to handle shields, Jr 46:9
who are **a** to handle and string Jr 46:9
No one will be **a** to retrieve a Jr 51:26
person won't be **a** to survive by Ezk 33:12
Are you **a** to tell me the dream I Dn 2:26

astrologer is **a** to make known to Dn 2:27
since you were **a** to reveal this Dn 2:47
god who is **a** to deliver like Dn 3:29
And He is **a** to humble those who Dn 4:37
continually been **a** to rescue you Dn 6:20
troops will not be **a** to resist. Dn 11:15
will not be **a** to rescue them Zph 1:18
And who will be **a** to stand when Mal 3:2
you that God is **a** to raise up Mt 3:9
but are not **a** to kill the soul Mt 10:28
Him who is **a** to destroy both Mt 10:28
Are you **a** to drink the cup that Mt 20:22
"We are **a**," they said to Him. Mt 20:22
No one was **a** to answer Him at Mt 22:46
they were not **a** to bring him to Mk 2:4
they were not even **a** to eat. Mk 3:20
as they were **a** to understand. Mk 4:33
No one was **a** to restrain him any Mk 5:3
So He was not **a** to do any Mk 6:5
Are you **a** to drink the cup I Mk 10:38
"We are **a**," they told Him. Mk 10:39
you that God is **a** to raise up Lk 3:8
If then you're not **a** to do even Lk 12:26
will try to enter and won't be **a** Lk 13:24
build and wasn't **a** to finish.' Lk 14:30
decide if he is **a** with 10,000 to Lk 14:31
but he was not **a** because of the Lk 19:3
They were not **a** to catch Him in Lk 20:26
adversaries will be **a** to resist Lk 21:15
The Son is not **a** to do anything Jn 5:19
wouldn't be **a** to do anything." Jn 9:33
one is **a** to snatch them out of Jn 10:29
you will not be **a** to overthrow Ac 5:39
nor we have been **a** to bear? Ac 15:10
which is **a** to build you up and Ac 20:32
he was not **a** to get reliable Ac 21:34
you will be **a** to discern all Ac 24:8
You are **a** to determine that it Ac 24:11
that they were not **a** to prove, Ac 25:7
we were barely **a** to get control Ac 27:16
He was also **a** to perform. Rm 4:21
For the Lord is **a** to make him Rm 14:4
and **a** to instruct one another. Rm 15:14
he is not **a** to know it since it 1Co 2:14
I was not **a** to speak to you as 1Co 3:1
were not yet **a** to receive it. 1Co 3:2
In fact, you are still not **a**, 1Co 3:2
you who will be **a** to arbitrate 1Co 6:5
tempted beyond what you are **a**, 1Co 10:13
so that you are **a** to bear it. 1Co 10:13
that we may be **a** to comfort 2Co 1:4
Israel were not **a** to look 2Co 3:7
And God is **a** to make every grace 2Co 9:8
For we are not **a** to do anything 2Co 13:8
given that was **a** to give life, Gl 3:21
this you are **a** to understand my Eph 3:4
may be **a** to comprehend with all Eph 3:18
Now to Him who is **a** to do above Eph 3:20
that you may be **a** to resist in Eph 6:13
it you will be **a** to extinguish Eph 6:16
I am **a** to do all things through Php 4:13
hospitable, an **a** teacher, 1Tm 3:2
that He is **a** to guard what has 2Tm 1:12
who will be **a** to teach others 2Tm 2:2
gentle to everyone, **a** to teach, 2Tm 2:24
learning and never **a** to come to 2Tm 3:7
which are **a** to instruct you for 2Tm 3:15
that he will be **a** both to Ti 1:9
He is **a** to help those who are Heb 2:18
is **a** to deal gently with those Heb 5:2
to the One who was **a** to save Him Heb 5:7
He is always **a** to save those who Heb 7:25
God to be **a** even to raise Heb 11:19
word, which is **a** to save you. Jms 1:21
man who is also **a** to control his Jms 3:2
and judge who is **a** to save and Jms 4:12
you may be **a** to recall these 2Pt 1:15
he is not **a** to sin, because he 1Jn 3:9
to Him who is **a** to protect you Jd 24
door that no one is **a** to close. Rv 3:8
the earth was **a** to open the Rv 5:3
And who is **a** to stand?" Rv 6:17
which are not **a** to see, hear, Rv 9:20
is **a** to wage war against him? Rv 13:4

ABLE-BODIED *(3)*

All the **a** men listened to Hamor Gn 34:24
and all the **a** men were Gn 34:24
Moabites, all strong and **a** men. Jdg 3:29

ABNER *(57)*

of his army was **A** son of Saul's 1Sm 14:50
he asked **A** the commander of the 1Sm 17:55
Whose son is this youth, **A**?" 1Sm 17:55
live, I don't know," **A** replied. 1Sm 17:55
A took him and brought him 1Sm 17:57
facing him and **A** took his place 1Sm 20:25
where Saul and **A** son of Ner, 1Sm 26:5
A and the troops were lying 1Sm 26:7
the troops and to **A** son of Ner: 1Sm 26:14
"Aren't you going to answer, **A**?" 1Sm 26:14
who calls to the king?" **A** asked. 1Sm 26:14
called to **A**, "You're a man, 1Sm 26:15
A son of Ner, commander of 2Sm 2:8
A son of Ner and soldiers of 2Sm 2:12
Then **A** said to Joab, "Let's have 2Sm 2:14
and **A** and the men of Israel were 2Sm 2:17
He chased **A** and did not turn to 2Sm 2:19
A glanced back and said, "Is 2Sm 2:20
A said to him, "Turn to your 2Sm 2:21
Once again, **A** warned Asahel, 2Sm 2:22
so **A** hit him in the stomach with 2Sm 2:23
but Joab and Abishai pursued **A**. 2Sm 2:24
The Benjaminites rallied to **A**; 2Sm 2:25
Then **A** called out to Joab: 2Sm 2:26
So **A** and his men marched through 2Sm 2:29
had turned back from pursuing **A**, 2Sm 2:30
A kept acquiring more power in 2Sm 3:6
and Ish-bosheth questioned **A**, 2Sm 3:7
A was very angry about 2Sm 3:8
May God punish **A** and do so 2Sm 3:9
could not answer **A** because he 2Sm 3:11
A sent messengers as his 2Sm 3:12
A said to him, "Go back." 2Sm 3:16
A conferred with the elders of 2Sm 3:17
A also informed the Benjaminites 2Sm 3:19
A and 20 men came to David 2Sm 3:20
A said to David, "Let me now go 2Sm 3:21
David dismissed **A**, and he went 2Sm 3:21
A was not with David in Hebron 2Sm 3:22
A son of Ner came to see the 2Sm 3:23
Look here, **A** came to you. 2Sm 3:24
You know that **A** son of Ner came 2Sm 3:25
and sent messengers after **A**. 2Sm 3:26
When **A** returned to Hebron, 2Sm 3:27
So **A** died in revenge for the 2Sm 3:27
the blood of **A** son of Ner. 2Sm 3:28
Abishai killed **A** because he had 2Sm 3:30
on sackcloth, and mourn over **A**." 2Sm 3:31
When they buried **A** in Hebron, 2Sm 3:32
the king sang a lament for **A**: 2Sm 3:33
Should **A** die as a fool dies? 2Sm 3:33
in the killing of **A** son of Ner. 2Sm 3:37
heard that **A** had died in Hebron, 2Sm 4:1
A son of Ner and Amasa son of 1Kg 2:5
Joab murdered **A** son of Ner, 1Kg 2:32
Saul son of Kish, **A** son of Ner, 1Ch 26:28
for Benjamin, Jaasiel son of **A**; 1Ch 27:21

ABNER'S *(4)*

A father was Ner son of Abiel. 1Sm 14:51
of the Benjaminites and **A** men. 2Sm 2:31
the king wept aloud at **A** tomb. 2Sm 3:32
buried it in **A** tomb in Hebron. 2Sm 4:12

ABNORMALLY *(1)*

all, as to one **a** born, He also 1Co 15:8

ABODE *(2)*

Sheol, far from their lofty **a**. Ps 49:14
for jackals, an **a** for ostriches. Is 34:13

ABOLISH *(1)*

They will **a** the daily sacrifice Dn 11:31

ABOLISHED *(7)*

I **a** the borders of nations and Is 10:13
The LORD has **a** appointed Lm 2:6
daily sacrifice is **a** and the Dn 12:11
dominion over the body may be **a**, Rm 6:6
The last enemy to be **a** is death. 1Co 15:26
offense of the cross has been **a**. Gl 5:11
who has **a** death and has brought 2Tm 1:10

ABOLISHES *(1)*

when He **a** all rule and all 1Co 15:24

ABOMINATION *(9)*

they have both committed an **a**. Lv 20:13
for Milcom, the **a** of the 2Kg 23:13
turned your beauty into an **a**. Ezk 16:25
you commits an **a** with his Ezk 22:11
And the **a** of desolation will be Dn 9:27
and set up the **a** of desolation. Dn 11:31
and the **a** of desolation is Dn 12:11
when you see the **a** that causes Mt 24:15
When you see the **a** that causes Mk 13:14

ABOMINATIONS *(48)*

must not commit any of these **a**— Lv 18:26
you have committed all these **a**, Lv 18:27
any of these **a** must be cut off Lv 18:29
imitated all the **a** of the 1Kg 14:24
imitating the **a** of the nations 2Kg 16:3
imitating the **a** of the nations 2Kg 21:2
has committed all these **a**— 2Kg 21:11
there are seven **a** in his heart. Pr 26:25
ways and delight in their **a**. Is 66:3
of all your **a**, I will do to you Ezk 5:9
your detestable practices and **a**. Ezk 5:11
they did, their **a** of every kind. Ezk 6:9
over all the evil **a** of the house Ezk 6:11
will punish you for all your **a**. Ezk 7:3
ways and for your **a** within you. Ezk 7:4
will punish you for all your **a**. Ezk 7:8
ways and for your **a** within you. Ezk 7:9
the great **a** that the house of Ezk 8:6
You will see even greater **a**." Ezk 8:6
see the terrible **a** they are Ezk 8:9
You will see even greater **a**, Ezk 8:13
see even greater **a** than these." Ezk 8:15
to commit the **a** they are Ezk 8:17
over all the **a** committed in it. Ezk 9:4
things and all its **a** from it. Ezk 11:18
for detestable things and **a**, Ezk 11:21
about all their **a** among the Ezk 12:16
your faces away from all your **a**. Ezk 14:6
explain Jerusalem's **a** to her. Ezk 16:2
In all your **a** and acts of Ezk 16:22
acts in addition to all your **a**? Ezk 16:43
their ways and practice their **a**? Ezk 16:47
multiplied your **a** beyond theirs Ezk 16:51
by all the **a** you have committed Ezk 16:51
of your indecency and **a**"— Ezk 16:58
eyes to the idols, commits **a**, Ezk 18:12
he has committed all these **a**, Ezk 18:13
the same **a** that the wicked do Ezk 18:24
to them the **a** of their fathers. Ezk 20:4
Then explain all her **a** to her. Ezk 22:2
Then declare their **a** to them. Ezk 23:36
have committed **a**, and each of Ezk 33:26
because of all the **a** they have Ezk 33:29
for your iniquities and **a**. Ezk 36:31
name by the **a** they committed. Ezk 43:8
have had enough of all your **a**, Ezk 44:6
My covenant with all your **a**. Ezk 44:7
of the **a** they committed. Ezk 44:13

ABOUND *(3)*

when their grain and new wine **a**. Ps 4:7
and prosperity **a** until the moon Ps 72:7
May your prosperity **a**. Dn 6:25

ABOUT *(1100)*

(See pp. xi-xii.)

ABOVE *(162)*

(See pp. xi-xii.)

ABRAHAM *(226)*

(AKA ABRAM)

name will be **A**, for I will make Gn 17:5
God also said to **A**, "As for you, Gn 17:9
God said to **A**, "As for your wife Gn 17:15
A fell to the ground, laughed, Gn 17:17
So **A** said to God, "If only Gn 17:18
with him, God withdrew from **A**. Gn 17:22
Then **A** took his son Ishmael and Gn 17:23
A was 99 years old when the Gn 17:24
On that same day **A** and his son Gn 17:26
LORD appeared to **A** at the oaks Gn 18:1
So **A** hurried into the tent and Gn 18:6
A ran to the herd and got a Gn 18:7
Then **A** took curds and milk, Gn 18:8
A and Sarah were old and getting Gn 18:11
the LORD asked **A**, "Why did Sarah Gn 18:13
and **A** was walking with them to Gn 18:16
I hide from **A** what I am about to Gn 18:17
A is to become a great and Gn 18:18
will fulfill to **A** what He Gn 18:19
Sodom while **A** remained standing Gn 18:22
A stepped forward and said, Gn 18:23
Then **A** answered, "Since I have Gn 18:27
had finished speaking with **A**, Gn 18:33
and **A** returned to his place. Gn 18:33

in the morning A went to the Gn 19:27
He remembered A and brought Lot Gn 19:29
From there A traveled to the Gn 20:1
A said about his wife Sarah, Gn 20:2
Abimelech called A in and said Gn 20:9
Abimelech also said to A, Gn 20:10
A replied, "I thought, 'There is Gn 20:11
gave them to A, and returned his Gn 20:14
Then A prayed to God, and God Gn 20:17
bore a son to A in his old age, Gn 21:2
A named his son who was born to Gn 21:3
days old, A circumcised him Gn 21:4
A was 100 years old when his son Gn 21:5
would have told A that Sarah Gn 21:7
and A held a great feast on the Gn 21:8
the Egyptian had borne to A, Gn 21:9
she said to A, "Drive out this Gn 21:10
thing for A because of his son Gn 21:11
But God said to A, "Do not be Gn 21:12
Early in the morning A got up, Gn 21:14
army, said to A, "God is with Gn 21:22
And A said, "I swear ⌊it⌋." Gn 21:24
But A complained to Abimelech Gn 21:25
Then A took sheep and cattle and Gn 21:27
But A had set apart seven ewe Gn 21:28
said to A, "Why have you Gn 21:29
A planted a tamarisk tree in Gn 21:33
A lived as a foreigner in the Gn 21:34
God tested A and said to him, Gn 22:1
Abraham and said to him, "A!" Gn 22:1
early in the morning A got up, Gn 22:3
On the third day A looked up and Gn 22:4
Then A said to his young men, Gn 22:5
A took the wood for the burnt Gn 22:6
spoke to his father A and said, Gn 22:7
A answered, "God Himself will Gn 22:8
A built the altar there and Gn 22:9
Then A reached out and took the Gn 22:10
heaven and said, "A, Abraham!" Gn 22:11
heaven and said, "Abraham, A!" Gn 22:11
A looked up and saw a ram caught Gn 22:13
So A went and took the ram and Gn 22:13
And A named that place The LORD Gn 22:14
LORD called to A a second time Gn 22:15
A went back to his young men, Gn 22:19
And A settled in Beer-sheba. Gn 22:19
after these things A was told, Gn 22:20
and A went in to mourn for Sarah Gn 23:2
A got up from beside his dead Gn 23:3
The Hittites replied to A, Gn 23:5
Then A rose and bowed down to Gn 23:7
Ephron the Hittite answered A: Gn 23:10
A bowed down to the people of Gn 23:12
answered A and said to him Gn 23:14
A agreed with Ephron, and Gn 23:16
and A weighed out to Ephron the Gn 23:16
A buried his wife Sarah in the Gn 23:19
the Hittites to A as a burial Gn 23:20
A was now old, getting on in Gn 24:1
A said to his servant, the elder Gn 24:2
A answered him, "Make sure that Gn 24:6
God of my master A," he prayed, Gn 24:12
show kindness to my master A. Gn 24:12
God of my master A, who has not Gn 24:27
God of my master A, if only You Gn 24:42
God of my master A, who guided Gn 24:48
Now A took another wife, whose Gn 25:1
A gave everything he owned to Gn 25:5
And A gave gifts to the sons of Gn 25:6
This was the field that A bought Gn 25:10
A was buried there with his wife Gn 25:10
Sarah's slave, bore to A. Gn 25:12
records of Isaac son of A. Gn 25:19
of Abraham. A fathered Isaac. Gn 25:19
that I swore to your father A. Gn 26:3
because A listened to My voice Gn 26:5
dug in the days of his father A, Gn 26:15
days of his father A and that Gn 26:18
had stopped up after A died. Gn 26:18
I am the God of your father A. Gn 26:24
because of My servant A." Gn 26:24
blessing of A so that you may Gn 28:4
alien, the land God gave to A." Gn 28:4
God of your father A and the God Gn 28:13
the God of A, the Fear of Isaac Gn 31:42
The God of A, and the gods of Gn 31:53
God of my father A and God of my Gn 32:9
I gave to A and Isaac I will Gn 35:12
where A and Isaac had stayed. Gn 35:27
whom my fathers A and Isaac Gn 48:15
names of my fathers A and Isaac, Gn 48:16
This is the field A purchased Gn 49:30
A and his wife Sarah are buried Gn 49:31
A had purchased as a burial Gn 50:13
land to the land He promised A, Gn 50:24
remembered His covenant with A, Ex 2:24
the God of A, the God of Isaac Ex 3:6
the God of A, the God of Isaac, Ex 3:15
the God of A, Isaac, and Jacob, Ex 3:16
the God of A, the God of Isaac, Ex 4:5
appeared to A, Isaac, and Jacob Ex 6:3
land that I swore to give to A, Ex 6:8
You swore to Your servants A, Ex 32:13
to the land I promised to A, Ex 33:1
Isaac and My covenant with A, Lv 26:42
the land I swore ⌊to give⌋ A, Nm 32:11
swore to give to your fathers A, Dt 1:8
land He swore to your fathers A, Dt 6:10
to your fathers, A, Isaac, and Dt 9:5
Your servants A, Isaac, and Dt 9:27
as He swore to your fathers A, Dt 29:13
swore to give to your fathers A, Dt 30:20
This is the land I promised A, Dt 34:4
the father of A and Nahor, Jos 24:2
your father A from the region Jos 24:3
LORD God of A, Isaac, and Israel 1Kg 18:36
because of His covenant with A, 2Kg 13:23
and Abram (that is, A). 1Ch 1:27
A fathered Isaac. Isaac's sons: 1Ch 1:34
⌊the covenant⌋ He made with A, 1Ch 16:16
God of A, Isaac, and Israel, 1Ch 29:18
descendants of A Your friend? 2Ch 20:7
return to the LORD God of A, 2Ch 30:6
and changed his name to A. Neh 9:7
the people of the God of A. Ps 47:9
You offspring of A His servant, Ps 105:6
⌊the covenant⌋ He made with A, Ps 105:9
holy promise to A His servant. Ps 105:42
who redeemed A says this about Is 29:22
descendant of A, My friend— Is 41:8
Look to A your father, and to Is 51:2
even though A does not know us Is 63:16
over the descendants of A, Jr 33:26
A was only one person, yet he Ezk 33:24
to Jacob and faithful love to A, Mc 7:20
the Son of David, the Son of A: Mt 1:1
A fathered Isaac, Isaac fathered Mt 1:2
from A to David were 14 Mt 1:17
'We have A as our father.' Mt 3:9
up children for A from these Mt 3:9
and recline at the table with A, Mt 8:11
I am the God of A and the God of Mt 22:32
I am the God of A and the God of Mk 12:26
A and his descendants forever. Lk 1:55
that He swore to our father A. Lk 1:73
'We have A as our father,' Lk 3:8
up children for A from these Lk 3:8
son⌋ of A, ⌊son⌋ of Terah Lk 3:34
a daughter of A, for 18 years— Lk 13:16
when you see A, Isaac, Jacob, Lk 13:28
up and saw A a long way off, Lk 16:23
'Father A!' he called out, 'Have Lk 16:24
'Son,' A said, 'remember that Lk 16:25
But A said, 'They have Moses and Lk 16:29
'No, father A,' he said. Lk 16:30
because he too is a son of A. Lk 19:9
Lord the God of A and the God Lk 20:37
"We are descendants of A," Jn 8:33
I know you are descendants of A, Jn 8:37
"Our father is A!" they replied. Jn 8:39
them, "you would do what A did. Jn 8:39
from God. A did not do this Jn 8:40
A died and so did the prophets. Jn 8:52
than our father A who died? Jn 8:53
Your father A was overjoyed that Jn 8:56
old yet, and You've seen A?" Jn 8:57
Before A was, I am." Jn 8:58
The God of A, Isaac, and Jacob, Ac 3:13
saying to A, And in your seed Ac 3:25
to our father A when he was Ac 7:2
the tomb that A had bought for Ac 7:16
promise that God had made to A, Ac 7:17
the God of A, of Isaac, and of Ac 7:32
What then can we say that A, Rm 4:1
If A was justified by works, Rm 4:2
A believed God, and it was Rm 4:3
was credited to A for Rm 4:9
our father A had while still Rm 4:12
For the promise to A or to his Rm 4:13
him was not written for A alone, Rm 4:23
descendant of A, from the tribe Rm 11:1
Are they the seed of A? 2Co 11:22
Just as A believed God, and it Gl 3:6
and foretold the good news to A, Gl 3:8
have faith are blessed with A, Gl 3:9
the blessing of A would come to Gl 3:14
spoken to A and to his seed. Gl 3:16
God granted it to A through the Gl 3:18
is written that A had two sons, Gl 4:22
when God made a promise to A, Heb 6:13
waiting patiently, A obtained Heb 6:15
who met A and blessed him as he Heb 7:1
and A gave him a tenth of Heb 7:2
whom even A the patriarch gave Heb 7:4
have ⌊also⌋ descended from A. Heb 7:5
tithes from A and blessed the Heb 7:6
has paid tithes through A, Heb 7:9
By faith A, when he was called, Heb 11:8
By faith A, when he was tested, Heb 11:17
Wasn't A our father justified by Jms 2:21
that says, A believed God, and Jms 2:23
as Sarah obeyed A, calling him 1Pt 3:6

ABRAHAM'S *(24)*

the members of A household— Gn 17:23
on account of Sarah, A wife. Gn 20:18
these eight to Nahor, A brother. Gn 22:23
A possession in the presence of Gn 23:18
his master A thigh and swore Gn 24:9
the wife of A brother Nahor— Gn 24:15
"I am A servant," he said. Gn 24:34
A servant heard their words, Gn 24:52
and A servant and his men. Gn 24:59
This is the length of A life: Gn 25:7
After A death, God blessed his Gn 25:11
family records of A son Ishmael, Gn 25:12
one that had occurred in A time. Gn 26:1
daughter of Ishmael, A son. Gn 28:9
A sons: Isaac and Ishmael. 1Ch 1:28
born to Keturah, A concubine: 1Ch 1:32
away by the angels to A side. Lk 16:22
"If you were A children," Jesus Jn 8:39
sons of A race, and those Ac 13:26
to those who are of A faith. Rm 4:16
because they are A descendants. Rm 9:7
those who have faith are A sons. Gl 3:7
then you are A seed, heirs Gl 3:29
angels, but to help A offspring. Heb 2:16

ABRAM *(54)*

(AKA ABRAHAM)

lived 70 years and fathered A, Gn 11:26
Terah fathered A, Nahor, and Gn 11:27
A and Nahor took wives: Gn 11:29
took his son A, his grandson Lot Gn 11:31
The LORD said to A: Go out from Gn 12:1
So A went, as the LORD had told Gn 12:4
A was 75 years old when he left Gn 12:4
A passed through the land to the Gn 12:6
the LORD appeared to A and said, Gn 12:7
Then A journeyed by stages to Gn 12:9
so A went down to Egypt to live Gn 12:10
When A entered Egypt, the Gn 12:14
treated A well because of her, Gn 12:16
and A acquired flocks and herds, Gn 12:16
So Pharaoh sent for A and said, Gn 12:18
Then A went up from Egypt to the Gn 13:1
A was very rich in livestock, Gn 13:2
And A worshiped the LORD there. Gn 13:4
traveling with A, also had Gn 13:5
Then A said to Lot, "Please, Gn 13:8
A lived in the land of Canaan, Gn 13:12
the LORD said to A, "Look from Gn 13:14
So A moved his tent and went to Gn 13:18
came and told A the Hebrew, Gn 14:13
were bound by a treaty with A. Gn 14:13
When A heard that his relative Gn 14:14
After A returned from defeating Gn 14:17
A is blessed by God Most High, Gn 14:19
And A gave him a tenth of Gn 14:20
the king of Sodom said to A, Gn 14:21
But A said to the king of Sodom, Gn 14:22
can never say, 'I made A rich.' Gn 14:23
the LORD came to A in a vision: Gn 15:1
not be afraid, A. I am your Gn 15:1
But A said, "Lord GOD, what can Gn 15:2

A continued, "Look, You have Gn 15:3
A believed the LORD, and He Gn 15:6
but A drove them away. Gn 15:11
sleep fell on A, and suddenly Gn 15:12
LORD said to A, "Know this for Gn 15:13
the LORD made a covenant with A, Gn 15:18
Sarai said to A, "Since the LORD Gn 16:2
And A agreed to what Sarai Gn 16:2
to her husband A as a wife for Gn 16:3
This happened⌋ after A had lived Gn 16:3
Then Sarai said to A, "You are Gn 16:5
A replied to Sarai, "Here, your Gn 16:6
and A gave the name Ishmael to Gn 16:15
A was 86 years old when Hagar Gn 16:16
A was 99 years old, the LORD Gn 17:1
Then A fell to the ground, Gn 17:3
Your name will no longer be A, Gn 17:5
and A (that is, Abraham). 1Ch 1:27
God who chose A and brought him Neh 9:7

ABRAM'S *(8)*

A wife was named Sarai, and Gn 11:29
Sarai, his son A wife, and they Gn 11:31
plagues because of A wife Sarai. Gn 12:17
the herdsmen of A livestock Gn 13:7
They also took A nephew Lot and Gn 14:12
A wife Sarai had not borne him Gn 16:1
So A wife Sarai took Hagar, Gn 16:3
So Hagar gave birth to A son, Gn 16:15

ABREK *(1)*

called out before him, "A!" Gn 41:43

ABROAD *(1)*

the earth; he has no name a. Jb 18:17

ABRONAH *(2)*

from Jotbathah and camped at A. Nm 33:34
departed from A and camped at Nm 33:35

ABSALOM *(96)*

the third was A, son of Maacah 2Sm 3:3
David's son A had a beautiful 2Sm 13:1
Her brother A said to her: 2Sm 13:20
in the house of her brother A. 2Sm 13:20
A didn't say anything to Amnon, 2Sm 13:22
and A invited all the king's 2Sm 13:23
king replied to A, "No, my son, 2Sm 13:25
Although A urged him, he wasn't 2Sm 13:25
"If not," A said, "please let my 2Sm 13:26
A urged him, so he sent Amnon 2Sm 13:27
A commanded his young men, 2Sm 13:28
Amnon just as A had commanded 2Sm 13:29
A struck down all the king's 2Sm 13:30
A has planned this ever since 2Sm 13:32
Meanwhile, A had fled. 2Sm 13:34
A fled and went to Talmai son 2Sm 13:37
A had fled and gone to Geshur 2Sm 13:38
King David longed to go to A, 2Sm 13:39
that the king's mind was on A. 2Sm 14:1
bring back the young man A." 2Sm 14:21
and brought A to Jerusalem. 2Sm 14:23
So A returned to his house, 2Sm 14:24
and highly praised as A. 2Sm 14:25
Three sons were born to A, 2Sm 14:27
A resided in Jerusalem two years 2Sm 14:28
Then A sent for Joab in order to 2Sm 14:29
Then A said to his servants, 2Sm 14:30
"Look," A explained to Joab, "I 2Sm 14:32
David summoned A, who came 2Sm 14:33
Then the king kissed A. 2Sm 14:33
After this, A got himself a 2Sm 15:1
A called out to him and asked, 2Sm 15:2
A said to him, "Look, your 2Sm 15:3
down to him, A reached out his 2Sm 15:5
A did this to all the Israelites 2Sm 15:6
So A stole the hearts of the men 2Sm 15:6
had passed, A said to the king 2Sm 15:7
A sent messengers throughout 2Sm 15:10
A has become king in Hebron! 2Sm 15:10
men from Jerusalem went with A. 2Sm 15:11
A sent for David's adviser 2Sm 15:12
people supporting A continued to 2Sm 15:12
the men of Israel are with A." 2Sm 15:13
or we will not escape from A! 2Sm 15:14
among the conspirators with A." 2Sm 15:31
return to the city and tell A, 2Sm 15:34
Jerusalem just as A was entering 2Sm 15:37
the kingdom over to your son A. 2Sm 16:8
A and all the Israelites came 2Sm 16:15
Hushai the Archite came to A, 2Sm 16:16
Hushai said to A, "Long live the 2Sm 16:16
to your friend?" A asked Hushai. 2Sm 16:17
"Not at all," Hushai answered A. 2Sm 16:18
Then A said to Ahithophel, 2Sm 16:20
replied to A, "Sleep with your 2Sm 16:21
a tent for A on the roof, 2Sm 16:22
that both David and A had for 2Sm 16:23
said to A, "Let me choose 2Sm 17:1
seemed good to A and all the 2Sm 17:4
Then A said, "Summon Hushai the 2Sm 17:5
Hushai came to A, and Absalom 2Sm 17:6
came to Absalom, and A told him: 2Sm 17:6
Hushai replied to A, "The advice 2Sm 17:7
among the people who follow A.' 2Sm 17:9
A and all the men of Israel said, 2Sm 17:14
advised A and the elders 2Sm 17:15
did see them and informed A. 2Sm 17:18
by the time A crossed the Jordan 2Sm 17:24
Now A had appointed Amasa 2Sm 17:25
And Israel and A camped in the 2Sm 17:26
the young man A gently for my 2Sm 18:5
to all the commanders about A. 2Sm 18:5
A was riding on his mule when he 2Sm 18:9
saw A hanging in an oak tree! 2Sm 18:10
the young man A for me.' 2Sm 18:12
armor-bearers surrounded A, 2Sm 18:15
They took A, threw him into a 2Sm 18:17
A had erected for himself a 2Sm 18:18
"Is the young man A all right?" 2Sm 18:29
"Is the young man A all right?" 2Sm 18:32
he walked, he cried, "My son A! 2Sm 18:33
My son, my son A! If only I had 2Sm 18:33
of you, A, my son, my son! 2Sm 18:33
He's mourning over A." 2Sm 19:1
the top of his voice, "My son A! 2Sm 19:4
son Absalom! A, my son, my son! 2Sm 19:4
I know that if A were alive and 2Sm 19:6
fled from the land because of A. 2Sm 19:9
But A, the man we anointed over 2Sm 19:10
will do more harm to us than A. 2Sm 20:6
handsome and was born after A. 1Kg 1:6
when I fled from your brother A. 1Kg 2:7
supported Adonijah but not A, 1Kg 2:28
A son of Maacah, daughter of 1Ch 3:2
he married Maacah daughter of A. 2Ch 11:20
daughter of A more than all his 2Ch 11:21

ABSALOM'S *(10)*

Tamar, my brother A sister." 2Sm 13:4
A sheepshearers were at 2Sm 13:23
A young men did to Amnon just 2Sm 13:29
So A servants set the field on 2Sm 14:30
Then Joab came to A house and 2Sm 14:31
in order to bring about A ruin, 2Sm 17:14
A servants came to the woman at 2Sm 17:20
A head was caught fast in the 2Sm 18:9
thrust them into A heart while 2Sm 18:14
still called A Monument today. 2Sm 18:18

ABSENCE *(3)*

asked the king for a leave of a Neh 13:6
men have made up for your a. 1Co 16:17
but now even more in my a, Php 2:12

ABSENT *(7)*

For though a in body but present 1Co 5:3
but bold toward you when a. 2Co 10:1
the words of our letters when a, 2Co 10:11
now while I am a—to those who 2Co 13:2
am writing these things while a, 2Co 13:10
I come and see you or am a, Php 1:27
For I may be a in body, but I am Col 2:5

ABSOLUTE *(3)*

"A futility," says the Teacher. Ec 1:2
says the Teacher. "A futility. Ec 1:2
"A futility," says the Teacher. Ec 12:8

ABSOLUTELY *(21)*

'There is a no fear of God in Gn 20:11
If her father a refuses to give Ex 22:17
You are a beautiful, my darling, Sg 4:7
He is a desirable. Sg 5:16
you will become a nothing. Is 41:12
I gave you a nothing to eat in Am 4:6
A not! God must be true, but Rm 3:4
A not! Otherwise, how will God Rm 3:6
law through faith? A not! On the Rm 3:31
A not! How can we who died to Rm 6:2
law but under grace? A not! Rm 6:15
Is the law sin? A not! On the Rm 7:7
cause my death? A not! On the Rm 7:13
there injustice with God? A not! Rm 9:14
His people? A not! For I too am Rm 11:1
so as to fall? A not! On the Rm 11:11
members of a prostitute? A not! 1Co 6:15
for us an a incomparable 2Co 4:17
then a promoter of sin? A not! Gl 2:17
God's promises? A not! For if a Gl 3:21
and there is a no darkness in 1Jn 1:5

ABSOLVE *(2)*

The LORD will a her because her Nm 30:5
them, and the LORD will a her. Nm 30:12

ABSOLVED *(1)*

they will be a of responsibility Dt 21:8

ABSTAIN *(5)*

he is to a from wine and beer. Nm 6:3
write to them to a from things Ac 15:20
that you a from food offered to Ac 15:29
that you a from sexual 1Th 4:3
residents to a from fleshly 1Pt 2:11

ABSTINENCE *(1)*

and demand a from foods that God 1Tm 4:3

ABSURD *(2)*

and you will say a things. Pr 23:33
How a is the one who says to Is 45:10

ABUNDANCE *(45)*

an a of grain and new wine. Gn 27:28
years of great a are coming Gn 41:29
and all the a in the land of Gn 41:30
The a in the land will not be Gn 41:31
during the seven years of a. Gn 41:34
seven years of a the land Gn 41:47
stored up grain in such a— Gn 41:49
the seven years of a in the land Gn 41:53
you had⌋ an a of everything, Dt 28:47
gold in great a, and precious 1Kg 10:2
sacrifices in a for all Israel. 1Ch 29:21
logs for me in a because the 2Ch 2:9
in such great a that the weight 2Ch 4:18
spices, gold in a, and precious 2Ch 9:1
he had riches and honor in a. 2Ch 17:5
had riches and honor in a, 2Ch 18:1
found among them an a of goods 2Ch 20:25
and gathered the money in a. 2Ch 24:11
this a is what is left over." 2Ch 31:10
and made an a of weapons and 2Ch 32:5
herds of sheep and cattle in a, 2Ch 32:29
An a of all kinds of wine was Neh 5:18
groves, and fruit trees in a. Neh 9:25
He gives food in a. Jb 36:31
house by the a of Your faithful Ps 5:7
gold—than an a of pure gold; Ps 19:10
filled from the a of Your house; Ps 36:8
has than the a of many wicked Ps 37:16
trusted in the a of his riches, Ps 52:7
but You brought us out to a. Ps 66:12
to the a of His faithful Ps 106:45
and with Him is redemption in a. Ps 130:7
the a of the rich permits him Ec 5:12
and the a of His faithful Is 63:7
the priests their fill with a, Jr 31:14
experience the a of peace and Jr 33:6
Through the a of your trade, Ezk 28:16
an a of every precious thing. Nah 2:9
silver, and clothing in great a. Zch 14:14
is not in the a of his Lk 12:15
may have life and have it in a. Jn 10:10
their a of joy and their deep 2Co 8:2
so that their a may also become 2Co 8:14
hungry, whether in a or in need. Php 4:12
in full, and I have an a. Php 4:18

ABUNDANT *(50)*

this evening and a bread in the Ex 16:8
and his seed will be by a water. Nm 24:7
hands, and you will have a joy. Dt 16:15
open for you His a storehouse, Dt 28:12
the sun and the a yield of the Dt 33:14
he made cedar as a as sycamore 1Kg 10:27
mules, and oxen—a provisions 1Ch 12:40
he made cedar as a as sycamore 2Ch 1:15
he made cedar as a as sycamore 2Ch 9:27
the burnt offerings were a, 2Ch 29:35
they brought an a tenth of 2Ch 31:5
Hezekiah had a riches and glory, 2Ch 32:27
for God gave him a possessions. 2Ch 32:29
In Your a compassion You gave Neh 9:27
in Your a compassion, You Neh 9:31
with Your a goodness You gave Neh 9:35

Its a harvest goes to the kings Neh 9:37
in keeping with Your a, Neh 13:22
wickedness a and aren't your Jb 22:5
in Your presence is a joy; Ps 16:11
and will enjoy a prosperity. Ps 37:11
and boast of their a riches. Ps 49:6
according to Your a compassion, Ps 51:1
You, God, showered a rain; Ps 68:9
In Your a, faithful love, God, Ps 69:13
them drink as a as the depths. Ps 78:15
sent them an a supply of food. Ps 78:25
a in faithful love to all who Ps 86:5
to anger and a in faithful love Ps 86:15
A peace belongs to those who Ps 119:165
praise Him for His a greatness. Ps 150:2
field of the poor yields a food, Pr 13:23
but an a harvest ⌊comes⌋ through Pr 14:4
and from the a milk they give he Is 7:22
who sow seed beside a waters, Is 32:20
Then a spoil will be divided, Is 33:23
Their waves roar like a waters; Jr 51:55
compassion according to His a, Lm 3:32
a willow, a plant by a waters. Ezk 17:5
good field by a waters in order Ezk 17:8
earth with your a wealth and Ezk 27:33
its roots extended to a water. Ezk 31:7
and ⌊its⌋ a waters were Ezk 31:15
its fruit was a, and on it was Dn 4:12
were beautiful and its fruit a— Dn 4:21
but based on Your a compassion. Dn 9:18
harvest is a, but the workers Mt 9:37
The harvest is a, but the Lk 10:2
should know the a love I have 2Co 2:4
But God, who is a in mercy, Eph 2:4

ABUNDANTLY *(7)*

you prosper a with children, Dt 28:11
you prosper a in all the work Dt 30:9
out and shower a on mankind. Jb 36:28
visit the earth and water it a, Ps 65:9
I will a bless its food; Ps 132:15
It will blossom a and will also Is 35:2
poured out on us a through Jesus Ti 3:6

ABUSE *(4)*

and the slave dies under his a, Ex 21:20
in my heart I carry ⌊a⌋ from all Ps 89:50
destruction and Israel to a. Is 43:28
hand me over to them to a me." Jr 38:19

ABUSED *(1)*

raped her and a her all night Jdg 19:25

ABUSIVE *(1)*

not dare bring an a condemnation Jd 9

ABYSS *(10)*

fire, into the a, never again to Ps 140:10
Him not to banish them to the a. Lk 8:31
"Who will go down into the a?" Rm 10:7
shaft of the a was given to him Rv 9:1
He opened the shaft of the a, Rv 9:2
their king the angel of the a; Rv 9:11
up out of the a will make war Rv 11:7
to come up from the a and go to Rv 17:8
the key to the a and a great Rv 20:1
threw him into the a, closed it, Rv 20:3

ACACIA *(32)*

red and manatee skins; a wood; Ex 25:5
are to make an ark of a wood, Ex 25:10
Make poles of a wood and overlay Ex 25:13
to construct a table of a wood, Ex 25:23
the poles of a wood and overlay Ex 25:28
make upright planks of a wood Ex 26:15
five crossbars of a wood for the Ex 26:26
posts of a wood that have gold Ex 26:32
Make five posts of a wood for Ex 26:37
construct the altar of a wood. Ex 27:1
altar, poles of a wood, and Ex 27:6
of incense; make it of a wood. Ex 30:1
the poles of a wood and overlay Ex 30:5
red and manatee skins; a wood; Ex 35:7
who possessed a wood useful for Ex 35:24
made upright planks of a wood Ex 36:20
five crossbars of a wood for the Ex 36:31
four posts of a wood and Ex 36:36
Bezalel made the ark of a wood, Ex 37:1
He made poles of a wood and Ex 37:4
constructed the table of a wood, Ex 37:10
the table from a wood and Ex 37:15
altar of incense out of a wood. Ex 37:25
the poles of a wood and overlaid Ex 37:28
of burnt offering from a wood. Ex 38:1
the poles of a wood and overlaid Ex 38:6
Israel was staying in A Grove, Nm 25:1
Beth-jeshimoth to A Meadows on Nm 33:49
So I made an ark of a wood, Dt 10:3
two men as spies from A Grove, Jos 2:1
morning and left A Grove with Jos 3:1
from A Grove to Gilgal, Mc 6:5

ACACIAS *(2)*

in the desert, a, myrtles, and Is 41:19
house, watering the Valley of A. Jl 3:18

ACCAD *(1)*

Babylon, Erech, A, and Calneh, Gn 10:10

ACCELERATED *(1)*

favor so that he a the process Est 2:9

ACCENT *(1)*

even your a gives you away. Mt 26:73

ACCENTED *(1)*

jewelry for you, a with silver. Sg 1:11

ACCEPT *(68)*

You are to a the seven ewe lambs Gn 21:30
A it from me, and let me bury my Gn 23:13
Its owner must a ⌊the oath⌋, Ex 22:11
a us as Your own possession." Ex 34:9
you do not a My discipline, Lv 26:23
A ⌊these⌋ from them to be used Nm 7:5
must a land in Canaan with you. Nm 32:30
are not to a a ransom for the Nm 35:31
Neither should you a a ransom Nm 35:32
Do not a a bribe, for it blinds Dt 16:19
and a the work of his hands. Dt 33:11
because he won't a boiled meat 1Sm 2:15
which you will a from them. 1Sm 10:4
A this gift your servant has 1Sm 25:27
then may He a an offering. 1Sm 26:19
"May the LORD your God a you." 2Sm 24:23
a a gift from your servant. 2Kg 5:15
Him. I will not a it." Naaman 2Kg 5:16
Naaman urged him to a it, 2Kg 5:16
"Please, a 150 pounds." 2Kg 5:23
Is it a time to a money and 2Kg 5:26
but he did not a ⌊them⌋. Est 4:4
Should we a only good from God Jb 2:10
Don't you a their reports? Jb 21:29
I will surely a his ⌊prayer⌋ and Jb 42:8
your offerings and a your burnt Ps 20:3
I will not a a bull from your Ps 50:9
please a my willing offerings of Ps 119:108
and did not a my correction, Pr 1:25
you a my words and store up my Pr 2:1
A my words, and you will live Pr 4:10
A my instruction instead of Pr 8:10
who grumble will a instruction. Is 29:24
they would not a discipline. Jr 2:30
they refused to a discipline. Jr 5:3
God and would not a discipline. Jr 7:28
So the LORD does not a them. Jr 14:10
offering, I will not a them. Jr 14:12
Will you not a discipline by Jr 35:13
There I will a them and will Ezk 20:40
will a you as a pleasing aroma. Ezk 20:41
live⌋ in you a bribes in order Ezk 22:12
on the altar, and I will a you." Ezk 43:27
flesh, the LORD does not a them. Hs 8:13
⌊our⌋ sin and a what is good, Hs 14:2
offerings, I will not a ⌊them⌋; Am 5:22
fear Me and a correction. Zph 3:7
and I will a no offering from Mal 1:10
Am I to a that from your hands?" Mal 1:13
if you're willing to a it, Mt 11:14
Not everyone can a this saying, Mt 19:11
Let anyone a this who can." Mt 19:12
but you do not a Our testimony. Jn 3:11
I do not a glory from men, Jn 5:41
name, yet you don't a Me. Jn 5:43
in his own name, you will a him. Jn 5:43
teaching is hard! Who can a it?" Jn 6:60
Me and doesn't a My sayings has Jn 12:48
they will not a your testimony Ac 22:18
these men themselves also a, Ac 24:15
A anyone who is weak in faith, Rm 14:1
Therefore a one another, just as Rm 15:7
do⌋, at least a me as a fool, so 2Co 11:16
you will not a any other view. Gl 5:10
because they did not a the love 2Th 2:10
Don't a an accusation against an 1Tm 5:19
me a partner, a him as you would Phm 17
If we a the testimony of men, 1Jn 5:9

ACCEPTABLE *(22)*

it have been a in the LORD's Lv 10:19
heard this, it was a to him. Lv 10:20
has to be unblemished to be a; Lv 22:21
but it is not a as a vow Lv 22:23
on, it will be a as a gift, a Lv 22:27
there they offer a sacrifices. Dt 33:19
of my heart be a to You, Ps 19:14
just is more a to the LORD than Pr 21:3
will be a on My altar, Is 56:7
a fast and a day a to the LORD? Is 58:5
on My altar as an a ⌊sacrifice⌋. Is 60:7
Your burnt offerings are not a; Jr 6:20
who has an ⌊a⌋ male in his flock Mal 1:14
does righteousness is a to Him. Ac 10:35
in this way is a to God and Rm 14:18
of the Gentiles may be a, Rm 15:16
may be a to the saints, Rm 15:31
Food will not make us a to God. 1Co 8:8
an a time, I heard you, and in 2Co 6:2
Look, now is the a time; 2Co 6:2
it is a according to what one 2Co 8:12
sacrifices a to God through 1Pt 2:5

ACCEPTABLY *(1)*

may serve God a, with reverence Heb 12:28

ACCEPTANCE *(4)*

they may find a with the LORD. Ex 28:38
what will their a mean but life Rm 11:15
and deserving of full a: 1Tm 1:15
trustworthy and deserves full a. 1Tm 4:9

ACCEPTED *(29)*

If you do right, won't you be a? Gn 4:7
God's face, since you have a me. Gn 33:10
So Jacob urged him until he a. Gn 33:11
so that he may be a by the LORD. Lv 1:3
so it can be a on his behalf to Lv 1:4
the third day, it will not be a. Lv 7:18
sacrifice it that you may be a. Lv 19:5
thing; it will not be a. Lv 19:7
goats in order for you to be a. Lv 22:19
it will not be a on your behalf. Lv 22:20
will not be a for you because Lv 22:25
it so that you may be a. Lv 22:29
the LORD so that you may be a; Lv 23:11
He wouldn't have a the burnt Jdg 13:23
David a what she had brought 1Sm 25:35
and the LORD a Job's ⌊prayer⌋. Jb 42:9
God has already a your works. Ec 9:7
she has not a discipline. Zph 3:2
No prophet is a in his hometown. Lk 4:24
So he a ⌊the offer⌋ and started Lk 22:6
The one who has a His testimony Jn 3:33
So those who a his message were Ac 2:41
who does, because God has a him. Rm 14:3
just as the Messiah also a you, Rm 15:7
For he a our urging and, being 2Co 8:17
you had not a, you put up with 2Co 11:4
with the prisoners and a with Heb 10:34
deceived those who a the mark of Rv 19:20
and who had not a the mark on Rv 20:4

ACCEPTING *(7)*

lightly by not a from him what 2Kg 5:20
not listening or a discipline. Jr 17:23
While a glory from one another, Jn 5:44
with patience, a one another in Eph 4:2
a one another and forgiving one Col 3:13
tortured, not a release, so that Heb 11:35
sake of the name, a nothing from 3Jn 7

ACCEPTS *(6)*

If it a your offer of peace and Dt 20:11
is the one who a a bribe to kill Dt 27:25
the LORD a my prayer. Ps 6:9
A wise heart a commands, but Pr 10:8
but the one who a rebuke will be Pr 13:18
yet no one a His testimony. Jn 3:32

ACCESS *(10)*

to deny anyone a to Judah's King 1Kg 15:17
in order to deny anyone's a— 2Ch 16:1
excluded from a to the LORD's 2Ch 26:21
who had personal a to the king Est 1:14
My roots will have a to water, Jb 29:19
also grant you a among these who Zch 3:7
we have obtained a by faith into Rm 5:2
we both have a by one Spirit to Eph 2:18

have boldness, a, and confidence Eph 3:12
claiming a to a visionary realm Col 2:18

ACCIDENTALLY *(4)*
his neighbor a without Dt 4:42
his neighbor a without Dt 19:4
or a may flee there. Jos 20:3
his neighbor a and did not hate Jos 20:5

ACCLAIMED *(1)*
synagogues, being a by everyone. Lk 4:15

ACCO *(1)*
the residents of A or of Sidon, Jdg 1:31

ACCOMMODATE *(2)*
was too small to a the burnt 1Kg 8:64
made could not a the burnt 2Ch 7:7

ACCOMPANIED *(19)*
commanders who had a him, Jos 10:24
to one of the men who had a him. Jdg 14:20
her to one of the men who a you. Jdg 15:2
a by her two daughters-in-law, Ru 1:7
a by 3,000 of the choice men of 1Sm 26:2
from Rogelim and a the king to 2Sm 19:31
1,000 commanders a by 37,000 1Ch 12:34
voices with joy a by musical 1Ch 15:16
who were to prophesy a by lyres, 1Ch 25:1
their⌋ voices, a by trumpets, 2Ch 5:13
a by the instruments of David 2Ch 29:27
temple servants a ⌊him⌋ to Ezr 7:7
and singing a by cymbals, Neh 12:27
out the capstone a by shouts Zch 4:7
turned back and no longer a Him. Jn 6:66
the men who have a us during the Ac 1:21
six brothers a me, and we went Ac 11:12
He was a by Sopater, son of Ac 20:4
the right to be a by a Christian 1Co 9:5

ACCOMPANIES *(1)*
but trouble a the income of the Pr 15:6

ACCOMPANIMENT *(1)*
prophesying to the a of lyres, 1Ch 25:3

ACCOMPANY *(8)*
they brought 30 men to a him. Jdg 14:11
descent must a the Levites when Neh 10:38
for this will a him in his labor Ec 8:15
with Him, and His gifts a Him. Is 40:10
not let anyone a Him except Mk 5:37
these signs will a those who Mk 16:17
a them with no doubts at all, Ac 10:20
the churches to a us with this 2Co 8:19

ACCOMPANYING *(4)*
will offer the a grain offering Nm 6:17
her five female servants a her, 1Sm 25:42
and half of the officials a me, Neh 12:40
the word by the a signs. Mk 16:20

ACCOMPLISH *(14)*
the LORD of Hosts will a this. 2Kg 19:31
He will certainly a what He has Jb 23:14
pleasure, "What does this a?" Ec 2:2
the LORD of Hosts will a this. Is 9:7
the LORD of Hosts will a this.' Is 37:32
he will a His will against Is 48:14
but it will a what I please, Is 55:11
I will a it quickly in its time. Is 60:22
I watch over My word to a it." Jr 1:12
morning light they a it because Mc 2:1
He was about to a in Jerusalem. Lk 9:31
the Father has given Me to a. Jn 5:36
the Lord, so that you can a it." Col 4:17
anger does not a God's Jms 1:20

ACCOMPLISHED *(22)*
all the work they had a. Ex 39:43
You have a this great victory Jdg 15:18
who a such a great deliverance 1Sm 14:45
this task had been a by our God. Neh 6:16
It will be a before his time, Jb 15:32
and a in the sight of everyone Ps 31:19
the work You a in their days, Ps 44:1
all that I had a and what I had Ec 2:11
for You have a wonders, plans Is 25:1
so My arm a victory for Me, Is 63:5
what the LORD our God has a. Jr 51:10
both planned and a what He has Jr 51:12
He has a His decree, which He Lm 2:17
what has been decreed will be a. Dn 11:36
the law until all things are a. Mt 5:18
about the Son of Man will be a. Lk 18:31
may be shown to be a by God." Jn 3:21
You've a nothing. Jn 12:19
was now a that the Scripture Jn 19:28
would be a in us who do not Rm 8:4
what Christ has a through me to Rm 15:18
beast until God's words are a. Rv 17:17

ACCOMPLISHES *(1)*
nor uncircumcision a anything; Gl 5:6

ACCOMPLISHING *(2)*
a everything He commands them Jb 37:12
Both hands are good at a evil: Mc 7:3

ACCOMPLISHMENTS *(28)*
with all his a and his wisdom, 1Kg 11:41
with all his a, are written 1Kg 14:29
with all his a, are written 1Kg 15:7
might, all his a, and the cities 1Kg 15:23
with all his a, are written 1Kg 15:31
along with all his a and might, 1Kg 16:5
with all his a, are written 1Kg 16:14
along with his a and the might 1Kg 16:27
with all his a, the ivory palace 1Kg 22:39
along with his a, are written 2Kg 1:18
with all his a, are written 2Kg 8:23
with all his a and all his might 2Kg 10:34
with all his a, are written 2Kg 12:19
with all his a and his might, 2Kg 13:8
with all his a and the power he 2Kg 13:12
along with his a, his might, and 2Kg 14:15
with all his a and the power he 2Kg 14:28
with all his a, are written 2Kg 15:6
with all his a, are written 2Kg 15:21
with all his a, they are written 2Kg 15:26
with all his a, they are written 2Kg 15:31
with all his a, are written 2Kg 15:36
along with his a, are written 2Kg 16:19
with all his a and the sin that 2Kg 21:17
along with his a, are written 2Kg 21:25
with all his a, are written 2Kg 23:28
with all his a, are written 2Kg 24:5
and magnificent a and the Est 10:2

ACCORDANCE *(4)*
Give me life in a with Your Ps 119:88
stand today in a with Your Ps 119:91
them in a with the news that Hs 7:12
spirit of faith in a with what 2Co 4:13

ACCORDING *(403)*
(See pp. xi-xii.)

ACCORDINGLY *(5)*
And we answered him a. Gn 43:7
they were divided ⌊a⌋: 1Ch 24:4
pleased the king, and he did a. Est 2:4
if we don't act a, may the LORD Jr 42:5
tell it to us, and we'll act a.' Jr 42:20

ACCOUNT *(45)*
life will be spared on your a." Gn 12:13
"I will not do ⌊it⌋ on a of 40." Gn 18:29
not destroy ⌊it⌋ on a of 20." Gn 18:31
not destroy ⌊it⌋ on a of 10." Gn 18:32
household on a of Sarah, Gn 20:18
will kill me on a of Rebekah, Gn 26:7
I might die on a of her." Gn 26:9
Now we must a for his blood!" Gn 42:22
him, "Are you jealous on my a? Nm 11:29
with me on a of you and would Dt 3:26
was angry with me on your a. Dt 4:21
to all these nations on your a, Jos 23:3
back on your a and drive them Jos 23:5
Gideon heard the a of the dream Jdg 7:15
is the a of the forced labor 1Kg 9:15
the LORD see and demand an a." 2Ch 24:22
and the detailed a of Mordecai's Est 10:2
earth be abandoned on your a, Jb 18:4
Him when He calls ⌊me⌋ to a? Jb 31:14
give Him an a of all my steps; Jb 31:37
"You will not demand an a." Ps 10:13
wickedness into a until nothing Ps 10:15
rebellion to a with the rod, Ps 89:32
and they do not take Me into a. Jr 9:3
a of the day that is coming to Jr 47:4
grew proud on a of its height, Ezk 31:10
I made Lebanon mourn on a of it, Ezk 31:15
he will die on a of this. Ezk 33:18
the nations on a of famine. Ezk 36:30
into exile on a of their Ezk 39:23
here is the summary of his a. Dn 7:1
So on your a, the skies have Hg 1:10
will have to a for every Mt 12:36
him in prison on a of Herodias, Mt 14:3
him in prison on a of Herodias, Mk 6:17
Give an a of your management, Lk 16:2
things to you on a of My name, Jn 15:21
to one's a when there is no Rm 5:13
us will give an a of himself to Rm 14:12
that is increasing to your a. Php 4:17
anything, charge that to my a. Phm 18
Him to whom we must give an a. Heb 4:13
as those who will give an a, Heb 13:17
will give an a to the One who 1Pt 4:5
been forgiven on a of His name. 1Jn 2:12

ACCOUNTABILITY *(1)*
There is no a, ⌊since⌋ God does Ps 10:4

ACCOUNTABLE *(8)*
You can hold me personally a! Gn 43:9
servant became a to my father Gn 44:32
will hold them a for their sin. Ex 32:34
I will hold a whoever does not Dt 18:19
hold us a if ⌊we intended Jos 22:23
LORD hold David's enemies a." 1Sm 20:16
the watchman a for their blood. Ezk 33:6
would be a to them so that Dn 6:2

ACCOUNTANT *(1)*
Where is the a? Where is the Is 33:18

ACCOUNTANTS *(1)*
of silver to the a for deposit Est 3:9

ACCOUNTING *(3)*
No a was required from the men 2Kg 12:15
But no a is to be required from 2Kg 22:7
One who seeks an a for bloodshed Ps 9:12

ACCOUNTS *(4)*
But on the day I settle a, Ex 32:34
to settle a with his slaves Mt 18:23
When he began to settle a, Mt 18:24
came and settled a with them. Mt 25:19

ACCUMULATE *(1)*
will a teachers for themselves 2Tm 4:3

ACCUMULATED *(3)*
all the possessions they had a, Gn 12:5
Solomon a 1,400 chariots and 1Kg 10:26
Solomon a 1,400 chariots and 2Ch 1:14

ACCUMULATING *(1)*
gathering and a in order to give Ec 2:26

ACCURATE *(3)*
back to me with a information, 1Sm 23:23
God weigh me with an a balance, Jb 31:6
but an a weight is His delight. Pr 11:1

ACCURATELY *(4)*
sayings and to a write words of Ec 12:10
taught the things about Jesus a, Ac 18:25
the way of God to him more a. Ac 18:26
Since Felix was a informed about Ac 24:22

ACCURSED *(4)*
proud, the a, who wander from Ps 119:21
and the a short measure Mc 6:10
doesn't know the law, is a!" Jn 7:49
trained in greed. A children! 2Pt 2:14

ACCUSATION *(11)*
Stay far away from a false a. Ex 23:7
But if this a is true and no Dt 22:20
the king make an a against your 1Sm 22:15
angry about Ish-bosheth's a. 2Sm 3:8
in the land wrote an a against Ezr 4:6
will refute any a raised against Is 54:17
from anyone by force or false a; Lk 3:14
who received an a that his Lk 16:1
though I had any a against my Ac 28:19
Who can bring an a against God's Rm 8:33
Don't accept an a against an 1Tm 5:19

ACCUSATIONS *(2)*
You record bitter a against me Jb 13:26
found out that the a were about Ac 23:29

ACCUSE *(22)*
but now you a me of wrongdoing 2Sm 3:8
will not a ⌊me⌋ as long as I Jb 27:6
will not always a ⌊us⌋ or be Ps 103:9
In return for my love they a me, Ps 109:4
Don't a anyone without cause, Pr 3:30
with ⌊their⌋ speech, a a person Is 29:21
For I will not a ⌊you⌋ forever, Is 57:16
and maliciously a the Jews. Dn 3:8
at his right side to a him. Zch 3:1
And in order to a Him they asked Mt 12:10
In order to a Him, they were Mk 3:2

priests began to **a** Him of many Mk 15:3
They began to **a** Him, saying, "We Lk 23:2
man with those things you **a** Him Lk 23:14
that I will **a** you to the Father Jn 5:45
might have evidence to **a** Him. Jn 8:6
began to **a** him and said: Ac 24:2
these things of which we **a** him." Ac 24:8
you go down with me and **a** him, Ac 25:5
nothing to what these men **a** me Ac 25:11
thoughts either **a** or excuse them Rm 2:15
no opportunity to **a** us. 1Tm 5:14

ACCUSED *(12)*
harshly to us and **a** us of spying Gn 42:30
who has falsely **a** his brother, Dt 19:18
has **a** her of shameful conduct, Dt 22:17
I **a** the nobles and officials, Neh 5:7
had maliciously **a** Daniel were Dn 6:24
He was being **a** by the chief Mt 27:12
Paul was being **a** by the Jews, Ac 22:30
man up before the **a** confronts Ac 25:16
I am **a** of by the Jews, Ac 26:2
hope I am being **a** by the Jews, Ac 26:7
children not **a** of wildness Ti 1:6
that when you are **a**, those who 1Pt 3:16

ACCUSER *(3)*
an **a** stand at his right hand. Ps 109:6
a is Moses, on whom you have Jn 5:45
because the **a** of our brothers Rv 12:10

ACCUSERS *(8)*
be the LORD's payment to my **a**, Ps 109:20
an object of ridicule to my **a**; Ps 109:25
My **a** will be clothed with Ps 109:29
ordered his **a** to state their Ac 23:30
whenever your **a** get here too." Ac 23:35
commanding his **a** to come to you. Ac 24:7
confronts the **a** face to face and Ac 25:16
the **a** stood up and brought no Ac 25:18

ACCUSES *(2)*
and **a** ⌊her⌋ of shameful conduct, Dt 22:14
one who **a** them before our God Rv 12:10

ACCUSING *(4)*
someone **a** him of a crime, Dt 19:16
how many things they are **a** You Mk 15:4
stood by, vehemently **a** Him. Lk 23:10
for which they were **a** him, Ac 23:28

ACCUSTOMED *(1)*
as young men were **a** to do. Jdg 14:10

ACHAIA *(10)*
While Gallio was proconsul of **A**, Ac 18:12
he wanted to cross over to **A**, Ac 18:27
Macedonia and **A** and go to Ac 19:21
Macedonia and **A** were pleased to Rm 15:26
firstfruits of **A** and have 1Co 16:15
the saints who are throughout **A**. 2Co 1:1
A has been prepared since last 2Co 9:2
be stopped in the regions of **A**. 2Co 11:10
believers in Macedonia and **A**. 1Th 1:7
not only in Macedonia and **A**, 1Th 1:8

ACHAICUS *(1)*
Fortunatus, and **A**, because these 1Co 16:17

ACHAN *(6)*
A son of Carmi, son of Zabdi, Jos 7:1
man by man, and **A** son of Carmi, Jos 7:18
Joshua said to **A**, "My son, give Jos 7:19
A replied to Joshua, "It is true. Jos 7:20
with him took **A** son of Zerah, Jos 7:24
Wasn't **A** son of Zerah unfaithful Jos 22:20

ACHAR *(1)*
A, who brought trouble on Israel 1Ch 2:7

ACHBOR *(7)*
Baal-hanan son of **A** ruled in his Gn 36:38
When Baal-hanan son of **A** died, Gn 36:39
of Shaphan, **A** son of Micaiah, 2Kg 22:12
the priest, Ahikam, **A**, Shaphan, 2Kg 22:14
Baal-hanan son of **A** ruled in his 1Ch 1:49
Elnathan son of **A** and ⌊certain Jr 26:22
Elnathan son of **A**, Gemariah son Jr 36:12

ACHIEVE *(3)*
so that they **a** no success. Jb 5:12
do not let them **a** their goals. Ps 140:8
and what I had labored to **a**, Ec 2:11

ACHIEVED *(3)*
LORD and your plans will be **a**. Pr 16:3
they had **a** their purpose; Ac 27:13
has not **a** the law. Rm 9:31

ACHIEVEMENTS *(1)*
I increased my **a**. Ec 2:4

ACHIM *(2)*
Zadok fathered **A**, Achim fathered Mt 1:14
Achim, **A** fathered Eliud, Mt 1:14

ACHISH *(20)*
and went to King **A** of Gath. 1Sm 21:10
very afraid of King **A** of Gath, 1Sm 21:12
A said to his servants. 1Sm 21:14
men and went to **A** son of Maoch, 1Sm 27:2
his men stayed with **A** in Gath. 1Sm 27:3
David said to **A**, "If I have 1Sm 27:5
That day **A** gave Ziklag to him, 1Sm 27:6
Then he came back to **A**, 1Sm 27:9
So **A** trusted David, thinking, 1Sm 27:12
A said to David, "You know, of 1Sm 28:1
replied to **A**, "Good, you will 1Sm 28:2
So **A** said to David, "Very well, 1Sm 28:2
in review⌋ behind them with **A**. 1Sm 29:2
A answered the Philistine 1Sm 29:3
enraged with **A** and told him, 1Sm 29:4
A summoned David and told him, 1Sm 29:6
David replied to **A**. 1Sm 29:8
A answered David, "I'm convinced 1Sm 29:9
ran away to **A** son of Maacah, 1Kg 2:39
and set out to **A** at Gath to 1Kg 2:40

ACHISH'S *(1)*
But **A** servants said to him, 1Sm 21:11

ACHOR *(5)*
them up to the Valley of **A**. Jos 7:24
the Valley of **A** to this day. Jos 7:26
to Debir from the Valley of **A**, Jos 15:7
and the Valley of **A** a place for Is 65:10
the Valley of **A** into a gateway Hs 2:15

ACHSAH *(5)*
give my daughter **A** as a wife to Jos 15:16
his daughter **A** to him as a wife Jos 15:17
my daughter **A** to him as a wife. Jdg 1:12
gave his daughter **A** to him as Jdg 1:13
Caleb's daughter was **A**. 1Ch 2:49

ACHSHAPH *(3)*
the kings of Shimron and **A**, Jos 11:1
one the king of **A** one Jos 12:20
Helkath, Hali, Beten, **A**, Jos 19:25

ACHZIB *(4)*
Keilah, **A**, and Mareshah—nine Jos 15:44
the sea, including Mahalab, **A**, Jos 19:29
or Ahlab, **A**, Helbah, Aphik, Jdg 1:31
the houses of **A** are a deception Mc 1:14

ACKNOWLEDGE *(18)*
He must **a** the firstborn, the son Dt 21:17
'Today I **a** to the LORD your God Dt 26:3
brothers and didn't **a** his sons, Dt 33:9
on the nations that don't **a** You, Ps 79:6
A that the LORD is God. Ps 100:3
Will you not **a** it? Is 48:6
a what you have done. Jr 2:23
Only **a** your guilt—you have Jr 3:13
We **a** our wickedness, LORD, the Jr 14:20
until you **a** that the Most High Dn 4:25
as soon as you **a** that Heaven Dn 4:26
until you **a** that the Most High Dn 4:32
greatly honor those who **a** him, Dn 11:39
so that you may **a** the LORD's Mc 6:5
who will **a** Me before men, Mt 10:32
I will also **a** him before My Mt 10:32
of Man will also **a** him before Lk 12:8
but will **a** his name before My Rv 3:5

ACKNOWLEDGED *(5)*
has sinned and **a** ⌊his⌋ guilt— Lv 6:4
Then I **a** my sin to You and did Ps 32:5
the sky until he **a** that the Most Dn 5:21
they **a** God's way of Lk 7:29
a the grace that had been given Gl 2:9

ACKNOWLEDGES *(3)*
on the day he **a** ⌊his⌋ guilt. Lv 6:5
and **a** the truth in his heart— Ps 15:2
anyone who **a** Me before men, Lk 12:8

ACQUAINTANCE *(1)*
disciple was an **a** of the high Jn 18:15

ACQUAINTANCES *(3)*
my **a** have abandoned me. Jb 19:13
and former **a** came to his house Jb 42:11
I am an object of dread to my **a**; Ps 31:11

ACQUIRE *(12)*
about, and **a** property in it. Gn 34:10
only land he didn't **a** was that Gn 47:22
he must not **a** many horses for Dt 17:16
back to Egypt to **a** many horses, Dt 17:16
He must not **a** many wives for Dt 17:17
He must not **a** very large amounts Dt 17:17
you will also **a** Ruth the Ru 4:5
will also **a** Ruth the Moabitess, Ru 4:10
A wisdom—how much better it is Pr 16:16
And **a** understanding—it is Pr 16:16
What you **a**, you cannot save, and Mc 6:14
as deacons **a** a good standing 1Tm 3:13

ACQUIRED *(20)*
the people he had **a** in Haran, Gn 12:5
and Abram **a** flocks and herds, Gn 12:16
he had **a** in Paddan-aram, Gn 31:18
the property he had **a** in Canaan; Gn 36:6
they had **a** in the land Gn 46:6
Joseph **a** all the land in Egypt Gn 47:20
that I have **a** you and your land Gn 47:23
They **a** property in it and became Gn 47:27
country of Ephraim **a** a woman Jdg 19:1
went to Ophir and **a** gold there— 1Kg 9:28
He **a** 18 wives and 60 concubines 2Ch 11:21
Abijah grew strong, **a** 14 wives, 2Ch 13:21
Jehoiada **a** two wives for him, 2Ch 24:3
and he **a** herds of sheep and 2Ch 32:29
my own hand has **a** ⌊so⌋ much, Jb 31:25
the mountain His right hand **a**. Ps 78:54
I **a** male and female servants and Ec 2:7
you have **a** wealth for yourself. Ezk 28:4
You have **a** gold and silver for Ezk 28:4
Now this man **a** a field with his Ac 1:18

ACQUIRES *(5)*
wisdom and who **a** understanding, Pr 3:13
to correction **a** good sense, Pr 15:32
of the discerning **a** knowledge, Pr 18:15
The one who **a** good sense loves Pr 19:8
a wise man, he **a** knowledge. Pr 21:11

ACQUIRING *(2)*
Abner kept **a** more power in the 2Sm 3:6
who have been **a** cattle and Ezk 38:12

ACQUIT *(3)*
I know You will not **a** me. Jb 9:28
and would not **a** me of my Jb 10:14
who **a** the guilty for a bribe and Is 5:23

ACQUITTED *(2)*
and such a talker be **a**? Jb 11:2
For by your words you will be **a**, Mt 12:37

ACQUITTING *(1)*
A the guilty and condemning the Pr 17:15

ACROSS *(83)*
(See pp. xi-xii.)

ACT *(83)*
so that this **a** will serve as my Gn 21:30
Pharaoh must not **a** deceptively Ex 8:29
is caught in the **a** of breaking Ex 22:2
must not **a** deceptively or lie Lv 19:11
You must not **a** unjustly when Lv 19:15
You must not **a** unfairly in Lv 19:35
If you **a** with hostility toward Lv 26:21
but **a** with hostility toward Me, Lv 26:23
then I will **a** with hostility Lv 26:24
not obey Me but **a** with hostility Lv 26:27
I will **a** with furious hostility Lv 26:28
she wasn't caught ⌊in the **a**⌋; Nm 5:13
He speak and not **a**, or promise Nm 23:19
not to **a** corruptly and make an Dt 4:16
and if you **a** corruptly, make Dt 4:25
can no longer **a** as your leader. Dt 31:2
Israelites would **a** even more Jdg 2:19
With one **a** of vengeance, let me Jdg 16:28
this one to **a** crazy around me? 1Sm 21:15
balsam trees, **a** decisively, for 2Sm 5:24
A like a woman who has been 2Sm 14:2
saying, "Why do you **a** this way?" 1Kg 1:6
A according to your wisdom, 1Kg 2:6
may You hear in heaven and **a**. 1Kg 8:32
You forgive, **a**, and repay the 1Kg 8:39
may You hear in heaven and **a**. 2Ch 6:23
officials ⌊to **a**⌋ against them to Ezr 4:5
about the queen's **a** will say Est 1:18
given to Mordecai for this ⌊**a**⌋?" Est 6:3
the Almighty ⌊to **a**⌋ unjustly. Jb 34:10
that God does not **a** wickedly Jb 34:12

I will no ⌊longer⌋ **a** wickedly. Jb 34:31
who **a** treacherously without Ps 25:3
trust in Him, and He will **a**, Ps 37:5
It is time for the LORD to **a**, Ps 119:126
it is ⌊an **a** of⌋ faithful love; Ps 141:5
than to **a** important but have no Pr 12:9
the wicked **a** disgustingly and Pr 13:5
because they refuse to **a** justly. Pr 21:7
a criminal **a** is not carried out Ec 8:11
will bring every **a** to judgment, Ec 12:14
the youth will **a** arrogantly Is 3:5
The treacherous **a** treacherously; Is 24:16
I **a**, and who can reverse it?" Is 43:13
will **a** for My own sake, indeed, Is 48:11
See, My servant will **a** wisely; Is 52:13
so I will **a** because of My Is 65:8
if you **a** justly toward one Jr 7:5
us, LORD, **a** for Your name's Jr 14:7
will continue to **a** according to Jr 18:12
this detestable **a** causing Judah Jr 32:35
if we don't **a** accordingly, Jr 42:5
to us, and we'll **a** accordingly.' Jr 42:20
and they will **a** foolishly. Jr 50:36
LORD, have spoken, and I will **a**. Ezk 22:14
not for your sake that I will **a**, Ezk 36:22
for your sake that I will **a**"— Ezk 36:32
Lord, listen and **a**! My God, for Dn 9:19
with him, he will **a** deceitfully. Dn 11:23
those who **a** wickedly toward Dn 11:32
but the wicked will **a** wickedly; Dn 12:10
will **a** the same way toward you. Hs 3:3
one **a** of bloodshed follows Hs 4:2
they **a** promiscuously in Hs 4:12
your daughters **a** promiscuously Hs 4:13
when they **a** promiscuously Hs 4:14
Israel, if you **a** promiscuously, Hs 4:15
Only to **a** justly, to love Mc 6:8
Why then do we **a** treacherously Mal 2:10
and do not **a** treacherously Mal 2:15
and do not **a** treacherously. Mal 2:16
and doesn't **a** on them will be Mt 7:26
and does not **a** is like a man who Lk 6:49
caught in the **a** of committing Jn 8:4
one righteous **a** there is Rm 5:18
committed this **a** might be 1Co 5:2
you **a** unjustly and cheat— 1Co 6:8
does not **a** improperly; is not 1Co 13:5
to will and to **a** for His good Php 2:13
people ought to **a** in God's 1Tm 3:15
Every generous **a** and every Jms 1:17
Speak and **a** as those who will be Jms 2:12
authority to **a** for 42 months. Rv 13:5

ACTED *(55)*

daughters. You have **a** foolishly. Gn 31:28
The Israelites **a** on Moses' word Ex 12:35
the Egyptians **a** arrogantly Ex 18:11
because he has **a** treacherously Ex 21:8
land of Egypt have **a** corruptly. Ex 32:7
They have **a** perversely; Lv 20:12
and how they **a** with hostility Lv 26:40
and I **a** with hostility toward Lv 26:41
out of Egypt have **a** corruptly. Dt 9:12
His people have **a** corruptly Dt 32:5
a deceptively. They gathered Jos 9:4
Now if you have **a** faithfully and Jdg 9:16
you have **a** faithfully and Jdg 9:19
He **a** like a madman around them, 1Sm 21:13
You **a** in secret, but I will do 2Sm 12:12
has sinned and **a** very wickedly. 1Ch 21:17
He **a** unfaithfully against the 2Ch 26:16
for you have **a** unfaithfully! 2Ch 26:18
We have **a** corruptly toward You Neh 1:7
But our ancestors **a** arrogantly; Neh 9:16
but they **a** arrogantly and would Neh 9:29
because You have **a** faithfully, Neh 9:33
while we have **a** wickedly. Neh 9:33
You who have **a** on our behalf. Ps 68:28
who hate You have **a** arrogantly. Ps 83:2
gone astray and have **a** wickedly. Ps 106:6
have spoken and **a** against the Is 3:8
heavens, for the LORD has **a**; Is 44:23
Suddenly I **a**, and they occurred. Is 48:3
when they **a** so abhorrently? Jr 6:15
when they **a** so abhorrently? Jr 8:12
inheritance has **a** toward Me like Jr 12:8
for she has **a** arrogantly against Jr 50:29
you have **a** according to the Ezk 11:12
they have **a** unfaithfully." Ezk 15:8
your beauty and **a** like a Ezk 16:15
But I **a** for the sake of My name, Ezk 20:9
But I **a** because of My name, Ezk 20:14
hand and **a** because of My name Ezk 20:22
who **a** like prostitutes in Egypt, Ezk 23:3
Oholah **a** like a prostitute even Ezk 23:5
youth when she **a** like a Ezk 23:19
you because you **a** like a Ezk 23:30
Because Edom **a** vengefully Ezk 25:12
the Philistines **a** in vengeance Ezk 25:15
done wrong, **a** wickedly, rebelled Dn 9:5
have sinned, we have **a** wickedly. Dn 9:15
conceived them and **a** shamefully. Hs 2:5
you have **a** promiscuously; Hs 5:3
for you have **a** promiscuously, Hs 9:1
have taunted and **a** arrogantly Zph 2:10
Judah has **a** treacherously, Mal 2:11
You have **a** treacherously against Mal 2:14
because he had **a** astutely. Lk 16:8
that I had **a** in unbelief, 1Tm 1:13

ACTING *(11)*

but he's **a** like a judge! Gn 19:9
has been **a** like a prostitute, Gn 38:24
You are still **a** arrogantly Ex 9:17
Jehu was **a** deceptively in order 2Kg 10:19
terrible evil and **a** unfaithfully Neh 13:27
has stopped **a** wisely and doing Ps 36:3
who has been **a** like a prophet Jr 29:27
against Me by **a** faithlessly, Ezk 14:13
My ordinances, **a** faithfully. Ezk 18:9
They are all **a** contrary to Ac 17:7
man thinks he is **a** improperly 1Co 7:36

ACTION *(14)*

Let us take **a** and build an altar Jos 22:26
Now take **a**, because the LORD has 2Sm 3:18
Be strong and take **a**!" Ezr 10:4
For the queen's **a** will become Est 1:17
hand is lifted up ⌊to take **a**⌋, Is 26:11
He will take **a** against them and Dn 11:7
he will take **a**, then return to Dn 11:28
the holy covenant and take **a**. Dn 11:30
God will be strong and take **a**. Dn 11:32
agreed with their plan and **a**. Lk 23:51
powerful in **a** and speech before Lk 24:19
Then the high priest took **a**. Ac 5:17
Your every ⌊**a**⌋ must be done with 1Co 16:14
get your minds ready for **a**, 1Pt 1:13

ACTIONS *(39)*

of your **a** in abandoning Me. Dt 28:20
of knowledge, and **a** are weighed 1Sm 2:3
about your evil **a** from all these 1Sm 2:23
a have been a great advantage 1Sm 19:4
see if Mordecai's **a** would be Est 3:4
from his⌋ **a** and suppress his Jb 33:17
their **a** are revolting. Ps 14:1
done and meditate on Your **a**. Ps 77:12
by their **a** and prostituted Ps 106:39
words and gracious in all His **a**. Ps 145:13
a young man is known by his **a**— Pr 20:11
who get what the **a** of the wicked Ec 8:14
get what the **a** of the righteous Ec 8:14
do not perceive the LORD's **a**, Is 5:12
of life and your **a** have brought Jr 4:18
change your ways and your **a**, Jr 7:5
according to what his **a** deserve. Jr 17:10
way of life, and correct your **a**. Jr 35:15
will bring their **a** down on their Ezk 9:10
will bring their **a** down on their Ezk 11:21
observe their conduct and **a**. Ezk 14:22
you see their conduct and **a**, Ezk 14:23
also bring your **a** down on your Ezk 16:43
sins are revealed in all your **a**, Ezk 21:24
brought their **a** down on their Ezk 22:31
it with their conduct and **a**. Ezk 36:17
to their conduct and **a**. Ezk 36:19
Their **a** do not allow ⌊them⌋ to Hs 5:4
because of their evil, wicked **a**. Hs 9:15
will repay him based on his **a**. Hs 12:2
God saw their **a**—that they had Jnh 3:10
and as a result of their **a**. Mc 7:13
more corrupt in all their **a**. Zph 3:7
greed, evil **a**, deceit, lewdness, Mk 7:22
powerful in his speech and **a**. Ac 7:22
we will be in **a** when present. 2Co 10:11
which ⌊leads to⌋ reckless **a**, Eph 5:18
in mind because of your evil **a**. Col 1:21
they did not repent of their **a**. Rv 16:11

ACTIVE *(3)*

the same God is **a** in everyone 1Co 12:6
same Spirit is **a** in all these, 1Co 12:11
that faith was **a** together with Jms 2:22

ACTIVITIES *(8)*

in all his **a** because the LORD 1Sm 18:14
out about your **a** and everything 2Sm 3:25
about their daily **a** because the 2Ch 15:5
Commit your **a** to the LORD and Pr 16:3
over the **a** of her household Pr 31:27
for a person to enjoy his **a**, Ec 3:22
And there are different **a**, 1Co 12:6
away while pursuing his **a**. Jms 1:11

ACTIVITY *(6)*

a of the wicked leads to sin. Pr 10:16
a time for every **a** under heaven: Ec 3:1
time for every **a** and every work. Ec 3:17
not seen the evil **a** that is done Ec 4:3
every **a** there is a right time Ec 8:6
to observe the **a** that is done Ec 8:16

ACTS *(89)*

arm and great **a** of judgment. Ex 6:6
of Egypt by great **a** of judgment. Ex 7:4
a person willfully **a** against his Ex 21:14
not forgive your **a** of rebellion, Ex 23:21
impurities and rebellious **a**. Lv 16:16
wrongdoings and rebellious **a**— Lv 16:21
person **a** unfaithfully toward Nm 5:6
penalty for your **a** of Nm 14:33
the person who **a** in error Nm 15:28
for the person who **a** in error, Nm 15:29
But the person who **a** defiantly, Nm 15:30
deeds and mighty **a** like Yours? Dt 3:24
The person who **a** arrogantly, Dt 17:12
such things and **a** unfairly is Dt 25:16
for all the mighty ⌊**a** of⌋ power Dt 34:12
the righteous **a** of the LORD, Jdg 5:11
the righteous **a** He has done for 1Sm 12:7
for them great and awesome **a**, 2Sm 7:23
most detestable **a** by going after 1Kg 21:26
my youth or my **a** of rebellion; Ps 25:7
He **a** violently against those at Ps 55:20
His **a** toward mankind are Ps 66:5
one who goes on in his guilty **a**. Ps 68:21
and my guilty **a** are not hidden Ps 69:5
of the mighty **a** of the Lord GOD; Ps 71:16
saving **a** on the earth. Ps 74:12
the former **a** of Your faithful Ps 89:49
No one who **a** deceitfully will Ps 101:7
LORD executes **a** of righteousness Ps 103:6
LORD's mighty **a** or proclaim all Ps 106:2
Your many **a** of faithful love; Ps 106:7
the LORD's **a** of faithful love. Ps 107:43
perform reckless **a** with men who Ps 141:4
the evil **a** of the wicked. Ps 141:5
and will proclaim Your mighty **a**. Ps 145:4
of Your mighty **a** and of the Ps 145:12
ways and gracious in all His **a**. Ps 145:17
Praise Him for His powerful **a**; Ps 150:2
the merciful **a** of the wicked are Pr 12:10
sensible person **a** knowledgeably, Pr 13:16
quick-tempered man **a** foolishly, Pr 14:17
and the one who **a** hastily sins. Pr 19:2
named "Mocker," **a** with excessive Pr 21:24
observed all the **a** of oppression Ec 4:1
for his arrogant **a** and the proud Is 10:12
treacherous one **a** treacherously, Is 21:2
land he **a** unjustly and does Is 26:10
violent **a** are in their hands. Is 59:6
and⌋ the LORD's praiseworthy **a**, Is 63:7
who **a** on behalf of the one who Is 64:4
all our righteous **a** are like a Is 64:6
anyone who **a** justly, who seeks Jr 5:1
their rebellious **a** are many, Jr 5:6
guilty **a** have diverted these Jr 5:25
doing all these detestable **a**! Jr 7:10
I have seen your detestable **a**. Jr 13:27
to you because of your evil **a**"— Jr 23:2
madman who **a** like a prophet. Jr 29:26
the detestable **a** you have Jr 44:22
the righteous **a** he did will not Ezk 3:20
and **a** of prostitution Ezk 16:22
in promiscuous **a** with Egyptian Ezk 16:26
the **a** of a brazen prostitute, Ezk 16:30
women in your **a** of prostitution; Ezk 16:34
by your **a** of prostitution Ezk 16:36
immoral **a** in addition to Ezk 16:43
the righteous **a** he did will be Ezk 18:24

your evil ways and corrupt a." Ezk 20:44
commit immoral a within you. Ezk 22:9
her promiscuous a worse than Ezk 23:11
multiplied her a of promiscuity, Ezk 23:19
with all Your righteous a, Dn 9:16
You based on our righteous a, Dn 9:18
the city and the a of oppression Am 3:9
Israel's a of rebellion can Mc 1:13
the LORD's righteous a. Mc 6:5
of Mine and a on them will be Mt 7:24
hears My words, and a on them: Lk 6:47
the magnificent a of God." Ac 2:11
good works and a of charity. Ac 9:36
and your a of charity have Ac 10:4
and your a of charity have been Ac 10:31
committed shameless a with males Rm 1:27
whose lawless a are forgiven Rm 4:7
in many a of thanksgiving to 2Co 9:12
their sins and their lawless a. Heb 10:17
hearer but a doer who a— Jms 1:25
Your righteous a have been Rv 15:4
the righteous a of the saints. Rv 19:8

ACTUAL *(1)*
and not the a form of those Heb 10:1

ACTUALLY *(10)*
is a found alive in his Ex 22:4
it was a torn apart ⌊by a wild Ex 22:13
We a did this from a specific Jos 22:24
You didn't a give ⌊the women⌋ to Jdg 21:22
A, Saul intended to cause 1Sm 18:25
A your servant said: 2Sm 19:26
Would he a violate the queen Est 7:8
This I a did in Jerusalem, Ac 26:10
is to him I am a speaking boldly Ac 26:26
happened to me has a resulted Php 1:12

ADADAH *(1)*
Kinah, Dimonah, A, Jos 15:22

ADAH *(8)*
one named A and the other named Gn 4:19
A bore Jabal; he was the father Gn 4:20
A and Zillah, hear my voice; Gn 4:23
A daughter of Elon the Hittite, Gn 36:2
A bore Eliphaz to Esau, Basemath Gn 36:4
Eliphaz son of Esau's wife A, Gn 36:10
were the sons of Esau's wife A. Gn 36:12
These are the sons of A. Gn 36:16

ADAIAH *(9)*
was Jedidah the daughter of A; 2Kg 22:1
Ethni, son of Zerah, son of A, 1Ch 6:41
A, Beraiah, and Shimrath were 1Ch 8:21
A son of Jeroham, son of Pashhur, 1Ch 9:12
son of A, and Elishaphat 2Ch 23:1
Malluch, A, Jashub, Sheal, Ezr 10:29
Shelemiah, Nathan, A, Ezr 10:39
son of A, son of Joiarib Neh 11:5
A son of Jeroham, son of Neh 11:12

ADALIA *(1)*
Poratha, A, Aridatha, Est 9:8

ADAM *(20)*
And He said to A, "Because you Gn 3:17
A named his wife Eve because she Gn 3:20
out of skins for A and his wife, Gn 3:21
A knew his wife Eve intimately, Gn 4:1
A knew his wife intimately again, Gn 4:25
records of the descendants of A. Gn 5:1
A was 130 years old when he Gn 5:3
A lived 800 years after the Gn 5:4
mass that extended as far as A, Jos 3:16
A, Seth, Enosh, 1Ch 1:1
Return, descendants of A." Ps 90:3
But they, like A, have violated Hs 6:7
Seth, ⌊son⌋ of A, ⌊son⌋ of God. Lk 3:38
death reigned from A to Moses, Rm 5:14
just as in A all die, so also 1Co 15:22
The first man A became a living 1Co 15:45
the last A became a life-giving 1Co 15:45
For A was created first, then 1Tm 2:13
And A was not deceived, but the 1Tm 2:14
the seventh ⌊generation⌋ from A, Jd 14

ADAM'S *(2)*
So A life lasted 930 years; Gn 5:5
the likeness of A transgression. Rm 5:14

ADAMAH *(1)*
A, Ramah, Hazor, Jos 19:36

ADAMI-NEKEB *(1)*
including A and Jabneel, as far Jos 19:33

ADAR *(9)*
of the month of A in the sixth Ezr 6:15
the twelfth month, the month A. Est 3:7
thirteenth day of A, the twelfth Est 3:13
the twelfth month, the month A. Est 8:12
the twelfth month, the month A. Est 9:1
of the month of A and killed 300 Est 9:15
day of the month of A and rested Est 9:17
day of the month of A as ⌊a time Est 9:19
days of the month A every year Est 9:21

ADBEEL *(2)*
then Kedar, A, Mibsam, Gn 25:13
firstborn, Kedar, A, Mibsam, 1Ch 1:29

ADD *(31)*
the LORD a another son to me. Gn 30:24
it and a a fifth of its value Lv 6:5
he must a a fifth to its value Lv 22:14
he must a a fifth to the Lv 27:13
he must a a fifth to the Lv 27:15
he must a a fifth to the Lv 27:19
must a one-fifth to its value. Lv 27:31
a a fifth of its value to it, Nm 5:7
the altar in it, and a incense. Nm 16:46
and a fresh water to them. Nm 19:17
You must not a anything to what Dt 4:2
do not a anything to it or take Dt 12:32
you are to a three more cities Dt 19:9
yoke, I will a to your yoke; 1Kg 12:11
but I will a to your yoke; 1Kg 12:14
I will a 15 years to your life. 2Kg 20:6
you will need to a more to them. 1Ch 22:14
but I will a to your yoke; 2Ch 10:11
yoke heavy, but I will a to it; 2Ch 10:14
from the LORD to a to our sins 2Ch 28:13
but ⌊now⌋ I can a nothing. Jb 40:5
A days to the king's life; Ps 61:6
A guilt to their guilt; do not Ps 69:27
the LORD a to ⌊your numbers⌋, Ps 115:14
Don't a to His words, or He will Pr 30:6
to those who a house to house Is 5:8
I am going to a 15 years to your Is 38:5
A your burnt offerings to your Jr 7:21
Can any of you a a single cubit Mt 6:27
Can any of you a a cubit to his Lk 12:25
God will a to him the plagues Rv 22:18

ADDAN *(1)*
(AKA ADDON)
Cherub, A, and Immer but were Ezr 2:59

ADDAR *(2)*
(AKA ARD, HAZAR-ADDAR)
ascended to A, and turned to Jos 15:3
Bela's sons: A, Gera, Abihud, 1Ch 8:3

ADDED *(25)*
And she a, "Examine them. Gn 38:25
After he a incense, he made Nm 16:47
inheritance and a to that of the Nm 36:3
inheritance will be a to that of Nm 36:4
mountain; He a nothing more. He Dt 5:22
we have a to all our sins the 1Sm 12:19
David a, "As the LORD lives, the 1Sm 26:10
the king a, "He may return 2Sm 14:24
He a, "If only someone would 2Sm 15:4
servant be an a burden to my 2Sm 19:35
So he a the gold overlay to the 1Kg 6:22
more," Haman a, "Queen Esther Est 5:12
years will be a to your life. Pr 9:11
You have a to the nation, LORD. Is 26:15
You have a to the nation; Is 26:15
other words like them were a. Jr 36:32
LORD has a misery to my pain! Jr 45:3
will be measured and a to you. Mk 4:24
a this to everything else— Lk 3:20
3,000 people were a to them. Ac 2:41
day the Lord a to them those who Ac 2:47
Believers were a to the Lord in Ac 5:14
of people were a to the Lord. Ac 11:24
as important a nothing to me. Gl 2:6
It was a because of Gl 3:19

ADDI *(1)*
son⌋ of A, ⌊son⌋ of Cosam Lk 3:28

ADDICTED *(3)*
not a to wine, not a bully but 1Tm 3:3
tempered, not a to wine, not Ti 1:7
slanderers, not a to much wine. Ti 2:3

ADDING *(9)*
they said, a, "This one came Gn 19:9

a a fifth of its value to it, Lv 5:16
valuation by a a fifth of its Lv 27:27
fathers' place a even more to Nm 32:14
a to the trouble Hadad ⌊had 1Kg 11:25
foreign women, a to Israel's Ezr 10:10
there is no a to it or taking Ec 3:14
a one thing to another to find Ec 7:27
they are always a to the number 1Th 2:16

ADDITION *(56)*
in the land in a to the one that Gn 26:1
and married, in a to his other Gn 28:9
In a the LORD said to him, Ex 4:6
in a to the thanksgiving Lv 7:12
on the altar in a to the morning Lv 9:17
These are in a to the offerings Lv 23:38
in a to the posts of the Nm 3:37
in a to the breast of the Nm 6:20
in a to whatever else he can Nm 6:21
a to those who died because of Nm 16:49
in a to the regular burnt Nm 28:10
in a to the regular burnt Nm 28:15
offerings in a to the regular Nm 28:31
These are in a to the monthly Nm 29:6
offerings are in a to the sin Nm 29:11
These are in a to the regular Nm 29:16
These are in a to the regular Nm 29:19
These are in a to the regular Nm 29:22
These are in a to the regular Nm 29:25
These are in a to the regular Nm 29:28
These are in a to the regular Nm 29:31
These are in a to the regular Nm 29:34
These are in a to the regular Nm 29:38
appointed times in a to your vow Nm 29:39
in a to these, give 42 ⌊other⌋ Nm 35:6
in a to the covenant He had made Dt 29:1
in a to the crescent ornaments Jdg 8:26
a, a shield-bearer was walking 1Sm 17:7
In a, every man who was 1Sm 22:2
In a, David brought the men who 2Sm 2:3
In a to Asahel, 19 of David's 2Sm 2:30
In a, David took away a large 2Sm 12:30
and in a, Ira the Jairite was 2Sm 20:26
In a, he was quite handsome and 1Kg 1:6
In a, I will give you what you 1Kg 3:13
In a, Hiram's fleet that carried 1Kg 10:11
foreign women in a to Pharaoh's 1Kg 11:1
This was in a to his sin he 2Kg 21:16
a, Josiah removed the mediums, 2Kg 23:24
in a to the sons by his 1Ch 3:9
in a to Jehoiada, leader of the 1Ch 12:27
a, their neighbors from as far 1Ch 12:40
In a, David took away a large 1Ch 20:2
In a, Hiram's servants and 2Ch 9:10
In a, ⌊they distributed it⌋ to 2Ch 31:16
in a to all that was given as a Ezr 1:6
In a, Your servant is warned by Ps 19:11
In a, the hearts of people are Ec 9:3
In a to the Teacher being a wise Ec 12:9
immoral acts in a to all your Ezk 16:43
In a, they sent for men who came Ezk 23:40
In a, the temple yard and the Ezk 41:13
In a, all the prophets who have Ac 3:24
In a, a multitude came together Ac 5:16
In a, we are found to be false 1Co 15:15
a to our comfort, we were made 2Co 7:13

ADDITIONAL *(6)*
We have brought a money with us Gn 43:22
If he takes an a wife, he must Ex 21:10
Make two a planks for the two Ex 26:23
also made two a planks for the Ex 36:28
ones and take a plaster to Lv 14:42
slaughtered an a 18,000 Jdg 20:25

ADDITIONS *(1)*
been ratified, or makes a to it. Gl 3:15

ADDON *(1)*
(AKA ADDAN)
Cherub, A, and Immer, Neh 7:61

ADDRESS *(7)*
to come forward and a the army. Dt 20:2
The officers are to a the army, Dt 20:5
continue to a the army and say Dt 20:8
has done this to a the issue 2Sm 14:20
He finished the a the LORD had Jr 26:8
delivered a public a to them. Ac 12:21
And if you a as Father the One 1Pt 1:17

ADDRESSED *(5)*
approached and a Moses and the Nm 36:1

Then Esther **a** the king again. Est 8:3
to release Jesus, **a** them again, Lk 23:20
Peter saw this, he **a** the people: Ac 3:12
a them in the Hebrew language: Ac 21:40

ADDRESSES *(2)*
When Pharaoh **a** you and asks, Gn 46:33
exhortation that **a** you as sons: Heb 12:5

ADDRESSING *(2)*
have finished **a** the army, Dt 20:9
heard that he was **a** them in the Ac 22:2

ADDS *(4)*
For he **a** rebellion to his sin; Jb 34:37
and struggle **a** nothing to it. Pr 10:22
⌊He **a**⌋: I will never again Heb 10:17
anyone **a** to them, God will add Rv 22:18

ADIEL *(3)*
Asaiah, **A**, Jesimiel, Benaiah 1Ch 4:36
son of **A**, son of Jahzerah, 1Ch 9:12
Azmaveth son of **A** was in charge 1Ch 27:25

ADIN *(1)*
Adonijah, Bigvai, **A**, Neh 10:16

ADIN'S *(3)*
A descendants 454 Ezr 2:15
of Jonathan from **A** descendants, Ezr 8:6
A descendants 655 Neh 7:20

ADINA *(1)*
A son of Shiza the Reubenite, 1Ch 11:42

ADITHAIM *(1)*
Shaaraim, **A**, Gederah, and Jos 15:36

ADJACENT *(5)*
of the room **a** to the great hall Ezk 41:4
a to the holy donation ⌊of land⌋. Ezk 45:6
a to the holy donation and the Ezk 45:7
most holy place **a** to the Ezk 48:12
own ⌊the land⌋ **a** to the ⌊tribal⌋ Ezk 48:21

ADJOURNED *(1)*
about the Way, he **a** the hearing, Ac 24:22

ADLAI *(1)*
Shaphat son of **A** was in charge 1Ch 27:29

ADMAH *(5)*
Gomorrah, **A**, and Zeboiim, as Gn 10:19
Shinab king of **A**, and Shemeber Gn 14:2
the king of **A**, the king of Gn 14:8
and Gomorrah, **A** and Zeboiim, Dt 29:23
How can I make you like **A**? Hs 11:8

ADMATHA *(1)*
Shethar, **A**, Tarshish, Meres, Est 1:14

ADMINISTER *(4)*
A justice every morning, and Jr 21:12
A justice and righteousness. Jr 22:3
wisely as king and **a** justice Jr 23:5
and He will **a** justice and Jr 33:15

ADMINISTERED *(5)*
You have **a** justice and Ps 99:4
He **a** justice and righteousness, Jr 22:15
gift that is being **a** by us for 2Co 8:19
this large sum **a** by us. 2Co 8:20
kingdoms, **a** justice, obtained Heb 11:33

ADMINISTERING *(2)*
a justice and righteousness for 2Sm 8:15
a justice and righteousness for 1Ch 18:14

ADMINISTRATION *(4)*
for the **a** of the days of Eph 1:10
about the **a** of God's grace that Eph 3:2
all about the **a** of the mystery Eph 3:9
to God's **a** that was given to Col 1:25

ADMINISTRATOR *(1)*
Without leader, **a**, or ruler, Pr 6:7

ADMINISTRATORS *(7)*
the royal civil **a** aided the Jews Est 9:3
officers and **a**, all of them Ezk 23:23
over them three **a**, including Dn 6:2
himself above the **a** and satraps Dn 6:3
The **a** and satraps, therefore, Dn 6:4
So the **a** and satraps went Dn 6:6
All the **a** of the kingdom, the Dn 6:7

ADMIRED *(4)*
his service, Saul **a** him greatly, 1Sm 16:21
I **a** the dead, who have already Ec 4:2
For what is highly **a** by people Lk 16:15
and to be **a** by all those who 2Th 1:10

ADMONISH *(2)*
My people, and I will **a** you. Ps 81:8
lead you in the Lord and **a** you, 1Th 5:12

ADMONISHED *(2)*
they **a** them, but they would not 2Ch 24:19
women will be **a** not to imitate Ezk 23:48

ADMONISHING *(1)*
teaching and **a** one another in Col 3:16

ADNA *(2)*
A, Chelal, Benaiah, Maaseiah, Ezr 10:30
A of Harim, Helkai of Meraioth, Neh 12:15

ADNAH *(2)*
A, Jozabad, Jediael, Michael, 1Ch 12:20
A the commander and 300,000 2Ch 17:14

ADONI-BEZEK *(3)*
They found **A** in Bezek, fought Jdg 1:5
When **A** fled, they pursued him, Jdg 1:6
A said, "Seventy kings with Jdg 1:7

ADONI-ZEDEK *(3)*
Now **A** king of Jerusalem heard Jos 10:1
So **A** and his people were greatly Jos 10:2
A king of Jerusalem sent Jos 10:3

ADONIJAH *(25)*
fourth was **A**, son of Haggith; 2Sm 3:4
A son of Haggith kept exalting 1Kg 1:5
the priest. They supported **A**, 1Kg 1:7
warriors did not side with **A**. 1Kg 1:8
A sacrificed sheep, oxen, and 1Kg 1:9
not heard that **A** son of Haggith 1Kg 1:11
So why has **A** become king?' 1Kg 1:13
Now look, **A** has become king. 1Kg 1:18
'**A** is to become king after me, 1Kg 1:24
saying, 'Long live King **A**!' 1Kg 1:25
A and all the invited guests who 1Kg 1:41
A said, "Come in, for you are an 1Kg 1:42
A was afraid of Solomon, so he 1Kg 1:50
Look, **A** fears King Solomon, and 1Kg 1:51
Now **A** son of Haggith came to 1Kg 2:13
Solomon to speak to him about **A**. 1Kg 2:19
to your brother **A** as a wife." 1Kg 2:21
Abishag the Shunammite for **A**? 1Kg 2:22
so severely if **A** has not made 1Kg 2:23
A will be put to death today! 1Kg 2:24
who struck down **A**, and he died. 1Kg 2:25
had supported **A** but not Absalom 1Kg 2:28
A son of Haggith was fourth; 1Ch 3:2
Jehonathan, **A**, Tobijah, 2Ch 17:8
A, Bigvai, Adin, Neh 10:16

ADONIJAH'S *(1)*
Then all of **A** guests got up 1Kg 1:49

ADONIKAM'S *(3)*
A descendants 666 Ezr 2:13
last ones, from **A** descendants, Ezr 8:13
A descendants 667 Neh 7:18

ADONIRAM *(2)*
and **A** son of Abda, in charge of 1Kg 4:6
A was in charge of the forced 1Kg 5:14

ADOPT *(1)*
us as Romans to **a** or practice." Ac 16:21

ADOPTED *(6)*
who is **a** by your father; Lv 18:11
Mordecai had **a** her as his own Est 2:7
who had **a** ⌊her⌋ as his own Est 2:15
the nations and **a** their ways. Ps 106:35
daughter **a** and raised him as Ac 7:21
us to be **a** through Jesus Christ Eph 1:5

ADOPTION *(4)*
you received the Spirit of **a**, Rm 8:15
waiting for **a**, the redemption Rm 8:23
to them belong the **a**, the glory, Rm 9:4
that we might receive **a** as sons. Gl 4:5

ADORAIM *(1)*
A, Lachish, Azekah, 2Ch 11:9

ADORAM *(2)*
A was in charge of forced labor; 2Sm 20:24
Then King Rehoboam sent **A**, 1Kg 12:18

ADORE *(3)*
No wonder young women **a** you. Sg 1:3
is only right that they **a** you. Sg 1:4
of Asia and the world **a**." Ac 19:27

ADORN *(4)*
Do you **a** his neck with a mane? Jb 39:19
A yourself with majesty and Jb 40:10
that you **a** yourself with gold Jr 4:30
so that they may **a** the teaching Ti 2:10

ADORNED *(14)*
They should be **a** with gold Ex 28:20
painted her eyes, **a** her head, 2Kg 9:30
He **a** the temple with precious 2Ch 3:6
the queen, **a** with gold from Ps 45:9
I **a** you with jewelry, putting Ezk 16:11
So you were **a** with gold and Ezk 16:13
and **a** yourself with jewelry for Ezk 23:40
his splendor was **a** like one of Mt 6:29
his splendor was **a** like one of Lk 12:27
how it was **a** with beautiful Lk 21:5
and scarlet, **a** with gold, Rv 17:4
and scarlet, **a** with gold, Rv 18:16
like a bride **a** for her husband. Rv 21:2
city wall were **a** with every kind Rv 21:19

ADORNMENT *(1)*
for you and **a** for your neck. Pr 3:22

ADORNS *(2)*
He **a** the humble with salvation. Ps 149:4
as a bride **a** herself with her Is 61:10

ADRAMMELECH *(3)*
in the fire to **A** and Anammelech, 2Kg 17:31
his sons **A** and Sharezer struck 2Kg 19:37
his sons **A** and Sharezer struck Is 37:38

ADRAMYTTIUM *(1)*
when we had boarded a ship of **A**, Ac 27:2

ADRIATIC *(1)*
we were drifting in the **A** Sea, Ac 27:27

ADRIEL *(2)*
was given to **A** the Meholathite 1Sm 18:19
had borne to **A** son of Barzillai 2Sm 21:8

ADULLAM *(8)*
of Libnah one the king of **A** one Jos 12:15
Jarmuth, **A**, Socoh, Azekah, Jos 15:35
took refuge in the cave of **A**. 1Sm 22:1
came to David at the cave of **A**, 2Sm 23:13
to the rock at the cave of **A**, 1Ch 11:15
Beth-zur, Soco, **A**, 2Ch 11:7
and **A** with their villages; Neh 11:30
of Israel will come to **A**. Mc 1:15

ADULLAMITE *(4)*
settled near an **A** named Hirah. Gn 38:1
friend Hirah the **A** went up to Gn 38:12
his friend the **A** in order to get Gn 38:20
So the **A** returned to Judah, Gn 38:22

ADULT *(2)*
as an **a** he wrestled with God. Hs 12:3
in evil and **a** in your thinking. 1Co 14:20

ADULTERER *(2)*
both the **a** and the adulteress Lv 20:10
offspring of an **a** and a Is 57:3

ADULTERER'S *(1)*
The **a** eye watches for twilight, Jb 24:15

ADULTERERS *(7)*
him, and you associate with **a**. Ps 50:18
for they are all **a**, a solemn Jr 9:2
For the land is full of **a**; Jr 23:10
witness against sorcerers and **a**; Mal 3:5
unrighteous, **a**, or even like Lk 18:11
idolaters, **a**, male prostitutes 1Co 6:9
will judge immoral people and **a**. Heb 13:4

ADULTERESS *(7)*
and the **a** must be put to Lv 20:10
but an **a** goes after ⌊your⌋ very Pr 6:26
This is the way of an **a**: Pr 30:20
city—what an **a** she has become! Is 1:21
by another man and is an **a**, Hs 3:1
living, she will be called an **a**. Rm 7:3
to another man, she is not an **a**. Rm 7:3

ADULTERESSES *(4)*
judge you the way **a** and those Ezk 16:38
them the way **a** and those who Ezk 23:45
for they are **a** and blood is on Ezk 23:45
A! Do you not know that Jms 4:4

ADULTERIES *(3)*
Your **a** and your ⌊lustful⌋ Jr 13:27
thoughts, murders, **a**, sexual Mt 15:19
a, greed, evil actions, deceit, Mk 7:22

ADULTEROUS *(4)*
You **a** wife, who receives Ezk 16:32
An evil and **a** generation demands Mt 12:39

An evil and a generation wants a Mt 16:4
of My words in this a and sinful Mk 8:38

ADULTERY (41)
Do not commit a. Ex 20:14
a man commits a with a married Lv 20:10
if he commits a with his Lv 20:10
Do not commit a. Dt 5:18
soon commit a with the foreign Dt 31:16
one who commits a lacks sense; Pr 6:32
had committed a that I had sent Jr 3:8
land and committed a with stone Jr 3:9
needs, yet they committed a; Jr 5:7
murder, commit a, swear falsely, Jr 7:9
They commit a and walk in lies. Jr 23:14
Israel by committing a with Jr 29:23
For they have committed a, Ezk 23:37
have committed a with their Ezk 23:37
this woman worn out by a: Ezk 23:43
face and her a from between her Hs 2:2
stealing, and a are rampant; Hs 4:2
your daughters-in-law commit a. Hs 4:13
when they commit a, Hs 4:14
All of them commit a; Hs 7:4
it was said, Do not commit a. Mt 5:27
committed a with her in his Mt 5:28
causes her to commit a. Mt 5:32
a divorced woman commits a. Mt 5:32
and marries another, commits a." Mt 19:9
not commit a; do not steal; do Mt 19:18
another commits a against her. Mk 10:11
marries another, she commits a." Mk 10:12
not commit a; do not steal; do Mk 10:19
marries another woman commits a, Lk 16:18
from her husband commits a. Lk 16:18
Do not commit a; do not murder; Lk 18:20
brought a woman caught in a, Jn 8:3
in the act of committing a. Jn 8:4
must not commit a"—do you Rm 2:22
adultery"—do you commit a? Rm 2:22
shall not commit a, you shall Rm 13:9
Do not commit a, also said, Do Jms 2:11
So if you do not commit a, Jms 2:11
eyes full of a and always 2Pt 2:14
those who commit a with her into Rv 2:22

ADUMMIM (2)
is opposite the ascent of A, Jos 15:7
is opposite the ascent of A, Jos 18:17

ADVANCE (24)
Rephaim at the a of the Dt 2:21
the people will a, each man Jos 6:5
around to a from behind them 2Ch 13:13
His troops a together; Jb 19:12
They a as through a gaping Jb 30:14
They a against me; now they Ps 17:11
destroys. A, Elam! Lay siege, Is 21:2
many peoples with you will a, Ezk 38:9
You will a against My people Ezk 38:16
They will a, sweeping through Dn 11:10
years he will a with a great Dn 11:13
all the men of war a and attack! Jl 3:9
the way⌋ will a before them; Mc 2:13
they stumble as they a. Nah 2:5
the trumpet and a with the Zch 9:14
I have told you in a. Mt 24:25
I have told you everything in a. Mk 13:23
My body in a for burial. Mk 14:8
of David spoke in a about Judas, Ac 1:16
Seeing this in a, he spoke Ac 2:31
a the obedience of faith among Rm 16:26
and arrange in a the generous 2Co 9:5
about which I tell you in a— Gl 5:21
He testified in a to the 1Pt 1:11

ADVANCED (19)
The people a into the city, Jos 6:20
joined forces, a with all their Jos 10:5
Joshua was now old, a in years, Jos 13:1
You have become old, a in years, Jos 13:1
day the Israelites a against the Jdg 20:24
they a and put the whole city to Jdg 20:37
the ark of the LORD a six steps, 2Sm 6:13
his troops a to fight against 2Sm 10:13
so King Jehoash of Israel a. 2Kg 14:11
They a and came to Jerusalem, 2Kg 18:17
of Babylon a against Jerusalem 2Kg 25:1
So King Jehoash of Israel a. 2Ch 25:21
assembled; they a together. Ps 48:4
king of Assyria a against all Is 36:1
of Babylon a against Jerusalem Jr 39:1
of Babylon a against Jerusalem Jr 52:4
the Amorite as Israel a; Am 2:9
staff in hand because of a age. Zch 8:4
and I a in Judaism beyond many Gl 1:14

ADVANCEMENT (2)
resulted in the a of the gospel, Php 1:12
all of you for your a and joy in Php 1:25

ADVANCES (2)
The LORD a like a warrior; Is 42:13
Look, he a like clouds; Jr 4:13

ADVANTAGE (21)
have been a great a to you. 1Sm 19:4
gained the a over us and came 2Sm 11:23
there is an a to wisdom over Ec 2:13
like the a of light over Ec 2:13
People have no a over animals, Ec 3:19
What a then does the wise man Ec 6:8
What ⌊a⌋ is there for the poor Ec 6:8
What is the a for man? Ec 6:11
and an a to those who see the Ec 7:11
and the a of knowledge is that Ec 7:12
a of wisdom is that it brings Ec 10:10
there is no a for the charmer Ec 10:11
that it is to your a that one Jn 11:50
So what a does the Jew have? Rm 3:1
they are enemies for your a, Rm 11:28
may not be taken a of by Satan; 2Co 2:11
Did I take a of you by anyone I 2Co 12:17
Did Titus take a of you? 2Co 12:18
to be used for His own a. Php 2:6
have no a over those who 1Th 4:15
people for their own a. Jd 16

ADVANTAGEOUS (1)
Jews that it was a that one man Jn 18:14

ADVERSARIES (35)
overthrew Your a by Your great Ex 15:7
vengeance on My a and repay Dt 32:41
He will take vengeance on His a; Dt 32:43
the loins of his a and enemies, Dt 33:11
You subdue my a beneath me. 2Sm 22:40
You exalt me above my a; 2Sm 22:49
righteousness, because of my a; Ps 5:8
up against the fury of my a; Ps 7:6
Because of Your a, You have Ps 8:2
he scoffs at all his a. Ps 10:5
You subdue my a beneath me. Ps 18:39
You exalt me above my a; Ps 18:48
Because of my a, show me Your Ps 27:11
by all my a and even by my Ps 31:11
My a taunt me, as if crushing my Ps 42:10
will repay my a for ⌊their⌋ evil Ps 54:5
a trample me all day, for many Ps 56:2
will let me look down on my a. Ps 59:10
You are aware of all my a. Ps 69:19
May my a be disgraced and Ps 71:13
Your a roared in the meeting Ps 74:4
not forget the clamor of Your a, Ps 74:23
raised up Rezin's a against him Is 9:11
fire for Your a will consume Is 26:11
and all your a—all of them— Jr 30:16
to avenge Himself against His a. Jr 46:10
them. Their a said: We're not Jr 50:7
Her a have become ⌊her⌋ masters; Lm 1:5
The a looked at her, laughing Lm 1:7
his neighbors should be his a. Lm 1:17
and exalting the horn of your a. Lm 2:17
be lifted up against your a, Mc 5:9
all His a were humiliated, Lk 13:17
none of your a will be able to Lk 21:15
a fire about to consume the a. Heb 10:27

ADVERSARY (16)
land against an a who is Nm 10:9
to become our a during the 1Sm 29:4
Have you become my a today? 2Sm 19:22
a and enemy is this evil Haman. Est 7:6
plundered my a without cause, Ps 7:4
them from the hand of the a; Ps 106:10
away as captives before the a. Lm 1:5
a has seized all her precious Lm 1:10
hand is positioned like an a. Lm 2:4
that an enemy or a could enter Lm 4:12
quickly with your a while you're Mt 5:25
or your a will hand you over to Mt 5:25
going with your a to the ruler, Lk 12:58
'Give me justice against my a.' Lk 18:3
and give the a no opportunity to 1Tm 5:14
Your a the Devil is prowling 1Pt 5:8

ADVERSARY'S (1)
her people fell into the a hand, Lm 1:7

ADVERSITIES (1)
Many a come to the one who is Ps 34:19

ADVERSITY (11)
and prosperity, death and a. Dt 30:15
only good from God and not a?" Jb 2:10
about all this a that had Jb 2:11
concerning all the a the LORD Jb 42:11
in His shelter in the day of a; Ps 27:5
not be disgraced in times of a; Ps 37:19
will save him in a day of a. Ps 41:1
as many years as we have seen a. Ps 90:15
but in the day of a, consider: Ec 7:14
Before the days of a come, Ec 12:1
Do not both a and good come from Lm 3:38

ADVICE (38)
give you some a, and God be with Ex 18:19
ones who, at Balaam's a, incited Nm 31:16
to Jonathan's a and swore an 1Sm 19:6
Ahithophel, "Give ⌊me⌋ your a. 2Sm 16:20
Now the a Ahithophel gave in 2Sm 16:23
Absalom had for Ahithophel's a. 2Sm 16:23
The a Ahithophel has given this 2Sm 17:7
Ahithophel's good a be 2Sm 17:14
The a of Hushai the Archite is 2Sm 17:14
is better than Ahithophel's a." 2Sm 17:14
has given this a against you." 2Sm 17:21
realized that his a had not been 2Sm 17:23
he rejected the a of the elders 1Kg 12:8
He rejected the a the elders had 1Kg 12:13
according to the young men's a: 1Kg 12:14
So the king sought a. 1Kg 12:28
he rejected the a of the elders 2Ch 10:8
Rehoboam rejected the elders' a 2Ch 10:13
according to the young men's a, 2Ch 10:14
for his mother gave him evil a. 2Ch 22:3
followed their a and went with 2Ch 22:5
and have not listened to my a." 2Ch 25:16
and he followed Memucan's a. Est 1:21
The a pleased Haman, so he had Est 5:14
waiting silently for my a. Jb 29:21
not follow the a of the wicked, Ps 1:1
I possess good a and competence; Pr 8:14
is gained by those who take a. Pr 13:10
wisest advisers give stupid a! Is 19:11
He gives wonderful a; Is 28:29
to Egypt without asking My a, Is 30:2
to their own a and according to Jr 7:24
I give you a, you won't listen Jr 38:15
and give wicked a in this city. Ezk 11:2
may my a seem good to you my Dn 4:27
gave Alexander a when the Jews Ac 19:33
already over, Paul gave his a Ac 27:9
have followed my a not to sail Ac 27:21

ADVISE (8)
I a that all Israel from Dan to 2Sm 17:11
please come and let me a you. 1Kg 1:12
How do you a me to respond to 1Kg 12:6
message do you a that we send 1Kg 12:9
How do you a me to respond to 2Ch 10:6
message do you a we send back to 2Ch 10:9
We a the king that if this city Ezr 4:16
I a you to buy from Me gold Rv 3:18

ADVISED (7)
⌊Someone⌋ a ⌊me⌋ to kill you, 1Sm 24:10
is what Ahithophel a Absalom 2Sm 17:15
of Israel, and this is what I a. 2Sm 17:15
elders who had a him and 1Kg 12:8
elders who had a him and 2Ch 10:8
a that tribute, duty, and land Ezr 7:24
the one who had a the Jews that Jn 18:14

ADVISER (4)
with Ahuzzath his a and Phicol Gn 26:26
sent for David's a Ahithophel 2Sm 15:12
David's personal a, entered 2Sm 15:37
a priest and a to the king; 1Kg 4:5

ADVISERS (12)
they were his a after the death 2Ch 22:4
His a and his wife Zeresh said Est 6:13
deprives trusted a of speech and Jb 12:20
but with many a they succeed. Pr 15:22
your a to their former state. Is 1:26
Pharaoh's wisest a give stupid Is 19:11

governors, **a**, treasurers, judges Dn 3:2
governors, **a**, treasurers, judges Dn 3:3
He said to his **a**, "Didn't we Dn 3:24
the king's **a** gathered around, Dn 3:27
a and my nobles sought me out, Dn 4:36
satraps, **a**, and governors Dn 6:7

ADVOCATE *(3)*
and my **a** is in the heights! Jb 16:19
have been an **a** for your sisters Ezk 16:52
we have an **a** with the Father— 1Jn 2:1

AENEAS *(2)*
There he found a man named **A**, Ac 9:33
said to him, "**A**, Jesus Christ Ac 9:34

AENON *(1)*
was baptizing in **A** near Salim, Jn 3:23

AFAR *(2)*
my knowledge from **a** and ascribe Jb 36:3
but He knows the haughty from **a**. Ps 138:6

AFFAIRS *(3)*
He set his **a** in order and hanged 2Sm 17:23
'Put your **a** in order, for you 2Kg 20:1
'Put your **a** in order, for you Is 38:1

AFFECT *(1)*
If you sin, how does it **a** God? Jb 35:6

AFFECTED *(1)*
incidents that **a** him and Israel 1Ch 29:30

AFFECTION *(7)*
family **a** to one another with Rm 12:10
And his **a** toward you is even 2Co 7:15
will have deep **a** for you because 2Co 9:14
you with the **a** of Christ Jesus Php 1:8
the Spirit, if any **a** and mercy, Php 2:1
godliness with brotherly **a**, 2Pt 1:7
and brotherly **a** with love. 2Pt 1:7

AFFECTIONS *(1)*
you are limited by your own **a**. 2Co 6:12

AFFECTS *(1)*
wickedness ⌊**a**⌋ a person like Jb 35:8

AFFIRM *(5)*
of my lord the king, so **a** it. 1Kg 1:36
I will never **a** that you are Jb 27:5
but the Pharisees **a** them all. Ac 23:8
I **a** by the pride in you that I 1Co 15:31
women who **a** that they worship 1Tm 2:10

AFFIRMED *(5)*
Today you have **a** that the LORD Dt 26:17
the LORD has **a** that you are His Dt 26:18
Jehoshaphat **a**, "The LORD's words 2Kg 3:12
they **a** the proposal and spread 2Ch 30:5
testimony has **a** that God is true Jn 3:33

AFFLICT *(13)*
they will **a** Asshur and Eber, Nm 24:24
The LORD will **a** you with wasting Dt 28:22
The LORD will **a** you with the Dt 28:27
LORD will **a** you with madness, Dt 28:28
LORD will **a** you on your knees Dt 28:35
He will **a** you again with all the Dt 28:60
will not **a** them as they have 2Sm 7:10
The enemy will not **a** him; Ps 89:22
they **a** Your heritage. Ps 94:5
You keep silent and **a** severely? Is 64:12
you, I will **a** you no longer. Nah 1:12
I will deal with all who **a** you. Zph 3:19
with affliction those who **a** you, 2Th 1:6

AFFLICTED *(64)*
man is **a** with a skin disease; Lv 13:44
The person **a** with an infectious Lv 13:45
the person **a** with a skin disease Lv 14:2
disappeared from the **a** person, Lv 14:3
the camp who is **a** with a skin Nm 5:2
hand to your **a** and poor brother Dt 15:11
Egyptians mistreated and **a** us, Dt 26:6
and the Almighty has **a** me?" Ru 1:21
He **a** the men of the city, from 1Sm 5:9
did not die were **a** with tumors, 1Sm 5:12
When He **a** them, didn't they send 1Sm 6:6
You rescue an **a** people, but Your 2Sm 22:28
The LORD **a** the king, and he had 2Kg 15:5
of Israel, **a** them, and handed 2Kg 17:20
in God's sight, so He **a** Israel. 1Ch 21:7
the LORD **a** him in his intestines 2Ch 21:18
out because the LORD had **a** him. 2Ch 26:20
the hardships that have **a** us, Neh 9:32
He heard the outcry of the **a**. Jb 34:28
but He gives justice to the **a**. Jb 36:6
God rescues the **a** by afflicting Jb 36:15
not forget the cry of the **a**. Ps 9:12
hope of the **a** will not perish Ps 9:18
relentlessly pursue the **a**; Ps 10:2
lurks in order to seize the **a**. Ps 10:9
He seizes the **a** and drags him in Ps 10:9
Do not forget the **a**. Ps 10:12
of the **a** and the groaning Ps 12:5
frustrate the plans of the **a**, Ps 14:6
For You rescue an **a** people, Ps 18:27
detested the torment of the **a**. Ps 22:24
to me, for I am alone and **a**. Ps 25:16
bring down the **a** and needy and Ps 37:14
am **a** and needy; the Lord thinks Ps 40:17
I am **a** and needy; hurry to me, Ps 70:5
and Your **a** ones with justice. Ps 72:2
vindicate the **a** among the people Ps 72:4
cry out and the **a** who have no Ps 72:12
they are not **a** like most people. Ps 73:5
For I am **a** all day long, and Ps 73:14
I have been **a** and near death. Ps 88:15
My heart is **a**, withered like Ps 102:4
when I said, "I am severely **a**." Ps 116:10
Before I was **a** I went astray, Ps 119:67
for me to be **a** so that I could Ps 119:71
and that You have **a** me fairly. Ps 119:75
I am severely **a**; LORD, give me Ps 119:107
The LORD helps the **a** but brings Ps 147:6
to deprive the **a** among my people Is 10:2
and His **a** people find refuge in Is 14:32
have compassion on His **a** ones. Is 49:13
listen to this, **a** and drunken Is 51:21
struck down by God, and **a**. Is 53:4
oppressed and **a**, yet He did not Is 53:7
and satisfy the **a** one, then your Is 58:10
Though I have **a** you, I will Nah 1:12
slaughter, the **a** of the flock. Zch 11:7
and so the **a** of the flock who Zch 11:11
to Him all those who were **a**, Mt 4:24
If we are **a**, it is for your 2Co 1:6
Instead, we were **a** in every way: 2Co 7:5
reward⌋ with rest you who are **a**, 2Th 1:7
feet, helped the **a**, and devoted 1Tm 5:10
destitute, **a**, and mistreated. Heb 11:37

AFFLICTING *(5)*
who were oppressing and **a** them. Jdg 2:18
terrorizing and **a** the people of 1Sm 5:6
sins because You are **a** them, 1Kg 8:35
sins because You are **a** them, 2Ch 6:26
rescues the afflicted by **a** them; Jb 36:15

AFFLICTION *(45)*
LORD has heard your ⌊cry of⌋ **a**. Gn 16:11
said, "The LORD has seen my **a**; Gn 29:32
God has seen my **a** and my hard Gn 31:42
fruitful in the land of my **a**." Gn 41:52
take notice of Your servant's **a**, 1Sm 1:11
have seen ⌊the **a** of⌋ My people, 1Sm 9:16
LORD will see my **a** and restore 2Sm 16:12
LORD saw that the **a** of Israel 2Kg 14:26
knowing his own **a** and suffering, 2Ch 6:29
possessions with a horrible **a**. 2Ch 21:14
with shame and aware of my **a**. Jb 10:15
and trapped by the cords of **a**, Jb 36:8
why you have been tested by **a**. Jb 36:21
You freed me from **a**; Ps 4:1
consider my **a** at the hands of Ps 9:13
Consider my **a** and trouble, Ps 25:18
love because You have seen my **a**. Ps 31:7
friends stand back from my **a**, Ps 38:11
and forget our **a** and oppression? Ps 44:24
suffered **a** because of their Ps 107:17
This is my comfort in my **a**: Ps 119:50
I would have died in my **a**. Ps 119:92
Consider my **a** and rescue me, Ps 119:153
the gloom of **a**, and they will Is 8:22
tested you in the furnace of **a**. Is 48:10
exile following **a** and harsh Lm 1:3
the days of her **a** and Lm 1:7
LORD, look on my **a**, for the Lm 1:9
man who has seen **a** under the rod Lm 3:1
Remember my **a** and my Lm 3:19
enjoy bringing **a** or suffering Lm 3:33
they suffer **a** because there is Zch 10:2
When **a** or persecution comes Mk 4:17
that she was cured of her **a**. Mk 5:29
peace and be free from your **a**." Mk 5:34
a and distress for every human Rm 2:9
we know that **a** produces Rm 5:3
Can **a** or anguish or persecution Rm 8:35
be patient in **a**; be persistent Rm 12:12
He comforts us in all our **a**, 2Co 1:4
those who are in any kind of **a**, 2Co 1:4
of our **a** that took place in the 2Co 1:8
momentary light **a** is producing 2Co 4:17
during a severe testing by **a**, 2Co 8:2
to repay with **a** those who 2Th 1:6

AFFLICTIONS *(12)*
troubles and **a** will come to them Dt 31:17
troubles and **a** come to them, Dt 31:21
from all your troubles and **a**. 1Sm 10:19
knowing his own **a** and spreading 1Kg 8:38
that chains and **a** are waiting Ac 20:23
but we also rejoice in our **a**, Rm 5:3
endurance, by **a**, by hardship, 2Co 6:4
overcome with joy in all our **a**. 2Co 7:4
over my **a** on your behalf, Eph 3:13
in Christ's **a** for His body, Col 1:24
persecutions and **a** you endure. 2Th 1:4
exposed to taunts and **a**, Heb 10:33

AFFORD *(11)*
But if he cannot **a** an animal Lv 5:7
if he cannot **a** two turtledoves Lv 5:11
he is poor and cannot **a** ⌊these⌋, Lv 14:21
whatever he can **a**, one to be a Lv 14:22
one type of what he can **a**, Lv 14:30
what he can **a** together with the Lv 14:31
and cannot **a** the cost of his Lv 14:32
the one making the vow can **a**. Lv 27:8
to whatever else he can **a**; Nm 6:21
you can **a** to your servants 1Sm 25:8
he can **a** with the lambs, Ezk 46:7

AFRAID *(196)*
and I was **a** because I was naked, Gn 3:10
Do not be **a**, Abram. I am your Gn 15:1
she said, because she was **a**. Gn 18:15
he was **a** to live in Zoar. Gn 19:30
Don't be **a**, for God has heard Gn 21:17
for he was **a** to say "my wife," Gn 26:7
Do not be **a**, for I am with you. Gn 26:24
He was **a** and said, "What an Gn 28:17
answered, "I was **a**, for I Gn 31:31
was greatly **a** and distressed; Gn 32:7
brother Esau, for I am **a** of him; Gn 32:11
to her, "Don't be **a**, for this is Gn 35:17
bags of money, they were **a**. Gn 42:35
But the men were **a** because they Gn 43:18
well. Don't be **a**. Your God and Gn 43:23
Do not be **a** to go down to Egypt, Gn 46:3
said to them, "Don't be **a**. Gn 50:19
Therefore don't be **a**. Gn 50:21
Then Moses became **a** and thought: Ex 2:14
because he was **a** to look at God. Ex 3:6
said to the people, "Don't be **a**. Ex 14:13
Don't be **a**, for God has come Ex 20:20
They were **a** to come near him. Ex 34:30
were you not **a** to speak against Nm 12:8
and don't be **a** of the people of Nm 14:9
is with us. Don't be **a** of them!" Nm 14:9
Do not be **a** or discouraged. Dt 1:21
Don't be terrified or **a** of them! Dt 1:29
They will be **a** of you, so you Dt 2:4
Don't be **a** of them, for the LORD Dt 3:22
because you were **a** of the fire Dt 5:5
do not be **a** of them. Be sure to Dt 7:18
I was **a** of the fierce anger the Dt 9:19
All Israel will hear and be **a**, Dt 13:11
about it⌋, be **a**, and no longer Dt 17:13
Do not be **a** of him. Dt 18:22
else will hear and be **a**, Dt 19:20
yours, do not be **a** of them, for Dt 20:1
Do not be **a**, alarmed, or Dt 20:3
man who is **a** or fainthearted? Dt 20:8
all Israel will hear and be **a**. Dt 21:21
don't be terrified or **a** of them. Dt 31:6
Do not be **a** or discouraged." Dt 31:8
Do not be **a** or discouraged, Jos 1:9
Do not be **a** or discouraged. Jos 8:1
Do not be **a** of them, for I Jos 10:8
Do not be **a** or discouraged. Jos 10:25
Do not be **a** of them, for at Jos 11:6
with me. Don't be **a**." So he went Jdg 4:18
be **a**, for you will not die. Jdg 6:23
he was too **a** of his father's Jdg 6:27
But if you are **a** to go to the Jdg 7:10
because he was **a**, for he was Jdg 8:20
Now don't be **a**, my daughter. Ru 3:11

He was **a** to tell Eli the vision, 1Sm 3:15
care of her said, "Don't be **a**. 1Sm 4:20
they were **a** because of the 1Sm 7:7
Samuel replied, "Don't be **a**. 1Sm 12:20
Because I was **a** of the people, 1Sm 15:24
Saul was **a** of David, because the 1Sm 18:12
he became even more **a** of David. 1Sm 18:29
Ahimelech was **a** to meet David, 1Sm 21:1
became very **a** of King Achish 1Sm 21:12
be **a**, for the one who wants 1Sm 22:23
Look, we're **a** here in Judah; 1Sm 23:3
Don't be **a**, for my father 1Sm 23:17
he was **a** and trembled violently. 1Sm 28:5
king said to her, "Don't be **a**. 1Sm 28:13
you were not **a** to lift your hand 2Sm 1:14
Abner because he was **a** of him. 2Sm 3:11
"Don't be **a**," David said to him, 2Sm 9:7
the Arameans were **a** to ever help 2Sm 10:19
servants were **a** to tell him the 2Sm 12:18
him. Don't be **a**. Am I not the 2Sm 13:28
the people have made me **a**. 2Sm 14:15
Adonijah was **a** of Solomon, 1Kg 1:50
Elijah said to her, "Don't be **a**; 1Kg 17:13
Elijah became **a** and immediately 1Kg 19:3
him. Don't be **a** of him." So he 2Kg 1:15
said, "Don't be **a**, for those who 2Kg 6:16
Don't be **a** because of the words 2Kg 19:6
Don't be **a** of the servants of 2Kg 25:24
they were **a** of the Chaldeans. 2Kg 25:26
Don't be **a** or discouraged. 1Ch 22:13
Don't be **a** or discouraged, 1Ch 28:20
Jehoshaphat was **a**, so he 2Ch 20:3
'Do not be **a** or discouraged 2Ch 20:15
Do not be **a** or discouraged. 2Ch 20:17
Don't be **a** or discouraged before 2Ch 32:7
Judah and made them **a** to build. Ezr 4:4
the people, "Don't be **a** of them. Neh 4:14
because they were **a** of Mordecai. Est 9:3
something dreadful, you are **a**. Jb 6:21
be **a** of the sword, because wrath Jb 19:29
consider ⌊this⌋, I am **a** of Him. Jb 23:15
I was timid and **a** to tell you Jb 32:6
fear, since he is **a** of nothing; Jb 39:22
I am not **a** of the thousands of Ps 3:6
my life—of whom should I be **a**? Ps 27:1
against me, my heart is not **a**; Ps 27:3
Therefore we will not be **a**, Ps 46:2
not be **a** when a man gets rich, Ps 49:16
I am **a**, I will trust in You. Ps 56:3
at him suddenly and are not **a**. Ps 64:4
safely, and they were not **a**; Ps 78:53
I will not be **a**. What can man do Ps 118:6
you lie down, you will not be **a**; Pr 3:24
She is not **a** for her household Pr 31:21
are **a** of heights and dangers Ec 12:5
Don't be **a** or fainthearted Is 7:4
I will trust ⌊Him⌋ and not be **a**. Is 12:2
his officers will be **a** because Is 31:9
The sinners in Zion are **a**; Is 33:14
Don't be **a** because of the words Is 37:6
Raise it, do not be **a**! Is 40:9
The islands see and are **a**, Is 41:5
do not be **a**, for I am your God. Is 41:10
Do not be startled or **a**. Is 44:8
Do not be **a**, for you will not be Is 54:4
you will certainly not be **a**; Is 54:14
not be **a** of anyone, for I will Jr 1:8
Judah was not **a** but also went Jr 3:8
will no longer be **a** or dismayed, Jr 23:4
Jacob, do not be **a**—⌊this is⌋ Jr 30:10
Don't be **a** to serve the Jr 40:9
be **a** of the king of Babylon Jr 42:11
don't be **a** of him'—⌊this is⌋ Jr 42:11
Jacob, do not be **a**, and do not Jr 46:27
Jacob, do not be **a**—⌊this is⌋ Jr 46:28
on You; You say: "Do not be **a**." Lm 3:57
do not be **a** of them or their Ezk 2:6
Don't be **a** of their words or be Ezk 2:6
be **a** of them or discouraged Ezk 3:9
I'm **a** ⌊of what would happen⌋ if Dn 1:10
"Don't be **a**, Daniel," he said to Dn 10:12
said, "Don't be **a**, you who are Dn 10:19
Don't be **a**, land; rejoice and be Jl 2:21
Don't be **a**, wild animals, for Jl 2:22
in a city, aren't people **a**? Am 3:6
sailors were **a**, and each cried Jnh 1:5
even more **a** and said to him, Jnh 1:10
with nothing to make ⌊them⌋ **a**. Zph 3:13
present among you; don't be **a**." Hg 2:5
Don't be **a**; let your hands be Zch 8:13
the house of Judah. Don't be **a**. Zch 8:15
Ashkelon will see it and be **a**; Zch 9:5
don't be **a** to take Mary as your Mt 1:20
Herod, he was **a** to go there. Mt 2:22
don't be **a** of them, since Mt 10:26
Don't be **a** therefore; Mt 10:31
courage! It is I. Don't be **a**." Mt 14:27
strength of the wind, he was **a**. Mt 14:30
and said, "Get up; don't be **a**." Mt 17:7
From men,' we're **a** of the crowd, Mt 21:26
So I was **a** and went off and hid Mt 25:25
Don't be **a**, because I know Mt 28:5
Jesus told them, "Do not be **a**. Mt 28:10
his right mind; and they were **a**. Mk 5:15
synagogue leader, "Don't be **a**. Mk 5:36
courage! It is I. Don't be **a**." Mk 6:50
and they were **a** to ask Him. Mk 9:32
those who followed Him were **a**. Mk 10:32
For they were **a** of Him, because Mk 11:18
they were **a** of the crowd, Mk 11:32
but they were **a** of the crowd. Mk 12:12
to anyone, since they were **a**. Mk 16:8
Do not be **a**, Zechariah, because Lk 1:13
Do not be **a**, Mary, for you have Lk 1:30
to them, "Don't be **a**, for look, Lk 2:10
"Don't be **a**," Jesus told Simon. Lk 5:10
his right mind. And they were **a**. Lk 8:35
He answered him, "Don't be **a**. Lk 8:50
They became **a** as they entered Lk 9:34
and they were **a** to ask Him about Lk 9:45
Don't be **a**; you are worth Lk 12:7
be **a**, little flock, because Lk 12:32
because I was **a** of you, for Lk 19:21
they were **a** of the people. Lk 22:2
near the boat, and they were **a**. Jn 6:19
to them, "It is I. Don't be **a**!" Jn 6:20
because they were **a** of the Jews, Jn 9:22
he was more **a** than ever. Jn 19:8
they were **a** the people might Ac 5:26
but they were all **a** of him, Ac 9:26
him, he became **a** and said, "What Ac 10:4
And they were **a** when they heard Ac 16:38
vision, "Don't be **a**, but keep on Ac 18:9
Felix became **a** and replied, Ac 24:25
saying, 'Don't be **a**, Paul. Ac 27:24
Do not be arrogant, but be **a**. Rm 11:20
do wrong, be **a**, because it does Rm 13:4
so that the rest will also be **a**. 1Tm 5:20
not being **a** of the king's anger, Heb 11:27
I will not be **a**. What can man do Heb 13:6
on me, and said, "Don't be **a**! Rv 1:17
Don't be **a** of what you are about Rv 2:10

AFTER *(799)*
(See pp. xi-xii.)

AFTERBIRTH *(1)*
a that comes out from between Dt 28:57

AFTERNOON *(8)*
waited until late **a** and the two Jdg 19:8
All **a**, they kept on raving until 1Kg 18:29
three in the **a** darkness came Mt 27:45
three in the **a** Jesus cried out Mt 27:46
whole land until three in the **a**. Mk 15:33
of prayer at three in the **a**. Ac 3:1
three in the **a** he distinctly saw Ac 10:3
at three in the **a**, I was praying Ac 10:30

AFTERWARD *(2)*
and **a** his brothers talked with Gn 45:15
a, at His coming, the people of 1Co 15:23

AFTERWARDS *(47)*
(See pp. xi-xii.)

AGABUS *(2)*
one of them, named **A**, stood up Ac 11:28
a prophet named **A** came down Ac 21:10

AGAG *(7)*
His king will be greater than **A**, Nm 24:7
He captured **A** king of Amalek 1Sm 15:8
Saul and the troops spared **A**, 1Sm 15:9
brought back **A**, king of Amalek, 1Sm 15:20
"Bring me **A** king of Amalek." 1Sm 15:32
A came to him trembling, 1Sm 15:32
he hacked **A** to pieces before 1Sm 15:33

AGAGITE *(5)*
Haman, son of Hammedatha the **A**. Est 3:1
Haman son of Hammedatha the **A**, Est 3:10
revoke the evil of Haman the **A**, Est 8:3
Haman son of Hammedatha the **A**, Est 8:5
Haman son of Hammedatha the **A**, Est 9:24

AGAIN *(446)*
(See pp. xi-xii.)

AGAINST *(1489)*
(See pp. xi-xii.)

AGATE *(2)*
a jacinth, an **a**, and an amethyst Ex 28:19
a jacinth, an **a**, and an amethyst Ex 39:12

AGE *(65)*
and be buried at a ripe old **a**. Gn 15:15
passed the **a** of childbearing. Gn 18:11
a son to Abraham in his old **a**, Gn 21:2
borne him a son in his old **a**." Gn 21:7
a son to my master in her old **a**, Gn 24:36
breath and died at a ripe old **a**, Gn 25:8
At 17 years of **a**, Joseph tended Gn 37:2
son ⌊born to him⌋ in his old **a**, Gn 37:3
seated before him in order by **a**, Gn 43:33
brother, the child of his old **a**. Gn 44:20
was poor because of old **a**; Gn 48:10
Joseph died at the **a** of 110. Gn 50:26
of Nun, died at the **a** of 110. Jos 24:29
the LORD, died at the **a** of 110. Jdg 2:8
at a ripe old **a** and was buried Jdg 8:32
and sustain you in your old **a**. Ru 4:15
in your family will reach old **a**. 1Sm 2:31
will ever again reach old **a**. 1Sm 2:32
his gaze was fixed due to his **a**. 1Kg 14:4
But in his old **a** he developed a 1Kg 15:23
at a good old **a**, full of days, 1Ch 29:28
thought that **a** should speak and Jb 32:7
Don't discard me in my old **a**: Ps 71:9
will still bear fruit in old **a**, Ps 92:14
be the same until ⌊your⌋ old **a**, Is 46:4
pride, a joy from **a** to age. Is 60:15
pride, a joy from age to **a**. Is 60:15
were indeed at the **a** for love. Ezk 16:8
of the other young men your **a**. Dn 1:10
the kingdom at the **a** of 62. Dn 5:31
in hand because of advanced **a**. Zch 8:4
either in this **a** or in the one Mt 12:32
worries of this **a** and the Mt 13:22
The harvest is the end of the **a**, Mt 13:39
it will be at the end of the **a**. Mt 13:40
it will be at the end of the **a**. Mt 13:49
In the Messianic **A**, when the Son Mt 19:28
coming and of the end of the **a**?" Mt 24:3
always, to the end of the **a**." Mt 28:20
but the worries of this **a**, Mk 4:19
eternal life in the **a** to come. Mk 10:30
conceived a son in her old **a**, Lk 1:36
sons of this **a** are more astute Lk 16:8
eternal life in the **a** to come." Lk 18:30
The sons of this **a** marry and are Lk 20:34
take part in that **a** and in the Lk 20:35
him; he's of **a**. He will speak Jn 9:21
his parents said, "He's of **a**; Jn 9:23
he was approaching the **a** of 40, Ac 7:23
Do not be conformed to this **a**, Rm 12:2
Where is the debater of this **a**? 1Co 1:20
but not a wisdom of this **a**, 1Co 2:6
or of the rulers of this **a**, 1Co 2:6
of the rulers of this **a** knew it, 1Co 2:8
you thinks he is wise in this **a**, 1Co 3:18
if she is past marriageable **a**, 1Co 7:36
god of this **a** has blinded the 2Co 4:4
us from this present evil **a**, Gl 1:4
not only in this **a** but also in Eph 1:21
according to this worldly **a**, Eph 2:2
in the present **a** not to be 1Tm 6:17
foundation for the **a** to come, 1Tm 6:19
and godly way in the present **a**, Ti 2:12
and the powers of the coming **a**, Heb 6:5
even though she was past the **a**, Heb 11:11

AGE-OLD *(1)*
The **a** mountains break apart; Hab 3:6

AGED *(5)*
count the men **a** 20 or under, 1Ch 27:23
man and virgin or elderly and **a**; 2Ch 36:17
a feast of **a** wine, choice meat, Is 25:6
choice meat, finely **a** wine. Is 25:6
assemble the **a**; gather the Jl 2:16

AGEE *(1)*
Shammah son of **A** the Hararite. 2Sm 23:11

AGENDA *(1)*
a prostitute, having a hidden **a**. Pr 7:10
AGENT *(1)*
was the king's **a** in every matter Neh 11:24
AGENTS *(10)*
Saul sent **a** to David's house to 1Sm 19:11
When Saul sent **a** to seize David, 1Sm 19:14
Saul sent the **a** ⌊back⌋ to see 1Sm 19:15
Saul sent **a** to seize David. 1Sm 19:20
Spirit of God came on Saul's **a**, 1Sm 19:20
he sent other **a**, and they also 1Sm 19:21
and sent a third group of **a**, 1Sm 19:21
kings of Aram through their **a**. 1Kg 10:29
kings of Aram through their **a**. 2Ch 1:17
your **a** have crossed the sea Is 23:2
AGES *(12)*
existed in the **a** before us. Ec 1:10
I have kept silent from **a** past; Is 42:14
those who have been dead for **a**. Lm 3:6
existed in **a** past and never Jl 2:2
secret kept silent for long **a**, Rm 16:25
before the **a** for our glory. 1Co 2:7
the ends of the **a** have come. 1Co 10:11
in the coming **a** He might display Eph 2:7
hidden for **a** in God who created Eph 3:9
to the purpose of the **a**, Eph 3:11
hidden for **a** and generations Col 1:26
the end of the **a**, for the Heb 9:26
AGGRAVATED *(1)*
was greatly **a**, and turning to Ac 16:18
AGGRAVATION *(1)*
but **a** from a fool outweighs them Pr 27:3
AGGRESSOR *(1)*
be a refuge for Moab from the **a**. Is 16:4
AGILE *(1)*
arms were made **a** by the hands Gn 49:24
AGING *(1)*
And what is old and **a** is about Heb 8:13
AGITATED *(4)*
Do not be **a** by evildoers; Ps 37:1
do not be **a** by one who prospers Ps 37:7
do not be **a**—it can only bring Ps 37:8
heard a bad report and are **a**; Jr 49:23
AGITATING *(1)*
a and disturbing the crowds. Ac 17:13
AGITATION *(1)*
released on her **a** and terrors. Jr 15:8
AGITATOR *(1)*
an **a** among all the Jews Ac 24:5
AGO *(41)*
'Long **a** your ancestors, Jos 24:2
away from you three days **a**, 1Sm 9:20
me when I got sick three days **a**. 1Sm 30:13
designed it long **a**; I planned it 2Kg 19:25
that was built many years **a**, Ezr 5:11
For long **a**, in the days of David Neh 12:46
in their days, in days long **a**: Ps 44:1
the One enthroned from long **a**, Ps 55:19
purchased long **a** and redeemed as Ps 74:2
a You established the earth, Ps 102:25
from long **a** and find comfort. Ps 119:52
Long **a** I learned from Your Ps 119:152
before His works of long **a**. Pr 8:22
was given its name long **a**, Ec 6:10
the One who created it long **a**. Is 22:11
formed⌋ long **a**, with perfect Is 25:1
designed it long **a**; I planned it Is 37:26
told you and declared it long **a**? Is 44:8
Who predicted this long **a**? Is 45:21
Remember what happened long **a**, Is 46:9
and from long **a** what is not yet Is 46:10
declared the past events long **a**; Is 48:3
I declared to you long **a**; Is 48:5
created now, and not long **a**; Is 48:7
as in generations of long **a**. Is 51:9
the foundations laid long **a**; Is 58:12
For long **a** I broke your yoke; Jr 2:20
to our fathers from days long **a**. Mc 7:20
in sackcloth and ashes long **a**! Mt 11:21
they would have repented long **a**, Lk 10:13
Not long **a** Theudas rose up, Ac 5:36
Four days **a** at this hour, Ac 10:30
have been known from long **a**. Ac 15:18
some time **a** and led 4,000 Ac 21:38
He promised long **a** through His Rm 1:2
who a year **a** began not only to 2Co 8:10
the third heaven 14 years **a**. 2Co 12:2
Long **a** God spoke to the fathers Heb 1:1
pronounced⌋ long **a**, is not idle, 2Pt 2:3
long **a** the heavens and the earth 2Pt 3:5
for this judgment long **a**, Jd 4
AGONIZE *(1)*
to **a** together with me in your Rm 15:30
AGONIZING *(1)*
relief from the **a** labor of our Gn 5:29
AGONY *(9)*
within me, **a** in my mind every Ps 13:2
a like that of a woman in labor, Ps 48:6
pain and **a** will seize ⌊them⌋; Is 13:8
I writhe in **a**! Oh, the pain in Jr 4:19
come on you, **a** like a woman Jr 22:23
home paralyzed, in terrible **a**!" Mt 8:6
I am in **a** in this flame!' Lk 16:24
here, while you are in **a**. Lk 16:25
in labor and **a** to give birth. Rv 12:2
AGREE *(20)*
We will **a** with you only on this Gn 34:15
the men will **a** to live with us Gn 34:22
let us **a** with them, and they Gn 34:23
They said, "We **a** to give them." Jdg 8:25
Please **a** to stay overnight and Jdg 19:6
Who can **a** to your proposal? 1Sm 30:24
of Zeruiah, do we **a** on anything? 2Sm 16:10
of Zeruiah, do we **a** on anything? 2Sm 19:22
to him, "Don't listen or **a**." 1Kg 20:8
of you on earth **a** about any Mt 18:19
Didn't you **a** with me on a Mt 20:13
but the testimonies did not **a**. Mk 14:56
did not **a** even on this. Mk 14:59
Why did you **a** to test the Spirit Ac 5:9
of the prophets **a** with this, Ac 15:15
a with the law that it is good. Rm 7:16
I joyfully **a** with God's law. Rm 7:22
except when you **a**, for a time, 1Co 7:5
urge Syntyche to **a** in the Lord. Php 4:2
and does not **a** with the sound 1Tm 6:3
AGREEABLE *(1)*
it will be **a** to God that you Nm 23:27
AGREED *(20)*
And Abram **a** to what Sarai said. Gn 16:2
Abraham **a** with Ephron, and Gn 23:16
that he had **a** to in the hearing Gn 23:16
⌊own⌋ flesh." His brothers **a**. Gn 37:27
Moses **a** to stay with the man, Ex 2:21
He **a** not to annihilate you. Dt 10:10
and **a** to stay with the man, Jdg 17:11
all that was **a** on by Israel 2Sm 3:19
So the priests **a** they would not 2Kg 12:8
the people **a** to the covenant. 2Kg 23:3
the whole assembly **a** to do it. 1Ch 13:4
So the Jews **a** to continue the Est 9:23
a with them in this matter and Dn 1:14
governors have **a** that the king Dn 6:7
with the elders and **a** on a plan, Mt 28:12
were glad and **a** to give him Lk 22:5
had not **a** with their plan and Lk 23:51
had already **a** that if anyone Jn 9:22
a with putting him to death. Ac 8:1
have **a** to ask you to bring Paul Ac 23:20
AGREEING *(3)*
walk together without **a** to meet? Am 3:3
After **a** with the workers on one Mt 20:2
⌊**a**⌋ that we should go to the Gl 2:9
AGREEMENT *(20)*
not break an **a** with me or with Gn 21:23
making a binding **a** in writing Neh 9:38
into an **a** with a stranger Pr 6:1
sense enters an **a** and puts up Pr 17:18
we have made an **a** with Sheol; Is 28:15
and your **a** with Sheol will not Is 28:18
An **a** has been broken, and cities Is 33:8
the purchase **a**—the sealed copy Jr 32:11
gave the purchase **a** to Baruch Jr 32:12
who were signing the purchase **a**, Jr 32:12
this purchase **a** with the sealed Jr 32:14
given the purchase **a** to Baruch, Jr 32:16
king of the North to seal the **a**. Dn 11:6
and will reach an **a** with him. Dn 11:17
Be in **a** with one another. Rm 12:16
grant you **a** with one another, Rm 15:5
What **a** does Christ have with 2Co 6:15
And what **a** does God's sanctuary 2Co 6:16
everything in **a** with the Eph 1:11
—and these three are in **a**. 1Jn 5:8
AGREEMENTS *(2)*
who hates such **a** is protected. Pr 11:15
be one of those who enter **a**, Pr 22:26
AGREES *(1)*
nations—and Geshem **a**—that Neh 6:6
AGRICULTURAL *(2)*
at the turn of the ⌊**a**⌋ year. Ex 34:22
offering in all our **a** towns. Neh 10:37
AGRICULTURE *(1)*
a place renowned for ⌊its⌋ **a**, Ezk 34:29
AGRIPPA *(11)*
King **A** and Bernice arrived in Ac 25:13
Then **A** said to Festus, "I would Ac 25:22
A and Bernice came with great Ac 25:23
King **A** and all men present with Ac 25:24
before you, King **A**, so that Ac 25:26
A said to Paul, "It is permitted Ac 26:1
fortunate, King **A**, that today I Ac 26:2
Therefore, King **A**, I was not Ac 26:19
King **A**, do you believe the Ac 26:27
Then **A** said to Paul, "Are you Ac 26:28
Then **A** said to Festus, "This man Ac 26:32
AGROUND *(4)*
they would run **a** on the Syrtis, Ac 27:17
must run **a** on a certain island. Ac 27:26
we might run **a** in some rocky Ac 27:29
a sandbar and ran the ship **a**. Ac 27:41
AGUR *(1)*
The words of **A** son of Jakeh. Pr 30:1
AH *(14)*
A, the smell of my son is like Gn 27:27
A, who can live when God does Nm 24:23
A, I will gain satisfaction Is 1:24
A! The roar of many peoples— Is 17:12
A! The land of buzzing insect Is 18:1
He warms himself and says, "**A**! Is 44:16
A, Lord GOD! You Yourself made Jr 32:17
A, sword of the LORD! How long Jr 47:6
But I said, "**A**, Lord GOD, I have Ezk 4:14
and cried out, "**A**, Lord GOD! Ezk 9:8
a loud voice: "**A**, Lord GOD! Will Ezk 11:13
Then I said, "**A**, Lord GOD, they Ezk 20:49
A, Lord—the great and Dn 9:4
"**A**!" His disciples said. "Now Jn 16:29
AHA *(7)*
against me and say, "**A**, aha! Ps 35:21
against me and say, "Aha, **a**! Ps 35:21
them say in their hearts, "**A**! Ps 35:25
those who say to me, "**A**, aha!" Ps 40:15
those who say to me, "Aha, **a**!" Ps 40:15
Let those who say, "**A**, aha!" Ps 70:3
Let those who say, "Aha, **a**!" Ps 70:3
AHAB *(87)*
His son **A** became king in his 1Kg 16:28
A son of Omri became king over 1Kg 16:29
A son of Omri reigned over 1Kg 16:29
But **A** son of Omri did what was 1Kg 16:30
A also made an Asherah pole. 1Kg 16:33
A did more to provoke the LORD 1Kg 16:33
said to **A**, "As the LORD God 1Kg 17:1
Go and present yourself to **A**. 1Kg 18:1
went to present himself to **A**. 1Kg 18:2
A called for Obadiah, who was in 1Kg 18:3
A said to Obadiah, "Go 1Kg 18:5
A went one way by himself, 1Kg 18:6
servant over to **A** to put me to 1Kg 18:9
I go report to **A** and he doesn't 1Kg 18:12
I will present myself to **A**." 1Kg 18:15
to meet **A** and report to him. 1Kg 18:16
Then **A** went to meet Elijah. 1Kg 18:16
When **A** saw Elijah, Ahab said to 1Kg 18:17
saw Elijah, **A** said to him, "Is 1Kg 18:17
So **A** summoned all the Israelites 1Kg 18:20
Elijah said to **A**, "Go up, eat 1Kg 18:41
So **A** went to eat and drink, 1Kg 18:42
said, "Go and tell **A**, 'Get ⌊your 1Kg 18:44
So **A** got in ⌊his chariot⌋ and 1Kg 18:45
ran ahead of **A** to the entrance 1Kg 18:46
A told Jezebel everything that 1Kg 19:1
the city to **A** king of Israel 1Kg 20:2
prophet came to **A** king of Israel 1Kg 20:13
A asked, "By whom?" And the 1Kg 20:14
A counted the young men of the 1Kg 20:15

and **A** had him come up into the 1Kg 20:33
⌊**A** responded⌋,"On the basis of 1Kg 20:34
the palace of **A** king of Samaria 1Kg 21:1
So **A** spoke to Naboth, saying, 1Kg 21:2
Naboth said to **A**, "I will never 1Kg 21:3
A went to his palace resentful 1Kg 21:4
she said to **A**, "Get up and take 1Kg 21:15
When **A** heard that Naboth was 1Kg 21:16
and go to meet **A** king of Israel, 1Kg 21:18
A said to Elijah, "So, you have 1Kg 21:20
He who belongs to **A** and dies in 1Kg 21:24
was no one like **A**, who devoted 1Kg 21:25
A heard these words, he tore 1Kg 21:27
you seen how **A** has humbled 1Kg 21:29
'Who will entice **A** to march up 1Kg 22:20
A rested with his fathers, 1Kg 22:40
fourth year of Israel's King **A**. 1Kg 22:41
Ahaziah son of **A** said to 1Kg 22:49
Ahaziah son of **A** became king 1Kg 22:51
the death of **A**, Moab rebelled 2Kg 1:1
Joram son of **A** became king over 2Kg 3:1
when **A** died, the king of Moab 2Kg 3:5
of Israel's King Joram son of **A**, 2Kg 8:16
as the house of **A** had done, 2Kg 8:18
of Israel's King Joram son of **A**, 2Kg 8:25
of the house of **A** and did what 2Kg 8:27
sight like the house of **A**, 2Kg 8:27
Joram son of **A** to fight against 2Kg 8:28
Joram son of **A** since Joram was 2Kg 8:29
of your master **A** so that I may 2Kg 9:7
whole house of **A** will perish, 2Kg 9:8
the house of **A** like the house 2Kg 9:9
by side behind his father **A**, 2Kg 9:25
of Joram son of **A** that Ahaziah 2Kg 9:29
Since **A** had 70 sons in Samaria, 2Kg 10:1
the house of **A** will fail, 2Kg 10:10
of the house of **A** in Jezreel— 2Kg 10:11
the house of⌋ **A** in Samaria until 2Kg 10:17
and said to them, "**A** served Baal 2Kg 10:18
the house of **A** all that was in 2Kg 10:30
as King **A** of Israel had done; 2Kg 21:3
level ⌊used on⌋ the house of **A**, 2Kg 21:13
alliance with **A** through marriage 2Ch 18:1
went down to visit **A** in Samaria. 2Ch 18:2
A sacrificed many sheep and 2Ch 18:2
Israel's King **A** asked Judah's 2Ch 18:3
'Who will entice **A** king of 2Ch 18:19
as the house of **A** had done, 2Ch 21:6
like the house of **A** prostituted 2Ch 21:13
in the ways of the house of **A**, 2Ch 22:3
sight like the house of **A**, 2Ch 22:4
Israel's King **A** to fight against 2Ch 22:5
Joram son of **A** since Joram was 2Ch 22:6
to destroy the house of **A**. 2Ch 22:7
judgment on the house of **A**, 2Ch 22:8
says to **A** son of Kolaiah and to Jr 29:21
make you like Zedekiah and **A**, Jr 29:22

AHAB'S *(9)*
letters in **A** name and sealed 1Kg 21:8
I will eliminate all of **A** males, 1Kg 21:21
rest of the events of **A** ⌊reign⌋, 1Kg 22:39
for **A** daughter was his wife. 2Kg 8:18
he was a son-in-law to **A** family. 2Kg 8:27
I will eliminate all of **A** males, 2Kg 9:8
and to the guardians of **A** sons, 2Kg 10:1
for **A** daughter was his wife. 2Ch 21:6
practices of **A** house have been Mc 6:16

AHARAH *(1)*
was ⌊born⌋ second, **A** third, 1Ch 8:1

AHARHEL *(1)*
the families of **A** son of Harum. 1Ch 4:8

AHASBAI *(1)*
Eliphelet son of **A** son of the 2Sm 23:34

AHASUERUS *(20)*
the beginning of the reign of **A**, Ezr 4:6
took place during the days of **A**, Est 1:1
those days King **A** reigned from Est 1:2
from the wine, **A** commanded Est 1:10
'King **A** ordered Queen Vashti Est 1:17
woman's turn to go to King **A**, Est 2:12
was taken to King **A** in the royal Est 2:16
and tried to assassinate King **A**. Est 2:21
place, King **A** honored Haman, Est 3:1
Then Haman informed King **A**, Est 3:8
name of King **A** and sealed with Est 3:12
planned to assassinate King **A**. Est 6:2
King **A** spoke up and asked Queen Est 7:5
same day King **A** awarded Queen Est 8:1
King **A** said to Esther the Queen Est 8:7
all the provinces of King **A**, Est 8:12
provinces of the kingdom of **A**, Est 9:30
King **A** imposed a tax throughout Est 10:1
Jew was second only to King **A**, Est 10:3
who was the son of **A**, was a Mede Dn 9:1

AHASUERUS' *(10)*
for the women of King **A** palace. Est 1:9
to obey King **A** command that was Est 1:15
every one of King **A** provinces. Est 1:16
is not to enter King **A** presence, Est 1:19
King **A** rage had cooled down, Est 2:1
the Jews, throughout **A** kingdom. Est 3:6
Nisan, in King **A** twelfth year, Est 3:7
wrote in King **A** name and sealed Est 8:10
In each of King **A** provinces the Est 9:2
Jews in all of King **A** provinces, Est 9:20

AHAVA *(3)*
at the river that flows to **A**, Ezr 8:15
a fast by the **A** River, Ezr 8:21
We set out from the **A** River on Ezr 8:31

AHAZ *(44)*
His son **A** became king in his 2Kg 15:38
A son of Jotham became king of 2Kg 16:1
A was 20 years old when he 2Kg 16:2
besieged **A** but were not able 2Kg 16:5
So **A** sent messengers to 2Kg 16:7
A also took the silver and gold 2Kg 16:8
King **A** went to Damascus to meet 2Kg 16:10
King **A** sent a model of the altar 2Kg 16:10
King **A** sent from Damascus 2Kg 16:11
the time King **A** came back from 2Kg 16:11
Then King **A** commanded Uriah 2Kg 16:15
everything King **A** commanded. 2Kg 16:16
Then King **A** cut off the frames 2Kg 16:17
A rested with his fathers and 2Kg 16:20
twelfth year of Judah's King **A**, 2Kg 17:1
Hezekiah son of **A** became king of 2Kg 18:1
his son **A**, his son Hezekiah, his 1Ch 3:13
Pithon, Melech, Tarea, and **A**. 1Ch 8:35
A fathered Jehoaddah, Jehoaddah 1Ch 8:36
Pithon, Melech, Tahrea, and **A**. 1Ch 9:41
A fathered Jarah; Jarah fathered 1Ch 9:42
His son **A** became king in his 2Ch 27:9
A was 20 years old when he 2Ch 28:1
God handed **A** over to the king 2Ch 28:5
A was also handed over to the 2Ch 28:5
that time King **A** asked the king 2Ch 28:16
because of King **A** of Judah, 2Ch 28:19
king of Assyria came against **A**; 2Ch 28:20
Although **A** plundered the LORD's 2Ch 28:21
King **A** himself became more 2Ch 28:22
Then **A** gathered up the utensils 2Ch 28:24
A rested with his fathers and 2Ch 28:27
that King **A** rejected during 2Ch 29:19
Uzziah, Jotham, **A**, and Hezekiah, Is 1:1
place during the reign of **A**, Is 7:1
the heart of **A** and the hearts of Is 7:2
Shear-jashub to meet **A** at the Is 7:3
Then the LORD spoke again to **A**: Is 7:10
But **A** replied, "I will not ask. Is 7:12
In the year that King **A** died, Is 14:28
Uzziah, Jotham, **A**, and Hezekiah, Hs 1:1
days of Jotham, **A**, and Hezekiah, Mc 1:1
Jotham fathered **A**, Ahaz fathered Mt 1:9
fathered Ahaz, **A** fathered Mt 1:9

AHAZ'S *(4)*
rest of the events of **A** ⌊reign⌋, 2Kg 16:19
it had descended on **A** stairway. 2Kg 20:11
A upper chamber that the kings 2Kg 23:12
goes down on **A** stairway return Is 38:8

AHAZIAH *(35)*
and his son **A** became king in his 1Kg 22:40
A son of Ahab said to 1Kg 22:49
A son of Ahab became king over 1Kg 22:51
A had fallen through the 2Kg 1:2
So King **A** sent a captain of 50 2Kg 1:9
Then Elijah said to King **A**, 2Kg 1:16
A died according to the word of 2Kg 1:17
and his son **A** became king in his 2Kg 8:24
A son of Jehoram became king of 2Kg 8:25
A was 22 years old when he 2Kg 8:26
A went with Joram son of Ahab to 2Kg 8:28
Judah's King **A** son of Jehoram 2Kg 8:29
up there and **A** king of Judah had 2Kg 9:16
of Israel and **A** king of Judah 2Kg 9:21
shouting to **A**, "It's treachery 2Kg 9:23
to Ahaziah, "It's treachery, **A**!" 2Kg 9:23
When King **A** of Judah saw ⌊what 2Kg 9:27
of Ahab that **A** had become king 2Kg 9:29
the relatives of **A** king of Judah 2Kg 10:13
Joash son of **A** from the king's 2Kg 11:2
and **A**—had consecrated, 2Kg 12:18
of Judah's King Joash son of **A**, 2Kg 13:1
Joash, son of **A**, at Beth-shemesh 2Kg 14:13
his son **A**, his son Joash, 1Ch 3:11
alliance with Israel's King **A**, 2Ch 20:35
you formed an alliance with **A**, 2Ch 20:37
inhabitants of Jerusalem made **A**, 2Ch 22:1
So **A** son of Jehoram became king 2Ch 22:1
A was 22 years old when he 2Ch 22:2
Judah's King **A** son of Jehoram 2Ch 22:6
God, for when **A** went, he went 2Ch 22:7
brothers who were serving **A**, 2Ch 22:8
Jehu looked for **A**, and Jehu's 2Ch 22:9
So the house of **A** had no one to 2Ch 22:9
Joash son of **A** from the king's 2Ch 22:11

AHAZIAH'S *(8)*
rest of the events of **A** ⌊reign⌋, 2Kg 1:18
answered, "We're **A** relatives. 2Kg 10:13
Athaliah, **A** mother, saw that 2Kg 11:1
Jehoram's daughter and **A** sister, 2Kg 11:2
going to Joram, **A** downfall was 2Ch 22:7
and the sons of **A** brothers who 2Ch 22:8
Athaliah, **A** mother, saw that 2Ch 22:10
Since she was **A** sister, she hid 2Ch 22:11

AHBAN *(1)*
who bore him **A** and Molid. 1Ch 2:29

AHEAD *(103)*
(See pp. xi-xii.)

AHER *(1)*
the Hushim were the sons of **A**. 1Ch 7:12

AHI *(2)*
A son of Abdiel, son of Guni, 1Ch 5:15
A, Rohgah, Hubbah, and Aram. 1Ch 7:34

AHIAH *(1)*
A, Hanan, Anan, Neh 10:26

AHIAM *(2)*
A son of Sharar the Hararite, 2Sm 23:33
A son of Sachar the Hararite, 1Ch 11:35

AHIAN *(1)*
A, Shechem, Likhi, and Aniam. 1Ch 7:19

AHIEZER *(6)*
A son of Ammishaddai from Dan; Nm 1:12
of the Danites is **A** son of Nm 2:25
On the tenth day **A** son of Nm 7:66
the offering of **A** son of Nm 7:71
A son of Ammishaddai was over Nm 10:25
Their chief was **A** son of Shemaah 1Ch 12:3

AHIHUD *(2)*
A son of Shelomi, a leader from Nm 34:27
was the father of Uzza and **A**. 1Ch 8:7

AHIJAH *(23)*
A, who was wearing an ephod, 1Sm 14:3
Saul told **A**, "Bring the ark of 1Sm 14:18
Elihoreph and **A** the sons of 1Kg 4:3
the prophet **A** the Shilonite met 1Kg 11:29
A had wrapped himself with a 1Kg 11:29
A took hold of the new cloak 1Kg 11:30
spoken through **A** the Shilonite 1Kg 12:15
A the prophet is there; 1Kg 14:2
Ahijah's house. **A** could not see; 1Kg 14:4
But the LORD had said to **A**, 1Kg 14:5
When **A** heard the sound of her 1Kg 14:6
His servant **A** the prophet. 1Kg 14:18
Baasha son of **A** of the house 1Kg 15:27
His servant **A** the Shilonite. 1Kg 15:29
Baasha son of **A** became king 1Kg 15:33
the house of Baasha son of **A**, 1Kg 21:22
the house of Baasha son of **A**. 2Kg 9:9
Bunah, Oren, Ozem, and **A**. 1Ch 2:25
Naaman, **A**, and Gera. Gera 1Ch 8:7
Mecherathite, **A** the Pelonite, 1Ch 11:36
A was in charge of the 1Ch 26:20
the Prophecy of **A** the Shilonite, 2Ch 9:29
spoken through **A** the Shilonite 2Ch 10:15

AHIJAH'S *(1)*
Shiloh and arrived at **A** house. 1Kg 14:4

AHIKAM *(20)*
the priest, **A** son of Shaphan, 2Kg 22:12
the priest, **A**, Achbor, Shaphan, 2Kg 22:14

appointed Gedaliah son of A, 2Kg 25:22
Hilkiah, A son of Shaphan, 2Ch 34:20
But A son of Shaphan supported Jr 26:24
him over to Gedaliah son of A, Jr 39:14
Return to Gedaliah son of A, Jr 40:5
to Gedaliah son of A at Mizpah, Jr 40:6
Gedaliah son of A over the land Jr 40:7
son of A, son of Shaphan Jr 40:9
had appointed Gedaliah son of A, Jr 40:11
Gedaliah son of A would not Jr 40:14
Gedaliah son of A responded to Jr 40:16
to Gedaliah son of A at Mizpah. Jr 41:1
struck down Gedaliah son of A, Jr 41:2
"Come to Gedaliah son of A!" Jr 41:6
had appointed Gedaliah son of A. Jr 41:10
had killed Gedaliah son of A— Jr 41:16
struck down Gedaliah son of A, Jr 41:18
son of A son of Shaphan, Jr 43:6

AHILUD *(5)*
Jehoshaphat son of A was court 2Sm 8:16
Jehoshaphat son of A was court 2Sm 20:24
Jehoshaphat son of A, historian; 1Kg 4:3
Baana son of A, in Taanach, 1Kg 4:12
Jehoshaphat son of A was court 1Ch 18:15

AHIMAAZ *(16)*
wife was Ahinoam daughter of A. 1Sm 14:50
your son A and Abiathar's son 2Sm 15:27
Zadok's son A and Abiathar's son 2Sm 15:36
Jonathan and A were staying at 2Sm 17:17
"Where are A and Jonathan?" 2Sm 17:20
A and Jonathan climbed out of 2Sm 17:21
A son of Zadok said, "Please let 2Sm 18:19
A son of Zadok persisted and 2Sm 18:22
So A ran by way of the plain and 2Sm 18:23
me like the way A son of Zadok 2Sm 18:27
A called out to the king, 2Sm 18:28
A replied, "When Joab sent the 2Sm 18:29
A, in Naphtali (he also had 1Kg 4:15
Zadok; Zadok fathered A; 1Ch 6:8
A fathered Azariah; Azariah 1Ch 6:9
his son Zadok, and his son A. 1Ch 6:53

AHIMAN *(4)*
to Hebron, where A, Sheshai, and Nm 13:22
Sheshai, A, and Talmai, Jos 15:14
down Sheshai, A, and Talmai. Jdg 1:10
Akkub, Talmon, A, and their 1Ch 9:17

AHIMELECH *(18)*
(AKA ABIMELECH)
David went to A the priest at 1Sm 21:1
A was afraid to meet David, 1Sm 21:1
David answered A the priest, 1Sm 21:2
David said to A, "Do you have a 1Sm 21:8
son come to A son of Ahitub at 1Sm 22:9
A inquired of the LORD for him 1Sm 22:10
to summon A the priest, 1Sm 22:11
A replied to the king: 1Sm 22:14
You will die, A—you and your 1Sm 22:16
of the sons of A son of Ahitub 1Sm 22:20
Abiathar son of A fled to David 1Sm 23:6
Then David asked A the Hittite 1Sm 26:6
the priest, son of A, "Bring me 1Sm 30:7
of Ahitub and A son of Abiathar 2Sm 8:17
of Ahitub and A son of Abiathar 1Ch 18:16
of Eleazar and A from the sons 1Ch 24:3
the priest, A son of Abiathar, 1Ch 24:6
David, Zadok, A, and the heads 1Ch 24:31

AHIMOTH *(1)*
Elkanah's sons: Amasai and A, 1Ch 6:25

AHINADAB *(1)*
A son of Iddo, ⌊in⌋ Mahanaim; 1Kg 4:14

AHINOAM *(7)*
of Saul's wife was A daughter of 1Sm 14:50
David also married A of Jezreel, 1Sm 25:43
A of Jezreel and Abigail of 1Sm 27:3
A the Jezreelite and Abigail the 1Sm 30:5
A the Jezreelite and Abigail, 2Sm 2:2
was Amnon, by A the Jezreelite; 2Sm 3:2
the firstborn, by A of Jezreel; 1Ch 3:1

AHIO *(6)*
Uzzah and A, sons of Abinadab, 2Sm 6:3
A walked in front of the ark. 2Sm 6:4
A, Shashak, and Jeremoth. 1Ch 8:14
Gedor, A, Zecher, 1Ch 8:31
A, Zechariah, and Mikloth. 1Ch 9:37
Uzzah and A were guiding the 1Ch 13:7

AHIRA *(5)*
A son of Enan from Naphtali. Nm 1:15
Naphtalites is A son of Enan. Nm 2:29
the twelfth day A son of Enan, Nm 7:78
the offering of A son of Enan. Nm 7:83
and A son of Enan was over the Nm 10:27

AHIRAM *(1)*
the Ahiramite clan from A; Nm 26:38

AHIRAMITE *(1)*
the A clan from Ahiram; Nm 26:38

AHISAMACH *(3)*
also selected Oholiab son of A, Ex 31:6
both him and Oholiab son of A, Ex 35:34
With him was Oholiab son of A, Ex 38:23

AHISHAHAR *(1)*
Zethan, Tarshish, and A. 1Ch 7:10

AHISHAR *(1)*
A, in charge of the palace; 1Kg 4:6

AHITHOPHEL *(16)*
David's adviser A the Gilonite, 2Sm 15:12
A is among the conspirators with 2Sm 15:31
counsel of A into foolishness! 2Sm 15:31
A was also with him. 2Sm 16:15
Absalom said to A, "Give ⌊me⌋ 2Sm 16:20
A replied to Absalom, "Sleep 2Sm 16:21
Now the advice A gave in those 2Sm 16:23
A said to Absalom, "Let me 2Sm 17:1
A offered this proposal. 2Sm 17:6
The advice A has given this time 2Sm 17:7
This is what A advised Absalom 2Sm 17:15
for A has given this advice 2Sm 17:21
When A realized that his advice 2Sm 17:23
Eliam son of A the Gilonite, 2Sm 23:34
A was the king's counselor. 1Ch 27:33
After A came Jehoiada son of 1Ch 27:34

AHITHOPHEL'S *(4)*
can counteract A counsel for me. 2Sm 15:34
and Absalom had for A advice. 2Sm 16:23
had decreed that A good advice 2Sm 17:14
is better than A advice." 2Sm 17:14

AHITUB *(14)*
He was the son of A, the brother 1Sm 14:3
to Ahimelech son of A at Nob. 1Sm 22:9
priest, son of A, and his 1Sm 22:11
Saul said, "Listen, son of A!" 1Sm 22:12
of Ahimelech son of A escaped. 1Sm 22:20
Zadok son of A and Ahimelech son 2Sm 8:17
Amariah; Amariah fathered A; 1Ch 6:7
A fathered Zadok; Zadok fathered 1Ch 6:8
Amariah; Amariah fathered A; 1Ch 6:11
A fathered Zadok; Zadok fathered 1Ch 6:12
his son Amariah, his son A, 1Ch 6:52
Meraioth, son of A, the chief 1Ch 9:11
Zadok son of A and Ahimelech 1Ch 18:16
Meraioth, son of A, the chief Neh 11:11

AHITUB'S *(1)*
son, Zadok's son, A son, Ezr 7:2

AHLAB *(1)*
of Sidon, or A, Achzib, Helbah Jdg 1:31

AHLAI *(2)*
Sheshan's descendant: A. 1Ch 2:31
the Hittite, Zabad son of A, 1Ch 11:41

AHOAH *(1)*
Abishua, Naaman, A, 1Ch 8:4

AHOHI *(1)*
son of Dodo son of A was among 2Sm 23:9

AHOHITE *(4)*
Zalmon the A, Maharai the 2Sm 23:28
son of Dodo the A was one of the 1Ch 11:12
the Hushathite, Ilai the A, 1Ch 11:29
Dodai the A was in charge of the 1Ch 27:4

AHUMAI *(1)*
and Jahath fathered A and Lahad. 1Ch 4:2

AHUZZAM *(1)*
bore him A, Hepher, Temeni 1Ch 4:6

AHUZZATH *(1)*
from Gerar with A his adviser Gn 26:26

AHZAI *(1)*
of Azarel, son of A, son of Neh 11:13

AI *(38)*
(AKA AIATH, AIJA)
on the west and A on the east. Gn 12:8
Bethel and A where his tent had Gn 13:3
sent men from Jericho to A, Jos 7:2
the men went up and scouted A. Jos 7:2
2,000 or 3,000 men to attack A. Jos 7:3
the people of A are so few, Jos 7:3
but they fled from the men of A. Jos 7:4
The men of A struck down about Jos 7:5
force with you and go attack A. Jos 8:1
over to you the king of A, Jos 8:1
Treat A and its king as you did Jos 8:2
force set out to attack A. Jos 8:3
and waited between Bethel and A, Jos 8:9
Bethel and Ai, to the west of A. Jos 8:9
Israel led the troops up to A. Jos 8:10
opposite A, and camped to Jos 8:11
in ambush between Bethel and A, Jos 8:12
When the king of A saw ⌊the Jos 8:14
the troops of A were summoned to Jos 8:16
man was left in A or Bethel who Jos 8:17
the sword in your hand toward A, Jos 8:18
The men of A turned and looked Jos 8:20
and struck down the men of A. Jos 8:21
and the men of A were ⌊trapped⌋ Jos 8:22
the king of A alive and brought Jos 8:23
living in A who had pursued Jos 8:24
returned to A and struck it down Jos 8:24
12,000—all the people of A. Jos 8:25
inhabitants of A were completely Jos 8:26
Joshua burned A and left it a Jos 8:28
the king of A on a tree until Jos 8:29
heard ⌊about Jericho and A⌋, Jos 9:1
had done to Jericho and A, Jos 9:3
had captured A and completely Jos 10:1
doing to A and its king as he Jos 10:1
was larger than A, and all its Jos 10:2
of Jericho one the king of A, Jos 12:9
Heshbon, for A is devastated; Jr 49:3

AI'S *(2)*
Bethel's and A men 223 Ezr 2:28
Bethel's and A men 123 Neh 7:32

AIAH *(5)*
Zibeon's sons: A and Anah. This Gn 36:24
name was Rizpah daughter of A, 2Sm 3:7
daughter of A had borne to Saul 2Sm 21:8
Rizpah, daughter of A, had done, 2Sm 21:11
Onam. Zibeon's sons: A and Anah. 1Ch 1:40

AIAH'S *(1)*
Rizpah, A daughter, took 2Sm 21:10

AIATH *(1)*
(AKA AI, AIJA)
has come to A and has gone Is 10:28

AID *(8)*
come to your a and bring you up Gn 50:24
When God comes to your a, Gn 50:25
will certainly come to your a; Ex 13:19
heavens to your a on the clouds Dt 33:26
son of Zeruiah came to his a, 2Sm 21:17
and small—and come to my a. Ps 35:2
Give us a against the foe, Ps 60:11
Give us a against the foe, Ps 108:12

AIDE *(2)*
Jehu said to Bidkar his a, 2Kg 9:25
message a fifth time by his a, Neh 6:5

AIDED *(1)*
administrators a the Jews Est 9:3

AIDES *(2)*
trusted royal a found in the 2Kg 25:19
trusted royal a found in the Jr 52:25

AIJA *(1)*
(AKA AI, AIATH)
Geba, Michmash, A, and Bethel— Neh 11:31

AIJALON *(9)*
and moon, over the valley of A." Jos 10:12
Shaalabbin, A, Ithlah, Jos 19:42
A with its pasturelands, and Jos 21:24
Har-heres, A, and Shaalbim. Jdg 1:35
was buried in A in the land of Jdg 12:12
from Michmash all the way to A. 1Sm 14:31
A and its pasturelands, and 1Ch 6:69
Zorah, A, and Hebron, which are 2Ch 11:10
Beth-shemesh, A, Gederoth, Soco 2Ch 28:18

AIJALON'S *(1)*
of families of A residents and 1Ch 8:13

AILMENT *(1)*
from whatever a he had. Jn 5:4

AIM *(7)*
taking special **a** and struck the 1Kg 22:34
taking special **a** and struck the 2Ch 18:33
flight when you **a** your bow at Ps 21:12
will **a** their useless arrows. Ps 58:7
like swords and **a** bitter words Ps 64:3
So my **a** is to evangelize where Rm 15:20
we make it our **a** to be pleasing 2Co 5:9

AIMED *(1)*
His plan is **a** at Babylon to Jr 51:11

AIMING *(1)*
it as if I'm **a** at a target. 1Sm 20:20

AIMLESSLY *(2)*
So they wandered **a**. Lm 4:15
do not run like one who runs **a**, 1Co 9:26

AIN *(5)*
(AKA ASHAN)
Shepham to Riblah east of **A**. Nm 34:11
Shilhim, **A**, and Rimmon—29 Jos 15:32
A, Rimmon, Ether, and Ashan— Jos 19:7
A with its pasturelands, Juttah Jos 21:16
were Etam, **A**, Rimmon, Tochen, 1Ch 4:32

AIR *(12)*
dust into the **a** and on his head. Jb 2:12
another that no **a** can pass Jb 41:16
panting for **a** like jackals. Jr 14:6
birds of the **a**—He has handed Dn 2:38
the birds of the **a** lived in its Dn 4:12
the birds of the **a** lived— Dn 4:21
and throwing dust into the **a**, Ac 22:23
or box like one who beats the **a**. 1Co 9:26
you will be speaking into the **a**. 1Co 14:9
to meet the Lord in the **a**; 1Th 4:17
the sun and the **a** were darkened Rv 9:2
poured out his bowl into the **a**, Rv 16:17

AKAN *(1)*
(AKA JAAKAN)
sons: Bilhan, Zaavan, and **A**. Gn 36:27

AKKUB *(5)*
Pelaiah, **A**, Johanan, Delaiah 1Ch 3:24
Shallum, **A**, Talmon, Ahiman, and 1Ch 9:17
Sherebiah, Jamin, **A**, Shabbethai, Neh 8:7
A, Talmon, and their relatives, Neh 11:19
and **A** were gatekeepers who Neh 12:25

AKKUB'S *(3)*
descendants, **A** descendants, Ezr 2:42
descendants, **A** descendants, Ezr 2:45
descendants, **A** descendants, Neh 7:45

AKRABBIM *(3)*
turn south of the Ascent of **A**, Nm 34:4
went south of the ascent of **A**, Jos 15:3
extended from the ascent of **A**, Jdg 1:36

ALABASTER *(4)*
His legs are **a** pillars set on Sg 5:15
Him with an **a** jar of very Mt 26:7
woman came with an **a** jar of pure Mk 14:3
She brought an **a** flask of Lk 7:37

ALAMOTH *(1)*
to play harps according to **A**; 1Ch 15:20

ALARM *(5)*
my **a** I had said, "I am cut off Ps 31:22
In my **a** I said, "Everyone is a Ps 116:11
Nebuchadnezzar jumped up in **a**. Dn 3:24
or its interpretation **a** you." Dn 4:19
sound the **a** on My holy mountain! Jl 2:1

ALARMED *(12)*
not be afraid, **a**, or terrified Dt 20:3
were greatly **a** because Gibeon Jos 10:2
the sea are **a** by your demise." Ezk 26:18
and visions in my mind **a** me. Dn 4:5
moment, and his thoughts **a** him. Dn 4:19
you are not **a**, because these Mt 24:6
and rumors of wars, don't be **a**; Mk 13:7
they were amazed and **a**. Mk 16:5
"Don't be **a**," he told them. Mk 16:6
wars and rebellions, don't be **a**. Lk 21:9
said, "Don't be **a**, for his life Ac 20:10
too was **a** when he realized Ac 22:29

ALARMING *(1)*
aren't frightened by anything **a**. 1Pt 3:6

ALAS *(3)*
preceded you. **A**, lord! will be Jr 34:5
may stumble. **A**! It is ready to Ezk 21:15
GOD says: Wail: **A** for the day! Ezk 30:2

ALCOHOLIC *(3)*
drink wine or other **a** beverages, Jdg 13:4
drink wine or other **a** beverages, Jdg 13:7
drink wine or other **a** beverages. Jdg 13:14

ALEMETH *(4)*
(AKA ALMON)
its pasturelands, **A** and its 1Ch 6:60
Abijah, Anathoth, and **A**; 1Ch 7:8
Jehoaddah fathered **A**, Azmaveth, 1Ch 8:36
Jarah fathered **A**, Azmaveth, and 1Ch 9:42

ALERT *(19)*
the watchman stays **a** in vain. Ps 127:1
Therefore be **a**, since you don't Mt 24:42
have stayed **a** and not let his Mt 24:43
Therefore be **a**, because you Mt 25:13
Watch! Be **a**! For you don't know Mk 13:33
the doorkeeper to be **a**. Mk 13:34
Therefore be **a**, since you don't Mk 13:35
you, I say to everyone: Be **a**!" Mk 13:37
master will find **a** when he comes Lk 12:37
and finds them **a**, those slaves Lk 12:38
But be **a** at all times, praying Lk 21:36
be on the **a**, remembering that Ac 20:31
a, stand firm in the faith, be 1Co 16:13
Spirit, and stay **a** in this, with Eph 6:18
stay **a** in it with thanksgiving. Col 4:2
Be on the **a**! Your adversary 1Pt 5:8
a and strengthen what remains, Rv 3:2
if you are not **a**, I will come Rv 3:3
is the one who is **a** and remains Rv 16:15

ALERTED *(1)*
they **a** the whole vicinity and Mt 14:35

ALEXANDER *(6)*
the father of **A** and Rufus. Mk 15:21
Caiaphas, John and **A**, and all Ac 4:6
of the crowd gave **A** advice when Ac 19:33
A wanted to make his defense to Ac 19:33
Hymenaeus and **A** are among them 1Tm 1:20
A the coppersmith did great harm 2Tm 4:14

ALEXANDRIAN *(3)*
a native **A**, an eloquent man Ac 18:24
found an **A** ship sailing for Ac 27:6
set sail in an **A** ship that had Ac 28:11

ALEXANDRIANS *(1)*
of both Cyrenians and **A**, Ac 6:9

ALGUM *(3)*
cypress, and **a** logs from Lebanon 2Ch 2:8
also brought **a** wood and precious 2Ch 9:10
The king made the **a** wood into 2Ch 9:11

ALIAN *(1)*
A, Manahath, Ebal, Shephi, and 1Ch 1:40

ALIEN *(12)*
where you are a resident **a**." Gn 21:23
I am a resident **a** among you. Gn 23:4
the land where you live as an **a**, Gn 28:4
it to a resident **a** within your Dt 14:21
if you no longer oppress the **a**, Jr 7:6
are You like an **a** in the land, Jr 14:8
exploit or brutalize the **a**, Jr 22:3
you stay as a resident **a**.' Jr 35:7
even stay in it as a resident **a**. Jr 49:18
even stay in it as a resident **a**. Jr 49:33
even stay in it as a resident **a**. Jr 50:40
be regarded as something **a**. Hs 8:12

ALIENATED *(2)*
by the law are **a** from Christ; Gl 5:4
And you were once **a** and hostile Col 1:21

ALIENATION *(1)*
cursed ⌊with **a**⌋ from the ground Gn 4:11

ALIENS *(2)*
there as **a** to this very day. 2Sm 4:3
I urge you as **a** and temporary 1Pt 2:11

ALIGNED *(3)*
So Israel **a** itself with Baal of Nm 25:3
of the men who **a** themselves with Nm 25:5
They **a** themselves with Baal of Ps 106:28

ALIKE *(18)*
the righteous and the wicked **a**. Gn 18:25
will be **a** before the LORD. Nm 15:15
listen to small and great **a**. Dt 1:17
citizen **a**, with their elders, Jos 8:33
because the sword devours all **a**. 2Sm 11:25
and their younger brothers **a**. 1Ch 24:31
the young and old **a**, the teacher 1Ch 25:8
young and old **a**, for each gate. 1Ch 26:13
all **a** have become corrupt. Ps 14:3
and dancers **a** ⌊will say⌋, Ps 87:7
the LORD—small and great **a**. Ps 115:13
darkness and light are **a** to You. Ps 139:12
day and a nagging wife are **a**. Pr 27:15
young and old **a**, naked and Is 20:4
people and priest **a**, servant and Is 24:2
fathers and sons **a**"—the LORD's Jr 13:14
and Judeans **a** have been Jr 50:33
sea, in summer and winter **a**. Zch 14:8

ALIVE *(91)*
female, to keep them **a** with you. Gn 6:19
you so that you can keep them **a**. Gn 6:20
to keep offspring **a** on the face Gn 7:3
while he was still **a** he sent Gn 25:6
'Is your father still **a**? Gn 43:7
told me about? Is he still **a**?" Gn 43:27
He is still **a**." And they bowed Gn 43:28
and to keep you **a** by a great Gn 45:7
Joseph is still **a**, and he is Gn 45:26
My son Joseph is still **a**. Gn 45:28
⌊and know⌋ you are still **a**!" Gn 46:30
actually found **a** in his Ex 22:4
be presented **a** before the LORD Lv 16:10
remained **a** of those men who Nm 14:38
that they go down **a** into Sheol, Nm 16:30
They went down **a** into Sheol with Nm 16:33
keep **a** for yourselves all the Nm 31:18
LORD your God are all **a** today. Dt 4:4
one of these cities and stay **a**: Dt 4:42
all of us who are **a** here today. Dt 5:3
I am still **a**, how much more Dt 31:27
the king of Ai **a** and brought him Jos 8:23
he left no one **a**. Then he burned Jos 11:11
them, leaving no one **a**. Jos 11:14
has kept me **a** ⌊these⌋ 45 years Jos 14:10
while the judge was still **a**. Jdg 2:18
they had kept **a** from Jdg 21:14
captured Agag king of Amalek **a**, 1Sm 15:8
did not leave a single person **a**, 1Sm 27:9
length ⌊of those⌋ to be kept **a**. 2Sm 8:2
the baby was **a**, we spoke to him 2Sm 12:18
While the baby was **a**, you fasted 2Sm 12:21
the baby was **a**, I fasted and 2Sm 12:22
he was still **a** in the oak tree, 2Sm 18:14
When he was **a**, Absalom had 2Sm 18:18
if Absalom were **a** and all of us 2Sm 19:6
my son who is **a**, and your son is 1Kg 3:23
son is dead, and my son is **a**.'" 1Kg 3:23
whose son was **a** spoke to the 1Kg 3:26
father Solomon when he was **a**, 1Kg 12:6
Jeroboam anyone **a** until he had 1Kg 15:29
said, "Look, your son is **a**." 1Kg 17:23
and mules **a** and not have to 1Kg 18:5
peace, take them **a**, and if they 1Kg 20:18
out for battle, take them **a**." 1Kg 20:18
So he said, "Is he still **a**? 1Kg 20:32
since Naboth isn't **a**, but dead." 1Kg 21:15
we will take them **a** and go into 2Kg 7:12
Jehu ordered, "Take them **a**." 2Kg 10:14
So they took them **a** and then 2Kg 10:14
father Solomon when he was **a**, 2Ch 10:6
the Judahites captured 10,000 **a**. 2Ch 25:12
while they are still **a**, Jb 21:8
He does not keep the wicked **a**, Jb 36:6
and to keep them **a** in famine. Ps 33:19
let them go down to Sheol **a**, Ps 55:15
He keeps us **a** and does not allow Ps 66:9
swallowed us **a** in their burning Ps 124:3
no one **a** is righteous in Your Ps 143:2
swallow them **a**, like Sheol, Pr 1:12
the living, who are still **a**. Ec 4:2
for food in order to stay **a**. Lm 1:11
me⌋, no one to keep me **a**. Lm 1:16
for food to keep themselves **a**. Lm 1:19
They dropped me **a** into a pit and Lm 3:53
as he and the buyer remain **a**. Ezk 7:13
wanted and kept **a** anyone he Dn 5:19
stone: Come **a**! Can it teach? Hab 2:19
cannot remain **a** because you have Zch 13:3
while this deceiver was still **a**, Mt 27:63
that He was **a** and had been seen Mk 16:11
of mine was dead and is **a** again; Lk 15:24
yours was dead and is **a** again; Lk 15:32
of angels who said He was **a**. Lk 24:23
him saying that his boy was **a**. Jn 4:51
Himself **a** to them by many Ac 1:3
and widows and presented her **a**. Ac 9:41

the boy home **a** and were greatly Ac 20:12
man whom Paul claimed to be **a**. Ac 25:19
but **a** to God in Christ Jesus. Rm 6:11
those who are **a** from the dead, Rm 6:13
Once I was **a** apart from the law, Rm 7:9
in Christ all will be made **a**. 1Co 15:22
made us **a** with the Messiah even Eph 2:5
He made you **a** with Him and Col 2:13
We who are still **a** at the Lord's 1Th 4:15
who are still **a** will be caught 1Th 4:17
but made **a** in the spiritual 1Pt 3:18
but look—I am **a** forever and Rv 1:18
have a reputation for being **a**, Rv 3:1
them were thrown **a** into the lake Rv 19:20

ALL *(4420)*
(See pp. xi-xii.)

ALL-POWERFUL *(1)*
God is wise and **a**. Jb 9:4

ALLAMMELECH *(1)*
A, Amad, and Mishal and reached Jos 19:26

ALLEGIANCE *(6)*
maintained their **a** to the house 1Ch 12:29
pledged their **a** to King Solomon. 1Ch 29:24
your **a** to the LORD, and come 2Ch 30:8
had made him swear **a** by God. 2Ch 36:13
every tongue will swear **a**. Is 45:23
were free from **a** to Rm 6:20

ALLEGING *(2)*
a that these things were so. Ac 24:9
a that the Day of the Lord has 2Th 2:2

ALLEYS *(1)*
the streets and **a** of the city, Lk 14:21

ALLIANCE *(16)*
a unified **a** to fight against Jos 9:2
having no **a** with anyone. Jdg 18:7
and they had no **a** with anyone. Jdg 18:28
Solomon made an **a** with Pharaoh 1Kg 3:1
and he made an **a** with Ahab 2Ch 18:1
made an **a** with Israel's King 2Ch 20:35
formed an **a** with him to make 2Ch 20:36
you formed an **a** with Ahaziah, 2Ch 20:37
they form an **a** against You— Ps 83:5
everything an **a** these people say Is 8:12
these people say is an **a**. Is 8:12
form a triple ⌊**a**⌋ with Egypt Is 19:24
They make an **a**, but against My Is 30:1
you with an **a** of nations and Ezk 23:24
some years they will form an **a**, Dn 11:6
After an **a** is made with him, Dn 11:23

ALLIES *(8)*
of these came as **a** to the Valley Gn 14:3
and all their **a** were handed over 1Ch 5:20
let it be a trap for ⌊their⌋ **a**. Ps 69:22
and against the **a** of evildoers. Is 31:2
and all its **a** are shattered. Ezk 30:8
As its **a** they had lived in its Ezk 31:17
of Sheol about him and his **a**: Ezk 32:21
Put and Libya were among her **a**. Nah 3:9

ALLOCATED *(1)*
on⌋ all that I had **a** to her. Zph 3:7

ALLON *(1)*
Shiphi, son of **A**, son of Jedaiah 1Ch 4:37

ALLOT *(2)*
You will **a** it as an inheritance Ezk 47:22
land you are to **a** as an Ezk 48:29

ALLOTMENT *(7)*
for it was their **a** from Pharaoh. Gn 47:22
lived off the **a** Pharaoh had Gn 47:22
Now the **a** for the tribe of the Jos 15:1
The **a** for the descendants of Jos 16:1
This was the **a** for the tribe of Jos 17:1
So the **a** was for the rest of Jos 17:2
only one tribal **a** as an Jos 17:14

ALLOTMENTS *(2)*
according to their tribal **a**. Jos 11:23
of Israel according to their **a**: Jos 12:7

ALLOTS *(1)*
He **a** our fields to traitors. Mc 2:4

ALLOTTED *(16)*
it will be **a** to you as an Nm 34:2
part of our **a** inheritance would Nm 36:3
their **a** territory lay between Jos 18:11
The **a** cities to the remaining Jos 21:20
12 cities were **a** to the clans Jos 21:40
I have **a** these remaining nations Jos 23:4
buried him in his **a** territory at Jos 24:30
took longer than the time **a** him. 2Sm 20:5
from the food **a** to the governor Neh 5:14
the food **a** to the governor Neh 5:18
the land **a** to the righteous, Ps 125:3
His hand **a** their portion with a Is 34:17
they will be **a** an inheritance Ezk 47:22
measures out the **a** land of my Mc 2:4
give them their **a** food at the Lk 12:42
number and was **a** a share in this Ac 1:17

ALLOW *(40)*
of Egypt will not **a** you to go, Ex 3:19
You must not **a** a sorceress to Ex 22:18
You are to **a** the redemption of Lv 25:24
Do not **a** the Kohathite tribal Nm 4:18
Edom refused to **a** Israel to Nm 20:21
you **a** to remain will become Nm 33:55
and did not **a** them to go down Jdg 1:34
and did not **a** anyone to cross Jdg 3:28
Please **a** me to make one more Jdg 6:39
me back and **a** me to see both it 2Sm 15:25
and don't **a** injustice to dwell Jb 11:14
against God and **a** such words to Jb 15:13
You will not **a** Your Faithful One Ps 16:10
him in his hand or **a** him to be Ps 37:33
He will never **a** the righteous to Ps 55:22
and does not **a** our feet to slip Ps 66:9
He will not **a** your foot to slip; Ps 121:3
I will not **a** my eyes to sleep or Ps 132:4
but God does not **a** him to enjoy Ec 6:2
will not **a** those who practice Ec 8:8
and I will **a** you to live in this Jr 7:3
I will **a** you to live in this Jr 7:7
I will **a** no mercy, pity, or Jr 13:14
on you and **a** you to return to Jr 42:12
If I **a** dangerous animals to pass Ezk 14:15
I will no longer **a** the insults Ezk 36:15
will no longer **a** it to be Ezk 39:7
actions do not **a** ⌊them⌋ to Hs 5:4
answered him, "**A** it for now, Mt 3:15
and you don't **a** those entering Mt 23:13
A the children to be satisfied Mk 7:27
A us to sit at Your right and at Mk 10:37
and would not **a** them to speak, Lk 4:41
or **a** Your Holy One to see decay. Ac 2:27
You will not **a** Your Holy One to Ac 13:35
Spirit of Jesus did not **a** them. Ac 16:7
wind did not **a** us to approach Ac 27:7
Justice does not **a** him to live!" Ac 28:4
and He will not **a** you to be 1Co 10:13
do not **a** a woman to teach or to 1Tm 2:12

ALLOWANCE *(4)*
for his **a**, a regular allowance 2Kg 25:30
a regular **a** was given to him by 2Kg 25:30
for his **a**, a regular allowance Jr 52:34
a regular **a** was given to him by Jr 52:34

ALLOWED *(14)*
Then you will be **a** to settle Gn 46:34
He **a** no one to oppress them; 1Ch 16:21
and have **a** us to survive— Ezr 9:13
I have not **a** my mouth to sin by Jb 31:30
up and have not **a** my enemies to Ps 30:1
He **a** no one to oppress them; Ps 105:14
and He has **a** him to enjoy them, Ec 5:19
a to remain with Gedaliah son Jr 43:6
Ephraim has **a** himself to get Hs 7:8
Then he **a** Him ⌊to be baptized⌋. Mt 3:15
generations He **a** all the nations Ac 14:16
"Am I **a** to say something to you?" Ac 21:37
Paul kindly and **a** him to go to Ac 27:3
which a man is not **a** to speak. 2Co 12:4

ALLOWING *(2)*
a him to return and live in the Nm 35:32
a the cavalry to go on with him. Ac 23:32

ALLOWS *(4)*
and then **a** his animals to go and Ex 22:5
behind someone who **a** me to?" Ru 2:2
Whoever **a** any of the men I am 2Kg 10:24
time with you, if the Lord **a**. 1Co 16:7

ALLY *(2)*
trouble by law—become Your **a**? Ps 94:20
and Sidon every remaining **a**. Jr 47:4

ALMIGHTY *(57)*
to him, saying, "I am God **A**. Gn 17:1
May God **A** bless you and make you Gn 28:3
to him: I am God **A**. Be fruitful Gn 35:11
May God **A** cause the man to be Gn 43:14
God **A** appeared to me at Luz in Gn 48:3
by the **A** who blesses you with Gn 49:25
Jacob as God **A**, but I did not Ex 6:3
who sees a vision from the **A**, Nm 24:4
who sees a vision from the **A**, Nm 24:16
for the **A** has made me very Ru 1:20
and the **A** has afflicted me?" Ru 1:21
reject the discipline of the **A**. Jb 5:17
arrows of the **A** have pierced me Jb 6:4
he abandons the fear of the **A**. Jb 6:14
the **A** pervert what is right? Jb 8:3
God and ask the **A** for mercy, Jb 8:5
or discover the limits of the **A**? Jb 11:7
to speak to the **A** and argue my Jb 13:3
has arrogantly opposed the **A**. Jb 15:25
Who is the **A**, that we should Jb 21:15
Does it delight the **A** if you are Jb 22:3
and "What can the **A** do to us?" Jb 22:17
you return to the **A**, you will be Jb 22:23
the **A** will be your gold and your Jb 22:25
delight in the **A** and lift up Jb 22:26
the **A** has terrified me. Jb 23:16
Why does the **A** not reserve times Jb 24:1
the **A** who has made me bitter, Jb 27:2
Will he delight in the **A**? Jb 27:10
conceal what the **A** has planned. Jb 27:11
the ruthless receive from the **A**. Jb 27:13
when the **A** was still with me and Jb 29:5
inheritance from the **A** on high? Jb 31:2
let the **A** answer me. Jb 31:35
breath of the **A** that give him Jb 32:8
breath of the **A** gives me life. Jb 33:4
and ⌊for⌋ the **A** ⌊to act⌋ Jb 34:10
and the **A** does not pervert Jb 34:12
and the **A** does not take note of Jb 35:13
The **A**—we cannot reach Him—He Jb 37:23
with the **A** correct ⌊Him⌋? Jb 40:2
When the **A** scattered kings in Ps 68:14
dwells in the shadow of the **A**. Ps 91:1
like destruction from the **A**. Is 13:6
the voice of the **A**, and a sound Ezk 1:24
voice of God **A** when He speaks. Ezk 10:5
come as devastation from the **A**. Jl 1:15
to Me, says the Lord **A**. 2Co 6:18
was, and who is coming, the **A**." Rv 1:8
God, the **A**, who was, who is, Rv 4:8
Lord God, the **A**, who is and who Rv 11:17
are Your works, Lord God, the **A**; Rv 15:3
Yes, Lord God, the **A**, true and Rv 16:7
of the great day of God, the **A**. Rv 16:14
our Lord God, the **A**, has begun Rv 19:6
the fierce anger of God, the **A**. Rv 19:15
Lord God the **A** and the Lamb are Rv 21:22

ALMIGHTY'S *(1)*
let him drink from the **A** wrath! Jb 21:20

ALMODAD *(2)*
And Joktan fathered **A**, Sheleph, Gn 10:26
Joktan fathered **A**, Sheleph, 1Ch 1:20

ALMON *(1)*
(AKA ALEMETH)
and **A** with its pasturelands— Jos 21:18

ALMON-DIBLATHAIM *(2)*
from Dibon-gad and camped at **A**. Nm 33:46
They departed from **A** and camped Nm 33:47

ALMOND *(9)*
fresh poplar, **a**, and plane wood Gn 30:37
cups shaped like **a** blossoms, Ex 25:33
cups shaped like **a** blossoms, Ex 25:33
four cups shaped like **a** blossoms Ex 25:34
cups shaped like **a** blossoms, Ex 37:19
cups shaped like **a** blossoms, Ex 37:19
cups shaped like **a** blossoms with Ex 37:20
the **a** tree blossoms, the Ec 12:5
"I see a branch of an **a** tree." Jr 1:11

ALMONDS *(2)*
gum and resin, pistachios and **a**. Gn 43:11
buds, blossomed, and produced **a**! Nm 17:8

ALMOST *(13)*
(See pp. xi-xii.)

ALMUG *(3)*
quantity of **a** wood and precious 1Kg 10:11
king made the **a** wood into steps 1Kg 10:12
before⌋ had such **a** wood come, 1Kg 10:12

ALOES *(5)*
like **a** the LORD has planted, Nm 24:6
Myrrh, **a**, and cassia ⌊perfume⌋ Ps 45:8
bed with myrrh, **a**, and cinnamon. Pr 7:17
myrrh and **a**, with all the best Sg 4:14
about 75 pounds of myrrh and **a**. Jn 19:39

ALONE *(131)*
is not good for the man to be **a**. Gn 2:18
seen that you ⌊**a**⌋ are righteous Gn 7:1
Jacob was left **a**, and a man Gn 32:24
is dead and he **a** is left. Gn 42:38
He let him **a**. At that time she Ex 4:26
Leave us **a** so that we may serve Ex 14:12
Why are you **a** sitting as judge, Ex 18:14
for you. You can't do it **a**. Ex 18:18
If he arrives **a**, he is to leave Ex 21:3
arrives alone, he is to leave **a**; Ex 21:3
and the man must leave **a**. Ex 21:4
except the LORD **a**, is to be set Ex 22:20
Moses **a** is to approach the LORD, Ex 24:2
Now leave Me **a**, so that My anger Ex 32:10
must live **a** in a place outside Lv 13:46
There is a people living **a**; Nm 23:9
live on bread **a** but on every Dt 8:3
Leave Me **a**, and I will destroy Dt 9:14
Pursue justice and justice **a**, Dt 16:20
The LORD **a** led him, with no help Dt 32:12
See now that I **a** am He; Dt 32:39
he was sitting **a** in his room Jdg 3:20
Why are you **a** and no one is with 1Sm 21:1
Leave him **a** and let him curse 2Sm 16:11
out and saw a man running **a**. 2Sm 18:24
said, "If he's **a**, he bears good 2Sm 18:25
Another man is running **a**!" 2Sm 18:26
also had a baby and we were **a**. 1Kg 3:18
You **a** know every human heart, 1Kg 8:39
two of them were **a** in the open 1Kg 11:29
except the tribe of Judah **a**. 1Kg 12:20
for this one **a** out of Jeroboam's 1Kg 14:13
because in him ⌊**a**⌋ out of the 1Kg 14:13
a am left, and they are looking 1Kg 19:10
I **a** am left, and they're looking 1Kg 19:14
said, "Leave her **a**—she is in 2Kg 4:27
You are God—You **a**—of all the 2Kg 19:15
You are the LORD God—You **a**." 2Kg 19:19
God has chosen him **a**—is young 1Ch 29:1
for You **a** know the human heart, 2Ch 6:30
since we **a** must build ⌊it⌋ for Ezr 4:3
of this house of God **a**. Ezr 6:7
You **a** are the LORD. You created Neh 9:6
not to do away with Mordecai **a**. Est 3:6
I **a** have escaped to tell you! Jb 1:15
I **a** have escaped to tell you! Jb 1:16
I **a** have escaped to tell you! Jb 1:17
I **a** have escaped to tell you! Jb 1:19
Leave me **a**, for my days are a Jb 7:16
or leave me **a** until I swallow my Jb 7:19
He **a** stretches out the heavens Jb 9:8
Leave me **a**, so that I can smile Jb 10:20
given to them **a** when no Jb 15:19
God: "Leave us **a**! We don't want Jb 21:14
who said to God, "Leave us **a**!" Jb 22:17
my few crumbs **a** without letting Jb 31:17
peace, for You **a**, LORD, make me Ps 4:8
to me, for I am **a** and afflicted. Ps 25:16
He **a** crafts their hearts; Ps 33:15
You—You **a**—I have sinned Ps 51:4
I am at rest in God **a**; Ps 62:1
a is my rock and my salvation, Ps 62:2
Rest in God **a**, my soul, for my Ps 62:5
a is my rock and my salvation, Ps 62:6
Your righteousness, Yours **a**. Ps 71:16
be praised, who **a** does wonders. Ps 72:18
May they know that You **a**— Ps 83:18
perform wonders; You **a** are God. Ps 86:10
He **a** does great wonders. Ps 136:4
for His name **a** is exalted. Ps 148:13
be for you **a** and not for you Pr 5:17
a will bear ⌊the consequences⌋ Pr 9:12
how can one person **a** keep warm? Ec 4:11
the LORD **a** will be exalted on Is 2:11
the LORD **a** will be exalted on Is 2:17
more room and you **a** are left in Is 5:8
but we remember Your name **a**. Is 26:13
until you **a** remain like a Is 30:17
You are God—You **a**—of all the Is 37:16
that You are the LORD—You **a**." Is 37:20
I **a** declared, saved, and Is 43:12
from today on I am He ⌊**a**⌋, Is 43:13
who **a** spread out the earth; Is 44:24
I trampled the winepress **a**, Is 63:3
Or can the skies **a** give showers? Jr 14:22
on me⌋, I sat **a**, for You filled Jr 15:17
even a gate bar; they live **a**. Jr 49:31
How she sits **a**, the city ⌊once⌋ Lm 1:1
Let him sit **a** and be silent, Lm 3:28
they were killing, I was left **a**. Ezk 9:8
They **a** would be delivered, Ezk 14:16
but they **a** would be delivered. Ezk 14:18
set apart for the priests ⌊**a**⌋. Ezk 48:10
I was left **a**, looking at this Dn 10:8
attached to idols; leave him **a**! Hs 4:17
will be for their appetites ⌊**a**⌋; Hs 9:4
They live **a** in a scrubland, Mc 7:14
earth—Yahweh **a**, and His name Zch 14:9
Yahweh alone, and His name **a**. Zch 14:9
live on bread **a** but on every Mt 4:4
boat to a remote place to be **a**. Mt 14:13
evening came, He was there **a**. Mt 14:23
Leave them **a**! They are blind Mt 15:14
saw no one except Him—Jesus **a**. Mt 17:8
the children **a**, and don't try to Mt 19:14
Who can forgive sins but God **a**?" Mk 2:7
When He was **a** with the Twelve, Mk 4:10
sea, and He was **a** on the land. Mk 6:47
mountain by themselves to be **a**. Mk 9:2
anyone with them except Jesus **a**. Mk 9:8
Then Jesus said, "Leave her **a**. Mk 14:6
Man must not live on bread **a**." Lk 4:4
Leave us **a**! What do You have to Lk 4:34
Who can forgive sins but God **a**?" Lk 5:21
sister has left me to serve **a**? Lk 10:40
His disciples had gone off **a**. Jn 6:22
because I am not **a**, but I and Jn 8:16
has not left Me **a**, because I Jn 8:29
Jesus answered, "Leave her **a**; Jn 12:7
home, and you will leave Me **a**. Jn 16:32
Yet I am not **a**, because the Jn 16:32
from these men and leave them **a**. Ac 5:38
was not written for Abraham **a**, Rm 4:23
for boasting in himself **a**, Gl 6:4
and receiving except you **a**. Php 4:15
These **a** of the circumcision are Col 4:11
better to be left **a** in Athens. 1Th 3:1
widow, left all **a**, has put her 1Tm 5:5
the high priest **a** enters the Heb 9:7
by works and not by faith **a**. Jms 2:24
Because You **a** are holy, because Rv 15:4

ALONG *(346)*
(See pp. xi-xii.)

ALONGSIDE *(5)*
The wheels rose **a** them, for the Ezk 1:20
the wheels rose **a** them, for the Ezk 1:21
a Hamath and extending from the Ezk 48:1
the length **a** the holy donation Ezk 48:18
It will run **a** the holy donation. Ezk 48:18

ALOOF *(1)*
the day you stood **a**, on the day Ob 11

ALOUD *(21)*
and read ⌊it⌋ **a** to the people. Ex 24:7
to read this law **a** before all Dt 31:11
Moses recited **a** every single Dt 31:30
Joshua read **a** all the words of Jos 8:34
terms to the people, all wept **a**. 1Sm 11:4
my son?" Then Saul wept **a** 1Sm 24:16
the king wept **a** at Abner's tomb. 2Sm 3:32
They wept **a**, and each man tore Jb 2:12
I cry **a** to the LORD, and He Ps 3:4
decided to say these things ⌊**a**⌋, Ps 73:15
cry **a** to God, aloud to God, and Ps 77:1
aloud to God, **a** to God, and He Ps 77:1
I cry **a** to the LORD; I plead Ps 142:1
I plead **a** to the LORD for mercy. Ps 142:1
Cry **a**, daughter of Gallim! Is 10:30
where Kedar dwells ⌊cry **a**⌋. Is 42:11
shouts, He roars **a**, He prevails Is 42:13
that you read all these words **a**. Jr 51:61
She weeps **a** during the night, Lm 1:2
reading the prophet Isaiah **a**. Ac 8:28
and he is read **a** in the Ac 15:21

ALPHA *(3)*
"I am the **A** and the Omega," Rv 1:8
I am the **A** and the Omega, the Rv 21:6
I am the **A** and the Omega, the Rv 22:13

ALPHAEUS *(5)*
the son of **A**, and Thaddaeus; Mt 10:3
Levi the son of **A** sitting at the Mk 2:14
the son of **A**, and Thaddaeus; Mk 3:18
James the son of **A**, and Simon Lk 6:15
James the son of **A**, Simon the Ac 1:13

ALREADY *(83)*
(See pp. xi-xii.)

ALSO *(1114)*
(See pp. xi-xii.)

ALTAR *(376)*
Noah built an **a** to the LORD. Gn 8:20
burnt offerings on the **a**. Gn 8:20
So he built an **a** there to the Gn 12:7
There he built an **a** to the LORD Gn 12:8
site where he had built the **a**. Gn 13:4
where he built an **a** to the LORD. Gn 13:18
Abraham built the **a** there and Gn 22:9
Isaac and placed him on the **a**, Gn 22:9
he built an **a** there, worshiped Gn 26:25
he set up an **a** there and called Gn 33:20
Build an **a** there to the God who Gn 35:1
I will build an **a** there to the Gn 35:3
built an **a** there and called Gn 35:7
Moses built an **a** and named it, Ex 17:15
make an earthen **a** for Me and Ex 20:24
If you make a stone **a** for Me, Ex 20:25
must not go up to My **a** on steps, Ex 20:26
take him from My **a** to be put to Ex 21:14
and set up an **a** and 12 pillars Ex 24:4
the blood he sprinkled on the **a**. Ex 24:6
construct the **a** of acacia wood. Ex 27:1
The **a** must be square, seven and Ex 27:1
the mesh comes halfway up the **a**. Ex 27:5
Then make poles for the **a**, Ex 27:6
two sides of the **a** when it is Ex 27:7
Construct the **a** with boards so Ex 27:8
or approach the **a** to minister Ex 28:43
horns of the **a** with your finger Ex 29:12
the blood at the base of the **a**. Ex 29:12
them, and burn ⌊them⌋ on the **a**. Ex 29:13
it⌋ on all sides of the **a**. Ex 29:16
head and its pieces ⌊on the **a**⌋. Ex 29:17
burn the whole ram on the **a**; Ex 29:18
blood on all sides of the **a**. Ex 29:20
blood that is on the **a** and some Ex 29:21
burn ⌊them⌋ on the **a** on top of Ex 29:25
Purify the **a** when you make Ex 29:36
for the **a** and consecrate it Ex 29:37
The **a** will become especially Ex 29:37
touches the **a** will become holy. Ex 29:37
regularly on the **a** every day: Ex 29:38
the tent of meeting and the **a**; Ex 29:44
are to make an **a** for the burning Ex 30:1
are to place the **a** in front of Ex 30:6
rite on the horns of the **a**. Ex 30:10
a is especially holy to the LORD. Ex 30:10
the tent of meeting and the **a**, Ex 30:18
or approach the **a** to minister by Ex 30:20
its utensils, the **a** of incense, Ex 30:27
the **a** of burnt offering with all Ex 30:28
its utensils, the **a** of incense, Ex 31:8
the **a** of burnt offering with all Ex 31:9
this⌋, he built an **a** before it; Ex 32:5
the **a** of incense with its poles; Ex 35:15
the **a** of burnt offering with its Ex 35:16
He made the **a** of incense out of Ex 37:25
constructed the **a** of burnt Ex 38:1
for the **a** a grate of bronze Ex 38:4
the sides of the **a** in order to Ex 38:7
constructed the **a** with boards so Ex 38:7
the bronze **a** and its bronze Ex 38:30
all the utensils for the **a**, Ex 38:30
the gold **a**; the anointing oil; Ex 39:38
the bronze **a** with its bronze Ex 39:39
Place the gold **a** for incense in Ex 40:5
Position the **a** of burnt offering Ex 40:6
the tent of meeting and the **a**, Ex 40:7
Anoint the **a** of burnt offering Ex 40:10
consecrate the **a** so that it will Ex 40:10
installed the gold **a** in the tent Ex 40:26
he placed the **a** of burnt Ex 40:29
meeting and the **a** and put water Ex 40:30
of meeting and approached the **a**, Ex 40:32
and the **a** and hung a screen Ex 40:33
on all sides of the **a** that is at Lv 1:5
a fire on the **a** and arrange wood Lv 1:7
of the burning wood on the **a**. Lv 1:8

all of it on the **a** as a burnt Lv 1:9
side of the **a** before the LORD. Lv 1:11
against the **a** on all sides. Lv 1:11
of the burning wood on the **a**. Lv 1:12
of it and burn ⌊it⌋ on the **a**; Lv 1:13
priest must bring it to the **a**, Lv 1:15
its head and burn ⌊it⌋ on the **a**; Lv 1:15
be drained at the side of the **a**. Lv 1:15
side of the **a** at the place for Lv 1:16
is to burn it on the **a** on top of Lv 1:17
memorial portion of it on the **a**, Lv 2:2
and he will take it to the **a**. Lv 2:8
offering and burn it on the **a**, Lv 2:9
offered on the **a** as a pleasing Lv 2:12
the blood on all sides of the **a**. Lv 3:2
will burn it on the **a** along with Lv 3:5
its blood on all sides of the **a**. Lv 3:8
will burn it on the **a** as food, Lv 3:11
its blood on all sides of the **a**. Lv 3:13
will burn them on the **a** as food, Lv 3:16
the horns of the **a** of fragrant Lv 4:7
the base of the **a** of burnt Lv 4:7
burn them on the **a** of burnt Lv 4:10
horns of the **a** that is before Lv 4:18
the base of the **a** of burnt Lv 4:18
from it and burn it on the **a**. Lv 4:19
the horns of the **a** of burnt Lv 4:25
the base of the **a** of burnt Lv 4:25
must burn all its fat on the **a**, Lv 4:26
the horns of the **a** of burnt Lv 4:30
its blood at the base of the **a**. Lv 4:30
burn ⌊it⌋ on the **a** as a pleasing Lv 4:31
the horns of the **a** of burnt Lv 4:34
its blood at the base of the **a**. Lv 4:34
burn it on the **a** along with the Lv 4:35
offering on the side of the **a**, Lv 5:9
out at the base of the **a**; Lv 5:9
burn ⌊it⌋ on the **a** along with Lv 5:12
fire of the **a** is kept burning Lv 6:9
the fire has consumed on the **a**, Lv 6:10
and place them beside the **a**. Lv 6:10
The fire on the **a** is to be kept Lv 6:12
burning on the **a** continually; Lv 6:13
the LORD in front of the **a**. Lv 6:14
portion on the **a** as a pleasing Lv 6:15
its blood on all sides of the **a**. Lv 7:2
burn them on the **a** as a fire Lv 7:5
is to burn the fat on the **a**, Lv 7:31
of the oil on the **a** seven times, Lv 8:11
anointing the **a** with all its Lv 8:11
the horns of the **a** on all sides, Lv 8:15
on all sides, purifying the **a**. Lv 8:15
base of the **a** and consecrated Lv 8:15
and he burned them on the **a**. Lv 8:16
the blood on all sides of the **a**. Lv 8:19
burned the entire ram on the **a**. Lv 8:21
the blood on all sides of the **a**. Lv 8:24
them⌋ on the **a** with the burnt Lv 8:28
that was on the **a** and sprinkled Lv 8:30
Approach the **a** and sacrifice Lv 9:7
approached the **a** and slaughtered Lv 9:8
it to the horns of the **a**. Lv 9:9
the blood at the base of the **a**. Lv 9:9
from the sin offering on the **a**, Lv 9:10
it on all sides of the **a**. Lv 9:12
and he burned ⌊them⌋ on the **a**. Lv 9:13
the burnt offering on the **a**. Lv 9:14
burned it on the **a** in addition Lv 9:17
it on all sides of the **a**. Lv 9:18
the fat portions on the **a**, Lv 9:20
and the fat portions on the **a**. Lv 9:24
without yeast beside the **a**, Lv 10:12
and the grain offering on the **a**. Lv 14:20
coals from the **a** before the LORD Lv 16:12
go out to the **a** that is before Lv 16:18
the horns on all sides of the **a**. Lv 16:18
meeting, and the **a**, he is to Lv 16:20
of the sin offering on the **a**. Lv 16:25
meeting and the **a** and will make Lv 16:33
on the LORD's **a** at the entrance Lv 17:6
on the **a** for your lives, Lv 17:11
the curtain or approach the **a**. Lv 21:23
of them on the **a** as a fire Lv 22:22
the tabernacle and the **a**, Nm 3:26
a blue cloth over the gold **a**, Nm 4:11
the ashes from the ⌊bronze⌋ **a**, Nm 4:13
all the equipment of the **a**. Nm 4:14
the tabernacle and the **a**, Nm 4:26

the LORD, and bring it to the **a**. Nm 5:25
portion and burn it on the **a**. Nm 5:26
along with the **a** and all its Nm 7:1
gift for the **a** when it was Nm 7:10
offerings in front of the **a**. Nm 7:10
for the dedication of the **a**." Nm 7:11
of Israel for the **a** when it was Nm 7:84
gift for the **a** after it was Nm 7:88
sheets as plating for the **a**, Nm 16:38
hammered into plating for the **a**, Nm 16:39
place fire from the **a** in it, Nm 16:46
sanctuary equipment or the **a**; Nm 18:3
and the **a** so that wrath may Nm 18:5
concerning the **a** and for what is Nm 18:7
blood on the **a** and burn their Nm 18:17
a bull and a ram on each **a**. Nm 23:2
a bull and a ram on each **a**." Nm 23:4
a bull and a ram on each **a**. Nm 23:14
a bull and a ram on each **a**. Nm 23:30
on the **a** of the LORD your Dt 12:27
beside the **a** of the LORD your Dt 12:27
next to the **a** you will build Dt 16:21
it before the **a** of the LORD your Dt 26:4
Build an **a** of stones there to Dt 27:5
to build the **a** of the LORD your Dt 27:6
whole burnt offerings on Your **a**. Dt 33:10
Joshua built an **a** on Mount Ebal Jos 8:30
an **a** of uncut stones on which no Jos 8:31
for the LORD's **a** at the place He Jos 9:27
a there by the Jordan. Jos 22:10
have built an **a** on the frontier Jos 22:11
building an **a** for yourselves, Jos 22:16
for yourselves an **a** other than Jos 22:19
other than the **a** of the LORD our Jos 22:19
for ourselves an **a** to turn away Jos 22:23
and build an **a** for ourselves, Jos 22:26
of the LORD's **a** that our fathers Jos 22:28
by building an **a** for burnt Jos 22:29
other than the **a** of the LORD our Jos 22:29
and Gadites named the **a**: Jos 22:34
Gideon built an **a** to the LORD Jdg 6:24
tear down the **a** of Baal that Jdg 6:25
a to the LORD your Jdg 6:26
they found Baal's **a** torn down, Jdg 6:28
offered up on the **a** that had Jdg 6:28
tore down Baal's **a** and cut down Jdg 6:30
someone tore down his **a**." Jdg 6:31
because he tore down his **a**. Jdg 6:32
went up from the **a** to the sky, Jdg 13:20
early, built an **a** there, and Jdg 21:4
to offer sacrifices on My **a**, 1Sm 2:28
cut off from My **a** will bring 1Sm 2:33
he had built an **a** to the LORD 1Sm 7:17
Saul built an **a** to the LORD; 1Sm 14:35
he had built an **a** to the LORD. 1Sm 14:35
up and set up an **a** to the LORD 2Sm 24:18
order to build an **a** to the LORD, 2Sm 24:21
He built an **a** to the LORD there 2Sm 24:25
take hold of the horns of the **a**. 1Kg 1:50
hold of the horns of the **a**, 1Kg 1:51
they took him down from the **a**. 1Kg 1:53
took hold of the horns of the **a**. 1Kg 2:28
and is now beside the **a**." 1Kg 2:29
1,000 burnt offerings on that **a**. 1Kg 3:4
He also overlaid the cedar **a**. 1Kg 6:20
the entire **a** that belongs 1Kg 6:22
the gold **a**; the gold table 1Kg 7:48
stood before the **a** of the LORD 1Kg 8:22
before Your **a** in this temple, 1Kg 8:31
before the **a** of the LORD, 1Kg 8:54
the bronze **a** before the LORD 1Kg 8:64
on the **a** he had built for 1Kg 9:25
He offered sacrifices on the **a**; 1Kg 12:32
sacrifices on the **a** he had set 1Kg 12:33
offered sacrifices on the **a**, 1Kg 12:33
beside the **a** to burn incense. 1Kg 13:1
against the **a** by a revelation 1Kg 13:2
A, altar, this is what the LORD 1Kg 13:2
Altar, **a**, this is what the LORD 1Kg 13:2
'The **a** will now be ripped apart, 1Kg 13:3
out against the **a** at Bethel, 1Kg 13:4
his hand from the **a** and said, 1Kg 13:4
The **a** was ripped apart, and the 1Kg 13:5
and the ashes spilled off the **a**, 1Kg 13:5
the LORD against the **a** in Bethel 1Kg 13:32
He set up an **a** for Baal in the 1Kg 16:32
around the **a** they had made. 1Kg 18:26
the LORD's **a** that had been torn 1Kg 18:30

he built an **a** with the stones 1Kg 18:32
around the **a** a large enough to 1Kg 18:32
the water ran all around the **a**; 1Kg 18:35
approached ⌊the **a**⌋ and said, 1Kg 18:36
by the **a** and by the temple. 2Kg 11:11
it beside the **a** on the right 2Kg 12:9
When he saw the **a** that was in 2Kg 16:10
a model of the **a** and complete 2Kg 16:10
built the **a** according to all 2Kg 16:11
from Damascus, he saw the **a**. 2Kg 16:12
approached the **a** and ascended it 2Kg 16:12
fellowship offerings on the **a**. 2Kg 16:13
the bronze **a** that was before 2Kg 16:14
between ⌊his⌋ **a** and the LORD's 2Kg 16:14
it on the north side of ⌊his⌋ **a**. 2Kg 16:14
on the great **a** the morning burnt 2Kg 16:15
Sprinkle on the **a** all the blood 2Kg 16:15
The bronze **a** will be for me to 2Kg 16:15
worship at this **a** in Jerusalem?' 2Kg 18:22
not come up to the **a** of the LORD 2Kg 23:9
even tore down the **a** at Bethel 2Kg 23:15
and he burned them on the **a**. 2Kg 23:16
have done to the **a** at Bethel." 2Kg 23:17
offerings on the **a** of burnt 1Ch 6:49
and on the **a** of incense to make 1Ch 6:49
the LORD on the **a** of burnt 1Ch 16:40
go and set up an **a** to the LORD 1Ch 21:18
I may build an **a** to the LORD on 1Ch 21:22
He built an **a** to the LORD there 1Ch 21:26
heaven on the **a** of burnt 1Ch 21:26
and the **a** of burnt offering were 1Ch 21:29
and this is the **a** of burnt 1Ch 22:1
gold for the **a** of incense; 1Ch 28:18
put the bronze **a**, which Bezalel 2Ch 1:5
on the bronze **a** at the tent of 2Ch 1:6
He made a bronze **a** 30 feet long, 2Ch 4:1
temple: the gold **a**; the tables 2Ch 4:19
were standing east of the **a**, 2Ch 5:12
stood before the **a** of the LORD 2Ch 6:12
before Your **a** in this temple, 2Ch 6:22
the bronze **a** that Solomon had 2Ch 7:7
of the **a** lasted seven days 2Ch 7:9
LORD on the LORD's **a** he had made 2Ch 8:12
renovated the **a** of the LORD that 2Ch 15:8
by the **a** and by the temple. 2Ch 23:10
burn incense on the incense **a**. 2Ch 26:16
temple beside the **a** of incense, 2Ch 26:19
the **a** of burnt offering and all 2Ch 29:18
in front of the **a** of the LORD." 2Ch 29:19
offer them on the **a** of the LORD. 2Ch 29:21
blood and sprinkled it on the **a**. 2Ch 29:22
sprinkled the blood on the **a**. 2Ch 29:22
sprinkled the blood on the **a**. 2Ch 29:22
blood on the **a** for a sin 2Ch 29:24
offering be offered on the **a**. 2Ch 29:27
You must worship before one **a**, 2Ch 32:12
He built the **a** of the LORD and 2Ch 33:16
offerings on the **a** of the LORD, 2Ch 35:16
to build the **a** of Israel's God Ezr 3:2
They set up the **a** on its Ezr 3:3
offer them on the **a** at the house Ezr 7:17
to burn on the **a** of the LORD our Neh 10:34
innocence and go around Your **a**, Ps 26:6
I will come to the **a** of God, Ps 43:4
bulls will be offered on Your **a**. Ps 51:19
cords to the horns of the **a**. Ps 118:27
had taken from the **a** with tongs. Is 6:6
there will be an **a** to the LORD Is 19:19
he makes all the **a** stones like Is 27:9
You are to worship at this **a**? Is 36:7
will be acceptable on My **a**, Is 56:7
go up on My **a** as an acceptable Is 60:7
The Lord has rejected His **a**, Lm 2:7
statue north of the **a** gate, Ezk 8:5
between the portico and the **a**, Ezk 8:16
and stood beside the bronze **a**. Ezk 9:2
who keep charge of the **a**. Ezk 40:46
a was in front of the temple. Ezk 40:47
The **a** was made of wood, five and Ezk 41:22
of the **a** in units of length Ezk 43:13
This is the base of the **a**. Ezk 43:13
a hearth is seven feet ⌊high⌋ Ezk 43:15
for the **a** on the day it is Ezk 43:18
it⌋ to the four horns of the **a**, Ezk 43:20
will purify the **a** and make Ezk 43:20
will purify the **a** just as they Ezk 43:22
for the **a** and cleanse it. Ezk 43:26
fellowship offerings on the **a**, Ezk 43:27

of the temple, south of the a. Ezk 47:1
wail, you ministers of the a. Jl 1:13
between the portico and the a. Jl 2:17
out beside every a on garments Am 2:8
horns of the a will be cut off Am 3:14
the LORD standing beside the a, Am 9:1
those⌋ at the corners of the a. Zch 9:15
sprinkling basins before the a. Zch 14:20
defiled food on My a." Mal 1:7
kindle a useless ⌊fire on⌋ My a! Mal 1:10
cover the LORD's a with tears, Mal 2:13
are offering your gift on the a, Mt 5:23
gift there in front of the a. Mt 5:24
'Whoever takes an oath by the a, Mt 23:18
gift or the a that sanctifies Mt 23:19
oath by the a takes an oath by Mt 23:20
between the sanctuary and the a. Mt 23:35
the right of the a of incense. Lk 1:11
between the a and the sanctuary. Lk 11:51
I even found an a on which was Ac 17:23
who serve at the a share in the 1Co 9:13
share in the offerings of the a? 1Co 9:13
sacrifices partners in the a? 1Co 10:18
no one has served at the a. Heb 7:13
contained the gold a of incense Heb 9:4
have an a from which those who Heb 13:10
offered Isaac his son on the a? Jms 2:21
I saw under the a the souls of Rv 6:9
burner, came and stood at the a. Rv 8:3
saints on the gold a in front of Rv 8:3
filled it with fire from the a, Rv 8:5
of the gold a that is before Rv 9:13
God's sanctuary and the a, Rv 11:1
came from the a, and he called Rv 14:18
I heard someone from the a say: Rv 16:7

ALTAR'S *(5)*

below, under the a ledge, so Ex 27:5
He made all the a utensils: Ex 38:3
remain on the a hearth all night Lv 6:9
The a steps face east." Ezk 43:17
the four corners of the a ledge, Ezk 45:19

ALTARS *(63)*

you must tear down their a, Ex 34:13
your incense a, and heap your Lv 26:30
lampstand, the a, the sanctuary Nm 3:31
Build me seven a here and Nm 23:1
arranged seven a and offered a Nm 23:4
built seven a, and offered a Nm 23:14
Build me seven a here and Nm 23:29
tear down their a, smash their Dt 7:5
Tear down their a, smash their Dt 12:3
you are to tear down their a. Jdg 2:2
down Your a, and killed Your 1Kg 19:10
down Your a, and killed Your 1Kg 19:14
They broke its a and images into 2Kg 11:18
the priest of Baal, at the a. 2Kg 11:18
high places and a Hezekiah has 2Kg 18:22
reestablished the a for Baal. 2Kg 21:3
He would build a in the LORD's 2Kg 21:4
He built a to the whole heavenly 2Kg 21:5
king tore down the a that were 2Kg 23:12
and the a that Manasseh had made 2Kg 23:12
on the a all the priests 2Kg 23:20
he burned human bones on the a. 2Kg 23:20
removed the pagan a and the high 2Ch 14:3
and the incense a from all the 2Ch 14:5
They broke its a and images into 2Ch 23:17
the priest of Baal, at the a. 2Ch 23:17
made himself a on every street 2Ch 28:24
to take away the a that were in 2Ch 30:14
the incense a and threw them 2Ch 30:14
high places and a throughout 2Ch 31:1
places and His a and say to 2Ch 32:12
the a for the Baals. 2Ch 33:3
He built a in the LORD's temple, 2Ch 33:4
He built a to the whole heavenly 2Ch 33:5
with all the a that he had built 2Ch 33:15
his presence the a of the Baals 2Ch 34:4
the incense a that were above 2Ch 34:4
bones of the priests on their a. 2Ch 34:5
tore down the a, and he smashed 2Ch 34:7
all the incense a throughout the 2Ch 34:7
near Your a, LORD of Hosts, Ps 84:3
not look to the a they made with Is 17:8
and incense a they made with Is 17:8
poles or incense a will remain Is 27:9
high places and a Hezekiah has Is 36:7
and the a you have set up to Jr 11:13
a to burn incense to Baal— Jr 11:13
and on the horns of their a, Jr 17:1
remember their a and their Jr 17:2
a will be desolated and your Ezk 6:4
and your incense a smashed. Ezk 6:4
your bones around your a. Ezk 6:5
so that your a will lie in ruins Ezk 6:6
incense a cut down, and your Ezk 6:6
their idols around their a, Ezk 6:13
multiplied his a for sin, Hs 8:11
they became his a for sinning. Hs 8:11
the more he increased the a. Hs 10:1
break down their a and demolish Hs 10:2
thistles will grow over their a. Hs 10:8
even their a will be like heaps Hs 12:11
I will punish the a of Bethel on Am 3:14
Your prophets, torn down Your a; Rm 11:3

ALTERNATE *(1)*

pomegranates a around the lower Ex 28:34

ALTERNATING *(1)*

and a pomegranate a all around Ex 39:26

ALTHOUGH *(54)*

(See pp. xi-xii.)

ALTOGETHER *(2)*

are reliable and a righteous. Ps 19:9
are righteous and a trustworthy. Ps 119:138

ALUSH *(2)*

from Dophkah and camped at A. Nm 33:13
departed from A and camped at Nm 33:14

ALVAH *(2)*

Chiefs Timna, A, Jetheth, Gn 36:40
chiefs: Timna, A, Jetheth, 1Ch 1:51

ALVAN *(1)*

A, Manahath, Ebal, Shepho, and Gn 36:23

ALWAYS *(118)*

I will a bear the guilt for Gn 44:32
you and will a believe you." Ex 19:9
It is a to be on his forehead, Ex 28:38
the Levites a have the right to Lv 25:32
for our prosperity a and for our Dt 6:24
your God and a keep His mandate Dt 11:1
is a watching over it from the Dt 11:12
so that you will a learn to fear Dt 14:23
stones will a be a memorial for Jos 4:7
so that you may a fear the LORD Jos 4:24
cursed and will a be slaves— Jos 9:23
a gave portions of the meat to 1Sm 1:4
as a when I go out ⌊to battle⌋. 1Sm 21:5
will a eat meals at my table. 2Sm 9:7
is a to eat at my table. 2Sm 9:10
because he a ate at the king's 2Sm 9:13
Hiram had a been friends with 1Kg 5:1
who a stand in your presence 1Kg 10:8
David will a have a lamp before 1Kg 11:36
are to be careful a to observe 2Kg 17:37
His strength; seek His face a. 1Ch 16:11
who a stand in your presence 2Ch 9:7
she a had while he raised her. Est 2:20
will not a be forgotten; Ps 9:18
His ways are a secure; Ps 10:5
I keep the LORD in mind a. Ps 16:8
My eyes are a on the LORD, Ps 25:15
His praise will a be on my lips. Ps 34:1
is a generous, always lending, Ps 37:26
generous, a lending, and his Ps 37:26
love and truth will a guard me. Ps 40:11
a helper who is a found in times Ps 46:1
and my sin is a before me. Ps 51:3
refuge for me, where I can a go. Ps 71:3
My praise is a about You. Ps 71:6
They are a at ease, and they Ps 73:12
Yet I am a with You; You hold my Ps 73:23
My hand will a be with him, Ps 89:21
I will a preserve My faithful Ps 89:28
He will not a accuse ⌊us⌋ or be Ps 103:9
His strength; seek His face a. Ps 105:4
Let their sins a remain before Ps 109:15
himself, like a belt he a wears. Ps 109:19
and I will a keep them. Ps 119:33
I will a keep Your law, forever Ps 119:44
my enemies, for it is a with me. Ps 119:98
let her breasts a satisfy you; Pr 5:19
A bind them to your heart; Pr 6:21
every day, a rejoicing before Pr 8:30
instead, a fear the LORD. Pr 23:17
is the one who is a reverent, Pr 28:14
and I will not a be angry; Is 57:16
LORD will a lead you, satisfy Is 58:11
Your gates will a be open; Is 60:11
Why is Jerusalem a turning away? Jr 8:5
after them, they will fear Me a. Jr 32:39
to have a man a before Me to Jr 33:18
have a man to a stand before Me Jr 35:19
and a put your hope in God. Hs 12:6
You a have the poor with you, Mt 26:11
you, but you do not a have Me. Mt 26:11
I am with you a, to the end of Mt 28:20
And a, night and day, he was Mk 5:5
You a have the poor with you, Mk 14:7
want, but you do not a have Me. Mk 14:7
said to him, 'you are a with me, Lk 15:31
them to pray a and not become Lk 18:1
Sir, give us this bread a!" Jn 6:34
but your time is a at hand. Jn 7:6
I a do what pleases Him." Jn 8:29
I know that You a hear Me, Jn 11:42
you a have the poor with you, Jn 12:8
but you do not a have Me." Jn 12:8
I have a taught in the synagogue Jn 18:20
You are a resisting the Holy Ac 7:51
She was a doing good works and Ac 9:36
people and a prayed to God. Ac 10:2
them a and in all places, Ac 24:3
I a do my best to have a clear Ac 24:16
a asking in my prayers that if Rm 1:10
I a thank my God for you because 1Co 1:4
a excelling in the Lord's work, 1Co 15:58
who a puts us on display in 2Co 2:14
We a carry the death of Jesus in 2Co 4:10
we who live are a given over to 2Co 4:11
though we are a confident and 2Co 5:6
as grieving yet a rejoicing; 2Co 6:10
a having everything you need, 2Co 9:8
we have a made that clear to you 2Co 11:6
Now it is a good to be Gl 4:18
giving thanks a for everything Eph 5:20
a praying with joy for all of Php 1:4
but that now as a, with all Php 1:20
just as you have a obeyed, Php 2:12
Rejoice in the Lord a. Php 4:4
a thank God, the Father of our Col 1:3
speech should a be gracious, Col 4:6
is a contending for you in his Col 4:12
We a thank God for all of you, 1Th 1:2
they are a adding to the number 1Th 2:16
that you a have good memories 1Th 3:6
and so we will a be with the 1Th 4:17
a pursue what is good for one 1Th 5:15
Rejoice a! 1Th 5:16
We must a thank God for you, 2Th 1:3
we a pray for you that our God 2Th 1:11
But we must a thank God for you, 2Th 2:13
give you peace a in every way. 2Th 3:16
a learning and never able to 2Tm 3:7
said, Cretans are a liars, evil Ti 1:12
a showing gentleness to all Ti 3:2
I a thank my God when I mention Phm 4
They a go astray in their Heb 3:10
Therefore He is a able to save Heb 7:25
since He a lives to intercede Heb 7:25
and a be ready to give a defense 1Pt 3:15
I will a remind you about 2Pt 1:12
adultery and a looking for sin 2Pt 2:14

AM *(1141)*

(See pp. xi-xii. See also I AM.)

AMAD *(1)*

Allammelech, A, and Mishal and Jos 19:26

AMAL *(1)*

Zophah, Imna, Shelesh, and A. 1Ch 7:35

AMALEK *(20)*

son Eliphaz, bore A to Eliphaz. Gn 36:12
Korah, Gatam, and A. These are Gn 36:16
A came and fought against Israel. Ex 17:8
for us, and go fight against A. Ex 17:9
fought against A, while Moses, Ex 17:10
put his hand down, A prevailed. Ex 17:11
Joshua defeated A and his army Ex 17:13
the memory of A under heaven." Ex 17:14
be at war with A from generation Ex 17:16
Balaam saw A and proclaimed Nm 24:20
A was first among the nations, Nm 24:20
the memory of A from under Dt 25:19
their roots in A ⌊came⌋ from Jdg 5:14

came to the city of **A** and set up 1Sm 15:5
captured Agag king of **A** alive, 1Sm 15:8
Agag, king of **A**, and I 1Sm 15:20
"Bring me Agag king of **A**." 1Sm 15:32
carry out His wrath against **A**; 1Sm 28:18
and Kenaz; and by Timna, **A**. 1Ch 1:36
Ammon, and **A**, Philistia with Ps 83:7

AMALEKITE *(4)*
the slave of an **A** man," he said. 1Sm 30:13
are you?' I told him: I'm an **A**. 2Sm 1:8
foreigner" he said. "I'm an **A**." 2Sm 1:13
For David had said to the **A**, 2Sm 1:16

AMALEKITES *(30)*
all the territory of the **A**, Gn 14:7
The **A** are living in the land of Nm 13:29
Since the **A** and Canaanites are Nm 14:25
The **A** and Canaanites are right Nm 14:43
Then the **A** and Canaanites who Nm 14:45
Remember what the **A** did to you Dt 25:17
and the **A** to join forces Jdg 3:13
the Midianites, **A**, and the Jdg 6:3
the Midianites, **A**, and Qedemites Jdg 6:33
Now the Midianites, **A**, and all Jdg 7:12
Sidonians, **A**, and Maonites Jdg 10:12
in the hill country of the **A**. Jdg 12:15
defeated the **A**, and delivered 1Sm 14:48
witnessed what the **A** did to the 1Sm 15:2
and attack the **A** and completely 1Sm 15:3
away from the **A**, or I'll sweep 1Sm 15:6
the Kenites withdrew from the **A**. 1Sm 15:6
struck down the **A** from Havilah 1Sm 15:7
them from the **A** and spared the 1Sm 15:15
completely destroy the sinful **A**. 1Sm 15:18
I completely destroyed the **A**. 1Sm 15:20
the Girzites, and the **A**. 1Sm 27:8
The **A** had raided the Negev and 1Sm 30:1
there were the **A**, spread out 1Sm 30:16
everything the **A** had taken; 1Sm 30:18
all the plunder the **A** had taken. 1Sm 30:19
defeating the **A** and stayed at 2Sm 1:1
Philistines, the **A**, and the 2Sm 8:12
remnant of the **A** who had escaped 1Ch 4:43
the Philistines, and the **A**. 1Ch 18:11

AMAM *(1)*
A, Shema, Moladah, Jos 15:26

AMANA *(1)*
Descend from the peak of **A**, Sg 4:8

AMARIAH *(15)*
Meraioth fathered **A**; 1Ch 6:7
Amariah; **A** fathered Ahitub, 1Ch 6:7
Azariah fathered **A**; Amariah 1Ch 6:11
Amariah; **A** fathered Ahitub; 1Ch 6:11
his son **A**, his son Ahitub, 1Ch 6:52
was first, **A** second, Jahaziel 1Ch 23:19
⌊the first⌋, **A** the second, 1Ch 24:23
Note that **A**, the chief priest, 2Ch 19:11
Shemaiah, **A**, and Shecaniah 2Ch 31:15
Shallum, **A**, and Joseph; Ezr 10:42
Pashhur, **A**, Malchijah, Neh 10:3
Zechariah, son of **A**, son of Neh 11:4
A, Malluch, Hattush, Neh 12:2
of Ezra, Jehohanan of **A**, Neh 12:13
son of **A**, son of Hezekiah Zph 1:1

AMARIAH'S *(1)*
A son, Azariah's son, Meraioth's Ezr 7:3

AMASA *(17)*
had appointed **A** over the army 2Sm 17:25
A was the son of a man named 2Sm 17:25
And tell **A**, 'Aren't you my flesh 2Sm 19:13
king said to **A**, "Summon the men 2Sm 20:4
A went to summon Judah, but he 2Sm 20:5
in Gibeon when **A** joined them. 2Sm 20:8
Joab asked **A**, "Are you well, my 2Sm 20:9
Joab grabbed **A** by the beard to 2Sm 20:9
A was not on guard against the 2Sm 20:10
stab him again for **A** was dead. 2Sm 20:10
men had stood over **A** saying, 2Sm 20:11
Now **A** was writhing in his blood 2Sm 20:12
he moved **A** from the highway to 2Sm 20:12
encountered **A** were stopping. 2Sm 20:12
son of Ner and **A** son of Jether. 1Kg 2:5
army, and **A** son of Jether, 1Kg 2:32
Shallum, and **A** son of Hadlai— 2Ch 28:12

AMASA'S *(1)*
A mother was Abigail, and his 1Ch 2:17

AMASAI *(5)*
Elkanah's sons: **A** and Ahimoth, 1Ch 6:25
son of Mahath, son of **A**, 1Ch 6:35
the Spirit took control of **A**, 1Ch 12:18
Nethanel, **A**, Zechariah, Benaiah 1Ch 15:24
Mahath son of **A** and Joel son of 2Ch 29:12

AMASHSAI *(1)*
A son of Azarel, son of Ahzai, Neh 11:13

AMASIAH *(1)*
next to him, **A** son of Zichri, 2Ch 17:16

AMASSED *(2)*
I have **a** wisdom far beyond all Ec 1:16
I also **a** silver and gold for Ec 2:8

AMASSES *(1)*
Woe to him who **a** what is not his Hab 2:6

AMAZED *(43)*
He was **a** that there was no one Is 59:16
I was **a** that no one assisted; Is 63:5
Jesus was **a** and said to those Mt 8:10
The men were **a** and asked, Mt 8:27
the crowds were **a**, saying, Mt 9:33
So the crowd was **a** when they saw Mt 15:31
it, they were **a** and said, "How Mt 21:20
they heard this, they were **a**. Mt 22:22
that the governor was greatly **a**. Mt 27:14
they were all **a**, so they began Mk 1:27
for him, and they were all **a**. Mk 5:20
And He was **a** at their unbelief. Mk 6:6
were **a** and ran to greet Him. Mk 9:15
And they were **a** at Him. Mk 12:17
anything, so Pilate was **a**. Mk 15:5
they were **a** and alarmed. Mk 16:5
a that he stayed so long in the Lk 1:21
IS JOHN And they were all **a**. Lk 1:63
who heard it were **a** at what the Lk 2:18
and mother were **a** at what was Lk 2:33
Him and were **a** by the gracious Lk 4:22
with him were **a** at the catch Lk 5:9
heard this and was **a** at him, Lk 7:9
They were fearful and **a**, Lk 8:25
everyone was **a** at all the things Lk 9:43
spoke, and the crowds were **a**. Lk 11:14
he was **a** that He did not first Lk 11:38
and being **a** at His answer, Lk 20:26
So he went home, **a** at what had Lk 24:12
of ⌊their⌋ joy and were **a**, Lk 24:41
Do not be **a** that I told you that Jn 3:7
and they were **a** that He was Jn 4:27
these so that you will be **a**. Jn 5:20
Do not be **a** at this, because a Jn 5:28
Then the Jews were **a** and said, Jn 7:15
and you are all **a**," Jesus Jn 7:21
And they were astounded and **a**, Ac 2:7
people, greatly **a**, ran toward Ac 3:11
Israel, why are you **a** at this? Ac 3:12
they were **a** and knew that they Ac 4:13
saw it, he was **a** at the sight. Ac 7:31
I am **a** that you are so quickly Gl 1:6
whole earth was **a** and followed Rv 13:3

AMAZEMENT *(1)*
struck with **a** and kept saying Lk 4:36

AMAZIAH *(42)*
and his son **A** became king in his 2Kg 12:21
wage war against Judah's King **A**, 2Kg 13:12
A son of Joash became king of 2Kg 14:1
A killed his servants who had 2Kg 14:5
A killed 10,000 Edomites in the 2Kg 14:7
A then sent messengers to 2Kg 14:8
sent ⌊word⌋ to **A** king of Judah, 2Kg 14:9
But **A** would not listen, so King 2Kg 14:11
He and King **A** of Judah faced off 2Kg 14:11
Judah's King **A** son of Joash, 2Kg 14:13
war against **A** king of Judah, 2Kg 14:15
Judah's King **A** son of Joash 2Kg 14:17
king in place of his father **A**. 2Kg 14:21
to Judah after ⌊**A**⌋ the king 2Kg 14:22
of Judah's King **A** son of Joash, 2Kg 14:23
Azariah son of **A** became king of 2Kg 15:1
just as his father **A** had done. 2Kg 15:3
his son **A**, his son Azariah, his 1Ch 3:12
Jamlech, Joshah son of **A**, 1Ch 4:34
son of **A**, son of Hilkiah, 1Ch 6:45
His son **A** became king in his 2Ch 24:27
A became king ⌊when he was⌋ 25 2Ch 25:1
Then **A** gathered Judah and 2Ch 25:5
Then **A** said to the man of God, 2Ch 25:9
So **A** released the division that 2Ch 25:10
A strengthened his position and 2Ch 25:11
division that **A** sent back so 2Ch 25:13
After **A** came from the attack on 2Ch 25:14
the LORD's anger was against **A**, 2Ch 25:15
King **A** of Judah took counsel and 2Ch 25:17
sent ⌊word⌋ to King **A** of Judah, 2Ch 25:18
But **A** would not listen, for this 2Ch 25:20
He and King **A** of Judah faced off 2Ch 25:21
Judah's King **A** son of Joash, 2Ch 25:23
Judah's King **A** son of Joash 2Ch 25:25
From the time **A** turned from 2Ch 25:27
king in place of his father **A**. 2Ch 26:1
to Judah after ⌊**A**⌋ the king 2Ch 26:2
sight as his father **A** had done. 2Ch 26:4
A the priest of Bethel sent Am 7:10
Then **A** said to Amos, "Go away, Am 7:12
So Amos answered **A**, "I was not a Am 7:14

AMAZIAH'S *(2)*
of the events of **A** ⌊reign⌋ are 2Kg 14:18
rest of the events of **A** ⌊reign⌋, 2Ch 25:26

AMAZING *(1)*
"This is an **a** thing," the man Jn 9:30

AMBASSADOR *(1)*
For this I am an **a** in chains. Eph 6:20

AMBASSADORS *(4)*
When the **a** of Babylon's rulers 2Ch 32:31
A will come from Egypt; Ps 68:31
sending his **a** to Egypt so they Ezk 17:15
Therefore, we are **a** for Christ; 2Co 5:20

AMBER *(3)*
fire, there was a gleam like **a**. Ezk 1:4
saw a gleam like **a**, with what Ezk 1:27
bright, like the gleam of **a**. Ezk 8:2

AMBITION *(2)*
and selfish **a** in your heart, Jms 3:14
where envy and selfish **a** exist, Jms 3:16

AMBITIONS *(2)*
anger, selfish **a**, slander, 2Co 12:20
anger, selfish **a**, dissensions, Gl 5:20

AMBUSH *(46)*
lies in **a** for him, attacks Dt 19:11
Set an **a** behind the city." Jos 8:2
in **a** behind the city, not too Jos 8:4
come out of your **a** and seize the Jos 8:7
went to the **a** site and waited Jos 8:9
and set them in **a** between Bethel Jos 8:12
there was an **a** ⌊waiting⌋ for him Jos 8:14
the men in **a** rose quickly from Jos 8:19
that the ⌊men in⌋ **a** had captured Jos 8:21
The men in the **a** came out of the Jos 8:22
mountains to **a** and rob everyone Jdg 9:25
to come wait in **a** in the Jdg 9:32
and waited in **a** for Shechem in Jdg 9:34
with him got up from their **a**. Jdg 9:35
and waited in **a** in the Jdg 9:43
and waited in **a** for him all that Jdg 16:2
While the men in **a** were waiting Jdg 16:9
while the men in **a** were waiting Jdg 16:12
set up an **a** around Gibeah. Jdg 20:29
the Israelites in **a** charged out Jdg 20:33
confident in the **a** they had set Jdg 20:36
The men in **a** had rushed quickly Jdg 20:37
signal with the men in **a**: Jdg 20:38
and set up an **a** in the wadi. 1Sm 15:5
own servant to wait in **a** for me, 1Sm 22:8
up against me and wait in **a**, 1Sm 22:13
had sent an **a** around to advance 2Ch 13:13
and the **a** was behind them. 2Ch 13:13
the LORD set an **a** against the 2Ch 20:22
enemy and from **a** along the way. Ezr 8:31
He waits in **a** near the villages; Ps 10:8
like a young lion lurking in **a**. Ps 17:12
They set an **a** for me. Ps 59:3
Let's set an **a** and kill someone. Pr 1:11
but they set an **a** to kill Pr 1:18
of the wicked are a deadly **a**, Pr 12:6
she sets an **a** like a robber and Pr 23:28
Don't set an **a**, wicked man, at Pr 24:15
but inwardly he sets up an **a**. Jr 9:8
prepare the **a**. For the LORD has Jr 51:12
He is a bear waiting in **a**, Lm 3:10
who wait in **a** for someone, Hs 6:9
of them wait in **a** to shed blood; Mc 7:2
about their **a**, came and entered Ac 23:16

40 of them arranging to **a** him, Ac 23:21
preparing an **a** along the road to Ac 25:3

AMBUSHED *(1)*
the mountains and **a** us in the Lm 4:19

AMEN *(58)*
the woman must reply, '**A**, Amen.' Nm 5:22
the woman must reply, 'Amen, **A**.' Nm 5:22
all the people will reply, '**A**!' Dt 27:15
all the people will say, '**A**!' Dt 27:16
all the people will say, '**A**!' Dt 27:17
all the people will say, '**A**!' Dt 27:18
all the people will say, '**A**!' Dt 27:19
all the people will say, '**A**!' Dt 27:20
And all the people will say '**A**!' Dt 27:21
all the people will say, '**A**!' Dt 27:22
all the people will say, '**A**!' Dt 27:23
all the people will say, '**A**!' Dt 27:24
all the people will say, '**A**!' Dt 27:25
all the people will say, '**A**!' Dt 27:26
"**A**," Benaiah son of Jehoiada 1Kg 1:36
"**A**" and "Praise the LORD." 1Ch 16:36
assembly said, "**A**," and they Neh 5:13
all the people said, "**A**, Amen!" Neh 8:6
all the people said, "Amen, **A**!" Neh 8:6
to everlasting. **A** and amen. Ps 41:13
to everlasting. Amen and **a**. Ps 41:13
with His glory. **A** and amen. Ps 72:19
with His glory. Amen and **a**. Ps 72:19
be praised forever. **A** and amen. Ps 89:52
be praised forever. Amen and **a**. Ps 89:52
Let all the people say, "**A**!" Ps 106:48
I answered, "**A**, LORD." Jr 11:5
The prophet Jeremiah said, "**A**! Jr 28:6
power and the glory forever. **A**. Mt 6:13
who is blessed forever. **A**. Rm 1:25
over all, blessed forever. **A**. Rm 9:5
To Him be the glory forever. **A**. Rm 11:36
of peace be with all of you. **A**. Rm 15:33
to Him be the glory forever! **A**. Rm 16:27
person say "**A**" at your giving 1Co 14:16
Therefore the "**A**" is also 2Co 1:20
the glory forever and ever. **A**. Gl 1:5
Christ be with your spirit. **A**. Gl 6:18
forever and ever. **A**. Eph 3:21
be glory forever and ever. **A**. Php 4:20
Jesus with all His saints. **A**. 1Th 3:13
and glory forever and ever. **A**. 1Tm 1:17
be honor and eternal might. **A**. 1Tm 6:16
the glory forever and ever! **A**. 2Tm 4:18
be glory forever and ever. **A**. Heb 13:21
the power forever and ever. **A**. 1Pt 4:11
Him be the dominion forever. **A**. 1Pt 5:11
and to the day of eternity. **A**. 2Pt 3:18
all time, now, and forever. **A**. Jd 25
dominion forever and ever. **A**. Rv 1:6
over Him. This is certain. **A**. Rv 1:7
The **A**, the faithful and true Rv 3:14
said, "**A**," and the elders Rv 5:14
saying: **A**! Blessing and glory Rv 7:12
to our God forever and ever. **A**. Rv 7:12
throne, saying: **A**! Hallelujah! Rv 19:4
coming quickly." **A**! Come, Lord Rv 22:20
Jesus be with all the saints. **A**. Rv 22:21

AMETHYST *(3)*
a jacinth, an agate, and an **a**; Ex 28:19
a jacinth, an agate, and an **a**; Ex 39:12
eleventh jacinth, the twelfth **a**. Rv 21:20

AMI'S *(1)*
(AKA AMON'S)
descendants, and **A** descendants. Ezr 2:57

AMID *(2)*
God ascends **a** shouts of joy, Ps 47:5
of joy, the LORD, **a** the sound of Ps 47:5

AMINADAB *(2)*
Aram fathered **A**, Aminadab Mt 1:4
Aminadab, **A** fathered Nahshon, Mt 1:4

AMITTAI *(2)*
Jonah son of **A** from Gath-hepher. 2Kg 14:25
the LORD came to Jonah son of **A**: Jnh 1:1

AMMAH *(1)*
gone as far as the hill of **A**, 2Sm 2:24

AMMIEL *(6)*
A son of Gemalli from the tribe Nm 13:12
the house of Machir son of **A**." 2Sm 9:4
of Machir son of **A** in Lo-debar. 2Sm 9:5
Machir son of **A** from Lo-debar, 2Sm 17:27
him⌋ by Bath-shua daughter of **A**. 1Ch 3:5
A the sixth, Issachar the 1Ch 26:5

AMMIHUD *(10)*
Elishama son of **A** from Ephraim, Nm 1:10
is Elishama son of **A**. Nm 2:18
seventh day Elishama son of **A**, Nm 7:48
offering of Elishama son of **A**. Nm 7:53
Elishama son of **A** was over Nm 10:22
Shemuel son of **A** from the tribe Nm 34:20
Pedahel son of **A**, a leader from Nm 34:28
and went to Talmai son of **A**, 2Sm 13:37
Ladan, his son **A**, his son 1Ch 7:26
Uthai son of **A**, son of Omri, son 1Ch 9:4

AMMINADAB *(14)*
daughter of **A** and sister of Ex 6:23
Nahshon son of **A** from Judah; Nm 1:7
of Judah is Nahshon son of **A**. Nm 2:3
Nahshon son of **A** from the tribe Nm 7:12
offering of Nahshon son of **A**. Nm 7:17
son of **A** was over Judah's Nm 10:14
fathered Ram, who fathered **A**. Ru 4:19
A fathered Nahshon, who fathered Ru 4:20
Ram fathered **A**, and Amminadab 1Ch 2:10
Amminadab, and **A** fathered 1Ch 2:10
son **A**, his son Korah, his son 1Ch 6:22
A the leader and 112 of his 1Ch 15:10
Joel, Shemaiah, Eliel, and **A**. 1Ch 15:11
⌊son⌋ of **A**, ⌊son⌋ of Ram, ⌊son⌋ Lk 3:33

AMMISHADDAI *(5)*
Ahiezer son of **A** from Dan; Nm 1:12
the Danites is Ahiezer son of **A**. Nm 2:25
the tenth day Ahiezer son of **A**, Nm 7:66
offering of Ahiezer son of **A**. Nm 7:71
Ahiezer son of **A** was over Dan's Nm 10:25

AMMIZABAD *(1)*
and his son **A** was in charge of 1Ch 27:6

AMMON *(5)*
women from Ashdod, **A**, and Neh 13:23
Gebal, **A**, and Amalek, Philistia Ps 83:7
for camels and **A** a sheepfold. Ezk 25:5
it along with **A** to the people Ezk 25:10
so that **A** will not be remembered Ezk 25:10

AMMONITE *(21)*
⌊but only up⌋ to the **A** border, Nm 21:24
No **A** or Moabite may enter the Dt 23:3
Nahash the **A** came up and laid 1Sm 11:1
Nahash the **A** replied, "I'll make 1Sm 11:2
they invaded the **A** camp and 1Sm 11:11
A leaders said to Hanun their 2Sm 10:3
the same to all the **A** cities. 2Sm 12:31
Zelek the **A**, Naharai the 2Sm 23:37
Moabite, **A**, Edomite, Sidonian, 1Kg 11:1
mother's name was Naamah the **A** 1Kg 14:21
mother's name was Naamah the **A** 1Kg 14:31
and **A** raiders against Jehoiakim. 2Kg 24:2
Zelek the **A**, Naharai the 1Ch 11:39
the **A** leaders said to Hanun, 1Ch 19:3
the same to all the **A** cities. 1Ch 20:3
mother's name was Naamah the **A** 2Ch 12:13
son of the **A** woman Shimeath, 2Ch 24:26
and Tobiah the **A** official heard Neh 2:10
Tobiah the **A** official, and Neh 2:19
Tobiah the **A**, who was beside Neh 4:3
it that no **A** or Moabite should Neh 13:1

AMMONITE'S *(1)*
murdered him with the **A** sword. 2Sm 12:9

AMMONITES *(94)*
is the father of the **A** of today. Gn 19:38
When you get close to the **A**, Dt 2:19
though the **A** called them Dt 2:20
Rephaim at the advance of the **A**, Dt 2:21
Isn't it in Rabbah of the **A**? Dt 3:11
River, the border of the **A**. Dt 3:16
River (the border of the **A**), Jos 12:2
Heshbon, to the border of the **A**; Jos 13:10
half the land of the **A** to Aroer, Jos 13:25
convinced the **A** and the Jdg 3:13
the gods of the **A** and the Jdg 10:6
to the Philistines and the **A**. Jdg 10:7
The **A** also crossed the Jordan to Jdg 10:9
Amorites, **A**, Philistines, Jdg 10:11
The **A** were called together, Jdg 10:17
lead the fight against the **A**? Jdg 10:18
the **A** fought against Israel. Jdg 11:4
When the **A** made war with Israel, Jdg 11:5
and let's fight against the **A**." Jdg 11:6
us, fight the **A**, and you will Jdg 11:8
back to fight the **A** and the LORD Jdg 11:9
messengers to the king of the **A**, Jdg 11:12
The king of the **A** said to Jdg 11:13
messengers to the king of the **A** Jdg 11:14
of Moab or the land of the **A**. Jdg 11:15
the Israelites and the **A**." Jdg 11:27
the king of the **A** would not Jdg 11:28
crossed over to the **A** from Jdg 11:29
You will hand over the **A** to me, Jdg 11:30
peace from the **A** will belong to Jdg 11:31
over to the **A** to fight against Jdg 11:32
So the **A** were subdued before the Jdg 11:33
on your enemies, the **A**." Jdg 11:36
against the **A** but didn't call Jdg 12:1
a serious conflict with the **A**. Jdg 12:2
hands and crossed over to the **A**, Jdg 12:3
king of the **A** was coming against 1Sm 12:12
Moab, the **A**, Edom, the kings 1Sm 14:47
Edom, Moab, the **A**, the 2Sm 8:12
later the king of the **A** died, 2Sm 10:1
arrived in the land of the **A**, 2Sm 10:2
When the **A** realized they had 2Sm 10:6
The **A** marched out and lined up 2Sm 10:8
formation to engage the **A**. 2Sm 10:10
if the **A** are too strong for you, 2Sm 10:11
the **A** saw that the Arameans 2Sm 10:14
attack against the **A** and went to 2Sm 10:14
afraid to ever help the **A** again. 2Sm 10:19
destroyed the **A** and besieged 2Sm 11:1
Rabbah of the **A** and captured 2Sm 12:26
of Nahash from Rabbah of the **A**, 2Sm 17:27
the detestable idol of the **A**. 1Kg 11:5
idol of the **A** on the hill across 1Kg 11:7
and to Milcom, the god of the **A**. 1Kg 11:33
the abomination of the **A**. 2Kg 23:13
Edom, Moab, the **A**, the 1Ch 18:11
King Nahash of the **A** died, 1Ch 19:1
land of the **A** to console him, 1Ch 19:2
the **A** realized they had made 1Ch 19:6
Hanun and the **A** sent 38 tons of 1Ch 19:6
The **A** also gathered from their 1Ch 19:7
The **A** marched out and lined up 1Ch 19:9
formation to engage the **A**. 1Ch 19:11
if the **A** are too strong for you, 1Ch 19:12
the **A** saw that the Arameans 1Ch 19:15
willing to help the **A** again. 1Ch 19:19
Moabites and **A**, together with 2Ch 20:1
here are the **A**, Moabites, and 2Ch 20:10
set an ambush against the **A**, 2Ch 20:22
A and Moabites turned against 2Ch 20:23
The **A** gave Uzziah tribute money, 2Ch 26:8
war against the king of the **A**. 2Ch 27:5
overpowered the **A**, and that year 2Ch 27:5
Jebusites, **A**, Moabites, Ezr 9:1
and the Arabs, **A**, and Ashdodites Neh 4:7
the **A** will be their subjects. Is 11:14
Edom, the **A**, Moab, all those Jr 9:26
Edom, Moab, and the **A**; Jr 25:21
the king of the **A**, the king of Jr 27:3
Moab and among the **A** and in Edom Jr 40:11
king of the **A**, has sent Ishmael Jr 40:14
set off to cross over to the **A**. Jr 41:10
eight men and went to the **A**. Jr 41:15
About the **A**, this is what the Jr 49:1
heard against Rabbah of the **A**. Jr 49:2
restore the fortunes of the **A**. Jr 49:6
to Rabbah of the **A** and to Judah Ezk 21:20
concerning the **A** and their Ezk 21:28
face toward the **A** and prophesy Ezk 25:2
Say to the **A**: Hear the word of Ezk 25:3
the prominent people of the **A**. Dn 11:41
punishing the **A** for three crimes Am 1:13
Moab and the insults of the **A**, Zph 2:8
Sodom and the **A** like Gomorrah— Zph 2:9

AMMONITES' *(3)*
give you any of the **A** land as a Dt 2:19
you did not go near the **A** land, Dt 2:37
army and destroyed the **A** land. 1Ch 20:1

AMNON *(25)*
his firstborn was **A**, by Ahinoam 2Sm 3:2
and David's son **A** was infatuated 2Sm 13:1
A was frustrated to the point of 2Sm 13:2
A had a friend named Jonadab, 2Sm 13:3
he asked **A**, "Why are you, the 2Sm 13:4
A replied, "I'm in love with 2Sm 13:4
A lay down and pretended to be 2Sm 13:6
came to see him, **A** said to him, 2Sm 13:6

house while **A** was lying down. 2Sm 13:8
A said, "Everyone leave me!" 2Sm 13:9
the bedroom," **A** told Tamar, "so 2Sm 13:10
A hated Tamar with such 2Sm 13:15
your brother **A** been with you? 2Sm 13:20
didn't say anything to **A**, 2Sm 13:22
because he hated **A** since he 2Sm 13:22
let my brother **A** go with us." 2Sm 13:26
so he sent **A** and all the king's 2Sm 13:27
Watch **A** until he is in a good 2Sm 13:28
When I order you to strike **A**, 2Sm 13:28
men did to **A** just as Absalom 2Sm 13:29
sons, because only **A** is dead. 2Sm 13:32
since the day **A** disgraced his 2Sm 13:32
sons are dead. Only **A** is dead." 2Sm 13:33
A was the firstborn, by Ahinoam 1Ch 3:1
A, Rinnah, Ben-hanan, and Tilon. 1Ch 4:20

AMNON'S *(4)*
to your brother **A** house and 2Sm 13:7
went to her brother **A** bedroom. 2Sm 13:10
A servant threw her out and 2Sm 13:18
finished grieving over **A** death. 2Sm 13:39

AMOK *(2)*
Sallu, **A**, Hilkiah, Jedaiah. Neh 12:7
Kallai of Sallai, Eber of **A**, Neh 12:20

AMON *(17)*
Micaiah and return him to **A**, 1Kg 22:26
His son **A** became king in his 2Kg 21:18
A was 22 years old when he 2Kg 21:19
against King **A** and made his son 2Kg 21:24
his son **A**, and his son Josiah. 1Ch 3:14
Micaiah and return him to **A**, 2Ch 18:25
His son **A** became king in his 2Ch 33:20
A was 22 years old when he 2Ch 33:21
A sacrificed to all the carved 2Ch 33:22
A increased ⌊his⌋ guilt. 2Ch 33:23
against King **A** and made his son 2Ch 33:25
of the reign of Josiah son of **A**, Jr 1:2
year of Josiah son of **A**, Jr 25:3
about to punish **A**, ⌊god⌋ of Jr 46:25
in the days of Josiah son of **A**, Zph 1:1
fathered **A**, Amon fathered Mt 1:10
Amon, **A** fathered Josiah, Mt 1:10

AMON'S *(3)*
(AKA AMI'S)
A servants conspired against the 2Kg 21:23
rest of the events of **A** ⌊reign⌋, 2Kg 21:25
descendants, **A** descendants. Neh 7:59

AMONG *(881)*
(See pp. xi-xii.)

AMORITE *(18)*
oaks belonging to Mamre the **A**, Gn 14:13
that extends from the **A** border, Nm 21:13
and lived in all these **A** cities, Nm 21:25
captivity to Sihon the **A** king. Nm 21:29
I have handed Sihon the **A**, Dt 2:24
land from the two **A** kings across Dt 3:8
the two **A** kings who were across Dt 4:47
—the Hittite, **A**, Canaanite, Dt 20:17
the two **A** kings you completely Jos 2:10
When all the **A** kings across the Jos 5:1
He did to the two **A** kings beyond Jos 9:10
So the five **A** kings—the kings Jos 10:5
all the **A** kings living in the Jos 10:6
out the two **A** kings before you Jos 24:12
father was an **A** and your mother Ezk 16:3
a Hittite and your father an **A**. Ezk 16:45
I destroyed the **A** as Israel Am 2:9
to possess the land of the **A**. Am 2:10

AMORITES *(69)*
Jebusites, the **A**, the Gn 10:16
as well as the **A** who lived in Gn 14:7
iniquity of the **A** has not yet Gn 15:16
A, Canaanites, Girgashites, and Gn 15:21
the hand of the **A** with my sword Gn 48:22
Hittites, **A**, Perizzites, Hivites Ex 3:8
Hittites, **A**, Perizzites, Hivites Ex 3:17
Hittites, **A**, Hivites, Ex 13:5
you to ⌊the land of⌋ the **A**, Ex 23:23
out the Canaanites, **A**, Hittites, Ex 33:2
to drive out before you the **A**, Ex 34:11
and **A** live in the hill country; Nm 13:29
border between Moab and the **A**. Nm 21:13
to say to Sihon king of the **A**: Nm 21:21
the city of Sihon king of the **A**, Nm 21:26
drove out the **A** who were there. Nm 21:32
you did to Sihon king of the **A**, Nm 21:34
that Israel had done to the **A**. Nm 22:2
king of the **A** and the kingdom Nm 32:33
drove out the **A** who were there. Nm 32:39
defeated Sihon king of the **A**, Dt 1:4
country of the **A** and their Dt 1:7
to the hill country of the **A**, Dt 1:19
the hill country of the **A**, Dt 1:20
the hands of the **A** so they would Dt 1:27
Then the **A** who lived there came Dt 1:44
you did to Sihon king of the **A**, Dt 3:2
Sirion, but the **A** call Senir, Dt 3:9
the land of Sihon king of the **A**. Dt 4:46
Girgashites, **A**, Canaanites, Dt 7:1
kings of the **A**, and their land Dt 31:4
Girgashites, **A**, and Jebusites Jos 3:10
us over to the **A** for our Jos 7:7
the Hittites, **A**, Canaanites, Jos 9:1
day the LORD gave the **A** over to Jos 10:12
east and west, the **A**, Hittites, Jos 11:3
king of the **A** lived in Heshbon Jos 12:2
of the Hittites, **A**, Canaanites, Jos 12:8
as far as the border of the **A**; Jos 13:4
cities of Sihon king of the **A**, Jos 13:10
kingdom of Sihon king of the **A**, Jos 13:21
the land of the **A** who lived Jos 24:8
as well as the **A**, Perizzites, Jos 24:11
the gods of the **A** in whose land Jos 24:15
including the **A** who lived in the Jos 24:18
A forced the Danites into the Jdg 1:34
A refused to leave Har-heres, Jdg 1:35
the **A** were made to serve as Jdg 1:35
The territory of the **A** extended Jdg 1:36
Hittites, **A**, Perizzites, Hivites Jdg 3:5
the gods of the **A** whose land you Jdg 6:10
in the land of the **A** in Gilead. Jdg 10:8
the Egyptians, **A**, Ammonites, Jdg 10:11
to Sihon king of the **A**, Jdg 11:19
land of the **A** who lived in that Jdg 11:21
territory of the **A** from the Jdg 11:22
driven out the **A** before His Jdg 11:23
peace between Israel and the **A**. 1Sm 7:14
but rather a remnant of the **A**. 2Sm 21:2
king of the **A** and of Og king 1Kg 4:19
peoples who remained of the **A**, 1Kg 9:20
going after idols as the **A** had, 1Kg 21:26
evil than the **A** who preceded him 2Kg 21:11
the Jebusites, **A**, Girgashites, 1Ch 1:14
of the Hittites, **A**, Perizzites, 2Ch 8:7
Moabites, Egyptians, and **A**. Ezr 9:1
Hittites, **A**, Perizzites, Neh 9:8
Sihon king of the **A**, Og king of Ps 135:11
Sihon king of the **A** His love is Ps 136:19

AMORITES' *(1)*
So Israel lived in the **A** land. Nm 21:31

AMOS *(8)*
The words of **A**, who was one of Am 1:1
asked me, "What do you see, **A**?" Am 7:8
A has conspired against you Am 7:10
for **A** has said this: 'Jeroboam Am 7:11
Amaziah said to **A**, "Go away, you Am 7:12
A answered Amaziah, "I was not Am 7:14
asked me, "What do you see, **A**?" Am 8:2
son⌋ of **A**, ⌊son⌋ of Nahum, Lk 3:25

AMOUNT *(18)*
gift, double the **a** of money, Gn 43:15
It was the full **a** of our money, Gn 43:21
life in the full **a** demanded from Ex 21:30
he must pay an **a** in silver equal Ex 22:17
to a greater **a** of years, Lv 25:16
to a lesser **a** of years, Lv 25:16
for him the **a** of the valuation Lv 27:23
that a great **a** of water gushed Nm 20:11
of the great **a** of plunder they 1Sm 30:16
brought a large **a** of plundered 2Sm 3:22
there was a large **a** of money in 2Kg 12:10
He did a great **a** of evil in the 2Kg 21:6
there was a large **a** of money, 2Ch 24:11
as the exact **a** of money Haman Est 4:7
lye and use a great **a** of soap, Jr 2:22
harvested a great **a** of wine and Jr 40:12
for a large **a** of money." Ac 22:28
was given a large **a** of incense Rv 8:3

AMOUNTED *(4)*
territory **a** to a year and four 1Sm 27:7
much, but then it **a** to little. Hg 1:9
20 measures, it ⌊only⌋ **a** to 10; Hg 2:16
from the vat, it ⌊only⌋ **a** to 20. Hg 2:16

AMOUNTS *(4)*
seven sabbatic years **a** to 49. Lv 25:8
very large **a** of silver and gold Dt 17:17
Samaria's dust **a** to a handful 1Kg 20:10
told about you **a** to nothing, Ac 21:24

AMOZ *(13)*
to the prophet Isaiah son of **A**. 2Kg 19:2
Isaiah son of **A** sent ⌊a message⌋ 2Kg 19:20
Isaiah son of **A** came and said to 2Kg 20:1
Isaiah son of **A** wrote about the 2Ch 26:22
Isaiah son of **A** prayed about 2Ch 32:20
of the Prophet Isaiah son of **A**, 2Ch 32:32
that Isaiah son of **A** saw during Is 1:1
Isaiah son of **A** saw concerning Is 2:1
that Isaiah son of **A** saw: Is 13:1
spoken through Isaiah son of **A**, Is 20:2
to the prophet Isaiah son of **A**. Is 37:2
Isaiah son of **A** sent ⌊a message⌋ Is 37:21
Isaiah son of **A** came and said to Is 38:1

AMPHIPOLIS *(1)*
traveled through **A** and Apollonia Ac 17:1

AMPHITHEATER *(2)*
rushed all together into the **a**, Ac 19:29
a chance by going into the **a**. Ac 19:31

AMPLE *(2)*
them with **a** food and sacred Is 23:18
worthy of an **a** honorarium, 1Tm 5:17

AMPLIATUS *(1)*
Greet **A**, my dear friend in the Rm 16:8

AMPLIFIED *(1)*
God's truth is **a** to His glory, Rm 3:7

AMPLY *(1)*
He is an **a** watered plant in the Jb 8:16

AMRAM *(10)*
A, Izhar, Hebron, and Uzziel. Ex 6:18
A married his father's sister Ex 6:20
and Moses. **A** lived 137 years Ex 6:20
sons by their clans were **A**, Nm 3:19
Kohath was the ancestor of **A**. Nm 26:58
She bore to **A**: Aaron, Moses, Nm 26:59
A, Izhar, Hebron, and Uzziel. 1Ch 6:2
A, Izhar, Hebron and Uzziel. 1Ch 6:18
A, Izhar, Hebron, and Uzziel— 1Ch 23:12
descendants: Maadai, **A**, Uel, Ezr 10:34

AMRAM'S *(4)*
The name of **A** wife was Jochebed, Nm 26:59
A children: Aaron, Moses, and 1Ch 6:3
A sons: Aaron and Moses. Aaron, 1Ch 23:13
sons: from **A** sons: Shubael; 1Ch 24:20

AMRAMITE *(1)*
The **A** clan, the Izharite clan, Nm 3:27

AMRAMITES *(1)*
From the **A**, the Izharites, the 1Ch 26:23

AMRAPHEL *(2)*
In those days **A** king of Shinar, Gn 14:1
king of Goiim, **A** king of Shinar, Gn 14:9

AMULETS *(1)*
sashes, perfume bottles, **a**, Is 3:20

AMZI *(2)*
son of **A**, son of Bani, son of 1Ch 6:46
Pelaliah, son of **A**, son of Neh 11:12

AN *(1255)*
(See pp. xi-xii.)

ANAB *(2)*
Hebron, Debir, **A**—all the hill Jos 11:21
A, Eshtemoh, Anim, Jos 15:50

ANAH *(11)*
daughter of **A** and granddaughter Gn 36:2
daughter of **A** and granddaughter Gn 36:14
wife Oholibamah daughter of **A**. Gn 36:18
Lotan, Shobal, Zibeon, **A**, Gn 36:20
sons: Aiah and **A**. This was the Gn 36:24
This was the **A** who found the hot Gn 36:24
These are the children of **A**: Gn 36:25
and Oholibamah daughter of **A**. Gn 36:25
Chiefs Lotan, Shobal, Zibeon, **A**, Gn 36:29
Shobal, Zibeon, **A**, Dishon, Ezer, 1Ch 1:38
Onam. Zibeon's sons: Aiah and **A**. 1Ch 1:40

ANAH'S *(1)*
A son: Dishon. Dishon's sons: 1Ch 1:41

ANAHARATH *(1)*
Hapharaim, Shion, **A**, Jos 19:19

ANAIAH (2)
Shema, **A**, Uriah, Hilkiah, Neh 8:4
Pelatiah, Hanan, **A**, Neh 10:22

ANAK (9)
descendants of **A**, were living. Nm 13:22
saw the descendants of **A** there. Nm 13:28
offspring of **A** were descended Nm 13:33
can stand up to the sons of **A**?' Dt 9:2
Arba was the father of **A**). Jos 15:13
from there the three sons of **A**: Jos 15:14
and Talmai, descendants of **A**. Jos 15:14
Arba was the father of **A**. Jos 21:11
three sons of **A** who lived there Jdg 1:20

ANAKIM (9)
the descendants of the **A** there.' Dt 1:28
people as tall as the **A**, Dt 2:10
Rephaim, like the **A**, though the Dt 2:11
numerous people, tall as the **A**. Dt 2:21
tall, the descendants of the **A**. Dt 9:2
exterminate the **A** from the hill Jos 11:21
A were left in the land of the Jos 11:22
heard then that the **A** are there, Jos 14:12
the greatest man among the **A**. Jos 14:15

ANALOGY (1)
I am using a human **a** because of Rm 6:19

ANAMIM (2)
fathered Ludim, **A**, Lehabim, Gn 10:13
fathered Ludim, **A**, Lehabim, 1Ch 1:11

ANAMMELECH (1)
the fire to Adrammelech and **A**, 2Kg 17:31

ANAN (1)
Ahiah, Hanan, **A**, Neh 10:26

ANANI (1)
Johanan, Delaiah, and **A**—seven. 1Ch 3:24

ANANIAH (2)
Maaseiah, son of **A**, made repairs Neh 3:23
Anathoth, Nob, **A**, Neh 11:32

ANANIAS (11)
But a man named **A**, with Sapphira Ac 5:1
Peter said, "**A**, why has Satan Ac 5:3
these words, **A** dropped dead, Ac 5:5
there was a disciple named **A**. Ac 9:10
said to him in a vision, "**A**!" Ac 9:10
has seen a man named **A** coming in Ac 9:12
"Lord," **A** answered, "I have Ac 9:13
So **A** left and entered the house. Ac 9:17
Someone named **A**, a devout man Ac 22:12
the high priest **A** ordered those Ac 23:2
five days **A** the high priest Ac 24:1

ANATH (2)
Shamgar son of **A** ⌊became judge⌋. Jdg 3:31
In the days of Shamgar son of **A**, Jdg 5:6

ANATHOTH (14)
A with its pasturelands, and Jos 21:18
priest, "Go to your fields in **A**. 1Kg 2:26
and **A** and its pasturelands. 1Ch 6:60
Abijah, **A**, and Alemeth; 1Ch 7:8
Hariph, **A**, Nebai, Neh 10:19
A, Nob, Ananiah, Neh 11:32
Listen, Laishah! **A** is miserable. Is 10:30
living in **A** in the territory Jr 1:1
the people of **A** who want to take Jr 11:21
on the people of **A** ⌊in⌋ the year Jr 11:23
Jeremiah of **A** who has been Jr 29:27
Buy my field in **A** for yourself, Jr 32:7
buy my field in **A** in the land Jr 32:8
the field in **A** from my cousin Jr 32:9

ANATHOTH'S (2)
A men 128 Ezr 2:23
A men 128 Neh 7:27

ANATHOTHITE (4)
Abiezer the **A**, Mebunnai the 2Sm 23:27
the Tekoite, Abiezer the **A**, 1Ch 11:28
Beracah, Jehu the **A**; 1Ch 12:3
Abiezer the **A**, a Benjaminite; 1Ch 27:12

ANCESTOR (22)
Kohath was the **a** of Amram. Nm 26:58
Leshem after their **a** Dan. Jos 19:47
after the name of their **a** Dan, Jdg 18:29
his God as his **a** David had been. 1Kg 15:3
eyes, as his **a** David had done. 1Kg 15:11
sight, but not like his **a** David. 2Kg 14:3
in the city of his **a** David. 2Kg 15:38
LORD his God like his **a** David 2Kg 16:2
just as his **a** David had done. 2Kg 18:3
LORD God of your **a** David says: 2Kg 20:5
in all the ways of his **a** David; 2Kg 22:2
the **a** of ⌊those in⌋ the Valley 1Ch 4:14
received from their **a** Aaron, 1Ch 24:19
LORD God of your **a** David says: 2Ch 21:12
just as his **a** David had done. 2Ch 29:2
in the ways of his **a** David; 2Ch 34:2
to seek the God of his **a** David, 2Ch 34:3
LORD God of your **a** David says: Is 38:5
son of our **a** Rechab, commanded: Jr 35:6
son of our **a** Rechab, in all he Jr 35:8
and done as our **a** Jonadab Jr 35:10
command of your **a** Jonadab and Jr 35:18

ANCESTOR'S (2)
have obeyed their **a** command. Jr 35:14
out their **a** command he gave Jr 35:16

ANCESTORS (113)
blessings of my **a** and the bounty Gn 49:26
fathers and **a** never saw since Ex 10:6
'Long ago your **a**, including Jos 24:2
the gods your **a** worshiped beyond Jos 24:14
was also gathered to their **a**. Jdg 2:10
brought your **a** up from the land 1Sm 12:6
He has done for you and your **a**. 1Sm 12:7
your **a** cried out to the LORD, 1Sm 12:8
who led your **a** out of Egypt and 1Sm 12:8
against you and against your **a**. 1Sm 12:15
made with our **a** when He brought 1Kg 8:21
to the land You gave their **a**. 1Kg 8:34
live on the land You gave our **a**. 1Kg 8:40
land that You gave their **a**, 1Kg 8:48
brought their **a** out of Egypt. 1Kg 8:53
be with us as He was with our **a**. 1Kg 8:57
which He commanded our **a**. 1Kg 8:58
brought their **a** out of the land 1Kg 9:9
all that their **a** had done with 1Kg 14:22
consecrated items that his **a**— 2Kg 12:18
commanded your **a** and sent to 2Kg 17:13
like their **a** who did not believe 2Kg 17:14
made with their **a** and the 2Kg 17:15
I gave to their **a** if only they 2Kg 21:8
the day their **a** came out of 2Kg 21:15
LORD God of his **a** and did not 2Kg 21:22
us because our **a** have not obeyed 2Kg 22:13
sight just as his **a** had done. 2Kg 23:32
sight just as his **a** had done. 2Kg 23:37
to the God of their **a**. 1Ch 5:25
Their **a** had been assigned to the 1Ch 9:19
may the God of our **a** look on it 1Ch 12:17
genealogical records of his **a**. 1Ch 26:31
Your presence as were all our **a**. 1Ch 29:15
and Israel, our **a**, keep this 1Ch 29:18
praised the LORD God of their **a**. 1Ch 29:20
land You gave them and their **a**. 2Ch 6:25
live on the land You gave our **a**. 2Ch 6:31
land that You gave their **a**, 2Ch 6:38
God of their **a** who brought them 2Ch 7:22
to the LORD God of their **a**. 2Ch 11:16
against the LORD God of your **a**, 2Ch 13:12
on the LORD, the God of their **a**. 2Ch 13:18
God of their **a** and to carry out 2Ch 14:4
God of their **a** with all their 2Ch 15:12
back to the LORD God of their **a**. 2Ch 19:4
LORD God of our **a**, are You not 2Ch 20:6
to worship⌋ the God of their **a**. 2Ch 20:33
abandoned the LORD God of his **a**. 2Ch 21:10
LORD God of their **a** and served 2Ch 24:18
the LORD God of their **a**. 2Ch 24:24
the LORD God of their **a**. 2Ch 28:6
God of your **a** handed them over 2Ch 28:9
he provoked the God of his **a**. 2Ch 28:25
of the LORD God of your **a**. 2Ch 29:5
God of their **a** so that He made 2Ch 30:7
LORD God of his **a**, even though 2Ch 30:19
to the LORD God of their **a**. 2Ch 30:22
land where I stationed your **a**, 2Ch 33:8
himself before the God of his **a**. 2Ch 33:12
of God, the God of their **a**. 2Ch 34:32
the LORD God of their **a**. 2Ch 34:33
God of their **a** sent word against 2Ch 36:15
city where my **a** are buried lies Neh 2:3
the city where my **a** are buried, Neh 2:5
oppression of our **a** in Egypt and Neh 9:9
arrogantly they treated our **a**. Neh 9:10
But our **a** acted arrogantly; Neh 9:16
You told their **a** to go in and Neh 9:23
our **a** and all Your people, Neh 9:32
and **a** did not obey Your law or Neh 9:34
land You gave our **a** so that they Neh 9:36
Didn't your **a** do the same, Neh 13:18
was not suppressed by their **a**, Jb 15:18
Your sons will succeed your **a**; Ps 45:16
I have given your **a** to inherit." Jr 3:18
I gave to your **a** forever and Jr 7:7
that I gave you and your **a**. Jr 7:14
I brought your **a** out of the land Jr 7:22
Since the day your **a** came out of Jr 7:25
they did more evil than their **a**. Jr 7:26
commanded your **a** when I brought Jr 11:4
the oath I swore to your **a**, Jr 11:5
warned your **a** when I brought Jr 11:7
sins of their **a** who refused to Jr 11:10
My covenant I made with their **a**. Jr 11:10
land that I gave to their **a**. Jr 16:15
just as I commanded your **a**. Jr 17:22
I gave to them and their **a**." Jr 24:10
to you and your **a** for ever and Jr 25:5
I gave to their **a** and they will Jr 30:3
made with their **a** when I took Jr 31:32
You swore ⌊to give⌋ to their **a**, Jr 32:22
with your **a** when I brought Jr 34:13
your **a** did not obey Me or pay Jr 34:14
land that I gave you and your **a**. Jr 35:15
I set before you and your **a**. Jr 44:10
the hope of their **a**, the LORD. Jr 50:7
and their **a** have transgressed Ezk 2:3
I swore to give it to your **a**. Ezk 47:14
days or in the days of your **a**? Jl 1:2
lies that their **a** followed have Am 2:4
was extremely angry with your **a**. Zch 1:2
Do not be like your **a**; Zch 1:4
Where are your **a** now? Zch 1:5
the prophets overtake your **a**? Zch 1:6
heard that it was said to our **a**, Mt 5:21
heard that it was said to our **a**, Mt 5:33
just as He spoke to our **a**, Lk 1:55
is the way their **a** used to treat Lk 6:23
is the way their **a** used to treat Lk 6:26
for the traditions of my **a**. Gl 1:14
For by it our **a** were approved. Heb 11:2

ANCESTRAL (83)
to his clan and his **a** property. Lv 25:41
their clans and their **a** houses, Nm 1:2
one the head of his **a** house. Nm 1:4
are leaders of their **a** tribes, Nm 1:16
their clans and their **a** houses, Nm 1:18
their clans and their **a** houses, Nm 1:20
their clans and their **a** houses, Nm 1:22
their clans and their **a** houses, Nm 1:24
their clans and their **a** houses, Nm 1:26
their clans and their **a** houses, Nm 1:28
their clans and their **a** houses, Nm 1:30
their clans and their **a** houses, Nm 1:32
their clans and their **a** houses, Nm 1:34
their clans and their **a** houses, Nm 1:36
their clans and their **a** houses, Nm 1:38
their clans and their **a** houses, Nm 1:40
their clans and their **a** houses, Nm 1:42
each represented his **a** house. Nm 1:44
registered by their **a** houses. Nm 1:45
with them by their **a** tribe. Nm 1:47
the flags of their **a** houses. Nm 2:2
registered by their **a** houses. Nm 2:32
by his clan and by his **a** house. Nm 2:34
by their **a** houses and their Nm 3:15
Levite clans by their **a** houses. Nm 3:20
their clans and their **a** houses, Nm 4:2
by their **a** houses and their Nm 4:22
their clans and their **a** houses. Nm 4:29
their clans and their **a** houses, Nm 4:34
their clans and their **a** houses, Nm 4:38
and their **a** houses numbered Nm 4:40
their clans and their **a** houses, Nm 4:42
their clans and their **a** houses, Nm 4:46
the heads of their **a** houses, Nm 7:2
from each of their **a** tribes." Nm 13:2
from them for each **a** house, Nm 17:2
the leaders of their **a** houses. Nm 17:2
for the head of each **a** house. Nm 17:3
the leaders of their **a** houses, Nm 17:6
and your **a** house will be Nm 18:1
of Levi, your **a** tribe, so they Nm 18:2
leader of a Simeonite **a** house. Nm 25:14
head of an **a** house in Midian. Nm 25:15
by their **a** houses of those 20 Nm 26:2
to the names of their **a** tribes. Nm 26:55

according to your a tribes. Nm 33:54
according to their a houses, Nm 34:14
the inheritance of our a tribe." Nm 36:4
within a clan of their a tribe. Nm 36:6
the inheritance of his a tribe. Nm 36:7
from the clan of her a tribe, Nm 36:8
Myself to your a house when it 1Sm 2:27
family and your a house would 1Sm 2:30
the strength of your a family, 1Sm 2:31
tribal heads and the a leaders 1Kg 8:1
a houses increased greatly. 1Ch 4:38
according to their a houses: 1Ch 5:13
was head of their a houses. 1Ch 5:15
the heads of their a houses: 1Ch 5:24
the heads of their a houses. 1Ch 7:2
records of their a houses, 1Ch 7:4
and heads of their a houses; 1Ch 7:7
to the heads of their a houses— 1Ch 7:9
the heads of their a houses, 1Ch 7:40
were heads of their a houses. 1Ch 9:9
from his own a house. 1Ch 12:28
famous men in their a houses. 1Ch 12:30
so they became an a house ⌊and 1Ch 23:11
sons of Levi by their a houses— 1Ch 23:24
16 heads of a houses were from 1Ch 24:4
eight ⌊heads⌋ of a houses were 1Ch 24:4
One a house was taken for 1Ch 24:6
according to their a houses. 1Ch 24:30
over their a houses because 1Ch 26:6
according to their a houses, 1Ch 26:13
the a chiefs of the Israelites— 2Ch 5:2
according to their a families. 2Ch 17:14
the priests by their a families 2Ch 31:17
Organize your a houses by your 2Ch 35:4
of the a houses for your 2Ch 35:5
divisions of the a houses of the 2Ch 35:12
to represent their a houses. Ezr 10:16
of wood by our a houses at the Neh 10:34

ANCESTRY (3)
recorded their a by their clans Nm 1:18
families and a were Israelite: Ezr 2:59
families and a were Israelite: Neh 7:61

ANCHOR (2)
they weighed a and sailed along Ac 27:13
a sure and firm a of the soul— Heb 6:19

ANCHORS (3)
dropped four a from the stern Ac 27:29
going to put out a from the bow. Ac 27:30
casting off the a, they left Ac 27:40

ANCIENT (45)
best products of the a mountains Dt 33:15
away, the a river, the river Jdg 5:21
From a times they had been the 1Sm 27:8
⌊names⌋ are from a records. 1Ch 4:22
revolts in it since a times. Ezr 4:15
against kings since a times, Ezr 4:19
continue on the a path that Jb 22:15
gates! Rise up, a doors! Then Ps 24:7
gates! Rise up, a doors! Then Ps 24:9
to Him who rides in the a, Ps 68:33
God my king is from a times, Ps 74:12
I will remember Your a wonders. Ps 77:11
I was formed before a times, Pr 8:23
Don't move an a property line Pr 22:28
Don't move an a property line, Pr 23:10
for the waters of the a pool, Is 22:11
whose origin was in a times, Is 23:7
I have established an a people. Is 44:7
Who announced it from a times? Is 45:21
of you will rebuild the a ruins; Is 58:12
They will rebuild the a ruins; Is 61:4
from a times, Your name is our Is 63:16
From a times no one has heard, Is 64:4
nation, an a nation, a nation Jr 5:15
Ask about the a paths: Jr 6:16
ways—in the a roads—to walk Jr 18:15
you and me from a times Jr 28:8
inhabited again as in a times." Jr 46:26
because of their⌋ a hatred, Ezk 25:15
the underworld like the a ruins, Ezk 26:20
maintained an a hatred and Ezk 35:5
The a heights have become our Ezk 36:2
and the A of Days took His seat. Dn 7:9
approached the A of Days and was Dn 7:13
until the A of Days arrived and Dn 7:22
Bashan and Gilead as in a times. Mc 7:14
the a hills sink down. Hab 3:6
sink down. His pathways are a. Hab 3:6
of His holy prophets in a times; Lk 1:70
that one of the a prophets had Lk 9:8
that one of the a prophets has Lk 9:19
For since a times, Moses has had Ac 15:21
if He didn't spare the a world, 2Pt 2:5
out—the a serpent, who is Rv 12:9
that a serpent who is the Devil Rv 20:2

AND (28,240)
(See pp. xi-xii.)

ANDREW (12)
called Peter, and his brother A. Mt 4:18
called Peter, and A his brother; Mt 10:2
saw Simon and A, Simon's brother Mk 1:16
A; Philip and Bartholomew; Mk 3:18
and A asked Him privately, Mk 13:3
named Peter, and A his brother; Lk 6:14
A, Simon Peter's brother, was Jn 1:40
the hometown of A and Peter. Jn 1:44
His disciples, A, Simon Peter's Jn 6:8
Philip went and told A; Jn 12:22
then A and Philip went and told Jn 12:22
John, James, A, Philip, Thomas, Ac 1:13

ANDREW'S (1)
Simon and A house with James Mk 1:29

ANDRONICUS (1)
Greet A and Junia, my fellow Rm 16:7

ANEM (1)
and A and its pasturelands. 1Ch 6:73

ANER (3)
(AKA TAANACH)
of Eshcol and the brother of A. Gn 14:13
came with me—A, Eshcol, and Gn 14:24
tribe of Manasseh, A and its 1Ch 6:70

ANGEL (192)
The A of the LORD found her by a Gn 16:7
Then the A of the LORD said to Gn 16:9
The A of the LORD also said to Gn 16:10
Then the A of the LORD said to Gn 16:11
and the a of God called to Hagar Gn 21:17
But the A of the LORD called to Gn 22:11
Then the A of the LORD called to Gn 22:15
He will send His a before you, Gn 24:7
send His a with you and make Gn 24:40
that dream the A of God said to Gn 31:11
the A who has redeemed me from Gn 48:16
Then the A of the LORD appeared Ex 3:2
Then the A of God, who was going Ex 14:19
going to send an A before you to Ex 23:20
For My A will go before you and Ex 23:23
see, My a will go before you. Ex 32:34
will send an a ahead of you and Ex 33:2
voice, sent an A, and brought us Nm 20:16
and the A of the LORD took His Nm 22:22
the donkey saw the A of the LORD Nm 22:23
Then the A of the LORD stood in Nm 22:24
donkey saw the A of the LORD Nm 22:25
The A of the LORD went ahead Nm 22:26
donkey saw the A of the LORD, Nm 22:27
and he saw the A of the LORD Nm 22:31
The A of the LORD asked him, Nm 22:32
said to the A of the LORD, Nm 22:34
Then the A of the LORD said to Nm 22:35
The A of the LORD went up from Jdg 2:1
the A of the LORD had spoken Jdg 2:4
says the A of the LORD, Jdg 5:23
The A of the LORD came, and He Jdg 6:11
Then the A of the LORD appeared Jdg 6:12
The A of God said to him, Jdg 6:20
The A of the LORD extended the Jdg 6:21
Then the A of the LORD vanished Jdg 6:21
that He was the A of the LORD, Jdg 6:22
I have seen the A of the LORD Jdg 6:22
A of the LORD appeared to the Jdg 13:3
like the awe-inspiring A of God. Jdg 13:6
and the A of GOD came again to Jdg 13:9
The A of the LORD answered Jdg 13:13
The A of the LORD said to him, Jdg 13:16
know He was the A of the LORD. Jdg 13:16
the A of the LORD asked him, Jdg 13:18
the A of the LORD went up in its Jdg 13:20
The A of the LORD did not appear Jdg 13:21
that it was the A of the LORD. Jdg 13:21
are as reliable as an a of God. 1Sm 29:9
and the bad like the A of God. 2Sm 14:17
like the wisdom of the A of God, 2Sm 14:20
the king is like the A of God, 2Sm 19:27
Then the a extended his hand 2Sm 24:16
and said to the a who was 2Sm 24:16
The a of the LORD was then at 2Sm 24:16
When David saw the a striking 2Sm 24:17
An a spoke to me by the word of 1Kg 13:18
Suddenly, an a touched him. 1Kg 19:5
a told him, "Get up and eat." 1Kg 19:5
Then the a of the LORD returned 1Kg 19:7
But the a of the LORD said to 2Kg 1:3
a of the LORD said to Elijah, 2Kg 1:15
night the a of the LORD went 2Kg 19:35
the a of the LORD bringing 1Ch 21:12
God sent an a to Jerusalem to 1Ch 21:15
but when the a was about to 1Ch 21:15
and said to the a who was 1Ch 21:15
The a of the LORD was then 1Ch 21:15
up and saw the a of the LORD 1Ch 21:16
So the a of the LORD ordered Gad 1Ch 21:18
when he turned and saw the a. 1Ch 21:20
Then the LORD spoke to the a, 1Ch 21:27
of the sword of the LORD's a. 1Ch 21:30
LORD sent an a who annihilated 2Ch 32:21
If there is an a on his side, Jb 33:23
The a of the LORD encamps around Ps 34:7
with the a of the LORD driving Ps 35:5
with the a of the LORD pursuing Ps 35:6
Then the a of the LORD went out Is 37:36
and the A of His Presence saved Is 63:9
He sent His a and rescued His Dn 3:28
sent His a and shut the lions' Dn 6:22
with the A and prevailed; Hs 12:4
The a who was talking to me Zch 1:9
reported to the A of the LORD Zch 1:11
the A of the LORD responded, Zch 1:12
words to the a who was speaking Zch 1:13
the a who was speaking with me Zch 1:14
I asked the a who was speaking Zch 1:19
Then the a who was speaking with Zch 2:3
and another a went out to meet Zch 2:3
before the A of the LORD, Zch 3:1
as he stood before the A. Zch 3:3
while the A of the LORD was Zch 3:5
Then the A of the LORD charged Zch 3:6
The a who was speaking with me Zch 4:1
I asked the a who was speaking Zch 4:4
replied the a who was speaking Zch 4:5
Then the a who was speaking with Zch 5:5
I asked the a who was speaking Zch 5:10
inquired of the a who was Zch 6:4
The a told me, "These are the Zch 6:5
God, like the A of the LORD, Zch 12:8
an a of the Lord suddenly Mt 1:20
as the Lord's a had commanded Mt 1:24
an a of the Lord suddenly Mt 2:13
an a of the Lord suddenly Mt 2:19
because an a of the Lord Mt 28:2
But the a told the women, Mt 28:5
a of the Lord appeared to him, Lk 1:11
But the a said to him: Lk 1:13
Zechariah asked the a. Lk 1:18
The a answered him, "I am Lk 1:19
the a Gabriel was sent by God to Lk 1:26
⌊the a⌋ came to her and said, Lk 1:28
Then the a told her: Do not be Lk 1:30
Mary asked the a, "How can this Lk 1:34
The a replied to her: The Holy Lk 1:35
Then the a left her. Lk 1:38
Then an a of the Lord stood Lk 2:9
But the a said to them, "Don't Lk 2:10
of the heavenly host with the a, Lk 2:13
name given by the a before He Lk 2:21
Then an a from heaven appeared Lk 22:43
because an a would go down into Jn 5:4
said, "An a has spoken to Him! Jn 12:29
But an a of the Lord opened the Ac 5:19
face was like the face of an a. Ac 6:15
an a appeared to him in the Ac 7:30
means of the a who appeared to Ac 7:35
with the a who spoke to him Ac 7:38
a of the Lord spoke to Philip: Ac 8:26
in a vision an a of God who came Ac 10:3
When the a who spoke to him had Ac 10:7
by a holy a to call you to his Ac 10:22
had seen the a standing in his Ac 11:13
Suddenly an a of the Lord Ac 12:7
Get dressed," the a told him, Ac 12:8
place through the a was real, Ac 12:9
and immediately the a left him. Ac 12:10

has sent His **a** and rescued me	Ac 12:11
Then they said, "It's his **a**!"	Ac 12:15
At once an **a** of the Lord struck	Ac 12:23
and no **a** or spirit,	Ac 23:8
a spirit or an **a** has spoken to	Ac 23:9
For this night an **a** of the God I	Ac 27:23
is disguised as an **a** of light.	2Co 11:14
even if we or an **a** from heaven	Gl 1:8
you received me as an **a** of God,	Gl 4:14
it through His **a** to His slave	Rv 1:1
To the **a** of the church in	Rv 2:1
To the **a** of the church in Smyrna	Rv 2:8
To the **a** of the church in	Rv 2:12
To the **a** of the church in	Rv 2:18
To the **a** of the church in Sardis	Rv 3:1
To the **a** of the church in	Rv 3:7
To the **a** of the church in	Rv 3:14
also saw a mighty **a** proclaiming	Rv 5:2
I saw another **a** rise up from	Rv 7:2
Another **a**, with a gold incense	Rv 8:3
The **a** took the incense burner,	Rv 8:5
The first ⌊**a**⌋ blew his trumpet,	Rv 8:7
The second **a** blew his trumpet,	Rv 8:8
The third **a** blew his trumpet,	Rv 8:10
The fourth **a** blew his trumpet,	Rv 8:12
The fifth **a** blew his trumpet,	Rv 9:1
their king the **a** of the abyss;	Rv 9:11
The sixth **a** blew his trumpet.	Rv 9:13
say to the sixth **a** who had the	Rv 9:14
saw another mighty **a** coming down	Rv 10:1
Then the **a** that I had seen	Rv 10:5
of the sound of the seventh **a**,	Rv 10:7
hand of the **a** who is standing	Rv 10:8
I went to the **a** and asked him to	Rv 10:9
The seventh **a** blew his trumpet,	Rv 11:15
Then I saw another **a** flying in	Rv 14:6
A second **a** followed, saying:	Rv 14:8
And a third **a** followed them and	Rv 14:9
Another **a** came out of the	Rv 14:15
Then another **a** who also had a	Rv 14:17
Yet another **a**, who had authority	Rv 14:18
So the **a** swung his sickle toward	Rv 14:19
I heard the **a** of the waters say:	Rv 16:5
Then the **a** said to me, "Why are	Rv 17:7
this I saw another **a** with great	Rv 18:1
a mighty **a** picked up a stone	Rv 18:21
Then I saw an **a** standing in the	Rv 19:17
Then I saw an **a** coming down from	Rv 20:1
measurement, which the **a** used.	Rv 21:17
has sent His **a** to show His	Rv 22:6
the feet of the **a** who had shown	Rv 22:8
have sent My **a** to attest these	Rv 22:16

ANGEL'S *(2)*

presence of God from the **a** hand.	Rv 8:4
from the **a** hand and ate it	Rv 10:10

ANGELS *(93)*

The two **a** entered Sodom in the	Gn 19:1
But the **a** reached out, brought	Gn 19:10
Then the **a** said to Lot, "Do you	Gn 19:12
crack of dawn the **a** urged Lot	Gn 19:15
As soon as the **a** got them	Gn 19:17
and God's **a** were going up and	Gn 28:12
on his way, and God's **a** met him.	Gn 32:1
He charges His **a** with	Jb 4:18
People ate the bread of **a**.	Ps 78:25
He will give His **a** orders	Ps 91:11
⌊all⌋ His **a** of great strength,	Ps 103:20
Praise Him, all His **a**;	Ps 148:2
He will give His **a** orders	Mt 4:6
and immediately **a** came and began	Mt 4:11
age, and the harvesters are **a**.	Mt 13:39
Son of Man will send out His **a**,	Mt 13:41
The **a** will go out, separate the	Mt 13:49
to come with His **a** in the glory	Mt 16:27
in heaven their **a** continually	Mt 18:10
but are like **a** in heaven.	Mt 22:30
will send out His **a** with a loud	Mt 24:31
neither the **a** in heaven, nor	Mt 24:36
and all the **a** with Him, then He	Mt 25:31
for the Devil and his **a**!	Mt 25:41
with more than 12 legions of **a**?	Mt 26:53
and the **a** began to serve Him.	Mk 1:13
of His Father with the holy **a**."	Mk 8:38
but are like **a** in heaven.	Mk 12:25
send out the **a** and gather His	Mk 13:27
neither the **a** in heaven nor the	Mk 13:32
When the **a** had left them and	Lk 2:15
He will give His **a** orders	Lk 4:10
of the Father and the holy **a**.	Lk 9:26
him before the **a** of God,	Lk 12:8
be denied before the **a** of God.	Lk 12:9
of God's **a** over one sinner	Lk 15:10
away by the **a** to Abraham's side	Lk 16:22
they are like **a** and are sons of	Lk 20:36
a vision of **a** who said He was	Lk 24:23
and the **a** of God ascending	Jn 1:51
She saw two **a** in white sitting	Jn 20:12
direction of **a** and yet have not	Ac 7:53
nor life, nor **a** nor rulers, nor	Rm 8:38
the world and to **a** and to men.	1Co 4:9
not know that we will judge **a**—	1Co 6:3
on her head: because of the **a**.	1Co 11:10
the languages of men and of **a**,	1Co 13:1
was ordered through **a** by means	Gl 3:19
practices and the worship of **a**,	Col 2:18
from heaven with His powerful **a**,	2Th 1:7
Spirit, seen by **a**, preached	1Tm 3:16
Christ Jesus and the elect **a**,	1Tm 5:21
higher in rank than the **a**,	Heb 1:4
which of the **a** did He ever say	Heb 1:5
all God's **a** must worship Him.	Heb 1:6
And about the **a** He says:	Heb 1:7
He makes His **a** winds, and His	Heb 1:7
to which of the **a** has He ever	Heb 1:13
spoken through **a** was legally	Heb 2:2
not subjected to **a** the world to	Heb 2:5
lower than the **a** for a short	Heb 2:7
lower than the **a** for a short	Heb 2:9
He does not reach out to help **a**,	Heb 2:16
to myriads of **a** in festive	Heb 12:22
have welcomed **a** as guests	Heb 13:2
A desire to look into these	1Pt 1:12
right hand, with **a**, authorities,	1Pt 3:22
didn't spare the **a** who sinned,	2Pt 2:4
however, **a**, who are greater in	2Pt 2:11
a who did not keep their own	Jd 6
stars are the **a** of the seven	Rv 1:20
My Father and before His **a**.	Rv 3:5
voice of many **a** around the	Rv 5:11
this I saw four **a** standing at	Rv 7:1
voice to the four **a** who were	Rv 7:2
All the **a** stood around the	Rv 7:11
Then I saw the seven **a** who stand	Rv 8:2
the seven **a** who had the seven	Rv 8:6
the three **a** are about to sound!	Rv 8:13
Release the four **a** bound at the	Rv 9:14
So the four **a** who were prepared	Rv 9:15
Michael and his **a** fought against	Rv 12:7
dragon and his **a** also fought,	Rv 12:7
to earth, and his **a** with him.	Rv 12:9
of the holy **a** and in the sight	Rv 14:10
seven **a** with the seven last	Rv 15:1
came the seven **a** with the seven	Rv 15:6
the seven **a** seven gold bowls	Rv 15:7
of the seven **a** were completed.	Rv 15:8
sanctuary saying to the seven **a**,	Rv 16:1
one of the seven **a** who had the	Rv 17:1
one of the seven **a**, who had held	Rv 21:9
Twelve **a** were at the gates;	Rv 21:12

ANGER *(238)*

your brother's **a** subsides—	Gn 27:44
For in their **a** they kill men,	Gn 49:6
Their **a** is cursed, for it is	Gn 49:7
Then the LORD's **a** burned against	Ex 4:14
Pharaoh's presence in fierce **a**.	Ex 11:8
break out ⌊in **a**⌋ against them."	Ex 19:22
break out ⌊in **a**⌋ against them."	Ex 19:24
My **a** will burn, and I will kill	Ex 22:24
so that My **a** can burn against	Ex 32:10
does Your **a** burn against Your	Ex 32:11
Your great **a** and change Your	Ex 32:12
slow to **a** and rich in faithful	Ex 34:6
LORD heard, His **a** burned, and	Nm 11:1
the LORD's **a** burned against the	Nm 11:33
LORD'S **a** burned against them,	Nm 12:9
The LORD is slow to **a** and rich	Nm 14:18
and the LORD's **a** burned against	Nm 25:3
that His burning **a** may turn away	Nm 25:4
So the LORD'S **a** burned that day,	Nm 32:10
The LORD'S **a** burned against	Nm 32:13
LORD's burning **a** against Israel.	Nm 32:14
your God, provoking Him to **a**,	Dt 4:25
Then the LORD's **a** will burn	Dt 7:4
sight and provoking Him to **a**.	Dt 9:18
of the fierce **a** the LORD had	Dt 9:19
Then the LORD's **a** will burn	Dt 11:17
from His burning **a** and grant you	Dt 13:17
the heat of his **a** might pursue	Dt 19:6
His **a** and jealousy will burn	Dt 29:20
LORD demolished in His fierce **a**.	Dt 29:23
Why this great outburst of **a**?'	Dt 29:24
the LORD's **a** burned against this	Dt 29:27
them from their land in ⌊His⌋ **a**,	Dt 29:28
My **a** will burn against them on	Dt 31:17
provoked ⌊to **a**⌋ by His sons and	Dt 32:19
because of My **a** and burns to	Dt 32:22
and the LORD's **a** burned against	Jos 7:1
LORD turned from His burning **a**.	Jos 7:26
the LORD's **a** will burn against	Jos 23:16
The LORD's **a** burned against	Jdg 2:14
The LORD'S **a** burned against	Jdg 2:20
The LORD's **a** burned against	Jdg 3:8
their **a** against him subsided.	Jdg 8:3
So the LORD's **a** burned against	Jdg 10:7
and his **a** burned furiously.	1Sm 11:6
table in fierce **a** and did not	1Sm 20:34
Then the LORD's **a** burned against	2Sm 6:7
if the king's **a** gets stirred up	2Sm 11:20
shook because He burned with **a**.	2Sm 22:8
The LORD's **a** burned against	2Sm 24:1
Him to jealous **a** more than all	1Kg 14:22
provoked ⌊My⌋ **a** and caused	1Kg 21:22
So the LORD's **a** burned against	2Kg 13:3
of His great wrath and **a**,	2Kg 23:26
of the LORD's **a**, it came to the	2Kg 24:20
Then the LORD's **a** burned against	1Ch 13:10
God burst out ⌊in **a**⌋ against us	1Ch 15:13
the LORD's **a** turned away from	2Ch 12:12
because of his **a** over this.	2Ch 16:10
So the LORD's **a** was against	2Ch 25:15
but His great **a** is against all	Ezr 8:22
to avert the fierce **a** of our God	Ezr 10:14
slow to **a** and rich in faithful	Neh 9:17
rekindling ⌊His⌋ **a** against	Neh 13:18
furious and his **a** burned within	Est 1:12
Then the king's **a** subsided.	Est 7:10
For **a** kills a fool, and jealousy	Jb 5:2
overturning them in His **a**.	Jb 9:5
God does not hold back His **a**;	Jb 9:13
and multiply Your **a** toward me.	Jb 10:17
conceal me until Your **a** passes,	Jb 14:13
as you turn your **a** against God	Jb 15:13
His **a** tears ⌊at me⌋, and He	Jb 16:9
You who tear yourself in **a**—	Jb 18:4
His **a** burns against me, and He	Jb 19:11
send His burning **a** against him,	Jb 20:23
away on the day of God's **a**.	Jb 20:28
apportion destruction in His **a**?	Jb 21:17
because God's **a** does not punish	Jb 35:15
have a godless heart harbor **a**;	Jb 36:13
Unleash your raging **a**;	Jb 40:11
to them in His **a** and terrifies	Ps 2:5
for His **a** may ignite at any	Ps 2:12
do not rebuke me in Your **a**;	Ps 6:1
Rise up, LORD, in Your **a**;	Ps 7:6
shook because He burned with **a**.	Ps 18:7
not turn Your servant away in **a**.	Ps 27:9
For His **a** lasts only a moment,	Ps 30:5
Refrain from **a** and give up	Ps 37:8
me in Your **a** or discipline me	Ps 38:1
on me and harass me in **a**.	Ps 55:3
Your burning **a** overtake them.	Ps 69:24
Why does Your **a** burn against the	Ps 74:1
He in **a** withheld His compassion?	Ps 77:9
and **a** flared up against Israel	Ps 78:21
God's **a** flared up against them,	Ps 78:31
often turned His **a** aside and did	Ps 78:38
sent His burning **a** against them:	Ps 78:49
He cleared a path for His **a**.	Ps 78:50
You turned from Your burning **a**.	Ps 85:3
You prolong Your **a** for all	Ps 85:5
slow to **a** and abundant in	Ps 86:15
Will Your **a** keep burning like	Ps 89:46
For we are consumed by Your **a**;	Ps 90:7
understands the power of Your **a**?	Ps 90:11
I swore in My **a**, 'They will not	Ps 95:11
slow to **a** and full of faithful	Ps 103:8
the LORD's **a** burned against His	Ps 106:40
crush kings on the day of His **a**.	Ps 110:5
My **a** overwhelms me because	Ps 119:139
in their burning **a** against us.	Ps 124:3
life from the **a** of my enemies.	Ps 138:7
slow to **a** and great in faithful	Ps 145:8
but his **a** falls on a disgraceful	Pr 14:35

A gentle answer turns away **a**, Pr 15:1
a man slow to **a** calms strife. Pr 15:18
with great **a** bears the penalty Pr 19:19
gift soothes **a**, and a covert Pr 21:14
Fury is cruel, and **a** is a flood, Pr 27:4
city, but the wise turn away **a**. Pr 29:8
A fool gives full vent to his **a**, Pr 29:11
stirring up **a** produces strife Pr 30:33
much sorrow, sickness, and **a**. Ec 5:17
for **a** abides in the heart of Ec 7:9
If the ruler's **a** rises against Ec 10:4
the LORD's **a** burns against His Is 5:25
all this, His **a** is not removed, Is 5:25
all this, His **a** is not removed, Is 9:12
all this, His **a** is not removed, Is 9:17
all this, His **a** is not removed, Is 9:21
all this, His **a** is not removed, Is 10:4
the rod of My **a**—the staff in Is 10:5
be spent and My **a** will turn to Is 10:25
Your **a** has turned away, and You Is 12:1
rage and burning **a**—to make the Is 13:9
on the day of His burning **a**. Is 13:13
the peoples in **a** with unceasing Is 14:6
His **a** burning and heavy with Is 30:27
His furious **a** and the power Is 42:25
I will delay My **a** for the honor Is 48:9
In a surge of **a** I hid My face Is 54:8
them in My **a** and ground them Is 63:3
I crushed nations in My **a**; Is 63:6
to execute His **a** with fury, Is 66:15
His **a** is sure to turn away from Jr 2:35
I will not look on you with **a**, Jr 3:12
LORD's burning **a** has not turned Jr 4:8
of the LORD and His burning **a**. Jr 4:26
so that they provoke Me to **a**. Jr 7:18
Look, My **a**—My burning wrath— Jr 7:20
provoked Me to **a** with their Jr 8:19
in Your **a**, or You will reduce Jr 10:24
provoking Me to **a** by burning Jr 11:17
because of the LORD's burning **a**. Jr 12:13
for My **a** will kindle a fire that Jr 15:14
for you have set My **a** on fire; Jr 17:4
to turn Your **a** from them. Jr 18:20
with them in the time of Your **a**. Jr 18:23
arm, with **a**, rage, and great Jr 21:5
or My **a** will flare up like fire Jr 21:12
The LORD's **a** will not turn back Jr 23:20
not provoke Me to **a** by the work Jr 25:6
provoke Me to **a** by the work of Jr 25:7
because of the LORD's burning **a**. Jr 25:37
because of His burning **a**. Jr 25:38
LORD's burning **a** will not turn Jr 30:24
other gods to provoke Me to **a**. Jr 32:29
but provoke Me to **a** by the work Jr 32:30
have done to provoke Me to **a**— Jr 32:32
for the **a** and fury that the LORD Jr 36:7
'Just as My **a** and fury were Jr 42:18
evil ways that provoked Me to **a**, Jr 44:3
provoking Me to **a** by the work of Jr 44:8
disaster on them, My burning **a**. Jr 49:37
from the LORD's burning **a**. Jr 51:45
of the LORD's **a**, it came to the Jr 52:3
on the day of His burning **a**? Lm 1:12
Daughter Zion with His **a**! Lm 2:1
footstool in the day of His **a**. Lm 2:1
in His burning **a** and withdrawn Lm 2:3
king and priest in His fierce **a**. Lm 2:6
them⌋ in the day of Your **a**, Lm 2:21
of the LORD's **a** no one escaped Lm 2:22
Yourself in **a** and pursued us; Lm 3:43
them⌋ in **a** and destroy them Lm 3:66
wrath, poured out His burning **a**; Lm 4:11
When My **a** is spent and I have Ezk 5:13
judgments against you in **a**, Ezk 5:15
I will send My **a** against you and Ezk 7:3
I will exhaust My **a** against you Ezk 7:8
and repeatedly provoke Me to **a**, Ezk 8:17
rain will come in My **a**, Ezk 13:13
prostitution to provoke Me to **a**. Ezk 16:26
exhausting My **a** against them Ezk 20:8
and exhausting My **a** against them Ezk 20:21
gather ⌊you⌋ in My **a** and wrath, Ezk 22:20
according to My **a** and wrath. Ezk 25:14
to the **a** and jealousy you Ezk 35:11
So I destroyed them in My **a**. Ezk 43:8
may Your **a** and wrath turn away Dn 9:16
though not in **a** or in battle. Dn 11:20
Their **a** smolders all night; Hs 7:6
My **a** burns against them. Hs 8:5
not vent the full fury of My **a**; Hs 11:9
Ephraim has provoked bitter **a**, Hs 12:14
you a king in My **a** and take away Hs 13:11
for My **a** will have turned from Hs 14:4
slow to **a**, rich in faithful love Jl 2:13
a tore ⌊at them⌋ continually, Am 1:11
His burning **a** so that we will Jnh 3:9
vengeance in **a** and wrath against Mc 5:15
not hold on to His **a** forever, Mc 7:18
LORD is slow to **a** but great in Nah 1:3
Who can endure His burning **a**? Nah 1:6
of the LORD's **a** overtakes you, Zph 2:2
of the LORD's **a** overtakes you. Zph 2:2
on the day of the LORD's **a**. Zph 2:3
on them, all My burning **a**; Zph 3:8
Therefore great **a** came from the Zch 7:12
your fathers provoked Me to **a**, Zch 8:14
a burns against the shepherds, Zch 10:3
at them with **a** and sorrow at Mk 3:5
Then in **a**, the master of the Lk 14:21
outbursts of **a**, selfish 2Co 12:20
outbursts of **a**, selfish Gl 5:20
let the sun go down on your **a**, Eph 4:26
All bitterness, **a** and wrath, Eph 4:31
stir up **a** in your children, Eph 6:4
a, wrath, malice, slander, and Col 3:8
hands without **a** or argument. 1Tm 2:8
I swore in My **a**, "They will not Heb 3:11
I swore in My **a**, they will not Heb 4:3
being afraid of the king's **a**, Heb 11:27
slow to speak, and slow to **a**, Jms 1:19
for man's **a** does not accomplish Jms 1:20
strength in the cup of His **a**. Rv 14:10
with the wine of His fierce **a**. Rv 16:19
of the fierce **a** of God, Rv 19:15

ANGERED *(4)*
our fathers **a** the God of heaven Ezr 5:12
A by this, the king arose from Est 7:7
They **a** ⌊the LORD⌋ at the waters Ps 106:32
fool is easily **a** and is careless Pr 14:16

ANGLE *(4)*
ascent to the armory at the **A**. Neh 3:19
from the **A** to the door of the Neh 3:20
Azariah to the **A** and the corner. Neh 3:24
opposite the **A** and tower that Neh 3:25

ANGRY *(104)*
the Lord not be **a**, and I will Gn 18:30
the Lord not be **a**, and I will Gn 18:32
Jacob became **a** with Rachel and Gn 30:2
don't be **a** that I cannot stand Gn 31:35
and were deeply grieved and **a**. Gn 34:7
Pharaoh was **a** with his two Gn 40:2
Pharaoh had been **a** with his Gn 41:10
Do not be **a** with your servant, Gn 44:18
be worried or **a** with yourselves Gn 45:5
Therefore Moses was **a** with them. Ex 16:20
will become **a** with the whole Lv 10:6
He was **a** with Eleazar and Lv 10:16
LORD was very **a**; Moses was also Nm 11:10
Why are You **a** with me, and why Nm 11:11
Then Moses became **a** and said to Nm 16:15
He grew **a** and swore an oath: Dt 1:34
The LORD was **a** with me also Dt 1:37
But the LORD was **a** with me on Dt 3:26
The LORD was **a** with me on your Dt 4:21
God will become **a** with you and Dt 6:15
and He was **a** enough with you to Dt 9:8
The LORD was **a** enough with Aaron Dt 9:20
He will be **a** with the entire Jos 22:18
to God, "Don't be **a** with me; Jdg 6:39
of Gaal son of Ebed, he was **a**. Jdg 9:30
against us, or **a** men will attack Jdg 18:25
Samuel became **a** and cried out to 1Sm 15:11
the men, and became **a** with him. 1Sm 17:28
if he becomes **a**, you will know 1Sm 20:7
Saul became **a** with Jonathan 1Sm 20:30
Abner was very **a** about 2Sm 3:8
was **a** because of the LORD's 2Sm 6:8
Why does this make you **a**? 2Sm 19:42
and You are **a** with them and hand 1Kg 8:46
The LORD was **a** with Solomon, 1Kg 11:9
left for home resentful and **a**, 1Kg 20:43
to his palace resentful and **a**, 1Kg 21:4
But Naaman got **a** and left, 2Kg 5:11
man of God was **a** with him and 2Kg 13:19
the LORD was very **a** with Israel, 2Kg 17:18
was **a** because of the LORD's 1Ch 13:11
and You are **a** with them and hand 2Ch 6:36
Asa was **a** with the seer and put 2Ch 16:10
But they got very **a** with Judah 2Ch 25:10
You become ⌊so⌋ **a** with us that Ezr 9:14
became extremely **a** when I heard Neh 5:6
from the family of Ram became **a**. Jb 32:2
He was **a** at Job because he had Jb 32:2
He was also **a** at Job's three Jb 32:3
not answer Job, he became **a**. Jb 32:5
I am **a** with you and your two Jb 42:7
or He will be **a**, and you will Ps 2:12
a and do not sin; on your bed, Ps 4:4
are worn out from **a** sorrow— Ps 31:9
Turn Your **a** gaze from me so that Ps 39:13
us; You have been **a**. Restore us! Ps 60:1
When You are **a**, who can stand Ps 76:7
Will You be **a** forever? Ps 79:5
long will You be **a** with Your Ps 80:4
Will You be **a** with us forever? Ps 85:5
accuse ⌊us⌋ or be **a** forever. Ps 103:9
man will see ⌊it⌋ and be **a**; Ps 112:10
make friends with an **a** man, Pr 22:24
a backbiting tongue, **a** looks. Pr 25:23
An **a** man stirs up conflict, Pr 29:22
should God be **a** with your words Ec 5:6
let your spirit rush to be **a**, Ec 7:9
My mother's sons were **a** with me; Sg 1:6
although You were **a** with me. Is 12:1
I am not **a**, but if it produces Is 27:4
arm striking in **a** wrath and a Is 30:30
The LORD is **a** with all the Is 34:2
I was **a** with My people; Is 47:6
I will not be **a** with you or Is 54:9
and I will not always be **a**; Is 57:16
of his sinful greed I was **a**, Is 57:17
him; I was **a** and hid; but he Is 57:17
we have sinned, and You were **a**; Is 64:5
not be terribly **a** or remember Is 64:9
I will not be **a** forever. Jr 3:12
The officials were **a** at Jeremiah Jr 37:15
us and are intensely **a** with us. Lm 5:22
bitterness and in an **a** spirit, Ezk 3:14
will be silent and no longer **a**. Ezk 16:42
violently **a** and gave orders Dn 2:12
slow to become **a**, rich in Jnh 4:2
"Is it right for you to be **a**?" Jnh 4:4
you to be **a** about the plant?" Jnh 4:9
is right. I'm **a** enough to die!" Jnh 4:9
Are You **a** at the rivers, LORD? Hab 3:8
LORD was extremely **a** with your Zch 1:2
You have been **a** with these 70 Zch 1:12
I am fiercely **a** with the nations Zch 1:15
I was a little **a**, but they made Zch 1:15
everyone who is **a** with his Mt 5:22
his master got **a** and handed him Mt 18:34
Then he became **a** and didn't want Lk 15:28
are you **a** at Me because I made a Jn 7:23
was **a** in His spirit and deeply Jn 11:33
Then Jesus, **a** in Himself again, Jn 11:38
had been very **a** with the Tyrians Ac 12:20
I will make you **a** by a nation Rm 10:19
Be **a** and do not sin. Don't let Eph 4:26
nations were **a**, but Your wrath Rv 11:18

ANGUISH *(29)*
you will bear children in **a**. Gn 3:16
be a great cry of **a** through all Ex 11:6
a will seize the inhabitants of Ex 15:14
and be in **a** because of you.' Dt 2:25
depth of my **a** and resentment. 1Sm 1:16
she is in severe **a**, and the LORD 2Kg 4:27
speak in the **a** of my spirit; Jb 7:11
because of the **a** of my heart. Ps 38:8
their courage melting away in **a**, Ps 107:26
they will be in **a** like a woman Is 13:8
Therefore I am filled with **a**. Is 21:3
they will be in **a** over the news Is 23:5
He will see ⌊it⌋ out of His **a**, Is 53:11
My **a**, my anguish! I writhe in Jr 4:19
My anguish, my **a**! I writhe in Jr 4:19
cry of⌋ **a** like one bearing her Jr 4:31
give them a heart filled with **a**. Lm 3:65
A is coming! They will seek Ezk 7:25
over you with deep **a** and bitter Ezk 27:31
and there will be **a** in Cush when Ezk 30:4
A will come over them on the day Ezk 30:9
Pelusium will writhe in **a**, Ezk 30:16
he cried out in **a** to Daniel. Dn 6:20
will cry out in **a** in all the Am 5:16

so that **a** grips you like a woman Mc 4:9
and there will be **a** on the earth Lk 21:25
Being in **a**, He prayed more Lk 22:44
affliction or **a** or persecution Rm 8:35
and continual **a** in my heart. Rm 9:2

ANGUISHED *(2)*
will cry out from an **a** heart, Is 65:14
troubled and **a** heart I wrote to 2Co 2:4

ANIAM *(1)*
Ahian, Shechem, Likhi, and **A**. 1Ch 7:19

ANIM *(1)*
Anab, Eshtemoh, **A**, Jos 15:50

ANIMAL *(103)*
ground each wild **a** and each bird Gn 2:19
of the sky, and to every wild **a**; Gn 2:20
and more than any wild **a**. Gn 3:14
and from every **a** that crawls on Gn 6:20
kind of clean **a** and every kind Gn 8:20
life of every **a** and every man Gn 9:5
say that a vicious **a** ate him. Gn 37:20
A vicious **a** has devoured him. Gn 37:33
Slaughter an **a** and prepare it, Gn 43:16
Every person and **a** that is in Ex 9:19
each select an **a** of the flock Ex 12:3
households, one **a** per household. Ex 12:3
is too small for a ⌊whole⌋ **a**, Ex 12:4
apportion the **a** according to Ex 12:4
You must have an unblemished **a**, Ex 12:5
select an **a** from the flock Ex 12:21
the Israelites, both man and **a**; Ex 13:2
of a donkey with a flock **a**, Ex 13:13
neither **a** or man will live. Ex 19:13
but the dead **a** will become his. Ex 21:34
must also divide the dead **a**. Ex 21:35
the dead **a** will become his. Ex 21:36
or any ⌊other⌋ **a** to care for, Ex 22:10
the **a** was stolen from his Ex 22:12
torn apart ⌊by a wild **a**⌋, Ex 22:13
a man borrows ⌊an **a**⌋ from his Ex 22:14
with an **a** must be put to Ex 22:19
meat of a mauled **a** ⌊found⌋ in Ex 22:31
presenting ⌊an **a**⌋ from the herd, Lv 3:1
a carcass of an unclean wild **a**, Lv 5:2
afford an **a** from the flock, Lv 5:7
an unclean **a**, or any unclean, Lv 7:21
The fat of an **a** that dies Lv 7:24
If anyone eats **a** fat from a fire Lv 7:25
eat the blood of any bird or **a**. Lv 7:26
You may eat any **a** with divided Lv 11:3
down a wild **a** or bird that may Lv 17:13
eats an **a** that died a natural Lv 17:15
sexual intercourse with any **a**, Lv 18:23
herself to an **a** to mate with it; Lv 18:23
sexual intercourse with an **a**, Lv 20:15
you are also to kill the **a**. Lv 20:15
comes near any **a** and mates with Lv 20:16
are to kill the woman and the **a**. Lv 20:16
the clean **a** from the unclean one Lv 20:25
detestable by any land **a**, Lv 20:25
He must not eat an **a** that died Lv 22:8
to present any ⌊**a**⌋ to the LORD Lv 22:22
offering any **a** from the herd Lv 22:23
to slaughter an **a** from the herd Lv 22:28
Whoever kills an **a** is to make Lv 24:18
Whoever kills an **a** is to make Lv 24:21
substitute one **a** for another, Lv 27:10
both that **a** and its substitute Lv 27:10
the **a** must be presented before Lv 27:11
whether an **a** from the herd or Lv 27:26
a person, an **a**, or his inherited Lv 27:28
Every tenth **a** from the herd or Lv 27:32
both the **a** and its substitute Lv 27:33
to Myself, both man and **a**; Nm 3:13
is Mine, both man and **a**. Nm 8:17
are to eat the **a** with unleavened Nm 9:11
thing, man or **a**, presented to Nm 18:15
the firstborn of an unclean **a**. Nm 18:15
the captives, both human and **a**. Nm 31:11
what was captured, human and **a**. Nm 31:26
may eat any **a** that has hooves Dt 14:6
if there is a defect in the **a**, Dt 15:21
God a Passover **a** from the herd Dt 16:2
the Passover **a** in any of the Dt 16:5
Passover **a** at the place where Dt 16:6
to bring the **a** to your home to Dt 22:2
sexual intercourse with any **a**.' Dt 27:21
Then a wild **a** that was in 2Kg 14:9
Then a wild **a** that was in 2Ch 25:18
The only **a** I took was the one I Neh 2:12
narrow for my **a** to go through. Neh 2:14
that some wild **a** may trample Jb 39:15
for every **a** of the forest is Ps 50:10
was an unthinking **a** toward You. Ps 73:22
as a burden for the weary ⌊**a**⌋. Is 46:1
out ⌊both⌋ man and **a** from it, Ezk 14:13
out ⌊both⌋ man and **a** from it, Ezk 14:17
out ⌊both⌋ man and **a** from it, Ezk 14:19
out ⌊both⌋ man and **a** from it! Ezk 14:21
cut off both man and **a** from it. Ezk 25:13
and wipe out man and **a** from you. Ezk 29:8
and no **a** foot will pass through Ezk 29:11
for every wild **a** since ⌊they⌋ Ezk 34:8
eat any bird or **a** that died Ezk 44:31
flock is one **a** out of every 200 Ezk 45:15
the mind of an **a** for seven Dn 4:16
No **a** could stand against him, Dn 8:4
I will sweep away man and **a**; Zph 1:3
of it, every kind of wild **a**. Zph 2:14
a blind ⌊**a**⌋ for sacrifice, Mal 1:8
you present a lame or sick ⌊**a**⌋, Mal 1:8
a defective ⌊**a**⌋ to the Lord. Mal 1:14
I will spread **a** waste over your Mal 2:3
Then he put him on his own **a**, Lk 10:34
And if even an **a** touches the Heb 12:20
we also guide the whole **a**. Jms 3:3
creature—**a** or bird, reptile Jms 3:7

ANIMAL'S *(2)*
man cares about his **a** health, Pr 12:10
was like an **a**, he lived with Dn 5:21

ANIMALS *(129)*
the sky, the **a**, all the earth, Gn 1:26
of all the wild **a** that the LORD Gn 3:1
with the **a**, creatures that Gn 6:7
of all the clean **a**, and two of Gn 7:2
and two of the **a** that are not Gn 7:2
From the clean **a**, unclean Gn 7:8
animals, unclean **a**, birds, and Gn 7:8
all the **a** of the earth that came Gn 9:10
passed between the divided ⌊**a**⌋. Gn 15:17
time for the **a** to be gathered. Gn 29:7
And whose ⌊**a**⌋ are these ahead of Gn 32:17
who was walking behind the **a**, Gn 32:19
Load your **a** and go on back to Gn 45:17
gnats were on the people and **a**. Ex 8:17
remained on the people and **a**. Ex 8:18
on people and **a** throughout the Ex 9:9
slaughter the **a** at twilight. Ex 12:6
allows his **a** to go and graze Ex 22:5
and the wild **a** may consume what Ex 23:11
wild **a** would multiply against Ex 23:29
eat all these ⌊kinds⌋ of land **a**. Lv 11:2
a that have hooves but do not Lv 11:26
the four-footed **a** that walk on Lv 11:27
If one of the **a** that you use for Lv 11:39
This is the law concerning **a**, Lv 11:46
between the **a** that may be eaten Lv 11:47
to your God from any of these **a**. Lv 22:25
and the wild **a** in your land. Lv 25:7
dangerous **a** from the land, Lv 26:6
will send wild **a** against you Lv 26:22
one of the **a** that may be brought Lv 27:9
of the unclean **a** that may not be Lv 27:11
Your **a** are to be unblemished. Nm 28:19
Your **a** are to be unblemished. Nm 28:31
⌊All⌋ your **a** are to be Nm 29:8
the prisoners, **a**, and spoils of Nm 31:12
and all our **a** will remain here Nm 32:26
flocks, and all their ⌊other⌋ **a**. Nm 35:3
the wild **a** will become too Dt 7:22
These are the **a** you may eat: Dt 14:4
women, children, **a**, and whatever Dt 20:14
sky and the wild **a** of the land, Dt 28:26
city, the **a**, and everything Jdg 20:48
by day and the wild **a** by night. 2Sm 21:10
taught about **a**, birds, reptiles 1Kg 4:33
water for the army or their **a**. 2Kg 3:9
you and your cattle and your **a**.' 2Kg 3:17
Levites were skinning the ⌊**a**⌋, 2Ch 35:11
and not fear the **a** of the earth. Jb 5:22
and the wild **a** will be at peace Jb 5:23
But ask the **a**, and they will Jb 12:7
than the **a** of the earth and Jb 35:11
The wild **a** enter ⌊their⌋ lairs Jb 37:8
⌊sorts of⌋ wild **a** play there. Jb 40:20
oxen, as well as **a** in the wild, Ps 8:7
he is like the **a** that perish. Ps 49:12
is like the **a** that perish. Ps 49:20
when all the forest **a** stir. Ps 104:20
of Egypt, both people and **a**. Ps 135:8
provides the **a** with their food Ps 147:9
wild **a** and all cattle, creatures Ps 148:10
that they are like **a**." Ec 3:18
and the fate of **a** is the same. Ec 3:19
People have no advantage over **a**, Ec 3:19
the spirit of **a** goes downward to Ec 3:21
But wild **a** will lie down there, Is 13:21
and a region for wild **a**, Is 14:23
and for the wild **a** of the land. Is 18:6
them, and all the **a**, the winter Is 18:6
oracle about the **a** of the Negev: Is 30:6
or its **a** enough for a burnt Is 40:16
a of the field will honor Me, Is 43:20
All you **a** of the field and Is 56:9
and for the wild **a** of the land, Jr 7:33
the birds of the sky to the **a**, Jr 9:10
a and birds have been swept away, Jr 12:4
Go, gather all the wild **a**; Jr 12:9
sky and the wild **a** of the land Jr 15:3
and for the wild **a** of the land. Jr 16:4
and for the wild **a** of the land. Jr 19:7
and **a** on the face of the earth. Jr 27:5
him the wild **a** to serve him. Jr 27:6
also put the wild **a** under him." Jr 28:14
and for the wild **a** of the land. Jr 34:20
and dangerous **a** against you. Ezk 5:17
dangerous **a** to pass through Ezk 14:15
⌊it⌋ for ⌊fear of⌋ the **a**, Ezk 14:15
dangerous **a**, and plague— Ezk 14:21
and all the **a** of the field gave Ezk 31:6
and all the **a** of the field were Ezk 31:13
given to wild **a** to be devoured, Ezk 33:27
all the wild **a** when they were Ezk 34:5
dangerous **a** in the land, Ezk 34:25
and the wild **a** of the land will Ezk 34:28
will fill you with people and **a**, Ezk 36:11
of the sky, the **a** of the field, Ezk 38:20
bird and to the wild **a**. Ezk 39:4
kind of bird and all the wild **a**: Ezk 39:17
live—or wild **a**, or birds of Dn 2:38
Wild **a** found shelter under it, Dn 4:12
Let the **a** flee from under it, Dn 4:14
plants of the earth with the **a**. Dn 4:15
under it the wild **a** lived, Dn 4:21
the wild **a** for seven periods Dn 4:23
people to live with the wild **a**. Dn 4:25
people to live with the wild **a**, Dn 4:32
and the wild **a** will eat them. Hs 2:12
for them with the wild **a**, Hs 2:18
with the wild **a** and the birds Hs 4:3
How the **a** groan! The herds of Jl 1:18
Even the wild **a** cry out to You, Jl 1:20
be afraid, wild **a**, for the Jl 2:22
their left, as well as many **a**?" Jnh 4:11
a lion among **a** of the forest, Mc 5:8
destruction of **a** will terrify Hab 2:17
a place for wild **a** to lie down! Zph 2:15
the people and **a**, and on all Hg 1:11
and all the **a** that are in those Zch 14:15
bring stolen, lame, or sick **a**. Mal 1:13
with the wild **a**, and the angels Mk 1:13
the four-footed **a** and reptiles Ac 10:12
the four-footed **a** of the earth, Ac 11:6
four-footed **a**, and reptiles. Rm 1:23
I fought wild **a** in Ephesus with 1Co 15:32
another for **a**, another for birds 1Co 15:39
bodies of those **a** whose blood is Heb 13:11
like irrational **a**—creatures of 2Pt 2:12
unreasoning **a**—they destroy Jd 10
and by the wild **a** of the earth. Rv 6:8

ANKLE *(3)*
jingling their **a** bracelets, Is 3:16
a bracelets, headbands, Is 3:18
headdresses, **a** jewelry, sashes, Is 3:20

ANKLES *(4)*
steps, and my **a** do not give way 2Sm 22:37
steps, and my **a** do not give way Ps 18:36
It came up to ⌊my⌋ **a**. Ezk 47:3
his feet and **a** became strong. Ac 3:7

ANNA *(1)*
also a prophetess, **A**, a daughter Lk 2:36

ANNAS *(4)*
priesthood of **A** and Caiaphas, Lk 3:2

they led Him to A, for he was Jn 18:13
A sent Him bound to Caiaphas Jn 18:24
A the high priest, Caiaphas, Ac 4:6

ANNIHILATE *(12)*

against you; you will a them. Dt 7:24
Lord GOD, do not a Your people, Dt 9:26
He agreed not to a you. Dt 10:10
I a those who hated me. 2Sm 22:41
Israelites were unable to a— 1Kg 9:21
she proceeded to a all the royal 2Kg 11:1
she proceeded to a all the royal 2Ch 22:10
and a all the Jewish people— Est 3:13
a every ethnic and provincial Est 8:11
I a those who hate me. Ps 18:40
of Your faithfulness, a them. Ps 54:5
fury to destroy and a many. Dn 11:44

ANNIHILATED *(12)*

the sword until they had a them, Jos 11:14
mercy, and be a, just as the Jos 11:20
until He has a you from this Jos 23:15
land, and I a them before you. Jos 24:8
them until you have a them.' 1Sm 15:18
for the man who a us and plotted 2Sm 21:5
be wiped out and a from the face 1Kg 13:34
until he had a his house, 2Kg 10:17
Seir and completely a them. 2Ch 20:23
sent an angel who a every brave 2Ch 32:21
those nations will be a. Is 60:12
plain will be a, as the LORD has Jr 48:8

ANNIHILATES *(2)*

the LORD your God a the nations Dt 12:29
LORD your God a the nations Dt 19:1

ANNOUNCE *(27)*

a to the people that both men Ex 11:2
and the verdict they a to you. Dt 17:11
Now a in the presence of the Jdg 7:3
don't a it in the streets of 2Sm 1:20
thanksgiving and a His works Ps 107:22
and a to her that her time of Is 40:2
a them to you before they occur. Is 42:9
like Me, can a ⌊the future⌋? Is 44:7
now on I will a new things to Is 48:6
a, "The LORD has redeemed His Is 48:20
that the LORD's mouth will a. Is 62:2
Go and a directly to Jerusalem Jr 2:2
A to them: Hear the word of the Jr 17:20
one moment I might a concerning Jr 18:7
another⌋ time I a that I will Jr 18:9
of Judah and a this word there. Jr 22:1
A it in Egypt, and proclaim it Jr 46:14
A to the nations; proclaim and Jr 50:2
to a to the king of Babylon that Jr 51:31
I a what is certain among the Hs 5:9
A a sacred fast; proclaim an Jl 1:14
horn in Zion! A a sacred fast; Jl 2:15
Don't a it in Gath, don't weep Mc 1:10
Then I will a to them, 'I never Mt 7:23
As you go, a this: Mt 10:7
feet of those who a the gospel Rm 10:15
eternal gospel to a to the Rv 14:6

ANNOUNCED *(21)*

and it was a to the king, 1Kg 1:23
He a, "Man of God, the king 2Kg 1:9
He took in the situation and a, 2Kg 1:11
He a, "May God punish me and do 2Kg 6:31
Elisha a, "You will in fact see 2Kg 7:2
For the LORD has a a seven-year 2Kg 8:1
so a law was a in Susa, and they Est 9:14
LORD previously a about Moab. Is 16:13
No one a it, no one told it, no Is 41:26
Who a it from ancient times? Is 45:21
a it to you before it occurred, Is 48:5
The LORD a to me, "Unfaithful Jr 3:11
He a, 'Turn, each of you, from Jr 25:5
Bring on the day You have a, Lm 1:21
went and a to the disciples, Jn 20:18
him, have also a these days. Ac 3:24
killed those who a beforehand Ac 7:52
but ran in and a that Peter was Ac 12:14
He a to us your deep longing, 2Co 7:7
have now been a to you through 1Pt 1:12
a to His servants the prophets. Rv 10:7

ANNOUNCEMENT *(2)*

then he made an a: Ex 32:5
nation I have made an a about, Jr 18:8

ANNOUNCES *(1)*

For a voice a from Dan, Jr 4:15

ANNOUNCING *(5)*

around it, a, "This one came Gn 38:28
Jerusalem, by a, 'You will have Jr 4:10
land of Babylon a in Zion the Jr 50:28
a the completion of the Ac 21:26
a the testimony of God to you, 1Co 2:1

ANNUAL *(7)*

there's an a festival to the Jdg 21:19
up to make the a sacrifice and 1Sm 1:21
to offer the a sacrifice. 1Sm 2:19
for an a sacrifice there 1Sm 20:6
man would bring his a tribute: 1Kg 10:25
and the three a appointed 2Ch 8:13
and mules—as an a tribute. 2Ch 9:24

ANNUALLY *(2)*

came to Solomon a was 25 tons, 1Kg 10:14
came to Solomon a was 25 tons, 2Ch 9:13

ANNULLED *(2)*

It was a on that day, and so the Zch 11:11
commandment is a because it was Heb 7:18

ANNULLING *(2)*

a the covenant I had made with Zch 11:10
a the brotherhood between Judah Zch 11:14

ANOINT *(28)*

then a, ordain, and consecrate Ex 28:41
⌊it⌋ on his head, and a him. Ex 29:7
and a it in order to consecrate Ex 29:36
With it you are to a the tent of Ex 30:26
A Aaron and his sons and Ex 30:30
and a the tabernacle and Ex 40:9
A the altar of burnt offering Ex 40:10
A the basin and its stand, Ex 40:11
the holy garments, a him, and Ex 40:13
A them just as you anointed Ex 40:15
but not a yourself with oil Dt 28:40
trees set out to a a king over Jdg 9:8
A him ruler over My people 1Sm 9:16
LORD sent me to a you as king 1Sm 15:1
You are to a for Me the one I 1Sm 16:3
the LORD said, "A him, for he is 1Sm 16:12
prophet are to a him as king 1Kg 1:34
you are to a Hazael as king over 1Kg 19:15
You are to a Jehu son of Nimshi 1Kg 19:16
"I a you king over Israel." ' 2Kg 9:3
'I a you king over the LORD's 2Kg 9:6
I a you king over Israel.' " 2Kg 9:12
You a my head with oil; Ps 23:5
and to a the most holy place. Dn 9:24
bowlful and a themselves with Am 6:6
olives but not a yourself with Mc 6:15
so they could go and a Him. Mk 16:1
You didn't a My head with oil, Lk 7:46

ANOINTED *(90)*

on it and a it with oil. Gn 35:14
that they can be a and ordained Ex 29:29
them just as you a their father, Ex 40:15
If the a priest sins, bringing Lv 4:3
The a priest must then take some Lv 4:5
The a priest will bring some of Lv 4:16
LORD on the day that he is a: Lv 6:20
sons and will be a to take his Lv 6:22
Israelites on the day He a them. Lv 7:36
oil and a the tabernacle Lv 8:10
head and a and consecrated Lv 8:12
priest who is a and ordained to Lv 16:32
sons, the a priests, who were Nm 3:3
he a and consecrated it and all Nm 7:1
After he a and consecrated these Nm 7:1
for the altar when it was a. Nm 7:10
for the altar when it was a: Nm 7:84
for the altar after it was a. Nm 7:88
priest who was a with the holy Nm 35:25
will lift up the horn of His a. 1Sm 2:10
walk before My a one for all 1Sm 2:35
Hasn't the LORD a you ruler over 1Sm 10:1
me before the LORD and His a: 1Sm 12:3
His a is a witness today that 1Sm 12:5
The LORD a you king over Israel 1Sm 15:17
the LORD's a one is here before 1Sm 16:6
a him in the presence of his 1Sm 16:13
thing to my lord, the LORD's a. 1Sm 24:6
since he is the LORD's a." 1Sm 24:6
lord, since he is the LORD's a. 1Sm 24:10
the LORD's a and be blameless? 1Sm 26:9
my hand against the LORD's a. 1Sm 26:11
protect your lord, the LORD's a. 1Sm 26:16
my hand against the LORD's a, 1Sm 26:23
hand to destroy the LORD's a?" 2Sm 1:14
'I killed the LORD's a.' " 2Sm 1:16
of Saul, no longer a with oil. 2Sm 1:21
and there they a David king over 2Sm 2:4
of Judah has a me king over them 2Sm 2:7
even though I am the a king, 2Sm 3:39
and they a David king over 2Sm 5:3
David had been a king over 2Sm 5:17
'I a you king over Israel, 2Sm 12:7
washed, a himself, changed his 2Sm 12:20
the man we a over us, has died 2Sm 19:10
he ridiculed the LORD's a?" 2Sm 19:21
He shows loyalty to His a, 2Sm 22:51
the one a by the God of Jacob, 2Sm 23:1
the tabernacle and a Solomon. 1Kg 1:39
the prophet have a him king in 1Kg 1:45
that he had been a king in his 1Kg 5:1
They a him and clapped their 2Kg 11:12
son of Josiah, a him, and made 2Kg 23:30
and they a David king over 1Ch 11:3
David had been a king over all 1Ch 14:8
not touch My a ones or harm My 1Ch 16:22
they a him as the LORD's ruler, 1Ch 29:22
God, do not reject Your a one; 2Ch 6:42
whom the LORD had a to destroy 2Ch 22:7
and his sons a him and cried, 2Ch 23:11
against the LORD and His A One: Ps 2:2
He shows loyalty to His a, Ps 18:50
the LORD gives victory to His a; Ps 20:6
of salvation for His a. Ps 28:8
your God, has a you, more than Ps 45:7
look on the face of Your a one. Ps 84:9
I have a him with My sacred oil. Ps 89:20
have become enraged with Your a. Ps 89:38
ridiculed every step of Your a. Ps 89:51
I have been a with oil. Ps 92:10
Do not touch My a ones, or harm Ps 105:15
David, do not reject Your a one. Ps 132:10
prepared a lamp for My a one. Ps 132:17
to Cyrus, His a, whose right Is 45:1
the LORD has a Me to bring good Is 61:1
The LORD's a, the breath of our Lm 4:20
your blood, and a you with oil. Ezk 16:9
You were an a guardian cherub, Ezk 28:14
Your people, to save Your a. Hab 3:13
"These are the two a ones," Zch 4:14
she has a My body in advance for Mk 14:8
because He has a Me to preach Lk 4:18
but she has a My feet with Lk 7:46
(which means "A One"), Jn 1:41
was the one who a the Lord with Jn 11:2
expensive nard—a Jesus' feet, Jn 12:3
holy Servant Jesus, whom You a, Ac 4:27
how God a Jesus of Nazareth with Ac 10:38
in Christ, and has a us, is God; 2Co 1:21
Your God, has a You, rather than Heb 1:9

ANOINTING *(31)*

spices for the a oil and for the Ex 25:6
Take the a oil, pour ⌊it⌋ on his Ex 29:7
the altar and some of the a oil, Ex 29:21
Prepare from these a holy a oil, Ex 30:25
it will be holy a oil. Ex 30:25
will be My holy a oil throughout Ex 30:31
for ⌊ordinary⌋ a on a person's Ex 30:32
the a oil, and the fragrant Ex 31:11
spices for the a oil and for the Ex 35:8
the a oil and the fragrant Ex 35:15
light, for the a oil, and for Ex 35:28
made the holy a oil and the pure Ex 37:29
gold altar; the a oil; the Ex 39:38
Take the a oil, and anoint the Ex 40:9
Their a will serve to inaugurate Ex 40:15
garments, the a oil, the bull Lv 8:2
took the a oil and anointed Lv 8:10
a the altar with all its Lv 8:11
some of the a oil on Aaron's Lv 8:12
took some of the a oil and some Lv 8:30
for the LORD's a oil is on you." Lv 10:7
who has had the a oil poured on Lv 21:10
of the a oil of his God is Lv 21:12
grain offering, and the a oil. Nm 4:16
you really are a me as king over Jdg 9:15
a many sick people with oil, Mk 6:13
kissing them and a them with the Lk 7:38
over him after a him with olive Jms 5:14

But you have an a from the Holy 1Jn 2:20
The a you received from Him 1Jn 2:27
His a teaches you about all 1Jn 2:27

ANOTHER (397)

has given me a child in place Gn 4:25
he had waited a seven days, Gn 8:12
Abraham took a wife, whose name Gn 25:1
There was a famine in the land Gn 26:1
Then they dug a well and Gn 26:21
He moved from there and dug a, Gn 26:22
yet a seven years for me. Gn 29:27
worked for Laban a seven years. Gn 29:30
"May the LORD add a son to me." Gn 30:24
for this is a son for you." Gn 35:17
Then he had a dream and told it Gn 37:9
said, "I had a dream, and this Gn 37:9
They said to one a, "Here comes Gn 37:19
gave birth to a son and named Gn 38:5
they turned to one a and said, Gn 42:28
the man that you had a brother?" Gn 43:6
Do you have ⌊a⌋ brother?' Gn 43:7
they said to one a, "If Joseph Gn 50:15
One person could not see a, Ex 10:23
first day and a sacred assembly Ex 12:16
they asked one a, "What is it?" Ex 16:15
decision between one man and a. Ex 18:16
wings, and are to face one a. Ex 25:20
never bow down to a god because Ex 34:14
quarantine him for a seven days. Lv 13:5
scaly outbreak for a seven days. Lv 13:33
quarantined for a seven days. Lv 13:54
act deceptively or lie to one a. Lv 19:11
a slave designated for ⌊a⌋ man, Lv 19:20
from him, do not cheat one a. Lv 25:14
You are not to cheat one a, Lv 25:17
not rule over one a harshly. Lv 25:46
over one a as if ⌊fleeing⌋ Lv 26:37
substitute one animal for a, Lv 27:10
or if he has sold it to a man, Lv 27:20
woman commits any sin against a, Nm 5:6
and sleeps with a, but it is Nm 5:13
said to one a, "Let's appoint Nm 14:4
come with me to a place where Nm 23:13
I will take you to a place. Nm 23:27
and strikes a man and he dies, Nm 35:17
to transfer from one tribe to a, Nm 36:9
as his own out of ⌊a⌋ nation, Dt 4:34
in battle and a man dedicate it Dt 20:5
in battle and a man enjoy its Dt 20:6
in battle and a man marry her.' Dt 20:7
relations with ⌊a⌋ man's wife, Dt 22:22
⌊a⌋ man encounters her in the Dt 22:23
goes and becomes a man's wife, Dt 24:2
to a woman, but a man will rape Dt 28:30
will be given to a people, Dt 28:32
threw them into a land where Dt 29:28
After them a generation rose up Jdg 2:10
rulers of Gilead said to one a, Jdg 10:18
you are the son of a woman." Jdg 11:2
wife and given her to a man." Jdg 15:6
I am too old to have a husband. Ru 1:12
and gather ⌊grain⌋ in a field, Ru 2:8
will happen to you in a field." Ru 2:22
If a man sins against a man, 1Sm 2:25
were standing on a hill with a 1Sm 17:3
for there isn't a one here." 1Sm 21:9
front of him and a behind him, 2Sm 10:9
give them to a before your very 2Sm 12:11
You may do it a day, but today 2Sm 18:20
watchman saw a man running. 2Sm 18:26
A man is running alone!" 2Sm 18:26
there was a battle with the 2Sm 21:18
Gath there was still a battle. 2Sm 21:20
So he went a way; he did not go 1Kg 13:10
Raise a army for yourself like 1Kg 20:25
prophet found a man and said to 1Kg 20:37
this and a was saying that 1Kg 22:20
So the king sent a captain of 50 2Kg 1:11
her son, "Bring me a container." 2Kg 4:6
came back and entered a tent, 2Kg 7:8
people and ⌊a one⌋ between 2Kg 11:17
with it from one end to a. 2Kg 21:16
Jerahmeel had a wife named 1Ch 2:26
A descendant was named 1Ch 7:15
and from one kingdom to a, 1Ch 16:20
front of him and a behind him, 1Ch 19:10
There was still a battle at Gath 1Ch 20:6
this and a was saying that 2Ch 18:19
made repairs to a section, Neh 3:11
made repairs to a section Neh 3:19
diligently repaired a section, Neh 3:20
made repairs to a section, Neh 3:21
made repairs to a section, Neh 3:24
made repairs to a section from Neh 3:27
made repairs to a section. Neh 3:30
far from one a along the wall. Neh 4:19
day and ⌊spent⌋ a fourth of the Neh 9:3
to be given to a woman who is Est 1:19
cosmetics for ⌊a⌋ six months. Est 2:12
the Jewish people from a place, Est 4:14
when they send gifts to one a. Est 9:19
gifts to one a and the poor. Est 9:22
speaking when a ⌊messenger⌋ came Jb 1:16
when ⌊yet⌋ a came and reported: Jb 1:17
speaking when a ⌊messenger⌋ came Jb 1:18
Yet a person dies with a bitter Jb 21:25
wife grind ⌊grain⌋ for a man, Jb 31:10
righteousness ⌊a⌋ human being. Jb 35:8
is so close to a that no air can Jb 41:16
are joined to one a, so closely Jb 41:17
They lie to one a; they speak Ps 12:2
of those who take a ⌊god⌋ for Ps 16:4
Your power to ⌊a⌋ generation, Ps 71:18
He brings down one and exalts a. Ps 75:7
and from one kingdom to a, Ps 105:13
let a take over his position. Ps 109:8
who sleeps with a man's wife; Pr 6:29
a withholds what is right, Pr 11:24
but a path leads to death. Pr 12:28
a pretends to be poor but has Pr 13:7
case seems right until a comes Pr 18:17
I'll look for a ⌊drink⌋." Pr 23:35
Let a praise you, and not your Pr 27:2
iron, and one man sharpens a. Pr 27:17
falls without a to lift him up. Ec 4:10
official protects a official, Ec 5:8
adding one thing to a to find Ec 7:27
authority over a to his harm. Ec 8:9
the one you love better than a, Sg 5:9
What makes him better than a, Sg 5:9
The people will oppress one a, Is 3:5
And one called to a: Is 6:3
one wild goat will call to a. Is 34:14
A said, "What should I cry out? Is 40:6
and says to a, "Take courage!" Is 41:6
I will not give My glory to a, Is 42:8
a will call ⌊himself⌋ by the Is 44:5
still a will write on his hand: Is 44:5
I will not give My glory to a. Is 48:11
will give His servants a name. Is 65:15
one New Moon to a, and from one Is 66:23
and from one Sabbath to a," Is 66:23
and she leaves him to marry a, Jr 3:1
if you act justly toward one a, Jr 7:5
they proceed from one evil to a, Jr 9:3
a lament and one a a dirge, Jr 9:20
he made it into a jar, as it Jr 18:4
At ⌊a⌋ time I announce that I Jr 18:9
pass by this city and ask one a: Jr 22:8
gave birth to you into a land, Jr 22:26
dreams that they tell one a, Jr 23:27
both near and far from one a; Jr 25:26
A man was also prophesying in Jr 26:20
Take a scroll, and once again Jr 36:28
Jeremiah took a scroll and gave Jr 36:32
one container to a or gone into Jr 48:11
year, and then a the next year. Jr 51:46
touching that of a and two wings Ezk 1:11
wings extended one toward a. Ezk 1:23
one disaster after a is coming! Ezk 7:5
There was a man among them, Ezk 9:2
your place to a place while they Ezk 12:3
But there was a great eagle with Ezk 17:7
she took a of her cubs and made Ezk 19:5
a wickedly defiles his Ezk 22:11
and ⌊yet⌋ a violates his sister, Ezk 22:11
sins and will groan to one a. Ezk 24:23
speaks to a, each saying to Ezk 33:30
judge between one sheep and a, Ezk 34:17
judge between one sheep and a. Ezk 34:22
Then take a stick and write on Ezk 37:16
and a beside the south gate, Ezk 40:44
one above a in three stories Ezk 41:6
the north and a to the south. Ezk 41:11
There will be ⌊a area⌋ eight and Ezk 45:5
He measured off a third ⌊of a Ezk 47:4
there will arise a kingdom, Dn 2:39
yours, and then a, a third Dn 2:39
mix with one a but will not hold Dn 2:43
will not be left to a people. Dn 2:44
Suddenly, a beast appeared, a Dn 7:5
was watching, a beast appeared. Dn 7:6
horns, suddenly a horn, a little Dn 7:8
A, different from the previous Dn 7:24
and a holy one said to the Dn 8:13
who is loved by a man and is Hs 3:1
one act of bloodshed follows a. Hs 4:2
on one city but no rain on a. Am 4:7
staggered to a city to drink Am 4:8
was placed on a in the LORD's Hg 2:15
a angel went out to meet him. Zch 2:3
love and compassion to one a. Zch 7:9
in your hearts against one a. Zch 7:10
Speak truth to one a; Zch 8:16
of one city will go to a, Zch 8:21
each will seize the hand of a, Zch 14:13
act treacherously against one a, Mal 2:10
And this is a thing you do: Mal 2:13
feared the LORD spoke to one a. Mal 3:16
to their own country by a route. Mt 2:12
goes; and to a, 'Come!' and he Mt 8:9
a of His disciples said, Mt 8:21
you in one town, escape to a. Mt 10:23
He presented a parable to them: Mt 13:24
He presented a parable to them: Mt 13:31
He told them a parable: Mt 13:33
marries a, commits adultery." Mt 19:9
Listen to a parable: Mt 21:33
beat one, killed a, and stoned a Mt 21:35
his own farm, a to his business Mt 22:5
be left here on a that will not Mt 24:2
betray one a and hate one Mt 24:10
one another and hate one a. Mt 24:10
five talents; to a, two; and to Mt 25:15
to a, one—to each according Mt 25:15
will separate them one from a, Mt 25:32
a woman saw him and told those Mt 26:71
they began to argue with one a, Mk 1:27
were terrified and asked one a, Mk 4:41
arguing with one a about who was Mk 9:34
and be at peace with one a." Mk 9:50
and marries a commits adultery Mk 10:11
her husband and marries a, Mk 10:12
saying to one a, "Then who can Mk 10:26
Again he sent a slave to them, Mk 12:4
Then he sent a, and they killed Mk 12:5
be left here on a that will not Mk 13:2
expressing indignation to one a: Mk 14:4
I will build a not made by hands Mk 14:58
mocking Him to one a and saying, Mk 15:31
They were saying to one a, Mk 16:3
the shepherds said to one a, Lk 2:15
and kept saying to one a, Lk 4:36
On a Sabbath He entered the Lk 6:6
with one a what they might do Lk 6:11
goes; and to a, 'Come!' and he Lk 7:8
from one town and village to a, Lk 8:1
asking one a, "Who can this be Lk 8:25
and they went to a village. Lk 9:56
Then He said to a, "Follow Me." Lk 9:59
A also said, "I will follow You, Lk 9:61
they were trampling on one a. Lk 12:1
one town and village after a, Lk 13:22
A said, 'I have bought five yoke Lk 14:19
And a said, 'I just got married, Lk 14:20
going to war against a king, Lk 14:31
Next he asked a, 'How much do Lk 16:7
wife and marries a woman commits Lk 16:18
And a came and said, 'Master, Lk 19:20
not leave one stone on a in you, Lk 19:44
He sent yet a slave, but they Lk 20:11
will be left on a that will not Lk 21:6
an hour later, a kept insisting, Lk 22:59
The disciples said to one a, Jn 4:33
'One sows and a reaps.' Jn 4:37
There is A who testifies about Jn 5:32
accepting glory from one a, Jn 5:44
Then the Jews said to one a, Jn 7:35
and asking one a as they stood Jn 11:56
the Pharisees said to one a, Jn 12:19
started looking at one a— Jn 13:22
love one a. Just as I have loved Jn 13:34
you, you must also love one a. Jn 13:34
if you have love for one a." Jn 13:35

will give you a Counselor to be Jn 14:16
love one a as I have loved you. Jn 15:12
what I command you: love one a. Jn 15:17
of His disciples said to one a, Jn 16:17
you asking one a about what I Jn 16:19
Jesus, as was a disciple. Jn 18:15
said to one a, "Let's not tear Jn 19:24
Also, a Scripture says: Jn 19:37
saying to one a, "What could Ac 2:12
about—himself or a person?" Ac 8:34
He also says in a passage, Ac 13:35
saying that there is a king— Ac 17:7
place after a in the Galatian Ac 18:23
shouting one thing and some a, Ac 19:32
bring charges against one a. Ac 19:38
we said good-bye to one a. Ac 21:6
shouting one thing and some a. Ac 21:34
they said to one a, "This man is Ac 28:4
in their lust for one a. Rm 1:27
when you judge a, you condemn Rm 2:1
then, who teach a, do you not Rm 2:21
gives herself to a man while her Rm 7:3
if she gives herself to a man, Rm 7:3
so that you may belong to a— Rm 7:4
for honor and a for dishonor? Rm 9:21
individually members of one a. Rm 12:5
to one a with brotherly Rm 12:10
Outdo one a in showing honor. Rm 12:10
Be in agreement with one a. Rm 12:16
to love one a, for the one who Rm 13:8
one who loves a has fulfilled Rm 13:8
one day to be above a day. Rm 14:5
us no longer criticize one a, Rm 14:13
peace and what builds up one a. Rm 14:19
grant you agreement with one a, Rm 15:5
accept one a, just as the Rm 15:7
and able to instruct one a. Rm 15:14
Greet one a with a holy kiss. Rm 16:16
with Paul," and a, "I'm with 1Co 3:4
foundation, and a builds on it. 1Co 3:10
in favor of one person over a. 1Co 4:6
you have lawsuits against one a. 1Co 6:7
not deprive one a—except when 1Co 7:5
from God, one this and a that. 1Co 7:7
freedom judged by a person's 1Co 10:29
is hungry while a is drunk! 1Co 11:21
together to eat, wait for one a. 1Co 11:33
the Spirit, to a, a message 1Co 12:8
to a, faith by the same Spirit, 1Co 12:9
same Spirit, to a, gifts of 1Co 12:9
a, the performing of miracles, 1Co 12:10
of miracles, to a, prophecy, to 1Co 12:10
prophecy, to a, distinguishing 1Co 12:10
spirits, to a, different kinds 1Co 12:10
languages, to a, interpretation 1Co 12:10
speaks in ⌊a⌋ language is not 1Co 14:2
speaks in ⌊a⌋ language builds 1Co 14:4
speaks in ⌊a⌋ language should 1Co 14:13
For if I pray in ⌊a⌋ language, 1Co 14:14
10,000 words in ⌊a⌋ language. 1Co 14:19
a revelation, ⌊a⌋ language, 1Co 14:26
person speaks in ⌊a⌋ language, 1Co 14:27
revealed to a person sitting 1Co 14:30
perhaps of wheat or a grain. 1Co 15:37
flesh for humans, a for animals, 1Co 15:39
for animals, a for birds, 1Co 15:39
for birds, and a for fish. 1Co 15:39
of the sun, a of the moon, 1Co 15:41
of the moon, and a of the stars; 1Co 15:41
Greet one a with a holy kiss. 1Co 16:20
come to you on a painful visit. 2Co 2:1
comes and preaches a Jesus, 2Co 11:4
Greet one a with a holy kiss. 2Co 13:12
not that there is a ⌊gospel⌋, Gl 1:7
but serve one a through love. Gl 5:13
if you bite and devour one a, Gl 5:15
you will be consumed by one a. Gl 5:15
provoking one a, envying one Gl 5:26
one another, envying one a. Gl 5:26
accepting one a in love, Eph 4:2
because we are members of one a. Eph 4:25
kind and compassionate to one a, Eph 4:32
forgiving one a, just as God Eph 4:32
speaking to one a in psalms, Eph 5:19
submitting to one a in the fear Eph 5:21
not have one grief on top of a. Php 2:27
not lie to one a, since you have Col 3:9
accepting one a and forgiving Col 3:13
forgiving one a if anyone has Col 3:13
has a complaint against a. Col 3:13
admonishing one a in all wisdom, Col 3:16
love for one a and for everyone 1Th 3:12
are taught by God to love one a. 1Th 4:9
one a with these words. 1Th 4:18
encourage one a and build each 1Th 5:11
is good for one a and for all. 1Th 5:15
of you for one a is increasing. 2Th 1:3
envy, hateful, detesting one a. Ti 3:3
have spoken later about a day. Heb 4:8
also said in a passage, You are Heb 5:6
was there for a priest to arise Heb 7:11
becomes clearer if a priest like Heb 7:15
yearly with the blood of a. Heb 9:25
about one a in order to promote Heb 10:24
begged that not a word be spoken Heb 12:19
Don't criticize one a, brothers. Jms 4:11
do not complain about one a, Jms 5:9
sins to one a and pray for one Jms 5:16
one another and pray for one a, Jms 5:16
love one a earnestly from a pure 1Pt 1:22
love for one a at full strength 1Pt 4:8
hospitable to one a without 1Pt 4:9
with humility toward one a, 1Pt 5:5
Greet one a with a kiss of love. 1Pt 5:14
we have fellowship with one a, 1Jn 1:7
we should love one a, 1Jn 3:11
and love one a as He commanded 1Jn 3:23
let us love one a, because love 1Jn 4:7
way, we also must love one a. 1Jn 4:11
If we love one a, God remains in 1Jn 4:12
beginning—that we love one a. 2Jn 5
Then a horse went out, a fiery Rv 6:4
people would slaughter one a. Rv 6:4
Then I saw a angel rise up from Rv 7:2
A angel, with a gold incense Rv 8:3
Then I saw a mighty angel coming Rv 10:1
and send gifts to one a, Rv 11:10
Then a sign appeared in heaven: Rv 12:3
Then I saw a beast coming up out Rv 13:11
Then I saw a angel flying in Rv 14:6
A angel came out of the Rv 14:15
a angel who also had a sharp Rv 14:17
Yet a angel, who had authority Rv 14:18
Then I saw a great and Rv 15:1
this I saw a angel with great Rv 18:1
I heard a voice from heaven: Rv 18:4
A book was opened, which is the Rv 20:12

ANOTHER'S *(5)*

not understand one a speech." Gn 11:7
without revealing a secret; Pr 25:9
also ought to wash one a feet. Jn 13:14
to criticize a household slave Rm 14:4
Carry one a burdens; Gl 6:2

ANSWER *(139)*

give Pharaoh a favorable a." Gn 41:16
were too terrified to a him. Gn 45:3
give you the a the LORD tells me Nm 22:8
people will a, 'It is because Dt 29:25
Her wisest princesses a her; Jdg 5:29
LORD won't a you on that day. 1Sm 8:18
But God did not a him that day. 1Sm 14:37
gave him the same a as before. 1Sm 17:30
"Aren't you going to a, Abner?" 1Sm 26:14
the LORD did not a him in dreams 1Sm 28:6
He doesn't a me any more, either 1Sm 28:15
could not a Abner because he was 2Sm 3:11
LORD, but He does not a them. 2Sm 22:42
and decide what a I should take 2Sm 24:13
the people didn't a him a word. 1Kg 18:21
noon, saying, "Baal, a us!" 1Kg 18:26
A me, LORD! Answer me so that 1Kg 18:37
A me so that this people will 1Kg 18:37
a man greets you, don't a him. 2Kg 4:29
command was, "Don't a him." 2Kg 18:36
Now decide what a I should 1Ch 21:12
please. Will anyone a you? Which Jb 5:1
he could not a God once in a Jb 9:3
How then can I a Him or choose Jb 9:14
in the right, I could not a. Jb 9:15
me, that I can a Him, that we Jb 9:32
and I will a, or I will speak Jb 13:22
would call, and I would a You. Jb 14:15
Does a wise man a with empty Jb 15:2
but he does not a, even if I beg Jb 19:16
thoughts compel me to a, Jb 20:2
I would learn how He would a me; Jb 23:5
for help, but You do not a me; Jb 30:20
How should I a Him when He calls Jb 31:14
let the Almighty a me. Jb 31:35
the three men could not a Job, Jb 32:5
dismayed and can no longer a; Jb 32:15
stand ⌊there⌋ and no longer a? Jb 32:16
I too will a; yes, I will tell Jb 32:17
you have something to say, a me; Jb 33:32
I will a you and your friends Jb 35:4
out, but He does not a, because Jb 35:12
Get ready to a Me like a man; Jb 38:3
who argues with God give an a. Jb 40:2
How can I a You? I place my hand Jb 40:4
Get ready to a Me like a man; Jb 40:7
A me when I call, God, who Ps 4:1
Consider me and a, LORD, my God. Ps 13:3
You, God, because You will a me; Ps 17:6
LORD, but He does not a them. Ps 18:41
May the LORD a you in a day of Ps 20:1
He will a him from His holy Ps 20:6
May He a us on the day that we Ps 20:9
but You do not a, by night, yet Ps 22:2
be gracious to me and a me. Ps 27:7
You will a, Lord my God. Ps 38:15
Pay attention to me and a me. Ps 55:2
right hand, and a me, so that Ps 60:5
You a us in righteousness, Ps 65:5
a me with Your sure salvation. Ps 69:13
A me, LORD, for Your faithful Ps 69:16
I am in distress. A me quickly! Ps 69:17
LORD, and a me, for I am poor Ps 86:1
my distress, for You will a me. Ps 86:7
calls out to Me, I will a him; Ps 91:15
a me quickly when I call. Ps 102:2
hand and a me so that those Ps 108:6
Then I can a the one who taunts Ps 119:42
all my heart; a me, LORD. I will Ps 119:145
and in Your righteousness a me. Ps 143:1
A me quickly, LORD; my spirit Ps 143:7
will call me, but I won't a; Pr 1:28
A gentle a turns away anger, Pr 15:1
A man takes joy in giving an a; Pr 15:23
but the a of the tongue is from Pr 16:1
one who gives an a before he Pr 18:13
gives an honest a gives a kiss Pr 24:26
Don't a a fool according to his Pr 26:4
A a fool according to his Pr 26:5
seven men who can a sensibly. Pr 26:16
that I can a anyone who taunts Pr 27:11
money is the a for everything. Ec 10:19
I called him, but he did not a. Sg 5:6
What a will be given to the Is 14:32
when He hears, He will a you. Is 30:19
silent and did not a him at all, Is 36:21
command was, "Don't a him." Is 36:21
I, the LORD, will a them; Is 41:17
cry out to it but it doesn't a; Is 46:7
I will a you in a time of favor, Is 49:8
there no one to a when I called? Is 50:2
when you call, the LORD will a; Is 58:9
I called and you did not a, Is 65:12
Even before they call, I will a; Is 65:24
to you, but you wouldn't a, Jr 7:13
to them, they will not a you. Jr 7:27
Then you will a them: Jr 16:11
They will a: Because they Jr 22:9
Me and I will a you and tell you Jr 33:3
to them, but they would not a." Jr 35:17
will a him appropriately. Ezk 14:4
⌊I will a him⌋ according to his Ezk 14:4
I, the LORD, will a him Myself. Ezk 14:7
The a marked Jerusalem appears Ezk 21:22
to give you an a to this Dn 3:16
of your petitions an a went out, Dn 9:23
is I who a and watch over him. Hs 14:8
LORD, but He will not a them. Mc 3:4
there will be no a from God. Mc 3:7
and the rafters will a them from Hab 2:11
their God, and I will a them. Zch 10:6
then he will a: The wounds I Zch 13:6
on My name, and I will a them. Zch 13:9
and if you a it for Me, then I Mt 21:24
No one was able to a Him at all, Mt 22:46
Then the righteous will a Him, Mt 25:37
And the King will a them, Mt 25:40
they too will a, 'Lord, when did Mt 25:44
Then He will a them, 'I assure Mt 25:45
You have an a to what these men Mt 26:62

priests and elders, He didn't **a**. Mt 27:12
But He didn't **a** him on even one Mt 27:14
then **a** Me, and I will tell you Mk 11:29
from heaven or from men? **A** Me." Mk 11:30
You have an **a** to what these men Mk 14:60
silent and did not **a** anything. Mk 14:61
Jesus still did not **a** anything, Mk 15:5
Then he will **a** from inside and Lk 11:7
He will **a** you, 'I don't know Lk 13:25
To this they could find no **a**. Lk 14:6
and being amazed at His **a**, Lk 20:26
if I ask you, you will not **a**. Lk 22:68
but Jesus did not **a** him. Lk 23:9
not refuse to **a**, but he declared Jn 1:20
need to give an **a** to those who Jn 1:22
the way you **a** the high priest? Jn 18:22
But Jesus did not give him an **a**. Jn 19:9
a servant named Rhoda came to **a**. Ac 12:13
how you should **a** each person. Col 4:6

ANSWERED *(364)*
(See pp. xi-xii.)

ANSWERING *(5)*
(See pp. xi-xii.)

ANSWERS *(10)*
answer her; she even **a** herself: Jdg 5:29
if your father **a** you harshly?" 1Sm 20:10
The God who **a** with fire, He is 1Kg 18:24
by calling on God, who **a** me. Jb 12:4
Your **a** are deceptive. Jb 21:34
because ⌊his⌋ **a** are ⌊like⌋ those Jb 34:36
and He **a** me from His holy Ps 3:4
but the rich one **a** roughly. Pr 18:23
that the LORD **a** you I will tell Jr 42:4
at His understanding and His **a**. Lk 2:47

ANT *(1)*
Go to the **a**, you slacker! Pr 6:6

ANTELOPE *(2)*
ibex, the **a**, and the mountain Dt 14:5
every street like an **a** in a net. Is 51:20

ANTHOTHIJAH *(1)*
Hananiah, Elam, **A**, 1Ch 8:24

ANTICHRIST *(4)*
have heard, "**A** is coming," even 1Jn 2:18
He is the **a**, the one who denies 1Jn 2:22
This is the spirit of the **a**; 1Jn 4:3
This is the deceiver and the **a**. 2Jn 7

ANTICHRISTS *(1)*
even now many **a** have come. 1Jn 2:18

ANTICIPATION *(1)*
waits with **a** for God's sons to Rm 8:19

ANTIMONY *(1)*
for⌋ mounting, **a**, stones of 1Ch 29:2

ANTIOCH *(19)*
Nicolaus, a proselyte from **A**. Ac 6:5
Cyprus, and **A**, speaking the Ac 11:19
who came to **A** and began speaking Ac 11:20
Barnabas to travel as far as **A**. Ac 11:22
found him he brought him to **A**. Ac 11:26
first called Christians in **A**. Ac 11:26
came down from Jerusalem to **A**. Ac 11:27
local church at **A** there were Ac 13:1
Perga and reached **A** in Pisidia. Ac 13:14
Jews came from **A** and Iconium, Ac 14:19
to Lystra, to Iconium, and to **A**, Ac 14:21
sailed back to **A** where they had Ac 14:26
and to send them to **A** with Paul Ac 15:22
from among the Gentiles in **A**, Ac 15:23
they went down to **A**, and after Ac 15:30
remained in **A** teaching and Ac 15:35
the church, and went down to **A**. Ac 18:22
But when Cephas came to **A**, Gl 2:11
sufferings that came to me in **A**, 2Tm 3:11

ANTIPAS *(1)*
in the days of **A**, My faithful Rv 2:13

ANTIPATRIS *(1)*
brought him to **A** as they were Ac 23:31

ANTIQUITY *(4)*
you know that ever since **a**, Jb 20:4
for they ⌊have existed⌋ from **a**. Ps 25:6
to the Pit, to the people of **a**. Ezk 26:20
origin is from **a**, from eternity. Mc 5:2

ANTS *(1)*
the **a** are not a strong people, Pr 30:25

ANUB *(1)*
Koz fathered **A**, Zobebah, and the 1Ch 4:8

ANVIL *(1)*
the one who strikes the **a**, Is 41:7

ANXIETY *(8)*
I will put **a** in the hearts of Lv 26:36
answered Gad, "I have great **a**. 2Sm 24:14
answered Gad, "I have great **a**. 1Ch 21:13
A in a man's heart weighs it Pr 12:25
the sea there is **a** that cannot Jr 49:23
your water with shaking and **a**. Ezk 12:18
bread with **a** and drink their Ezk 12:19
Samaria will have **a** over the Hs 10:5

ANXIOUS *(6)*
because he was **a** about the ark 1Sm 4:13
I store up **a** concerns within Ps 13:2
I am **a** because of my sin. Ps 38:18
dream and am **a** to understand it. Dn 2:3
should drink, and don't be **a**. Lk 12:29
him again and I may be less **a**. Php 2:28

ANXIOUSLY *(3)*
They will **a** eat bread ⌊rationed⌋ Ezk 4:16
of Maroth **a** wait for something Mc 1:12
I have been **a** searching for You. Lk 2:48

ANY *(535)*
(See pp. xi-xii.)

ANYMORE *(3)*
Don't bother the Teacher **a**." Lk 8:49
they cannot die **a**, because they Lk 20:36
I do not call you slaves **a**, Jn 15:15

ANYONE *(366)*
(See pp. xi-xii.)

ANYONE'S *(7)*
(See pp. xi-xii.)

ANYTHING *(225)*
(See pp. xi-xii.)

ANYWAY *(1)*
you won't listen to me **a**." Jr 38:15

ANYWHERE *(14)*
(See pp. xi-xii.)

APART *(87)*
Abraham had set **a** seven ewe Gn 21:28
have you set **a** these seven ewe Gn 21:29
his own stock **a** and didn't put Gn 30:40
actually torn **a** ⌊by a wild Ex 22:13
is to be set **a** for destruction. Ex 22:20
I am the LORD who sets you **a**. Ex 31:13
cleanse and set it **a** from the Lv 16:19
I am the LORD who sets you **a**. Lv 20:8
God who set you **a** from the Lv 20:24
have set these **a** as unclean for Lv 20:25
have set you **a** from the nations Lv 20:26
LORD who sets you **a**, am holy. Lv 21:8
I am the LORD who sets him **a**." Lv 21:15
I am the LORD who sets them **a**." Lv 21:23
I am the LORD who sets them **a**. Lv 22:9
I am the LORD who sets them **a**." Lv 22:16
I am the LORD who sets you **a**, Lv 22:32
like a field permanently set **a**; Lv 27:21
permanently sets **a** to the LORD Lv 27:28
everything set **a** is especially Lv 27:28
has been set **a** ⌊for destruction Lv 27:29
Him, who is set **a**, and ⌊the one⌋ Nm 16:5
will be the one who is set **a**. Nm 16:7
Then Moses set **a** three cities Dt 4:41
will be set **a** for destruction Dt 7:26
it is set **a** for destruction. Dt 7:26
the LORD set **a** the tribe of Levi Dt 10:8
Nothing set **a** for destruction is Dt 13:17
are to set **a** three cities for Dt 19:2
you to set **a** three cities for Dt 19:7
in it are set **a** to the LORD for Jos 6:17
from the things set **a**, Jos 6:18
will be set **a** for destruction Jos 6:18
will set **a** the camp of Israel Jos 6:18
things set **a** for destruction. Jos 7:1
took some of what was set **a**, Jos 7:1
taken some of what was set **a**. Jos 7:11
have been set **a** for destruction. Jos 7:12
remove from you what is set **a**. Jos 7:12
among you, Israel, things set **a**. Jos 7:13
until you remove what is set **a**. Jos 7:13
the things set **a** must be burned, Jos 7:15
the cities set **a** for the Jos 16:9
what was set **a** for destruction, Jos 22:20
he tore the lion **a** with his bare Jdg 14:6
The Israelites, **a** from Benjamin, Jdg 20:17
what was set **a** for destruction 1Sm 15:21
I will break them **a** there, 1Kg 5:9
have set them **a** as Your 1Kg 8:53
'The altar will now be ripped **a**, 1Kg 13:3
was ripped **a**, and the ashes 1Kg 13:5
and set them **a** for destruction, 1Ch 4:41
was set **a** forever to consecrate 1Ch 23:13
army also set **a** some of the sons 1Ch 25:1
LORD has set **a** the faithful for Ps 4:3
ripping me **a**, with no one to Ps 7:2
will tear you **a**, and there will Ps 50:22
gloom and broke their chains **a**. Ps 107:14
us be ripped **a** by their teeth. Ps 124:6
who can enjoy life **a** from Him? Ec 2:25
will set them **a** for destruction Is 34:2
I have set **a** for destruction. Is 34:5
set you **a** before you were born. Jr 1:5
⌊them⌋ **a** for war against her; Jr 6:4
and set them **a** for the day of Jr 12:3
was it **a** from our husbands' Jr 44:19
set **a** the nations against her. Jr 51:27
Set **a** the nations for battle Jr 51:28
LORD who sets them **a** as holy. Ezk 20:12
will be set **a** for the priests Ezk 48:10
you are to set **a** the holy Ezk 48:20
the ship threatened to break **a**. Jnh 1:4
and the valleys will split **a**, Mc 1:4
The age-old mountains break **a**; Hab 3:6
and **a** from Him not one thing was Jn 1:3
One the Father set **a** and sent Jn 10:36
Set **a** for Me Barnabas and Saul Ac 13:2
Paul might be torn **a** by them and Ac 23:10
But now, **a** from the law, God's Rm 3:21
by faith **a** from works of law Rm 3:28
righteousness **a** from works: Rm 4:6
For **a** from the law sin is dead. Rm 7:8
Once I was alive **a** from the law, Rm 7:9
womb set me **a** and called me by Gl 1:15
instrument, set **a**, useful to the 2Tm 2:21
Father and set **a** by the Spirit 1Pt 1:2
but set **a** the Messiah as Lord in 1Pt 3:15

APELLES *(1)*
Greet **A**, who is approved in Rm 16:10

APES *(2)*
silver, ivory, **a**, and peacocks. 1Kg 10:22
silver, ivory, **a**, and peacocks. 2Ch 9:21

APHEK *(8)*
(AKA APHIK)
the king of **A** one the king of Jos 12:18
the Sidonians to **A** and as far as Jos 13:4
Ummah, **A**, and Rehob—22 cities, Jos 19:30
the Philistines camped at **A**. 1Sm 4:1
together at **A** while Israel was 1Sm 29:1
and went up to **A** to battle 1Kg 20:26
fled into the city of **A**, 1Kg 20:30
the Arameans in **A** until you have 2Kg 13:17

APHEKAH *(1)*
Janim, Beth-tappuah, **A**, Jos 15:53

APHIAH *(1)*
of Becorath, son of **A**, son of a 1Sm 9:1

APHIK *(1)*
(AKA APHEK)
Achzib, Helbah, **A**, or Rehob. Jdg 1:31

APIECE *(1)*
food, four quarts **a**, and all the Ex 16:22

APOLLONIA *(1)*
Amphipolis and **A** and came to Ac 17:1

APOLLOS *(10)*
A Jew named **A**, a native Ac 18:24
While **A** was in Corinth, Paul Ac 19:1
or "I'm with **A**," or "I'm with 1Co 1:12
I'm with **A**," are you not 1Co 3:4
So, what is **A**? And what is Paul? 1Co 3:5
I planted, **A** watered, but God 1Co 3:6
whether Paul or **A** or Cephas or 1Co 3:22
myself and **A** for your benefit, 1Co 4:6
About our brother **A**: 1Co 16:12
the lawyer and **A** on their Ti 3:13

APOLLYON *(1)*
and in Greek he has the name **A**. Rv 9:11

APOLOGIZED *(1)*
So they came and **a** to them, Ac 16:39

APOSTASIES (2)
your own **a** will reprimand you. Jr 2:19
from all their **a** by which they Ezk 37:23

APOSTASY (2)
I will heal their **a**; Hs 14:4
come unless the **a** comes first 2Th 2:3

APOSTLE (19)
called as an **a** and singled out Rm 1:1
that I am an **a** to the Gentiles, Rm 11:13
called as an **a** of Christ Jesus 1Co 1:1
Am I not an **a**? Have I not seen 1Co 9:1
If I am not an **a** to others, 1Co 9:2
unworthy to be called an **a**, 1Co 15:9
an **a** of Christ Jesus by God's 2Co 1:1
The signs of an **a** were performed 2Co 12:12
Paul, an **a**—not from men or by Gl 1:1
an **a** of Christ Jesus by God's Eph 1:1
an **a** of Christ Jesus by God's Col 1:1
a of Christ Jesus according to 1Tm 1:1
a herald, an **a** (I am telling 1Tm 2:7
an **a** of Christ Jesus by God's 2Tm 1:1
a herald, **a**, and teacher, 2Tm 1:11
and an **a** of Jesus Christ for the Ti 1:1
the **a** and high priest of our Heb 3:1
Peter, an **a** of Jesus Christ: 1Pt 1:1
slave and an **a** of Jesus Christ: 2Pt 1:1

APOSTLES (52)
These are the names of the 12 **a**: Mt 10:2
also named them **a**—to be with Mk 3:14
The **a** gathered around Jesus and Mk 6:30
of them—He also named them **a**: Lk 6:13
When the **a** returned, they Lk 9:10
'I will send them prophets and **a**, Lk 11:49
a said to the Lord, "Increase Lk 17:5
the table, and the **a** with Him. Lk 22:14
were telling the **a** these things. Lk 24:10
Spirit to the **a** whom He had Ac 1:2
he was numbered with the 11 **a**. Ac 1:26
to Peter and the rest of the **a**: Ac 2:37
being performed through the **a**. Ac 2:43
great power the **a** were giving Ac 4:33
whom the **a** named Barnabas, Ac 4:36
through the hands of the **a**. Ac 5:12
they arrested the **a** and put them Ac 5:18
But Peter and the **a** replied, Ac 5:29
called in the **a** and had them Ac 5:40
had them stand before the **a**, Ac 6:6
all except the **a** were scattered Ac 8:1
When the **a** who were at Jerusalem Ac 8:14
him to the **a** and explained to Ac 9:27
The **a** and the brothers who were Ac 11:1
the Jews and some with the **a**. Ac 14:4
The **a** Barnabas and Paul tore Ac 14:14
to go up to the **a** and elders Ac 15:2
church, the **a**, and the elders Ac 15:4
Then the **a** and the elders Ac 15:6
Then the **a** and the elders, Ac 15:22
From the **a** and the elders, Ac 15:23
reached by the **a** and elders at Ac 16:4
are outstanding among the **a**, Rm 16:7
us, the **a**, in last place, 1Co 4:9
like the other **a**, the Lord's 1Co 9:5
first **a**, second prophets, third 1Co 12:28
Are all **a**? Are all prophets? Are 1Co 12:29
to James, then to all the **a**. 1Co 15:7
For I am the least of the **a**, 1Co 15:9
For such people are false **a**, 2Co 11:13
themselves as **a** of Christ. 2Co 11:13
who had become **a** before me; Gl 1:17
any of the other **a** except James, Gl 1:19
of the **a** and prophets, Eph 2:20
to His holy **a** and prophets Eph 3:5
He personally gave some to be **a**, Eph 4:11
been a burden as Christ's **a**, 1Th 2:7
Savior ⌊given⌋ through your **a**. 2Pt 3:2
foretold by the **a** of our Lord Jd 17
call themselves **a** and are not, Rv 2:2
and you saints, **a**, and prophets, Rv 18:20
the 12 names of the Lamb's 12 **a**. Rv 21:14

APOSTLES' (5)
themselves to the **a** teaching, Ac 2:42
and laid them at the **a** feet. Ac 4:35
and laid it at the **a** feet. Ac 4:37
of it and laid it at the **a** feet. Ac 5:2
the laying on of the **a** hands, Ac 8:18

APOSTLESHIP (3)
grace and **a** through Him to Rm 1:5
the seal of my **a** in the Lord. 1Co 9:2
with Peter in the **a** to the Gl 2:8

APOSTOLIC (1)
the place in this **a** service that Ac 1:25

APPAIM (1)
sons: Seled and **A**. Seled died 1Ch 2:30

APPAIM'S (1)
A son: Ishi. Ishi's son: Sheshan. 1Ch 2:31

APPALLED (11)
to live there will be **a** by it. Lv 26:32
will be **a** and will hiss. 1Kg 9:8
passerby will be **a** and will say: 2Ch 7:21
The upright are **a** at this, Jb 17:8
in the west are **a** at his fate, Jb 18:20
Just as many were **a** at You— Is 52:14
be shocked and utterly **a**. Jr 2:12
continually, and be **a** at you. Ezk 26:16
coasts and islands are **a** at you. Ezk 27:35
among the nations are **a** at you. Ezk 28:19
many nations to be **a** at you, Ezk 32:10

APPAREL (2)
One who is splendid in His **a**, Is 63:1
gold, pearls, or expensive **a**, 1Tm 2:9

APPARENT (1)
For no ⌊**a**⌋ reason, my enemies Lm 3:52

APPEAL (14)
go very far. Make an **a** for me." Ex 8:28
said, "I will **a** to the LORD, Ex 8:29
Make an **a** to the LORD. Ex 9:28
and make an **a** to the LORD your Ex 10:17
went to **a** to the king for her 2Kg 8:3
life came to **a** to the king for 2Kg 8:5
I would **a** to God and would Jb 5:8
He has heard my **a** for mercy. Ps 116:1
me up to them. I **a** to Caesar!" Ac 25:11
I was compelled to **a** to Caesar; Ac 28:19
with Him, we also **a** to you: 2Co 6:1
make a personal **a** to you by the 2Co 10:1
I **a**, instead, on the basis of Phm 9
a to you for my child, whom I Phm 10

APPEALED (9)
presence and **a** to the LORD. Ex 8:30
presence and **a** to the LORD. Ex 10:18
So Moses **a** to the LORD, Nm 27:15
against Paul to him; and they **a**, Ac 25:2
replied, "You have **a** to Caesar; Ac 25:12
But when Paul **a** to be held for Ac 25:21
Jewish community has **a** to me, Ac 25:24
he himself **a** to the Emperor, Ac 25:25
if he had not **a** to Caesar." Ac 26:32

APPEALING (1)
that God is **a** through us, 2Co 5:20

APPEALS (2)
keep on making **a** to the king?" 2Sm 19:28
prayers and **a**, with loud cries Heb 5:7

APPEAR (51)
place, and let the dry land **a**." Gn 1:9
The LORD did not **a** to you'?" Ex 4:1
No one is to **a** before Me Ex 23:15
males are to **a** before the Lord Ex 23:17
No one is to **a** before Me Ex 34:20
males are to **a** before the Lord Ex 34:23
times a year to **a** before the Ex 34:24
LORD is going to **a** to you.'" Lv 9:4
glory of the LORD may **a** to you." Lv 9:6
and does not **a** to be deeper than Lv 13:4
if it does not **a** to be deeper Lv 13:31
and it does not **a** to be deeper Lv 13:32
and does not **a** to be deeper than Lv 13:34
indentations that **a** to be Lv 14:37
because I **a** in the cloud above Lv 16:2
are to **a** before the LORD Nm 16:16
your males are to **a** three times Dt 16:16
No one is to **a** before the LORD Dt 16:16
Everyone ⌊must **a**⌋ with a gift Dt 16:17
LORD did not **a** again to Manoah Jdg 13:21
I'll take him to **a** in the LORD's 1Sm 1:22
LORD continued to **a** in Shiloh, 1Sm 3:21
Do not **a** before me unless you 2Sm 3:13
summoned to **a** before the king Est 4:11
May it not **a** among the days of Jb 3:6
godless person can **a** before Him. Jb 13:16
really want to **a** superior to me Jb 19:5
like a fiery furnace when you **a**; Ps 21:9
can I come and **a** before God? Ps 42:2
vengeance—God of vengeance, **a**. Ps 94:1
He will **a** in His glory. Ps 102:16
The blossoms **a** in the Sg 2:12
When you come to **a** before Me, Is 1:12
the glory of the LORD will **a**, Is 40:5
your light will **a** like the dawn, Is 58:8
and His glory will **a** over you. Is 60:2
⌊Now⌋ they **a** darker than soot; Lm 4:8
your sisters **a** righteous by all Ezk 16:51
For they **a** more righteous than Ezk 16:52
made your sisters **a** righteous. Ezk 16:52
Then the LORD will **a** over them, Zch 9:14
a beautiful on the outside, Mt 23:27
Son of Man will **a** in the sky, Mt 24:30
God was going to **a** right away. Lk 19:11
things in which I will **a** to you. Ac 26:16
of Jesse will **a**, the One who Rm 15:12
For we must all **a** before the 2Co 5:10
not that we may **a** to pass the 2Co 13:7
even though we ⌊may **a**⌋ to fail. 2Co 13:7
He might now **a** in the presence Heb 9:24
of many, will **a** a second time, Heb 9:28

APPEARANCE (40)
tree pleasing in **a** and good for Gn 2:9
their **a** was as bad as it had Gn 41:21
The **a** of the LORD's glory to the Ex 24:17
like the **a** of a skin disease on Lv 13:43
If the **a** of the contaminated Lv 13:55
and its **a** was like that of Nm 11:7
look at his **a** or his stature, 1Sm 16:7
eyes and a healthy, handsome **a**. 1Sm 16:12
but I could not recognize its **a**; Jb 4:16
You change his **a** and send him Jb 14:20
His **a** was so disfigured that He Is 52:14
no **a** that we should desire Him. Is 53:2
coral, their **a** ⌊like⌋ sapphire. Lm 4:7
And this was their **a**: Ezk 1:5
was like the **a** of burning coals Ezk 1:13
The **a** of the wheels and their Ezk 1:16
Their **a** and craftsmanship was Ezk 1:16
throne with the **a** of sapphire Ezk 1:26
was a form with the **a** of a human Ezk 1:26
The **a** of the brilliant light all Ezk 1:28
This was the **a** of the form of Ezk 1:28
a form that had the **a** of a man. Ezk 8:2
a, all four had the same form, Ezk 10:10
a man whose **a** was like bronze Ezk 40:3
of the sanctuary had the same **a**. Ezk 41:21
Then examine our **a** and the Dn 1:13
and the **a** of the young men Dn 1:13
you, and its **a** was terrifying. Dn 2:31
His **a** is as sure as the dawn. Hs 6:3
Their **a** is like that of horses, Jl 2:4
how to read the **a** of the sky, Mt 16:3
a was like lightning, and his Mt 28:3
day of his public **a** to Israel. Lk 1:80
Him in a physical **a** like a dove. Lk 3:22
the **a** of His face changed, Lk 9:29
to interpret the **a** of the earth Lk 12:56
in the outward **a** rather than 2Co 5:12
And the **a** was so terrifying that Heb 12:21
its beautiful **a** is destroyed. Jms 1:11
The **a** of the locusts was like Rv 9:7

APPEARANCES (1)
judging according to outward **a**; Jn 7:24

APPEARED (94)
the LORD **a** to Abram and said, Gn 12:7
to the LORD who had **a** to him. Gn 12:7
a flaming torch **a** and passed Gn 15:17
old, the LORD **a** to him, saying, Gn 17:1
Then the LORD **a** to Abraham at Gn 18:1
The LORD **a** to him and said, Gn 26:2
and the LORD **a** to him that night Gn 26:24
to the God who **a** to you when you Gn 35:1
God **a** to Jacob again after he Gn 35:9
God Almighty **a** to me at Luz in Gn 48:3
of the LORD **a** to him in a flame Ex 3:2
and Jacob, has **a** to me and said: Ex 3:16
the God of Jacob, has **a** to you." Ex 4:5
I **a** to Abraham, Isaac, and Jacob Ex 6:3
in a cloud, the LORD's glory **a**. Ex 16:10
of the LORD **a** to all the people Lv 9:23
contamination has **a** in my house. Lv 14:35
and it **a** like fire above the Nm 9:15
glory of the LORD **a** to all the Nm 14:10
glory of the LORD **a** to the whole Nm 16:19
it, and the LORD's glory **a**. Nm 16:42
the glory of the LORD **a** to them. Nm 20:6

the LORD **a** at the tent in a Dt 31:15
from Sinai and **a** to them from Dt 33:2
of Him who **a** in the ⌊burning Dt 33:16
of the LORD **a** to him and said: Jdg 6:12
Angel of the LORD **a** to the woman Jdg 13:3
ate and no longer **a** downcast. 1Sm 1:18
At Gibeon the LORD **a** to Solomon 1Kg 3:5
the LORD **a** to Solomon a second 1Kg 9:2
just as He had **a** to him at 1Kg 9:2
Israel, who had **a** to him twice. 1Kg 11:9
of fire suddenly **a** and separated 2Kg 2:11
That night God **a** to Solomon and 2Ch 1:7
the LORD had **a** to his father 2Ch 3:1
Then the LORD **a** to Solomon at 2Ch 7:12
the LORD **a** to him from far away. Jr 31:3
stretched out what **a** to be a Ezk 8:3
of a throne that **a** above them. Ezk 10:1
The cherubim **a** to have the form Ezk 10:8
looked, tendons **a** on them, flesh Ezk 37:8
watching, a colossal statue **a**. Dn 2:31
of a man's hand **a** and began Dn 5:5
another beast **a**, a second one, Dn 7:5
I was watching, another beast **a**. Dn 7:6
a fourth beast **a**, frightening Dn 7:7
reign, a vision **a** to me, Daniel, Dn 8:1
one that had **a** to me earlier. Dn 8:1
a male goat **a**, coming from the Dn 8:5
me someone who **a** to be a man. Dn 8:15
It **a** in a night and perished in Jnh 4:10
Lord suddenly **a** to him in a Mt 1:20
them the exact time the star **a**. Mt 2:7
the Lord suddenly **a** to Joseph in Mt 2:13
the Lord suddenly **a** in a dream Mt 2:19
than John the Baptist has **a**, Mt 11:11
grain, then the weeds also **a**. Mt 13:26
Moses and Elijah **a** to them, Mt 17:3
the holy city, and **a** to many. Mt 27:53
Elijah **a** to them with Moses, Mk 9:4
A cloud **a**, overshadowing them, Mk 9:7
He **a** first to Mary Magdalene, Mk 16:9
He **a** in a different form to two Mk 16:12
He **a** to the Eleven themselves as Mk 16:14
An angel of the Lord **a** to him, Lk 1:11
that Elijah had **a**, and others Lk 9:8
a in glory and were speaking Lk 9:31
a cloud **a** and overshadowed them. Lk 9:34
an angel from heaven **a** to Him, Lk 22:43
raised, and has **a** to Simon!" Lk 24:34
time Jesus **a** to the disciples Jn 21:14
a to them and rested on each one Ac 2:3
The God of glory **a** to our father Ac 7:2
an angel **a** to him in the desert Ac 7:30
of the angel who **a** to him in the Ac 7:35
Philip **a** in Azotus, and passing Ac 8:40
a to you on the road you were Ac 9:17
Suddenly an angel of the Lord **a**, Ac 12:7
and He **a** for many days to those Ac 13:31
the night a vision **a** to Paul: Ac 16:9
For I have **a** to you for this Ac 26:16
days neither sun nor stars **a**, Ac 27:20
and that He **a** to Cephas, then to 1Co 15:5
Then He **a** to over 500 brothers 1Co 15:6
Then He **a** to James, then to all 1Co 15:7
born, He also **a** to me. 1Co 15:8
For the grace of God has **a**, Ti 2:11
and love for man **a** from God our Ti 3:4
the Messiah has **a**, high priest Heb 9:11
But now He has **a** one time, Heb 9:26
of His covenant **a** in His Rv 11:19
A great sign **a** in heaven: Rv 12:1
Then another sign **a** in heaven: Rv 12:3
One of his heads **a** to be fatally Rv 13:3

APPEARING *(7)*
would cover it, a like fire at Nm 9:16
a to them during 40 days and Ac 1:3
blame until the **a** of our Lord 1Tm 6:14
through the **a** of our Savior 2Tm 1:10
and by His **a** and His kingdom, 2Tm 4:1
all those who have loved His **a**. 2Tm 4:8
hope and the **a** of the glory of Ti 2:13

APPEARS *(19)*
and the bow **a** in the clouds, Gn 9:14
the infection **a** to be deeper Lv 13:3
But whenever raw flesh **a** on him, Lv 13:14
When a boil **a** on the skin of Lv 13:18
and the spot **a** to be deeper than Lv 13:25
If it **a** to be deeper than the Lv 13:30
of beauty, God **a** in radiance. Ps 50:2
each **a** before God in Zion. Ps 84:7
and new growth **a** and the grain Pr 27:25
When Moab **a** on the high place, Is 16:12
My salvation **a**, and My arms will Is 51:5
marked Jerusalem **a** in his right Ezk 21:22
All their evil **a** at Gilgal, Hs 9:15
a great and strong people ⌊**a**⌋, Jl 2:2
will be able to stand when He **a**? Mal 3:2
bit of smoke that **a** for a little Jms 4:14
And when the chief Shepherd **a**, 1Pt 5:4
so that when He **a** we may have 1Jn 2:28
that when He **a**, we will be like 1Jn 3:2

APPEASE *(1)*
I want to **a** Esau with the gift Gn 32:20

APPEASED *(3)*
He will not be **a** by anything or Pr 6:35
My wrath on them, I will be **a**. Ezk 5:13
yet we have not **a** the LORD our Dn 9:13

APPEASES *(1)*
of death, but a wise man **a** it. Pr 16:14

APPETITE *(9)*
But now our **a** is gone; Nm 11:6
his **a** is never satisfied, Jb 20:20
or satisfy the **a** of young lions Jb 38:39
people have an **a** for violence. Pr 13:2
A worker's **a** works for him Pr 16:26
your throat if you have a big **a**; Pr 23:2
yet the **a** is never satisfied. Ec 6:7
they have an **a** for their Hs 4:8
He enlarges his **a** like Sheol, Hab 2:5

APPETITES *(4)*
These dogs have fierce **a**; Is 56:11
satisfy their **a** or fill their Ezk 7:19
will be for their **a** ⌊alone⌋; Hs 9:4
our Lord Christ but their own **a**, Rm 16:18

APPHIA *(1)*
A our sister, to Archippus our Phm 2

APPIUS *(1)*
far as Forum of **A** and Three Ac 28:15

APPLAUD *(1)*
but even **a** others who practice Rm 1:32

APPLAUDED *(1)*
the streets, to be **a** by people. Mt 6:2

APPLE *(2)*
Guard me as the **a** of Your eye; Ps 17:8
palm, and the **a**—all the trees Jl 1:12

APPLES *(1)*
is like golden **a** on a silver Pr 25:11

APPLIED *(9)*
and **a** it with his finger to the Lv 8:15
the blood and **a** it to the horns Lv 9:9
them with gold **a** evenly over the 1Kg 6:35
brought it and **a** it to his 2Kg 20:7
I **a** my mind to seek and explore Ec 1:13
I **a** my mind to know wisdom and Ec 1:17
When I **a** my mind to know wisdom Ec 8:16
has been **a** and no splint put Ezk 30:21
I have **a** these things to myself 1Co 4:6

APPLIES *(3)*
know that one law **a** to every man Est 4:11
the judgment **a** to you because Hs 5:1
He **a** His justice morning by Zph 3:5

APPLY *(17)*
The same law will **a** to both the Ex 12:49
bull's blood and **a** ⌊it⌋ to the Ex 29:12
The priest must **a** some of the Lv 4:7
He is to **a** some of the blood to Lv 4:18
his finger and **a** it to the horns Lv 4:25
his finger and **a** it to the horns Lv 4:30
his finger and **a** it to the horns Lv 4:34
the priest will **a** this entire Nm 5:30
You are to **a** the same statute to Nm 9:14
same ordinance will **a** to both Nm 15:16
will not **a** their hands to Ps 125:3
and **a** your mind to my knowledge. Pr 22:17
A yourself to instruction and Pr 23:12
lump of figs and **a** it to his Is 38:21
its blood and **a** ⌊it⌋ to the four Ezk 43:20
sin offering and **a** ⌊it⌋ to the Ezk 45:19
the dream **a** to those who hate Dn 4:19

APPLYING *(1)*
a my mind to all the work that Ec 8:9

APPOINT *(44)*
him **a** overseers over the land Gn 41:34
will **a** a place for you where he Ex 21:13
I will **a** My blessing for you in Lv 25:21
A the Levites over the Nm 1:50
You are to **a** Aaron and his sons Nm 3:10
Let's **a** a leader and go back to Nm 14:4
you also have to **a** yourself as Nm 16:13
a a man over the community Nm 27:16
A for yourselves wise, Dt 1:13
A judges and officials for your Dt 16:18
'We want to **a** a king over us Dt 17:14
you are to **a** over you the king Dt 17:15
A a king from your brothers. Dt 17:15
they will **a** military commanders Dt 20:9
A for yourselves three men from Jos 18:4
Please **a** me to some priestly 1Sm 2:36
a a king to judge us the same as 1Sm 8:5
He can **a** them for his use as 1Sm 8:12
"**A** a king for them." 1Sm 8:22
I will **a** you as my permanent 1Sm 28:2
whole family to **a** me ruler over 2Sm 6:21
only someone would **a** me judge in 2Sm 15:4
I will **a** you, and you will reign 1Kg 11:37
his position and **a** captains in 1Kg 20:24
the Levites to **a** their relatives 1Ch 15:16
will **a** him over My house and My 1Ch 17:14
a magistrates and judges to Ezr 7:25
Let the king **a** commissioners in Est 2:3
that You would **a** a time for me Jb 14:13
a faithful love and truth to Ps 61:7
I will **a** you to be a covenant Is 49:8
I will **a** peace as your guard and Is 60:17
I will **a** destroyers against you, Jr 22:7
I will **a** whoever is chosen for Jr 49:19
I will **a** whoever is chosen for Jr 50:44
A a marshal against her; Jr 51:27
I will **a** over them a single Ezk 34:23
They will **a** men on a full-time Ezk 39:14
decided to **a** 120 satraps over Dn 6:1
They will **a** for themselves a Hs 1:11
whom we can **a** to this duty. Ac 6:3
to **a** you as a servant and a Ac 26:16
For God did not **a** us to wrath, 1Th 5:9
to **a** elders in every town: Ti 1:5

APPOINTED *(170)*
the **a** time I will come back to Gn 18:14
at the **a** time God had told him. Gn 21:2
one You have **a** for Your servant Gn 24:14
the LORD has **a** for my master's Gn 24:44
statute at its **a** time from year Ex 13:10
days at the **a** time in the month Ex 23:15
I have **a** by name Bezalel son of Ex 31:2
days at the **a** time in the month Ex 34:18
the LORD has **a** by name Bezalel Ex 35:30
by the man **a** for the task. Lv 16:21
and I have **a** it to you to make Lv 17:11
These are My **a** times, the times Lv 23:2
These are the LORD's **a** times, Lv 23:4
to proclaim at their **a** times. Lv 23:4
are the LORD's **a** times that you Lv 23:37
declared the LORD's **a** times to Lv 23:44
the Passover at its **a** time. Nm 9:2
observe it at its **a** time on the Nm 9:3
offering at its **a** time with the Nm 9:7
LORD's offering at its **a** time. Nm 9:13
occasions, your **a** festivals, Nm 10:10
or at your **a** festivals—to Nm 15:3
to Me at its **a** time My offering Nm 28:2
the LORD at your **a** times in Nm 29:39
king that you have **a** to a nation Dt 28:36
the **a** time in the year of debt Dt 31:10
My covenant that I **a** for them. Jos 7:11
These are the cities **a** for all Jos 20:9
he **a** his sons as judges over 1Sm 8:1
who **a** Moses and Aaron and who 1Sm 12:6
days for the **a** time that Samuel 1Sm 13:8
didn't come within the **a** days 1Sm 13:11
and the LORD has **a** him as ruler 1Sm 13:14
the field for the **a** meeting with 1Sm 20:35
Now Absalom had **a** Amasa over 2Sm 17:25
his troops and **a** commanders of 2Sm 18:1
You have **a** me the head of 2Sm 22:44
that morning until the **a** time, 2Sm 24:15
Then the king **a** Benaiah son of 1Kg 2:35
and he **a** Zadok the priest in 1Kg 2:35
he **a** him over the entire labor 1Kg 11:28
a you ruler over My people 1Kg 14:7
The king had **a** the captain, 2Kg 7:17
So the king **a** a court official 2Kg 8:6

control and **a** their own king. 2Kg 8:20
Jehoiada⌋ the priest **a** guards 2Kg 11:18
but they also **a** from their 2Kg 17:32
of Judah had **a** to burn incense 2Kg 23:5
had been **a** over the warriors; 2Kg 25:19
king of Babylon **a** Gedaliah son 2Kg 25:22
king of Babylon had **a** Gedaliah, 2Kg 25:23
the seer had **a** them to their 1Ch 9:22
So the Levites **a** Heman son of 1Ch 15:17
David **a** some of the Levites to 1Ch 16:4
and he **a** stonemasons to cut 1Ch 22:2
New Moons, and **a** festivals, they 1Ch 23:31
father had **a** him as the first 1Ch 26:10
King David **a** them over the 1Ch 26:32
and the **a** festivals of the LORD 2Ch 2:4
and Jerusalem, **a** by my father 2Ch 2:7
the three annual **a** festivals: 2Ch 8:13
a the divisions of the priests 2Ch 8:14
Jeroboam **a** his own priests for 2Ch 11:15
Rehoboam **a** Abijah son of 2Ch 11:22
He **a** judges in all the fortified 2Ch 19:5
Jehoshaphat also **a** in Jerusalem 2Ch 19:8
people and **a** some to sing for 2Ch 20:21
domination and **a** their own king. 2Ch 21:8
David had **a** over the LORD's 2Ch 23:18
They ate the **a** feast for seven 2Ch 30:22
Moons, and of the **a** feasts, as 2Ch 31:3
He **a** the priests to their 2Ch 35:2
earth and has **a** me to build Him 2Ch 36:23
earth and has **a** me to build Him Ezr 1:2
all the LORD's **a** holy occasions, Ezr 3:5
They **a** the Levites who were 20 Ezr 3:8
They also **a** the priests by their Ezr 6:18
who had been **a** by David and the Ezr 8:20
foreign women come at **a** times, Ezr 10:14
King Artaxerxes **a** me to be their Neh 5:14
singers, and Levites were **a**. Neh 7:1
stiff-necked and **a** a leader to Neh 9:17
offerings, the **a** festivals, the Neh 10:33
houses at the **a** times each year. Neh 10:34
and I **a** two large processions Neh 12:31
I **a** as treasurers over the Neh 13:13
of wood at the **a** times and for Neh 13:31
and according to the time **a**. Est 9:27
the place **a** for all who live. Jb 30:23
Who has **a** His way for Him, Jb 36:23
You have **a** me the head of Ps 18:43
to her—the **a** time has come. Ps 102:13
the LORD has **a** the blessing— Ps 133:3
The fool is **a** to great heights, Ec 10:6
I have **a** trustworthy witnesses— Is 8:2
stroke of the **a** staff that the Is 30:32
I have **a** watchmen on your walls; Is 62:6
a you a prophet to the nations. Jr 1:5
a watchmen over you ⌊and said:⌋ Jr 6:17
I have **a** you to be an assayer Jr 6:27
The LORD has **a** you priest in Jr 29:26
of Babylon has **a** over the cities Jr 40:5
of Babylon had **a** Gedaliah son Jr 40:7
in Judah and had **a** Gedaliah son Jr 40:11
of Babylon had **a** in the land. Jr 41:2
had **a** Gedaliah son of Ahikam. Jr 41:10
of Babylon had **a** in the land. Jr 41:18
had been **a** over the warriors; Jr 52:25
no one comes to the **a** festivals. Lm 1:4
LORD has abolished **a** festivals Lm 2:6
as on the day of an **a** festival. Lm 2:7
as if ⌊for⌋ an **a** festival day; Lm 2:22
He **a** His beautiful ornaments for Ezk 7:20
have **a** a sword for slaughter at Ezk 21:15
cherub, for I had **a** you. Ezk 28:14
A sword is **a**! They drag her Ezk 32:20
during its **a** festivals. Ezk 36:38
in the place **a** for the temple. Ezk 43:21
things but have **a** ⌊others⌋ to Ezk 44:8
regarding all My **a** festivals, Ezk 44:24
for all the **a** times of the house Ezk 45:17
before the LORD at the **a** times, Ezk 46:9
At the festivals and **a** times, Ezk 46:11
the king **a** Shadrach, Meshach Dn 2:49
some Jews you have **a** to manage Dn 3:12
a him chief of the diviners, Dn 5:11
refers to the **a** time of the end Dn 8:19
the end will come at the **a** time. Dn 11:27
At the **a** time he will come again Dn 11:29
will still come at the **a** time. Dn 11:35
A harvest is also **a** for you, Hs 6:11
They have **a** leaders, but without Hs 8:4
Then the LORD **a** a great fish to Jnh 1:17
Then the LORD God **a** a plant, Jnh 4:6
God **a** a worm that attacked the Jnh 4:7
God **a** a scorching east wind. Jnh 4:8
You **a** them to execute judgment; Hab 1:12
vision is yet for the **a** time; Hab 2:3
driven from the **a** festivals; Zph 3:18
also **a** 12—He also named them Mk 3:14
He **a** the Twelve: To Simon, He Mk 3:16
this, the Lord **a** 70 others, and Lk 10:1
who **a** Me a judge or arbitrator Lk 12:14
I **a** you that you should go out Jn 15:16
who has been **a** Messiah for you. Ac 3:20
a him governor over Egypt and Ac 7:10
Who **a** you a ruler and a judge Ac 7:27
Who **a** you a ruler and a judge? Ac 7:35
witnesses **a** beforehand by God, Ac 10:41
that He is the One **a** by God to Ac 10:42
So on an **a** day, dressed in royal Ac 12:21
I have **a** you as a light for the Ac 13:47
who had been **a** to eternal life Ac 13:48
When they had **a** elders in every Ac 14:23
has determined their **a** times and Ac 17:26
by the Man He has **a**. Ac 17:31
Holy Spirit has **a** you as Ac 20:28
fathers has **a** you to know His Ac 22:14
helpless, at the **a** moment, Rm 5:6
he was also **a** by the churches 2Co 8:19
His feet and **a** Him as head over Eph 1:22
that I am **a** for the defense Php 1:16
know that we are **a** to this. 1Th 3:3
For this I was **a** a herald, 1Tm 2:7
this ⌊gospel⌋ I was **a** a herald, 2Tm 1:11
whom He has **a** heir of all things Heb 1:2
faithful to the One who **a** Him, Heb 3:2
from men is **a** in service to God Heb 5:1
high priest is **a** to offer gifts Heb 8:3
just as it is **a** for people to Heb 9:27

APPOINTING *(2)*
from among them, **a** him as their Ezk 33:2
faithful, **a** me to the ministry 1Tm 1:12

APPOINTMENT *(2)*
Shimei by **a** of King Hezekiah 2Ch 31:13
governor by the **a** of King Cyrus. Ezr 5:14

APPOINTS *(4)*
He promised and **a** you ruler over 1Sm 25:30
you say when He **a** close friends Jr 13:21
the law **a** as high priests men Heb 7:28
after the law, ⌊**a**⌋ a Son, who Heb 7:28

APPORTION *(4)*
should **a** the animal according Ex 12:4
Does He **a** destruction in His Jb 21:17
I will **a** the Valley of Succoth. Ps 60:6
I will **a** the Valley of Succoth. Ps 108:7

APPORTIONED *(1)*
a their inheritance by lot and Ps 78:55

APPREHENDED *(3)*
and he **a** Jeremiah the prophet, Jr 37:13
to him but **a** Jeremiah and took Jr 37:14
so we **a** him and wanted to judge Ac 24:6

APPROACH *(30)*
Moses alone is to **a** the LORD, Ex 24:2
but the others are not to **a**, Ex 24:2
tent of meeting or **a** the altar Ex 28:43
tent of meeting or **a** the altar Ex 30:20
A the altar and sacrifice your Lv 9:7
near the curtain or **a** the altar. Lv 21:23
when they **a** the sanctuary." Nm 8:19
of Aaron should **a** to offer Nm 16:40
When you **a** a city to fight Dt 20:10
who are with me will **a** the city. Jos 8:5
a King David and say to him, 1Kg 1:13
and instruct her to **a** the king, Est 4:8
You will **a** the grave in full Jb 5:26
I would **a** Him like a prince. Jb 31:37
that one should **a** Him in court. Jb 34:23
and the years **a** when you will Ec 12:1
these people **a** Me with their Is 29:13
Let them **a**, then let them Is 41:1
tremble. They **a** and arrive. Is 41:5
A Me and listen to this. Is 48:16
Me, and he will **a** Me, for who Jr 30:21
otherwise risk his life to **a** Me? Jr 30:21
of Levi who may **a** the LORD to Ezk 40:46
the priests who **a** the LORD will Ezk 42:13
before they **a** the public area." Ezk 42:14
who **a** Me in order to serve Me." Ezk 43:19
They must not **a** Me to serve Me Ezk 44:13
from Me, will **a** Me to serve Me. Ezk 44:15
wind did not allow us to **a** it, Ac 27:7
Therefore let us **a** the throne of Heb 4:16

APPROACHED *(85)*
Now Abimelech had not **a** her, Gn 20:4
times until he **a** his brother. Gn 33:3
their children **a** ⌊him⌋ and bowed Gn 33:6
children also **a** and bowed down, Gn 33:7
and Rachel **a** and bowed down. Gn 33:7
So they **a** Joseph's steward and Gn 43:19
But Judah **a** him and said, Gn 44:18
As Pharaoh **a**, the Israelites Ex 14:10
distance as Moses **a** the thick Ex 20:21
he **a** the camp and saw the calf Ex 32:19
tent of meeting and **a** the altar, Ex 40:32
So Aaron **a** the altar and Lv 9:8
sons when they **a** the presence Lv 16:1
The daughters of Zelophehad **a**; Nm 27:1
and of hundreds, **a** Moses Nm 31:48
Then they **a** him and said, Nm 32:16
sons of Joseph **a** and addressed Nm 36:1
Then all of you **a** me and said, Dt 1:22
All of you **a** me with your tribal Dt 5:23
Joshua **a** Him and asked, "Are You Jos 5:13
with him went up and **a** the city, Jos 8:11
of Judah **a** Joshua at Gilgal, Jos 14:6
Levite families **a** Eleazar the Jos 21:1
Then Ehud **a** him while he was Jdg 3:20
he **a** its entrance to set it on Jdg 9:52
Saul **a** Samuel in the gate area 1Sm 9:18
his hand, he **a** the Philistine. 1Sm 17:40
David **a** the men, he greeted 1Sm 30:21
When a person **a** to bow down to 2Sm 15:5
he was yelling curses as he **a**. 2Sm 16:5
As he **a**, ⌊the sword⌋ fell out. 2Sm 20:8
As the time **a** for David to die, 1Kg 2:1
Then Elijah **a** all the people and 1Kg 18:21
So all the people **a** him. 1Kg 18:30
Elijah the prophet **a** ⌊the altar⌋ 1Kg 18:36
The prophet **a** the king of Israel 1Kg 20:22
Then the man of God **a** and said 1Kg 20:28
his servants **a** and said to him 2Kg 5:13
Then he **a** the altar and ascended 2Kg 16:12
people with him **a** the Arameans 1Ch 19:14
a Zerubbabel and the leaders Ezr 4:2
the leaders **a** me and said: Ezr 9:1
and she **a** and touched the tip of Est 5:2
the least to the greatest, **a** Jr 42:1
Nebuchadnezzar then **a** the door Dn 3:26
So they **a** the king and asked Dn 6:12
He **a** the Ancient of Days and was Dn 7:13
I **a** one of those who were Dn 7:16
So he **a** where I was standing; Dn 8:17
The captain **a** him and said, Jnh 1:6
it has **a** the gate of my people, Mc 1:9
Then the tempter **a** Him and said, Mt 4:3
A scribe **a** Him and said, Mt 8:19
for 12 years **a** from behind Mt 9:20
the blind men **a** Him, and Jesus Mt 9:28
His disciples **a** Him and said, Mt 13:36
the disciples **a** Him and said, Mt 14:15
So His disciples **a** Him and urged Mt 15:23
The Pharisees and Sadducees **a**, Mt 16:1
a man **a** and knelt down before Mt 17:14
the disciples **a** Jesus privately Mt 17:19
tax **a** Peter and said, Mt 17:24
Pharisees **a** Him to test Him. Mt 19:3
Zebedee's sons **a** Him with her Mt 20:20
When they **a** Jerusalem and came Mt 21:1
disciples **a** Him privately and Mt 24:3
who had received five talents **a**, Mt 25:20
the man with two talents also **a**. Mt 25:22
one talent also **a** and said, Mt 25:24
a woman **a** Him with an alabaster Mt 26:7
A servant **a** him and she said, Mt 26:69
standing there **a** and said to Mt 26:73
He **a** Pilate and asked for Jesus' Mt 27:58
from heaven and **a** ⌊the tomb⌋. Mt 28:2
His disciples **a** Him and said, Mk 6:35
Pharisees **a** Him to test Him. Mk 10:2
sons of Zebedee, **a** Him and said, Mk 10:35
When they **a** Jerusalem, at Mk 11:1
One of the scribes **a**. Mk 12:28
a from behind and touched the Lk 8:44
the Twelve **a** and said to Him, Lk 9:12
As He **a** Bethphage and Bethany, Lk 19:29

He **a** and saw the city, He wept Lk 19:41
He **a** Pilate and asked for Jesus' Lk 23:52
all the widows **a** him, weeping Ac 9:39

APPROACHES *(5)*
uncleanness yet **a** the holy Lv 22:3
evening **a**, he must wash with Dt 23:11
Anyone who **a** the ranks is to be 2Kg 11:8
man or woman who **a** the king in Est 4:11
as one **a** the entrance of the Ezk 40:40

APPROACHING *(15)*
of mourning for my father are **a**; Gn 27:41
The time of your death is now **a**. Dt 31:14
saw Jehu's troops **a** and shouted, 2Kg 9:17
the cattle also, the **a** ⌊storm⌋. Jb 36:33
My love ⌊is **a**⌋. Look! Here he Sg 2:8
I saw him **a** the ram, and Dn 8:7
is near, near and rapidly **a**. Zph 1:14
and see what this is that is **a**." Zch 5:5
a measuring basket that is **a**." Zch 5:6
saw two women **a** with the wind Zch 5:9
the boy was still **a**, the demon Lk 9:42
sinners were **a** to listen to Him Lk 15:1
As he was **a** the age of 40, Ac 7:23
As he was **a** to look at it, Ac 7:31
thought they were **a** land. Ac 27:27

APPROPRIATE *(13)*
of lashes⌋ **a** for his crime. Dt 25:2
to observe it at the **a** time, 2Ch 30:3
of the righteous know what is **a**, Pr 10:32
is not **a** on a fool's lips; Pr 17:7
Luxury is not **a** for a fool— Pr 19:10
made everything **a** in its time. Ec 3:11
it is **a** to eat, drink, and Ec 5:18
or awaken love until the **a** time. Sg 2:7
or awaken love until the **a** time. Sg 3:5
or awaken love until the **a** time. Sg 8:4
and do not **a** their possessions Ob 13
did not think it **a** to take along Ac 15:38
own persons the **a** penalty for Rm 1:27

APPROPRIATELY *(2)*
rewarded him **a** for what he did Jdg 9:16
I, the LORD, will answer him **a**. Ezk 14:4

APPROVAL *(12)*
Naphtali, enjoying **a**, full of Dt 33:23
it without the LORD's ⌊**a**⌋? 2Kg 18:25
If it meets the king's **a**, Est 1:19
Esther won **a** in the sight of Est 2:15
more favor and **a** from him than Est 2:17
in the courtyard, she won his **a**. Est 5:2
If I have obtained your **a**, Est 7:3
and I have found **a** before him, Est 8:5
it without the LORD's ⌊**a**⌋? Is 36:10
leaders, but without My **a**. Hs 8:4
has set His seal of **a** on Him." Jn 6:27
Do good and you will have its **a**. Rm 13:3

APPROVE *(4)*
followers, who **a** of their words. Ps 49:13
Lord does not **a** ⌊of these things Lm 3:36
that you **a** the deeds of your Lk 11:48
and **a** the things that are Rm 2:18

APPROVED *(12)*
his counselors **a** the proposal, Est 1:21
acceptable to God and **a** by men. Rm 14:18
Apelles, who is **a** in Christ. Rm 16:10
so that the **a** among you may be 1Co 11:19
one commending himself who is **a** 2Co 10:18
as we have been **a** by God to be 1Th 2:4
to present yourself **a** to God, 2Tm 2:15
For by it our ancestors were **a**. Heb 11:2
By this he was **a** as a righteous Heb 11:4
man, because God **a** his gifts, Heb 11:4
to his transformation he was **a**, Heb 11:5
All these were **a** through their Heb 11:39

APPROVES *(3)*
If the king **a**, let an order be Est 3:9
If the king **a** of me and if it Est 5:8
condemn himself by what he **a**. Rm 14:22

APPROVING *(1)*
I myself was standing by and **a**, Ac 22:20

APRICOT *(2)*
Like an **a** tree among the trees Sg 2:3
I awakened you under the **a** tree. Sg 8:5

APRICOTS *(2)*
refresh me with **a**, for I am Sg 2:5
fragrance of your breath like **a**. Sg 7:8

APRONS *(1)*
or work **a** that had touched Ac 19:12

AQUEDUCT *(1)*
position by the **a** of the upper 2Kg 18:17

AQUILA *(6)*
he found a Jewish man named **A**, Ac 18:2
Priscilla and **A** were with him. Ac 18:18
After Priscilla and **A** heard him, Ac 18:26
my greetings to Prisca and **A**, Rm 16:3
A and Priscilla greet you 1Co 16:19
Greet Prisca and **A**, and the 2Tm 4:19

AR *(6)*
to the site of **A** and lie along Nm 21:15
It consumed **A** of Moab, the lords Nm 21:28
I have given **A** as a possession Dt 2:9
cross the border of Moab at **A**. Dt 2:18
and the Moabites who live in **A**, Dt 2:29
A in Moab is devastated, Is 15:1

ARA *(1)*
Jephunneh, Pispa, and **A**. 1Ch 7:38

ARAB *(3)*
A, Dumah, Eshan, Jos 15:52
and Geshem the **A** heard ⌊about Neh 2:19
Geshem the **A**, and the rest Neh 6:1

ARABAH *(22)*
in the **A** opposite Suph, Dt 1:1
and their neighbors in the **A**, Dt 1:7
away from the **A** road and from Dt 2:8
A and Jordan are also borders Dt 3:17
as far as the Sea of the **A**, Dt 3:17
and all the **A** on the east side Dt 4:49
who live in the **A**, opposite Dt 11:30
downstream into the Sea of the **A** Jos 3:16
including all the **A** eastward: Jos 12:1
the **A** east of the Sea of Jos 12:3
Chinnereth to the Sea of the **A** Jos 12:3
near Maon in the **A** south of 1Sm 23:24
through the **A** all that night. 2Sm 2:29
by way of the **A** all night. 2Sm 4:7
as far as the Sea of the **A**, 2Kg 14:25
way along the route to the **A**, 2Kg 25:4
will be like a juniper in the **A**; Jr 17:6
left along the route to the **A**. Jr 39:4
a dry land, a wilderness, an **A**. Jr 50:12
way along the route to the **A**. Jr 52:7
region and goes down to the **A**. Ezk 47:8
of Hamath to the Brook of the **A**. Am 6:14

ARABIA *(5)*
oracle against **A**: You will camp Is 21:13
all the kings of **A**, and all the Jr 25:24
A and all the princes of Kedar Ezk 27:21
I went to **A** and came back to Gl 1:17
Mount Sinai in **A** and corresponds Gl 4:25

ARABIAN *(2)*
all the **A** kings and governors 1Kg 10:15
All the **A** kings and governors of 2Ch 9:14

ARABS *(6)*
and the **A** brought him flocks: 2Ch 17:11
and the **A** who live near 2Ch 21:16
come with the **A** to the camp had 2Ch 22:1
the **A** that live in Gur-baal, 2Ch 26:7
Tobiah, and the **A**, Ammonites, Neh 4:7
Cretans and **A**—we hear them Ac 2:11

ARAD *(5)*
When the Canaanite king of **A**, Nm 21:1
time the Canaanite king of **A**, Nm 33:40
of Hormah one the king of **A** one Jos 12:14
which was in the Negev of **A**. Jdg 1:16
Zebadiah, **A**, Eder, 1Ch 8:15

ARAH *(3)*
from **A** of the Sidonians to Aphek Jos 13:4
Ulla's sons: **A**, Hanniel, and 1Ch 7:39
of Shecaniah son of **A**, Neh 6:18

ARAH'S *(2)*
A descendants 775 Ezr 2:5
A descendants 652 Neh 7:10

ARAM *(70)*
(AKA RAM, SYRIA)
Asshur, Arpachshad, Lud, and **A**. Gn 10:22
Buz, Kemuel the father of **A**, Gn 22:21
Balak brought me from **A**; Nm 23:7
king of **A** of the Two Rivers, Jdg 3:8
king of **A** to him, Jdg 3:10
the gods of **A**, Sidon, and Moab, Jdg 10:6
garrisons in **A** of Damascus, 2Sm 8:6
vow when I lived in Geshur of **A**, 2Sm 15:8
to the kings of **A** through their 1Kg 10:29
He ruled over **A**, but he loathed 1Kg 11:25
of Hezion king of **A** who lived in 1Kg 15:18
to anoint Hazael as king over **A**. 1Kg 19:15
Ben-hadad king of **A** assembled 1Kg 20:1
Ben-hadad king of **A** escaped on a 1Kg 20:20
a great slaughter on **A**. 1Kg 20:21
the king of **A** will march up 1Kg 20:22
war between **A** and Israel. 1Kg 22:1
from the hand of the king of **A**?" 1Kg 22:3
the king of **A** had ordered his 1Kg 22:31
of the army for the king of **A**, 2Kg 5:1
the LORD had given victory to **A**. 2Kg 5:1
A had gone on raids and brought 2Kg 5:2
the king of **A** said, "Go and I 2Kg 5:5
master, ⌊the king of **A**⌋, goes 2Kg 5:18
When the king of **A** was waging 2Kg 6:8
king of **A** was enraged because 2Kg 6:11
Ben-hadad of **A** brought all his 2Kg 6:24
Ben-hadad king of **A** was sick, 2Kg 8:7
king of **A**, has sent me to 2Kg 8:9
that you will be king over **A**." 2Kg 8:13
Hazael king of **A** in 2Kg 8:28
guard against Hazael king of **A**. 2Kg 9:14
time Hazael king of **A** marched up 2Kg 12:17
sent ⌊them⌋ to Hazael king of **A**. 2Kg 12:18
of Hazael king of **A** and his son 2Kg 13:3
the king of **A** inflicted on 2Kg 13:4
the king of **A** had destroyed them 2Kg 13:7
the arrow of victory over **A**. 2Kg 13:17
have struck down **A** until you had 2Kg 13:19
only strike down **A** three times." 2Kg 13:19
king of **A** oppressed Israel 2Kg 13:22
King Hazael of **A** died, and his 2Kg 13:24
Rezin king of **A** and Pekah son 2Kg 15:37
Rezin king of **A** recovered Elath 2Kg 16:6
Elath for **A** and expelled 2Kg 16:6
of the king of **A** and of the king 2Kg 16:7
Lud, **A**, Uz, Hul, Gether 1Ch 1:17
But Geshur and **A** captured Jair's 1Ch 2:23
Ahi, Rohgah, Hubbah, and **A**. 1Ch 7:34
garrisons in **A** of Damascus, 1Ch 18:6
to the kings of **A** through their 2Ch 1:17
on the king of **A** and have not 2Ch 16:7
of the king of **A** has escaped 2Ch 16:7
the king of **A** had ordered his 2Ch 18:30
Hazael, king of **A**, in 2Ch 22:5
Ahaz over to the king of **A**. 2Ch 28:5
of the kings of **A** are helping 2Ch 28:23
Rezin king of **A**, along with Is 7:1
of David that **A** had occupied Is 7:2
Rezin of **A**, and the son Is 7:4
A, along with Ephraim and the Is 7:5
The head of **A** is Damascus, Is 7:8
A from the east and Philistia Is 9:12
remnant of **A** will be like the Is 17:3
the daughters of **A** and all those Ezk 16:57
A was your trading partner Ezk 27:16
Jacob fled to the land of **A**. Hs 12:12
The people of **A** will be exiled Am 1:5
Hezron, Hezron fathered **A**, Mt 1:3
A fathered Aminadab, Aminadab Mt 1:4

ARAM'S *(7)*
A sons: Uz, Hul, Gether, and Gn 10:23
Now the king of **A** servants said 1Kg 20:23
he fought against **A** King Hazael. 2Kg 8:29
he fought against **A** King Hazael. 2Kg 9:15
Then **A** King Rezin and Israel's 2Kg 16:5
and sent it to **A** King Ben-hadad, 2Ch 16:2
he fought against **A** King Hazael. 2Ch 22:6

ARAM-MAACAH *(1)*
Aram-naharaim, **A**, and Zobah. 1Ch 19:6

ARAM-NAHARAIM *(3)*
out for the town of Nahor, **A**. Gn 24:10
from Pethor in **A** was hired to Dt 23:4
chariots and horsemen from **A**, 1Ch 19:6

ARAMAIC *(4)*
speak to your servants in **A**, 2Kg 18:26
was written in **A** and translated. Ezr 4:7
speak to your servants in **A**, Is 36:11
to the king (**A** begins here): Dn 2:4

ARAMEAN *(19)*
(AKA SYRIAN)
of Bethuel the **A** from Gn 25:20
and sister of Laban the **A**. Gn 25:20
to Laban son of Bethuel the **A**, Gn 28:5

And Jacob deceived Laban the A, Gn 31:20
came to Laban the A in a dream Gn 31:24
My father was a wandering A. Dt 26:5
David struck down 22,000 A men. 2Sm 8:5
has let this A Naaman off 2Kg 5:20
The A raiders did not come into 2Kg 6:23
had caused the A camp to hear 2Kg 7:6
We went to the A camp and no one 2Kg 7:10
king sent them after the A army, 2Kg 7:14
out and plundered the A camp. 2Kg 7:16
LORD sent Chaldean, A, Moabite, 2Kg 24:2
sons through his A concubine: 1Ch 7:14
David struck down 22,000 A men. 1Ch 18:5
an A army went to war against 2Ch 24:23
Although the A army came with 2Ch 24:24
from the Chaldean and A armies. Jr 35:11

ARAMEANS *(47)*
When the A of Damascus came to 2Sm 8:5
the A became David's subjects 2Sm 8:6
from the A of Beth-rehob 2Sm 10:6
gate while the A of Zobah and 2Sm 10:8
formation to engage the A. 2Sm 10:9
"If the A are too strong for me," 2Sm 10:11
advanced to fight against the A, 2Sm 10:13
saw that the A had fled, 2Sm 10:14
the A saw that they had been 2Sm 10:15
to bring the A who were across 2Sm 10:16
Then the A lined up in formation 2Sm 10:17
But the A fled before Israel, 2Sm 10:18
the A were afraid to ever help 2Sm 10:19
So the A fled and Israel pursued 1Kg 20:20
mobilized the A and went up to 1Kg 20:26
the A filled the landscape. 1Kg 20:27
'Because the A have said: 1Kg 20:28
Israelites struck down the A— 1Kg 20:29
will gore the A with these until 1Kg 22:11
up in his chariot facing the A. 1Kg 22:35
for the A are going down there." 2Kg 6:9
When the A came against him, 2Kg 6:18
The A had said to each other, 2Kg 7:6
you what the A have done to us. 2Kg 7:12
equipment the A had thrown off 2Kg 7:15
and the A wounded Joram. 2Kg 8:28
wounds that the A had inflicted 2Kg 8:29
wounds that the A had inflicted 2Kg 9:15
escaped from the power of the A. 2Kg 13:5
strike down the A in Aphek until 2Kg 13:17
Then the A came to Elath, and 2Kg 16:6
When the A of Damascus came to 1Ch 18:5
the A became David's subjects 1Ch 18:6
formation to engage the A. 1Ch 19:10
"If the A are too strong for me," 1Ch 19:12
him approached the A for battle, 1Ch 19:14
saw that the A had fled, 1Ch 19:15
When the A realized that they 1Ch 19:16
bring out the A who were across 1Ch 19:16
up to engage the A in battle, 1Ch 19:17
But the A fled before Israel, 1Ch 19:18
the A were never willing to help 1Ch 19:19
will gore the A with these until 2Ch 18:10
facing the A until evening. 2Ch 18:34
The A wounded Joram, 2Ch 22:5
When the A saw that Joash had 2Ch 24:25
Caphtor, and the A from Kir? Am 9:7

ARAMEANS' *(2)*
Let's go to the A camp. 2Kg 7:4
at twilight to go to the A camp. 2Kg 7:5

ARAN *(2)*
are Dishan's sons: Uz and A. Gn 36:28
Jaakan. Dishan's sons: Uz and A. 1Ch 1:42

ARARAT *(4)*
month, on the mountains of A. Gn 8:4
and escaped to the land of A. 2Kg 19:37
and escaped to the land of A. Is 37:38
against her—A, Minni, and Jr 51:27

ARAUNAH *(7)*
(AKA ORNAN)
floor of A the Jebusite. 2Sm 24:16
floor of A the Jebusite." 2Sm 24:18
A looked down and saw the king 2Sm 24:20
A said, "Why has my lord the 2Sm 24:21
A said to David, "My lord the 2Sm 24:22
A gives everything here to the 2Sm 24:23
king answered A, "No, I insist 2Sm 24:24

ARBA *(3)*
A was the greatest man among the Jos 14:15
A was the father of Anak). Jos 15:13
A was the father of Anak. Jos 21:11

ARBATHITE *(2)*
Abi-albon the A, Azmaveth the 2Sm 23:31
the wadis of Gaash, Abiel the A, 1Ch 11:32

ARBITE *(1)*
the Carmelite, Paarai the A, 2Sm 23:35

ARBITRATE *(2)*
someone might a between a man Jb 16:21
will be able to a between his 1Co 6:5

ARBITRATION *(2)*
and provide a for many peoples. Is 2:4
and provide a for strong nations Mc 4:3

ARBITRATOR *(1)*
Me a judge or a over you?" Lk 12:14

ARCHANGEL *(1)*
Yet Michael the a, when he was Jd 9

ARCHANGEL'S *(1)*
shout, with the a voice, and 1Th 4:16

ARCHELAUS *(1)*
he heard that A was ruling over Mt 2:22

ARCHER *(5)*
the wilderness and became an a. Gn 21:20
like an a who wounds everyone. Pr 26:10
sound of the horseman and the a. Jr 4:29
Don't let the a string his bow; Jr 51:3
a will not stand ⌊his ground⌋ Am 2:15

ARCHERS *(14)*
The a attacked him, shot at him, Gn 49:23
the a caught up with him and 1Sm 31:3
the a shot down on your soldiers 2Sm 11:24
Ulam's sons were warriors and a. 1Ch 8:40
the a found him and severely 1Ch 10:3
They were a who, using either 1Ch 12:2
The a shot King Josiah, and he 2Ch 35:23
His a surround me. He pierces my Jb 16:13
that they can flee before the a. Ps 60:4
The Ephraimite a turned back on Ps 78:9
remaining Kedarite a will be few Is 21:17
Lud (who are a), Tubal, Javan, Is 66:19
around Babylon, all you a! Jr 50:14
Summon the a to Babylon, all who Jr 50:29

ARCHIPPUS *(2)*
tell A, "Pay attention to the Col 4:17
our sister, to A our fellow Phm 2

ARCHITE *(5)*
was Hushai the A with his robe 2Sm 15:32
Hushai the A came to Absalom, 2Sm 16:16
Summon Hushai the A also. 2Sm 17:5
of Hushai the A is better than 2Sm 17:14
Hushai the A was the king's 1Ch 27:33

ARCHITECT *(1)*
whose a and builder is God. Heb 11:10

ARCHITES *(1)*
the border of the A by Ataroth. Jos 16:2

ARCHIVES *(2)*
of the royal a in Babylon be Ezr 5:17
the library of Babylon in the a. Ezr 6:1

ARD *(3)*
(AKA ADDAR)
Rosh, Muppim, Huppim, and A. Gn 46:21
descendants ⌊from⌋ A and Naaman: Nm 26:40
the Ardite clan ⌊from⌋ A; Nm 26:40

ARDENT *(1)*
a love is as unrelenting as Sg 8:6

ARDITE *(1)*
the A clan ⌊from⌋ Ard; Nm 26:40

ARDON *(1)*
Jesher, Shobab, and A. 1Ch 2:18

ARE *(3917)*
(See pp. xi-xii.)

AREA *(42)*
of the young women of the a. Gn 34:1
illuminate the a in front of it. Ex 25:37
minister in the sanctuary ⌊a⌋, Ex 28:43
sin offering in the sanctuary a? Lv 10:17
eaten it in the sanctuary ⌊a⌋, Lv 10:18
but not shave the scaly a. Lv 13:33
in the sanctuary a where the sin Lv 14:13
to the LORD in the sanctuary a. Nm 28:7
and Gadites ⌊the a extending⌋ Dt 3:12
and Gadites ⌊the a extending⌋ Dt 3:16
and clear ⌊an a⌋ for yourselves Jos 17:15
the valley a have iron chariots Jos 17:16
Samuel in the gate a and asked, 1Sm 9:18
Hebrews from the a who had 1Sm 14:21
spread out over the entire a, 1Sm 30:16
the surrounding a made repairs. Neh 3:22
and from the a around Jerusalem Jr 17:26
them and the a around My hill Ezk 34:26
a of free space was eight and Ezk 41:11
out from the holy a to the outer Ezk 42:14
they approach the public a." Ezk 42:14
In this a there will be a square Ezk 45:2
measure off an a eight and Ezk 45:3
will be a holy a of the land to Ezk 45:4
well as a holy a for the Ezk 45:4
will be ⌊another a⌋ eight and Ezk 45:5
must set aside an a one and Ezk 45:6
will have the a on each side Ezk 45:7
will have an a⌋ eight and Ezk 48:13
The remaining ⌊a⌋, one and Ezk 48:15
city property as a square ⌊a⌋. Ezk 48:20
The remaining ⌊a⌋ on both sides Ezk 48:21
the middle of the a belonging to Ezk 48:22
the a between the territory of Ezk 48:22
a planting a for a vineyard. Mc 1:6
spread throughout that whole a. Mt 9:26
Him throughout that whole a. Mt 9:31
withdrew to the a of Tyre and Mt 15:21
Now in the a around that place Ac 28:7
measure of the a ⌊of ministry⌋ 2Co 10:13
our a ⌊of ministry⌋ will be 2Co 10:15
someone else's a ⌊of ministry⌋. 2Co 10:16

AREAS *(7)*
its outlying a will be yours. Jos 17:18
Judah and in the a surrounding 2Kg 23:5
the wall, at the vulnerable a. Neh 4:13
cultivated a of the Nile will Is 19:7
in the a surrounding Jerusalem, Jr 32:44
All four corner a had the same Ezk 46:22
through those a and exhorted Ac 20:2

ARELI *(2)*
Shuni, Ezbon, Eri, Arodi, and A. Gn 46:16
the Arelite clan from A. Nm 26:17

ARELITE *(1)*
the A clan from Areli. Nm 26:17

AREN'T *(39)*
(See pp. xi-xii.)

AREOPAGITE *(1)*
among whom were Dionysius the A Ac 17:34

AREOPAGUS *(2)*
him and brought him to the A, Ac 17:19
in the middle of the A and said: Ac 17:22

ARETAS *(1)*
under King A guarded the city 2Co 11:32

ARGOB *(5)*
entire region of A, the kingdom Dt 3:4
entire region of A, the whole Dt 3:13
entire region of A as far as the Dt 3:14
and he had the region of A, 1Kg 4:13
down, as well as A and Arieh, 2Kg 15:25

ARGUE *(16)*
to them, "Don't a on the way." Gn 45:24
Almighty and a my case before Jb 13:3
to Him or a the case in His Jb 13:8
Should he a with useless talk or Jb 15:3
The LORD rises to a the case and Is 3:13
let us a our case together. Is 43:26
let no one a, for My case is Hs 4:4
and He will a it against Israel. Mc 6:2
He will not a or shout, and no Mt 12:19
They began to a among Mt 21:25
they began to a with one another Mk 1:27
out and began to a with Him, Mk 8:11
began to a among themselves: Mk 11:31
they began to a among themselves Lk 22:23
but don't a about doubtful Rm 14:1
if anyone wants to a about this, 1Co 11:16

ARGUED *(6)*
And they a with him violently. Jdg 8:1
So they a before the king. 1Kg 3:22
the Jews a among themselves, Jn 6:52
circumcision a with him, Ac 11:2
Stoic philosophers a with him. Ac 17:18
party got up and a vehemently: Ac 23:9

ARGUES *(3)*
Let him who a with God give an Jb 40:2

the one who a with his Maker— Is 45:9
LORD's rage until He a my case Mc 7:9

ARGUING *(6)*
all the tribes of Israel were a: 2Sm 19:9
"What are you a with them about?" Mk 9:16
were you a about on the way? Mk 9:33
they had been a with one another Mk 9:34
they were discussing and a, Lk 24:15
without grumbling and a, Php 2:14

ARGUMENT *(6)*
Hear now my a, and listen to my Jb 13:6
has not directed his a to me, Jb 32:14
Then an a started among them Lk 9:46
them in serious a and debate, Ac 15:2
say? I use a human a: Is God Rm 3:5
holy hands without anger or a. 1Tm 2:8

ARGUMENTS *(11)*
Him or choose my a against Him? Jb 9:14
Him and fill my mouth with a. Jb 23:4
not one of you refuted his a. Jb 32:12
not respond to him with your a. Jb 32:14
For my a are without flaw; Jb 36:4
hear and has no a in his mouth. Ps 38:14
"Present your a," says Jacob's Is 41:21
of strongholds. We demolish a 2Co 10:4
no one deceive you with empty a, Eph 5:6
deceive you with persuasive a. Col 2:4
in disputes and a over words. 1Tm 6:4

ARID *(3)*
of a massive rock in an a land. Is 32:2
A wolf from an a plain will Jr 5:6
a dry and a land, a land where Jr 51:43

ARIDAI *(1)*
Arisai, A, and Vaizatha. Est 9:9

ARIDATHA *(1)*
Poratha, Adalia, A, Est 9:8

ARIEH *(1)*
as Argob and A, in Samaria at 2Kg 15:25

ARIEL *(8)*
(AKA JERUSALEM)
killed two sons of A of Moab, 2Sm 23:20
killed two ⌊sons of⌋ A of Moab, 1Ch 11:22
Eliezer, A, Shemaiah, Elnathan, Ezr 8:16
Woe to A, Ariel, the city where Is 29:1
Woe to Ariel, A, the city where Is 29:1
I will oppress A, and there will Is 29:2
and she will be to Me like an A. Is 29:2
going out to battle against A— Is 29:7

ARIMATHEA *(4)*
a rich man from A named Joseph Mt 27:57
Joseph of A, a prominent member Mk 15:43
was from A, a Judean town, and Lk 23:51
this, Joseph of A, who was a Jn 19:38

ARIOCH *(7)*
of Shinar, A king of Ellasar Gn 14:1
of Shinar, and A king of Ellasar Gn 14:9
with tact and discretion to A, Dn 2:14
He asked A, the king's officer, Dn 2:15
Then A explained the situation Dn 2:15
Therefore Daniel went to A, Dn 2:24
Then A quickly brought Daniel Dn 2:25

ARISAI *(1)*
Parmashta, A, Aridai, and Est 9:9

ARISE *(23)*
would say: A, LORD! Let Your Nm 10:35
a scepter will a from Israel. Nm 24:17
A Barak, and take hold of your Jdg 5:12
A, LORD God, ⌊come⌋ to Your 2Ch 6:41
A, God, defend Your cause! Ps 74:22
You will a and have compassion Ps 102:13
A, LORD, come to Your resting Ps 132:8
calls to me: A, my darling. Come Sg 2:10
their fragrance. A, my darling. Sg 2:13
I will a now and go about the Sg 3:2
A, shine, for your light has Is 60:1
A, cry out in the night, from Lm 2:19
thoughts that a in your mind. Ezk 11:5
thoughts will a in your mind, Ezk 38:10
there will a another kingdom, Dn 2:39
more kings will a in Persia, Dn 11:2
Then a warrior king will a; Dn 11:3
place one will a who will send Dn 11:20
place a despised person will a; Dn 11:21
Won't your creditors suddenly a, Hab 2:7
prophets will a and perform Mt 24:24
why do doubts a in your hearts? Lk 24:38
another priest to a in the order Heb 7:11

ARISEN *(1)*
No prophet has a again in Israel Dt 34:10

ARISES *(6)*
who has dreams a among you Dt 13:1
God a. His enemies scatter, and Ps 68:1
that no prophet a from Galilee." Jn 7:52
priest like Melchizedek a, Heb 7:15
the fiery ordeal a among you to 1Pt 4:12
morning star a in your hearts. 2Pt 1:19

ARISING *(1)*
Lord, when a, You will despise Ps 73:20

ARISTARCHUS *(5)*
dragging along Gaius and A, Ac 19:29
A and Secundus from Thessalonica, Ac 20:4
A, a Macedonian of Thessalonica, Ac 27:2
A, my fellow prisoner, greets Col 4:10
Mark, A, Demas, and Luke, my Phm 24

ARISTOBULUS *(1)*
belong to the household of A. Rm 16:10

ARK *(223)*
yourself an a of gofer wood. Gn 6:14
Make rooms in the a, and cover Gn 6:14
The a will be 450 feet long, Gn 6:15
the sides of the a⌋ to within 18 Gn 6:16
put a door in the side of the a. Gn 6:16
will enter the a with your sons, Gn 6:18
to bring into the a two of every Gn 6:19
Noah, "Enter the a, you and all Gn 7:1
wives entered the a because of Gn 7:7
entered the a with Noah, just as Gn 7:9
wives entered the a with him. Gn 7:13
in it entered the a with Noah. Gn 7:15
lifted up the a so that it rose Gn 7:17
and the a floated on the surface Gn 7:18
that were with him in the a. Gn 7:23
that were with him in the a. Gn 8:1
a came to rest in the seventh Gn 8:4
window of the a that he had made Gn 8:6
to him in the a because water Gn 8:9
her into the a to himself. Gn 8:9
out the dove from the a again. Gn 8:10
out of the a, you, your wife Gn 8:16
out of the a by their groups Gn 8:19
earth that came out of the a. Gn 9:10
who came out of the a were Shem, Gn 9:18
are to make an a of acacia wood, Ex 25:10
the sides of the a in order to Ex 25:14
order to carry the a with them. Ex 25:14
to remain in the rings of the a; Ex 25:15
that I will give you into the a. Ex 25:16
seat on top of the a and put the Ex 25:21
that I will give you into the a. Ex 25:21
are over the a of the testimony Ex 25:22
and bring the a of the testimony Ex 26:33
seat on the a of the testimony Ex 26:34
the veil by the a of the Ex 30:6
of meeting, the a of the Ex 30:26
of meeting, the a of the Ex 31:7
the a with its poles, the mercy Ex 35:12
made the a of acacia wood, Ex 37:1
the sides of the a for carrying Ex 37:5
of the ark for carrying the a. Ex 37:5
the a of the testimony with its Ex 39:35
the a of the testimony there, Ex 40:3
screen off the a with the veil. Ex 40:3
in front of the a of the Ex 40:5
and placed ⌊it⌋ in the a, Ex 40:20
and attached the poles to the a. Ex 40:20
the mercy seat on top of the a. Ex 40:20
He brought the a into the Ex 40:21
off the a of the testimony Ex 40:21
seat on the a or else he will Lv 16:2
Their duties involved the a, Nm 3:31
and cover the a of the testimony Nm 4:5
that was on the a of the Nm 7:89
the a of the LORD's covenant Nm 10:33
Whenever the a set out, Moses Nm 10:35
even though the a of the LORD's Nm 14:44
mountain and make a wooden a. Dt 10:1
you are to place them in the a.' Dt 10:2
So I made an a of acacia wood, Dt 10:3
the tablets in the a I had made. Dt 10:5
to carry the a of the LORD's Dt 10:8
who carried the a of the LORD's Dt 31:9
who carried the a of the LORD's Dt 31:25
it beside the a of the covenant Dt 31:26
you see the a of the covenant Jos 3:3
between yourselves and the a. Jos 3:4
Take the a of the covenant and Jos 3:6
carried the a of the covenant Jos 3:6
the a of the covenant: Jos 3:8
when the a of the covenant of Jos 3:11
who carry the a of the LORD, Jos 3:13
carried the a of the covenant Jos 3:14
carrying the a reached the Jos 3:15
carrying the a of the LORD's Jos 3:17
across to the a of the LORD your Jos 4:5
in front of the a of the LORD's Jos 4:7
carried the a of the covenant Jos 4:9
the a continued standing Jos 4:10
priests with the a of the LORD Jos 4:11
who carry the a of the testimony Jos 4:16
carrying the a of the LORD's Jos 4:18
trumpets in front of the a. Jos 6:4
Take up the a of the covenant Jos 6:6
in front of the a of the LORD." Jos 6:6
go ahead of the a of the LORD." Jos 6:7
the a of the LORD's covenant Jos 6:8
rear guard went behind the a. Jos 6:9
So the a of the LORD was carried Jos 6:11
priests took the a of the LORD, Jos 6:12
in front of the a of the LORD. Jos 6:13
went behind the a of the LORD. Jos 6:13
fell before the a of the LORD Jos 7:6
side of the a of the LORD's Jos 8:33
the a of the covenant of God was Jdg 20:27
LORD where the a of God was 1Sm 3:3
Let's bring the a of the LORD's 1Sm 4:3
bring back the a of the covenant 1Sm 4:4
there with the a of the covenant 1Sm 4:4
When the a of the covenant of 1Sm 4:5
that the a of the LORD had 1Sm 4:6
The a of God was captured, 1Sm 4:11
was anxious about the a of God. 1Sm 4:13
the a of God has been captured. 1Sm 4:17
When he mentioned the a of God, 1Sm 4:18
capture of God's a and the 1Sm 4:19
capture of the a of God and to 1Sm 4:21
because the a of God has been 1Sm 4:22
had captured the a of God, 1Sm 5:1
ground before the a of the LORD. 1Sm 5:3
ground before the a of the LORD. 1Sm 5:4
The a of Israel's God must not 1Sm 5:7
do with the a of Israel's God? 1Sm 5:8
The a of Israel's God should 1Sm 5:8
the men of Ashdod moved the a. 1Sm 5:8
then sent the a of God to Ekron, 1Sm 5:10
moved the a of Israel's God 1Sm 5:10
Send the a of Israel's God away. 1Sm 5:11
When the a of the LORD had been 1Sm 6:1
we do with the a of the LORD? 1Sm 6:2
you send the a of Israel's God 1Sm 6:3
Take the a of the LORD, place it 1Sm 6:8
Then they put the a of the LORD 1Sm 6:11
they looked up and saw the a, 1Sm 6:13
removed the a of the LORD, 1Sm 6:15
on which the a of the LORD was 1Sm 6:18
looked inside the a of the LORD. 1Sm 6:19
should the a go to from here? 1Sm 6:20
have returned the a of the LORD. 1Sm 6:21
came for the a of the LORD and 1Sm 7:1
passed since the a had been 1Sm 7:2
Bring the a of God," for it 1Sm 14:18
set out to bring the a of God 2Sm 6:2
The a is called by the Name, 2Sm 6:2
They set the a of God on a new 2Sm 6:3
brought it with the a of God 2Sm 6:4
Ahio walked in front of the a. 2Sm 6:4
out to the a of God and took 2Sm 6:6
died there next to the a of God. 2Sm 6:7
How can the a of the LORD ever 2Sm 6:9
to move the a of the LORD to 2Sm 6:10
a of the LORD remained in his 2Sm 6:11
to him because of the a of God." 2Sm 6:12
and had the a of God brought 2Sm 6:12
those carrying the a of the LORD 2Sm 6:13
bringing up the a of the LORD 2Sm 6:15
the a of the LORD was entering 2Sm 6:16
They brought the a of the LORD 2Sm 6:17
house while the a of God sits 2Sm 7:2
David, "The a, Israel, and Judah 2Sm 11:11
carrying the a of the covenant 2Sm 15:24
They set the a of God down, 2Sm 15:24

Return the **a** of God to the city. 2Sm 15:25
returned the **a** of God to 2Sm 15:29
carried the **a** of the Lord GOD 1Kg 2:26
stood before the **a** of the Lord's 1Kg 3:15
to put the **a** of the LORD's 1Kg 6:19
to bring the **a** of the LORD's 1Kg 8:1
and the priests picked up the **a**. 1Kg 8:3
brought the **a** of the LORD, 1Kg 8:4
were with him in front of the **a**, 1Kg 8:5
brought the **a** of the LORD's 1Kg 8:6
wings over the place of the **a**, 1Kg 8:7
covered the **a** and its poles 1Kg 8:7
was in the **a** except the two 1Kg 8:9
a place there for the **a**, 1Kg 8:21
temple after the **a** came to rest 1Ch 6:31
us bring back the **a** of our God, 1Ch 13:3
to bring the **a** of God from 1Ch 13:5
to take from there the **a** of God, 1Ch 13:6
they set the **a** of God on a new 1Ch 13:7
Uzzah reached out to hold the **a**, 1Ch 13:9
he had reached out to the **a**. 1Ch 13:10
ever bring the **a** of God to me?" 1Ch 13:12
did not move the **a** of God home 1Ch 13:13
The **a** of God remained with 1Ch 13:14
a place for the **a** of God and 1Ch 15:1
Levites may carry the **a** of God, 1Ch 15:2
them to carry the **a** of the LORD 1Ch 15:2
to bring the **a** of the LORD to 1Ch 15:3
may bring the **a** of the LORD God 1Ch 15:12
bring up the **a** of the LORD God 1Ch 15:14
carried the **a** of God the way 1Ch 15:15
to be gatekeepers for the **a**. 1Ch 15:23
trumpets before the **a** of God. 1Ch 15:24
to be gatekeepers for the **a**. 1Ch 15:24
to bring the **a** of the covenant 1Ch 15:25
carrying the **a** of the covenant 1Ch 15:26
Levites who were carrying the **a**, 1Ch 15:27
bringing the **a** of the covenant 1Ch 15:28
As the **a** of the covenant of the 1Ch 15:29
They brought the **a** of God and 1Ch 16:1
before the **a** of the LORD, 1Ch 16:4
before the **a** of the covenant 1Ch 16:6
there before the **a** of the LORD's 1Ch 16:37
before the **a** according to 1Ch 16:37
house while the **a** of the LORD's 1Ch 17:1
may bring the **a** of the LORD's 1Ch 22:19
place for the **a** of the LORD's 1Ch 28:2
and cover the **a** of the LORD's 1Ch 28:18
David had brought the **a** of God 2Ch 1:4
to bring the **a** of the covenant 2Ch 5:2
and the Levites picked up the **a**. 2Ch 5:4
They brought up the **a**, the tent 2Ch 5:5
in front of the **a** sacrificing 2Ch 5:6
brought the **a** of the LORD's 2Ch 5:7
the place of the **a** so that the 2Ch 5:8
cover above the **a** and its poles. 2Ch 5:8
was in the **a** except the two 2Ch 5:10
have put the **a** there, where the 2Ch 6:11
You and the **a** ⌊that shows⌋ Your 2Ch 6:41
to which the **a** of the LORD has 2Ch 8:11
Put the holy **a** in the temple 2Ch 35:3
heard of ⌊the **a**⌋ in Ephrathah; Ps 132:6
You and the **a** ⌊that shows⌋ Your Ps 132:8
The **a** of the LORD's covenant. Jr 3:16
the day Noah boarded the **a**. Mt 24:38
the day Noah boarded the **a**, Lk 17:27
and the **a** of the covenant Heb 9:4
built an **a** to deliver his Heb 11:7
of Noah while an **a** was being 1Pt 3:20
and the **a** of His covenant Rv 11:19

ARK'S *(1)*

Noah removed the **a** cover and saw Gn 8:13

ARKITES *(2)*

the Hivites, the **A**, the Sinites, Gn 10:17
Hivites, **A**, Sinites, 1Ch 1:15

ARM *(55)*

an outstretched **a** and great acts Ex 6:6
of Your powerful **a** until Your Ex 15:16
But we will **a** ourselves and be Nm 32:17
if you **a** yourselves for battle Nm 32:20
hand and an outstretched **a**, Dt 4:34
hand and an outstretched **a**. Dt 5:15
strong hand and outstretched **a**, Dt 7:19
great power and outstretched **a**. Dt 9:29
strong hand, and outstretched **a**; Dt 11:2
hand and an outstretched **a**, Dt 26:8
tears off an **a** or even a head. Dt 33:20
the armband that was on his **a**, 2Sm 1:10
outstretched **a**, and will come 1Kg 8:42
power and an outstretched **a**. 2Kg 17:36
mighty hand and outstretched **a**: 2Ch 6:32
delivered the **a** that is weak! Jb 26:2
and my **a** be pulled from its Jb 31:22
help from the **a** of the mighty. Jb 35:9
and the **a** raised ⌊in violence⌋ Jb 38:15
Do you have an **a** like God's? Jb 40:9
Break the **a** of the wicked and Ps 10:15
their **a** did not bring them Ps 44:3
hand, Your **a**, and the light Ps 44:3
enemies with Your powerful **a**. Ps 89:10
You have a mighty **a**; Your hand Ps 89:13
and My **a** will strengthen him. Ps 89:21
hand and holy **a** have won Him Ps 98:1
strong hand and outstretched **a**. Ps 136:12
your heart, as a seal on your **a**. Sg 8:6
one eats the flesh of his own **a**. Is 9:20
his **a** harvesting the heads of Is 17:5
and reveal His **a** striking in Is 30:30
and works it with his strong **a**. Is 44:12
and His **a** ⌊will be against⌋ the Is 48:14
displayed His holy **a** in the Is 52:10
And who has the **a** of the LORD Is 53:1
so His own **a** brought salvation, Is 59:16
His right hand and His strong **a**: Is 62:8
so My **a** accomplished victory for Is 63:5
His glorious **a** at Moses' right Is 63:12
hand and a mighty **a**, Jr 21:5
strength and outstretched **a**, Jr 27:5
and with Your outstretched **a**. Jr 32:17
hand and an outstretched **a**, Jr 32:21
off; his **a** is shattered." Jr 48:25
of Jerusalem with your **a** bared, Ezk 4:7
an outstretched **a**, and outpoured Ezk 20:33
an outstretched **a**, and outpoured Ezk 20:34
broken the **a** of Pharaoh king Ezk 30:21
sword strike his **a** and his right Zch 11:17
May his **a** wither away and his Zch 11:17
done a mighty deed with His **a**; Lk 1:51
And who has the **a** of the Lord Jn 12:38
them out of it with a mighty **a**. Ac 13:17
a yourselves also with the same 1Pt 4:1

ARMAGEDON *(1)*

at the place called in Hebrew **A**. Rv 16:16

ARMBAND *(1)*

head and the **a** that was on his 2Sm 1:10

ARMED *(22)*

every one of your **a** men crosses Nm 32:21
and have the **a** troops go ahead Jos 6:7
a troops went in front of the Jos 6:9
the **a** troops went in front of Jos 6:13
Zorah and Eshtaol **a** with weapons Jdg 18:11
a with their weapons of war. Jdg 18:16
with the 600 men **a** with weapons Jdg 18:17
400,000 **a** foot soldiers. Jdg 20:2
rallied 26,000 **a** men from their Jdg 20:15
rallied 400,000 **a** men, every one Jdg 20:17
on the field; all were **a** men. Jdg 20:25
men of Benjamin; all were **a** men. Jdg 20:35
died that day were 25,000 **a** men; Jdg 20:46
touches them must be **a** with iron 2Sm 23:7
numbers of the **a** troops who came 1Ch 12:23
6,800 **a** troops bearing shields 1Ch 12:24
200,000 with him **a** with bow and 2Ch 17:17
out in front of the **a** forces, 2Ch 20:21
with all his **a** forces besieged 2Ch 32:9
huge company **a** with shields and Ezk 38:4
a large number of **a** forces. Dn 11:10
strong man, fully **a**, guards his Lk 11:21

ARMIES *(27)*

advanced with all their **a**, Jos 10:5
They went out with all their **a**— Jos 11:4
should defy the **a** of the living 1Sm 17:26
has defied the **a** of the living 1Sm 17:36
God of Israel's **a**—you have 1Sm 17:45
commanders of his **a** against the 1Kg 15:20
all the commanders of the **a**— 2Kg 25:23
commanders of his **a** to the 2Ch 16:4
You do not march out with our **a**. Ps 44:9
You do not march out with our **a**. Ps 60:10
The kings of the **a** flee— Ps 68:12
LORD, all His **a**, His servants Ps 103:21
You do not march out with our **a**. Ps 108:11
furious with all their **a**. Is 34:2
from the Chaldean and Aramean **a**. Jr 35:11
of the **a** in the field— Jr 40:7
of the **a** in the field came Jr 40:13
of the **a** with him heard Jr 41:11
commanders of the **a** with him Jr 41:16
all the commanders of the **a**, Jr 42:1
of the **a** who were with him Jr 42:8
commanders of the **a** did not obey Jr 43:4
of the **a** took the whole Jr 43:5
see Jerusalem surrounded by **a**, Lk 21:20
and put foreign **a** to flight. Heb 11:34
The **a** that were in heaven Rv 19:14
and their **a** gathered together to Rv 19:19

ARMLETS *(1)*

each man found—**a**, bracelets, Nm 31:50

ARMONI *(1)*

the king took **A** and Mephibosheth 2Sm 21:8

ARMOR *(23)*

that for body **a** so that it does Ex 28:32
that for body **a** with a collar Ex 39:23
bronze scale **a** that weighed 125 1Sm 17:5
There was bronze **a** on his shins, 1Sm 17:6
head and had him put on **a**. 1Sm 17:38
stripped off his **a**, and sent 1Sm 31:9
they put his **a** in the temple 1Sm 31:10
pounds and who wore new **a**, 2Sm 21:16
who puts on his **a** boast like the 1Kg 20:11
through the joints of his **a**. 1Kg 22:34
his head, took his **a**, and sent 1Ch 10:9
they put his **a** in the temple 1Ch 10:10
through the joints of his **a**. 2Ch 18:33
spears, helmets, **a**, bows and 2Ch 26:14
spears, shields, bows, and **a**. Neh 4:16
penetrate his double layer of **a**? Jb 41:13
on! Polish the lances; put on **a**! Jr 46:4
don't let him put on his **a**. Jr 51:3
and put on the **a** of light. Rm 13:12
Put on the full **a** of God so that Eph 6:11
must take up the full **a** of God, Eph 6:13
like **a** on your chest, Eph 6:14
and put the **a** of faith and love 1Th 5:8

ARMOR-BEARER *(19)*

called his **a** and said to him, Jdg 9:54
So his **a** thrust him through, Jdg 9:54
His **a** responded, "Do what is in 1Sm 14:7
called to Jonathan and his **a**. 1Sm 14:12
told his **a**, "for the LORD 1Sm 14:12
and feet, with his **a** behind him. 1Sm 14:13
and his **a** followed and finished 1Sm 14:13
Jonathan and his **a** struck down 1Sm 14:14
Jonathan and his **a** were gone. 1Sm 14:17
greatly, and David became his **a**. 1Sm 16:21
Saul said to his **a**, "Draw your 1Sm 31:4
But his **a** would not do it 1Sm 31:4
When his **a** saw that Saul was 1Sm 31:5
three sons, his **a**, and all his 1Sm 31:6
the **a** for Joab son of Zeruiah, 2Sm 23:37
Saul said to his **a**, "Draw your 1Ch 10:4
But his **a** wouldn't do it 1Ch 10:4
When his **a** saw that Saul was 1Ch 10:5
the **a** for Joab son of Zeruiah, 1Ch 11:39

ARMOR-BEARERS *(1)*

who were Joab's **a** surrounded 2Sm 18:15

ARMORY *(6)*

back to the royal escorts' **a**. 1Kg 14:28
oil—and his **a**, and everything 2Kg 20:13
back to the royal escorts' **a**. 2Ch 12:11
ascent to the **a** at the Angle. Neh 3:19
and all his **a**, and everything Is 39:2
LORD opened His **a** and brought Jr 50:25

ARMPITS *(1)*

between your **a** and the ropes." Jr 38:12

ARMRESTS *(4)*

a on either side of the seat, 1Kg 10:19
two lions standing beside the **a**. 1Kg 10:19
a on either side of the seat, 2Ch 9:18
two lions standing beside the **a**. 2Ch 9:18

ARMS *(44)*

slave in your **a**, and ever since Gn 16:5
him, threw his **a** around him, Gn 33:4
threw his **a** around Benjamin Gn 45:14
to him, threw his **a** around him, Gn 46:29
and his strong **a** were made agile Gn 49:24
are the everlasting **a**. Dt 33:27
that were on his **a** became like Jdg 15:14
ropes off his **a** like a thread. Jdg 16:12
it slept in his **a**, and it was 2Sm 12:3
your master's wives into your **a**, 2Sm 12:8

my **a** can bend a bow of bronze. 2Sm 22:35
she put her dead son in my **a**. 1Kg 3:20
So he took him from her **a**, 1Kg 17:19
who could bear **a**, from the 2Kg 3:21
you will have a son in your **a**." 2Kg 4:16
my **a** can bend a bow of bronze. Ps 18:34
For the **a** of the wicked will be Ps 37:17
reaper or the **a** of the one who Ps 129:7
little folding of the **a** to rest, Pr 6:10
little folding of the **a** to rest, Pr 24:33
reveals that her **a** are strong. Pr 31:17
fool folds his **a** and consumes Ec 4:5
His **a** are rods of gold set with Sg 5:14
spread out his **a** in the middle Is 25:11
spreads out ⌊his **a**⌋ to swim. Is 25:11
the lambs in His **a** and carries Is 40:11
will bring your sons in their **a**, Is 49:22
and My **a** will bring justice to Is 51:5
away in the **a** of their mothers Lm 2:12
I will tear them from your **a**. Ezk 13:20
will break his **a**, both the Ezk 30:22
strengthen the **a** of Babylon's Ezk 30:24
I will break the **a** of Pharaoh, Ezk 30:24
strengthen the **a** of Babylon's Ezk 30:25
but Pharaoh's **a** will fall. Ezk 30:25
its chest and **a** were silver, Dn 2:32
his **a** and feet like the gleam of Dn 10:6
and strengthened their **a**, Hs 7:15
them in My **a**, but they never Hs 11:3
the woman who lies in your **a**. Mc 7:5
him in His **a**, He said to them Mk 9:36
After taking them in His **a**, Mk 10:16
Simeon took Him up in his **a**, Lk 2:28
threw his **a** around his neck, Lk 15:20

ARMY *(210)*

Phicol the commander of his **a**, Gn 21:22
commander of his **a**, left and Gn 21:32
Phicol the commander of his **a**. Gn 26:26
means of Pharaoh and all his **a**, Ex 14:4
and his **a**—chased after Ex 14:9
Pharaoh, all his **a**, and his Ex 14:17
the entire **a** of Pharaoh, that Ex 14:28
chariots and his **a** into the sea; Ex 15:4
Amalek and his **a** with the sword. Ex 17:13
who can serve in Israel's **a**. Nm 1:3
who could serve in the **a**, Nm 1:20
who could serve in the **a**, Nm 1:22
who could serve in the **a**, Nm 1:24
who could serve in the **a**, Nm 1:26
who could serve in the **a**, Nm 1:28
who could serve in the **a**, Nm 1:30
who could serve in the **a**, Nm 1:32
who could serve in the **a**, Nm 1:34
who could serve in the **a**, Nm 1:36
who could serve in the **a**, Nm 1:38
who could serve in the **a**, Nm 1:40
who could serve in the **a**, Nm 1:42
who could serve in Israel's **a**, Nm 1:45
his whole **a** and went out to Nm 21:23
with his whole **a** to do battle at Nm 21:33
with his whole **a** and his land. Nm 21:34
and his whole **a** until no one was Nm 21:35
who can serve in Israel's **a**." Nm 26:2
the plunder the **a** had taken Nm 31:32
over the thousands of the **a**, Nm 31:48
and his whole **a** came out against Dt 2:32
him, his sons, and his whole **a**. Dt 2:33
with his whole **a**, came out Dt 3:1
with his whole **a** and his land. Dt 3:2
of Bashan and his whole **a** to us. Dt 3:3
He did to Egypt's **a**, its horses Dt 11:4
and an **a** larger than yours, Dt 20:1
come forward and address the **a**. Dt 20:2
officers are to address the **a**, Dt 20:5
to address the **a** and say, Dt 20:8
have finished addressing the **a**, Dt 20:9
go out with the **a** or be liable Dt 24:5
as commander of the LORD's **a**." Jos 5:14
of the Lord's **a** said to Joshua, Jos 5:15
and his **a** at the Wadi Kishon ⌊to Jdg 4:7
all his **a** into confusion with Jdg 4:15
chariots and the **a** as far as Jdg 4:16
and the whole **a** of Sisera fell Jdg 4:16
the entire ⌊Midianite⌋ **a** fled, Jdg 7:21
each man in the **a** against each Jdg 7:22
we should give bread to your **a**?" Jdg 8:6
them was their **a** of about 15,000 Jdg 8:10
of the entire **a** of the Qedemites Jdg 8:10
attacked their **a** while the army Jdg 8:11
army while the **a** was Jdg 8:11
Midian and routed the entire **a**. Jdg 8:12
"Gather your **a** and come out." Jdg 9:29
the Israelite **a** rallied and Jdg 20:22
whole Israelite **a** went to Bethel Jdg 20:26
commander of the **a** of Hazor, 1Sm 12:9
commander of his **a** was Abner 1Sm 14:50
the camp as the **a** was marching 1Sm 17:20
Abner the commander of the **a**, 1Sm 17:55
David marched out ⌊with the **a**⌋, 1Sm 18:5
general of his **a**, had lain down. 1Sm 26:5
into one **a** to fight against 1Sm 28:1
march out in the **a** with me." 1Sm 28:1
will hand Israel's **a** over to the 1Sm 28:19
of Saul's **a**, took Saul's son 2Sm 2:8
When Joab and all his **a** arrived, 2Sm 3:23
the entire **a** of Hadadezer, 2Sm 8:9
son of Zeruiah was over the **a**; 2Sm 8:16
commander of Hadadezer's **a**, 2Sm 10:16
Shobach commander of their **a**, 2Sm 10:18
over the **a** in Joab's place. 2Sm 17:25
commander of the **a** from now on 2Sm 19:13
commanded the whole **a** of Israel; 2Sm 20:23
of his **a**, "Go through all 2Sm 24:2
and the commanders of the **a**. 2Sm 24:4
of the **a** left the king's 2Sm 24:4
and Joab the commander of the **a**, 1Kg 1:19
commanders of the **a**, and 1Kg 1:25
two commanders of Israel's **a**, 1Kg 2:5
of Israel's **a**, and Amasa son 1Kg 2:32
Jether, commander of Judah's **a**. 1Kg 2:32
in Joab's place over the **a**, 1Kg 2:35
of Jehoiada, in charge of the **a**; 1Kg 4:4
commander of the **a**, had gone to 1Kg 11:15
of the **a**, was dead, Hadad 1Kg 11:21
made Omri, the **a** commander, 1Kg 16:16
of Aram assembled his entire **a**. 1Kg 20:1
leaders and the **a** behind them 1Kg 20:19
Raise another **a** for yourself 1Kg 20:25
yourself like the **a** you lost— 1Kg 20:25
out in the **a** as the sun set, 1Kg 22:36
water for the **a** or their animals 2Kg 3:9
or to the commander of the **a**?'" 2Kg 4:13
commander of the **a** for the king 2Kg 5:1
chariots, and a massive **a** there. 2Kg 6:14
he discovered an **a** with horses 2Kg 6:15
chariots, horses, and a great **a**. 2Kg 7:6
sent them after the Aramean **a**, 2Kg 7:14
the **a** commanders were sitting 2Kg 9:5
of hundreds in charge of the **a**, 2Kg 11:15
Jehoahaz did not have an **a** left, 2Kg 13:7
with a massive **a**, from Lachish 2Kg 18:17
Jerusalem with his entire **a**. 2Kg 25:1
the Chaldean **a** pursued him and 2Kg 25:5
Zedekiah's entire **a** was 2Kg 25:5
The whole Chaldean **a** ⌊with⌋ the 2Kg 25:10
of the commander of the **a**, 2Kg 25:19
and the commanders of the **a**, 2Kg 25:26
who could serve in the **a**— 1Ch 5:18
17,200 who could serve in the **a**. 1Ch 7:11
saw that the **a** had run away 1Ch 10:7
the Philistine **a** was encamped 1Ch 11:15
Gadites were **a** commanders; 1Ch 12:14
and commanders in the **a**. 1Ch 12:21
David until there was a great **a**, 1Ch 12:22
a great army, like an **a** of God. 1Ch 12:22
50,000 who could serve in the **a**, 1Ch 12:33
40,000 who could serve in the **a**, 1Ch 12:36
the Philistine **a** from Gibeon to 1Ch 14:16
the entire **a** of King Hadadezer 1Ch 18:9
son of Zeruiah was over the **a**; 1Ch 18:15
the king of Maacah with his **a**, 1Ch 19:7
and the entire **a** of warriors. 1Ch 19:8
commander of Hadadezer's **a**, 1Ch 19:16
Shophach, commander of the **a**. 1Ch 19:18
Joab led the **a** and destroyed the 1Ch 20:1
officers of the **a** also set apart 1Ch 25:1
and by the **a** commanders. 1Ch 26:26
chief of all the **a** commanders 1Ch 27:3
The third **a** commander, as chief 1Ch 27:5
the commander of the king's **a**. 1Ch 27:34
Abijah set his **a** of warriors in 2Ch 13:3
his mighty **a** of 800,000 choice 2Ch 13:3
Asa had an **a** of 300,000 from 2Ch 14:8
them with an **a** of one million 2Ch 14:9
the LORD and before His **a**. 2Ch 14:13
the **a** of the king of Aram has 2Ch 16:7
Libyans a vast **a** with very many 2Ch 16:8
charge of the **a**, saying, "Take 2Ch 23:14
an Aramean **a** went to war against 2Ch 24:23
the Aramean **a** came with only a 2Ch 24:24
over a vast **a** to them because 2Ch 24:24
men who could serve in the **a**, 2Ch 25:5
not let Israel's **a** go with you, 2Ch 25:7
Uzziah had an **a** equipped for 2Ch 26:11
authority was an **a** of 307,500 2Ch 26:13
the entire **a** with shields, 2Ch 26:14
out to meet the **a** that came to 2Ch 28:9
The **a** left the captives and the 2Ch 28:14
the **a** of Persia and Media, Est 1:3
provincial **a** hostile to them, Est 8:11
Though an **a** deploy against me, Ps 27:3
king is not saved by a large **a**; Ps 33:16
Pharaoh and his **a** into the Red Ps 136:15
and a king at the head of his **a**. Pr 30:31
as an **a** with banners. Sg 6:4
as an **a** with banners? Sg 6:10
is mobilizing an **a** for war. Is 13:4
with a massive **a**, from Lachish Is 36:2
a and the mighty one together Is 43:17
an **a** is coming from a northern Jr 6:22
the **a** of the king of Babylon was Jr 32:2
all his **a**, all the earthly Jr 34:1
of Babylon's **a** was attacking Jr 34:7
king of Babylon's **a** that is Jr 34:21
Pharaoh's **a** had left Egypt, Jr 37:5
Pharaoh's **a**, which has come out Jr 37:7
entire Chaldean **a** that is Jr 37:10
the Chaldean **a** withdrew from Jr 37:11
because of Pharaoh's **a**, Jr 37:11
over to the king of Babylon's **a**, Jr 38:3
with his entire **a** and laid siege Jr 39:1
the Chaldean **a** pursued them and Jr 39:5
commanders of the **a** with him, Jr 41:13
Egypt and the **a** of Pharaoh Neco, Jr 46:2
the enemy⌋ will come with an **a**; Jr 46:22
completely destroy her entire **a**! Jr 51:3
Jerusalem with his entire **a**. Jr 52:4
The Chaldean **a** pursued the king Jr 52:8
Zedekiah's entire **a** was Jr 52:8
whole Chaldean **a** with the Jr 52:14
of the commander of the **a**, Jr 52:25
has summoned an **a** against me to Lm 1:15
like the noise of an **a**. Ezk 1:24
give him horses and a large **a**. Ezk 17:15
⌊his⌋ great **a** and vast horde Ezk 17:17
your gates as ⌊an **a**⌋ entering a Ezk 26:10
Put were in your **a**, ⌊serving⌋ as Ezk 27:10
Babylon made his **a** labor Ezk 29:18
but he and his **a** received no Ezk 29:18
and all his **a**, slain by the Ezk 32:31
stood on their feet, a vast **a**. Ezk 37:10
bring you out with all your **a**, Ezk 38:4
a mighty horde, a huge **a**? Ezk 38:15
soldiers in his **a** to tie up Dn 3:20
He wants with the **a** of heaven Dn 4:35
up, come against the **a**, and Dn 11:7
a great **a** and many supplies. Dn 11:13
With a large **a** he will stir up Dn 11:25
extremely large and powerful **a**, Dn 11:25
his **a** will be swept away, and Dn 11:26
a mighty **a** deployed for war. Jl 2:5
voice in the presence of His **a**. Jl 2:11
My great **a** that I sent against Jl 2:25
camp at My house against an **a**, Zch 9:8
on the horse and against His **a**. Rv 19:19

ARMY'S *(1)*

This will be his **a** compensation. Ezk 29:19

ARNAN *(1)*

sons of Rephaiah, **A**, Obadiah, 1Ch 3:21

ARNON *(24)*

the other side of the **A** ⌊River⌋, Nm 21:13
because the **A** was the Moabite Nm 21:13
Suphah and the ravines of the **A**, Nm 21:14
land from the **A** to the Jabbok, Nm 21:24
of all his land as far as the **A**. Nm 21:26
city on the **A** border at the edge Nm 22:36
out, and cross the **A** Valley. Dt 2:24
on the rim of the **A** Valley, Dt 2:36
the **A** Valley as far as Mount Dt 3:8
from Aroer by the **A** Valley, Dt 3:12
from Gilead to the **A** Valley Dt 3:16
the rim of the **A** Valley as far Dt 4:48
and from the **A** Valley to Mount Jos 12:1
on the rim of the **A** Valley, Jos 12:2

on the rim of the **A** Valley, Jos 13:9
on the rim of the **A** Valley, Jos 13:16
my land from the **A** to the Jabbok Jdg 11:13
side of the **A** but did not enter Jdg 11:18
for the **A** was the boundary of Jdg 11:18
Amorites from the **A** to the Jdg 11:22
that are on the banks of the **A**, Jdg 11:26
which is by the **A** Valley through 2Kg 10:33
will be at the fords of the **A**. Is 16:2
Declare by the **A** that Moab is Jr 48:20

ARNON'S *(1)*
of Moab, the lords of **A** heights. Nm 21:28

AROD *(1)*
the Arodite clan from **A**; Nm 26:17

ARODI *(1)*
Shuni, Ezbon, Eri, **A**, and Areli. Gn 46:16

ARODITE *(1)*
the **A** clan from Arod; Nm 26:17

AROER *(16)*
rebuilt Dibon, Ataroth, **A**, Nm 32:34
from **A** on the rim of the Arnon Dt 2:36
extending⌋ from **A** by the Arnon Dt 3:12
from **A** on the rim of the Arnon Dt 4:48
the territory⌋ from **A** on the rim Jos 12:2
From **A** on the rim of the Arnon Jos 13:9
From **A** on the rim of the Arnon Jos 13:16
the land of the Ammonites to **A**, Jos 13:25
villages, in **A** and its villages Jdg 11:26
slaughter from **A** all the way to Jdg 11:33
to those in **A**, in Siphmoth, and 1Sm 30:28
the Jordan and camped in **A**, 2Sm 24:5
from **A** which is by the Arnon 2Kg 10:33
They settled in **A** as far as Nebo 1Ch 5:8
The cities of **A** are forsaken; Is 17:2
highway and look, resident of **A**! Jr 48:19

AROERITE *(1)*
Jeiel the sons of Hotham the **A**, 1Ch 11:44

AROMA *(43)*
the LORD smelled the pleasing **a**, Gn 8:21
is a pleasing **a**, a fire offering Ex 29:18
as a pleasing **a** before the LORD; Ex 29:25
as a pleasing **a**, a fire offering Ex 29:41
of a pleasing **a** to the LORD. Lv 1:9
of a pleasing **a** to the LORD. Lv 1:13
of a pleasing **a** to the LORD. Lv 1:17
of a pleasing **a** to the LORD. Lv 2:2
of a pleasing **a** to the LORD. Lv 2:9
on the altar as a pleasing **a**. Lv 2:12
of a pleasing **a** to the LORD. Lv 3:5
fire offering for a pleasing **a**. Lv 3:16
as a pleasing **a** to the LORD. Lv 4:31
as a pleasing **a** to the LORD. Lv 6:15
a pleasing **a** to the LORD. Lv 6:21
burnt offering for a pleasing **a**, Lv 8:21
offering for a pleasing **a**, Lv 8:28
fat as a pleasing **a** to the LORD. Lv 17:6
LORD, a pleasing **a**, and its Lv 23:13
of a pleasing **a** to the LORD. Lv 23:18
smell the pleasing **a** of your Lv 26:31
a pleasing **a** for the LORD, Nm 15:3
as a pleasing **a** to the LORD. Nm 15:7
of pleasing **a** to the LORD. Nm 15:10
as a pleasing **a** to the LORD. Nm 15:13
as a pleasing **a** to the LORD, Nm 15:14
as a pleasing **a** to the LORD, Nm 15:24
for a pleasing **a** to the LORD. Nm 18:17
offering, a pleasing **a** to Me. Nm 28:2
at Mount Sinai for a pleasing **a**, Nm 28:6
a pleasing **a** to the LORD. Nm 28:8
a pleasing **a**, a fire offering to Nm 28:13
a pleasing **a** to the LORD. Nm 28:24
for a pleasing **a** to the LORD: Nm 28:27
as a pleasing **a** to the LORD: Nm 29:2
a pleasing **a**, a fire offering Nm 29:6
to the LORD, a pleasing **a**: Nm 29:8
as a pleasing **a** to the LORD: Nm 29:13
as a pleasing **a** to the LORD: Nm 29:36
of pleasing **a** to the God of Ezr 6:10
same, and his **a** hasn't changed. Jr 48:11
as a pleasing **a** the food I gave Ezk 16:19
will accept you as a pleasing **a**. Ezk 20:41

AROMAS *(2)*
offered pleasing **a** to all their Ezk 6:13
their pleasing **a** and poured out Ezk 20:28

AROMATIC *(5)*
camels were carrying **a** gum, Gn 37:25
and some honey, **a** gum and resin, Gn 43:11
not bought Me **a** cane with silver Is 43:24
and **a** cane were ⌊exchanged⌋ for Ezk 27:19
linen cloths with the **a** spices, Jn 19:40

AROSE *(16)*
So Moses **a** with his assistant Ex 24:13
Early the next morning they **a**, Ex 32:6
officials of Moab **a**, returned to Nm 22:14
Balaam then **a** and went back to Nm 24:25
I, Deborah, I **a**, a mother in Jdg 5:7
so he **a** against them and struck Jdg 9:43
and no one like him **a** after him. 2Kg 23:25
the king **a** from where they were Est 7:7
violent storm **a** on the sea that Jnh 1:4
a violent storm **a** on the sea, Mt 8:24
fierce windstorm **a**, and the Mk 4:37
dispute also **a** among them about Lk 22:24
Then **a** dispute **a** between John's Jn 3:25
Then a high wind **a**, and the sea Jn 6:18
there **a** a complaint by the Ac 6:1
⌊This issue **a**⌋ because of false Gl 2:4

AROUND *(358)*
(See pp. xi-xii.)

ARPACHSHAD *(9)*
Elam, Asshur, **A**, Lud, and Aram. Gn 10:22
A fathered Shelah, and Shelah Gn 10:24
and fathered **A** two years after Gn 11:10
he fathered **A**, Shem lived 500 Gn 11:11
A lived 35 years and fathered Gn 11:12
A lived 403 years and fathered Gn 11:13
Elam, Asshur, **A**, Lud, Aram, Uz, 1Ch 1:17
A fathered Shelah, and Shelah 1Ch 1:18
Shem, **A**, Shelah, 1Ch 1:24

ARPAD *(6)*
are the gods of Hamath and **A**? 2Kg 18:34
Hamath, the king of **A**, the king 2Kg 19:13
Hamath like **A**? Isn't Samaria Is 10:9
are the gods of Hamath and **A**? Is 36:19
Hamath, the king of **A**, the king Is 37:13
Hamath and **A** are put to shame, Jr 49:23

ARPHAXAD *(1)*
son⌋ of **A**, ⌊son⌋ of Shem, Lk 3:36

ARRANGE *(6)*
the altar and **a** wood on the fire Lv 1:7
the priests are to **a** the pieces, Lv 1:8
the priest will **a** them on top Lv 1:12
He is to **a** the burnt offering on Lv 6:12
A them in two rows, six to a row, Lv 24:6
on ahead to you and **a** in advance 2Co 9:5

ARRANGED *(13)*
the altar there and **a** the wood. Gn 22:9
with its lamps **a** and all its Ex 39:37
He **a** the bread on it before the Ex 40:23
I have **a** seven altars and Nm 23:4
flax that she had **a** on the roof. Jos 2:6
Next, he **a** the wood, cut up the 1Kg 18:33
Jeroboam **a** his mighty army of 2Ch 13:3
also **a** for the donation of wood Neh 13:31
couches ⌊were **a**⌋ on a mosaic Est 1:6
explored, and **a** many proverbs. Ec 12:9
side rooms were **a** one above Ezk 41:6
For they were **a** in three stories Ezk 42:6
they **a** for Paul and Barnabas and Ac 15:2

ARRANGEMENT *(2)*
in the table and lay out its **a**; Ex 40:4
Jonathan and David knew the **a**. 1Sm 20:39

ARRANGEMENTS *(1)*
Make **a**! Put up security for me. Jb 17:3

ARRANGING *(2)*
than 40 of them **a** to ambush him, Ac 23:21
After **a** a day with him, many Ac 28:23

ARRAY *(2)*
stars—all the **a** of heaven—do Dt 4:19
served in an **a** of gold goblets, Est 1:7

ARRAYED *(2)*
God's terrors are **a** against me. Jb 6:4
a with God's glory. Her radiance Rv 21:11

ARREST *(19)*
We have come to **a** Samson and Jdg 15:10
We've come to **a** you and hand Jdg 15:12
the altar and said, "**A** him!" 1Kg 13:4
were looking for a way to **a** Him, Mt 21:46
and they conspired to **a** Jesus in Mt 26:4
I kiss, He's the One; **a** Him!" Mt 26:48
complex, and you didn't **a** Me. Mt 26:55
given orders to **a** John and to Mk 6:17
were looking for a way to **a** Him, Mk 12:12
So when they **a** you and hand you Mk 13:11
way to **a** and kill Him. Mk 14:1
a Him and take Him away under Mk 14:44
complex, and you didn't **a** Me. Mk 14:49
sent temple police to **a** Him. Jn 7:32
report it so they could **a** Him. Jn 11:57
chief priests to **a** all who call Ac 9:14
he proceeded to **a** Peter too, Ac 12:3
the **a**, he put him in prison Ac 12:4
the Damascenes in order to **a** me, 2Co 11:32

ARRESTED *(13)*
So they **a** her, and she went out 2Kg 11:16
king of Assyria **a** him and put 2Kg 17:4
So they **a** her, and she went by 2Ch 23:15
of Jericho, **a** him, and brought Jr 39:5
He heard that John had been **a**, Mt 4:12
For Herod had **a** John, chained Mt 14:3
took hold of Jesus, and **a** Him. Mt 26:50
Those who had **a** Jesus led Him Mt 26:57
After John was **a**, Jesus went to Mk 1:14
they took hold of Him and **a** Him. Mk 14:46
temple police **a** Jesus and tied Jn 18:12
a guide to those who **a** Jesus. Ac 1:16
So they **a** the apostles and put Ac 5:18

ARRIVAL *(7)*
gift for Joseph's **a** at noon. Gn 43:25
to prepare for his **a** at Goshen. Gn 46:28
was to be set up before their **a**. Nm 10:21
about their **a** and ⌊the local Ru 1:19
Now the day before Saul's **a**, 1Sm 9:15
Israel, since their **a** is near. Ezk 36:8
On **a**, they went into the Ac 17:10

ARRIVE *(9)*
When you **a** at the city, you will 1Sm 10:5
of spices **a** as those the queen 1Kg 10:10
Tarshish would **a** bearing gold, 1Kg 10:22
When you **a**, you are to anoint 1Kg 19:15
Tarshish would **a** bearing gold, 2Ch 9:21
When they **a** there, they are Jb 6:20
tremble. They approach and **a**. Is 41:5
When they **a** there, they will Ezk 11:18
And when I **a**, I will send those 1Co 16:3

ARRIVED *(86)*
When they **a** at the place that Gn 22:9
brother Esau **a** from the hunt. Gn 27:30
a safely at the Canaanite city Gn 33:18
before the years of famine **a**. Gn 41:50
some shepherds **a** and drove them Ex 2:17
gods that had just **a**, which your Dt 32:17
she **a**, she persuaded Othniel Jos 15:18
she **a**, she persuaded Othniel Jdg 1:14
After he **a**, he sounded the ram's Jdg 3:27
When Barak **a** in pursuit of Jdg 4:22
When Gideon **a**, there was a man Jdg 7:13
of Ephraim and **a** at Micah's Jdg 18:13
departed, and **a** opposite Jebus Jdg 19:10
They **a** in Bethlehem at the Ru 1:22
when Boaz **a** from Bethlehem, Ru 2:4
When he **a**, there was Eli sitting 1Sm 4:13
and his attendant **a** at Gibeah, 1Sm 10:10
the burnt offering, Samuel **a**. 1Sm 13:10
When they **a**, Samuel saw Eliab 1Sm 16:6
a at the perimeter of the camp 1Sm 17:20
When he **a**, he asked his brothers 1Sm 17:22
Before the wedding day **a**, 1Sm 18:26
the messengers **a**, to their 1Sm 19:16
David and his men **a** in Ziklag on 1Sm 30:1
David and his men **a** at the town, 1Sm 30:3
When they **a** at Jabesh, they 1Sm 31:12
all morning, and **a** at Mahanaim. 2Sm 2:29
When Joab and all his army **a**, 2Sm 3:23
set out and **a** at Ish-bosheth's 2Sm 4:5
After he **a** from Hebron, David 2Sm 5:13
when they **a** in the land of the 2Sm 10:2
When he **a**, he reported to David 2Sm 11:22
When he **a**, he said to him: 2Sm 12:1
Besides, you only **a** yesterday; 2Sm 15:20
the people with him **a** exhausted, 2Sm 16:14
David had **a** at Mahanaim by the 2Sm 17:24
When he **a** at the Jordan, Judah 2Sm 19:15
the king, Nathan the prophet **a**, 1Kg 1:22
Abiathar the priest, suddenly **a**. 1Kg 1:42
When Rehoboam **a** in Jerusalem, 1Kg 12:21
to Shiloh and **a** at Ahijah's 1Kg 14:4
When he **a** at the city gate, 1Kg 17:10

When he **a**, the army commanders 2Kg 9:5
David's emissaries **a** in the land 1Ch 19:2
When Rehoboam **a** in Jerusalem, 2Ch 11:1
After they **a** at the LORD's house Ezr 2:68
year after they **a** at God's house Ezr 3:8
first month and **a** in Jerusalem Ezr 7:9
So we **a** at Jerusalem and rested Ezr 8:32
of my brothers, **a** with men from Neh 1:2
After I **a** in Jerusalem and had Neh 2:11
the Jews who lived nearby **a**, Neh 4:12
of the king **a** and rushed Haman Est 6:14
the day has **a**. Let the buyer Ezk 7:12
evening before the fugitive **a**, Ezk 33:22
Ancient of Days **a** and a judgment Dn 7:22
who have **a** from Babylon, Zch 6:10
men from the east **a** unexpectedly Mt 2:1
gone to buy some, the groom **a**. Mt 25:10
one of the Twelve, suddenly **a**. Mt 26:47
the towns and **a** ahead of them. Mk 6:33
came, He **a** with the Twelve Mk 14:17
one of the Twelve, suddenly **a**. Mk 14:43
when he **a** at the place and saw Lk 10:32
When they **a** at the place called Lk 23:33
They **a** early at the tomb, Lk 24:22
Just then His disciples **a**, Jn 4:27
has not yet **a**, but your time Jn 7:6
When Jesus **a**, He found that Jn 11:17
When they **a**, they went to the Ac 1:13
When the day of Pentecost had **a**, Ac 2:1
and those who were with him **a**, Ac 5:21
When he **a** in Jerusalem, he tried Ac 9:26
When he **a**, they led him to the Ac 9:39
me from Caesarea **a** at the house Ac 11:11
When he **a** and saw the grace of Ac 11:23
After they **a** and gathered the Ac 14:27
When they **a** at Jerusalem, they Ac 15:4
in the Scriptures, **a** in Ephesus. Ac 18:24
After he **a**, he greatly helped Ac 18:27
the next day we **a** off Chios. Ac 20:15
on to Syria and **a** at Tyre, Ac 21:3
I **a** with my troops and rescued Ac 23:27
after Festus **a** in the province, Ac 25:1
When he **a**, the Jews who had come Ac 25:7
and Bernice **a** in Caesarea Ac 25:13

ARRIVES *(5)*
If he **a** alone, he is to leave Ex 21:3
if he **a** with a wife, his wife is Ex 21:3
she **a**, she will be disguised. 1Kg 14:5
When this letter **a**, since your 2Kg 10:2
And when it **a**, it finds ⌊the Mt 12:44

ARRIVING *(2)*
the city, **a** opposite Ai, Jos 8:11
A in Salamis, they proclaimed Ac 13:5

ARROGANCE *(14)*
know your **a** and your evil heart 1Sm 17:28
Me and your **a** have reached My 2Kg 19:28
Though his **a** reaches heaven, Jb 20:6
In **a** the wicked relentlessly Ps 10:2
A leads to nothing but strife, Pr 13:10
They will say with pride and **a**: Is 9:9
his pride, his **a**, and his empty Is 16:6
Me and your **a** has reached My Is 37:29
his insolence, **a**, pride, and Jr 48:29
has blossomed; **a** has bloomed. Ezk 7:10
Israel's **a** testifies against Hs 5:5
Israel's **a** testifies against Hs 7:10
gossip, **a**, and disorder. 2Co 12:20
as it is, you boast in your **a**. Jms 4:16

ARROGANT *(40)*
let **a** ⌊words⌋ come out of your 1Sm 2:3
he grew **a** and it led to his own 2Ch 26:16
loyal, but fully repays the **a**. Ps 31:23
the foot of the **a** come near me Ps 36:11
those who are **a** toward me when I Ps 38:16
is the way of those who are **a**, Ps 49:13
For I envied the **a**; Ps 73:3
a people have attacked me; Ps 86:14
They pour out **a** words; Ps 94:4
with haughty eyes or an **a** heart. Ps 101:5
The **a** constantly ridicule me, Ps 119:51
The **a** have smeared me with lies, Ps 119:69
Let the **a** be put to shame for Ps 119:78
The **a** have dug pits for me; Ps 119:85
do not let the **a** oppress me. Ps 119:122
scorn from the **a** ⌊and⌋ contempt Ps 123:4
a eyes, a lying tongue, hands Pr 6:17
hate **a** pride, evil conduct, and Pr 8:13
and an **a** spirit before a fall. Pr 16:18
haughty eyes and an **a** heart— Pr 21:4
The proud and **a** person, named Pr 21:24
his youth will become **a** later Pr 29:21
Assyria for his **a** acts and the Is 10:12
the pride of the **a** and humiliate Is 13:11
all the other **a** men responded to Jr 43:2
you, you **a** one—⌊this is⌋ Jr 50:31
The **a** will stumble and fall with Jr 50:32
exalted and his spirit became **a**, Dn 5:20
sound of the **a** words the horn Dn 7:11
he will become **a** and cause tens Dn 11:12
an **a** man is never at rest. Hab 2:5
consider the **a** to be fortunate Mal 3:15
when all the **a** and everyone who Mal 4:1
God-haters, **a**, proud, boastful, Rm 1:30
Do not be **a**, but be afraid. Rm 11:20
a persecutor, and an **a** man. 1Tm 1:13
age not to be **a** or to set their 1Tm 6:17
be blameless, not **a**, not quick Ti 1:7
Bold, **a** people! They do 2Pt 2:10
their mouths utter **a** words, Jd 16

ARROGANTLY *(21)*
are still acting **a** against My Ex 9:17
acted **a** against Israel. Ex 18:11
person who acts **a**, refusing to Dt 17:12
afraid, and no longer behave **a**. Dt 17:13
You knew how **a** they treated our Neh 9:10
But our ancestors acted **a**; Neh 9:16
but they acted **a** and would not Neh 9:29
against God and has **a** opposed Jb 15:25
have done and how **a** they have Jb 36:9
scheming, the wicked **a** thinks: Ps 10:4
their mouths speak **a**. Ps 17:10
they speak **a** against the Ps 31:18
for many **a** fight against me. Ps 56:2
they **a** threaten oppression. Ps 73:8
against heaven or speak **a**.'" Ps 75:5
those who hate You have acted **a**. Ps 83:2
youth will act **a** toward the Is 3:5
she has acted **a** against the LORD Jr 50:29
and it had a mouth that spoke **a**. Dn 7:8
mouth that spoke **a**, and that was Dn 7:20
taunted and acted **a** against the Zph 2:10

ARROW *(20)*
Jonathan shot an **a** beyond him. 1Sm 20:36
location of the **a** that Jonathan 1Sm 20:37
and said, "The **a** is beyond you, 1Sm 20:37
picked up the **a** and returned to 1Sm 20:38
The **a** went through his heart, 2Kg 9:24
The LORD's **a** of victory, yes, 2Kg 13:17
the **a** of victory over Aram. 2Kg 13:17
city or shoot an **a** there or come 2Kg 19:32
⌊an **a** from⌋ a bronze bow will Jb 20:24
nor will a spear, dart, or **a**. Jb 41:26
No **a** can make him flee; Jb 41:28
they put the **a** on the bowstring Ps 11:2
the night, the **a** that flies by Ps 91:5
until an **a** pierces its liver, Pr 7:23
a club, a sword, or a sharp **a**. Pr 25:18
city or shoot an **a** there or come Is 37:33
He made me like a sharpened **a**; Is 49:2
Do not spare an **a**, for she has Jr 50:14
set me as the target for His **a**. Lm 3:12
and His **a** will fly like Zch 9:14

ARROWS *(44)*
will be stoned or shot ⌊with **a**⌋, Ex 19:13
will strike ⌊them⌋ with his **a**. Nm 24:8
I will use up My **a** against them. Dt 32:23
will make My **a** drunk with blood Dt 32:42
shoot three **a** beside it as if 1Sm 20:20
and say⌋, 'Go and find the **a**!' 1Sm 20:21
the **a** are on this side of you— 1Sm 20:21
'Look, the **a** are beyond you!' 1Sm 20:22
and find the **a** I'm shooting." 1Sm 20:36
He shot **a** and scattered them; 2Sm 22:15
responded, "Take a bow and **a**." 2Kg 13:15
So he got a bow and **a**. 2Kg 13:15
Then Elisha said, "Take the **a**!" 2Kg 13:18
sling⌋ or ⌊shoot⌋ **a** with a bow. 1Ch 12:2
to shoot **a** and ⌊catapult⌋ 2Ch 26:15
Surely the **a** of the Almighty Jb 6:4
He tips His **a** with fire. Ps 7:13
shot His **a** and scattered them; Ps 18:14
For Your **a** have sunk into me, Ps 38:2
Your **a** pierce the hearts of the Ps 45:5
Their teeth are spears and **a**; Ps 57:4
they will aim their useless **a**. Ps 58:7
and aim bitter words like **a**, Ps 64:3
But God will shoot them with **a**; Ps 64:7
He shatters the bow's flaming **a**, Ps 76:3
Your **a** flashed back and forth. Ps 77:17
warrior's sharp **a**, with burning Ps 120:4
Like **a** in the hand of a warrior Ps 127:4
shoot Your **a** and rout them. Ps 144:6
flaming darts and deadly **a**, Pr 26:18
Their **a** are sharpened, and all Is 5:28
with bow and **a** because the whole Is 7:24
Their tongues are deadly **a**— Jr 9:8
Their **a** will be like those of a Jr 50:9
Sharpen the **a**! Fill the quivers! Jr 51:11
pierced my kidneys with His **a**. Lm 3:13
I shoot deadly **a** of famine at Ezk 5:16
a for destruction that I will Ezk 5:16
he shakes the **a**, consults the Ezk 21:21
and make your **a** drop from your Ezk 39:3
the bows and **a**, the clubs and Ezk 39:9
the **a** are ready to be used with Hab 3:9
at the flash of Your flying **a**, Hab 3:11
the flaming **a** of the evil one. Eph 6:16

ART *(1)*
by human **a** and imagination. Ac 17:29

ARTAXERXES *(14)*
the time of ⌊King⌋ **A** of Persia, Ezr 4:7
his colleagues wrote to King **A**. Ezr 4:7
a letter to King **A** concerning Ezr 4:8
To King **A** from your servants, Ezr 4:11
Darius, and King **A** of Persia. Ezr 6:14
the reign of King **A** of Persia, Ezr 7:1
in the seventh year of King **A**. Ezr 7:7
the letter King **A** gave to Ezra Ezr 7:11
A, king of kings, to Ezra the Ezr 7:12
I, King **A**, issue a decree to all Ezr 7:21
during the reign of King **A**: Ezr 8:1
in the twentieth year of King **A**, Neh 2:1
the day King **A** appointed me to Neh 5:14
returned to King **A** of Babylon Neh 13:6

ARTAXERXES' *(1)*
text of King **A** letter was read Ezr 4:23

ARTEMAS *(1)*
When I send **A** to you, or Ti 3:12

ARTEMIS *(5)*
who made silver shrines of **A**, Ac 19:24
great goddess **A** may be despised Ac 19:27
"Great is **A** of the Ephesians!" Ac 19:28
"Great is **A** of the Ephesians!" Ac 19:34
temple guardian of the great **A**, Ac 19:35

ARTICLE *(8)*
or any leather **a**, it is a mildew Lv 13:49
linen, or any leather **a**, which Lv 13:52
warp or woof, or any leather **a**, Lv 13:53
contaminated **a** has not changed Lv 13:55
or any leather **a**, it has broken Lv 13:57
any leather **a**, which have been Lv 13:58
or any leather **a**, in order to Lv 13:59
goat hair, and every **a** of wood." Nm 31:20

ARTICLES *(48)*
the tabernacle and all its **a**, Nm 1:50
of the silver **a** was 60 pounds Nm 7:85
of the gold **a** each man found— Nm 31:50
them all the **a** made out of gold Nm 31:51
and the **a** of bronze and iron, Jos 6:19
and gold and the **a** of bronze and Jos 6:24
or any **a** of gold or silver were 2Kg 12:13
temple all the **a** made for Baal, 2Kg 23:4
all the gold **a** that Solomon king 2Kg 24:13
the bronze **a** used in ⌊temple⌋ 2Kg 25:14
of all these **a** was beyond 2Kg 25:16
the pillars, and the bronze **a**. 1Ch 18:8
and the holy **a** of God to the 1Ch 22:19
all the **a** of service of the 1Ch 28:13
for all the **a** for every kind 1Ch 28:14
all the silver **a** for every kind 1Ch 28:14
gold for the gold ⌊**a**⌋, silver 1Ch 29:2
made **a** for the LORD's temple 2Ch 24:14
a for ministry and for making 2Ch 24:14
and ladles and **a** of gold and 2Ch 24:14
all the **a** of God's temple, 2Ch 36:18
supported them with silver **a**, Ezr 1:6
brought out the **a** of the LORD's Ezr 1:7
silver bowls, and 1,000 other **a**. Ezr 1:10
gold and silver **a** totaled 5,400. Ezr 1:11
gold and silver **a** of God's house Ezr 5:14
him, 'Take these **a**, put them Ezr 5:15

gold and silver a of God's house Ezr 6:5
all the a given to you for Ezr 7:19
the gold, and the a—the Ezr 8:25
silver a weighing 7,500 pounds, Ezr 8:26
and two a of fine gleaming Ezr 8:27
to the LORD, and the a are holy. Ezr 8:28
and the a that had been weighed Ezr 8:30
the a were weighed out in the Ezr 8:33
where the a of the sanctuary are Neh 10:39
the a, and the tenths Neh 13:5
and I had the a of the house of Neh 13:9
and a of fine gold cannot be Jb 28:17
soon now the a of the LORD's Jr 27:16
not to let the a that remain Jr 27:18
the rest of the a that still Jr 27:19
says about the a that remain in Jr 27:21
place all the a of the LORD's Jr 28:3
He restore the a of the LORD's Jr 28:6
the bronze a used in ⌊temple⌋ Jr 52:18
of all these a was beyond Jr 52:20
their precious a of silver and Dn 11:8

ARTIFICIAL *(1)*
as far as the a pool and the Neh 3:16

ARTISANS *(2)*
money to the stonecutters and a, Ezr 3:7
all the work of skilled a. Jr 10:9

ARTISTIC *(4)*
to design a works in gold, Ex 31:4
to design a works in gold, Ex 35:32
work in every kind of a craft. Ex 35:33
of craft and design a designs. Ex 35:35

ARTISTICALLY *(2)*
The a woven waistband that is on Ex 28:8
The a woven waistband that was Ex 39:5

ARUBBOTH *(1)*
Ben-hesed, in A (he had Socoh 1Kg 4:10

ARUMAH *(1)*
stayed in A, and Zebul drove Jdg 9:41

ARVAD *(2)*
of Sidon and A were your rowers. Ezk 27:8
Men of A and Helech were Ezk 27:11

ARVADITES *(2)*
the A, the Zemarites, and the Gn 10:18
A, Zemarites, and Hamathites. 1Ch 1:16

ARZA *(1)*
himself drunk in the house of A, 1Kg 16:9

AS *(3569)*
(See pp. xi-xii.)

ASA *(56)*
His son A became king in his 1Kg 15:8
King Jeroboam, A became king of 1Kg 15:9
A did what was right in the 1Kg 15:11
A chopped down her obscene 1Kg 15:13
war between A and Baasha king 1Kg 15:16
anyone access to Judah's King A. 1Kg 15:17
So A withdrew all the silver and 1Kg 15:18
Then King A sent them to 1Kg 15:18
listened to King A and sent the 1Kg 15:20
Then King A gave a command to 1Kg 15:22
Then King A built Geba of 1Kg 15:22
Then A rested with his fathers 1Kg 15:24
second year of Judah's King A; 1Kg 15:25
third year of Judah's King A, 1Kg 15:28
war between A and Baasha king 1Kg 15:32
third year of Judah's King A, 1Kg 15:33
year of Judah's King A, 1Kg 16:8
year of Judah's King A, 1Kg 16:10
year of Judah's King A, 1Kg 16:15
year of Judah's King A, 1Kg 16:23
year of Judah's King A; 1Kg 16:29
son of A became king over 1Kg 22:41
in all the ways of his father A; 1Kg 22:43
from the days of his father A. 1Kg 22:46
was Abijah, his son A, his son 1Ch 3:10
son of A, son of Elkanah 1Ch 9:16
His son A became king in his 2Ch 14:1
A did what was good and right in 2Ch 14:2
A built fortified cities in 2Ch 14:6
A had an army of 300,000 from 2Ch 14:8
So A marched out against him and 2Ch 14:10
Then A cried out to the LORD his 2Ch 14:11
Cushites before A and before 2Ch 14:12
Then A and the people who were 2Ch 14:13
out to meet A and said to him 2Ch 15:2
A and all Judah and Benjamin, 2Ch 15:2
When A heard these words and the 2Ch 15:8
King A also removed Maacah, 2Ch 15:16
A chopped down her obscene 2Ch 15:16
A was wholehearted his entire 2Ch 15:17
In the thirty-sixth year of A, 2Ch 16:1
or coming—to Judah's King A. 2Ch 16:1
So A brought out the silver and 2Ch 16:2
listened to King A and sent the 2Ch 16:4
Then King A brought all Judah, 2Ch 16:6
came to King A of Judah and said 2Ch 16:7
A was angry with the seer and 2Ch 16:10
And A mistreated some of the 2Ch 16:10
A developed a disease in his 2Ch 16:12
A died in the forty-first year 2Ch 16:13
that his father A had captured. 2Ch 17:2
in the way of A his father; 2Ch 20:32
in the ways of A king of Judah 2Ch 21:12
a large one that King A had made Jr 41:9
Abijah, Abijah fathered A, Mt 1:7
A fathered Jehoshaphat, Mt 1:8

ASA'S *(5)*
but A heart was completely with 1Kg 15:14
of all the events of A ⌊reign⌋, 1Kg 15:23
the fifteenth year of A reign. 2Ch 15:10
thirty-fifth year of A reign. 2Ch 15:19
that the events of A ⌊reign⌋, 2Ch 16:11

ASAHEL *(19)*
Joab, Abishai, and A. 2Sm 2:18
A was a fast runner, like one of 2Sm 2:18
back and said, "Is that you, A?" 2Sm 2:20
"Yes it is," A replied. 2Sm 2:20
But A would not stop chasing 2Sm 2:21
Abner warned A, "Stop chasing me 2Sm 2:22
But A refused to turn away, 2Sm 2:23
to the place where A had fallen 2Sm 2:23
In addition to A, 19 of David's 2Sm 2:30
they carried A to his father's 2Sm 2:32
in revenge for the death of A, 2Sm 3:27
had put their brother A to death 2Sm 3:30
Joab's brother A, Elhanan son of 2Sm 23:24
Abishai, Joab, and A. 1Ch 2:16
Joab's brother A, Elhanan son of 1Ch 11:26
Joab's brother A, and his son 1Ch 27:7
Zebadiah, A, Shemiramoth, 2Ch 17:8
Azaziah, Nahath, A, Jerimoth, 2Ch 31:13
Jonathan son of A and Jahzeiah Ezr 10:15

ASAIAH *(8)*
and the king's servant A: 2Kg 22:12
and A went to the prophetess 2Kg 22:14
Jeshohaiah, A, Adiel, Jesimiel, 1Ch 4:36
his son Haggiah, and his son A. 1Ch 6:30
A the firstborn and his sons; 1Ch 9:5
A the leader and 220 of his 1Ch 15:6
Uriel, A, Joel, Shemaiah, 1Ch 15:11
and the king's servant A, 2Ch 34:20

ASAPH *(28)*
and Joah son of A, the court 2Kg 18:18
and Joah son of A, the court 2Kg 18:37
relative was A, who stood at his 1Ch 6:39
A son of Berechiah, son of 1Ch 6:39
Mica, son of Zichri, son of A; 1Ch 9:15
his relatives, A son of 1Ch 15:17
singers Heman, A, and Ethan were 1Ch 15:19
A was the chief and Zechariah 1Ch 16:5
while A ⌊sounded⌋ the cymbals 1Ch 16:5
to the LORD by A and his 1Ch 16:7
David left A and his relatives 1Ch 16:37
set apart some of the sons of A, 1Ch 25:1
sons of A, under Asaph's 1Ch 25:2
A, Jeduthun, and Heman were 1Ch 25:6
first lot for A fell to Joseph, 1Ch 25:9
of Kore, one of the sons of A. 1Ch 26:1
the Levitical singers of A, 2Ch 5:12
of David and of A the seer. 2Ch 29:30
descendants of A, were at their 2Ch 35:15
command of David, A, Heman, 2Ch 35:15
the Levites descended from A, Ezr 3:10
have⌋ a letter ⌊written⌋ to A, Neh 2:8
Zabdi, son of A, the leader who Neh 11:17
descendants of A, who were Neh 11:22
son of Zaccur, son of A, Neh 12:35
in the days of David and A, Neh 12:46
and Joah son of A, the record Is 36:3
and Joah son of A, the record Is 36:22

ASAPH'S *(5)*
From A sons: Zaccur, Joseph, 1Ch 25:2
of Asaph, under A authority, who 1Ch 25:2
a Levite from A descendants 2Ch 20:14
included⌋: A descendants 128 Ezr 2:41
included⌋: A descendants 148 Neh 7:44

ASAPHITES *(1)*
and Mattaniah from the A; 2Ch 29:13

ASAREL *(1)*
Ziph, Ziphah, Tiria, and A. 1Ch 4:16

ASARELAH *(1)*
(AKA JESARELAH)
Nethaniah, and A, sons of Asaph, 1Ch 25:2

ASCEND *(5)*
Who may a the mountain of the Ps 24:3
I will a to the heavens; Is 14:13
I will a above the highest Is 14:14
Babylon should a to the heavens Jr 51:53
Saviors will a Mount Zion to Ob 21

ASCENDED *(24)*
cry for help a to God because Ex 2:23
a to the south of Kadesh-barnea, Jos 15:3
passed Hezron, a to Addar, and Jos 15:3
It a to Beth-hoglah, proceeded Jos 15:6
and a to the stone of Bohan son Jos 15:6
Then the border a to Debir from Jos 15:7
there the border a the Valley of Jos 15:8
a to the top of the hill that Jos 15:8
a to the slope of Jericho on the Jos 18:12
of Olives, weeping as he a. 2Sm 15:30
and went up, weeping as they a. 2Sm 15:30
approached the altar and a it. 2Kg 16:12
a to the heights, taking away Ps 68:18
She has a every high hill and Jr 3:6
The cherubim a; these were the Ezk 10:15
and when they a, the wheels Ezk 10:17
the wheels a with them, for Ezk 10:17
their wings and a from the earth Ezk 10:19
No one has a into heaven except Jn 3:13
I have not yet a to the Father. Jn 20:17
not David who a into the heavens Ac 2:34
When He a on high, He took Eph 4:8
what does "He a" mean except Eph 4:9
as the One who a far above all Eph 4:10

ASCENDING *(5)*
the wilderness a from Jericho Jos 16:1
of Shallecheth on the a highway. 1Ch 26:16
angels of God a and descending Jn 1:51
the Son of Man a to where He was Jn 6:62
them that I am a to My Father Jn 20:17

ASCENDS *(4)*
Halak, which a to Seir, as far Jos 11:17
Mount Halak, which a toward Seir Jos 12:7
God a amid shouts of joy, the Ps 47:5
Her smoke a forever and ever! Rv 19:3

ASCENT *(12)*
turn south of the A of Akrabbim, Nm 34:4
through the a of Beth-horon, Jos 10:10
went south of the a of Akrabbim, Jos 15:3
is opposite the a of Adummim, Jos 15:7
is opposite the a of Adummim, Jos 18:17
extended from the a of Akrabbim, Jdg 1:36
the battle by the a of Heres. Jdg 8:13
see them coming up the a of Ziz, 2Ch 20:16
was buried on the a to the tombs 2Ch 32:33
opposite the a to the armory at Neh 3:19
of David on the a of the wall Neh 12:37
For on the a to Luhith they will Jr 48:5

ASCETIC *(2)*
insisting on a practices and the Col 2:18
wisdom by promoting a practices, Col 2:23

ASCRIBE *(8)*
A to the LORD, families of the 1Ch 16:28
a to the LORD glory and strength. 1Ch 16:28
A to the LORD the glory of His 1Ch 16:29
from afar and a righteousness to Jb 36:3
A power to God. His majesty is Ps 68:34
A to the LORD, you families of Ps 96:7
a to the LORD glory and strength. Ps 96:7
A to the LORD the glory of His Ps 96:8

ASENATH *(3)*
and gave him a wife, A daughter Gn 41:45
A daughter of Potiphera, priest Gn 41:50
were born to him by A daughter Gn 46:20

ASH *(3)*
outside the camp to the a heap, Lv 4:12
is to be burned at the a heap. Lv 4:12
sayings are proverbs of a; Jb 13:12

ASHAMED *(66)*
at him until Hazael was **a**. 2Kg 8:11
powerless, dismayed, and **a**. 2Kg 19:26
The priests and Levites were **a**, 2Ch 30:15
because I was **a** to ask the king Ezr 8:22
am **a** and embarrassed to lift my Ezr 9:6
They are **a** because they had been Jb 6:20
enemies will be **a** and shake with Ps 6:10
their faces will never be **a**. Ps 34:5
to harm me be turned back and **a**. Ps 35:4
I would not be **a** when I think Ps 119:6
before kings and not be **a**. Ps 119:46
do not let me be **a** of my hope. Ps 119:116
they will be **a** of the sacred Is 1:29
boast will be dismayed and **a**. Is 20:5
a Sidon, the stronghold of the Is 23:4
no longer be **a** and his face will Is 29:22
everyone will be **a** because of a Is 30:5
Lebanon is **a** and decayed. Is 33:9
powerless, dismayed, and **a**. Is 37:27
you will be **a** and disgraced; Is 41:11
be turned back⌊and⌋ utterly **a**— Is 42:17
a prostitute and refuse to be **a**. Jr 3:3
Were they **a** when they acted so Jr 6:15
They weren't at all **a**. Jr 6:15
Were they **a** when they acted so Jr 8:12
They weren't at all **a**. Jr 8:12
We are greatly **a**, for we have Jr 9:19
They are **a** and humiliated; Jr 14:3
The farmers are **a**; they cover Jr 14:4
she was **a** and humiliated. Jr 15:9
you will be **a** and humiliated Jr 22:22
I was **a** and humiliated because I Jr 31:19
his back! He is **a**. Moab will Jr 48:39
We are **a** because we have heard Jr 51:51
be **a** and bear your disgrace, Ezk 16:52
disgrace and be **a** of all you did Ezk 16:54
ways and be **a** when you receive Ezk 16:61
you will remember and be **a**, Ezk 16:63
Be **a** and humiliated because of Ezk 36:32
that they may be **a** of their Ezk 43:10
they will be **a** of all that they Ezk 43:11
and they will be **a** of their Hs 4:19
Israel will be **a** of its counsel. Hs 10:6
Be **a**, you farmers, wail, you Jl 1:11
seers will be **a** and the diviners Mc 3:7
will see and be **a** of all their Mc 7:16
prophet will be **a** of his vision Zch 13:4
For whoever is **a** of Me and of My Mk 8:38
Man will also be **a** of him when Mk 8:38
For whoever is **a** of Me and My Lk 9:26
of Man will be **a** of him when He Lk 9:26
enough to dig; I'm **a** to beg. Lk 16:3
For I am not **a** of the gospel, Rm 1:16
from the things you are now **a** Rm 6:21
tearing you down, I am not **a**. 2Co 10:8
I will not be **a** about anything, Php 1:20
with him, so that he may be **a**. 2Th 3:14
So don't be **a** of the testimony 2Tm 1:8
But I am not **a**, because I know 2Tm 1:12
me and was not **a** of my chains. 2Tm 1:16
worker who doesn't need to be **a**, 2Tm 2:15
so that the opponent will be **a**, Ti 2:8
is why He is not **a** to call them Heb 2:11
God is not **a** to be called their Heb 11:16
he should not be **a**, but should 1Pt 4:16
and not be **a** before Him at His 1Jn 2:28

ASHAN *(4)*
(AKA AIN)
Libnah, Ether, **A**, Jos 15:42
Ether, and **A**—four cities, Jos 19:7
Tochen, and **A**—five cities, 1Ch 4:32
A and its pasturelands, and 1Ch 6:59

ASHBEL *(3)*
Bela, Becher, **A**, Gera, Naaman, Gn 46:21
the Ashbelite clan from **A**; Nm 26:38
A was⌊born⌋ second, Aharah 1Ch 8:1

ASHBELITE *(1)*
the **A** clan from Ashbel; Nm 26:38

ASHDOD *(22)*
(AKA AZOTUS)
remaining in Gaza, Gath, and **A**. Jos 11:22
of Gaza, **A**, Ashkelon, Gath Jos 13:3
the cities⌋ near **A**, with their Jos 15:46
A, with its towns and villages; Jos 15:47
they took it from Ebenezer to **A**, 1Sm 5:1
the people of **A** got up early 1Sm 5:3
temple of Dagon in **A** do not step 1Sm 5:5
oppressed the people of **A**, 1Sm 5:6
people of **A** and its territory 1Sm 5:6
When the men of **A** saw what was 1Sm 5:7
So the men of **A** moved the ark. 1Sm 5:8
A, Gaza, Ashkelon, Gath, and 1Sm 6:17
of Jabneh, and the wall of **A**. 2Ch 26:6
in⌊the vicinity of⌋ **A** and among 2Ch 26:6
who had married women from **A**, Neh 13:23
spoke the language of **A** or of Neh 13:24
came to **A** and attacked and Is 20:1
Ekron, and the remnant of **A**; Jr 25:20
I will cut off the ruler from **A**, Am 1:8
on the citadels in **A** and on the Am 3:9
A will be driven out at noon, Zph 2:4
A mongrel people will live in **A**, Zch 9:6

ASHDODITES *(1)*
and **A** heard that the repair to Neh 4:7

ASHER *(35)*
me happy," so she named him **A**. Gn 30:13
slave Zilpah were Gad and **A**. Gn 35:26
Dan and Naphtali; Gad and **A**. Ex 1:4
Pagiel son of Ochran from **A**; Nm 1:13
descendants of **A**: according to Nm 1:40
the tribe of **A** numbered 41,500 Nm 1:41
The tribe of **A** will camp next to Nm 2:27
the division of the tribe of **A**, Nm 10:26
of Michael from the tribe of **A**; Nm 13:13
a leader from the tribe of **A**; Nm 34:27
Reuben, Gad, **A**, Zebulun, Dan, Dt 27:13
said about **A**: May Asher be the Dt 33:24
May **A** be the most blessed of the Dt 33:24
went from **A** to Michmethath Jos 17:7
They reached **A** on the north and Jos 17:10
Issachar and **A**, Manasseh had Jos 17:11
on the south, **A** on the west, Jos 19:34
of Issachar, **A**, Naphtali, and Jos 21:6
From the tribe of **A**⌊they gave⌋: Jos 21:30
A failed to drive out the Jdg 1:31
A remained at the seashore and Jdg 5:17
sent messengers throughout **A**, Jdg 6:35
from Naphtali, **A**, and Manasseh, Jdg 7:23
over Gilead, **A**, Jezreel, Ephraim 2Sm 2:9
son of Hushai, in **A** and Bealoth; 1Kg 4:16
Benjamin, Naphtali, Gad, and **A**. 1Ch 2:2
tribes of Issachar, **A**, Naphtali, 1Ch 6:62
the tribe of **A**⌊they received⌋ 1Ch 6:74
From **A**: 40,000 who could serve 1Ch 12:36
But some from **A**, Manasseh, and 2Ch 30:11
west, will be **A**—one⌊portion⌋ Ezk 48:2
Next to the territory of **A**, Ezk 48:3
one, the gate of **A**; and one, the Ezk 48:34
of Phanuel, of the tribe of **A**. Lk 2:36
12,000 from the tribe of **A**, Rv 7:6

ASHER'S *(8)*
A sons: Imnah, Ishvah, Ishvi, Gn 46:17
A food will be rich, and he will Gn 49:20
A descendants by their clans: Nm 26:44
And the name of **A** daughter was Nm 26:46
for the tribe of **A** descendants Jos 19:24
of the tribe of **A** descendants by Jos 19:31
A sons: Imnah, Ishvah, Ishvi, 1Ch 7:30
All these were **A** sons. 1Ch 7:40

ASHERAH *(38)*
and chop down their **A** poles. Ex 34:13
cut down their **A** poles, and burn Dt 7:5
burn up their **A** poles, cut down Dt 12:3
Do not set up an **A** of any kind Dt 16:21
cut down the **A** pole beside it. Jdg 6:25
wood of the **A** pole you cut down. Jdg 6:26
the **A** pole beside it cut down, Jdg 6:28
cut down the **A** pole beside it. Jdg 6:30
because they made their **A** poles, 1Kg 14:15
and **A** poles on every high hill 1Kg 14:23
had made an obscene image of **A**. 1Kg 15:13
Ahab also made an **A** pole. 1Kg 16:33
the 400 prophets of **A** who eat at 1Kg 18:19
and the **A** pole also remained 2Kg 13:6
pillars and **A** poles on every 2Kg 17:10
even two calves—and an **A** pole. 2Kg 17:16
and cut down the **A**⌊poles⌋. 2Kg 18:4
He made an **A**, as King Ahab of 2Kg 21:3
the carved image of **A** he made in 2Kg 21:7
made for Baal, **A**, and the whole 2Kg 23:4
He brought out the **A** pole from 2Kg 23:6
were weaving tapestries for **A**. 2Kg 23:7
down the **A** poles, then filled 2Kg 23:14
it to dust, and burned the **A**. 2Kg 23:15
and chopped down their **A** poles. 2Ch 14:3
had made an obscene image of **A**. 2Ch 15:16
high places and **A** poles from 2Ch 17:6
have removed the **A** poles from 2Ch 19:3
and served the **A** poles and the 2Ch 24:18
down the **A** poles, and tore 2Ch 31:1
made **A** poles, and he worshiped 2Ch 33:3
and set up **A** poles and carved 2Ch 33:19
high places, the **A** poles, the 2Ch 34:3
The **A** poles, the carved images, 2Ch 34:4
and he smashed the **A** poles and 2Ch 34:7
A poles or incense altars will Is 27:9
their altars and their **A** poles, Jr 17:2
pull up the **A** poles from among Mc 5:14

ASHERAHS *(2)*
worshiped the Baals and the **A**. Jdg 3:7
hands or to the **A** and incense Is 17:8

ASHERITE *(1)*
were the **A** clans⌊numbered⌋ Nm 26:47

ASHERITES *(3)*
leader of the **A** is Pagiel son Nm 2:27
leader of the **A**,⌊presented Nm 7:72
The **A** lived among the Canaanites Jdg 1:32

ASHES *(35)*
even though I am dust and **a**— Gn 18:27
Make its pots for removing **a**, Ex 27:3
of the altar at the place for **a**. Lv 1:16
is to remove the **a** of the burnt Lv 6:10
and bring the **a** outside the camp Lv 6:11
to remove the **a** from the⌊bronze Nm 4:13
up the cow's **a** and deposit them Nm 19:9
The **a** must be kept by the Nm 19:9
up the cow's **a** must wash his Nm 19:10
some of the **a** of the burnt sin Nm 19:17
Tamar put **a** on her head and tore 2Sm 13:19
and the **a** that are on it will be 1Kg 13:3
and the **a** spilled off the altar, 1Kg 13:5
and carried their **a** to Bethel. 2Kg 23:4
on sackcloth and **a**, went into Est 4:1
and many lay on sackcloth and **a**. Est 4:3
while he sat among the **a**. Jb 2:8
I have become like dust and **a**. Jb 30:19
words⌋ and repent in dust and **a**. Jb 42:6
I eat **a** like bread and mingle my Ps 102:9
He scatters frost like **a**; Ps 147:16
The peoples will be burned to **a**, Is 33:12
He feeds on **a**.⌊His⌋ deceived Is 44:20
to spread out sackcloth and **a**? Is 58:5
a crown of beauty instead of **a**, Is 61:3
the corpses, the **a**, and all the Jr 31:40
on their heads; they roll in **a**. Ezk 27:30
I reduced you to **a** on the ground Ezk 28:18
with fasting, sackcloth, and **a**. Dn 9:3
put on sackcloth, and sat in **a**. Jnh 3:6
they will be **a** under the soles Mal 4:3
in sackcloth and **a** long ago! Mt 11:21
sitting in sackcloth and **a**! Lk 10:13
and bulls and the **a** of a heifer Heb 9:13
and Gomorrah to **a** and condemned 2Pt 2:6

ASHHUR *(1)*
Abijah bore him **A** the father of 1Ch 2:24

ASHIMA *(1)*
the men of Hamath made **A**, 2Kg 17:30

ASHKELON *(13)*
Gaza, Ashdod, **A**, Gath, and Ekron Jos 13:3
its territory, **A** and its Jdg 1:18
he went down to **A** and killed 30 Jdg 14:19
Gaza, **A**, Gath, and Ekron. 1Sm 6:17
announce it in the streets of **A**, 2Sm 1:20
Philistines—**A**, Gaza, Ekron, Jr 25:20
A will become silent, a remnant Jr 47:5
it against **A** and the shore Jr 47:7
who wields the scepter from **A**. Am 1:8
be abandoned, and **A** will become Zph 2:4
evening among the houses of **A**, Zph 2:7
A will see it and be afraid; Zch 9:5
and **A** will become uninhabited. Zch 9:5

ASHKENAZ *(3)*
A, Riphath, and Togarmah. Gn 10:3
A, Riphath, and Togarmah. 1Ch 1:6
her—Ararat, Minni, and **A**. Jr 51:27

ASHNAH *(2)*
foothills: Eshtaol, Zorah, **A**, Jos 15:33
Iphtah, **A**, Nezib, Jos 15:43

ASHORE *(6)*
they dragged it **a**, sat down, Mt 13:48
As He stepped **a**, He saw a huge Mt 14:14
as He stepped **a**, He saw a huge Mk 6:34
got up and hauled the net **a**, Jn 21:11
to run the ship **a** if they could. Ac 27:39
Safely **a**, we then learned that Ac 28:1

ASHPENAZ *(1)*
The king ordered **A**, the chief of Dn 1:3

ASHTAROTH *(6)*
(AKA ASHTEROTH-KARNAIM, BEESHTERAH, KARNAIM)
who lived in **A**, at Edrei. Dt 1:4
Og king of Bashan, who was in **A**. Jos 9:10
Rephaim, lived in **A** and Edrei. Jos 12:4
who reigned in **A** and Edrei; Jos 13:12
in Bashan—**A** and Edrei—are Jos 13:31
and **A** and its pasturelands from 1Ch 6:71

ASHTERATHITE *(1)*
Uzzia the **A**, Shama and Jeiel the 1Ch 11:44

ASHTEROTH-KARNAIM *(1)*
(AKA ASHTAROTH, BEESHTERAH, KARNAIM)
and defeated the Rephaim in **A**, Gn 14:5

ASHTORETH *(3)*
Solomon followed **A**, the goddess 1Kg 11:5
they have bowed the knee to **A**, 1Kg 11:33
king of Israel had built for **A**, 2Kg 23:13

ASHTORETHS *(6)*
and worshiped Baal and the **A**. Jdg 2:13
worshiped the Baals and the **A**, Jdg 10:6
gods and the **A** that are among 1Sm 7:3
the Baals and the **A** and only 1Sm 7:4
worshiped the Baals and the **A**. 1Sm 12:10
temple of the **A** and hung his 1Sm 31:10

ASHURBANIPAL *(1)*
and illustrious **A** deported and Ezr 4:10

ASHVATH *(1)*
Pasach, Bimhal, and **A**. 1Ch 7:33

ASIA *(19)*
and Cappadocia, Pontus and **A**, Ac 2:9
and some from Cilicia and **A**, Ac 6:9
message in the province of **A**. Ac 16:6
of the province of **A**, Ac 19:10
the province of **A** for a while. Ac 19:22
almost the whole province of **A**, Ac 19:26
province of **A** and the world Ac 19:27
the provincial officials of **A**, Ac 19:31
Tychicus and Trophimus from **A**. Ac 20:4
spend time in the province of **A**, Ac 20:16
the first day I set foot in **A**, Ac 20:18
from the province of **A** saw him Ac 21:27
the province of **A** found me Ac 24:18
the coast of the province of **A**. Ac 27:2
first convert to Christ from **A**. Rm 16:5
took place in the province of **A**: 2Co 1:8
all those in **A** have turned away 2Tm 1:15
Cappadocia, **A**, and Bithynia, 1Pt 1:1
churches in the province of **A**. Rv 1:4

ASIAN *(1)*
churches of the **A** province greet 1Co 16:19

ASIDE *(51)*
(See pp. xi-xii.)

ASIEL *(1)*
son of Seraiah, son of **A**, 1Ch 4:35

ASK *(172)*
(See pp. xi-xii.)

ASKED *(457)*
(See pp. xi-xii.)

ASKING *(43)*
(See pp. xi-xii.)

ASKS *(34)*
(See pp. xi-xii.)

ASLEEP *(28)*
He fell **a** and dreamed a second Gn 41:5
the men fell **a**, she went up Jos 2:8
let him fall **a** on her lap and Jdg 16:19
was lying there **a** in the inner 1Sm 26:7
all remained **a** because a deep 1Sm 26:12
side while your servant was **a**. 1Kg 3:20
I would be **a**. Then I would be Jb 3:13
they will fall **a** forever and Jr 51:39
they will fall **a** forever and Jr 51:57
What are you doing sound **a**? Jnh 1:6
all became drowsy and fell **a**. Mt 25:5
The child is not dead but **a**." Mk 5:39
as they were sailing He fell **a**. Lk 8:23
for she is not dead but **a**." Lk 8:52
Our friend Lazarus has fallen **a**, Jn 11:11
if he has fallen **a**, he will get Jn 11:12
And saying this, he fell **a**. Ac 7:60
plan, fell **a**, was buried with Ac 13:36
you, and many have fallen **a**. 1Co 11:30
present, but some have fallen **a**. 1Co 15:6
who have fallen **a** in Christ have 1Co 15:18
of those who have fallen **a**. 1Co 15:20
not all fall **a**, but we will all 1Co 15:51
concerning those who are **a**, 1Th 4:13
who have fallen **a** through Jesus. 1Th 4:14
over those who have fallen **a**. 1Th 4:15
that whether we are awake or **a**, 1Th 5:10
ever since the fathers fell **a**, 2Pt 3:4

ASNAH'S *(1)*
A descendants, Meunim's Ezr 2:50

ASPATHA *(1)*
Parshandatha, Dalphon, **A**, Est 9:7

ASPHALT *(3)*
for stone and **a** for mortar. Gn 11:3
of Siddim contained many **a** pits, Gn 14:10
and coated it with **a** and pitch. Ex 2:3

ASPIRE *(1)*
they now **a** to a better land— Heb 11:16

ASPIRES *(1)*
If anyone **a** to be an overseer, 1Tm 3:1

ASRIEL *(3)*
The Asrielite clan ⌊from⌋ **A**; Nm 26:31
Abiezer, Helek, **A**, Shechem, Jos 17:2
A and Machir the father of 1Ch 7:14

ASRIELITE *(1)*
The **A** clan ⌊from⌋ Asriel; Nm 26:31

ASS *(1)*
man will be ⌊like⌋ a wild **a**. Gn 16:12

ASSAILANTS *(1)*
A I did not know tore at me and Ps 35:15

ASSASSINATE *(2)*
and tried to **a** King Ahasuerus. Est 2:21
planned to **a** King Ahasuerus. Est 6:2

ASSASSINS *(1)*
and led 4,000 **A** into the desert? Ac 21:38

ASSAULT *(10)*
every dispute and ⌊case of⌋ **a**. Dt 21:5
made a frontal **a** against Gibeah, Jdg 20:34
In that first **a** Jonathan and his 1Sm 14:14
Do not make a frontal **a**. 2Sm 5:23
They built an **a** ramp against the 2Sm 20:15
build up an **a** ramp against it. 2Kg 19:32
Hardships **a** me, wave after wave. Jb 10:17
build up an **a** ramp against it. Is 37:33
build up an **a** ramp, and capture Dn 11:15
rulers, to **a** and stone them, Ac 14:5

ASSAULTS *(2)*
lawsuits, or **a**—cases disputed Dt 17:8
The one who **a** his father and Pr 19:26

ASSAY *(1)*
you may know and **a** their way of Jr 6:27

ASSAYER *(1)*
you to be an **a** among My people— Jr 6:27

ASSEMBLE *(26)*
Go and **a** the elders of Israel Ex 3:16
A the surrounding courtyard and Ex 40:8
and **a** the whole community at the Lv 8:3
tent of meeting and **a** the entire Nm 8:9
the staff and **a** the community. Nm 20:8
said to me, '**A** the people before Dt 4:10
A all your tribal elders and Dt 31:28
hand, and they **a** at Your feet. Dt 33:3
Now therefore, **a** the rest of the 2Sm 12:28
it into my mind to **a** the nobles, Neh 7:5
so that they may **a** all the Est 2:3
Go and **a** all the Jews who can be Est 4:16
city the right to **a** and defend Est 8:11
They all will **a** and stand; Is 44:11
All of you, **a** and listen! Is 48:14
A yourselves, and let's flee to Jr 4:5
A yourselves to come against her. Jr 49:14
from the peoples and **a** you from Ezk 11:17
wild animals: **A** and come! Gather Ezk 39:17
sent word to **a** the satraps, Dn 3:2
for war and **a** a large number Dn 11:10
congregation; **a** the aged; gather Jl 2:16
A on the mountains of Samaria Am 3:9
I will **a** the lame and gather the Mc 4:6
nations, to **a** kingdoms, in order Zph 3:8
whole world to **a** them for the Rv 16:14

ASSEMBLED *(62)*
prisoner, he **a** his 318 trained Gn 14:14
Aaron went and **a** all the elders Ex 4:29
Moses **a** the entire Israelite Ex 35:1
the community **a** at the entrance Lv 8:4
and they **a** the whole community Nm 1:18
Korah **a** the whole community Nm 16:19
the community **a** against them, Nm 16:42
so they **a** against Moses and Nm 20:2
community **a** at Shiloh where it Jos 18:1
community **a** at Shiloh to go to Jos 22:12
a all the tribes of Israel Jos 24:1
the Israelites **a** and camped at Jdg 10:17
and the community **a** as one body Jdg 20:1
troops with him **a** and marched to 1Sm 14:20
and all Israel **a** to mourn for 1Sm 25:1
David again **a** all the choice men 2Sm 6:1
So David **a** all the troops and 2Sm 12:29
Philistines had **a** ⌊in formation⌋ 2Sm 23:11
He also **a** chariots, cavalry, 1Kg 1:5
that time Solomon **a** the elders 1Kg 8:1
of Israel were **a** in the presence 1Kg 8:2
king of Aram **a** his entire army. 1Kg 20:1
So David **a** all Israel, from the 1Ch 13:5
David **a** all Israel at Jerusalem 1Ch 15:3
David **a** in Jerusalem all the 1Ch 28:1
that time Solomon **a** at Jerusalem 2Ch 5:2
of Israel were **a** in the king's 2Ch 5:3
They **a** in the Valley of Beracah 2Ch 20:26
Judah and **a** them according to 2Ch 25:5
a before Ezra the scribe to Neh 8:13
of this month the Israelites **a**; Neh 9:1
young women were **a** together for Est 2:19
the Jews **a** in their cities to Est 9:2
The Jews in Susa **a** again on the Est 9:15
Jews in the royal provinces **a**, Est 9:16
Jews in Susa had **a** on the Est 9:18
the peoples have **a** ⌊with⌋ the Ps 47:9
Look! The kings **a**; they advanced Ps 48:4
and kingdoms are **a** to serve the Ps 102:22
together, and the peoples are **a**. Is 43:9
the people **a** against Jeremiah Jr 26:9
up and said to all the **a** people, Jr 26:17
Have you **a** your hordes to carry Ezk 38:13
of the provinces **a** for the Dn 3:3
nations have now **a** against you; Mc 4:11
he **a** all the chief priests and Mt 2:4
of the people **a** in the palace Mt 26:3
priests had **a** with the elders Mt 28:12
whole town was **a** at the door, Mk 1:33
and scribes **a** in Jerusalem Ac 4:5
the rulers **a** together against Ac 4:26
a together against Your holy Ac 4:27
where they were **a** was shaken, Ac 4:31
where many had **a** and were Ac 12:12
the whole town **a** to hear the Ac 13:44
the elders **a** to consider this Ac 15:6
When he had **a** them, as well as Ac 19:25
the week, we **a** to break bread. Ac 20:7
room upstairs where we were **a**, Ac 20:8
when they had **a** here, I did not Ac 25:17
when you are **a**, along with my 1Co 5:4
So they **a** them at the place Rv 16:16

ASSEMBLES *(2)*
all Israel **a** in the presence Dt 31:11
if the whole church **a** together, 1Co 14:23

ASSEMBLIES *(8)*
you will proclaim as sacred **a**. Lv 23:2
the sacred **a** you are to proclaim Lv 23:4
as sacred **a** for presenting Lv 23:37
I will praise the LORD in the **a**. Ps 26:12
Praise God in the **a**; Ps 68:26
and the calling of solemn **a**— Is 1:13
of Mount Zion and over its **a**. Is 4:5
the stench of your solemn **a**. Am 5:21

ASSEMBLY *(137)*
that you become an **a** of peoples. Gn 28:3
indeed an **a** of nations, will Gn 35:11
may I never join their **a**. Gn 49:6
the whole **a** of the community Ex 12:6
hold a sacred **a** on the first day Ex 12:16

another sacred **a** on the seventh Ex 12:16
this whole **a** die of hunger!" Ex 16:3
escapes the notice of the **a**, Lv 4:13
then the **a** must present a young Lv 4:14
elders of the **a** are to lay their Lv 4:15
is the sin offering for the **a**. Lv 4:21
and the whole **a** of Israel. Lv 16:17
and all the people of the **a**. Lv 16:33
of complete rest, a sacred **a**. Lv 23:3
day you are to hold a sacred **a**; Lv 23:7
day there will be a sacred **a**; Lv 23:8
and hold a sacred **a**. Lv 23:21
and jubilation—a sacred **a**. Lv 23:24
to hold a sacred **a** and practice Lv 23:27
to be a sacred **a** on the first Lv 23:35
to hold a sacred **a** and present a Lv 23:36
When calling the **a** together, Nm 10:7
of the whole **a** of the Israelite Nm 14:5
a is to have the same statute Nm 15:15
and representatives in the **a**, Nm 16:2
yourselves above the LORD's **a**?" Nm 16:3
and they vanished from the **a**. Nm 16:33
ran into the middle of the **a**, Nm 16:47
off from the **a** because he has Nm 19:20
brought the LORD's **a** into this Nm 20:4
presence of the **a** to the doorway Nm 20:6
Aaron summoned the **a** in front of Nm 20:10
not bring this **a** into the land I Nm 20:12
got up from the **a**, took a spear Nm 25:7
day there is to be a sacred **a**; Nm 28:18
day you are to hold a sacred **a**; Nm 28:25
hold a sacred **a** when you present Nm 28:26
hold a sacred **a** in the seventh Nm 29:1
to hold a sacred **a** on the tenth Nm 29:7
hold a sacred **a** on the fifteenth Nm 29:12
day you are to hold a solemn **a**; Nm 29:35
he stands trial before the **a**. Nm 35:12
the **a** is to judge between the Nm 35:24
The **a** is to protect the one who Nm 35:25
Then the **a** will return him to Nm 35:25
to your entire **a** from the fire, Dt 5:22
the day of the **a** the LORD gave Dt 9:10
the day of the **a**, the LORD wrote Dt 10:4
to be a solemn **a** to the LORD Dt 16:8
day of the **a** when you said, Dt 18:16
cut off may enter the LORD's **a**. Dt 23:1
birth may enter the LORD's **a**; Dt 23:2
may enter the LORD's **a**. Dt 23:2
Moabite may enter the LORD's **a**; Dt 23:3
may ever enter the LORD's **a**. Dt 23:3
may enter the LORD's **a**. Dt 23:8
song to the entire **a** of Israel: Dt 31:30
a possession for the **a** of Jacob. Dt 33:4
before the entire **a** of Israel, Jos 8:35
trial before the **a** and until the Jos 20:6
until he stands before the **a**. Jos 20:9
in the **a** of God's people: Jdg 20:2
come to the LORD with the **a**?" Jdg 21:5
had come to the camp and the **a**. Jdg 21:8
and this whole **a** will know that 1Sm 17:47
him—a great **a**, from the 1Kg 8:65
and the whole **a** of Israel came 1Kg 12:3
him to the **a** and made him king 1Kg 12:20
"Consecrate a solemn **a** for Baal." 2Kg 10:20
said to the whole **a** of Israel, 1Ch 13:2
the whole **a** agreed to do it. 1Ch 13:4
all Israel, the **a** of the LORD, 1Ch 28:8
King David said to all the **a**, 1Ch 29:1
LORD in the sight of all the **a**. 1Ch 29:10
Then David said to the whole **a**, 1Ch 29:20
So the whole **a** praised the LORD 1Ch 29:20
and the whole **a** with him went to 2Ch 1:3
and the **a** inquired of Him 2Ch 1:5
a very great **a**, from the 2Ch 7:8
eighth day they held a sacred **a**, 2Ch 7:9
stood in the **a** of Judah and 2Ch 20:5
Then the whole **a** made a covenant 2Ch 23:3
Moses and the **a** of Israel for 2Ch 24:6
The whole **a** was worshiping, 2Ch 29:28
A very large **a** of people was 2Ch 30:13
were many in the **a** who had not 2Ch 30:17
Then the whole **a** of Judah with 2Ch 30:25
the whole **a** that came from 2Ch 30:25
of the whole **a** (for they had 2Ch 31:18
combined **a** numbered 42,360 Ezr 2:64
extremely large **a** of Israelite Ezr 10:1
from the **a** of the exiles. Ezr 10:8
Then all the **a** responded with a Ezr 10:12
leaders represent the entire **a**. Ezr 10:14
I called a large **a** against them Neh 5:7
The whole **a** said, "Amen," and Neh 5:13
combined **a** numbered 42,360 Neh 7:66
the law before the **a** of men, Neh 8:2
the eighth day there was an **a**, Neh 8:18
should ever enter the **a** of God, Neh 13:1
I stood in the **a** and cried out Jb 30:28
Let the **a** of peoples gather Ps 7:7
righteousness in the great **a**; Ps 40:9
love and truth from the great **a**. Ps 40:10
the rulers of Judah in their **a**, Ps 68:27
taken His place in the divine **a**; Ps 82:1
in the **a** of the holy ones. Ps 89:5
it covered the **a** of Abiram. Ps 106:17
Fire blazed throughout their **a**; Ps 106:18
exalt Him in the **a** of the people Ps 107:32
my heart in the **a** of the upright Ps 111:1
praise in the **a** of the godly. Ps 149:1
to rest in the **a** of the departed Pr 21:16
evil will be revealed in the **a**. Pr 26:26
on the mount of the ⌊gods'⌋ **a**, Is 14:13
solemn **a** of treacherous people. Jr 9:2
will return here as a great **a**! Jr 31:8
by—a great **a**—and all the Jr 44:15
Babylon an **a** of great nations Jr 50:9
had forbidden to enter Your **a**. Lm 1:10
Summon an **a** against them and Ezk 23:46
The **a** will stone them and cut Ezk 23:47
you with an **a** of many peoples Ezk 32:3
the news that reaches their **a**. Hs 7:12
fast; proclaim an **a**! Gather the Jl 1:14
a sacred fast; proclaim an **a**. Jl 2:15
no one in the **a** of the LORD to Mc 2:5
the whole **a** of the people was Lk 1:10
Then their whole **a** rose up and Lk 23:1
Then the whole **a** fell silent and Ac 15:12
and after gathering the **a**, Ac 15:30
bring them out to the public **a**. Ac 17:5
because the **a** was in confusion, Ac 19:32
it must be decided in a legal **a**. Ac 19:39
saying this, he dismissed the **a**. Ac 19:41
and the **a** was divided. Ac 23:7
to the **a** of the firstborn whose Heb 12:23

ASSERT *(4)*
and unable to **a** himself against 2Ch 13:7
saying you can **a** yourselves 2Ch 13:8
say, and Israel, why do you **a**: Is 40:27
own people will **a** themselves to Dn 11:14

ASSES *(1)*
the joy of wild **a**, and a pasture Is 32:14

ASSESS *(1)*
the priest will **a** its value, Lv 27:14

ASSESSES *(1)*
stand just as the priest **a** it. Lv 27:14

ASSESSING *(1)*
oil that you have been **a** them." Neh 5:11

ASSESSMENT *(1)*
pay according to judicial **a**. Ex 21:22

ASSESSOR *(1)*
to take from his **a** and repair 2Kg 12:5

ASSESSORS *(1)*
take any money from your **a**; 2Kg 12:7

ASSETS *(3)*
despite ⌊his⌋ **a**, man will not Ps 49:12
So he distributed the **a** to them. Lk 15:12
devoured your **a** with prostitutes Lk 15:30

ASSHUR *(7)*
sons were Elam, **A**, Arpachshad, Gn 10:22
Egypt as you go toward **A**. Gn 25:18
destroyed when **A** takes you Nm 24:22
they will afflict **A** and Eber, Nm 24:24
Elam, **A**, Arpachshad, Lud, Aram, 1Ch 1:17
A fathered Tekoa and had two 1Ch 4:5
of Sheba, **A**, and Chilmad traded Ezk 27:23

ASSHURIM *(1)*
sons were the **A**, Letushim, Gn 25:3

ASSIGN *(7)*
A the Levites to Aaron and his Nm 3:9
are to go in and **a** each man his Nm 4:19
you are to **a** to them all that Nm 4:27
You are to **a** by name the items Nm 4:32
will **a** his inheritance there. Ezk 47:23
to pieces and **a** him a place with Mt 24:51
to pieces and **a** him a place with Lk 12:46

ASSIGNED *(43)*
of the guard **a** Joseph to them, Gn 40:4
the Egyptians **a** taskmasters over Ex 1:11
Finish your **a** work each day, Ex 5:13
have **a** it as their portion from Lv 6:17
and have **a** them to Aaron the Lv 7:34
have been **a** to you and your Lv 10:14
and He has **a** it to you to take Lv 10:17
they have been **a** exclusively to Nm 3:9
The **a** duties of Merari's Nm 3:36
have been exclusively **a** to Me Nm 8:16
a by the LORD to work at the Nm 18:6
portion was **a** there for him. Dt 33:21
return to the place you **a** him. 1Sm 29:4
the Levites were **a** to all the 1Ch 6:48
the places **a** to Aaron's sons 1Ch 6:54
of Manasseh ⌊were **a**⌋ by lot. 1Ch 6:61
Gershomites ⌊were **a**⌋ 13 towns 1Ch 6:62
Merarites ⌊were **a**⌋ by lot 12 1Ch 6:63
They **a** by lot the towns named 1Ch 6:65
were **a** to guard the thresholds 1Ch 9:19
had been **a** to the LORD's camp 1Ch 9:19
their sons were **a** to the gates 1Ch 9:23
to the **a** duties of their 1Ch 24:3
These had their **a** duties for 1Ch 24:19
had **a** duties in Israel west of 1Ch 26:30
so he **a** 70,000 men as porters, 2Ch 2:2
and peoples and **a** them to be a Neh 9:22
foreign and **a** specific duties to Neh 13:30
He **a** seven hand-picked female Est 2:9
of the king's eunuchs **a** to her, Est 4:5
nights have been **a** to me. Jb 7:3
the morning or **a** the dawn its Jb 38:12
He has **a** it against Ashkelon and Jr 47:7
For I have **a** you the years of Ezk 4:5
I have **a** you 40 days, a day for Ezk 4:6
The king **a** them daily provisions Dn 1:5
My lord the king **a** your food and Dn 1:10
chief official had **a** to Daniel, Dn 1:11
whom the king had **a** to destroy Dn 2:24
him in prison and **a** four squads Ac 12:4
that is **a** for you to do.' Ac 22:10
the Lord **a** when God called 1Co 7:17
ministry⌋ that God has **a** to us, 2Co 10:13

ASSIGNMENT *(3)*
and his **a** was as the LORD Nm 4:49
place according to his **a**. 1Kg 4:28
house ⌊and received⌋ a single **a**. 1Ch 23:11

ASSIGNMENTS *(1)*
according to the their **a**, 2Ch 26:11

ASSIR *(4)*
A, Elkanah, and Abiasaph. Ex 6:24
his son Korah, his son **A**, 1Ch 6:22
his son Ebiasaph, his son **A**, 1Ch 6:23
Tahath, son of **A**, son of 1Ch 6:37

ASSIST *(8)*
of the men who are to **a** you: Nm 1:5
to Aaron the priest to **a** him. Nm 3:6
He may **a** his brothers to fulfill Nm 8:26
came to **a** King Hadadezer 2Sm 8:5
came to **a** King Hadadezer 1Ch 18:5
duty will be to **a** the sons of 1Ch 23:28
son of Mattaniah to **a** them, Neh 13:13
and **a** her in whatever matter she Rm 16:2

ASSISTANCE *(3)*
with ⌊the **a** of⌋ the 12 leaders Nm 1:44
as we looked⌋ in vain for **a**; Lm 4:17
one came to my **a**, but everyone 2Tm 4:16

ASSISTANT *(4)*
Moses arose with his **a** Joshua, Ex 24:13
camp, but his **a**, the young man Ex 33:11
a to Moses since his youth, Nm 11:28
They also had John as their **a**. Ac 13:5

ASSISTANTS *(1)*
Rahab's **a** cringe in fear beneath Jb 9:13

ASSISTED *(4)*
be **a** by the men of that region Ezr 1:4
and I was amazed that no one **a**; Is 63:5
for Me, and My wrath **a** Me. Is 63:5
sending two of those who **a** him, Ac 19:22

ASSOCIATE *(14)*
that you do not **a** with these Jos 23:7
intermarry or **a** with them and Jos 23:12
worthless or **a** with hypocrites Ps 26:4
and you **a** with adulterers. Ps 50:18
Don't **a** with those who drink too Pr 23:20

king, and don't a with rebels, Pr 24:21
against the man who is My a— Zch 13:7
Jews do not a with Samaritans Jn 4:9
tried to a with the disciples, Ac 9:26
a Jewish man to a with or visit Ac 10:28
instead, a with the humble. Rm 12:16
a letter not to a with sexually 1Co 5:9
you not to a with anyone who 1Co 5:11
don't a with him, so that he may 2Th 3:14

ASSOCIATED *(3)*

and the Israelites a with him. Ezk 37:16
the house of Israel a with him. Ezk 37:16
the tribes of Israel a with him, Ezk 37:19

ASSOCIATES *(1)*

I and my a never ate from the Neh 5:14

ASSOS *(2)*

to the ship and sailed for A, Ac 20:13
When he met us at A, we took him Ac 20:14

ASSUME *(2)*

Don't a that I came to destroy Mt 5:17
Don't a that I came to bring Mt 10:34

ASSUMED *(3)*

When Saul a the kingship over 1Sm 14:47
they a they would get more, Mt 20:10
He a his brothers would Ac 7:25

ASSUMING *(4)*

A He was in the traveling party, Lk 2:44
a you heard Him and were taught Eph 4:21
emptied Himself by a the form of Php 2:7
a that I will somehow reach the Php 3:11

ASSURANCE *(4)*

Go in the a the two of us 1Sm 20:42
up, they have no a of life. Jb 24:22
Holy Spirit, and with much a. 1Th 1:5
a true heart in full a of faith, Heb 10:22

ASSURE *(76)*

against my pursuers, and a me: Ps 35:3
For I a you: Until heaven and Mt 5:18
I a you: You will never get out Mt 5:26
by people. I a you: They've got Mt 6:2
by people. I a you: They've got Mt 6:5
to people. I a you: They've got Mt 6:16
those following Him, "I a you: Mt 8:10
I a you: It will be more Mt 10:15
another. For I a you: You will Mt 10:23
he is a disciple—I a you: Mt 10:42
I a you: Among those born of Mt 11:11
For I a you: Many prophets and Mt 13:17
I a you: There are some standing Mt 16:28
them. "For I a you: If you have Mt 17:20
"I a you," He said, "unless you Mt 18:3
And if he finds it, I a you: Mt 18:13
I a you: Whatever you bind on Mt 18:18
Again, I a you: If two of you on Mt 18:19
said to His disciples, "I a you: Mt 19:23
Jesus said to them, "I a you: Mt 19:28
Jesus answered them, "I a you: Mt 21:21
Jesus said to them, "I a you: Mt 21:31
I a you: All these things will Mt 23:36
these things? I a you: Not one Mt 24:2
I a you: This generation will Mt 24:34
I a you: He will put him in Mt 24:47
But he replied, 'I a you: Mt 25:12
King will answer them, 'I a you: Mt 25:40
He will answer them, 'I a you: Mt 25:45
I a you: Wherever this gospel is Mt 26:13
were eating, He said, "I a you: Mt 26:21
"I a you," Jesus said to him, Mt 26:34
I a you: People will be forgiven Mk 3:28
demand a sign? I a you: No sign Mk 8:12
Then He said to them, "I a you: Mk 9:1
belong to the Messiah—I a you: Mk 9:41
a you: Whoever does not welcome Mk 10:15
"I a you," Jesus said, "there is Mk 10:29
I a you: If anyone says to this Mk 11:23
He said to them, "I a you: Mk 12:43
I a you: This generation will Mk 13:30
I a you: Wherever the gospel is Mk 14:9
eating, Jesus said, "I a you: Mk 14:18
I a you: I will no longer drink Mk 14:25
"I a you," Jesus said to him, Mk 14:30
He also said, "I a you: Lk 4:24
be blessed. I a you: He will get Lk 12:37
a you: Whoever does not welcome Lk 18:17
So He said to them, "I a you: Lk 18:29
I a you: This generation will Lk 21:32
And He said to him, "I a you: Lk 23:43
Then He said, "I a you: Jn 1:51
Jesus replied, "I a you: Jn 3:3
Jesus answered, "I a you: Jn 3:5
I a you: We speak what We know Jn 3:11
Then Jesus replied, "I a you: Jn 5:19
I a you: Anyone who hears My Jn 5:24
I a you: An hour is coming, and Jn 5:25
Jesus answered, "I a you: Jn 6:26
Jesus said to them, "I a you: Jn 6:32
I a you: Anyone who believes has Jn 6:47
So Jesus said to them, "I a you: Jn 6:53
Jesus responded, "I a you: Jn 8:34
a you: If anyone keeps My word, Jn 8:51
Jesus said to them, "I a you: Jn 8:58
I a you: Anyone who doesn't Jn 10:1
So Jesus said again, "I a you: Jn 10:7
I a you: Unless a grain of wheat Jn 12:24
I a you: A slave is not greater Jn 13:16
I a you: The one who receives Jn 13:20
spirit and testified, "I a you: Jn 13:21
life for Me? I a you: A rooster Jn 13:38
I a you: The one who believes in Jn 14:12
I a you: You will weep and wail, Jn 16:20
Me anything. "I a you: Anything Jn 16:23
I a you: When you were young, Jn 21:18

ASSURED *(8)*

a us the donkeys had been found. 1Sm 10:16
heart is a; he will not fear. Ps 112:8
Be a that the wicked will not go Pr 11:21
be a, he will not go unpunished. Pr 16:5
his food provided, his water a. Is 33:16
you, the promises a to David. Is 55:3
the riches of a understanding, Col 2:2
mature and fully a in everything Col 4:12

ASSUREDLY *(2)*

A, I will set you free and care Jr 15:11
A, I will intercede for you in a Jr 15:11

ASSURING *(2)*

and their men, a them, "Don't be 2Kg 25:24
and their men, a them, "Don't be Jr 40:9

ASSYRIA *(135)*

which flows to the east of A. Gn 2:14
land he went to A and built Gn 10:11
Pul king of A invaded the land, 2Kg 15:19
Israel to give to the king of A. 2Kg 15:20
the king of A withdrew and did 2Kg 15:20
king of A came and captured Ijon 2Kg 15:29
and deported the people to A. 2Kg 15:29
to Tiglath-pileser king of A, 2Kg 16:7
to the king of A as a gift. 2Kg 16:8
So the king of A listened to him 2Kg 16:9
meet Tiglath-pileser king of A. 2Kg 16:10
the king of A, he removed 2Kg 16:18
king of A attacked him, 2Kg 17:3
But the king of A discovered a 2Kg 17:4
to the king of A as in previous 2Kg 17:4
the king of A arrested him and 2Kg 17:4
Then the king of A invaded the 2Kg 17:5
the king of A captured Samaria. 2Kg 17:6
Israelites to A and settled them 2Kg 17:6
has been exiled to A from their 2Kg 17:23
the king of A brought ⌊people 2Kg 17:24
settlers spoke to the king of A, 2Kg 17:26
the king of A issued a command 2Kg 17:27
the king of A and did not serve 2Kg 18:7
king of A marched against 2Kg 18:9
The king of A deported the 2Kg 18:11
the Israelites to A and put them 2Kg 18:11
king of A attacked all 2Kg 18:13
to the king of A at Lachish, 2Kg 18:14
The king of A demanded from 2Kg 18:14
and gave it to the king of A. 2Kg 18:16
the king of A sent the Tartan 2Kg 18:17
king, the king of A, says: 2Kg 18:19
with my master the king of A. 2Kg 18:23
the great king, the king of A. 2Kg 18:28
handed over to the king of A.' 2Kg 18:30
is what the king of A says: 2Kg 18:31
from the power of the king of A? 2Kg 18:33
master the king of A sent to 2Kg 19:4
the king of A had left Lachish 2Kg 19:8
be handed over to the king of A. 2Kg 19:10
the kings of A have done to all 2Kg 19:11
the kings of A have devastated 2Kg 19:17
about Sennacherib king of A.' 2Kg 19:20
LORD says about the king of A: 2Kg 19:32
king of A broke camp and left 2Kg 19:36
from the hand of the king of A. 2Kg 20:6
to the king of A at the 2Kg 23:29
king of A took him into exile. 1Ch 5:6
of A to take the Reubenites, 1Ch 5:26
asked the king of A for help. 2Ch 28:16
king of A came against Ahaz; 2Ch 28:20
the plunder to the king of A, 2Ch 28:21
the grasp of the kings of A. 2Ch 30:6
king of A came and entered 2Ch 32:1
the kings of A come and find 2Ch 32:4
the king of A or before all 2Ch 32:7
king of A with all his armed 2Ch 32:9
King Sennacherib of A says: 2Ch 32:10
the power of the king of A"? 2Ch 32:11
in the camp of the king of A. 2Ch 32:21
So the king of A returned with 2Ch 32:21
Sennacherib of A and from the 2Ch 32:22
commanders of the king of A. 2Ch 33:11
Esar-haddon of A brought us here. Ezr 4:2
Even A has joined them; Ps 83:8
the king of A ⌊is coming⌋. Is 7:17
bee that is in the land of A. Is 7:18
the king of A—to shave the Is 7:20
carried off to the king of A." Is 8:4
the king of A and all his glory. Is 8:7
Woe to A, the rod of My anger— Is 10:5
the king of A for his arrogant Is 10:12
disease on the well-fed of A, Is 10:16
Zion, do not fear A, though he Is 10:24
A has come to Aiath and has gone Is 10:28
recover—from A, Egypt, Pathros Is 11:11
people who will survive from A, Is 11:16
I will break A in My land; Is 14:25
be a highway from Egypt to A. Is 19:23
A will go to Egypt, Egypt to Is 19:23
Egypt, Egypt to A, and Egypt Is 19:23
and Egypt will worship with A. Is 19:23
alliance⌋ with Egypt and A— Is 19:24
Egypt My people, A My handiwork, Is 19:25
Sargon king of A, came to Ashdod Is 20:1
so the king of A will lead the Is 20:4
rescue ⌊us⌋ from the king of A! Is 20:6
A destined it for wild beasts. Is 23:13
lost in the land of A will come, Is 27:13
A will be shattered by the voice Is 30:31
Then A will fall, but not by Is 31:8
king of A advanced against Is 36:1
Then the king of A sent the Is 36:2
the king of A, says this: Is 36:4
with my master, the king of A. Is 36:8
the great king, the king of A! Is 36:13
handed over to the king of A.'" Is 36:15
For the king of A says: Is 36:16
from the hand of the king of A? Is 36:18
the king of A, sent to mock Is 37:4
that the king of A was fighting Is 37:8
be handed over to the king of A. Is 37:10
the kings of A have done to all Is 37:11
the kings of A have devastated Is 37:18
Me about Sennacherib king of A, Is 37:21
LORD says about the king of A: Is 37:33
king of A broke camp and left Is 37:37
from the hand of the king of A; Is 38:6
then A oppressed them without Is 52:4
along the way to A to drink the Jr 2:18
as you were put to shame by A. Jr 2:36
devoured him was the king of A; Jr 50:17
as I punished the king of A. Jr 50:18
a treaty with Egypt and with A, Lm 5:6
all of them were the elite of A. Ezk 23:7
Think of A, a cedar in Lebanon, Ezk 31:3
A is there with all her company; Ezk 32:22
Ephraim went to A and sent ⌊a Hs 5:13
call to Egypt, and they go to A. Hs 7:11
have gone up to A ⌊like⌋ a wild Hs 8:9
they will eat unclean food in A. Hs 9:3
be taken to A as an offering Hs 10:6
of Egypt and A will be his king Hs 11:5
like doves from the land of A. Hs 11:11
He makes a covenant with A, Hs 12:1
A will not save us, we will not Hs 14:3
When A invades our land, when it Mc 5:5
the land of A with the sword, Mc 5:6
rescue us from A when it invades Mc 5:6
to you from A and the cities Mc 7:12
King of A, your shepherds Nah 3:18
against the north and destroy A; Zph 2:13

of Egypt and gather them from **A**. Zch 10:10
The pride of **A** will be brought Zch 10:11

ASSYRIA'S *(3)*
the king of **A** attendants have 2Kg 19:6
it will burn up **A** thorns and Is 10:17
the king of **A** attendants have Is 37:6

ASSYRIAN *(4)*
changed the **A** king's attitude Ezr 6:22
the days of the **A** kings until Neh 9:32
The **A** stood near the conduit of Is 36:2
with the **A** men because you were Ezk 16:28

ASSYRIANS *(7)*
The **A** captured it at the end of 2Kg 18:10
185,000 in the camp of the **A**. 2Kg 19:35
185,000 in the camp of the **A**. Is 37:36
lusted after her lovers, the **A**: Ezk 23:5
lovers, the **A** she lusted for. Ezk 23:9
She lusted after the **A**: Ezk 23:12
and all the **A** with them— Ezk 23:23

ASTONISHED *(17)*
don't be **a** at the situation, Ec 5:8
Stop and be **a**; blind yourselves Is 29:9
crowds were **a** at His teaching Mt 7:28
so that they were **a** and said, Mt 13:54
they were utterly **a** and asked, Mt 19:25
they were **a** at His teaching. Mt 22:33
They were **a** at His teaching Mk 1:22
and many who heard Him were **a**. Mk 6:2
They were extremely **a** and said, Mk 7:37
disciples were **a** at His words. Mk 10:24
were even more **a**, saying to one Mk 10:26
They were **a**, but those who Mk 10:32
crowd was **a** by His teaching Mk 11:18
Him, they were **a**, and His mother Lk 2:48
They were **a** at His teaching Lk 4:32
they were all **a** at the greatness Lk 9:43
and was **a** at the teaching Ac 13:12

ASTONISHING *(1)*
Her downfall was **a**; Lm 1:9

ASTONISHMENT *(3)*
men looked at each other in **a**. Gn 43:33
and **a** overwhelmed them. Mk 16:8
filled with awe and **a** at what Ac 3:10

ASTOUNDED *(21)*
sky tremble, **a** at His rebuke. Jb 26:11
and observe—be utterly **a**! Hab 1:5
all the crowds were **a** and said, Mt 12:23
they were all **a** and gave glory Mk 2:12
At this they were utterly **a**. Mk 5:42
They were completely **a**, Mk 6:51
who heard Him were **a** at His Lk 2:47
everyone was **a**, and they were Lk 5:26
Her parents were **a**, but He Lk 8:56
some women from our group **a** us. Lk 24:22
And they were **a** and amazed, Ac 2:7
they were all **a** and perplexed, Ac 2:12
in that city and **a** the Samaritan Ac 8:9
because he had **a** them with his Ac 8:11
Philip and was **a** as he observed Ac 8:13
who heard him were **a** and said, Ac 9:21
who had come with Peter were **a**, Ac 10:45
door and saw him, they were **a**. Ac 12:16
When I saw her, I was utterly **a**. Rv 17:6
said to me, "Why are you **a**? Rv 17:7
world will be **a** when they see Rv 17:8

ASTRAY *(53)*
man's wife goes **a**, is unfaithful Nm 5:12
you have not gone **a** and become Nm 5:19
you have gone **a** while under your Nm 5:20
when a wife goes **a** and defiles Nm 5:29
do not be led **a** to bow down and Dt 4:19
the inhabitants of their city **a**, Dt 13:13
so that his heart won't go **a**. Dt 17:17
a blind person **a** on the road.' Dt 27:18
and you are led **a** to bow down to Dt 30:17
themselves, and he led Judah **a**. 2Ch 21:11
being led **a**, for what he gets Jb 15:31
let a large ransom lead you **a**. Jb 36:18
The wicked go **a** from the womb; Ps 58:3
my steps nearly went **a**. Ps 73:2
are a people whose hearts go **a**; Ps 95:10
we have gone **a** and have acted Ps 106:6
Before I was afflicted I went **a**, Ps 119:67
who rejects correction goes **a**. Pr 10:17
ways of wicked men lead them **a**. Pr 12:26
Don't those who plan evil go **a**? Pr 14:22
own foolishness leads him **a**, Pr 19:3
chieftains have led Egypt **a**. Is 19:13
of the peoples to lead ⌊them⌋ **a**. Is 30:28
Even the fool will not go **a**. Is 35:8
deceived mind has led him **a**, Is 44:20
wisdom and knowledge led you **a**. Is 47:10
We all went **a** like sheep; Is 53:6
Baal and led My people Israel **a**. Jr 23:13
leading My people **a** with their Jr 23:32
your own selves **a** because you Jr 42:20
their shepherds have led them **a**, Jr 50:6
have led My people **a** saying: Ezk 13:10
My flock went **a** on all the Ezk 34:6
away from Me when Israel went **a**, Ezk 44:10
the Israelites went **a** from Me, Ezk 44:15
and did not go **a** as the Levites Ezk 48:11
did when the Israelites went **a**. Ezk 48:11
of promiscuity leads them **a**; Hs 4:12
followed have led them **a**. Am 2:4
prophets who lead my people **a**, Mc 3:5
let what is going **a** go astray; Zch 11:9
let what is going astray go **a**; Zch 11:9
care for those who are going **a**, Zch 11:16
of them goes **a**, won't he leave Mt 18:12
over the 99 that did not go **a**. Mt 18:13
signs and wonders to lead **a**, Mt 24:24
signs and wonders to lead **a**, Mk 13:22
led to dumb idols—being led **a**. 1Co 12:2
They always go **a** in their hearts Heb 3:10
are ignorant and are going **a**, Heb 5:2
Don't be led **a** by various kinds Heb 13:9
For you were like sheep going **a**, 1Pt 2:25
they have gone **a** and have 2Pt 2:15

ASTROLOGER *(1)*
a is able to make known to the Dn 2:27

ASTROLOGERS *(4)*
save you—the **a**, who observe Is 47:13
Chaldeans, and **a** came in, I told Dn 4:7
the mediums, Chaldeans, and **a**. Dn 5:7
mediums, Chaldeans, and **a**. Dn 5:11

ASTUTE *(1)*
age are more **a** than the sons Lk 16:8

ASTUTELY *(1)*
manager because he had acted **a**. Lk 16:8

ASYNCRITUS *(1)*
Greet **A**, Phlegon, Hermes, Rm 16:14

AT *(2111)*
(See pp. xi-xii.)

ATAD *(2)*
the threshing floor of **A**, Gn 50:10
at the threshing floor of **A**, Gn 50:11

ATARAH *(1)*
had another wife named **A**, 1Ch 2:26

ATAROTH *(4)*
territory of⌋ **A**, Dibon, Jazer, Nm 32:3
Gadites rebuilt Dibon, **A**, Aroer, Nm 32:34
the border of the Archites by **A**. Jos 16:2
it descended to **A** and Naarah, Jos 16:7

ATAROTH-ADDAR *(2)*
went from **A** on the east of Upper Jos 16:5
went down by **A**, over the hill Jos 18:13

ATE *(107)*
some of its fruit and **a** ⌊it⌋; Gn 3:6
was⌋ with her, and he **a** ⌊it⌋. Gn 3:6
fruit⌋ from the tree, and I **a**." Gn 3:12
He deceived me, and I **a**." Gn 3:13
wife's voice and **a** from the tree Gn 3:17
them as they **a** under the tree. Gn 18:8
bread for them, and they **a**. Gn 19:3
the men with him **a** and drank and Gn 24:54
he **a**, drank, got up, and went Gn 25:34
for them, and they **a** and drank. Gn 26:30
brought it to him, and he **a**; Gn 27:25
I **a** it all before you came in, Gn 27:33
then **a** there by the mound. Gn 31:46
So they **a** a meal and spent the Gn 31:54
say that a vicious animal **a** him. Gn 37:20
anything except the food he **a**. Gn 39:6
sickly, thin cows **a** the healthy, Gn 41:4
ugly cows **a** the first seven Gn 41:20
of meat and **a** all the bread we Ex 16:3
The Israelites **a** manna for 40 Ex 16:35
They **a** manna until they reached Ex 16:35
saw Him, and they **a** and drank. Ex 24:11
the free fish we **a** in Egypt, Nm 11:5
and the people **a** and bowed in Nm 25:2
a the fat of their sacrifices Dt 32:38
Passover they **a** unleavened bread Jos 5:11
after they **a** from the produce Jos 5:12
a from the crops of the land Jos 5:12
and as they **a** and drank, they Jdg 9:27
his hands and **a** ⌊it⌋ as he went Jdg 14:9
some⌋ to them and they **a** ⌊it⌋. Jdg 14:9
They **a**, drank, and spent the Jdg 19:4
the two of them **a** and drank Jdg 19:6
afternoon and the two of them **a**. Jdg 19:8
their feet and **a** and drank. Jdg 19:21
She **a** and was satisfied and had Ru 2:14
After Boaz **a**, drank, and was in Ru 3:7
got up after they **a** and drank at 1Sm 1:9
she **a** and no longer appeared 1Sm 1:18
So Saul **a** with Samuel that 1Sm 9:24
but none of them **a** any of it 1Sm 14:26
When he **a** the honey, he had 1Sm 14:27
and **a** ⌊meat⌋ with the blood 1Sm 14:32
and his servants, and they **a**. 1Sm 28:25
After he **a** he revived, for he 1Sm 30:12
So Mephibosheth **a** at David's 2Sm 9:11
because he always **a** at the 2Sm 9:13
they served him food, and he **a**. 2Sm 12:20
he died, you got up and **a** food." 2Sm 12:21
back with him, **a** bread in his 1Kg 13:19
went back and **a** bread and drank 1Kg 13:22
her household **a** for many days. 1Kg 17:15
So he **a** and drank and lay down 1Kg 19:6
So he got up, **a**, and drank. 1Kg 19:8
it to the people, and they **a**. 1Kg 19:21
but when they **a** the stew they 2Kg 4:40
they **a** and had some left over. 2Kg 4:44
So we boiled my son and **a** him, 2Kg 6:29
Then he went in, **a** and drank, 2Kg 9:34
they **a** unleavened bread with 2Kg 23:9
They **a** and drank with great joy 1Ch 29:22
They **a** the appointed feast for 2Ch 30:22
had returned from exile **a** ⌊it⌋, Ezr 6:21
associates never **a** from the food Neh 5:14
They **a**, were filled, became Neh 9:25
trusted, one who **a** my bread, has Ps 41:9
People **a** the bread of angels. Ps 78:25
They **a** and were completely Ps 78:29
Baal of Peor and **a** sacrifices Ps 106:28
its coals, I roasted meat and **a**. Is 44:19
All who **a** of it found themselves Jr 2:3
words were found, and I **a** them. Jr 15:16
They **a** a meal together there in Jr 41:1
So I **a** ⌊it⌋, and it was as Ezk 3:3
a fine flour, honey, and oil. Ezk 16:13
He **a** grass like cattle, and his Dn 4:33
that the swarming locust **a**, Jl 2:25
and they **a** the sacred bread, Mt 12:4
the birds came and **a** them up. Mt 13:4
Everyone **a** and was filled. Mt 14:20
Now those who **a** were about 5,000 Mt 14:21
They all **a** and were filled. Mt 15:37
Now those who **a** were 4,000 men, Mt 15:38
his waist and **a** locusts and wild Mk 1:6
high priest and **a** the sacred Mk 2:26
and the birds came and **a** it up. Mk 4:4
Everyone **a** and was filled. Mk 6:42
Now those who **a** the loaves were Mk 6:44
a and were filled. Then they Mk 8:8
He **a** nothing during those days, Lk 4:2
and took and **a** the sacred bread, Lk 6:4
the birds of the sky **a** it up. Lk 8:5
Everyone **a** and was filled. Lk 9:17
'We **a** and drank in Your presence, Lk 13:26
He took it and **a** in their Lk 24:43
where they **a** the bread after Jn 6:23
but because you **a** the loaves and Jn 6:26
Our fathers **a** the manna in the Jn 6:31
Your fathers **a** the manna in the Jn 6:49
like the manna your fathers **a**— Jn 6:58
After ⌊Judas **a**⌋ the piece of Jn 13:27
They **a** their food with gladness Ac 2:46
who **a** and drank with Him after Ac 10:41
men and **a** with them!" Ac 11:3
They all **a** the same spiritual 1Co 10:3
from the angel's hand and **a** it. Rv 10:10
but when I **a** it, my stomach Rv 10:10

ATER *(1)*
A, Hezekiah, Azzur, Neh 10:17

ATER'S *(4)*
A descendants: Hezekiah's 98 Ezr 2:16

descendants, **A** descendants, Ezr 2:42
A descendants: of Hezekiah 98 Neh 7:21
descendants, **A** descendants, Neh 7:45

ATHACH *(1)*
Hormah, in Bor-ashan, and in **A**; 1Sm 30:30

ATHAIAH *(1)*
A son of Uzziah, son of Neh 11:4

ATHALIAH *(17)*
name was **A**, granddaughter 2Kg 8:26
When **A**, Ahaziah's mother, saw 2Kg 11:1
was hidden from **A** and was not 2Kg 11:2
six years while **A** ruled over the 2Kg 11:3
When **A** heard the noise from the 2Kg 11:13
A tore her clothes and screamed 2Kg 11:14
for they had put **A** to death by 2Kg 11:20
Shamsherai, Shehariah, **A**, 1Ch 8:26
name was **A**, granddaughter 2Ch 22:2
When **A**, Ahaziah's mother, saw 2Ch 22:10
hid Joash from **A** so that she did 2Ch 22:11
While **A** ruled over the land, 2Ch 22:12
When **A** heard the noise from the 2Ch 23:12
A tore her clothes and screamed, 2Ch 23:13
for they had put **A** to death by 2Ch 23:21
sons of that wicked **A** broke into 2Ch 24:7
Jeshaiah son of **A** from Elam's Ezr 8:7

ATHARIM *(1)*
Israel was coming on the **A** road, Nm 21:1

ATHENIANS *(1)*
Now all the **A** and the foreigners Ac 17:21

ATHENS *(5)*
Paul brought him as far as **A**, Ac 17:15
Paul was waiting for them in **A**, Ac 17:16
said: "Men of **A**! I see that you Ac 17:22
he left from **A** and went to Ac 18:1
better to be left alone in **A**. 1Th 3:1

ATHLAI *(1)*
Hananiah, Zabbai, and **A**; Ezr 10:28

ATHLETE *(2)*
like an **a** running a course Ps 19:5
if anyone competes as an **a**, 2Tm 2:5

ATMOSPHERIC *(1)*
to the ruler of the **a** domain, Eph 2:2

ATONE *(5)*
to the LORD to **a** for your lives. Ex 30:15
the LORD to **a** for your lives." Ex 30:16
sin offerings to **a** for Israel, Neh 10:33
only You can **a** for our Ps 65:3
Deliver us and **a** for our sins, Ps 79:9

ATONED *(3)*
He **a** for ⌊their⌋ guilt and did Ps 78:38
Wickedness is **a** for by loyalty Pr 16:6
removed, and your sin is **a** for. Is 6:7

ATONEMENT *(81)*
things by which **a** was made at Ex 29:33
a sin offering each day for **a**. Ex 29:36
altar when you make **a** for it, Ex 29:36
you must make **a** for the altar Ex 29:37
blood of the sin offering for **a**. Ex 30:10
Take the **a** money from the Ex 30:16
on his behalf to make **a** for him. Lv 1:4
will make **a** on their behalf Lv 4:20
priest will make **a** on his behalf Lv 4:26
will make **a** on his behalf, Lv 4:31
priest will make **a** on his behalf Lv 4:35
priest will make **a** on his behalf Lv 5:6
priest will make **a** on his behalf Lv 5:10
priest will make **a** on his behalf Lv 5:13
priest will make **a** on his behalf Lv 5:16
priest will make **a** on his behalf Lv 5:18
priest will make **a** on his behalf Lv 6:7
meeting to make **a** in the holy Lv 6:30
the priest who makes **a** with it. Lv 7:7
it by making **a** for it. Lv 8:15
in order to make **a** for you. Lv 8:34
make **a** for yourself and the Lv 9:7
offering and make **a** for them, Lv 9:7
and make **a** for them before Lv 10:17
LORD and make **a** on her behalf; Lv 12:7
will make **a** on her behalf, Lv 12:8
will make **a** for him before Lv 14:18
and make **a** for the one to be Lv 14:19
The priest will make **a** for him, Lv 14:20
in order to make **a** for him, Lv 14:21
cleansed to make **a** for him Lv 14:29
will make **a** before the LORD Lv 14:31
he will make **a** for the house, Lv 14:53
will make **a** for him before Lv 15:15
will make **a** for her before Lv 15:30
offering and make **a** for himself Lv 16:6
offering and makes **a** for himself Lv 16:11
enters to make **a** in the ⌊most⌋ Lv 16:17
after he has made **a** for himself, Lv 16:17
the LORD and make **a** for it. Lv 16:18
he will make **a** for himself and Lv 16:24
the ⌊most⌋ holy place to make **a**, Lv 16:27
A will be made for you on this Lv 16:30
place of his father will make **a**. Lv 16:32
and will make **a** for the priests Lv 16:33
make **a** for the Israelites once Lv 16:34
to you to make **a** on the altar Lv 17:11
is the lifeblood that makes **a**. Lv 17:11
priest will make **a** on his behalf Lv 19:22
seventh month is the Day of **A**. Lv 23:27
it is a Day of **A** to make Lv 23:28
to make **a** for yourselves Lv 23:28
your land on the Day of **A**. Lv 25:9
along with the **a** ram by which Nm 5:8
will make **a** for the ⌊guilty Nm 5:8
offering to make **a** on behalf Nm 6:11
to make **a** for the Levites. Nm 8:12
and to make **a** on their behalf, Nm 8:19
Aaron also made **a** for them to Nm 8:21
must then make **a** for the entire Nm 15:25
must then make **a** before the LORD Nm 15:28
and when he makes **a** for him, Nm 15:28
community and make **a** for them, Nm 16:46
he made **a** for the people. Nm 16:47
his God and made **a** for the Nm 25:13
to make **a** for yourselves. Nm 28:22
goat to make **a** for yourselves. Nm 28:30
to make **a** for yourselves. Nm 29:5
to the sin offering of **a**. Nm 29:11
to make **a** for ourselves before Nm 31:50
there can be no **a** for the land Nm 35:33
of incense to make **a** for Israel 1Ch 6:49
and the room for the place of **a**. 1Ch 28:11
to make **a** for all Israel, 2Ch 29:24
good LORD provide **a** on behalf 2Ch 30:18
when I make **a** for all you have Ezk 16:63
the altar and make **a** for it. Ezk 43:20
are to make **a** for the altar Ezk 43:26
to make **a** for the people." Ezk 45:15
offerings to make **a** on behalf of Ezk 45:17
you will make **a** for the temple. Ezk 45:20

ATOP *(1)*
⌊you **a**⌋ the rocky plateau— Jr 21:13

ATROCITIES *(1)*
road to Shechem. They commit **a**. Hs 6:9

ATROTH-BETH-JOAB *(1)*
the Netophathites, **A**, and half 1Ch 2:54

ATROTH-SHOPHAN *(1)*
A, Jazer, Jogbehah, Nm 32:35

ATTACH *(7)*
and **a** the rings to the four Ex 25:26
and **a** the cord chains to the Ex 28:14
breastpiece and **a** them to its Ex 28:23
Then **a** the two gold cords to the Ex 28:24
A the other ends of the two Ex 28:25
and in this way **a** ⌊them⌋ to the Ex 28:25
gold rings and **a** them to the Ex 28:27

ATTACHED *(14)*
will become **a** to me because I Gn 29:34
shoulder pieces **a** to its two Ex 28:7
rings for it and **a** the rings to Ex 37:13
gold rings and **a** the two rings Ex 39:16
Then they **a** the two gold cords Ex 39:17
They **a** the other ends of the two Ex 39:18
a ⌊them⌋ to the ephod's shoulder Ex 39:18
gold rings and **a** them to the Ex 39:20
of pure gold and **a** the bells Ex 39:25
Then they **a** a cord of blue yarn Ex 39:31
and **a** the poles to the ark. Ex 40:20
and what was **a** to it and set it 1Sm 9:24
was deeply **a** to these women 1Kg 11:2
Ephraim is **a** to idols; Hs 4:17

ATTACHING *(1)*
made shoulder pieces for **a** it; Ex 39:4

ATTACK *(63)*
may come and **a** me, the mothers Gn 32:11
they unite against me and **a** me, Gn 34:30
but he will **a** their heels. Gn 49:19
A the Midianites and strike them Nm 25:17
2,000 or 3,000 men to **a** Ai. Jos 7:3
force with you and go **a** Ai. Jos 8:1
military force set out to **a** Ai. Jos 8:3
the Israelites did not **a** them, Jos 9:18
We will **a** Gibeon, because they Jos 10:4
enemies and **a** them from behind Jos 10:19
the waters of Merom to **a** Israel. Jos 11:5
Abimelech came to **a** the tower, Jdg 9:52
or angry men will **a** you, and you Jdg 18:25
They began to **a** the people as Jdg 20:31
Now go and **a** the Amalekites and 1Sm 15:3
started forward to **a** him, 1Sm 17:48
I launch an **a** against these 1Sm 23:2
Launch an **a** against the 1Sm 23:2
behind them and **a** them opposite 2Sm 5:23
out ahead of you to **a** the camp 2Sm 5:24
withdrew from the **a** against the 2Sm 10:14
will **a** him while he is weak and 2Sm 17:2
Then we will **a** David wherever 2Sm 17:12
With You I can **a** a barrier, 2Sm 22:30
Then you must **a** every fortified 2Kg 3:19
and the kings of Egypt to **a** us." 2Kg 7:6
he set out to **a** the Edomites who 2Kg 8:21
Then he planned to **a** Jerusalem. 2Kg 12:17
'**A** this land and destroy it.'" 2Kg 18:25
from them and **a** them opposite 1Ch 14:14
out ahead of you to **a** the camp 1Ch 14:15
So they turned to **a** him, 2Ch 18:31
he set out to **a** the Edomites who 2Ch 21:9
near the Cushites to **a** Jehoram. 2Ch 21:16
came from the **a** on the Edomites, 2Ch 25:14
you turn, ⌊they⌋ **a** us." Neh 4:12
their cities to **a** those who Est 9:2
There are many who **a** me. Ps 3:1
With You I can **a** a barrier, Ps 18:29
evil for good **a** me for pursuing Ps 38:20
Powerful men **a** me, but not Ps 59:3
Will all of you **a** as if he were Ps 62:3
hear evildoers when they **a** me. Ps 92:11
words and **a** me without cause Ps 109:3
Wipe out all those who **a** me, Ps 143:12
Let's **a** some innocent person Pr 1:11
they **a** their own lives. Pr 1:18
you repel ⌊the **a** of even⌋ the Is 36:9
'**A** this land and destroy it.'" Is 36:10
They will **a** all her surrounding Jr 1:15
rise up, let's **a** at noon. Jr 6:4
Rise up, let's **a** by night. Jr 6:5
neighbors who **a** the inheritance Jr 12:14
and boast⌋: Who can **a** me? Jr 49:4
my opponents **a** me all day long Lm 3:62
I will **a** them like a bear robbed Hs 13:8
They **a** as warriors ⌊attack⌋; Jl 2:7
They attack as warriors ⌊**a**⌋; Jl 2:7
the men of war advance and **a**! Jl 3:9
Now daughter ⌊who is⌋ under **a**, Mc 5:1
joined in the **a** against them, Ac 16:22
made a united **a** against Paul Ac 18:12
The Jews also joined in the **a**, Ac 24:9

ATTACKED *(54)*
Cain **a** his brother Abel and Gn 4:8
them by night, **a** them, and Gn 14:15
Gad will be **a** by ⌊marauding⌋ Gn 49:19
The archers **a** him, shot at him, Gn 49:23
came down, **a** them, and routed Nm 14:45
they **a** you with the treachery Nm 25:18
along the way and **a** all your Dt 25:18
They laid siege to it and **a** it. Jos 10:31
They laid siege to it and **a** it. Jos 10:34
from Eglon to Hebron and **a** it. Jos 10:36
turned toward Debir and **a** it. Jos 10:38
the waters of Merom and **a** them. Jos 11:7
When Judah **a**, the LORD handed Jdg 1:4
house of Joseph also **a** Bethel, Jdg 1:22
a and defeated Israel and took Jdg 3:13
eastern peoples came and **a** them. Jdg 6:3
and **a** their army while the army Jdg 8:11
and now you have **a** my father's Jdg 9:18
Judah said, "Why have you **a** us?" Jdg 15:10
Jonathan **a** the Philistine 1Sm 13:3
Saul has **a** the Philistine 1Sm 13:4
Whenever David **a** the land, 1Sm 27:9
the Negev and **a** and burned down 1Sm 30:1
of the city came out and **a** Joab, 2Sm 11:17
ground⌋ and **a** the Philistines 2Sm 23:10
king of Egypt had **a** and captured 1Kg 9:16
a Ijon, Dan, Abel-beth-maacah, 1Kg 15:20

marched out and **a** the cavalry 1Kg 20:21
the Israelites **a** them, and they 2Kg 3:24
surrounded ⌊the city⌋ and **a** it. 2Kg 3:25
Tirzah, Menahem **a** Tiphsah, all 2Kg 15:16
a ⌊it and⌋ ripped open all the 2Kg 15:16
He **a** him, killed him, and became 2Kg 15:30
king of Assyria **a** him, 2Kg 17:3
king of Assyria **a** all the 2Kg 18:13
Have I **a** this place to destroy 2Kg 18:25
king of Babylon **a**, 2Kg 24:1
a the Hamites' tents and the 1Ch 4:41
Joab **a** Rabbah and demolished it. 1Ch 20:1
they **a** all the cities around 2Ch 14:14
They also **a** the tents of the 2Ch 14:15
They **a** Ijon, Dan, Abel-maim, and 2Ch 16:4
He **a** him and took many captives 2Ch 28:5
came again, **a** Judah, and took 2Ch 28:17
king of Babylon **a** him and bound 2Ch 36:6
gallows because he **a** the Jews. Est 8:7
arrogant people have **a** me; Ps 86:14
been on our side when men **a** us, Ps 124:2
my youth they have often **a** me— Ps 129:1
my youth they have often **a** me, Ps 129:2
to Ashdod and **a** and captured it Is 20:1
Have I **a** this land to destroy it Is 36:10
a worm that **a** the plant, Jnh 4:7
Herod cruelly **a** some who Ac 12:1

ATTACKERS *(2)*
Ariel—all the **a**, the Is 29:7
You summoned my **a** on every side, Lm 2:22

ATTACKING *(4)*
"Why are you **a** your neighbor?" Ex 2:13
an adversary who is **a** you, Nm 10:9
army was **a** Jerusalem and all Jr 34:7
A Jason's house, they searched Ac 17:5

ATTACKS *(8)*
Esau comes to one camp and **a** it, Gn 32:8
ambush for him, **a** him, and Dt 19:11
in which a man **a** his neighbor Dt 22:26
Whoever **a** the Jebusites must go 2Sm 5:8
he is at peace, a robber **a** him. Jb 15:21
If anyone **a** you, it is not from Is 54:15
whoever **a** you will fall before Is 54:15
than he **a** and overpowers Lk 11:22

ATTAI *(4)*
Jarha, and she bore him **A**. 1Ch 2:35
A fathered Nathan, and Nathan 1Ch 2:36
A sixth, Eliel seventh, 1Ch 12:11
bore him Abijah, **A**, Ziza, and 2Ch 11:20

ATTAIN *(1)*
tribes hope to **a** as they Ac 26:7

ATTAINED *(2)*
beautiful and **a** royalty. Ezk 16:13
to whatever ⌊truth⌋ we have **a**. Php 3:16

ATTALIA *(1)*
in Perga, they went down to **A**. Ac 14:25

ATTEMPT *(1)*
When an **a** was made by both the Ac 14:5

ATTEMPTED *(5)*
a god ⌊ever⌋ **a** to go and take Dt 4:34
Jews, but they **a** to kill him. Ac 9:29
Jewish exorcists **a** to pronounce Ac 19:13
God and **a** to establish their Rm 10:3
When the Egyptians **a** to do this, Heb 11:29

ATTEMPTS *(1)*
pursues you and **a** to take your 1Sm 25:29

ATTEND *(6)*
She is to **a** the king and be his 1Kg 1:2
I will **a** to you because of your Jr 23:2
there until I **a** to them again.' Jr 27:22
I will **a** to you and will confirm Jr 29:10
he will stay until I **a** to him'— Jr 32:5
provinces to **a** the dedication Dn 3:2

ATTENDANT *(24)*
sight and became his personal **a**. Gn 39:4
and he became their personal **a**. Gn 40:4
Saul and his **a** went through the 1Sm 9:4
said to the **a** who was with him 1Sm 9:5
"Look," the **a** said, "there's a 1Sm 9:6
Saul said to his **a**, "what do we 1Sm 9:7
The **a** answered Saul: 1Sm 9:8
"Good," Saul replied to his **a**. 1Sm 9:10
Saul and his **a** were entering the 1Sm 9:14
Samuel took Saul and his **a**, 1Sm 9:22
Tell the **a** to go on ahead of us, 1Sm 9:27
So the **a** went on. 1Sm 9:27
Saul and his **a** arrived at Gibeah 1Sm 10:10
uncle asked him and his **a**, 1Sm 10:14
said to the **a** who carried his 1Sm 14:1
said to the **a** who carried his 1Sm 14:6
summoned Saul's **a** Ziba and said 2Sm 9:9
an **a** from the house of Saul, 2Sm 19:17
He ordered his **a** Gehazi, "Call 2Kg 4:12
he said to his **a** Gehazi, "Look, 2Kg 4:25
He said to his **a**, "Put on the 2Kg 4:38
But Elisha's **a** asked, "What? 2Kg 4:43
the **a** of Elisha the man of God, 2Kg 5:20
it back to the **a**, and sat down. Lk 4:20

ATTENDANTS *(10)*
composure in front of all his **a**, Gn 45:1
silence, and all his **a** left him. Jdg 3:19
one of the **a** with you and go 1Sm 9:3
of Assyria's **a** have blasphemed 2Kg 19:6
The king's personal **a** suggested, Est 2:2
The king's personal **a** replied, Est 6:3
The king's **a** answered him, Est 6:5
of Assyria's **a** have blasphemed Is 37:6
scatter all the **a** who surround Ezk 12:14
Then the king told the **a**, Mt 22:13

ATTENDANTS' *(2)*
his **a** service and their attire, 1Kg 10:5
his **a** service and their attire, 2Ch 9:4

ATTENDED *(4)*
of Hachmoni **a** the king's sons 1Ch 27:32
all Israel who had **a** went out to 2Ch 31:1
them, and have not **a** to them. Jr 23:2
who was one of those who **a** him. Ac 10:7

ATTENDING *(3)*
of meeting by **a** to the service Nm 3:7
Israelites by **a** to the service Nm 3:8
continually **a** to these tasks. Rm 13:6

ATTENDS *(1)*
of Nun, who **a** you, will enter Dt 1:38

ATTENTION *(120)*
of Lamech, pay **a** to my words. Gn 4:23
have paid close **a** to you and to Ex 3:16
LORD had paid **a** to them and that Ex 4:31
it and not pay **a** to deceptive Ex 5:9
His eyes, pay **a** to His commands Ex 15:26
Pay strict **a** to everything I Ex 23:13
of Zippor, pay **a** to what I say! Nm 23:18
your requests or pay **a** to you. Dt 1:45
a, heavens, and I will speak; Dt 32:1
them: "Pay **a**. Lie in ambush Jos 8:4
kings! Pay **a**, princes! I will Jdg 5:3
LORD had paid **a** to His people's Ru 1:6
LORD paid **a** to Hannah's ⌊need⌋ 1Sm 2:21
not respond, and did not pay **a**. 1Sm 4:20
pay **a** ⌊is better⌋ than the fat 1Sm 15:22
should pay no **a** to this 1Sm 25:25
they will not pay any **a** to us. 2Sm 18:3
will not pay any **a** to us because 2Sm 18:3
no one answered, no one paid **a**. 1Kg 18:29
of him and pay so much **a** to him? Jb 7:17
and pay **a** to what their fathers Jb 8:8
He would pay **a** to what I said. Jb 9:16
Pay close **a** to my words; Jb 13:17
Pay close **a** to my words; Jb 21:2
He will certainly pay **a** to me. Jb 23:6
yet God pays no **a** to this crime. Jb 24:12
I paid close **a** to you. Jb 32:12
now, Job, pay **a** to my speech, Jb 33:1
Pay **a**, Job, and listen to me. Jb 33:31
He does not pay **a** to Jb 35:15
Pay **a** to the sound of my cry, Ps 5:2
just cause; pay **a** to my cry; Ps 17:1
daughter, pay **a** and consider: Ps 45:10
Pay **a** to me and answer me. Ps 55:2
pay **a** to my prayer. Ps 61:1
increases, pay no **a** to it. Ps 62:10
He has paid **a** to the sound of my Ps 66:19
The God of Jacob doesn't pay **a**." Ps 94:7
Pay **a**, you stupid people! Ps 94:8
I will pay **a** to the way of Ps 101:2
He will pay **a** to the prayer of Ps 102:17
is wise pay **a** to these things Ps 107:43
my hand and no one paid **a**, Pr 1:24
and pay **a** so that you may gain Pr 4:1
My son, pay **a** to my words; Pr 4:20
My son, pay **a** to my wisdom; Pr 5:1
and pay **a** to the words of my Pr 7:24
a liar pays **a** to a destructive Pr 17:4
pay **a** to the words of the wise, Pr 22:17
stop giving your **a** to it. Pr 23:4
flock, and pay **a** to your herds, Pr 27:23
no longer pays **a** to warnings. Ec 4:13
Don't pay **a** to everything people Ec 7:21
heavens, and pay **a**, earth, for Is 1:2
pay **a**, all you distant lands; Is 8:9
riders on camels—pay close **a**." Is 21:7
Pay **a** and hear what I say. Is 28:23
Pay **a** to what I say, you Is 32:9
you peoples, pay **a**! Is 34:1
among you will pay **a** to this? Is 42:23
it burned him, but he paid no **a**. Is 42:25
pay no **a** to things of old. Is 43:18
you had paid **a** to My commands. Is 48:18
distant peoples, pay **a**. Is 49:1
Pay **a** to Me, My people, and Is 51:4
Pay **a** and come to Me; Is 55:3
pay **a** to the word of the LORD! Jr 2:31
and wounds keep coming to My **a**. Jr 6:7
so they cannot pay **a**. Jr 6:10
they have paid no **a** to My word. Jr 6:19
listen or pay **a** but walked Jr 7:24
listen to Me or pay **a** but became Jr 7:26
I have paid careful **a**. Jr 8:6
Pay **a** to the word of His mouth. Jr 9:20
they would not obey or pay **a**; Jr 11:8
Listen and pay **a**. Do not be Jr 13:15
listen or pay **a** but became Jr 17:23
and pay no **a** to all his words. Jr 18:18
Pay **a** to me, LORD. Jr 18:19
Who has paid **a** to His word and Jr 23:18
have not obeyed or even paid **a**. Jr 25:4
Hosts says: Pay **a**! Disaster goes Jr 25:32
did not obey Me or pay any **a**. Jr 34:14
you would not pay **a** or obey Me. Jr 35:15
Now pay **a** ⌊to what I say⌋. Jr 40:4
they did not listen or pay **a**; Jr 44:5
it will draw **a** to ⌊their⌋ guilt Ezk 21:23
you have drawn **a** to your guilt, Ezk 21:24
a to their sin of turning Ezk 29:16
and pay **a** to everything I am Ezk 40:4
Son of man, pay **a**; Ezk 44:5
So I turned my **a** to the Lord God Dn 9:3
and paying **a** to Your truth. Dn 9:13
he will turn his **a** to the coasts Dn 11:18
He will turn his **a** back to the Dn 11:19
Pay **a**, house of Israel! Hs 5:1
pay **a**, earth and everyone in it! Mc 1:2
Pay **a** to the rod and the One who Mc 6:9
did not listen or pay **a** to Me"— Zch 1:4
they refused to pay **a** and turned Zch 7:11
he pays no **a** to them, tell the Mt 18:17
if he doesn't pay **a** even to the Mt 18:17
they paid no **a** and went away, Mt 22:5
and called His **a** to the temple Mt 24:1
to them, "Pay **a** to what you hear Mk 4:24
to you and pay **a** to my words. Ac 2:14
The crowds paid **a** with one mind Ac 8:6
They all paid **a** to him, from the Ac 8:10
Before He came to public **a**, Ac 13:24
her heart to pay **a** to what was Ac 16:14
centurion paid **a** to the captain Ac 27:11
Pay careful **a**, then, to how you Eph 5:15
Pay **a** to the ministry you have Col 4:17
or to pay **a** to myths and endless 1Tm 1:4
paying **a** to deceitful spirits 1Tm 4:1
give your **a** to public reading, 1Tm 4:13
may not pay **a** to Jewish myths Ti 1:14
pay even more **a** to what we have Heb 2:1
since his **a** was on the reward. Heb 11:26
You will do well to pay **a** to it, 2Pt 1:19

ATTENTIVE *(8)*
Be **a** to Him and listen to His Ex 23:21
and Your ears **a** to the prayer 2Ch 6:40
and My ears **a** to prayer from 2Ch 7:15
and Your ears be **a** to hear Your Neh 1:6
let Your ear be **a** to the prayer Neh 1:11
let Your ears be **a** to my cry for Ps 130:2
so will I be **a** to build and to Jr 31:28
They were **a** to him because he Ac 8:11

ATTENTIVELY *(1)*
people listened **a** to the book Neh 8:3

ATTEST *(1)*
My angel to **a** these things to Rv 22:16

ATTESTED *(1)*
a by the Law and the Prophets Rm 3:21

ATTIRE *(7)*
attendants' service and their **a**, 1Kg 10:5
clothed in royal **a**, were each 1Kg 22:10
but you wear your royal **a**." 1Kg 22:30
attendants' service and their **a**, 2Ch 9:4
his cupbearers and their **a**, 2Ch 9:4
clothed in royal **a**, were each 2Ch 18:9
but you wear your royal **a**." 2Ch 18:29

ATTITUDE *(5)*
face that his **a** toward him was Gn 31:2
face that his **a** toward me is not Gn 31:5
Assyrian king's **a** toward them, Ezr 6:22
Render service with a good **a**, Eph 6:7
Make your own **a** that of Christ Php 2:5

ATTRACTED *(2)*
is strongly **a** to your daughter. Gn 34:8
of the census and **a** a following. Ac 5:37

ATTRACTIVE *(2)*
of the wise makes knowledge **a**, Pr 15:2
the **a** mistress of sorcery, Nah 3:4

ATTRACTS *(1)*
Wealth **a** many friends, but a Pr 19:4

ATTRIBUTES *(1)*
of the world His invisible **a**, Rm 1:20

AUDIENCE *(2)*
world wanted an **a** with Solomon 1Kg 10:24
world wanted an **a** with Solomon 2Ch 9:23

AUDITORIUM *(1)*
and entered the **a** with the Ac 25:23

AUGUSTUS *(1)*
out from Caesar **A** that the whole Lk 2:1

AUNT *(2)*
intercourse; she is your **a**. Lv 18:14
If a man sleeps with his **a**, Lv 20:20

AUTHORITATIVE *(1)*
king's word is **a**, and who can Ec 8:4

AUTHORITIES *(11)*
synagogues and rulers and **a**, Lk 12:11
it be true that the **a** know He is Jn 7:26
into the marketplace to the **a**. Ac 16:19
must submit to the governing **a**, Rm 13:1
since the ⌊**a**⌋ are God's public Rm 13:6
the rulers and **a** in the heavens. Eph 3:10
against the **a**, against the world Eph 6:12
or dominions or rulers or **a**— Col 1:16
the rulers and **a** and disgraced Col 2:15
be submissive to rulers and **a**, Ti 3:1
hand, with angels, **a**, and powers 1Pt 3:22

AUTHORITY *(119)*
They are placed under your **a**. Gn 9:2
all that he owned under his **a**. Gn 39:4
that he owned under Joseph's **a**; Gn 39:6
put all that he owns under my **a**. Gn 39:8
in the prison under Joseph's **a**, Gn 39:22
with anything under Joseph's **a**, Gn 39:23
under Pharaoh's **a** as food in the Gn 41:35
while under your husband's **a**, Nm 5:19
while under your husband's **a**, Nm 5:20
while under her husband's **a**, Nm 5:29
some of your **a** on him so that Nm 27:20
and judges in **a** at the time. Dt 19:17
under Asaph's **a**, who prophesied 1Ch 25:2
under the **a** of the king. 1Ch 25:2
under the **a** of their father 1Ch 25:3
own fathers' **a** for the music 1Ch 25:6
Heman were under the king's **a**. 1Ch 25:6
officer under the **a** of Hananiah, 2Ch 26:11
Under their **a** was an army of 2Ch 26:13
deputies under the **a** of Conaniah 2Ch 31:13
under his **a** to their brothers 2Ch 31:15
and exercised **a** over the whole Ezr 4:20
were under the **a** of the governor Neh 3:7
letter with full **a** to confirm Est 9:29
Who gave Him **a** over the earth? Jb 34:13
Can you impose its **a** on earth? Jb 38:33
No one has **a** over the wind to Ec 8:8
and there is no **a** over the day Ec 8:8
one man has **a** over another to Ec 8:9
I will put your **a** into his hand, Is 22:21
the priests rule by their own **a**. Jr 5:31
lands under the **a** of My servant Jr 27:6
men under your **a** and pull Jr 38:10
the men under his **a** and went to Jr 38:11
heads and was given **a** to rule. Dn 7:6
their **a** to rule was removed, Dn 7:12
He was given **a** to rule, and Dn 7:14
them like one who had **a**, Mt 7:29
For I too am a man under **a**, Mt 8:9
the Son of Man has **a** on earth to Mt 9:6
God who had given such **a** to men. Mt 9:8
He gave them **a** over unclean Mt 10:1
By what **a** are You doing these Mt 21:23
Who gave You this **a**?" Mt 21:23
tell you by what **a** I do these Mt 21:24
tell you by what **a** I do these Mt 21:27
All **a** has been given to Me in Mt 28:18
teaching them as one having **a**. Mk 1:22
A new teaching with **a**! Mk 1:27
the Son of Man has **a** on earth to Mk 2:10
and to have **a** to drive out Mk 3:15
and gave them **a** over unclean Mk 6:7
By what **a** are You doing these Mk 11:28
Who gave You this **a** to do these Mk 11:28
you by what **a** I am doing these Mk 11:29
tell you by what **a** I do these Mk 11:33
his house, gave **a** to his slaves, Mk 13:34
their splendor and all this **a**, Lk 4:6
because His message had **a**. Lk 4:32
spirits with **a** and power, Lk 4:36
the Son of Man has **a** on earth to Lk 5:24
I too am a man placed under **a**, Lk 7:8
them power and **a** over all the Lk 9:1
have given you the **a** to trample Lk 10:19
Him who has **a** to throw ⌊people Lk 12:5
for himself **a** to be king and Lk 19:12
received the **a** to be king, Lk 19:15
matter, have **a** over 10 towns.' Lk 19:17
by what **a** are You doing these Lk 20:2
Who is it who gave You this **a**?" Lk 20:2
tell you by what **a** I do these Lk 20:8
to the governor's rule and **a**. Lk 20:20
those who have **a** over them are Lk 22:25
What sign ⌊of **a**⌋ will You show Jn 2:18
You gave Him **a** over all flesh; Jn 17:2
that I have the **a** to release You Jn 19:10
You and the **a** to crucify You?" Jn 19:10
would have no **a** over Me at all, Jn 19:11
the Father has set by His own **a**. Ac 1:7
And he has **a** here from the chief Ac 9:14
let the men of **a** among you go Ac 25:5
since I had received **a** for that Ac 26:10
Damascus with **a** and a commission Ac 26:12
the law has **a** over someone as Rm 7:1
there is no **a** except from God Rm 13:1
who resists the **a** is opposing Rm 13:2
want to be unafraid of the **a**? Rm 13:3
does not have **a** over her own 1Co 7:4
does not have **a** over his own 1Co 7:4
If others share this **a** over you, 1Co 9:12
we have not used this **a**; 1Co 9:12
full use of my **a** in the gospel. 1Co 9:18
⌊a symbol of⌋ **a** on her head: 1Co 11:10
all rule and all **a** and power. 1Co 15:24
I boast some more about our **a**, 2Co 10:8
with the **a** the Lord gave me 2Co 13:10
far above every ruler and **a**, Eph 1:21
the head over every ruler and **a**. Col 2:10
and all those who are in **a**, 1Tm 2:2
teach or to have **a** over a man; 1Tm 2:12
encourage and rebuke with all **a**. Ti 2:15
to the Emperor as the supreme **a**, 1Pt 2:13
of the flesh and despise **a**. 2Pt 2:10
flesh, despise **a**, and blaspheme Jd 8
power, and **a** before all time, Jd 25
I will give him **a** over the Rv 2:26
A was given to them over a Rv 6:8
our God and the **a** of His Messiah Rv 12:10
power, his throne, and great **a**. Rv 13:2
because he gave **a** to the beast. Rv 13:4
was also given **a** to act for 42 Rv 13:5
was also given **a** over every Rv 13:7
exercises all the **a** of the first Rv 13:12
angel, who had **a** over fire, came Rv 14:18
will receive **a** as kings with Rv 17:12
their power and **a** to the beast. Rv 17:13
angel with great **a** coming down Rv 18:1
had performed signs on his **a**, Rv 19:20
them who were given **a** to judge. Rv 20:4

AUTHORIZATION *(2)*
according to the **a** ⌊given⌋ them Ezr 3:7
whom we gave no **a** went out from Ac 15:24

AUTHORIZED *(2)*
a you to carve out a tomb for Is 22:16
more than what you have been **a**." Lk 3:13

AUTHORIZING *(1)*
be drawn up **a** their destruction Est 3:9

AUTUMN *(4)*
even the **a** rain will cover it Ps 84:6
He gives you the **a** rain for your Jl 2:23
a and spring rain as before. Jl 2:23
trees in late **a**—fruitless, Jd 12

AVAIL *(1)*
at the same table but to no **a**, Dn 11:27

AVAILABLE *(2)*
surplus is ⌊**a**⌋ for their need 2Co 8:14
also become ⌊**a**⌋ for your need, 2Co 8:14

AVEN *(2)*
high places of **A**, the sin of Hs 10:8
the ruler from the Valley of **A**, Am 1:5

AVENGE *(12)*
for He will **a** the blood of His Dt 32:43
of peace to **a** blood shed in war 1Kg 2:5
so that I may **a** the blood shed 2Kg 9:7
could be ready to **a** themselves Est 8:13
Don't say, "I will **a** this evil!" Pr 20:22
Should I not **a** Myself on such a Jr 5:9
Should I not **a** Myself on such a Jr 5:29
A me against my persecutors. Jr 15:15
vengeance to **a** Himself against Jr 46:10
while I will **a** the bloodshed Hs 1:4
Friends, do not **a** yourselves; Rm 12:19
until You judge and **a** our blood Rv 6:10

AVENGED *(4)*
Cain is to be **a** seven times over Gn 4:24
would be **a** on their brother Jdg 9:24
his rescue and **a** the oppressed Ac 7:24
and He has **a** the blood of His Rv 19:2

AVENGER *(17)*
cities as a refuge from the **a**, Nm 35:12
a of blood himself is to kill Nm 35:19
The **a** of blood is to kill the Nm 35:21
slayer and the **a** of blood Nm 35:24
from the hand of the **a** of blood. Nm 35:25
and the **a** of blood finds him Nm 35:27
the **a** will not be guilty of Nm 35:27
a of blood in the heat of his Dt 19:6
him over to the **a** of blood and Dt 19:12
your refuge from the **a** of blood. Jos 20:3
And if the **a** of blood pursues Jos 20:5
the hand of the **a** of blood until Jos 20:9
so that the **a** of blood will not 2Sm 14:11
to silence the enemy and the **a**. Ps 8:2
because of the enemy and **a**. Ps 44:16
a that brings wrath on the one Rm 13:4
the Lord is an **a** of all these 1Th 4:6

AVENGING *(3)*
bloodshed and **a** yourself by your 1Sm 25:26
bloodshed and **a** myself by my 1Sm 25:33
The LORD is a jealous and **a** God; Nah 1:2

AVERT *(2)*
order to **a** the fierce anger of Ezr 10:14
you will not know how to **a** it. Is 47:11

AVITH *(2)*
the name of his city was **A**. Gn 36:35
Hadad's town was named **A**. 1Ch 1:46

AVOID *(12)*
be careful to **a** anything Dt 23:9
A it; don't travel on it. Turn Pr 4:15
so that he may **a** going down to Pr 15:24
a someone with a big mouth. Pr 20:19
and a time to **a** embracing; Ec 3:5
his eyes to **a** endorsing evil— Is 33:15
you have learned. **A** them; Rm 16:17
but only to **a** being persecuted Gl 6:12
But **a** irreverent, empty speech, 2Tm 2:16
its power. **A** these people! 2Tm 3:5
no one, to **a** fighting, and to Ti 3:2
But **a** foolish debates, Ti 3:9

AVOIDED *(1)*
Your lips I have **a** the ways of Ps 17:4

AVOIDING *(1)*
to you, **a** irreverent, empty 1Tm 6:20

AVOIDS *(2)*
highway of the upright **a** evil; Pr 16:17
things hates the light and **a** it, Jn 3:20

AVVA *(1)*
(AKA IVVAH)
from Babylon, Cuthah, **A**, Hamath 2Kg 17:24

AVVIM *(2)*
destroyed the **A**, who lived in Dt 2:23
A, Parah, Ophrah, Jos 18:23

AVVITES *(2)*
Gath, and Ekron, as well as the **A** Jos 13:3
the **A** made Nibhaz and Tartak, 2Kg 17:31

AWAIT *(3)*
If I **a** Sheol as my home, spread Jb 17:13
and snare ⌊**a**⌋ you who dwell on Is 24:17
pit, and trap **a** you, resident Jr 48:43

AWAITS *(2)*
extinguished. A graveyard **a** me. Jb 17:1
but destruction **a** the malicious. Pr 10:29

AWAKE *(22)*
A! Awake, Deborah! Awake! Awake Jdg 5:12
Awake! **A**, Deborah! Awake! Awake Jdg 5:12
Awake, Deborah! **A**! Awake, sing a Jdg 5:12
Deborah! Awake! **A**, sing a song! Jdg 5:12
my adversaries; **a** for me; You Ps 7:6
when I **a**, I will be satisfied Ps 17:15
A to help me, and take notice. Ps 59:4
I stay **a**; I am like a solitary Ps 102:7
I am **a** through each watch of the Ps 119:148
I sleep, but my heart is **a**. Sg 5:2
A and sing, you who dwell in the Is 26:19
in the dust of the earth will **a**, Dn 12:2
Sword, **a** against My shepherd, Zch 13:7
Remain here and stay **a** with Me." Mt 26:38
you stay **a** with Me one hour Mt 26:40
Stay **a** and pray, so that you Mt 26:41
Remain here and stay **a**." Mk 14:34
Couldn't you stay **a** one hour? Mk 14:37
a and pray so that you won't Mk 14:38
and when they became fully **a**, Lk 9:32
but we must stay **a** and be sober. 1Th 5:6
that whether we are **a** or asleep, 1Th 5:10

AWAKEN *(5)*
do not stir up or **a** love until Sg 2:7
do not stir up or **a** love until Sg 3:5
A, north wind—come, south wind. Sg 4:16
do not stir up or **a** love until Sg 8:4
I **a** your pure understanding with 2Pt 3:1

AWAKENED *(4)*
I **a** you under the apricot tree. Sg 8:5
nation will be **a** from the remote Jr 6:22
It has **a** against you. Ezk 7:6
roused me as one **a** out of sleep. Zch 4:1

AWAKENS *(2)*
He **a** ⌊Me⌋ each morning; Is 50:4
He **a** My ear to listen like those Is 50:4

AWARDED *(1)*
King Ahasuerus **a** Queen Esther Est 8:1

AWARE *(18)*
without being **a** of it, he is Lv 5:2
without being **a** of it, but Lv 5:3
without being **a** of it, but Lv 5:4
Am I not **a** that today I'm king 2Sm 19:22
with shame and **a** of my Jb 10:15
If I had been **a** of malice in my Ps 66:18
You are **a** of all my adversaries. Ps 69:19
You are **a** of all my ways. Ps 139:3
and crane are **a** of their Jr 8:7
a that I will put cords on you Ezk 4:8
When Jesus became **a** of this, Mt 12:15
A of this, Jesus said, "You of Mt 16:8
But Jesus, **a** of this, said to Mt 26:10
A of this, He said to them, "Why Mk 8:17
you are **a** that in the early days Ac 15:7
we are **a** that it is spoken Ac 28:22
a that our brother Timothy has Heb 13:23
First, be **a** of this: scoffers 2Pt 3:3

AWARENESS *(1)*
without the community's **a**, Nm 15:24

AWAY *(755)*
(See pp. xi-xii.)

AWE *(20)*
and they will stand in **a** of you. Dt 28:10
and they stood in **a** of the king 1Kg 3:28
the LORD with reverential **a**, Ps 2:11
temple in reverential **a** of You. Ps 5:7
of the world stand in **a** of Him. Ps 33:8
look on with **a** and will ridicule Ps 52:6
I tremble in **a** of You; I fear Ps 119:120
that people will be in **a** of Him. Ec 3:14
only He should be held in **a**. Is 8:13
Jacob and stand in **a** of the God Is 29:23
we will be in **a** and perceive. Is 41:23
tremble with **a** because of all Jr 33:9
will come with **a** to the LORD and Hs 3:5
they will stand in **a** of You. Mc 7:17
I stand in **a** of Your deeds. Hab 3:2
Me and stood in **a** of My name. Mal 2:5
Herod was in **a** of John and was Mk 6:20
were filled with **a** and said, Lk 5:26
filled with **a** and astonishment Ac 3:10
with reverence and **a**; Heb 12:28

AWE-INSPIRING *(24)*
what I am doing with you is **a**. Ex 34:10
looked like the **a** Angel of God. Jdg 13:6
great and **a** God who keeps His Neh 1:5
Remember the great and **a** Lord, Neh 4:14
and **a** God who keeps His gracious Neh 9:32
right hand show your **a** deeds. Ps 45:4
For the LORD Most High is **a**, Ps 47:2
with **a** works, God of our Ps 65:5
to God, "How **a** are Your works! Ps 66:3
His acts toward mankind are **a**. Ps 66:5
You are **a** in Your sanctuaries. Ps 68:35
Him bring tribute to the **a** One. Ps 76:11
a than all who surround Him. Ps 89:7
praise Your great and **a** name. Ps 99:3
land of Ham, **a** deeds at the Red Ps 106:22
His name is holy and **a**. Ps 111:9
the power of Your **a** works, Ps 145:6
a as an army with banners. Sg 6:4
a as an army with banners? Sg 6:10
with a gleam like **a** crystal, Ezk 1:22
great and **a** God who keeps His Dn 9:4
the great and **a** Day of the LORD Jl 2:31
great and **a** sign in heaven: Rv 15:1
Great and **a** are Your works, Rv 15:3

AWED *(1)*
far away are **a** by Your signs; Ps 65:8

AWESOME *(10)*
said, "What an **a** place this is! Gn 28:17
God, a great and **a** God, is among Dt 7:21
mighty, and **a** God, showing no Dt 10:17
these great and **a** works your Dt 10:21
this glorious and **a** name— Dt 28:58
for them great and **a** acts, 2Sm 7:23
great and **a** deeds by driving 1Ch 17:21
a majesty surrounds Him. Jb 37:22
When You did **a** deeds that we did Is 64:3
the great and **a** Day of the LORD Mal 4:5

AWESTRUCK *(1)*
they were **a** and gave glory to Mt 9:8

AWFUL *(1)*
How **a** that day will be! Jr 30:7

AWHILE *(1)*
you stay for **a**, and I'll reveal 1Sm 9:27

AWL *(2)*
must pierce his ear with an **a**, Ex 21:6
take an **a** and pierce through his Dt 15:17

AWNING *(1)*
Your **a** was of blue and purple Ezk 27:7

AWOKE *(6)*
When Noah **a** from his drinking Gn 9:24
When Jacob **a** from his sleep, Gn 28:16
He **a** from his sleep and pulled Jdg 16:14
When he **a** from his sleep, Jdg 16:20
the Lord **a** as if from sleep, Ps 78:65
At this I **a** and looked around. Jr 31:26

AX *(8)*
hand swings the **a** to chop down a Dt 19:5
trees by putting an **a** to them, Dt 20:19
Abimelech took his **a** in his hand Jdg 9:48
the iron ⌊**a** head⌋ fell into the 2Kg 6:5
Does an **a** exalt itself above the Is 10:15
of the forest with an **a**, Is 10:34
now the **a** is ready to strike Mt 3:10
now the **a** is ready to strike Lk 3:9

AXE *(1)*
If the **a** is dull, and one does Ec 10:10

AXES *(6)*
mattocks, **a**, and sickles. 1Sm 13:20
a shekel⌋ for pitchforks and **a**, 1Sm 13:21
picks, and iron **a**, and to labor 2Sm 12:31
with saws, iron picks, and **a**. 1Ch 20:3
a thicket of trees, wielding **a**, Ps 74:5
with **a** they will come against Jr 46:22

AXLES *(3)*
bronze wheels with bronze **a**. 1Kg 7:30
and the wheel **a** were part of the 1Kg 7:32
their **a**, rims, spokes, and hubs 1Kg 7:33

AYYAH *(1)*
as far as **A** and its villages, 1Ch 7:28

AZAL *(1)*
the mountains will extend to **A**. Zch 14:5

AZALIAH *(2)*
secretary Shaphan son of **A**, 2Kg 22:3
Josiah sent Shaphan son of **A**, 2Ch 34:8

AZANIAH *(1)*
Jeshua son of **A**, Binnui of the Neh 10:9

AZAREL *(6)*
Elkanah, Isshiah, **A**, Joezer, and 1Ch 12:6
the eleventh ⌊to⌋ **A**, his sons, 1Ch 25:18
for Dan, **A** son of Jeroham. 1Ch 27:22
A, Shelemiah, Shemariah, Ezr 10:41
Amashsai son of **A**, son of Ahzai, Neh 11:13
Shemaiah, **A**, Milalai, Gilalai, Neh 12:36

AZARIAH *(47)*
(AKA ABEDNEGO, JAAZANIAH, JEZANIAH, SERIAH, UZZIAH)
A son of Zadok, priest; 1Kg 4:2
A son of Nathan, in charge of 1Kg 4:5
all the people of Judah took **A**, 2Kg 14:21
A son of Amaziah became king of 2Kg 15:1
A did what was right in the 2Kg 15:3
A rested with his fathers, 2Kg 15:7
year of Judah's King **A**, 2Kg 15:8
year of Judah's King **A**, 2Kg 15:17
fiftieth year of Judah's King **A**, 2Kg 15:23
year of Judah's King **A**, 2Kg 15:27
Ethan's son: **A**. 1Ch 2:8
Jehu, and Jehu fathered **A**. 1Ch 2:38
A fathered Helez, and Helez 1Ch 2:39
his son **A**, his son Jotham 1Ch 3:12
Ahimaaz fathered **A**; Azariah 1Ch 6:9
Azariah; **A** fathered Johanan 1Ch 6:9
Johanan fathered **A**, who served 1Ch 6:10
A fathered Amariah; Amariah 1Ch 6:11
Hilkiah; Hilkiah fathered **A**; 1Ch 6:13
A fathered Seraiah; and Seraiah 1Ch 6:14
of Joel, son of **A**, son of 1Ch 6:36
A son of Hilkiah, son of 1Ch 9:11
of God came on **A** son of Oded. 2Ch 15:1
the prophecy of ⌊**A** son of⌋ Oded 2Ch 15:8
A, Jehiel, Zechariah, Azariah, 2Ch 21:2
Jehiel, Zechariah, **A**, Michael, 2Ch 21:2
A son of Jeroham, Ishmael son of 2Ch 23:1
son of Jehohanan, **A** son of Obed, 2Ch 23:1
A the priest, along with 80 2Ch 26:17
Then **A** the chief priest and all 2Ch 26:20
Ephraimites—**A** son of Johanan, 2Ch 28:12
and Joel son of **A** from the 2Ch 29:12
son of Abdi and **A** son of 2Ch 29:12
A, the chief priest of the 2Ch 31:10
Hezekiah and of **A** the ruler of 2Ch 31:13
Beside them **A** son of Maaseiah, Neh 3:23
from the house of **A** to the Angle Neh 3:24
Jeshua, Nehemiah, **A**, Raamiah, Neh 7:7
Kelita, **A**, Jozabad, Hanan, Neh 8:7
Seraiah, **A**, Jeremiah, Neh 10:2
A, Ezra, Meshullam, Neh 12:33
then **A** son of Hoshaiah, Johanan Jr 43:2
Hananiah, Mishael, and **A**. Dn 1:6
Meshach; and to **A**, Abednego. Dn 1:7
Hananiah, Mishael, and **A**, Dn 1:11
Hananiah, Mishael, and **A**. Dn 1:19
Mishael, and **A** about the matter, Dn 2:17

AZARIAH'S *(3)*
rest of the events of **A** ⌊reign⌋, 2Kg 15:6
Seraiah's son, **A** son, Hilkiah's Ezr 7:1
Amariah's son, **A** son, Meraioth's Ezr 7:3

AZAZ *(1)*
and Bela son of **A**, son of Shema, 1Ch 5:8

AZAZEL *(4)*
the LORD and the other for **A**, Lv 16:8
chosen by lot for **A** is to be Lv 16:10
it into the wilderness for **A**. Lv 16:10
the goat for **A** is to wash his Lv 16:26

AZAZIAH *(3)*
A were to lead the music with 1Ch 15:21
Ephraimites, Hoshea son of **A**; 1Ch 27:20
Jehiel, **A**, Nahath, Asahel, 2Ch 31:13

AZBUK *(1)*
After him Nehemiah son of **A**, Neh 3:16

AZEKAH *(7)*
down as far as **A** and Makkedah. Jos 10:10
of Beth-horon all the way to **A**, Jos 10:11
Jarmuth, Adullam, Socoh, **A**, Jos 15:35
Socoh and **A** in Ephes-dammim. 1Sm 17:1
Adoraim, Lachish, **A**, 2Ch 11:9
its fields and **A** and its Neh 11:30
Lachish and **A**, for only they Jr 34:7

AZEL *(4)*
his son Eleasah, and his son **A**. 1Ch 8:37
A had six sons, and these were 1Ch 8:38
his son Eleasah, and his son **A**. 1Ch 9:43
A had six sons, and these were 1Ch 9:44

AZEL'S *(2)*
All these were **A** sons. 1Ch 8:38
and Hanan. These were **A** sons. 1Ch 9:44

AZGAD *(1)*
Bunni, **A**, Bebai, Neh 10:15

AZGAD'S *(3)*
A descendants 1,222 Ezr 2:12
of Hakkatan from **A** descendants, Ezr 8:12
A descendants 2,322 Neh 7:17

AZIEL *(1)*
(AKA JAAZIEL)
Zechariah, **A**, Shemiramoth, 1Ch 15:20

AZIZA *(1)*
Jeremoth, Zabad, and **A**; Ezr 10:27

AZMAVETH *(7)*
(AKA BETH-AZMAVETH'S)
the Arbathite, **A** the Barhumite, 2Sm 23:31
fathered Alemeth, **A**, and Zimri, 1Ch 8:36
fathered Alemeth, **A**, and Zimri; 1Ch 9:42
A the Baharumite, Eliahba the 1Ch 11:33
Jeziel and Pelet sons of **A**; 1Ch 12:3
A son of Adiel was in charge of 1Ch 27:25
from the fields of Geba and **A**, Neh 12:29

AZMAVETH'S *(1)*
A people 42 Ezr 2:24

AZMON *(3)*
to Hazar-addar and proceed to **A**. Nm 34:4
will turn from **A** to the Brook of Nm 34:5
It proceeded to **A** and to the Jos 15:4

AZNOTH-TABOR *(1)*
boundary turned to **A** and went Jos 19:34

AZOR *(2)*
Eliakim, Eliakim fathered **A**, Mt 1:13
A fathered Zadok, Zadok fathered Mt 1:14

AZOTUS *(1)*
(AKA ASHDOD)
appeared in **A**, and passing Ac 8:40

AZRIEL *(3)*
Ishi, Eliel, **A**, Jeremiah, 1Ch 5:24
for Naphtali, Jerimoth son of **A**; 1Ch 27:19
Seraiah son of **A**, and Shelemiah Jr 36:26

AZRIKAM *(6)*
Hizkiah, and **A**—three. 1Ch 3:23
A, Bocheru, Ishmael, Sheariah, 1Ch 8:38
Hasshub, son of **A**, son of 1Ch 9:14
A, Bocheru, Ishmael, Sheariah, 1Ch 9:44
king's son Maaseiah, **A** governor 2Ch 28:7
Hasshub, son of **A**, son of Neh 11:15

AZUBAH *(4)*
mother's name was **A** daughter of 1Kg 22:42
by ⌊his⌋ wife **A** and by Jerioth. 1Ch 2:18
When **A** died, Caleb married 1Ch 2:19
mother's name was **A** daughter of 2Ch 20:31

AZUBAH'S *(1)*
These were **A** sons: Jesher, 1Ch 2:18

AZZAN *(1)*
Paltiel son of **A**, a leader from Nm 34:26

AZZUR *(3)*
Ater, Hezekiah, **A**, Neh 10:17
Hananiah son of **A** from Gibeon Jr 28:1
them I saw Jaazaniah son of **A**, Ezk 11:1

B

BAAL *(63)*
aligned itself with **B** of Peor, Nm 25:3
themselves with **B** of Peor." Nm 25:5
of you who followed **B** of Peor. Dt 4:3
Him and worshiped **B** and the Jdg 2:13
the altar of **B** that belongs to Jdg 6:25
"Let **B** plead his case with him," Jdg 6:32
to serve **B** and worship him. 1Kg 16:31
up an altar for **B** in the temple 1Kg 16:32
in the temple of **B** that he had 1Kg 16:32
450 prophets of **B** and the 400 1Kg 18:19
Him. But if **B**, follow him." 1Kg 18:21
said to the prophets of **B**, 1Kg 18:25
on the name of **B** from morning 1Kg 18:26
noon, saying, "**B**, answer us!" 1Kg 18:26
them, "Seize the prophets of **B**! 1Kg 18:40
not bowed to **B** and every mouth 1Kg 19:18
He served **B** and worshiped him. 1Kg 22:53
sacred pillar of **B** his father 2Kg 3:2
Ahab served **B** a little, but Jehu 2Kg 10:18
to me all the prophets of **B**, 2Kg 10:19
I have a great sacrifice for **B**. 2Kg 10:19
to destroy the servants of **B**. 2Kg 10:19
a solemn assembly for **B**." 2Kg 10:20
and all the servants of **B** came; 2Kg 10:21
They entered the temple of **B**, 2Kg 10:21
for all the servants of **B**." 2Kg 10:22
Rechab entered the temple of **B**, 2Kg 10:23
Jehu said to the servants of **B**, 2Kg 10:23
among you—only servants of **B**." 2Kg 10:23
inner room of the temple of **B**. 2Kg 10:25
the temple of **B** and burned them 2Kg 10:26
and tore down the pillar of **B**. 2Kg 10:27
down the temple of **B** and made it 2Kg 10:27
Jehu eliminated **B** ⌊worship⌋ from 2Kg 10:28
the temple of **B** and tore it down 2Kg 11:18
the priest of **B**, at the altars. 2Kg 11:18
heavenly host and served **B**. 2Kg 17:16
reestablished the altars for **B**. 2Kg 21:3
all the articles made for **B**, 2Kg 23:4
They had burned incense to **B**, 2Kg 23:5
villages as far as **B**. 1Ch 4:33
his son Reaiah, his son **B**, 1Ch 5:5
son, then Zur, Kish, **B**, Nadab, 1Ch 8:30
then Zur, Kish, **B**, Ner, Nadab, 1Ch 9:36
the temple of **B** and tore it down 2Ch 23:17
the priest of **B**, at the altars. 2Ch 23:17
themselves with **B** of Peor and Ps 106:28
prophesied by **B** and followed Jr 2:8
burn incense to **B**, and follow Jr 7:9
altars to burn incense to **B**— Jr 11:13
anger by burning incense to **B**." Jr 11:17
taught My people to swear by **B**— Jr 12:16
places to **B** on which to burn Jr 19:5
fire as burnt offerings to **B**, Jr 19:5
prophesied by **B** and led My Jr 23:13
My name through **B** worship. Jr 23:27
been burned to **B** on their Jr 32:29
high places of **B** in the Valley Jr 32:35
on her, which they used for **B**. Hs 2:8
and no longer call Me: My **B**. Hs 2:16
guilt through **B** and died. Hs 13:1
this place every vestige of **B**, Zph 1:4
who have not bowed down to **B**. Rm 11:4

BAAL'S *(4)*
they found **B** altar torn down, Jdg 6:28
tore down **B** altar and cut down Jdg 6:30
Would you plead **B** case for him? Jdg 6:31
but **B** prophets are 450 men. 1Kg 18:22

BAAL-BERITH *(2)*
the Baals and made **B** their god. Jdg 8:33
of silver from the temple of **B**. Jdg 9:4

BAAL-GAD *(3)*
as far as **B** in the Valley of Jos 11:17
from **B** in the valley of Lebanon Jos 12:7
Lebanon east from **B** below Mount Jos 13:5

BAAL-HAMON *(1)*
Solomon owned a vineyard in **B**. Sg 8:11

BAAL-HANAN *(5)*
B son of Achbor ruled in his Gn 36:38
When **B** son of Achbor died, Gn 36:39
B son of Achbor ruled in his 1Ch 1:49
When **B** died, Hadad ruled in his 1Ch 1:50
B the Gederite was in charge of 1Ch 27:28

BAAL-HAZOR *(1)*
were at **B** near Ephraim, 2Sm 13:23

BAAL-HERMON *(2)*
(AKA HERMAN, SENIR, SION, SIRION)
mountains from Mount **B** as far as Jdg 3:3
in the land from Bashan to **B** 1Ch 5:23

BAAL-MEON *(3)*
(AKA BEON, BETH-BAAL-MEON, BETH-MEON)
well as Nebo and **B** (whose names Nm 32:38
in Aroer as far as Nebo and **B**. 1Ch 5:8
B, and Kiriathaim Ezk 25:9

BAAL-PEOR *(2)*
seen what the LORD did at **B**, Dt 4:3
But they went to **B**, consecrated Hs 9:10

BAAL-PERAZIM *(2)*
So David went to **B** and defeated 2Sm 5:20
So the Israelites went up to **B**, 1Ch 14:11

BAAL-SHALISHAH *(1)*
A man from **B** came to the man of 2Kg 4:42

BAAL-TAMAR *(1)*
their battle positions at **B**, Jdg 20:33

BAAL-ZEBUB *(4)*
(AKA BEELZEBUL, DEVIL, SATAN)
Go inquire of **B**, the god of 2Kg 1:2
you are going to inquire of **B**, 2Kg 1:3
these men⌋ to inquire of **B**, 2Kg 1:6
sent messengers to inquire of **B**, 2Kg 1:16

BAAL-ZEPHON *(3)*
you must camp in front of **B**, Ex 14:2
Pi-hahiroth, in front of **B**. Ex 14:9
which faces **B**, and they camped Nm 33:7

BAALAH *(5)*
(AKA KIRIATH, KIRIATHARIM, KIRIATH-BAAL, KIRIATH-JEARIM)
and then curved to **B** (that is, Jos 15:9
westward from **B** to Mount Seir, Jos 15:10
to Mount **B**, went to Jabneel, Jos 15:11
B, Iim, Ezem, Jos 15:29
David and all Israel went to **B** 1Ch 13:6

BAALATH *(3)*
Eltekeh, Gibbethon, **B**, Jos 19:44
B, Tamar in the Wilderness of 1Kg 9:18
B, all the storage cities that 2Ch 8:6

BAALATH-BEER *(1)*
these cities as far as **B** Jos 19:8

BAALE-JUDAH *(1)*
to bring the ark of God from **B**. 2Sm 6:2

BAALIS *(1)*
Don't you realize that **B**, Jr 40:14

BAALS *(18)*
sight. They worshiped the **B** Jdg 2:11
worshiped the **B** and the Asherahs Jdg 3:7
themselves with the **B** and made Jdg 8:33
worshiped the **B** and the Jdg 10:6
our God and worshiped the **B**." Jdg 10:10
removed the **B** and the Ashtoreths 1Sm 7:4
and worshiped the **B** and the 1Sm 12:10
and followed the **B**. 1Kg 18:18
David. He did not seek the **B** 2Ch 17:3
of the LORD's temple for the **B**." 2Ch 24:7
and made cast images of the **B**. 2Ch 28:2
the altars for the **B**. 2Ch 33:3
altars of the **B** were torn down, 2Ch 34:4
I have not followed the **B**? Jr 2:23
of their hearts and the **B**, Jr 9:14
days of the **B** when she burned Hs 2:13
names of the **B** from her mouth; Hs 2:17
sacrificing to the **B** and burning Hs 11:2

BAANA *(3)*
B son of Ahilud, in Taanach, 1Kg 4:12
B son of Hushai, in Asher and 1Kg 4:16
Zadok son of **B** made repairs. Neh 3:4

BAANAH *(10)*
named **B** and the other Rechab, 2Sm 4:2
Rechab and **B**, the sons of Rimmon 2Sm 4:5
and his brother **B** escaped. 2Sm 4:6
Rechab and his brother **B**, 2Sm 4:9
and they killed Rechab and **B**. 2Sm 4:12
Heleb son of **B** the Netophahite, 2Sm 23:29
Heled son of **B** the Netophathite, 1Ch 11:30
Mispar, Bigvai, Rehum, and **B**. Ezr 2:2
Mispereth, Bigvai, Nehum, and **B**. Neh 7:7
Malluch, Harim, **B**. Neh 10:27

BAARA *(1)*
divorced his wives Hushim and **B**. 1Ch 8:8

BAASEIAH *(1)*
Michael, son of **B**, son of 1Ch 6:40

BAASHA *(29)*
between Asa and **B** king of Israel 1Kg 15:16
Israel's King **B** went to war 1Kg 15:17
treaty with **B** king of Israel 1Kg 15:19
When **B** heard ⌊about it⌋, he quit 1Kg 15:21
and the timbers **B** had built it 1Kg 15:22
B son of Ahijah of the house 1Kg 15:27
and **B** struck him down at 1Kg 15:27
B killed Nadab and reigned in 1Kg 15:28
When **B** became king, he struck 1Kg 15:29
between Asa and **B** king of Israel 1Kg 15:32
B son of Ahijah became king over 1Kg 15:33
to Jehu son of Hanani against **B**: 1Kg 16:1
will sweep away **B** and his house, 1Kg 16:3
who belongs to **B** and dies in the 1Kg 16:4
B rested with his fathers and 1Kg 16:6
came against **B** and against his 1Kg 16:7
because **B** had struck down the 1Kg 16:7
Elah son of **B** became king over 1Kg 16:8
down the entire house of **B**. 1Kg 16:11
the entire house of **B**, 1Kg 16:12
spoken against **B** through Jehu 1Kg 16:12
all the sins of **B** and the sins 1Kg 16:13
the house of **B** son of Ahijah, 1Kg 21:22
the house of **B** son of Ahijah. 2Kg 9:9
Israel's King **B** went to war 2Ch 16:1
Israel's King **B** so that he will 2Ch 16:3
When **B** heard ⌊about it⌋, he quit 2Ch 16:5
and the timbers **B** had built it 2Ch 16:6
encounter with **B** king of Israel. Jr 41:9

BAASHA'S *(1)*
rest of the events of **B** ⌊reign⌋, 1Kg 16:5

BABBLE *(1)*
don't **b** like the idolaters, Mt 6:7

BABBLING *(1)*
Should your **b** put others to Jb 11:3

BABIES *(2)*
B removed from the breast? Is 28:9
of the flesh, as **b** in Christ. 1Co 3:1

BABY *(21)*
I really have a **b** when I'm old?' Gn 18:13
a nursing woman carries a **b**,' Nm 11:12
like a dead ⌊**b**⌋ whose flesh is Nm 12:12
LORD struck the **b** that Uriah's 2Sm 12:15
On the seventh day the **b** died. 2Sm 12:18
to tell him the **b** was dead. 2Sm 12:18
Look, while the **b** was alive, we 2Sm 12:18
can we tell him the **b** is dead? 2Sm 12:18
he guessed that the **b** was dead. 2Sm 12:19
his servants, "Is the **b** dead?" 2Sm 12:19
the **b** was alive, you fasted 2Sm 12:21
While the **b** was alive, I fasted 2Sm 12:22
and I had a **b** while she was in 1Kg 3:17
she also had a **b** and we were 1Kg 3:18
her the living **b**," she said, 1Kg 3:26
Give the living **b** to the first 1Kg 3:27
Will I bring a **b** to the point of Is 66:9
greeting, the **b** leaped inside Lk 1:41
the **b** leaped for joy inside me! Lk 1:44
you will find a **b** wrapped snugly Lk 2:12
and the **b** who was lying in the Lk 2:16

BABYLON *(280)*
(AKA SHESHACH, SHINAR)
His kingdom started with **B**, Gn 10:10
Therefore its name is called **B**, Gn 11:9
spoils a beautiful cloak from **B**, Jos 7:21
Assyria brought ⌊people⌋ from **B**, 2Kg 17:24
men of **B** made Succoth-benoth, 2Kg 17:30
Baladan, king of **B**, sent letters 2Kg 20:12
from a distant country, from **B**." 2Kg 20:14
day will be carried off to **B**; 2Kg 20:17
the palace of the king of **B**.'" 2Kg 20:18
king of **B** attacked, 2Kg 24:1
the king of **B** took everything 2Kg 24:7
king of **B** marched up to 2Kg 24:10
of **B** came to the city 2Kg 24:11
surrendered to the king of **B**. 2Kg 24:12
So the king of **B** took him 2Kg 24:12
deported Jehoiachin to **B**. 2Kg 24:15
into exile from Jerusalem to **B**. 2Kg 24:15
The king of **B** also brought 2Kg 24:16
into **B** all 7,000 fighting 2Kg 24:16
the king of **B** made Mattaniah, 2Kg 24:17
rebelled against the king of **B**. 2Kg 24:20
of **B** advanced against 2Kg 25:1
up to the king of **B** at Riblah, 2Kg 25:6
the king of **B** blinded Zedekiah, 2Kg 25:7
chains⌋, and took him to **B**. 2Kg 25:7
king of **B**, Nebuzaradan, 2Kg 25:8
a servant of the king of **B**, 2Kg 25:8
had defected to the king of **B**, 2Kg 25:11
and carried the bronze to **B**. 2Kg 25:13
them to the king of **B** at Riblah. 2Kg 25:20
The king of **B** put them to death 2Kg 25:21
king of **B** appointed Gedaliah son 2Kg 25:22
that the king of **B** had appointed 2Kg 25:23
land and serve the king of **B**, 2Kg 25:24
king of **B**, in the year he 2Kg 25:27
kings who were with him in **B**. 2Kg 25:28
of the king of **B** for the rest of 2Kg 25:29
was exiled to **B** because of their 1Ch 9:1
shackles⌋, and took him to **B**. 2Ch 33:11
king of **B** attacked him and bound 2Ch 36:6
shackles⌋ to take him to **B**. 2Ch 36:6
LORD's temple to **B** and put them 2Ch 36:7
and put them in his temple in **B**. 2Ch 36:7
and brought him to **B** along with 2Ch 36:10
everything to **B**—all the 2Ch 36:18
from the sword he deported to **B**, 2Ch 36:20
went up from **B** to Jerusalem. Ezr 1:11
of **B** had deported to Ezr 2:1
of Babylon had deported to **B**. Ezr 2:1
Persia, Erech, **B**, Susa (that is, Ezr 4:9
to King Nebuchadnezzar of **B**, Ezr 5:12
and deported the people to **B**. Ezr 5:12
first year of Cyrus king of **B**, Ezr 5:13
from the temple in **B** the gold Ezr 5:14
them⌋ to the temple in **B**. Ezr 5:14
the temple in **B** to a man named Ezr 5:14
archives in **B** be conducted ⌊to Ezr 5:17
the library of **B** in the archives Ezr 6:1
and carried to **B** must also be Ezr 6:5
—came up from **B**. He was a Ezr 7:6
journey from **B** on the first day Ezr 7:9
throughout the province of **B**, Ezr 7:16
with me from **B** during the reign Ezr 8:1
by King Nebuchadnezzar of **B**. Neh 7:6
King Artaxerxes of **B** in the Neh 13:6
Nebuchadnezzar of **B** took King Est 2:6
Rahab, **B**, Philistia, Tyre, and Ps 87:4
the rivers of **B**—there we sat Ps 137:1
Daughter **B**, doomed to Ps 137:8
oracle against **B** that Isaiah son Is 13:1
B, the jewel of the kingdoms, Is 13:19
about the king of **B** and say: Is 14:4
cut off from **B** her reputation, Is 14:22
saying, "**B** has fallen, has Is 21:9
Baladan, king of **B**, sent letters Is 39:1
from a distant country, from **B**." Is 39:3
day will be carried off to **B**; Is 39:6
the palace of the king of **B**.'" Is 39:7
will send to **B** and bring all of Is 43:14
in the dust, Virgin Daughter **B**. Is 47:1
accomplish His will against **B**, Is 48:14
B, flee from the Chaldeans! Is 48:20
Judah over to the king of **B**, Jr 20:4
deport them to **B** and put them to Jr 20:4
them, and carry them off to **B**. Jr 20:5
You will go to **B**. There you will Jr 20:6
king of **B** is making war against Jr 21:2
the king of **B** and the Chaldeans Jr 21:4
to King Nebuchadnezzar of **B**, Jr 21:7
be handed over to the king of **B**, Jr 21:10
king of **B** and the Chaldeans. Jr 22:25
king of **B** had deported Jeconiah Jr 24:1
and had brought them to **B**, Jr 24:1
year of Nebuchadnezzar king of **B** Jr 25:1
Nebuchadnezzar king of **B**, Jr 25:9
the king of **B** for 70 years. Jr 25:11
the king of **B** and that nation' Jr 25:12
Nebuchadnezzar, king of **B**. Jr 27:6
king of **B** and does not place its Jr 27:8
under the yoke of the king of **B**, Jr 27:8
Don't serve the king of **B**! Jr 27:9
of the king of **B** and serve him, Jr 27:11
under the yoke of the king of **B**, Jr 27:12
does not serve the king of **B**? Jr 27:13
must not serve the king of **B**,' Jr 27:14
will be brought back from **B**. Jr 27:16
Serve the king of **B** and live! Jr 27:17
and in Jerusalem go to **B**.' Jr 27:18
king of **B** did not take when he Jr 27:20
Jerusalem to **B** along with all Jr 27:20
be brought to **B** and will remain Jr 27:22
the yoke of the king of **B**. Jr 28:2
king of **B** took from here Jr 28:3
from here and transported to **B**. Jr 28:3
from Judah who went to **B**'— Jr 28:4
the yoke of the king of **B**.'" Jr 28:4
the exiles from **B** to this place! Jr 28:6
king of **B**, from the neck of all Jr 28:11
serve Nebuchadnezzar king of **B**, Jr 28:14
deported from Jerusalem to **B**. Jr 29:1
had sent to **B** to Nebuchadnezzar Jr 29:3
to Nebuchadnezzar king of **B**. Jr 29:3
I deported from Jerusalem to **B**: Jr 29:4
70 years for **B** are complete, Jr 29:10
raised up prophets for us in **B**!" Jr 29:15
I have sent from Jerusalem to **B**. Jr 29:20
to Nebuchadnezzar king of **B**, Jr 29:21
Judah who are in **B** will create a Jr 29:22
whom the king of **B** roasted in Jr 29:22
he has sent ⌊word⌋ to us in **B**, Jr 29:28
of the king of **B** was besieging Jr 32:2
take Zedekiah to **B** where he will Jr 32:5
king of **B**, all his army, all Jr 34:1
this city over to the king of **B**, Jr 34:2
meet the king of **B** eye to eye Jr 34:3
face to face; you will go to **B**. Jr 34:3
king of **B** marched into the land Jr 35:11
king of **B** will certainly come Jr 36:29
king of **B** made him king. Jr 37:1
handed over to the king of **B**." Jr 37:17
'The king of **B** will not come Jr 37:19
the officials of the king of **B**, Jr 38:17
the officials of the king of **B**, Jr 38:18
of the king of **B** and will say: Jr 38:22
by the king of **B** and this city Jr 38:23
of **B** advanced against Jr 39:1
of the king of **B** entered and sat Jr 39:3
Riblah the king of **B** slaughtered Jr 39:6
bronze chains to take him to **B**. Jr 39:7
deported to **B** the rest of the Jr 39:9
Nebuchadnezzar of **B** gave orders Jr 39:11
the captains of the king of **B** Jr 39:13
who were being exiled to **B**. Jr 40:1
you to come with me to **B**, Jr 40:4
to you to come with me to **B**, Jr 40:4
whom the king of **B** has appointed Jr 40:5
that the king of **B** had appointed Jr 40:7
who had not been deported to **B**, Jr 40:7
land and serve the king of **B**, Jr 40:9
that the king of **B** had left a Jr 40:11
one the king of **B** had appointed Jr 41:2
whom the king of **B** had appointed Jr 41:18
of the king of **B** whom you now Jr 42:11
to death or to deport us to **B**!" Jr 43:3
Nebuchadnezzar king of **B**, Jr 43:10
king of **B** in the fourth year Jr 46:2
king of **B** to defeat the land Jr 46:13
king of **B** and his officers. Jr 46:26
king of **B** has drawn up a plan Jr 49:30
The word the LORD spoke about **B**, Jr 50:1
nothing. Say: **B** is captured; Bel Jr 50:2
Escape from **B**; depart from the Jr 50:8
and bring against **B** an assembly Jr 50:9
passes through **B** will be Jr 50:13
up in battle formation around **B**, Jr 50:14
the sower from **B** as well as him Jr 50:16
was Nebuchadnezzar king of **B**. Jr 50:17
the king of **B** and his land just Jr 50:18
What a horror **B** has become among Jr 50:23
B, I laid a trap for you, and Jr 50:24
from the land of **B** announcing in Jr 50:28
the archers to **B**, all who string Jr 50:29
turmoil to those who live in **B**. Jr 50:34
against those who live in **B**, Jr 50:35
against you, Daughter of **B**. Jr 50:42
The king of **B** has heard reports Jr 50:43
I will chase **B** away from her Jr 50:44
drawn up against **B** and the Jr 50:45
wind against **B** and against Jr 51:1
strangers to **B** who will scatter Jr 51:2
Leave **B**; save your lives, each Jr 51:6
B was a golden cup in the LORD's Jr 51:7
Suddenly **B** fell and was Jr 51:8
tried to heal **B**, but she could Jr 51:9
is aimed at **B** to destroy her, Jr 51:11

flag against the walls of **B**; Jr 51:12
against those who live in **B**. Jr 51:12
I will repay **B** and all the Jr 51:24
LORD's purposes against **B** stand: Jr 51:29
the land of **B** an uninhabited Jr 51:29
to the king of **B** that his city Jr 51:31
The daughter of **B** is like a Jr 51:33
of **B** has devoured me; Jr 51:34
me and my family ⌊be done⌋ to **B**. Jr 51:35
B will become a heap of rubble, Jr 51:37
What a horror **B** has become among Jr 51:41
The sea has risen over **B**; Jr 51:42
I will punish Bel in **B**. Jr 51:44
shout for joy over **B** because the Jr 51:48
B must fall ⌊because of⌋ the Jr 51:49
all the earth fell because of **B**. Jr 51:49
Even if **B** should ascend to the Jr 51:53
The sound of a cry from **B**! Jr 51:54
LORD is going to devastate **B**; Jr 51:55
coming against her, against **B**. Jr 51:56
when he went to **B** with Zedekiah Jr 51:59
disaster that would come to **B**; Jr 51:60
words were written against **B**. Jr 51:60
When you get to **B**, see that you Jr 51:61
B will sink and never rise again Jr 51:64
rebelled against the king of **B**. Jr 52:3
of **B** advanced against Jr 52:4
him to the king of **B** at Riblah Jr 52:9
Riblah the king of **B** slaughtered Jr 52:10
The king of **B** brought Zedekiah Jr 52:11
Babylon brought Zedekiah to **B**, Jr 52:11
king of **B**—Nebuzaradan, Jr 52:12
representative of the king of **B**. Jr 52:12
had defected to the king of **B**, Jr 52:15
and carried all the bronze to **B**. Jr 52:17
them to the king of **B** at Riblah. Jr 52:26
The king of **B** put them to death Jr 52:27
king of **B**, in the ⌊first⌋ year Jr 52:31
kings who were with him in **B**. Jr 52:32
of the king of **B** for the rest of Jr 52:33
given to him by the king of **B**, Jr 52:34
I will bring him to **B**, the land Ezk 12:13
The king of **B** came to Jerusalem, Ezk 17:12
brought them back with him to **B**. Ezk 17:12
he will die in **B**, in the land Ezk 17:16
will bring him to **B** and execute Ezk 17:20
led him away to the king of **B**. Ezk 19:9
For the king of **B** stands at the Ezk 21:21
The king of **B** has laid siege to Ezk 24:2
bring King Nebuchadnezzar of **B**, Ezk 26:7
king of **B** made his army labor Ezk 29:18
to Nebuchadnezzar king of **B**, Ezk 29:19
of Nebuchadnezzar king of **B**. Ezk 30:10
king of **B** came to Jerusalem Dn 1:1
carried them to the land of **B**, Dn 1:2
destroy all the wise men of **B**. Dn 2:12
to execute the wise men of **B**. Dn 2:14
to destroy the wise men of **B**. Dn 2:24
Don't kill the wise men of **B**! Dn 2:24
province of **B** and chief governor Dn 2:48
over all the wise men of **B**. Dn 2:48
to manage the province of **B**. Dn 2:49
of Dura in the province of **B**. Dn 3:1
to manage the province of **B**: Dn 3:12
Abednego in the province of **B**. Dn 3:30
the wise men of **B** to me in order Dn 4:6
roof of the royal palace in **B**, Dn 4:29
Is this not **B** the Great that I Dn 4:30
He said to these wise men of **B**, Dn 5:7
year of Belshazzar king of **B**, Dn 7:1
You will go to **B**; there you will Mc 4:10
who are living with Daughter **B**." Zch 2:7
arrived from **B**, and go that same Zch 6:10
at the time of the exile to **B**. Mt 1:11
the exile to **B** Jechoniah Mt 1:12
from David until the exile to **B**, Mt 1:17
the exile to **B** until the Messiah Mt 1:17
So I will deport you beyond **B**! Ac 7:43
She who is in **B**, also chosen, 1Pt 5:13
It has fallen, **B** the Great has Rv 14:8
B the Great was remembered in Rv 16:19
B THE GREAT THE MOTHER OF Rv 17:5
It has fallen, **B** the Great has Rv 18:2
the great city, **B**, the mighty Rv 18:10
B the great city will be thrown Rv 18:21

BABYLON'S *(25)*

ambassadors of **B** rulers were 2Ch 32:31
B time is almost up; Is 13:22
hand this city over to **B** king, Jr 32:3
be handed over to **B** king. Jr 32:4
the Chaldeans, to **B** king Jr 32:28
handed over to **B** king through Jr 32:36
while the king of **B** army was Jr 34:7
to the king of **B** army that is Jr 34:21
over to the king of **B** army, Jr 38:3
rest of the officials of **B** king. Jr 39:3
Nebuchadnezzar, **B** king, at Jr 39:5
King Zedekiah to **B** King Jr 44:30
B king, defeated, Jr 49:28
At the sound of **B** conquest the Jr 50:46
B warriors have stopped fighting; Jr 51:30
B homes have been set ablaze, Jr 51:30
even **B** wall will fall. Jr 51:44
I will punish **B** carved images. Jr 51:47
B thick walls will be totally Jr 51:58
the sword of **B** king can take. Ezk 21:19
the arms of **B** king and place My Ezk 30:24
strengthen the arms of **B** king, Ezk 30:25
in the hand of **B** king and he Ezk 30:25
The sword of **B** king will come Ezk 32:11
with the rest of **B** wise men. Dn 2:18

BABYLONIANS *(4)*

who have sworn an oath to the **B**, Ezk 21:23
a depiction of the **B** in Chaldea, Ezk 23:15
Then the **B** came to her, to the Ezk 23:17
the **B** and all the Chaldeans; Ezk 23:23

BACA *(1)*

pass through the Valley of **B**, Ps 84:6

BACK *(500)*

It went **b** and forth until the Gn 8:7
Then they came **b** to invade Gn 14:7
He brought **b** all the goods and Gn 14:16
You must go **b** to your mistress Gn 16:9
certainly come **b** to you in about Gn 18:10
time I will come **b** to you, Gn 18:14
Don't look **b** and don't stop Gn 19:17
his wife looked **b** and became a Gn 19:26
then we'll come **b** to you." Gn 22:5
Abraham went **b** to his young men, Gn 22:19
your son go **b** to the land you Gn 24:5
you don't take my son **b** there. Gn 24:6
don't let my son go **b** there." Gn 24:8
woman will not come **b** with me?' Gn 24:39
you and bring you **b** from there. Gn 27:45
I will bring you **b** to this land, Gn 28:15
was then placed **b** on the well's Gn 29:3
Go **b** to the land of your fathers Gn 31:3
'Go **b** to your land and to your Gn 32:9
started on his way **b** to Seir, Gn 33:16
doing, and bring word **b** to me." Gn 37:14
He went **b** to his brothers and Gn 37:30
and put her widow's clothes **b** Gn 38:19
in order to get **b** the items he Gn 38:20
But then he pulled his hand **b**, Gn 38:29
Then he turned **b** and spoke to Gn 42:24
Bring **b** your youngest brother to Gn 42:34
then give your brother **b** to you, Gn 42:34
if I don't bring him **b** to you. Gn 42:37
they had brought **b** from Egypt, Gn 43:2
"Go **b** and buy us some food." Gn 43:2
not bring him **b** to you and set Gn 43:9
could have come **b** twice by now." Gn 43:10
and go **b** at once to the man. Gn 43:13
we have brought it **b** with us. Gn 43:21
even brought **b** to you from the Gn 44:8
when we went **b** to your servant Gn 44:24
Let him go **b** with his brothers. Gn 44:33
For how can I go **b** to my father Gn 44:34
animals and go on **b** to the land Gn 45:17
households, and come **b** to me. Gn 45:18
and I will also bring you **b**. Gn 46:4
and will bring you **b** to the land Gn 48:21
have you come **b** so quickly today Ex 2:18
your hand **b** inside your cloak. Ex 4:7
He put his hand **b** inside his Ex 4:7
Then Moses went **b** to his Ex 4:18
When you go **b** to Egypt, make Ex 4:21
So Moses went **b** to the LORD and Ex 5:22
Aaron were brought **b** to Pharaoh. Ex 10:8
to turn **b** and camp in front Ex 14:2
the sea ⌊**b**⌋ with a powerful Ex 14:21
waters may come **b** on the Ex 14:26
waters came **b** and covered the Ex 14:28
waters of the sea **b** over them. Ex 15:19
wife, after he had sent her **b**, Ex 18:2
After Moses came **b**, He summoned Ex 19:7
people's words **b** to the LORD. Ex 19:8
Go down and come **b** with Aaron. Ex 19:24
You must not hold **b** ⌊offerings Ex 22:29
down over the **b** of the Ex 26:12
planks for the two **b** corners of Ex 26:23
for the planks of the **b** side of Ex 26:27
sides—inscribed front and **b**. Ex 32:15
go **b** and forth through the camp Ex 32:27
you will see My **b**, but My face Ex 33:23
planks for the two **b** corners of Ex 36:28
for those at the **b** of the Ex 36:32
its head at the **b** of the neck Lv 5:8
the front or **b** ⌊of the fabric⌋ Lv 13:55
field will transfer **b** to him. Lv 27:19
after that she may be brought **b** Nm 12:14
on until Miriam was brought **b** Nm 12:15
b some fruit from the land. Nm 13:20
The men went **b** to Moses, Aaron, Nm 13:26
They brought **b** a report for them Nm 13:26
better for us to go **b** to Egypt?" Nm 14:3
a leader and go **b** to Egypt." Nm 14:4
turn **b** tomorrow and head for the Nm 14:25
Put Aaron's rod **b** in front of Nm 17:10
officials, "Go **b** to your land, Nm 22:13
in Your sight, I will go **b**." Nm 22:34
Now I am going **b** to my people, Nm 24:14
and went **b** to his homeland, Nm 24:25
has turned **b** My wrath from the Nm 25:11
them and come **b** in before them, Nm 27:17
and come **b** in at his command. Nm 27:21
you turn **b** from following Him, Nm 32:15
and turned **b** to Pi-hahiroth, Nm 33:7
us and bring us **b** a report about Dt 1:22
and brought us **b** a report: Dt 1:25
you are to turn **b** and head for Dt 1:40
Then we turned **b** and headed for Dt 2:1
He directly pays **b** and destroys Dt 7:10
to directly pay **b** the one who Dt 7:10
So I went **b** down the mountain, Dt 9:15
and I went **b** down the mountain Dt 10:5
or send the people **b** to Egypt to Dt 17:16
never to go **b** that way again. Dt 17:16
field, do not go **b** to get it. Dt 24:19
will take you **b** in ships to Dt 28:68
you and bring you **b** from there. Dt 30:4
has turned its **b** ⌊and run⌋ from Jos 7:8
to be beaten **b** by them and fled Jos 8:15
men of Ai turned and looked **b**, Jos 8:20
they turned **b** and struck down Jos 8:21
did not draw **b** his hand that was Jos 8:26
At that time Joshua turned **b**, Jos 11:10
I brought **b** an honest report. Jos 14:7
turned **b** to Hosah and ended at Jos 19:29
and brought **b** a report to them. Jos 22:32
force them **b** on your account Jos 23:5
may turn **b** and leave Mount Jdg 7:3
22,000 of the people turned **b**, Jdg 7:3
of Joash went **b** to live at his Jdg 8:29
brothers, God turned **b** on him. Jdg 9:56
you are bringing me **b** to fight Jdg 11:9
you take them **b** at that time? Jdg 11:26
the LORD and cannot take ⌊it⌋ **b**. Jdg 11:35
and brought **b** 30 wives for his Jdg 12:9
to me today has just come **b**!" Jdg 13:10
went **b** and told his father and Jdg 14:2
and pay him **b** for what he did to Jdg 15:10
began to grow **b** after it had Jdg 16:22
let me pay **b** the Philistines for Jdg 16:28
carried him **b**, and buried him Jdg 16:31
the men went **b** to their clans at Jdg 18:8
and Micah turned to go **b** home, Jdg 18:26
kindly to her and bring her **b**. Jdg 19:3
made her way **b**, and as it was Jdg 19:26
of Israel turned **b** against the Jdg 20:48
They went **b** to their own Jdg 21:23
the road leading **b** to the land Ru 1:7
Each of you go **b** to your Ru 1:8
has gone **b** to her people and to Ru 1:15
leave you or go **b** and not follow Ru 1:16
the LORD has brought me **b** empty. Ru 1:21
So Naomi came **b** from the land of Ru 1:22
'Don't go **b** to your Ru 3:17
Buy ⌊it⌋ **b** in the presence of Ru 4:4
"Buy **b** ⌊the property⌋ yourself." Ru 4:8
to Shiloh to bring **b** the ark of 1Sm 4:4
we can send it **b** to its place." 1Sm 6:2
should we send **b** to Him?" 1Sm 6:4
had sent **b** one gold tumor for 1Sm 6:17

Each of you, go **b** to your city.” 1Sm 8:22
on, let’s go **b**, or my father 1Sm 9:5
brought **b** Agag, king of Amalek, 1Sm 15:20
Come **b** with me so I can bow 1Sm 15:30
Samuel went **b**, following Saul 1Sm 15:31
David kept going **b** and forth 1Sm 17:15
The servants reported **b** to Saul, 1Sm 18:24
sent the agents ⌊**b**⌋ to see David 1Sm 19:15
Jonathan answered his father **b**: 1Sm 20:32
Go, take it **b** to the city.” 1Sm 20:40
Then come **b** to me with accurate 1Sm 23:23
staying in the **b** of the cave, 1Sm 24:3
Saul went **b** home, and David 1Sm 24:22
yet he paid me **b** evil for good. 1Sm 25:21
evil deeds **b** on his own head.” 1Sm 25:39
Come **b**, my son David, I will 1Sm 26:21
Then he came **b** to Achish, 1Sm 27:9
Send that man **b** and let him 1Sm 29:4
Now go **b** quietly and you won’t 1Sm 29:7
David got everything **b**. 1Sm 30:19
Abner glanced **b** and said, 2Sm 2:20
Joab had turned **b** from pursuing 2Sm 2:30
Saul, “Give me **b** my wife, Michal 2Sm 3:14
Abner said to him, “Go **b**.” 2Sm 3:16
to him, “Go back.” So he went **b**. 2Sm 3:16
They brought him **b** from the well 2Sm 3:26
⌊to battle⌋ and brought us **b**. 2Sm 5:2
until your beards grow **b**; 2Sm 10:5
and tomorrow I will send you **b**. 2Sm 11:12
Can I bring him **b** again? 2Sm 12:23
has not brought **b** his own 2Sm 14:13
bring **b** the young man Absalom.” 2Sm 14:21
Why have I come **b** from Geshur? 2Sm 14:32
really brings me **b** to Jerusalem, 2Sm 15:8
b and stay with the king since 2Sm 15:19
Go **b** and take your brothers with 2Sm 15:20
will bring me **b** and allow me to 2Sm 15:25
has paid you **b** for all the blood 2Sm 16:8
bring all the people **b** to you. 2Sm 17:3
Come **b**, you and all your 2Sm 19:14
I do not turn **b** until they are 2Sm 22:38
Then the troops came **b** to him, 2Sm 23:10
They brought it **b** to David, 2Sm 23:16
I should take **b** to the One who 2Sm 24:13
took a message **b** to the king, 1Kg 2:30
LORD will bring **b** his own blood 1Kg 2:32
blood will come **b** on Joab’s head 1Kg 2:33
and brought them **b** from Gath. 1Kg 2:40
LORD has brought **b** your evil on 1Kg 2:44
top at the **b** of the throne, 1Kg 10:19
you to want to go **b** to your own 1Kg 11:22
that we send **b** to these people 1Kg 12:9
heard that Jeroboam had come **b**, 1Kg 12:20
said and went **b** as He had told 1Kg 12:24
murder me and go **b** to the king 1Kg 12:27
could not pull it **b** to himself. 1Kg 13:4
water or go **b** the way you came. 1Kg 13:9
did not go **b** by the way he had 1Kg 13:10
I cannot go **b** with you, eat 1Kg 13:16
there or go **b** by the way you 1Kg 13:17
‘Bring him **b** with you to your 1Kg 13:18
the man of God went **b** with him, 1Kg 13:19
prophet who had brought him **b**, 1Kg 13:20
but you went **b** and ate bread and 1Kg 13:22
the prophet he had brought **b**. 1Kg 13:23
had brought him **b** from his way 1Kg 13:26
on the donkey and brought it **b**. 1Kg 13:29
you have flung Me behind your **b**. 1Kg 14:9
would take them **b** to the royal 1Kg 14:28
You have turned their hearts **b**.” 1Kg 18:37
Seven times Elijah said, “Go **b**.” 1Kg 18:43
“Go on **b**,” he replied, “for 1Kg 19:20
So he turned **b** from following 1Kg 19:21
left and took word **b** to him. 1Kg 20:9
water until I come **b** safely.’ ” 1Kg 22:27
they turned **b** from pursuing him. 1Kg 22:33
them, “Why have you come **b**?” 2Kg 1:5
‘Go **b** to the king who sent you 2Kg 1:6
off Elijah and went **b** and stood 2Kg 2:13
the man of God and then come **b**.” 2Kg 4:22
so he went **b** to meet Elisha and 2Kg 4:31
house, and paced **b** and forth. 2Kg 4:35
Then he came **b** and cut them up 2Kg 4:39
raids and brought **b** from the 2Kg 5:2
company went **b** to the man of God 2Kg 5:15
They came **b** and entered another 2Kg 7:8
them but hasn’t started **b**.” 2Kg 9:18
them but hasn’t started **b**. 2Kg 9:20

So they went **b** and told him, 2Kg 9:36
Jehoahaz took **b** from Ben-hadad 2Kg 13:25
They carried him **b** on horses, 2Kg 14:20
Ahaz came **b** from Damascus, 2Kg 16:11
the king came **b** from Damascus, 2Kg 16:12
Send **b** one of the priests you 2Kg 17:27
can you drive **b** a single officer 2Kg 18:24
shakes ⌊her⌋ head behind your **b**. 2Kg 19:21
make you go **b** the way you came 2Kg 19:28
He will go **b** on the road that he 2Kg 19:33
Go **b** and tell Hezekiah, the 2Kg 20:5
10 steps or go **b** 10 steps?” 2Kg 20:9
let the shadow go **b** 10 steps.” 2Kg 20:10
the shadow **b** the 10 steps it 2Kg 20:11
⌊to battle⌋ and brought us **b**. 1Ch 11:2
They brought it **b** to David, 1Ch 11:18
let us bring **b** the ark of our 1Ch 13:3
until your beards grow **b**; 1Ch 19:5
I should take **b** to the One who 1Ch 21:12
put his sword **b** into its sheath 1Ch 21:27
advise we send **b** to this people 2Ch 10:9
said and turned **b** from going 2Ch 11:4
and take them **b** to the royal 2Ch 12:11
water until I come **b** safely.’ ” 2Ch 18:26
they turned **b** from pursuing him. 2Ch 18:32
brought them **b** to the LORD God 2Ch 19:4
turned **b** with Jehoshaphat 2Ch 20:27
to bring them **b** to the LORD; 2Ch 24:19
Amaziah sent **b** so they would not 2Ch 25:13
They carried him **b** on horses and 2Ch 25:28
and brought him **b** to Jerusalem, 2Ch 33:13
heading **b**, I entered through Neh 2:15
these burnt stones **b** to life Neh 4:2
our best to buy **b** our Jewish Neh 5:8
and we have to buy them **b**.” Neh 5:8
of those who came **b** first, Neh 7:5
and bring **b** branches of olive Neh 8:15
went out, brought **b** ⌊branches⌋, Neh 8:16
them to turn them **b** to You. Neh 9:26
them to turn **b** to Your law, Neh 9:29
had gone **b** to his own field Neh 13:10
God does not hold **b** His anger; Jb 9:13
dies, will he come **b** to life? Jb 14:14
and if I hold **b**, what have I Jb 16:6
But come **b** ⌊and try⌋ again, Jb 17:10
hands must give **b** his wealth. Jb 20:10
out of his **b**, the flashing tip Jb 20:25
the miners swing **b** and forth. Jb 28:4
shoulder blade fall from my **b**, Jb 31:22
to turn him **b** from the Pit, Jb 33:30
you can lead it **b** to its border? Jb 38:20
Therefore I take **b** ⌊my words⌋ Jb 42:6
they will turn **b** and suddenly be Ps 6:10
trouble comes **b** on his own head Ps 7:16
I do not turn **b** until they are Ps 18:37
give them **b** what they deserve. Ps 28:4
harm me be turned **b** and ashamed. Ps 35:4
and friends stand **b** from my Ps 38:11
harm be driven **b** and humiliated. Ps 40:14
Through You we drive **b** our foes; Ps 44:5
Our hearts have not turned **b**; Ps 44:18
and turn your **b** on My words. Ps 50:17
will bring ⌊them⌋ **b** from Bashan; Ps 68:22
bring ⌊them⌋ **b** from the depths Ps 68:22
harm be driven **b** and humiliated. Ps 70:2
Why do You hold **b** Your hand? Ps 74:11
Your arrows flashed **b** and forth. Ps 77:17
archers turned **b** on the day of Ps 78:9
He beat **b** His foes; He gave them Ps 78:66
Pay **b** sevenfold to our neighbors Ps 79:12
let them go **b** to foolish ways Ps 85:8
also turned **b** his sharp sword Ps 89:43
will pay them **b** for their sins Ps 94:23
they go **b** and lie down in their Ps 104:22
an oath and will not take it **b**: Ps 110:4
and fled; the Jordan turned **b**. Ps 114:3
Jordan, that you turned **b**? Ps 114:5
my steps **b** to Your decrees Ps 119:59
will surely come **b** with shouts Ps 126:6
Plowmen plowed over my **b**; Ps 129:3
Zion be driven **b** in disgrace. Ps 129:5
one who pays you **b** what you have Ps 137:8
Go away! Come **b** later. I’ll give Pr 3:28
rod is for the **b** of the one who Pr 10:13
even bring it **b** to his mouth. Pr 19:24
righteous give and don’t hold **b**. Pr 21:26
a stone—it will come **b** on him. Pr 26:27
silver, its **b** of gold, and its Sg 3:10

How can I put it **b** on? I have Sg 5:3
Come **b**, come back, Shulammite! Sg 6:13
Come back, come **b**, Shulammite! Sg 6:13
Come **b**, come back, that we may Sg 6:13
Come back, come **b**, that we may Sg 6:13
minds, turn **b**, and be healed. Is 6:10
so who can turn it **b**? Is 14:27
want to ask, ask! Come **b** again.” Is 21:12
and she will go **b** into business, Is 23:17
those who turn **b** the battle at Is 28:6
does not go **b** on what He says; Is 31:2
time of paying **b** ⌊Edom⌋ for its Is 34:8
shakes ⌊her⌋ head behind your **b**. Is 37:22
make you go **b** the way you came Is 37:29
He will go **b** on the road that he Is 37:34
shadow went **b** the 10 steps it Is 38:8
all my sins behind Your **b**. Is 38:17
will be turned **b** ⌊and⌋ utterly Is 42:17
no one saying “Give ⌊it⌋ **b**!” Is 42:22
not hold ⌊them⌋ **b**! Bring My sons Is 43:6
to bring Jacob **b** to Him so that Is 49:5
rebellious; I did not turn **b**. Is 50:5
gave My **b** to those who beat Me, Is 50:6
You made your **b** like the ground, Is 51:23
out; do not hold **b**; lengthen Is 54:2
but I will take you **b** with great Is 54:7
went on turning **b** to the desires Is 57:17
Cry out loudly, don’t hold **b**! Is 58:1
Justice is turned **b**, and Is 59:14
paying **b** His enemies what they Is 66:6
have turned their **b** to Me and Jr 2:27
not relent or turn **b** from it. Jr 4:28
I am tired of holding it **b**. Jr 6:11
have turned your **b**, so I have Jr 15:6
show them ⌊My⌋ **b** and not ⌊My⌋ Jr 18:17
Jeremiah came **b** from Topheth, Jr 19:14
and none turns his **b** on evil. Jr 23:14
will not turn **b** until He has Jr 23:20
turned them **b** from their evil Jr 23:22
there. Do not hold **b** a word. Jr 26:2
will be brought **b** from Babylon. Jr 27:16
will not turn **b** until He has Jr 30:24
will bring them **b** with Jr 31:9
their minds and took **b** their Jr 34:11
Each has taken **b** his male and Jr 34:16
will bring them **b** to this city. Jr 34:22
Don’t send me **b** to the house of Jr 37:20
whom he brought **b** from Gibeon. Jr 41:16
they never look **b**, terror is on Jr 46:5
too will turn **b**; together they Jr 46:21
will not turn **b** for their sons, Jr 47:3
be restless? Go **b** to your Jr 47:6
How Moab has turned his **b**! Jr 48:39
run **b** and forth within your Jr 49:3
Run! Turn **b**! Lie low, residents Jr 49:8
net for my feet and turned me **b**. Lm 1:13
ways, and turn **b** to the LORD. Lm 3:40
will pay them **b** what they Lm 3:64
with fire flashing **b** and forth Ezk 1:4
Fire was moving **b** and forth Ezk 1:13
were darting **b** and forth like Ezk 1:14
was written on the front and **b**; Ezk 2:10
at his side reported **b**, Ezk 9:11
and brought them **b** with him to Ezk 17:12
Me and cast Me behind your **b**, Ezk 23:35
They brought **b** ivory tusks and Ezk 27:15
and bring them **b** to the land Ezk 29:14
I held **b** the rivers of the deep, Ezk 31:15
injured, brought **b** the strays, Ezk 34:4
the lost, bring **b** the strays, Ezk 34:16
I bring them **b** from the peoples Ezk 39:27
were set **b** from the ground Ezk 42:6
man then brought me **b** toward the Ezk 44:1
he brought me **b** to the entrance Ezk 47:1
Then he led me **b** to the bank of Ezk 47:6
who can hold **b** His hand or say Dn 4:35
four wings of a bird on its **b**. Dn 7:6
his attention **b** to the Dn 11:19
will go **b** to my former husband, Hs 2:7
I will take **b** My grain in its Hs 2:9
her vineyards **b** to her and make Hs 2:15
I will not turn **b** to destroy Hs 11:9
you paying Me **b** or trying to get Jl 3:4
rowed hard to get **b** to dry land, Jnh 1:13
they dart **b** and forth like Nah 2:4
⌊they cry,⌋ but no one turns **b**. Nah 2:8
those who turn **b** from following Zph 1:6
He has turned **b** your enemy. Zph 3:15

At that time I will bring you **b**, Zph 3:20
Now, reflect **b** from this day: Hg 2:15
I will bring them ⌊**b**⌋ to live in Zch 8:8
those who march **b** and forth, Zch 9:8
will bring them **b** from the land Zch 10:10
report **b** to me so that I too can Mt 2:8
in a dream not to go **b** to Herod, Mt 2:12
'I'll go **b** to my house that I Mt 12:44
with their hearts and turn **b**— Mt 13:15
Since he had no way to pay it **b**, Mt 18:25
with me, and I will pay you **b**.' Mt 18:29
give **b** to Caesar the things that Mt 22:21
field must not go **b** to get his Mt 24:18
my money **b** with interest. Mt 25:27
Put your sword **b** in place Mt 26:52
He rolled **b** the stone and was Mt 28:2
they might turn **b**—and be Mk 4:12
Go **b** home to your own people, Mk 5:19
When she went **b** to her home, Mk 7:30
will send it **b** here right away. Mk 11:3
Give **b** to Caesar the things that Mk 12:17
field must not go **b** to get his Mk 13:16
were completed, he went **b** home. Lk 1:23
gave it **b** to the attendant, Lk 4:20
don't hold **b** your shirt either. Lk 6:29
things, don't ask for them **b**. Lk 6:30
it will be measured **b** to you." Lk 6:38
Since they could not pay it **b**, Lk 7:42
Go **b** to your home, and tell all Lk 8:39
ancient prophets has come **b**." Lk 9:19
and gave him **b** to his father. Lk 9:42
the plow and looks **b** is fit for Lk 9:62
When I come **b** I'll reimburse you Lk 10:35
'I'll go **b** to my house where I Lk 11:24
because they might invite you **b**, Lk 14:12
So the slave came **b** and reported Lk 14:21
he has him **b** safe and sound.' Lk 15:27
and comes **b** to you seven times, Lk 17:4
is in the field must not turn **b**. Lk 17:31
I'll pay **b** four times as much!" Lk 19:8
in business until I come **b**.' Lk 19:13
give **b** to Caesar the things that Lk 20:25
you have turned **b**, strengthen Lk 22:32
robe, and sent Him **b** to Pilate. Lk 23:11
because he sent Him **b** to us. Lk 23:15
we're getting **b** what we deserve Lk 23:41
He told her, "and come **b** here." Jn 4:16
disciples turned **b** and no longer Jn 6:66
left, washed, and came **b** seeing. Jn 9:7
she went **b** and called her sister Jn 11:28
and that He was going **b** to God. Jn 13:3
So he leaned **b** against Jesus and Jn 13:25
I will come **b** and receive you to Jn 14:3
they stepped **b** and fell to the Jn 18:6
Then Pilate went **b** into the Jn 18:33
They shouted **b**, "Not this man, Jn 18:40
He went **b** into the headquarters Jn 19:9
who had leaned **b** against Jesus Jn 21:20
Therefore repent and turn **b**, Ac 3:19
he kept **b** part of the proceeds Ac 5:2
Spirit and keep **b** part of the Ac 5:3
were carried **b** to Shechem, Ac 7:16
their hearts turned **b** to Egypt. Ac 7:39
they traveled **b** to Jerusalem, Ac 8:25
them and went **b** to Jerusalem. Ac 13:13
they sailed **b** to Antioch where Ac 14:26
they were sent **b** in peace by the Ac 15:33
Let's go **b** and visit the Ac 15:36
I'll come **b** to you again, Ac 18:21
was made to go **b** through Ac 20:3
did not shrink **b** from Ac 20:20
did not shrink **b** from declaring Ac 20:27
After I came **b** to Jerusalem and Ac 22:17
of slavery to fall **b** into fear, Rm 8:15
anyone who talks **b** to God? Rm 9:20
Arabia and came **b** to Damascus. Gl 1:17
how can you turn **b** again to the Gl 4:9
receive this **b** from the Lord. Eph 6:8
be paid **b** for whatever wrong Col 3:25
be well-pleasing, not talking **b** Ti 2:9
a part of myself—**b** to you. Phm 12
you might get him **b** permanently, Phm 15
and if he draws **b**, My soul has Heb 10:38
those who draw **b** and are Heb 10:39
he also got him **b** as an Heb 11:19
truth, and someone turns him **b**, Jms 5:19
not paying **b** evil for evil or 1Pt 3:9
to turn **b** from the holy 2Pt 2:21
with eyes in front and in **b**. Rv 4:6
on the inside and on the **b**, Rv 5:1
Pay her **b** the way she also paid, Rv 18:6

BACKBITING *(1)*
rain, and a **b** tongue, angry Pr 25:23

BACKBONE *(1)*
he is to remove close to the **b**. Lv 3:9

BACKGROUND *(2)*
her ethnic **b** or her birthplace Est 2:10
her birthplace or her ethnic **b**, Est 2:20

BACKS *(14)*
turn their **b** to you in retreat Ex 23:27
and you will tread on their **b**. Dt 33:29
will turn their **b** ⌊and run⌋ from Jos 7:12
and turned their **b** on Him. 2Ch 29:6
behind their **b** and killed Your Neh 9:26
You placed burdens on our **b**. Ps 66:11
and beatings for the **b** of fools. Pr 19:29
and a rod for the **b** of fools. Pr 26:3
have turned their **b** ⌊on Him⌋. Is 1:4
their wealth on the **b** of donkeys Is 30:6
have turned their **b** to Me and Jr 32:33
their **b** to the LORD's temple Ezk 8:16
including their **b**, hands, wings, Ezk 10:12
and their **b** be bent continually. Rm 11:10

BACKWARD *(1)*
They went **b** and not forward. Jr 7:24

BACKWARDS *(4)*
walking **b**, they covered their Gn 9:23
heels so that its rider falls **b**. Gn 49:17
Eli fell **b** off the chair by the 1Sm 4:18
go stumbling **b**, to be broken, Is 28:13

BAD *(54)*
to Jacob, either good or **b**." Gn 31:24
to Jacob, either good or **b**.' Gn 31:29
and he brought a **b** report about Gn 37:2
was as **b** as it had been Gn 41:21
river smelled so **b** the Egyptians Ex 7:21
the people heard this **b** news, Ex 33:4
either good for **b**, or bad for Lv 27:10
good for bad, or **b** for good. Lv 27:10
inspect whether it is good or **b**, Lv 27:33
the land they live in good or **b**? Nm 13:19
by spreading a **b** report about Nm 14:36
good or **b** of my own will? Nm 24:13
gives her a **b** name, saying, Dt 22:14
an Israelite virgin a **b** name. Dt 22:19
on you every **b** thing until He Jos 23:15
nothing **b** will happen to you 1Sm 28:10
either good or **b**, because he 2Sm 13:22
good and the **b** like the Angel 2Sm 14:17
I have **b** news for you. 1Kg 14:6
the water is **b** and the land 2Kg 2:19
there was nothing **b** in the pot. 2Kg 4:41
sin, and get a **b** reputation, in Neh 6:13
He will not fear **b** news; Ps 112:7
wealth was lost in a **b** venture, Ec 5:14
and don't persist in a **b** cause, Ec 8:3
good and the **b**, for the clean Ec 9:2
reject what is **b** and choose what Is 7:15
reject what is **b** and choose what Is 7:16
good or **b**, then we will be Is 41:23
basket contained very **b** figs, Jr 24:2
very bad figs, so **b** they were Jr 24:2
the **b** figs are extremely bad, Jr 24:3
the bad figs are extremely **b**, Jr 24:3
bad, so **b** they are inedible Jr 24:3
But as for the **b** figs, so bad Jr 24:8
the bad figs, so **b** they are Jr 24:8
inedible because they are so **b**. Jr 29:17
have heard a **b** report and are Jr 49:23
your eye is **b**, your whole body Mt 6:23
but a **b** tree produces bad fruit. Mt 7:17
but a bad tree produces **b** fruit. Mt 7:17
good tree can't produce **b** fruit; Mt 7:18
neither can a **b** tree produce Mt 7:18
or make the tree **b** and its fruit Mt 12:33
the tree bad and its fruit **b**; Mt 12:33
tree doesn't produce **b** fruit; Lk 6:43
a **b** tree doesn't produce good Lk 6:43
But when it is **b**, your body is Lk 11:34
as Lazarus received **b** things, Lk 16:25
yet or done anything good or **b**, Rm 9:11
to good conduct, but to **b**. Rm 13:3
B company corrupts good morals. 1Co 15:33
in the body, whether good or **b**. 2Co 5:10
nothing **b** to say about us. Ti 2:8

BADLY *(7)*
treated us and our fathers **b**. Nm 20:15
the battle, for I am **b** wounded!" 1Kg 22:34
the battle, for I am **b** wounded!" 2Ch 18:33
⌊it will go⌋ **b** ⌊for them⌋, Is 3:11
them only the **b** wounded men, Jr 37:10
to treat you **b** when your fathers Zch 8:14
the living. You are **b** deceived." Mk 12:27

BAFFLED *(1)*
they were **b** about them, as to Ac 5:24

BAG *(20)*
money there at the top of the **b**. Gn 42:27
It's here in my **b**." Their hearts Gn 42:28
man's sack was his **b** of money! Gn 42:35
money was at the top of his **b**! Gn 43:21
one's money at the top of his **b**. Gn 44:1
the top of the youngest one's **b**, Gn 44:2
two different weights in your **b**, Dt 25:13
the pouch, in his shepherd's **b**. 1Sm 17:40
David put his hand in the **b**, 1Sm 17:49
would be sealed up in a **b**, Jb 14:17
carrying the **b** of seed, he will Ps 126:6
took a **b** of money with him and Pr 7:20
in the **b** are His concern. Pr 16:11
wages into a **b** with a hole in it Hg 1:6
take a traveling **b** for the road, Mt 10:10
no traveling **b**, no money in Mk 6:8
no traveling **b**, no bread, no Lk 9:3
traveling **b**, or sandals; Lk 10:4
traveling **b**, or sandals, did you Lk 22:35
take it, and also a traveling **b**. Lk 22:36

BAGS *(21)*
father saw their **b** of money, Gn 42:35
to you⌋ in the top of your **b**. Gn 43:12
in our **b** the first time. Gn 43:18
night and opened our **b** of grain, Gn 43:21
who put our money in the **b**." Gn 43:22
have put treasure in your **b**. Gn 43:23
Fill the men's **b** with as much Gn 44:1
we found at the top of our **b**. Gn 44:8
silver in two **b** with two changes 2Kg 5:23
found there and tie it up in **b**. 2Kg 12:10
pour out their **b** of gold and Is 46:6
your **b** for exile, inhabitant Jr 46:19
your **b** for exile and go into Ezk 12:3
bring out your **b** like an exile's Ezk 12:4
an exile's **b** while they look Ezk 12:4
and take the ⌊**b**⌋ out through it. Ezk 12:5
lift ⌊the **b**⌋ to ⌊your⌋ shoulder Ezk 12:6
brought out my **b** like an exile's Ezk 12:7
an exile's **b** in the daytime. Ezk 12:7
lift ⌊his **b**⌋ to his shoulder Ezk 12:12
wicked scales or **b** of deceptive Mc 6:11

BAHARUMITE *(1)*
(AKA BARHUMITE)
Azmaveth the **B**, Eliahba the 1Ch 11:33

BAHURIM *(5)*
her, weeping all the way to **B**. 2Sm 3:16
David got to **B**, a man belonging 2Sm 16:5
came to the house of a man in **B**. 2Sm 17:18
Benjaminite from **B**, hurried 2Sm 19:16
from **B** who is with you 1Kg 2:8

BAILIFF *(2)*
judge hand you over to the **b**, Lk 12:58
and the **b** throw you into prison. Lk 12:58

BAIT *(1)*
ground if there is no **b** for it? Am 3:5

BAKBAKKAR *(1)*
B, Heresh, Galal, and Mattaniah, 1Ch 9:15

BAKBUK'S *(2)*
B descendants, Hakupha's Ezr 2:51
B descendants, Hakupha's Neh 7:53

BAKBUKIAH *(3)*
B, second among his relatives; Neh 11:17
B, Unni, and their relatives Neh 12:9
Mattaniah, **B**, and Obadiah. Neh 12:25

BAKE *(6)*
B what you want to bake, and Ex 16:23
you want to **b**, and boil what Ex 16:23
fine flour and **b** it into 12 Lv 24:5
10 women will **b** your bread in a Lv 26:26
barley cake and **b** it over dried Ezk 4:12
where they will **b** the grain Ezk 46:20

BAKED *(15)*
a feast and **b** unleavened bread Gn 19:3
all sorts of **b** goods for Pharaoh Gn 40:17
The people **b** the dough they had Ex 12:39
a grain offering **b** in an oven, Lv 2:4
It must not be **b** with yeast; Lv 6:17
as a grain offering of **b** pieces, Lv 6:21
offering that is **b** in an oven, Lv 7:9
of fine flour, **b** with yeast, as Lv 23:17
kneaded it, and **b** unleavened 1Sm 28:24
in his presence, and **b** them. 2Sm 13:8
have anything **b**—only a handful 1Kg 17:12
loaf of bread **b** over hot stones 1Kg 19:6
is dried up like **b** clay; Ps 22:15
I also **b** bread on its coals, Is 44:19
unturned bread, **b** on a griddle. Hs 7:8

BAKER *(8)*
and his **b** offended their Gn 40:1
chief cupbearer and the chief **b**, Gn 40:2
cupbearer and the **b** of the king Gn 40:5
When the chief **b** saw that the Gn 40:16
chief cupbearer and the chief **b**: Gn 40:20
but he hanged the chief **b**, Gn 40:22
and the chief **b** in the custody Gn 41:10
oven heated by a **b** who stops Hs 7:4

BAKER'S *(1)*
day from the **b** street until all Jr 37:21

BAKERS *(1)*
become perfumers, cooks, and **b**. 1Sm 8:13

BAKES *(1)*
he kindles a fire and **b** bread; Is 44:15

BAKING *(2)*
was entrusted with **b** the bread. 1Ch 9:31
bread, the **b**, the mixing, and 1Ch 23:29

BALAAM *(62)*
messengers to **B** son of Beor at Nm 22:5
They came to **B** and reported Nm 22:7
officials of Moab stayed with **B**. Nm 22:8
Then God came to **B** and asked, Nm 22:9
B replied to God, "Balak son of Nm 22:10
God said to **B**, "You are not to Nm 22:12
So **B** got up the next morning and Nm 22:13
"**B** refused to come with us." Nm 22:14
They came to **B** and said to him, Nm 22:16
But **B** responded to the servants Nm 22:18
God came to **B** at night and said Nm 22:20
B saddled his donkey and went Nm 22:21
was incensed that **B** was going, Nm 22:22
B was riding his donkey, and his Nm 22:22
B hit her to return her to the Nm 22:23
she crouched down under **B**. Nm 22:27
and she asked **B**, "What have I Nm 22:28
B answered the donkey, "You Nm 22:29
B knelt and bowed with his face Nm 22:31
B said to the Angel of the LORD, Nm 22:34
the Angel of the LORD said to **B**, Nm 22:35
So **B** went with Balak's Nm 22:35
Balak heard that **B** was coming, Nm 22:36
Balak asked **B**, "Did I not send Nm 22:37
B said to him, "Look, I have Nm 22:38
So **B** went with Balak, and they Nm 22:39
and sent for **B** and the officials Nm 22:40
Balak took **B** and brought him to Nm 22:41
Then **B** said to Balak, "Build me Nm 23:1
So Balak did as **B** directed, Nm 23:2
B said to Balak, "Stay here by Nm 23:3
met with him and **B** said to Him, Nm 23:4
B proclaimed his poem: Nm 23:7
Balak asked **B**. "I brought you Nm 23:11
B said to Balak, "Stay here by Nm 23:15
LORD met with **B** and put a Nm 23:16
B proclaimed his poem: Nm 23:18
Then Balak told **B**, "Don't curse Nm 23:25
But **B** answered him, "Didn't I Nm 23:26
Balak said to **B**, "Please come. Nm 23:27
So Balak took **B** to the top of Nm 23:28
B told Balak, "Build me seven Nm 23:29
So Balak did as **B** said and Nm 23:30
Since **B** saw that it pleased the Nm 24:1
When **B** looked up and saw Israel Nm 24:2
The oracle of **B** son of Beor, Nm 24:3
Balak became furious with **B**, Nm 24:10
B answered Balak, "Didn't I Nm 24:12
The oracle of **B** son of Beor, Nm 24:15
B saw Amalek and proclaimed Nm 24:20
B then arose and went back to Nm 24:25
also killed **B** son of Beor with Nm 31:8
and because **B** son of Beor from Dt 23:4
your God would not listen to **B**, Dt 23:5
the diviner, **B** son of Beor, with Jos 13:22
He sent for **B** son of Beor to Jos 24:9
but I would not listen to **B**. Jos 24:10
they hired **B** against them to Neh 13:2
what **B** son of Beor answered him, Mc 6:5
and have followed the path of **B**, 2Pt 2:15
to the error of **B** for profit, Jd 11
who hold to the teaching of **B**, Rv 2:14

BALAAM'S *(4)*
squeezing **B** foot against it. Nm 22:25
Then the LORD opened **B** eyes, Nm 22:31
a message in **B** mouth and said, Nm 23:5
ones who, at **B** advice, incited Nm 31:16

BALADAN *(2)*
time Merodach-baladan son of **B**, 2Kg 20:12
time Merodach-baladan son of **B**, Is 39:1

BALAH *(1)*
Hazar-shual, **B**, Ezem, Jos 19:3

BALAK *(41)*
Now **B** son of Zippor saw all that Nm 22:2
Since **B** son of Zippor was Nm 22:4
of his people. **B** said to him: Nm 22:5
to God, "**B** son of Zippor, Nm 22:10
returned to **B**, and reported, Nm 22:14
B sent officials again who were Nm 22:15
This is what **B** son of Zippor Nm 22:16
responded to the servants of **B**, Nm 22:18
If **B** were to give me his house Nm 22:18
When **B** heard that Balaam was Nm 22:36
B asked Balaam, "Did I not send Nm 22:37
Balaam went with **B**, and they Nm 22:39
B sacrificed cattle and sheep, Nm 22:40
B took Balaam and brought him to Nm 22:41
Balaam said to **B**, "Build me Nm 23:1
So **B** did as Balaam directed, Nm 23:2
Balaam said to **B**, "Stay here by Nm 23:3
to **B** and say what I tell you. Nm 23:5
he returned to **B**, who was Nm 23:6
B brought me from Aram; Nm 23:7
done to me?" **B** asked Balaam. "I Nm 23:11
Then **B** said to him, "Please come Nm 23:13
B took him to Lookout Field on Nm 23:14
Balaam said to **B**, "Stay here by Nm 23:15
to **B** and say what I tell you. Nm 23:16
he returned to **B**, who was Nm 23:17
B asked him, "What did the LORD Nm 23:17
his poem: **B**, get up and listen; Nm 23:18
Then **B** told Balaam, "Don't curse Nm 23:25
Again **B** said to Balaam, "Please Nm 23:27
So **B** took Balaam to the top of Nm 23:28
Balaam told **B**, "Build me seven Nm 23:29
So **B** did as Balaam said and Nm 23:30
Then **B** became furious with Nm 24:10
Balaam answered **B**, "Didn't I Nm 24:12
If **B** were to give me his house Nm 24:13
homeland, and **B** also went his Nm 24:25
B son of Zippor, king of Moab, Jos 24:9
any better than **B** son of Zippor, Jdg 11:25
remember what **B** king of Moab Mc 6:5
taught **B** to place a stumbling Rv 2:14

BALAK'S *(3)*
and reported **B** words to him. Nm 22:7
morning and said to **B** officials, Nm 22:13
So Balaam went with **B** officials. Nm 22:35

BALANCE *(6)*
repay the **b** to the man he sold Lv 25:27
God weigh me with an accurate **b**, Jb 31:6
On a **b** scale, they go up; Ps 62:9
mountains in a **b** and the hills Is 40:12
weighed in the **b** and found Dn 5:27
on it had a **b** scale in his hand. Rv 6:5

BALANCES *(3)*
have honest **b**, honest weights, Lv 19:36
Honest **b** and scales are the Pr 16:11
must have honest **b**, an honest Ezk 45:10

BALCONIES *(1)*
and the **b** all around with their Ezk 41:16

BALD *(11)*
his head, he is **b**, but he is Lv 13:40
he is **b** on his forehead Lv 13:41
on the **b** head or forehead Lv 13:42
on his **b** head or forehead Lv 13:43
may not make **b** spots on their Lv 21:5
or make a **b** spot on your head Dt 14:1
every head is **b** and every beard Jr 48:37
and all their heads will be **b**. Ezk 7:18
head was made **b** and every Ezk 29:18
yourselves **b** and cut off your Mc 1:16
yourselves as **b** as an eagle, Mc 1:16

BALDNESS *(2)*
of beautifully styled hair, **b**; Is 3:24
B is coming to Gaza. Jr 47:5

BALDY *(2)*
him, chanting, "Go up, **b**! 2Kg 2:23
Go up, baldy! Go up, **b**!" 2Kg 2:23

BALL *(1)*
you up into a **b**, and sling you Is 22:18

BALM *(4)*
Is there no **b** in Gilead? Jr 8:22
Go up to Gilead and get **b**, Jr 46:11
b for her wound—perhaps she Jr 51:8
oil, and **b** for your goods. Ezk 27:17

BALSAM *(7)*
aromatic gum, **b**, and resin, Gn 37:25
a gift—some **b** and some honey, Gn 43:11
them opposite the **b** trees. 2Sm 5:23
in the tops of the **b** trees, 2Sm 5:24
them opposite the **b** trees. 1Ch 14:14
in the tops of the **b** trees, 1Ch 14:15
of your perfume than any **b**. Sg 4:10

BAMOTH *(2)*
to Nahaliel, from Nahaliel to **B**, Nm 21:19
from **B** to the valley in the Nm 21:20

BAMOTH-BAAL *(2)*
Balaam and brought him to **B**. Nm 22:41
Dibon, **B**, Beth-baal-meon Jos 13:17

BAN *(1)*
They will **b** you from the Jn 16:2

BAND *(11)*
He put the woven **b** of the ephod Lv 8:7
the cart was a **b** nine inches 1Kg 7:35
suddenly they saw a marauding **b**, 2Kg 13:21
and calamity—a **b** of deadly Ps 78:49
They **b** together against the life Ps 94:21
B together, peoples, and be Is 8:9
its prey when a **b** of shepherds Is 31:4
sat with the **b** of revelers, Jr 15:17
and with a **b** of iron and bronze Dn 4:15
ground and with a **b** of iron and Dn 4:23
a **b** of priests murders on the Hs 6:9

BANDAGE *(4)*
himself with a **b** over his eyes. 1Kg 20:38
removed the **b** from his eyes. 1Kg 20:41
splint put on to **b** it so that it Ezk 30:21
back the strays, **b** the injured, Ezk 34:16

BANDAGED *(4)*
not cleansed, **b**, or soothed with Is 1:6
has not been **b**—⌊no⌋ medicine Ezk 30:21
healed the sick, **b** the injured, Ezk 34:4
over to him and **b** his wounds, Lk 10:34

BANDAGES *(1)*
day that the LORD **b** His people's Is 30:26

BANDED *(2)*
courtyard are to be **b** with Ex 27:17
courtyard were **b** with silver. Ex 38:17

BANDIT *(2)*
a robber, your need, like a **b**. Pr 6:11
a robber, your need, like a **b**. Pr 24:34

BANDS *(14)*
be attacked by ⌊marauding⌋ **b**, Gn 49:19
hooks and **b** of the posts must Ex 27:10
hooks and **b** of the posts must Ex 27:11
the posts and their **b** with gold, Ex 36:38
hooks and **b** of the posts were Ex 38:10
hooks and **b** of the posts were Ex 38:11
hooks and **b** of the posts were Ex 38:12
hooks and **b** of the posts were Ex 38:17
and the **b** as well as the plating Ex 38:19
tops, and supplied **b** for them. Ex 38:28
marauding **b** of Moabites used 2Kg 13:20
The Chaldeans formed three **b**, Jb 1:17
who sew ⌊magic⌋ **b** on the wrist Ezk 13:18
your ⌊magic⌋ **b** that you ensnare Ezk 13:20

BANI *(12)*
(AKA BINNUI)
Nathan from Zobah, **B** the Gadite, 2Sm 23:36
Amzi, son of **B**, son of Shemer, 1Ch 6:46
of Imri, son of **B**, a descendant 1Ch 9:4

B, Binnui, Shimei, Ezr 10:38
repairs ⌊under⌋ Rehum son of **B**. Neh 3:17
Jeshua, **B**, Sherebiah, Jamin, Neh 8:7
Jeshua, **B**, Kadmiel, Shebaniah, Neh 9:4
Bunni, Sherebiah, **B**, and Chenani Neh 9:4
Jeshua, Kadmiel, **B**, Hashabneiah, Neh 9:5
Hodiah, **B**, and Beninu. Neh 10:13
Pahath-moab, Elam, Zattu, **B**, Neh 10:14
in Jerusalem was Uzzi son of **B**, Neh 11:22

BANI'S *(4)*
B descendants 642 Ezr 2:10
of Josiphiah from **B** descendants, Ezr 8:10
B descendants: Meshullam, Ezr 10:29
B descendants: Maadai, Amram, Ezr 10:34

BANISH *(10)*
My name I will **b** from My 2Ch 7:20
Didn't you **b** the priests of the 2Ch 13:9
you **b** injustice from your tent Jb 22:23
not **b** me from Your presence or Ps 51:11
the LORD will **b** them with the Ps 125:5
I will **b** you, and you will Jr 27:10
I will **b** you, and you will Jr 27:15
nations where I will **b** them." Ezk 4:13
far from you and **b** him to a dry Jl 2:20
Him not to **b** them to the abyss Lk 8:31

BANISHED *(28)*
not brought back his own **b** one. 2Sm 14:13
so that the one **b** from Him does 2Sm 14:14
from Him does not remain **b**. 2Sm 14:14
So Solomon **b** Abiathar from being 1Kg 2:27
He **b** the male shrine prostitutes 1Kg 15:12
now He has not **b** them from His 2Kg 13:23
until He had **b** them from His 2Kg 17:20
that He finally **b** them from His 2Kg 24:20
your exiles were **b** to the ends Neh 1:9
for⌋ success has been **b** from me. Jb 6:13
remain wherever I have **b** them." Jr 8:3
other lands where He had **b** them. Jr 16:15
My flock, **b** them, and have not Jr 23:2
the lands where I have **b** them, Jr 23:3
countries where I had **b** them. Jr 23:8
cursing, wherever I have **b** them. Jr 24:9
and places where I **b** you"— Jr 29:14
where I will have **b** them. Jr 29:18
where I have **b** them in My wrath Jr 32:37
where they had been **b** and came Jr 40:12
they had been **b** to live in the Jr 43:5
the nations where I have **b** you, Jr 46:28
will be **b**, each man headlong, Jr 49:5
to which Elam's **b** ones will not Jr 49:36
that He finally **b** them from His Jr 52:3
of God, and **b** you, guardian Ezk 28:16
b it because of its wickedness. Ezk 31:11
I have been **b** from Your sight, Jnh 2:4

BANISHING *(2)*
Since You are **b** me today from Gn 4:14
with her by **b** and driving her Is 27:8

BANISHMENT *(1)*
whether death, **b**, confiscation Ezr 7:26

BANK *(14)*
cows along the **b** of the Nile. Gn 41:3
standing on the **b** of the Nile, Gn 41:17
the reeds by the **b** of the Nile. Ex 2:3
meet him by the **b** of the Nile. Ex 7:15
all along the **b** of the Jabbok Dt 2:37
stood on the **b** of the Jordan. 2Kg 2:13
north by the **b** of the Euphrates Jr 46:6
me back to the **b** of the river. Ezk 47:6
standing on the **b** of the great Dn 10:4
one on this **b** of the river and Dn 12:5
down the steep **b** into the sea Mt 8:32
down the steep **b** into the sea Mk 5:13
down the steep **b** into the lake Lk 8:33
you put my money in the **b**? Lk 19:23

BANKERS *(1)*
deposited my money with the **b**. Mt 25:27

BANKRUPT *(1)*
to the weak and **b** elemental Gl 4:9

BANKS *(6)*
overflows its **b** throughout Jos 3:15
over all the **b** as before. Jos 4:18
that are on the **b** of the Arnon, Jdg 11:26
it was overflowing all its **b**, 1Ch 12:15
and spill over all its **b**. Is 8:7
grow along both **b** of the river. Ezk 47:12

BANNED *(3)*
he was still **b** from the presence 1Ch 12:1
would be **b** from the synagogue. Jn 9:22
they would not be **b** from the Jn 12:42

BANNER *(19)*
named it, "The LORD Is My **B**." Ex 17:15
his encampment and under his **b**. Nm 1:52
the sunrise under their **b**. Nm 2:3
on the south side under their **b**. Nm 2:10
on the west side under their **b**. Nm 2:18
on the north side under their **b**. Nm 2:25
with their **b** set out first, Nm 10:14
of Reuben with their **b** set out, Nm 10:18
of Ephraim with their **b** set out, Nm 10:22
of Dan with their **b** set out, Nm 10:25
lift the **b** in the name of our Ps 20:5
stand as a **b** for the peoples Is 11:10
will lift up a **b** for the nations Is 11:12
up a **b** on a barren mountain. Is 13:2
when a **b** is raised on the Is 18:3
a mountaintop or a **b** on a hill. Is 30:17
and raise My **b** to the peoples. Is 49:22
Raise a **b** for the peoples. Is 62:10
Egypt, and served as your **b**. Ezk 27:7

BANNERS *(6)*
respective **b** beside the flags Nm 2:2
each in his place, with their **b**. Nm 2:17
to move out last, with their **b**." Nm 2:31
camped by their **b** in this way Nm 2:34
awe-inspiring as an army with **b**. Sg 6:4
awe-inspiring as an army with **b**? Sg 6:10

BANQUET *(29)*
So he prepared a **b** for them, Gn 26:30
brought them to the **b** hall, 1Sm 9:22
David held a **b** for him and his 2Sm 3:20
held a week-long **b** in the garden Est 1:5
king held a great **b** for all his Est 2:18
It was Esther's **b**. He freed his Est 2:18
today to the **b** I have prepared Est 5:4
Haman went to the **b** Esther had Est 5:5
come to the **b** I will prepare Est 5:8
the king at the **b** she had Est 5:12
Then go to the **b** with the king Est 5:14
Haman to the **b** Esther had Est 6:14
He brought me to the **b** hall, Sg 2:4
the queen came to the **b** hall. Dn 5:10
gave a wedding **b** for his son. Mt 22:2
summon those invited to the **b**, Mt 22:3
Come to the wedding **b**.' Mt 22:4
his slaves, 'The **b** is ready, but Mt 22:8
everyone you find to the **b**.' Mt 22:9
The wedding **b** was filled with Mt 22:10
in with him to the wedding **b**, Mt 25:10
Herod gave a **b** for his nobles, Mk 6:21
hosted a grand **b** for Him at his Lk 5:29
the wedding **b** so that when he Lk 12:36
by someone to a wedding **b**, Lk 14:8
when you host a **b**, invite those Lk 14:13
giving a large **b** and invited Lk 14:16
the time of the **b**, he sent his Lk 14:17
were invited will enjoy my **b**!' " Lk 14:24

BANQUETING *(1)*
Whenever a round of **b** was over, Jb 1:5

BANQUETS *(4)*
sons used to have **b**, each at his Jb 1:4
love the place of honor at **b**, Mt 23:6
and the places of honor at **b**. Mk 12:39
and the places of honor at **b**. Lk 20:46

BAPTISM *(21)*
coming to the place of his **b**, Mt 3:7
Where did John's **b** come from? Mt 21:25
and preaching a **b** of repentance Mk 1:4
with the **b** I am baptized Mk 10:38
with the **b** I am baptized Mk 10:39
Was John's **b** from heaven or from Mk 11:30
preaching a **b** of repentance for Lk 3:3
had been baptized with John's **b**. Lk 7:29
But I have a **b** to be baptized Lk 12:50
was the **b** of John from heaven or Lk 20:4
from the **b** of John until Ac 1:22
Galilee after the **b** that John Ac 10:37
proclaimed a **b** of repentance to Ac 13:24
although he knew only John's **b**. Ac 18:25
Then with what ⌊**b**⌋ were you Ac 19:3
"With John's **b**," they replied. Ac 19:3
baptized with a **b** of repentance, Ac 19:4
buried with Him by **b** into death, Rm 6:4
one Lord, one faith, one **b**, Eph 4:5
been buried with Him in **b**, Col 2:12
B, which corresponds to this, 1Pt 3:21

BAPTIST *(11)*
In those days John the **B** came, Mt 3:1
than John the **B** has appeared, Mt 11:11
days of John the **B** until now, Mt 11:12
"This is John the **B**!" Mt 14:2
they said, "Some say John the **B**; Mt 16:14
spoke to them about John the **B**. Mt 17:13
John the **B** has been raised from Mk 6:14
They answered Him, "John the **B**; Mk 8:28
John the **B** sent us to ask You, Lk 7:20
For John the **B** did not come Lk 7:33
They answered, "John the **B**; Lk 9:19

BAPTIST'S *(3)*
Give me John the **B** head here on Mt 14:8
"John the **B** head!" Mk 6:24
give me John the **B** head on a Mk 6:25

BAPTIZE *(10)*
I **b** you with water for Mt 3:11
He Himself will **b** you with the Mt 3:11
but He will **b** you with the Holy Mk 1:8
them all, "I **b** you with water, Lk 3:16
He will **b** you with the Holy Lk 3:16
Why then do you **b** if you aren't Jn 1:25
"I **b** with water," John answered Jn 1:26
who sent me to **b** with water told Jn 1:33
b the household of Stephanas; 1Co 1:16
For Christ did not send me to **b**, 1Co 1:17

BAPTIZED *(54)*
and they were **b** by him in the Mt 3:6
at the Jordan, to be **b** by him. Mt 3:13
I need to be **b** by You, and yet Mt 3:14
Then he allowed Him ⌊to be **b**⌋. Mt 3:15
After Jesus was **b**, He went up Mt 3:16
and they were **b** by him in the Mk 1:5
I have **b** you with water, but He Mk 1:8
Galilee and was **b** in the Jordan Mk 1:9
drink or to be **b** with the Mk 10:38
with the baptism I am **b** with?" Mk 10:38
and you will be **b** with the Mk 10:39
with the baptism I am **b** with. Mk 10:39
believes and is **b** will be saved, Mk 16:16
who came out to be **b** by him, Lk 3:7
collectors also came to be **b**, Lk 3:12
When all the people were **b**, Lk 3:21
were baptized, Jesus also was **b**. Lk 3:21
they had been **b** with John's Lk 7:29
the law had not been **b** by him, Lk 7:30
I have a baptism to be **b** with, Lk 12:50
He spent time with them and **b**. Jn 3:22
People were coming and being **b**, Jn 3:23
for John **b** with water, but you Ac 1:5
but you will be **b** with the Holy Ac 1:5
to them, "and be **b**, each of you, Ac 2:38
who accepted his message were **b**, Ac 2:41
both men and women were **b**. Ac 8:12
after he was **b**, he went around Ac 8:13
they had only been **b** in the name Ac 8:16
would keep me from being **b**?" Ac 8:36
into the water, and he **b** him. Ac 8:38
Then he got up and was **b**. Ac 9:18
and prevent these from being **b**, Ac 10:47
them to be **b** in the name of Ac 10:48
how He said, 'John **b** with water, Ac 11:16
but you will be **b** with the Holy Ac 11:16
she and her household were **b**, Ac 16:15
he and all his family were **b**. Ac 16:33
they heard, believed and were **b**. Ac 18:8
with what ⌊baptism⌋ were you **b**?" Ac 19:3
John **b** with a baptism of Ac 19:4
they were **b** in the name of the Ac 19:5
Get up and be **b**, and wash away Ac 22:16
of us who were **b** into Christ Rm 6:3
Jesus were **b** into His death? Rm 6:3
Or were you **b** in Paul's name? 1Co 1:13
thank God that I **b** none of you 1Co 1:14
say you had been **b** in my name. 1Co 1:15
I don't know if I **b** anyone else. 1Co 1:16
and all were **b** into Moses in the 1Co 10:2
For we were all **b** by one Spirit 1Co 12:13
do who are being **b** for the dead? 1Co 15:29
then why are people **b** for them? 1Co 15:29
as have been **b** into Christ have Gl 3:27

BAPTIZES *(1)*
is the One who **b** with the Holy Jn 1:33

BAPTIZING *(9)*
b them in the name of the Father Mt 28:19
John came b in the wilderness Mk 1:4
the Jordan, where John was b. Jn 1:28
but I came b with water so He Jn 1:31
John also was b in Aenon near Jn 3:23
the Jordan, is b—and everyone Jn 3:26
was making and b more disciples Jn 4:1
though Jesus Himself was not b, Jn 4:2
where John had been b earlier, Jn 10:40

BAR *(8)*
and a b of gold weighing 50 Jos 7:21
cloak, and the b of gold, his Jos 7:24
and pulled them out, b and all. Jdg 16:3
took the yoke b from the neck Jr 28:10
broken the yoke b from the neck Jr 28:12
You broke a wooden yoke b, Jr 28:13
you will make an iron yoke b. Jr 28:13
no doors, not even a gate b; Jr 49:31

BAR-JESUS *(1)*
(AKA ELYMAS)
a Jewish false prophet named B. Ac 13:6

BARABBAS *(11)*
a notorious prisoner called B. Mt 27:16
for you—B, or Jesus who is Mt 27:17
to ask for B and to execute Mt 27:20
for you?" "B!" they answered. Mt 27:21
Then he released B to them. Mt 27:26
was one named B, who was in Mk 15:7
would release B to them instead Mk 15:11
Pilate released B to them. Mk 15:15
this man away! Release B to us!" Lk 23:18
back, "Not this man, but B!" Jn 18:40
Now B was a revolutionary. Jn 18:40

BARACHEL *(2)*
Then Elihu son of B the Buzite Jb 32:2
So Elihu son of B the Buzite Jb 32:6

BARAK *(15)*
(AKA BEDAN)
She summoned B son of Abinoam Jdg 4:6
B said to her, "If you will go Jdg 4:8
up and went with B to Kedesh. Jdg 4:9
B summoned Zebulun and Naphtali Jdg 4:10
to Sisera that B son of Abinoam Jdg 4:12
Deborah said to B, "Move on, for Jdg 4:14
So B came down from Mount Tabor Jdg 4:14
with the sword before B. Jdg 4:15
B pursued the chariots and the Jdg 4:16
When B arrived in pursuit of Jdg 4:22
day Deborah and B son of Abinoam Jdg 5:1
Arise B, and take hold of your Jdg 5:12
was with B. They set out at Jdg 5:15
sent Jerubbaal, B, Jephthah, 1Sm 12:11
about Gideon, B, Samson, Heb 11:32

BARBARIAN *(1)*
uncircumcision, b, Scythian, Col 3:11

BARBARIANS *(4)*
the fortress of b is no longer a Is 25:2
You subdue the uproar of b. Is 25:5
You will no longer see the b, Is 33:19
obligated both to Greeks and b, Rm 1:14

BARBED *(4)*
discipline you with b whips.'" 1Kg 12:11
discipline you with b whips." 1Kg 12:14
whips, but I, with b whips.'" 2Ch 10:11
whips, but I, with b whips." 2Ch 10:14

BARBER'S *(1)*
use it as you would a b razor, Ezk 5:1

BARBS *(1)*
Death, where are your b? Hs 13:14

BARE *(16)*
your vineyard b or gather its Lv 19:10
apart with his b hands as he Jdg 14:6
it under Jehu on the b steps. 2Kg 9:13
and strips the woodlands b. Ps 29:9
will shave their foreheads b. Is 3:17
the earth b and making it Is 24:1
completely b and will be totally Is 24:3
Strip yourselves b and put Is 32:11
your⌊ skirt, b your thigh, wade Is 47:2
from going b and your throat Jr 2:25
But I will strip Esau b; Jr 49:10
her and strip her land b, Jr 51:2
She put it out on the b rock; Ezk 24:7
put her blood on the b rock, Ezk 24:8
her and turn her into a b rock. Ezk 26:4
I will turn you into a b rock, Ezk 26:14

BARED *(2)*
and barefoot, with b buttocks, Is 20:4
of Jerusalem with your arm b, Ezk 4:7

BAREFOOT *(7)*
covered, and he was walking b. 2Sm 15:30
counselors away b and makes Jb 12:17
priests away b and overthrows Jb 12:19
he did so, going naked and b— Is 20:2
gone naked and b three years as Is 20:3
alike, naked and b, with bared Is 20:4
I will walk b and naked. Mc 1:8

BARELY *(6)*
they could ⌊b⌋ recognize him. Jb 2:12
They are b planted, barely sown, Is 40:24
barely planted, b sown, their Is 40:24
they b stopped the crowds from Ac 14:18
we were b able to get control of Ac 27:16
people who have b escaped from 2Pt 2:18

BARGAIN *(3)*
So now make a b with my master 2Kg 18:23
Will traders b for him or divide Jb 41:6
you have made a b for yourself Is 57:8

BARHUMITE *(1)*
(AKA BAHARUMITE)
the Arbathite, Azmaveth the B, 2Sm 23:31

BARIAH *(1)*
Hattush, Igal, B, Neariah, and 1Ch 3:22

BARK *(3)*
and peeled ⌊the b⌋, exposing Gn 30:37
are mute dogs, they cannot b; Is 56:10
stripped off its b and thrown it Jl 1:7

BARKOS'S *(2)*
B descendants, Sisera's Ezr 2:53
B descendants, Sisera's Neh 7:55

BARLEY *(38)*
flax and the b were destroyed Ex 9:31
because the b was ripe and the Ex 9:31
every⌋ five bushels of b seed. Lv 27:16
her of two quarts of b flour. Nm 5:15
a land of wheat, b, vines, figs, Dt 8:8
a loaf of b bread came tumbling Jdg 7:13
the beginning of the b harvest. Ru 1:22
and it was about 26 quarts of b. Ru 2:17
Where did you gather ⌊b⌋ today, Ru 2:19
grain⌋ until the b and the wheat Ru 2:23
be winnowing b on the threshing Ru 3:2
at the end of the pile of b. Ru 3:7
measures⌋ of b into her shawl, Ru 3:15
me these six ⌊measures⌋ of b, Ru 3:17
to mine, and he has b there. 2Sm 14:30
brought⌋ wheat, b, flour, 2Sm 17:28
the beginning of the b harvest. 2Sm 21:9
man brought the b and the straw 1Kg 4:28
of 20 loaves of b bread from the 2Kg 4:42
12 quarts of b ⌊will sell⌋ for 2Kg 7:1
and 12 quarts of b ⌊sold⌋ for a 2Kg 7:16
12 quarts of b ⌊will sell⌋ for 2Kg 7:18
of ground full of b was there, 1Ch 11:13
bushels of b, 110,000 gallons 2Ch 2:10
send the wheat, b, oil, and wine 2Ch 2:15
wheat, and 50,000 bushels of b. 2Ch 27:5
and stinkweed instead of b. Jb 31:40
wheat in rows and b in plots, Is 28:25
—wheat, b, oil, and honey! Jr 41:8
take wheat, b, beans, lentils Ezk 4:9
you would⌋ a b cake and bake it Ezk 4:12
for handfuls of b and scraps of Ezk 13:19
quarts from five bushels of b. Ezk 45:13
of silver and five bushels of b. Hs 3:2
the wheat and the b, because the Jl 1:11
who has five b loaves and two Jn 6:9
from the five b loaves that were Jn 6:13
three quarts of b for a denarius Rv 6:6

BARN *(4)*
and gather His wheat into the b. Mt 3:12
but store the wheat in my b.'" Mt 13:30
and gather the wheat into His b, Lk 3:17
don't have a storeroom or a b; Lk 12:24

BARNABAS *(28)*
(AKA JOSEPH)
whom the apostles named B, Ac 4:36
B, however, took him and brought Ac 9:27
they sent out B to travel as far Ac 11:22
elders by means of B and Saul. Ac 11:30
And B and Saul returned to Ac 12:25
B, Simeon who was called Niger, Ac 13:1
Set apart for Me B and Saul for Ac 13:2
This man summoned B and Saul and Ac 13:7
proselytes followed Paul and B, Ac 13:43
Then Paul and B boldly said: Ac 13:46
against Paul and B and expelled Ac 13:50
And they started to call B, Ac 14:12
The apostles B and Paul tore Ac 14:14
day he left with B for Derbe. Ac 14:20
after Paul and B had engaged Ac 15:2
for Paul and B and some others Ac 15:2
and listened to B and Paul Ac 15:12
them to Antioch with Paul and B: Ac 15:22
with our beloved B and Paul, Ac 15:25
But Paul and B, along with many Ac 15:35
Paul said to B, "Let's go back Ac 15:36
B wanted to take along John Mark. Ac 15:37
and B took Mark with him and Ac 15:39
is it only B and I who have no 1Co 9:6
up again to Jerusalem with B, Gl 2:1
hand of fellowship to me and B, Gl 2:9
so that even B was carried away Gl 2:13
you, as does Mark, B' cousin Col 4:10

BARNS *(3)*
then your b will be completely Pr 3:10
sow or reap or gather into b, Mt 6:26
tear down my b and build bigger Lk 12:18

BARRACKS *(6)*
him to be taken into the b. Ac 21:34
about to be brought into the b, Ac 21:37
him to be brought into the b, Ac 22:24
them, and bring him into the b. Ac 23:10
and entered the b and reported Ac 23:16
they returned to the b, allowing Ac 23:32

BARRED *(1)*
entering a town with b gates." 1Sm 23:7

BARREN *(30)*
Sarai was b; she had no child. Gn 11:30
of his wife because she was b. Gn 25:21
her womb; but Rachel was b. Gn 29:31
miscarry or be b in your land. Ex 23:26
So he went to a b hill. Nm 23:3
land, in a b, howling wilderness Dt 32:10
his wife was b and had no Jdg 13:2
true that you are b and have no Jdg 13:3
b woman gives birth to seven, 1Sm 2:5
Yes, may that night be b; Jb 3:7
of the godless will be b, Jb 15:34
prey on the b, childless woman Jb 24:21
Sheol; a b womb; earth, which is Pr 30:16
up a banner on a b mountain. Is 13:2
will become b places forever, Is 32:14
open rivers on the b heights, Is 41:18
will be on all the b heights. Is 49:9
deprived of my children and b, Is 49:21
Rejoice, b one, who did not give Is 54:1
Look to the b heights and see. Jr 3:2
sound is heard on the b heights, Jr 3:21
wind ⌊blows⌋ from the b heights Jr 4:11
up a dirge on the b heights, Jr 7:29
Over all the b heights in the Jr 12:12
stand on the b heights panting Jr 14:6
in your field will not be b," Mal 3:11
month for her who was called b. Lk 1:36
Blessed are the b, the wombs Lk 23:29
O b woman who does not give Gl 4:27
when she was b, received power Heb 11:11

BARRIER *(4)*
With You I can attack a b, 2Sm 22:30
With You I can attack a b, Ps 18:29
an enduring b that it cannot Jr 5:22
There was a b of 21 inches in Ezk 40:12

BARRIERS *(1)*
have built b between you and Is 59:2

BARS *(24)*
I broke the b of your yoke and Lv 26:13
gates, and b, besides a large Dt 3:5
cities with walls and bronze b 1Kg 4:13
with walls, gates, and b— 2Ch 8:5
and towers, with doors and b. 2Ch 14:7
its doors, bolts, and b. Neh 3:3
its doors, bolts, and b. Neh 3:6
bolts, and b, and repaired 500 Neh 3:13
its doors, bolts, and b. Neh 3:14

its doors, bolts, and **b**. Neh 3:15
and put ⌊its⌋ **b** and doors in Jb 38:10
those with **b** of silver. Ps 68:30
and cut through the iron **b**. Ps 107:16
strengthens the **b** of your gates Ps 147:13
are like the **b** of a fortress. Pr 18:19
doors and cut the iron **b** in two. Is 45:2
fetters and yoke **b** for yourself Jr 27:2
her gate **b** are shattered. Jr 51:30
shattered the **b** on her ⌊gates⌋. Lm 2:9
when I break the **b** of their yoke Ezk 34:27
walls and without **b** or gates— Ezk 38:11
and devour the **b** of his gates, Hs 11:6
with its prison **b** closed behind Jnh 2:6
devour the **b** ⌊of your gates⌋ Nah 3:13

BARSABBAS *(2)*
(AKA JOSEPH, JUDAS, JUSTUS)
Joseph, called **B**, who was also Ac 1:23
Judas, called **B**, and Silas, both Ac 15:22

BARTER *(2)*
came to you to **b** for your goods. Ezk 27:9
those who **b** for your goods, Ezk 27:27

BARTERED *(1)*
they **b** a boy for a prostitute Jl 3:3

BARTHOLOMEW *(4)*
(AKA NATHANAEL)
Philip and **B**; Thomas and Matthew Mt 10:3
Andrew; Philip and **B**; Matthew Mk 3:18
James and John; Philip and **B**; Lk 6:14
Philip, Thomas, **B**, Matthew, Ac 1:13

BARTIMAEUS *(1)*
and a large crowd, **B** (the son of Mk 10:46

BARUCH *(26)*
After him **B** son of Zabbai Neh 3:20
Daniel, Ginnethon, **B**, Neh 10:6
Maaseiah son of **B**, son of Neh 11:5
agreement to **B** son of Neriah, Jr 32:12
I instructed **B** in their sight, Jr 32:13
the purchase agreement to **B**, Jr 32:16
summoned **B** son of Neriah. Jr 36:4
B wrote on a scroll all the Jr 36:4
Then Jeremiah commanded **B**, Jr 36:5
B son of Neriah did everything Jr 36:8
B read Jeremiah's words from the Jr 36:10
had heard when **B** read from the Jr 36:13
sent ⌊word⌋ to **B** through Jehudi Jr 36:14
So **B** son of Neriah took the Jr 36:14
So **B** read ⌊it⌋ in their Jr 36:15
other in fear and said to **B**, Jr 36:16
Then they asked **B**, "Tell us— Jr 36:17
B said to them, "At his Jr 36:18
officials said to **B**, "You and Jr 36:19
of Abdeel to seize **B** the scribe Jr 36:26
with the words **B** had written at Jr 36:27
and gave it to **B** son of Neriah, Jr 36:32
B son of Neriah is inciting you Jr 43:3
prophet and **B** son of Neriah— Jr 43:6
prophet spoke to **B** son of Neriah Jr 45:1
God of Israel, says to you, **B**: Jr 45:2

BARZILLAI *(13)*
and **B** the Gileadite from Rogelim 2Sm 17:27
B the Gileadite had come down 2Sm 19:31
B was a very old man—80 years 2Sm 19:32
The king said to **B**, "Cross over 2Sm 19:33
B replied to the king, "How many 2Sm 19:34
king kissed **B** and blessed him 2Sm 19:39
and **B** returned to his home. 2Sm 19:39
Adriel son of **B** the Meholathite 2Sm 21:8
to the sons of **B** the Gileadite 1Kg 2:7
descendants of **B**—who had taken Ezr 2:61
the daughters of **B** the Gileadite Ezr 2:61
and the descendants of **B**— Neh 7:63
the daughters of **B** the Gileadite Neh 7:63

BASE *(21)*
on the mountain or touch its **b**. Ex 19:12
Israel at the **b** of the mountain Ex 24:4
b and shaft, its ⌊ornamental⌋ Ex 25:31
the blood at the **b** of the altar. Ex 29:12
them at the **b** of the mountain. Ex 32:19
b and shaft, its ⌊ornamental⌋ Ex 37:17
pounds, 75 pounds for each **b**. Ex 38:27
blood at the **b** of the altar Lv 4:7
the blood at the **b** of the altar Lv 4:18
pour out at the **b** of the altar Lv 4:25
its blood at the **b** of the altar. Lv 4:30
its blood at the **b** of the altar. Lv 4:34
out at the **b** of the altar; Lv 5:9
the blood at the **b** of the altar Lv 8:15
the blood at the **b** of the altar. Lv 9:9
hammered from its **b** to its Nm 8:4
stood at the **b** of the mountain Dt 4:11
cannot hold the **b** of the mast Is 33:23
At the **b** of these chambers there Ezk 42:9
This is the **b** of the altar. Ezk 43:13
built at the **b** of the walls Ezk 46:23

BASED *(40)*
to select one **b** on the combined Ex 12:4
and his sons **b** on all I have Ex 29:35
with Israel **b** on these words. Ex 34:27
are to work **b** on everything Ex 36:1
your neighbor **b** on the number Lv 25:15
to sell to you **b** on the number Lv 25:15
to them **b** on his purchase Lv 25:51
sins 40 years **b** on the number Nm 14:34
an inheritance **b** on the number Nm 26:53
to be put to death **b** on the word Nm 35:30
be put to death **b** on the Nm 35:30
of Judah **b** on the LORD's Jos 15:13
he built Samaria **b** on the name 1Kg 16:24
B on what they could give, Ezr 2:69
b on the number specified by Ezr 3:4
Your servant **b** on Your faithful Ps 119:124
has done for them **b** on His Is 63:7
B on ⌊what happens to⌋ them, Jr 29:22
your servants **b** on what you see. Dn 1:13
before You **b** on our righteous Dn 9:18
but **b** on Your abundant Dn 9:18
will repay him **b** on his actions. Hs 12:2
not be cut off ⌊**b** on⌋ all that I Zph 3:7
such things is **b** on the truth. Rm 2:2
might not be **b** on men's wisdom 1Co 2:5
by me is not **b** on a human point Gl 1:11
But the law is not **b** on faith; Gl 3:12
from God **b** on faith. Php 3:9
and empty deceit **b** on human Col 2:8
b on the elemental forces of the Col 2:8
the world, and not **b** on Christ. Col 2:8
lawless one⌋ is **b** on Satan's 2Th 2:9
b on the glorious gospel of the 1Tm 1:11
become a ⌊priest⌋ **b** on a legal Heb 7:16
descent but **b** on the power Heb 7:16
b on the testimony of two or Heb 10:28
a short time **b** on what seemed Heb 12:10
impartially **b** on each one's work 1Pt 1:17
B on the gift they have received, 1Pt 4:10
b on His promise, we wait for 2Pt 3:13

BASEMATH *(7)*
and **B** daughter of Elon the Gn 26:34
and **B** daughter of Ishmael and Gn 36:3
Eliphaz to Esau, **B** bore Reuel, Gn 36:4
and Reuel son of Esau's wife **B**. Gn 36:10
were the sons of Esau's wife **B**. Gn 36:13
are the sons of Esau's wife **B**. Gn 36:17
a daughter of Solomon—**B**); 1Kg 4:15

BASES *(52)*
and make 40 silver **b** under the Ex 26:19
two **b** under the first plank for Ex 26:19
and two **b** under the next plank Ex 26:19
along with their 40 silver **b**, Ex 26:21
two **b** under the first plank and Ex 26:21
and two **b** under each plank; Ex 26:21
planks with their silver **b**: Ex 26:25
bases: 16 **b**; two bases under Ex 26:25
two **b** under the first plank and Ex 26:25
and two **b** under each plank. Ex 26:25
that stand⌋ on four silver **b**. Ex 26:32
to cast five bronze **b** for them. Ex 26:37
to be 20 posts and 20 bronze **b**. Ex 27:10
to be 20 posts and 20 bronze **b**. Ex 27:11
their 10 posts and 10 **b**. Ex 27:12
three posts and their three **b**. Ex 27:14
three posts and their three **b**. Ex 27:15
posts including their four **b**. Ex 27:16
have silver hooks and bronze **b**. Ex 27:17
The **b** of the posts must be Ex 27:18
its crossbars, its posts and **b**; Ex 35:11
its posts and **b**, and the screen Ex 35:17
he made 40 silver **b** to put under Ex 36:24
two **b** under the first plank for Ex 36:24
and two **b** under each of the Ex 36:24
their 40 silver **b**, two bases Ex 36:26
two **b** under the first plank and Ex 36:26
first plank and two **b** under each Ex 36:26
planks with their 16 silver **b**, Ex 36:30
bases, two **b** under each one. Ex 36:30
four silver **b** for the posts. Ex 36:36
but their five **b** were bronze. Ex 36:38
their 20 posts and 20 bronze **b**. Ex 38:10
their 20 posts and 20 bronze **b**. Ex 38:11
their 10 posts and 10 **b**. Ex 38:12
their three posts and three **b**. Ex 38:14
posts and three **b** on both sides Ex 38:15
The **b** for the posts were bronze; Ex 38:17
including their four bronze **b**. Ex 38:19
to cast the **b** of the sanctuary Ex 38:27
and the **b** of the veil— Ex 38:27
the veil—100 **b** from 7,500 Ex 38:27
with it the **b** for the entrance Ex 38:30
the **b** for the surrounding Ex 38:31
the **b** for the gate of the Ex 38:31
crossbars, and its posts and **b**; Ex 39:33
its posts and **b**, the screen for Ex 39:40
he laid its **b**, positioned its Ex 40:18
crossbars, posts, **b**, all its Nm 3:36
courtyard with their **b**, Nm 3:37
its crossbars, posts, and **b**, Nm 4:31
courtyard with their **b**, Nm 4:32

BASHAN *(60)*
and went up the road to **B**, Nm 21:33
Og king of **B** came out against Nm 21:33
and the kingdom of Og king of **B**, Nm 32:33
and Og king of **B**, who lived in Dt 1:4
and went up the road to **B**, Dt 3:1
and Og king of **B**, with his whole Dt 3:1
over Og king of **B** and his whole Dt 3:3
Argob, the kingdom of Og in **B**. Dt 3:4
and **B** as far as Salecah and Dt 3:10
cities of Og's kingdom in **B**. Dt 3:10
Only Og king of **B** was left of Dt 3:11
the rest of Gilead and all **B**, Dt 3:13
territory of **B**, used to be Dt 3:13
He called **B** by his own name, Dt 3:14
or Golan in **B**, belonging to the Dt 4:43
and the land of Og king of **B**, Dt 4:47
Og king of **B** came out against Dt 29:7
rams from **B**, and goats, with Dt 32:14
a young lion, leaping out of **B**. Dt 33:22
of Heshbon and Og king of **B**, Jos 9:10
Og king of **B**, of the remnant of Jos 12:4
all **B** up to the Geshurite and Jos 12:5
Hermon, and all **B** to Salecah— Jos 13:11
the whole kingdom of Og in **B**, Jos 13:12
From Mahanaim through all **B**— Jos 13:30
all the kingdom of Og king of **B**, Jos 13:30
Jair's Villages that are in **B**— Jos 13:30
and Og's royal cities in **B**— Jos 13:31
Gilead and **B** came to Machir, Jos 17:1
the land of Gilead and **B**, Jos 17:5
and Golan in **B** from Manasseh's Jos 20:8
half the tribe of Manasseh in **B**. Jos 21:6
with its pasturelands in **B**, Jos 21:27
half the tribe of Manasseh in **B**, Jos 22:7
which is in **B**, 60 great cities 1Kg 4:13
Amorites and of Og king of **B**. 1Kg 4:19
Valley through Gilead to **B**. 2Kg 10:33
in the land of **B** as far as 1Ch 5:11
Janai, and Shaphat in **B**. 1Ch 5:12
in Gilead, in **B** and its towns, 1Ch 5:16
the land from **B** to Baal-hermon 1Ch 5:23
and Manasseh in **B** according to 1Ch 6:62
Golan in **B** and its pasturelands, 1Ch 6:71
and of the land of Og king of **B**. Neh 9:22
strong ones of **B** encircle me. Ps 22:12
Mount **B** is God's towering Ps 68:15
Mount **B** is a mountain of many Ps 68:15
I will bring ⌊them⌋ back from **B**; Ps 68:22
Og king of **B**, and all the kings Ps 135:11
and Og king of **B**—His love is Ps 136:20
against all the oaks of **B**, Is 2:13
B and Carmel shake off ⌊their⌋ Is 33:9
raise your voice in **B**; Jr 22:20
he will feed on Carmel and **B**; Jr 50:19
made your oars of oaks from **B**. Ezk 27:6
all of them fatlings of **B**. Ezk 39:18
cows of **B** who are on the hill Am 4:1
Let them graze in **B** and Gilead Mc 7:14
rivers run dry. **B** and Carmel Nah 1:4
Wail, oaks of **B**, for the stately Zch 11:2

BASIC *(1)*
you again the **b** principles of Heb 5:12

BASIN *(32)*
in the blood that is in the **b**, Ex 12:22

with some of the blood in the **b**. Ex 12:22
Make a bronze **b** for washing and Ex 30:18
their hands and feet from the **b**. Ex 30:19
and the **b** with its stand. Ex 30:28
utensils, the **b** with its stand Ex 31:9
utensils; the **b** with its stand; Ex 35:16
made the bronze **b** and its stand Ex 38:8
utensils; the **b** with its stand; Ex 39:39
Place the **b** between the tent of Ex 40:7
Anoint the **b** and its stand, Ex 40:11
He set the **b** between the tent of Ex 40:30
and the **b** with its stand, Lv 8:11
and one silver **b** weighing one Nm 7:13
and one silver **b** weighing one Nm 7:19
and one silver **b** weighing one Nm 7:25
and one silver **b** weighing one Nm 7:31
and one silver **b** weighing one Nm 7:37
and one silver **b** weighing one Nm 7:43
and one silver **b** weighing one Nm 7:49
and one silver **b** weighing one Nm 7:55
and one silver **b** weighing one Nm 7:61
and one silver **b** weighing one Nm 7:67
and one silver **b** weighing one Nm 7:73
and one silver **b** weighing one Nm 7:79
and each **b** one and three-quarter Nm 7:85
corners of the **b** were cast 1Kg 7:30
each **b** holding 220 gallons and 1Kg 7:38
one **b** for each of the 10 water 1Kg 7:38
removed the bronze **b** from ⌊each 2Kg 16:17
be as full as the sprinkling **b**, Zch 9:15
water into a **b** and began to wash Jn 13:5

BASING *(1)*

'What are you **b** your confidence Is 36:4

BASINS *(23)*

half the blood and set it in **b**; Ex 24:6
and its shovels, **b**, meat forks, Ex 27:3
pots, shovels, **b**, meat forks, Ex 38:3
shovels, and **b**—all the Nm 4:14
dishes, 12 silver **b**, and 12 gold Nm 7:84
brought beds, **b**, and pottery 2Sm 17:28
Then he made 10 bronze **b**— 1Kg 7:38
Hiram made the **b**, the shovels, 1Kg 7:40
shovels, and the sprinkling **b**. 1Kg 7:40
the 10 **b** on the water carts; 1Kg 7:43
pots, shovels, and sprinkling **b**. 1Kg 7:45
trimmers, sprinkling **b**, ladles, 1Kg 7:50
sprinkling **b**, trumpets, or any 2Kg 12:13
firepans and the sprinkling **b**— 2Kg 25:15
sprinkling **b**, and pitchers; 1Ch 28:17
He made 10 **b** for washing and he 2Ch 4:6
carts and the **b** on the water 2Ch 4:14
trimmers, sprinkling **b**, ladles, 2Ch 4:22
30 gold **b**, 1,000 silver basins, Ezr 1:9
silver **b**, 29 silver knives, Ezr 1:9
sprinkling **b**, the dishes, and Jr 52:18
the sprinkling **b**, the pots, Jr 52:19
the sprinkling **b** before the Zch 14:20

BASIS *(3)*

On the **b** of this treaty, I 1Kg 20:34
on a full-time **b** to pass through Ezk 39:14
instead, on the **b** of love. Phm 9

BASKET *(34)*

In the top **b** were all sorts of Gn 40:17
them out of the **b** on my head." Gn 40:17
she got a papyrus **b** for him and Ex 2:3
Seeing the **b** among the reeds, Ex 2:5
put them in a **b**, and bring them Ex 29:3
bring them in the **b**, along with Ex 29:3
wafer from the **b** of unleavened Ex 29:23
that is in the **b** at the entrance Ex 29:32
and the **b** of unleavened bread, Lv 8:2
From the **b** of unleavened bread Lv 8:26
that is in the **b** for the Lv 8:31
and a **b** of unleavened cakes made Nm 6:15
with the **b** of unleavened Nm 6:17
one unleavened cake from the **b**, Nm 6:19
Your **b** and kneading bowl will be Dt 28:5
Your **b** and kneading bowl will be Dt 28:17
the meat in a **b** and the broth Jdg 6:19
freed from ⌊carrying⌋ the **b**. Ps 81:6
b ⌊contained⌋ very good figs, Jr 24:2
but the other **b** contained very Jr 24:2
me this: A **b** of summer fruit. Am 8:1
I replied, "A **b** of summer fruit. Am 8:2
It's a measuring **b** that is Zch 5:6
a woman sitting inside the **b**. Zch 5:7
her down into the **b** and pushed Zch 5:8
lifted up the **b** between earth Zch 5:9
"Where are they taking the **b**?" Zch 5:10
⌊the **b**⌋ will be placed there on Zch 5:11
a lamp and puts it under a **b**, Mt 5:15
be put under a **b** or under a bed? Mk 4:21
it with a **b** or puts it under Lk 8:16
it in the cellar or under a **b**, Lk 11:33
him in a large **b** through ⌊an Ac 9:25
let down in a **b** through a window 2Co 11:33

BASKETS *(14)*

Three **b** of white bread were on Gn 40:16
The three **b** are three days. Gn 40:18
their heads in **b**, and sent them 2Kg 10:7
showed me two **b** of figs placed Jr 24:1
picked up 12 **b** full of leftover Mt 14:20
pieces—seven large **b** full. Mt 15:37
and how many **b** you collected? Mt 16:9
how many large **b** you collected? Mt 16:10
picked up 12 **b** full of pieces Mk 6:43
large **b** of leftover pieces. Mk 8:8
how many **b** full of pieces of Mk 8:19
how many large **b** full of pieces Mk 8:20
they picked up 12 **b** of leftover Lk 9:17
and filled 12 **b** with the pieces Jn 6:13

BAT *(2)*

of heron, the hoopoe, and the **b**. Lv 11:19
of heron, the hoopoe, and the **b**. Dt 14:18

BATCH *(7)*

from your first **b** of dough as Nm 15:20
from the first **b** of your dough. Nm 15:21
from our first **b** of dough to Neh 10:37
to give your first **b** of dough to Ezk 44:30
up are holy, so is the whole **b**. Rm 11:16
permeates the whole **b** of dough? 1Co 5:6
so that you may be a new **b**, 1Co 5:7

BATH-RABBIM *(1)*

in Heshbon by the gate of **B**. Sg 7:4

BATH-SHUA *(2)*
(AKA BATHSHEBA)

born to him by **B** the Canaanite 1Ch 2:3
born to him⌋ by **B** daughter of 1Ch 3:5

BATHE *(24)*

went down to **b** at the Nile while Ex 2:5
all his hair, and **b** with water; Lv 14:8
his clothes and **b** himself with Lv 14:9
his clothes and **b** with water, Lv 15:5
his clothes and **b** with water, Lv 15:6
his clothes and **b** with water, Lv 15:7
his clothes and **b** with water, Lv 15:8
his clothes and **b** with water, Lv 15:10
his clothes and **b** with water, Lv 15:11
and **b** his body in fresh water; Lv 15:13
he is to **b** himself completely Lv 15:16
of them are to **b** with water, Lv 15:18
his clothes and **b** with water, Lv 15:21
his clothes and **b** with water, Lv 15:22
his clothes and **b** with water, Lv 15:27
he must **b** his body with water Lv 16:4
He will **b** his body with water in Lv 16:24
his clothes and **b** his body with Lv 16:26
his clothes and **b** himself with Lv 16:28
his clothes and **b** with water, Lv 17:15
⌊his clothes⌋ and **b** himself, Lv 17:16
his clothes and **b** his body in Nm 19:7
his clothes and **b** his body in Nm 19:8
wash his clothes and **b** in water, Nm 19:19

BATHED *(5)*

unless he has **b** his body with Lv 22:6
and the prostitutes **b** ⌊in it⌋, 1Kg 22:38
when my feet were **b** in cream and Jb 29:6
You **b**, painted your eyes, and Ezk 23:40
"One who has **b**," Jesus told him, Jn 13:10

BATHING *(1)*

From the roof he saw a woman **b** 2Sm 11:2

BATHSHEBA *(10)*
(AKA BATH-SHUA)

This is **B**, daughter of Eliam 2Sm 11:3
Then David comforted his wife **B** 2Sm 12:24
Nathan said to **B**, Solomon's 1Kg 1:11
So **B** went to the king in his 1Kg 1:15
B bowed down and paid homage to 1Kg 1:16
by saying, "Call in **B** for me." 1Kg 1:28
B bowed with her face to the 1Kg 1:31
son of Haggith came to **B**, 1Kg 2:13
"Very well," **B** replied. 1Kg 2:18
So **B** went to King Solomon to 1Kg 2:19

BATS *(1)*

worship, to the moles and the **b**. Is 2:20

BATTERED *(3)*

mile from land, **b** by the waves, Mt 14:24
saw them being **b** as they rowed, Mk 6:48
being severely **b** by the storm, Ac 27:18

BATTERING *(5)*

Joab were **b** the wall to make 2Sm 20:15
and place **b** rams against it on Ezk 4:2
that he should set up **b** rams, Ezk 21:22
set **b** rams against the gates, Ezk 21:22
the blows of his **b** rams against Ezk 26:9

BATTERS *(1)*

He **b** me with a whirlwind and Jb 9:17

BATTLE *(200)*

and lined up for **b** in the Valley Gn 14:8
land of Egypt in **b** formation. Ex 13:18
you enter into **b** in your land Nm 10:9
his whole army to do **b** at Edrei. Nm 21:33
the soldiers who had gone to **b**, Nm 31:21
for **b** before the LORD, Nm 32:20
to the **b** as my lord orders. Nm 32:27
every man in **b** formation before Nm 32:29
across with you in **b** formation, Nm 32:30
cross over in **b** formation before Nm 32:32
and do not provoke them to **b**, Dt 2:9
of it⌋; engage him in **b**. Dt 2:24
out against us for **b** at Jahaz. Dt 2:32
out against us for **b** at Edrei. Dt 3:1
cross over in **b** formation ahead Dt 3:18
you are about to engage in **b**, Dt 20:2
to engage in **b** with your enemies Dt 20:3
he may die in **b** and another man Dt 20:5
he may die in **b** and another man Dt 20:6
he may die in **b** and another man Dt 20:7
Bashan came out against us in **b**, Dt 29:7
cross over in **b** formation ahead Jos 1:14
Manasseh went in **b** formation in Jos 4:12
engage Israel in **b** at a suitable Jos 8:14
all of them were taken in **b**. Jos 11:19
they would engage Israel in **b**, Jos 11:20
My strength for **b** and for daily Jos 14:11
Israelites ⌊how to fight in⌋ **b**, Jdg 3:2
went out to **b**, and the LORD Jdg 3:10
returned from the **b** by the Jdg 8:13
and took their **b** positions Jdg 20:20
and again took their **b** positions Jdg 20:22
and took their **b** positions Jdg 20:30
and took their **b** positions at Jdg 20:33
Gibeah, and the **b** was fierce, Jdg 20:34
of Israel would return to the **b**. Jdg 20:39
as they were in the first **b**." Jdg 20:39
but the **b** overtook them, Jdg 20:42
wives for each of them in the **b**. Jdg 21:22
Philistines in **b** and camped at 1Sm 4:1
lined up in **b** formation against 1Sm 4:2
and as the **b** intensified, 1Sm 4:2
man ran from the **b** and came to 1Sm 4:12
I'm the one who came from the **b**. 1Sm 4:16
on the day of **b** not a sword or 1Sm 13:22
assembled and marched to the **b**, 1Sm 14:20
Saul and Jonathan in the **b**. 1Sm 14:22
b extended beyond Beth-aven, 1Sm 14:23
they lined up in **b** formation to 1Sm 17:2
and shouted to the **b** formations: 1Sm 17:8
out to line up in **b** formation?" 1Sm 17:8
out to its **b** formation shouting 1Sm 17:20
formation shouting their **b** cry. 1Sm 17:20
lined up in **b** formation facing 1Sm 17:21
and ran to the **b** line. 1Sm 17:22
Philistine **b** line and shouted 1Sm 17:23
you came down to see the **b**!" 1Sm 17:28
saves, for the **b** is the LORD's. 1Sm 17:47
quickly to the **b** line to meet 1Sm 17:48
shouting their **b** cry, and chased 1Sm 17:52
as always when I go out ⌊to **b**⌋. 1Sm 21:5
or he will go into **b** and perish. 1Sm 26:10
with us into **b** only to become 1Sm 29:4
our adversary during the **b**. 1Sm 29:4
'He must not go into **b** with us.' 1Sm 29:9
who goes into **b** is to be the 1Sm 30:24
When the **b** intensified against 1Sm 31:3
"The troops fled from the **b**," 2Sm 1:4
have fallen in the thick of **b**! 2Sm 1:25
The **b** that day was extremely 2Sm 2:17
to death in the **b** at Gibeon. 2Sm 3:30
led us out ⌊to **b**⌋ and brought us 2Sm 5:2

and lined up in **b** formation at 2Sm 10:8
that there was a **b** line in front 2Sm 10:9
and lined up in **b** formation to 2Sm 10:9
who lined up in **b** formation to 2Sm 10:10
engage David in **b** and fought 2Sm 10:17
David's soldiers fell ⌊in **b**⌋; 2Sm 11:17
David all the details of the **b**. 2Sm 11:18
king all the details of the **b**— 2Sm 11:19
that you personally go into **b**. 2Sm 17:11
the field to engage Israel in **b**, 2Sm 18:6
The **b** spread over the entire 2Sm 18:8
humiliated after fleeing in **b**. 2Sm 19:3
anointed over us, has died in **b**. 2Sm 19:10
never again go out with us to **b**. 2Sm 21:17
there was another **b** with the 2Sm 21:18
again there was a **b** with the 2Sm 21:19
Gath there was still another **b**. 2Sm 21:20
clothed me with strength for **b**; 2Sm 22:40
place they had gathered for **b**, 2Sm 23:9
asked, "Who is to start the **b**?" 1Kg 20:14
if they have marched out for **b**, 1Kg 20:18
went up to Aphek to **b** Israel. 1Kg 20:26
seventh day, the **b** took place, 1Kg 20:29
out into the midst of the **b**. 1Kg 20:39
disguise myself and go into **b**, 1Kg 22:30
himself and went into **b**. 1Kg 22:30
around and take me out of the **b**, 1Kg 22:34
The **b** raged throughout that day, 1Kg 22:35
saw that the **b** was too fierce 2Kg 3:26
He took Sela in **b** and called it 2Kg 14:7
they cried out to God in **b**. 1Ch 5:20
killed because it was God's **b**. 1Ch 5:22
36,000 troops for **b** according to 1Ch 7:4
When the **b** intensified against 1Ch 10:3
led us out ⌊to **b**⌋ and brought us 1Ch 11:2
had gathered there for **b**. 1Ch 11:13
warriors who helped him in **b**. 1Ch 12:1
men, trained for **b**, expert with 1Ch 12:8
trained for **b** with all kinds of 1Ch 12:33
28,600 trained for **b**. 1Ch 12:35
in the army, trained for **b**. 1Ch 12:36
lined up in **b** formation, came to 1Ch 12:38
march out to **b**, for God will 1Ch 14:15
their cities and came for the **b**. 1Ch 19:7
and lined up in **b** formation at 1Ch 19:9
that there was a **b** line in front 1Ch 19:10
and lined up in **b** formation to 1Ch 19:10
they lined up in **b** formation to 1Ch 19:11
approached the Arameans for **b**, 1Ch 19:14
and lined up in **b** formation 1Ch 19:17
up to engage the Arameans in **b**, 1Ch 19:17
again there was a **b** with the 1Ch 20:5
still another **b** at Gath where 1Ch 20:6
men in **b** formation against 2Ch 13:3
that the **b** was in front 2Ch 13:14
men of Judah raised the **b** cry. 2Ch 13:15
men of Judah raised the **b** cry, 2Ch 13:15
him and lined up in **b** formation 2Ch 14:10
⌊we will be⌋ with you in the **b**." 2Ch 18:3
disguise myself and go into **b**, 2Ch 18:29
himself, and they went into **b**. 2Ch 18:29
around and take me out of the **b**, 2Ch 18:33
The **b** raged throughout that day, 2Ch 18:34
for the **b** is not yours, 2Ch 20:15
do not have to fight this ⌊**b**⌋. 2Ch 20:17
Be strong for **b**! ⌊But⌋ God will 2Ch 25:8
would not go with him into **b**, 2Ch 25:13
death, and in **b**, from the power Jb 5:20
him like a king prepared for **b**. Jb 15:24
for the day of warfare and **b**? Jb 38:23
his strength; He charges into **b**. Jb 39:21
He smells the **b** from a distance; Jb 39:25
officers' shouts and the **b** cry. Jb 39:25
remember the **b** and never repeat Jb 41:8
clothed me with strength for **b**; Ps 18:39
mighty, the LORD, mighty in **b**. Ps 24:8
redeem me from my **b** unharmed. Ps 55:18
turned back on the day of **b**. Ps 78:9
and have not let him stand in **b**. Ps 89:43
will volunteer on Your day of **b**. Ps 110:3
shield my head on the day of **b**. Ps 140:7
my hands for **b** and my fingers Ps 144:1
is prepared for the day of **b**, Pr 21:31
who keep the law **b** against them. Pr 28:4
there is no furlough in **b**, Ec 8:8
swift, or the **b** to the strong, Ec 9:11
the sword, your warriors in **b**. Is 3:25
boot of **b** and the bloodied Is 9:5
bent bow, from the stress of **b**. Is 21:15
they were not killed in **b**. Is 22:2
who turn back the **b** at the gate. Is 28:6
going out to **b** against Ariel— Is 29:7
nations who go to **b** against Is 29:8
the ram's horn—the shout of **b**. Jr 4:19
up like men in **b** formation Jr 6:23
like a horse rushing into **b**. Jr 8:6
struck down by the sword in **b**. Jr 18:21
and large; draw near for **b**! Jr 46:3
mighty men ⌊ready⌋ for **b**? Jr 48:14
the shout of **b** heard against Jr 49:2
will line up in **b** formation Jr 50:9
Line up in **b** formation around Jr 50:14
up like men in **b** formation Jr 50:42
You are My **b** club, My weapons of Jr 51:20
the nations for **b** against her— Jr 51:28
might stand in **b** on the day of Ezk 13:5
great army and vast horde in **b**, Ezk 17:17
raise a **b** cry, set battering Ezk 21:22
though not in anger or in **b**. Dn 11:20
will prepare for **b** with an Dn 11:25
the South will engage him in **b**, Dn 11:40
the roar of **b** will rise against Hs 10:14
on the day of **b** and a violent Am 1:14
the day of its ⌊**b**⌋ preparations, Nah 2:3
⌊blast⌋ and **b** cry against Zph 1:16
like His majestic steed in **b**. Zch 10:3
from them the **b** bow, from them Zch 10:4
warriors in **b** trampling down Zch 10:5
nations against Jerusalem for **b**. Zch 14:2
as He fights on a day of **b**. Zch 14:3
sound, who will prepare for **b**? 1Co 14:8
For our **b** is not against flesh Eph 6:12
you may strongly engage in **b**, 1Tm 1:18
mighty in **b**, and put foreign Heb 11:34
was like horses equipped for **b**. Rv 9:7
with many horses rushing into **b**; Rv 9:9
them for the **b** of the great day Rv 16:14
and Magog, to gather them for **b**. Rv 20:8

BATTLEFIELD *(2)*
also, on the heights of the **b**. Jdg 5:18
down about 4,000 men on the **b**. 1Sm 4:2

BATTLEMENTS *(1)*
I will make your **b** of rubies, Is 54:12

BATTLES *(5)*
out before us, and fight our **b**." 1Sm 8:20
for me and fight the LORD's **b**." 1Sm 18:17
because he fights the LORD's **b**. 1Sm 25:28
from their **b** for the repair 1Ch 26:27
to help us and to fight our **b**." 2Ch 32:8

BAY *(4)*
of the Dead Sea on the south **b** Jos 15:2
side was from the **b** of the sea Jos 15:5
the northern **b** of the Dead Sea Jos 18:19
but sighted a **b** with a beach. Ac 27:39

BAZLITH'S *(1)*
(AKA BAZLUTH'S)
B descendants, Mehida's Neh 7:54

BAZLUTH'S *(1)*
(AKA BAZLITH'S)
B descendants, Mehida's Ezr 2:52

BDELLIUM *(2)*
b and onyx are also there. Gn 2:12
appearance was like that of **b**. Nm 11:7

BE *(4935)*
(See pp. xi-xii.)

BEACH *(3)*
kneeling down on the **b** to pray, Ac 21:5
but sighted a bay with a **b**. Ac 27:39
the wind and headed for the **b**. Ac 27:40

BEACHED *(1)*
at Gennesaret and **b** the boat. Mk 6:53

BEAK *(2)*
a plucked olive leaf in her **b**. Gn 8:11
no **b** opened or chirped. Is 10:14

BEALIAH *(1)*
Eluzai, Jerimoth, **B**, Shemariah, 1Ch 12:5

BEALOTH *(2)*
Ziph, Telem, **B**, Jos 15:24
son of Hushai, in Asher and **B**; 1Kg 4:16

BEAM *(5)*
shaft was like a weaver's **b**, 1Sm 17:7
his spear was like a weaver's **b**. 2Sm 21:19
in his hand like a weaver's **b**, 1Ch 11:23
his spear was like a weaver's **b**. 1Ch 20:5
Let a **b** be torn from his house Ezr 6:11

BEAMS *(12)*
its stones, its **b**, and all its Lv 14:45
to the temple with cedar **b**; 1Kg 6:10
and a row of trimmed cedar **b**. 1Kg 6:36
with cedar **b** on top of the 1Kg 7:2
and a row of trimmed cedar **b**. 1Kg 7:12
temple—the **b**, the thresholds 2Ch 3:7
for joining and to make **b**— 2Ch 34:11
and its **b** are being set in the Ezr 5:8
built it with **b** and installed Neh 3:3
built it with **b** and installed Neh 3:6
laying the **b** of His palace on Ps 104:3
the **b** of our house are cedars, Sg 1:17

BEANS *(2)*
roasted grain, **b**, lentils, 2Sm 17:28
wheat, barley, **b**, lentils, Ezk 4:9

BEAR *(114)*
you will **b** children in anguish. Gn 3:16
My punishment is too great to **b**! Gn 4:13
wife Sarah will **b** you a son, Gn 17:19
whom Sarah will **b** to you at this Gn 17:21
so that they could **b** children, Gn 20:17
can't ⌊**b** to⌋ watch the boy die! Gn 21:16
and she'll **b** ⌊children⌋ for me Gn 30:3
I will always **b** the guilt for Gn 44:32
I could not **b** to see the grief Gn 44:34
his shoulder to **b** a load and Gn 49:15
and they will **b** ⌊it⌋ with you. Ex 18:22
so that Aaron may **b** the guilt Ex 28:38
he will **b** his punishment." Lv 17:16
eats it will **b** his punishment, Lv 19:8
take revenge or **b** a grudge Lv 19:18
he will **b** his punishment. Lv 20:17
people will **b** their punishment Lv 20:19
they will **b** their guilt and die Lv 20:20
and have them **b** the penalty of Lv 22:16
will **b** the consequences of his Lv 24:15
of the field will **b** their fruit. Lv 26:4
the land will not **b** their fruit. Lv 26:20
that woman will **b** the Nm 5:31
That man will **b** the consequences Nm 9:13
They will help you **b** the burden Nm 11:17
do not have to **b** it by yourself. Nm 11:17
40 years and **b** the penalty for Nm 14:33
You will **b** the consequences of Nm 14:34
and they will **b** the Nm 18:23
I can't **b** ⌊the responsibility Dt 1:9
But how can I **b** your troubles, Dt 1:12
and the unloved **b** him sons, Dt 21:15
a husband tonight and to **b** sons, Ru 1:12
a lion or a **b** came and carried 1Sm 17:34
the paw of the **b** will rescue me 1Sm 17:37
a wild **b** robbed of her cubs. 2Sm 17:8
all who could **b** arms, from the 2Kg 3:21
downward and **b** fruit upward. 2Kg 19:30
how could I **b** to see the evil Est 8:6
How could I **b** to see the Est 8:6
the **B**, Orion, the Pleiades, and Jb 9:9
B with me while I speak; Jb 21:3
and lead the **B** and her cubs? Jb 38:32
a burden too heavy for me to **b**. Ps 38:4
me—otherwise I could **b** it; Ps 55:12
They will still **b** fruit in old Ps 92:14
you alone will **b** ⌊the Pr 9:12
a man to meet a **b** robbed of her Pr 17:12
a roaring lion or a charging **b**. Pr 28:15
it cannot **b** up under four: Pr 30:21
from his roots will **b** fruit. Is 11:1
The cow and the **b** will graze, Is 11:7
downward and **b** fruit upward. Is 37:31
and I will **b** ⌊you⌋ up when you Is 46:4
I will **b** and save ⌊you⌋. Is 46:4
their shoulder and **b** it along; Is 46:7
success or **b** children ⌊destined Is 65:23
Will He **b** a grudge forever? Jr 3:5
suffering, but I must **b** it." Jr 10:19
the mothers who **b** them and the Jr 16:3
so that they may **b** sons and Jr 29:6
This city will **b** on My behalf a Jr 33:9
can no longer **b** your evil deeds Jr 44:22
He is a **b** waiting in ambush, Lm 3:10
for a man to **b** the yoke while he Lm 3:27
but we **b** their punishment. Lm 5:7
will **b** their iniquity for the Ezk 4:4
you will **b** the iniquity of the Ezk 4:5
and **b** the iniquity of the house Ezk 4:6

They will **b** their punishment— Ezk 14:10
You must also **b** your disgrace, Ezk 16:52
be ashamed and **b** your disgrace, Ezk 16:52
so you will **b** your disgrace and Ezk 16:54
yourself must **b** the consequences Ezk 16:58
branches, **b** fruit, and become Ezk 17:8
so that it may **b** branches, Ezk 17:23
you must **b** the consequences of Ezk 23:35
and you will **b** the consequences Ezk 23:49
They **b** their disgrace with those Ezk 32:24
They **b** their disgrace with those Ezk 32:25
They **b** their disgrace with those Ezk 32:30
branches and **b** your fruit for My Ezk 36:8
will **b** the consequences of their Ezk 44:10
that they would **b** the Ezk 44:12
They will **b** their disgrace and Ezk 44:13
month they will **b** fresh fruit Ezk 47:12
one, that looked like a **b**. Dn 7:5
cannot **b** fruit. Even if they Hs 9:16
Even if they **b** children, I will Hs 9:16
now they must **b** their guilt. Hs 10:2
them like a **b** robbed of her cubs Hs 13:8
Samaria will **b** her guilt because Hs 13:16
green, the trees **b** their fruit, Jl 2:22
only to have a **b** confront him. Am 5:19
will **b** the scorn of My people. Mc 6:16
to **b** witness to them and to the Mt 10:18
who does **b** fruit and yields: Mt 13:23
do not **b** false witness; Mt 19:18
do not **b** false witness; Mk 10:19
wife Elizabeth will **b** you a son, Lk 1:13
to it and by enduring, **b** fruit. Lk 8:15
it will **b** fruit next year Lk 13:9
Whoever does not **b** his own cross Lk 14:27
do not **b** false witness; Lk 18:20
you, but you can't **b** them now. Jn 16:12
nor we have been able to **b**? Ac 15:10
that we may **b** fruit for God. Rm 7:4
obligation to **b** the weaknesses Rm 15:1
so that you are able to **b** it. 1Co 10:13
we will also **b** the image of the 1Co 15:49
offered once to **b** the sins of Heb 9:28
time, not to **b** sin, but to bring Heb 9:28
they could not **b** what was Heb 12:20
the noble name that you **b**? Jms 2:7

BEAR'S *(1)*

were like a **b**, and his mouth Rv 13:2

BEARD *(12)*

his head, his **b**, his eyebrows, Lv 14:9
head or mar the edge of your **b**. Lv 19:27
letting saliva run down his **b**. 1Sm 21:13
Amasa by the **b** to kiss him. 2Sm 20:9
of the hair from my head and **b**, Ezr 9:3
down on the **b**, running down Ps 133:2
down Aaron's **b**, on his robes. Ps 133:2
and to remove the **b** as well. Is 7:20
is shaved; every **b** is cut off. Is 15:2
to those who tore out My **b**. Is 50:6
is bald and every **b** clipped; Jr 48:37
and shave your head and **b**. Ezk 5:1

BEARDED *(2)*

the eagle, the **b** vulture, the Lv 11:13
the eagle, the **b** vulture, the Dt 14:12

BEARDS *(5)*

shave the edge of their **b**, Lv 21:5
off half their **b**, cut their 2Sm 10:4
Jericho until your **b** grow back; 2Sm 10:5
Jericho until your **b** grow back; 1Ch 19:5
Samaria who had shaved their **b**, Jr 41:5

BEARER *(1)*

thought he was a **b** of good news, 2Sm 4:10

BEARING *(18)*

on the earth **b** fruit with seed Gn 1:11
kinds and trees **b** fruit with Gn 1:12
prevented me from **b** children, Gn 16:2
that she was not **b** Jacob ⌊any Gn 30:1
root among you **b** poisonous and Dt 29:18
with camels **b** spices, gold 1Kg 10:2
of Tarshish would arrive **b** gold, 1Kg 10:22
armed troops **b** shields and 1Ch 12:24
with camels **b** spices, gold 2Ch 9:1
of Tarshish would arrive **b** gold, 2Ch 9:21
from Judah **b** large shields 2Ch 14:8
from Benjamin **b** regular shields 2Ch 14:8
in the army, **b** spear and shield 2Ch 25:5
like one **b** her first child Jr 4:31
It is **b** fruit and growing all Col 1:6
b fruit in every good work and Col 1:10
the camp, **b** His disgrace. Heb 13:13
the tree of life **b** 12 kinds of Rv 22:2

BEARS *(17)*

set free that **b** beautiful fawns Gn 49:21
him a wife and she **b** him sons or Ex 21:4
he **b** the consequences of his Lv 5:17
The first son she **b** will carry Dt 25:6
her legs and the children she **b**, Dt 28:57
servant has killed lions and **b**; 1Sm 17:36
If he's alone, he **b** good news." 2Sm 18:25
Then two female **b** came out of 2Kg 2:24
of water that **b** its fruit in Ps 1:3
Day after day He **b** our burdens; Ps 68:19
with great anger **b** the penalty; Pr 19:19
all growl like **b** and moan like Is 59:11
on the city that **b** My name, Jr 25:29
with anyone who **b** the name of 1Co 5:11
b all things, believes all 1Co 13:7
from Mount Sinai and **b** children Gl 4:24
that falsely **b** that name. 1Tm 6:20

BEAST *(67)*

festering boils on man and **b**. Ex 9:10
on man and **b** and every plant of Ex 9:22
in the field, both man and **b**. Ex 9:25
whether man or **b**, not ⌊even⌋ a Ex 11:7
land of Egypt, both man and **b**. Ex 12:12
the form of any **b** on the earth, Dt 4:17
LORD, You preserve man and **b**. Ps 36:6
Rebuke the **b** in the reeds, Ps 68:30
supply water for every wild **b**; Ps 104:11
and no vicious **b** will go up on Is 35:9
place, on man and **b**, on the tree Jr 7:20
of this city, both man and **b**. Jr 21:6
seed of man and the seed of **b**. Jr 31:27
a desolation without man or **b**; Jr 32:43
without man or **b**—that is, Jr 33:10
and without **b**—there will be Jr 33:10
without man or **b**—and in all Jr 33:12
cause it to be without man or **b**? Jr 36:29
both man and **b** will escape. Jr 50:3
one will live in it—man or **b**. Jr 51:62
Suddenly, another **b** appeared, a Dn 7:5
watching, another **b** appeared. Dn 7:6
visions, a fourth **b** appeared, Dn 7:7
the **b** was killed and its body Dn 7:11
true meaning of the fourth **b**, Dn 7:19
'The fourth **b** will be a fourth Dn 7:23
a wild **b** that would rip them Hs 13:8
man or **b**, herd or flock, is to Jnh 3:7
both man and **b** must be covered Jnh 3:8
neither man nor **b** had wages. Zch 8:10
the foal of a **b** of burden." Mt 21:5
the **b** that comes up out of the Rv 11:7
And I saw a **b** coming up out of Rv 13:1
The **b** I saw was like a leopard, Rv 13:2
was amazed and followed the **b**. Rv 13:3
he gave authority to the **b**. Rv 13:4
worshiped the **b**, saying, "Who is Rv 13:4
saying, "Who is like the **b**? Rv 13:4
I saw another **b** coming up out Rv 13:11
of the first **b** on his behalf Rv 13:12
on it to worship the first **b**, Rv 13:12
to perform on behalf of the **b**, Rv 13:14
an image of the **b** who had the Rv 13:14
a spirit to the image of the **b**, Rv 13:15
image of the **b** could both speak Rv 13:15
the image of the **b** to be killed. Rv 13:15
calculate the number of the **b**, Rv 13:18
worships the **b** and his image Rv 14:9
who worship the **b** and his image, Rv 14:11
had won the victory from the **b**, Rv 15:2
the mark of the **b** and who Rv 16:2
his bowl on the throne of the **b**, Rv 16:10
on a scarlet **b** that was covered Rv 17:3
of the woman and of the **b**, Rv 17:7
The **b** that you saw was, and is Rv 17:8
when they see the **b** that was, Rv 17:8
The **b** that was and is not, Rv 17:11
kings with the **b** for one hour. Rv 17:12
power and authority to the **b**. Rv 17:13
you saw, and the **b**, will hate Rv 17:16
kingdom to the **b** until God's Rv 17:17
every unclean and despicable **b**. Rv 18:2
Then I saw the **b**, the kings of Rv 19:19
But the **b** was taken prisoner, Rv 19:20
the mark of the **b** and those who Rv 19:20
worshiped the **b** or his image, Rv 20:4
sulfur where the **b** and the false Rv 20:10

BEAST'S *(2)*

the **b** name or the number of his Rv 13:17
mouth, from the **b** mouth, Rv 16:13

BEASTS *(25)*

any of the flock torn by wild **b**; Gn 31:39
mauled by wild **b** may be used for Lv 7:24
mauled by wild **b** is to wash his Lv 17:15
or was mauled by wild **b**, Lv 22:8
on them wild **b** with fangs, Dt 32:24
of the sky and the wild **b**!" 1Sm 17:44
Proud **b** have never walked on it; Jb 28:8
he is king over all the proud **b**. Jb 41:34
give the life of Your dove to **b**; Ps 74:19
ones to the **b** of the earth. Ps 79:2
is mightiest among **b** and doesn't Pr 30:30
Assyria destined it for wild **b**. Is 23:13
The wild **b** will meet hyenas, Is 34:14
are consigned to **b** and cattle. Is 46:1
or was mauled by wild **b**. Ezk 4:14
creatures and **b**, as well as all Ezk 8:10
given you to the **b** of the earth Ezk 29:5
you and let the **b** of the entire Ezk 32:4
or was mauled by wild **b**. Ezk 44:31
huge **b** came up from the sea, Dn 7:3
from all the **b** before it, Dn 7:7
the rest of the **b**, their Dn 7:12
'These huge **b**, four in number, Dn 7:17
earth, the wild **b**, the reptiles, Ac 11:6
liars, evil **b**, lazy gluttons. Ti 1:12

BEAT *(29)*

The hail **b** down every plant of Ex 9:25
furious and **b** the donkey with Nm 22:27
the house and **b** on the door. Jdg 19:22
She **b** out what she had gathered, Ru 2:17
the Kidron Valley, **b** it to dust, 2Kg 23:6
cursed them, **b** some of their men Neh 13:25
He **b** back His foes; He gave them Ps 78:66
or to **b** a noble for his honesty. Pr 17:26
if you **b** him with a rod, he will Pr 23:13
They **b** me, but I didn't know it! Pr 23:35
found me. They **b** and wounded me; Sg 5:7
B your breasts ⌊in mourning⌋ for Is 32:12
gave My back to those who **b** Me, Is 50:6
at Jeremiah and **b** him and placed Jr 37:15
The sun **b** down on Jonah's head Jnh 4:8
They will **b** their swords into Mc 4:3
of doves, and **b** their breasts. Nah 2:7
took his slaves, **b** one, killed Mt 21:35
and starts to **b** his fellow Mt 24:49
they spit in His face and **b** Him; Mt 26:67
they took him, **b** him, and sent Mk 12:3
b some and they killed some. Mk 12:5
Him, and to **b** Him, saying, Mk 14:65
stripped him, **b** him up, and fled Lk 10:30
and starts to **b** the male and Lk 12:45
But the farmers **b** him and sent Lk 20:10
slave, but they **b** that one too, Lk 20:11
They **b** us in public without a Ac 16:37
b him in front of the judge's Ac 18:17

BEATEN *(20)*

people, were **b** and asked, "Why Ex 5:14
your servants are being **b**, Ex 5:16
in, and he is **b** to death, no one Ex 22:2
you pure oil of **b** olives for the Lv 24:2
that you have **b** me these three Nm 22:28
Why have you **b** your donkey Nm 22:32
with a quart of **b** olive oil. Nm 28:5
pretended to be **b** back by them Jos 8:15
and 110,000 gallons of **b** oil. 1Kg 5:11
and were **b** down by their sin. Ps 106:43
as if an olive tree had been **b**— Is 17:6
black cumin is **b** out with a Is 28:27
B silver is brought from Jr 10:9
the prophet **b** and put him Jr 20:2
or do it will be severely **b**. Lk 12:47
of blows will be **b** lightly. Lk 12:48
ordered them to be **b** with rods. Ac 16:22
in You imprisoned and **b**. Ac 22:19
Three times I was **b** with rods. 2Co 11:25
endure when you sin and are **b**? 1Pt 2:20

BEATING *(5)*

He saw an Egyptian **b** a Hebrew, Ex 2:11
He will get a **b** and dishonor, Pr 6:33
and his mouth provokes a **b**. Pr 18:6

Jesus started mocking and **b** Him. Lk 22:63
soldiers, they stopped **b** Paul. Ac 21:32

BEATINGS *(5)*

and **b** for the backs of fools. Pr 19:29
and **b** cleanse the innermost Pr 20:30
Why do you want more **b**? Is 1:5
b, by imprisonments, by riots, 2Co 6:5
far worse **b**, near death many 2Co 11:23

BEATS *(1)*

or box like one who **b** the air. 1Co 9:26

BEAUTIFIED *(1)*

hoped in God also **b** themselves 1Pt 3:5

BEAUTIFUL *(89)*

the daughters of man were **b**, Gn 6:2
I know what a **b** woman you are. Gn 12:11
saw that the woman was very **b**. Gn 12:14
girl was very **b**, a young woman Gn 24:16
Rebekah, for she is a **b** woman." Gn 26:7
but Rachel was shapely and **b**. Gn 29:17
doe set free that bears **b** fawns. Gn 49:21
when she saw that he was **b**, Ex 2:2
b are your tents, Jacob, your Nm 24:5
over and see the **b** land on the Dt 3:25
with⌋ large and **b** cities that Dt 6:10
and build **b** houses to live in, Dt 8:12
if you see a **b** woman among the Dt 21:11
the spoils a **b** cloak from Jos 7:21
sister more **b** than she is? Jdg 15:2
He had **b** eyes and a healthy, 1Sm 16:12
The woman was intelligent and **b**, 1Sm 25:3
woman bathing—a very **b** woman. 2Sm 11:2
son Absalom had a **b** sister named 2Sm 13:1
Tamar, who was a **b** woman. 2Sm 14:27
searched for a **b** girl throughout 1Kg 1:3
because she was very **b**. Est 1:11
be made for **b** young virgins for Est 2:2
all the **b** young virgins to Est 2:3
woman had a **b** figure and was Est 2:7
No women as **b** as Job's daughters Jb 42:15
indeed, I have a **b** inheritance. Ps 16:6
praise from the upright is **b**. Ps 33:1
A **b** woman who rejects good sense Pr 11:22
every precious and **b** treasure. Pr 24:4
not know, most **b** of women, Sg 1:8
Your cheeks are **b** with jewelry, Sg 1:10
How **b** you are, my darling. Sg 1:15
How very **b**! Your eyes are Sg 1:15
Come away, my **b** one. Sg 2:10
Come away, my **b** one. Sg 2:13
How **b** you are, my darling. Sg 4:1
How very **b**! Behind your veil Sg 4:1
are absolutely **b**, my darling, Sg 4:7
than another, most **b** of women? Sg 5:9
your love gone, most **b** of women? Sg 6:1
You are as **b** as Tirzah, my Sg 6:4
the dawn—as **b** as the moon, Sg 6:10
How **b** are your sandaled feet, Sg 7:1
How **b** you are and how pleasant, Sg 7:6
the LORD will be **b** and glorious, Is 4:2
you will plant **b** plants and set Is 17:10
fading flower of its **b** splendor, Is 28:1
fading flower of his **b** splendor, Is 28:4
like a **b** person, to dwell Is 44:13
Put on your **b** garments, Is 52:1
How **b** on the mountains are the Is 52:7
I will glorify My **b** house. Is 60:7
Your lofty home—holy and **b**. Is 63:15
Our holy and **b** temple, where our Is 64:11
most **b** inheritance of all the Jr 3:19
⌊Though she is⌋ **b** and delicate, Jr 6:2
olive tree, **b** with well-formed Jr 11:16
Egypt is a **b** young cow, but a Jr 46:20
He appointed His **b** ornaments for Ezk 7:20
and matured and became very **b**. Ezk 16:7
and a **b** tiara on your head. Ezk 16:12
became extremely **b** and attained Ezk 16:13
also took your **b** jewelry made Ezk 16:17
take your **b** jewelry, and leave Ezk 16:39
honey, the most **b** of all lands. Ezk 20:6
them⌋—the most **b** of all lands, Ezk 20:15
clothes and take your **b** jewelry. Ezk 23:26
hands and **b** crowns on their Ezk 23:42
and tear down your **b** homes. Ezk 26:12
with **b** branches and shady Ezk 31:3
It was **b** in its greatness, Ezk 31:7
I made it **b** with its many limbs, Ezk 31:9
who has a **b** voice and plays Ezk 33:32
Its leaves were **b**, its fruit was Dn 4:12
leaves were **b** and its fruit Dn 4:21
the east and toward the **b** land. Dn 8:9
himself in the **b** land with total Dn 11:16
He will also invade the **b** land, Dn 11:41
the sea and the **b** holy mountain, Dn 11:45
In that day the **b** young women, Am 8:13
How lovely and **b** they will be! Zch 9:17
which appear **b** on the outside, Mt 23:27
adorned with **b** stones and gifts Lk 21:5
day at the temple gate called **B**, Ac 3:2
and beg at the **B** Gate of the Ac 3:10
born, and he was **b** before God. Ac 7:20
they saw that the child was **b**, Heb 11:23
and its **b** appearance is Jms 1:11

BEAUTIFULLY *(1)*

instead of **b** styled hair, Is 3:24

BEAUTIFY *(2)*

to **b** the place of My sanctuary, Is 60:13
You **b** yourself for nothing. Jr 4:30

BEAUTY *(35)*

brother Aaron, for glory and **b**. Ex 28:2
sons to ⌊give them⌋ glory and **b**. Ex 28:40
The girl was of unsurpassed **b**, 1Kg 1:4
with precious stones for **b**, 2Ch 3:6
to show off her **b** to the people Est 1:11
them the required **b** treatments. Est 2:3
the process of the **b** treatments Est 2:9
her to receive **b** treatments with Est 2:12
the heavens gained their **b**; Jb 26:13
gazing on the **b** of the LORD and Ps 27:4
and the king will desire your **b**. Ps 45:11
the perfection of **b**, God appears Ps 50:2
holiness is the **b** of Your house Ps 93:5
strength and **b** are in His Ps 96:6
she will give you a crown of **b**." Pr 4:9
your heart for her **b** or let her Pr 6:25
is deceptive and **b** is fleeting, Pr 31:30
instead of **b**, branding. Is 3:24
desecrate all ⌊its⌋ glorious **b**, Is 23:9
become a crown of **b** and a diadem Is 28:5
eyes will see the king in his **b**; Is 33:17
them a crown of **b** instead of Is 61:3
was called the perfection of **b**, Lm 2:15
the nations because of your **b**, Ezk 16:14
in your **b** and acted like Ezk 16:15
passed by. Your **b** became his. Ezk 16:15
and turned your **b** into an Ezk 16:25
you declared: I am perfect in **b**. Ezk 27:3
your builders perfected your **b**. Ezk 27:4
they perfected your **b**. Ezk 27:11
full of wisdom and perfect in **b**. Ezk 28:12
became proud because of your **b**; Ezk 28:17
God could compare with it in **b**. Ezk 31:8
B is stripped, she is carried Nah 2:7
Your **b** should not consist of 1Pt 3:3

BEBAI *(2)*

Zechariah son of **B** from Bebai's Ezr 8:11
Bunni, Azgad, **B**, Neh 10:15

BEBAI'S *(4)*

B descendants 623 Ezr 2:11
son of Bebai from **B** descendants, Ezr 8:11
B descendants: Jehohanan, Ezr 10:28
B descendants 628 Neh 7:16

BECAME *(400)*

and the man **b** a living being. Gn 2:7
it divided and **b** the source of Gn 2:10
Abel **b** a shepherd of a flock, Gn 4:2
Then Cain **b** the builder of a Gn 4:17
some of the wine, **b** drunk, and Gn 9:21
with Hagar, and she **b** pregnant. Gn 16:4
looked back and **b** a pillar of Gn 19:26
Lot's daughters **b** pregnant by Gn 19:36
of my mother, and she **b** my wife. Gn 20:12
Sarah **b** pregnant and bore a son Gn 21:2
the wilderness and **b** an archer. Gn 21:20
the boundaries of the field—**b** Gn 23:17
grew up, Esau **b** an expert hunter Gn 25:27
and the man **b** rich and kept Gn 26:13
Jacob **b** angry with Rachel and Gn 30:2
And the man **b** very rich. Gn 30:43
Jacob **b** incensed and brought Gn 31:36
He **b** infatuated with Dinah, Gn 34:3
and he **b** a successful man, Gn 39:2
sight and **b** his personal Gn 39:4
and he **b** their personal Gn 40:4
Your servant **b** accountable to my Gn 44:32
The land **b** Pharaoh's, Gn 47:20
in it and **b** fruitful and very Gn 47:27
bear a load and **b** a forced Gn 49:15
and **b** extremely numerous so that Ex 1:7
multiplied and **b** very numerous. Ex 1:20
The woman **b** pregnant and gave Ex 2:2
daughter, and he **b** her son. Ex 2:10
Then Moses **b** afraid and Ex 2:14
on the ground, and it **b** a snake. Ex 4:3
and it **b** a staff in his hand. Ex 4:4
officials, and it **b** a serpent. Ex 7:10
his staff, and it **b** a serpent. Ex 7:12
of the earth **b** gnats throughout Ex 8:17
and it **b** festering boils on man Ex 9:10
water, the water **b** drinkable. Ex 15:25
Moses **b** enraged and threw the Ex 32:19
the tabernacle **b** a single unit. Ex 36:13
his consecrated hair **b** defiled. Nm 6:12
skin⌋ suddenly **b** diseased, Nm 12:10
Then Moses **b** angry and said to Nm 16:15
but the people **b** impatient Nm 21:4
So he **b** furious and beat the Nm 22:27
Balak **b** furious with Balaam, Nm 24:10
But Moses **b** furious with the Nm 31:14
Eleazar his son **b** priest in his Dt 10:6
There he **b** a great, powerful, Dt 26:5
Then Jeshurun **b** fat and rebelled Dt 32:15
rebelled—you **b** fat, bloated, Dt 32:15
He **b** King in Jeshurun when the Dt 33:5
hearts melted and **b** like water. Jos 7:5
wilderness now **b** the pursuers. Jos 8:20
So the Gibeonites **b** woodcutters Jos 9:21
of Joseph **b** two tribes, Jos 14:4
Israel **b** stronger, they made Jdg 1:28
until they **b** worried and saw Jdg 3:25
country, and he **b** their leader. Jdg 3:27
Moab **b** subject to Israel that Jdg 3:30
Shamgar son of Anath ⌊**b** judge⌋. Jdg 3:31
So Israel **b** poverty stricken Jdg 6:6
and it **b** a snare to Gideon and Jdg 8:27
son of Dodo ⌊**b** judge⌋ and began Jdg 10:1
but He **b** weary of Israel's Jdg 10:16
Now it **b** a custom in Israel Jdg 11:39
on his arms **b** like burnt flax Jdg 15:14
He **b** very thirsty and called out Jdg 15:18
the young man **b** like one of his Jdg 17:11
and the young man **b** his priest Jdg 17:12
took Ruth and she **b** his wife. Ru 4:13
b a popular saying. 1Sm 10:12
was 30 years old when he **b** king, 1Sm 13:1
So Samuel **b** angry and cried out 1Sm 15:11
and David **b** his armor-bearer. 1Sm 16:21
the men, and **b** angry with him. 1Sm 17:28
and he **b** even more afraid of 1Sm 18:29
So his name **b** very famous. 1Sm 18:30
Then Saul **b** angry with Jonathan 1Sm 20:30
this to heart and **b** very afraid 1Sm 21:12
him, and he **b** their leader. 1Sm 22:2
had a seizure and **b** paralyzed. 1Sm 25:37
And so she **b** his wife. 1Sm 25:42
and the two of them **b** his wives. 1Sm 25:43
to flee, he fell and **b** lame. 2Sm 4:4
David **b** more and more powerful, 2Sm 5:10
So the Moabites **b** David's 2Sm 8:2
the Arameans **b** David's subjects 2Sm 8:6
his son Hanun **b** king in his 2Sm 10:1
Israel and **b** their subjects. 2Sm 10:19
She **b** his wife and bore him a 2Sm 11:27
borne to David, and he **b** ill. 2Sm 12:15
but David **b** exhausted. 2Sm 21:15
The depths of the sea **b** visible, 2Sm 22:16
b their commander even though 2Sm 23:19
and she **b** the king's caregiver. 1Kg 1:4
He **b** captain of a raiding party 1Kg 11:24
there, and **b** king in Damascus 1Kg 11:24
His son Rehoboam **b** king in his 1Kg 11:43
to him and **b** as it had been at 1Kg 13:6
and they **b** priests of the high 1Kg 13:33
Abijah son of Jeroboam **b** sick. 1Kg 14:1
his son Nadab **b** king in his 1Kg 14:20
was 41 years old when he **b** king; 1Kg 14:21
His son Abijam **b** king in his 1Kg 14:31
Nebat, Abijam **b** king over Judah 1Kg 15:1
His son Asa **b** king in his place. 1Kg 15:8
Jeroboam, Asa **b** king of Judah; 1Kg 15:9
son Jehoshaphat **b** king in his 1Kg 15:24
son of Jeroboam **b** king over 1Kg 15:25
When Baasha **b** king, he struck 1Kg 15:29

son of Ahijah **b** king over all	1Kg 15:33
son Elah **b** king in his place.	1Kg 16:6
son of Baasha **b** king over Israel	1Kg 16:8
Then Zimri **b** king in his place.	1Kg 16:10
When he **b** king, as soon as he	1Kg 16:11
Zimri **b** king for seven days in	1Kg 16:15
So Tibni died and Omri **b** king.	1Kg 16:22
King Asa, Omri **b** king over	1Kg 16:23
son Ahab **b** king in his place.	1Kg 16:28
son of Omri **b** king over Israel	1Kg 16:29
woman who owned the house **b** ill	1Kg 17:17
His illness **b** very severe until	1Kg 17:17
Then Elijah **b** afraid and	1Kg 19:3
his son Ahaziah **b** king in his	1Kg 22:40
son of Asa **b** king over Judah	1Kg 22:41
was 35 years old when he **b** king;	1Kg 22:42
His son Jehoram **b** king in his	1Kg 22:50
son of Ahab **b** king over Israel	1Kg 22:51
Joram **b** king in his place.	2Kg 1:17
son of Ahab **b** king over Israel	2Kg 3:1
him, the boy's flesh **b** warm.	2Kg 4:34
restored ⌊and **b**⌋ like the skin	2Kg 5:14
of Jehoshaphat **b** king of Judah,	2Kg 8:16
was 32 years old when he **b** king;	2Kg 8:17
his son Ahaziah **b** king in his	2Kg 8:24
son of Jehoram **b** king of Judah.	2Kg 8:25
was 22 years old when he **b** king;	2Kg 8:26
His son Jehoahaz **b** king in his	2Kg 10:35
seven years old when he **b** king.	2Kg 12:21
year of Jehu, Joash **b** king;	2Kg 12:1
his son Amaziah **b** king in his	2Kg 12:21
son of Jehu **b** king over Israel	2Kg 13:1
His son Jehoash **b** king in his	2Kg 13:9
son of Jehoahaz **b** king over	2Kg 13:10
When Elisha **b** sick with the	2Kg 13:14
son Ben-hadad **b** king in his	2Kg 13:24
son of Joash **b** king of Judah.	2Kg 14:1
was 25 years old when he **b** king;	2Kg 14:2
His son Jeroboam **b** king in his	2Kg 14:16
son of Jehoash **b** king of Israel	2Kg 14:23
son Zechariah **b** king in his	2Kg 14:29
son of Amaziah **b** king of Judah.	2Kg 15:1
was 16 years old when he **b** king;	2Kg 15:2
His son Jotham **b** king in his	2Kg 15:7
son of Jeroboam **b** king over	2Kg 15:8
killed him, and **b** king in his	2Kg 15:10
Shallum son of Jabesh **b** king;	2Kg 15:13
killed him and **b** king in his	2Kg 15:14
son of Gadi **b** king over Israel;	2Kg 15:17
his son Pekahiah **b** king in his	2Kg 15:22
of Menahem **b** king over Israel	2Kg 15:23
Pekahiah and **b** king in his place	2Kg 15:25
son of Remaliah **b** king over	2Kg 15:27
and **b** king in his place in the	2Kg 15:30
son of Uzziah **b** king of Judah.	2Kg 15:32
was 25 years old when he **b** king;	2Kg 15:33
son Ahaz **b** king in his place.	2Kg 15:38
son of Jotham **b** king of Judah.	2Kg 16:1
was 20 years old when he **b** king;	2Kg 16:2
his son Hezekiah **b** king in his	2Kg 16:20
son of Elah **b** king over Israel	2Kg 17:1
and Hoshea **b** his vassal and paid	2Kg 17:3
they **b** obstinate like their	2Kg 17:14
worthless idols and **b** worthless	2Kg 17:15
son of Ahaz **b** king of Judah.	2Kg 18:1
was 25 years old when he **b** king;	2Kg 18:2
son Esar-haddon **b** king in his	2Kg 19:37
days Hezekiah **b** terminally ill.	2Kg 20:1
his son Manasseh **b** king in his	2Kg 20:21
was 12 years old when he **b** king;	2Kg 21:1
son Amon **b** king in his place.	2Kg 21:18
was 22 years old when he **b** king;	2Kg 21:19
his son Josiah **b** king in his	2Kg 21:26
eight years old when he **b** king;	2Kg 22:1
was 23 years old when he **b** king;	2Kg 23:31
was 25 years old when he **b** king;	2Kg 23:36
and Jehoiakim **b** his vassal for	2Kg 24:1
son Jehoiachin **b** king in his	2Kg 24:6
was 18 years old when he **b** king;	2Kg 24:8
was 21 years old when he **b** king;	2Kg 24:18
in the year he **b** king, pardoned	2Kg 25:27
their cities until David **b** king.	1Ch 4:31
Although Judah **b** strong among	1Ch 5:2
up first, so he **b** the chief.	1Ch 11:6
the Three and **b** their commander	1Ch 11:21
and he **b** the father of more sons	1Ch 14:3
and they **b** David's subjects and	1Ch 18:2
the Arameans **b** David's subjects	1Ch 18:6
and his son **b** king in his place.	1Ch 19:1
with David and **b** his subjects.	1Ch 19:19
they **b** an ancestral house ⌊and	1Ch 23:11
his son Solomon **b** king in his	1Ch 29:28
His son Rehoboam **b** king in his	2Ch 9:31
was 41 years old when he **b** king;	2Ch 12:13
His son Abijah **b** king in his	2Ch 12:16
Abijah **b** king over Judah	2Ch 13:1
His son Asa **b** king in his place.	2Ch 14:1
and his disease **b** increasingly	2Ch 16:12
son Jehoshaphat **b** king in his	2Ch 17:1
Jehoshaphat **b** king over Judah.	2Ch 20:31
was 35 years old when he **b** king;	2Ch 20:31
His son Jehoram **b** king in his	2Ch 21:1
was 32 years old when he **b** king;	2Ch 21:5
was 32 years old when he **b** king;	2Ch 21:20
son of Jehoram **b** king of Judah.	2Ch 22:1
was 22 years old when he **b** king;	2Ch 22:2
seven years old when he **b** king;	2Ch 24:1
His son Amaziah **b** king in his	2Ch 24:27
Amaziah **b** king ⌊when he was⌋ 25	2Ch 25:1
was 16 years old when he **b** king;	2Ch 26:3
helped until he **b** strong.	2Ch 26:15
But when he **b** strong, he grew	2Ch 26:16
But when he **b** enraged with the	2Ch 26:19
His son Jotham **b** king in his	2Ch 26:23
was 25 years old when he **b** king;	2Ch 27:1
was 25 years old when he **b** king;	2Ch 27:8
son Ahaz **b** king in his place.	2Ch 27:9
was 20 years old when he **b** king;	2Ch 28:1
Ahaz himself **b** more unfaithful	2Ch 28:22
his son Hezekiah **b** king in his	2Ch 28:27
was 25 years old when he **b** king;	2Ch 29:1
his reign when he **b** unfaithful	2Ch 29:19
Hezekiah **b** sick to the point	2Ch 32:24
His son Manasseh **b** king in his	2Ch 32:33
was 12 years old when he **b** king;	2Ch 33:1
son Amon **b** king in his place.	2Ch 33:20
was 22 years old when he **b** king;	2Ch 33:21
eight years old when he **b** king;	2Ch 34:1
was 23 years old when he **b** king;	2Ch 36:2
was 25 years old when he **b** king;	2Ch 36:5
Jehoiachin **b** king in his place	2Ch 36:8
was 18 years old when he **b** king;	2Ch 36:9
was 21 years old when he **b** king;	2Ch 36:11
He **b** obstinate and hardened his	2Ch 36:13
and they **b** servants to him and	2Ch 36:20
farther down it **b** too narrow for	Neh 2:14
the wall, he **b** furious.	Neh 4:1
being closed, they **b** furious.	Neh 4:7
I **b** extremely angry when I heard	Neh 5:6
they **b** stiff-necked and did not	Neh 9:16
b stiff-necked and appointed	Neh 9:17
ate, were filled, **b** prosperous,	Neh 9:25
The king **b** furious and his anger	Est 1:12
and edict **b** public knowledge	Est 2:8
b infuriated and tried to	Est 2:21
provinces as he **b** more and more	Est 9:4
and it **b** a day of feasting and	Est 9:17
and it **b** a day of feasting and	Est 9:18
from the family of Ram **b** angry.	Jb 32:2
not answer Job, he **b** angry.	Jb 32:5
The depths of the sea **b** visible,	Ps 18:15
my bones **b** brittle from my	Ps 32:3
When I **b** embittered and my	Ps 73:21
the LORD heard and **b** furious;	Ps 78:21
they **b** warped like a faulty bow.	Ps 78:57
God heard and **b** furious;	Ps 78:59
they **b** manure for the ground.	Ps 83:10
darkness, and it **b** dark—for	Ps 105:28
idols, which **b** a snare to them.	Ps 106:36
so the land **b** polluted with	Ps 106:38
Judah **b** His sanctuary, Israel,	Ps 114:2
I **b** great and surpassed all who	Ec 2:9
When it **b** known to the house of	Is 7:2
We **b** pregnant, we writhed in	Is 26:18
son Esar-haddon **b** king in his	Is 37:38
days Hezekiah **b** terminally ill.	Is 38:1
You **b** weary on your many	Is 57:10
and He **b** their Savior.	Is 63:8
So He **b** their enemy ⌊and⌋ fought	Is 63:10
and **b** worthless themselves?	Jr 2:5
pay attention but **b** obstinate;	Jr 7:26
Your words **b** a delight to me and	Jr 15:16
pay attention but **b** obstinate,	Jr 17:23
making from the clay **b** flawed in	Jr 18:4
so that they **b** the desolate ruin	Jr 44:6
was 21 years old when he **b** king;	Jr 52:1
they **b** their food during the	Lm 4:10
matured and **b** very beautiful.	Ezk 16:7
with you, and you **b** Mine."	Ezk 16:8
You **b** extremely beautiful and	Ezk 16:13
passed by. Your beauty **b** his.	Ezk 16:15
It sprouted and **b** a spreading	Ezk 17:6
So it **b** a vine, produced	Ezk 17:6
her cubs, and he **b** a young lion.	Ezk 19:3
lions, and he **b** a young lion.	Ezk 19:6
They **b** Mine and gave birth to	Ezk 23:4
she **b** notorious among women.	Ezk 23:10
So you **b** full and heavily loaded	Ezk 27:25
Your heart **b** proud because of	Ezk 28:17
the cedar **b** greater in height	Ezk 31:5
Since it **b** great in height and	Ezk 31:10
they **b** food for all the wild	Ezk 34:5
because it **b** a desolation,	Ezk 35:15
so that you **b** a possession for	Ezk 36:3
that its pastureland **b** plunder.	Ezk 36:5
their idols and **b** a sinful	Ezk 44:12
the king **b** violently angry and	Dn 2:12
were shattered and **b** like chaff	Dn 2:35
the statue **b** a great mountain	Dn 2:35
King Belshazzar **b** even more	Dn 5:9
and his spirit **b** arrogant,	Dn 5:20
whatever he wanted and **b** great.	Dn 8:4
Then the male goat **b** very great,	Dn 8:8
great, but when he **b** powerful,	Dn 8:8
they **b** his altars for sinning.	Hs 8:11
to Shame, and **b** detestable, like	Hs 9:10
had pasture, they **b** satisfied;	Hs 13:6
and their hearts **b** proud.	Hs 13:6
Then the LORD **b** jealous for His	Jl 2:18
displeased and **b** furious.	Jnh 4:1
she **b** an exile; she went into	Nah 3:10
they **b** more corrupt in all their	Zph 3:7
b impatient with them, and they	Zch 11:8
When Jesus **b** aware of this,	Mt 12:15
Even His clothes **b** as white as	Mt 17:2
they **b** indignant with the two	Mt 20:24
they all **b** drowsy and fell	Mt 25:5
him that they **b** like dead men.	Mt 28:4
On the contrary, she **b** worse.	Mk 5:26
and His clothes **b** dazzling—	Mk 9:3
The boy **b** like a corpse, so that	Mk 9:26
child grew up and **b** spiritually	Lk 1:80
The boy grew up and **b** strong,	Lk 2:40
Judas Iscariot, who **b** a traitor.	Lk 6:16
His clothes **b** dazzling white.	Lk 9:29
and when they **b** fully awake,	Lk 9:32
They **b** afraid as they entered	Lk 9:34
just as Jonah **b** a sign to the	Lk 11:30
It grew and **b** a tree, and the	Lk 13:19
Then he **b** angry and didn't want	Lk 15:28
heard this, he **b** extremely sad,	Lk 18:23
that he **b** sad, Jesus said,	Lk 18:24
at His answer, they **b** silent.	Lk 20:26
and His sweat **b** like drops of	Lk 22:44
day Herod and Pilate **b** friends.	Lk 23:12
The Word **b** flesh and took up	Jn 1:14
who **b** a guide to those who	Ac 1:16
b known to all the residents	Ac 1:19
his feet and ankles **b** strong.	Ac 3:7
group of priests **b** obedient to	Ac 6:7
The patriarchs **b** jealous of	Ac 7:9
Joseph's family **b** known to	Ac 7:13
Moses fled and **b** an exile in the	Ac 7:29
but their plot **b** known to Saul.	Ac 9:24
those days she **b** sick and died.	Ac 9:37
This **b** known throughout all	Ac 9:42
at him, he **b** afraid and said,	Ac 10:4
Then he **b** hungry and wanted to	Ac 10:10
they heard this they **b** silent.	Ac 11:18
and he **b** infected with worms and	Ac 12:23
But the Jews **b** jealous, and when	Ac 17:5
But when some **b** hardened and	Ac 19:9
This **b** known to everyone who	Ac 19:17
language, they **b** even quieter.	Ac 22:2
When the dispute **b** violent,	Ac 23:10
Felix **b** afraid and replied,	Ac 24:25
They all **b** encouraged and took	Ac 27:36
their thinking **b** nonsense,	Rm 1:21
Claiming to be wise, they **b**	Rm 1:22
And he **b** the father of the	Rm 4:12
so that he **b** the father of many	Rm 4:18
you **b** enslaved to righteousness.	Rm 6:18
when Rebekah **b** pregnant by Isaac	Rm 9:10
who for us **b** wisdom from God,	1Co 1:30

To the Jews I **b** like a Jew, 1Co 9:20
the weak I **b** weak, in order to 1Co 9:22
these things **b** examples for us 1Co 10:6
When I **b** a man, I put aside 1Co 13:11
first man Adam **b** a living being; 1Co 15:45
the last Adam **b** a life-giving 1Co 15:45
for your sake He **b** poor, so that 2Co 8:9
like me, for I also **b** like you. Gl 4:12
They **b** callous and gave Eph 4:19
and you **b** imitators of us and of 1Th 1:6
you **b** an example to all the 1Th 1:7
b imitators of God's churches in 1Th 2:14
So He **b** higher in rank than the Heb 1:4
He **b** the source of eternal Heb 5:9
b companions with the Holy Heb 6:4
For others **b** priests without an Heb 7:20
condemned the world and **b** an Heb 11:7
being weak, **b** mighty in battle Heb 11:34
the entire moon **b** like blood; Rv 6:12
So a third of the sea **b** blood, Rv 8:8
third of the waters **b** wormwood. Rv 8:11
I ate it, my stomach **b** bitter. Rv 10:10
of water, and they **b** blood. Rv 16:4
on the earth **b** drunk on the wine Rv 17:2
things, who **b** rich from her, Rv 18:15
ships on the sea **b** rich from her Rv 18:19

BECAUSE *(2042)*
(See pp. xi-xii.)

BECHER *(3)*
(AKA BERED)
Bela, **B**, Ashbel, Gera, Naaman, Gn 46:21
the Becherite clan from **B**; Nm 26:35
Bela, **B**, and Jediael. 1Ch 7:6

BECHER'S *(2)*
B sons: Zemirah, Joash, Eliezer, 1Ch 7:8
all these were **B** sons. 1Ch 7:8

BECHERITE *(1)*
the **B** clan from Becher; Nm 26:35

BECOME *(472)*
his wife, and they **b** one flesh. Gn 2:24
Since man has **b** like one of Us, Gn 3:22
Your presence and **b** a restless Gn 4:14
will never again **b** a deluge to Gn 9:15
you will **b** the father of many Gn 17:4
After I have **b** shriveled up and Gn 18:12
Abraham is to **b** a great and Gn 18:18
my master, and he has **b** rich. Gn 24:35
may you **b** thousands upon ten Gn 24:60
you so that you **b** an assembly of Gn 28:3
my husband will **b** attached to me Gn 29:34
and now I have **b** two camps. Gn 32:10
live with you, and **b** one people. Gn 34:16
and all their livestock **b** ours? Gn 34:23
we will **b** a laughingstock. Gn 38:23
we also will **b** my lord's slaves Gn 44:9
you have will **b** destitute." ' Gn 45:11
our land will **b** Pharaoh's slaves Gn 47:19
that the land won't **b** desolate." Gn 47:19
too will **b** a tribe, and he too Gn 48:19
offspring will **b** a populous Gn 48:19
I have **b** a stranger in a foreign Ex 2:22
it had again **b** like the rest of Ex 4:7
from the Nile will **b** blood on Ex 4:9
It will **b** a serpent." Ex 7:9
and they will **b** blood. Ex 7:19
and it will **b** gnats throughout Ex 8:16
It will **b** fine dust over the Ex 9:9
It will **b** festering boils on Ex 9:9
Egypt since it had **b** a nation. Ex 9:24
he will **b** like a native of the Ex 12:48
He has **b** my salvation. Ex 15:2
but the dead animal will **b** his. Ex 21:34
the dead animal will **b** his. Ex 21:36
the land would **b** desolate, Ex 23:29
until you have **b** numerous and Ex 23:30
he and his garments will **b** holy, Ex 29:21
altar will **b** especially holy; Ex 29:37
touches the altar will **b** holy. Ex 29:37
they will **b** a snare among you. Ex 34:12
by which one can **b** defiled— Lv 5:3
the offerings will **b** holy." Lv 6:18
touches its flesh will **b** holy, Lv 6:27
and the LORD will **b** angry with Lv 10:6
everything in it will **b** unclean; Lv 11:33
unclean⌋ water will **b** unclean, Lv 11:34
in any container will **b** unclean. Lv 11:34
falls on will **b** unclean. Lv 11:35
carcass ⌊in it⌋ will **b** unclean. Lv 11:36
Do not **b** contaminated by any Lv 11:43
do not **b** unclean or defiled by Lv 11:43
his clothes and will **b** clean. Lv 13:6
her menstruation will **b** unclean, Lv 15:20
she sits on will **b** unclean. Lv 15:20
bed he lies on will **b** unclean. Lv 15:24
The land has **b** defiled, so I am Lv 18:25
and the land has **b** defiled. Lv 18:27
set, he will **b** clean, and then Lv 22:7
These may **b** your property. Lv 25:45
So your land will **b** desolate, Lv 26:33
and your cities will **b** ruins. Lv 26:33
gone astray and **b** defiled while Nm 5:19
She will **b** a curse among her Nm 5:27
little children will **b** plunder. Nm 14:3
whom you said would **b** plunder Nm 14:31
obey them and not **b** unfaithful Nm 15:39
the LORD and **b** like Korah and Nm 16:40
person touches will **b** unclean, Nm 19:22
Edom will **b** a possession; Nm 24:18
Seir will **b** a possession of its Nm 24:18
to remain will **b** thorns in your Nm 33:55
your God will **b** angry with you Dt 6:15
animals will **b** too numerous for Dt 7:22
heart doesn't **b** proud and you Dt 8:14
and he will **b** your slave for Dt 15:17
and you will not **b** guilty of Dt 19:10
Has any man **b** engaged to a woman Dt 20:7
in it will **b** forced laborers Dt 20:11
and she must **b** his wife because Dt 22:29
This day you have **b** the people Dt 27:9
You will **b** engaged to a woman, Dt 28:30
You will **b** an object of horror, Dt 28:37
so that they will **b** easy prey. Dt 31:17
my death you will **b** completely Dt 31:29
I will see what will **b** of them, Dt 32:20
not die though his people **b** few. Dt 33:6
him, "You have **b** old, advanced Jos 13:1
They will **b** a snare and a trap Jos 23:13
and you will **b** leader of all the Jdg 11:8
I will **b** weak and be like any Jdg 16:7
I will **b** weak and be like any Jdg 16:11
I will **b** weak and be like any Jdg 16:17
a Levite has **b** my priest." Jdg 17:13
sons who could **b** your husbands? Ru 1:11
May your house **b** like the house Ru 4:12
your daughters to **b** perfumers, 1Sm 8:13
yourselves can **b** his servants. 1Sm 8:17
have you not **b** the leader of the 1Sm 15:17
that I should **b** the king's 1Sm 18:18
you should **b** the king's 1Sm 18:22
in your sight to **b** the king's 1Sm 18:23
he was pleased to **b** the king's 1Sm 18:26
full payment to the king to **b** 1Sm 18:27
from you and has **b** your enemy, 1Sm 28:16
battle only to **b** our adversary 1Sm 29:4
and You, LORD, have **b** their God. 2Sm 7:24
realized they had **b** repulsive to 2Sm 10:6
'Absalom has **b** king in Hebron!' 2Sm 15:10
is for those who **b** exhausted to 2Sm 16:2
you have **b** repulsive to your 2Sm 16:21
May what has **b** of the young man 2Sm 18:32
if you don't **b** commander of the 2Sm 19:13
Have you **b** my adversary today? 2Sm 19:22
he did not **b** one of the Three 2Sm 23:19
but he did not **b** one of the 2Sm 23:23
of Haggith has **b** king and our 1Kg 1:11
Solomon is to **b** king after me, 1Kg 1:13
So why has Adonijah **b** king?' 1Kg 1:13
Solomon is to **b** king after me, 1Kg 1:17
Now look, Adonijah has **b** king. 1Kg 1:18
'Adonijah is to **b** king after me, 1Kg 1:24
Solomon is to **b** king after me, 1Kg 1:30
one who is to **b** king in my place 1Kg 1:35
Israel will **b** an object of scorn 1Kg 9:7
jar will not **b** empty and the oil 1Kg 17:14
The flour jar did not **b** empty, 1Kg 17:16
'I will go and **b** a lying spirit 1Kg 22:22
who was to **b** king in his place, 2Kg 3:27
Ahaziah had **b** king over Judah 2Kg 9:29
and you have **b** overconfident. 2Kg 14:10
inhabitants have **b** powerless, 2Kg 19:26
and they will **b** eunuchs in the 2Kg 20:18
They will **b** plunder and spoil to 2Kg 21:14
that they would **b** a desolation 2Kg 22:19
the first to **b** a great warrior 1Ch 1:10
family did not **b** as numerous as 1Ch 4:27
first to kill a Jebusite will **b** 1Ch 11:6
he did not **b** one of the Three 1Ch 11:21
but he did not **b** one of the 1Ch 11:25
and You, LORD, have **b** their God. 1Ch 17:22
they will **b** his servants so that 2Ch 12:8
seven rams may **b** a priest of 2Ch 13:9
'I will go and **b** a lying spirit 2Ch 18:21
and you have **b** overconfident 2Ch 25:19
Don't **b** obstinate now like your 2Ch 30:8
the holy people has **b** mixed with Ezr 9:2
Wouldn't You **b** ⌊so⌋ angry with Ezr 9:14
reports, you are to **b** their king Neh 6:6
They will **b** discouraged in the Neh 6:9
had **b** a son-in-law to Sanballat Neh 13:28
action will **b** public knowledge Est 1:17
to you, you have **b** exhausted. Jb 4:5
and **b** darkened because of ice, Jb 6:16
is what you have now **b** ⌊to me⌋. Jb 6:21
that I have **b** a burden to You? Jb 7:20
if they **b** insignificant, he is Jb 14:21
destined to **b** piles of rubble. Jb 15:28
me up—it has **b** a witness; Jb 16:8
I have **b** a man people spit at. Jb 17:6
whole body has **b** but a shadow. Jb 17:7
I have **b** an object of scorn to Jb 30:9
I have **b** like dust and ashes. Jb 30:19
have **b** a brother to jackals and Jb 30:29
or **b** excited when trouble came Jb 31:29
slingstones **b** like stubble to Jb 41:28
today I have **b** Your Father. Ps 2:7
all alike have **b** corrupt. Ps 14:3
They have **b** hardened; Ps 17:10
they have all **b** corrupt. Ps 53:3
they will **b** the jackals' prey. Ps 63:10
I have **b** a stranger to my Ps 69:8
have **b** an ominous sign to many, Ps 71:7
suddenly they **b** a desolation! Ps 73:19
We have **b** an object of reproach Ps 79:4
us quickly, for we have **b** weak. Ps 79:8
You have **b** enraged with Your Ps 89:38
has **b** a joke to his neighbors. Ps 89:41
trouble by law—**b** Your ally? Ps 94:20
have **b** an object of ridicule to Ps 109:25
He has **b** my salvation. Ps 118:14
me and have **b** my salvation. Ps 118:21
rejected has **b** the cornerstone. Ps 118:22
Though I have **b** like a wineskin Ps 119:83
light around me will **b** night"— Ps 139:11
⌊Otherwise,⌋ they will **b** proud. Ps 140:8
Observe its ways and **b** wise. Pr 6:6
what is right, only to **b** poor. Pr 11:24
walks with the wise will **b** wise, Pr 13:20
love sleep, or you will **b** poor; Pr 20:13
the inexperienced **b** wiser; Pr 21:11
pleasure will **b** a poor man; Pr 21:17
and the glutton will **b** poor, Pr 23:21
or he'll **b** wise in his own eyes. Pr 26:5
his youth will **b** arrogant later Pr 29:21
you, and you will **b** guilty. Pr 30:10
his eyes I have **b** like one who Sg 8:10
They have **b** a burden to Me; Is 1:14
what an adulteress she has **b**! Is 1:21
Your silver has **b** dross, your Is 1:22
For you will **b** like an oak whose Is 1:30
The strong one will **b** tinder, Is 1:31
many houses will **b** desolate, Is 5:9
roots will **b** like something Is 5:24
of silver, will **b** thorns and Is 7:23
famished, they will **b** enraged, Is 8:21
Israel's Light will **b** a fire, Is 10:17
my song, He has **b** my salvation." Is 12:2
everyone's hands will **b** weak, Is 13:7
and how the raging has **b** quiet! Is 14:4
You too have **b** as weak as we Is 14:10
as we are; you have **b** like us! Is 14:10
Moab's splendor will **b** an object Is 16:14
It has **b** a ruined heap. Is 17:1
healthy body will **b** emaciated. Is 17:4
its inhabitants have **b** guilty; Is 24:6
of Hosts will **b** a crown of Is 28:5
your shackles will **b** stronger. Is 28:22
while Lebanon will **b** an orchard, Is 29:17
protection will **b** your shame, Is 30:3
watchtower will **b** barren places Is 32:14
the desert will **b** an orchard, Is 32:15
her land will **b** burning pitch. Is 34:9
She will **b** a dwelling for Is 34:13
ground will **b** a pool of water, Is 35:7

inhabitants have **b** powerless, Is 37:27
the uneven ground will **b** smooth, Is 40:4
with you will **b** as nothing and Is 41:11
against you will **b** absolutely Is 41:12
They have **b** plunder, with no one Is 42:22
Israel, you have **b** weary of Me. Is 43:22
Their webs cannot **b** clothing, Is 59:6
riches of the sea will **b** yours, Is 60:5
The least will **b** a thousand, Is 60:22
We have **b** like those You never Is 63:19
All of us have **b** like something Is 64:6
holy cities have **b** a wilderness; Is 64:10
Zion has **b** a wilderness, Is 64:10
Why else has he **b** a prey? Jr 2:14
look for her will not **b** tired; Jr 2:24
such a land **b** totally defiled? Jr 3:1
The prophets **b** ⌊only⌋ wind, Jr 5:13
to make My words **b** fire in your Jr 5:14
They have **b** fat and sleek. Jr 5:28
the LORD has **b** contemptible to Jr 6:10
b a den of robbers in your view? Jr 7:11
Topheth will **b** a cemetery, Jr 7:32
these people will **b** food for the Jr 7:33
the land will **b** a desolate waste Jr 7:34
buried but will **b** like manure Jr 8:2
Why has my pain **b** unending, Jr 15:18
You truly have **b** like a mirage Jr 15:18
corpses will **b** food for the Jr 16:4
Don't **b** a terror to me. Jr 17:17
Let their wives **b** childless and Jr 18:21
of Judah will **b** impure like that Jr 19:13
for they have **b** obstinate, Jr 19:15
the LORD has **b** for me constant Jr 20:8
I **b** tired of holding it in, Jr 20:9
"that this house will **b** a ruin." Jr 22:5
They will **b** fruitful and Jr 23:3
I have **b** like a drunkard, like a Jr 23:9
Their way of life has **b** evil, Jr 23:10
land will **b** a desolate ruin Jr 25:11
will fall and **b** shattered like Jr 25:34
land will **b** lifeless because Jr 25:37
their land has **b** a desolation Jr 25:38
'This temple will **b** like Shiloh Jr 26:9
this city will **b** an uninhabited Jr 26:9
Jerusalem will **b** ruins, and the Jr 26:18
Why should this city **b** a ruin? Jr 27:17
Your despoilers will **b** spoil, Jr 30:16
forced them to **b** slaves ⌊again⌋. Jr 34:11
corpses will **b** food for the Jr 34:20
servants did not **b** terrified or Jr 36:24
You will **b** an object of Jr 42:18
will be cut off and **b** an object Jr 44:8
They have not **b** humble to this Jr 44:10
Then they will **b** an object of Jr 44:12
so your land has **b** a waste, Jr 44:22
For Memphis will **b** a desolation, Jr 46:19
Ashkelon will **b** silent, a Jr 47:5
her towns will **b** a desolation, Jr 48:9
he will also **b** a laughingstock Jr 48:26
of Nimrim have **b** desolate. Jr 48:34
Moab will **b** a laughingstock and Jr 48:39
It will **b** a desolate mound, Jr 49:2
Bozrah will **b** a desolation, Jr 49:13
cities will **b** ruins forever." Jr 49:13
Edom will **b** a desolation. Jr 49:17
Damascus has **b** weak; she has Jr 49:24
Their camels will **b** plunder, Jr 49:32
herds of cattle will **b** spoil. Jr 49:32
Hazor will **b** a jackals' den, Jr 49:33
The Chaldeans will **b** plunder; Jr 50:10
she will **b** a desolation, every Jr 50:13
Babylon has **b** among the nations Jr 50:23
you will **b** desolate forever Jr 51:26
they have **b** like women. Jr 51:30
Babylon will **b** a heap of rubble, Jr 51:37
Babylon has **b** among the nations Jr 51:41
Her cities have **b** a desolation, Jr 51:43
May you not **b** faint-hearted and Jr 51:46
the nations has **b** like a widow. Lm 1:1
the provinces has **b** a slave. Lm 1:1
they have **b** her enemies. Lm 1:2
have **b** ⌊her⌋ masters; Lm 1:5
she has **b** an object of scorn. Lm 1:8
and see how I have **b** despised. Lm 1:11
Jerusalem has **b** something impure Lm 1:17
so that they may **b** like me. Lm 1:21
them⌋ and have **b** depressed. Lm 3:20
How the gold has **b** tarnished, Lm 4:1

tarnished, the fine gold **b** dull! Lm 4:1
my dear people have **b** cruel like Lm 4:3
it has **b** dry like wood. Lm 4:8
We have **b** orphans, fatherless; Lm 5:3
All their hands will **b** weak, Ezk 7:17
the land will **b** a desolation. Ezk 12:20
fruit, and **b** a splendid vine Ezk 17:8
fruit, and **b** a majestic cedar. Ezk 17:23
and every hand will **b** weak. Ezk 21:7
of Israel has **b** dross to Me. Ezk 22:18
Because all of you have **b** dross, Ezk 22:19
She will **b** a place in the sea to Ezk 26:5
She will **b** plunder for the Ezk 26:5
you have **b** an object of horror Ezk 27:36
your heart has **b** proud because Ezk 28:5
You have **b** an object of horror Ezk 28:19
water would **b** great in height Ezk 31:14
of Israel will **b** desolate, Ezk 33:28
My flock has **b** ⌊prey and⌋ food Ezk 34:8
and you will **b** a desolation. Ezk 35:4
you will **b** a desolation, Mount Ezk 35:15
heights have **b** our possession,' Ezk 36:2
which have **b** plunder and a Ezk 36:4
desolate has **b** like the garden Ezk 36:35
so that they **b** one in your hand Ezk 37:17
so that they **b** one in My hand. Ezk 37:19
It will **b** their property by Ezk 46:16
Since the water will **b** fresh, Ezk 47:9
These will **b** places where nets Ezk 47:10
For you have **b** great and strong: Dn 4:22
and Your people have **b** an object Dn 9:16
will **b** arrogant and cause tens Dn 11:12
don't let Judah **b** guilty! Hs 4:15
Ephraim will **b** a desolation on Hs 5:9
So Ephraim has **b** like a silly, Hs 7:11
all who eat it **b** defiled. Hs 9:4
they will **b** wanderers among the Hs 9:17
How rich I have **b**; I made it all Hs 12:8
Egypt will **b** desolate, and Edom Jl 3:19
temple songs will **b** wailing"— Am 8:3
God, slow to **b** angry, rich in Jnh 4:2
Jerusalem will **b** ruins, and the Mc 3:12
the earth will **b** a wasteland Mc 7:13
and their ears will **b** deaf. Mc 7:16
You also will **b** drunk; Nah 3:11
Then you will **b** spoil for them. Hab 2:7
wealth will **b** plunder and their Zph 1:13
and Ashkelon will **b** a ruin. Zph 2:4
seacoast will **b** pasturelands Zph 2:6
What a desolation she has **b**, Zph 2:15
never have enough to **b** drunk. Hg 1:6
any other food, does it **b** holy?" Hg 2:12
of these, does it **b** defiled?" Hg 2:13
they will **b** plunder for their Zch 2:9
on that day and **b** My people. Zch 2:11
Zerubbabel you will **b** a plain. Zch 4:7
the tenth will **b** times of joy, Zch 8:19
and Ashkelon will **b** uninhabited. Zch 9:5
they too will **b** a remnant for Zch 9:7
they will **b** like a clan in Judah Zch 9:7
the LORD because I have **b** rich! Zch 11:5
day Yahweh will **b** king over all Zch 14:9
wickedness will **b** stubble. Mal 4:1
the virgin will **b** pregnant and Mt 1:23
tell these stones to **b** bread." Mt 4:3
a disciple to **b** like his teacher Mt 10:25
converted and **b** like children, Mt 18:3
and the two will **b** one flesh? Mt 19:5
wants to **b** great among you Mt 20:26
rejected has **b** the cornerstone. Mt 21:42
outside of it may also **b** clean. Mt 23:26
himself had also **b** a disciple of Mt 27:57
Jesus' name had **b** well known. Mk 6:14
and the two will **b** one flesh. Mk 10:8
wants to **b** great among you Mk 10:43
this has **b** the cornerstone. Mk 12:10
You will **b** silent and unable to Lk 1:20
"What then will this child **b**?" Lk 1:66
the crooked will **b** straight, Lk 3:5
tell this stone to **b** bread." Lk 4:3
always and not **b** discouraged: Lk 18:1
this has **b** the cornerstone? Lk 20:17
among you must **b** like the Lk 22:26
after it had **b** wine), he did not Jn 2:9
give him will **b** a well of water Jn 4:14
can You say, 'You will **b** free'?" Jn 8:33
don't want to **b** His disciples Jn 9:27
those who do see will **b** blind." Jn 9:39

that you may **b** sons of light." Jn 12:36
You will **b** sorrowful, but your Jn 16:20
Let his dwelling **b** desolate; Ac 1:20
that one **b** a witness with us Ac 1:22
who has **b** the cornerstone. Ac 4:11
we don't know what's **b** of him. Ac 7:40
and murderers you have now **b**. Ac 7:52
to what could have **b** of Peter. Ac 12:18
today I have **b** Your Father. Ac 13:33
many who had **b** believers came Ac 19:18
persuade me to **b** a Christian so Ac 26:28
to me today might **b** as I am— Ac 26:29
has **b** uncircumcision. Rm 2:25
together they have **b** useless; Rm 3:12
whole world may **b** subject to Rm 3:19
from sin and **b** enslaved to God, Rm 6:22
sin might **b** sinful beyond Rm 7:13
we would have **b** like Sodom, Rm 9:29
their feasting **b** a snare and a Rm 11:9
say that Christ has **b** a servant Rm 15:8
each one's work will **b** obvious, 1Co 3:13
he must **b** foolish so that he can 1Co 3:18
foolish so that he can **b** wise. 1Co 3:18
we have **b** a spectacle to the 1Co 4:9
says, The two will **b** one flesh. 1Co 6:16
But if you can **b** free, by all 1Co 7:21
do not **b** slaves of men. 1Co 7:23
I have **b** all things to all 1Co 9:22
that I may **b** a partner in its 1Co 9:23
Don't **b** idolaters as some of 1Co 10:7
B right-minded and stop sinning, 1Co 15:34
—did not **b** "Yes and no"; 2Co 1:19
so that we might **b** the 2Co 5:21
by His poverty you might **b** rich. 2Co 8:9
may also **b** ⌊available⌋ for 2Co 8:14
have **b** a fool; you forced it on 2Co 12:11
those who had **b** apostles before Gl 1:17
or rather have **b** known by God, Gl 4:9
b like me, for I also became Gl 4:12
Have I now **b** your enemy by Gl 4:16
We must not **b** conceited, Gl 5:26
do not **b** their partners. Eph 5:7
and the two will **b** one flesh. Eph 5:31
that it has **b** known throughout Php 1:13
I, Paul, have **b** a minister of it Col 1:23
I have **b** its minister, according Col 1:25
wives and don't **b** bitter against Col 3:19
so they won't **b** discouraged. Col 3:21
because you had **b** dear to us. 1Th 2:8
or he might **b** conceited and fall 1Tm 3:6
and imposters will **b** worse, 2Tm 3:13
we may **b** heirs with the hope of Ti 3:7
in the faith may **b** effective Phm 6
today I have **b** Your Father, Heb 1:5
that He could **b** a merciful and Heb 2:17
For we have **b** companions of the Heb 3:14
Himself to **b** a high priest, Heb 5:5
today I have **b** Your Father, Heb 5:5
since you have **b** slow to Heb 5:11
so that you won't **b** lazy, but Heb 6:12
because He has **b** a "high priest Heb 6:20
who doesn't **b** a ⌊priest⌋ based Heb 7:16
Jesus has also **b** the guarantee Heb 7:22
Now many have **b** ⌊Levitical⌋ Heb 7:23
yourselves and **b** judges with Jms 2:4
Not many should **b** teachers, Jms 3:1
this One has **b** the cornerstone, 1Pt 2:7
You have **b** her children when you 1Pt 3:6
what will **b** of the ungodly and 1Pt 4:18
I have **b** wealthy, and need Rv 3:17
of the world has **b** the ⌊kingdom⌋ Rv 11:15
She has **b** a dwelling for demons, Rv 18:2

BECOMES *(48)*

we'll see what **b** of his dreams!" Gn 37:20
regard to the command **b** known, Lv 4:14
Whoever touches them **b** unclean. Lv 11:26
falls on anything it **b** unclean— Lv 11:32
a woman **b** pregnant and gives Lv 12:2
and it **b** a disease on the skin Lv 13:2
by the burn **b** a reddish-white Lv 13:24
nothing in the house **b** unclean. Lv 14:36
priest's daughter **b** widowed or Lv 22:13
If your brother **b** destitute and Lv 25:25
If your brother **b** destitute and Lv 25:35
brother among you **b** destitute Lv 25:39
living⌋ near him **b** destitute and Lv 25:47
it **b** the priest's property. Lv 27:21
husband and he **b** jealous because Nm 5:14

over him and he **b** jealous of her Nm 5:14
husband and he **b** jealous of his Nm 5:30
nostrils and **b** nauseating to you Nm 11:20
but she **b** displeasing to him Dt 24:1
she goes and **b** another man's Dt 24:2
safe, but if he **b** angry, you 1Sm 20:7
and a wadi **b** parched and dry, Jb 14:11
and by night he **b** a thief. Jb 24:14
nothing when he **b** God's friend." Jb 34:9
when water **b** as hard as stone, Jb 38:30
meditate; my spirit **b** weak. Ps 77:3
and it **b** night, when all Ps 104:20
who is reckless only **b** poor. Pr 21:5
One who **b** stiff-necked, after Pr 29:1
servant when he **b** king, a fool Pr 30:22
and the blossom **b** a ripening Is 18:5
His message **b** a fire burning in Jr 20:9
each man's word **b** his burden and Jr 23:36
it so that it **b** desolate, Ezk 14:15
coals so that it **b** hot and its Ezk 24:11
person so that he **b** defiled. Ezk 44:25
the water ⌊of the sea⌋ **b** fresh. Ezk 47:8
answered, "It **b** defiled." Hg 2:13
the word, and it **b** unfruitful. Mt 13:22
the vegetables and **b** a tree, Mt 13:32
and when he **b** one, you make him Mt 23:15
as its branch **b** tender and Mt 24:32
the word, and it **b** unfruitful. Mk 4:19
grinds his teeth, and **b** rigid. Mk 9:18
as its branch **b** tender and Mk 13:28
yours in no way **b** a stumbling 1Co 8:9
And this **b** clearer if another Heb 7:15
world's friend **b** God's enemy. Jms 4:4

BECOMING *(7)*
of semen, **b** unclean by it; Lv 15:32
and the house of Saul **b** weaker. 2Sm 3:1
told about me **b** king over this 1Kg 14:2
growing old and **b** powerful? Jb 21:7
the north and **b** an overflowing Jr 47:2
of the law by **b** a curse for us, Gl 3:13
humbled Himself by **b** obedient to Php 2:8

BECORATH *(1)*
Zeror, son of **B**, son of Aphiah, 1Sm 9:1

BED *(79)*
Before they went to **b**, the men Gn 19:4
he refused to go to **b** with her. Gn 39:10
in thanks⌋ at the head of his **b**. Gn 47:31
his strength and sat up in **b**. Gn 48:2
your father's **b** and you defiled Gn 49:4
defiled it—he got into my **b**. Gn 49:4
his feet into the **b** and died. Gn 49:33
into your bedroom and on your **b**, Ex 8:3
not die but is confined to **b**, Ex 21:18
Any **b** the man with the discharge Lv 15:4
who touches his **b** is to wash his Lv 15:5
who touches her **b** is to wash his Lv 15:21
is on the **b** or the furniture Lv 15:23
and every **b** he lies on will Lv 15:24
b she lies on during the days Lv 15:26
be like her **b** during menstrual Lv 15:26
Rephaim. His **b** was made of iron Dt 3:11
violate his father's marriage **b**. Dt 22:30
his father's marriage **b**.' Dt 27:20
and went to **b** with her. Jdg 16:1
stayed in **b** until midnight Jdg 16:3
idol and put it on the **b**, 1Sm 19:13
Bring him on his **b** so I can kill 1Sm 19:15
was on the **b** with some goats' 1Sm 19:16
off the ground and sat on the **b**. 1Sm 28:23
lying on his **b** in his bedroom 2Sm 4:7
in his own house on his own **b**! 2Sm 4:11
got up from his **b** and strolled 2Sm 11:2
Lie down on your **b** and pretend 2Sm 13:5
king bowed in worship on his **b**. 1Kg 1:47
and laid him on his own **b**. 1Kg 17:19
lay down on his **b**, turned his 1Kg 21:4
small room upstairs and put a **b**, 2Kg 4:10
laid him on the **b** of the man of 2Kg 4:21
the boy lying dead on his **b**. 2Kg 4:32
Reuben defiled his father's **b**. 1Ch 5:1
him on his **b**, because he had 2Ch 24:25
My **b** will comfort me, and my Jb 7:13
spread out my **b** in darkness, Jb 17:13
disciplined on his **b** with pain Jb 33:19
on your **b**, reflect in your heart Ps 4:4
and drench my **b** every night. Ps 6:6
Even on his **b** he makes malicious Ps 36:4
heal him on the **b** where he lies. Ps 41:3
When, on my **b**, I think of You, I Ps 63:6
enter my house or get into my **b**, Ps 132:3
if I make my **b** in Sheol, You are Ps 139:8
How long will you stay in **b**, Pr 6:9
I've spread coverings on my **b**— Pr 7:16
I've perfumed my **b** with myrrh, Pr 7:17
even your **b** will be taken from Pr 22:27
hinge, and a slacker, on his **b**. Pr 26:14
She makes her own **b** coverings; Pr 31:22
Our **b** is lush with foliage; Sg 1:16
my **b** at night I sought the one Sg 3:1
b is too short to stretch out Is 28:20
have placed your **b** on a high and Is 57:7
up, and made your **b** wide, and Is 57:8
loved their **b**; you have gazed Is 57:8
to him from its planting **b**, Ezk 17:7
wither on the **b** where it Ezk 17:10
came to her, to the **b** of love, Ezk 23:17
⌊as you lay⌋ in **b** were these: Dn 2:28
were in your **b**, thoughts came Dn 2:29
while in my **b**, the images and Dn 4:5
of my mind as I was lying in **b**, Dn 4:10
I was lying in my **b**, I also saw Dn 4:13
mind as he was lying in his **b**. Dn 7:1
the corner of a **b** or the cushion Am 3:12
lying in **b** with a fever. Mt 8:14
was lying in **b** with a fever, Mk 1:30
put under a basket or under a **b**? Mk 4:21
found her child lying on the **b**, Mk 7:30
a basket or puts it under a **b**, Lk 8:16
children and I have gone to **b**. Lk 11:7
that night two will be in one **b**: Lk 17:34
Get up and make your own **b**," Ac 9:34
father was in **b** suffering from Ac 28:8
the marriage **b** kept undefiled, Heb 13:4

BEDAD *(2)*
Hadad son of **B** ruled in his Gn 36:35
Hadad son of **B**, who defeated 1Ch 1:46

BEDAN *(1)*
(AKA BARAK)
Ulam's son: **B**. These were the 1Ch 7:17

BEDCLOTHES *(1)*
they covered him with **b**, 1Kg 1:1

BEDEIAH *(1)*
Benaiah, **B**, Cheluhi, Ezr 10:35

BEDRIDDEN *(1)*
and had been **b** for eight years. Ac 9:33

BEDROLL *(5)*
"pick up your **b** and walk!" Jn 5:8
picked up his **b**, and started to Jn 5:9
for you to pick up your **b**." Jn 5:10
'Pick up your **b** and walk.' " Jn 5:11
'Pick up ⌊your **b**⌋ and walk?' " Jn 5:12

BEDROOM *(11)*
into your **b** and on your bed, Ex 8:3
on his bed in his **b** and stabbed 2Sm 4:7
"Bring the meal to the **b**," 2Sm 13:10
went to her brother Amnon's **b**. 2Sm 13:10
went to the king in his **b**. 1Kg 1:15
the words you speak in your **b**." 2Kg 6:12
put⌋ him and his nurse in a **b**. 2Kg 11:2
put him and his nurse in a **b**. 2Ch 22:11
a rich person even in your **b**, Ec 10:20
Let the bridegroom leave his **b**, Jl 2:16
was in charge of the king's **b**, Ac 12:20

BEDS *(11)*
brought **b**, basins, and pottery 2Sm 17:28
as they slumber on ⌊their⌋ **b**, Jb 33:15
them shout for joy on their **b**. Ps 149:5
His cheeks are like **b** of spice, Sg 5:13
his garden, to **b** of spice, to Sg 6:2
they will rest on their **b**— Is 57:2
rather, they wail on their **b**. Hs 7:14
for the river **b** are dried up, Jl 1:20
They lie on **b** ⌊inlaid with⌋ Am 6:4
prepare evil ⌊plans⌋ on their **b**! Mc 2:1
and lay them on **b** and pallets so Ac 5:15

BEE *(1)*
Nile and to the **b** that is in the Is 7:18

BEELIADA *(1)*
Elishama, **B**, and Eliphelet. 1Ch 14:7

BEELZEBUL *(7)*
(AKA BAAL-ZEBUB, DEVIL, SATAN)
the head of the house '**B**,' Mt 10:25
man drives out demons only by **B**, Mt 12:24
And if I drive out demons by **B**, Mt 12:27
said, "He has **B** in Him!" Mk 3:22
He drives out demons by **B**, Lk 11:15
you say I drive out demons by **B**. Lk 11:18
And if I drive out demons by **B**, Lk 11:19

BEEN *(778)*
(See pp. xi-xii.)

BEER *(21)*
(See also BEER proper noun.)
drink wine or **b** when you enter Lv 10:9
is to abstain from wine and **b**. Nm 6:3
made from wine or from **b**. Nm 6:3
the offering of **b** to the LORD Nm 28:7
sheep, wine, **b**, or anything you Dt 14:26
eat bread or drink wine or **b**— Dt 29:6
I haven't had any wine or **b**; 1Sm 1:15
is a mocker, **b** is a brawler, Pr 20:1
or for rulers ⌊to desire⌋ **b**. Pr 31:4
Give **b** to one who is dying, Pr 31:6
your **b** is diluted with water. Is 1:22
in the morning in pursuit of **b**, Is 5:11
who are fearless at mixing **b**, Is 5:22
b is bitter to those who drink Is 24:9
under the influence of **b**: Is 28:7
prophet stagger because of **b**, Is 28:7
They stumble because of **b**, Is 28:7
they stagger, but not with **b**. Is 29:9
wine, let's guzzle ⌊some⌋ **b**; Is 56:12
preach to you about wine and **b**," Mc 2:11
and will never drink wine or **b**. Lk 1:15

BEER (proper noun) *(2)*
From there ⌊they went⌋ to **B**, Nm 21:16
escaping to **B**, and lived there Jdg 9:21

BEER-ELIM *(1)*
(AKA BEER)
their wailing reaches **B**. Is 15:8

BEER-LAHAI-ROI *(2)*
Now Isaac was returning from **B**, Gn 24:62
his son Isaac, who lived near **B**. Gn 25:11

BEER-SHEBA *(34)*
(AKA SHEBA)
wandered in the Wilderness of **B**. Gn 21:14
place was called **B** because it Gn 21:31
they had made a covenant at **B**, Gn 21:32
planted a tamarisk tree in **B**, Gn 21:33
got up and went together to **B**. Gn 22:19
And Abraham settled in **B**. Gn 22:19
From there he went up to **B**, Gn 26:23
of the city is **B** to this day. Gn 26:33
Jacob left **B** and went toward Gn 28:10
all that he had and came to **B**, Gn 46:1
Jacob left **B**. The sons of Israel Gn 46:5
Hazar-shual, **B**, Biziothiah, Jos 15:28
B (or Sheba), Moladah, Jos 19:2
from Dan to **B** and from the land Jdg 20:1
from Dan to **B** knew that Samuel 1Sm 3:20
They were judges in **B**. 1Sm 8:2
Israel and Judah from Dan to **B**." 2Sm 3:10
that all Israel from Dan to **B**— 2Sm 17:11
from Dan to **B** and register 2Sm 24:2
went to the Negev of Judah at **B**. 2Sm 24:7
from Dan to **B** 70,000 men died 2Sm 24:15
lived in safety from Dan to **B**, 1Kg 4:25
When he came to **B** that belonged 1Kg 19:3
name was Zibiah, who was from **B**. 2Kg 12:1
the high places from Geba to **B**, 2Kg 23:8
They lived in **B**, Moladah, 1Ch 4:28
Israel from **B** to Dan and bring 1Ch 21:2
the people from **B** to the hill 2Ch 19:4
⌊she was⌋ from **B**. 2Ch 24:1
Israel, from **B** to Dan, to come 2Ch 30:5
and **B** and its villages Neh 11:27
settled from **B** to the Valley Neh 11:30
or go to Gilgal or journey to **B**, Am 5:5
or "As the way of **B** lives"— Am 8:14

BEERA *(1)*
Shamma, Shilshah, Ithran, and **B**. 1Ch 7:37

BEERAH *(2)*
and his son **B**. Beerah was a 1Ch 5:6
B was a leader of the Reubenites, 1Ch 5:6

BEERI *(2)*
daughter of **B** the Hittite, Gn 26:34
to Hosea son of **B** during the Hs 1:1

BEEROTH *(4)*
(AKA BENE-JAAKAN)
traveled from **B** Bene-jaakan to Dt 10:6

Gibeon, Chephirah, **B**, and Jos 9:17
Gibeon, Ramah, **B**, Jos 18:25
B is also considered part of 2Sm 4:2

BEEROTH'S *(2)*
Chephirah's, and **B** people 743 Ezr 2:25
Chephirah's, and **B** men 743 Neh 7:29

BEEROTHITE *(5)*
sons of Rimmon the **B** of the 2Sm 4:2
sons of Rimmon the **B**, set out 2Sm 4:5
of Rimmon the **B**, "As surely as 2Sm 4:9
Naharai the **B**, the armor-bearer 2Sm 23:37
Naharai the **B**, the armor-bearer 1Ch 11:39

BEEROTHITES *(1)*
and the **B** fled to Gittaim and 2Sm 4:3

BEES *(3)*
chased you like a swarm of **b**. Dt 1:44
was a swarm of **b** with honey Jdg 14:8
They surrounded me like **b**; Ps 118:12

BEESHTERAH *(1)*
(AKA ASHTAROTH, ASHTEROTH-KARNAIM, KARNAIM)
and **B** with its pasturelands— Jos 21:27

BEFORE *(1138)*
(See pp. xi-xii.)

BEFOREHAND *(5)*
and did not hate him **b**. Jos 20:5
don't worry **b** what you will say. Mk 13:11
those who announced **b** the coming Ac 7:52
witnesses appointed **b** by God, Ac 10:41
that He prepared **b** for glory— Rm 9:23

BEG *(20)*
remained to **b** Queen Esther for Est 7:7
I could only **b** my judge for Jb 9:15
even if I **b** him with my own Jb 19:16
children will **b** from the poor, Jb 20:10
Will he **b** you for mercy or speak Jb 41:3
their time of disaster they **b**: Jr 2:27
and do not **b** Me, for I will not Jr 7:16
Little children **b** for bread, Lm 4:4
b You before God, don't torment Mk 5:7
they began to **b** Him to leave Mk 5:17
I **b** You, don't torment me!" Lk 8:28
I **b** You to look at my son, Lk 9:38
enough to dig; I'm ashamed to **b**. Lk 16:3
'then I **b** you to send him to my Lk 16:27
he could **b** from those entering Ac 3:2
used to sit and **b** at the Ac 3:10
I **b** you in your graciousness to Ac 24:4
Therefore I **b** you to listen to Ac 26:3
I **b** you that when I am present I 2Co 10:2
I **b** you, brothers: become like Gl 4:12

BEGAN *(191)*
that time people **b** to call on Gn 4:26
When mankind **b** to multiply on Gn 6:1
and the water **b** to subside. Gn 8:1
Isaac **b** to tremble Gn 27:33
Ephrath, Rachel **b** to give birth, Gn 35:16
the Nile and **b** to graze among Gn 41:2
the Nile and **b** to graze among Gn 41:18
and the seven years of famine **b**, Gn 41:54
As they **b** emptying their sacks, Gn 42:35
Now the people **b** complaining Nm 11:1
the people **b** to have sexual Nm 25:1
Moses **b** to explain this law, Dt 1:5
They **b** to worship other gods, Dt 29:26
southern border **b** at the tip Jos 15:2
the north side **b** at the Jordan, Jos 18:12
The south side **b** at the edge of Jos 18:15
judge⌋ and **b** to deliver Israel Jdg 10:1
of the LORD **b** to direct him Jdg 13:25
his hair **b** to grow back after Jdg 16:22
They **b** to attack the people as Jdg 20:31
the column of smoke **b** to go up Jdg 20:40
house of Israel **b** to seek the 1Sm 7:2
And Samuel ⌊**b** to lead⌋ the 1Sm 7:6
from the LORD **b** to torment him, 1Sm 16:14
and he **b** to rave inside the 1Sm 18:10
and they also **b** prophesying. 1Sm 19:21
and even they **b** prophesying. 1Sm 19:21
this incident **b** and stay beside 1Sm 20:19
old when he **b** his reign over 2Sm 2:10
years old when he **b** his reign; 2Sm 5:4
Solomon ⌊**b** to⌋ build the temple 1Kg 6:1
days the LORD **b** to reduce the 2Kg 10:32
days the LORD **b** sending Rezin 2Kg 15:37
and he **b** to teach them how they 2Kg 17:28
son of Zeruiah **b** to count them, 1Ch 27:24
Then Solomon **b** to build the 2Ch 3:1
b to build on the second ⌊day⌋ 2Ch 3:2
The moment they **b** ⌊their⌋ shouts 2Ch 20:22
They **b** the consecration on the 2Ch 29:17
When the burnt offerings **b**, 2Ch 29:27
of the LORD and the trumpets **b**, 2Ch 29:27
third month they **b** building up 2Ch 31:7
Since they **b** bringing the 2Ch 31:10
deed that he **b** in the service 2Ch 31:21
Josiah **b** to seek the God of his 2Ch 34:3
twelfth year he **b** to cleanse 2Ch 34:3
and his brothers **b** to build the Ezr 3:2
month they **b** to offer burnt Ezr 3:6
the captivity, **b** ⌊to build⌋. Ezr 3:8
of Jozadak **b** to rebuild God's Ezr 5:2
He **b** the journey from Babylon on Ezr 7:9
his fellow priests **b** rebuilding Neh 3:1
all the people **b** to eat and Neh 8:12
leader who **b** the thanksgiving Neh 11:17
When shadows **b** to fall on the Neh 13:19
After this Job **b** to speak and Jb 3:1
them, ⌊the rest⌋ **b** to seek Him; Ps 78:34
before a single one of them **b**. Ps 139:16
beginning, before the earth **b**. Pr 8:23
So I **b** to give myself over to Ec 2:20
So they **b** with the elders who Ezk 9:6
her promiscuity that **b** in Egypt, Ezk 23:8
which **b** in the land of Egypt, Ezk 23:27
So they **b** to serve in the king's Dn 1:19
hand appeared and **b** writing on Dn 5:5
spring crop first **b** to sprout— Am 7:1
They **b** work on the house of Hg 1:14
angels came and **b** to serve Him. Mt 4:11
From then on Jesus **b** to preach, Mt 4:17
Then He **b** to teach them, saying: Mt 5:2
she got up and **b** to serve Him. Mt 8:15
Jesus **b** to speak to the crowds Mt 11:7
were hungry and **b** to pick and Mt 12:1
His hometown and **b** to teach them Mt 13:54
then on Jesus **b** to point out to Mt 16:21
Him aside and **b** to rebuke Him, Mt 16:22
When he **b** to settle accounts, Mt 18:24
fell down and **b** begging him, Mt 18:29
they **b** to complain to the Mt 20:11
They **b** to argue among Mt 21:25
each one **b** to say to Him, Mt 26:22
He **b** to be sorrowful and deeply Mt 26:37
and the angels **b** to serve Him. Mk 1:13
on the Sabbath and **b** to teach. Mk 1:21
so they **b** to argue with one Mk 1:27
her, and she **b** to serve them. Mk 1:31
they **b** bringing to Him all those Mk 1:32
he went out and **b** to proclaim it Mk 1:45
His disciples **b** to make their Mk 2:23
Again He **b** to teach by the sea, Mk 4:1
Then they **b** to beg Him to leave Mk 5:17
So he went out and **b** to proclaim Mk 5:20
the girl got up and **b** to walk. Mk 5:42
He **b** to teach in the synagogue, Mk 6:2
Twelve and **b** to send them out Mk 6:7
Then He **b** to teach them many Mk 6:34
vicinity and **b** to carry the sick Mk 6:55
and he **b** to speak clearly. Mk 7:35
out and **b** to argue with Him, Mk 8:11
Then He **b** to teach them that the Mk 8:31
Him aside and **b** to rebuke Him. Mk 8:32
Then they **b** to question Him, Mk 9:11
He **b** teaching them once more. Mk 10:1
Peter **b** to tell Him, "Look, we Mk 10:28
b to tell them the things that Mk 10:32
b to be indignant with James Mk 10:41
Nazarene, he **b** to cry out, "Son Mk 10:47
he could see and **b** to follow Him Mk 10:52
complex and **b** to throw out those Mk 11:15
Then He **b** to teach them: Mk 11:17
b to argue among themselves: Mk 11:31
Then He **b** to speak to them in Mk 12:1
Then Jesus **b** by telling them: Mk 13:5
And they **b** to scold her. Mk 14:5
They **b** to be distressed and to Mk 14:19
and He **b** to be deeply distressed Mk 14:33
and **b** to pray that if it were Mk 14:35
Then some **b** to spit on Him, Mk 14:65
him again she **b** to tell those Mk 14:69
thought about it, he **b** to weep. Mk 14:72
chief priests **b** to accuse Him Mk 15:3
came up and **b** to ask ⌊Pilate⌋ Mk 15:8
And they **b** to salute Him, Mk 15:18
set free⌋, and he **b** to speak, Lk 1:64
she came up and **b** to thank God Lk 2:38
they **b** looking for Him among Lk 2:44
He **b** ⌊His ministry⌋, Jesus was Lk 3:23
b by saying to them, "Today as Lk 4:21
news about Him **b** to go out to Lk 4:37
immediately and **b** to serve them. Lk 4:39
fish, and their nets **b** to tear. Lk 5:6
so full that they **b** to sink. Lk 5:7
and the Pharisees **b** to reason: Lk 5:21
he got up and **b** to follow Him. Lk 5:28
dead man sat up and **b** to speak, Lk 7:15
b to speak to the crowds about Lk 7:24
and **b** to wash His feet with her Lk 7:38
table with Him **b** to say among Lk 7:49
were increasing, He **b** saying: Lk 11:29
the Pharisees **b** to oppose Him Lk 11:53
He **b** to say to His disciples Lk 12:1
restored and **b** to glorify God. Lk 13:13
they all **b** to make excuses. Lk 14:18
So they **b** to celebrate. Lk 15:24
see, and he **b** to follow Him, Lk 18:43
All who saw it **b** to complain, Lk 19:7
of the disciples **b** to praise God Lk 19:37
complex and **b** to throw out those Lk 19:45
He **b** to tell the people this Lk 20:9
So they **b** to argue among Lk 22:23
knelt down, and **b** to pray, Lk 22:41
b to accuse Him, saying, "We Lk 23:2
hanging there **b** to yell insults Lk 23:39
happened, he **b** to glorify God, Lk 23:47
came near and **b** to walk along Lk 24:15
Then they **b** to describe what had Lk 24:35
the Jews **b** persecuting Jesus Jn 5:16
is why the Jews **b** trying all the Jn 5:18
arose, and the sea **b** to churn. Jn 6:18
temple complex and **b** to teach. Jn 7:14
He sat down and **b** to teach them. Jn 8:2
into a basin and **b** to wash His Jn 13:5
all that Jesus **b** to do and teach Ac 1:1
the Holy Spirit and **b** to speak Ac 2:4
Holy Spirit and **b** to speak God's Ac 4:31
at daybreak and **b** to teach. Ac 5:21
Moses **b** to tremble and did not Ac 7:32
of the city and **b** to stone him. Ac 7:58
Immediately he **b** proclaiming Ac 9:20
Then Peter **b** to speak: Ac 10:34
Peter **b** to explain to them in an Ac 11:4
As I **b** to speak, the Holy Spirit Ac 11:15
came to Antioch and **b** speaking Ac 11:20
The populace **b** to shout, "It's Ac 12:22
jealousy and **b** to oppose what Ac 13:45
down from Judea and **b** to teach Ac 15:1
the dead, some **b** to ridicule him Ac 17:32
He **b** to speak boldly in the Ac 18:26
and they **b** to speak with ⌊other⌋ Ac 19:6
with rage and **b** to cry out, Ac 19:28
Tertullus **b** to accuse him and Ac 24:2
out his hand and **b** his defense: Ac 26:1
they **b** to jettison the cargo the Ac 27:18
he had broken it, he **b** to eat. Ac 27:35
they **b** to lighten the ship by Ac 27:38
but the stern **b** to break up with Ac 27:41
they **b** to leave after Paul made Ac 28:25
who a year ago **b** not only to do 2Co 8:10
in Christ Jesus before time **b**. 2Tm 1:9
lie, promised before time **b**, Ti 1:2
b to speak blasphemies against Rv 13:6

BEGGAR *(2)*
Timaeus), a blind **b**, was sitting Mk 10:46
had seen him as a **b** said, Jn 9:8

BEGGARS *(1)*
Let his children wander as **b**, Ps 109:10

BEGGED *(21)*
At that time I **b** the LORD: Dt 3:23
Then he **b** me, 'Stand over me and 2Sm 1:9
in front of Elijah and **b** him, 2Kg 1:13
and **b** him to revoke the evil of Est 8:3
out," the demons **b** Him, "send us Mt 8:31
b Him to leave their region. Mt 8:34
all that debt because you **b** me. Mt 18:32
to Him and, on his knees, **b** Him: Mk 1:40
demons **b** Him, "Send us to the Mk 5:12
marketplaces and **b** Him that they Mk 6:56
and **b** Jesus to lay His hand on Mk 7:32
man to Him and **b** Him to touch Mk 8:22
Jesus, fell facedown, and **b** Him: Lk 5:12

they **b** Him not to banish them Lk 8:31
The demons **b** Him to permit them Lk 8:32
I **b** Your disciples to drive it Lk 9:40
sent two men to him who **b** him, Ac 9:38
they **b** that these matters be Ac 13:42
local people **b** him not to go up Ac 21:12
they **b** us insistently for the 2Co 8:4
who heard it **b** that not another Heb 12:19

BEGGING *(10)*
or his children **b** bread. Ps 37:25
Israel weeping and **b** for mercy, Jr 3:21
They were **b** Him that they might Mt 14:36
fell down and began **b** him, Mt 18:29
And he kept **b** Him not to send Mk 5:10
kept **b** Him to be with Him. Mk 5:18
and kept **b** Him, "My little Mk 5:23
departed kept **b** Him to be with Lk 8:38
man was sitting by the road **b**. Lk 18:35
"Isn't this the man who sat **b**?" Jn 9:8

BEGIN *(15)*
the east will **b** at the east end Nm 34:3
B to take possession ⌊of it⌋; Dt 2:24
Today I will **b** to put the fear Dt 2:25
B to take possession of it.' Dt 2:31
Today I will **b** to exalt you in Jos 3:7
he will **b** to save Israel from Jdg 13:5
Now **b** the work, and may the LORD 1Ch 22:16
Now **b** at My sanctuary." Ezk 9:6
and they will **b** to decrease in Hs 8:10
onlookers will **b** to make fun of Lk 14:29
these things **b** to take place, Lk 21:28
Then they will **b** to say to the Lk 23:30
and the Sabbath was about to **b**. Lk 23:54
For, to **b** with, I hear that when 1Co 11:18
for judgment to **b** with God's 1Pt 4:17

BEGINNING *(89)*
In the **b** God created the heavens Gn 1:1
b with the oldest and ending Gn 44:12
is to be the **b** of months for you Ex 12:2
the **b** of each of your months. Nm 10:10
At the **b** of each of your months Nm 28:11
over it from the **b** to the end of Dt 11:12
the camp at the **b** of the middle Jdg 7:19
Bethlehem at the **b** of the barley Ru 1:22
about his family, from **b** to end. 1Sm 3:12
harvest at the **b** of the barley 2Sm 21:9
rock from the **b** of the harvest 2Sm 21:10
reign⌋, from **b** to end, note that 1Ch 29:29
reign⌋, from **b** to end, are 2Ch 9:29
reign⌋, from **b** to end, are 2Ch 12:15
reign⌋, from **b** to end, are 2Ch 16:11
reign⌋ from **b** to end are written 2Ch 20:34
reign⌋, from **b** to end, are 2Ch 25:26
Uzziah's ⌊reign⌋, from **b** to end. 2Ch 26:22
ways, from **b** to end, they are 2Ch 28:26
his words, from **b** to end, are 2Ch 35:27
offerings for the **b** of each Ezr 3:5
At the **b** of the reign of Ezr 4:6
has been established from the **b**; Ps 93:2
of the LORD is the **b** of wisdom; Ps 111:10
the LORD is the **b** of knowledge; Pr 1:7
me at the **b** of His creation, Pr 8:22
times, from the **b**, before the Pr 8:23
of the LORD is the **b** of wisdom, Pr 9:10
work God has done from **b** to end. Ec 3:11
a matter is better than its **b**; Ec 7:8
The **b** of the words of his mouth Ec 10:13
been declared to you from the **b**? Is 40:21
the generations from the **b**? Is 41:4
Who told about this from the **b**, Is 41:26
I declare the end from the **b**, Is 46:10
From the **b** I have not spoken in Is 48:16
on high from the **b** is the place Jr 17:12
At the **b** of the reign of Jr 26:1
the **b** of the reign of Zedekiah Jr 27:1
the **b** of the reign of Zedekiah Jr 28:1
about Elam at the **b** of the reign Jr 49:34
Moab's flank **b** with its frontier Ezk 25:9
our exile, at the **b** of the year, Ezk 40:1
entrance at the **b** of the Ezk 42:12
At the **b** of your petitions an Dn 9:23
This was the **b** of sin for Mc 1:13
And **b** to sink he cried out, Mt 14:30
them in the **b** made them male Mt 19:4
it was not like that from the **b**. Mt 19:8
events are the **b** of birth pains. Mt 24:8
place from the **b** of the world Mt 24:21
The **b** of the gospel of Jesus Mk 1:1
But from the **b** of creation God Mk 10:6
These are the **b** of birth pains. Mk 13:8
been from the **b** of the world, Mk 13:19
Then **b** with Moses and all the Lk 24:27
all the nations, **b** at Jerusalem. Lk 24:47
In the **b** was the Word, and the Jn 1:1
He was with God in the **b**. Jn 1:2
knew from the **b** those who would Jn 6:64
telling you from the very **b**," Jn 8:25
from the **b** and has not stood Jn 8:44
have been with Me from the **b**. Jn 15:27
you these things from the **b**, Jn 16:4
b from the baptism of John until Ac 1:22
of His holy prophets from the **b**. Ac 3:21
news about Jesus, **b** from that Ac 8:35
b from Galilee after the baptism Ac 10:37
on them, just as on us at the **b**. Ac 11:15
spent from the **b** among my own Ac 26:4
Are we **b** to commend ourselves 2Co 3:1
After **b** with the Spirit, are you Gl 3:3
He is the **b**, the firstborn from Col 1:18
because from the **b** God has 2Th 2:13
In the **b**, Lord, You established Heb 1:10
having neither **b** of days nor end Heb 7:3
been since the **b** of creation." 2Pt 3:4
was from the **b**, what we have 1Jn 1:1
that you have had from the **b**. 1Jn 2:7
know the One who is from the **b**. 1Jn 2:13
know the One who is from the **b**. 1Jn 2:14
heard from the **b** must remain in 1Jn 2:24
heard from the **b** remains in you, 1Jn 2:24
the Devil has sinned from the **b**. 1Jn 3:8
you have heard from the **b**: 1Jn 3:11
but one we have had from the **b**— 2Jn 5
as you have heard it from the **b**: 2Jn 6
the Omega, the **B** and the End. Rv 21:6
and the Last, the **B** and the End. Rv 22:13

BEGINNINGS *(1)*
even if your **b** were modest, Jb 8:7

BEGINS *(4)*
to the LORD **b** on the fifteenth Lv 23:34
festival ⌊that **b**⌋ on the Ezk 45:25
to the king (Aramaic **b** here): Dn 2:4
and if it **b** with us, what will 1Pt 4:17

BEGRUDGE *(1)*
will **b** the husband she embraces, Dt 28:56

BEGUN *(15)*
they have **b** to do this, then Gn 11:6
the LORD; the plague has **b**." Nm 16:46
the plague had **b** among the Nm 16:47
I have **b** to give Sihon and his Dt 2:31
have **b** to show Your greatness Dt 3:24
vineyard and not **b** to enjoy its Dt 20:6
Benjamin had **b** to strike them Jdg 20:39
before whom you have **b** to fall, Est 6:13
the practice they had **b**, Est 9:23
I have **b** to strike you severely, Mc 6:13
I have already **b** to curse them Mal 2:2
You have **b** to reign as kings 1Co 4:8
just as he had **b**, so he should 2Co 8:6
great power and have **b** to reign. Rv 11:17
the Almighty, has **b** to reign! Rv 19:6

BEHALF *(69)*
ask Ephron son of Zohar on my **b** Gn 23:8
to the LORD on **b** of his wife Gn 25:21
accepted on his **b** to make Lv 1:4
will make atonement on their **b**, Lv 4:20
atonement on his **b** for that Lv 4:26
will make atonement on his **b**, Lv 4:31
atonement on his **b** for the sin Lv 4:35
atonement on his **b** for his sin. Lv 5:6
atonement on his **b** for the sin Lv 5:10
atonement on his **b** concerning Lv 5:13
atonement on his **b** with the ram Lv 5:16
on his **b** for the error he Lv 5:18
on his **b** before the LORD Lv 6:7
and make atonement on her **b**; Lv 12:7
will make atonement on her **b**, Lv 12:8
on his **b** before the LORD Lv 19:22
will not be accepted on your **b**. Lv 22:20
as a service on **b** of the Nm 3:38
atonement on **b** of the Nazirite, Nm 6:11
to make atonement on their **b**, Nm 8:19
the LORD on **b** of the person who Nm 15:28
on your head on **b** of the dead, Dt 14:1
pray to the LORD on your **b**." 1Sm 7:5
out to the LORD on **b** of Israel, 1Sm 7:9
things to Nabal on David's **b**, 1Sm 25:9
will issue a command on your **b**." 2Sm 14:8
prayer on **b** of the land, 2Sm 24:25
speak on your **b** to the king or 2Kg 4:13
He rebuked kings on their **b**: 1Ch 16:21
LORD provide atonement on **b** 2Ch 30:18
Jerusalem to proclaim on your **b**: Neh 6:7
Eliashib had done on **b** of Tobiah Neh 13:7
told the king on Mordecai's **b**. Est 2:22
even now on your **b** and restore Jb 8:6
unjustly on God's **b** or speak Jb 13:7
more to be said on God's **b**. Jb 36:2
Your **b** my heart says, "Seek My Ps 27:8
You who have acted on our **b**. Ps 68:28
He rebuked kings on their **b**: Ps 105:14
the dead on **b** of the living? Is 8:19
who acts on **b** of the one who Is 64:4
a cry or a prayer on their **b**, Jr 7:16
up a cry or a prayer on their **b**, Jr 11:14
You to speak good on their **b**, Jr 18:20
Ask the LORD on our **b**, since Jr 21:2
Pray to the LORD on its **b**, Jr 29:7
will bear on My **b** a name of joy, Jr 33:9
to the LORD your God on our **b**, Jr 42:2
on **b** of this entire remnant Jr 42:2
to the LORD our God on our **b**, Jr 42:20
and take vengeance on your **b**; Jr 51:36
What can I say on your **b**? Lm 2:13
gap before Me on **b** of the land Ezk 22:30
make atonement on **b** of the house Ezk 45:17
a sin offering on **b** of himself Ezk 45:22
to the Father on your **b**. Jn 16:26
be dishonored on **b** of the name. Ac 5:41
the nations, on **b** of His name, Rm 1:5
circumcised on **b** of the truth Rm 15:8
in your prayers to God on my **b**: Rm 15:30
by many on our **b** for the gift 2Co 1:11
on Christ's **b**, "Be reconciled 2Co 5:20
Jesus on **b** of you Gentiles Eph 3:1
over my afflictions on your **b**, Eph 3:13
to you on Christ's **b** not only to Php 1:29
of the Messiah on your **b**, Col 1:7
there on our **b** as a forerunner, Heb 6:20
first beast on his **b** and compels Rv 13:12
to perform on **b** of the beast, Rv 13:14

BEHAVE *(2)*
and no longer **b** arrogantly. Dt 17:13
you see how they **b** in the cities Jr 7:17

BEHAVED *(4)*
You **b** more wickedly than all who 1Kg 14:9
the people still **b** corruptly. 2Ch 27:2
time before you **b** more corruptly Ezk 16:47
have not **b** as you and your Ezk 16:48

BEHAVING *(1)*
b promiscuously in their youth. Ezk 23:3

BEHAVIOR *(14)*
shameful **b** toward David. 1Sm 20:34
denounce his **b** to his face? Jb 21:31
He profit if you perfect your **b**? Jb 22:3
refuge in his destructive **b**." Ps 52:7
Wicked **b** is detestable to kings, Pr 16:12
by whether his **b** is pure and Pr 20:11
but the **b** of the innocent is Pr 21:8
Look at your **b** in the valley; Jr 2:23
embarrassed by your indecent **b**. Ezk 16:27
not to imitate your indecent **b**. Ezk 23:48
Their **b** before Me was like Ezk 36:17
women are to be reverent in **b**, Ti 2:3
carrying on in unrestrained **b**, 1Pt 4:3
unrestrained **b** of the immoral 2Pt 2:7

BEHEADED *(6)*
Then they **b** him, took his head, 2Sm 4:7
and had John **b** in the prison. Mt 14:10
John, the one I **b**, has been Mk 6:16
So he went and **b** him in prison, Mk 6:27
"I **b** John," Herod said, "but who Lk 9:9
who had been **b** because of their Rv 20:4

BEHEMOTH *(2)*
Look at **B**, which I made along Jb 40:15
the river rages, **B** is unafraid; Jb 40:23

BEHIND *(107)*
(See pp. xi-xii.)

BEHOLD *(1)*
That man will **b** His face with a Jb 33:26

BEING *(187)*
and the man became a living **b**. Gn 2:7

As she was **b** brought out, she Gn 38:25
that we are **b** punished for what Gn 42:21
your servants are **b** beaten, Ex 5:16
the LORD, **b** jealous by nature Ex 34:14
without **b** aware of it, he is Lv 5:2
defiled—without **b** aware of it, Lv 5:3
an oath—without **b** aware of it, Lv 5:4
the one **b** purified must wash his Nm 19:19
keep you from **b** defeated by your Dt 1:42
Israel by **b** promiscuous in her Dt 22:21
destroyed every living **b**, Jos 10:40
has stopped **b** concerned about 1Sm 10:2
you from **b** king over Israel. 1Sm 15:26
that women are **b** kept from us, 1Sm 21:5
Abiathar from **b** the LORD's 1Kg 2:27
the temple while it was **b** built. 1Kg 6:7
Maacah from **b** queen mother 1Kg 15:13
his hands and **b** like the house 1Kg 16:7
If you see me **b** taken from you, 2Kg 2:10
the king's sons were **b** cared for 2Kg 10:6
sons who were **b** killed and ⌊put⌋ 2Kg 11:2
b responsible for the courts and 1Ch 23:28
from **b** queen mother because she 2Ch 15:16
sons who were **b** killed and put 2Ch 22:11
It is **b** built with cut stones, Ezr 5:8
its beams are **b** set in the walls Ezr 5:8
This work is **b** done diligently Ezr 5:8
wives away, and **b** guilty, ⌊they Ezr 10:19
and that the gaps were **b** closed, Neh 4:7
kinds of goods were **b** brought to Neh 13:15
things, **b** led astray, for Jb 15:31
righteousness ⌊another⌋ human **b**. Jb 35:8
whole **b** is shaken with terror. Ps 6:3
sorrow—my whole **b** as well. Ps 31:9
He spoke, and it came into **b**; Ps 33:9
and my innermost **b** was wounded, Ps 73:21
praises with the whole of my **b**. Ps 108:1
gaining wisdom and **b** instructed; Pr 1:2
goes down to one's innermost **b**. Pr 18:8
My innermost **b** will cheer when Pr 23:16
Rescue those **b** taken off to Pr 24:11
goes down to one's innermost **b**. Pr 26:22
of oppression **b** done under the Ec 4:1
to the Teacher **b** a wise man, Ec 12:9
nations **b** gathered together! Is 13:4
my innermost **b** for Kir-heres. Is 16:11
listen like those **b** instructed. Is 50:4
did not resemble a human **b**— Is 52:14
with their kings **b** led ⌊in Is 60:11
Instead of your **b** deserted and Is 60:15
and so they all came into **b**. Is 66:2
they themselves ⌊**b** provoked⌋ to Jr 7:19
my innermost **b** will weep in Jr 13:17
run away from **b** Your shepherd, Jr 17:16
My inner **b** yearns for him; Jr 31:20
Judah who were **b** exiled to Jr 40:1
no human **b** will even stay in it Jr 49:18
no human **b** will even stay in it Jr 49:33
no human **b** will even stay in it Jr 50:40
where no human **b** passes through. Jr 51:43
For you are not **b** sent to a Ezk 3:5
⌊You are⌋ not ⌊**b** sent⌋ to many Ezk 3:6
instead of one **b** paid to you, Ezk 16:34
stop you from **b** a prostitute, Ezk 16:41
and every human **b** on the face of Ezk 38:20
each unit **b** the standard length Ezk 43:13
gates of the city **b** named for Ezk 48:31
him, and **b** intimidated, he Dn 11:30
came into **b** until that time. Dn 12:1
Joseph, **b** a righteous man Mt 1:19
And **b** warned in a dream not to Mt 2:12
And **b** warned in a dream, he Mt 2:22
that the boat was **b** swamped by Mt 8:24
can you escape **b** condemned to Mt 23:33
Son of Man is **b** betrayed into Mt 26:45
while He was **b** accused by the Mt 27:12
He saw the heavens **b** torn open Mk 1:10
40 days, **b** tempted by Satan. Mk 1:13
the boat was already **b** swamped. Mk 4:37
He saw them **b** battered as they Mk 6:48
The Son of Man is **b** betrayed Mk 9:31
concerning the dead **b** raised— Mk 12:26
Son of Man is **b** betrayed into Mk 14:41
these things were **b** talked about Lk 1:65
at what was **b** said about Him. Lk 2:33
b rebuked by him about Herodias, Lk 3:19
in their synagogues, **b** acclaimed Lk 4:15
a dead man was **b** carried out. Lk 7:12
they were **b** swamped and were in Lk 8:23
Him, "are there few **b** saved?" Lk 13:23
And **b** in torment in Hades, Lk 16:23
B asked by the Pharisees when Lk 17:20
and **b** amazed at His answer, Lk 20:26
B in anguish, He prayed more Lk 22:44
were coming and **b** baptized, Jn 3:23
Him previously, **b** one of them— Jn 7:50
because You—**b** a man—make Jn 10:33
but **b** high priest that year he Jn 11:51
and signs were **b** performed Ac 2:43
to them those who were **b** saved. Ac 2:47
If we are **b** examined today about Ac 4:9
wonders were **b** done among the Ac 5:12
their widows were **b** overlooked Ac 6:1
This **b** so, he fathered Isaac and Ac 7:8
he saw one of them **b** mistreated, Ac 7:24
miracles that were **b** performed. Ac 8:13
would keep me from **b** baptized?" Ac 8:36
b built up and walking in the Ac 9:31
a large sheet **b** lowered to the Ac 10:11
prevent these from **b** baptized, Ac 10:47
a large sheet **b** lowered from Ac 11:5
but prayer was **b** made earnestly Ac 12:5
B sent out by the Holy Spirit, Ac 13:4
of sins is **b** proclaimed to you, Ac 13:38
Then, **b** sent off, they went down Ac 15:30
after **b** commended to the grace Ac 15:40
B God's offspring, then, we Ac 17:29
and **b** of the same occupation, Ac 18:3
b fervent in spirit, he spoke Ac 18:25
we run a risk of **b** charged with Ac 19:40
B zealous for God, just as all Ac 22:3
Your witness Stephen was **b** shed, Ac 22:20
why Paul was **b** accused by the Ac 22:30
am **b** judged because of the hope Ac 23:6
'Today I am **b** judged before you Ac 24:21
of this hope I am **b** accused by Ac 26:7
B greatly enraged at them, Ac 26:11
Because we were **b** severely Ac 27:18
your faith is **b** reported in all Rm 1:8
b understood through what He has Rm 1:20
for every human **b** who does evil, Rm 2:9
b instructed from the law, Rm 2:18
For if their **b** rejected is world Rm 11:15
to us who are **b** saved it is 1Co 1:18
conscience, **b** weak, is defiled 1Co 8:7
the law—not **b** outside God's 1Co 9:21
to dumb idols—**b** led astray. 1Co 12:2
other person is not **b** built up. 1Co 14:17
they do who are **b** baptized for 1Co 15:29
man Adam became a living **b**; 1Co 15:45
those who are **b** saved and among 2Co 2:15
the Lord and are **b** transformed 2Co 3:18
our outer person is **b** destroyed, 2Co 4:16
inner person is **b** renewed day by 2Co 4:16
as **b** chastened yet not killed; 2Co 6:9
our urging and, **b** very diligent, 2Co 8:17
this gift that is **b** administered 2Co 8:19
the law no human **b** will be Gl 2:16
only to avoid **b** persecuted for Gl 6:12
building is **b** fitted together Eph 2:21
you also are **b** built together Eph 2:22
b rooted and firmly established Eph 3:17
you are **b** renewed in the spirit Eph 4:23
work only⌋ while **b** watched, Eph 6:6
not **b** frightened in any way by Php 1:28
His sufferings, **b** conformed to Php 3:10
the secret ⌊of **b** content⌋— Php 4:12
what is destroyed by **b** used up; Col 2:22
who is **b** renewed in knowledge Col 3:10
don't work only while **b** watched, Col 3:22
and our **b** gathered to Him: 2Th 2:1
to the point of **b** bound like a 2Tm 2:9
worse, deceiving and **b** deceived. 2Tm 3:13
For I am already **b** poured out as 2Tm 4:6
and sins, **b** self-condemned. Ti 3:11
be described as **b** in the order Heb 7:11
point of what is **b** said is this: Heb 8:1
they have stopped **b** offered, Heb 10:2
after **b** warned about what was Heb 11:7
b afraid of the king's anger, Heb 11:27
fell down after **b** encircled for Heb 11:30
gained strength after **b** weak, Heb 11:34
say, "I am **b** tempted by God." Jms 1:13
who are **b** protected by God's 1Pt 1:5
for action, **b** self-disciplined 1Pt 1:13
are **b** built into a spiritual 1Pt 2:5
after **b** put to death in the 1Pt 3:18
while an ark was **b** prepared; 1Pt 3:20
but **b** examples to the flock. 1Pt 5:3
sufferings are **b** experienced by 1Pt 5:9
will keep you from **b** useless or 2Pt 1:8
b kept until the day of judgment 2Pt 3:7
have a reputation for **b** alive, Rv 3:1
like a scroll **b** rolled up; Rv 6:14
the filthy go on **b** made filthy; Rv 22:11
let the holy go on **b** made holy." Rv 22:11

BEINGS *(5)*
you heavenly **b**—give the LORD Ps 29:1
the heavenly **b** is like the LORD Ps 89:6
praise before the heavenly **b**. Ps 138:1
will give human **b** in your place, Is 43:4
and blaspheme glorious **b**. Jd 8

BEL *(3)*
(AKA MARDUK, MERODACH)
B crouches; Nebo cowers. Their Is 46:1
is captured; **B** is put to shame; Jr 50:2
I will punish **B** in Babylon. Jr 51:44

BELA *(11)*
(AKA ZOAR)
the king of **B** (that is, Zoar) Gn 14:2
the king of **B** (that is, Zoar) Gn 14:8
B son of Beor ruled in Edom; Gn 36:32
When **B** died, Jobab son of Zerah Gn 36:33
B, Becher, Ashbel, Gera, Naaman, Gn 46:21
the Belaite clan from **B**; Nm 26:38
the Israelites: **B** son of Beor. 1Ch 1:43
When **B** died, Jobab son of Zerah 1Ch 1:44
and **B** son of Azaz, son of Shema, 1Ch 5:8
B, Becher, and Jediael. 1Ch 7:6
fathered **B**, his firstborn; 1Ch 8:1

BELA'S *(4)*
B descendants ⌊from⌋ Ard and Nm 26:40
B town was named Dinhabah. 1Ch 1:43
B sons: Ezbon, Uzzi, Uzziel, 1Ch 7:7
B sons: Addar, Gera, Abihud, 1Ch 8:3

BELAITE *(1)*
the **B** clan from Bela; Nm 26:38

BELIAL *(1)*
does Christ have with **B**? 2Co 6:15

BELIEF *(1)*
and through **b** in the truth. 2Th 2:13

BELIEVE *(162)*
stunned, for he did not **b** them. Gn 45:26
if they won't **b** me and will not Ex 4:1
so they will **b** that the LORD, Ex 4:5
they will not **b** you and will not Ex 4:8
they may **b** the evidence of the Ex 4:8
if they don't **b** even these two Ex 4:9
with you and will always **b** you." Ex 19:9
You did not **b** or obey Him. Dt 9:23
do you really **b** he's showing 2Sm 10:3
But I didn't **b** the reports until 1Kg 10:7
did not **b** the LORD their God. 2Kg 17:14
do you really **b** he's showing 1Ch 19:3
But I didn't **b** their reports 2Ch 9:6
B in the LORD your God, and you 2Ch 20:20
b in His prophets, and you will 2Ch 20:20
Don't **b** him, for no god of any 2Ch 32:15
do not **b** He would pay attention Jb 9:16
He doesn't **b** he will return from Jb 15:22
at them, they couldn't **b** ⌊it⌋; Jb 29:24
they did not **b** God or rely on Ps 78:22
and did not **b** His wonderful Ps 78:32
land and did not **b** His promise. Ps 106:24
The inexperienced **b** anything, Pr 14:15
don't **b** him, for there Pr 26:25
you may know and **b** Me and Is 43:10
son of Ahikam would not **b** them. Jr 40:14
did not **b** that an enemy Lm 4:12
you will not **b** when you hear Hab 1:5
"Do you **b** that I can do this?" Mt 9:28
these little ones who **b** in Me— Mt 18:6
And if you **b**, you will receive Mt 21:22
'Then why didn't you **b** him?' Mt 21:25
and you didn't **b** him. Mt 21:32
and prostitutes did **b** him, Mt 21:32
your minds then and **b** him. Mt 21:32
or, 'Over here!' do not **b** it! Mt 24:23
the inner rooms!' do not **b** it. Mt 24:26
the cross, and we will **b** in Him. Mt 27:42
Repent and **b** in the good news!" Mk 1:15
Don't be afraid. Only **b**." Mk 5:36

of the boy cried out, "I do **b**! Mk 9:24
these little ones who **b** in Me— Mk 9:42
b that you have received them, Mk 11:24
'Then why didn't you **b** him?' Mk 11:31
Look—there!' do not **b** it! Mk 13:21
so that we may see and **b**." Mk 15:32
seen by her, they did not **b** it. Mk 16:11
who did not **b** them either. Mk 16:13
they did not **b** those who saw Him Mk 16:14
whoever does not **b** will be Mk 16:16
will accompany those who **b**: Mk 16:17
because you did not **b** my words, Lk 1:20
they may not **b** and be saved. Lk 8:12
these **b** for a while and depart Lk 8:13
b, and she will be made well. Lk 8:50
say, 'Why didn't you **b** him?' Lk 20:5
I do tell you, you will not **b**. Lk 22:67
and they did not **b** the women. Lk 24:11
slow you are to **b** in your hearts Lk 24:25
still could not **b** because of Lk 24:41
so that all might **b** through him. Jn 1:7
to those who **b** in His name, Jn 1:12
Do you **b** ⌊only⌋ because I told Jn 1:50
happen on earth and you don't **b**, Jn 3:12
how will you **b** if I tell you Jn 3:12
who does not **b** is already judged Jn 3:18
who refuses to **b** in the Son will Jn 3:36
Jesus told her, "**B** Me, woman, an Jn 4:21
We no longer **b** because of what Jn 4:42
and wonders, you will not **b**." Jn 4:48
you don't **b** the One He sent. Jn 5:38
How can you **b**? While accepting Jn 5:44
Moses, you would **b** Me, because Jn 5:46
But if you don't **b** his writings, Jn 5:47
how will you **b** My words?" Jn 5:47
you **b** in the One He has sent. Jn 6:29
to do so we may see and **b** You?" Jn 6:30
seen Me, and yet you do not **b**. Jn 6:36
are some among you who don't **b**." Jn 6:64
who would not **b** and the one who Jn 6:64
We have come to **b** and know that Jn 6:69
if you do not **b** that I am ⌊He⌋, Jn 8:24
tell the truth, you do not **b** Me. Jn 8:45
the truth, why don't you **b** Me? Jn 8:46
Jews did not **b** this about him Jn 9:18
"Do you **b** in the Son of Man?" Jn 9:35
He, Sir, that I may **b** in Him?" Jn 9:36
"I **b**, Lord!" he said, and he Jn 9:38
"I did tell you and you don't **b**," Jn 10:25
But you don't **b** because you are Jn 10:26
My Father's works, don't **b** Me. Jn 10:37
doing them and you don't **b** Me, Jn 10:38
don't believe Me, **b** the works. Jn 10:38
wasn't there so that you may **b**. Jn 11:15
die—ever. Do you **b** this?" Jn 11:26
she told Him, "I **b** You are the Jn 11:27
so they may **b** You sent Me." Jn 11:42
way, everybody will **b** in Him! Jn 11:48
b in the light so that you may Jn 12:36
presence, they did not **b** in Him. Jn 12:37
is why they were unable to **b**, Jn 12:39
many did **b** in Him even among the Jn 12:42
you will **b** that I am ⌊He⌋. Jn 13:19
be troubled. **B** in God; believe Jn 14:1
Believe in God; **b** also in Me. Jn 14:1
Don't you **b** that I am in the Jn 14:10
B Me that I am in the Father and Jn 14:11
b because of the works Jn 14:11
when it does happen you may **b**. Jn 14:29
because they do not **b** in Me; Jn 16:9
we **b** that You came from God. Jn 16:30
to them, "Do you now **b**? Jn 16:31
for those who **b** in Me through Jn 17:20
so the world may **b** You sent Me. Jn 17:21
so that you also may **b**. Jn 19:35
into His side, I will never **b**!" Jn 20:25
Those who **b** without seeing are Jn 20:29
so that you may **b** Jesus is the Jn 20:31
If you **b** with all your heart you Ac 8:37
I **b** that Jesus Christ is the Son Ac 8:37
they did not **b** he was a disciple Ac 9:26
a work that you will never **b**, Ac 13:41
Jews who refused to **b** stirred up Ac 14:2
hear the gospel message and **b**. Ac 15:7
we **b** we are saved through the Ac 15:11
So they said, "**B** on the Lord Ac 16:31
that they should **b** in the One Ac 19:4
became hardened and would not **b**, Ac 19:9
Agrippa, do you **b** the prophets? Ac 26:27
the prophets? I know you **b**." Ac 26:27
because I **b** God that it will be Ac 27:25
he said, but others did not **b**. Ac 28:24
If some did not **b**, will their Rm 3:3
to all who **b**, since there is no Rm 3:22
father of all who **b** but are not Rm 4:11
to us who **b** in Him who raised Rm 4:24
we **b** that we will also live with Rm 6:8
and **b** in your heart that God Rm 10:9
how can they **b** without hearing Rm 10:14
to save those who **b** through the 1Co 1:21
among you, and in part I **b** it. 1Co 11:18
spoke, we also **b**, and therefore 2Co 4:13
might be given to those who **b**. Gl 3:22
of His power to us who **b**, Eph 1:19
behalf not only to **b** in Him, Php 1:29
Since we **b** that Jesus died and 1Th 4:14
that they will **b** what is false, 2Th 2:11
those who did not **b** the truth 2Th 2:12
those who would **b** in Him for 1Tm 1:16
by those who **b** and know the 1Tm 4:3
especially of those who **b**. 1Tm 4:10
to Him must **b** that He exists Heb 11:6
You **b** that God is one; Jms 2:19
The demons also **b**—and they Jms 2:19
you **b** in Him and rejoice with 1Pt 1:8
So the honor is for you who **b**; 1Pt 2:7
that we **b** in the name of His Son 1Jn 3:23
friends, do not **b** every spirit, 1Jn 4:1
to know and to **b** the love that 1Jn 4:16
who does not **b** God has made Him 1Jn 5:10
things to you who **b** in the name 1Jn 5:13
destroyed those who did not **b**; Jd 5

BELIEVED *(74)*

b the LORD, and He credited Gn 15:6
people **b**, and when they heard Ex 4:31
the LORD and **b** in Him and in His Ex 14:31
they **b** His promises and sang Ps 106:12
I **b**, even when I said, "I am Ps 116:10
Who has **b** what we have heard? Is 53:1
The men of Nineveh **b** in God. Jnh 3:5
you have **b**, let it be done for Mt 8:13
She who has **b** is blessed because Lk 1:45
and His disciples **b** in Him. Jn 2:11
And they **b** the Scripture and the Jn 2:22
because he has not **b** in the name Jn 3:18
from that town **b** in Him because Jn 4:39
Many more **b** because of what He Jn 4:41
The man **b** what Jesus said to Jn 4:50
Then he himself **b**, along with Jn 4:53
For if you **b** Moses, you would Jn 5:46
not even His brothers **b** in Him. Jn 7:5
the crowd **b** in Him and said, Jn 7:31
whom those who **b** in Him were Jn 7:39
Have any of the rulers **b** in Him? Jn 7:48
these things, many **b** in Him. Jn 8:30
said to the Jews who had **b** Him, Jn 8:31
And many **b** in Him there. Jn 10:42
you that if you **b** you would see Jn 11:40
and saw what He did **b** in Him. Jn 11:45
Lord, who has **b** our message? Jn 12:38
loved Me and have **b** that I came Jn 16:27
They have **b** that You sent Me. Jn 17:8
entered the tomb, saw, and **b**. Jn 20:8
you have seen Me, you have **b**. Jn 20:29
those who heard the message **b**, Ac 4:4
of those who **b** were of one heart Ac 4:32
But when they **b** Philip, as he Ac 8:12
Then even Simon himself **b**. Ac 8:13
Joppa, and many **b** in the Lord. Ac 9:42
to us when we **b** on the Lord Ac 11:17
large number who **b** turned to the Ac 11:21
b and was astonished at the Ac 13:12
appointed to eternal life **b**. Ac 13:48
of both Jews and Greeks **b**. Ac 14:1
to the Lord in whom they had **b**. Ac 14:23
because he had **b** God with his Ac 16:34
many of them **b**, including a Ac 17:12
some men joined him and **b**, Ac 17:34
the synagogue, **b** the Lord, along Ac 18:8
when they heard, **b** and were Ac 18:8
those who had **b** through grace. Ac 18:27
the Holy Spirit when you **b**?" Ac 19:2
of Jews there are who have **b**, Ac 21:20
to the Gentiles who have **b**, Ac 21:25
I had those who **b** in You Ac 22:19
Abraham **b** God, and it was Rm 4:3
He **b** in God, who gives life to Rm 4:17
with hope he **b**, so that he Rm 4:18
on Him in whom they have not **b**? Rm 10:14
Lord, who has **b** our message? Rm 10:16
is nearer than when we first **b**. Rm 13:11
are servants through whom you **b**, 1Co 3:5
unless you **b** to no purpose. 1Co 15:2
so we preach and so you have **b**. 1Co 15:11
is written, I **b**, therefore I 2Co 4:13
And we have **b** in Christ Jesus, Gl 2:16
Just as Abraham **b** God, and it Gl 3:6
in Him when you **b**—were sealed Eph 1:13
admired by all those who have **b**, 2Th 1:10
our testimony among you was **b**. 2Th 1:10
the Gentiles, **b** on in the world, 1Tm 3:16
whom I have **b** and am persuaded 2Tm 1:12
you have learned and firmly **b**, 2Tm 3:14
those who have **b** God might be Ti 3:8
for we who have **b** enter the rest Heb 4:3
says, Abraham **b** God, and it was Jms 2:23
he has not **b** in the testimony 1Jn 5:10

BELIEVER *(3)*

be an unbeliever, but a **b**." Jn 20:27
you consider me a **b** in the Lord, Ac 16:15
Or what does a **b** have in common 2Co 6:15

BELIEVERS *(17)*

Now all the **b** were together and Ac 2:44
B were added to the Lord in Ac 5:14
The circumcised **b** who had come Ac 10:45
But some of the **b** from the party Ac 15:5
had become **b** came confessing Ac 19:18
we found **b** and were invited Ac 28:14
Now the **b** from there had heard Ac 28:15
not to **b** but to unbelievers. 1Co 14:22
not for unbelievers but for **b**. 1Co 14:22
the saints and **b** in Christ Jesus Eph 1:1
to all the **b** in Macedonia 1Th 1:7
conducted ourselves with you **b**. 1Th 2:10
also works effectively in you **b**. 1Th 2:13
an example to the **b** in speech, 1Tm 4:12
service are **b** and dearly loved 1Tm 6:2
who through Him are **b** in God, 1Pt 1:21
should love **b**, and be 1Pt 3:8

BELIEVES *(33)*

one who **b** will be unshakable. Is 28:16
is possible to the one who **b**." Mk 9:23
but **b** that what he says will Mk 11:23
Whoever **b** and is baptized will Mk 16:16
everyone who **b** in Him will have Jn 3:15
everyone who **b** in Him will not Jn 3:16
Anyone who **b** in Him is not Jn 3:18
The one who **b** in the Son has Jn 3:36
My word and **b** Him who sent Me Jn 5:24
and no one who **b** in Me will ever Jn 6:35
the Son and **b** in Him may have Jn 6:40
Anyone who **b** has eternal life. Jn 6:47
The one who **b** in Me, as the Jn 7:38
The one who **b** in Me, even if he Jn 11:25
who lives and **b** in Me will never Jn 11:26
The one who **b** in Me believes not Jn 12:44
who believes in Me **b** not in Me, Jn 12:44
everyone who **b** in Me would not Jn 12:46
The one who **b** in Me will also do Jn 14:12
name everyone who **b** in Him will Ac 10:43
and everyone who **b** in Him is Ac 13:39
for salvation to everyone who **b**, Rm 1:16
but **b** on Him who declares Rm 4:5
the one who **b** on Him will not Rm 9:33
righteousness to everyone who **b**. Rm 10:4
With the heart one **b**, resulting Rm 10:10
No one who **b** on Him will be put Rm 10:11
person **b** he may eat anything, Rm 14:2
all things, **b** all things, hopes 1Co 13:7
and the one who **b** in Him will 1Pt 2:6
Everyone who **b** that Jesus is the 1Jn 5:1
but the one who **b** that Jesus is 1Jn 5:5
The one who **b** in the Son of God 1Jn 5:10

BELIEVING *(7)*

deserting them and **b** in Jesus. Jn 12:11
by **b** you may have life in His Jn 20:31
the son of a **b** Jewish woman, Ac 16:1
b all the things that are Ac 24:14
you with all joy and peace in **b**, Rm 15:13
If any **b** woman has widows, 1Tm 5:16
those who have **b** masters should 1Tm 6:2

BELL *(1)*

b and a pomegranate alternating Ex 39:26

BELLIES *(1)*
You fill their **b** with what You Ps 17:14

BELLOWS *(1)*
The **b** blow, blasting the lead Jr 6:29

BELLS *(5)*
Put gold **b** between them all the Ex 28:33
that⌋ gold **b** and pomegranates Ex 28:34
They made **b** of pure gold and Ex 39:25
gold and attached the **b** between Ex 39:25
will be on the **b** of the horses. Zch 14:20

BELLY *(12)*
move on your **b** and eat dust all Gn 3:14
moves on its **b** or walks on all Lv 11:42
thigh shrivel and your **b** swell. Nm 5:21
causing ⌊your⌋ **b** to swell and Nm 5:22
her **b** will swell, and her thigh Nm 5:27
and the woman—through her **b**. Nm 25:8
and plunged it into Eglon's **b**. Jdg 3:21
withdraw the sword from his **b**. Jdg 3:22
power in the muscles of his **b**. Jb 40:16
he filled his **b** with my Jr 51:34
out for help in the **b** of Sheol; Jnh 2:2
Jonah was in the **b** of the great Mt 12:40

BELONG *(74)*
a land that does not **b** to them; Gn 15:13
you and asks, 'Who do you **b** to? Gn 32:17
'They **b** to your servant Jacob. Gn 32:18
the man to whom these items **b**." Gn 38:25
Don't interpretations **b** to God? Gn 40:8
land does not **b** to Pharaoh. Gn 47:26
and Manasseh **b** to me just as Gn 48:5
her children **b** to her master, Ex 21:4
will **b** to Aaron and his sons Ex 29:28
garments that **b** to Aaron are to Ex 29:29
to Aaron are to **b** to his sons Ex 29:29
offering will **b** to Aaron and his Lv 2:3
offering will **b** to Aaron and his Lv 2:10
The rest will **b** to the priest, Lv 5:13
It will **b** to the priest who Lv 7:14
It will **b** permanently to you and Lv 10:15
divisions who **b** to Judah's Nm 2:9
divisions who **b** to Reuben's Nm 2:16
divisions who **b** to Ephraim's Nm 2:24
total number who **b** to Dan's Nm 2:31
the womb. The Levites **b** to Me, Nm 3:12
cattle. The Levites **b** to Me; I Nm 3:45
that the Levites will **b** to Me. Nm 8:14
bring to the LORD, **b** to you. Nm 18:13
And this land will **b** to you as a Nm 32:22
This will **b** to them as Nm 35:5
heavens, **b** to the LORD your Dt 10:14
hidden things **b** to the LORD our Dt 29:29
revealed things **b** to us and our Dt 29:29
and Urim **b** to Your faithful Dt 33:8
and all who **b** to them, and save Jos 2:13
Ammonites will **b** to the LORD, Jdg 11:31
said to him, "Who do you **b** to? 1Sm 30:13
Jerusalem, where they **b**, and put Ezr 6:5
and vineyards **b** to others." Neh 5:5
Wisdom and strength **b** to God; Jb 12:13
True wisdom and power **b** to Him. Jb 12:16
Dominion and dread **b** to Him, Jb 25:2
its inhabitants, **b** to the LORD; Ps 24:1
leaders of the earth **b** to God; Ps 47:9
for all the nations **b** to You. Ps 82:8
of the heart **b** to man, Pr 16:1
sayings⌋ also **b** to the wise: Pr 24:23
b to my love, and his desire is Sg 7:10
for they do not **b** to the LORD. Jr 5:10
life of the son—both **b** to Me. Ezk 18:4
to the LORD⌋ will **b** to them. Ezk 44:29
gifts will **b** to the priests. Ezk 44:30
it will **b** to his sons. Ezk 46:16
it will **b** to that servant until Ezk 46:17
property will **b** to the prince. Ezk 48:21
Benjamin will **b** to the prince. Ezk 48:22
for wisdom and power **b** to Him. Dn 2:20
forgiveness **b** to the Lord our Dn 9:9
be promiscuous or **b** to any man, Hs 3:3
coastland will **b** to the remnant Zph 2:7
"The silver and gold **b** to Me"— Hg 2:8
since you **b** to the Messiah— Mk 9:41
of the God I **b** to and serve Ac 27:23
so that you may **b** to another— Rm 7:4
of Christ, he does not **b** to Him. Rm 8:9
and to them **b** the adoption, Rm 9:4
live or die, we **b** to the Lord. Rm 14:8
Greet those who **b** to the Rm 16:10
Greet those who **b** to the Rm 16:11
and you **b** to Christ, and Christ 1Co 3:23
a hand, I don't **b** to the body," 1Co 12:15
an eye, I don't **b** to the body," 1Co 12:16
Now those who **b** to Christ Jesus Gl 5:24
for those who **b** to the household Gl 6:10
To Him **b** the glory and the power 1Pt 4:11
the things that **b** to the world. 1Jn 2:15
us, but they did not **b** to us; 1Jn 2:19
glory, and power **b** to our God, Rv 19:1

BELONGED *(32)*
that the weak sheep **b** to Laban Gn 30:42
from what **b** to our father." Gn 31:1
Sheol with all that **b** to them. Nm 16:33
brothers, and all who **b** to her. Jos 6:23
all who **b** to her, because she Jos 6:25
Hebron has **b** to Caleb son of Jos 14:14
The land of Gilead **b** to the rest Jos 17:6
region of Tappuah **b** to Manasseh, Jos 17:8
Manasseh's border **b** to the Jos 17:8
cities **b** to Ephraim among Jos 17:9
was in Ophrah, which **b** to Joash, Jdg 6:11
and the priest that **b** to him, Jdg 18:27
a valley that **b** to Beth-rehob. Jdg 18:28
of land that **b** to our brother Ru 4:3
everything that **b** to Elimelech, Ru 4:9
was in Egypt and **b** to Pharaoh's 1Sm 2:27
everything that **b** to this man 1Sm 25:21
all that **b** to Saul and his 2Sm 9:9
cities that **b** to Solomon, 1Kg 9:19
to Beer-sheba that **b** to Judah, 1Kg 19:3
since it **b** to the priests. 2Kg 12:16
which had **b** to Judah—are 2Kg 14:28
everything that **b** to the king of 2Kg 24:7
cities that **b** to Solomon, 2Ch 8:6
while the land **b** to a powerful Jb 22:8
the boats, which **b** to Simon, and Lk 5:3
those who **b** to the party of the Ac 5:17
he found any who **b** to the Way, Ac 9:2
some who **b** to the church, Ac 12:1
as if you still **b** to the world? Col 2:20
things are said **b** to a different Heb 7:13
for if they had **b** to us, they 1Jn 2:19

BELONGING *(23)*
who was at the oaks **b** to Mamre Gn 14:13
number of persons **b** to Jacob— Gn 46:26
An inheritance **b** to the Nm 36:7
plateau land, **b** to the Dt 4:43
in Gilead, **b** to the Gadites; Dt 4:43
Golan in Bashan, **b** to the Dt 4:43
a holy people **b** to the LORD your Dt 7:6
a holy people **b** to the LORD your Dt 14:2
a holy people **b** to the LORD your Dt 14:21
the portion of land **b** to Boaz, Ru 2:3
a man **b** to the family of the 2Sm 16:5
the plot of ground **b** to Naboth 2Kg 9:25
who were warriors **b** to all the 1Ch 7:5
the heads of families **b** to Ladan 1Ch 26:21
all the lands **b** to the 2Ch 34:33
a day **b** to the LORD of Hosts is Is 2:12
a day **b** to the LORD is near. Ezk 30:3
B to Judah and the Israelites Ezk 37:16
B to Joseph—the stick of Ezk 37:16
35 ⌊foot space⌋ **b** to the inner Ezk 42:3
the paved surface **b** to the outer Ezk 42:3
of the area **b** to the prince, Ezk 48:22
was an estate **b** to the leading Ac 28:7

BELONGINGS *(9)*
not be concerned about your **b**, Gn 45:20
the things⌋ with their own **b**. Jos 7:11
their wealth and **b** over the Wadi Is 15:7
up your **b** from the ground, Jr 10:17
her precious **b** that were ⌊hers Lm 1:7
has seized all her precious **b**. Lm 1:10
their precious **b** for food in Lm 1:11
your **b** and give to the poor, Mt 19:21
housetop, whose **b** are in the Lk 17:31

BELONGS *(77)*
strap or anything that **b** to you, Gn 14:23
else in the city who **b** to you? Gn 19:12
cave of Machpelah that **b** to him; Gn 23:9
from our father **b** to us and to Gn 31:16
all our livestock **b** to our lord. Gn 47:18
of the produce⌋ **b** to Pharaoh. Gn 47:26
of the peoples **b** to Him. Gn 49:10
anything that **b** to your neighbor Ex 20:17
male from every womb **b** to Me, Ex 34:19
All fat **b** to the LORD. Lv 3:16
It **b** to the priest who makes Lv 7:7
he has presented **b** to him; Lv 7:8
b to the priest who presents it; Lv 7:9
b equally to all of Aaron's sons. Lv 7:10
the breast **b** to Aaron and his Lv 7:31
offering **b** to the priest; Lv 14:13
It **b** to Aaron and his sons, Lv 24:9
already⌋ **b** to the LORD. Lv 27:26
from the trees, **b** to the LORD; Lv 27:30
because every firstborn **b** to Me. Nm 3:13
LORD will reveal who **b** to Him, Nm 16:5
touch anything that **b** to them, Nm 16:26
with all that **b** to them so that Nm 16:30
of their gifts also **b** to you. Nm 18:11
⌊to the LORD⌋ **b** to you. Nm 18:14
presented to the LORD **b** to you. Nm 18:15
But their meat **b** to you. Nm 18:18
It **b** to you like the breast of Nm 18:18
LORD from what **b** to the fighting Nm 31:28
anyone, for judgment **b** to God. Dt 1:17
anything that **b** to your neighbor Dt 5:21
of everything that **b** to him, Dt 21:17
Vengeance **b** to Me; I will repay. Dt 32:35
of Baal that **b** to your father Jdg 6:25
and it still **b** to the kings of 1Sm 27:6
I a dog's head who **b** to Judah?" 2Sm 3:8
and all that **b** to him because 2Sm 6:12
All that **b** to Mephibosheth is 2Sm 16:4
entire altar that **b** in the inner 1Kg 6:22
Anyone who **b** to Jeroboam and 1Kg 14:11
Anyone who **b** to Baasha and dies 1Kg 16:4
go to Zarephath that **b** to Sidon, 1Kg 17:9
He who **b** to Ahab and dies in the 1Kg 21:24
at Beth-shemesh that **b** to Judah. 2Kg 14:11
which **b** to Judah, to take 1Ch 13:6
the LORD what **b** to you or offer 1Ch 21:24
heavens and on earth **b** to You. 1Ch 29:11
everything **b** to You. 1Ch 29:16
from our lands **b** to the Levites, Neh 10:37
Everything under heaven **b** to Me. Jb 41:11
Salvation **b** to the LORD; Ps 3:8
for kingship **b** to the LORD; Ps 22:28
this twice: strength **b** to God, Ps 62:11
and faithful love **b** to You, Ps 62:12
from death **b** to the Lord GOD. Ps 68:20
Surely our shield **b** to the LORD, Ps 89:18
the dew of Your youth **b** to You. Ps 110:3
Abundant peace **b** to those who Ps 119:165
That day **b** to the Lord, the GOD Jr 46:10
Look, every life **b** to Me. Ezk 18:4
His inheritance **b** only to his Ezk 46:17
righteousness **b** to You, but this Dn 9:7
this day public shame **b** to us: Dn 9:7
public shame **b** to us, our kings Dn 9:8
it **b** to those for whom it has Mt 20:23
kingdom of God **b** to such as Mk 10:14
with what **b** to someone else, Lk 16:12
kingdom of God **b** to such as Lk 18:16
Vengeance **b** to Me; I will Rm 12:19
of this it still **b** to the body. 1Co 12:15
of this it still **b** to the body. 1Co 12:16
confident that he **b** to Christ, 2Co 10:7
as he **b** to Christ, so do we. 2Co 10:7
said, Vengeance **b** to Me, I will Heb 10:30
everything that **b** to the world— 1Jn 2:15
clear that none of them **b** to us. 1Jn 2:19
Salvation **b** to our God, who is Rv 7:10

BELOVED *(16)*
The LORD's **b** rests securely on Dt 33:12
right⌋ does My **b** have to be in Jr 11:15
heaven: This is My **b** Son. I take Mt 3:17
My **b** in whom My soul delights; Mt 12:18
said: This is My **b** Son. I take Mt 17:5
heaven: You are My **b** Son; I take Mk 1:11
This is My **b** Son; listen to Mk 9:7
still had one to send, a **b** son. Mk 12:6
heaven: You are My **b** Son. I take Lk 3:22
I will send my **b** son. Lk 20:13
along with our **b** Barnabas and Ac 15:25
and she who is "Unloved," "**B**." Rm 9:25
who is my **b** and faithful child 1Co 4:17
He favored us with in the **B**. Eph 1:6
Glory: This is My **b** Son. I take 2Pt 1:17
of the saints, the **b** city. Rv 20:9

BELOW *(27)*
(See pp. xi-xii.)

BELSHAZZAR *(7)*
King **B** held a great feast for Dn 5:1
B gave orders to bring in the Dn 5:2
Then King **B** became even more Dn 5:9
his successor, **B**, have not Dn 5:22
Then **B** gave an order, and they Dn 5:29
That very night **B** the king of Dn 5:30
first year of **B** king of Babylon Dn 7:1

BELSHAZZAR'S *(1)*
the third year of King **B** reign, Dn 8:1

BELT *(19)*
his sword, his bow, and his **b**. 1Sm 18:4
you 10 silver pieces and a **b**!" 2Sm 18:11
over it was a **b** around his waist 2Sm 20:8
mantle under his **b** and ran ahead 1Kg 18:46
a leather **b** around his waist. 2Kg 1:8
Tuck your mantle under your **b**, 2Kg 4:29
Tuck your mantle under your **b**, 2Kg 9:1
or loosen the **b** of Orion? Jb 38:31
like a **b** he always wears Ps 109:19
instead of a **b**, a rope; Is 3:24
No **b** is loose, and no sandal Is 5:27
will be a **b** around His waist. Is 11:5
with a **b** of gold from Uphaz Dn 10:5
with a leather **b** around his Mt 3:4
a leather **b** around his waist Mk 1:6
would tie your **b** and walk Jn 21:18
us, took Paul's **b**, tied his own Ac 21:11
bind the man who owns this **b**, Ac 21:11
truth like a **b** around your waist Eph 6:14

BELTESHAZZAR *(10)*
(AKA DANIEL)
to Daniel, he gave the name **B**; Dn 1:7
whose name was **B**, "Are you able Dn 2:26
named **B** after the name of my god Dn 4:8
B, head of the diviners, because Dn 4:9
Now, **B**, tell me the Dn 4:18
whose name is **B**, was stunned for Dn 4:19
The king said, "**B**, don't let the Dn 4:19
B answered, "My lord, may the Dn 4:19
the king named **B**, was found to Dn 5:12
to Daniel, who was named **B**. Dn 10:1

BELTS *(3)*
she delivers **b** to the merchants. Pr 31:24
wearing **b** on their waists and Ezk 23:15
bag, no money in their **b**. Mk 6:8

BEN-ABINADAB *(1)*
B, in all Naphath-dor (Taphath 1Kg 4:11

BEN-AMMI *(1)*
to a son, and she named him **B**. Gn 19:38

BEN-DEKER *(1)*
B, in Makaz, Shaalbim, 1Kg 4:9

BEN-GEBER *(1)*
B, in Ramoth-gilead (he had the 1Kg 4:13

BEN-HADAD *(26)*
sent them to **B** son of Tabrimmon 1Kg 15:18
B listened to King Asa and sent 1Kg 15:20
Now **B** king of Aram assembled his 1Kg 20:1
to him, "This is what **B** says: 1Kg 20:2
and said, "This is what **B** says: 1Kg 20:5
Then **B** sent ⌊messengers⌋ to him 1Kg 20:10
When **B** heard this response, 1Kg 20:12
at noon while **B** and the 32 kings 1Kg 20:16
Then **B** sent out scouts, and they 1Kg 20:17
but **B** king of Aram escaped on a 1Kg 20:20
B mobilized the Arameans and 1Kg 20:26
B also fled and went into an 1Kg 20:30
Your servant **B** says, 'Please 1Kg 20:32
and said, "Yes, your brother **B**." 1Kg 20:33
So **B** came out to him, and Ahab 1Kg 20:33
Then **B** said to him, "The cities 1Kg 20:34
King **B** of Aram brought all his 2Kg 6:24
Damascus while **B** king of Aram 2Kg 8:7
said, "Your son, **B** king of Aram, 2Kg 8:9
B died, and Hazael reigned 2Kg 8:15
Aram and his son **B** during their 2Kg 13:3
and his son **B** became king in his 2Kg 13:24
took back from **B** son of Hazael 2Kg 13:25
Jehoash defeated **B** three times 2Kg 13:25
and sent it to Aram's King **B**, 2Ch 16:2
B listened to King Asa and sent 2Ch 16:4

BEN-HADAD'S *(3)*
So he said to **B** messengers, 1Kg 20:9
it will devour **B** citadels. Jr 49:27
and it will consume **B** citadels. Am 1:4

BEN-HAIL *(1)*
his officials—**B**, Obadiah, 2Ch 17:7

BEN-HANAN *(1)*
Amnon, Rinnah, **B**, and Tilon. 1Ch 4:20

BEN-HESED *(1)*
B, in Arubboth (he had Socoh and 1Kg 4:10

BEN-HUR *(1)*
B, in the hill country of 1Kg 4:8

BEN-ONI *(1)*
she named him **B**, but his father Gn 35:18

BEN-ZOHETH *(1)*
Ishi's sons: Zoheth and **B**. 1Ch 4:20

BENAIAH *(46)*
B son of Jehoiada ⌊was over⌋ the 2Sm 8:18
B son of Jehoiada was over the 2Sm 20:23
B son of Jehoiada was the son of 2Sm 23:20
B killed two sons of Ariel of 2Sm 23:20
B went down to him with a club, 2Sm 23:21
exploits of **B** son of Jehoiada 2Sm 23:22
B the Pirathonite, Hiddai from 2Sm 23:30
the priest, **B** son of Jehoiada, 1Kg 1:8
the prophet, **B**, the warriors, 1Kg 1:10
the priest or **B** son of Jehoiada 1Kg 1:26
and **B** son of Jehoiada for me." 1Kg 1:32
B son of Jehoiada replied to 1Kg 1:36
the prophet, **B** son of Jehoiada, 1Kg 1:38
the prophet, **B** son of Jehoiada, 1Kg 1:44
the order to **B** son of Jehoiada, 1Kg 2:25
Solomon sent **B** son of Jehoiada 1Kg 2:29
So **B** went to the tabernacle and 1Kg 2:30
So **B** took a message back to the 1Kg 2:30
B son of Jehoiada went up, 1Kg 2:34
king appointed **B** son of Jehoiada 1Kg 2:35
commanded **B** son of Jehoiada, 1Kg 2:46
B son of Jehoiada, in charge of 1Kg 4:4
Asaiah, Adiel, Jesimiel, **B**, 1Ch 4:36
B son of Jehoiada was the son of 1Ch 11:22
B killed two ⌊sons of⌋ Ariel of 1Ch 11:22
B went down to him with a club, 1Ch 11:23
exploits of **B** son of Jehoiada 1Ch 11:24
Benjaminites, **B** the Pirathonite 1Ch 11:31
Unni, Eliab, **B**, Maaseiah, 1Ch 15:18
and **B** were to play harps 1Ch 15:20
Zechariah, **B**, and Eliezer, were 1Ch 15:24
Mattithiah, Eliab, **B**, Obed-edom, 1Ch 16:5
and the priests **B** and Jahaziel 1Ch 16:6
B son of Jehoiada was over the 1Ch 18:17
B son of Jehoiada the priest; 1Ch 27:5
This **B** was a mighty man among 1Ch 27:6
was **B** the Pirathonite from the 1Ch 27:14
came Jehoiada son of **B**, 1Ch 27:34
son of **B**, son of Jeiel, 2Ch 20:14
and **B** were deputies under the 2Ch 31:13
Eleazar, Malchijah, and **B**; Ezr 10:25
Adna, Chelal, **B**, Maaseiah, Ezr 10:30
B, Bedeiah, Cheluhi, Ezr 10:35
Zebina, Jaddai, Joel, and **B**. Ezr 10:43
and Pelatiah son of **B**, leaders Ezk 11:1
Pelatiah son of **B** died. Ezk 11:13

BENCH *(7)*
he was sitting on the judge's **b**, Mt 27:19
on the judge's **b** in a place Jn 19:13
brought him to the judge's **b**. Ac 18:12
drove them from the judge's **b**. Ac 18:16
him in front of the judge's **b**. Ac 18:17
at the judge's **b**, he commanded Ac 25:6
sat at the judge's **b** and ordered Ac 25:17

BEND *(3)*
my arms can **b** a bow of bronze. 2Sm 22:35
my arms can **b** a bow of bronze. Ps 18:34
For I will **b** Judah ⌊as My bow⌋; Zch 9:13

BENDS *(1)*
He crouches and **b** down; Ps 10:10

BENE-BERAK *(1)*
Jehud, **B**, Gath-rimmon, Jos 19:45

BENE-JAAKAN *(3)*
(AKA BEEROTH)
from Moseroth and camped at **B**. Nm 33:31
departed from **B** and camped at Nm 33:32
from Beeroth **B** to Moserah. Dt 10:6

BENEATH *(32)*
(See pp. xi-xii.)

BENEFACTOR *(1)*
she has been a **b** of many— Rm 16:2

BENEFACTORS *(1)*
over them are called '**B**.' Lk 22:25

BENEFICIAL *(2)*
person to produce what is **b**: 1Co 12:7
but godliness is **b** in every way, 1Tm 4:8

BENEFIT *(27)*
for my son's **b** to make a carved Jdg 17:3
to the **b** that had come to 2Ch 32:25
You, and what **b** comes to me, if Jb 35:3
you are wise for your own **b**; Pr 9:12
They are of no **b**, they are no Is 30:5
Myself for your **b** and ⌊for⌋ My Is 48:9
who teaches you for ⌊your⌋ **b**, Is 48:17
worthless idols of no **b** at all." Jr 16:19
they are of no **b** at all to these Jr 23:32
Whatever **b** you might have Mt 15:5
What will it **b** a man if he gains Mt 16:26
Whatever **b** you might have Mk 7:11
For what does it **b** a man to gain Mk 8:36
It is for your **b** that I go away, Jn 16:7
place for the **b** of this nation Ac 24:2
what is the **b** of circumcision? Rm 3:1
for the **b** of my brothers, Rm 9:3
myself and Apollos for your **b**, 1Co 4:6
I am saying this for your own **b**, 1Co 7:35
how will I **b** you unless I speak 1Co 14:6
so you could have a double **b**, 2Co 1:15
Christ will not **b** you at all. Gl 5:2
we were among you for your **b**, 1Th 1:5
of the body has a limited **b**, 1Tm 4:8
since those who **b** from their 1Tm 6:2
they heard did not **b** them, Heb 4:2
does it for our **b**, so that we Heb 12:10

BENEFITED *(3)*
What is a man **b** if he gains the Lk 9:25
you have **b** from their labor." Jn 4:38
involved in them have not **b**. Heb 13:9

BENEFITS *(5)*
and do not forget all His **b**. Ps 103:2
kind man **b** himself, but a cruel Pr 11:17
For circumcision **b** you if you Rm 2:25
shared in their spiritual **b**, Rm 15:27
I may become a partner in its **b**. 1Co 9:23

BENINU *(1)*
Hodiah, Bani, and **B**. Neh 10:13

BENJAMIN *(118)*
but his father called him **B**. Gn 35:18
Rachel's sons were Joseph and **B**. Gn 35:24
Joseph's brother **B** with his Gn 42:4
Now you want to take **B**. Gn 42:36
your other brother and **B** to you. Gn 43:14
the amount of money, and **B**. Gn 43:15
When Joseph saw **B** with them, Gn 43:16
looked up and saw his brother **B**, Gn 43:29
his arms around **B** and wept, Gn 45:14
and **B** wept on his shoulder. Gn 45:14
but he gave **B** 300 pieces of Gn 45:22
wife Rachel: Joseph and **B**. Gn 46:19
B is a wolf; he tears ⌊his prey.⌋ Gn 49:27
Issachar, Zebulun, and **B**; Ex 1:3
Abidan son of Gideoni from **B**; Nm 1:11
The descendants of **B**: Nm 1:36
the tribe of **B** numbered 35,400 Nm 1:37
The tribe of **B** ⌊will be next⌋. Nm 2:22
the division of the tribe of **B**. Nm 10:24
of Raphu from the tribe of **B**; Nm 13:9
of Chislon from the tribe of **B**; Nm 34:21
Judah, Issachar, Joseph, and **B**. Dt 27:12
He said about **B**: The LORD's Dt 33:12
tribes of Judah, Simeon, and **B**. Jos 21:4
From the tribe of **B** ⌊they gave⌋: Jos 21:17
B ⌊came with⌋ your people after Jdg 5:14
against Judah, **B**, and the house Jdg 10:9
set as they neared Gibeah in **B**. Jdg 19:14
to Gibeah in **B** with my concubine Jdg 20:4
go to Gibeah in **B** to punish them Jdg 20:10
men throughout the tribe of **B**, Jdg 20:12
apart from **B**, rallied 400,000 Jdg 20:17
fight against **B** and took their Jdg 20:20
LORD defeated **B** in the presence Jdg 20:35
slaughtered 25,100 men of **B**; Jdg 20:35
Israel had retreated before **B**, Jdg 20:36
When **B** had begun to strike them Jdg 20:39
from the city, **B** looked behind Jdg 20:40
and the men of **B** were terrified Jdg 20:41
18,000 men who died from **B**; Jdg 20:44
Then **B** turned and fled toward Jdg 20:45

B returned at that time, and Jdg 21:14
The people had compassion on **B**, Jdg 21:15
since the women of **B** have been Jdg 21:16
be heirs for the survivors of **B**, Jdg 21:17
Shiloh, and go to the land of **B**. Jdg 21:21
man of **B** named Kish son 1Sm 9:1
you a man from the land of **B**. 1Sm 9:16
at Zelzah in the land of **B**. 1Sm 10:2
and the tribe of **B** was selected. 1Sm 10:20
had the tribe of **B** come forward 1Sm 10:21
with Jonathan in Gibeah of **B**. 1Sm 13:2
went from Gilgal to Gibeah in **B**. 1Sm 13:15
them were staying in Geba of **B**, 1Sm 13:16
watchmen in Gibeah of **B** looked, 1Sm 14:16
his servants, "Listen, men of **B**: 1Sm 22:7
Ephraim, **B**—over all Israel 2Sm 2:9
12 for **B** and Ish-bosheth son of 2Sm 2:15
Israel and the whole house of **B**. 2Sm 3:19
is also considered part of **B**, 2Sm 4:2
were 1,000 men from **B** with him. 2Sm 19:17
in the land of **B** in the tomb 2Sm 21:14
Shimei son of Ela, in **B**; 1Kg 4:18
the tribe of **B** to fight against 1Kg 12:21
the whole house of Judah and **B**, 1Kg 12:23
built Geba of **B** and Mizpah with 1Kg 15:22
Dan, Joseph, **B**, Naphtali, Gad, 1Ch 2:2
the tribe of **B** ⌊they were given 1Ch 6:60
Jeush, **B**, Ehud, Chenaanah, 1Ch 7:10
B fathered Bela, his firstborn; 1Ch 8:1
of Judah, **B**, Ephraim, 1Ch 9:3
were Saul's relatives from **B**: 1Ch 12:2
include Levi and **B** in the count 1Ch 21:6
for **B**, Jaasiel son of Abner; 1Ch 27:21
the house of Judah and **B**— 2Ch 11:1
to all Israel in Judah and **B**, 2Ch 11:3
cities in Judah and in **B**. 2Ch 11:10
So Judah and **B** were his. 2Ch 11:12
regions of Judah and **B** and to 2Ch 11:23
280,000 from **B** bearing regular 2Ch 14:8
and all Judah and **B**, hear me. 2Ch 15:2
land of Judah and **B** and from the 2Ch 15:8
he gathered all Judah and **B**, 2Ch 15:9
from **B**, Eliada, a brave warrior, 2Ch 17:17
old or more for all Judah and **B**. 2Ch 25:5
altars throughout Judah and **B**, 2Ch 31:1
and from all Judah, **B**, and the 2Ch 34:9
in Jerusalem and **B** enter ⌊the 2Ch 34:32
family leaders of Judah and **B**, Ezr 1:5
enemies of Judah and **B** heard Ezr 4:1
the men of Judah and **B** gathered Ezr 10:9
B, Malluch, and Shemariah; Ezr 10:32
After them **B** and Hasshub made Neh 3:23
Judah and **B** settled in Jerusalem Neh 11:4
divisions of Levites were in **B**. Neh 11:36
B, Shemaiah, and Jeremiah. Neh 12:34
is **B**, the youngest, leading Ps 68:27
of Ephraim, **B**, and Manasseh. Ps 80:2
Anathoth in the territory of **B**. Jr 1:1
from the land of **B** and from the Jr 17:26
at the Upper **B** Gate in the Jr 20:2
in Anathoth in the land of **B**, Jr 32:8
be called on in the land of **B**, Jr 32:44
Negev, the land of **B**—the Jr 33:13
go to the land of **B** to claim his Jr 37:12
But when he was at the **B** Gate, Jr 37:13
king was sitting at the **B** Gate, Jr 38:7
and that of **B** will belong to Ezk 48:22
west, will be **B**—one ⌊portion⌋ Ezk 48:23
Next to the territory of **B**, Ezk 48:24
one, the gate of **B**; Ezk 48:32
cry in Beth-aven: After you, **B**! Hs 5:8
while **B** will possess Gilead. Ob 19
site from the **B** Gate to the Zch 14:10
of the tribe of **B**, for 40 years. Ac 13:21
of Abraham, from the tribe of **B**. Rm 11:1
of the tribe of **B**, a Hebrew born Php 3:5
sealed from the tribe of **B**. Rv 7:8

BENJAMIN'S *(13)*
and **B** portion was five times Gn 43:34
and the cup was found in **B** sack. Gn 44:12
and my brother **B** eyes can see Gn 45:12
B sons: Bela, Becher, Ashbel, Gn 46:21
B descendants by their clans: Nm 26:38
for the tribe of **B** descendants Jos 18:11
inheritance of **B** descendants, Jos 18:20
of the tribe of **B** descendants by Jos 18:21
inheritance for **B** descendants Jos 18:28
Three of **B** ⌊sons⌋: 1Ch 7:6
All these were among **B** sons. 1Ch 8:40
These were **B** descendants: Neh 11:7
B descendants: from Geba, Neh 11:31

BENJAMINITE *(15)*
These were the **B** clans numbered Nm 26:41
a left-handed **B**, as a deliverer Jdg 3:15
daughter to a **B** in marriage." Jdg 21:1
gives a wife to a **B** is cursed." Jdg 21:18
a **B** man ran from the battle and 1Sm 4:12
son of Aphiah, son of a **B**. 1Sm 9:1
through the **B** region but still 1Sm 9:4
Am I not a **B** from the smallest 1Sm 9:21
of all the clans of the **B** tribe? 1Sm 9:21
how much more now this **B**! 2Sm 16:11
son of Gera, a **B** from Bahurim, 2Sm 19:16
a **B** named Sheba son of Bichri, 2Sm 20:1
the **B** from Bahurim who is with 1Kg 2:8
Abiezer the Anathothite, a **B**; 1Ch 27:12
son of Shimei, son of Kish, a **B**. Est 2:5

BENJAMINITES *(39)*
leader of the **B** is Abidan son Nm 2:22
leader of the **B**, ⌊presented Nm 7:60
same time the **B** did not drive Jdg 1:21
lived among the **B** in Jerusalem Jdg 1:21
the men of that place were **B**. Jdg 19:16
The **B** heard that the Israelites Jdg 20:3
But the **B** would not obey their Jdg 20:13
the **B** gathered together from Jdg 20:14
On that day the **B** rallied 26,000 Jdg 20:15
to fight for us against the **B**?" Jdg 20:18
The **B** came out of Gibeah and Jdg 20:21
against our brothers the **B**?" Jdg 20:23
advanced against the **B**. Jdg 20:24
same day the **B** came out from Jdg 20:25
the **B** or should we stop? Jdg 20:28
against the **B** and took their Jdg 20:30
Then the **B** came out against the Jdg 20:31
The **B** said, "We are defeating Jdg 20:32
but the **B** did not know that Jdg 20:34
the **B** realized they had been Jdg 20:36
surrounded the **B**, pursued them, Jdg 20:43
All the **B** who died that day were Jdg 20:46
the ⌊other⌋ **B** and killed them Jdg 20:48
brothers, the **B**, and said, "Today Jdg 21:6
peace to the **B** who were at the Jdg 21:13
Then they commanded the **B**: Jdg 21:20
The **B** did this and took the Jdg 21:23
The **B** rallied to Abner; 2Sm 2:25
360 of the **B** and Abner's men. 2Sm 2:31
also informed the **B** and went to 2Sm 3:19
Rimmon the Beerothite of the **B**. 2Sm 4:2
of Ribai from Gibeah of the **B**, 2Sm 23:29
Judahites, Simeonites, and **B**. 1Ch 6:65
The **B**: Sallu son of Meshullam, 1Ch 9:7
of Ribai from Gibeah of the **B**, 1Ch 11:31
Other **B** and men from Judah also 1Ch 12:16
From the **B**, the relatives of 1Ch 12:29
majority of the **B** maintained 1Ch 12:29
Run for cover, **B**, out of Jr 6:1

BENT *(13)*
While he **b** down over him, the 2Kg 4:34
he went up and **b** down over him 2Kg 4:35
I am **b** over and brought low; Ps 38:6
sword, and from the **b** bow, from Is 21:15
b their tongues ⌊like⌋ their Jr 9:3
Like an enemy He has **b** His bow; Lm 2:4
He **b** His bow and set me as the Lm 3:12
And this vine **b** its roots toward Ezk 17:7
whose hearts are **b** on evil, Dn 11:27
I **b** down to give them food. Hs 11:4
My people are **b** on turning from Hs 11:7
She was **b** over and could not Lk 13:11
their backs be **b** continually. Rm 11:10

BEON *(1)*
(AKA BAAL-MEON, BETH-BAAL-MEON, BETH-MEON)
Elealeh, Sebam, Nebo, and **B**, Nm 32:3

BEOR *(10)*
Bela son of **B** ruled in Edom; Gn 36:32
to Balaam son of **B** at Pethor, Nm 22:5
The oracle of Balaam son of **B**, Nm 24:3
The oracle of Balaam son of **B**, Nm 24:15
Balaam son of **B** with the sword. Nm 31:8
Balaam son of **B** from Pethor Dt 23:4
Balaam son of **B**, with the sword. Jos 13:22
Balaam son of **B** to curse you, Jos 24:9
Bela son of **B**. Bela's town was 1Ch 1:43
Balaam son of **B** answered him, Mc 6:5

BEQUEATHED *(1)*
that I **b** to My people, Jr 12:14

BERA *(1)*
war against **B** king of Sodom, Gn 14:2

BERACAH *(3)*
B, Jehu the Anathothite; 1Ch 12:3
in the Valley of **B** on the fourth 2Ch 20:26
called the Valley of **B** today. 2Ch 20:26

BERAIAH *(1)*
Adaiah, **B**, and Shimrath were 1Ch 8:21

BEREAVE *(1)*
I will **b** them of each one. Hs 9:12

BERECHIAH *(12)*
Hashubah, Ohel, **B**, Hasadiah, 1Ch 3:20
Asaph son of **B**, son of Shimea, 1Ch 6:39
and **B** son of Asa, son of Elkanah 1Ch 9:16
his relatives, Asaph son of **B**; 1Ch 15:17
B and Elkanah were to be 1Ch 15:23
son of Johanan, **B** son of 2Ch 28:12
Beside them Meshullam son of **B**, Neh 3:4
Meshullam son of **B** made repairs Neh 3:30
daughter of Meshullam son of **B**. Neh 6:18
the prophet Zechariah son of **B**, Zch 1:1
the prophet Zechariah son of **B**, Zch 1:7
Zechariah, son of **B**, whom you Mt 23:35

BERED *(2)*
(AKA BECHER)
is located between Kadesh and **B**. Gn 16:14
and his son **B**, his son Tahath, 1Ch 7:20

BERI *(1)*
Harnepher, Shual, **B**, Imrah, 1Ch 7:36

BERIAH *(7)*
Ishvah, Ishvi, **B**, and their Gn 46:17
the Beriite clan from **B**. Nm 26:44
So he named him **B**, because there 1Ch 7:23
Ishvi, and **B**, with their sister 1Ch 7:30
B and Shema, who were the heads 1Ch 8:13
Jahath, Zizah, Jeush, and **B**. 1Ch 23:10
Jeush and **B** did not have many 1Ch 23:11

BERIAH'S *(4)*
B sons were Heber and Malchiel. Gn 46:17
From **B** descendants: Nm 26:45
B sons: Heber, and Malchiel, who 1Ch 7:31
Ishpah, and Joha were **B** sons. 1Ch 8:16

BERIITE *(1)*
the **B** clan from Beriah. Nm 26:44

BERITES *(1)*
All the **B** came together and 2Sm 20:14

BERNICE *(3)*
King Agrippa and **B** arrived in Ac 25:13
Agrippa and **B** came with great Ac 25:23
the governor, **B**, and those Ac 26:30

BEROEA *(3)*
sent Paul and Silas off to **B**. Ac 17:10
been proclaimed by Paul at **B**, Ac 17:13
of Pyrrhus, from **B**, Aristarchus Ac 20:4

BEROTHAH *(1)*
B, and Sibraim (which is between Ezk 47:16

BEROTHAI *(1)*
of bronze from Betah and **B**, 2Sm 8:8

BERRIES *(1)*
two or three **b** at the very top Is 17:6

BERRY *(1)*
and the caper **b** has no effect; Ec 12:5

BERYL *(6)*
the fourth row, a **b**, an onyx, Ex 28:20
the fourth row, a **b**, an onyx, Ex 39:13
was like the gleam of **b**, Ezk 1:16
wheels was like the gleam of **b**. Ezk 10:9
and diamond, **b**, onyx, and jasper Ezk 28:13
the eighth **b**, the ninth topaz, Rv 21:20

BESAI'S *(2)*
descendants, **B** descendants, Ezr 2:49
B descendants, Meunim's Neh 7:52

BESIDE *(102)*
(See pp. xi-xii.)

BESIDES *(34)*
(See pp. xi-xii.)

BESIEGE *(9)*
They will **b** you within all your Dt 28:52

They will **b** you within all your Dt 28:52
at Keilah and **b** David and his 1Sm 23:8
and marched up to **b** Samaria. 2Kg 6:24
their enemies **b** them in the 2Ch 6:28
the bones of those who **b** you. Ps 53:5
I will **b** you with earth ramps, Is 29:3
Those who **b** are coming from a Jr 4:16
it is under siege, and **b** it. Ezk 4:3

BESIEGED *(11)*
all their armies, **b** Gibeon, and Jos 10:5
the Ammonites and **b** Rabbah, 2Sm 11:1
troops came and **b** Sheba in Abel 2Sm 20:15
up from Gibbethon and **b** Tirzah. 1Kg 16:17
He marched up, **b** Samaria, and 1Kg 20:1
They **b** Ahaz but were not able to 2Kg 16:5
to Samaria, and **b** it for three 2Kg 17:5
against Samaria and **b** it. 2Kg 18:9
He came to Rabbah and **b** it, 1Ch 20:1
all his armed forces **b** Lachish, 2Ch 32:9
a cucumber field, like a **b** city. Is 1:8

BESIEGES *(1)*
when their enemy **b** them in the 1Kg 8:37

BESIEGING *(7)*
When Joab was **b** the city, he put 2Sm 11:16
and all Israel were **b** Gibbethon. 1Kg 15:27
while his servants were **b** it. 2Kg 24:11
Chaldeans who are **b** you outside Jr 21:4
Chaldeans who are **b** you will Jr 21:9
king of Babylon was **b** Jerusalem, Jr 32:2
who were **b** Jerusalem, heard Jr 37:5

BESODEIAH *(1)*
son of **B** repaired the Old Neh 3:6

BESOR *(3)*
him went as far as the Wadi **B**. 1Sm 30:9
exhausted to cross the Wadi **B**. 1Sm 30:10
and had been left at the Wadi **B**, 1Sm 30:21

BEST *(52)*
Rebekah took the **b** clothes of Gn 27:15
some of the **b** products of the Gn 43:11
will give you the **b** of the land Gn 45:18
for the **b** of all the land of Gn 45:20
the **b** products of Egypt, Gn 45:23
brothers in the **b** part of the Gn 47:6
property in the **b** part of the Gn 47:11
took 600 of the **b** chariots and Ex 14:7
with the **b** of his own field Ex 22:5
Bring the **b** of the firstfruits Ex 23:19
Bring the **b** firstfruits of your Ex 34:26
you all the **b** of the fresh olive Nm 18:12
The **b** part of the tenth is to be Nm 18:29
presented the **b** part of the Nm 18:30
have presented the **b** part of it, Nm 18:32
with the **b** products of the Dt 33:15
He chose the **b** ⌊part⌋ for Dt 33:21
and wear your ⌊**b**⌋ clothes. Ru 3:3
you think is **b**, and stay here 1Sm 1:23
fat with the **b** part of all 1Sm 2:29
He can take your **b** fields, 1Sm 8:14
servants, your **b** young men, and 1Sm 8:16
Agag, and the **b** of the sheep, 1Sm 15:9
rams and the **b** of everything 1Sm 15:9
spared the **b** sheep and cattle 1Sm 15:15
the **b** of what was set apart for 1Sm 15:21
he knew the **b** ⌊enemy⌋ soldiers 2Sm 11:16
do whatever you think is **b**," 2Sm 18:4
so do whatever you think **b**. 2Sm 19:27
your **b** wives and children are 1Kg 20:3
So to the **b** of my ability I've 1Ch 29:2
liberally of the **b** of the grain, 2Ch 31:5
whatever seems **b** to you and your Ezr 7:18
have done our **b** to buy back our Neh 5:8
to the harem's **b** quarters. Est 2:9
not in the king's **b** interest to Est 3:8
All of my **b** friends despise me, Jb 19:19
He killed some of their **b** men. Ps 78:31
feed Israel with the **b** wheat. Ps 81:16
Even the **b** of them are struggle Ps 90:10
aloes, with all the **b** spices. Sg 4:14
Your **b** valleys were full of Is 22:7
vine from the very **b** seed. Jr 2:21
and the **b** of its young men have Jr 48:15
gold, the **b** of all spices, Ezk 27:22
the choice and **b** of Lebanon, Ezk 31:16
The **b** of all the firstfruits of Ezk 44:30
The **b** of them is like a brier; Mc 7:4
would choose the **b** places for Lk 14:7
don't recline at the **b** place, Lk 14:8
Bring out the **b** robe and put it Lk 15:22
I always do my **b** to have a clear Ac 24:16

BESTOW *(1)*
I **b** on you a kingdom, just as My Lk 22:29

BESTOWED *(4)*
all Israel and **b** on him such 1Ch 29:25
as had not been ⌊**b**⌋ on any king 1Ch 29:25
splendor, which I had **b** on you." Ezk 16:14
just as My Father **b** one on Me, Lk 22:29

BESTOWER *(1)*
Tyre, the **b** of crowns, whose Is 23:8

BETAH *(1)*
(AKA TIBHATH)
of bronze from **B** and Berothai, 2Sm 8:8

BETEN *(1)*
Helkath, Hali, **B**, Achshaph, Jos 19:25

BETH-ANATH *(3)*
Horem, **B**, and Beth-shemesh Jos 19:38
or the residents of **B**. Jdg 1:33
and **B** served as their Jdg 1:33

BETH-ANOTH *(1)*
Maarath, **B**, and Eltekon—six Jos 15:59

BETH-ARABAH *(3)*
north of **B**, and ascended to Jos 15:6
B, Middin, Secacah, Jos 15:61
B, Zemaraim, Bethel, Jos 18:22

BETH-ARBEL *(1)*
like Shalman's destruction of **B**. Hs 10:14

BETH-ASHBEA *(1)*
the guild of linen workers at **B**, 1Ch 4:21

BETH-AVEN *(7)*
(AKA BETHEL)
which is near **B**, east of Bethel Jos 7:2
ended at the wilderness of **B**. Jos 18:12
camped at Michmash, east of **B**. 1Sm 13:5
The battle extended beyond **B**, 1Sm 14:23
or make a pilgrimage to **B**, Hs 4:15
raise the war cry in **B**: Hs 5:8
have anxiety over the calf of **B**. Hs 10:5

BETH-AZMAVETH'S *(1)*
(AKA AZMAVETH)
B men 42 Neh 7:28

BETH-BAAL-MEON *(1)*
(AKA BAAL-MEON, BEON, BETH-MEON)
plateau—Dibon, Bamoth-baal, **B**, Jos 13:17

BETH-BARAH *(2)*
them as far as **B** and the Jordan. Jdg 7:24
as far as **B** and the Jordan. Jdg 7:24

BETH-BIRI *(1)*
(AKA BETH-LEBAOTH, LEBAOTH)
Hazar-susim, **B**, and Shaaraim. 1Ch 4:31

BETH-CAR *(1)*
all the way to a place below **B**. 1Sm 7:11

BETH-DAGON *(2)*
Gederoth, **B**, Naamah, and Jos 15:41
eastward to **B**, passed Zebulun Jos 19:27

BETH-DIBLATHAIM *(1)*
Dibon, Nebo, **B**, Jr 48:22

BETH-EDEN *(1)*
who wields the scepter from **B**. Am 1:5

BETH-EKED *(2)*
while he was at **B** of the 2Kg 10:12
them at the pit of **B**— 2Kg 10:14

BETH-EMEK *(1)*
north toward **B** and Neiel, and Jos 19:27

BETH-EZEL *(1)*
not come out. **B** is lamenting; Mc 1:11

BETH-GADER *(1)*
and Hareph fathered **B**. 1Ch 2:51

BETH-GAMUL *(1)*
Kiriathaim, **B**, Beth-meon, Jr 48:23

BETH-GILGAL *(1)*
from **B**, and from the fields of Neh 12:29

BETH-HACCHEREM *(2)*
ruler over the district of **B**, Neh 3:14
raise a smoke signal over **B**, Jr 6:1

BETH-HAGGAN *(1)*
he fled up the road toward **B**. 2Kg 9:27

BETH-HARAM *(1)*
(AKA BETH-HARAN)
B, Beth-nimrah, Succoth, and Jos 13:27

BETH-HARAN *(1)*
(AKA BETH-HARAM)
and **B** as fortified cities, Nm 32:36

BETH-HOGLAH *(3)*
ascended to **B**, proceeded north Jos 15:6
the north slope of **B** and ended Jos 18:19
Jericho, **B**, Emek-keziz, Jos 18:21

BETH-HORON *(14)*
them through the ascent of **B**, Jos 10:10
the descent of **B** all the way to Jos 10:11
as far as the border of lower **B**, Jos 16:3
on the east of Upper **B**. Jos 16:5
over the hill south of Lower **B**. Jos 18:13
the hill facing **B** on the south, Jos 18:14
and **B** with its pasturelands— Jos 21:22
headed toward the **B** road, 1Sm 13:18
Solomon rebuilt Gezer, Lower **B**, 1Kg 9:17
its pasturelands, **B** and its 1Ch 6:68
Lower and Upper **B** and 1Ch 7:24
He built Upper **B** and Lower 2Ch 8:5
Upper Beth-horon and Lower **B**— 2Ch 8:5
of Judah from Samaria to **B**, 2Ch 25:13

BETH-JESHIMOTH *(4)*
the Jordan from **B** to Acacia Nm 33:49
eastward through **B** and southward Jos 12:3
the slopes of Pisgah, and **B**— Jos 13:20
B, Baal-meon, and Kiriathaim. Ezk 25:9

BETH-LEAPHRAH *(1)*
In **B** roll in the dust. Mc 1:10

BETH-LEBAOTH *(1)*
(AKA BETH-BIRI, LEBAOTH)
B, and Sharuhen—13 cities, Jos 19:6

BETH-MAACAH *(2)*
tribes of Israel to Abel of **B**. 2Sm 20:14
and besieged Sheba in Abel of **B**. 2Sm 20:15

BETH-MARCABOTH *(2)*
Ziklag, **B**, Hazar-susah, Jos 19:5
B, Hazar-susim, Beth-biri, and 1Ch 4:31

BETH-MEON *(1)*
(AKA BAAL-MEON, BEON, BETH-BAAL-MEON)
Kiriathaim, Beth-gamul, **B**, Jr 48:23

BETH-MILLO *(4)*
Shechem and of **B** gathered Jdg 9:6
the lords of Shechem and **B**, Jdg 9:20
of Shechem and **B** and consume Jdg 9:20
killed him at **B** ⌊on the road 2Kg 12:20

BETH-NIMRAH *(2)*
(AKA NIMRAH)
B, and Beth-haran as fortified Nm 32:36
Beth-haram, **B**, Succoth, and Jos 13:27

BETH-PAZZEZ *(1)*
En-gannim, En-haddah, **B**. Jos 19:21

BETH-PELET *(2)*
Hazar-gaddah, Heshmon, **B**, Jos 15:27
in Jeshua, Moladah, **B**, Neh 11:26

BETH-PEOR *(4)*
stayed in the valley facing **B**. Dt 3:29
the valley facing **B** in the land Dt 4:46
in the land of Moab facing **B**, Dt 34:6
B, the slopes of Pisgah, and Jos 13:20

BETH-RAPHA *(1)*
Eshton fathered **B**, Paseah, and 1Ch 4:12

BETH-REHOB *(2)*
in a valley that belonged to **B**. Jdg 18:28
the Arameans of **B** and Zobah, 2Sm 10:6

BETH-SHAN *(3)*
hung his body on the wall of **B**. 1Sm 31:10
of his sons from the wall of **B**. 1Sm 31:12
the public square of **B** where the 2Sm 21:12

BETH-SHEAN *(6)*
Manasseh had **B** with its towns, Jos 17:11
both at **B** with its towns and in Jos 17:16
possession of **B** and its villages Jdg 1:27
and all **B** which is beside 1Kg 4:12
Jezreel, from **B** to Abel-meholah, 1Kg 4:12
of Manasseh, **B** and its villages 1Ch 7:29

BETH-SHEMESH *(22)*
descended to **B**, and proceeded to Jos 15:10
Shahazumah, and **B**, and ended at Jos 19:22
Beth-anath, and **B**—19 cities, Jos 19:38
and **B** with its pasturelands— Jos 21:16
residents of **B** or the residents Jdg 1:33
residents of **B** and Beth-anath Jdg 1:33

road to its homeland toward **B**, 1Sm 6:9
went straight up the road to **B**. 1Sm 6:12
them to the territory of **B**. 1Sm 6:12
The people of **B** were harvesting 1Sm 6:13
of Joshua of **B** and stopped there 1Sm 6:14
day the men of **B** offered burnt 1Sm 6:15
of Joshua of **B** to this day. 1Sm 6:18
down the men of **B** because they 1Sm 6:19
The men of **B** asked, "Who is able 1Sm 6:20
in Makaz, Shaalbim, **B**, and 1Kg 4:9
faced off at **B** that belongs to 2Kg 14:11
of Joash, son of Ahaziah, at **B**. 2Kg 14:13
and **B** and its pasturelands. 1Ch 6:59
Judah faced off at **B** in Judah. 2Ch 25:21
of Joash, son of Jehoahaz, at **B**. 2Ch 25:23
Negev of Judah and captured **B**, 2Ch 28:18

BETH-SHITTAH *(1)*
They fled to **B** in the direction Jdg 7:22

BETH-TAPPUAH *(1)*
Janim, **B**, Aphekah, Jos 15:53

BETH-TOGARMAH *(2)*
Those from **B** exchanged horses, Ezk 27:14
and **B** from the remotest parts of Ezk 38:6

BETH-ZUR *(4)*
Halhul, **B**, Gedor, Jos 15:58
was Maon, and Maon fathered **B**. 1Ch 2:45
B, Soco, Adullam, 2Ch 11:7
over half the district of **B**, Neh 3:16

BETHANY *(12)*
went out of the city to **B**, Mt 21:17
Jesus was in **B** at the house Mt 26:6
Bethphage and **B** near the Mount Mk 11:1
went out to **B** with the Twelve. Mk 11:11
day when they came out from **B**, Mk 11:12
While He was in **B** at the house Mk 14:3
He approached Bethphage and **B**, Lk 19:29
He led them out as far as **B**, Lk 24:50
this happened in **B** across the Jn 1:28
Lazarus, from **B**, the village Jn 11:1
B was near Jerusalem (about two Jn 11:18
Jesus came to **B** where Lazarus Jn 12:1

BETHEL *(69)*
(AKA BETH-AVEN, BETHUEL, LUZ)
country east of **B** and pitched Gn 12:8
with **B** on the west and Ai on the Gn 12:8
by stages from the Negev to **B**, Gn 13:3
place between **B** and Ai where his Gn 13:3
named the place **B**, though Gn 28:19
I am the God of **B**, where you Gn 31:13
Go to **B** and settle there. Gn 35:1
We must get up and go to **B**. Gn 35:3
to Luz (that is, **B**) in the land Gn 35:6
place God of **B** because it was Gn 35:7
buried under the oak south of **B**. Gn 35:8
where God had spoken with him **B**. Gn 35:15
set out from **B**. When they were Gn 35:16
east of **B**, and told them, Jos 7:2
and waited between **B** and Ai, Jos 8:9
them in ambush between **B** and Ai, Jos 8:12
left in Ai or **B** who did not go Jos 8:17
of Ai, which is next to **B** one Jos 12:9
Makkedah one the king of **B** one Jos 12:16
into the hill country of **B**. Jos 16:1
From **B** it went to Luz and Jos 16:2
slope of Luz (that is, **B**); Jos 18:13
Beth-arabah, Zemaraim, **B**, Jos 18:22
house of Joseph also attacked **B**, Jdg 1:22
sent spies to **B** (the town was Jdg 1:23
between Ramah and **B** in the hill Jdg 4:5
set out, went to **B**, and inquired Jdg 20:18
army went to **B** where they wept Jdg 20:26
goes up to **B** and the other to Jdg 20:31
people went to **B** and sat there Jdg 21:2
which is north of **B**, east of the Jdg 21:19
that goes up from **B** to Shechem, Jdg 21:19
he would go on a circuit to **B**, 1Sm 7:16
up to God at **B** will meet you 1Sm 10:3
⌊He sent gifts⌋ to those in **B**, 1Sm 30:27
He set up one in **B**, and put the 1Kg 12:29
offering in **B** to sacrifice to 1Kg 12:32
stationed in **B** the priests for 1Kg 12:32
had set up in **B** on the fifteenth 1Kg 12:33
from Judah to **B** by a revelation 1Kg 13:1
out against the altar at **B**, 1Kg 13:4
by the way he had come to **B**. 1Kg 13:10
old prophet was living in **B**. 1Kg 13:11
of God had done that day in **B**. 1Kg 13:11
the altar in **B** and against all 1Kg 13:32
the LORD is sending me on to **B**." 2Kg 2:2
So they went down to **B**. 2Kg 2:2
who were at **B** came out to Elisha 2Kg 2:3
From there Elisha went up to **B**. 2Kg 2:23
calves that were in **B** and Dan. 2Kg 10:29
deported came and lived in **B**, 2Kg 17:28
and carried their ashes to **B**. 2Kg 23:4
down the altar at **B** and the high 2Kg 23:15
have done to the altar at **B**." 2Kg 23:17
to them that he had done at **B**. 2Kg 23:19
were **B** and its villages 1Ch 7:28
B and its villages, Jeshanah and 2Ch 13:19
Aija, and **B**—and its villages Neh 11:31
shame because of **B** that they Jr 48:13
be done to you, **B**, because of Hs 10:15
He found him at **B**, and there He Hs 12:4
the altars of **B** on the day I Am 3:14
Come to **B** and rebel; rebel even Am 4:4
Do not seek **B** or go to Gilgal or Am 5:5
and **B** will come to nothing. Am 5:5
with no one at **B** to extinguish Am 5:6
the priest of **B** sent ⌊word⌋ to Am 7:10
don't ever prophesy at **B** again, Am 7:13
the people of⌋ **B** had sent Zch 7:2

BETHEL'S *(3)*
Michmash and in **B** hill country, 1Sm 13:2
B and Ai's men 223 Ezr 2:28
B and Ai's men 123 Neh 7:32

BETHELITE *(1)*
reign, Hiel the **B** built Jericho. 1Kg 16:34

BETHESDA *(1)*
a pool, called **B** in Hebrew, Jn 5:2

BETHLEHEM *(50)*
(AKA EPHRATH)
way to Ephrath (that is, **B**). Gn 35:19
way to Ephrath," (that is, **B**). Gn 48:7
Idalah, and **B**—12 cities, with Jos 19:15
who was from **B**, judged Israel Jdg 12:8
he died, he was buried in **B**. Jdg 12:10
a Levite, from **B** in Judah, who Jdg 17:7
left the town of **B** in Judah to Jdg 17:8
I am a Levite from **B** in Judah, Jdg 17:9
a woman from **B** in Judah as his Jdg 19:1
father's house in **B** in Judah. Jdg 19:2
traveling from **B** in Judah to Jdg 19:18
went to **B** in Judah, and now I'm Jdg 19:18
A man left **B** in Judah with his Ru 1:1
Ephrathites from **B** in Judah. Ru 1:2
traveled until they came to **B**. Ru 1:19
they entered **B**, the whole town Ru 1:19
They arrived in **B** at the Ru 1:22
Boaz arrived from **B**, he said to Ru 2:4
in Ephrathah and famous in **B**. Ru 4:11
you to Jesse of **B** because I have 1Sm 16:1
the LORD directed and went to **B**. 1Sm 16:4
son of Jesse of **B** who knows how 1Sm 16:18
Ephrathite from **B** of Judah 1Sm 17:12
to tend his father's flock in **B**. 1Sm 17:15
son of your servant Jesse of **B**," 1Sm 17:58
go to his town **B** for an annual 1Sm 20:6
for my permission to go to **B**. 1Sm 20:28
tomb in **B** and buried him. 2Sm 2:32
a Philistine garrison was at **B**. 2Sm 23:14
the well at the city gate of **B**!" 2Sm 23:15
from the well at the gate of **B**. 2Sm 23:16
Elhanan son of Dodo of **B**, 2Sm 23:24
Salma fathered **B**, and Hareph 1Ch 2:51
B, the Netophathites, 1Ch 2:54
firstborn and the father of **B**: 1Ch 4:4
a Philistine garrison was at **B**. 1Ch 11:16
the well at the city gate of **B**!" 1Ch 11:17
from the well at the gate of **B**. 1Ch 11:18
Elhanan son of Dodo of **B**, 1Ch 11:26
He built up **B**, Etam, Tekoa, 2Ch 11:6
which is near **B**, in order to Jr 41:17
B Ephrathah, you are small among Mc 5:2
Jesus was born in **B** of Judea in Mt 2:1
"In **B** of Judea," they told him, Mt 2:5
you, **B**, in the land of Judah, Mt 2:6
He sent them to **B** and said, Mt 2:8
in and around **B** who were two Mt 2:16
which is called **B**, because he Lk 2:4
straight to **B** and see what has Lk 2:15
and from the town of **B**, Jn 7:42

BETHLEHEM'S *(2)*
B people 123 Ezr 2:21
B and Netophah's men 188 Neh 7:26

BETHLEHEMITE *(1)*
Jaare-oregim the **B** killed 2Sm 21:19

BETHPHAGE *(3)*
and came to **B** at the Mount Mt 21:1
at **B** and Bethany near the Mount Mk 11:1
As He approached **B** and Bethany, Lk 19:29

BETHSAIDA *(7)*
Woe to you, **B**! For if the Mt 11:21
the other side, to **B**, while He Mk 6:45
Then they came to **B**. Mk 8:22
privately to a town called **B**. Lk 9:10
Woe to you, **B**! For if the Lk 10:13
Philip was from **B**, the hometown Jn 1:44
who was from **B** in Galilee, Jn 12:21

BETHUEL *(10)*
(AKA BETHEL, BETHUL)
Hazo, Pildash, Jidlaph, and **B**." Gn 22:22
And **B** fathered Rebekah. Gn 22:23
daughter of **B** son of Milcah, Gn 24:15
the daughter of **B** son of Milcah, Gn 24:24
'The daughter of **B** son of Nahor, Gn 24:47
Laban and **B** answered, "This is Gn 24:50
daughter of **B** the Aramean Gn 25:20
to the house of **B**, your mother's Gn 28:2
to Laban son of **B** the Aramean, Gn 28:5
B, Hormah, Ziklag, 1Ch 4:30

BETHUL *(1)*
(AKA BETHEL, BETHUEL)
Eltolad, **B**, Hormah, Jos 19:4

BETONIM *(1)*
Heshbon to Ramath-mizpeh and **B**, Jos 13:26

BETRAY *(21)*
have come to **b** me to my enemies 1Ch 12:17
from him or **b** My faithfulness Ps 89:33
do not **b** the one who flees. Is 16:3
betraying, they will **b** you. Is 33:1
as a woman may **b** her lover, Jr 3:20
Brother will **b** brother to death, Mt 10:21
b one another and hate one Mt 24:10
for a good opportunity to **b** Him. Mt 26:16
One of you will **b** Me." Mt 26:21
Me in the bowl—he will **b** Me. Mt 26:23
brother will **b** brother to death Mk 13:12
for a good opportunity to **b** Him. Mk 14:11
One of you will **b** Me—one who Mk 14:18
opportunity to **b** Him to them Lk 22:6
and the one who would **b** Him. Jn 6:64
because he was going to **b** Him. Jn 6:71
who was about to **b** Him), said, Jn 12:4
Simon Iscariot's son, to **b** Him. Jn 13:2
For He knew who would **b** Him. Jn 13:11
One of you will **b** Me!" Jn 13:21
the one that's going to **b** You?" Jn 21:20

BETRAYED *(24)*
"my servant ⌊Ziba⌋ **b** me. 2Sm 19:26
You or **b** Your covenant. Ps 44:17
I would have **b** Your people. Ps 73:15
destroyed, you traitor never **b**! Is 33:1
lover, so you have **b** Me, house Jr 3:20
All her friends have **b** her; Lm 1:2
to my lovers, but they **b** me. Lm 1:19
They **b** the LORD; indeed, they Hs 5:7
there they have **b** Me. Hs 6:7
Judas Iscariot, who also **b** Him. Mt 10:4
is about to be **b** into the hands Mt 17:22
man by whom the Son of Man is **b**! Mt 26:24
of Man is being **b** into the hands Mt 26:45
Judas Iscariot, who also **b** Him. Mk 3:19
of Man is being **b** into the hands Mk 9:31
by whom the Son of Man is **b**! Mk 14:21
of Man is being **b** into the hands Mk 14:41
is about to be **b** into the hands Lk 9:44
You will even be **b** by parents, Lk 21:16
to that man by whom He is **b**!" Lk 22:22
of Man must be **b** into the hands Lk 24:7
Judas, who **b** Him, also knew the Jn 18:2
Judas, who **b** Him, was also Jn 18:5
on the night when He was **b**, 1Co 11:23

BETRAYER *(6)*
Then Judas, His **b**, replied, Mt 26:25
See—My **b** is near." Mt 26:46
His **b** had given them a sign: Mt 26:48
Then Judas, His **b**, seeing that Mt 27:3

See—My **b** is near." Mk 14:42
His **b** had given them a signal. Mk 14:44

BETRAYERS *(1)*
whose **b** and murderers you have Ac 7:52

BETRAYING *(4)*
have finished **b**, they will Is 33:1
have sinned by **b** innocent blood, Mt 27:4
hand of the one **b** Me is at the Lk 22:21
b the Son of Man with a kiss? Lk 22:48

BETRAYS *(3)*
Each one **b** his friend; Jr 9:5
b nations by her prostitution Nah 3:4
Moreover, wine **b**; an arrogant Hab 2:5

BETTER *(135)*
B that I give her to you than to Gn 29:19
have been **b** for us to serve Ex 14:12
Wouldn't it be **b** for us to go Nm 14:3
of Ephraim **b** than the vintage Jdg 8:2
'Is it **b** for you that 70 men, Jdg 9:2
Now are you any **b** than Balak son Jdg 11:25
Is it **b** for you to be a priest Jdg 18:19
loves you and is **b** to you than Ru 4:15
Am I not **b** to you than 10 sons?" 1Sm 1:8
How much **b** if the troops had 1Sm 14:30
to obey is **b** than sacrifice, 1Sm 15:22
attention ⌊is **b**⌋ than the fat 1Sm 15:22
your neighbor who is **b** than you. 1Sm 15:28
the harp, and you will feel **b**." 1Sm 16:16
relieved, feel **b**, and the evil 1Sm 16:23
There is nothing **b** for me than 1Sm 27:1
What **b** way could he regain his 1Sm 29:4
be **b** off if I were still there. 2Sm 14:32
the Archite is **b** than 2Sm 17:14
it is **b** if you support us from 2Sm 18:3
more righteous and **b** than he, 1Kg 2:32
for I'm no **b** than my fathers." 1Kg 19:4
will give you a **b** vineyard in 1Kg 21:2
b than all the waters of Israel? 2Kg 5:12
family, who were **b** than you, 2Ch 21:13
B the little that the righteous Ps 37:16
faithful love is **b** than life. Ps 63:3
B a day in Your courts than a Ps 84:10
It is **b** to take refuge in the Ps 118:8
It is **b** to take refuge in the Ps 118:9
from Your lips is **b** for me than Ps 119:72
and her revenue is **b** than gold. Pr 3:14
For wisdom is **b** than precious Pr 8:11
My fruit is **b** than solid gold, Pr 8:19
B to be dishonored, yet have a Pr 12:9
B a little with the fear of the Pr 15:16
B a meal of vegetables where Pr 15:17
B a little with righteousness Pr 16:8
how much **b** it is than gold! Pr 16:16
B to be lowly of spirit with the Pr 16:19
Patience is **b** than power, and Pr 16:32
B a dry crust with peace than a Pr 17:1
B for a man to meet a bear Pr 17:12
B a poor man who walks in Pr 19:1
b to be a poor man than a Pr 19:22
B to live on the corner of a Pr 21:9
B to live in a wilderness than Pr 21:19
favor is **b** than silver and gold. Pr 22:1
wise warrior is **b** than a strong Pr 24:5
for it is **b** for him to say to Pr 25:7
B to live on the corner of a Pr 25:24
B an open reprimand than Pr 27:5
of a friend is **b** than Pr 27:9
b a neighbor nearby than a Pr 27:10
B a poor man who lives with Pr 28:6
is nothing **b** for man than to Ec 2:24
is nothing **b** for them than to Ec 3:12
there is nothing **b** than for a Ec 3:22
But **b** than either of them is the Ec 4:3
B one handful with rest, than Ec 4:6
Two are **b** than one because they Ec 4:9
B is a poor but wise youth than Ec 4:13
B to draw near in obedience than Ec 5:1
B that you do not vow than that Ec 5:5
child is **b** off than he. Ec 6:3
B what the eyes see than Ec 6:9
A good name is **b** than fine Ec 7:1
It is **b** to go to a house of Ec 7:2
Grief is **b** than laughter, for Ec 7:3
It is **b** to listen to rebuke from Ec 7:5
of a matter is **b** than its Ec 7:8
patient spirit is **b** than a proud Ec 7:8
the former days **b** than these?" Ec 7:10
there is nothing **b** for man under Ec 8:15
live dog is **b** than a dead lion. Ec 9:4
Wisdom is **b** than strength, Ec 9:16
Wisdom is **b** than weapons of war, Ec 9:18
Your love is much **b** than wine, Sg 4:10
the one you love **b** than another, Sg 5:9
What makes him **b** than another, Sg 5:9
memorial and a name **b** than sons Is 56:5
will be like today, only far **b**!" Is 56:12
the sword are **b** off than those Lm 4:9
and make ⌊you⌋ **b** off than you Ezk 36:11
days they looked **b** and healthier Dn 1:15
found them 10 times **b** than all Dn 1:20
then it was **b** for me than now Hs 2:7
The **b** his land produced, the Hs 10:1
the **b** they made the sacred Hs 10:1
Are you **b** than these kingdoms? Am 6:2
for it is **b** for me to die than Jnh 4:3
b for me to die than to live. Jnh 4:8
Are you **b** than Thebes that sat Nah 3:8
For it is **b** that you lose one of Mt 5:29
For it is **b** that you lose one of Mt 5:30
it would be **b** for him if a heavy Mt 18:6
It is **b** for you to enter life Mt 18:8
It is **b** for you to enter life Mt 18:9
like this, it's **b** not to marry!" Mt 19:10
would have been **b** for that man Mt 26:24
it would be **b** for him if a heavy Mk 9:42
It is **b** for you to enter life Mk 9:43
It is **b** for you to enter life Mk 9:45
It is **b** for you to enter the Mk 9:47
would have been **b** for that man Mk 14:21
he says, 'The old is **b**.' " Lk 5:39
It would be **b** for him if a Lk 17:2
them at what time he got **b**. Jn 4:52
Are we any **b**? Not at all! For Rm 3:9
brag that you are **b** than those Rm 11:18
it is **b** to marry than to burn 1Co 7:9
he who does not marry will do **b**. 1Co 7:38
and we are not **b** if we do eat. 1Co 8:8
For it would be **b** for me to die 1Co 9:15
not for the **b** but for the worse. 1Co 11:17
parts have a **b** presentation. 1Co 12:23
I will show you an even **b** way. 1Co 12:31
like a madman—I'm a **b** one: 2Co 11:23
with Christ—which is far **b**— Php 1:23
thought it was **b** to be left 1Th 3:1
serve them **b**, since those who 1Tm 6:2
of the **b** things connected Heb 6:9
but a **b** hope is introduced, Heb 7:19
the guarantee of a **b** covenant. Heb 7:22
is the mediator of a **b** covenant, Heb 8:6
legally enacted on **b** promises. Heb 8:6
purified⌋ with **b** sacrifices than Heb 9:23
yourselves have a **b** and enduring Heb 10:34
offered to God a **b** sacrifice Heb 11:4
they now aspire to a **b** land— Heb 11:16
might gain a **b** resurrection, Heb 11:35
had provided something **b** for us, Heb 11:40
which says **b** things than the Heb 12:24
For it is **b** to suffer for doing 1Pt 3:17
would have been **b** for them not 2Pt 2:21

BETWEEN *(216)*
(See pp. xi-xii.)

BEVELED *(4)*
made windows with **b** frames for 1Kg 6:4
pilasters had **b** windows all Ezk 40:16
the thresholds, the **b** windows, Ezk 41:16
There were **b** windows and palm Ezk 41:26

BEVERAGES *(4)*
drink wine or other alcoholic **b**, Jdg 13:4
drink wine or other alcoholic **b**, Jdg 13:7
drink wine or other alcoholic **b**. Jdg 13:14
B were served in an array of Est 1:7

BEWARE *(12)*
⌊**B**⌋ that Hezekiah does not Is 36:18
B! I am against you, you who sit Jr 21:13
B, I am against you—the Nah 2:13
B of false prophets who come to Mt 7:15
in their synagogues, **b** of them. Mt 10:17
Watch out and **b** of the yeast of Mt 16:6
'**B** of the yeast of the Pharisees Mt 16:11
not tell them to **b** of the yeast Mt 16:12
B of the yeast of the Pharisees Mk 8:15
His teaching, "**B** of the scribes, Mk 12:38
B of the scribes, who want to go Lk 20:46
So **b** that what is said in the Ac 13:40

BEWILDERED *(2)*
pale, and his nobles were **b**. Dn 5:9
among nations **b** by the roaring Lk 21:25

BEWILDERMENT *(1)*
and **b** in the Valley of Vision— Is 22:5

BEYOND *(68)*
(See pp. xi-xii.)

BEZAI *(1)*
Hodiah, Hashum, **B**, Neh 10:18

BEZAI'S *(2)*
B descendants 323 Ezr 2:17
B descendants 324 Neh 7:23

BEZALEL *(12)*
appointed by name **B** son of Uri, Ex 31:2
appointed by name **B** son of Uri, Ex 35:30
B, Oholiab, and all the skilled Ex 36:1
Moses summoned **B**, Oholiab, and Ex 36:2
B made them of finely spun linen, Ex 36:8
B made the ark of acacia wood, Ex 37:1
B constructed the altar of burnt Ex 38:1
B son of Uri, son of Hur, of the Ex 38:22
B made the ephod of gold, of Ex 39:2
Uri, and Uri fathered **B**. 1Ch 2:20
altar, which **B** son of Uri, son 2Ch 1:5
Maaseiah, Mattaniah, **B**, Binnui, Ezr 10:30

BEZEK *(3)*
struck down 10,000 men in **B**. Jdg 1:4
They found Adoni-bezek in **B**, Jdg 1:5
Saul counted them at **B**. 1Sm 11:8

BEZER *(5)*
B in the wilderness on the Dt 4:43
selected **B** on the wilderness Jos 20:8
B with its pasturelands, Jahzah Jos 21:36
⌊they received⌋ **B** in the desert 1Ch 6:78
B, Hod, Shamma, Shilshah, Ithran, 1Ch 7:37

BICHRI *(8)*
named Sheba son of **B**, 2Sm 20:1
and followed Sheba son of **B**, 2Sm 20:2
Sheba son of **B** will do more harm 2Sm 20:6
to pursue Sheba son of **B**. 2Sm 20:7
Abishai pursued Sheba son of **B**. 2Sm 20:10
Joab to pursue Sheba son of **B**. 2Sm 20:13
is a man named Sheba son of **B**, 2Sm 20:21
Sheba son of **B** and threw it to 2Sm 20:22

BIDKAR *(1)*
Jehu said to **B** his aide, "Pick 2Kg 9:25

BIG *(12)*
and on the **b** toes of their right Ex 29:20
and on the **b** toe of his right Lv 8:23
and on the **b** toes of their right Lv 8:24
and on the **b** toe of his right Lv 14:14
and on the **b** toe of his right Lv 14:17
and on the **b** toe of his right Lv 14:25
and on the **b** toe of his right Lv 14:28
cut off his thumbs and **b** toes. Jdg 1:6
their thumbs and **b** toes cut off Jdg 1:7
servant, I saw a **b** disturbance, 2Sm 18:29
avoid someone with a **b** mouth. Pr 20:19
throat if you have a **b** appetite; Pr 23:2

BIGGER *(1)*
down my barns and build **b** ones, Lk 12:18

BIGTHA *(1)*
Harbona, **B**, Abagtha, Zethar Est 1:10

BIGTHAN *(1)*
King's Gate, **B** and Teresh, two Est 2:21

BIGTHANA *(1)*
had informed on **B** and Teresh, Est 6:2

BIGVAI *(3)*
Bilshan, Mispar, **B**, Rehum, and Ezr 2:2
Mispereth, **B**, Nehum, and Baanah Neh 7:7
Adonijah, **B**, Adin, Neh 10:16

BIGVAI'S *(3)*
B descendants 2,056 Ezr 2:14
and Zaccur from **B** descendants, Ezr 8:14
B descendants 2,067 Neh 7:19

BILDAD *(5)*
the Temanite, **B** the Shuhite, Jb 2:11
Then **B** the Shuhite replied: Jb 8:1
Then **B** the Shuhite replied: Jb 18:1
Then **B** the Shuhite replied: Jb 25:1
the Temanite, **B** the Shuhite, Jb 42:9

BILE *(1)*
and pours my **b** on the ground. Jb 16:13

BILEAM *(1)*
(AKA GATH-RIMMON, IBLEAM)
and **B** and its pasturelands ⌊were 1Ch 6:70

BILGAH *(3)*
fifteenth to **B**, the sixteenth 1Ch 24:14
Mijamin, Maadiah, **B**, Neh 12:5
Shammua of **B**, Jehonathan of Neh 12:18

BILGAI *(1)*
Maaziah, **B**, and Shemaiah. Neh 10:8

BILHAH *(10)*
gave his slave **B** to his daughter Gn 29:29
she said, "Here is my slave **B**. Gn 30:3
gave her slave **B** to Jacob as a Gn 30:4
B conceived and bore Jacob a son. Gn 30:5
Rachel's slave **B** conceived again Gn 30:7
with his father's concubine **B**, Gn 35:22
of Rachel's slave **B** were Dan and Gn 35:25
with the sons of **B** and Zilpah, Gn 37:2
the sons of **B**, whom Laban gave Gn 46:25
B, Ezem, Tolad, 1Ch 4:29

BILHAH'S *(1)*
Jezer, and Shallum—**B** sons. 1Ch 7:13

BILHAN *(3)*
are Ezer's sons: **B**, Zaavan, and Gn 36:27
B, Zaavan, and Jaakan. 1Ch 1:42
Jediael's son: **B**. Bilhan's sons: 1Ch 7:10

BILHAN'S *(1)*
son: Bilhan. **B** sons: Jeush, 1Ch 7:10

BILLOWS *(3)*
Smoke **b** from his nostrils as Jb 41:20
and Your **b** have swept over Ps 42:7
and Your **b** swept over me. Jnh 2:3

BILSHAN *(2)*
Mordecai, **B**, Mispar, Bigvai, Ezr 2:2
Mordecai, **B**, Mispereth, Bigvai Neh 7:7

BIMHAL *(1)*
Pasach, **B**, and Ashvath. 1Ch 7:33

BIND *(10)*
B them as a sign on your hand Dt 6:8
b them as a sign on your hands, Dt 11:18
B the festival sacrifice with Ps 118:27
Always **b** them to your heart; Pr 6:21
B up the testimony. Seal up the Is 8:16
on you and **b** you with them so Ezk 3:25
and He will **b** up our wounds. Hs 6:1
and whatever you **b** on earth is Mt 16:19
Whatever you **b** on earth is Mt 18:18
Jerusalem will **b** the man who Ac 21:11

BINDING *(20)*
b sheaves of grain in the field. Gn 37:7
she put herself under are **b**. Nm 30:4
she put herself under are **b**. Nm 30:5
she herself made are **b**, Nm 30:6
out, her vows are **b**, and the Nm 30:7
she put herself under are **b**. Nm 30:7
her vow that is **b** or the rash Nm 30:8
put herself under is **b** on her. Nm 30:9
all her vows are **b**, and every Nm 30:11
she put herself under is **b**. Nm 30:11
vows or her obligation, is **b**. Nm 30:12
and obligations, which are **b**. Nm 30:14
matter ⌊legally⌋ **b** concerning Ru 4:7
of⌋ legally **b** a transaction Ru 4:7
we are making a **b** agreement in Neh 9:38
b his officials at will and Ps 105:22
b their kings with chains and Ps 149:8
to a fool is like **b** a stone in a Pr 26:8
b and putting both men and women Ac 22:4
through angels was legally **b**, Heb 2:2

BINDS *(5)*
For He crushes but also **b** up; Jb 5:18
even when God **b** them, they do Jb 36:13
arms of the one who **b** sheaves. Ps 129:7
and **b** up their wounds. Ps 147:3
with the peace that **b** ⌊us⌋. Eph 4:3

BINEA *(2)*
Moza fathered **B**. His son was 1Ch 8:37
Moza fathered **B**. His son was 1Ch 9:43

BINNUI *(7)*
(AKA BANI)
Noadiah son of **B** were also with Ezr 8:33
Bezalel, **B**, and Manasseh; Ezr 10:30
Bani, **B**, Shimei, Ezr 10:38
⌊under⌋ **B** son of Henadad, Neh 3:18
After him **B** son of Henadad made Neh 3:24
son of Azaniah, **B** of the sons of Neh 10:9
Jeshua, **B**, Kadmiel, Sherebiah, Neh 12:8

BINNUI'S *(1)*
B descendants 648 Neh 7:15

BIRD *(44)*
every winged **b** according to its Gn 1:21
earth, for every **b** of the sky, Gn 1:30
animal and each **b** of the sky, Gn 2:19
livestock, every **b**, and every Gn 8:19
of clean **b** and offered burnt Gn 8:20
the earth, every **b** of the sky, Gn 9:2
wings without dividing ⌊the **b**⌋. Lv 1:17
prepare the second ⌊**b**⌋ as a Lv 5:10
the blood of any **b** or animal. Lv 7:26
to take the live **b** together with Lv 14:6
the blood of the **b** that was Lv 14:6
release the live **b** over the open Lv 14:7
yarn, and the live **b**, dip them Lv 14:51
the slaughtered **b** and the fresh Lv 14:51
house with the blood of the **b**, Lv 14:52
the live **b**, the cedar wood Lv 14:52
release the live **b** into the open Lv 14:53
a wild animal or **b** that may be Lv 17:13
and the unclean **b** from the clean Lv 20:25
any land animal, **b**, or whatever Lv 20:25
You may eat every clean **b**, Dt 14:11
No **b** of prey knows that path; Jb 28:7
play with him like a **b** or put Jb 41:5
Escape to the mountain like a **b**! Ps 11:1
know every **b** of the mountains , Ps 50:11
am like a solitary **b** on a roof. Ps 102:7
escaped like a **b** from the Ps 124:7
a net where any **b** can see it, Pr 1:17
like a **b** from a fowler's trap. Pr 6:5
like a **b** darting into a snare— Pr 7:23
home is like a **b** wandering from Pr 27:8
for a **b** of the sky may carry the Ec 10:20
one rises at the sound of a **b**, Ec 12:4
Like a **b** fleeing, forced from Is 16:2
call a **b** of prey from the east, Is 46:11
my enemies hunted me like a **b**. Lm 3:52
of predatory **b** and to the wild Ezk 39:4
every kind of **b** and all the wild Ezk 39:17
may not eat any **b** or animal that Ezk 44:31
four wings of a **b** on its back. Dn 7:6
glory will fly away like a **b**: Hs 9:11
Does a **b** land in a trap on the Am 3:5
animal or **b**, reptile or fish— Jms 3:7
a haunt for every unclean **b**, Rv 18:2

BIRD'S *(1)*
come across a **b** nest with chicks Dt 22:6

BIRDS *(90)*
and let **b** fly above the earth Gn 1:20
let the **b** multiply on the earth. Gn 1:22
of the sea, the **b** of the sky, Gn 1:26
of the sea, the **b** of the sky, Gn 1:28
livestock, to the **b** of the sky, Gn 2:20
that crawl, and **b** of the sky— Gn 6:7
from the **b** according to their Gn 6:20
female, of the **b** of the sky— Gn 7:3
unclean animals, **b**, and every Gn 7:8
to its kind, all **b**, every fowl, Gn 7:14
on the earth, **b**, livestock, Gn 7:21
that crawl, to the **b** of the sky, Gn 7:23
that is with you—**b**, livestock, Gn 8:17
that is with you—**b**, livestock, Gn 9:10
but he did not cut up the **b**. Gn 15:10
B of prey came down on the Gn 15:11
but the **b** were eating them out Gn 40:17
Then the **b** will eat the flesh Gn 40:19
LORD is a burnt offering of **b**, Lv 1:14
You are to detest these **b**. Lv 11:13
concerning animals, **b**, all Lv 11:46
order that two live clean **b**, Lv 14:4
that one of the **b** be slaughtered Lv 14:5
He is to take two **b**, cedar wood, Lv 14:49
one of the **b** over a clay pot Lv 14:50
be food for all the **b** of the sky Dt 28:26
your flesh to the **b** of the sky 1Sm 17:44
camp to the **b** of the sky 1Sm 17:46
She kept the **b** of the sky from 2Sm 21:10
about animals, **b**, reptiles, and 1Kg 4:33
the **b** of the sky will eat, 1Kg 14:11
the **b** of the sky will eat. 1Kg 16:4
the **b** of the sky will eat.' " 1Kg 21:24
⌊ask⌋ the **b** of the sky, and they Jb 12:7
concealed from the **b** of the sky. Jb 28:21
us wiser than the **b** of the sky?" Jb 35:11
b of the sky, and fish of the Ps 8:8
winged **b** like the sand of the Ps 78:27
servants to the **b** of the sky for Ps 79:2
b of the sky live beside ⌊the Ps 104:12
There the **b** make their nests; Ps 104:17
that crawl and flying **b**, Ps 148:10
or like **b** caught in a trap, Ec 9:12
all be left for the **b** of prey on Is 18:6
The **b** will spend the summer on Is 18:6
Like hovering **b**, so the LORD of Is 31:5
the **b** of prey will gather there, Is 34:15
all the **b** of the sky had fled. Jr 4:25
cage full of **b**, so their houses Jr 5:27
food for the **b** of the sky and Jr 7:33
From the **b** of the sky to the Jr 9:10
animals and **b** have been swept Jr 12:4
Are **b** of prey circling her? Jr 12:9
the **b** of the sky and the wild Jr 15:3
food for the **b** of the sky and Jr 16:4
as food for the **b** of the sky and Jr 19:7
food for the **b** of the sky and Jr 34:20
you ensnare people with like **b**, Ezk 13:20
people you have ensnared like **b**. Ezk 13:20
B of every kind will nest under Ezk 17:23
the earth and the **b** of the sky Ezk 29:5
All the **b** of the sky nested in Ezk 31:6
All the **b** of the sky nested on Ezk 31:13
cause all the **b** of the sky to Ezk 32:4
of the sea, the **b** of the sky, Ezk 38:20
animals, or **b** of the air—He Dn 2:38
the **b** of the air lived in its Dn 4:12
and the **b** from its branches. Dn 4:14
branches the **b** of the air lived Dn 4:21
wild animals, the **b** of the sky, Hs 2:18
animals and the **b** of the sky; Hs 4:3
them down like **b** of the sky. Hs 7:12
be roused like **b** from Egypt and Hs 11:11
will sweep away the **b** of the sky Zph 1:3
Look at the **b** of the sky: Mt 6:26
have dens and **b** of the sky have Mt 8:20
and the **b** came and ate them up. Mt 13:4
that the **b** of the sky come and Mt 13:32
and the **b** came and ate it up. Mk 4:4
that the **b** of the sky can nest Mk 4:32
and the **b** of the sky ate it up. Lk 8:5
and **b** of the sky have nests, Lk 9:58
you worth much more than the **b**? Lk 12:24
and the **b** of the sky nested in Lk 13:19
the earth, and the **b** of the sky. Ac 10:12
reptiles, and the **b** of the sky. Ac 11:6
mortal man, **b**, four-footed Rm 1:23
another for **b**, and another for 1Co 15:39
saying to all the **b** flying in Rv 19:17
and all the **b** were filled with Rv 19:21

BIRDS' *(1)*
and his nails like **b** ⌊claws⌋. Dn 4:33

BIRSHA *(1)*
king of Sodom, **B** king of Gn 14:2

BIRTH *(149)*
conceived and gave **b** to Cain. Gn 4:1
she also gave **b** to his brother Gn 4:2
conceived and gave **b** to Enoch. Gn 4:17
she gave **b** to a son and named Gn 4:25
800 years after the **b** of Seth, Gn 5:4
807 years after the **b** of Enosh, Gn 5:7
815 years after the **b** of Kenan, Gn 5:10
years after the **b** of Mahalalel, Gn 5:13
830 years after the **b** of Jared, Gn 5:16
800 years after the **b** of Enoch, Gn 5:19
And after the **b** of Methuselah, Gn 5:22
782 years after the **b** of Lamech, Gn 5:26
lived 595 years after Noah's **b**, Gn 5:30
So Hagar gave **b** to Abram's son, Gn 16:15
ninety-year-old woman, give **b**?" Gn 17:17
firstborn gave **b** to a son and Gn 19:37
younger also gave **b** to a son, Gn 19:38
When her time came to give **b**, Gn 25:24
conceived, gave **b** to a son, and Gn 29:32
gave **b** to a son, and said, Gn 29:33
gave **b** to a son, and said, Gn 29:34
gave **b** to a son, and said, Gn 29:35
After Rachel gave **b** to Joseph, Gn 30:25
began to give **b**, and her labor Gn 35:16
conceived and gave **b** to a son, Gn 38:3
again, gave **b** to a son, and Gn 38:4
She gave **b** to another son and Gn 38:5
Chezib that she gave **b** to him. Gn 38:5

the time came for her to give **b**, Gn 38:27
she was giving **b**, one of them Gn 38:28
help the Hebrew women give **b**, Ex 1:16
and give **b** before a midwife Ex 1:19
pregnant and gave **b** to a son; Ex 2:2
gave **b** to a son whom he named Ex 2:22
stone, in the order of their **b**. Ex 28:10
and gives **b** to a male child, Lv 12:2
But if she gives **b** to a female Lv 12:5
is the law for a woman giving **b**, Lv 12:7
Did I give them **b** so You should Nm 11:12
one of illegitimate **b** may enter Dt 23:2
ignored the Rock who gave you **b**; Dt 32:18
conceive and give **b** to a son. Jdg 13:3
conceive and give **b** to a son. Jdg 13:5
be a Nazirite to God from **b**. Jdg 13:5
conceive and give a **b** to a son. Jdg 13:7
to God from **b** until the day of Jdg 13:7
So the woman gave **b** to a son and Jdg 13:24
I am a Nazirite to God from **b**. Jdg 16:17
land of your **b**, and ⌊how⌋ you Ru 2:11
and she gave **b** to a son. Ru 4:13
seven sons, has given **b** to him." Ru 4:15
conceived and gave **b** to a son. 1Sm 1:20
barren woman gives **b** to seven, 1Sm 2:5
and gave **b** to three sons 1Sm 2:21
pregnant and about to give **b**. 1Sm 4:19
and gave **b** because her labor 1Sm 4:19
You've given **b** to a son!" 1Sm 4:20
gave **b** to a son and named him 2Sm 12:24
On the third day after I gave **b**, 1Kg 3:18
he was not the son I gave **b** to." 1Kg 3:21
sister gave **b** to Hadad's son 1Kg 11:20
conceived and gave **b** to a son at 2Kg 4:17
have come to the point of **b**, 2Kg 19:3
"I gave **b** to him in pain." 1Ch 4:9
wife Bithiah gave **b** to Miriam, 1Ch 4:17
Judean wife gave **b** to Jered the 1Ch 4:18
wife Maacah gave **b** to a son, 1Ch 7:16
Hammolecheth gave **b** to Ishhod, 1Ch 7:18
conceived and gave **b** to a son. 1Ch 7:23
trouble and give **b** to evil; Jb 15:35
gave **b** to the frost of heaven Jb 38:29
know when mountain goats give **b**? Jb 39:1
can know the time they give **b**? Jb 39:2
down to give **b** to their young; Jb 39:3
trouble, and gives **b** to deceit. Ps 7:14
I was given over to You at **b**; Ps 22:10
makes the deer give **b** and strips Ps 29:9
from the womb; liars err from **b**. Ps 58:3
I have leaned on You from **b**; Ps 71:6
before You gave **b** to the earth Ps 90:2
her who gave **b** to you rejoice. Pr 23:25
a time to give **b** and a time to Ec 3:2
death than the day of one's **b**. Ec 7:1
to the one who gave her **b**. Sg 6:9
she conceived and gave you **b**. Sg 8:5
conceived and gave **b** to a son. Is 8:3
not been in labor or given **b**. Is 23:4
to give **b** writhes and cries Is 26:17
pain; we gave **b** to wind. We have Is 26:18
you will give **b** to stubble. Is 33:11
children come to the point of **b**, Is 37:3
Maker who shaped you from **b**; Is 44:2
What are you giving **b** to?" Is 45:10
the womb, carried along since **b**. Is 46:3
were known as a rebel from **b**. Is 48:8
Sarah who gave **b** to you in pain. Is 51:2
barren one, who did not give **b**; Is 54:1
trouble and give **b** to iniquity. Is 59:4
Zion was in labor, she gave **b**; Is 66:7
labor, she gave **b** to her sons. Is 66:8
the point of **b** and not deliver Is 66:9
stone: You gave **b** to me. For Jr 2:27
the field gives **b** and abandons Jr 14:5
that you gave **b** to me, a man who Jr 15:10
mother who gave **b** to you into Jr 22:26
see whether a male can give **b**. Jr 30:6
and those about to give **b**. Jr 31:8
people and to the land of our **b**, Jr 46:16
origin and your **b** were in the Ezk 16:3
As for your **b**, your umbilical Ezk 16:4
became Mine and gave **b** to sons Ezk 23:4
in Chaldea, the land of their **b**. Ezk 23:15
of the field gave **b** beneath its Ezk 31:6
was a Mede by **b**, and was ruler Dn 9:1
again and gave **b** to a daughter, Hs 1:6
conceived and gave **b** to a son. Hs 1:8
as she was on the day of her **b**. Hs 2:3
they gave **b** to illegitimate Hs 5:7
no **b**, no gestation, no Hs 9:11
she who is in labor has given **b**; Mc 5:3
gave **b** to Jesus who is called Mt 1:16
The **b** of Jesus Christ came about Mt 1:18
will give **b** to a son, and you Mt 1:21
pregnant and give **b** to a son, Mt 1:23
until she gave **b** to a son. Mt 1:25
are the beginning of **b** pains. Mt 24:8
Syrophoenician by **b**, and she Mk 7:26
are the beginning of **b** pains. Mk 13:8
and many will rejoice at his **b**. Lk 1:14
conceive and give **b** to a son, Lk 1:31
come for Elizabeth to give **b**, Lk 1:57
the time came for her to give **b**. Lk 2:6
Then she gave **b** to her firstborn Lk 2:7
He saw a man blind from **b**. Jn 9:1
when she has given **b** to a child, Jn 16:21
a Levite and a Cypriot by **b**, Ac 4:36
feet, lame from **b**, and who had Ac 14:8
powerful, not many of noble **b**. 1Co 1:26
are Jews by **b** and not "Gentile Gl 2:15
woman who does not give **b**. Gl 4:27
it gives **b** to sin, and when Jms 1:15
grown, it gives **b** to death. Jms 1:15
gave us a new **b** by the message Jms 1:18
given us a new **b** into a living 1Pt 1:3
in labor and agony to give **b**. Rv 12:2
woman who was about to give **b**, Rv 12:4
she did give **b** he might devour Rv 12:4
But she gave **b** to a Son—a male Rv 12:5
woman who gave **b** to the male. Rv 12:13

BIRTHDAY *(3)*
was Pharaoh's **b**, he gave a feast Gn 40:20
when Herod's **b** celebration came Mt 14:6
an opportune time came on his **b**, Mk 6:21

BIRTHPLACE *(2)*
her ethnic background or her **b**, Est 2:10
not revealed her **b** or her ethnic Est 2:20

BIRTHRIGHT *(9)*
replied, "First sell me your **b**." Gn 25:31
so what good is a **b** to me?" Gn 25:32
to Jacob and sold his **b** to him. Gn 25:33
So Esau despised his **b**. Gn 25:34
He took my **b**, and look, now he Gn 27:36
but his **b** was given to the sons 1Ch 5:1
in the genealogy according to **b**. 1Ch 5:1
the **b** was given to Joseph. 1Ch 5:2
who sold his **b** in exchange for Heb 12:16

BIRZAITH *(1)*
and Malchiel, who fathered **B**. 1Ch 7:31

BISHLAM *(1)*
of Persia, **B**, Mithredath, Tabeel Ezr 4:7

BIT *(8)*
will bring a **b** of bread so that Gn 18:5
and they **b** them so that many Nm 21:6
in the jar and a **b** of oil in the 1Kg 17:12
nose and My **b** in your mouth; 2Kg 19:28
be controlled with **b** and bridle, Ps 32:9
nose and My **b** in your mouth; Is 37:29
a desolation, every **b** of her. Jr 50:13
For you are a **b** of smoke that Jms 4:14

BITE *(5)*
tongues as sharp as a snake's **b**; Ps 140:3
They will **b** you. ⌊This is⌋ Jr 8:17
wall only to have a snake **b** him. Am 5:19
the ⌊sea⌋ serpent to **b** them. Am 9:3
But if you **b** and devour one Gl 5:15

BITES *(3)*
that **b** the horses' heels so that Gn 49:17
In the end it **b** like a snake and Pr 23:32
If the snake **b** before it is Ec 10:11

BITHIAH *(2)*
Mered's wife **B** gave birth to 1Ch 4:17
sons of Pharaoh's daughter **B**; 1Ch 4:18

BITHYNIA *(2)*
to go into **B**, but the Spirit Ac 16:7
Cappadocia, Asia, and **B**, chosen 1Pt 1:1

BITS *(3)*
stones like crushed **b** of chalk, Is 27:9
of Samaria will be smashed to **b**! Hs 8:6
when we put **b** into the mouths Jms 3:3

BITTEN *(3)*
anyone who is **b** looks at it, Nm 21:8
someone was **b**, and he looked at Nm 21:9
a wall may be **b** by a snake. Ec 10:8

BITTER *(49)*
They made life **b** for Isaac and Gn 26:35
with a loud and **b** cry and said Gn 27:34
their lives **b** with difficult Ex 1:14
unleavened bread and **b** herbs. Ex 12:8
at Marah because it was **b**— Ex 15:23
is to hold the **b** water that Nm 5:18
by this **b** water that brings Nm 5:19
⌊them⌋ off into the **b** water. Nm 5:23
to drink the **b** water that brings Nm 5:24
enter her and cause **b** suffering. Nm 5:24
enter her and cause **b** suffering; Nm 5:27
unleavened bread and **b** herbs; Nm 9:11
bearing poisonous and **b** fruit. Dt 29:18
by pestilence and **b** plague; Dt 32:24
their clusters are **b**. Dt 32:32
is much too **b** for you ⌊to share Ru 1:13
the Almighty has made me very **b**. Ru 1:20
were all very **b** over ⌊the loss 1Sm 30:6
affliction of Israel was very **b**. 2Kg 14:26
to those whose existence is **b**, Jb 3:20
but soaks me with **b** experiences. Jb 9:18
For You record **b** accusations Jb 13:26
person dies with a **b** soul, Jb 21:25
Today also my complaint is **b**. Jb 23:2
the Almighty who has made me **b**, Jb 27:2
swords and aim **b** words like Ps 64:3
the end she's as **b** as wormwood Pr 5:4
person, any **b** thing is sweet. Pr 27:7
and wine to one whose life is **b**. Pr 31:6
And I find more **b** than death the Ec 7:26
who substitute **b** for sweet and Is 5:20
for sweet and sweet for **b**. Is 5:20
beer is **b** to those who drink it. Is 24:9
how evil and **b** it is for you to Jr 2:19
It is very **b**, because it has Jr 4:18
for⌋ an only son, a **b** lament, Jr 6:26
a lament with **b** weeping—Rachel Jr 31:15
grieve, and she herself is **b**. Lm 1:4
deep anguish and **b** mourning. Ezk 27:31
Ephraim has provoked **b** anger, Hs 12:14
and its outcome like a **b** day. Am 8:10
Chaldeans, that **b**, impetuous Hab 1:6
there the warrior's cry is **b**. Zph 1:14
and don't become **b** against them. Col 3:19
pour out sweet and **b** water from Jms 3:11
But if you have **b** envy and Jms 3:14
because they had been made **b**. Rv 8:11
it will be **b** in your stomach, Rv 10:9
I ate it, my stomach became **b**. Rv 10:10

BITTERLY *(15)*
Angel of the LORD, "**B** curse her Jdg 5:23
They wept loudly and **b**, Jdg 21:2
all his servants also wept **b**. 2Sm 13:36
And Hezekiah wept **b**. 2Kg 20:3
The people also wept **b**. Ezr 10:1
city, and cried loudly and **b**. Est 4:1
me! Let me weep **b**! Do not try to Is 22:4
the messengers of peace weep **b**. Is 33:7
And Hezekiah wept **b**. Is 38:3
Weep **b** for the one who has gone Jr 22:10
b with a broken heart right Ezk 21:6
voices over you and cry out **b**. Ezk 27:30
child and weep **b** for Him as one Zch 12:10
And he went outside and wept **b**. Mt 26:75
And he went outside and wept **b**. Lk 22:62

BITTERNESS *(15)*
the **b** of death has come. 1Sm 15:32
realize this will only end in **b**? 2Sm 2:26
complain in the **b** of my soul. Jb 7:11
and speak in the **b** of my soul. Jb 10:1
The heart knows its own **b**, Pr 14:10
his father and **b** to the one who Pr 17:25
because of the **b** of my soul, Is 38:15
welfare that I had such great **b**; Is 38:17
me with **b** and hardship. Lm 3:5
filled me with **b**, sated me with Lm 3:15
I left in **b** and in an angry Ezk 3:14
you are poisoned by **b** and bound Ac 8:23
mouth is full of cursing and **b**. Rm 3:14
All **b**, anger and wrath, insult Eph 4:31
that no root of **b** springs up, Heb 12:15

BIZIOTHIAH *(1)*
Hazar-shual, Beer-sheba, **B**, Jos 15:28

BIZTHA *(1)*
Mehuman, **B**, Harbona, Bigtha, Est 1:10

BLACK *(19)*
or any lambs that are not **b**, Gn 30:33
land so that the land was **b**, Ex 10:15
bearded vulture, the **b** vulture, Lv 11:13
and there is no **b** hair in it, Lv 13:31
unchanged and **b** hair has grown Lv 13:37
enveloped in a dense, **b** cloud. Dt 4:11
bearded vulture, the **b** vulture, Dt 14:12
hair is wavy and **b** as a raven. Sg 5:11
scatter cumin and sow **b** cumin? Is 28:25
Certainly **b** cumin is not Is 28:27
But **b** cumin is beaten out with a Is 28:27
the heavens in **b** and make Is 50:3
set your stones in **b** mortar, Is 54:11
daylight will turn **b** over them. Mc 3:6
the second chariot **b** horses, Zch 6:2
one with the **b** horses is going Zch 6:6
make a single hair white or **b**. Mt 5:36
looked, and there was a **b** horse. Rv 6:5
the sun turned **b** like sackcloth Rv 6:12

BLACKENED *(1)*
I walk about **b**, but not by the Jb 30:28

BLACKENS *(1)*
My skin **b** and flakes off, and my Jb 30:30

BLACKNESS *(3)*
is⌋ a land of **b** like the deepest Jb 10:22
gloom, a day of clouds and **b**, Zph 1:15
is reserved the **b** of darkness Jd 13

BLACKSMITH *(1)*
No **b** could be found in all the 1Sm 13:19

BLACKSMITHS *(1)*
b and coppersmiths to repair 2Ch 24:12

BLADE *(6)*
but the **b** flies off the handle Dt 19:5
the handle went in after the **b**, Jdg 3:22
let my shoulder **b** fall from my Jb 31:22
wherever your **b** is directed. Ezk 21:16
land of Nimrod with a drawn **b**. Mc 5:6
first the **b**, then the head, Mk 4:28

BLADES *(1)*
in Gibeon, is named Field of **B**. 2Sm 2:16

BLAME *(7)*
may any **b** be on me and my 2Sm 14:9
did not sin or **b** God for Jb 1:22
who is to **b** for this trouble Jnh 1:7
us who is to **b** for this trouble Jnh 1:8
that I'm to **b** for this violent Jnh 1:12
living without **b** according to Lk 1:6
without spot or **b** until the 1Tm 6:14

BLAMED *(2)*
that the ministry will not be **b**. 2Co 6:3
this, so that they won't be **b**. 1Tm 5:7

BLAMELESS *(36)*
b among his contemporaries; Gn 6:9
and the rest of you will be **b**." Gn 44:10
You must be **b** before the LORD Dt 18:13
the LORD's anointed and be **b**?" 1Sm 26:9
I was **b** before Him and kept 2Sm 22:24
the **b** man You prove Yourself 2Sm 22:26
man You prove Yourself **b**; 2Sm 22:26
if I were **b**, my mouth would Jb 9:20
Though I am **b**, I no longer care Jb 9:21
both the **b** and the wicked." Jb 9:22
I was **b** toward Him and kept Ps 18:23
the **b** man You prove Yourself Ps 18:25
man You prove Yourself **b**; Ps 18:25
over the **b** all their days, Ps 37:18
Watch the **b** and observe the Ps 37:37
You are **b** when You judge. Ps 51:4
happy are those whose way is **b**, Ps 119:1
May my heart be **b** regarding Your Ps 119:80
of the **b** clears his path, Pr 11:5
but those with **b** conduct are His Pr 11:20
but the **b** will inherit what is Pr 28:10
created you were **b** in your ways Ezk 28:15
b in the day of our Lord Jesus 1Co 1:8
to be holy and **b** in His sight. Eph 1:4
any such thing, but holy and **b**. Eph 5:27
and can be pure and **b** in the day Php 1:10
so that you may be **b** and pure, Php 2:15
that is in the law, **b**. Php 3:6
faultless, and **b** before Him— Col 1:22
make your hearts **b** in holiness 1Th 3:13
kept sound and **b** for the coming 1Th 5:23
if they prove **b**, then they can 1Tm 3:10
someone who is **b**, the husband of Ti 1:6
must be **b**, not arrogant, Ti 1:7
of His glory, **b** and with great Jd 24
in their mouths; they are **b**. Rv 14:5

BLAMELESSLY *(1)*
b we conducted ourselves with 1Th 2:10

BLAND *(1)*
Is **b** food eaten without salt? Jb 6:6

BLANKET *(1)*
and thick darkness its **b**, Jb 38:9

BLANKETS *(1)*
sit on saddle **b**, and who travel Jdg 5:10

BLASPHEME *(9)*
You must not **b** God or curse a Ex 22:28
whatever blasphemies they may **b**. Mk 3:28
to make them **b** by punishing them Ac 26:11
they may be taught not to **b**. 1Tm 1:20
Don't they **b** the noble name that Jms 2:7
when they **b** the glorious ones 2Pt 2:10
and **b** glorious beings. Jd 8
But these people **b** anything they Jd 10
to **b** His name and His dwelling— Rv 13:6

BLASPHEMED *(15)*
Her son cursed and **b** the Name, Lv 24:11
attendants have **b** Me with. 2Kg 19:6
Who is it you mocked and **b**? 2Kg 19:22
attendants have **b** Me with. Is 37:6
Who is it you have mocked and **b**? Is 37:23
is continually **b** all day long. Is 52:5
your fathers **b** Me by committing Ezk 20:27
his robes and said, "He has **b**! Mt 26:65
But when they resisted and **b**, Ac 18:6
name of God is **b** among the Rm 2:24
and His teaching will not be **b**. 1Tm 6:1
them the way of truth will be **b**. 2Pt 2:2
they **b** the name of God who had Rv 16:9
and **b** the God of heaven because Rv 16:11
and they **b** God for the plague of Rv 16:21

BLASPHEMER *(1)*
was formerly a **b**, a persecutor, 1Tm 1:13

BLASPHEMERS *(2)*
robbers or **b** of our goddess. Ac 19:37
proud, **b**, disobedient to 2Tm 3:2

BLASPHEMES *(5)*
Whoever **b** the name of the LORD Lv 24:16
he **b** the Name, he is to be put Lv 24:16
or foreign resident, **b** the LORD. Nm 15:30
But whoever **b** against the Holy Mk 3:29
but the one who **b** against the Lk 12:10

BLASPHEMIES *(9)*
they had committed terrible **b**, Neh 9:18
They committed terrible **b**. Neh 9:26
have heard all the **b** you uttered Ezk 35:12
thefts, false testimonies, **b**. Mt 15:19
sins and whatever **b** they may Mk 3:28
Who is this man who speaks **b**? Lk 5:21
speak **b** about things they don't 2Pt 2:12
to him to speak boasts and **b**. Rv 13:5
He began to speak **b** against God: Rv 13:6

BLASPHEMING *(3)*
said among themselves, "He's **b**!" Mt 9:3
like this? He's **b**! Who can Mk 2:7
'You are **b**' to the One the Jn 10:36

BLASPHEMOUS *(5)*
many other **b** things against Lk 22:65
him speaking **b** words against Ac 6:11
stop speaking **b** words against Ac 6:13
and on his heads were **b** names. Rv 13:1
that was covered with **b** names, Rv 17:3

BLASPHEMY *(6)*
be forgiven every sin and **b**, Mt 12:31
the **b** against the Spirit will Mt 12:31
Look, now you've heard the **b**! Mt 26:65
lewdness, stinginess, **b**, pride, Mk 7:22
You have heard the **b**! Mk 14:64
but for **b**, because You— Jn 10:33

BLAST *(12)*
up at the **b** of Your nostrils Ex 15:8
the ram's horn sounds a long **b**, Ex 19:13
is a prolonged **b** of the horn and Jos 6:5
they heard the **b** of the trumpet, Jos 6:20
at the **b** of the breath of His 2Sm 22:16
a ⌊single⌋ **b** from God and come Jb 4:9
Your words are a **b** of wind. Jb 8:2
at the **b** of the breath of Your Ps 18:15
trumpets and the **b** of the ram's Ps 98:6
Praise Him with trumpet **b**; Ps 150:3
of trumpet ⌊**b**⌋ and battle cry Zph 1:16
to the **b** of a trumpet, and the Heb 12:19

BLASTED *(2)*
the rooftops, **b** by the east wind 2Kg 19:26
the rooftops, **b** by the east wind Is 37:27

BLASTING *(1)*
bellows blow, **b** the lead with Jr 6:29

BLASTS *(9)*
When both are sounded in long **b**, Nm 10:3
you sound short **b**, the camps Nm 10:5
you sound short **b** a second time, Nm 10:6
Short **b** are to be sounded for Nm 10:6
to sound long **b**, not short ones Nm 10:7
sound short **b** on the trumpets, Nm 10:9
It **b** at him without mercy, Jb 27:22
When the trumpet **b**, he snorts Jb 39:25
trumpet **b** that the three Rv 8:13

BLASTUS *(1)*
having won over **B**, who was in Ac 12:20

BLATANT *(1)*
and cleansed from **b** rebellion. Ps 19:13

BLAZE *(1)*
I am warm, I see the **b**." Is 44:16

BLAZED *(4)*
fire from the LORD **b** among them Nm 11:1
LORD's fire had **b** among them. Nm 11:3
b throughout their assembly; Ps 106:18
He has **b** against Jacob like a Lm 2:3

BLAZES *(2)*
as a flame **b** through mountains, Ps 83:14
the morning it **b** like a flaming Hs 7:6

BLAZING *(20)*
a mountain **b** with fire into the Dt 4:11
the mountain was **b** with fire. Dt 5:23
while it was **b** with fire, and Dt 9:15
onward with hail and **b** coals. Ps 18:12
columns into the **b** fire until Jr 36:23
The **b** flame will not be Ezk 20:47
into a furnace of **b** fire." Dn 3:6
thrown into a furnace of **b** fire. Dn 3:11
into a furnace of **b** fire— Dn 3:15
us from the furnace of **b** fire, Dn 3:17
them into the furnace of **b** fire. Dn 3:20
into the furnace of **b** fire. Dn 3:21
into the furnace of **b** fire. Dn 3:23
the furnace of **b** fire and called Dn 3:26
its wheels were **b** fire. Dn 7:9
of Jacob will be a ⌊**b**⌋ fire, Ob 18
them into the **b** furnace where Mt 13:42
throw them into the **b** furnace. Mt 13:50
be touched, to a **b** fire, to Heb 12:18
a great star, **b** like a torch, Rv 8:10

BLEEDING *(6)*
from her **b** for 33 days. Lv 12:4
from her **b** for 66 days. Lv 12:5
had suffered from **b** for 12 years Mt 9:20
suffering from **b** for 12 years Mk 5:25
suffering from **b** for 12 years, Lk 8:43
Instantly her **b** stopped. Lk 8:44

BLEMISH *(10)*
one without **b** before the LORD. Lv 3:1
a male or female without **b**. Lv 3:6
both without **b**, and present Lv 9:2
yearlings without **b**, for a burnt Lv 9:3
male lamb without **b** as a burnt Lv 23:12
seven rams without **b** as a burnt Ezk 45:23
six lambs and a ram without **b**. Ezk 46:6
Himself without **b** to God, Heb 9:14
of a lamb without defect or **b**. 1Pt 1:19
without spot or **b** before Him. 2Pt 3:14

BLEMISHES *(1)*
They are blots and **b**, delighting 2Pt 2:13

BLEND *(1)*
oil, a scented **b**, the work of a Ex 30:25

BLENDED *(3)*
Prepare expertly **b** incense from Ex 30:35
and expertly **b** incense. Ex 37:29
full of wine **b** with spices, Ps 75:8

BLENDS *(1)*
Anyone who **b** something like it Ex 30:33

BLESS *(98)*

nation, I will **b** you, I will	Gn 12:2
I will **b** those who bless you,	Gn 12:3
I will bless those who **b** you,	Gn 12:3
will **b** her; indeed, I will give	Gn 17:16
I will **b** her, and she will	Gn 17:16
I will certainly **b** him;	Gn 17:20
will indeed **b** you and make your	Gn 22:17
I will be with you and **b** you.	Gn 26:3
I will **b** you and multiply your	Gn 26:24
that I can **b** you before I die.	Gn 27:4
so that I can **b** you in the	Gn 27:7
so that he may **b** you before he	Gn 27:10
my game so that you may **b** me."	Gn 27:19
son's game so that I can **b** you."	Gn 27:25
and those who **b** you will be	Gn 27:29
game, so that you may **b** me."	Gn 27:31
his father, "**B** me—me too, my	Gn 27:34
B me—me too, my father!"	Gn 27:38
God Almighty **b** you and make you	Gn 28:3
not let You go unless You **b** me."	Gn 32:26
them to me and I will **b** them."	Gn 48:9
all harm—may He **b** these boys.	Gn 48:16
come to you and **b** you in every	Ex 20:24
He will **b** your bread and your	Ex 23:25
how you are to **b** the Israelites.	Nm 6:23
The LORD **b** you and protect you;	Nm 6:24
Israelites, and I will **b** them."	Nm 6:27
that those you **b** are blessed	Nm 22:6
received ⌊a command⌋ to **b**;	Nm 23:20
curse them and don't **b** them!"	Nm 23:25
it pleased the LORD to **b** Israel,	Nm 24:1
Those who **b** you will be blessed,	Nm 24:9
and **b** you as He promised you.	Dt 1:11
will love you, **b** you, and	Dt 7:13
He will **b** your descendants,	Dt 7:13
Him, and to **b** in His name, as	Dt 10:8
LORD your God will **b** you in all	Dt 14:29
is certain to **b** you in the land	Dt 15:4
your God will **b** you in all your	Dt 15:10
your God will **b** you in	Dt 15:18
your God will **b** you in all your	Dt 16:15
your God may **b** you in everything	Dt 23:20
he will sleep in it and **b** you,	Dt 24:13
LORD your God may **b** you in all	Dt 24:19
and **b** Your people Israel and the	Dt 26:15
Mount Gerizim to **b** the people:	Dt 27:12
He will **b** you in the land the	Dt 28:8
its season and to **b** all the work	Dt 28:12
he may **b** himself in his mind,	Dt 29:19
your God may **b** you in the land	Dt 30:16
LORD, **b** his possessions, and	Dt 33:11
to **b** the people of Israel.	Jos 8:33
"The LORD **b** you," they replied.	Ru 2:4
May ⌊the LORD⌋ **b** the man who	Ru 2:19
May the LORD **b** you, my daughter.	Ru 3:10
would **b** Elkanah and his wife:	1Sm 2:20
because he must **b** the sacrifice;	1Sm 9:13
Saul said, "May the LORD **b** you.	1Sm 15:13
them, "The LORD **b** you, because	2Sm 2:5
home⌋ to **b** his household,	2Sm 6:20
please **b** Your servant's house so	2Sm 7:29
to go, though he did **b** him.	2Sm 13:25
only You would **b** me, extend my	1Ch 4:10
⌊home⌋ to **b** his household.	1Ch 16:43
been pleased to **b** Your servant's	1Ch 17:27
Levites stood to **b** the people,	2Ch 30:27
B the LORD your God from	Neh 9:5
if he did not **b** me while warming	Jb 31:20
For You, LORD, **b** the righteous	Ps 5:12
Your people, **b** Your possession,	Ps 28:9
they **b** with their mouths, but	Ps 62:4
with showers and **b** its growth,	Ps 65:10
God be gracious to us and **b** us;	Ps 67:1
God will **b** us, and all the ends	Ps 67:7
Though they curse, You will **b**.	Ps 109:28
remembers us and will **b** ⌊us⌋.	Ps 115:12
He will **b** the house of Israel;	Ps 115:12
He will **b** the house of Aaron;	Ps 115:12
will **b** those who fear the LORD	Ps 115:13
the house of the LORD we **b** you.	Ps 118:26
May the LORD **b** you from Zion,	Ps 128:5
We **b** you in the name of the	Ps 129:8
I will abundantly **b** its food;	Ps 132:15
and earth, **b** you from Zion.	Ps 134:3
You, LORD; the godly will **b** You.	Ps 145:10
and does not **b** its mother.	Pr 30:11
The LORD of Hosts will **b** them,	Is 19:25
May the LORD **b** you, righteous	Jr 31:23
from this day on I will **b** you."	Hg 2:19
b those who curse you, pray for	Lk 6:28
first to you to **b** you by turning	Ac 3:26
B those who persecute you;	Rm 12:14
persecute you; **b** and do not	Rm 12:14
When we are reviled, we **b**;	1Co 4:12
The cup of blessing that we **b**,	1Co 10:16
if you **b** with the spirit,	1Co 14:16
I will most certainly **b** you,	Heb 6:14
it we **b** our Lord and Father,	Jms 3:9

BLESSED *(210)*

So God **b** them, "Be fruitful,	Gn 1:22
b them, and God said to them,	Gn 1:28
God **b** the seventh day and	Gn 2:3
He **b** them and called them man.	Gn 5:2
God **b** Noah and his sons and said	Gn 9:1
on earth will be **b** through you.	Gn 12:3
He **b** him and said: Abram is	Gn 14:19
Abram is **b** by God Most High,	Gn 14:19
the earth will be **b** through him.	Gn 18:18
earth will be **b** by your	Gn 22:18
and the LORD had **b** him in	Gn 24:1
you who are **b** by the LORD.	Gn 24:31
LORD has greatly **b** my master,	Gn 24:35
They **b** Rebekah, saying to her:	Gn 24:60
death, God **b** his son Isaac, who	Gn 25:11
earth will be **b** by your	Gn 26:4
what was sown⌋. The LORD **b** him,	Gn 26:12
You are now **b** by the LORD."	Gn 26:29
his brother Esau; so he **b** him.	Gn 27:23
his clothes, he **b** him and said:	Gn 27:27
of a field that the LORD has **b**.	Gn 27:27
those who bless you will be **b**.	Gn 27:29
before you came in, and I **b** him.	Gn 27:33
Indeed, he will be **b**!"	Gn 27:33
summoned Jacob, **b** him, and	Gn 28:1
that Isaac **b** Jacob and sent him	Gn 28:6
When he **b** him, Isaac commanded	Gn 28:6
on earth will be **b** through you	Gn 28:14
the LORD has **b** me because of you	Gn 30:27
LORD has **b** you because of me.	Gn 30:30
and daughters, and **b** them.	Gn 31:55
And He **b** him there.	Gn 32:29
from Paddan-aram, and He **b** him.	Gn 35:9
the LORD **b** the Egyptian's house	Gn 39:5
Pharaoh, and Jacob **b** Pharaoh.	Gn 47:7
So Jacob **b** Pharaoh and departed	Gn 47:10
in the land of Canaan and **b** me.	Gn 48:3
Then he **b** Joseph and said:	Gn 48:15
So he **b** them that day with these	Gn 48:20
He **b** them, and he blessed each	Gn 49:28
he **b** each one with a suitable	Gn 49:28
"**B** is the LORD," Jethro	Ex 18:10
the LORD **b** the Sabbath day	Ex 20:11
commanded. Then Moses **b** them.	Ex 39:43
toward the people and **b** them.	Lv 9:22
came out, they **b** the people,	Lv 9:23
you bless are **b** and those you	Nm 22:6
this people, for they are **b**."	Nm 22:12
look, you have only **b** ⌊them⌋!"	Nm 23:11
since He has **b**, I cannot change	Nm 23:20
Those who bless you will be **b**,	Nm 24:9
you have **b** ⌊them these three	Nm 24:10
LORD your God has **b** you in all	Dt 2:7
You will be **b** above all peoples;	Dt 7:14
the LORD your God has **b** you.	Dt 12:7
the LORD your God has **b** you,	Dt 14:24
LORD your God has **b** you with.	Dt 15:14
how the LORD your God has **b** you.	Dt 16:10
You will be **b** in the city and	Dt 28:3
the city and **b** in the country.	Dt 28:3
Your descendants will be **b**,	Dt 28:4
and kneading bowl will be **b**.	Dt 28:5
You will be **b** when you come in	Dt 28:6
come in and **b** when you go out	Dt 28:6
May his land be **b** by the LORD	Dt 33:13
Gad's ⌊territory⌋ will be **b**.	Dt 33:20
Asher be the most **b** of the sons;	Dt 33:24
Then Joshua **b** Caleb son of	Jos 14:13
the LORD has greatly **b** us."	Jos 17:14
Joshua **b** them and sent them on	Jos 22:6
them to their homes and **b** them,	Jos 22:7
he repeatedly **b** you, and I	Jos 24:10
is most **b** of women, the wife	Jdg 5:24
is most **b** among tent-dwelling	Jdg 5:24
boy grew, and the LORD **b** him.	Jdg 13:24
My son, you are **b** by the LORD!"	Jdg 17:2
May he be **b** by the LORD, who has	Ru 2:20
"May you be **b** by the LORD,"	1Sm 23:21
B is your discernment, and	1Sm 25:33
your discernment, and **b** are you.	1Sm 25:33
him, "You are **b**, my son David.	1Sm 26:25
the LORD **b** Obed-edom and his	2Sm 6:11
The LORD has **b** Obed-edom's	2Sm 6:12
he **b** the people in the name of	2Sm 6:18
house will be **b** forever."	2Sm 7:29
king kissed Barzillai and **b** him,	2Sm 19:39
but King Solomon will be **b**,	1Kg 2:45
turned around and **b** the entire	1Kg 8:14
and he stood and **b** the whole	1Kg 8:55
So they **b** the king and went home	1Kg 8:66
the LORD **b** his family and all	1Ch 13:14
he **b** the people in the name of	1Ch 16:2
You, LORD, have **b** it, and it is	1Ch 17:27
it, and it is **b** forever."	1Ch 17:27
the eighth, for God **b** him.	1Ch 26:5
the king turned and **b** the entire	2Ch 6:3
the LORD has **b** His people;	2Ch 31:10
Ezra **b** the LORD, the great God,	Neh 8:6
have **b** the work of his hands,	Jb 1:10
heard me, they **b** me, and when	Jb 29:11
The dying man **b** me, and I made	Jb 29:13
So the LORD **b** the latter part of	Jb 42:12
Those who are **b** by Him will	Ps 37:22
he will be **b** in the land.	Ps 41:2
Therefore God has **b** you forever.	Ps 45:2
and may he be **b** all day long.	Ps 72:15
all nations be **b** by him and call	Ps 72:17
blessed by him and call him **b**.	Ps 72:17
of the upright will be **b**.	Ps 112:2
May you be **b** by the LORD, the	Ps 115:15
B is he who comes in the name of	Ps 118:26
who fears the LORD will be **b**.	Ps 128:4
your fountain be **b**, and take	Pr 5:18
will not be **b** ultimately.	Pr 20:21
A generous person will be **b**,	Pr 22:9
Her sons rise up and call her **b**.	Pr 31:28
B are you, land, when your king	Ec 10:17
them, saying, "**B** be Egypt My	Is 19:25
I **b** him and made him many.	Is 51:2
are a people the LORD has **b**.	Is 61:9
Whoever is **b** in the land will be	Is 65:16
the land will be **b** by the God of	Is 65:16
will be a people **b** by the LORD	Is 65:23
nations will be **b** by Him and	Jr 4:2
B is the man who trusts in the	Jr 17:7
bore me—let it never be **b**.	Jr 20:14
B is the one who waits for and	Dn 12:12
B are the poor in spirit,	Mt 5:3
B are those who mourn, because	Mt 5:4
B are the gentle, because they	Mt 5:5
B are those who hunger and	Mt 5:6
B are the merciful, because they	Mt 5:7
B are the pure in heart, because	Mt 5:8
B are the peacemakers, because	Mt 5:9
B are those who are persecuted	Mt 5:10
B are you when they insult you	Mt 5:11
because of Me, he is **b**."	Mt 11:6
your eyes are **b** because they do	Mt 13:16
looking up to heaven, He **b** them.	Mt 14:19
are **b** because flesh and blood	Mt 16:17
B is He who comes in the name of	Mt 21:9
B is He who comes in the name of	Mt 23:39
you who are **b** by My Father,	Mt 25:34
took bread, **b** and broke it,	Mt 26:26
He **b** and broke the loaves.	Mk 6:41
and when He had **b** them, He said	Mk 8:7
His hands on them and **b** them.	Mk 10:16
B is He who comes in the name of	Mk 11:9
B is the coming kingdom of our	Mk 11:10
He took bread, **b** and broke it,	Mk 14:22
Messiah, the Son of the **B** One?"	Mk 14:61
You are the most **b** of women,	Lk 1:42
women, and your child will be **b**!	Lk 1:42
has believed is **b** because what	Lk 1:45
all generations will call me **b**,	Lk 1:48
Then Simeon **b** them and told His	Lk 2:34
B are you who are poor, because	Lk 6:20
B are you who are hungry now,	Lk 6:21
B are you who weep now, because	Lk 6:21
B are you when people hate you,	Lk 6:22
offended because of Me is **b**."	Lk 7:23
to heaven, He **b** and broke them.	Lk 9:16
see the things you see are **b**!	Lk 10:23
the one who nursed You are **b**!"	Lk 11:27

word of God and keep it are **b**!” Lk 11:28
alert when he comes will be **b**. Lk 12:37
them alert, those slaves are **b**. Lk 12:38
B is He who comes in the name of Lk 13:35
And you will be **b**, because they Lk 14:14
in the kingdom of God is **b**!” Lk 14:15
B is the King who comes in the Lk 19:38
will say, ‘**B** are the barren, Lk 23:29
took the bread, **b** and broke it, Lk 24:30
lifting up His hands He **b** them. Lk 24:50
B is He who comes in the name of Jn 12:13
you are **b** if you do them. Jn 13:17
believe without seeing are **b**.” Jn 20:29
families of the earth will be **b**. Ac 3:25
‘It is more **b** to give than to Ac 20:35
the Creator, who is **b** forever. Rm 1:25
who is God over all, **b** forever. Rm 9:5
B is the man who does not Rm 14:22
B be the God and Father of our 2Co 1:3
The eternally **b** One, the God and 2Co 11:31
the nations will be **b** in you. Gl 3:8
have faith are **b** with Abraham, Gl 3:9
B be the God and Father of our Eph 1:3
has **b** us with every spiritual Eph 1:3
gospel of the **b** God that was 1Tm 1:11
⌊He is⌋ the **b** and only Sovereign, 1Tm 6:15
while we wait for the **b** hope and Ti 2:13
met Abraham and **b** him as he Heb 7:1
Abraham and **b** the one who had Heb 7:6
inferior is **b** by the superior Heb 7:7
By faith Isaac **b** Jacob and Esau Heb 11:20
b each of the sons of Joseph, Heb 11:21
B is a man who endures trials, Jms 1:12
will be **b** in what he does. Jms 1:25
we count as **b** those who have Jms 5:11
B be the God and Father of our 1Pt 1:3
for righteousness, you are **b**. 1Pt 3:14
Christ, you are **b**, because the 1Pt 4:14
B is the one who reads and Rv 1:3
who reads and **b** are those who Rv 1:3
B are the dead who die in the Rv 14:13
B is the one who is alert and Rv 16:15
B are those invited to the Rv 19:9
B and holy is the one who shares Rv 20:6
B is the one who keeps the Rv 22:7
B are those who wash their Rv 22:14

BLESSEDNESS *(1)*

happened to this **b** of yours? Gl 4:15

BLESSES *(8)*

the Almighty who **b** you with Gn 49:25
LORD your God **b** you as He has Dt 15:6
LORD **b** His people with peace. Ps 29:11
its harvest; God, our God, **b** us. Ps 67:6
He **b** them, and they multiply Ps 107:38
your gates and **b** your children Ps 147:13
but He **b** the home of the Pr 3:33
one **b** his neighbor with a loud Pr 27:14

BLESSING *(67)*

name great, and you will be a **b**. Gn 12:2
rather than a **b** on myself.” Gn 27:12
had finished **b** Jacob and Jacob Gn 27:30
deceitfully and took your **b**.” Gn 27:35
look, now he has taken my **b**.” Gn 27:36
“Haven’t you saved a **b** for me?” Gn 27:36
you only have one **b**, my father? Gn 27:38
because of the **b** his father had Gn 27:41
offspring the **b** of Abraham so Gn 28:4
The LORD’s **b** was on all that he Gn 39:5
each one with a suitable **b**. Gn 49:28
this will also be a **b** to me.” Ex 12:32
have brought a **b** on yourselves Ex 32:29
I will appoint My **b** for you in Lv 25:21
set before you a **b** and a curse: Dt 11:26
⌊there will be⌋ a **b**, if you obey Dt 11:27
to proclaim the **b** at Mount Dt 11:29
according to the **b** the LORD your Dt 12:15
according to the **b** the LORD your Dt 16:17
curse into a **b** for you because Dt 23:5
will grant you a **b** on your Dt 28:8
you life and death, **b** and curse. Dt 30:19
This is the **b** that Moses, the Dt 33:1
of the LORD’s **b**, take possession Dt 33:23
She replied, “Give me a **b**. Jos 15:19
She answered him, “Give me a **b**. Jdg 1:15
and with Your **b** Your servant’s 2Sm 7:29
you will bring a **b** on the LORD’s 2Sm 21:3
exalted above all **b** and praise. Neh 9:5
God turned the curse into a **b**. Neh 13:2
may Your **b** be on Your people. Ps 3:8
my portion and my cup ⌊of **b**⌋; Ps 16:5
He will receive **b** from the LORD, Ps 24:5
and his children are a **b**. Ps 37:26
no delight in **b**—let it be far Ps 109:17
“May the LORD’s **b** be on you.” Ps 129:8
the LORD has appointed the **b**— Ps 133:3
of the righteous is a **b**, Pr 10:7
The LORD’s **b** enriches, and Pr 10:22
up by the **b** of the upright, Pr 11:11
but a **b** will come to the one who Pr 11:26
and a generous **b** will come to Pr 24:25
Assyria—a **b** within the land Is 19:24
and My **b** on your offspring Is 44:3
and the area around My hill a **b**: Ezk 34:26
in their season—showers of **b**. Ezk 34:26
so that a **b** may rest on your Ezk 44:30
relent and leave a **b** behind Him, Jl 2:14
and you take My **b** from their Mc 2:9
save you, and you will be a **b**. Zch 8:13
and pour out a **b** for you without Mal 3:10
And while He was **b** them, He left Lk 24:51
in the temple complex **b** God. Lk 24:53
speaks of the **b** of the man to Rm 4:6
Is this **b** only for the Rm 4:9
the fullness of the **b** of Christ. Rm 15:29
The cup of **b** that we bless, 1Co 10:16
was that the **b** of Abraham would Gl 3:14
spiritual **b** in the heavens, Eph 1:3
for, receives a **b** from God. Heb 6:7
when he wanted to inherit the **b**, Heb 12:17
same mouth come **b** and cursing. Jms 3:10
giving a **b**, since you were 1Pt 3:9
so that you can inherit a **b**. 1Pt 3:9
and honor and glory and **b**! Rv 5:12
B and honor and glory and Rv 5:13
B and glory and wisdom and Rv 7:12

BLESSINGS *(19)*

Israel will invoke **b** by you, Gn 48:20
you with **b** of the heavens Gn 49:25
b of the deep that lies below, Gn 49:25
and **b** of the breasts and the Gn 49:25
The **b** of your father excel the Gn 49:26
excel the **b** of my ancestors Gn 49:26
and pronounce **b** in the LORD’s Dt 21:5
All these **b** will come and Dt 28:2
the **b** and curses I have set Dt 30:1
the **b** as well as the curses— Jos 8:34
and to pronounce **b** in His name 1Ch 23:13
For You meet him with rich **b**; Ps 21:3
You give him **b** forever; Ps 21:6
rain will cover it with **b**. Ps 84:6
are the people with such ⌊**b**⌋. Ps 144:15
B are on the head of the Pr 10:6
A faithful man will have many **b**, Pr 28:20
you, and I will curse your **b**. Mal 2:2
covenant **b** made to David. Ac 13:34

BLEW *(28)*

the locusts and **b** them into the Ex 10:19
But You **b** with Your breath, Ex 15:10
the LORD came up and **b** quail in Nm 11:31
forward and **b** the trumpets; Jos 6:8
the priests who **b** the trumpets, Jos 6:9
the priests **b** the trumpets, Jos 6:16
and he **b** the ram’s horn and the Jdg 6:34
They **b** their trumpets and broke Jdg 7:19
three companies **b** their trumpets Jdg 7:20
When Gideon’s men **b** their 300 Jdg 7:22
So Saul **b** the ram’s horn 1Sm 13:3
Then Joab **b** the ram’s horn, 2Sm 2:28
Joab **b** the ram’s horn, 2Sm 18:16
He **b** the ram’s horn and shouted: 2Sm 20:1
So he **b** the ram’s horn, and they 2Sm 20:22
Then they **b** the ram’s horn, 1Kg 1:39
They **b** the ram’s horn and 2Kg 9:13
and Jahaziel ⌊**b**⌋ the trumpets 1Ch 16:6
Then the priests **b** the trumpets, 2Ch 13:14
and the winds **b** and pounded that Mt 7:25
the winds **b** and pounded that Mt 7:27
The first ⌊angel⌋ **b** his trumpet, Rv 8:7
The second angel **b** his trumpet, Rv 8:8
The third angel **b** his trumpet, Rv 8:10
The fourth angel **b** his trumpet, Rv 8:12
The fifth angel **b** his trumpet, Rv 9:1
The sixth angel **b** his trumpet. Rv 9:13
The seventh angel **b** his trumpet, Rv 11:15

BLIGHT *(5)*

heat, drought, **b**, and mildew; Dt 28:22
when there is **b**, mildew, locust, 1Kg 8:37
when there is **b**, mildew, locust, 2Ch 6:28
I struck you with **b** and mildew; Am 4:9
hands—with **b**, mildew, and hail Hg 2:17

BLIGHTED *(1)*

Ephraim is **b**; their roots are Hs 9:16

BLIND *(81)*

him mute or deaf, seeing or **b**? Ex 4:11
block in front of the **b**, Lv 19:14
no man who is **b**, lame, facially Lv 21:18
animal⌋ to the LORD that is **b**, Lv 22:22
if it is lame or **b** or has any Dt 15:21
one who leads a **b** person astray Dt 27:18
you will grope as a **b** man gropes Dt 28:29
the **b** and lame can repel you, 2Sm 5:6
lame and the **b** who are despised 2Sm 5:8
The **b** and the lame will never 2Sm 5:8
I was eyes to the **b** and feet to Jb 29:15
or let the widow’s eyes go **b**, Jb 31:16
LORD opens ⌊the eyes of⌋ the **b**. Ps 146:8
their ears and **b** their eyes; Is 6:10
b yourselves and be blind! Is 29:9
blind yourselves and be **b**! Is 29:9
the eyes of the **b** will see. Is 29:18
eyes of the **b** will be opened, Is 35:5
order to open **b** eyes, to bring Is 42:7
I will lead the **b** by a way they Is 42:16
you **b**, so that you may see. Is 42:18
Who is **b** but My servant, or deaf Is 42:19
is **b** like ⌊My⌋ dedicated one, Is 42:19
or **b** like the servant of the Is 42:19
Bring out a people who are **b**, Is 43:8
watchmen are **b**, all of them, Is 56:10
grope along a wall like the **b**; Is 59:10
the **b** and the lame will be with Jr 31:8
B, they stumbled in the streets, Lm 4:14
walk like the **b** because they Zph 1:17
his right eye go completely **b**!” Zch 11:17
When you present a **b** ⌊animal⌋ Mal 1:8
from there, two **b** men followed Mt 9:27
the house, the **b** men approached Mt 9:28
the **b** see, the lame walk, those Mt 11:5
who was **b** and unable to speak Mt 12:22
alone! They are **b** guides. And if Mt 15:14
And if the **b** guide the blind, Mt 15:14
And if the blind guide the **b**, Mt 15:14
the lame, the **b**, the deformed, Mt 15:30
lame walking, and the **b** seeing. Mt 15:31
There were two **b** men sitting by Mt 20:30
The **b** and the lame came to Him Mt 21:14
Woe to you, **b** guides, who say, Mt 23:16
B fools! For which is greater, Mt 23:17
B people! For which is greater, Mt 23:19
B guides! You strain out a gnat, Mt 23:24
B Pharisee! First clean the Mt 23:26
They brought a **b** man to Him and Mk 8:22
took the **b** man by the hand and Mk 8:23
son of Timaeus), a **b** beggar, was Mk 10:46
they called the **b** man and said Mk 10:49
Rabbouni,” the **b** man told Him, Mk 10:51
and recovery of sight to the **b**, Lk 4:18
Can the **b** guide the blind? Lk 6:39
Can the blind guide the **b**? Lk 6:39
granted sight to many **b** people. Lk 7:21
The **b** receive their sight, Lk 7:22
are poor, maimed, lame, or **b**. Lk 14:13
the poor, maimed, **b**, and lame!’ Lk 14:21
a **b** man was sitting by the road Lk 18:35
of the sick—**b**, lame, and Jn 5:3
He saw a man **b** from birth. Jn 9:1
parents, that he was born **b**?” Jn 9:2
who used to be **b** to the Jn 9:13
Again they asked the **b** man, Jn 9:17
that he was **b** and received sight Jn 9:18
⌊the one⌋ you say was born **b**? Jn 9:19
our son and that he was born **b**,” Jn 9:20
man who had been **b** and told him, Jn 9:24
I was **b**, and now I can see!” Jn 9:25
the eyes of a person born **b**. Jn 9:32
those who do see will become **b**.” Jn 9:39
Him, “We aren’t **b** too, are we?” Jn 9:40
“If you were **b**,” Jesus told them, Jn 9:41
a demon open the eyes of the **b**?” Jn 10:21
who opened the **b** man’s eyes also Jn 11:37
are going to be **b**, and will not Ac 13:11
that you are a guide for the **b**, Rm 2:19
these things is **b** and 2Pt 1:9
pitiful, poor, **b**, and naked, Rv 3:17

BLINDED *(6)*
the king of Babylon **b** Zedekiah, 2Kg 25:7
Then he **b** Zedekiah and put him Jr 39:7
Then he **b** Zedekiah and bound him Jr 52:11
He has **b** their eyes and hardened Jn 12:40
god of this age has **b** the minds 2Co 4:4
the darkness has **b** his eyes. 1Jn 2:11

BLINDFOLD *(1)*
spit on Him, to **b** Him, and to Mk 14:65

BLINDFOLDING *(1)*
After **b** Him, they kept asking, Lk 22:64

BLINDFOLDS *(1)*
the wicked; He **b** its judges. If Jb 9:24

BLINDING *(1)*
with a **b** light so that they were Gn 19:11

BLINDNESS *(4)*
you with madness, **b**, and mental Dt 28:28
strike this nation with **b**." 2Kg 6:18
So He struck them with **b**, 2Kg 6:18
horses of the nations with **b**. Zch 12:4

BLINDS *(2)*
for a bribe **b** the clear-sighted Ex 23:8
it **b** the eyes of the wise and Dt 16:19

BLOATED *(1)*
you became fat, **b**, and gorged. Dt 32:15

BLOCK *(14)*
or put a stumbling **b** in front of Lv 19:14
I will bow down to a **b** of wood." Is 44:19
a stumbling **b** in front of him Ezk 3:20
stumbling **b** before his face Ezk 14:4
stumbling **b** before his face Ezk 14:7
a stumbling **b** that causes your Ezk 18:30
It will **b** those who travel Ezk 39:11
a sinful stumbling **b** to them, Ezk 44:12
I will **b** her way with thorns; Hs 2:6
of the ground and **b** the path of Am 2:7
put a stumbling **b** or pitfall in Rm 14:13
a stumbling **b** to the Jews and 1Co 1:23
a stumbling **b** to the weak. 1Co 8:9
place a stumbling **b** in front of Rv 2:14

BLOCKED *(2)*
This same Hezekiah **b** the outlet 2Ch 32:30
He has **b** my way so that I cannot Jb 19:8

BLOCKS *(3)*
place stumbling **b** before these Jr 6:21
the stumbling **b** that brought Ezk 7:19
sinful stumbling **b** before their Ezk 14:3

BLOOD *(396)*
Your brother's **b** cries out to Me Gn 4:10
your brother's **b** you have shed. Gn 4:11
man for your life and your **b**. Gn 9:5
sheds man's **b**, his blood will be Gn 9:6
his **b** will be shed by man, Gn 9:6
you are my own flesh and **b**." Gn 29:14
said to them, "Don't shed **b**. Gn 37:22
our brother and cover up his **b**? Gn 37:26
and dipped the robe in its **b**. Gn 37:31
Now we must account for his **b**!" Gn 42:22
his robes in the **b** of grapes. Gn 49:11
will become **b** on the ground." Ex 4:9
are a bridegroom of **b** to me!" Ex 4:25
"You are a bridegroom of **b**," Ex 4:26
my hand, and it will turn to **b**. Ex 7:17
and they will become **b**. Ex 7:19
There will be **b** throughout the Ex 7:19
in the Nile was turned to **b**. Ex 7:20
There was **b** throughout the land Ex 7:21
take some of the **b** and put it on Ex 12:7
b on the houses where you are Ex 12:13
when I see the **b**, I will pass Ex 12:13
dip it in the **b** that is in the Ex 12:22
with some of the **b** in the basin. Ex 12:22
and sees the **b** on the lintel Ex 12:23
not offer the **b** of My sacrifices Ex 23:18
Moses took half the **b** and set it Ex 24:6
half of the **b** he sprinkled Ex 24:6
Moses took the **b**, sprinkled it Ex 24:8
This is the **b** of the covenant Ex 24:8
of the bull's **b** and apply ⌊it⌋ Ex 29:12
the ⌊rest⌋ of the **b** at the base Ex 29:12
ram, take its **b**, and sprinkle Ex 29:16
take some of its **b**, and put it Ex 29:20
the ⌊remaining⌋ **b** on all sides Ex 29:20
Take some of the **b** that is on Ex 29:21
with the **b** of the sin offering Ex 30:10
not present the **b** for My Ex 34:25
to present the **b** and sprinkle it Lv 1:5
sprinkle its **b** against the altar Lv 1:11
its **b** should be drained at the Lv 1:15
will sprinkle the **b** on all sides Lv 3:2
will sprinkle its **b** on all sides Lv 3:8
will sprinkle its **b** on all sides Lv 3:13
must not eat any fat or any **b**." Lv 3:17
some of the bull's **b** and bring Lv 4:5
finger in the **b** and sprinkle Lv 4:6
apply some of the **b** to the horns Lv 4:7
rest of the bull's **b** at the base Lv 4:7
of the bull's **b** into the tent Lv 4:16
finger in the **b** and sprinkle ⌊it Lv 4:17
apply some of the **b** to the horns Lv 4:18
the rest of the **b** at the base Lv 4:18
take some of the **b** from the sin Lv 4:25
The rest of its **b** he must pour Lv 4:25
some of its **b** with his finger Lv 4:30
the rest of its **b** at the base Lv 4:30
take some of the **b** of the sin Lv 4:34
the rest of its **b** at the base Lv 4:34
some of the **b** of the sin Lv 5:9
the rest of the **b** is to be Lv 5:9
and if any of its **b** spatters on Lv 6:27
be eaten if its **b** has been Lv 6:30
to sprinkle its **b** on all sides Lv 7:2
sprinkles the **b** of the Lv 7:14
must not eat the **b** of any bird Lv 7:26
Whoever eats any **b**, that person Lv 7:27
who presents the **b** of the Lv 7:33
it⌋, took the **b**, and applied it Lv 8:15
He poured out the **b** at the base Lv 8:15
and sprinkled the **b** on all sides Lv 8:19
took some of its **b**, and put ⌊it⌋ Lv 8:23
put some of the **b** on their right Lv 8:24
sprinkled the **b** on all sides Lv 8:24
oil and some of the **b** that was Lv 8:30
sons brought the **b** to him, Lv 9:9
finger in the **b** and applied it Lv 9:9
He poured out the **b** at the base Lv 9:9
Aaron's sons brought him the **b**, Lv 9:12
Aaron's sons brought him the **b**, Lv 9:18
Since its **b** was not brought Lv 10:18
clean from her discharge of **b**. Lv 12:7
all into the **b** of the bird that Lv 14:6
sprinkle ⌊the **b**⌋ seven times Lv 14:7
to take some of the **b** from the Lv 14:14
on top of the **b** of the Lv 14:17
take some of the **b** of the Lv 14:25
place as the **b** of the Lv 14:28
dip them in the **b** of the Lv 14:51
house with the **b** of the bird, Lv 14:52
it consists of **b** from her body, Lv 15:19
and ⌊**b** from⌋ her menstruation Lv 15:24
of her **b** for many days, Lv 15:25
of the bull's **b** and sprinkle ⌊it Lv 16:14
some of the **b** with his finger Lv 16:14
brings its **b** inside the veil, Lv 16:15
same with its **b** as he did with Lv 16:15
as he did with the bull's **b**: Lv 16:15
some of the bull's **b** and some of Lv 16:18
of the goat's **b** and put ⌊it⌋ Lv 16:18
some of the **b** on it with his Lv 16:19
whose **b** was brought into the Lv 16:27
has shed **b** and must be cut off Lv 17:4
sprinkle the **b** on the LORD's Lv 17:6
live among them who eats any **b**, Lv 17:10
person who eats **b** and cut him Lv 17:10
life of a creature is in the **b**, Lv 17:11
who lives among you may eat **b**. Lv 17:12
must drain its **b** and cover it Lv 17:13
life of every creature is its **b**, Lv 17:14
not eat the **b** of any creature Lv 17:14
life of every creature is its **b**; Lv 17:14
eat ⌊anything⌋ with **b** ⌊in it⌋. Lv 19:26
his **b** is on his own hands. Lv 20:9
their **b** is on their own hands. Lv 20:11
their **b** is on their own hands. Lv 20:12
their **b** is on their own hands. Lv 20:13
their ⌊own⌋ **b** is on them. Lv 20:16
uncovered the source of her **b**. Lv 20:18
exposing one's own **b** relative; Lv 20:19
their **b** is on their own hands." Lv 20:27
to sprinkle their **b** on the altar Nm 18:17
some of its **b** with his finger Nm 19:4
hide, flesh, and **b**, are to be Nm 19:5
and drink the **b** of the slain. Nm 23:24
The avenger of **b** himself is to Nm 35:19
The avenger of **b** is to kill the Nm 35:21
the avenger of **b** according to Nm 35:24
the hand of the avenger of **b**. Nm 35:25
the avenger of **b** finds him Nm 35:27
because of the **b** that is shed on Nm 35:33
except by the **b** of the person Nm 35:33
but you must not eat the **b**; Dt 12:16
don't eat the **b**, since the blood Dt 12:23
blood, since the **b** is the life, Dt 12:23
Do not eat **b**; pour it on the Dt 12:24
the meat and **b** of your burnt Dt 12:27
The **b** of your ⌊other⌋ sacrifices Dt 12:27
But you must not eat its **b**; Dt 15:23
the avenger of **b** in the heat of Dt 19:6
innocent **b** will not be shed, Dt 19:10
the avenger of **b** and he will die Dt 19:12
guilt of shedding innocent **b**, Dt 19:13
'Our hands did not shed this **b**; Dt 21:7
of innocent **b** against them.' Dt 21:8
guilt of shedding innocent **b**, Dt 21:9
drunk with **b** while My sword Dt 32:42
the **b** of the slain and the Dt 32:42
avenge the **b** of His servants Dt 32:43
his **b** will be on his own head, Jos 2:19
his **b** will be on our heads. Jos 2:19
refuge from the avenger of **b**. Jos 20:3
if the avenger of **b** pursues him, Jos 20:5
the avenger of **b** until he stands Jos 20:9
that I am your own flesh and **b**." Jdg 9:2
and their **b** would be avenged Jdg 9:24
meat⌋ with the **b** ⌊still in it.⌋ 1Sm 14:32
meat⌋ with the **b** ⌊still in it.⌋" 1Sm 14:33
meat⌋ with the **b** ⌊in it.⌋'" 1Sm 14:34
innocent **b** by killing David 1Sm 19:5
So don't let my **b** fall to the 1Sm 26:20
Your **b** is on your own head 2Sm 1:16
from the **b** of the slain, 2Sm 1:22
concerning the **b** of Abner son of 2Sm 3:28
require his **b** from your hands 2Sm 4:11
we are, your own flesh and **b**. 2Sm 5:1
the avenger of **b** will not 2Sm 14:11
back for all the **b** of the house 2Sm 16:8
own flesh and **b**, intends to take 2Sm 16:11
are my brothers, my flesh and **b**. 2Sm 19:12
'Aren't you my flesh and **b**? 2Sm 19:13
writhing in his **b** in the middle 2Sm 20:12
is because of the **b** shed by Saul 2Sm 21:1
Is this not the **b** of men who 2Sm 23:17
peace to avenge **b** shed in war. 1Kg 2:5
He spilled that **b** on his own 1Kg 2:5
gray head down to Sheol with **b**." 1Kg 2:9
house the **b** that Joab shed 1Kg 2:31
back his own **b** on his own head 1Kg 2:32
Their **b** will come back on Joab's 1Kg 2:33
b will be on your own head." 1Kg 2:37
until **b** gushed out on them. 1Kg 18:28
the dogs licked Naboth's **b**, 1Kg 21:19
dogs will also lick your **b**!'" 1Kg 21:19
and **b** from his wound flowed into 1Kg 22:35
dogs licked up his **b**, and the 1Kg 22:38
across from them was red like **b**. 2Kg 3:22
"This is **b**!" they exclaimed. "The 2Kg 3:23
may avenge the **b** shed by the 2Kg 9:7
b of My servants the prophets 2Kg 9:7
surely as I saw the **b** of Naboth 2Kg 9:26
of Naboth and the **b** of his sons 2Kg 9:26
and some of her **b** splattered on 2Kg 9:33
sprinkled the **b** of his 2Kg 16:13
the altar all the **b** of the burnt 2Kg 16:15
and all the **b** of sacrifice. 2Kg 16:15
much innocent **b** that he filled 2Kg 21:16
all the innocent **b** he had shed. 2Kg 24:4
Jerusalem with innocent **b**, 2Kg 24:4
we are, your own flesh and **b**. 1Ch 11:1
can I drink the **b** of these men 1Ch 11:19
have shed much **b** and waged great 1Ch 22:8
shed so much **b** on the ground 1Ch 22:8
a man of war and have shed **b**.' 1Ch 28:3
he had shed the **b** of the sons of 2Ch 24:25
received the **b** and sprinkled it 2Ch 29:22
sprinkled the **b** on the altar. 2Ch 29:22
sprinkled the **b** on the altar. 2Ch 29:22
and put their **b** on the altar for 2Ch 29:24
sprinkled the **b** ⌊received⌋ 2Ch 30:16
sprinkled the **b** they had been 2Ch 35:11
Earth, do not cover my **b**; Jb 16:18
brood gulps down **b**, and wherever Jb 39:30

out their drink offerings of **b**, Ps 16:4
bulls or drink the **b** of goats? Ps 50:13
his feet in the **b** of the wicked. Ps 58:10
may wade in **b** and your dogs' Ps 68:23
He turned their rivers into **b**, Ps 78:44
poured out their **b** like water Ps 79:3
for the shed **b** of Your servants Ps 79:10
waters into **b** and caused their Ps 105:29
They shed innocent **b**—the blood Ps 106:38
b of their sons and daughters Ps 106:38
the land became polluted with **b**. Ps 106:38
hands that shed innocent **b**, Pr 6:17
and twisting a nose draws **b**, Pr 30:33
no desire for the **b** of bulls, Is 1:11
Your hands are covered with **b**. Is 1:15
waters of Dibon are full of **b**, Is 15:9
will reveal the **b** shed on it and Is 26:21
the mountains flow with their **b**. Is 34:3
LORD's sword is covered with **b**. Is 34:6
with the **b** of lambs and goats, Is 34:6
land will be soaked with **b**, Is 34:7
with their own **b** as with sweet Is 49:26
ignore your own flesh ⌊and **b**⌋? Is 58:7
your hands are defiled with **b**, Is 59:3
they rush to shed innocent **b**. Is 59:7
their **b** spattered My garments, Is 63:3
out their **b** on the ground. Is 63:6
offering, one offers swine's **b**; Is 66:3
with the **b** of the innocent Jr 2:34
shed innocent **b** in this place Jr 7:6
with the **b** of the innocent. Jr 19:4
shed innocent **b** in this place. Jr 22:3
innocent **b** and committing Jr 22:17
bring innocent **b** on yourselves, Jr 26:15
will drink its fill of their **b**, Jr 46:10
Let my **b** be on the inhabitants Jr 51:35
who shed the **b** of the righteous Lm 4:13
defiled by this **b**, so that no Lm 4:14
hold you responsible for his **b**. Ezk 3:18
hold you responsible for his **b**. Ezk 3:20
you and saw you lying in your **b**, Ezk 16:6
to you ⌊as you lay⌋ in your **b**: Ezk 16:6
to you ⌊as you lay⌋ in your **b**: Ezk 16:6
rinsed off your **b**, and anointed Ezk 16:9
stark naked and lying in your **b**. Ezk 16:22
idols and the **b** of your children Ezk 16:36
and those who shed **b** are judged. Ezk 16:38
sheds **b** and does any of these Ezk 18:10
die. His **b** will be on him. Ezk 18:13
Your **b** will be ⌊spilled⌋ in the Ezk 21:32
judgment against the city of **b**? Ezk 22:2
city that sheds **b** within her Ezk 22:3
guilty of the **b** you have shed, Ezk 22:4
has used his strength to shed **b**. Ezk 22:6
who slander in order to shed **b**. Ezk 22:9
bribes in order to shed **b**. Ezk 22:12
against the **b** shed among you. Ezk 22:13
prey, shedding **b**, and destroying Ezk 22:27
adultery, and **b** is on their Ezk 23:37
and those who shed **b** are judged, Ezk 23:45
adulteresses and **b** is on their Ezk 23:45
For the **b** she shed is in her Ezk 24:7
I have put her **b** on the bare Ezk 24:8
land with the flow of your **b**, Ezk 32:6
his **b** will be on his own head. Ezk 33:4
his **b** is on his own hands. Ezk 33:5
accountable for their **b**. Ezk 33:6
hold you responsible for his **b**. Ezk 33:8
You eat ⌊meat⌋ with **b** ⌊in it⌋, Ezk 33:25
eyes to your idols, and shed **b**. Ezk 33:25
because of the **b** they had shed Ezk 36:18
you will eat flesh and drink **b**. Ezk 39:17
and drink the **b** of the earth's Ezk 39:18
and drink **b** until you are drunk Ezk 39:19
on it and **b** may be sprinkled Ezk 43:18
some of its **b** and apply ⌊it⌋ Ezk 43:20
My food—the fat and the **b**. Ezk 44:7
Me to offer Me fat and **b**." Ezk 44:15
take some of the **b** from the sin Ezk 45:19
b, fire, and columns of smoke. Jl 2:30
and the moon to **b** before the Jl 2:31
whose land they shed innocent **b**. Jl 3:19
don't charge us with innocent **b**! Jnh 1:14
them wait in ambush to shed **b**; Mc 7:2
to the city of **b**, totally Nah 3:1
Their **b** will be poured out like Zph 1:17
will remove the **b** from their Zch 9:7
because of the **b** of your Zch 9:11
flesh and **b** did not reveal Mt 16:17
in shedding the prophets' **b**.' Mt 23:30
the righteous **b** shed on the Mt 23:35
from the **b** of righteous Abel to Mt 23:35
Abel to the **b** of Zechariah, Mt 23:35
For this is My **b** ⌊that Mt 26:28
sinned by betraying innocent **b**," Mt 27:4
treasury, since it is **b** money." Mt 27:6
been called "**B** Field" to this Mt 27:8
I am innocent of this man's **b**. Mt 27:24
b be on us and on our children! Mt 27:25
Instantly her flow of **b** ceased, Mk 5:29
This is My **b** ⌊that establishes⌋ Mk 14:24
for the **b** of all the prophets Lk 11:50
from the **b** of Abel to the blood Lk 11:51
of Abel to the **b** of Zechariah, Lk 11:51
Galileans whose **b** Pilate had Lk 13:1
covenant ⌊established by⌋ My **b**; Lk 22:20
became like drops of **b** falling Lk 22:44
born, not of **b**, or of the will Jn 1:13
the Son of Man and drink His **b**, Jn 6:53
drinks My **b** has eternal life, Jn 6:54
food and My **b** is real drink. Jn 6:55
and drinks My **b** lives in Me, Jn 6:56
at once **b** and water came out. Jn 19:34
Hakeldama, that is, Field of **B**. Ac 1:19
b and fire and a cloud of smoke. Ac 2:19
and the moon to **b**, before the Ac 2:20
to bring this man's **b** on us!" Ac 5:28
has been strangled, and from **b**. Ac 15:20
to idols, from **b**, from eating Ac 15:29
Your **b** is on your own heads! Ac 18:6
I am innocent of everyone's **b**, Ac 20:26
He purchased with His own **b**. Ac 20:28
to idols, from **b**, from what is Ac 21:25
And when the **b** of Your witness Ac 22:20
Their feet are swift to shed **b**; Rm 3:15
through faith in His **b**, Rm 3:25
declared righteous by His **b**, Rm 5:9
a sharing in the **b** of Christ? 1Co 10:16
cup is the new covenant in My **b**. 1Co 11:25
the body and **b** of the Lord. 1Co 11:27
flesh and **b** cannot inherit the 1Co 15:50
have redemption through His **b**, Eph 1:7
near by the **b** of the Messiah. Eph 2:13
is not against flesh and **b**, Eph 6:12
through the **b** of His cross— Col 1:20
have flesh and **b** in common, Heb 2:14
never without **b**, which he offers Heb 9:7
by the **b** of goats and calves, Heb 9:12
by His own **b**, having obtained Heb 9:12
For if the **b** of goats and bulls Heb 9:13
more will the **b** of the Messiah, Heb 9:14
covenant was inaugurated with **b**. Heb 9:18
he took the **b** of calves and Heb 9:19
This is the **b** of the covenant Heb 9:20
the vessels of worship with **b**. Heb 9:21
everything is purified with **b**, Heb 9:22
the shedding of **b** there is no Heb 9:22
yearly with the **b** of another. Heb 9:25
for the **b** of bulls and goats Heb 10:4
through the **b** of Jesus, Heb 10:19
as profane the **b** of the covenant Heb 10:29
and the sprinkling of the **b**, Heb 11:28
to the point of shedding your **b**. Heb 12:4
to the sprinkled **b**, which says Heb 12:24
things than the ⌊**b**⌋ of Abel. Heb 12:24
those animals whose **b** is brought Heb 13:11
the people by His own **b**. Heb 13:12
with the **b** of the everlasting Heb 13:20
with the **b** of Jesus Christ. 1Pt 1:2
with the precious **b** of Christ, 1Pt 1:19
and the **b** of Jesus His Son 1Jn 1:7
the One who came by water and **b**; 1Jn 5:6
only, but by water and by **b**. 1Jn 5:6
water, and the **b**—and these 1Jn 5:8
us free from our sins by His **b**, Rv 1:5
for God by Your **b** from every Rv 5:9
and avenge our **b** from those who Rv 6:10
the entire moon became like **b**; Rv 6:12
them white in the **b** of the Lamb. Rv 7:14
mixed with **b**, were hurled to Rv 8:7
So a third of the sea became **b**, Rv 8:8
the waters to turn them into **b**, Rv 11:6
him by the **b** of the Lamb Rv 12:11
and **b** flowed out of the press up Rv 14:20
turned to **b** like a dead man's, Rv 16:3
of water, and they became **b**. Rv 16:4
poured out the **b** of the saints Rv 16:6
You also gave them **b** to drink; Rv 16:6
was drunk on the **b** of the saints Rv 17:6
and on the **b** of the witnesses Rv 17:6
the **b** of prophets and saints, Rv 18:24
avenged the **b** of His servants Rv 19:2
He wore a robe stained with **b**, Rv 19:13

BLOODGUILT *(6)*
you don't bring **b** on your house Dt 22:8
it regards differences of **b**, 2Ch 19:10
A man burdened by **b** will be a Pr 28:17
cleansed the **b** from the heart Is 4:4
leave his **b** on him and repay Hs 12:14
pardon their **b**, ⌊which⌋ I have Jl 3:21

BLOODIED *(1)*
battle and the **b** garments of war Is 9:5

BLOODLINE *(1)*
not corrupt his **b** among his Lv 21:15

BLOODSHED *(34)*
to death, no one is guilty of **b**. Ex 22:2
sunrise, there is guilt of **b**. Ex 22:3
avenger will not be guilty of **b**, Nm 35:27
you are, for **b** defiles the land Nm 35:33
you—concerning **b**, lawsuits, Dt 17:8
become guilty of **b** in the land Dt 19:10
of responsibility for **b**. Dt 21:8
participating in **b** and avenging 1Sm 25:26
of needless **b** or my lord's 1Sm 25:31
participating in **b** and avenging 1Sm 25:33
abhors a man of **b** and treachery. Ps 5:6
accounting for **b** remembers them; Ps 9:12
or my life along with men of **b** Ps 26:9
Save me from the guilt of **b**, Ps 51:14
men of **b** and treachery will not Ps 55:23
and save me from men of **b**. Ps 59:2
who withholds his sword from **b**. Jr 48:10
Plague and **b** will sweep through Ezk 5:17
land is filled with crimes of **b**, Ezk 7:23
land is full of **b**, and the city Ezk 9:9
wrath on it with **b** to wipe out Ezk 14:19
bring about your **b** in wrath and Ezk 16:38
to the city of **b**, the pot that Ezk 24:6
Woe to the city of **b**! Ezk 24:9
her and **b** in her streets; Ezk 28:23
I will destine you for **b**, Ezk 35:6
did not hate **b**, it will pursue Ezk 35:6
on him with plague and **b**. Ezk 38:22
will avenge the **b** of Jezreel on Hs 1:4
one act of **b** follows another. Hs 4:2
build Zion with **b** and Jerusalem Mc 3:10
because of human **b** and violence Hab 2:8
a city with **b** and founds a town Hab 2:12
of ⌊your⌋ human **b** and violence Hab 2:17

BLOODTHIRSTY *(2)*
wicked—you **b** men, stay away Ps 139:19
B men hate an honest person, Pr 29:10

BLOODY *(1)*
tracked with **b** footprints. Hs 6:8

BLOOM *(3)*
for our vineyards are in **b**. Sg 2:15
if the pomegranates are in **b**. Sg 7:12
will blossom and **b** and fill the Is 27:6

BLOOMED *(1)*
has blossomed; arrogance has **b**. Ezk 7:10

BLOOMING *(1)*
budding and the pomegranates **b**. Sg 6:11

BLOOMS *(1)*
he **b** like a flower of the field; Ps 103:15

BLOSSOM *(9)*
brim of a cup or of a lily **b**. 1Kg 7:26
the brim of a cup or a lily **b**. 2Ch 4:5
budded, if the **b** has opened, if Sg 7:12
is over and the **b** becomes a Is 18:5
Israel will **b** and bloom and fill Is 27:6
will rejoice and **b** like a rose. Is 35:1
It will **b** abundantly and will Is 35:2
he will **b** like the lily and take Hs 14:5
grow grain and **b** like the vine. Hs 14:7

BLOSSOMED *(2)*
formed buds, **b**, and produced Nm 17:8
out. The rod has **b**; arrogance Ezk 7:10

BLOSSOMING *(2)*
the **b** vines give off their Sg 2:13
when the **b** is over and the Is 18:5

BLOSSOMS *(19)*
its **b** came out and its clusters Gn 40:10
three cups shaped like almond **b**, Ex 25:33
three cups shaped like almond **b**, Ex 25:33
like almond **b** on the lampstand Ex 25:34
three cups shaped like almond **b**, Ex 37:19
three cups shaped like almond **b**, Ex 37:19
like almond **b** with its calyxes Ex 37:20
ornamental⌋ gourds and flower **b**. 1Kg 6:18
trees and flower **b**—in both the 1Kg 6:29
trees and flower **b** on them and 1Kg 6:32
trees and flower **b** on them and 1Kg 6:35
b like a flower, then withers; Jb 14:2
an olive tree that sheds its **b**. Jb 15:33
the almond tree **b**, the Ec 12:5
is a cluster of henna **b** to me, Sg 1:14
The **b** appear in the countryside. Sg 2:12
to see the **b** of the valley, Sg 6:11
the night among the henna **b**. Sg 7:11
rotten and their **b** will blow Is 5:24

BLOT *(9)*
will completely **b** out the memory Ex 17:14
destroy them and **b** out their Dt 9:14
b out the memory of Amalek from Dt 25:19
The LORD will **b** out his name Dt 29:20
to pieces and **b** out the memory Dt 32:26
not said He would **b** out the name 2Kg 14:27
compassion, **b** out my rebellion. Ps 51:1
my sins and **b** out all my guilt Ps 51:9
do not **b** out their sin before Jr 18:23

BLOTS *(1)*
They are **b** and blemishes, 2Pt 2:13

BLOTTED *(3)*
will not be **b** out from Israel Dt 25:6
their name be **b** out in the next Ps 109:13
let his mother's sin be **b** out. Ps 109:14

BLOW *(27)*
this people with a single **b**, Nm 14:15
the priests **b** the trumpets. Jos 6:4
everyone with me **b** our trumpets, Jdg 7:18
you are also to **b** your trumpets Jdg 7:18
You are to **b** the ram's horn and 1Kg 1:34
were to **b** trumpets before the 1Ch 15:24
struck them with a mighty **b**, 2Ch 13:17
away, so You **b** ⌊them⌋ away. Ps 68:2
the east wind **b** in the skies Ps 78:26
B the horn during the new moon Ps 81:3
B on my garden, and spread the Sg 4:16
blossoms will **b** away like dust, Is 5:24
will wither, **b** away, and vanish Is 19:7
B the ram's horn throughout the Jr 4:5
The bellows **b**, blasting the lead Jr 6:29
b a ram's horn among the nations; Jr 51:27
I will **b** the fire of My fury on Ezk 21:31
the furnace to **b** fire on them Ezk 22:20
you together and **b** on you with Ezk 22:21
away from you with a fatal **b**. Ezk 24:16
but doesn't **b** the trumpet, Ezk 33:6
B the horn in Gibeah, the Hs 5:8
B the horn in Zion; sound the Jl 2:1
B the horn in Zion! Announce a Jl 2:15
no wind could **b** on the earth Rv 7:1
trumpets prepared to **b** them. Rv 8:6
when he will **b** his trumpet, Rv 10:7

BLOWING *(9)*
While the trumpets were **b**, Jos 6:9
While the trumpets were **b**, Jos 6:13
were rejoicing and **b** trumpets. 2Kg 11:14
were 120 priests **b** trumpets. 2Ch 5:12
the priests were **b** trumpets, 2Ch 7:6
rejoicing and **b** trumpets while 2Ch 23:13
the song, and **b** the trumpets— 2Ch 29:28
of the ruthless, like **b** chaff. Is 29:5
And when the south wind is **b**, Lk 12:55

BLOWN *(6)*
As smoke is **b** away, so You blow Ps 68:2
day a great trumpet will be **b**, Is 27:13
They have **b** the trumpet and Ezk 7:14
like chaff **b** from a threshing Hs 13:3
If a ram's horn is **b** in a city, Am 3:6
the waves and **b** around by every Eph 4:14

BLOWS *(13)*
rod and with **b** from others. 2Sm 7:14
like chaff that the wind **b** away. Ps 1:4
with the rod, their sin with **b**. Ps 89:32
in anger with unceasing **b**. Is 14:6
breath of the LORD **b** on them; Is 40:7
ground when He **b** on them and Is 40:24
craftsman who **b** on the charcoal Is 54:16
A searing wind ⌊**b**⌋ from the Jr 4:11
will direct the **b** of his Ezk 26:9
the land and **b** his trumpet to Ezk 33:3
deserving of **b** will be beaten Lk 12:48
The wind **b** where it pleases, Jn 3:8
had inflicted many **b** on them, Ac 16:23

BLUE *(48)*
b, purple, and scarlet yarn; Ex 25:4
spun linen, and **b**, purple, and Ex 26:1
Make loops of **b** yarn on the edge Ex 26:4
You are to make a veil of **b**, Ex 26:31
a screen embroidered with **b**, Ex 26:36
screen embroidered with **b**, Ex 27:16
b, purple, and scarlet yarn; Ex 28:5
with gold, and with **b**, purple, Ex 28:6
of gold, of **b**, purple, and Ex 28:8
make it of gold, of **b**, purple, Ex 28:15
the ephod with a cord of **b** yarn, Ex 28:28
of the ephod entirely of **b** yarn. Ex 28:31
pomegranates of **b**, purple, and Ex 28:33
it to a cord of **b** yarn so it can Ex 28:37
b, purple, and scarlet yarn; Ex 35:6
who had in his possession **b**, Ex 35:23
b, purple, and scarlet yarn, and Ex 35:25
an embroiderer in **b**, purple, and Ex 35:35
linen, as well as **b**, purple, and Ex 36:8
made loops of **b** yarn on the edge Ex 36:11
Then he made the veil with **b**, Ex 36:35
a screen embroidered with **b**, Ex 36:37
was embroidered with **b**, Ex 38:18
and an embroiderer with **b**, Ex 38:23
garments for Aaron from the **b**, Ex 39:1
ephod of gold, of **b**, purple, and Ex 39:2
them⌋ to interweave with the **b**, Ex 39:3
of gold, of **b**, purple, and Ex 39:5
ephod of gold, of **b**, purple, and Ex 39:8
the ephod with a cord of **b** yarn, Ex 39:21
of the ephod entirely of **b** yarn. Ex 39:22
pomegranates of finely spun **b**, Ex 39:24
spun linen of embroidered **b**, Ex 39:29
attached a cord of **b** yarn to it Ex 39:31
spread a solid **b** cloth on top, Nm 4:6
are to spread a **b** cloth over the Nm 4:7
are to take a **b** cloth and cover Nm 4:9
are to spread a **b** cloth over the Nm 4:11
place ⌊them⌋ in a **b** cloth, Nm 4:12
put a **b** cord on the tassel at Nm 15:38
purple, crimson, and **b** yarn. 2Ch 2:7
with purple, **b**, crimson yarn, 2Ch 2:14
He made the veil of **b**, purple, 2Ch 3:14
Their clothing is **b** and purple, Jr 10:9
dressed in **b**, governors and Ezk 23:6
awning was of **b** and purple Ezk 27:7
cloaks of **b** and embroidered Ezk 27:24
red, hyacinth **b**, and sulfur Rv 9:17

BLURTS *(2)*
of fools **b** out foolishness. Pr 15:2
of the wicked **b** out evil things. Pr 15:28

BOANERGES *(1)*
gave the name "**B**" (that is, Mk 3:17

BOAR *(1)*
The **b** from the forest gnaws at Ps 80:13

BOARD *(8)*
not threshed with a threshing **b**, Is 28:27
you into a sharp threshing **b**, Is 41:15
with all the other people on **b**, Ezk 27:27
got on **b** ⌊the boat⌋ again, Mk 8:13
were willing to take Him on **b**, Jn 6:21
intending to take Paul on **b**. Ac 20:13
we took him on **b** and came to Ac 20:14
for Italy and put us on **b**. Ac 27:6

BOARDED *(6)*
until the day Noah **b** the ark. Mt 24:38
until the day Noah **b** the ark, Lk 17:27
Jesus had not **b** the boat with Jn 6:22
to Phoenicia, we **b** and set sail. Ac 21:2
Then we **b** the ship, and they Ac 21:6
So when we had **b** a ship of Ac 27:2

BOARDS *(6)*
the altar with **b** so that it is Ex 27:8
the altar with **b** so that it was Ex 38:7
he paneled it with **b** and planks 1Kg 6:9
temple walls with cedar **b**; 1Kg 6:15
the floor with cypress **b**. 1Kg 6:15
with cedar **b** from the floor to 1Kg 6:16

BOAST *(55)*
protects you, the sword you **b** Dt 33:29
Do not **b** so proudly, or let 1Sm 2:3
on his armor **b** like the one who 1Kg 20:11
who love Your name **b** about You. Ps 5:11
I will rejoice and **b** about You; Ps 9:2
I will **b** in the LORD; the humble Ps 34:2
We **b** in God all day long; Ps 44:8
their wealth and **b** of their Ps 49:6
all who swear by Him will **b**, Ps 63:11
boastful, 'Do not **b**,' and to the Ps 75:4
words; all the evildoers **b**. Ps 94:4
those who **b** in idols, will be Ps 97:7
and **b** about Your heritage. Ps 106:5
Don't **b** about tomorrow, for you Pr 27:1
and Egypt their **b** will be Is 20:5
you will **b** in the Holy One of Is 41:16
and you will **b** in their riches. Is 61:6
wise must not **b** in his wisdom; Jr 9:23
mighty must not **b** in his might; Jr 9:23
rich must not **b** in his riches. Jr 9:23
one who boasts should **b** in this, Jr 9:24
It is empty. His **b** is empty. Jr 48:30
trust in your treasures ⌊and **b**⌋: Jr 49:4
rest in the law, and **b** in God, Rm 2:17
You who **b** in the law, do you Rm 2:23
have reason to **b** in Christ Jesus Rm 15:17
no one can **b** in His presence 1Co 1:29
who boasts must **b** in the Lord. 1Co 1:31
So no one should **b** in men, 1Co 3:21
why do you **b** as if you hadn't 1Co 4:7
anyone to deprive me of my **b**! 1Co 9:15
have no reason to **b**, because an 1Co 9:16
For our **b** is this: the testimony 2Co 1:12
I have made any **b** to him about 2Co 7:14
For if I **b** some more about our 2Co 10:8
will not **b** beyond measure, 2Co 10:13
who boasts must **b** in the Lord. 2Co 10:17
a fool, so I too may **b** a little. 2Co 11:16
Since many **b** from a human 2Co 11:18
perspective, I will also **b**. 2Co 11:18
whatever anyone dares ⌊to **b**⌋— 2Co 11:21
I will **b** about my weaknesses. 2Co 11:30
is necessary to **b**; it is not 2Co 12:1
I will **b** about this person, 2Co 12:5
For if I want to **b**, I will not 2Co 12:6
will most gladly **b** all the more 2Co 12:9
in order to **b** about your flesh. Gl 6:13
I will never **b** about anything Gl 6:14
works, so that no one can **b**. Eph 2:9
I can **b** in the day of Christ Php 2:16
of God, **b** in Christ Jesus, Php 3:3
we ourselves **b** about you among 2Th 1:4
should **b** in his exaltation; Jms 1:9
is rich ⌊should **b**⌋ in his Jms 1:10
as it is, you **b** in your Jms 4:16

BOASTED *(1)*
b against Me with your mouth, Ezk 35:13

BOASTFUL *(6)*
The **b** cannot stand in Your Ps 5:5
I say to the **b**, 'Do not boast,' Ps 75:4
I will remove your **b** braggarts Zph 3:11
arrogant, proud, **b**, inventors of Rm 1:30
not envy; is not **b**; is not 1Co 13:4
lovers of money, **b**, proud, 2Tm 3:2

BOASTFULLY *(2)*
and the tongue that speaks **b**. Ps 12:3
do not **b** mock in the day of Ob 12

BOASTING *(15)*
his arrogance, and his empty **b**. Is 16:6
their falsehoods and their **b**. Jr 23:32
Where then is **b**? It is excluded. Rm 3:27
Your **b** is not good. 1Co 5:6
our **b** to Titus has also turned 2Co 7:14
love and of our **b** about you. 2Co 8:24
the brothers so our **b** about you 2Co 9:3
b about what has already been 2Co 10:16
this **b** of mine will not be 2Co 11:10
we are in what they are **b** about. 2Co 11:12
What I say in this matter of **b**, 2Co 11:17
If **b** is necessary, I will boast 2Co 11:30
a reason for **b** in himself alone Gl 6:4
or crown of **b** in the presence of 1Th 2:19
All such **b** is evil. Jms 4:16

BOASTS (9)
My mouth **b** over my enemies, 1Sm 2:1
the wicked one **b** about his own Ps 10:3
The man who **b** about a gift that Pr 25:14
But the one who **b** should boast Jr 9:24
like rivers. He **b**: I will go up, Jr 46:8
The one who **b** must boast in the 1Co 1:31
So the one who **b** must boast in 2Co 10:17
of the body⌋, it **b** great things. Jms 3:5
him to speak **b** and blasphemies Rv 13:5

BOAT (44)
They were in a **b** with Zebedee Mt 4:21
they left the **b** and their father Mt 4:22
He got into the **b**, His disciples Mt 8:23
so that the **b** was being swamped Mt 8:24
He got into a **b**, crossed over, Mt 9:1
He got into a **b** and sat down, Mt 13:2
there by **b** to a remote place Mt 14:13
get into the **b** and go ahead of Mt 14:22
the **b** was already over a mile Mt 14:24
And climbing out of the **b**, Mt 14:29
got into the **b**, the wind ceased Mt 14:32
Then those in the **b** worshiped Mt 14:33
got into the **b** and went to the Mt 15:39
were in their **b** mending their Mk 1:19
Zebedee in the **b** with the hired Mk 1:20
to have a small **b** ready for Him, Mk 3:9
He got into a **b** on the sea and Mk 4:1
since He was ⌊already⌋ in the **b**. Mk 4:36
waves were breaking over the **b**, Mk 4:37
so that the **b** was already being Mk 4:37
As soon as He got out of the **b**, Mk 5:2
As He was getting into the **b**, Mk 5:18
over again by **b** to the other Mk 5:21
away in the **b** by themselves to Mk 6:32
get into the **b** and go ahead of Mk 6:45
the **b** was in the middle of the Mk 6:47
He got into the **b** with them, Mk 6:51
at Gennesaret and beached the **b**. Mk 6:53
got out of the **b**, people Mk 6:54
into the **b** with His disciples Mk 8:10
got on board ⌊the **b**⌋ again, Mk 8:13
one loaf with them in the **b**. Mk 8:14
teaching the crowds from the **b**. Lk 5:3
in the other **b** to come and help Lk 5:7
and His disciples got into a **b**, Lk 8:22
getting into the **b**, He returned. Lk 8:37
got into a **b**, and started across Jn 6:17
coming near the **b**, and they were Jn 6:19
and at once the **b** was at the Jn 6:21
knew there had been only one **b**. Jn 6:22
not boarded the **b** with His Jn 6:22
went out and got into the **b**, Jn 21:3
net on the right side of the **b**," Jn 21:6
other disciples came in the **b**, Jn 21:8

BOATS (8)
sweep by like **b** made of papyrus, Jb 9:26
And other **b** were with Him. Mk 4:36
He saw two **b** at the edge of the Lk 5:2
one of the **b**, which belonged Lk 5:3
and filled both **b** so full that Lk 5:7
Then they brought the **b** to land, Lk 5:11
Some **b** from Tiberias came near Jn 6:23
they got into the **b** and went to Jn 6:24

BOAZ (29)
on her husband's side named **B**. Ru 2:1
portion of land belonging to **B**, Ru 2:3
when **B** arrived from Bethlehem, Ru 2:4
B asked his servant who was in Ru 2:5
Then **B** said to Ruth, "Listen, my Ru 2:8
B answered her, "Everything you Ru 2:11
At mealtime **B** told her, "Come Ru 2:14
gather ⌊grain⌋, **B** ordered his Ru 2:15
man I worked with today is **B**." Ru 2:19
Now isn't **B** our relative? Ru 3:2
After **B** ate, drank, and was in Ru 3:7
At midnight, **B** was startled, Ru 3:8
Then **B** said, "Don't let it be Ru 3:14
B went to the gate ⌊of the town⌋ Ru 4:1
family redeemer **B** had spoken Ru 4:1
B called him by name and said, Ru 4:1
Then **B** took 10 men of the city's Ru 4:2
Then **B** said, "On the day you buy Ru 4:5
his sandal and said to **B**, Ru 4:8
B said to the elders and all the Ru 4:9
B took Ruth and she became his Ru 4:13
Salmon fathered **B**, who fathered Ru 4:21
the left pillar and named it **B**. 1Kg 7:21
Salma, and Salma fathered **B**. 1Ch 2:11
B fathered Obed, and Obed 1Ch 2:12
and the one on the left **B**. 2Ch 3:17
Salmon fathered **B** by Rahab, Mt 1:5
Boaz by Rahab, **B** fathered Obed Mt 1:5
Obed, ⌊son⌋ of **B**, ⌊son⌋ of Lk 3:32

BOAZ'S (1)
stayed close to **B** young women Ru 2:23

BOCHERU (2)
Azrikam, **B**, Ishmael, Sheariah, 1Ch 8:38
Azrikam, **B**, Ishmael, Sheariah, 1Ch 9:44

BOCHIM (2)
up from Gilgal to **B** and said, Jdg 2:1
named that place **B** and offered Jdg 2:5

BODIES (58)
lord except our **b** and our land. Gn 47:18
to cover ⌊their⌋ naked **b**; Ex 28:42
gashes on your **b** for the dead or Lv 19:28
or make gashes on their **b**. Lv 21:5
heap your dead **b** on the lifeless Lv 26:30
on the lifeless **b** of your idols; Lv 26:30
their entire **b** and wash their Nm 8:7
burned their **b**, threw stones Jos 7:25
threadbare clothing on their **b**. Jos 9:5
hung their **b** on five trees and Jos 10:26
Philistine **b** were strewn all 1Sm 17:52
young men's **b** are consecrated 1Sm 21:5
course their **b** are consecrated 1Sm 21:5
of Saul and the **b** of his sons 1Sm 31:12
Jabesh, they burned the **b** there. 1Sm 31:12
slain, from the **b** of the mighty. 2Sm 1:22
and hung ⌊their **b**⌋ by the pool 2Sm 4:12
down from heaven on the **b**. 2Sm 21:10
threw ⌊the **b**⌋ out and went 2Kg 10:25
there were all the dead **b**! 2Kg 19:35
of Saul and the **b** of his sons 1Ch 10:12
of goods on the **b** and valuable 2Ch 20:25
rule over our **b** and our Neh 9:37
and may ⌊the **b** of⌋ Haman's 10 Est 9:13
they hung ⌊the **b** of⌋ Haman's 10 Est 9:14
our **b** cling to the ground. Ps 44:25
die, and their **b** are well-fed. Ps 73:4
live; their **b** will rise. Awake Is 26:19
the heavenly **b** will dissolve. Is 34:4
there were all the dead **b**! Is 37:36
see the dead **b** of the men who Is 66:24
⌊their⌋ **b** were more ruddy than Lm 4:7
had two wings covering their **b**. Ezk 1:23
Their entire **b**, including their Ezk 10:12
stone from their **b** and give them Ezk 11:19
no effect on the **b** of these men: Dn 3:27
Many dead **b**, thrown everywhere! Am 8:3
of corpses, dead **b** without end— Nah 3:3
opened and many **b** of the saints Mt 27:52
did not want the **b** to remain Jn 19:31
that ⌊their **b**⌋ be taken away. Jn 19:31
so that their **b** were degraded Rm 1:24
your mortal **b** to life through Rm 8:11
the redemption of our **b**. Rm 8:23
to present your **b** as a living Rm 12:1
know that your **b** are the members 1Co 6:15
are heavenly **b** and earthly 1Co 15:40
heavenly bodies and earthly **b**, 1Co 15:40
of the heavenly **b** is different 1Co 15:40
love their wives as their own **b**. Eph 5:28
whose **b** fell in the desert? Heb 3:17
and our **b** washed in pure Heb 10:22
For the **b** of those animals whose Heb 13:11
among the parts of our ⌊**b**⌋; Jms 3:6
Their dead **b** will lie in the Rv 11:8
will view their **b** for three and Rv 11:9
and not permit their **b** to be put Rv 11:9
and human **b** and souls. Rv 18:13

BODILY (4)
anyone who has a ⌊**b**⌋ discharge, Nm 5:2
because of a **b** emission during Dt 23:10
of God's nature dwells **b**, Col 2:9
you yourselves were suffering **b**. Heb 13:3

BODY (210)
your own **b** will be your heir. Gn 15:4
will eat the flesh from your **b**." Gn 40:19
it is the clothing for his **b**. Ex 22:27
like that for **b** armor so that it Ex 28:32
anointing on a person's **b**, Ex 30:32
robe like that for **b** armor with Ex 39:23
or spot on the skin of his **b**, Lv 13:2
a disease on the skin of his **b**, Lv 13:2
infection on the skin of his **b**. Lv 13:3
deeper than the skin of his **b**, Lv 13:3
the skin of his **b** is white and Lv 13:4
disease on the skin of his **b**, Lv 13:11
has covered his entire **b**, Lv 13:13
skin of one's **b** and it heals, Lv 13:18
skin of one's **b** produced by fire Lv 13:24
spots on the skin of the **b**, Lv 13:38
skin of the **b** are dull white, Lv 13:39
of a skin disease on his **b**, Lv 13:43
man has a discharge from his **b**, Lv 15:2
Whether his **b** secretes the Lv 15:3
the days that his **b** secretes or Lv 15:3
touches the **b** of the man with Lv 15:7
and bathe his **b** in fresh water; Lv 15:13
it consists of blood from her **b**, Lv 15:19
are to be on his **b**. Lv 16:4
must bathe his **b** with water Lv 16:4
will bathe his **b** with water in Lv 16:24
and bathe his **b** with water; Lv 16:26
he has bathed his **b** with water. Lv 22:6
go near a dead **b** during the time Nm 6:6
and bathe his **b** in water; Nm 19:7
and bathe his **b** in water, Nm 19:8
who touches a **b** of a person who Nm 19:13
and you hang his **b** on a tree, Dt 21:22
hung ⌊the **b** of⌋ the king of Ai Jos 8:29
they take his **b** down from the Jos 8:29
as one **b** before the LORD Jdg 20:1
and hung his **b** on the wall 1Sm 31:10
and retrieved the **b** of Saul and 1Sm 31:12
The spear went through his **b**, 2Sm 2:23
who will come from your **b**, 2Sm 7:12
over his **b**, and fasted. 1Kg 21:27
carried his dead **b** in a chariot, 2Kg 23:30
out and retrieved the **b** of Saul 1Ch 10:12
rather than life in this **b**. Jb 7:15
of his own **b** and mourns only Jb 14:22
and my whole **b** has become but a Jb 17:7
terrified and my **b** trembles in Jb 21:6
His **b** is well-fed, and his bones Jb 21:24
my **b** also rests securely. Ps 16:9
soundness in my **b** because of Ps 38:3
and there is no health in my **b**. Ps 38:7
my **b** faints for You in a land Ps 63:1
it enter his **b** like water and Ps 109:18
fasting, and my **b** is emaciated. Ps 109:24
healing for your **b** and Pr 3:8
and health to one's whole **b**. Pr 4:22
your physical **b** has been Pr 5:11
tranquil heart is life to the **b**, Pr 14:30
the taste and health to the **b**. Pr 16:24
how to let my **b** enjoy life with Ec 2:3
and much study wearies the **b**. Ec 12:12
His **b** is an ivory panel covered Sg 5:14
and his healthy **b** will become Is 17:4
of your **b** like its grains; Is 48:19
stripped off, your **b** ravished. Jr 13:22
and two wings covering its **b**. Ezk 1:11
and his **b** was drenched with dew Dn 4:33
and his **b** was drenched with dew Dn 5:21
was killed and its **b** destroyed Dn 7:11
oil ⌊on my **b**⌋ until the three Dn 10:3
His **b** was like topaz, his face Dn 10:6
child of my **b** for my own sin? Mc 6:7
parts of your **b** than for your Mt 5:29
for your whole **b** to be thrown Mt 5:29
parts of your **b** than for your Mt 5:30
your whole **b** to go into hell! Mt 5:30
The eye is the lamp of the **b**. Mt 6:22
your whole **b** will be full of Mt 6:22
your whole **b** will be full of Mt 6:23
or about your **b**, what you will Mt 6:25
than food and the **b** more than Mt 6:25
who kill the **b** but are not able Mt 10:28
destroy both soul and **b** in hell. Mt 10:28
this fragrant oil on My **b**, Mt 26:12
Take and eat it; this is My **b**." Mt 26:26
Pilate and asked for Jesus' **b**. Mt 27:58
So Joseph took the **b**, wrapped it Mt 27:59
she sensed in her **b** that she was Mk 5:29
has anointed My **b** in advance for Mk 14:8
said, "Take ⌊it⌋; this is My **b**." Mk 14:22
wrapped around his naked **b**, Mk 14:51
Pilate and asked for Jesus' **b**. Mk 15:43
Your eye is the lamp of the **b**. Lk 11:34
your whole **b** is also full of Lk 11:34
your **b** is also full of darkness. Lk 11:34

your whole **b** is full of light, Lk 11:36
the whole **b** will be full of Lk 11:36
don't fear those who kill the **b**, Lk 12:4
or about the **b**, what you will Lk 12:22
than food and the **b** more than Lk 12:23
was a man whose **b** was swollen Lk 14:2
This is My **b**, which is given Lk 22:19
Pilate and asked for Jesus' **b**. Lk 23:52
tomb and how His **b** was placed. Lk 23:55
did not find the **b** of the Lord Lk 24:3
and when they didn't find His **b**, Lk 24:23
about the sanctuary of His **b**. Jn 2:21
that he might remove Jesus' **b**. Jn 19:38
so he came and took His **b** away. Jn 19:38
they took Jesus' **b** and wrapped Jn 19:40
where Jesus' **b** had been lying. Jn 20:12
up, wrapped ⌊his **b**⌋, carried him Ac 5:6
and turning toward the **b** said, Ac 9:40
his own **b** to be already dead Rm 4:19
over the **b** may be abolished Rm 6:6
let sin reign in your mortal **b**, Rm 6:12
⌊crucified⌋ **b** of the Messiah, Rm 7:4
law in the parts of my **b**, Rm 7:23
law of sin in the parts of my **b**. Rm 7:23
rescue me from this **b** of death? Rm 7:24
the **b** is dead because of sin, Rm 8:10
put to death the deeds of the **b**, Rm 8:13
as we have many parts in one **b**, Rm 12:4
who are many are one **b** in Christ Rm 12:5
though absent in **b** but present 1Co 5:3
The **b** is not for sexual 1Co 6:13
Lord, and the Lord for the **b**. 1Co 6:13
a prostitute is one **b** with her? 1Co 6:16
can commit is outside the **b**," 1Co 6:18
immoral sins against his own **b**. 1Co 6:18
know that your **b** is a sanctuary 1Co 6:19
therefore glorify God in your **b**. 1Co 6:20
have authority over her own **b**, 1Co 7:4
have authority over his own **b**, 1Co 7:4
be holy both in **b** and in spirit. 1Co 7:34
I discipline my **b** and bring it 1Co 9:27
a sharing in the **b** of Christ? 1Co 10:16
we who are many are one **b**, 1Co 10:17
This is My **b**, which is for you 1Co 11:24
sin against the **b** and blood of 1Co 11:27
without recognizing the **b**, 1Co 11:29
For as the **b** is one and has many 1Co 12:12
and all the parts of that **b**, 1Co 12:12
many, are one **b**—so also is 1Co 12:12
by one Spirit into one **b**— 1Co 12:13
So the **b** is not one part but 1Co 12:14
belong to the **b**," in spite of 1Co 12:15
this it still belongs to the **b**. 1Co 12:15
belong to the **b**," in spite of 1Co 12:16
this it still belongs to the **b**. 1Co 12:16
If the whole **b** were an eye, 1Co 12:17
in the **b** just as He wanted. 1Co 12:18
same part, where would the **b** be? 1Co 12:19
there are many parts, yet one **b**. 1Co 12:20
parts of the **b** that seem to be 1Co 12:22
parts of the **b** that we think to 1Co 12:23
God has put the **b** together, 1Co 12:24
would be no division in the **b**, 1Co 12:25
Now you are the **b** of Christ, 1Co 12:27
and if I give my **b** to be burned, 1Co 13:3
What kind of **b** will they have 1Co 15:35
you are not sowing the future **b**, 1Co 15:37
God gives it a **b** as He wants, 1Co 15:38
to each of the seeds its own **b**. 1Co 15:38
sown a natural **b**, raised a 1Co 15:44
body, raised a spiritual **b**. 1Co 15:44
is a natural **b**, there is also 1Co 15:44
there is also a spiritual **b**. 1Co 15:44
the death of Jesus in our **b**, 2Co 4:10
may also be revealed in our **b**. 2Co 4:10
are at home in the **b** we are away 2Co 5:6
be out of the **b** and at home with 2Co 5:8
for what he has done in the **b**, 2Co 5:10
he was in the **b** or out of the 2Co 12:2
was in the body or out of the **b**, 2Co 12:2
whether in the **b** or out of the 2Co 12:3
or out of the **b** I do not know, 2Co 12:3
the marks of Jesus on my **b**. Gl 6:17
which is His **b**, the fullness of Eph 1:23
to God in one **b** through the Eph 2:16
of the same **b**, and partners Eph 3:6
There is one **b** and one Spirit, Eph 4:4
to build up the **b** of Christ, Eph 4:12
Him the whole **b**, fitted and knit Eph 4:16
growth of the **b** for building up Eph 4:16
He is the Savior of the **b**. Eph 5:23
since we are members of His **b**. Eph 5:30
will be highly honored in my **b**, Php 1:20
transform the **b** of our humble Php 3:21
the likeness of His glorious **b**, Php 3:21
He is also the head of the **b**, Col 1:18
by His physical **b** through His Col 1:22
Christ's afflictions for His **b**, Col 1:24
be absent in **b**, but I am with Col 2:5
by putting off the **b** of flesh, Col 2:11
whom the whole **b**, nourished and Col 2:19
and severe treatment of the **b**, Col 2:23
you were also called in one **b**, Col 3:15
b be kept sound and blameless 1Th 5:23
training of the **b** has a limited 1Tm 4:8
but You prepared a **b** for Me. Heb 10:5
offering of the **b** of Jesus Heb 10:10
give them what the **b** needs, Jms 2:16
For just as the **b** without the Jms 2:26
able to control his whole **b**. Jms 3:2
is a small part ⌊of the **b**⌋, Jms 3:5
the whole **b**, sets the course Jms 3:6
our sins in His **b** on the tree, 1Pt 2:24
in a debate about Moses' **b**, Jd 9

BODYGUARD *(4)*
captain of your **b**, and honored 1Sm 22:14
appoint you as my permanent **b**." 1Sm 28:2
put him in charge of his **b**. 2Sm 23:23
put him in charge of his **b**. 1Ch 11:25

BOHAN *(2)*
to the stone of **B** son of Reuben. Jos 15:6
down to the Stone of **B**, Jos 18:17

BOIL *(14)*
and **b** what you want to boil, Ex 16:23
and boil what you want to **b**, Ex 16:23
You must not **b** a young goat in Ex 23:19
of ordination and **b** its flesh in Ex 29:31
You must not **b** a young goat in Ex 34:26
B the meat at the entrance to Lv 8:31
When a **b** appears on the skin of Lv 13:18
spot develops where the **b** was, Lv 13:19
that has broken out in the **b**. Lv 13:20
is ⌊only⌋ the scar from the **b**. Lv 13:23
You must not **b** a young goat in Dt 14:21
and fire causes water to **b**— Is 64:2
Bring it to a **b** and cook the Ezk 24:5
priests will **b** the restitution Ezk 46:20

BOILED *(7)*
offering is **b** must be broken; Lv 6:28
if it is **b** in a bronze vessel, Lv 6:28
is to take the **b** shoulder from Nm 6:19
then **b** ⌊it⌋ in a cooking pot and Nm 11:8
won't accept **b** meat from you— 1Sm 2:15
So we **b** my son and ate him, 2Kg 6:29
They **b** the holy ⌊sacrifices⌋ in 2Ch 35:13

BOILING *(4)*
of it raw or cooked in **b** water, Ex 12:9
meat fork while the meat was **b** 1Sm 2:13
as from a **b** pot or ⌊burning⌋ Jb 41:20
I see a **b** pot, its mouth Jr 1:13

BOILS *(7)*
become festering **b** on people and Ex 9:9
festering **b** on man and beast Ex 9:10
before Moses because of the **b**, Ex 9:11
for the **b** were on the magicians Ex 9:11
afflict you with the **b** of Egypt, Dt 28:27
and incurable **b** from the sole of Dt 28:35
with incurable **b** from the sole Jb 2:7

BOLD *(6)*
A wicked man puts on a **b** face, Pr 21:29
righteous are as **b** as a lion. Pr 28:1
but **b** toward you when absent. 2Co 10:1
not need to be **b** with the 2Co 10:2
that I might be **b** enough in Him Eph 6:20
authority. **B**, arrogant people! 2Pt 2:10

BOLDLY *(11)*
came and **b** went in to Pilate and Mk 15:43
he had spoken **b** in the name of Ac 9:27
speaking **b** in the name of the Ac 9:28
Then Paul and Barnabas **b** said: Ac 13:46
there for some time and spoke **b**, Ac 14:3
began to speak **b** in the Ac 18:26
and spoke **b** over a period Ac 19:8
to him I am actually speaking **b**. Ac 26:26
And Isaiah says **b**: I was found Rm 10:20
to you more **b** on some points Rm 15:15
Therefore, we may **b** say: Heb 13:6

BOLDNESS *(13)*
observed the **b** of Peter and John Ac 4:13
Your message with complete **b**, Ac 4:29
to speak God's message with **b**. Ac 4:31
Christ with full **b** and without Ac 28:31
such a hope, we use great **b**— 2Co 3:12
in whom we have **b**, access, and Eph 3:12
to make known with **b** the mystery Eph 6:19
with all **b**, Christ will be Php 1:20
and great **b** in the faith that is 1Tm 3:13
I have great **b** in Christ to Phm 8
the throne of grace with **b**, Heb 4:16
since we have **b** to enter the Heb 10:19
we may have **b** and not be ashamed 1Jn 2:28

BOLT *(2)*
woman out and **b** the door behind 2Sm 13:17
myrrh on the handles of the **b**. Sg 5:5

BOLTED *(1)*
her out and **b** the door behind 2Sm 13:18

BOLTS *(10)*
May the **b** of your gate be iron Dt 33:25
lightning **b** and routed them. 2Sm 22:15
its doors, **b**, and bars. Neh 3:3
its doors, **b**, and bars. Neh 3:6
its doors, **b**, and bars, Neh 3:13
its doors, **b**, and bars. Neh 3:14
its doors, **b**, and bars. Neh 3:15
Can you send out lightning **b**, Jb 38:35
lightning **b** and routed them Ps 18:14
and their cattle to lightning **b**. Ps 78:48

BOMBASTIC *(1)*
uttering **b**, empty words, they 2Pt 2:18

BOND *(4)*
help Israel, neither **b** nor free. 2Kg 14:26
you into the **b** of the covenant. Ezk 20:37
taking a security **b** from Jason Ac 17:9
love—the perfect **b** of unity. Col 3:14

BONDAGE *(3)*
to put them in **b** for their two Hs 10:10
from this **b** on the Sabbath Lk 13:16
free from the **b** of corruption Rm 8:21

BONDS *(6)*
and mother and **b** with his wife, Gn 2:24
burnt flax and his **b** fell off Jdg 15:14
releases the **b** put on by kings Jb 12:18
You have loosened my **b**. Ps 116:16
Remove the **b** from your neck, Is 52:2
as well as **b** and imprisonment. Heb 11:36

BONE *(8)*
one, at last, is **b** of my bone, Gn 2:23
is bone of my **b**, and flesh of my Gn 2:23
died, or a human **b**, or a grave, Nm 19:16
the one who touched a **b**, Nm 19:18
a gentle tongue can break a **b**. Pr 25:15
bones came together, **b** to bone. Ezk 37:7
bones came together, bone to **b**. Ezk 37:7
and one of them sees a human **b**, Ezk 39:15

BONES *(93)*
are to carry my **b** up from here." Gn 50:25
you may not break any of its **b**. Ex 12:46
Moses took the **b** of Joseph with Ex 13:19
you must take my **b** with you from Ex 13:19
morning or break any of its **b**. Nm 9:12
enemy nations and gnaw their **b**; Nm 24:8
Joseph's **b**, which the Israelites Jos 24:32
took their **b** and buried them 1Sm 31:13
and got the **b** of Saul and his 2Sm 21:12
David had the **b** brought from 2Sm 21:13
gathered up the **b** of Saul's 2Sm 21:13
buried the **b** of Saul and his 2Sm 21:14
Human **b** will be burned on you.' 1Kg 13:2
lay my **b** beside his bones, 1Kg 13:31
lay my bones beside his **b**, 1Kg 13:31
When he touched Elisha's **b**, 2Kg 13:21
their places with human **b**. 2Kg 23:14
to take the **b** out of the tombs, 2Kg 23:16
Don't let anyone disturb his **b**." 2Kg 23:18
they left his **b** undisturbed with 2Kg 23:18
with the **b** of the prophet who 2Kg 23:18
he burned human **b** on the altars. 2Kg 23:20
They buried their **b** under the 1Ch 10:12
burned the **b** of the priests on 2Ch 34:5
hand and strike his flesh and **b**, Jb 2:5

over me and made all my **b** shake. Jb 4:14
me together with **b** and tendons. Jb 10:11
skin and my flesh cling to my **b**; Jb 19:20
His **b** may be full of youthful Jb 20:11
and his **b** are full of marrow. Jb 21:24
pierces my **b**, and my gnawing Jb 30:17
off, and my **b** burn with fever. Jb 30:30
and constant distress in his **b**, Jb 33:19
and his unseen **b** stick out. Jb 33:21
His **b** are bronze tubes; Jb 40:18
me, LORD, for my **b** are shaking; Ps 6:2
and all my **b** are disjointed; Ps 22:14
can count all my **b**; people look Ps 22:17
sinfulness, and my **b** waste away. Ps 31:10
my **b** became brittle from my Ps 32:3
He protects all his **b**; Ps 34:20
very **b** will say, "LORD, who is Ps 35:10
no health in my **b** because of my Ps 38:3
if crushing my **b**, while all day Ps 42:10
let the **b** You have crushed Ps 51:8
will scatter the **b** of those who Ps 53:5
and my **b** burn like a furnace. Ps 102:3
my flesh sticks to my **b**. Ps 102:5
and go into his **b** like oil. Ps 109:18
My **b** were not hidden from You Ps 139:15
so our **b** have been scattered at Ps 141:7
and strengthening for your **b**. Pr 3:8
is like rottenness in his **b**. Pr 12:4
jealousy is rottenness to the **b**. Pr 14:30
good news strengthens the **b**. Pr 15:30
a broken spirit dries up the **b**. Pr 17:22
how **b** ⌊develop⌋ in the womb of Ec 11:5
will break all my **b** like a lion; Is 38:13
land, and strengthen your **b**. Is 58:11
the **b** of the kings of Judah, Jr 8:1
Judah, the **b** of her officials, Jr 8:1
officials, the **b** of the priests, Jr 8:1
priests, the **b** of the prophets Jr 8:1
and the **b** of the residents of Jr 8:1
⌊Their **b**⌋ will not be collected Jr 8:2
in my heart, shut up in my **b**. Jr 20:9
within me, and all my **b** tremble. Jr 23:9
has crunched his **b** was Jr 50:17
fire from on high into my **b**; Lm 1:13
He has shattered my **b**. Lm 3:4
skin has shriveled on their **b**; Lm 4:8
and scatter your **b** around your Ezk 6:5
Fill it with choice **b**. Ezk 24:4
to a boil and cook the **b** in it." Ezk 24:5
the spices! Let the **b** be burned! Ezk 24:10
their sins rested on their **b**, Ezk 32:27
of the valley; it was full of **b**. Ezk 37:1
Son of man, can these **b** live?" Ezk 37:3
these **b** and say to them Ezk 37:4
b, hear the word of the LORD! Ezk 37:4
the Lord GOD says to these **b**: Ezk 37:5
sound, and the **b** came together, Ezk 37:7
these **b** are the whole house of Ezk 37:11
Our **b** are dried up, and our hope Ezk 37:11
them and crushed all their **b**. Dn 6:24
burned to lime the **b** of the king Am 2:1
strip⌋ their flesh from their **b**. Mc 3:2
from them and break their **b**. Mc 3:3
Rottenness entered my **b**; Hab 3:16
of dead men's **b** and every Mt 23:27
have flesh and **b** as you can see Lk 24:39
Not one of His **b** will be broken. Jn 19:36
instructions concerning his **b**. Heb 11:22

BOOK *(91)*

me from the **b** You have written. Ex 32:32
Me I will erase from My **b**. Ex 32:33
is stated in the **B** of the LORD's Nm 21:14
recorded in the **b** of this law, Dt 28:61
written in this **b** of the law. Dt 29:21
curse written in this **b** on it. Dt 29:27
are written in this **b** of the law Dt 30:10
Take this **b** of the law and place Dt 31:26
This **b** of instruction must not Jos 1:8
written in the **b** of the law of Jos 8:31
is written in the **b** of the law. Jos 8:34
this written in the **B** of Jashar? Jos 10:13
written in the **b** of the law of Jos 23:6
things in the **b** of the law of Jos 24:26
is written in the **B** of Jashar: 2Sm 1:18
about in the **B** of Solomon's 1Kg 11:41
written in the **b** of the law of 2Kg 14:6
I have found the **b** of the law in 2Kg 22:8
and he gave the **b** to Shaphan, 2Kg 22:8
the priest has given me a **b**," 2Kg 22:10
the words of the **b** of the law, 2Kg 22:11
in this **b** that has been found 2Kg 22:13
words of this **b** in order to do 2Kg 22:13
the words of the **b** that the king 2Kg 22:16
words of the **b** of the covenant 2Kg 23:2
that were written in this **b**; 2Kg 23:3
in the **b** of the covenant. 2Kg 23:21
written in the **b** that Hilkiah 2Kg 23:24
about in the **B** of the Kings 1Ch 9:1
about in the **B** of the Kings 2Ch 16:11
⌊having⌋ the **b** of the LORD's 2Ch 17:9
recorded in the **B** of Israel's 2Ch 20:34
Writing of the **B** of the Kings. 2Ch 24:27
Law, in the **b** of Moses, where 2Ch 25:4
about in the **B** of the Kings 2Ch 25:26
about in the **B** of the Kings 2Ch 27:7
about in the **B** of the Kings 2Ch 28:26
and in the **B** of the Kings of 2Ch 32:32
priest found the **b** of the law 2Ch 34:14
I have found the **b** of the law in 2Ch 34:15
and he gave the **b** to Shaphan. 2Ch 34:15
Shaphan took the **b** to the king, 2Ch 34:16
"Hilkiah the priest gave me a **b**," 2Ch 34:18
words of the **b** that was found. 2Ch 34:21
everything written in this **b**." 2Ch 34:21
written in the **b** that they read 2Ch 34:24
words of the **b** of the covenant 2Ch 34:30
the covenant written in this **b**. 2Ch 34:31
is written in the **b** of Moses; 2Ch 35:12
about in the **B** of the Kings 2Ch 35:27
in the **B** of Israel's Kings. 2Ch 36:8
is written in the **b** of Moses. Ezr 6:18
to bring the **b** of the law of Neh 8:1
attentively to the **b** of the law. Neh 8:3
Ezra opened the **b** in full view Neh 8:5
They read the **b** of the law of Neh 8:8
read out of the **b** of the law of Neh 8:18
they read from the **b** of the law Neh 9:3
recorded in the **B** of the Neh 12:23
At that time the **b** of Moses was Neh 13:1
he ordered the **b** recording daily Est 6:1
erased from the **b** of life and Ps 69:28
written in Your **b** and planned Ps 139:16
written in this **b** that Jeremiah Jr 25:13
is recorded in the **b** of truth. Dn 10:21
written in the **b** will escape. Dn 12:1
and seal the **b** until the time Dn 12:4
The **b** of the vision of Nahum the Nah 1:1
a **b** of remembrance was written Mal 3:16
you read in the **b** of Moses, Mk 12:26
is written in the **b** of the words Lk 3:4
himself says in the **B** of Psalms: Lk 20:42
that are not written in this **b**. Jn 20:30
is written in the **B** of Psalms: Ac 1:20
written in the **b** of the prophets Ac 7:42
written in the **b** of the law. Gl 3:10
names are in the **b** of life. Php 4:3
his name from the **b** of life, Rv 3:5
world in the **b** of life of the Rv 13:8
not written in the **b** of life Rv 17:8
Another **b** was opened, which is Rv 20:12
opened, which is the **b** of life, Rv 20:12
written in the **b** of life was Rv 20:15
written in the Lamb's **b** of life. Rv 21:27
the prophetic words of this **b**." Rv 22:7
who keep the words of this **b**. Rv 22:9
the prophetic words of this **b**, Rv 22:10
the prophetic words of this **b**: Rv 22:18
that are written in this **b**. Rv 22:18
the words of this prophetic **b**, Rv 22:19
holy city, written in this **b**. Rv 22:19

BOOKS *(9)*

made in your fathers' record **b**. Ezr 4:15
In these record **b** you will Ezr 4:15
no end to the making of many **b**, Ec 12:12
convened, and the **b** were opened. Dn 7:10
from the **b** according to Dn 9:2
could contain the **b** that would Jn 21:25
collected their **b** and burned Ac 19:19
the throne, and **b** were opened. Rv 20:12
by what was written in the **b**. Rv 20:12

BOOT *(1)*

the trampling **b** of battle and Is 9:5

BOOTH *(4)*

cocoon⌋ or a **b** set up by a Jb 27:18
there will be a **b** for shade from Is 4:6
as if ⌊it were⌋ a garden ⌊**b**⌋, Lm 2:6
restore the fallen **b** of David: Am 9:11

BOOTHS *(16)*

(Festival of, AKA Festival of INGATHERING, Festival of TABERNACLES)

The Festival of **B** to the LORD Lv 23:34
are to live in **b** for seven days. Lv 23:42
of Israel must live in **b**, Lv 23:42
live in **b** when I brought Lv 23:43
the Festival of **B** for seven days Dt 16:13
of Weeks, and the Festival of **B**. Dt 16:16
during the Festival of **B**, Dt 31:10
of Weeks, and the Festival of **B**. 2Ch 8:13
the Festival of **B** as prescribed, Ezr 3:4
should dwell in **b** during the Neh 8:14
other⌋ leafy trees to make **b**, Neh 8:15
made **b** for themselves on each Neh 8:16
from exile made **b** and lived in Neh 8:17
to celebrate the Festival of **B**. Zch 14:16
to celebrate the Festival of **B**. Zch 14:18
to celebrate the Festival of **B**. Zch 14:19

BOR-ASHAN *(1)*

in Hormah, in **B**, and in Athach; 1Sm 30:30

BORDER *(105)*

The Canaanite **b** went from Sidon Gn 10:19
they reached the **b** of the land Ex 16:35
to the inner **b** of the ephod. Ex 28:26
to the inner **b** of the ephod. Ex 39:19
a city on the **b** of your Nm 20:16
Mount Hor on the **b** of the land Nm 20:23
that extends from the Amorite **b**, Nm 21:13
was the Moabite **b** between Moab Nm 21:13
Ar and lie along the **b** of Moab. Nm 21:15
⌊but only up⌋ to the Ammonite **b**, Nm 21:24
city on the Arnon **b** at the edge Nm 22:36
at Iye-abarim on the **b** of Moab. Nm 33:44
Your southern **b** on the east will Nm 34:3
Your **b** will turn south of the Nm 34:4
b will turn from Azmon to the Nm 34:5
Your western **b** will be the Nm 34:6
this will be your western **b**. Nm 34:6
This will be your northern **b**: Nm 34:7
and the **b** will reach Zedad. Nm 34:8
Then the **b** will go to Ziphron Nm 34:9
This will be your northern **b**. Nm 34:9
For your eastern **b**, draw a line Nm 34:10
The **b** will go down from Shepham Nm 34:11
Then the **b** will go down to the Nm 34:12
goes outside the **b** of the city Nm 35:26
him outside the **b** of his city of Nm 35:27
to cross the **b** of Moab at Ar. Dt 2:18
far as the **b** of the Geshurites Dt 3:14
middle of the valley was the **b** Dt 3:16
River, the **b** of the Ammonites Dt 3:16
River (the **b** of the Ammonites Jos 12:2
the Geshurite and Maacathite **b**, Jos 12:5
of Gilead to the **b** of Sihon, Jos 12:5
east of Egypt to the **b** of Ekron Jos 13:3
as far as the **b** of the Amorites Jos 13:4
to the **b** of the Ammonites; Jos 13:10
The **b** of the Reubenites was the Jos 13:23
from Mahanaim to the **b** of Debir; Jos 13:26
of Zin to the **b** of Edom. Jos 15:1
Their southern **b** began at the Jos 15:2
of Egypt and so the **b** ended at Jos 15:4
This is your southern **b**. Jos 15:4
Now the eastern **b** was along the Jos 15:5
The **b** on the north side was from Jos 15:5
the **b** ascended to Debir from Jos 15:7
The **b** proceeded to the waters of Jos 15:7
From there the **b** ascended the Jos 15:8
top of the hill the **b** curved to Jos 15:9
b turned westward from Baalah Jos 15:10
Then the **b** reached to the slope Jos 15:11
Now the western **b** was the Jos 15:12
of Judah toward the **b** of Edom in Jos 15:21
to the **b** of the Archites Jos 16:2
westward to the **b** of the Jos 16:3
as far as the **b** of lower Jos 16:3
The **b** of their inheritance went Jos 16:5
In the north the **b** went westward Jos 16:6
From Tappuah the **b** went westward Jos 16:8
b of Manasseh went from Asher Jos 17:7
on Manasseh's **b** belonged to Jos 17:8
From there the **b** descended to Jos 17:9
Manasseh's **b** was on the north Jos 17:9
north, with the Sea as its **b**. Jos 17:10
Their **b** on the north side began Jos 18:12

there the **b** went toward Luz, Jos 18:13
the south, the **b** curved, turning Jos 18:14
was the west side ⌊of their **b**⌋. Jos 18:14
and the **b** extended westward; Jos 18:15
The **b** descended to the foot of Jos 18:16
The **b** continued to the north Jos 18:19
This was the southern **b**. Jos 18:19
formed the **b** on the east side Jos 18:20
their **b** went up westward to Jos 19:11
along the **b** of Chisloth-tabor Jos 19:12
The **b** then circled around Neah Jos 19:14
The **b** reached Tabor, Shahazumah, Jos 19:22
made the Jordan a **b** between us Jos 22:25
as far as the **b** of Abel-meholah Jdg 7:22
headed down the **b** road that 1Sm 13:18
and as far as the **b** of Egypt. 1Kg 4:21
and took their stand at the **b**. 2Kg 3:21
Israel's **b** from Lebo-hamath 2Kg 14:25
me, extend my **b**, let Your hand 1Ch 4:10
and as far as the **b** of Egypt. 2Ch 9:26
you can lead it back to its **b**? Jb 38:20
a pillar to the LORD near her **b**. Is 19:19
in plots, with spelt as their **b**. Is 28:25
judge you at the **b** of Israel. Ezk 11:10
judge you at the **b** of Israel, Ezk 11:11
Syene, as far as the **b** of Cush. Ezk 29:10
This is the **b** you will ⌊use to⌋ Ezk 47:13
This is to be the **b** of the land: Ezk 47:15
is between the **b** of Damascus Ezk 47:16
of Damascus and the **b** of Hamath Ezk 47:16
which is on the **b** of Hauran. Ezk 47:16
the **b** will run from the sea to Ezk 47:17
Hazar-enon at the **b** of Damascus, Ezk 47:17
the ⌊northern⌋ **b** to the eastern Ezk 47:18
Mediterranean Sea will be the **b**, Ezk 47:20
the ⌊southern⌋ **b** up to a point Ezk 47:20
at the northern **b** of Damascus, Ezk 48:1
far as the eastern **b** and next to Ezk 48:21
as far as the western **b**. Ezk 48:21
the **b** will run from Tamar to the Ezk 48:28
you will drive you to the **b**; Ob 7

BORDERS *(17)*

I will set your **b** from the Red Ex 23:31
wilderness that **b** Moab on the Nm 21:11
as an inheritance with these **b**: Nm 34:2
defined⌋ by its **b** on all sides." Nm 34:12
are also **b** from Chinnereth Dt 3:17
according to its surrounding **b**. Jos 18:20
peace on all his surrounding **b**. 1Kg 4:24
as far as Gaza and its **b**, 2Kg 18:8
and along the **b** of the sons of 1Ch 7:29
I abolished the **b** of nations and Is 10:13
expanded all the **b** of the land. Is 26:15
will be gone from⌋ your **b**. Is 60:18
sins, and within all your **b**. Jr 15:13
high places within all your **b**. Jr 17:3
on them across all their **b**. Jr 49:32
Hamath, which **b** it, as well as Zch 9:2
⌊even⌋ beyond the **b** of Israel. Mal 1:5

BORE *(66)*

Adah **b** Jabal; he was the father Gn 4:20
Zillah **b** Tubal-cain, who made Gn 4:22
of man, who **b** children to them. Gn 6:4
old when Hagar **b** Ishmael to him. Gn 16:16
pregnant and **b** a son to Abraham Gn 21:2
the one Sarah **b** to him—Isaac. Gn 21:3
Milcah **b** these eight to Nahor, Gn 22:23
was Reumah, also **b** Tebah, Gaham Gn 22:24
of Milcah, whom she **b** to Nahor." Gn 24:24
b a son to my master in her old Gn 24:36
of Nahor, whom Milcah **b** to him.' Gn 24:47
and she **b** him Zimran, Jokshan, Gn 25:2
Sarah's slave, **b** to Abraham. Gn 25:12
conceived and **b** Jacob a son. Gn 30:5
again and **b** Jacob a second son Gn 30:7
slave Zilpah **b** Jacob a son. Gn 30:10
slave Zilpah **b** Jacob a second Gn 30:12
conceived and **b** Jacob a fifth Gn 30:17
again and **b** Jacob a sixth son. Gn 30:19
Leah **b** a daughter and named her Gn 30:21
She conceived and **b** a son, Gn 30:23
of the branches and **b** streaked, Gn 30:39
beasts; I myself **b** the loss. You Gn 31:39
daughter whom she **b** to Jacob, Gn 34:1
Adah **b** Eliphaz to Esau, Basemath Gn 36:4
to Esau, Basemath **b** Reuel, Gn 36:4
and Oholibamah **b** Jeush, Jalam, Gn 36:5
son Eliphaz, **b** Amalek to Eliphaz Gn 36:12
She **b** Jeush, Jalam, and Korah to Gn 36:14
priest at On, **b** ⌊them⌋ to him. Gn 41:50
know that my wife **b** me two sons. Gn 44:27
Leah—that she **b** to Jacob: Gn 46:18
Rachel. She **b** to Jacob: seven Gn 46:25
and she **b** him Aaron and Moses. Ex 6:20
She **b** him Nadab and Abihu, Ex 6:23
Putiel and she **b** him Phinehas. Ex 6:25
in Egypt. She **b** to Amram: Aaron, Nm 26:59
was in Shechem also **b** him a son, Jdg 8:31
Gilead's wife **b** him sons, and Jdg 11:2
son Tamar **b** to Judah, because Ru 4:12
became his wife and **b** him a son. 2Sm 11:27
Tamar **b** him Perez and Zerah. 1Ch 2:4
Ephrath, and she **b** him Hur. 1Ch 2:19
years old, and she **b** him Segub. 1Ch 2:21
his wife Abijah **b** him Ashhur the 1Ch 2:24
who **b** him Ahban and Molid. 1Ch 2:29
Jarha, and she **b** him Attai. 1Ch 2:35
Naarah **b** him Ahuzzam, Hepher, 1Ch 4:6
b him sons: Jeush, Shemariah, 2Ch 11:19
She **b** him Abijah, Attai, Ziza, 2Ch 11:20
bitterness to the one who **b** him. Pr 17:25
Yet He Himself **b** our sicknesses, Is 53:4
yet He **b** the sin of many and Is 53:12
day my mother **b** me—let it Jr 20:14
because I **b** the disgrace of my Jr 31:19
she who **b** you will be put to Jr 50:12
and daughters you **b** to Me and Ezk 16:20
the children they **b** to Me pass Ezk 23:37
she conceived and **b** him a son. Hs 1:3
his mother who **b** him will say to Zch 13:3
his mother who **b** him will pierce Zch 13:3
equal to us who **b** the burden Mt 20:12
The womb that **b** You and the one Lk 11:27
that never **b**, and the breasts Lk 23:29
of us and **b** fruit for death. Rm 7:5
Himself **b** our sins in His body 1Pt 2:24

BORED *(1)*

took a chest, **b** a hole in its 2Kg 12:9

BORN *(147)*

Irad was **b** to Enoch, Irad Gn 4:18
A son was **b** to Seth also, and he Gn 4:26
and daughters were **b** to them, Gn 6:1
trained men, **b** in his household Gn 14:14
so a slave **b** in my house will be Gn 15:3
includes a slave **b** in your house Gn 17:12
a slave **b** in your house, as well Gn 17:13
Can a child be **b** to a Gn 17:17
all the slaves **b** in his house Gn 17:23
both slaves **b** in his house and Gn 17:27
named his son who was **b** to him— Gn 21:3
when his son Isaac was **b** to him. Gn 21:5
60 years old when they were **b**. Gn 25:26
all the sheep were **b** spotted. Gn 31:8
all the sheep were **b** streaked. Gn 31:8
were **b** to him in Paddan-aram. Gn 35:26
who were **b** to him in the land of Gn 36:5
was a son ⌊**b** to him⌋ in his Gn 37:3
Two sons were **b** to Joseph before Gn 41:50
were Leah's sons **b** to Jacob Gn 46:15
and Ephraim were **b** to Joseph in Gn 46:20
They were **b** to him by Asenath Gn 46:20
sons who were **b** to Jacob: Gn 46:22
sons who were **b** to him in Egypt: Gn 46:27
Your two sons **b** to you in the Gn 48:5
Children **b** to you after them Gn 48:6
throw every son **b** to the Hebrews Ex 1:22
children are **b** ⌊prematurely⌋, Ex 21:22
whether **b** at home or born Lv 18:9
born at home or **b** elsewhere. Lv 18:9
and those **b** in his house may eat Lv 22:11
or goat is **b**, it must remain Lv 22:27
you—those **b** in your land. Lv 25:45
of Levi, **b** to Levi in Egypt. Nm 26:59
and Ithamar were **b** to Aaron, Nm 26:60
The children **b** to them in the Dt 23:8
of the people **b** in the Jos 5:5
do for the boy who will be **b**." Jdg 13:8
Dan, who was **b** to Israel. Jdg 18:29
"A son has been **b** to Naomi," Ru 4:17
Sons were **b** to David in Hebron: 2Sm 3:2
These were **b** to David in Hebron. 2Sm 3:5
and daughters were **b** to him. 2Sm 5:13
the names of those **b** to him in 2Sm 5:14
the son **b** to you will die." 2Sm 12:14
Three sons were **b** to Absalom, 2Sm 14:27
and was **b** after Absalom. 1Kg 1:6
'A son will be **b** to the house of 1Kg 13:2
Two sons were **b** to Eber. 1Ch 1:19
The sons **b** to Keturah, Abraham's 1Ch 1:32
⌊These⌋ three were **b** to him by 1Ch 2:3
sons, who were **b** to him: 1Ch 2:9
Abinadab was ⌊**b**⌋ second, Shimea 1Ch 2:13
who were **b** to him in Hebron: 1Ch 3:1
was ⌊**b**⌋ second, by Abigail 1Ch 3:1
Six sons were **b** to David in 1Ch 3:4
These ⌊sons⌋ were **b** to him in 1Ch 3:5
These four were ⌊**b** to him⌋ by 1Ch 3:5
of Gath who were **b** in the land 1Ch 7:21
Ashbel was ⌊**b**⌋ second, Aharah 1Ch 8:1
of the children **b** to him in 1Ch 14:4
But a son will be **b** to you; 1Ch 22:9
Shemaiah were **b** sons who ruled 1Ch 26:6
and cursed the day he was **b**. Jb 3:1
May the day I was **b** perish, Jb 3:3
But mankind is **b** for trouble as Jb 5:7
since we were ⌊**b** only⌋ yesterday Jb 8:9
as a wild donkey is **b** a man! Jb 11:12
Man **b** of woman is short of days Jb 14:1
you the first person ever **b**, Jb 15:7
be pure, or one **b** of woman, that Jb 15:14
How can one **b** of woman be pure? Jb 25:4
the day I was **b** I guided the Jb 31:18
were already **b**; you have lived Jb 38:21
a people yet to be **b** about His Ps 22:31
I was guilty ⌊when I⌋ was **b**; Ps 51:5
yet to be **b**—might know. Ps 78:6
Cush—each one was **b** there." Ps 87:4
one and that one were **b** in her." Ps 87:5
record, "This one was **b** there." Ps 87:6
Before the mountains were **b**, Ps 90:2
are the sons **b** in one's youth. Ps 127:4
a brother is **b** for a difficult Pr 17:17
slaves who were **b** in my house. Ec 2:7
even though he was **b** poor in his Ec 4:14
For a child will be **b** for us, Is 9:6
LORD called me before I was **b**. Is 49:1
Can a land be **b** in one day, Is 66:8
set you apart before you were **b**. Jr 1:5
a slave? Was he **b** into slavery? Jr 2:14
and daughters **b** in this place as Jr 16:3
be the day on which I was **b**. Jr 20:14
"A male child is **b** to you," Jr 20:15
where neither of you were **b**, Jr 22:26
cut on the day you were **b**, Ezk 16:4
despised on the day you were **b**. Ezk 16:5
time comes, he will not be **b**. Hs 13:13
After Jesus was **b** in Bethlehem Mt 2:1
He who has been **b** King of the Mt 2:2
where the Messiah would be **b**. Mt 2:4
Among those **b** of women no one Mt 11:11
eunuchs who were **b** that way from Mt 19:12
that man if he had not been **b**." Mt 26:24
that man if he had not been **b**." Mk 14:21
holy One to be **b** will be called Lk 1:35
was **b** for you in the city of Lk 2:11
among those **b** of women no one is Lk 7:28
who were **b**, not of blood, or of Jn 1:13
Unless someone is **b** again, Jn 3:3
can anyone be **b** when he is old? Jn 3:4
womb a second time and be **b**?" Jn 3:4
Unless someone is **b** of water and Jn 3:5
Whatever is **b** of the flesh is Jn 3:6
and whatever is **b** of the Spirit Jn 3:6
you that you must be **b** again. Jn 3:7
with everyone **b** of the Spirit." Jn 3:8
weren't **b** of sexual immorality, Jn 8:41
parents, that he was **b** blind?" Jn 9:2
⌊the one⌋ you say was **b** blind? Jn 9:19
son and that he was **b** blind," Jn 9:20
the eyes of a person **b** blind. Jn 9:32
"You were **b** entirely in sin," Jn 9:34
has been **b** into the world. Jn 16:21
I was **b** for this, and I have Jn 18:37
this time Moses was **b**, and he Ac 7:20
am a Jewish man, **b** in Tarsus of Ac 22:3
"But I myself was **b** a citizen," Ac 22:28
they had not been **b** yet or done Rm 9:11
one abnormally **b**, He also 1Co 15:8
sent His Son, **b** of a woman, born Gl 4:4
of a woman, **b** under the law, Gl 4:4
by the slave was **b** according to Gl 4:23
free woman was **b** as the result Gl 4:23
as then the child **b** according to Gl 4:29
persecuted the one **b** according Gl 4:29

Benjamin, a Hebrew **b** of Hebrews; Php 3:5
after he was **b**, was hidden by Heb 11:23
since you have been **b** again— 1Pt 1:23
of instinct **b** to be caught 2Pt 2:12
what is right has been **b** of Him. 1Jn 2:29
who has been **b** of God does not 1Jn 3:9
because he has been **b** of God. 1Jn 3:9
has been **b** of God and knows 1Jn 4:7
the Messiah has been **b** of God, 1Jn 5:1
has been **b** of God conquers 1Jn 5:4
who has been **b** of God does not 1Jn 5:18
the One who is **b** of God keeps 1Jn 5:18

BORNE *(12)*
Sarai had not **b** him children. Gn 16:1
I have **b** him a son in his old Gn 21:7
the Egyptian had **b** to Abraham. Gn 21:9
Milcah also has **b** sons to your Gn 22:20
because I have **b** him three sons. Gn 29:34
because I have **b** him six sons," Gn 30:20
or for the children they have **b**? Gn 31:43
Uriah's wife had **b** to David, 2Sm 12:15
daughter of Aiah had **b** to Saul, 2Sm 21:8
of Saul had **b** to Adriel son 2Sm 21:8
of the wives had **b** children. Ezr 10:44
And just as we have **b** the image 1Co 15:49

BORROW *(5)*
lend to many nations but not **b**; Dt 15:6
nations, but you will not **b**. Dt 28:12
Go and **b** empty containers from 2Kg 4:3
did not lend or **b**, yet everyone Jr 15:10
the one who wants to **b** from you. Mt 5:42

BORROWED *(2)*
"Oh, my master, it was **b**!" 2Kg 6:5
We have **b** money to pay the Neh 5:4

BORROWER *(2)*
and the **b** is a slave to the Pr 22:7
seller, lender and **b**, creditor Is 24:2

BORROWS *(2)*
When a man **b** ⌊an animal⌋ from Ex 22:14
The wicked **b** and does not repay, Ps 37:21

BOSOR *(1)*
Balaam, the son of **B**, who loved 2Pt 2:15

BOTH *(301)*
(See pp. xi-xii.)

BOTHER *(4)*
warden did not **b** with anything Gn 39:23
Why **b** the Teacher any more?" Mk 5:35
Don't **b** the Teacher anymore." Lk 8:49
inside and say, 'Don't **b** me! Lk 11:7

BOTHERED *(1)*
conscience **b** him because he had 1Sm 24:5

BOTHERING *(2)*
Why are you **b** this woman? Mt 26:10
Why are you **b** her? Mk 14:6

BOTTLE *(1)*
Put my tears in Your **b**. Ps 56:8

BOTTLES *(1)*
sashes, perfume **b**, amulets, Is 3:20

BOTTOM *(9)*
They are to be paired at the **b**, Ex 26:24
them to the **b** of the ephod's two Ex 28:27
were paired at the **b** and joined Ex 36:29
ledge, halfway up from the **b**. Ex 38:4
them to the **b** of the ephod's two Ex 39:20
into the **b** of the chariot. 1Kg 22:35
not reached the **b** of the den Dn 6:24
was split in two from top to **b**; Mt 27:51
was split in two from top to **b**. Mk 15:38

BOUGHS *(6)*
palm fronds, **b** of leafy trees, Lv 23:40
and its **b** grew long as it spread Ezk 31:5
field gave birth beneath its **b**; Ezk 31:6
the plane trees match its **b**. Ezk 31:8
its **b** lay broken in all the Ezk 31:12
of the field were among its **b**. Ezk 31:13

BOUGHT *(26)*
that Abraham **b** from the Hittites Gn 25:10
b him from the Ishmaelites who Gn 39:1
will return to the one he **b** it Lv 27:24
small ewe lamb that he had **b**. 2Sm 12:3
David **b** the threshing floor and 2Sm 24:24
king's traders **b** them from Kue 1Kg 10:28
then he **b** the hill of Samaria 1Kg 16:24
who cannot be **b** off with silver Is 13:17
You have not **b** Me aromatic cane Is 43:24
So I **b** underwear as the LORD Jr 13:2
that you **b** and are wearing, Jr 13:4
I **b** the field in Anathoth from Jr 32:9
will again be **b** in this land.' Jr 32:15
Fields will be **b** in this land Jr 32:43
So I **b** her for 15 shekels of Hs 3:2
everything he had, and **b** it. Mt 13:46
together and **b** the potter's Mt 27:7
After he **b** some fine linen, Mk 15:46
and Salome **b** spices, so they Mk 16:1
to him, 'I have **b** a field, and I Lk 14:18
'I have **b** five yoke of oxen, Lk 14:19
that Abraham had **b** for a sum of Ac 7:16
I **b** this citizenship for a large Ac 22:28
for you were **b** at a price; 1Co 6:20
You were **b** at a price; 1Co 7:23
denying the Master who **b** them, 2Pt 2:1

BOUNCED *(1)*
⌊her⌋ hip, and **b** on ⌊her⌋ lap. Is 66:12

BOUND *(45)*
They were **b** by a treaty with Gn 14:13
b his son Isaac and placed him Gn 22:9
them and had him **b** before their Gn 42:24
to Gaza and **b** him with bronze Jdg 16:21
hands were not **b**, your feet not 2Sm 3:34
Zedekiah, **b** him in bronze 2Kg 25:7
b him with bronze ⌊shackles⌋, 2Ch 33:11
attacked him and **b** him in bronze 2Ch 36:6
in Judah were **b** by oath to him, Neh 6:18
the Jews **b** themselves, their Est 9:27
If people are **b** with chains and Jb 36:8
Who has **b** up the waters in a Pr 30:4
he had been **b** in chains with Jr 40:1
Zedekiah and **b** him with bronze Jr 52:11
which were **b** and secured with Ezk 27:24
Abednego fell, **b**, into the Dn 3:23
three men, **b**, into the fire? Dn 3:24
They **b** on the tops of the Jl 2:5
all her nobles were **b** in chains. Nah 3:10
on earth is already **b** in heaven, Mt 16:19
on earth is already **b** in heaven, Mt 18:18
the sanctuary is **b** by his oath.' Mt 23:16
that is on it is **b** by his oath.' Mt 23:18
often had been **b** with shackles Mk 5:4
he was guarded, **b** by chains and Lk 8:29
Satan has **b** this woman, a Lk 13:16
man came out **b** hand and foot Jn 11:44
Annas sent Him **b** to Caiaphas Jn 18:24
bitterness and **b** by iniquity." Ac 8:23
two soldiers, **b** with two chains, Ac 12:6
to Jerusalem, **b** in my spirit, Ac 20:22
For I am ready not only to be **b**, Ac 21:13
him to be **b** with two chains. Ac 21:33
Roman citizen and he had **b** him. Ac 22:29
conspiracy and **b** themselves Ac 23:12
We have **b** ourselves under a Ac 23:14
men who have **b** themselves under Ac 23:21
is legally **b** to her husband Rm 7:2
a sister is not **b** in such cases. 1Co 7:15
Are you **b** to a wife? Do not seek 1Co 7:27
A wife is **b** as long as her 1Co 7:39
of being **b** like a criminal; 2Tm 2:9
but God's message is not **b**. 2Tm 2:9
the four angels **b** at the great Rv 9:14
and **b** him for 1,000 years. Rv 20:2

BOUNDARIES *(6)*
within the **b** of the field— Gn 23:17
Put **b** for the people all around Ex 19:12
He set the **b** of the peoples Dt 32:8
I determined its **b** and put ⌊its⌋ Jb 38:10
You set all the **b** of the earth; Ps 74:17
times and the **b** of where they Ac 17:26

BOUNDARY *(20)*
Put a **b** around the mountain and Ex 19:23
of Zin along the **b** of Edom. Nm 34:3
move your neighbor's **b** marker, Dt 19:14
moves his neighbor's **b** marker.' Dt 27:17
was the **b** of the descendants Jos 15:12
Their **b** included Helkath, Hali, Jos 19:25
b then turned to Ramah as far Jos 19:29
Their **b** went from Heleph and Jos 19:33
the **b** turned to Aznoth-tabor and Jos 19:34
for the Arnon was the **b** of Moab. Jdg 11:18
and assigned them to be a **b**. Neh 9:22
The wicked displace **b** markers. Jb 24:2
waters at the **b** between light Jb 26:10
The **b** lines have fallen for me Ps 16:6
You set a **b** they cannot cross; Ps 104:9
the sand as the **b** of the sea, Jr 5:22
the western **b** to the eastern Ezk 45:7
boundary to the eastern **b**. Ezk 45:7
like those who move **b** markers; Hs 5:10
that day ⌊your⌋ **b** will be Mc 7:11

BOUNDING *(2)*
like a deer **b** toward a trap Pr 7:22
the mountains, **b** over the hills. Sg 2:8

BOUNTIFUL *(1)*
with the **b** harvest from the sun Dt 33:14

BOUNTY *(8)*
and the **b** of the eternal Gn 49:26
dew of heaven's **b** and the watery Dt 33:13
and the **b** of the eternal Dt 33:15
given her out of his royal **b**. 1Kg 10:13
freely, according to the king's **b** Est 1:7
gifts worthy of the king's **b**. Est 2:18
land to eat its fruit and **b**, Jr 2:7
have withheld ⌊My⌋ **b** from you, Jr 5:25

BOW *(118)*
have placed My **b** in the clouds, Gn 9:13
the earth and the **b** appears in Gn 9:14
The **b** will be in the clouds, Gn 9:16
your quiver and **b**, and go out Gn 27:3
you and nations **b** down to you. Gn 27:29
mother's sons **b** down to you. Gn 27:29
and I going to **b** down to the Gn 37:10
Amorites with my sword and **b**." Gn 48:22
sons will **b** down to you. Gn 49:8
Yet his **b** remained steady, Gn 49:24
come down to me and **b** before me, Ex 11:8
You must not **b** down to them or Ex 20:5
must not **b** down to their gods Ex 23:24
and **b** in worship at a distance. Ex 24:1
stand up, then **b** in worship, Ex 33:10
are to never **b** down to another Ex 34:14
in your land to **b** down to it, Lv 26:1
led astray to **b** down and worship Dt 4:19
You must not **b** down to them or Dt 5:9
to worship and **b** down to them, Dt 8:19
worship, and **b** down to other Dt 11:16
your God and **b** down to Him. Dt 26:10
led astray to **b** down to other Dt 30:17
worship them or **b** down to them. Jos 23:7
other gods, and **b** down to them, Jos 23:16
It was not by your sword or **b**. Jos 24:12
to worship and **b** down to them. Jdg 2:19
got up early to **b** and to worship 1Sm 1:19
will come and **b** down to him for 1Sm 2:36
with me so I can **b** and worship 1Sm 15:30
his sword, his **b**, and his belt. 1Sm 18:4
be taught ⌊The Song of⌋ the **B**. 2Sm 1:18
Jonathan's **b** never retreated, 2Sm 1:22
approached to **b** down to him, 2Sm 15:5
"I **b** ⌊before you⌋," Ziba said. 2Sm 16:4
my arms can bend a **b** of bronze. 2Sm 22:35
a man drew his **b** without taking 1Kg 22:34
b in the temple of Rimmon— 2Kg 5:18
I **b** in the temple of Rimmon, 2Kg 5:18
with your sword or your **b**? 2Kg 6:22
Jehu drew his **b** and shot Joram 2Kg 9:24
"Take a **b** and arrows." 2Kg 13:15
So he got a **b** and arrows. 2Kg 13:15
"Put your hand on the **b**." 2Kg 13:16
gods; do not **b** down to them; do 2Kg 17:35
are to **b** down to Him, and you 2Kg 17:36
sword, drew the **b**, and were 1Ch 5:18
or ⌊shoot⌋ arrows with a **b**. 1Ch 12:2
shields and drawing the **b**. 2Ch 14:8
him armed with **b** and shield; 2Ch 17:17
a man drew his **b** without taking 2Ch 18:33
would not **b** down or pay homage Est 3:2
a bronze **b** will pierce him. Jb 20:24
and my **b** will be renewed in my Jb 29:20
I **b** down toward Your holy temple Ps 5:7
has strung His **b** and made it Ps 7:12
look, the wicked string the **b**; Ps 11:2
my arms can bend a **b** of bronze. Ps 18:34
you aim your **b** at their faces. Ps 21:12
nations will **b** down before You Ps 22:27
on earth will eat and **b** down; Ps 22:29
and strung the **b** to bring down Ps 37:14
For I do not trust in my **b**, Ps 44:6
B down to him, for he is your Ps 45:11
And let all kings **b** down to him, Ps 72:11

became warped like a faulty **b**. Ps 78:57
you must not **b** down to a foreign Ps 81:9
will come and **b** down before You, Ps 86:9
let us worship and **b** down; Ps 95:6
b in worship at His footstool. Ps 99:5
b in worship at His holy Ps 99:9
I will **b** down toward Your holy Ps 138:2
The evil **b** before those who are Pr 14:19
they **b** down to the work of their Is 2:8
go there with **b** and arrows Is 7:24
from the bent **b**, from the stress Is 21:15
together, captured without a **b**. Is 22:3
wind-driven stubble ⌊with⌋ his **b**. Is 41:2
will **b** down to a block of wood. Is 44:19
in chains; and **b** down to you. Is 45:14
Every knee will **b** to Me, every Is 45:23
they kneel and **b** down to it. Is 46:6
and princes will **b** down, because Is 49:7
They will **b** down to you with Is 49:23
to **b** his head like a reed, Is 58:5
will come and **b** down to you; Is 60:14
They grasp **b** and javelin. Jr 6:23
able to handle and string the **b**. Jr 46:9
I am about to shatter Elam's **b**, Jr 49:35
Babylon, all who string the **b**; Jr 50:29
They grasp **b** and javelin. Jr 50:42
let the archer string his **b**; Jr 51:3
Like an enemy He has bent His **b**; Lm 2:4
He bent His **b** and set me as the Lm 3:12
will knock your **b** from your left Ezk 39:3
He will **b** in worship at the Ezk 46:2
land will also **b** in worship Ezk 46:3
day I will break the **b** of Israel Hs 1:5
I will not deliver them by **b**, Hs 1:7
I will shatter **b**, sword, and Hs 2:18
they are like a faulty **b**. Hs 7:16
that you will not **b** down again Mc 5:13
when I come to **b** before God on Mc 6:6
You took the sheath from Your **b**; Hab 3:9
those who **b** in worship on the Zph 1:5
those who **b** and pledge loyalty Zph 1:5
the nations will **b** in worship to Zph 2:11
The **b** of war will be removed, Zch 9:10
For I will bend Judah ⌊as My **b**⌋; Zch 9:13
I will fill that **b** with Ephraim. Zch 9:13
them the battle **b**, from them Zch 10:4
to put out anchors from the **b**. Ac 27:30
The **b** jammed fast and remained Ac 27:41
every knee will **b** to Me, and Rm 14:11
this reason I **b** my knees before Eph 3:14
of Jesus every knee should **b**— Php 2:10
them come and **b** down at your Rv 3:9
The horseman on it had a **b**; Rv 6:2

BOW'S *(1)*

shatters the **b** flaming arrows, Ps 76:3

BOWED *(63)*

meet them and **b** to the ground. Gn 18:2
He **b** ⌊with his⌋ face to the Gn 19:1
Abraham rose and **b** down to the Gn 23:7
Abraham **b** down to the people of Gn 23:12
Then the man **b** down, worshiped Gn 24:26
Then I **b** down, worshiped the Gn 24:48
he **b** to the ground before the Gn 24:52
on ahead and **b** to the ground Gn 33:3
approached ⌊him⌋ and **b** down. Gn 33:6
also approached and **b** down, Gn 33:7
Rachel approached and **b** down. Gn 33:7
it and **b** down to my sheaf. Gn 37:7
came and **b** down before him Gn 42:6
and they **b** to the ground before Gn 43:26
And they **b** down to honor him. Gn 43:28
Then Israel **b** ⌊in thanks⌋ at the Gn 47:31
knees and **b** with his face to Gn 48:12
came to him, **b** down before him, Gn 50:18
they **b** down and worshiped. Ex 4:31
So the people **b** down and Ex 12:27
father-in-law, **b** down, and then Ex 18:7
They have **b** down to it, Ex 32:8
Moses immediately **b** down to the Ex 34:8
Balaam knelt and **b** with his face Nm 22:31
people ate and **b** in worship to Nm 25:2
Then Joshua **b** with his face to Jos 5:14
peoples and **b** down to them. Jdg 2:12
interpretation, he **b** in worship. Jdg 7:15
b with her face to the ground Ru 2:10
Then he **b** and worshiped the 1Sm 1:28
and Saul **b** down to the LORD. 1Sm 15:31
the ground, and **b** three times. 1Sm 20:41
David **b** to the ground in homage. 1Sm 24:8
She **b** her face to the ground and 1Sm 25:41
and he **b** his face to the ground 1Sm 28:14
b down to the ground and paid 2Sm 9:6
Mephibosheth **b** down and said, 2Sm 9:8
to the king and **b** down with his 2Sm 14:33
The Cushite **b** to Joab and took 2Sm 18:21
and then **b** down to the king 2Sm 18:28
he went out and **b** to the king 2Sm 24:20
Bathsheba **b** down and paid 1Kg 1:16
presence and **b** to him with his 1Kg 1:23
Bathsheba **b** with her face to the 1Kg 1:31
Then the king **b** in worship on 1Kg 1:47
to greet her, **b** to her, sat down 1Kg 2:19
they have **b** the knee to 1Kg 11:33
He **b** down to the ground and put 1Kg 18:42
that has not **b** to Baal and every 1Kg 19:18
to meet him and **b** down to the 2Kg 2:15
his feet, and **b** to the ground; 2Kg 4:37
floor and **b** to David with his 1Ch 21:21
They **b** down and paid homage to 1Ch 29:20
They **b** down with their faces to 2Ch 7:3
Jehoshaphat **b** with his face to 2Ch 20:18
present with him **b** down and 2Ch 29:29
rejoicing and **b** down and 2Ch 29:30
Then they **b** down and worshiped Neh 8:6
the King's Gate **b** down and paid Est 3:2
was **b** down with grief, like one Ps 35:14
Jerusalem have **b** their heads to Lm 2:10
terrified and **b** down to the Lk 24:5
who have not **b** down to Baal. Rm 11:4

BOWING *(7)*

and 11 stars were **b** down to me." Gn 37:9
other gods by **b** down to the sun, Dt 17:3
b down to gods they had not Dt 29:26
with other gods, **b** down to them. Jdg 2:17
Mordecai was not **b** down or Est 3:5
They were **b** to the east in Ezk 8:16
Then **b** His head, He gave up His Jn 19:30

BOWL *(35)*

to take holy water in a clay **b**, Nm 5:17
one gold **b** weighing four ounces, Nm 7:14
one gold **b** weighing four ounces, Nm 7:20
one gold **b** weighing four ounces, Nm 7:26
one gold **b** weighing four ounces, Nm 7:32
one gold **b** weighing four ounces, Nm 7:38
one gold **b** weighing four ounces, Nm 7:44
one gold **b** weighing four ounces, Nm 7:50
one gold **b** weighing four ounces, Nm 7:56
one gold **b** weighing four ounces, Nm 7:62
one gold **b** weighing four ounces, Nm 7:68
one gold **b** weighing four ounces, Nm 7:74
one gold **b** weighing four ounces, Nm 7:80
and kneading **b** will be blessed. Dt 28:5
and kneading **b** will be cursed. Dt 28:17
curdled milk in a majestic **b**. Jdg 5:25
of it, filling a **b** with water. Jdg 6:38
me a new **b** and put salt in it. 2Kg 2:20
clean as one wipes a **b**— 2Kg 21:13
the weight of each silver **b**; 1Ch 28:17
buries his hand in the **b**; Pr 19:24
buries his hand in the **b**; Pr 26:15
and the golden **b** is broken, Ec 12:6
Your navel is a rounded **b**; Sg 7:2
there with a **b** on its top. Zch 4:2
the right of the **b** and the other Zch 4:3
his hand with Me in the **b**— Mt 26:23
⌊bread⌋ with Me in the **b**. Mk 14:20
poured out his **b** on the earth, Rv 16:2
poured out his **b** into the sea. Rv 16:3
poured out his **b** into the rivers Rv 16:4
poured out his **b** on the sun. Rv 16:8
poured out his **b** on the throne Rv 16:10
poured out his **b** on the great Rv 16:12
poured out his **b** into the air, Rv 16:17

BOWLFUL *(1)*

drink wine by the **b** and anoint Am 6:6

BOWLS *(34)*

into your ovens and kneading **b**. Ex 8:3
their kneading **b** wrapped up in Ex 12:34
its pitchers and **b** for pouring Ex 25:29
well as its **b** and pitchers for Ex 37:16
well as the **b** and pitchers for Nm 4:7
12 silver basins, and 12 gold **b**. Nm 7:84
12 gold **b** full of incense each Nm 7:86
of the gold **b** was three pounds. Nm 7:86
b for the capitals that were on 1Kg 7:41
covering both **b** of the capitals 1Kg 7:41
both capitals' **b** on top of the 1Kg 7:42
the pure gold ceremonial **b**, 1Kg 7:50
no silver **b**, wick trimmers, 2Kg 12:13
He also made 100 gold **b**. 2Ch 4:8
pots, the shovels, and the **b**. 2Ch 4:11
the **b** and the capitals on top of 2Ch 4:12
covering both **b** of the capitals 2Ch 4:12
both capitals' **b** on top of the 2Ch 4:13
in pots, in kettles, and in **b**; 2Ch 35:13
30 gold **b**, 410 various silver Ezr 1:10
various silver **b**, and 1,000 Ezr 1:10
gold **b** worth 1,000 gold coins, Ezr 8:27
drachmas, 50 **b**, and 530 priestly Neh 7:70
from **b** to every kind of jar. Is 22:24
polluted broth in their **b**. Is 65:4
Fortune and fill **b** of mixed wine Is 65:11
of the guards took away the **b**, Jr 52:19
and the drink offering **b**— Jr 52:19
are not only gold and silver **b**, 2Tm 2:20
a harp and gold **b** filled with Rv 5:8
angels seven gold **b** filled with Rv 15:7
out the seven **b** of God's wrath Rv 16:1
had the seven **b** came and spoke Rv 17:1
had held the seven **b** filled with Rv 21:9

BOWS *(13)*

b of the warriors are broken, 1Sm 2:4
armor, **b** and slingstones 2Ch 26:14
their swords, spears, and **b**. Neh 4:13
spears, shields, **b**, and armor. Neh 4:16
and their **b** will be broken. Ps 37:15
He shatters **b** and cuts spears to Ps 46:9
and all their **b** strung. Is 5:28
⌊Their⌋ **b** will cut young men to Is 13:18
it an idol and **b** down to it. Is 44:15
He **b** down to it and worships; Is 44:17
their tongues ⌊like⌋ their **b**; Jr 9:3
captured, their **b** shattered, for Jr 51:56
and shields, the **b** and arrows, Ezk 39:9

BOWSHOT *(1)*

nearby, about a **b** away, for she Gn 21:16

BOWSTRING *(2)*

has loosened my **b** and oppressed Jb 30:11
put the arrow on the **b** to shoot Ps 11:2

BOWSTRINGS *(3)*

with seven fresh **b** that have not Jdg 16:7
her seven fresh **b** that had not Jdg 16:8
But he snapped the **b** as a strand Jdg 16:9

BOX *(5)*

gold objects in a **b** beside it, 1Sm 6:8
along with the **b** ⌊containing⌋ 1Sm 6:11
along with the **b** containing the 1Sm 6:15
elms and **b** trees together, Is 41:19
or **b** like one who beats the air. 1Co 9:26

BOXED *(1)*

the wilderness has **b** them in. Ex 14:3

BOY *(69)*

me, a **b** for striking me. Gn 4:23
about the **b** and your slave. Gn 21:12
and sent her and the **b** away. Gn 21:14
she left the **b** under one of the Gn 21:15
⌊bear to⌋ watch the **b** die!" Gn 21:16
God heard the voice of the **b**, Gn 21:17
voice of the **b** from the place Gn 21:17
up, help the **b** up, and sustain Gn 21:18
and gave the **b** a drink. Gn 21:19
God was with the **b**, and he grew; Gn 21:20
The **b** and I will go over there Gn 22:5
a hand on the **b** or do anything Gn 22:12
and said, "The **b** is gone! Gn 37:30
I tell you not to harm the **b**? Gn 42:22
Israel, "Send the **b** with me. Gn 43:8
'The **b** cannot leave his father. Gn 44:22
father and the **b** is not with us Gn 44:30
sees that the **b** is not with us, Gn 44:31
to my father for the **b**, Gn 44:32
lord's slave, in place of the **b**. Gn 44:33
back to my father without the **b**? Gn 44:34
the child—a little **b**, crying. Ex 2:6
Hebrews to nurse the **b** for you?" Ex 2:7
woman took the **b** and nursed him. Ex 2:9
because the **b** will be a Nazirite Jdg 13:5
because the **b** will be a Nazirite Jdg 13:7
do for the **b** who will be born. Jdg 13:8
The **b** grew, and the LORD blessed Jdg 13:24
Though the **b** was ⌊still⌋ young, 1Sm 1:24

bull and brought the **b** to Eli. 1Sm 1:25
I prayed for this **b**, and since 1Sm 1:27
I now give the **b** to the LORD. 1Sm 1:28
but the **b** served the LORD in the 1Sm 2:11
b Samuel served in the LORD's 1Sm 2:18
the **b** Samuel grew up in the 1Sm 2:21
the **b** Samuel grew in stature and 1Sm 2:26
The **b** Samuel served the LORD in 1Sm 3:1
that the LORD was calling the **b**. 1Sm 3:8
She named the **b** Ichabod, saying, 1Sm 4:21
pleaded with God for the **b**. 2Sm 12:16
Cut the living **b** in two and give 1Kg 3:25
At the time Hadad was a small **b**. 1Kg 11:17
you what will happen to the **b**." 1Kg 14:3
enter the city, the **b** will die. 1Kg 14:12
of the house, the **b** died. 1Kg 14:17
out over the **b** three times. 1Kg 17:21
Elijah took the **b**, brought him 1Kg 17:23
him, "The **b** didn't wake up." 2Kg 4:31
discovered the **b** lying dead on 2Kg 4:32
he went up and lay on the **b**: 2Kg 4:34
The **b** sneezed seven times and 2Kg 4:35
like the skin of a small **b**, 2Kg 5:14
they said, "A **b** is conceived." Jb 3:3
For before the **b** knows to reject Is 7:16
for before the **b** knows how to Is 8:4
was in pain, she delivered a **b**. Is 66:7
they bartered a **b** for a Jl 3:3
that moment the **b** was healed. Mt 17:18
it immediately convulsed the **b**. Mk 9:20
the father of the **b** cried out, Mk 9:24
The **b** became like a corpse, Mk 9:26
The **b** grew up and became strong, Lk 2:40
the **b** Jesus stayed behind in Lk 2:43
As the **b** was still approaching, Lk 9:42
spirit, cured the **b**, and gave Lk 9:42
"come down before my **b** dies!" Jn 4:49
him saying that his **b** was alive. Jn 4:51
There's a **b** here who has five Jn 6:9
They brought the **b** home alive Ac 20:12

BOY'S *(10)*
The **b** brother is dead. Gn 44:20
is wrapped up with the **b** life— Gn 44:30
went and called the **b** mother. Ex 2:8
what will the **b** responsibilities Jdg 13:12
let this **b** life return to him! 1Kg 17:21
and the **b** life returned to him, 1Kg 17:22
place my staff on the **b** face." 2Kg 4:29
The **b** mother said ⌊to Elisha⌋, 2Kg 4:30
placed the staff on the **b** face, 2Kg 4:31
over him, the **b** flesh became 2Kg 4:34

BOYS *(9)*
When the **b** grew up, Esau became Gn 25:27
all harm—may He bless these **b**. Gn 48:16
told them; they let the **b** live. Ex 1:17
done this and let the **b** live?" Ex 1:18
"This is one of the Hebrew **b**." Ex 2:6
small **b** came out of the city 2Kg 2:23
Even young **b** scorn me. When I Jb 19:18
b stumble under ⌊loads of⌋ wood. Lm 5:13
be filled with **b** and girls Zch 8:5

BOZEZ *(1)*
One was named **B** and the other 1Sm 14:4

BOZKATH *(2)*
Lachish, **B**, Eglon, Jos 15:39
of Adaiah; ⌊she was⌋ from **B**. 2Kg 22:1

BOZRAH *(8)*
son of Zerah from **B** ruled in his Gn 36:33
son of Zerah from **B** ruled in his 1Ch 1:44
the LORD has a sacrifice in **B**, Is 34:6
garments from **B**— Is 63:1
Kerioth, **B**, and all the towns of Jr 48:24
B will become a desolation, Jr 49:13
and spreading its wings over **B**. Jr 49:22
will consume the citadels of **B**. Am 1:12

BRACE *(1)*
Watch the road! **B** yourself! Nah 2:1

BRACED *(1)*
and **b** the knees that were Jb 4:4

BRACELETS *(9)*
for her wrists two **b** weighing 10 Gn 24:22
the **b** on his sister's wrists, Gn 24:30
nose and the **b** on her wrists. Gn 24:47
armlets, **b**, rings, earrings Nm 31:50
steps, jingling their ankle **b**, Is 3:16
ankle **b**, headbands, crescents, Is 3:18
pendants, **b**, veils, Is 3:19
putting **b** on your wrists and a Ezk 16:11
They put **b** on the women's hands Ezk 23:42

BRACES *(2)*
its **b** and its frames were one 1Kg 7:35
plates of its **b** and on its 1Kg 7:36

BRAG *(9)*
you, or else Israel might **b**: Jdg 7:2
Why **b** about evil, you hero! Ps 52:1
Don't **b** about yourself before Pr 25:6
Why do you **b** about your valleys, Jr 49:4
he has something to **b** about— Rm 4:2
not **b** that you are better than Rm 11:18
But if you do **b**—you do not Rm 11:18
and I **b** about you to the 2Co 9:2
don't **b** and lie in defiance of Jms 3:14

BRAGGARTS *(1)*
your boastful **b** from among you, Zph 3:11

BRAGGING *(1)*
are not **b** beyond measure about 2Co 10:15

BRAIDED *(3)*
will make them of **b** cord work, Ex 28:14
You are to make **b** chains of pure Ex 28:22
They made **b** chains of pure gold Ex 39:15

BRAIDS *(3)*
weave the seven **b** on my head Jdg 16:13
fastened the **b** with a pin and Jdg 16:14
off the seven **b** on his head. Jdg 16:19

BRAMBLE *(4)*
all the trees said to the **b**, Jdg 9:14
The **b** said to the trees, "If you Jdg 9:15
come out from the **b** and consume Jdg 9:15
or grapes picked from a **b** bush. Lk 6:44

BRANCH *(31)*
on the first **b**, and three cups Ex 25:33
calyx and petals, on the next **b**. Ex 25:33
on the first **b**, and three cups Ex 37:19
calyx and petals, on the next **b**. Ex 37:19
they cut down a **b** with a single Nm 13:23
hand and cut a **b** from the trees. Jdg 9:48
picked up the **b**, put it on his Jdg 9:48
also cut his own **b** and followed Jdg 9:49
and his **b** will not flourish. Jb 15:32
On that day the **b** of the LORD Is 4:2
palm **b** and reed in a single day. Is 9:14
and a **b** from his roots will bear Is 11:1
like a worthless **b**, covered by Is 14:19
they are the **b** I planted, the Is 60:21
"I see a **b** of an almond tree." Jr 1:11
raise up a righteous **B** of David. Jr 23:5
will cause a **B** of righteousness Jr 33:15
putting the **b** to their nose? Ezk 8:17
that **b** among the trees of the Ezk 15:2
from its main **b** and has devoured Ezk 19:14
it no longer has a strong **b**, Ezk 19:14
to bring My servant, the **B**. Zch 3:8
Here is a man whose name is **B**; Zch 6:12
He will **b** out from His place and Zch 6:12
As soon as its **b** becomes tender Mt 24:32
As soon as its **b** becomes tender Mk 13:28
Every **b** in Me that does not Jn 15:2
He prunes every **b** that produces Jn 15:2
Just as a **b** is unable to produce Jn 15:4
aside like a **b** and he withers. Jn 15:6
a wild olive **b**, were grafted Rm 11:17

BRANCHES *(82)*
then took **b** of fresh poplar Gn 30:37
exposing white stripes on the **b**. Gn 30:37
set the peeled **b** in the troughs Gn 30:38
in front of the **b** and bore Gn 30:39
placed the **b** in the troughs, Gn 30:41
would breed in front of the **b**. Gn 30:41
he did not put out the **b**. Gn 30:42
On the vine were three **b**. Gn 40:10
The three **b** are three days. Gn 40:12
its **b** climb over the wall. Gn 49:22
Six **b** are to extend from its Ex 25:32
three **b** of the lampstand from Ex 25:32
and three **b** of the lampstand Ex 25:32
way for the six **b** that extend Ex 25:33
For the six **b** that extend from Ex 25:35
the ⌊first⌋ pair of **b** from it, Ex 25:35
the ⌊second⌋ pair of **b** from it, Ex 25:35
the ⌊third⌋ pair of **b** from it. Ex 25:35
calyxes and **b** are to be of one Ex 25:36
Six **b** extended from its sides, Ex 37:18
three **b** of the lampstand from Ex 37:18
and three **b** of the lampstand Ex 37:18
way for the six **b** that extended Ex 37:19
For the six **b** that extended from Ex 37:21
the first pair of **b** from it, Ex 37:21
the second pair of **b** from it, Ex 37:21
the third pair of **b** from it. Ex 37:21
calyxes and **b** were of one piece Ex 37:22
must not go over the **b** again. Dt 24:20
They put the **b** against the inner Jdg 9:49
the tangled **b** of a large oak 2Sm 18:9
and bring back **b** of olive, Neh 8:15
brought back ⌊**b**⌋, and made Neh 8:16
and his **b** above wither away. Jb 18:16
dew will rest on my **b** all night. Jb 29:19
the mighty cedars with its **b**. Ps 80:10
Your **b** are a paradise of Sg 4:13
chop off the **b** with terrifying Is 10:33
four or five on its fruitful **b**. Is 17:6
and tear away and remove the **b**. Is 18:5
will spread out and strip its **b**. Is 27:10
When its **b** dry out, they will be Is 27:11
a grape gatherer over the **b**. Jr 6:9
and its **b** are consumed with a Jr 11:16
height with its **b** turned toward Ezk 17:6
vine, produced **b**, and sent forth Ezk 17:6
out its **b** to him from its Ezk 17:7
waters in order to produce **b**, Ezk 17:8
mountain so that it may bear **b**, Ezk 17:23
shelter in the shade of its **b**. Ezk 17:23
and full of **b** because of Ezk 19:10
It had strong **b**, ⌊fit⌋ for the Ezk 19:11
height as well as its many **b**. Ezk 19:11
Its strong **b** were torn off and Ezk 19:12
with beautiful **b** and shady Ezk 31:3
Its **b** multiplied, and its boughs Ezk 31:5
of the sky nested in its **b**, Ezk 31:6
couldn't compare with its **b**, Ezk 31:8
put forth your **b** and bear your Ezk 36:8
birds of the air lived in its **b**, Dn 4:12
the tree and chop off its **b**; Dn 4:14
it, and the birds from its **b**. Dn 4:14
in its **b** the birds of the air Dn 4:21
His new **b** will spread, and his Hs 14:6
its **b** have turned white. Jl 1:7
them and ruined their vine **b**. Nah 2:2
the two olive **b** beside the two Zch 4:12
not leaving them root or **b**. Mal 4:1
the sky come and nest in its **b**." Mt 13:32
were cutting **b** from the trees Mt 21:8
produces large **b**, so that the Mk 4:32
spread leafy **b** cut from the Mk 11:8
of the sky nested in its **b**." Lk 13:19
they took palm **b** and went out to Jn 12:13
vine; you are the **b**. The one who Jn 15:5
the root is holy, so are the **b**. Rm 11:16
some of the **b** were broken off, Rm 11:17
you are better than those **b**. Rm 11:18
B were broken off so that I Rm 11:19
God did not spare the natural **b**, Rm 11:21
the natural **b**—be grafted Rm 11:24
with palm **b** in their hands. Rv 7:9

BRANDING *(1)*
instead of beauty, **b**. Is 3:24

BRANDISH *(2)*
of Hosts will **b** a whip against Is 10:26
you when I **b** My sword in front Ezk 32:10

BRANDISHED *(3)*
b by the hand of a drunkard. Pr 26:9
against him with **b** weapons. Is 30:32
and the spears are **b**. Nah 2:3

BRANDISHING *(1)*
bucklers, all of them **b** swords. Ezk 38:4

BRASS *(1)*
expensive wood, **b**, iron, and Rv 18:12

BRAVE *(30)*
sent out five **b** men from all Jdg 18:2
sent 12,000 **b** warriors there Jdg 21:10
and **b** men whose hearts God had 1Sm 10:26
noticed any strong or **b** man, 1Sm 14:52
all their **b** men set out, 1Sm 31:12
even a **b** man with the heart of a 2Sm 17:10
the son of a **b** man from Kabzeel 2Sm 23:20
of the earth. Be strong and **b**, 1Kg 2:2
The man was a **b** warrior, but he 2Kg 5:1
were **b** warriors, famous men, 1Ch 5:24
all their **b** men set out and 1Ch 10:12

the son of a **b** man from Kabzeel 1Ch 11:22
for they were all **b** warriors and 1Ch 12:21
7,100 **b** warriors ready for war. 1Ch 12:25
Zadok, a young **b** warrior, with 1Ch 12:28
b warriors who were famous 1Ch 12:30
men, and all the **b** warriors. 1Ch 28:1
All these were **b** warriors. 2Ch 14:8
He had fighting men, **b** warriors, 2Ch 17:13
and 300,000 **b** warriors with him; 2Ch 17:14
and 200,000 **b** warriors with him; 2Ch 17:16
Benjamin, Eliada, a **b** warrior, 2Ch 17:17
he hired 100,000 **b** warriors from 2Ch 25:6
families was 2,600 **b** warriors. 2Ch 26:12
along with 80 **b** priests of the 2Ch 26:17
in one day—all **b** men—because 2Ch 28:6
who annihilated every **b** warrior, 2Ch 32:21
Remember this and be **b**; Is 46:8
the **b** will not save his life. Am 2:14
in the faith, be **b** and strong. 1Co 16:13

BRAVE-HEARTED *(1)*
The **b** have been plundered; Ps 76:5

BRAVELY *(1)*
He fought **b**, defeated the 1Sm 14:48

BRAWLER *(1)*
mocker, beer is a **b**, and whoever Pr 20:1

BRAY *(2)*
a wild donkey **b** over fresh grass Jb 6:5
They **b** among the shrubs; Jb 30:7

BRAZEN *(2)*
You have the **b** look of a Jr 3:3
the acts of a **b** prostitute, Ezk 16:30

BRAZENLY *(1)*
kisses him; she **b** says to him, Pr 7:13

BRAZIER *(1)*
consumed by the fire in the **b**. Jr 36:23

BREACH *(4)*
advance as through a gaping **b**; Jb 30:14
Him in the **b** to turn His wrath Ps 106:23
will be no **b** ⌊in the walls⌋, Ps 144:14
will be like a spreading **b**, Is 30:13

BREACHED *(2)*
as ⌊an army⌋ entering a **b** city, Ezk 26:10
Thebes will be **b**, and Memphis Ezk 30:16

BREACHES *(2)*
there were many **b** in ⌊the walls Is 22:9
will go through **b** in the wall, Am 4:3

BREAD *(292)*
You will eat **b** by the sweat of Gn 3:19
Salem, brought out **b** and wine; Gn 14:18
bring a bit of **b** so that you may Gn 18:5
of fine flour and make **b**." Gn 18:6
and baked unleavened **b** for them, Gn 19:3
got up, took **b** and a waterskin, Gn 21:14
Jacob gave **b** and lentil stew Gn 25:34
food and the **b** she had made to Gn 27:17
of white **b** were on my head Gn 40:16
with unleavened **b** and bitter Ex 12:8
eat unleavened **b** for seven days. Ex 12:15
of⌋ Unleavened **B** because on this Ex 12:17
to eat unleavened **b** in the first Ex 12:18
unleavened **b** in all your homes. Ex 12:20
days you must eat unleavened **b**, Ex 13:6
Unleavened **b** is to be eaten for Ex 13:7
and ate all the **b** we wanted. Ex 16:3
going to rain **b** from heaven for Ex 16:4
and abundant **b** in the morning, Ex 16:8
you will eat **b** until you are Ex 16:12
It is the **b** the LORD has given Ex 16:15
give you two days' worth of **b**. Ex 16:29
that they may see the **b** I fed Ex 16:32
the Festival of Unleavened **B**. Ex 23:15
eat unleavened **b** for seven days Ex 23:15
bless your **b** and your water. Ex 23:25
Put the **b** of the Presence on the Ex 25:30
with unleavened **b**, unleavened Ex 29:2
take one loaf of **b**, one cake of Ex 29:23
one cake of **b** ⌊made⌋ with oil, Ex 29:23
of unleavened **b** that is before Ex 29:23
of the ram and the **b** that is in Ex 29:32
or any of the **b** is left until Ex 29:34
the Festival of Unleavened **B**. Ex 34:18
eat unleavened **b** for seven days Ex 34:18
he did not eat **b** or drink water. Ex 34:28
and the **b** of the Presence; Ex 35:13
and the **b** of the Presence; Ex 39:36
He arranged the **b** on it before Ex 40:23
be unleavened **b** ⌊made⌋ of fine Lv 2:5
as unleavened **b** in a holy place; Lv 6:16
offering cakes of leavened **b**, Lv 7:13
and the basket of unleavened **b**, Lv 8:2
of unleavened **b** that was before Lv 8:26
took one cake of unleavened **b**, Lv 8:26
one cake of **b** ⌊made⌋ with oil, Lv 8:26
it there with the **b** that is in Lv 8:31
what remains of the meat and **b**. Lv 8:32
of Unleavened **B** to the LORD is Lv 23:6
days you must eat unleavened **b**. Lv 23:6
must not eat **b**, roasted grain, Lv 23:14
Bring two loaves of **b** from your Lv 23:17
present with the **b** seven Lv 23:18
lambs with the **b** of firstfruits Lv 23:20
the **b** and the two lambs will be Lv 23:20
portion for the **b** and a fire Lv 24:7
b is to be set out before the Lv 24:8
When I cut off your supply of **b**, Lv 26:26
bake your **b** in a single oven Lv 26:26
and ration out your **b** by weight, Lv 26:26
The regular **b** ⌊offering⌋ is to Nm 4:7
with the basket of unleavened **b**. Nm 6:17
with unleavened **b** and bitter Nm 9:11
There is no **b** or water, and we Nm 21:5
unleavened **b** is to be eaten for Nm 28:17
does not live on **b** alone but on Dt 8:3
I did not eat **b** or drink water. Dt 9:9
I did not eat **b** or drink water Dt 9:18
must not eat leavened **b** with it. Dt 16:3
are to eat unleavened **b** with it, Dt 16:3
with it, the **b** of hardship— Dt 16:3
eat unleavened **b** for six days. Dt 16:8
at the Festival of Unleavened **B**, Dt 16:16
you did not eat **b** or drink wine Dt 29:6
ate unleavened **b** and roasted Jos 5:11
provision of **b** was dry and Jos 9:5
This **b** of ours was warm when we Jos 9:12
and unleavened **b** from a half Jdg 6:19
the meat with the unleavened **b**, Jdg 6:20
the meat and the unleavened **b**. Jdg 6:21
the meat and the unleavened **b**. Jdg 6:21
a loaf of barley **b** came tumbling Jdg 7:13
some loaves of **b** to the people Jdg 8:5
we should give **b** to your army?" Jdg 8:6
we should give **b** to your Jdg 8:15
donkeys, and **b** and wine for me Jdg 19:19
here and have some **b** and dip it Ru 2:14
piece of silver or a loaf of **b**. 1Sm 2:36
can have a piece of **b** to eat.'" 1Sm 2:36
one bringing three loaves of **b**, 1Sm 10:3
and give you two ⌊loaves of⌋ **b**, 1Sm 10:4
took a donkey loaded with **b**, 1Sm 16:20
these loaves of **b** for your 1Sm 17:17
five loaves of **b** or whatever can 1Sm 21:3
There is no ordinary **b** on hand. 1Sm 21:4
is consecrated **b**, but the young 1Sm 21:4
gave him the consecrated ⌊**b**⌋, 1Sm 21:6
for there was no **b** there except 1Sm 21:6
except the **b** of the Presence 1Sm 21:6
When the **b** was removed, it had 1Sm 21:6
had been replaced with warm **b**. 1Sm 21:6
You gave him **b** and a sword and 1Sm 22:13
Am I supposed to take my **b**, 1Sm 25:11
200 loaves of **b**, two skins of 1Sm 25:18
it, and baked unleavened **b**. 1Sm 28:24
gave him some **b** to eat and water 1Sm 30:11
urge David to eat **b** while it was 2Sm 3:35
if I taste **b** or anything else 2Sm 3:35
Then he distributed a loaf of **b**, 2Sm 6:19
loaded with 200 loaves of **b**, 2Sm 16:1
the **b** and summer fruit are for 2Sm 16:2
table that the **b** of the Presence 1Kg 7:48
I wouldn't eat **b** or drink water 1Kg 13:8
must not eat **b** or drink water 1Kg 13:9
"Come home with me and eat **b**." 1Kg 13:15
with you, eat **b**, or drink water 1Kg 13:16
must not eat **b** or drink water 1Kg 13:17
he may eat **b** and drink water. 1Kg 13:18
with him, ate **b** in his house, 1Kg 13:19
back and ate **b** and drank water 1Kg 13:22
Do not eat **b** and do not drink 1Kg 13:22
he had eaten **b** and after he had 1Kg 13:23
Take with you 10 loaves of **b**, 1Kg 14:3
kept bringing him **b** and meat in 1Kg 17:6
me a piece of **b** in your hand." 1Kg 17:11
was a loaf of **b** baked over hot 1Kg 19:6
feed him only **b** and water until 1Kg 22:27
loaves of barley **b** from the 2Kg 4:42
from the first **b** of the harvest. 2Kg 4:42
a land of **b** and vineyards, 2Kg 18:32
ate unleavened **b** with their 2Kg 23:9
was entrusted with baking the **b**. 1Ch 9:31
the rows of the **b** ⌊of the 1Ch 9:32
women, a loaf of **b**, a date cake, 1Ch 16:3
rows ⌊of the **b** of the Presence⌋ 1Ch 23:29
the wafers of unleavened **b**, 1Ch 23:29
rows ⌊of the **b** of the Presence 1Ch 28:16
rows ⌊of the **b** of the Presence 2Ch 2:4
to put⌋ the **b** of the Presence; 2Ch 4:19
the Festival of Unleavened **B**, 2Ch 8:13
the rows of the **b** ⌊of the 2Ch 13:11
feed him only **b** and water until 2Ch 18:26
rows ⌊of the **b** of the Presence 2Ch 29:18
of Unleavened **B** in the second 2Ch 30:13
of Unleavened **B** seven days with 2Ch 30:21
of Unleavened **B** for seven days. 2Ch 35:17
of Unleavened **B** for seven days Ezr 6:22
You provided **b** from heaven for Neh 9:15
the **b** displayed before the LORD, Neh 10:33
that he detests **b**, and his soul Jb 33:20
my people as they consume **b**; Ps 14:4
or his children begging **b**. Ps 37:25
one who ate my **b**, has lifted up Ps 41:9
My people as they consume **b**; Ps 53:4
also provide **b** or furnish meat Ps 78:20
People ate the **b** of angels. Ps 78:25
You fed them the **b** of tears and Ps 80:5
I eat ashes like **b** and mingle my Ps 102:9
and **b** that sustains man's heart. Ps 104:15
them with **b** from heaven. Ps 105:40
I will satisfy its needy with **b**. Ps 132:15
They eat the **b** of wickedness and Pr 4:17
fee is only a loaf of **b**, Pr 6:26
Come, eat my **b**, and drink the Pr 9:5
b ⌊eaten⌋ secretly is tasty!" Pr 9:17
Don't eat a stingy person's **b**, Pr 23:6
a man may sin for a piece of **b**. Pr 28:21
Go, eat your **b** with pleasure, Ec 9:7
to the strong, or **b** to the wise, Ec 9:11
Send your **b** on the surface of Ec 11:1
entire supply of **b** and water, Is 3:1
eat our own **b** and provide our Is 4:1
B grain is crushed, but is not Is 28:28
give you meager **b** and water Is 30:20
a land of **b** and vineyards. Is 36:17
he kindles a fire and bakes **b**; Is 44:15
I also baked **b** on its coals, Is 44:19
to share your **b** with the hungry Is 58:7
was given a loaf of **b** each day Jr 37:21
street until all the **b** was gone Jr 37:21
there is no more **b** in the city." Jr 38:9
groan while they search for **b**. Lm 1:11
Little children beg for **b**, Lm 4:4
make them into **b** for yourself. Ezk 4:9
Israelites will eat their **b**— Ezk 4:13
you can make your **b** over that." Ezk 4:15
the supply of **b** in Jerusalem. Ezk 4:16
will anxiously eat **b** ⌊rationed⌋ Ezk 4:16
So they will lack **b** and water; Ezk 4:17
and cut off your supply of **b**. Ezk 5:16
eat your **b** with trembling and Ezk 12:18
will eat their **b** with anxiety Ezk 12:19
of barley and scraps of **b**; Ezk 13:19
it to cut off its supply of **b**, Ezk 14:13
gives his **b** to the hungry and Ezk 18:7
He gives his **b** to the hungry and Ezk 18:16
or eat the **b** of mourners." Ezk 24:17
or eat the **b** of mourners. Ezk 24:22
unleavened **b** will be eaten. Ezk 45:21
is unturned **b**, baked on a Hs 7:8
will be like the **b** of mourners; Hs 9:4
For their **b** will be for their Hs 9:4
Offer leavened **b** as a thank Am 4:5
a famine of **b** or a thirst for Am 8:11
who eat your **b** will set a trap Ob 7
and with his fold touches **b**, Hg 2:12
tell these stones to become **b**." Mt 4:3
must not live on **b** alone but on Mt 4:4
Give us today our daily **b**. Mt 6:11
if his son asks him for **b**, Mt 7:9
and they ate the sacred **b**, Mt 12:4
the children's **b** and throw it to Mt 15:26
we get enough **b** in this desolate Mt 15:33
they had forgotten to take **b**. Mt 16:5

We didn't bring any **b**." Mt 16:7
that you do not have **b**? Mt 16:8
Sadducees,' it wasn't about **b**?" Mt 16:11
to beware of the yeast in **b**, Mt 16:12
of Unleavened **B** the disciples Mt 26:17
Jesus took **b**, blessed and broke Mt 26:26
priest and ate the sacred **b**— Mk 2:26
no **b**, no traveling bag, no money Mk 6:8
denarii worth of **b** and give them Mk 6:37
full of pieces of **b** and fish. Mk 6:43
eating their **b** with unclean— Mk 7:2
of eating **b** with ritually Mk 7:5
the children's **b** and throw it to Mk 7:27
anyone get enough **b** here in this Mk 8:4
to take **b** and had only one Mk 8:14
that they did not have any **b**. Mk 8:16
that you do not have any **b**? Mk 8:17
of pieces of **b** did you collect? Mk 8:19
of pieces of **b** did you collect? Mk 8:20
the Festival of Unleavened **B**. Mk 14:1
the first day of Unleavened **B**, Mk 14:12
one who is dipping ⌊**b**⌋ with Me Mk 14:20
eating, He took **b**, blessed and Mk 14:22
tell this stone to become **b**." Lk 4:3
Man must not live on **b** alone." Lk 4:4
and took and ate the sacred **b**, Lk 6:4
not come eating **b** or drinking Lk 7:33
traveling bag, no **b**, no money; Lk 9:3
Give us each day our daily **b**. Lk 11:3
lend me three loaves of **b**, Lk 11:5
who will eat **b** in the kingdom Lk 14:15
The Festival of Unleavened **B**, Lk 22:1
Day of Unleavened **B** came when Lk 22:7
He took **b**, gave thanks, broke Lk 22:19
with them that He took the **b**, Lk 24:30
them in the breaking of the **b**. Lk 24:35
will we buy **b** so these people Jn 6:5
denarii worth of **b** wouldn't be Jn 6:7
they ate the **b** after the Lord Jn 6:23
gave them **b** from heaven to eat. Jn 6:31
give you the **b** from heaven, Jn 6:32
you the real **b** from heaven. Jn 6:32
For the **b** of God is the One who Jn 6:33
Sir, give us this **b** always!" Jn 6:34
"I am the **b** of life," Jesus told Jn 6:35
I am the **b** that came down from Jn 6:41
I am the **b** of life. Jn 6:48
This is the **b** that comes down Jn 6:50
I am the living **b** that came down Jn 6:51
eats of this **b** he will live Jn 6:51
The **b** that I will give for the Jn 6:51
is the **b** that came down from Jn 6:58
who eats this **b** will live Jn 6:58
one who eats My **b** has raised his Jn 13:18
the piece of **b** to after I have Jn 13:26
When He had dipped the **b**, Jn 13:26
⌊Judas ate⌋ the piece of **b**, Jn 13:27
After receiving the piece of **b**, Jn 13:30
with fish lying on it, and **b**. Jn 21:9
came, took the **b**, and gave it to Jn 21:13
breaking of **b**, and to prayers Ac 2:42
and broke **b** from house to house. Ac 2:46
during the days of Unleavened **B**. Ac 12:3
after the days of Unleavened **B**. Ac 20:6
week, we assembled to break **b**. Ac 20:7
breaking the **b**, and eating, he Ac 20:11
things and had taken some **b**, Ac 27:35
the unleavened **b** of sincerity 1Co 5:8
The **b** that we break, is it not a 1Co 10:16
there is one **b**, we who are many 1Co 10:17
for all of us share that one **b**. 1Co 10:17
betrayed, the Lord Jesus took **b**, 1Co 11:23
as you eat this **b** and drink the 1Co 11:26
whoever eats the **b** or drinks the 1Co 11:27
should eat of the **b** and drink of 1Co 11:28
the sower and **b** for food will 2Co 9:10
eat anyone's **b** free of charge; 2Th 3:8
they may eat their own **b**. 2Th 3:12

BREAK *(79)*

and came up to **b** down the door. Gn 19:9
you will not **b** an agreement with Gn 21:23
you will **b** his yoke from your Gn 27:40
and you may not **b** any of its Ex 12:46
do not redeem it, **b** its neck. Ex 13:13
Tell the Israelites to **b** camp. Ex 14:15
people not to **b** through to see Ex 19:21
the LORD will **b** out ⌊in anger⌋ Ex 19:22
people must not **b** through to Ex 19:24
or He will **b** out ⌊in anger⌋ Ex 19:24
do not redeem ⌊it⌋, **b** its neck. Ex 34:20
B it into pieces and pour oil on Lv 2:6
become unclean; you must **b** it. Lv 11:33
commands—and **b** My covenant, Lv 26:15
I will **b** down your strong pride. Lv 26:19
them and **b** My covenant with Lv 26:44
morning or **b** any of its bones Nm 9:12
he must not **b** his word; Nm 30:2
and they will **b** the cow's neck Dt 21:4
abandon Me and **b** the covenant I Dt 31:16
you must **b** camp and follow it. Jos 3:3
you **b** the covenant of the LORD Jos 23:16
I will never **b** My covenant with Jdg 2:1
I will **b** them apart there, 1Kg 5:9
Go and **b** your treaty with Baasha 1Kg 15:19
with him to try to **b** through to 2Kg 3:26
Go **b** your treaty with Israel's 2Ch 16:3
and intended to **b** into them. 2Ch 32:1
should we **b** Your commandments Ezr 9:14
would **b** down their stone wall! Neh 4:3
In the dark they **b** into houses; Jb 24:16
You will **b** them with a rod of Ps 2:9
You **b** the teeth of the wicked. Ps 3:7
B the arm of the wicked and evil Ps 10:15
though war **b** out against me, Ps 27:3
a gentle tongue can **b** a bone. Pr 25:15
I will **b** Assyria in My land; Is 14:25
continuously⌋ **b** up and cultivate Is 28:24
He will **b** all my bones like a Is 38:13
He will not **b** a bruised reed, Is 42:3
B out into singing, mountains, Is 44:23
Mountains **b** into joyful shouts! Is 49:13
the hills will **b** into singing Is 55:12
To **b** the chains of wickedness, Is 58:6
B up the unplowed ground; Jr 4:3
wrath will **b** out like fire and Jr 4:4
covenant with us; do not **b** it. Jr 14:21
'for I will **b** the yoke of the Jr 28:4
two years I will **b** the yoke Jr 28:11
I will **b** his yoke from your neck Jr 30:8
you can **b** My covenant with the Jr 33:20
Can he **b** a covenant and ⌊still⌋ Ezk 17:15
when I **b** the yoke of Egypt there Ezk 30:18
I will **b** his arms, both the Ezk 30:22
I will **b** the arms of Pharaoh, Ezk 30:24
the LORD when I **b** the bars of Ezk 34:27
You saw a stone **b** off from the Dn 2:45
that day I will **b** the bow of Hs 1:5
LORD will **b** down their altars Hs 10:2
So lawsuits **b** out like poisonous Hs 10:4
b up your untilled ground. Hs 10:12
I will **b** down the gates of Am 1:5
the ship threatened to **b** apart. Jnh 1:4
they will **b** out, pass through Mc 2:13
from them and **b** their bones. Mc 3:3
For I will now **b** off his yoke Nah 1:13
The age-old mountains **b** apart; Hab 3:6
must not **b** your oath, but you Mt 5:33
where thieves **b** in and steal. Mt 6:19
thieves don't **b** in and steal. Mt 6:20
He will not **b** a bruised reed, Mt 12:20
Your disciples **b** the tradition Mt 15:2
And why do you **b** God's Mt 15:3
they did not **b** His legs since Jn 19:33
week, we assembled to **b** bread. Ac 20:7
the stern began to **b** up with the Ac 27:41
The bread that we **b**, is it not a 1Co 10:16
B forth and shout, you who are Gl 4:27
the scroll and **b** its seals?" Rv 5:2

BREAKERS *(3)*

all Your **b** and Your billows have Ps 42:7
the mighty **b** of the sea— Ps 93:4
Your **b** and Your billows swept Jnh 2:3

BREAKFAST *(2)*

"Come and have **b**," Jesus told Jn 21:12
they had eaten **b**, Jesus asked Jn 21:15

BREAKING *(17)*

thief is caught in the act of **b** Ex 22:2
a skin disease **b** out on his head Lv 13:42
despising Me and **b** My covenant. Dt 31:20
not guilty ⌊of **b** your oath⌋.'" Jdg 21:22
may it not see the **b** of dawn. Jb 3:9
not catch them **b** and entering. Jr 2:34
the oath by **b** the covenant. Ezk 16:59
the oath by **b** the covenant. Ezk 17:18
the waves were **b** over the boat, Mk 4:37
to them in the **b** of the bread. Lk 24:35
not only was He **b** the Sabbath, Jn 5:18
to the **b** of bread, and to Ac 2:42
going upstairs, **b** the bread, and Ac 20:11
doing, weeping and **b** my heart? Ac 21:13
you dishonor God by **b** the law? Rm 2:23
point, is guilty of ⌊**b** it⌋ all. Jms 2:10
sin is the **b** of law. 1Jn 3:4

BREAKS *(15)*

and if war **b** out, they may join Ex 1:10
skin disease **b** out completely Lv 13:12
He **b** through my defenses again Jb 16:14
voice of the LORD **b** the cedars; Ps 29:5
one plows and **b** up the soil, Ps 141:7
a devious tongue **b** the spirit. Pr 15:4
the dispute before it **b** out. Pr 17:14
and the one who **b** through a wall Ec 10:8
Before the day **b** and the shadows Sg 2:17
Before the day **b** and the shadows Sg 4:6
a lamb, one **b** a dog's neck; Is 66:3
fraud; a thief **b** in; a gang Hs 7:1
One who **b** open ⌊the way⌋ will Mc 2:13
whoever **b** one of the least of Mt 5:19
who commits sin also **b** the law; 1Jn 3:4

BREAST *(20)*

Take the **b** from the ram of Ex 29:26
and his sons the **b** of the Ex 29:27
the fat together with the **b**. Lv 7:30
The **b** is to be waved as a Lv 7:30
but the **b** belongs to Aaron and Lv 7:31
the Israelites the **b** of the Lv 7:34
He also took the **b** and waved it Lv 8:29
eat the **b** of the presentation Lv 10:14
and the **b** of the presentation Lv 10:15
in addition to the **b** of the Nm 6:20
them at your **b**, as a nursing Nm 11:12
to you like the **b** of the Nm 18:18
laid him at her **b**, and she put 1Kg 3:20
infant is snatched from the **b**; Jb 24:9
secure while at my mother's **b**. Ps 22:9
or embrace the **b** of a stranger? Pr 5:20
Babies removed from the **b**? Is 28:9
and nurse at the **b** of kings; Is 60:16
comforting **b** and drink deeply Is 66:11
even those nursing at the **b**. Jl 2:16

BREASTPIECE *(23)*

for mounting on the ephod and **b**. Ex 25:7
a **b**, an ephod, a robe, a Ex 28:4
an embroidered **b** for decisions. Ex 28:15
pure gold cord work for the **b**. Ex 28:22
rings for the **b** and attach them Ex 28:23
rings at the corners of the **b**. Ex 28:24
corners of the **b** on the edge Ex 28:26
are to tie the **b** from its rings Ex 28:28
so that the **b** is above the Ex 28:28
heart on the **b** for decisions, Ex 28:29
Thummim in the **b** for decisions, Ex 28:30
the ephod itself, and the **b**; Ex 29:5
to mount on the ephod and **b**. Ex 35:9
to mount on the ephod and **b**, Ex 35:27
the embroidered **b** with the same Ex 39:8
made the **b** square and folded Ex 39:9
of pure gold cord for the **b**. Ex 39:15
rings on the corners of the **b**. Ex 39:17
corners of the **b** on the edge Ex 39:19
they tied the **b** from its rings Ex 39:21
so that the **b** was above the Ex 39:21
Then he put the **b** on him and Lv 8:8
the Urim and Thummim into the **b**. Lv 8:8

BREASTPLATE *(1)*

put on righteousness like a **b**, Is 59:17

BREASTPLATES *(2)*

they had chests like iron **b**; Rv 9:9
horsemen had **b** that were fiery Rv 9:17

BREASTS *(24)*

blessings of the **b** and the womb. Gn 49:25
and placed these on the **b**. Lv 9:20
but he waved the **b** and the right Lv 9:21
were there **b** for me to nurse? Jb 3:12
let her **b** always satisfy you; Pr 5:19
spending the night between my **b**. Sg 1:13
Your **b** are like two fawns, Sg 4:5
Your **b** are like two fawns, Sg 7:3
your **b** are clusters ⌊of fruit⌋. Sg 7:7
May your **b** be like clusters of Sg 7:8
one who nursed at my mother's **b**, Sg 8:1
she has no **b**. What will we do Sg 8:8
am a wall and my **b** like towers. Sg 8:10

Beat your **b** ⌊in mourning⌋ for Is 32:12
yourselves from her glorious **b**. Is 66:11
offer ⌊their⌋ **b** to nurse their Lm 4:3
Your **b** were formed and your hair Ezk 16:7
Their **b** were fondled there, Ezk 23:3
to enjoy your youthful **b**. Ezk 23:21
broken pieces, and tear your **b**. Ezk 23:34
her adultery from between her **b**. Hs 2:2
miscarries and **b** that are dry! Hs 9:14
of doves, and beat their **b**. Nah 2:7
and the **b** that never nursed!' Lk 23:29

BREATH *(65)*
having the **b** of life in it. Gn 1:30
breathed the **b** of life into his Gn 2:7
heaven with the **b** of life in it. Gn 6:17
that has the **b** of life in it Gn 7:15
with the **b** of the spirit Gn 7:22
He took his last **b** and died at a Gn 25:8
He took his last **b** and died, Gn 25:17
With her last **b**—for she was Gn 35:18
He took his last **b** and died, Gn 35:29
blew with Your **b**, and the sea Ex 15:10
blast of the **b** of His nostrils 2Sm 22:16
temple, it took her **b** away. 1Kg 10:5
until no **b** remained in him 1Kg 17:17
temple, it took her **b** away. 2Ch 9:4
an end by the **b** of His nostrils Jb 4:9
that my life is ⌊but⌋ a **b**. Jb 7:7
me alone, for my days are a **b**. Jb 7:16
let me catch my **b** but soaks me Jb 9:18
as well as the **b** of all mankind. Jb 12:10
depart by the **b** of God's mouth. Jb 15:30
My **b** is offensive to my wife, Jb 19:17
b came out of your ⌊mouth⌋? Jb 26:4
His **b** the heavens gained their Jb 26:13
as long as my **b** is still in me Jb 27:3
in me and the **b** from God remains Jb 27:3
in man and the **b** of the Almighty Jb 32:8
and the **b** of the Almighty gives Jb 33:4
the spirit and **b** He ⌊gave⌋, Jb 34:14
Ice is formed by the **b** of God, Jb 37:10
His **b** sets coals ablaze, and Jb 41:21
blast of the **b** of Your nostrils Ps 18:15
stars, by the **b** of His mouth. Ps 33:6
when You take away their **b**, Ps 104:29
You send Your **b**, they are Ps 104:30
there is no **b** in their mouths. Ps 135:17
Man is like a **b**; his days are Ps 144:4
his **b** leaves him, he returns Ps 146:4
A person's **b** is the lamp of the Pr 20:27
they all have the same **b**. Ec 3:19
of your **b** like apricots. Sg 7:8
has only the **b** in his nostrils Is 2:22
the **b** of the violent is like Is 25:4
His **b** is like an overflowing Is 30:28
b of the LORD, like a torrent Is 30:33
Your **b** is fire that will consume Is 33:11
when the **b** of the LORD blows Is 40:7
who gives **b** to the people on it Is 42:5
of them off, a **b** will take them Is 57:13
Me, even the **b** ⌊of man⌋, which I Is 57:16
of Daughter Zion gasping for **b**, Jr 4:31
there is no **b** in them. Jr 10:14
she breathed her ⌊last⌋ **b**. Jr 15:9
there is no **b** in them. Jr 51:17
anointed, the **b** of our life, was Lm 4:20
I will cause **b** to enter you, Ezk 37:5
I will put **b** in you so that you Ezk 37:6
but there was no **b** in them. Ezk 37:8
Prophesy to the **b**, prophesy, son Ezk 37:9
B, come from the four winds and Ezk 37:9
b entered them, and they came Ezk 37:10
and there is no **b** in me." Dn 10:17
yet there is no **b** in it at all. Hab 2:19
life and **b** and all things. Ac 17:25
him with the **b** of His mouth 2Th 2:8
the **b** of life from God entered Rv 11:11

BREATHE *(1)*
winds and **b** into these slain Ezk 37:9

BREATHED *(6)*
the ground and **b** the breath of Gn 2:7
she **b** her ⌊last⌋ breath. Jr 15:9
out a loud cry and **b** His last. Mk 15:37
saw the way He **b** His last, Mk 15:39
Saying this, He **b** His last. Lk 23:46
saying this, He **b** on them and Jn 20:22

BREATHES *(2)*
he **b** his last—where is he? Jb 14:10
that **b** praise the LORD Ps 150:6

BREATHING *(2)*
rise up against me, **b** violence. Ps 27:12
still **b** threats and murder Ac 9:1

BREATHLESSLY *(1)*
a woman in labor, gasping **b**. Is 42:14

BRED *(4)*
And the sheep **b** when they came Gn 30:38
The flocks **b** in front of the Gn 30:39
and it **b** worms and smelled. Ex 16:20
fast horses **b** from the royal Est 8:10

BREED *(3)*
and they would **b** in front of the Gn 30:41
Their bulls **b** without fail; Jb 21:10
knowing that they **b** quarrels. 2Tm 2:23

BREEDER *(1)*
Mesha of Moab was a sheep **b**. 2Kg 3:4

BREEDERS *(1)*
one of the sheep **b** from Tekoa— Am 1:1

BREEDING *(15)*
stronger of the flock were **b**, Gn 30:41
the flocks were **b**, I saw in a Gn 31:10
rams, five male **b** goats, and Nm 7:17
rams, five male **b** goats, and Nm 7:23
rams, five male **b** goats, and Nm 7:29
rams, five male **b** goats, and Nm 7:35
rams, five male **b** goats, and Nm 7:41
rams, five male **b** goats, and Nm 7:47
rams, five male **b** goats, and Nm 7:53
rams, five male **b** goats, and Nm 7:59
rams, five male **b** goats, and Nm 7:65
rams, five male **b** goats, and Nm 7:71
rams, five male **b** goats, and Nm 7:77
rams, five male **b** goats, and Nm 7:83
60 rams, 60 male **b** goats, and 60 Nm 7:88

BREEZE *(1)*
at the time of the evening **b**, Gn 3:8

BRIBE *(18)*
must not take a **b**, for a bribe Ex 23:8
for a **b** blinds the clear-sighted Ex 23:8
no partiality and taking no **b**. Dt 10:17
Do not accept a **b**, for it blinds Dt 16:19
one who accepts a **b** to kill an Dt 27:25
have I taken a **b** to overlook 1Sm 12:3
or Pay a **b** for me from your Jb 6:22
interest or take a **b** against the Ps 15:5
A **b** seems like a magic stone to Pr 17:8
secretly takes a **b** to subvert Pr 17:23
and a covert **b**, fierce rage. Pr 21:14
and a **b** destroys the mind. Ec 7:7
the guilty for a **b** and deprive Is 5:23
whose hand never takes a **b**, Is 33:15
a price or a **b**," says the LORD Is 45:13
righteous, take a **b**, and deprive Am 5:12
leaders issue rulings for a **b**, Mc 3:11
and the judge demand a **b**; Mc 7:3

BRIBED *(2)*
They also **b** officials ⌊to act⌋ Ezr 4:5
You **b** them to come to you from Ezk 16:33

BRIBES *(8)*
trustworthy, and hating **b**. Ex 18:21
gain, took **b**, and perverted 1Sm 8:3
or taking **b** with the LORD our 2Ch 19:7
the tents of those who offer **b**. Jb 15:34
right hands are filled with **b**. Ps 26:10
the one who hates **b** will live. Pr 15:27
love graft and chase after **b**. Is 1:23
in you accept **b** in order to shed Ezk 22:12

BRICK *(4)*
They had **b** for stone and Gn 11:3
difficult labor in **b** and mortar, Ex 1:14
mortar of the **b** pavement that is Jr 43:9
man, take a **b**, set it in front Ezk 4:1

BRICK-MOLD *(1)*
take hold of the **b**! Nah 3:14

BRICKMAKING *(1)*
iron axes, and to labor at **b**. 2Sm 12:31

BRICKS *(9)*
let us make oven-fired **b**." Gn 11:3
people with straw for making **b**, Ex 5:7
same quota of **b** from them as Ex 5:8
number of **b** yesterday or today, Ex 5:14
yet they say to us, 'Make **b**!' Ex 5:16
produce the same quantity of **b**." Ex 5:18
reduce your daily quota of **b**." Ex 5:19
The **b** have fallen, but we will Is 9:10
gardens, burning incense on **b**, Is 65:3

BRIDAL *(3)*
pay the **b** price for her to Ex 22:16
equal to the **b** price for virgins Ex 22:17
groom coming from the **b** chamber; Ps 19:5

BRIDE *(22)*
a man takes a **b**, he must not go Dt 24:5
me from Lebanon, my **b**—with me Sg 4:8
my heart, my sister, my **b**. Sg 4:9
your love is, my sister, my **b**. Sg 4:10
like⌋ the honeycomb, my **b**. Sg 4:11
My sister, my **b**, ⌊you are⌋ a Sg 4:12
to my garden—my sister, my **b**. Sg 5:1
and put them on as a **b** does. Is 49:18
turban and as a **b** adorns herself Is 61:10
rejoices over ⌊his⌋ **b**, Is 62:5
your love as a **b**—how you Jr 2:2
jewelry or a **b** her wedding sash Jr 2:32
of the bridegroom and the **b**, Jr 7:34
of the bridegroom and the **b**. Jr 16:9
of the bridegroom and the **b**, Jr 25:10
of the bridegroom and the **b**, Jr 33:11
and the **b** her honeymoon chamber. Jl 2:16
He who has the **b** is the groom. Jn 3:29
of a groom and **b** will never be Rv 18:23
prepared like a **b** adorned for Rv 21:2
I will show you the **b**, the wife Rv 21:9
Both the Spirit and the **b** say, Rv 22:17

BRIDE-PRICE *(1)*
desires no other **b** except 100 1Sm 18:25

BRIDEGROOM *(9)*
"You are a **b** of blood to me!" Ex 4:25
said, "You are a **b** of blood," Ex 4:26
as a **b** wears a turban and as a Is 61:10
and as a **b** rejoices over ⌊his⌋ Is 62:5
voices of the **b** and the bride, Jr 7:34
voice of the **b** and the bride. Jr 16:9
voice of the **b** and the bride, Jr 25:10
voice of the **b** and the bride, Jr 33:11
Let the **b** leave his bedroom, Jl 2:16

BRIDES *(1)*
daughters ⌊as **b**⌋ for your sons. Ex 34:16

BRIDLE *(3)*
be controlled with bit and **b**, Ps 32:9
the horse, a **b** for the donkey, Pr 26:3
and to put a **b** on the jaws Is 30:28

BRIDLES *(1)*
to the horses' **b** for about 180 Rv 14:20

BRIEF *(5)*
But now, for a **b** moment, grace Ezr 9:8
wicked has been **b** and the Jb 20:5
I deserted you for a **b** moment, Is 54:7
to give us a **b** hearing. Ac 24:4
from you⌋ for a **b** time, Phm 15

BRIEFLY *(2)*
as I have **b** written above. Eph 3:3
have written **b**, encouraging you 1Pt 5:12

BRIER *(2)*
instead of the **b**, a myrtle will Is 55:13
The best of them is like a **b**; Mc 7:4

BRIERS *(12)*
on thorns and **b** from the Jdg 8:7
as some thorns and **b** from the Jdg 8:16
thorns and **b** will grow up. Is 5:6
will become thorns and **b**. Is 7:23
whole land will be thorns and **b**. Is 7:24
for fear of the thorns and **b**. Is 7:25
consumes thorns and **b** and Is 9:18
it produces thorns and **b** for Me, Is 27:4
my people growing thorns and **b**, Is 32:13
cities, with thistles and **b**. Is 34:13
though **b** and thorns are beside Ezk 2:6
by prickling **b** or painful thorns Ezk 28:24

BRIGHT *(12)*
B eyes cheer the heart; Pr 15:30
as the moon, **b** as the sun, Sg 6:10
will be as **b** as the sunlight, Is 30:26
shines like a **b** light, Is 62:1
it was **b**, with lightning coming Ezk 1:13
up was something that looked **b**, Ezk 8:2
will shine like the **b** expanse Dn 12:3

suddenly a **b** cloud covered them, Mt 17:5
in clean, **b** linen, with gold Rv 15:6
to wear fine linen, **b** and pure. Rv 19:8
a jasper stone, **b** as crystal. Rv 21:11
of David, the **B** Morning Star." Rv 22:16

BRIGHTENS *(1)*
A man's wisdom **b** his face, Ec 8:1

BRIGHTER *(6)*
life will be **b** than noonday; Jb 11:17
shining **b** and brighter until Pr 4:18
brighter and **b** until midday. Pr 4:18
sunlight will be seven times **b**— Is 30:26
dignitaries were **b** than snow, Lm 4:7
from heaven **b** than the sun, Ac 26:13

BRIGHTLY *(1)*
light of the righteous shines **b**, Pr 13:9

BRIGHTNESS *(9)*
Restore **b** to my eyes; Ps 13:3
for **b**, but we live in the night. Is 59:9
kings to the **b** of your radiance Is 60:3
and the **b** of the moon will not Is 60:19
filled with the **b** of the LORD's Ezk 10:4
even gloom without any **b** in it? Am 5:20
at the **b** of Your shining spear. Hab 3:11
because of the **b** of that light, Ac 22:11
with the **b** of His coming. 2Th 2:8

BRILLIANCE *(3)*
face like the **b** of lightning, Dn 10:6
⌊His⌋ **b** is like light; Hab 3:4
did not come with **b** of speech or 1Co 2:1

BRILLIANT *(4)*
and forth and **b** light all around Ezk 1:4
There was a **b** light all around Ezk 1:27
of the **b** light all around Ezk 1:28
dressed Him in a **b** robe, and Lk 23:11

BRIM *(8)*
feet from **b** to brim, perfectly 1Kg 7:23
from brim to **b**, perfectly round 1Kg 7:23
gourds encircled it below the **b**, 1Kg 7:24
fashioned like the **b** of a cup or 1Kg 7:26
feet from **b** to brim, perfectly 2Ch 4:2
from brim to **b**, perfectly round 2Ch 4:2
like the **b** of a cup or a lily 2Ch 4:5
So they filled them to the **b**. Jn 2:7

BRIMSTONE *(2)*
like a torrent of **b**, kindles it. Is 30:33
fire, and **b** on him, as well as Ezk 38:22

BRING *(625)*
This one will **b** us relief from Gn 5:29
You are also to **b** into the ark Gn 6:19
B out every living thing of all Gn 8:17
B me a three-year-old cow, Gn 15:9
I will **b** a bit of bread so that Gn 18:5
I'll **b** them out to you, and you Gn 19:8
I love and **b** it to me to eat Gn 27:4
the field to hunt some game to **b** Gn 27:5
'**B** me some game and make some Gn 27:7
to the flock and **b** me two choice Gn 27:9
and I will **b** a curse rather than Gn 27:12
send for you and **b** you back from Gn 27:45
I will **b** you back to this land, Gn 28:15
I did not **b** you any of the flock Gn 31:39
him and could not **b** themselves Gn 37:4
doing, and **b** word back to me. Gn 37:14
is pregnant." "**B** her out!" Judah Gn 38:24
B your youngest brother to me so Gn 42:20
B back your youngest brother to Gn 42:34
if I don't **b** him back to you Gn 42:37
you will **b** my gray hairs down to Gn 42:38
would say, '**B** your brother here' Gn 43:7
I do not **b** him back to you and Gn 43:9
'**B** him to me so that I can see Gn 44:21
you will **b** my gray hairs down to Gn 44:29
And **b** my father here quickly." Gn 45:13
your wives, and **b** your father Gn 45:19
and I will also **b** you back. Gn 46:4
B them to me and I will bless Gn 48:9
with you and will **b** you back to Gn 48:21
it for good to **b** about the Gn 50:20
to your aid and **b** you up from Gn 50:24
Egyptians and to **b** them from Ex 3:8
that I should **b** the Israelites Ex 3:11
when you **b** the people out of Ex 3:12
that I will **b** you up from the Ex 3:17
I will **b** you to the land that I Ex 6:8
of Egypt to **b** the Israelites Ex 6:13
B the Israelites out of the land Ex 6:26
in order to **b** the Israelites Ex 6:27
on Egypt and **b** out the ranks Ex 7:4
and **b** out the Israelites from Ex 7:5
hand will **b** a severe plague Ex 9:3
give orders to **b** your livestock Ex 9:19
tomorrow I will **b** locusts into Ex 10:4
I will **b** one more plague on Ex 11:1
because He would **b** them out of Ex 12:42
will **b** them in and plant them Ex 15:17
they prepare what they **b** in, Ex 16:5
did you ever **b** us out of Egypt Ex 17:3
before God and **b** their cases to Ex 18:19
Then they can **b** you every Ex 18:22
cases they would **b** to Moses, Ex 18:26
his master is to **b** him to the Ex 21:6
judges and then **b** him to the Ex 21:6
he is to **b** it as evidence; Ex 22:13
B the best of the firstfruits of Ex 23:19
the way and **b** you to the place Ex 23:20
before you and **b** you to ⌊the Ex 23:23
under the clasps and **b** the ark Ex 26:33
the Israelites to **b** you pure oil Ex 27:20
in a basket, and **b** them in the Ex 29:3
B Aaron and his sons to the Ex 29:4
You must also **b** his sons, clothe Ex 29:8
You are to **b** the bull to the Ex 29:10
daughters and **b** ⌊them⌋ to me." Ex 32:2
said He would **b** on His people. Ex 32:14
B the best firstfruits of your Ex 34:26
heart is willing **b** this as the Ex 35:5
them to **b** ⌊something⌋ for Ex 35:29
continued to **b** freewill Ex 36:3
Then **b** in the table and lay out Ex 40:4
also **b** in the lampstand and set Ex 40:4
Then **b** Aaron and his sons to the Ex 40:12
you may **b** your offering from the Lv 1:2
he is to **b** an unblemished male. Lv 1:3
He must **b** it to the entrance to Lv 1:3
priest must **b** it to the altar Lv 1:15
and **b** it to Aaron's sons the Lv 2:2
When you **b** to the LORD the grain Lv 2:8
He must **b** the bull to the Lv 4:4
blood and **b** it into the tent Lv 4:5
must **b** to a ceremonially clean Lv 4:12
they are to **b** it before the tent Lv 4:14
priest will **b** some of the bull's Lv 4:16
Then he will **b** the bull outside Lv 4:21
he is to **b** an unblemished male Lv 4:23
then he is to **b** an unblemished Lv 4:28
is to **b** an unblemished female. Lv 4:32
must **b** his restitution for the Lv 5:6
then he may **b** to the LORD two Lv 5:7
He is to **b** them to the priest, Lv 5:8
may **b** two quarts of fine flour Lv 5:11
He is to **b** it to the priest, Lv 5:12
he must **b** his restitution Lv 5:15
must **b** an unblemished ram from Lv 5:18
Then he must **b** his restitution Lv 6:6
and **b** the ashes outside the camp Lv 6:11
you are to **b** it well-kneaded. Lv 6:21
the LORD must **b** an offering to Lv 7:29
own hands will **b** the fire Lv 7:30
He will **b** the fat together with Lv 7:30
They are to **b** the thigh of the Lv 10:15
she is to **b** to the priest at the Lv 12:6
day he is to **b** these things for Lv 14:23
young pigeons and **b** them to the Lv 15:29
and **b** ⌊them⌋ inside the veil. Lv 16:12
Israelites will **b** to the LORD Lv 17:5
They are to **b** them to the priest Lv 17:5
does not **b** it to the entrance Lv 17:9
he must **b** his ram as a Lv 19:21
you are to **b** the first sheaf of Lv 23:10
B two loaves of bread from your Lv 23:17
the Israelites to **b** you pure oil Lv 24:2
B the one who has cursed to the Lv 24:14
I will **b** terror on you—wasting Lv 26:16
I will **b** a sword against you to Lv 26:25
B the tribe of Levi near and Nm 3:6
then the man is to **b** his wife to Nm 5:15
He is also to **b** an offering for Nm 5:15
The priest is to **b** her forward Nm 5:16
the LORD, and **b** it to the altar. Nm 5:25
day he is to **b** two turtledoves Nm 6:10
LORD and to **b** a year-old male Nm 6:12
B the Levites before the tent of Nm 8:9
B Me 70 men from Israel known Nm 11:16
B back some fruit from the land." Nm 13:20
He will **b** us into this land, Nm 14:8
wasn't able to **b** this people Nm 14:16
I will **b** him into the land where Nm 14:24
I will **b** your children whom you Nm 14:31
They are to **b** their offering, Nm 15:25
community to **b** you near to Nm 16:9
didn't **b** us to a land flowing Nm 16:14
also **b** your brothers with you Nm 18:2
land, which they **b** to the LORD, Nm 18:13
the Israelites to **b** you an Nm 19:2
from Egypt to **b** us to this evil Nm 20:5
You will **b** out water for them Nm 20:8
Must we **b** water out of this rock Nm 20:10
will not **b** this assembly into Nm 20:12
son Eleazar and **b** them up Mount Nm 20:25
who will **b** them out and bring Nm 27:17
will bring them out and **b** them Nm 27:17
B me any case too difficult for Dt 1:17
land for us and **b** us back a Dt 1:22
you and to **b** you in and give Dt 4:38
You must not **b** any abhorrent Dt 7:26
wasn't able to **b** them into the Dt 9:28
You are to **b** there your burnt Dt 12:6
B there everything I command you: Dt 12:11
b a tenth of all your produce Dt 14:28
must **b** out to your gates that Dt 17:5
that city will **b** the cow down to Dt 21:4
are to **b** her into your house. Dt 21:12
hold of him and **b** him to the Dt 21:19
you are to **b** the animal to your Dt 22:2
that you don't **b** bloodguilt on Dt 22:8
virginity and **b** ⌊it⌋ to the city Dt 22:15
will **b** the woman to the door Dt 22:21
Do not **b** a female prostitute's Dt 23:18
You must not **b** guilt on the land Dt 24:4
so that he can **b** joy to the wife Dt 24:5
The LORD will **b** you and your Dt 28:36
LORD will **b** a nation from far Dt 28:49
He will **b** extraordinary plagues Dt 28:59
gather you and **b** you back from Dt 30:4
your God will **b** you into the Dt 30:5
When I **b** them into the land I Dt 31:20
even before I **b** them into the Dt 31:21
for you will **b** the Israelites Dt 31:23
I **b** death and I give life; Dt 32:39
Judah's cry and **b** him to his Dt 33:7
B out the men who came to you Jos 2:3
B your father, mother, brothers, Jos 2:18
and **b** disaster on it. Jos 6:18
house and **b** the woman out of Jos 6:22
why did You ever **b** these people Jos 7:7
and **b** those five kings to me out Jos 10:22
they are to **b** him into the city Jos 20:4
so He will **b** on you every bad Jos 23:15
Let me **b** my gift and set it Jdg 6:18
said to Joash, "**B** out your son. Jdg 6:30
"**B** Samson here to entertain us." Jdg 16:25
kindly to her and **b** her back. Jdg 19:3
B out the man who came to your Jdg 19:22
let me **b** out my virgin daughter Jdg 19:24
B the shawl you're wearing and Ru 3:15
My altar will **b** grief and 1Sm 2:33
Let's **b** the ark of the LORD's 1Sm 4:3
men⌋ to Shiloh to **b** back the ark 1Sm 4:4
him and did not **b** him a gift, 1Sm 10:27
B charges against me before the 1Sm 12:3
B me the burnt offering and the 1Sm 13:9
told Ahijah, "**B** the ark of God," 1Sm 14:18
'Each man must **b** me his ox or 1Sm 14:34
"**B** me Agag king of Amalek." 1Sm 15:32
who plays well and **b** him to me." 1Sm 16:17
brothers and **b** a confirmation 1Sm 17:18
B him on his bed so I can kill 1Sm 19:15
father intends to **b** evil on you, 1Sm 20:13
send for him and **b** him to me— 1Sm 20:31
I didn't even **b** my sword or my 1Sm 21:8
Why did you **b** him to me? 1Sm 21:14
the priest, "**B** the ephod." 1Sm 23:9
David sent us to **b** you to him as 1Sm 25:40
B up for me the one I tell you." 1Sm 28:8
you want me to **b** up for you?" 1Sm 28:11
"**B** up Samuel for me," he 1Sm 28:11
of Ahimelech, "**B** me the ephod." 1Sm 30:7
me unless you **b** Saul's daughter 2Sm 3:13
set out to **b** the ark of God 2Sm 6:2
and you are to **b** in ⌊the crops⌋ 2Sm 9:10
messengers⌋ to **b** the Arameans 2Sm 10:16

man could not **b** himself to take 2Sm 12:4
'I am going to **b** disaster on you 2Sm 12:11
Can I **b** him back again? 2Sm 12:23
"**B** the meal to the bedroom," 2Sm 13:10
to Tekoa to **b** a clever woman 2Sm 14:2
the king said, "**b** him to me. 2Sm 14:10
of my lord the king **b** relief, 2Sm 14:17
b back the young man Absalom." 2Sm 14:21
a grievance to **b** before the king 2Sm 15:2
will **b** me back and allow me to 2Sm 15:25
b all the people back to you. 2Sm 17:3
all Israel will **b** ropes to that 2Sm 17:13
in order to **b** about Absalom's 2Sm 17:14
the Jordan to **b** the king's 2Sm 19:18
so that you will **b** a blessing 2Sm 21:3
Will He not **b** about my whole 2Sm 23:5
someone would **b** me water to 2Sm 23:15
deal with him to **b** his gray head 1Kg 2:9
The LORD will **b** back his own 1Kg 2:32
king continued, "**B** me a sword." 1Kg 3:24
servants will **b** ⌊the logs⌋ down 1Kg 5:9
in order to **b** the ark of the 1Kg 8:1
Every man would **b** his annual 1Kg 10:25
'**B** him back with you to your 1Kg 13:18
I am about to **b** disaster on the 1Kg 14:10
Please **b** me a little water in a 1Kg 17:10
Please **b** me a piece of bread in 1Kg 17:11
loaf from it and **b** it out to me. 1Kg 17:13
Then he said, "Go and **b** him." 1Kg 20:33
'I am about to **b** disaster on you 1Kg 21:21
I will not **b** the disaster during 1Kg 21:29
I will **b** the disaster on his 1Kg 21:29
B me a new bowl and put salt in 2Kg 2:20
Now, **b** me a musician." 2Kg 3:15
said to her son, "**B** me another 2Kg 4:6
b me the heads of your master's 2Kg 10:6
B out the garments for all the 2Kg 10:22
"**B** a lump of pressed figs." 2Kg 20:7
'I am about to **b** such disaster 2Kg 21:12
I am about to **b** disaster on this 2Kg 22:16
doorkeepers to **b** out of the 2Kg 23:4
only someone would **b** me water 1Ch 11:17
Then let us **b** back the ark of 1Ch 13:3
to **b** the ark of God from 1Ch 13:5
How can I ever **b** the ark of God 1Ch 13:12
at Jerusalem to **b** the ark of the 1Ch 15:3
so that you may **b** the ark of the 1Ch 15:12
themselves to **b** up the ark of 1Ch 15:14
went with rejoicing to **b** the ark 1Ch 15:25
b an offering and come before 1Ch 16:29
messengers to **b** out the Arameans 1Ch 19:16
to Dan and **b** ⌊a report⌋ to me so 1Ch 21:2
should he **b** guilt on Israel?" 1Ch 21:3
so that you may **b** the ark of the 1Ch 22:19
b them to you as rafts by sea 2Ch 2:16
in order to **b** the ark of the 2Ch 5:2
of them would **b** his own gift— 2Ch 9:24
the Levites to **b** from Judah 2Ch 24:6
them prophets to **b** them back to 2Ch 24:19
You must not **b** the captives 2Ch 28:13
for you plan to **b** guilt on us 2Ch 28:13
Come near and **b** sacrifices and 2Ch 29:31
I am about to **b** disaster on this 2Ch 34:24
so they could **b** cedar wood from Ezr 3:7
⌊You are⌋ also to **b** the silver Ezr 7:15
they should **b** us ministers for Ezr 8:17
to **b** ⌊them⌋ to the house of our Ezr 8:30
from there and **b** them to the Neh 1:9
Can they **b** these burnt stones Neh 4:2
Ezra the scribe to **b** the book of Neh 8:1
hill country and **b** back branches Neh 8:15
peoples **b** merchandise or any Neh 10:31
They are to **b** ⌊the wood⌋ to our Neh 10:34
⌊We will⌋ **b** the firstfruits of Neh 10:35
⌊We will also **b**⌋ the firstborn Neh 10:36
and will **b** the firstborn of our Neh 10:36
will **b** ⌊a loaf⌋ from our first Neh 10:37
will also **b** the firstfruits of Neh 10:37
Levites are to **b** the Neh 10:39
b Queen Vashti before him with Est 1:11
Have them **b** a royal garment that Est 6:8
It would still **b** me comfort, Jb 6:10
did You **b** me out of the womb? Jb 10:18
Will You **b** me into judgment Jb 14:3
from my lips would **b** relief. Jb 16:5
that he may **b** to light what is Jb 28:11
deeds, and He **b** his ways on him Jb 34:11
b rain on an uninhabited land, Jb 38:26

Can you **b** out the constellations Jb 38:32
your grain and **b** ⌊it⌋ to your Jb 39:12
Confront him; **b** him down. With Ps 17:13
b me out of my sufferings. Ps 25:17
agitated—it can only **b** harm. Ps 37:8
strung the bow to **b** down the Ps 37:14
Let them **b** me to Your holy Ps 43:3
arm did not **b** them victory— Ps 44:3
my sword does not **b** me victory. Ps 44:6
ivory palaces harps **b** you joy. Ps 45:8
is why God will **b** you down Ps 52:5
For they **b** down disaster on me Ps 55:3
will **b** them down to the pit of Ps 55:23
b down the nations in wrath. Ps 56:7
wanderers and **b** them down, Ps 59:11
Who will **b** me to the fortified Ps 60:9
only plan to **b** him down from his Ps 62:4
You choose and **b** near to live Ps 65:4
I will **b** ⌊them⌋ back from Ps 68:22
I will **b** ⌊them⌋ back from the Ps 68:22
kings will **b** tribute to You. Ps 68:29
will **b** me up again, even from Ps 71:20
May the mountains **b** prosperity Ps 72:3
coasts and islands **b** tribute, Ps 72:10
that fools **b** against You all Ps 74:22
who are around Him **b** tribute to Ps 76:11
B joy to Your servant's life, Ps 86:4
b an offering and enter His Ps 96:8
You **b** darkness, and it becomes Ps 104:20
Who will **b** me to the fortified Ps 108:10
Do not **b** Your servant into Ps 143:2
for they will **b** you many days, Pr 3:2
a mocker will **b** dishonor on Pr 9:7
but diligent hands **b** riches. Pr 10:4
he doesn't even **b** it back to his Pr 19:24
warriors and **b** down its mighty Pr 21:22
what disaster these two can **b**? Pr 24:22
too weary to **b** it to his mouth Pr 26:15
don't know what a day might **b**. Pr 27:1
Oil and incense **b** joy to the Pr 27:9
my son, and **b** my heart joy, so Pr 27:11
let your mouth **b** guilt on you, Ec 5:6
For many dreams **b** futility, Ec 5:7
God will **b** you to judgment Ec 11:9
For God will **b** every act to Ec 12:14
the king would **b** me to his Sg 1:4
was to **b** for his fruit 1,000 Sg 8:11
The LORD will **b** on you, your Is 7:17
will certainly **b** against them Is 8:7
future He will **b** honor to the Is 9:1
I will **b** disaster on the world, Is 13:11
escort Israel and **b** it to its Is 14:2
but I will **b** on Dibon even more Is 15:9
B water for the thirsty. Is 21:14
the earth will **b** forth the Is 26:19
will **b** judgment on Leviathan, Is 27:1
will **b** it across the land with Is 28:2
will **b** justice to the nations. Is 42:1
He will faithfully **b** justice. Is 42:3
to **b** out prisoners from the Is 42:7
I will **b** your descendants from Is 43:5
B My sons from far away, and My Is 43:6
B out a people who are blind, Is 43:8
to Babylon and **b** all of them as Is 43:14
so I will also **b** it about. Is 46:11
to **b** Jacob back to Him so that Is 49:5
They will **b** your sons in their Is 49:22
I will **b** it about quickly. Is 51:4
My arms will **b** justice to the Is 51:5
will **b** them to My holy mountain Is 56:7
to **b** the poor and homeless into Is 58:7
b your children from far away, Is 60:9
I will **b** gold instead of bronze; Is 60:17
I will **b** silver instead of iron, Is 60:17
has anointed Me to **b** good news Is 61:1
and I will **b** on them what they Is 66:4
Will I **b** a baby to the point of Is 66:9
They will **b** all your brothers Is 66:20
as the Israelites **b** an offering Is 66:20
I will **b** a case against you Jr 2:9
I will **b** a case against your Jr 2:9
Why do you **b** a case against Me? Jr 2:29
and I will **b** you to Zion. Jr 3:14
am about to **b** a nation from far Jr 5:15
am about to **b** disaster on these Jr 6:19
them and **b** them to an end. Jr 8:13
I am about to **b** on them disaster Jr 11:11
for I will **b** disaster on the Jr 11:23

even if I **b** a case against You. Jr 12:1
b them to devour ⌊her⌋. Jr 12:9
idols of the nations **b** rain? Jr 14:22
B on them the day of disaster; Jr 17:18
up a load and **b** it in through Jr 17:21
and do not **b** loads through the Jr 17:24
will not **b** the disaster on it I Jr 18:8
I will not **b** the good I had said Jr 18:10
I am about to **b** harm to you and Jr 18:11
You suddenly **b** raiders against Jr 18:22
I am going to **b** such disaster on Jr 19:3
'I am about to **b** on this city— Jr 19:15
I will **b** them into the center Jr 21:4
this city to ⌊**b**⌋ disaster and Jr 21:10
for I will **b** disaster on them, Jr 23:12
will **b** on you everlasting shame Jr 23:40
of your hands and **b** disaster on Jr 25:7
and I will **b** them against this Jr 25:9
I will **b** on that land all My Jr 25:13
you will **b** innocent blood on Jr 26:15
We are about to **b** great harm on Jr 26:19
'Then I will **b** them up and Jr 27:22
that I will **b** to My people"— Jr 29:32
I will **b** destruction on all the Jr 30:11
I will not destruction on you. Jr 30:11
But I will **b** you health and will Jr 30:17
I am going to **b** them from the Jr 31:8
but I will **b** them back with Jr 31:9
and ⌊**b**⌋ happiness out of grief. Jr 31:13
them by the hand to **b** them out Jr 31:32
so am I about to **b** on them all Jr 32:42
I will certainly **b** health and Jr 33:6
peace I will **b** about for them. Jr 33:9
as they **b** thank offerings Jr 33:11
and I will **b** them back to this Jr 34:22
b them to one of the chambers Jr 35:2
will certainly **b** to Judah and to Jr 35:17
I am planning to **b** on them, Jr 36:3
B the scroll that you read in Jr 36:14
I will **b** on them, on the Jr 36:31
offerings to **b** to the temple Jr 41:5
you sent me to **b** your petition Jr 42:9
the disaster I will **b** on them.' Jr 42:17
against you to ⌊**b**⌋ disaster, Jr 44:11
I am about to **b** disaster on Jr 45:5
I will **b** destruction on all the Jr 46:28
but I will not **b** destruction on Jr 46:28
for I will **b** against Moab the Jr 48:44
I am about to **b** terror on you— Jr 49:5
for I will **b** Esau's calamity on Jr 49:8
from there I will **b** you down. Jr 49:16
I will **b** calamity on them across Jr 49:32
I will **b** the four winds against Jr 49:36
I will **b** disaster on them, Jr 49:37
stir up and **b** against Babylon Jr 50:9
so that He might **b** rest to the Jr 50:34
with you I will **b** kingdoms to Jr 51:20
b up horses like a swarm of Jr 51:27
I will **b** them down like lambs to Jr 51:40
B on the day You have announced, Lm 1:21
My eyes **b** me grief because of Lm 3:51
I will **b** a sword against you. Ezk 5:17
I am about to **b** a sword against Ezk 6:3
not threaten to **b** this disaster Ezk 6:10
So I will **b** the most evil of Ezk 7:24
I will **b** their actions down on Ezk 9:10
I will **b** the sword against you. Ezk 11:8
I will **b** you out of the city and Ezk 11:9
Will You **b** to an end the remnant Ezk 11:13
I will **b** their actions down on Ezk 11:21
b out your bags like an exile's Ezk 12:4
the wall to **b** ⌊him⌋ out through Ezk 12:12
will **b** him to Babylon, the land Ezk 12:13
a message and **b** it to pass." Ezk 12:25
Or if I **b** a sword against that Ezk 14:17
They will **b** you consolation when Ezk 14:23
Then I will **b** about your Ezk 16:38
They will **b** a mob against you to Ezk 16:40
I will also **b** your actions down Ezk 16:43
will **b** down on his head My oath Ezk 17:19
I will **b** him to Babylon and Ezk 17:20
I **b** down the tall tree, and make Ezk 17:24
them that I would **b** them out of Ezk 20:6
that I would not **b** them into the Ezk 20:15
and did not **b** them to an end Ezk 20:17
that did not **b** them life. Ezk 20:25
will **b** you from the peoples and Ezk 20:34
the rod and will **b** you into the Ezk 20:37

I will **b** them out of the land Ezk 20:38
When I **b** you from the peoples Ezk 20:41
lowly and **b** down the exalted. Ezk 21:26
I will **b** them against you from Ezk 23:22
B it to a boil and cook the Ezk 24:5
I am about to **b** King Ezk 26:7
then I will **b** you down ⌊to be⌋ Ezk 26:20
am about to **b** strangers against Ezk 28:7
They will **b** you down to the Pit, Ezk 28:8
I am going to **b** a sword against Ezk 29:8
of Egypt and **b** them back to the Ezk 29:14
I will **b** desolation on the land Ezk 30:12
will **b** darkness on your land. Ezk 32:8
when I **b** about your destruction Ezk 32:9
hordes of Egypt and **b** Egypt and Ezk 32:18
Suppose I **b** the sword against a Ezk 33:2
I will **b** them out from the Ezk 34:13
and **b** them into their own land. Ezk 34:13
the lost, **b** back the strays, Ezk 34:16
and will **b** you into your own Ezk 36:24
and will not **b** famine on you. Ezk 36:29
your graves and **b** you up from Ezk 37:12
your graves and **b** you up from Ezk 37:13
all around and **b** them into their Ezk 37:21
b you out with all your army, Ezk 38:4
I will **b** you against My land Ezk 38:16
that I would **b** you against them Ezk 38:17
I will **b** you against the Ezk 39:2
When I **b** them back from the Ezk 39:27
that they do not **b** ⌊them⌋ into Ezk 46:20
to **b** some of the Israelites from Dn 1:3
B me before the king, and I will Dn 2:24
kingdoms and **b** them to an end, Dn 2:44
gave orders to **b** in Shadrach, Dn 3:13
a decree to **b** all the wise men Dn 4:6
gave orders to **b** in the gold and Dn 5:2
called out to **b** in the mediums, Dn 5:7
to **b** the rebellion to an end, Dn 9:24
to **b** in everlasting Dn 9:24
I will **b** them down like birds of Hs 7:12
so Ephraim will **b** out his Hs 9:13
I will quickly **b** retribution on Jl 3:4
I will **b** retribution on your Jl 3:7
B down Your warriors there, Jl 3:11
"**B** us something to drink." Am 4:1
B your sacrifices every morning, Am 4:4
of the evil day and **b** in a reign Am 6:3
from there I will **b** them down. Am 9:2
Didn't I **b** Israel from the land Am 9:7
Who can **b** me down to the ground? Ob 3
from there I will **b** you down. Ob 4
I will again **b** a conqueror Mc 1:15
Don't My words **b** good to the one Mc 2:7
will **b** them together like sheep Mc 2:12
What should I **b** before the LORD Mc 6:6
He will **b** me into the light; Mc 7:9
He will **b** ⌊it⌋ to complete Nah 1:9
I will **b** distress on mankind, Zph 1:17
will **b** an offering to Me. Zph 3:10
He will **b** ⌊you⌋ quietness with Zph 3:17
At that time I will **b** you back, Zph 3:20
into the hills, **b** down lumber, Hg 1:8
that I am about to **b** My servant, Zch 3:8
And he will **b** out the capstone Zch 4:7
I will **b** them ⌊back⌋ to live in Zch 8:8
I will **b** them back from the land Zch 10:10
I will **b** them to the land of Zch 10:10
B it to your governor! Mal 1:8
You **b** stolen, lame, or sick Mal 1:13
You **b** this as an offering! Mal 1:13
B the full 10 percent into the Mal 3:10
And do not **b** us into temptation, Mt 6:13
that I came to **b** peace on the Mt 10:34
I did not come to **b** peace, Mt 10:34
"**B** them here to Me," He said. Mt 14:18
We didn't **b** any bread." Mt 16:7
up with you? **B** him here to Me. Mt 17:17
Untie them and **b** them to Me. Mt 21:2
were not able to **b** him to Jesus Mk 2:4
commanded him to **b** John's head. Mk 6:27
I put up with you? **B** him to Me." Mk 9:19
Untie it and **b** it here. Mk 11:2
B Me a denarius to look at." Mk 12:15
They tried to **b** him in and set Lk 5:18
find a way to **b** him in because Lk 5:19
up with you? **B** your son here." Lk 9:41
do not **b** us into temptation." Lk 11:4
Whenever they **b** you before Lk 12:11
I came to **b** fire on the earth, Lk 12:49
the city, and **b** in here the poor Lk 14:21
B out the best robe and put it Lk 15:22
Then **b** the fattened calf and Lk 15:23
b here these enemies of mine, Lk 19:27
Untie it and **b** it here. Lk 19:30
this day what ⌊would **b**⌋ peace— Lk 19:42
must **b** them also, and they will Jn 10:16
do you **b** against this man? Jn 18:29
B some of the fish you've just Jn 21:10
determined to **b** this man's blood Ac 5:28
Did you **b** Me offerings and Ac 7:42
he might **b** them as prisoners to Ac 9:2
intending to **b** him out to the Ac 12:4
Herod was to **b** him out ⌊for Ac 12:6
b salvation to the ends of the Ac 13:47
for them to **b** them out to Ac 17:5
Let them **b** charges against one Ac 19:38
to Damascus to **b** those who were Ac 22:5
and **b** him into the barracks. Ac 23:10
that he **b** him down to you Ac 23:15
and asked me to **b** this young man Ac 23:18
to ask you to **b** Paul down to Ac 23:20
Paul on them and **b** him safely to Ac 23:24
of what they now **b** against me. Ac 24:13
I came to **b** charitable gifts and Ac 24:17
be here before you to **b** charges, Ac 24:19
through Him to **b** about the Rm 1:5
dead will also **b** your mortal Rm 8:11
Who can **b** an accusation against Rm 8:33
that is, to **b** Christ down Rm 10:6
to **b** Christ up from the dead. Rm 10:7
more will their full number **b**! Rm 11:12
who oppose it will **b** judgment on Rm 13:2
so He might **b** to nothing the 1Co 1:28
who will both **b** to light what is 1Co 4:5
my body and **b** it under strict 1Co 9:27
to **b** everything together in the Eph 1:10
Messiah might **b** praise to His Eph 1:12
b them up in the training and Eph 6:4
way God will **b** with Him those 1Th 4:14
mouth and will **b** him to nothing 2Th 2:8
which God will **b** about in His 1Tm 6:15
B Mark with you, for he is 2Tm 4:11
b the cloak I left in Troas with 2Tm 4:13
work and will **b** me safely into 2Tm 4:18
but to **b** salvation to those who Heb 9:28
even know what tomorrow will **b**— Jms 4:14
that He might **b** you to God, 1Pt 3:18
will secretly **b** in destructive 2Pt 2:1
and will **b** swift destruction on 2Pt 2:1
do not **b** a slanderous charge 2Pt 2:11
a sin that does not **b** death, 1Jn 5:16
commit sin that doesn't **b** death. 1Jn 5:16
is sin that does not **b** death. 1Jn 5:17
and does not **b** this teaching, 2Jn 10
did not dare **b** an abusive Jd 9
of the earth will **b** their glory Rv 21:24
They will **b** the glory and honor Rv 21:26

BRINGING *(61)*

that I am **b** a deluge— Gn 6:17
done to us by **b** us out of Egypt Ex 14:11
b the consequences of the Ex 34:7
The people are **b** more than is Ex 36:5
priest sins, **b** guilt on the Lv 4:3
instead of **b** it to the entrance Lv 17:4
of Canaan, where I am **b** you. Lv 18:3
land where I am **b** you to live Lv 20:22
Why is the LORD **b** us into this Nm 14:3
b the consequences of the Nm 14:18
enter the land where I am **b** you, Nm 15:18
man came **b** a Midianite woman Nm 25:6
your God is **b** you into a good Dt 8:7
b wrath on the entire community Jos 22:20
If you are **b** me back to fight Jdg 11:9
there, one **b** three goats, one 1Sm 10:3
one **b** three loaves of bread, 1Sm 10:3
bread, and one **b** a skin of wine. 1Sm 10:3
you disturbed me by **b** me up?" 1Sm 28:15
house of Israel were **b** up the 2Sm 6:15
"This one is also **b** good news," 2Sm 18:26
and you must be **b** good news." 1Kg 1:42
the wicked by **b** what he has done 1Kg 8:32
The ravens kept **b** him bread and 1Kg 17:6
they kept **b** her ⌊containers⌋, 2Kg 4:5
that I am **b** on this place.'" 2Kg 22:20
Naphtali came **b** food on donkeys 1Ch 12:40
So all Israel was **b** the ark of 1Ch 15:28
of the LORD **b** destruction to 1Ch 21:12
the wicked by **b** what he has done 2Ch 6:23
They were **b** horses for Solomon 2Ch 9:28
they began **b** the offering to 2Ch 31:10
Many were **b** an offering to the 2Ch 32:23
that I am **b** on this place 2Ch 34:28
They were also **b** in stores of Neh 13:15
merchant ships, **b** her food from Pr 31:14
Stop **b** useless offerings. Is 1:13
I am **b** My justice near; Is 46:13
For I am **b** disaster from the Jr 4:6
other gods, **b** harm on yourselves Jr 7:6
at this time and **b** them such Jr 10:18
from the Negev **b** burnt offerings Jr 17:26
born to you," **b** him great joy. Jr 20:15
For I am already **b** disaster on Jr 25:29
'I was **b** before the king my Jr 38:26
of the disaster I am **b** on her. Jr 51:64
He does not enjoy **b** affliction Lm 3:33
to Israel by **b** them out of Egypt Ezk 20:9
our rulers by **b** on us so great Dn 9:12
b desolation because of your Mc 6:13
the feet of one **b** good news and Nah 1:15
they began to **b** to Him all those Mk 1:32
they came to Him **b** a paralytic, Mk 2:3
people were **b** little children Mk 10:13
people were even **b** infants to Lk 18:15
b the spices they had prepared. Lk 24:1
I'm **b** Him outside to you to let Jn 19:4
b a mixture of about 75 pounds Jn 19:39
b sick people and those who were Ac 5:16
And **b** them before the chief Ac 16:20
was fitting, in **b** many sons to Heb 2:10

BRINGS *(74)*

the LORD **b** you into the land Ex 13:5
When the LORD **b** you into the Ex 13:11
When any of you **b** an offering to Lv 1:2
offering that he **b** as a sin Lv 4:32
offering and **b** its blood inside Lv 16:15
remembrance that **b** sin to mind. Nm 5:15
the bitter water that **b** a curse. Nm 5:18
bitter water that **b** a curse. Nm 5:19
this water that **b** a curse enter Nm 5:22
the bitter water that **b** a curse, Nm 5:24
the water that **b** a curse will Nm 5:27
if the LORD **b** about something Nm 16:30
LORD your God **b** you into the Dt 6:10
LORD your God **b** you into the Dt 7:1
LORD your God **b** you into the Dt 11:29
the loan to **b** the security out Dt 24:11
The LORD **b** death and gives life; 1Sm 2:6
The LORD **b** poverty and gives 1Sm 2:7
If the LORD really **b** me back to 2Sm 15:8
When disaster **b** sudden death, Jb 9:23
the darkness and **b** the deepest Jb 12:22
because wrath ⌊**b**⌋ punishment by Jb 19:29
the south wind **b** calm to the Jb 37:17
Evil **b** death to the sinner, Ps 34:21
who **b** devastation on the earth. Ps 46:8
meditation ⌊**b**⌋ understanding. Ps 49:3
b down one and exalts another. Ps 75:7
cares, Your comfort **b** me joy. Ps 94:19
of Your words **b** light and gives Ps 119:130
for the rain and **b** the wind from Ps 135:7
the afflicted but **b** the wicked Ps 147:6
A wise son **b** joy to his father, Pr 10:1
but a cruel man **b** disaster on Pr 11:17
The one who **b** ruin on his Pr 11:29
tongue of the wise ⌊**b**⌋ healing. Pr 12:18
trustworthy courier ⌊**b**⌋ healing. Pr 13:17
speech of a fool ⌊**b**⌋ a rod ⌊of Pr 14:3
A wise son **b** joy to his father, Pr 15:20
Foolishness **b** joy to one without Pr 15:21
his lips **b** about evil. Pr 16:30
doors for a man and **b** him before Pr 18:16
He **b** the wicked to ruin. Pr 21:12
more so when he **b** it with Pr 21:27
who loves wisdom **b** joy to his Pr 29:3
By justice a king **b** stability to Pr 29:4
of wisdom is that it **b** success. Ec 10:10
The LORD **b** ⌊this⌋ charge against Is 3:14
city. He **b** it down; He brings it Is 26:5
He **b** it down to the ground; Is 26:5
that the LORD **b** down on him will Is 30:32
He also is wise and **b** disaster. Is 31:2
He **b** out the starry host by Is 40:26
who **b** out the chariot and horse, Is 43:17
who **b** news of good things, Is 52:7

as the earth **b** forth its growth Is 61:11
for the rain and **b** the wind from Jr 10:13
your God before He **b** darkness, Jr 13:16
but He **b** darkest gloom and makes Jr 13:16
the LORD **b** a case against Jr 25:31
the town that **b** Me joy? Jr 49:25
for the rain and **b** the wind from Jr 51:16
He **b** destruction on the strong, Am 5:9
defilement **b** destruction— Mc 2:10
off it goes and **b** with it seven Mt 12:45
a landowner who **b** out of his Mt 13:52
Then it goes and **b** seven other Lk 11:26
if their stumbling **b** riches for Rm 11:12
an avenger that **b** wrath on the Rm 13:4
When He again **b** His firstborn Heb 1:6
For it ⌊**b**⌋ favor if, because of 1Pt 2:19
you endure, it **b** favor with God. 1Pt 2:20
There is sin that **b** death. 1Jn 5:16
immorality, which **b** wrath." Rv 14:8
immorality, which **b** wrath. Rv 18:3

BRITTLE *(2)*
my bones became **b** from my Ps 32:3
be strong, and part will be **b**. Dn 2:42

BROAD *(11)*
Look, it is still **b** daylight. Gn 29:7
execute them in **b** daylight Nm 25:4
all Israel and in **b** daylight.' " 2Sm 12:12
the land was **b**, peaceful, and 1Ch 4:40
Jerusalem as far as the **B** Wall. Neh 3:8
of the Ovens to the **B** Wall, Neh 12:38
a place of rivers and **b** streams, Is 33:21
will face foes in **b** daylight. Ezk 30:16
and the road is **b** that leads to Mt 7:13
b street of the city was pure Rv 21:21
the middle of the **b** street ⌊of Rv 22:2

BROADCAST *(1)*
lips of the wise **b** knowledge, Pr 15:7

BROADEN *(1)*
for You **b** my understanding. Ps 119:32

BROADNESS *(1)*
for the temple's **b** as it rose. Ezk 41:7

BROILED *(1)*
gave Him a piece of a **b** fish, Lk 24:42

BROKE *(63)*
the first tablets, which you **b**. Ex 34:1
fight **b** out in the camp between Lv 24:10
I **b** the bars of your yoke and Lv 26:13
community **b** into loud cries Nm 14:1
were on the first tablets you **b**, Dt 10:2
For ⌊both of⌋ you **b** faith with Dt 32:51
When the people **b** camp to cross Jos 3:14
trumpets and **b** the pitchers that Jdg 7:19
heavy, his neck **b** and he died. 1Sm 4:18
When war **b** out again, David went 1Sm 19:8
So Saul **b** off his pursuit of 1Sm 23:28
and the troops **b** off their 2Sm 18:16
three of the warriors **b** through 2Sm 23:16
b its altars and images into 2Kg 11:18
Jerusalem and **b** down 200 yards 2Kg 14:13
b into pieces the bronze snake 2Kg 18:4
king of Assyria **b** camp and left. 2Kg 19:36
He **b** the sacred pillars into 2Kg 23:14
Now the Chaldeans **b** into pieces 2Kg 25:13
So the Three **b** through the 1Ch 11:18
a war **b** out with the Philistines 1Ch 20:4
b its altars and images into 2Ch 23:17
Athaliah **b** into the LORD's 2Ch 24:7
Jerusalem and **b** down 200 yards 2Ch 25:23
a skin disease **b** out on his 2Ch 26:19
of Judah and **b** up the sacred 2Ch 31:1
then fire **b** out against Jacob, Ps 78:21
and a plague **b** out against them. Ps 106:29
He **b** their spirits with hard Ps 107:12
and gloom and **b** their chains Ps 107:14
the watery depths **b** open, Pr 3:20
He **b** up the soil, cleared it of Is 5:2
king of Assyria **b** camp and left. Is 37:37
For long ago I **b** your yoke; Jr 2:20
house of Judah **b** My covenant I Jr 11:10
Jeremiah the prophet and **b** it. Jr 28:10
You **b** a wooden yoke bar, but in Jr 28:13
a covenant they **b** even though I Jr 31:32
Now the Chaldeans **b** into pieces Jr 52:17
and whose covenant he **b**. Ezk 17:16
and My covenant that he **b**. Ezk 17:19
You **b** My covenant with all your Ezk 44:7
a stone **b** off without a hand Dn 2:34
of exiles to Edom and **b** a treaty Am 1:9
He **b** the loaves and gave them to Mt 14:19
He gave thanks, **b** them, and kept Mt 15:36
blessed and **b** it, gave it to Mt 26:26
He blessed and **b** the loaves. Mk 6:41
He gave thanks, **b** the ⌊loaves⌋, Mk 8:6
When I **b** the five loaves for the Mk 8:19
When I **b** the seven loaves for Mk 8:20
She **b** the jar and poured it on Mk 14:3
blessed and **b** it, gave it to Mk 14:22
heaven, He blessed and **b** them. Lk 9:16
gave thanks, **b** it, gave it to Lk 22:19
blessed and **b** it, and gave it to Lk 24:30
soldiers came and **b** the legs of Jn 19:32
and **b** bread from house to house. Ac 2:46
severe persecution **b** out against Ac 8:1
a dispute **b** out between the Ac 23:7
gave thanks, **b** it, and said, 1Co 11:24
Then war **b** out in heaven: Rv 12:7
painful sores **b** out on the Rv 16:2

BROKEN *(93)*
he has **b** My covenant." Gn 17:14
said, "You have **b** out ⌊first⌋!" Gn 38:29
of their **b** spirit and hard Ex 6:9
offering is boiled must be **b**; Lv 6:28
that has **b** out in the boil Lv 13:20
that has **b** out in the burn Lv 13:25
rash that has **b** out on the skin Lv 13:39
article, it has **b** out again. Lv 13:57
the discharge touches must be **b**, Lv 15:12
no man who has a **b** foot or hand, Lv 21:19
LORD's word and **b** His command; Nm 15:31
heifer whose neck has been **b**. Dt 21:6
I am a woman with a **b** heart. 1Sm 1:15
The bows of the warriors are **b**, 1Sm 2:4
his hands were **b** off and lying 1Sm 5:4
Then the city was **b** into, and 2Kg 25:4
has **b** up what you have made. 2Ch 20:37
wall has been **b** down, Neh 1:3
that had been **b** down and its Neh 2:13
took a piece of **b** pottery to Jb 2:8
the fangs of young lions are **b**. Jb 4:10
My spirit is **b**. My days are Jb 17:1
So injustice is **b** like a tree. Jb 24:20
arm raised ⌊in violence⌋ is **b**. Jb 38:15
a dead person—like **b** pottery. Ps 31:12
not one of them is **b**. Ps 34:20
and their bows will be **b**. Ps 37:15
arms of the wicked will be **b**, Ps 37:17
pleasing to God is a **b** spirit. Ps 51:17
not despise a **b** and humbled Ps 51:17
You have **b** out against us; Ps 60:1
Insults have **b** my heart, and I Ps 69:20
Why have You **b** down its walls so Ps 80:12
You have **b** down all his walls; Ps 89:40
He has **b** my strength in Ps 102:23
For He has **b** down the bronze Ps 107:16
⌊for⌋ they have **b** Your law. Ps 119:126
sad heart ⌊produces⌋ a **b** spirit. Pr 15:13
but a **b** spirit dries up the Pr 17:22
but who can survive a **b** spirit? Pr 18:14
a city whose wall is **b** down. Pr 25:28
reprimands will be **b** suddenly— Pr 29:1
three strands is not easily **b**. Ec 4:12
golden bowl is **b**, and the jar is Ec 12:6
the wheel is **b** into the well; Ec 12:6
is loose, and no sandal strap **b**. Is 5:27
together, peoples, and be **b**; Is 8:9
prepare for war, and be **b**; Is 8:9
prepare for war, and be **b**. Is 8:9
they will fall and be **b**; Is 8:15
yoke will be **b** because of ⌊his Is 10:27
The LORD has **b** the staff of the Is 14:5
of the one who struck you is **b**. Is 14:29
and **b** the everlasting covenant. Is 24:5
dry out, they will be **b** off. Is 27:11
backwards, to be **b**, trapped, and Is 28:13
agreement has been **b**, and cities Is 33:8
called the repairer of **b** walls, Is 58:12
will lament out of a **b** spirit. Is 65:14
have also **b** your skull. Jr 2:16
these also had **b** the yoke and Jr 5:5
I am **b** by the brokenness of my Jr 8:21
My heart is **b** within me, and all Jr 23:9
'I have **b** the yoke of the king Jr 28:2
the prophet had **b** the yoke bar Jr 28:12
David may be **b** so that he will Jr 33:21
day of the month, the city was **b** Jr 39:2
How **b** it is! They wail! How Moab Jr 48:39
Then the city was **b** into, and Jr 52:7
and the Lord has **b** my strength. Lm 1:14
my heart is **b**, for I have been Lm 1:20
bitterly with a **b** heart right Ezk 21:6
then you will gnaw its **b** pieces, Ezk 23:34
I have **b** the arm of Pharaoh king Ezk 30:21
one and the one ⌊already⌋ **b**, Ezk 30:22
its boughs lay **b** in all the Ezk 31:12
All Israel has **b** Your law and Dn 9:11
kingdom will be **b** up and divided Dn 11:4
and the granaries are **b** down, Jl 1:17
not seek the lost or heal the **b**. Zch 11:16
this stone will be **b** to pieces; Mt 21:44
alert and not let his house be **b** Mt 24:43
And when they had **b** through, Mk 2:4
not have let his house be **b** Lk 12:39
that stone will be **b** to pieces, Lk 20:18
the law of Moses won't be **b**, Jn 7:23
and the Scripture cannot be **b**— Jn 10:35
the men's legs **b** and that ⌊their Jn 19:31
Not one of His bones will be **b**. Jn 19:36
and when he had **b** it, he began Ac 27:35
some of the branches were **b** off, Rm 11:17
Branches were **b** off so that I Rm 11:19
they were **b** off by unbelief, Rm 11:20

BROKEN-DOWN *(1)*
the entire **b** wall and 2Ch 32:5

BROKENHEARTED *(4)*
The LORD is near the **b**; Ps 34:18
poor and the **b** in order to put Ps 109:16
heals the **b** and binds up their Ps 147:3
He has sent Me to heal the **b**, Is 61:1

BROKENNESS *(4)*
My people's **b** superficially, Jr 6:14
the **b** of My dear people Jr 8:11
am broken by the **b** of my dear Jr 8:21
Woe to me because of my **b**— Jr 10:19

BRONZE *(157)*
all kinds of **b** and iron tools. Gn 4:22
from them: gold, silver, and **b**; Ex 25:3
Make 50 **b** clasps; put the clasps Ex 26:11
to cast five **b** bases for them. Ex 26:37
of one piece. Overlay it with **b**. Ex 27:2
make all its utensils of **b**. Ex 27:3
a grate for it of **b** mesh, Ex 27:4
make four **b** rings on the mesh Ex 27:4
wood, and overlay them with **b**. Ex 27:6
to be 20 posts and 20 **b** bases. Ex 27:10
to be 20 posts and 20 **b** bases. Ex 27:11
have silver hooks and **b** bases. Ex 27:17
bases of the posts must be **b**. Ex 27:18
courtyard are to be made of **b**. Ex 27:19
Make a **b** basin for washing and a Ex 30:18
washing and a **b** stand for it. Ex 30:18
works in gold, silver, and **b**, Ex 31:4
offering: gold, silver, and **b**; Ex 35:5
burnt offering with its **b** grate, Ex 35:16
of silver or **b** brought it to the Ex 35:24
works in gold, silver, and **b**, Ex 35:32
He made 50 **b** clasps to join the Ex 36:18
but their five bases were **b**. Ex 36:38
Then he overlaid it with **b**. Ex 38:2
he made all its utensils of **b**. Ex 38:3
altar a grate of **b** mesh under Ex 38:4
corners of the **b** grate he cast Ex 38:5
wood and overlaid them with **b**. Ex 38:6
made the **b** basin and its stand Ex 38:8
its stand from the ⌊**b**⌋ mirrors Ex 38:8
their 20 posts and 20 **b** bases. Ex 38:10
their 20 posts and 20 **b** bases. Ex 38:11
The bases for the posts were **b**; Ex 38:17
including their four **b** bases. Ex 38:19
surrounding courtyard were **b**. Ex 38:20
The **b** of the presentation Ex 38:29
b altar and its bronze grate, Ex 38:30
bronze altar and its **b** grate, Ex 38:30
the **b** altar with its bronze Ex 39:39
bronze altar with its **b** grate, Ex 39:39
if it is boiled in a **b** vessel, Lv 6:28
like iron and your land like **b**, Lv 26:19
the ashes from the ⌊**b**⌋ altar, Nm 4:13
priest took the **b** firepans that Nm 16:39
So Moses made a **b** snake and Nm 21:9
and he looked at the **b** snake, Nm 21:9
the gold, silver, **b**, iron, tin, Nm 31:22

The sky above you will be **b**, Dt 28:23
of your gate be iron and **b**, Dt 33:25
and the articles of **b** and iron, Jos 6:19
and the articles of **b** and iron Jos 6:24
and silver, gold, **b**, iron, and a Jos 22:8
and bound him with **b** shackles, Jdg 16:21
and wore a **b** helmet and bronze 1Sm 17:5
helmet and **b** scale armor that 1Sm 17:5
There was **b** armor on his shins, 1Sm 17:6
and a **b** sword was slung between 1Sm 17:6
put a **b** helmet on David's head 1Sm 17:38
feet not placed in **b** ⌊shackles⌋. 2Sm 3:34
huge quantities of **b** from Betah 2Sm 8:8
of silver, gold, and **b** with him. 2Sm 8:10
b spear weighed about eight 2Sm 21:16
my arms can bend a bow of **b**. 2Sm 22:35
cities with walls and **b** bars 1Kg 4:13
a man of Tyre, a **b** craftsman. 1Kg 7:14
to do every kind of **b** work. 1Kg 7:14
He cast two ⌊hollow⌋ **b** pillars: 1Kg 7:15
capitals of cast **b** to set on top 1Kg 7:16
Then he made 10 **b** water carts. 1Kg 7:27
cart had four **b** wheels with 1Kg 7:30
four bronze wheels with **b** axles. 1Kg 7:30
Then he made 10 **b** basins— 1Kg 7:38
were made⌋ of burnished **b**. 1Kg 7:45
the weight of the **b** was not 1Kg 7:47
since the **b** altar before 1Kg 8:64
Rehoboam made **b** shields in their 1Kg 14:27
He took the **b** altar that was 2Kg 16:14
The **b** altar will be for me to 2Kg 16:15
and removed the **b** basin from 2Kg 16:17
from the **b** oxen that were 2Kg 16:17
into pieces the **b** snake that 2Kg 18:4
bound him in **b** ⌊chains⌋, and 2Kg 25:7
into pieces the **b** pillars of the 2Kg 25:13
carts, and the **b** reservoir, 2Kg 25:13
and carried the **b** to Babylon. 2Kg 25:13
and all the **b** articles used in 2Kg 25:14
the weight of the **b** of all these 2Kg 25:16
tall and had a **b** capital on top 2Kg 25:17
a grating and pomegranates of **b**, 2Kg 25:17
were to sound the **b** cymbals; 1Ch 15:19
also took huge quantities of **b**, 1Ch 18:8
Solomon made the **b** reservoir, 1Ch 18:8
the pillars, and the **b** articles. 1Ch 18:8
of items of gold, silver, and **b**. 1Ch 18:10
an immeasurable quantity of **b**, 1Ch 22:3
and **b** and iron that can't be 1Ch 22:14
in gold, silver, **b**, and iron— 1Ch 22:16
the silver, **b** for the bronze, 1Ch 29:2
bronze for the **b**, iron for the 1Ch 29:2
675 tons of **b**, and 4,000 tons 1Ch 29:7
but he put the **b** altar, which 2Ch 1:5
presence on the **b** altar at the 2Ch 1:6
with gold, silver, **b**, and iron, 2Ch 2:7
gold, silver, **b**, iron, stone, 2Ch 2:14
He made a **b** altar 30 feet long, 2Ch 4:1
He overlaid the doors with **b**. 2Ch 4:9
these were made⌋ of polished **b**. 2Ch 4:16
the weight of the **b** was not 2Ch 4:18
had made a **b** platform seven 2Ch 6:13
since the **b** altar that Solomon 2Ch 7:7
Rehoboam made **b** shields in their 2Ch 12:10
bound him with **b** ⌊shackles⌋, 2Ch 33:11
and bound him in **b** ⌊shackles⌋ to 2Ch 36:6
two articles of fine gleaming **b**, Ezr 8:27
of stone, or my flesh made of **b**? Jb 6:12
arrow from⌋ a **b** bow will pierce Jb 20:24
His bones are **b** tubes; Jb 40:18
as straw, and **b** as rotten wood. Jb 41:27
my arms can bend a bow of **b**. Ps 18:34
broken down the **b** gates and cut Ps 107:16
will shatter the **b** doors and cut Is 45:2
is iron and your forehead **b**, Is 48:4
I will bring gold instead of **b**; Is 60:17
of iron, **b** instead of wood Is 60:17
and **b** walls against the whole Jr 1:18
⌊They are⌋ **b** and iron; Jr 6:28
iron, iron from the north, or **b**? Jr 15:12
wall of **b** to this people. Jr 15:20
and put him in chains to take Jr 39:7
and bound him with **b** chains. Jr 52:11
into pieces the **b** pillars for Jr 52:17
carts and the **b** reservoir that Jr 52:17
carried all the **b** to Babylon. Jr 52:17
and all the **b** articles used in Jr 52:18
and the 12 **b** bulls under the Jr 52:20
the weight of the **b** of all these Jr 52:20
had a **b** capital on top of it. Jr 52:22
encircled by **b** latticework and Jr 52:22
like the gleam of polished **b**. Ezk 1:7
and stood beside the **b** altar. Ezk 9:2
slaves and **b** utensils for your Ezk 27:13
man whose appearance was like **b**, Ezk 40:3
its stomach and thighs were **b**, Dn 2:32
fired clay, the **b**, the silver, Dn 2:35
kingdom, of **b**, which will rule Dn 2:39
crushed the iron, **b**, fired clay, Dn 2:45
a band of iron and **b** around it, Dn 4:15
a band of iron and **b** around it, Dn 4:23
gold and silver, **b**, iron, wood, Dn 5:4
silver and gold, **b**, iron, wood, Dn 5:23
with iron teeth and **b** claws, Dn 7:19
like the gleam of polished **b**, Dn 10:6
horns iron and your hooves **b**, Mc 4:13
the mountains were made of **b**. Zch 6:1
feet like fine **b** fired in a Rv 1:15
whose feet are like fine **b** says: Rv 2:18
gold, silver, **b**, stone, and wood Rv 9:20

BROOCHES *(1)*

had willing hearts brought **b**, Ex 35:22

BROOD *(8)*

And here you, a **b** of sinners, Nm 32:14
Its **b** gulps down blood, and Jb 39:30
with iniquity, **b** of evildoers, Is 1:4
will gather ⌊her **b**⌋ under her Is 34:15
he said to them, "**B** of vipers! Mt 3:7
B of vipers! How can you speak Mt 12:34
Snakes! **B** of vipers! How can you Mt 23:33
baptized by him, "**B** of vipers! Lk 3:7

BROOK *(18)*

from the **b** of Egypt to the Gn 15:18
willows of the **b**—and rejoice Lv 23:40
from Azmon to the **B** of Egypt, Nm 34:5
and to the **B** of Egypt and so Jos 15:4
to the **B** of Egypt and the Jos 15:47
along the **B** of Kanah and ended Jos 16:8
descended to the **B** of Kanah; Jos 17:9
south of the **b**, cities belonged Jos 17:9
north side of the **b** and ended at Jos 17:9
and met the **b** east of Jokneam. Jos 19:11
of Hamath to the **B** of Egypt— 1Kg 8:65
from the **B** of Egypt to the 2Kg 24:7
to Hamath to the **B** of Egypt— 2Ch 7:8
willows by the **b** surround him. Jb 40:22
drink from the **b** by the road; Ps 110:7
on to the **B** ⌊of Egypt⌋ as far Ezk 47:19
to the **B** ⌊of Egypt⌋, and out to Ezk 48:28
Hamath to the **B** of the Arabah. Am 6:14

BROOM *(4)*

down under a **b** tree and prayed 1Kg 19:4
down and slept under the **b** tree. 1Kg 19:5
roots of the **b** tree were their Jb 30:4
away with a **b** of destruction. Is 14:23

BROTH *(3)*

in a basket and the **b** in a pot. Jdg 6:19
stone, and pour the **b** ⌊on it⌋." Jdg 6:20
polluted **b** in their bowls. Is 65:4

BROTHER *(341)*

also gave birth to his **b** Abel. Gn 4:2
said to his **b** Abel, "Let's go Gn 4:8
attacked his **b** Abel and killed Gn 4:8
to Cain, "Where is your **b** Abel?" Gn 4:9
His **b** was named Jubal; Gn 4:21
of each man's **b** for a man's life Gn 9:5
Japheth's older **b**, also had Gn 10:21
his **b** was named Joktan. Gn 10:25
the **b** of Eshcol and the brother Gn 14:13
of Eshcol and the **b** of Aner. Gn 14:13
she herself said, 'He is my **b**.' Gn 20:5
say about me: 'He's my **b**.'" Gn 20:13
I am giving your **b** 1,000 pieces Gn 20:16
has borne sons to your **b** Nahor: Gn 22:20
his firstborn, his **b** Buz, Kemuel Gn 22:21
eight to Nahor, Abraham's **b**. Gn 22:23
the wife of Abraham's **b** Nahor— Gn 24:15
Rebekah had a **b** named Laban, Gn 24:29
of my master's **b** for his son. Gn 24:48
gifts to her **b** and her mother. Gn 24:53
But her **b** and mother said, Gn 24:55
his **b** came out grasping Esau's Gn 25:26
father talking with your **b** Esau. Gn 27:6
Look, my **b** Esau is a hairy Gn 27:11
hairy like those of his **b** Esau; Gn 27:23
b Esau arrived from the hunt. Gn 27:30
Your **b** came deceitfully and took Gn 27:35
and you will serve your **b**. Gn 27:40
then I will kill my **b** Jacob." Gn 27:41
your **b** Esau is consoling himself Gn 27:42
at once to my **b** Laban in Haran, Gn 27:43
of Laban, your mother's **b**. Gn 28:2
the Aramean, the **b** of Rebekah, Gn 28:5
of him to his **b** Esau in the land Gn 32:3
said, "We went to your **b** Esau; Gn 32:6
me from the hand of my **b** Esau, Gn 32:11
him as a gift for his **b** Esau: Gn 32:13
When my **b** Esau meets you and Gn 32:17
times until he approached his **b**. Gn 33:3
enough, my **b**," Esau replied. Gn 33:9
when you fled from your **b** Esau." Gn 35:1
when he was fleeing from his **b**. Gn 35:7
to a land away from his **b** Jacob. Gn 36:6
we kill our **b** and cover up his Gn 37:26
he is our **b**, our ⌊own⌋ flesh. Gn 37:27
produce offspring for your **b**." Gn 38:8
not produce offspring for his **b**. Gn 38:9
He might die too, like his **b**." Gn 38:11
hand back, and his **b** came out. Gn 38:29
Then his **b**, who had the scarlet Gn 38:30
send Joseph's **b** Benjamin with Gn 42:4
your youngest **b** comes here. Gn 42:15
of your number to get your **b**. Gn 42:16
your youngest **b** to me so that Gn 42:20
for what we did to our **b**. Gn 42:21
Leave one **b** with me, take ⌊food Gn 42:33
back your youngest **b** to me, Gn 42:34
then give your **b** back to you, Gn 42:34
for his **b** is dead and he alone Gn 42:38
unless your **b** is with you.' Gn 43:3
If you will send our **b** with us, Gn 43:4
unless your **b** is with you.'" Gn 43:5
the man that you had another **b**?" Gn 43:6
Do you have ⌊another⌋ **b**?' Gn 43:7
would say, 'Bring your **b** here'?" Gn 43:7
Take your **b** also, and go back at Gn 43:13
your other **b** and Benjamin to Gn 43:14
up and saw his **b** Benjamin, Gn 43:29
your youngest **b** that you told me Gn 43:29
overcome with emotion for his **b**, Gn 43:30
'Do you have a father or a **b**?' Gn 44:19
an elderly father and a young **b**, Gn 44:20
The boy's **b** is dead. Gn 44:20
'If your younger **b** does not come Gn 44:23
our younger **b** goes with us. Gn 44:26
if our younger **b** isn't with us, Gn 44:26
"I am Joseph, your **b**," he said, Gn 45:4
eyes and my **b** Benjamin's eyes Gn 45:12
his younger **b** will be greater Gn 48:19
Isn't Aaron the Levite your **b**? Ex 4:14
and Aaron your **b** will be your Ex 7:1
then Aaron your **b** must declare Ex 7:2
Have your **b** Aaron, with his Ex 28:1
holy garments for your **b** Aaron, Ex 28:2
garments for your **b** Aaron and Ex 28:4
these on your **b** Aaron and his Ex 28:41
and each of you kill his **b**, Ex 32:27
went against his son and his **b**. Ex 32:29
Tell your **b** Aaron that he may Lv 16:2
your father's **b** by coming near Lv 18:14
it will shame your **b**. Lv 18:16
not hate your **b** in your heart. Lv 19:17
He has shamed his **b**; Lv 20:21
father, son, daughter, or **b**. Lv 21:2
If your **b** becomes destitute and Lv 25:25
and redeem what his **b** has sold. Lv 25:25
If your **b** becomes destitute and Lv 25:35
and let your **b** live among you. Lv 25:36
If your **b** among you becomes Lv 25:39
but your **b** ⌊living⌋ near him Lv 25:47
mother, or his **b** or sister, when Nm 6:7
and your **b** Aaron are to speak Nm 20:8
is what your **b** Israel says, Nm 20:14
people, as Aaron your **b** was. Nm 27:13
LORD to give our **b** Zelophehad's Nm 36:2
a man and his **b** or a foreign Dt 1:16
If your **b**, the son of your Dt 13:6
from his neighbor or **b**, Dt 15:2
whatever your **b** owes you. Dt 15:3
tightfisted toward your poor **b**. Dt 15:7
toward your poor **b** and give him Dt 15:9
and poor **b** in your land.' Dt 15:11
who has falsely accused his **b**, Dt 19:18

as he intended to do to his **b**. Dt 19:19
sure you return it to your **b**. Dt 22:1
If your **b** does not live near you Dt 22:2
you until your **b** comes looking Dt 22:2
anything your **b** has lost and you Dt 22:3
Edomite, because he is your **b**. Dt 23:7
not charge your **b** interest on Dt 23:19
must not charge your **b** interest, Dt 23:20
your **b** will be degraded in your Dt 25:3
carry on the name of the dead **b**, Dt 25:6
will look grudgingly at his **b**, Dt 28:54
just as your **b** Aaron died on Dt 32:50
So Othniel son of Caleb's **b**, Jos 15:17
Judah said to his **b** Simeon, Jdg 1:3
Caleb's youngest **b**, captured it, Jdg 1:13
Judah went with his **b** Simeon, Jdg 1:17
youngest **b** as a deliverer Jdg 3:9
for they said, "He is our **b**." Jdg 9:3
Shechem 'because he is your **b**'— Jdg 9:18
because of his **b** Abimelech. Jdg 9:21
be avenged on their **b** Abimelech, Jdg 9:24
belonged to our **b** Elimelech. Ru 4:3
b of Ichabod son of Phinehas, 1Sm 14:3
David's oldest **b** Eliab listened 1Sm 17:28
my **b** has told me to be there. 1Sm 20:29
Hittite and Joab's **b** Abishai son 1Sm 26:6
I grieve for you, Jonathan my **b**. 2Sm 1:26
look your **b** Joab in the face? 2Sm 2:22
the death of Asahel, Joab's **b**. 2Sm 3:27
Joab and his **b** Abishai killed 2Sm 3:30
had put their **b** Asahel to death 2Sm 3:30
Rechab and his **b** Baanah escaped. 2Sm 4:6
Rechab and his **b** Baanah, 2Sm 4:9
command of his **b** Abishai who 2Sm 10:10
a son of David's **b** Shimeah. 2Sm 13:3
Tamar, my **b** Absalom's sister. 2Sm 13:4
Please go to your **b** Amnon's 2Sm 13:7
went to her **b** Amnon's bedroom 2Sm 13:10
"Don't, my **b**!" she cried. "Don't 2Sm 13:12
Her **b** Absalom said to her: 2Sm 13:20
your **b** Amnon been with you? 2Sm 13:20
He is your **b**. Don't take this 2Sm 13:20
in the house of her **b** Absalom. 2Sm 13:20
let my **b** Amnon go with us. 2Sm 13:26
son of David's **b** Shimeah, spoke 2Sm 13:32
who killed his **b** so we may put 2Sm 14:7
the life of the **b** he murdered. 2Sm 14:7
third under Joab's **b** Abishai son 2Sm 18:2
Amasa, "Are you well, my **b**?" 2Sm 20:9
Joab and his **b** Abishai pursued 2Sm 20:10
son of David's **b** Shimei, killed 2Sm 21:21
Joab's **b** and son of Zeruiah, 2Sm 23:18
Joab's **b** Asahel, Elhanan son of 2Sm 23:24
the warriors, or his **b** Solomon. 1Kg 1:10
when I fled from your **b** Absalom. 1Kg 2:7
was turned over to my **b**, 1Kg 2:15
be given to your **b** Adonijah as a 1Kg 2:21
he is my elder **b**, you might as 1Kg 2:22
towns you've given me, my **b**?" 1Kg 9:13
mourned over him: "Oh, my **b**!" 1Kg 13:30
Is he still alive? He is my **b**." 1Kg 20:32
said, "Yes, your **b** Ben-hadad." 1Kg 20:33
the name of his **b** was Joktan. 1Ch 1:19
The sons of Jada **b** of Shammai: 1Ch 2:32
sons of Caleb **b** of Jerahmeel: 1Ch 2:42
Chelub **b** of Shuhah fathered 1Ch 4:11
His **b** was named Sheresh, and his 1Ch 7:16
b Helem's sons: Zophah, Imna, 1Ch 7:35
His **b** Eshek's sons: Ulam was his 1Ch 8:39
Abishai, Joab's **b**, was the 1Ch 11:20
Joab's **b** Asahel, Elhanan son of 1Ch 11:26
Joel the **b** of Nathan, Mibhar son 1Ch 11:38
Shimri and his **b** Joha the Tizite 1Ch 11:45
Then there was his **b** Joash; 1Ch 12:3
the command of his **b** Abishai, 1Ch 19:11
fled before Joab's **b** Abishai and 1Ch 19:15
killed Lahmi the **b** of Goliath 1Ch 20:5
son of David's **b** Shimei, killed 1Ch 20:7
Micah's **b**: Isshiah; from 1Ch 24:25
Zetham and his **b** Joel, were in 1Ch 26:22
was Joab's **b** Asahel, and his 1Ch 27:7
and his **b** Shimei was second. 2Ch 31:12
of Conaniah and his **b** Shimei by 2Ch 31:13
made Jehoahaz's **b** Eliakim king 2Ch 36:4
But Neco took his **b** Jehoahaz and 2Ch 36:4
His **b** Jehoiachin became king in 2Ch 36:8
Jehoiachin's **b** Zedekiah king 2Ch 36:10
Then I put my **b** Hanani in charge Neh 7:2
I have become a **b** to jackals and Jb 30:29
as if for my friend or **b**; Ps 35:14
maligning your **b**, slandering Ps 50:20
and a **b** is born for a difficult Pr 17:17
in his work is **b** to a vandal. Pr 18:9
An offended **b** is ⌊harder to Pr 18:19
who stays closer than a **b**. Pr 18:24
nearby than a **b** far away. Pr 27:10
a son or **b**, and though there Ec 4:8
I could treat you like my **b**, Sg 8:1
even seize his **b** in his father's Is 3:6
No one has compassion on his **b**. Is 9:19
against his **b** and each against Is 19:2
Don't trust any **b**, for every Jr 9:4
for every **b** will certainly Jr 9:4
for him, ⌊saying,⌋ Woe, my **b**! Jr 22:18
say to his friend and to his **b**: Jr 23:35
one teach his neighbor or his **b**, Jr 31:34
and no one enslave his Judean **b**. Jr 34:9
free his Hebrew **b** who sold Jr 34:14
each man for his **b** and for his Jr 34:17
robbed ⌊his⌋ **b**, and did what was Ezk 18:18
another, each saying to his **b**: Ezk 33:30
sword will be against his **b**. Ezk 38:21
a daughter, a **b**, or an unmarried Ezk 44:25
he pursued his **b** with the sword. Am 1:11
violence done to your **b** Jacob. Ob 10
gloat over your **b** in the day of Ob 12
"Wasn't Esau Jacob's **b**?" Mal 1:2
called Peter, and his **b** Andrew. Mt 4:18
son of Zebedee, and his **b** John. Mt 4:21
angry with his **b** will be subject Mt 5:22
And whoever says to his **b**, Mt 5:22
that your **b** has something Mt 5:23
and be reconciled with your **b**, Mt 5:24
Or how can you say to your **b**, Mt 7:4
called Peter, and Andrew his **b**; Mt 10:2
son of Zebedee, and John his **b**; Mt 10:2
B will betray brother to death, Mt 10:21
Brother will betray **b** to death, Mt 10:21
that person is My **b** and sister Mt 12:50
Herodias, his **b** Philip's wife, Mt 14:3
James, and his **b** John, and led Mt 17:1
If your **b** sins against you, Mt 18:15
to you, you have won your **b**. Mt 18:15
times could my **b** sin against me Mt 18:21
forgive his **b** from his heart. Mt 18:35
his **b** is to marry his wife and Mt 22:24
raise up offspring for his **b**. Mt 22:24
he left his wife to his **b**. Mt 22:25
saw Simon and Andrew, Simon's **b**. Mk 1:16
son of Zebedee and his **b** John. Mk 1:19
and to his **b** John, He gave Mk 3:17
will of God is My **b** and sister Mk 3:35
James, and John, James' **b**. Mk 5:37
Mary, and the **b** of James, Joses Mk 6:3
Herodias, his **b** Philip's wife, Mk 6:17
for us that if a man's **b** dies, Mk 12:19
his **b** should take the wife and Mk 12:19
and produce offspring for his **b**. Mk 12:19
Then **b** will betray brother to Mk 13:12
brother will betray **b** to death, Mk 13:12
his **b** Philip tetrarch of the Lk 3:1
named Peter, and Andrew his **b**; Lk 6:14
Or how can you say to your **b**, Lk 6:42
your brother, '**B**, let me take Lk 6:42
tell my **b** to divide the Lk 12:13
'Your **b** is here,' he told him, Lk 15:27
because this **b** of yours was dead Lk 15:32
If your **b** sins, rebuke him, and Lk 17:3
us that if a man's **b** has a wife, Lk 20:28
his **b** should take the wife and Lk 20:28
and produce offspring for his **b**. Lk 20:28
Simon Peter's **b**, was one of the Jn 1:40
found his own **b** Simon and told Jn 1:41
Simon Peter's **b**, said to Him, Jn 6:8
and it was her **b** Lazarus who was Jn 11:2
to comfort them about their **b**. Jn 11:19
been here, my **b** wouldn't have Jn 11:21
"Your **b** will rise again," Jesus Jn 11:23
my **b** would not have died!" Jn 11:32
him and said, "**B** Saul, the Lord Ac 9:17
James, John's **b**, with the sword. Ac 12:2
said, "You see, **b**, how many Ac 21:20
me, and said, '**B** Saul, regain Ac 22:13
why do you criticize your **b**? Rm 14:10
why do you look down on your **b**? Rm 14:10
if your **b** is hurt by what you Rm 14:15
that makes your **b** stumble. Rm 14:21
and our **b** Quartus greet you. Rm 16:23
God's will, and our **b** Sosthenes: 1Co 1:1
the name of **b** who is sexually 1Co 5:11
b goes to law against brother, 1Co 6:6
brother goes to law against **b**, 1Co 6:6
any **b** has an unbelieving wife, 1Co 7:12
A **b** or a sister is not bound in 1Co 7:15
the **b** for whom Christ died, 1Co 8:11
if food causes my **b** to fall, 1Co 8:13
that I won't cause my **b** to fall. 1Co 8:13
About our **b** Apollos: 1Co 16:12
God's will, and Timothy our **b**: 2Co 1:1
I did not find my **b** Titus, 2Co 2:13
have sent the **b** who is praised 2Co 8:18
with them our **b** whom we have 2Co 8:22
and I sent the **b** with him. 2Co 12:18
except James, the Lord's **b**. Gl 1:19
our dearly loved **b** and faithful Eph 6:21
Epaphroditus—my **b**, co-worker, Php 2:25
God's will, and Timothy our **b**: Col 1:1
Tychicus, a loved **b**, a faithful Col 4:7
and loved **b**, who is one of you Col 4:9
our **b** and God's co-worker in the 1Th 3:2
defraud his **b** in this matter, 1Th 4:6
keep away from every **b** who walks 2Th 3:6
an enemy, but warn him as a **b**. 2Th 3:15
Jesus, and Timothy, our **b**: Phm 1
been refreshed through you, **b**. Phm 7
a slave—as a dearly loved **b**. Phm 16
Yes, **b**, may I have joy from you Phm 20
and each his **b**, saying, 'Know Heb 8:11
aware that our **b** Timothy has Heb 13:23
The **b** of humble circumstances Jms 1:9
If a **b** or sister is without Jms 2:15
who criticizes a **b** or judges his Jms 4:11
or judges his **b** criticizes the Jms 4:11
whom I consider a faithful **b**, 1Pt 5:12
as our dear **b** Paul, according 2Pt 3:15
but hates his **b** is in the 1Jn 2:9
one who loves his **b** remains in 1Jn 2:10
one who hates his **b** is in the 1Jn 2:11
the one who does not love his **b**. 1Jn 3:10
the evil one and murdered his **b**. 1Jn 3:12
who hates his **b** is a murderer, 1Jn 3:15
and sees his **b** in need but shuts 1Jn 3:17
yet hates his **b**, he is a liar. 1Jn 4:20
not love his **b** whom he has seen 1Jn 4:20
loves God must also love his **b**. 1Jn 4:21
anyone sees his **b** committing a 1Jn 5:16
Jesus Christ, and a **b** of James: Jd 1
your **b** and partner in the Rv 1:9

BROTHER'S *(26)*

"Am I my **b** guardian?" Gn 4:9
b blood cries out to Me from Gn 4:10
to receive your **b** blood you have Gn 4:11
days until your **b** anger subsides Gn 27:44
until your **b** rage turns away Gn 27:45
Onan, "Sleep with your **b** wife. Gn 38:8
he slept with his **b** wife, Gn 38:9
intercourse with your **b** wife; Lv 18:16
If a man marries his **b** wife, Lv 20:21
If you see your **b** ox or sheep Dt 22:1
If you see your **b** donkey or ox Dt 22:4
preserve his **b** name in Israel. Dt 25:7
will not build up his **b** house.' Dt 25:9
wine in their oldest **b** house, Jb 1:13
wine in their oldest **b** house. Jb 1:18
don't go to your **b** house in your Pr 27:10
the womb he grasped his **b** heel, Hs 12:3
will fall, each by his **b** sword. Hg 2:22
speck in your **b** eye but don't Mt 7:3
the speck out of your **b** eye. Mt 7:5
for you to have your **b** wife!" Mk 6:18
Herodias, his **b** wife, and about Lk 3:19
look at the speck in your **b** eye, Lk 6:41
out the speck in your **b** eye. Lk 6:42
block or pitfall in your **b** way. Rm 14:13
evil, and his **b** were righteous. 1Jn 3:12

BROTHER-IN-LAW *(5)*

your duty as her **b** and produce Gn 38:8
b is to take her as his wife, Dt 25:5
perform the duty of a **b** for her. Dt 25:5
'My **b** refuses to preserve his Dt 25:7
perform the duty of a **b** for me.' Dt 25:7

BROTHERHOOD *(3)*

to Edom and broke a treaty of **b**. Am 1:9

annulling the **b** between Judah Zch 11:14
Love the **b**. Fear God. Honor 1Pt 2:17

BROTHERLY *(5)*

to one another with **b** love. Rm 12:10
About **b** love: you don't need me 1Th 4:9
Let **b** love continue. Heb 13:1
godliness with **b** affection, 2Pt 1:7
and **b** affection with love. 2Pt 1:7

BROTHERS *(464)*

and told his two **b** outside. Gn 9:22
the lowest of slaves to his **b**. Gn 9:25
live at odds with all his **b**. Gn 16:12
Don't do ⌊this⌋ evil, my **b**. Gn 19:7
in opposition to all his **b**. Gn 25:18
Be master over your **b**; Gn 27:29
the men at the well, "My **b**! Gn 29:4
and Laban and his **b** also pitched Gn 31:25
said to Dinah's father and **b**, Gn 34:11
and Levi, Dinah's **b**, took their Gn 34:25
Joseph tended sheep with his **b**. Gn 37:2
When his **b** saw that their father Gn 37:4
loved him more than all his **b**, Gn 37:4
told it to his **b**, they hated him Gn 37:5
his **b** asked him. Gn 37:8
dream and told it to his **b**. Gn 37:9
his father and **b**, but his father Gn 37:10
your mother and **b** and I going to Gn 37:10
His **b** were jealous of him, Gn 37:11
His **b** had gone to pasture their Gn 37:12
Joseph, "Your **b**, you know, are Gn 37:13
see how your **b** and the flocks Gn 37:14
looking for my **b**," Joseph said. Gn 37:16
out after his **b** and found them Gn 37:17
When Joseph came to his **b**, Gn 37:23
Then Judah said to his **b**, Gn 37:26
our ⌊own⌋ flesh." His **b** agreed. Gn 37:27
He went back to his **b** and said, Gn 37:30
Judah left his **b** and settled Gn 38:1
10 of Joseph's **b** went down to Gn 42:3
brother Benjamin with his **b**, Gn 42:4
His **b** came and bowed down before Gn 42:6
Joseph saw his **b**, he recognized Gn 42:7
Joseph recognized his **b**, Gn 42:8
were 12 **b**, the sons of one Gn 42:13
He said to his **b**, "My money has Gn 42:28
We were 12 **b**, sons of the same Gn 42:32
by himself, his **b** by themselves, Gn 43:32
Judah and his **b** reached Joseph's Gn 44:14
Let him go back with his **b**. Gn 44:33
revealed his identity to his **b**. Gn 45:1
said to his **b**, "I am Joseph! Gn 45:3
But his **b** were too terrified to Gn 45:3
Then Joseph said to his **b**, Gn 45:4
kissed each of his **b** as he wept, Gn 45:15
afterward his **b** talked with him Gn 45:15
house, "Joseph's **b** have come," Gn 45:16
Joseph, "Tell your **b**, 'Do this: Gn 45:17
gave each of the **b** changes of Gn 45:22
Joseph sent his **b** on their way, Gn 45:24
Joseph said to his **b** and to his Gn 46:31
My **b** and my father's household, Gn 46:31
My father and my **b**, with their Gn 47:1
took five of his **b** and presented Gn 47:2
Then Pharaoh asked his **b**, Gn 47:3
your father and **b** have come to Gn 47:5
your father and **b** in the best Gn 47:6
his father and **b** in the land of Gn 47:11
his father, his **b**, and all his Gn 47:12
names of their **b** with regard to Gn 48:6
above what I am giving your **b**, Gn 48:22
Simeon and Levi are **b**; Gn 49:5
Judah, your **b** will praise you. Gn 49:8
crown of the prince of his **b**. Gn 49:26
household, his **b**, and his Gn 50:8
Egypt with his **b** and all who had Gn 50:14
When Joseph's **b** saw that their Gn 50:15
Then his **b** also came to him, Gn 50:18
said to his **b**, "I am about to Gn 50:24
Joseph and all his **b** and all Ex 1:6
However, your **b**, the whole house Lv 10:6
who is highest among his **b**, Lv 21:10
your **b**, the Israelites Lv 25:46
One of his **b** may redeem him. Lv 25:48
He may assist his **b** to fulfill Nm 8:26
But also bring your **b** with you Nm 18:2
when our **b** perished before Nm 20:3
property among our father's **b**." Nm 27:4
their father's **b** and transfer Nm 27:7
give his inheritance to his **b**. Nm 27:9
If he has no **b**, give his Nm 27:10
inheritance to his father's **b**. Nm 27:10
If his father has no **b**, give his Nm 27:11
Should your **b** go to war while Nm 32:6
Hear ⌊the cases⌋ between your **b**, Dt 1:16
Our **b** have discouraged us, Dt 1:28
through the territory of your **b**, Dt 2:4
we bypassed our **b**, the Dt 2:8
ahead of your **b** the Israelites. Dt 3:18
rest to your **b** as He has to you Dt 3:20
or inheritance like his **b**; Dt 10:9
one of your **b** within any of your Dt 15:7
Appoint a king from your **b**. Dt 17:15
has no inheritance among his **b**, Dt 18:2
like me from among your own **b**. Dt 18:15
like you from among their **b**. Dt 18:18
one of his Israelite **b**, Dt 24:7
whether one of your **b** or one of Dt 24:14
When **b** live on the same property Dt 25:5
He disregarded his **b** and didn't Dt 33:9
crown of the prince of his **b**. Dt 33:16
among his **b** and dip his foot Dt 33:24
ahead of your **b** and help them Jos 1:14
until the LORD gives our **b** rest, Jos 1:15
father, mother, **b**, sisters, and Jos 2:13
father, mother, **b**, and all your Jos 2:18
father, mother, **b**, and all who Jos 6:23
My **b** who went with me caused the Jos 14:8
among their father's **b**, Jos 17:4
deserted your **b** even once this Jos 22:3
that He has given your **b** rest, Jos 22:4
half, with their **b**, on the west Jos 22:7
of your enemies with your **b**." Jos 22:8
They were my **b**, the sons of my Jdg 8:19
to his mother's **b** at Shechem and Jdg 9:1
in Ophrah and killed his 70 **b**, Jdg 9:5
who had helped him kill his **b**. Jdg 9:24
Ebed came with his **b** and crossed Jdg 9:26
Ebed, with his **b**, have come to Jdg 9:31
Gaal and his **b** from Shechem. Jdg 9:41
killing his 70 **b**, God turned Jdg 9:56
fled from his **b** and lived in the Jdg 11:3
Then his **b** and his father's Jdg 16:31
the land of Laish told their **b**, Jdg 18:14
No, don't do ⌊this⌋ evil, my **b**. Jdg 19:23
against our **b** the Benjaminites? Jdg 20:23
against our **b** the Benjaminites Jdg 20:28
had compassion on their **b**, Jdg 21:6
their fathers or **b** come to us Jdg 21:22
him in the presence of his **b**, 1Sm 16:13
of bread for your **b** and hurry to 1Sm 17:17
the welfare of your **b** and bring 1Sm 17:18
he asked his **b** how they were. 1Sm 17:22
let me go so I can see my **b**.' 1Sm 20:29
When David's **b** and his father's 1Sm 22:1
David said, "My **b**, you must not 1Sm 30:23
to stop pursuing their **b**?" 2Sm 2:26
pursuing their **b** until morning." 2Sm 2:27
Saul, to his **b**, and to his 2Sm 3:8
back and take your **b** with you. 2Sm 15:20
are my **b**, my flesh and blood. 2Sm 19:12
Why did our **b**, the men of Judah 2Sm 19:41
all his royal **b** and all the men 1Kg 1:9
up and fight against your **b**, 1Kg 12:24
was more honorable than his **b**. 1Ch 4:9
but his **b** did not have many 1Ch 4:27
among his **b** and a ruler came 1Ch 5:2
heads and their younger **b** alike. 1Ch 24:31
his sons, and his **b**—12⌊⌊to⌋ 1Ch 25:9
him, his **b**, and his sons—12 1Ch 25:9
Zaccur, his sons, and his **b**—12 1Ch 25:10
Izri, his sons, and his **b**—12 1Ch 25:11
his sons, and his **b**—12 1Ch 25:12
Bukkiah, his sons, and his **b**— 1Ch 25:13
his sons, and his **b**—12 1Ch 25:14
his sons, and his **b**—12 1Ch 25:15
his sons, and his **b**—12 1Ch 25:16
Shimei, his sons, and his **b**—12 1Ch 25:17
Azarel, his sons, and his **b**—12 1Ch 25:18
his sons, and his **b**—12 1Ch 25:19
Shubael, his sons, and his **b**— 1Ch 25:20
his sons, and his **b**—12 1Ch 25:21
his sons, and his **b**—12 1Ch 25:22
his sons, and his **b**—12 1Ch 25:23
his sons, and his **b**—12 1Ch 25:24
Hanani, his sons, and his **b**—12 1Ch 25:25
his sons, and his **b**—12 1Ch 25:26
his sons, and his **b**—12 1Ch 25:27
Hothir, his sons, and his **b**—12 1Ch 25:28
his sons, and his **b**—12 1Ch 25:29
his sons, and his **b**—12 1Ch 25:30
his sons, and his **b**—12. 1Ch 25:31
his **b** Elihu and Semachiah were 1Ch 26:7
Obed-edom with their sons and **b**; 1Ch 26:8
had sons and **b** who were capable 1Ch 26:9
The sons and **b** of Hosah were 13 1Ch 26:11
temple, just as their **b** did. 1Ch 26:12
and his **b** were in charge 1Ch 26:26
the care of Shelomith and his **b**. 1Ch 26:28
Judah, Elihu, one of David's **b**; 1Ch 27:18
to me, my **b** and my people. 1Ch 28:2
up and fight against your **b**. 2Ch 11:4
leader among his **b**, intending to 2Ch 11:22
to you from your **b** who dwell in 2Ch 19:10
will not come on you and your **b**. 2Ch 19:10
He had **b**, sons of Jehoshaphat: 2Ch 21:2
sword all his **b** as well as some 2Ch 21:4
and also have killed your **b**, 2Ch 21:13
of Ahaziah's **b** who were serving 2Ch 22:8
200,000 captives from their **b**— 2Ch 28:8
captives you took from your **b**, 2Ch 28:11
City of Palms, among their **b**. 2Ch 28:15
They gathered their **b** together, 2Ch 29:15
so their Levite **b** helped them 2Ch 29:34
fathers and your **b** who were 2Ch 30:7
your **b** and your sons ⌊will 2Ch 30:9
to their **b** by divisions, 2Ch 31:15
the ancestral houses for your **b**, 2Ch 35:5
for your **b** to carry out the word 2Ch 35:6
Conaniah and his **b** Shemaiah and 2Ch 35:9
Because their Levite **b** had made 2Ch 35:15
Jozadak and his **b** the priests Ezr 3:2
and his **b** began to build Ezr 3:2
the rest of their **b**, including Ezr 3:8
Jeshua with his sons and **b**, Ezr 3:9
their sons and **b**, the Levites, Ezr 3:9
their priestly **b**, and all the Ezr 6:20
to you and your **b** with the rest Ezr 7:18
a message for him and his **b**, Ezr 8:17
along with his sons and **b**, Ezr 8:18
and his **b** and their sons, Ezr 8:19
Hashabiah, and 10 of their **b**. Ezr 8:24
Jeshua son of Jozadak and his **b**: Ezr 10:18
one of my **b**, arrived with men Neh 1:2
And I, my **b**, my men, and the Neh 4:23
as well as my **b** and my servants, Neh 5:10
and their **b** Shebaniah, Hodiah, Neh 10:10
with their noble **b** and commit Neh 10:29
My **b** are as treacherous as a Jb 6:15
He has removed my **b** from me; Jb 19:13
from your **b** without cause, Jb 22:6
All his **b**, sisters, and former Jb 42:11
an inheritance with their **b**. Jb 42:15
will proclaim Your name to my **b**; Ps 22:22
stranger to my **b** and a foreigner Ps 69:8
Because of my **b** and friends, Ps 122:8
it is when **b** can live together! Ps 133:1
who stirs up trouble among **b**. Pr 6:19
share an inheritance among **b**. Pr 17:2
the **b** of a poor man hate him; Pr 19:7
Your **b** who hate and exclude you Is 66:5
will bring all your **b** from all Is 66:20
as I drove out all of your **b**, Jr 7:15
Even your **b**—your own father's Jr 12:6
concerning your **b** who did not go Jr 29:16
and his **b** and all his sons— Jr 35:3
Call your **b**: My People and your Hs 2:1
he flourishes among ⌊his⌋ **b**, Hs 13:15
the rest of His **b** will return to Mc 5:3
Jacob fathered Judah and his **b**, Mt 1:2
Jechoniah and his **b** at the time Mt 1:11
He saw two **b**, Simon, who was Mt 4:18
saw two other **b**, James the son Mt 4:21
And if you greet only your **b**, Mt 5:47
His mother and **b** were standing Mt 12:46
mother and Your **b** are standing Mt 12:47
is My mother and who are My **b**?" Mt 12:48
Here are My mother and My **b**! Mt 12:49
Mary, and His **b** James, Joseph, Mt 13:55
has left houses, **b** or sisters, Mt 19:29
became indignant with the two **b**. Mt 20:24
Now there were seven **b** among us. Mt 22:25
one Teacher, and you are all **b**. Mt 23:8
of the least of these **b** of Mine, Mt 25:40
Go and tell My **b** to leave for Mt 28:10

Then His mother and His **b** came, Mk 3:31
mother, Your **b**, and Your sisters Mk 3:32
"Who are My mother and My **b**?" Mk 3:33
Here are My mother and My **b**! Mk 3:34
has left house, **b** or sisters, Mk 10:29
time—houses, **b** and sisters, Mk 10:30
There were seven **b**. Mk 12:20
His mother and **b** came to Him, Lk 8:19
mother and Your **b** are standing Lk 8:20
My mother and My **b** are those who Lk 8:21
friends, your **b**, your relatives, Lk 14:12
and children, **b** and sisters— Lk 14:26
I have five **b**—to warn them, so Lk 16:28
a house, wife or **b**, parents or Lk 18:29
Now there were seven **b**. Lk 20:29
by parents, **b**, relatives, Lk 21:16
turned back, strengthen your **b**." Lk 22:32
His mother, His **b**, and His Jn 2:12
His **b** said to Him, "Leave here Jn 7:3
not even His **b** believed in Him. Jn 7:5
After His **b** had gone up to the Jn 7:10
go to My **b** and tell them that Jn 20:17
spread to the **b** that this Jn 21:23
the mother of Jesus, and His **b**. Ac 1:14
Peter stood up among the **b**— Ac 1:15
B, the Scripture had to be Ac 1:16
B, I can confidently speak to Ac 2:29
"**B**, what must we do?" Ac 2:37
And now, **b**, I know that you did Ac 3:17
like me from among your **b**. Ac 3:22
Therefore, **b**, select from among Ac 6:3
"**B** and fathers," he said, Ac 7:2
Joseph was revealed to his **b**, Ac 7:13
he decided to visit his **b**, Ac 7:23
assumed his **b** would understand Ac 7:25
saying, 'Men, you are **b**. Ac 7:26
like me from among your **b**. Ac 7:37
When the **b** found out, they took Ac 9:30
some of the **b** from Joppa went Ac 10:23
apostles and the **b** who were Ac 11:1
These six **b** accompanied me, Ac 11:12
relief to the **b** who lived in Ac 11:29
things to James and the **b**," Ac 12:17
them, saying, "**B**, if you have Ac 13:15
B, sons of Abraham's race, and Ac 13:26
be known to you, **b**, that through Ac 13:38
of the Gentiles against the **b**. Ac 14:2
Judea and began to teach the **b**: Ac 15:1
great joy among all the **b**. Ac 15:3
B, you are aware that in the Ac 15:7
responded: "**B**, listen to me! Ac 15:13
both leading men among the **b**. Ac 15:22
elders, your **b**, To the brothers Ac 15:23
To the **b** from among the Gentiles Ac 15:23
the **b** and strengthened Ac 15:32
in peace by the **b** to those who Ac 15:33
and visit the **b** in every town Ac 15:36
the grace of the Lord by the **b**. Ac 15:40
b at Lystra and Iconium spoke Ac 16:2
they saw and encouraged the **b**, Ac 16:40
some of the **b** before the city Ac 17:6
the **b** sent Paul and Silas off to Ac 17:10
Then the **b** immediately sent Paul Ac 17:14
good-bye to the **b** and sailed Ac 18:18
the **b** wrote to the disciples Ac 18:27
we greeted the **b** and stayed with Ac 21:7
Jerusalem, the **b** welcomed us Ac 21:17
B and fathers, listen now to my Ac 22:1
letters from them to the **b**, Ac 22:5
and said, "**B**, I have lived my Ac 23:1
"I did not know, **b**," Paul said, Ac 23:5
the Sanhedrin, "**B**, I am a Ac 23:6
with the Twin **B** as its Ac 28:11
B, although I have done nothing Ac 28:17
none of the **b** has come and Ac 28:21
you to know, **b**, that I often Rm 1:13
understand law, **b**, are you Rm 7:1
Therefore, my **b**, you also were Rm 7:4
So then, **b**, we are not obligated Rm 8:12
be the firstborn among many **b**. Rm 8:29
Messiah for the benefit of my **b**, Rm 9:3
B, my heart's desire and prayer Rm 10:1
be conceited, **b**, I do not want Rm 11:25
Therefore, **b**, by the mercies of Rm 12:1
my **b**, I myself am convinced Rm 15:14
I implore you, **b**, through the Rm 15:30
and the **b** who are with them. Rm 16:14
I implore you, **b**, watch out for Rm 16:17
Now I urge you, **b**, in the name 1Co 1:10
me about you, my **b**, by members 1Co 1:11
B, consider your calling: 1Co 1:26
I came to you, **b**, announcing 1Co 2:1
B, I was not able to speak to 1Co 3:1
Now, **b**, I have applied these 1Co 4:6
able to arbitrate between his **b**? 1Co 6:5
and cheat—and this to **b**! 1Co 6:8
B, each person should remain 1Co 7:24
And I say this, **b**: the time is 1Co 7:29
against the **b** and wound their 1Co 8:12
the Lord's **b**, and Cephas? 1Co 9:5
you to know, **b**, that our fathers 1Co 10:1
Therefore, my **b**, when you come 1Co 11:33
b, I do not want you to be 1Co 12:1
But now, **b**, if I come to you 1Co 14:6
B, don't be childish in your 1Co 14:20
How is it then, **b**? Whenever you 1Co 14:26
Therefore, my **b**, be eager to 1Co 14:39
Now **b**, I want to clarify for you 1Co 15:1
to over 500 **b** at one time, 1Co 15:6
B, I tell you this: 1Co 15:50
my dear **b**, be steadfast, 1Co 15:58
I am expecting him with the **b**. 1Co 16:11
him to come to you with the **b**, 1Co 16:12
B, you know the household of 1Co 16:15
All the **b** greet you. 1Co 16:20
to be unaware, **b**, of our 2Co 1:8
you to know, **b**, about the grace 2Co 8:1
as for our **b**, they are the 2Co 8:23
But I sent the **b** so our boasting 2Co 9:3
to urge the **b** to go on ahead to 2Co 9:5
the **b** who came from Macedonia 2Co 11:9
and dangers among false **b**; 2Co 11:26
Finally, **b**, rejoice. 2Co 13:11
and all the **b** who are with me: Gl 1:2
you to know, **b**, that the gospel Gl 1:11
because of false **b** smuggled Gl 2:4
B, I'm using a human Gl 3:15
beg you, **b**: become like me, for Gl 4:12
Now you, **b**, like Isaac, are Gl 4:28
Therefore, **b**, we are not Gl 4:31
Now **b**, if I still preach Gl 5:11
you are called to freedom, **b**; Gl 5:13
B, if someone is caught in any Gl 6:1
B, the grace of our Lord Jesus Gl 6:18
Peace to the **b**, and love with Eph 6:23
you to know, **b**, that what has Php 1:12
Most of the **b** in the Lord have Php 1:14
Finally, my **b**, rejoice in the Php 3:1
B, I do not consider myself to Php 3:13
in imitating me, **b**, and observe Php 3:17
my dearly loved **b**, my joy and Php 4:1
Finally **b**, whatever is true, Php 4:8
Those **b** who are with me greet Php 4:21
saints and faithful **b** in Christ Col 1:2
greetings to the **b** in Laodicea, Col 4:15
your election, **b** loved by God. 1Th 1:4
know, **b**, that our visit 1Th 2:1
our labor and hardship, **b**. 1Th 2:9
For you, **b**, became imitators of 1Th 2:14
But as for us, **b**, after we were 1Th 2:17
Therefore, **b**, in all our 1Th 3:7
Finally then, **b**, we ask and 1Th 4:1
toward all the **b** in the entire 1Th 4:10
encourage you, **b**, to do so even 1Th 4:10
be uninformed, **b**, concerning 1Th 4:13
b, you do not need anything to 1Th 5:1
But you, **b**, are not in the dark, 1Th 5:4
Now we ask you, **b**, to give 1Th 5:12
And we exhort you, **b**: 1Th 5:14
B, pray for us also. 1Th 5:25
all the **b** with a holy kiss. 1Th 5:26
letter be read to all the **b**. 1Th 5:27
God for you, **b**, which is fitting 2Th 1:3
gathered to Him: we ask you, **b**, 2Th 2:1
God for you, **b** loved by the Lord 2Th 2:13
Therefore, **b**, stand firm and 2Th 2:15
pray for us, **b**, that the Lord's 2Th 3:1
command you, **b**, in the name of 2Th 3:6
B, do not grow weary in doing 2Th 3:13
point these things out to the **b**, 1Tm 4:6
as a father, younger men as **b**, 1Tm 5:1
to them because they are **b**, 1Tm 6:2
Linus, Claudia, and all the **b**. 2Tm 4:21
is not ashamed to call them **b**, Heb 2:11
will proclaim Your name to My **b**; Heb 2:12
to be like His **b** in every way, Heb 2:17
holy **b** and companions in a Heb 3:1
out, **b**, so that there won't Heb 3:12
is, from their **b**—though they Heb 7:5
Therefore, **b**, since we have Heb 10:19
B, I urge you to receive this Heb 13:22
a great joy, my **b**, whenever you Jms 1:2
be deceived, my dearly loved **b**. Jms 1:16
My dearly loved **b**, understand Jms 1:19
My **b**, hold your faith in our Jms 2:1
Listen, my dear **b**: Didn't God Jms 2:5
is it, my **b**, if someone says Jms 2:14
teachers, my **b**, knowing that we Jms 3:1
My **b**, these things should not be Jms 3:10
olives, my **b**, or a grapevine Jms 3:12
Don't criticize one another, **b**. Jms 4:11
Therefore, **b**, be patient until Jms 5:7
B, do not complain about one Jms 5:9
B, take the prophets who spoke Jms 5:10
above all, my **b**, do not swear, Jms 5:12
My **b**, if any among you strays Jms 5:19
for sincere love of the **b**, 1Pt 1:22
by your **b** in the world. 1Pt 5:9
Therefore, **b**, make every effort 2Pt 1:10
be surprised, **b**, if the world 1Jn 3:13
to life because we love our **b**. 1Jn 3:14
lay down our lives for our **b**. 1Jn 3:16
glad when some **b** came and 3Jn 3
by whatever you do for the **b**, 3Jn 5
to welcome the **b** himself, 3Jn 10
their fellow slaves and their **b**, Rv 6:11
accuser of our **b** has been thrown Rv 12:10
with you and your **b** who have the Rv 19:10
with you, your **b** the prophets, Rv 22:9

BROTHERS' *(2)*

forgive your **b** transgression Gn 50:17
so that his **b** hearts won't melt Dt 20:8

BROUGHT *(683)*

The earth **b** forth vegetation: Gn 1:12
b each to the man to see what Gn 2:19
a woman and **b** her to the man. Gn 2:22
reached out and **b** her into the Gn 8:9
He **b** back all the goods and also Gn 14:16
king of Salem, **b** out bread and Gn 14:18
I am the LORD who **b** you from Ur Gn 15:7
So he **b** all these to Him, split Gn 15:10
little water be **b**, that you may Gn 18:4
b Lot into the house with them, Gn 19:10
And they **b** him out and left him Gn 19:16
Abraham and **b** Lot out of the Gn 19:29
of Gerar had Sarah **b** to him. Gn 20:2
that you have **b** such enormous Gn 20:9
and water was **b** to wash his feet Gn 24:32
Then he **b** out objects of silver Gn 24:53
And Isaac **b** her into the tent of Gn 24:67
you would have **b** guilt on us." Gn 26:10
and got them and **b** them to his Gn 27:14
Jacob **b** it to him, and he ate; Gn 27:25
he **b** him wine, and he drank. Gn 27:25
food and **b** it to his father. Gn 27:31
who hunted game and **b** it to me? Gn 27:33
When he **b** them to his mother Gn 30:14
incensed and **b** charges against Gn 31:36
of what he had **b** with him as a Gn 32:13
He took them and **b** them across Gn 32:23
my present that was **b** to you, Gn 33:11
You have **b** trouble on me, Gn 34:30
and he **b** a bad report about them Gn 37:2
As she was being **b** out, she sent Gn 38:25
Ishmaelites who had **b** him there. Gn 39:1
my husband **b** a Hebrew man to us Gn 39:14
slave you **b** to us came to me Gn 39:17
and they quickly **b** him from the Gn 41:14
they had **b** back from Egypt, Gn 43:2
had said and **b** them to Joseph's Gn 43:17
We have been **b** here because of Gn 43:18
and we have **b** it back with us. Gn 43:21
We have **b** additional money with Gn 43:22
Then he **b** Simeon out to them. Gn 43:23
The man **b** the men into Joseph's Gn 43:24
they **b** him the gift they had Gn 43:26
We even **b** back to you from the Gn 44:8
will have **b** the gray hairs Gn 44:31
offspring, he **b** with him to Gn 46:7
They have **b** their sheep and Gn 46:32
Joseph then **b** his father Jacob Gn 47:7
and he **b** the money to Pharaoh's Gn 47:14
So they **b** their livestock to Gn 47:17
Joseph **b** them to him, and he Gn 48:10

right—and **b** them to Israel. Gn 48:13
she **b** him to Pharaoh's daughter, Ex 2:10
practices and **b** frogs up onto Ex 8:7
that He had **b** against Pharaoh. Ex 8:12
field and not **b** inside will die Ex 9:19
Aaron were **b** back to Pharaoh. Ex 10:8
east wind had **b** in the locusts. Ex 10:13
this very day I **b** your ranks out Ex 12:17
dough they had **b** out of Egypt Ex 12:39
day the LORD **b** the Israelites Ex 12:51
for the LORD **b** you out of here Ex 13:3
for the LORD **b** you out of Egypt Ex 13:9
hand the LORD **b** us out of Egypt, Ex 13:14
for the LORD **b** us out of Egypt Ex 13:16
the LORD **b** the waters of the sea Ex 15:19
you **b** us into this wilderness to Ex 16:3
the LORD who **b** you out of the Ex 16:6
wilderness when I **b** you out of Ex 16:32
how the LORD had **b** Israel out of Ex 18:1
b a burnt offering and Ex 18:12
eagles' wings and **b** you to Me. Ex 19:4
So Moses **b** the people's words Ex 19:8
Then Moses **b** the people out of Ex 19:17
who **b** you out of the land of Ex 20:2
who **b** them out of the land of Ex 29:46
man who **b** us up from the land Ex 32:1
their ears and **b** ⌊them⌋ to Aaron Ex 32:3
b you up from the land of Egypt! Ex 32:4
your people you **b** up from the Ex 32:7
who **b** you up from the land of Ex 32:8
people You **b** out of the land Ex 32:11
'He **b** them out with an evil Ex 32:12
man who **b** us up from the land Ex 32:23
Therefore you have **b** a blessing Ex 32:29
people you **b** up from the land Ex 33:1
him came and **b** an offering to Ex 35:21
had willing hearts **b** brooches, Ex 35:22
red or manatee skins, **b** ⌊them⌋. Ex 35:23
or bronze **b** it to the LORD. Ex 35:24
for any task in the work **b** ⌊it⌋. Ex 35:24
yarn⌋ with her hands and **b** it: Ex 35:25
The leaders **b** onyx and gemstones Ex 35:27
So the Israelites **b** a freewill Ex 35:29
Israelites had **b** for the task Ex 36:3
Then they **b** the tabernacle to Ex 39:33
b the ark into the tabernacle, Ex 40:21
blood has been **b** into the tent Lv 6:30
Then he **b** the bull near for the Lv 8:14
They **b** what Moses had commanded Lv 9:5
Aaron's sons **b** the blood to him, Lv 9:9
Aaron's sons **b** him the blood, Lv 9:12
They **b** him the burnt offering Lv 9:13
Aaron's sons **b** him the blood, Lv 9:18
also **b** the fat portions from Lv 9:19
its blood was not **b** inside the Lv 10:18
who **b** you up from the land of Lv 11:45
is to be **b** to Aaron the priest Lv 13:2
he is to be **b** to the priest. Lv 13:9
He is to be **b** to the priest, Lv 14:2
and hyssop be **b** for the one who Lv 14:4
blood was **b** into the ⌊most⌋ Lv 16:27
must be **b** outside the camp and Lv 16:27
who **b** you out of the land of Lv 19:36
One who **b** you out of the land Lv 22:33
and you have **b** the offering of Lv 23:14
the day you **b** the sheaf of the Lv 23:15
in booths when I **b** them out of Lv 23:43
Name, and they **b** him to Moses. Lv 24:11
they **b** the one who had cursed to Lv 24:23
who **b** you out of the land of Lv 25:38
My slaves I **b** out of the land Lv 25:42
My slaves I **b** out of the land Lv 25:55
who **b** you out of the land of Lv 26:13
toward them and **b** them into the Lv 26:41
I **b** out of the land of Egypt Lv 26:45
that may be **b** as an offering to Lv 27:9
that may not be **b** as an offering Lv 27:11
If the one who **b** it decides to Lv 27:13
he must be **b** to the entrance to Nm 6:13
They **b** as their offering before Nm 7:3
Why have You **b** such trouble on Nm 11:11
He **b** 70 men from the elders of Nm 11:24
that she may be **b** back in." Nm 12:14
move on until Miriam was **b** back Nm 12:15
They **b** back a report for them Nm 13:26
strength You **b** up this people Nm 14:13
gathering wood **b** him to Moses, Nm 15:33
entire community **b** him outside Nm 15:36

LORD your God who **b** you out of Nm 15:41
He has **b** you near, and all your Nm 16:10
enough that you **b** us up from a Nm 16:13
Moses then **b** out all the staffs Nm 17:9
of the contributions **b** to Me. Nm 18:8
he will have it **b** outside the Nm 19:3
Why have you **b** the LORD's Nm 20:4
an Angel, and **b** us out of Egypt. Nm 20:16
took Balaam and **b** him to Nm 22:41
Balak **b** me from Aram; Nm 23:7
I **b** you to curse my enemies, Nm 23:11
God **b** them out of Egypt; Nm 23:22
God **b** him out of Egypt; Nm 24:8
Moses **b** their case before the Nm 27:5
They **b** the prisoners, animals, Nm 31:12
of hundreds and **b** it into the Nm 31:54
until we have **b** them into their Nm 32:17
down to us, and **b** us back a Dt 1:25
'The LORD **b** us out of the land Dt 1:27
selected you and **b** you out of Dt 4:20
them and **b** you out of Egypt Dt 4:37
who **b** you out of the land of Dt 5:6
LORD your God **b** you out of there Dt 5:15
the LORD who **b** you out of the Dt 6:12
but the LORD **b** us out of Egypt Dt 6:21
but He **b** us from there in order Dt 6:23
He **b** you out with a strong hand Dt 7:8
the LORD your God **b** you out. Dt 7:19
LORD your God who **b** you out of Dt 8:14
He **b** water out of the flintlike Dt 8:15
'The LORD **b** me in to take Dt 9:4
your people you **b** out of Egypt Dt 9:12
greatness and **b** out of Egypt Dt 9:26
in the land you **b** us from will Dt 9:28
b them out to kill them in the Dt 9:28
whom You **b** out by Your great Dt 9:29
LORD your God who **b** you out of Dt 13:5
LORD your God who **b** you out of Dt 13:10
LORD your God **b** you out of Egypt Dt 16:1
who **b** you out of the land of Dt 20:1
Then the LORD **b** us out of Egypt Dt 26:8
I have now **b** the first of the Dt 26:10
with them when He **b** them out of Dt 29:25
and He **b** every curse written in Dt 29:27
forgot the God who **b** you forth. Dt 32:18
went in and **b** out Rahab and her Jos 6:23
They **b** out her whole family and Jos 6:23
b them to Joshua and all the Jos 7:23
and **b** them up to the Valley of Jos 7:24
of Ai alive and **b** him to Joshua. Jos 8:23
They **b** the five kings of Jos 10:23
they had **b** the kings to him, Jos 10:24
and I **b** back an honest report. Jos 14:7
portions of land and **b** it to me, Jos 18:6
which **b** a plague on the LORD's Jos 22:17
of Canaan and **b** back a report to Jos 22:32
and afterwards I **b** you out. Jos 24:5
When I **b** your fathers out of Jos 24:6
Egyptians, and **b** the sea over Jos 24:7
I **b** you to the land of the Jos 24:8
the LORD our God **b** us and our Jos 24:17
Israelites had **b** up from Egypt, Jos 24:32
They **b** him to Jerusalem, Jdg 1:7
I **b** you out of Egypt and led you Jdg 2:1
who had **b** them out of Egypt. Jdg 2:12
against them and **b** disaster ⌊on Jdg 2:15
and **b** the tribute to Eglon king Jdg 3:17
She **b** him curdled milk in a Jdg 5:25
'I **b** you out of Egypt and out of Jdg 6:8
the LORD **b** us out of Egypt Jdg 6:13
b them out and offered them to Jdg 6:19
So he **b** the people down to the Jdg 7:5
b the heads of Oreb and Zeeb Jdg 7:25
You have **b** great misery on me. Jdg 11:35
for the LORD **b** vengeance on your Jdg 11:36
tribe and **b** back 30 wives for Jdg 12:9
they **b** 30 men to accompany him. Jdg 14:11
leaders **b** her seven fresh Jdg 16:8
came to her and **b** the money with Jdg 16:18
b him down to Gaza and bound Jdg 16:21
So they **b** Samson from prison, Jdg 16:25
him and asked, "Who **b** you here? Jdg 18:3
So she **b** him to her father's Jdg 19:3
So he **b** him to his house and fed Jdg 19:21
and they **b** them to the camp at Jdg 21:12
the LORD has **b** me back empty. Ru 1:21
Then she **b** out what she had left Ru 2:18
the bull and **b** the boy to Eli. 1Sm 1:25

whatever the meat fork **b** up. 1Sm 2:14
b it into the temple of Dagon 1Sm 5:2
since the day I **b** them out of 1Sm 8:8
b them to the banquet hall, 1Sm 9:22
'I **b** Israel out of Egypt, and I 1Sm 10:18
Aaron and who **b** your ancestors 1Sm 12:6
My father has **b** trouble to the 1Sm 14:29
of the troops **b** his ox that 1Sm 14:34
The troops **b** them from the 1Sm 15:15
I **b** back Agag, king of Amalek, 1Sm 15:20
Saul, so he had David **b** to him. 1Sm 17:31
head and **b** it to Jerusalem, 1Sm 17:54
took him and **b** him before Saul 1Sm 17:57
He **b** their foreskins and 1Sm 18:27
and the LORD **b** about a great 1Sm 19:5
Then Jonathan **b** David to Saul, 1Sm 19:7
you have **b** me into a covenant 1Sm 20:8
people that you **b** this one to 1Sm 21:15
and he **b** an ephod with him. 1Sm 23:6
your servant has **b** to my lord, 1Sm 25:27
what she had **b** him and said, 1Sm 25:35
The LORD **b** Nabal's evil deeds 1Sm 25:39
or woman live to be **b** to Gath, 1Sm 27:11
the Philistines **b** their military 1Sm 28:1
The Philistines **b** all their 1Sm 29:1
So Abiathar **b** it to him, 1Sm 30:7
open country and **b** him to David. 1Sm 30:11
man who had **b** him the report, 2Sm 1:5
I've **b** them here to my lord." 2Sm 1:10
man who had **b** him the report, 2Sm 1:13
David **b** the men who were with 2Sm 2:3
from a raid and **b** a large amount 2Sm 3:22
They **b** him back from the well of 2Sm 3:26
They **b** Ish-bosheth's head to 2Sm 4:8
out ⌊to battle⌋ and **b** us back. 2Sm 5:2
b it with the ark of God from 2Sm 6:4
had the ark of God **b** up from 2Sm 6:12
They **b** the ark of the LORD and 2Sm 6:17
From the time I **b** the Israelites 2Sm 7:6
that You have **b** me this far? 2Sm 7:18
David's subjects and **b** tribute. 2Sm 8:2
David's subjects and **b** tribute. 2Sm 8:6
and **b** them to Jerusalem. 2Sm 8:7
David had him **b** from the house 2Sm 9:5
David had her **b** to his house. 2Sm 11:27
She **b** the pan and set it down in 2Sm 13:9
When she **b** ⌊them⌋ to him to eat, 2Sm 13:11
The king has not **b** back his own 2Sm 14:13
and **b** Absalom to Jerusalem. 2Sm 14:23
b beds, basins, and pottery 2Sm 17:28
⌊They also **b**⌋ wheat, barley, 2Sm 17:28
had the bones **b** from there. 2Sm 21:13
b me out to a wide-open place; 2Sm 22:20
The LORD **b** about a great victory 2Sm 23:10
So the LORD **b** about a great 2Sm 23:12
They **b** it back to David, but he 2Sm 23:16
and **b** her to the king. 1Kg 1:3
He went and **b** them back from 1Kg 2:40
the LORD has **b** back your evil on 1Kg 2:44
Solomon **b** her to the city of 1Kg 3:1
So they **b** the sword to the 1Kg 3:24
Each man **b** the barley and the 1Kg 4:28
Solomon had Hiram **b** from Tyre. 1Kg 7:13
Solomon **b** in the consecrated 1Kg 7:51
and the Levites **b** the ark of the 1Kg 8:4
The priests **b** the ark of the 1Kg 8:6
Since the day I **b** My people 1Kg 8:16
ancestors when He **b** them out of 1Kg 8:21
You **b** them out of Egypt, out of 1Kg 8:51
Moses when You **b** their ancestors 1Kg 8:53
their God who **b** their ancestors 1Kg 9:9
LORD **b** all this ruin on them. 1Kg 9:9
gold from Ophir **b** from Ophir a 1Kg 10:11
is your God who **b** you out of the 1Kg 12:28
the prophet who had **b** him back, 1Kg 13:20
for the prophet he had **b** back. 1Kg 13:23
prophet who had **b** him back from 1Kg 13:26
it on the donkey and **b** it back. 1Kg 13:29
He **b** his father's consecrated 1Kg 15:15
b him up to the upper room where 1Kg 17:19
have You also **b** tragedy on the 1Kg 17:20
b him down from the upper room 1Kg 17:23
and Elijah **b** them down to the 1Kg 18:40
turned aside and **b** someone to me 1Kg 20:39
king died and was **b** to Samaria. 1Kg 22:37
After they had **b** him one, 2Kg 2:20
gone on raids and **b** back from 2Kg 5:2
He **b** the letter to the king of 2Kg 5:6

accepting from him what he **b**.	2Kg 5:20
of Aram **b** all his military	2Kg 6:24
They have **b** the heads of the	2Kg 10:8
Then Jehu **b** all the people	2Kg 10:18
So he **b** out their garments.	2Kg 10:22
They **b** out the pillars of the	2Kg 10:26
messengers⌋ and **b** in the	2Kg 11:4
They each **b** their men—those	2Kg 11:9
He **b** out the king's son, put the	2Kg 11:12
and they **b** the king from the	2Kg 11:19
dedicated money **b** to the LORD's	2Kg 12:4
all the money **b** into the LORD's	2Kg 12:9
the money **b** into the temple.	2Kg 12:13
offering was not **b** to the LORD's	2Kg 12:16
their God who had **b** them out of	2Kg 17:7
the king of Assyria **b** ⌊people⌋	2Kg 17:24
who **b** you from the land of Egypt	2Kg 17:36
I have now **b** it to pass, and you	2Kg 19:25
So they **b** it and applied it to	2Kg 20:7
and He **b** the shadow back the 10	2Kg 20:11
and the tunnel and **b** water into	2Kg 20:20
up the money **b** into the LORD's	2Kg 22:4
He **b** out the Asherah pole from	2Kg 23:6
Then Josiah **b** all the priests	2Kg 23:8
in a chariot, **b** him into	2Kg 23:30
of Babylon also **b** captive into	2Kg 24:16
the king and **b** him up to the	2Kg 25:6
took them and **b** them to the king	2Kg 25:20
who **b** trouble on Israel when he	1Ch 2:7
when they **b** them in and when	1Ch 9:28
his sons and **b** them to Jabesh.	1Ch 10:12
out ⌊to battle⌋ and **b** us back.	1Ch 11:2
They **b** it back to David, but he	1Ch 11:18
For they **b** it at the risk of	1Ch 11:19
They **b** the ark of God and placed	1Ch 16:1
From the time I **b** Israel out of	1Ch 17:5
that You have **b** me this far?	1Ch 17:16
David's subjects and **b** tribute.	1Ch 18:2
David's subjects and **b** tribute.	1Ch 18:6
and **b** them to Jerusalem.	1Ch 18:7
⌊Hadoram **b**⌋ all kinds of items	1Ch 18:10
He **b** out the people who were in	1Ch 20:3
and Tyrians had **b** a large	1Ch 22:4
David had **b** the ark of God from	2Ch 1:4
Then Solomon **b** the consecrated	2Ch 5:1
They **b** up the ark, the tent of	2Ch 5:5
and the Levites **b** them up.	2Ch 5:5
The priests **b** the ark of the	2Ch 5:7
Since the day I **b** My people	2Ch 6:5
their ancestors who **b** them out	2Ch 7:22
He **b** all this ruin on them.	2Ch 7:22
b the daughter of Pharaoh	2Ch 8:11
servants who **b** gold from Ophir	2Ch 9:10
from Ophir also **b** algum wood	2Ch 9:10
more than she had **b** the king.	2Ch 9:12
what was **b** by the merchants	2Ch 9:14
the land also **b** gold and silver	2Ch 9:14
from all the plunder they had **b**.	2Ch 15:11
He **b** his father's consecrated	2Ch 15:18
So Asa **b** out the silver and gold	2Ch 16:2
Then King Asa **b** all Judah,	2Ch 16:6
Then all Judah **b** him tribute,	2Ch 17:5
also **b** gifts and silver	2Ch 17:11
and the Arabs **b** him flocks:	2Ch 17:11
Ephraim and **b** them back to the	2Ch 19:4
they **b** him to Jehu, and they	2Ch 22:9
They each **b** their men—those	2Ch 23:8
They **b** out the king's son,	2Ch 23:11
of the land and **b** the king down	2Ch 23:20
the wilderness be **b** to the LORD.	2Ch 24:9
people rejoiced, **b** ⌊the tax⌋,	2Ch 24:10
the chest was **b** by the Levites	2Ch 24:11
b the gods of the Seirites and	2Ch 25:14
from them and **b** it to Samaria.	2Ch 28:8
Israelites **b** them to Jericho,	2Ch 28:15
Then he **b** in the priests and	2Ch 29:4
They **b** seven bulls, seven rams,	2Ch 29:21
Then they **b** the sin offering	2Ch 29:23
So the congregation **b** sacrifices	2Ch 29:31
hearts **b** burnt offerings.	2Ch 29:31
the congregation **b** was 70 bulls,	2Ch 29:32
themselves and **b** burnt offerings	2Ch 30:15
and they **b** an abundant tenth of	2Ch 31:5
they also ⌊**b**⌋ a tenth of the	2Ch 31:6
things were **b** faithfully.	2Ch 31:12
He **b** against them the military	2Ch 33:11
and **b** him back to Jerusalem,	2Ch 33:13
he **b** it around the Ophel, and he	2Ch 33:14
him the money **b** into God's	2Ch 34:9
When they **b** out the money that	2Ch 34:14
and they quickly **b** ⌊them⌋ to the	2Ch 35:13
chariot, and **b** him to Jerusalem.	2Ch 35:24
Jehoahaz and **b** him to Egypt.	2Ch 36:4
for him⌋ and **b** him to Babylon	2Ch 36:10
So He **b** up against them the king	2Ch 36:17
King Cyrus also **b** out the	Ezr 1:7
of Persia had them **b** out under	Ezr 1:8
Sheshbazzar **b** all of them when	Ezr 1:11
offerings **b** to the LORD.	Ezr 3:5
of Assyria **b** us here."	Ezr 4:2
They are to be **b** to the temple	Ezr 6:5
was on us, they **b** us Sherebiah—	Ezr 8:18
Ezra the priest **b** the law before	Neh 8:2
went out, **b** back ⌊branches⌋	Neh 8:16
chose Abram and **b** him out of Ur	Neh 9:7
You **b** them water from the rock	Neh 9:15
your God who **b** you out of Egypt,	Neh 9:18
of heaven and **b** them to the land	Neh 9:23
they lived and **b** them to	Neh 12:27
Then I **b** the leaders of Judah up	Neh 12:31
Then all Judah **b** a tenth of the	Neh 13:12
goods were being **b** to Jerusalem	Neh 13:15
so that our God **b** all this	Neh 13:18
Queen Vashti **b** before him,	Est 1:17
daily events to be **b** and read to	Est 6:1
matter was **b** before the king,	Est 9:25
A word was **b** to me in secret;	Jb 4:12
are quickly **b** to an end.	Jb 5:13
or were you **b** forth before the	Jb 15:7
they are **b** low and shrivel up	Jb 24:24
adversity the LORD had **b** on him.	Jb 42:11
b me out to a wide-open place;	Ps 18:19
LORD, You **b** me up from Sheol;	Ps 30:3
I am bent over and **b** low;	Ps 38:6
He **b** me up from a desolate pit,	Ps 40:2
her companions, are **b** to you.	Ps 45:14
but You **b** us out to abundance.	Ps 66:12
of women **b** the good news:	Ps 68:11
and fasted, but it **b** me insults.	Ps 69:10
split the sea and **b** them across;	Ps 78:13
b streams out of the stone and	Ps 78:16
He **b** them to His holy land,	Ps 78:54
He **b** him from tending ewes to be	Ps 78:71
who **b** you up from the land of	Ps 81:10
Then He **b** Israel out with silver	Ps 105:37
He **b** quail and satisfied them	Ps 105:40
He **b** His people out with	Ps 105:43
He **b** them out of darkness and	Ps 107:14
and He **b** them out of their	Ps 107:28
and **b** Israel out from among them	Ps 136:11
she has **b** many down to death;	Pr 7:26
I was **b** forth when there were no	Pr 8:24
I was **b** forth before the	Pr 8:25
He **b** me to the banquet hall,	Sg 2:4
him go until I **b** him to my	Sg 3:4
raised children and **b** them up,	Is 1:2
So humanity is **b** low, and man is	Is 2:9
loftiness of men will be **b** low;	Is 2:11
So human pride will be **b** low,	Is 2:17
For they have **b** evil on	Is 3:9
Humanity is **b** low, man is	Is 5:15
has been **b** down to Sheol,	Is 14:11
But you will be **b** down to Sheol	Is 14:15
a gift will be **b** to the LORD	Is 18:7
men ⌊or⌋ **b** up young women."	Is 23:4
pride will be **b** low, along with	Is 25:11
fortress will be **b** down,	Is 25:12
You will be **b** down; you will	Is 29:4
I have now **b** it to pass, and you	Is 37:26
I **b** you from the ends of the	Is 41:9
You have not **b** Me your sheep for	Is 43:23
have **b** him, and he will succeed	Is 48:15
wandering—but who **b** them up?	Is 49:21
all the offspring she has **b** up.	Is 51:18
so His own arm **b** salvation,	Is 59:16
the nations may be **b** into you,	Is 60:11
Where is He who **b** them up out of	Is 63:11
is the LORD who **b** us from the	Jr 2:6
I **b** you to a fertile land to eat	Jr 2:7
Have you not **b** this on yourself	Jr 2:17
your actions have **b** this on you.	Jr 4:18
for when I **b** your ancestors out	Jr 7:22
Jerusalem will be **b** out of their	Jr 8:1
silver is **b** from Tarshish,	Jr 10:9
ancestors when I **b** them out of	Jr 11:4
ancestors when I **b** them out of	Jr 11:7
So I **b** on them all the curses of	Jr 11:8
house of Judah **b** on themselves,	Jr 11:17
I **b** against the mother of young	Jr 15:8
LORD lives who **b** the Israelites	Jr 16:14
LORD lives who **b** the Israelites	Jr 16:15
be the man who **b** the news to my	Jr 20:15
LORD lives who **b** the Israelites	Jr 23:7
who **b** and led the descendants of	Jr 23:8
and had **b** them to Babylon,	Jr 24:1
They **b** Uriah out of Egypt and	Jr 26:23
temple will be **b** back from	Jr 27:16
'They will be **b** to Babylon and	Jr 27:22
You **b** Your people Israel out of	Jr 32:21
and so You have **b** all this	Jr 32:23
Just as I have **b** all this great	Jr 32:42
ancestors when I **b** them out of	Jr 34:13
and I **b** them into the temple of	Jr 35:4
king will be **b** out to the	Jr 38:22
and sons will be **b** out to the	Jr 38:23
and **b** him to Nebuchadnezzar,	Jr 39:5
had Jeremiah **b** from the guard's	Jr 39:14
whom he **b** back from Gibeon	Jr 41:16
disaster that I have **b** on you.	Jr 42:10
the disaster I **b** against	Jr 44:2
them? He **b** this to mind.	Jr 44:21
His armory and **b** out His weapons	Jr 50:25
The LORD has **b** about our	Jr 51:10
the king and **b** him to the king	Jr 52:9
king of Babylon **b** Zedekiah to	Jr 52:11
took them and **b** them to the king	Jr 52:26
He **b** ⌊them⌋ to the ground and	Lm 2:2
blocks that **b** about their	Ezk 7:19
Then He **b** me to the entrance of	Ezk 8:7
He **b** me to the entrance of the	Ezk 8:14
So He **b** me to the inner court of	Ezk 8:16
lifted me up and **b** me to the	Ezk 11:1
lifted me up and **b** me to Chaldea	Ezk 11:24
I **b** out my bags like an exile's	Ezk 12:7
and daughters who will be **b** out.	Ezk 14:22
I have **b** on Jerusalem,	Ezk 14:22
about all I have **b** on it.	Ezk 14:22
b it to the land of merchants,	Ezk 17:4
and **b** them back with him to	Ezk 17:12
She **b** up one of her cubs, and he	Ezk 19:3
They **b** him into the fortresses	Ezk 19:9
So I **b** them out of the land of	Ezk 20:10
in whose sight I had **b** them out.	Ezk 20:14
in whose sight I **b** them out.	Ezk 20:22
When I **b** them into the land that	Ezk 20:28
You have **b** your ⌊judgment⌋ days	Ezk 22:4
I have **b** their actions down on	Ezk 22:31
Drunkards from the desert were **b**	Ezk 23:42
b back ivory tusks and ebony	Ezk 27:15
Your rowers have **b** you onto the	Ezk 27:26
be **b** in to destroy the land.	Ezk 30:11
You also will be **b** down to the	Ezk 31:18
the injured, **b** back the strays,	Ezk 34:4
He **b** me out by His Spirit and	Ezk 37:1
were **b** out from the peoples,	Ezk 38:8
was on me, and He **b** me there.	Ezk 40:1
He **b** me there, and I saw a man	Ezk 40:3
you have been **b** here so that I	Ezk 40:4
Then he **b** me into the outer	Ezk 40:17
He **b** me to the south side,	Ezk 40:24
Then he **b** me to the inner court	Ezk 40:28
Then he **b** me to the inner court	Ezk 40:32
Then he **b** me to the north gate.	Ezk 40:35
Then he **b** me to the portico of	Ezk 40:48
Next he **b** me into the great hall	Ezk 41:1
He **b** me to the group of chambers	Ezk 42:1
me up and **b** me to the inner	Ezk 43:5
man then **b** me back toward the	Ezk 44:1
Then the man **b** me by way of the	Ezk 44:4
When you **b** in foreigners,	Ezk 44:7
he **b** me through the entrance	Ezk 46:19
he **b** me into the outer court	Ezk 46:21
he **b** me back to the entrance	Ezk 47:1
Next he **b** me out by way of the	Ezk 47:2
Arioch quickly **b** Daniel before	Dn 2:25
these men were **b** before the king	Dn 3:13
So they **b** in the gold vessels	Dn 5:3
Daniel was **b** before the king	Dn 5:13
the king **b** from Judah?	Dn 5:13
and mediums were **b** before me to	Dn 5:15
from His house were **b** to you,	Dn 5:23
your kingdom and **b** it to an end.	Dn 5:26
and they **b** Daniel and threw him	Dn 6:16
stone was **b** and placed over the	Dn 6:17

No diversions were **b** to him, Dn 6:18
accused Daniel were **b** and thrown Dn 6:24
disaster in mind and **b** it on us, Dn 9:14
b Your people out of the land Dn 9:15
The LORD **b** Israel from Egypt by Hs 12:13
And I **b** you from the land of Am 2:10
clan that I **b** from the land Am 3:1
b you up from the land of Egypt Mc 6:4
When you **b** ⌊the harvest⌋ to your Hg 1:9
pride of Assyria will be **b** down, Zch 10:11
So they **b** to Him all those who Mt 4:24
they **b** to Him many who were Mt 8:16
then some men **b** to Him a Mt 9:2
unable to speak was **b** to Him. Mt 9:32
will even be **b** before governors Mt 10:18
unable to speak was **b** to Him. Mt 12:22
His head was **b** on a platter and Mt 14:11
vicinity and **b** to Him all who Mt 14:35
I **b** him to Your disciples, Mt 17:16
10,000 talents was **b** before him. Mt 18:24
children were **b** to Him so He Mt 19:13
They **b** the donkey and the colt; Mt 21:7
So they **b** Him a denarius. Mt 22:19
Is a lamp **b** in to be put under a Mk 4:21
b his head on a platter, and Mk 6:28
b to Him a deaf man who also Mk 7:32
They **b** a blind man to Him and Mk 8:22
man by the hand and **b** him out of Mk 8:23
"Teacher, I **b** my son to You. Mk 9:17
So they **b** him to Him. Mk 9:20
Then they **b** the donkey to Jesus Mk 11:7
So they **b** one. "Whose image and Mk 12:16
And they **b** Jesus to the place Mk 15:22
they **b** Him up to Jerusalem to Lk 2:22
When the parents **b** in the child Lk 2:27
where He had been **b** up. Lk 4:16
b Him to the edge of the hill Lk 4:29
various diseases **b** them to Him. Lk 4:40
Then they **b** the boats to land, Lk 5:11
She **b** an alabaster flask of Lk 7:37
his own animal, **b** him to an inn, Lk 10:34
commanded that he be **b** to Him. Lk 18:40
Then they **b** it to Jesus, and Lk 19:35
and you will be **b** before kings Lk 21:12
and **b** Him into the high priest's Lk 22:54
convened and **b** Him before their Lk 22:66
rose up and **b** Him before Pilate. Lk 23:1
You have **b** me this man as one Lk 23:14
and he **b** ⌊Simon⌋ to Jesus. Jn 1:42
someone have **b** Him something to Jn 4:33
them, "Why haven't you **b** Him?" Jn 7:45
the Pharisees **b** a woman caught Jn 8:3
They **b** the man who used to be Jn 9:13
When he has **b** all his own Jn 10:4
was the doorkeeper and **b** Peter Jn 18:16
these words, he **b** Jesus outside. Jn 19:13
b the proceeds of the things Ac 4:34
a field he owned, **b** the money, Ac 4:37
and **b** a portion of it and laid Ac 5:2
during the night, **b** them out, Ac 5:19
to the jail to have them **b**. Ac 5:21
police and **b** them in without Ac 5:26
When they had **b** them in, they Ac 5:27
this Moses who **b** us out of the Ac 7:40
with Joshua **b** it in when they Ac 7:45
took him and **b** him to the Ac 9:27
found him he **b** him to Antioch. Ac 11:26
the Lord had **b** him out of the Ac 12:17
the promise, God **b** the Savior, Ac 13:23
b oxen and garlands to the gates. Ac 14:13
He **b** them up into his house, Ac 16:34
when they had **b** together some Ac 17:5
who escorted Paul **b** him as far Ac 17:15
They took him and **b** him to the Ac 17:19
against Paul and **b** him to the Ac 18:12
his skin were **b** to the sick, Ac 19:12
you have **b** these men here who Ac 19:37
They **b** the boy home alive and Ac 20:12
went with us and **b** us to Mnason, Ac 21:16
he also **b** Greeks into the temple Ac 21:28
that Paul had **b** him into the Ac 21:29
was about to be **b** into the Ac 21:37
b up in this city at the feet Ac 22:3
him to be **b** into the barracks Ac 22:24
Then he **b** Paul down and placed Ac 22:30
So he took him, **b** him to the Ac 23:18
I **b** him down before their Ac 23:28
Paul and **b** him to Antipatris Ac 23:31
he commanded Paul to be **b** in. Ac 25:6
around him and **b** many serious Ac 25:7
and ordered the man to be **b** Ac 25:17
stood up and **b** no charge of the Ac 25:18
gave the command, Paul was **b** Ac 25:23
I have **b** him before all of you, Ac 25:26
I will not be **b** under the 1Co 6:12
away have been **b** near by the Eph 2:13
us from you and **b** us good news 1Th 3:6
is, if she has **b** up children, 1Tm 5:10
For we **b** nothing into the world, 1Tm 6:7
death and has **b** life and 2Tm 1:10
whose blood is **b** into the holy Heb 13:11
who **b** up from the dead our Lord Heb 13:20
on the grace to be **b** to you at 1Pt 1:13
when He **b** a flood on the world 2Pt 2:5

BROW *(3)*
sweat of your **b** until you return Gn 3:19
your **b** is like a slice of Sg 4:3
your **b** is like a slice of Sg 6:7

BRUISE *(2)*
burn for burn, **b** for bruise, Ex 21:25
bruise for **b**, wound for wound Ex 21:25

BRUISED *(3)*
to the LORD anything that has **b**, Lv 22:24
He will not break a **b** reed, Is 42:3
He will not break a **b** reed, Mt 12:20

BRUSH *(1)*
and **b** the lintel and the two Ex 12:22

BRUSHING *(1)*
creatures' wings **b** against each Ezk 3:13

BRUSHWOOD *(2)*
kindles the **b**, and fire causes Is 64:2
gathered a bundle of **b** and put Ac 28:3

BRUTAL *(2)*
I will hand you over to **b** men, Ezk 21:31
self-control, **b**, without love 2Tm 3:3

BRUTALIZE *(1)*
Don't exploit or **b** the alien, Jr 22:3

BRUTALLY *(1)*
on a loan⌋ and **b** extort your Ezk 22:12

BUCKET *(2)*
nations are like a drop in a **b**; Is 40:15
even have a **b**, and the well is Jn 4:11

BUCKETS *(1)*
Water will flow from his **b**, Nm 24:7

BUCKLERS *(4)*
A thousand **b** are hung on it— Sg 4:4
with shields, **b**, and helmets. Ezk 23:24
armed with shields and **b**, Ezk 38:4
the weapons—the **b** and shields, Ezk 39:9

BUCKLING *(1)*
braced the knees that were **b**. Jb 4:4

BUD *(1)*
tree does not **b** and there is no Hab 3:17

BUDDED *(3)*
As soon as it **b**, its blossoms Gn 40:10
let's see if the vine has **b**, Sg 7:12
rod that **b**, and the tablets Heb 9:4

BUDDING *(2)*
was ripe and the flax was **b**, Ex 9:31
if the vines were **b** and the Sg 6:11

BUDGE *(1)*
it does not **b** from its place. Is 46:7

BUDS *(1)*
sprouted, formed **b**, blossomed, Nm 17:8

BUILD *(136)*
let us **b** ourselves a city and a Gn 11:4
her I too can **b** ⌊a family⌋." Gn 30:3
B an altar there to the God who Gn 35:1
I will **b** an altar there to the Gn 35:3
you must not **b** it out of cut Ex 20:25
B me seven altars here and Nm 23:1
B me seven altars here and Nm 23:29
We want to **b** sheepfolds here for Nm 32:16
B cities for your dependents and Nm 32:24
cities that you did not **b**, Dt 6:10
and **b** beautiful houses to live Dt 8:12
altar you will **b** for the LORD Dt 16:21
cut them down to **b** siege works Dt 20:20
If you **b** a new house, make a Dt 22:8
who will not **b** up his brother's Dt 25:9
B an altar of stones there to Dt 27:5
Use uncut stones to **b** the altar Dt 27:6
You will **b** a house but not live Dt 28:30
take action and **b** an altar for Jos 22:26
you did not **b**, though you live Jos 24:13
B a well-constructed altar to Jdg 6:26
Are you to **b** a house for Me to 2Sm 7:5
He will **b** a house for My name, 2Sm 7:13
'I will **b** a house for you.' 2Sm 7:27
in order to **b** an altar to the 2Sm 24:21
B a house for yourself in 1Kg 2:36
was not able to **b** a temple for 1Kg 5:3
So I plan to **b** a temple for the 1Kg 5:5
and he will **b** the temple for My 1Kg 5:5
began to⌋ **b** the temple for 1Kg 6:1
chosen a city to **b** a temple in 1Kg 8:16
father David to **b** a temple for 1Kg 8:17
your desire to **b** a temple for My 1Kg 8:18
Yet you are not the one to **b** it; 1Kg 8:19
will **b** it for My name. 1Kg 8:19
had imposed to **b** the LORD's 1Kg 9:15
desired to **b** in Jerusalem, 1Kg 9:19
I will **b** you a lasting dynasty 1Kg 11:38
a log and can **b** ourselves a 2Kg 6:2
with a shield or **b** up an assault 2Kg 19:32
He would **b** altars in the LORD's 2Kg 21:4
carpenters to **b** a palace for him 1Ch 14:1
not the one to **b** Me a house to 1Ch 17:4
Himself will **b** a house for you. 1Ch 17:10
He will **b** a house for Me, and I 1Ch 17:12
that You will **b** him a house, 1Ch 17:25
plot so that I may **b** an altar to 1Ch 21:22
instructed him to **b** a house for 1Ch 22:6
was in my heart to **b** a house for 1Ch 22:7
You are not to **b** a house for My 1Ch 22:8
the one who will **b** a house for 1Ch 22:10
was in my heart to **b** a house as 1Ch 28:2
I had made preparations to **b**, 1Ch 28:2
'You are not to **b** a house for My 1Ch 28:3
one who is to **b** My house and My 1Ch 28:6
has chosen you to **b** a house for 1Ch 28:10
and to **b** the temple for which I 1Ch 29:19
Solomon decided to **b** a temple 2Ch 2:1
him cedars to **b** him a house to 2Ch 2:3
who is able to **b** a temple for 2Ch 2:6
that I should **b** a house for Him 2Ch 2:6
who will **b** a temple for the LORD 2Ch 2:12
Solomon began to **b** the LORD's 2Ch 3:1
began to **b** on the second ⌊day⌋ 2Ch 3:2
chosen a city to **b** a temple in 2Ch 6:5
father David to **b** a temple for 2Ch 6:7
your desire to **b** a temple for My 2Ch 6:8
are not the one to **b** the temple, 2Ch 6:9
will **b** the temple for My name." 2Ch 6:9
desired to **b** in Jerusalem, 2Ch 8:6
Let's **b** these cities and 2Ch 14:7
appointed me to **b** Him a temple 2Ch 36:23
appointed me to **b** Him a house at Ezr 1:2
in Judah and **b** the house of the Ezr 1:3
brothers began to **b** the altar of Ezr 3:2
the captivity, began ⌊to **b**⌋. Ezr 3:8
them, "Let us **b** with you, for we Ezr 4:2
we alone must **b** ⌊it⌋ for the Ezr 4:3
Judah and made them afraid to **b**. Ezr 4:4
Have them **b** a gallows 75 feet Est 5:14
he seized a house he did not **b**. Jb 20:19
b the walls of Jerusalem. Ps 51:18
save Zion and **b** up the cities Ps 69:35
forever and **b** up your throne for Ps 89:4
afterwards, **b** your house. Pr 24:27
to tear down and a time to **b**; Ec 3:3
will **b** a silver parapet on it. Sg 8:9
with a shield or **b** up an assault Is 37:33
He said, "**B** it up, build it up, Is 57:14
Build it up, **b** it up, prepare Is 57:14
Foreigners will **b** up your walls, Is 60:10
B it up, build up the highway; Is 62:10
Build it up, **b** up the highway; Is 62:10
People will **b** houses and live Is 65:21
They will not **b** and others live Is 65:22
could you possibly **b** for Me? Is 66:1
and demolish, to **b** and plant. Jr 1:10
that I will **b** and plant a nation Jr 18:9
will **b** myself a massive palace, Jr 22:14
will **b** them up and not demolish Jr 24:6
B houses and live ⌊in them⌋. Jr 29:5
B houses and settle down. Jr 29:28
Again I will **b** you so that you Jr 31:4
be attentive to **b** and to plant Jr 31:28

You must not **b** a house or sow Jr 35:7
a siege wall, **b** a ramp, pitch Ezk 4:2
Isn't the time near to **b** houses? Ezk 11:3
against the gates, **b** a ramp, and Ezk 21:22
and will **b** a ramp and raise a Ezk 26:8
there securely, **b** houses, and Ezk 28:26
North will come, **b** up an assault Dn 11:15
who **b** Zion with bloodshed and Mc 3:10
fortress and **b** siege ramps to Hab 1:10
will **b** houses but never live Zph 1:13
down lumber, and **b** the house. Hg 1:8
To **b** a shrine for it in the land Zch 5:11
His place and **b** the LORD's Zch 6:12
He will **b** the LORD's temple; Zch 6:13
will come and **b** the LORD's Zch 6:15
They may **b**, but I will demolish. Mal 1:4
on this rock I will **b** My church, Mt 16:18
You **b** the tombs of the prophets Mt 23:29
days I will **b** another not made Mk 14:58
sanctuary and **b** it in three days Mk 15:29
You **b** monuments to the prophets, Lk 11:47
and you **b** their monuments. Lk 11:48
down my barns and **b** bigger ones, Lk 12:18
you, wanting to **b** a tower, Lk 14:28
man started to **b** and wasn't able Lk 14:30
enemies will **b** an embankment Lk 19:43
sanctuary took 46 years to **b**, Jn 2:20
sort of house will you **b** for Me? Ac 7:49
which is able to **b** you up and to Ac 20:32
his good, in order to **b** him up. Rm 15:2
to **b** up the body of Christ, Eph 4:12
one another and **b** each other up 1Th 5:11

BUILDER (4)

Cain became the **b** of a city, Gn 4:17
a skilled master **b** I have laid 1Co 3:10
as the **b** has more honor than Heb 3:3
whose architect and **b** is God. Heb 11:10

BUILDERS (17)

So Solomon's **b** and Hiram's 1Kg 5:18
builders and Hiram's **b**, 1Kg 5:18
temple—the carpenters, the **b**, 2Kg 12:11
the carpenters, **b**, and masons to 2Kg 22:6
carpenters and **b** and ⌊also used 2Ch 34:11
When the **b** had laid the Ezr 3:10
they have provoked the **b**. Neh 4:5
Each of the **b** had his sword Neh 4:18
stone that the **b** rejected has Ps 118:22
its **b** labor over it in vain; Ps 127:1
Your **b** hurry; those who destroy Is 49:17
your **b** perfected your beauty. Ezk 27:4
stone that the **b** rejected has Mt 21:42
The stone that the **b** rejected— Mk 12:10
The stone that the **b** rejected— Lk 20:17
is The stone despised by you **b**, Ac 4:11
The stone that the **b** rejected— 1Pt 2:7

BUILDING (53)

the tower that the men were **b**. Gn 11:5
and they stopped **b** the city. Gn 11:8
from the LORD and **b** an altar for Jos 22:16
against us by **b** for yourselves Jos 22:19
from Him today by **b** an altar for Jos 22:29
until he finished **b** his palace, 1Kg 3:1
When he finished **b** the temple, 1Kg 6:9
As for this temple you are **b**— 1Kg 6:12
Solomon finished **b** the temple, 1Kg 6:14
Solomon finished **b** the temple 1Kg 9:1
he quit **b** Ramah and stayed in 1Kg 15:21
stones for **b** God's house. 1Ch 22:2
may you succeed in **b** the house 1Ch 22:11
Get started **b** the LORD God's 1Ch 22:19
provided for **b** You a house for 1Ch 29:16
Now I myself am **b** a temple for 2Ch 2:4
that I am **b** will be great, 2Ch 2:5
the temple I am **b** will be great 2Ch 2:9
foundations for **b** God's temple: 2Ch 3:3
he quit **b** Ramah and stopped his 2Ch 16:5
month they began **b** up the piles, 2Ch 31:7
exiles were **b** a temple for Ezr 4:1
part with us in **b** a house for Ezr 4:3
who are constructing this **b**?" Ezr 5:4
with the **b** under the prophesying Ezr 6:14
They finished the **b** according to Ezr 6:14
will start **b**, but you have no Neh 2:20
⌊After **b** the wall⌋ to the Tower Neh 3:1
fox climbed up what they are **b**, Neh 4:3
around his waist while he was **b**, Neh 4:18
the reason you are **b** the wall. Neh 6:6
b your mound at the head of Ezk 16:31
Now the **b** that faced the temple Ezk 41:12
The wall of the **b** was eight and Ezk 41:12
the temple yard and the **b**, Ezk 41:13
length of the **b** facing the Ezk 41:15
and opposite the **b** to the north. Ezk 42:1
and middle stories of the **b**. Ezk 42:5
temple yard and the ⌊western⌋ **b**, Ezk 42:10
He is like a man **b** a house, Lk 6:48
buying, selling, planting, **b**. Lk 17:28
I will not be **b** on someone Rm 15:20
You are God's field, God's **b**. 1Co 3:9
to excel in **b** up the church. 1Co 14:12
we have a **b** from God, a house 2Co 5:1
Lord gave for **b** you up and not 2Co 10:8
dear friends, is for **b** you up. 2Co 12:19
Lord gave me for **b** up and not 2Co 13:10
The whole **b** is being fitted Eph 2:21
of the body for **b** up itself in Eph 4:16
is good for the **b** up of someone Eph 4:29
b yourselves up in your most Jd 20
The **b** material of its wall was Rv 21:18

BUILDING'S (1)

and the **b** length was 157 and a Ezk 41:12

BUILDINGS (8)

All of these ⌊**b**⌋ were of costly 1Kg 7:9
only the **b** of Kir-hareseth were 2Kg 3:25
of the temple⌋ and its **b**, 1Ch 28:11
overlaying the walls of the **b**, 1Ch 29:4
for the **b** that Judah's Kings had 2Ch 34:11
His attention to the temple **b**. Mt 24:1
What impressive **b**!" Mk 13:1
Do you see these great **b**? Mk 13:2

BUILDS (15)

Unless the LORD **b** a house, Ps 127:1
Every wise woman **b** her house, Pr 14:1
one who **b** a high threshold Pr 17:19
for the one who **b** his palace Jr 22:13
for when someone **b** a wall they Ezk 13:10
He **b** His upper chambers in the Am 9:6
Woe to him who **b** a city with Hab 2:12
peace and what **b** up one another. Rm 14:19
foundation, and another **b** on it. 1Co 3:10
must be careful how he **b** on it, 1Co 3:10
If anyone **b** on the foundation 1Co 3:12
with pride, but love **b** up. 1Co 8:1
but not everything **b** up. 1Co 10:23
another⌋ language **b** himself up, 1Co 14:4
who prophesies **b** up the church. 1Co 14:4

BUILT (186)

Noah **b** an altar to the LORD. Gn 8:20
went to Assyria and **b** Nineveh, Gn 10:11
So he **b** an altar there to the Gn 12:7
There he **b** an altar to the LORD Gn 12:8
site where he had **b** the altar. Gn 13:4
where he **b** an altar to the LORD. Gn 13:18
Abraham **b** the altar there and Gn 22:9
he **b** an altar there, worshiped Gn 26:25
father's and has **b** this wealth Gn 31:1
He **b** a house for himself and Gn 33:17
b an altar there and called Gn 35:7
They **b** Pithom and Rameses as Ex 1:11
And Moses **b** an altar and named Ex 17:15
saw ⌊this⌋, he **b** an altar before Ex 32:5
Hebron was **b** seven years before Nm 13:22
top of Pisgah, **b** seven altars, Nm 23:14
cities, and ⌊**b**⌋ sheepfolds. Nm 32:36
'Has any man **b** a new house and Dt 20:5
house that was ⌊**b**⌋ into the wall Jos 2:15
that time Joshua **b** an altar on Jos 8:30
He **b** it according to what is Jos 8:31
the tribe of Manasseh **b** a large, Jos 22:10
of Manasseh have **b** an altar Jos 22:11
that we have **b** for ourselves an Jos 22:23
of the Hittites, **b** a town, and Jdg 1:26
So Gideon **b** an altar to the LORD Jdg 6:24
up on the altar that had been **b**. Jdg 6:28
got up early, **b** an altar there, Jdg 21:4
who together **b** the house of Ru 4:11
he had **b** an altar to the LORD 1Sm 7:17
Saul **b** an altar to the LORD; 1Sm 14:35
first time he had **b** an altar to 1Sm 14:35
He **b** it up all the way around 2Sm 5:9
and they **b** a palace for David. 2Sm 5:11
Why haven't you **b** Me a house of 2Sm 7:7
They **b** an assault ramp against 2Sm 20:15
He **b** an altar to the LORD there 2Sm 24:25
the LORD's name had not been **b**. 1Kg 3:2
King Solomon **b** for the LORD was 1Kg 6:2
He then **b** a chambered structure 1Kg 6:5
the temple while it was being **b**. 1Kg 6:7
He **b** the chambers along the 1Kg 6:10
he **b** the interior as an inner 1Kg 6:16
He **b** the inner courtyard with 1Kg 6:36
So he **b** it in seven years. 1Kg 6:38
He **b** the House of the Forest of 1Kg 7:2
I have indeed **b** an exalted 1Kg 8:13
I have **b** the temple for the name 1Kg 8:20
much less this temple I have **b**. 1Kg 8:27
temple I have **b** is called by 1Kg 8:43
temple I have **b** for Your name, 1Kg 8:44
temple I have **b** for Your name, 1Kg 8:48
this temple you have **b**, 1Kg 9:3
Solomon had **b** the two houses, 1Kg 9:10
that Solomon had **b** for her; 1Kg 9:24
he then **b** the terraces. 1Kg 9:24
the altar he had **b** for the LORD, 1Kg 9:25
wisdom, the palace he had **b**, 1Kg 10:4
Solomon **b** a high place for 1Kg 11:7
Solomon had **b** the supporting 1Kg 11:27
dynasty just as I **b** for David, 1Kg 11:38
Jeroboam **b** Shechem in the hill 1Kg 12:25
there he went out and **b** Penuel. 1Kg 12:25
Jeroboam also **b** shrines on the 1Kg 12:31
They also **b** for themselves high 1Kg 14:23
He **b** Ramah in order to deny 1Kg 15:17
timbers Baasha had **b** it with. 1Kg 15:22
King Asa **b** Geba of Benjamin 1Kg 15:22
and the cities he **b**, are written 1Kg 15:23
of silver, and he **b** up the hill. 1Kg 16:24
the city he **b** Samaria based 1Kg 16:24
Baal that he had **b** in Samaria. 1Kg 16:32
Hiel the Bethelite **b** Jericho. 1Kg 16:34
he **b** an altar with the stones 1Kg 18:32
ivory palace he **b**, and all the 1Kg 22:39
all the cities he **b**, are written 1Kg 22:39
Jotham who **b** the Upper Gate 2Kg 15:35
b the altar according to all 2Kg 16:11
canopy they had **b** in the palace, 2Kg 16:18
They **b** high places in all their 2Kg 17:9
b altars to the whole heavenly 2Kg 21:5
of Israel had **b** for Ashtoreth, 2Kg 23:13
to the city and **b** a siege wall 2Kg 25:1
that Solomon **b** in Jerusalem; 1Ch 6:10
Solomon **b** the LORD's temple 1Ch 6:32
b Lower and Upper Beth-horon 1Ch 7:24
Shemed who **b** Ono and Lod and 1Ch 8:12
He **b** up the city all the way 1Ch 11:8
David **b** houses for himself in 1Ch 15:1
Why haven't you **b** Me a house of 1Ch 17:6
He **b** an altar to the LORD there 1Ch 21:26
is to be **b** for the LORD must 1Ch 22:5
that is to be **b** for the name 1Ch 22:19
but I have **b** an exalted temple 2Ch 6:2
I have **b** the temple for the name 2Ch 6:10
much less this temple I have **b**. 2Ch 6:18
temple I have **b** is called by 2Ch 6:33
that I have **b** for Your name, 2Ch 6:34
temple I have **b** for Your name, 2Ch 6:38
Solomon had **b** the LORD's temple 2Ch 8:1
He **b** Tadmor in the wilderness 2Ch 8:4
cities that he **b** in Hamath. 2Ch 8:4
He **b** Upper Beth-horon and Lower 2Ch 8:5
to the house he had **b** for her, 2Ch 8:11
wisdom, the palace he had **b**, 2Ch 9:3
He **b** up Bethlehem, Etam, Tekoa, 2Ch 11:6
Asa **b** fortified cities in Judah. 2Ch 14:6
So they **b** and succeeded. 2Ch 14:7
He **b** Ramah in order to deny 2Ch 16:1
timbers Baasha had **b** it with. 2Ch 16:6
Then he **b** Geba and Mizpah with 2Ch 16:6
He **b** fortresses and storage 2Ch 17:12
land and have **b** You a sanctuary 2Ch 20:8
Jehoram also **b** high places in 2Ch 21:11
he **b** cities in ⌊the vicinity 2Ch 26:6
Uzziah **b** towers in Jerusalem at 2Ch 26:9
b towers in the desert and dug 2Ch 26:10
Jotham **b** the Upper Gate of the 2Ch 27:3
and he **b** extensively on the wall 2Ch 27:3
He also **b** cities in the hill 2Ch 27:4
b altars in the LORD's temple, 2Ch 33:4
b altars to the whole heavenly 2Ch 33:5
he **b** the outer wall of the city 2Ch 33:14
that he had **b** on the mountain 2Ch 33:15
He **b** the altar of the LORD and 2Ch 33:16
the sites where he **b** high places 2Ch 33:19

in the temple **b** by Solomon son 2Ch 35:3
It is being **b** with cut stones, Ezr 5:8
that was **b** many years ago, Ezr 5:11
king of Israel **b** and finished. Ezr 5:11
men of Jericho **b** next to Neh 3:2
to them Zaccur son of Imri **b**. Neh 3:2
of Hassenaah **b** the Fish Gate. Neh 3:3
They **b** it with beams and Neh 3:3
They **b** it with beams and Neh 3:6
and no houses had been **b** yet. Neh 7:4
platform ⌊**b**⌋ for the Levites Neh 9:4
for they had **b** villages for Neh 12:29
The house he **b** is like a moth's Jb 27:18
He **b** His sanctuary like the Ps 78:69
Faithful love is **b** up forever; Ps 89:2
Jerusalem, **b** as a city ⌊should Ps 122:3
Wisdom has **b** her house; Pr 9:1
city is **b** up by the blessing of Pr 11:11
house is **b** by wisdom, and it is Pr 24:3
I **b** houses and planted vineyards Ec 2:4
and **b** large siege works against Ec 9:14
He **b** a tower in the middle of it Is 5:2
iniquities have **b** barriers Is 59:2
They have **b** the high places of Jr 7:31
they will be **b** up among My Jr 12:16
They have **b** high places to Baal Jr 19:5
from the day it was **b** until now. Jr 32:31
They have **b** the high places of Jr 32:35
also have not **b** houses to live Jr 35:9
What I have **b** I am about to Jr 45:4
to the city and **b** a siege wall Jr 52:4
places should not have been **b**, Ezk 16:16
you **b** yourself a mound and made Ezk 16:24
You **b** your elevated place at the Ezk 16:25
when ramps are **b** and siege walls Ezk 17:17
with ovens **b** at the base of the Ezk 46:23
that I have **b** by my vast power Dn 4:30
his Maker and **b** palaces; Hs 8:14
houses of cut stone you have **b**; Am 5:11
Tyre has **b** herself a fortress; Zch 9:3
sensible man who **b** his house on Mt 7:24
a foolish man who **b** his house on Mt 7:26
in it, and **b** a watchtower. Mt 21:33
a winepress, and **b** a watchtower. Mk 12:1
of the hill their town was **b** Lk 4:29
shake it, because it was well **b**. Lk 6:48
is like a man who **b** a house on Lk 6:49
and has **b** us a synagogue." Lk 7:5
was Solomon who **b** Him a house. Ac 7:47
being **b** up and walking in the Ac 9:31
work that he has **b** survives, 1Co 3:14
so that the church may be **b** up. 1Co 14:5
other person is not being **b** up. 1Co 14:17
b on the foundation of the Eph 2:20
also are being **b** together for Eph 2:22
rooted and **b** up in Him and Col 2:7
Now every house is **b** by someone, Heb 3:4
but the One who **b** everything is Heb 3:4
in reverence **b** an ark to deliver Heb 11:7
are being **b** into a spiritual 1Pt 2:5

BUKKI *(4)*
B son of Jogli, a leader from Nm 34:22
fathered **B**; Bukki fathered 1Ch 6:5
fathered Bukki; **B** fathered Uzzi; 1Ch 6:5
his son **B**, his son Uzzi, his son 1Ch 6:51

BUKKI'S *(1)*
son, Uzzi's son, **B** son, Ezr 7:4

BUKKIAH *(2)*
B, Mattaniah, Uzziel, Shebuel, 1Ch 25:4
the sixth ⌊to⌋ **B**, his sons, and 1Ch 25:13

BUL *(1)*
the month of **B**, the temple was 1Kg 6:38

BULGE *(2)*
Their eyes **b** out from fatness; Ps 73:7
b in a high wall whose collapse Is 30:13

BULGES *(1)*
fat and his waistline **b** with it, Jb 15:27

BULL *(83)*
Take a young **b** and two Ex 29:1
along with the **b** and two rams. Ex 29:3
are to bring the **b** to the front Ex 29:10
Slaughter the **b** before the LORD Ex 29:11
Sacrifice a **b** as a sin offering Ex 29:36
slaughter the **b** before the LORD Lv 1:5
unblemished **b** as a sin offering Lv 4:3
must bring the **b** to the entrance Lv 4:4
the fat from the **b** of the sin Lv 4:8
the hide of the **b** and all its Lv 4:11
rest⌋ of the **b**—he must bring Lv 4:12
present a young **b** as a sin Lv 4:14
to offer this **b** just as he did Lv 4:20
as he did with the **b** in the sin Lv 4:20
will bring the **b** outside the Lv 4:21
just as he burned the first **b**. Lv 4:21
the **b** of the sin offering, Lv 8:2
brought the **b** near for the sin Lv 8:14
on the head of the **b** for the sin Lv 8:14
burned up the **b** with its hide, Lv 8:17
Take a young **b** for a sin Lv 9:2
a young **b** for a sin offering Lv 16:3
will present the **b** for his sin Lv 16:6
Aaron presents the **b** for his sin Lv 16:11
will slaughter the **b** for his sin Lv 16:11
The **b** for the sin offering and Lv 16:27
old, one young **b**, and two rams. Lv 23:18
one young **b**, one ram, and one Nm 7:15
one young **b**, one ram, and one Nm 7:21
one young **b**, one ram, and one Nm 7:27
one young **b**, one ram, and one Nm 7:33
one young **b**, one ram, and one Nm 7:39
one young **b**, one ram, and one Nm 7:45
one young **b**, one ram, and one Nm 7:51
one young **b**, one ram, and one Nm 7:57
one young **b**, one ram, and one Nm 7:63
one young **b**, one ram, and one Nm 7:69
one young **b**, one ram, and one Nm 7:75
one young **b**, one ram, and one Nm 7:81
to take a young **b** and its grain Nm 8:8
a second young **b** for a sin Nm 8:8
prepare a young **b** as a burnt Nm 15:8
must be presented with the **b**. Nm 15:9
prepare one young **b** for a burnt Nm 15:24
they offered a **b** and a ram on Nm 23:2
offered a **b** and a ram on each Nm 23:4
offered a **b** and a ram on each Nm 23:14
and offered a **b** and a ram on Nm 23:30
as a grain offering for each **b**, Nm 28:12
two quarts of wine with each **b**, Nm 28:14
with each **b** and four quarts Nm 28:20
quarts with each **b**, four quarts Nm 28:28
one young **b**, one ram, seven male Nm 29:2
quarts with the **b**, four quarts Nm 29:3
one young **b**, one ram, and seven Nm 29:8
quarts with the **b**, four quarts Nm 29:9
one **b**, one ram, seven male lambs Nm 29:36
His firstborn **b** has splendor, Dt 33:17
father's young **b** and a second Jdg 6:25
and a second **b** seven years old. Jdg 6:25
Take the second **b** and offer it Jdg 6:26
and the second **b** offered up on Jdg 6:28
as well as a three-year-old **b**, 1Sm 1:24
slaughtered the **b** and brought 1Sm 1:25
to choose one **b** for themselves, 1Kg 18:23
prepare the other **b** and place it 1Kg 18:23
yourselves one **b** and prepare it 1Kg 18:25
So they took the **b** that he gave 1Kg 18:26
wood, cut up the **b**, and placed 1Kg 18:33
with a young **b** and seven rams 2Ch 13:9
will not accept a **b** from your Ps 50:9
more than a **b** with horns and Ps 69:31
are to give a **b** from the herd as Ezk 43:19
must take away the **b** for the sin Ezk 43:21
just as they did with the **b**. Ezk 43:22
unblemished **b** and an Ezk 43:23
A young **b** and a ram from the Ezk 43:25
unblemished **b** and purify the Ezk 45:18
will provide a **b** as a sin Ezk 45:22
a bushel per **b** and half a bushel Ezk 45:24
unblemished **b**, as well as six Ezk 46:6
of half a bushel with the **b**, Ezk 46:7
be half a bushel with the **b**, Ezk 46:11

BULL'S *(11)*
lay their hands on the **b** head. Ex 29:10
some of the **b** blood and apply Ex 29:12
burn up the **b** flesh, its hide Ex 29:14
lay his hand on the **b** head, Lv 4:4
some of the **b** blood and bring Lv 4:5
the rest of the **b** blood at the Lv 4:7
their hands on the **b** head before Lv 4:15
bring some of the **b** blood into Lv 4:16
take some of the **b** blood and Lv 16:14
as he did with the **b** blood: Lv 16:15
some of the **b** blood and some Lv 16:18

BULLS *(70)*
40 cows, 10 **b**, 20 female donkeys Gn 32:15
and sacrificed **b** as fellowship Ex 24:5
and two **b**, five rams, five male Nm 7:17
and two **b**, five rams, five male Nm 7:23
and two **b**, five rams, five male Nm 7:29
and two **b**, five rams, five male Nm 7:35
and two **b**, five rams, five male Nm 7:41
and two **b**, five rams, five male Nm 7:47
and two **b**, five rams, five male Nm 7:53
and two **b**, five rams, five male Nm 7:59
and two **b**, five rams, five male Nm 7:65
and two **b**, five rams, five male Nm 7:71
and two **b**, five rams, five male Nm 7:77
and two **b**, five rams, five male Nm 7:83
the burnt offering totaled 12 **b**, Nm 7:87
sacrifice totaled 24 **b**, Nm 7:88
hands on the heads of the **b**. Nm 8:12
prepare seven **b** and seven rams Nm 23:1
prepare seven **b** and seven rams Nm 23:29
two young **b**, one ram, seven male Nm 28:11
two young **b**, one ram, and seven Nm 28:19
two young **b**, one ram, and seven Nm 28:27
young **b**, two rams, and 14 male Nm 29:13
quarts with each of the 13 **b**, Nm 29:14
second day ⌊present⌋ 12 young **b**, Nm 29:17
and drink offerings for the **b**, Nm 29:18
On the third day ⌊present⌋ 11 **b**, Nm 29:20
and drink offerings for the **b**, Nm 29:21
the fourth day ⌊present⌋ 10 **b**, Nm 29:23
and drink offerings for the **b**, Nm 29:24
the fifth day ⌊present⌋ nine **b**, Nm 29:26
and drink offerings for the **b**, Nm 29:27
the sixth day ⌊present⌋ eight **b**, Nm 29:29
and drink offerings for the **b**, Nm 29:30
seventh day ⌊present⌋ seven **b**, Nm 29:32
and drink offerings for the **b**, Nm 29:33
and drink offerings for the **b**, Nm 29:37
Let two **b** be given to us. 1Kg 18:23
seven **b** and seven rams. 1Ch 15:26
1,000 **b**, 1,000 rams, and 1,000 1Ch 29:21
brought seven **b**, seven rams, 2Ch 29:21
So they slaughtered the **b**, 2Ch 29:22
congregation brought was 70 **b**, 2Ch 29:32
Six hundred **b** and 3,000 sheep 2Ch 29:33
1,000 **b** and 7,000 sheep 2Ch 30:24
1,000 **b** and 10,000 sheep 2Ch 30:24
plus 3,000 **b** from his own 2Ch 35:7
and 300 **b** for the priests. 2Ch 35:8
for the Levites, plus 500 **b**. 2Ch 35:9
⌊they did⌋ the same with the **b**. 2Ch 35:12
needed—young **b**, rams, and Ezr 6:9
God's house they offered 100 **b**, Ezr 6:17
buy with this money as many **b**, Ezr 7:17
b for all Israel, 96 rams, and Ezr 8:35
Their **b** breed without fail; Jb 21:10
Now take seven **b** and seven rams, Jb 42:8
Many **b** surround me; strong ones Ps 22:12
eat the flesh of **b** or drink the Ps 50:13
then **b** will be offered on Your Ps 51:19
the herd of **b** with the calves of Ps 68:30
no desire for the blood of **b**, Is 1:11
and young **b** with the mighty Is 34:7
young bulls with the mighty **b**. Is 34:7
all her young **b** to the sword; Jr 50:27
the 12 bronze **b** under the water Jr 52:20
male goats, and **b**, all of them Ezk 39:18
provide seven **b** and seven rams Ezk 45:23
They sacrifice **b** in Gilgal; Hs 12:11
of goats and **b** and the ashes Heb 9:13
for the blood of **b** and goats to Heb 10:4

BULLY *(2)*
to wine, not a **b** but gentle, not 1Tm 3:3
to wine, not a **b**, not greedy for Ti 1:7

BUNAH *(1)*
his firstborn, **B**, Oren, Ozem, 1Ch 2:25

BUNCH *(1)*
wine is found in a **b** of grapes, Is 65:8

BUNCHES *(1)*
raisins, 100 ⌊**b**⌋ of summer fruit 2Sm 16:1

BUNDLE *(1)*
Paul gathered a **b** of brushwood Ac 28:3

BUNDLES *(4)*
grain among the **b** behind the Ru 2:7
her gather ⌊grain⌋ among the **b**, Ru 2:15
from the **b** for her and leave Ru 2:16
and tie them in **b** to burn them, Mt 13:30

BUNNI *(3)*
Shebaniah, **B**, Sherebiah, Bani, Neh 9:4
B, Azgad, Bebai, Neh 10:15
son of Hashabiah, son of **B**; Neh 11:15

BURDEN *(39)*
and why do You **b** me with all Nm 11:11
you bear the **b** of the people, Nm 11:17
or we would be a **b** to you." 2Sm 13:25
with me, you'll be a **b** to me, 2Sm 15:33
be an added **b** to my lord the 2Sm 19:35
because the **b** on the people was Neh 5:18
that I have become a **b** to You? Jb 7:20
they are a **b** too heavy for me to Ps 38:4
Cast your **b** on the LORD, and He Ps 55:22
his shoulder from the **b**; Ps 81:6
and sand, a **b**, but aggravation Pr 27:3
They have become a **b** to Me; Is 1:14
On that day his **b** will fall from Is 10:27
and his **b** will be removed from Is 14:25
him the whole **b** of his father's Is 22:24
as a **b** for the weary ⌊animal⌋. Is 46:1
are not able to rescue the **b**, Is 46:2
What is the **b** of the LORD? Jr 23:33
What is the **b**? I will throw you Jr 23:33
The **b** of the LORD, I will punish Jr 23:34
refer to the **b** of the LORD, Jr 23:36
becomes his **b** and you pervert Jr 23:36
The **b** of the LORD, then this is Jr 23:38
have said, The **b** of the LORD, Jr 23:38
not to say, The **b** of the LORD, Jr 23:38
number under the **b** of the king Hs 8:10
yoke is easy and My **b** is light." Mt 11:30
to us who bore the **b** of the day Mt 20:12
the foal of a beast of **b**." Mt 21:5
put no greater **b** on you than Ac 15:28
I will not **b** you any further Ac 24:4
in need, I did not **b** anyone, for 2Co 11:9
that I personally did not **b** you? 2Co 12:13
I will not **b** you, for I am not 2Co 12:14
could have been a **b** as Christ's 1Th 2:7
that we would not **b** any of you, 1Th 2:9
would not be a **b** to any of you. 2Th 3:8
Now His commands are not a **b**, 1Jn 5:3
I do not put any other **b** on you. Rv 2:24

BURDENED *(12)*
my father **b** you with a heavy 1Kg 12:11
my father **b** you with a heavy 2Ch 10:11
me had heavily **b** the people, Neh 5:15
light given to one **b** with grief, Jb 3:20
A man **b** by bloodguilt will be a Pr 28:17
I have not **b** you with offerings Is 43:23
you have **b** Me with your sins; Is 43:24
all of you who are weary and **b**, Mt 11:28
this tent groan, **b** as we are, 2Co 5:4
Now granted, I have not **b** you; 2Co 12:16
and the church should not be **b**, 1Tm 5:16
idle women **b** down with sins, 2Tm 3:6

BURDENING *(2)*
wouldn't be worth **b** the king." Est 7:4
myself, from **b** you in any way. 2Co 11:9

BURDENS *(6)*
your troubles, **b**, and disputes Dt 1:12
You placed **b** on our backs. Ps 66:11
Day after day He bears our **b**; Ps 68:19
people with **b** that are hard to Lk 11:46
touch these **b** with one of your Lk 11:46
Carry one another's **b**; Gl 6:2

BURDENSOME *(1)*
shattered their **b** yoke and the Is 9:4

BURIAL *(23)*
Give me a **b** site among you so Gn 23:4
your dead in our finest **b** place. Gn 23:6
from you his **b** place for burying Gn 23:6
the full price, as a **b** place." Gn 23:9
to Abraham as a **b** place. Gn 23:20
and bury me in their **b** place." Gn 47:30
Ephron the Hittite as a **b** site. Gn 49:30
purchased as a **b** site from Gn 50:13
his fathers in the **b** ground of 2Ch 26:23
does not even have a proper **b**, Ec 6:3
You will not join them in **b**, Is 14:20
He⌋ will destroy the ⌊**b**⌋ shroud, Is 25:7
there will be no other **b** place. Jr 7:32
will die in this land without **b**. Jr 16:6
corpse into the **b** place of the Jr 26:23
taken away or gathered ⌊for **b**⌋. Ezk 29:5
is all around her **b** place. Ezk 32:23
I will give Gog a **b** place there Ezk 39:11
she has prepared Me for **b**. Mt 26:12
field with it as a **b** place for Mt 27:7
My body in advance for **b**. Mk 14:8
has kept it for the day of My **b**. Jn 12:7
according to the **b** custom of the Jn 19:40

BURIED *(109)*
in peace and be **b** at a ripe old Gn 15:15
Abraham **b** his wife Sarah in the Gn 23:19
and Ishmael **b** him in the cave Gn 25:9
Abraham was **b** there with his Gn 25:10
died and was **b** under the oak Gn 35:8
died and was **b** on the way to Gn 35:19
His sons Esau and Jacob **b** him. Gn 35:29
I **b** her there along the way to Gn 48:7
and his wife Sarah are **b** there, Gn 49:31
his wife Rebekah are **b** there, Gn 49:31
there, and I **b** Leah there. Gn 49:31
of Canaan and **b** him in the cave Gn 50:13
After Joseph **b** his father, Gn 50:14
there they **b** the people who had Nm 11:34
Miriam died and was **b** there. Nm 20:1
Aaron died and was **b** there, Dt 10:6
He **b** him in the valley in the Dt 34:6
They **b** him in his allotted Jos 24:30
were **b** at Shechem in the parcel Jos 24:32
died, and they **b** him at Gibeah, Jos 24:33
They **b** him in the territory of Jdg 2:9
old age and was **b** in the tomb of Jdg 8:32
when he died, was **b** in Shamir. Jdg 10:2
Jair died, he was **b** in Kamon. Jdg 10:5
he was **b** in one of the cities of Jdg 12:7
he died, he was **b** in Bethlehem. Jdg 12:10
he was **b** in Aijalon in the land Jdg 12:12
he was **b** in Pirathon in the land Jdg 12:15
and **b** him between Zorah and Jdg 16:31
will die, and there I will be **b**. Ru 1:17
and they **b** him by his home in 1Sm 25:1
for him and **b** him in Ramah, 1Sm 28:3
their bones and **b** them under 1Sm 31:13
of Jabesh-gilead who **b** Saul." 2Sm 2:4
Saul your lord when you **b** him. 2Sm 2:5
tomb in Bethlehem and **b** him. 2Sm 2:32
When they **b** Abner in Hebron, 2Sm 3:32
head and **b** it in Abner's tomb 2Sm 4:12
died and was **b** in his father's 2Sm 17:23
They ⌊also⌋ **b** the bones of Saul 2Sm 21:14
fathers and was **b** in the city 1Kg 2:10
He was **b** at his house in the 1Kg 2:34
fathers and was **b** in the city of 1Kg 11:43
After he had **b** him, he said to 1Kg 13:31
grave where the man of God is **b**; 1Kg 13:31
He was **b**, and all Israel mourned 1Kg 14:18
fathers and was **b** with his 1Kg 14:31
fathers and was **b** in the city 1Kg 15:8
fathers and was **b** in the city of 1Kg 15:24
his fathers and was **b** in Tirzah. 1Kg 16:6
fathers and was **b** in Samaria. 1Kg 16:28
They **b** the king in Samaria. 1Kg 22:37
fathers and was **b** with his 1Kg 22:50
fathers and was **b** with his 2Kg 8:24
in a chariot and **b** him in his 2Kg 9:28
and he was **b** in Samaria. 2Kg 10:35
Then they **b** him with his fathers 2Kg 12:21
and he was **b** in Samaria. 2Kg 13:9
Jehoash was **b** in Samaria with 2Kg 13:13
Then Elisha died and was **b**. 2Kg 13:20
and he was **b** in Samaria with the 2Kg 14:16
and he was **b** in Jerusalem with 2Kg 14:20
and he was **b** with his fathers in 2Kg 15:7
and he was **b** with his fathers in 2Kg 15:38
fathers and was **b** with his 2Kg 16:20
fathers and was **b** in the garden 2Kg 21:18
He was **b** in his tomb in the 2Kg 21:26
and **b** him in his own tomb. 2Kg 23:30
They **b** their bones under the oak 1Ch 10:12
fathers and was **b** in the city of 2Ch 9:31
fathers and was **b** in the city 2Ch 12:16
fathers and was **b** in the city 2Ch 14:1
He was **b** in his own tomb that he 2Ch 16:14
fathers and was **b** with his 2Ch 21:1
regret and was **b** in the city of 2Ch 21:20
They **b** him, for they said, "He 2Ch 22:9
He was **b** in the city of David 2Ch 24:16
and they **b** him in the city of 2Ch 24:25
back on horses and **b** him with 2Ch 25:28
and he was **b** with his fathers in 2Ch 26:23
fathers and was **b** in the city 2Ch 27:9
fathers and was **b** in the city, 2Ch 28:27
fathers and was **b** on the ascent 2Ch 32:33
and he was **b** in his own house. 2Ch 33:20
they **b** him in the tomb of his 2Ch 35:24
my ancestors are **b** lies in ruins Neh 2:3
city where my ancestors are **b**, Neh 2:5
have **b** my strength in the dust. Jb 16:15
him will be **b** by the plague, Jb 27:15
I saw the wicked **b**. Ec 8:10
collected and **b** but will become Jr 8:2
be mourned or **b** but will be like Jr 16:4
you will be **b**, you and all your Jr 20:6
He will be **b** ⌊like⌋ a donkey, Jr 22:19
not be mourned, gathered, or **b**. Jr 25:33
all his hordes will be **b** there. Ezk 39:11
buriers have **b** it in the Valley Ezk 39:15
like treasure, **b** in a field, Mt 13:44
the corpse, **b** it, and went Mt 14:12
rich man also died and was **b**. Lk 16:22
both dead and **b**, and his tomb is Ac 2:29
carried him out, and **b** him. Ac 5:6
those who have **b** your husband Ac 5:9
and **b** her beside her husband. Ac 5:10
But devout men **b** Stephen and Ac 8:2
asleep, was **b** with his fathers Ac 13:36
Therefore we were **b** with Him by Rm 6:4
He was **b**, that He was raised 1Co 15:4
Having been **b** with Him in Col 2:12

BURIERS *(1)*
to it until the **b** have buried it Ezk 39:15

BURIES *(2)*
The slacker **b** his hand in the Pr 19:24
The slacker **b** his hand in the Pr 26:15

BURN *(128)*
must **b** up any part of it that Ex 12:10
b for burn, bruise for bruise, Ex 21:25
burn for **b**, bruise for bruise, Ex 21:25
My anger will **b**, and I will kill Ex 22:24
and **b** ⌊them⌋ on the altar. Ex 29:13
But **b** up the bull's flesh, Ex 29:14
Then **b** the whole ram on the Ex 29:18
their hands and **b** ⌊them⌋ on the Ex 29:25
until morning, **b** up what is left Ex 29:34
Aaron must **b** fragrant incense on Ex 30:7
he must **b** it every morning when Ex 30:7
at twilight, he must **b** incense. Ex 30:8
that My anger can **b** against them Ex 32:10
does Your anger **b** against Your Ex 32:11
Then the priest will **b** all of it Lv 1:9
all of it and **b** ⌊it⌋ on the Lv 1:13
off its head and **b** ⌊it⌋ on the Lv 1:15
priest is to **b** it on the altar Lv 1:17
and will **b** this memorial portion Lv 2:2
offering and **b** it on the altar, Lv 2:9
you are not to **b** any yeast or Lv 2:11
priest will then **b** some of its Lv 2:16
sons will **b** it on the altar Lv 3:5
priest will **b** it on the altar Lv 3:11
the priest will **b** them on the Lv 3:16
The priest is to **b** them on the Lv 4:10
and must **b** it on a wood fire. Lv 4:12
from it and **b** it on the altar Lv 4:19
the camp and **b** it just as he Lv 4:21
He must **b** all its fat on the Lv 4:26
The priest is to **b** ⌊it⌋ on the Lv 4:31
priest will **b** it on the altar Lv 4:35
portion and **b** ⌊it⌋ on the altar Lv 5:12
the priest will **b** wood on the Lv 6:12
on the fire and **b** the fat Lv 6:12
b its memorial portion on the Lv 6:15
The priest will **b** them on the Lv 7:5
priest is to **b** the fat on the Lv 7:31
must **b** up what remains of the Lv 8:32
When there is a **b** on the skin of Lv 13:24
patch made raw by the **b** becomes Lv 13:24
that has broken out in the **b**. Lv 13:25
it is the swelling from the **b**. Lv 13:28
is ⌊only⌋ the scar from the **b**. Lv 13:28
He is to **b** the fabric, the warp Lv 13:52
you must **b** up the fabric. Lv 13:55
You must **b** up whatever is Lv 13:57
He is to **b** the fat of the sin Lv 16:25
tent of meeting and **b** the fat as Lv 17:6
that the lamp will **b** regularly. Lv 24:2
portion and **b** it on the altar. Nm 5:26
on the altar and **b** their fat as Nm 18:17
LORD's anger will **b** against you, Dt 7:4
and **b** up their carved images. Dt 7:5

You must **b** up the carved images Dt 7:25
LORD's anger will **b** against you. Dt 11:17
sacred pillars, **b** up their Dt 12:3
They even **b** their sons and Dt 12:31
and completely **b** up the city and Dt 13:16
and jealousy will **b** against that Dt 29:20
My anger will **b** against them on Dt 31:17
horses and **b** up their chariots. Jos 11:6
Israel did not **b** any of the Jos 11:13
LORD's anger will **b** against you, Jos 23:16
will **b** your house down with you Jdg 12:1
or we will **b** you and your Jdg 14:15
My altar, to **b** incense, and to 1Sm 2:28
beside the altar to **b** incense. 1Kg 13:1
appointed to **b** incense at the 2Kg 23:5
to **b** incense in the presence of 1Ch 23:13
as a place to **b** incense before 2Ch 2:6
pure gold to **b** in front of the 2Ch 4:20
LORD's sanctuary to **b** incense on 2Ch 26:16
lamps, did not **b** incense, and 2Ch 29:7
and you must **b** incense on it"? 2Ch 32:12
God's house to **b** on the altar Neh 10:34
and my bones **b** with fever. Jb 30:30
will make them ⌊**b**⌋ like a fiery Ps 21:9
does Your anger **b** against the Ps 74:1
and my bones **b** like a furnace. Ps 102:3
you and will **b** away your dross Is 1:25
both will **b** together, with no Is 1:31
one day it will **b** up Assyria's Is 10:17
trample it, and **b** it to the Is 27:4
and the flame will not **b** you. Is 43:2
who **b** with lust among the oaks, Is 57:5
abandoned Me to **b** incense to Jr 1:16
like fire and **b** with no one to Jr 4:4
falsely, **b** incense to Baal, Jr 7:9
will **b** and not be quenched. Jr 7:20
Hinnom in order to **b** their sons Jr 7:31
altars to **b** incense to Baal— Jr 11:13
a fire that will **b** against you. Jr 15:14
on fire; it will **b** forever. Jr 17:4
They **b** incense to false ⌊idols⌋ Jr 18:15
on which to **b** their children Jr 19:5
Babylon, who will **b** it down.' Jr 21:10
up like fire and **b** unquenchably Jr 21:12
and **b** it along with the houses Jr 32:29
offerings, to **b** grain offerings, Jr 33:18
Babylon, and he will **b** it down. Jr 34:2
it, capture it, and **b** it down. Jr 34:22
the king not to **b** the scroll, Jr 36:25
will capture it and **b** it down. Jr 37:8
get up and **b** this city down. Jr 37:10
They will **b** it down, and you Jr 38:18
and this city will **b** down.'" Jr 38:23
and he will **b** them and take them Jr 43:12
of Egypt and **b** down the temples Jr 43:13
b incense to the queen of heaven Jr 44:17
time we ceased to **b** incense to Jr 44:18
we have made to **b** incense to the Jr 44:25
are to **b** up one third ⌊of it⌋ Ezk 5:2
into the fire, and **b** them in it. Ezk 5:4
they will **b** down your houses Ezk 16:41
daughters and **b** their houses Ezk 23:47
fires, and **b** the weapons— Ezk 39:9
and they **b** offerings on the Hs 4:13
dragnet and **b** incense to their Hab 1:16
chaff He will **b** up with fire Mt 3:12
tie them in bundles to **b** them, Mt 13:30
of the Lord and **b** incense. Lk 1:9
chaff He will **b** up with a fire Lk 3:17
to marry than to **b** with desire. 1Co 7:9
and I do not **b** with indignation? 2Co 11:29
elements will **b** and be dissolved 2Pt 3:10
the power to **b** people with fire Rv 16:8
her flesh, and **b** her up with Rv 17:16

BURNED *(161)*

"Let her be **b** ⌊to death⌋!" Gn 38:24
LORD's anger **b** against Moses, Ex 4:14
full restitution for what was **b**. Ex 22:6
they had made, **b** ⌊it⌋ up, and Ex 32:20
and **b** fragrant incense on it, Ex 40:27
It is to be **b** at the ash heap. Lv 4:12
it just as he **b** the first bull. Lv 4:21
be completely **b** as a permanent Lv 6:22
the holy place; it must be **b** up. Lv 6:30
by the third day must be **b** up. Lv 7:17
it is to be **b** up. Everyone who Lv 7:19
and he **b** them on the altar. Lv 8:16
He **b** up the bull with its hide, Lv 8:17
ram into pieces and **b** the head, Lv 8:20
He then **b** the entire ram on the Lv 8:21
their hands and **b** ⌊them⌋ on the Lv 8:28
He **b** the fat, the kidneys, and Lv 9:10
He **b** up the flesh and the hide Lv 9:11
and he **b** ⌊them⌋ on the altar. Lv 9:13
and the shanks and **b** them with Lv 9:14
b it on the altar in addition Lv 9:17
Aaron **b** the fat portions on the Lv 9:20
presence and **b** them to death Lv 10:2
but it had already been **b** up. Lv 10:16
harmful mildew it must be **b** up. Lv 13:52
hide, flesh, and dung **b** up. Lv 16:27
on the third day must be **b** up. Lv 19:6
he and they must be **b** with fire, Lv 20:14
her father; she must be **b** up. Lv 21:9
heard, His anger **b**, and the fire Nm 11:1
the LORD's anger **b** against the Nm 11:33
The LORD'S anger **b** against them, Nm 12:9
those who were **b** had presented, Nm 16:39
The cow must be **b** in his sight. Nm 19:5
are to be **b** along with its dung. Nm 19:5
The one who **b** the cow must also Nm 19:8
LORD's anger **b** against Israel. Nm 25:3
Then they **b** all the cities where Nm 31:10
So the LORD'S anger **b** that day, Nm 32:10
LORD'S anger **b** against Israel, Nm 32:13
you had made, **b** it up, and Dt 9:21
the LORD's anger **b** against this Dt 29:27
b up the city and everything Jos 6:24
and the LORD's anger **b** against Jos 7:1
the things set apart must be **b**, Jos 7:15
b their bodies, threw stones Jos 7:25
Joshua **b** Ai and left it a Jos 8:28
their horses and **b** up their Jos 11:9
Then he **b** down Hazor. Jos 11:11
except Hazor, which Joshua **b**. Jos 11:13
LORD's anger **b** against Israel, Jdg 2:14
LORD'S anger **b** against Israel, Jdg 2:20
LORD's anger **b** against Israel, Jdg 3:8
LORD's anger **b** against Israel, Jdg 10:7
He **b** up the piles of grain and Jdg 15:5
father and **b** ⌊them⌋ to death. Jdg 15:6
swords and **b** down the city. Jdg 18:27
They also **b** down all the cities Jdg 20:48
Even before the fat was **b**, 1Sm 2:15
him, "The fat must be **b** first; 1Sm 2:16
and his anger **b** furiously. 1Sm 11:6
and attacked and **b** down Ziklag. 1Sm 30:1
the town, they found it **b** down. 1Sm 30:3
of Caleb, and we **b** down Ziklag." 1Sm 30:14
at Jabesh, they **b** the bodies 1Sm 31:12
LORD's anger **b** against Uzzah, 2Sm 6:7
shook because He **b** with anger. 2Sm 22:8
be completely **b** up on the spot. 2Sm 23:7
LORD's anger **b** against Israel 2Sm 24:1
sacrificed and **b** incense on the 1Kg 3:3
He then **b** it down, killed the 1Kg 9:16
he **b** incense with them in the 1Kg 9:25
on the altar, and **b** incense. 1Kg 12:33
bones will be **b** on you.'" 1Kg 13:2
image and **b** it in the Kidron 1Kg 15:13
palace and **b** down the royal 1Kg 16:18
to be **b** and on the wood. 1Kg 18:33
sacrificed and **b** incense on the 1Kg 22:43
of the temple of Baal and **b** them 2Kg 10:26
LORD's anger **b** against Israel, 2Kg 13:3
He sacrificed and **b** incense on 2Kg 16:4
They **b** incense on all the high 2Kg 17:11
the Sepharvites **b** their children 2Kg 17:31
the Israelites **b** incense to it 2Kg 18:4
Me and **b** incense to other 2Kg 22:17
He **b** them outside Jerusalem in 2Kg 23:4
They had **b** incense to Baal, 2Kg 23:5
He **b** it at the Kidron Valley, 2Kg 23:6
where the priests had **b** incense. 2Kg 23:8
and he **b** up the chariots of the 2Kg 23:11
he **b** the high place, crushed 2Kg 23:15
it to dust, and **b** the Asherah. 2Kg 23:15
and he **b** them on the altar. 2Kg 23:16
and he **b** human bones on the 2Kg 23:20
which **b** against Judah because of 2Kg 23:26
He **b** the LORD's temple, the 2Kg 25:9
he **b** down all the great houses. 2Kg 25:9
LORD's anger **b** against Uzzah, 1Ch 13:10
that they be **b** in the fire. 1Ch 14:12
crushed it and **b** it in the 2Ch 15:16
them and **b** incense to them 2Ch 25:14
He **b** incense in the Valley of 2Ch 28:3
of Hinnom and **b** his children 2Ch 28:3
He sacrificed and **b** incense on 2Ch 28:4
He **b** the bones of the priests on 2Ch 34:5
Me and **b** incense to other 2Ch 34:25
the Chaldeans **b** God's temple. 2Ch 36:19
Jerusalem's wall, **b** down all its 2Ch 36:19
and its gates have been **b** down." Neh 1:3
and its gates have been **b** down. Neh 2:17
and his anger **b** within him. Est 1:12
It **b** up the sheep and the Jb 1:16
shook because He **b** with anger. Ps 18:7
as I mused, a fire **b**. Ps 39:3
They **b** down every place Ps 74:8
It was cut down and **b** up; Ps 80:16
the LORD's anger **b** against His Ps 106:40
fire and his clothes not be **b**? Pr 6:27
your cities **b** with fire; Is 1:7
in the land, it will be **b** again. Is 6:13
of war will be **b** as fuel for the Is 9:5
earth's inhabitants have been **b**, Is 24:6
The peoples will be **b** to ashes, Is 33:12
thorns cut down and **b** in a fire. Is 33:12
it **b** him, but he paid no Is 42:25
I **b** half of it in the fire, Is 44:19
You, has been **b** with fire, and Is 64:11
Because they **b** incense on the Is 65:7
They have **b** incense in it to Jr 19:4
rooftops they have **b** incense to Jr 19:13
has been **b** to Baal on their Jr 32:29
the king had **b** the scroll with Jr 36:27
that Jehoiakim king of Judah **b**. Jr 36:28
You have **b** the scroll, saying: Jr 36:29
Judah's king, had **b** in the fire. Jr 36:32
this city will not be **b** down, Jr 38:17
Chaldeans next **b** down the king's Jr 39:8
poured forth and **b** in Judah's Jr 44:6
When we **b** incense to the queen Jr 44:19
the incense you **b** in Judah's Jr 44:21
Because you **b** incense and sinned Jr 44:23
and its villages will be **b** down. Jr 49:2
He **b** the LORD's temple, the Jr 52:13
the spices! Let the bones be **b**! Ezk 24:10
and it must be **b** outside the Ezk 43:21
when she **b** incense to them, Hs 2:13
because he **b** to lime the bones Am 2:1
her wages will be **b** in the fire, Mc 1:7
are gathered and **b** in the fire, Mt 13:40
and **b** down their city. Mt 22:7
into the fire, and they are **b**. Jn 15:6
their books and **b** them in front Ac 19:19
anyone's work is **b** up, it will 1Co 3:15
and if I give my body to be **b**, 1Co 13:3
and will be **b** at the end. Heb 6:8
offering are **b** outside the camp Heb 13:11
a third of the earth was **b** up, Rv 8:7
a third of the trees were **b** up, Rv 8:7
all the green grass was **b** up. Rv 8:7
and people were **b** by the intense Rv 16:9
She will be **b** up with fire, Rv 18:8

BURNED-OUT *(1)*

and turn you into a **b** mountain. Jr 51:25

BURNER *(4)*

had an incense **b** in his hand, Ezk 8:11
relative and a **b**, will remove Am 6:10
a gold incense **b**, came and stood Rv 8:3
The angel took the incense **b**, Rv 8:5

BURNERS *(1)*

His ministers and **b** of incense." 2Ch 29:11

BURNING *(93)*

LORD rained **b** sulfur on Sodom Gn 19:24
Why isn't the bush **b** up? Ex 3:3
You unleashed Your **b** wrath; Ex 15:7
to keep the lamp **b** continually. Ex 27:20
an altar for the **b** of incense; Ex 30:1
to minister by **b** up an offering Ex 30:20
on top of the **b** wood on the Lv 1:8
on top of the **b** wood on the Lv 1:12
the altar on top of the **b** wood. Lv 1:17
offering that is on the **b** wood, Lv 3:5
of the altar is kept **b** on it. Lv 6:9
on the altar is to be kept **b**; Lv 6:12
Fire must be kept **b** on the altar Lv 6:13
the firepans from the **b** debris, Nm 16:37
the fire where the cow is **b**. Nm 19:6
so that His **b** anger may turn Nm 25:4
to the LORD's **b** anger against Nm 32:14

turn from His **b** anger and grant Dt 13:17
inflammation, **b** heat, drought, Dt 28:22
soil will be a **b** waste of sulfur Dt 29:23
who appeared in the ⌊**b**⌋ bush. Dt 33:16
LORD turned from His **b** anger. Jos 7:26
who were **b** incense and offering 1Kg 11:8
places who are **b** incense on you. 1Kg 13:2
sacrificing and **b** incense on the 2Kg 12:3
sacrificing and **b** incense on the 2Kg 14:4
sacrificing and **b** incense on the 2Kg 15:4
sacrificing and **b** incense on the 2Kg 15:35
it to Him for **b** sweet incense 2Ch 2:4
B sulfur is scattered over his Jb 18:15
will send His **b** anger against Jb 20:23
from a boiling pot or ⌊**b**⌋ reeds. Jb 41:20
He will rain **b** coals and sulfur Ps 11:6
For my loins are full of **b** pain, Ps 38:7
green or **b**—He will sweep Ps 58:9
and let Your **b** anger overtake Ps 69:24
sent His **b** anger against them: Ps 78:49
Your jealousy keep **b** like fire? Ps 79:5
You turned from Your **b** anger. Ps 85:3
Your anger keep **b** like fire? Ps 89:46
sharp arrows, with **b** charcoal! Ps 120:4
alive in their **b** anger against Ps 124:3
crackling of ⌊**b**⌋ thorns under Ec 7:6
of judgment and a spirit of **b**. Is 4:4
will kindle a **b** fire under its Is 10:16
with rage and **b** anger—to make Is 13:9
on the day of His **b** anger. Is 13:13
anger **b** and heavy with smoke. Is 30:27
her land will become **b** pitch. Is 34:9
in gardens, **b** incense on bricks, Is 65:3
for the LORD's **b** anger has not Jr 4:8
of the LORD and His **b** anger. Jr 4:26
My anger—My **b** wrath—is about Jr 7:20
they have been **b** incense to, Jr 11:12
to anger by **b** incense to Baal. Jr 11:17
because of the LORD's **b** anger. Jr 12:13
becomes a fire **b** in my heart, Jr 20:9
because of the LORD's **b** anger. Jr 25:37
because of His **b** anger. Jr 25:38
The LORD's **b** anger will not turn Jr 30:24
There will be a **b** ceremony for Jr 34:5
just like the **b** ceremonies for Jr 34:5
with a fire **b** in front of him. Jr 36:22
going and **b** incense to serve Jr 44:3
evil or stop **b** incense to other Jr 44:5
You are **b** incense to other gods Jr 44:8
wives were **b** incense to other Jr 44:15
disaster on them, My **b** anger. Jr 49:37
of you, from the LORD's **b** anger. Jr 51:45
on the day of His **b** anger? Lm 1:12
of Israel in His **b** anger and Lm 2:3
wrath, poured out His **b** anger; Lm 4:11
appearance of **b** coals of fire Ezk 1:13
Certainly in My **b** zeal I speak Ezk 36:5
I speak in My **b** zeal because you Ezk 36:6
and given over to the **b** fire. Dn 7:11
to the Baals and **b** offerings to Hs 11:2
you were like a **b** stick snatched Am 4:11
the house of Joseph a ⌊**b**⌋ flame, Ob 18
turn from His **b** anger so that we Jnh 3:9
Who can endure His **b** anger? Nah 1:6
before the **b** of the LORD's anger Zph 2:2
on them, all My **b** anger; Zph 3:8
this man a **b** stick snatched Zch 3:2
day is coming, **b** like a furnace, Mal 4:1
of the day and the **b** heat!' Mt 20:12
in the passage about the **b** bush, Mk 12:26
about the **b** bush that the dead Lk 20:37
John was a **b** and shining lamp, Jn 5:35
Sinai, in the flame of a **b** bush. Ac 7:30
B before the throne were seven Rv 4:5
they see the smoke of her **b**. Rv 18:9
smoke from her **b** and kept crying Rv 18:18

BURNISHED *(1)*

temple ⌊were made⌋ of **b** bronze. 1Kg 7:45

BURNS *(16)*

one who **b** them is to wash his Lv 16:28
of My anger and **b** to the depths Dt 32:22
His anger **b** against me, and He Jb 19:11
to pieces; He **b** up the chariots. Ps 46:9
As fire **b** a forest, as a flame Ps 83:14
before Him and **b** up His foes Ps 97:3
the LORD's anger **b** against His Is 5:25
wickedness **b** like a fire that Is 9:18
He **b** half of it in a fire, Is 44:16
stubble; fire **b** them up. They Is 47:14
a fire that **b** all day long. Is 65:5
high place and **b** incense to his Jr 48:35
My anger **b** against them. Hs 8:5
anger **b** against the shepherds, Zch 10:3
lake of fire that **b** with sulfur. Rv 19:20
be in the lake that **b** with fire Rv 21:8

BURNT *(295)*

bird and offered **b** offerings on Gn 8:20
him there as a **b** offering on one Gn 22:2
wood for a **b** offering and set Gn 22:3
the wood for the **b** offering and Gn 22:6
is the lamb for the **b** offering?" Gn 22:7
the lamb for the **b** offering, Gn 22:8
offered it as a **b** offering in Gn 22:13
sacrifices and **b** offerings to Ex 10:25
brought a **b** offering and Ex 18:12
sacrifice on it your **b** offerings Ex 20:24
and they offered **b** offerings and Ex 24:5
it is a **b** offering to the LORD. Ex 29:18
altar on top of the **b** offering. Ex 29:25
will be a regular **b** offering Ex 29:42
on it, or a **b** or grain offering Ex 30:9
the altar of **b** offering with all Ex 30:28
the altar of **b** offering with all Ex 31:9
they arose, offered **b** offerings, Ex 32:6
the altar of **b** offering with its Ex 35:16
the altar of **b** offering from Ex 38:1
the altar of **b** offering in front Ex 40:6
the altar of **b** offering and all Ex 40:10
placed the altar of **b** offering Ex 40:29
and offered the **b** offering and Ex 40:29
If his gift is a **b** offering from Lv 1:3
the head of the **b** offering so it Lv 1:4
must skin the **b** offering and cut Lv 1:6
it on the altar as a **b** offering, Lv 1:9
if his gift for a **b** offering is Lv 1:10
it is a **b** offering, a fire Lv 1:13
to the LORD is a **b** offering of Lv 1:14
It is a **b** offering, a fire Lv 1:17
along with the **b** offering that Lv 3:5
of the altar of **b** offering that Lv 4:7
them on the altar of **b** offering. Lv 4:10
of the altar of **b** offering that Lv 4:18
the place where the **b** offering Lv 4:24
of the altar of **b** offering. Lv 4:25
base of the altar of **b** offering. Lv 4:25
at the place of the **b** offering. Lv 4:29
of the altar of **b** offering. Lv 4:30
the place where the **b** offering Lv 4:33
of the altar of **b** offering. Lv 4:34
and the other as a **b** offering. Lv 5:7
bird⌋ as a **b** offering according Lv 5:10
is the law of the **b** offering; Lv 6:9
b offering itself must remain Lv 6:9
the ashes of the **b** offering the Lv 6:10
is to arrange the **b** offering on Lv 6:12
will be a whole **b** offering; Lv 6:23
the place where the **b** offering Lv 6:25
the place where the **b** offering Lv 7:2
presents someone's **b** offering, Lv 7:8
hide of the **b** offering he has Lv 7:8
is the law for the **b** offering, Lv 7:37
the ram for the **b** offering, Lv 8:18
It was a **b** offering for a Lv 8:21
the altar with the **b** offering. Lv 8:28
and a ram for a **b** offering, Lv 9:2
blemish, for a **b** offering; Lv 9:3
offering and your **b** offering; Lv 9:7
he slaughtered the **b** offering. Lv 9:12
brought him the **b** offering piece Lv 9:13
burned them with the **b** offering Lv 9:14
He presented the **b** offering and Lv 9:16
to the morning **b** offering. Lv 9:17
sin offering, the **b** offering, Lv 9:22
and consumed the **b** offering and Lv 9:24
and their **b** offering before Lv 10:19
male lamb for a **b** offering, Lv 12:6
one for a **b** offering and the Lv 12:8
sin offering and **b** offering are Lv 14:13
will slaughter the **b** offering. Lv 14:19
is to offer the **b** offering and Lv 14:20
and the other a **b** offering. Lv 14:22
and the other as a **b** offering, Lv 14:31
and the other as a **b** offering. Lv 15:15
and the other as a **b** offering. Lv 15:30
and a ram for a **b** offering. Lv 16:3
and one ram for a **b** offering. Lv 16:5
out and sacrifice his **b** offering Lv 16:24
and the people's **b** offering; Lv 16:24
them who offers a **b** offering or Lv 17:8
to the LORD as **b** offerings— Lv 22:18
blemish as a **b** offering to the Lv 23:12
They will be a **b** offering to the Lv 23:18
b offerings and grain offerings, Lv 23:37
other as a **b** offering to make Nm 6:11
male lamb as a **b** offering, Nm 6:14
sin offering and **b** offering. Nm 6:16
a year old, for a **b** offering; Nm 7:15
a year old, for a **b** offering; Nm 7:21
a year old, for a **b** offering; Nm 7:27
a year old, for a **b** offering; Nm 7:33
a year old, for a **b** offering; Nm 7:39
a year old, for a **b** offering; Nm 7:45
a year old, for a **b** offering; Nm 7:51
a year old, for a **b** offering; Nm 7:57
a year old, for a **b** offering; Nm 7:63
a year old, for a **b** offering; Nm 7:69
a year old, for a **b** offering; Nm 7:75
a year old, for a **b** offering; Nm 7:81
for the **b** offering totaled Nm 7:87
and the other as a **b** offering to Nm 8:12
over your **b** offerings and your Nm 10:10
either a **b** offering or a Nm 15:3
offering with the **b** offering or Nm 15:5
young bull as a **b** offering or as Nm 15:8
young bull for a **b** offering as Nm 15:24
the ashes of the **b** sin offering, Nm 19:17
here by your **b** offering while I Nm 23:3
there by his **b** offering with all Nm 23:6
here by your **b** offering while I Nm 23:15
there by his **b** offering with Nm 23:17
lambs as a regular **b** offering. Nm 28:3
It is a regular **b** offering Nm 28:6
It is the **b** offering for every Nm 28:10
the regular **b** offering and its Nm 28:10
months present a **b** offering to Nm 28:11
It is a **b** offering, a pleasing Nm 28:13
the monthly **b** offering for all Nm 28:14
to the regular **b** offering with Nm 28:15
a fire offering, a **b** offering to Nm 28:19
the morning **b** offering that is Nm 28:23
part of the regular **b** offering. Nm 28:23
and the regular **b** offering. Nm 28:24
Present a **b** offering for a Nm 28:27
the regular **b** offering and its Nm 28:31
Offer a **b** offering as a pleasing Nm 29:2
and regular **b** offerings with Nm 29:6
a **b** offering to the LORD, Nm 29:8
The regular **b** offering with its Nm 29:11
Present a **b** offering, a fire Nm 29:13
to the regular **b** offering with Nm 29:16
to the regular **b** offering with Nm 29:19
to the regular **b** offering with Nm 29:22
to the regular **b** offering with Nm 29:25
to the regular **b** offering with Nm 29:28
to the regular **b** offering with Nm 29:31
to the regular **b** offering with Nm 29:34
Present a **b** offering, a fire Nm 29:36
to the regular **b** offering with Nm 29:38
whether **b**, grain, drink, Nm 29:39
to bring there your **b** offerings Dt 12:6
your **b** offerings, sacrifices, Dt 12:11
to offer your **b** offerings in all Dt 12:13
must offer your **b** offerings only Dt 12:14
and blood of your **b** offerings on Dt 12:27
your God and offer **b** offerings Dt 27:6
and whole **b** offerings on Your Dt 33:10
Then they offered **b** offerings to Jos 8:31
intended⌋ to offer **b** offerings Jos 22:23
but not for **b** offering or Jos 22:26
presence with our **b** offerings, Jos 22:27
not for **b** offering or sacrifice, Jos 22:28
an altar for **b** offering, Jos 22:29
offer it as a **b** offering with Jdg 6:26
will offer it as a **b** offering." Jdg 11:31
want to prepare a **b** offering, Jdg 13:16
have accepted the **b** offering and Jdg 13:23
arms became like **b** flax and his Jdg 15:14
evening and offered **b** offerings Jdg 20:26
and offered **b** offerings and Jdg 21:4
the cows as a **b** offering to the 1Sm 6:14
offered **b** offerings and made 1Sm 6:15
it as a whole **b** offering to the 1Sm 7:9
was offering the **b** offering as 1Sm 7:10
to you to offer **b** offerings and 1Sm 10:8

Bring me the **b** offering and the 1Sm 13:9
Then he offered the **b** offering. 1Sm 13:9
offering the **b** offering, 1Sm 13:10
myself to offer the **b** offering." 1Sm 13:12
take pleasure in **b** offerings 1Sm 15:22
Then David offered **b** offerings 2Sm 6:17
finished offering the **b** offering 2Sm 6:18
are the oxen for a **b** offering 2Sm 24:22
the LORD my God **b** offerings that 2Sm 24:24
there and offered **b** offerings 2Sm 24:25
He offered 1,000 **b** offerings on 1Kg 3:4
and offered **b** offerings and 1Kg 3:15
where he offered the **b** offering, 1Kg 8:64
to accommodate the **b** offerings, 1Kg 8:64
year Solomon offered **b** offerings 1Kg 9:25
and the **b** offerings he offered 1Kg 10:5
and consumed the **b** offering, 1Kg 18:38
offered him as a **b** offering on 2Kg 3:27
no longer offer a **b** offering 2Kg 5:17
sacrifices and **b** offerings. 2Kg 10:24
offering the **b** offering, 2Kg 10:25
offered his **b** offering and his 2Kg 16:13
altar the morning **b** offering, 2Kg 16:15
the king's **b** offering and his 2Kg 16:15
offer⌋ the **b** offering of all 2Kg 16:15
blood of the **b** offering and all 2Kg 16:15
on the altar of **b** offerings 1Ch 6:49
Then they offered **b** offerings 1Ch 16:1
offering the **b** offerings 1Ch 16:2
to offer **b** offerings regularly, 1Ch 16:40
on the altar of **b** offerings and 1Ch 16:40
the oxen for the **b** offerings, 1Ch 21:23
to you or offer **b** offerings that 1Ch 21:24
there and offered **b** offerings 1Ch 21:26
on the altar of **b** offering. 1Ch 21:26
the altar of **b** offering were at 1Ch 21:29
is the altar of **b** offering for 1Ch 22:1
Whenever **b** offerings are offered 1Ch 23:31
to the LORD and **b** offerings to 1Ch 29:21
offered 1,000 **b** offerings on it 2Ch 1:6
⌊sacrificing⌋ **b** offerings for 2Ch 2:4
The parts of the **b** offering were 2Ch 4:6
and consumed the **b** offering 2Ch 7:1
where he offered the **b** offerings 2Ch 7:7
not accommodate the **b** offering, 2Ch 7:7
Solomon offered **b** offerings to 2Ch 8:12
and the **b** offerings he offered 2Ch 9:4
They offer a **b** offering and 2Ch 13:11
to offer **b** offerings to the LORD 2Ch 23:18
and for making **b** offerings, 2Ch 24:14
regularly offered **b** offerings 2Ch 24:14
and did not offer **b** offerings in 2Ch 29:7
the altar of **b** offering and all 2Ch 29:18
said that the **b** offering and sin 2Ch 29:24
ordered that the **b** offering be 2Ch 29:27
When the **b** offerings began, 2Ch 29:27
until the **b** offering was 2Ch 29:28
When the **b** offerings were 2Ch 29:29
hearts brought **b** offerings. 2Ch 29:31
The number of **b** offerings the 2Ch 29:32
these were for a **b** offering to 2Ch 29:32
to skin all the **b** offerings, 2Ch 29:34
the **b** offerings were abundant, 2Ch 29:35
offerings for the **b** offering. 2Ch 29:35
and brought **b** offerings to 2Ch 30:15
and Levites for the **b** offerings 2Ch 31:2
morning and evening **b** offerings, 2Ch 31:3
the **b** offerings of the Sabbaths, 2Ch 31:3
They removed the **b** offerings so 2Ch 35:12
busy offering up **b** offerings and 2Ch 35:14
and for offering **b** offerings on 2Ch 35:16
order to offer **b** offerings on it Ezr 3:2
and offered **b** offerings for Ezr 3:3
and ⌊offered⌋ **b** offerings each Ezr 3:4
offered⌋ the regular **b** offering Ezr 3:5
began to offer **b** offerings to Ezr 3:6
and lambs for **b** offerings to the Ezr 6:9
captivity offered **b** offerings to Ezr 8:35
this was a **b** offering for the Ezr 8:35
they bring these **b** stones back Neh 4:2
the regular **b** offering, the Neh 10:33
morning to offer **b** offerings for Jb 1:5
and offer a **b** offering for Jb 42:8
and accept your **b** offering. Ps 20:3
ask for a whole **b** offering or a Ps 40:6
or for your **b** offerings, Ps 50:8
not pleased with a **b** offering. Ps 51:16
sacrifices, whole **b** offerings; Ps 51:19
Your house with **b** offerings; Ps 66:13
fattened sheep as **b** offerings, Ps 66:15
had enough of **b** offerings and Is 1:11
animals enough for a **b** offering. Is 40:16
Me your sheep for **b** offerings or Is 43:23
Their **b** offerings and sacrifices Is 56:7
Your **b** offerings are not Jr 6:20
Add your **b** offerings to your Jr 7:21
them concerning **b** offering and Jr 7:22
If they offer **b** offering and Jr 14:12
the Negev bringing **b** offerings Jr 17:26
in the fire as **b** offerings to Jr 19:5
before Me to offer **b** offerings, Jr 33:18
The **b** offering was to be washed Ezk 40:38
to slaughter the **b** offering, Ezk 40:39
of cut stone for the **b** offering, Ezk 40:42
to slaughter the **b** offerings and Ezk 40:42
so that **b** offerings may be Ezk 43:18
sacrifice them as a **b** offering Ezk 43:24
will offer your **b** offerings Ezk 43:27
will slaughter the **b** offerings Ezk 44:11
grain offerings, **b** offerings, Ezk 45:15
Then the **b** offerings, grain Ezk 45:17
grain offerings, **b** offerings, Ezk 45:17
blemish as a **b** offering to the Ezk 45:23
offerings, **b** offerings, grain Ezk 45:25
sacrifice his **b** offerings Ezk 46:2
The **b** offering that the prince Ezk 46:4
⌊the **b** offering⌋ is to be a Ezk 46:6
whether a **b** offering or a Ezk 46:12
He is to offer his **b** offering or Ezk 46:12
lamb as a daily **b** offering to Ezk 46:13
morning as a regular **b** offering. Ezk 46:15
of God rather than **b** offerings. Hs 6:6
offer Me your **b** offerings and Am 5:22
before Him with **b** offerings, Mc 6:6
than all the **b** offerings Mk 12:33
delight in whole **b** offerings and Heb 10:6
whole **b** offerings and sin Heb 10:8

BURST *(12)*
of the watery depths **b** open, Gn 7:11
the LORD has **b** out against my 2Sm 5:20
has used me to **b** out against my 1Ch 14:11
LORD our God **b** out ⌊in anger⌋ 1Ch 15:13
clouds do not **b** beneath their Jb 26:8
it is about to **b** like new Jb 32:19
doors when it **b** from the womb, Jb 38:8
b into song and shout, you who Is 54:1
the skins **b**, the wine spills out Mt 9:17
the wine will **b** the skins, Mk 2:22
the new wine will **b** the skins, Lk 5:37
headfirst, he **b** open in the Ac 1:18

BURSTING *(2)*
said, "Like a **b** flood, the LORD 2Sm 5:20
said, "Like a **b** flood, God has 1Ch 14:11

BURSTS *(2)*
named that place the Lord **B** Out. 2Sm 5:20
named that place the Lord **B** Out. 1Ch 14:11

BURY *(35)*
you so that I can **b** my dead." Gn 23:4
B your dead in our finest burial Gn 23:6
willing ⌊for me⌋ to **b** my dead, Gn 23:8
of my people. **B** your dead." Gn 23:11
and let me **b** my dead there." Gn 23:13
you and me? **B** your dead." Gn 23:15
love. Do not **b** me in Egypt. Gn 47:29
from Egypt and **b** me in their Gn 47:30
B me with my fathers in the cave Gn 49:29
You must **b** me there in the tomb Gn 50:5
Now let me go and **b** my father. Gn 50:5
Go and **b** your father in keeping Gn 50:6
Joseph went to **b** his father, Gn 50:7
gone with him to **b** his father. Gn 50:14
but are to **b** him that day, Dt 21:23
him down and **b** him in order to 1Kg 2:31
had gone to **b** the dead and had 1Kg 11:15
the city to mourn and to **b** him. 1Kg 13:29
you must **b** me in the grave where 1Kg 13:31
will mourn for him and **b** him, 1Kg 14:13
Jezreel—no one will **b** her.'" 2Kg 9:10
of this cursed woman and **b** her, 2Kg 9:34
But when they went out to **b** her, 2Kg 9:35
they did not **b** him in the tombs 2Ch 24:25
there was no one to **b** ⌊them⌋. Ps 79:3
There will be no one to **b** them— Jr 14:16
They will **b** in Topheth until Jr 19:11
there is no place left to **b**. Jr 19:11
the land will **b** ⌊them⌋ and their Ezk 39:13
the land and **b** the invaders who Ezk 39:14
them, and Memphis will **b** them. Hs 9:6
"first let me go **b** my father." Mt 8:21
let the dead **b** their own dead. Mt 8:22
"first let me go **b** my father." Lk 9:59
Let the dead **b** their own dead, Lk 9:60

BURYING *(4)*
burial place for **b** your dead." Gn 23:6
Egyptians were **b** every firstborn Nm 33:4
as the Israelites were **b** a man, 2Kg 13:21
seven months **b** them in order to Ezk 39:12

BUSH *(11)*
in a flame of fire within a **b**. Ex 3:2
saw that the **b** was on fire but Ex 3:2
Why isn't the **b** burning up? Ex 3:3
called out to him from the **b**, Ex 3:4
who appeared in the ⌊burning⌋ **b**. Dt 33:16
like a juniper **b** in the Jr 48:6
the passage about the burning **b**, Mk 12:26
grapes picked from a bramble **b**. Lk 6:44
the burning **b** that the dead are Lk 20:37
in the flame of a burning **b**. Ac 7:30
who appeared to him in the **b**. Ac 7:35

BUSHEL *(15)*
bread from a half **b** of flour. Jdg 6:19
sheep, a **b** of roasted grain, 1Sm 25:18
of seed will yield only ⌊one⌋ **b**. Is 5:10
dry measure ⌊holding⌋ half a **b**. Ezk 45:11
of half a **b** per bull and half Ezk 45:24
per bull and half a **b** per ram, Ezk 45:24
gallon of oil for every half **b**. Ezk 45:24
will be half a **b** with the ram, Ezk 46:5
gallon of oil for every half **b**. Ezk 46:5
of half a **b** with the bull, Ezk 46:7
the bull, half a **b** with the ram, Ezk 46:7
gallon of oil for every half **b**. Ezk 46:7
will be half a **b** with the bull, Ezk 46:11
the bull, half a **b** with the ram, Ezk 46:11
gallon of oil for every half **b**. Ezk 46:11

BUSHELS *(14)*
every⌋ five **b** of barley seed. Lv 27:16
took the least gathered 33 **b**— Nm 11:32
one day were 150 **b** of fine flour 1Kg 4:22
of fine flour and 300 **b** of meal, 1Kg 4:22
with 100,000 **b** of wheat as food 1Kg 5:11
trees, 100,000 **b** of wheat flour, 2Ch 2:10
flour, 100,000 **b** of barley, 2Ch 2:10
silver, 50,000 **b** of wheat, and 2Ch 27:5
wheat, and 50,000 **b** of barley. 2Ch 27:5
of silver, 500 **b** of wheat, 550 Ezr 7:22
and 10 **b** of seed will yield only Is 5:10
quarts from five **b** of wheat and Ezk 45:13
quarts from five **b** of barley. Ezk 45:13
of silver and five **b** of barley. Hs 3:2

BUSHES *(1)*
left the boy under one of the **b**. Gn 21:15

BUSINESS *(18)*
A man in Maon had a **b** in Carmel; 1Sm 25:2
and conducts his **b** fairly. Ps 112:5
and she will go back into **b**, Is 23:17
does the LORD's **b** deceitfully, Jr 48:10
of Kedar were your **b** partners, Ezk 27:21
up and went about the king's **b**. Dn 8:27
What is your **b** and where are you Jnh 1:8
to do what I want with my **b**? Mt 20:15
his own farm, another to his **b**. Mt 22:5
'Engage in **b** until I come back.' Lk 19:13
out how much they had made in **b**. Lk 19:15
a great deal of **b** for the Ac 19:24
engaged in this type of **b**, Ac 19:25
is derived from this **b**. Ac 19:25
a risk that our **b** may be Ac 19:27
to mind your own **b**, and to work 1Th 4:11
there and do **b** and make a profit Jms 4:13
and all who do **b** by sea, stood Rv 18:17

BUSY *(4)*
servant was **b** here and there, 1Kg 20:40
were **b** offering up burnt 2Ch 35:14
forsaken, the **b** city abandoned. Is 32:14
each of you is **b** with his own Hg 1:9

BUSYBODIES *(1)*
but are also gossips and **b**, 1Tm 5:13

BUT *(3880)*
(See pp. xi-xii.)

BUTCHER *(1)*
the wool, and **b** the fatlings, Ezk 34:3

BUTCHERED *(2)*
my meat that I **b** for my shearers 1Sm 25:11
of wine, five **b** sheep, a bushel 1Sm 25:18

BUTCHERING *(1)*
joy and gladness, **b** of cattle, Is 22:13

BUTCHERS *(1)*
or a sheep and **b** it or sells it, Ex 22:1

BUTTED *(1)*
and shoulder and **b** all the weak Ezk 34:21

BUTTER *(4)*
the churning of milk produces **b**, Pr 30:33
he will be eating **b** and honey. Is 7:15
milk they give he will eat **b**, Is 7:22
the land will eat **b** and honey. Is 7:22

BUTTERY *(1)*
His **b** words are smooth, but war Ps 55:21

BUTTOCKS *(1)*
with bared **b**, to Egypt's shame. Is 20:4

BUTTRESS *(1)*
and the corner **b**, and he 2Ch 26:9

BUY *(52)*
to Joseph in Egypt to **b** grain, Gn 41:57
down there and **b** some for us so Gn 42:2
went down to **b** grain from Egypt. Gn 42:3
among those who came to **b** grain, Gn 42:5
the land of Canaan to **b** food," Gn 42:7
servants have come to **b** food," Gn 42:10
"Go back and **b** us some food." Gn 43:2
will go down and **b** food for you. Gn 43:4
the first time only to **b** food. Gn 43:20
money with us to **b** food. Gn 43:22
Go again, and **b** us some food.' Gn 44:25
B us and our land in exchange Gn 47:19
When you **b** a Hebrew slave, Ex 21:2
and **b** water from them to drink. Dt 2:6
but no one will **b** ⌊you⌋." Dt 28:68
B ⌊it⌋ back in the presence of Ru 4:4
On the day you **b** the land from Ru 4:5
"**B** back ⌊the property⌋ yourself." Ru 4:8
To **b** the threshing floor from 2Sm 24:21
would use it⌋ to **b** timber and 2Kg 12:12
and masons to **b** timber and 2Kg 22:6
used it⌋ to **b** quarried stone 2Ch 34:11
you are to **b** with this money as Ezr 7:17
our best to **b** back our Jewish Neh 5:8
and we have to **b** them back." Neh 5:8
the work. We didn't **b** any land. Neh 5:16
we will not **b** from them on the Neh 10:31
B—and do not sell—truth, Pr 23:23
without money, come, **b**, and eat! Is 55:1
b wine and milk without money Is 55:1
Go and **b** yourself linen Jr 13:1
Go, **b** a potter's clay jug. Jr 19:1
B my field in Anathoth for Jr 32:7
right of redemption to **b** it.' Jr 32:7
'Please **b** my field in Anathoth Jr 32:8
redemption. **B** it for yourself. Jr 32:8
B the field with silver and call Jr 32:25
can **b** the poor with silver and Am 8:6
Those who **b** them slaughter them Zch 11:5
the villages and **b** food for Mt 14:15
and **b** oil for yourselves.' Mt 25:9
When they had gone to **b** some, Mt 25:10
and villages to **b** themselves Mk 6:36
Should we go and **b** 200 denarii Mk 6:37
unless we go and **b** food for all Lk 9:13
should sell his robe and **b** one. Lk 22:36
had gone into town to **b** food. Jn 4:8
Where will we **b** bread so these Jn 6:5
B what we need for the festival, Jn 13:29
those who **b** as though they did 1Co 7:30
I advise you to **b** from Me gold Rv 3:18
that no one can **b** or sell unless Rv 13:17

BUYER *(4)*
the **b** says, but after he is on Pr 20:14
and mistress, **b** and seller, Is 24:2
Let the **b** not rejoice and the Ezk 7:12
as he and the **b** remain alive. Ezk 7:13

BUYING *(6)*
today that I am **b** from Naomi Ru 4:9
I insist on **b** it from you for a 2Sm 24:24
with no intention of **b** wisdom? Pr 17:16
out all those **b** and selling Mt 21:12
to throw out those **b** and selling Mk 11:15
eating, drinking, **b**, selling, Lk 17:28

BUYS *(3)*
She evaluates a field and **b** it; Pr 31:16
he has and **b** that field. Mt 13:44
because no one **b** their Rv 18:11

BUZ *(3)*
his brother **B**, Kemuel the father Gn 22:21
son of Jahdo, son of **B**. 1Ch 5:14
Dedan, Tema, **B**, and all those Jr 25:23

BUZI *(1)*
priest, the son of **B**, in the Ezk 1:3

BUZITE *(2)*
Barachel the **B** from the family Jb 32:2
son of Barachel the **B** replied: Jb 32:6

BUZZING *(1)*
land of **b** insect wings beyond Is 18:1

BY *(2497)*
(See pp. xi-xii.)

BYPASS *(2)*
the Red Sea to **b** the land of Nm 21:4
and you **b** justice and love for Lk 11:42

BYPASSED *(1)*
So we **b** our brothers, the Dt 2:8

BYPASSING *(1)*
So, **b** Mysia, they came down to Ac 16:8

C

CABBON *(1)*
C, Lahmam, Chitlish, Jos 15:40

CABUL *(2)*
and Neiel, and went north to **C**, Jos 19:27
So he called them the Land of **C**, 1Kg 9:13

CAESAR *(19)*
(See also AUGUSTUS, TIBERIUS.)
to pay taxes to **C** or not?" Mt 22:17
give back to **C** the things that Mt 22:21
lawful to pay taxes to **C** or not? Mk 12:14
Give back to **C** the things that Mk 12:17
went out from **C** Augustus that Lk 2:1
year of the reign of Tiberius **C**, Lk 3:1
us to pay taxes to **C** or not?" Lk 20:22
give back to **C** the things that Lk 20:25
opposing payment of taxes to **C**, Lk 23:2
makes himself a king opposes **C**!" Jn 19:12
"We have no king but **C**!" Jn 19:15
against **C** have I sinned at all. Ac 25:8
me up to them. I appeal to **C**!" Ac 25:11
"You have appealed to **C**; Ac 25:12
to Caesar; to **C** you will go!" Ac 25:12
until I could send him to **C**." Ac 25:21
if he had not appealed to **C**." Ac 26:32
You must stand before **C**. Ac 27:24
I was compelled to appeal to **C**; Ac 28:19

CAESAR'S *(10)*
"**C**," they said to Him. Mt 22:21
to Caesar the things that are **C**, Mt 22:21
He asked them. "**C**," they said. Mk 12:16
to Caesar the things that are **C**, Mk 12:17
does it have?" "**C**," they said. Lk 20:24
the things that are **C** and to God Lk 20:25
this man, you are not **C** friend. Jn 19:12
acting contrary to **C** decrees, Ac 17:7
I am standing at **C** tribunal, Ac 25:10
those from **C** household. Php 4:22

CAESAREA *(17)*
to the region of **C** Philippi, Mt 16:13
to the villages of **C** Philippi. Mk 8:27
the towns until he came to **C**. Ac 8:40
him down to **C** and sent him off Ac 9:30
was a man in **C** named Cornelius, Ac 10:1
The following day he entered **C**. Ac 10:24
sent to me from **C** arrived at the Ac 11:11
from Judea to **C** and stayed there Ac 12:19
On landing at **C**, he went up and Ac 18:22
next day we left and came to **C**, Ac 21:8
disciples from **C** also went with Ac 21:16
to go to **C** at nine tonight. Ac 23:23
men entered **C** and delivered Ac 23:33
he went up to Jerusalem from **C**. Ac 25:1
that Paul should be kept at **C**, Ac 25:4
among them, he went down to **C**. Ac 25:6
Bernice arrived in **C** and paid a Ac 25:13

CAGE *(2)*
Like a **c** full of birds, so their Jr 5:27
open the rib **c** over their hearts Hs 13:8

CAIAPHAS *(9)*
high priest, who was called **C**, Mt 26:3
Him away to **C** the high priest Mt 26:57
high priesthood of Annas and **C**, Lk 3:2
One of them, **C**, who was high Jn 11:49
he was the father-in-law of **C**, Jn 18:13
C was the one who had advised Jn 18:14
Him bound to **C** the high priest. Jn 18:24
took Jesus from **C** to the Jn 18:28
the high priest, **C**, John and Ac 4:6

CAIN *(20)*
conceived and gave birth to **C**. Gn 4:1
but **C** cultivated the land. Gn 4:2
course of time **C** presented some Gn 4:3
have regard for **C** and his Gn 4:5
C was furious, and he was Gn 4:5
the LORD said to **C**, "Why are you Gn 4:6
C said to his brother Abel, Gn 4:8
C attacked his brother Abel and Gn 4:8
LORD said to **C**, "Where is your Gn 4:9
But **C** answered the LORD, "My Gn 4:13
whoever kills **C** will suffer Gn 4:15
a mark on **C** so that whoever Gn 4:15
Then **C** went out from the LORD's Gn 4:16
C knew his wife intimately, Gn 4:17
Then **C** became the builder of a Gn 4:17
C is to be avenged seven times Gn 4:24
of Abel, since **C** killed him." Gn 4:25
a better sacrifice than **C** ⌊did⌋. Heb 11:4
unlike **C**, who was of the evil 1Jn 3:12
have traveled in the way of **C**, Jd 11

CAINAN *(2)*
⌊son⌋ of **C**, ⌊son⌋ of Arphaxad, Lk 3:36
son⌋ of Mahalaleel, ⌊son⌋ of **C**, Lk 3:37

CAKE *(9)*
one **c** of bread ⌊made⌋ with oil, Ex 29:23
LORD he took one **c** of unleavened Lv 8:26
one **c** of bread ⌊made⌋ with oil, Lv 8:26
unleavened **c** from the basket, Nm 6:19
of bread, a date **c**, and a raisin 2Sm 6:19
a raisin **c** to each one of the 2Sm 6:19
of bread, a date **c**, and a raisin 1Ch 16:3
a date cake, and a raisin **c**. 1Ch 16:3
would⌋ a barley **c** and bake it Ezk 4:12

CAKES *(18)*
unleavened **c** mixed with oil, Ex 29:2
unleavened **c** mixed with oil Lv 2:4
unleavened **c** mixed with olive Lv 7:12
and well-kneaded **c** of fine flour Lv 7:12
as his offering **c** of leavened Lv 7:13
From the **c** he must present one Lv 7:14
of unleavened **c** made from fine Nm 6:15
pot and shaped it into **c**. Nm 11:8
and 200 **c** of pressed figs, 1Sm 25:18
a couple of **c** in my presence 2Sm 13:6
it, made **c** in his presence 2Sm 13:8
Tamar took the **c** she had made 2Sm 13:10
of bread, some **c**, and a jar of 1Kg 14:3
of flour, fig **c**, raisins, wine 1Ch 12:40
the raisin **c** of Kir-hareseth. Is 16:7
dough to make **c** for the queen Jr 7:18
made sacrificial **c** in her image Jr 44:19
other gods and love raisin **c**." Hs 3:1

CALAH *(2)*
built Nineveh, Rehoboth-ir, **C**, Gn 10:11
Nineveh and the great city **C**. Gn 10:12

CALAMITIES *(1)*
He will rescue you from six **c**; Jb 5:19

CALAMITY *(15)*
is at ease holds **c** in contempt Jb 12:5
to generation without **c**." Ps 10:6
indignation, and **c**—a band of Ps 78:49
in turn, will laugh at your **c**. Pr 1:26
a storm and your **c** comes like Pr 1:27
Therefore **c** will strike him Pr 6:15
house in your time of **c**; Pr 27:10
My⌋ face on the day of their **c**. Jr 18:17
the day of their **c** is coming on Jr 46:21
Moab's **c** is near at hand; Jr 48:16
will bring Esau's **c** on him at Jr 49:8
will bring **c** on them across all Jr 49:32
brother in the day of his **c**; Ob 12
c has come from the LORD to the Mc 1:12

No **c** will overtake us.” Mc 3:11

CALAMUS *(1)*

and saffron, **c** and cinnamon, Sg 4:14

CALCOL *(2)*

and Heman, **C**, and Darda, sons 1Kg 4:31
Ethan, Heman, **C**, and Dara—five 1Ch 2:6

CALCULATE *(7)*

he may **c** the years since its Lv 25:27
purchased him is to **c** ⌊the time⌋ Lv 25:50
he will **c** and pay the price of Lv 25:52
the priest will **c** the price for Lv 27:18
the priest will **c** for him the Lv 27:23
sit down and **c** the cost to see Lk 14:28
understanding must **c** the number Rv 13:18

CALCULATED *(1)*

So they **c** their value, and found Ac 19:19

CALDRON *(3)*

or kettle or **c** or cooking pot. 1Sm 2:14
the depths seethe like a **c**; Jb 41:31
cooking pot, like meat in a **c**.” Mc 3:3

CALEB *(31)*
(AKA CHELUBAI)

C son of Jephunneh from the Nm 13:6
Then **C** quieted the people in the Nm 13:30
son of Nun and **C** son of Nm 14:6
My servant **C** has a different Nm 14:24
except **C** son of Jephunneh and Nm 14:30
of Nun and **C** son of Jephunneh Nm 14:38
was left except **C** son of Nm 26:65
none except **C** son of Jephunneh Nm 32:12
C son of Jephunneh from the Nm 34:19
except **C** the son of Jephunneh. Dt 1:36
and **C** son of Jephunneh the Jos 14:6
blessed **C** son of Jephunneh Jos 14:13
has belonged to **C** son of Jos 14:14
He gave **C** son of Jephunneh ⌊the Jos 15:13
C drove out from there the three Jos 15:14
and **C** said, “I will give my Jos 15:16
and **C** gave his daughter Achsah Jos 15:17
off her donkey, **C** asked her, Jos 15:18
the city to **C** son of Jephunneh Jos 21:12
C said, “Whoever strikes down Jdg 1:12
and **C** gave his daughter Achsah Jdg 1:13
off her donkey, **C** asked her, Jdg 1:14
So **C** gave her both the upper Jdg 1:15
gave Hebron to **C**, just as Moses Jdg 1:20
Then **C** drove out the three sons Jdg 1:20
and the south country of **C**, 1Sm 30:14
C son of Hezron had children by 1Ch 2:18
Azubah died, **C** married Ephrath, 1Ch 2:19
The sons of **C** brother of 1Ch 2:42
The sons of **C** son of Jephunneh: 1Ch 4:15
were given to **C** son of Jephunneh 1Ch 6:56

CALEB'S *(7)*

So Othniel son of **C** brother, Jos 15:17
of Kenaz, **C** youngest brother, Jdg 1:13
C youngest brother as a Jdg 3:9
C concubine Ephah was the mother 1Ch 2:46
C concubine Maacah was the 1Ch 2:48
C daughter was Achsah. 1Ch 2:49
These were **C** descendants. 1Ch 2:50

CALEB-EPHRATHAH *(1)*

After Hezron's death in **C**, 1Ch 2:24

CALEBITE *(1)*

but the man, a **C**, was harsh and 1Sm 25:3

CALENDAR *(1)*

the year or be listed in the **c**. Jb 3:6

CALF *(31)*

herd and got a tender, choice **c**. Gn 18:7
and the **c** that he had prepared, Gn 18:8
made it into an image of a **c**. Ex 32:4
for themselves an image of a **c**. Ex 32:8
and saw the **c** and the dancing Ex 32:19
he took the **c** they had made, Ex 32:20
into the fire, out came this **c**!” Ex 32:24
did with the **c** Aaron had made. Ex 32:35
a **c** and a lamb, male yearlings Lv 9:3
slaughtered the **c** as a sin Lv 9:8
you had made a **c** image for Dt 9:16
took the sinful **c** you had made, Dt 9:21
had a fattened **c** at her house, 1Sm 28:24
an ox and a fattened **c**. 2Sm 6:13
an image of a **c** for themselves Neh 9:18
He makes Lebanon skip like a **c**, Ps 29:6
they made a **c** and worshiped Ps 106:19
than a fattened **c** with hatred. Pr 15:17
The **c**, the young lion, and the Is 11:6
disciplined like an untrained **c**. Jr 31:18
them like the **c** they cut in two Jr 34:18
between the pieces of the **c** Jr 34:19
were like the hooves of a **c**, Ezk 1:7
The **c** of Samaria will be smashed Hs 8:6
anxiety over the **c** of Beth-aven. Hs 10:5
The **c** itself will be taken to Hs 10:6
the fattened **c** and slaughter it Lk 15:23
fattened **c** because he has him Lk 15:27
the fattened **c** for him.’ Lk 15:30
even made a **c** in those days, Ac 7:41
living creature was like a **c**; Rv 4:7

CALF-IDOL *(1)*

Your **c** is rejected, Samaria. Hs 8:5

CALL *(170)*

man to see what he would **c** it. Gn 2:19
people began to **c** on the name Gn 4:26
Sarai, do not **c** her Sarai, for Gn 17:15
Let's **c** the girl and ask her Gn 24:57
that the women **c** me happy,” Gn 30:13
Should I go and **c** a woman from Ex 2:7
to a public **c** to testify, Lv 5:1
which the Sidonians **c** Sirion, Dt 3:9
but the Amorites **c** Senir, Dt 3:9
is ⌊to us⌋ whenever we **c** to Him? Dt 4:7
c heaven and earth as witnesses Dt 4:26
c heaven and earth as witnesses Dt 30:19
C Joshua and present yourselves Dt 31:14
to them and **c** heaven and earth Dt 31:28
Do not **c** on the names of their Jos 23:7
but didn't **c** us to go with you? Jdg 12:1
“Don't **c** me Naomi. Call me Mara,” Ru 1:20
C me Mara,” she answered, “for Ru 1:20
Why do you **c** me Naomi, since the Ru 1:21
“I didn't **c**,” Eli replied. 1Sm 3:5
“I didn't **c**, my son,” he 1Sm 3:6
I will **c** on the LORD and He will 1Sm 12:17
C the roll and determine who has 1Sm 14:17
saying, “**C** in Bathsheba for me. 1Kg 1:28
David then said, “**C** in Zadok the 1Kg 1:32
to them whenever they **c** to You. 1Kg 8:52
Then you **c** on the name of your 1Kg 18:24
and I will **c** on the name of 1Kg 18:24
Then **c** on the name of your god 1Kg 18:25
who went to **c** Micaiah instructed 1Kg 22:13
“**C** this Shunammite woman.” 2Kg 4:12
“**C** her,” Elisha said. So Gehazi 2Kg 4:15
and said, “**C** the Shunammite 2Kg 4:36
and **c** on the name of Yahweh 2Kg 5:11
to the LORD; **c** on His name; 1Ch 16:8
who went to **c** Micaiah instructed 2Ch 18:12
C out if you please. Will anyone Jb 5:1
Then **c**, and I will answer, or I Jb 13:22
You would **c**, and I would answer Jb 14:15
I **c** for help, but there is no Jb 19:7
I **c** for my servant, but he does Jb 19:16
Will he **c** on God at all times? Jb 27:10
Answer me when I **c**, God, who Ps 4:1
LORD will hear when I **c** to Him. Ps 4:3
c his wickedness into account Ps 10:15
they do not **c** on the LORD. Ps 14:4
c on You, God, because You will Ps 17:6
answer us on the day that we **c**. Ps 20:9
LORD, hear my voice when I **c**; Ps 27:7
LORD, I **c** to You; my rock, do Ps 28:1
me be disgraced when I **c** on You. Ps 31:17
C on Me in a day of trouble; Ps 50:15
bread; they do not **c** on God. Ps 53:4
I **c** to God, and the LORD will Ps 55:16
retreat on the day when I **c**. Ps 56:9
I **c** to God Most High, to God who Ps 57:2
I **c** to You from the ends of the Ps 61:2
by him and **c** him blessed. Ps 72:17
that don't **c** on Your name, Ps 79:6
and we will **c** on Your name. Ps 80:18
for I **c** to You all day long. Ps 86:3
love to all who **c** on You. Ps 86:5
I **c** on You in the day of my Ps 86:7
But I **c** to You for help, LORD; Ps 88:13
He will **c** to Me, ‘You are my Ps 89:26
then I will **c** their rebellion to Ps 89:32
answer me quickly when I **c**. Ps 102:2
to the LORD, **c** on His name; Ps 105:1
I will **c** ⌊out to Him⌋ as long as Ps 116:2
c with all my heart; answer me, Ps 119:145
I **c** to You; save me, and I will Ps 119:146
Out of the depths I **c** to You, Ps 130:1
LORD, I **c** on You; hurry to Ps 141:1
to my voice when I **c** on You. Ps 141:1
is near all who **c** out to Him, Ps 145:18
all who **c** out to Him with Ps 145:18
Then they will **c** me, but I won't Pr 1:28
if you **c** out to insight and lift Pr 2:3
and **c** understanding ⌊your⌋ Pr 7:4
Doesn't Wisdom **c** out? Doesn't Pr 8:1
People, I **c** out to you; Pr 8:4
himself also **c** out and not be Pr 21:13
sons rise up and **c** her blessed. Pr 31:28
Woe to those who **c** evil good and Is 5:20
boy knows how to **c** out father or Is 8:4
Do not **c** everything an alliance Is 8:12
barren mountain. **C** out to them. Is 13:2
day I will **c** for my servant, Is 22:20
therefore, I **c** her: Rahab Who Is 30:7
cloths, and **c** them filth. Is 30:22
one wild goat will **c** to another. Is 34:14
another will **c** ⌊himself⌋ by the Is 44:5
God of Israel **c** you by your name Is 45:3
I **c** you by your name, because of Is 45:4
c a bird of prey from the east, Is 46:11
c to Him while He is near. Is 55:6
Will you **c** this a fast and a day Is 58:5
time, when you **c**, the LORD will Is 58:9
if you **c** the Sabbath a delight, Is 58:13
They will **c** you the City of the Is 60:14
before they **c**, I will answer; Is 65:24
You will **c** Me, my Father, and Jr 3:19
strong for this comes at My **c**. Jr 4:12
LORD and there **c** out this word: Jr 7:2
When you **c** to them, they will Jr 7:27
that don't **c** on Your name, Jr 10:25
when they **c** out to Me at Jr 11:14
The LORD does not **c** you Pashhur, Jr 20:3
You will **c** to Me and come and Jr 29:12
for they **c** you The Outcast, Jr 30:17
watchmen will **c** out in the hill Jr 31:6
with silver and **c** in witnesses— Jr 32:25
C to Me and I will answer you Jr 33:3
They will **c** out to them: Jr 49:29
Yet I **c** this to mind, and Lm 3:21
You come near when I **c** on You; Lm 3:57
I will **c** for a sword against him Ezk 38:21
C your brothers: My People and Hs 2:1
declaration—you will **c** ⌊Me⌋: Hs 2:16
My husband, and no longer **c** Me: Hs 2:16
they **c** to Egypt, and they go to Hs 7:11
Though they **c** to Him on high, Hs 11:7
I **c** to You, LORD, for fire has Jl 1:19
will **c** to someone in the inner Am 6:10
asleep? Get up! **C** to your god. Jnh 1:6
everyone must **c** out earnestly to Jnh 3:8
must I **c** for help and You do not Hab 1:2
all of them may **c** on the name Zph 3:9
They will **c** on My name, and I Zch 13:9
didn't come to **c** the righteous, Mt 9:13
marketplaces who **c** out to each Mt 11:16
‘**C** the workers and give them Mt 20:8
Do not **c** anyone on earth your Mt 23:9
that I cannot **c** on My Father, Mt 26:53
didn't come to **c** the righteous, Mk 2:17
“Why do you **c** Me good?” Mk 10:18
Jesus stopped and said, “**C** him.” Mk 10:49
with the One you **c** the King of Mk 15:12
and you will **c** His name JESUS. Lk 1:31
generations will **c** me blessed, Lk 1:48
not come to **c** the righteous, Lk 5:32
Why do you **c** Me ‘Lord, Lord,’ Lk 6:46
do You want us to **c** down fire Lk 9:54
“Why do you **c** Me good?” Lk 18:19
“Go **c** your husband,” He told her, Jn 4:16
You **c** Me Teacher and Lord. Jn 13:13
I do not **c** you slaves anymore, Jn 15:15
as the Lord our God will **c**.” Ac 2:39
arrest all who **c** on Your name.” Ac 9:14
men to Joppa and **c** for Simon, Ac 10:5
clean, you must not **c** common.” Ac 10:15
a holy angel to **c** you to his Ac 10:22
that I must not **c** any person Ac 10:28
clean, you must not **c** common.’ Ac 11:9
to Joppa, and **c** for Simon, who Ac 11:13
And they started to **c** Barnabas, Ac 14:12
Way, which they **c** a sect, so I Ac 24:14
I find time I'll **c** for you.” Ac 24:25
and paid a courtesy **c** on Festus. Ac 25:13

Now if you **c** yourself a Jew, Rm 2:17
I will **c** "Not-My-People," Rm 9:25
all is rich to all who **c** on Him. Rm 10:12
how can they **c** on Him in whom Rm 10:14
in every place who **c** on the name 1Co 1:2
I **c** on God as a witness against 2Co 1:23
God's heavenly **c** in Christ Jesus Php 3:14
with those who **c** on the Lord 2Tm 2:22
not ashamed to **c** them brothers, Heb 2:11
should **c** for the elders of the Jms 5:14
tested those who **c** themselves Rv 2:2

CALLED *(428)*

God **c** the light "day," and He Gn 1:5
and He **c** the darkness "night." Gn 1:5
God **c** the expanse "sky." Gn 1:8
God **c** the dry land "earth," Gn 1:10
and He **c** the gathering of the Gn 1:10
whatever the man **c** a living Gn 2:19
this one will be **c** woman, for Gn 2:23
So the LORD God **c** out to the man Gn 3:9
He blessed them and **c** them man. Gn 5:2
Therefore its name is **c** Babylon, Gn 11:9
They **c** out to Lot and said, Gn 19:5
c all his servants together, Gn 20:8
Then Abimelech **c** Abraham in and Gn 20:9
the angel of God **c** to Hagar from Gn 21:17
that place was **c** Beer-sheba Gn 21:31
Angel of the LORD **c** to him from Gn 22:11
Angel of the LORD **c** to Abraham a Gn 22:15
They **c** Rebekah and said to her, Gn 24:58
He **c** it Oath. Therefore the name Gn 26:33
he **c** his older son Esau and said Gn 27:1
Rachel and Leah **c** to the field Gn 31:4
the place was **c** Galeed, Gn 31:48
So he **c** that place Mahanaim. Gn 32:2
is why the place was **c** Succoth. Gn 33:17
up an altar there and **c** it "God, Gn 33:20
altar there and **c** the place God Gn 35:7
but his father **c** him Benjamin. Gn 35:18
she **c** the household servants. Gn 39:14
and ⌊servants⌋ **c** out before him, Gn 41:43
attendants, so he **c** out, "Send Gn 45:1
he **c** his son Joseph and said to Gn 47:29
And may they be **c** by my name Gn 48:16
Then Jacob **c** his sons and said, Gn 49:1
girl went and **c** the boy's mother Ex 2:8
God **c** out to him from the bush, Ex 3:4
But then Pharaoh **c** the wise men Ex 7:11
and the LORD **c** to him from the Ex 19:3
On the seventh day He **c** to Moses Ex 24:16
he **c** it the tent of meeting. Ex 33:7
Moses **c** out to them, so Aaron Ex 34:31
These are the men **c** from the Nm 1:16
That place was **c** the Valley of Nm 13:24
villages and **c** it Nobah after Nm 32:42
though the Moabites **c** them Emim. Dt 2:11
the Ammonites **c** them Zamzummim, Dt 2:20
used to be **c** the land of the Dt 3:13
He **c** Bashan by his own name, Dt 3:14
Israel will be **c** 'The house of Dt 25:10
So we **c** out to the LORD, the God Dt 26:7
see that you are **c** by the LORD's Dt 28:10
place has been **c** Gilgal to this Jos 5:9
place has been **c** the Valley of Jos 7:26
The king **c** for silence, and all Jdg 3:19
LORD there and **c** it Yahweh Jdg 6:24
Gideon's father **c** him Jerubbaal, Jdg 6:32
of Israel were **c** from Naphtali, Jdg 7:23
the men of Ephraim were **c** out, Jdg 7:24
raised his voice, and **c** to them: Jdg 9:7
quickly **c** his armor-bearer and Jdg 9:54
which are **c** Jair's Villages to Jdg 10:4
The Ammonites were **c** together, Jdg 10:17
men of Ephraim were **c** together Jdg 12:1
So I **c** for you, but you didn't Jdg 12:2
thirsty and **c** out to the LORD Jdg 15:18
in her room, she **c** out to him, Jdg 16:9
braids with a pin and **c** to him, Jdg 16:14
on her lap and **c** a man to shave Jdg 16:19
He **c** out to the LORD: Jdg 16:28
the place is **c** the Camp of Dan Jdg 18:12
c to the Danites, who turned Jdg 18:23
Boaz **c** him by name and said, Ru 4:1
Then the LORD **c** Samuel, and he 1Sm 3:4
Here I am; you **c** me." "I didn't 1Sm 3:5
Once again the LORD **c**, "Samuel!" 1Sm 3:6
Here I am; you **c** me." "I didn't 1Sm 3:6
third time, the LORD **c** Samuel. 1Sm 3:8

Here I am; you **c** me." Then Eli 1Sm 3:8
stood there, and **c** as before, 1Sm 3:10
but Eli **c** him and said, "Samuel, 1Sm 3:16
So they **c** all the Philistine 1Sm 5:8
The Ekronites **c** all the 1Sm 5:11
today was formerly **c** the seer. 1Sm 9:9
Samuel **c** to Saul on the roof, 1Sm 9:26
Samuel **c** on the LORD, and on 1Sm 12:18
the garrison **c** to Jonathan and 1Sm 14:12
They **c** the roll and saw that 1Sm 14:17
Jesse **c** Abinadab and presented 1Sm 16:8
the Philistine **c** to David, 1Sm 17:44
but Jonathan **c** to him and said, 1Sm 20:37
Then Jonathan **c** to him, "Hurry 1Sm 20:38
from Keilah, he **c** off the 1Sm 23:13
of the cave, and **c** to Saul, "My 1Sm 24:8
David **c** to Abner, "You're a man, 1Sm 26:15
So I've **c** on you to tell me what 1Sm 28:15
and saw me, he **c** out to me, so I 2Sm 1:7
Then Abner **c** out to Joab: 2Sm 2:26
The ark is **c** by the Name, the 2Sm 6:2
c to the servant who waited on 2Sm 13:17
Absalom **c** out to him and asked, 2Sm 15:2
It is still **c** Absalom's Monument 2Sm 18:18
He **c** out and told the king. 2Sm 18:25
He **c** out to the gatekeeper, 2Sm 18:26
Ahimaaz **c** out to the king, 2Sm 18:28
wise woman **c** out from the city, 2Sm 20:16
c to the LORD, who is worthy of 2Sm 22:4
I **c** to the LORD in my distress; 2Sm 22:7
in my distress; I **c** to my God. 2Sm 22:7
I have built is **c** by Your name. 1Kg 8:43
So he **c** them the Land of Cabul, 1Kg 9:13
as they are ⌊still **c**⌋ today. 1Kg 9:13
Elijah **c** to her and said, 1Kg 17:10
to get it, he **c** to her and said, 1Kg 17:11
Ahab **c** for Obadiah, who was in 1Kg 18:3
and **c** on the name of Baal from 1Kg 18:26
king of Israel **c** for all the 1Kg 20:7
the king of Israel **c** an officer 1Kg 22:9
So he **c** her and she stood 2Kg 4:12
Gehazi **c** her, and she stood in 2Kg 4:15
Elisha **c** Gehazi and said, 2Kg 4:36
He **c** her and she came. 2Kg 4:36
and he **c** his servants and 2Kg 6:11
men went and **c** to the city's 2Kg 7:10
The gatekeepers **c** out, and ⌊the 2Kg 7:11
prophet Elisha **c** one of the sons 2Kg 9:1
for Baal." So they **c** one. 2Kg 10:20
So King Joash **c** Jehoiada the 2Kg 12:7
in battle and **c** it Joktheel, 2Kg 14:7
to that time. He **c** it Nehushtan. 2Kg 18:4
Then they **c** for the king, but 2Kg 18:18
Rabshakeh stood and **c** out loudly 2Kg 18:28
the prophet **c** out to the LORD, 2Kg 20:11
c out to the God of Israel: 1Ch 4:10
A Levite **c** Mattithiah, the 1Ch 9:31
it was **c** the city of David. 1Ch 11:7
which is **c** by the name of the 1Ch 13:6
c on the LORD, and He answered 1Ch 21:26
I have built is **c** by Your name. 2Ch 6:33
people who are **c** by My name 2Ch 7:14
the king of Israel **c** an officer 2Ch 18:8
that place is still **c** the Valley 2Ch 20:26
So the king **c** Jehoiada the high 2Ch 24:6
Then they **c** out loudly in Hebrew 2Ch 32:18
and was **c** by their name. Ezr 2:61
So I **c** a large assembly against Neh 5:7
and was **c** by their name. Neh 7:63
reason these days are **c** Purim, Est 9:26
in gold or **c** fine gold my trust, Jb 31:24
c to the LORD, who is worthy of Ps 18:3
I **c** to the LORD in my distress, Ps 18:6
LORD, I **c** to You; I sought favor Ps 30:8
You **c** out in distress, and I Ps 81:7
They **c** to the LORD, and He Ps 99:6
c down famine against the land Ps 105:16
I **c** on the name of the LORD: Ps 116:4
I **c** to the LORD in distress; Ps 118:5
In my distress I **c** to the LORD, Ps 120:1
On the day I **c**, You answered me; Ps 138:3
Since I **c** out and you refused, Pr 1:24
a wise heart is **c** discerning, Pr 16:21
plots evil will be **c** a schemer. Pr 24:8
I **c** him, but he did not answer. Sg 5:6
will be **c** the Righteous City, Is 1:26
Just let us be **c** by your name. Is 4:1
in Jerusalem will be **c** holy— Is 4:3

And one **c** to another: Is 6:3
I have also **c** My warriors, Is 13:3
the cities will be **c** the City of Is 19:18
Lord GOD of Hosts **c** for weeping, Is 22:12
shepherds is **c** out against it, Is 31:4
will no longer be **c** a noble, Is 32:5
it will be **c** the Holy Way. Is 35:8
Rabshakeh stood and **c** out loudly Is 36:13
of the earth and **c** you from its Is 41:9
have **c** you for a righteous Is 42:6
I have **c** you by your name; Is 43:1
everyone **c** by My name and Is 43:7
you have not **c** on Me, because, Is 43:22
will no longer be **c** pampered and Is 47:1
will no longer be **c** mistress of Is 47:5
those who are **c** by the name Is 48:1
and Israel, the one **c** by Me: Is 48:12
yes, I have **c** him; I have Is 48:15
The LORD **c** me before I was born. Is 49:1
there no one to answer when I **c**? Is 50:2
When I **c** him, he was only one; Is 51:2
is **c** the God of all the earth. Is 54:5
the LORD has **c** you, like a wife Is 54:6
My house will be **c** a house of Is 56:7
you will be **c** the repairer of Is 58:12
they will be **c** righteous trees Is 61:3
But you will be **c** the LORD's Is 61:6
You will be **c** by a new name that Is 62:2
will no longer be **c** Deserted, Is 62:4
land will not be **c** Desolate; Is 62:4
you will be **c** My Delight is in Is 62:4
they will be **c** the Holy People Is 62:12
and you will be **c** Cared For, Is 62:12
like those not **c** by Your name. Is 63:19
that was not **c** by My name. Is 65:1
because I **c** and you did not Is 65:12
because I **c** and no one answered; Is 66:4
Have you not lately **c** Me: Jr 3:4
that time Jerusalem will be **c**, Jr 3:17
They are **c** rejected silver, Jr 6:30
in this house **c** by My name and Jr 7:10
house, which is **c** by My name, Jr 7:11
and I have **c** to you, but you Jr 7:13
the house that is **c** by My name— Jr 7:14
the house that is **c** by My name Jr 7:30
will no longer be **c** Topheth and Jr 7:32
and we are **c** by Your name. Jr 14:9
heart, for I am **c** by Your name, Jr 15:16
will no longer be **c** Topheth and Jr 19:6
sealed it, **c** in witnesses, Jr 32:10
the house that is **c** by My name Jr 32:34
will be **c** on in the land Jr 32:44
Me at the temple **c** by My name. Jr 34:15
and I have **c** to them, but they Jr 35:17
I **c** to my lovers, but they Lm 1:19
city that was **c** the perfection Lm 2:15
I **c** on Your name, Yahweh, from Lm 3:55
Then He **c** to me directly with a Ezk 9:1
He **c** to the man clothed in linen Ezk 9:3
wheels were **c** "the wheelwork. Ezk 10:13
And it is **c** High Place to this Ezk 20:29
So ⌊it⌋ will be **c** the Valley of Ezk 39:11
furnace of blazing fire and **c**: Dn 3:26
He **c** out loudly: Cut down the Dn 4:14
The king **c** out to bring in the Dn 5:7
and the city **c** by Your name. Dn 9:18
Your people are **c** by Your name. Dn 9:19
not My people, they will be **c**: Hs 1:10
and out of Egypt I **c** My son. Hs 11:1
The more⌋ they **c** them, ⌊the more Hs 11:2
farmer will be **c** on to mourn, Am 5:16
nations that are **c** by My name— Am 9:12
So they **c** out to the LORD: Jnh 1:14
I **c** to the LORD in my distress, Jnh 2:2
Just as He had **c**, and they would Zch 7:13
so when they **c**, I would not Zch 7:13
will be **c** the Faithful City Zch 8:3
I took my staff **c** Favor and cut Zch 11:10
They will be **c** a wicked country Mal 1:4
it **c** for reverence, and he Mal 2:5
to Jesus who is **c** the Messiah. Mt 1:16
Out of Egypt I **c** My Son. Mt 2:15
settled in a town **c** Nazareth to Mt 2:23
that He will be **c** a Nazarene. Mt 2:23
Simon, who was **c** Peter, and his Mt 4:18
their nets, and He **c** them. Mt 4:21
they will be **c** sons of God. Mt 5:9
to do so will be **c** least in the Mt 5:19

will be **c** great in the kingdom Mt 5:19
Simon, who is **c** Peter, and Mt 10:2
they **c** the head of the house Mt 10:25
Isn't His mother **c** Mary, and His Mt 13:55
Then He **c** a child to Him and had Mt 18:2
But Jesus **c** them over and said, Mt 20:25
Jesus stopped, **c** them, and said, Mt 20:32
My house will be **c** a house of Mt 21:13
and to be **c** 'Rabbi' by people. Mt 23:7
you, do not be **c** 'Rabbi,' Mt 23:8
And do not be **c** masters either, Mt 23:10
came up and **c** His attention to Mt 24:1
He **c** his own slaves and turned Mt 25:14
high priest, who was **c** Caiaphas, Mt 26:3
the man **c** Judas Iscariot— Mt 26:14
them to a place **c** Gethsemane, Mt 26:36
field has been **c** "Blood Field" Mt 27:8
a notorious prisoner **c** Barabbas. Mt 27:16
or Jesus who is **c** Messiah?" Mt 27:17
with Jesus, who is **c** Messiah?" Mt 27:22
they came to a place **c** Golgotha Mt 27:33
Immediately He **c** them, and they Mk 1:20
sent ⌊word⌋ to Him and **c** Him. Mk 3:31
c the Twelve and said to them, Mk 9:35
Jesus **c** them over and said to Mk 10:42
So they **c** the blind man and Mk 10:49
My house will be **c** a house of Mk 11:17
c the whole company together. Mk 15:16
Jesus to the place **c** Golgotha Mk 15:22
to a town in Galilee **c** Nazareth, Lk 1:26
great and will be **c** the Son of Lk 1:32
born will be **c** the Son of God. Lk 1:35
month for her who was **c** barren. Lk 1:36
No! He will be **c** John." Lk 1:60
out what he wanted him to be **c**. Lk 1:62
you will be **c** a prophet of the Lk 1:76
David, which is **c** Bethlehem, Lk 2:4
and Simon **c** the Zealot; Lk 6:15
was on His way to a town **c** Nain. Lk 7:11
Mary, **c** Magdalene (seven demons Lk 8:2
said this, He **c** out, "Anyone who Lk 8:8
took her by the hand and **c** out, Lk 8:54
privately to a town **c** Bethsaida. Lk 9:10
Jesus saw her, He **c** out to her, Lk 13:12
longer worthy to be **c** your son. Lk 15:19
longer worthy to be **c** your son.' Lk 15:21
he **c** the manager in and asked, Lk 16:2
he **c** out, 'Have mercy on me Lk 16:24
So he **c** out, "Jesus, Son of Lk 18:38
He **c** 10 of his slaves, gave them Lk 19:13
at the place **c** the Mount of Lk 19:29
night on what is **c** the Mount of Lk 21:37
Bread, which is **c** Passover, was Lk 22:1
entered Judas, **c** Iscariot, who Lk 22:3
over them are **c** 'Benefactors.' Lk 22:25
Pilate **c** together the chief Lk 23:13
at the place **c** The Skull, Lk 23:33
And Jesus **c** out with a loud Lk 23:46
their way to a village **c** Emmaus, Lk 24:13
You will be **c** Cephas" (which Jn 1:42
Before Philip **c** you, when you Jn 1:48
the water knew. He **c** the groom Jn 2:9
a town of Samaria **c** Sychar near Jn 4:5
is coming" (who is **c** Christ). Jn 4:25
there is a pool, **c** Bethesda in Jn 5:2
The man **c** Jesus made mud, Jn 9:11
If He **c** those whom the word of Jn 10:35
Then Thomas (**c** "Twin") said to Jn 11:16
went back and **c** her sister Mary Jn 11:28
wilderness, to a town **c** Ephraim. Jn 11:54
with Him when He **c** Lazarus out Jn 12:17
I have **c** you friends, because I Jn 15:15
bench in a place **c** the Stone Jn 19:13
out to what is **c** Skull Place, Jn 19:17
which in Hebrew is **c** Golgotha. Jn 19:17
Twelve, Thomas (**c** "Twin"), was Jn 20:24
Peter, Thomas (**c** "Twin"), Jn 21:2
"Men," Jesus **c** to them, "you Jn 21:5
from the mount **c** Olive Grove, Ac 1:12
that field is **c** Hakeldama, Ac 1:19
Joseph, **c** Barsabbas, who was Ac 1:23
at the temple gate **c** Beautiful, Ac 3:2
them in what is **c** Solomon's Ac 3:11
So they **c** for them and ordered Ac 4:18
After they **c** in the apostles and Ac 5:40
from what is **c** the Freedmen's Ac 6:9
stoning Stephen as he **c** out: Ac 7:59
This man is **c** the Great Power of Ac 8:10
go to the street **c** Straight," Ac 9:11
those who **c** on this name, Ac 9:21
Then he **c** the saints and widows Ac 9:41
of what was **c** the Italian Ac 10:1
he **c** two of his household slaves Ac 10:7
They **c** out, asking if Simon, who Ac 10:18
them and had **c** together his Ac 10:24
were first **c** Christians Ac 11:26
Simeon who was **c** Niger, Lucius Ac 13:1
the work that I have **c** them to." Ac 13:2
Then Saul—also **c** Paul—filled Ac 13:9
Lycaonian towns **c** Lystra and Ac 14:6
Gentiles who are **c** by My name, Ac 15:17
Judas, **c** Barsabbas, and Silas, Ac 15:22
that God had **c** us to evangelize Ac 16:10
But Paul **c** out in a loud voice, Ac 16:28
Then the jailer **c** for lights, Ac 16:29
to Ephesus and **c** for the elders Ac 20:17
Paul **c** one of the centurions Ac 23:17
prisoner Paul **c** me and asked me Ac 23:18
he was **c** in, Tertullus began Ac 24:2
came to a place **c** Fair Havens Ac 27:8
fierce wind **c** the "northeaster" Ac 27:14
of a little island **c** Cauda, Ac 27:16
that the island was **c** Malta. Ac 28:1
After three days he **c** together Ac 28:17
c as an apostle and singled out Rm 1:1
Rome, loved by God, **c** as saints. Rm 1:7
she will be **c** an adulteress. Rm 7:3
those who are **c** according to His Rm 8:28
those He predestined, He also **c**; Rm 8:30
and those He **c**, He also Rm 8:30
in Isaac your seed will be **c**. Rm 9:7
on us whom He also **c**, not only Rm 9:24
they will be **c** sons of the Rm 9:26
c as an apostle of Christ Jesus 1Co 1:1
in Christ Jesus and **c** as saints, 1Co 1:2
Him you were **c** into fellowship 1Co 1:9
to those who are **c**, both Jews 1Co 1:24
God has **c** you to peace. 1Co 7:15
Lord assigned when God **c** him. 1Co 7:17
circumcised when he was **c**? 1Co 7:18
anyone **c** while uncircumcised? 1Co 7:18
situation in which he was **c**. 1Co 7:20
Were you **c** while a slave? 1Co 7:21
For he who is **c** by the Lord as a 1Co 7:22
he who is **c** as a free man is 1Co 7:22
in whatever situation he was **c**. 1Co 7:24
unworthy to be **c** an apostle, 1Co 15:9
from Him who **c** you by the grace Gl 1:6
me apart and **c** me by His grace Gl 1:15
did not come from Him who **c** you. Gl 5:8
For you are **c** to freedom, Gl 5:13
c "the uncircumcised" by those Eph 2:11
by those **c** "the circumcised," Eph 2:11
just as you were **c** to one hope Eph 4:4
you were also **c** in one body, Col 3:15
so does Jesus who is **c** Justus. Col 4:11
God has not **c** us to impurity, 1Th 4:7
He **c** you to this through our 2Th 2:14
which you were **c** and have made 1Tm 6:12
saved us and **c** us with a holy 2Tm 1:9
while it is still **c** today, Heb 3:13
a person is **c** by God, just as Heb 5:4
which is **c** "the holy place," Heb 9:2
the tabernacle was **c** "the holy Heb 9:3
those who are **c** might receive Heb 9:15
when he was **c**, obeyed and went Heb 11:8
not ashamed to be **c** their God, Heb 11:16
In Isaac your seed will be **c**. Heb 11:18
refused to be **c** the son of Heb 11:24
and he was **c** God's friend. Jms 2:23
as the One who **c** you is holy, 1Pt 1:15
of the One who **c** you out of 1Pt 2:9
For you were **c** to this, because 1Pt 2:21
since you were **c** for this, 1Pt 3:9
who **c** you to His eternal glory 1Pt 5:10
of Him who **c** us by His own glory 2Pt 1:3
we should be **c** God's children. 1Jn 3:1
those who are the **c**, loved by Jd 1
on the island **c** Patmos because Rv 1:9
city, which is **c**, prophetically, Rv 11:8
who is **c** the Devil and Satan, Rv 12:9
he **c** with a loud voice to the Rv 14:18
them at the place **c** in Hebrew Rv 16:16
Those with Him are **c** and elect Rv 17:14
rider is **c** Faithful and True, Rv 19:11
His name is **c** the Word of God Rv 19:13

CALLING *(29)*

When **c** the assembly together, Nm 10:7
not **c** us when you went to fight Jdg 8:1
that the LORD was **c** the boy. 1Sm 3:8
to my friends, by **c** on God, who Jb 12:4
was among those **c** on His name. Ps 99:6
c to those who pass by, who go Pr 9:15
and the **c** of solemn assemblies— Is 1:13
c the generations from the Is 41:4
a human voice **c** from the middle Dn 8:16
Lord GOD was **c** for a judgment Am 7:4
c one Favor and the other Union, Zch 11:7
they said, "He's **c** for Elijah!" Mt 27:47
Get up; He's **c** for you." Mk 10:49
said, "Look, He's **c** for Elijah!" Mk 15:35
marketplace and **c** to each other: Lk 7:32
but He was even **c** God His own Jn 5:18
is here and is **c** for you." Jn 11:28
your sins by **c** on His name.' Ac 22:16
are also Jesus Christ's by **c**: Rm 1:6
gifts and **c** are irrevocable. Rm 11:29
Brothers, consider your **c**: 1Co 1:26
know what is the hope of His **c**, Eph 1:18
worthy of the **c** you have Eph 4:1
called to one hope at your **c**; Eph 4:4
consider you worthy of His **c**, 2Th 1:11
us and called us with a holy **c**, 2Tm 1:9
and companions in a heavenly **c**, Heb 3:1
obeyed Abraham, **c** him lord. 1Pt 3:6
to confirm your **c** and election, 2Pt 1:10

CALLOUS *(3)*

this people's heart has grown **c**; Mt 13:15
this people's heart has grown **c**, Ac 28:27
became **c** and gave themselves Eph 4:19

CALLS *(33)*

If He **c** you, say, 'Speak, LORD, 1Sm 3:9
Who are you who **c** to the king?" 1Sm 26:14
Him when He **c** ⌊me⌋ to account? Jb 31:14
Deep **c** to deep in the roar of Ps 42:7
When he **c** out to Me, I will Ps 91:15
Wisdom **c** out in the street; Pr 1:20
c out from the highest points Pr 9:3
My love **c** to me: Arise, my Sg 2:10
c to me from Seir, "Watchman, Is 21:11
He **c** all of them by name. Is 40:26
He **c** righteousness to his feet. Is 41:2
No one **c** on Your name, striving Is 64:7
c out with a shout, like those Jr 25:30
not one of them **c** on Me. Hs 7:7
Then everyone who **c** on the name Jl 2:32
among the survivors the LORD **c**. Jl 2:32
of the LORD **c** out to the city Mc 6:9
⌊Their⌋ **c** will sound from the Zph 2:14
by the Spirit, **c** Him 'Lord': Mt 22:43
If David **c** Him 'Lord,' how then Mt 22:45
David himself **c** Him 'Lord'; Mk 12:37
he **c** his friends and neighbors Lk 15:6
she **c** her women friends and Lk 15:9
where he **c** the Lord the God of Lk 20:37
David **c** Him 'Lord'; how then can Lk 20:44
He **c** his own sheep by name and Jn 10:3
then whoever **c** on the name of Ac 2:21
life to the dead and **c** things Rm 4:17
works but from the One who **c** Rm 9:12
For everyone who **c** on the name Rm 10:13
who **c** you into His own kingdom 1Th 2:12
He who **c** you is faithful, who 1Th 5:24
who **c** herself a prophetess, Rv 2:20

CALM *(12)*

south wind brings **c** to the land, Jb 37:17
The **c** words of the wise are Ec 9:17
Say to him: **C** down and be quiet. Is 7:4
All the earth is **c** and at rest; Is 14:7
return and have **c** and quiet with Jr 30:10
return and have **c** and quiet with Jr 46:27
do to you to **c** this sea that's Jnh 1:11
the whole earth is **c** and quiet." Zch 1:11
And there was a great **c**. Mt 8:26
ceased, and there was a great **c**. Mk 4:39
they ceased, and there was a **c**. Lk 8:24
you must keep **c** and not do Ac 19:36

CALMED *(3)*

I have **c** and quieted myself like Ps 131:2
is anxiety that cannot be **c**. Jr 49:23
city clerk had **c** the crowd down, Ac 19:35

CALMNESS *(1)*

for **c** puts great offenses to Ec 10:4

CALMS *(1)*
a man slow to anger **c** strife. Pr 15:18

CALNEH *(2)*
Erech, Accad, and **C**, in the land Gn 10:10
Cross over to **C** and see; Am 6:2

CALNO *(1)*
Isn't **C** like Carchemish? Is 10:9

CALVE *(1)*
cows **c** and do not miscarry. Jb 21:10

CALVES *(19)*
but take their **c** away and pen 1Sm 6:7
and confined their **c** in the pen. 1Sm 6:10
cattle, and **c**, slaughtered them 1Sm 14:32
made two gold **c**, and he said to 1Kg 12:28
one of the **c** all the way to 1Kg 12:30
to the **c** he had set up. 1Kg 12:32
the golden **c** that were in Bethel 2Kg 10:29
even two **c**—and an Asherah 2Kg 17:16
and the ⌊gold⌋ **c** he had made. 2Ch 11:15
you the golden **c** that Jeroboam 2Ch 13:8
bulls with the **c** of the peoples. Ps 68:30
C will graze there, and there Is 27:10
among her are like stall-fed **c**. Jr 46:21
men who sacrifice kiss the **c**." Hs 13:2
the flock and **c** from the stall. Am 6:4
offerings, with year-old **c**? Mc 6:6
jump like **c** from the stall. Mal 4:2
not by the blood of goats and **c**, Heb 9:12
took the blood of **c** and goats, Heb 9:19

CALYX *(10)*
each with a **c** and petals, Ex 25:33
each with a **c** and petals, Ex 25:33
a **c** must be under the ⌊first⌋ Ex 25:35
a **c** under the ⌊second⌋ pair of Ex 25:35
and a **c** under the ⌊third⌋ pair Ex 25:35
each with a **c** and petals, Ex 37:19
each with a **c** and petals, Ex 37:19
a **c** was under the first pair of Ex 37:21
a **c** under the second pair of Ex 37:21
and a **c** under the third pair of Ex 37:21

CALYXES *(6)*
cups, and its **c** and petals. Ex 25:31
along with its **c** and petals. Ex 25:34
Their **c** and branches are to be Ex 25:36
cups, and its **c** and petals. Ex 37:17
blossoms with its **c** and petals. Ex 37:20
Their **c** and branches were of one Ex 37:22

CAME *(1276)*
Evening **c**, and then morning: Gn 1:5
Evening **c**, and then morning: Gn 1:8
Evening **c**, and then morning: Gn 1:13
Evening **c**, and then morning: Gn 1:19
Evening **c**, and then morning: Gn 1:23
Evening **c**, and then morning: Gn 1:31
the sons of God **c** to the Gn 6:4
when the deluge **c** ⌊and⌋ water Gn 7:6
of the deluge **c** on the earth. Gn 7:10
The ark **c** to rest in the seventh Gn 8:4
When the dove **c** to him at Gn 8:11
and his sons' wives, **c** out. Gn 8:18
on the earth **c** out of the ark Gn 8:19
the earth that **c** out of the ark. Gn 9:10
Noah's sons who **c** out of the ark Gn 9:18
the Philistines **c** from them Gn 10:14
the LORD **c** down to look over Gn 11:5
But when they **c** to Haran, they Gn 11:31
When they **c** to the land of Gn 12:5
All of these **c** as allies to the Gn 14:3
who were with him **c** and defeated Gn 14:5
Then they **c** back to invade Gn 14:7
the survivors **c** and told Abram Gn 14:13
share of the men who **c** with me— Gn 14:24
word of the LORD **c** to Abram in a Gn 15:1
the word of the LORD **c** to him: Gn 15:4
Birds of prey **c** down on the Gn 15:11
the men who **c** to you tonight? Gn 19:5
This one **c** here as a foreigner, Gn 19:9
on Lot and **c** up to break down Gn 19:9
the firstborn **c** and slept with Gn 19:33
God **c** to Abimelech in a dream Gn 20:3
The LORD **c** to Sarah as He had Gn 21:1
the Hittites who **c** to the gate Gn 23:10
the Hittites who **c** to the gate Gn 23:18
son go back to the land you **c** Gn 24:5
filled her jug, and **c** up. Gn 24:16
So the man **c** to the house, Gn 24:32
Today when I **c** to the spring, Gn 24:42
When her time **c** to give birth, Gn 25:24
The first one **c** out reddish, Gn 25:25
brother **c** out grasping Esau's Gn 25:26
stew, Esau **c** in from the field, Gn 25:29
Then Abimelech **c** to him from Gn 26:26
Isaac's slaves **c** to tell him Gn 26:32
he **c** to his father, he said, Gn 27:18
So Jacob **c** closer to his father Gn 27:22
So he **c** closer and kissed him. Gn 27:27
I ate it all before you **c** in, Gn 27:33
Your brother **c** deceitfully and Gn 27:35
c with her father's sheep, Gn 29:9
When morning **c**, there was Leah! Gn 29:25
When Jacob **c** in from the field Gn 30:16
you had very little before I **c**, Gn 30:30
where the sheep **c** to drink. Gn 30:38
sheep bred when they **c** to drink. Gn 30:38
But God **c** to Laban the Aramean Gn 31:24
After Jacob **c** from Paddan-aram, Gn 33:18
father Hamor **c** to speak with Gn 34:6
other⌋ sons **c** to the slaughter Gn 34:27
from God **c** over the cities Gn 35:5
all who were with him **c** to Luz Gn 35:6
Jacob **c** to his father Isaac at Gn 35:27
When Joseph **c** to his brothers, Gn 37:23
When the time **c** for her to give Gn 38:27
This one **c** out first." Gn 38:28
back, and his brother **c** out. Gn 38:29
tied to his hand, **c** out, and was Gn 38:30
c to me so he could sleep with Gn 39:14
her until his master **c** home. Gn 39:16
brought to us **c** to me to make Gn 39:17
When Joseph **c** to them in the Gn 40:6
its blossoms **c** out and its Gn 40:10
well-fed cows **c** up from the Nile Gn 41:2
c up from the Nile and stood Gn 41:3
and good, **c** up on one stalk. Gn 41:5
When morning **c**, he was troubled, Gn 41:8
cows **c** up from the Nile Gn 41:18
very sickly, and thin—**c** up. Gn 41:19
ugly cows that **c** up after them Gn 41:27
the land of Egypt **c** to an end, Gn 41:53
Extreme hunger **c** to all the land Gn 41:55
The whole world **c** to Joseph in Gn 41:57
among those who **c** to buy grain, Gn 42:5
His brothers **c** and bowed down Gn 42:6
When we **c** to the place where we Gn 43:21
When Joseph **c** home, they brought Gn 43:26
he washed his face and **c** out. Gn 43:31
come near me," and they **c** near. Gn 45:4
from Egypt and **c** to their father Gn 45:25
that he had and **c** to Beer-sheba, Gn 46:1
Jacob's sons—who **c** to Egypt: Gn 46:26
When they **c** to the land of Gn 46:28
the Egyptians **c** to Joseph and Gn 47:15
they **c** the next year and said to Gn 47:18
Egypt before I **c** to you in Egypt Gn 48:5
when their message **c** to him. Gn 50:17
Then his brothers also **c** to him, Gn 50:18
of Israel who **c** to Egypt with Ex 1:1
each **c** with his family: Ex 1:1
known Joseph, **c** to power in Ex 1:8
so that the Egyptians **c** to dread Ex 1:12
They **c** to draw water and filled Ex 2:16
but Moses **c** to their rescue and Ex 2:17
the wilderness and **c** to Horeb, Ex 3:1
the frogs **c** up and covered the Ex 8:6
day when you **c** out of Egypt, Ex 13:3
for me when I **c** out of Egypt.' Ex 13:8
It **c** between the Egyptian and Ex 14:20
neither group **c** near the other Ex 14:20
waters **c** back and covered the Ex 14:28
They **c** to Marah, but they could Ex 15:23
Then they **c** to Elim, where there Ex 15:27
Elim and **c** to the Wilderness Ex 16:1
at evening quail **c** and covered Ex 16:13
of the community **c** and reported Ex 16:22
until they **c** to an inhabited Ex 16:35
Amalek **c** and fought against Ex 17:8
c to him in the wilderness where Ex 18:5
and Aaron **c** with all the elders Ex 18:12
After Moses **c** back, He summoned Ex 19:7
Then Moses **c** down from the Ex 19:14
day, when morning **c**, there was Ex 19:16
because the LORD **c** down on it in Ex 19:18
The LORD **c** down on Mount Sinai, Ex 19:20
because you **c** out of Egypt in Ex 23:15
Moses **c** and told the people all Ex 24:3
into the fire, out **c** this calf!" Ex 32:24
The LORD **c** down in a cloud, Ex 34:5
For you **c** out of Egypt in the Ex 34:18
all the Israelites **c** near, Ex 34:32
remove the veil until he **c** out. Ex 34:34
After he **c** out, he would tell Ex 34:34
prompted him **c** and brought Ex 35:21
Both men and women **c**; all who Ex 35:22
for the sanctuary **c** one by one Ex 36:4
whenever they **c** to the tent Ex 40:32
whole community **c** forward and Lv 9:5
He **c** down after sacrificing the Lv 9:22
When they **c** out, they blessed Lv 9:23
Fire **c** out from the LORD and Lv 9:24
So they **c** forward and carried Lv 10:5
Shimeite clan **c** from Gershon; Nm 3:21
Uzzielite clan **c** from Kohath; Nm 3:27
the Mushite clan **c** from Merari; Nm 3:33
person who **c** near ⌊it⌋ was to be Nm 3:38
the Levites **c** to do their work Nm 8:22
These men **c** before Moses and Nm 9:6
When it **c** to rest, he would say: Nm 10:36
sent by the LORD **c** up and blew Nm 11:31
When the two of them **c** forward, Nm 12:5
the Negev and **c** to Hebron, Nm 13:22
When they **c** to the Valley of Nm 13:23
of the⌋ hill country **c** down, Nm 14:45
They **c** together against Moses Nm 16:3
and Abiram **c** out and stood at Nm 16:27
Fire also **c** out from the LORD Nm 16:35
And they **c** out to confront them Nm 20:20
community **c** to Mount Hor. Nm 20:22
Moses and Eleazar **c** down from Nm 20:28
The people then **c** to Moses and Nm 21:7
When he **c** to Jahaz, he fought Nm 21:23
For fire **c** out of Heshbon, Nm 21:28
king of Bashan **c** out against Nm 21:33
They **c** to Balaam and reported Nm 22:7
Then God **c** to Balaam and asked, Nm 22:9
c to Balaam and said to him, Nm 22:16
c to Balaam at night and said Nm 22:20
Look, I **c** out to oppose you, Nm 22:32
and they **c** to Kiriath-huzoth. Nm 22:39
An Israelite man **c** bringing a Nm 25:6
the day the plague **c** at Peor." Nm 25:18
Israelites who **c** out of the land Nm 26:4
nothing that **c** from her lips, Nm 30:12
that the plague **c** against the Nm 31:16
and Reubenites **c** to Moses, Nm 32:2
old or more who **c** up from Egypt Nm 32:11
from Marah and **c** to Elim. Nm 33:9
hill country and **c** to the Valley Dt 1:24
lived there **c** out against you Dt 1:44
Caphtorim, who **c** from Caphtor, Dt 2:23
his whole army **c** out against us Dt 2:32
c out against us for battle at Dt 3:1
You **c** near and stood at the base Dt 4:11
them after they **c** out of Egypt, Dt 4:45
him after they **c** out of Egypt. Dt 4:46
into the stream that **c** down from Dt 9:21
after you **c** out of Egypt, Dt 23:4
king of Bashan **c** out against us Dt 29:7
Moses **c** with Joshua son of Nun Dt 32:44
The LORD **c** from Sinai and Dt 33:2
Mount Paran and **c** with ten Dt 33:2
He **c** ⌊with⌋ the leaders of the Dt 33:21
mourning for Moses **c** to an end. Dt 34:8
and they **c** to the house of a Jos 2:1
out the men who **c** to you and Jos 2:3
for they **c** to investigate the Jos 2:3
you when you **c** out of Egypt, Jos 2:10
c down from the hill country, Jos 2:23
LORD's covenant **c** up from the Jos 4:18
The people **c** up from the Jordan Jos 4:19
people who **c** out of Egypt who Jos 5:4
all the people who **c** out were Jos 5:5
of war who **c** out of Egypt had Jos 5:6
in the ambush **c** out of the city Jos 8:22
the fighting men, **c** from Gilgal. Jos 10:7
the commanders **c** forward and put Jos 10:24
they **c** together and camped at Jos 11:5
Gilead and Bashan **c** to Machir, Jos 17:1
c before Eleazar the priest, Jos 17:4
The lot **c** up for the tribe of Jos 18:11
The second lot **c** out for Simeon, Jos 19:1
The third lot **c** up for Zebulun's Jos 19:10
The fourth lot **c** out for the Jos 19:17

fifth lot **c** out for the tribe Jos 19:24
The sixth lot **c** out for Jos 19:32
The seventh lot **c** out for the Jos 19:40
The lot **c** out for the Kohathite Jos 21:4
c from the tribe of Ephraim. Jos 21:20
When they **c** to the region of the Jos 22:10
the Jordan and **c** to Jericho. Jos 24:11
And Eglon's insides **c** out. Jdg 3:22
was gone when Eglon's servants **c** Jdg 3:24
The Israelites **c** down with him Jdg 3:27
So Barak **c** down from Mount Jdg 4:14
LORD, when You **c** from Seir, when Jdg 5:4
The survivors **c** down to the Jdg 5:13
LORD's people **c** down to me with Jdg 5:13
in Amalek ⌊**c**⌋ from Ephraim; Jdg 5:14
Benjamin ⌊**c** with⌋ your people Jdg 5:14
The leaders **c** down from Machir, Jdg 5:14
staff ⌊**c**⌋ from Zebulun. Jdg 5:14
Kings **c** and fought. Then the Jdg 5:19
eastern peoples **c** and attacked Jdg 6:3
the Midianites **c** with their Jdg 6:5
of the LORD **c**, and He sat under Jdg 6:11
Fire **c** up from the rock and Jdg 6:21
who ⌊also⌋ **c** to meet him. Jdg 6:35
loaf of barley bread **c** tumbling Jdg 7:13
and the 300 men **c** to the Jordan Jdg 8:4
Gaal son of Ebed **c** with his Jdg 9:26
When Abimelech **c** to attack the Jdg 9:52
son of Jerubbaal **c** on them. Jdg 9:57
After him **c** Jair the Gileadite, Jdg 10:3
When Israel **c** from Egypt, Jdg 11:13
But when they **c** from Egypt, Jdg 11:16
to the Red Sea and **c** to Kadesh. Jdg 11:16
They **c** to the east side of the Jdg 11:18
of the LORD **c** on Jephthah, Jdg 11:29
husband, "A man of God **c** to me. Jdg 13:6
didn't ask Him where He **c** from, Jdg 13:6
the Angel of GOD **c** again to the Jdg 13:9
The man who **c** to me today has Jdg 13:10
When he **c** to the man, he asked, Jdg 13:11
mother and **c** to the vineyards Jdg 14:5
a young lion **c** roaring at him, Jdg 14:5
of the eater **c** something to eat Jdg 14:14
of the strong **c** something sweet Jdg 14:14
So Samson's wife **c** to him, Jdg 14:16
When he **c** to Lehi, the Jdg 15:14
the Philistines **c** to meet him Jdg 15:14
at Lehi, and water **c** out of it. Jdg 15:19
leaders **c** to her and brought Jdg 16:18
and his father's family **c** down, Jdg 16:31
On his way he **c** to Micah's home Jdg 17:8
They **c** to the hill country of Jdg 18:2
five men left and **c** to Laish. Jdg 18:7
an old man **c** in from his work in Jdg 19:16
out the man who **c** to your house Jdg 19:22
the Israelites **c** out of the land Jdg 19:30
from the land of Gilead **c** out, Jdg 20:1
The Benjaminites **c** out of Gibeah Jdg 20:21
Benjaminites **c** out from Gibeah Jdg 20:25
the Benjaminites **c** out against Jdg 20:31
those who **c** out of the cities Jdg 20:42
until they **c** to Bethlehem. Ru 1:19
So Naomi **c** back from the land of Ru 1:22
She **c** and has remained from Ru 2:7
and ⌊how⌋ you **c** to a people you Ru 2:11
that a woman **c** to the threshing Ru 3:14
redeemer Boaz had spoken about **c** Ru 4:1
who **c** there to Shiloh. 1Sm 2:14
man of God **c** to Eli and said to 1Sm 2:27
The LORD **c**, stood there, and 1Sm 3:10
Samuel's words **c** to all Israel. 1Sm 4:1
from the battle and **c** to Shiloh. 1Sm 4:12
The man quickly **c** and reported 1Sm 4:14
the one who **c** from the battle 1Sm 4:16
her labor pains **c** on her. 1Sm 4:19
cart **c** to the field of Joshua 1Sm 6:14
of Kiriath-jearim **c** for the ark 1Sm 7:1
When they **c** to the land of Zuph, 1Sm 9:5
he just now **c** to the city, 1Sm 9:12
all the signs **c** about that day. 1Sm 10:9
the Ammonite **c** up and laid siege 1Sm 11:1
When the messengers **c** to Gibeah, 1Sm 11:4
Saul **c** to the city of Amalek and 1Sm 15:5
when they **c** out of Egypt, 1Sm 15:6
word of the LORD **c** to Samuel: 1Sm 15:10
When Samuel **c** to him, Saul said, 1Sm 15:13
Agag **c** to him trembling, 1Sm 15:32
David **c** to Saul and entered 1Sm 16:21

c out from the Philistine camp. 1Sm 17:4
Philistine **c** forward and took 1Sm 17:16
c forward from the Philistine 1Sm 17:23
you **c** down to see the battle!" 1Sm 17:28
lion or a bear **c** and carried off 1Sm 17:34
The Philistine **c** closer and 1Sm 17:41
the women **c** out from all the 1Sm 18:6
commanders **c** out to fight, 1Sm 18:30
from the LORD **c** on Saul as he 1Sm 19:9
Spirit of God **c** on Saul's agents 1Sm 19:20
He **c** to the large cistern at 1Sm 19:22
The Spirit of God also **c** on him, 1Sm 19:23
in Ramah and **c** to Jonathan 1Sm 20:1
c to the location of the arrow 1Sm 20:37
All of them **c** to the king. 1Sm 22:11
son Jonathan **c** to David in 1Sm 23:16
Some Ziphites **c** up to Saul at 1Sm 23:19
a messenger **c** to Saul saying, 1Sm 23:27
When Saul **c** to the sheep pens 1Sm 24:3
David's servants **c** to Abigail at 1Sm 25:40
the Ziphites **c** to Saul at Gibeah 1Sm 26:1
and Abishai **c** to the troops, 1Sm 26:7
sleep from the LORD **c** over them. 1Sm 26:12
of the people **c** to destroy him? 1Sm 26:15
Then he **c** back to Achish, 1Sm 27:9
The Philistines **c** together and 1Sm 28:4
They **c** to the woman at night, 1Sm 28:8
woman **c** over to Saul, and she 1Sm 28:21
from the day you **c** to me until 1Sm 29:6
servants who **c** with you. 1Sm 29:10
When David **c** to the 200 men 1Sm 30:21
they **c** out to meet him and to 1Sm 30:21
us the raiders who **c** against us. 1Sm 30:23
When David **c** to Ziklag, he sent 1Sm 30:26
So the Philistines **c** and settled 1Sm 31:7
the Philistines **c** to strip the 1Sm 31:8
on his head **c** from Saul's camp 2Sm 1:2
When he **c** to David, he fell to 2Sm 1:2
men of Judah **c**, and there they 2Sm 2:4
all who **c** to the place where 2Sm 2:23
Abner and 20 men **c** to David at 2Sm 3:20
son of Ner **c** to see the king 2Sm 3:23
Look here, Abner **c** to you. 2Sm 3:24
Abner son of Ner **c** to deceive 2Sm 3:25
Then they **c** to urge David to eat 2Sm 3:35
and Jonathan **c** from Jezreel. 2Sm 4:4
tribes of Israel **c** to David at 2Sm 5:1
elders of Israel **c** to the king 2Sm 5:3
the Philistines **c** and spread out 2Sm 5:18
The Philistines **c** up again and 2Sm 5:22
When they **c** to Nacon's threshing 2Sm 6:6
Michal **c** out to meet him 2Sm 6:20
word of the LORD **c** to Nathan: 2Sm 7:4
God **c** to one nation on earth in 2Sm 7:23
of Damascus **c** to assist King 2Sm 8:5
Jonathan son of Saul **c** to David, 2Sm 9:6
they **c** to Helam with Shobach, 2Sm 10:16
and when she **c** to him, he slept 2Sm 11:4
When Uriah **c** to him, David asked 2Sm 11:7
men of the city **c** out and 2Sm 11:17
over us and **c** out against us 2Sm 11:23
a traveler **c** to the rich man, 2Sm 12:4
When the king **c** to see him, 2Sm 13:6
woman from Tekoa **c** to the king, 2Sm 14:4
Then Joab **c** to Absalom's house 2Sm 14:31
who **c** to the king and bowed 2Sm 14:33
Israelites who **c** to the king for 2Sm 15:6
Then an informer **c** to David and 2Sm 15:13
men who **c** with him from Gath 2Sm 15:18
When David **c** to the summit 2Sm 15:32
the Israelites **c** to Jerusalem. 2Sm 16:15
Hushai the Archite **c** to Absalom, 2Sm 16:16
So Hushai **c** to Absalom, and 2Sm 17:6
left quickly and **c** to the house 2Sm 17:18
servants **c** to the woman at 2Sm 17:20
When David **c** to Mahanaim, 2Sm 17:27
As the first runner **c** closer, 2Sm 18:25
then the Cushite **c** and said, 2Sm 18:31
Then they all **c** into the king's 2Sm 19:8
Judah **c** to Gilgal to meet the 2Sm 19:15
When he **c** from Jerusalem to 2Sm 19:25
the men of Israel **c** to the king. 2Sm 19:41
When David **c** to his palace in 2Sm 20:3
All the Berites **c** together and 2Sm 20:14
Joab's troops **c** and besieged 2Sm 20:15
son of Zeruiah **c** to his aid, 2Sm 21:17
fire ⌊**c**⌋ from His mouth 2Sm 22:9
parted the heavens and **c** down, 2Sm 22:10

Then the troops **c** back to him, 2Sm 23:10
harvest time and **c** to David at 2Sm 23:13
Gad **c** to David that day and said 2Sm 24:18
He **c** into the king's presence 1Kg 1:23
So she **c** into the king's 1Kg 1:28
So they **c** into the king's 1Kg 1:32
He **c** and paid homage to King 1Kg 1:53
But he **c** down to meet me at the 1Kg 2:8
son of Haggith **c** to Bathsheba, 1Kg 2:13
were prostitutes **c** to the king 1Kg 3:16
for everyone who **c** to King 1Kg 4:27
People **c** from everywhere, 1Kg 4:34
the Israelites **c** out from the 1Kg 6:1
word of the LORD **c** to Solomon: 1Kg 6:11
So he **c** to King Solomon and 1Kg 7:14
All the elders of Israel **c**, 1Kg 8:3
when they **c** out of the land 1Kg 8:9
the priests **c** out of the holy 1Kg 8:10
of the LORD and **c** to test him 1Kg 10:1
She **c** to Jerusalem with a very 1Kg 10:2
c to Solomon and spoke to him 1Kg 10:2
reports until I **c** and saw with 1Kg 10:7
of gold that **c** to Solomon 1Kg 10:14
besides what **c** from merchants, 1Kg 10:15
as Jeroboam **c** out of Jerusalem 1Kg 11:29
assembly of Israel **c** and spoke 1Kg 12:3
and all the people **c** to Rehoboam 1Kg 12:12
turn of events **c** from the LORD 1Kg 12:15
from God **c** to Shemaiah, 1Kg 12:22
A man of God **c** from Judah to 1Kg 13:1
or go back the way you **c**.' " 1Kg 13:9
His son **c** and told him all the 1Kg 13:11
man of God who **c** from Judah?" 1Kg 13:14
a message **c** to me by the word 1Kg 13:17
or go back by the way you **c**.' " 1Kg 13:17
of the LORD **c** to the prophet 1Kg 13:20
The old prophet **c** into to the 1Kg 13:29
word of the LORD **c** to Jehu son 1Kg 16:1
the LORD also **c** against Baasha 1Kg 16:7
from the LORD **c** to him: 1Kg 17:2
the word of the LORD **c** to him: 1Kg 17:8
the word of the LORD **c** to Elijah 1Kg 18:1
When he **c** to Beer-sheba that 1Kg 19:3
the word of the LORD **c** to him, 1Kg 19:9
a voice **c** to him and said, 1Kg 19:13
by the way you **c** to the 1Kg 19:15
A prophet **c** to Ahab king of 1Kg 20:13
So Ben-hadad **c** out to him, 1Kg 20:33
wife Jezebel **c** to him and said 1Kg 21:5
The two wicked men **c** in and sat 1Kg 21:13
the word of the LORD **c** to Elijah 1Kg 21:17
the word of the LORD **c** to Elijah 1Kg 21:28
Then a spirit **c** forward, stood 1Kg 22:21
Zedekiah son of Chenaanah **c** up, 1Kg 22:24
A man **c** to meet us and said, 2Kg 1:6
What sort of man **c** up to meet 2Kg 1:7
Then fire **c** down from heaven 2Kg 1:10
a divine fire **c** down from heaven 2Kg 1:12
were at Bethel **c** out to Elisha 2Kg 2:3
were in Jericho **c** up to Elisha 2Kg 2:5
of the prophets **c** and stood 2Kg 2:7
They **c** to meet him and bowed 2Kg 2:15
small boys **c** out of the city 2Kg 2:23
female bears **c** out of the woods 2Kg 2:24
the LORD's hand **c** on Elisha. 2Kg 3:15
water suddenly **c** from the 2Kg 3:20
the Moabites **c** to Israel's camp 2Kg 3:24
One day he **c** there and stopped 2Kg 4:11
When she **c** up to the man of God 2Kg 4:27
Gehazi **c** to push her away, 2Kg 4:27
He called her and she **c**. 2Kg 4:36
She **c**, fell at his feet, and 2Kg 4:37
Then he **c** back and cut them up 2Kg 4:39
Baal-shalishah **c** to the man of 2Kg 4:42
So Naaman **c** with his horses and 2Kg 5:9
When Gehazi **c** to the hill, 2Kg 5:24
c and stood by his master. 2Kg 5:25
and when they **c** to the Jordan, 2Kg 6:4
When the Arameans **c** against him, 2Kg 6:18
the messenger **c** down to him. 2Kg 6:33
When they **c** to the camp's edge, 2Kg 7:5
When these men **c** to the edge of 2Kg 7:8
They **c** back and entered another 2Kg 7:8
when the king **c** to him. 2Kg 7:17
restored to life **c** to appeal to 2Kg 8:5
Elisha **c** to Damascus while 2Kg 8:7
When he **c** and stood before him, 2Kg 8:9
When Jehu **c** out to his master's 2Kg 9:11

When Jehu **c** to Jezreel, Jezebel 2Kg 9:30
When the letter **c** to them, 2Kg 10:7
the messenger **c** and told him, 2Kg 10:8
Jehu **c** to Samaria, he struck 2Kg 10:17
and all the servants of Baal **c**; 2Kg 10:21
son of Gadi **c** up from Tirzah to 2Kg 15:14
king of Assyria **c** and captured 2Kg 15:29
son of Remaliah **c** to wage war 2Kg 16:5
Then the Arameans **c** to Elath, 2Kg 16:6
time King Ahaz **c** back from 2Kg 16:11
When the king **c** back from 2Kg 16:12
they had deported **c** and lived in 2Kg 17:28
advanced and **c** to Jerusalem, 2Kg 18:17
court historian, **c** out to them. 2Kg 18:18
c to Hezekiah with their clothes 2Kg 18:37
I **c** to its farthest outpost, 2Kg 19:23
make you go back the way you **c**. 2Kg 19:28
road that he **c** and he will not 2Kg 19:33
son of Amoz **c** and said to him, 2Kg 20:1
the word of the LORD **c** to him: 2Kg 20:4
Isaiah **c** to King Hezekiah 2Kg 20:14
They **c** from a distant country, 2Kg 20:14
their ancestors **c** out of Egypt 2Kg 21:15
the man of God who **c** from Judah 2Kg 23:17
the prophet who **c** from Samaria. 2Kg 23:18
and the city **c** under siege. 2Kg 24:10
of Babylon **c** to the city while 2Kg 24:11
it **c** to the point in Jerusalem 2Kg 24:20
they **c** to Gedaliah at Mizpah. 2Kg 25:23
c with 10 men and struck down 2Kg 25:25
the Philistines **c** from them 1Ch 1:12
the Kenites who **c** from Hammath, 1Ch 2:55
recorded by name **c** in the days 1Ch 4:41
brothers and a ruler **c** from him, 1Ch 5:2
after the ark **c** to rest there. 1Ch 6:31
his relatives **c** to comfort him. 1Ch 7:22
Their relatives **c** from their 1Ch 9:25
So the Philistines **c** and settled 1Ch 10:7
the Philistines **c** to strip the 1Ch 10:8
All Israel **c** together to David 1Ch 11:1
elders of Israel **c** to the king 1Ch 11:3
were the men who **c** to David at 1Ch 12:1
c day after day to help David 1Ch 12:22
armed troops who **c** to David at 1Ch 12:23
c to Hebron with wholehearted 1Ch 12:38
and Naphtali **c** bringing food on 1Ch 12:40
they **c** to Chidon's threshing 1Ch 13:9
the word of God **c** to Nathan: 1Ch 17:3
You **c** to one nation on earth to 1Ch 17:21
of Damascus **c** to assist King 1Ch 18:5
Someone **c** and reported to David 1Ch 19:5
who **c** and camped near Medeba. 1Ch 19:7
cities and **c** for the battle. 1Ch 19:7
He **c** up to them and lined up in 1Ch 19:17
He **c** to Rabbah and besieged it, 1Ch 20:1
David **c** to Ornan, and when 1Ch 21:21
the word of the LORD **c** to me: 1Ch 22:8
and his lot **c** out for the north 1Ch 26:14
After Ahithophel **c** Jehoiada son 1Ch 27:34
Solomon's horses **c** from Egypt 2Ch 1:16
All the elders of Israel **c**, 2Ch 5:4
when they **c** out of Egypt. 2Ch 5:10
the priests **c** out of the holy 2Ch 5:11
of the LORD **c** on the temple. 2Ch 7:3
so she **c** to test Solomon with 2Ch 9:1
She **c** to Solomon and spoke with 2Ch 9:1
reports until I **c** and saw with 2Ch 9:6
of gold that **c** to Solomon 2Ch 9:13
and all Israel **c** and spoke to 2Ch 10:3
and all the people **c** to Rehoboam 2Ch 10:12
the turn of events **c** from God, 2Ch 10:15
word of the LORD **c** to Shemaiah, 2Ch 11:2
people who **c** with him from Egypt 2Ch 12:3
of Judah and **c** as far as 2Ch 12:4
LORD's message **c** to Shemaiah: 2Ch 12:7
the Cushite **c** against them with 2Ch 14:9
They **c** as far as Mareshah. 2Ch 14:9
Spirit of God **c** on Azariah son 2Ch 15:1
Hanani the seer **c** to King Asa of 2Ch 16:7
Then a spirit **c** forward, stood 2Ch 18:20
Zedekiah son of Chenaanah **c** up, 2Ch 18:23
c ⌊to fight⌋ against Jehoshaphat. 2Ch 20:1
People **c** and told Jehoshaphat, 2Ch 20:2
They even **c** from all the cities 2Ch 20:4
when Israel **c** out of the land 2Ch 20:10
Spirit of the LORD **c** on Jahaziel 2Ch 20:14
Mount Seir who **c** ⌊to fight⌋ 2Ch 20:22
When Judah **c** to a place 2Ch 20:24

So they **c** into Jerusalem to the 2Ch 20:28
Then a letter **c** to Jehoram from 2Ch 21:12
his intestines **c** out because of 2Ch 21:19
Israel, and they **c** to Jerusalem. 2Ch 23:2
priest's deputy **c** and emptied 2Ch 24:11
of Judah **c** and paid homage 2Ch 24:17
Aramean army **c** with only a few 2Ch 24:24
a man of God **c** to him and said, 2Ch 25:7
the division that **c** to him from 2Ch 25:10
After Amaziah **c** from the attack 2Ch 25:14
meet the army that **c** to Samaria 2Ch 28:9
The Edomites **c** again, attacked 2Ch 28:17
king of Assyria **c** against Ahaz; 2Ch 28:20
the month they **c** to the 2Ch 29:17
themselves and **c** to Jerusalem. 2Ch 30:11
assembly that **c** from Israel, 2Ch 30:25
foreigners who **c** from the land 2Ch 30:25
and their prayer **c** into His holy 2Ch 30:27
and his officials **c** and viewed 2Ch 31:8
king of Assyria **c** and entered 2Ch 32:1
So Manasseh **c** to know that the 2Ch 33:13
the province who **c** from those Ezr 2:1
They **c** with Zerubbabel, Jeshua, Ezr 2:2
are those who **c** from Tel-melah, Ezr 2:59
the Jews who **c** from you have Ezr 4:12
their colleagues **c** to the Jews Ezr 5:3
this same Sheshbazzar **c** and laid Ezr 5:16
—**c** up from Babylon. He was a Ezr 7:6
Ezra **c** to Jerusalem in the fifth Ezr 7:8
daybreak until the stars **c** out. Neh 4:21
Tobiah's ⌊letters⌋ **c** to them. Neh 6:17
of those who **c** back first, Neh 7:5
They **c** with Zerubbabel, Jeshua, Neh 7:7
are those who **c** from Tel-melah, Neh 7:61
the seventh month **c** and the Neh 8:1
You **c** down on Mount Sinai, Neh 9:13
When her turn **c** to go to the Est 2:15
the king's command and edict **c**. Est 4:3
and her eunuchs **c** and reported Est 4:4
c and repeated Mordecai's Est 4:9
king and Haman **c** to feast with Est 7:1
day the sons of God **c** to present Jb 1:6
and Satan also **c** with them. Jb 1:6
a messenger **c** to Job and Jb 1:14
messenger⌋ **c** and reported: Jb 1:16
yet⌋ another **c** and reported: Jb 1:17
messenger⌋ **c** and reported: Jb 1:18
Naked I **c** from my mother's womb, Jb 1:21
the sons of God **c** again to Jb 2:1
and Satan also **c** with them to Jb 2:1
each of them **c** from his home. Jb 2:11
I die as I **c** from the womb? Jb 3:11
and trembling **c** over me and made Jb 4:14
breath **c** out of your ⌊mouth⌋ Jb 26:4
when I hoped for good, evil **c**; Jb 30:26
I looked for light, darkness **c**. Jb 30:26
excited when trouble **c** his way? Jb 31:29
acquaintances **c** to his house Jb 42:11
fire ⌊**c**⌋ from His mouth Ps 18:8
parted the heavens and **c** down, Ps 18:9
When evildoers **c** against me to Ps 27:2
He spoke, and it **c** into being; Ps 33:9
and it **c** into existence. Ps 33:9
the time his prediction **c** true, Ps 105:19
and insects **c**—gnats throughout Ps 105:31
and locusts **c**—young locusts Ps 105:34
all food and **c** near the gates Ps 107:18
When Israel **c** out of Egypt— Ps 114:1
This **c** from the LORD; it is Ps 118:23
A woman **c** to meet him, dressed Pr 7:10
I **c** out to meet you, to search Pr 7:15
no memory of those who **c** before; Ec 1:11
For he **c** from prison to be king, Ec 4:14
As he **c** from his mother's womb, Ec 5:15
he will go again, naked as he **c**; Ec 5:15
They **c** and went from the holy Ec 8:10
A great king **c** against it, Ec 9:14
I **c** down to the walnut grove to Sg 6:11
Jacob; it **c** against Israel. Is 9:8
when they **c** up from the land Is 11:16
King Ahaz died, this oracle **c**: Is 14:28
c to Ashdod and attacked and Is 20:1
the word of the LORD **c** to them: Is 28:13
the record keeper, **c** out to him. Is 36:3
c to Hezekiah with their clothes Is 36:22
Hezekiah's servants **c** to Isaiah, Is 37:5
I **c** to its remotest heights, Is 37:24
make you go back the way you **c**. Is 37:29

road that he **c** and he will not Is 37:34
son of Amoz **c** and said to him, Is 38:1
word of the LORD **c** to Isaiah: Is 38:4
the prophet **c** to King Hezekiah Is 39:3
men who **c** to you—where were Is 39:3
They **c** to me from a distant Is 39:3
they **c** out of My mouth; Is 48:3
Why was no one there when I **c**? Is 50:2
and the year of My redemption **c**. Is 63:4
we did not expect, You **c** down, Is 64:3
and so they all **c** into being. Is 66:2
The word of the LORD **c** to him in Jr 1:2
It also **c** throughout the days of Jr 1:3
The word of the LORD **c** to me: Jr 1:4
the word of the LORD **c** to me, Jr 1:11
of the LORD **c** to me inquiring Jr 1:13
The word of the LORD **c** to me: Jr 2:1
disaster **c** on them." ⌊This Jr 2:3
is⌋ the word that **c** to Jeremiah Jr 7:1
your ancestors **c** out of the land Jr 7:25
is⌋ the word that **c** to Jeremiah Jr 11:1
of the LORD **c** to me a second Jr 13:3
the word of the LORD **c** to me: Jr 13:8
of the LORD that **c** to Jeremiah Jr 14:1
The word of the LORD **c** to me: Jr 16:1
is⌋ the word that **c** to Jeremiah Jr 18:1
The word of the LORD **c** to me: Jr 18:5
Jeremiah **c** back from Topheth, Jr 19:14
is⌋ the word that **c** to Jeremiah Jr 21:1
The word of the LORD **c** to me: Jr 24:4
is⌋ the word that **c** to Jeremiah Jr 25:1
this word **c** from the LORD: Jr 26:1
this word **c** to Jeremiah from the Jr 27:1
word of the LORD **c** to Jeremiah Jr 28:12
word of the LORD **c** to Jeremiah: Jr 29:30
is⌋ the word that **c** to Jeremiah Jr 30:1
is⌋ the word that **c** to Jeremiah Jr 32:1
The word of the LORD **c** to me: Jr 32:6
Hanamel ⌊**c**⌋ to the guard's Jr 32:8
word of the LORD **c** to Jeremiah: Jr 32:26
word of the LORD **c** to Jeremiah a Jr 33:1
word of the LORD **c** to Jeremiah: Jr 33:19
word of the LORD **c** to Jeremiah: Jr 33:23
is⌋ the word that **c** to Jeremiah Jr 34:1
is⌋ the word that **c** to Jeremiah Jr 34:8
word of the LORD **c** to Jeremiah Jr 34:12
is⌋ the word that **c** to Jeremiah Jr 35:1
word of the LORD **c** to Jeremiah: Jr 35:12
this word **c** to Jeremiah from the Jr 36:1
Then they **c** to the king at the Jr 36:20
word of the LORD **c** to Jeremiah: Jr 36:27
word of the LORD **c** to Jeremiah Jr 37:6
all the officials **c** to Jeremiah Jr 38:27
is⌋ the word that **c** to Jeremiah Jr 40:1
they **c** to Gedaliah at Mizpah. Jr 40:8
been banished and **c** to the land Jr 40:12
in the field **c** to Gedaliah at Jr 40:13
c with 10 men to Gedaliah son of Jr 41:1
80 men **c** from Shechem, Shiloh, Jr 41:5
of Nethaniah **c** out of Mizpah to Jr 41:6
to meet them, weeping as he **c**. Jr 41:6
But when they **c** into the city, Jr 41:7
word of the LORD **c** to Jeremiah, Jr 42:7
word of the LORD **c** to Jeremiah Jr 43:8
the word that **c** to Jeremiah for Jr 44:1
of the LORD that **c** to Jeremiah Jr 46:1
of the LORD that **c** to Jeremiah Jr 47:1
If grape harvesters **c** to you, Jr 49:9
of the LORD that **c** to Jeremiah Jr 49:34
it **c** to the point in Jerusalem Jr 52:3
word of the LORD **c** directly to Ezk 1:3
four living creatures **c** from it. Ezk 1:5
A voice **c** from above the expanse Ezk 1:25
I **c** to the exiles at Tel-abib, Ezk 3:15
the word of the LORD **c** to me: Ezk 3:16
The word of the LORD **c** to me: Ezk 6:1
the word of the LORD **c** to me: Ezk 7:1
of the Lord GOD **c** down on me. Ezk 8:1
They **c** and stood beside the Ezk 9:2
the Spirit of the LORD **c** on me, Ezk 11:5
word of the LORD **c** to me again: Ezk 11:14
The word of the LORD **c** to me: Ezk 12:1
word of the LORD **c** to me in the Ezk 12:8
The word of the LORD **c** to me: Ezk 12:17
the word of the LORD **c** to me: Ezk 12:21
The word of the LORD **c** to me: Ezk 12:26
The word of the LORD **c** to me: Ezk 13:1
elders of Israel **c** to me and sat Ezk 14:1

the word of the LORD **c** to me:	Ezk 14:2
The word of the LORD **c** to me:	Ezk 14:12
the word of the LORD **c** to me:	Ezk 15:1
word of the LORD **c** to me again:	Ezk 16:1
The word of the LORD **c** to me:	Ezk 17:1
of many colors **c** to Lebanon and	Ezk 17:3
The word of the LORD **c** to me:	Ezk 17:11
king of Babylon **c** to Jerusalem,	Ezk 17:12
The word of the LORD **c** to me:	Ezk 18:1
of Israel's elders **c** to consult	Ezk 20:1
the word of the LORD **c** to me:	Ezk 20:2
The word of the LORD **c** to me:	Ezk 20:45
word of the LORD **c** to me again:	Ezk 21:1
The word of the LORD **c** to me:	Ezk 21:8
the word of the LORD **c** to me:	Ezk 21:18
The word of the LORD **c** to me:	Ezk 22:1
The word of the LORD **c** to me:	Ezk 22:17
The word of the LORD **c** to me:	Ezk 22:23
word of the LORD **c** to me again:	Ezk 23:1
Then the Babylonians **c** to her,	Ezk 23:17
sent for men who **c** from far away	Ezk 23:40
And look how they **c**! You bathed,	Ezk 23:40
word of the LORD **c** to me in the	Ezk 24:1
the word of the LORD **c** to me:	Ezk 24:15
The word of the LORD **c** to me:	Ezk 24:20
the word of the LORD **c** to me:	Ezk 25:1
the word of the LORD **c** to me:	Ezk 26:1
The word of the LORD **c** to me:	Ezk 27:1
their sailors **c** to you to barter	Ezk 27:9
The word of the LORD **c** to me:	Ezk 28:1
The word of the LORD **c** to me:	Ezk 28:11
The word of the LORD **c** to me:	Ezk 28:20
the word of the LORD **c** to me:	Ezk 29:1
the word of the LORD **c** to me:	Ezk 29:17
The word of the LORD **c** to me:	Ezk 30:1
the word of the LORD **c** to me:	Ezk 30:20
the word of the LORD **c** to me:	Ezk 31:1
the word of the LORD **c** to me:	Ezk 32:1
the word of the LORD **c** to me:	Ezk 32:17
The word of the LORD **c** to me:	Ezk 33:1
from Jerusalem **c** to me and	Ezk 33:21
before the man **c** to me in the	Ezk 33:22
the word of the LORD **c** to me:	Ezk 33:23
The word of the LORD **c** to me:	Ezk 34:1
The word of the LORD **c** to me:	Ezk 35:1
The word of the LORD **c** to me:	Ezk 36:16
When they **c** to the nations where	Ezk 36:20
and the bones **c** together, bone	Ezk 37:7
and they **c** to life and stood on	Ezk 37:10
The word of the LORD **c** to me:	Ezk 37:15
The word of the LORD **c** to me:	Ezk 38:1
Then he **c** to the gate that faced	Ezk 40:6
I had seen when He **c** to destroy	Ezk 43:3
It **c** up to ⌊my⌋ ankles.	Ezk 47:3
water. It **c** up to ⌊my⌋ knees.	Ezk 47:4
the water⌋. It **c** up to ⌊my⌋	Ezk 47:4
king of Babylon **c** to Jerusalem	Dn 1:1
When they **c** and stood before the	Dn 2:2
c and said to him, "Don't kill	Dn 2:24
visions ⌊that **c** into⌋ your mind	Dn 2:28
thoughts **c** ⌊to your mind⌋ about	Dn 2:29
and Abednego **c** out of the fire.	Dn 3:26
astrologers **c** in, I told them	Dn 4:7
gods is in him—**c** before me.	Dn 4:8
mouth, a voice **c** from heaven:	Dn 4:31
and even more greatness **c** to me.	Dn 4:36
So all the king's wise men **c** in,	Dn 5:8
the queen **c** to the banquet hall.	Dn 5:10
huge beasts **c** up from the sea	Dn 7:3
a little one, **c** up among them,	Dn 7:8
about the other horn that **c** up,	Dn 7:20
and the longer one **c** up last.	Dn 8:3
He **c** toward the two-horned ram I	Dn 8:6
horns **c** up in its place,	Dn 8:8
when he **c** near, I was terrified	Dn 8:17
c to me in my extreme weariness,	Dn 9:21
c to help me after I had been	Dn 10:13
since nations **c** into being until	Dn 12:1
of the LORD that **c** to Hosea son	Hs 1:1
in the day she **c** out of the land	Hs 2:15
for there I **c** to hate them.	Hs 9:15
of the LORD that **c** to Joel son	Jl 1:1
thieves **c** to you, if marauders	Ob 5
If grape pickers **c** to you,	Ob 5
word of the LORD **c** to Jonah son	Jnh 1:1
My prayer **c** to You, to Your holy	Jnh 2:7
word of the LORD **c** to Jonah a	Jnh 3:1
When dawn **c** the next day, God	Jnh 4:7
word of the LORD that **c** to Micah	Mc 1:1
the LORD that **c** to Zephaniah son	Zph 1:1
of the LORD **c** through Haggai	Hg 1:1
of the LORD **c** through Haggai	Hg 1:3
of the LORD **c** through Haggai	Hg 2:1
to you when you **c** out of Egypt,	Hg 2:5
the word of the LORD **c** to Haggai	Hg 2:10
When someone **c** to a ⌊grain⌋ heap	Hg 2:16
when one **c** to the winepress to	Hg 2:16
word of the LORD **c** to Haggai a	Hg 2:20
of the LORD **c** to the prophet	Zch 1:1
of the LORD **c** to the prophet	Zch 1:7
the word of the LORD **c** to me:	Zch 4:8
with me **c** forward and told	Zch 5:5
The word of the LORD **c** to me:	Zch 6:9
word of the LORD **c** to Zechariah	Zch 7:1
of the LORD of Hosts **c** to me:	Zch 7:4
word of the LORD **c** to Zechariah:	Zch 7:8
great anger **c** from the LORD	Zch 7:12
The word of the LORD of Hosts **c**:	Zch 8:1
enemy for anyone who **c** or went,	Zch 8:10
of the LORD of Hosts **c** to me:	Zch 8:18
the nations that **c** against	Zch 14:16
Jesus Christ **c** about this way:	Mt 1:18
before they **c** together that she	Mt 1:18
them until it **c** and stopped	Mt 2:9
those days John the Baptist **c**,	Mt 3:1
Jesus **c** from Galilee to John	Mt 3:13
And there **c** a voice from heaven:	Mt 3:17
angels **c** and began to serve	Mt 4:11
down, His disciples **c** to Him.	Mt 5:1
assume that I **c** to destroy the	Mt 5:17
He **c** down from the mountain,	Mt 8:1
skin disease **c** up and knelt	Mt 8:2
a centurion **c** to Him, pleading	Mt 8:5
When evening **c**, they brought to	Mt 8:16
the disciples **c** and woke Him up	Mt 8:25
met Him as they **c** out of the	Mt 8:28
over, and **c** to His own town.	Mt 9:1
and sinners **c** as guests to eat	Mt 9:10
Then John's disciples **c** to Him,	Mt 9:14
of the leaders **c** and knelt down	Mt 9:18
When Jesus **c** to the leader's	Mt 9:23
assume that I **c** to bring peace	Mt 10:34
I **c** to turn a man against his	Mt 10:35
The Son of Man **c** eating and	Mt 11:19
because she **c** from the ends of	Mt 12:42
go back to my house that I **c**	Mt 12:44
and the birds **c** and ate them up.	Mt 13:4
But when the sun **c** up they were	Mt 13:6
and the thorns **c** up and choked	Mt 13:7
the disciples **c** up and asked Him	Mt 13:10
his enemy **c**, sowed weeds among	Mt 13:25
slaves **c** to him and said,	Mt 13:27
Herod's birthday celebration **c**,	Mt 14:6
Then his disciples **c**, removed	Mt 14:12
When evening **c**, the disciples	Mt 14:15
When evening **c**, He was there	Mt 14:23
He **c** toward them walking on the	Mt 14:25
on the water and **c** toward Jesus.	Mt 14:29
they **c** to land at Gennesaret.	Mt 14:34
and scribes **c** from Jerusalem to	Mt 15:1
the disciples **c** up and told Him,	Mt 15:12
that region **c** and kept crying	Mt 15:22
But she **c**, knelt before Him, and	Mt 15:25
and large crowds **c** to Him,	Mt 15:30
When Jesus **c** to the region of	Mt 16:13
Then Jesus **c** up, touched them,	Mt 17:7
the demon, and it **c** out of him,	Mt 17:18
When they **c** to Capernaum, those	Mt 17:24
the disciples **c** to Jesus and	Mt 18:1
Then Peter **c** to Him and said,	Mt 18:21
then someone **c** up and asked Him	Mt 19:16
When evening **c**, the owner of the	Mt 20:8
who were hired about five **c**,	Mt 20:9
the first ones **c**, they assumed	Mt 20:10
Jerusalem and **c** to Bethphage at	Mt 21:1
blind and the lame **c** to Him in	Mt 21:14
of the people **c** up to Him as He	Mt 21:23
For John **c** to you in the way of	Mt 21:32
This **c** from the Lord and is	Mt 21:42
But when the king **c** in to view	Mt 22:11
c up to Him and questioned Him:	Mt 22:23
they **c** together in the same	Mt 22:34
disciples **c** up and called His	Mt 24:1
until the flood **c** and swept them	Mt 24:39
the virgins also **c** and said,	Mt 25:11
of those slaves **c** and settled	Mt 25:19
the disciples **c** to Jesus and	Mt 26:17
When evening **c**, He was reclining	Mt 26:20
Jesus **c** with them to a place	Mt 26:36
Then He **c** to the disciples and	Mt 26:40
And He **c** again and found them	Mt 26:43
Then He **c** to the disciples and	Mt 26:45
Then they **c** up, took hold of	Mt 26:50
many false witnesses **c** forward.	Mt 26:60
Finally, two who **c** forward	Mt 26:60
When daybreak **c**, all the chief	Mt 27:1
When they **c** to a place called	Mt 27:33
darkness **c** over the whole	Mt 27:45
they **c** out of the tombs after	Mt 27:53
from Arimathea named Joseph **c**,	Mt 27:57
They **c** up, took hold of His	Mt 28:9
of the guard **c** into the city	Mt 28:11
'His disciples **c** during the	Mt 28:13
Then Jesus **c** near and said to	Mt 28:18
John **c** baptizing in the	Mk 1:4
those days Jesus **c** from Nazareth	Mk 1:9
As soon as He **c** up out of the	Mk 1:10
And a voice **c** from heaven:	Mk 1:11
a loud voice, and **c** out of him.	Mk 1:26
When evening **c**, after the sun	Mk 1:32
a serious skin disease **c** to Him	Mk 1:40
Then they **c** to Him bringing a	Mk 2:3
People **c** and asked Him, "Why do	Mk 2:18
great multitude **c** to Him because	Mk 3:8
He wanted, and they **c** to Him.	Mk 3:13
His mother and His brothers **c**,	Mk 3:31
and the birds **c** and ate it up.	Mk 4:4
When the sun **c** up, it was	Mk 4:6
and the thorns **c** up and choked	Mk 4:7
Then they **c** to the other side of	Mk 5:1
unclean spirit **c** out of the	Mk 5:2
spirits **c** out and entered	Mk 5:13
They **c** to Jesus and saw the man	Mk 5:15
named Jairus, **c**, and when he saw	Mk 5:22
c behind Him in the crowd and	Mk 5:27
c with fear and trembling,	Mk 5:33
people **c** from the synagogue	Mk 5:35
They **c** to the leader's house,	Mk 5:38
there and **c** to His hometown,	Mk 6:1
When the Sabbath **c**, He began to	Mk 6:2
opportune time **c** on his birthday	Mk 6:21
own daughter **c** in and danced,	Mk 6:22
they **c** and removed his corpse	Mk 6:29
When evening **c**, the boat was in	Mk 6:47
in the morning He **c** toward them	Mk 6:48
they **c** to land at Gennesaret and	Mk 6:53
unclean spirit **c** and fell at His	Mk 7:25
The Pharisees **c** out and began to	Mk 8:11
Then they **c** to Bethsaida.	Mk 8:22
and a voice **c** from the cloud:	Mk 9:7
When they **c** to the disciples,	Mk 9:14
Then it **c** out, shrieking and	Mk 9:26
Then they **c** to Capernaum.	Mk 9:33
They **c** to Jericho. And as He was	Mk 10:46
coat, jumped up, and **c** to Jesus.	Mk 10:50
day when they **c** out from Bethany	Mk 11:12
He **c** to it, He found nothing	Mk 11:13
They **c** to Jerusalem, and He went	Mk 11:15
whenever evening **c**, they would	Mk 11:19
They **c** again to Jerusalem.	Mk 11:27
and the elders **c** and asked Him,	Mk 11:27
This **c** from the Lord and is	Mk 12:11
When they **c**, they said to Him,	Mk 12:14
c to Him and questioned Him:	Mk 12:18
And a poor widow **c** and dropped	Mk 12:42
a woman **c** with an alabaster jar	Mk 14:3
When evening **c**, He arrived with	Mk 14:17
Then they **c** to a place named	Mk 14:32
Then He **c** and found them	Mk 14:37
And He **c** again and found them	Mk 14:40
Then He **c** a third time and said	Mk 14:41
when he **c**, he went right up to	Mk 14:45
of the high priest's servants **c**.	Mk 14:66
The crowd **c** up and began to ask	Mk 15:8
darkness **c** over the whole land	Mk 15:33
c and boldly went in to Pilate	Mk 15:43
the angel⌋ **c** to her and said	Lk 1:28
When they **c** to circumcise the	Lk 1:59
Fear **c** on all those who lived	Lk 1:65
time **c** for her to give birth.	Lk 2:6
she **c** up and began to thank God	Lk 2:38
down with them and **c** to Nazareth	Lk 2:51
God's word **c** to John the son of	Lk 3:2
to the crowds who **c** out to be	Lk 3:7

also **c** to be baptized,	Lk 3:12
And a voice **c** from heaven:	Lk 3:22
He **c** to Nazareth, where He had	Lk 4:16
words that **c** from His mouth,	Lk 4:22
a great famine **c** over all the	Lk 4:25
the demon **c** out of him without	Lk 4:35
They **c** to Him and tried to keep	Lk 4:42
they **c** and filled both boats so	Lk 5:7
Just then some men **c**, carrying	Lk 5:18
When daylight **c**, He summoned His	Lk 6:13
They **c** to hear Him and to be	Lk 6:18
When the flood **c**, the river	Lk 6:48
He **c** up and touched the open	Lk 7:14
Then fear **c** over everyone,	Lk 7:16
kissing My feet since I **c**	Lk 7:45
mother and brothers **c** to Him,	Lk 8:19
windstorm **c** down on the lake	Lk 8:23
They **c** and woke Him up, saying,	Lk 8:24
The demons **c** out of the man and	Lk 8:33
They **c** to Jesus and found the	Lk 8:35
Just then, a man named Jairus **c**.	Lk 8:41
she **c** trembling and fell down	Lk 8:47
someone **c** from the synagogue	Lk 8:49
After He **c** to the house, He let	Lk 8:51
Then a voice **c** from the cloud,	Lk 9:35
when they **c** down from the	Lk 9:37
on his journey **c** up to him,	Lk 10:33
tasks, and she **c** up and asked,	Lk 10:40
When the demon **c** out, the man	Lk 11:14
go back to my house where I **c**	Lk 11:24
because she **c** from the ends of	Lk 11:31
of many thousands **c** together,	Lk 12:1
I **c** to bring fire on the earth,	Lk 12:49
you think that I **c** here to give	Lk 12:51
some people **c** and reported to	Lk 13:1
He **c** looking for fruit on it and	Lk 13:6
some Pharisees **c** and told Him,	Lk 13:31
So the slave **c** back and reported	Lk 14:21
he **c** to his senses, he said,	Lk 15:17
as he **c** near the house, he heard	Lk 15:25
So his father **c** out and pleaded	Lk 15:28
But when this son of yours **c**,	Lk 15:30
and the flood **c** and destroyed	Lk 17:27
When Jesus **c** to the place,	Lk 19:5
he quickly **c** down and welcomed	Lk 19:6
The first **c** forward and said,	Lk 19:16
The second **c** and said, 'Master,	Lk 19:18
And another **c** and said, 'Master,	Lk 19:20
Now He **c** near the path down the	Lk 19:37
scribes, with the elders, **c** up	Lk 20:1
no resurrection, **c** up and	Lk 20:27
Unleavened Bread **c** when the	Lk 22:7
When the hour **c**, He reclined at	Lk 22:14
from prayer and **c** to the	Lk 22:45
He **c** near Jesus to kiss Him,	Lk 22:47
When daylight **c**, the elders of	Lk 22:66
They **c** offering Him sour wine	Lk 23:36
and darkness **c** over the whole	Lk 23:44
the morning, they **c** to the tomb,	Lk 24:1
Jesus Himself **c** near and began	Lk 24:15
they **c** and reported that they	Lk 24:23
They **c** near the village where	Lk 24:28
He **c** as a witness to testify	Jn 1:7
but he **c** to testify about the	Jn 1:8
He **c** to His own, and His own	Jn 1:11
grace and truth **c** through Jesus	Jn 1:17
but I **c** baptizing with water so	Jn 1:31
did not know where it **c** from—	Jn 2:9
This man **c** to Him at night and	Jn 3:2
So they **c** to John and told him,	Jn 3:26
so He **c** to a town of Samaria	Jn 4:5
of Samaria **c** to draw water.	Jn 4:7
when the Samaritans **c** to Him,	Jn 4:40
after He **c** from Judea to	Jn 4:54
When evening **c**, His disciples	Jn 6:16
from Tiberias **c** near the place	Jn 6:23
the bread that **c** down from	Jn 6:41
bread that **c** down from heaven	Jn 6:51
the bread that **c** down from	Jn 6:58
the temple police **c** to the chief	Jn 7:45
the one who **c** to Him previously,	Jn 7:50
I know where I **c** from and where	Jn 8:14
because I **c** from God and I am	Jn 8:42
⌊This **c** about⌋ so that God's	Jn 9:3
left, washed, and **c** back seeing.	Jn 9:7
I **c** into this world for	Jn 9:39
All who **c** before Me are thieves	Jn 10:8
the word of God **c** to 'gods'—	Jn 10:35
Many **c** to Him and said, "John	Jn 10:41
When Mary **c** to where Jesus was	Jn 11:32
in Himself again, **c** to the tomb.	Jn 11:38
dead man **c** out bound hand and	Jn 11:44
the Jews who **c** to Mary and saw	Jn 11:45
Jesus **c** to Bethany where Lazarus	Jn 12:1
c not only because of Jesus,	Jn 12:9
they **c** to Philip, who was from	Jn 12:21
that is why I **c** to this hour.	Jn 12:27
Then a voice **c** from heaven:	Jn 12:28
This voice **c**, not for Me, but	Jn 12:30
He **c** to Simon Peter, who asked	Jn 13:6
have believed that I **c** from God.	Jn 16:27
c from the Father and have come	Jn 16:28
we believe that You **c** from God."	Jn 16:30
for certain that I **c** from You.	Jn 17:8
the Pharisees and **c** there with	Jn 18:3
Then Pilate **c** out to them and	Jn 18:29
they repeatedly **c** up to Him and	Jn 19:3
Then Jesus **c** out wearing the	Jn 19:5
So the soldiers **c** and broke the	Jn 19:32
When they **c** to Jesus, they did	Jn 19:33
at once blood and water **c** out.	Jn 19:34
so he **c** and took His body away.	Jn 19:38
Him at night) also **c**, bringing a	Jn 19:39
Mary Magdalene **c** to the tomb	Jn 20:1
him, Simon Peter **c** also.	Jn 20:6
Then Jesus **c**, stood among them,	Jn 20:19
was not with them when Jesus **c**.	Jn 20:24
Jesus **c** and stood among them.	Jn 20:26
When daybreak **c**, Jesus stood on	Jn 21:4
other disciples **c** in the boat,	Jn 21:8
Jesus **c**, took the bread, and	Jn 21:13
rushing wind **c** from heaven,	Ac 2:2
the multitude **c** together and was	Ac 2:6
Then fear **c** over everyone,	Ac 2:43
of the men **c** to about 5,000.	Ac 4:4
a great fear **c** on all who heard	Ac 5:5
then his wife **c** in, not knowing	Ac 5:7
the young men **c** in, they found	Ac 5:10
Then great fear **c** on the whole	Ac 5:11
and pallets so that when Peter **c**	Ac 5:15
a multitude **c** together from the	Ac 5:16
Someone **c** and reported to them,	Ac 5:25
were dispersed and **c** to nothing.	Ac 5:36
c forward and disputed with	Ac 6:9
so they **c** up, dragged him off,	Ac 6:12
Then he **c** out of the land of the	Ac 7:4
a famine **c** over all of Egypt	Ac 7:11
he **c** to his rescue and avenged	Ac 7:24
at it, the voice of the Lord **c**:	Ac 7:31
c out of many who were possessed,	Ac 8:7
the road, they **c** to some water.	Ac 8:36
When they **c** up out of the water,	Ac 8:39
towns until he **c** to Caesarea.	Ac 8:40
and then **c** here for the purpose	Ac 9:21
he also **c** down to the saints who	Ac 9:32
angel of God who **c** in and said	Ac 10:3
That's why I **c** without any	Ac 10:29
the Holy Spirit **c** down on all	Ac 10:44
four corners, and it **c** to me.	Ac 11:5
the Holy Spirit **c** down on them,	Ac 11:15
who **c** to Antioch and began	Ac 11:20
days some prophets **c** down from	Ac 11:27
they **c** to the iron gate that	Ac 12:10
Peter **c** to himself and said,	Ac 12:11
servant named Rhoda **c** to answer.	Ac 12:13
Spirit, they **c** down to Seleucia	Ac 13:4
as Paphos, they **c** across a	Ac 13:6
sail from Paphos and **c** to Perga	Ac 13:13
Before He **c** to public attention,	Ac 13:24
days to those who **c** up with Him	Ac 13:31
Then some Jews **c** from Antioch	Ac 14:19
Pisidia and **c** to Pamphylia.	Ac 14:24
Some men **c** down from Judea and	Ac 15:1
When they **c** to Mysia, they tried	Ac 16:7
Mysia, they **c** down to Troas.	Ac 16:8
And it **c** out right away.	Ac 16:18
and everyone's chains **c** loose.	Ac 16:26
When daylight **c**, the chief	Ac 16:35
they **c** and apologized to them,	Ac 16:39
they **c** to Lydia's house where	Ac 16:40
Apollonia and **c** to Thessalonica	Ac 17:1
at Beroea, they **c** there too,	Ac 17:13
to leave Rome. Paul **c** to them,	Ac 18:2
Silas and Timothy **c** down from	Ac 18:5
regions and **c** to Ephesus.	Ac 19:1
the Holy Spirit **c** on them,	Ac 19:6
the evil spirits **c** out of them.	Ac 19:12
become believers **c** confessing	Ac 19:18
them at length, he **c** to Greece	Ac 20:2
him on board and **c** to Mitylene.	Ac 20:14
the day after, we **c** to Miletus.	Ac 20:15
And when they **c** to him, he said	Ac 20:18
the trials that **c** to me through	Ac 20:19
we **c** by a direct route to Cos,	Ac 21:1
day we left and **c** to Caesarea,	Ac 21:8
named Agabus **c** down from Judea.	Ac 21:10
He **c** to us, took Paul's belt,	Ac 21:11
Then the commander **c** up, took	Ac 21:33
with me, and **c** into Damascus.	Ac 22:11
c to me, stood by me, and said,	Ac 22:13
After I **c** back to Jerusalem and	Ac 22:17
The commander **c** and said to him,	Ac 22:27
c and entered the barracks and	Ac 23:16
the high priest **c** down with some	Ac 24:1
the commander **c** and took him	Ac 24:7
c to bring charitable gifts and	Ac 24:17
when Felix **c** with his wife	Ac 24:24
and Bernice **c** with great pomp	Ac 25:23
we **c** with difficulty as far as	Ac 27:7
and **c** to a place called Fair	Ac 27:8
When the fourteenth night **c**,	Ac 27:27
When daylight **c**, they did not	Ac 27:39
viper **c** out because of the heat	Ac 28:3
diseases also **c** and were cured.	Ac 28:9
the second day we **c** to Puteoli.	Ac 28:13
seven days. And so we **c** to Rome.	Ac 28:14
many **c** to him at his lodging.	Ac 28:23
from one sin **c** the judgment,	Rm 5:16
from many trespasses **c** the gift,	Rm 5:16
The law **c** along to multiply the	Rm 5:20
but when the commandment **c**,	Rm 7:9
descent, **c** the Messiah, who	Rm 9:5
Christ died and **c** to life for	Rm 14:9
When I **c** to you, brothers,	1Co 2:1
woman, but woman **c** from man;	1Co 11:8
For just as woman **c** from man,	1Co 11:12
For since death **c** through a man,	1Co 15:21
the gift that **c** to us through	2Co 1:11
so that when I **c** I wouldn't have	2Co 2:3
When I **c** to Troas for the gospel	2Co 2:12
on stones, **c** with glory, so	2Co 3:7
fact, when we **c** into Macedonia,	2Co 7:5
brothers who **c** from Macedonia	2Co 11:9
but it **c** by a revelation from	Gl 1:12
to Arabia and **c** back to Damascus	Gl 1:17
who **c** in secretly to spy on our	Gl 2:4
But when Cephas **c** to Antioch,	Gl 2:11
before certain men **c** from James.	Gl 2:12
However, when they **c**, he	Gl 2:12
law, which **c** 430 years later,	Gl 3:17
this faith **c**, we were confined	Gl 3:23
the completion of the time **c**,	Gl 4:4
When ⌊Christ⌋ **c**, He proclaimed	Eph 2:17
because he **c** close to death for	Php 2:30
Christ Jesus **c** into the world to	1Tm 1:15
sufferings that **c** to me in	2Tm 3:11
no one **c** to my assistance,	2Tm 4:16
it really all who **c** out of Egypt	Heb 3:16
perfection **c** through the	Heb 7:11
that our Lord **c** from Judah,	Heb 7:14
the oath, which **c** after the law,	Heb 7:28
c offspring as numerous as the	Heb 11:12
remembering that land they **c**	Heb 11:15
a voice **c** to Him from the	2Pt 1:17
voice when it **c** from heaven	2Pt 1:18
prophecy ever **c** by the will of	2Pt 1:21
He is the One who **c** by water and	1Jn 5:6
some brothers **c** and testified to	3Jn 3
from His mouth **c** a sharp	Rv 1:16
One who was dead and **c** to life,	Rv 2:8
From the throne **c** flashes of	Rv 4:5
c and took ⌊the scroll⌋ out of	Rv 5:7
incense burner, **c** and stood at	Rv 8:3
and smoke **c** up out of the shaft	Rv 9:2
smoke locusts **c** to the earth,	Rv 9:3
and from their mouths **c** fire,	Rv 9:17
the sulfur that **c** from their	Rv 9:18
Another angel **c** out of the	Rv 14:15
had a sharp sickle **c** out of the	Rv 14:17
over fire, **c** from the altar,	Rv 14:18
the sanctuary **c** the seven angels	Rv 15:6
and a loud voice **c** out of the	Rv 16:17
the seven bowls **c** and spoke with	Rv 17:1
A voice **c** from the throne,	Rv 19:5

From His mouth **c** a sharp sword, Rv 19:15
the sword that **c** from the mouth Rv 19:21
They **c** to life and reigned with Rv 20:4
They **c** up over the surface of Rv 20:9
Then fire **c** down from heaven and Rv 20:9
last plagues, **c** and spoke with Rv 21:9

CAMEL *(9)*

Isaac, she got down from her **c** Gn 24:64
them in the saddlebag of the **c**, Gn 31:34
the **c**, though it chews the cud, Lv 11:4
the **c**, the hare, and the hyrax, Dt 14:7
are⌋ a swift young **c** twisting Jr 2:23
is easier for a **c** to go through Mt 19:24
out a gnat, yet gulp down a **c**! Mt 23:24
is easier for a **c** to go through Mk 10:25
is easier for a **c** to go through Lk 18:25

CAMEL-HAIR *(2)*

himself had a **c** garment with Mt 3:4
John wore a **c** garment with a Mk 1:6

CAMEL-LOADS *(1)*

40 **c** of all kinds of goods from 2Kg 8:9

CAMELS *(50)*

male and female slaves, and **c**. Gn 12:16
of his master's **c** and departed Gn 24:10
made the **c** kneel beside a well Gn 24:11
and I'll water your **c** also'— Gn 24:14
water for your **c** until they have Gn 24:19
She drew water for all his **c** Gn 24:20
After the **c** had finished Gn 24:22
there by the **c** at the spring. Gn 24:30
house and a place for the **c**." Gn 24:31
house, and the **c** were unloaded. Gn 24:32
and feed were given to the **c**, Gn 24:32
slaves, and **c** and donkeys. Gn 24:35
draw water for your **c** also'— Gn 24:44
and I'll water your **c** also.' Gn 24:46
and she also watered the **c**. Gn 24:46
up, mounted the **c**, and followed Gn 24:61
and looking up, he saw **c** coming. Gn 24:63
slaves, and **c** and donkeys. Gn 30:43
his children and wives on the **c**. Gn 31:17
with the flocks, cattle, and **c**. Gn 32:7
30 milk **c** with their young, Gn 32:15
Their **c** were carrying aromatic Gn 37:25
horses, donkeys, **c**, herds, and Ex 9:3
They and their **c** were without Jdg 6:5
and their **c** were as innumerable Jdg 7:12
were on the necks of their **c**. Jdg 8:21
chains on the necks of their **c**. Jdg 8:26
oxen and sheep, **c** and donkeys.' 1Sm 15:3
herds, donkeys, **c**, and clothing. 1Sm 27:9
young men who got on **c** and fled. 1Sm 30:17
retinue, with **c** bearing spices, 1Kg 10:2
of their **c**, 250,000 sheep, 1Ch 5:21
on donkeys, **c**, mules, and oxen 1Ch 12:40
was in charge of the **c**. 1Ch 27:30
retinue, with **c** bearing spices, 2Ch 9:1
and captured many sheep and **c**. 2Ch 14:15
435 **c**, and 6,720 donkeys. Ezr 2:67
435 **c**, and 6,720 donkeys. Neh 7:69
sheep, 3,000 **c**, 500 yoke of oxen Jb 1:3
a raid on the **c**, and took them Jb 1:17
sheep, 6,000 **c**, 1,000 yoke of Jb 42:12
donkeys, riders on **c**—pay close Is 21:7
treasures on the humps of **c**, Is 30:6
Caravans of **c** will cover your Is 60:6
young **c** of Midian and Ephah— Is 60:6
and on mules and **c**, to My holy Is 66:20
take their **c** for themselves. Jr 49:29
Their **c** will become plunder, Jr 49:32
Rabbah a pasture for **c** and Ammon Ezk 25:5
horses, mules, **c**, donkeys, and Zch 14:15

CAMP *(187)*

Jacob said, "This is God's **c**." Gn 32:2
comes to one **c** and attacks it, Gn 32:8
he remained in the **c** that night. Gn 32:21
to turn back and **c** in front of Ex 14:2
you must **c** in front of Ex 14:2
Tell the Israelites to break **c**. Ex 14:15
quail came and covered the **c**. Ex 16:13
a layer of dew all around the **c**. Ex 16:13
the people in the **c** shuddered. Ex 19:16
people out of the **c** to meet God, Ex 19:17
and its dung outside the **c**; Ex 29:14
is a sound of war in the **c**." Ex 32:17
approached the **c** and saw the Ex 32:19
through the **c** from entrance to Ex 32:27
and set it up outside the **c**, Ex 33:7
the camp, far away from the **c**; Ex 33:7
meeting that was outside the **c**. Ex 33:7
Moses would return to the **c**, Ex 33:11
a proclamation throughout the **c**: Ex 36:6
outside the **c** to the ash heap, Lv 4:12
outside the **c** and burn it just Lv 4:21
outside the **c** to a ceremonially Lv 6:11
outside the **c**, as the LORD had Lv 8:17
and the hide outside the **c**. Lv 9:11
to ⌊a place⌋ outside the **c**." Lv 10:4
in their tunics outside the **c**, Lv 10:5
alone in a place outside the **c**. Lv 13:46
outside the **c** and examine ⌊him⌋ Lv 14:3
Afterwards he may enter the **c**, Lv 14:8
afterwards he may reenter the **c**. Lv 16:26
outside the **c** and their hide, Lv 16:27
afterwards he may reenter the **c**. Lv 16:28
or goat in the **c**, or slaughters Lv 17:3
slaughters ⌊it⌋ outside the **c**, Lv 17:3
broke out in the **c** between the Lv 24:10
outside of the **c** and have all Lv 24:14
outside of the **c** and stoned him. Lv 24:23
care of it, and **c** around it. Nm 1:50
are to **c** by their military Nm 1:52
The Levites are to **c** around the Nm 1:53
Israelites are to **c** under their Nm 2:2
They are to **c** around the tent of Nm 2:2
divisions will **c** on the east Nm 2:3
of Issachar will **c** next to it. Nm 2:5
divisions will **c** on the south Nm 2:10
of Simeon will **c** next to it. Nm 2:12
to move out with the Levites' **c**, Nm 2:17
are to move out just as they **c**, Nm 2:17
divisions will **c** on the west Nm 2:18
divisions will **c** on the north Nm 2:25
of Asher will **c** next to it. Nm 2:27
Whenever the **c** is about to move Nm 4:5
whenever the **c** is to move Nm 4:15
anyone from the **c** who is Nm 5:2
them outside the **c**, so that they Nm 5:3
sending them outside the **c**. Nm 5:4
They would **c** at the LORD's Nm 9:20
divisions of the **c** of Judah with Nm 10:14
divisions of the **c** of Reuben Nm 10:18
of the **c** of Ephraim with Nm 10:22
divisions of the **c** of Dan with Nm 10:25
where we should **c** in the Nm 10:31
when they set out from the **c**. Nm 10:34
consumed the outskirts of the **c**. Nm 11:1
the dew fell on the **c** at night, Nm 11:9
Two men had remained in the **c**, Nm 11:26
and they prophesied in the **c**. Nm 11:26
Medad are prophesying in the **c**." Nm 11:27
returned to the **c** along with the Nm 11:30
them⌋ at the **c** all around, Nm 11:31
them out all around the **c**. Nm 11:32
outside the **c** for seven days; Nm 12:14
outside the **c** for seven days, Nm 12:15
and Moses did not leave the **c**. Nm 14:44
is to stone him outside the **c**." Nm 15:35
him outside the **c** and stoned him Nm 15:36
outside the **c** and slaughtered Nm 19:3
after that he may enter the **c**, Nm 19:7
them outside the **c** in a Nm 19:9
the outskirts of the people's **c**. Nm 22:41
see the outskirts of their **c**; Nm 23:13
community at the **c** on the plains Nm 31:12
went to meet them outside the **c**. Nm 31:13
outside the **c** for seven days. Nm 31:19
After that you may enter the **c**." Nm 31:24
seek out a place for you to **c**. Dt 1:33
men had perished from the **c**, Dt 2:14
them from the **c** until they had Dt 2:15
whole Israelite ⌊**c**⌋ the earth Dt 11:6
night, he must go outside the **c**; Dt 23:10
not come anywhere inside the **c**. Dt 23:10
sets he may come inside the **c**. Dt 23:11
outside the **c** and go there ⌊to Dt 23:12
throughout your **c** to protect you Dt 23:14
Go through the **c** and tell the Jos 1:11
the officers went through the **c** Jos 3:2
you must break **c** and follow it. Jos 3:3
the people broke **c** to cross the Jos 3:14
them to the **c** and set them down Jos 4:8
they were in the **c** until they Jos 5:8
returned to the **c** and spent the Jos 6:11
city once and returned to the **c**. Jos 6:14
set apart the **c** of Israel for Jos 6:18
them outside the **c** of Israel. Jos 6:23
the main **c** to the north of the Jos 8:13
to Joshua in the **c** at Gilgal and Jos 9:6
to Joshua in the **c** at Gilgal: Jos 10:6
him returned to the **c** at Gilgal. Jos 10:15
to Joshua in the **c** at Makkedah. Jos 10:21
all Israel to the **c** at Gilgal. Jos 10:43
to Joshua at the **c** in Shiloh. Jos 18:9
The **c** of Midian was north of Jdg 7:1
The **c** of Midian was below him in Jdg 7:8
Get up and go into the **c**, Jdg 7:9
you are afraid to go to the **c**, Jdg 7:10
be strengthened to go to the **c**." Jdg 7:11
of the troops who were in the **c**. Jdg 7:11
tumbling into the Midianite **c**, Jdg 7:13
entire Midianite **c** over to him." Jdg 7:14
returned to Israel's **c** and said, Jdg 7:15
the Midianite **c** over to you." Jdg 7:15
I come to the outpost of the **c**, Jdg 7:17
your trumpets all around the **c**. Jdg 7:18
of the **c** at the beginning Jdg 7:19
took his position around the **c**, Jdg 7:21
to direct him in the **C** of Dan, Jdg 13:25
is called the **C** of Dan to this Jdg 18:12
had come to the **c** and the Jdg 21:8
brought them to the **c** at Shiloh Jdg 21:12
the troops returned to the **c**, 1Sm 4:3
of the LORD entered the **c**, 1Sm 4:5
loud shout in the Hebrews' **c**?" 1Sm 4:6
of the LORD had entered the **c**, 1Sm 4:6
"The gods have entered their **c**!" 1Sm 4:7
the Ammonite **c** and slaughtered 1Sm 11:11
the Philistine **c** in three 1Sm 13:17
the ⌊Philistine⌋ **c** and the open 1Sm 14:15
in the Philistine **c** increased in 1Sm 14:19
gone earlier into the **c** to join 1Sm 14:21
came out from the Philistine **c**. 1Sm 17:4
brothers and hurry to their **c**. 1Sm 17:17
of the **c** as the army was 1Sm 17:20
of the Philistine **c** to the birds 1Sm 17:46
circle of the **c** with the troops 1Sm 26:5
go with me into the **c** to Saul?" 1Sm 26:6
circle of the **c** with his spear 1Sm 26:7
When Saul saw the Philistine **c**, 1Sm 28:5
you working with me in the **c**, 1Sm 29:6
on his head came from Saul's **c**. 2Sm 1:2
escaped from the Israelite **c**." 2Sm 1:3
you to attack the **c** of the 2Sm 5:24
the Philistine **c** and drew water 2Sm 23:16
Israel that very day in the **c**. 1Kg 16:16
the Moabites came to Israel's **c**, 2Kg 3:24
My **c** will be at such and such a 2Kg 6:8
Let's go to the Arameans' **c**. 2Kg 7:4
to go to the Arameans' **c**. 2Kg 7:5
the Aramean **c** to hear the sound 2Kg 7:6
The **c** was intact, and they had 2Kg 7:7
men came to the edge of the **c**, 2Kg 7:8
to the Aramean **c** and no one was 2Kg 7:10
they have left the **c** to hide in 2Kg 7:12
out and plundered the Aramean **c**. 2Kg 7:16
185,000 in the **c** of the 2Kg 19:35
of Assyria broke **c** and left. 2Kg 19:36
from the **c** of the Levites. 1Ch 9:18
to the LORD's **c** as guardians 1Ch 9:19
the Philistine **c** and drew water 1Ch 11:18
you to attack the **c** of the 1Ch 14:15
Arabs to the **c** had killed all 2Ch 22:1
the gates of the **c** of the LORD, 2Ch 31:2
commander in the **c** of the king 2Ch 32:21
against me and **c** around my tent. Jb 19:12
He made ⌊them⌋ fall in His **c**, Ps 78:28
In the **c** they were envious of Ps 106:16
at the **c** of the righteous man; Pr 24:15
You will **c** for the night in the Is 21:13
I will **c** in a circle around you; Is 29:3
185,000 in the **c** of the Is 37:36
of Assyria broke **c** and left. Is 37:37
the bow; **c** all around her; Jr 50:29
His army. His **c** is very large; Jl 2:11
stench of your **c** to fill your Am 4:10
the city and **c** in the open Mc 4:10
I will set up **c** at My house Zch 9:8
are burned outside the **c**. Heb 13:11
us then go to Him outside the **c**, Heb 13:13

CAMP'S *(2)*

stood at the **c** entrance and said Ex 32:26
When they came to the **c** edge, 2Kg 7:5

CAMPAIGN *(2)*
returning from the military **c**. Nm 31:14
kings and their land in one **c**, Jos 10:42

CAMPED *(101)*
left there, **c** in the valley Gn 26:17
city of Shechem and **c** in front Gn 33:18
from Succoth and **c** at Etham on Ex 13:20
them as they **c** by the sea beside Ex 14:9
and they **c** there by the waters. Ex 15:27
They **c** at Rephidim, but there Ex 17:1
where he was **c** at the mountain Ex 18:5
Sinai and **c** in the wilderness, Ex 19:2
and Israel **c** there in front of Ex 19:2
they **c** by their banners in this Nm 2:34
Gershonite clans **c** behind the Nm 3:23
the Kohathites **c** on the south Nm 3:29
they **c** on the north side of the Nm 3:35
c in front of the tabernacle on Nm 3:38
stopped, there the Israelites **c**. Nm 9:17
at the LORD's command they **c**. Nm 9:18
over the tabernacle, they **c**. Nm 9:18
the Israelites **c** and did not set Nm 9:22
They **c** at the LORD's command, Nm 9:23
Hazeroth and **c** in the Wilderness Nm 12:16
set out and **c** at Oboth. Nm 21:10
from Oboth and **c** at Iye-abarim Nm 21:11
they went and **c** at Zered Valley. Nm 21:12
from there and **c** on the other Nm 21:13
traveled on and **c** in the plains Nm 22:1
from Rameses and **c** at Succoth. Nm 33:5
from Succoth and **c** at Etham, Nm 33:6
and they **c** before Migdol. Nm 33:7
of Etham and **c** at Marah. Nm 33:8
palms at Elim, so they **c** there. Nm 33:9
from Elim and **c** by the Red Sea. Nm 33:10
the Red Sea and **c** in the Nm 33:11
of Sin and **c** in Dophkah. Nm 33:12
from Dophkah and **c** at Alush. Nm 33:13
from Alush and **c** at Rephidim, Nm 33:14
Rephidim and **c** in the Wilderness Nm 33:15
of Sinai and **c** at Nm 33:16
and **c** at Hazeroth. Nm 33:17
from Hazeroth and **c** at Rithmah. Nm 33:18
Rithmah and **c** at Rimmon-perez Nm 33:19
Rimmon-perez and **c** at Libnah. Nm 33:20
from Libnah and **c** at Rissah. Nm 33:21
from Rissah and **c** at Kehelathah. Nm 33:22
Kehelathah and **c** at Mount Nm 33:23
Mount Shepher and **c** at Haradah. Nm 33:24
from Haradah and **c** at Makheloth. Nm 33:25
from Makheloth and **c** at Tahath. Nm 33:26
from Tahath and **c** at Terah. Nm 33:27
from Terah and **c** at Mithkah. Nm 33:28
Mithkah and **c** at Hashmonah. Nm 33:29
Hashmonah and **c** at Moseroth. Nm 33:30
Moseroth and **c** at Bene-jaakan. Nm 33:31
Bene-jaakan and **c** at Nm 33:32
and **c** at Jotbathah. Nm 33:33
from Jotbathah and **c** at Abronah. Nm 33:34
Abronah and **c** at Ezion-geber. Nm 33:35
Ezion-geber and **c** in the Nm 33:36
from Kadesh and **c** at Mount Hor Nm 33:37
Mount Hor and **c** at Zalmonah. Nm 33:41
from Zalmonah and **c** at Punon. Nm 33:42
from Punon and **c** at Oboth. Nm 33:43
from Oboth and **c** at Iye-abarim Nm 33:44
from Iyim and **c** at Dibon-gad. Nm 33:45
from Dibon-gad and **c** at Nm 33:46
and **c** in the Abarim ⌊range Nm 33:47
range⌋ and **c** on the plains Nm 33:48
They **c** by the Jordan from Nm 33:49
and **c** at Gilgal on the eastern Jos 4:19
While the Israelites **c** at Gilgal Jos 5:10
opposite Ai, and **c** to the north Jos 8:11
together and **c** at the waters Jos 11:5
and **c** in the Valley of Jezreel. Jdg 6:33
got up early and **c** beside the Jdg 7:1
went to Thebez, **c** against it, Jdg 9:50
together, and they **c** in Gilead. Jdg 10:17
assembled and **c** at Mizpah. Jdg 10:17
land of Moab and **c** on the other Jdg 11:18
all his people, **c** at Jahaz, and Jdg 11:20
went up, **c** in Judah, and raided Jdg 15:9
They went up and **c** at Jdg 18:12
set out and **c** near Gibeah. Jdg 20:19
battle and **c** at Ebenezer while 1Sm 4:1
the Philistines **c** at Aphek. 1Sm 4:1
They went up and **c** at Michmash, 1Sm 13:5
Philistines were **c** at Michmash. 1Sm 13:16
in Judah and **c** between Socoh 1Sm 17:1
gathered and **c** in the Valley 1Sm 17:2
Saul **c** beside the road at the 1Sm 26:3
to the place where Saul had **c**. 1Sm 26:5
with the troops **c** around him. 1Sm 26:5
came together and **c** at Shunem. 1Sm 28:4
Israel, and they **c** at Gilboa. 1Sm 28:4
while Israel was **c** by the spring 1Sm 29:1
Israel and Absalom **c** in the land 2Sm 17:26
the Jordan and **c** in Aroer, 2Sm 24:5
Israelites **c** in front of them 1Kg 20:27
They **c** opposite each other for 1Kg 20:29
who came and **c** near Medeba. 1Ch 19:7
and we **c** there for three days. Ezr 8:15
kinds of goods **c** outside Neh 13:20
Ariel, the city where David **c**! Is 29:1

CAMPING *(3)*
his soldiers are **c** in the open 2Sm 11:11
Philistines was **c** in the Valley 2Sm 23:13
Why are you **c** in front of the Neh 13:21

CAMPS *(14)*
the people with him into two **c**, Gn 32:7
and now I have become two **c**. Gn 32:10
which is in the middle of the **c**. Nm 2:17
in the **c** by their military Nm 2:32
not defile their **c** where I dwell Nm 5:3
and have the **c** set out. Nm 10:2
the **c** pitched on the east are to Nm 10:5
the **c** pitched on the south are Nm 10:6
as rearguard for all the **c**, Nm 10:25
in your **c** who cut your wood Dt 29:11
they plundered their **c**. 1Sm 17:53
look⌋ at the dance of the two **c**? Sg 6:13
pitch military **c**, and place Ezk 4:2
the animals that are in those **c**. Zch 14:15

CAMPSITE *(2)*
at an overnight **c**, it happened Ex 4:24
whenever it is to stop at a **c**, Nm 1:51

CAN *(756)*
so that you **c** keep them alive Gn 6:20
to you, so you **c** never say, 'I Gn 14:23
Mamre—they **c** take their share. Gn 14:24
Lord GOD, what **c** You give me, Gn 15:2
c I know that I will possess it? Gn 15:8
I **c** have children by her. Gn 16:2
C a child be born to a Gn 17:17
C Sarah, a ninety-year-old woman, Gn 17:17
Later, you **c** continue on." Gn 18:5
'**C** I really have a baby when I'm Gn 18:13
Then you **c** get up early and go Gn 19:2
us so we **c** have sex with them! Gn 19:5
and you **c** do whatever you want Gn 19:8
it?—so that I **c** survive." Gn 19:20
wine so that we **c** sleep with him Gn 19:32
tonight so you **c** go sleep with Gn 19:34
with him and we **c** preserve our Gn 19:34
you so that I **c** bury my dead." Gn 23:4
and you **c** take a wife for my son Gn 24:7
about 10 days. Then she **c** go." Gn 24:55
that I **c** bless you before I die. Gn 27:4
me to eat so that I **c** bless you Gn 27:7
come closer so I **c** touch you, Gn 27:21
game so that I **c** bless you." Gn 27:25
then **c** I do for you, my son? Gn 27:37
her I too **c** build ⌊a family⌋. Gn 30:3
you **c** sleep with him tonight in Gn 30:15
my way so that I **c** return to my Gn 30:25
I **c** see from your father's face Gn 31:5
But what **c** I do today for these Gn 31:43
the remaining one **c** escape." Gn 32:8
After that, I **c** face him, and Gn 32:20
C you tell me where they are Gn 37:16
We **c** say that a vicious animal Gn 37:20
and no one **c** interpret it. Gn 41:15
you that you **c** hear a dream Gn 41:15
no one **c** tell me what it means. Gn 41:24
C we find anyone like this, Gn 41:38
that your words **c** be tested to Gn 42:16
that your words **c** be confirmed; Gn 42:20
and you **c** trade in the country.' Gn 42:34
You **c** kill my two sons if I Gn 42:37
You **c** hold me personally Gn 43:9
as much food as they **c** carry, Gn 44:1
"What **c** we say to my lord?" Gn 44:16
replied. "How **c** we plead? How Gn 44:16
How **c** we justify ourselves? Gn 44:16
The rest of you **c** go in peace to Gn 44:17
him to me so that I **c** see him.' Gn 44:21
For how **c** I go back to my father Gn 44:34
You **c** settle in the land of Gn 45:10
eyes **c** see that it is I Gn 45:12
and you **c** eat from the richness Gn 45:18
At last I **c** die, now that I Gn 46:30
They **c** live in the land of Gn 47:6
seed so that we **c** live and not Gn 47:19
before a midwife **c** get to them." Ex 1:19
I know that he **c** speak well. Ex 4:14
wherever you **c** find it, Ex 5:11
people go and they **c** sacrifice Ex 8:8
a darkness that **c** be felt." Ex 10:21
the Israelites **c** go through the Ex 14:16
Then they **c** bring you every Ex 18:22
if he **c** ⌊later⌋ get up and walk Ex 21:19
if the slave **c** stand up after a Ex 21:21
he **c** pay a redemption price for Ex 21:30
that the table **c** be carried by Ex 25:28
edges so that it **c** be joined Ex 28:7
blue yarn so it **c** be placed on Ex 28:37
so that they **c** be anointed and Ex 29:29
so that My anger **c** burn against Ex 32:10
them and I **c** destroy them. Ex 32:10
for no one **c** see Me and live." Ex 33:20
They **c** do every kind of craft Ex 35:35
so that he **c** serve Me as a Ex 40:13
offering so it **c** be accepted on Lv 1:4
by which one **c** become defiled— Lv 5:3
feet so far as the priest **c** see, Lv 13:12
But if as far as he **c** see, Lv 13:37
whatever he **c** afford, one to be Lv 14:22
one type of what he **c** afford, Lv 14:30
what he **c** afford together with Lv 14:31
Sabbath year **c** be food for you Lv 25:6
so that you **c** eat, be satisfied Lv 25:19
one of the Levites **c** redeem— Lv 25:33
so that he **c** continue to live Lv 25:35
you **c** make them slaves for life. Lv 25:46
the one making the vow **c** afford. Lv 27:8
But no one **c** consecrate a Lv 27:26
it **c** be sold according to your Lv 27:27
landholding, **c** be sold or Lv 27:28
everyone who **c** serve in Israel's Nm 1:3
to whatever else he **c** afford; Nm 6:21
and you **c** serve as our eyes. Nm 10:31
Where **c** I get meat to give all Nm 11:13
land because we **c** certainly Nm 13:30
but **c** I say anything I want? Nm 22:38
c I curse someone God has not Nm 23:8
c I denounce someone the LORD Nm 23:8
place where you **c** see them. Nm 23:13
to God that you **c** put a curse on Nm 23:27
who **c** live when God does this? Nm 24:23
old or more who **c** serve in Nm 26:2
everything that **c** withstand fire Nm 31:23
and there **c** be no atonement for Nm 35:33
But how **c** I bear your troubles, Dt 1:12
Where **c** we go? Our brothers have Dt 1:28
You **c** sell us food in exchange Dt 2:28
or on earth who **c** perform deeds Dt 3:24
Then you **c** tell us everything Dt 5:27
how **c** I drive them out?' Dt 7:17
'Who **c** stand up to the sons of Dt 9:2
'How **c** we recognize a message Dt 18:21
manslaughter **c** flee to these Dt 19:3
you **c** get food from them. Dt 20:19
then you **c** return it to him. Dt 22:2
anything that **c** earn interest. Dt 23:19
so that he **c** bring joy to the Dt 24:5
c no longer act as your leader. Dt 31:2
No one **c** rescue ⌊anyone⌋ from My Dt 32:39
and you **c** catch up with them!" Jos 2:5
so that you **c** see the way to go, Jos 3:4
What **c** I say, Lord, now that Jos 7:8
took them. You **c** see for Jos 7:21
c we make a treaty with you?" Jos 9:7
You **c** also drive out the Jos 17:18
so that you **c** take possession of Jos 23:5
Lord, how **c** I deliver Israel Jdg 6:15
you, 'This one **c** go with you,' Jdg 7:4
one can go with you,' he **c** go. Jdg 7:4
do to him whatever you **c**." Jdg 9:33
If you **c** explain it to me during Jdg 14:12
from, so we **c** overpower him, Jdg 16:5
tell me how you **c** be tied up?" Jdg 16:10
Tell me how you **c** be tied up." Jdg 16:13

"How **c** you say, 'I love you,' "	Jdg 16:15
Lead me where I **c** feel the	Jdg 16:26
so I **c** lean against them."	Jdg 16:26
wherever I **c** find a place.	Jdg 17:9
How **c** you say to me, 'What's the	Jdg 18:24
strength and then you **c** go."	Jdg 19:5
then you **c** get up early tomorrow	Jdg 19:9
house so we **c** have sex with him!	Jdg 19:22
in Gibeah so we **c** put them to	Jdg 20:13
exclaimed, "**C** this be Naomi?"	Ru 1:19
you **c** take whatever you want	1Sm 2:16
another man, God **c** intercede for	1Sm 2:25
LORD, who **c** intercede for him?	1Sm 2:25
office so I **c** have a piece	1Sm 2:36
Tell us how we **c** send it back to	1Sm 6:2
He **c** take your sons and put them	1Sm 8:11
He **c** appoint them for his use as	1Sm 8:12
He **c** take your daughters to	1Sm 8:13
He **c** take your best fields,	1Sm 8:14
He **c** take a tenth of your grain	1Sm 8:15
He **c** take your male servants,	1Sm 8:16
c take a tenth of your flocks,	1Sm 8:17
and you yourselves **c** become his	1Sm 8:17
you **c** catch up with him before	1Sm 9:13
after that, the guests **c** eat.	1Sm 9:13
you **c** find him now."	1Sm 9:13
said, "How **c** this guy save us?	1Sm 10:27
c do whatever you want to us.	1Sm 11:10
us those men so we **c** kill them!"	1Sm 11:12
we **c** renew the kingship there.	1Sm 11:14
you **c** see that the king is	1Sm 12:2
Nothing **c** keep the LORD from	1Sm 14:6
here and then you **c** eat.	1Sm 14:34
with me so I **c** worship the LORD.	1Sm 15:25
with me so I **c** bow and worship	1Sm 15:30
Samuel asked, "How **c** I go?	1Sm 16:2
that person **c** play the harp,	1Sm 16:16
a man so we **c** fight each other!	1Sm 17:10
more **c** he have but the kingdom?	1Sm 18:8
"You **c** now be my son-in-law."	1Sm 18:21
him on his bed so I **c** kill him."	1Sm 19:15
me go so I **c** see my brothers.	1Sm 20:29
bread or whatever **c** be found."	1Sm 21:3
You **c** see the man is crazy,"	1Sm 21:14
to you so you **c** do to him	1Sm 24:4
c see with your own eyes that	1Sm 24:10
whatever you **c** afford to your	1Sm 25:8
fool nobody **c** talk to him!"	1Sm 25:17
who **c** lift a hand against the	1Sm 26:9
towns, so I **c** live there.	1Sm 27:5
out what your servant **c** do."	1Sm 28:2
so I **c** go and consult her."	1Sm 28:7
so you **c** go on your way.	1Sm 28:22
Who **c** agree to your proposal?	1Sm 30:24
whatever you **c** get from him."	2Sm 2:21
you **c** be certain I am on your	2Sm 3:12
or a man who **c** only work a	2Sm 3:29
the blind and lame **c** repel you,"	2Sm 5:6
How **c** the ark of the LORD ever	2Sm 6:9
What more **c** David say to You?	2Sm 7:20
Saul's family I **c** show kindness	2Sm 9:1
Saul's family I **c** show the	2Sm 9:3
c I enter my house to eat and	2Sm 11:11
So how **c** we tell him the baby is	2Sm 12:18
C I bring him back again?	2Sm 12:23
my presence so I **c** watch and eat	2Sm 13:5
so I **c** eat from her hand.	2Sm 13:6
"so I **c** eat from your hand."	2Sm 13:10
no one **c** turn to the right or	2Sm 14:19
today while I go wherever I **c**?	2Sm 15:20
c do with me whatever pleases	2Sm 15:26
then you **c** counteract	2Sm 15:34
Therefore, who **c** say, 'Why did	2Sm 16:10
even a pebble **c** be found there.	2Sm 17:13
C I discern what is pleasant and	2Sm 19:35
C your servant taste what he	2Sm 19:35
C I still hear the voice of male	2Sm 19:35
How **c** I wipe out this guilt so	2Sm 21:3
With You I **c** attack a barrier,	2Sm 22:30
with my God I **c** leap over a wall	2Sm 22:30
my arms **c** bend a bow of bronze.	2Sm 22:35
they **c** never be picked up by	2Sm 23:6
troops so I **c** know their number.	2Sm 24:2
there, and you **c** take them away.	1Kg 5:9
You then **c** meet my needs by	1Kg 5:9
so I **c** go to my own country."	1Kg 11:21
my son so we **c** eat it and die.	1Kg 17:12
grass so we **c** keep the horses	1Kg 18:5
your vineyard so I **c** have it for	1Kg 21:2
one man who **c** ask the LORD,	1Kg 22:8
Tell ⌊me⌋ what I **c** do for you	2Kg 2:9
though our lord **c** see that the	2Kg 2:19
asked her, "What **c** I do for you?	2Kg 4:2
and your sons **c** live on the rest	2Kg 4:7
he comes, he **c** stay there."	2Kg 4:10
for us. What **c** ⌊we⌋ do for you?	2Kg 4:13
C ⌊we⌋ speak on your behalf to	2Kg 4:13
so I **c** hurry to the man of God	2Kg 4:22
Jordan where we **c** each get a log	2Kg 6:2
get a log and **c** build ourselves	2Kg 6:2
I **c** send ⌊men⌋ to capture him.	2Kg 6:13
of them so they **c** eat and drink	2Kg 6:22
where **c** I get help for you?	2Kg 6:27
as a foreigner wherever you **c**.	2Kg 8:1
What peace **c** there be as long as	2Kg 9:22
stand against him; how **c** we?"	2Kg 10:4
live there so he **c** teach them	2Kg 17:27
How then **c** you drive back a	2Kg 18:24
How **c** I drink the blood of these	1Ch 11:19
How **c** I ever bring the ark of	1Ch 13:12
What more **c** David say to You for	1Ch 17:18
to me so I **c** know their number.	1Ch 21:2
who **c** judge this great people	2Ch 1:10
You **c** then take them up to	2Ch 2:16
are saying you **c** assert	2Ch 13:8
one man who **c** ask the LORD,	2Ch 18:7
and no one **c** stand against You.	2Ch 20:6
of the Jews **c** rebuild this house	Ezr 6:8
so that they **c** offer sacrifices	Ezr 6:10
that we **c** rebuild the house of	Ezr 9:9
what **c** we say in light of this?	Ezr 9:10
though no one **c** stand in Your	Ezr 9:15
something that **c** be done in a	Ezr 10:13
C they restore ⌊it⌋ by	Neh 4:2
C they bring these burnt stones	Neh 4:2
among them and **c** kill them and	Neh 4:11
so that they **c** stand guard by	Neh 4:22
so that we **c** eat and live."	Neh 5:2
How **c** I enter the temple and	Neh 6:11
the Jews who **c** be found in Susa	Est 4:16
get Haman so we **c** do as Esther	Est 5:5
Yet who **c** keep from speaking?	Jb 4:2
C a person be more righteous	Jb 4:17
How painful honest words **c** be!	Jb 6:25
think that you **c** disprove ⌊my⌋	Jb 6:26
or **c** I not recognize lies?	Jb 6:30
but how **c** a person be justified	Jb 9:2
something⌋, who **c** stop Him?	Jb 9:12
Who **c** ask Him, "What are You	Jb 9:12
then **c** I answer Him or choose	Jb 9:14
of justice, who **c** summon Him?	Jb 9:19
like me, that I **c** answer Him,	Jb 9:32
that we **c** take each other to	Jb 9:32
no one who **c** deliver from Your	Jb 10:7
so that I **c** smile a little	Jb 10:20
so that you **c** keep on ridiculing	Jb 11:3
C you fathom the depths of God	Jb 11:7
the heavens—what **c** you do?	Jb 11:8
than Sheol—what **c** you know?	Jb 11:8
a court, who **c** stop Him?	Jb 11:10
godless person **c** appear before	Jb 13:16
C anyone indict me? If so, I	Jb 13:19
speak, and You **c** respond to me.	Jb 13:22
c produce something pure from	Jb 14:4
rest so that he **c** enjoy his day	Jb 14:6
Who **c** see ⌊any⌋ hope for me?	Jb 17:15
some sense, and then we **c** talk.	Jb 18:2
C anyone teach God knowledge,	Jb 21:22
how **c** you offer me such futile	Jb 21:34
C a man be of ⌊any⌋ use to God?	Jb 22:2
C even a wise man be of use to	Jb 22:2
C He judge through thick	Jb 22:13
"What **c** the Almighty do to us?	Jb 22:17
who **c** oppose Him? He	Jb 23:13
so they **c** rely ⌊on it⌋,	Jb 24:23
then who **c** prove me a liar and	Jb 24:25
C His troops be numbered?	Jb 25:3
How **c** a person be justified	Jb 25:4
How **c** one born of woman be pure?	Jb 25:4
Who **c** understand His mighty	Jb 26:14
But where **c** wisdom be found,	Jb 28:12
man **c** know its value, since it	Jb 28:13
dismayed and **c** no longer answer	Jb 32:15
speak so that I **c** find relief;	Jb 32:20
Refute me if you **c**. Prepare your	Jb 33:5
evildoers **c** hide themselves	Jb 34:22
who **c** declare ⌊Him⌋ guilty?	Jb 34:29
hides ⌊His⌋ face, who **c** see Him?	Jb 34:29
C your wealth or all ⌊your⌋	Jb 36:19
C anyone understand how the	Jb 36:29
c you help God spread out the	Jb 37:18
C a man speak when he is	Jb 37:20
so you **c** lead it back to its	Jb 38:20
C you fasten the chains of the	Jb 38:31
C you bring out the	Jb 38:32
C you impose its authority on	Jb 38:33
C you command the clouds so that	Jb 38:34
C you send out lightning bolts,	Jb 38:35
Or who **c** tilt the water jars of	Jb 38:37
C you hunt prey for a lioness or	Jb 38:39
C you count the months they are	Jb 39:2
pregnant so you **c** know the time	Jb 39:2
C you hold the wild ox by its	Jb 39:10
C you depend on it because of	Jb 39:11
C you trust the wild ox to	Jb 39:12
How **c** I answer You? I	Jb 40:4
but ⌊now⌋ I **c** add nothing.	Jb 40:5
C you thunder with a voice like	Jb 40:9
own right hand **c** deliver you.	Jb 40:14
⌊only⌋ his Maker **c** draw the	Jb 40:19
C anyone capture him while he	Jb 40:24
C you pull in Leviathan with a	Jb 41:1
C you put a cord through his	Jb 41:2
you so that you **c** take him as a	Jb 41:4
C you play with him like a bird	Jb 41:5
C you fill his hide with	Jb 41:7
who then **c** stand against Me?	Jb 41:10
Who **c** strip off his outer	Jb 41:13
Who **c** penetrate his double layer	Jb 41:13
Who **c** open his jaws, surrounded	Jb 41:14
that no air **c** pass between them	Jb 41:16
No arrow **c** make him flee;	Jb 41:28
know that You **c** do anything and	Jb 42:2
no plan of Yours **c** be thwarted.	Jb 42:2
"Who **c** show us anything good?"	Ps 4:6
who **c** thank You in Sheol?	Ps 6:5
How **c** you say to me, "Escape to	Ps 11:1
what **c** the righteous do?	Ps 11:3
our own—who **c** be our master?"	Ps 12:4
LORD, who **c** dwell in Your tent?	Ps 15:1
c live on Your holy mountain?	Ps 15:1
With You I **c** attack a barrier,	Ps 18:29
with my God I **c** leap over a wall	Ps 18:29
my arms **c** bend a bow of bronze.	Ps 18:34
I **c** count all my bones; people	Ps 22:17
so that I **c** sing to You and not	Ps 30:12
agitated—it **c** only bring harm	Ps 37:8
none **c** compare with You.	Ps 40:5
they are more than **c** be told.	Ps 40:5
When **c** I come and appear before	Ps 42:2
so that you **c** tell a future	Ps 48:13
For one **c** see that wise men die;	Ps 49:10
not fear. What **c** man do to me?	Ps 56:4
not fear. What **c** man do to me?	Ps 56:11
Before your pots **c** feel the heat	Ps 58:9
so that they **c** flee before the	Ps 60:4
only You **c** atone for our	Ps 65:3
for me, where I **c** always go.	Ps 71:3
They say, "How **c** God know?	Ps 73:11
so I **c** tell about all You do.	Ps 73:28
are angry, who **c** stand before	Ps 76:7
But **c** He also provide bread or	Ps 78:20
who in the skies **c** compare with	Ps 89:6
What man **c** live and never see	Ps 89:48
c save himself from the power	Ps 89:48
C the One who shaped the ear not	Ps 94:9
C a corrupt throne—one that	Ps 94:20
Who **c** declare the LORD's mighty	Ps 106:2
a city where they **c** live.	Ps 107:36
How **c** I repay the LORD all the	Ps 116:12
be afraid. What **c** man do to me?	Ps 118:6
How **c** a young man keep his way	Ps 119:9
so that I **c** meditate on Your	Ps 119:27
Then I **c** answer the one who	Ps 119:42
so that I **c** learn Your commands.	Ps 119:73
me so that I **c** be safe and be	Ps 119:117
when brothers **c** live together!	Ps 133:1
How **c** we sing the LORD's song on	Ps 137:4
Where **c** I go to escape Your	Ps 139:7
Where **c** I flee from Your	Ps 139:7
so that I **c** praise Your name	Ps 142:7
Who **c** withstand His cold?	Ps 147:17
a net where any bird **c** see it,	Pr 1:17
C a man embrace fire and his	Pr 6:27

C a man walk on coals without Pr 6:28
desirable **c** compare with it. Pr 8:11
man's spirit **c** endure sickness, Pr 18:14
but who **c** survive a broken Pr 18:14
but any fool **c** get himself into Pr 20:3
who **c** find a trustworthy man? Pr 20:6
Who **c** say, "I have kept my heart Pr 20:9
so how **c** anyone understand his Pr 20:24
what disaster these two **c** bring? Pr 24:22
A ruler **c** be persuaded through Pr 25:15
a gentle tongue **c** break a bone. Pr 25:15
seven men who **c** answer sensibly. Pr 26:16
but who **c** withstand jealousy? Pr 27:4
so that I **c** answer anyone who Pr 27:11
a lizard **c** be caught in your Pr 30:28
drink so that he **c** forget his Pr 31:7
Who **c** find a capable wife? Pr 31:10
and she **c** laugh at the time to Pr 31:25
C one say about anything, Ec 1:10
For who **c** eat and who can enjoy Ec 2:25
can eat and who **c** enjoy life Ec 2:25
For who **c** enable him to see what Ec 3:22
his companion **c** lift him up; Ec 4:10
down together, they **c** keep warm; Ec 4:11
but how **c** one person alone keep Ec 4:11
one person, two **c** resist him. Ec 4:12
efforts that he **c** carry in his Ec 5:15
Who **c** tell man what will happen Ec 6:12
for who **c** straighten out what He Ec 7:13
very deep. Who **c** discover it? Ec 7:24
and who **c** say to him, "What are Ec 8:4
because who **c** tell him what will Ec 8:7
but one sinner **c** destroy much Ec 9:18
and who **c** tell anyone what will Ec 10:14
my clothing. How **c** I put it back Sg 5:3
my feet. How **c** I get them dirty? Sg 5:3
quickly so that we **c** see it! Is 5:19
place so that we **c** know it!" Is 5:19
off, and no one **c** rescue ⌊it⌋. Is 5:29
Then we **c** install Tabeel's son Is 7:6
so that widows **c** be their spoil Is 10:2
their spoil and they **c** plunder Is 10:2
therefore, who **c** stand in its Is 14:27
so who **c** turn it back? Is 14:27
How **c** you say to Pharaoh, Is 19:11
what he opens, no one **c** close; Is 22:22
what he closes, no one **c** open. Is 22:22
so a righteous nation **c** come Is 26:2
given to one who **c** read and he Is 29:11
How **c** what is made say about its Is 29:16
How **c** what is formed say about Is 29:16
Who among us **c** dwell with a Is 33:14
Who among us **c** dwell with Is 33:14
horses if you **c** put riders on Is 36:8
How then **c** you repel ⌊the attack Is 36:9
What **c** I say? He has spoken to Is 38:15
only the living **c** thank You, Is 38:19
Who among them **c** declare this, Is 43:9
no one **c** take ⌊anything⌋ from Is 43:13
I act, and who **c** reverse it?" Is 43:13
Who, like Me, **c** announce ⌊the Is 44:7
his own way; no one **c** save you. Is 47:15
My own, for how **c** I be defiled? Is 48:11
C a woman forget her nursing Is 49:15
C the prey be taken from the Is 49:24
for you? How **c** I comfort you? Is 51:19
Lie down, so we **c** walk over you. Is 51:23
so that we **c** see your joy! Is 66:5
C a land be born in one day, Is 66:8
How **c** you protest: I am not Jr 2:23
Who **c** control her passion? Jr 2:24
your time of disaster if they **c**, Jr 2:28
C a young woman forget her Jr 2:32
marry another, **c** he ever return Jr 3:1
many partners—**c** you return to Jr 3:1
Who **c** I speak to and give such a Jr 6:10
They **c** no longer feel Jr 6:15
c you claim: We are wise; the Jr 8:8
They **c** no longer feel Jr 8:12
for what else **c** I do because of Jr 9:7
so no one **c** pass through? Jr 9:12
them for they **c** do no harm— Jr 10:5
C holy meat prevent your Jr 11:15
your disaster so you **c** rejoice? Jr 11:15
how **c** you compete with horses? Jr 12:5
siege; no one **c** help ⌊them⌋. All Jr 13:19
C the Cushite change his skin, Jr 13:23
C any of the worthless idols of Jr 14:22

Or **c** the skies alone give Jr 14:22
C anyone smash iron, iron from Jr 15:12
C one make gods for himself? Jr 16:20
sick—who **c** understand it? Jr 17:9
c I not treat you as this potter Jr 18:6
jar that **c** never again be Jr 19:11
Who **c** come down against us? Jr 21:13
Who **c** enter our hiding places? Jr 21:13
C a man hide himself in secret Jr 23:24
see whether a male **c** give birth. Jr 30:6
have nothing that **c** heal you. Jr 30:13
the heavens above **c** be measured Jr 31:37
happened. Look, You **c** see it! Jr 32:24
If you **c** break My covenant with Jr 33:20
go well for you and you **c** live. Jr 38:20
as you **c** see with your own eyes Jr 42:2
The LORD **c** no longer bear your Jr 44:22
How **c** it rest when the LORD has Jr 47:7
How **c** you say, We are warriors— Jr 48:14
and boast⌋: Who **c** attack me? Jr 49:4
c you possibly remain unpunished? Jr 49:12
shepherd who **c** stand against Me? Jr 49:19
How **c** the city of praise not be Jr 49:25
shepherd who **c** stand against Me? Jr 50:44
wound—perhaps she **c** be healed. Jr 51:8
What **c** I say on your behalf? Lm 2:13
what **c** I compare you, Daughter Lm 2:13
What **c** I liken you to, so that I Lm 2:13
vast as the sea. Who **c** heal you? Lm 2:13
that no prayer **c** pass through. Lm 3:44
"They **c** stay here no longer." Lm 4:15
you **c** make your bread over that. Ezk 4:15
plague so they **c** tell about all Ezk 12:16
C wood be taken from it to make Ezk 15:3
c anyone make a peg from it to Ezk 15:3
C it be useful for anything? Ezk 15:4
How much less **c** it ever be made Ezk 15:5
C he break a covenant and Ezk 17:15
sword of Babylon's king **c** take. Ezk 21:19
that the sword **c** take to Rabbah Ezk 21:20
it so that it **c** grow strong Ezk 30:21
of them! How then **c** we survive? Ezk 33:10
Son of man, **c** these bones live? Ezk 37:3
whatever he **c** afford with the Ezk 46:7
I will know you **c** give me its Dn 2:9
one on earth **c** make known what Dn 2:10
that no one **c** make it known to Dn 2:11
exiles who **c** let the king know Dn 2:25
is the god who **c** rescue you from Dn 3:15
then He **c** rescue us from the Dn 3:17
He **c** rescue us from the power Dn 3:17
wise men of my kingdom **c** make Dn 4:18
But you **c**, because you have the Dn 4:18
is no one who **c** hold back His Dn 4:35
about you that you **c** give Dn 5:16
if you **c** read this inscription Dn 5:16
king establishes **c** be changed." Dn 6:15
How **c** someone like me, your Dn 10:17
wants, and no one **c** oppose him. Dn 11:16
C the LORD now shepherd them Hs 4:16
and no one **c** rescue ⌊them⌋. Hs 5:14
raise us up so we **c** live in His Hs 6:2
What **c** a king do for us?" Hs 10:3
How **c** I give you up, Ephraim? Hs 11:8
How **c** I surrender you, Israel? Hs 11:8
How **c** I make you like Admah? Hs 11:8
How **c** I treat you like Zeboiim? Hs 11:8
no one **c** find any crime in me Hs 12:8
in me that I **c** be punished for! Hs 12:8
and dreadful—who **c** endure it? Jl 2:11
⌊so you **c**⌋ offer grain and wine Jl 2:14
C two walk together without Am 3:3
We **c** reduce the measure while Am 8:5
c buy the poor with silver and Am 8:6
Who **c** bring me down to the Ob 3
of rebellion **c** be traced to you Mc 1:13
so you **c** crush many peoples. Mc 4:13
C I excuse wicked scales or bags Mc 6:11
Who **c** withstand His indignation? Nah 1:6
Who **c** endure His burning anger? Nah 1:6
Where **c** I find anyone to comfort Nah 3:7
Come alive! **C** it teach? Look! It Hab 2:19
But who **c** endure the day of His Mal 3:2
But you ask: "How **c** we return?" Mal 3:7
so that I too **c** go and worship Mt 2:8
its taste, how **c** it be made Mt 5:13
No one **c** be a slave of two Mt 6:24
C any of you add a single cubit Mt 6:27

how **c** you say to your brother, Mt 7:4
neither **c** a bad tree produce Mt 7:18
willing, You **c** make me clean." Mt 8:2
C the wedding guests be sad Mt 9:15
If I **c** just touch His robe, Mt 9:21
you believe that I **c** do this?" Mt 9:28
How **c** someone enter a strong Mt 12:29
Then he **c** rob his house. Mt 12:29
How **c** you speak good things when Mt 12:34
crowds away so they **c** go into Mt 14:15
of heaven **c** be compared to Mt 18:23
Not everyone **c** accept this Mt 19:11
Let anyone accept this who **c**." Mt 19:12
asked, "Then who **c** be saved?" Mt 19:25
how then **c** the Messiah be his Mt 22:45
c you escape being condemned Mt 23:33
'I **c** demolish God's sanctuary Mt 26:61
willing, You **c** make me clean." Mk 1:40
c forgive sins but God alone? Mk 2:7
the groom is with them, **c** they? Mk 2:19
How **c** Satan drive out Satan? Mk 3:23
no one **c** enter a strong man's Mk 3:27
How **c** we illustrate the kingdom Mk 4:30
or what parable **c** we use to Mk 4:30
of the sky **c** nest in its shade. Mk 4:32
her so she **c** get well and live. Mk 5:23
If I **c** just touch His robes, Mk 5:28
they **c** go into the surrounding Mk 6:36
from outside **c** defile him, Mk 7:15
from the outside **c** defile him? Mk 7:18
Where **c** anyone get enough bread Mk 8:4
What **c** a man give in exchange Mk 8:37
But if You **c** do anything, have Mk 9:22
Jesus said to him, " 'If You **c**?' Mk 9:23
This kind **c** come out by nothing Mk 9:29
in My name who **c** soon afterwards Mk 9:39
its flavor, how **c** you make it Mk 9:50
another, "Then who **c** be saved?" Mk 10:26
How **c** the scribes say that the Mk 12:35
then **c** the Messiah be his Son? Mk 12:37
and you **c** do good for them Mk 14:7
"How **c** I know this?" Zechariah Lk 1:18
the angel, "How **c** this be, since Lk 1:34
You **c** dismiss Your slave in Lk 2:29
I **c** give it to anyone I want. Lk 4:6
willing, You **c** make me clean." Lk 5:12
c forgive sins but God alone? Lk 5:21
the groom is with them, **c** you? Lk 5:34
C the blind guide the blind? Lk 6:39
how **c** you say to your brother, Lk 6:42
one another, "Who **c** this be? Lk 8:25
they **c** go into the surrounding Lk 9:12
after that **c** do nothing more. Lk 12:4
C any of you add a cubit to his Lk 12:25
they **c** open ⌊the door⌋ for him Lk 12:36
if not, you **c** cut it down.' " Lk 13:9
and what **c** I compare it to? Lk 13:18
What **c** I compare the kingdom of Lk 13:20
because you **c** no longer be ⌊my⌋ Lk 16:2
household slave **c** be the slave Lk 16:13
neither **c** those from there cross Lk 16:26
you **c** say to this mulberry tree, Lk 17:6
later you **c** eat and drink'? Lk 17:8
asked, "Then who **c** be saved?" Lk 18:26
How **c** they say that the Messiah Lk 20:41
then **c** the Messiah be his Son? Lk 20:44
out ⌊leaves⌋ you **c** see for Lk 21:30
meal for us, so we **c** eat it." Lk 22:8
room where I **c** eat the Passover Lk 22:11
and bones as you **c** see I have." Lk 24:39
c you tell us about yourself? Jn 1:22
C anything good come out of Jn 1:46
But how **c** anyone be born when he Jn 3:4
C he enter his mother's womb a Jn 3:4
"How **c** these things be?" Jn 3:9
No one **c** receive a single thing Jn 3:27
You yourselves **c** testify that I Jn 3:28
and reaper **c** rejoice together Jn 4:36
I **c** do nothing on My own. Jn 5:30
How **c** you believe? While Jn 5:44
bread so these people **c** eat?" Jn 6:5
What **c** we do to perform the Jn 6:28
How **c** He now say, 'I have come Jn 6:42
No one **c** come to Me unless the Jn 6:44
How **c** this man give us His flesh Jn 6:52
is hard! Who **c** accept it?" Jn 6:60
you that no one **c** come to Me Jn 6:65
Your disciples **c** see Your works Jn 7:3

C it be true that the Jn 7:26
How **c** You say, 'You will become Jn 8:33
Who among you **c** convict Me of Jn 8:46
is coming when no one **c** work. Jn 9:4
them. "I washed and I **c** see." Jn 9:15
How **c** a sinful man perform such Jn 9:16
I was blind, and now I **c** see!" Jn 9:25
C a demon open the eyes of the Jn 10:21
how **c** You say, 'The Son of Man Jn 12:34
going. How **c** we know the way? Jn 14:5
How **c** you say, 'Show us the Jn 14:9
so neither **c** you unless you Jn 15:4
because you **c** do nothing without Jn 15:5
I **c** confidently speak to you Ac 2:29
whom we **c** appoint to this duty. Ac 6:3
"How **c** I," he said, "unless Ac 8:31
C anyone withhold water and Ac 10:47
for the people, you **c** speak." Ac 13:15
that we **c** give as a reason for Ac 19:40
of elders **c** testify about me Ac 22:5
mounts so they **c** put Paul on Ac 23:24
Neither **c** they provide evidence Ac 24:13
as even you **c** see very well. Ac 25:10
no one **c** give me up to them. Ac 25:11
I **c** see that this voyage is Ac 27:10
since what **c** be known about God Rm 1:19
What then **c** we say that Abraham, Rm 4:1
How **c** we who died to sin still Rm 6:2
c bring an accusation against Rm 8:33
Who **c** separate us from the love Rm 8:35
C affliction or anguish or Rm 8:35
For who **c** resist His will?" Rm 9:19
I **c** testify about them that they Rm 10:2
But how **c** they call on Him in Rm 10:14
And how **c** they believe without Rm 10:14
And how **c** they hear without a Rm 10:14
how **c** they preach unless they Rm 10:15
I **c** somehow make my own people Rm 11:14
that no one **c** say you had been 1Co 1:15
so that no one **c** boast in His 1Co 1:29
person, however, **c** evaluate 1Co 2:15
because no one **c** lay any other 1Co 3:11
so that he **c** become wise. 1Co 3:18
you **c** have 10,000 instructors 1Co 4:15
C it be that there is not one 1Co 6:5
sin a person **c** commit is outside 1Co 6:18
But if you **c** become free, by all 1Co 7:21
it must be, he **c** do what he 1Co 7:36
not sinning; they **c** get married. 1Co 7:36
so that you **c** come together and 1Co 11:34
and no one **c** say, "Jesus is Lord 1Co 12:3
so that I **c** move mountains, 1Co 13:2
should pray that he **c** interpret. 1Co 14:13
For you **c** all prophesy one by 1Co 14:31
the dead, how **c** some of you say, 1Co 15:12
way in peace so he **c** come to me, 1Co 16:11
And you **c** join in helping with 2Co 1:11
than what you **c** read and also 2Co 1:13
so no one **c** find fault with us 2Co 8:20
so that no one **c** credit me with 2Co 12:6
c you compel Gentiles to live Gl 2:14
how **c** you turn back again to the Gl 4:9
works, so that no one **c** boast. Eph 2:9
God so that you **c** stand against Eph 6:11
so that you **c** determine what Php 1:10
really matters and **c** be pure and Php 1:10
Then I **c** boast in the day of Php 2:16
so that you **c** stand mature and Col 4:12
so that you **c** accomplish it." Col 4:17
How **c** we thank God for you in 1Th 3:9
then they **c** serve as deacons. 1Tm 3:10
so that it **c** help those who are 1Tm 5:16
and we **c** take nothing out. 1Tm 6:7
of mankind has seen or **c** see, 1Tm 6:16
c never perfect the worshipers Heb 10:1
which **c** never take away sins. Heb 10:11
And what more **c** I say? Time is Heb 11:32
so that we **c** share His holiness. Heb 12:10
removal of what **c** be shaken— Heb 12:27
be afraid. What **c** man do to me? Heb 13:6
so that they **c** do this with joy Heb 13:17
not have works? **C** his faith save Jms 2:14
but no man **c** tame the tongue. Jms 3:8
C a fig tree produce olives, Jms 3:12
Neither **c** a saltwater spring Jms 3:12
that you **c** inherit a blessing. 1Pt 3:9
looking for anyone he **c** devour. 1Pt 5:8
so that you **c** remember the words 2Pt 3:2
the Son **c** have the Father; 1Jn 2:23
how **c** God's love reside in him? 1Jn 3:17
and **c** receive whatever we ask 1Jn 3:22
so that we **c** be co-workers with 3Jn 8
so that no one **c** buy or sell Rv 13:17

CAN'T (37)

'You **c** eat from any tree in the Gn 3:1
But I **c** run to the mountains; Gn 19:19
I **c** ⌊bear to⌋ watch the boy die! Gn 21:16
they replied, "We **c**, until all Gn 29:8
for you. You **c** do it alone. Ex 18:18
I **c** carry all these people by Nm 11:14
We **c** go up against the people Nm 13:31
c bear ⌊the responsibility for⌋ Dt 1:9
C you find a young woman among Jdg 14:3
But if you **c** explain it to me, Jdg 14:13
But we **c** give them our daughters Jdg 21:18
replied, "I **c** redeem ⌊it⌋ myself Ru 4:6
because I **c** redeem it." Ru 4:6
things that **c** profit or deliver 1Sm 12:21
You **c** go fight this Philistine. 1Sm 17:33
"I **c** walk in these," David said 1Sm 17:39
from me? This **c** be ⌊true⌋." 1Sm 20:2
thinking, "David **c** get in here." 2Sm 5:6
ground, which **c** be recovered. 2Sm 14:14
he **c** deliver you from my hand. 2Kg 18:29
and iron that **c** be weighed 1Ch 22:14
and **c** even fill the hands of the Ps 129:7
they **c** sleep unless they have Pr 4:16
beyond me; four I **c** understand: Pr 30:18
he will say, "I **c** read it, Is 29:11
it, he will say, "I **c** read." Is 29:12
because of a people who **c** help. Is 30:5
since the king **c** do anything Jr 38:5
I **c** stand the stench of your Am 5:21
A good tree **c** produce bad fruit; Mt 7:18
but you **c** read the signs of the Mt 16:3
You **c** make the wedding guests Lk 5:34
c get up to give you anything.' Lk 11:7
You **c** be slaves to both God and Lk 16:13
asked, "why **c** I follow You now Jn 13:37
you, but you **c** bear them now. Jn 16:12
but you **c** have many fathers. 1Co 4:15

CANA (4)

took place in **C** of Galilee. Jn 2:1
this first sign in **C** of Galilee. Jn 2:11
He went again to **C** of Galilee, Jn 4:46
Nathanael from **C** of Galilee, Jn 21:2

CANAAN (85)

Ham was the father of **C**. Gn 9:18
the father of **C**, saw his father Gn 9:22
he said: **C** will be cursed. He Gn 9:25
the God of Shem; **C** will be his Gn 9:26
tents of Shem; **C** will be his Gn 9:27
Cush, Egypt, Put, and **C**. Gn 10:6
C fathered Sidon his firstborn, Gn 10:15
to go to the land of **C**. Gn 11:31
they set out for the land of **C**. Gn 12:5
When they came to the land of **C**, Gn 12:5
Abram lived in the land of **C**, Gn 13:12
lived in the land of **C** 10 years. Gn 16:3
the land of **C**—as an eternal Gn 17:8
in the land of **C**, and Abraham Gn 23:2
is, Hebron) in the land of **C**. Gn 23:19
land of his father Isaac in **C**. Gn 31:18
is, Bethel) in the land of **C**. Gn 35:6
born to him in the land of **C**. Gn 36:5
property he had acquired in **C**; Gn 36:6
had stayed, the land of **C**. Gn 37:1
the famine was in the land of **C**. Gn 42:5
"From the land of **C** to buy food," Gn 42:7
of one man in the land of **C**. Gn 42:13
father Jacob in the land of **C**, Gn 42:29
our father in the land of **C**. Gn 42:32
from the land of **C** the money we Gn 44:8
and go on back to the land of **C**. Gn 45:17
father Jacob in the land of **C**. Gn 45:25
had acquired in the land of **C**. Gn 46:6
and Onan died in the land of **C**. Gn 46:12
who were in the land of **C**, Gn 46:31
from the land of **C** and are now Gn 47:1
the land of **C** has been severe. Gn 47:4
and the land of **C** were exhausted Gn 47:13
the land of **C** in exchange for Gn 47:14
and the land of **C** was gone, Gn 47:15
in the land of **C** and blessed me. Gn 48:3
from Ephrath in the land of **C**. Gn 48:7
near Mamre, in the land of **C**. Gn 49:30
for myself in the land of **C**.' Gn 50:5
to the land of **C** and buried him Gn 50:13
them to give them the land of **C**, Ex 6:4
the inhabitants of **C** will panic; Ex 15:15
the border of the land of **C**. Ex 16:35
the land of **C** that I am giving Lv 14:34
the practices of the land of **C**, Lv 18:3
you the land of **C** and to be your Lv 25:38
out the land of **C** I am giving to Nm 13:2
them to scout out the land of **C**, Nm 13:17
but they died in the land of **C**. Nm 26:19
must accept land in **C** with you." Nm 32:30
the LORD into the land of **C**, Nm 32:32
in the Negev in the land of **C**, Nm 33:40
the Jordan into the land of **C**, Nm 33:51
When you enter the land of **C**, Nm 34:2
the Israelites in the land of **C**. Nm 34:29
the Jordan into the land of **C**, Nm 35:10
in the land of **C** to be cities Nm 35:14
view the land of **C** I am giving Dt 32:49
of the land of **C** that year. Jos 5:12
gave them in the land of **C**. Jos 14:1
them at Shiloh in the land of **C**: Jos 21:2
in the land of **C** to go to their Jos 22:9
of the Jordan in the land of **C**, Jos 22:10
of the land of **C** at the region Jos 22:11
the land of **C** and brought back Jos 22:32
him throughout the land of **C**, Jos 24:3
in any of the wars with **C**. Jdg 3:1
the hand of Jabin king of **C**, Jdg 4:2
Jabin king of **C** before the Jdg 4:23
Jabin king of **C** until they Jdg 4:24
the kings of **C** fought at Taanach Jdg 5:19
camp at Shiloh in the land of **C**. Jdg 21:12
Cush, Mizraim, Put, and **C**. 1Ch 1:8
C fathered Sidon, his firstborn, 1Ch 1:13
the land of **C** to you as your 1Ch 16:18
and temporary residents in **C** 1Ch 16:19
the land of **C** to you as your Ps 105:11
and temporary residents in **C**, Ps 105:12
sacrificed to the idols of **C**; Ps 106:38
Bashan, and all the kings of **C**. Ps 135:11
the language of **C** and swear Is 19:18
LORD is against you, **C**, land of Zph 2:5
came over all of Egypt and **C**, Ac 7:11
seven nations in the land of **C**, Ac 13:19

CANAANITE (20)

the **C** clans scattered. Gn 10:18
The **C** border went from Sidon Gn 10:19
take a wife from the **C** women. Gn 28:1
Jacob not to marry a **C** woman. Gn 28:6
disapproved of the **C** women, Gn 28:8
safely at the **C** city of Shechem Gn 33:18
took his wives from the **C** women: Gn 36:2
the daughter of a **C** named Shua; Gn 38:2
and Shaul, the son of a **C** woman. Gn 46:10
When the **C** inhabitants of the Gn 50:11
and Shaul, the son of a **C** woman. Ex 6:15
When the **C** king of Arad, who Nm 21:1
At that time the **C** king of Arad, Nm 33:40
Hittite, Amorite, **C**, Perizzite, Dt 20:17
west and all the **C** kings near Jos 5:1
considered to be **C** territory Jos 13:3
to him by Bath-shua the **C** woman. 1Ch 2:3
that the **C** fortresses be Is 23:11
no longer be a **C** in the house Zch 14:21
Just then a **C** woman from that Mt 15:22

CANAANITES (58)

that time the **C** were in the land Gn 12:6
At that time the **C** and the Gn 13:7
Amorites, **C**, Girgashites, and Gn 15:21
daughters of the **C** among whom I Gn 24:3
of the **C** in whose land I Gn 24:37
of the land, the **C** and the Gn 34:30
territory of the **C**, Hittites, Ex 3:8
of Egypt to the land of the **C**, Ex 3:17
you into the land of the **C**, Ex 13:5
you into the land of the **C**, Ex 13:11
Perizzites, **C**, Hivites, Ex 23:23
the Hivites, **C**, and Hittites Ex 23:28
of you and will drive out the **C**, Ex 33:2
you the Amorites, **C**, Hittites, Ex 34:11
and the **C** live by the sea and Nm 13:29
the Amalekites and **C** are living Nm 14:25
Amalekites and **C** are right in Nm 14:43
Amalekites and **C** who lived in Nm 14:45
request, the **C** were defeated, Nm 21:3
the land of the **C** and to Lebanon Dt 1:7

Amorites, **C**, Perizzites, Hivites Dt 7:1
road in the land of the **C**, Dt 11:30
dispossess before you the **C**, Jos 3:10
When the **C** and all who live in Jos 7:9
Amorites, **C**, Perizzites, Jos 9:1
the **C** in the east and west, Jos 11:3
Amorites, **C**, Perizzites, Jos 12:8
all the land of the **C**: Jos 13:4
not drive out the **C** who lived in Jos 16:10
So the **C** live in Ephraim to this Jos 16:10
because the **C** were determined to Jos 17:12
labor on the **C** but did not drive Jos 17:13
and all the **C** who inhabit the Jos 17:16
You can also drive out the **C**, Jos 17:18
Perizzites, **C**, Hittites, Jos 24:11
to fight for us against the **C**?" Jdg 1:1
and let us fight against the **C**. Jdg 1:3
LORD handed the **C** and Perizzites Jdg 1:4
down the **C** and Perizzites. Jdg 1:5
against the **C** who were living Jdg 1:9
against the **C** who were living Jdg 1:10
struck the **C** who were living in Jdg 1:17
But the **C** refused to leave this Jdg 1:27
they made the **C** serve as forced Jdg 1:28
drive out the **C** who were living Jdg 1:29
the **C** have lived among them in Jdg 1:29
so the **C** lived among them and Jdg 1:30
among the **C** who were living Jdg 1:32
among the **C** who were living Jdg 1:33
Philistines and all of the **C**, Jdg 3:3
But they settled among the **C**, Jdg 3:5
the cities of the Hivites and **C**. 2Sm 24:7
killed the **C** who lived in the 1Kg 9:16
are like those of the **C**, Ezr 9:1
him to give the land of the **C**, Neh 9:8
You subdued the **C** who inhabited Neh 9:24
birth were in the land of the **C**. Ezk 16:3
who are among the **C** as far as Ob 20

CANAL *(11)*
the exiles by the Chebar **C**, Ezk 1:1
the Chaldeans by the Chebar **C**. Ezk 1:3
who were living by the Chebar **C**, Ezk 3:15
I had seen by the Chebar **C**, Ezk 3:23
I had seen by the Chebar **C**. Ezk 10:15
God of Israel by the Chebar **C**, Ezk 10:20
I had seen by the Chebar **C**. Ezk 10:22
ones I had seen by the Chebar **C**. Ezk 43:3
that I was beside the Ulai **C**. Dn 8:2
was a ram standing beside the **c**. Dn 8:3
beside the **c** and rushed at him Dn 8:6

CANALS *(3)*
their rivers, **c**, ponds, and all Ex 7:19
over the rivers, **c**, and ponds, Ex 8:5
and Egypt's **c** will be parched. Is 19:6

CANCEL *(9)*
will **c** her vow that is binding Nm 30:8
may confirm or **c** any vow or any Nm 30:13
seven years you must **c** debts. Dt 15:1
This is how to **c** debt: Dt 15:2
creditor is to **c** what he has Dt 15:2
year and will **c** every debt. Neh 10:31
their unbelief **c** God's Rm 3:3
Do we then **c** the law through Rm 3:31
by God, so as to **c** the promise. Gl 3:17

CANCELED *(2)*
Her husband has **c** them, and the Nm 30:12
made empty and the promise is **c**. Rm 4:14

CANCELING *(1)*
the year of **c** debts, is near,' Dt 15:9

CANCELLATION *(1)*
time in the year of debt **c**, Dt 31:10

CANCELS *(2)*
if her husband **c** them on the day Nm 30:12
But if he **c** them after he hears Nm 30:15

CANDACE *(1)*
a eunuch and high official of **C**, Ac 8:27

CANE *(4)*
a quarter pounds of fragrant **c**, Ex 30:23
Me aromatic **c** with silver, Is 43:24
Sheba or sweet **c** from a distant Jr 6:20
and aromatic **c** were ⌊exchanged⌋ Ezk 27:19

CANNEH *(1)*
Haran, **C**, Eden, the merchants of Ezk 27:23

CANNOT *(221)*
I **c** do anything until you get Gn 19:22
be angry that I **c** stand up in Gn 31:35
the sea, which **c** be counted.' " Gn 32:12
"We **c** do this thing," they said Gn 34:14
'The boy **c** leave his father. Gn 44:22
'We **c** go down unless our younger Gn 44:26
with us, we **c** see the man.' Gn 44:26
We **c** hide from our lord that the Gn 47:18
You **c** reduce your daily quota of Ex 5:19
The people **c** come up Mount Ex 19:23
answered, "You **c** see My face, Ex 33:20
But if he **c** afford an animal Lv 5:7
But if he **c** afford two Lv 5:11
he is poor and **c** afford ⌊these⌋, Lv 14:21
disease and **c** afford the cost Lv 14:32
But if he **c** obtain enough to Lv 25:28
destitute and **c** sustain himself Lv 25:35
be holy; they **c** be redeemed." Lv 27:33
He has blessed, I **c** change it. Nm 23:20
Anything that **c** withstand fire, Nm 31:23
stone, which **c** see, hear, eat, Dt 4:28
One witness **c** establish any Dt 19:15
he **c** divorce her as long as he Dt 22:19
He **c** divorce her as long as he Dt 22:29
from which you **c** be cured. Dt 28:27
so that they **c** rise again. Dt 33:11
the Israelites **c** stand against Jos 7:12
Israel, and now we **c** touch them. Jos 9:19
This one **c** go with you,' he Jdg 7:4
cannot go with you,' he **c** go." Jdg 7:4
the LORD and **c** take ⌊it⌋ back. Jdg 11:35
and we **c** put anyone to death in 2Sm 21:4
highest heaven, **c** contain You, 1Kg 8:27
he answered, "I **c** go back with 1Kg 13:16
do, but this thing I **c** do.' " 1Kg 20:9
established; it **c** be shaken. 1Ch 16:30
highest heaven **c** contain Him? 2Ch 2:6
highest heaven, **c** contain You, 2Ch 6:18
a great work and **c** come down. Neh 6:3
Media, so that it **c** be revoked: Est 1:19
royal signet ring **c** be revoked." Est 8:8
I **c** relax or be still; Jb 3:26
Since I **c** help myself, ⌊the hope Jb 6:13
righteous, I **c** lift up my head Jb 10:15
He tears down **c** be rebuilt; Jb 12:14
He imprisons **c** be released. Jb 12:14
You have set limits he **c** pass, Jb 14:5
my way so that I **c** pass through; Jb 19:8
so you **c** see, and a flood Jb 22:11
veil Him so that He **c** see, Jb 22:14
if I go west, I **c** perceive Him. Jb 23:8
work to the north, I **c** see Him; Jb 23:9
He turns south, I **c** find Him. Jb 23:9
since it **c** be found in the land Jb 28:13
Gold **c** be exchanged for it, Jb 28:15
and silver **c** be weighed out for Jb 28:15
Wisdom **c** be valued in the gold Jb 28:16
of fine gold **c** be exchanged for Jb 28:17
from Cush **c** compare with it Jb 28:19
and it **c** be valued in pure gold. Jb 28:19
I am churning within and **c** rest; Jb 30:27
Teach me what I **c** see; Jb 34:32
of His years **c** be counted. Jb 36:26
things that we **c** comprehend. Jb 37:5
we **c** prepare ⌊our case⌋ because Jb 37:19
Now men **c** ⌊even⌋ look at the sun Jb 37:21
Almighty—we **c** reach Him—He Jb 37:23
c stand still at the trumpet's Jb 39:24
I **c** be silent about his limbs, Jb 41:12
connected they **c** be separated. Jb 41:17
evil **c** lodge with You. Ps 5:4
The boastful **c** stand in Your Ps 5:5
I crush them, and they **c** get up; Ps 18:38
even the one who **c** preserve his Ps 22:29
been thrown down and **c** rise. Ps 36:12
Yet these **c** redeem a person or Ps 49:7
long, though I **c** sum them up. Ps 71:15
I am troubled and **c** speak. Ps 77:4
I am shut in and **c** go out. Ps 88:8
established; it **c** be shaken. Ps 93:1
established; it **c** be shaken. He Ps 96:10
I **c** tolerate anyone with haughty Ps 101:5
You set a boundary they **c** cross; Ps 104:9
have mouths, but **c** speak, eyes, Ps 115:5
cannot speak, eyes, but **c** see. Ps 115:5
have ears, but **c** hear, noses, Ps 115:6
cannot hear, noses, but **c** smell. Ps 115:6
have hands, but **c** feel, feet, Ps 115:7
cannot feel, feet, but **c** walk. Ps 115:7
They **c** make a sound with their Ps 115:7
Mount Zion. It **c** be shaken; it Ps 125:1
have mouths, but **c** speak, eyes, Ps 135:16
cannot speak, eyes, but **c** see. Ps 135:16
They have ears, but **c** hear; Ps 135:17
in nobles, in man, who **c** save. Ps 146:3
Man **c** be made secure by Pr 12:3
of kings **c** be investigated Pr 25:3
A servant **c** be disciplined by Pr 29:19
it **c** bear up under four: Pr 30:21
is crooked **c** be straightened Ec 1:15
what is lacking **c** be counted. Ec 1:15
but man **c** discover the work God Ec 3:11
so that man **c** discover anything Ec 7:14
to explore it, he **c** find it; Ec 8:17
Mighty waters **c** extinguish love; Sg 8:7
rivers **c** sweep it away. Sg 8:7
I **c** stand iniquity with a Is 1:13
who **c** be bought off with silver Is 13:17
given to one who **c** read and he Is 29:12
they **c** hold the base of the mast Is 33:23
you, for he **c** deliver you. Is 36:14
For Sheol **c** thank You; Is 38:18
thank You; Death **c** praise You. Is 38:18
down to the Pit **c** hope for Your Is 38:18
not comprehend and **c** understand, Is 44:18
shut their eyes so they **c** see, Is 44:18
minds so they **c** understand. Is 44:18
and he **c** deliver himself, Is 44:20
and pray to a god who **c** save, Is 45:20
They **c** deliver themselves from Is 47:14
them are mute dogs, they **c** bark; Is 56:10
sea, for it **c** be still, and its Is 57:20
You **c** fast as ⌊you do⌋ today, Is 58:4
Their webs **c** become clothing, Is 59:6
and they **c** cover themselves with Is 59:6
square, and honesty **c** enter. Is 59:14
cisterns that **c** hold water. Jr 2:13
heart pounds; I **c** be silent. For Jr 4:19
barrier that it **c** cross? Jr 5:22
waves surge, but they **c** prevail. Jr 5:22
They roar but **c** pass over it. Jr 5:22
so they **c** pay attention. Jr 6:10
in deceitful words that **c** help. Jr 7:8
vipers that **c** be charmed. Jr 8:17
patch, their idols **c** speak. Jr 10:5
be carried because they **c** walk. Jr 10:5
harm—and they **c** do any good. Jr 10:5
the nations **c** endure His rage Jr 10:10
disaster that they **c** escape. Jr 11:11
"He **c** see what our end will be." Jr 12:4
he **c** see when good comes but Jr 17:6
holding it in, and I **c** prevail. Jr 20:9
places where I **c** see him?" Jr 23:24
hosts of heaven **c** be counted; Jr 33:22
sand of the sea **c** be measured. Jr 33:22
c enter the temple of the LORD, Jr 36:5
swift **c** flee, and the warrior Jr 46:6
flee, and the warrior **c** escape! Jr 46:6
than locusts; they **c** be counted. Jr 46:23
is anxiety that **c** be calmed. Jr 49:23
me over to those I **c** withstand. Lm 1:14
has walled me in so I **c** escape; Lm 3:7
whose words you **c** understand. Ezk 3:6
with them so you **c** go out among Ezk 3:25
you so you **c** turn from side to Ezk 4:8
face so that you **c** see the land. Ezk 12:6
his face so he **c** see the land Ezk 12:12
them so small they **c** rule over Ezk 29:15
irrevocable and **c** be changed." Dn 6:8
which **c** be measured or counted. Hs 1:10
so that she **c** find her paths. Hs 2:6
But he **c** cure you or heal your Hs 5:13
withered; they **c** bear fruit. Hs 9:16
The land **c** endure all his words, Am 7:10
120,000 people who **c** distinguish Jnh 4:11
you **c** free your necks from it. Mc 2:3
acquire, you **c** save, and what Mc 6:14
and You **c** tolerate wrongdoing. Hab 1:13
it and makes idols that **c** speak. Hab 2:18
You **c** remain alive because you Zch 13:3
situated on a hill **c** be hidden. Mt 5:14
because you **c** make a single hair Mt 5:36
You **c** be slaves of God and of Mt 6:24
this **c** pass unless I drink it, Mt 26:42
you think that I **c** call on My Mt 26:53
others, but He **c** save Himself! Mt 27:42
The wedding guests **c** fast while Mk 2:19

groom with them, they **c** fast. Mk 2:19
itself, that kingdom **c** stand. Mk 3:24
itself, that house **c** stand. Mk 3:25
he **c** stand but is finished! Mk 3:26
saved others; He **c** save Himself! Mk 15:31
because they **c** repay you; Lk 14:14
own life—he **c** be My disciple. Lk 14:26
come after Me **c** be My disciple. Lk 14:27
the foundation and **c** finish it, Lk 14:29
possessions **c** be My disciple. Lk 14:33
to pass over from here to you **c**; Lk 16:26
For they **c** die anymore, because Lk 20:36
he **c** see the kingdom of God." Jn 3:3
he **c** enter the kingdom of God. Jn 3:5
world **c** hate you, but it does Jn 7:7
and where I am, you **c** come." Jn 7:34
and where I am, you **c** come'?" Jn 7:36
Where I'm going, you **c** come." Jn 8:21
Where I'm going, you **c** come'?" Jn 8:22
Because you **c** listen to My word. Jn 8:43
and the Scripture **c** be broken— Jn 10:35
'Where I am going you **c** come,' Jn 13:33
I am going you **c** follow Me now, Jn 13:36
through them, and we **c** deny it! Ac 4:16
by Moses, you **c** be saved!" Ac 15:1
in the ship, you **c** be saved." Ac 27:31
eyes that **c** see and ears that Rm 11:8
cannot see and ears that **c** hear, Rm 11:8
eyes be darkened so they **c** see, Rm 11:10
yet he himself **c** be evaluated by 1Co 2:15
You **c** drink the cup of the Lord 1Co 10:21
You **c** share in the Lord's table 1Co 10:21
So the eye **c** say to the hand, 1Co 12:21
flesh and blood **c** inherit the 1Co 15:50
and corruption **c** inherit 1Co 15:50
so they **c** see the light 2Co 4:4
not ⌊obvious⌋ **c** remain hidden. 1Tm 5:25
faithful, for He **c** deny Himself. 2Tm 2:13
that God, who **c** lie, promised Ti 1:2
are offered that **c** perfect the Heb 9:9
a kingdom that **c** be shaken, Heb 12:28
murder and covet and **c** obtain. Jms 4:2
he has seen **c** love God whom he 1Jn 4:20
and that you **c** tolerate evil. Rv 2:2

CANOPIES *(1)*
rooms of the temple, and the **c**. Ezk 41:26

CANOPY *(7)*
made darkness a **c** around Him, 2Sm 22:12
and a **c** with pillars were in 1Kg 7:6
the Sabbath **c** they had built 2Kg 16:18
storm clouds His **c** around Him. Ps 18:11
spreading out the sky like a **c**, Ps 104:2
there will be a **c** over all the Is 4:5
There was a wooden **c** outside, Ezk 41:25

CAPABLE *(20)*
know of any **c** men among them, Gn 47:6
hand a stone **c** of causing death Nm 35:17
a wooden object **c** of causing Nm 35:18
Now the man Jeroboam was **c**, 1Kg 11:28
They were **c** men employed in the 1Ch 9:13
because they were strong, **c** men. 1Ch 26:6
and Semachiah were also **c** men. 1Ch 26:7
they were **c** men with strength 1Ch 26:8
and brothers who were **c** men— 1Ch 26:9
relatives, 1,700 **c** men, had 1Ch 26:30
c men were found among them at 1Ch 26:31
2,700 **c** men who were heads of 1Ch 26:32
in Jerusalem, was 468 **c** men. Neh 11:6
and their relatives, **c** men: Neh 11:14
A **c** wife is her husband's crown, Pr 12:4
Who can find a **c** wife? Pr 31:10
Many women are **c**, but you Pr 31:29
and done, the evil you are **c** Jr 3:5
and **c** of serving in the king's Dn 1:4
But Saul grew more **c**, and kept Ac 9:22

CAPACITY *(3)*
the standard larger **c** measure. Ezk 45:11
one standard larger **c** measure, Ezk 45:14
one standard larger **c** measure. Ezk 45:14

CAPER *(1)*
and the **c** berry has no effect; Ec 12:5

CAPERNAUM *(16)*
went to live in **C** by the sea, Mt 4:13
When He entered **C**, a centurion Mt 8:5
And you, **C**, will you be exalted Mt 11:23
When they came to **C**, those who Mt 17:24
they went into **C**, and right away Mk 1:21
When He entered **C** again after Mk 2:1
Then they came to **C**. Mk 9:33
heard that took place in **C**, Lk 4:23
He went down to **C**, a town in Lk 4:31
of the people, He entered **C**. Lk 7:1
And you, **C**, will you be exalted Lk 10:15
He went down to **C**, together with Jn 2:12
official whose son was ill at **C**. Jn 4:46
and started across the sea to **C**. Jn 6:17
and went to **C** looking for Jesus Jn 6:24
teaching in the synagogue in **C**. Jn 6:59

CAPES *(1)*
robes, **c**, cloaks, purses, Is 3:22

CAPHTOR *(3)*
who came from **C**, destroyed the Dt 2:23
the remnant of the islands of **C**. Jr 47:4
Philistines from **C**, and the Am 9:7

CAPHTORIM *(3)*
came from them), and **C**. Gn 10:14
The **C**, who came from Caphtor, Dt 2:23
came from them), and **C**. 1Ch 1:12

CAPITAL *(13)*
was the height of the first **c**, 1Kg 7:16
also the height of the second **c**. 1Kg 7:16
for the first **c** and seven for 1Kg 7:17
grating to cover the **c** on top; 1Kg 7:18
did the same for the second **c**. 1Kg 7:18
were in rows encircling each **c**. 1Kg 7:20
and had a bronze **c** on top of it. 2Kg 25:17
c, encircled by a grating and 2Kg 25:17
The **c** on top of each was seven 2Ch 3:15
and had a bronze **c** on top of it. Jr 52:22
One **c**, encircled by bronze Jr 52:22
⌊Each **c** had⌋ 96 pomegranates all Jr 52:23
I had not committed a **c** offense. Ac 28:18

CAPITALS *(10)*
also made two **c** of cast bronze 1Kg 7:16
The **c** on top of the pillars had 1Kg 7:17
And the **c** on top of the pillars 1Kg 7:19
The **c** on the two pillars were 1Kg 7:20
bowls for the **c** that were on top 1Kg 7:41
bowls of the **c** that were on top 1Kg 7:41
bowls and the **c** on top of the 2Ch 4:12
bowls of the **c** that were on top 2Ch 4:12
Strike the **c** of the pillars so Am 9:1
roost in the **c** of its pillars. Zph 2:14

CAPITALS' *(2)*
covering both **c** bowls on top 1Kg 7:42
covering both **c** bowls on top 2Ch 4:13

CAPPADOCIA *(2)*
in Judea and **C**, Pontus and Asia, Ac 2:9
Pontus, Galatia, **C**, Asia, and 1Pt 1:1

CAPSTONE *(1)*
will bring out the **c** accompanied Zch 4:7

CAPTAIN *(28)*
Pharaoh and the **c** of the guard. Gn 37:36
Pharaoh and the **c** of the guard, Gn 39:1
the house of the **c** of the guard, Gn 40:3
The **c** of the guard assigned Gn 40:4
custody of the **c** of the guard. Gn 41:10
a slave of the **c** of the guards, Gn 41:12
son-in-law, **c** of your bodyguard 1Sm 22:14
He became **c** of a raiding party 1Kg 11:24
Ahaziah sent a **c** of 50 with his 2Kg 1:9
When the **c** went up to him, 2Kg 1:9
responded to the **c** of the 50, 2Kg 1:10
sent another **c** of 50 with his 50 2Kg 1:11
sent a third **c** of 50 with his 50 2Kg 1:13
The third **c** of 50 went up and 2Kg 1:13
the **c**, the king's right-hand 2Kg 7:2
The king had appointed the **c**, 2Kg 7:17
this **c** had answered the man of 2Kg 7:19
Nebuzaradan, **c** of the guard, Jr 39:11
Nebuzaradan, **c** of the guard, Jr 39:13
Nebuzaradan, **c** of the guard, Jr 40:1
The **c** of the guard took Jeremiah Jr 40:2
So the **c** of the guard gave him Jr 40:5
Nebuzaradan, **c** of the guard, had Jr 41:10
Nebuzaradan, **c** of the guard, had Jr 43:6
The **c** approached him and said, Jnh 1:6
the **c** of the temple police and Ac 5:24
Then the **c** went with the temple Ac 5:26
attention to the **c** and the owner Ac 27:11

CAPTAINS *(7)*
commanders, his **c**, and 1Kg 9:22
the care of the **c** of the royal 1Kg 14:27
and appoint **c** in their place. 1Kg 20:24
the first two **c** of 50 with their 2Kg 1:14
of his **c**, and commanders 2Ch 8:9
the care of the **c** of the royal 2Ch 12:10
and all the **c** of the king of Jr 39:13

CAPTIVATE *(2)*
beauty or let her **c** you with her Pr 6:25
away from me, for they **c** me. Sg 6:5

CAPTIVATED *(1)*
the people were **c** by what they Lk 19:48

CAPTIVE *(24)*
when Asshur takes you **c**. Nm 24:22
women and their children **c**, Nm 31:9
their enemies who took them **c**, 1Kg 8:48
took him ⌊**c**⌋ in the eighth 2Kg 24:12
also brought **c** into Babylon all 2Kg 24:16
The sons of Jeconiah the **c**: 1Ch 3:17
where they were taken **c**, 2Ch 6:38
came from those **c** exiles King Ezr 2:1
from among the **c** exiles deported Neh 7:6
the LORD restores His **c** people, Ps 14:7
When God restores His **c** people, Ps 53:6
could be held **c** in your tresses. Sg 7:5
your neck, **c** Daughter Zion." Is 52:2
LORD's flock has been taken **c**. Jr 13:17
Ishmael took **c** all the remnant Jr 41:10
took them **c** and set off to Jr 41:10
Ishmael had taken **c** from Mizpah Jr 41:14
it will be taken **c**. The fortress Jr 48:1
have been taken **c** and your Jr 48:46
nations where they are taken **c**, Ezk 6:9
take even their gods **c** to Egypt, Dn 11:8
sword and be led **c** into all the Lk 21:24
every thought **c** to the obedience 2Co 10:5
no one takes you **c** through Col 2:8

CAPTIVES *(26)*
all the spoils of war and the **c**, Nm 31:11
Then divide the **c** between the Nm 31:27
The **c** remaining from the plunder Nm 31:32
a beautiful woman among the **c**, Dt 21:11
blood of the slain and the **c**, Dt 32:42
hold of your **c**, son of Abinoam! Jdg 5:12
fighting men, 10,000 **c**, and all 2Kg 24:14
him and took many **c** to Damascus. 2Ch 28:5
took 200,000 **c** from their 2Ch 28:8
and return the **c** you took from 2Ch 28:11
You must not bring the **c** here, 2Ch 28:13
army left the **c** and the plunder 2Ch 28:14
charge of the **c** and provided 2Ch 28:15
attacked Judah, and took **c**. 2Ch 28:17
with the other **c** when King Est 2:6
The **c** are completely at ease; Jb 3:18
to the heights, taking away **c**; Ps 68:18
will make **c** of their captors Is 14:2
Assyria will lead the **c** of Egypt Is 20:4
or the **c** of the righteous be Is 49:24
Even the **c** of a mighty man will Is 49:25
to proclaim liberty to the **c**, Is 61:1
have gone away as **c** before the Lm 1:5
exile as the first of the **c**, Am 6:7
freedom to the **c** and recovery of Lk 4:18
c of various passions and Ti 3:3

CAPTIVITY *(29)*
daughters into **c** to Sihon the Nm 21:29
land of their **c** where they were 2Ch 6:38
wives are in **c** because of this 2Ch 29:9
to Jerusalem from the **c**, Ezr 3:8
returned from the **c** offered Ezr 8:35
and to the sword, **c**, plundering, Ezr 9:7
taken as plunder to a land of **c**. Neh 4:4
His strength to **c** and His Ps 78:61
no going ⌊into **c**⌋, and no cry of Ps 144:14
but they themselves go into **c**. Is 46:2
destined⌋ for **c**, to captivity. Jr 15:2
destined⌋ for captivity, to **c**. Jr 15:2
your house, you will go into **c**. Jr 20:6
and your lovers will go into **c**. Jr 22:22
from the land of their **c**! Jr 30:10
destined⌋ for **c**, to captivity; Jr 43:11
destined⌋ for captivity, to **c**; Jr 43:11
from the land of their **c**! Jr 46:27
your daughters have gone into **c**. Jr 48:46
men and women have gone into **c**. Lm 1:18
they will go into exile, into **c**. Ezk 12:11
and those cities will go into **c**. Ezk 30:17
and its villages will go into **c**. Ezk 30:18
When I return My people from **c**, Hs 6:11

driven by their enemies into **c**, Am 9:4
she went into **c**. Her children Nah 3:10
high, He took prisoners into **c**; Eph 4:8
If anyone is destined for **c**, Rv 13:10
for captivity, into **c** he goes. Rv 13:10

CAPTORS (8)
and their **c** deport them to the 1Kg 8:46
in the eyes of their **c**, 1Kg 8:50
and their **c** deport them to a 2Ch 6:36
of their **c** and will return 2Ch 30:9
to be pitied before all their **c**. Ps 106:46
for our **c** there asked us for Ps 137:3
captives of their **c** and will Is 14:2
All their **c** hold them fast; Jr 50:33

CAPTORS' (2)
petition You in their **c** land: 1Kg 8:47
petition You in their **c** land, 2Ch 6:37

CAPTURE (26)
against it in order to **c** it, Dt 20:19
news about the **c** of God's ark 1Sm 4:19
referring to the **c** of the ark of 1Sm 4:21
on David and his men to **c** them. 1Sm 23:26
Yet David did **c** the stronghold 2Sm 5:7
lay siege to the city, and **c** it. 2Sm 12:28
I will be the one to **c** the city, 2Sm 12:28
so I can send ⌊men⌋ to **c** him." 2Kg 6:13
Yet David did **c** the stronghold 1Ch 11:5
order that he might **c** the city. 2Ch 32:18
Can anyone **c** him while he looks Jb 40:24
Your hand will **c** all your Ps 21:8
have dug a pit to **c** me and have Jr 18:22
king, and he will **c** it. Jr 32:3
come against the city to **c** it, Jr 32:24
and he will **c** it. Jr 32:28
against it, **c** it, and burn it Jr 34:22
They will **c** it and burn it down. Jr 37:8
army, and he will **c** it.' " Jr 38:3
and **c** a well-fortified city. Dn 11:15
coasts and islands and **c** many. Dn 11:18
Didn't we **c** Karnaim for Am 6:13
and build siege ramps to **c** it. Hab 1:10
if I were a criminal, to **c** Me? Mt 26:55
I were a criminal, to **c** Me? Mk 14:48
households and **c** idle women 2Tm 3:6

CAPTURED (104)
They **c** all their possessions, Gn 34:29
Israel and **c** some prisoners. Nm 21:1
Israel **c** its villages and drove Nm 21:32
to take a count of what was **c**, Nm 31:26
went to Gilead, **c** it, and drove Nm 32:39
went and **c** their villages, Nm 32:41
Nobah went and **c** Kenath with its Nm 32:42
At that time we **c** all his cities Dt 2:34
the cities we **c** as plunder for Dt 2:35
c all his cities at that time. Dt 3:4
ahead, and they **c** the city. Jos 6:20
entered the city, **c** it, and Jos 8:19
in⌋ ambush had **c** the city and Jos 8:21
but they **c** the king of Ai alive Jos 8:23
that Joshua had **c** Ai and Jos 10:1
that day Joshua **c** Makkedah and Jos 10:28
and Joshua **c** it on the second Jos 10:32
that day they **c** it and struck it Jos 10:35
They **c** it and struck down its Jos 10:37
He **c** it—its king and all its Jos 10:39
Joshua **c** all these kings and Jos 10:42
turned back, **c** Hazor, and struck Jos 11:10
Joshua **c** all these kings and Jos 11:12
He **c** all their kings and struck Jos 11:17
brother, Kenaz, **c** it, and Caleb Jos 15:17
against Leshem, **c** it, and struck Jos 19:47
against Jerusalem and **c** it. Jdg 1:8
youngest brother, **c** it, and Jdg 1:13
Judah **c** Gaza and its territory, Jdg 1:18
c the fords of the Jordan Jdg 3:28
They **c** Oreb and Zeeb, the two Jdg 7:25
He **c** these two kings of Midian Jdg 8:12
He **c** a youth from the men of Jdg 8:14
entire day, **c** it, and killed Jdg 9:45
camped against it, and **c** it. Jdg 9:50
Gileadites **c** the fords of the Jdg 12:5
had been **c** ⌊by them⌋ among Jdg 18:1
ark of God was **c**, and Eli's two 1Sm 4:11
and the ark of God has been **c**." 1Sm 4:17
the ark of God has been **c**." 1Sm 4:22
had **c** the ark of God, 1Sm 5:1
He **c** Agag king of Amalek alive, 1Sm 15:8
c 1,700 horsemen and 20,000 2Sm 8:4
the Ammonites and **c** the royal 2Sm 12:26
have also **c** the water supply. 2Sm 12:27
he fought against it and **c** it. 2Sm 12:29
Egypt had attacked and **c** Gezer. 1Kg 9:16
Zimri saw that the city was **c**, 1Kg 16:18
those you have **c** with your sword 2Kg 6:22
fought against Gath and **c** it. 2Kg 12:17
Jehoash of Israel **c** Judah's King 2Kg 14:13
king of Assyria came and **c** Ijon, 2Kg 15:29
marched up to Damascus and **c** it. 2Kg 16:9
the king of Assyria **c** Samaria. 2Kg 17:6
The Assyrians **c** it at the end of 2Kg 18:10
King Hoshea, Samaria was **c**. 2Kg 18:10
cities of Judah and **c** them. 2Kg 18:13
and Aram **c** Jair's Villages 1Ch 2:23
They **c** the Hagrites' livestock— 1Ch 5:21
David **c** 1,000 chariots, 7,000 1Ch 18:4
He **c** the fortified cities of 2Ch 12:4
Jeroboam and **c** ⌊some⌋ cities 2Ch 13:19
of the herdsmen and **c** many sheep 2Ch 14:15
the cities he had **c** in the hill 2Ch 15:8
that his father Asa had **c**. 2Ch 17:2
and Jehu's soldiers **c** him 2Ch 22:9
the Judahites **c** 10,000 alive. 2Ch 25:12
Jehoash of Israel **c** Judah's King 2Ch 25:23
of Judah and **c** Beth-shemesh, 2Ch 28:18
They **c** Manasseh with hooks, 2Ch 33:11
They **c** fortified cities and Neh 9:25
but the sinner will be **c** by her. Ec 7:26
You have **c** my heart, my sister, Sg 4:9
You have **c** my heart with one Sg 4:9
they will be snared and **c**. Is 8:15
Ashdod and attacked and **c** it— Is 20:1
fled together, **c** without a bow. Is 22:3
your fugitives were **c** together; Is 22:3
to be broken, trapped, and **c**. Is 28:13
cities of Judah and **c** them. Is 36:1
both husband and wife will be **c**, Jr 6:11
certain to be **c** and handed over Jr 34:3
until the day Jerusalem was **c**, Jr 38:28
live in the cities you have **c**." Jr 40:10
treasures, you will be **c** also. Jr 48:7
The towns have been **c**, and the Jr 48:41
the pit will be **c** in the trap, Jr 48:44
Say: Babylon is **c**; Bel is put to Jr 50:2
from there she will be **c**. Jr 50:9
were found and **c** because you Jr 50:24
city has been **c** from end ⌊to end Jr 51:31
Sheshach has been **c**, the praise Jr 51:41
warriors will be **c**, their bows Jr 51:56
our life, was **c** in their traps; Lm 4:20
and he will be **c** in My snare. Ezk 17:20
guilt so that they will be **c**. Ezk 21:23
this, you will be **c** by them. Ezk 21:24
year after Jerusalem had been **c**, Ezk 40:1
and be **c** and plundered for a Dn 11:33
unless it has **c** ⌊something⌋? Am 3:4
sword, along with your **c** horses. Am 4:10
the day strangers **c** his wealth, Ob 11
The city will be **c**, the houses Zch 14:2
having been **c** by him to do his 2Tm 2:26

CAPTURES (3)
down and **c** Kiriath-sepher. Jos 15:16
down and **c** Kiriath-sepher, Jdg 1:12
you, if someone **c** you, if 2Co 11:20

CAPTURING (2)
hope of ⌊**c**⌋ him proves false. Jb 41:9
one's temper, than **c** a city. Pr 16:32

CARAVAN (2)
and there was a **c** of Ishmaelites Gn 37:25
Gideon traveled on the **c** route, Jdg 8:11

CARAVANS (4)
C turn away from their routes, Jb 6:18
The **c** of Tema look ⌊for these Jb 6:19
the desert, you **c** of Dedanites. Is 21:13
C of camels will cover your land Is 60:6

CARCASS (12)
make restitution for the torn **c**. Ex 22:13
a **c** of an unclean wild animal, Lv 5:2
who touches a **c** ⌊in it⌋ will Lv 11:36
touches its **c** will be unclean Lv 11:39
eats some of its **c** must wash his Lv 11:40
who carries its **c** must wash his Lv 11:40
You are not to eat any **c**; Dt 14:21
the road⌋ to see the lion's **c**, Jdg 14:8
of bees with honey in the **c**. Jdg 14:8
the honey from the lion's **c**. Jdg 14:9
fill the valleys with your **c**. Ezk 32:5
Wherever the **c** is, there the Mt 24:28

CARCASSES (11)
of prey came down on the **c**, Gn 15:11
of their meat or touch their **c**— Lv 11:8
and you must detest their **c**. Lv 11:11
touches their **c** will be unclean Lv 11:24
any of their **c** must wash his Lv 11:25
touches their **c** will be unclean Lv 11:27
carries their **c** must wash his Lv 11:28
one of their **c** falls on will Lv 11:35
If one of their **c** falls on any Lv 11:37
and one of their **c** falls on it, Lv 11:38
eat their meat or touch their **c**. Dt 14:8

CARCHEMISH (3)
up to fight at **C** by the 2Ch 35:20
Isn't Calno like **C**? Is 10:9
was defeated at **C** on the Jr 46:2

CARE (57)
Put him in my **c**, and I will Gn 42:37
I will take **c** of you and your Gn 50:21
or any ⌊other⌋ animal to **c** for, Ex 22:10
articles, take **c** of it, and camp Nm 1:50
They are to take **c** of all the Nm 3:8
in whose **c** were the holy objects Nm 31:6
I'll take **c** of everything you Jdg 19:20
so that you will be taken **c** of? Ru 3:1
on her lap, and took **c** of him. Ru 4:16
the women taking **c** of her said, 1Sm 4:20
his son Eleazar to take **c** of it. 1Sm 7:1
his supplies in the **c** of the 1Sm 17:22
left them in the **c** of the king 1Sm 22:4
to take **c** of the palace. 2Sm 15:16
he left to take **c** of the palace. 2Sm 16:21
He had not taken **c** of his feet, 2Sm 19:24
had left to take **c** of the palace 2Sm 20:3
them into the **c** of the captains 1Kg 14:27
Take **c** of this cursed woman and 2Kg 9:34
were in the **c** of Shelomith and 1Ch 26:28
house under the **c** of Jehiel 1Ch 29:8
them into the **c** of the captains 2Ch 12:10
our God into the **c** of Meremoth Ezr 8:33
⌊Put them⌋ under the **c** of Hegai, Est 2:3
of Susa under Hegai's **c**. Est 2:8
and placed under the **c** of Hegai, Est 2:8
May God above not **c** about it, Jb 3:4
I no longer **c** about myself; Jb 9:21
and Your **c** has guarded my life. Jb 10:12
what does he **c** about his family Jb 21:21
and see; take **c** of this vine, Ps 80:14
and who are cut off from Your **c**. Ps 88:5
pasture, the sheep under His **c**. Ps 95:7
man, that You **c** for him, the son Ps 144:3
but the upright **c** about him. Pr 29:10
will set you free and **c** for you. Jr 15:11
come, and I will take **c** of you. Jr 40:4
and I took **c** of sycamore figs. Am 7:14
Should I not **c** about the great Jnh 4:11
house and take **c** of My courts; Zch 3:7
who will not **c** for those who are Zch 11:16
I was sick and you took **c** of Me; Mt 25:36
and you didn't take **c** of Me.' Mt 25:43
Don't you **c** that we're going to Mk 4:38
take **c** how you listen. Lk 8:18
to an inn, and took **c** of him. Lk 10:34
and said, 'Take **c** of him. Lk 10:35
don't You **c** that my sister has Lk 10:40
Take **c** then, that the light in Lk 11:35
and doesn't **c** about the sheep Jn 10:13
his friends to receive their **c**. Ac 27:3
my **c** for all the churches. 2Co 11:28
who will genuinely **c** about your Php 2:20
you have renewed your **c** for me. Php 4:10
will he take **c** of God's church? 1Tm 3:5
son of man, that You **c** for him? Heb 2:6
casting all your **c** upon Him, 1Pt 5:7

CARED (7)
surrounded him, **c** for him, and Dt 32:10
sons were being **c** for by the 2Kg 10:6
and you will be called **C** For, Is 62:12
one **c** ⌊enough⌋ about you to do Ezk 16:5
said, "You **c** about the plant Jnh 4:10
this because he **c** about the poor Jn 12:6
c so much for you that we were 1Th 2:8

CAREFREE (1)
sound of a **c** crowd was there. Ezk 23:42

CAREFUL *(58)*
Be **c** that you don't go up on the Ex 19:12
Be **c** to make ⌊everything⌋ Ex 25:40
Be **c** not to make a treaty with Ex 34:12
of you, so you must be very **c**. Dt 2:4
Be extremely **c** for your own good Dt 4:15
Be **c** not to forget the covenant Dt 4:23
c to dedicate the Sabbath day, Dt 5:12
Be **c** to do as the LORD your God Dt 5:32
and be **c** to follow ⌊them⌋, Dt 6:3
be **c** not to forget the LORD who Dt 6:12
ours if we are **c** to follow every Dt 6:25
listen to and are **c** to keep Dt 7:12
Be **c** that you don't forget the Dt 8:11
⌊be **c**⌋ that your heart doesn't Dt 8:14
Be **c** that you are not enticed to Dt 11:16
be **c** to follow all the statutes Dt 11:32
Be **c** to follow these statutes Dt 12:1
Be **c** not to offer your burnt Dt 12:13
and be **c** not to neglect the Dt 12:19
Be **c** to obey all these things I Dt 12:28
be **c** not to be ensnared by their Dt 12:30
You must be **c** to do everything I Dt 12:32
God and are **c** to follow every Dt 15:5
c that there isn't this wicked Dt 15:9
Be **c** to do exactly as they Dt 17:10
are to make a **c** investigation, Dt 19:18
c to avoid anything offensive. Dt 23:9
Be **c** to do whatever comes from Dt 23:23
Be **c** in a case of infectious Dt 24:8
Be **c** to do as I have commanded Dt 24:8
must be **c** to follow them with Dt 26:16
your God and are **c** to follow all Dt 28:1
today and are **c** to follow ⌊them⌋ Dt 28:13
If you are not **c** to obey all the Dt 28:58
your God and be **c** to follow all Dt 31:12
please be **c** not to drink wine Jdg 13:4
'If your sons are **c** to walk 1Kg 2:4
Be **c** passing by this place, 2Kg 6:9
Jehu was not **c** to follow with 2Kg 10:31
are to be **c** always to observe 2Kg 17:37
they will be **c** to do all I have 2Kg 21:8
they will be **c** to do all that I 2Ch 33:8
Be **c** that no one lures you with Jb 36:18
Be **c** that you do not turn to Jb 36:21
man is **c** in dealing with Pr 12:26
I have paid **c** attention. Jr 8:6
Take **c** note of the entrance of Ezk 44:5
Be **c** not to practice your Mt 6:1
be **c** about what you're going to Ac 5:35
are also **c** about observing Ac 21:24
a somewhat more **c** inquiry about Ac 23:20
each one must be **c** how he builds 1Co 3:10
be **c** that this right of yours 1Co 8:9
he stands must be **c** not to fall! 1Co 10:12
c attention, then, to how you Eph 5:15
Be **c** that no one takes you Col 2:8
God might be **c** to devote Ti 3:8
Be **c** that you make everything Heb 8:5

CAREFULLY *(50)*
(See pp. xi-xii.)

CAREGIVER *(2)*
to attend the king and be his **c**. 1Kg 1:2
and she became the king's **c**. 1Kg 1:4

CARELESS *(2)*
fool is easily angered and is **c**. Pr 14:16
for every **c** word they speak. Mt 12:36

CARES *(11)*
a land the LORD your God **c** for. Dt 11:12
None of you **c** about me or tells 1Sm 22:8
abandon me, the LORD **c** for me. Ps 27:10
Happy is one who **c** for the poor; Ps 41:1
I am filled with **c**, Your comfort Ps 94:19
for me; no one **c** about me. Ps 142:4
A righteous man **c** about his Pr 12:10
that Zion no one **c** about. Jr 30:17
c for those who take refuge in Nah 1:7
but provides and **c** for it, Eph 5:29
Him, because He **c** about you. 1Pt 5:7

CARESSED *(3)*
and their virgin nipples **c**. Ezk 23:3
her in her youth, **c** her virgin Ezk 23:8
the Egyptians **c** your nipples to Ezk 23:21

CARESSING *(1)*
to see Isaac **c** his wife Rebekah. Gn 26:8

CARGO *(4)*
the ship's **c** into the sea to Jnh 1:5
ship was to unload its **c** there. Ac 21:3
not only of the **c** and the ship, Ac 27:10
to jettison the **c** the next day. Ac 27:18

CARITES *(2)*
hundreds, the **C**, and the guards 2Kg 11:4
of hundreds, the **C**, the guards, 2Kg 11:19

CARKAS *(1)*
Zethar, and **C**, the seven eunuchs Est 1:10

CARMEL *(24)*
one the king of Jokneam in **C** one Jos 12:22
Maon, **C**, Ziph, Juttah, Jos 15:55
westward to **C** and Shihor-libnath Jos 19:26
Saul went to **C** where he set up a 1Sm 15:12
man in Maon had a business in **C**; 1Sm 25:2
and was shearing his sheep in **C**. 1Sm 25:2
them, "Go up to **C**, and when you 1Sm 25:5
the whole time they were in **C**. 1Sm 25:7
servants came to Abigail at **C**, 1Sm 25:40
of Jezreel and Abigail of **C**, 1Sm 27:3
Israel to meet me at Mount **C**, 1Kg 18:19
the prophets at Mount **C**. 1Kg 18:20
went up to the summit of **C**. 1Kg 18:42
there Elisha went to Mount **C**, 2Kg 2:25
to the man of God at Mount **C**. 2Kg 4:25
born⌋ second, by Abigail of **C**; 1Ch 3:1
head crowns you like Mount **C**, Sg 7:5
Bashan and **C** shake off ⌊their⌋ Is 33:9
the splendor of **C** and Sharon. Is 35:2
mountains and like **C** by the sea. Jr 46:18
he will feed on **C** and Bashan; Jr 50:19
and the summit of **C** withers. Am 1:2
hide themselves on the top of **C**, Am 9:3
dry. Bashan and **C** wither; even Nah 1:4

CARMELITE *(5)*
the widow of Nabal the **C**, 1Sm 30:5
the widow of Nabal the **C**. 2Sm 2:2
the widow of Nabal the **C**; 2Sm 3:3
Hezro the **C**, Paarai the Arbite, 2Sm 23:35
the **C**, Naarai son of Ezbai, 1Ch 11:37

CARMI *(7)*
Hanoch, Pallu, Hezron, and **C**. Gn 46:9
Hanoch and Pallu, Hezron and **C**. Ex 6:14
the Carmite clan from **C**. Nm 26:6
Achan son of **C**, son of Zabdi, Jos 7:1
Achan son of **C**, son of Zabdi, Jos 7:18
Perez, Hezron, **C**, Hur, and 1Ch 4:1
Hanoch, Pallu, Hezron, and **C**. 1Ch 5:3

CARMI'S *(1)*
C son: Achar, who brought 1Ch 2:7

CARMITE *(1)*
the **C** clan from Carmi. Nm 26:6

CARNELIAN *(5)*
first row should be a row of **c**, Ex 28:17
The first row was a row of **c**, Ex 39:10
c, topaz, and diamond, beryl, Ezk 28:13
looked like jasper and **c** stone. Rv 4:3
the sixth **c**, the seventh Rv 21:20

CAROB *(1)*
fill from the **c** pods the pigs Lk 15:16

CAROUSE *(2)*
crowds, and those who **c** in her! Is 5:14
a pleasure to **c** in the daytime. 2Pt 2:13

CAROUSERS *(1)*
All the **c** now groan. Is 24:7

CAROUSING *(4)*
minds are not dulled from **c**, Lk 21:34
not in **c** and drunkenness; Rm 13:13
drunkenness, **c**, and anything Gl 5:21
orgies, **c**, and lawless 1Pt 4:3

CARPENTER *(1)*
Isn't this the **c**, the son of Mk 6:3

CARPENTER'S *(1)*
Isn't this the **c** son? Mt 13:55

CARPENTERS *(7)*
cedar logs, **c**, and stonemasons 2Sm 5:11
temple—the **c**, the builders, 2Kg 12:11
⌊They are to give it⌋ to the **c**, 2Kg 22:6
and **c** to build a palace for him. 1Ch 14:1
masons, **c**, and people skilled 1Ch 22:15
hiring masons and **c** to renovate 2Ch 24:12
gave it to the **c** and builders 2Ch 34:11

CARPET *(1)*
a table, and spread out a **c**! Is 21:5

CARPETS *(1)*
and multicolored **c**, which were Ezk 27:24

CARPUS *(1)*
cloak I left in Troas with **C**, 2Tm 4:13

CARRIAGES *(1)*
horses and **c**; and human bodies Rv 18:13

CARRIED *(108)*
This order was **c** out. Gn 42:25
gift they had **c** into the house, Gn 43:26
They **c** him to the land of Canaan Gn 50:13
it **c** off the locusts and blew Ex 10:19
and how I **c** you on eagles' Ex 19:4
that the table can be **c** by them. Ex 25:28
sides of the altar when it is **c**. Ex 27:7
came forward and **c** them in their Lv 10:5
the holy objects **c** on their Nm 7:9
the Israelites **c** out the LORD's Nm 9:19
c out the LORD's requirement Nm 9:23
was **c** on a pole by two men. Nm 13:23
their hands, **c** ⌊it⌋ down to us Dt 1:25
the LORD your God **c** you as a man Dt 1:31
who **c** the ark of the LORD's Dt 31:9
the Levites who **c** the ark of the Dt 31:25
he **c** out the LORD's justice and Dt 33:21
LORD your God **c** by the Levitical Jos 3:3
So they **c** the ark of the Jos 3:6
the priests **c** the ark of the Jos 3:14
They **c** them to the camp and set Jos 4:8
where the priests who **c** the ark Jos 4:9
the LORD was **c** around the city Jos 6:11
the Levitical priests who **c** it. Jos 8:33
time but have **c** out the Jos 22:3
the people who had **c** it. Jdg 3:18
family came down, **c** him back, Jdg 16:31
the attendant who **c** his weapons, 1Sm 14:1
the attendant who **c** his weapons, 1Sm 14:6
has not **c** out My instructions. 1Sm 15:11
I have **c** out the LORD's 1Sm 15:13
or a bear came and **c** off a lamb 1Sm 17:34
one but had **c** them off as they 1Sm 30:2
they **c** Asahel to his father's 2Sm 2:32
David and his men **c** them off. 2Sm 5:21
since you **c** the ark of the Lord 1Kg 2:26
Solomon and **c** out all his work 1Kg 7:14
fleet that **c** gold from Ophir 1Kg 10:11
and they **c** away the stones of 1Kg 15:22
of the LORD has **c** him away and 2Kg 2:16
his young men who **c** them ahead 2Kg 5:23
his servants **c** him to Jerusalem 2Kg 9:28
They **c** him back on horses, 2Kg 14:20
day will be **c** off to Babylon; 2Kg 20:17
the Kidron and **c** their ashes to 2Kg 23:4
his servants **c** his dead body 2Kg 23:30
He also **c** off from there all the 2Kg 24:13
and **c** the bronze to Babylon. 2Kg 25:13
men who **c** shield and sword, 1Ch 5:18
Then the Levites **c** the ark of 1Ch 15:15
gold shields **c** by Hadadezer's 1Ch 18:7
and gold he had **c** off from all 1Ch 18:11
work was **c** out from the day 2Ch 8:16
people of Judah **c** off a great 2Ch 14:13
and they **c** away the stones of 2Ch 16:6
and **c** out great works in the 2Ch 17:13
They **c** off all the possessions 2Ch 21:17
They **c** him back on horses and 2Ch 25:28
of Jerusalem **c** out the covenant 2Ch 34:32
c him in his second chariot, 2Ch 35:24
in Jerusalem and **c** ⌊them⌋ to the Ezr 5:14
Jerusalem and **c** to Babylon must Ezr 6:5
Let it be **c** out diligently. Ezr 6:12
diligently **c** out what King Ezr 6:13
laborers who **c** the loads worked Neh 4:17
Each **c** his weapon, even when Neh 4:23
but had been **c** from the womb to Jb 10:19
is **c** to the grave, and someone Jb 21:32
it will be **c** out, and light will Jb 22:28
act is not **c** out quickly, Ec 8:11
Samaria will be **c** off to the Is 8:4
day will be **c** off to Babylon; Is 39:6
from the womb, **c** along since Is 46:3
daughters will be **c** on their Is 49:22
sicknesses, and He **c** our pains; Is 53:4
daughters will be **c** on the hip. Is 60:4
them up and **c** them all the days Is 63:9
nurse and be **c** on ⌊her⌋ hip, Is 66:12

They must be **c** because they Jr 10:5
having **c** out so many evil Jr 11:15
son of Rechab, have been **c** out. Jr 35:14
son of Rechab **c** out their Jr 35:16
and **c** all the bronze to Babylon. Jr 52:17
and heaven and **c** me in visions Ezk 8:3
Nebuchadnezzar **c** them to the Dn 1:2
The wind **c** them away, and not a Dn 2:35
killed those men who **c** Shadrach, Dn 3:22
He has **c** out His words that He Dn 9:12
When the multitude is **c** off, Dn 11:12
and olive oil is **c** to Egypt. Hs 12:1
and gold and **c** My finest Jl 3:5
is stripped, she is **c** away; Nah 2:7
weaknesses and **c** our diseases. Mt 8:17
the girl, who **c** it to her mother Mt 14:11
a paralytic, **c** by four men. Mk 2:3
a dead man was being **c** out. Lk 7:12
man died and was **c** away by the Lk 16:22
them and was **c** up into heaven. Lk 24:51
womb was **c** there and placed Ac 3:2
his body⌋, **c** him out, and buried Ac 5:6
found her dead, **c** her out, and Ac 5:10
were **c** back to Shechem, and were Ac 7:16
of the Lord **c** Philip away, Ac 8:39
he had to be **c** by the soldiers Ac 21:35
Barnabas was **c** away by their Gl 2:13
clouds **c** along by winds; Jd 12
So he **c** me away in the Spirit to Rv 17:3
He then **c** me away in the Spirit Rv 21:10

CARRIERS *(4)*

and water **c** for the whole Jos 9:21
and water **c** for the house of my Jos 9:23
them woodcutters and water **c**— Jos 9:27
were the **c** for your goods. Ezk 27:25

CARRIES *(12)*

and whoever **c** any of their Lv 11:25
and anyone who **c** their carcasses Lv 11:28
Anyone who **c** its carcass must Lv 11:40
and whoever **c** such things is to Lv 15:10
as a nursing woman **c** a baby,' Nm 11:12
you as a man **c** his son all along Dt 1:31
it **c** him away from his place. Jb 27:21
by the man who **c** out evil plans. Ps 37:7
in His arms and **c** ⌊them⌋ in the Is 40:11
and a whirlwind **c** them away like Is 40:24
wrongdoing and **c** out true Ezk 18:8
and the 10 horns, that **c** her. Rv 17:7

CARRY *(122)*

and He will soon **c** it out. Gn 41:32
with as much food as they can **c**, Gn 44:1
Pharaoh had sent to **c** him, Gn 46:5
c me away from Egypt and bury Gn 47:30
are to **c** my bones up from here. Gn 50:25
you must **c** out this ritual in Ex 13:5
ark in order to **c** the ark with Ex 25:14
for the poles to **c** the table. Ex 25:27
Aaron will **c** their names on his Ex 28:12
Aaron is to **c** the names of Ex 28:29
will continually **c** the ⌊means Ex 28:30
for the poles to **c** it with. Ex 30:4
for the poles to **c** the table. Ex 37:14
for the poles to **c** it with. Ex 37:27
in order to **c** it with them. Ex 38:7
Come here and **c** your relatives Lv 10:4
The goat will **c** on it all their Lv 16:22
and his sons to **c** out their Nm 3:10
Kohathites will come and **c** them, Nm 4:15
They will **c** out everything that Nm 4:26
that they are responsible to **c**. Nm 4:27
responsible to **c** as the whole Nm 4:31
that they are responsible to **c**. Nm 4:32
should tell me, '**C** them at your Nm 11:12
I can't **c** all these people by Nm 11:14
your sons will **c** out your Nm 18:7
the tribe of Levi to **c** the ark Dt 10:8
is too great for you to **c** it, Dt 14:24
son she bears will **c** on the name Dt 25:6
of the priests who **c** the ark of Jos 3:13
are standing, **c** them with you, Jos 4:3
Command the priests who **c** the Jos 4:16
seven priests **c** seven ram's-horn Jos 6:4
seven priests **c** seven trumpets Jos 6:6
so that we may **c** out the worship Jos 22:27
those who **c** a marshal's staff Jdg 5:14
that day I will **c** out against 1Sm 3:12
LORD and did not **c** out His wrath 1Sm 28:18
Should we **c** out his proposal? 2Sm 17:6
the LORD will **c** out His promise 1Kg 2:4
was in him to **c** out justice. 1Kg 3:28
made you king to **c** out justice 1Kg 10:9
My eyes and to **c** out My statutes 1Kg 11:33
from the LORD to **c** out His word, 1Kg 12:15
escorts would **c** the shields, 1Kg 14:28
the LORD may **c** you off to some 1Kg 18:12
his servant, "**C** him to his 2Kg 4:19
and to **c** out the words of this 2Kg 23:3
this in order to **c** out the words 2Kg 23:24
Levites may **c** the ark of God, 1Ch 15:2
has chosen them to **c** the ark of 1Ch 15:2
longer need to **c** the tabernacle 1Ch 23:26
They are to **c** out their 1Ch 23:32
to keep and to **c** out all Your 1Ch 29:19
them as king to **c** out justice 2Ch 9:8
the LORD might **c** out His word 2Ch 10:15
escorts would **c** the shields 2Ch 12:11
ancestors and to **c** out the 2Ch 14:4
until nobody could **c** any more. 2Ch 20:25
one heart to **c** out the command 2Ch 30:12
soul in order to **c** out the words 2Ch 34:31
you do not have to **c** it on your 2Ch 35:3
your brothers to **c** out the word 2Ch 35:6
tomorrow to **c** out today's law Est 9:13
They **c** sheaves but go hungry. Jb 24:10
I would surely **c** it on my Jb 31:36
them, and **c** them forever. Ps 28:9
in my heart I **c** ⌊abuse⌋ from all Ps 89:50
salvation and **c** out Your Ps 119:166
that he can **c** in his hands. Ec 5:15
of the sky may **c** the message, Ec 10:20
seize their prey and **c** ⌊it⌋ off, Is 5:29
So they **c** their wealth and Is 15:7
through, it will **c** you away; Is 28:19
They **c** out a plan, but not Mine, Is 30:1
they **c** their wealth on the backs Is 30:6
and a wind will **c** them away, Is 41:16
Those who **c** their wooden idols, Is 45:20
The ⌊images⌋ you **c** are loaded, Is 46:1
made ⌊you⌋, and I will **c** ⌊you⌋; Is 46:4
you who **c** the vessels of the Is 52:11
and He will **c** their iniquities. Is 53:11
The wind will **c** all of them off, Is 57:13
will **c** gold and frankincense Is 60:6
our iniquities **c** us away like Is 64:6
of this covenant and **c** them out. Jr 11:6
must not **c** a load out of your Jr 17:22
and **c** them off to Babylon. Jr 20:5
conscientiously **c** out this word, Jr 22:4
who will **c** off its wealth, Ezk 29:19
seize spoil and **c** off plunder, Ezk 38:12
your hordes to **c** off plunder, Ezk 38:13
its statutes and may **c** them out. Ezk 43:11
with its wings will **c** them off, Hs 4:19
I will **c** ⌊them⌋ off, and no one Hs 5:14
Those who **c** out His command are Jl 2:11
no offspring to **c** on your name. Nah 1:14
who **c** out what He commands. Zph 2:3
that are hard to **c** and put them Mt 23:4
forced this man to **c** His cross. Mt 27:32
vicinity and began to **c** the sick Mk 6:55
permit anyone to **c** goods through Mk 11:16
passing by, to **c** Jesus' cross. Mk 15:21
Don't **c** a money-bag, traveling Lk 10:4
with burdens that are hard to **c**, Lk 11:46
cross on him to **c** behind Jesus. Lk 23:26
and you want to **c** out your Jn 8:44
will tie you and **c** you where you Jn 21:18
door, and they will **c** you out!" Ac 5:9
they would **c** the sick out into Ac 5:15
instrument to **c** My name before Ac 9:15
who will **c** out all My will.' Ac 13:22
it does not **c** the sword for no Rm 13:4
letter to **c** your gracious gift 1Co 16:3
always **c** the death of Jesus in 2Co 4:10
you will not **c** out the desire Gl 5:16
C one another's burdens; Gl 6:2
will have to **c** his own load. Gl 6:5
because I **c** the marks of Jesus Gl 6:17
work in you will **c** it on to Php 1:6
you really **c** out the royal law Jms 2:8
their hearts to **c** out His plan Rv 17:17

CARRYING *(38)*

camels were **c** aromatic gum, Gn 37:25
donkeys **c** the best products of Gn 45:23
and 10 female donkeys **c** grain, Gn 45:23
sides of the ark for **c** the ark. Ex 37:5
made the poles for **c** the table Ex 37:15
and put ⌊them⌋ on the **c** frame. Nm 4:10
and put ⌊them⌋ on a **c** frame. Nm 4:12
Command the priests **c** the ark of Jos 3:8
as the priests **c** the ark reached Jos 3:15
The priests **c** the ark of the Jos 3:17
The priests **c** the ark continued Jos 4:10
When the priests **c** the ark of Jos 4:18
seven priests **c** seven trumpets Jos 6:8
seven priests **c** seven trumpets Jos 6:13
the staff he was **c** and dipped it 1Sm 14:27
the end of the staff I was **c**. 1Sm 14:43
When those **c** the ark of the LORD 2Sm 6:13
Levites with him were **c** the ark 2Sm 15:24
done well in **c** out what is right 2Kg 10:30
the Levites who were **c** the ark 1Ch 15:26
the Levites who were **c** the ark, 1Ch 15:27
We are **c** out the requirements of 2Ch 13:11
were freed from ⌊**c**⌋ the basket. Ps 81:6
weeping, **c** the bag of seed, Ps 126:6
shouts of joy, **c** his sheaves. Ps 126:6
c out the judgment decreed Ps 149:9
GOD of Hosts is **c** out a Is 10:23
Sabbath day by not **c** a load Jr 17:27
and who were **c** grain and incense Jr 41:5
c ⌊them⌋ on my shoulder in their Ezk 12:7
a man is **c** consecrated meat in Hg 2:12
a man **c** a water jug will meet Mk 14:13
c on a stretcher a man who was Lk 5:18
a man **c** a water jug will meet Lk 22:10
C His own cross, He went out to Jn 19:17
kept them from **c** out their plan Ac 27:43
c out the inclinations of our Eph 2:3
c on in unrestrained behavior, 1Pt 4:3

CARSHENA *(1)*

The most trusted ones were **C**, Est 1:14

CART *(22)*

c from every two leaders and an Nm 7:3
prepare one new **c** and two milk 1Sm 6:7
cows to the **c**, but take their 1Sm 6:7
place it on the **c**, and put the 1Sm 6:8
them to the **c**, and confined 1Sm 6:10
the ark of the LORD on the **c**, 1Sm 6:11
c came to the field of Joshua 1Sm 6:14
chopped up the **c** and offered 1Sm 6:14
God on a new **c** and transported 2Sm 6:3
of Abinadab, were guiding the **c** 2Sm 6:3
Each water **c** was six feet long, 1Kg 7:27
Each **c** had four bronze wheels 1Kg 7:30
axles were part of the water **c**; 1Kg 7:32
four corners of each water **c**; 1Kg 7:34
was one piece with the water **c**. 1Kg 7:34
the top of the **c** was a band nine 1Kg 7:35
at the top of the **c**, its braces 1Kg 7:35
set the ark of God on a new **c**. 1Ch 13:7
and Ahio were guiding the **c**. 1Ch 13:7
pull⌋ sin along with **c** ropes, Is 5:18
and a **c** wheel is not rolled over Is 28:27
of ⌊the farmer's⌋ **c** rumbles, Is 28:28

CART'S *(1)*

And the water **c** opening inside 1Kg 7:31

CARTS *(19)*

LORD six covered **c** and 12 oxen, Nm 7:3
Moses took the **c** and oxen and Nm 7:6
Gershonites two **c** and four oxen Nm 7:7
Merarites four **c** and eight oxen Nm 7:8
Then he made 10 bronze water **c**. 1Kg 7:27
This was the design of the **c**: 1Kg 7:28
the 10 water **c** using the same 1Kg 7:37
for each of the 10 water **c**. 1Kg 7:38
set five water **c** on the right 1Kg 7:39
the 10 water **c**; the 10 basins on 1Kg 7:43
the 10 basins on the water **c**; 1Kg 7:43
of the water **c** and removed 2Kg 16:17
the water **c**, and the bronze 2Kg 25:13
and the water **c** that Solomon had 2Kg 25:16
made the water **c** and the basins 2Ch 4:14
and the basins on the water **c**. 2Ch 4:14
sea, the water **c**, and the rest Jr 27:19
and the water **c** and the bronze Jr 52:17
under the water **c** that King Jr 52:20

CARVE *(4)*

and to **c** wood for work in every Ex 31:5
and to **c** wood for work in every Ex 35:33
They **c** ⌊meat⌋ on the right, Is 9:20
you to **c** out a tomb for Is 22:16

CARVED *(48)*
up a **c** image or sacred pillar Lv 26:1
and burn up their **c** images. Dt 7:5
burn up the **c** images of their Dt 7:25
cut down the **c** images of their Dt 12:3
who makes a **c** idol or cast image Dt 27:15
At the **c** images near Gilgal he Jdg 3:19
Jordan⌋ near the **c** images and Jdg 3:26
to make a **c** image overlaid Jdg 17:3
made it into a **c** image overlaid Jdg 17:4
and a **c** image overlaid with Jdg 18:14
in and took the **c** image overlaid Jdg 18:17
and took the **c** image overlaid Jdg 18:18
idols, and **c** image, and went Jdg 18:20
Danites set up the **c** image for Jdg 18:30
Micah's **c** image that he had Jdg 18:31
the temple was **c** with 1Kg 6:18
He **c** all the surrounding temple 1Kg 6:29
temple walls with **c** engravings— 1Kg 6:29
He **c** cherubim, palm trees and 1Kg 6:32
He **c** cherubim, palm trees and 1Kg 6:35
set up the **c** image of Asherah he 2Kg 21:7
and he **c** cherubim on the walls. 2Ch 3:7
set up a **c** image of the idol 2Ch 33:7
poles and **c** images before he 2Ch 33:19
to all the **c** images that his 2Ch 33:22
Asherah poles, the **c** images, and 2Ch 34:3
Asherah poles, the **c** images, and 2Ch 34:4
and the **c** images to powder. 2Ch 34:7
jealousy with their **c** images. Ps 78:58
who serve **c** images, those who Ps 97:7
pillars that are **c** in the palace Ps 144:12
she has **c** out her seven pillars. Pr 9:1
my **c** image and cast idol control Is 48:5
put to shame by ⌊his⌋ **c** image, Jr 10:14
For it is a land of **c** images, Jr 50:38
put to shame by ⌊his⌋ **c** image, Jr 51:17
will punish Babylon's **c** images. Jr 51:47
when I will punish her **c** images, Jr 51:52
saw male figures **c** on the wall, Ezk 23:14
c with cherubim and palm trees. Ezk 41:18
were **c** throughout the temple Ezk 41:19
trees were **c** from the ground Ezk 41:20
palm trees were **c** on the doors Ezk 41:25
hall like those **c** on the walls. Ezk 41:25
All her **c** images will be smashed Mc 1:7
will remove your **c** images and Mc 5:13
eliminate the **c** idol and cast Nah 1:14
What use is a **c** idol after its Hab 2:18

CARVES *(1)*
idol after its craftsman **c** it? Hab 2:18

CARVING *(2)*
gold applied evenly over the **c**. 1Kg 6:35
c your tomb on the height and Is 22:16

CARVINGS *(2)*
On it were **c**, but their frames 1Kg 7:31
smashing all the **c** with hatchets Ps 74:6

CASCADING *(4)*
water **c** down a mountainside. Mc 1:4
like the sound of **c** waters. Rv 1:15
the sound of **c** waters and like Rv 14:2
like the sound of **c** waters, Rv 19:6

CASE *(90)*
him, "In that **c**, whoever kills Gn 4:15
important **c** but judge every Ex 18:22
judge every minor **c** themselves. Ex 18:22
but every minor **c** they would Ex 18:26
In any **c** of wrongdoing involving Ex 22:9
the **c** between the two parties is Ex 22:9
same in the **c** involving their Nm 25:18
brought their **c** before the LORD, Nm 27:5
Bring me any **c** too difficult for Dt 1:17
If a **c** is too difficult for you Dt 17:8
give you a verdict in the **c**. Dt 17:9
concerning a **c** of someone who Dt 19:4
dispute and ⌊**c** of⌋ assault. Dt 21:5
This **c** is just like one in which Dt 22:26
Be careful in a **c** of infectious Dt 24:8
the judges will hear their **c**. Dt 25:1
and states his **c** before the Jos 20:4
you plead Baal's **c** for him? Jdg 6:31
pleads his **c** will be put to Jdg 6:31
plead his own **c**, because someone Jdg 6:31
"Let Baal plead his **c** with him," Jdg 6:32
for me, as ⌊is the **c**⌋ today." 1Sm 22:8
in ambush, as ⌊is the **c**⌋ today." 1Sm 22:13
and plead my **c** and deliver me 1Sm 24:15
and would present my **c** to Him. Jb 5:8
is not the **c**; I am on my own Jb 9:35
and declare His **c** against you, Jb 11:5
and argue my **c** before God. Jb 13:3
or argue the **c** in His defense? Jb 13:8
then, I have prepared ⌊my⌋ **c**; Jb 13:18
would plead my **c** before Him and Jb 23:4
examined the **c** of the stranger. Jb 29:16
have dismissed the **c** of my male Jb 31:13
I had someone to hear my ⌊**c**⌋! Jb 31:35
Prepare your **c** against me; Jb 33:5
Would I lie about my **c**? Jb 34:6
⌊that your⌋ **c** is before Him and Jb 35:14
prepare ⌊our **c**⌋ because of our Jb 37:19
I plead my **c** to You and watch Ps 5:3
and lay out the **c** before you. Ps 50:21
to state his **c** seems right until Pr 18:17
take up their **c** and will plunder Pr 22:23
take up their **c** against you. Pr 23:11
Make your **c** with your opponent Pr 25:9
and the widow's **c** never comes Is 1:23
to argue the **c** and stands to Is 3:13
"Submit your **c**," says the LORD. Is 41:21
let us argue our **c** together. Is 43:26
State your ⌊**c**⌋, so that you may Is 43:26
say so and make a **c** before Me, Is 44:7
Speak up and present ⌊your **c**⌋— Is 45:21
Who has a **c** against Me? Is 50:8
I will bring a **c** against you Jr 2:9
I will bring a **c** against your Jr 2:9
Why do you bring a **c** against Me? Jr 2:29
such as the **c** of orphans, so Jr 5:28
I have presented my **c** to You. Jr 11:20
even if I bring a **c** against You. Jr 12:1
I have presented my **c** to You. Jr 20:12
He took up the **c** of the poor and Jr 22:16
the LORD brings a **c** against the Jr 25:31
takes up the **c** for your sores. Jr 30:13
Yourself, as ⌊is the **c**⌋ today. Jr 32:20
plead their **c** so that He might Jr 50:34
to plead your **c** and take Jr 51:36
wrong done to me; judge my **c**. Lm 3:59
and decide the **c** according to My Ezk 44:24
for the LORD has a **c** against the Hs 4:1
for My **c** is against you priests. Hs 4:4
Is this not the **c**, Israelites? Am 2:11
plead ⌊your⌋ **c** before the Mc 6:1
the LORD has a **c** against His Mc 6:2
He argues my **c** and establishes Mc 7:9
except in a **c** of sexual Mt 5:32
in this **c** the saying is true: Jn 4:37
him have a **c** against anyone, Ac 19:38
his **c** more thoroughly Ac 23:15
to state their **c** against him in Ac 23:30
presented their **c** against Paul Ac 24:1
down, I will decide your **c**." Ac 24:22
presented their **c** against Paul Ac 25:2
presented Paul's **c** to the king, Ac 25:14
presented their **c** and asked for Ac 25:15
glorious in this **c** because of 2Co 3:10
In that **c** the offense of the Gl 5:11
In any **c**, we should live up to Php 3:16
your **c** we are confident of the Heb 6:9
In the one **c**, men who will die Heb 7:8
but in the other **c**, ⌊Scripture⌋ Heb 7:8
so that in a **c** where they speak 1Pt 2:12

CASES *(11)*
God and bring their **c** to Him. Ex 18:19
the hard **c** they would bring to Ex 18:26
incurs guilt in one of these **c**, Lv 5:5
has committed in any of these **c**, Lv 5:13
Hear ⌊the **c**⌋ between your Dt 1:16
or assaults—**c** disputed at your Dt 17:8
not taken up **c**, such as the case Jr 5:28
to judge the smallest **c**? 1Co 6:2
So if you have **c** pertaining to 1Co 6:4
a sister is not bound in such **c**. 1Co 7:15
good works for **c** of urgent need, Ti 3:14

CASINGS *(1)*
seeds lie shriveled in their **c**. Jl 1:17

CASIPHIA *(2)*
the leader at **C**, with a message Ezr 8:17
servants at **C**, that they should Ezr 8:17

CASLUHIM *(2)*
Pathrusim, **C** (the Philistines Gn 10:14
Pathrusim, **C** (the Philistines 1Ch 1:12

CASSIA *(3)*
12 and a half pounds of **c** Ex 30:24
and **c** ⌊perfume⌋ all your Ps 45:8
wrought iron, **c**, and aromatic Ezk 27:19

CAST *(79)*
C four gold rings for it and Ex 25:12
and you are to **c** five bronze Ex 26:37
Do not make **c** images of gods for Ex 34:17
And he **c** four silver bases for Ex 36:36
c four gold rings for it to be Ex 37:3
He **c** four gold rings for it and Ex 37:13
bronze grate he **c** four rings as Ex 38:5
of silver ⌊used⌋ to **c** the bases Ex 38:27
idols or make **c** images of gods Lv 19:4
their stone images and **c** images, Nm 33:52
they have made a **c** image for Dt 9:12
c spells, consult a medium or a Dt 18:11
makes a carved idol or **c** image, Dt 27:15
will **c** lots for you here in the Jos 18:6
I will then **c** lots for you here Jos 18:8
Joshua **c** lots for them at Shiloh Jos 18:10
C ⌊the lot⌋ between me and my 1Sm 14:42
c two ⌊hollow⌋ bronze pillars: 1Kg 7:15
two capitals of **c** bronze to set 1Kg 7:16
He made the **c** ⌊metal⌋ reservoir, 1Kg 7:23
The gourds were **c** in two rows 1Kg 7:24
rows when the reservoir was **c**. 1Kg 7:24
of the basin were **c** supports, 1Kg 7:30
and hubs were all of **c** metal. 1Kg 7:33
king had them **c** in clay molds 1Kg 7:46
other gods and **c** images, 1Kg 14:9
They also **c** lots the same way as 1Ch 24:31
c lots impartially for their 1Ch 25:8
They **c** lots according to their 1Ch 26:13
They also **c** lots for his son 1Ch 26:14
Then he made the **c** ⌊metal⌋ 2Ch 4:2
The oxen were **c** in two rows when 2Ch 4:3
rows when the reservoir was **c**. 2Ch 4:3
king had them **c** in clay molds 2Ch 4:17
of Israel and made **c** images of 2Ch 28:2
carved images, and the **c** images. 2Ch 34:3
and the **c** images he shattered, 2Ch 34:4
after they had **c** an image of a Neh 9:18
have **c** lots among the priests, Neh 10:34
of the people **c** lots for one out Neh 11:1
was **c** before Haman for each day Est 3:7
He **c** the Pur (that is, the lot) Est 9:24
certain⌋ days **c** a spell on it, Jb 3:8
No doubt you would **c** ⌊lots⌋ for Jb 6:27
they have **c** off restraint in my Jb 30:11
if I ever **c** my vote against a Jb 31:21
as hard as a **c** metal mirror? Jb 37:18
dust hardens like **c** metal and Jb 38:38
and they **c** lots for my clothing. Ps 22:18
C your burden on the LORD, Ps 55:22
and worshiped the **c** metal image. Ps 106:19
The lot is **c** into the lap, Pr 16:33
All those who **c** hooks into the Is 19:8
carved image and **c** idol control Is 48:5
for his **c** images are a lie; Jr 10:14
hurled out and **c** into a land Jr 22:28
for his **c** images are a lie; Jr 51:17
forgotten Me and **c** Me behind Ezk 23:35
should not be **c** for its contents Ezk 24:6
and make themselves a **c** image, Hs 13:2
They **c** lots for My people; Jl 3:3
his gate and **c** lots for Ob 11
other. "Let's **c** lots. Then we Jnh 1:7
So they **c** lots, and the lot Jnh 1:7
You will **c** all our sins into the Mc 7:19
the carved idol and **c** image from Nah 1:14
They **c** lots for her dignitaries, Nah 3:10
is ⌊only⌋ a **c** image, a teacher Hab 2:18
impoverish her and **c** her wealth Zch 9:4
go to the sea, **c** in a fishhook, Mt 17:27
divided His clothes and **c** lots. Lk 23:34
comes to Me I will never **c** out. Jn 6:37
of this world will be **c** out. Jn 12:31
and they **c** lots for My clothing. Jn 19:24
C the net on the right side of Jn 21:6
Then they **c** lots for them, Ac 1:26
to death, I **c** my vote against Ac 26:10
or shadow **c** by turning. Jms 1:17
c their crowns before the throne, Rv 4:10

CASTING *(9)*
10 water carts using the same **c**, 1Kg 7:37
⌊**C**⌋ the lot ends quarrels and Pr 18:18
to divide the land by **c** lots. Mc 2:5

They were **c** a net into the sea, Mt 4:18
divided His clothes by **c** lots. Mt 27:35
They were **c** a net into the sea, Mk 1:16
c lots for them to decide what Mk 15:24
After **c** off the anchors, they Ac 27:40
c all your care upon Him, 1Pt 5:7

CASTRATED *(1)*
you might also get themselves **c**! Gl 5:12

CASTS *(4)*
After Aaron **c** lots for the two Lv 16:8
vengeance and **c** down peoples 2Sm 22:48
⌊something that⌋ a smelter **c**, Is 40:19
makes a god or **c** a metal image Is 44:10

CASUALTIES *(1)*
was vast that day—20,000 ⌊**c**⌋. 2Sm 18:7

CATAPULT *(1)*
arrows and ⌊**c**⌋ large stones for 2Ch 26:15

CATASTROPHES *(1)*
in insults, in **c**, in 2Co 12:10

CATASTROPHIC *(1)*
rise, for he has done **c** things. Jl 2:20

CATCH *(16)*
your sin will **c** up with you. Nm 32:23
and you can **c** up with them!" Jos 2:5
the vineyards and **c** a wife for Jdg 21:21
you can **c** up with him before he 1Sm 9:13
doesn't let me **c** my breath but Jb 9:18
chase him and **c** him, for there Ps 71:11
C the foxes for us—the little Sg 2:15
You did not **c** them breaking and Jr 2:34
They set a trap; they **c** men. Jr 5:26
her lovers but not **c** them; Hs 2:7
up with a hook, **c** them in their Hab 1:15
and **c** the first fish that comes Mt 17:27
and let down your nets for a **c**." Lk 5:4
amazed at the **c** of fish they Lk 5:9
so they could **c** Him in what He Lk 20:20
were not able to **c** Him in what Lk 20:26

CATCHES *(4)*
His wings, **c** him, and lifts him Dt 32:11
lion dies if ⌊it **c**⌋ no prey, Jb 4:11
A trap **c** ⌊him⌋ by the heel; Jb 18:9
c the wise in their craftiness 1Co 3:19

CATCHING *(1)*
now on you will be **c** people!" Lk 5:10

CATERPILLAR *(1)*
crops to the **c** and the fruit Ps 78:46

CATTLE *(90)*
took sheep and **c** and male and Gn 20:14
took sheep and **c** and gave them Gn 21:27
He has given him sheep and **c**, Gn 24:35
sheep, herds of **c**, and many Gn 26:14
with the flocks, **c**, and camels. Gn 32:7
and I have nursing sheep and **c**. Gn 33:13
himself and stalls for his **c**; Gn 33:17
were with his **c** in the field, Gn 34:5
took their sheep, **c**, donkeys, Gn 34:28
your sheep, **c**, and all you have. Gn 45:10
took their **c** and possessions Gn 46:6
their sheep and **c** and all that Gn 46:32
their sheep and **c** and all that Gn 47:1
the herds of **c**, and the donkeys. Gn 47:17
their **c** were left in the land Gn 50:8
and goats, as well as your **c**. Ex 20:24
must repay five **c** for the ox or Ex 22:1
same with your **c** and your flock. Ex 22:30
the firstborn of **c** or sheep. Ex 34:19
an unblemished male from the **c**, Lv 22:19
and the Levites' **c** in place of Nm 3:41
among the Israelites' **c**." Nm 3:41
and the Levites' **c** in place of Nm 3:45
cattle in place of their **c**. Nm 3:45
Balak sacrificed **c** and sheep, Nm 22:40
and they plundered all their **c**, Nm 31:9
500 humans, **c**, donkeys, sheep, Nm 31:28
the people, **c**, donkeys, sheep Nm 31:30
72,000 **c**, Nm 31:33
from the 36,000 **c**, the tribute Nm 31:38
36,000 **c**, Nm 31:44
c, sheep, wine, beer, or Dt 14:26
only the **c** and spoil of that Jos 8:27
the spoils and **c** of these cities Jos 11:14
for their **c** and livestock. Jos 14:4
a huge number of **c**, and silver, Jos 22:8
with their **c** and their tents Jdg 6:5
took sheep, **c**, and calves, 1Sm 14:32
of the sheep, **c**, and fatlings, 1Sm 15:9
sound of sheep and **c** I hear?" 1Sm 15:14
best sheep and **c** in order to 1Sm 15:15
sheep and **c** from the plunder 1Sm 15:21
He took all the sheep and **c**, 1Sm 30:20
a large number of sheep and **c**, 2Sm 12:2
own sheep or **c** to prepare for 2Sm 12:4
and fattened **c** near the stone of 1Kg 1:9
oxen, fattened **c**, and sheep. 1Kg 1:19
oxen, fattened **c**, and sheep. 1Kg 1:25
sheep and **c** that could not be 1Kg 8:5
22,000 **c** and 120,000 sheep. 1Kg 8:63
and not have to destroy any **c**." 1Kg 18:5
and your **c** and your animals.' 2Kg 3:17
they went down to raid their **c**. 1Ch 7:21
the property and **c** of the king 1Ch 28:1
sheep and **c** that could not be 2Ch 5:6
of 22,000 **c** and 120,000 sheep. 2Ch 7:5
the LORD 700 **c** and 7,000 sheep 2Ch 15:11
many sheep and **c** for him and for 2Ch 18:2
Since he had many **c** both in the 2Ch 26:10
a tenth of the **c** and sheep, 2Ch 31:6
and stalls for all kinds of **c**, 2Ch 32:28
of sheep and **c** in abundance, 2Ch 32:29
we regarded as **c**, as stupid in Jb 18:3
the **c** also, the approaching Jb 36:33
the **c** on a thousand hills. Ps 50:10
to hail and their **c** to lightning Ps 78:48
Our **c** will be well fed. Ps 144:14
animals and all **c**, creatures Ps 148:10
many herds of **c** and flocks, Ec 2:7
rams and the fat of well-fed **c**; Is 1:11
butchering of **c**, slaughtering of Is 22:13
On that day your **c** will graze in Is 30:23
are consigned to beasts and **c**. Is 46:1
Like **c** that go down into the Is 63:14
Achor a place for **c** to lie down, Is 65:10
The sound of **c** is no longer Jr 9:10
massive herds of **c** will become Jr 49:32
all its **c** that are beside Ezk 32:13
and no **c** hooves will disturb Ezk 32:13
been acquiring **c** and possessions Ezk 38:12
to take **c** and possessions, Ezk 38:13
on grass like **c** and be drenched Dn 4:25
on grass like **c** for seven Dn 4:32
ate grass like **c**, and his body Dn 4:33
fed grass like **c**, and his body Dn 5:21
The herds of **c** wander in Jl 1:18
offerings of fattened **c**. Am 5:22
the pen and no **c** in the stalls, Hab 3:17
my oxen and fattened **c** have been Mt 22:4
and grain; **c** and sheep; horses Rv 18:13

CAUDA *(1)*
of a little island called **C**, Ac 27:16

CAUGHT *(50)*
up and saw a ram **c** by its horns Gn 22:13
stretched out his hand and **c** it, Ex 4:4
after them and **c** up with them as Ex 14:9
If a thief is **c** in the act of Ex 22:2
the thief, if **c**, must repay Ex 22:7
If the thief is not **c**, the owner Ex 22:8
and she wasn't **c** ⌊in the act⌋; Nm 5:13
fish in the sea were **c** for them, Nm 11:22
The one who is **c** with the things Jos 7:15
So Joshua **c** them by surprise, Jos 10:9
So he went out and **c** 300 foxes. Jdg 15:4
it mobilized and **c** up with the Jdg 18:22
needed from the dancers they **c**. Jdg 21:23
the archers **c** up with him and 1Sm 31:3
head was **c** fast in the tree. 2Sm 18:9
So, you have **c** me, my enemy." 1Kg 21:20
I have **c** you because you devoted 1Kg 21:20
my ears **c** a whisper of it. Jb 4:12
wronged me and **c** me in His net. Jb 19:6
their foot is **c** in the net they Ps 9:15
them be **c** in the schemes they Ps 10:2
so let them be **c** in their pride. Ps 59:12
Still, if **c**, he must pay seven Pr 6:31
An evil man is **c** by sin, but the Pr 29:6
a lizard can be **c** in your hands, Pr 30:28
like fish **c** in a cruel net, Ec 9:12
or like birds **c** in a trap, Ec 9:12
and whoever is **c** will die by the Is 13:15
the pit will be **c** in a snare. Is 24:18
shame of a thief when he is **c**, Jr 2:26
and you were **c**, but you did not Jr 50:24
and he will be **c** in My snare. Ezk 12:13
him, he was **c** in their pit. Ezk 19:4
he was **c** in their pit. Ezk 19:8
ground when it has **c** nothing? Am 3:5
out His hand, **c** hold of him, and Mt 14:31
Him. They **c** hold of him, Mk 14:51
all night long and **c** nothing! Lk 5:5
they **c** a great number of fish, Lk 5:6
brought a woman **c** in adultery, Jn 8:3
this woman was **c** in the act of Jn 8:4
but that night they **c** nothing. Jn 21:3
some of the fish you've just **c**," Jn 21:10
the ship was **c** and was unable to Ac 27:15
Christ who was **c** up into the 2Co 12:2
was **c** up into paradise. 2Co 12:4
if someone is **c** in any Gl 6:1
alive will be **c** up together with 1Th 4:17
born to be **c** and destroyed— 2Pt 2:12
her child was **c** up to God and to Rv 12:5

CAUSE *(105)*
and I will **c** you to prosper,' Gn 32:9
said, 'I will **c** you to prosper, Gn 32:12
did you **c** me so much trouble? Gn 43:6
May God Almighty **c** the man to be Gn 43:14
and **c** the frogs to come up onto Ex 8:5
place where I **c** My name to be Ex 20:24
I will **c** the people ahead of you Ex 23:27
I will **c** all My goodness to pass Ex 33:19
their gods and **c** your sons to Ex 34:16
fever that will **c** your eyes to Lv 26:16
enter her and **c** bitter suffering Nm 5:24
enter her and **c** bitter suffering Nm 5:27
end He might **c** you to prosper. Dt 8:16
The LORD will **c** the enemies who Dt 28:7
The LORD will **c** you to be Dt 28:25
until they **c** you to perish. Dt 28:51
was glad to **c** you to prosper Dt 28:63
also be glad to **c** you to perish Dt 28:63
He will **c** you to prosper and Dt 30:5
He fights for his **c** with his own Dt 33:7
may **c** our descendants Jos 22:25
intended to **c** David's death at 1Sm 18:25
championed my **c** against Nabal's 1Sm 25:39
that Joab shed without just **c**. 1Kg 2:31
in heaven and uphold their **c**. 1Kg 8:45
and petition and uphold their **c**. 1Kg 8:49
His servant's **c** and the cause of 1Kg 8:59
cause and the **c** of His people 1Kg 8:59
land where I will **c** him to fall 2Kg 19:7
I will never again **c** the feet of 2Kg 21:8
so that I will not **c** any pain." 1Ch 4:10
in heaven and uphold their **c**. 2Ch 6:35
petitions and uphold their **c**. 2Ch 6:39
the women and **c** them to despise Est 1:17
to destroy him without just **c**." Jb 2:3
multiplies my wounds without **c**. Jb 9:17
from your brothers without **c**, Jb 22:6
wasteland and **c** the grass to Jb 38:27
my adversary without **c**, Ps 7:4
For You have upheld my just **c**; Ps 9:4
hear a just **c**; pay attention to Ps 17:1
without **c** will be disgraced. Ps 25:3
hid their net for me without **c**; Ps 35:7
they dug a pit for me without **c**. Ps 35:7
who hate me without **c** look at me Ps 35:19
defense, to my **c**, my God and my Ps 35:23
and defend my **c** against an Ps 43:1
triumphantly in the **c** of truth, Ps 45:4
I will **c** your name to be Ps 45:17
pleasure, **c** Zion to prosper; Ps 51:18
hate me without **c** are more Ps 69:4
Arise, God, defend Your **c**! Ps 74:22
words and attack me without **c**. Ps 109:3
Defend my **c**, and redeem me; Ps 119:154
have persecuted me without **c**, Ps 119:161
their lips **c** overwhelm ⌊them⌋. Ps 140:9
upholds the just **c** of the poor, Ps 140:12
Don't accuse anyone without **c**, Pr 3:30
against your neighbor without **c**. Pr 24:28
defend the **c** of the oppressed Pr 31:9
and don't persist in a bad **c**, Ec 8:3
fatherless. Plead the widow's **c**. Is 1:17
Only terror will **c** you to Is 28:19
and without **c** deprive the Is 29:21
where I will **c** him to fall by Is 37:7
oppressed them without **c**. Is 52:4
Lord GOD will **c** righteousness Is 61:11
by them or I will **c** you to cower Jr 1:17
they make plans to **c** My people Jr 23:27

destroy, and to **c** disaster, so Jr 31:28
at that time I will **c** a Branch Jr 33:15
this land and **c** it to be without Jr 36:29
to the terror you **c**, your Jr 49:16
You defend my **c**, Lord; Lm 3:58
was not without **c** that I have Ezk 14:23
I **c** the green tree to wither and Ezk 17:24
that day I will **c** a horn to Ezk 29:21
will **c** all the birds of the sky Ezk 32:4
I will **c** many nations to be Ezk 32:10
wicked person **c** him to stumble Ezk 33:12
I will **c** people, My people Ezk 36:12
will no longer **c** your nation to Ezk 36:15
within you and **c** you to follow Ezk 36:27
I will **c** the cities to be Ezk 36:33
I will **c** breath to enter you, Ezk 37:5
He will **c** terrible destruction Dn 8:24
He will **c** deceit to prosper Dn 8:25
arrogant and **c** tens of thousands Dn 11:12
I will **c** everyone to wear Am 8:10
is destined to **c** the fall and Lk 2:34
than for him to **c** one of these Lk 17:2
we should not **c** difficulties for Ac 15:19
did what is good **c** my death? Rm 7:13
for a man to **c** stumbling by what Rm 14:20
out for those who **c** dissensions Rm 16:17
so that I won't **c** my brother to 1Co 8:13
together and not **c** judgment. 1Co 11:34
For if I **c** you pain, then who 2Co 2:2
may **c** thanksgiving to overflow 2Co 4:15
now on, let no one **c** me trouble, Gl 6:17
seeking to **c** ⌊me⌋ trouble in my Php 1:17
inflated without **c** by his Col 2:18
may the Lord **c** you to increase 1Th 3:12
and there is no **c** for stumbling 1Jn 2:10
both speak and **c** whoever would Rv 13:15

CAUSED *(64)*
LORD God **c** to grow out of the Gn 2:9
the LORD God **c** a deep sleep to Gn 2:21
c by the ground the LORD has Gn 5:29
God **c** a wind to pass over the Gn 8:1
us for all the wrong we **c** him." Gn 50:15
sin—the wrong they **c** you.' Gn 50:17
why have You **c** trouble for this Ex 5:22
name he has **c** trouble for this Ex 5:23
He **c** their chariot wheels to Ex 14:25
yet God **c** it to happen by his Ex 21:13
c desolation as far as Nophah, Nm 21:30
who went with me **c** the people's Jos 14:8
Wherever he turned, he **c** havoc. 1Sm 14:47
to the trouble Hadad ⌊had **c**⌋. 1Kg 11:25
the sin that **c** it to be wiped 1Kg 13:34
and **c** Israel to commit. 1Kg 14:16
the sin he had **c** Israel to 1Kg 15:26
and had **c** Israel to commit 1Kg 15:30
the sin he had **c** Israel to 1Kg 15:34
and have **c** My people Israel 1Kg 16:2
committed and **c** Israel to commit 1Kg 16:13
and the sin he **c** Israel to 1Kg 16:19
and the sins he **c** Israel to 1Kg 16:26
My⌋ anger and **c** Israel to sin. 1Kg 21:22
Nebat, who had **c** Israel to sin. 1Kg 22:52
of Nebat had **c** Israel to commit 2Kg 3:3
the Lord had **c** the Aramean camp 2Kg 7:6
of Nebat had **c** Israel to commit 2Kg 10:29
Jeroboam had **c** Israel to commit 2Kg 10:31
of Nebat had **c** Israel to commit 2Kg 13:2
of Jeroboam had **c** Israel to 2Kg 13:6
of Nebat had **c** Israel to commit 2Kg 13:11
of Nebat had **c** Israel to commit 2Kg 14:24
of Nebat had **c** Israel to commit 2Kg 15:9
of Nebat had **c** Israel to commit 2Kg 15:18
of Nebat had **c** Israel to commit 2Kg 15:24
of Nebat had **c** Israel to commit 2Kg 15:28
the LORD and **c** them to commit 2Kg 17:21
Manasseh **c** them to stray so that 2Kg 21:9
idols has also **c** Judah to sin, 2Kg 21:11
to his sin he **c** Judah to commit 2Kg 21:16
of Nebat, who **c** Israel to sin, 2Kg 23:15
and the LORD **c** all the nations 1Ch 14:17
and he **c** the inhabitants of 2Ch 21:11
have **c** Judah and the inhabitants 2Ch 21:13
So Manasseh **c** Judah and the 2Ch 33:9
May the God who **c** His name to Ezr 6:12
c the poor to cry out to Him, Jb 34:28
You **c** me to experience many Ps 71:20
into blood and **c** their fish to Ps 105:29
c them to be pitied before all Ps 106:46
He has **c** His wonderful works to Ps 111:4
this the man who **c** the earth to Is 14:16
claim: My idol **c** them; my carved Is 48:5
are glad that You have **c** ⌊it⌋. Lm 1:21
though I have not **c** him grief, Ezk 13:22
The waters **c** it to grow; Ezk 31:4
c grieving on the day the cedar Ezk 31:15
I **c** the stench of your camp to Am 4:10
You have **c** many to stumble by Mal 2:8
If anyone has **c** pain, he has not 2Co 2:5
pain, he has not **c** pain to me, 2Co 2:5
the Spirit He has **c** to live in Jms 4:5
like the torment **c** by a scorpion Rv 9:5

CAUSES *(33)*
He **c** this to happen for Jb 37:13
c the springs to gush into the Ps 104:10
He **c** grass to grow for the Ps 104:14
He **c** the hungry to settle there, Ps 107:36
He **c** the clouds to rise from the Ps 135:7
c grass to grow on the hills. Ps 147:8
A sly wink of the eye **c** grief, Pr 10:10
but a wife who **c** shame is like Pr 12:4
and a flattering mouth **c** ruin. Pr 26:28
he stands up for noble **c**. Is 32:8
the cup that ⌊**c** people⌋ to Is 51:17
and fire **c** water to boil— Is 64:2
and He **c** the clouds to rise from Jr 10:13
and He **c** the clouds to rise from Jr 51:16
Even if He **c** suffering, He will Lm 3:32
block that **c** your punishment. Ezk 18:30
a cup that **c** staggering for Zch 12:2
If your right eye **c** you to sin, Mt 5:29
if your right hand **c** you to sin, Mt 5:30
immorality, **c** her to commit Mt 5:32
For He **c** His sun to rise on the Mt 5:45
everything that **c** sin and those Mt 13:41
But whoever **c** the downfall of Mt 18:6
or your foot **c** your downfall, Mt 18:8
And if your eye **c** your downfall, Mt 18:9
abomination that **c** desolation, Mt 24:15
But whoever **c** the downfall of Mk 9:42
if your hand **c** your downfall, Mk 9:43
if your foot **c** your downfall, Mk 9:45
And if your eye **c** your downfall, Mk 9:47
abomination that **c** desolation Mk 13:14
if food **c** my brother to fall, 1Co 8:13
A stone that **c** men to stumble, 1Pt 2:8

CAUSING *(9)*
why are you **c** the people to Ex 5:4
c ⌊your⌋ belly to swell and Nm 5:22
stone capable of **c** death and he Nm 35:17
capable of **c** death and he dies Nm 35:18
city of Gath, **c** a great panic. 1Sm 5:9
detestable act **c** Judah to sin! Jr 32:35
with anyone or **c** a disturbance Ac 24:12
springs up, **c** trouble and by it, Heb 12:15
even **c** fire to come down from Rv 13:13

CAUTIOUS *(1)*
A wise man is **c** and turns from Pr 14:16

CAVALRY *(16)*
chariots and the **c** were closing 2Sm 1:6
chariots, **c**, and 50 men to run 1Kg 1:5
chariot cities, the **c** cities, 1Kg 9:19
of his chariots and his **c**. 1Kg 9:22
escaped on a horse with the **c**. 1Kg 20:20
and attacked the **c** and the 1Kg 20:21
chariot cities, the **c** cities, 2Ch 8:6
of his chariots and his **c**. 2Ch 8:9
for infantry and **c** to protect us Ezr 8:22
of the infantry and **c** with me. Neh 2:9
Rise up, you **c**! Race furiously, Jr 46:9
horses, chariots, **c**, and a vast Ezk 26:7
will shake from the noise of **c**, Ezk 26:10
or war, or by horses and **c**. Hs 1:7
ready with 70 **c** and 200 spearmen Ac 23:23
the **c** to go on with him. Ac 23:32

CAVALRYMEN *(1)*
chariots, 60,000 **c**, and 2Ch 12:3

CAVE *(34)*
his two daughters lived in a **c**. Gn 19:30
to give me the **c** of Machpelah Gn 23:9
I give you the **c** that is in it. Gn 23:11
field with its **c** and all the Gn 23:17
Sarah in the **c** of the field at Gn 23:19
The field with its **c** passed from Gn 23:20
him in the **c** of Machpelah near Gn 25:9
my fathers in the **c** in the field Gn 49:29
The **c** is in the field of Gn 49:30
The field and the **c** in it ⌊were Gn 49:32
buried him in the **c** at Machpelah Gn 50:13
themselves in the **c** at Makkedah. Jos 10:16
hiding in the **c** at Makkedah." Jos 10:17
against the mouth of the **c**, Jos 10:18
mouth of the **c**, and bring those Jos 10:22
Eglon to Joshua out of the **c**. Jos 10:23
thrown into the **c** where they had Jos 10:27
against the mouth of the **c**, Jos 10:27
and stayed in the **c** at the rock Jdg 15:8
Judah went to the **c** at the rock Jdg 15:11
took refuge in the **c** of Adullam. 1Sm 22:1
the road, a **c** was there, and he 1Sm 24:3
staying in the back of the **c**, 1Sm 24:3
Saul left the **c** and went on his 1Sm 24:7
went out of the **c**, and called to 1Sm 24:8
you over to me today in the **c**. 1Sm 24:10
to David at the **c** of Adullam, 2Sm 23:13
them, 50 men to a **c**, and 1Kg 18:4
50 men to a **c**, and I provided 1Kg 18:13
He entered a **c** there and spent 1Kg 19:9
stood at the entrance of the **c**. 1Kg 19:13
to the rock at the **c** of Adullam, 1Ch 11:15
nests inside the mouth of a **c**. Jr 48:28
was a **c**, and a stone was lying Jn 11:38

CAVES *(10)*
the mountains, **c**, and Jdg 6:2
They hid in **c**, thickets, among 1Sm 13:6
in one of the **c** or some other 2Sm 17:9
Because of laziness the roof **c** Ec 10:18
will go into **c** in the rocks Is 2:19
will go into the **c** of the rocks Is 2:21
strongholds and **c** will die by Ezk 33:27
pasturelands with **c** for Zph 2:6
deserts, mountains, **c**, and holes Heb 11:38
person hid in the **c** and among Rv 6:15

CEASE *(18)*
and day and night will not **c**." Gn 8:22
thunder will **c**, and there will Ex 9:29
there will never **c** to be poor Dt 15:11
should the work **c** while I leave Neh 6:3
the wicked **c** to make trouble Jb 3:17
He makes wars **c** throughout the Ps 46:9
made his splendor **c** and have Ps 89:44
lawsuits and dishonor will **c**. Pr 22:10
women who grind **c** because they Ec 12:3
Ephraim's envy will **c**; Is 11:13
They will **c** to follow the Jr 3:17
of drought or **c** producing fruit. Jr 17:8
descendants will **c** to be a Jr 31:36
day and night **c** to come at their Jr 33:20
and the stars **c** their shining. Jl 2:10
the stars will **c** their shining. Jl 3:15
There will **c** to be a king in Zch 9:5
as for languages, they will **c**; 1Co 13:8

CEASED *(13)*
Then the thunder and hail **c**, Ex 9:33
and thunder had **c**, he sinned Ex 9:34
of the land, the manna **c**. Jos 5:12
Has His faithful love **c** forever? Ps 77:8
The joyful tambourines have **c**. Is 24:8
The joyful lyre has **c**. Is 24:8
travel has **c**. An agreement has Is 33:8
the time we **c** to burn incense Jr 44:18
got into the boat, the wind **c**. Mt 14:32
The wind **c**, and there was a Mk 4:39
Instantly her flow of blood **c**, Mk 5:29
boat with them, and the wind **c**. Mk 6:51
So they **c**, and there was a calm. Lk 8:24

CEASES *(1)*
otherwise grace **c** to be grace. Rm 11:6

CEASING *(1)*
the LORD by **c** to pray for you. 1Sm 12:23

CEDAR *(53)*
clean birds, **c** wood, scarlet Lv 14:4
bird together with the **c** wood, Lv 14:6
take two birds, **c** wood, scarlet Lv 14:49
will take the **c** wood, the hyssop Lv 14:51
live bird, the **c** wood, the Lv 14:52
The priest is to take **c** wood, Nm 19:6
⌊he also sent⌋ **c** logs, 2Sm 5:11
I am living in a **c** house while 2Sm 7:2
you built Me a house of **c**?' 2Sm 7:7
from the **c** in Lebanon to the 1Kg 4:33
regarding the **c** and cypress 1Kg 5:8
all the **c** and cypress timber 1Kg 5:10

it with boards and planks of **c**. 1Kg 6:9
to the temple with **c** beams; 1Kg 6:10
temple walls with **c** boards; 1Kg 6:15
of the temple with **c** boards from 1Kg 6:16
The **c** paneling inside the temple 1Kg 6:18
Everything was **c**; not a stone 1Kg 6:18
He also overlaid the **c** altar. 1Kg 6:20
and a row of trimmed **c** beams. 1Kg 6:36
high on four rows of **c** pillars, 1Kg 7:2
with **c** beams on top of the 1Kg 7:2
paneled above with **c** at the top 1Kg 7:3
paneled with **c** from the floor 1Kg 7:7
cut to size, as well as **c** wood. 1Kg 7:11
and a row of trimmed **c** beams. 1Kg 7:12
him with **c** and cypress logs 1Kg 9:11
and he made **c** as abundant as 1Kg 10:27
a message⌋ to the **c** that was in 2Kg 14:9
along with **c** logs, stonemasons 1Ch 14:1
I am living in a **c** house while 1Ch 17:1
you built Me a house of **c**?' 1Ch 17:6
and innumerable **c** logs, because 1Ch 22:4
quantity of **c** logs to David. 1Ch 22:4
and he made **c** as abundant as 2Ch 1:15
Also, send me **c**, cypress, and 2Ch 2:8
and he made **c** as abundant as 2Ch 9:27
a message⌋ to the **c** that was in 2Ch 25:18
they could bring **c** wood from Ezr 3:7
stiffens his tail like a **c** tree; Jb 40:17
grow like a **c** tree in Lebanon Ps 92:12
will enclose it with **c** planks. Sg 8:9
be paneled with **c** and painted Jr 22:14
a king because you excel in **c**? Jr 22:15
and took the top of the **c**. Ezk 17:3
top of the **c** and plant ⌊it⌋. Ezk 17:22
fruit, and become a majestic **c**. Ezk 17:23
They took a **c** from Lebanon to Ezk 27:5
of Assyria, a **c** in Lebanon, with Ezk 31:3
Therefore the **c** became greater Ezk 31:5
on the day the **c** went down to Ezk 31:15
for He will expose the **c** work. Zph 2:14
cypress, for the **c** has fallen; Zch 11:2

CEDARS *(24)*
planted, like **c** beside the water Nm 24:6
and consume the **c** of Lebanon." Jdg 9:15
command that **c** from Lebanon be 1Kg 5:6
down its tallest **c**, its choice 2Kg 19:23
You sent him **c** to build him a 2Ch 2:3
voice of the LORD breaks the **c**; Ps 29:5
LORD shatters the **c** of Lebanon. Ps 29:5
and the mighty **c** with its Ps 80:10
c of Lebanon that He planted. Ps 104:16
hills, fruit trees and all **c**, Ps 148:9
the beams of our house are **c**, Sg 1:17
Lebanon, as majestic as the **c**. Sg 5:15
against all the **c** of Lebanon, Is 2:13
we will replace them with **c**." Is 9:10
cypresses and the **c** of Lebanon Is 14:8
down its tallest **c**, its choice Is 37:24
I will plant **c** in the desert, Is 41:19
He cuts down **c** for his use, Is 44:14
choicest of your **c** and throw Jr 22:7
nestled among the **c**, how you Jr 22:23
The **c** in God's garden could not Ezk 31:8
root like ⌊the **c** of⌋ Lebanon. Hs 14:5
his height was like the **c**, Am 2:9
and fire will consume your **c**. Zch 11:1

CEILING *(3)*
the surface of the **c** he overlaid 1Kg 6:15
floor to the surface of the **c**, 1Kg 6:16
and he overlaid the **c** with gold. 2Ch 3:9

CELEBRATE *(33)*
and you must **c** it as a festival Ex 12:14
You are to **c** it throughout your Ex 12:14
community of Israel must **c** it. Ex 12:47
you and wants to **c** the LORD's Ex 12:48
C a festival in My honor three Ex 23:14
You are to **c** the LORD's festival Lv 23:39
You are to **c** it as a festival to Lv 23:41
you must **c** it in the seventh Lv 23:41
are to **c** a seven-day festival Nm 29:12
of Abib and **c** the Passover to Dt 16:1
You are to **c** the Festival of Dt 16:10
You are to **c** the Festival of Dt 16:13
I will **c** before the LORD, 2Sm 6:21
to **c** the LORD God of Israel, 1Ch 16:4
to Jerusalem to **c** the joyous Neh 12:27
them to **c** the fourteenth Est 9:21
not fail to **c** these two days Est 9:27
before God and **c** with joy. Ps 68:3
Let Israel **c** its Maker; Ps 149:2
Let the godly **c** in triumphal Ps 149:5
doing evil and **c** perversity, Pr 2:14
C His deeds among the peoples. Is 12:4
and I did not **c** ⌊with them⌋. Jr 15:17
you are to **c** the Passover, Ezk 45:21
C your festivals, Judah; Nah 1:15
and to **c** the Festival of Booths. Zch 14:16
do not go up to **c** the Festival Zch 14:18
do not go up to **c** the Festival Zch 14:19
it, and let's **c** with a feast, Lk 15:23
So they began to **c**. Lk 15:24
so I could **c** with my friends Lk 15:29
But we had to **c** and rejoice, Lk 15:32
over them and **c** and send gifts Rv 11:10

CELEBRATED *(8)*
As they **c**, the women sang: 1Sm 18:7
They **c** the Festival of Booths as Ezr 3:4
c the dedication of this house Ezr 6:16
They had not **c** like this from Neh 8:17
The Israelites **c** the feast for Neh 8:18
The women and children also **c**, Neh 12:43
and the Jews **c** with gladness, Est 8:16
are remembered and **c** by every Est 9:28

CELEBRATING *(7)*
c it throughout their Ex 31:16
c because of the great amount 1Sm 30:16
of Israel were **c** before the LORD 2Sm 6:5
all Israel were **c** with all their 1Ch 13:8
saw King David dancing and **c**, 1Ch 15:29
am **c** the Passover at your place Mt 26:18
and were **c** what their hands had Ac 7:41

CELEBRATION *(9)*
this week ⌊of wedding **c**⌋, Gn 29:27
He finished the week ⌊of **c**⌋, Gn 29:28
trod the grapes and held a **c**. Jdg 9:27
and have a great **c**, because they Neh 8:12
There was a **c** and a holiday. Est 8:17
come out of them, a sound of **c**. Jr 30:19
Joy and **c** are taken from the Jr 48:33
on the mountains and not **c**. Ezk 7:7
when Herod's birthday **c** came, Mt 14:6

CELEBRATIONS *(1)*
I will put an end to all her **c**: Hs 2:11

CELESTIAL *(3)*
and the **c** powers will be shaken. Mt 24:29
and the **c** powers will be shaken. Mk 13:25
because the **c** powers will be Lk 21:26

CELL *(2)*
went into a **c** in the dungeon Jr 37:16
and a light shone in the **c**. Ac 12:7

CELLAR *(1)*
puts it in the **c** or under a Lk 11:33

CELLARS *(1)*
of the vineyards for the wine **c**. 1Ch 27:27

CEMETERY *(2)*
burial ground of the kings' **c**, 2Ch 26:23
will become a **c**, because there Jr 7:32

CENCHREAE *(2)*
his head at **C**, because he had Ac 18:18
is a servant of the church in **C**. Rm 16:1

CENSER *(1)*
with a **c** in his hand to offer 2Ch 26:19

CENSUS *(15)*
When you take a **c** of the Ex 30:12
Take a **c** of the entire Israelite Nm 1:2
register or take a **c** of the Nm 1:49
take a **c** of the Kohathites by Nm 4:2
Take a **c** of the Gershonites Nm 4:22
who were registered ⌊in the **c**⌋, Nm 14:29
Take a **c** of the entire Israelite Nm 26:2
⌊Take a **c** of⌋ those 20 years old Nm 26:4
have taken a **c** of the fighting Nm 31:49
he had taken a **c** of the troops. 2Sm 24:10
LORD's temple, **c** money, money 2Kg 12:4
Israel because of this ⌊**c**⌋, 1Ch 27:24
Solomon took a **c** of all the 2Ch 2:17
the **c** that his father David 2Ch 2:17
the days of the **c** and attracted Ac 5:37

CENT *(1)*
until you have paid the last **c**." Lk 12:59

CENTER *(13)*
at its top in the **c** of it. Ex 28:32
opening in the **c** of the robe Ex 39:23
side, with the city in the **c**. Nm 35:5
hindquarters were toward the **c**. 1Kg 7:25
hindquarters were toward the **c**. 2Ch 4:4
to the LORD in the **c** of the land Is 19:19
them into the **c** of this city. Jr 21:4
In the **c** of the fire, there was Ezk 1:4
in the **c** of the nations, Ezk 5:5
who live at the **c** of the world. Ezk 38:12
making her stand in the **c**. Jn 8:3
left, with the woman in the **c**. Jn 8:9
who is at the **c** of the throne Rv 7:17

CENTRAL *(3)*
The **c** crossbar is to run through Ex 26:28
He made the **c** crossbar run Ex 36:33
from the **c** part of the land, Jdg 9:37

CENTURION *(20)*
Capernaum, a **c** came to Him, Mt 8:5
"Lord," the **c** replied, "I am not Mt 8:8
Then Jesus told the **c**, "Go. Mt 8:13
When the **c** and those with him, Mt 27:54
When the **c**, who was standing Mk 15:39
Summoning the **c**, he asked him Mk 15:44
When he found out from the **c**, Mk 15:45
When the **c** heard about Jesus, Lk 7:3
the **c** sent friends to tell Him, Lk 7:6
When the **c** saw what happened, Lk 23:47
a **c** of what was called the Ac 10:1
said, "Cornelius, a **c**, an Ac 10:22
Paul said to the **c** standing by, Ac 22:25
When the **c** heard this, he went Ac 22:26
that the **c** keep Paul under Ac 24:23
prisoners to a **c** named Julius, Ac 27:1
There the **c** found an Alexandrian Ac 27:6
But the **c** paid attention to the Ac 27:11
said to the **c** and the soldiers Ac 27:31
the **c** kept them from carrying Ac 27:43

CENTURION'S *(1)*
A **c** slave, who was highly valued Lk 7:2

CENTURIONS *(3)*
Taking along soldiers and **c**, Ac 21:32
called one of the **c** and said, Ac 23:17
summoned two of his **c** and said, Ac 23:23

CEPHAS *(9)*
(AKA PETER, SIMEON, SIMON)
will be called **C**" (which means Jn 1:42
or "I'm with **C**," or "I'm with 1Co 1:12
or Apollos or **C** or the world 1Co 3:22
the Lord's brothers, and **C**? 1Co 9:5
and that He appeared to **C**, 1Co 15:5
to Jerusalem to get to know **C**, Gl 1:18
When James, **C**, and John, Gl 2:9
But when **C** came to Antioch, Gl 2:11
I told **C** in front of everyone, Gl 2:14

CEREMONIAL *(1)*
the pure gold **c** bowls, wick 1Kg 7:50

CEREMONIALLY *(15)*
he must bring to a **c** clean place Lv 4:12
the camp to a **c** clean place. Lv 6:11
in any **c** clean place, Lv 10:14
to make himself **c** unclean for a Lv 21:1
Israelites and **c** cleanse them. Nm 8:6
once you have **c** cleansed them Nm 8:15
for them to **c** cleanse them. Nm 8:21
But the man who is **c** clean, Nm 9:13
Every **c** clean person in your Nm 18:11
he will remain **c** unclean until Nm 19:7
the camp in a **c** clean place. Nm 19:9
he must be **c** unclean—yes, 1Sm 20:26
Presence⌋ on the **c** clean table. 2Ch 13:11
and Levites were **c** clean, Ezr 6:20
their bread—**c** unclean—among Ezk 4:13

CEREMONIES *(1)*
the burning **c** for your fathers Jr 34:5

CEREMONY *(1)*
be a burning **c** for you just like Jr 34:5

CERTAIN *(46)*
said to Abram, "Know this for **c**: Gn 15:13
He reached a **c** place and spent Gn 28:11
the LORD is **c** to bless you Dt 15:4
and day, never **c** of survival. Dt 28:66
know for **c** that the LORD your Jos 23:13
There was a **c** man from Zorah, Jdg 13:2
my⌋ young men at a **c** place. 1Sm 21:2
Now I know for **c** you will be 1Sm 24:20
because there is **c** to be trouble 1Sm 25:17
for the LORD is **c** to make a 1Sm 25:28

and knew for **c** that Saul had 1Sm 26:4
and you can be **c** I am on your 2Sm 3:12
There were two men in a **c** city, 2Sm 12:1
I'm **c** my lord the king would not 1Kg 1:27
Now a **c** old prophet was living 1Kg 13:11
of Samaria is **c** to happen." 1Kg 13:32
because your downfall is **c**." Est 6:13
those who curse ⌊**c**⌋ days cast a Jb 3:8
am **c** that I will see the LORD's Ps 27:13
Then **c** ones said, "Come, let's Jr 18:18
But know for **c** that if you put Jr 26:15
for it is **c** the LORD has sent me Jr 26:15
of Achbor and ⌊**c** other⌋ men with Jr 26:22
hand but are **c** to be captured Jr 34:3
Know for **c** that I have warned Jr 42:19
know for **c** that by the sword, Jr 42:22
I know for **c** you are trying to Dn 2:8
and its interpretation **c**." Dn 2:45
to them for a **c** period of time. Dn 7:12
what is **c** among the tribes Hs 5:9
"Go into the city to a **c** man," Mt 26:18
a **c** young man, having a linen Mk 14:51
Know this for **c**: the kingdom of Lk 10:11
He was praying in a **c** place, Lk 11:1
There was a **c** royal official Jn 4:46
and have known for **c** that I came Jn 17:8
Now I know for **c** that the Lord Ac 12:11
religion and about a **c** Jesus, Ac 25:19
must run aground on a **c** island." Ac 27:26
c that God is appealing through 2Co 5:20
to challenge **c** people who think 2Co 10:2
Gentiles before **c** men came from Gl 2:12
you may command **c** people not to 1Tm 1:3
He specifies a **c** day—today— Heb 4:7
For **c** men, who were designated Jd 4
mourn over Him. This is **c**. Amen. Rv 1:7

CERTAINLY *(121)*
(See pp. xi-xii.)

CERTAINTY *(2)*
you may know the **c** of the things Lk 1:4
Israel know with **c** that God has Ac 2:36

CERTIFICATE *(5)*
he may write her a divorce **c**, Dt 24:1
a divorce **c**, hands it to her, Dt 24:3
mother's divorce **c** that I used Is 50:1
had given her a **c** of divorce. Jr 3:8
erased the **c** of debt, with its Col 2:14

CHAFED *(1)*
made bald and every shoulder **c**, Ezk 29:18

CHAFF *(12)*
like **c** a storm sweeps away? Jb 21:18
they are like **c** that the wind Ps 1:4
the wind like **c** on the hills Is 17:13
of the ruthless, like blowing **c**. Is 29:5
will conceive **c**; you will give Is 33:11
them⌋, and make hills like **c**. Is 41:15
like drifting **c** before the Jr 13:24
became like **c** from the summer Dn 2:35
like **c** blown from a threshing Hs 13:3
and the day passes like **c**, Zph 2:2
But the **c** He will burn up with Mt 3:12
but the **c** He will burn up with a Lk 3:17

CHAIN *(10)*
placed a gold **c** around his neck Gn 41:42
and a ⌊gold⌋ **c** around your neck Pr 1:9
Forge the **c**, for the land is Ezk 7:23
wrists and a **c** around your neck Ezk 16:11
have a gold **c** around his neck, Dn 5:7
have a gold **c** around your neck, Dn 5:16
placed⌋ a gold **c** around his neck Dn 5:29
John and to **c** him in prison Mk 6:17
Israel that I'm wearing this **c**." Ac 28:20
abyss and a great **c** in his hand. Rv 20:1

CHAINED *(1)*
arrested John, **c** him, and put Mt 14:3

CHAINS *(40)*
and two **c** of pure gold; Ex 28:14
the cord **c** to the settings Ex 28:14
to make braided **c** of pure gold Ex 28:22
made braided **c** of pure gold cord Ex 39:15
and the **c** on the necks of their Jdg 8:26
he hung gold **c** across the front 1Kg 6:21
him in bronze ⌊**c**⌋, and took him 2Kg 25:7
decorated with palm trees and **c**. 2Ch 3:5
are bound with **c** and trapped Jb 36:8
you fasten the **c** of the Pleiades Jb 38:31
us tear off their **c** and free Ps 2:3
gloom—prisoners in cruel **c**— Ps 107:10
gloom and broke their **c** apart. Ps 107:14
their kings with **c** and their Ps 149:8
heart a net, and her hands **c**. Ec 7:26
you, they will come over in **c**; Is 45:14
To break the **c** of wickedness, Is 58:6
him in bronze **c** to take him to Jr 39:7
had been bound in **c** with all the Jr 40:1
free from the **c** that were on Jr 40:4
and bound him with bronze **c**. Jr 52:11
He has weighed me down with **c**. Lm 3:7
all her nobles were bound in **c**. Nah 3:10
him any more—even with **c**— Mk 5:3
been bound with shackles and **c**, Mk 5:4
snapped off the **c** and smashed Mk 5:4
bound by **c** and shackles, he Lk 8:29
bound with two **c**, while the Ac 12:6
Then the **c** fell off his wrists. Ac 12:7
and everyone's **c** came loose. Ac 16:26
to me that **c** and afflictions are Ac 20:23
him to be bound with two **c**. Ac 21:33
charge that merited death or **c**. Ac 23:29
as I am—except for these **c**." Ac 26:29
that deserves death or **c**." Ac 26:31
this I am an ambassador in **c**. Eph 6:20
me and was not ashamed of my **c**. 2Tm 1:16
whom I fathered while in **c**— Phm 10
to be kept in **c** of darkness 2Pt 2:4
with eternal **c** in darkness for Jd 6

CHAINWORK *(3)*
wreaths made of **c**—seven for 1Kg 7:17
He had made **c** in the inner 2Ch 3:16
and fastened them into the **c**. 2Ch 3:16

CHAIR *(6)*
sitting on a **c** by the doorpost 1Sm 1:9
sitting on his **c** beside the road 1Sm 4:13
off the **c** by the city gate 1Sm 4:18
bed, a table, a **c**, and a lamp 2Kg 4:10
made a sedan **c** for himself with Sg 3:9
are seated in the **c** of Moses. Mt 23:2

CHAIRS *(2)*
and the **c** of those selling Mt 21:12
and the **c** of those selling Mk 11:15

CHALCEDONY *(1)*
the third **c**, the fourth emerald Rv 21:19

CHALDEA *(8)*
(AKA LEB-QAMAI)
without a throne, Daughter **C**! Is 47:1
Daughter **C**, sit in silence and Is 47:5
the residents of **C** for all their Jr 51:24
be on the inhabitants of **C**," Jr 51:35
brought me to **C** and to the Ezk 11:24
extended your prostitution to **C**, Ezk 16:29
of the Babylonians in **C**, Ezk 23:15
sent messengers to them in **C**. Ezk 23:16

CHALDEAN *(13)*
The LORD sent **C**, Aramean, 2Kg 24:2
the **C** army pursued him and 2Kg 25:5
The whole **C** army ⌊with⌋ the 2Kg 25:10
of Babylon, the **C**, who destroyed Ezr 5:12
get away from the **C** and Aramean Jr 35:11
down the entire **C** army that is Jr 37:10
When the **C** army withdrew from Jr 37:11
the **C** army pursued them and Jr 39:5
as well as the **C** soldiers who Jr 41:3
The **C** army pursued the king and Jr 52:8
The whole **C** army with the Jr 52:14
and to teach them the **C** language Dn 1:4
diviner-priest, medium, or **C**. Dn 2:10

CHALDEANS *(72)*
in Ur of the **C**, during his Gn 11:28
from Ur of the **C** to go to the Gn 11:31
Ur of the **C** to give you this Gn 15:7
even though the **C** surrounded the 2Kg 25:4
C seized the king and brought 2Kg 25:6
Now the **C** broke into pieces the 2Kg 25:13
afraid of the servants of the **C**. 2Kg 25:24
the Jews and the **C** who were with 2Kg 25:25
for they were afraid of the **C**. 2Kg 25:26
against them the king of the **C**, 2Ch 36:17
Then the **C** burned God's temple. 2Ch 36:19
brought him out of Ur of the **C**, Neh 9:7
The **C** formed three bands, Jb 1:17
the glory of the pride of the **C**, Is 13:19
at the land of **C**—a people who Is 23:13
even the **C** in the ships in which Is 43:14
His arm ⌊will be against⌋ the **C**. Is 48:14
Leave Babylon, flee from the **C**! Is 48:20
Babylon and the **C** who are Jr 21:4
to the **C** who are besieging Jr 21:9
king of Babylon and the **C**. Jr 22:25
this place to the land of the **C**. Jr 24:5
the land of the **C**, for their Jr 25:12
will not escape from the **C**; Jr 32:4
will fight the **C**, but you will Jr 32:5
over to the **C** who are fighting Jr 32:24
has been handed over to the **C**!" Jr 32:25
to hand this city over to the **C**, Jr 32:28
The **C** who are going to fight Jr 32:29
has been handed over to the **C**! Jr 32:43
coming to fight the **C** will fill Jr 33:5
and when the **C**, who were Jr 37:5
The **C** will then return and fight Jr 37:8
The **C** will leave us for good, Jr 37:9
"You are deserting to the **C**." Jr 37:13
"I am not deserting to the **C**!" Jr 37:14
surrenders to the **C** will live. Jr 38:2
will be handed over to the **C**. Jr 38:18
who have deserted to the **C**. Jr 38:19
will be brought out to the **C**. Jr 38:23
C next burned down the king's Jr 39:8
Don't be afraid to serve the **C**. Jr 40:9
before the **C** who come to us. Jr 40:10
away from the **C**. For they feared Jr 41:18
us over to the **C** to put us to Jr 43:3
the land of the **C**, through Jr 50:1
The **C** will become plunder; Jr 50:10
of Hosts in the land of the **C**. Jr 50:25
sword is over the **C**—⌊this is⌋ Jr 50:35
against the land of the **C**: Jr 50:45
will fall in the land of the **C**, Jr 51:4
from the land of the **C**! Jr 51:54
the **C** surrounded the city. Jr 52:7
C seized the king and brought Jr 52:9
Now the **C** broke into pieces the Jr 52:17
the land of the **C** by the Chebar Ezk 1:3
the land of the **C**, yet he will Ezk 12:13
wall, images of the **C**, engraved Ezk 23:14
the Babylonians and all the **C**; Ezk 23:23
and **C** to tell the king his Dn 2:2
The **C** spoke to the king (Aramaic Dn 2:4
The king replied to the **C**, Dn 2:5
The **C** answered the king, "No one Dn 2:10
C took this occasion to come Dn 3:8
mediums, **C**, and astrologers came Dn 4:7
in the mediums, **C**, and Dn 5:7
mediums, **C**, and astrologers. Dn 5:11
the king of the **C** was killed, Dn 5:30
over the kingdom of the **C**— Dn 9:1
raising up the **C**, that bitter, Hab 1:6
The **C** pull them all up with a Hab 1:15
of the land of the **C** and settled Ac 7:4

CHALDEANS' *(1)*
depart from the **C** land. Jr 50:8

CHALK *(1)*
stones like crushed bits of **c**, Is 27:9

CHALLENGE *(2)*
Would you really **c** My justice? Jb 40:8
which I plan to **c** certain people 2Co 10:2

CHALLENGING *(2)*
c the one who tramples me. Ps 57:3
how they keep **c** me, "Where is Jr 17:15

CHAMBER *(27)*
entered the inner **c** of the Jdg 9:46
against the inner **c** and set it Jdg 9:49
went up to the gate **c** and wept. 2Sm 18:33
lowest **c** was seven and a half 1Kg 6:6
the lowest side **c** was on the 1Kg 6:8
up a stairway to the middle ⌊**c**⌋, 1Kg 6:8
in an inner **c** on that day." 1Kg 22:25
by the **c** of Nathan-melech 2Kg 23:11
Ahaz's upper **c** that the kings of 2Kg 23:12
in an inner **c** on that day." 2Ch 18:24
walked to the **c** of Jehohanan son Ezr 10:6
The windstorm comes from its **c**, Jb 37:9
groom coming from the bridal **c**; Ps 19:5
⌊her **c**⌋, the royal daughter is Ps 45:13
the **c** of the one who conceived Sg 3:4
of the LORD to a **c** ⌊occupied by⌋ Jr 35:4
who had a **c** near the officials' Jr 35:4
a chamber near the officials' **c**, Jr 35:4
was above the **c** of Maaseiah son Jr 35:4
in the **c** of Gemariah son of Jr 36:10

the horse under the **c** of one of Est 6:9
put him in **c** of Haman's estate Est 8:2
Who put Him in **c** of the entire Jb 34:13
the LORD does not **c** with sin, Ps 32:2
of Jerusalem, I **c** you, by the Sg 2:7
of Jerusalem, I **c** you, by the Sg 3:5
women of Jerusalem, I **c** you: Sg 5:8
that you would give us this **c**? Sg 5:9
women of Jerusalem, I **c** you: Sg 8:4
brings ⌊this⌋ **c** against the Is 3:14
who is in **c** of the palace, Is 22:15
who was in **c** of the palace, Is 36:3
who was in **c** of the palace, Is 36:22
who was in **c** of the palace, Is 37:2
learn what ⌊the **c**⌋ is against Jr 6:18
The wind will take **c** of all your Jr 22:22
he had put him in **c** of the men, Jr 40:7
who keep **c** of the temple. Ezk 40:45
priests who keep **c** of the altar. Ezk 40:46
have not kept **c** of My holy Ezk 44:8
to keep **c** of My sanctuary Ezk 44:8
who kept **c** of My sanctuary when Ezk 44:15
who kept My **c** and did not go Ezk 48:11
to find a **c** against Daniel Dn 6:4
could find no **c** or corruption, Dn 6:4
never find any **c** against this Dn 6:5
and don't **c** us with innocent Jnh 1:14
Their horsemen **c** ahead; Hab 1:8
You have received free of **c**; Mt 10:8
free of charge; give free of **c**. Mt 10:8
has put in **c** of his household Mt 24:45
He will put him in **c** of all his Mt 24:47
put you in **c** of many things. Mt 25:21
put you in **c** of many things. Mt 25:23
didn't answer him on even one **c**, Mt 27:14
they put up the **c** against Him Mt 27:37
of the **c** written against Mk 15:26
they could find a **c** against Him. Lk 6:7
will put in **c** of his household Lk 12:42
he will put him in **c** of all his Lk 12:44
no grounds to **c** this man with Lk 23:14
He was in **c** of the money-bag and Jn 12:6
What **c** do you bring against this Jn 18:29
do not **c** them with this sin!" Ac 7:60
who was in **c** of her entire Ac 8:27
who was in **c** of the king's Ac 12:20
to know the **c** for which they Ac 23:28
that there was no **c** that merited Ac 23:29
give a defense concerning the **c**. Ac 25:16
and brought no **c** of the sort I Ac 25:18
the Lord will never **c** with sin! Rm 4:8
gospel and offer it free of **c**, 1Co 9:18
gospel of God to you free of **c**? 2Co 11:7
I **c** you by the Lord that this 1Th 5:27
eat anyone's bread free of **c**; 2Th 3:8
I solemnly **c** you, before God and 1Tm 5:21
before Pontius Pilate, I **c** you 1Tm 6:13
His kingdom, I solemnly **c** you: 2Tm 4:1
you anything, **c** that to my Phm 18
bring a slanderous **c** against 2Pt 2:11

CHARGED *(8)*

person will be **c** with murder. Lv 17:4
in ambush **c** out of their places Jdg 20:33
men of Israel **c** out of Mizpah 1Sm 7:11
the Angel of the LORD **c** Joshua: Zch 3:6
on the earth will be **c** to you, Mt 23:35
a risk of being **c** with rioting Ac 19:40
have previously **c** that both Jews Rm 3:9
sin is not **c** to one's account Rm 5:13

CHARGES *(11)*

and brought **c** against Laban. Gn 31:36
Bring **c** against me before the 1Sm 12:3
servants and He **c** His angels Jb 4:18
He **c** at me like a warrior. Jb 16:14
his strength; He **c** into battle. Jb 39:21
He **c** ahead with trembling rage; Jb 39:24
Let them bring **c** against one Ac 19:38
be here before you to bring **c**, Ac 24:19
many serious **c** that they were Ac 25:7
be tried before me on these **c**?" Ac 25:9
to indicate the **c** against him." Ac 25:27

CHARGING *(11)*

Each of you is **c** his countrymen Neh 5:7
let us stop **c** this interest. Neh 5:10
like a roaring lion or a **c** bear. Pr 28:15
and by **c** the poor during a Is 32:7
I saw the ram **c** to the west, Dn 8:4
C horseman, flashing sword, Nah 3:3

find no grounds for **c** this man." Lk 23:4
I find no grounds for **c** Him. Jn 18:38
I find no grounds for **c** Him." Jn 19:4
I find no grounds for **c** Him." Jn 19:6
c them before God not to fight 2Tm 2:14

CHARIOT *(68)*

had Joseph ride in his second **c**, Gn 41:43
horses to⌋ his **c** and went up to Gn 46:29
So he got his **c** ready and took Ex 14:6
He caused their **c** wheels to Ex 14:25
Sisera left his **c** and fled on Jdg 4:15
Why is his **c** so long in coming? Jdg 5:28
got himself a **c**, horses, and 50 2Sm 15:1
straw for the **c** teams and the 1Kg 4:28
was similar to that of **c** wheels: 1Kg 7:33
to Solomon, the **c** cities, the 1Kg 9:19
them in the **c** cities and with 1Kg 10:26
A **c** was imported from Egypt for 1Kg 10:29
to get into the **c** and flee to 1Kg 12:18
Get ⌊your **c**⌋ ready and go down 1Kg 18:44
Ahab got in ⌊his **c**⌋ and went to 1Kg 18:45
horse for horse, **c** for chariot— 1Kg 20:25
chariot for **c**—and let's fight 1Kg 20:25
Ahab had him come up into the **c**. 1Kg 20:33
had ordered his 32 **c** commanders, 1Kg 22:31
When the **c** commanders saw 1Kg 22:32
When the **c** commanders saw that 1Kg 22:33
propped up in his **c** facing the 1Kg 22:35
flowed into the bottom of the **c**. 1Kg 22:35
someone washed the **c** at the pool 1Kg 22:38
a **c** of fire with horses of fire 2Kg 2:11
got down from the **c** to meet him 2Kg 5:21
got down from his **c** to meet you? 2Kg 5:26
him and the **c** commanders, 2Kg 8:21
Jehu got into his **c** and went to 2Kg 9:16
and they harnessed his **c**. 2Kg 9:21
each in his own **c**, and met Jehu 2Kg 9:21
and he slumped down in his **c**. 2Kg 9:24
shot him in his **c** at Gur Pass 2Kg 9:27
Jerusalem in a **c** and buried him 2Kg 9:28
him up into the **c** with him. 2Kg 10:15
let him ride with him in his **c**. 2Kg 10:16
carried his dead body in a **c**, 2Kg 23:30
the plans for the **c** of the gold 1Ch 28:18
in the **c** cities and with 2Ch 1:14
A **c** could be imported from Egypt 2Ch 1:17
Solomon, all the **c** cities, the 2Ch 8:6
them in the **c** cities and with 2Ch 9:25
to get up into the **c** to flee to 2Ch 10:18
had ordered his **c** commanders, 2Ch 18:30
When the **c** commanders saw 2Ch 18:31
When the **c** commanders saw that 2Ch 18:32
himself up in his **c** facing the 2Ch 18:34
him and the **c** commanders. 2Ch 21:9
took him out of the war **c**, 2Ch 35:24
carried him in his second **c**, 2Ch 35:24
take pride in a **c**, and others Ps 20:7
both **c** and horse lay still. Ps 76:6
the clouds His **c**, walking on the Ps 104:3
their ⌊**c**⌋ wheels are like a Is 5:28
who brings out the **c** and horse, Is 43:17
will smash the **c** and its rider. Jr 51:21
Harness the horses to the **c**, Mc 1:13
fittings of the **c** flash like Nah 2:3
galloping horse and jolting **c**! Nah 3:2
Your horses, Your victorious **c**? Hab 3:8
The first **c** had red horses, Zch 6:2
the second **c** black horses, Zch 6:2
third **c** white horses, and the Zch 6:3
the fourth **c** dappled horses— Zch 6:3
will cut off the **c** from Ephraim Zch 9:10
in his **c** on his way home, Ac 8:28
Philip, "Go and join that **c**." Ac 8:29
Then he ordered the **c** to stop, Ac 8:38

CHARIOTEER *(2)*

he said to his **c**, "Turn around 1Kg 22:34
he said to the **c**, "Turn around 2Ch 18:33

CHARIOTEERS *(4)*

Sisera, all his **c**, and all his Jdg 4:15
700 of their **c** and 40,000 foot 2Sm 10:18
7,000 of their **c** and 40,000 foot 1Ch 19:18
and in the great strength of **c**. Is 31:1

CHARIOTRY *(2)*

horses and **c**, were with him. 1Kg 20:1
attacked the cavalry and the **c**. 1Kg 20:21

CHARIOTS *(90)*

Horses and **c** went up with him; Gn 50:9

600 of the best **c** and all the Ex 14:7
all the rest of the **c** of Egypt, Ex 14:7
all Pharaoh's horses and **c**, Ex 14:9
army, and his **c** and horsemen. Ex 14:17
his **c**, and his horsemen. Ex 14:18
his **c**, and his horsemen— Ex 14:23
on their **c** and horsemen." Ex 14:26
and covered the **c** and horsemen, Ex 14:28
threw Pharaoh's **c** and his army Ex 15:4
horses with his **c** and horsemen Ex 15:19
its horses and **c**, when He made Dt 11:4
and see horses, **c**, and an army Dt 20:1
a vast number of horses and **c**. Jos 11:4
horses and burn up their **c**." Jos 11:6
horses and burned up their **c**. Jos 11:9
the valley area have iron **c**, Jos 17:16
have iron **c** and are strong." Jos 17:18
fathers with **c** and horsemen as Jos 24:6
because those people had iron **c**. Jdg 1:19
because Jabin had 900 iron **c**, Jdg 4:3
forces, his **c**, and his army at Jdg 4:7
all his 900 iron **c** and all the Jdg 4:13
pursued the **c** and the army as Jdg 4:16
put them to his use in his **c**, 1Sm 8:11
or running in front of his **c**. 1Sm 8:11
war or the equipment for his **c**. 1Sm 8:12
3,000 **c**, 6,000 horsemen, and 1Sm 13:5
moment the **c** and the cavalry 2Sm 1:6
the horses, and he kept 100 **c**. 2Sm 8:4
also assembled **c**, cavalry, and 1Kg 1:5
stalls of horses for his **c**, 1Kg 4:26
of his **c** and his cavalry. 1Kg 9:22
accumulated 1,400 **c** and 12,000 1Kg 10:26
of half his **c**, conspired against 1Kg 16:9
the **c** and horsemen of Israel!" 2Kg 2:12
his horses and **c** and stood at 2Kg 5:9
he sent horses, **c**, and a massive 2Kg 6:14
with horses and **c** surrounding 2Kg 6:15
with horses and **c** of fire all 2Kg 6:17
camp to hear the sound of **c**, 2Kg 7:6
took two **c** with horses, 2Kg 7:14
over to Zair with all his **c**. 2Kg 8:21
are with you and you have **c**, 2Kg 10:2
50 horsemen, 10 **c**, and 10,000 2Kg 13:7
the **c** and horsemen of Israel!" 2Kg 13:14
in Egypt for **c** and for horsemen 2Kg 18:24
With my many **c** I have gone up 2Kg 19:23
he burned up the **c** of the sun. 2Kg 23:11
1,000 **c**, 7,000 horsemen, 1Ch 18:4
the horses, and he kept 100 **c**. 1Ch 18:4
of silver to hire **c** and horsemen 1Ch 19:6
They hired 32,000 **c** and the king 1Ch 19:7
accumulated 1,400 **c** and 12,000 2Ch 1:14
of his **c** and his cavalry. 2Ch 8:9
4,000 stalls for horses and **c**, 2Ch 9:25
with 1,200 **c**, 60,000 cavalrymen, 2Ch 12:3
of one million men and 300 **c**. 2Ch 14:9
with very many **c** and horsemen? 2Ch 16:8
his commanders and all his **c**. 2Ch 21:9
to pieces; He burns up the **c**. Ps 46:9
God's **c** are tens of thousands, Ps 68:17
to a mare among Pharaoh's **c**. Sg 1:9
me ⌊among⌋ the **c** of my noble Sg 6:12
there is no limit to their **c**. Is 2:7
up a quiver with **c** and horsemen, Is 22:6
best valleys were full of **c**, Is 22:7
there your glorious **c** will be— Is 22:18
the number of **c** and in the great Is 31:1
in Egypt for **c** and horsemen? Is 36:9
With my many **c** I have gone up to Is 37:24
His **c** are like the whirlwind— Is 66:15
to the LORD on horses and **c**, Is 66:20
his **c** are like a storm. Jr 4:13
riding in **c** and on horses with Jr 17:25
palace riding on **c** and horses— Jr 22:4
Race furiously, you **c**! Jr 46:9
rumbling of his **c**, and the Jr 47:3
his horses and **c** and against all Jr 50:37
and with weapons, **c**, and wagons. Ezk 23:24
north with horses, **c**, cavalry, Ezk 26:7
noise of cavalry, wagons, and **c**. Ezk 26:10
will storm against him with **c**, Dn 11:40
sound is like the sound of **c**, Jl 2:5
from you and wreck your **c**. Mc 5:10
The **c** dash madly through the Nah 2:4
will make your **c** go up in smoke Nah 2:13
I will overturn **c** and their Hg 2:22

again and saw four c coming from Zch 6:1
the sound of c with many horses Rv 9:9

CHARITABLE (2)
He did many c deeds for the Ac 10:2
I came to bring c gifts and Ac 24:17

CHARITY (4)
But give to c what is within, Lk 11:41
doing good works and acts of c. Ac 9:36
your acts of c have come up as Ac 10:4
and your acts of c have been Ac 10:31

CHARM (1)
C is deceptive and beauty is Pr 31:30

CHARMED (2)
the snake bites before it is c, Ec 10:11
vipers that cannot be c. Jr 8:17

CHARMER (1)
there is no advantage for the c. Ec 10:11

CHARMERS (1)
sound of the c who skillfully Ps 58:5

CHARRED (2)
its ends, and the middle is c. Ezk 15:4
has devoured it and it is c! Ezk 15:5

CHASE (12)
draw a sword ⌊to c⌋ after you. Lv 26:33
C after them quickly, and you Jos 2:5
Will You c after dry straw? Jb 13:25
they c my dignity away like the Jb 30:15
c him and catch him, for there Ps 71:11
love graft and c after bribes. Is 1:23
I will c Edom away from her Jr 49:19
I will c Babylon away from her Jr 50:44
draw a sword ⌊to c⌋ after them. Ezk 5:2
draw a sword ⌊to c⌋ after them. Ezk 5:12
draw a sword ⌊to c⌋ after them. Ezk 12:14
and He will c His enemies into Nah 1:8

CHASED (10)
c after them and caught up with Ex 14:9
against you and c you like a Dt 1:44
36 of them and c them from Jos 7:5
c them through the ascent of Jos 10:10
and c the Philistines to the 1Sm 17:52
He c Abner and did not turn to 2Sm 2:19
to darkness and c from the Jb 18:18
he will be c away like a vision Jb 20:8
is a stray lamb, c by lions. Jr 50:17
Those who c us were swifter than Lm 4:19

CHASES (3)
but whoever c fantasies lacks Pr 12:11
whoever c fantasies will have Pr 28:19
Ephraim c the wind and pursues Hs 12:1

CHASING (3)
What are you c after? 1Sm 24:14
But Asahel would not stop c him. 2Sm 2:21
Abner warned Asahel, "Stop c me. 2Sm 2:22

CHASM (1)
a great c has been fixed between Lk 16:26

CHASTENED (1)
as being c yet not killed; 2Co 6:9

CHEAT (5)
from him, do not c one another. Lv 25:14
You are not to c one another, Lv 25:17
the price and c with dishonest Am 8:5
and c the wage earner Mal 3:5
act unjustly and c—and this to 1Co 6:8

CHEATED (3)
For he has c me twice now. Gn 27:36
and that he has c me and changed Gn 31:7
Why not rather be c? 1Co 6:7

CHEBAR (8)
among the exiles by the C Canal, Ezk 1:1
of the Chaldeans by the C Canal. Ezk 1:3
who were living by the C Canal, Ezk 3:15
glory I had seen by the C Canal, Ezk 3:23
I had seen by the C Canal. Ezk 10:15
God of Israel by the C Canal, Ezk 10:20
faces I had seen by the C Canal. Ezk 10:22
ones I had seen by the C Canal. Ezk 43:3

CHECK (4)
when you come to c on my wages, Gn 30:33
C on the welfare of your 1Sm 17:18
Go and c again. Investigate and 1Sm 23:22
but a wise man holds it in c. Pr 29:11

CHEDORLAOMER (5)
king of Ellasar, C king of Elam, Gn 14:1
were subject to C for 12 years, Gn 14:4
fourteenth year C and the kings Gn 14:5
against C king of Elam, Tidal Gn 14:9
from defeating C and the kings Gn 14:17

CHEEK (5)
strike all my enemies on the c; Ps 3:7
him offer ⌊his⌋ c to the one who Lm 3:30
of Israel on the c with a rod. Mc 5:1
slaps you on your right c, Mt 5:39
If anyone hits you on the c, Lk 6:29

CHEEKS (5)
and strike my c with contempt; Jb 16:10
Your c are beautiful with Sg 1:10
His c are like beds of spice, Sg 5:13
and My c to those who tore out Is 50:6
the night, with tears on her c. Lm 1:2

CHEER (4)
You c him with joy in Your Ps 21:6
Bright eyes c the heart; Pr 15:30
being will c when your lips say Pr 23:16
then who will c me other than 2Co 2:2

CHEERED (1)
that I may be c up before I die Ps 39:13

CHEERFUL (7)
your God with joy and a c heart, Dt 28:47
A joyful heart makes a face c, Pr 15:13
but a c heart has a continual Pr 15:15
drink your wine with a c heart, Ec 9:7
and c festivals for the house of Zch 8:19
for God loves a c giver. 2Co 9:7
pray. Is anyone c? He should Jms 5:13

CHEERFULNESS (1)
showing mercy, with c. Rm 12:8

CHEERING (1)
in the temple complex c, Mt 21:15

CHEERS (2)
my wine that c both God and man, Jdg 9:13
down, but a good word c it up. Pr 12:25

CHEESE (3)
10 portions of c to the field 1Sm 17:18
c from the herd for David and 2Sm 17:29
like milk and curdle me like c? Jb 10:10

CHELAL (1)
Adna, C, Benaiah, Maaseiah, Ezr 10:30

CHELUB (2)
C brother of Shuhah fathered 1Ch 4:11
Ezri son of C was in charge of 1Ch 27:26

CHELUBAI (1)
(AKA CALEB)
Jerahmeel, Ram, and C. 1Ch 2:9

CHELUHI (1)
Benaiah, Bedeiah, C, Ezr 10:35

CHEMOSH (8)
been destroyed, people of C! Nm 21:29
your god C drives out for Jdg 11:24
built a high place for C, 1Kg 11:7
Sidonians, to C, the god of Moab 1Kg 11:33
for C, the detestable idol of 2Kg 23:13
C will go into exile with his Jr 48:7
be put to shame because of C, Jr 48:13
The people of C have perished Jr 48:46

CHENAANAH (5)
Zedekiah son of C made iron 1Kg 22:11
Then Zedekiah son of C came up, 1Kg 22:24
Benjamin, Ehud, C, Zethan, 1Ch 7:10
Zedekiah son of C made iron 2Ch 18:10
Then Zedekiah son of C came up, 2Ch 18:23

CHENANI (1)
C stood on the raised platform Neh 9:4

CHENANIAH (3)
C, the leader of the Levites in 1Ch 15:22
as well as the singers and C, 1Ch 15:27
C and his sons had the outside 1Ch 26:29

CHEPHAR-AMMONI (1)
C, Ophni, and Geba—12 cities, Jos 18:24

CHEPHIRAH (2)
cities were Gibeon, C, Beeroth, Jos 9:17
Mizpeh, C, Mozah, Jos 18:26

CHEPHIRAH'S (2)
Kiriatharim's, C, and Beeroth's Ezr 2:25
C, and Beeroth's Neh 7:29

CHERAN (2)
Hemdan, Eshban, Ithran, and C. Gn 36:26
Hamran, Eshban, Ithran, and C. 1Ch 1:41

CHERETHITES (10)
the south country of the C, 1Sm 30:14
was over⌋ the C and the 2Sm 8:18
Then all the C, the Pelethites, 2Sm 15:18
men, the C, the Pelethites 2Sm 20:7
was over the C and Pelethites; 2Sm 20:23
of Jehoiada, the C, and the 1Kg 1:38
of Jehoiada, the C, and the 1Kg 1:44
was over the C and the 1Ch 18:17
cutting off the C and wiping out Ezk 25:16
the seacoast, nation of the C! Zph 2:5

CHERISH (1)
C her, and she will exalt you; Pr 4:8

CHERISHES (1)
though he c it and will not let Jb 20:13

CHERITH (2)
at the Wadi C where it enters 1Kg 17:3
by the Wadi C where it enters 1Kg 17:5

CHERUB (16)
(See also Cherub proper noun.)
Make one c at one end and one Ex 25:19
one end and one c at the other Ex 25:19
one c at one end and one cherub Ex 37:8
one end and one c at the other Ex 37:8
He rode on a c and flew, soaring 2Sm 22:11
wing of the ⌊first⌋ c was seven 1Kg 6:24
The second c also was 15 feet; 1Kg 6:25
the wing of the other c. 2Ch 3:11
wing of the other c was seven 2Ch 3:12
the wing of the other c. 2Ch 3:12
He rode on a c and flew, soaring Ps 18:10
one wheel beside each c. Ezk 10:9
the first face was that of a c, Ezk 10:14
You were an anointed guardian c, Ezk 28:14
you, guardian c, from among the Ezk 28:16
Each c had two faces: Ezk 41:18

CHERUB (proper noun) (2)
Tel-harsha, C, Addan, and Immer Ezr 2:59
Tel-harsha, C, Addon, and Immer, Neh 7:61

CHERUB'S (3)
The first c height was 15 feet 1Kg 6:26
15 feet and so was the second c. 1Kg 6:26
while the second c wing touched 1Kg 6:27

CHERUBIM (66)
He stationed c with a flaming, Gn 3:24
Make two c of gold; Ex 25:18
Make the c of one piece with the Ex 25:19
The c are to have wings spread Ex 25:20
faces of the c should be toward Ex 25:20
between the two c that are over Ex 25:22
a design of c worked into them Ex 26:1
a design of c worked into it. Ex 26:31
a design of c worked into them Ex 36:8
a design of c worked into it. Ex 36:35
He made two c of gold; Ex 37:7
made the c ⌊of one piece⌋ with Ex 37:8
mercy seat, ⌊a c⌋ at each end. Ex 37:8
The faces of the c were looking Ex 37:9
from between the two c. Nm 7:89
who dwells ⌊between⌋ the c. 1Sm 4:4
who dwells ⌊between⌋ the c. 2Sm 6:2
he made two c 15 feet high out 1Kg 6:23
both c had the same size and 1Kg 6:25
Then he put the c inside the 1Kg 6:27
also overlaid the c with gold. 1Kg 6:28
carved engravings—c, palm 1Kg 6:29
He carved c, palm trees and 1Kg 6:32
gold over the c and palm trees. 1Kg 6:32
He carved c, palm trees and 1Kg 6:35
were lions, oxen, and c. 1Kg 7:29
He engraved c, lions, and palm 1Kg 7:36
beneath the wings of the c. 1Kg 8:6
For the c were spreading their 1Kg 8:7
that the c covered the ark and 1Kg 8:7
who is enthroned ⌊above⌋ the c, 2Kg 19:15
LORD who dwells ⌊between⌋ the c. 1Ch 13:6
of the gold c that spread out 1Ch 28:18
and he carved c on the walls. 2Ch 3:7
made two c of sculptured work, 2Ch 3:10
the wings of the c was 30 feet: 2Ch 3:11
wingspan of these c was 30 feet. 2Ch 3:13
linen, and he wove c into it. 2Ch 3:14
beneath the wings of the c. 2Ch 5:7

the **c** spread their wings over 2Ch 5:8
ark so that the **c** formed a cover 2Ch 5:8
who sit enthroned ⌊on⌋ the **c**, Ps 80:1
He is enthroned above the **c**. Ps 99:1
who is enthroned above the **c**, Is 37:16
from above the **c** where it had Ezk 9:3
the heads of the **c** was something Ezk 10:1
the wheelwork beneath the **c**. Ezk 10:2
from among the **c** and scatter Ezk 10:2
Now the **c** were standing to the Ezk 10:3
above the **c** to the threshold Ezk 10:4
from among the **c**," the man went Ezk 10:6
Then one of the **c** reached out Ezk 10:7
The **c** appeared to have the form Ezk 10:8
were four wheels beside the **c**, Ezk 10:9
The **c** ascended; these were the Ezk 10:15
When the **c** moved, the wheels Ezk 10:16
When the **c** stood still, the Ezk 10:17
temple and stood above the **c**. Ezk 10:18
The **c** lifted their wings and Ezk 10:19
I recognized that they were **c**. Ezk 10:20
Then the **c**, with the wheels Ezk 11:22
carved with **c** and palm trees. Ezk 41:18
tree between each pair of **c**. Ezk 41:18
C and palm trees were carved Ezk 41:20
C and palm trees were carved on Ezk 41:25
The **c** of glory were above it Heb 9:5

CHERUBIM'S *(1)*
The sound of the **c** wings could Ezk 10:5

CHESALON *(1)*
(AKA JEARIM)
Jearim (that is, **C**), descended Jos 15:10

CHESED *(1)*
C, Hazo, Pildash, Jidlaph, and Gn 22:22

CHESIL *(1)*
Eltolad, **C**, Hormah, Jos 15:30

CHEST *(12)*
Jehoiada the priest took a **c**, 2Kg 12:9
large amount of money in the **c**, 2Kg 12:10
king's command a **c** was made and 2Ch 24:8
put it in the **c** until it was 2Ch 24:10
Whenever the **c** was brought by 2Ch 24:11
deputy came and emptied the **c**, 2Ch 24:11
at this and leaps from my **c**. Jb 37:1
its **c** and arms were silver, Dn 2:32
What are these wounds on your **c**? Zch 13:6
striking his **c** and saying, Lk 18:13
like armor on your **c**, Eph 6:14
gold sash wrapped around His **c**. Rv 1:13

CHESTS *(4)*
went home, striking their **c**. Lk 23:48
of faith and love on our **c**, 1Th 5:8
they had **c** like iron Rv 9:9
sashes wrapped around their **c**. Rv 15:6

CHESULLOTH *(1)*
and ⌊included⌋ **C**, Shunem, Jos 19:18

CHEW *(6)*
the ones that **c** the cud or have Lv 11:4
does not **c** the cud—it is Lv 11:7
hoof and do not **c** the cud are Lv 11:26
the ones that **c** the cud or have Dt 14:7
though they **c** the cud, they do Dt 14:7
it does not ⌊**c**⌋ the cud—it is Dt 14:8

CHEWED *(1)*
before it was **c**, the LORD's Nm 11:33

CHEWS *(5)*
hooves and that **c** the cud. Lv 11:3
camel, though it **c** the cud, does Lv 11:4
hyrax, though it **c** the cud, does Lv 11:5
hare, though it **c** the cud, does Lv 11:6
divided in two and **c** the cud. Dt 14:6

CHEZIB *(1)*
It was at **C** that she gave birth Gn 38:5

CHICKS *(4)*
a bird's nest with **c** or eggs, Dt 22:6
is sitting on the **c** or eggs, Dt 22:6
gathers her **c** under her wings Mt 23:37
gathers her **c** under her wings Lk 13:34

CHIDON'S *(1)*
(AKA NACON)
they came to **C** threshing floor, 1Ch 13:9

CHIEF *(133)*
the **c** cupbearer and the chief Gn 40:2
chief cupbearer and the **c** baker, Gn 40:2
the **c** cupbearer told his dream Gn 40:9
When the **c** baker saw that the Gn 40:16
up the heads of the **c** cupbearer Gn 40:20
chief cupbearer and the **c** baker: Gn 40:20
he restored the **c** cupbearer to Gn 40:21
but he hanged the **c** baker, Gn 40:22
Yet the **c** cupbearer did not Gn 40:23
Then the **c** cupbearer said to Gn 41:9
he put me and the **c** baker in the Gn 41:10
The **c** of the Levite leaders was Nm 3:32
Doeg the Edomite, **c** of Saul's 1Sm 21:7
David's sons were **c** officials. 2Sm 8:18
was **c** of the officers 2Sm 23:8
took away Seraiah the **c** priest, 2Kg 25:18
Jeiel the **c**, Zechariah, 1Ch 5:7
Joel the **c**, Shapham the second 1Ch 5:12
the **c** official of God's temple; 1Ch 9:11
relatives. Shallum was their **c**; 1Ch 9:17
but the four **c** gatekeepers, 1Ch 9:26
up first, so he became the **c**. 1Ch 11:6
of Hachmoni was **c** of the Thirty; 1Ch 11:11
Three of the 30 **c** men went down 1Ch 11:15
the Reubenite, **c** of the 1Ch 11:42
Their **c** was Ahiezer son of 1Ch 12:3
Ezer was the **c**, Obadiah second, 1Ch 12:9
of Amasai, **c** of the Thirty, 1Ch 12:18
Asaph was the **c** and Zechariah 1Ch 16:5
sons were the **c** officials at 1Ch 18:17
of Perez and **c** of all the army 1Ch 27:3
commander, as **c** for the third 1Ch 27:5
of Zichri was the **c** official; 1Ch 27:16
Abijah son of Maacah as **c**, 2Ch 11:22
Amariah, the **c** priest, is over 2Ch 19:11
Then Azariah the **c** priest and 2Ch 26:20
the **c** priest of the household of 2Ch 31:10
Rehum the **c** deputy and Shimshai Ezr 4:8
⌊From⌋ Rehum the **c** deputy, Ezr 4:9
a reply to his **c** deputy Rehum, Ezr 4:17
son, Aaron the **c** priest's son Ezr 7:5
the **c** official of God's house, Neh 11:11
son of Haggedolim, was their **c**. Neh 11:14
their course and presided as **c**. Jb 29:25
of Immer and **c** officer in the Jr 20:1
the priest to be the **c** officer Jr 29:26
shout for the **c** of the nations! Jr 31:7
one of the king's **c** officers, Jr 41:1
took away Seraiah the **c** priest, Jr 52:24
the **c** prince of Meshech and Ezk 38:2
c prince of Meshech and Tubal. Ezk 38:3
c prince of Meshech and Tubal. Ezk 39:1
the **c** of his court officials, Dn 1:3
The **c** official gave them Dn 1:7
from the **c** official not to Dn 1:8
compassion from the **c** official, Dn 1:9
guard whom the **c** official had Dn 1:11
the **c** official presented them to Dn 1:18
of Babylon and **c** governor over Dn 2:48
appointed him **c** of the diviners, Dn 5:11
one of the **c** princes, came to Dn 10:13
assembled all the **c** priests and Mt 2:4
from the elders, **c** priests, and Mt 16:21
handed over to the **c** priests and Mt 20:18
When the **c** priests and the Mt 21:15
the **c** priests and the elders of Mt 21:23
When the **c** priests and the Mt 21:45
the **c** priests and the elders Mt 26:3
Iscariot—went to the **c** priests Mt 26:14
with him from the **c** priests and Mt 26:47
The **c** priests and the whole Mt 26:59
all the **c** priests and the elders Mt 27:1
of silver to the **c** priests and Mt 27:3
c priests took the silver and Mt 27:6
accused by the **c** priests and Mt 27:12
The **c** priests and the elders, Mt 27:20
In the same way the **c** priests, Mt 27:41
the **c** priests and the Pharisees Mt 27:62
reported to the **c** priests Mt 28:11
the elders, the **c** priests, and Mk 8:31
be handed over to the **c** priests Mk 10:33
Then the **c** priests and the Mk 11:18
temple complex, the **c** priests, Mk 11:27
The **c** priests and the scribes Mk 14:1
went to the **c** priests to hand Mk 14:10
and clubs, from the **c** priests, Mk 14:43
and all the **c** priests, the Mk 14:53
The **c** priests and the whole Mk 14:55
the **c** priests had a meeting with Mk 15:1
the **c** priests began to accuse Mk 15:3
of envy that the **c** priests had Mk 15:10
But the **c** priests stirred up the Mk 15:11
the **c** priests with the scribes Mk 15:31
by the elders, **c** priests, and Lk 9:22
who was a **c** tax collector, Lk 19:2
The **c** priests, the scribes, and Lk 19:47
the **c** priests and the scribes, Lk 20:1
scribes and the **c** priests looked Lk 20:19
The **c** priests and the scribes Lk 22:2
with the **c** priests and temple Lk 22:4
Jesus said to the **c** priests, Lk 22:52
both the **c** priests and the Lk 22:66
Pilate then told the **c** priests Lk 23:4
The **c** priests and the scribes Lk 23:10
called together the **c** priests, Lk 23:13
how our **c** priests and leaders Lk 24:20
and take it to the **c** servant." Jn 2:8
the **c** servant tasted the water Jn 2:9
so the **c** priests and the Jn 7:32
police came to the **c** priests and Jn 7:45
So the **c** priests and the Jn 11:47
The **c** priests and the Pharisees Jn 11:57
Therefore the **c** priests decided Jn 12:10
temple police from the **c** priests Jn 18:3
nation and the **c** priests handed Jn 18:35
the **c** priests and the temple Jn 19:6
the **c** priests answered. Jn 19:15
the **c** priests of the Jews said Jn 19:21
reported all that the **c** priests Ac 4:23
police and the **c** priests heard Ac 5:24
from the **c** priests to arrest Ac 9:14
as prisoners to the **c** priests?" Ac 9:21
them before the **c** magistrates, Ac 16:20
and the **c** magistrates stripped Ac 16:22
c magistrates sent the police Ac 16:35
Sceva, a Jewish **c** priest, were Ac 19:14
instructed the **c** priests and all Ac 22:30
men went to the **c** priests and Ac 23:14
Then the **c** priests and the Ac 25:2
the **c** priests and the elders of Ac 25:15
for that from the **c** priests. Ac 26:10
a commission from the **c** priests. Ac 26:12
And when the **c** Shepherd appears, 1Pt 5:4

CHIEFS *(27)*
These are the **c** of Esau's sons: Gn 36:15
C Teman, Omar, Zepho, Kenaz, Gn 36:15
These are the **c** of Eliphaz in Gn 36:16
C Nahath, Zerah, Shammah, and Gn 36:17
These are the **c** of Reuel in the Gn 36:17
C Jeush, Jalam, and Korah. Gn 36:18
These are the **c** of Esau's wife Gn 36:18
Edom), and these are their **c**. Gn 36:19
These are the **c** of the Horites, Gn 36:21
These are the **c** of the Horites: Gn 36:29
C Lotan, Shobal, Zibeon, Anah, Gn 36:29
These are the **c** of the Horites, Gn 36:30
These are the names of Esau's **c**, Gn 36:40
C Timna, Alvah, Jetheth, Gn 36:40
These are Edom's **c**, according to Gn 36:43
Then the **c** of Edom will be Ex 15:15
killed him and the **c** of Midian— Jos 13:21
died. Edom's **c**: Timna, Alvah, 1Ch 1:51
and Iram. These were Edom's **c**. 1Ch 1:54
All five of them were **c**. 1Ch 7:3
warriors, and **c** among the 1Ch 7:40
c according to their genealogies, 1Ch 8:28
c according to their genealogies, 1Ch 9:34
following were the **c** of David's 1Ch 11:10
c of thousands in Manasseh. 1Ch 12:20
200 **c** with all their relatives 1Ch 12:32
ancestral **c** of the Israelites 2Ch 5:2

CHIEFTAINS *(1)*
Her tribal **c** have led Egypt Is 19:13

CHILD *(97)*
had a male **c** with the LORD's Gn 4:1
me another **c** in place of Abel Gn 4:25
he fathered ⌊a **c**⌋ in his Gn 5:3
Sarai was barren; she had no **c**. Gn 11:30
Can a **c** be born to a Gn 17:17
The **c** grew and was weaned, Gn 21:8
brother, the **c** of his old age. Gn 44:20
If the **c** is a son, kill him, but Ex 1:16
She placed the **c** in it and set Ex 2:3
she saw the **c**—a little boy, Ex 2:6
Take this **c** and nurse him for Ex 2:9
When the **c** grew older, she Ex 2:10
any widow or fatherless **c**. Ex 22:22
and gives birth to a male **c**, Lv 12:2
she gives birth to a female **c**, Lv 12:5

resident ⌊or⌋ fatherless **c**, Dt 24:17
a fatherless **c**, or a widow.' Dt 27:19
was his only **c**; he had no other Jdg 11:34
Naomi took the **c**, placed him on Ru 4:16
After the **c** is weaned, I'll 1Sm 1:22
Michal had no **c** to the day of 2Sm 6:23
The **c** grew and one day went out 2Kg 4:18
The **c** sat on her lap until noon 2Kg 4:20
not hidden like a miscarried **c**, Jb 3:16
for a fatherless **c** and negotiate Jb 6:27
the nursing **c** of the poor is Jb 24:9
the fatherless **c** who had no one Jb 29:12
a fatherless **c** when I saw that I Jb 31:21
like a woman's miscarried ⌊**c**⌋, Ps 58:8
little weaned **c** with its mother Ps 131:2
mother; I am like a little **c**. Ps 131:2
that a stillborn **c** is better off Ec 6:3
Though a stillborn **c** does not Ec 6:5
For a **c** will be born for us, Is 9:6
number that a **c** could count them Is 10:19
and a **c** will lead them. Is 11:6
a woman forget her nursing **c**, Is 49:15
for the **c** of her womb? Is 49:15
like one bearing her first **c**. Jr 4:31
"A male **c** is born to you," Jr 20:15
son to Me, a delightful **c**? Jr 31:20
off man and woman, **c** and infant Jr 44:7
Israel was a **c**, I loved him, Hs 11:1
the **c** of my body for my own sin? Mc 6:7
for an only **c** and weep bitterly Zch 12:10
and search carefully for the **c**. Mt 2:8
above the place where the **c** was. Mt 2:9
they saw the **c** with Mary His Mt 2:11
Take the **c** and His mother, Mt 2:13
search for the **c** to destroy Him. Mt 2:13
took the **c** and His mother during Mt 2:14
Take the **c** and His mother and go Mt 2:20
took the **c** and His mother, Mt 2:21
to death, and a father his **c**. Mt 10:21
Then He called a **c** to Him and Mt 18:2
humbles himself like this **c**— Mt 18:4
welcomes one **c** like this in My Mt 18:5
The **c** is not dead but asleep." Mk 5:39
the place where the **c** was. Mk 5:40
Then He took the **c** by the hand Mk 5:41
found her **c** lying on the bed, Mk 7:30
Then He took a **c**, had him stand Mk 9:36
one little **c** such as this in My Mk 9:37
like a little **c** will never enter Mk 10:15
and leaves no **c**, his brother Mk 12:19
to death, and a father his **c**. Mk 13:12
and your **c** will be blessed! Lk 1:42
circumcise the **c** on the eighth Lk 1:59
"What then will this **c** become?" Lk 1:66
And **c**, you will be called a Lk 1:76
The **c** grew up and became Lk 1:80
they were told about this **c**, Lk 2:17
in the **c** Jesus to perform Lk 2:27
this **c** is destined to cause the Lk 2:34
and called out, "**C**, get up!" Lk 8:54
son, because he's my only ⌊**c**⌋. Lk 9:38
a little **c** and had him stand Lk 9:47
this little **c** in My name Lk 9:48
like a little **c** will never enter Lk 18:17
when she has given birth to a **c**, Jn 16:21
and faithful **c** in the Lord. 1Co 4:17
When I was a **c**, I spoke like a 1Co 13:11
I spoke like a **c**, I thought like 1Co 13:11
thought like a **c**, I reasoned 1Co 13:11
a child, I reasoned like a **c**. 1Co 13:11
that as long as the heir is a **c**, Gl 4:1
as then the **c** born according Gl 4:29
Timothy, my true **c** in the faith. 1Tm 1:2
Timothy, my **c**, I am giving you 1Tm 1:18
To Timothy, my dearly loved **c**. 2Tm 1:2
You, therefore, my **c**, be strong 2Tm 2:1
my true **c** in our common faith. Ti 1:4
to you for my **c**, whom I fathered Phm 10
saw that the **c** was beautiful, Heb 11:23
the parent also loves his **c**. 1Jn 5:1
birth he might devour her **c**. Rv 12:4
and her **c** was caught up to God Rv 12:5

CHILD'S *(3)*

who sought the **c** life are dead." Mt 2:20
took the **c** father, mother, and Mk 5:40
and the **c** father and mother. Lk 8:51

CHILDBEARING *(2)*

Sarah had passed the age of **c**. Gn 18:11
But she will be saved through **c**, 1Tm 2:15

CHILDBIRTH *(1)*

in the pains of **c** for you until Gl 4:19

CHILDHOOD *(2)*

"From **c**," he said. Mk 9:21
and that from **c** you have known 2Tm 3:15

CHILDISH *(2)*

a man, I put aside **c** things. 1Co 13:11
don't be **c** in your thinking, 1Co 14:20

CHILDLESS *(14)*

since I am **c** and the heir of my Gn 15:2
will bear their guilt and die **c**. Lv 20:20
his brother; they will be **c**. Lv 20:21
had children, but Hannah was **c**. 1Sm 1:2
your sword has made women **c**, 1Sm 15:33
mother will be **c** among women. 1Sm 15:33
c woman and do not deal kindly Jb 24:21
gives the **c** woman a household, Ps 113:9
I made ⌊them⌋ **c**; I destroyed My Jr 15:7
wives become **c** and widowed, Jr 18:21
this man as **c**, a man who will Jr 22:30
will leave you **c**, ⌊Jerusalem⌋. Ezk 5:17
a wife, and dies **c**, his brother Lk 20:28
after him, even though he was **c**. Ac 7:5

CHILDREN *(396)*

you will bear **c** in anguish. Gn 3:16
of man, who bore **c** to them. Gn 6:4
older brother, also had **c**. Gn 10:21
the father of all the **c** of Eber. Gn 10:21
wife Sarai had not borne him **c**. Gn 16:1
has prevented me from bearing **c**, Gn 16:2
perhaps I can have **c** by her." Gn 16:2
will command his **c** and his house Gn 18:19
so that they could bear **c**, Gn 20:17
that Sarah would nurse **c**? Gn 21:7
me or with my **c** and descendants. Gn 21:23
But the **c** inside her struggled Gn 25:22
Then Leah stopped having **c**. Gn 29:35
was not bearing Jacob ⌊any **c**⌋, Gn 30:1
who has withheld **c** from you?" Gn 30:2
she'll bear ⌊**c**⌋ for me so that Gn 30:3
that she had stopped having **c**, Gn 30:9
my wives and my **c** that I have Gn 30:26
belongs to us and to our **c**. Gn 31:16
got up and put his **c** and wives Gn 31:17
or for the **c** they have borne Gn 31:43
me, the mothers, and their **c**. Gn 32:11
So he divided the **c** among Leah, Gn 33:1
up and saw the women and **c**, Gn 33:5
The **c** God has graciously given Gn 33:5
and their **c** approached ⌊him Gn 33:6
Leah and her **c** also approached Gn 33:7
lord knows that the **c** are weak, Gn 33:13
to the livestock and the **c**, Gn 33:14
their possessions, **c**, and wives, Gn 34:29
These are the **c** of Anah: Gn 36:25
neither we, nor you, nor our **c**. Gn 43:8
me—you, your **c**, and Gn 45:10
land of Egypt for your young **c**, Gn 45:19
with their **c** and their wives Gn 46:5
and all his **c** with him went to Gn 46:6
C born to you after them will be Gn 48:6
Only their **c**, their sheep, and Gn 50:8
When your **c** ask you, 'What does Ex 12:26
kill us and our **c** and our Ex 17:3
punishing the **c** for the fathers' Ex 20:5
the wife and her **c** belong to her Ex 21:4
my master, my wife, and my **c**; Ex 21:5
woman so that her **c** are born Ex 21:22
be widows and your **c** fatherless. Ex 22:24
on the **c** and grandchildren Ex 34:7
to you and your **c** from the Lv 10:14
permanently to you and your **c**, Lv 10:15
make any of your **c** pass through Lv 18:21
gives any of his **c** to Molech Lv 20:2
gives any of his **c** to Molech, Lv 20:4
has no **c**, and returns to Lv 22:13
Then he and his **c** are to be Lv 25:41
he and his **c** are to be released Lv 25:54
that will deprive you of your **c**, Lv 26:22
and will be able to conceive **c**. Nm 5:28
wives and little **c** will become Nm 14:3
wrongdoing on the **c** to the third Nm 14:18
will bring your **c** whom you said Nm 14:31
Your **c** will be shepherds in the Nm 14:33
their wives, **c**, and infants. Nm 16:27
women and their **c** captive, Nm 31:9
all the male **c** and kill every Nm 31:17
Our little **c**, wives, livestock, Nm 32:26
Your little **c** who you said would Dt 1:39
including the women and **c**. Dt 2:34
men, women, and **c** of every city. Dt 3:6
wives, young **c**, and livestock— Dt 3:19
Teach them to your **c** and your Dt 4:9
earth and may instruct their **c**.' Dt 4:10
When you have **c** and Dt 4:25
that you and your **c** after you Dt 4:40
punishing the **c** for the fathers' Dt 5:9
they and their **c** will prosper Dt 5:29
Repeat them to your **c**. Dt 6:7
it is not your **c** who experienced Dt 11:2
them to your **c**, talking about Dt 11:19
and those of your **c** may be many Dt 11:21
you and your **c** after you will Dt 12:25
that you and your **c** after you Dt 12:28
may take the women, **c**, animals, Dt 20:14
The **c** born to them in the third Dt 23:8
for ⌊their⌋ **c** or children for Dt 24:16
their⌋ children or **c** for ⌊their⌋ Dt 24:16
you prosper abundantly with **c**, Dt 28:11
You will eat your **c**, the flesh Dt 28:53
embraces, and the rest of his **c**, Dt 28:54
her legs and the **c** she bears, Dt 28:57
your **c**, your wives, and the Dt 29:11
of your **c** who follow you Dt 29:22
belong to us and our **c** forever, Dt 29:29
and you and your **c** return to the Dt 30:2
the work of your hands with **c**, Dt 30:9
men, women, **c**, and foreigners Dt 31:12
their **c** who do not know ⌊the Dt 31:13
they are not His **c** but a devious Dt 32:5
generation—unfaithful **c**. Dt 32:20
the sword will take their **c**, Dt 32:25
may command your **c** to carefully Dt 32:46
wives, young **c**, and livestock Jos 1:14
when your **c** ask you, 'What do Jos 4:6
When your **c** ask their fathers in Jos 4:21
tell your **c**, 'Israel crossed Jos 4:22
women, little **c**, and foreigners Jos 8:35
wife was barren and had no **c**. Jdg 13:2
you are barren and have no **c**, Jdg 13:3
their small **c**, livestock, Jdg 18:21
sword, including women and **c**. Jdg 21:10
without her two **c** and without Ru 1:5
Peninnah had **c**, but Hannah was 1Sm 1:2
LORD give you **c** by this woman 1Sm 2:20
men and women, **c** and infants, 1Sm 15:3
men and women, **c** and infants, 1Sm 22:19
for each man's wife and **c**. 1Sm 30:22
and grew up with him and his **c**. 2Sm 12:3
his men and the **c** who were with 2Sm 15:22
best wives and **c** are mine as 1Kg 20:3
your **c** you are to give to me. 1Kg 20:5
wives, my **c**, my silver, and my 1Kg 20:7
to take my two **c** as his slaves." 2Kg 4:1
did not put the **c** of the 2Kg 14:6
be put to death because of **c**, 2Kg 14:6
and **c** must not be put to death 2Kg 14:6
burned their **c** in the fire to 2Kg 17:31
Their **c** and grandchildren 2Kg 17:41
for **c** have come to the point of 2Kg 19:3
of Hezron had **c** by ⌊his⌋ wife 1Ch 2:18
Seled died without **c**. 1Ch 2:30
Jether died without **c**. 1Ch 2:32
brothers did not have many **c**, 1Ch 4:27
Amram's **c**: Aaron, Moses, and 1Ch 6:3
for they had many wives and **c**. 1Ch 7:4
the names of the **c** born to him 1Ch 14:4
their wives, and their **c**. 2Ch 20:13
he did not put their **c** to death, 2Ch 25:4
must not die because of **c**, 2Ch 25:4
and **c** must not die because of 2Ch 25:4
and burned his **c** in the fire, 2Ch 28:3
some of his own **c** cut him down 2Ch 32:21
for us, our **c**, and all our Ezr 8:21
and **c** gathered around him. Ezr 10:1
the ⌊foreign⌋ wives and their **c**, Ezr 10:3
some of the wives had borne **c**. Ezr 10:44
We and our **c** are ⌊just⌋ like our Neh 5:5
like our countrymen and their **c**, Neh 5:5
The women and **c** also celebrated, Neh 12:43
Half of their **c** spoke the Neh 13:24
old, women and **c**—and plunder Est 3:13

women and **c**, and to take their	Est 8:11
⌊for his **c**⌋ and purify them,	Jb 1:5
Perhaps my **c** have sinned, having	Jb 1:5
His **c** are far from safety.	Jb 5:4
Since your **c** sinned against Him,	Jb 8:4
the eyes of his **c** will fail.	Jb 17:5
He has no **c** or descendants among	Jb 18:19
and my own **c** find me repulsive.	Jb 19:17
His **c** will beg from the poor,	Jb 20:10
Their **c** are established while	Jb 21:8
their **c** skip about,	Jb 21:11
a person's punishment for his **c**.	Jb 21:19
nourishment for their **c**.	Jb 24:5
Even if his **c** increase, they are	Jb 27:14
with me and my **c** were around me,	Jb 29:5
this and saw his **c** and their	Jb 42:16
and their **c** to the fourth	Jb 42:16
from the mouths of **c** and nursing	Ps 8:2
leave their surplus to their **c**.	Ps 17:14
Come, **c**, listen to me;	Ps 34:11
or his **c** begging bread.	Ps 37:25
and his **c** are a blessing.	Ps 37:26
but the **c** of the wicked will be	Ps 37:28
must not hide them from their **c**,	Ps 78:4
our fathers to teach to their **c**	Ps 78:5
generation—**c** yet to be born—	Ps 78:6
were to rise and tell their **c**	Ps 78:6
and Your splendor by their **c**.	Ps 90:16
Your servants' **c** will dwell	Ps 102:28
father has compassion on his **c**,	Ps 103:13
Let his **c** be fatherless and his	Ps 109:9
Let his **c** wander as beggars,	Ps 109:10
be gracious to his fatherless **c**.	Ps 109:12
her⌋ the joyful mother of **c**.	Ps 113:9
from the LORD, **c**, a reward.	Ps 127:3
and will see your children's **c**!	Ps 128:6
and blesses your **c** within you.	Ps 147:13
let the **c** of Zion rejoice in	Ps 149:2
and his **c** have a refuge.	Pr 14:26
his **c** who come after him will be	Pr 20:7
father a hundred **c** and live many	Ec 6:3
I have raised **c** and brought them	Is 1:2
brood of evildoers, depraved **c**!	Is 1:4
I am with the **c** the LORD has	Is 8:18
Their **c** will be smashed ⌊to	Is 13:16
will not look with pity on **c**.	Is 13:18
he sees his **c**, the work of My	Is 29:23
Woe to the rebellious **c**!	Is 30:1
deceptive **c**, children who do	Is 30:9
c who do not obey the LORD's	Is 30:9
⌊as⌋ when **c** come to the point of	Is 37:3
Your faithfulness known to **c**	Is 38:19
a widow or know the loss of **c**.	Is 47:8
loss of **c** and widowhood.	Is 47:9
will wear all your **c** as jewelry,	Is 49:18
c that you have been deprived	Is 49:20
was deprived of my **c** and barren,	Is 49:21
you, and I will save your **c**.	Is 49:25
among all the **c** she has raised;	Is 51:18
Your **c** have fainted;	Is 51:20
For the **c** of the forsaken one	Is 54:1
more than the **c** of the married	Is 54:1
Then all your **c** will be taught	Is 54:13
you rebellious **c**, you race of	Is 57:4
who slaughter **c** in the wadis	Is 57:5
or from the mouth of your **c**,	Is 59:21
the mouth of your children's **c**,	Is 59:21
to bring your **c** from far away,	Is 60:9
c who will not be disloyal,"	Is 63:8
success or bear **c** ⌊destined⌋ for	Is 65:23
case against your children's **c**.	Jr 2:9
have struck down your **c** in vain;	Jr 2:30
you faithless **c**"—⌊this is⌋	Jr 3:14
the **c** of Israel weeping and	Jr 3:21
Return, you faithless **c**.	Jr 3:22
They are foolish **c**, without	Jr 4:22
Your **c** have abandoned Me and	Jr 5:7
it⌋ out on the **c** in the street,	Jr 6:11
cutting off **c** from the streets,	Jr 9:21
while their **c** remember their	Jr 17:2
hand their **c** over to famine,	Jr 18:21
to burn their **c** in the fire as	Jr 19:5
His **c** will be as in past days;	Jr 30:20
weeping for her **c**, refusing to	Jr 31:15
for her **c** because they are	Jr 31:15
and your **c** will return from the	Jr 31:16
and your **c** will return to their	Jr 31:17
men, women, and **c**, the poorest	Jr 40:7
soldiers, women, **c**, and court	Jr 41:16
the men, women, **c**, king's	Jr 43:6
Her **c** have gone away as captives	Lm 1:5
My **c** are desolate because the	Lm 1:16
Outside, the sword takes the **c**;	Lm 1:20
because **c** and infants faint in	Lm 2:11
lives of your **c** who are fainting	Lm 2:19
Should women eat their own **c**,	Lm 2:20
Little **c** beg for bread, but no	Lm 4:4
women have cooked their own **c**;	Lm 4:10
The **c** are obstinate and	Ezk 2:4
the ⌊older⌋ women and little **c**,	Ezk 9:6
slaughtered My **c** and gave them	Ezk 16:21
blood of your **c** that you gave to	Ezk 16:36
who despised her husband and **c**.	Ezk 16:45
despised their husbands and **c**.	Ezk 16:45
I said to their **c** in the	Ezk 20:18
But the **c** rebelled against Me.	Ezk 20:21
making your **c** pass through the	Ezk 20:31
even made the **c** they bore to Me	Ezk 23:37
their **c** for their idols,	Ezk 23:39
deprive them of ⌊their⌋ **c**.	Ezk 36:12
and deprive your nation of **c**,	Ezk 36:13
and deprive your nation of **c**."	Ezk 36:14
with their **c** and grandchildren	Ezk 37:25
who have fathered **c** among you.	Ezk 47:22
they, their **c**, and their wives	Dn 6:24
and ⌊have⌋ **c** of promiscuity,	Hs 1:2
on her **c** because they are	Hs 2:4
they are the **c** of promiscuity.	Hs 2:4
gave birth to illegitimate **c**.	Hs 5:7
if they raise **c**, I will bereave	Hs 9:12
bring out his **c** to the	Hs 9:13
Even if they bear **c**, I will kill	Hs 9:16
to pieces along with ⌊their⌋ **c**.	Hs 10:14
His **c** will come trembling from	Hs 11:10
Tell your **c** about it, and let	Jl 1:3
and let your **c** tell their	Jl 1:3
let your children tell their **c**,	Jl 1:3
and their **c** the next generation.	Jl 1:3
gather the **c**, even those nursing	Jl 2:16
C of Zion, rejoice and be glad	Jl 2:23
in sorrow for your precious **c**;	Mc 1:16
blessing from their **c** forever.	Mc 2:9
Her **c** were also dashed to pieces	Nah 3:10
Their **c** will see it and be glad;	Zch 10:7
they and their **c** will live and	Zch 10:9
to ⌊their⌋ **c** and the hearts	Mal 4:6
the hearts of **c** to their fathers	Mal 4:6
all the male **c** in and around	Mt 2:16
Rachel weeping for her **c**;	Mt 2:18
able to raise up **c** for Abraham	Mt 3:9
to give good gifts to your **c**,	Mt 7:11
C will even rise up against	Mt 10:21
It's like **c** sitting in the	Mt 11:16
5,000 men, besides women and **c**.	Mt 14:21
4,000 men, besides women and **c**.	Mt 15:38
are converted and become like **c**,	Mt 18:3
his wife, his **c**, and everything	Mt 18:25
Then **c** were brought to Him so He	Mt 19:13
Leave the **c** alone, and don't	Mt 19:14
father or mother, **c**, or fields	Mt 19:29
He did and the **c** in the temple	Mt 21:15
hear what these ⌊**c**⌋ are saying?"	Mt 21:16
from the mouths of **c** and nursing	Mt 21:16
dies, having no **c**, his brother	Mt 22:24
to gather your **c** together,	Mt 23:37
blood be on us and on our **c**!"	Mt 27:25
Allow the **c** to be satisfied	Mk 7:27
bringing little **c** to Him so He	Mk 10:13
Let the little **c** come to Me.	Mk 10:14
said to them, "**C**, how hard it is	Mk 10:24
mother or father, **c**, or fields	Mk 10:29
mothers and **c**, and fields, with	Mk 10:30
C will rise up against parents	Mk 13:12
But they had no **c** because	Lk 1:7
hearts of fathers to their **c**,	Lk 1:17
able to raise up **c** for Abraham	Lk 3:8
They are like **c** sitting in the	Lk 7:32
is vindicated by all her **c**."	Lk 7:35
and my **c** and I have gone to bed.	Lk 11:7
to give good gifts to your **c**,	Lk 11:13
to gather your **c** together,	Lk 13:34
and mother, wife and **c**, brothers	Lk 14:26
Let the little **c** come to Me,	Lk 18:16
parents or **c** because of the	Lk 18:29
you and your **c** within you to	Lk 19:44
took a wife and died without **c**.	Lk 20:29
all seven died and left no **c**.	Lk 20:31
weep for yourselves and your **c**.	Lk 23:28
them the right to be **c** of God,	Jn 1:12
"If you were Abraham's **c**,"	Jn 8:39
to unite the scattered **c** of God.	Jn 11:52
C, I am with you a little while	Jn 13:33
is for you and for your **c**,	Ac 2:39
this to us their **c** by raising up	Ac 13:33
their wives and **c**, escorted us	Ac 21:5
circumcise their **c** or to walk in	Ac 21:21
our spirit that we are God's **c**,	Rm 8:16
and if **c**, also heirs—heirs of	Rm 8:17
the glorious freedom of God's **c**.	Rm 8:21
are they all **c** because they are	Rm 9:7
it is not the **c** by physical	Rm 9:8
descent who are God's **c**,	Rm 9:8
but the **c** of the promise are	Rm 9:8
but to warn you as my dear **c**.	1Co 4:14
Otherwise your **c** would be	1Co 7:14
speak as to **c**—you also should	2Co 6:13
For **c** are not obligated to save	2Co 12:14
but parents for their **c**.	2Co 12:14
when we were **c**, were in slavery	Gl 4:3
My **c**, again I am in the pains of	Gl 4:19
Sinai and bears **c** into slavery—	Gl 4:24
she is in slavery with her **c**.	Gl 4:25
for the **c** of the desolate are	Gl 4:27
like Isaac, are **c** of promise.	Gl 4:28
we are not **c** of the slave but of	Gl 4:31
by nature we were **c** under wrath,	Eph 2:3
we will no longer be little **c**,	Eph 4:14
of God, as dearly loved **c**.	Eph 5:1
Walk as **c** of light—	Eph 5:8
C, obey your parents in the Lord,	Eph 6:1
don't stir up anger in your **c**,	Eph 6:4
c of God who are faultless in a	Php 2:15
C, obey your parents in	Col 3:20
exasperate your **c**, so they won't	Col 3:21
mother nurtures her own **c**.	1Th 2:7
like a father with his own **c**,	1Th 2:11
having his **c** under control with	1Tm 3:4
managing their **c** and their own	1Tm 3:12
any widow has **c** or grandchildren	1Tm 5:4
has brought up **c**, shown	1Tm 5:10
to marry, have **c**, manage their	1Tm 5:14
having faithful **c** not accused of	Ti 1:6
to love their husbands and **c**,	Ti 2:4
I am with the **c** God gave Me.	Heb 2:13
Now since the **c** have flesh and	Heb 2:14
are illegitimate **c** and not sons.	Heb 12:8
As obedient **c**, do not be	1Pt 1:14
have become her **c** when you do	1Pt 3:6
trained in greed. Accursed **c**!	2Pt 2:14
My little **c**, I am writing you	1Jn 2:1
to you, little **c**, because your	1Jn 2:12
written to you, **c**, because you	1Jn 2:14
C, it is the last hour.	1Jn 2:18
So now, little **c**, remain in Him,	1Jn 2:28
we should be called God's **c**.	1Jn 3:1
we are God's **c** now, and what we	1Jn 3:2
c, let no one deceive you!	1Jn 3:7
is how God's **c**—and the Devil's	1Jn 3:10
and the Devil's **c**—are made	1Jn 3:10
Little **c**, we must not love in	1Jn 3:18
from God, little **c**, and you have	1Jn 4:4
we love God's **c** when we love God	1Jn 5:2
Little **c**, guard yourselves from	1Jn 5:21
To the elect lady and her **c**,	2Jn 1
some of your **c** walking in truth	2Jn 4
The **c** of your elect sister send	2Jn 13
to hear that my **c** are walking in	3Jn 4
will kill her **c** with the plague	Rv 2:23

CHILDREN'S *(11)*

any of them his **c** flesh that he	Dt 28:55
thirsty pant for his **c** wealth.	Jb 5:5
numbers⌋, both yours and your **c**.	Ps 115:14
and will see your **c** children!	Ps 128:6
the mouth of your **c** children,	Is 59:21
a case against your **c** children.	Jr 2:9
and the **c** teeth are set on edge.	Jr 31:29
and the **c** teeth are set on edge?	Ezk 18:2
to take the **c** bread and throw	Mt 15:26
to take the **c** bread and throw	Mk 7:27
the table eat the **c** crumbs."	Mk 7:28

CHILEAB *(1)*

(AKA DANIEL)

second was **C**, by Abigail, the	2Sm 3:3

CHILION *(3)*
his two sons were Mahlon and **C**. Ru 1:2
both Mahlon and **C** also died, Ru 1:5
to Elimelech, **C**, and Mahlon. Ru 4:9

CHILMAD *(1)*
Asshur, and **C** traded with you. Ezk 27:23

CHIMHAM *(4)*
But here is your servant **C**: 2Sm 19:37
C will cross over with me, 2Sm 19:38
to Gilgal, and **C** went with him. 2Sm 19:40
in Geruth **C**, which is near Jr 41:17

CHIN *(2)*
an infection on the head or **c**, Lv 13:29
a skin disease of the head or **c**. Lv 13:30

CHINNERETH *(6)*
(AKA GALILEE, GENNESARET)
eastern slope of the Sea of **C**. Nm 34:11
borders from **C** as far as the Sea Dt 3:17
the plain south of **C**, the Judean Jos 11:2
east of the Sea of **C** to the Sea Jos 12:3
of the Sea of **C** on the east side Jos 13:27
Zer, Hammath, Rakkath, **C**, Jos 19:35

CHINNEROTH *(1)*
all **C**, and the whole land 1Kg 15:20

CHIOS *(1)*
the next day we arrived off **C**. Ac 20:15

CHIRP *(2)*
spiritists who **c** and mutter," Is 8:19
I **c** like a swallow ⌊or⌋ a crane; Is 38:14

CHIRPED *(1)*
no beak opened or **c**. Is 10:14

CHISEL *(3)*
you use your **c** on it, you will Ex 20:25
that no hammer, **c**, or any iron 1Kg 6:7
hands of a craftsman with a **c**. Jr 10:3

CHISELED *(1)*
ministry of death, **c** in letters 2Co 3:7

CHISELS *(1)*
shapes it with **c** and outlines it Is 44:13

CHISLEV *(2)*
the month of **C** in the twentieth Neh 1:1
of the ninth month, which is **C**. Zch 7:1

CHISLON *(1)*
Elidad son of **C** from the tribe Nm 34:21

CHISLOTH-TABOR *(1)*
sunrise along the border of **C**, Jos 19:12

CHITLISH *(1)*
Cabbon, Lahmam, **C**, Jos 15:40

CHLOE'S *(1)*
by members of **C** household, 1Co 1:11

CHOICE *(42)*
herd and got a tender, **c** calf. Gn 18:7
we have no **c** in the matter. Gn 24:50
and bring me two **c** young goats, Gn 27:9
of his donkey to the **c** vine. Gn 49:11
Make the **c** rather than me ⌊by Ex 8:9
and all your **c** offerings you vow Dt 12:11
with the **c** gifts of the land and Dt 33:16
besides 700 **c** men rallied by the Jdg 20:15
There were 700 **c** men who were Jdg 20:16
10,000 **c** men from all Israel Jdg 20:34
of Israel's **c** men and went to 1Sm 24:2
by 3,000 of the **c** men of Israel, 1Sm 26:2
all the **c** men in Israel, 2Sm 6:1
he mobilized 180,000 **c** warriors 1Kg 12:21
fortified city and every **c** city. 2Kg 3:19
cedars, its **c** cypress trees. 2Kg 19:23
the LORD says: 'Take your ⌊**c**⌋— 1Ch 21:11
180,000 **c** warriors—to 2Ch 11:1
in order with 400,000 **c** men. 2Ch 13:3
army of 800,000 **c** men in battle 2Ch 13:3
and 500,000 **c** men of Israel were 2Ch 13:17
to be 300,000 **c** men who could 2Ch 25:5
killed their **c** young men with 2Ch 36:17
one ox, six **c** sheep, and some Neh 5:18
table was spread with **c** food. Jb 36:16
down Israel's **c** young men. Ps 78:31
words are like **c** food that goes Pr 18:8
don't desire his **c** food, for Pr 23:3
and don't desire his **c** food, Pr 23:6
words are like **c** food that goes Pr 26:22
have trampled its **c** vines that Is 16:8
aged wine, **c** meat, finely aged Is 25:6
cedars, its **c** cypress trees. Is 37:24
c vine from the very best seed. Jr 2:21
Fill it with **c** bones. Ezk 24:4
your merchants in **c** garments, Ezk 27:24
the **c** and best of Lebanon, Ezk 31:16
transfer this **c** ⌊part⌋ of the Ezk 48:14
Mary has made the right **c**, Lk 10:42
days God made a **c** among you, Ac 15:7
went out to you by his own **c**. 2Co 8:17
By His own **c**, He gave us a new Jms 1:18

CHOICES *(3)*
I am offering you three ⌊**c**⌋. 2Sm 24:12
told him ⌊the **c**⌋, and asked him, 2Sm 24:13
I am offering you three ⌊**c**⌋. 1Ch 21:10

CHOICEST *(7)*
with the **c** grains of wheat; Dt 32:14
of pomegranates with **c** fruits, Sg 4:13
his garden and eat its **c** fruits. Sg 4:16
you will enjoy the **c** of foods. Is 55:2
cut down the **c** of your cedars Jr 22:7
your contributions and **c** gifts, Ezk 20:40
Take the **c** of the flock and also Ezk 24:5

CHOKE *(2)*
seduction of wealth **c** the word, Mt 13:22
things enter in and **c** the word, Mk 4:19

CHOKED *(4)*
the thorns came up and **c** them. Mt 13:7
and the thorns came up and **c** it, Mk 4:7
sprang up with it and **c** it. Lk 8:7
way and are **c** with worries, Lk 8:14

CHOKES *(1)*
He **c** me by the neck of my Jb 30:18

CHOKING *(1)*
him, started **c** him, and said, Mt 18:28

CHOOSE *(38)*
of the man I **c** will sprout, Nm 17:5
your God will **c** the place to Dt 12:11
C life so that you and your Dt 30:19
Now **c** 12 men from the tribes of Jos 3:12
C 12 men from the people, Jos 4:2
altar at the place He would **c**. Jos 9:27
c for yourselves today the one Jos 24:15
heart. You **c**. I'm right here 1Sm 14:7
C one of your men and have him 1Sm 17:8
Absalom, "Let me **c** 12,000 men, 2Sm 17:1
C one of them, and I will do it 2Sm 24:12
They are to **c** one bull for 1Kg 18:23
c for yourselves one bull and 1Kg 18:25
C a rider and send him to meet 2Kg 9:17
C one of them for yourself, 1Ch 21:10
I answer Him or **c** my arguments Jb 9:14
and you **c** the language of the Jb 15:5
His⌋? You must **c**, not I! So Jb 34:33
show him the way he should **c**. Ps 25:12
is the one You **c** and bring near Ps 65:4
When I **c** a time, I will judge Ps 75:2
Joseph and did not **c** the tribe Ps 78:67
didn't **c** to fear the LORD, Pr 1:29
violent man or **c** any of his ways Pr 3:31
what is bad and **c** what is good, Is 7:15
what is bad and **c** what is good, Is 7:16
Jacob and will **c** Israel again. Is 14:1
Sabbaths, and **c** what pleases Me Is 56:4
Will the fast I **c** be like this: Is 58:5
Isn't the fast I **c**: To break the Is 58:6
So I will **c** their punishment, Is 66:4
Zion and again **c** Jerusalem." Zch 1:17
He will once again **c** Jerusalem. Zch 2:12
how they would **c** the best places Lk 14:7
Didn't I **c** you, the Twelve Jn 6:70
You did not **c** Me, but I chose Jn 15:16
don't know which one I should **c**. Php 1:22
Didn't God **c** the poor in this Jms 2:5

CHOOSES *(27)*
Or if he **c** her for his son, Ex 21:9
let the one He **c** come near Him. Nm 16:5
man the LORD **c** will be the one Nm 16:7
LORD your God **c** from all your Dt 12:5
place the LORD **c** in one of your Dt 12:14
the place the LORD your God **c**— Dt 12:18
LORD your God **c** to put His name Dt 12:21
and go to the place the LORD **c**. Dt 12:26
place where He **c** to have His Dt 14:23
LORD your God **c** to put His name Dt 14:24
the place the LORD your God **c**. Dt 14:25
God in the place the LORD **c**. Dt 15:20
where the LORD **c** to have His Dt 16:2
LORD your God **c** to have His name Dt 16:6
the place the LORD your God **c**, Dt 16:7
place where He **c** to have His Dt 16:11
LORD your God in the place He **c**, Dt 16:15
LORD your God in the place He **c**: Dt 16:16
the place the LORD your God **c**. Dt 17:8
you at the place the LORD **c**. Dt 17:10
the king the LORD your God **c**. Dt 17:15
to go to the place the LORD **c**, Dt 18:6
LORD your God **c** to have His name Dt 26:2
LORD your God at the place He **c**, Dt 31:11
He **c** for us our inheritance— Ps 47:4
He directs it wherever He **c**. Pr 21:1
Anyone who **c** you is detestable. Is 41:24

CHOOSING *(1)*
a pedestal, **c** wood that does not Is 40:20

CHOP *(5)*
and **c** down their Asherah poles. Ex 34:13
swings the ax to **c** down a tree, Dt 19:5
of Hosts will **c** off the branches Is 10:33
the tree and **c** off its branches Dn 4:14
You **c** them up like flesh for the Mc 3:3

CHOPPED *(8)*
people of the city **c** up the cart 1Sm 6:14
Asa **c** down her obscene image 1Kg 15:13
pillars and **c** down their Asherah 2Ch 14:3
Asa **c** down her obscene image, 2Ch 15:16
sacred pillars, **c** down the 2Ch 31:1
that were above them he **c** down. 2Ch 34:4
He **c** down all the incense altars 2Ch 34:7
Moab's horn is **c** off; Jr 48:25

CHOPS *(1)*
above the one who **c** with it? Is 10:15

CHORAZIN *(2)*
Woe to you, **C**! Woe to you, Mt 11:21
Woe to you, **C**! Woe to you, Lk 10:13

CHOSE *(37)*
they took any they **c** as wives Gn 6:2
Lot **c** the entire Jordan Valley Gn 13:11
So Moses **c** able men from all Ex 18:25
master, who **c** her for himself Ex 21:8
c their descendants after them Dt 4:37
was devoted to you and **c** you, Dt 7:7
c their descendants after them Dt 10:15
⌊He **c**⌋ you out of all the Dt 10:15
c the best ⌊part⌋ for himself, Dt 33:21
Israel **c** new gods, then war was Jdg 5:8
He **c** 3,000 men from Israel for 1Sm 13:2
in his hand and **c** five smooth 1Sm 17:40
the LORD who **c** me over your 2Sm 6:21
he **c** some men out of all the 2Sm 10:9
because of Jerusalem that I **c**." 1Kg 11:13
the city I **c** out of all the 1Kg 11:32
whom I **c** and who kept My 1Kg 11:34
the city I **c** for Myself to put 1Kg 11:36
he **c** some men out of all the 1Ch 19:10
God of Israel **c** me out of all my 1Ch 28:4
For He **c** Judah as leader, and 1Ch 28:4
place where I **c** to have My name Neh 1:9
the LORD God who **c** Abram and Neh 9:7
He **c** instead the tribe of Judah, Ps 78:68
He **c** David His servant and took Ps 78:70
in My sight and **c** what I did not Is 65:12
in My sight and **c** what I didn't Is 66:4
I **c** you before I formed you in Jr 1:5
the day I **c** Israel, I swore an Ezk 20:5
because of the elect, whom He **c**. Mk 13:20
and He **c** 12 of them—He Lk 6:13
did not choose Me, but I **c** you. Jn 15:16
So they **c** Stephen, a man full of Ac 6:5
people Israel **c** our forefathers, Ac 13:17
Then Paul **c** Silas and departed, Ac 15:40
for He **c** us in Him, before the Eph 1:4
and **c** to suffer with the people Heb 11:25

CHOSEN *(105)*
For I have **c** him so that he will Gn 18:19
You are God's **c** one among us. Gn 23:6
present the goat **c** by lot for Lv 16:9
But the goat **c** by lot for Azazel Lv 16:10
and Abiram, **c** by the community, Nm 26:9
your God has **c** you to be His own Dt 7:6
The LORD has **c** you to be His Dt 14:2
your God has **c** him and his sons Dt 18:5
your God has **c** them to serve Him Dt 21:5
yourselves have **c** to worship the Jos 24:22
cry out to the gods you have **c**. Jdg 10:14

king you've **c** for yourselves, 1Sm 8:18
you see the one the LORD has **c**? 1Sm 10:24
Now here is the king you've **c**, 1Sm 12:13
LORD hasn't **c** this one either 1Sm 16:8
LORD hasn't **c** this one either 1Sm 16:9
"The LORD hasn't **c** any of these." 1Sm 16:10
all the men of Israel have **c**. 2Sm 16:18
Gibeah of Saul, the LORD's **c**." 2Sm 21:6
is among Your people You have **c**, 1Kg 3:8
I have not **c** a city to build a 1Kg 8:16
But I have **c** David to rule My 1Kg 8:16
city You have **c** and the temple I 1Kg 8:44
city You have **c**, and the temple 1Kg 8:48
city the LORD had **c** from all the 1Kg 14:21
which I have **c** out of all the 2Kg 21:7
that I have **c**, and the temple 2Kg 23:27
houses, **c** men, warriors, 1Ch 7:40
number of those **c** to be 1Ch 9:22
the LORD has **c** them to carry 1Ch 15:2
descendants—His **c** ones. 1Ch 16:13
rest who were **c** and designated 1Ch 16:41
has **c** my son Solomon to sit on 1Ch 28:5
for I have **c** him to be My son, 1Ch 28:6
that the LORD has **c** you to build 1Ch 28:10
God has **c** him alone—is 1Ch 29:1
I have not **c** a city to build a 2Ch 6:5
and I have not **c** a man to be 2Ch 6:5
But I have **c** Jerusalem so that 2Ch 6:6
and I have **c** David to be over My 2Ch 6:6
city You have **c** and the temple 2Ch 6:34
the city You have **c**, and toward 2Ch 6:38
prayer and have **c** this place for 2Ch 7:12
And I have now **c** and consecrated 2Ch 7:16
city the LORD had **c** from all the 2Ch 12:13
for the LORD has **c** you to stand 2Ch 29:11
which I have **c** out of all the 2Ch 33:7
that God has **c** to overlook some Jb 11:6
people He has **c** to be His own Ps 33:12
Fire consumed His **c** young men, Ps 78:63
made a covenant with My **c** one; Ps 89:3
exalted one **c** from the people Ps 89:19
descendants—His **c** ones. Ps 105:6
and Aaron, whom He had **c**. Ps 105:26
His **c** ones with shouts of joy. Ps 105:43
the prosperity of Your **c** ones, Ps 106:5
if Moses His **c** one had not stood Ps 106:23
I have **c** the way of truth; Ps 119:30
for I have **c** Your precepts. Ps 119:173
For the LORD has **c** Zion; Ps 132:13
For the LORD has **c** Jacob for Ps 135:4
name is to be **c** over great Pr 22:1
of the gardens you have **c**. Is 1:29
I have commanded My **c** ones; Is 13:3
Jacob, whom I have **c**, descendant Is 41:8
I have **c** you and not rejected Is 41:9
Him, ⌊this is⌋ My **C** One; Is 42:1
and My servant whom I have **c**, Is 43:10
to give drink to My **c** people. Is 43:20
servant, Israel whom I have **c**. Is 44:1
My servant; I have **c** Jeshurun. Is 44:2
My servant and Israel My **c** one. Is 45:4
of Israel—and He has **c** you." Is 49:7
My **c** ones will possess it, Is 65:9
behind as a curse for My **c** ones, Is 65:15
My **c** ones will fully enjoy the Is 65:22
all these have **c** their ways and Is 66:3
Death will be **c** over life by all Jr 8:3
the two families He had **c**. Jr 33:24
appoint whoever is **c** for her. Jr 49:19
appoint whoever is **c** for her. Jr 50:44
signet ring, for I have **c** you." Hg 2:23
LORD who has **c** Jerusalem rebuke Zch 3:2
is My Servant whom I have **c**, Mt 12:18
are invited, but few are **c**." Mt 22:14
happened that he was **c** by lot, Lk 1:9
This is My Son, the **C** One; Lk 9:35
is God's Messiah, the **C** One!" Lk 23:35
I know those I have **c**. Jn 13:18
but I have **c** you out of it, Jn 15:19
to the apostles whom He had **c**. Ac 1:2
which of these two You have **c** Ac 1:24
this man is My **c** instrument to Ac 9:15
time a remnant **c** by grace. Rm 11:5
Greet Rufus, **c** in the Lord; Rm 16:13
God has **c** the world's foolish 1Co 1:27
and God has **c** the world's weak 1Co 1:27
God has **c** the world's 1Co 1:28
Therefore, God's **c** ones, holy Col 3:12
God has **c** you for salvation 2Th 2:13
Cappadocia, Asia, and Bithynia, **c** 1Pt 1:1
by men but **c** and valuable to God 1Pt 2:4
a **c** and valuable cornerstone, 1Pt 2:6
But you are a **c** race, a royal 1Pt 2:9
is in Babylon, also **c**, sends you 1Pt 5:13

CHRIST *(406)*
(AKA MESSIAH)

historical record of Jesus **C**, Mt 1:1
birth of Jesus **C** came about this Mt 1:18
of the gospel of Jesus **C**, Mk 1:1
and truth came through Jesus **C**. Jn 1:17
is coming" (who is called **C**). Jn 4:25
the One You have sent—Jesus **C**. Jn 17:3
name of Jesus **C** the Nazarene, Ac 3:6
name of Jesus **C** the Nazarene— Ac 4:10
of God and the name of Jesus **C**, Ac 8:12
that Jesus **C** is the Son of God. Ac 8:37
him, "Aeneas, Jesus **C** heals you. Ac 9:34
news of peace through Jesus **C**— Ac 10:36
baptized in the name of Jesus **C**. Ac 10:48
we believed on the Lord Jesus **C**, Ac 11:17
the name of our Lord Jesus **C**. Ac 15:26
the name of Jesus **C** to come out Ac 16:18
the subject of faith in **C** Jesus. Ac 24:24
the Lord Jesus **C** with full Ac 28:31
a slave of **C** Jesus, called as Rm 1:1
His Son, Jesus **C** our Lord, who Rm 1:3
our Father and the Lord Jesus **C**. Rm 1:7
through Jesus **C** for all of you Rm 1:8
to my gospel through **C** Jesus. Rm 2:16
through faith in Jesus **C**, Rm 3:22
redemption that is in **C** Jesus. Rm 3:24
God through our Lord Jesus **C**. Rm 5:1
appointed moment, **C** died for the Rm 5:6
still sinners **C** died for us! Rm 5:8
in God through our Lord Jesus **C**, Rm 5:11
grace of the one man, Jesus **C**. Rm 5:15
through the one man, Jesus **C**. Rm 5:17
life through Jesus **C** our Lord. Rm 5:21
were baptized into **C** Jesus were Rm 6:3
just as **C** was raised from the Rm 6:4
if we died with **C**, we believe Rm 6:8
we know that **C**, having been Rm 6:9
but alive to God in **C** Jesus. Rm 6:11
life in **C** Jesus our Lord. Rm 6:23
God through Jesus **C** our Lord! Rm 7:25
now exists for those in **C** Jesus, Rm 8:1
law of life in **C** Jesus has set Rm 8:2
does not have the Spirit of **C**, Rm 8:9
Now if **C** is in you, the body is Rm 8:10
He who raised **C** from the dead Rm 8:11
of God and co-heirs with **C**— Rm 8:17
C Jesus is the One who died, Rm 8:34
separate us from the love of **C**? Rm 8:35
God that is in **C** Jesus our Lord! Rm 8:39
the truth in **C**—I am not lying Rm 9:1
For **C** is the end of the law for Rm 10:4
that is, to bring **C** down Rm 10:6
to bring **C** up from the dead. Rm 10:7
through the message about **C**. Rm 10:17
are one body in **C** and Rm 12:5
But put on the Lord Jesus **C**, Rm 13:14
C died and came to life for this: Rm 14:9
that one for whom **C** died. Rm 14:15
another, according to **C** Jesus, Rm 15:5
our Lord Jesus **C** with a united Rm 15:6
Now I say that **C** has become a Rm 15:8
to be a minister of **C** Jesus to Rm 15:16
to boast in **C** Jesus regarding Rm 15:17
except what **C** has accomplished Rm 15:18
evangelize where **C** has not been Rm 15:20
fullness of the blessing of **C**. Rm 15:29
the Lord Jesus **C** and through the Rm 15:30
my co-workers in **C** Jesus, Rm 16:3
first convert to **C** from Asia. Rm 16:5
they were also in **C** before me. Rm 16:7
our co-worker in **C**, and my dear Rm 16:9
Apelles, who is approved in **C**. Rm 16:10
the churches of **C** send you Rm 16:16
serve our Lord **C** but their own Rm 16:18
our Lord Jesus **C** be with you all Rm 16:24
and the proclamation of Jesus **C**, Rm 16:25
God, through Jesus **C**—to Him be Rm 16:27
an apostle of **C** Jesus by God's 1Co 1:1
sanctified in **C** Jesus and called 1Co 1:2
the name of Jesus **C** our Lord— 1Co 1:2
our Father and the Lord Jesus **C**. 1Co 1:3
grace given to you in **C** Jesus, 1Co 1:4
testimony about **C** was confirmed 1Co 1:6
revelation of our Lord Jesus **C**. 1Co 1:7
in the day of our Lord Jesus **C**. 1Co 1:8
with His Son, Jesus **C** our Lord. 1Co 1:9
in the name of our Lord Jesus **C**, 1Co 1:10
with Cephas," or "I'm with **C**." 1Co 1:12
C divided? Was it Paul who was 1Co 1:13
C did not send me to baptize, 1Co 1:17
that the cross of **C** will not be 1Co 1:17
but we preach **C** crucified, 1Co 1:23
C is God's power and God's 1Co 1:24
But from Him you are in **C** Jesus, 1Co 1:30
you except Jesus **C** and Him 1Co 2:2
But we have the mind of **C**. 1Co 2:16
of the flesh, as babies in **C**. 1Co 3:1
been laid—that is, Jesus **C**. 1Co 3:11
you belong to **C**, and Christ to 1Co 3:23
belong to Christ, and **C** to God. 1Co 3:23
as servants of **C** and managers of 1Co 4:1
We are fools for **C**, but you are 1Co 4:10
Christ, but you are wise in **C**! 1Co 4:10
have 10,000 instructors in **C**, 1Co 4:15
fathered you in **C** Jesus through 1Co 4:15
you about my ways in **C** Jesus, 1Co 4:17
For **C** our Passover has been 1Co 5:7
the Lord Jesus **C** and by the 1Co 6:11
bodies are the members of **C**? 1Co 6:15
the members of **C** and make them 1Co 6:15
one Lord, Jesus **C**, through whom 1Co 8:6
the brother for whom **C** died, 1Co 8:11
you are sinning against **C**. 1Co 8:12
will not hinder the gospel of **C**. 1Co 9:12
the law of **C**—to win those 1Co 9:21
them, and that rock was **C**. 1Co 10:4
us not tempt **C** as some of them 1Co 10:9
not a sharing in the blood of **C**? 1Co 10:16
not a sharing in the body of **C**? 1Co 10:16
of me, as I also am of **C**. 1Co 11:1
you to know that **C** is the head 1Co 11:3
woman, and God is the head of **C**. 1Co 11:3
are one body—so also is **C**. 1Co 12:12
Now you are the body of **C**, 1Co 12:27
that **C** died for our sins 1Co 15:3
Now if **C** is preached as raised 1Co 15:12
then **C** has not been raised; 1Co 15:13
and if **C** has not been raised, 1Co 15:14
about God that He raised up **C**— 1Co 15:15
are not raised, **C** has not been 1Co 15:16
And if **C** has not been raised, 1Co 15:17
fallen asleep in **C** have also 1Co 15:18
our hope in **C** for this life only 1Co 15:19
But now **C** has been raised from 1Co 15:20
so also in **C** all will be made 1Co 15:22
his own order: **C**, the 1Co 15:23
at His coming, the people of **C**. 1Co 15:23
that I have in **C** Jesus our Lord: 1Co 15:31
through our Lord Jesus **C**! 1Co 15:57
be with all of you in **C** Jesus. 1Co 16:24
an apostle of **C** Jesus by God's 2Co 1:1
our Father and the Lord Jesus **C**. 2Co 1:2
and Father of our Lord Jesus **C**, 2Co 1:3
sufferings of **C** overflow to us, 2Co 1:5
our comfort overflows through **C**. 2Co 1:5
of God, Jesus **C**, who was 2Co 1:19
who confirms us with you in **C**, 2Co 1:21
is for you in the presence of **C**, 2Co 2:10
to Troas for the gospel of **C**, 2Co 2:12
always puts us on display in **C**, 2Co 2:14
fragrance of **C** among those who 2Co 2:15
we speak in **C**, as from God 2Co 2:17
confidence toward God through **C**: 2Co 3:4
it is set aside ⌊only⌋ in **C**. 2Co 3:14
of the gospel of the glory of **C**, 2Co 4:4
ourselves but Jesus **C** as Lord, 2Co 4:5
glory in the face of Jesus **C**. 2Co 4:6
before the judgment seat of **C**, 2Co 5:10
if we have known **C** in a purely 2Co 5:16
Therefore if anyone is in **C**, 2Co 5:17
to Himself through **C** and gave us 2Co 5:18
that is, in **C**, God was 2Co 5:19
we are ambassadors for **C**; 2Co 5:20
agreement does **C** have with 2Co 6:15
the grace of our Lord Jesus **C**: 2Co 8:9
of the churches, the glory of **C**. 2Co 8:23
confession of the gospel of **C**, 2Co 9:13
and graciousness of **C**— 2Co 10:1
captive to the obedience of **C**. 2Co 10:5

confident that he belongs to **C**, 2Co 10:7
as he belongs to **C**, so do we. 2Co 10:7
to you with the gospel of **C**. 2Co 10:14
to present a pure virgin to **C**. 2Co 11:2
complete and pure devotion to **C**. 2Co 11:3
As the truth of **C** is in me, 2Co 11:10
themselves as apostles of **C**. 2Co 11:13
Are they servants of **C**? 2Co 11:23
I know a man in **C** who was caught 2Co 12:2
So because of **C**, I am pleased in 2Co 12:10
of God we are speaking in **C**, 2Co 12:19
seek proof of **C** speaking in me. 2Co 13:3
that Jesus **C** is in you? 2Co 13:5
The grace of the Lord Jesus **C**, 2Co 13:13
by Jesus **C** and God the Father Gl 1:1
the Father and our Lord Jesus **C**, Gl 1:3
called you by the grace of **C**, Gl 1:6
want to change the gospel of **C**. Gl 1:7
I would not be a slave of **C**. Gl 1:10
by a revelation from Jesus **C**. Gl 1:12
to the Judean churches in **C**; Gl 1:22
freedom that we have in **C** Jesus, Gl 2:4
the law but by faith in Jesus **C**. Gl 2:16
And we have believed in **C** Jesus, Gl 2:16
by faith in **C** and not by the Gl 2:16
seeking to be justified by **C**, Gl 2:17
is **C** then a promoter of sin? Gl 2:17
I have been crucified with **C**; Gl 2:19
longer live, but **C** lives in me. Gl 2:20
law, then **C** died for nothing. Gl 2:21
whose eyes Jesus **C** was vividly Gl 3:1
C has redeemed us from the curse Gl 3:13
come to the Gentiles in **C** Jesus, Gl 3:14
referring to one, who is **C**. Gl 3:16
faith in Jesus **C** might be given Gl 3:22
guardian until **C**, so that we Gl 3:24
of God through faith in **C** Jesus. Gl 3:26
baptized into **C** have put on Gl 3:27
into Christ have put on **C**. Gl 3:27
for you are all one in **C** Jesus. Gl 3:28
of God, as **C** Jesus ⌊Himself⌋ Gl 4:14
you until **C** is formed in you. Gl 4:19
C has liberated us into freedom. Gl 5:1
C will not benefit you at all. Gl 5:2
by the law are alienated from **C**; Gl 5:4
For in **C** Jesus neither Gl 5:6
those who belong to **C** Jesus have Gl 5:24
you will fulfill the law of **C**. Gl 6:2
persecuted for the cross of **C**. Gl 6:12
the cross of our Lord Jesus **C**, Gl 6:14
of our Lord Jesus **C** be with your Gl 6:18
an apostle of **C** Jesus by God's Eph 1:1
believers in **C** Jesus at Ephesus Eph 1:1
our Father and the Lord Jesus **C**. Eph 1:2
and Father of our Lord Jesus **C**, Eph 1:3
blessing in the heavens, in **C**; Eph 1:3
through Jesus **C** for Himself, Eph 1:5
the God of our Lord Jesus **C**, Eph 1:17
Him in the heavens, in **C** Jesus, Eph 2:6
His⌋ kindness to us in **C** Jesus. Eph 2:7
created in **C** Jesus for good Eph 2:10
But now in **C** Jesus, you who were Eph 2:13
When ⌊**C**⌋ came, He proclaimed the Eph 2:17
with **C** Jesus Himself as the Eph 2:20
prisoner of **C** Jesus on behalf Eph 3:1
the promise in **C** Jesus through Eph 3:6
the church and in **C** Jesus to all Eph 3:21
to build up the body of **C**, Eph 4:12
into Him who is the head—**C**. Eph 4:15
as God also forgave you in **C**. Eph 4:32
in the name of our Lord Jesus **C**, Eph 5:20
to one another in the fear of **C**. Eph 5:21
of the wife as also **C** is head of Eph 5:23
Now as the church submits to **C**, Eph 5:24
just as also **C** loved the church Eph 5:25
just as **C** does for the church, Eph 5:29
talking about **C** and the church. Eph 5:32
of your heart, as to **C**. Eph 6:5
as slaves of **C**, do God's will Eph 6:6
the Father and the Lord Jesus **C**. Eph 6:23
love for our Lord Jesus **C**. Eph 6:24
and Timothy, slaves of **C** Jesus: Php 1:1
the saints in **C** Jesus who are Php 1:1
our Father and the Lord Jesus **C**. Php 1:2
until the day of **C** Jesus. Php 1:6
with the affection of **C** Jesus. Php 1:8
and blameless in the day of **C**, Php 1:10
that ⌊comes⌋ through Jesus **C**, Php 1:11

that my imprisonment is for **C**. Php 1:13
preach **C** out of envy and strife, Php 1:15
proclaim **C** out of rivalry, Php 1:17
or true, **C** is proclaimed. Php 1:18
help from the Spirit of Jesus **C**. Php 1:19
C will be highly honored in my Php 1:20
living is **C** and dying is gain. Php 1:21
desire to depart and be with **C**— Php 1:23
may grow in **C** Jesus when I come Php 1:26
worthy of the gospel of **C**. Php 1:27
there is any encouragement in **C**, Php 2:1
own attitude that of **C** Jesus, Php 2:5
confess that Jesus **C** is Lord, Php 2:11
the day of **C** that I didn't run Php 2:16
interests, not those of Jesus **C**. Php 2:21
to death for the work of **C**, Php 2:30
of God, boast in **C** Jesus, and do Php 3:3
to be a loss because of **C**. Php 3:7
of knowing **C** Jesus my Lord. Php 3:8
them filth, so that I may gain **C** Php 3:8
one that is through faith in **C**— Php 3:9
been taken hold of by **C** Jesus. Php 3:12
God's heavenly call in **C** Jesus. Php 3:14
as enemies of the cross of **C**. Php 3:18
for a Savior, the Lord Jesus **C**. Php 3:20
and your minds in **C** Jesus. Php 4:7
His riches in glory in **C** Jesus. Php 4:19
Greet every saint in **C** Jesus. Php 4:21
of the Lord Jesus **C** be with your Php 4:23
an apostle of **C** Jesus by God's Col 1:1
brothers in **C** in Colossae. Col 1:2
the Father of our Lord Jesus **C**, Col 1:3
of your faith in **C** Jesus and of Col 1:4
which is **C** in you, the hope Col 1:27
present everyone mature in **C**. Col 1:28
knowledge of God's mystery—**C**. Col 2:2
the strength of your faith in **C**. Col 2:5
have received **C** Jesus the Lord, Col 2:6
the world, and not based on **C**. Col 2:8
you died with **C** to the elemental Col 2:20
but **C** is all and in all. Col 3:11
the Lord—you serve the Lord **C**. Col 3:24
you, a slave of **C** Jesus, greets Col 4:12
the Father and the Lord Jesus **C**. 1Th 1:1
of hope in our Lord Jesus **C**, 1Th 1:3
churches in **C** Jesus that are 1Th 2:14
co-worker in the gospel of **C**, 1Th 3:2
the dead in **C** will rise first 1Th 4:16
through our Lord Jesus **C**, 1Th 5:9
God's will for you in **C** Jesus. 1Th 5:18
the coming of our Lord Jesus **C**. 1Th 5:23
of our Lord Jesus **C** be with you! 1Th 5:28
our Father and the Lord Jesus **C**. 2Th 1:1
our Father and the Lord Jesus **C**. 2Th 1:2
of our God and the Lord Jesus **C**. 2Th 1:12
our Lord Jesus **C** and our being 2Th 2:1
the glory of our Lord Jesus **C**. 2Th 2:14
our Lord Jesus **C** Himself and God 2Th 2:16
in the name of our Lord Jesus **C**, 2Th 3:6
the Lord Jesus **C**, that quietly 2Th 3:12
of our Lord Jesus **C** be with all 2Th 3:18
an apostle of **C** Jesus according 1Tm 1:1
God our Savior and of **C** Jesus, 1Tm 1:1
the Father and **C** Jesus our Lord. 1Tm 1:2
give thanks to **C** Jesus our Lord 1Tm 1:12
and love that are in **C** Jesus. 1Tm 1:14
C Jesus came into the world to 1Tm 1:15
C Jesus might demonstrate the 1Tm 1:16
God and man, a man, **C** Jesus, 1Tm 2:5
in the faith that is in **C** Jesus. 1Tm 3:13
be a good servant of **C** Jesus, 1Tm 4:6
are drawn away from **C** by desire, 1Tm 5:11
before God and **C** Jesus and the 1Tm 5:21
of our Lord Jesus **C** and with the 1Tm 6:3
all, and before **C** Jesus, who 1Tm 6:13
appearing of our Lord Jesus **C**, 1Tm 6:14
an apostle of **C** Jesus by God's 2Tm 1:1
the promise of life in **C** Jesus: 2Tm 1:1
the Father and **C** Jesus our Lord. 2Tm 1:2
given to us in **C** Jesus before 2Tm 1:9
appearing of our Savior **C** Jesus, 2Tm 1:10
and love that are in **C** Jesus. 2Tm 1:13
in the grace that is in **C** Jesus. 2Tm 2:1
as a good soldier of **C** Jesus. 2Tm 2:3
Keep in mind Jesus **C**, risen from 2Tm 2:8
is in **C** Jesus, with eternal 2Tm 2:10
a godly life in **C** Jesus will be 2Tm 3:12
through faith in **C** Jesus. 2Tm 3:15

Before God and **C** Jesus, who is 2Tm 4:1
apostle of Jesus **C** for the faith Ti 1:1
the Father and **C** Jesus our Ti 1:4
great God and Savior, Jesus **C**. Ti 2:13
through Jesus **C** our Savior, Ti 3:6
a prisoner of **C** Jesus, and Phm 1
our Father and the Lord Jesus **C**. Phm 3
is in us for ⌊the glory of⌋ **C**. Phm 6
boldness in **C** to command you to Phm 8
also as a prisoner of **C** Jesus, Phm 9
refresh my heart in **C**. Phm 20
my fellow prisoner in **C** Jesus, Phm 23
of the Lord Jesus **C** be with your Phm 25
But **C** was faithful as a Son over Heb 3:6
body of Jesus **C** once and for all Heb 10:10
Jesus **C** is the same yesterday, Heb 13:8
through Jesus **C**, to whom be Heb 13:21
of God and of the Lord Jesus **C**: Jms 1:1
Lord Jesus **C** without showing Jms 2:1
Peter, an apostle of Jesus **C**: 1Pt 1:1
with the blood of Jesus **C**. 1Pt 1:2
and Father of our Lord Jesus **C**. 1Pt 1:3
of Jesus **C** from the dead, 1Pt 1:3
at the revelation of Jesus **C**. 1Pt 1:7
the Spirit of **C** within them was 1Pt 1:11
at the revelation of Jesus **C**. 1Pt 1:13
with the precious blood of **C**, 1Pt 1:19
to God through Jesus **C**. 1Pt 2:5
because **C** also suffered for you, 1Pt 2:21
C also suffered for sins once 1Pt 3:18
the resurrection of Jesus **C**. 1Pt 3:21
since **C** suffered in the flesh, 1Pt 4:1
be glorified through Jesus **C**. 1Pt 4:11
are ridiculed for the name of **C**, 1Pt 4:14
to His eternal glory in **C** Jesus, 1Pt 5:10
to all of you who are in **C**. 1Pt 5:14
slave and an apostle of Jesus **C**: 2Pt 1:1
of our God and Savior Jesus **C**. 2Pt 1:1
knowledge of our Lord Jesus **C**. 2Pt 1:8
Savior Jesus **C** will be richly 2Pt 1:11
our Lord Jesus **C** has also shown 2Pt 1:14
and coming of our Lord Jesus **C**; 2Pt 1:16
of our Lord and Savior Jesus **C**, 2Pt 2:20
of our Lord and Savior Jesus **C**. 2Pt 3:18
Father and with His Son Jesus **C**. 1Jn 1:3
Jesus **C** the righteous One. 1Jn 2:1
in the name of His Son Jesus **C**, 1Jn 3:23
confesses that Jesus **C** has come 1Jn 4:2
Jesus **C**—He is the One who came 1Jn 5:6
that is, in His Son Jesus **C**. 1Jn 5:20
God the Father and from Jesus **C**, 2Jn 3
coming of Jesus **C** in the flesh. 2Jn 7
remain in the teaching about **C**, 2Jn 9
slave of Jesus **C**, and a brother Jd 1
the Father and kept by Jesus **C**. Jd 1
only Master and Lord, Jesus **C**. Jd 4
apostles of our Lord Jesus **C**; Jd 17
our Lord Jesus **C** for eternal Jd 21
through Jesus **C** our Lord, be Jd 25
of Jesus **C** that God gave Him Rv 1:1
to the testimony about Jesus **C**, Rv 1:2
and from Jesus **C**, the faithful Rv 1:5

CHRIST'S *(12)*

who are also Jesus **C** by calling: Rm 1:6
called as a free man is **C** slave. 1Co 7:22
is plain that you are **C** letter, 2Co 3:3
For **C** love compels us, since we 2Co 5:14
us, we plead on **C** behalf, "Be 2Co 5:20
that **C** power may reside in me. 2Co 12:9
And if you are **C**, then you are Gl 3:29
stature measured by **C** fullness. Eph 4:13
given to you on **C** behalf not Php 1:29
is lacking in **C** afflictions for Col 1:24
been a burden as **C** apostles, 1Th 2:7
to God's love and **C** endurance. 2Th 3:5

CHRISTIAN *(6)*

me to become a **C** so easily?" Ac 26:28
is sanctified by the **C** husband. 1Co 7:14
to be accompanied by a **C** wife, 1Co 9:5
if some disobey the ⌊**C**⌋ message, 1Pt 3:1
denounce your **C** life will be put 1Pt 3:16
But if ⌊anyone suffers⌋ as a **C**, 1Pt 4:16

CHRISTIANS *(1)*

were first called **C** in Antioch. Ac 11:26

CHRONIC *(2)*

it is a **c** disease on the skin of Lv 13:11
and terrible and **c** sicknesses. Dt 28:59

CHRYSOLITE *(1)*
the seventh **c**, the eighth beryl, Rv 21:20
CHRYSOPRASE *(1)*
topaz, the tenth **c**, the eleventh Rv 21:20
CHURCH *(73)*
on this rock I will build My **c**, Mt 16:18
attention to them, tell the **c**. Mt 18:17
pay attention even to the **c**, Mt 18:17
on the whole **c** and on all who Ac 5:11
out against the **c** in Jerusalem, Ac 8:1
was ravaging the **c**, and he would Ac 8:3
So the **c** throughout all Judea, Ac 9:31
the ears of the **c** in Jerusalem, Ac 11:22
met with the **c** and taught large Ac 11:26
some who belonged to the **c**, Ac 12:1
to God for him by the **c**. Ac 12:5
In the local **c** at Antioch there Ac 13:1
elders in every **c** and prayed Ac 14:23
and gathered the **c** together, Ac 14:27
been sent on their way by the **c**, Ac 15:3
they were welcomed by the **c**, Ac 15:4
with the whole **c**, decided to Ac 15:22
he went up and greeted the **c**, Ac 18:22
called for the elders of the **c**. Ac 20:17
to shepherd the **c** of God, which Ac 20:28
a servant of the **c** in Cenchreae. Rm 16:1
Greet also the **c** that meets in Rm 16:5
host to me and to the whole **c**, Rm 16:23
To God's **c** at Corinth, to those 1Co 1:2
I teach everywhere in every **c**. 1Co 4:17
no standing in the **c** to judge? 1Co 6:4
or the Greeks or the **c** of God, 1Co 10:32
come together as a **c** there are 1Co 11:18
look down on the **c** of God and 1Co 11:22
God has placed these in the **c**: 1Co 12:28
who prophesies builds up the **c**. 1Co 14:4
so that the **c** may be built up. 1Co 14:5
to excel in building up the **c**. 1Co 14:12
in the **c** I would rather speak 1Co 14:19
if the whole **c** assembles 1Co 14:23
keep silent in the **c** and speak 1Co 14:28
woman to speak in the **c** meeting. 1Co 14:35
I persecuted the **c** of God. 1Co 15:9
along with the **c** that meets in 1Co 16:19
To God's **c** at Corinth, with all 2Co 1:1
persecuted God's **c** to an extreme Gl 1:13
head over everything for the **c**, Eph 1:22
through the **c** to the rulers Eph 3:10
be glory in the **c** and in Christ Eph 3:21
as also Christ is head of the **c**. Eph 5:23
Now as the **c** submits to Christ, Eph 5:24
loved the **c** and gave Himself Eph 5:25
this to present the **c** to Himself Eph 5:27
just as Christ does for the **c**, Eph 5:29
talking about Christ and the **c**. Eph 5:32
as to zeal, persecuting the **c**; Php 3:6
c shared with me in the matter Php 4:15
the head of the body, the **c**; Col 1:18
for His body, that is, the **c**. Col 1:24
Nympha and the **c** in her house. Col 4:15
read also in the **c** of the Col 4:16
To the **c** of the Thessalonians in 1Th 1:1
To the **c** of the Thessalonians in 2Th 1:1
will he take care of God's **c**? 1Tm 3:5
is the **c** of the living God, 1Tm 3:15
the **c** should not be burdened, 1Tm 5:16
and to the **c** that meets in your Phm 2
call for the elders of the **c**, Jms 5:14
to your love before the **c**. 3Jn 6
I wrote something to the **c**, 3Jn 9
so and expels them from the **c**. 3Jn 10
angel of the **c** in Ephesus write Rv 2:1
angel of the **c** in Smyrna write Rv 2:8
the angel of the **c** in Pergamum Rv 2:12
the angel of the **c** in Thyatira Rv 2:18
angel of the **c** in Sardis write Rv 3:1
angel of the **c** in Philadelphia Rv 3:7
the angel of the **c** in Laodicea Rv 3:14
CHURCHES *(36)*
Cilicia, strengthening the **c**. Ac 15:41
the **c** were strengthened in the Ac 16:5
but so do all the Gentile **c**. Rm 16:4
All the **c** of Christ send you Rm 16:16
is what I command in all the **c**. 1Co 7:17
custom, nor do the **c** of God. 1Co 11:16
As in all the **c** of the saints, 1Co 14:33
women should be silent in the **c**, 1Co 14:34
as I instructed the Galatian **c**. 1Co 16:1
c of the Asian province greet 1Co 16:19
granted to the **c** of Macedonia: 2Co 8:1
throughout the **c** for his gospel 2Co 8:18
by the **c** to accompany us 2Co 8:19
are the messengers of the **c**, 2Co 8:23
before the **c**, show them the 2Co 8:24
I robbed other **c** by taking pay 2Co 11:8
my care for all the **c**. 2Co 11:28
treated worse than the other **c**, 2Co 12:13
To the **c** of Galatia. Gl 1:2
to the Judean **c** in Christ; Gl 1:22
of God's **c** in Christ Jesus 1Th 2:14
boast about you among God's **c**— 2Th 1:4
the seven **c** in the province of Rv 1:4
see and send it to the seven **c**: Rv 1:11
are the angels of the seven **c**, Rv 1:20
lampstands are the seven **c**. Rv 1:20
The Letters to the Seven **C** Rv 1:20
what the Spirit says to the **c**. Rv 2:7
what the Spirit says to the **c**. Rv 2:11
what the Spirit says to the **c**. Rv 2:17
Then all the **c** will know that I Rv 2:23
what the Spirit says to the **c**. Rv 2:29
what the Spirit says to the **c**. Rv 3:6
what the Spirit says to the **c**. Rv 3:13
what the Spirit says to the **c**." Rv 3:22
these things to you for the **c**. Rv 22:16
CHURN *(6)*
and its waters **c** up mire and Is 57:20
like rivers whose waters **c**? Jr 46:7
and its waters **c** like rivers. Jr 46:8
c up the waters with your feet, Ezk 32:2
No human foot will **c** them again, Ezk 32:13
arose, and the sea began to **c**. Jn 6:18
CHURNING *(6)*
like a stone into **c** waters. Neh 9:11
I am **c** within and cannot rest; Jb 30:27
For the **c** of milk produces Pr 30:33
A **c** storm, it will whirl about Jr 30:23
distress. I am **c** within; my Lm 1:20
weeping; I am **c** within. My heart Lm 2:11
CHUZA *(1)*
the wife of **C**, Herod's steward; Lk 8:3
CILICIA *(8)*
and some from **C** and Asia, came Ac 6:9
in Antioch, Syria, and **C**: Ac 15:23
He traveled through Syria and **C**, Ac 15:41
a Jewish man from Tarsus of **C**, Ac 21:39
in Tarsus of **C**, but brought up Ac 22:3
when he learned he was from **C**, Ac 23:34
open sea off **C** and Pamphylia, Ac 27:5
to the regions of Syria and **C**. Gl 1:21
CINNAMON *(4)*
of fragrant **c**, six and a quarter Ex 30:23
my bed with myrrh, aloes, and **c**. Pr 7:17
calamus and **c**, with all the Sg 4:14
c, spice, incense, myrrh, and Rv 18:13
CIRCLE *(8)*
the inner **c** of the camp with 1Sm 26:5
in the inner **c** of the camp with 1Sm 26:7
C around behind them and attack 2Sm 5:23
C down away from them and 1Ch 14:14
He walks on the **c** of the sky." Jb 22:14
I will camp in a **c** around you; Is 29:3
above the **c** of the earth; Is 40:22
were sitting in a **c** around Him, Mk 3:34
CIRCLED *(1)*
The border then **c** around Neah on Jos 19:14
CIRCLES *(1)*
the heavens and **c** to their other Ps 19:6
CIRCLING *(3)*
the men of war, **c** the city one Jos 6:3
around the city, **c** it once. Jos 6:11
Are birds of prey **c** her? Jr 12:9
CIRCUIT *(4)*
he would go on a **c** to Bethel, 1Sm 7:16
They made a **c** throughout Judah. 2Ch 23:2
around the villages in a **c**, Mk 6:6
making a **c** along the coast, Ac 28:13
CIRCULATED *(1)*
They **c** a proclamation throughout Ezr 10:7
CIRCUMCISE *(9)*
You must **c** the flesh of your Gn 17:11
c your hearts and don't be Dt 10:16
LORD your God will **c** your heart Dt 30:6
flint knives and **c** the Israelite Jos 5:2
C yourselves to the LORD; Jr 4:4
When they came to **c** the child on Lk 1:59
and you **c** a man on the Sabbath. Jn 7:22
It is necessary to **c** them and to Ac 15:5
them not to **c** their children Ac 21:21
CIRCUMCISED *(51)*
one of your males must be **c**. Gn 17:10
at eight days old is to be **c**. Gn 17:12
purchased with money, must be **c**. Gn 17:13
any male is not **c** in the flesh Gn 17:14
and he **c** the flesh of their Gn 17:23
the flesh of his foreskin was **c**, Gn 17:24
the flesh of his foreskin was **c**. Gn 17:25
and his son Ishmael were **c**. Gn 17:26
a foreigner—were **c** with him. Gn 17:27
old, Abraham **c** him, as God had Gn 21:4
all your males are **c** as we are. Gn 34:15
will not listen to us and be **c**, Gn 34:17
all our men are **c** as they are. Gn 34:22
all the able-bodied men were **c**. Gn 34:24
eat it, after you have **c** him. Ex 12:44
male in his household must be **c**, Ex 12:48
foreskin must be **c** on the eighth Lv 12:3
flint knives and **c** the Israelite Jos 5:3
is the reason Joshua **c** ⌊them⌋: Jos 5:4
the people who came out were **c**, Jos 5:5
the way were **c** after they had Jos 5:5
it was these he **c**. Jos 5:7
had not been **c** along the way. Jos 5:7
the entire nation had been **c**, Jos 5:8
punish all the **c** yet Jr 9:25
Isaac and **c** him on the eighth Ac 7:8
c believers who had come with Ac 10:45
Unless you are **c** according to Ac 15:1
so he took him and **c** him because Ac 16:3
who will justify the **c** by faith Rm 3:30
Is this blessing only for the **c**, Rm 4:9
he was **c**, or uncircumcised? Rm 4:10
Not while he was **c**, but Rm 4:10
all who believe but are not **c**, Rm 4:11
he became the father of the **c**, Rm 4:12
not only to those who are **c**, Rm 4:12
a servant of the **c** on behalf of Rm 15:8
anyone already **c** when he was 1Co 7:18
He should not get **c**. 1Co 7:18
a Greek, was compelled to be **c**. Gl 2:3
just as Peter was for the **c**. Gl 2:7
to the **c** was also at work Gl 2:8
the Gentiles and they to the **c**. Gl 2:9
tell you that if you get **c**, Gl 5:2
every man who gets **c** that he is Gl 5:3
who would compel you to be **c**— Gl 6:12
even the **c** don't keep the law Gl 6:13
want you to be **c** in order to Gl 6:13
by those called "the **c**," Eph 2:11
c the eighth day; Php 3:5
Him you were also **c** with a Col 2:11
CIRCUMCISION *(25)*
of blood," referring to the **c**. Ex 4:26
days were completed for His **c**, Lk 2:21
has given you **c**—not that it Jn 7:22
a man receives **c** on the Sabbath Jn 7:23
He gave him the covenant of **c**. Ac 7:8
who stressed **c** argued with him, Ac 11:2
c benefits you if you observe Rm 2:25
c has become uncircumcision. Rm 2:25
not be counted as **c**? Rm 2:26
the letter ⌊of the law⌋ and **c**. Rm 2:27
and ⌊true⌋ **c** is not something Rm 2:28
inwardly, and **c** is of the heart Rm 2:29
Or what is the benefit of **c**? Rm 3:1
received the sign of **c** as a seal Rm 4:11
He should not undo his **c**. 1Co 7:18
C does not matter and 1Co 7:19
feared those from the **c** party. Gl 2:12
Jesus neither **c** nor Gl 5:6
I still preach **c**, why am I still Gl 5:11
For both **c** and uncircumcision Gl 6:15
For we are the **c**, the ones who Php 3:3
with a **c** not done with Col 2:11
flesh, in the **c** of the Messiah. Col 2:11
Greek and Jew, **c** and Col 3:11
alone of the **c** are my co-workers Col 4:11
CIRCUMFERENCE *(4)*
27 feet high and 18 feet in **c**. 1Kg 7:15
half feet high and 45 feet in **c**. 1Kg 7:23

feet high, and 45 feet in **c**. 2Ch 4:2
tall, had a **c** of 18 feet, was Jr 52:21

CIRCUMSTANCES *(9)*
whatever your **c** require because 1Sm 10:7
In such **c**, I saw the wicked Ec 8:10
In these **c**, a crowd of many Lk 12:1
Under these **c** I was traveling to Ac 26:12
tested, in many **c**, and found 2Co 8:22
be content in whatever **c** I am. Php 4:11
In any and all **c** I have learned Php 4:12
brother of humble **c** should boast Jms 1:9
what time or what **c** the Spirit 1Pt 1:11

CISTERN *(16)*
A spring or **c** containing water Lv 11:36
He came to the large **c** at Secu, 1Sm 19:22
may drink water from his own **c** 2Kg 18:31
Drink water from your own **c**, Pr 5:15
hearth or scoop water from a **c**." Is 30:14
and drink water from his own **c** Is 36:16
him into the **c** of Malchiah Jr 38:6
There was no water in the **c**, Jr 38:6
had been put into the **c**. Jr 38:7
him into the **c** where he will die Jr 38:9
up from the **c** before he dies." Jr 38:10
by ropes to Jeremiah in the **c**. Jr 38:11
and lifted him out of the **c**, Jr 38:13
them and threw them into a **c**. Jr 41:7
Now the **c** where Ishmael had Jr 41:9
prisoners from the waterless **c**. Zch 9:11

CISTERNS *(5)*
among rocks, and in holes and **c**. 1Sm 13:6
rock-hewn **c**, vineyards, olive Neh 9:25
water, and dug **c** for themselves, Jr 2:13
c that cannot hold water. Jr 2:13
They go to the **c**; they find no Jr 14:3

CITADEL *(3)*
he entered the **c** of the royal 1Kg 16:18
Samaria at the **c** of the king's 2Kg 15:25
every **c** will stand on its proper Jr 30:18

CITADELS *(17)*
known as a stronghold in its **c**. Ps 48:3
tour its **c** so that you can tell Ps 48:13
will consume the **c** of Jerusalem Jr 17:27
it will devour Ben-hadad's **c**. Jr 49:27
and it will consume their **c**. Hs 8:14
it will consume Ben-hadad's **c**. Am 1:4
and it will consume its **c**. Am 1:7
and it will consume its **c**. Am 1:10
it will consume the **c** of Bozrah. Am 1:12
and it will consume its **c**. Am 1:14
will consume the **c** of Kerioth. Am 2:2
will consume the **c** of Jerusalem. Am 2:5
Proclaim on the **c** in Ashdod and Am 3:9
Ashdod and on the **c** in the land Am 3:9
and destruction in their **c**. Am 3:10
strongholds and plunder your **c**. Am 3:11
Jacob's pride and hate his **c**, Am 6:8

CITIES *(391)*
Lot lived in the **c** of the valley Gn 13:12
overthrew these **c**, the entire Gn 19:25
all the inhabitants of the **c**, Gn 19:25
destroyed the **c** of the plain, Gn 19:29
He overthrew the **c** where Lot had Gn 19:29
God came over the **c** around them, Gn 35:5
authority as food in the **c**, Gn 41:35
years and placed it in the **c**. Gn 41:48
the people to the **c** from one end Gn 47:21
Rameses as supply **c** for Pharaoh. Ex 1:11
Concerning the Levitical **c**, Lv 25:32
houses in the **c** they possess. Lv 25:32
in the Levitical **c** are their Lv 25:33
around their **c** may not be sold, Lv 25:34
Though you withdraw into your **c**, Lv 26:25
will reduce your **c** to ruins and Lv 26:31
and your **c** will become ruins. Lv 26:33
Are the **c** they live in Nm 13:19
and the **c** are large and Nm 13:28
completely destroy their **c**." Nm 21:2
destroyed them and their **c**. Nm 21:3
took all the **c** and lived in all Nm 21:25
lived in all these Amorite **c**, Nm 21:25
they burned all the **c** where the Nm 31:10
our livestock and **c** for our Nm 32:16
in the fortified **c** because Nm 32:17
Build **c** for your dependents and Nm 32:24
remain here in the **c** of Gilead, Nm 32:26
land including its **c** with the Nm 32:33
and Beth-haran as fortified **c**, Nm 32:36
names to the **c** they rebuilt. Nm 32:38
Israelites to give **c** out of Nm 35:2
in and pastureland around the **c**. Nm 35:2
The **c** will be for them to live Nm 35:3
of the **c** you are to give Nm 35:4
them as pasturelands for the **c**. Nm 35:5
The **c** you give the Levites will Nm 35:6
will include six **c** of refuge, Nm 35:6
to these, give 42 ⌊other⌋ **c**. Nm 35:6
The total number of **c** you give Nm 35:7
Of the **c** that you give from the Nm 35:8
some of its **c** to the Levites Nm 35:8
designate **c** to serve as cities Nm 35:11
to serve as **c** of refuge for you Nm 35:11
You will have the **c** as a refuge Nm 35:12
c you select will be your six Nm 35:13
will be your six **c** of refuge. Nm 35:13
Select three **c** across the Jordan Nm 35:14
Jordan and three **c** in the land Nm 35:14
of Canaan to be **c** of refuge. Nm 35:14
These six **c** will serve as a Nm 35:15
up and the **c** we will come to.' Dt 1:22
c are large, fortified to the Dt 1:28
all his **c** and completely Dt 2:34
spoil from the **c** we captured as Dt 2:35
River and the **c** of the hill Dt 2:37
captured all his **c** at that time. Dt 3:4
c, the entire region of Argob, Dt 3:4
spoil from the **c** as plunder for Dt 3:7
the **c** of the plateau, Gilead, Dt 3:10
c of Og's kingdom in Bashan. Dt 3:10
of Gilead along with its **c**. Dt 3:12
remain in the **c** I have given you Dt 3:19
set apart three **c** across the Dt 4:41
one of these **c** and stay alive: Dt 4:42
and beautiful **c** that you did not Dt 6:10
you ⌊with⌋ large **c** fortified to Dt 9:1
one of your **c** the LORD your God Dt 13:12
and live in their **c** and houses, Dt 19:1
set apart three **c** for yourselves Dt 19:2
can flee to these **c**. Dt 19:3
flee to one of these **c** and live. Dt 19:5
apart three **c** for yourselves. Dt 19:7
add three more **c** to these three. Dt 19:9
and flees to one of these **c**, Dt 19:11
to treat all the **c** that are far Dt 20:15
not among the **c** of these nations Dt 20:15
among the **c** of these people Dt 20:16
from the victim to the nearby **c**. Dt 21:2
Gibeonite **c** on the third day. Jos 9:17
Now their **c** were Gibeon, Jos 9:17
city like one of the royal **c**; Jos 10:2
Don't let them enter their **c**, Jos 10:19
ran away to the fortified **c**. Jos 10:20
kings and their **c** and struck Jos 11:12
burn any of the **c** that stood on Jos 11:13
of these **c** for themselves. Jos 11:14
destroyed them with their **c**. Jos 11:21
and all the **c** of Sihon king of Jos 13:10
and all its **c** on the plateau— Jos 13:17
the **c** of the plateau, and all Jos 13:21
with the **c** and their villages. Jos 13:23
Jazer and all the **c** of Gilead, Jos 13:25
with the **c** and their villages. Jos 13:28
that are in Bashan—60 **c**. Jos 13:30
and Og's royal **c** in Bashan— Jos 13:31
to the Levites except **c** to live Jos 14:4
as well as large fortified **c**. Jos 14:12
went to the **c** of Mount Ephron, Jos 15:9
the outermost **c** of the tribe Jos 15:21
and Rimmon—29 **c** in all, with Jos 15:32
Gederothaim—14 **c**, with their Jos 15:36
and Makkedah—16 **c**, with their Jos 15:41
Mareshah—nine **c**, with their Jos 15:44
sea, all ⌊the **c**⌋ near Ashdod, Jos 15:46
and Giloh—11 **c**, with their Jos 15:51
and Zior—nine **c**, with their Jos 15:54
and Timnah—10 **c**, with their Jos 15:57
and Eltekon—six **c**, with their Jos 15:59
and Rabbah—two **c**, with their Jos 15:60
and En-gedi—six **c**, with their Jos 15:62
the **c** set apart for the Jos 16:9
all these **c** with their villages. Jos 16:9
c belonged to Ephraim among Jos 17:9
to Ephraim among Manasseh's **c**. Jos 17:9
—the three ⌊**c**⌋ of Naphath. Jos 17:11
could not possess these **c**, Jos 17:12
These were the **c** of the tribe of Jos 18:21
and Geba—12 **c**, with their Jos 18:24
and Kiriath—14 **c**, with their Jos 18:28
and Sharuhen—13 **c**, with their Jos 19:6
and Ashan—four **c**, with their Jos 19:7
surrounding these **c** as far as Jos 19:8
and Bethlehem—12 **c**, with their Jos 19:15
their clans, these **c**, with their Jos 19:16
at the Jordan—16 **c**, with their Jos 19:22
their clans, the **c**, with their Jos 19:23
and Rehob—22 **c**, with their Jos 19:30
these **c** with their villages. Jos 19:31
The fortified **c** were Ziddim, Jos 19:35
Beth-shemesh—19 **c**, with their Jos 19:38
the **c** with their villages. Jos 19:39
these **c** with their villages. Jos 19:48
'Select your **c** of refuge, as I Jos 20:2
someone flees to one of these **c**, Jos 20:4
These are the **c** appointed for Jos 20:9
Moses that we be given **c** to live Jos 21:2
the Levites these **c** with their Jos 21:3
priest received 13 **c** by lot from Jos 21:4
Kohath received 10 **c** by lot from Jos 21:5
received 13 **c** by lot from the Jos 21:6
received 12 **c** for their clans Jos 21:7
gave these **c** with their Jos 21:8
Israelites gave these **c** by name Jos 21:9
nine **c** from these two tribes. Jos 21:16
with its pasturelands—four **c**. Jos 21:18
All 13 **c** with their pasturelands Jos 21:19
The allotted **c** to the remaining Jos 21:20
with its pasturelands—four **c**. Jos 21:22
with its pasturelands—four **c**. Jos 21:24
with its pasturelands—two **c**. Jos 21:25
All 10 **c** with their pasturelands Jos 21:26
with its pasturelands—two **c**. Jos 21:27
with its pasturelands—four **c**. Jos 21:29
with its pasturelands—four **c**. Jos 21:31
with its pasturelands—three **c**. Jos 21:32
All 13 **c** with their pasturelands Jos 21:33
with its pasturelands—four **c**. Jos 21:35
with its pasturelands—four **c**. Jos 21:37
pasturelands—four **c** in all. Jos 21:39
All 12 **c** were allotted to the Jos 21:40
were 48 **c** in all with their Jos 21:41
Each of these **c** had its own Jos 21:42
this was true for all the **c**. Jos 21:42
labor for, and **c** you did not Jos 24:13
and in all the **c** that are on the Jdg 11:26
20 of their **c** with a great Jdg 11:33
in one of the **c** of Gilead. Jdg 12:7
from their **c** to Gibeah to go out Jdg 20:14
26,000 armed men from their **c**, Jdg 20:15
came out of the **c** slaughtered Jdg 20:42
down all the **c** that remained. Jdg 20:48
rebuilt their **c**, and lived in Jdg 21:23
of Philistine **c** of the five 1Sm 6:18
the fortified **c** and the outlying 1Sm 6:18
The **c** from Ekron to Gath, which 1Sm 7:14
out from all the **c** of Israel to 1Sm 18:6
they abandoned the **c** and fled. 1Sm 31:7
and Berothai, Hadadezer's **c**. 2Sm 8:8
people and for the **c** of our God. 2Sm 10:12
the same to all the Ammonite **c**. 2Sm 12:31
find fortified **c** and elude us." 2Sm 20:6
and all the **c** of the Hivites 2Sm 24:7
60 great **c** with walls and bronze 1Kg 4:13
the region of their fortified **c**, 1Kg 8:37
all the storage **c** that belonged 1Kg 9:19
the chariot **c**, the cavalry 1Kg 9:19
the cavalry **c**, and whatever 1Kg 9:19
in the chariot **c** and with the 1Kg 10:26
living in the **c** of Judah. 1Kg 12:17
places in the **c** of Samaria is 1Kg 13:32
armies against the **c** of Israel. 1Kg 15:20
and the **c** he built, are written 1Kg 15:23
The **c** that my father took from 1Kg 20:34
and all the **c** he built, are 1Kg 22:39
destroyed the **c**, and each of 2Kg 3:25
of Hazael the **c** that Hazael had 2Kg 13:25
and recovered the **c** of Israel. 2Kg 13:25
and in the **c** of the Medes. 2Kg 17:6
Israelites in the **c** of Samaria. 2Kg 17:24
of Samaria and lived in its **c**. 2Kg 17:24
placed in the **c** of Samaria do 2Kg 17:26
in the **c** where they lived, 2Kg 17:29
and in the **c** of the Medes, 2Kg 18:11
all the fortified **c** of Judah and 2Kg 18:13

crushed fortified **c** into piles 2Kg 19:25
high places in the **c** of Judah 2Kg 23:5
the priests from the **c** of Judah, 2Kg 23:8
that were in the **c** of Samaria, 2Kg 23:19
These were their **c** until David 1Ch 4:31
Tochen, and Ashan—five **c**, 1Ch 4:32
they abandoned their **c** and fled. 1Ch 10:7
Levites in their **c** with 1Ch 13:2
Hadadezer's **c**, David also took 1Ch 18:8
from their **c** and came for 1Ch 19:7
people and for the **c** of our God. 1Ch 19:13
the same to all the Ammonite **c**. 1Ch 20:3
country, in the **c**, in the 1Ch 27:25
in the chariot **c** and with the 2Ch 1:14
the region of their fortified **c**, 2Ch 6:28
rebuilt the **c** Hiram gave him 2Ch 8:2
all the storage **c** that he built 2Ch 8:4
fortified **c** with walls, gates, 2Ch 8:5
all the storage **c** that belonged 2Ch 8:6
all the chariot **c**, the cavalry 2Ch 8:6
the cavalry **c**, and everything 2Ch 8:6
in the chariot **c** and with the 2Ch 9:25
living in the **c** of Judah, 2Ch 10:17
and he fortified **c** in Judah. 2Ch 11:5
which are fortified **c** in Judah 2Ch 11:10
and to all the fortified **c**. 2Ch 11:23
fortified **c** of Judah and came 2Ch 12:4
and captured ⌊some⌋ **c** from him: 2Ch 13:19
altars from all the **c** of Judah, 2Ch 14:5
Asa built fortified **c** in Judah. 2Ch 14:6
build these **c** and surround them 2Ch 14:7
attacked all the **c** around Gerar 2Ch 14:14
They also plundered all the **c**, 2Ch 14:14
and from the **c** he had captured 2Ch 15:8
his armies to the **c** of Israel. 2Ch 16:4
all the storage **c** of Naphtali. 2Ch 16:4
and in the **c** of Ephraim that 2Ch 17:2
to teach in the **c** of Judah. 2Ch 17:7
fortresses and storage **c** in 2Ch 17:12
the fortified **c** throughout all 2Ch 17:19
all the fortified **c** of the land 2Ch 19:5
brothers who dwell in their **c**— 2Ch 19:10
from all the **c** of Judah to seek 2Ch 20:4
along with fortified **c** in Judah, 2Ch 21:3
Levites from all the **c** of Judah 2Ch 23:2
Go out to the **c** of Judah and 2Ch 24:5
they raided the **c** of Judah from 2Ch 25:13
Then he built **c** in ⌊the vicinity 2Ch 26:6
He also built **c** in the hill 2Ch 27:4
also raided the **c** of the Judean 2Ch 28:18
went out to the **c** of Judah and 2Ch 31:1
Israelites returned to their **c**, 2Ch 31:1
who lived in the **c** of Judah, 2Ch 31:6
Shecaniah in the **c** of the 2Ch 31:15
in the common fields of their **c**, 2Ch 31:19
the fortified **c** and intended to 2Ch 32:1
He made **c** for himself, and he 2Ch 32:29
in all the fortified **c** of Judah. 2Ch 33:14
the same⌋ in the **c** of Manasseh, 2Ch 34:6
and settled in the **c** of Samaria Ezr 4:10
fortified **c** and fertile land Neh 9:25
in their **c** to attack those Est 9:2
rebuilt ruined **c** for themselves, Jb 3:14
he will dwell in ruined **c**, Jb 15:28
uprooted the **c**, and the very Ps 9:6
and build up the **c** of Judah. Ps 69:35
flourish in the **c** like the grass Ps 72:16
his fortified **c** to ruins. Ps 89:40
desolate, your **c** burned with Is 1:7
Until **c** lie in ruins without Is 6:11
who trampled its **c** and would not Is 14:17
the surface of the earth with **c**. Is 14:21
The **c** of Aroer are forsaken; Is 17:2
day their strong **c** will be like Is 17:9
that day five **c** in the land of Is 19:18
One of the **c** will be called the Is 19:18
has been broken, and **c** despised. Is 33:8
her fortified **c**, with thistles Is 34:13
all the fortified **c** of Judah and Is 36:1
crushed fortified **c** into piles Is 37:26
Say to the **c** of Judah, "Here is Is 40:9
Let the desert and its **c** shout, Is 42:11
and to the **c** of Judah: Is 44:26
and inhabit the desolate **c**. Is 54:3
they will renew the ruined **c**, Is 61:4
Your holy **c** have become a Is 64:10
and all the other **c** of Judah. Jr 1:15
His **c** are in ruins, without Jr 2:15
gods are as numerous as your **c**, Jr 2:28
let's flee to the fortified **c**. Jr 4:5
Your **c** will be reduced to Jr 4:7
voices against the **c** of Judah. Jr 4:16
All its **c** were torn down because Jr 4:26
keeps watch over their **c**. Jr 5:6
your fortified **c** in which you Jr 5:17
they behave in the **c** of Judah Jr 7:17
will remove from the **c** of Judah Jr 7:34
the fortified **c** and there suffer Jr 8:14
I will make the **c** of Judah a Jr 9:11
The **c** of Judah will be made Jr 10:22
these words in the **c** of Judah Jr 11:6
Then the **c** of Judah and the Jr 11:12
indeed as numerous as your **c**, Jr 11:13
The **c** of the Negev are under Jr 13:19
will come from the **c** of Judah Jr 17:26
man be like the **c** the LORD Jr 20:16
a wilderness, uninhabited **c**. Jr 22:6
and the ⌊other⌋ **c** of Judah, Jr 25:18
to all Judah's **c** that are coming Jr 26:2
Return to these **c** of yours. Jr 31:21
the land of Judah and in its **c**: Jr 31:23
and all its **c** will live in it Jr 31:24
and in Judah's **c**—the cities of Jr 32:44
the **c** of the hill country, Jr 32:44
the **c** of the Judean foothills, Jr 32:44
and the **c** of the Negev— Jr 32:44
in Judah's **c** and Jerusalem's Jr 33:10
and in all its **c** there will once Jr 33:12
counts them in the **c** of the hill Jr 33:13
the **c** of the Judean foothills, Jr 33:13
foothills, the **c** of the Negev, Jr 33:13
the **c** surrounding Jerusalem and Jr 33:13
Jerusalem and Judah's **c**, Jr 33:13
and all its surrounding **c**: Jr 34:1
and all of Judah's remaining **c**— Jr 34:7
left among Judah's fortified **c**. Jr 34:7
make Judah's **c** a desolation, Jr 34:22
who are coming from their **c**. Jr 36:6
in from Judah's **c** into Jerusalem Jr 36:9
appointed over the **c** of Judah, Jr 40:5
live in the **c** you have captured. Jr 40:10
Jerusalem and all Judah's **c**; Jr 44:2
in Judah's **c** and Jerusalem's Jr 44:6
did in Judah's **c** and in Jr 44:17
burned in Judah's **c** and in Jr 44:21
I will destroy **c** with their Jr 46:8
the **c** and their inhabitants. Jr 47:2
his people settled in their **c**? Jr 49:1
and all her **c** will become ruins Jr 49:13
set fire to his **c**, and it will Jr 50:32
Her **c** have become a desolation, Jr 51:43
the fortified **c** of Daughter Lm 2:2
and destroyed its fortified **c**. Lm 2:5
virgins in the **c** of Judah. Lm 5:11
you live the **c** will be in ruins Ezk 6:6
The inhabited **c** will be Ezk 12:20
and destroyed their **c**. Ezk 19:7
beginning with its frontier **c**, Ezk 25:9
city like ⌊other⌋ deserted **c**, Ezk 26:19
and its **c** will be a desolation Ezk 29:12
among ruined **c** for 40 years. Ezk 29:12
their **c** will lie among ruined Ezk 30:7
cities will lie among ruined **c**. Ezk 30:7
and those **c** will go into Ezk 30:17
I will turn your **c** into ruins, Ezk 35:4
your **c** will not be inhabited. Ezk 35:9
desolate ruins and abandoned **c**, Ezk 36:4
The **c** will be inhabited and the Ezk 36:10
will cause the **c** to be inhabited Ezk 36:33
The **c** that were once ruined, Ezk 36:35
So the ruined **c** will be filled Ezk 36:38
of Israel's **c** will go out, Ezk 39:9
make plans against fortified **c**, Dn 11:24
has also multiplied fortified **c**. Hs 8:14
I will send fire on their **c**, Hs 8:14
sword will whirl through his **c**; Hs 11:6
he may save you in all your **c**, Hs 13:10
nothing to eat in all your **c**, Am 4:6
Two or three **c** staggered to Am 4:8
rebuild and occupy ruined **c**, Am 9:14
will possess the **c** of the Negev. Ob 20
I will remove the **c** of your land Mc 5:11
among you and demolish your **c**. Mc 5:14
from Assyria and the **c** of Egypt, Mc 7:12
against lands, **c**, and all who Hab 2:8
against lands, **c**, and all who Hab 2:17
cry against the fortified **c**, Zph 1:16
Their **c** lie devastated, without Zph 3:6
and the **c** of Judah that You Zch 1:12
My **c** will again overflow with Zch 1:17
along with its surrounding **c**, Zch 7:7
come, the residents of many **c**; Zch 8:20
even pursued them to foreign **c**. Ac 26:11
if He reduced the **c** of Sodom and 2Pt 2:6
Gomorrah and the **c** around them Jd 7
and the **c** of the nations fell. Rv 16:19

CITIZEN *(10)*

foreigner and **c** alike, with Jos 8:33
Cry out and sing, **c** of Zion, for Is 12:6
of Cilicia, a **c** of an important Ac 21:39
who is a Roman **c** and is Ac 22:25
For this man is a Roman **c**." Ac 22:26
Tell me—are you a Roman **c**?" Ac 22:27
"But I myself was born a **c**," Ac 22:28
was a Roman **c** and he had bound Ac 22:29
I learned that he is a Roman **c**. Ac 23:27
will not teach his fellow **c**, Heb 8:11

CITIZENS *(8)*

C of Gibeah ganged up on me and Jdg 20:5
the **c** of Keilah hand me over 1Sm 23:11
Will the **c** of Keilah hand me and 1Sm 23:12
Station the **c** of Jerusalem as Neh 7:3
one of the **c** of that country, Lk 15:15
we are Roman **c**, and threw us in Ac 16:37
Paul and Silas were Roman **c**. Ac 16:38
but fellow **c** with the saints, Eph 2:19

CITIZENSHIP *(3)*

I bought this **c** for a large Ac 22:28
excluded from the **c** of Israel, Eph 2:12
but our **c** is in heaven, from Php 3:20

CITY *(781)*

Cain became the builder of a **c**, Gn 4:17
he named the **c** Enoch after his Gn 4:17
Nineveh and the great **c** Calah. Gn 10:12
ourselves a **c** and a tower with Gn 11:4
to look over the **c** and the tower Gn 11:5
and they stopped building the **c**. Gn 11:8
50 righteous people in the **c**? Gn 18:24
50 righteous people in the **c**, Gn 18:26
the whole **c** for lack of five? Gn 18:28
the men of the **c** of Sodom, Gn 19:4
else in the **c** who belongs to you Gn 19:12
LORD is about to destroy the **c**!" Gn 19:14
in the punishment of the **c**." Gn 19:15
out and left him outside the **c**. Gn 19:16
the name of the **c** is Zoar. Gn 19:22
who came to the gate of his **c**, Gn 23:10
who came to the gate of his **c**. Gn 23:18
the name of the **c** is Beer-sheba Gn 26:33
previously the **c** was named Luz. Gn 28:19
the Canaanite **c** of Shechem and Gn 33:18
and camped in front of the **c**. Gn 33:18
the gate of their **c** and spoke to Gn 34:20
went into the unsuspecting **c**, Gn 34:25
plundered the **c** because their Gn 34:27
was in the **c** and in the field. Gn 34:28
the name of his **c** was Dinhabah. Gn 36:32
the name of his **c** was Avith. Gn 36:35
His **c** was Pau, and his wife's Gn 36:39
food in every **c** from the fields Gn 41:48
far from the **c** when Joseph said Gn 44:4
donkey and returned to the **c**. Gn 44:13
I have left the **c**, I will extend Ex 9:29
went out from Pharaoh and the **c**, Ex 9:33
an unclean place outside the **c**. Lv 14:40
an unclean place outside the **c**. Lv 14:41
outside the **c** to an unclean Lv 14:45
open countryside outside the **c**. Lv 14:53
sells a residence in a walled **c**, Lv 25:29
in the walled **c** is permanently Lv 25:30
house sold in a **c** they possess— Lv 25:33
a **c** on the border of your Nm 20:16
Heshbon was the **c** of Sihon king Nm 21:26
let the **c** of Sihon be restored. Nm 21:27
a flame from the **c** of Sihon. Nm 21:28
at the Moabite **c** on the Arnon Nm 22:36
extend⌋ from the **c** wall 500 Nm 35:4
outside the **c** for the east side Nm 35:5
side, with the **c** in the center. Nm 35:5
him to the **c** of refuge he fled Nm 35:25
border of the **c** of refuge he Nm 35:26
border of his **c** of refuge and Nm 35:27
to live in his **c** of refuge until Nm 35:28

who flees to his **c** of refuge, Nm 35:32
destroyed the people of every **c**, Dt 2:34
There was no **c** that was Dt 2:36
along with the **c** in the valley, Dt 2:36
There wasn't a **c** that we didn't Dt 3:4
women, and children of every **c**. Dt 3:6
inhabitants of their **c** astray, Dt 13:13
of that **c** with the sword. Dt 13:15
the middle of the **c** square and Dt 13:16
burn up the **c** and all its spoil Dt 13:16
The **c** must remain a mound of Dt 13:16
elders of his **c** must send ⌊for Dt 19:12
approach a **c** to fight against Dt 20:10
and whatever else is in the **c**— Dt 20:14
siege to a **c** for a long time, Dt 20:19
against the **c** that is waging Dt 20:20
The elders of the **c** nearest to Dt 21:3
elders of that **c** will bring the Dt 21:4
the elders of the **c** nearest to Dt 21:6
him to the elders of his **c**, Dt 21:19
say to the elders of his **c**, Dt 21:20
the men of his **c** will stone him Dt 21:21
bring ⌊it⌋ to the **c** elders at Dt 22:15
the cloth before the **c** elders. Dt 22:17
elders of that **c** will take the Dt 22:18
the men of her **c** will stone her Dt 22:21
her in the **c** and has sex with Dt 22:23
gate of that **c** and stone them Dt 22:24
not cry out in the **c** and the man Dt 22:24
elders at the ⌊**c**⌋ gate and say, Dt 25:7
elders of his **c** will summon him Dt 25:8
be blessed in the **c** and blessed Dt 28:3
be cursed in the **c** and cursed Dt 28:16
of Jericho, the **C** of Palms, as Dt 34:3
built⌋ into the wall of the **c**. Jos 2:15
far as Adam, a **c** next to Jos 3:16
around the **c** with all the men Jos 6:3
of war, circling the **c** one time. Jos 6:3
march around the **c** seven times, Jos 6:4
Then the **c** wall will collapse, Jos 6:5
march around the **c**, and have the Jos 6:7
LORD was carried around the **c**, Jos 6:11
around the **c** once and returned Jos 6:14
marched around the **c** seven times Jos 6:15
around the **c** seven times. Jos 6:15
the LORD has given you the **c**. Jos 6:16
But the **c** and everything in it Jos 6:17
The people advanced into the **c**, Jos 6:20
ahead, and they captured the **c**. Jos 6:20
in the **c** with the sword— Jos 6:21
burned up the **c** and everything Jos 6:24
the rebuilding of this **c**, Jos 6:26
of Ai, his people, **c**, and land. Jos 8:1
Set an ambush behind the **c**." Jos 8:2
Lie in ambush behind the **c**, Jos 8:4
are with me will approach the **c**. Jos 8:5
have drawn them away from the **c**, Jos 8:6
of your ambush and seize the **c**, Jos 8:7
taking the **c**, set it on fire Jos 8:8
went up and approached the **c**, Jos 8:11
a valley between them and the **c**. Jos 8:11
and Ai, to the west of the **c**. Jos 8:12
the north of the **c** and its rear Jos 8:13
rear guard to the west of the **c**. Jos 8:13
men of the **c** hurried and went Jos 8:14
waiting⌋ for him behind the **c**. Jos 8:14
and were drawn away from the **c**. Jos 8:16
leaving the **c** exposed while they Jos 8:17
I will hand the **c** over to you." Jos 8:18
ran, entered the **c**, captured it, Jos 8:19
smoke from the **c** was rising to Jos 8:20
captured the **c** and that smoke Jos 8:21
came out of the **c** against them, Jos 8:22
spoil of that **c** for themselves, Jos 8:27
entrance of the **c** gate and put Jos 8:29
Gibeon was a large **c** like one of Jos 10:2
No **c** made peace with the Jos 11:19
along with the **c** in the middle Jos 13:9
along with the **c** in the middle Jos 13:16
Nibshan, the **C** of Salt, and Jos 15:62
a **c** of the descendants of Judah. Jos 18:14
far as the fortified **c** of Tyre; Jos 19:29
gave him the **c** Timnath-serah Jos 19:50
rebuilt the **c** and lived in it. Jos 19:50
at the entrance of the **c** gate, Jos 20:4
before the elders of that **c**, Jos 20:4
bring him into the **c** and give Jos 20:4
stay in that **c** until he stands Jos 20:6
to his own **c** from which he fled. Jos 20:6
villages of the **c** to Caleb son Jos 21:12
the **c** of refuge for the one who Jos 21:13
the **c** of refuge for the one who Jos 21:21
the **c** of refuge for the one who Jos 21:27
the **c** of refuge for the one who Jos 21:32
the **c** of refuge for the one who Jos 21:38
They put the **c** to the sword and Jdg 1:8
of Judah from the **C** of Palms to Jdg 1:16
possession of the **C** of Palms. Jdg 3:13
and the men of the **c** to do it in Jdg 6:27
When the men of the **c** got up in Jdg 6:28
the men of the **c** said to Joash, Jdg 6:30
So he took the elders of the **c**, Jdg 8:16
and killed the men of the **c**. Jdg 8:17
ruler of the **c**, heard the words Jdg 9:30
are turning the **c** against you. Jdg 9:31
and at sunrise, charge the **c**. Jdg 9:33
at the entrance of the **c** gate. Jdg 9:35
people were coming out of the **c**, Jdg 9:43
at the entrance of the **c** gate. Jdg 9:44
against the **c** that entire day, Jdg 9:45
he tore down the **c** and sowed it Jdg 9:45
was a strong tower inside the **c**, Jdg 9:51
and lords of the **c** fled there. Jdg 9:51
the men of the **c** said to him: Jdg 14:18
all that night at the **c** gate. Jdg 16:2
doors of the **c** gate along with Jdg 16:3
swords and burned down the **c**. Jdg 18:27
rebuilt the **c** and lived in it Jdg 18:28
They named the **c** Dan, after the Jdg 18:29
The **c** was formerly named Laish. Jdg 18:29
at this Jebusite **c** and spend the Jdg 19:11
at a foreign **c** where there are Jdg 19:12
in and sat down in the **c** square, Jdg 19:15
the traveler in the **c** square, Jdg 19:17
men of the **c** surrounded the Jdg 19:22
gathered united against the **c**. Jdg 20:11
and were drawn away from the **c**. Jdg 20:31
away from the **c** to the highways. Jdg 20:32
put the whole **c** to the sword. Jdg 20:37
great cloud of smoke from the **c**, Jdg 20:38
smoke began to go up from the **c**, Jdg 20:40
and the whole **c** was going up in Jdg 20:40
the entire **c**, the animals, Jdg 20:48
Which **c** among the tribes of Jdg 21:8
the grain⌋ and went into the **c**, Ru 2:18
shawl, and she went into the **c**. Ru 3:15
man entered the **c** to give a 1Sm 4:13
report, the entire **c** cried out. 1Sm 4:13
off the chair by the **c** gate, 1Sm 4:18
hand was against the **c** of Gath, 1Sm 5:9
He afflicted the men of the **c**, 1Sm 5:9
fear of death pervaded the **c**; 1Sm 5:11
outcry of the **c** went up to 1Sm 5:12
The people of the **c** chopped up 1Sm 6:14
back one gold tumor for each **c**: 1Sm 6:17
Each of you, go back to your **c**." 1Sm 8:22
of God in this **c** who is highly 1Sm 9:6
they went to the **c** where the man 1Sm 9:10
were climbing the hill to the **c**, 1Sm 9:11
he just now came to the **c**, 1Sm 9:12
So they went up toward the **c**. 1Sm 9:14
were entering the **c** when they 1Sm 9:14
from the high place to the **c**, 1Sm 9:25
going down to the edge of the **c**, 1Sm 9:27
arrive at the **c**, you will meet 1Sm 10:5
Saul came to the **c** of Amalek and 1Sm 15:5
Go, take it back to the **c**." 1Sm 20:40
and Jonathan went into the **c**. 1Sm 20:42
down Nob, the **c** of the priests, 1Sm 22:19
live in the royal **c** with you?" 1Sm 27:5
in Ramah, his **c**, and Saul had 1Sm 28:3
of Zion, the **c** of David. 2Sm 5:7
which he named the **c** of David. 2Sm 5:9
of the LORD to the **c** of David; 2Sm 6:10
house to the **c** of David with 2Sm 6:12
was entering the **c** of David, 2Sm 6:16
in order to scout out the **c**, 2Sm 10:3
the entrance to the **c** gate while 2Sm 10:8
Abishai and entered the **c**. 2Sm 10:14
When Joab was besieging the **c**, 2Sm 11:16
Then the men of the **c** came out 2Sm 11:17
get so close to the **c** to fight? 2Sm 11:20
against the **c** and demolish it. 2Sm 11:25
were two men in a certain **c**, 2Sm 12:1
siege to the **c**, and capture it 2Sm 12:28
be the one to capture the **c**, 2Sm 12:28
quantity of plunder from the **c**. 2Sm 12:30
who were in the **c** and put ⌊them 2Sm 12:31
the road leading to the **c** gate. 2Sm 15:2
him and asked, "What **c** are you 2Sm 15:2
Gilonite, from his **c** of Giloh. 2Sm 15:12
and strike the **c** with the edge 2Sm 15:14
Return the ark of God to the **c**. 2Sm 15:25
return to the **c** in peace and 2Sm 15:27
return to the **c** and tell Absalom 2Sm 15:34
as Absalom was entering the **c**. 2Sm 15:37
to some **c**, all Israel will 2Sm 17:13
will bring ropes to that **c**, 2Sm 17:13
not be seen entering the **c**. 2Sm 17:17
if you support us from the **c**." 2Sm 18:3
returned to the **c** quietly that 2Sm 19:3
die in my own **c** near the tomb 2Sm 19:37
against the outer wall of the **c**. 2Sm 20:15
woman called out from the **c**, 2Sm 20:16
to destroy a **c** that is like 2Sm 20:19
and I will withdraw from the **c**." 2Sm 20:21
and they dispersed from the **c**, 2Sm 20:22
well at the **c** gate of Bethlehem! 2Sm 23:15
was buried in the **c** of David. 1Kg 2:10
her to the **c** of David until he 1Kg 3:1
from Zion, the **c** of David. 1Kg 8:1
not chosen a **c** to build a temple 1Kg 8:16
of the **c** You have chosen 1Kg 8:44
the **c** You have chosen, 1Kg 8:48
Canaanites who lived in the **c**, 1Kg 9:16
moved from the **c** of David to the 1Kg 9:24
the wall of the **c** of his father 1Kg 11:27
the **c** I chose out of all the 1Kg 11:32
the **c** I chose for Myself to put 1Kg 11:36
buried in the **c** of his father 1Kg 11:43
about it⌋ in the **c** where the old 1Kg 13:25
into to the **c** to mourn and to 1Kg 13:29
to Jeroboam and dies in the **c**, 1Kg 14:11
When your feet enter the **c**, 1Kg 14:12
the **c** the LORD had chosen from 1Kg 14:21
his fathers in the **c** of David. 1Kg 14:31
was buried in the **c** of David. 1Kg 15:8
buried in the **c** of his 1Kg 15:24
to Baasha and dies in the **c**, 1Kg 16:4
saw that the **c** was captured, 1Kg 16:18
He named the **c** he built Samaria 1Kg 16:24
When he arrived at the **c** gate, 1Kg 17:10
into the **c** to Ahab king 1Kg 20:2
their⌋ positions against the **c**. 1Kg 20:12
them marched out from the **c**, 1Kg 20:19
fled into the **c** of Aphek, 1Kg 20:30
into an inner room in the **c**. 1Kg 20:30
who lived with Naboth in his **c**. 1Kg 21:8
The men of his **c**, the elders and 1Kg 21:11
and nobles who lived in his **c**, 1Kg 21:11
him outside the **c** and stoned him 1Kg 21:13
to Ahab and dies in the **c**, 1Kg 21:24
governor of the **c**, and to Joash, 1Kg 22:26
man to his own **c**, and each man 1Kg 22:36
fathers in the **c** of his 1Kg 22:50
the men of the **c** said to Elisha, 2Kg 2:19
came out of the **c** and harassed 2Kg 2:23
every fortified **c** and every 2Kg 3:19
city and every choice **c**. 2Kg 3:19
surrounded ⌊the **c**⌋ and attacked 2Kg 3:25
a burnt offering on the **c** wall. 2Kg 3:27
by night and surrounded the **c**. 2Kg 6:14
and chariots surrounding the **c**. 2Kg 6:15
the way, and this is not the **c**. 2Kg 6:19
Let's go into the **c**,' we will 2Kg 7:4
because the famine is in the **c**, 2Kg 7:4
'When they come out of the **c**, 2Kg 7:12
alive and go into the **c**.'" 2Kg 7:12
horses that are left in the **c**. 2Kg 7:13
his fathers in the **c** of David, 2Kg 8:24
escape from the **c** to go tell 2Kg 9:15
fathers' tomb in the **c** of David. 2Kg 9:28
a fortified **c**, and weaponry, 2Kg 10:2
overseer of the **c**, the elders, 2Kg 10:5
and the **c** was quiet, for 2Kg 11:20
his fathers in the **c** of David, 2Kg 12:21
his fathers in the **c** of David. 2Kg 14:20
his fathers in the **c** of David. 2Kg 15:7
fathers in the **c** of his ancestor 2Kg 15:38
his fathers in the **c** of David, 2Kg 16:20
from watchtower to fortified **c**. 2Kg 17:9
from watchtower to fortified **c**. 2Kg 18:8
This **c** will not be handed over 2Kg 18:30
the king of the **c** of Sepharvaim, 2Kg 19:13

not enter this **c** or shoot an 2Kg 19:32
and he will not enter this **c**, 2Kg 19:33
will defend this **c** and rescue it 2Kg 19:34
you and this **c** from the hand 2Kg 20:6
I will defend this **c** for My sake 2Kg 20:6
and brought water into the **c**, 2Kg 20:20
of Joshua the governor of the **c** 2Kg 23:8
(on the left at the **c** gate). 2Kg 23:8
The men of the **c** told him, 2Kg 23:17
I will reject this **c** Jerusalem, 2Kg 23:27
and the **c** came under siege. 2Kg 24:10
came to the **c** while his servants 2Kg 24:11
siege to the **c** and built a siege 2Kg 25:1
The **c** was under siege until King 2Kg 25:2
severe in the **c** that the people 2Kg 25:3
Then the **c** was broken into, 2Kg 25:4
the Chaldeans surrounded the **c**. 2Kg 25:4
people who were left in the **c**, 2Kg 25:11
From the **c** he took a court 2Kg 25:19
royal aides found in the **c**; 2Kg 25:19
who were found within the **c**. 2Kg 25:19
Hadad's **c** was named Pai, and his 1Ch 1:50
around the **c** were given to Caleb 1Ch 6:56
Hebron (a **c** of refuge), Libnah 1Ch 6:57
Shechem (a **c** of refuge) with its 1Ch 6:67
Zion (that is, the **c** of David). 1Ch 11:5
it was called the **c** of David. 1Ch 11:7
He built up the **c** all the way 1Ch 11:8
Joab restored the rest of the **c**. 1Ch 11:8
well at the **c** gate of Bethlehem! 1Ch 11:17
of God home to the **c** of David; 1Ch 13:13
for himself in the **c** of David, 1Ch 15:1
was entering the **c** of David, 1Ch 15:29
entrance of the **c** while the 1Ch 19:9
Abishai and entered the **c**. 1Ch 19:15
quantity of plunder from the **c**. 1Ch 20:2
was about to destroy the **c**, 1Ch 21:15
the LORD up from the **c** of David, 2Ch 5:2
not chosen a **c** to build a temple 2Ch 6:5
of this **c** You have chosen 2Ch 6:34
and the **c** You have chosen, 2Ch 6:38
Pharaoh from the **c** of David to 2Ch 8:11
buried in the **c** of his father 2Ch 9:31
each and every **c** to make them 2Ch 11:12
the **c** the LORD had chosen from 2Ch 12:13
was buried in the **c** of David. 2Ch 12:16
was buried in the **c** of David. 2Ch 14:1
crushed by nation and **c** by city, 2Ch 15:6
crushed by nation and city by **c**, 2Ch 15:6
for himself in the **c** of David. 2Ch 16:14
every fortified **c** of Judah and 2Ch 17:2
governor of the **c**, and to Joash, 2Ch 18:25
of the land of Judah, **c** by city. 2Ch 19:5
of the land of Judah, city by **c**. 2Ch 19:5
his fathers in the **c** of David. 2Ch 21:1
buried in the **c** of David but not 2Ch 21:20
and the **c** was quiet, for 2Ch 23:21
buried in the **c** of David with 2Ch 24:16
buried him in the **c** of David, 2Ch 24:25
his fathers in the **c** of Judah. 2Ch 25:28
was buried in the **c** of David. 2Ch 27:9
Jericho, the **C** of Palms, among 2Ch 28:15
places in every **c** of Judah to 2Ch 28:25
fathers and was buried in the **c**, 2Ch 28:27
gathered the **c** officials, and 2Ch 29:20
traveled from **c** to city in the 2Ch 30:10
from city to **c** in the land 2Ch 30:10
cities, in each and every **c**. 2Ch 31:19
springs that were outside the **c**, 2Ch 32:3
terraces of the **c** of David, 2Ch 32:5
in the square of the **c** gate. 2Ch 32:6
that he might capture the **c**. 2Ch 32:18
and westward to the **c** of David. 2Ch 32:30
outer wall of the **c** of David 2Ch 33:14
and he threw them outside the **c**. 2Ch 33:15
governor of the **c** and the 2Ch 34:8
that rebellious and evil **c**, Ezr 4:12
king that if that **c** is rebuilt Ezr 4:13
that the **c** is a rebellious Ezr 4:15
that the city is a rebellious **c**, Ezr 4:15
is why this **c** was destroyed. Ezr 4:15
king that if this **c** is rebuilt Ezr 4:16
that this **c** has had uprisings Ezr 4:19
so that this **c** will not be Ezr 4:21
I was in the fortress **c** of Susa, Neh 1:1
be sad when the **c** where my Neh 2:3
Judah and to the **c** where my Neh 2:5
fortress, the **c** wall, and the Neh 2:8

descend from the **c** of David. Neh 3:15
The **c** was large and spacious, Neh 7:4
the holy **c**, while the other Neh 11:1
second in command over the **c**. Neh 11:9
All the Levites in the holy **c**: Neh 11:18
the steps of the **c** of David on Neh 12:37
disaster on us and on this **c**? Neh 13:18
while the **c** of Susa was in Est 3:15
went into the middle of the **c**, Est 4:1
Mordecai in the **c** square in Est 4:6
the horse through the **c** square, Est 6:9
him through the **c** square, Est 6:11
in each and every **c** the right to Est 8:11
The **c** of Susa shouted and Est 8:15
In every province and every **c**, Est 8:17
province, and **c**, so that these Est 9:28
are crushed at the ⌊**c**⌋ gate, Jb 5:4
From the **c**, men groan; the Jb 24:12
went out to the **c** gate and took Jb 29:7
C officials stopped talking and Jb 29:9
I had support in the ⌊**c**⌋ gate, Jb 31:21
love to me in a **c** under siege. Ps 31:21
streams delight the **c** of God, Ps 46:4
praised in the **c** of our God. Ps 48:1
the north is the **c** of the great Ps 48:2
have seen in the **c** of the LORD Ps 48:8
of Hosts, in the **c** of our God; Ps 48:8
violence and strife in the **c**; Ps 55:9
dogs and prowling around the **c**. Ps 59:6
dogs and prowling around the **c**. Ps 59:14
bring me to the fortified **c**? Ps 60:9
who sit at the **c** gate talk about Ps 69:12
are said about you, **c** of God. Ps 87:3
all evildoers from the LORD's **c**. Ps 101:8
no way to a **c** where they could Ps 107:4
path to go to a **c** where they Ps 107:7
they establish a **c** where they Ps 107:36
bring me to the fortified **c**? Ps 108:10
built as a **c** ⌊should be⌋, Ps 122:3
the LORD watches over a **c**, Ps 127:1
their⌋ enemies at the **c** gate. Ps 127:5
at the entrance of the **c** gates: Pr 1:21
the gates at the entry to the **c**, Pr 8:3
the highest points of the **c**: Pr 9:3
at the highest point of the **c**, Pr 9:14
man's wealth is his fortified **c**; Pr 10:15
thrive, a **c** rejoices, and when Pr 11:10
A **c** is built up by the blessing Pr 11:11
temper, than capturing a **c**. Pr 16:32
man's wealth is his fortified **c**; Pr 18:11
to reach⌋ than a fortified **c**, Pr 18:19
The wise conquer a **c** of warriors Pr 21:22
temper is like a **c** whose wall is Pr 25:28
Mockers inflame a **c**, but the Pr 29:8
husband is known at the **c** gates, Pr 31:23
works praise her at the **c** gates. Pr 31:31
stronger than ten rulers of a **c**. Ec 7:19
praised in the **c** where they did Ec 8:10
There was a small **c** with few men Ec 9:14
wise man was found in the **c**, Ec 9:15
delivered the **c** by his wisdom. Ec 9:15
don't know how to go to the **c**. Ec 10:15
arise now and go about the **c**, Sg 3:2
who go about the **c** found me. Sg 3:3
who go about the **c** found me. Sg 5:7
field, like a besieged **c**. Is 1:8
The faithful **c**—what an Is 1:21
will be called the Righteous **C**, Is 1:26
Righteous City, a Faithful **C**." Is 1:26
gates! Cry out, **c**! Tremble with Is 14:31
Damascus is no longer a **c**. Is 17:1
his friend, **c** against city, Is 19:2
city against **c**, kingdom against Is 19:2
will be called the **C** of the Sun. Is 19:18
The noisy **c**, the jubilant town, Is 22:2
⌊the walls of⌋ the **c** of David. Is 22:9
Is this your jubilant ⌊**c**⌋, Is 23:7
stroll through the **c**, prostitute Is 23:16
The **c** of chaos is shattered; Is 24:10
desolation remains in the **c**; Is 24:12
have turned the **c** into a pile Is 25:2
a fortified **c**, into a ruin; Is 25:2
of barbarians is no longer a **c**; Is 25:2
A **c** of violent people will fear Is 25:3
We have a strong **c**. Salvation is Is 26:1
places—an inaccessible **c**. Is 26:5
the fortified **c** will be deserted Is 27:10
Ariel, Ariel, the **c** where David Is 29:1

joyous house in the joyful **c**. Is 32:13
forsaken, the busy **c** abandoned. Is 32:14
and the **c** will sink into the Is 32:19
the **c** of our festival times. Is 33:20
This **c** will not be handed over Is 36:15
the king of the **c** of Sepharvaim, Is 37:13
not enter this **c** or shoot an Is 37:33
and he will not enter this **c**. Is 37:34
defend this **c** and rescue it, Is 37:35
you and this **c** from the hand Is 38:6
Assyria; I will defend this **c**. Is 38:6
will rebuild My **c**, and set My Is 45:13
they are named after the Holy **C**, Is 48:2
garments, Jerusalem, the Holy **C**! Is 52:1
will call you the **C** of the LORD, Is 60:14
Cared For, A **C** Not Deserted. Is 62:12
A sound of uproar from the **c**! Is 66:6
who has made you a fortified **c**, Jr 1:18
one from a **c** and two from a Jr 3:14
Every **c** flees at the sound of Jr 4:29
rocks. Every **c** is abandoned; no Jr 4:29
This **c** must be punished. Jr 6:6
the **c** and all its residents. Jr 8:16
If I enter the **c**, look—those Jr 14:18
gates of this **c** on the Sabbath Jr 17:24
through the gates of this **c**. Jr 17:25
c will be inhabited forever. Jr 17:25
I will make this **c** desolate, Jr 19:8
shatter these people and this **c**, Jr 19:11
making this **c** like Topheth. Jr 19:12
'I am about to bring on this **c**— Jr 19:15
away all the wealth of this **c**, Jr 20:5
them into the center of this **c**. Jr 21:4
strike the residents of this **c**, Jr 21:6
those in this **c** who survive the Jr 21:7
stays in this **c** will die by the Jr 21:9
against this **c** to ⌊bring⌋ Jr 21:10
will pass by this **c** and ask one Jr 22:8
do such a thing to this great **c**? Jr 22:8
you and the **c** that I gave you Jr 23:39
disaster on the **c** that bears My Jr 25:29
I will make this **c** an object of Jr 26:6
Shiloh and this **c** will become Jr 26:9
has prophesied against this **c**, Jr 26:11
heard against this temple and **c**. Jr 26:12
yourselves, on this **c**, and on Jr 26:15
against this **c** and against this Jr 26:20
Why should this **c** become a ruin? Jr 27:17
that still remain in this **c**, Jr 27:19
welfare of the **c** I have deported Jr 29:7
the people living in this **c**— Jr 29:16
Every **c** will be rebuilt on its Jr 30:18
when the **c** from the Tower of Jr 31:38
to hand this **c** over to Babylon's Jr 32:3
against the **c** to capture it, Jr 32:24
it, and the **c**, as a result Jr 32:24
though the **c** has been handed Jr 32:25
about to hand this **c** over to the Jr 32:28
fight against this **c** will come, Jr 32:29
come, set this **c** on fire, and Jr 32:29
for this **c** has been up against Jr 32:31
says to this **c** about which you Jr 32:36
houses of this **c** and the palaces Jr 33:4
face from this **c** because of all Jr 33:5
This **c** will bear on My behalf a Jr 33:9
to hand this **c** over to the king Jr 34:2
will bring them back to this **c**. Jr 34:22
return and fight against this **c**. Jr 37:8
get up and burn this **c** down." Jr 37:10
the bread was gone from the **c**. Jr 37:21
stays in this **c** will die by the Jr 38:2
'This **c** will most certainly be Jr 38:3
who remain in this **c** and of all Jr 38:4
is no more bread in the **c**." Jr 38:9
this **c** will not be burned down, Jr 38:17
then this **c** will be handed over Jr 38:18
and this **c** will burn down. Jr 38:23
of the month, the **c** was broken Jr 39:2
They left the **c** at night by way Jr 39:4
remained in the **c** and those Jr 39:9
and not for good against this **c**. Jr 39:16
But when they came into the **c**, Jr 41:7
How can the **c** of praise not be Jr 49:25
Babylon that his **c** has been Jr 51:31
siege to the **c** and built a siege Jr 52:4
The **c** was under siege until King Jr 52:5
severe in the **c** that the people Jr 52:6
Then the **c** was broken into, Jr 52:7

They left the c by night by way Jr 52:7
the Chaldeans surrounded the c. Jr 52:7
people who were left in the c, Jr 52:15
From the c he took a court Jr 52:25
royal aides found in the c; Jr 52:25
who were found within the c. Jr 52:25
c ⌊once⌋ crowded with people! Lm 1:1
in the c while searching Lm 1:19
faint in the streets of the c. Lm 2:11
wounded in the streets of the c, Lm 2:12
this the c that was called the Lm 2:15
fate of⌋ all the women in my c. Lm 3:51
The elders have left the c gate, Lm 5:14
and draw the c of Jerusalem on Ezk 4:1
wall between yourself and the c. Ezk 4:3
of it⌋ in the c when the days Ezk 5:2
with the sword all around the c; Ezk 5:2
will devour whoever is in the c. Ezk 7:15
and the c is filled with Ezk 7:23
of the c, each ⌊of you⌋ with Ezk 9:1
throughout the c of Jerusalem," Ezk 9:4
Pass through the c after him and Ezk 9:5
out killing ⌊people⌋ in the c. Ezk 9:7
and the c full of perversity. Ezk 9:9
and scatter ⌊them⌋ over the c." Ezk 10:2
give wicked advice in this c. Ezk 11:2
The c is the pot, and we are the Ezk 11:3
multiplied your slain in this c, Ezk 11:6
meat, and the c is the pot, but Ezk 11:7
you out of the c and hand you Ezk 11:9
The c will not be a pot for you, Ezk 11:11
up from within the c and stood Ezk 11:23
on the mountain east of the c. Ezk 11:23
The c will fall, and you will be Ezk 13:14
and set it in a c of traders. Ezk 17:4
fork in the road to ⌊each⌋ c. Ezk 21:19
judgment against the c of blood? Ezk 22:2
A c that sheds blood within her Ezk 22:3
you will be melted within the c. Ezk 22:21
you will be melted inside the c. Ezk 22:22
Woe to the c of bloodshed, Ezk 24:6
Woe to the c of bloodshed! Ezk 24:9
an army⌋ entering a breached c, Ezk 26:10
have perished, c of renown, you Ezk 26:17
make you a ruined c like ⌊other⌋ Ezk 26:19
comes to an end in the c. Ezk 30:18
"The c has been taken!" Ezk 33:21
about you near the ⌊c⌋ walls and Ezk 33:30
will even be a c named Hamonah Ezk 39:16
was a structure resembling a c. Ezk 40:2
when He came to destroy the c, Ezk 43:3
As the property of the c, Ezk 45:6
will be for common use by the c, Ezk 48:15
The c will be in the middle of Ezk 48:15
food for the workers of the c. Ezk 48:18
along with the c property as a Ezk 48:20
donation and the c property will Ezk 48:21
property and the c property in Ezk 48:22
These are the exits of the c: Ezk 48:30
gates of the c being named for Ezk 48:31
perimeter ⌊of the c⌋ will be six Ezk 48:35
the name of the c from that day Ezk 48:35
I was in the fortress c of Susa, Dn 8:2
turn away from Your c Jerusalem, Dn 9:16
and the c called by Your name Dn 9:18
because Your c and Your people Dn 9:19
your people and your holy c— Dn 9:24
will destroy the c and the Dn 9:26
and capture a well-fortified c. Dn 11:15
Gilead is a c of evildoers, Hs 6:8
They storm the c; they run on Jl 2:9
If a ram's horn is blown in a c, Am 3:6
If a disaster occurs in a c, Am 3:6
turmoil in the c and the acts Am 3:9
I sent rain on one c but no rain Am 4:7
to another c to drink water Am 4:8
c that marches out a thousand Am 5:3
at the c gate and despise Am 5:10
hand over the c and everything Am 6:8
will be a prostitute in the c, Am 7:17
Go to the great c of Nineveh and Jnh 1:2
Go to the great c of Nineveh and Jnh 3:2
was an extremely large c, Jnh 3:3
walk in the c and proclaimed, Jnh 3:4
Jonah left the c and sat down Jnh 4:5
see what would happen to the c. Jnh 4:5
about the great c of Nineveh, Jnh 4:11
you will leave the c and camp in Mc 4:10
of the LORD calls out to the c Mc 6:9
the wealthy of the c are full of Mc 6:12
Woe to the c of blood, totally Nah 3:1
who builds a c with bloodshed Hab 2:12
is the self-assured c that lives Zph 2:15
Woe to the c that is rebellious Zph 3:1
and defiled, the oppressive c! Zph 3:1
will be called the Faithful C, Zch 8:3
streets of the c will be filled Zch 8:5
residents of one c will go to Zch 8:21
the peoples who surround the c. Zch 12:2
The c will be captured, the Zch 14:2
Half the c will go into exile, Zch 14:2
will not be removed from the c. Zch 14:2
Devil took Him to the holy c, Mt 4:5
A c situated on a hill cannot be Mt 5:14
it is the c of the great King Mt 5:35
went into the c and reported Mt 8:33
no c or house divided against Mt 12:25
the whole c was shaken, saying, Mt 21:10
went out of the c to Bethany, Mt 21:17
as He was returning to the c, Mt 21:18
and burned down their c. Mt 22:7
the roads exit the c and invite Mt 22:9
The c who kills the prophets and Mt 23:37
"Go into the c to a certain man," Mt 26:18
the holy c, and appeared to Mt 27:53
came into the c and reported to Mt 28:11
they would go out of the c. Mk 11:19
them, "Go into the c, and a man Mk 14:13
out, entered the c, and found it Mk 14:16
Judea, to the c of David, which Lk 2:4
born for you in the c of David. Lk 2:11
crowd from the c was also with Lk 7:12
The c who kills the prophets and Lk 13:34
the streets and alleys of the c, Lk 14:21
As He approached and saw the c, Lk 19:41
inside the c must leave it, Lk 21:21
when you've entered the c, Lk 22:10
that had taken place in the c, Lk 23:19
stay in the c until you are Lk 24:49
was crucified was near the c, Jn 19:20
in this c both Herod and Pontius Ac 4:27
and put them in the c jail. Ac 5:18
him out of the c and began to Ac 7:58
went down to a c in Samaria Ac 8:5
there was great joy in that c. Ac 8:8
sorcery in that c and astounded Ac 8:9
But get up and go into the c, Ac 9:6
traveling and nearing the c, Ac 10:9
iron gate that leads into the c, Ac 12:10
and the leading men of the c. Ac 13:50
people of the c were divided, Ac 14:4
they dragged him out of the c, Ac 14:19
has had in every c those who Ac 15:21
is a leading c of that district Ac 16:12
We stayed in that c for a number Ac 16:12
went outside the c gate by the Ac 16:13
cloth from the c of Thyatira, Ac 16:14
are seriously disturbing our c. Ac 16:20
they set the c in an uproar. Ac 17:5
brothers before the c officials, Ac 17:6
crowd and the c officials who Ac 17:8
he saw that the c was full of Ac 17:16
I have many people in this c." Ac 18:10
So the c was filled with Ac 19:29
when the c clerk had calmed the Ac 19:35
know that the c of the Ephesians Ac 19:35
escorted us out of the c. Ac 21:5
the Ephesian in the c with him, Ac 21:29
The whole c was stirred up, Ac 21:30
a citizen of an important c. Ac 21:39
brought up in this c at the feet Ac 22:3
or anywhere in the c. Ac 24:12
and prominent men of the c. Ac 25:23
Fair Havens near the c of Lasea. Ac 27:8
Erastus, the c treasurer, and Rm 16:23
dangers in the c, dangers in the 2Co 11:26
guarded the c of the Damascenes 2Co 11:32
forward to the c that has Heb 11:10
He has prepared a c for them. Heb 11:16
to the c of the living God Heb 12:22
we do not have an enduring c; Heb 13:14
such and such a c and spend a Jms 4:13
the name of the c of My God— Rv 3:12
the holy c for 42 months. Rv 11:2
public square of the great c, Rv 11:8
a tenth of the c fell, and 7,000 Rv 11:13
was trampled outside the c, Rv 14:20
The great c split into three Rv 16:19
saw is the great c that has an Rv 17:18
Woe, woe, the great c, Babylon, Rv 18:10
city, Babylon, the mighty c! Rv 18:10
woe, the great c, clothed in Rv 18:16
"Who is like the great c?" Rv 18:18
woe, the great c, where all Rv 18:19
the great c will be thrown Rv 18:21
of the saints, the beloved c. Rv 20:9
saw the Holy C, new Jerusalem, Rv 21:2
and showed me the holy c, Rv 21:10
⌊The c⌋ had a massive high wall, Rv 21:12
The c wall had 12 foundations, Rv 21:14
measuring rod to measure the c, Rv 21:15
The c is laid out in a square; Rv 21:16
measured the c with the rod at Rv 21:16
and the c was pure gold like Rv 21:18
of the c wall were adorned Rv 21:19
street of the c was pure gold, Rv 21:21
The c does not need the sun or Rv 21:23
of the broad street ⌊of the c⌋. Rv 22:2
of the Lamb will be in the c, Rv 22:3
may enter the c by the gates. Rv 22:14
the tree of life and the holy c, Rv 22:19

CITY'S *(11)*

he will destroy the c survivors. Nm 24:19
10 men of the c elders and said, Ru 4:2
see that the c location is good 2Kg 2:19
and called to the c gatekeepers 2Kg 7:10
for by the c prominent men. 2Kg 10:6
of land⌋ and the c property, Ezk 45:7
donation and the c property, Ezk 45:7
These are the c measurements: Ezk 48:16
The c open space will extend: Ezk 48:17
c workers from all the tribes Ezk 48:19
place and the c residents an Mc 6:16

CIVIL *(1)*

and the royal c administrators Est 9:3

CLAIM *(14)*

The priest would c for himself 1Sm 2:14
have a greater ⌊c⌋ to David than 2Sm 19:43
or historic c in Jerusalem." Neh 2:20
So do not c, "We have found Jb 32:13
and my c is ignored by my God"? Is 40:27
it occurred, so you could not c: Is 48:5
you could not c, "I already knew Is 48:7
Why do My people c: We will go Jr 2:31
you c: I am innocent. His anger Jr 2:35
How can you c: We are wise; the Jr 8:8
of Benjamin to c his portion Jr 37:12
divinations. They c: ⌊This is⌋ Ezk 13:6
people slanderously c we say, Rm 3:8
who c to be Jews and are not, Rv 3:9

CLAIMED *(3)*

the forest c more people than 2Sm 18:8
will be with you, as you have c. Am 5:14
man whom Paul c to be alive. Ac 25:19

CLAIMING *(9)*

brokenness superficially, c: Jr 6:14
brokenness of My dear people, c: Jr 8:11
They are prophesying to you, c: Jr 27:16
sent ⌊word⌋ to us in Babylon, c: Jr 29:28
prophesied to you, c, 'The king Jr 37:19
rose up, c to be somebody, Ac 5:36
while c to be somebody great. Ac 8:9
C to be wise, they became fools Rm 1:22
c access to a visionary realm Col 2:18

CLAIMS *(5)*

else⌋ lost, and someone c: Ex 22:9
your c are good and right, 2Sm 15:3
if the wise man c to know it, Ec 8:17
No one makes c justly; Is 59:4
has died is freed from sin's c. Rm 6:7

CLAMOR *(1)*

Do not forget the c of Your Ps 74:23

CLAN *(102)*

and each of you to his c. Lv 25:10
return to his c and his Lv 25:41
a member of the foreigner's c, Lv 25:47
from his c may redeem him. Lv 25:49
each man by his c and by his Nm 2:34
The Libnite c and the Shimeite Nm 3:21
and the Shimeite c came from Nm 3:21
The Amramite c, the Izharite Nm 3:27
the Izharite c, the Hebronite Nm 3:27

the Hebronite **c**, and the Nm 3:27
the Uzzielite **c** came from Kohath Nm 3:27
The Mahlite **c** and the Mushite Nm 3:33
and the Mushite **c** came from Nm 3:33
the Hanochite **c** ⌊from⌋ Hanoch; Nm 26:5
the Palluite **c** from Pallu; Nm 26:5
the Hezronite **c** from Hezron; Nm 26:6
the Carmite **c** from Carmi. Nm 26:6
the Nemuelite **c** from Nemuel; Nm 26:12
the Jaminite **c** from Jamin; Nm 26:12
the Jachinite **c** from Jachin; Nm 26:12
the Zerahite **c** from Zerah; Nm 26:13
the Shaulite **c** from Shaul. Nm 26:13
the Zephonite **c** from Zephon; Nm 26:15
the Haggite **c** from Haggi; Nm 26:15
the Shunite **c** from Shuni; Nm 26:15
the Oznite **c** from Ozni; Nm 26:16
from Ozni; the Erite **c** from Eri; Nm 26:16
the Arodite **c** from Arod; Nm 26:17
the Arelite **c** from Areli. Nm 26:17
the Shelanite **c** from Shelah; Nm 26:20
the Perezite **c** from Perez; Nm 26:20
the Zerahite **c** from Zerah. Nm 26:20
the Hezronite **c** from Hezron; Nm 26:21
the Hamulite **c** from Hamul. Nm 26:21
the Tolaite **c** from Tola; Nm 26:23
the Punite **c** from Puvah; Nm 26:23
the Jashubite **c** from Jashub; Nm 26:24
the Shimronite **c** from Shimron. Nm 26:24
the Seredite **c** from Sered; Nm 26:26
the Elonite **c** from Elon; Nm 26:26
the Jahleelite **c** from Jahleel. Nm 26:26
the Machirite **c** from Machir. Nm 26:29
the Gileadite **c** from Gilead. Nm 26:29
the Iezerite **c** ⌊from⌋ Iezer; Nm 26:30
the Helekite **c** from Helek; Nm 26:30
The Asrielite **c** ⌊from⌋ Asriel; Nm 26:31
the Shechemite **c** ⌊from⌋ Shechem; Nm 26:31
the Shemidaite **c** ⌊from⌋ Shemida; Nm 26:32
the Hepherite **c** ⌊from⌋ Hepher; Nm 26:32
Shuthelahite **c** from Shuthelah; Nm 26:35
the Becherite **c** from Becher; Nm 26:35
the Tahanite **c** from Tahan. Nm 26:35
the Eranite **c** from Eran. Nm 26:36
the Belaite **c** from Bela; Nm 26:38
the Ashbelite **c** from Ashbel; Nm 26:38
the Ahiramite **c** from Ahiram; Nm 26:38
the Shuphamite **c** from Shupham; Nm 26:39
the Huphamite **c** from Hupham. Nm 26:39
the Ardite **c** ⌊from⌋ Ard; Nm 26:40
the Naamite **c** from Naaman. Nm 26:40
the Shuhamite **c** from Shuham. Nm 26:42
the Imnite **c** from Imnah; Nm 26:44
the Ishvite **c** from Ishvi; Nm 26:44
the Beriite **c** from Beriah. Nm 26:44
the Heberite **c** from Heber; Nm 26:45
the Malchielite **c** from Malchiel. Nm 26:45
the Jahzeelite **c** from Jahzeel; Nm 26:48
the Gunite **c** from Guni; Nm 26:48
the Jezerite **c** from Jezer; Nm 26:49
the Shillemite **c** from Shillem. Nm 26:49
the Gershonite **c** from Gershon; Nm 26:57
the Kohathite **c** from Kohath; Nm 26:57
the Merarite **c** from Merari. Nm 26:57
the Libnite **c**, the Hebronite Nm 26:58
the Hebronite **c**, the Mahlite Nm 26:58
the Mahlite **c**, the Mushite clan Nm 26:58
the Mushite **c**, and the Korahite Nm 26:58
clan, and the Korahite **c**. Nm 26:58
father be taken away from his **c**? Nm 27:4
the nearest relative of his **c**, Nm 27:11
Gilead to ⌊the **c** of⌋ Machir son Nm 32:40
a large **c** and decrease it for Nm 33:54
leaders from the **c** of the Nm 36:1
marry within a **c** of their Nm 36:6
from the **c** of her ancestral Nm 36:8
the tribe of their father's **c**. Nm 36:12
no man, woman, **c**, or tribe among Dt 29:18
is to come forward **c** by clan. Jos 7:14
is to come forward clan by **c**. Jos 7:14
c the LORD selects is to come Jos 7:14
and the Zerahite **c** was selected. Jos 7:17
had the Zerahite **c** come forward Jos 7:17
his maternal grandfather's **c**, Jdg 9:1
resided within the **c** of Judah. Jdg 17:7
and isn't my **c** the least 1Sm 9:21
and the Matrite **c** was selected. 1Sm 10:21
or my father's **c** in Israel that 1Sm 18:18
there involving the whole **c**.' 1Sm 20:6
me go because our **c** is holding 1Sm 20:29
Now the whole **c** has risen up 2Sm 14:7
the entire **c** that I brought Am 3:1
become like a **c** in Judah and Zch 9:7

CLANGING *(1)*

a sounding gong or a **c** cymbal. 1Co 13:1

CLANS *(147)*

are ⌊Japheth's sons⌋ by their **c**, Gn 10:5
the Canaanite **c** scattered. Gn 10:18
sons, by their **c**, according to Gn 10:20
are Shem's sons by their **c**, Gn 10:31
These are the **c** of Noah's sons, Gn 10:32
12 leaders of their **c**. Gn 25:16
These are the **c** of Reuben. Ex 6:14
These are the **c** of Simeon. Ex 6:15
Libni and Shimei, by their **c**. Ex 6:17
These are the **c** of the Levites Ex 6:19
are the **c** of the Korahites. Ex 6:24
the Levite families by their **c**. Ex 6:25
community by their **c** and their Nm 1:2
the heads of Israel's **c**." Nm 1:16
ancestry by their **c** and their Nm 1:18
records by their **c** and their Nm 1:20
records by their **c** and their Nm 1:22
records by their **c** and their Nm 1:24
records by their **c** and their Nm 1:26
records by their **c** and their Nm 1:28
records by their **c** and their Nm 1:30
records by their **c** and their Nm 1:32
records by their **c** and their Nm 1:34
records by their **c** and their Nm 1:36
records by their **c** and their Nm 1:38
records by their **c** and their Nm 1:40
records by their **c** and their Nm 1:42
ancestral houses and their **c**. Nm 3:15
of Gershon's sons by their **c**: Nm 3:18
sons by their **c** were Amram, Nm 3:19
sons by their **c** were Mahli and Nm 3:20
were the Levite **c** by their Nm 3:20
these were the Gershonite **c**. Nm 3:21
The Gershonite **c** camped behind Nm 3:23
The **c** of the Kohathites camped Nm 3:29
of the Kohathite **c** was Elizaphan Nm 3:30
these were the Merarite **c**. Nm 3:33
of the Merarite **c** was Zuriel son Nm 3:35
by their **c** at the LORD's Nm 3:39
by their **c** and their ancestral Nm 4:2
tribal **c** to be wiped out Nm 4:18
ancestral houses and their **c**. Nm 4:22
the Gershonite **c** regarding work Nm 4:24
of the Gershonite **c** at the tent Nm 4:28
them by their **c** and their Nm 4:29
of the Merarite **c** regarding all Nm 4:33
by their **c** and their ancestral Nm 4:34
by their **c** numbered 2,750. Nm 4:36
men of the Kohathite **c**, Nm 4:37
by their **c** and their ancestral Nm 4:38
by their **c** and their ancestral Nm 4:40
men of the Gershonite **c**. Nm 4:41
the Merarite **c** were registered Nm 4:42
by their **c** and their ancestral Nm 4:42
by their **c** numbered 3,200. Nm 4:44
men of the Merarite **c**; Nm 4:45
Levites by their **c** and their Nm 4:46
of Israel's **c**, are to gather Nm 10:4
These were the Reubenite **c**, Nm 26:7
Simeon's descendants by their **c**: Nm 26:12
These were the Simeonite **c**, Nm 26:14
Gad's descendants by their **c**: Nm 26:15
were the Gadite **c** ⌊numbered⌋ by Nm 26:18
Judah's descendants by their **c**: Nm 26:20
These were Judah's **c** ⌊numbered⌋ Nm 26:22
descendants by their **c**: Nm 26:23
were Issachar's **c** ⌊numbered⌋ by Nm 26:25
descendants by their **c**: Nm 26:26
the Zebulunite **c** ⌊numbered⌋ by Nm 26:27
by their **c** ⌊from⌋ Manasseh Nm 26:28
were Manasseh's **c**, numbered by Nm 26:34
descendants by their **c**: Nm 26:35
the Ephraimite **c** ⌊numbered⌋ by Nm 26:37
Joseph's descendants by their **c**. Nm 26:37
descendants by their **c**: Nm 26:38
the Benjaminite **c** numbered by Nm 26:41
Dan's descendants by their **c**: Nm 26:42
These were the **c** of Dan by their Nm 26:42
the clans of Dan by their **c**. Nm 26:42
All the Shuhamite **c** ⌊numbered⌋ Nm 26:43
Asher's descendants by their **c**: Nm 26:44
were the Asherite **c** ⌊numbered⌋ Nm 26:47
descendants by their **c**: Nm 26:48
the Naphtali **c** numbered by their Nm 26:50
Levites registered by their **c**: Nm 26:57
Manasseh from the **c** of Manasseh, Nm 27:1
by lot according to your **c**. Nm 33:54
one of the **c** of the sons of Nm 36:1
men⌋ from the **c** of the Nm 36:12
He had the **c** of Judah come Jos 7:17
of the Reubenites by their **c**, Jos 13:15
of the Reubenites by their **c**, Jos 13:23
tribe of the Gadites by their **c**, Jos 13:24
of the Gadites by their **c**, Jos 13:28
descendants by their **c**, Jos 13:29
of Machir by their **c**. Jos 13:31
of Judah by their **c** was in the Jos 15:1
of Judah around their **c**. Jos 15:12
descendants of Judah by their **c**. Jos 15:20
of Ephraim by their **c**: Jos 16:5
of Ephraim by their **c**, Jos 16:8
descendants by their **c**, Jos 17:2
son of Joseph, by their **c**. Jos 17:2
descendants by their **c**, Jos 18:11
by their **c**, according to its Jos 18:20
descendants by their **c**: Jos 18:21
descendants by their **c**. Jos 18:28
of his descendants by their **c**, Jos 19:1
Simeon's descendants by their **c**. Jos 19:8
descendants by their **c**. Jos 19:10
descendants by their **c**. Jos 19:16
descendants by their **c**. Jos 19:17
descendants by their **c**, Jos 19:23
Asher's descendants by their **c**. Jos 19:24
Asher's descendants by their **c**, Jos 19:31
descendants by their **c**. Jos 19:32
descendants by their **c**, Jos 19:39
for the Danite tribe by its **c**. Jos 19:40
of the Danite tribe by its **c**, Jos 19:48
came out for the Kohathite **c**: Jos 21:4
by lot from the **c** of the tribes Jos 21:5
by lot from the **c** of the tribes Jos 21:6
for their **c** from the tribes Jos 21:7
the Kohathite **c** of the Levites, Jos 21:10
to the remaining **c** of Kohath's Jos 21:20
were for the **c** of Kohath's other Jos 21:26
who were one of the Levite **c**: Jos 21:27
for the Gershonites by their **c**. Jos 21:33
they gave⌋ to the **c** of the Jos 21:34
allotted to the **c** of Merari's Jos 21:40
the remaining Levite **c**. Jos 21:40
families among the **c** of Israel. Jos 22:14
the leaders of the Israelite **c**, Jos 22:21
of Israel's **c** who were with him Jos 22:30
of heart among the **c** of Reuben. Jdg 5:15
of heart among the **c** of Reuben. Jdg 5:16
five brave men from all their **c**, Jdg 18:2
went back to their **c** at Zorah Jdg 18:8
of all the **c** of the Benjaminite 1Sm 9:21
the LORD by your tribes and **c**." 1Sm 10:19
Benjamin come forward by its **c**, 1Sm 10:21
him among all the **c** of Judah." 1Sm 23:23
contempt of the **c** terrified me, Jb 31:34
to summon all the **c** and kingdoms Jr 1:15
out of all the **c** of the earth; Am 3:2
are small among the **c** of Judah; Mc 5:2
prostitution and **c** by her Nah 3:4

CLAP *(9)*

C your hands, all you peoples; Ps 47:1
Let the rivers **c** their hands; Ps 98:8
the field will **c** ⌊their⌋ hands. Is 55:12
by ⌊scornfully⌋ **c** their hands at Lm 2:15
C your hands, stamp your feet, Ezk 6:11
prophesy and **c** ⌊your⌋ hands Ezk 21:14
I also will **c** My hands together, Ezk 21:17
c My hands together against the Ezk 22:13
about you will **c** their hands Nah 3:19

CLAPPED *(2)*

anointed him and **c** their hands 2Kg 11:12
Because you **c** ⌊your⌋ hands, Ezk 25:6

CLAPS *(2)*

It **c** its hands at him and scorns Jb 27:23
scornfully⌋ **c** in our presence Jb 34:37

CLARIFY *(1)*

I want to **c** for you the gospel I 1Co 15:1

CLASHED *(1)*

The kings have **c** swords and 2Kg 3:23

CLASHING *(1)*
praise Him with **c** cymbals. Ps 150:5

CLASPS *(9)*
Also make 50 gold **c** and join the Ex 26:6
curtains together with the **c**, Ex 26:6
Make 50 bronze **c**; put the clasps Ex 26:11
put the **c** through the loops and Ex 26:11
veil under the **c** and bring the Ex 26:33
covering, its **c** and planks, its Ex 35:11
also made 50 gold **c** and joined Ex 36:13
made 50 bronze **c** to join the Ex 36:18
its **c**, its planks, its Ex 39:33

CLASS *(2)*
from every **c** of people who were 1Kg 12:31
from every **c** of people for 1Kg 13:33

CLASSIFIED *(1)*
them are to be **c** as open fields. Lv 25:31

CLASSIFY *(1)*
For we don't dare **c** or compare 2Co 10:12

CLATTER *(1)*
and the **c** of their wheels, Jr 47:3

CLAUDIA *(1)*
as do Pudens, Linus, **C**, and all 2Tm 4:21

CLAUDIUS *(3)*
took place during the time of **C**. Ac 11:28
because **C** had ordered all Ac 18:2
C Lysias, To the most excellent Ac 23:26

CLAWS *(2)*
and his nails like birds' ⌊**c**⌋. Dn 4:33
with iron teeth and bronze **c**, Dn 7:19

CLAY *(39)*
c pot in which the sin offering Lv 6:28
of them falls into any **c** pot, Lv 11:33
over fresh water in a **c** pot. Lv 14:5
birds over a **c** pot containing Lv 14:50
Any **c** pot that the man with the Lv 15:12
to take holy water in a **c** bowl, Nm 5:17
had them cast in **c** molds in the 1Kg 7:46
had them cast in **c** molds in the 2Ch 4:17
those who dwell in **c** houses, Jb 4:19
that You formed me like **c**. Jb 10:9
your defenses are made of **c**. Jb 13:12
and heaps up a wardrobe like **c**— Jb 27:16
pinched off from ⌊a piece of⌋ **c**. Jb 33:6
is changed as **c** is by a seal; Jb 38:14
is dried up like baked **c**; Ps 22:15
of the muddy **c**, and set my feet Ps 40:2
them down like **c** in the streets. Is 10:6
potter were the same as the **c**. Is 29:16
like a potter who treads the **c**. Is 41:25
Maker—one **c** pot among many. Is 45:9
c say to the one forming it: Is 45:9
we are the **c**, and You are our Is 64:8
making from the **c** became flawed Jr 18:4
as this potter ⌊treats his **c**⌋?" Jr 18:6
Just like **c** in the potter's Jr 18:6
Go, buy a potter's **c** jug. Jr 19:1
how they are regarded as **c** jars, Lm 4:2
partly iron and partly fired **c**. Dn 2:33
on its feet of iron and fired **c**, Dn 2:34
iron, the fired **c**, the bronze, Dn 2:35
a potter's fired **c** and partly of Dn 2:41
You saw the iron mixed with **c**, Dn 2:41
part iron and part fired **c**— Dn 2:42
You saw the iron mixed with **c**— Dn 2:43
iron does not mix with fired **c**. Dn 2:43
bronze, fired **c**, silver, and Dn 2:45
Step into the **c** and tread the Nah 3:14
the potter no right over His **c**, Rm 9:21
we have this treasure in **c** jars, 2Co 4:7

CLEAN *(115)*
of all the **c** animals, and two Gn 7:2
of the animals that are not **c**, Gn 7:2
From the **c** animals, unclean Gn 7:8
every kind of **c** animal and every Gn 8:20
every kind of **c** bird and offered Gn 8:20
a clear conscience and **c** hands." Gn 20:5
a ceremonially **c** place outside Lv 4:12
camp to a ceremonially **c** place. Lv 6:11
Everyone who is **c** may eat any Lv 7:19
and the **c** and the unclean, Lv 10:10
in any ceremonially **c** place, Lv 10:14
evening; then it will be **c**. Lv 11:32
containing water will remain **c**, Lv 11:36
that is to be sown, it is **c**; Lv 11:37
between the unclean and the **c**, Lv 11:47
she will be **c** from her discharge Lv 12:7
her behalf, and she will be **c**." Lv 12:8
priest is to pronounce him **c**; Lv 13:6
his clothes and will become **c**. Lv 13:6
pronounce the infected person **c**. Lv 13:13
turned totally white, he is **c**. Lv 13:13
pronounce the infected person **c**; Lv 13:17
infected person clean; he is **c**. Lv 13:17
priest is to pronounce him **c**. Lv 13:23
priest is to pronounce him **c**, Lv 13:28
is to pronounce the person **c**. Lv 13:34
his clothes, and he will be **c**. Lv 13:34
healed; he is **c**. The priest is Lv 13:37
is to pronounce the person **c**. Lv 13:37
on the skin; the person is **c**. Lv 13:39
head, he is bald, but he is **c**. Lv 13:40
on his forehead, but he is **c**. Lv 13:41
washed again, and it will be **c**. Lv 13:58
to pronounce it **c** or unclean." Lv 13:59
order that two live **c** birds, Lv 14:4
to pronounce him **c** and release Lv 14:7
water; he is **c**. Afterwards he Lv 14:8
himself with water; he is **c**. Lv 14:9
for him, and he will be **c**. Lv 14:20
to pronounce the house **c** because Lv 14:48
for the house, and it will be **c**. Lv 14:53
when something is unclean or **c**. Lv 14:57
spits on anyone who is **c**, Lv 15:8
in fresh water; he will be **c**. Lv 15:13
and after that she will be **c**. Lv 15:28
and you will be **c** from all your Lv 16:30
until evening; he will be **c**. Lv 17:15
must distinguish the **c** animal Lv 20:25
the unclean bird from the **c** one. Lv 20:25
holy offerings until he is **c**. Lv 22:4
will become **c**, and then he may Lv 22:7
the man who is ceremonially **c**, Nm 9:13
ceremonially **c** person in your Nm 18:11
Every **c** person in your house may Nm 18:13
A man who is **c** is to gather up Nm 19:9
camp in a ceremonially **c** place. Nm 19:9
he will be **c**. But if he does Nm 19:12
seventh days, he will not be **c**. Nm 19:12
A person who is **c** is to take Nm 19:18
The one who is **c** is to sprinkle Nm 19:19
and he will be **c** by evening. Nm 19:19
through fire, and it will be **c**. Nm 31:23
your clothes, and you will be **c**. Nm 31:24
Those who are **c** or unclean may Dt 12:15
both the **c** and the unclean may Dt 12:22
You may eat every **c** bird, Dt 14:11
may eat every **c** flying creature Dt 14:20
person and the **c** ⌊may eat it⌋, Dt 15:22
be restored and you will be **c**." 2Kg 5:10
I not wash in them and be **c**?" 2Kg 5:12
he tells you, 'Wash and be **c**'?" 2Kg 5:13
of a small boy, and he was **c**. 2Kg 5:14
wipe Jerusalem **c** as one wipes a 2Kg 21:13
on the ceremonially **c** table. 2Ch 13:11
and Levites were ceremonially **c**, Ezr 6:20
whose hands are **c** will grow Jb 17:9
I am **c** and have no guilt. Jb 33:9
The one who has **c** hands and a Ps 24:4
me with hyssop, and I will be **c**; Ps 51:7
create a **c** heart for me and Ps 51:10
for the **c** and the unclean, Ec 9:2
an offering in a **c** vessel to the Is 66:20
He will **c** the land of Egypt as a Jr 43:12
you weren't washed **c** with water. Ezk 16:4
between the **c** and the unclean. Ezk 22:26
also sprinkle **c** water on you, Ezk 36:25
water on you, and you will be **c**. Ezk 36:25
between the **c** and the unclean. Ezk 44:23
them put a **c** turban on his head. Zch 3:5
So a **c** turban was placed on his Zch 3:5
are willing, You can make me **c**." Mt 8:2
willing; be made **c**." Immediately Mt 8:3
You **c** the outside of the cup and Mt 23:25
First **c** the inside of the cup, Mt 23:26
outside of it may also become **c**. Mt 23:26
wrapped it in **c**, fine linen, Mt 27:59
are willing, You can make me **c**." Mk 1:40
He told him. "Be made **c**." Mk 1:41
a result, He made all foods **c**. Mk 7:19
are willing, You can make me **c**." Lk 5:12
be made **c**," and immediately the Lk 5:13
Now you Pharisees **c** the outside Lk 11:39
then everything is **c** for you. Lk 11:41
feet, but he is completely **c**. Jn 13:10
You are **c**, but not all of you." Jn 13:10
He said, "You are not all **c**." Jn 13:11
You are already **c** because of the Jn 15:3
What God has made **c**, you must Ac 10:15
What God has made **c**, you must Ac 11:9
own heads! I am **c**. From now on I Ac 18:6
Everything is **c**, but it is wrong Rm 14:20
C out the old yeast so that you 1Co 5:7
wash ourselves **c** from every 2Co 7:1
hearts sprinkled ⌊**c**⌋ from an Heb 10:22
dressed in **c**, bright linen, with Rv 15:6

CLEANNESS *(4)*
according to the **c** of my hands. 2Sm 22:21
according to my **c** in His sight. 2Sm 22:25
according to the **c** of my hands. Ps 18:20
according to the **c** of my hands Ps 18:24

CLEANSE *(25)*
times to **c** and set it apart Lv 16:19
for you on this day to **c** you, Lv 16:30
and ceremonially **c** them. Nm 8:6
for them to ceremonially **c** them. Nm 8:21
of the LORD to **c** the LORD's 2Ch 29:15
of the LORD's temple to **c** it. 2Ch 29:16
year he began to **c** Judah and 2Ch 34:3
in order to **c** the land and the 2Ch 34:8
with snow, and **c** my hands with Jb 9:30
C me from my hidden faults. Ps 19:12
my guilt, and **c** me from my sin. Ps 51:2
and beatings **c** the innermost Pr 20:30
Wash yourselves. **C** yourselves. Is 1:16
I will **c** you from all your Ezk 36:25
On the day I **c** you from all your Ezk 36:33
they sinned, and I will **c** them. Ezk 37:23
them in order to **c** the land. Ezk 39:12
of the ground, in order to **c** it. Ezk 39:14
So they will **c** the land. Ezk 39:16
for the altar and **c** it. Ezk 43:26
c those with skin diseases, Mt 10:8
lawlessness and to **c** for Himself Ti 2:14
c our consciences from dead Heb 9:14
C your hands, sinners, and Jms 4:8
us our sins and to **c** us from all 1Jn 1:9

CLEANSED *(24)*
for the one who is to be **c**. Lv 14:4
one who is to be **c** from the skin Lv 14:7
one who is to be **c** must wash his Lv 14:8
place the person who is to be **c**, Lv 14:11
right ear of the one to be **c**, Lv 14:14
right ear of the one to be **c**, Lv 14:17
on the head of the one to be **c**. Lv 14:18
earlobe of the one to be **c**, Lv 14:25
earlobe of the one to be **c**, Lv 14:28
of the one to be **c** to make Lv 14:29
the LORD for the one to be **c**. Lv 14:31
have ceremonially **c** them and Nm 8:15
we have not **c** ourselves from Jos 22:17
We have **c** the whole temple of 2Ch 29:18
So he **c** Judah and Jerusalem. 2Ch 34:5
and **c** from blatant rebellion. Ps 19:13
I am **c** from my sin"? Pr 20:9
and festering sores not **c**, Is 1:6
of Zion and **c** the bloodguilt Is 4:4
are a land that has not been **c**, Ezk 22:24
After he is **c**, he is to count Ezk 44:26
and **c** until the time of the end, Dn 11:35
be purified, **c**, and refined, Dn 12:10
Then Jesus said, "Were not 10 **c**? Lk 17:17

CLEANSES *(1)*
Jesus His Son **c** us from all sin 1Jn 1:7

CLEANSING *(13)*
himself to the priest for his **c**, Lv 13:7
further on the skin after his **c**, Lv 13:35
disease on the day of his **c**. Lv 14:2
performs the **c** will place the Lv 14:11
things for his **c** to the priest Lv 14:23
afford the cost of his **c**." Lv 14:32
to count seven days for his **c**, Lv 15:13
a refiner's fire and like **c** lye. Mal 3:2
Moses prescribed for your **c**, Mk 1:44
for your **c** as a testimony to Lk 5:14
us and them, **c** their hearts Ac 15:9
c her in the washing of water by Eph 5:26
forgotten the **c** from his past 2Pt 1:9

CLEAR *(37)*
I did this with a **c** conscience Gn 20:5
did this with a **c** conscience. Gn 20:6

stone, as c as the sky itself Ex 24:10
order them to c the house before Lv 14:36
could be made c to them. Lv 24:12
year and will c out the old to Lv 26:10
They will c the innocent and Dt 25:1
the forest and c ⌊an area⌋ for Jos 17:15
c it and its outlying areas will Jos 17:18
you have made it c that the 2Sm 19:6
that is not ⌊c⌋ to us? Jb 15:9
All of them are c to the Pr 8:9
You c a straight path for the Is 26:7
the highway; c away the stones Is 62:10
that you drink the c water? Ezk 34:18
and he will c the way before Me. Mal 3:1
He will c His threshing floor Mt 3:12
in His hand to c His threshing Lk 3:17
best to have a c conscience Ac 24:16
what a desire to c yourselves, 2Co 7:11
always made that c to you in 2Co 11:6
Now it is c that no one is Gl 3:11
exposed by the light is made c, Eph 5:13
makes everything c is light. Eph 5:14
It is a c evidence of God's 2Th 1:5
the faith with a c conscience. 1Tm 3:9
serve with a c conscience as my 2Tm 1:3
understanding will be c to all, 2Tm 3:9
keep a c head about everything, 2Tm 4:5
For it is c that He does not Heb 2:16
was making it c that the way Heb 9:8
things make it c that they are Heb 11:14
that we have a c conscience, Heb 13:18
keeping your conscience c, 1Pt 3:16
is c⌋ what sort of people you 2Pt 3:11
it might be made c that none of 1Jn 2:19
city was pure gold like c glass. Rv 21:18

CLEAR-HEADED *(1)*
be c and disciplined for prayer. 1Pt 4:7

CLEAR-SIGHTED *(1)*
bribe blinds the c and corrupts Ex 23:8

CLEARED *(5)*
troops were c ⌊of the charge⌋ 1Sm 14:41
swept through and c them away. Jb 37:21
He c a path for His anger. Ps 78:50
You c ⌊a place⌋ for it; Ps 80:9
up the soil, c it of stones, Is 5:2

CLEARER *(1)*
And this becomes c if another Heb 7:15

CLEARING *(1)*
He is c the thickets of the Is 10:34

CLEARLY *(14)*
(See pp. xi-xii.)

CLEARS *(2)*
flooding rain or c the way for Jb 38:25
of the blameless c his path, Pr 11:5

CLEFTS *(6)*
dove, in the c of the rock, in Sg 2:14
ravines, in the c of the rocks, Is 7:19
wadis below the c of the rocks? Is 57:5
and out of the c of the rocks, Jr 16:16
who live in the c of the rock, Jr 49:16
you who live in c of the rock in Ob 3

CLEMENT *(1)*
along with C and the rest of my Php 4:3

CLEOPAS *(1)*
The one named C answered Him, Lk 24:18

CLERK *(1)*
when the city c had calmed the Ac 19:35

CLEVER *(5)*
to bring a c woman from there 2Sm 14:2
They devise c schemes against Ps 83:3
own opinion and c in their own Is 5:21
strength and wisdom, for I am c. Is 10:13
not with c words, so that 1Co 1:17

CLEVERLY *(1)*
did not follow c contrived myths 2Pt 1:16

CLEVERNESS *(1)*
cunning with c in the techniques Eph 4:14

CLIFF *(5)*
to the top of a c where they 2Ch 25:12
It lives on a c where it spends Jb 39:28
be thrown off the sides of a c, Ps 141:6
crevices of the c, let me see Sg 2:14
to hurl Him over the c. Lk 4:29

CLIFFS *(9)*
them from the top of rocky c, Nm 23:9
your nest is set in the c. Nm 24:21
shattering c before the LORD, 1Kg 19:11
the c are a refuge for hyraxes. Ps 104:18
they make their homes in the c; Pr 30:26
rocks and the crevices in the c, Is 2:21
in the c, residents of Moab! Jr 48:28
down from the c, and turn you Jr 51:25
down, the c will collapse, Ezk 38:20

CLIMB *(5)*
its branches c over the wall. Gn 49:22
I will c the palm tree and take Sg 7:8
thickets and c among the rocks Jr 4:29
they c into the houses; Jl 2:9
if they c up to heaven, from Am 9:2

CLIMBED *(12)*
in his hand, he c Mount Sinai, Ex 34:4
they c Mount Hor in the sight Nm 20:27
Aaron the priest c Mount Hor and Nm 33:38
and c the mountain with the two Dt 10:3
c to the top of Mount Gerizim, Jdg 9:7
and they c down into it. 2Sm 17:18
and Jonathan c out of the well 2Sm 17:21
even if a fox c up what they are Neh 4:3
Fountain Gate they c the steps Neh 12:37
for Death has c through our Jr 9:21
that faced east and c its steps. Ezk 40:6
he c up a sycamore tree to see Lk 19:4

CLIMBING *(3)*
As they were c the hill to the 1Sm 9:11
David was c the slope of the 2Sm 15:30
And c out of the boat, Peter Mt 14:29

CLIMBS *(2)*
and he who c from the pit will Jr 48:44
by the door but c in some other Jn 10:1

CLING *(14)*
make pestilence c to you until Dt 28:21
dreaded, and they will c to you. Dt 28:60
you turn away and c to the rest Jos 23:12
disease will c to you and your 2Kg 5:27
skin and my flesh c to my bones; Jb 19:20
I will c to my righteousness and Jb 27:6
our bodies c to the ground. Ps 44:25
it will not c to me. Ps 101:3
c to Your decrees; LORD, do not Ps 119:31
your streams c to your scales. Ezk 29:4
streams will c to your scales. Ezk 29:4
Those who c to worthless idols Jnh 2:8
"Don't c to Me," Jesus told her, Jn 20:17
Detest evil; c to what is good. Rm 12:9

CLINGS *(3)*
as underwear c to one's waist, Jr 13:11
infant's tongue c to the roof of Lm 4:4
of your town that c to our feet. Lk 10:11

CLIP *(1)*
those who c the hair on their Jr 9:26

CLIPPED *(1)*
head is bald and every beard c; Jr 48:37

CLOAK *(23)*
Japheth took a c and placed it Gn 9:23
"Put your hand inside your c." Ex 4:6
So he put his hand inside his c, Ex 4:6
your hand back inside your c." Ex 4:7
put his hand back inside his c, Ex 4:7
your neighbor's c as collateral, Ex 22:26
a beautiful c from Babylon, Jos 7:21
with the money under the c." Jos 7:21
there was the c, concealed in Jos 7:22
the silver, the c, and the bar Jos 7:24
Spread your c over me, for you Ru 3:9
wrapped himself with a new c, 1Kg 11:29
took hold of the new c he had 1Kg 11:30
or a needy person without a c, Jb 31:19
will wear their shame like a c. Ps 109:29
has bound up the waters in a c? Pr 30:4
they took my c from me—the Sg 5:7
You have a c—you be our Is 3:6
Himself in zeal as in a c. Is 59:17
not put on a hairy c in order to Zch 13:4
"Wrap your c around you," he Ac 12:8
bring the c I left in Troas with 2Tm 4:13
You will roll them up like a c, Heb 1:12

CLOAKS *(2)*
festive robes, capes, c, purses, Is 3:22
c of blue and embroidered Ezk 27:24

CLODS *(1)*
metal and the c ⌊of dirt⌋ stick Jb 38:38

CLOPAS *(1)*
Mary the wife of C, and Mary Jn 19:25

CLOSE *(48)*
this town is c enough for me to Gn 19:20
I have paid c attention to you Ex 3:16
on its front, c to its seam, Ex 28:27
on its front, c to its seam, Ex 39:20
is to remove c to the backbone Lv 3:9
to come near any c relative for Lv 18:6
she is your father's c relative. Lv 18:12
she is your mother's c relative. Lv 18:13
her. They are c relatives; it is Lv 18:17
or any of his c relatives from Lv 25:49
When you get c to the Ammonites, Dt 2:19
will c the sky, and there will Dt 11:17
when the gate was about to c, Jos 2:5
but stay here c to my young Ru 2:8
The man is a c relative. Ru 2:20
Ruth stayed c to Boaz's young Ru 2:23
did you get so c to the city to 2Sm 11:20
did you get so c to the wall?' 2Sm 11:21
his great men, c friends, and 2Kg 10:11
If I c the sky so there is no 2Ch 7:13
Pay c attention to my words; Jb 13:17
and my c friends have forgotten Jb 19:14
Pay c attention to my words; Jb 21:2
I paid c attention to you. Jb 32:12
scale is so c to another that Jb 41:16
We used to have c fellowship; Ps 55:14
I follow c to You; Your right Ps 63:8
let the Pit c its mouth over me Ps 69:15
they c in on me from every side. Ps 88:17
Israelites, the people c to Him. Ps 148:14
one's eyes do not c in sleep day Ec 8:16
on camels—pay c attention." Is 21:7
what he opens, no one can c; Is 22:22
your rooms and c your doors Is 26:20
I who deliver, c ⌊the womb⌋?" Is 66:9
when He appoints c friends as Jr 13:21
A c relative and a burner, Am 6:10
don't trust in a c companion. Mc 7:5
were coming to a c for Him to be Lk 9:51
was reclining c beside Jesus. Jn 13:23
his relatives and c friends. Ac 10:24
c friend of Herod the tetrarch, Ac 13:1
because he came c to death for Php 2:30
the time for my departure is c. 2Tm 4:6
who opens and no one will c, Rv 3:7
door that no one is able to c. Rv 3:8
the power to c the sky so that Rv 11:6
will never c because it will Rv 21:25

CLOSED *(26)*
of his ribs and c the flesh at Gn 2:21
floodgates of the sky were c, Gn 8:2
had completely c all the wombs Gn 20:18
The earth c over them, and they Nm 16:33
and Eglon's fat c in over it, Jdg 3:22
c the door behind the two of 2Kg 4:33
⌊he c⌋ the outer entrance for 2Kg 16:18
They also c the doors of the 2Ch 29:7
and that the gaps were being c, Neh 4:7
the gates be c and not opened Neh 13:19
You have c their minds to Jb 17:4
of evildoers has c in on me; Ps 22:16
I do not keep my mouth c— Ps 40:9
every house is c to entry. Is 24:10
of those who see will not be c, Is 32:3
I c off the underground deep Ezk 31:15
that faced east, and it was c. Ezk 44:1
This gate will remain c. Ezk 44:2
Therefore it will remain c. Ezk 44:2
east must be c during the six Ezk 46:1
must not be c until evening. Ezk 46:2
gate must be c after he leaves Ezk 46:12
its prison bars c behind me Jnh 2:6
they c their ears so they could Zch 7:11
But their minds were c. 2Co 3:14
into the abyss, c it, and put a Rv 20:3

CLOSELY *(24)*
I looked c at him I realized 1Kg 3:21
Listen c, LORD, and hear; 2Kg 19:16
of scales, c sealed together Jb 41:15
so c connected they cannot be Jb 41:17
me; listen c to me; hear what Ps 17:6
Listen c to me; rescue me Ps 31:2

listen **c** to me and save me. Ps 71:2
trouble. Listen **c** to me; answer Ps 102:2
listening **c** to wisdom and Pr 2:2
listen **c** to my sayings. Pr 4:20
listen **c** to my understanding Pr 5:1
or listen **c** to my mentors. Pr 5:13
Listen **c**, pay attention to the Pr 22:17
they will look **c** at you: Is 14:16
Listen **c**, LORD, and hear; Is 37:17
Our steps were **c** followed, Lm 4:18
We are **c** pursued; we are tired, Lm 5:5
watching Him **c** to see whether He Mk 3:2
Pharisees were watching Him **c**, Lk 6:7
they were watching Him **c**. Lk 14:1
They watched **c** and sent spies Lk 20:20
and looked **c** at him, she said, Lk 22:56
When I looked **c** and considered Ac 11:6
observing him **c** and seeing that Ac 14:9

CLOSER *(11)*

Please come **c** so I can touch Gn 27:21
So Jacob came **c** to his father Gn 27:22
Please come **c** and kiss me, Gn 27:26
So he came **c** and kissed him. Gn 27:27
"Do not come **c**," He said. Ex 3:5
Come **c** and listen to the words Jos 3:9
there is a redeemer **c** than I am. Ru 3:12
Philistine came **c** and closer to 1Sm 17:41
came closer and **c** to David, 1Sm 17:41
As the first runner came **c**, 2Sm 18:25
who stays **c** than a brother. Pr 18:24

CLOSES *(2)*

what he **c**, no one can open. Is 22:22
and **c** and no one opens says: Rv 3:7

CLOSEST *(1)*

your **c** friend secretly entices Dt 13:6

CLOSING *(4)*

c and locking the doors of the Jdg 3:23
and his men were **c** in on David 1Sm 23:26
the cavalry were **c** in on him. 2Sm 1:6
You have kept me from **c** my eyes; Ps 77:4

CLOTH *(26)*

spread a solid blue **c** on top, Nm 4:6
spread a blue **c** over the table Nm 4:7
to spread a scarlet **c** over them, Nm 4:8
are to take a blue **c** and cover Nm 4:9
to spread a blue **c** over the gold Nm 4:11
them⌋ in a blue **c**, cover them Nm 4:12
spread a purple **c** over it, Nm 4:13
spread out the **c** before the city Dt 22:17
wrapped in a **c** behind the ephod. 1Sm 21:9
next day Hazael took a heavy **c**, 2Kg 8:15
kings and ties a **c** around their Jb 12:18
of your head like purple **c**— Sg 7:5
like thin **c** and spreads them Is 40:22
embroidered **c** and provided you Ezk 16:10
linen, silk, and embroidered **c**. Ezk 16:13
and embroidered **c**, fine linen, Ezk 27:16
an old garment with unshrunk **c**, Mt 9:16
of unshrunk **c** on an old garment Mk 2:21
patch pulls away from the old **c**, Mk 2:21
having a linen **c** wrapped around Mk 14:51
left the linen **c** behind and ran Mk 14:52
Him snugly in **c** and laid Him Lk 2:7
wrapped snugly in **c** and lying in Lk 2:12
have kept it hidden away in a **c** Lk 19:20
with his face wrapped in a **c**. Jn 11:44
dealer in purple **c** from the city Ac 16:14

CLOTHE *(19)*

garments and **c** Aaron with the Ex 29:5
bring his sons, **c** them with Ex 29:8
C Aaron with the holy garments, Ex 40:13
forward and **c** them in tunics. Ex 40:14
Have them **c** the man the king Est 6:9
and **c** yourself with honor and Jb 40:10
You will **c** Yourself with their Ps 76:10
I will **c** its priests with Ps 132:16
I will **c** his enemies with shame, Ps 132:18
will **c** ⌊them⌋ in rags. Pr 23:21
I will **c** him with your robe and Is 22:21
to **c** the naked when you see him, Is 58:7
C yourselves with sackcloth, Jr 49:3
They will **c** themselves with Ezk 26:16
will **c** you with splendid robes. Zch 3:4
or without clothes and **c** You? Mt 25:38
I was naked and you didn't **c** Me, Mt 25:43
we **c** these with greater honor, 1Co 12:23
And all of you **c** yourselves with 1Pt 5:5

CLOTHED *(51)*

and his wife, and He **c** them. Gn 3:21
c him with fine linen garments, Gn 41:42
sash around him, **c** him with the Lv 8:7
sons, **c** them with tunics, Lv 8:13
the feeble are **c** with strength. 1Sm 2:4
for Saul, who **c** you in scarlet, 2Sm 1:24
You have **c** me with strength for 2Sm 22:40
of Judah, **c** in royal attire, 1Kg 22:10
and the elders, **c** in sackcloth, 1Ch 21:16
LORD God, be **c** with salvation, 2Ch 6:41
of Judah, **c** in royal attire, 2Ch 18:9
They **c** them, gave them sandals, 2Ch 28:15
He **c** Mordecai and paraded him Est 6:11
presence **c** in royal purple Est 8:15
My flesh is **c** with maggots and Jb 7:5
enemies will be **c** with shame; Jb 8:22
You **c** me with skin and flesh, Jb 10:11
I **c** myself in righteousness, Jb 29:14
You have **c** me with strength for Ps 18:39
sackcloth and **c** me with gladness Ps 30:11
over me be **c** with shame Ps 35:26
The pastures are **c** with flocks, Ps 65:13
You are **c** with majesty and Ps 104:1
will be **c** with disgrace; Ps 109:29
Your priests be **c** with Ps 132:9
in her household are doubly **c**. Pr 31:21
He has **c** me with the garments Is 61:10
the prince will be **c** in grief; Ezk 7:27
man among them, **c** in linen, with Ezk 9:2
called to the man **c** in linen Ezk 9:3
Then the man **c** in linen with the Ezk 9:11
spoke to the man **c** in linen and Ezk 10:2
commanded the man **c** in linen, Ezk 10:6
the hands of the man **c** in linen, Ezk 10:7
I **c** you in embroidered cloth and Ezk 16:10
will be **c** in purple, Dn 5:7
you will be **c** in purple, have a Dn 5:16
and they **c** Daniel in purple, Dn 5:29
and they **c** him in garments while Zch 3:5
will be **c** in splendor and will Zch 6:13
I was naked and you **c** Me; Mt 25:36
are poorly **c**, roughly treated, 1Co 4:11
corruptible must be **c** with 1Co 15:53
mortal must be **c** with 1Co 15:53
this corruptible is **c** with 1Co 15:54
this mortal is **c** with 1Co 15:54
when we are **c**, we will not be 2Co 5:3
not want to be unclothed but **c**, 2Co 5:4
a woman **c** with the sun, with the Rv 12:1
and remains **c** so that he may Rv 16:15
the great city, **c** in fine linen, Rv 18:16

CLOTHES *(167)*

took the best **c** of her older son Gn 27:15
smelled his **c**, he blessed him Gn 27:27
yourselves and change your **c**. Gn 35:2
was not there, he tore his **c**. Gn 37:29
Jacob tore his **c**, put sackcloth Gn 37:34
So she took off her widow's **c**, Gn 38:14
veil and put her widow's **c** back Gn 38:19
changed his **c**, and went to Gn 41:14
they tore their **c**, and each one Gn 44:13
of the brothers changes of **c**, Gn 45:22
of silver and five changes of **c**. Gn 45:22
He washes his **c** in wine, and his Gn 49:11
up in their **c** on their shoulders Ex 12:34
They must wash their **c** Ex 19:10
them, and they washed their **c**. Ex 19:14
put on other **c**, and bring the Lv 6:11
must wash his **c** and will be Lv 11:25
must wash his **c** and will be Lv 11:28
must wash his **c** and will be Lv 11:40
must wash his **c** and will be Lv 11:40
is to wash his **c** and will become Lv 13:6
is to wash his **c**, and he will be Lv 13:34
is to have his **c** torn and his Lv 13:45
to be cleansed must wash his **c**, Lv 14:8
is to wash his **c** and bathe Lv 14:9
in the house is to wash his **c**, Lv 14:47
eats in it is to wash his **c**. Lv 14:47
is to wash his **c** and bathe with Lv 15:5
is to wash his **c** and bathe with Lv 15:6
is to wash his **c** and bathe with Lv 15:7
is to wash his **c** and bathe with Lv 15:8
is to wash his **c** and bathe with Lv 15:10
is to wash his **c** and bathe with Lv 15:11
wash his **c**, and bathe his body Lv 15:13
is to wash his **c** and bathe with Lv 15:21
is to wash his **c** and bathe with Lv 15:22
must wash his **c** and bathe with Lv 15:27
a holy place and put on his **c**. Lv 16:24
is to wash his **c** and bathe his Lv 16:26
is to wash his **c** and bathe Lv 16:28
is to wash his **c** and bathe with Lv 17:15
not wash ⌊his **c**⌋ and bathe Lv 17:16
entire bodies and wash their **c**, Nm 8:7
themselves and washed their **c**; Nm 8:21
out the land, tore their **c** Nm 14:6
must wash his **c** and bathe his Nm 19:7
also wash his **c** and bathe his Nm 19:8
the cow's ashes must wash his **c**, Nm 19:10
must wash his **c** and bathe in Nm 19:19
for impurity is to wash his **c**, Nm 19:21
On the seventh day wash your **c**, Nm 31:24
remove the **c** she was wearing Dt 21:13
Do not wear **c** made of both wool Dt 22:11
your **c** and the sandals on your Dt 29:5
tore his **c** and fell before Jos 7:6
And these **c** and sandals of ours Jos 9:13
to his right thigh under his **c** Jdg 3:16
he tore his **c** and said, "No! Jdg 11:35
garments and 30 changes of **c**. Jdg 14:12
garments and 30 changes of **c**." Jdg 14:13
gave their **c** to those who had Jdg 14:19
oil, and wear your ⌊best⌋ **c**. Ru 3:3
His **c** were torn, and there was 1Sm 4:12
his own military **c** put on David. 1Sm 17:38
the military **c** and tried to walk 1Sm 17:39
then removed his **c** and also 1Sm 19:24
on different **c** and set out with 1Sm 28:8
man with torn **c** and dust on his 2Sm 1:2
hold of his **c** and tore them, 2Sm 1:11
him, "Tear your **c**, put on 2Sm 3:31
cut their **c** in half at the hips, 2Sm 10:4
changed his **c**, went to the 2Sm 12:20
up, tore his **c**, and lay down 2Sm 13:31
stood by with their **c** torn. 2Sm 13:31
dress in mourning **c** and don't 2Sm 14:2
or washed his **c** from the day the 2Sm 19:24
he tore his **c**, put sackcloth 1Kg 21:27
hold of his own **c** and tore them 2Kg 2:12
of gold, and 10 changes of **c**. 2Kg 5:5
he tore his **c** and asked, "Am I 2Kg 5:7
the king of Israel tore his **c**, 2Kg 5:8
Why have you torn your **c**? 2Kg 5:8
silver and two changes of **c**.'" 2Kg 5:22
two bags with two changes of **c**. 2Kg 5:23
it a time to accept money and **c**, 2Kg 5:26
woman's words, he tore his **c**. 2Kg 6:30
under his **c** next to his skin. 2Kg 6:30
littered with **c** and equipment 2Kg 7:15
Athaliah tore her **c** and screamed 2Kg 11:14
with their **c** torn and reported 2Kg 18:37
he tore his **c**, covered himself 2Kg 19:1
book of the law, he tore his **c**. 2Kg 22:11
have torn your **c** and wept before 2Kg 22:19
Jehoiachin changed his prison **c**, 2Kg 25:29
cut their **c** in half at the hips, 1Ch 19:4
tore her **c** and screamed, 2Ch 23:13
and provided **c** for their naked 2Ch 28:15
words of the law, he tore his **c**. 2Ch 34:19
you tore your **c** and wept before 2Ch 34:27
with me never took off our **c**. Neh 4:23
Their **c** did not wear out, and Neh 9:21
he tore his **c**, put on sackcloth Est 4:1
She sent **c** for Mordecai to wear Est 4:4
mud⌋, and my own **c** despise me! Jb 9:31
off their **c** and leaving them Jb 22:6
You whose **c** get hot when the Jb 37:17
He **c** me with strength and makes Ps 18:32
fire and his **c** not be burned? Pr 6:27
your **c** be white all the time, Ec 9:8
garments, linen **c**, turbans, and Is 3:23
instead of fine **c**, sackcloth; Is 3:24
to Hezekiah with their **c** torn, Is 36:22
he tore his **c**, put on sackcloth, Is 37:1
and splendid **c** instead of Is 61:3
and all My **c** were stained. Is 63:3
and worn-out **c** and lowered them Jr 38:11
these old rags and **c** between Jr 38:12
Jehoiachin changed his prison **c**, Jr 52:33
They will strip off your **c**, Ezk 16:39
strip off your **c** and take your Ezk 23:26
have removed the **c** they minister Ezk 42:14
to put on other **c** before they Ezk 42:14
take off the **c** they have been Ezk 44:19

dress in other **c** so that they do Ezk 44:19
to the people through their **c**. Ezk 44:19
and other **c**, were tied up Dn 3:21
not just your **c**, and return to Jl 2:13
You put on **c** but never have Hg 1:6
with filthy **c** as he stood before Zch 3:3
Him, "Take off his filthy **c**!" Zch 3:4
And why do you worry about **c**? Mt 6:28
If that's how God **c** the grass of Mt 6:30
A man dressed in soft **c**? Mt 11:8
who wear soft **c** are in kings' Mt 11:8
Even His **c** became as white as Mt 17:2
get in here without wedding **c**?' Mt 22:12
must not go back to get his **c**. Mt 24:18
or without **c** and clothe You? Mt 25:38
stranger, or without **c**, or sick, Mt 25:44
robe, put His **c** on Him, and led Mt 27:31
divided His **c** by casting lots Mt 27:35
and His **c** became dazzling— Mk 9:3
must not go back to get his **c**. Mk 13:16
robe, put His **c** on Him, and led Mk 15:20
crucified Him and divided His **c**, Mk 15:24
had worn no **c** and did not stay Lk 8:27
and His **c** became dazzling white. Lk 9:29
If that's how God **c** the grass, Lk 12:28
divided His **c** and cast lots. Lk 23:34
men stood by them in dazzling **c**. Lk 24:4
they took His **c** and divided them Jn 19:23
They divided My **c** among Jn 19:24
men in white **c** stood by them. Ac 1:10
the robes and **c** that Dorcas had Ac 9:39
off their **c** and ordered them Ac 16:22
shook out his **c** and told them, Ac 18:6
and I guarded the **c** of those who Ac 22:20
dressed in fine **c**, and a poor Jms 2:2
dressed in dirty **c** also comes Jms 2:2
the fine **c** so that you say Jms 2:3
is without **c** and lacks daily Jms 2:15
your **c** are moth-eaten; Jms 5:2
of gold ornaments or fine **c**; 1Pt 3:3
who have not defiled their **c**, Rv 3:4
will be dressed in white **c**, Rv 3:5
and white **c** so that you may be Rv 3:18
24 elders dressed in white **c**, Rv 4:4

CLOTHING *(58)*

LORD God made **c** out of skins for Gn 3:21
with food to eat and **c** to wear, Gn 28:20
jewelry, and **c**, and you will put Ex 3:22
and gold jewelry and for **c**. Ex 12:35
reduce the food, **c**, or marital Ex 21:10
it is the **c** for his body. Ex 22:27
any item of wood, **c**, leather, Lv 11:32
for mildew in **c** or on a house, Lv 14:55
Any **c** or leather on which there Lv 15:17
c did not wear out, and your Dt 8:4
resident, giving him food and **c**. Dt 10:18
A woman is not to wear male **c**, Dt 22:5
threadbare **c** on their bodies. Jos 9:5
and a large quantity of **c**. Jos 22:8
with your **c** and provisions. Jdg 17:10
herds, donkeys, camels, and **c**. 1Sm 27:9
and gold, **c**, weapons, spices 1Kg 10:25
and **c** and went off and hid them. 2Kg 7:8
and gold, **c**, weapons, spices 2Ch 9:24
up in her royal **c** and stood in Est 5:1
Without **c**, they spend the night Jb 24:7
Without **c**, they wander about Jb 24:10
My **c** is distorted with great Jb 30:18
for lack of **c** or a needy person Jb 31:19
and they cast lots for my **c**. Ps 22:18
were sick, my **c** was sackcloth; Ps 35:13
her **c** embroidered with gold. Ps 45:13
sackcloth as my **c**, and I was a Ps 69:11
of them will wear out like **c**. Ps 102:26
like taking off **c** on a cold day, Pr 25:20
lambs will provide your **c**, Pr 27:26
her **c** is fine linen and purple. Pr 31:22
Strength and honor are her **c**, Pr 31:25
I have taken off my **c**. Sg 5:3
even have food or **c** in my house. Is 3:7
own bread and provide our own **c**. Is 4:1
with ample food and sacred **c**. Is 23:18
and make sackcloth their **c**. Is 50:3
Their webs cannot become **c**, Is 59:6
on garments of vengeance for **c**, Is 59:17
Why is Your **c** red, and Your Is 63:2
Their **c** is blue and purple, Jr 10:9
and your **c** was ⌊made⌋ of fine Ezk 16:13
and covers the naked with **c**. Ezk 18:7
and covers the naked with **c**. Ezk 18:16
His **c** was white like snow, Dn 7:9
who are dressed in foreign **c**. Zph 1:8
gold, silver, and **c** in great Zch 14:14
food and the body more than **c**? Mt 6:25
you in sheep's **c** but inwardly Mt 7:15
food and the body more than **c**. Lk 12:23
and they cast lots for My **c**. Jn 19:24
anyone's silver or gold or **c**. Ac 20:33
parts have no need ⌊of **c**⌋. 1Co 12:24
food, cold, and lacking **c**. 2Co 11:27
to dress themselves in modest **c**, 1Tm 2:9
But if we have food and **c**, 1Tm 6:8
They will all wear out like **c**; Heb 1:11

CLOTHS *(7)*

them away like menstrual **c**, Is 30:22
with salt or wrapped in **c**. Ezk 16:4
in, he saw only the linen **c**. Lk 24:12
it in linen **c** with the aromatic Jn 19:40
he saw the linen **c** lying there, Jn 20:5
and saw the linen **c** lying there. Jn 20:6
with the linen **c** but was folded Jn 20:7

CLOUD *(104)*

in a pillar of **c** to lead them Ex 13:21
The pillar of **c** by day and the Ex 13:22
The pillar of **c** moved from in Ex 14:19
The **c** was there ⌊in⌋ the Ex 14:20
from the pillar of fire and **c**, Ex 14:24
and there, in a **c**, the LORD's Ex 16:10
to come to you in a dense **c**, Ex 19:9
a thick **c** on the mountain, Ex 19:16
the mountain, the **c** covered it. Ex 24:15
and the **c** covered it for six Ex 24:16
He called to Moses from the **c**. Ex 24:16
Moses entered the **c** as he went Ex 24:18
the pillar of **c** would come down Ex 33:9
saw the pillar of **c** remaining at Ex 33:10
The LORD came down in a **c**, Ex 34:5
The **c** covered the tent of Ex 40:34
because the **c** rested on it, Ex 40:35
out whenever the **c** was taken up Ex 40:36
If the **c** was not taken up, Ex 40:37
For the **c** of the LORD was over Ex 40:38
a fire inside the **c** by night, Ex 40:38
appear in the **c** above the mercy Lv 16:2
so that the **c** of incense covers Lv 16:13
the **c** covered the tabernacle, Nm 9:15
the **c** would cover it, appearing Nm 9:16
Whenever the **c** was lifted up Nm 9:17
the place where the **c** stopped, Nm 9:17
As long as the **c** stayed over the Nm 9:18
Even when the **c** stayed over the Nm 9:19
Sometimes the **c** remained over Nm 9:20
Sometimes the **c** remained ⌊only⌋ Nm 9:21
the **c** lifted in the morning, Nm 9:21
moved out when the **c** lifted. Nm 9:21
out as long as the **c** stayed over Nm 9:22
the **c** was lifted up above the Nm 10:11
to the next until the **c** stopped Nm 10:12
the **c** of the LORD was over them Nm 10:34
in the **c** and spoke to him Nm 11:25
LORD descended in a pillar of **c**, Nm 12:5
As the **c** moved away from the Nm 12:10
how Your **c** stands over them, Nm 14:14
them in a pillar of **c** by day and Nm 14:14
and suddenly the **c** covered it, Nm 16:42
and in the **c** by day to guide Dt 1:33
enveloped in a dense, black **c**. Dt 4:11
from the fire, **c**, and thick Dt 5:22
at the tent in a pillar of **c**, Dt 31:15
and the **c** stood at the entrance Dt 31:15
they sent up a great **c** of smoke Jdg 20:38
a dark **c** beneath His feet. 2Sm 22:10
the **c** filled the LORD's temple, 1Kg 8:10
because of the **c**, the priests 1Kg 8:11
There's a **c** as small as a man's 1Kg 18:44
temple, was filled with a **c**. 2Ch 5:13
because of the **c**, the priests 2Ch 5:14
them with a pillar of **c** by day, Neh 9:12
the pillar of **c** never turned Neh 9:19
it, and a **c** settle over it. Jb 3:5
As a **c** fades away and vanishes, Jb 7:9
throne, spreading His **c** over it. Jb 26:9
has passed by like a **c**. Jb 30:15
a dark **c** beneath His feet. Ps 18:9
them with a **c** by day and with Ps 78:14
spoke to them in a pillar of **c**; Ps 99:7
He spread a **c** as a covering and Ps 105:39
hail, snow and **c**, powerful wind Ps 148:8
favor is like a **c** with spring Pr 16:15
will create a **c** of smoke by day Is 4:5
For a **c** of dust is coming from Is 14:31
like a rain **c** in harvest heat. Is 18:4
on a swift **c** and is coming to Is 19:1
the shade of a **c** ⌊cools⌋ the Is 25:5
your transgressions like a **c**, Is 44:22
Who are these who fly like a **c**, Is 60:8
Yourself with a **c** so that no Lm 3:44
great **c** with fire flashing back Ezk 1:4
a rainbow in a **c** on a rainy day. Ezk 1:28
and a fragrant **c** of incense was Ezk 8:11
the **c** filled the inner court. Ezk 10:3
temple was filled with the **c**, Ezk 10:4
A **c** will cover Tehaphnehes, Ezk 30:18
I will cover the sun with a **c**, Ezk 32:7
will be like a **c** covering the Ezk 38:9
Israel like a **c** covering the Ezk 38:16
a bright **c** covered them, Mt 17:5
and a voice from the **c** said: Mt 17:5
c appeared, overshadowing them, Mk 9:7
and a voice came from the **c**: Mk 9:7
a **c** appeared and overshadowed Lk 9:34
afraid as they entered the **c**. Lk 9:34
Then a voice came from the **c**, Lk 9:35
When you see a **c** rising in the Lk 12:54
of Man coming in a **c** with power Lk 21:27
a **c** received Him out of their Ac 1:9
blood and fire and a **c** of smoke. Ac 2:19
fathers were all under the **c**, 1Co 10:1
Moses in the **c** and in the sea. 1Co 10:2
have such a large **c** of witnesses Heb 12:1
surrounded by a **c**, with a Rv 10:1
They went up to heaven in a **c**, Rv 11:12
there was a white **c**, and One Rv 14:14
Son of Man was seated on the **c**, Rv 14:14
the One who was seated on the **c**, Rv 14:15
seated on the **c** swung His sickle Rv 14:16

CLOUDLESS *(1)*

the sun rises on a **c** morning, 2Sm 23:4

CLOUDS *(65)*

I have placed My bow in the **c**, Gn 9:13
Whenever I form **c** over the earth Gn 9:14
and the bow appears in the **c**, Gn 9:14
be in the **c**, and I will look Gn 9:16
numbered the dust **c** of Israel? Nm 23:10
aid on the **c** in His majesty. Dt 33:26
rain⌋, the **c** poured water. Jdg 5:4
gathering of water and thick **c**. 2Sm 22:12
sky grew dark with **c** and wind, 1Kg 18:45
and his head touches the **c**, Jb 20:6
C veil Him so that He cannot see, Jb 22:14
He enfolds the waters in His **c**, Jb 26:8
yet the **c** do not burst beneath Jb 26:8
gaze at the **c** high above you. Jb 35:5
which the **c** pour out and shower Jb 36:28
how the **c** spread out or how Jb 36:29
He saturates **c** with moisture; Jb 37:11
God directs His **c** or makes their Jb 37:15
you understand how the **c** float, Jb 37:16
when I made the **c** its garment Jb 38:9
command the **c** so that a flood Jb 38:34
has the wisdom to number the **c**? Jb 38:37
dark storm **c** His canopy around Ps 18:11
His **c** swept onward with hail and Ps 18:12
faithfulness reaches to the **c**. Ps 57:10
Exalt Him who rides on the **c**— Ps 68:4
Israel, His power among the **c**. Ps 68:34
The **c** poured down water. Ps 77:17
The storm **c** thundered; Ps 77:17
command to the **c** above and Ps 78:23
C and thick darkness surround Ps 97:2
making the **c** His chariot, Ps 104:3
Your faithfulness reaches the **c**. Ps 108:4
He causes the **c** to rise from the Ps 135:7
who covers the sky with **c**, Ps 147:8
and the **c** dripped with dew. Pr 3:20
exist is like **c** and wind without Pr 25:14
the **c** are full, they will pour Ec 11:3
looks at the **c** will not reap. Ec 11:4
and the **c** return after the rain; Ec 12:2
orders to the **c** that rain should Is 5:6
light will be obscured by **c**. Is 5:30
will ascend above the highest **c**; Is 14:14
Look, he advances like **c**; Jr 4:13
and He causes the **c** to rise from Jr 10:13

sky and reaches as far as the **c**. Jr 51:9
and He causes the **c** to rise from Jr 51:16
its height towered among the **c**. Ezk 19:11
be a day of **c**, a time ⌊of doom Ezk 30:3
Its top was among the **c**. Ezk 31:3
and set its top among the **c**, Ezk 31:10
and set their tops among the **c**, Ezk 31:14
man coming with the **c** of heaven. Dn 7:13
a day of **c** and dense overcast, Jl 2:2
and **c** are the dust beneath His Nah 1:3
your scribes like **c** of locusts, Nah 3:17
gloom, a day of **c** and blackness, Zph 1:15
The LORD makes the rain **c**, Zch 10:1
coming on the **c** of heaven with Mt 24:30
and coming on the **c** of heaven." Mt 26:64
Man coming in **c** with great power Mk 13:26
coming with the **c** of heaven." Mk 14:62
them in the **c** to meet the Lord 1Th 4:17
are waterless **c** carried along Jd 12
coming with the **c**, and every eye Rv 1:7

CLOUDY *(1)*
scattered on a **c** and dark day. Ezk 34:12

CLUB *(6)*
went down to him with a **c**, 2Sm 23:21
went down to him with a **c**, 1Ch 11:23
A **c** is regarded as stubble, Jb 41:29
his neighbor is like a **c**, Pr 25:18
You are My battle **c**, My weapons Jr 51:20
each with a war **c** in his hand. Ezk 9:2

CLUBS *(6)*
and arrows, the **c** and spears. Ezk 39:9
with swords and **c**, was with him Mt 26:47
you come out with swords and **c**, Mt 26:55
swords and **c**, from the chief Mk 14:43
you come out with swords and **c**, Mk 14:48
with swords and **c** as if I were Lk 22:52

CLUNG *(5)*
mother-in-law, but Ruth **c** to her. Ru 1:14
They **c** to other gods and 1Kg 9:9
c to the sins that Jeroboam 2Kg 3:3
the mountain, she **c** to his feet. 2Kg 4:27
They **c** to other gods and 2Ch 7:22

CLUSTER *(5)*
Take a **c** of hyssop, dip it in Ex 12:22
with a single **c** of grapes, Nm 13:23
because of the **c** ⌊of grapes⌋ Nm 13:24
My love is a **c** of henna blossoms Sg 1:14
⌊finds⌋ no grape **c** to eat, Mc 7:1

CLUSTERS *(8)*
came out and its **c** ripened into Gn 40:10
their **c** are bitter. Dt 32:32
roasted grain, 100 **c** of raisins, 1Sm 25:18
figs and two **c** of raisins. 1Sm 30:12
of bread, 100 **c** of raisins, 100 2Sm 16:1
your breasts are **c** ⌊of fruit⌋. Sg 7:7
breasts be like **c** of grapes, Sg 7:8
and gather the **c** of grapes Rv 14:18

CLUTCHES *(4)*
and from the **c** of the powerful. Jb 5:15
LORD, from the **c** of the wicked. Ps 140:4
and from the **c** of those who hate Lk 1:71
rescued from our enemies' **c**, Lk 1:74

CNIDUS *(1)*
with difficulty as far as **C**. Ac 27:7

CO-HEIR *(1)*
not be a **c** with my son Isaac! Gn 21:10

CO-HEIRS *(4)*
heirs of God and **c** with Christ— Rm 8:17
the Gentiles are **c**, members of Eph 3:6
Isaac and Jacob, **c** of the same Heb 11:9
them honor as **c** of the grace of 1Pt 3:7

CO-WORKER *(6)*
Urbanus, our **c** in Christ, and my Rm 16:9
my **c**, and Lucius, Jason, Rm 16:21
is my partner and **c** serving you; 2Co 8:23
my brother, **c**, and fellow Php 2:25
brother and God's **c** in the 1Th 3:2
Philemon, our dear friend and **c**, Phm 1

CO-WORKERS *(6)*
Aquila, my **c** in Christ Jesus, Rm 16:3
For we are God's **c**. 1Co 3:9
the rest of my **c** whose names are Php 4:3
are my **c** for the kingdom Col 4:11
Demas, and Luke, my **c**. Phm 24
that we can be **c** with the truth. 3Jn 8

COAL *(2)*
was a glowing **c** that he had Is 6:6
This is not a **c** for warming Is 47:14

COALS *(16)*
full of fiery **c** from the altar Lv 16:12
c were set ablaze by it. 2Sm 22:9
flaming **c** were ignited. 2Sm 22:13
His breath sets **c** ablaze, and Jb 41:21
will rain burning **c** and sulfur Ps 11:6
c were set ablaze by it. Ps 18:8
onward with hail and blazing **c**. Ps 18:12
Let hot **c** fall on them. Ps 140:10
a man walk on **c** without Pr 6:28
for you will heap **c** on his head, Pr 25:22
ironworker labors over the **c**, Is 44:12
I also baked bread on its **c**, Is 44:19
of burning **c** of fire and torches Ezk 1:13
your hands with hot **c** from among Ezk 10:2
empty pot on its **c** so that it Ezk 24:11
be heaping fiery **c** on his head. Rm 12:20

COARSE *(1)*
And **c** and foolish talking or Eph 5:4

COAST *(7)*
will come from the **c** of Kittim; Nm 24:24
Negev and the sea **c**—to the Dt 1:7
and all along the **c** of the Jos 9:1
along the **c** of the province Ac 27:2
the northern **c** of Cyprus because Ac 27:4
we sailed along the **c**, Ac 27:8
making a circuit along the **c**, Ac 28:13

COASTAL *(1)*
what remains of the **c** peoples. Ezk 25:16

COASTLAND *(5)*
The **c** peoples spread out into Gn 10:5
of this **c** will say on that Is 20:6
of the **c**, you merchants Is 23:2
wail, inhabitants of the **c**! Is 23:6
The **c** will belong to the remnant Zph 2:7

COASTLANDS *(7)*
C, listen to me; distant peoples, Is 49:1
The **c** will put their hope in Me, Is 51:5
foes, and He will repay the **c**. Is 59:18
kings of the **c** across the sea; Jr 25:22
and tell it among the far off **c**! Jr 31:10
Now the **c** tremble on the day of Ezk 26:18
all the distant **c** of the nations Zph 2:11

COASTLINE *(3)*
border will be the **c** of the Nm 34:6
border was the **c** of the Jos 15:12
of Egypt and the **c** of the Jos 15:47

COASTS *(11)*
Tarshish and the **c** and islands Ps 72:10
let the many **c** and islands be Ps 97:1
the **c** and islands of the west Is 11:11
Won't the **c** and islands quake at Ezk 26:15
peoples to many **c** and islands: Ezk 27:3
wood from the **c** of Cyprus, Ezk 27:6
fabric from the **c** of Elishah. Ezk 27:7
many **c** and islands were your Ezk 27:15
of the **c** and islands are Ezk 27:35
securely on the **c** and islands. Ezk 39:6
attention to the **c** and islands Dn 11:18

COAT *(7)*
covered with hair like a fur **c**, Gn 25:25
But you **c** ⌊the truth⌋ with lies; Jb 13:4
He wore cursing like his **c**— Ps 109:18
Where is the **c** of whitewash that Ezk 13:12
let him have your **c** as well. Mt 5:40
He threw off his **c**, jumped up, Mk 10:50
And if anyone takes away your **c**, Lk 6:29

COATED *(5)*
for him and **c** it with asphalt Ex 2:3
unleavened wafers **c** with oil. Ex 29:2
or unleavened wafers **c** with oil. Lv 2:4
unleavened wafers **c** with oil, Lv 7:12
unleavened wafers **c** with oil. Nm 6:15

COBRA *(2)*
like the deaf **c** that stops up Ps 58:4
tread on the lion and the **c**; Ps 91:13

COBRA'S *(1)*
will play beside the **c** pit, Is 11:8

COBRAS *(2)*
venom, the deadly poison of **c**. Dt 32:33
He will suck the poison of **c**; Jb 20:16

COBRAS' *(1)*
turns into **c** venom inside him. Jb 20:14

COCOON *(1)*
like a moth's ⌊**c**⌋ or a booth set Jb 27:18

COFFIN *(3)*
and placed him in a **c** in Egypt. Gn 50:26
him out in a **c** that was full 2Ch 16:14
came up and touched the open **c**, Lk 7:14

COIN *(4)*
open its mouth you'll find a **c**. Mt 17:27
Show Me the **c** used for the tax." Mt 22:19
she loses one **c**, does not light Lk 15:8
have found the silver **c** I lost!' Lk 15:9

COINS *(6)*
gave 61,000 gold **c**, 6,250 pounds Ezr 2:69
gold bowls worth 1,000 gold **c**, Ezr 8:27
in two tiny **c** worth very little Mk 12:42
what woman who has 10 silver **c**, Lk 15:8
widow dropping in two tiny **c**. Lk 21:2
money changers' **c** and overturned Jn 2:15

COL-HOZEH *(2)*
Shallun son of **C**, ruler over the Neh 3:15
Baruch, son of **C**, son of Hazaiah Neh 11:5

COLD *(16)*
and harvest, **c** and heat, summer Gn 8:22
no covering against the **c**. Jb 24:7
and the **c** from the driving north Jb 37:9
Who can withstand His **c**? Ps 147:17
taking off clothing on a **c** day, Pr 25:20
is like **c** water to a parched Pr 25:25
Or does **c** water flowing from a Jr 18:14
settle on the walls on a **c** day; Nah 3:17
just a cup of **c** water to one Mt 10:42
the love of many will grow **c**. Mt 24:12
charcoal fire, because it was **c**. Jn 18:18
rain was falling and it was **c**. Ac 28:2
without food, **c**, and lacking 2Co 11:27
that you are neither **c** nor hot. Rv 3:15
I wish that you were **c** or hot. Rv 3:15
neither hot nor **c**, I am going to Rv 3:16

COLLAPSE *(14)*
Then the city wall will **c**, Jos 6:5
battering the wall to make it **c**, 2Sm 20:15
a person not **c** at the very sight Jb 41:9
They **c** and fall, but we rise and Ps 20:8
high wall whose **c** will come very Is 30:13
c will be like the shattering Is 30:14
they will **c**, says the LORD. Jr 6:15
they will **c**, says the LORD. Jr 8:12
and its proud strength will **c**. Ezk 30:6
cliffs will **c**, and every wall Ezk 38:20
Yet it didn't **c**, because its Mt 7:25
And its **c** was great!" Mt 7:27
they might **c** on the way." Mt 15:32
they will **c** on the way, Mk 8:3

COLLAPSED *(13)*
a great shout, and the wall **c**. Jos 6:20
c, he fell, he lay down at her Jdg 5:27
he **c**, he fell at her feet; Jdg 5:27
he **c**, there he fell—dead. Jdg 5:27
tent upside down so that it **c**." Jdg 7:13
c at the doorway of the man's Jdg 19:26
c near the doorway of the house Jdg 19:27
she **c** and gave birth because her 1Sm 4:19
c ⌊and lay⌋ naked all that day 1Sm 19:24
It **c** on the young people so that Jb 1:19
its gate has **c** in ruins. Is 24:12
pounded that house, and it **c**. Mt 7:27
it, and immediately it **c**. Lk 6:49

COLLAPSES *(1)*
But as a mountain **c** and crumbles Jb 14:18

COLLAR *(4)*
be a woven **c** with an opening Ex 28:32
body armor with a **c** around the Ex 39:23
his neck was put in an iron **c**. Ps 105:18
him in stocks and an iron **c**. Jr 29:26

COLLATERAL *(11)*
take your neighbor's cloak as **c**, Ex 22:26
you took **c** from your brothers Jb 22:6
and take the widow's ox as **c**. Jb 24:3
of the poor is seized as **c**. Jb 24:9
get **c** if it is for foreigners. Pr 20:16
get **c** if it is for foreigners. Pr 27:13
but returns his **c** to the debtor. Ezk 18:7
does not return **c**, and ⌊when⌋ he Ezk 18:12

anyone, hold **c**, or commit Ezk 18:16
he returns **c**, makes restitution Ezk 33:15
altar on garments taken as **c**, Am 2:8

COLLEAGUES *(13)*
away from his **c**, and take him to 2Kg 9:2
the rest of his **c** wrote to King Ezr 4:7
the rest of their **c**—the judges Ezr 4:9
rest of their **c** living in Ezr 4:17
and their **c**, they immediately Ezr 4:23
and their **c** came to the Jews and Ezr 5:3
and their **c**, the officials Ezr 5:6
and your **c**, the officials Ezr 6:6
and their **c** diligently carried Ezr 6:13
before his **c** and the powerful Neh 4:2
for the distribution to their **c**. Neh 13:13
you and your **c** sitting before Zch 3:8
He and all his **c**, those who Ac 5:17

COLLECT *(20)*
c five shekels for each person, Nm 3:47
He is not to **c** ⌊anything⌋ from Dt 15:2
You may **c** ⌊something⌋ from a Dt 15:3
his house to **c** what he offers as Dt 24:10
of Judah and **c** money from all 2Ch 24:5
Levites are to **c** the one-tenth Neh 10:37
Levites when they **c** the tenth, Neh 10:38
He will **c** the scattered of Judah Is 11:12
I will **c** the remnant of Israel. Mc 2:12
Don't **c** for yourselves treasures Mt 6:19
But **c** for yourselves treasures Mt 6:20
earthly kings **c** tariffs or taxes Mt 17:25
to the farmers to **c** his fruit. Mt 21:34
of pieces of bread did you **c**?" Mk 8:19
of pieces of bread did you **c**?" Mk 8:20
the farmers to **c** some of the Mk 12:2
Don't **c** any more than what you Lk 3:13
c what you didn't deposit and Lk 19:21
C the leftovers so that nothing Jn 6:12
to the law to **c** a tenth from the Heb 7:5

COLLECTED *(19)*
Joseph **c** all the money to be Gn 47:14
So Moses **c** the redemption money Nm 3:49
c the money from the firstborn Nm 3:50
have **c** from the people 2Kg 22:4
the doorkeepers had **c** ⌊money⌋ 2Ch 34:9
You **c** water from the lower pool. Is 22:9
bones⌋ will not be **c** and buried Jr 8:2
Since she **c** the wages of a Mc 1:7
surrounding nations will be **c**: Zch 14:14
It **c** every kind ⌊of fish⌋, Mt 13:47
they **c** the leftover pieces— Mt 15:37
and how many baskets you **c**? Mt 16:9
how many large baskets you **c**? Mt 16:10
those who **c** the double-drachma Mt 17:24
Then they **c** seven large baskets Mk 8:8
would have **c** it with interest!' Lk 19:23
So they **c** them and filled 12 Jn 6:13
practiced magic **c** their books Ac 19:19
this lineage **c** tithes from Heb 7:6

COLLECTING *(1)*
c what I didn't deposit and Lk 19:22

COLLECTION *(2)*
let your **c** ⌊of idols⌋ deliver Is 57:13
Now about the **c** for the saints: 1Co 16:1

COLLECTIONS *(2)*
masters of **c** are like firmly Ec 12:11
that no **c** will need to be made 1Co 16:2

COLLECTOR *(9)*
Where is the tribute **c**? Is 33:18
send out a tax **c** for the glory Dn 11:20
Thomas and Matthew the tax **c**; Mt 10:3
unbeliever and a tax **c** to you. Mt 18:17
out and saw a tax **c** named Levi Lk 5:27
Pharisee and the other a tax **c**. Lk 18:10
or even like this tax **c**. Lk 18:11
But the tax **c**, standing far off, Lk 18:13
Zacchaeus who was a chief tax **c**, Lk 19:2

COLLECTORS *(15)*
even the tax **c** do the same? Mt 5:46
many tax **c** and sinners came as Mt 9:10
eat with tax **c** and sinners?" Mt 9:11
a friend of tax **c** and sinners!' Mt 11:19
Tax **c** and prostitutes are Mt 21:31
c and prostitutes did believe Mt 21:32
many tax **c** and sinners were also Mk 2:15
eating with sinners and tax **c**, Mk 2:16
He eat with tax **c** and sinners?" Mk 2:16
Tax **c** also came to be baptized, Lk 3:12
crowd of tax **c** and others who Lk 5:29
drink with tax **c** and sinners?" Lk 5:30
the tax **c**, heard this, they Lk 7:29
a friend of tax **c** and sinners!' Lk 7:34
All the tax **c** and sinners were Lk 15:1

COLLECTS *(2)*
interest **c** it for one who is Pr 28:8
c all the peoples for himself. Hab 2:5

COLONNADE *(3)*
temple complex in Solomon's **C**. Jn 10:23
in what is called Solomon's **C**. Ac 3:11
would all meet in Solomon's **C**. Ac 5:12

COLONNADES *(1)*
in Hebrew, which has five **c**. Jn 5:2

COLONY *(1)*
Philippi, a Roman **c**, which is a Ac 16:12

COLORED *(2)*
the spoil of **c** garments for Jdg 5:30
richly **c** linen from Egypt. Pr 7:16

COLORFUL *(2)*
In **c** garments she is led to the Ps 45:14
and made **c** high places for Ezk 16:16

COLORS *(5)*
made a robe of many **c** for him. Gn 37:3
the robe of many **c** that he had Gn 37:23
robe of many **c** to their father Gn 37:32
stones of various **c**, all kinds 1Ch 29:2
of many **c** came to Lebanon Ezk 17:3

COLOSSAE *(1)*
brothers in Christ in **C**. Col 1:2

COLOSSAL *(1)*
watching, a **c** statue appeared Dn 2:31

COLT *(6)*
and the **c** of his donkey to the Gn 49:11
on a donkey, on a **c**, the foal of Zch 9:9
tied there, and a **c** with her. Mt 21:2
a donkey, even on a **c**, the foal Mt 21:5
brought the donkey and the **c**; Mt 21:7
coming, sitting on a donkey's **c**. Jn 12:15

COLUMN *(2)*
But when the **c** of smoke began to Jdg 20:40
that they go up in a **c** of smoke. Is 9:18

COLUMNS *(6)*
were sharp **c** of rock on both 1Sm 14:4
to silver rods on marble **c**. Est 1:6
the wilderness like **c** of smoke, Sg 3:6
would read three or four **c**, Jr 36:23
and throw the **c** into the blazing Jr 36:23
blood, fire, and **c** of smoke. Jl 2:30

COMB *(1)*
than honey dripping from the **c**. Ps 19:10

COMBAT *(2)*
equipped for **c** that went out to 2Ch 26:11
army of 307,500 equipped for **c**, 2Ch 26:13

COMBERS *(1)*
c and weavers will turn pale. Is 19:9

COMBINED *(3)*
based on the **c** number of people Ex 12:4
The whole **c** assembly numbered Ezr 2:64
The whole **c** assembly numbered Neh 7:66

COME *(1303)*
But water would **c** out of the Gn 2:6
a deep sleep to **c** over the man, Gn 2:21
will **c** to you so that you can Gn 6:20
C out of the ark, you, your Gn 8:16
to each other, "**C**, let us make Gn 11:3
And they said, "**C**, let us build Gn 11:4
C, let Us go down there and Gn 11:7
where have you **c** from, and where Gn 16:8
nations and kings **c** from you. Gn 17:6
of peoples will **c** from her." Gn 17:16
I will certainly **c** back to you Gn 18:10
time I will **c** back to you, Gn 18:14
the cry that has **c** up to Me. Gn 18:21
because they have **c** under the Gn 19:8
C, let's get our father to drink Gn 19:32
then we'll **c** back to you." Gn 22:5
Laban said, "**C**, you who are Gn 24:31
woman will not **c** back with me?' Gn 24:39
people will ⌊**c**⌋ from you and be Gn 25:23
to them, "Why have you **c** to me? Gn 26:27
Please **c** closer so I can touch Gn 27:21
Please **c** closer and kiss me, Gn 27:26
said, "You must **c** with me, for I Gn 30:16
future when you **c** to check on my Gn 30:33
C now, let's make a covenant, Gn 31:44
he may **c** and attack me, Gn 32:11
until I **c** to my lord at Seir." Gn 33:14
of nations, will **c** from you, and Gn 35:11
C on, let's kill him and throw Gn 37:20
C, let's sell him to the Gn 37:27
her and said, "**C**, let me sleep Gn 38:16
Where do you **c** from?" he asked. Gn 42:7
You have **c** to see the weakness Gn 42:9
servants have **c** to buy food," Gn 42:10
You have **c** to see the weakness Gn 42:12
why this trouble has **c** to us." Gn 42:21
could have **c** back twice by now. Gn 43:10
we really did **c** down here the Gn 43:20
does not **c** down with you, Gn 44:23
if I **c** to your servant my father Gn 44:30
Please, **c** near me," and they Gn 45:4
C down to me without delay. Gn 45:9
"Joseph's brothers have **c**," Gn 45:16
households, and **c** back to me. Gn 45:18
household who had **c** to Egypt: Gn 46:27
land of Canaan, have **c** to me. Gn 46:31
have **c** from the land of Canaan Gn 47:1
We have **c** to live in the land Gn 47:4
and brothers have **c** to you, Gn 47:5
"Your son Joseph has **c** to you," Gn 48:2
make many nations ⌊**c** from⌋ you, Gn 48:4
to your descendants to **c**.' Gn 48:4
happen to you in the days to **c**. Gn 49:1
C together and listen, sons of Gn 49:2
God will certainly **c** to your aid Gn 50:24
Why have you **c** back so quickly Ex 2:18
"Do not **c** closer," He said. Ex 3:5
have **c** down to rescue them from Ex 3:8
cry for help has **c** to Me, Ex 3:9
they will **c** up and go into your Ex 8:3
The frogs will **c** up on you, Ex 8:4
the frogs to **c** up onto the land Ex 8:5
locusts will **c** up over it and Ex 10:12
of yours will **c** down to me and Ex 11:8
will certainly **c** to your aid; Ex 13:19
that the waters may **c** back on Ex 14:26
community, '**C** before the LORD, Ex 16:9
water will **c** out of it and the Ex 17:6
the people **c** to me to inquire Ex 18:15
I am going to **c** to you in a Ex 19:9
the LORD will **c** down on Mount Ex 19:11
the priests who **c** near the LORD Ex 19:22
people cannot **c** up Mount Sinai, Ex 19:23
Go down and **c** back with Aaron. Ex 19:24
through to **c** up to the LORD, Ex 19:24
for God has **c** to test you, Ex 20:20
I will **c** to you and bless you in Ex 20:24
parties is to **c** before the Ex 22:9
If you **c** across your enemy's Ex 23:4
all the nations you **c** to. Ex 23:27
C up to Me on the mountain and Ex 24:12
c to you from the Israelites to Ex 28:1
and does not **c** loose from the Ex 28:28
no plague will **c** on them as they Ex 30:12
said to him, "**C**, make us a god Ex 32:1
is for the LORD, ⌊**c**⌋ to me." Ex 32:26
of cloud would **c** down and remain Ex 33:9
C up Mount Sinai in the morning Ex 34:2
They were afraid to **c** near him. Ex 34:30
among you **c** and make everything Ex 35:10
to **c** to the work and do it. Ex 36:2
and did not **c** loose from the Ex 39:21
Have his sons **c** forward and Ex 40:14
C here and carry your relatives Lv 10:4
the house is to **c** and tell the Lv 14:35
the priest will **c** to examine the Lv 14:36
priest must **c** and examine it. Lv 14:44
c before the LORD at the Lv 15:14
that he may not **c** whenever he Lv 16:2
You are not to **c** near any close Lv 18:6
You are not to **c** near a woman Lv 18:19
When you **c** into the land and Lv 19:23
defect is to **c** near to present Lv 21:17
who has any defect is to **c** near: Lv 21:18
a defect is to **c** near to present Lv 21:21
and is not to **c** near to present Lv 21:21
relative may **c** and redeem what Lv 25:25
your enemies who **c** to live there Lv 26:32
will **c** and carry them, Nm 4:15
die when they **c** near the most Nm 4:19

the Levites may c to serve ⌊at⌋	Nm 8:15
place of all who c first from	Nm 8:16
that no plague will c against	Nm 8:19
C with us, and we will treat	Nm 10:29
If you c with us, whatever good	Nm 10:32
I will c down and speak with	Nm 11:17
You three c out to the tent of	Nm 12:4
They will c to an end in the	Nm 14:35
the one⌋ He will let c near Him.	Nm 16:5
the one He chooses c near Him.	Nm 16:5
but they said, "We will not c!	Nm 16:12
of these men? We will not c!"	Nm 16:14
wrath has c from the LORD;	Nm 16:46
They must not c near the	Nm 18:3
person may c near you.	Nm 18:4
must never again c near the tent	Nm 18:22
we will c out and confront you	Nm 20:18
C to Heshbon, let it be rebuilt;	Nm 21:27
a people has c out of Egypt;	Nm 22:5
Please c and put a curse on	Nm 22:6
a people has c out of Egypt,	Nm 22:11
c and put a curse on them for	Nm 22:11
"Balaam refused to c with us."	Nm 22:14
So please c and put a curse on	Nm 22:17
these men have c to summon you,	Nm 22:20
Why didn't you c to me?	Nm 22:37
Look, I have c to you, but can I	Nm 22:38
C, put a curse on Jacob for me;	Nm 23:7
Jacob for me; c, denounce Israel	Nm 23:7
Please c with me to another	Nm 23:13
Balak said to Balaam, "Please c.	Nm 23:27
A star will c from Jacob, and a	Nm 24:17
Ships will c from the coast of	Nm 24:24
they too will c to destruction.	Nm 24:24
before them and c back in before	Nm 27:17
will go out and c back in at his	Nm 27:21
up and the cities we will c to.'	Dt 1:22
first ones and c to Me on the	Dt 10:1
you have c, where you sowed	Dt 11:10
have not yet c into the resting	Dt 12:9
widow within your gates may c,	Dt 14:29
message does not c true or is	Dt 18:22
the priest is to c forward and	Dt 20:2
field human, to c under siege by	Dt 20:19
judges must c out and measure	Dt 21:2
sons of Levi, will c forward,	Dt 21:5
If you c across a bird's nest	Dt 22:6
he may not c anywhere inside the	Dt 23:10
sets he may c inside the camp	Dt 23:11
When you c before the priest who	Dt 26:3
blessings will c and overtake	Dt 28:2
when you c in and blessed	Dt 28:6
curses will c and overtake you	Dt 28:15
cursed when you c in and cursed	Dt 28:19
these curses will c, pursue, and	Dt 28:45
c down throughout your land.	Dt 28:52
and you c to your senses ⌊while	Dt 30:1
and afflictions will c to them.	Dt 31:17
these troubles c to us because	Dt 31:17
and afflictions c to them,	Dt 31:21
Disaster will c to you in the	Dt 31:29
men have c here tonight to	Jos 2:2
Yes, the men did c to me, but I	Jos 2:4
C closer and listen to the words	Jos 3:9
c to rest in the Jordan's waters,	Jos 3:13
the testimony to c up from the	Jos 4:16
priests, "C up from the Jordan.	Jos 4:17
after they had c out of Egypt.	Jos 5:4
after they had c out of Egypt.	Jos 5:5
I have now c as commander of the	Jos 5:14
let one word c out of your mouth	Jos 6:10
selects is to c forward clan	Jos 7:14
selects is to c forward family	Jos 7:14
selects is to c forward man by	Jos 7:14
He had Israel c forward tribe by	Jos 7:16
the clans of Judah c forward,	Jos 7:17
Zerahite clan c forward by heads	Jos 7:17
Zabdi's family c forward man by	Jos 7:18
When they c out against us as	Jos 8:5
They will c after us until we	Jos 8:6
you are to c out of your ambush	Jos 8:7
We have c from a distant land.	Jos 9:6
Who are you and where do you c	Jos 9:8
servants have c from a far away	Jos 9:9
on the day we left to c to you.	Jos 9:12
C up and help me. We will attack	Jos 10:4
servants. C quickly and save	Jos 10:6
C here and put your feet on the	Jos 10:24
God promised you has c about,	Jos 23:15
C with me to my territory,	Jdg 1:3
and said to him, "C in, my lord.	Jdg 4:18
in, my lord. C in with me. Don't	Jdg 4:18
C and I will show you the man	Jdg 4:22
they did not c to help the LORD	Jdg 5:23
When I c to the outpost of the	Jdg 7:17
C down to intercept the	Jdg 7:24
the fig tree, "C and reign over	Jdg 9:10
the grapevine, "C and reign over	Jdg 9:12
bramble, "C and reign over us.	Jdg 9:14
c and find refuge in my shade.	Jdg 9:15
may fire c out from the bramble	Jdg 9:15
may fire c from Abimelech and	Jdg 9:20
and may fire c from the lords of	Jdg 9:20
of Jerubbaal might c to justice	Jdg 9:24
"Gather your army and c out."	Jdg 9:29
c to Shechem and are turning	Jdg 9:31
with you are to c wait in ambush	Jdg 9:32
are with him c out against you	Jdg 9:33
said to him, "C, be our	Jdg 11:6
then have you c to me now when	Jdg 11:7
C with us, fight the Ammonites,	Jdg 11:8
that you have c to fight against	Jdg 11:12
then have you c today to fight	Jdg 12:3
man of God you sent c again to	Jdg 13:8
to me today has just c back!"	Jdg 13:10
Your words c true, what will	Jdg 13:12
You when Your words c true?"	Jdg 13:17
We have c to arrest Samson and	Jdg 15:10
We've c to arrest you and hand	Jdg 15:12
does your great strength ⌊c	Jdg 16:6
C one more time, for he has told	Jdg 16:18
"Where do you c from?" Micah	Jdg 17:9
They answered, "C on, let's go	Jdg 18:9
you will c to an unsuspecting	Jdg 18:10
C with us and be a father and a	Jdg 18:19
"C on," he said, "let's try to	Jdg 19:13
you going, and where do you c	Jdg 19:17
this man has c into my house.	Jdg 19:23
Israel didn't c to the LORD with	Jdg 21:5
who had not c to the LORD at	Jdg 21:5
Israel didn't c to the LORD at	Jdg 21:8
Jabesh-gilead had c to the camp	Jdg 21:8
women of Shiloh c out to perform	Jdg 21:21
or brothers c to us and protest	Jdg 21:22
wings you have c for refuge."	Ru 2:12
C over here and have some bread	Ru 2:14
"C over here and sit down."	Ru 4:1
arrogant ⌊words⌋ c out of your	1Sm 2:3
servant would c with a	1Sm 2:13
servant would c and say to the	1Sm 2:15
sign that will c to you	1Sm 2:34
family will c and bow down to	1Sm 2:36
of the LORD. C down and get it.	1Sm 6:21
was with him, "C on, let's go	1Sm 9:5
he says is sure to c true.	1Sm 9:6
God would say, "C, let's go to	1Sm 9:9
his attendant. "C on, let's go."	1Sm 9:10
for their cry has c to Me."	1Sm 9:16
there until you c to the oak of	1Sm 10:3
that you will c to the Hill of	1Sm 10:5
I will c to you to offer burnt	1Sm 10:8
days until I c to you and show	1Sm 10:8
the tribes of Israel c forward,	1Sm 10:20
of Benjamin c forward by its	1Sm 10:21
LORD, "Has the man c here yet?"	1Sm 10:22
told the messengers who had c,	1Sm 11:9
we will c out, and you can	1Sm 11:10
to the people, "C, let's go to	1Sm 11:14
but Samuel didn't c to Gilgal,	1Sm 13:8
me and you didn't c within the	1Sm 13:11
his weapons, "C on, let's cross	1Sm 14:1
his weapons, "C on, let's cross	1Sm 14:6
But if they say, 'C on up,' then	1Sm 14:10
C on up, and we'll teach you a	1Sm 14:12
leaders of the troops, c here.	1Sm 14:38
C back with me so I can bow and	1Sm 15:30
the bitterness of death has c."	1Sm 15:32
'I have c to sacrifice to the	1Sm 16:2
and asked, "Do you c in peace?"	1Sm 16:4
I've c to sacrifice to the LORD.	1Sm 16:5
yourselves and c with me to the	1Sm 16:5
Why do you c out to line up in	1Sm 17:8
and have him c down against me	1Sm 17:8
"Why did you c down here?"	1Sm 17:28
a dog that you c against me with	1Sm 17:43
"C here," the Philistine called	1Sm 17:44
You c against me with a dagger,	1Sm 17:45
but I c against you in the name	1Sm 17:45
you have c to look favorably	1Sm 20:3
David, "C on, let's go out	1Sm 20:11
them,' then c, because as the	1Sm 20:21
Jesse's son c to the meal either	1Sm 20:27
why he didn't c to the king's	1Sm 20:29
one going to c into my house?"	1Sm 21:15
saw Jesse's son c to Ahimelech	1Sm 22:9
that Saul intends to c to Keilah	1Sm 23:10
Will Saul c down as Your servant	1Sm 23:11
answered, "He will c down."	1Sm 23:11
that Saul had c out to take his	1Sm 23:15
the king wants to c down,	1Sm 23:20
to come down, let him c down.	1Sm 23:20
Then c back to me with accurate	1Sm 23:23
Saul saying, "C quickly, because	1Sm 23:27
has the king of Israel c after?	1Sm 24:14
and when you c to Nabal, greet	1Sm 25:5
for we have c on a feast day.	1Sm 25:8
if you had not c quickly to meet	1Sm 25:34
Saul had c there after him.	1Sm 26:3
for certain that Saul had c.	1Sm 26:4
his day will c and he will die,	1Sm 26:10
of Israel has c out to search	1Sm 26:20
C back, my son David, I will	1Sm 26:21
the young men c over and get it	1Sm 26:22
men will c and run me through	1Sm 31:4
asked him, "Where have you c	2Sm 1:3
and said, "C here and kill him!	2Sm 1:15
here when you c to see me."	2Sm 3:13
ark of the LORD ever c to me?"	2Sm 6:9
who will c from your body,	2Sm 7:12
for you, I'll c to help you.	2Sm 10:11
you just c from a journey?	2Sm 11:10
the traveler who had c to him.	2Sm 12:4
my sister Tamar c and give me	2Sm 13:5
my sister Tamar c and make a	2Sm 13:6
her and said, "C sleep with me,	2Sm 13:11
please c with your servant?	2Sm 13:24
Look, the king's sons have c!	2Sm 13:35
I've c to present this matter to	2Sm 14:15
but Joab was unwilling to c.	2Sm 14:29
time, but he still wouldn't c.	2Sm 14:29
sent for you and said, 'C here.	2Sm 14:32
Why have I c back from Geshur?	2Sm 14:32
or dispute could c to me,	2Sm 15:4
girl would c and pass along	2Sm 17:17
day like people c in when they	2Sm 19:3
that has c to you from your	2Sm 19:7
C back, you and all your	2Sm 19:14
of Joseph to c down to meet my	2Sm 19:20
why didn't you c with me?"	2Sm 19:25
the king has c to his palace	2Sm 19:30
Gileadite had c down from	2Sm 19:31
tell Joab to c here and let me	2Sm 20:16
he had c near her, the woman	2Sm 20:17
lose heart and c trembling from	2Sm 22:46
the LORD had c to the prophet	2Sm 24:11
of famine to c on your land,	2Sm 24:13
lord the king c to his servant?	2Sm 24:21
Now please c and let me advise	1Kg 1:12
I'll c in after you and confirm	1Kg 1:14
You are to c up after him,	1Kg 1:35
and he is to c in and sit on my	1Kg 1:35
Adonijah said, "C in, for you	1Kg 1:42
asked, "Do you c peacefully?"	1Kg 2:13
the king says: 'C out!' " But	1Kg 2:30
blood will c back on Joab's	1Kg 2:33
Israel but has c from a distant	1Kg 8:41
and will c and pray toward this	1Kg 8:42
and when they c to their senses	1Kg 8:47
before⌋ had such almug wood c,	1Kg 10:12
heard that Jeroboam had c back,	1Kg 12:20
the man of God, "C home with me,	1Kg 13:7
by the way he had c to Bethel.	1Kg 13:10
man of God who had c from	1Kg 13:12
"C home with me and eat bread."	1Kg 13:15
man of God who had c from	1Kg 13:21
the door, he said, "C in, wife	1Kg 14:6
sons⌋ will c to the grave,	1Kg 14:13
Have you c to remind me of my	1Kg 17:18
to all the people, "C near me."	1Kg 18:30
the word of the LORD had c,	1Kg 18:31
and Ahab had him c up into the	1Kg 20:33
water until I c back safely.' "	1Kg 22:27
them, "Why have you c back?"	2Kg 1:5
the king declares, 'C down!' "	2Kg 1:9

may fire **c** down from heaven and 2Kg 1:10
'**C** down immediately!' " 2Kg 1:11
may fire **c** down from heaven and 2Kg 1:12
fire has **c** down from heaven 2Kg 1:14
The time had **c** for the LORD to 2Kg 2:1
that the kings had **c** up to fight 2Kg 3:21
the man of God and then **c** back." 2Kg 4:22
Have him **c** to me, and he will 2Kg 5:8
He will surely **c** out, stand and 2Kg 5:11
the prophets have **c** to me from 2Kg 5:22
"Please **c** with your servants." 2Kg 6:3
"I'll **c**," he answered. 2Kg 6:3
raiders did not **c** into Israel's 2Kg 6:23
die. So now, **c** on. Let's go to 2Kg 7:4
'When they **c** out of the city, 2Kg 7:12
it has already **c** to the land." 2Kg 8:1
"The man of God has **c** here." 2Kg 8:7
did this crazy person **c** to you?" 2Kg 9:11
ask, '⌊Do you **c** in⌋ peace?' " 2Kg 9:17
'⌊Do you **c** in⌋ peace?' " 2Kg 9:18
'⌊Do you **c** in⌋ peace?' " 2Kg 9:19
"⌊Do you **c** in⌋ peace, Jehu? 2Kg 9:22
said, "⌊Do you **c** in⌋ peace, 2Kg 9:31
We've **c** down to greet the king's 2Kg 10:13
C with me and see my zeal for 2Kg 10:16
not a man left who did not **c**. 2Kg 10:21
He had them **c** to him in the 2Kg 11:4
one third of you who **c** on duty 2Kg 11:5
Moabites used to **c** into the land 2Kg 13:20
Israel, saying, "**C**, let us meet 2Kg 14:8
until I **c** and take you away to a 2Kg 18:32
for children have **c** to the point 2Kg 19:3
arrow there or **c** before it with 2Kg 19:32
where did they **c** to you from? 2Kg 20:14
will certainly **c** when everything 2Kg 20:17
descendants who **c** from you will 2Kg 20:18
did not **c** up to the altar of the 2Kg 23:9
men will **c** and torture me!" 1Ch 10:4
If you have **c** in peace to help 1Ch 12:17
but if you have **c** to betray me 1Ch 12:17
name to **c** and make David king 1Ch 12:31
Philistines had **c** and made a 1Ch 14:9
an offering and **c** before Him. 1Ch 16:29
kings who had **c** were in the 1Ch 19:9
He has **c** to stay in Jerusalem 1Ch 23:25
Riches and honor **c** from You, 1Ch 29:12
to my father David now **c** true. 2Ch 1:9
Israel but has **c** from a distant 2Ch 6:32
and when they **c** to their senses 2Ch 6:37
⌊**c**⌋ to Your resting place, 2Ch 6:41
ark of the LORD has **c** are holy." 2Ch 8:11
this incident has **c** from Me.' " 2Ch 11:4
Your name we have **c** against this 2Ch 14:11
water until I **c** back safely.' " 2Ch 18:26
wrath will not **c** on you and your 2Ch 19:10
and from Edom has **c** ⌊to fight⌋ 2Ch 20:2
your intestines **c** out day after 2Ch 21:15
troops that had **c** with the Arabs 2Ch 22:1
Israel, saying, "**C**, let us meet 2Ch 25:17
C near and bring sacrifices and 2Ch 29:31
for it had **c** about suddenly. 2Ch 29:36
and Manasseh to **c** to the LORD's 2Ch 30:1
to **c** to observe the Passover of 2Ch 30:5
and **c** to His sanctuary that He 2Ch 30:8
Sennacherib had **c** and that he 2Ch 32:2
of Assyria **c** and find plenty 2Ch 32:4
the benefit that had **c** to him. 2Ch 32:25
wrath didn't **c** on them during 2Ch 32:26
I have not **c** against you today 2Ch 35:21
grace has **c** from the LORD our Ezr 9:8
Whoever did not **c** within three Ezr 10:8
foreign women **c** at appointed Ezr 10:14
that someone had **c** to seek the Neh 2:10
C, let's rebuild Jerusalem's Neh 2:17
together to **c** and fight against Neh 4:8
C, let's meet together in the Neh 6:2
a great work and cannot **c** down. Neh 6:3
So **c**, let's confer together. Neh 6:7
concerning all that has **c** on us, Neh 9:33
one out of ten to **c** and live in Neh 11:1
that they did not **c** again on the Neh 13:21
refused to **c** at the king's Est 1:12
before him, but she did not **c**.' Est 1:17
deliverance will **c** to the Jewish Est 4:14
you have **c** to the kingdom Est 4:14
king and Haman **c** today to the Est 5:4
king and Haman **c** to the banquet Est 5:8
evil that would **c** on my people? Est 8:6

asked Satan, "Where have you **c** Jb 1:7
asked Satan, "Where have you **c** Jb 2:2
it does not **c**, and search for Jb 3:21
blast from God and **c** to an end Jb 4:9
they **c** to an end without hope. Jb 7:6
opposed Him and **c** out unharmed? Jb 9:4
dies, will he **c** back to life? Jb 14:14
But **c** back ⌊and try⌋ again, Jb 17:10
success distress will **c** to him; Jb 20:22
his liver. Terrors **c** over him. Jb 20:25
Does disaster **c** on them? Jb 21:17
C to terms with God and be at Jb 22:21
in this way good will **c** to you. Jb 22:21
Food may **c** from the earth, Jb 28:5
Where then does wisdom **c** from, Jb 28:20
Doesn't disaster **c** to the wicked Jb 31:3
My words ⌊**c** from⌋ my upright Jb 33:3
You may **c** this far, but no Jb 38:11
Whose womb did the ice **c** from? Jb 38:29
evil of the wicked **c** to an end, Ps 7:9
The enemy has **c** to eternal ruin; Ps 9:6
deliverance would **c** from Zion! Ps 14:7
Let my vindication **c** from You, Ps 17:2
lose heart and **c** trembling from Ps 18:45
My strength, **c** quickly to help Ps 22:19
They will **c** and tell a people Ps 22:31
the King of glory will **c** in. Ps 24:7
the King of glory will **c** in. Ps 24:9
floodwaters **c**, they will not Ps 32:6
or else it will not **c** near you. Ps 32:9
Many pains **c** to the wicked, Ps 32:10
C, children, listen to me; Ps 34:11
Many adversities **c** to the one Ps 34:19
and small—and **c** to my aid. Ps 35:2
Let ruin **c** on him unexpectedly, Ps 35:8
Malicious witnesses **c** forward; Ps 35:11
of the arrogant **c** near me or the Ps 36:11
Then I said, "See, I have **c**; Ps 40:7
When can I **c** and appear before Ps 42:2
Then I will **c** to the altar of Ps 43:4
C, see the works of the LORD, Ps 46:8
deliverance would **c** from Zion! Ps 53:6
faithful God will **c** to meet me; Ps 59:10
All humanity will **c** to You, Ps 65:2
C and see the works of God; Ps 66:5
C and listen, all who fear God, Ps 66:16
Ambassadors will **c** from Egypt; Ps 68:31
I have **c** into deep waters, Ps 69:2
c because of the mighty acts of Ps 71:16
strength to all who are to **c**. Ps 71:18
They **c** to an end, swept away by Ps 73:19
does not **c** from the east, Ps 75:6
Your compassion **c** to us quickly, Ps 79:8
Your power and **c** to save us. Ps 80:2
They say, "**C**, let us wipe them Ps 83:4
have made will **c** and bow down Ps 86:9
no harm will **c** to you; no plague Ps 91:10
no plague will **c** near your tent. Ps 91:10
house for all the days to **c**. Ps 93:5
C, let us shout joyfully to the Ps 95:1
C, let us worship and bow down; Ps 95:6
c before Him with joyful songs. Ps 100:2
When will You **c** to me? I will Ps 101:2
my cry for help **c** before You. Ps 102:1
her—the appointed time has **c**. Ps 102:13
C to me with Your salvation Ps 106:4
throughout all generations to **c**. Ps 106:31
Good will **c** to a man who lends Ps 112:5
of the wicked will **c** to nothing. Ps 112:10
Let Your faithful love **c** to me, Ps 119:41
Your compassion **c** to me so that Ps 119:77
who pursue evil plans **c** near; Ps 119:150
Where will my help **c** from? Ps 121:1
will surely **c** back with shouts Ps 126:6
Arise, LORD, **c** to Your resting Ps 132:8
I **c** to You for protection. Ps 143:9
part Your heavens and **c** down. Ps 144:5
If they say—"**C** with us! Pr 1:11
from His mouth **c** knowledge and Pr 2:6
Go away! **C** back later. I'll Pr 3:28
poverty will **c** like a robber, Pr 6:11
C, let's drink deeply of Pr 7:18
him and will **c** home at the time Pr 7:20
C, eat my bread, and drink the Pr 9:5
the wicked dreads will **c** to him, Pr 10:24
a blessing will **c** to the one who Pr 11:26
for trouble, it will **c** to him. Pr 11:27
and disgrace ⌊**c** to⌋ those who Pr 13:18

children who **c** after him will Pr 20:7
the way of wisdom will **c** to rest Pr 21:16
destruction will **c** suddenly; Pr 24:22
blessing will **c** to them. Pr 24:25
Thistles had **c** up everywhere, Pr 24:31
poverty will **c** like a robber, Pr 24:34
him to say to you, "**C** up here!" Pr 25:7
a stone—it will **c** back on him. Pr 26:27
but when the wicked **c** to power, Pr 28:12
know that poverty will **c** to him. Pr 28:22
When the wicked **c** to power, Pr 28:28
gone up to heaven and **c** down? Pr 30:4
she can laugh at the time to **c**. Pr 31:25
those who will **c** after there Ec 1:11
in the days to **c** both will be Ec 2:16
all **c** from dust, and all return Ec 3:20
yet those who **c** later will not Ec 4:16
anything that will **c** after him. Ec 7:14
Before the days of adversity **c**, Ec 12:1
C away, my beautiful one. Sg 2:10
The time of singing has **c**, Sg 2:12
C away, my beautiful one. Sg 2:13
C out, young women of Zion, and Sg 3:11
C with me from Lebanon, my bride Sg 4:8
north wind—**c**, south wind. Sg 4:16
Let my love **c** to his garden and Sg 4:16
I have **c** to my garden—my Sg 5:1
C back, come back, Shulammite! Sg 6:13
Come back, **c** back, Shulammite! Sg 6:13
C back, come back, that we may Sg 6:13
Come back, **c** back, that we may Sg 6:13
C, my love, let's go to the Sg 7:11
When you **c** to appear before Me, Is 1:12
"**C**, let us discuss this," says Is 1:18
and many peoples will **c** and say, Is 2:3
come and say, "**C**, let us go up Is 2:3
c and let us walk in the LORD's Is 2:5
how quickly and swiftly they **c**! Is 5:26
All of them will **c** and settle in Is 7:19
Assyria has **c** to Aiath and has Is 10:28
It will **c** like destruction from Is 13:6
no woodcutter has **c** against us." Is 14:8
a viper will **c** out of the root Is 14:29
Look, riders **c**—horsemen in Is 21:9
Morning has **c**, and also night. Is 21:12
want to ask, ask! **C** back again." Is 21:12
so a righteous nation can **c** Is 26:2
In days to **c**, Jacob will take Is 27:6
Women will **c** and make fires with Is 27:11
in the land of Assyria will **c**, Is 27:13
and your words will **c** from low Is 29:4
collapse will **c** very suddenly. Is 30:13
of Hosts will **c** down to fight Is 31:4
fail and the harvest will not **c**. Is 32:10
You nations, **c** here and listen; Is 34:1
it will then **c** down on Edom Is 34:5
her princes will **c** to nothing. Is 34:12
will return and **c** to Zion with Is 35:10
until I **c** and take you away to a Is 36:17
when children **c** to the point Is 37:3
arrow there or **c** before it with Is 37:33
will certainly **c** when everything Is 39:6
descendants who **c** from you will Is 39:7
let us **c** together for the trial. Is 41:1
Let them **c** and tell us what will Is 41:22
north, and he has **c**, one from Is 41:25
will **c** over to you and will be Is 45:14
they will **c** over in chains; Is 45:14
C, gather together, and draw Is 45:20
against Him will **c** to Him and be Is 45:24
C out, and to those who are in Is 49:9
these will **c** from far away, Is 49:12
together; they **c** to you. As I Is 49:18
but these, where did they **c** Is 49:21
against Me? Let him **c** near Me! Is 50:8
for instruction will **c** from Me, Is 51:4
will return and **c** to Zion with Is 51:11
will certainly not **c** near you. Is 54:14
C, everyone who is thirsty, come Is 55:1
who is thirsty, **c** to the waters; Is 55:1
without money, **c**, buy, and eat! Is 55:1
C, buy wine and milk without Is 55:1
Pay attention and **c** to Me; Is 55:3
a cypress will **c** up, and instead Is 55:13
the brier, a myrtle will **c** up; Is 55:13
the field and forest, **c** and eat! Is 56:9
C, let me get ⌊some⌋ wine, let's Is 56:12
But **c** here, you sons of a Is 57:3

your recovery will **c** quickly. Is 58:8
for He will **c** like a rushing Is 59:19
The Redeemer will **c** to Zion, Is 59:20
your light has **c**, and the glory Is 60:1
Nations will **c** to your light, Is 60:3
they all gather and **c** to you; Is 60:4
your sons will **c** from far away, Is 60:4
of the nations will **c** to you. Is 60:5
all of them will **c** from Sheba. Is 60:6
glory of Lebanon will **c** to you— Is 60:13
oppressors will **c** and bow down Is 60:14
the heavens open ⌊and⌋ **c** down, Is 64:1
yourself, don't **c** near me, for I Is 65:5
not be remembered or **c** to mind. Is 65:17
the LORD will **c** with fire— Is 66:15
I have **c** to gather all nations Is 66:18
they will **c** and see My glory. Is 66:18
mankind will **c** to worship Me, Is 66:23
will **c**, and each ⌊king⌋ will Jr 1:15
we will no longer **c** to You? Jr 2:31
is why the showers haven't **c**— Jr 3:3
It will never **c** to mind, and no Jr 3:16
they will **c** together from the Jr 3:18
Harm won't **c** to us; we won't Jr 5:12
their flocks will **c** against her; Jr 6:3
the destroyer will **c** on us. Jr 6:26
Then do you **c** and stand before Jr 7:10
They **c** to devour the land and Jr 8:16
of my dear people not **c** about? Jr 8:22
Let them **c** quickly to raise a Jr 9:18
the destroyers have **c**, Jr 12:12
the nations will **c** to You from Jr 16:19
the word of the LORD? Let it **c**!" Jr 17:15
people⌋ will **c** from the cities Jr 17:26
ones said, "**C**, let's make plans Jr 18:18
C, let's denounce him and pay no Jr 18:18
did I **c** out of the womb to see Jr 20:18
Who can **c** down against us? Jr 21:13
groan when labor pains **c** on you, Jr 22:23
said, No harm will **c** to you." Jr 23:17
In time to **c** you will understand Jr 23:20
word of the LORD has **c** to me, Jr 25:3
days of your slaughter have **c**, Jr 25:34
have prophesied **c** true and may Jr 28:6
call to Me and **c** and pray to Me, Jr 29:12
Thanksgiving will **c** out of them, Jr 30:19
In time to **c** you will understand Jr 30:24
They will **c** weeping, but I will Jr 31:9
They will **c** and shout for joy on Jr 31:12
reward for your work will **c**— Jr 31:16
ramps have **c** against the city Jr 32:24
fight against this city will **c**, Jr 32:29
cease to **c** at their regular Jr 33:20
C, let's go into Jerusalem to Jr 35:11
petition will **c** before the LORD, Jr 36:7
hearing of the people, and **c**." Jr 36:14
certainly **c** and destroy this Jr 36:29
which has **c** out to help you, Jr 37:7
Babylon will not **c** against you Jr 37:19
May my petition **c** before you. Jr 37:20
with you and **c** and demand of you Jr 38:25
and don't let any harm **c** to him; Jr 39:12
of the LORD had **c** to Jeremiah Jr 39:15
it pleases you to **c** with me to Jr 40:4
to Babylon, **c**, and I will take Jr 40:4
wrong to you to **c** with me to Jr 40:4
the Chaldeans who **c** to us. Jr 40:10
"**C** to Gedaliah son of Ahikam!" Jr 41:6
May our petition **c** before you; Jr 42:2
He will **c** and strike down the Jr 43:11
this disaster has **c** to you, Jr 44:23
you will certainly **c** to pass. Jr 44:29
He will **c** like Tabor among the Jr 46:18
the enemy⌋ will **c** with an army; Jr 46:22
they will **c** against her like Jr 46:22
C, let's cut her off from Jr 48:2
of Moab and its towns has **c** up, Jr 48:15
C down from glory; sit on Jr 48:18
of Moab has **c** against you; Jr 48:18
Judgment has **c** to the land of Jr 48:21
fire has **c** out from Heshbon Jr 48:45
Were thieves to **c** in the night, Jr 49:9
yourselves to **c** against her. Jr 49:14
the north will **c** against her; Jr 50:3
and Judeans will **c** together, Jr 50:4
weeping as they **c**, and will seek Jr 50:4
They will **c** and join themselves Jr 50:5
C against her from the most Jr 50:26

their day has **c**, the time of Jr 50:27
your day has **c**, the time when I Jr 50:31
A drought will **c** on her waters, Jr 50:38
for they will **c** against her from Jr 51:2
c, let's tell in Zion what the Jr 51:10
your end has **c**, your life thread Jr 51:13
while her harvest time will **c**. Jr 51:33
C out from among her, My people! Jr 51:45
for the report will **c** one year, Jr 51:46
the north will **c** against her. Jr 51:48
let Jerusalem **c** to your mind. Jr 51:50
destroyers will **c** against her Jr 51:53
that would **c** to Babylon; Jr 51:60
their wickedness **c** before You, Lm 1:22
and good **c** from the mouth Lm 3:38
You **c** near when I call on You; Lm 3:57
our time ran out. Our end had **c**! Lm 4:18
end has **c** on the four corners Ezk 7:2
An end has **c**; the end has come! Ezk 7:6
the end has **c**! It has awakened Ezk 7:6
Doom has **c** on you, inhabitants Ezk 7:7
The time has **c**; the day is near Ezk 7:7
The time has **c**; the day has Ezk 7:12
Disaster after disaster will **c**, Ezk 7:26
a loud voice, "**C** near, Ezk 9:1
but do not **c** near anyone who has Ezk 9:6
rain will **c**, and I will send Ezk 13:11
rain will **c** in My anger, Ezk 13:13
Indeed, they will **c** out to you, Ezk 14:22
bribed them to **c** to you from all Ezk 16:33
neighbor's wife or **c** near a Ezk 18:6
will therefore **c** out of its Ezk 21:4
day has **c** for your punishment. Ezk 21:25
⌊the time⌋ has **c** to put you to Ezk 21:29
the day has **c** for your Ezk 21:29
of judgment has **c** and who makes Ezk 22:3
near and have **c** to your years Ezk 22:4
They will **c** against you with an Ezk 23:24
and whose rust will not **c** off! Ezk 24:6
its thick rust will not **c** off. Ezk 24:12
a fugitive will **c** to you and Ezk 24:26
A sword will **c** against Egypt, Ezk 30:4
Anguish will **c** over them on the Ezk 30:9
king will **c** against you! Ezk 32:11
allies: They have **c** down; the Ezk 32:21
proud strength will **c** to an end. Ezk 33:28
C and hear what the message is Ezk 33:30
So My people **c** to you in crowds, Ezk 33:31
and it will definitely **c**— Ezk 33:33
off from it those who **c** and go. Ezk 35:7
in you so that you **c** to life. Ezk 37:6
c from the four winds and Ezk 37:9
I will **c** against a tranquil Ezk 38:11
Have you **c** to seize spoil? Ezk 38:13
and **c** from your place in the Ezk 38:15
Assemble and **c**! Gather from all Ezk 39:17
as priests or **c** near any of My Ezk 44:13
A priest may not **c** ⌊near⌋ a dead Ezk 44:25
of the land **c** before the LORD at Ezk 46:9
took this occasion to **c** forward Dn 3:8
of the Most High God—**c** out!" Dn 3:26
for the time had **c**, and the holy Dn 7:22
intrigue, will **c** to the throne. Dn 8:23
all this disaster has **c** on us, Dn 9:13
I've **c** now to give you Dn 9:22
out, and I have **c** to give it, Dn 9:23
The end will **c** with a flood, Dn 9:26
have **c** because of your prayers. Dn 10:12
Now I have **c** to help you Dn 10:14
Do you know why I've **c** to you? Dn 10:20
the prince of Greece will **c**. Dn 10:20
rise up, **c** against the army, Dn 11:7
the king of the North will **c**, Dn 11:15
will resolve to **c** with the force Dn 11:17
but he will **c** during a time of Dn 11:21
he will **c** into the richest parts Dn 11:24
the end will **c** at the appointed Dn 11:27
time he will **c** again to the Dn 11:29
of Kittim will **c** against him, Dn 11:30
it will still **c** at the appointed Dn 11:35
They will **c** with awe to the LORD Hs 3:5
C, let us return to the LORD. Hs 6:1
He will **c** to us like the rain, Hs 6:3
The days of punishment have **c**; Hs 9:7
the days of retribution have **c**. Hs 9:7
among you; I will not **c** in rage. Hs 11:9
His children will **c** trembling Hs 11:10
will certainly **c** to nothing. Hs 12:11

Labor pains **c** on him. He is not Hs 13:13
an east wind will **c**, a wind from Hs 13:15
C and spend the night in Jl 1:13
near and will **c** as devastation Jl 1:15
in all the generations to **c**. Jl 2:2
C quickly, all you surrounding Jl 3:11
be roused and **c** to the Valley Jl 3:12
C and trample ⌊the grapes⌋ Jl 3:13
great houses will **c** to an end— Am 3:15
C to Bethel and rebel; rebel Am 4:4
and Bethel will **c** to nothing. Am 5:5
who sprawl out will **c** to an end. Am 6:7
The end has **c** for My people Am 8:2
"**C** on!" the sailors said to each Jnh 1:7
of Zaanan will not **c** out. Mc 1:11
calamity has **c** from the LORD to Mc 1:12
of Israel will **c** to Adullam. Mc 1:15
and many nations will **c** and say, Mc 4:2
come and say, "**C**, let us go up Mc 4:2
the former rule will **c** to you, Mc 4:8
sovereignty will **c** to Daughter Mc 4:8
One will **c** from you to be ruler Mc 5:2
the LORD when I **c** to bow before Mc 6:6
Should I **c** before Him with burnt Mc 6:6
A day will **c** for rebuilding your Mc 7:11
day people will **c** to you from Mc 7:12
they will **c** trembling out of Mc 7:17
their horsemen **c** from distant Hab 1:8
All of them **c** to do violence; Hab 1:9
will certainly **c** and not be late Hab 2:3
right hand will **c** around to you, Hab 2:16
to mute stone: **C** alive! Can it Hab 2:19
You **c** out to save Your people, Hab 3:13
of distress to **c** against the Hab 3:16
The time has not **c** for the house Hg 1:2
of all the nations will **c**, Hg 2:7
have **c** to terrify them Zch 1:21
are far off will **c** and build the Zch 6:15
will yet **c**, the residents Zch 8:20
nations will **c** to seek the LORD Zch 8:22
them will **c** the cornerstone, Zch 10:4
of Egypt will **c** to an end. Zch 10:11
the nations that **c** against Zch 12:9
my God will **c** and all the holy Zch 14:5
sacrifices will **c** and take some Zch 14:21
this has **c** from your hands Mal 1:9
will suddenly **c** to His temple, Mal 3:1
I will **c** to you in judgment, Mal 3:5
will **c** and strike the land with Mal 4:6
east and have **c** to worship Him. Mt 2:2
out of you will **c** a leader who Mt 2:6
kingdom of heaven has **c** near!" Mt 3:2
by You, and yet You **c** to me?" Mt 3:14
kingdom of heaven has **c** near!" Mt 4:17
I did not **c** to destroy but to Mt 5:17
and then **c** and offer your gift. Mt 5:24
kingdom **c**. Your will be done Mt 6:10
prophets who **c** to you in sheep's Mt 7:15
"I will **c** and heal him," He told Mt 8:7
to have You **c** under my roof. Mt 8:8
to another, '**C**!' and he comes; Mt 8:9
that many will **c** from east and Mt 8:11
When He had **c** to the other side, Mt 8:28
Have You **c** here to torment us Mt 8:29
So when they had **c** out, they Mt 8:32
For I didn't **c** to call the Mt 9:13
The days will **c** when the groom Mt 9:15
but **c** and lay Your hand on her, Mt 9:18
kingdom of heaven has **c** near.' Mt 10:7
I did not **c** to bring peace, Mt 10:34
Are You the One who is to **c**, Mt 11:3
he is the Elijah who is to **c**. Mt 11:14
For John did not **c** eating or Mt 11:18
C to Me, all of you who are Mt 11:28
the kingdom of God has **c** to you. Mt 12:28
in this age or in the one to **c**. Mt 12:32
where did the weeds **c** from?' Mt 13:27
of the sky **c** and nest in its Mt 13:32
and these miracles **c** to Him? Mt 13:54
me to **c** to You on the water. Mt 14:28
"**C**!" He said. And climbing out Mt 14:29
from the heart **c** evil thoughts, Mt 15:19
If anyone wants to **c** with Me, Mt 16:24
is going to **c** with His angels Mt 16:27
say that Elijah must **c** first?" Mt 17:10
has already **c**, and they didn't Mt 17:12
this kind does not **c** out except Mt 17:21
offenses must **c**, but woe to that Mt 18:7

Son of Man has **c** to save the Mt 18:11
in heaven. Then **c**, follow Me." Mt 19:21
of Man did not **c** to be served, Mt 20:28
no fruit ever **c** from you again! Mt 21:19
Where did John's baptism **c** from? Mt 21:25
C, let's kill him and take his Mt 21:38
but they didn't want to **c**. Mt 22:3
C to the wedding banquet.' Mt 22:4
these things will **c** on this Mt 23:36
For many will **c** in My name, Mt 24:5
And then the end will **c**. Mt 24:14
housetop must not **c** down to get Mt 24:17
master will **c** on a day he does Mt 24:50
the groom! **C** out to meet him. Mt 25:6
on His right, '**C**, you who are Mt 25:34
asked him, "why have you **c**?" Mt 26:50
Have you **c** out with swords and Mt 26:55
the Son of God, **c** down from the Mt 27:40
Let Him **c** down now from the Mt 27:42
His disciples may **c**, steal Him, Mt 27:64
C and see the place where He lay. Mt 28:6
powerful than I will **c** after me. Mk 1:7
the kingdom of God has **c** near. Mk 1:15
Have You **c** to destroy us? Mk 1:24
Be quiet, and **c** out of him!" Mk 1:25
too. This is why I have **c**." Mk 1:38
and they would **c** to Him from Mk 1:45
didn't **c** to call the righteous, Mk 2:17
the time will **c** when the groom Mk 2:20
scribes who had **c** down from Mk 3:22
hidden except to **c** to light. Mk 4:22
sickle, because harvest has **c**." Mk 4:29
evening had **c**, He told them, Mk 4:35
had told him, "**C** out of the man, Mk 5:8
C and lay Your hands on her so Mk 5:23
C away by yourselves to a remote Mk 6:31
scribes who had **c** from Jerusalem Mk 7:1
they **c** from the marketplace, Mk 7:4
things that **c** out of a person Mk 7:15
hearts, **c** evil thoughts, Mk 7:21
these evil things **c** from within Mk 7:23
of them have **c** a long distance. Mk 8:3
the kingdom of God **c** in power." Mk 9:1
say that Elijah must **c** first?" Mk 9:11
Elijah does **c** first and restores Mk 9:12
you that Elijah really has **c**, Mk 9:13
c out of him and never enter him Mk 9:25
This kind can **c** out by nothing Mk 9:29
Let the little children **c** to Me. Mk 10:14
in heaven. Then **c**, follow Me." Mk 10:21
eternal life in the age to **c**. Mk 10:30
of Man did not **c** to be served, Mk 10:45
C, let's kill him, and the Mk 12:7
will **c** and destroy the farmers Mk 12:9
will **c** in My name, saying, Mk 13:6
must not **c** down or go in to Mk 13:15
he might **c** suddenly and find you Mk 13:36
The time has **c**. Look, the Son Mk 14:41
Have you **c** out with swords and Mk 14:48
c down now from the cross, Mk 15:32
other women had **c** up with Him to Mk 15:41
When he did **c** out, he could not Lk 1:22
The Holy Spirit will **c** upon you, Lk 1:35
of my Lord should **c** to me? Lk 1:43
the time had **c** for Elizabeth to Lk 1:57
Have You **c** to destroy us? Lk 4:34
"Be quiet and **c** out of him!" Lk 4:35
and power, and they **c** out!" Lk 4:36
other boat to **c** and help them; Lk 5:7
crowds would **c** together to hear Lk 5:15
there who had **c** from every Lk 5:17
I have not **c** to call the Lk 5:32
the days will **c** when the groom Lk 5:35
Him to **c** and save the life Lk 7:3
to have You **c** under my roof. Lk 7:6
myself worthy to **c** to You. Lk 7:7
to another, '**C**!' and he comes; Lk 7:8
Are You the One who is to **c**, Lk 7:19
'Are You the One who is to **c**, Lk 7:20
Baptist did not **c** eating bread Lk 7:33
The Son of Man has **c** eating and Lk 7:34
seven demons had **c** out of her Lk 8:2
so that those who **c** in may see Lk 8:16
be made known and **c** to light. Lk 8:17
spirit to **c** out of the man. Lk 8:29
with Him to **c** to his house, Lk 8:41
ancient prophets has **c** back." Lk 9:19
If anyone wants to **c** with Me, Lk 9:23

kingdom of God has **c** near you.' Lk 10:9
the kingdom of God has **c** near.' Lk 10:11
When I **c** back I'll reimburse you Lk 10:35
honored as holy. Your kingdom **c**. Lk 11:2
mine on a journey has **c** to me, Lk 11:6
the kingdom of God has **c** to you. Lk 11:20
that those who **c** in may see its Lk 11:33
table, then **c** and serve them. Lk 12:37
master will **c** on a day he does Lk 12:46
years I have **c** looking for fruit Lk 13:7
therefore **c** on those days and be Lk 13:14
They will **c** from east and west, Lk 13:29
of you may **c** and say to you, Lk 14:9
who were invited, '**C**, because Lk 14:17
and therefore I'm unable to **c**.' Lk 14:20
and lanes and make them **c** Lk 14:23
own cross and **c** after Me cannot Lk 14:27
the dogs would **c** and lick his Lk 16:21
they won't also **c** to this place Lk 16:28
Offenses will certainly **c**, Lk 17:1
woe to the one they **c** through! Lk 17:1
'**C** at once and sit down to eat'? Lk 17:7
when the kingdom of God will **c**, Lk 17:20
must not **c** down to get them. Lk 17:31
Let the little children **c** to Me, Lk 18:16
in heaven. Then **c**, follow Me." Lk 18:22
eternal life in the age to **c**." Lk 18:30
hurry and **c** down, because today Lk 19:5
salvation has **c** to this house," Lk 19:9
Son of Man has **c** to seek and to Lk 19:10
in business until I **c** back.' Lk 19:13
the days will **c** on you when your Lk 19:43
He will **c** and destroy those Lk 20:16
the days will **c** when not one Lk 21:6
For many will **c** in My name, Lk 21:8
but the end won't **c** right away." Lk 21:9
that its desolation has **c** near. Lk 21:20
or that day will **c** on you Lk 21:34
For it will **c** on all who live on Lk 21:35
the people would **c** early in the Lk 21:38
the elders who had **c** for Him, Lk 22:52
Have you **c** out with swords and Lk 22:52
me when You **c** into Your kingdom! Lk 23:42
women who had **c** with Him from Lk 23:55
"**C** and you'll see," He replied. Jn 1:39
anything good **c** out of Nazareth? Jn 1:46
"**C** and see," Philip answered. Jn 1:46
"My hour has not yet **c**." Jn 2:4
know that You have **c** from God as Jn 3:2
the light has **c** into the world, Jn 3:19
and **c** here to draw water. Jn 4:15
He told her, "and **c** back here." Jn 4:16
C, see a man who told me Jn 4:29
that Jesus had **c** from Judea Jn 4:47
with Him to **c** down and heal his Jn 4:47
"**c** down before my boy dies!" Jn 4:49
and will not **c** under judgment Jn 5:24
and **c** out—those who have done Jn 5:29
not willing to **c** to Me that you Jn 5:40
I have **c** in My Father's name, Jn 5:43
who was to **c** into the world!" Jn 6:14
they were about to **c** and take Jn 6:15
but Jesus had not yet **c** to them. Jn 6:17
Father gives Me will **c** to Me, Jn 6:37
For I have **c** down from heaven, Jn 6:38
I have **c** down from heaven'?" Jn 6:42
No one can **c** to Me unless the Jn 6:44
that no one can **c** to Me unless Jn 6:65
We have **c** to believe and know Jn 6:69
My time has not yet fully **c**." Jn 7:8
Yet I have not **c** on My own, Jn 7:28
because His hour had not yet **c**. Jn 7:30
and where I am, you cannot **c**." Jn 7:34
and where I am, you cannot **c**'?" Jn 7:36
he should **c** to Me and drink! Jn 7:37
Messiah doesn't **c** from Galilee, Jn 7:41
know where I **c** from or where I'm Jn 8:14
because His hour had not **c**. Jn 8:20
Where I'm going, you cannot **c**." Jn 8:21
I'm going, you cannot **c**'?" Jn 8:22
For I didn't **c** on My own, but He Jn 8:42
saved and will **c** in and go out Jn 10:9
I have **c** that they may have life Jn 10:10
of the Jews had **c** to Martha and Jn 11:19
who was to **c** into the world." Jn 11:27
had not yet **c** into the village Jn 11:30
Jews who had **c** with her crying Jn 11:33
they told Him, "**c** and see." Jn 11:34

a loud voice, "Lazarus, **c** out!" Jn 11:43
Romans will **c** and remove both Jn 11:48
He won't **c** to the festival, Jn 11:56
crowd that had **c** to the festival Jn 12:12
The hour has **c** for the Son of Jn 12:23
I have **c** as a light into the Jn 12:46
for I did not **c** to judge the Jn 12:47
that His hour had **c** to depart Jn 13:1
that He had **c** from God, and that Jn 13:3
'Where I am going you cannot **c**,' Jn 13:33
I will **c** back and receive you to Jn 14:3
We will **c** to him and make Our Jn 14:23
If I had not **c** and spoken to Jn 15:22
the Counselor will not **c** to you. Jn 16:7
declare to you what is to **c**. Jn 16:13
has pain because her time has **c**. Jn 16:21
and have **c** into the world. Jn 16:28
coming, and has **c**, when each of Jn 16:32
Father, the hour has **c**. Jn 17:1
and I have **c** into the world for Jn 18:37
had previously **c** to Him at night Jn 19:39
"**C** and have breakfast," Jesus Jn 21:12
I want him to remain until I **c**," Jn 21:22
I want him to remain until I **c**, Jn 21:23
So when they had **c** together, Ac 1:6
the Holy Spirit has **c** upon you, Ac 1:8
will **c** in the same way that you Ac 1:11
refreshing may **c** from the Ac 3:19
as to what could **c** of this. Ac 5:24
and **c** to the land that I will Ac 7:3
they will **c** out and worship Me Ac 7:7
and have **c** down to rescue Ac 7:34
And now, **c**, I will send you to Ac 7:34
For He had not yet **c** down on any Ac 8:16
He had **c** to worship in Jerusalem Ac 8:27
Philip to **c** up and sit with Ac 8:31
of charity have **c** up as a Ac 10:4
that many had **c** together there. Ac 10:27
who had **c** with Peter were Ac 10:45
The gods have **c** down to us in Ac 14:11
in the Lord, **c** and stay at my Ac 16:15
Jesus Christ to **c** out of her!" Ac 16:18
So **c** out now and go in peace." Ac 16:36
let them **c** themselves and escort Ac 16:37
upside down have **c** here too, Ac 17:6
and Timothy to **c** to him as Ac 17:15
had recently **c** from Italy with Ac 18:2
I'll **c** back to you again, Ac 18:21
the One who would **c** after him, Ac 19:4
her magnificence **c** to the verge Ac 19:27
know why they had **c** together. Ac 19:32
wolves will **c** in among you, Ac 20:29
certainly hear that you've **c**. Ac 21:22
his accusers to **c** to you. Ac 24:7
the judgment to **c**, Felix became Ac 24:25
the Jews who had **c** down from Ac 25:7
and prayed for daylight to **c**. Ac 27:29
about us and had **c** to meet us as Ac 28:15
the brothers has **c** and reported Ac 28:21
that I often planned to **c** to you Rm 1:13
us do evil so that good may **c**"? Rm 3:8
nor things to **c**, nor powers, Rm 8:38
time I will **c**, and Sarah will Rm 9:9
salvation has **c** to the Gentiles Rm 11:11
and have **c** to share in the rich Rm 11:17
hardening has **c** to Israel until Rm 11:25
number of the Gentiles has **c** Rm 11:25
The Liberator will **c** from Zion; Rm 11:26
for many years to **c** to you Rm 15:23
But I know that when I **c** to you, Rm 15:29
I will **c** in the fullness of the Rm 15:29
I may **c** to you with joy and be Rm 15:32
I did not **c** with brilliance of 1Co 2:1
what has never **c** into a man's 1Co 2:9
things present or things to **c**— 1Co 3:22
then praise will **c** to each one 1Co 4:5
But I will **c** to you soon, if the 1Co 4:19
Should I **c** to you with a rod, 1Co 4:21
prayer. Then **c** together again; 1Co 7:5
the ends of the ages have **c**. 1Co 10:11
For man did not **c** from woman, 1Co 11:8
and all things **c** from God. 1Co 11:12
since you **c** together not for the 1Co 11:17
hear that when you **c** together as 1Co 11:18
when you **c** together in one 1Co 11:20
when you **c** together to eat, 1Co 11:33
so that you can **c** together and 1Co 11:34
the other matters whenever I **c**. 1Co 11:34

they will c to an end; 1Co 13:8
knowledge, it will c to an end. 1Co 13:8
the partial will c to an end. 1Co 13:10
I c to you speaking in ⌊other⌋ 1Co 14:6
are uninformed or unbelievers c 1Co 14:23
Whenever you c together, each 1Co 14:26
you, or did it c to you only? 1Co 14:36
will they have when they c?" 1Co 15:35
sow does not c to life unless 1Co 15:36
will need to be made when I c. 1Co 16:2
I will c to you after I pass 1Co 16:5
way in peace so he can c to me, 1Co 16:11
urged him to c to you with 1Co 16:12
was not at all willing to c now. 1Co 16:12
when he has time, he will c. 1Co 16:12
I planned to c to you first, 2Co 1:15
then c to you again from 2Co 1:16
Yes" has c about in Him. 2Co 1:19
you that I did not c to Corinth. 2Co 1:23
not to c to you on another 2Co 2:1
and look, new things have c. 2Co 5:17
c out from among them and be 2Co 6:17
should c with me and find 2Co 9:4
since we have c to you with the 2Co 10:14
am ready to c to you this third 2Co 12:14
I urged Titus ⌊to c⌋, and I sent 2Co 12:18
perhaps when I c I will not find 2Co 12:20
fear that when I c my God will 2Co 12:21
if I c again, I will not be 2Co 13:2
Abraham would c to the Gentiles Gl 3:14
the promise was made would c. Gl 3:19
But since that faith has c, Gl 3:25
persuasion did not c from Him Gl 5:8
age but also in the one to c. Eph 1:21
talk should c from your mouth, Eph 4:29
Jesus when I c to you again. Php 1:26
whether I c and see you or am Php 1:27
when He had c as a man in His Php 2:7
I myself will also c quickly. Php 2:24
the gospel that has c to you. Col 1:6
so that He might c to have first Col 1:18
are a shadow of what was to c; Col 2:17
gospel did not c to you in word 1Th 1:5
exhortation didn't c from error 1Th 2:3
So we wanted to c to you— 1Th 2:18
now Timothy has c to us from you 1Th 3:6
of the Lord will c just like a 1Th 5:2
that the Day of the Lord has c. 2Th 2:2
that day⌋ will not c unless the 2Th 2:3
be saved and to c to the 1Tm 2:4
to you, hoping to c to you soon. 1Tm 3:14
life and also for the life to c. 1Tm 4:8
Until I c, give your attention 1Tm 4:13
From these c envy, quarreling, 1Tm 6:4
foundation for the age to c, 1Tm 6:19
Then they may c to their senses 2Tm 2:26
times will c in the last days. 2Tm 3:1
never able to c to a knowledge 2Tm 3:7
the time will c when they will 2Tm 4:3
every effort to c to me soon, 2Tm 4:9
When you c, bring the cloak I 2Tm 4:13
every effort to c before winter. 2Tm 4:21
every effort to c to me in Ti 3:12
the world to c that we are Heb 2:5
save those who c to God through Heb 7:25
of the good things that have c. Heb 9:11
shadow of the good things to c, Heb 10:1
See, I have c—it is written Heb 10:7
See, I have c to do Your will. Heb 10:9
Coming One will c and not delay. Heb 10:37
and Esau concerning things to c. Heb 11:20
you have not c to what could be Heb 12:18
you have c to Mount Zion, to Heb 12:22
instead, we seek the one to c. Heb 13:14
of the same mouth c blessing and Jms 3:10
does not c down from above Jms 3:15
Don't they c from the cravings Jms 4:1
C now, you who say, "Today or Jms 4:13
C now, you rich people! Jms 5:1
that would c to you searched 1Pt 1:10
the time has c for judgment to 1Pt 4:17
scoffers will c in the last days 2Pt 3:3
but all to c to repentance. 2Pt 3:9
of the Lord will c like a thief; 2Pt 3:10
sure that we have c to know Him: 1Jn 2:3
says, "I have c to know Him," 1Jn 2:4
you have c to know the One 1Jn 2:13
because you have c to know the 1Jn 2:14
you have c to know the One 1Jn 2:14
now many antichrists have c. 1Jn 2:18
is how we have c to know love: 1Jn 3:16
Christ has c in the flesh is 1Jn 4:2
And we have c to know and to 1Jn 4:16
Son of God has c and has given 1Jn 5:20
all who have c to know the truth 2Jn 1
is why, if I c, I will remind 3Jn 10
long ago, have c in by stealth; Jd 4
I will c to you and remove your Rv 2:5
will c to you quickly and fight Rv 2:16
on to what you have until I c. Rv 2:25
alert, I will c like a thief, Rv 3:3
what hour I will c against you. Rv 3:3
will make them c and bow down at Rv 3:9
is going to c over the whole Rv 3:10
I will c in to him and have Rv 3:20
trumpet said, "C up here, and I Rv 4:1
with a voice like thunder, "C!" Rv 6:1
second living creature say, "C!" Rv 6:3
third living creature say, "C!" Rv 6:5
fourth living creature say, "C!" Rv 6:7
great day of Their wrath has c! Rv 6:17
and where did they c from?" Rv 7:13
two more woes to c after this. Rv 9:12
saying to them, "C up here." Rv 11:12
angry, but Your wrath has c. Rv 11:18
The time has c for the dead to Rv 11:18
the time has c to destroy those Rv 11:18
of His Messiah have now c, Rv 12:10
the Devil has c down to you with Rv 12:12
causing fire to c down from Rv 13:13
the hour of His judgment has c. Rv 14:7
for the time to reap has c, Rv 14:15
the nations will c and worship Rv 15:4
C, I will show you the judgment Rv 17:1
and is about to c up from the Rv 17:8
other has not yet c, and when he Rv 17:10
C out of her, My people, so that Rv 18:4
her plagues will c in one day— Rv 18:8
single hour your judgment has c. Rv 18:10
the marriage of the Lamb has c, Rv 19:7
in mid-heaven, "C, gather Rv 19:17
the dead did not c to life until Rv 20:5
C, I will show you the bride, Rv 21:9
Spirit and the bride say, "C!" Rv 22:17
who hears should say, "C!" Rv 22:17
the one who is thirsty should c. Rv 22:17
quickly." Amen! C, Lord Jesus! Rv 22:20

COMES *(254)*

who c from your own body will Gn 15:4
the virgin who c out to draw Gn 24:43
If Esau c to one camp and Gn 32:8
another, "Here c that dreamer! Gn 37:19
your youngest brother c here. Gn 42:15
right it is c and the obedience Gn 49:10
When God c to your aid, you are Gn 50:25
a dispute, it c to me, and I Ex 18:16
that the mesh c halfway up the Ex 27:5
whenever he c before the LORD. Ex 28:30
the priest c and examines it Lv 14:48
If a woman c near any animal and Lv 20:16
to the LORD c in the first month Lv 23:5
ninth year when its harvest c Lv 25:22
person who c near ⌊it⌋ must be Nm 1:51
who c near ⌊the sanctuary⌋ Nm 3:10
of jealousy c over the husband Nm 5:14
of jealousy c over him and he Nm 5:14
of jealousy c over a husband Nm 5:30
until it c out of your nostrils Nm 11:20
eaten away when he c out of his Nm 12:12
Anyone who c near the LORD's Nm 17:13
who c near ⌊the sanctuary⌋ Nm 18:7
One who c from Jacob will rule; Nm 24:19
to the LORD c in the first month Nm 28:16
When the Jubilee c for the Nm 36:4
every word that c from the mouth Dt 8:3
he has promised you c about, Dt 13:2
your brother c looking for it; Dt 22:2
with her, and c to hate her, Dt 22:13
to do whatever c from your lips, Dt 23:23
afterbirth that c out from Dt 28:57
foreigner who c from a distant Dt 29:22
If a man c and asks you, 'Is Jdg 4:20
whatever c out of the doors of Jdg 11:31
eat anything that c from the Jdg 13:14
you where his great strength c Jdg 16:5
When that day c, you will cry 1Sm 8:18
eat until he c because he must 1Sm 9:13
coming out? He c to defy Israel. 1Sm 17:25
'Wickedness c from wicked 1Sm 24:13
When your time c and you rest 2Sm 7:12
When your father c to see you, 2Sm 13:5
until word c from you to inform 2Sm 15:28
he c with good news," the king 2Sm 18:27
and he c to take an oath before 1Kg 8:31
he c, he can stay there. 2Kg 4:10
When this letter c to you, 2Kg 5:6
the messenger c, shut the door 2Kg 6:32
When your time c to be with your 1Ch 17:11
For everything c from You, 1Ch 29:14
You only what c from Your own 1Ch 29:14
Your holy name c from Your hand 1Ch 29:16
an oath and he c to take an oath 2Ch 6:22
when he c and prays toward this 2Ch 6:32
Whoever c to ordain himself with 2Ch 13:9
dispute that c to you from your 2Ch 19:10
If disaster c on us—sword or 2Ch 20:9
multitude that c ⌊to fight⌋ 2Ch 20:12
your strength ⌊c from⌋ rejoicing Neh 8:10
I have no rest, for trouble c. Jb 3:26
not fear destruction when it c. Jb 5:21
understanding c with long life. Jb 12:12
Let whatever c happen to me. Jb 13:13
my struggle until my relief c. Jb 14:14
his cry when distress c on him? Jb 27:9
and what benefit c to me, if I Jb 35:3
rumbling that c from His mouth. Jb 37:2
Then there c a roaring sound; Jb 37:4
windstorm c from its chamber, Jb 37:9
Yet out of the north He c, Jb 37:22
His trouble c back on his own Ps 7:16
When one ⌊of them⌋ c to visit, Ps 41:6
my salvation c from Him. Ps 62:1
my soul, for my hope c from Him. Ps 62:5
Blessed is he who c in the name Ps 118:26
My help c from the LORD, the Ps 121:2
your calamity c like a whirlwind Pr 1:27
ruin of the wicked when it c, Pr 3:25
of the wicked c to nothing. Pr 10:28
When pride c, disgrace follows, Pr 11:2
but with humility c wisdom. Pr 11:2
his expectation c to nothing, Pr 11:7
an abundant harvest ⌊c⌋ through Pr 14:4
but knowledge ⌊c⌋ easily to the Pr 14:6
and humility c before honor. Pr 15:33
Pride c before destruction, Pr 16:18
a wicked man c, shame does also Pr 18:3
but before honor c humility. Pr 18:12
until another c and Pr 18:17
but victory c from the LORD. Pr 21:31
victory c with many counselors. Pr 24:6
goes and a generation c, Ec 1:4
be like who c after the king? Ec 2:12
that one fate c to them both. Ec 2:14
it to the man who c after me. Ec 2:18
exactly as he c, so he will go. Ec 5:16
For he c in futility and he goes Ec 6:4
be many. All that c is futile. Ec 11:8
Here he c, leaping over the Sg 2:8
case never c before them." Is 1:23
devastation c from far away? Is 10:3
from its egg c a flying serpent Is 14:29
himself out and c to his Is 16:12
the Negev, it c from the desert, Is 21:1
This also c from the LORD of Is 28:29
Look, Yahweh c from far away, Is 30:27
⌊He c⌋ to sift the nations in a Is 30:28
world and all that c from it. Is 34:1
the Lord GOD c with strength, Is 40:10
the earth and what c from it, Is 42:5
so My word that c from My mouth Is 55:11
falsehood c from the hills, Jr 3:23
⌊It c⌋ not to winnow or to sift; Jr 4:11
strong for this c at My call. Jr 4:12
see when good c but dwells Jr 17:6
it doesn't fear when heat c, Jr 17:8
the time for his own land c, Jr 27:7
word of the prophet c true will Jr 28:9
A people c from the north. Jr 50:41
for no one c to the appointed Lm 1:4
our wood c at a price. Lm 5:4
and then c to the prophet, Ezk 14:4
and then c to the prophet to Ezk 14:7
this will not happen until He c; Ezk 21:27
its proud strength c to an end Ezk 30:18

and the sword **c** and takes him Ezk 33:4
and the sword **c** and takes away Ezk 33:6
message is that **c** from the LORD! Ezk 33:30
Yet when it **c**—and it will Ezk 33:33
day when Gog **c** against the land Ezk 38:18
because the water ⌊**c**⌋ from the Ezk 47:12
the North who **c** against him will Dn 11:16
like an eagle **c** against the Hs 8:1
the LORD until He **c** and sends Hs 10:12
when the time **c**, he will not be Hs 13:13
pine tree; your fruit **c** from Me. Hs 14:8
awe-inspiring Day of the LORD **c**. Jl 2:31
those the house of Israel **c** to. Am 6:1
a man of spirit **c** and invents Mc 2:11
justice **c** out perverted. Hab 1:4
God **c** from Teman, the Holy One Hab 3:3
and awesome Day of the LORD **c**. Mal 4:5
every word that **c** from the mouth Mt 4:4
and he **c**; and to my slave, Mt 8:9
Israel before the Son of Man **c**. Mt 10:23
unclean spirit **c** out of a man, Mt 12:43
the evil one **c** and snatches away Mt 13:19
or persecution **c** because of the Mt 13:21
but what **c** out of the mouth, Mt 15:11
what **c** out of the mouth comes Mt 15:18
of the mouth **c** from the heart, Mt 15:18
When evening **c** you say, 'It will Mt 16:2
catch the first fish that **c** up. Mt 17:27
that man by whom the offense **c**. Mt 18:7
Blessed is He who **c** in the name Mt 21:9
the owner of the vineyard **c**, Mt 21:40
Blessed is He who **c** in the name Mt 23:39
as the lightning **c** from the east Mt 24:27
working when he **c** will be Mt 24:46
the Son of Man **c** in His glory, Mt 25:31
see if Elijah **c** to save Him!" Mt 27:49
outside, everything **c** in Mk 4:11
Satan **c** and takes away Mk 4:15
or persecution **c** because of the Mk 4:17
c up and grows taller than all Mk 4:32
He said, "What **c** out of a person Mk 7:20
of him when He **c** in the glory of Mk 8:38
Blessed is He who **c** in the name Mk 11:9
if Elijah **c** to take Him down! Mk 15:36
someone is like who **c** to Me, Lk 6:47
and he **c**; and to my slave, Lk 7:8
Then the Devil **c** and takes away Lk 8:12
him when He **c** in His glory and Lk 9:26
unclean spirit **c** out of a man, Lk 11:24
where no thief **c** near and no Lk 12:33
so that when he **c** and knocks, Lk 12:36
alert when he **c** will be blessed. Lk 12:37
If he **c** in the middle of the Lk 12:38
working when he **c** will be Lk 12:43
until the time **c** when you say, Lk 13:35
Blessed is He who **c** in the name Lk 13:35
when the one who invited you **c**, Lk 14:10
If anyone **c** to Me and does not Lk 14:26
the one who **c** against him with Lk 14:31
and **c** back to you seven times, Lk 17:4
to him when he **c** in from the Lk 17:7
the Son of Man **c**, will He find Lk 18:8
is the King who **c** in the name of Lk 19:38
until the kingdom of God **c**." Lk 22:18
'After me **c** a man who has Jn 1:30
know where it **c** from or where it Jn 3:8
by the truth **c** to the light, Jn 3:21
One who **c** from above is above Jn 3:31
The One who **c** from heaven is Jn 3:31
When He **c**, He will explain Jn 4:25
months, then **c** the harvest'? Jn 4:35
someone else **c** in his own name Jn 5:43
the glory that **c** from the only Jn 5:44
the One who **c** down from heaven Jn 6:33
No one who **c** to Me will ever be Jn 6:35
and the one who **c** to Me I will Jn 6:37
from the Father **c** to Me— Jn 6:45
the bread that **c** down from Jn 6:50
that it **c** from Moses but from Jn 7:22
When the Messiah **c**, nobody will Jn 7:27
When the Messiah **c**, He won't Jn 7:31
that the Messiah **c** from David's Jn 7:42
A thief **c** only to steal and to Jn 10:10
Blessed is He who **c** in the name Jn 12:13
No one **c** to the Father except Jn 14:6
the Counselor **c**, the One I will Jn 15:26
when their time **c** you may Jn 16:4
When He **c**, He will convict the Jn 16:8
When the Spirit of truth **c**, Jn 16:13
remarkable day of the Lord **c**; Ac 2:20
the faith that **c** through Him has Ac 3:16
Lysias the commander **c** down, Ac 24:22
obtained help that **c** from God, Ac 26:22
the law ⌊**c**⌋ the knowledge Rm 3:20
righteousness that **c** by faith. Rm 4:13
righteousness that **c** from faith. Rm 9:30
that **c** from faith speaks Rm 10:6
So faith **c** from what is heard, Rm 10:17
and what is heard **c** through the Rm 10:17
not welcome what **c** from God's 1Co 2:14
before the Lord **c**, who will both 1Co 4:5
man, so man **c** through woman, 1Co 11:12
the Lord's death until He **c**. 1Co 11:26
when the perfect **c**, the partial 1Co 13:10
or uninformed person **c** 1Co 14:24
the dead also **c** through a man. 1Co 15:21
Then **c** the end, when He hands 1Co 15:24
If Timothy **c**, see that he has 1Co 16:10
For if a person **c** and preaches 2Co 11:4
righteousness **c** through the law Gl 2:21
that ⌊**c**⌋ through Jesus Php 1:11
wrath **c** on the disobedient, Col 3:6
if he **c** to you, welcome him), Col 4:10
sudden destruction **c** on them, 1Th 5:3
day when He **c** to be glorified 2Th 1:10
the apostasy **c** first and the man 2Th 2:3
righteousness that **c** by faith. Heb 11:7
If he **c** soon enough, he will be Heb 13:23
suppose a man **c** into your Jms 2:2
dressed in dirty clothes also **c** Jms 2:2
of Scripture **c** from one's own 2Pt 1:20
because no lie **c** from the truth. 1Jn 2:21
If anyone **c** to you and does not 2Jn 10
The Lord **c** with thousands of His Jd 14
which **c** down out of heaven from Rv 3:12
fire **c** from their mouths and Rv 11:5
the beast that **c** up out of the Rv 11:7
and when he **c**, he must remain Rv 17:10

COMFORT *(49)*

and daughters tried to **c** him, Gn 37:35
and his relatives came to **c** him. 1Ch 7:22
and offer sympathy and **c** to him. Jb 2:11
It would still bring me **c**, Jb 6:10
My bed will **c** me, and my couch Jb 7:13
can you offer me such futile **c**? Jb 21:34
sympathy and **c** concerning all Jb 42:11
rod and Your staff—they **c** me. Ps 23:4
my honor and **c** me once again. Ps 71:21
cares, Your **c** brings me joy. Ps 94:19
This is my **c** in my affliction: Ps 119:50
from long ago and find **c**. Ps 119:52
May Your faithful love **c** me, Ps 119:76
I ask, "When will You **c** me?" Ps 119:82
son, and he will give you **c**; Pr 29:17
they have no one to **c** them. Ec 4:1
they have no one to **c** them. Ec 4:1
Do not try to **c** me about the Is 22:4
"**C**, comfort My people," says Is 40:1
"Comfort, **c** My people," says Is 40:1
For the LORD will **c** Zion; Is 51:3
He will **c** all her waste places, Is 51:3
grieve for you? How can I **c** you? Is 51:19
will lead him and **c** him and his Is 57:18
vengeance; to **c** all who mourn, Is 61:2
son, so I will **c** you, and you Is 66:13
for the mourner to **c** him because Jr 16:7
There is no one to offer her **c**, Lm 1:2
there was no one to **c** her. Lm 1:9
is no one nearby to **c** ⌊me⌋, Lm 1:16
there is no one to **c** her. Lm 1:17
but there is no one to **c** me. Lm 1:21
can I find anyone to **c** you? Nah 3:7
will once more **c** Zion and again Zch 1:17
empty dreams and offer empty **c**. Zch 10:2
you have received your **c**. Lk 6:24
and Mary to **c** them about their Jn 11:19
of mercies and the God of all **c**. 2Co 1:3
may be able to **c** those who are 2Co 1:4
through the **c** we ourselves 2Co 1:4
so our **c** overflows through 2Co 1:5
it is for your **c** and salvation; 2Co 1:6
it is for your **c**, which is 2Co 1:6
so you will share in the **c**. 2Co 1:7
forgive and **c** him instead; 2Co 2:7
but also by the **c** he received 2Co 7:7
addition to our **c**, we were made 2Co 7:13
and they have been a **c** to me. Col 4:11
who are lazy, **c** the discouraged, 1Th 5:14

COMFORTABLE *(2)*

plenty of food, and **c** security, Ezk 16:49
My people out of their **c** homes, Mc 2:9

COMFORTABLY *(1)*

the men who settle down **c**, Zph 1:12

COMFORTED *(22)*

and he was **c** after his mother's Gn 24:67
him, but he refused to be **c**. Gn 37:35
And he **c** them and spoke kindly Gn 50:21
for you have **c** and encouraged Ru 2:13
Then David **c** his wife Bathsheba; 2Sm 12:24
I refused to be **c**. Ps 77:2
You, LORD, have helped and **c** me. Ps 86:17
For the LORD has **c** His people, Is 49:13
For the LORD has **c** His people; Is 52:9
and not **c**, I will set your Is 54:11
and you will be **c** in Jerusalem. Is 66:13
to be **c** for her children Jr 31:15
of all you did when you **c** them. Ezk 16:54
of Lebanon, were **c** in the Ezk 31:16
see them and be **c** over all his Ezk 32:31
mourn, because they will be **c**. Mt 5:4
but now he is **c** here, while you Lk 16:25
home alive and were greatly **c**. Ac 20:12
if we are **c**, it is for your 2Co 1:6
c us by the coming of Titus, 2Co 7:6
For this reason we have been **c**. 2Co 7:13
we encouraged, **c**, and implored 1Th 2:12

COMFORTERS *(2)*

You are all miserable **c**. Jb 16:2
for **c**, but found no one. Ps 69:20

COMFORTING *(2)*

from her **c** breast and drink Is 66:11
with kind and **c** words to the Zch 1:13

COMFORTS *(5)*

like one who **c** those who mourn. Jb 29:25
I—I am the One who **c** you. Is 51:12
As a mother **c** her son, so I will Is 66:13
He **c** us in all our affliction, 2Co 1:4
But God, who **c** the humble, 2Co 7:6

COMING *(310)*

of the town are **c** out to draw Gn 24:13
c with a jug on her shoulder. Gn 24:15
there was Rebekah **c** with her jug Gn 24:45
and looking up, he saw camels **c**. Gn 24:63
man in the field **c** to meet us?" Gn 24:65
Rachel, **c** with his sheep. Gn 29:6
he is **c** to meet you—and he has Gn 32:6
and saw Esau **c** toward him with Gn 33:1
of Ishmaelites **c** from Gilead. Gn 37:25
and good, **c** up on one stalk. Gn 41:22
abundance are **c** throughout the Gn 41:29
these good years that are **c**, Gn 41:35
saw the Egyptians **c** after them. Ex 14:10
am **c** to you with your wife and Ex 18:6
Moses delayed in **c** down from Ex 32:1
edible food **c** into contact with Lv 11:34
brother by **c** near his wife to Lv 18:14
that Israel was **c** on the Atharim Nm 21:1
nothing keep you from **c** to me, Nm 22:16
Balak heard that Balaam was **c**, Nm 22:36
heard the Israelites were **c**. Nm 33:40
and their doom is **c** quickly." Dt 32:35
spies saw a man **c** out of the Jdg 1:24
Why is his chariot so long in **c**? Jdg 5:28
people are **c** down from the Jdg 9:36
people are **c** down from the Jdg 9:37
and one unit is **c** from the Jdg 9:37
people were **c** out of the city Jdg 9:43
c out to meet him with Jdg 11:34
said to him, "Look, night is **c**. Jdg 19:9
the days are **c** when I will cut 1Sm 2:31
some young women **c** out to draw 1Sm 9:11
they saw Samuel **c** toward them on 1Sm 9:14
group of prophets **c** down from 1Sm 10:5
then Saul was **c** in from the 1Sm 11:5
the Ammonites was **c** against you, 1Sm 12:12
the Hebrews are **c** out of the 1Sm 14:11
way as they were **c** out of Egypt. 1Sm 15:2
see this man who keeps **c** out? 1Sm 17:25
David and his men **c** toward her 1Sm 25:20
a spirit form **c** up out of the 1Sm 28:13
An old man is **c** up," she replied 1Sm 28:14
many people **c** from the road 2Sm 13:34

house of Saul was just c out. 2Sm 16:5
and his servants c toward him, 2Sm 24:20
wife is c soon to ask you 1Kg 14:5
as a man's hand c from the sea." 1Kg 18:44
the creditor is c to take my two 2Kg 4:1
son of Rechab ⌊c⌋ to meet him. 2Kg 10:15
those c on duty on the Sabbath 2Kg 11:9
your going out and your c in, 2Kg 19:27
for He is c to judge the earth. 1Ch 16:33
going or c—to Judah's King 2Ch 16:1
repay us by c to drive us out 2Ch 20:11
will see them c up the ascent 2Ch 20:16
and Levites who are c on duty on 2Ch 23:4
those c on duty on the Sabbath 2Ch 23:8
to those c from the war. 2Ch 28:12
because they are c to kill you. Neh 6:10
They are c to kill you tonight! Neh 6:10
relatives stop c by, and my Jb 19:14
like a groom c from the bridal Ps 19:5
He sees that his day is c. Ps 37:13
Our God is c; He will not be Ps 50:3
and majestic ⌊c down⌋ from the Ps 76:4
LORD, for He is c—for He is Ps 96:13
for He is c to judge the earth. Ps 96:13
for He is c to judge the earth. Ps 98:9
protect your c and going both Ps 121:8
What is this c up from the Sg 3:6
shorn ⌊sheep⌋ c up from washing, Sg 4:2
flock of ewes c up from washing Sg 6:6
Who is this c up from the Sg 8:5
of Hosts is ⌊c⌋ against all that Is 2:12
the king of Assyria ⌊is c⌋. Is 7:17
They are c from a far land, Is 13:5
the day of the LORD is c— Is 13:9
below is eager to greet your c. Is 14:9
of dust is c from the north, Is 14:31
a swift cloud and is c to Egypt. Is 19:1
the LORD is c from His place to Is 26:21
God; vengeance is c. God's Is 35:4
God's retribution is c; Is 35:4
your going out and your c in, Is 37:28
Tell us the c events, then we Is 41:23
even now it is c. Do you not see Is 43:19
these gods declare the c things, Is 44:7
for My salvation is c soon, Is 56:1
salvation is c, His reward is Is 62:11
Who is this c from Edom in Is 63:1
Here we are, c to You, for You Jr 3:22
who besiege are c from a distant Jr 4:16
wounds keep c to My attention Jr 6:7
an army is c from a northern Jr 6:22
Days are c"—the LORD's Jr 7:32
"The days are c"—the LORD's Jr 9:25
A noise—it is c—a great Jr 10:22
and see those c from the north. Jr 13:20
The days are c"—the LORD's Jr 16:14
The days are c"—⌊this is⌋ the Jr 19:6
"The days are c"—⌊this is⌋ the Jr 23:5
The days are c"—the LORD's Jr 23:7
cities that are c to worship Jr 26:2
who are c to Zedekiah king Jr 27:3
for the days are certainly c"— Jr 30:3
"The days are c"—⌊this is⌋ the Jr 31:27
Look, the days are c"—⌊this Jr 31:31
the days are c"—the LORD's Jr 31:38
Shallum, is c to you to say: Jr 32:7
The people c to fight the Jr 33:5
Look, the days are c"—⌊this Jr 33:14
Judeans who are c from their Jr 36:6
and all those c in from Judah's Jr 36:9
about the c of Nebuchadnezzar Jr 46:13
from the north is c against her. Jr 46:20
of their calamity is c on them, Jr 46:21
the day that is c to destroy all Jr 47:4
Baldness is c to Gaza. Jr 47:5
look, the days are c—⌊this is⌋ Jr 48:12
look, the days are c—⌊this is⌋ Jr 49:2
will be like a lion c up from Jr 49:19
will be like a lion c up from Jr 50:44
days are c when I will punish Jr 51:47
look, the days are c—⌊this is⌋ Jr 51:52
a destroyer is c against her, Jr 51:56
a whirlwind c from the north, Ezk 1:4
with lightning c out of it. Ezk 1:13
one disaster after another is c! Ezk 7:5
against you. Look, it is c! Ezk 7:6
Look, the day is c! Doom has Ezk 7:10
Anguish is c! They will seek Ezk 7:25

And I saw six men c from the Ezk 9:2
Are you c to consult Me? Ezk 20:3
Because of the news that is c. Ezk 21:7
it is c and it will happen." Ezk 21:7
It is c, and I will do it! Ezk 24:14
doom⌋. For indeed it is c." Ezk 30:9
sees the sword c against the Ezk 33:3
the sword c but doesn't blow Ezk 33:6
you will advance, c like a Ezk 38:9
it is c, and it will happen. Ezk 39:8
God of Israel c from the east. Ezk 43:2
The water was c down from under Ezk 47:1
a holy one, c down from heaven. Dn 4:13
c down from heaven and saying, Dn 4:23
fire was flowing, c out from His Dn 7:10
a son of man c with the clouds Dn 7:13
c from the west across the Dn 8:5
The people of the c prince will Dn 9:26
for the Day of the LORD is c; Jl 2:1
the days are c when you will be Am 4:2
The days are c—⌊this is⌋ the Am 8:11
The days are c—the LORD's Am 9:13
His place and c down to trample Mc 1:3
day of⌋ your punishment, is c; Mc 7:4
scatters is c up against you. Nah 2:1
asked, "What are they c to do?" Zch 1:21
for I am c to dwell among you"— Zch 2:10
He is c from His holy dwelling. Zch 2:13
four chariots c from between two Zch 6:1
them, with no one c or going. Zch 7:14
See, your King is c to you; Zch 9:9
of the LORD is c when your Zch 14:1
see, He is c," says the LORD Mal 3:1
who can endure the day of His c? Mal 3:2
the day is c, burning like Mal 4:1
The c day will consume them," Mal 4:1
and Sadducees c to the place of Mt 3:7
you to flee from the c wrath? Mt 3:7
One who is c after me is more Mt 3:11
like a dove and c down on Him. Mt 3:16
Son of Man c in His kingdom." Mt 16:28
As they were c down from the Mt 17:9
Elijah is c and will restore Mt 17:11
try to keep them from c to Me, Mt 19:14
your King is c to you, gentle, Mt 21:5
sign of Your c and of the end Mt 24:3
so will be the c of the Son of Mt 24:27
the Son of Man c on the clouds Mt 24:30
so the c of the Son of Man will Mt 24:37
is the way the c of the Son of Mt 24:39
know what day your Lord is c. Mt 24:42
known what time the thief was c, Mt 24:43
Son of Man is c at an hour you Mt 24:44
of the Power and c on the clouds Mt 26:64
The whole crowd was c to Him, Mk 2:13
many people were c and going, Mk 6:31
As they were c down from the Mk 9:9
a crowd was rapidly c together, Mk 9:25
Blessed is the c kingdom of our Mk 11:10
the Son of Man c in clouds with Mk 13:26
don't know when the time is ⌊c⌋. Mk 13:33
the master of the house is c— Mk 13:35
the Power and c with the clouds Mk 14:62
They forced a man c in from the Mk 15:21
save Yourself by c down from the Mk 15:30
you to flee from the c wrath? Lk 3:7
One is c who is more powerful Lk 3:16
demons were c out of many, Lk 4:41
After c down with them, He stood Lk 6:17
because power was c out from Him Lk 6:19
the days were c to a close for Lk 9:51
at what hour the thief was c, Lk 12:39
Son of Man is c at an hour that Lk 12:40
'My master is delaying his c,' Lk 12:45
A storm is c,' and so it does Lk 12:54
and c home, he calls his friends Lk 15:6
of the estate I have c to me.' Lk 15:12
of God is not c with something Lk 17:20
The days are c when you will Lk 17:22
in that town kept c to him, Lk 18:3
me out by her persistent c.' " Lk 18:5
things that are c on the world, Lk 21:26
the Son of Man c in a cloud with Lk 21:27
about Me is c to its fulfillment Lk 22:37
who was c in from the country, Lk 23:26
the days are c when they will Lk 23:29
everyone, was c into the world. Jn 1:9
'The One c after me has Jn 1:15

He is the One c after me, whose Jn 1:27
day John saw Jesus c toward him Jn 1:29
saw Nathanael c toward Him and Jn 1:47
were c and being baptized, Jn 3:23
an hour is c when you will Jn 4:21
But an hour is c, and is now Jn 4:23
"I know that Messiah is c" Jn 4:25
up, but while I'm c, someone Jn 5:7
An hour is c, and is now here, Jn 5:25
a time is c when all who are Jn 5:28
a huge crowd c toward Him, Jn 6:5
He was c near the boat, and they Jn 6:19
all the people were c to Him. Jn 8:2
Night is c when no one can work. Jn 9:4
runs away when he sees a wolf c. Jn 10:12
Martha heard that Jesus was c, Jn 11:20
that Jesus was c to Jerusalem, Jn 12:12
your King is c, sitting on a Jn 12:15
you as orphans; I am c to you. Jn 14:18
going away and I am c to you.' Jn 14:28
the ruler of the world is c. Jn 14:30
time is c when anyone who kills Jn 16:2
time is c when I will no longer Jn 16:25
An hour is c, and has come, when Jn 16:32
in the world, and I am c to You. Jn 17:11
Now I am c to You, and I speak Jn 17:13
"We're c with you," they told Jn 21:3
beforehand the c of the Ac 7:52
named Ananias c in and placing Ac 9:12
Saul was c and going with them Ac 9:28
"Don't delay in c with us." Ac 9:38
and an object c down that Ac 10:11
you did the right thing in c. Ac 10:33
an object c down that resembled Ac 11:5
Someone is c after me, and I am Ac 13:25
now at last succeed in c to you. Rm 1:10
He is a prototype of the C One. Rm 5:14
many times from c to you. Rm 15:22
this age, who are c to nothing. 1Co 2:6
as though I were not c to you. 1Co 4:18
afterward, at His c, the people 1Co 15:23
anything as c from ourselves, 2Co 3:5
comforted us by the c of Titus, 2Co 7:6
and not only by his c, but also 2Co 7:7
is the third time I am c to you. 2Co 13:1
until the c faith was revealed. Gl 3:23
so that in the c ages He might Eph 2:7
God's wrath is c on the Eph 5:6
who rescues us from the c wrath. 1Th 1:10
of our Lord Jesus at His c? 1Th 2:19
Father at the c of our Lord 1Th 3:13
at the Lord's c will certainly 1Th 4:15
for the c of our Lord Jesus 1Th 5:23
concerning the c of our Lord 2Th 2:1
with the brightness of His c. 2Th 2:8
The c ⌊of the lawless one⌋ is 2Th 2:9
and the powers of the c age, Heb 6:5
the days are c," says the Lord, Heb 8:8
as He was c into the world, Heb 10:5
the C One will come and not Heb 10:37
c down from the Father of lights; Jms 1:17
the miseries that are c on you. Jms 5:1
be patient until the Lord's c. Jms 5:7
because the Lord's c is near. Jms 5:8
C to Him, a living stone— 1Pt 2:4
the power and c of our Lord 2Pt 1:16
Where is the promise of His c? 2Pt 3:4
desire the c of the day of God, 2Pt 3:12
Antichrist is c," even now many 1Jn 2:18
be ashamed before Him at His c. 1Jn 2:28
you have heard that he is c, 1Jn 4:3
confess the c of Jesus Christ 2Jn 7
who is, who was, and who is c; Rv 1:4
He is c with the clouds, and Rv 1:7
and who is c, the Almighty." Rv 1:8
I am c quickly. Hold on to what Rv 3:11
who was, who is, and who is c. Rv 4:8
are the ones c out of the great Rv 7:14
mighty angel c down from heaven, Rv 10:1
the third woe is c quickly! Rv 11:14
I saw a beast c up out of the Rv 13:1
another beast c up out of the Rv 13:11
like frogs ⌊c⌋ from the dragon's Rv 16:13
Look, I am c like a thief. Rv 16:15
great authority c down from Rv 18:1
saw an angel c down from heaven Rv 20:1
c down out of heaven from God, Rv 21:2
c down out of heaven from God, Rv 21:10

Look, I am **c** quickly! Rv 22:7
I am **c** quickly, and My reward is Rv 22:12
says, "Yes, I am **c** quickly." Rv 22:20

COMMAND *(227)*

so that he will **c** his children Gn 18:19
because you have obeyed My **c**." Gn 22:18
he died your father gave a **c**: Gn 50:16
You must say whatever I **c** you; Ex 7:2
Keep this **c** permanently as a Ex 12:24
next according to the LORD's **c**. Ex 17:1
about all that I **c** you regarding Ex 25:22
You are to **c** the Israelites to Ex 27:20
Observe what I **c** you today. Ex 34:11
that was recorded at Moses' **c**. Ex 38:21
regard to the **c** becomes known, Lv 4:14
C Aaron and his sons: Lv 6:9
C the Israelites to bring you Lv 24:2
at the LORD's **c** was 22,000. Nm 3:39
done⌋ at the **c** of Aaron and his Nm 4:27
at the LORD's **c** through Moses. Nm 4:37
At the LORD's **c** Moses and Aaron Nm 4:41
at the LORD's **c** through Moses. Nm 4:45
At the LORD's **c** they were Nm 4:49
C the Israelites to send away Nm 5:2
At the LORD's **c** the Israelites Nm 9:18
and at the LORD's **c** they camped. Nm 9:18
at the LORD's **c** and set out at Nm 9:20
and set out at the LORD's **c**. Nm 9:20
They camped at the LORD's **c**, Nm 9:23
they set out at the LORD's **c**. Nm 9:23
to His **c** through Moses. Nm 9:23
to the LORD's **c** through Moses. Nm 10:13
of Paran at the LORD's **c**. Nm 13:3
you going against the LORD's **c**? Nm 14:41
LORD's word and broken His **c**; Nm 15:31
against My **c** at the waters Nm 20:24
go against the **c** of the LORD my Nm 22:18
indeed received ⌊a **c**⌋ to bless; Nm 23:20
not go against the LORD's **c**, Nm 24:13
against My **c** to show My holiness Nm 27:14
out and come back in at his **c**." Nm 27:21
C the Israelites and say to Nm 28:2
of the fighting men under our **c**, Nm 31:49
the LORD's **c**, Moses wrote down Nm 33:2
the LORD's **c**, Aaron the priest Nm 33:38
C the Israelites and say to Nm 34:2
C the Israelites to give cities Nm 35:2
against the **c** of the LORD your Dt 1:26
the LORD's **c** and defiantly went Dt 1:43
C the people: You are about to Dt 2:4
anything to what I **c** you or take Dt 4:2
and I will tell you every **c**— Dt 5:31
This is the **c**—the statutes and Dt 6:1
So keep the **c**—the statutes and Dt 7:11
follow every **c** I am giving you Dt 8:1
God by failing to keep His **c**— Dt 8:11
against the **c** of the LORD your Dt 9:23
Keep every **c** I am giving you Dt 11:8
from the path I **c** you today Dt 11:28
Bring there everything I **c** you: Dt 12:11
you must do everything I **c** you. Dt 12:14
obey all these things I **c** you, Dt 12:28
to do everything I **c** you; Dt 12:32
I am giving you this **c** today. Dt 15:15
turn from this **c** to the right Dt 17:20
tell them everything I **c** him. Dt 18:18
Keep every **c** I am giving you Dt 27:1
This **c** that I give you today is Dt 30:11
so that you may **c** your children Dt 32:46
words in all that you **c** him, Jos 1:18
C the priests carrying the ark Jos 3:8
and **c** them, 'Take 12 stones from Jos 4:3
C the priests who carry the ark Jos 4:16
the LORD's **c**—see ⌊that you Jos 8:8
the LORD's **c** that He had given Jos 8:27
By the LORD's **c**, they gave him Jos 19:50
the LORD's **c**, gave the Levites Jos 21:3
of the **c** of the LORD your Jos 22:3
obey the **c** and instruction Jos 22:5
to the LORD's **c** through Moses. Jos 22:9
rebel against the LORD's **c**, 1Sm 12:14
LORD and rebel against His **c**, 1Sm 12:15
not kept the **c** which the LORD 1Sm 13:13
the LORD's **c** and your words. 1Sm 15:24
our lord **c** your servants here 1Sm 16:16
put him in **c** of the soldiers 1Sm 18:5
under the **c** of his brother 2Sm 10:10
you despised the **c** of the LORD 2Sm 12:9
will issue a **c** on your behalf." 2Sm 14:8
For we heard the king **c** you, 2Sm 18:12
marched out under Abishai's **c**; 2Sm 20:7
went up in obedience to Gad's **c**, 2Sm 24:19
oath and the **c** that I gave you?" 1Kg 2:43
c that cedars from Lebanon be 1Kg 5:6
you obey all I **c** you, walk in My 1Kg 11:38
against the **c** of the LORD and 1Kg 13:21
who disobeyed the **c** of the LORD. 1Kg 13:26
King Asa gave a **c** to everyone 1Kg 15:22
these years except by my **c**!" 1Kg 17:1
according to the **c** of the man of 2Kg 5:14
the king of Assyria issued a **c**: 2Kg 17:27
for the king's **c** was, "Don't 2Kg 18:36
but at Pharaoh's **c** he taxed the 2Kg 23:35
at the LORD's **c** to remove them 2Kg 24:3
Shapham the second ⌊in **c**⌋, 1Ch 5:12
their relatives under their **c**. 1Ch 12:32
under the **c** of his brother 1Ch 19:11
the king's **c** was detestable to 1Ch 21:6
This **c** was also evil in God's 1Ch 21:7
went up at Gad's **c** spoken in the 1Ch 21:19
the people are at your every **c**." 1Ch 28:21
or if I **c** the grasshopper to 2Ch 7:13
this had been the **c** of David, 2Ch 8:14
from the king's **c** regarding the 2Ch 8:15
out the instruction and the **c**. 2Ch 14:4
At the king's **c** a chest was made 2Ch 24:8
at the king's **c** in the courtyard 2Ch 24:21
to the king's **c** by the words 2Ch 29:15
according to the **c** of David, 2Ch 29:25
For the **c** was from the LORD 2Ch 29:25
and according to the king's **c**, 2Ch 30:6
to carry out the **c** of the king 2Ch 30:12
according to the king's **c**. 2Ch 35:10
according to the **c** of David, 2Ch 35:15
to the **c** of King Josiah. 2Ch 35:16
the prophet at the LORD's **c**. 2Ch 36:12
according to the **c** of the God of Ezr 6:14
was second in **c** over the city. Neh 11:9
For there was a **c** of the king Neh 11:23
The **c** was found written in it Neh 13:1
at the king's **c** that was Est 1:12
King Ahasuerus' **c** that was Est 1:15
When the king's **c** and edict Est 2:8
you disobeying the king's **c**?" Est 3:3
on by royal **c**, and the law was Est 3:15
the king's **c** and edict came. Est 4:3
haste, at the king's urgent **c**. Est 8:14
the king's **c** and his law reached Est 8:17
The king's **c** and law went into Est 9:1
So Esther's **c** confirmed these Est 9:32
Can you **c** the clouds so that a Jb 38:34
soar at your **c** and make its nest Jb 39:27
The Lord gave the **c**; Ps 68:11
Give the **c** to save me, for You Ps 71:3
He gave a **c** to the clouds above Ps 78:23
do His word, obedient to His **c**. Ps 103:20
but Your **c** is without limit. Ps 119:96
Your **c** makes me wiser than my Ps 119:98
He sends His **c** throughout the Ps 147:15
wind that executes His **c**, Ps 148:8
your father's **c**, and don't Pr 6:20
waters would not violate His **c**, Pr 8:29
who respects a **c** will be Pr 13:13
Keep the king's **c**. Concerning an Ec 8:2
one who keeps a **c** will not Ec 8:5
I will **c** him ⌊to go⌋ against a Is 10:6
wicked with a **c** from His lips. Is 11:4
will hear this **c** behind you: Is 30:21
for the king's **c** was, "Don't Is 36:21
them everything that I **c** you. Jr 1:17
with them or **c** them concerning Jr 7:22
However, I did give them this **c**: Jr 7:23
in every way I **c** you so that it Jr 7:23
the fire, a thing I did not **c**; Jr 7:31
and do everything that I **c** you, Jr 11:4
nor did I **c** them or speak to Jr 14:14
C them ⌊to go⌋ to their masters, Jr 27:4
My name, which I did not **c** them. Jr 29:23
I am about to give the **c**"— Jr 34:22
have obeyed their ancestor's **c**. Jr 35:14
their ancestor's **c** he gave them, Jr 35:16
have obeyed the **c** of your Jr 35:18
when the LORD has given it a **c**? Jr 47:7
I have rebelled against His **c**. Lm 1:18
Since the king's **c** was so urgent Dn 3:22
the king's **c** and risked their Dn 3:28
the matter is a **c** from the holy Dn 4:17
As for the **c** to leave the tree's Dn 4:26
then gave the **c**, and those men Dn 6:24
carry out His **c** are powerful. Jl 2:11
there I will **c** the ⌊sea⌋ serpent Am 9:3
there I will **c** the sword to kill Am 9:4
for I am about to give the **c**, Am 9:9
according to the LORD's **c**. Jnh 3:3
having soldiers under my **c**. Mt 8:9
c me to come to You on the water. Mt 14:28
did Moses **c** ⌊us⌋ to give divorce Mt 19:7
When the young man heard that **c**, Mt 19:22
Disregarding the **c** of God, Mk 7:8
invalidate God's **c** in order to Mk 7:9
mute and deaf spirit, I **c** you: Mk 9:25
to them, "What did Moses **c** you?" Mk 10:3
having soldiers under my **c**. Lk 7:8
received this **c** from My Father." Jn 10:18
Me has given Me a **c** as to what I Jn 12:49
know that His **c** is eternal life Jn 12:50
This is My **c**: love one another Jn 15:12
friends if you do what I **c** you. Jn 15:14
This is what I **c** you: Jn 15:17
them and to **c** them to keep the Ac 15:5
I **c** you in the name of Jesus Ac 16:18
I **c** you by the Jesus whom Paul Ac 19:13
Festus gave the **c**, Paul was Ac 25:23
authority is opposing God's **c**, Rm 13:2
according to the **c** of the Rm 16:26
as a concession, not as a **c**. 1Co 7:6
I **c** the married—not I, but the 1Co 7:10
This is what I **c** in all the 1Co 7:17
I have no **c** from the Lord, 1Co 7:25
I write to you is the Lord's **c**. 1Co 14:37
I am not saying this as a **c**. 2Co 8:8
are doing and will do what we **c**. 2Th 3:4
Now we **c** you, brothers, in the 2Th 3:6
Now we **c** and exhort such people, 2Th 3:12
according to the **c** of God our 1Tm 1:1
so that you may **c** certain people 1Tm 1:3
C and teach these things. 1Tm 4:11
C this, so that they won't be 1Tm 5:7
with by the **c** of God our Savior: Ti 1:3
in Christ to **c** you to do what is Phm 8
based on a legal **c** concerning Heb 7:16
I am not writing you a new **c**, 1Jn 2:7
but an old **c** that you have had 1Jn 2:7
old **c** is the message you have 1Jn 2:7
Yet I am writing you a new **c**, 1Jn 2:8
Now this is His **c**: that we 1Jn 3:23
And we have this **c** from Him: 1Jn 4:21
keeping with a **c** we have 2Jn 4
if I were writing you a new **c**, 2Jn 5
This is the **c** as you have heard 2Jn 6
you have kept My **c** to endure, Rv 3:10

COMMANDED *(350)*

And the LORD God **c** the man, Gn 2:16
tree that I had **c** you not to eat Gn 3:11
the tree about which I **c** you, Gn 3:17
everything that God had **c** him. Gn 6:22
everything that the LORD **c** him. Gn 7:5
Noah, just as God had **c** him. Gn 7:9
entered just as God had **c** him. Gn 7:16
him, as God had **c** him. Gn 21:4
Jacob, blessed him, and **c** him: Gn 28:1
Isaac **c** Jacob not to marry a Gn 28:6
He **c** them, "You are to say to my Gn 32:4
Then Joseph **c** his steward: Gn 44:1
You are also **c**, 'Do this: Gn 45:19
them wagons as Pharaoh had **c**, Gn 45:21
of Rameses, as Pharaoh had **c**. Gn 47:11
Then he **c** them: "I am about to Gn 49:29
He **c** his servants who were Gn 50:2
did for him what he had **c** them. Gn 50:12
Pharaoh then **c** all his people: Ex 1:22
the signs He had **c** him ⌊to do⌋. Ex 4:28
That day Pharaoh **c** the overseers Ex 5:6
did just as the LORD **c** them. Ex 7:6
and did just as the LORD had **c**. Ex 7:10
did just as the LORD had **c**; Ex 7:20
the LORD had **c** Moses and Aaron Ex 12:28
the LORD had **c** Moses and Aaron Ex 12:50
This is what the LORD has **c**: Ex 16:16
aside until morning as Moses **c**, Ex 16:24
This is what the LORD has **c**: Ex 16:32
the LORD **c** Moses, Aaron placed Ex 16:34
words that the LORD had **c** him. Ex 19:7
As I **c** you, you are to eat Ex 23:15

something I had not **c** them. Jr 32:35
son of our ancestor Rechab, **c**: Jr 35:6
ancestor Rechab, in all he **c** us. Jr 35:8
as our ancestor Jonadab **c** us. Jr 35:10
He **c** his sons not to drink wine, Jr 35:14
and have done all that he **c** you, Jr 35:18
Then Jeremiah **c** Baruch, "I am Jr 36:5
Jeremiah the prophet had **c** him. Jr 36:8
Then the king **c** Jerahmeel the Jr 36:26
So the king **c** Ebed-melech, Jr 38:10
words to them the king had **c**, Jr 38:27
do everything I have **c** you. Jr 50:21
the prophet **c** Seraiah son Jr 51:59
"I have done as You **c** me." Ezk 9:11
After the LORD **c** the man clothed Ezk 10:6
So I did just as I was **c**. Ezk 12:7
morning I did just as I was **c**. Ezk 24:18
So I prophesied as I had been **c**. Ezk 37:7
So I prophesied as He **c** me; Ezk 37:10
nation and language, you are **c**: Dn 3:4
and he **c** some of the strongest Dn 3:20
drink wine and **c** the prophets: Am 2:12
Then the LORD **c** the fish, and it Jnh 2:10
My statutes that I **c** My servants Zch 1:6
ordinances I **c** him at Horeb for Mal 4:4
as the Lord's angel had **c** him. Mt 1:24
he **c** that it be granted because Mt 14:9
Then He **c** the crowds to sit down Mt 14:19
mountain, Jesus **c** them, "Don't Mt 17:9
back, his master **c** that he, his Mt 18:25
observe everything I have **c** you. Mt 28:20
executioner and **c** him to bring Mk 6:27
Then He **c** the crowd to sit down Mk 8:6
Then he **c** them: "Watch out! Mk 8:15
c the doorkeeper to be alert. Mk 13:34
For He had **c** the unclean spirit Lk 8:29
slave because he did what was **c**? Lk 17:9
have done all that you were **c**, Lk 17:10
Jesus stopped and **c** that he be Lk 18:40
the law Moses **c** us to stone such Jn 8:5
as the Father **c** Me, so I do. Jn 14:31
c them not to leave Jerusalem, Ac 1:4
spoke to Moses **c** him to make it Ac 7:44
you have been **c** by the Lord." Ac 10:33
He **c** us to preach to the people, Ac 10:42
And he **c** them to be baptized in Ac 10:48
this is what the Lord has **c** us: Ac 13:47
he **c** Paul to be brought in. Ac 25:6
the Lord has **c** that those who 1Co 9:14
your own hands, as we **c** you, 1Th 4:11
with you, this is what we **c** you: 2Th 3:10
covenant that God has **c** for you. Heb 9:20
they could not bear what was **c**: Heb 12:20
and love one another as He **c** us. 1Jn 3:23

COMMANDER *(85)*

with Phicol the **c** of his army, Gn 21:22
and Phicol, the **c** of his army, Gn 21:32
and Phicol the **c** of his army. Gn 26:26
have now come as **c** of the LORD's Jos 5:14
The **c** of the Lord's army said to Jos 5:15
The **c** of his forces was Sisera Jdg 4:2
will lure Sisera **c** of Jabin's Jdg 4:7
Come, be our **c**, and let's fight Jdg 11:6
over themselves as leader and **c**, Jdg 11:11
over to Sisera **c** of the army 1Sm 12:9
name of the **c** of his army was 1Sm 14:50
of cheese to the field **c**. 1Sm 17:18
asked Abner the **c** of the army, 1Sm 17:55
and made him **c** over 1,000 men. 1Sm 18:13
son of Ner, **c** of Saul's army, 2Sm 2:8
with Shobach, **c** of Hadadezer's 2Sm 10:16
down Shobach **c** of their army, 2Sm 10:18
you don't become **c** of the army 2Sm 19:13
He became their **c** even though he 2Sm 23:19
to Joab, the **c** of his army, "Go 2Sm 24:2
and Joab the **c** of the army, 1Kg 1:19
son of Ner, **c** of Israel's army 1Kg 2:32
of Jether, **c** of Judah's army. 1Kg 2:32
Edom, Joab, the **c** of the army, 1Kg 11:15
that Joab, the **c** of the army, 1Kg 11:21
His servant Zimri, **c** of half his 1Kg 16:9
Omri, the army **c**, king over 1Kg 16:16
king or to the **c** of the army?' " 2Kg 4:13
c of the army for the king of 2Kg 5:1
I have a message for you, **c**." 2Kg 9:5
He answered, "For you, **c**." 2Kg 9:5
the **c** of the guards, 2Kg 25:8
army ⌊with⌋ the **c** of the guards 2Kg 25:10
the **c** of the guards, 2Kg 25:11
the **c** of the guards left some 2Kg 25:12
c of the guards took away the 2Kg 25:15
The **c** of the guards also took 2Kg 25:18
secretary of the **c** of the army, 2Kg 25:19
the **c** of the guards, 2Kg 25:20
and became their **c** even though 1Ch 11:21
with Shophach, **c** of Hadadezer's 1Ch 19:16
killed Shophach, **c** of the army. 1Ch 19:18
The third army **c**, as chief for 1Ch 27:5
The fourth ⌊**c**⌋, for the fourth 1Ch 27:7
son Zebadiah ⌊was **c**⌋ after him; 1Ch 27:7
was the **c** Shamhuth the Izrahite; 1Ch 27:8
Joab was the **c** of the king's 1Ch 27:34
Adnah the **c** and 300,000 brave 2Ch 17:14
Jehohanan the **c** and 280,000 with 2Ch 17:15
and **c** in the camp of the king of 2Ch 32:21
Hananiah, **c** of the fortress, Neh 7:2
the **c** of 50 and the dignitary, Is 3:3
a leader and **c** for the peoples, Is 55:4
the **c** of the guards, Jr 39:9
the **c** of the guards, Jr 39:10
the **c** of the guards, Jr 52:12
army with the **c** of the guards Jr 52:14
the **c** of the guards, Jr 52:15
the **c** of the guards, Jr 52:16
c of the guards took away the Jr 52:19
The **c** of the guards also took Jr 52:24
secretary of the **c** of the army, Jr 52:25
the **c** of the guards, Jr 52:26
the **c** of the guards, Jr 52:30
the **c** of the king's guard, Dn 2:14
But a **c** will put an end to his Dn 11:18
soldiers, the **c**, and the Jewish Jn 18:12
the **c** of the temple guard, Ac 4:1
went up to the **c** of the regiment Ac 21:31
Seeing the **c** and the soldiers, Ac 21:32
the **c** came up, took him into Ac 21:33
said to the **c**, "Am I allowed Ac 21:37
the **c** ordered him to be brought Ac 22:24
he went and reported to the **c**, Ac 22:26
The **c** came and said to him, Ac 22:27
The **c** replied, "I bought this Ac 22:28
The **c** too was alarmed when he Ac 22:29
the **c** feared that Paul might be Ac 23:10
a request to the **c** that he bring Ac 23:15
Take this young man to the **c**, Ac 23:17
brought him to the **c**, and said, Ac 23:18
Then the **c** took him by the hand, Ac 23:19
So the **c** dismissed the young man Ac 23:22
But Lysias the **c** came and took Ac 24:7
When Lysias the **c** comes down, Ac 24:22

COMMANDER-IN-CHIEF *(2)*

kill a Jebusite will become **c**." 1Ch 11:6
year that the **c**, sent by Sargon Is 20:1

COMMANDERS *(98)*

c of thousands and commanders Nm 31:14
of thousands and **c** of hundreds, Nm 31:14
the **c** of thousands and of Nm 31:48
from the **c** of thousands and of Nm 31:52
the gold from the **c** of thousands Nm 31:54
appoint military **c** to lead it. Dt 20:9
to the military **c** who had Jos 10:24
So the **c** came forward and put Jos 10:24
for his use as **c** of thousands 1Sm 8:12
of thousands or **c** of fifties, 1Sm 8:12
the Philistine **c** came out to 1Sm 18:30
make all of you **c** of thousands 1Sm 22:7
of thousands and **c** of hundreds? 1Sm 22:7
Then the Philistine **c** asked, 1Sm 29:3
answered the Philistine **c**, 1Sm 29:3
The Philistine **c**, however, were 1Sm 29:4
the Philistine **c** have said, 1Sm 29:9
and appointed **c** of hundreds 2Sm 18:1
to all the **c** about Absalom. 2Sm 18:5
clear that the **c** and soldiers 2Sm 19:6
over Joab and the **c** of the army. 2Sm 24:4
So Joab and the **c** of the army 2Sm 24:4
of the king, the **c** of the army, 1Kg 1:25
did to the two **c** of Israel's 1Kg 2:5
servants, his **c**, his captains, 1Kg 9:22
and **c** of his chariots and his 1Kg 9:22
Asa and sent the **c** of his armies 1Kg 15:20
had ordered his 32 chariot **c**, 1Kg 22:31
the chariot **c** saw Jehoshaphat 1Kg 22:32
the chariot **c** saw that he was 1Kg 22:33
him and the chariot **c**, 2Kg 8:21
the army **c** were sitting there, 2Kg 9:5
you ⌊**c**⌋ wish ⌊to make me king⌋ 2Kg 9:15
brought in the **c** of hundreds, 2Kg 11:4
So the **c** of hundreds did 2Kg 11:9
gave to the **c** of hundreds King 2Kg 11:10
The **c** and the trumpeters were by 2Kg 11:14
priest ordered the **c** of hundreds 2Kg 11:15
with him⌋ the **c** of hundreds, 2Kg 11:19
his servants, his **c**, and his 2Kg 24:12
and all the **c** and all the 2Kg 24:14
When all the **c** of the armies— 2Kg 25:23
⌊The **c** included⌋ Ishmael son of 2Kg 25:23
oldest, and the **c** of the army, 2Kg 25:26
These Gadites were army **c**; 1Ch 12:14
warriors and **c** in the army. 1Ch 12:21
with 22 **c** from his own ancestral 1Ch 12:28
1,000 **c** accompanied by 37,000 1Ch 12:34
the **c** of hundreds and of 1Ch 13:1
and the **c** of the thousands went 1Ch 15:25
to Joab and the **c** of the troops, 1Ch 21:2
who were the **c** of the thousands 1Ch 26:26
the hundreds, and by the army **c**. 1Ch 26:26
the **c** of thousands and the 1Ch 27:1
thousands and the **c** of hundreds, 1Ch 27:1
of all the army **c** for the first 1Ch 27:3
the **c** of thousands and the 1Ch 28:1
thousands and the **c** of hundreds, 1Ch 28:1
the **c** of thousands and of 1Ch 29:6
to the **c** of thousands and of 2Ch 1:2
soldiers, **c** of his captains, 2Ch 8:9
and **c** of his chariots and his 2Ch 8:9
and sent the **c** of his armies to 2Ch 16:4
For Judah, the **c** of thousands: 2Ch 17:14
Aram had ordered his chariot **c**, 2Ch 18:30
the chariot **c** saw Jehoshaphat 2Ch 18:31
the chariot **c** saw that he was 2Ch 18:32
into Edom⌋ with his **c** and all 2Ch 21:9
him and the chariot **c**. 2Ch 21:9
and took the **c** of hundreds 2Ch 23:1
So the **c** of hundreds did 2Ch 23:8
gave to the **c** of hundreds King 2Ch 23:9
The **c** and the trumpeters were by 2Ch 23:13
sent out the **c** of hundreds, 2Ch 23:14
with him⌋ the **c** of hundreds, 2Ch 23:20
according to **c** of thousands, 2Ch 25:5
and according to **c** of hundreds. 2Ch 25:5
Hananiah, one of the king's **c**. 2Ch 26:11
set military **c** over the people 2Ch 32:6
them the military **c** of the king 2Ch 33:11
placed military **c** in all the 2Ch 33:14
Aren't all my **c** kings? Is 10:8
When all the **c** of the armies in Jr 40:7
⌊The **c** included⌋ Ishmael son of Jr 40:8
and all the **c** of the armies Jr 40:13
and all the **c** of the armies with Jr 41:11
and all the **c** of the army with Jr 41:13
and all the **c** of the armies with Jr 41:16
Then all the **c** of the armies, Jr 42:1
all the **c** of the armies who were Jr 42:8
and all the **c** of the armies did Jr 43:4
and all the **c** of the armies took Jr 43:5
also slaughtered the Judean **c**. Jr 52:10
but one of his **c** will grow more Dn 11:5
military **c**, and the leading Mk 6:21
with the **c** and prominent men Ac 25:23
the military **c**, the rich, Rv 6:15
kings, the flesh of **c**, the flesh Rv 19:18

COMMANDING *(10)*

is why I am **c** you, 'You must Dt 15:11
is why I am **c** you to set apart Dt 19:7
Therefore I am **c** you to do this. Dt 24:18
Therefore I am **c** you to do this. Dt 24:22
your God is **c** you this day to Dt 26:16
Ebal, as I am **c** you today, and Dt 27:4
all the things I am **c** you today, Dt 28:14
For I am **c** you today to love the Dt 30:16
After **c** the crowd to sit down on Mt 15:35
c his accusers to come to you. Ac 24:7

COMMANDMENT *(30)*

did not keep the **c** that the LORD 1Kg 13:21
and the **c** He wrote for you; 2Kg 17:37
according to the **c** of Moses for 2Ch 8:13
of bloodguilt, law, **c**, statutes, 2Ch 19:10
law and in the **c**, in order to 2Ch 31:21
who tremble at the **c** of our God. Ezr 10:3
the **c** of the LORD is radiant, Ps 19:8
For a **c** is a lamp, teaching is a Pr 6:23
break God's **c** because of your Mt 15:3
c in the law is the greatest? Mt 22:36

greatest and most important **c**. Mt 22:38
He wrote this **c** for you because Mk 10:5
Which **c** is the most important of Mk 12:28
There is no other **c** greater than Mk 12:31
the Sabbath according to the **c**. Lk 23:56
I give you a new **c**: Jn 13:34
an opportunity through the **c**, Rm 7:8
but when the **c** came, sin sprang Rm 7:9
The **c** that was meant for life Rm 7:10
an opportunity through the **c**, Rm 7:11
and the **c** is holy and just and Rm 7:12
through the **c** sin might become Rm 7:13
and if there is any other **c**— Rm 13:9
is the first **c** with a promise— Eph 6:2
to keep the **c** without spot or 1Tm 6:14
office have a **c** according to the Heb 7:5
So the previous **c** is annulled Heb 7:18
For when every **c** had been Heb 9:19
from the holy **c** delivered to 2Pt 2:21
and the **c** of our Lord and Savior 2Pt 3:2

COMMANDMENTS *(49)*

of the covenant—the Ten **C**. Ex 34:28
you to follow the Ten **C**, Dt 4:13
the Ten **C** that He had spoken to Dt 10:4
keep His statutes, **c**, judgments, 1Kg 2:3
My statutes and **c** just as your 1Kg 3:14
and keep all My **c** by walking in 1Kg 6:12
who kept My **c** and My statutes 1Kg 11:34
statutes and My **c** as My servant 1Kg 11:38
who kept My **c** and followed Me 1Kg 14:8
the LORD's **c** and followed 1Kg 18:18
ways and keep My **c** and statutes 2Kg 17:13
all the **c** of the LORD their 2Kg 17:16
did not keep the **c** of the LORD 2Kg 17:19
law and **c** the LORD commanded 2Kg 17:34
Him but kept the **c** the LORD had 2Kg 18:6
the LORD and to keep His **c**, 2Kg 23:3
keeping My **c** and My ordinances 1Ch 28:7
after all the **c** of the LORD your 1Ch 28:8
and to carry out all Your **c**, 1Ch 29:19
the LORD and to keep His **c**, 2Ch 34:31
of the LORD's **c** and statutes for Ezr 7:11
For we have abandoned the **c** Ezr 9:10
we break Your **c** again and Ezr 9:14
and good decrees and **c**. Neh 9:13
them, and gave them **c**, statutes, Neh 9:14
and would not obey Your **c**. Neh 9:29
listen to Your **c** and warnings Neh 9:34
the following⌋ **c** on ourselves: Neh 10:32
God's works, but keep His **c**. Ps 78:7
statutes and do not keep My **c**, Ps 89:31
taking great delight in His **c**. Ps 112:1
I love Your **c** more than gold, Ps 119:127
for all Your **c** are righteous. Ps 119:172
who love Him and keep His **c**— Dn 9:4
away from Your **c** and ordinances. Dn 9:5
least of these **c** and teaches Mt 5:19
teaches ⌊these **c**⌋ will be called Mt 5:19
to enter into life, keep the **c**." Mt 19:17
Prophets depend on these two **c**." Mt 22:40
You know the **c**: Mk 10:19
to all the **c** and requirements Lk 1:6
You know the **c**: Lk 18:20
you love Me, you will keep My **c**. Jn 14:15
The **c**: You shall not commit Rm 13:9
but keeping God's **c** does. 1Co 7:19
the law of the **c** in regulations, Eph 2:15
and the **c** of men who reject Ti 1:14
who keep the **c** of God and have Rv 12:17
who keep the **c** of God and the Rv 14:12

COMMANDS *(130)*

My mandate, My **c**, My statutes, Gn 26:5
all my people will obey your **c**. Gn 41:40
and gave them **c** concerning both Ex 6:13
attention to His **c**, and keep all Ex 15:26
to keep My **c** and instructions Ex 16:28
those who love Me and keep My **c**. Ex 20:6
the people all the **c** of the LORD Ex 24:3
the law and **c** I have written Ex 24:12
of the LORD's **c** and does Lv 4:2
of the LORD's **c** and incur guilt Lv 4:13
any of the **c** of the LORD his God Lv 4:22
violating one of the LORD's **c**, Lv 4:27
any of the LORD's **c** concerning Lv 5:17
are to keep My **c** and do them; Lv 22:31
and faithfully observe My **c**, Lv 26:3
Me and observe all these **c**— Lv 26:14
and do not observe all My **c**— Lv 26:15
These are the **c** the LORD gave Lv 27:34
I hear what the LORD **c** for you." Nm 9:8
obey all these **c** that the LORD Nm 15:22
the LORD issued the **c** and onward Nm 15:23
all the LORD's **c** and obey them Nm 15:39
and obey all My **c** and be holy to Nm 15:40
will do just as my lord **c**. Nm 32:25
These are the **c** and ordinances Nm 36:13
may keep the **c** of the LORD your Dt 4:2
His statutes and **c**, which I am Dt 4:40
those who love Me and keep My **c**. Dt 5:10
spoke these **c** in a loud voice Dt 5:22
to fear Me and keep all My **c**, Dt 5:29
statutes and **c** I am giving you Dt 6:2
observe the **c** of the LORD your Dt 6:17
one of these **c** before the LORD Dt 6:25
who love Him and keep His **c**. Dt 7:9
or not you would keep His **c**. Dt 8:2
So keep the **c** of the LORD your Dt 8:6
Keep the LORD's **c** and statutes I Dt 10:13
His statutes, ordinances, and **c**. Dt 11:1
obey My **c** I am giving you Dt 11:13
one of these **c** I am giving you Dt 11:22
if you obey the **c** of the LORD Dt 11:27
do not obey the **c** of the LORD Dt 11:28
must keep His **c** and listen to Dt 13:4
keeping all His **c** I am giving Dt 13:18
one of these **c** I am giving you Dt 15:5
one of these **c** I am giving you Dt 19:9
to all the **c** You gave me. Dt 26:13
violated or forgotten Your **c**. Dt 26:13
His statutes, **c**, and ordinances, Dt 26:17
that you are to keep all His **c**, Dt 26:18
and follow His **c** and statutes I Dt 27:10
follow all His **c** I am giving you Dt 28:1
if you obey the **c** of the LORD Dt 28:9
LORD your God's **c** I am giving Dt 28:13
all His **c** and statutes I am Dt 28:15
and keep the **c** and statutes He Dt 28:45
follow all His **c** I am giving you Dt 30:8
by keeping His **c** and statutes Dt 30:10
and to keep His **c**, statutes, Dt 30:16
before you, and **c**, "Destroy!" Dt 33:27
ways, keep His **c**, remain Jos 22:5
in obedience to the LORD's **c**. Jdg 2:17
keep the LORD's **c** He had given Jdg 3:4
will do all my lord the king **c**." 2Sm 9:11
all His ways and to keep His **c**, 1Kg 8:58
ordinances and to keep His **c**, 1Kg 8:61
Me and do not keep My **c**— 1Kg 9:6
statutes and My **c** that I have 2Ch 7:19
his father and walked by His **c**, 2Ch 17:4
the LORD's **c** and you do not 2Ch 24:20
who love Him and keep His **c**, Neh 1:5
You and have not kept the **c**, Neh 1:7
Me and carefully observe My **c**, Neh 1:9
and did not listen to Your **c**. Neh 9:16
and to carefully obey all the **c**, Neh 10:29
He **c** the sun not to shine and Jb 9:7
departed from the **c** of His lips; Jb 23:12
lightning and **c** it to hit its Jb 36:32
everything He **c** them over the Jb 37:12
for did they not defy His **c**? Ps 105:28
against God's **c** and despised Ps 107:11
when I think about all Your **c**. Ps 119:6
don't let me wander from Your **c**. Ps 119:10
do not hide Your **c** from me. Ps 119:19
who wander from Your **c**. Ps 119:21
I pursue the way of Your **c**, Ps 119:32
me stay on the path of Your **c**, Ps 119:35
delight in Your **c**, which I love. Ps 119:47
will lift up my hands to Your **c**, Ps 119:48
not hesitating to keep Your **c**. Ps 119:60
for I rely on Your **c**. Ps 119:66
so that I can learn Your **c**. Ps 119:73
All Your **c** are true; Ps 119:86
so that I may obey my God's **c**. Ps 119:115
mouth because I long for Your **c**. Ps 119:131
but Your **c** are my delight. Ps 119:143
LORD, and all Your **c** are true. Ps 119:151
salvation and carry out Your **c**. Ps 119:166
for I do not forget Your **c**. Ps 119:176
and store up my **c** within you, Pr 2:1
but let your heart keep my **c**; Pr 3:1
Keep my **c** and live. Pr 4:4
my words, and treasure my **c**. Pr 7:1
Keep my **c** and live; Pr 7:2
heart accepts **c**, but foolish Pr 10:8
one who keeps **c** preserves Pr 19:16
God and keep His **c**, because this Ec 12:13
you had paid attention to My **c**. Is 48:18
kept all his **c** and have done all Jr 35:18
For the LORD **c**: The large house Am 6:11
earth, who carry out what He **c**. Zph 2:3
as doctrines the **c** of men." Mt 15:9
He **c** even the unclean spirits, Mk 1:27
as doctrines the **c** of men. Mk 7:7
He **c** the unclean spirits with Lk 4:36
He **c** even the winds and the Lk 8:25
one who has My **c** and keeps them Jn 14:21
If you keep My **c** you will remain Jn 15:10
kept My Father's **c** and remain in Jn 15:10
God now **c** all people everywhere Ac 17:30
they are human **c** and doctrines. Col 2:22
For you know what **c** we gave you 1Th 4:2
to know Him: by keeping His **c**. 1Jn 2:3
keeping His **c**, is a liar, 1Jn 2:4
we keep His **c** and do what is 1Jn 3:22
who keeps His **c** remains in Him, 1Jn 3:24
when we love God and obey His **c**. 1Jn 5:2
is: to keep His **c**. Now His 1Jn 5:3
Now His **c** are not a burden, 1Jn 5:3
that we walk according to His **c**. 2Jn 6

COMMEMORATE *(1)*

of Israel would **c** the daughter Jdg 11:40

COMMEMORATION *(1)*

complete rest, **c** and jubilation Lv 23:24

COMMEND *(5)*

I **c** to you our sister Phoebe, Rm 16:1
beginning to **c** ourselves again 2Co 3:1
in God's sight we **c** ourselves to 2Co 4:2
God's ministers, we **c** ourselves: 2Co 6:4
with some who **c** themselves. 2Co 10:12

COMMENDABLE *(1)*

whatever is **c**—if there is any Php 4:8

COMMENDED *(3)*

So I **c** enjoyment, because there Ec 8:15
after being **c** to the grace of Ac 15:40
way you have **c** yourselves to be 2Co 7:11

COMMENDING *(2)*

We are not **c** ourselves to you 2Co 5:12
is not the one **c** himself who is 2Co 10:18

COMMENDS *(1)*

but the one the Lord **c**. 2Co 10:18

COMMENTED *(1)*

with good news," the king **c**. 2Sm 18:27

COMMERCIAL *(1)*

of silver at the current **c** rate. Gn 23:16

COMMISSION *(4)*

community, and **c** him in their Nm 27:19
But **c** Joshua and encourage and Dt 3:28
meeting, so that I may **c** him." Dt 31:14
authority and a **c** from the chief Ac 26:12

COMMISSIONED *(2)*

on him, and **c** him, as the LORD Nm 27:23
The LORD **c** Joshua son of Nun, Dt 31:23

COMMISSIONERS *(1)*

king appoint **c** in each province Est 2:3

COMMIT *(64)*

Do not **c** adultery. Ex 20:14
You must not **c** any of these Lv 18:26
Do not **c** adultery. Dt 5:18
people will soon **c** adultery with Dt 31:16
and caused Israel to **c**." 1Kg 14:16
sin he had caused Israel to **c**. 1Kg 15:26
caused Israel to **c** in the 1Kg 15:30
sin he had caused Israel to **c**. 1Kg 15:34
and caused Israel to **c**, 1Kg 16:13
the sin he caused Israel to **c**. 1Kg 16:19
the sins he caused Israel to **c**, 1Kg 16:26
of Nebat had caused Israel to **c**. 2Kg 3:3
Nebat had caused Israel to **c**— 2Kg 10:29
Jeroboam had caused Israel to **c**. 2Kg 10:31
of Nebat had caused Israel to **c**; 2Kg 13:2
Jeroboam had caused Israel to **c**. 2Kg 13:6
of Nebat had caused Israel to **c**, 2Kg 13:11
of Nebat had caused Israel to **c**. 2Kg 14:24
of Nebat had caused Israel to **c**. 2Kg 15:9
of Nebat had caused Israel to **c**. 2Kg 15:18
of Nebat had caused Israel to **c**. 2Kg 15:24
of Nebat had caused Israel to **c**. 2Kg 15:28
and caused them to **c** great sin. 2Kg 17:21
caused Judah to **c** so that they 2Kg 21:16

the peoples who **c** these Ezr 9:14
brothers and **c** themselves with Neh 10:29
C your way to the LORD; Ps 37:5
acts with men who **c** sin. Ps 141:4
and they hurry to **c** murder. Pr 1:16
C your activities to the LORD Pr 16:3
with the desire⌋ to **c** crime. Ec 8:11
steal, murder, **c** adultery, swear Jr 7:9
c adultery and walk in lies. Jr 23:14
of Judah to **c** the abominations Ezk 8:17
Samaria did not **c** ⌊even⌋ half Ezk 16:51
He does not **c** robbery, but gives Ezk 18:7
hold collateral, or **c** robbery. Ezk 18:16
they **c** immoral acts within you. Ezk 22:9
daughters-in-law **c** adultery. Hs 4:13
when they **c** adultery, Hs 4:14
to Shechem. They **c** atrocities. Hs 6:9
All of them **c** adultery; Hs 7:4
only do those who **c** wickedness Mal 3:15
it was said, Do not **c** adultery. Mt 5:27
causes her to **c** adultery. Mt 5:32
murder; do not **c** adultery; do Mt 19:18
murder; do not **c** adultery; do Mk 10:19
Do not **c** adultery; do not Lk 18:20
And now I **c** you to God and to Ac 20:32
"You must not **c** adultery"— Rm 2:22
adultery"—do you **c** adultery? Rm 2:22
You shall not **c** adultery, you Rm 13:9
a person can **c** is outside the 1Co 6:18
Let us not **c** sexual immorality 1Co 10:8
Or did I **c** a sin by humbling 2Co 11:7
c to faithful men who will be 2Tm 2:2
you **c** sin and are convicted by Jms 2:9
said, Do not **c** adultery, also Jms 2:11
So if you do not **c** adultery, Jms 2:11
He did not **c** sin, and no deceit 1Pt 2:22
to those who **c** sin that doesn't 1Jn 5:16
to idols and to **c** sexual Rv 2:14
My slaves to **c** sexual immorality Rv 2:20
those who **c** adultery with her Rv 2:22

COMMITMENT *(5)*

or the rash **c** she herself made Nm 30:6
or the rash **c** she herself made, Nm 30:8
will be responsible for her **c**." Nm 30:15
with them ⌊to a **c**⌋ that they Est 9:27
waiting for a **c** from you." Ac 23:21

COMMITS *(26)*

If a man **c** adultery with a Lv 20:10
if he **c** adultery with his Lv 20:10
a man or woman **c** any sin against Nm 5:6
that anyone who **c** manslaughter Dt 19:3
for the one who **c** manslaughter, Jos 21:13
for the one who **c** manslaughter, Jos 21:21
for the one who **c** manslaughter, Jos 21:27
for the one who **c** manslaughter, Jos 21:32
for the one who **c** manslaughter, Jos 21:38
The one who **c** adultery lacks Pr 6:32
a sinner **c** crime a hundred Ec 8:12
poor and needy, **c** robbery, and Ezk 18:12
to the idols, **c** abominations, Ezk 18:12
man within you **c** an abomination Ezk 22:11
righteousness and **c** iniquity, Ezk 33:13
righteousness and **c** iniquity, Ezk 33:18
everyone who **c** wickedness will Mal 4:1
a divorced woman **c** adultery. Mt 5:32
marries another, **c** adultery." Mt 19:9
marries another **c** adultery Mk 10:11
another, she **c** adultery." Mk 10:12
another woman **c** adultery, Lk 16:18
from her husband **c** adultery. Lk 16:18
Everyone who **c** sin is a slave of Jn 8:34
Everyone who **c** sin also breaks 1Jn 3:4
The one who **c** sin is of the 1Jn 3:8

COMMITTED *(107)*

For Shechem had **c** an outrage Gn 34:7
people, "You have **c** a great sin. Ex 32:30
this people has **c** a great sin; Ex 32:31
offering for the sin he has **c**. Lv 4:3
the sin they have **c** in regard to Lv 4:14
him about the sin he has **c**, Lv 4:23
him about the sin he has **c**, Lv 4:28
for the sin that he has **c**. Lv 4:28
his behalf for the sin he has **c**, Lv 4:35
is to confess he has **c** that sin. Lv 5:5
the sin he has **c** to the LORD: Lv 5:6
his behalf for the sin he has **c**, Lv 5:10
the sin he has **c** in any of these Lv 5:13
error he has **c** unintentionally Lv 5:18
prior to you have **c** all these Lv 18:27
offering for the sin he has **c**, Lv 19:22
be forgiven for the sin he **c**. Lv 19:22
they have both **c** an abomination. Lv 20:13
is to confess the sin he has **c**. Nm 5:7
this sin we have so foolishly **c**. Nm 12:11
could flee who **c** manslaughter Dt 4:42
because of all the sin you **c**, Dt 9:18
the one who **c** manslaughter, Dt 19:6
For she has **c** an outrage in Dt 22:21
LORD's covenant and **c** an outrage Jos 7:15
hand the one who **c** manslaughter Jos 20:5
the one who **c** manslaughter may Jos 20:6
you have **c** today against Jos 22:16
you have not **c** this treachery Jos 22:31
because they **c** a horrible shame Jdg 20:6
a great evil you **c** in the LORD's 1Sm 12:17
though you have **c** all this evil, 1Sm 12:20
Jonathan **c** himself to David, 1Sm 18:1
I've **c** a grave error." 1Sm 26:21
sins that he **c** and caused Israel 1Kg 14:16
had done with the sins they **c**. 1Kg 14:22
their place and **c** them into the 1Kg 14:27
sins he had **c** and had caused 1Kg 15:30
which they **c** and caused Israel 1Kg 16:13
his sin he **c** by doing what was 1Kg 16:19
What sin have I **c**, that you are 1Kg 18:9
He **c** the most detestable acts by 1Kg 21:26
that Jeroboam **c** and did not turn 2Kg 17:22
king of Judah has **c** all these 2Kg 21:11
and the sin that he **c**, 2Kg 21:17
their place and **c** them into the 2Ch 12:10
the sins we have **c** against You. Neh 1:6
and they had **c** terrible Neh 9:18
They **c** terrible blasphemies. Neh 9:26
just as they had **c** themselves Est 9:31
iniquities and sins have I **c**? Jb 13:23
my ways were **c** to keeping Your Ps 119:5
My people have **c** a double evil: Jr 2:13
Israel had **c** adultery that I had Jr 3:8
the land and **c** adultery with Jr 3:9
needs, yet they **c** adultery; Jr 5:7
that we have **c** against the LORD Jr 16:10
because they have **c** an outrage Jr 29:23
wrongs they have **c** against Me, Jr 33:8
wrongs they have **c** against Me, Jr 33:8
wives that were **c** in the land of Jr 44:9
the detestable acts you have **c**, Jr 44:22
all the abominations **c** in it." Ezk 9:4
Haven't you **c** immoral acts in Ezk 16:43
all the abominations you have **c**. Ezk 16:51
which you **c** more abhorrently Ezk 16:52
the treachery he **c** against Me. Ezk 17:20
Since he has **c** all these Ezk 18:13
all the sins his father has **c**, Ezk 18:14
from all the sins he has **c**, Ezk 18:21
he has **c** will be held against Ezk 18:22
engaged in and the sin he has **c**. Ezk 18:24
he has **c** and does what is Ezk 18:27
all the transgressions he had **c**; Ezk 18:28
the transgressions you have **c**, Ezk 18:31
extortion and **c** robbery. Ezk 22:29
For they have **c** adultery, and Ezk 23:37
they have **c** adultery with their Ezk 23:37
of the iniquity he has **c**. Ezk 33:13
of the sins he **c** will be held Ezk 33:16
swords, you have **c** abominations, Ezk 33:26
the abominations they have **c**. Ezk 33:29
they **c** against Me, Ezk 39:26
name by the abominations they **c**. Ezk 43:8
of the abominations they **c**. Ezk 44:13
I have not **c** a crime against you Dn 6:22
of the crimes they have **c**. Mc 3:4
her has already **c** adultery with Mt 5:28
me is a gift ⌊**c** to the temple⌋" Mt 15:5
is, a gift ⌊**c** to the temple⌋ Mk 7:11
rebels who had **c** murder during Mk 15:7
they **c** them to the Lord in whom Ac 14:23
since I had not **c** a capital Ac 28:18
c shameless acts with males Rm 1:27
over the sins previously **c**. Rm 3:25
that he who has **c** this act might 1Co 5:2
and He has **c** the message of 2Co 5:19
be **c** to them, so that your 1Tm 4:15
of the people **c** in ignorance. Heb 9:7
transgressions ⌊**c**⌋ under the Heb 9:15
and if he has **c** sins, he will be Jms 5:15
but **c** Himself to the One who 1Pt 2:23
around them **c** sexual immorality Jd 7
So be **c** and repent. Rv 3:19
of the earth **c** sexual immorality Rv 17:2
the earth have **c** sexual Rv 18:3
earth who have **c** sexual Rv 18:9

COMMITTING *(9)*

innocent blood and **c** extortion Jr 22:17
in Israel by **c** adultery with Jr 29:23
the house of Israel is **c** here, Ezk 8:6
abominations they are **c** here." Ezk 8:9
abominations, which they are **c**." Ezk 8:13
c the same abominations that the Ezk 18:24
blasphemed Me by **c** treachery Ezk 20:27
caught in the act of **c** adultery. Jn 8:4
his brother **c** a sin that does 1Jn 5:16

COMMON *(39)*

Now if any of the **c** people sins Lv 4:27
between the holy and the **c**, Lv 10:10
lizard, the **c** lizard, the skink Lv 11:30
I am a poor man who is **c**." 1Sm 18:23
made silver as **c** in Jerusalem as 1Kg 10:27
of God, what do we have in **c**? 1Kg 17:18
Israel, "We have nothing in **c**. 2Kg 3:13
Then the **c** people executed all 2Kg 21:24
on the graves of the **c** people. 2Kg 23:6
Then the **c** people took Jehoahaz 2Kg 23:30
men from the **c** people who were 2Kg 25:19
and gold as **c** in Jerusalem as 2Ch 1:15
made silver as **c** in Jerusalem as 2Ch 9:27
in the **c** fields of their cities, 2Ch 31:19
Then the **c** people executed all 2Ch 33:25
Then the **c** people took Jehoahaz 2Ch 36:1
develop **c** sense, you who are Pr 8:5
and the poor have this in **c**: Pr 22:2
the oppressor have this in **c**: Pr 29:13
burial place of the **c** people. Jr 26:23
men from the **c** people who were Jr 52:25
between the holy and the **c**, Ezk 22:26
brought in, along with **c** men. Ezk 23:42
to separate the holy from the **c**. Ezk 42:20
between the holy and the **c**, Ezk 44:23
will be for **c** use by the city, Ezk 48:15
and had everything in **c**. Ac 2:44
they held everything in **c**. Ac 4:32
By **c** consent they would all meet Ac 5:12
eaten anything **c** and unclean!" Ac 10:14
clean, you must not call **c**." Ac 10:15
call any person **c** or unclean. Ac 10:28
'For nothing **c** or unclean has Ac 11:8
clean, you must not call **c**.' Ac 11:9
except what is **c** to humanity. 1Co 10:13
believer have in **c** with an 2Co 6:15
my true child in our **c** faith. Ti 1:4
have flesh and blood in **c**, Heb 2:14
write you about our **c** salvation, Jd 3

COMMOTION *(8)*

outcry and asked, "Why this **c**?" 1Sm 4:14
She cries out above the **c**; Pr 1:21
from the hills, **c** from the Jr 3:23
a great **c** from the land to the Jr 10:22
and a sound of **c** like the noise Ezk 1:24
and He saw a **c**—people weeping Mk 5:38
are you making a **c** and weeping? Mk 5:39
there was a great **c** among the Ac 12:18

COMMUNICATE *(1)*

after night they **c** knowledge. Ps 19:2

COMMUNICATES *(1)*

powerful man **c** his evil desire Mc 7:3

COMMUNITIES *(1)*

shortage of food in all your **c**, Am 4:6

COMMUNITY *(112)*

Tell the whole **c** of Israel that Ex 12:3
assembly of the **c** of Israel will Ex 12:6
be cut off from the **c** of Israel. Ex 12:19
The whole **c** of Israel must Ex 12:47
entire Israelite **c** departed from Ex 16:1
Israelite **c** grumbled against Ex 16:2
Say to the entire Israelite **c**, Ex 16:9
to the entire Israelite **c**, Ex 16:10
leaders of the **c** came and Ex 16:22
entire Israelite **c** left the Ex 17:1
of the **c** returned to him, Ex 34:31
Israelite **c** and said to them Ex 35:1
said to the entire Israelite **c**, Ex 35:4
entire Israelite **c** left Moses' Ex 35:20
from those of the **c** who were Ex 38:25

if the whole **c** of Israel errs, Lv 4:13
the whole **c** at the entrance to Lv 8:3
and the **c** assembled at the Lv 8:4
and the whole **c** came forward and Lv 9:5
become angry with the whole **c**. Lv 10:6
the guilt of the **c** and make Lv 10:17
the Israelite **c** two male goats Lv 16:5
Israelite **c** and tell them: Lv 19:2
against members of your **c**, Lv 19:18
then have the whole **c** stone him. Lv 24:14
the whole **c** must stone him. Lv 24:16
entire Israelite **c** by their Nm 1:2
are the men called from the **c**; Nm 1:16
the whole **c** on the first day Nm 1:18
will fall on the Israelite **c**." Nm 1:53
and the entire **c** before the tent Nm 3:7
the leaders of the **c** registered Nm 4:34
assemble the entire Israelite **c**. Nm 8:9
entire Israelite **c** did ⌊this⌋ to Nm 8:20
to summon the **c** and have the Nm 10:2
the entire **c** is to gather before Nm 10:3
entire Israelite **c** in the Nm 13:26
report for them and the whole **c**, Nm 13:26
Then the whole **c** broke into loud Nm 14:1
and the whole **c** told them, Nm 14:2
assembly of the Israelite **c**. Nm 14:5
said to the entire Israelite **c**: Nm 14:7
While the whole **c** threatened to Nm 14:10
I endure⌋ this evil **c** that keeps Nm 14:27
the entire evil **c** that has Nm 14:35
the entire **c** to complain about Nm 14:36
the entire **c** is to prepare one Nm 15:24
Israelite **c** so that they may Nm 15:25
entire Israelite **c** and the Nm 15:26
Moses, Aaron, and the entire **c**. Nm 15:33
The entire **c** is to stone him Nm 15:35
So the entire **c** brought him Nm 15:36
leaders of the **c** and Nm 16:2
in the entire **c** is holy, Nm 16:3
the Israelite **c** to bring you Nm 16:9
stand before the **c** to minister Nm 16:9
the whole **c** against them at Nm 16:19
LORD appeared to the whole **c**. Nm 16:19
from this **c** so I may consume Nm 16:21
vent Your wrath on the whole **c**?" Nm 16:22
Tell the **c**: Get away from the Nm 16:24
He warned the **c**, "Get away now Nm 16:26
Israelite **c** complained about Nm 16:41
When the **c** assembled against Nm 16:42
away from this **c** so that I may Nm 16:45
Go quickly to the **c** and make Nm 16:46
the Israelite **c** for ⌊preparing⌋ Nm 19:9
The entire Israelite **c** entered Nm 20:1
There was no water for the **c**, Nm 20:2
the staff and assemble the **c**. Nm 20:8
for the **c** and their livestock. Nm 20:8
and the **c** and their livestock Nm 20:11
entire Israelite **c** came to Mount Nm 20:22
Hor in the sight of the whole **c**. Nm 20:27
When the whole **c** saw that Aaron Nm 20:29
whole Israelite **c** while they Nm 25:6
entire Israelite **c** by their Nm 26:2
chosen by the **c**, who fought Nm 26:9
and the entire **c** at the entrance Nm 27:2
When the **c** quarreled in the Nm 27:14
flesh, appoint a man over the **c** Nm 27:16
that the LORD's **c** won't be like Nm 27:17
the priest and the whole **c**, Nm 27:19
entire Israelite **c** will obey Nm 27:20
even the entire **c**, will go out Nm 27:21
the priest and the entire **c**, Nm 27:22
and the Israelite **c** at the camp Nm 31:12
leaders of the **c** went to meet Nm 31:13
came against the LORD's **c**. Nm 31:16
leaders of the **c** are to take a Nm 31:26
out to war and the entire **c**. Nm 31:27
the leaders of the **c** and said: Nm 32:2
down before the **c** of Israel, Nm 32:4
leaders of the **c** swore an oath Jos 9:15
leaders of the **c** had sworn an Jos 9:18
the whole **c** grumbled against Jos 9:18
water carriers for the whole **c**, Jos 9:21
for the **c** and for the LORD's Jos 9:27
entire Israelite **c** assembled at Jos 18:1
entire Israelite **c** assembled at Jos 22:12
what the LORD's entire **c** says: Jos 22:16
a plague on the LORD's **c**, Jos 22:17
with the entire **c** of Israel. Jos 22:18
wrath on the entire **c** of Israel? Jos 22:20
the priest and the **c** leaders, Jos 22:30
and the **c** assembled as one body Jdg 20:1
The whole **c** that had returned Neh 8:17
not be in the **c** of the righteous Ps 1:5
ruin before the entire **c**." Pr 5:14
because they exiled a whole **c**, Am 1:6
over a whole **c** of exiles to Edom Am 1:9
whole Jewish **c** has appealed to Ac 25:24

COMMUNITY'S *(2)*

without the **c** awareness, Nm 15:24
c half was: 337,500 sheep and Nm 31:43

COMPANIES *(3)*

men into three **c** and gave each Jdg 7:16
The three **c** blew their trumpets Jdg 7:20
divided them into three **c**, Jdg 9:43

COMPANION *(11)*

to jackals and a **c** of ostriches. Jb 30:29
my peer, my **c** and good friend! Ps 55:13
who abandons the **c** of her youth Pr 2:17
but a **c** of fools will suffer Pr 13:20
and don't be a **c** of a Pr 22:24
but a **c** of gluttons humiliates Pr 28:7
is a **c** to a man who destroys. Pr 28:24
There is a person without a **c**, Ec 4:8
falls, his **c** can lift him up; Ec 4:10
My Father, my youthful **c**? Jr 3:4
don't trust in a close **c**. Mc 7:5

COMPANIONS *(14)*

more than your **c**, with the oil Ps 45:7
virgins, her **c**, are brought to Ps 45:14
beside the flocks of your **c**? Sg 1:7
c are listening for your voice— Sg 8:13
kill them along with their **c**. Jr 41:8
Simon and his **c** went searching Mk 1:36
and also gave some to his **c**?" Mk 2:26
Paul and his **c** set sail from Ac 13:13
who were Paul's traveling **c**. Ac 19:29
rather than Your **c**, with the oil Heb 1:9
brothers and **c** in a heavenly Heb 3:1
we have become **c** of the Messiah Heb 3:14
became **c** with the Holy Spirit, Heb 6:4
times you were **c** of those who Heb 10:33

COMPANY *(19)*

while a **c** of Philistines was 2Sm 23:13
and his whole **c** went back to the 2Kg 5:15
For the **c** of the godless will be Jb 15:34
He keeps **c** with evildoers and Jb 34:8
a great **c** of women brought the Ps 68:11
cavalry, and a vast **c** of troops. Ezk 26:7
Assyria is there with all her **c**; Ezk 32:22
and her **c** is all around her Ezk 32:23
a huge **c** armed with shields and Ezk 38:4
you and all your **c** who have been Ezk 38:7
gathered the whole **c** around Him. Mt 27:27
and called the whole **c** together. Mk 15:16
Judas took a **c** of soldiers and Jn 18:3
Then the **c** of soldiers, the Jn 18:12
the whole **c** of the disciples Ac 6:2
proposal pleased the whole **c**. Ac 6:5
disagreement that they parted **c**, Ac 15:39
enjoyed your **c** for a while. Rm 15:24
"Bad **c** corrupts good morals." 1Co 15:33

COMPARE *(20)*

Gold and glass do not **c** with it, Jb 28:17
from Cush cannot **c** with it, Jb 28:19
none can **c** with You. Ps 40:5
the skies can **c** with the LORD? Ps 89:6
nothing desirable can **c** with it. Pr 8:11
I **c** you, my darling, to a mare Sg 1:9
Who will you **c** God with? Is 40:18
What likeness will you **c** Him to? Is 40:18
Who will you **c** Me to, or who is Is 40:25
Who will you **c** Me or make Me Is 46:5
To what can I **c** you, Daughter Lm 2:13
of the forest, **c** to any other Ezk 15:2
trees couldn't **c** with its Ezk 31:8
of God could **c** with it in beauty Ezk 31:8
You **c** yourself to a lion of the Ezk 32:2
what should I **c** this generation Mt 11:16
then should I **c** the people of Lk 7:31
like, and what can I **c** it to? Lk 13:18
What can I **c** the kingdom of God Lk 13:20
classify or **c** ourselves with 2Co 10:12

COMPARED *(6)*

What have I done now **c** to you? Jdg 8:2
What was I able to do **c** to you?" Jdg 8:3
for what is straw ⌊**c**⌋ to grain?" Jr 23:28
of heaven may be **c** to a man who Mt 13:24
of heaven can be **c** to a king who Mt 18:23
of heaven may be **c** to a king who Mt 22:2

COMPARES *(1)*

nothing you desire **c** with her. Pr 3:15

COMPARING *(2)*

are not worth **c** with the glory Rm 8:18
themselves and **c** themselves to 2Co 10:12

COMPASS *(1)*

and outlines it with a **c**. Is 44:13

COMPASSION *(104)*

because of the LORD's **c** for him, Gn 19:16
and I will have **c** on whom I will Ex 33:19
on whom I will have **c**." Ex 33:19
mercy, show you **c**, and multiply Dt 13:17
fortunes, have **c** on you, and Dt 30:3
and have **c** on His servants Dt 32:36
Israelites had **c** on their Jdg 21:6
The people had **c** on Benjamin, Jdg 21:15
she felt great **c** for her son. 1Kg 3:26
may You give them **c** in the eyes 1Kg 8:50
to them and had **c** on them and 2Kg 13:23
for He had **c** on His people and 2Ch 36:15
have **c** on him in the presence Neh 1:11
because of Your great **c**. Neh 9:19
In Your abundant **c** You gave them Neh 9:27
them many times in Your **c**. Neh 9:28
in Your abundant **c**, You did not Neh 9:31
on me with **c** in keeping with Neh 13:22
Your **c** and Your faithful love, Ps 25:6
do not withhold Your **c** from me; Ps 40:11
according to Your abundant **c**, Ps 51:1
in keeping with Your great **c**, Ps 69:16
Has He in anger withheld His **c**?" Ps 77:9
let Your **c** come to us quickly, Ps 79:8
and have **c** on Your servants. Ps 90:13
will arise and have **c** on Zion, Ps 102:13
you with faithful love and **c**. Ps 103:4
a father has **c** on his children Ps 103:13
so the LORD has **c** on those who Ps 103:13
May Your **c** come to me so that I Ps 119:77
and have **c** on His servants Ps 135:14
c ⌊rests⌋ on all He has made. Ps 145:9
men and has no **c** on its Is 9:17
No one has **c** on his brother. Is 9:19
away, and You have had **c** on me. Is 12:1
will have no **c** on little ones; Is 13:18
LORD will have **c** on Jacob and Is 14:1
Maker will not have **c** on them, Is 27:11
and is rising up to show you **c**, Is 30:18
and will have **c** on His afflicted Is 49:13
or lack **c** for the child of her Is 49:15
will take you back with great **c**. Is 54:7
but I will have **c** on you with Is 54:8
so He may have **c** on him, and to Is 55:7
them because of His love and **c**; Is 63:9
yearning and Your **c** are withheld Is 63:15
once again have **c** on them and Jr 12:15
c ⌊to keep Me⌋ from destroying Jr 13:14
I am tired of showing **c**. Jr 15:6
well as My⌋ faithful love and **c**. Jr 16:5
the LORD overthrew without **c**. Jr 20:16
spare them or show pity or **c**.' Jr 21:7
tents and show **c** on his Jr 30:18
I will truly have **c** on him. Jr 31:20
fortunes and have **c** on them." Jr 33:26
I will grant you **c**, and he will Jr 42:12
he will have **c** on you and allow Jr 42:12
Without **c** the Lord has swallowed Lm 2:2
He has demolished without **c**, Lm 2:17
anger, slaughtering without **c**. Lm 2:21
He will show **c** according to His Lm 3:32
You have killed without **c**. Lm 3:43
these things out of **c** for you. Ezk 16:5
of Jacob and have **c** on the whole Ezk 39:25
Daniel favor and **c** from the Dn 1:9
C and forgiveness belong to the Dn 9:9
but based on Your abundant **c**. Dn 9:18
Name her No **C**, for I will no Hs 1:6
no longer have **c** on the house Hs 1:6
But I will have **c** on the house Hs 1:7
After Gomer had weaned No **C**, Hs 1:8
My People and your sisters: **C**. Hs 2:1
I will have no **c** on her children Hs 2:4
justice, love, and **c**. Hs 2:19

and I will have **c** on No Hs 2:23
I will have compassion on No **C**; Hs 2:23
of heart; My **c** is stirred! Hs 11:8
C is hidden from My eyes. Hs 13:14
fatherless receives **c** in You." Hs 14:3
He stifled his **c**, his anger tore Am 1:11
He will again have **c** on us; Mc 7:19
love and **c** to one another. Zch 7:9
them because I have **c** on them, Zch 10:6
shepherds have no **c** for them. Zch 11:5
no longer have **c** on the Zch 11:6
I will have **c** on them as a man Mal 3:17
as a man has **c** on his son who Mal 3:17
crowds, He felt **c** for them, Mt 9:36
a huge crowd, felt **c** for them, Mt 14:14
said, "I have **c** on the crowd, Mt 15:32
the master of that slave had **c**, Mt 18:27
with **c**, Jesus touched their Mt 20:34
Moved with **c**, Jesus reached out Mk 1:41
a huge crowd and had **c** on them, Mk 6:34
I have **c** on the crowd, because Mk 8:2
have **c** on us and help us." Mk 9:22
Because of our God's merciful **c**, Lk 1:78
He had **c** on her and said, Lk 7:13
when he saw ⌊the man⌋, he had **c**. Lk 10:33
saw him and was filled with **c**. Lk 15:20
and I will have **c** on whom I have Rm 9:15
compassion on whom I have **c**. Rm 9:15
put on heartfelt **c**, kindness, Col 3:12
but shuts off his **c** from him— 1Jn 3:17

COMPASSIONATE *(21)*
I will listen because I am **c**. Ex 22:27
Yahweh is a **c** and gracious God, Ex 34:6
the LORD your God is a **c** God. Dt 4:31
so that they may be **c** to them. 1Kg 8:50
gracious and **c**, slow to anger Neh 9:17
You are a gracious and **c** God. Neh 9:31
Yet He was **c**; He atoned for Ps 78:38
Lord, are a **c** and gracious God Ps 86:15
The LORD is **c** and gracious, Ps 103:8
The LORD is gracious and **c**. Ps 111:4
is gracious, **c**, and righteous. Ps 112:4
and righteous; our God is **c**. Ps 116:5
The LORD is gracious and **c**, Ps 145:8
for their **c** One will guide them, Is 49:10
be shaken," says your **c** LORD. Is 54:10
The hands of **c** women have cooked Lm 4:10
gracious and **c**, slow to anger, Jl 2:13
You are a merciful and **c** God, Jnh 4:2
be kind and **c** to one another, Eph 4:32
the Lord is very **c** and merciful. Jms 5:11
believers, and be **c** and humble, 1Pt 3:8

COMPASSIONS *(3)*
Your **c** are many, LORD; Ps 119:156
based on His **c** and the abundance Is 63:7
My **c** would not ⌊reach out⌋ to Jr 15:1

COMPEL *(3)*
thoughts **c** me to answer, Jb 20:2
how can you **c** Gentiles to live Gl 2:14
the ones who would **c** you to be Gl 6:12

COMPELLED *(2)*
I was **c** to appeal to Caesar; Ac 28:19
was a Greek, was **c** to be Gl 2:3

COMPELS *(3)*
and my spirit **c** me ⌊to speak⌋. Jb 32:18
Christ's love **c** us, since we 2Co 5:14
his behalf and **c** the earth and Rv 13:12

COMPENSATE *(1)*
it, he must **c** fully, ox for ox; Ex 21:36

COMPENSATION *(9)*
Set for me the **c** and the gift; Gn 34:12
slave go free in **c** for his eye. Ex 21:26
go free in **c** for his tooth. Ex 21:27
owner of the pit must give **c**; Ex 21:34
He is to pay full **c**, add a fifth Nm 5:7
has no relative to receive **c**, Nm 5:8
the **c** goes to the LORD for the Nm 5:8
army received no **c** from Tyre for Ezk 29:18
This will be his army's **c**. Ezk 29:19

COMPETE *(2)*
get up and **c** in front of us." 2Sm 2:14
how can you **c** with horses? Jr 12:5

COMPETENCE *(3)*
⌊your⌋ **c** and discretion. Pr 3:21
I possess good advice and **c**; Pr 8:14
but our **c** is from God. 2Co 3:5

COMPETENT *(3)*
And who is **c** for this? 2Co 2:16
not that we are **c** in ourselves 2Co 3:5
He has made us **c** to be ministers 2Co 3:6

COMPETENTLY *(2)*
who manages his own household **c**, 1Tm 3:4
and their own households **c**. 1Tm 3:12

COMPETES *(3)*
Now everyone who **c** exercises 1Co 9:25
if anyone **c** as an athlete, 2Tm 2:5
crowned unless he **c** according to 2Tm 2:5

COMPETING *(1)*
and their **c** thoughts either Rm 2:15

COMPILE *(1)*
undertaken to **c** a narrative Lk 1:1

COMPLACENCY *(1)*
and the **c** of fools will destroy Pr 1:32

COMPLACENT *(2)*
Stand up, you **c** women; Is 32:9
Shudder, you **c** ones; Is 32:11

COMPLAIN *(12)*
who are we that you **c** about us?" Ex 16:7
entire community to **c** about him Nm 14:36
he that you should **c** about him?" Nm 16:11
I will **c** in the bitterness of my Jb 7:11
less when you **c** that you do not Jb 35:14
I **c** and groan morning, noon, and Ps 55:17
God, hear my voice when I **c**. Ps 64:1
should ⌊any⌋ living person **c**, Lm 3:39
began to **c** to the landowner: Mt 20:11
All who saw it began to **c**, Lk 19:7
Nor should we **c** as some of them 1Co 10:10
do not **c** about one another, Jms 5:9

COMPLAINED *(8)*
But Abraham **c** to Abimelech Gn 21:25
So the people **c** to Moses: Ex 17:2
because the Israelites **c**, Ex 17:7
All the Israelites **c** about Moses Nm 14:2
because you have **c** about Me. Nm 14:29
Israelite community **c** about Nm 16:41
to David," he **c**, "but they only 1Sm 18:8
⌊Suddenly⌋, he **c** to his father, 2Kg 4:19

COMPLAINING *(9)*
"Why are you **c** to me?" Ex 17:2
the people began **c** openly before Nm 11:1
community that keeps **c** about Me? Nm 14:27
scribes were **c** to His disciples Lk 5:30
Pharisees and scribes were **c**, Lk 15:2
the Jews started **c** about Him, Jn 6:41
them, "Stop **c** among yourselves. Jn 6:43
His disciples were **c** about this, Jn 6:61
to one another without **c**. 1Pt 4:9

COMPLAINT *(12)*
and my couch will ease my **c**, Jb 7:13
I will forget my **c**, change my Jb 9:27
I will express my **c** and speak in Jb 10:1
for me, is my **c** against a man? Jb 21:4
Today also my **c** is bitter. Jb 23:2
when they made a **c** against me, Jb 31:13
and in turmoil with my **c**, Ps 55:2
I pour out my **c** before Him; Ps 142:2
what I should reply about my **c**. Hab 2:1
there arose a **c** by the Ac 6:1
you who has a **c** against someone 1Co 6:1
anyone has a **c** against another Col 3:13

COMPLAINTS *(10)*
He has heard your **c** about Him. Ex 16:7
He has heard the **c** that you are Ex 16:8
Your **c** are not against us but Ex 16:8
for He has heard your **c**.'" Ex 16:9
I have heard the **c** of the Ex 16:12
the Israelites' **c** that they make Nm 14:27
the Israelites' **c** that they have Nm 17:5
put an end to their **c** before Me, Nm 17:10
heard their outcry and these **c**. Neh 5:6
Who has **c**? Who has wounds Pr 23:29

COMPLETE *(49)*
C this week ⌊of wedding Gn 29:27
They took 40 days to **c** this, Gn 50:3
'Tomorrow is a day of **c** rest, Ex 16:23
provide for ⌊his⌋ **c** recovery. Ex 21:19
must be a Sabbath of **c** rest, Ex 31:15
a Sabbath of **c** rest to the LORD. Ex 35:2
her days of purification are **c**, Lv 12:6
is a Sabbath of **c** rest for you, Lv 16:31
must be a Sabbath of **c** rest, Lv 23:3
to count seven **c** weeks starting Lv 23:15
you are to have a day of **c** rest, Lv 23:24
be a Sabbath of **c** rest for you, Lv 23:32
will be **c** rest on the first Lv 23:39
the first day and **c** rest on the Lv 23:39
be a Sabbath of **c** rest for the Lv 25:4
be a year of **c** rest for the land Lv 25:5
of the altar and **c** plans for its 2Kg 16:10
count them, but he didn't **c** it. 1Ch 27:24
on the verge of **c** ruin before Pr 5:14
C your outdoor work, and prepare Pr 24:27
The princes of Zoan are **c** fools; Is 19:11
When 70 years for Babylon are **c**, Jr 29:10
Zion, your punishment is **c**; Lm 4:22
its **c** design along with all its Ezk 43:11
may observe its **c** design and all Ezk 43:11
c the days ⌊of purification⌋. Ezk 43:27
bring ⌊it⌋ to **c** destruction; Nah 1:9
He will make a **c**, yes, a Zph 1:18
house, and his hands will **c** it. Zch 4:9
third day I will **c** My work.' Lk 13:32
to see if he has enough to **c** it? Lk 14:28
So this joy of mine is **c**. Jn 3:29
be in you and your joy may be **c**. Jn 15:11
receive, that your joy may be **c**. Jn 16:24
Your message with **c** boldness, Ac 4:29
sanctification **c** in the fear of 2Co 7:1
that I have **c** confidence in you 2Co 7:16
he should also **c** this grace to 2Co 8:6
once your obedience is **c**. 2Co 10:6
corrupted from a **c** and pure 2Co 11:3
going to be made **c** by the flesh? Gl 3:3
to face and to **c** what is lacking 1Th 3:10
so that the man of God may be **c**, 2Tm 3:17
was about to **c** the tabernacle. Heb 8:5
endurance must do its **c** work, Jms 1:4
so that you may be mature and **c**, Jms 1:4
things so that our joy may be **c**. 1Jn 1:4
face so that our joy may be **c**. 2Jn 12
your works **c** before My God. Rv 3:2

COMPLETED *(38)*
and everything in them were **c**. Gn 2:1
God **c** His work that He had done, Gn 2:2
me my wife, for my time is **c**. Gn 29:21
your days of ordination are **c**, Lv 8:33
the time is **c** during which he Nm 6:5
his time of consecration is **c**, Nm 6:13
everything was **c** that the LORD Jos 4:10
the temple was **c** in every detail 1Kg 6:38
Solomon **c** his entire 1Kg 7:1
the work of the pillars was **c**. 1Kg 7:22
did in the LORD's temple was **c**. 1Kg 7:51
So he **c** the temple. 1Kg 9:25
did for the LORD's temple was **c**. 2Ch 5:1
So the LORD's temple was **c**. 2Ch 8:16
until the burnt offering was **c**. 2Ch 29:28
When the burnt offerings were **c**, 2Ch 29:29
all this was **c**, all Israel who 2Ch 31:1
now, yet it has not been **c**. Ezr 5:16
This house was **c** on the third Ezr 6:15
The wall was **c** in 52 days, Neh 6:15
70 years are **c**, I will punish Jr 25:12
When you have **c** these days, Ezk 4:6
until the time of wrath is **c**, Dn 11:36
all these things will be **c**. Dn 12:7
the days of his ministry were **c**, Lk 1:23
the eight days were **c** for His Lk 2:21
When they had **c** everything Lk 2:39
they may have My joy **c** in them. Jn 17:13
after they had **c** their relief Ac 12:25
of God for the work they had **c**. Ac 14:26
When we **c** our voyage from Tyre, Ac 21:7
as they had been, would be **c**. Rv 6:11
God's hidden plan will be **c**, Rv 10:7
them, God's wrath will be **c**. Rv 15:1
of the seven angels were **c**. Rv 15:8
until the 1,000 years were **c**. Rv 20:3
until the 1,000 years were **c**. Rv 20:5
When the 1,000 years are **c**, Rv 20:7

COMPLETELY *(114)*
(See pp. xi-xii.)

COMPLETING *(4)*
the sanctuary until **c** her days Lv 12:4
on the earth by **c** the work You Jn 17:4
as John was **c** his life work, Ac 13:25
and I am **c** in my flesh what is Col 1:24

COMPLETION (4)
announcing the c of the Ac 21:26
may also be a c from what you 2Co 8:11
But when the c of the time came, Gl 4:4
carry it on to c until the day Php 1:6

COMPLEX (56)
measuring inside the temple c, Ezk 42:15
and measured all around the c. Ezk 42:15
the temple c on all four sides. Ezk 42:20
into the temple c and drove out Mt 21:12
came to Him in the temple c, Mt 21:14
in the temple c cheering, Mt 21:15
When He entered the temple c, Mt 21:23
was going out of the temple c, Mt 24:1
in the temple c, and you didn't Mt 26:55
Jerusalem and into the temple c. Mk 11:11
into the temple c and began to Mk 11:15
goods through the temple c. Mk 11:16
He was walking in the temple c, Mk 11:27
as He taught in the temple c, Mk 12:35
was going out of the temple c, Mk 13:1
Olives across from the temple c, Mk 13:3
in the temple c, and you didn't Mk 14:49
Spirit, he entered the temple c. Lk 2:27
She did not leave the temple c, Lk 2:37
in the temple c sitting among Lk 2:46
went up to the temple c to pray, Lk 18:10
into the temple c and began to Lk 19:45
He was teaching in the temple c. Lk 19:47
in the temple c and proclaiming Lk 20:1
were talking about the temple c, Lk 21:5
He was teaching in the temple c, Lk 21:37
to hear Him in the temple c. Lk 21:38
I was with you in the temple c, Lk 22:53
in the temple c blessing God. Lk 24:53
In the temple c He found people Jn 2:14
of the temple c with their sheep Jn 2:15
in the temple c and said to him Jn 5:14
into the temple c and began to Jn 7:14
He was teaching in the temple c, Jn 7:28
He went to the temple c again, Jn 8:2
while teaching in the temple c. Jn 8:20
and went out of the temple c. Jn 8:59
in the temple c in Solomon's Jn 10:23
as they stood in the temple c: Jn 11:56
synagogue and in the temple c, Jn 18:20
together in the temple c, Ac 2:46
to the temple c at the hour of Ac 3:1
those entering the temple c. Ac 3:2
about to enter the temple c, Ac 3:3
entered the temple c with them— Ac 3:8
Beautiful Gate of the temple c. Ac 3:10
Go and stand in the temple c, Ac 5:20
entered the temple c at daybreak Ac 5:21
in the temple c and teaching Ac 5:25
Every day in the temple c, Ac 5:42
of Asia saw him in the temple c, Ac 21:27
brought him into the temple c. Ac 21:29
dragged him out of the temple c, Ac 21:30
and was praying in the temple c, Ac 22:17
in the temple c or in the Ac 24:12
in the temple c and were trying Ac 26:21

COMPLIANT (1)
gentle, c, full of mercy Jms 3:17

COMPOSE (1)
Let my Opponent c ⌊His⌋ Jb 31:35

COMPOSED (2)
Solomon c 3,000 proverbs, and 1Kg 4:32
c of both Cyrenians and Ac 6:9

COMPOSURE (2)
Regaining his c, he said, "Serve Gn 43:31
longer keep his c in front of Gn 45:1

COMPREHEND (6)
great things that we cannot c. Jb 37:5
Your thoughts are for me ⌊to c⌋; Ps 139:17
whose speech is difficult to c— Is 33:19
Such people do not c and cannot Is 44:18
Do you not yet understand or c? Mk 8:17
may be able to c with all the Eph 3:18

COMPREHENDED (1)
Have you c the extent of the Jb 38:18

COMPRESSES (1)
the one who c his lips brings Pr 16:30

COMPULSION (2)
who is under no c, but has 1Co 7:37
overseeing out of c but freely, 1Pt 5:2

CONANIAH (3)
C the Levite was the officer in 2Ch 31:12
authority of C and his brother 2Ch 31:13
C and his brothers Shemaiah and 2Ch 35:9

CONCEAL (12)
don't c it from me!" 2Sm 14:18
me in Sheol and c me until Your Jb 14:13
I will not c what the Almighty Jb 27:11
For He will c me in His shelter Ps 27:5
You c them in a shelter from the Ps 31:20
You and did not c my iniquity. Ps 32:5
I did not c Your constant love Ps 40:10
the glory of God to c a matter Pr 25:2
They do not c it. Woe to them Is 3:9
and will no longer c her slain. Is 26:21
if they c themselves from My Am 9:3
your freedom as a way to c evil. 1Pt 2:16

CONCEALED (14)
but it is c from her husband, Nm 5:13
They are c in the ground inside Jos 7:21
was the cloak, c in his tent, Jos 7:22
Yet You c these ⌊thoughts⌋ in Jb 10:13
living thing and c from the Jb 28:21
caught in the net they have c. Ps 9:15
shooting from c places at the Ps 64:4
his hatred is c by deception, Pr 26:26
an open reprimand than c love. Pr 27:5
are not c from Me, and their Jr 16:17
perhaps you will be c on the day Zph 2:3
For nothing is c except to be Mk 4:22
For nothing is c that won't be Lk 8:17
it was c from them so that they Lk 9:45

CONCEALS (8)
his mouth and he c it under his Jb 20:12
Who is this who c ⌊My⌋ counsel Jb 42:3
mouth of the wicked c violence. Pr 10:6
mouth of the wicked c violence. Pr 10:11
The one who c hatred has lying Pr 10:18
A shrewd person c knowledge, Pr 12:23
Whoever c an offense promotes Pr 17:9
The one who c his sins will not Pr 28:13

CONCEDE (1)
our Rock; even our enemies c. Dt 32:31

CONCEIT (1)
Do nothing out of rivalry or c, Php 2:3

CONCEITED (6)
So that you will not be c, Rm 11:25
envy; is not boastful; is not c; 1Co 13:4
must not become c, provoking one Gl 5:26
or he might become c and fall 1Tm 3:6
he is c, understanding nothing, 1Tm 6:4
reckless, c, lovers of pleasure 2Tm 3:4

CONCEIVE (13)
and will be able to c children. Nm 5:28
Did I c all these people? Nm 11:12
but you will c and give birth to Jdg 13:3
you will c and give birth to a Jdg 13:5
'You will c and give a birth to Jdg 13:7
the LORD enabled her to c, Ru 4:13
They c trouble and give birth to Jb 15:35
The virgin will c, have a son, Is 7:14
You will c chaff; you will give Is 33:11
they c trouble and give birth to Is 59:4
because Elizabeth could not c, Lk 1:7
You will c and give birth to a Lk 1:31
received power to c offspring, Heb 11:11

CONCEIVED (35)
she c and gave birth to Cain. Gn 4:1
and she c and gave birth to Gn 4:17
You have c and will have a son. Gn 16:11
prayer, and his wife Rebekah c. Gn 25:21
Leah c, gave birth to a son, and Gn 29:32
c again, gave birth to a son, Gn 29:33
c again, gave birth to a son, Gn 29:34
And she c again, gave birth to a Gn 29:35
Bilhah c and bore Jacob a son. Gn 30:5
slave Bilhah c again and bore Gn 30:7
and she c and bore Jacob a fifth Gn 30:17
Then Leah c again and bore Jacob Gn 30:19
She c and bore a son, and said, Gn 30:23
She c and gave birth to a son, Gn 38:3
c again, gave birth to a son, Gn 38:4
c and gave birth to a son. 1Sm 1:20
she c and gave birth to three 1Sm 2:21
The woman c and sent word to 2Sm 11:5
The woman c and gave birth to a 2Kg 4:17
and she c and gave birth to a 1Ch 7:23
when they said, "A boy is c." Jb 3:3
was sinful when my mother c me. Ps 51:5
the chamber of the one who c me. Sg 3:4
There your mother c you; Sg 8:5
there she c and gave you birth. Sg 8:5
and she c and gave birth to a Is 8:3
and she c and bore him a son. Hs 1:3
She c again and gave birth to a Hs 1:6
she c and gave birth to a son. Hs 1:8
she c them and acted shamefully. Hs 2:5
what has been c in her is by the Mt 1:20
Elizabeth c and kept herself Lk 1:24
even she has c a son in her old Lk 1:36
by the angel before He was c. Lk 2:21
desire has c, it gives birth Jms 1:15

CONCEIVES (1)
with evil, c trouble, and gives Ps 7:14

CONCEIVING (3)
the LORD had kept her from c. 1Sm 1:5
the LORD had kept Hannah from c. 1Sm 1:6
c and uttering lying words from Is 59:13

CONCEPTION (1)
no birth, no gestation, no c. Hs 9:11

CONCERN (8)
he did not c himself with Gn 39:6
master does not c himself with Gn 39:8
from a specific c that in the Jos 22:24
weights in the bag are His c. Pr 16:11
Then I had c for My holy name, Ezk 36:21
What has this c of yours to do Jn 2:4
It should not be a c to you. 1Co 7:21
have the same c for each other. 1Co 12:25

CONCERNED (12)
Do not be c about the boy and Gn 21:12
Do not be c about your Gn 45:20
stopped being c about the 1Sm 10:2
be safe and be c with Your Ps 119:117
none of these things c Gallio. Ac 18:17
man is c about the things 1Co 7:32
married man is c about the 1Co 7:33
a virgin is c about the things 1Co 7:34
woman is c about the things 1Co 7:34
Is God really c with oxen? 1Co 9:9
You were, in fact, c about me, Php 4:10
let us be c about one another Heb 10:24

CONCERNING (139)
(See pp. xi-xii.)

CONCERNS (14)
the valuation c a male from 20 Lv 27:3
tent of meeting c the most holy Nm 4:4
sinned, my mistake c only me. Jb 19:4
I store up anxious c within me, Ps 13:2
test me and know my c. Ps 139:23
one does not understand these c. Pr 29:7
vision that he sees c many years Ezk 12:27
not thinking about God's c, Mt 16:23
not thinking about God's c, Mk 8:33
offer my defense in what c me. Ac 24:10
men knows the c of a man except 1Co 2:11
no one knows the c of God except 1Co 2:11
I want you to be without c. 1Co 7:32
in the c of everyday life 2Tm 2:4

CONCESSION (1)
I say this as a c, not as a 1Co 7:6

CONCLUDE (1)
For we c that a man is justified Rm 3:28

CONCLUDED (6)
⌊David c,⌋ "By the LORD's hand 1Ch 28:19
Hezekiah c, "Now you are 2Ch 29:31
The words of Job are c. Jb 31:40
of David son of Jesse are c. Ps 72:20
work of God ⌊and c⌋ that man is Ec 8:17
When He had c all His sayings in Lk 7:1

CONCLUDING (2)
about the offer, c, "That is 1Sm 17:27
c that God had called us to Ac 16:10

CONCLUSION (3)
been heard, the c of the matter Ec 12:13
will happen at the c of the time Dn 8:19
since we have reached this c: 2Co 5:14

CONCLUSIONS (1)
Look, I waited for your c; Jb 32:11

CONCUBINE (21)
His c, whose name was Reumah, Gn 22:24

with his father's **c** Bilhah, Gn 35:22
a **c** of Esau's son Eliphaz, Gn 36:12
His **c** who was in Shechem also Jdg 8:31
Bethlehem in Judah as his **c**. Jdg 19:1
to go with his **c** and his servant Jdg 19:9
donkeys and his **c** with him. Jdg 19:10
daughter and the man's **c** now. Jdg 19:24
man seized his **c** and took her Jdg 19:25
the woman, his **c**, collapsed near Jdg 19:27
hold of his **c**, cut her into 12 Jdg 19:29
Benjamin with my **c** to spend the Jdg 20:4
they raped my **c**, and she died. Jdg 20:5
Then I took my **c** and cut her in Jdg 20:6
Now Saul had a **c** whose name was 2Sm 3:7
you sleep with my father's **c**?" 2Sm 3:7
to David what Saul's **c** Rizpah, 2Sm 21:11
born to Keturah, Abraham's **c**: 1Ch 1:32
Caleb's **c** Ephah was the mother 1Ch 2:46
Caleb's **c** Maacah was the mother 1Ch 2:48
sons through his Aramean **c**: 1Ch 7:14

CONCUBINES *(18)*
gave gifts to the sons of his **c**, Gn 25:6
David took more **c** and wives in 2Sm 5:13
he left behind 10 **c** to take care 2Sm 15:16
your father's **c** he left to take 2Sm 16:21
with his father's **c** in the sight 2Sm 16:22
your wives, and your **c**. 2Sm 19:5
he took the 10 **c** he had left to 2Sm 20:3
who were princesses and 300 **c**, 1Kg 11:3
addition to the sons by his **c**. 1Ch 3:9
more than all his wives and **c**. 2Ch 11:21
18 wives and 60 **c** and was the 2Ch 11:21
eunuch in charge of the **c**. Est 2:14
myself, and many **c**, the delights Ec 2:8
queens and 80 **c** and young women Sg 6:8
queens and **c** also, and they sing Sg 6:9
and **c** could drink from them. Dn 5:2
wives, and **c** drank from them. Dn 5:3
and **c** drank wine from them, Dn 5:23

CONDEMN *(20)*
one the judges **c** must repay Ex 22:9
the innocent and **c** the guilty. Dt 25:1
right, my own mouth would **c** me; Jb 9:20
Will you **c** the mighty Righteous Jb 34:17
righteous and **c** the innocent to Ps 94:21
him from those who would **c** him. Ps 109:31
who is he who will **c** Me? Is 50:9
with this generation and **c** it, Mt 12:41
with this generation and **c** it, Mt 12:42
and they will **c** Him to death. Mt 20:18
and they will **c** Him to death. Mk 10:33
Do not **c**, and you will not be Lk 6:37
of this generation and **c** them, Lk 11:31
with this generation and **c** it, Lk 11:32
"Neither do I **c** you," said Jesus. Jn 8:11
another, you **c** yourself, since Rm 2:1
who does not **c** himself by what Rm 14:22
I don't say this to **c** you, 2Co 7:3
because if our hearts **c** us, 1Jn 3:20
our hearts do not **c** ⌊us⌋ we have 1Jn 3:21

CONDEMNATION *(9)*
Their **c** is deserved! Rm 3:8
resulting in **c**, but from many Rm 5:16
there is **c** for everyone, Rm 5:18
no **c** now exists for those in Rm 8:1
if the ministry of **c** had glory, 2Co 3:9
fall into the **c** of the Devil. 1Tm 3:6
receive **c** because they have 1Tm 5:12
Their **c**, ⌊pronounced⌋ long ago, 2Pt 2:3
bring an abusive **c** against him, Jd 9

CONDEMNED *(23)*
The one **c** to die is to be Dt 17:6
refute ⌊him⌋, and yet had **c** him. Jb 32:3
allow him to be **c** when he is Ps 37:33
power, preserve those **c** to die. Ps 79:11
to set free those **c** to die, Ps 102:20
for the LORD our God has **c** us. Jr 8:14
would not have **c** the innocent. Mt 12:7
by your words you will be **c**." Mt 12:37
can you escape being **c** to hell? Mt 23:33
seeing that He had been **c**, Mt 27:3
And they all **c** Him to be Mk 14:64
does not believe will be **c**. Mk 16:16
condemn, and you will not be **c**. Lk 6:37
Has no one **c** you?" Jn 8:10
He **c** sin in the flesh by sending Rm 8:3
doubts stands **c** if he eats, Rm 14:23
last place, like men **c** to die: 1Co 4:9
we may not be **c** with the world. 1Co 11:32
to his face because he stood **c**. Gl 2:11
all will be **c**—those who did 2Th 2:12
this he **c** the world and became Heb 11:7
You have **c**—you have murdered— Jms 5:6
to ashes and **c** them to ruin, 2Pt 2:6

CONDEMNING *(4)*
c the wicked by bringing what he 1Kg 8:32
c the wicked by bringing what he 2Ch 6:23
the guilty and **c** the just— Pr 17:15
fulfilled their words by **c** Him. Ac 13:27

CONDEMNS *(3)*
Your own mouth **c** you, not I; Jb 15:6
but He **c** a man who schemes. Pr 12:2
Who is the one who **c**? Rm 8:34

CONDITION *(9)*
agree with you only on this **c**: Gn 34:15
be one people only on this **c**: Gn 34:22
make one with you on this **c**: 1Sm 11:2
Know well the **c** of your flock, Pr 27:23
that man's last **c** is worse than Mt 12:45
on the humble **c** of His slave. Lk 1:48
that man's last **c** is worse than Lk 11:26
my physical **c** was a trial for Gl 4:14
of our humble **c** into the Php 3:21

CONDITIONS *(2)*
Besides that, **c** were good in 2Ch 12:12
its terms and **c** and the open Jr 32:11

CONDOLENCES *(2)*
has sent men with **c** for you, 2Sm 10:3
has sent men with **c** for you, 1Ch 19:3

CONDONED *(1)*
that is not even **c** among the 1Co 5:1

CONDUCT *(23)*
and accuses ⌊her⌋ of shameful **c**, Dt 22:14
has accused her of shameful **c**, Dt 22:17
orders his **c**, I will show him Ps 50:23
pride, evil **c**, and perverse Pr 8:13
As shameful **c** is pleasure for a Pr 10:23
blameless **c** are His delight. Pr 11:20
will get what their **c** deserves, Pr 14:14
A guilty man's **c** is crooked, Pr 21:8
knows how to **c** himself before Ec 6:8
them according to their own **c**, Ezk 7:27
observe their **c** and actions. Ezk 14:22
you see their **c** and actions, Ezk 14:23
it with their **c** and actions. Ezk 36:17
to their **c** and actions. Ezk 36:19
are not a terror to good **c**, Rm 13:3
in speech, in **c**, in love, in 1Tm 4:12
my teaching, **c**, purpose, faith, 2Tm 3:10
wanting to **c** ourselves honorably Heb 13:18
works by good **c** with wisdom's Jms 3:13
are to be holy in all your **c**; 1Pt 1:15
you are to **c** yourselves in 1Pt 1:17
C yourselves honorably among the 1Pt 2:12
be in holy **c** and godliness 2Pt 3:11

CONDUCTED *(5)*
that his father David had **c**, 2Ch 2:17
a decree and a search was **c**. Ezr 4:19
Babylon be **c** ⌊to see⌋ if it is Ezr 5:17
that we have **c** ourselves in the 2Co 1:12
blamelessly we **c** ourselves with 1Th 2:10

CONDUCTING *(2)*
c trade on the vast waters. Ps 107:23
c discussions every day in the Ac 19:9

CONDUCTS *(1)*
generously and **c** his business Ps 112:5

CONDUIT *(2)*
the end of the **c** of the upper Is 7:3
stood near the **c** of the upper Is 36:2

CONDUITS *(1)*
branches beside the two gold **c**, Zch 4:12

CONFER *(4)*
C some of your authority on him Nm 27:20
So come, let's **c** together. Neh 6:7
procedure to **c** with experts in Est 1:13
You **c** majesty and splendor on Ps 21:5

CONFERRED *(5)*
Abner **c** with the elders of 2Sm 3:17
Israel, he **c** with his servants 2Kg 6:8
they **c** together and bought the Mt 27:7
Sanhedrin, they **c** among Ac 4:15
After Festus **c** with his council, Ac 25:12

CONFESS *(18)*
he is to **c** he has committed that Lv 5:5
the live goat and **c** over it all Lv 16:21
But if they will **c** their sin and Lv 26:40
person is to **c** the sin he has Nm 5:7
I **c** the sins we have committed Neh 1:6
Then I will **c** to you that your Jb 40:14
I will **c** my transgressions to Ps 32:5
So I **c** my guilt; I am anxious Ps 38:18
you. They will **c** to you: God is Is 45:14
Pharisees they did not **c** Him, Jn 12:42
But I **c** this to you: Ac 24:14
if you **c** with your mouth, Rm 10:9
should **c** that Jesus Christ Php 2:11
of our lips that **c** His name. Heb 13:15
c your sins to one another and Jms 5:16
If we **c** our sins, He is faithful 1Jn 1:9
who does not **c** Jesus is not 1Jn 4:3
do not **c** the coming of Jesus 2Jn 7

CONFESSED *(8)*
there they **c**, "We have sinned 1Sm 7:6
Ezra prayed and **c**, weeping and Ezr 10:1
and they stood and **c** their sins Neh 9:2
prayed to the LORD my God and **c**: Dn 9:4
River as they **c** their sins. Mt 3:6
River as they **c** their sins. Mk 1:5
that if anyone **c** Him as Messiah, Jn 9:22
and **c** that they were foreigners Heb 11:13

CONFESSES *(5)*
but whoever **c** and renounces them Pr 28:13
with the mouth one **c**, resulting Rm 10:10
he who **c** the Son has the Father 1Jn 2:23
Every spirit who **c** that Jesus 1Jn 4:2
Whoever **c** that Jesus is the Son 1Jn 4:15

CONFESSING *(2)*
c my sin and the sin of my Dn 9:20
believers came **c** and disclosing Ac 19:18

CONFESSION *(9)*
of Israel, and make a **c** to Him. Jos 7:19
make a **c** to the LORD God of your Ezr 10:11
of the day in **c** and worship Neh 9:3
obedience to the **c** of the gospel 2Co 9:13
have made a good **c** before many 1Tm 6:12
who gave a good **c** before Pontius 1Tm 6:13
and high priest of our **c**; Heb 3:1
let us hold fast to the **c**. Heb 4:14
us hold on to the **c** of our hope Heb 10:23

CONFIDENCE *(34)*
intimidated and lost their **c**, Neh 6:16
your piety your **c**, and the Jb 4:6
His source of **c** is fragile; Jb 8:14
If I placed my **c** in gold or Jb 31:24
Lord GOD, my **c** from my youth. Ps 71:5
might put their **c** in God and not Ps 78:7
will be your **c** and will keep Pr 3:26
but the trustworthy keeps a **c**. Pr 11:13
has strong **c** and his children Pr 14:26
so that your **c** may be in the Pr 22:19
strength will lie in quiet **c**. Is 30:15
will be quiet **c** forever. Is 32:17
'What are you basing your **c** on? Is 36:4
Do not have **c** in them, though Jr 12:6
whose **c** indeed is the LORD. Jr 17:7
In this **c**, I planned to come to 2Co 1:15
have this kind of **c** toward God 2Co 3:4
I have great **c** in you; 2Co 7:4
that I have complete **c** in you. 2Co 7:16
because of his great **c** in you. 2Co 8:22
bold with the **c** by which I plan 2Co 10:2
Lord I have **c** in you that you Gl 5:10
and **c** through faith in Him. Eph 3:12
Lord have gained **c** from my Php 1:14
your **c** may grow in Christ Jesus Php 1:26
and do not put **c** in the flesh— Php 3:3
I once had **c** in the flesh too. Php 3:4
has grounds for **c** in the flesh, Php 3:4
We have **c** in the Lord about you, 2Th 3:4
courage and the **c** of our hope. Heb 3:6
So don't throw away your **c**, Heb 10:35
us⌋ we have **c** before God, 1Jn 3:21
so that we may have **c** in the day 1Jn 4:17
Now this is the **c** we have before 1Jn 5:14

CONFIDENT *(17)*
because they were **c** in the Jdg 20:36
had been **c** ⌊of finding water⌋ Jb 6:20
You will be **c**, because there is Jb 11:18
he remains **c**, even if the Jordan Jb 40:23

out against me, still I am **c**. Ps 27:3
My heart is **c**, God, my heart is Ps 57:7
confident, God, my heart is **c**. Ps 57:7
My heart is **c**, God; Ps 108:1
his heart is **c**, trusting in the Ps 112:7
But you were **c** in your beauty Ezk 16:15
Me in ships to terrify **c** Cush. Ezk 30:9
because I am **c** about all of you 2Co 2:3
we are always **c** and know that 2Co 5:6
yet we are **c** and satisfied to be 2Co 5:8
anyone is **c** that he belongs to 2Co 10:7
Since I am **c** of your obedience, Phm 21
your case we are **c** of the better Heb 6:9

CONFIDENTLY *(2)*
those who are passing through **c**, Mc 2:8
I can **c** speak to you about the Ac 2:29

CONFINE *(1)*
You must **c** him in stocks and an Jr 29:26

CONFINED *(13)*
the king's prisoners were **c**. Gn 39:20
the prison where Joseph was **c**. Gn 40:3
Egypt, who were **c** in the prison, Gn 40:5
one of you be **c** to the Gn 42:19
does not die but is **c** to bed, Ex 21:18
her be **c** outside the camp for Nm 12:14
So Miriam was **c** outside the camp Nm 12:15
and **c** their calves in the pen. 1Sm 6:10
They were **c** until the day of 2Sm 20:3
They will be **c** to a dungeon; Is 24:22
he was still **c** in the guard's Jr 33:1
when he was **c** in the guard's Jr 39:15
came, we were **c** under the law, Gl 3:23

CONFIRM *(21)*
I **c** My covenant with you that Gn 9:11
I will **c** My covenant with him as Gn 17:19
But I will **c** My covenant with Gn 17:21
and I will **c** the oath that I Gn 26:3
and **c** My covenant with you. Lv 26:9
Her husband may **c** or cancel any Nm 30:13
in order to **c** His covenant He Dt 8:18
May the LORD **c** your word." 1Sm 1:23
in after you and **c** your words." 1Kg 1:14
please **c** what You promised to 1Kg 8:26
and **c** their hearts toward You. 1Ch 29:18
please **c** what You promised to 2Ch 6:17
authority to **c** the letter about Est 9:29
order to **c** these days of Purim Est 9:31
C what You said to Your servant, Ps 119:38
to you and will **c** My promise Jr 29:10
⌊Go ahead,⌋ **c** your vows! Jr 44:25
c the promises to the fathers, Rm 15:8
He will also **c** you to the end, 1Co 1:8
urge you to **c** your love to him. 2Co 2:8
every effort to **c** your calling 2Pt 1:10

CONFIRMATION *(1)*
and bring a **c** from them. 1Sm 17:18

CONFIRMED *(13)*
that I have **c** between Me and all Gn 9:17
me so that your words can be **c**; Gn 42:20
He has **c** them because he said Nm 30:14
that Samuel was a **c** prophet of 1Sm 3:20
and **c** to Jacob as a decree, 1Ch 16:17
and his house be **c** forever, 1Ch 17:23
Let your name be **c** and magnified 1Ch 17:24
Esther's command **c** these customs Est 9:32
and **c** to Jacob as a decree and Ps 105:10
about Christ was **c** among you, 1Co 1:6
witnesses every word will be **c**. 2Co 13:1
Lord and was **c** to us by those Heb 2:3
the prophetic word strongly **c**. 2Pt 1:19

CONFIRMING *(3)*
that I am **c** My covenant with you Gn 9:9
working with them and **c** the word Mk 16:20
and for them a **c** oath ends every Heb 6:16

CONFIRMS *(5)*
he **c** all her vows and Nm 30:14
You, as all we have heard **c**. 2Sm 7:22
You, as all we have heard **c**. 1Ch 17:20
who **c** the message of His servant Is 44:26
Now the One who **c** us with you in 2Co 1:21

CONFISCATION *(2)*
banishment, **c** of property, Ezr 7:26
with joy the **c** of your Heb 10:34

CONFLICT *(12)*
I had a serious **c** with the Jdg 12:2
The **c** with the Philistines was 1Sm 14:52
A hot-tempered man stirs up **c**, Pr 15:18
man spreads **c**, and a gossip Pr 16:28
To start a **c** is to release a Pr 17:14
out a mocker, and **c** goes too; Pr 22:10
without a gossip, **c** dies down. Pr 26:20
A greedy person provokes **c**, Pr 28:25
angry man stirs up **c**, and a Pr 29:22
dispute and **c** in all the land. Jr 15:10
true and was about a great **c**. Dn 10:1
is ongoing, and **c** escalates. Hab 1:3

CONFLICTS *(3)*
of the lands had many **c**. 2Ch 15:5
Hatred stirs up **c**, but love Pr 10:12
sorrow? Who has **c**? Who has Pr 23:29

CONFORMED *(4)*
predestined to be **c** to the image Rm 8:29
Do not be **c** to this age, but be Rm 12:2
being **c** to His death, Php 3:10
do not be **c** to the desires of 1Pt 1:14

CONFOUND *(2)*
confuse and **c** their speech, Ps 55:9
I will again **c** these people with Is 29:14

CONFOUNDED *(4)*
take my life be disgraced and **c**. Ps 40:14
seek my life be disgraced and **c**; Ps 70:2
adversaries be disgraced and **c**; Ps 71:13
my harm will be disgraced and **c**. Ps 71:24

CONFOUNDING *(1)*
and kept **c** the Jews who lived in Ac 9:22

CONFOUNDS *(1)*
who **c** the wise and makes their Is 44:25

CONFRONT *(14)*
will come out and **c** you with the Nm 20:18
they came out to **c** them with a Nm 20:20
army and went out to **c** Israel in Nm 21:23
standing in the path to **c** me. Nm 22:34
morning Samuel got up to **c** Saul, 1Sm 15:12
going out to **c** the Philistine, 1Sm 17:55
King Josiah went to **c** him, 2Kg 23:29
went out to **c** him and said to 2Ch 19:2
and Josiah went out to **c** him. 2Ch 35:20
days of suffering **c** me. Jb 30:27
Rise up, LORD! **C** him; bring him Ps 17:13
Let us **c** each other. Is 50:8
lion only to have a bear **c** him. Am 5:19
will never overtake or **c** us, Am 9:10

CONFRONTED *(10)*
that the LORD **c** him and sought Ex 4:24
Pharaoh, they **c** Moses and Aaron, Ex 5:20
that **c** them on the way, Ex 18:8
the snares of death **c** me. 2Sm 22:6
They **c** me in the day of my 2Sm 22:19
Who **c** Me, that I should repay Jb 41:11
the snares of death **c** me. Ps 18:5
They **c** me in the day of my Ps 18:18
their wickedness has **c** Me." Jnh 1:2
guard, and the Sadducees **c** them, Ac 4:1

CONFRONTS *(1)*
the accused **c** the accusers face Ac 25:16

CONFUSE *(3)*
down there and **c** their language Gn 11:7
c and confound their speech, Ps 55:9
they **c** the direction of your Is 3:12

CONFUSED *(5)*
there the LORD **c** the language Gn 11:9
Can a man speak when he is **c**? Jb 37:20
of beer, they are **c** by wine. Is 28:7
Those who are **c** will gain Is 29:24
and was **c** because each one Ac 2:6

CONFUSION *(16)*
wandering around the land in **c**; Ex 14:3
cloud, and threw them into **c**. Ex 14:24
and throw into **c** all the nations Ex 23:27
them into great **c** until they are Dt 7:23
against you curses, **c**, and Dt 28:20
blindness, and mental **c**, Dt 28:28
threw them into **c** before Israel. Jos 10:10
his army into **c** with the sword Jdg 4:15
them into such **c** that they fled 1Sm 7:10
against each other in great **c**! 1Sm 14:20
Jerusalem and throw it into **c**. Neh 4:8
while the city of Susa was in **c**. Est 3:15
mixed within her a spirit of **c**. Is 19:14
wander in **c** since they have Jl 1:18
So the city was filled with **c**; Ac 19:29
because the assembly was in **c**, Ac 19:32

CONGEALED *(1)*
The watery depths **c** in the heart Ex 15:8

CONGRATULATE *(3)*
greet him and to **c** him because 2Sm 8:10
also gone to **c** our lord King 1Kg 1:47
greet him and to **c** him because 1Ch 18:10

CONGREGATE *(1)*
all the Jews **c**, and I haven't Jn 18:20

CONGREGATION *(30)*
The **c** sent 12,000 brave warriors Jdg 21:10
The whole **c** sent a message of Jdg 21:13
The elders of the **c** said, Jdg 21:16
and the entire **c** of Israel, 1Kg 8:5
the entire **c** of Israel while 1Kg 8:14
front of the entire **c** of Israel 1Kg 8:22
the whole **c** of Israel with 1Kg 8:55
and the entire **c** of Israel who 2Ch 5:6
the entire **c** of Israel while 2Ch 6:3
front of the entire **c** of Israel 2Ch 6:12
front of the entire **c** of Israel, 2Ch 6:13
the midst of the **c**, the Spirit 2Ch 20:14
of the officers and the **c**. 2Ch 28:14
presence of the king and the **c**, 2Ch 29:23
So the **c** brought sacrifices and 2Ch 29:31
offerings the **c** brought was 70 2Ch 29:32
and the entire **c** in Jerusalem 2Ch 30:2
pleased the king and the **c**, 2Ch 30:4
The whole **c** decided to observe 2Ch 30:23
bulls and 7,000 sheep for the **c**. 2Ch 30:24
and 10,000 sheep for the **c**, 2Ch 30:24
I will praise You in the **c**. Ps 22:22
in the great **c** because of You; Ps 22:25
will praise You in the great **c**; Ps 35:18
Remember Your **c**, which You Ps 74:2
of the upright and in the **c**. Ps 111:1
his **c** will be established in My Jr 30:20
sanctify the **c**; Jl 2:16
who was in the **c** in the desert Ac 7:38
will sing hymns to You in the **c**. Heb 2:12

CONIAH *(2)*
(AKA JECHONIAH, JEHOIACHIN)
though you, **C** son of Jehoiakim, Jr 22:24
Is this man **C** a despised, Jr 22:28

CONNECTED *(6)*
plank must be **c** together with Ex 26:17
bear the guilt **c** with the holy Ex 28:38
were two tenons **c** to each other Ex 36:22
Solomon's fame **c** with the name 1Kg 10:1
so closely **c** they cannot be Jb 41:17
better things **c** with salvation. Heb 6:9

CONQUER *(11)*
because we can certainly **c** it!" Nm 13:30
Ahaz but were not able to **c** him. 2Kg 16:5
wise **c** a city of warriors and Pr 21:22
it, and **c** it for ourselves Is 7:6
with you will deceive and **c** you. Ob 7
consume and **c** with slingstones Zch 9:15
by evil, but **c** evil with good. Rm 12:21
he went out as a victor to **c**. Rv 6:2
war with them, **c** them, and kill Rv 11:7
the saints and to **c** them. Rv 13:7
the Lamb will **c** them because He Rv 17:14

CONQUERED *(8)*
So Joshua **c** the whole region— Jos 10:40
Joshua **c** everyone from Jos 10:41
I have **c** the world." Jn 16:33
Do not be **c** by evil, but conquer Rm 12:21
who by faith **c** kingdoms, Heb 11:33
and you have **c** them, because the 1Jn 4:4
victory that has **c** the world: 1Jn 5:4
They **c** him by the blood of the Rv 12:11

CONQUEROR *(1)*
again bring a **c** against you who Mc 1:15

CONQUERS *(2)*
been born of God **c** the world. 1Jn 5:4
who is the one who **c** the world 1Jn 5:5

CONQUEST *(1)*
of Babylon's **c** the earth will Jr 50:46

CONSCIENCE *(33)*
with a clear **c** and clean hands. Gn 20:5
you did this with a clear **c**. Gn 20:6
David's **c** bothered him because 1Sm 24:5
or a troubled **c** for my lord 1Sm 25:31

David's **c** troubled him after he 2Sm 24:10
c will not accuse ⌊me⌋ as long Jb 27:6
even at night my **c** instructs me. Ps 16:7
lips, but far from their **c**. Jr 12:2
in all good **c** until this day. Ac 23:1
to have a clear **c** toward God and Ac 24:16
c is testifying to me with the Rm 9:1
but also because of your **c**. Rm 13:5
an idol, their **c**, being weak, is 1Co 8:7
won't his weak **c** be encouraged 1Co 8:10
brothers and wound their weak **c**, 1Co 8:12
asking no questions for **c**' sake, 1Co 10:25
without raising questions of **c**. 1Co 10:27
who told you, and for **c**' sake. 1Co 10:28
mean your own **c**, but the other 1Co 10:29
judged by another person's **c**? 1Co 10:29
testimony of our **c** that we have 2Co 1:12
to every person's **c** by an open 2Co 4:2
heart, a good **c**, and a sincere 1Tm 1:5
having faith and a good **c**. 1Tm 1:19
of the faith with a clear **c**. 1Tm 3:9
with a clear **c** as my forefathers 2Tm 1:3
their mind and **c** are defiled. Ti 1:15
perfect the worshiper's **c**. Heb 9:9
from an evil **c** and our bodies Heb 10:22
that we have a clear **c**, Heb 13:18
if, because of **c** toward God, 1Pt 2:19
keeping your **c** clear, so that 1Pt 3:16
pledge of a good **c** toward God 1Pt 3:21

CONSCIENCES *(4)*
Their **c** testify in support of Rm 2:15
open to your **c** as well. 2Co 5:11
of liars whose **c** are seared. 1Tm 4:2
cleanse our **c** from dead works to Heb 9:14

CONSCIENTIOUS *(2)*
were more **c** to consecrate 2Ch 29:34
Be **c** about yourself and your 1Tm 4:16

CONSCIENTIOUSLY *(1)*
if you **c** carry out this word, Jr 22:4

CONSCIOUS *(3)*
For I am **c** of my rebellion, Ps 51:3
not see the sun and is not **c**, Ec 6:5
For I am not **c** of anything 1Co 4:4

CONSCIOUSNESS *(1)*
no longer have any **c** of sins? Heb 10:2

CONSECRATE *(43)*
C every firstborn male to Me, Ex 13:2
the Israelites **c** as all their Ex 28:38
ordain, and **c** them, so that they Ex 28:41
do for them to **c** them to serve Ex 29:1
C for Aaron and his sons the Ex 29:27
and anoint it in order to **c** it. Ex 29:36
for the altar and **c** it. Ex 29:37
I will **c** the tent of meeting and Ex 29:44
I will also **c** Aaron and his sons Ex 29:44
C them and they will be Ex 30:29
his sons and **c** them to serve Me Ex 30:30
c it along with all its Ex 40:9
c the altar so that it will be Ex 40:10
basin and its stand, and **c** it. Ex 40:11
anoint him, and **c** him, so that Ex 40:13
and everything in it to **c** them. Lv 8:10
basin with its stand, to **c** them. Lv 8:11
so you must **c** yourselves and be Lv 11:44
C yourselves and be holy, for I Lv 20:7
the Israelites **c** to the LORD, Lv 22:3
You are to **c** the fiftieth year Lv 25:10
But no one can **c** a firstborn of Lv 27:26
a Nazirite vow, to **c** himself to Nm 6:2
day he must **c** his head ⌊again⌋ Nm 6:11
You must **c** to the LORD your God Dt 15:19
told the people, "**C** yourselves, Jos 3:5
Go and **c** the people. Jos 7:13
Tell them to **c** themselves Jos 7:13
I personally **c** the silver to the Jdg 17:3
C yourselves and come with me to 1Sm 16:5
"**C** a solemn assembly for Baal." 2Kg 10:20
relatives must **c** yourselves so 1Ch 15:12
apart forever to **c** the most holy 1Ch 23:13
will volunteer to **c** himself to 1Ch 29:5
C yourselves now and consecrate 2Ch 29:5
yourselves now and **c** the temple 2Ch 29:5
to **c** themselves than 2Ch 29:34
person to **c** ⌊the lambs⌋ to 2Ch 30:17
Passover ⌊lambs⌋, **c** yourselves, 2Ch 35:6
but you must **c** the Sabbath day, Jr 17:22
Sabbath day and **c** the Sabbath Jr 17:24
listen to Me to **c** the Sabbath Jr 17:27
In this way they will **c** it Ezk 43:26

CONSECRATED *(64)*
to the people and **c** them, Ex 19:14
place will be **c** by My glory. Ex 29:43
Whatever touches them will be **c**. Ex 30:29
head and anointed and **c** him. Lv 8:12
of the altar and **c** it by making Lv 8:15
In this way he **c** Aaron and his Lv 8:30
its fruit must be **c** as a praise Lv 19:24
that they have **c** to Me, Lv 22:2
if the one who **c** his house Lv 27:15
If the one who **c** the field Lv 27:19
I **c** every firstborn in Israel to Nm 3:13
because the hair **c** to his God is Nm 6:7
defiling his **c** head of hair, Nm 6:9
because his **c** hair became Nm 6:12
is to shave his **c** head at the Nm 6:18
after he has shaved his **c** head. Nm 6:19
he anointed and **c** it and all its Nm 7:1
he anointed and **c** these things, Nm 7:1
I **c** them to Myself on the day I Nm 8:17
part of the tenth is to be **c**. Nm 18:29
have taken the **c** portion out of Dt 26:13
c the Levite, and the young Jdg 17:12
They **c** his son Eleazar to take 1Sm 7:1
Then he **c** Jesse and his sons 1Sm 16:5
However, there is **c** bread, but 1Sm 21:4
men's bodies are **c** even on an 1Sm 21:5
their bodies are **c** today." 1Sm 21:5
priest gave him the **c** ⌊bread⌋, 1Sm 21:6
brought in the **c** things of his 1Kg 7:51
the king **c** the middle of the 1Kg 8:64
I have **c** this temple you have 1Kg 9:3
his father's **c** gifts and his own 1Kg 15:15
gifts and his own **c** gifts into 1Kg 15:15
took all the **c** items that his 2Kg 12:18
Ahaziah—had **c**, along with his 2Kg 12:18
with his own **c** items and all 2Kg 12:18
and the Levites **c** themselves to 1Ch 15:14
brought the **c** things of his 2Ch 5:1
were present had **c** themselves 2Ch 5:11
Solomon **c** the middle of the 2Ch 7:7
now chosen and **c** this temple so 2Ch 7:16
his father's **c** gifts and his own 2Ch 15:18
and his own **c** gifts into God's 2Ch 15:18
the LORD—only the **c** priests, 2Ch 26:18
brothers together, **c** themselves, 2Ch 29:15
They **c** the LORD's temple for 2Ch 29:17
unfaithful we have set up and **c**. 2Ch 29:19
Now you are **c** to the LORD. 2Ch 29:31
bulls and 3,000 sheep were **c**. 2Ch 29:33
until the priests **c** themselves. 2Ch 29:34
of the priests had **c** themselves 2Ch 30:3
sanctuary that He has **c** forever. 2Ch 30:8
they **c** themselves and brought 2Ch 30:15
who had not **c** themselves, 2Ch 30:17
and many priests **c** themselves. 2Ch 30:24
things that were **c** to the LORD 2Ch 31:6
to the LORD and the **c** things. 2Ch 31:14
had faithfully **c** themselves as 2Ch 31:18
that He had **c** in Jerusalem. 2Ch 36:14
I have **c** My King on Zion, Ps 2:6
is for the **c** priests, the sons Ezk 48:11
to Baal-peor, **c** themselves to Hs 9:10
He has **c** His guests. Zph 1:7
man is carrying **c** meat in the Hg 2:12

CONSECRATES *(7)*
When a man **c** his house as holy Lv 27:14
If a man **c** to the LORD any part Lv 27:16
he **c** his field during the Year Lv 27:17
But if he **c** his field after the Lv 27:18
If a person **c** to the LORD a Lv 27:22
during which he **c** himself to the Nm 6:5
during the time he **c** himself to Nm 6:6

CONSECRATING *(1)*
garments for **c** him to serve Me Ex 28:3

CONSECRATION *(9)*
time of⌋ their ordination and **c**. Ex 29:33
for the **c** of the anointing oil Lv 21:12
the time of his vow of **c**. Nm 6:5
the LORD during the time of **c**. Nm 6:8
his time of **c** to the LORD and to Nm 6:12
day his time of **c** is completed, Nm 6:13
offering to the LORD for his **c**, Nm 6:21
with the ritual for his **c**." Nm 6:21
They began the **c** on the first 2Ch 29:17

CONSENT *(3)*
ground without your Father's **c**. Mt 10:29
By common **c** they would all meet Ac 5:12
to do anything without your **c**, Phm 14

CONSENTED *(1)*
And they **c** to this. Gn 42:20

CONSEQUENCES *(15)*
bringing the **c** of the fathers' Ex 34:7
he bears the **c** of his guilt. Lv 5:17
he will bear the **c** of his sin. Lv 24:15
will bear the **c** of her guilt." Nm 5:31
man will bear the **c** of his sin. Nm 9:13
bringing the **c** of the fathers' Nm 14:18
will bear the **c** of your sins 40 Nm 14:34
will bear the ⌊**c**⌋ of their sin. Nm 18:23
you alone will bear ⌊the **c**⌋." Pr 9:12
bear the **c** of your indecency Ezk 16:58
must bear the **c** of your Ezk 23:35
will bear the **c** for your sins Ezk 23:49
will bear the **c** of their sin. Ezk 44:10
would bear the **c** of their sin. Ezk 44:12
disgrace and the **c** of the Ezk 44:13

CONSEQUENTLY *(4)*
C, the king of Israel sent 2Kg 6:10
C, Hilkiah told Shaphan the 2Ch 34:15
C, no king, however great and Dn 2:10
C, many of them believed, Ac 17:12

CONSIDER *(93)*
the mountain and **c** it holy." Ex 19:23
Now **c** that this nation is Your Ex 33:13
are to **c** the fruit forbidden. Lv 19:23
You are to **c** him holy since he Lv 21:8
it does not **c** itself among the Nm 23:9
c the years long past. Dt 32:7
c carefully what you must do, 1Sm 25:17
so may the LORD **c** my life 1Sm 26:24
the LORD by doing what I **c** evil? 2Sm 12:9
then **c** what you should do, 1Kg 20:22
servants said to him, "**C** this: 1Kg 20:31
to the judges, "**C** what you are 2Ch 19:6
C: who has perished when he was Jb 4:7
Your face and **c** me Your enemy? Jb 13:24
when I **c** ⌊this⌋, I am afraid of Jb 23:15
Stop and **c** God's wonders. Jb 37:14
to my words, LORD; **c** my sighing. Ps 5:1
c my affliction at the hands of Ps 9:13
C me and answer, LORD, my God. Ps 13:3
C my affliction and trouble, Ps 25:18
C my enemies; they are numerous, Ps 25:19
they do not **c** what the LORD has Ps 28:5
daughter, pay attention and **c**: Ps 45:10
C the covenant, for the dark Ps 74:20
c days of old, years long past. Ps 77:5
C our shield, God; look on the Ps 84:9
things and **c** the LORD's acts Ps 107:43
C my affliction and rescue me, Ps 119:153
C how I love Your precepts; Ps 119:159
I **c** them my enemies. Ps 139:22
Don't **c** yourself to be wise; Pr 3:7
Carefully **c** the path for your Pr 4:26
She doesn't **c** the path of life; Pr 5:6
man's wisdom is to **c** his way, Pr 14:8
c carefully what is before you, Pr 23:1
won't He who weighs hearts **c** it? Pr 24:12
Then I turned to **c** wisdom, Ec 2:12
does not often **c** the days of his Ec 5:20
C the work of God; for who can Ec 7:13
but in the day of adversity, **c**: Ec 7:14
or **c** the One who created it long Is 22:11
see and know, **c** and understand, Is 41:20
to Kedar and **c** carefully; Jr 2:10
C, and summon the women who Jr 9:17
and **c** who You have done this Lm 2:20
So **c** the message and understand Dn 9:23
But they never **c** that I remember Hs 7:2
this god will **c** us, and we won't Jnh 1:6
C carefully from this day Hg 2:18
temple was laid; **c** it carefully. Hg 2:18
nations will **c** you fortunate, Mal 3:12
So now we **c** the arrogant to be Mal 3:15
C the sower who went out to sow. Mt 13:3
C the sower who went out to sow. Mk 4:3
And **c** your relative Elizabeth— Lk 1:36
I didn't even **c** myself worthy to Lk 7:7
C the ravens: they don't sow or Lk 12:24
C how the wildflowers grow: Lk 12:27
C this: Moses has given you Jn 7:22

And now, Lord, c their threats, Ac 4:29
and c yourselves unworthy of Ac 13:46
assembled to c this matter. Ac 15:6
If you c me a believer in the Ac 16:15
I c myself fortunate, King Ac 26:2
we c it suitable to hear from Ac 28:22
too c yourselves dead to sin, Rm 6:11
For I c that the sufferings of Rm 8:18
c God's kindness and severity: Rm 11:22
Brothers, c your calling: 1Co 1:26
person should c us in this way: 1Co 4:1
Therefore I c this to be good 1Co 7:26
in ourselves to c anything as 2Co 3:5
For c how much diligence this 2Co 7:11
Such a person should c this: 2Co 10:11
I c myself in no way inferior 2Co 11:5
no one should c me a fool. 2Co 11:16
but in humility c others as more Php 2:3
did not c equality with God as Php 2:6
I also c everything to be a loss Php 3:8
of all things and c them filth, Php 3:8
I do not c myself to have taken Php 3:13
our God will c you worthy of His 2Th 1:11
C what I say, for the Lord will 2Tm 2:7
So if you c me a partner, accept Phm 17
heavenly calling, c Jesus, the Heb 3:1
Now c how great this man was, Heb 7:4
For c Him who endured such Heb 12:3
C it a great joy, my brothers, Jms 1:2
And c ships: though very large Jms 3:4
C how large a forest a small Jms 3:5
whom I c a faithful brother, 1Pt 5:12
I c it right, as long as I am in 2Pt 1:13
They c it a pleasure to carouse 2Pt 2:13

CONSIDERABLE (6)

was a c space between them. 1Sm 26:13
been with me a c period of time. 1Sm 29:3
And they spent a c time with the Ac 14:28
and misled a c number of people Ac 19:26
conversed a c time until dawn. Ac 20:11
C in every way. Rm 3:2

CONSIDERABLY (1)

Ophel, and he heightened it c. 2Ch 33:14

CONSIDERATION (2)

he has no c for his neighbor. Pr 21:10
out of c for the one who told 1Co 10:28

CONSIDERED (41)

black, they will be c stolen." Gn 30:33
c to be Canaanite territory Jos 13:3
Samuel c their demand sinful, 1Sm 8:6
Although you once c yourself 1Sm 15:17
today you c my life precious 1Sm 26:21
Just as I c your life valuable 1Sm 26:24
Beeroth is also c part of 2Sm 4:2
the LORD c what David had done 2Sm 11:27
since it was c as nothing in 1Kg 10:21
since it was c as nothing in 2Ch 9:20
because they were c trustworthy. Neh 13:13
Have you c My servant Job? Jb 1:8
Have you c My servant Job? Jb 2:3
He c wisdom and evaluated it; Jb 28:27
LORD, if You c sins, Lord, who Ps 130:3
Even a fool is c wise when he Pr 17:28
When I c all that I had Ec 2:11
they are c as a speck of dust on Is 40:15
they are c by Him as nothingness Is 40:17
Have you not c the foundations Is 40:21
and who c His fate? Is 53:8
She never c her end. Lm 1:9
So I c pouring out My wrath on Ezk 20:8
So I c pouring out My wrath on Ezk 20:13
So I c pouring out My wrath on Ezk 20:21
But after he had c these things, Mt 1:20
who should be c the greatest. Lk 22:24
When I looked closely and c it, Ac 11:6
Why is it c incredible by any of Ac 26:8
pay is not c as a gift, but as Rm 4:4
He c his own body to be already Rm 4:19
of the promise are c seed. Rm 9:8
Therefore I c it necessary to 2Co 9:5
But I c it necessary to send you Php 2:25
I have c to be a loss because of Php 3:7
me, because He c me faithful, 1Tm 1:12
leaders should be c worthy of an 1Tm 5:17
For Jesus is c worthy of more Heb 3:3
since she c that the One who had Heb 11:11
c God to be able even to raise Heb 11:19
For he c reproach for the sake Heb 11:26

CONSIDERING (4)

c the great things He has done 1Sm 12:24
After seriously c the matter, Neh 5:7
While I was c the horns, Dn 7:8
You're not c that it is to your Jn 11:50

CONSIDERS (10)

He c no disaster for Jacob; Nm 23:21
He c all their works. Ps 33:15
eyes, and He c all his paths. Pr 5:21
The Righteous One c the house of Pr 21:12
but the upright man c his way. Pr 21:29
For a son c his father a fool, Mc 7:6
One person c one day to be above Rm 14:5
Someone else c every day to be Rm 14:5
to someone who c a thing to be Rm 14:14
For if anyone c himself to be Gl 6:3

CONSIGN (4)

Solomon did not c the Israelites 1Kg 9:22
Solomon did not c the Israelites 2Ch 8:9
and c your gold to the dust, Jb 22:24
against them and c them to Ezk 23:46

CONSIGNED (3)

Isn't mankind c to forced labor Jb 7:1
Their idols are c to beasts and Is 46:1
they have all been c to death, Ezk 31:14

CONSIST (4)

his gift must c of fine flour. Lv 2:1
Their fish will c of many Ezk 47:10
should not c of outward things 1Pt 3:3
⌊it should c of⌋ the hidden 1Pt 3:4

CONSISTENT (3)

produce fruit c with repentance. Mt 3:8
produce fruit c with repentance. Lk 3:8
must speak what is c with sound Ti 2:1

CONSISTING (1)

to the LORD ⌊c of⌋ its fat Lv 3:9

CONSISTS (4)

of the house c of green or red Lv 14:37
and it c of blood from her body, Lv 15:19
their worship ⌊c of⌋ man-made Is 29:13
c in this: not that we loved 1Jn 4:10

CONSOLATION (9)

and the c from my lips would Jb 16:5
let this be the c you offer. Jb 21:2
A cup of c won't be given him Jr 16:7
I will bring them back with c. Jr 31:9
joy, give them c, and ⌊bring⌋ Jr 31:13
will bring you c when you see Ezk 14:23
looking forward to Israel's c, Lk 2:25
encouragement, and c. 1Co 14:3
Christ, if any c of love, if any Php 2:1

CONSOLATIONS (1)

Are God's c not enough for you, Jb 15:11

CONSOLE (4)

emissaries to c Hanun concerning 2Sm 10:2
messengers to c him concerning 1Ch 19:2
land of the Ammonites to c him, 1Ch 19:2
to, so that I may c you, Virgin Lm 2:13

CONSOLED (2)

Then you will be c about the Ezk 14:22
refused to be c, because they Mt 2:18

CONSOLING (2)

brother Esau is c himself by Gn 27:42
her in the house c her saw that Jn 11:31

CONSORTS (1)

but one who c with prostitutes Pr 29:3

CONSPICUOUS (3)

So it was c for its height as Ezk 19:11
goat had a c horn between his Dn 8:5
Four c horns came up in its Dn 8:8

CONSPIRACY (11)

So the c grew strong, and the 2Sm 15:12
along with the c that he 1Kg 16:20
A c was formed against him in 2Kg 14:19
along with the c that he formed, 2Kg 15:15
Elah organized a c against Pekah 2Kg 15:30
discovered a c by Hoshea— 2Kg 17:4
a c was formed against him in 2Ch 25:27
A c has been discovered among Jr 11:9
The c of her prophets within her Ezk 22:25
there is a c with traitors. Hs 7:5
the Jews formed a c and bound Ac 23:12

CONSPIRATORS (1)

is among the c with Absalom." 2Sm 15:31

CONSPIRE (3)

and Jesse's son c against me? 1Sm 22:13
the rulers c together against Ps 2:2
they c against Your treasured Ps 83:3

CONSPIRED (25)

community that has c against Me. Nm 14:35
who have c against the LORD! Nm 16:11
all of you have c against me! 1Sm 22:8
c with Joab son of Zeruiah and 1Kg 1:7
of Issachar c against Nadab, 1Kg 15:27
c against him while Elah was in 1Kg 16:9
Zimri had not only c but had 1Kg 16:16
son of Nimshi, c against Joram. 2Kg 9:14
It was I who c against my master 2Kg 10:9
Joash's servants c against him 2Kg 12:20
son of Jabesh c against 2Kg 15:10
c against him and struck him 2Kg 15:25
Amon's servants c against the 2Kg 21:23
those who had c against King 2Kg 21:24
they c against him and stoned 2Ch 24:21
His servants c against him, 2Ch 24:25
Those who c against him were 2Ch 24:26
his servants c against him and 2Ch 33:24
those who c against King Amon 2Ch 33:25
When they c against me, they Ps 31:13
For they have c with one mind; Ps 83:5
You have c to tell me something Dn 2:9
Amos has c against you ⌊right Am 7:10
and they c to arrest Jesus in a Mt 26:4
passed, the Jews c to kill him, Ac 9:23

CONSTANT (10)

with pain and c distress in his Jb 33:19
conceal Your c love and truth Ps 40:10
c love and truth will always Ps 40:11
God's faithful love is c. Ps 52:1
Your name for Your c love and Ps 138:2
reveals secrets is a c gossip; Pr 20:19
You are in c dread all day long Is 51:13
has become for me c disgrace and Jr 20:8
not experienced your c cruelty? Nah 3:19
and c disagreement among men 1Tm 6:5

CONSTANTLY (15)

fall, and my pain is c with me. Ps 38:17
Your opponents that goes up c. Ps 74:23
They c tested God and provoked Ps 78:41
The arrogant c ridicule me, Ps 119:51
My life is c in danger, yet I do Ps 119:109
heart—he stirs up trouble c. Pr 6:14
and if they are c on your lips. Pr 22:18
c taught the people knowledge; Ec 12:9
you are, c changing your way Jr 2:36
he went around c with Philip and Ac 8:13
my witness that I c mention you, Rm 1:9
you c in our prayers. 1Th 1:2
this is why we c thank God, 1Th 2:13
Pray c. 1Th 5:17
when I c remember you in my 2Tm 1:3

CONSTELLATIONS (4)

the sun, moon, c, and the whole 2Kg 23:5
and the c of the southern sky. Jb 9:9
bring out the c in their season Jb 38:32
the sky and its c will not give Is 13:10

CONSTRUCT (10)

You are to c a table of acacia Ex 25:23
You are to c the tabernacle Ex 26:1
You are to c the altar of acacia Ex 27:1
C a grate for it of bronze mesh, Ex 27:4
C the altar with boards so that Ex 27:8
to the LORD to c the tent of Ex 35:21
c a ramp against me and camp Jb 19:12
my feet and c their siege ramp Jb 30:12
c a siege wall, build a ramp, Ezk 4:2
a ramp, and c a siege wall. Ezk 21:22

CONSTRUCTED (10)

He c the table of acacia wood, Ex 37:10
Bezalel c the altar of burnt Ex 38:1
He c for the altar a grate of Ex 38:4
He c the altar with boards so Ex 38:7
Haman, so he had the gallows c. Est 5:14
I c reservoirs of water for Ec 2:6
the tower of David, c in layers. Sg 4:4
siege walls c to destroy many Ezk 17:17
They c all your planking with Ezk 27:5
the altar on the day it is c, Ezk 43:18

CONSTRUCTING *(2)*
the work of **c** the sanctuary." Ex 36:1
who are **c** this building?" Ezr 5:4

CONSTRUCTION *(10)*
is needed for the **c** of the work Ex 36:5
and stone for the temple's **c**. 1Kg 5:18
The temple's **c** used finished 1Kg 6:7
after 13 years of **c**. 1Kg 7:1
the hall, was of similar **c**. 1Kg 7:8
plans for its **c** to Uriah the 2Kg 16:10
Now the **c** of God's house in Ezr 4:24
has been under **c** from that time Ezr 5:16
Leave the **c** of this house of God Ezr 6:7
myself to the **c** of the wall, Neh 5:16

CONSULT *(18)*
who wanted to **c** the LORD would Ex 33:7
turn to mediums or **c** spiritists, Lv 19:31
who will **c** the LORD for him Nm 27:21
c a medium or a familiar spirit, Dt 18:11
said, "We must **c** God here." 1Sm 14:36
medium, so I can go and **c** her." 1Sm 28:7
Saul said, "**C** a spirit for me 1Sm 28:8
priest who could **c** the Urim and Ezr 2:63
priest who could **c** the Urim and Neh 7:65
he will not **c** the wise. Pr 15:12
C the spirits of the dead and Is 8:19
shouldn't a people **c** their God? Is 8:19
⌊Should they **c**⌋ the dead on Is 8:19
Who did He **c** with? Who gave Him Is 40:14
elders came to **c** the LORD, Ezk 20:1
Are you coming to **c** Me? Ezk 20:3
people **c** their wooden ⌊idols⌋, Hs 4:12
not immediately **c** with anyone. Gl 1:16

CONSULTATION *(1)*
following **c**, sent David away 1Ch 12:19

CONSULTATIONS *(1)*
are worn out with your many **c**. Is 47:13

CONSULTED *(17)*
King Rehoboam **c** with the elders 1Kg 12:6
advised him and **c** with the young 1Kg 12:8
and **c** mediums and spiritists. 2Kg 21:6
He even **c** a medium for guidance, 1Ch 10:13
David **c** with all his leaders, 1Ch 13:1
King Rehoboam **c** with the elders 2Ch 10:6
advised him and **c** with the young 2Ch 10:8
Then he **c** with the people and 2Ch 20:21
so he **c** with his officials and 2Ch 32:3
and **c** mediums and spiritists. 2Ch 33:6
The king **c** the wise men who Est 1:13
you never **c** those who travel Jb 21:29
Should I be **c** by them at all? Ezk 14:3
I live, I will not be **c** by you." Ezk 20:3
should I be **c** by you, house of Ezk 20:31
GOD—"I will not be **c** by you! Ezk 20:31
that the king **c** them about, Dn 1:20

CONSULTS *(1)*
shakes the arrows, **c** the idols, Ezk 21:21

CONSUME *(54)*
animals may **c** what they leave Ex 23:11
so I may **c** them instantly." Nm 16:21
so that I may **c** them instantly." Nm 16:45
great fire will **c** us and we will Dt 5:25
the bramble and **c** the cedars Jdg 9:15
from Abimelech and **c** the lords Jdg 9:20
and Beth-millo and **c** Abimelech." Jdg 9:20
heaven and **c** you and your 50 2Kg 1:10
heaven and **c** you and your 50 2Kg 1:12
the grasshopper to **c** the land, 2Ch 7:13
The hungry **c** his harvest, even Jb 5:5
and fire will **c** the tents of Jb 15:34
Nothing is left for him to **c**; Jb 20:21
by human hands⌋ will **c** him; Jb 20:26
They **c** my people as they consume Ps 14:4
my people as they **c** bread; Ps 14:4
They **c** My people as they consume Ps 53:4
My people as they **c** bread; Ps 53:4
C ⌊them⌋ in rage; consume ⌊them⌋ Ps 59:13
c ⌊them⌋ until they are gone. Ps 59:13
the ones who **c** them multiply; Ec 5:11
but the lips of a fool **c** him. Ec 10:12
Your adversaries will **c** them! Is 26:11
breath is fire that will **c** you. Is 33:11
wood, and the fire will **c** them. Jr 5:14
will **c** your harvest and your Jr 5:17
They will **c** your sons and your Jr 5:17
They will **c** your flocks and your Jr 5:17
They will **c** your vines and your Jr 5:17
and it will **c** the citadels of Jr 17:27
forest that will **c** everything Jr 21:14
it will **c** everything around him. Jr 50:32
but it will ⌊still⌋ **c** them. Ezk 15:7
polished to **c**, to flash like Ezk 21:28
of the land will not **c** them. Ezk 34:28
oven, and they **c** their rulers. Hs 7:7
Foreigners **c** his strength, Hs 7:9
and it will **c** their citadels. Hs 8:14
and it will **c** Ben-hadad's Am 1:4
and it will **c** its citadels. Am 1:7
and it will **c** its citadels. Am 1:10
and it will **c** the citadels of Am 1:12
and it will **c** its citadels. Am 1:14
and it will **c** the citadels of Am 2:2
and it will **c** the citadels of Am 2:5
it will **c** ⌊everything,⌋ with no Am 5:6
set them on fire and **c** them. Ob 18
They will **c** and conquer with Zch 9:15
and fire will **c** your cedars. Zch 11:1
they will **c** all the peoples Zch 12:6
The coming day will **c** them," Mal 4:1
fire from heaven to **c** them?" Lk 9:54
Zeal for Your house will **c** Me. Jn 2:17
fire about to **c** the adversaries Heb 10:27

CONSUMED *(50)*
the heat **c** me by day and the Gn 31:40
bush was on fire but was not **c**. Ex 3:2
and they **c** all the plants on the Ex 10:15
it **c** them like stubble. Ex 15:7
the fire has **c** on the altar, Lv 6:10
from the LORD and **c** the burnt Lv 9:24
among them and **c** the outskirts Nm 11:1
the LORD and **c** the 250 men who Nm 16:35
It **c** Ar of Moab, the lords of Nm 21:28
died and the fire **c** 250 men. Nm 26:10
up from the rock and **c** the meat Jdg 6:21
fire fell and **c** the burnt 1Kg 18:38
from heaven and **c** him and his 50 2Kg 1:10
from heaven and **c** him and his 50 2Kg 1:12
from heaven and **c** the first two 2Kg 1:14
from heaven and **c** the burnt 2Ch 7:1
has **c** what they left behind. Jb 22:20
if I have **c** its produce without Jb 31:39
my life is **c** with grief, and my Ps 31:10
zeal for Your house has **c** me, Ps 69:9
Fire **c** His chosen young men, Ps 78:63
For we are **c** by Your anger; Ps 90:7
in their land and **c** the produce Ps 105:35
flames **c** the wicked. Ps 106:18
your physical body has been **c**, Pr 5:11
its hedge, and it will be **c**; Is 5:5
the west have **c** Israel with open Is 9:12
a curse has **c** the earth, Is 24:6
one has **c** what our fathers Jr 3:24
name, for they have **c** Jacob; Jr 10:25
they have **c** him and finished him Jr 10:25
its branches are **c** with a great Jr 11:16
entire scroll was **c** by the fire Jr 36:23
and her high gates **c** by fire. Jr 51:58
and it has **c** her foundations. Lm 4:11
plague and be **c** by famine within Ezk 5:12
off and dried up; fire **c** them. Ezk 19:12
on them and **c** them with the fire Ezk 22:31
descendants will be **c** by fire. Ezk 23:25
its rust will be **c**. Ezk 24:11
from within you, and it **c** you. Ezk 28:18
for fire has **c** the pastures of Jl 1:19
and fire has **c** the pastures of Jl 1:20
It **c** the great deep and devoured Am 7:4
they will be **c** like entangled Nah 1:10
earth will be **c** by the fire of Zph 1:18
earth will be **c** by the fire of Zph 3:8
she herself will be **c** by fire. Zch 9:4
or you will be **c** by one another. Gl 5:15
down from heaven and **c** them. Rv 20:9

CONSUMES *(11)*
and **c** stacks of cut grain, Ex 22:6
death's firstborn **c** his limbs. Jb 18:13
is a fire that **c** down to Abaddon Jb 31:12
wise, but a foolish man **c** them. Pr 21:20
his arms and **c** his own flesh. Ec 4:5
tongue of fire **c** straw and as Is 5:24
like a fire that **c** thorns and Is 9:18
as a sickness **c** a person. Is 10:18
flaming fire that **c** everything Lm 2:3
and how it **c** Me until it is Lk 12:50
mouths and **c** their enemies; Rv 11:5

CONSUMING *(13)*
Israelites was like a **c** fire on Ex 24:17
the LORD your God is a **c** fire, Dt 4:24
over ahead of you as a **c** fire; Dt 9:3
c fire ⌊came⌋ from His mouth; 2Sm 22:9
of his labor without **c** ⌊it⌋; Jb 20:18
c fire ⌊came⌋ from His mouth; Ps 18:8
c like a moth what is precious Ps 39:11
tempest, and a flame of **c** fire. Is 29:6
and His tongue is like a **c** fire. Is 30:27
wrath and a flame of **c** fire, Is 30:30
us can dwell with a **c** fire? Is 33:14
sound of fiery flames **c** stubble, Jl 2:5
for our God is a **c** fire. Heb 12:29

CONTACT *(2)*
food coming into **c** with ⌊that Lv 11:34
defiled by ⌊**c** with⌋ a corpse Hg 2:13

CONTAIN *(4)*
heaven, cannot **c** You, much less 1Kg 8:27
the highest heaven cannot **c** Him? 2Ch 2:6
heaven, cannot **c** You, much less 2Ch 6:18
itself could **c** the books that Jn 21:25

CONTAINED *(6)*
Valley of Siddim **c** many asphalt Gn 14:10
The plans **c** everything he had in 1Ch 28:12
One basket ⌊**c**⌋ very good figs, Jr 24:2
other basket **c** very bad figs, Jr 24:2
Each **c** 20 or 30 gallons. Jn 2:6
It **c** the gold altar of incense Heb 9:4

CONTAINER *(12)*
Take a **c** and put two quarts of Ex 16:33
liquid in any **c** will become Lv 11:34
any open **c** without a lid tied Nm 19:15
must not put ⌊any⌋ in your **c**. Dt 23:24
giving you and put ⌊it⌋ in a **c**. Dt 26:2
will take the **c** from your hand Dt 26:4
then place the **c** before the LORD Dt 26:10
She opened a **c** of milk, gave Jdg 4:19
plunge it into the **c** or kettle 1Sm 2:14
her son, "Bring me another **c**." 2Kg 4:6
poured from one **c** to another or Jr 48:11
them in a single **c** and make them Ezk 4:9

CONTAINERS *(8)*
to fill their **c** with grain, Gn 42:25
even in wooden and stone ⌊**c**⌋." Ex 7:19
borrow empty **c** from everyone— 2Kg 4:3
and pour oil into all these **c**. 2Kg 4:4
they kept bringing her ⌊**c**⌋, 2Kg 4:5
their **c** return empty. Jr 14:3
will empty his **c** and smash his Jr 48:12
gathered the good ⌊fish⌋ into **c**, Mt 13:48

CONTAINING *(9)*
or cistern **c** water will remain Lv 11:36
over a clay pot **c** fresh water. Lv 14:50
with the box ⌊**c**⌋ the gold mice 1Sm 6:11
with the box **c** the gold objects 1Sm 6:15
sealed document ⌊**c** the names of⌋ Neh 9:38
of sapphire, **c** flecks of gold. Jb 28:6
liquid measure **c** five and a half Ezk 45:11
written a letter **c** our decision Ac 21:25
was a gold jar **c** the manna, Heb 9:4

CONTAINS *(1)*
every tree whose fruit **c** seed. Gn 1:29

CONTAMINATED *(9)*
Do not become **c** by any creature Lv 11:43
If a fabric is **c** with mildew— Lv 13:47
quarantine the **c** fabric for Lv 13:50
any leather article, which is **c**. Lv 13:52
order whatever is **c** to be washed Lv 13:54
of the **c** article has not Lv 13:55
he must cut the **c** section out of Lv 13:56
You must burn up whatever is **c**. Lv 13:57
they are like **c** food. Jb 6:7

CONTAMINATION *(21)*
and if the **c** is green or red in Lv 13:49
it is a mildew **c** and is to be Lv 13:49
to examine the **c** and quarantine Lv 13:50
reexamine the **c** on the seventh Lv 13:51
it is used, the **c** is harmful Lv 13:51
if the **c** has not spread in the Lv 13:53
priest is to reexamine the **c**. Lv 13:55
though the **c** has not spread, Lv 13:55
and the **c** has faded after it has Lv 13:56
But if the **c** disappears from the Lv 13:58

a mildew **c** in wool or linen Lv 13:59
I place a mildew **c** in a house Lv 14:34
like mildew **c** has appeared in my Lv 14:35
he enters to examine the **c**, Lv 14:36
and if the **c** in the walls of the Lv 14:37
If the **c** has spread on the walls Lv 14:39
stones with the **c** be pulled out Lv 14:40
If the **c** reappears in the house Lv 14:43
the **c** has spread in the house, Lv 14:44
if the **c** has not spread in the Lv 14:48
because the **c** has disappeared. Lv 14:48

CONTEMPLATE *(2)*

Your temple, we **c** Your faithful Ps 48:9
me, but I **c** Your decrees. Ps 119:95

CONTEMPORARIES *(2)*

man, blameless among his **c**; Gn 6:9
beyond many **c** among my people, Gl 1:14

CONTEMPT *(34)*

those who treat you with **c**, Gn 12:3
the LORD's offering with **c**. 1Sm 2:17
LORD with such **c** in this matter, 2Sm 12:14
resulting in more **c** and fury. Est 1:18
calamity in **c** ⌊and thinks⌋ it Jb 12:5
He pours out **c** on nobles and Jb 12:21
me and strike my cheeks with **c**; Jb 16:10
and the **c** of the clans terrified Jb 31:34
or shown **c** for its tenants Jb 31:39
the righteous with pride and **c**. Ps 31:18
He pours **c** on nobles and makes Ps 107:40
Take insult and **c** away from me, Ps 119:22
we've had more than enough **c**. Ps 123:3
arrogant ⌊and⌋ **c** from the proud. Ps 123:4
Whoever shows **c** for his neighbor Pr 11:12
one who has **c** for instruction Pr 13:13
this song ⌊of **c**⌋ about the king Is 14:4
will become an object of **c**, Is 16:14
are treated with **c** and no longer Jr 33:24
you with **c** from every side Ezk 16:57
the Ammonites and their **c**. Ezk 21:28
and mother are treated with **c**, Ezk 22:7
of Israel with wholehearted **c**, Ezk 25:6
and took revenge with deep **c**, Ezk 25:15
neighbors who treat them with **c**. Ezk 28:24
neighbors who treat them with **c**. Ezk 28:26
rejoicing and utter **c**, Ezk 36:5
and some to shame and eternal **c**. Dn 12:2
on him and repay him for his **c**. Hs 12:14
city's residents an object of **c**; Mc 6:16
on you and treat you with **c**; Nah 3:6
things and be treated with **c**? Mk 9:12
treated Him with **c**, mocked Him, Lk 23:11
of God and holding Him up to **c**. Heb 6:6

CONTEMPTIBLE *(5)*

C people among them had a strong Nm 11:4
the LORD has become **c** to them— Jr 6:10
your grave, for you are **c**. Nah 1:14
"The LORD's table is **c**." Mal 1:7
its product, its food, is **c**." Mal 1:12

CONTEND *(8)*

Did he ever **c** with Israel or Jdg 11:25
he is not able to **c** with the One Ec 6:10
those who **c** with you will become Is 41:11
look for those who **c** with you, Is 41:12
I will **c** with the one who Is 49:25
near; who will **c** with Me? Let us Is 50:8
Yet, I wish to **c** with You: Jr 12:1
exhort you to **c** for the faith Jd 3

CONTENDED *(2)*

him at Massah and **c** with him at Dt 33:8
women who have **c** for the gospel Php 4:3

CONTENDING *(1)*

He is always **c** for you in his Col 4:12

CONTENDS *(2)*

Will the one who **c** with the Jb 40:2
with the one who **c** with you, Is 49:25

CONTENT *(5)*

If only we had been **c** to remain Jos 7:7
are still not **c** with riches. Ec 4:8
have learned to be **c** in whatever Php 4:11
the secret ⌊of being **c**⌋— Php 4:12
we will be **c** with these. 1Tm 6:8

CONTENTED *(1)*

old age, old and **c**, and he was Gn 25:8

CONTENTION *(1)*

You fast ⌊with⌋ **c** and strife to Is 58:4

CONTENTMENT *(1)*

with **c** is a great gain. 1Tm 6:6

CONTENTS *(1)*

should not be cast for its **c**. Ezk 24:6

CONTINUAL *(4)*

as a **c** reminder before the LORD. Ex 28:29
a cheerful heart has a **c** feast. Pr 15:15
Because of the **c** prostitution of Nah 3:4
sorrow and **c** anguish in my Rm 9:2

CONTINUALLY *(38)*

(See pp. xi-xii.)

CONTINUE *(61)*

Later, you can **c** on." Gn 18:5
I will **c** to shepherd and keep Gn 30:31
I will **c** on slowly, at a pace Gn 33:14
Don't **c** to supply the people Ex 5:7
She will **c** in purification from Lv 12:4
She will **c** in purification from Lv 12:5
so that he can **c** to live among Lv 25:35
threshing will **c** until grape Lv 26:5
harvest will **c** until sowing time Lv 26:5
It will **c** down and reach the Nm 34:11
C your journey ahead of the Dt 10:11
his sons will **c** ruling many Dt 17:20
'Let us not **c** to hear the voice Dt 18:16
The officers will **c** to address Dt 20:8
c obeying all that is written Jos 23:6
God will not **c** to drive these Jos 23:13
if you **c** to do what is evil, 1Sm 12:25
I **c** to live, treat me with the 1Sm 20:14
so that it will **c** before You 2Sm 7:29
were not able to **c** ministering, 1Kg 8:11
grandchildren **c** doing as their 2Kg 17:41
will not **c** to oppress them as 1Ch 17:9
house that it may **c** before You 1Ch 17:27
were not able to **c** ministering, 2Ch 5:14
Jews agreed to **c** the practice Est 9:23
I have that I should **c** to hope? Jb 6:11
you that you **c** testifying? Jb 16:3
have spoken, you may **c** mocking. Jb 21:3
Why do the wicked **c** to live, Jb 21:7
Will you **c** on the ancient path Jb 22:15
Should I **c** to wait now that they Jb 32:16
and I will **c** to see the light." Jb 33:28
May he **c** while the sun endures, Ps 72:5
His offspring will **c** forever, Ps 89:36
Your years **c** through all Ps 102:24
they accuse me, but I **c** to pray. Ps 109:4
David camped! **C** year after year; Is 29:1
and I will **c** to follow them. Jr 2:25
are free to **c** doing all these Jr 7:10
We will **c** to follow our plans, Jr 18:12
each of us will **c** to act Jr 18:12
long will this **c** in the minds Jr 23:26
you **c** to defile yourselves with Ezk 20:31
The scepter will not **c**. Ezk 21:13
Now they **c** to sin and make Hs 13:2
so My covenant with Levi may **c**," Mal 2:4
Him, "If you **c** in My word, you Jn 8:31
If we let Him **c** in this way, Jn 11:48
persuading them to **c** in the Ac 13:43
them to **c** in the faith, Ac 14:22
over, we left to **c** our journey, Ac 21:5
Should we **c** in sin in order that Rm 6:1
But I will **c** to do what I am 2Co 11:12
who does not **c** doing everything Gl 3:10
will remain and **c** with all of Php 1:25
Don't **c** drinking only water, 1Tm 5:23
c in what you have learned and 2Tm 3:14
—and you **c** to serve them. Heb 6:10
they did not **c** in My covenant, Heb 8:9
Let brotherly love **c**. Heb 13:1
all things **c** as they have been 2Pt 3:4

CONTINUED *(59)*

The deluge **c** 40 days on the Gn 7:17
The waters **c** to recede until the Gn 8:5
Abram **c**, "Look, You have given Gn 15:3
Then He **c**, "I am the God of your Ex 3:6
take place," He **c**, "so they will Ex 4:5
Moses **c**, "The LORD will give you Ex 16:8
the people **c** to bring freewill Ex 36:3
You **c** to provoke the LORD at Dt 9:22
Moses **c** to speak these words Dt 31:1
carrying the ark **c** standing in Jos 4:10
c down to the Stone of Bohan, Jos 18:17
The border **c** to the north slope Jos 18:19
of the Israelites **c** to increase Jdg 4:24
So they **c** on their journey, Jdg 19:14
Naomi **c**, "The man is a close Ru 2:20
The LORD **c** to appear in Shiloh, 1Sm 3:21
Samuel **c**, "Although you once 1Sm 15:17
c to be successful in all his 1Sm 18:14
Then he **c**, "Why is my lord 1Sm 26:18
and 400 of the men **c** in pursuit. 1Sm 30:10
pursued Israel or **c** to fight. 2Sm 2:28
Absalom **c** to increase. 2Sm 15:12
Hushai **c**, "You know your father 2Sm 17:8
He **c**, "May the LORD your God 2Sm 18:28
Hittites and **c** on to Dan-jaan 2Sm 24:6
You have **c** this great and 1Kg 3:6
The king **c**, "Bring me a sword." 1Kg 3:24
As they **c** walking and talking, 2Kg 2:11
and they **c** the siege against it 2Kg 6:25
the people **c** sacrificing and 2Kg 12:3
and the people **c** sacrificing and 2Kg 14:4
the people **c** sacrificing and 2Kg 15:4
the people **c** sacrificing and 2Kg 15:35
listen but **c** practicing their 2Kg 17:40
This **c** day after day until two 2Ch 21:19
all of this ⌊**c**⌋ until the burnt 2Ch 29:28
Jewish elders **c** successfully Ezr 6:14
So we **c** the work, while half of Neh 4:21
He **c** to seek good for his people Est 10:3
Job **c** his discourse, saying: Jb 27:1
Job **c** his discourse, saying: Jb 29:1
Then Elihu **c**, saying: Jb 34:1
Then Elihu **c**, saying: Jb 35:1
Then Elihu **c**, saying: Jb 36:1
But they **c** to sin against Him, Ps 78:17
but they **c** to rebel deliberately Ps 106:43
I have **c** to extend faithful love Jr 31:3
responded, and he **c**, "You will Jr 37:17
but he **c** to stay in the guard's Jr 38:13
So the guard **c** to remove their Dn 1:16
c watching until its wings were Dn 7:4
As I **c** watching, the beast was Dn 7:11
I **c** watching in the night Dn 7:13
And he **c**, "This is their Zch 5:6
down again and **c** writing on the Jn 8:8
him from the dead, **c** to testify. Jn 12:17
they **c** teaching and proclaiming Ac 5:42
They **c** their journey from Perga Ac 13:14
c, "I am a Jewish man, born in Ac 22:3

CONTINUES *(6)*

month and **c** for seven days. Lv 23:34
Israel ⌊and it **c**⌋ to this very 1Sm 30:25
He **c** to stumble. Indeed, each Jr 46:16
Jerusalem **c** to be inhabited Zch 12:6
if she **c** in faith, love, 1Tm 2:15
hope in God and **c** night and day 1Tm 5:5

CONTINUOUSLY *(3)*

It remained that way **c**: Nm 9:16
of the bread of the Presence⌋ **c**, 2Ch 2:4
Does he ⌊**c**⌋ break up and Is 28:24

CONTORTED *(1)*

⌊their⌋ faces are **c**. Ezk 27:35

CONTRACTIONS *(2)*

the heart of a woman with **c**. Jr 48:41
the heart of a woman with **c**. Jr 49:22

CONTRADICT *(2)*

will be able to resist or **c**. Lk 21:15
and to refute those who **c** it. Ti 1:9

CONTRADICTED *(1)*

They have **c** the LORD and Jr 5:12

CONTRADICTIONS *(1)*

empty speech and **c** from the 1Tm 6:20

CONTRARY *(41)*

eaten the Passover **c** to what was 2Ch 30:18
A **c** man spreads conflict, and a Pr 16:28
On the **c**, if anyone slaps you on Mt 5:39
On the **c**, they did whatever they Mt 17:12
On the **c**, he went and threw him Mt 18:30
the **c**, whoever wants to become Mt 20:26
On the **c**, she became worse. Mk 5:26
the **c**, whoever wants to become Mk 10:43
On the **c**, whatever is given to Mk 13:11
On the **c**, when you host a Lk 14:13
On the **c**, whoever is greatest Lk 22:26
No, on the **c**, He's deceiving Jn 7:12
On the **c**, I honor My Father and Jn 8:49
On the **c**, ⌊I am going away⌋ so Jn 14:31
the **c**, this is what was spoken Ac 2:16
the **c**, we believe we are saved Ac 15:11

On the **c**, let them come Ac 16:37
are all acting **c** to Caesar's Ac 17:7
to worship God **c** to the law!" Ac 18:13
On the **c**, I'm speaking words of Ac 26:25
On the **c**, a person is a Jew who Rm 2:29
No, on the **c**, by a law of faith. Rm 3:27
On the **c**, we uphold the law. Rm 3:31
On the **c**, I would not have known Rm 7:7
On the **c**, sin, in order to be Rm 7:13
the **c**, in Isaac your seed will Rm 9:7
On the **c**, what does it say? Rm 10:8
On the **c**, by their stumbling, Rm 11:11
On the **c**, as it is written, The Rm 15:3
and pitfalls **c** to the doctrine Rm 16:17
On the **c**, we speak God's hidden 1Co 2:7
On the **c**, all the more, those 1Co 12:22
the **c**, "Yes" has come about in 2Co 1:19
to you a gospel **c** to what you Gl 1:9
On the **c**, they saw that I had Gl 2:7
law therefore **c** to God's Gl 3:21
On the **c**, you received me as an Gl 4:14
the **c**, after we had previously 1Th 2:2
whatever else is **c** to the sound 1Tm 1:10
the **c**, when he was in Rome, he 2Tm 1:17
but, on the **c**, giving a blessing 1Pt 3:9

CONTRAST *(1)*
By **c**, the boy Samuel grew in 1Sm 2:26

CONTRIBUTE *(1)*
c to my destruction, without Jb 30:13

CONTRIBUTED *(4)*
king of Judah **c** 1,000 bulls and 2Ch 30:24
the officials **c** 1,000 bulls and 2Ch 30:24
The king **c** from his own 2Ch 31:3
all Israel **c** the daily portions Neh 12:47

CONTRIBUTION *(32)*
thigh of the **c** that is lifted Ex 29:27
the Israelites, for it is a **c**. Ex 29:28
be the Israelites' **c** from their Ex 29:28
sacrifices, their **c** to the LORD. Ex 29:28
half shekel is a **c** to the LORD. Ex 30:13
must give this **c** to the LORD. Ex 30:14
when giving the **c** to the LORD to Ex 30:15
who offered a **c** of silver or Ex 35:24
offering as a **c** to the LORD. Lv 7:14
to the priest as a **c** from your Lv 7:32
the thigh of the **c** from their Lv 7:34
the thigh of the **c** in any Lv 10:14
thigh of the **c** and the breast Lv 10:15
Every holy **c** the Israelites Nm 5:9
one's holy **c** is his ⌊to give⌋ Nm 5:10
offering and the thigh of the **c**. Nm 6:20
to offer a **c** to the LORD when Nm 15:19
first batch of dough as a **c**; Nm 15:20
it just like a **c** from the Nm 15:20
give the LORD a **c** from the first Nm 15:21
The **c** of their gifts also Nm 18:11
to the LORD as a **c** for ⌊their⌋ Nm 18:24
the priest as a **c** to the LORD. Nm 31:29
the priest as a **c** for the LORD, Nm 31:41
the gold of the **c** they offered Nm 31:52
to give a **c** for the priests 2Ch 31:4
to distribute the **c** to the LORD 2Ch 31:14
the **c** for the house of our God Ezr 8:25
every kind and **c** of every kind Ezk 44:30
This is the **c** you are to offer: Ezk 45:13
part in this **c** for the prince Ezk 45:16
to make a **c** to the poor among Rm 15:26

CONTRIBUTIONS *(13)*
presence all the **c** that the Ex 36:3
is not to eat from the holy **c**. Lv 22:12
charge of the **c** brought to Me. Nm 18:8
all the holy **c** that the Nm 18:19
your tenths and personal **c**, Dt 12:6
tenth, personal **c**, and all your Dt 12:11
or your personal **c**. Dt 12:17
are to bring the **c** of grain, Neh 10:39
the supplies, **c**, firstfruits, Neh 12:44
with the **c** for the priests. Neh 13:5
who demands⌋ "**c**" demolishes it. Pr 29:4
will require your **c** and choicest Ezk 20:40
of 10 percent and the **c**. Mal 3:8

CONTRIVE *(1)*
but **c** deceitful schemes against Ps 35:20

CONTRIVED *(1)*
follow cleverly **c** myths when we 2Pt 1:16

CONTROL *(43)*
When a fire gets out of **c**, Ex 22:6
of the land under your **c**, Ex 23:31
that the people were out of **c**, Ex 32:25
Aaron had let them get out of **c**, Ex 32:25
and had taken **c** of all his land Nm 21:26
Danites slipped out of their **c**, Jos 19:47
and take **c** of the watercourses Jdg 7:24
and they took **c** of the Jdg 7:24
of the LORD took **c** of him, Jdg 14:6
of the LORD took **c** of him, Jdg 14:19
of the LORD took **c** of him, Jdg 15:14
territories from Philistine **c**. 1Sm 7:14
Spirit of the LORD will **c** you, 1Sm 10:6
the Spirit of God took **c** of him, 1Sm 10:10
of God suddenly took **c** of him, 1Sm 11:6
garrison took **c** of the pass at 1Sm 13:23
of the LORD took **c** of David from 1Sm 16:13
spirit from God took **c** of Saul, 1Sm 18:10
Metheg-ammah from Philistine **c**. 2Sm 8:1
restore his **c** at the Euphrates 2Sm 8:3
against Judah's **c** and appointed 2Kg 8:20
against Judah's **c** today. 2Kg 8:22
the Spirit took **c** of Amasai, 1Ch 12:18
its villages from Philistine **c**. 1Ch 18:1
establish his **c** at the Euphrates 1Ch 18:3
of God took **c** of Zechariah son 2Ch 24:20
man who does not **c** his temper is Pr 25:28
of rubble will be under your **c**." Is 3:6
and I placed them under your **c**. Is 47:6
image and cast idol **c** them. Is 48:5
Who can **c** her passion? Jr 2:24
you from the **c** of the ruthless. Jr 15:21
earthly kingdoms under his **c**, Jr 34:1
He will get **c** over the hidden Dn 11:43
able to get **c** of the skiff. Ac 27:16
brought under the **c** of anything. 1Co 6:12
but has **c** over his own will 1Co 7:37
and bring it under strict **c**, 1Co 9:27
are under the **c** of the prophets, 1Co 14:32
that we have **c** of your faith, 2Co 1:24
in one body, **c** your hearts. Col 3:15
children under **c** with all 1Tm 3:4
also able to **c** his whole body. Jms 3:2

CONTROLLED *(2)*
Yet Haman **c** himself and went Est 5:10
that must be **c** with bit and Ps 32:9

CONTROLLING *(2)*
than power, and **c** one's temper, Pr 16:32
without **c** his tongue but Jms 1:26

CONTROLS *(4)*
but the one who **c** his lips is Pr 10:19
The one who **c** her controls the Pr 27:16
who controls her **c** the wind and Pr 27:16
hand and who **c** the whole course Dn 5:23

CONTROVERSIES *(1)*
in all the Jewish customs and **c**. Ac 26:3

CONTROVERSY *(1)*
in Jerusalem concerning this **c**. Ac 15:2

CONVENE *(2)*
the court will **c**, and his Dn 7:26
and all the Sanhedrin to **c**. Ac 22:30

CONVENED *(7)*
They **c** on the first day of the Ezr 10:16
The court was **c**, and the books Dn 7:10
scribes and the elders had **c**. Mt 26:57
the elders, and the scribes **c**. Mk 14:53
c and brought Him before their Lk 22:66
the Pharisees **c** the Sanhedrin Jn 11:47
arrived, they **c** the Sanhedrin— Ac 5:21

CONVENES *(1)*
someone⌋ in prison or **c** a court, Jb 11:10

CONVENIENT *(1)*
persist in it whether **c** or not; 2Tm 4:2

CONVERGED *(1)*
Then crowds **c** on Him again and, Mk 10:1

CONVERSED *(3)*
He **c** and debated with the Ac 9:29
he **c** a considerable time until Ac 20:11
him quite often and **c** with him. Ac 24:26

CONVERSION *(1)*
in detail the **c** of the Gentiles, Ac 15:3

CONVERT *(3)*
foreigners who **c** to the LORD, Is 56:6
is the first **c** to Christ from Rm 16:5
must not be a new **c**, or he might 1Tm 3:6

CONVERTED *(4)*
foreigner who has **c** to the LORD Is 56:3
unless you are **c** and become like Mt 18:3
hearts, and be **c**, and I would Jn 12:40
heart, and be **c**—and I would Ac 28:27

CONVICT *(4)*
with those who **c** the guilty, Pr 24:25
Who among you can **c** Me of sin? Jn 8:46
He will **c** the world about sin, Jn 16:8
and to **c** them of all their Jd 15

CONVICTED *(2)*
he is **c** by all and is judged by 1Co 14:24
sin and are **c** by the law as Jms 2:9

CONVICTION *(1)*
understanding and the same **c**. 1Co 1:10

CONVICTS *(1)*
the one who **c** ⌊the guilty⌋ at Am 5:10

CONVINCE *(1)*
and will **c** our hearts in His 1Jn 3:19

CONVINCED *(12)*
After Eglon **c** the Ammonites and Jdg 3:13
I'm **c** that you are as reliable 1Sm 29:9
all Israel were **c** that the king 2Sm 3:37
because they are **c** that John was Lk 20:6
For I'm not **c** that any of these Ac 26:26
and are **c** that you are a guide Rm 2:19
he was fully **c** that what He had Rm 4:21
must be fully **c** in his own mind Rm 14:5
I myself am **c** about you that you Rm 15:14
And I am **c** in the Lord that I Php 2:24
and that I am **c** is in you also. 2Tm 1:5
we are **c** that we have a clear Heb 13:18

CONVINCING *(1)*
alive to them by many **c** proofs, Ac 1:3

CONVULSED *(2)*
And the unclean spirit **c** him, Mk 1:26
Him, it immediately **c** the boy. Mk 9:20

CONVULSING *(1)*
shrieking and **c** him violently. Mk 9:26

CONVULSIONS *(2)*
throws him into **c** until he foams Lk 9:39
and threw him into severe **c**. Lk 9:42

COOING *(1)*
turtledove's **c** is heard in our Sg 2:12

COOK *(7)*
You are to **c** and eat ⌊it⌋ in the Dt 16:7
Then Samuel said to the **c**, 1Sm 9:23
The **c** picked up the thigh and 1Sm 9:24
to a boil and **c** the bones in it. Ezk 24:5
C the meat well and mix in the Ezk 24:10
the temple will **c** the people's Ezk 46:24
and take some of the pots to **c** Zch 14:21

COOKED *(4)*
of it raw or **c** in boiling water Ex 12:9
like a pastry **c** with the finest Nm 11:8
he **c** the meat and gave it to the 1Kg 19:21
women have **c** their own children; Lm 4:10

COOKING *(4)*
Once when Jacob was **c** a stew, Gn 25:29
⌊it⌋ in a **c** pot and shaped Nm 11:8
or kettle or caldron or **c** pot. 1Sm 2:14
up like flesh for the **c** pot, Mc 3:3

COOKS *(1)*
become perfumers, **c**, and bakers. 1Sm 8:13

COOL *(4)*
room upstairs ⌊where it was⌋ **c**. Jdg 3:20
relieving himself in the **c** room. Jdg 3:24
one who keeps a **c** head is a man Pr 17:27
finger in water and **c** my tongue, Lk 16:24

COOLED *(1)*
King Ahasuerus' rage had **c** down, Est 2:1

COOLNESS *(1)*
is like the **c** of snow on a Pr 25:13

COOLS *(1)*
shade of a cloud ⌊**c**⌋ the heat of Is 25:5

COPIED *(2)*
Joshua **c** the law of Moses, Jos 8:32
of Hezekiah, king of Judah, **c**. Pr 25:1

COPIES *(1)*
necessary for the **c** of the Heb 9:23

COPING *(1)*
from foundation to **c** and from 1Kg 7:9

COPPER *(7)*
whose hills you will mine **c**. Dt 8:9
and **c** is smelted from ore. Jb 28:2
of them are **c**, tin, iron, and Ezk 22:18
gathers silver, **c**, iron, lead, Ezk 22:20
it becomes hot and its **c** glows. Ezk 24:11
or **c** for your money-belts. Mt 10:9
of cups, jugs, **c** utensils, and Mk 7:4

COPPERSMITH *(1)*
Alexander the **c** did great harm 2Tm 4:14

COPPERSMITHS *(1)*
blacksmiths and **c** to repair the 2Ch 24:12

COPY *(9)*
he is to write a **c** of this Dt 17:18
A **c** of the text, issued as law Est 3:14
also gave him a **c** of the written Est 4:8
A **c** of the document was to be Est 8:13
the sealed **c** with its terms and Jr 32:11
and conditions and the open **c**— Jr 32:11
with the sealed **c** and this open Jr 32:14
sealed copy and this open **c**— Jr 32:14
These serve as a **c** and shadow of Heb 8:5

COR *(2)*
will be one percent of every **c**. Ezk 45:14
c equals⌋ 10 liquid measures Ezk 45:14

CORAL *(3)*
C and quartz are not worth Jb 28:18
bodies were more ruddy than **c**, Lm 4:7
fine linen, **c**, and rubies for Ezk 27:16

CORBAN *(1)*
have received from me is **C**'" Mk 7:11

CORD *(21)*
ring, your **c**, and the staff Gn 38:18
signet ring, **c**, and staff are Gn 38:25
make them of braided **c** work, Ex 28:14
and attach the **c** chains to the Ex 28:14
chains of pure gold **c** work for Ex 28:22
the ephod with a **c** of blue yarn, Ex 28:28
Fasten it to a **c** of blue yarn so Ex 28:37
of pure gold **c** for the Ex 39:15
the ephod with a **c** of blue yarn, Ex 39:21
they attached a **c** of blue yarn Ex 39:31
put a blue **c** on the tassel at Nm 15:38
tie this scarlet **c** to the window Jos 2:18
the scarlet **c** to the window. Jos 2:21
he measured them off with a **c**. 2Sm 8:2
every two **c** lengths ⌊of those 2Sm 8:2
Can you put a **c** through his nose Jb 41:2
A **c** of three strands is not Ec 4:12
before the silver **c** is snapped, Ec 12:6
Your lips are like a scarlet **c**, Sg 4:3
your umbilical **c** wasn't cut on Ezk 16:4
with a linen **c** and a measuring Ezk 40:3

CORDS *(15)*
the two gold **c** to the two gold Ex 28:24
ends of the two **c** to the two Ex 28:25
the two gold **c** to the two gold Ex 39:17
ends of the two **c** to the two Ex 39:18
purple linen **c** to silver rods Est 1:6
Are their tent **c** not pulled up? Jb 4:21
trapped by the **c** of affliction, Jb 36:8
sacrifice with **c** to the horns Ps 118:27
wickedness with **c** of deceit and Is 5:18
will any of its **c** be loosened. Is 33:20
all my tent **c** are snapped. Jr 10:20
that I will put **c** on you so you Ezk 4:8
and secured with **c** in your Ezk 27:24
them with human **c**, with ropes Hs 11:4
After making a whip out of **c**, Jn 2:15

CORIANDER *(2)*
It resembled **c** seed, was white, Ex 16:31
The manna resembled **c** seed, Nm 11:7

CORINTH *(6)*
left from Athens and went to **C**, Ac 18:1
Apollos was in **C**, Paul traveled Ac 19:1
God's church at **C**, to those who 1Co 1:2
To God's church at **C**, with all 2Co 1:1
you that I did not come to **C**. 2Co 1:23
Erastus has remained at **C**; 2Tm 4:20

CORINTHIANS *(2)*
and many of the **C**, when they Ac 18:8
We have spoken openly to you, **C**; 2Co 6:11

CORMORANT *(2)*
owl, the **c**, the long-eared Lv 11:17
desert owl, the osprey, the **c**, Dt 14:17

CORNELIUS *(8)*
was a man in Caesarea named **C**, Ac 10:1
came in and said to him, "**C**!" Ac 10:3
the men who had been sent by **C**, Ac 10:17
They said, "**C**, a centurion, an Ac 10:22
Now **C** was expecting them and Ac 10:24
Peter entered, **C** met him, fell Ac 10:25
C replied, "Four days ago at Ac 10:30
and said, '**C**, your prayer has Ac 10:31

CORNER *(27)*
cord on the tassel at ⌊each⌋ **c**. Nm 15:38
cut off the **c** of Saul's robe. 1Sm 24:4
cut off the **c** of Saul's robe. 1Sm 24:5
Look at the **c** of your robe in my 1Sm 24:11
the Ephraim Gate to the **C** Gate. 2Kg 14:13
the Ephraim Gate to the **C** Gate. 2Ch 25:23
in Jerusalem at the **C** Gate, 2Ch 26:9
Gate, and the **c** buttress, and he 2Ch 26:9
on every street **c** in Jerusalem. 2Ch 28:24
Azariah to the Angle and the **c**. Neh 3:24
far as the upper room of the **c**. Neh 3:31
room of the **c** and the Sheep Neh 3:32
like **c** pillars that are carved Ps 144:12
Crossing the street near her **c**, Pr 7:8
squares, she lurks at every **c**. Pr 7:12
to live on the **c** of a roof than Pr 21:9
to live on the **c** of a roof than Pr 25:24
of Hananel to the **C** Gate will be Jr 31:38
Valley to the **c** of the Horse Jr 31:40
hunger on the **c** of every street. Lm 2:19
at the **c** of every street Lm 4:1
All four **c** areas had the same Ezk 46:22
with ⌊only⌋ the **c** of a bed or Am 3:12
and against the high **c** towers. Zph 1:16
their **c** towers are destroyed. Zph 3:6
the First Gate, to the **C** Gate, Zch 14:10
since this was not done in a **c**! Ac 26:26

CORNERS *(38)*
to the four **c** at its four legs Ex 25:26
for the two back **c** of the Ex 26:23
they will serve as the two **c**. Ex 26:24
Make horns for it on its four **c**; Ex 27:2
rings on the mesh at its four **c**. Ex 27:4
and attach them to its two **c**. Ex 28:23
gold rings at the **c** of the Ex 28:24
at the two other **c** of the Ex 28:26
for the two back **c** of the Ex 36:28
with both of them for the two **c**. Ex 36:29
to the four **c** at its four legs Ex 37:13
made horns for it on its four **c**; Ex 38:2
the four **c** of the bronze grate Ex 38:5
the two rings to its two **c**. Ex 39:16
gold rings on the **c** of the Ex 39:17
at the two other **c** of the Ex 39:19
tassels for the **c** of their Nm 15:38
on the four **c** of the outer Dt 22:12
the four **c** of the basin were 1Kg 7:30
were at the four **c** of each water 1Kg 7:34
use on the towers and on the **c**. 2Ch 26:15
struck the four **c** of the house. Jb 1:19
from the four **c** of the earth. Is 11:12
called you from its farthest **c**. Is 41:9
from the four **c** of the heavens, Jr 49:36
come on the four **c** of the land. Ezk 7:2
It had **c**, and its length and Ezk 41:22
altar, the four **c** of the ledge, Ezk 43:20
the four **c** of the altar's ledge, Ezk 45:19
and led me past its four **c**. Ezk 46:21
court in each of its **c**. Ezk 46:21
In the four **c** of the ⌊outer⌋ Ezk 46:22
those⌋ at the **c** of the altar. Zch 9:15
and on the street **c** to be seen Mt 6:5
to the earth by its four **c**. Ac 10:11
from heaven by its four **c**, Ac 11:5
at the four **c** of the earth, Rv 7:1
at the four **c** of the earth, Rv 20:8

CORNERSTONE *(12)*
Or who laid its **c** Jb 38:6
rejected has become the **c**. Ps 118:22
stone, a precious **c**, a sure Is 28:16
to retrieve a **c** or a foundation Jr 51:26
From them will come the **c**, Zch 10:4
rejected has become the **c**. Mt 21:42
—this has become the **c**. Mk 12:10
—this has become the **c**? Lk 20:17
builders, who has become the **c**. Ac 4:11
Christ Jesus Himself as the **c**. Eph 2:20
and valuable **c**, and the one who 1Pt 2:6
this One has become the **c**, 1Pt 2:7

CORPSE *(28)*
who is defiled because of a **c**. Nm 5:2
he sinned because of the **c**. Nm 6:11
unclean because of a human **c**, Nm 9:6
unclean because of a human **c**. Nm 9:7
of a **c** or is on a distant Nm 9:10
any human **c** will be unclean Nm 19:11
a grave, a **c**, or a person who Nm 19:18
not to leave his **c** on the tree Dt 21:23
c will never reach the grave 1Kg 13:22
His **c** was thrown on the road, 1Kg 13:24
was standing beside the **c** too. 1Kg 13:24
by who saw the **c** thrown on the 1Kg 13:25
and found the **c** of the man of 1Kg 13:28
the lion standing beside the **c**. 1Kg 13:28
not eaten the **c** or mauled the 1Kg 13:28
lifted the **c** of the man of God 1Kg 13:29
he laid the **c** in his own grave 1Kg 13:30
Jezebel's **c** will be like manure 2Kg 9:37
a rocky pit like a trampled **c**. Is 14:19
and threw his **c** into the burial Jr 26:23
and his **c** will be thrown out ⌊to Jr 36:30
remove his **c** from the house. Am 6:10
⌊contact with⌋ a **c** touches any Hg 2:13
came, removed the **c**, buried it, Mt 14:12
and removed his **c** and placed it Mk 6:29
became like a **c**, so that many Mk 9:26
he gave the **c** to Joseph. Mk 15:45
them, "Where the **c** is, there Lk 17:37

CORPSES *(23)*
Your **c** will fall in this Nm 14:29
your **c** will fall in this Nm 14:32
until all your **c** lie ⌊scattered⌋ Nm 14:33
Your **c** will be food for all the Dt 28:26
and give the **c** of the Philistine 1Sm 17:46
and there were **c** lying on the 2Ch 20:24
and wherever **c** lie, it is there. Jb 39:30
They gave the **c** of Your servants Ps 79:2
judge the nations, heaping up **c**; Ps 110:6
and their **c** were like garbage in Is 5:25
the stench of their **c** will rise; Is 34:3
c of these people will become Jr 7:33
Human **c** will fall like manure on Jr 9:22
Their **c** will become food for the Jr 16:4
will provide their **c** as food for Jr 19:7
whole valley—the **c**, the ashes, Jr 31:40
houses with the **c** of ⌊their own⌋ Jr 33:5
Their **c** will become food for the Jr 34:20
thrown all the **c** of the men he Jr 41:9
I will lay the **c** of the Ezk 6:5
and by the **c** of their kings at Ezk 43:7
and the **c** of their kings far Ezk 43:9
slain, mounds of **c**, dead bodies Nah 3:3

CORRECT *(9)*
Zelophehad's daughters say is **c**. Nm 27:7
Does He **c** you and take you to Jb 22:4
with the Almighty **c** ⌊Him⌋? Jb 40:2
Seek justice. **C** the oppressor. Is 1:17
C your ways and your deeds, Jr 7:3
and **c** your ways and your deeds. Jr 18:11
c your ways and deeds and obey Jr 26:13
way of life, and **c** your actions. Jr 35:15
rebuke, **c**, and encourage with 2Tm 4:2

CORRECTING *(1)*
rebuking, for **c**, for training 2Tm 3:16

CORRECTION *(13)*
their ears to **c** and insists they Jb 36:10
counsel and did not accept my **c**, Pr 1:25
counsel, and rejected all my **c**, Pr 1:30
and how my heart despised **c**. Pr 5:12
one who rejects **c** goes astray. Pr 10:17
but one who hates **c** is stupid. Pr 12:1
person who heeds **c** is sensible. Pr 15:5
the one who hates **c** will die. Pr 15:10
listens to **c** acquires good Pr 15:32
Don't withhold **c** from a youth; Pr 23:13
A wise **c** to a receptive ear is Pr 25:12
A rod of **c** imparts wisdom, Pr 29:15
certainly fear Me and accept **c**. Zph 3:7

CORRECTIVE *(1)*
and **c** instructions are the way Pr 6:23

CORRECTLY *(11)*
he could not pronounce it **c**, Jdg 12:6
You have seen **c**, for I watch Jr 1:12
prophesied **c** about you when he Mt 15:7
Isaiah prophesied **c** about you Mk 7:6
You have **c** said that He is One, Mk 12:32
You have judged **c**," He told him. Lk 7:43
You've answered **c**," He told him. Lk 10:28
know that You speak and teach **c**, Lk 20:21
You have **c** said, 'I don't have a Jn 4:17
The Holy Spirit **c** spoke through Ac 28:25
c teaching the word of truth. 2Tm 2:15

CORRECTS *(3)*
See how happy the man is God **c**; Jb 5:17
one who **c** a mocker will bring Pr 9:7
doesn't love one who **c** him; Pr 15:12

CORRESPOND *(2)*
12 stones are to **c** to the names Ex 28:21
⌊Its⌋ length will **c** to one of Ezk 45:7

CORRESPONDED *(4)*
The 12 stones **c** to the names of Ex 39:14
gold mice also ⌊**c**⌋ to the number 1Sm 6:18
its length **c** to the width of the 2Ch 3:8
the gates and **c** to the length Ezk 40:18

CORRESPONDING *(7)*
the edge of the ⌊**c**⌋ curtain of Ex 26:10
the edge of the ⌊**c**⌋ curtain in Ex 36:17
four oxen **c** to their service, Nm 7:7
and eight oxen **c** to their Nm 7:8
five gold mice ⌊**c** to⌋ the number 1Sm 6:4
each division **c** to his service 2Ch 31:2
in front of the **c** wall as one Ezk 42:12

CORRESPONDS *(2)*
in Arabia and **c** to the present Gl 4:25
Baptism, which **c** to this, now 1Pt 3:21

CORRODED *(1)*
your silver and gold are **c**, Jms 5:3

CORROSION *(1)*
and their **c** will be a witness Jms 5:3

CORRUPT *(17)*
forever, because they are **c**. Gn 6:3
the earth was **c** in God's sight, Gn 6:11
God saw how **c** the earth was, Gn 6:12
that he does not **c** his bloodline Lv 21:15
become completely **c** and turn Dt 31:29
less one who is revolting and **c**, Jb 15:16
exist." They are **c**; their Ps 14:1
all alike have become **c**. Ps 14:3
They are **c**, and they do vile Ps 53:1
they have all become **c**. Ps 53:3
a **c** throne—one that creates Ps 94:20
and iron; all of them are **c**. Jr 6:28
to your evil ways and **c** acts." Ezk 20:44
flattery he will **c** those who act Dn 11:32
they became more **c** in all their Zph 3:7
saved from this **c** generation!" Ac 2:40
men who are **c** in mind, worthless 2Tm 3:8

CORRUPTED *(7)*
for all flesh had **c** its way on Gn 6:12
your splendor you **c** your wisdom. Ezk 28:17
They have deeply **c** themselves as Hs 9:9
wronged no one, **c** no one, 2Co 7:2
minds may be **c** from a complete 2Co 11:3
old man that is **c** by deceitful Eph 4:22
prostitute who **c** the earth with Rv 19:2

CORRUPTIBLE *(2)*
Because this **c** must be clothed 1Co 15:53
Now when this **c** is clothed with 1Co 15:54

CORRUPTION *(8)*
they could find no charge or **c**, Dn 6:4
negligence or **c** was found in him Dn 6:4
the bondage of **c** into the Rm 8:21
Sown in **c**, raised in 1Co 15:42
and **c** cannot inherit 1Co 15:50
will reap **c** from the flesh, Gl 6:8
escaping the **c** that is in the 2Pt 1:4
they themselves are slaves of **c**, 2Pt 2:19

CORRUPTLY *(9)*
the land of Egypt have acted **c**. Ex 32:7
to act **c** and make an idol for Dt 4:16
and if you act **c**, make an idol Dt 4:25
out of Egypt have acted **c**. Dt 9:12
people have acted **c** toward Him; Dt 32:5
act even more **c** than their Jdg 2:19
the people still behaved **c**. 2Ch 27:2
We have acted **c** toward You and Neh 1:7
behaved more **c** than they did. Ezk 16:47

CORRUPTS *(2)*
clear-sighted and **c** the words Ex 23:8
"Bad company **c** good morals." 1Co 15:33

COS *(1)*
we came by a direct route to **C**, Ac 21:1

COSAM *(1)*
Addi, ⌊son⌋ of **C**, ⌊son⌋ of Lk 3:28

COSMETICS *(1)*
perfumes and **c** for ⌊another⌋ six Est 2:12

COST *(16)*
afford the **c** of his cleansing. Lv 14:32
who sinned at the **c** of their own Nm 16:38
at the **c** of⌋ his firstborn Jos 6:26
gates ⌊at the **c** of⌋ his youngest Jos 6:26
offerings that **c** ⌊me⌋ nothing." 2Sm 24:24
request at the **c** of his life. 1Kg 2:23
the **c** of Abiram his firstborn, 1Kg 16:34
and at the **c** of Segub his 1Kg 16:34
offerings that **c** ⌊me⌋ nothing." 1Ch 21:24
The **c** is to be paid from the Ezr 6:4
The **c** is to be paid in full to Ezr 6:8
keeps his word whatever the **c**, Ps 15:4
know it will **c** him his life. Pr 7:23
without money and without **c**! Is 55:1
plunder, without **c**, for all your Jr 15:13
calculate the **c** to see if he has Lk 14:28

COSTLY *(6)*
c stones to lay the foundation 1Kg 5:17
buildings⌋ were of **c** stones, 1Kg 7:9
c stones 12 and 15 feet long. 1Kg 7:10
Above were also **c** stones, cut to 1Kg 7:11
price of redeeming him is too **c**, Ps 49:8
gold, silver, **c** stones, wood, 1Co 3:12

COT *(1)*
lie down on his **c** with his 2Sm 11:13

COUCH *(5)*
falling on the **c** where Esther Est 7:8
and my **c** will ease my complaint, Jb 7:13
While the king is on his **c**, Sg 1:12
on a luxurious **c** with a table Ezk 23:41
of a bed or the cushion of a **c**. Am 3:12

COUCHES *(3)*
and silver **c** ⌊were arranged⌋ Est 1:6
on their **c**, and dine on lambs Am 6:4
copper utensils, and dining **c**. Mk 7:4

COULD *(289)*
(See pp. xi-xii.)

COULDN'T *(17)*
(See pp. xi-xii.)

COUNCIL *(9)*
May I never enter their **c**; Gn 49:6
you listen in on the **c** of God, Jb 15:8
in the **c** of the holy ones, Ps 89:7
Him in the **c** of the elders. Ps 107:32
has stood in the **c** of the LORD Jr 23:18
they had really stood in My **c**, Jr 23:22
and the whole **c** of elders can Ac 22:5
Festus conferred with his **c**, Ac 25:12
on of hands by the **c** of elders. 1Tm 4:14

COUNSEL *(41)*
but did not seek the LORD's **c**. Jos 9:14
please turn the **c** of Ahithophel 2Sm 15:31
Ahithophel's **c** for me. 2Sm 15:34
used to say, 'Seek **c** in Abel,' 2Sm 20:18
all the people with her wise **c**, 2Sm 20:22
of Judah took **c** and sent ⌊word⌋ 2Ch 25:17
according to the **c** of my lord Ezr 10:3
c and understanding are His. Jb 12:13
with empty **c** or fill himself Jb 15:2
The **c** of the wicked is far from Jb 21:16
The **c** of the wicked is far from Jb 22:18
obscures ⌊My⌋ **c** with ignorant Jb 38:2
conceals ⌊My⌋ **c** with ignorance? Jb 42:3
The secret **c** of the LORD is for Ps 25:14
My eye on you, I will give **c**. Ps 32:8
frustrates the **c** of the nations; Ps 33:10
c of the LORD stands forever, Ps 33:11
me with Your **c**, and afterwards Ps 73:24
and would not wait for His **c**. Ps 106:13
despised the **c** of the Most High Ps 107:11
neglected all my **c** and did not Pr 1:25
were not interested in my **c**, Pr 1:30
whoever listens to **c** is wise. Pr 12:15
Plans fail when there is no **c**, Pr 15:22
Listen to **c** and receive Pr 19:20
C in a man's heart is deep water; Pr 20:5
plans through **c**, and wage war Pr 20:18
and no **c** ⌊will prevail⌋ against Pr 21:30
sayings about **c** and knowledge, Pr 22:20
a Spirit of **c** and strength, Is 11:2
Give us **c** and make a decision. Is 16:3
the LORD, or who gave Him His **c**? Is 40:13
and fulfills the **c** of His Is 44:26
yes, let them take **c** together. Is 45:21
the priest, or **c** from the wise, Jr 18:18
the One great in **c** and mighty in Jr 32:19
Has **c** perished from the prudent? Jr 49:7
priests and **c** from the elders Ezk 7:26
Israel will be ashamed of its **c**. Hs 10:6
revealing His **c** to His servants Am 3:7
be peaceful **c** between the two Zch 6:13

COUNSELED *(1)*
How you have **c** the unwise and Jb 26:3

COUNSELOR *(14)*
insightful **c**, and his lot came 1Ch 26:14
David's uncle Jonathan was a **c**; 1Ch 27:32
Ahithophel was the king's **c**. 1Ch 27:33
Have we made you the king's **c**? 2Ch 25:16
dignitary, the **c**, cunning Is 3:3
He will be named Wonderful **C**, Is 9:6
there is no **c** among them; Is 41:28
Has your **c** perished, so that Mc 4:9
the LORD, and is a wicked **c**. Nah 1:11
give you another **C** to be with Jn 14:16
But the **C**, the Holy Spirit—the Jn 14:26
When the **C** comes, the One I will Jn 15:26
go away the **C** will not come to Jn 16:7
Or who has been His **c**? Rm 11:34

COUNSELORS *(10)*
and his seven **c** to evaluate Ezr 7:14
king and his **c** have willingly Ezr 7:15
the king, his **c**, and all his Ezr 7:28
the king, his **c**, his leaders, Ezr 8:25
The king and his **c** approved the Est 1:21
the kings and **c** of the earth, Jb 3:14
He leads **c** away barefoot and Jb 12:17
decrees are my delight and my **c**. Ps 119:24
but with many **c** there is Pr 11:14
victory comes with many **c**. Pr 24:6

COUNSELS *(1)*
will praise the LORD who **c** me— Ps 16:7

COUNT *(31)*
so that if one could **c** the dust Gn 13:16
Look at the sky and **c** the stars, Gn 15:5
if you are able to **c** them." Gn 15:5
and they will be too many to **c**." Gn 16:10
he is to **c** seven days for his Lv 15:13
she is to **c** seven days, Lv 15:28
You are to **c** seven complete Lv 23:15
You are to **c** 50 days until the Lv 23:16
You are to **c** seven sabbatic Lv 25:8
do not **c** the previous period, Nm 6:12
are to take a **c** of what was Nm 31:26
You are to **c** seven weeks, Dt 16:9
c ⌊the people of⌋ Israel and 2Sm 24:1
temple and **c** the money found 2Kg 12:10
They would **c** them when they 1Ch 9:28
incited David to **c** ⌊the people 1Ch 21:1
Go and **c** Israel from Beer-sheba 1Ch 21:2
Benjamin in the **c** because the 1Ch 21:6
gave the order to **c** the people? 1Ch 21:17
David didn't **c** the men aged 20 1Ch 27:23
son of Zeruiah began to **c** them, 1Ch 27:24
then You would **c** my steps but Jb 14:16
Can you **c** the months they are Jb 39:2
can **c** all my bones; people look Ps 22:17
Zion, encircle it; **c** its towers, Ps 48:12
search and a time to **c** as lost; Ec 3:6
that a child could **c** them. Is 10:19
he is to **c** off seven days for Ezk 44:26
But I **c** my life of no value to Ac 20:24
we **c** as blessed those who have Jms 5:11
and ⌊**c**⌋ those who worship there. Rv 11:1

COUNTED *(41)*
then your offspring could be **c**. Gn 13:16
the sea, which cannot be **c**.'" Gn 32:12
Who has **c** the dust of Jacob or Nm 23:10
and it will be **c** against you as Dt 23:21
it will not be **c** against you as Dt 23:22
this will be **c** as righteousness Dt 24:13

For when the people were **c**, Jdg 21:9
Saul **c** them at Bezek. 1Sm 11:8
the troops and **c** them at Telaim: 1Sm 15:4
So they got up and were **c** off— 2Sm 2:15
numerous to be numbered or **c**. 1Kg 3:8
that could not be **c** or numbered, 1Kg 8:5
So Ahab **c** the young men of the 1Kg 20:15
them he **c** all the Israelite 1Kg 20:15
they would put the **c** money into 2Kg 12:11
30 years old and above were **c**; 1Ch 23:3
years old or more were to be **c**— 1Ch 23:27
that could not be **c** or numbered 2Ch 5:6
c them out to Sheshbazzar the Ezr 1:8
number of His years cannot be **c**. Jb 36:26
we are **c** as sheep to be Ps 44:22
I am **c** among those going down to Ps 88:4
and let his prayer be **c** as sin. Ps 109:7
I **c** them, they would outnumber Ps 139:18
it will be **c** as a curse to him. Pr 27:14
what is lacking cannot be **c**. Ec 1:15
You **c** the houses of Jerusalem so Is 22:10
and was **c** among the rebels; Is 53:12
The hosts of heaven cannot be **c**; Jr 33:22
than locusts; they cannot be **c**. Jr 46:23
of the earth are **c** as nothing, Dn 4:35
which cannot be measured or **c**. Hs 1:10
of your head have all been **c**. Mt 10:30
And He was **c** among outlaws. Mk 15:28
hairs of your head are all **c**. Lk 12:7
those who are **c** worthy to take Lk 20:35
And He was **c** among the outlaws. Lk 22:37
that they were **c** worthy to be Ac 5:41
not be **c** as circumcision? Rm 2:26
you will be **c** worthy of God's 2Th 1:5
May it not be **c** against them. 2Tm 4:16

COUNTENANCE *(2)*
thrilled at the light of my **c**. Jb 29:24
perish at the rebuke of Your **c**. Ps 80:16

COUNTERACT *(1)*
then you can **c** Ahithophel's 2Sm 15:34

COUNTERATTACKED *(1)*
we **c** right up to the entrance 2Sm 11:23

COUNTING *(19)*
c the names of every male one by Nm 1:2
c one by one the names of those Nm 1:18
c one by one the names of every Nm 1:20
those registered **c** one by one Nm 1:22
c the names of those 20 years Nm 1:24
c the names of those 20 years Nm 1:26
c the names of those 20 years Nm 1:28
c the names of those 20 years Nm 1:30
c the names of those 20 years Nm 1:32
c the names of those 20 years Nm 1:34
c the names of those 20 years Nm 1:36
c the names of those 20 years Nm 1:38
c the names of those 20 years Nm 1:40
c the names of those 20 years Nm 1:42
c every male one month old or Nm 3:22
C every male one month old or Nm 3:28
c every male one month old or Nm 3:34
c the weeks from the time the Dt 16:9
not **c** their trespasses against 2Co 5:19

COUNTLESS *(9)*
They piled them in **c** heaps, Ex 8:14
to the **c** thousands of Israel. Nm 10:36
and **c** people who came with him 2Ch 12:3
How **c** are Your works, LORD! Ps 104:24
her victims are **c**. Pr 7:26
even if you offer **c** prayers, Is 1:15
have been as ⌊**c**⌋ as the sand, Is 48:19
have forgotten Me for **c** days. Jr 2:32
Their number was **c** thousands, Rv 5:11

COUNTRIES *(31)*
Assyria have done to all the **c**: 2Kg 19:11
from Egypt and from all the **c**. 2Ch 9:28
Assyria have done to all the **c**; Is 37:11
all these **c** and their lands Is 37:18
from all the other **c** where I had Jr 23:8
nations, with **c** all around her. Ezk 5:5
more than the **c** that surround Ezk 5:6
throughout the **c** there will be Ezk 6:8
and scattered them among the **c**, Ezk 11:16
them in the **c** where they have Ezk 11:16
you from the **c** where you have Ezk 11:17
and scatter them among the **c**. Ezk 12:15
and scatter them among the **c**. Ezk 20:23
like the peoples of ⌊other⌋ **c**, Ezk 20:32
you from the **c** where you were Ezk 20:34
you from the **c** where you have Ezk 20:41
and scatter you among the **c**; Ezk 22:15
and eliminate you from the **c**. Ezk 25:7
and scatter them across the **c**. Ezk 29:12
and scatter them among the **c**. Ezk 30:23
and scatter them among the **c**. Ezk 30:26
nations, in **c** you do not know Ezk 32:9
them from the **c**, and bring them Ezk 34:13
they were scattered among the **c**. Ezk 36:19
and gather you from all the **c**, Ezk 36:24
from the **c** of their enemies, Ezk 39:27
in all the **c** where You have Dn 9:7
He will invade **c** and sweep Dn 11:40
extend his power against the **c**, Dn 11:42
in foreign **c** and divided up My Jl 3:2
fuel the fire and **c** exhaust Hab 2:13

COUNTRY *(171)*
to Sephar, the eastern hill **c**. Gn 10:30
on to the hill **c** east of Bethel Gn 12:8
me and with the **c** where you are Gn 21:23
and went to the eastern **c**. Gn 29:1
headed for the hill **c** of Gilead. Gn 31:21
pitched his tent in the hill **c**, Gn 31:25
tents⌋ in the hill **c** of Gilead. Gn 31:25
the land of Seir, the **c** of Edom. Gn 32:3
Then the **c** will not be wiped out Gn 41:36
There was famine in every **c**, Gn 41:54
had spread across the whole **c**, Gn 41:56
Joseph was in charge of the **c**; Gn 42:6
the lord of the **c** spoke harshly Gn 42:30
accused us of spying on the **c**. Gn 42:30
the lord of the **c** said to us, Gn 42:33
and you can trade in the **c**.'" Gn 42:34
against us, and leave the **c**." Ex 1:10
to your God within the **c**." Ex 8:25
send them quickly out of the **c**, Ex 12:33
been offering in the open **c**. Lv 17:5
people of the **c** are to stone him Lv 20:2
people of the **c** look the other Lv 20:4
then go up into the hill **c**. Nm 13:17
and Amorites live in the hill **c**; Nm 13:29
went up the ridge of the hill **c**, Nm 14:40
go up the ridge of the hill **c**, Nm 14:44
part of the⌋ hill **c** came down, Nm 14:45
go to the hill **c** of the Amorites Dt 1:7
the hill **c**, the lowlands, Dt 1:7
to the hill **c** of the Amorites Dt 1:19
the hill **c** of the Amorites Dt 1:20
up into the hill **c** and came to Dt 1:24
easy to go up into the hill **c**. Dt 1:41
went up into the hill **c**. Dt 1:43
around the hill **c** of Seir for Dt 2:1
around this hill **c** long enough; Dt 2:3
Esau the hill **c** of Seir as ⌊his⌋ Dt 2:5
and the cities of the hill **c**, Dt 2:37
half the hill **c** of Gilead along Dt 3:12
that good hill **c** and Lebanon. Dt 3:25
the engaged woman in the open **c**, Dt 22:25
the city and blessed in the **c**. Dt 28:3
in the city and cursed in the **c**. Dt 28:16
from a distant **c** will see the Dt 29:22
Go to the hill **c** so that the men Jos 2:16
into the hill **c** and stayed there Jos 2:22
came down from the hill **c**, Jos 2:23
pursued them into the open **c**, Jos 8:24
of the Jordan in the hill **c**, Jos 9:1
in the hill **c** have joined forces Jos 10:6
region—the hill **c**, the Negev, Jos 10:40
of the north in the hill **c**, Jos 11:2
and Jebusites in the hill **c**, Jos 11:3
—the hill **c**, all the Negev, Jos 11:16
the hill **c** of Israel with its Jos 11:16
the Anakim from the hill **c**— Jos 11:21
all the hill **c** of Judah and of Jos 11:21
hill **c**, the Judean foothills, Jos 12:8
of the hill **c** from Lebanon to Jos 13:6
me this hill **c** the LORD promised Jos 14:12
In the hill **c**: Shamir, Jattir, Jos 15:48
into the hill **c** of Bethel. Jos 16:1
Ephraim's hill **c** is too small Jos 17:15
The hill **c** is not enough for us, Jos 17:16
because the hill **c** will be yours Jos 17:18
through the hill **c** westward, Jos 18:12
in the hill **c** of Ephraim, Jos 19:50
Kedesh in the hill **c** of Naphtali Jos 20:7
in the hill **c** of Ephraim, Jos 20:7
Hebron) in the hill **c** of Judah. Jos 20:7
in the hill **c** of Judah. Jos 21:11
in the hill **c** of Ephraim, Jos 21:21
gave the hill **c** of Seir to Esau Jos 24:4
the hill **c** of Ephraim north of Jos 24:30
in the hill **c** of Ephraim. Jos 24:33
who were living in the hill **c**, Jdg 1:9
take possession of the hill **c**, Jdg 1:19
the hill **c** and did not allow Jdg 1:34
in the hill **c** of Ephraim, north Jdg 2:9
the hill **c** of Ephraim. Jdg 3:27
down with him from the hill **c**, Jdg 3:27
Bethel in the hill **c** of Ephraim, Jdg 4:5
the hill **c** of Ephraim with Jdg 7:24
Shamir in the hill **c** of Ephraim. Jdg 10:1
through your land to our **c**,' Jdg 11:19
Amorites who lived in that **c**. Jdg 11:21
in the hill **c** of the Amalekites. Jdg 12:15
from the hill **c** of Ephraim named Jdg 17:1
home in the hill **c** of Ephraim. Jdg 17:8
came to the hill **c** of Ephraim as Jdg 18:2
traveled to the hill **c** of Jdg 18:13
part of the hill **c** of Ephraim Jdg 19:1
was from the hill **c** of Ephraim Jdg 19:16
to the remote hill **c** of Ephraim, Jdg 19:18
to Gibeah through the open **c**. Jdg 20:31
in the hill **c** of Ephraim. 1Sm 1:1
through the hill **c** of Ephraim 1Sm 9:4
Michmash and in Bethel's hill **c**, 1Sm 13:2
in the hill **c** of Ephraim heard 1Sm 14:22
and in the hill **c** of the 1Sm 23:14
replied, "The south **c** of Judah," 1Sm 27:10
south **c** of the Jerahmeelites, 1Sm 27:10
the south **c** of the Kenites." 1Sm 27:10
in the open **c** and brought him to 1Sm 30:11
raided the south **c** of the 1Sm 30:14
and the south **c** of Caleb, and we 1Sm 30:14
from the hill **c** of Ephraim, 2Sm 20:21
in the hill **c** of Ephraim; 1Kg 4:8
the **c** of Sihon king of the 1Kg 4:19
deport them to the enemy's **c**— 1Kg 8:46
heard in my own **c** about your 1Kg 10:6
servants, returned to her own **c**. 1Kg 10:13
leave, so I can go to my own **c**." 1Kg 11:21
want to go back to your own **c**?" 1Kg 11:22
Shechem in the hill **c** of Ephraim 1Kg 12:25
gods are gods of the hill **c**. 1Kg 20:23
me from the hill **c** of Ephraim. 2Kg 5:22
the camp to hide in the open **c**, 2Kg 7:12
day she left the **c** until now." 2Kg 8:6
They came from a distant **c**, 2Kg 20:14
Midian in the **c** of Moab, 1Ch 1:46
in the hill **c** of Ephraim, 1Ch 6:67
had sons in the **c** of Moab after 1Ch 8:8
of the storehouses in the **c**, 1Ch 27:25
them to a distant or nearby **c**, 2Ch 6:36
heard in my own **c** about your 2Ch 9:5
servants, returned to her own **c**. 2Ch 9:12
is in the hill **c** of Ephraim, 2Ch 13:4
in the hill **c** of Ephraim. 2Ch 15:8
to the hill **c** of Ephraim and 2Ch 19:4
cities in the hill **c** of Judah 2Ch 27:4
out to the hill **c** and bring back Neh 8:15
a man in the **c** of Uz named Job Jb 1:1
came—gnats throughout their **c**. Ps 105:31
wrath—to destroy the whole **c**. Is 13:5
came to me from a distant **c**, Is 39:3
man for My purpose from a far **c**. Is 46:11
from the hill **c** and from the Jr 17:26
out in the hill **c** of Ephraim: Jr 31:6
cities of the hill **c**, the cities Jr 32:44
in the cities of the hill **c**, Jr 33:13
great nations from the north **c**. Jr 50:9
in the hill **c** of Ephraim Jr 50:19
from the hill **c** of Esau? Ob 8
from the hill **c** of Esau will be Ob 9
will possess the hill **c** of Esau; Ob 19
to rule over the hill **c** of Esau, Ob 21
What is your **c** and what people Jnh 1:8
while I was still in my own **c**? Jnh 4:2
called a wicked **c** and the people Mal 1:4
to their own **c** by another route. Mt 2:12
towns, or the **c**, they laid the Mk 6:56
a man coming in from the **c**, Mk 15:21
walking on their way into the **c**. Mk 16:12
to a town in the hill **c** of Judah Lk 1:39
throughout the hill **c** of Judea. Lk 1:65
had and traveled to a distant **c**, Lk 15:13
a severe famine struck that **c**, Lk 15:14

one of the citizens of that **c**, Lk 15:15
to a far **c** to receive for Lk 19:12
who are in the **c** must not enter Lk 21:21
who was coming in from the **c**, Lk 23:26
has no honor in his own **c**. Jn 4:44
Jerusalem from the **c** to purify Jn 11:55
Get out of your **c** and away from Ac 7:3
be strangers in a foreign **c**, Ac 7:6
both the Judean **c** and in Ac 10:39
because their **c** was supplied Ac 12:20
with food from the king's **c**. Ac 12:20
in the open **c**, dangers on the 2Co 11:26
from people of your own **c**, 1Th 2:14

COUNTRYMAN *(1)*
Greet Herodion, my fellow **c**. Rm 16:11

COUNTRYMEN *(10)*
will not be exalted above his **c**, Dt 17:20
and fight for your **c**, your sons Neh 4:14
wives against their Jewish **c**. Neh 5:1
⌊just⌋ like our **c** and their Neh 5:5
you is charging his **c** interest." Neh 5:7
back our Jewish **c** who were sold Neh 5:8
but now you sell your own **c**, Neh 5:8
of my brothers, my **c** by physical Rm 9:3
fellow **c** and fellow prisoners. Rm 16:7
my fellow **c**, greet you. Rm 16:21

COUNTRYSIDE *(22)*
the live bird over the open **c**. Lv 14:7
into the open **c** outside the city Lv 14:53
went out to the **c** and harvested Jdg 9:27
to come wait in ambush in the **c**. Jdg 9:32
when the people went into the **c**, Jdg 9:42
and waited in ambush in the **c**. Jdg 9:43
were in the **c** and struck them Jdg 9:44
Everyone in the **c** was weeping 2Sm 15:23
The blossoms appear in the **c**. Sg 2:12
My mountains in the **c**. Jr 17:3
c shakes at the sound of your Ezk 27:28
wood from the **c** or cut ⌊it⌋ down Ezk 39:10
devoured all the trees of the **c**. Jl 1:19
a heap of ruins in the **c**, Mc 1:6
The whole Judean **c** and all the Mk 1:5
it in the town and the **c**, Mk 5:14
the surrounding **c** and villages Mk 6:36
it in the town and in the **c**. Lk 8:34
villages and **c** to find food and Lk 9:12
disciples went to the Judean **c**, Jn 3:22
from there to the **c** near the Jn 11:54
Derbe, and to the surrounding **c**. Ac 14:6

COUNTS *(4)*
He **c** the number of the stars; Ps 147:4
as a hired worker **c** years, Is 16:14
as a hired worker **c** years, Is 21:16
of the one who **c** them in the Jr 33:13

COUPLE *(3)*
servant and a **c** of donkeys were Jdg 19:3
come and make a **c** of cakes in my 2Sm 13:6
I am gathering a **c** of sticks in 1Kg 17:12

COURAGE *(28)*
and everyone's **c** failed because Jos 2:11
heart and their **c** failed because Jos 5:1
Show some **c** and be men, 1Sm 4:9
they lost their **c** and were 1Sm 17:11
in Hebron, his **c** failed, and all 2Sm 4:1
has found the **c** to pray this 2Sm 7:27
has found ⌊**c**⌋ to pray in Your 1Ch 17:25
he took **c** and removed the 2Ch 15:8
Jehoiada summoned his **c** and took 2Ch 23:1
So I took **c** because I was Ezr 7:28
of my head, and my **c** leaves me. Ps 40:12
their **c** melting away in anguish, Ps 107:26
and says to another, "Take **c**!" Is 41:6
the officials will lose their **c**. Jr 4:9
Will your **c** endure or your hands Ezk 22:14
No one has the **c** to support me Dn 10:21
power and his **c** against the king Dn 11:25
justice and **c**, to proclaim to Mc 3:8
Have **c**, son, your sins Mt 9:2
"Have **c**, daughter," He said. Mt 9:22
to them. "Have **c**! It is I. Don't Mt 14:27
with them and said, "Have **c**! Mk 6:50
man and said to him, "Have **c**! Mk 10:49
stood by him and said, "Have **c**! Ac 23:11
you to take **c**, because there Ac 27:22
Therefore, take **c**, men, because Ac 27:25
he thanked God and took **c**. Ac 28:15
we hold on to the **c** and the Heb 3:6

COURAGEOUS *(18)*
it or not? Be **c**. Bring back some Nm 13:20
Be strong and **c**; don't be Dt 31:6
Be strong and **c**, for you will go Dt 31:7
Be strong and **c**, for you will Dt 31:23
Be strong and **c**, for you will Jos 1:6
strong and very **c** to carefully Jos 1:7
be strong and **c**? Do not be Jos 1:9
Above all, be strong and **c**!" Jos 1:18
Be strong and **c**, for the LORD Jos 10:25
be strong and **c**, for though Saul 2Sm 2:7
Be strong and **c**!" 2Sm 13:28
Be strong and **c**. Don't be afraid 1Ch 22:13
strong and **c**, and do the work. 1Ch 28:20
Be strong and **c**! 2Ch 32:7
be **c** and let your heart be Ps 27:14
Be strong and **c**, all you who put Ps 31:24
Even the most **c** of the warriors Am 2:16
this world. Be **c**! I have Jn 16:33

COURIER *(1)*
a trustworthy **c** ⌊brings⌋ healing Pr 13:17

COURIERS *(6)*
So the **c** went throughout Israel 2Ch 30:6
The **c** traveled from city to city 2Ch 30:10
were sent by **c** to each of the Est 3:13
The **c** left, spurred on by royal Est 3:15
sent the documents by mounted **c**, Est 8:10
horses, the **c** rode out in haste Est 8:14

COURSE *(17)*
In the **c** of time Cain presented Gn 4:3
of the Jordan resumed their **c**, Jos 4:18
so of **c** their bodies are 1Sm 21:5
God for him? Of **c** not! Please 1Sm 22:15
know, of **c**, that you and your 1Sm 28:1
directed their **c** and presided as Jb 29:25
like an athlete running a **c**. Ps 19:5
The **c** of my life is in Your Ps 31:15
to subvert the **c** of justice. Pr 17:23
keep your mind on the right **c**. Pr 23:19
has stayed his **c** like a horse Jr 8:6
"Yes, of **c**, Your Majesty," they Dn 3:24
the whole **c** of your life. Dn 5:23
and they do not change their **c**. Jl 2:7
ran a straight **c** to Samothrace, Ac 16:11
I may finish my **c** and the Ac 20:24
sets the **c** of life on fire, Jms 3:6

COURSES *(1)*
fought with Sisera from their **c**. Jdg 5:20

COURT *(99)*
are to go to **c**, and the judges Dt 25:1
son of Ahilud was **c** historian; 2Sm 8:16
Seraiah was **c** secretary; 2Sm 8:17
son of Ahilud was **c** historian; 2Sm 20:24
Sheva was **c** secretary; 2Sm 20:25
appointed a **c** official for her 2Kg 8:6
Shebnah the **c** secretary, and 2Kg 18:18
of Asaph, the **c** historian, came 2Kg 18:18
palace, Shebna the **c** secretary, 2Kg 18:37
of Asaph, the **c** historian, came 2Kg 18:37
palace, Shebna the **c** secretary, 2Kg 19:2
king sent the **c** secretary 2Kg 22:3
told Shaphan the **c** secretary, 2Kg 22:8
Shaphan the **c** secretary went 2Kg 22:9
Shaphan the **c** secretary told 2Kg 22:10
Shaphan the **c** secretary, 2Kg 22:12
of Nathan-melech the **c** official, 2Kg 23:11
city he took a **c** official who 2Kg 25:19
son of Ahilud was **c** historian; 1Ch 18:15
Shavsha was **c** secretary; 1Ch 18:16
As for the **c** on the west, there 1Ch 26:18
at the highway and two at the **c**. 1Ch 26:18
along with the **c** officials, 1Ch 28:1
of the priests and the large **c**, 2Ch 4:9
court, and doors for the **c**. 2Ch 4:9
feet high and put it in the **c**. 2Ch 6:13
by Jeiel the **c** secretary 2Ch 26:11
told Shaphan the **c** secretary, 2Ch 34:15
Shaphan the **c** secretary told 2Ch 34:18
Micah, Shaphan the **c** secretary, 2Ch 34:20
the **c** of the house of God, Neh 8:16
recorded in the **c** records of Est 2:23
king asked, "Who's in the **c**?" Est 6:4
the outer **c** of the palace to Est 6:4
Haman is standing in the **c**." Est 6:5
written in the **c** record of daily Est 10:2
If one wanted to take Him to **c**, Jb 9:3
we can take each other to **c**. Jb 9:32
in prison or convenes a **c**, Jb 11:10
take you to **c** because of your Jb 22:4
you take Him to **c** for not Jb 33:13
one should approach Him in **c**. Jb 34:23
take a matter to **c** hastily. Pr 25:8
wise man goes to **c** with a fool, Pr 29:9
Take Me to **c**; let us argue our Is 43:26
raised against you in **c**. Is 54:17
queen mother, the **c** officials, Jr 29:2
and Jerusalem, the **c** officials, Jr 34:19
a Cushite **c** official employed in Jr 38:7
and **c** officials whom he brought Jr 41:16
city he took a **c** official who Jr 52:25
me to the entrance of the **c**, Ezk 8:7
me to the inner **c** of the LORD's Ezk 8:16
the cloud filled the inner **c**. Ezk 10:3
and the **c** was filled with the Ezk 10:4
be heard as far as the outer **c**; Ezk 10:5
around to the pilaster of the **c**. Ezk 40:14
he brought me into the outer **c**, Ezk 40:17
laid out all around the **c**. Ezk 40:17
exterior front of the inner **c**; Ezk 40:19
of the outer **c** facing north, Ezk 40:20
inner **c** had a gate facing the Ezk 40:23
The inner **c** had a gate on the Ezk 40:27
me to the inner **c** through the Ezk 40:28
Its portico faced the outer **c**, Ezk 40:31
me to the inner **c** on the east Ezk 40:32
Its portico faced the outer **c**, Ezk 40:34
Its portico faced the outer **c**, Ezk 40:37
within the inner **c**, there were Ezk 40:44
Next he measured the **c**. Ezk 40:47
and the porticoes of the **c**— Ezk 41:15
the north gate into the outer **c**. Ezk 42:1
to the inner **c** and opposite the Ezk 42:3
belonging to the outer **c**, Ezk 42:3
to them, toward the outer **c**; Ezk 42:7
the outer **c** were 87 and a half Ezk 42:8
enters them from the outer **c**. Ezk 42:9
the wall of the **c** toward the Ezk 42:10
to the outer **c** until they have Ezk 42:14
and brought me to the inner **c**, Ezk 43:5
of the inner **c** they must wear Ezk 44:17
of the inner **c** and within ⌊it⌋. Ezk 44:17
they go out to the outer **c**, Ezk 44:19
before he enters the inner **c**. Ezk 44:21
into the inner **c** to minister in Ezk 44:27
of the gate to the inner **c**. Ezk 45:19
of the inner **c** that faces east Ezk 46:1
into the outer **c** and transmit Ezk 46:20
into the outer **c** and led me past Ezk 46:21
a ⌊separate⌋ **c** in each of its Ezk 46:21
of the ⌊outer⌋ **c** there were Ezk 46:22
the chief of his **c** officials, Dn 1:3
were to serve in the king's **c**. Dn 1:5
began to serve in the king's **c**. Dn 1:19
Daniel remained at the king's **c**. Dn 2:49
c was convened, and the books Dn 7:10
But the **c** will convene, and his Dn 7:26
Your **c** officials are like the Nah 3:17
by you or by a human **c**. 1Co 4:3

COURTESY *(1)*
and paid a **c** call on Festus. Ac 25:13

COURTROOM *(1)*
his royal throne in the royal **c**, Est 5:1

COURTS *(19)*
for the **c** and the chambers, 1Ch 23:28
is to build My house and My **c**, 1Ch 28:6
in mind for the **c** of the LORD's 1Ch 28:12
a room in the **c** of God's house. Neh 13:7
bring near to live in Your **c**! Ps 65:4
and yearn for the **c** of the LORD; Ps 84:2
a day in Your **c** than a thousand Ps 84:10
an offering and enter His **c**. Ps 96:8
and His **c** with praise. Ps 100:4
in the **c** of the LORD's house— Ps 116:19
the **c** of the house of our God. Ps 135:2
you—⌊this⌋ trampling of My **c**? Is 1:12
drink ⌊the wine⌋ in My holy **c**. Is 62:9
and fill the **c** with the slain. Ezk 9:7
like the pillars of the **c**; Ezk 42:6
court there were enclosed **c**, Ezk 46:22
My house and take care of My **c**; Zch 3:7
anyone, the **c** are in session, Ac 19:38
you and drag you into the **c**? Jms 2:6

COURTYARD *(78)*
are to make the **c** for the Ex 27:9

the south of the **c** out of finely Ex 27:9
hangings of the **c** on the west Ex 27:12
hangings of the **c** on the east Ex 27:13
The gate of the **c** is to have a Ex 27:16
around the **c** are to be banded Ex 27:17
length of the **c** is to be 150 Ex 27:18
pegs of the **c** are to be made Ex 27:19
the hangings of the **c**, its posts Ex 35:17
screen for the gate of the **c**; Ex 35:17
and the tent pegs for the **c**, Ex 35:18
Then he made the **c**. Ex 38:9
side of the **c** were of finely Ex 38:9
on both sides of the **c** gate. Ex 38:15
around the **c** were of finely spun Ex 38:16
posts of the **c** were banded with Ex 38:17
gate of the **c** was embroidered Ex 38:18
and like the hangings of the **c**, Ex 38:18
the surrounding **c** were bronze. Ex 38:20
the bases for the surrounding **c**, Ex 38:31
the bases for the gate of the **c**, Ex 38:31
tent pegs for the surrounding **c**. Ex 38:31
the hangings of the **c**, its posts Ex 39:40
screen for the gate of the **c**, Ex 39:40
the surrounding **c** and hang the Ex 40:8
screen for the gate of the **c**. Ex 40:8
the surrounding **c** for the Ex 40:33
a screen for the gate of the **c**. Ex 40:33
to eat it in the **c** of the tent Lv 6:16
in the **c** of the tent of meeting. Lv 6:26
hangings of the **c**, the screen Nm 3:26
entrance to the **c** that surrounds Nm 3:26
the surrounding **c** with their Nm 3:37
hangings of the **c**, the screen Nm 4:26
the gate of the **c** that surrounds Nm 4:26
the surrounding **c** with their Nm 4:32
a well in his **c**, and they 2Sm 17:18
built the inner **c** with three 1Kg 6:36
in the other **c** behind the hall, 1Kg 7:8
from the outside to the great **c**. 1Kg 7:9
Around the great **c**, as well as 1Kg 7:12
as the inner **c** of the LORD's 1Kg 7:12
middle of the **c** that was in 1Kg 8:64
out of the inner **c** when the word 2Kg 20:4
He made the **c** of the priests and 2Ch 4:9
middle of the **c** that was in 2Ch 7:7
LORD's temple before the new **c**. 2Ch 20:5
command in the **c** of the LORD's 2Ch 24:21
sanctuary to the **c** of the LORD's 2Ch 29:16
the king, by the **c** of the guard. Neh 3:25
in the garden **c** of the royal Est 1:5
of the harem's **c** to learn how Est 2:11
in the inner **c** and who has not Est 4:11
in the inner **c** of the palace Est 5:1
Queen Esther standing in the **c**, Est 5:2
stood in the **c** of the LORD's Jr 19:14
Stand in the **c** of the LORD's Jr 26:2
the guard's **c** in the palace of Jr 32:2
to the guard's **c** as the LORD had Jr 32:8
sitting in the guard's **c**. Jr 32:12
still confined in the guard's **c**, Jr 33:1
in the upper **c** at the opening of Jr 36:10
they came to the king at the **c**, Jr 36:20
was placed in the guard's **c**. Jr 37:21
remained in the guard's **c**. Jr 37:21
which was in the guard's **c**, Jr 38:6
to stay in the guard's **c**. Jr 38:13
in the guard's **c** until the day Jr 38:28
from the guard's **c** and turned Jr 39:14
was confined in the guard's **c**: Jr 39:15
right to the high priest's **c**. Mt 26:58
was sitting outside in the **c**. Mt 26:69
right into the high priest's **c**. Mk 14:54
While Peter was in the **c** below, Mk 14:66
soldiers led Him away into the **c** Mk 15:16
the middle of the **c** and sat down Lk 22:55
Jesus into the high priest's **c**. Jn 18:15
But exclude the **c** outside the Rv 11:2

COURTYARDS *(7)*

in the houses, **c**, and fields Ex 8:13
host in both **c** of the LORD's 2Kg 21:5
made in the two **c** of the LORD's 2Kg 23:12
will be in the **c** of the LORD's 2Ch 23:5
host in both **c** of the LORD's 2Ch 33:5
their rooftops, and **c**, the court Neh 8:16
they thrive in the **c** of our God. Ps 92:13

COUSIN *(6)*

His uncle or **c** may redeem him, Lv 25:49
legal guardian of his **c** Hadassah Est 2:7
Then my **c** Hanamel ⌊came⌋ to the Jr 32:8
in Anathoth from my **c** Hanamel, Jr 32:9
in the sight of my **c** Hanamel, Jr 32:12
Barnabas' **c** (concerning whom Col 4:10

COUSINS *(2)*

c on their father's side. Nm 36:11
Their **c**, the sons of Kish, 1Ch 23:22

COVENANT *(302)*

I will establish My **c** with you, Gn 6:18
am confirming My **c** with you and Gn 9:9
I confirm My **c** with you that Gn 9:11
is the sign of the **c** I am making Gn 9:12
a **c** for all future generations: Gn 9:12
be a sign of the **c** between Me Gn 9:13
will remember My **c** between Me Gn 9:15
everlasting **c** between God and Gn 9:16
is the sign of the **c** that I have Gn 9:17
the LORD made a **c** with Abram, Gn 15:18
will establish My **c** between Me Gn 17:2
As for Me, My **c** is with you, and Gn 17:4
I will keep My **c** between Me and Gn 17:7
an everlasting **c** to be your God Gn 17:7
generations are to keep My **c**. Gn 17:9
This is My **c**, which you are to Gn 17:10
a sign of the **c** between Me and Gn 17:11
My **c** will be in your flesh as an Gn 17:13
your flesh as an everlasting **c**. Gn 17:13
he has broken My **c**." Gn 17:14
I will confirm My **c** with him as Gn 17:19
an everlasting **c** for his Gn 17:19
I will confirm My **c** with Isaac, Gn 17:21
and the two of them made a **c**. Gn 21:27
they had made a **c** at Beer-sheba, Gn 21:32
Let us make a **c** with you: Gn 26:28
now, let's make a **c**, you and I. Gn 31:44
remembered His **c** with Abraham, Ex 2:24
established My **c** with them to Ex 6:4
and I have remembered My **c**. Ex 6:5
to Me and carefully keep My **c**, Ex 19:5
must not make a **c** with them or Ex 23:32
then took the **c** scroll and read Ex 24:7
the blood of the **c** that the LORD Ex 24:8
generations as a perpetual **c**. Ex 31:16
Look, I am making a **c**. Ex 34:10
I have made a **c** with you and Ex 34:27
the tablets the words of the **c**— Ex 34:28
the salt of the **c** with your God. Lv 2:13
day as a perpetual **c** obligation Lv 24:8
and confirm My **c** with you. Lv 26:9
My commands—and break My **c**, Lv 26:15
execute the vengeance of the **c**. Lv 26:25
I will remember My **c** with Jacob. Lv 26:42
also remember My **c** with Isaac Lv 26:42
Isaac and My **c** with Abraham, Lv 26:42
them and break My **c** with them, Lv 26:44
will remember the **c** with their Lv 26:45
of the LORD's **c** traveling ahead Nm 10:33
of the LORD's **c** and Moses did Nm 14:44
is a perpetual **c** of salt before Nm 18:19
I grant him My **c** of peace. Nm 25:12
It will be a **c** of perpetual Nm 25:13
He declared His **c** to you. Dt 4:13
to forget the **c** of the LORD your Dt 4:23
forget the **c** with your fathers Dt 4:31
our God made a **c** with us at Dt 5:2
not make this **c** with our fathers Dt 5:3
keeps His gracious **c** loyalty for Dt 7:9
will keep His **c** loyalty with you Dt 7:12
confirm His **c** He swore to your Dt 8:18
tablets of the **c** the LORD made Dt 9:9
the tablets of the **c**, at the end Dt 9:11
tablets of the **c** were in my Dt 9:15
carry the ark of the LORD's **c**, Dt 10:8
your God and violating His **c** Dt 17:2
the words of the **c** the LORD Dt 29:1
addition to the **c** He had made Dt 29:1
words of this **c** and follow them Dt 29:9
enter into the **c** of the LORD Dt 29:12
I am making this **c** and this oath Dt 29:14
curses of the **c** written in this Dt 29:21
abandoned the **c** of the LORD, Dt 29:25
carried the ark of the LORD's **c**, Dt 31:9
and break the **c** I have made with Dt 31:16
despising Me and breaking My **c**. Dt 31:20
carried the ark of the LORD's **c**, Dt 31:25
ark of the **c** of the LORD your Dt 31:26
Your word and maintained Your **c**. Dt 33:9
ark of the **c** of the LORD your Jos 3:3
the ark of the **c** and go on ahead Jos 3:6
the ark of the **c** and went ahead Jos 3:6
carrying the ark of the **c**: Jos 3:8
the ark of the **c** of the Lord of Jos 3:11
the ark of the **c** ahead of the Jos 3:14
ark of the LORD's **c** stood firmly Jos 3:17
of the ark of the LORD's **c**. Jos 4:7
the ark of the **c** were standing. Jos 4:9
the ark of the LORD's **c** came up Jos 4:18
the ark of the **c** and have seven Jos 6:6
of the LORD's **c** followed them. Jos 6:8
violated My **c** that I appointed Jos 7:11
the LORD's **c** and committed Jos 7:15
ark of the LORD's **c** facing the Jos 8:33
you break the **c** of the LORD your Jos 23:16
Joshua made a **c** for the people Jos 24:25
will never break My **c** with you. Jdg 2:1
not to make a **c** with the people Jdg 2:2
has violated My **c** that I made Jdg 2:20
the ark of the **c** of God was Jdg 20:27
ark of the LORD's **c** from Shiloh. 1Sm 4:3
the ark of the **c** of the LORD 1Sm 4:4
with the ark of the **c** of God. 1Sm 4:4
the ark of the **c** of the LORD 1Sm 4:5
Jonathan made a **c** with David 1Sm 18:3
me into a **c** before the LORD 1Sm 20:8
Jonathan made a **c** with the house 1Sm 20:16
own son makes a **c** with Jesse's 1Sm 22:8
of them made a **c** in the LORD's 1Sm 23:18
Make your **c** with me, and you can 2Sm 3:12
Good, I will make a **c** with you. 2Sm 3:13
They will make a **c** with you, 2Sm 3:21
King David made a **c** with them at 2Sm 5:3
the ark of the **c** of God. 2Sm 15:24
an everlasting **c** with me, 2Sm 23:5
before the ark of the Lord's **c**, 1Kg 3:15
the ark of the LORD's **c** there. 1Kg 6:19
ark of the LORD's **c** from Zion, 1Kg 8:1
of the LORD's **c** to its place, 1Kg 8:6
the LORD made a **c** with the 1Kg 8:9
the LORD's **c** is that He made 1Kg 8:21
gracious **c** with Your servants 1Kg 8:23
not keep My **c** and My statutes 1Kg 11:11
have abandoned Your **c**, 1Kg 19:10
have abandoned Your **c**, 1Kg 19:14
where he made a **c** with them and 2Kg 11:4
Jehoiada made a **c** between the 2Kg 11:17
because of His **c** with Abraham, 2Kg 13:23
and His **c** He had made with 2Kg 17:15
The LORD made a **c** with them 2Kg 17:35
not forget the **c** that I have 2Kg 17:38
their God but violated His **c**— 2Kg 18:12
the book of the **c** that had been 2Kg 23:2
and made a **c** in the presence 2Kg 23:3
words of this **c** that were 2Kg 23:3
all the people agreed to the **c**. 2Kg 23:3
written in the book of the **c**." 2Kg 23:21
David made a **c** with them at 1Ch 11:3
the ark of the **c** of the LORD 1Ch 15:25
the ark of the **c** of the LORD, 1Ch 15:26
the ark of the **c** of the LORD up 1Ch 15:28
the ark of the **c** of the LORD was 1Ch 15:29
before the ark of the **c** of God. 1Ch 16:6
Remember His **c** forever—the 1Ch 16:15
⌊the **c**⌋ He made with Abraham, 1Ch 16:16
to Israel as an everlasting **c**: 1Ch 16:17
ark of the LORD's **c** to minister 1Ch 16:37
of the LORD's **c** is under tent 1Ch 17:1
ark of the LORD's **c** and the holy 1Ch 22:19
ark of the LORD's **c** and as a 1Ch 28:2
cover the ark of the LORD's **c**. 1Ch 28:18
the ark of the **c** of the LORD up 2Ch 5:2
of the LORD's **c** to its place, 2Ch 5:7
LORD had made a **c** with the 2Ch 5:10
the LORD's **c** is that He made 2Ch 6:11
gracious **c** with Your servants 2Ch 6:14
forever by a **c** of salt? 2Ch 13:5
entered into a **c** to seek the 2Ch 15:12
because of the **c** the LORD had 2Ch 21:7
of hundreds into a **c** with him: 2Ch 23:1
assembly made a **c** with the king 2Ch 23:3
made a **c** between himself 2Ch 23:16
to make a **c** with the LORD God 2Ch 29:10
the book of the **c** that had been 2Ch 34:30
post and made a **c** in the LORD's 2Ch 34:31
words of the **c** written in this 2Ch 34:31
and Benjamin enter ⌊the **c**⌋. 2Ch 34:32
carried out the **c** of God, 2Ch 34:32

therefore make a **c** before our Ezr 10:3
His gracious **c** with those who Neh 1:5
made a **c** with him to give the Neh 9:8
God who keeps His gracious **c**— Neh 9:32
as well as the **c** of the Neh 13:29
will have a **c** with the stones Jb 5:23
I have made a **c** with my eyes. Jb 31:1
he make a **c** with you so that Jb 41:4
who keep His **c** and decrees. Ps 25:10
and He reveals His **c** to them. Ps 25:14
You or betrayed Your **c**. Ps 44:17
those who made a **c** with Me by Ps 50:5
and to take My **c** on your lips? Ps 50:16
with him; he violates his **c**. Ps 55:20
Consider the **c**, for the dark Ps 74:20
not keep God's **c** and refused to Ps 78:10
they were unfaithful to His **c**. Ps 78:37
I have made a **c** with My chosen Ps 89:3
and My **c** with him will endure. Ps 89:28
not violate My **c** or change what Ps 89:34
repudiated the **c** with Your Ps 89:39
who keep His **c**, who remember to Ps 103:18
He forever remembers His **c**, Ps 105:8
⌊the **c**⌋ He made with Abraham, Ps 105:9
to Israel as an everlasting **c**: Ps 105:10
remembered His **c** with them, Ps 106:45
He remembers His **c** forever. Ps 111:5
He has ordained His **c** forever. Ps 111:9
sons keep My **c** and My decrees Ps 132:12
and forgets the **c** of her God; Pr 2:17
should be loyalty to the **c**; Pr 19:22
and broken the everlasting **c**. Is 24:5
I make you a **c** for the people Is 42:6
you to be a **c** for the people, Is 49:8
from you and My **c** of peace will Is 54:10
make an everlasting **c** with you, Is 55:3
Me, and hold firmly to My **c**, Is 56:4
and who hold firmly to My **c**— Is 56:6
Me, this is My **c** with them," Is 59:21
make an everlasting **c** with them. Is 61:8
The ark of the LORD's **c**. Jr 3:16
Listen to the words of this **c**, Jr 11:2
not obey the words of this **c**, Jr 11:3
words of this **c** and carry them Jr 11:6
them all the curses of this **c**, Jr 11:8
Judah broke My **c** I made with Jr 11:10
Remember Your **c** with us; Jr 14:21
abandoned the **c** of the LORD Jr 22:9
will make a new **c** with the house Jr 31:31
not be like the **c** I made with Jr 31:32
a **c** they broke even though I had Jr 31:32
this is the **c** I will make with Jr 31:33
make with them an everlasting **c**: Jr 32:40
you can break My **c** with the day Jr 33:20
the day and My **c** with the night Jr 33:20
then also My **c** with My servant Jr 33:21
do not ⌊keep⌋ My **c** with the day Jr 33:25
Zedekiah made a **c** with all the Jr 34:8
who entered into **c** to free their Jr 34:10
I made a **c** with your ancestors Jr 34:13
You made a **c** before Me at the Jr 34:15
As for those who disobeyed My **c**, Jr 34:18
terms of the **c** they made before Jr 34:18
an everlasting **c** that will never Jr 50:5
entered into a **c** with you, Ezk 16:8
the oath by breaking the **c**. Ezk 16:59
remember the **c** I made with you Ezk 16:60
an everlasting **c** with you. Ezk 16:60
but not because of your **c**. Ezk 16:61
I will establish My **c** with you, Ezk 16:62
family and made a **c** with him, Ezk 17:13
might keep his **c** in order to Ezk 17:14
Can he break a **c** and ⌊still⌋ Ezk 17:15
despised and whose **c** he broke. Ezk 17:16
the oath by breaking the **c**. Ezk 17:18
despised and My **c** that he broke. Ezk 17:19
you into the bond of the **c**. Ezk 20:37
the men of the **c** land will fall Ezk 30:5
I will make a **c** of peace with Ezk 34:25
I will make a **c** of peace with Ezk 37:26
be an everlasting **c** with them. Ezk 37:26
You broke My **c** with all your Ezk 44:7
His gracious **c** with those who Dn 9:4
will make a firm **c** with many for Dn 9:27
as well as the **c** prince. Dn 11:22
will be set against the holy **c**; Dn 11:28
the holy **c** and take action Dn 11:30
those who abandon the holy **c**. Dn 11:30
who act wickedly toward the **c**, Dn 11:32
I will make a **c** for them with Hs 2:18
like Adam, have violated the **c**; Hs 6:7
transgress My **c** and rebel Hs 8:1
He makes a **c** with Assyria, Hs 12:1
because of the blood of your **c**, Zch 9:11
annulling the **c** I had made with Zch 11:10
this decree so My **c** with Levi Mal 2:4
My **c** with him was one of life Mal 2:5
have violated the **c** of Levi," Mal 2:8
profaning the **c** of our fathers? Mal 2:10
partner and your wife by **c**. Mal 2:14
Messenger of the **c** you desire— Mal 3:1
blood ⌊that establishes⌋ the **c**; Mt 26:28
blood ⌊that establishes⌋ the **c**; Mk 14:24
and remembered His holy **c**— Lk 1:72
is the new **c** ⌊established by⌋ Lk 22:20
and of the **c** that God made with Ac 3:25
gave him the **c** of circumcision Ac 7:8
the faithful **c** blessings made Ac 13:34
And this will be My **c** with them, Rm 11:27
cup is the new **c** in My blood. 1Co 11:25
to be ministers of a new **c**, 2Co 3:6
at the reading of the old **c**, 2Co 3:14
even a human **c** that has been Gl 3:15
does not revoke a **c** that was Gl 3:17
the guarantee of a better **c**. Heb 7:22
is the mediator of a better **c**, Heb 8:6
For if that first ⌊**c**⌋ had been Heb 8:7
will make a new **c** with the house Heb 8:8
not like the **c** that I made with Heb 8:9
they did not continue in My **c**, Heb 8:9
But this is the **c** that I will Heb 8:10
saying, a new ⌊**c**⌋, He has Heb 8:13
Now the first ⌊**c**⌋ also had Heb 9:1
of incense and the ark of the **c**, Heb 9:4
and the tablets of the **c**. Heb 9:4
He is the mediator of a new **c**, Heb 9:15
committed⌋ under the first **c**. Heb 9:15
even the first **c** was inaugurated Heb 9:18
the blood of the **c** that God has Heb 9:20
This is the **c** that I will make Heb 10:16
blood of the **c** by which he was Heb 10:29
mediator of a new **c**), and to Heb 12:24
the blood of the everlasting **c**, Heb 13:20
the ark of His **c** appeared in His Rv 11:19

COVENANTS *(4)*

false oaths while making **c**. Hs 10:4
the glory, the **c**, the giving of Rm 9:4
the women represent the two **c**. Gl 4:24
to the **c** of the promise, Eph 2:12

COVER *(72)*

and **c** it with pitch inside and Gn 6:14
removed the ark's **c** and saw that Gn 8:13
our brother and **c** up his blood? Gn 37:26
They will **c** the surface of the Ex 10:5
pit, and does not **c** it, and an Ex 21:33
on either side to **c** it. Ex 26:13
undergarments to **c** ⌊their⌋ naked Ex 28:42
of the rock and **c** you with My Ex 33:22
and he must **c** his mouth and cry Lv 13:45
its blood and **c** it with dirt. Lv 17:13
and **c** the ark of the testimony Nm 4:5
c them with a covering made of Nm 4:8
a blue cloth and **c** the lampstand Nm 4:9
c it with a covering made of Nm 4:11
c them with a covering made of Nm 4:12
the cloud would **c** it, appearing Nm 9:16
they **c** the surface of the land Nm 22:5
and they **c** the surface of the Nm 22:11
hole with it and **c** up your Dt 23:13
large stones and **c** them with Dt 27:2
and you are to **c** them with Dt 27:4
wife took the **c**, placed it over 2Sm 17:19
one grating to **c** the capital on 1Kg 7:18
between them in order to **c** it. 1Kg 18:6
threw stones to **c** every good 2Kg 3:25
their wings⌋ and **c** the ark of 1Ch 28:18
cherubim formed a **c** above the 2Ch 5:8
not **c** their guilt or let their Neh 4:5
You would **c** over my iniquity. Jb 14:17
Earth, do not **c** my blood; Jb 16:18
in the dust, and worms **c** them. Jb 21:26
Lotus plants **c** him with their Jb 40:22
hide me under the **c** of His tent; Ps 27:5
C their faces with shame so that Ps 83:16
autumn rain will **c** it with Ps 84:6
He will **c** you with His feathers; Ps 91:4
will never **c** the earth again Ps 104:9
person sees danger and takes **c**, Pr 22:3
sensible see danger and take **c**; Pr 27:12
out under you, and worms **c** you." Is 14:11
and its **c** too small to wrap up Is 28:20
they cannot **c** themselves with Is 59:6
of camels will **c** your land— Is 60:6
let our disgrace **c** us. Jr 3:25
Zion. Run for **c**! Don't stand Jr 4:6
Run for **c**, Benjaminites, out of Jr 6:1
humiliated; they **c** their heads. Jr 14:3
are ashamed; they **c** their heads. Jr 14:4
will go up, I will **c** the earth; Jr 46:8
Shame will **c** all ⌊their⌋ faces, Ezk 7:18
c your face so that you cannot Ezk 12:6
He will **c** his face so he cannot Ezk 12:12
embroidered garments to **c** them, Ezk 16:18
on the ground to **c** it with dust. Ezk 24:7
do not **c** ⌊your⌋ mustache or eat Ezk 24:17
You will not **c** ⌊your⌋ mustache Ezk 24:22
that their dust will **c** you. Ezk 26:10
so that the mighty waters **c** you, Ezk 26:19
A cloud will **c** Tehaphnehes, Ezk 30:18
I will **c** the heavens and darken Ezk 32:7
I will **c** the sun with a cloud, Ezk 32:7
on you, and **c** you with skin. Ezk 37:6
which were to **c** her nakedness. Hs 2:9
say to the mountains, "**C** us!" Hs 10:8
They will all **c** their mouths Mc 3:7
glory, as the waters **c** the sea. Hab 2:14
disgrace will **c** your glory. Hab 2:16
Then a lead **c** was lifted, and Zch 5:7
you **c** the LORD's altar with Mal 2:13
and to the hills, '**C** us!' Lk 23:30
fact, should not **c** his head, 1Co 11:7
from death and **c** a multitude of Jms 5:20

COVERED *(92)*

darkness **c** the surface of the Gn 1:2
came ⌊and⌋ water **c** the earth. Gn 7:6
under the whole sky were **c**. Gn 7:19
mountains were **c** as the waters Gn 7:20
ark because water **c** the surface Gn 8:9
water ⌊that had **c**⌋ the earth was Gn 8:13
they **c** their father's nakedness. Gn 9:23
she took her veil and **c** herself. Gn 24:65
c with hair like a fur coat, Gn 25:25
A large stone **c** the opening of Gn 29:2
her face⌋, **c** herself, and sat Gn 38:14
for she had **c** her face. Gn 38:15
came up and **c** the land of Egypt Ex 8:6
They **c** the surface of the whole Ex 10:15
came back and **c** the chariots Ex 14:28
The floods **c** them; they sank to Ex 15:5
Your breath, and the sea **c** them. Ex 15:10
quail came and **c** the camp. Ex 16:13
the loss is **c** by its rental Ex 22:15
up the mountain, the cloud **c** it. Ex 24:15
and the cloud **c** it for six days. Ex 24:16
The cloud **c** the tent of meeting, Ex 40:34
disease has **c** his entire body Lv 13:13
the LORD six **c** carts and 12 oxen Nm 7:3
the cloud **c** the tabernacle, Nm 9:15
and suddenly the cloud **c** it, Nm 16:42
tent, and she **c** him with a rug. Jdg 4:18
him a drink, and **c** him ⌊again⌋. Jdg 4:19
on its head, and **c** it with a 1Sm 19:13
His head was **c**, and he was 2Sm 15:30
people with him **c** their heads 2Sm 15:30
Although they **c** him with 1Kg 1:1
the cherubim **c** the ark and its 1Kg 8:7
the mountain was **c** with horses 2Kg 6:17
tore his clothes, **c** himself with 2Kg 19:1
the priests, **c** with sackcloth, 2Kg 19:2
was a footstool **c** in gold for 2Ch 9:18
off for home with his head **c**. Est 6:12
mouth, Haman's face was **c**. Est 7:8
his face is **c** with fat and his Jb 15:27
talking and **c** their mouths with Jb 29:9
Have I **c** my transgressions as Jb 31:33
You have **c** the heavens with Your Ps 8:1
is forgiven, whose sin is **c**! Ps 32:1
long, and shame has **c** my face, Ps 44:15
and have **c** us with deepest Ps 44:19
and the valleys **c** with grain. Ps 65:13
of a dove are **c** with silver, Ps 68:13
of You, and shame has **c** my face. Ps 69:7
seek my harm be **c** with disgrace Ps 71:13
but the sea **c** their enemies. Ps 78:53

mountains were **c** by its shade, Ps 80:10
You **c** all their sin. Ps 85:2
You have **c** him with shame. Ps 89:45
You **c** it with the deep as if it Ps 104:6
Water **c** their foes; not one of Ps 106:11
it **c** the assembly of Abiram. Ps 106:17
everywhere, weeds **c** the ground, Pr 24:31
an ivory panel **c** with sapphires. Sg 5:14
Your hands are **c** with blood. Is 1:15
with two he **c** his face, with two Is 6:2
face, with two he **c** his feet, Is 6:2
c by those slain with the sword Is 14:19
For you will be **c** with the Is 26:19
their tables are **c** with vomit; Is 28:8
the prophets, and **c** your heads— Is 29:10
LORD's sword is **c** with blood. Is 34:6
and **c** you in the shadow of My Is 51:16
she is **c** with its turbulent Jr 51:42
You have **c** Yourself in anger and Lm 3:43
You have **c** Yourself with a cloud Lm 3:44
over you and **c** your nakedness. Ezk 16:8
fine linen and **c** you with silk. Ezk 16:10
so that it would not be **c**. Ezk 24:8
kind of precious stone **c** you: Ezk 28:13
grew, and skin **c** them, but there Ezk 37:8
(but the windows were **c**), Ezk 41:16
You will be **c** with shame and Ob 10
beast must be **c** with sackcloth, Jnh 3:8
and she will be **c** with shame, Mc 7:10
You will not have **c** the towns of Mt 10:23
there is nothing **c** that won't be Mt 10:26
suddenly a bright cloud **c** them, Mt 17:5
There is nothing **c** that won't be Lk 12:2
named Lazarus, **c** with sores, was Lk 16:20
forgiven and whose sins are **c**! Rm 4:7
So if a woman's head is not **c**, 1Co 11:6
head shaved, she should be **c**. 1Co 11:6
the covenant, **c** with gold on all Heb 9:4
living creatures **c** with eyes in Rv 4:6
they were **c** with eyes around and Rv 4:8
that was **c** with blasphemous Rv 17:3

COVERING *(36)*
For it is his only **c**; Ex 22:27
c the mercy seat with their Ex 25:20
Make a **c** for the tent from ram Ex 26:14
and a **c** of manatee skins on top Ex 26:14
tail, the fat **c** the entrails, Ex 29:22
its tent and **c**, its clasps and Ex 35:11
He also made a **c** for the tent Ex 36:19
red and a **c** of manatee skins Ex 36:19
c the mercy seat with their Ex 37:9
the **c** of ram skins dyed red and Ex 39:34
red and the **c** of manatee skins Ex 39:34
and put the **c** of the tent on top Ex 40:19
the tent, its **c**, the screen for Nm 3:25
over this a **c** made of manatee Nm 4:6
them with a **c** made of manatee Nm 4:8
inside a **c** made of manatee Nm 4:10
it with a **c** made of manatee Nm 4:11
them with a **c** made of manatee Nm 4:12
to spread a **c** made of manatee Nm 4:14
are to finish **c** the holy objects Nm 4:15
with its **c** and the covering Nm 4:25
and the **c** made of manatee Nm 4:25
two gratings for **c** both bowls 1Kg 7:41
each grating **c** both capitals' 1Kg 7:42
two gratings for **c** both bowls 2Ch 4:12
each grating **c** both capitals' 2Ch 4:13
having no **c** against the cold. Jb 24:7
God, and Abaddon has no **c**. Jb 26:6
Who can strip off his outer **c**? Jb 41:13
a cloud as a **c** and ⌊gave⌋ a fire Ps 105:39
the sheet **c** all the nations; Is 25:7
and two wings **c** its body. Ezk 1:11
had two wings **c** their bodies. Ezk 1:23
will be like a cloud **c** the land. Ezk 38:9
Israel like a cloud **c** the land. Ezk 38:16
her hair is given to her as a **c**. 1Co 11:15

COVERINGS *(3)*
I've spread **c** on my bed—richly Pr 7:16
She makes her own bed **c**; Pr 31:22
head **c**, and other clothes, Dn 3:21

COVERS *(22)*
all the fat that **c** the entrails, Ex 29:13
skin so that it **c** all the skin Lv 13:12
cloud of incense **c** the mercy Lv 16:13
the shadow of death **c** my eyes, Jb 16:16
and a flood of water **c** you. Jb 22:11
thick darkness that **c** my face. Jb 23:17
will see me, he **c** ⌊his⌋ face. Jb 24:15
around Him and **c** the depths of Jb 36:30
He **c** ⌊His⌋ hands with lightning Jb 36:32
so that a flood of water **c** you? Jb 38:34
and violence **c** them like a Ps 73:6
who **c** the sky with clouds, Ps 147:8
His majesty **c** heaven and earth. Ps 148:13
but love **c** all offenses. Pr 10:12
For look, darkness **c** the earth, Is 60:2
Humiliation **c** our faces because Jr 51:51
the hungry and **c** the naked with Ezk 18:7
the hungry and **c** the naked with Ezk 18:16
His splendor **c** the heavens, Hab 3:3
he **c** his garment with injustice, Mal 2:16
c it with a basket or puts it Lk 8:16
love **c** a multitude of sins. 1Pt 4:8

COVERT *(1)*
anger, and a **c** bribe, fierce Pr 21:14

COVET *(10)*
Do not **c** your neighbor's house. Ex 20:17
Do not **c** your neighbor's wife, Ex 20:17
No one will **c** your land when you Ex 34:24
wife or **c** your neighbor's Dt 5:21
Don't **c** the silver and gold on Dt 7:25
They **c** fields and seize them; Mc 2:2
what it is to **c** if the law had Rm 7:7
had not said, You shall not **c**. Rm 7:7
you shall not **c**, and if there is Rm 13:9
You murder and **c** and cannot Jms 4:2

COVETED *(2)*
50 shekels, I **c** them and took Jos 7:21
I have not **c** anyone's silver or Ac 20:33

COVETING *(1)*
produced in me **c** of every kind. Rm 7:8

COW *(16)*
Bring me a three-year-old **c**, Gn 15:9
unblemished red **c** that has no Nm 19:2
The **c** must be burned in his Nm 19:5
the fire where the **c** is burning. Nm 19:6
who burned the **c** must also wash Nm 19:8
are to get a **c** that has not been Dt 21:3
city will bring the **c** down to a Dt 21:4
hadn't plowed with my young **c**, Jdg 14:18
Take a young **c** with you and say, 1Sm 16:2
raise a young **c** and two sheep, Is 7:21
The **c** and the bear will graze, Is 11:7
Egypt is a beautiful young **c**, Jr 46:20
like a young **c** treading grain Jr 50:11
let you ⌊use⌋ **c** dung instead Ezk 4:15
is as obstinate as a stubborn **c**. Hs 4:16
young **c** that loves to Hs 10:11

COW'S *(3)*
to gather up the **c** ashes and Nm 19:9
gathers up the **c** ashes must wash Nm 19:10
they will break the **c** neck there Dt 21:4

COWARDS *(1)*
But the **c**, unbelievers, vile, Rv 21:8

COWER *(3)*
gods **c**; they crouch together; Is 46:2
will cause you to **c** before them. Jr 1:17
and made me **c** in the dust. Lm 3:16

COWERS *(1)*
crouches; Nebo **c**. Their idols Is 46:1

COWS *(19)*
their young, 40 **c**, 10 bulls, 20 Gn 32:15
well-fed **c** came up from the Nile Gn 41:2
seven other **c**, sickly and thin Gn 41:3
beside those **c** along the bank Gn 41:3
sickly, thin **c** ate the healthy Gn 41:4
ate the healthy, well-fed **c**. Gn 41:4
healthy-looking **c** came up from Gn 41:18
them, seven other **c**—ugly, very Gn 41:19
ugly **c** ate the first seven Gn 41:20
ate the first seven well-fed **c**. Gn 41:20
seven good **c** are seven years, Gn 41:26
ugly **c** that came up after them Gn 41:27
and two milk **c** that have never 1Sm 6:7
Hitch the **c** to the cart, but 1Sm 6:7
took two milk **c**, hitched them to 1Sm 6:10
The **c** went straight up the road 1Sm 6:12
and offered the **c** as a burnt 1Sm 6:14
their **c** calve and do not Jb 21:10
you **c** of Bashan who are on the Am 4:1

COZBI *(2)*
the slain Midianite woman was **C**, Nm 25:15
case involving their sister **C**, Nm 25:18

COZEBA *(1)*
Jokim, the men of **C**; and Joash 1Ch 4:22

CRACK *(3)*
the **c** of dawn the angels urged Gn 19:15
c one open, and a viper is Is 59:5
The **c** of the whip and rumble of Nah 3:2

CRACKED *(4)*
and old wineskins, **c** and mended. Jos 9:4
them, but look, they are **c**. Jos 9:13
c cisterns that cannot hold Jr 2:13
The ground is **c** since no rain Jr 14:4

CRACKLING *(1)*
For like the **c** of ⌊burning⌋ Ec 7:6

CRAFT *(5)*
and ability in every **c** Ex 31:3
carve wood for work in every **c**. Ex 31:5
and ability in every kind of **c** Ex 35:31
in every kind of artistic **c**. Ex 35:33
do every kind of **c** and design Ex 35:35

CRAFTED *(1)*
and settings were **c** in gold; Ezk 28:13

CRAFTINESS *(3)*
wise in their **c** so that the Jb 5:13
detecting their **c**, He said to Lk 20:23
He catches the wise in their **c**— 1Co 3:19

CRAFTS *(2)*
He alone **c** their hearts; Ps 33:15
For the one who **c** its shape Hab 2:18

CRAFTSMAN *(13)*
every skilled **c** in order to make Ex 31:6
the work of a **c**, and sets ⌊it⌋ Dt 27:15
was a man of Tyre, a bronze **c**. 1Kg 7:14
send me a **c** who is skilled in 2Ch 2:7
I was a skilled **c** beside Him. Pr 8:30
a skilled **c** to set up an idol Is 40:20
c encourages the metalworker; Is 41:7
have created the **c** who blows on Is 54:16
the hands of a **c** with a chisel. Jr 10:3
of a goldsmith, the work of a **c**. Jr 10:9
from Israel—a **c** made it, and Hs 8:6
idol after its **c** carves it? Hab 2:18
no **c** of any trade will ever be Rv 18:22

CRAFTSMANSHIP *(2)*
wheels and their **c** was like the Ezk 1:16
appearance and **c** was like a Ezk 1:16

CRAFTSMEN *(23)*
to instruct all the skilled **c**, Ex 28:3
The **c** are to tie the breastpiece Ex 28:28
all the skilled **c** among you come Ex 35:10
Then all the **c** who were doing Ex 36:4
All the skilled **c** among those Ex 36:8
and all the **c** and metalsmiths. 2Kg 24:14
and 1,000 **c** and metalsmiths— 2Kg 24:16
of ⌊those in⌋ the Valley of **C**, 1Ch 4:14
of Craftsmen, for they were **c**. 1Ch 4:14
the work to be done by the **c**. 1Ch 29:5
work⌋ with the **c** who are with me 2Ch 2:7
to be with your **c** and the 2Ch 2:14
craftsmen and the **c** of my lord, 2Ch 2:14
and Ono, the valley of the **c**. Neh 11:35
to shame, and the **c** are humans. Is 44:11
and the **c** and metalsmiths from Jr 24:1
and Jerusalem, the **c**, and the Jr 29:2
Babylon, and the rest of the **c**. Jr 52:15
all of them the work of **c**. Hs 13:2
Then the LORD showed me four **c**. Zch 1:20
These ⌊**c**⌋ have come to terrify Zch 1:21
deal of business for the **c**. Ac 19:24
and the **c** who are with him Ac 19:38

CRAFTY *(2)*
schemes of the **c** so that they Jb 5:12
choose the language of the **c**. Jb 15:5

CRAG *(1)*
its stronghold is on a rocky **c**. Jb 39:28

CRAGS *(1)*
ever leave the highland **c**? Jr 18:14

CRANE *(2)*
I chirp like a swallow ⌊or⌋ a **c**; Is 38:14
and **c** are aware of their Jr 8:7

CRASHED *(2)*
the river **c** against that house Lk 6:48
The river **c** against it, and Lk 6:49

CRASHING *(1)*
and a loud **c** from the hills. Zph 1:10

CRAVE *(2)*
denies the wicked what they **c**. Pr 10:3
to eat, no early fig, which I **c**. Mc 7:1

CRAVED *(4)*
the people who had **c** ⌊the meat⌋. Nm 11:34
demanding the food they **c**. Ps 78:18
for He gave them what they **c**. Ps 78:29
The fruit you **c** has left you. Rv 18:14

CRAVES *(1)*
The slacker **c**, yet has nothing, Pr 13:4

CRAVING *(5)*
had a strong **c** ⌊for other food⌋ Nm 11:4
were seized with **c** in the Ps 106:14
A slacker's **c** will kill him Pr 21:25
is filled with **c** all day long, Pr 21:26
of evil, and by **c** it, some have 1Tm 6:10

CRAVINGS *(3)*
one boasts about his own **c**; Ps 10:3
over in the **c** of their hearts Rm 1:24
come from the **c** that are at war Jms 4:1

CRAWL *(9)*
creatures that **c**, and the Gn 1:24
creatures that **c** on the ground Gn 1:25
creatures that **c** on the earth." Gn 1:26
creatures that **c**, and birds of Gn 6:7
creatures that **c** on the earth, Gn 7:21
creatures that **c**, to the birds Gn 7:23
creatures that **c** on the ground— Gn 8:17
creatures that **c** and flying Ps 148:10
creatures that **c** on the ground. Hs 2:18

CRAWLING *(1)*
detestable thing, **c** creatures Ezk 8:10

CRAWLS *(11)*
creature that **c** on the earth." Gn 1:28
creature that **c** on the earth— Gn 1:30
animal that **c** on the ground Gn 6:20
creature that **c** on the ground, Gn 7:8
creature that **c** on the earth Gn 7:14
creature that **c** on the earth Gn 8:19
creature that **c** on the ground, Gn 9:2
creature that **c** on the ground. Lv 11:44
or whatever **c** on the ground; Lv 20:25
creature that **c** on the ground, Dt 4:18
creature that **c** on the ground, Ezk 38:20

CRAZY *(6)*
You can see the man is **c**," 1Sm 21:14
a shortage of **c** people that you 1Sm 21:15
this one to act **c** around me? 1Sm 21:15
did this **c** person come to you? 2Kg 9:11
He has a demon and He's **c**! Jn 10:20
"You're **c**!" they told her. But Ac 12:15

CREAM *(3)*
c from the herd and milk from Dt 32:14
rivers flowing with honey and **c**. Jb 20:17
were bathed in **c** and the rock Jb 29:6

CREATE *(11)*
c a clean heart for me and renew Ps 51:10
the LORD will **c** a cloud of smoke Is 4:5
I form light and **c** darkness, Is 45:7
I make success and **c** disaster; Is 45:7
He did not **c** it to be empty, Is 45:18
For I will **c** a new heaven and a Is 65:17
for I will **c** Jerusalem to be a Is 65:18
in Babylon will **c** a curse that Jr 29:22
Didn't one God **c** us? Why then do Mal 2:10
that He might **c** in Himself one Eph 2:15
These people **c** divisions and are Jd 19

CREATED *(55)*
the beginning God **c** the heavens Gn 1:1
So God **c** the large sea-creatures Gn 1:21
⌊He also **c**⌋ every winged bird Gn 1:21
So God **c** man in His own image; Gn 1:27
He **c** him in the image of God; Gn 1:27
He **c** them male and female. Gn 1:27
On the day that God **c** man, Gn 5:1
He **c** them male and female. Gn 5:2
they were **c**, He blessed them Gn 5:2
man, whom I **c**, together with the Gn 6:7
the day God **c** man on the earth Dt 4:32
You **c** the heavens, the highest Neh 9:6
North and south—You **c** them. Ps 89:12
Have You **c** everyone for nothing? Ps 89:47
and a newly **c** people will praise Ps 102:18
breath, they are **c**, and You Ps 104:30
was You who **c** my inward parts; Ps 139:13
He commanded, and they were **c**. Ps 148:5
the One who **c** it long ago. Is 22:11
up and see: who **c** these? He Is 40:26
the Holy One of Israel has **c** it. Is 41:20
who **c** the heavens and stretched Is 42:5
says—the One who **c** you, Jacob, Is 43:1
by My name and **c** for My glory. Is 43:7
I, the LORD, have **c** it. Is 45:8
made the earth, and **c** man on it. Is 45:12
They have been **c** now, and not Is 48:7
I have **c** the craftsman who blows Is 54:16
and I have **c** the destroyer to Is 54:16
in the place where you were **c**, Ezk 21:30
prepared on the day you were **c**. Ezk 28:13
the day you were **c** you were Ezk 28:15
that He who **c** them in the Mt 19:4
world, which God **c**, until now Mk 13:19
All things were **c** through Him, Jn 1:3
one thing was **c** that has been Jn 1:3
was created that has been **c**. Jn 1:3
and the world was **c** through Him, Jn 1:10
and they **c** great joy among all Ac 15:3
and served something **c** instead Rm 1:25
nor any other **c** thing will have Rm 8:39
and man was not **c** for woman, 1Co 11:9
c in Christ Jesus for good works, Eph 2:10
ages in God who **c** all things. Eph 3:9
the one **c** according to God's Eph 4:24
because by Him everything was **c**, Col 1:16
things have been **c** through Him Col 1:16
For Adam was **c** first, then Eve. 1Tm 2:13
foods that God **c** to be received 1Tm 4:3
For everything **c** by God is good, 1Tm 4:4
the universe was **c** by the word Heb 11:3
that is, **c** things—so that Heb 12:27
because You have **c** all things, Rv 4:11
Your will they exist and were **c**. Rv 4:11
who **c** heaven and what is in it, Rv 10:6

CREATES *(3)*
one that **c** trouble by law— Ps 94:20
For the LORD **c** something new in Jr 31:22
forms the mountains, **c** the wind, Am 4:13

CREATING *(2)*
c words of praise." Is 57:19
rejoice forever in what I am **c**; Is 65:18

CREATION *(18)*
it He rested from His work of **c**. Gn 2:3
their **c** at the time that Gn 2:4
me at the beginning of His **c**, Pr 8:22
the beginning of **c** God made them Mk 10:6
the gospel to the whole **c**. Mk 16:15
From the **c** of the world His Rm 1:20
For the **c** eagerly waits with Rm 8:19
For the **c** was subjected to Rm 8:20
that the **c** itself will also be Rm 8:21
that the whole **c** has been Rm 8:22
is in Christ, there is a new **c**; 2Co 5:17
matters⌋ instead is a new **c**. Gl 6:15
For we are His **c**—created in Eph 2:10
God, the firstborn over all **c**; Col 1:15
in all **c** under heaven, Col 1:23
hands (that is, not of this **c**), Heb 9:11
been since the beginning of **c**." 2Pt 3:4
the Originator of God's **c** says: Rv 3:14

CREATOR *(11)*
God Most High, **C** of heaven and Gn 14:19
God Most High, **C** of heaven and Gn 14:22
Isn't He your Father and **C**? Dt 32:6
remember your **C** in the days of Ec 12:1
and their **C** will not be gracious Is 27:11
God, the **C** of the whole earth. Is 40:28
Holy One, the **C** of Israel, your Is 43:15
God is the **C** of the heavens. Is 45:18
created instead of the **C**, Rm 1:25
according to the image of his **C**. Col 3:10
themselves to a faithful **C**. 1Pt 4:19

CREATURE *(48)*
every living **c** that moves and Gn 1:21
c that crawls on the earth. Gn 1:28
and for every **c** that crawls on Gn 1:30
the man called a living **c**, Gn 2:19
and every **c** that crawls on the Gn 7:8
every **c** that crawls on the earth Gn 7:14
and every **c** that crawls on the Gn 8:19
in every living **c** on the earth, Gn 9:2
every **c** that crawls on the Gn 9:2
Every living **c** will be food for Gn 9:3
every living **c** that is with you Gn 9:10
you and every living **c** with you, Gn 9:12
and every living **c** of all flesh: Gn 9:15
and every living **c** of all flesh Gn 9:16
or an unclean swarming **c**— Lv 5:2
detestable **c**, and eats meat Lv 7:21
by any **c** that swarms; Lv 11:43
by any swarming **c** that crawls on Lv 11:44
the life of a **c** is in the blood Lv 17:11
life of every **c** is its blood, Lv 17:14
must not eat the blood of any **c**, Lv 17:14
life of every **c** is its blood; Lv 17:14
any swarming **c** that makes him Lv 22:5
any winged **c** that flies in the Dt 4:17
any **c** that crawls on the ground, Dt 4:18
may eat every clean flying **c**. Dt 14:20
on earth—a **c** devoid of fear! Jb 41:33
He gives food to every **c**. Ps 136:25
and a winged **c** may report the Ec 10:20
disaster on every living **c**'— Jr 45:5
Each **c** went straight ahead. Ezk 1:12
beside each **c** that had four Ezk 1:15
Each **c** went straight ahead. Ezk 10:22
every **c** that crawls on the Ezk 38:20
kind of⌋ living **c** that swarms Ezk 47:9
and every **c** was fed from it. Dn 4:12
people saw the **c** hanging from Ac 28:4
he shook the **c** off into the fire Ac 28:5
No **c** is hidden from Him, but all Heb 4:13
For every **c**—animal or bird, Jms 3:7
first living **c** was like a lion Rv 4:7
second living **c** was like a calf Rv 4:7
third living **c** had a face like Rv 4:7
fourth living **c** was like a Rv 4:7
I heard every **c** in heaven, Rv 5:13
I heard the second living **c** say, Rv 6:3
I heard the third living **c** say, Rv 6:5
of the fourth living **c** say, Rv 6:7

CREATURES *(62)*
the water swarm with living **c**, Gn 1:20
produce living **c** according to Gn 1:24
livestock, **c** that crawl, and the Gn 1:24
and **c** that crawl on the ground Gn 1:25
the **c** that crawl on the earth. Gn 1:26
with the animals, **c** that crawl, Gn 6:7
c that crawl on the earth, Gn 7:21
and all **c** that swarm on the Gn 7:21
livestock, to **c** that crawl, to Gn 7:23
c that crawl on the ground— Gn 8:17
other⌋ living **c** in the water. Lv 11:10
These **c** that swarm on the ground Lv 11:29
you among all the swarming **c**. Lv 11:31
All the **c** that swarm on the Lv 11:41
not eat any of the **c** that swarm Lv 11:42
all living **c** that move in the Lv 11:46
and all **c** that swarm on the Lv 11:46
the sky and the **c** of the earth. 1Sm 17:46
and the **c** of the field are Mine. Ps 50:11
fed him to the **c** of the desert. Ps 74:14
and **c** of the field feed on it. Ps 80:13
the earth is full of Your **c**. Ps 104:24
teeming with **c** beyond number— Ps 104:25
c that crawl and flying birds, Ps 148:10
desert **c** will live with jackals, Jr 50:39
of four living **c** came from it. Ezk 1:5
c did not turn as they moved; Ezk 1:9
form of the living **c** was like Ezk 1:13
and forth between the living **c**; Ezk 1:13
c were darting back and forth Ezk 1:14
When I looked at the living **c**, Ezk 1:15
So when the living **c** moved, Ezk 1:19
and when the **c** rose from the Ezk 1:19
the **c** went in the direction the Ezk 1:20
of the living **c** was in the Ezk 1:20
When the **c** moved, the wheels Ezk 1:21
when the **c** stood still, the Ezk 1:21
and when the **c** rose from the Ezk 1:21
of the living **c** was in the Ezk 1:21
over the heads of the living **c**. Ezk 1:22
thing, crawling **c** and beasts, as Ezk 8:10
were the living **c** I had seen Ezk 10:15
of the living **c** was in them. Ezk 10:17
were the living **c** I had seen Ezk 10:20

and the **c** that crawl on the Hs 2:18
marine **c** that have no ruler. Hab 1:14
be the firstfruits of His **c**. Jms 1:18
c of instinct born to be caught 2Pt 2:12
were four living **c** covered with Rv 4:6
the four living **c** had six wings; Rv 4:8
the living **c** give glory, Rv 4:9
and the four living **c** and among Rv 5:6
the four living **c** and the 24 Rv 5:8
of the living **c**, and of the Rv 5:11
The four living **c** said, "Amen," Rv 5:14
the four living **c** say with a Rv 6:1
among the four living **c** say, Rv 6:6
the four living **c**, and they fell Rv 7:11
of the living **c** in the sea died, Rv 8:9
four living **c** and the elders, Rv 14:3
the four living **c** gave the seven Rv 15:7
and the four living **c** fell down Rv 19:4

CREATURES' *(1)*
of the living **c** wings brushing Ezk 3:13

CREDIT *(5)*
love you, what **c** is that to you? Lk 6:32
to you, what **c** is that to you? Lk 6:33
receive, what **c** is that to you? Lk 6:34
that no one can **c** me with 2Co 12:6
what **c** is there if you endure 1Pt 2:20

CREDITED *(17)*
and He **c** it to him as Gn 15:6
It will not be **c** to the one who Lv 7:18
will be **c** to you as if ⌊it Nm 18:27
it is **c** to you Levites as the Nm 18:30
c tens of thousands to David, 1Sm 18:8
but they only **c** me with 1Sm 18:8
It was **c** to him as righteousness Ps 106:31
and it was **c** to him for Rm 4:3
faith is **c** for righteousness. Rm 4:5
Faith was **c** to Abraham for Rm 4:9
How then was it **c**—while he was Rm 4:10
may be **c** to them also. Rm 4:11
it was **c** to him for Rm 4:22
Now it was **c** to him was not Rm 4:23
will be **c** to us who believe in Rm 4:24
and it was **c** to him for Gl 3:6
and it was **c** to him for Jms 2:23

CREDITOR *(5)*
Every **c** is to cancel what he has Dt 15:2
Now the **c** is coming to take my 2Kg 4:1
Let a **c** seize all he has; Ps 109:11
and borrower, **c** and debtor. Is 24:2
A **c** had two debtors. Lk 7:41

CREDITORS *(2)*
Or who were My **c** that I sold you Is 50:1
Won't your **c** suddenly arise, Hab 2:7

CREDITS *(1)*
man to whom God **c** righteousness Rm 4:6

CRESCENS *(1)*
C has gone to Galatia, Titus to 2Tm 4:10

CRESCENT *(2)*
and took the **c** ornaments that Jdg 8:21
addition to the **c** ornaments and Jdg 8:26

CRESCENTS *(1)*
ankle bracelets, headbands, **c**, Is 3:18

CRETANS *(2)*
C and Arabs—we hear them Ac 2:11
prophets said, **C** are always Ti 1:12

CRETE *(5)*
the south side of **C** off Salmone. Ac 27:7
a harbor on **C** open to the Ac 27:12
and sailed along the shore of **C**. Ac 27:13
to sail from **C** and sustain this Ac 27:21
I left you in **C** was to set right Ti 1:5

CREVICE *(2)*
put you in the **c** of the rock Ex 33:22
River and hide it in a rocky **c**." Jr 13:4

CREVICES *(2)*
the rock, in the **c** of the cliff, Sg 2:14
rocks and the **c** in the cliffs, Is 2:21

CREWS *(1)*
him ships with **c** of experienced 2Ch 8:18

CRICKET *(1)*
kinds of **c**, and the various Lv 11:22

CRIED *(112)*
he **c** out with a loud and bitter Gn 27:34
and the people **c** out to Pharaoh Gn 41:55
difficult labor, and they **c** out; Ex 2:23
went in and **c** for help to Ex 5:15
Moses **c** out to the LORD for help Ex 8:12
terrified and **c** out to the LORD Ex 14:10
So he **c** out to the LORD, and the Ex 15:25
Then Moses **c** out to the LORD, Ex 17:4
Then the people **c** out to Moses, Nm 11:2
The Israelites **c** again and said, Nm 11:4
because you **c** before the LORD Nm 11:18
is among you, and **c** to Him: Nm 11:20
Then Moses **c** out to the LORD, Nm 12:13
When we **c** out to the LORD, Nm 20:16
engaged woman **c** out, but there Dt 22:27
Your fathers **c** out to the LORD, Jos 24:7
Israelites **c** out to the LORD. Jdg 3:9
Israelites **c** out to the LORD, Jdg 3:15
Israelites **c** out to the LORD, Jdg 4:3
Israelites **c** out to the LORD. Jdg 6:6
the Israelites **c** out to Him Jdg 6:7
fled, and **c** out as they ran. Jdg 7:21
so they **c** out to the LORD, Jdg 10:10
you, and you **c** out to Me, did I Jdg 10:12
Then she **c**, "Samson, the Jdg 16:20
and **c** out, "Why, LORD God of Jdg 21:3
a report, the entire city **c** out. 1Sm 4:13
the Ekronites **c** out, "They've 1Sm 5:10
c out to the LORD on behalf of 1Sm 7:9
ancestors **c** out to the LORD, 1Sm 12:8
Then they **c** out to the LORD and 1Sm 12:10
angry and **c** out to the LORD 1Sm 15:11
my brother!" she **c**. "Don't 2Sm 13:12
"No," she **c**, "sending me away is 2Sm 13:16
walked, he **c**, "My son Absalom 2Sm 18:33
his face and **c** out at the top 2Sm 19:4
The man of God **c** out against the 1Kg 13:2
the man of God had **c** out against 1Kg 13:4
and the prophet **c** out to the man 1Kg 13:21
the word that he **c** out by a 1Kg 13:32
Then he **c** out to the LORD and 1Kg 17:20
He **c** out to the LORD and said, 1Kg 17:21
he **c** out to the king and said, 1Kg 20:39
him, but Jehoshaphat **c** out. 1Kg 22:32
of the prophets **c** out to Elisha, 2Kg 4:1
they ate the stew they **c** out, 2Kg 4:40
into the water, and he **c** out: 2Kg 6:5
wall, a woman **c** out to him, "My 2Kg 6:26
and clapped their hands and **c**, 2Kg 11:12
because they **c** out to God in 1Ch 5:20
so they **c** out to the LORD. 2Ch 13:14
Then Asa **c** out to the LORD his 2Ch 14:11
but Jehoshaphat **c** out and the 2Ch 18:31
and his sons anointed him and **c**, 2Ch 23:11
about this and **c** out to heaven, 2Ch 32:20
the Levites and **c** out loudly to Neh 9:4
of distress, they **c** out to You, Neh 9:27
When they **c** out to You again, Neh 9:28
and **c** loudly and bitterly. Est 4:1
the poor man who **c** out for help, Jb 29:12
the assembly and **c** out for help. Jb 30:28
and I **c** to my God for help. Ps 18:6
They **c** to You and were set free; Ps 22:5
when he **c** to Him for help Ps 22:24
my God, I **c** to You for help, Ps 30:2
when I **c** to You for help Ps 31:22
This poor man **c**, and the LORD Ps 34:6
I **c** out to Him with my mouth, Ps 66:17
Then they **c** out to the LORD in Ps 107:6
Then they **c** out to the LORD in Ps 107:13
Then they **c** out to the LORD in Ps 107:19
Then they **c** out to the LORD in Ps 107:28
double, and they **c** out, "Disgrace Is 61:7
they have **c** out loudly after Jr 12:6
the Cushite **c** out to Jeremiah, Jr 38:12
And I fell facedown and **c** out, Ezk 9:8
facedown and **c** out with a loud Ezk 11:13
he **c** out in anguish to Daniel. Dn 6:20
and each **c** out to his god. Jnh 1:5
I **c** out for help in the belly of Jnh 2:2
they said, and **c** out in fear. Mt 14:26
And beginning to sink he **c** out, Mt 14:30
by, they **c** out, "Lord, have Mt 20:30
but they **c** out all the more, Mt 20:31
afternoon Jesus **c** out with a Mt 27:46
in their synagogue. He **c** out, Mk 1:23
fell down before Him and **c** out, Mk 3:11
And he **c** out with a loud voice, Mk 5:7
it was a ghost and **c** out; Mk 6:49
the father of the boy **c** out, Mk 9:24
at three Jesus **c** out with a loud Mk 15:34
spirit who **c** out with a loud Lk 4:33
saw Jesus, he **c** out, fell down Lk 8:28
then a man from the crowd **c** out, Lk 9:38
Then they all **c** out together, Lk 23:18
complex, Jesus **c** out, "You know Jn 7:28
Jesus stood up and **c** out, Jn 7:37
Then Jesus **c** out, "The one who Jn 12:44
knelt down and **c** out with a loud Ac 7:60
followed Paul and us she **c** out, Ac 16:17
he **c** out in the Sanhedrin, Ac 23:6
one statement I **c** out while Ac 24:21
And I **c** and cried because no one Rv 5:4
And I cried and **c** because no one Rv 5:4
They **c** out with a loud voice: Rv 6:10
He **c** out in a loud voice to the Rv 7:2
And they **c** out in a loud voice: Rv 7:10
and he **c** out with a loud voice Rv 10:3
he **c** out, the seven thunders Rv 10:3
was pregnant and **c** out in labor Rv 12:2
He **c** in a mighty voice: Rv 18:2
and he **c** out in a loud voice, Rv 19:17

CRIES *(20)*
Your brother's blood **c** out to Me Gn 4:10
And if he **c** out to Me, I will Ex 22:27
community broke into loud **c**, Nm 14:1
At their **c**, all ⌊the people of Nm 16:34
man when he **c** out to him for Jb 30:24
If my land **c** out against me and Jb 31:38
does not listen to empty ⌊**c**⌋, Jb 35:13
She **c** out above the commotion; Pr 1:21
at the main entrance, she **c** out: Pr 8:3
but heard **c** of wretchedness. Is 5:7
My heart **c** out over Moab, whose Is 15:5
writhes and **c** out in her pains Is 26:17
A voice **c** out from Horonaim: Jr 48:3
will be heard **c** of distress over Jr 48:5
at the sound of your sailors' **c**. Ezk 27:28
Israel **c** out to Me: My God, we Hs 8:2
because she **c** out after us." Mt 15:23
But Isaiah **c** out concerning Rm 9:27
with loud **c** and tears, to Heb 5:7
who reaped your fields **c** out, Jms 5:4

CRIME *(13)*
What is my **c**?" he said to Laban Gn 31:36
someone accusing him of a **c**, Dt 19:16
lashes⌋ appropriate for his **c**. Dt 25:2
that the **c** against the 70 sons Jdg 9:24
God pays no attention to this **c**. Jb 24:12
it would be a **c** deserving Jb 31:11
would also be a **c** deserving Jb 31:28
C and trouble are within it; Ps 55:10
with the desire⌋ to commit **c**. Ec 8:11
sinner commits **c** a hundred times Ec 8:12
not committed a **c** against you my Dn 6:22
can find any **c** in me that I can Hs 12:8
a matter of a **c** or of moral evil Ac 18:14

CRIMES *(17)*
out because of their many **c**, Ps 5:10
devise **c** ⌊and say,⌋ "We have Ps 64:6
is filled with **c** of bloodshed, Ezk 7:23
Ephraim and the **c** of Samaria Hs 7:1
them in bondage for their two **c**. Hs 10:10
punishing Damascus for three **c**, Am 1:3
from punishing Gaza for three **c**, Am 1:6
from punishing Tyre for three **c**, Am 1:9
from punishing Edom for three **c**, Am 1:11
the Ammonites for three **c**, Am 1:13
from punishing Moab for three **c**, Am 2:1
punishing Judah for three **c**, Am 2:4
punishing Israel for three **c**, Am 2:6
day I punish Israel for its **c**; Am 3:14
For I know your **c** are many and Am 5:12
because of the **c** they have Mc 3:4
and God has remembered her **c**. Rv 18:5

CRIMINAL *(6)*
against a **c** act is not carried Ec 8:11
as if I were a **c**, to capture Me? Mt 26:55
I were a **c**, to capture Me? Mk 14:48
and clubs as if I were a **c**? Lk 22:52
man weren't a **c**, we wouldn't Jn 18:30
point of being bound like a **c**; 2Tm 2:9

CRIMINALS *(8)*
like one who falls victim to **c**. 2Sm 3:34
Solomon will be regarded as **c**." 1Kg 1:21
Then two **c** were crucified with Mt 27:38
same way even the **c** who were Mt 27:44

They crucified two **c** with Him, Mk 15:27
Two others—**c**—were also led Lk 23:32
along with the **c**, one on the Lk 23:33
Then one of the **c** hanging there Lk 23:39

CRIMSON *(5)*
hyssop, and **c** yarn, and throw Nm 19:6
with purple, **c**, and blue yarn. 2Ch 2:7
purple, blue, **c** yarn, and fine 2Ch 2:14
and **c** yarn and fine linen, 2Ch 3:14
though they are as red as **c**, Is 1:18

CRIMSON-STAINED *(1)*
coming from Edom in **c** garments Is 63:1

CRINGE *(3)*
Your enemies will **c** before you, Dt 33:29
assistants **c** in fear beneath Jb 9:13
Your enemies will **c** before You Ps 66:3

CRIPPLED *(1)*
had a son whose feet were **c**. 2Sm 4:4

CRISIS *(1)*
there is no enemy or **c**. 1Kg 5:4

CRISPUS *(2)*
C, the leader of the synagogue, Ac 18:8
none of you except **C** and Gaius, 1Co 1:14

CRITICIZE *(5)*
not eat must not **c** one who does, Rm 14:3
Who are you to **c** another's Rm 14:4
why do you **c** your brother? Rm 14:10
let us no longer **c** one another, Rm 14:13
Don't **c** one another, brothers. Jms 4:11

CRITICIZED *(1)*
Miriam and Aaron **c** Moses because Nm 12:1

CRITICIZES *(2)*
He who **c** a brother or judges his Jms 4:11
his brother **c** the law and judges Jms 4:11

CRITICIZING *(1)*
to all generously and without **c**, Jms 1:5

CROOKED *(14)*
but a devious and **c** generation. Dt 32:5
with the **c** You prove Yourself 2Sm 22:27
with the **c** You prove Yourself Ps 18:26
those who turn aside to **c** ways, Ps 125:5
whose paths are **c**, and whose Pr 2:15
A guilty man's conduct is **c**, Pr 21:8
and snares on the path of the **c**; Pr 22:5
is **c** cannot be straightened; Ec 1:15
out what He has made **c**? Ec 7:13
to those enacting **c** statutes and Is 10:1
They have made their roads **c**; Is 59:8
He has made my paths **c**. Lm 3:9
the **c** will become straight, Lk 3:5
faultless in a **c** and perverted Php 2:15

CROP *(14)*
grows by itself from your **c**, Lv 25:5
will produce a **c** sufficient for Lv 25:21
both the **c** you plant and the Dt 22:9
time the spring **c** first began to Am 7:1
though the olive **c** fails and the Hab 3:17
good ground, and produced a **c**: Mt 13:8
and it didn't produce a **c**. Mk 4:7
and produced a **c** that increased Mk 4:8
welcome it, and produce a **c**: Mk 4:20
soil produces a **c** by itself— Mk 4:28
But as soon as the **c** is ready, Mk 4:29
it sprang up, it produced a **c**: Lk 8:8
it dies, it produces a large **c**. Jn 12:24
do so in hope of sharing the **c**. 1Co 9:10

CROPS *(13)*
since they are later **c**. Ex 9:32
they ate from the **c** of the land Jos 5:12
the Israelites planted **c**, Jdg 6:3
to bring in ⌊the **c**⌋ so your 2Sm 9:10
sown, and let my **c** be uprooted. Jb 31:8
May its **c** be like Lebanon. Ps 72:16
He gave their **c** to the Ps 78:46
and our land will yield its **c**. Ps 85:12
and ⌊provides⌋ **c** for man to Ps 104:14
the dew and the land its **c**. Hg 1:10
of rain and **c** in the field for Zch 10:1
have anywhere to store my **c**? Lk 12:17
first to get a share of the **c**. 2Tm 2:6

CROSS *(87)*
Don't make us **c** the Jordan." Nm 32:5
and Reubenites **c** the Jordan with Nm 32:29
We will **c** over in battle Nm 32:32
When you **c** the Jordan into the Nm 33:51
When you **c** the Jordan into the Nm 35:10
Now get up and **c** the Zered Dt 2:13
you are going to **c** the border of Dt 2:18
move out, and **c** the Arnon Valley Dt 2:24
until we **c** the Jordan into the Dt 2:29
men will **c** over in battle Dt 3:18
Please let me **c** over and see the Dt 3:25
for you will not **c** this Jordan. Dt 3:27
for he will **c** over ahead of the Dt 3:28
are about to **c** into and possess Dt 4:14
that I would not **c** the Jordan Dt 4:21
you are about to **c** over and take Dt 4:22
you are about to **c** the Jordan to Dt 4:26
are about to **c** the Jordan to go Dt 9:1
your God will **c** over ahead of Dt 9:3
the strength to **c** into and Dt 11:8
you are about to **c** the Jordan to Dt 11:31
When you **c** the Jordan and live Dt 12:10
the time you **c** the Jordan into Dt 27:2
stones after you **c** to enter the Dt 27:3
ask, 'Who will **c** the sea, get it Dt 30:13
'You will not **c** this Jordan.' Dt 31:2
the One who will **c** ahead of you. Dt 31:3
the one who will **c** ahead of you, Dt 31:3
but you will not **c** into it." Dt 34:4
prepare to **c** over the Jordan Jos 1:2
men must **c** over in battle Jos 1:14
broke camp to **c** the Jordan, Jos 3:14
c over to the land the LORD Jos 22:19
did not allow anyone to **c** over. Jdg 3:28
said, "Let me **c** over," the Jdg 12:5
let's **c** over to the Philistine 1Sm 14:1
Jonathan intended to **c** to reach 1Sm 14:4
let's **c** over to the garrison of 1Sm 14:6
we'll **c** over to the men and then 1Sm 14:8
exhausted to **c** the Wadi Besor. 1Sm 30:10
but be sure to **c** over, or the 2Sm 17:16
to Barzillai, "**C** over with me, 2Sm 19:33
let him **c** over with my lord the 2Sm 19:37
Chimham will **c** over with me, 2Sm 19:38
you do leave and **c** the Kidron 1Kg 2:37
they will **c** the river ⌊of death⌋ Jb 36:12
set a boundary they cannot **c**; Ps 104:9
C over to Tarshish; wail, Is 23:6
Get up and **c** over to Cyprus— Is 23:12
C over to Cyprus and take a look. Jr 2:10
barrier that it cannot **c**? Jr 5:22
and set off to **c** over to the Jr 41:10
that I could not **c** ⌊on foot⌋. Ezk 47:5
C over to Calneh and see; Am 6:2
take up his **c** and follow Me is Mt 10:38
take up his **c**, and follow Me. Mt 16:24
forced this man to carry His **c**. Mt 27:32
of God, come down from the **c**!" Mt 27:40
Him come down now from the **c**, Mt 27:42
Let's **c** over to the other side Mk 4:35
take up his **c**, and follow Me. Mk 8:34
passing by, to carry Jesus' **c**. Mk 15:21
by coming down from the **c**!" Mk 15:30
now from the **c**, so that we may Mk 15:32
Let's **c** over to the other side Lk 8:22
take up his **c** daily, and follow Lk 9:23
bear his own **c** and come after Lk 14:27
those from there **c** over to us.' Lk 16:26
and laid the **c** on him to carry Lk 23:26
His own **c**, He went out to Jn 19:17
sign lettered and put on the **c**. Jn 19:19
Standing by the **c** of Jesus were Jn 19:25
remain on the **c** on the Sabbath Jn 19:31
to nail Him to a **c** and kill Him. Ac 2:23
C over to Macedonia and help us! Ac 16:9
he wanted to **c** over to Achaia, Ac 18:27
so that the **c** of Christ will not 1Co 1:17
message of the **c** is foolishness, 1Co 1:18
offense of the **c** has been Gl 5:11
persecuted for the **c** of Christ. Gl 6:12
except the **c** of our Lord Jesus Gl 6:14
one body through the **c** and put Eph 2:16
of death—even to death on a **c**. Php 2:8
as enemies of the **c** of Christ. Php 3:18
through the blood of His **c**— Col 1:20
the way by nailing it to the **c**. Col 2:14
Him endured a **c** and despised Heb 12:2

CROSS-EXAMINE *(1)*
fiercely and to **c** Him about many Lk 11:53

CROSS-EXAMINES *(1)*
until another comes and **c** him. Pr 18:17

CROSS-PIECES *(3)*
the frames were between the **c**, 1Kg 7:28
frames between the **c** were lions, 1Kg 7:29
On the **c** there was a pedestal 1Kg 7:29

CROSSBAR *(2)*
The central **c** is to run through Ex 26:28
made the central **c** run through Ex 36:33

CROSSBARS *(15)*
to make five **c** of acacia wood Ex 26:26
five **c** for the planks on the Ex 26:27
and five **c** for the planks of the Ex 26:27
gold as the holders for the **c**. Ex 26:29
Also overlay the **c** with gold. Ex 26:29
and planks, its **c**, its posts and Ex 35:11
made five **c** of acacia wood for Ex 36:31
five **c** for the planks on the Ex 36:32
and five **c** for those at the back Ex 36:32
holders for the **c** out of gold. Ex 36:34
also overlaid the **c** with gold. Ex 36:34
its planks, its **c**, and its posts Ex 39:33
inserted its **c**, and set up its Ex 40:18
supports, **c**, posts, bases, all Nm 3:36
with its **c**, posts, and bases, Nm 4:31

CROSSBREED *(1)*
You must not **c** two different Lv 19:19

CROSSED *(63)*
possessions, **c** the Euphrates, Gn 31:21
I **c** over this Jordan with my Gn 32:10
his 11 sons, and **c** the ford of Gn 32:22
or more who had **c** over to the Ex 38:26
Pi-hahiroth and **c** through the Nm 33:8
So we **c** the Zered Valley. Dt 2:13
until we **c** the Zered Valley was Dt 2:14
When you have **c** the Jordan, Dt 27:4
When you have **c** the Jordan, Dt 27:12
country, and **c** ⌊the Jordan⌋. Jos 2:23
and the people **c** opposite Jos 3:16
while all Israel **c** on dry ground Jos 3:17
When it **c** the Jordan, the Jos 4:7
ark of the LORD **c** in the sight Jos 4:11
equipped for war **c** to the plains Jos 4:13
'Israel **c** the Jordan on dry Jos 4:22
before you until you had **c** over, Jos 4:23
before us until we had **c** over. Jos 4:23
until they had **c** over, Jos 5:1
Israel with him **c** from Makkedah Jos 10:29
Israel with him **c** to Lachish. Jos 10:31
Then Joshua **c** from Lachish to Jos 10:34
You then **c** the Jordan and came Jos 24:11
He **c** over ⌊the Jordan⌋ near the Jdg 3:26
together, **c** over ⌊the Jordan⌋ Jdg 6:33
men came to the Jordan and **c** it. Jdg 8:4
his brothers and **c** into Shechem, Jdg 9:26
Ammonites also **c** the Jordan to Jdg 10:9
He **c** over to the Ammonites from Jdg 11:29
Jephthah **c** over to the Ammonites Jdg 11:32
together and **c** ⌊the Jordan⌋ to Jdg 12:1
Why have you **c** over to fight Jdg 12:1
my own hands and **c** over to the Jdg 12:3
Some Hebrews even **c** the Jordan 1Sm 13:7
David **c** to the other side and 1Sm 26:13
They **c** the Jordan, marched all 2Sm 2:29
all Israel, **c** the Jordan, and 2Sm 10:17
him got up and **c** the Jordan. 2Sm 17:22
no one who had not **c** the Jordan. 2Sm 17:22
time Absalom **c** the Jordan with 2Sm 17:24
Shimei son of Gera **c** the Jordan, 2Sm 19:18
So all the people **c** the Jordan, 2Sm 19:39
the Jordan, and then the king **c**. 2Sm 19:39
They **c** the Jordan and camped in 2Sm 24:5
the two of them **c** over on dry 2Kg 2:8
After they had **c** over, Elijah 2Kg 2:9
and the left, and Elisha **c** over. 2Kg 2:14
So Jehoram **c** over to Zair with 2Kg 8:21
are the men who **c** the Jordan 1Ch 12:15
all Israel and **c** the Jordan. 1Ch 19:17
Jehoram **c** ⌊into Edom⌋ with his 2Ch 21:9
and they **c** through it on dry Neh 9:11
and they **c** the river on foot. Ps 66:6
They **c** over at the ford, saying, Is 10:29
your agents have **c** the sea Is 23:2
that could not be **c** ⌊on foot⌋. Ezk 47:5
into a boat, **c** over, and came Mt 9:1
Once they **c** over, they came to Mt 14:34
When Jesus had **c** over again by Mk 5:21
When they had **c** over, they came Mk 6:53
Jesus **c** the Sea of Galilee Jn 6:1

day we **c** over to Samos, Ac 20:15
By faith they **c** the Red Sea as Heb 11:29

CROSSES *(1)*
your armed men **c** the Jordan Nm 32:21

CROSSING *(15)*
younger, and **c** his hands, put Gn 48:14
Israelites from **c** into the land Nm 32:7
won't be **c** the Jordan because I Dt 4:22
the land you are **c** the Jordan to Dt 31:13
the land you are **c** the Jordan to Dt 32:47
you will be **c** the Jordan to go Jos 1:11
and stayed there before **c**. Jos 3:1
had finished **c** the Jordan. Jos 3:17
had finished **c** the Jordan, Jos 4:1
after everyone had finished **c**, Jos 4:11
As the king was **c** the Kidron 2Sm 15:23
she was **c** the threshold of the 1Kg 14:17
his life from **c** the river ⌊of Jb 33:18
C the street near her corner, Pr 7:8
Finding a ship **c** over to Ac 21:2

CROSSROADS *(2)*
road, at the **c**, she takes her Pr 8:2
stand at the **c** to cut off their Ob 14

CROUCH *(4)*
when they **c** in their dens and Jb 38:40
They **c** down to give birth to Jb 39:3
to do⌋ except **c** among the Is 10:4
cower; they **c** together; they Is 46:2

CROUCHED *(1)*
of the LORD, she **c** down under Nm 22:27

CROUCHES *(4)*
you return from the kill—he **c**; Gn 49:9
c, he lies down like a lion or Nm 24:9
He **c** and bends down; Ps 10:10
Bel **c**; Nebo cowers. Their idols Is 46:1

CROUCHING *(1)*
do right, sin is **c** at the door. Gn 4:7

CROW *(2)*
will not **c** today until you Lk 22:34
rooster will not **c** until you Jn 13:38

CROWD *(113)*
diverse **c** also went up with Ex 12:38
not follow a **c** in wrongdoing. Ex 23:2
go along with a **c** to pervert Ex 23:2
from the guard ⌊and⌋ the **c**, 2Kg 11:13
hate a **c** of evildoers, and I do Ps 26:5
walked with the **c** into the house Ps 55:14
sound of a carefree **c** was there. Ezk 23:42
and a **c** lamenting loudly. Mt 9:23
But when the **c** had been put Mt 9:25
while the whole **c** stood on the Mt 13:2
him, he feared the **c**, since they Mt 14:5
He saw a huge **c**, felt compassion Mt 14:14
Summoning the **c**, He told them, Mt 15:10
the **c** was amazed when they saw Mt 15:31
I have compassion on the **c**, Mt 15:32
place to fill such a **c**?" Mt 15:33
commanding the **c** to sit down Mt 15:35
they reached the **c**, a man Mt 17:14
Jericho, a large **c** followed Him. Mt 20:29
The **c** told them to keep quiet, Mt 20:31
very large **c** spread their robes Mt 21:8
of the **c**, because everyone Mt 21:26
release to the **c** a prisoner they Mt 27:15
his hands in front of the **c**, Mt 27:24
him to Jesus because of the **c**, Mk 2:4
The whole **c** was coming to Him, Mk 2:13
so the **c** would not crush Him. Mk 3:9
and the **c** gathered again so that Mk 3:20
A **c** was sitting around Him and Mk 3:32
a very large **c** gathered around Mk 4:1
while the whole **c** was on the Mk 4:1
So they left the **c** and took Him Mk 4:36
a large **c** gathered around Him Mk 5:21
and a large **c** was following and Mk 5:24
Him in the **c** and touched His Mk 5:27
turned around in the **c** and said, Mk 5:30
You see the **c** pressing against Mk 5:31
He saw a huge **c** and had Mk 6:34
while He dismissed the **c**. Mk 6:45
Summoning the **c** again, He told Mk 7:14
into the house away from the **c**, Mk 7:17
him away from the **c** privately. Mk 7:33
days there was again a large **c**, Mk 8:1
I have compassion on the **c**, Mk 8:2
He commanded the **c** to sit down Mk 8:6
served the ⌊loaves⌋ to the **c**. Mk 8:6
Summoning the **c** along with His Mk 8:34
they saw a large **c** around them Mk 9:14
when the whole **c** saw Him, they Mk 9:15
Out of the **c**, one man answered Mk 9:17
Jesus saw that a **c** was rapidly Mk 9:25
His disciples and a large **c**, Mk 10:46
the whole **c** was astonished Mk 11:18
they were afraid of the **c**, Mk 11:32
but they were afraid of the **c**. Mk 12:12
And the large **c** was listening Mk 12:37
watched how the **c** dropped money Mk 12:41
The **c** came up and began to ask Mk 15:8
stirred up the **c** so that he Mk 15:11
gratify the **c**, Pilate released Mk 15:15
through the **c** and went on His Lk 4:30
the **c** was pressing in on Jesus Lk 5:1
bring him in because of the **c**, Lk 5:19
middle of the **c** before Jesus. Lk 5:19
was a large **c** of tax collectors Lk 5:29
with a large **c** of His disciples Lk 6:17
The whole **c** was trying to touch Lk 6:19
turning to the **c** following Him, Lk 7:9
a large **c** were traveling with Lk 7:11
A large **c** from the city was also Lk 7:12
As a large **c** was gathering, Lk 8:4
meet with Him because of the **c**. Lk 8:19
returned, the **c** welcomed Him, Lk 8:40
Him, "Send the **c** away, so they Lk 9:12
disciples to set before the **c**. Lk 9:16
the mountain, a large **c** met Him. Lk 9:37
then a man from the **c** cried out, Lk 9:38
woman from the **c** raised her Lk 11:27
a **c** of many thousands came Lk 12:1
Someone from the **c** said to Him, Lk 12:13
responded by telling the **c**, Lk 13:14
but the whole **c** was rejoicing Lk 13:17
Hearing a **c** passing by, he Lk 18:36
was not able because of the **c**, Lk 19:3
and the whole **c** of the disciples Lk 19:37
Pharisees from the **c** told Him, Lk 19:39
them when the **c** was not present Lk 22:6
away into the **c** that was there. Jn 5:13
And a huge **c** was following Him Jn 6:2
noticed a huge **c** coming toward Jn 6:5
the **c** that had stayed on the Jn 6:22
the **c** saw that neither Jesus Jn 6:24
a demon!" the **c** responded. "Who Jn 7:20
many from the **c** believed in Him Jn 7:31
heard the **c** muttering these Jn 7:32
some from the **c** heard these Jn 7:40
among the **c** because of Him. Jn 7:43
But this **c**, which doesn't know Jn 7:49
because of the **c** standing here I Jn 11:42
Then a large **c** of the Jews Jn 12:9
when the large **c** that had come Jn 12:12
Meanwhile the **c**, which had been Jn 12:17
This is also why the **c** met Him, Jn 12:18
c standing there heard it and Jn 12:29
Then the **c** replied to Him, Jn 12:34
this and rushed into the **c**, Ac 14:14
stirred up the **c** and the city Ac 17:8
the Way in front of the **c**, Ac 19:9
some of the **c** gave Alexander Ac 19:33
clerk had calmed the **c** down, Ac 19:35
up the whole **c**, and seized him, Ac 21:27
a disturbance among the **c**, Ac 24:12
without a **c** and without any Ac 24:18

CROWDED *(1)*
the city ⌊once⌋ **c** with people! Lm 1:1

CROWDS *(62)*
because I greatly feared the **c**, Jb 31:34
her masses, her **c**, and those who Is 5:14
will wipe out the **c** of Thebes. Ezk 30:15
So My people come to you in **c**, Ezk 33:31
Large **c** followed Him from Mt 4:25
When He saw the **c**, He went up on Mt 5:1
the **c** were astonished at His Mt 7:28
mountain, large **c** followed Him. Mt 8:1
Jesus saw large **c** around Him, Mt 8:18
When the **c** saw this, they were Mt 9:8
And the **c** were amazed, saying, Mt 9:33
When He saw the **c**, He felt Mt 9:36
to speak to the **c** about John: Mt 11:7
Huge **c** followed Him, and He Mt 12:15
And all the **c** were astounded and Mt 12:23
speaking to the **c** when suddenly Mt 12:46
Such large **c** gathered around Him Mt 13:2
told the **c** all these things Mt 13:34
Then He dismissed the **c** and went Mt 13:36
When the **c** heard this, they Mt 14:13
Send the **c** away so they can go Mt 14:15
He commanded the **c** to sit down Mt 14:19
disciples ⌊gave them⌋ to the **c**. Mt 14:19
side, while He dismissed the **c**. Mt 14:22
dismissing the **c**, He went up Mt 14:23
and large **c** came to Him, having Mt 15:30
disciples ⌊gave them⌋ to the **c**. Mt 15:36
After dismissing the **c**, He got Mt 15:39
Large **c** followed Him, and He Mt 19:2
Then the **c** who went ahead of Him Mt 21:9
And the **c** kept saying, "This is Mt 21:11
they feared the **c**, because they Mt 21:46
And when the **c** heard this, Mt 22:33
Jesus spoke to the **c** and to His Mt 23:1
that time Jesus said to the **c**, Mt 26:55
persuaded the **c** to ask for Mt 27:20
Then **c** converged on Him again Mk 10:1
said to the **c** who came out to Lk 3:7
the **c** were asking him. Lk 3:10
the **c** were searching for Him. Lk 4:42
teaching the **c** from the boat. Lk 5:3
and large **c** would come together Lk 5:15
to speak to the **c** about John: Lk 7:24
the **c** were nearly crushing Him. Lk 8:42
the **c** are hemming You in and Lk 8:45
When the **c** found out, they Lk 9:11
"Who do the **c** say that I am?" Lk 9:18
spoke, and the **c** were amazed. Lk 11:14
As the **c** were increasing, He Lk 11:29
He also said to the **c**: Lk 12:54
Now great **c** were traveling with Lk 14:25
the chief priests and the **c**, Lk 23:4
All the **c** that had gathered for Lk 23:48
about Him among the **c**. Jn 7:12
numbers—**c** of both men Ac 5:14
The **c** paid attention with one Ac 8:6
But when the Jews saw the **c**, Ac 13:45
When the **c** saw what Paul had Ac 14:11
He, with the **c**, intended to Ac 14:13
stopped the **c** from sacrificing Ac 14:18
won over the **c** and stoned Paul Ac 14:19
agitating and disturbing the **c**. Ac 17:13

CROWED *(5)*
Immediately a rooster **c**, Mt 26:74
the entryway, and a rooster **c**. Mk 14:68
a rooster **c** a second time, Mk 14:72
was still speaking, a rooster **c**. Lk 22:60
Immediately a rooster **c**. Jn 18:27

CROWING *(1)*
or at the **c** of the rooster Mk 13:35

CROWN *(50)*
on the **c** of the prince of his Gn 49:26
on the **c** of the prince of his Dt 33:16
took the **c** that was on his head 2Sm 1:10
He took the **c** from the head of 2Sm 12:30
The **c** weighed 75 pounds of gold, 2Sm 12:30
inside the **c** on top was 18 1Kg 7:31
son, put the **c** on him, gave him 2Kg 11:12
David took the **c** from the head 1Ch 20:2
discovered the **c** weighed 75 1Ch 20:2
son, put the **c** on him, gave him 2Ch 23:11
before him with her royal **c**. Est 1:11
placed the royal **c** on her head Est 2:17
a great golden **c** and a purple Est 8:15
and removed the **c** from my head. Jb 19:9
shoulder and wear it like a **c**. Jb 31:36
place a **c** of pure gold on his Ps 21:3
You **c** the year with Your Ps 65:11
completely dishonored his **c**. Ps 89:39
the **c** he wears will be glorious. Ps 132:18
will give you a **c** of beauty." Pr 4:9
capable wife is her husband's **c**, Pr 12:4
The **c** of the wise is their Pr 14:24
Gray hair is a glorious **c**; Pr 16:31
are the **c** of the elderly, Pr 17:6
not even a **c** lasts for all time. Pr 27:24
wearing the **c** his mother placed Sg 3:11
to the majestic **c** of Ephraim's Is 28:1
The majestic **c** of Ephraim's Is 28:3
Hosts will become a **c** of beauty Is 28:5
to give them a **c** of beauty Is 61:3
be a glorious **c** in the LORD's Is 62:3
The **c** has fallen from our head. Lm 5:16
the turban, and take off the **c**. Ezk 21:26
The **c** will reside in the LORD's Zch 6:14

for they are like jewels in a **c**, Zch 9:16
twisted together a **c** of thorns, Mt 27:29
twisted together a **c** of thorns, Mk 15:17
twisted together a **c** of thorns, Jn 19:2
came out wearing the **c** of thorns Jn 19:5
do it to receive a perishable **c**, 1Co 9:25
my joy and **c**, stand firm Php 4:1
or **c** of boasting in the presence 1Th 2:19
for me the **c** of righteousness, 2Tm 4:8
receive the **c** of life that He Jms 1:12
receive the unfading **c** of glory. 1Pt 5:4
I will give you the **c** of life. Rv 2:10
so that no one takes your **c**. Rv 3:11
c was given to him, and he went Rv 6:2
and a **c** of 12 stars on her head. Rv 12:1
with a gold **c** on His head and a Rv 14:14

CROWNED *(7)*
than God and **c** him with glory Ps 8:5
sensible are **c** with knowledge. Pr 14:18
with singing, **c** with unending Is 35:10
with singing, **c** with unending Is 51:11
he is not **c** unless he competes 2Tm 2:5
You **c** him with glory and honor Heb 2:7
c with glory and honor because Heb 2:9

CROWNS *(10)*
He **c** you with faithful love and Ps 103:4
Your head **c** you like Mount Sg 7:5
the bestower of **c**, whose traders Is 23:8
for your glorious **c** have fallen Jr 13:18
and beautiful **c** on their heads. Ezk 23:42
c and place them on the head Zch 6:11
with gold **c** on their heads. Rv 4:4
cast their **c** before the throne, Rv 4:10
were something like gold **c**; Rv 9:7
and on His head were many **c**. Rv 19:12

CROWS *(5)*
the rooster **c**, you will deny Me Mt 26:34
the rooster **c**, you will deny Me Mt 26:75
before the rooster **c** twice, Mk 14:30
Before the rooster **c** twice, Mk 14:72
Before the rooster **c** today, Lk 22:61

CRUCIBLE *(2)*
A **c** is for silver and a smelter Pr 17:3
Silver is ⌊tested⌋ in a **c**, Pr 27:21

CRUCIFIED *(36)*
flogged, and **c**, and He will be Mt 20:19
will be handed over to be **c**." Mt 26:2
he handed Him over to be **c**. Mt 27:26
two criminals were **c** with Him, Mt 27:38
who were **c** with Him kept Mt 27:44
are looking for Jesus who was **c**. Mt 28:5
he handed Him over to be **c**. Mk 15:15
Then they **c** Him and divided His Mk 15:24
in the morning when they **c** Him. Mk 15:25
They **c** two criminals with Him, Mk 15:27
those who were **c** with Him were Mk 15:32
Jesus the Nazarene, who was **c**. Mk 16:6
with loud voices that He be **c**. Lk 23:23
The Skull, they **c** Him there, Lk 23:33
of sinful men, be **c**, and rise on Lk 24:7
to death, and they **c** Him. Lk 24:20
he handed Him over to be **c**. Jn 19:16
There they **c** Him and two others Jn 19:18
where Jesus was **c** was near the Jn 19:20
When the soldiers **c** Jesus, Jn 19:23
one who had been **c** with Him. Jn 19:32
in the place where He was **c**. Jn 19:41
Jesus, whom you **c**, both Lord Ac 2:36
whom you **c** and whom God raised Ac 4:10
our old self was **c** with Him in Rm 6:6
law through the ⌊**c**⌋ body of the Rm 7:4
Was it Paul who was **c** for you? 1Co 1:13
we preach Christ **c**, a stumbling 1Co 1:23
except Jesus Christ and Him **c**. 1Co 2:2
would not have **c** the Lord of 1Co 2:8
In fact, He was **c** in weakness, 2Co 13:4
I have been **c** with Christ; Gl 2:19
was vividly portrayed as **c**? Gl 3:1
Jesus have **c** the flesh with Gl 5:24
whom the world has been **c** to me, Gl 6:14
where also their Lord was **c**. Rv 11:8

CRUCIFY *(15)*
of them you will kill and **c**, Mt 23:34
They all answered, "**C** Him!" Mt 27:22
But they kept shouting, "**C** Him!" Mt 27:23
and led Him away to **c** Him. Mt 27:31
Again they shouted, "**C** Him!" Mk 15:13
But they shouted, "**C** Him!" Mk 15:14
Him, and led Him out to **c** Him. Mk 15:20
but they kept shouting, "**C**! Lk 23:21
kept shouting, "Crucify! **C** Him!" Lk 23:21
saw Him, they shouted, "**C**! Jn 19:6
Crucify! **C**!" Pilate responded Jn 19:6
Take Him and **c** Him yourselves, Jn 19:6
You and the authority to **c** You?" Jn 19:10
Take Him away! **C** Him!" Pilate Jn 19:15
to them, "Should I **c** your king?" Jn 19:15

CRUCIFYING *(1)*
After **c** Him they divided His Mt 27:35

CRUDE *(1)*
talking or **c** joking are not Eph 5:4

CRUEL *(15)*
and their fury, for it is **c**! Gn 49:7
gloom—prisoners in **c** chains— Ps 107:10
and are humbled by **c** oppression Ps 107:39
and your years to someone **c**; Pr 5:9
but a **c** man brings disaster on Pr 11:17
acts of the wicked are **c**. Pr 12:10
a **c** messenger will be sent Pr 17:11
Fury is **c**, and anger is a flood, Pr 27:4
like fish caught in a **c** net, Ec 9:12
LORD is coming—**c**, with rage Is 13:9
They are **c** and show no mercy. Jr 6:23
the discipline of someone **c**, Jr 30:14
They are **c** and show no mercy. Jr 50:42
have become **c** like ostriches Lm 4:3
and gentle but also to the **c**. 1Pt 2:18

CRUELLY *(2)*
My daughter is **c** tormented by a Mt 15:22
time King Herod **c** attacked some Ac 12:1

CRUELTY *(3)*
have turned against me with **c**; Jb 30:21
ruled them with violence and **c**. Ezk 34:4
not experienced your constant **c**? Nah 3:19

CRUMBLES *(1)*
collapses and **c** and a rock is Jb 14:18

CRUMBLY *(2)*
of bread was dry and **c**. Jos 9:5
a look, it is now dry and **c**. Jos 9:12

CRUMBS *(4)*
eaten my few **c** alone without Jb 31:17
He throws His hailstones like **c**. Ps 147:17
dogs eat the **c** that fall from Mt 15:27
the table eat the children's **c**." Mk 7:28

CRUNCHED *(1)*
this last who has **c** his bones Jr 50:17

CRUSH *(29)*
I wipe them out and **c** them, 2Sm 22:39
I **c** them and trample them like 2Sm 22:43
is, the lot) to **c** and destroy Est 9:24
that He would decide to **c** me, Jb 6:9
torment me and **c** me with words? Jb 19:2
weight of misery will **c** him. Jb 20:22
They **c** olives in their presses; Jb 24:11
that a foot may **c** them or that Jb 39:15
c them, and they cannot get up; Ps 18:38
the poor, and **c** the oppressor. Ps 72:4
I will **c** his foes before him and Ps 89:23
LORD, they **c** Your people; Ps 94:5
will **c** kings on the day of His Ps 110:5
will **c** leaders over the entire Ps 110:6
and don't **c** the oppressed at the Pr 22:22
Why do you **c** My people and grind Is 3:15
rumbles, his horses do not **c** it. Is 28:28
the LORD was pleased to **c** Him, Is 53:10
against me to **c** my young Lm 1:15
it will **c** and smash all the Dn 2:40
It will **c** all these kingdoms and Dn 2:44
trample it down, and **c** it. Dn 7:23
I am about to **c** ⌊you⌋ in your Am 2:13
the poor and **c** the needy, Am 4:1
so you can **c** many peoples. Mc 4:13
You **c** the leader of the house of Hab 3:13
so the crowd would not **c** Him. Mk 3:9
will **c** you and your children Lk 19:44
peace will soon **c** Satan under Rm 16:20

CRUSHED *(47)*
you pure oil from **c** olives for Ex 27:20
with one quart of **c** olive oil, Ex 29:40
heads of grain, **c** kernels, Lv 2:14
some of its **c** kernels and oil Lv 2:16
rash, scabs, or a **c** testicle. Lv 21:20
has bruised, **c**, torn, or severed Lv 22:24
stones or **c** ⌊it⌋ in a mortar, Nm 11:8
it up, and **c** it, thoroughly Dt 9:21
have been **c** or whose penis has Dt 23:1
be oppressed and **c** continually. Dt 28:33
Sisera—she **c** his head; Jdg 5:26
shattered and **c** the Israelites Jdg 10:8
and you have **c** fortified cities 2Kg 19:25
high place, **c** it to dust, and 2Kg 23:15
for they were **c** before the LORD 2Ch 14:13
Nation was **c** by nation and city 2Ch 15:6
then **c** it and burned it in the 2Ch 15:16
images he shattered, **c** to dust, 2Ch 34:4
the dust, who are **c** like a moth! Jb 4:19
They are **c** at the ⌊city⌋ gate, Jb 5:4
of the fatherless was **c**. Jb 22:9
by His understanding He **c** Rahab. Jb 26:12
them⌋ by night, and they are **c**. Jb 34:25
He saves those **c** in spirit. Ps 34:18
I am faint and severely **c**; Ps 38:8
settle them, You **c** the peoples. Ps 44:2
But You have **c** us in a haunt of Ps 44:19
the bones You have **c** rejoice. Ps 51:8
You **c** the heads of Leviathan; Ps 74:14
You **c** Rahab like one who is Ps 89:10
I was **c** that he had left. Sg 5:6
stones like **c** bits of chalk, Is 27:9
Bread grain is **c**, but is not Is 28:28
a potter's jar, **c** to pieces, so Is 30:14
and you have **c** fortified cities Is 37:26
c because of our iniquities; Is 53:5
I **c** nations in My anger; Is 63:6
for all your lovers have been **c**. Jr 22:20
their warriors are **c**, they flee Jr 46:5
me; he has **c** me. He has set me Jr 51:34
how I was **c** by their promiscuous Ezk 6:9
iron and fired clay, and **c** them. Dn 2:34
it, and it **c** the iron, bronze, Dn 2:45
them and **c** all their bones. Dn 6:24
It devoured and **c**, and it Dn 7:7
is oppressed, **c** in judgment, for Hs 5:11
in every way but not **c**; 2Co 4:8

CRUSHES *(5)*
For He **c** but also binds up; Jb 5:18
Surely God **c** the heads of His Ps 68:21
A lying tongue hates those it **c**, Pr 26:28
for iron **c** and shatters Dn 2:40
wagon full of sheaves **c** ⌊grain⌋. Am 2:13

CRUSHING *(5)*
me, as if **c** my bones, while Ps 42:10
has pursued me, **c** me to the Ps 143:3
C all the prisoners of the land Lm 3:34
devouring, **c**, and trampling Dn 7:19
the crowds were nearly **c** Him. Lk 8:42

CRUST *(1)*
Better a dry **c** with peace than a Pr 17:1

CRY *(164)*
heard your ⌊**c** of⌋ affliction. Gn 16:11
justifies the **c** that has come up Gn 18:21
loud and bitter **c** and said to Gn 27:34
and their **c** for help ascended to Ex 2:23
The Israelites' **c** for help has Ex 3:9
will be a great **c** of anguish Ex 11:6
they will no doubt **c** to Me, Ex 22:23
I will certainly hear their **c**. Ex 22:23
of a victory **c** and not the sound Ex 32:18
not the sound of a **c** of defeat; Ex 32:18
cover his mouth and **c** out, Lv 13:45
will **c** out to the LORD against Dt 15:9
she did not **c** out in the city Dt 22:24
he will **c** out to the LORD Dt 24:15
LORD heard our **c** and saw our Dt 26:7
hear Judah's **c** and bring him to Dt 33:7
and **c** out to the gods you have Jdg 10:14
sound of the war **c** and asked, 1Sm 4:6
you will **c** out because of the 1Sm 8:18
for their **c** has come to Me." 1Sm 9:16
shouting their battle **c**. 1Sm 17:20
their battle **c**, and chased 1Sm 17:52
and my **c** for help ⌊reached⌋ His 2Sm 22:7
may hear the **c** and the prayer 1Kg 8:28
Then the **c** rang out in the army 1Kg 22:36
may hear the **c** and the prayer 2Ch 6:19
of Judah raised the battle **c**. 2Ch 13:15
of Judah raised the battle **c**, 2Ch 13:15
We will **c** out to You because of 2Ch 20:9
heard their **c** at the Red Sea. Neh 9:9

my **c** for help find no resting Jb 16:18
I **c** out: Violence! but get no Jb 19:7
the mortally wounded **c** for help, Jb 24:12
God hear his **c** when distress Jb 27:9
I **c** out to You for help, but You Jb 30:20
caused the poor to **c** out to Him, Jb 34:28
People **c** out because of severe Jb 35:9
There they **c** out, but He does Jb 35:12
them, they do not **c** for help. Jb 36:13
food when its young **c** out to God Jb 38:41
shouts and the battle **c**. Jb 39:25
I **c** aloud to the LORD, and He Ps 3:4
attention to the sound of my **c**, Ps 5:2
not forget the **c** of the Ps 9:12
attention to my **c**; listen to my Ps 17:1
my **c** to Him reached His ears. Ps 18:6
They **c** for help, but there is no Ps 18:41
them⌋—they **c**⌋ to the LORD, but Ps 18:41
My God, I **c** by day, but You do Ps 22:2
when I **c** to You for help Ps 28:2
In His temple all **c**, "Glory!" Ps 29:9
are open to their **c** for help. Ps 34:15
righteous **c** out, and the LORD Ps 34:17
and listen to my **c** for help; Ps 39:12
to me and heard my **c** for help. Ps 40:1
shout to God with a jubilant **c**. Ps 47:1
God, hear my **c**; pay attention to Ps 61:1
rescue the poor who **c** out and Ps 72:12
I **c** aloud to God, aloud to God, Ps 77:1
heart and flesh **c** out for the Ps 84:2
c out before You day and night. Ps 88:1
Your presence; listen to my **c**. Ps 88:2
I **c** out to You all day long; Ps 88:9
let my **c** for help come before Ps 102:1
He heard their **c**, He took note Ps 106:44
before dawn and **c** out for help; Ps 119:147
Let my **c** reach You, LORD; Ps 119:169
be attentive to my **c** for help. Ps 130:2
Listen, LORD, to my **c** for help. Ps 140:6
I **c** aloud to the LORD; I plead Ps 142:1
c to You, LORD; I say, "You are Ps 142:5
Listen to my **c**, for I am very Ps 142:6
and no **c** of lament in our public Ps 144:14
He hears their **c** for help and Ps 145:19
young ravens, what they **c** for. Ps 147:9
out to you; my **c** is to mankind. Pr 8:4
his ears to the **c** of the poor Pr 21:13
On that day he will **c** out, Is 3:7
C aloud, daughter of Gallim! Is 10:30
C out and sing, citizen of Zion, Is 12:6
people shout with a ringing **c**. Is 14:7
Wail, you gates! **C** out, city! Is 14:31
Heshbon and Elealeh **c** out; Is 15:4
the soldiers of Moab **c** out, Is 15:4
they raise a **c** of destruction on Is 15:5
their **c** echoes throughout the Is 15:8
When they **c** out to the LORD Is 19:20
In the streets they **c** for wine. Is 24:11
and will never **c** again. Is 30:19
to you at the sound of your **c**; Is 30:19
Their warriors **c** loudly in the Is 33:7
A voice was saying, "**C** out!" Is 40:6
said, "What should I **c** out?" Is 40:6
He will not **c** out or shout or Is 42:2
where Kedar dwells ⌊**c** aloud⌋. Is 42:11
let them **c** out from the Is 42:11
They **c** out to it but it doesn't Is 46:7
When you **c** out, let your Is 57:13
C out loudly, don't hold back! Is 58:1
when you **c** out, He will say: Is 58:9
but you will **c** out from an Is 65:14
the land. **C** out loudly and say: Jr 4:5
hear a **c** like a woman in labor, Jr 4:31
c of⌋ anguish like one bearing Jr 4:31
The **c** of Daughter Zion gasping Jr 4:31
Do not offer a **c** or a prayer on Jr 7:16
the **c** of my dear people from a Jr 8:19
will **c** out to Me, but I will Jr 11:11
will go and **c** out to the gods Jr 11:12
Do not raise up a **c** or a prayer Jr 11:14
Jerusalem's **c** rises up. Jr 14:2
not hear their **c** of despair. Jr 14:12
Let a **c** be heard from their Jr 18:22
I speak, I **c** out—I proclaim: Jr 20:8
morning and a war **c** at noontime Jr 20:16
Go up to Lebanon and **c** out; Jr 22:20
c out from Abarim, for all your Jr 22:20
Wail, you shepherds, and **c** out. Jr 25:34
the sound of the shepherds' **c**, Jr 25:36
We have heard a **c** of terror, Jr 30:5
Why do you **c** out about your Jr 30:15
There they will **c** out: Pharaoh Jr 46:17
The people will **c** out, and every Jr 47:2
her little ones will **c** out. Jr 48:4
dismayed. Wail and **c** out! Jr 48:20
will **c** out for Moab, all of it; Jr 48:31
There is a **c** from Heshbon to Jr 48:34
c out, daughters of Rabbah! Jr 49:3
sound of her **c** will be heard at Jr 49:21
Raise a war **c** against her on Jr 50:15
a **c** will be heard among the Jr 50:46
The sound of a **c** from Babylon! Jr 51:54
They **c** out to their mothers: Lm 2:12
of the people **c** out to the Lord. Lm 2:18
Arise, **c** out in the night, from Lm 2:19
Even when I **c** out and plead for Lm 3:8
Do not ignore my **c** for relief. Lm 3:56
and **c** out over all the evil Ezk 6:11
Though they **c** out in My ears Ezk 8:18
C out and wail, son of man, for Ezk 21:12
raise a battle **c**, set battering Ezk 21:22
over you and **c** out bitterly. Ezk 27:30
raise the war **c** in Beth-aven: Hs 5:8
They do not **c** to Me from their Hs 7:14
your God, and **c** out to the LORD. Jl 1:14
the wild animals **c** out to You, Jl 1:20
they will **c** out in anguish in Am 5:16
they will **c** out to the LORD, Mc 3:4
Writhe and **c** out, Daughter Zion, Mc 4:10
⌊they **c**,⌋ but no one turns Nah 2:8
or **c** out to You about violence Hab 1:2
the stones will **c** out from the Hab 2:11
there the warrior's **c** is bitter. Zph 1:14
blast⌋ and battle **c** against the Zph 1:16
began to **c** out, "Son of David, Mk 10:47
out a loud **c** and breathed His Mk 15:37
she exclaimed with a loud **c**: Lk 1:42
on her and said, "Don't **c**." Lk 7:13
His elect who **c** out to Him day Lk 18:7
silent, the stones would **c** out!" Lk 19:40
going to the tomb to **c** there. Jn 11:31
with rage and began to **c** out, Ac 19:28
a united **c** went up from all of Ac 19:34
by whom we **c** out, "Abba, Father! Rm 8:15

CRYING *(40)*

saw the child—a little boy, **c**. Ex 2:6
have heard them **c** out because Ex 3:7
that is why they are **c** out, Ex 5:8
Moses, "Why are you **c** out to Me? Ex 14:15
c at the entrance of their tents. Nm 11:10
For they are **c** to me: Nm 11:13
through the lattice, **c** out: Jdg 5:28
"Hannah, why are you **c**?" 1Sm 1:8
Don't stop **c** out to the LORD our 1Sm 7:8
he kept **c** out, "My father 2Kg 2:12
city square, **c** out before him, Est 6:11
I am weary from my **c**; Ps 69:3
My eyes are worn out from **c**. Ps 88:9
shouting and **c** to the mountains; Is 22:5
there will be mourning and **c**, Is 29:2
A voice of one **c** out: Is 40:3
of weeping and **c** will no longer Is 65:19
A voice of one **c** out in the Mt 3:3
that region came and kept **c** out, Mt 15:22
A voice of one **c** out in the Mk 1:3
he was **c** out among the tombs and Mk 5:5
but he was **c** out all the more, Mk 10:48
A voice of one **c** out in the Lk 3:4
Everyone was **c** and mourning for Lk 8:52
He said, "Stop **c**, for she is not Lk 8:52
but he kept **c** out all the more, Lk 18:39
I am a voice of one **c** out in the Jn 1:23
Jesus saw her **c**, and the Jews Jn 11:33
Jews who had come with her **c**, Jn 11:33
outside facing the tomb, **c**. Jn 20:11
she was **c**, she stooped to look Jn 20:11
to her, "Woman, why are you **c**?" Jn 20:13
said to her, "why are you **c**? Jn 20:15
spirits, **c** out with a loud Ac 8:7
our hearts, **c**, "Abba , Father! Gl 4:6
the elders said to me, "Stop **c**. Rv 5:5
c out in a loud voice to the One Rv 14:15
from her burning and kept **c** out: Rv 18:18
on their heads and kept **c** out, Rv 18:19
grief, **c**, and pain will exist no Rv 21:4

CRYPT *(1)*

and cutting a **c** for yourself out Is 22:16

CRYPTIC *(1)*

her forehead a **c** name was Rv 17:5

CRYSTAL *(4)*

a gleam like awe-inspiring **c**, Ezk 1:22
a sea of glass, similar to **c**. Rv 4:6
a jasper stone, bright as **c**. Rv 21:11
water, sparkling like **c**, flowing Rv 22:1

CUB *(1)*

and the lion's **c**, with nothing Nah 2:11

CUBIT *(2)*

you add a single **c** to his height Mt 6:27
any of you add a **c** to his height Lk 12:25

CUBITS *(1)*

144 **c** according to human Rv 21:17

CUBS *(10)*

a wild bear robbed of her **c**. 2Sm 17:8
and the **c** of the lioness are Jb 4:11
and lead the Bear and her **c**? Jb 38:32
robbed of her **c** than a fool in Pr 17:12
they will growl like lion **c**. Jr 51:38
she reared her **c** among the young Ezk 19:2
She brought up one of her **c**, Ezk 19:3
another of her **c** and made him Ezk 19:5
robbed of her **c** and tear open Hs 13:8
mauled whatever its **c** needed and Nah 2:12

CUCUMBER *(2)*

like a shack in a **c** field, Is 1:8
Like scarecrows in a **c** patch, Jr 10:5

CUCUMBERS *(1)*

along with the **c**, melons, leeks, Nm 11:5

CUD *(11)*

hooves and that chews the **c**. Lv 11:3
that chew the **c** or have hooves Lv 11:4
it chews the **c**, does not have Lv 11:4
it chews the **c**, does not have Lv 11:5
it chews the **c**, does not have Lv 11:6
not chew the **c**—it is unclean Lv 11:7
not chew the **c** are unclean for Lv 11:26
divided in two and chews the **c**. Dt 14:6
that chew the **c** or have divided Dt 14:7
chew the **c**, they do not have Dt 14:7
it does not ⌊chew⌋ the **c**— Dt 14:8

CULT *(7)*

Where is the **c** prostitute who Gn 38:21
has been no **c** prostitute here, Gn 38:21
has been no **c** prostitute here. Gn 38:22
woman is to be a **c** prostitute, Dt 23:17
man is to be a **c** prostitute. Dt 23:17
ends⌋ among male **c** prostitutes. Jb 36:14
sacrifices with **c** prostitutes. Hs 4:14

CULTIVATE *(4)*

will plant and **c** vineyards but Dt 28:39
provides⌋ crops for man to **c**, Ps 104:14
break up and **c** the soil? Is 28:24
the tribes of Israel will **c** it. Ezk 48:19

CULTIVATED *(6)*

of a flock, but Cain **c** the land. Gn 4:2
and all the **c** areas of the Nile Is 19:7
land will be **c** instead of lying Ezk 36:34
rich root of the **c** olive tree, Rm 11:17
grafted into a **c** olive tree, Rm 11:24
useful to those it is **c** for, Heb 6:7

CUMIN *(7)*

not then scatter **c** and sow black Is 28:25
scatter cumin and sow black **c**? Is 28:25
Certainly black **c** is not Is 28:27
wheel is not rolled over the **c**. Is 28:27
But black **c** is beaten out with a Is 28:27
with a stick, and **c** with a rod. Is 28:27
mint, dill, and **c**, yet you have Mt 23:23

CUN *(1)*

From Tibhath and **C**, Hadadezer's 1Ch 18:8

CUNNING *(6)*

was the most **c** of all the wild Gn 3:1
they tell me he is extremely **c**. 1Sm 23:22
the counselor, **c** magician, and Is 3:3
prosper through his **c** and by his Dn 8:25
serpent deceived Eve by his **c**, 2Co 11:3
human **c** with cleverness in the Eph 4:14

CUP *(67)*

Pharaoh's **c** was in my hand, Gn 40:11
squeezed them into Pharaoh's **c**, Gn 40:11

and placed the **c** in Pharaoh's Gn 40:11
will put Pharaoh's **c** in his hand Gn 40:13
he placed the **c** in Pharaoh's Gn 40:21
Put my **c**, the silver one, at the Gn 44:2
Isn't this the **c** that my master Gn 44:5
the **c** was found in Benjamin's Gn 44:12
possession the **c** was found." Gn 44:16
possession the **c** was found will Gn 44:17
food and drank from his **c**; 2Sm 12:3
the brim of a **c** or of a lily 1Kg 7:26
water in a **c** and let me drink. 1Kg 17:10
a **c** of dove's dung ⌊sold for⌋ 2Kg 6:25
the brim of a **c** or a lily 2Ch 4:5
portion and my **c** ⌊of blessing⌋; Ps 16:5
head with oil; my **c** overflows. Ps 23:5
For there is a **c** in the LORD's Ps 75:8
I will take the **c** of salvation Ps 116:13
it gleams in the **c** and goes down Pr 23:31
who have drunk the **c** of His fury Is 51:17
the **c** that ⌊causes people⌋ to Is 51:17
have removed the **c** of staggering Is 51:22
that goblet, the **c** of My fury. Is 51:22
c of consolation won't be given Jr 16:7
Take this **c** of the wine of wrath Jr 25:15
So I took the **c** from the LORD's Jr 25:17
to take the **c** from you and drink Jr 25:28
to drink the **c** must drink it, Jr 49:12
a golden **c** in the LORD's hand Jr 51:7
Yet the **c** will pass to you as Lm 4:21
I will put her **c** in your hand." Ezk 23:31
You will drink your sister's **c**, Ezk 23:32
with a **c** of devastation and Ezk 23:33
the **c** of your sister Samaria. Ezk 23:33
The **c** in the LORD's right hand Hab 2:16
make Jerusalem a **c** that causes Zch 12:2
gives just a **c** of cold water to Mt 10:42
to drink the **c** that I am about Mt 20:22
You will indeed drink My **c**. Mt 20:23
the outside of the **c** and dish, Mt 23:25
First clean the inside of the **c**, Mt 23:26
Then He took a **c**, and after Mt 26:27
let this **c** pass from Me. Mt 26:39
gives you a **c** of water to drink Mk 9:41
to drink the **c** I drink or to be Mk 10:38
You will drink the **c** I drink, Mk 10:39
Then He took a **c**, and after Mk 14:23
Take this **c** away from Me. Mk 14:36
the outside of the **c** and dish, Lk 11:39
Then He took a **c**, and after Lk 22:17
He also took the **c** after supper Lk 22:20
This **c** is the new covenant Lk 22:20
take this **c** away from Me— Lk 22:42
to drink the **c** the Father has Jn 18:11
The **c** of blessing that we bless, 1Co 10:16
cannot drink the **c** of the Lord 1Co 10:21
of the Lord and the **c** of demons. 1Co 10:21
same way ⌊He⌋ also ⌊took⌋ the **c**, 1Co 11:25
This **c** is the new covenant in My 1Co 11:25
eat this bread and drink the **c**, 1Co 11:26
bread or drinks the **c** of the 1Co 11:27
of the bread and drink of the **c**. 1Co 11:28
strength in the **c** of His anger. Rv 14:10
gave her the **c** filled with the Rv 16:19
She had a gold **c** in her hand Rv 17:4
In the **c** in which she mixed, Rv 18:6

CUPBEARER *(11)*
king of Egypt's **c** and his baker Gn 40:1
the chief **c** and the chief baker, Gn 40:2
The **c** and the baker of the king Gn 40:5
So the chief **c** told his dream to Gn 40:9
you used to when you were his **c**. Gn 40:13
of the chief **c** and the chief Gn 40:20
the chief **c** to his position as Gn 40:21
cupbearer to his position as **c**, Gn 40:21
Yet the chief **c** did not remember Gn 40:23
the chief **c** said to Pharaoh, Gn 41:9
the time,⌋ I was the king's **c**. Neh 1:11

CUPBEARERS *(2)*
attire, his **c**, and the burnt 1Kg 10:5
attire, his **c** and their attire 2Ch 9:4

CUPS *(15)*
also to make its plates and **c**, Ex 25:29
ornamental⌋ **c**, and its calyxes Ex 25:31
are to be three **c** shaped like Ex 25:33
and three **c** shaped like almond Ex 25:33
are to be four **c** shaped like Ex 25:34
its plates and **c**, as well as its Ex 37:16
ornamental⌋ **c**, and its calyxes Ex 37:17
There were three **c** shaped like Ex 37:19
and three **c** shaped like almond Ex 37:19
there were four **c** shaped like Ex 37:20
place the plates and **c** on it, Nm 4:7
Solomon's drinking **c** were gold, 1Kg 10:21
Solomon's drinking **c** were gold, 2Ch 9:20
wine and some **c** before the sons Jr 35:5
the washing of **c**, jugs, copper Mk 7:4

CURDLE *(1)*
like milk and **c** me like cheese? Jb 10:10

CURDLED *(1)*
She brought him **c** milk in a Jdg 5:25

CURDS *(2)*
Then Abraham took **c** and milk, Gn 18:8
honey, **c**, sheep, and cheese from 2Sm 17:29

CURE *(7)*
would **c** him of his skin disease. 2Kg 5:3
for you to **c** him of his skin 2Kg 5:6
expects me to **c** a man of his 2Kg 5:7
the spot and **c** the skin disease 2Kg 5:11
Your pain has no **c**! I have done Jr 30:15
But he cannot **c** you or heal your Hs 5:13
turn back—and I would **c** them. Mt 13:15

CURED *(14)*
the discharge has been **c** of it, Lv 15:13
When she is **c** of her discharge, Lv 15:28
from which you cannot be **c**. Dt 28:27
word, and my servant will be **c**. Mt 8:8
his servant was **c** that very Mt 8:13
that moment her daughter was **c**. Mt 15:28
that she was **c** of her affliction Mk 5:29
was **c** and could see everything Mk 8:25
word, and my servant will be **c**. Lk 7:7
Him and how she was instantly **c**. Lk 8:47
and **c** those who needed healing. Lk 9:11
unclean spirit, **c** the boy, and Lk 9:42
the man who was **c** did not know Jn 5:13
diseases also came and were **c**. Ac 28:9

CURING *(1)*
doing good and **c** all who were Ac 10:38

CURRENT *(3)*
silver at the **c** commercial rate Gn 23:16
the seas, and the **c** overcame me. Jnh 2:3
world in its **c** form is passing 1Co 7:31

CURRENTLY *(1)*
you know what **c** restrains ⌊him⌋ 2Th 2:6

CURRENTS *(2)*
the **c** stood firm like a dam. Ex 15:8
through the **c** of the seas. Ps 8:8

CURSE *(101)*
will never again **c** the ground Gn 8:21
will **c** those who treat you with Gn 12:3
and I will bring a **c** rather than Gn 27:12
to him, "Your **c** be on me, my son Gn 27:13
Those who **c** you will be cursed, Gn 27:29
blaspheme God or **c** a leader Ex 22:28
You must not **c** the deaf or put a Lv 19:14
bitter water that brings a **c**. Nm 5:18
bitter water that brings a **c**. Nm 5:19
take the oath with the sworn **c**, Nm 5:21
that brings a **c** enter your Nm 5:22
bitter water that brings a **c**, Nm 5:24
that brings a **c** will enter her Nm 5:27
will become a **c** among her people Nm 5:27
come and put a **c** on these people Nm 22:6
and those you **c** are cursed." Nm 22:6
come and put a **c** on them for me. Nm 22:11
You are not to **c** this people, Nm 22:12
come and put a **c** on these people Nm 22:17
Come, put a **c** on Jacob for me; Nm 23:7
How can I **c** someone God has not Nm 23:8
I brought you to **c** my enemies, Nm 23:11
there, put a **c** on them for me." Nm 23:13
is no magic **c** against Jacob Nm 23:23
Don't **c** them and don't bless Nm 23:25
you can put a **c** on them for me Nm 23:27
and those who **c** you will be Nm 24:9
you to put a **c** on my enemies, Nm 24:10
before you a blessing and a **c**: Dt 11:26
and a **c**, if you do not obey the Dt 11:28
Gerizim and the **c** at Mount Ebal. Dt 11:29
on a tree⌋ is under God's **c**. Dt 21:23
was hired to **c** you. Dt 23:4
He turned the **c** into a blessing Dt 23:5
on Mount Ebal to deliver the **c**: Dt 27:13
and every **c** written in this Dt 29:20
brought every **c** written in this Dt 29:27
life and death, blessing and **c**. Dt 30:19
that time Joshua imposed this **c**: Jos 6:26
for Balaam son of Beor to **c** you, Jos 24:9
"**C** Meroz," says the Angel of the Jdg 5:23
Bitterly **c** her inhabitants, Jdg 5:23
So the **c** of Jotham son of Jdg 9:57
I heard you utter a **c** about— Jdg 17:2
dead dog **c** my lord the king? 2Sm 16:9
the LORD told him, '**C** David!' 2Sm 16:10
him alone and let him **c** ⌊me⌋; 2Sm 16:11
become a desolation and a **c**, 2Kg 22:19
Balaam against them to **c** them, Neh 13:2
turned the **c** into a blessing. Neh 13:2
will surely **c** You to Your face. Jb 1:11
will surely **c** You to Your face. Jb 2:5
your integrity? **C** God and die!" Jb 2:9
Let those who **c** ⌊certain⌋ days Jb 3:8
pronounced a **c** on his home. Jb 5:3
by asking for his life with a **c**. Jb 31:30
mouths, but they **c** inwardly. Ps 62:4
they ridicule and **c** me. Ps 102:8
Though they **c**, You will bless. Ps 109:28
The LORD's **c** is on the household Pr 3:33
People will **c** anyone who hoards Pr 11:26
people will **c** him, and tribes Pr 24:24
an undeserved **c** goes nowhere. Pr 26:2
will be counted as a **c** to him. Pr 27:14
he hears the **c** but will not Pr 29:24
or he will **c** you, and you will Pr 30:10
Do not **c** the king even in your Ec 10:20
and do not **c** a rich person even Ec 10:20
will **c** their king and their God. Is 8:21
Therefore a **c** has consumed the Is 24:6
name behind as a **c** for My chosen Is 65:15
Let a **c** be on the man who does Jr 11:3
land mourns because of the **c**, Jr 23:10
the earth—a **c** and a desolation Jr 29:18
will create a **c** that says: Jr 29:22
a ruin, and a **c**, and all her Jr 49:13
May Your **c** be on them! Lm 3:65
promised **c** written in the law Dn 9:11
This is the **c** that is going out Zch 5:3
you have been a **c** among the Zch 8:13
there be a **c** of destruction. Zch 14:11
I will send a **c** among you, Mal 2:2
and I will **c** your blessings. Mal 2:2
begun to **c** them because you Mal 2:2
You are suffering under a **c**, Mal 3:9
and strike the land with a **c**." Mal 4:6
he started to **c** and to swear Mt 26:74
he started to **c** and to swear Mk 14:71
bless those who **c** you, pray for Lk 6:28
and bound themselves under a **c**: Ac 23:12
under a solemn **c** that we won't Ac 23:14
themselves under a **c** not to eat Ac 23:21
you; bless and do not **c**. Rm 12:14
love the Lord, a **c** be on him. 1Co 16:22
preached to you, a **c** be on him! Gl 1:8
you received, a **c** be on him! Gl 1:9
works of the law are under a **c**, Gl 3:10
redeemed us from the **c** of the Gl 3:13
the law by becoming a **c** for us, Gl 3:13
with it we **c** men who are made Jms 3:9
there will no longer be any **c**. Rv 22:3

CURSED *(68)*
are **c** more than any livestock Gn 3:14
The ground is **c** because of you. Gn 3:17
So now you are **c** ⌊with Gn 4:11
by the ground the LORD has **c**." Gn 5:29
Canaan will be **c**. He will be Gn 9:25
Those who curse you will be **c**, Gn 27:29
Their anger is **c**, for it is Gn 49:7
He has **c** his father or mother; Lv 20:9
Her son **c** and blasphemed the Lv 24:11
the one who has **c** to the outside Lv 24:14
the one who had **c** to the outside Lv 24:23
and those you curse are **c**." Nm 22:6
I curse someone God has not **c**? Nm 23:8
those who curse you will be **c**. Nm 24:9
'**C** is the person who makes a Dt 27:15
'**C** is the one who dishonors his Dt 27:16
'**C** is the one who moves his Dt 27:17
'**C** is the one who leads a blind Dt 27:18
'**C** is the one who denies justice Dt 27:19
'**C** is the one who sleeps with Dt 27:20
'**C** is the one who has sexual Dt 27:21
'**C** is the one who sleeps with Dt 27:22

‘C is the one who sleeps with Dt 27:23
‘C is the one who kills his Dt 27:24
‘C is the one who accepts a Dt 27:25
‘C is anyone who does not put Dt 27:26
You will be c in the city and Dt 28:16
the city and c in the country. Dt 28:16
and kneading bowl will be c. Dt 28:17
Your descendants will be c, Dt 28:18
You will be c when you come in Dt 28:19
come in and c when you go out Dt 28:19
C before the LORD is the man who Jos 6:26
you are c and will always Jos 9:23
ate and drank, they c Abimelech. Jdg 9:27
a wife to a Benjaminite is c.” Jdg 21:18
C is the man who eats food 1Sm 14:24
‘C is the man who eats food 1Sm 14:28
Then he c David by his gods. 1Sm 17:43
may they be c in the presence of 1Sm 26:19
Shimei said as he c: 2Sm 16:7
Shimei went, he c ⌊David⌋, and 2Sm 16:13
“You have c God and king!” 1Kg 21:10
“Naboth has c God and king!” 1Kg 21:13
and c them in the name of the 2Kg 2:24
care of this c woman and bury 2Kg 9:34
rebuked them, c them, beat some Neh 13:25
having c God in their hearts. Jb 1:5
to speak and c the day he was Jb 3:1
Their section of the land is c, Jb 24:18
but those c by Him will be Ps 37:22
a man c by the LORD will fall Pr 22:14
you yourself have c others. Ec 7:22
a hundred years will be c. Is 65:20
C is the man who trusts in Jr 17:5
C be the day on which I was born. Jr 20:14
C be the man who brought the Jr 20:15
C is the one who does the LORD’s Jr 48:10
and c is the one who withholds Jr 48:10
people the LORD has c forever. Mal 1:4
The deceiver is c who has an Mal 1:14
Me, you who are c, into the Mt 25:41
tree that You c is withered.” Mk 11:21
that I myself were c and cut off Rm 9:3
says, “Jesus is c,” and no one 1Co 12:3
C is everyone who does not Gl 3:10
C is everyone who is hung on a Gl 3:13
is worthless and about to be c, Heb 6:8

CURSES *(24)*

Whoever c his father or his Ex 21:17
If anyone c his father or Lv 20:9
anyone c his God, he will bear Lv 24:15
is to write these c on a scroll Nm 5:23
all these c will come and Dt 28:15
LORD will send against you c, Dt 28:20
All these c will come, pursue, Dt 28:45
These c will be a sign and a Dt 28:46
to all the c of the covenant Dt 29:21
blessings and c I have set Dt 30:1
put all these c on your enemies Dt 30:7
the blessings as well as the c— Jos 8:34
he was yelling c as he 2Sm 16:5
He c ⌊me⌋ this way because the 2Sm 16:10
me instead of Shimei’s c today.” 2Sm 16:12
uttered malicious c against me 1Kg 2:8
all the c written in the book 2Ch 34:24
one who is greedy c and despises Ps 10:3
They utter c and lies. Ps 59:12
Whoever c his father or mother— Pr 20:20
eyes away will receive many c. Pr 28:27
a generation that c its father Pr 30:11
on them all the c of this Jr 11:8
or borrow, yet everyone c me. Jr 15:10

CURSING *(16)*

of your people’s c and swearing Nm 5:21
C, deceit, and violence fill his Ps 10:7
He loved c—let it fall on him; Ps 109:17
He wore c like his coat—let it Ps 109:18
you may hear your servant c you; Ec 7:21
ridicule, and c, wherever I have Jr 24:9
an object of scorn and c— Jr 25:18
city an object of c for all the Jr 26:6
scorn, c, and disgrace, Jr 42:18
an object of c and insult among Jr 44:8
of scorn, of c, and of disgrace. Jr 44:12
and an object of c, without Jr 44:22
C, lying, murder, stealing, and Hs 4:2
of the c of their tongue. Hs 7:16
is full of c and bitterness. Rm 3:14
same mouth come blessing and c. Jms 3:10

CURTAIN *(29)*

length of each c should be 42 Ex 26:2
the width of each c six feet. Ex 26:2
of the last c in the ⌊first⌋ Ex 26:4
of the outermost c in the second Ex 26:4
loops on the one c and make 50 Ex 26:5
the edge of the c in the second Ex 26:5
length of each c should be 45 Ex 26:8
the width of each c six feet. Ex 26:8
fold the sixth c double at the Ex 26:9
loops on the edge of the one c, Ex 26:10
corresponding⌋ c of the second Ex 26:10
leftover half c is to hang down Ex 26:12
length of each c was 42 feet, Ex 36:9
the width of each c six feet; Ex 36:9
of the last c in the first set Ex 36:11
of the outermost c in the second Ex 36:11
loops on the one c and 50 loops Ex 36:12
the edge of the c in the second Ex 36:12
length of each c was 45 feet, Ex 36:15
the width of each c six feet. Ex 36:15
the outermost c in the ⌊first⌋ Ex 36:17
corresponding⌋ c in the second Ex 36:17
not go near the c or approach Lv 21:23
the c of the sanctuary was split Mt 27:51
Then the c of the sanctuary was Mk 15:38
The c of the sanctuary was split Lk 23:45
inner sanctuary behind the c. Heb 6:19
the second c, the tabernacle Heb 9:3
us, through the c (that is, His Heb 10:20

CURTAINS *(29)*

the tabernacle itself with 10 c. Ex 26:1
all the c are to have the same Ex 26:2
Five of the c should be joined Ex 26:3
other⌋ five c joined together Ex 26:3
and join the c together with Ex 26:6
You are to make c of goat hair Ex 26:7
make 11 of these c. Ex 26:7
All 11 c are to have the same Ex 26:8
five of the c by themselves, Ex 26:9
the ⌊other⌋ six c by themselves. Ex 26:9
is left over from the tent c, Ex 26:12
of the tent c should be hanging Ex 26:13
made the tabernacle with 10 c. Ex 36:8
all the c had the same Ex 36:9
five of the c to each other, Ex 36:10
the ⌊other⌋ five c he joined to Ex 36:10
and joined the c to each other, Ex 36:13
made c of goat hair for a tent Ex 36:14
All 11 c had the same Ex 36:15
joined five of the c together, Ex 36:16
to transport the tabernacle c, Nm 4:25
ark of God sits inside tent c.” 2Sm 7:2
covenant is under tent c.” 1Ch 17:1
lovely like the c of Solomon. Sg 1:5
let your tent c be stretched out Is 54:2
my tent c, in a moment. Jr 4:20
tent again or to hang up my c. Jr 10:20
with their tent c and all their Jr 49:29
the tent c of the land of Midian Hab 3:7

CURVED *(5)*

hill the border c to the spring Jos 15:9
and then c to Baalah (that Jos 15:9
north of Ekron, c to Shikkeron, Jos 15:11
south, the border c, turning Jos 18:14
It c northward and went to Jos 18:17

CURVES *(1)*

The c of your thighs are like Sg 7:1

CURVING *(1)*

to Rimmon, c around to Neah. Jos 19:13

CUSH *(27)*

encircles the entire land of C. Gn 2:13
C, Egypt, Put, and Canaan. Gn 10:6
C fathered Nimrod, who was the Gn 10:8
this about Tirhakah king of C: 2Kg 19:9
C, Mizraim, Put, and Canaan. 1Ch 1:8
C fathered Nimrod, who was the 1Ch 1:10
127 provinces from India to C. Est 1:1
127 provinces from India to C. Est 8:9
Topaz from C cannot compare with Jb 28:19
C will stretch out its hands to Ps 68:31
Tyre, and C—each one was born Ps 87:4
Egypt, Pathros, C, Elam, Shinar, Is 11:11
wings beyond the rivers of C Is 18:1
and omen against Egypt and C, Is 20:3
of Egypt and the exiles of C, Is 20:4
Those who made C their hope and Is 20:5
this about Tirhakah, king of C: Is 37:9
ransom for you, C and Seba in Is 43:3
of C and the Sabeans, Is 45:14
go forth—C and Put, who are Jr 46:9
as far as the border of C. Ezk 29:10
be anguish in C when the slain Ezk 30:4
C, Put, and Lud, and all the Ezk 30:5
in ships to terrify confident C. Ezk 30:9
C, and Put are with them, Ezk 38:5
C and Egypt were her endless Nah 3:9
the rivers of C My supplicants, Zph 3:10

CUSH’S *(2)*

C sons: Seba, Havilah, Sabtah, Gn 10:7
C sons: Seba, Havilah, Sabta, 1Ch 1:9

CUSHAN *(1)*

see the tents of C in distress; Hab 3:7

CUSHAN-RISHATHAIM *(2)*

He sold them to C king of Aram Jdg 3:8
handed over C king of Aram to Jdg 3:10

CUSHI *(2)*

son of C, saying, “Bring Jr 36:14
that came to Zephaniah son of C, Zph 1:1

CUSHION *(2)*

of a bed or the c of a couch. Am 3:12
in the stern, sleeping on the c. Mk 4:38

CUSHITE *(15)*

(AKA ETHIOPIAN)

of the C woman he married Nm 12:1
for he had married a C woman Nm 12:1
then said to the C, “Go tell the 2Sm 18:21
The C bowed to Joab and took 2Sm 18:21
let me run too behind the C!” 2Sm 18:22
of the plain and outran the C. 2Sm 18:23
Just then the C came and said, 2Sm 18:31
king asked the C, “Is the young 2Sm 18:32
The C replied, “May what has 2Sm 18:32
Then Zerah the C came against 2Ch 14:9
Can the C change his skin, Jr 13:23
a C court official employed in Jr 38:7
the C, “Take from here Jr 38:10
Ebed-melech the C cried out to Jr 38:12
Go tell Ebed-melech the C: Jr 39:16

CUSHITES *(8)*

the LORD routed the C before Asa 2Ch 14:12
before Judah, and the C fled. 2Ch 14:12
The C fell until they had no 2Ch 14:13
not the C and Libyans a vast 2Ch 16:8
live near the C to attack 2Ch 21:16
The Libyans and C will also be Dn 11:43
are you not like the C to Me? Am 9:7
You C will also be slain by My Zph 2:12

CUSTODIAN *(1)*

said to the c of the wardrobe, 2Kg 10:22

CUSTODY *(11)*

and put them in c in the house Gn 40:3
they were in c for some time. Gn 40:4
who were in c with him in his Gn 40:7
baker in the c of the captain Gn 41:10
animal was stolen from his c, Ex 22:12
They put him in c until the Lv 24:12
placed him in c, because it had Nm 15:34
he kept him in c until his dying Jr 52:11
and put them in c until the next Ac 4:3
took him into c, and ordered him Ac 21:33
to be kept in c until I could Ac 25:21

CUSTOM *(22)*

⌊as is⌋ the c of all the land. Gn 19:31
It is not the c in this place to Gn 29:26
It was her c to sit under the Jdg 4:5
Now it became a c in Israel Jdg 11:39
was David’s c during the whole 1Sm 27:11
according to their c, until 1Kg 18:28
the pillar according to the c. 2Kg 11:14
do not know the c of the God of 2Kg 17:26
don’t know the c of the God 2Kg 17:26
can teach them the c of the God 2Kg 17:27
according to the c of the 2Kg 17:33
practicing their former c. 2Kg 17:40
the governor’s c was to release Mt 27:15
it was Pilate’s c to release for Mk 15:6
to do for them as was his c. Mk 15:8
according to the c of the Lk 1:9
to the c of the festival Lk 2:42
You have a c that I release one Jn 18:39
to the burial c of the Jews. Jn 19:40
according to the c prescribed by Ac 15:1

the Romans' **c** to give any man Ac 25:16
we have no other **c**, nor do the 1Co 11:16

CUSTOMARY *(3)*
her according to the **c** treatment Ex 21:9
seven times more than was **c**, Dn 3:19
Him what was **c** under the law, Lk 2:27

CUSTOMS *(15)*
You must not follow their **c**. Lv 18:3
of the detestable **c** that were Lv 18:30
the detestable **c** of those Dt 18:9
according to the **c** of the 2Kg 17:8
Israelites and the **c** the kings 2Kg 17:8
according to the **c** Israel had 2Kg 17:19
the former **c** to this day. 2Kg 17:34
confirmed these **c** of Purim, Est 9:32
for the **c** of the peoples are Jr 10:3
are many other **c** they have Mk 7:4
and change the **c** that Moses Ac 6:14
and are promoting **c** that are not Ac 16:21
children or to walk in our **c**. Ac 21:21
all the Jewish **c** and Ac 26:3
our people or the **c** of our Ac 28:17

CUT *(255)*
but he did not **c** up the birds. Gn 15:10
that man will be **c** off from his Gn 17:14
took a flint, **c** off her son's Ex 4:25
day must be **c** off from Israel. Ex 12:15
must be **c** off from the community Ex 12:19
not build it out of **c** stones. Ex 20:25
and consumes stacks of **c** grain, Ex 22:6
C the ram into pieces. Wash its Ex 29:17
must be **c** off from his people. Ex 30:33
fragrance must be **c** off from his Ex 30:38
to **c** gemstones for mounting, Ex 31:5
person must be **c** off from his Ex 31:14
C two stone tablets like the Ex 34:1
Moses **c** two stone tablets like Ex 34:4
to **c** gemstones for mounting, Ex 35:33
and he **c** threads ⌊from them⌋ to Ex 39:3
offering and **c** it into pieces. Lv 1:6
will **c** it into pieces with its Lv 1:12
person must be **c** off from his Lv 7:20
person must be **c** off from his Lv 7:21
eats ⌊it⌋ must be **c** off from his Lv 7:25
person must be **c** off from his Lv 7:27
Moses **c** the ram into pieces and Lv 8:20
he must **c** the contaminated Lv 13:56
blood and must be **c** off from his Lv 17:4
person must be **c** off from his Lv 17:9
eats blood and **c** him off from Lv 17:10
whoever eats it must be **c** off. Lv 17:14
must be **c** off from his people Lv 18:29
person must be **c** off from his Lv 19:8
You are not to **c** off the hair at Lv 19:27
that man and **c** him off from his Lv 20:3
and **c** off from their people both Lv 20:5
that person and **c** him off from Lv 20:6
They must be **c** off publicly from Lv 20:17
of them must be **c** off from their Lv 20:18
that person will be **c** off from Lv 22:3
must be **c** off from his people. Lv 23:29
When I **c** off your supply of Lv 26:26
c down your incense altars, Lv 26:30
You must not **c** his hair Nm 6:5
Passover is to be **c** off from his Nm 9:13
they **c** down a branch with a Nm 13:23
grapes⌋ the Israelites **c** there. Nm 13:24
person is to be **c** off from his Nm 15:30
He will certainly be **c** off, Nm 15:31
will be **c** off from Israel. Nm 19:13
that person will be **c** off from Nm 19:20
c down their Asherah poles, Dt 7:5
'**C** two stone tablets like the Dt 10:1
c two stone tablets like the Dt 10:3
c down the carved images of Dt 12:3
do not **c** yourselves or make a Dt 14:1
with his neighbor to **c** timber, Dt 19:5
You must not **c** them down. Dt 20:19
You may **c** them down to build Dt 20:20
penis has been **c** off may enter Dt 23:1
you are to **c** off her hand. Dt 25:12
your camps who **c** your wood and Dt 29:11
I will **c** them to pieces and blot Dt 32:26
its waters will be **c** off. Jos 3:13
was completely **c** off, and the Jos 3:16
the Jordan were **c** off in front Jos 4:7
the Jordan's waters were **c** off.' Jos 4:7
and **c** off his thumbs and big Jdg 1:6
and big toes **c** off used to pick Jdg 1:7
your father and **c** down the Jdg 6:25
of the Asherah pole you **c** down." Jdg 6:26
Asherah pole beside it **c** down, Jdg 6:28
altar and **c** down the Asherah Jdg 6:30
ax in his hand and **c** a branch Jdg 9:48
person also **c** his own branch Jdg 9:49
You must never **c** his hair, Jdg 13:5
My hair has never been **c**, Jdg 16:17
of his concubine, **c** her into 12 Jdg 19:29
concubine and **c** her in pieces, Jdg 20:6
tribe has been **c** off from Israel Jdg 21:6
and his hair will never be **c**." 1Sm 1:11
when I will **c** off your strength 1Sm 2:31
family⌋ I do not **c** off from My 1Sm 2:33
team of oxen, **c** them in pieces, 1Sm 11:7
Jonathan **c** them down, and his 1Sm 14:13
you down, **c** your head off, 1Sm 17:46
him. Then he **c** off his head. 1Sm 17:51
up and secretly **c** off the corner 1Sm 24:4
because he had **c** off the corner 1Sm 24:5
in my hand, for I **c** it off, but 1Sm 24:11
that you will not **c** off my 1Sm 24:21
They **c** off Saul's head, stripped 1Sm 31:9
They **c** off their hands and feet 2Sm 4:12
c their clothes in half at the 2Sm 10:4
me go over and **c** his head off!" 2Sm 16:9
and they **c** off the head of Sheba 2Sm 20:22
C the living boy in two and give 1Kg 3:25
mine or yours. **C** ⌊him in two⌋!" 1Kg 3:26
from Lebanon be **c** down for me. 1Kg 5:6
us knows how to **c** timber like 1Kg 5:6
finished stones **c** at the quarry 1Kg 6:7
c to size and sawed with saws on 1Kg 7:9
costly stones, **c** to size, as 1Kg 7:11
will **c** off Israel from the land 1Kg 9:7
for themselves, **c** it in pieces, 1Kg 18:23
and **c** themselves with knives and 1Kg 18:28
the wood, **c** up the bull, 1Kg 18:33
You must **c** down every good tree 2Kg 3:19
of water and **c** down every good 2Kg 3:25
he came back and **c** them up into 2Kg 4:39
the Jordan, they **c** down trees. 2Kg 6:4
the man of God **c** a stick, threw 2Kg 6:6
sent ⌊someone⌋ to **c** off my head? 2Kg 6:32
Then King Ahaz **c** off the frames 2Kg 16:17
pillars and **c** down the Asherah 2Kg 18:4
I **c** down its tallest cedars, 2Kg 19:23
into pieces, **c** down the Asherah 2Kg 23:14
he **c** into pieces all the gold 2Kg 24:13
stripped Saul, **c** off his head, 1Ch 10:9
c their clothes in half at the 1Ch 19:4
stonemasons to **c** finished stones 1Ch 22:2
know how to **c** the trees of 2Ch 2:8
the woodcutters who **c** the trees, 2Ch 2:10
We will **c** logs from Lebanon, 2Ch 2:16
God's temple, **c** them into pieces 2Ch 28:24
his own children **c** him down with 2Ch 32:21
It is being built with **c** stones, Ezr 5:8
three layers of **c** stones and one Ezr 6:4
unleash His power and **c** me off! Jb 6:9
way of escape will be **c** off, Jb 11:20
If it is **c** down, it will sprout Jb 14:7
man have when he is **c** off, Jb 27:8
the LORD **c** off all flattering Ps 12:3
"I am **c** off from Your sight." Ps 31:22
rain that falls on the **c** grass, Ps 72:6
I will **c** off all the horns of Ps 75:10
It was **c** down and burned up; Ps 80:16
who are **c** off from Your care. Ps 88:5
gates and **c** through the iron Ps 107:16
of his descendants be **c** off; Ps 109:13
and let Him **c** off ⌊all⌋ memory Ps 109:15
has **c** the ropes of the wicked. Ps 129:4
wicked will be **c** off from the Pr 2:22
years of the wicked are **c** short. Pr 10:27
a perverse tongue will be **c** out. Pr 10:31
we will rebuild with **c** stones; Is 9:10
the sycamores have been **c** down, Is 9:10
So the LORD **c** off Israel's head Is 9:14
destroy and to **c** off many Is 10:7
the tall ⌊trees⌋ will be **c** down, Is 10:33
⌊Their⌋ bows will **c** young men to Is 13:18
you have been **c** down to the Is 14:12
and I will **c** off from Babylon Is 14:22
is shaved; every beard is **c** off. Is 15:2
He will **c** off the shoots with a Is 18:5
give way, be **c** off, and fall, Is 22:25
We have **c** a deal with Death, Is 28:15
like thorns **c** down and burned in Is 33:12
I **c** down its tallest cedars, Is 37:24
bronze doors and **c** the iron bars Is 45:2
would not be **c** off or eliminated Is 48:19
the rock from which you were **c**, Is 51:1
For He was **c** off from the land Is 53:8
name that will never be **c** off. Is 56:5
of Hosts says: **C** down the trees; Jr 6:6
C off the hair of your sacred Jr 7:29
like newly **c** grain after the Jr 9:22
let's **c** him off from the land of Jr 11:19
nor will anyone **c** himself or Jr 16:6
They will **c** down the choicest of Jr 22:7
He will **c** windows in it, and it Jr 22:14
the calf they **c** in two in order Jr 34:18
Jehoiakim would **c** the scroll Jr 36:23
you will be **c** off and become an Jr 44:8
disaster, to **c** off all Judah. Jr 44:11
her like those who **c** trees. Jr 46:22
They will **c** down her forest— Jr 46:23
to **c** off from Tyre and Sidon Jr 47:4
let's **c** her off from nationhood. Jr 48:2
C off the sower from Babylon as Jr 50:16
whole earth is **c** down and Jr 50:23
has come, your life thread is **c**. Jr 51:13
threatened to **c** off this place Jr 51:62
has **c** off every horn of Israel Lm 2:3
walled in my ways with **c** stones; Lm 3:9
am going to **c** off the supply of Ezk 4:16
I am going to **c** ⌊you⌋ off and Ezk 5:11
against you and **c** off your Ezk 5:16
your incense altars **c** down, Ezk 6:6
I will **c** him off from among My Ezk 14:8
against it to **c** off its supply Ezk 14:13
wasn't **c** on the day you were Ezk 16:4
to stone you and **c** you to pieces Ezk 16:40
from its sheath and **c** off both Ezk 21:3
Since I will **c** off ⌊both⌋ the Ezk 21:4
They will **c** off your nose and Ezk 23:25
stone them and **c** them down with Ezk 23:47
will **c** you off from the peoples Ezk 25:7
against Edom and **c** off both man Ezk 25:13
c it down and left it lying. Ezk 31:12
waste and will **c** off from it Ezk 35:7
hope has perished; we are **c** off. Ezk 37:11
the countryside or **c** ⌊it⌋ down Ezk 39:10
four tables of **c** stone for the Ezk 40:42
C down the tree and chop off its Dn 4:14
'**C** down the tree and destroy it, Dn 4:23
Messiah will be **c** off and will Dn 9:26
the prophets to **c** them down; Hs 6:5
have been **c** off from the house Jl 1:9
the food been **c** off before our Jl 1:16
I will **c** off the ruler from the Am 1:5
I will **c** off the ruler from Am 1:8
I will **c** off the judge from the Am 2:3
altar will be **c** off and fall to Am 3:14
the houses of **c** stone you have Am 5:11
the crossroads to **c** off their Ob 14
bald and **c** off your hair Mc 1:16
I will **c** off your prey from the Nah 2:13
the sword will **c** you down. Nah 3:15
I will **c** off mankind from the Zph 1:3
I will **c** off from this place Zph 1:4
with silver will be **c** off. Zph 1:11
I have **c** off nations; their Zph 3:6
would not be **c** off ⌊based on⌋ Zph 3:7
c off the horns of the nations Zch 1:21
I will **c** off the chariot from Zch 9:10
called Favor and **c** it in two, Zch 11:10
Then I **c** in two my second staff, Zch 11:14
two-thirds will be **c** off and die, Zch 13:8
may the LORD **c** off any Mal 2:12
fruit will be **c** down and thrown Mt 3:10
c it off and throw it away. Mt 5:30
good fruit is **c** down and thrown Mt 7:19
c it off and throw it away. Mt 18:8
He will **c** him to pieces and Mt 24:51
slave and **c** off his ear. Mt 26:51
which he had **c** into the rock. Mt 27:60
causes your downfall, **c** it off. Mk 9:43
causes your downfall, **c** it off. Mk 9:45
branches **c** from the fields. Mk 11:8
slave, and **c** off his ear. Mk 14:47
Him in a tomb **c** out of the rock, Mk 15:46
fruit will be **c** down and thrown Lk 3:9
He will **c** him to pieces and Lk 12:46

D

of Lebanon looking toward **D**. Sg 7:4
The head of Aram is **D**, the head Is 7:8
the head of **D** is Rezin (within Is 7:8
the wealth of **D** and the spoils Is 8:4
Isn't Samaria like **D**? Is 10:9
An oracle against **D**: Is 17:1
Look, **D** is no longer a city. Is 17:1
Ephraim, and a kingdom from **D**. Is 17:3
About **D**: Hamath and Arpad are Jr 49:23
D has become weak; she has Jr 49:24
will set fire to the wall of **D**; Jr 49:27
D was also your trading partner Ezk 27:18
the border of **D** and the border Ezk 47:16
Hazar-enon at the border of **D**, Ezk 47:17
will run between Hauran and **D**, Ezk 47:18
at the northern border of **D**, Ezk 48:1
from punishing **D** for three Am 1:3
will break down the gates of **D**. Am 1:5
send you into exile beyond **D**." Am 5:27
and **D** is its resting place— Zch 9:1
from him to the synagogues in **D**, Ac 9:2
he traveled and was nearing **D**, Ac 9:3
by the hand and led him into **D**. Ac 9:8
Now in **D** there was a disciple Ac 9:10
disciples in **D** for some days. Ac 9:19
who lived in **D** by proving that Ac 9:22
how in **D** he had spoken boldly Ac 9:27
traveling to **D** to bring those Ac 22:5
As I was traveling and near **D**, Ac 22:6
up and go into **D**, and there you Ac 22:10
were with me, and came into **D**. Ac 22:11
traveling to **D** with authority Ac 26:12
I preached to those in **D** first, Ac 26:20
In **D**, the governor under King 2Co 11:32
to Arabia and came back to **D**. Gl 1:17

DAMPEN *(1)*
with my tears I **d** my pillow and Ps 6:6

DAMS *(1)*
He **d** up the streams from flowing Jb 28:11

DAN *(52)*
(AKA LAISH, LESHEM)
went in pursuit as far as **D**. Gn 14:14
me a son," and she named him **D**. Gn 30:6
Bilhah were **D** and Naphtali. Gn 35:25
D will judge his people as one Gn 49:16
D and Naphtali; Gad and Asher. Ex 1:4
the tribe of **D**, to be with him Ex 31:6
of the tribe of **D**, ⌊the ability⌋ Ex 35:34
of the tribe of **D**, a gem cutter, Ex 38:23
of Dibri of the tribe of **D**. Lv 24:11
son of Ammishaddai from **D**; Nm 1:12
descendants of **D**: according to Nm 1:38
the tribe of **D** numbered 62,700 Nm 1:39
of the camp of **D** with their Nm 10:25
of Gemalli from the tribe of **D**; Nm 13:12
the clans of **D** by their clans. Nm 26:42
a leader from the tribe of **D**; Nm 34:22
Asher, Zebulun, **D**, and Naphtali. Dt 27:13
He said about **D**: Dan is a young Dt 33:22
D is a young lion, leaping out Dt 33:22
the land: Gilead as far as **D**, Dt 34:1
Leshem after their ancestor **D**. Jos 19:47
tribes of Ephraim, **D**, and half Jos 21:5
From the tribe of **D** ⌊they gave⌋: Jos 21:23
D, why did you linger at the Jdg 5:17
the family of **D**, whose name was Jdg 13:2
to direct him in the Camp of **D**, Jdg 13:25
the Camp of **D** to this day; Jdg 18:12
named the city **D**, after the name Jdg 18:29
the name of their ancestor **D**, Jdg 18:29
Israelites from **D** to Beer-sheba Jdg 20:1
All Israel from **D** to Beer-sheba 1Sm 3:20
and Judah from **D** to Beer-sheba." 2Sm 3:10
Israel from **D** to Beer-sheba— 2Sm 17:11
of Israel from **D** to Beer-sheba 2Sm 24:2
and from **D** to Beer-sheba 70,000 2Sm 24:15
in safety from **D** to Beer-sheba, 1Kg 4:25
Bethel, and put the other in **D**. 1Kg 12:29
of the calves all the way to **D**. 1Kg 12:30
attacked Ijon, **D**, 1Kg 15:20
that were in Bethel and **D**. 2Kg 10:29
D, Joseph, Benjamin, Naphtali, 1Ch 2:2
from Beer-sheba to **D** and bring 1Ch 21:2
for **D**, Azarel son of Jeroham. 1Ch 27:22
a woman from the daughters of **D**. 2Ch 2:14
attacked Ijon, **D**, Abel-maim, and 2Ch 16:4
from Beer-sheba to **D**, to come to 2Ch 30:5
For a voice announces from **D**, Jr 4:15
From **D** is heard the snorting of Jr 8:16
sea, will be **D**—one portion. Ezk 48:1
Next to the territory of **D**, Ezk 48:2
and one, the gate of **D**. Ezk 48:32
your god lives, **D**," or "As the Am 8:14

DAN'S *(5)*
D son: Hashum. Gn 46:23
D military divisions will camp Nm 2:25
who belong to **D** encampment is Nm 2:31
Ammishaddai was over **D** division Nm 10:25
were **D** descendants by their Nm 26:42

DAN-JAAN *(1)*
continued on to **D** and around to 2Sm 24:6

DANCE *(6)*
their lame **d** around the altar 1Kg 18:26
Him with tambourine and **d**; Ps 150:4
a time to mourn and a time to **d**; Ec 3:4
look⌋ at the **d** of the two camps Sg 6:13
flute for you, but you didn't **d**; Mt 11:17
flute for you, but you didn't **d**; Lk 7:32

DANCED *(2)*
Herodias' daughter **d** before them Mt 14:6
own daughter came in and **d**, Mk 6:22

DANCERS *(2)*
needed from the **d** they caught. Jdg 21:23
Singers and **d** alike ⌊will say⌋, Ps 87:7

DANCES *(4)*
come out to perform the **d**, Jdg 21:21
sing about him during their **d**: 1Sm 21:11
they sing about during their **d**: 1Sm 29:5
neck, and dismay **d** before him. Jb 41:22

DANCING *(14)*
her with tambourines and **d**. Ex 15:20
camp and saw the calf and the **d**, Ex 32:19
meet him with tambourines and **d**! Jdg 11:34
singing and **d** with tambourines, 1Sm 18:6
David was **d** with all his might 2Sm 6:14
leaping and **d** before the LORD, 2Sm 6:16
I was **d** before the LORD who 2Sm 6:21
King David **d** and celebrating, 1Ch 15:29
You turned my lament into **d**; Ps 30:11
His name with **d** and make music Ps 149:3
again and go forth in joyful **d**. Jr 31:4
the virgin will rejoice with **d**, Jr 31:13
our **d** has turned to mourning. Lm 5:15
the house, he heard music and **d**. Lk 15:25

DANGER *(12)*
I fear no **d**, for You are with Ps 23:4
of Your wings until **d** passes. Ps 57:1
My life is constantly in **d**, Ps 119:109
If I walk in the thick of **d**, Ps 138:7
and be free from the fear of **d**." Pr 1:33
Don't fear sudden **d** or the ruin Pr 3:25
will sleep at night without **d**. Pr 19:23
person sees **d** and takes cover, Pr 22:3
sensible see **d** and take cover; Pr 27:12
being swamped and were in **d**. Lk 8:23
or nakedness or **d** or sword? Rm 8:35
Why are we in **d** every hour? 1Co 15:30

DANGEROUS *(7)*
I will remove **d** animals from the Lv 26:6
famine and **d** animals against Ezk 5:17
If I allow **d** animals to pass Ezk 14:15
sword, famine, **d** animals, and Ezk 14:21
them and eliminate **d** animals in Ezk 34:25
and the voyage was already **d**. Ac 27:9
who are like **d** reefs at your Jd 12

DANGERS *(9)*
of heights and **d** on the road; Ec 12:5
I faced⌋ **d** from rivers, 2Co 11:26
from rivers, **d** from robbers, 2Co 11:26
from robbers, **d** from my own 2Co 11:26
my own people, **d** from the 2Co 11:26
the Gentiles, **d** in the city, 2Co 11:26
in the city, **d** in the open 2Co 11:26
the open country, **d** on the sea, 2Co 11:26
and **d** among false brothers; 2Co 11:26

DANIEL *(78)*
(AKA CHILEAB, BELTESHAZZAR)
D was ⌊born⌋ second, by Abigail 1Ch 3:1
D, from Ithamar's descendants; Ezr 8:2
D, Ginnethon, Baruch, Neh 10:6
men—Noah, **D**, and Job—were Ezk 14:14
even ⌊if⌋ Noah, **D**, and Job were Ezk 14:20
Yes, you are wiser than **D**; Ezk 28:3
of Judah, were **D**, Hananiah, Dn 1:6
to **D**, he gave the name Dn 1:7
D determined that he would not Dn 1:8
God had granted **D** favor and Dn 1:9
yet he said to **D**, "My lord the Dn 1:10
So **D** said to the guard whom the Dn 1:11
official had assigned to **D**, Dn 1:11
D also understood visions and Dn 1:17
no one was found equal to **D**, Dn 1:19
D remained there until the first Dn 1:21
searched for **D** and his friends, Dn 2:13
Then **D** responded with tact and Dn 2:14
explained the situation to **D**. Dn 2:15
So **D** went and asked the king to Dn 2:16
D went to his house and told Dn 2:17
D and his friends would not be Dn 2:18
then revealed to **D** in a vision Dn 2:19
and **D** praised the God of heaven Dn 2:19
Therefore **D** went to Arioch, Dn 2:24
quickly brought **D** before the Dn 2:25
The king said in reply to **D**, Dn 2:26
D answered the king: Dn 2:27
homage to **D**, and gave orders Dn 2:46
The king said to **D**, "Your God is Dn 2:47
king promoted **D** and gave him Dn 2:48
But **D** remained at the king's Dn 2:49
Finally **D**, named Belteshazzar Dn 4:8
Then **D**, whose name is Dn 4:19
this⌋ because **D**, the one the Dn 5:12
summon **D**, and he will give Dn 5:12
Then **D** was brought before the Dn 5:13
to him, "Are you **D**, one of the Dn 5:13
Then **D** answered the king, Dn 5:17
and they clothed **D** in purple, Dn 5:29
administrators, including **D**. Dn 6:2
D distinguished himself above Dn 6:3
a charge against **D** regarding the Dn 6:4
against this **D** unless we find Dn 6:5
When **D** learned that the document Dn 6:10
a group and found **D** petitioning Dn 6:11
to the king, "**D**, one of the Dn 6:13
on rescuing **D** and made every Dn 6:14
and they brought **D** and threw him Dn 6:16
king said to **D**, "May your God, Dn 6:16
in regard to **D** could be changed. Dn 6:17
he cried out in anguish to **D**. Dn 6:20
"**D**, servant of the living God," Dn 6:20
Then **D** spoke with the king: Dn 6:21
orders to take **D** out of the den. Dn 6:23
So **D** was taken out of the den, Dn 6:23
accused **D** were brought Dn 6:24
in fear before the God of **D**: Dn 6:26
He has rescued **D** from the power Dn 6:27
So **D** prospered during the reign Dn 6:28
D had a dream with visions in Dn 7:1
D said, "In my vision at night I Dn 7:2
As for me, **D**, my spirit was Dn 7:15
As for me, **D**, my thoughts Dn 7:28
appeared to me, **D**, after the one Dn 8:1
While I, **D**, was watching the Dn 8:15
I, **D**, was overcome and lay sick Dn 8:27
of his reign, I, **D**, understood Dn 9:2
D, I've come now to give you Dn 9:22
a message was revealed to **D**, Dn 10:1
In those days I, **D**, was mourning Dn 10:2
Only I, **D**, saw the vision. Dn 10:7
He said to me, "**D**, you are a man Dn 10:11
be afraid, **D**," he said to me Dn 10:12
But you, **D**, keep these words Dn 12:4
I, **D**, looked, and two others Dn 12:5
Go on your way, **D**, for the words Dn 12:9
spoken of by the prophet **D**, Mt 24:15

DANIEL'S *(1)*
At **D** request, the king appointed Dn 2:49

DANITE *(5)*
came out for the **D** tribe by its Jos 19:40
of the **D** tribe by its clans Jos 19:48
and the **D** tribe was looking for Jdg 18:1
The 600 **D** men were standing by Jdg 18:16
priests for the **D** tribe until Jdg 18:30

DANITES *(12)*
leader of the **D** is Ahiezer son Nm 2:25
leader of the **D**, ⌊presented an Nm 7:66
territory of the **D** slipped out Jos 19:47
forced the **D** into the hill Jdg 1:34
So the **D** sent out five brave men Jdg 18:2
hundred **D** departed from Zorah Jdg 18:11
and caught up with the **D**. Jdg 18:22

called to the **D**, who turned to Jdg 18:23
The **D** said to him, "Don't raise Jdg 18:25
The **D** went on their way, and Jdg 18:26
D set up the carved image for Jdg 18:30
From the **D**: 28,600 trained for 1Ch 12:35

DANNAH *(1)*
D, Kiriath-sannah (that is, Debir) Jos 15:49

DAPPLED *(2)*
the fourth chariot **d** horses— Zch 6:3
the **d** horses are going to the Zch 6:6

DARA *(1)*
(AKA DARDA)
Calcol, and **D**—five in all. 1Ch 2:6

DARDA *(1)*
(AKA DARA)
Calcol, and **D**, sons of Mahol. 1Kg 4:31

DARE *(10)*
How **d** you prophesy in the name Jr 26:9
tremble and did not **d** to look. Ac 7:32
Do you **d** revile God's high Ac 23:4
someone might even **d** to die. Rm 5:7
For I would not **d** say anything Rm 15:18
against someone **d** go to law 1Co 6:1
For we don't **d** classify or 2Co 10:12
am talking foolishly—I also **d**: 2Co 11:21
imprisonment and **d** even more to Php 1:14
did not **d** bring an abusive Jd 9

DARED *(8)*
But they **d** to go up the ridge of Nm 14:44
because they **d** not be seen 2Sm 17:17
so that no one **d** to touch their Lm 4:14
that day no one **d** to question Mt 22:46
And no one **d** to question Him Mk 12:34
And they no longer **d** to ask Him Lk 20:40
None of the disciples **d** ask Him, Jn 21:12
None of the rest **d** to join them, Ac 5:13

DARES *(4)*
a lioness—who **d** to rouse him? Nm 24:9
the prophet who **d** to speak in My Dt 18:20
king or people who **d** to harm or Ezr 6:12
whatever anyone **d** ⌊to boast⌋— 2Co 11:21

DARIUS *(25)*
the reign of King **D** of Persia. Ezr 4:5
the reign of King **D** of Persia. Ezr 4:24
until a report was sent to **D**, Ezr 5:5
in the region, sent to King **D**. Ezr 5:6
To King **D**: All greetings. Ezr 5:7
King **D** gave the order, and they Ezr 6:1
I, **D**, have issued the decree. Ezr 6:12
out what King **D** had decreed. Ezr 6:13
decrees of Cyrus, **D**, and King Ezr 6:14
year of the reign of King **D**. Ezr 6:15
recorded while **D** the Persian Neh 12:22
and **D** the Mede received the Dn 5:31
D decided to appoint 120 satraps Dn 6:1
him, "May King **D** live forever. Dn 6:6
So King **D** signed the document. Dn 6:9
Then King **D** wrote to those of Dn 6:25
the reign of **D** and the reign Dn 6:28
first year of **D**, who was the son Dn 9:1
In the first year of **D** the Mede, Dn 11:1
In the second year of King **D**, Hg 1:1
in the second year of King **D**. Hg 1:15
the second year of **D**, the word Hg 2:10
the second year of **D**, the word Zch 1:1
the second year of **D**, the word Zch 1:7
In the fourth year of King **D**, Zch 7:1

DARK *(35)*
the sun had set and it was **d**, Gn 15:17
completely **d** sheep in Laban's Gn 30:40
as a blind man gropes in the **d**. Dt 28:29
but got up while it was still **d**. Ru 3:14
a **d** cloud beneath His feet. 2Sm 22:10
the sky grew **d** with clouds and 1Kg 18:45
May its morning stars grow **d**. Jb 3:9
The light in his tent grows **d**, Jb 18:6
In the **d** they break into houses; Jb 24:16
a **d** cloud beneath His feet. Ps 18:9
d storm clouds His canopy around Ps 18:11
Let their way be **d** and slippery, Ps 35:6
for the **d** places of the land are Ps 74:20
and it became **d**—for did they Ps 105:28
the darkness is not **d** to You. Ps 139:12
evening, in the **d** of the night. Pr 7:9
I am **d** like the tents of Kedar, Sg 1:5
not stare at me because I am **d**, Sg 1:6
The sun will be **d** when it rises, Is 13:10
shade that is as **d** as night. Is 16:3
All joy grows **d**; earth's Is 24:11
the skies above will grow **d**. Jr 4:28
and take ⌊them⌋ out in the **d**; Ezk 12:6
I took ⌊them⌋ out in the **d**, Ezk 12:7
shoulder in the **d** and go out. Ezk 12:12
day will be **d** in Tehaphnehes, Ezk 30:18
scattered on a cloudy and **d** day. Ezk 34:12
and moon grow **d**, and the stars Jl 2:10
The sun and moon will grow **d**, Jl 3:15
it will grow **d** for you—without Mc 3:6
tell you in the **d**, speak in the Mt 10:27
it was still **d**, He got up, went Mk 1:35
have said in the **d** will be heard Lk 12:3
early, while it was still **d**. Jn 20:1
are not in the **d**, so that this 1Th 5:4

DARK-COLORED *(2)*
every **d** sheep among the lambs, Gn 30:32
and every **d** sheep among the Gn 30:35

DARKEN *(3)*
the heavens and **d** their stars. Ezk 32:7
I will **d** all the shining lights Ezk 32:8
will **d** the land in the daytime. Am 8:9

DARKENED *(9)*
and become **d** because of ice, Jb 6:16
the sun and the light are **d**, Ec 12:2
The sun will be **d**, and the moon Mt 24:29
The sun will be **d**, and the moon Mk 13:24
their senseless minds were **d**. Rm 1:21
their eyes be **d** so they cannot Rm 11:10
They are **d** in their Eph 4:18
so that a third of them were **d**. Rv 8:12
and the air were **d** by the smoke Rv 9:2

DARKENS *(1)*
into dawn and **d** day into night, Am 5:8

DARKER *(2)*
eyes are **d** than wine, and his Gn 49:12
⌊Now⌋ they appear **d** than soot; Lm 4:8

DARKEST *(4)*
when I go through the **d** valley, Ps 23:4
of the Pit, in the **d** places, in Ps 88:6
the wicked is like the **d** gloom; Pr 4:19
but He brings **d** gloom and makes Jr 13:16

DARKNESS *(165)*
d covered the surface of the Gn 1:2
separated the light from the **d**. Gn 1:4
and He called the **d** "night." Gn 1:5
and to separate light from **d**. Gn 1:18
and great **d** descended on him Gn 15:12
there will be **d** over the land Ex 10:21
of Egypt, a **d** that can be felt. Ex 10:21
there was thick **d** throughout the Ex 10:22
The cloud was there ⌊in⌋ the **d**, Ex 14:20
the thick **d** where God was. Ex 20:21
and thick **d** on the mountain; Dt 5:22
the voice from the **d** and while Dt 5:23
so He put **d** between you and the Jos 24:7
the wicked are silenced in **d**, 1Sm 2:9
He made **d** a canopy around Him, 2Sm 22:12
the LORD illuminates my **d**. 2Sm 22:29
that He would dwell in thick **d**, 1Kg 8:12
said He would dwell in thick **d**, 2Ch 6:1
only that day had turned to **d**! Jb 3:4
May **d** and gloom reclaim it, Jb 3:5
If only **d** had taken that night Jb 3:6
encounter **d** by day, and they Jb 5:14
I go to a land of **d** and gloom, Jb 10:21
of blackness like the deepest **d**, Jb 10:22
even the light is like the **d**. Jb 10:22
⌊its⌋ **d** will be like the morning. Jb 11:17
mysteries from the **d** and brings Jb 12:22
the deepest **d** into the light. Jb 12:22
grope around in **d** without light; Jb 12:25
believe he will return from **d**; Jb 15:22
knows the day of **d** is at hand. Jb 15:23
He will not escape from the **d**; Jb 15:30
seem⌋ near in the face of **d**. Jb 17:12
my home, spread out my bed in **d**, Jb 17:13
from light to **d** and chased Jb 18:18
He has veiled my paths with **d**. Jb 19:8
Total **d** is reserved for his Jb 20:26
or **d**, so you cannot see, and a Jb 22:11
Can He judge through thick **d**? Jb 22:13
Yet I am not destroyed by the **d**, Jb 23:17
by the thick **d** that covers my Jb 23:17
boundary between light and **d**. Jb 26:10
A miner puts an end to the **d**; Jb 28:3
for ore in the gloomy **d**. Jb 28:3
I walked through **d** by His light! Jb 29:3
when I looked for light, **d** came. Jb 30:26
There is no **d**, no deep darkness, Jb 34:22
no deep **d**, where evildoers Jb 34:22
our case⌋ because of our **d**. Jb 37:19
garment and thick **d** its blanket, Jb 38:9
⌊Do you know⌋ where **d** lives, Jb 38:19
He made **d** His hiding place, Ps 18:11
my God illuminates my **d**. Ps 18:28
have covered us with deepest **d**. Ps 44:19
they wander in **d**. All the Ps 82:5
Your wonders be known in the **d**, Ps 88:12
d is my ⌊only⌋ friend. Ps 88:18
the plague that stalks in **d**, Ps 91:6
Clouds and thick **d** surround Him; Ps 97:2
You bring **d**, and it becomes Ps 104:20
He sent **d**, and it became dark— Ps 105:28
Others sat in **d** and gloom— Ps 107:10
them out of **d** and gloom and Ps 107:14
shines in the **d** for the upright. Ps 112:4
Surely the **d** will hide me, Ps 139:11
even the **d** is not dark to You. Ps 139:12
d and light are alike to You. Ps 139:12
me live in **d** like those long Ps 143:3
paths to walk in ways of **d**, Pr 2:13
his lamp will go out in deep **d**. Pr 20:20
the advantage of light over **d**. Ec 2:13
head, but the fool walks in **d**. Ec 2:14
he eats in **d** all his days, Ec 5:17
in futility and he goes in **d**, Ec 6:4
and his name is shrouded in **d**. Ec 6:4
let him remember the days of **d**, Ec 11:8
who substitute **d** for light and Is 5:20
for light and light for **d**, Is 5:20
there will be **d** and distress; Is 5:30
only distress, **d**, and the gloom Is 8:22
will be driven into thick **d**. Is 8:22
walking in **d** have seen a great Is 9:2
those living in the land of **d**, Is 9:2
⌊They do⌋ their works in **d**, Is 29:15
and out of a deep **d** the eyes of Is 29:18
sitting in **d** from the prison Is 42:7
I will turn **d** to light in front Is 42:16
the treasures of **d** and riches Is 45:3
I form light and create **d**, Is 45:7
somewhere in a land of **d**. Is 45:19
sit in silence and go into **d**. Is 47:5
and to those who are in **d**: Is 49:9
Who ⌊among you⌋ walks in **d**, Is 50:10
your light will shine in the **d**, Is 58:10
hope for light, but there is **d**; Is 59:9
look, **d** covers the earth, and Is 60:2
earth, and total **d** the peoples; Is 60:2
through a land of drought and **d**, Jr 2:6
to Israel or a land of dense **d**? Jr 2:31
your God before He brings **d**, Jr 13:16
darkest gloom and makes thick **d**. Jr 13:16
me⌋ to walk in **d** instead of Lm 3:2
made me dwell in **d** like those Lm 3:6
of Israel are doing in the **d**, Ezk 8:12
and will bring **d** on your land. Ezk 32:8
He knows what is in the **d**, Dn 2:22
a day of **d** and gloom, a day of Jl 2:2
be turned to **d** and the moon to Jl 2:31
the dawn out of **d** and strides Am 4:13
turns **d** into dawn and darkens Am 5:8
It will be **d** and not light. Am 5:18
of the LORD be **d** rather than Am 5:20
though I sit in **d**, the LORD will Mc 7:8
will chase His enemies into **d**. Nah 1:8
a day of **d** and gloom, a day Zph 1:15
who live in **d** have seen a great Mt 4:16
whole body will be full of **d**. Mt 6:23
if the light within you is **d**— Mt 6:23
darkness—how deep is that **d**! Mt 6:23
will be thrown into the outer **d**. Mt 8:12
and throw him into the outer **d**, Mt 22:13
slave into the outer **d**. Mt 25:30
in the afternoon **d** came over the Mt 27:45
d came over the whole land until Mk 15:33
who live in **d** and the shadow Lk 1:79
your body is also full of **d**. Lk 11:34
that the light in you is not **d**. Lk 11:35
part of it in **d**, the whole body Lk 11:36
hour—and the dominion of **d**." Lk 22:53

and **d** came over the whole land Lk 23:44
That light shines in the **d**, Jn 1:5
yet the **d** did not overcome it. Jn 1:5
and people loved **d** rather than Jn 3:19
D had already set in, but Jesus Jn 6:17
never walk in the **d** but will Jn 8:12
light so that **d** doesn't overtake Jn 12:35
one who walks in **d** doesn't know Jn 12:35
in Me would not remain in **d**. Jn 12:46
The sun will be turned to **d**, Ac 2:20
a mist and **d** fell on him, Ac 13:11
they may turn from **d** to light Ac 26:18
blind, a light to those in **d**, Rm 2:19
the deeds of **d** and put on the Rm 13:12
what is hidden in **d** and reveal 1Co 4:5
"Light shall shine out of **d**"— 2Co 4:6
does light have with **d**? 2Co 6:14
you were once **d**, but now ⌊you Eph 5:8
in the fruitless works of **d**, Eph 5:11
the world powers of this **d**, Eph 6:12
the domain of **d** and transferred Col 1:13
We're not of the night or of **d**. 1Th 5:5
blazing fire, to **d**, gloom, and Heb 12:18
called you out of **d** into His 1Pt 2:9
in chains of **d** until judgment; 2Pt 2:4
The gloom of **d** has been reserved 2Pt 2:17
there is absolutely no **d** in Him. 1Jn 1:5
Him," and walk in **d**, we are 1Jn 1:6
because the **d** is passing away 1Jn 2:8
brother is in the **d** until now. 1Jn 2:9
hates his brother is in the **d**, 1Jn 2:11
walks in the **d**, and doesn't know 1Jn 2:11
because the **d** has blinded his 1Jn 2:11
chains in **d** for the judgment Jd 6
the blackness of **d** forever! Jd 13
his kingdom was plunged into **d**. Rv 16:10

DARKON'S *(2)*
descendants, **D** descendants, Ezr 2:56
descendants, **D** descendants, Neh 7:58

DARLING *(9)*
compare you, my **d**, to a mare Sg 1:9
How beautiful you are, my **d**. Sg 1:15
is my **d** among the young women. Sg 2:2
me: Arise, my **d**. Come away, my Sg 2:10
Arise, my **d**. Come away, my Sg 2:13
How beautiful you are, my **d**. Sg 4:1
beautiful, my **d**, with no Sg 4:7
me, my sister, my **d**, my dove, my Sg 5:2
as Tirzah, my **d**, lovely as Sg 6:4

DART *(2)*
nor will a spear, **d**, or arrow. Jb 41:26
they **d** back and forth like Nah 2:4

DARTING *(2)*
like a bird **d** into a snare— Pr 7:23
creatures were **d** back and forth Ezk 1:14

DARTS *(1)*
throws flaming **d** and deadly Pr 26:18

DASH *(2)*
You will **d** their little ones to 2Kg 8:12
The chariots **d** madly through the Nah 2:4

DASHED *(4)*
all of them were **d** to pieces. 2Ch 25:12
Mothers will be **d** to pieces Hs 10:14
little ones will be **d** to pieces, Hs 13:16
children were also **d** to pieces Nah 3:10

DASHES *(1)*
little ones and **d** them against Ps 137:9

DATE *(6)*
springs of water and 70 **d** palms, Ex 15:27
of water and 70 **d** palms at Elim, Nm 33:9
loaf of bread, a **d** cake, and a 2Sm 6:19
loaf of bread, a **d** cake, and a 1Ch 16:3
down today's **d**, this very day. Ezk 24:2
pomegranate, the **d** palm, and the Jl 1:12

DATHAN *(10)*
of Levi, with **D** and Abiram, sons Nm 16:1
Moses sent for **D** and Abiram, Nm 16:12
of Korah, **D**, and Abiram." Nm 16:24
got up and went to **D** and Abiram, Nm 16:25
of Korah, **D**, and Abiram. Nm 16:27
D and Abiram came out and stood Nm 16:27
were Nemuel, **D**, and Abiram. Nm 26:9
It was **D** and Abiram, chosen by Nm 26:9
and what He did to **D** and Abiram, Dt 11:6
earth opened up and swallowed **D**; Ps 106:17

DAUGHTER *(279)*
She was the **d** of Haran, the Gn 11:29
d of my father though not the Gn 20:12
though not the **d** of my mother, Gn 20:12
d of Bethuel son of Milcah, Gn 24:15
"Whose **d** are you?" he asked. Gn 24:23
I am the **d** of Bethuel son of Gn 24:24
asked her: Whose **d** are you? She Gn 24:47
'The **d** of Bethuel son of Nahor, Gn 24:47
way to take the **d** of my master's Gn 24:48
as his wife Rebekah **d** of Bethuel Gn 25:20
as his wives Judith **d** of Beeri Gn 26:34
and Basemath **d** of Elon the Gn 26:34
wives, Mahalath **d** of Ishmael, Gn 28:9
and here is his **d** Rachel, Gn 29:6
uncle Laban's **d** Rachel with his Gn 29:10
for your younger **d** Rachel." Gn 29:18
Laban took his **d** Leah and gave Gn 29:23
Zilpah to his **d** Leah as her Gn 29:24
give the younger ⌊**d** in marriage⌋ Gn 29:26
gave him his **d** Rachel as his Gn 29:28
Bilhah to his **d** Rachel as her Gn 29:29
Leah bore a **d** and named her Gn 30:21
Leah's **d** whom she bore to Jacob, Gn 34:1
with Dinah, **d** of Jacob. Gn 34:3
Shechem had defiled his **d** Dinah, Gn 34:5
by sleeping with Jacob's **d**, Gn 34:7
is strongly attracted to your **d**. Gn 34:8
then we will take our **d** and go." Gn 34:17
he was delighted with Jacob's **d**. Gn 34:19
Adah **d** of Elon the Hittite, Gn 36:2
Oholibamah **d** of Anah and Gn 36:2
and Basemath **d** of Ishmael and Gn 36:3
Esau's wife Oholibamah **d** of Anah Gn 36:14
wife Oholibamah **d** of Anah. Gn 36:18
Dishon and Oholibamah **d** of Anah. Gn 36:25
was Mehetabel **d** of Matred Gn 36:39
of Matred **d** of Me-zahab. Gn 36:39
Judah saw the **d** of a Canaanite Gn 38:2
wife, the **d** of Shua, died. Gn 38:12
a wife, Asenath **d** of Potiphera, Gn 41:45
Asenath **d** of Potiphera, priest Gn 41:50
as well as his **d** Dinah. Gn 46:15
whom Laban gave to his **d** Leah— Gn 46:18
him by Asenath **d** of Potiphera, Gn 46:20
whom Laban gave to his **d** Rachel. Gn 46:25
but if it's a **d**, she may live." Ex 1:16
the Nile, but let every **d** live." Ex 1:22
Pharaoh's **d** went down to bathe Ex 2:5
his sister said to Pharaoh's **d**, Ex 2:7
Pharaoh's **d** told her. Ex 2:8
Then Pharaoh's **d** said to her, Ex 2:9
she brought him to Pharaoh's **d**, Ex 2:10
he gave his **d** Zipporah to Moses Ex 2:21
d of Amminadab and sister of Ex 6:23
you, your son or **d**, your male or Ex 20:10
a man sells his **d** as a slave, Ex 21:7
gores a son or a **d**, he is to be Ex 21:31
for a son or **d**, she is to bring Lv 12:6
father's **d** or your mother's, Lv 18:9
with your son's **d** or your Lv 18:10
daughter or your daughter's **d**, Lv 18:10
with your father's wife's **d**, Lv 18:11
with a woman and her **d**. Lv 18:17
marry her son's **d** or her Lv 18:17
her daughter's **d** and have sex Lv 18:17
not debase your **d** by making her Lv 19:29
his father's **d** or his mother's Lv 20:17
daughter or his mother's **d**, Lv 20:17
father, son, **d**, or brother. Lv 21:2
If a priest's **d** defiles herself Lv 21:9
If the priest's **d** is married to Lv 22:12
the priest's **d** becomes widowed Lv 22:13
d of Dibri of the tribe of Dan. Lv 24:11
Cozbi, the **d** of Zur, a tribal Nm 25:15
d of the Midianite leader who Nm 25:18
the name of Asher's **d** was Serah. Nm 26:46
his inheritance to his **d**. Nm 27:8
If he has no **d**, give his Nm 27:9
a father and his **d** in his house Nm 30:16
Any **d** who possesses an Nm 36:8
you, your son or **d**, your male or Dt 5:14
you, your son and **d**, your male Dt 12:18
your son or **d**, or the wife you Dt 13:6
you, your son and **d**, your male Dt 16:11
you, your son and **d**, your male Dt 16:14
make his son or **d** pass through Dt 18:10
'I gave my **d** to this man as a Dt 22:16
his father's **d** or his mother's Dt 27:22
daughter or his mother's **d**.' Dt 27:22
embraces, her son, and her **d**, Dt 28:56
I will give my **d** Achsah as a Jos 15:16
Caleb gave his **d** Achsah to him Jos 15:17
will give my **d** Achsah to him as Jdg 1:12
Caleb gave his **d** Achsah to him Jdg 1:13
there was his **d**, coming out to Jdg 11:34
no other son or **d** besides her. Jdg 11:34
said, "No! ⌊Not⌋ my **d**! You have Jdg 11:35
commemorate the **d** of Jephthah Jdg 11:40
out my virgin **d** and the man's Jdg 19:24
will give his **d** to a Benjaminite Jdg 21:1
answered her, "Go ahead, my **d**." Ru 2:2
said to Ruth, "Listen, my **d**. Ru 2:8
Ruth, "My **d**, it is good for you Ru 2:22
said to her, "My **d**, shouldn't I Ru 3:1
May the LORD bless you, my **d**. Ru 3:10
Now don't be afraid, my **d**. Ru 3:11
her⌋, "How did it go, my **d**?" Ru 3:16
"Wait, my **d**," she said, "until Ru 3:18
wife was Ahinoam **d** of Ahimaaz. 1Sm 14:50
rich and will give him his **d**. 1Sm 17:25
Here is my oldest **d** Merab. 1Sm 18:17
to give Saul's **d** Merab to David, 1Sm 18:19
Saul's **d** Michal loved David, 1Sm 18:20
Saul gave his **d** Michal to David 1Sm 18:27
and that his **d** Michal loved him 1Sm 18:28
But Saul gave his **d** Michal, 1Sm 25:44
of Maacah the **d** of King Talmai 2Sm 3:3
whose name was Rizpah **d** of Aiah, 2Sm 3:7
bring Saul's **d** Michal here when 2Sm 3:13
Saul's **d** Michal looked down from 2Sm 6:16
Saul's **d** Michal came out to meet 2Sm 6:20
And Saul's **d** Michal had no child 2Sm 6:23
d of Eliam and wife of Uriah the 2Sm 11:3
and it was like a **d** to him. 2Sm 12:3
Absalom, and a **d** named Tamar, 2Sm 14:27
had married Abigail **d** of Nahash. 2Sm 17:25
sons whom Rizpah **d** of Aiah had 2Sm 21:8
sons whom Merab **d** of Saul had 2Sm 21:8
Rizpah, Aiah's **d**, took sackcloth 2Sm 21:10
Rizpah, **d** of Aiah, had done 2Sm 21:11
Egypt by marrying Pharaoh's **d**. 1Kg 3:1
Taphath **d** of Solomon was his 1Kg 4:11
had married a **d** of Solomon— 1Kg 4:15
like this hall for Pharaoh's **d**, 1Kg 7:8
and gave it as a dowry to his **d**, 1Kg 9:16
Pharaoh's **d** moved from the city 1Kg 9:24
in addition to Pharaoh's **d**: 1Kg 11:1
name was Maacah **d** of Abishalom. 1Kg 15:2
was Maacah **d** of Abishalom. 1Kg 15:10
the **d** of Ethbaal king of the 1Kg 16:31
name was Azubah **d** of Shilhi. 1Kg 22:42
for Ahab's **d** was his wife. 2Kg 8:18
her, since she's a king's **d**." 2Kg 9:34
King Jehoram's **d** and Ahaziah's 2Kg 11:2
'Give your **d** to my son as a wife. 2Kg 14:9
name was Jerusha **d** of Zadok. 2Kg 15:33
name was Abi **d** of Zechariah. 2Kg 18:2
young woman, **D** Zion, despises 2Kg 19:21
D Jerusalem shakes ⌊her⌋ head 2Kg 19:21
was Meshullemeth **d** of Haruz; 2Kg 21:19
was Jedidah the **d** of Adaiah; 2Kg 22:1
his son or his **d** pass through 2Kg 23:10
name was Hamutal **d** of Jeremiah; 2Kg 23:31
name was Zebidah **d** of Pedaiah; 2Kg 23:36
name was Nehushta **d** of Elnathan; 2Kg 24:8
name was Hamutal **d** of Jeremiah; 2Kg 24:18
name was Mehetabel **d** of Matred, 1Ch 1:50
of Matred, **d** of Me-zahab. 1Ch 1:50
slept with the **d** of Machir the 1Ch 2:21
Sheshan gave his **d** in marriage 1Ch 2:35
Caleb's **d** was Achsah. 1Ch 2:49
d of King Talmai of Geshur, 1Ch 3:2
him⌋ by Bath-shua **d** of Ammiel. 1Ch 3:5
the sons of Pharaoh's **d** Bithiah; 1Ch 4:18
His **d** was Sheerah, who built 1Ch 7:24
Saul's **d** Michal looked down 1Ch 15:29
Solomon brought the **d** of Pharaoh 2Ch 8:11
d of David's son Jerimoth and of 2Ch 11:18
and of Abihail **d** of Jesse's son 2Ch 11:18
he married Maacah **d** of Absalom. 2Ch 11:20
loved Maacah **d** of Absalom more 2Ch 11:21
name was Micaiah **d** of Uriel; 2Ch 13:2
name was Azubah **d** of Shilhi. 2Ch 20:31
for Ahab's **d** was his wife. 2Ch 21:6
the king's **d**, rescued Joash son 2Ch 22:11

was the **d** of King Jehoram 2Ch 22:11
'Give your **d** to my son as a wife. 2Ch 25:18
name was Jerushah **d** of Zadok. 2Ch 27:1
name was Abijah **d** of Zechariah. 2Ch 29:1
had married the **d** of Meshullam Neh 6:18
had adopted her as his own **d**. Est 2:7
Esther was the **d** of Abihail, Est 2:15
had adopted ⌊her⌋ as his own **d**. Est 2:15
Queen Esther **d** of Abihail, Est 9:29
He named his first ⌊**d**⌋ Jemimah, Jb 42:14
within the gates of **D** Zion. Ps 9:14
Listen, **d**, pay attention and Ps 45:10
The **d** of Tyre, the wealthy Ps 45:12
the royal **d** is all glorious, Ps 45:13
D Babylon, doomed to destruction, Ps 137:8
D Zion is abandoned like a Is 1:8
Cry aloud, **d** of Gallim! Is 10:30
fist at the mountain of **D** Zion, Is 10:32
to the mountain of **D** Zion. Is 16:1
like the Nile, **d** of Tarshish; Is 23:10
young woman, **d** of Sidon. Is 23:12
young woman, **D** Zion, despises Is 37:22
D Jerusalem shakes ⌊her⌋ head Is 37:22
in the dust, Virgin **D** Babylon. Is 47:1
without a throne, **D** Chaldea! Is 47:1
D Chaldea, sit in silence and go Is 47:5
from your neck, captive **D** Zion." Is 52:2
of the earth, "Say to **D** Zion: Is 62:11
The cry of **D** Zion gasping for Jr 4:31
delicate, I will destroy **D** Zion. Jr 6:2
formation against you, **D** Zion. Jr 6:23
the virgin **d** of my people has Jr 14:17
here and there, faithless **d**? Jr 31:22
and get balm, Virgin **D** Egypt! Jr 46:11
exile, inhabitant of **D** Egypt! Jr 46:19
D Egypt will be put to shame, Jr 46:24
resident of the **d** of Dibon, Jr 48:18
flowing valley, you faithless **d**? Jr 49:4
against you, **D** of Babylon. Jr 50:42
The **d** of Babylon is like a Jr 51:33
name was Hamutal **d** of Jeremiah; Jr 52:1
has vanished from **D** Zion. Lm 1:6
trampled Virgin **D** Judah ⌊like Lm 1:15
has overshadowed **D** Zion with His Lm 2:1
the fortified cities of **D** Judah. Lm 2:2
like fire on the tent of **D** Zion. Lm 2:4
and lamentation within **D** Judah. Lm 2:5
to destroy the wall of **D** Zion. Lm 2:8
The elders of **D** Zion sit on the Lm 2:10
can I compare you, **D** Jerusalem? Lm 2:13
may console you, Virgin **D** Zion? Lm 2:13
their heads at **D** Jerusalem: Lm 2:15
Wall of **D** Zion, let ⌊your⌋ tears Lm 2:18
be glad, **D** Edom, you resident Lm 4:21
D Zion, your punishment is Lm 4:22
your iniquity, **D** Edom, and will Lm 4:22
not deliver ⌊their⌋ son or **d**. Ezk 14:20
Like mother, like **d**. Ezk 16:44
You are the **d** of your mother, Ezk 16:45
his sister, his father's **d**. Ezk 22:11
a mother, a son, a **d**, a brother, Ezk 44:25
and the **d** of the king of the Dn 11:6
will give him a **d** in marriage to Dn 11:17
and married Gomer **d** of Diblaim, Hs 1:3
again and gave birth to a **d**, Hs 1:6
the beginning of sin for **D** Zion, Mc 1:13
hill of **D** Zion, the former Mc 4:8
will come to **D** Jerusalem. Mc 4:8
and cry out, **D** Zion, like a Mc 4:10
and thresh, **D** Zion, for I will Mc 4:13
Now **d** ⌊who is⌋ under attack, Mc 5:1
father a fool, a **d** opposes her Mc 7:6
Sing for joy, **D** Zion; Zph 3:14
all ⌊your⌋ heart, **D** Jerusalem! Zph 3:14
who are living with **D** Babylon." Zch 2:7
D Zion, shout for joy and be Zch 2:10
Rejoice greatly, **D** Zion! Zch 9:9
Shout in triumph, **D** Jerusalem! Zch 9:9
has married the **d** of a foreign Mal 2:11
saying, "My **d** is near death, Mt 9:18
"Have courage, **d**," He said. Mt 9:22
his father, a **d** against her Mt 10:35
loves son or **d** more than Me is Mt 10:37
Herodias' **d** danced before them Mt 14:6
d is cruelly tormented by a demon. Mt 15:22
that moment her **d** was cured. Mt 15:28
Tell **D** Zion, "See, your King is Mt 21:5
My little **d** is at death's door. Mk 5:23
"**D**," He said to her, "your faith Mk 5:34
house and said, "Your **d** is dead. Mk 5:35
Herodias' own **d** came in and Mk 6:22
whose little **d** had an unclean Mk 7:25
to drive the demon out of her **d**. Mk 7:26
demon has gone out of your **d**." Mk 7:29
Anna, a **d** of Phanuel, Lk 2:36
he had an only **d** about 12 years Lk 8:42
"**D**," He said to her, "your faith Lk 8:48
house⌋, saying, "Your **d** is dead. Lk 8:49
mother against **d**, daughter Lk 12:53
daughter, **d** against mother, Lk 12:53
this woman, a **d** of Abraham, for Lk 13:16
Fear no more, **D** Zion; Jn 12:15
Pharaoh's **d** adopted and raised Ac 7:21
be called the son of Pharaoh's **d** Heb 11:24

DAUGHTER'S *(4)*

daughter or your **d** daughter, Lv 18:10
daughter or her **d** daughter and Lv 18:17
evidence of your **d** virginity, Dt 22:17
the evidence of my **d** virginity.' Dt 22:17

DAUGHTER-IN-LAW *(17)*

son), and his **d** Sarai, his son Gn 11:31
Then Judah said to his **d** Tamar, Gn 38:11
did not know that she was his **d**. Gn 38:16
Your **d** has been acting like a Gn 38:24
sexual intercourse with your **d**. Lv 18:15
If a man sleeps with his **d**, Lv 20:12
of Moab with her **d** Ruth the Ru 1:22
Then Naomi said to her **d**, Ru 2:20
So Naomi said to her **d** Ruth, Ru 2:22
Indeed, your **d**, who loves you Ru 4:15
Eli's **d**, the wife of Phinehas, 1Sm 4:19
Judah's **d** Tamar bore him Perez 1Ch 2:4
another wickedly defiles his **d**; Ezk 22:11
and a **d** is against her Mc 7:6
a **d** against her mother-in-law; Mt 10:35
mother-in-law against her **d**, Lk 12:53
and **d** against mother-in-law." Lk 12:53

DAUGHTERS *(211)*

and he fathered sons and **d**. Gn 5:4
and he fathered sons and **d**. Gn 5:7
and he fathered sons and **d**. Gn 5:10
and he fathered sons and **d**. Gn 5:13
and he fathered sons and **d**. Gn 5:16
and he fathered sons and **d**. Gn 5:19
years and fathered sons and **d**. Gn 5:22
and he fathered sons and **d**. Gn 5:26
and he fathered sons and **d**. Gn 5:30
on the earth and **d** were born to Gn 6:1
God saw that the **d** of man were Gn 6:2
of God came to the **d** of man, Gn 6:4
and fathered ⌊other⌋ sons and **d**. Gn 11:11
and fathered ⌊other⌋ sons and **d**. Gn 11:13
and fathered ⌊other⌋ sons and **d**. Gn 11:15
and fathered ⌊other⌋ sons and **d**. Gn 11:17
and fathered ⌊other⌋ sons and **d**. Gn 11:19
and fathered ⌊other⌋ sons and **d**. Gn 11:21
and fathered ⌊other⌋ sons and **d**. Gn 11:23
and fathered ⌊other⌋ sons and **d**. Gn 11:25
I've got two **d** who haven't had Gn 19:8
your sons and **d**, or anyone else Gn 19:12
who were going to marry his **d**. Gn 19:14
and your two **d** who are here, Gn 19:15
and the hands of his two **d**. Gn 19:16
mountains along with his two **d**, Gn 19:30
and his two **d** lived in a cave. Gn 19:30
both of Lot's **d** became pregnant Gn 19:36
my son from the **d** of the Gn 24:3
spring where the **d** of the men Gn 24:13
my son from the **d** of the Gn 24:37
Marry one of the **d** of Laban, Gn 28:2
Now Laban had two **d**: Gn 29:16
me and taken my **d** away like Gn 31:26
kiss my grandchildren and my **d**. Gn 31:28
would take your **d** from me by Gn 31:31
for your two **d** and six years for Gn 31:41
Jacob, "The **d** are my daughters; Gn 31:43
Jacob, "The daughters are my **d**; Gn 31:43
today for these **d** of mine or for Gn 31:43
you mistreat my **d** or take other Gn 31:50
kissed his grandsons and **d**, Gn 31:55
give your **d** to us, and take our Gn 34:9
and take our **d** for yourselves. Gn 34:9
Then we will give you our **d**, Gn 34:16
take your **d** for ourselves, Gn 34:16
Let us take their **d** as our wives Gn 34:21
wives and give our **d** to them. Gn 34:21
his wives, sons, **d**, and all the Gn 36:6
his sons and **d** tried to comfort Gn 37:35
grandsons, his **d** and Gn 46:7
priest of Midian had seven **d**. Ex 2:16
he asked his **d**. Ex 2:20
put them on your sons and **d**. Ex 3:22
one of the **d** of Putiel and she Ex 6:25
with our sons and **d** and with our Ex 10:9
and she bears him sons or **d**, Ex 21:4
to the customary treatment of **d**. Ex 21:9
your **d** and bring ⌊them⌋ to me. Ex 32:2
some of their **d** ⌊as brides⌋ for Ex 34:16
Their **d** will prostitute Ex 34:16
sons and your **d** may eat the Lv 10:14
will eat the flesh of your **d**. Lv 26:29
your sons and **d** as a perpetual Nm 18:11
to your sons and **d** all the holy Nm 18:19
his **d** into captivity to Sihon Nm 21:29
of Hepher had no sons—only **d**. Nm 26:33
of Zelophehad's **d** were Mahlah, Nm 26:33
The **d** of Zelophehad approached; Nm 27:1
These were the names of his **d**: Nm 27:1
Zelophehad's **d** say is correct. Nm 27:7
inheritance to his **d**. Nm 36:2
concerning Zelophehad's **d**: Nm 36:6
The **d** of Zelophehad did as the Nm 36:10
and Noah, the **d** of Zelophehad, Nm 36:11
Do not give your **d** to their sons Dt 7:3
or take their **d** for your sons, Dt 7:3
you, your sons and **d**, your male Dt 12:12
their sons and **d** in the fire to Dt 12:31
Your sons and **d** will be given to Dt 28:32
You will father sons and **d**, Dt 28:41
of your sons and **d** the LORD your Dt 28:53
to anger⌋ by His sons and **d**. Dt 32:19
his sons and **d**, his ox, donkey, Jos 7:24
Manasseh, had no sons, only **d**. Jos 17:3
These are the names of his **d**: Jos 17:3
because Manasseh's **d** received an Jos 17:6
took their **d** as wives for Jdg 3:6
gave their own **d** to their sons, Jdg 3:6
He gave his 30 **d** in marriage ⌊to Jdg 12:9
them any of our **d** as wives." Jdg 21:7
can't give them our **d** as wives." Jdg 21:18
replied, "Return home, my **d**. Ru 1:11
Return home, my **d**. Ru 1:12
No, my **d**, ⌊my life⌋ is much too Ru 1:13
and to each of her sons and **d**. 1Sm 1:4
birth to three sons and two **d**. 1Sm 2:21
He can take your **d** to become 1Sm 8:13
The names of his two **d** were: 1Sm 14:49
wives, sons, and **d** had been 1Sm 30:3
the loss of⌋ their sons and **d**. 1Sm 30:6
the sons and **d**, of all the 1Sm 30:19
or the **d** of the Philistines will 2Sm 1:20
and the **d** of the uncircumcised 2Sm 1:20
D of Israel, weep for Saul, who 2Sm 1:24
more sons and **d** were born to him 2Sm 5:13
what the king's virgin **d** wore. 2Sm 13:18
the lives of your sons and **d**, 2Sm 19:5
their sons and **d** pass through 2Kg 17:17
no sons, only **d**, but he did have 1Ch 2:34
Shimei had 16 sons and six **d**, 1Ch 4:27
Zelophehad, but he had only **d**. 1Ch 7:15
the father of more sons and **d**. 1Ch 14:3
died having no sons, only **d**. 1Ch 23:22
Heman fourteen sons and three **d**. 1Ch 25:5
of a woman from the **d** of Dan. 2Ch 2:14
the father of 28 sons and 60 **d**. 2Ch 11:21
and fathered 22 sons and 16 **d**. 2Ch 13:21
he was the father of sons and **d**. 2Ch 24:3
brothers—women, sons, and **d**. 2Ch 28:8
our sons, our **d**, and our wives 2Ch 29:9
wives, sons, and **d**—of the 2Ch 31:18
a wife from the **d** of Barzillai Ezr 2:61
some of their **d** as wives for Ezr 9:2
do not give your **d** to their sons Ezr 9:12
or take their **d** for your sons. Ezr 9:12
made repairs—he and his **d**. Neh 3:12
your sons and **d**, your wives and Neh 4:14
sons, and our **d** are numerous. Neh 5:2
our sons and **d** to slavery. Neh 5:5
Some of our **d** are already Neh 5:5
a wife from the **d** of Barzillai Neh 7:63
sons, and **d**, everyone who is Neh 10:28
not give our **d** in marriage to Neh 10:30
take their **d** as wives for our Neh 10:30
not give your **d** in marriage to Neh 13:25

or take their **d** as wives for Neh 13:25
He had seven sons and three **d**. Jb 1:2
Job's sons and **d** were eating Jb 1:13
Your sons and **d** were eating and Jb 1:18
also had seven sons and three **d**. Jb 42:13
as Job's **d** could be found Jb 42:15
Kings' **d** are among your honored Ps 45:9
their sons and **d** to demons. Ps 106:37
of their sons and **d** whom they Ps 106:38
their youth, our **d**, like corner Ps 144:12
The leech has two **d**: Pr 30:15
all the **d** of song grow faint. Ec 12:4
D of Jerusalem, I am dark like Sg 1:5
Because the **d** of Zion are Is 3:16
on the heads of the **d** of Zion, Is 3:17
the filth of the **d** of Zion and Is 4:4
the **d** of Moab will be at the Is 16:2
what I say, you overconfident **d**. Is 32:9
and My **d** from the ends of the Is 43:6
and your **d** will be carried on Is 49:22
a name better than sons and **d**. Is 56:5
your **d** will be carried on the Is 60:4
herds, their sons and their **d**. Jr 3:24
consume your sons and your **d**. Jr 5:17
their sons and **d** in the fire, Jr 7:31
Teach your **d** a lament and one Jr 9:20
their sons and **d** will die by Jr 11:22
wives, their sons, and their **d**. Jr 14:16
or have sons or **d** in this place. Jr 16:2
sons and **d** born in this place Jr 16:3
flesh of their sons and their **d**, Jr 19:9
Take wives and have sons and **d**. Jr 29:6
sons and give your **d** to men ⌊in Jr 29:6
that they may bear sons and **d**. Jr 29:6
their sons and **d** pass through Jr 32:35
our wives, our sons, and our **d**. Jr 35:8
including the **d** of the king— Jr 41:10
children, king's **d**, and everyone Jr 43:6
captive and your **d** have gone Jr 48:46
cry out, **d** of Rabbah! Jr 49:3
not deliver ⌊their⌋ sons or **d**. Ezk 14:16
not deliver ⌊their⌋ sons or **d**, Ezk 14:18
sons and **d** who will be brought Ezk 14:22
your sons and **d** you bore to Me Ezk 16:20
lived with her **d** to the north Ezk 16:46
lived with her **d** to the south Ezk 16:46
Sodom and her **d** have not Ezk 16:48
behaved as you and your **d** have. Ezk 16:48
she and her **d** had pride, plenty Ezk 16:49
of Sodom and her **d** and those of Ezk 16:53
and those of Samaria and her **d**. Ezk 16:53
Sodom and her **d** and Samaria and Ezk 16:55
Samaria and her **d** will return to Ezk 16:55
You and your **d** will also return Ezk 16:55
scorned by the **d** of Aram and all Ezk 16:57
by the **d** of the Philistines— Ezk 16:57
I will give them to you as **d**, Ezk 16:61
were two women, **d** of the same Ezk 23:2
and gave birth to sons and **d**. Ezk 23:4
her sons and **d**, and killed her Ezk 23:10
They will seize your sons and **d**, Ezk 23:25
their sons and **d** and burn their Ezk 23:47
the sons and **d** you left behind Ezk 24:21
⌊as well as⌋ their sons and **d**, Ezk 24:25
and the **d** of mighty nations Ezk 32:18
And so your **d** act promiscuously Hs 4:13
not punish your **d** when they act Hs 4:14
sons and your **d** will prophesy, Jl 2:28
your sons and **d** into the hands Jl 3:8
your sons and **d** will fall by the Am 7:17
wife was from the **d** of Aaron, Lk 1:5
Jesus said, "**D** of Jerusalem, do Lk 23:28
sons and your **d** will prophesy, Ac 2:17
four virgin **d** who prophesied. Ac 21:9
you will be sons and **d** to Me, 2Co 6:18

DAUGHTERS-IN-LAW *(4)*

She and her **d** prepared to leave Ru 1:6
by her two **d**, and traveled along Ru 1:7
and your **d** commit adultery. Hs 4:13
or your **d** when they commit Hs 4:14

DAVID *(949)*

of Jesse, the father of **D**. Ru 4:17
fathered Jesse, who fathered **D**. Ru 4:22
took control of **D** from that day 1Sm 16:13
Send me your son **D**, who is with 1Sm 16:19
sent them by his son **D** to Saul. 1Sm 16:20
When **D** came to Saul and entered 1Sm 16:21
and **D** became his armor-bearer. 1Sm 16:21
Let **D** remain in my service, 1Sm 16:22
D would pick up his harp and 1Sm 16:23
Now **D** was the son of the 1Sm 17:12
and **D** was the youngest. 1Sm 17:14
but **D** kept going back and forth 1Sm 17:15
Jesse had told his son **D**, 1Sm 17:17
D got up early in the morning, 1Sm 17:20
D left his supplies in the care 1Sm 17:22
his usual words, which **D** heard. 1Sm 17:23
D spoke to the men who were 1Sm 17:26
now?" protested **D**. "It was just 1Sm 17:29
What **D** said was overheard and 1Sm 17:31
so he had **D** brought to him. 1Sm 17:31
D said to Saul, "Don't let 1Sm 17:32
D answered Saul, "Your servant 1Sm 17:34
Then **D** said, "The LORD who 1Sm 17:37
Saul said to **D**, "Go, and may 1Sm 17:37
own military clothes put on **D**. 1Sm 17:38
D strapped his sword on over the 1Sm 17:39
walk in these," **D** said to Saul, 1Sm 17:39
to them." So **D** took them off. 1Sm 17:39
came closer and closer to **D**, 1Sm 17:41
the Philistine looked and saw **D**, 1Sm 17:42
He said to **D**, "Am I a dog that 1Sm 17:43
Then he cursed **D** by his gods. 1Sm 17:43
the Philistine called to **D**, 1Sm 17:44
D said to the Philistine, 1Sm 17:45
D ran quickly to the battle line 1Sm 17:48
D put his hand in the bag, 1Sm 17:49
D defeated the Philistine with a 1Sm 17:50
Even though **D** had no sword, 1Sm 17:50
D ran and stood over him. 1Sm 17:51
D took Goliath's head and 1Sm 17:54
When Saul had seen **D** going out 1Sm 17:55
When **D** returned from killing the 1Sm 17:57
Jesse of Bethlehem," **D** answered. 1Sm 17:58
D had finished speaking with 1Sm 18:1
Jonathan committed himself to **D**, 1Sm 18:1
Saul kept **D** with him from that 1Sm 18:2
a covenant with **D** because he 1Sm 18:3
he was wearing and gave it to **D**, 1Sm 18:4
D marched out ⌊with the army⌋, 1Sm 18:5
As **D** was returning from killing 1Sm 18:6
but **D** his tens of thousands. 1Sm 18:7
tens of thousands to **D**," 1Sm 18:8
So Saul watched **D** jealously from 1Sm 18:9
D was playing ⌊the harp⌋ as 1Sm 18:10
I'll pin **D** to the wall." 1Sm 18:11
But **D** got away from him twice. 1Sm 18:11
was afraid of **D**, because the 1Sm 18:12
the LORD was with **D** but had left 1Sm 18:12
Saul reassigned **D** and made him 1Sm 18:13
over 1,000 men. **D** led the troops 1Sm 18:13
Saul observed that **D** was very 1Sm 18:15
Judah loved **D** because he was 1Sm 18:16
Saul told **D**, "Here is my oldest 1Sm 18:17
Then **D** responded, "Who am I, 1Sm 18:18
give Saul's daughter Merab to **D**, 1Sm 18:19
Saul's daughter Michal loved **D**, 1Sm 18:20
So Saul said to **D** a second time, 1Sm 18:21
Speak to **D** in private and tell 1Sm 18:22
these words directly to **D**, 1Sm 18:23
"These are the words **D** spoke." 1Sm 18:24
Saul replied, "Say this to **D**: 1Sm 18:25
reported these terms to **D**, 1Sm 18:26
D and his men went out and 1Sm 18:27
Michal to **D** as his wife. 1Sm 18:27
the LORD was with **D** and that his 1Sm 18:28
he became even more afraid of **D**. 1Sm 18:29
D was more successful than all 1Sm 18:30
and all his servants to kill **D**. 1Sm 19:1
son Jonathan liked **D** very much, 1Sm 19:1
spoke well of **D** to his father 1Sm 19:4
not sin against his servant **D**. 1Sm 19:4
by killing **D** for no reason?" 1Sm 19:5
the LORD lives, **D** will not be 1Sm 19:6
summoned **D** and told him all 1Sm 19:7
Then Jonathan brought **D** to Saul, 1Sm 19:7
D went out and fought against 1Sm 19:8
D was playing ⌊the harp⌋, 1Sm 19:9
tried to pin **D** to the wall with 1Sm 19:10
D eluded Saul and escaped. 1Sm 19:10
But his wife Michal warned **D**: 1Sm 19:11
she lowered **D** from the window, 1Sm 19:12
Saul sent agents to seize **D**, 1Sm 19:14
agents ⌊back⌋ to see **D** and said, 1Sm 19:15
D fled and escaped and went to 1Sm 19:18
to Saul that **D** was at Naioth 1Sm 19:19
Saul sent agents to seize **D**. 1Sm 19:20
"Where are Samuel and **D**?" 1Sm 19:22
D fled from Naioth in Ramah and 1Sm 20:1
But **D** said, "Your father 1Sm 20:3
D also swore, "As surely as 1Sm 20:3
Jonathan said to **D**, "Whatever 1Sm 20:4
D told him, "Look, tomorrow is 1Sm 20:5
'**D** urgently requested my 1Sm 20:6
So **D** asked Jonathan, "Who will 1Sm 20:10
answered **D**, "Come on, let's go 1Sm 20:11
a covenant with the house of **D**, 1Sm 20:16
again swore to **D** in his love for 1Sm 20:17
So **D** hid in the field. 1Sm 20:24
D asked for my permission to go 1Sm 20:28
father was determined to kill **D**. 1Sm 20:33
shameful behavior toward **D**. 1Sm 20:34
the appointed meeting with **D**. 1Sm 20:35
only Jonathan and **D** knew the 1Sm 20:39
D got up from the south side of 1Sm 20:41
each other, though **D** wept more. 1Sm 20:41
then said to **D**, "Go in the 1Sm 20:42
Then **D** left, and Jonathan went 1Sm 20:42
D went to Ahimelech the priest 1Sm 21:1
Ahimelech was afraid to meet **D**, 1Sm 21:1
D answered Ahimelech the priest, 1Sm 21:2
D answered him, "I swear that 1Sm 21:5
D said to Ahimelech, "Do you 1Sm 21:8
none like it!" **D** said. "Give it 1Sm 21:9
D fled that day from Saul's 1Sm 21:10
to him, "Isn't this **D**, the king 1Sm 21:11
but **D** his tens of thousands?" 1Sm 21:11
D took this to heart and became 1Sm 21:12
D left Gath and took refuge in 1Sm 22:1
From there **D** went to Mizpeh of 1Sm 22:3
him the whole time **D** was in the 1Sm 22:4
Then the prophet Gad said to **D**, 1Sm 22:5
So **D** left and went to the 1Sm 22:5
Saul heard that **D** and his men 1Sm 22:6
servants is as faithful as **D**? 1Sm 22:14
LORD because they sided with **D**. 1Sm 22:17
was Abiathar, and he fled to **D**. 1Sm 22:20
Abiathar told **D** that Saul had 1Sm 22:21
Then **D** said to Abiathar, "I knew 1Sm 22:22
It was reported to **D**: 1Sm 23:1
So **D** inquired of the LORD: 1Sm 23:2
The LORD answered **D**, "Launch 1Sm 23:2
Once again, **D** inquired of the 1Sm 23:4
Then **D** and his men went to 1Sm 23:5
So **D** rescued the inhabitants of 1Sm 23:5
Ahimelech fled to **D** at Keilah, 1Sm 23:6
to Saul that **D** had gone to 1Sm 23:7
and besiege **D** and his men. 1Sm 23:8
When **D** learned that Saul was 1Sm 23:9
D said, "LORD God of Israel, 1Sm 23:10
Then **D** asked, "Will the citizens 1Sm 23:12
D and his men, numbering about 1Sm 23:13
to Saul that **D** had escaped 1Sm 23:13
D then stayed in the wilderness 1Sm 23:14
God did not hand **D** over to him. 1Sm 23:14
D was in the Wilderness of Ziph 1Sm 23:15
Jonathan came to **D** in Horesh 1Sm 23:16
D remained in Horesh, 1Sm 23:18
D is hiding among us in the 1Sm 23:19
Now **D** and his men were in the 1Sm 23:24
D was told about it, he went 1Sm 23:25
of this and pursued **D** there. 1Sm 23:25
mountain and **D** and his men 1Sm 23:26
Even though **D** was hurrying to 1Sm 23:26
closing in on **D** and his men to 1Sm 23:26
his pursuit of **D** and went to 1Sm 23:28
From there **D** went up and stayed 1Sm 23:29
D is in the wilderness near 1Sm 24:1
went to look for **D** and his men 1Sm 24:2
D and his men were staying in 1Sm 24:3
Then **D** got up and secretly cut 1Sm 24:4
With these words **D** persuaded his 1Sm 24:7
After that, **D** got up, went out 1Sm 24:8
D bowed to the ground in homage. 1Sm 24:8
D said to Saul, "Why do you 1Sm 24:9
say, 'Look, **D** intends to harm 1Sm 24:9
When **D** finished saying these 1Sm 24:16
Is that your voice, **D** my son?" 1Sm 24:16
and said to **D**, "You are more 1Sm 24:17
So **D** swore to Saul. Then Saul 1Sm 24:22
and **D** and his men went up to the 1Sm 24:22
D then went down to the 1Sm 25:1
While **D** was in the wilderness, 1Sm 25:4
so **D** sent 10 young men 1Sm 25:5

servants and to your son **D**.' " 1Sm 25:8
Nabal asked them, "Who is **D**? 1Sm 25:10
So **D** and all his men put on 1Sm 25:13
men followed **D** while 200 stayed 1Sm 25:13
D sent messengers from the 1Sm 25:14
she saw **D** and his men coming 1Sm 25:20
D had just said, "I guarded 1Sm 25:21
Abigail saw **D**, she quickly got 1Sm 25:23
to the ground in front of **D**. 1Sm 25:23
Then **D** said to Abigail, "Praise 1Sm 25:32
Then **D** accepted what she had 1Sm 25:35
D heard that Nabal was dead, 1Sm 25:39
Then **D** sent messengers to speak 1Sm 25:39
D sent us to bring you to him as 1Sm 25:40
D also married Ahinoam of 1Sm 25:43
D is hiding on the hill of 1Sm 26:1
of Ziph to search for **D** there. 1Sm 26:2
D was living in the wilderness 1Sm 26:3
So **D** sent out spies and knew for 1Sm 26:4
D went to the place where Saul 1Sm 26:5
Then **D** asked Ahimelech the 1Sm 26:6
D and Abishai came to the troops, 1Sm 26:7
Abishai said to **D**, "Today God 1Sm 26:8
But **D** said to Abishai, "Don't 1Sm 26:9
D added, "As the LORD lives, the 1Sm 26:10
D took the spear and the water 1Sm 26:12
D crossed to the other side and 1Sm 26:13
Then **D** shouted to the troops and 1Sm 26:14
D called to Abner, "You're a man, 1Sm 26:15
Is that your voice, my son **D**?" 1Sm 26:17
my lord and king," **D** said. 1Sm 26:17
back, my son **D**, I will never 1Sm 26:21
D answered, "Here is the king's 1Sm 26:22
him, "You are blessed, my son **D**. 1Sm 26:25
Then **D** went on his way, and 1Sm 26:25
D said to himself, "One of these 1Sm 27:1
D set out with his 600 men and 1Sm 27:2
D and his men stayed with Achish 1Sm 27:3
with him, and **D** had his two 1Sm 27:3
to Saul that **D** had fled to Gath, 1Sm 27:4
Now **D** said to Achish, "If I have 1Sm 27:5
The time that **D** stayed in the 1Sm 27:7
D and his men went up and raided 1Sm 27:8
Whenever **D** attacked the land, 1Sm 27:9
D replied, "The south country 1Sm 27:10
D did not let a man or woman 1Sm 27:11
and say, 'This is what **D** did.' " 1Sm 27:11
Achish trusted **D**, thinking, 1Sm 27:12
So Achish said to **D**, "You know, 1Sm 28:1
D replied to Achish, "Good, you 1Sm 28:2
Achish said to **D**, "Very well, I 1Sm 28:2
and given it to your neighbor **D**. 1Sm 28:17
D and his men were passing ⌊in 1Sm 29:2
That is **D**, servant of King 1Sm 29:3
Isn't this the **D** they sing about 1Sm 29:5
but **D** his tens of thousands?" 1Sm 29:5
Achish summoned **D** and told him, 1Sm 29:6
D replied to Achish. 1Sm 29:8
answered **D**, "I'm convinced 1Sm 29:9
So **D** and his men got up early in 1Sm 29:11
D and his men arrived in Ziklag 1Sm 30:1
When **D** and his men arrived at 1Sm 30:3
D and the troops with him wept 1Sm 30:4
D was in a difficult position 1Sm 30:6
But **D** found strength in the LORD 1Sm 30:6
D said to Abiathar the priest, 1Sm 30:7
and **D** asked the LORD: 1Sm 30:8
D and the 600 men with him went 1Sm 30:9
D and 400 of the men continued 1Sm 30:10
country and brought him to **D**. 1Sm 30:11
Then **D** said to him, "Who do you 1Sm 30:13
D then asked him, "Will you lead 1Sm 30:15
D slaughtered them from twilight 1Sm 30:17
D recovered everything the 1Sm 30:18
D got everything back. 1Sm 30:19
When **D** came to the 200 men 1Sm 30:21
When **D** approached the men, 1Sm 30:21
who had gone with **D** retorted, 1Sm 30:22
But **D** said, "My brothers, you 1Sm 30:23
D established ⌊this policy⌋ as a 1Sm 30:25
When **D** came to Ziklag, he sent 1Sm 30:26
places where **D** and his men had 1Sm 30:31
D returned from defeating the 2Sm 1:1
When he came to **D**, he fell to 2Sm 1:2
D asked him, "Where have you 2Sm 1:3
Tell me," **D** asked him. 2Sm 1:4
D asked the young man who had 2Sm 1:5
Then **D** took hold of his clothes 2Sm 1:11

D inquired of the young man who 2Sm 1:13
D questioned him, "How is it 2Sm 1:14
Then **D** summoned one of his 2Sm 1:15
For **D** had said to the Amalekite, 2Sm 1:16
D sang the following lament for 2Sm 1:17
Some time later, **D** inquired of 2Sm 2:1
Then **D** asked, "Where should I 2Sm 2:1
So **D** went there with his two 2Sm 2:2
D brought the men who were with 2Sm 2:3
they anointed **D** king over the 2Sm 2:4
They told **D**: "It was the men 2Sm 2:4
D sent messengers to the men of 2Sm 2:5
of Judah, however, followed **D**. 2Sm 2:10
of time that **D** was king in 2Sm 2:11
and the house of **D** was long and 2Sm 3:1
with **D** growing stronger and the 2Sm 3:1
Sons were born to **D** in Hebron: 2Sm 3:2
These were born to **D** in Hebron. 2Sm 3:5
of Saul and the house of **D**, 2Sm 3:6
haven't handed you over to **D**, 2Sm 3:8
I don't do for **D** what the LORD 2Sm 3:9
the throne of **D** over Israel and 2Sm 3:10
his representatives to say to **D**, 2Sm 3:12
D replied, "Good, I will make a 2Sm 3:13
Then **D** sent messengers to say to 2Sm 3:14
you wanted **D** to be king over 2Sm 3:17
LORD has spoken concerning **D**: 2Sm 3:18
My servant **D** I will save My 2Sm 3:18
Hebron to inform **D** about all 2Sm 3:19
and 20 men came to **D** at Hebron, 2Sm 3:20
D held a banquet for him and his 2Sm 3:20
Abner said to **D**, "Let me now go 2Sm 3:21
So **D** dismissed Abner, and he 2Sm 3:21
was not with **D** in Hebron because 2Sm 3:22
Hebron because **D** had dismissed 2Sm 3:22
Then Joab left **D** and sent 2Sm 3:26
of Sirah, but **D** was unaware of 2Sm 3:26
D heard ⌊about it⌋ later and 2Sm 3:28
D then ordered Joab and all the 2Sm 3:31
And King **D** walked behind the 2Sm 3:31
they came to urge **D** to eat bread 2Sm 3:35
still day, but **D** took an oath: 2Sm 3:35
head to **D** at Hebron and said to 2Sm 4:8
But **D** answered Rechab and his 2Sm 4:9
So **D** gave orders to the young 2Sm 4:12
Israel came to **D** at Hebron and 2Sm 5:1
King **D** made a covenant with them 2Sm 5:3
they anointed **D** king over Israel 2Sm 5:3
D was 30 years old when he began 2Sm 5:4
The Jebusites had said to **D**: 2Sm 5:6
you," thinking, "**D** can't get in 2Sm 5:6
Yet **D** did capture the stronghold 2Sm 5:7
of Zion, the city of **D**. 2Sm 5:7
blind who are despised by **D**." 2Sm 5:8
D took up residence in the 2Sm 5:9
which he named the city of **D**. 2Sm 5:9
D became more and more powerful 2Sm 5:10
Hiram of Tyre sent envoys to **D**; 2Sm 5:11
and they built a palace for **D**. 2Sm 5:11
Then **D** knew that the LORD had 2Sm 5:12
D took more concubines and wives 2Sm 5:13
heard that **D** had been anointed 2Sm 5:17
they all went in search of **D**, 2Sm 5:17
Then **D** inquired of the LORD: 2Sm 5:19
LORD replied to **D**, "Go, for I 2Sm 5:19
So **D** went to Baal-perazim and 2Sm 5:20
and **D** and his men carried them 2Sm 5:21
So **D** inquired of the LORD, 2Sm 5:23
So **D** did exactly as the LORD 2Sm 5:25
D again assembled all the choice 2Sm 6:1
D and the whole house of Israel 2Sm 6:5
D was angry because of the 2Sm 6:8
D feared the LORD that day and 2Sm 6:9
of the LORD to the city of **D**; 2Sm 6:10
It was reported to King **D**: 2Sm 6:12
So **D** went and had the ark of 2Sm 6:12
to the city of **D** with rejoicing. 2Sm 6:12
D was dancing with all his might 2Sm 6:14
LORD was entering the city of **D**, 2Sm 6:16
and saw King **D** leaping and 2Sm 6:16
inside the tent **D** had set up for 2Sm 6:17
Then **D** offered burnt offerings 2Sm 6:17
When **D** had finished offering the 2Sm 6:18
When **D** returned ⌊home⌋ to bless 2Sm 6:20
D replied to Michal, "I was 2Sm 6:21
Go to My servant **D** and say, 2Sm 7:5
are to say to My servant **D**: 2Sm 7:8
and this entire vision to **D**. 2Sm 7:17

Then King **D** went in, sat in the 2Sm 7:18
What more can **D** say to You? 2Sm 7:20
of Your servant **D** will be 2Sm 7:26
D defeated the Philistines, 2Sm 8:1
D also defeated Hadadezer son of 2Sm 8:3
D captured 1,700 horsemen and 2Sm 8:4
D struck down 22,000 Aramean 2Sm 8:5
The LORD made **D** victorious 2Sm 8:6
D took the gold shields of 2Sm 8:7
King **D** also took huge quantities 2Sm 8:8
Hamath heard that **D** had defeated 2Sm 8:9
son Joram to King **D** to greet him 2Sm 8:10
him because **D** had fought against 2Sm 8:10
King **D** also dedicated these to 2Sm 8:11
D made a reputation for himself 2Sm 8:13
the Edomites were subject to **D**. 2Sm 8:14
The LORD made **D** victorious 2Sm 8:14
So **D** reigned over all Israel, 2Sm 8:15
D asked, "Is there anyone 2Sm 9:1
summoned him to **D**, and the king 2Sm 9:2
So King **D** had him brought from 2Sm 9:5
Jonathan son of Saul came to **D**, 2Sm 9:6
D said, "Mephibosheth!" 2Sm 9:6
Don't be afraid," **D** said to him, 2Sm 9:7
Then **D** said, "I'll show kindness 2Sm 10:2
So **D** sent his emissaries to 2Sm 10:2
Just because **D** has sent men with 2Sm 10:3
hasn't **D** sent his emissaries in 2Sm 10:3
When this was reported to **D**, 2Sm 10:5
they had become repulsive to **D**, 2Sm 10:6
D heard about it and sent Joab 2Sm 10:7
When this was reported to **D**, 2Sm 10:17
formation to engage **D** in battle 2Sm 10:17
and **D** killed 700 of their 2Sm 10:18
D sent Joab with his officers 2Sm 11:1
but **D** remained in Jerusalem. 2Sm 11:1
evening **D** got up from his bed 2Sm 11:2
So **D** sent someone to inquire 2Sm 11:3
D sent messengers to get her, 2Sm 11:4
and sent word to inform **D**: 2Sm 11:5
D sent orders to Joab: 2Sm 11:6
So Joab sent Uriah to **D**. 2Sm 11:6
D asked how Joab and the troops 2Sm 11:7
When it was reported to **D**, 2Sm 11:10
go home," **D** questioned Uriah 2Sm 11:10
Uriah answered **D**, "The ark, 2Sm 11:11
today also," **D** said to Uriah, 2Sm 11:12
Then **D** invited Uriah to eat and 2Sm 11:13
with him, and **D** got him drunk. 2Sm 11:13
next morning **D** wrote a letter 2Sm 11:14
to report to **D** all the details 2Sm 11:18
he reported to **D** all that Joab 2Sm 11:22
The messenger reported to **D**, 2Sm 11:23
D told the messenger, "Say this 2Sm 11:25
D had her brought to his house. 2Sm 11:27
considered what **D** had done to be 2Sm 11:27
So the LORD sent Nathan to **D**. 2Sm 12:1
D was infuriated with the man 2Sm 12:5
replied to **D**, "You are the man 2Sm 12:7
D responded to Nathan, "I have 2Sm 12:13
Then Nathan replied to **D**, 2Sm 12:13
Uriah's wife had borne to **D**, 2Sm 12:15
D pleaded with God for the boy. 2Sm 12:16
D saw that his servants were 2Sm 12:19
Then **D** got up from the ground. 2Sm 12:20
Then **D** comforted his wife 2Sm 12:24
sent messengers to **D** to say, 2Sm 12:27
D assembled all the troops and 2Sm 12:29
D took away a large quantity of 2Sm 12:30
D sent word to Tamar at the 2Sm 13:7
King **D** heard about all these 2Sm 13:21
on the way, a report reached **D**: 2Sm 13:30
And **D** mourned for his son every 2Sm 13:37
Then King **D** longed to go to 2Sm 13:39
for **D** had finished grieving over 2Sm 13:39
So **D** summoned Absalom, who 2Sm 14:33
informer came to **D** and reported, 2Sm 15:13
D said to all the servants with 2Sm 15:14
"March on," **D** replied to Ittai. 2Sm 15:22
D was climbing the slope of the 2Sm 15:30
Then someone reported to **D**: 2Sm 15:31
"LORD," **D** pleaded, "please turn 2Sm 15:31
When **D** came to the summit 2Sm 15:32
D said to him, "If you go away 2Sm 15:33
When **D** had gone a little beyond 2Sm 16:1
When King **D** got to Bahurim, 2Sm 16:5
He threw stones at **D** and at all 2Sm 16:6
the LORD told him, 'Curse **D**!' 2Sm 16:10

Then **D** said to Abishai and all 2Sm 16:11
D and his men proceeded along 2Sm 16:13
went, he cursed ⌊**D**⌋, and threw 2Sm 16:13
that both **D** and Absalom had 2Sm 16:23
set out in pursuit of **D** tonight. 2Sm 17:1
will attack **D** wherever we find 2Sm 17:12
someone quickly and tell **D**, 2Sm 17:16
would go and inform King **D**, 2Sm 17:17
and went and informed King **D**. 2Sm 17:21
So **D** and all the people with him 2Sm 17:22
D had arrived at Mahanaim by 2Sm 17:24
When **D** came to Mahanaim, 2Sm 17:27
the herd for **D** and the people 2Sm 17:29
D reviewed his troops and 2Sm 18:1
D was sitting between the two 2Sm 18:24
King **D** sent word to the priests, 2Sm 19:11
the men of Judah to meet King **D**. 2Sm 19:16
D answered, "Sons of Zeruiah, do 2Sm 19:22
a greater ⌊claim⌋ to **D** than you. 2Sm 19:43
no portion in **D**, no inheritance 2Sm 20:1
Israel deserted **D** and followed 2Sm 20:2
When **D** came to his palace in 2Sm 20:3
So **D** said to Abishai, "Sheba son 2Sm 20:6
Joab and whoever is for **D**, 2Sm 20:11
who has rebelled against King **D**. 2Sm 20:21
so **D** inquired of the LORD. 2Sm 21:1
So **D** summoned the Gibeonites 2Sm 21:2
D spared Mephibosheth, the son 2Sm 21:7
that was between **D** and Jonathan, 2Sm 21:7
it was reported to **D** what Saul's 2Sm 21:11
D had the bones brought from 2Sm 21:13
D went down with his soldiers, 2Sm 21:15
but **D** became exhausted 2Sm 21:15
new armor, intended to kill **D**. 2Sm 21:16
were killed by **D** and his 2Sm 21:22
D spoke the words of this song 2Sm 22:1
D and his descendants forever. 2Sm 22:51
These are the last words of **D**: 2Sm 23:1
proclamation of **D** son of Jesse, 2Sm 23:1
warriors with **D** when they defied 2Sm 23:9
time and came to **D** at the cave 2Sm 23:13
At that time **D** was in the 2Sm 23:14
D was extremely thirsty and said, 2Sm 23:15
They brought it back to **D**, 2Sm 23:16
D said, "LORD, I would never do 2Sm 23:17
D put him in charge of his 2Sm 23:23
it stirred up **D** against them to 2Sm 24:1
When **D** got up in the morning, 2Sm 24:11
Go and say to **D**, 'This is what 2Sm 24:12
So Gad went to **D**, told him ⌊the 2Sm 24:13
D answered Gad, "I have great 2Sm 24:14
When **D** saw the angel striking 2Sm 24:17
Gad came to **D** that day and said 2Sm 24:18
D went up in obedience to Gad's 2Sm 24:19
D replied, "To buy the 2Sm 24:21
Araunah said to **D**, "My lord the 2Sm 24:22
D bought the threshing floor 2Sm 24:24
Now King **D** was old and getting 1Kg 1:1
and our lord **D** does not know ⌊it 1Kg 1:11
King **D** and say to him, 1Kg 1:13
King **D** responded by saying, 1Kg 1:28
my lord King **D** live forever!" 1Kg 1:31
King **D** then said, "Call in Zadok 1Kg 1:32
the throne of my lord King **D**." 1Kg 1:37
lord King **D** has made Solomon 1Kg 1:43
to congratulate our lord King **D**, 1Kg 1:47
time approached for **D** to die, 1Kg 2:1
Then **D** rested with his fathers 1Kg 2:10
and was buried in the city of **D**. 1Kg 2:10
length of⌋ time **D** reigned over 1Kg 2:11
on the throne of his father **D**, 1Kg 2:12
me on the throne of my father **D**, 1Kg 2:24
of my father **D** and you suffered 1Kg 2:26
but for **D**, his descendants 1Kg 2:33
that you did to my father **D**. 1Kg 2:44
to the city of **D** until he 1Kg 3:1
in the statutes of his father **D**, 1Kg 3:3
my father **D**, because he walked 1Kg 3:6
just as your father **D** did, 1Kg 3:14
had always been friends with **D**. 1Kg 5:1
know my father **D** was not able to 1Kg 5:3
the LORD promised my father **D**: 1Kg 5:5
He has given **D** a wise son to be 1Kg 5:7
which I made to your father **D**. 1Kg 6:12
things of his father **D**— 1Kg 7:51
from Zion, the city of **D**. 1Kg 8:1
spoke directly to my father **D**, 1Kg 8:15
I have chosen **D** to rule My 1Kg 8:16
of my father **D** to build a temple 1Kg 8:17
the LORD said to my father **D**, 1Kg 8:18
taken the place of my father **D**, 1Kg 8:20
to Your servant, my father **D**. 1Kg 8:24
to Your servant, my father **D**: 1Kg 8:25
to Your servant, my father **D**. 1Kg 8:26
for His servant **D** and for His 1Kg 8:66
Me as your father **D** walked, 1Kg 9:4
as I promised your father **D**: 1Kg 9:5
from the city of **D** to the house 1Kg 9:24
unlike his father **D**, he did not 1Kg 11:6
because of your father **D**; 1Kg 11:12
of my servant **D** and because 1Kg 11:13
Earlier, when **D** was in Edom, 1Kg 11:15
in Egypt that **D** rested with his 1Kg 11:21
raiding party when **D** killed the 1Kg 11:24
of the city of his father **D**. 1Kg 11:27
of my servant **D** and because 1Kg 11:32
judgments as his father **D** did. 1Kg 11:33
life because of My servant **D**, 1Kg 11:34
that My servant **D** will always 1Kg 11:36
as My servant **D** did, 1Kg 11:38
dynasty just as I built for **D**, 1Kg 11:38
in the city of his father **D**. 1Kg 11:43
What portion do we have in **D**? 1Kg 12:16
D, now look after your own house 1Kg 12:16
the house of **D** until today. 1Kg 12:19
the house of **D** except the tribe 1Kg 12:20
might return to the house of **D**. 1Kg 12:26
will be born to the house of **D**, 1Kg 13:2
away from the house of **D**, 1Kg 14:8
you were not like My servant **D**, 1Kg 14:8
his fathers in the city of **D**. 1Kg 14:31
God as his ancestor **D** had been. 1Kg 15:3
But because of **D**, the LORD his 1Kg 15:4
because **D** did what was right in 1Kg 15:5
and was buried in the city of **D**. 1Kg 15:8
as his ancestor **D** had done. 1Kg 15:11
in the city of his forefather **D**. 1Kg 15:24
in the city of his forefather **D**. 1Kg 22:50
Judah because of His servant **D**, 2Kg 8:19
give a lamp to **D** and to his sons 2Kg 8:19
his fathers in the city of **D**, 2Kg 8:24
fathers' tomb in the city of **D**. 2Kg 9:28
his fathers in the city of **D**, 2Kg 12:21
but not like his ancestor **D**. 2Kg 14:3
his fathers in the city of **D**. 2Kg 14:20
his fathers in the city of **D**. 2Kg 15:7
in the city of his ancestor **D**. 2Kg 15:38
LORD his God like his ancestor **D** 2Kg 16:2
his fathers in the city of **D**, 2Kg 16:20
tore Israel from the house of **D**, 2Kg 17:21
just as his ancestor **D** had done. 2Kg 18:3
for the sake of My servant **D**. 2Kg 19:34
God of your ancestor **D** says: 2Kg 20:5
the sake of My servant **D**.'" 2Kg 20:6
spoken about to **D** and his son 2Kg 21:7
all the ways of his ancestor **D**; 2Kg 22:2
Ozem sixth, and **D** seventh. 1Ch 2:15
sons were born to **D** in Hebron, 1Ch 3:4
cities until **D** became king. 1Ch 4:31
are the men **D** put in charge 1Ch 6:31
D and Samuel the seer had 1Ch 9:22
kingdom over to **D** son of Jesse. 1Ch 10:14
came together to **D** at Hebron and 1Ch 11:1
D made a covenant with them at 1Ch 11:3
they anointed **D** king over Israel 1Ch 11:3
D and all Israel marched to 1Ch 11:4
inhabitants of Jebus said to **D**, 1Ch 11:5
Yet **D** did capture the 1Ch 11:5
Zion (that is, the city of **D**). 1Ch 11:5
D said, "Whoever is the first to 1Ch 11:6
Then **D** took up residence in the 1Ch 11:7
it was called the city of **D**. 1Ch 11:7
D steadily grew more powerful, 1Ch 11:9
He was with **D** at Pas-dammim 1Ch 11:13
But Eleazar and **D** took their 1Ch 11:14
the 30 chief men went down to **D**, 1Ch 11:15
At that time **D** was in the 1Ch 11:16
D was extremely thirsty and said, 1Ch 11:17
They brought it back to **D**, 1Ch 11:18
D said, "I would never do such a 1Ch 11:19
D put him in charge of his 1Ch 11:25
who came to **D** at Ziklag while 1Ch 12:1
defected to **D** at his stronghold 1Ch 12:8
also went to **D** at the stronghold 1Ch 12:16
D went out to meet them and said 1Ch 12:17
⌊We are⌋ yours, **D**, ⌊we are⌋ with 1Ch 12:18
D received them and made them 1Ch 12:18
defected to **D** when he went with 1Ch 12:19
consultation, sent **D** away. 1Ch 12:19
When **D** went to Ziklag, some 1Ch 12:20
They helped **D** against the 1Ch 12:21
day to help **D** until there was 1Ch 12:22
who came to **D** at Hebron to turn 1Ch 12:23
name to come and make **D** king. 1Ch 12:31
singleness of purpose to help **D**. 1Ch 12:33
to make **D** king over all Israel 1Ch 12:38
also of one mind to make **D** king. 1Ch 12:38
there with **D** for three days, 1Ch 12:39
D consulted with all his leaders, 1Ch 13:1
So **D** assembled all Israel, 1Ch 13:5
D and all Israel went to Baalah 1Ch 13:6
D and all Israel were 1Ch 13:8
D was angry because of the 1Ch 13:11
D feared God that day, and said, 1Ch 13:12
So **D** did not move the ark of God 1Ch 13:13
of God home to the city of **D**; 1Ch 13:13
Hiram of Tyre sent envoys to **D**, 1Ch 14:1
Then **D** knew that the LORD had 1Ch 14:2
D took more wives in Jerusalem, 1Ch 14:3
heard that **D** had been anointed 1Ch 14:8
they all went in search of **D**; 1Ch 14:8
when **D** heard of this, he went 1Ch 14:8
so **D** inquired of God, "Should I 1Ch 14:10
and **D** defeated the Philistines 1Ch 14:11
Then **D** said, "Like a bursting 1Ch 14:11
D ordered that they be burned 1Ch 14:12
So **D** again inquired of God, 1Ch 14:14
D did exactly as God commanded 1Ch 14:16
D built houses for himself in 1Ch 15:1
for himself in the city of **D**, 1Ch 15:1
Then **D** said, "No one but the 1Ch 15:2
D assembled all Israel at 1Ch 15:3
D summoned the priests Zadok 1Ch 15:11
Then **D** told the leaders of the 1Ch 15:16
D, the elders of Israel, and the 1Ch 15:25
Now **D** was dressed in a robe of 1Ch 15:27
D also wore a linen ephod. 1Ch 15:27
LORD was entering the city of **D**, 1Ch 15:29
window and saw King **D** dancing 1Ch 15:29
inside the tent **D** had pitched 1Ch 16:1
When **D** had finished offering the 1Ch 16:2
D appointed some of the Levites 1Ch 16:4
On that day **D** decreed for the 1Ch 16:7
D left Asaph and his relatives 1Ch 16:37
⌊**D** left⌋ Zadok the priest and 1Ch 16:39
and **D** returned ⌊home⌋ to bless 1Ch 16:43
When **D** had settled into his 1Ch 17:1
Nathan told **D**, "Do all that is 1Ch 17:2
Go to **D** My servant and say, 1Ch 17:4
you will say to My servant **D**: 1Ch 17:7
and this entire vision to **D**. 1Ch 17:15
Then King **D** went in, sat in the 1Ch 17:16
What more can **D** say to You for 1Ch 17:18
of Your servant **D** be established 1Ch 17:24
D defeated the Philistines, 1Ch 18:1
D also defeated King Hadadezer 1Ch 18:3
D captured 1,000 chariots, 1Ch 18:4
D struck down 22,000 Aramean 1Ch 18:5
The LORD made **D** victorious 1Ch 18:6
D took the gold shields carried 1Ch 18:7
D also took huge quantities of 1Ch 18:8
Hamath heard that **D** had defeated 1Ch 18:9
Hadoram to King **D** to greet him 1Ch 18:10
him because **D** had fought against 1Ch 18:10
King **D** also dedicated these to 1Ch 18:11
the Edomites were subject to **D**. 1Ch 18:13
The LORD made **D** victorious 1Ch 18:13
So **D** reigned over all Israel, 1Ch 18:14
Then **D** said, "I'll show kindness 1Ch 19:2
So **D** sent messengers to console 1Ch 19:2
Just because **D** has sent men with 1Ch 19:3
hasn't **D** sent his emissaries in 1Ch 19:3
and reported to **D** about his men, 1Ch 19:5
made themselves repulsive to **D**, 1Ch 19:6
D heard about this and sent Joab 1Ch 19:8
When this was reported to **D**, 1Ch 19:17
When **D** lined up to engage the 1Ch 19:17
and **D** killed 7,000 of their 1Ch 19:18
made peace with **D** and became 1Ch 19:19
but **D** remained in Jerusalem. 1Ch 20:1
Then **D** took the crown from the 1Ch 20:2
D took away a large quantity of 1Ch 20:2
D did the same to all the 1Ch 20:3
Gath killed by **D** and his 1Ch 20:8

Israel and incited **D** to count 1Ch 21:1
So **D** said to Joab and the 1Ch 21:2
Joab gave **D** the total of the 1Ch 21:5
D said to God, "I have sinned 1Ch 21:8
Go and say to **D**, 'This is what 1Ch 21:10
Gad went to **D** and said to him, 1Ch 21:11
D answered Gad, "I have great 1Ch 21:13
When **D** looked up and saw the 1Ch 21:16
Jerusalem, **D** and the elders, 1Ch 21:16
D said to God, "Wasn't I the one 1Ch 21:17
Gad to tell **D** to go and set up 1Ch 21:18
D went up at Gad's command 1Ch 21:19
D came to Ornan, and when 1Ch 21:21
when Ornan looked and saw **D**, 1Ch 21:21
and bowed to **D** with his face to 1Ch 21:21
Then **D** said to Ornan, "Give me 1Ch 21:22
Ornan said to **D**, "Take it! 1Ch 21:23
King **D** answered Ornan, "No, I 1Ch 21:24
D gave Ornan 15 pounds of gold 1Ch 21:25
D saw that the LORD answered 1Ch 21:28
but **D** could not go before it to 1Ch 21:30
Then **D** said, "This is the house 1Ch 22:1
So **D** gave orders to gather the 1Ch 22:2
D supplied a great deal of iron 1Ch 22:3
quantity of cedar logs to **D**. 1Ch 22:4
D said, "My son Solomon is young 1Ch 22:5
So **D** made lavish preparations 1Ch 22:5
"My son," **D** said to Solomon, "It 1Ch 22:7
Then **D** ordered all the leaders 1Ch 22:17
When **D** was old and full of days, 1Ch 23:1
"Of these," ⌊**D** said⌋, "24,000 1Ch 23:4
Then **D** divided them into 1Ch 23:6
For **D** said, "The LORD God of 1Ch 23:25
to the last words of **D**, 1Ch 23:27
D divided them according to the 1Ch 24:3
did in the presence of King **D**, 1Ch 24:31
D and the officers of the army 1Ch 25:1
had been dedicated by King **D**, 1Ch 26:26
King **D** appointed them over the 1Ch 26:32
D didn't count the men aged 20 1Ch 27:23
the Historical Record of King **D**. 1Ch 27:24
D assembled in Jerusalem all the 1Ch 28:1
Then King **D** rose to his feet and 1Ch 28:2
Then **D** gave his son Solomon the 1Ch 28:11
⌊**D** concluded,⌋ "By the LORD's 1Ch 28:19
Then **D** said to his son Solomon, 1Ch 28:20
Then King **D** said to all the 1Ch 29:1
King **D** also rejoiced greatly. 1Ch 29:9
Then **D** praised the LORD in the 1Ch 29:10
D said, "May You be praised, 1Ch 29:10
Then **D** said to the whole 1Ch 29:20
king in place of his father **D**. 1Ch 29:23
D son of Jesse was king over all 1Ch 29:26
Solomon son of **D** strengthened 2Ch 1:1
D had brought the ark of God 2Ch 1:4
faithful love to my father **D**, 2Ch 1:8
to my father **D** now come true. 2Ch 1:9
what you did for my father **D**. 2Ch 2:3
appointed by my father **D**. 2Ch 2:7
He gave King **D** a wise son with 2Ch 2:12
of my lord, your father **D**. 2Ch 2:14
that his father **D** had conducted, 2Ch 2:17
had appeared to his father **D**, 2Ch 3:1
the site **D** had prepared on the 2Ch 3:1
things of his father **D**— 2Ch 5:1
the LORD up from the city of **D**, 2Ch 5:2
spoke directly to my father **D**, 2Ch 6:4
and I have chosen **D** to be over 2Ch 6:6
of my father **D** to build a temple 2Ch 6:7
the LORD said to my father **D**, 2Ch 6:8
place of my father **D** and I sit 2Ch 6:10
to Your servant, my father **D**. 2Ch 6:15
to Your servant, my father **D**: 2Ch 6:16
You promised to Your servant **D**. 2Ch 6:17
the loyalty of Your servant **D**. 2Ch 6:42
which King **D** had made to praise 2Ch 7:6
when **D** offered praise with them. 2Ch 7:6
the LORD had done for **D**, 2Ch 7:10
Me as your father **D** walked, 2Ch 7:17
as I promised your father **D**: 2Ch 7:18
the city of **D** to the house he 2Ch 8:11
in the house of **D** king of Israel 2Ch 8:11
the ordinances of his father **D**, 2Ch 8:14
this had been the command of **D**, 2Ch 8:14
in the city of his father **D**. 2Ch 9:31
What portion do we have in **D**? 2Ch 10:16
D, look after your own house now 2Ch 10:16
the house of **D** until today. 2Ch 10:19
in the way of **D** and Solomon for 2Ch 11:17
and was buried in the city of **D**. 2Ch 12:16
over Israel to **D** and his 2Ch 13:5
a servant of Solomon son of **D**, 2Ch 13:6
and was buried in the city of **D**. 2Ch 14:1
for himself in the city of **D**. 2Ch 16:14
the former ways of his father **D**. 2Ch 17:3
his fathers in the city of **D**. 2Ch 21:1
the LORD had made with **D**, 2Ch 21:7
house of **D** since the LORD had 2Ch 21:7
give a lamp to **D** and to his sons 2Ch 21:7
God of your ancestor **D** says: 2Ch 21:12
in the city of **D** but not in the 2Ch 21:20
whom **D** had appointed over the 2Ch 23:18
and song ordained by **D**. 2Ch 23:18
in the city of **D** with the kings 2Ch 24:16
buried him in the city of **D**, 2Ch 24:25
and was buried in the city of **D**. 2Ch 27:9
sight like his forefather **D**, 2Ch 28:1
just as his ancestor **D** had done. 2Ch 29:2
according to the command of **D**, 2Ch 29:25
stood with the instruments of **D**, 2Ch 29:26
instruments of **D** king of Israel. 2Ch 29:27
in the words of **D** and of Asaph 2Ch 29:30
the days of Solomon son of **D**, 2Ch 30:26
terraces of the city of **D**, 2Ch 32:5
and westward to the city of **D**. 2Ch 32:30
God had said to **D** and his son 2Ch 33:7
of the city of **D** from west of 2Ch 33:14
in the ways of his ancestor **D**; 2Ch 34:2
seek the God of his ancestor **D**, 2Ch 34:3
Solomon son of **D** king of Israel. 2Ch 35:3
instruction of **D** king of Israel 2Ch 35:4
according to the command of **D**, 2Ch 35:15
as King **D** of Israel had Ezr 3:10
appointed by **D** and the leaders Ezr 8:20
that descend from the city of **D**. Neh 3:15
point⌋ opposite the tombs of **D**, Neh 3:16
as **D** the man of God had Neh 12:24
the musical instruments of **D**, Neh 12:36
of the city of **D** on the ascent Neh 12:37
the house of **D** to the Water Gate Neh 12:37
as **D** and his son Solomon had Neh 12:45
in the days of **D** and Asaph, Neh 12:46
D and his descendants forever. Ps 18:50
Concerning **D**, when he pretended Ps 34:1
prayers of **D** son of Jesse are Ps 72:20
He chose **D** His servant and took Ps 78:70
sworn an oath to **D** My servant: Ps 89:3
I have found **D** My servant; Ps 89:20
holiness; I will not lie to **D**. Ps 89:35
that You swore to **D** in Your Ps 89:49
thrones of the house of **D**. Ps 122:5
remember **D** and all the hardships Ps 132:1
Because of Your servant **D**, Ps 132:10
The LORD swore an oath to **D**, Ps 132:11
I will make a horn grow for **D**; Ps 132:17
His servant **D** from the deadly Ps 144:10
proverbs of Solomon son of **D**, Pr 1:1
Teacher, son of **D**, king in Ec 1:1
neck is like the tower of **D**, Sg 4:4
to the house of **D** that Aram had Is 7:2
said, "Listen, house of **D**! Is 7:13
on the throne of **D** and over his Is 9:7
the tent of **D** a throne will be Is 16:5
in ⌊the walls of⌋ the city of **D**. Is 22:9
the House of **D** on his shoulder Is 22:22
Ariel, the city where **D** camped! Is 29:1
and because of My servant **D**.' " Is 37:35
God of your ancestor **D** says: Is 38:5
the promises assured to **D**. Is 55:3
who reign for **D** on his throne, Jr 13:13
will sit on the throne of **D**, Jr 17:25
House of **D**, this is what the Jr 21:12
you who sit on the throne of **D**— Jr 22:2
the throne of **D** or ruling again Jr 22:30
up a righteous Branch of **D**. Jr 23:5
I will raise up **D** their king for Jr 30:9
to sprout up for **D**, Jr 33:15
D will never fail to have a man Jr 33:17
with My servant **D** may be broken Jr 33:21
of My servant **D** and the Levites Jr 33:22
of Jacob and of My servant **D**— Jr 33:26
My servant **D**, and he will Ezk 34:23
My servant **D** will be a prince Ezk 34:24
My servant **D** will be king over Ezk 37:24
and My servant **D** will be their Ezk 37:25
LORD their God and **D** their king. Hs 3:5
own musical instruments like **D**. Am 6:5
restore the fallen booth of **D**: Am 9:11
them will be like **D** on that day, Zch 12:8
the house of **D** will be like God Zch 12:8
on the house of **D** and the Zch 12:10
for the house of **D** and for the Zch 13:1
Christ, the Son of **D**, the Son of Mt 1:1
and Jesse fathered King **D**. Mt 1:6
Then **D** fathered Solomon by Mt 1:6
from Abraham to **D** were 14 Mt 1:17
and from **D** until the exile to Mt 1:17
Joseph, son of **D**, don't be Mt 1:20
Have mercy on us, Son of **D**!" Mt 9:27
you read what **D** did when he and Mt 12:3
"Perhaps this is the Son of **D**!" Mt 12:23
mercy on me, Lord, Son of **D**! Mt 15:22
have mercy on us, Son of **D**!" Mt 20:30
have mercy on us, Son of **D**!" Mt 20:31
Hosanna to the Son of **D**! Mt 21:9
"Hosanna to the Son of **D**!" Mt 21:15
How is it then that **D**, inspired Mt 22:43
If **D** calls Him 'Lord,' how then Mt 22:45
never read what **D** and those who Mk 2:25
cry out, "Son of **D**, Jesus, have Mk 10:47
Have mercy on me, Son of **D**!" Mk 10:48
coming kingdom of our father **D**! Mk 11:10
the Messiah is the Son of **D**? Mk 12:35
D himself says by the Holy Mk 12:36
D himself calls Him 'Lord'; Mk 12:37
named Joseph, of the house of **D**. Lk 1:27
Him the throne of His father **D**. Lk 1:32
in the house of His servant **D**, Lk 1:69
the city of **D**, which is called Lk 2:4
the house and family line of **D**, Lk 2:4
born for you in the city of **D**. Lk 2:11
son⌋ of Nathan, ⌊son⌋ of **D**, Lk 3:31
you read what **D** and those who Lk 6:3
Son of **D**, have mercy on me! Lk 18:38
more, "Son of **D**, have mercy on Lk 18:39
the Messiah is the Son of **D**? Lk 20:41
For **D** himself says in the Book Lk 20:42
D calls Him 'Lord'; how then can Lk 20:44
Bethlehem, where **D** once lived?" Jn 7:42
the mouth of **D** spoke in advance Ac 1:16
D says of Him: I saw the Lord Ac 2:25
to you about the patriarch **D**: Ac 2:29
For it was not **D** who ascended Ac 2:34
of our father **D** Your servant: Ac 4:25
fathers, until the days of **D**. Ac 7:45
He raised up **D** as their king, Ac 13:22
'I have found **D** the son of Jesse, Ac 13:22
covenant blessings made to **D**. Ac 13:34
For **D**, after serving his own Ac 13:36
a descendant of **D** according to Rm 1:3
D also speaks of the blessing of Rm 4:6
And **D** says: Let their feasting Rm 11:9
descended from **D**, according to 2Tm 2:8
speaking through **D** after such a Heb 4:7
D and Samuel and the prophets, Heb 11:32
the One who has the key of **D**, Rv 3:7
Judah, the Root of **D**, has been Rv 5:5
the Root and the Offspring of **D**, Rv 22:16

DAVID'S *(100)*

D oldest brother Eliab listened 1Sm 17:28
helmet on **D** head and had him 1Sm 17:38
intended to cause **D** death at the 1Sm 18:25
Saul was **D** enemy from then on. 1Sm 18:29
sent agents to **D** house to watch 1Sm 19:11
off every one of **D** enemies from 1Sm 20:15
May the LORD hold **D** enemies 1Sm 20:16
Saul, but **D** place was empty 1Sm 20:25
D place was ⌊still⌋ empty, 1Sm 20:27
When **D** brothers and his father's 1Sm 22:1
But **D** men said to him, "Look, 1Sm 23:3
D conscience bothered him 1Sm 24:5
D young men went and said all 1Sm 25:9
things to Nabal on **D** behalf, 1Sm 25:9
D men retraced their steps. 1Sm 25:12
When **D** servants came to Abigail 1Sm 25:40
donkey following **D** messengers. 1Sm 25:42
daughter Michal, **D** wife, to 1Sm 25:44
recognized **D** voice and asked 1Sm 26:17
This was **D** custom during the 1Sm 27:11
D two wives, Ahinoam the 1Sm 30:5
shouted, "This is **D** plunder!" 1Sm 30:20
Zeruiah and **D** soldiers marched 2Sm 2:13
of Saul, and 12 from **D** soldiers. 2Sm 2:15
were defeated by **D** soldiers. 2Sm 2:17

19 of **D** soldiers were missing, 2Sm 2:30
was Ithream, by **D** wife Eglah. 2Sm 3:5
Just then **D** soldiers and Joab 2Sm 3:22
the Moabites became **D** subjects 2Sm 8:2
the Arameans became **D** subjects 2Sm 8:6
and **D** sons were chief officials. 2Sm 8:18
ate at **D** table just like one 2Sm 9:11
So Hanun took **D** emissaries, 2Sm 10:4
of the men from **D** soldiers fell 2Sm 11:17
But **D** servants were afraid to 2Sm 12:18
and it was ⌊placed⌋ on **D** head. 2Sm 12:30
D son Absalom had a beautiful 2Sm 13:1
and **D** son Amnon was infatuated 2Sm 13:1
a son of **D** brother Shimeah. 2Sm 13:3
son of **D** brother Shimeah 2Sm 13:32
Absalom sent for **D** adviser 2Sm 15:12
So Hushai, **D** personal adviser, 2Sm 15:37
warriors on **D** right and left. 2Sm 16:6
When **D** friend Hushai the 2Sm 16:16
Then **D** forces marched into the 2Sm 18:6
were defeated by **D** soldiers, 2Sm 18:7
he happened to meet **D** soldiers. 2Sm 18:9
along with all of **D** men?" 2Sm 19:41
Ira the Jairite was **D** priest. 2Sm 20:26
D reign there was a famine 2Sm 21:1
Then **D** men swore to him: 2Sm 21:17
son of **D** brother Shimei, 2Sm 21:21
are the names of **D** warriors: 2Sm 23:8
D conscience troubled him after 2Sm 24:10
come to the prophet Gad, **D** seer: 2Sm 24:11
and **D** warriors did not side with 1Kg 1:8
had Solomon ride on King **D** mule, 1Kg 1:38
without my father **D** knowledge. 1Kg 2:32
and **D** throne will remain 1Kg 2:45
king in my father **D** place. 1Kg 3:7
as his father **D** heart had been. 1Kg 11:4
I will humble **D** descendants, 1Kg 11:39
of hundreds King **D** spears and 2Kg 11:10
These were **D** sons who were born 1Ch 3:1
Ithream, by **D** wife Eglah, was 1Ch 3:3
⌊**D** other sons⌋: Ibhar, Elishua, 1Ch 3:6
These⌋ were all **D** sons, with 1Ch 3:9
During **D** reign, 22,600 1Ch 7:2
the chiefs of **D** warriors who, 1Ch 11:10
This is the list of **D** warriors: 1Ch 11:11
Then **D** fame spread throughout 1Ch 14:17
and they became **D** subjects and 1Ch 18:2
the Arameans became **D** subjects 1Ch 18:6
and **D** sons were the chief 1Ch 18:17
when **D** emissaries arrived in the 1Ch 19:2
So Hanun took **D** emissaries, 1Ch 19:4
and it was ⌊placed⌋ on **D** head. 1Ch 20:2
son of **D** brother Shimei, 1Ch 20:7
the LORD instructed Gad, **D** seer, 1Ch 21:9
fortieth year of **D** reign a 1Ch 26:31
Judah, Elihu, one of **D** brothers; 1Ch 27:18
in charge of King **D** property. 1Ch 27:31
D uncle Jonathan was a counselor; 1Ch 27:32
they made **D** son Solomon king; 1Ch 29:22
and all of King **D** sons as well, 1Ch 29:24
the events of King **D** ⌊reign⌋, 1Ch 29:29
daughter of **D** son Jerimoth and 2Ch 11:18
in the hand of ⌊one of⌋ **D** sons. 2Ch 13:8
LORD promised concerning **D** sons. 2Ch 23:3
of hundreds King **D** spears, 2Ch 23:9
to the tombs of **D** descendants. 2Ch 32:33
Hattush, from **D** descendants, Ezr 8:2
kings sitting on **D** throne will Jr 22:4
the king sitting on **D** throne and Jr 29:16
have no one to sit on **D** throne, Jr 36:30
that the glory of **D** house and Zch 12:7
the family of **D** house by itself Zch 12:12
"**D**," they told Him. Mt 22:42
Messiah comes from **D** offspring Jn 7:42
return and will rebuild **D** tent, Ac 15:16

DAWN *(33)*

At the crack of **d** the angels Gn 19:15
they started at **d** and marched Jos 6:15
they said, "Let us wait until **d**; Jdg 16:2
and just before **d**, Samuel called 1Sm 9:26
night and reached Hebron at **d**. 2Sm 2:32
it not see the breaking of **d**. Jb 3:9
to pieces from **d** to dusk; Jb 4:20
and I toss and turn until **d**. Jb 7:4
rises at **d** to kill the poor Jb 24:14
or assigned the **d** its place, Jb 38:12
his eyes are like the rays of **d**. Jb 41:18
righteousness shine like the **d**, Ps 37:6
and lyre! I will wake up the **d**. Ps 57:8
and lyre! I will wake up the **d**. Ps 108:2
the womb of the **d**, the dew of Ps 110:3
I rise before **d** and cry out for Ps 119:147
is like the light of **d**, Pr 4:18
is this who shines like the **d**— Sg 6:10
there will be no **d** for them. Is 8:20
light will appear like the **d**, Is 58:8
first light of **d** the king got up Dn 6:19
appearance is as sure as the **d**. Hs 6:3
At **d** the king of Israel will be Hs 10:15
like the **d** spreading over the Jl 2:2
who makes the **d** out of darkness Am 4:13
darkness into **d** and darkens day Am 5:8
When **d** came the next day, God Jnh 4:7
not fail at **d**, yet the one who Zph 3:5
the **D** from on high will visit us Lk 1:78
or even near **d**, and finds them Lk 12:38
At **d** He went to the temple Jn 8:2
a considerable time until **d**. Ac 20:11
From **d** to dusk he expounded and Ac 28:23

DAWNED *(2)*

land of darkness, a light has **d**. Is 9:2
of death, light has **d**. Mt 4:16

DAWNING *(1)*

the first day of the week was **d**, Mt 28:1

DAWNS *(3)*

help her when the morning **d**. Ps 46:5
Light **d** for the righteous, Ps 97:11
until the day **d** and the morning 2Pt 1:19

DAY *(1394)*

the light "**d**," and He called Gn 1:5
and then morning: the first **d**. Gn 1:5
and then morning: the second **d**. Gn 1:8
and then morning: the third **d**. Gn 1:13
separate the **d** from the night. Gn 1:14
over the **d** and the lesser Gn 1:16
to dominate the **d** and the night, Gn 1:18
and then morning: the fourth **d**. Gn 1:19
and then morning: the fifth **d**. Gn 1:23
and then morning: the sixth **d**. Gn 1:31
By the seventh **d**, God completed Gn 2:2
on the seventh **d** from all His Gn 2:2
the seventh **d** and declared it Gn 2:3
for on the **d** you eat from it, Gn 2:17
On the **d** that God created man, Gn 5:1
the seventeenth **d** of the month, Gn 7:11
on that **d** all the sources of the Gn 7:11
On that same **d** Noah along with Gn 7:13
the seventeenth **d** of the month, Gn 8:4
on the first **d** of the month, Gn 8:5
on the first **d** of the month, Gn 8:13
twenty-seventh **d** of the second Gn 8:14
and **d** and night will not cease." Gn 8:22
On that **d** the LORD made a Gn 15:18
their foreskin on that very **d**, Gn 17:23
On that same **d** Abraham and his Gn 17:26
tent during the heat of the **d**. Gn 18:1
The next **d** the firstborn said to Gn 19:34
feast on the **d** Isaac was weaned Gn 21:8
On the third **d** Abraham looked up Gn 22:4
On that same **d** Isaac's slaves Gn 26:32
city is Beer-sheba to this **d**. Gn 26:33
do not know the **d** of my death. Gn 27:2
I lose you both in one **d**?" Gn 27:45
d Laban removed the streaked Gn 30:35
On the third **d** Laban was told Gn 31:22
was stolen by **d** or by night. Gn 31:39
consumed me by **d** and the frost Gn 31:40
why, to this **d**, the Israelites Gn 32:32
they are driven hard for one **d**, Gn 33:13
that **d** Esau started on his way Gn 33:16
On the third **d**, when they were Gn 34:25
answered me in my **d** of distress. Gn 35:3
at Rachel's grave to this **d**. Gn 35:20
she spoke to Joseph **d** after day, Gn 39:10
she spoke to Joseph day after **d**, Gn 39:10
Now one **d** he went into the house Gn 39:11
On the third **d**, which was Gn 40:20
On the third **d** Joseph said to Gn 42:18
shepherd all my life to this **d**, Gn 48:15
them that **d** with these words Gn 48:20
The next **d** he went out and saw Ex 2:13
That **d** Pharaoh commanded the Ex 5:6
your assigned work each **d**, Ex 5:13
On the **d** the LORD spoke to Moses Ex 6:28
on that **d** I will give special Ex 8:22
The LORD did this the next **d**. Ex 9:6
Egypt from the **d** it was founded Ex 9:18
the land all that **d** and through Ex 10:13
for on the **d** you see my face, Ex 10:28
on the tenth **d** of this month Ex 12:3
the fourteenth **d** of this month; Ex 12:6
This **d** is to be a memorial for Ex 12:14
On the first **d** you must remove Ex 12:15
from the first **d** through the Ex 12:15
the seventh **d** must be cut off Ex 12:15
the first **d** and another sacred Ex 12:16
assembly on the seventh **d**. Ex 12:16
on this very **d** I brought your Ex 12:17
observe this **d** throughout your Ex 12:17
of the fourteenth **d** of the month Ex 12:18
evening of the twenty-first **d**. Ex 12:18
on that same **d**, all the Ex 12:41
On that same **d** the LORD brought Ex 12:51
Remember this **d** when you came Ex 13:3
on the seventh **d** there is to be Ex 13:6
On that **d** explain to your son, Ex 13:8
way during the **d** and in a pillar Ex 13:21
they could travel **d** or night. Ex 13:21
of cloud by **d** and the pillar Ex 13:22
d the LORD saved Israel from Ex 14:30
on the fifteenth **d** of the second Ex 16:1
to go out each **d** and gather Ex 16:4
and gather enough for that **d**. Ex 16:4
the sixth **d**, when they prepare Ex 16:5
On the sixth **d** they gathered Ex 16:22
'Tomorrow is a **d** of complete Ex 16:23
on the seventh **d**, the Sabbath, Ex 16:26
on the seventh **d** some of the Ex 16:27
on the sixth **d** He will give you Ex 16:29
his place on the seventh **d**." Ex 16:29
people rested on the seventh **d**. Ex 16:30
The next **d** Moses sat down to Ex 18:13
the same **d** ⌊of the month⌋ that Ex 19:1
and be prepared by the third **d**, Ex 19:11
for on the third **d** the LORD will Ex 19:11
Be prepared by the third **d**. Ex 19:15
On the third **d**, when morning Ex 19:16
to dedicate the Sabbath **d**: Ex 20:8
but the seventh **d** is a Sabbath Ex 20:10
then He rested on the seventh **d**. Ex 20:11
the Sabbath **d** and declared it Ex 20:11
can stand up after a **d** or two, Ex 21:21
on the eighth **d** you are to give Ex 22:30
on the seventh **d** so that your ox Ex 23:12
On the seventh **d** He called to Ex 24:16
offering each **d** for atonement. Ex 29:36
regularly on the altar every **d**: Ex 29:38
on the seventh **d** there must be Ex 31:15
on the Sabbath **d** must be put to Ex 31:15
on the seventh **d** He rested and Ex 31:17
fell dead that **d** among the Ex 32:28
following **d** Moses said to the Ex 32:30
But on the **d** I settle accounts, Ex 32:34
you must rest on the seventh **d**; Ex 34:21
on the seventh **d** you are to have Ex 35:2
day you are to have a holy **d**, Ex 35:2
of your homes on the Sabbath **d**." Ex 35:3
on the first **d** of the first Ex 40:2
on the first ⌊**d**⌋ of the month. Ex 40:17
out until the **d** it was taken up Ex 40:37
was over the tabernacle by **d**, Ex 40:38
owner on the **d** he acknowledges Lv 6:5
to the LORD on the **d** that he is Lv 6:20
be eaten on the **d** he offers it; Lv 7:15
eaten on the **d** he presents his Lv 7:16
over may be eaten on the next **d**. Lv 7:16
by the third **d** must be burned up Lv 7:17
is eaten on the third **d**, Lv 7:18
his sons since the **d** they were Lv 7:35
on the **d** He anointed them Lv 7:36
Sinai on the **d** He commanded Lv 7:38
tent of meeting **d** and night for Lv 8:35
On the eighth **d** Moses summoned Lv 9:1
be circumcised on the eighth **d**. Lv 12:3
reexamine him on the seventh **d**. Lv 13:5
him again on the seventh **d**. Lv 13:6
reexamine him on the seventh **d**. Lv 13:27
the infection on the seventh **d**. Lv 13:32
scaly outbreak on the seventh **d**, Lv 13:34
contamination on the seventh **d**. Lv 13:51
disease on the **d** of his Lv 14:2
hair ⌊again⌋ on the seventh **d**: Lv 14:9
On the eighth **d** he must take two Lv 14:10

On the eighth **d** he is to bring Lv 14:23
on the seventh **d** and examine it. Lv 14:39
young pigeons on the eighth **d**, Lv 15:14
the eighth **d** she must take two Lv 15:29
the tenth ⌊**d**⌋ of the month you Lv 16:29
you on this **d** to cleanse you, Lv 16:30
be eaten on the **d** you sacrifice Lv 19:6
sacrifice ⌊it⌋ or on the next **d**, Lv 19:6
the third **d** must be burned up. Lv 19:6
If any is eaten on the third **d**, Lv 19:7
from the eighth **d** on, it will be Lv 22:27
on the same **d** as its young. Lv 22:28
It is to be eaten on the same **d**. Lv 22:30
on the seventh **d** there must be Lv 23:3
the fourteenth **d** of the month. Lv 23:5
on the fifteenth **d** of the same Lv 23:6
On the first **d** you are to hold a Lv 23:7
On the seventh **d** there will be a Lv 23:8
wave it on the **d** after the Lv 23:11
On the **d** you wave the sheaf, Lv 23:12
new grain until this very **d**, Lv 23:14
from the **d** after the Sabbath Lv 23:15
the **d** you brought the sheaf of Lv 23:15
days until the **d** after the Lv 23:16
On that same **d** you are to make a Lv 23:21
on the first ⌊**d**⌋ of the month, Lv 23:24
are to have a **d** of complete rest Lv 23:24
The tenth ⌊**d**⌋ of this seventh Lv 23:27
month is the **D** of Atonement. Lv 23:27
this particular **d** you are not to Lv 23:28
for it is a **D** of Atonement to Lv 23:28
self-denial on this particular **d**, Lv 23:29
does any work on this same **d**. Lv 23:30
of the ninth ⌊**d**⌋ of the month Lv 23:32
the fifteenth **d** of this seventh Lv 23:34
sacred assembly on the first **d**; Lv 23:35
On the eighth **d** you are to hold Lv 23:36
each on its ⌊designated⌋ **d**. Lv 23:37
the fifteenth **d** of the seventh Lv 23:39
on the first **d** and complete rest Lv 23:39
complete rest on the eighth **d**. Lv 23:39
On the first **d** you are to take Lv 23:40
every Sabbath **d** as a perpetual Lv 24:8
on the tenth ⌊**d**⌋ of the month; Lv 25:9
your land on the **D** of Atonement. Lv 25:9
valuation on that **d** as a holy Lv 27:23
on the first ⌊**d**⌋ of the second Nm 1:1
on the first **d** of the second Nm 1:18
his head on the **d** of his Nm 6:9
is to shave it on the seventh **d**. Nm 6:9
On the eighth **d** he is to bring Nm 6:10
On that **d** he must consecrate his Nm 6:11
the **d** his time of consecration Nm 6:13
On the **d** Moses finished setting Nm 7:1
Each **d** have one leader present Nm 7:11
on the first **d** was Nahshon son Nm 7:12
On the second **d** Nethanel son of Nm 7:18
On the third **d** Eliab son of Nm 7:24
On the fourth **d** Elizur son of Nm 7:30
On the fifth **d** Shelumiel son of Nm 7:36
On the sixth **d** Eliasaph son of Nm 7:42
On the seventh **d** Elishama son of Nm 7:48
On the eighth **d** Gamaliel son of Nm 7:54
On the ninth **d** Abidan son of Nm 7:60
On the tenth **d** Ahiezer son of Nm 7:66
On the eleventh **d** Pagiel son of Nm 7:72
On the twelfth **d** Ahira son of Nm 7:78
to Myself on the **d** I struck down Nm 8:17
the fourteenth **d** of this month Nm 9:3
on the fourteenth **d** at twilight Nm 9:5
observe the Passover on that **d**. Nm 9:6
Moses and Aaron the same **d** Nm 9:6
on the fourteenth **d** at twilight. Nm 9:11
On the **d** the tabernacle was set Nm 9:15
if it remained a **d** and a night, Nm 9:21
the twentieth ⌊**d**⌋ of the month, Nm 10:11
was over them by **d** when they set Nm 10:34
eat, not for one **d**, or two days, Nm 11:19
were up all that **d** and night and Nm 11:32
and all the next **d** gathering the Nm 11:32
of cloud by **d** and in a pillar Nm 14:14
the land, a year for each **d**. Nm 14:34
from the **d** the LORD issued the Nm 15:23
gathering wood on the Sabbath **d**. Nm 15:32
The next **d** the entire Israelite Nm 16:41
next **d** Moses entered the tent Nm 17:8
on the third **d** and the seventh Nm 19:12
the third day and the seventh **d**; Nm 19:12

on the third **d** and the seventh Nm 19:19
the third day and the seventh **d**. Nm 19:19
unclean person on the seventh **d**, Nm 19:19
was killed the **d** the plague came Nm 25:18
Each **d** ⌊present⌋ two unblemished Nm 28:3
On the Sabbath **d** ⌊present⌋ two Nm 28:9
the fourteenth **d** of the month. Nm 28:16
On the fifteenth **d** of this month Nm 28:17
On the first **d** there is to be a Nm 28:18
same food each **d** for seven days Nm 28:24
On the seventh **d** you are to hold Nm 28:25
On the **d** of firstfruits, you are Nm 28:26
on the first ⌊**d**⌋ of the month, Nm 29:1
This will be a **d** of jubilation Nm 29:1
on the tenth ⌊**d**⌋ of this seventh Nm 29:7
the fifteenth **d** of the seventh Nm 29:12
On the second **d** ⌊present⌋ 12 Nm 29:17
On the third **d** ⌊present⌋ 11 Nm 29:20
On the fourth **d** ⌊present⌋ 10 Nm 29:23
On the fifth **d** ⌊present⌋ nine Nm 29:26
On the sixth **d** ⌊present⌋ eight Nm 29:29
On the seventh **d** ⌊present⌋ seven Nm 29:32
On the eighth **d** you are to hold Nm 29:35
her on the **d** he hears ⌊about it⌋ Nm 30:5
them on the **d** he hears ⌊about it Nm 30:12
at all to her from **d** to day, Nm 30:14
at all to her from day to **d**, Nm 30:14
on the third **d** and the seventh Nm 31:19
the third day and the seventh **d**. Nm 31:19
On the seventh **d** wash your Nm 31:24
the LORD'S anger burned that **d**, Nm 32:10
on the fifteenth **d** of the month. Nm 33:3
On the **d** after the Passover the Nm 33:3
on the first ⌊**d**⌋ of the fifth Nm 33:38
in the cloud by **d** to guide you Dt 1:33
The **d** you stood before the LORD Dt 4:10
any form on the **d** the LORD spoke Dt 4:15
from the **d** God created man on Dt 4:32
to dedicate the Sabbath **d**, Dt 5:12
but the seventh **d** is a Sabbath Dt 5:14
you to keep the Sabbath **d**. Dt 5:15
LORD from the **d** you left the Dt 9:7
the **d** of the assembly the LORD Dt 9:10
Then, on the **d** of the assembly, Dt 10:4
of your life the **d** you left the Dt 16:3
the first **d** is to remain until Dt 16:4
same⌋ time ⌊of **d**⌋ you departed Dt 16:6
On the seventh **d** there is to be Dt 16:8
Horeb on the **d** of the assembly Dt 18:16
but are to bury him that **d**, Dt 21:23
his wages each **d** before the sun Dt 24:15
you this **d** to follow these Dt 26:16
d you have become the people Dt 27:9
On that **d** Moses commanded the Dt 27:11
weary looking for them every **d**. Dt 28:32
will be in dread night and **d**, Dt 28:66
Yet to this **d** the LORD has not Dt 29:4
burn against them on that **d**; Dt 31:17
that **d** they will say, 'Haven't Dt 31:17
My face on that **d** because of all Dt 31:18
song on that **d** and taught it to Dt 31:22
for their **d** of disaster is near, Dt 32:35
On that same **d** the LORD spoke to Dt 32:48
He shields him all **d** long, Dt 33:12
no one to this **d** knows where his Dt 34:6
are to recite it **d** and night, Jos 1:8
The stones are there to this **d**. Jos 4:9
that **d** the LORD exalted Joshua Jos 4:14
on the tenth **d** of the first Jos 4:19
been called Gilgal to this **d**. Jos 5:9
the fourteenth **d** of the month. Jos 5:10
The **d** after Passover they ate Jos 5:11
the **d** after they ate from the Jos 5:12
on the seventh **d**, march around Jos 6:4
On the second **d** they marched Jos 6:14
the seventh **d**, they started at Jos 6:15
That was the only **d** they marched Jos 6:15
she lives in Israel to this **d**. Jos 6:25
of rocks that remains to this **d**. Jos 7:26
the Valley of Achor to this **d**. Jos 7:26
total of those who fell that **d**, Jos 8:25
ruin, desolate to this **d**. Jos 8:28
it, which remains to this **d**. Jos 8:29
as food on the **d** we left to come Jos 9:12
Gibeonite cities on the third **d**. Jos 9:17
On that **d** he made them Jos 9:27
On the **d** the LORD gave the Jos 10:12
its setting almost a full **d**. Jos 10:13

has been no **d** like it before Jos 10:14
the stones are there to this **d**. Jos 10:27
On that **d** Joshua captured Jos 10:28
captured it on the second **d**. Jos 10:32
On that **d** they captured it and Jos 10:35
completely destroyed it that **d**, Jos 10:35
live in Israel to this **d**. Jos 13:13
On that **d** Moses promised me, Jos 14:9
as I was the **d** Moses sent me out Jos 14:11
LORD promised ⌊me⌋ on that **d**, Jos 14:12
as an inheritance to this **d**, Jos 14:14
descendants of Judah to this **d**. Jos 15:63
live in Ephraim to this **d**, Jos 16:10
from it even to this **d**, Jos 22:17
as you have done to this **d**. Jos 23:8
to stand against you to this **d**. Jos 23:9
On that **d** Joshua made a covenant Jos 24:25
in Jerusalem to this **d**. Jdg 1:21
That is its name to this **d**. Jdg 1:26
became subject to Israel that **d**, Jdg 3:30
for this is the **d** the LORD has Jdg 4:14
That **d** God subdued Jabin king of Jdg 4:23
On that **d** Deborah and Barak son Jdg 5:1
That **d**, Gideon's father called Jdg 6:32
Jerubbaal and his house this **d**, Jdg 9:19
The next **d** when the people went Jdg 9:42
against the city that entire **d**, Jdg 9:45
Jair's Villages to this **d**. Jdg 10:4
birth until the **d** of his death.' Jdg 13:7
On the fourth **d** they said to Jdg 14:15
the seventh **d**, he explained it Jdg 14:17
On the seventh **d** before sunset, Jdg 14:18
which is in Lehi to this **d**. Jdg 15:19
she nagged him **d** after day and Jdg 16:16
day after **d** and pled with him Jdg 16:16
the Camp of Dan to this **d**; Jdg 18:12
On the fourth **d**, they got up Jdg 19:5
morning of the fifth **d** to leave, Jdg 19:8
See, the **d** is almost over. Jdg 19:9
Jebus and the **d** was almost gone, Jdg 19:11
seen since the **d** the Israelites Jdg 19:30
of the land of Egypt to this **d**. Jdg 19:30
On that **d** the Benjaminites Jdg 20:15
of Israel on the field that **d**. Jdg 20:21
themselves on the first **d**. Jdg 20:22
On the second **d** the Israelites Jdg 20:24
same **d** the Benjaminites came Jdg 20:25
They fasted that **d** until evening Jdg 20:26
On the third **d** the Israelites Jdg 20:30
and on that **d** the Israelites Jdg 20:35
died that **d** were 25,000 armed Jdg 20:46
The next **d** the people got up Jdg 21:4
On the **d** you buy the land from Ru 4:5
of them will die on the same **d**. 1Sm 2:34
One **d** Eli, whose eyesight was 1Sm 3:2
On that **d** I will carry out 1Sm 3:12
That same **d**, a Benjaminite man 1Sm 4:12
is why, to this **d**, the priests 1Sm 5:5
That **d** the men of Beth-shemesh 1Sm 6:15
returned to Ekron that same **d**. 1Sm 6:16
of Beth-shemesh to this **d**. 1Sm 6:18
fasted that **d**, and there they 1Sm 7:6
Philistines that **d** and threw 1Sm 7:10
since the **d** I brought them out 1Sm 8:8
them out of Egypt until this **d**, 1Sm 8:8
When that **d** comes, you will cry 1Sm 8:18
won't answer you on that **d**." 1Sm 8:18
One **d** the donkeys of Saul's 1Sm 9:3
Now the **d** before Saul's arrival, 1Sm 9:15
So Saul ate with Samuel that **d**. 1Sm 9:24
all the signs came about that **d**. 1Sm 10:9
The next **d** Saul organized the 1Sm 11:11
them until the heat of the **d**. 1Sm 11:11
No one will be executed this **d**, 1Sm 11:13
and on that **d** the LORD sent 1Sm 12:18
on the **d** of battle not a sword 1Sm 13:22
That same **d** Saul's son Jonathan 1Sm 14:1
So the LORD saved Israel that **d**. 1Sm 14:23
of Israel were worn out that **d**, 1Sm 14:24
Philistines that **d** from Michmash 1Sm 14:31
God did not answer him that **d**. 1Sm 14:37
Even to the **d** of his death, 1Sm 15:35
of David from that **d** forward. 1Sm 16:13
⌊One **d**⌋, Jesse had told his son 1Sm 17:17
him from that **d** on and did not 1Sm 18:2
jealously from that **d** forward. 1Sm 18:9
The next **d** an evil spirit from 1Sm 18:10
Before the wedding **d** arrived, 1Sm 18:26

naked all that **d** and all that 1Sm 19:24
or the next **d** and I find out 1Sm 20:12
The following **d** hurry down and 1Sm 20:19
you hid on the **d** this incident 1Sm 20:19
say anything that **d** because he 1Sm 20:26
However, the **d** after the New 1Sm 20:27
Moon, the second **d**, David's 1Sm 20:27
Every **d** Jesse's son lives on 1Sm 20:31
that second **d** of the New Moon 1Sm 20:34
the LORD, was there that **d**. 1Sm 21:7
David fled that **d** from Saul's 1Sm 21:10
On that **d**, he killed 85 men who 1Sm 22:18
was there that **d** and that he was 1Sm 22:22
Saul searched for him every **d**, 1Sm 23:14
this is the **d** the LORD told you 1Sm 24:4
for we have come on a feast **d**. 1Sm 25:8
around us, both **d** and night, 1Sm 25:16
either his **d** will come and he 1Sm 26:10
d Achish gave Ziklag to him, 1Sm 27:6
any food all **d** and all night. 1Sm 28:20
From the **d** he defected until 1Sm 29:3
in you from the **d** you came to me 1Sm 29:6
From the first **d** I was with you 1Sm 29:8
in Ziklag on the third **d**. 1Sm 30:1
until the evening of the next **d**. 1Sm 30:17
has been so from that **d** forward. 1Sm 30:25
it continues⌋ to this very **d**. 1Sm 30:25
So on that **d**, Saul died together 1Sm 31:6
The next **d** when the Philistines 1Sm 31:8
On the third **d** a man with torn 2Sm 1:2
The battle that **d** was extremely 2Sm 2:17
eat bread while it was still **d**, 2Sm 3:35
On that **d** all the troops and all 2Sm 3:37
there as aliens to this very **d**. 2Sm 4:3
the heat of the **d** while the king 2Sm 4:5
He said that **d**, "Whoever attacks 2Sm 5:8
feared the LORD that **d** and said, 2Sm 6:9
no child to the **d** of her death. 2Sm 6:23
since the **d** I ordered judges 2Sm 7:11
Jerusalem that **d** and the next. 2Sm 11:12
On the seventh **d** the baby died. 2Sm 12:18
ever since the **d** Amnon disgraced 2Sm 13:32
mourned for his son every **d**. 2Sm 13:37
there was vast that **d**— 2Sm 18:7
and that **d** the forest claimed 2Sm 18:8
do it another **d**, but today you 2Sm 18:20
because on that **d** the troops 2Sm 19:2
quietly that **d** like people come 2Sm 19:3
on the **d** my lord the king 2Sm 19:19
clothes from the **d** the king left 2Sm 19:24
left until the **d** he returned 2Sm 19:24
until the **d** of their death, 2Sm 20:3
sky from them by **d** and the wild 2Sm 21:10
hung them the **d** the Philistines 2Sm 21:12
the LORD on the **d** the LORD 2Sm 22:1
me in the **d** of my distress, 2Sm 22:19
about a great victory that **d**. 2Sm 23:10
a pit on a snowy **d** and killed a 2Sm 23:20
to David that **d** and said to him, 2Sm 24:18
what I will do this very **d**." 1Kg 1:30
against me the **d** I went to 1Kg 2:8
On the **d** you do leave and cross 1Kg 2:37
'On the **d** you leave and go 1Kg 2:42
On the third **d** after I gave 1Kg 3:18
for one **d** were 150 bushels 1Kg 4:22
they are there to this **d**. 1Kg 8:8
Since the **d** I brought My people 1Kg 8:16
over this temple night and **d**, 1Kg 8:29
the LORD our God **d** and night, 1Kg 8:59
Israel, as each **d** requires, 1Kg 8:59
On the same **d**, the king 1Kg 8:64
On the fifteenth **d** he sent the 1Kg 8:66
⌊again⌋ even to this very **d**. 1Kg 10:12
came to Rehoboam on the third **d**, 1Kg 12:12
"Return to me on the third **d**." 1Kg 12:12
on the fifteenth **d** of the month, 1Kg 12:32
on the fifteenth **d** of the eighth 1Kg 12:33
a sign that **d**. He said, "This 1Kg 13:3
God had done that **d** in Bethel. 1Kg 13:11
This is the **d**, yes, even today! 1Kg 14:14
Israel that very **d** in the camp. 1Kg 16:16
dry until the **d** the LORD sends 1Kg 17:14
the seventh **d**, the battle took 1Kg 20:29
100,000 foot soldiers in one **d**. 1Kg 20:29
in an inner chamber on that **d**." 1Kg 22:25
battle raged throughout that **d**, 1Kg 22:35
to this very **d** according to 2Kg 2:22
One **d** Elisha went to Shunem. 2Kg 4:8
One **d** he came there and stopped 2Kg 4:11
grew and one **d** went out to his 2Kg 4:18
and I said to her the next **d**, 2Kg 6:29
Today is a **d** of good news. 2Kg 7:9
field from the **d** she left the 2Kg 8:6
The next **d** Hazael took a heavy 2Kg 8:15
which it is⌋ to this **d**. 2Kg 10:27
is its name⌋ to this very **d**. 2Kg 14:7
until the **d** of his death. 2Kg 15:5
the former customs to this **d**. 2Kg 17:34
'Today is a **d** of distress, 2Kg 19:3
One **d**, while he was worshiping 2Kg 19:37
On the third **d** ⌊from now⌋ you 2Kg 20:5
LORD's temple on the third **d**?" 2Kg 20:8
up until this **d** will be carried 2Kg 20:17
Me from the **d** their ancestors 2Kg 21:15
on the tenth **d** of the tenth 2Kg 25:1
By the ninth **d** of the ⌊fourth⌋ 2Kg 25:3
On the seventh **d** of the fifth 2Kg 25:8
twenty-seventh **d** of the twelfth 2Kg 25:27
portion for each **d**, for the rest 2Kg 25:30
they were on duty **d** and night. 1Ch 9:33
The next **d** when the Philistines 1Ch 10:8
a pit on a snowy **d** and killed a 1Ch 11:22
men came **d** after day to help 1Ch 12:22
came day after **d** to help David 1Ch 12:22
God that **d**, and said, "How 1Ch 13:12
On that **d** David decreed for the 1Ch 16:7
His salvation from **d** to day. 1Ch 16:23
His salvation from day to **d**. 1Ch 16:23
since the **d** I ordered judges 1Ch 17:10
six Levites each **d** on the east, 1Ch 26:17
east, four each **d** on the north, 1Ch 26:17
north, four each **d** on the south, 1Ch 26:17
The following **d** they offered 1Ch 29:21
in the LORD's presence that **d**. 1Ch 29:22
on the second ⌊**d**⌋ of the second 2Ch 3:2
they are there to this very **d**. 2Ch 5:9
Since the **d** I brought My people 2Ch 6:5
over this temple **d** and night, 2Ch 6:20
On the eighth **d** they held a 2Ch 7:9
twenty-third **d** of the seventh 2Ch 7:10
out from the **d** the foundation 2Ch 8:16
came to Rehoboam on the third **d**, 2Ch 10:12
"Return to me on the third **d**." 2Ch 10:12
in an inner chamber on that **d**." 2Ch 18:24
battle raged throughout that **d**, 2Ch 18:34
of Beracah on the fourth **d**, 2Ch 20:26
come out **d** after day because 2Ch 21:15
come out day after **d** because of 2Ch 21:15
This continued **d** after day until 2Ch 21:19
day after **d** until two full 2Ch 21:19
120,000 in Judah in one **d**— 2Ch 28:6
on the first **d** of the first 2Ch 29:17
on the eighth **d** of the month 2Ch 29:17
on the sixteenth **d** of the first 2Ch 29:17
the fourteenth **d** of the second 2Ch 30:15
praised the LORD **d** after day 2Ch 30:21
the LORD day after **d** with loud 2Ch 30:21
on the fourteenth **d** of the first 2Ch 35:1
established that **d** for observing 2Ch 35:16
in their dirges to this very **d**. 2Ch 35:25
offered⌋ burnt offerings each **d**, Ezr 3:4
ordinance for each festival **d**. Ezr 3:4
On the first **d** of the seventh Ezr 3:6
to them every **d** without fail, Ezr 6:9
on the third **d** of the month of Ezr 6:15
on the fourteenth **d** of the first Ezr 6:19
the first **d** of the first month Ezr 7:9
on the first **d** of the fifth Ezr 7:9
on the twelfth ⌊**d**⌋ of the first Ezr 8:31
On the fourth **d** the silver, Ezr 8:33
the twentieth ⌊**d**⌋ of the ninth Ezr 10:9
that can be done in a **d** or two, Ezr 10:13
the first **d** of the tenth month Ezr 10:16
and by the first **d** of the first Ezr 10:17
now pray to You **d** and night for Neh 1:6
because of them **d** and night. Neh 4:9
From that **d** on, half of my men Neh 4:16
guard by night and work by **d**." Neh 4:22
from the **d** King Artaxerxes Neh 5:14
d, one ox, six choice sheep, Neh 5:18
the twenty-fifth **d** of the month Neh 6:15
On the first **d** of the seventh Neh 8:2
This **d** is holy to the LORD your Neh 8:9
On the second **d**, the family Neh 8:13
Joshua son of Nun until that **d**. Neh 8:17
book of the law of God every **d**, Neh 8:18
from the first **d** to the last. Neh 8:18
and on the eighth **d** there was an Neh 8:18
twenty-fourth **d** of this month Neh 9:1
a fourth of the **d** and ⌊spent⌋ Neh 9:3
fourth of the **d** in confession Neh 9:3
Yourself that endures to this **d**. Neh 9:10
with a pillar of cloud by **d**, Neh 9:12
During the **d** the pillar of cloud Neh 9:19
grain to sell on the Sabbath **d**, Neh 10:31
them on the Sabbath or a holy **d**. Neh 10:31
On that **d** they offered great Neh 12:43
that same **d** men were placed in Neh 12:44
to Jerusalem on the Sabbath **d**. Neh 13:15
against selling food on that **d**. Neh 13:15
doing—profaning the Sabbath **d**? Neh 13:17
enter during the Sabbath **d**. Neh 13:19
to keep the Sabbath **d** holy. Neh 13:22
On the seventh **d**, when the king Est 1:10
⌊Before⌋ this **d** ⌊is over⌋, Est 1:18
Every **d** Mordecai took a walk in Est 2:11
had warned him **d** after day and Est 3:4
him day after **d** and he still Est 3:4
Haman for each **d** in each month, Est 3:7
on the thirteenth **d** of the first Est 3:12
their possessions on a single **d**, Est 3:13
day, the thirteenth **d** of Adar, Est 3:13
they might get ready for that **d**. Est 3:14
for three days, night and **d**. Est 4:16
the third **d**, Esther dressed up Est 5:1
That **d** Haman left full of joy Est 5:9
on the second **d** while drinking Est 7:2
That same **d** King Ahasuerus Est 8:1
the twenty-third **d** of the third Est 8:9
on a single **d** throughout all Est 8:12
the thirteenth **d** of the twelfth Est 8:12
against their enemies on that **d**. Est 8:13
the thirteenth **d** of the twelfth Est 9:1
On the **d** when the Jews' enemies Est 9:1
On that **d** the number of people Est 9:11
on the fourteenth **d** of the month Est 9:15
on the thirteenth **d** of the month Est 9:17
it became a **d** of feasting and Est 9:17
on the fifteenth **d** of the month, Est 9:18
it became a **d** of feasting and Est 9:18
the fourteenth **d** of the month of Est 9:19
One **d** the sons of God came to Jb 1:6
One **d** when Job's sons and Jb 1:13
One **d** the sons of God came again Jb 2:1
and cursed the **d** he was born. Jb 3:1
May the **d** I was born perish, Jb 3:3
If only that **d** had turned to Jb 3:4
They encounter darkness by **d**, Jb 5:14
he can enjoy his **d** like a hired Jb 14:6
He knows the **d** of darkness is Jb 15:23
night into **d** and ⌊made⌋ light Jb 17:12
away on the **d** of God's anger. Jb 20:28
spared from the **d** of disaster, Jb 21:30
rescued from the **d** of wrath. Jb 21:30
by **d** they lock themselves in, Jb 24:16
and since the **d** I was born I Jb 31:18
for the **d** of warfare and battle? Jb 38:23
he meditates on it **d** and night. Ps 1:2
who executes justice every **d**. Ps 7:11
me, agony in my mind every **d**? Ps 13:2
me in the **d** of my distress, Ps 18:18
D after day they pour out speech; Ps 19:2
after **d** they pour out speech; Ps 19:2
answer you in a **d** of trouble; Ps 20:1
answer us on the **d** that we call. Ps 20:9
God, I cry by **d**, but You do not Ps 22:2
I wait for You all **d** long. Ps 25:5
shelter in the **d** of adversity; Ps 27:5
from my groaning all **d** long. Ps 32:3
For **d** and night Your hand was Ps 32:4
Your praise all **d** long. Ps 35:28
He sees that his **d** is coming. Ps 37:13
all **d** long I go around in Ps 38:6
they plot treachery all **d** long. Ps 38:12
save him in a **d** of adversity. Ps 41:1
have been my food **d** and night, Ps 42:3
while all **d** long people say to Ps 42:3
send His faithful love by **d**; Ps 42:8
while all **d** long they say to me, Ps 42:10
We boast in God all **d** long; Ps 44:8
is before me all **d** long, Ps 44:15
of You we are slain all **d** long; Ps 44:22
Call on Me in a **d** of trouble; Ps 50:15
d and night they make the rounds Ps 55:10

and oppresses me all **d** long. Ps 56:1
My adversaries trample me all **d**, Ps 56:2
They twist my words all **d** long; Ps 56:5
retreat on the **d** when I call. Ps 56:9
a refuge in my **d** of trouble. Ps 59:16
fulfilling my vows **d** by day. Ps 61:8
fulfilling my vows day by **d**. Ps 61:8
D after day He bears our burdens; Ps 68:19
after **d** He bears our burdens; Ps 68:19
and honor to You all **d** long. Ps 71:8
and Your salvation all **d** long, Ps 71:15
Your righteousness all **d** long, Ps 71:24
may he be blessed all **d** long. Ps 72:15
For I am afflicted all **d** long, Ps 73:14
The **d** is Yours, also the night; Ps 74:16
bring against You all **d** long. Ps 74:22
In my **d** of trouble I sought the Ps 77:2
turned back on the **d** of battle. Ps 78:9
with a cloud by **d** and with a Ps 78:14
shown⌋ on the **d** He redeemed them Ps 78:42
moon, on the **d** of our feast. Ps 81:3
Better a **d** in Your courts than a Ps 84:10
for I call to You all **d** long. Ps 86:3
on You in the **d** of my distress, Ps 86:7
cry out before You **d** and night. Ps 88:1
I cry out to You all **d** long; Ps 88:9
me like water all **d** long; Ps 88:17
rejoice in Your name all **d** long, Ps 89:16
the arrow that flies by **d**, Ps 91:5
as on that **d** at Massah in the Ps 95:8
His salvation from **d** to day. Ps 96:2
His salvation from day to **d**. Ps 96:2
face from me in my **d** of trouble. Ps 102:2
My enemies taunt me all **d** long; Ps 102:8
volunteer on Your **d** of battle. Ps 110:3
kings on the **d** of His anger. Ps 110:5
This is the **d** the LORD has made; Ps 118:24
It is my meditation all **d** long. Ps 119:97
You seven times a **d** for Your Ps 119:164
sun will not strike you by **d**, Ps 121:6
the sun to rule by **d**, His love Ps 136:8
said that **d** at Jerusalem: Ps 137:7
On the **d** I called, You answered Ps 138:3
The night shines like the **d**; Ps 139:12
They stir up wars all **d** long. Ps 140:2
my head on the **d** of battle. Ps 140:7
I will praise You every **d**; Ps 145:2
on that **d** his plans die. Ps 146:4
I was His delight every **d**, Pr 8:30
watching at my doors every **d**, Pr 8:34
not profitable on a **d** of wrath, Pr 11:4
wicked for the **d** of disaster. Pr 16:4
filled with craving all **d** long, Pr 21:26
is prepared for the **d** of battle, Pr 21:31
coolness of snow on a harvest **d**; Pr 25:13
taking off clothing on a cold **d**, Pr 25:20
don't know what a **d** might bring. Pr 27:1
on a rainy **d** and a nagging wife Pr 27:15
the **d** of one's death than the Ec 7:1
death than the **d** of one's birth. Ec 7:1
the **d** of prosperity be joyful, Ec 7:14
but in the **d** of adversity, Ec 7:14
authority over the **d** of death; Ec 8:8
do not close in sleep **d** or night Ec 8:16
on the **d** when the guardians of Ec 12:3
Before the **d** breaks and the Sg 2:17
on him the **d** of his wedding— Sg 3:11
the **d** of his heart's rejoicing. Sg 3:11
Before the **d** breaks and the Sg 4:6
sister on the **d** she is spoken Sg 8:8
alone will be exalted on that **d**. Is 2:11
For a **d** belonging to the LORD of Is 2:12
alone will be exalted on that **d**. Is 2:17
that **d** people will throw their Is 2:20
On that **d** he will cry out, Is 3:7
On that **d** the Lord will strip Is 3:18
On that **d** seven women will seize Is 4:1
On that **d** the branch of the LORD Is 4:2
of smoke by **d** and a glowing Is 4:5
booth for shade from heat by **d**, Is 4:6
that **d** they will roar over it, Is 5:30
On that **d** the LORD will whistle Is 7:18
On that **d** the Lord will use a Is 7:20
On that **d** a man will raise a Is 7:21
And on that **d** every place where Is 7:23
as ⌊You did⌋ on the **d** of Midian. Is 9:4
branch and reed in a single **d**. Is 9:14
you do on the **d** of punishment Is 10:3

In one **d** it will burn up Is 10:17
On that **d** the remnant of Israel Is 10:20
On that **d** his burden will fall Is 10:27
On that **d** the root of Jesse will Is 11:10
On that **d** the Lord will ⌊extend⌋ Is 11:11
On that **d** you will say: Is 12:1
and on that **d** you will say: Is 12:4
For the **d** of the LORD is near. Is 13:6
the **d** of the LORD is coming— Is 13:9
on the **d** of His burning anger. Is 13:13
On that **d** the splendor of Jacob Is 17:4
On that **d** people will look to Is 17:7
On that **d** their strong cities Is 17:9
the **d** that you plant, you will Is 17:11
will vanish on the **d** of disease Is 17:11
On that **d** Egypt will be like Is 19:16
that **d** five cities in the land Is 19:18
On that **d** there will be an altar Is 19:19
will know the LORD on that **d**. Is 19:21
that **d** there will be a highway Is 19:23
that **d** Israel will form a triple Is 19:24
coastland will say on that **d**: Is 20:6
I stand on the watchtower all **d**, Is 21:8
GOD of Hosts had a **d** of tumult, Is 22:5
On that **d** you looked to the Is 22:8
On that **d** the Lord GOD of Hosts Is 22:12
On that **d** I will call for my Is 22:20
On that **d**"—the declaration of Is 22:25
On that **d** Tyre will be forgotten Is 23:15
On that **d** the LORD will punish Is 24:21
cloud ⌊cools⌋ the heat of the **d**, Is 25:5
On that **d** it will be said, Is 25:9
On that **d** this song will be sung Is 26:1
On that **d** the LORD with His Is 27:1
On that **d** sing about a desirable Is 27:2
it night and **d** so that no one Is 27:3
storm on the **d** of the east wind. Is 27:8
On that **d** the LORD will thresh Is 27:12
that **d** a great trumpet will be Is 27:13
On that **d** the LORD of Hosts will Is 28:5
every **d** and every night Is 28:19
plow every **d** to plant seed? Is 28:24
On that **d** the deaf will hear the Is 29:18
On that **d** your cattle will graze Is 30:23
hill on the **d** of great slaughter Is 30:25
on the **d** that the LORD bandages Is 30:26
For on that **d**, each one will Is 31:7
the LORD has a **d** of vengeance, Is 34:8
will never go out—**d** or night. Is 34:10
'Today is a **d** of distress, Is 37:3
One **d**, while he was worshiping Is 37:38
an end of me from **d** until night. Is 38:12
make an end of me **d** and night. Is 38:13
up until this **d** will be carried Is 39:6
to you suddenly, in one **d**: Is 47:9
help you in the **d** of salvation. Is 49:8
constant dread all **d** long Is 51:13
blasphemed all **d** long. Is 52:5
know⌋ on that **d** that I am He who Is 52:6
They seek Me **d** after day and Is 58:2
Me day after **d** and delight to Is 58:2
please on the **d** of your fast, Is 58:3
d for a person to deny himself, Is 58:5
this a fast and a **d** acceptable Is 58:5
whatever you want on My holy **d**; Is 58:13
and the holy ⌊**d**⌋ of the LORD Is 58:13
never be shut **d** or night so that Is 60:11
no longer be your light by **d**, Is 60:19
the **d** of our God's vengeance; Is 61:2
never be silent, **d** or night. Is 62:6
I planned the **d** of vengeance, Is 63:4
out My hands all **d** long to a Is 65:2
a fire that burns all **d** long. Is 65:5
Can a land be born in one **d**, Is 66:8
of our youth even to this **d**. Jr 3:25
"On that **d**"—⌊this is⌋ the Jr 4:9
Woe to us, for the **d** is passing; Jr 6:4
Since the **d** your ancestors came Jr 7:25
the land of Egypt until this **d**, Jr 7:25
would weep **d** and night over the Jr 9:1
them apart for the **d** of killing. Jr 12:3
d and night may ⌊they⌋ not stop, Jr 14:17
sun set while it was still **d**; Jr 15:9
other gods both **d** and night, Jr 16:13
have not longed for the fatal **d**. Jr 17:16
my refuge in the **d** of disaster. Jr 17:17
Bring on them the **d** of disaster; Jr 17:18
of Jerusalem on the Sabbath **d**. Jr 17:21

on the Sabbath **d** or do any work, Jr 17:22
must consecrate the Sabbath **d**, Jr 17:22
on the Sabbath **d** and consecrate Jr 17:24
the Sabbath **d** and do no work on Jr 17:24
the Sabbath **d** by not carrying a Jr 17:27
of Jerusalem on the Sabbath **d**, Jr 17:27
My⌋ face on the **d** of their Jr 18:17
next **d**, when Pashhur released Jr 20:3
Cursed be the **d** on which I was Jr 20:14
The **d** my mother bore me—let it Jr 20:14
until this very **d**—23 years— Jr 25:3
LORD on that **d** will be ⌊spread Jr 25:33
How awful that **d** will be! Jr 30:7
"On that **d**"—⌊this is⌋ the Jr 30:8
there will be a **d** when watchmen Jr 31:6
gives the sun for light by **d**, Jr 31:35
so to this very **d** both in Israel Jr 32:20
and fury from the **d** it was built Jr 32:31
with the **d** and My covenant Jr 33:20
night so that **d** and night cease Jr 33:20
covenant with the **d** and with the Jr 33:25
to this very **d** because they have Jr 35:14
of the LORD on a **d** of fasting. Jr 36:6
the heat of **d** and the frost of Jr 36:30
of bread each **d** from the baker's Jr 37:21
until the **d** Jerusalem was Jr 38:28
on the ninth **d** of the month, Jr 39:2
before your eyes on that **d**. Jr 39:16
I will rescue you on that **d**"— Jr 39:17
On the second **d** after he had Jr 41:4
not become humble to this **d**, Jr 44:10
That **d** belongs to the Lord, Jr 46:10
a **d** of vengeance to avenge Jr 46:10
for the **d** of their calamity is Jr 46:21
account of the **d** that is coming Jr 47:4
In that **d** the heart of Moab's Jr 48:41
In that **d** the hearts of Edom's Jr 49:22
will be silenced in that **d**. Jr 49:26
because their **d** has come, the Jr 50:27
will be silenced in that **d**. Jr 50:30
because your **d** has come, the Jr 50:31
every side in the **d** of disaster. Jr 51:2
on the tenth **d** of the tenth Jr 52:4
By the ninth **d** of the fourth Jr 52:6
in custody until his dying **d**. Jr 52:11
the tenth **d** of the fifth month Jr 52:12
twenty-fifth **d** of the twelfth Jr 52:31
portion for each **d** until the day Jr 52:34
day until the **d** of his death, Jr 52:34
suffer on the **d** of His burning Lm 1:12
me desolate, sick all **d** long. Lm 1:13
Bring on the **d** You have Lm 1:21
footstool in the **d** of His anger. Lm 2:1
LORD as on the **d** of an appointed Lm 2:7
is the **d** we have waited for! Lm 2:16
down like a river **d** and night. Lm 2:18
them⌋ in the **d** of Your anger, Lm 2:21
⌊for⌋ an appointed festival **d**; Lm 2:22
on the **d** of the LORD's anger no Lm 2:22
His hand against me all **d** long. Lm 3:3
by their songs all **d** long. Lm 3:14
opponents attack me all **d** long. Lm 3:62
on the fifth ⌊**d**⌋ of the month, Ezk 1:1
On the fifth ⌊**d**⌋ of the month— Ezk 1:2
rainbow in a cloud on a rainy **d**. Ezk 1:28
against Me to this **d**. Ezk 2:3
you 40 days, a **d** for each year. Ezk 4:6
you eat each **d** will be eight Ezk 4:10
has come; the **d** is near. There Ezk 7:7
Look, the **d** is coming! Doom has Ezk 7:10
has come; the **d** has arrived. Let Ezk 7:12
save them in the **d** of the LORD's Ezk 7:19
on the fifth ⌊**d**⌋ of the month, Ezk 8:1
in their sight during the **d**. Ezk 12:3
During the **d**, bring out your Ezk 12:4
in battle on the **d** of the LORD. Ezk 13:5
cut on the **d** you were born, Ezk 16:4
despised on the **d** you were born. Ezk 16:5
on the tenth ⌊**d**⌋ of the month, Ezk 20:1
On the **d** I chose Israel, I swore Ezk 20:5
On that **d** I swore to them that I Ezk 20:6
is called High Place to this **d**. Ezk 20:29
with all your idols to this **d**. Ezk 20:31
d has come for your punishment. Ezk 21:25
the **d** has come for your Ezk 21:29
rain in the **d** of indignation. Ezk 22:24
on that same **d** and profaned My Ezk 23:38
On the same **d** they slaughtered Ezk 23:39

on the tenth ⌊**d**⌋ of the month: Ezk 24:1
down today's date, this very **d**. Ezk 24:2
siege to Jerusalem this very **d**. Ezk 24:2
know that on the **d** I take their Ezk 24:25
that **d** a fugitive will come to Ezk 24:26
that **d** your mouth will be opened Ezk 24:27
on the first ⌊**d**⌋ of the month, Ezk 26:1
tremble on the **d** of your Ezk 26:18
the sea on the **d** of your Ezk 27:27
prepared on the **d** you were Ezk 28:13
From the **d** you were created you Ezk 28:15
on the twelfth ⌊**d**⌋ of the month, Ezk 29:1
on the first ⌊**d**⌋ of the month, Ezk 29:17
In that **d** I will cause a horn to Ezk 29:21
GOD says: Wail: Alas for the **d**! Ezk 30:2
For a **d** is near; a day belonging Ezk 30:3
a **d** belonging to the LORD is Ezk 30:3
It will be a **d** of clouds, a time Ezk 30:3
that **d**, messengers will go out Ezk 30:9
them on the **d** of Egypt's ⌊doom Ezk 30:9
The **d** will be dark in Ezk 30:18
on the seventh ⌊**d**⌋ of the month, Ezk 30:20
on the first ⌊**d**⌋ of the month, Ezk 31:1
grieving on the **d** the cedar went Ezk 31:15
on the first ⌊**d**⌋ of the month, Ezk 32:1
the **d** of your downfall each of Ezk 32:10
the fifteenth ⌊**d**⌋ of the month, Ezk 32:17
not save him on the **d** of his Ezk 33:12
stumble on the **d** he turns from Ezk 33:12
righteousness on the **d** he sins. Ezk 33:12
on the fifth ⌊**d**⌋ of the month, Ezk 33:21
sheep on the **d** he is among his Ezk 34:12
on a cloudy and dark **d**. Ezk 34:12
On the **d** I cleanse you from all Ezk 36:33
that **d**, thoughts will arise in Ezk 38:10
On that **d** when My people Israel Ezk 38:14
Now on that **d**, the day when Gog Ezk 38:18
the **d** when Gog comes against the Ezk 38:18
On that **d** there will be a great Ezk 38:19
This is the **d** I have spoken Ezk 39:8
Now on that **d** I will give Gog a Ezk 39:11
spread on the **d** I display My Ezk 39:13
From that **d** forward the house of Ezk 39:22
on the tenth **d** of the month in Ezk 40:1
on that very **d** the LORD's hand Ezk 40:1
the altar on the **d** it is Ezk 43:18
On the second **d** you are to Ezk 43:22
offering each **d** for seven days. Ezk 43:25
on the eighth **d** and afterwards, Ezk 43:27
On the **d** he goes into the Ezk 44:27
on the first ⌊**d**⌋ of the month, Ezk 45:18
on the seventh ⌊**d**⌋ of the month Ezk 45:20
the fourteenth **d** of the month, Ezk 45:21
that **d** the prince will provide Ezk 45:22
a male goat each **d** for a sin Ezk 45:23
the fifteenth **d** of the seventh Ezk 45:25
on the Sabbath **d** and opened on Ezk 46:1
opened on the **d** of the New Moon Ezk 46:1
on the Sabbath **d** is to be six Ezk 46:4
On the **d** of the New Moon, Ezk 46:6
as he does on the Sabbath **d**. Ezk 46:12
the city from that **d** on will be: Ezk 48:35
and three times a **d** he got down Dn 6:10
for he prays three times a **d**." Dn 6:13
but this **d** public shame belongs Dn 9:7
name ⌊renowned⌋ as it is this **d**, Dn 9:15
the twenty-fourth **d** of the first Dn 10:4
from the first **d** that you Dn 10:12
that **d** I will break the bow of Hs 1:5
For the **d** of Jezreel will be Hs 1:11
she was on the **d** of her birth. Hs 2:3
as in the **d** she came out of the Hs 2:15
In that **d**—the LORD's Hs 2:16
On that **d** I will make a covenant Hs 2:18
On that **d** I will respond— Hs 2:21
will stumble by **d**; the prophet Hs 4:5
on the **d** of punishment; Hs 5:9
on the third **d** He will raise us Hs 6:2
the **d** of our king, the princes Hs 7:5
will you do on a festival **d**, Hs 9:5
on the **d** of the LORD's feast? Hs 9:5
be demolished in a **d** of war, Hs 10:14
because of that **d**! For the Day Jl 1:15
the **D** of the LORD is near and Jl 1:15
for the **D** of the LORD is coming; Jl 2:1
a **d** of darkness and gloom, Jl 2:2
d of clouds and dense overcast, Jl 2:2
D of the LORD is terrible and Jl 2:11
awe-inspiring **D** of the LORD Jl 2:31
For the **D** of the LORD is near in Jl 3:14
that **d** the mountains will drip Jl 3:18
be shouting on the **d** of battle Am 1:14
wind on the **d** of the storm. Am 1:14
will flee naked on that **d**— Am 2:16
Bethel on the **d** I punish Israel Am 3:14
dawn and darkens **d** into night, Am 5:8
who long for the **D** of the LORD! Am 5:18
What will the **D** of the LORD be Am 5:18
Won't the **D** of the LORD be Am 5:20
thought of the evil **d** and bring Am 6:3
In that **d** the temple songs will Am 8:3
And in that **d**—⌊this is⌋ the Am 8:9
and its outcome like a bitter **d**. Am 8:10
In that **d** the beautiful young Am 8:13
In that **d** I will restore the Am 9:11
In that **d**—the LORD's Ob 8
On the **d** you stood aloof, on the Ob 11
on the **d** strangers captured his Ob 11
in the **d** of his calamity; Ob 12
of Judah in the **d** of their Ob 12
mock in the **d** of distress. Ob 12
My people in the **d** of their Ob 13
in the **d** of their disaster Ob 13
in the **d** of their disaster Ob 13
survivors in the **d** of distress. Ob 14
For the **D** of the LORD is near, Ob 15
out on the first **d** of his walk Jnh 3:4
When dawn came the next **d**, Jnh 4:7
In that **d** one will take up a Mc 2:4
On that **d**—⌊this is⌋ the LORD's Mc 4:6
In that **d**—the LORD's Mc 5:10
The **d** of your watchmen, ⌊the day Mc 7:4
⌊the **d** of⌋ your punishment, Mc 7:4
d will come for rebuilding your Mc 7:11
that **d** ⌊your⌋ boundary will be Mc 7:11
that **d** people will come to you Mc 7:12
a stronghold in a **d** of distress; Nah 1:7
fire on the **d** of its ⌊battle⌋ Nah 2:3
settle on the walls on a cold **d**; Nah 3:17
wait for the **d** of distress to Hab 3:16
for the **D** of the LORD is near. Zph 1:7
On the **d** of the LORD's sacrifice Zph 1:8
On that **d** I will punish all who Zph 1:9
On that **d**—the LORD's Zph 1:10
The great **D** of the LORD is near, Zph 1:14
Listen, the **D** of the LORD— Zph 1:14
That **d** is a day of wrath, a day Zph 1:15
That day is a **d** of wrath, a day Zph 1:15
a **d** of trouble and distress, Zph 1:15
a **d** of destruction and Zph 1:15
a **d** of darkness and gloom, Zph 1:15
a **d** of clouds and blackness, Zph 1:15
d of trumpet ⌊blast⌋ and battle Zph 1:16
them on the **d** of the LORD's Zph 1:18
effect and the **d** passes like Zph 2:2
before the **d** of the LORD's anger Zph 2:2
concealed on the **d** of the LORD's Zph 2:3
until the **d** I rise up for Zph 3:8
On that **d** you will not be put to Zph 3:11
On that **d** it will be said to Zph 3:16
on the first **d** of the sixth Hg 1:1
the twenty-fourth **d** of the sixth Hg 1:15
twenty-first **d** of the seventh Hg 2:1
the twenty-fourth **d** of the ninth Hg 2:10
Now, reflect back from this **d**: Hg 2:15
carefully from this **d** forward; Hg 2:18
the twenty-fourth **d** of the ninth Hg 2:18
from the **d** the foundation of the Hg 2:18
from this **d** on I will bless you. Hg 2:19
twenty-fourth **d** of the month: Hg 2:20
On that **d**"—the declaration of Hg 2:23
twenty-fourth **d** of the eleventh Zch 1:7
the LORD on that **d** and become My Zch 2:11
of this land in a single **d**. Zch 3:9
On that **d**, each of you will Zch 3:10
scorns the **d** of small things? Zch 4:10
and go that same **d** to the house Zch 6:10
on the fourth **d** of the ninth Zch 7:1
save them on that **d** as the flock Zch 9:16
It was annulled on that **d**, Zch 11:11
On that **d** I will make Jerusalem Zch 12:3
On that **d**"—the LORD's Zch 12:4
that **d** I will make the leaders Zch 12:6
On that **d** the LORD will defend Zch 12:8
will be like David on that **d**, Zch 12:8
On that **d** I will set out to Zch 12:9
On that **d** the mourning in Zch 12:11
On that **d** a fountain will be Zch 13:1
On that **d**"—the declaration of Zch 13:2
On that **d** every prophet will be Zch 13:4
A **d** of the LORD is coming when Zch 14:1
as He fights on a **d** of battle. Zch 14:3
On that **d** His feet will stand on Zch 14:4
that **d** there will be no light; Zch 14:6
It will be a **d** known ⌊only⌋ to Zch 14:7
to Yahweh, without **d** or night, Zch 14:7
On that **d** living water will flow Zch 14:8
that **d** Yahweh will become king Zch 14:9
On that **d** a great panic from the Zch 14:13
On that **d**, ⌊the words⌋ HOLY TO Zch 14:20
And on that **d** there will no Zch 14:21
can endure the **d** of His coming? Mal 3:2
on the **d** I am preparing. Mal 3:17
For indeed, the **d** is coming, Mal 4:1
The coming **d** will consume them," Mal 4:1
feet on the **d** I am preparing, Mal 4:3
and awesome **D** of the LORD comes Mal 4:5
Each **d** has enough trouble of its Mt 6:34
On that **d** many will say to Me, Mt 7:22
on the **d** of judgment for Mt 10:15
Sidon on the **d** of judgment than Mt 11:22
of Sodom on the **d** of judgment Mt 11:24
you that on the **d** of judgment Mt 12:36
On that **d** Jesus went out of the Mt 13:1
and be raised the third **d**. Mt 16:21
and on the third **d** He will be Mt 17:23
on one denarius for the **d**, Mt 20:2
here all **d** doing nothing?' Mt 20:6
burden of the **d** and the burning Mt 20:12
be resurrected on the third **d**." Mt 20:19
The same **d** some Sadducees, Mt 22:23
and from that **d** no one dared to Mt 22:46
concerning that **d** and hour no Mt 24:36
the **d** Noah boarded the ark. Mt 24:38
don't know what **d** your Lord is Mt 24:42
will come on a **d** he does not Mt 24:50
know either the **d** or the hour. Mt 25:13
On the first **d** of Unleavened Mt 26:17
vine until that **d** when I drink Mt 26:29
Every **d** I used to sit, teaching Mt 26:55
called "Blood Field" to this **d**. Mt 27:8
The next **d**, which followed the Mt 27:62
followed the preparation **d**, Mt 27:62
made secure until the third **d**. Mt 27:64
as the first **d** of the week was Mt 28:1
among Jewish people to this **d**. Mt 28:15
then they will fast in that **d**. Mk 2:20
rises—night and **d**, and the Mk 4:27
that **d**, when evening had come, Mk 4:35
night and **d**, he was crying Mk 5:5
The next **d** when they came out Mk 11:12
concerning that **d** or hour no one Mk 13:32
On the first **d** of Unleavened Mk 14:12
vine until that **d** when I drink Mk 14:25
d I was among you, teaching Mk 14:49
because it was preparation **d** Mk 15:42
day (that is, the **d** before the Mk 15:42
on the first **d** of the week, Mk 16:2
on the first **d** of the week, Mk 16:9
speak until the **d** these things Lk 1:20
the child on the eighth **d**, Lk 1:59
until the **d** of his public Lk 1:80
God night and **d** with fastings Lk 2:37
on the Sabbath **d** and stood up to Lk 4:16
When it was **d**, He went out and Lk 4:42
Rejoice in that **d** and leap for Lk 6:23
One **d** He and His disciples got Lk 8:22
Late in the **d**, the Twelve Lk 9:12
and be raised the third **d**." Lk 9:22
The next **d**, when they came down Lk 9:37
on that **d** it will be more Lk 10:12
The next **d** he took out two Lk 10:35
Give us each **d** our daily bread. Lk 11:3
will come on a **d** he does not Lk 12:46
and not on the Sabbath **d**." Lk 13:14
this bondage on the Sabbath **d**?" Lk 13:16
on the third **d** I will complete Lk 13:32
the next **d**, because it is not Lk 13:33
pull him out on the Sabbath **d**?" Lk 14:5
feasting lavishly every **d**. Lk 16:19
One **d** the poor man died and was Lk 16:22
against you seven times in a **d**, Lk 17:4
the Son of Man will be in His **d**. Lk 17:24
marriage until the **d** Noah Lk 17:27

But on the **d** Lot left Sodom, Lk 17:29
like that on the **d** the Son of Lk 17:30
that **d**, a man on the housetop, Lk 17:31
who cry out to Him **d** and night? Lk 18:7
He will rise on the third **d**." Lk 18:33
If you knew this **d** what ⌊would Lk 19:42
Every **d** He was teaching in the Lk 19:47
One **d** as He was teaching the Lk 20:1
or that **d** will come on you Lk 21:34
During the **d**, He was teaching in Lk 21:37
Then the **D** of Unleavened Bread Lk 22:7
Every **d** while I was with you in Lk 22:53
That very **d** Herod and Pilate Lk 23:12
was preparation **d**, and the Lk 23:54
On the first **d** of the week, Lk 24:1
and rise on the third **d**'?" Lk 24:7
Now that same **d** two of them were Lk 24:13
it's the third **d** since these Lk 24:21
and now the **d** is almost over." Lk 24:29
rise from the dead the third **d**, Lk 24:46
The next **d** John saw Jesus coming Jn 1:29
Again the next **d**, John was Jn 1:35
and they stayed with Him that **d**. Jn 1:39
The next **d** He decided to leave Jn 1:43
On the third **d** a wedding took Jn 2:1
Now that **d** was the Sabbath, Jn 5:9
The next **d**, the crowd that had Jn 6:22
raise them up on the last **d**. Jn 6:39
raise him up on the last **d**." Jn 6:40
will raise him up on the last **d**. Jn 6:44
will raise him up on the last **d**, Jn 6:54
important **d** of the festival, Jn 7:37
that he would see My **d**; Jn 8:56
Him who sent Me while it is **d**. Jn 9:4
d that Jesus made the mud and Jn 9:14
"Aren't there 12 hours in a **d**?" Jn 11:9
If anyone walks during the **d**, Jn 11:9
the resurrection at the last **d**." Jn 11:24
from that **d** on they plotted to Jn 11:53
kept it for the **d** of My burial. Jn 12:7
The next **d**, when the large crowd Jn 12:12
will judge him on the last **d**. Jn 12:48
that **d** you will know that I am Jn 14:20
In that **d** you will not ask Me Jn 16:23
In that **d** you will ask in My Jn 16:26
the preparation **d** for the Jn 19:14
Since it was the preparation **d**, Jn 19:31
for that Sabbath was a special **d** Jn 19:31
On the first **d** of the week Mary Jn 20:1
of that first **d** of the week, Jn 20:19
until the **d** He was taken up, Ac 1:2
John until the **d** He was taken up Ac 1:22
When the **d** of Pentecost had Ac 2:1
and remarkable **d** of the Lord Ac 2:20
his tomb is with us to this **d**. Ac 2:29
and that **d** about 3,000 people Ac 2:41
every **d** they devoted themselves Ac 2:46
And every **d** the Lord added to Ac 2:47
and placed every **d** at the temple Ac 3:2
in custody until the next **d**, Ac 4:3
next **d**, their rulers, elders, Ac 4:5
Every **d** in the temple complex, Ac 5:42
circumcised him on the eighth **d**; Ac 7:8
The next **d** he showed up while Ac 7:26
On that **d** a severe persecution Ac 8:1
watching the gates **d** and night Ac 9:24
The next **d**, as they were Ac 10:9
The next **d** he got up and set out Ac 10:23
The following **d** he entered Ac 10:24
man on the third **d** and permitted Ac 10:40
on an appointed **d**, dressed in Ac 12:21
On the Sabbath **d** they went into Ac 13:14
The next **d** he left with Barnabas Ac 14:20
the synagogues every Sabbath **d**." Ac 15:21
the next **d** to Neapolis, Ac 16:11
On the Sabbath **d** we went outside Ac 16:13
every **d** with those who Ac 17:17
He has set a **d** on which He is Ac 17:31
every **d** in the lecture Ac 19:9
On the first **d** of the week, Ac 20:7
was about to depart the next **d**, Ac 20:7
the next **d** we arrived off Chios. Ac 20:15
The following **d** we crossed over Ac 20:15
Samos, and the **d** after, we came Ac 20:15
for the **d** of Pentecost. Ac 20:16
from the first **d** I set foot in Ac 20:18
to you this **d** that I am innocent Ac 20:26
that night and **d** for three years Ac 20:31
to Cos, the next **d** to Rhodes, Ac 21:1
and stayed with them one **d**. Ac 21:7
The next **d** we left and came to Ac 21:8
following **d** Paul went in with Ac 21:18
Then the next **d**, Paul took the Ac 21:26
The next **d**, since he wanted to Ac 22:30
good conscience until this **d**." Ac 23:1
When it was **d**, the Jews formed a Ac 23:12
The next **d**, they returned to the Ac 23:32
next **d**, seated at the judge's Ac 25:6
The next **d** I sat at the judge's Ac 25:17
So the next **d**, Agrippa and Ac 25:23
earnestly serve Him night and **d**. Ac 26:7
to this **d** I stand and testify to Ac 26:22
The next **d** we put in at Sidon, Ac 27:3
jettison the cargo the next **d**. Ac 27:18
On the third **d**, they threw the Ac 27:19
the fourteenth **d** that you have Ac 27:33
After one **d** a south wind sprang Ac 28:13
and the second **d** we came to Ac 28:13
After arranging a **d** with him, Ac 28:23
for yourself in the **d** of wrath, Rm 2:5
on the **d** when God judges what Rm 2:16
All **d** long I have spread out My Rm 10:21
that cannot hear, to this **d**. Rm 11:8
considers one **d** to be above Rm 14:5
one day to be above another **d**. Rm 14:5
every **d** to be the same. Rm 14:5
observes the **d**, observes it to Rm 14:6
blameless in the **d** of our Lord 1Co 1:8
for the **d** will disclose it, 1Co 3:13
be saved in the **D** of the Lord. 1Co 5:5
and in a single **d** 23,000 people 1Co 10:8
on the third **d** according to 1Co 15:4
Jesus our Lord: I die every **d**! 1Co 15:31
On the first **d** of the week, 1Co 16:2
in the **d** of our Lord Jesus. 2Co 1:14
For to this **d**, at the reading of 2Co 3:14
to this **d**, whenever Moses 2Co 3:15
is being renewed **d** by day. 2Co 4:16
is being renewed day by **d**. 2Co 4:16
and in the **d** of salvation, 2Co 6:2
now is the **d** of salvation. 2Co 6:2
a night and a **d** in the depths 2Co 11:25
you for the **d** of redemption. Eph 4:30
be able to resist in the evil **d**, Eph 6:13
from the first **d** until now. Php 1:5
until the **d** of Christ Jesus. Php 1:6
blameless in the **d** of Christ, Php 1:10
boast in the **d** of Christ that I Php 2:16
circumcised the eighth **d**; Php 3:5
you since the **d** you heard it Col 1:6
since the **d** we heard this, Col 1:9
or a new moon or a sabbath **d**. Col 2:16
night and **d** so that we would 1Th 2:9
night and **d** to see you face to 1Th 3:10
well that the **D** of the Lord will 1Th 5:2
that this **d** would overtake you 1Th 5:4
sons of light and sons of the **d**. 1Th 5:5
But since we are of the **d**, 1Th 5:8
in that **d** when He comes to be 2Th 1:10
that the **D** of the Lord has 2Th 2:2
⌊that **d**⌋ will not come unless 2Th 2:3
night and **d**, so that we would 2Th 3:8
night and **d** in her petitions 1Tm 5:5
you in my prayers night and **d**. 2Tm 1:3
entrusted to me until that **d**. 2Tm 1:12
mercy from the Lord on that **d**. 2Tm 1:18
give me on that **d**, and not only 2Tm 4:8
on the **d** of testing in the Heb 3:8
about the seventh **d** in this way: Heb 4:4
And on the seventh **d** God rested Heb 4:4
He specifies a certain **d**— Heb 4:7
spoken later about another **d**. Heb 4:8
to offer sacrifices every **d**, Heb 7:27
fathers on the **d** I took them by Heb 8:9
every priest stands **d** after day Heb 10:11
stands day after **d** ministering Heb 10:11
as you see the **d** drawing near. Heb 10:25
hearts for the **d** of slaughter. Jms 5:5
God in a **d** of visitation. 1Pt 2:12
the **d** dawns and the morning 2Pt 1:19
tormented himself **d** by day with 2Pt 2:8
day by **d** with the lawless 2Pt 2:8
until the **d** of judgment, 2Pt 2:9
kept until the **d** of judgment 2Pt 3:7
the Lord one **d** is like 1,000 2Pt 3:8
and 1,000 years like one **d**. 2Pt 3:8
But the **D** of the Lord will come 2Pt 3:10
that ⌊**d**⌋ the heavens will pass 2Pt 3:10
the coming of the **d** of God, 2Pt 3:12
now and to the **d** of eternity. 2Pt 3:18
confidence in the **d** of judgment; 1Jn 4:17
for the judgment of the great **d**, Jd 6
in the Spirit on the Lord's **d**, Rv 1:10
D and night they never stop, Rv 4:8
the great **d** of Their wrath Rv 6:17
they serve Him **d** and night in Rv 7:15
A third of the **d** was without Rv 8:12
for the hour, **d**, month, and year Rv 9:15
them before our God **d** and night. Rv 12:10
There is no rest **d** or night for Rv 14:11
battle of the great **d** of God, Rv 16:14
her plagues will come in one **d**— Rv 18:8
be tormented **d** and night forever Rv 20:10
d its gates will never close Rv 21:25

DAY'S *(5)*

about a **d** journey in every Nm 11:31
That **d** victory was turned into 2Sm 19:2
but he went on a **d** journey into 1Kg 19:4
party, they went a **d** journey. Lk 2:44
a Sabbath **d** journey away. Ac 1:12

DAYBREAK *(12)*

a man wrestled with him until **d**. Gn 32:24
Jacob, "Let Me go, for it is **d**." Gn 32:26
and at **d** the sea returned to its Ex 14:27
At **d** they let her go. Jdg 19:25
By **d**, there was no one who had 2Sm 17:22
spears from **d** until the stars Neh 4:21
out of it from **d** until noon Neh 8:3
At **d**, LORD, You hear my voice; Ps 5:3
at **d** I plead my case to You and Ps 5:3
When **d** came, all the chief Mt 27:1
When **d** came, Jesus stood on the Jn 21:4
temple complex at **d** and began to Ac 5:21

DAYLIGHT *(16)*

"Look, it is still broad **d**. Gn 29:7
them in broad **d** before the LORD Nm 25:4
all Israel and in broad **d**.' " 2Sm 12:12
May it wait for **d** but have none; Jb 3:9
like infants who never see **d**? Jb 3:16
will face foes in broad **d**. Ezk 30:16
and the **d** will turn black over Mc 3:6
When **d** came, He summoned His Lk 6:13
When **d** came, the elders of the Lk 22:66
d, there was a great commotion Ac 12:18
When **d** came, the chief Ac 16:35
stern and prayed for **d** to come. Ac 27:29
was just about **d**, Paul urged Ac 27:33
When **d** came, they did not Ac 27:39
over, and the **d** is near, so let Rm 13:12
walk with decency, as in the **d**: Rm 13:13

DAYS *(667)*

festivals and for **d** and years. Gn 1:14
eat dust all the **d** of your life. Gn 3:14
labor all the **d** of your life. Gn 3:17
Their **d** will be 120 years." Gn 6:3
both in those **d** and afterwards, Gn 6:4
Seven **d** from now I will make it Gn 7:4
on the earth 40 **d** and 40 nights, Gn 7:4
Seven **d** later the waters of the Gn 7:10
on the earth 40 **d** and 40 nights. Gn 7:12
continued 40 **d** on the earth; Gn 7:17
surged on the earth 150 **d**. Gn 7:24
the end of 150 **d** the waters had Gn 8:3
40 **d** Noah opened the window Gn 8:6
waited seven more **d** and sent out Gn 8:10
he had waited another seven **d**, Gn 8:12
for during his **d** the earth was Gn 10:25
In those **d** Amraphel king of Gn 14:1
among you at eight **d** old is to Gn 17:12
his son Isaac was eight **d** old, Gn 21:4
of the Philistines for many **d**. Gn 21:34
stay with us for about 10 **d**. Gn 24:55
had dug in the **d** of his father Gn 26:15
been dug in the **d** of his father Gn 26:18
The **d** of mourning for my father Gn 27:41
with him for a few **d** until your Gn 27:44
like only a few **d** to him because Gn 29:20
pursued Jacob for seven **d**, Gn 31:23
his people, old and full of **d**. Gn 35:29
and mourned for his son many **d**. Gn 37:34
The three branches are three **d**. Gn 40:12
just three **d** Pharaoh will lift Gn 40:13
The three baskets are three **d**. Gn 40:18

just three **d** Pharaoh will lift Gn 40:19
them together for three **d**. Gn 42:17
happen to you in the **d** to come. Gn 49:1
They took 40 **d** to complete this, Gn 50:3
Egyptians mourned for him 70 **d**. Gn 50:3
the **d** of mourning were over, Gn 50:4
mourned seven **d** for his father. Gn 50:10
Seven **d** passed after the LORD Ex 7:25
distance of three **d** into the Ex 8:27
the land of Egypt for three **d**. Ex 10:22
for three **d** they did not move Ex 10:23
unleavened bread for seven **d**. Ex 12:15
be done on those ⌊**d**⌋ except for Ex 12:16
in your houses for seven **d**. Ex 12:19
For seven **d** you must eat Ex 13:6
to be eaten for those seven **d**. Ex 13:7
for three **d** in the wilderness Ex 15:22
much as they gather on other **d**.” Ex 16:5
For six **d** you may gather it, Ex 16:26
to labor six **d** and do all your Ex 20:9
and everything in them in six **d**; Ex 20:11
with their mothers for seven **d**, Ex 22:30
Do your work for six **d** but rest Ex 23:12
bread for seven **d** at the Ex 23:15
you⌋ the full number of your **d**. Ex 23:26
the cloud covered it for six **d**. Ex 24:16
the mountain 40 **d** and 40 nights. Ex 24:18
must wear them for seven **d**. Ex 29:30
Ordain them for seven **d**. Ex 29:35
For seven **d** you must make Ex 29:37
For six **d** work may be done, Ex 31:15
for in six **d** the LORD made the Ex 31:17
bread for seven **d** at the Ex 34:18
are to labor six **d** but you must Ex 34:21
the LORD 40 **d** and 40 nights; Ex 34:28
For six **d** work is to be done, Ex 35:2
the tent of meeting for seven **d**, Lv 8:33
time your **d** of ordination are Lv 8:33
will take seven **d** to ordain you. Lv 8:33
night for seven **d** and keep the Lv 8:35
she will be unclean seven **d**, Lv 12:2
is during the **d** of her menstrual Lv 12:2
from her bleeding for 33 **d**. Lv 12:4
her **d** of purification. Lv 12:4
from her bleeding for 66 **d**. Lv 12:5
When her **d** of purification are Lv 12:6
the infected person for seven **d**. Lv 13:4
him for another seven **d**. Lv 13:5
must quarantine him seven **d**. Lv 13:21
must quarantine him seven **d**. Lv 13:26
the scaly infection for seven **d**. Lv 13:31
outbreak for another seven **d**. Lv 13:33
contaminated fabric for seven **d**. Lv 13:50
quarantined for another seven **d**. Lv 13:54
outside his tent for seven **d**. Lv 14:8
the house for seven **d**. Lv 14:38
during any of the **d** the priest Lv 14:46
All the **d** that his body secretes Lv 15:3
to count seven **d** for his Lv 15:13
of her menstruation for seven **d**. Lv 15:19
he will be unclean for seven **d**, Lv 15:24
of her blood for many **d**, Lv 15:25
unclean all the **d** of her unclean Lv 15:25
she is⌋ during the **d** of her Lv 15:25
on during the **d** of her discharge Lv 15:26
to count seven **d**, and after that Lv 15:28
with its mother for seven **d**; Lv 22:27
For six **d** work may be done, Lv 23:3
For seven **d** you must eat Lv 23:6
to the LORD for seven **d**. Lv 23:8
are to count 50 **d** until the day Lv 23:16
month and continues for seven **d**. Lv 23:34
to the LORD for seven **d**. Lv 23:36
month for seven **d** after you have Lv 23:39
the LORD your God for seven **d**. Lv 23:40
to the LORD seven **d** each year. Lv 23:41
to live in booths for seven **d**. Lv 23:42
over the tabernacle many **d**, Nm 9:19
tabernacle for ⌊only⌋ a few **d**. Nm 9:20
Whether it was two **d**, a month, Nm 9:22
ahead of them for the three **d**. Nm 10:33
one day, or two **d**, or five days, Nm 11:19
two days, or five **d**, or 10 days, Nm 11:19
five days, or 10 **d**, or 20 days, Nm 11:19
five days, or 10 days, or 20 **d**, Nm 11:19
remain in disgrace for seven **d**? Nm 12:14
outside the camp for seven **d**; Nm 12:14
outside the camp for seven **d**, Nm 12:15

At the end of 40 **d** they returned Nm 13:25
of the 40 **d** that you scouted Nm 14:34
will be unclean for seven **d**. Nm 19:11
on the third and seventh **d**, Nm 19:12
will be unclean for seven **d**, Nm 19:14
will be unclean for seven **d**. Nm 19:16
of Israel mourned for him 30 **d**. Nm 20:29
is to be eaten for seven **d**. Nm 28:17
day for seven **d** as a fire Nm 28:24
outside the camp for seven **d**. Nm 31:19
hill country of Seir for many **d**. Dt 2:1
fear Me all the **d** they live on Dt 4:10
God in later **d** and obey Him. Dt 4:30
the earlier **d** that preceded you Dt 4:32
to labor six **d** and do all your Dt 5:13
your God all the **d** of your life Dt 6:2
the mountain 40 **d** and 40 nights. Dt 9:9
end of the 40 **d** and 40 nights. Dt 9:11
the LORD for 40 **d** and 40 nights; Dt 9:18
of the LORD 40 **d** and 40 nights Dt 9:25
the mountain 40 **d** and 40 nights Dt 10:10
d and those of your children Dt 11:21
to possess all the **d** you live on Dt 12:1
For seven **d** you are to eat Dt 16:3
in your territory for seven **d**, Dt 16:4
eat unleavened bread for six **d**. Dt 16:8
Booths for seven **d** when you have Dt 16:13
from it all the **d** of his life, Dt 17:19
Remember the **d** of old; consider Dt 32:7
in the plains of Moab 30 **d**. Dt 34:8
Then the **d** of weeping and Dt 34:8
for within three **d** you will be Jos 1:11
there for three **d** until they Jos 2:16
there three **d** until the pursuers Jos 2:22
After three **d** the officers went Jos 3:2
one time. Do this for six **d**. Jos 6:3
They did this for six **d**. Jos 6:14
Three **d** after making the treaty Jos 9:16
the **d** of Shamgar son of Anath, Jdg 5:6
of Anath, in the **d** of Jael, the Jdg 5:6
40 years during the **d** of Gideon. Jdg 8:28
⌊that⌋ four **d** each year the Jdg 11:40
during the seven **d** of the feast Jdg 14:12
After three **d**, they were unable Jdg 14:14
the whole seven **d** of the feast, Jdg 14:17
20 years in the **d** of the Jdg 15:20
In those **d** there was no king in Jdg 17:6
In those **d**, there was no king in Jdg 18:1
In those **d**, when there was no Jdg 19:1
he stayed with him for three **d**. Jdg 19:4
In those **d**, the ark of the Jdg 20:27
In those **d** there was no king in Jdg 21:25
the LORD all the **d** of his life, 1Sm 1:11
the **d** are coming when I will cut 1Sm 2:31
In those **d** the word of the LORD 1Sm 3:1
away from you three **d** ago, 1Sm 9:20
Wait seven **d** until I come to you 1Sm 10:8
do anything to us for seven **d**,” 1Sm 11:3
He waited seven **d** for the 1Sm 13:8
the appointed **d** and the 1Sm 13:11
was fierce all of Saul’s **d**, 1Sm 14:52
evening for 40 **d** the Philistine 1Sm 17:16
slaves these **d** are running away 1Sm 25:10
10 **d** later, the LORD struck 1Sm 25:38
One of these **d** I’ll be swept 1Sm 27:1
water for three **d** and three 1Sm 30:12
me when I got sick three **d** ago. 1Sm 30:13
in Jabesh and fasted seven **d**. 1Sm 31:13
and stayed at Ziklag two **d**. 2Sm 1:1
gave in those **d** was like someone 2Sm 16:23
to me within three **d** and be here 2Sm 20:4
in the first **d** of the harvest at 2Sm 21:9
the end of nine months and 20 **d**. 2Sm 24:8
a plague in your land three **d**? 2Sm 24:13
Solomon all the **d** of his life. 1Kg 4:21
may fear You all the **d** they live 1Kg 8:40
our God, seven **d**, and seven 1Kg 8:65
and seven ⌊more⌋ **d**—14 days. 1Kg 8:65
and seven ⌊more⌋ days—14 **d**. 1Kg 8:65
be ruler all the **d** of his life 1Kg 11:34
home for three **d** and then return 1Kg 12:5
him all the **d** of his life, 1Kg 15:5
Jeroboam all the **d** of Rehoboam’s 1Kg 15:6
king for seven **d** in Tirzah. 1Kg 16:15
her household ate for many **d**. 1Kg 17:15
he walked 40 **d** and 40 nights to 1Kg 19:8
opposite each other for seven **d**. 1Kg 20:29
left from the **d** of his father 1Kg 22:46

for three **d** but did not find 2Kg 2:17
indirect route for seven **d**, 2Kg 3:9
In those **d** the LORD began to 2Kg 10:32
the **d** of Pekah king of Israel, 2Kg 15:29
those **d** the LORD began sending 2Kg 15:37
I planned it in **d** gone by. 2Kg 19:25
In those **d** Hezekiah became 2Kg 20:1
came in the **d** of King Hezekiah 1Ch 4:41
times to be with them seven **d**, 1Ch 9:25
in Jabesh and fasted seven **d**. 1Ch 10:12
there with David for three **d**, 1Ch 12:39
not inquire of Him in Saul’s **d**.” 1Ch 13:3
or three **d** of the sword of the 1Ch 21:12
David was old and full of **d**, 1Ch 23:1
d on earth are like a shadow, 1Ch 29:15
old age, full of **d**, riches, and 1Ch 29:28
in Your ways all the **d** they live 2Ch 6:31
at that time for seven **d**. 2Ch 7:8
lasted seven **d** and the festival 2Ch 7:9
days and the festival seven **d**. 2Ch 7:9
“Return to me in three **d**.” 2Ch 10:5
him in those **d** because the LORD 2Ch 14:6
for three **d** because there was 2Ch 20:25
when he was old and full of **d**; 2Ch 24:15
the LORD’s temple for eight **d**, 2Ch 29:17
Bread seven **d** with great joy, 2Ch 30:21
the appointed feast for seven **d**, 2Ch 30:22
decided to observe seven more **d**, 2Ch 30:23
they observed seven **d** with joy, 2Ch 30:23
since the **d** of Solomon son 2Ch 30:26
In those **d** Hezekiah became sick 2Ch 32:24
of Unleavened Bread for seven **d**. 2Ch 35:17
in Israel since the **d** of Samuel 2Ch 35:18
months and 10 **d** in Jerusalem. 2Ch 36:9
rest all the **d** of the desolation 2Ch 36:21
Bread for seven **d** with joy, Ezr 6:22
and we camped there for three **d**. Ezr 8:15
and rested there for three **d**. Ezr 8:32
from the **d** of our fathers Ezr 9:7
within three **d** would forfeit all Ezr 10:8
in Jerusalem within the three **d**. Ezr 10:9
I mourned for a number of **d**, Neh 1:4
and had been there three **d**, Neh 2:11
wine was ⌊provided⌋ every 10 **d**. Neh 5:18
The wall was completed in 52 **d**, Neh 6:15
During those **d**, the nobles of Neh 6:17
this from the **d** of Joshua son Neh 8:17
the feast for seven **d**, Neh 8:18
from the **d** of the Assyrian kings Neh 9:32
relatives in the **d** of Jeshua. Neh 12:7
In the **d** of Joiakim, the leaders Neh 12:12
In the **d** of Eliashib, Joiada, Neh 12:22
during the **d** of Johanan son Neh 12:23
served⌋ in the **d** of Joiakim son Neh 12:26
and in the **d** of Nehemiah the Neh 12:26
in the **d** of David and Asaph, Neh 12:46
So in the **d** of Zerubbabel and Neh 12:47
In those **d** I also saw Jews who Neh 13:23
place during the **d** of Ahasuerus, Est 1:1
those **d** King Ahasuerus reigned Est 1:2
greatness for a total of 180 **d**. Est 1:4
During those **d** while Mordecai Est 2:21
the king for the last 30 **d**.” Est 4:11
Don’t eat or drink for three **d**, Est 4:16
the fourteenth **d** of the month. Est 9:18
fifteenth **d** of the month Adar Est 9:21
during those **d** the Jews got rid Est 9:22
They were to be **d** of feasting, Est 9:22
reason these **d** are called Purim Est 9:26
these two **d** each and every year Est 9:27
These **d** are remembered and Est 9:28
that these **d** of Purim will not Est 9:28
to confirm these **d** of Purim at Est 9:31
with him seven **d** and nights, Jb 2:13
appear among the **d** of the year Jb 3:6
curse ⌊certain⌋ **d** cast a spell Jb 3:8
Are not his **d** like those of a Jb 7:1
My **d** pass more swiftly than a Jb 7:6
me alone, for my **d** are a breath. Jb 7:16
your final **d** will be full of Jb 8:7
Our **d** on earth are but a shadow. Jb 8:9
d fly by faster than a runner; Jb 9:25
Your **d** like those of a human, Jb 10:5
Are my **d** not few? Stop ⌊it⌋! Jb 10:20
woman is short of **d** and full of Jb 14:1
Since man’s **d** are determined and Jb 14:5
wait all the **d** of my struggle Jb 14:14
man writhes in pain all his **d**; Jb 15:20

broken. My **d** are extinguished. Jb 17:1
My **d** have slipped by; my plans Jb 17:11
They spend their **d** in prosperity Jb 21:13
who know Him never see His **d**? Jb 24:1
in the **d** when God watched over Jb 29:2
as I was in the **d** of my youth Jb 29:4
and multiply ⌊my⌋ **d** as the sand. Jb 29:18
and **d** of suffering have seized Jb 30:16
d of suffering confront me. Jb 30:27
return to the **d** of his youthful Jb 33:25
will end their **d** in prosperity Jb 36:11
Job died, old and full of **d**. Jb 42:17
length of **d** forever and ever. Ps 21:4
pursue me all the **d** of my life, Ps 23:6
the LORD all the **d** of my life, Ps 27:4
over the blameless all their **d**, Ps 37:18
be satisfied in **d** of hunger. Ps 37:19
my life and the number of my **d**. Ps 39:4
have made my **d** short in length, Ps 39:5
You accomplished in their **d**, Ps 44:1
in their days, in **d** long ago: Ps 44:1
will not live out half their **d**. Ps 55:23
Add **d** to the king's life; Ps 61:6
the righteous flourish in his **d**, Ps 72:7
I consider **d** of old, years long Ps 77:5
He made their **d** end in futility, Ps 78:33
shortened the **d** of his youth; Ps 89:45
all our **d** ebb away under Your Ps 90:9
us to number our **d** carefully so Ps 90:12
with joy and be glad all our **d**. Ps 90:14
for as many **d** as You have Ps 90:15
house for all the **d** to come. Ps 93:5
For my **d** vanish like smoke, Ps 102:3
My **d** are like a lengthening Ps 102:11
He has shortened my **d**. Ps 102:23
As for man, his **d** are like grass Ps 103:15
Let his **d** be few; let another Ps 109:8
How many **d** ⌊must⌋ Your servant Ps 119:84
all the **d** of your life, Ps 128:5
all ⌊my⌋ **d** were written in Your Ps 139:16
I remember the **d** of old; Ps 143:5
his **d** are like a passing shadow. Ps 144:4
for they will bring you many **d**, Pr 3:2
by Wisdom your **d** will be many, Pr 9:11
All the **d** of the oppressed are Pr 15:15
not evil, all the **d** of her life. Pr 31:12
during the few **d** of their lives. Ec 2:3
since in the **d** to come both will Ec 2:16
For all his **d** are filled with Ec 2:23
he eats in darkness all his **d**, Ec 5:17
during the few **d** of his life God Ec 5:18
often consider the **d** of his life Ec 5:20
in the few **d** of his futile life Ec 6:12
the former **d** better than these? Ec 7:10
lengthen their **d** like a shadow, Ec 8:13
years of his **d** that God gives Ec 8:15
love all the **d** of your fleeting Ec 9:9
the sun, all your fleeting **d**. Ec 9:9
after many **d** you may find it. Ec 11:1
him remember the **d** of darkness, Ec 11:8
be glad in the **d** of your youth. Ec 11:9
Creator in the **d** of your youth: Ec 12:1
Before the **d** of adversity come, Ec 12:1
the last **d** the mountain of the Is 2:2
almost up; her **d** are almost over Is 13:22
after many **d** they will be Is 24:22
In **d** to come, Jacob will take Is 27:6
like the light of seven **d**— Is 30:26
I planned it in **d** gone by. Is 37:26
In those **d** Hezekiah became Is 38:1
all the **d** of our lives at Is 38:20
Wake up as in **d** past, as in Is 51:9
will prolong His **d**, and the will Is 53:10
is like the **d** of Noah to Me: Is 54:9
and the **d** of your sorrow will be Is 60:20
them all the **d** of the past. Is 63:9
He remembered the **d** of the past, Is 63:11
⌊the **d**⌋ of Moses ⌊and⌋ his Is 63:11
no longer live only a few **d**, Is 65:20
an old man not live out his **d**. Is 65:20
throughout the **d** of Jehoiakim Jr 1:3
forgotten Me for countless **d**. Jr 2:32
In the **d** of King Josiah the LORD Jr 3:6
land, in those **d**"—the LORD's Jr 3:16
In those **d** the house of Judah Jr 3:18
"But even in those **d**"—⌊this Jr 5:18
D are coming"—the LORD's Jr 7:32
"The **d** are coming"—the LORD's Jr 9:25

The **d** are coming"—the LORD's Jr 16:14
middle of his **d** ⌊his riches⌋ Jr 17:11
d are coming"—⌊this is⌋ the Jr 19:6
"The **d** are coming"—⌊this is⌋ Jr 23:5
In His **d** Judah will be saved, Jr 23:6
The **d** are coming"—the LORD's Jr 23:7
Because the **d** of your slaughter Jr 25:34
in the **d** of Hezekiah king Jr 26:18
the **d** are certainly coming"— Jr 30:3
children will be as in past **d**; Jr 30:20
"The **d** are coming"—⌊this is⌋ Jr 31:27
In those **d**, it will never again Jr 31:29
"Look, the **d** are coming"—⌊this Jr 31:31
house of Israel after those **d**"— Jr 31:33
"Look, the **d** are coming"—the Jr 31:38
"Look, the **d** are coming"—⌊this Jr 33:14
In those **d** and at that time I Jr 33:15
In those **d** Judah will be saved, Jr 33:16
the LORD in the **d** of Jehoiakim Jr 35:1
dungeon and stayed there many **d**. Jr 37:16
Now at the end of 10 **d**, the word Jr 42:7
look, the **d** are coming—⌊this Jr 48:12
fortunes of Moab in the last **d**. Jr 48:47
look, the **d** are coming—⌊this Jr 49:2
the last **d**, I will restore the Jr 49:39
In those **d** and at that time— Jr 50:4
In those **d** and at that time— Jr 50:20
the **d** are coming when I will Jr 51:47
look, the **d** are coming—⌊this Jr 51:52
During the **d** of her affliction Lm 1:7
that were ⌊hers⌋ in **d** of old. Lm 1:7
which He ordained in **d** of old. Lm 2:17
renew our **d** as in former times, Lm 5:21
I sat there stunned for seven **d**. Ezk 3:15
the end of seven **d** the word of Ezk 3:16
the number of **d** you lie on your Ezk 4:4
the number of **d** ⌊you lie down⌋, Ezk 4:5
of days ⌊you lie down⌋, 390 **d**; Ezk 4:5
When you have completed these **d**, Ezk 4:6
assigned you 40 **d**, a day for Ezk 4:6
finished the **d** of your siege. Ezk 4:8
the number of **d** you lie on your Ezk 4:9
you lie on your side, 390 **d**. Ezk 4:9
city when the **d** of the siege Ezk 5:2
The **d** keep passing by, and every Ezk 12:22
The **d** draw near, as well as the Ezk 12:23
For in your **d**, rebellious house, Ezk 12:25
not remember the **d** of your youth Ezk 16:22
not remember the **d** of your youth Ezk 16:43
with you in the **d** of your youth, Ezk 16:60
your ⌊judgment⌋ **d** near and have Ezk 22:4
strong in the **d** when I deal with Ezk 22:14
remembering the **d** of her youth Ezk 23:19
It will happen in the last **d**, Ezk 38:16
offering each day for seven **d**. Ezk 43:25
For seven **d** the priests are to Ezk 43:26
complete the **d** ⌊of purification Ezk 43:27
count off seven **d** for himself. Ezk 44:26
of seven **d** ⌊during which⌋ Ezk 45:21
the seven **d** of the festival Ezk 45:23
the LORD on each of the seven **d**, Ezk 45:23
the same things for seven **d**— Ezk 45:25
closed during the six **d** of work, Ezk 46:1
test your servants for 10 **d**. Dn 1:12
matter and tested them for 10 **d**. Dn 1:14
At the end of 10 **d** they looked Dn 1:15
what will happen in the last **d**. Dn 2:28
In the **d** of those kings, the God Dn 2:44
But at the end of those **d**, Dn 4:34
In the **d** of your predecessor he Dn 5:11
numbered ⌊the **d** of⌋ your kingdom Dn 5:26
enforce an edict that for 30 **d**, Dn 6:7
edict that for 30 **d** any man who Dn 6:12
the Ancient of **D** took His seat. Dn 7:9
Ancient of **D** and was escorted Dn 7:13
until the Ancient of **D** arrived Dn 7:22
to many **d** ⌊in the future⌋. Dn 8:26
was overcome and lay sick for **d**. Dn 8:27
In those **d** I, Daniel, was Dn 10:2
of Persia opposed me for 21 **d**. Dn 10:13
to your people in the last **d**, Dn 10:14
the vision refers to those **d**." Dn 10:14
but within a few **d** he will be Dn 11:20
set up, there will be 1,290 **d**. Dn 12:11
waits for and reaches 1,335 **d**. Dn 12:12
destiny at the end of the **d**." Dn 12:13
her for the **d** of the Baals when Hs 2:13
she did⌋ in the **d** of her youth, Hs 2:15

You must live with me many **d**. Hs 3:3
must live many **d** without king or Hs 3:4
to His goodness in the last **d**. Hs 3:5
He will revive us after two **d**, Hs 6:2
The **d** of punishment have come; Hs 9:7
the **d** of retribution have come. Hs 9:7
as in the **d** of Gibeah. Hs 9:9
sinned since the **d** of Gibeah; Hs 10:9
again, as in the festival **d**. Hs 12:9
happened in your **d** or in the Jl 1:2
days or in the **d** of your Jl 1:2
and female slaves in those **d**. Jl 2:29
in those **d** and at that time, Jl 3:1
Israel in the **d** of Uzziah, Am 1:1
the **d** are coming when you will Am 4:2
your tenths every three **d**. Am 4:4
such a time, for the **d** are evil. Am 5:13
The **d** are coming—⌊this is⌋ the Am 8:11
rebuild it as in the **d** of old, Am 9:11
The **d** are coming—the LORD's Am 9:13
the fish three **d** and three Jnh 1:17
40 **d** Nineveh will be overthrown! Jnh 3:4
Jerusalem in the **d** of Jotham, Mc 1:1
the last **d** the mountain of the Mc 4:1
deeds as in the **d** of your exodus Mc 7:15
to our fathers from **d** long ago. Mc 7:20
of water from her ⌊first⌋ **d**, Nah 2:8
place in your **d** that you will Hab 1:5
in the **d** of Josiah son of Amon, Zph 1:1
of this people in those **d**, Zch 8:6
prior to those **d** neither man nor Zch 8:10
people as in the former **d**"— Zch 8:11
again in these **d** to do what is Zch 8:15
In those **d**, 10 men from nations Zch 8:23
in the **d** of Uzziah king Zch 14:5
LORD as in **d** of old and years Mal 3:4
Since the **d** of your fathers, Mal 3:7
of Judea in the **d** of King Herod, Mt 2:1
those **d** John the Baptist came, Mt 3:1
had fasted 40 **d** and 40 nights, Mt 4:2
The **d** will come when the groom Mt 9:15
From the **d** of John the Baptist Mt 11:12
that on Sabbath **d** the priests Mt 12:5
fish three **d** and three nights Mt 12:40
the earth three **d** and three Mt 12:40
with Me three **d** and have nothing Mt 15:32
After six **d** Jesus took Peter, Mt 17:1
lived in the **d** of our fathers, Mt 23:30
and nursing mothers in those **d**! Mt 24:19
Unless those **d** were limited, Mt 24:22
But those **d** will be limited Mt 24:22
the tribulation of those **d**: Mt 24:29
As the **d** of Noah were, so the Mt 24:37
For in those **d** before the flood Mt 24:38
takes place after two **d**, Mt 26:2
and rebuild it in three **d**.'" Mt 26:61
and rebuild it in three **d**, Mt 27:40
'After three **d** I will rise again. Mt 27:63
In those **d** Jesus came from Mk 1:9
He was in the wilderness 40 **d**, Mk 1:13
Capernaum again after some **d**, Mk 2:1
In those **d** there was again a Mk 8:1
with Me three **d** and have nothing Mk 8:2
killed, and rise after three **d**. Mk 8:31
After six **d** Jesus took Peter, Mk 9:2
He will rise three **d** later." Mk 9:31
and He will rise after three **d**." Mk 10:34
and nursing mothers in those **d**! Mk 13:17
those will be **d** of tribulation, Mk 13:19
Unless the Lord limited those **d**, Mk 13:20
limited those **d** because of the Mk 13:20
But in those **d**, after that Mk 13:24
After two **d** it was the Passover Mk 14:1
and in three **d** I will build Mk 14:58
and build it in three **d**, Mk 15:29
In the **d** of King Herod of Judea, Lk 1:5
When the **d** of his ministry were Lk 1:23
After these **d** his wife Elizabeth Lk 1:24
favor in these **d** to take away my Lk 1:25
In those **d** Mary set out and Lk 1:39
in His presence all our **d**. Lk 1:75
those **d** a decree went out from Lk 2:1
When the eight **d** were completed Lk 2:21
And when the **d** of their Lk 2:22
After those **d** were over, as they Lk 2:43
After three **d**, they found Him in Lk 2:46
for 40 **d** to be tempted by the Lk 4:2
He ate nothing during those **d**, Lk 4:2

widows in Israel in Elijah's **d**, Lk 4:25
On one of those **d** while He was Lk 5:17
But the **d** will come when the Lk 5:35
then they will fast in those **d**." Lk 5:35
During those **d** He went out to Lk 6:12
About eight **d** after these words, Lk 9:28
and in those **d** told no one what Lk 9:36
the **d** were coming to a close Lk 9:51
There are six **d** when work should Lk 13:14
come on those **d** and be healed Lk 13:14
many **d** later, the younger son Lk 15:13
The **d** are coming when you will Lk 17:22
see one of the **d** of the Son of Lk 17:22
Just as it was in the **d** of Noah, Lk 17:26
will be in the **d** of the Son of Lk 17:26
same as it was in the **d** of Lot: Lk 17:28
For the **d** will come on you when Lk 19:43
the **d** will come when not one Lk 21:6
these are **d** of vengeance to Lk 21:22
and nursing mothers in those **d**, Lk 21:23
in Jerusalem during those **d**. Lk 23:7
the **d** are coming when they will Lk 23:29
that happened there in these **d**?" Lk 24:18
they stayed there only a few **d**. Jn 2:12
I will raise it up in three **d**." Jn 2:19
You raise it up in three **d**?" Jn 2:20
and He stayed there two **d**. Jn 4:40
After two **d** He left there for Jn 4:43
stayed two more **d** in the place Jn 11:6
already been in the tomb four **d**. Jn 11:17
stinks. It's been four **d**." Jn 11:39
Six **d** before the Passover, Jn 12:1
After eight **d** His disciples were Jn 20:26
to them during 40 **d** and speaking Ac 1:3
Spirit not many **d** from now." Ac 1:5
During these **d** Peter stood up Ac 1:15
And it will be in the last **d**, Ac 2:17
and female slaves in those **d**, Ac 2:18
have also announced these **d**. Ac 3:24
rose up in the **d** of the census Ac 5:37
In those **d**, as the number of the Ac 6:1
even made a calf in those **d**, Ac 7:41
fathers, until the **d** of David. Ac 7:45
was unable to see for three **d**, Ac 9:9
in Damascus for some **d**. Ac 9:19
After many **d** had passed, the Ac 9:23
In those **d** she became sick and Ac 9:37
stayed on many **d** in Joppa with Ac 9:43
replied, "Four **d** ago at this Ac 10:30
asked him to stay for a few **d**. Ac 10:48
In those **d** some prophets came Ac 11:27
the **d** of Unleavened Bread. Ac 12:3
for many **d** to those who came Ac 13:31
I am doing a work in your **d**, Ac 13:41
in the early **d** God made a choice Ac 15:7
in that city for a number of **d**. Ac 16:12
And she did this for many **d**. Ac 16:18
on three Sabbath **d** reasoned with Ac 17:2
having stayed on for many **d**, Ac 18:18
after the **d** of Unleavened Ac 20:6
In five **d** we reached them at Ac 20:6
Troas, where we spent seven **d**. Ac 20:6
and stayed there seven **d**. Ac 21:4
When our **d** there were over, Ac 21:5
we were staying there many **d**, Ac 21:10
After these **d** we got ready and Ac 21:15
the purification **d** when the Ac 21:26
the seven **d** were about to end, Ac 21:27
After five **d** Ananias the high Ac 24:1
more than 12 **d** since I went up Ac 24:11
After some **d**, when Felix came Ac 24:24
Three **d** after Festus arrived in Ac 25:1
than eight or 10 **d** among them, Ac 25:6
After some **d** had passed, King Ac 25:13
Since they stayed there many **d**, Ac 25:14
Sailing slowly for many **d**, Ac 27:7
For many **d** neither sun nor stars Ac 27:20
us hospitably for three **d**. Ac 28:7
at Syracuse, we stayed three **d**. Ac 28:12
to stay with them for seven **d**. Ac 28:14
After three **d** he called together Ac 28:17
and I stayed with him 15 **d**. Gl 1:18
special⌋ **d**, months, seasons Gl 4:10
of the **d** of fulfillment— Eph 1:10
time, because the **d** are evil. Eph 5:16
in the early **d** of the gospel, Php 4:15
times will come in the last **d**. 2Tm 3:1
these last **d**, He has spoken to Heb 1:2
beginning of **d** nor end of life, Heb 7:3
"Look, the **d** are coming," says Heb 8:8
house of Israel after those **d**," Heb 8:10
make with them after those **d**, Heb 10:16
Remember the earlier **d** when, Heb 10:32
being encircled for seven **d**. Heb 11:30
up treasure in the last **d**! Jms 5:3
and to see good **d** must keep his 1Pt 3:10
waited in the **d** of Noah while an 1Pt 3:20
come in the last **d** to scoff, 2Pt 3:3
will have tribulation for 10 **d**. Rv 2:10
Me, even in the **d** of Antipas, My Rv 2:13
those **d** people will seek death Rv 9:6
but in the **d** of the sound of the Rv 10:7
they will prophesy for 1,260 **d**, Rv 11:3
rain during the **d** of their Rv 11:6
and a half **d** and not permit Rv 11:9
after the three and a half **d**, Rv 11:11
to be fed there for 1,260 **d**. Rv 12:6

DAYS' *(1)*

give you two **d** worth of bread. Ex 16:29

DAYTIME *(4)*

of the city to do it in the **d**, Jdg 6:27
like an exile's bags in the **d**. Ezk 12:7
I will darken the land in the **d**. Am 8:9
a pleasure to carouse in the **d**. 2Pt 2:13

DAZZLING *(5)*

statue, tall and **d**, was standing Dn 2:31
and His clothes became **d**— Mk 9:3
and His clothes became **d** white. Lk 9:29
men stood by them in **d** clothes. Lk 24:4
then a man in a **d** robe stood Ac 10:30

DEACONS *(5)*

including the overseers and **d**. Php 1:1
D, likewise, should be worthy of 1Tm 3:8
then they can serve as **d**. 1Tm 3:10
D must be husbands of one wife, 1Tm 3:12
served well as **d** acquire a good 1Tm 3:13

DEAD *(298)*

of Siddim (that is, the **D** Sea). Gn 14:3
from beside his **d** ⌊wife⌋ and Gn 23:3
you so that I can bury my **d**." Gn 23:4
Bury your **d** in our finest burial Gn 23:6
place for burying your **d**." Gn 23:6
willing ⌊for me⌋ to bury my **d**, Gn 23:8
of my people. Bury your **d**." Gn 23:11
and let me bury my **d** there." Gn 23:13
you and me? Bury your **d**." Gn 23:15
his brother is **d** and he alone is Gn 42:38
The boy's brother is **d**. Gn 44:20
saw that their father was **d**, Gn 50:15
struck the Egyptian **d** and hid Ex 2:12
who wanted to kill you are **d**." Ex 4:19
the Israelite livestock was **d**. Ex 9:7
a house without someone **d**. Ex 12:30
the Egyptians **d** on the seashore Ex 14:30
the **d** animal will become his. Ex 21:34
must also divide the **d** animal. Ex 21:35
the **d** animal will become his. Ex 21:36
3,000 men fell **d** that day among Ex 32:28
when they are **d** will be unclean Lv 11:31
bodies for the **d** or put tattoo Lv 19:28
unclean for a ⌊**d**⌋ person among Lv 21:1
not go near any **d** person or make Lv 21:11
made unclean by a **d** person or by Lv 22:4
and heap your **d** bodies on the Lv 26:30
must not go near a **d** body during Nm 6:6
let her be like a **d** ⌊baby⌋ whose Nm 12:12
between the **d** and the living, Nm 16:48
who was struck **d** with the Nm 25:14
Midianites and strike them **d**. Nm 25:17
or touched the **d** are to purify Nm 31:19
at the east end of the **D** Sea. Nm 34:3
the Jordan and end at the **D** Sea. Nm 34:12
of the Arabah, the **D** Sea, under Dt 3:17
as far as the **D** Sea below the Dt 4:49
on your head on behalf of the **d**, Dt 14:1
spirit, or inquire of the **d**. Dt 18:11
is great, and strike him **d**. Dt 19:6
the wife of the **d** man may not Dt 25:5
on the name of the **d** brother, Dt 25:6
or offered any of it for the **d**. Dt 26:14
will you rebel⌋ after I am **d**! Dt 31:27
Moses My servant is **d**. Jos 1:2
of the Arabah (the **D** Sea) was Jos 3:16
all of them over **d** to Israel. Jos 11:6
that is, the **D** Sea), eastward Jos 12:3
the tip of the **D** Sea on the Jos 15:2
was along the **D** Sea to the mouth Jos 15:5
the northern bay of the **D** Sea, Jos 18:19
their lord lying **d** on the floor! Jdg 3:25
Sisera lying **d** with a tent peg Jdg 4:22
he collapsed, there he fell—**d**. Jdg 5:27
saw that Abimelech was **d**, Jdg 9:55
land and who multiplied our **d**. Jdg 16:24
And the **d** he killed at his death Jdg 16:30
Gidom and struck 2,000 more **d**. Jdg 20:45
have shown to the **d** and to me. Ru 1:8
to the living or the **d**." Ru 2:20
Phinehas, are both **d**, and the 1Sm 4:17
saw that their hero was **d**, 1Sm 17:51
you will be **d** tomorrow!" 1Sm 19:11
chasing after? A **d** dog? A flea? 1Sm 24:14
later, the LORD struck Nabal **d**. 1Sm 25:38
David heard that Nabal was **d**, 1Sm 25:39
saw that Saul was **d**, 1Sm 31:5
that Saul and his sons were **d**, 1Sm 31:7
three sons **d** on Mount Gilboa. 1Sm 31:8
troops have fallen and are **d**. 2Sm 1:4
and his son Jonathan are **d**." 2Sm 1:4
and his son Jonathan are **d**?" 2Sm 1:5
for though Saul your lord is **d**, 2Sm 2:7
Look, Saul is **d**,' he thought he 2Sm 4:10
God struck him **d** on the spot for 2Sm 6:7
an interest in a **d** dog like me?" 2Sm 9:8
Uriah the Hittite is **d** also.' " 2Sm 11:21
Uriah the Hittite is also **d**." 2Sm 11:24
to tell him the baby was **d**. 2Sm 12:18
can we tell him the baby is **d**? 2Sm 12:18
he guessed that the baby was **d**. 2Sm 12:19
his servants, "Is the baby **d**?" 2Sm 12:19
"He is **d**," they replied. 2Sm 12:19
now that he is **d**, why should I 2Sm 12:23
sons, because only Amnon is **d**. 2Sm 13:32
says all the king's sons are **d**. 2Sm 13:33
sons are dead. Only Amnon is **d**." 2Sm 13:33
for the **d** for a long time 2Sm 14:2
Why should this **d** dog curse my 2Sm 16:9
because the king's son is **d**." 2Sm 18:20
were alive and all of us were **d**, 2Sm 19:6
stab him again for Amasa was **d**. 2Sm 20:10
but only to plunder the **d**. 2Sm 23:10
she put her **d** son in my arms. 1Kg 3:20
my son, I discovered he was **d**. 1Kg 3:21
your son is the **d** one." 1Kg 3:22
"No, your son is the **d** one; 1Kg 3:22
and your son is **d**,' but that 1Kg 3:23
No, your son is **d**, and my son is 1Kg 3:23
to bury the **d** and had struck 1Kg 11:15
the army, was **d**, Hadad said to 1Kg 11:21
Naboth isn't alive, but **d**." 1Kg 21:15
Ahab heard that Naboth was **d**, 1Kg 21:16
the boy lying **d** on his bed. 2Kg 4:32
restored the **d** ⌊son⌋ to life, 2Kg 8:5
her son was **d**, she proceeded 2Kg 11:1
there were all the **d** bodies! 2Kg 19:35
carried his **d** body in a chariot, 2Kg 23:30
saw that Saul was **d**, 1Ch 10:5
that Saul and his sons were **d**, 1Ch 10:7
and his sons **d** on Mount Gilboa. 1Ch 10:8
He struck him **d** because he had 1Ch 13:10
from beyond the **D** Sea and from 2Ch 20:2
her son was **d**, she proceeded 2Ch 22:10
about his family once he is **d**, Jb 21:21
from memory like a **d** person— Ps 31:12
abandoned among the **d**. I am like Ps 88:5
Do You work wonders for the **d**? Ps 88:10
It is not the **d** who praise the Ps 115:17
in darkness like those long **d**. Ps 143:3
So I admired the **d**, who have Ec 4:2
after that they go to the **d**. Ec 9:3
dog is better than a **d** lion. Ec 9:4
but the **d** don't know anything. Ec 9:5
D flies make a perfumer's oil Ec 10:1
spirits of the **d** and the Is 8:19
they consult⌋ the **d** on behalf of Is 8:19
out and reached the **D** Sea. Is 16:8
hills and like **d** thistles before Is 17:13
of the **d**, and spiritists. Is 19:3
Your **d** did not die by the sword; Is 22:2
The **d** do not live; departed Is 26:14
Your **d** will live; their bodies Is 26:19
there were all the **d** bodies! Is 37:36
are⌋ like the **d** among those who Is 59:10
will see the **d** bodies of the men Is 66:24

to comfort him because of the **d**. Jr 16:7
not weep for the **d**; do not mourn Jr 22:10
those who have been **d** for ages. Lm 3:6
filling its streets with the **d**. Ezk 11:6
mourning rites for the **d**. Ezk 24:17
come ⌊near⌋ a **d** person so that Ezk 44:25
his front ranks into the **D** Sea, Jl 2:20
Many **d** bodies, thrown Am 8:3
of corpses, **d** bodies without end Nah 3:3
they stumble over their **d**. Nah 3:3
sought the child's life are **d**." Mt 2:20
let the **d** bury their own dead. Mt 8:22
let the dead bury their own **d**." Mt 8:22
because the girl isn't **d**, Mt 9:24
sick, raise the **d**, cleanse those Mt 10:8
the deaf hear, the **d** are raised, Mt 11:5
He has been raised from the **d**, Mt 14:2
of Man is raised from the **d**." Mt 17:9
the resurrection of the **d**, Mt 22:31
He is not the God of the **d**, Mt 22:32
inside are full of **d** men's bones Mt 23:27
'He has been raised from the **d**.' Mt 27:64
him that they became like **d** men. Mt 28:4
'He has been raised from the **d**. Mt 28:7
and said, "Your daughter is **d**. Mk 5:35
The child is not **d** but asleep." Mk 5:39
has been raised from the **d**, Mk 6:14
Son of Man had risen from the **d**. Mk 9:9
what "rising from the **d**" meant. Mk 9:10
so that many said, "He's **d**." Mk 9:26
For when they rise from the **d**, Mk 12:25
concerning the **d** being raised— Mk 12:26
not God of the **d** but of the Mk 12:27
surprised that He was already **d**. Mk 15:44
a **d** man was being carried out. Lk 7:12
The **d** man sat up and began to Lk 7:15
the deaf hear, the **d** are raised, Lk 7:22
saying, "Your daughter is **d**. Lk 8:49
for she is not **d** but asleep." Lk 8:52
because they knew she was **d**. Lk 8:53
John had been raised from the **d**, Lk 9:7
Let the **d** bury their own dead, Lk 9:60
Let the dead bury their own **d**, Lk 9:60
and fled, leaving him half **d**. Lk 10:30
son of mine was **d** and is alive Lk 15:24
of yours was **d** and is alive Lk 15:32
someone from the **d** goes to them, Lk 16:30
if someone rises from the **d**.' " Lk 16:31
from the **d** neither marry nor are Lk 20:35
bush that the **d** are raised, Lk 20:37
not God of the **d** but of the Lk 20:38
for the living among the **d**?" Lk 24:5
rise from the **d** the third day, Lk 24:46
when He was raised from the **d**, Jn 2:22
raises the **d** and gives them Jn 5:21
when the **d** will hear the voice Jn 5:25
Martha, the **d** man's sister, told Jn 11:39
d man came out bound hand and Jn 11:44
one Jesus had raised from the **d**. Jn 12:1
one He had raised from the **d**. Jn 12:9
tomb and raised him from the **d**, Jn 12:17
they saw that He was already **d**. Jn 19:33
that He must rise from the **d**. Jn 20:9
after He was raised from the **d**. Jn 21:14
he is both **d** and buried, and his Ac 2:29
whom God raised from the **d**; Ac 3:15
the resurrection from the **d**. Ac 4:2
and whom God raised from the **d**— Ac 4:10
Ananias dropped **d**, and a great Ac 5:5
she dropped **d** at his feet. Ac 5:10
they found her **d**, carried her Ac 5:10
Him after He rose from the **d**. Ac 10:41
Judge of the living and the **d**. Ac 10:42
But God raised Him from the **d**, Ac 13:30
Since He raised Him from the **d**, Ac 13:34
of the city, thinking he was **d**. Ac 14:19
to suffer and rise from the **d**, Ac 17:3
by raising Him from the **d**." Ac 17:31
about resurrection of the **d**, Ac 17:32
story, and was picked up **d**. Ac 20:9
of the resurrection of the **d**!" Ac 23:6
the resurrection of the **d**.' " Ac 24:21
a **d** man whom Paul claimed to be Ac 25:19
of you that God raises the **d**? Ac 26:8
as the first to rise from the **d**, Ac 26:23
swell up or suddenly drop **d**. Ac 28:6
from the **d** according to Rm 1:4
life to the **d** and calls things Rm 4:17
his own body to be already **d** Rm 4:19
Jesus our Lord from the **d**. Rm 4:24
raised from the **d** by the glory Rm 6:4
having been raised from the **d**, Rm 6:9
consider yourselves **d** to sin, Rm 6:11
those who are alive from the **d**, Rm 6:13
Him who was raised from the **d**— Rm 7:4
For apart from the law sin is **d**. Rm 7:8
the body is **d** because of sin, Rm 8:10
Jesus from the **d** lives in you, Rm 8:11
Christ from the **d** will also Rm 8:11
to bring Christ up from the **d**. Rm 10:7
that God raised Him from the **d**, Rm 10:9
mean but life from the **d**? Rm 11:15
over both the **d** and the living. Rm 14:9
single day 23,000 people fell **d**. 1Co 10:8
preached as raised from the **d**, 1Co 15:12
is no resurrection of the **d**"? 1Co 15:12
is no resurrection of the **d**, 1Co 15:13
if in fact the **d** are not raised. 1Co 15:15
For if the **d** are not raised, 1Co 15:16
has been raised from the **d**, 1Co 15:20
of the **d** also comes through 1Co 15:21
are being baptized for the **d**? 1Co 15:29
If the **d** are not raised at all, 1Co 15:29
If the **d** are not raised, Let us 1Co 15:32
will say, "How are the **d** raised? 1Co 15:35
with the resurrection of the **d**: 1Co 15:42
and the **d** will be raised 1Co 15:52
but in God who raises the **d**. 2Co 1:9
who raised Him from the **d**— Gl 1:1
Him from the **d** and seating Him Eph 1:20
you were **d** in your trespasses Eph 2:1
though we were **d** in trespasses. Eph 2:5
up from the **d**, and the Messiah Eph 5:14
resurrection from among the **d**. Php 3:11
from the **d**, so that He might Col 1:18
who raised Him from the **d**. Col 2:12
when you were **d** in trespasses Col 2:13
whom He raised from the **d**— 1Th 1:10
and the **d** in Christ will rise 1Th 4:16
is **d** even while she 1Tm 5:6
risen from the **d**, descended from 2Tm 2:8
to judge the living and the **d**, 2Tm 4:1
of repentance from **d** works, Heb 6:1
the resurrection of the **d**, Heb 6:2
consciences from **d** works to Heb 9:14
though he is **d**, he still speaks Heb 11:4
as good as **d**—came offspring Heb 11:12
to raise someone from the **d**, Heb 11:19
received their **d** raised to life Heb 11:35
up from the **d** our Lord Jesus— Heb 13:20
have works, is **d** by itself. Jms 2:17
body without the spirit is **d**, Jms 2:26
also faith without works is **d**. Jms 2:26
of Jesus Christ from the **d**, 1Pt 1:3
Him from the **d** and gave Him 1Pt 1:21
to judge the living and the **d**. 1Pt 4:5
to ⌊those who are now⌋ **d**, 1Pt 4:6
fruitless, twice **d**, pulled out Jd 12
from the **d** and the ruler Rv 1:5
I fell at His feet like a **d** man. Rv 1:17
I was **d**, but look—I am alive Rv 1:18
the One who was **d** and came to Rv 2:8
for being alive, but you are **d**. Rv 3:1
Their **d** bodies will lie in the Rv 11:8
has come for the **d** to be judged, Rv 11:18
Blessed are the **d** who die in the Rv 14:13
turned to blood like a **d** man's, Rv 16:3
The rest of the **d** did not come Rv 20:5
I also saw the **d**, the great and Rv 20:12
and the **d** were judged according Rv 20:12
Then the sea gave up its **d**, Rv 20:13
Death and Hades gave up their **d**; Rv 20:13

DEADLY *(14)*

venom, the **d** poison of cobras. Dt 32:33
He has prepared His **d** weapons; Ps 7:13
my **d** enemies who surround me. Ps 17:9
a band of **d** messengers. Ps 78:49
servant David from the **d** sword. Ps 144:10
of the wicked are a **d** ambush, Pr 12:6
flaming darts and **d** arrows, Pr 26:18
Their tongues are **d** arrows— Jr 9:8
They will die from **d** diseases. Jr 16:4
husbands slain by **d** disease, Jr 18:21
know all their **d** plots against Jr 18:23
When I shoot **d** arrows of famine Ezk 5:16
if they should drink anything **d**, Mk 16:18
restless evil, full of **d** poison. Jms 3:8

DEADNESS *(1)*

and the **d** of Sarah's womb, Rm 4:19

DEAF *(18)*

him mute or **d**, seeing or blind Ex 4:11
not curse the **d** or put a Lv 19:14
my rock, do not be **d** to me. Ps 28:1
I am like a **d** person; I do not Ps 38:13
like the **d** cobra that stops up Ps 58:4
Do not be **d**, God; do not be Ps 83:1
On that day the **d** will hear the Is 29:18
and the ears of the **d** unstopped. Is 35:5
Listen, you **d**! Look, you blind, Is 42:18
or **d** like My messenger I am Is 42:19
eyes, and are **d**, yet have ears. Is 43:8
His ear is not too **d** to hear. Is 59:1
and their ears will become **d**. Mc 7:16
are healed, the **d** hear, the dead Mt 11:5
to Him a **d** man who also had Mk 7:32
He even makes **d** people hear, Mk 7:37
You mute and **d** spirit, I command Mk 9:25
are healed, the **d** hear, the dead Lk 7:22

DEAFEN *(1)*

d their ears and blind their Is 6:10

DEAL *(50)*

me⌋ that you will **d** with me in Gn 47:29
Let us **d** shrewdly with them; Ex 1:10
he must **d** with her according to Ex 21:9
and his sons to **d** respectfully Lv 22:2
how you are to **d** with the Nm 8:26
The LORD will **d** with them as He Dt 31:4
a great **d** of the land remains Jos 13:1
D with us as You see fit; Jdg 10:15
D faithfully with your servant, 1Sm 20:8
You know how to **d** with him to 1Kg 2:9
a great **d** of iron to make 1Ch 22:3
there was a great **d** of plunder 2Ch 14:14
and took a great **d** of plunder. 2Ch 25:13
also took a great **d** of plunder 2Ch 28:8
He did a great **d** of evil in the 2Ch 33:6
the words that ⌊**d**⌋ gently with Jb 15:11
woman and do not **d** kindly with Jb 24:21
let God **d** with him, not man." Jb 32:13
prayer⌋ and not **d** with you as Jb 42:8
D with them as ⌊You did⌋ with Ps 83:9
people and to **d** deceptively with Ps 105:25
d ⌊kindly⌋ with me because of Ps 109:21
D generously with Your servant Ps 119:17
D with Your servant based on Ps 119:124
me because You **d** generously with Ps 142:7
the treacherous **d** very Is 24:16
We have cut a **d** with Death, Is 28:15
Your **d** with Death will be Is 28:18
Now make a **d** with my master, Is 36:8
d with them in the time of Your Jr 18:23
this way I will **d** with Zedekiah Jr 24:8
d with them as You have dealt Lm 1:22
I will **d** with them according to Ezk 7:27
I will **d** with you according to Ezk 16:59
in the days when I **d** with you? Ezk 22:14
they will **d** with you in wrath. Ezk 23:25
and they will **d** with Edom Ezk 25:14
he would surely **d** with it. Ezk 31:11
so I will **d** with you: Ezk 35:15
and **d** with your servants based Dn 1:13
He will **d** with the strongest Dn 11:39
that time I will **d** with all who Zph 3:19
purposed to **d** with us for our Zch 1:6
sold for a great **d** and given to Mt 26:9
we will **d** with him and keep you Mt 28:14
a great **d** of business for Ac 19:24
There was a great **d** of weeping Ac 20:37
is able to **d** gently with those Heb 5:2
We have a great **d** to say about Heb 5:11
and only **d** with food, Heb 9:10

DEALER *(1)*

d in purple cloth from the city Ac 16:14

DEALING *(3)*

is careful in **d** with his Pr 12:26
of light ⌊in **d**⌋ with their own Lk 16:8
God is **d** with you as sons. Heb 12:7

DEALINGS *(1)*

was harsh and evil in ⌊his⌋ **d**. 1Sm 25:3

DEALS *(2)*
to priest, everyone **d** falsely. Jr 6:13
to priest, everyone **d** falsely. Jr 8:10

DEALT *(15)*
how severely I **d** with the Ex 10:2
he is to be **d** with according to Ex 21:31
month they had **d** with all the Ezr 10:17
He has not **d** with us as our sins Ps 103:10
have **d** very treacherously with Jr 5:11
mine, which was **d** out to me, Lm 1:12
as You have **d** with me because Lm 1:22
when I have **d** with you because Ezk 20:44
Javan from Uzal **d** in your Ezk 27:19
because they **d** unfaithfully with Ezk 39:23
I **d** with them according to their Ezk 39:24
who has **d** wondrously with you. Jl 2:26
and deeds, so He has **d** with us." Zch 1:6
He has **d** mercifully with our Lk 1:72
He **d** deceitfully with our race Ac 7:19

DEAR *(51)*
even the things **d** to my heart. Jb 17:11
the destruction of my **d** people." Is 22:4
and all that was **d** to us lies in Is 64:11
on the way to My **d** people. Jr 4:11
My **d** people, dress yourselves in Jr 6:26
the brokenness of My **d** people, Jr 8:11
cry of my **d** people from a far Jr 8:19
the brokenness of my **d** people. Jr 8:21
healing of my **d** people not come Jr 8:22
over the slain of my **d** people. Jr 9:1
can I do because of My **d** people? Jr 9:7
the destruction of my **d** people, Lm 2:11
the destruction of my **d** people. Lm 3:48
my **d** people have become cruel Lm 4:3
punishment of my **d** people is Lm 4:6
the destruction of my **d** people. Lm 4:10
Greet my **d** friend Epaenetus, Rm 16:5
Ampliatus, my **d** friend in the Rm 16:8
Christ, and my **d** friend Stachys. Rm 16:9
Greet my **d** friend Persis, who Rm 16:12
to warn you as my **d** children. 1Co 4:14
Therefore, my **d** friends, flee 1Co 10:14
Therefore, my **d** brothers, be 1Co 15:58
Therefore **d** friends, since we 2Co 7:1
everything, **d** friends, is for 2Co 12:19
So then, my **d** friends, just as Php 2:12
firm in the Lord, **d** friends. Php 4:1
because you had become **d** to us. 1Th 2:8
our **d** friend and co-worker, Phm 1
this way, **d** friends, in your Heb 6:9
Listen, my **d** brothers: Didn't Jms 2:5
D friends, I urge you as aliens 1Pt 2:11
D friends, when the fiery ordeal 1Pt 4:12
D friends, this is now the 2Pt 3:1
D friends, don't let this one 2Pt 3:8
Therefore, **d** friends, while you 2Pt 3:14
just as our **d** brother Paul, 2Pt 3:15
Therefore, **d** friends, since you 2Pt 3:17
D friends, I am not writing you 1Jn 2:7
D friends, we are God's children 1Jn 3:2
D friends, if our hearts do not 1Jn 3:21
D friends, do not believe every 1Jn 4:1
D friends, let us love one 1Jn 4:7
D friends, if God loved us in 1Jn 4:11
my **d** friend Gaius, whom I love 3Jn 1
D friend, I pray that you may 3Jn 2
D friend, you are showing your 3Jn 5
D friend, do not imitate what is 3Jn 11
D friends, although I was eager Jd 3
But you, **d** friends, remember the Jd 17
But you, **d** friends, building Jd 20

DEARLY *(8)*
of God, as **d** loved children. Eph 5:1
our **d** loved brother and faithful Eph 6:21
this way, my **d** loved brothers, Php 4:1
are believers and **d** loved. 1Tm 6:2
To Timothy, my **d** loved child. 2Tm 1:2
a slave—as a **d** loved brother. Phm 16
deceived, my **d** loved brothers. Jms 1:16
My **d** loved brothers, understand Jms 1:19

DEATH *(393)*
after his mother's ⌊**d**⌋. Gn 24:67
After Abraham's **d**, God blessed Gn 25:11
and do not know the day of my **d**. Gn 27:2
and the LORD put him to **d**. Gn 38:7
sight, so He put him to **d** also. Gn 38:10
"Let her be burned ⌊to **d**⌋!" Gn 38:24
him and sought to put him to **d**. Ex 4:24
will take this **d** away from me." Ex 10:17
the mountain will be put to **d**. Ex 19:12
that he dies must be put to **d**. Ex 21:12
from My altar to be put to **d**. Ex 21:14
or his mother must be put to **d**. Ex 21:15
a person must be put to **d**, Ex 21:16
or his mother must be put to **d**. Ex 21:17
ox gores a man or a woman to **d**, Ex 21:28
its owner must also be put to **d**. Ex 21:29
he is beaten to **d**, no one is Ex 22:2
with an animal must be put to **d**. Ex 22:19
profanes it must be put to **d**. Ex 31:14
Sabbath day must be put to **d**. Ex 31:15
them to **d** before the LORD. Lv 10:2
Moses after the **d** of two of Lv 16:1
died a natural **d** or was mauled Lv 17:15
They are not to be put to **d**, Lv 19:20
to Molech must be put to **d**; Lv 20:2
Molech, and do not put him to **d**, Lv 20:4
or mother, he must be put to **d**. Lv 20:9
the adulteress must be put to **d**. Lv 20:10
Both of them must be put to **d**; Lv 20:11
both of them must be put to **d**. Lv 20:12
They must be put to **d**; Lv 20:13
an animal, he must be put to **d**; Lv 20:15
They must be put to **d**; Lv 20:16
or a spiritist must be put to **d**. Lv 20:27
of the LORD is to be put to **d**; Lv 24:16
is to be put to **d**, whether the Lv 24:16
anyone, he must be put to **d**. Lv 24:17
a person is to be put to **d**. Lv 24:21
ransomed; he must be put to **d**. Lv 27:29
near ⌊it⌋ must be put to **d**. Nm 1:51
sanctuary⌋ must be put to **d**." Nm 3:10
near ⌊it⌋ was to be put to **d**. Nm 3:38
The man is to be put to **d**. Nm 15:35
the camp and stoned him to **d**, Nm 15:36
sanctuary⌋ will be put to **d**." Nm 18:7
Let me die the **d** of the upright; Nm 23:10
an iron object and **d** results, Nm 35:16
the murderer must be put to **d**. Nm 35:16
capable of causing **d** and strikes Nm 35:17
the murderer must be put to **d**. Nm 35:17
of causing **d** and he dies, Nm 35:18
the murderer must be put to **d**. Nm 35:18
who struck him must be put to **d**; Nm 35:21
there until the **d** of the high Nm 35:25
refuge until the **d** of the high Nm 35:28
Only after the **d** of the high Nm 35:28
is to be put to **d** based on the Nm 35:30
one is to be put to **d** based on Nm 35:30
someone; he must be put to **d**. Nm 35:31
land before the **d** of the ⌊high⌋ Nm 35:32
or dreamer must be put to **d**, Dt 13:5
against him to put him to **d**, Dt 13:9
Stone him to **d** for trying to Dt 13:10
evil thing and stone them to **d**. Dt 17:5
the first in putting him to **d**, Dt 17:7
of his city will stone him to **d**. Dt 21:21
deserving the **d** penalty and is Dt 21:22
of her city will stone her to **d**. Dt 22:21
that city and stone them to **d**— Dt 22:24
of an offense deserving **d**. Dt 22:26
not to be put to **d** for ⌊their⌋ Dt 24:16
be put to **d** for his own sin. Dt 24:16
and prosperity, **d** and adversity. Dt 30:15
have set before you life and **d**, Dt 30:19
The time of your **d** is now Dt 31:14
that after my **d** you will become Dt 31:29
I bring **d** and I give life; Dt 32:39
the Israelites before his **d**. Dt 33:1
After the **d** of Moses the LORD's Jos 1:1
command him, will be put to **d**. Jos 1:18
to them, and save us from **d**." Jos 2:13
So all Israel stoned him to **d**. Jos 7:25
them down, putting them to **d**. Jos 11:17
those the Israelites put to **d**, Jos 13:22
and until the **d** of the high Jos 20:6
After the **d** of Joshua, the Jdg 1:1
will be put to **d** by morning! Jdg 6:31
birth until the day of his **d**.' " Jdg 13:7
your father's household to **d**. Jdg 14:15
father and burned ⌊them⌋ to **d**. Jdg 15:6
killed at his **d** were more than Jdg 16:30
can put them to **d** and eradicate Jdg 20:13
would certainly be put to **d**. Jdg 21:5
if anything but **d** separates you Ru 1:17
your husband's **d** has been fully Ru 2:11
LORD brings **d** and gives life; 1Sm 2:6
For the fear of **d** pervaded the 1Sm 5:11
the bitterness of **d** has come." 1Sm 15:32
the day of his **d**, Samuel never 1Sm 15:35
to cause David's **d** at the hands 1Sm 18:25
is but a step between me and **d**." 1Sm 20:3
After the **d** of Saul, David 2Sm 1:1
were not parted in life or in **d**. 2Sm 1:23
in revenge for the **d** of Asahel, 2Sm 3:27
Asahel to **d** in the battle at 2Sm 3:30
him and put him to **d** at Ziklag. 2Sm 4:10
no child to the day of her **d**. 2Sm 6:23
to be put to **d** and one length 2Sm 8:2
grieving over Amnon's **d**. 2Sm 13:39
we may put him to **d** for the life 2Sm 14:7
whether it means life or **d**, 2Sm 15:21
Shimei be put to **d** for this, 2Sm 19:21
family deserves **d** from my lord 2Sm 19:28
until the day of their **d**, 2Sm 20:3
put anyone to **d** in Israel." 2Sm 21:4
For the waves of **d** engulfed me; 2Sm 22:5
the snares of **d** confronted me. 2Sm 22:6
will be put to **d** today!" 1Kg 2:24
I will not put you to **d** today, 1Kg 2:26
down Joab, and put him to **d**. 1Kg 2:34
or the **d** of your enemies 1Kg 3:11
he remained until Solomon's **d**. 1Kg 11:40
but all Israel stoned him to **d**. 1Kg 12:18
over to Ahab to put me to **d**? 1Kg 18:9
will put to **d** whoever escapes 1Kg 19:17
will put to **d** whoever escapes 1Kg 19:17
take him out and stone him to **d**. 1Kg 21:10
and stoned him to **d** with stones. 1Kg 21:13
"Naboth has been stoned to **d**." 1Kg 21:14
Naboth had been stoned to **d**, 1Kg 21:15
After the **d** of Ahab, Moab 2Kg 1:1
No longer will **d** or 2Kg 2:21
out, "There's **d** in the pot, man 2Kg 4:40
the ranks is to be put to **d**. 2Kg 11:8
follows her to **d** by the sword," 2Kg 11:15
not to be put to **d** in the LORD's 2Kg 11:15
palace, where she was put to **d**. 2Kg 11:16
put Athaliah to **d** by the sword 2Kg 11:20
children of the murderers to **d**, 2Kg 14:6
must not be put to **d** because of 2Kg 14:6
not be put to **d** because of 2Kg 14:6
be put to **d** for his own sin. 2Kg 14:6
years after the **d** of Israel's 2Kg 14:17
and they put him to **d** there. 2Kg 14:19
disease until the day of his **d**. 2Kg 15:5
to Kir but put Rezin to **d**. 2Kg 16:9
Babylon put them to **d** at Riblah 2Kg 25:21
sight, so He put him to **d**. 1Ch 2:3
After Hezron's **d** in 1Ch 2:24
the LORD put him to **d** and turned 1Ch 10:14
for it before his **d**. 1Ch 22:5
the Israelites stoned him to **d**. 2Ch 10:18
God of Israel would be put to **d**, 2Ch 15:13
after the **d** of his father, 2Ch 22:4
the temple is to be put to **d**. 2Ch 23:7
follows her to **d** by the sword," 2Ch 23:14
Don't put her to **d** in the LORD's 2Ch 23:14
palace, where they put her to **d**. 2Ch 23:15
put Athaliah to **d** by the sword. 2Ch 23:21
he was 130 years old at his **d**. 2Ch 24:15
did not put their children to **d**, 2Ch 25:4
years after the **d** of Israel's 2Ch 25:25
and they put him to **d** there. 2Ch 25:27
diseased to the time of his **d**. 2Ch 26:21
to give you over to **d** by famine 2Ch 32:11
became sick to the point of **d**, 2Ch 32:24
paid him honor at his **d**. 2Ch 32:33
and put him to **d** in his own 2Ch 33:24
him, whether **d**, banishment, Ezr 7:26
summoned—⌊the⌋ **d** ⌊penalty⌋. Est 4:11
to destruction, **d**, and Est 7:4
who wait for **d**, but it does not Jb 3:21
He will redeem you from **d**, Jb 5:20
d rather than life in this body. Jb 7:15
When disaster brings sudden **d**, Jb 9:23
the shadow of **d** covers my eyes, Jb 16:16
Abaddon and **D** say, "We have Jb 28:22
that You will lead me to **d**— Jb 30:23
from crossing the river ⌊of **d**⌋. Jb 33:18
the river ⌊of **d**⌋ and die without Jb 36:12
the gates of **d** been revealed to Jb 38:17
is no remembrance of You in **d**; Ps 6:5

Lift me up from the gates of **d**, Ps 9:13
otherwise, I will sleep in **d**, Ps 13:3
The ropes of **d** were wrapped Ps 18:4
the snares of **d** confronted me. Ps 18:5
You put me into the dust of **d**. Ps 22:15
What gain is there in my **d**, Ps 30:9
them from **d** and to keep them Ps 33:19
Evil brings **d** to the sinner, Ps 34:21
for Sheol; **D** will shepherd Ps 49:14
terrors of **d** sweep over me. Ps 55:4
Let **d** take them by surprise; Ps 55:15
For You delivered me from **d**, Ps 56:13
and escape from **d** belongs to the Ps 68:20
He did not spare them from **d**, Ps 78:50
have been afflicted and near **d**. Ps 88:15
man can live and never see **d**? Ps 89:48
soon rest in the silence ⌊of **d**⌋. Ps 94:17
and condemn the innocent to **d**. Ps 94:21
and came near the gates of **d**. Ps 107:18
in order to put them to **d**. Ps 109:16
into the silence ⌊of **d**⌋. Ps 115:17
The ropes of **d** were wrapped Ps 116:3
rescued me from **d**, my eyes from Ps 116:8
The **d** of His faithful ones is Ps 116:15
but did not give me over to **d**. Ps 118:18
sinks down to **d** and her ways to Pr 2:18
Her feet go down to **d**; Pr 5:5
she has brought many down to **d**; Pr 7:26
descending to the chambers of **d**. Pr 7:27
all who hate me love **d**." Pr 8:36
righteousness rescues from **d**. Pr 10:2
righteousness rescues from **d**. Pr 11:4
but pursuing evil ⌊leads⌋ to **d**. Pr 11:19
but another path leads to **d**. Pr 12:28
away from the snares of **d**. Pr 13:14
but its end is the way to **d**. Pr 14:12
people from the snares of **d**. Pr 14:27
king's fury is a messenger of **d**, Pr 16:14
in the end it is the way of **d**. Pr 16:25
Life and **d** are in the power of Pr 18:21
vanishing mist, a pursuit of **d**. Pr 21:6
those being taken off to **d**, Pr 24:11
will be a fugitive until **d**. Pr 28:17
the day of one's **d** than the day Ec 7:1
bitter than **d** the woman who is Ec 7:26
no authority over the day of **d**; Ec 8:8
For love is as strong as **d**; Sg 8:6
be smashed ⌊to **d**⌋ before their Is 13:16
He will destroy **d** forever. Is 25:8
We have cut a deal with **D**, Is 28:15
Your deal with **D** will be Is 28:18
thank You; **D** cannot praise You Is 38:18
and with a rich man at His **d**, Is 53:9
He submitted Himself to **d**, Is 53:12
D will be chosen over life by Jr 8:3
for **D** has climbed through our Jr 9:21
⌊destined⌋ for **d**, to death; Jr 15:2
⌊destined⌋ for death, to **d**; Jr 15:2
way of life and the way of **d**. Jr 21:8
deserves the **d** sentence because Jr 26:11
certain that if you put me to **d**, Jr 26:15
doesn't deserve the **d** sentence, Jr 26:16
people of⌋ Judah put him to **d**? Jr 26:19
the king tried to put him to **d**. Jr 26:21
to the people to be put to **d**. Jr 26:24
put us to **d** or to deport us to Jr 43:3
⌊destined⌋ for **d**, to death; Jr 43:11
⌊destined⌋ for death, to **d**; Jr 43:11
Babylon put them to **d** at Riblah Jr 52:27
each day until the day of his **d**, Jr 52:34
children; inside, there is **d**. Lm 1:20
in the **d** of the wicked?" Ezk 18:23
take no pleasure in anyone's **d**." Ezk 18:32
die a violent **d** in the heart Ezk 28:8
You will die the **d** of the Ezk 28:10
have all been consigned to **d**, Ezk 31:14
pleasure in the **d** of the wicked, Ezk 33:11
I will redeem them from **d**. Hs 13:14
D, where are your barbs? Hs 13:14
like **D** he is never satisfied. Hab 2:5
He stayed there until Herod's **d**, Mt 2:15
living in the shadowland of **d**, Mt 4:16
daughter is near **d**, but come and Mt 9:18
will betray brother to **d**, Mt 10:21
parents and have them put to **d**. Mt 10:21
or mother must be put to **d**. Mt 15:4
will not taste **d** until they see Mt 16:28
and they will condemn Him to **d**. Mt 20:18
in sorrow—to the point of **d**. Mt 26:38
so they could put Him to **d**. Mt 26:59
They answered, "He deserves **d**!" Mt 26:66
against Jesus to put Him to **d**. Mt 27:1
or mother must be put to **d**. Mk 7:10
will not taste **d** until they see Mk 9:1
and they will condemn Him to **d**. Mk 10:33
will betray brother to **d**, Mk 13:12
parents and put them to **d**. Mk 13:12
in sorrow—to the point of **d**. Mk 14:34
against Jesus to put Him to **d**, Mk 14:55
Him to be deserving of **d**. Mk 14:64
in darkness and the shadow of **d**, Lk 1:79
he would not see **d** before he saw Lk 2:26
will not taste **d** until they see Lk 9:27
and were speaking of His **d**, Lk 9:31
⌊people⌋ into hell after **d**. Lk 12:5
for a way to put Him to **d**, Lk 22:2
You both to prison and to **d**!" Lk 22:33
has done nothing to deserve **d**. Lk 23:15
no grounds for the **d** penalty. Lk 23:22
Him over to be sentenced to **d**, Lk 24:20
but has passed from **d** to life. Jn 5:24
he will never see **d**—ever!" Jn 8:51
he will never taste **d**—ever!' Jn 8:52
will not end in **d** but is for the Jn 11:4
about his **d**, but they thought Jn 11:13
what kind of **d** He was about to Jn 12:33
for us to put anyone to **d**," Jn 18:31
what sort of **d** He was going to Jn 18:32
by what kind of **d** he would Jn 21:19
the pains of **d**, because it was Ac 2:24
agreed with putting him to **d**. Ac 8:1
no grounds for the **d** penalty, Ac 13:28
I persecuted this Way to the **d**, Ac 22:4
charge that merited **d** or chains. Ac 23:29
done anything deserving of **d**, Ac 25:11
done anything deserving of **d**, Ac 25:25
were put to **d**, I cast my vote Ac 26:10
that deserves **d** or chains." Ac 26:31
to God through the **d** of His Son, Rm 5:10
one man, and **d** through sin, in Rm 5:12
in this way **d** spread to all men, Rm 5:12
d reigned from Adam to Moses, Rm 5:14
d reigned through that one man, Rm 5:17
sin reigned in **d**, so also grace Rm 5:21
Jesus were baptized into His **d**? Rm 6:3
with Him by baptism into **d**, Rm 6:4
Him in the likeness of His **d**, Rm 6:5
D no longer rules over Him. Rm 6:9
sin leading to **d** or of obedience Rm 6:16
the end of those things is **d**. Rm 6:21
For the wages of sin is **d**, Rm 6:23
also were put to **d** in relation Rm 7:4
part of us and bore fruit for **d**. Rm 7:5
for life resulted in **d** for me. Rm 7:10
did what is good cause my **d**? Rm 7:13
was producing **d** in me through Rm 7:13
rescue me from this body of **d**? Rm 7:24
from the law of sin and of **d**. Rm 8:2
the mind-set of the flesh is **d**, Rm 8:6
Spirit you put to **d** the deeds of Rm 8:13
that neither **d** nor life, Rm 8:38
world or life or **d** or things 1Co 3:22
the Lord's **d** until He comes. 1Co 11:26
For since **d** came through a man, 1Co 15:21
last enemy to be abolished is **d**. 1Co 15:26
D has been swallowed up in 1Co 15:54
O **D**, where is your victory? 1Co 15:55
O **D**, where is your sting? 1Co 15:55
Now the sting of **d** is sin, 1Co 15:56
had a **d** sentence within 2Co 1:9
us from such a terrible **d**, 2Co 1:10
are a scent of **d** leading to 2Co 2:16
a scent of death leading to **d**, 2Co 2:16
the ministry of **d**, chiseled in 2Co 3:7
carry the **d** of Jesus in our 2Co 4:10
over to **d** because of Jesus, 2Co 4:11
So **d** works in us, but life in 2Co 4:12
but worldly grief produces **d**. 2Co 7:10
beatings, near **d** many times. 2Co 11:23
put the hostility to **d** by it. Eph 2:16
body, whether by life or by **d**. Php 1:20
obedient to the point of **d**— Php 2:8
of death—even to **d** on a cross. Php 2:8
he came close to **d** for the work Php 2:30
being conformed to His **d**, Php 3:10
His physical body through His **d**, Col 1:22
put to **d** whatever in you is Col 3:5
has abolished **d** and has brought 2Tm 1:10
He might taste **d** for everyone— Heb 2:9
because of the suffering of **d**. Heb 2:9
through His **d** He might destroy Heb 2:14
the one holding the power of **d**— Heb 2:14
their lives by the fear of **d**. Heb 2:15
who was able to save Him from **d**, Heb 5:7
prevented by **d** from remaining Heb 7:23
because a **d** has taken place for Heb 9:15
the **d** of the testator must be Heb 9:16
so that he did not experience **d**, Heb 11:5
grown, it gives birth to **d**. Jms 1:15
save his life from **d** and cover a Jms 5:20
being put to **d** in the fleshly 1Pt 3:18
passed from **d** to life because 1Jn 3:14
who does not love remains in **d**. 1Jn 3:14
a sin that does not bring **d**, 1Jn 5:16
commit sin that doesn't bring **d**. 1Jn 5:16
There is sin that brings **d**. 1Jn 5:16
is sin that does not bring **d**. 1Jn 5:17
I hold the keys of **d** and Hades. Rv 1:18
faithful until **d**, and I will Rv 2:10
never be harmed by the second **d**. Rv 2:11
The horseman on it was named **D**, Rv 6:8
people will seek **d** and will not Rv 9:6
but **d** will flee from them. Rv 9:6
their lives in the face of **d**. Rv 12:11
come in one day—**d**, and grief, Rv 18:8
The second **d** has no power over Rv 20:6
and **D** and Hades gave up their Rv 20:13
D and Hades were thrown into the Rv 20:14
is the second **d**, the lake of Rv 20:14
D will exist no longer; Rv 21:4
sulfur, which is the second **d**." Rv 21:8

DEATH'S *(6)*

d firstborn consumes his limbs. Jb 18:13
is like **d** shadow to them. Jb 24:17
with the terrors of **d** shadow! Jb 24:17
you seen the gates of **d** shadow? Jb 38:17
My little daughter is at **d** door. Mk 5:23
old, and she was at **d** door. Lk 8:42

DEATHLY *(1)*

my face grew **d** pale, and I was Dn 10:8

DEATHS *(2)*

of God's ark and the **d** of her 1Sm 4:19
ark of God and to ⌊the **d** of⌋ her 1Sm 4:21

DEBASE *(1)*

Do not **d** your daughter by making Lv 19:29

DEBATE *(4)*

them in serious argument and **d**, Ac 15:2
After there had been much **d**, Ac 15:7
in a prolonged **d** among Ac 28:29
the Devil in a **d** about Moses' Jd 9

DEBATED *(1)*

He conversed and **d** with the Ac 9:29

DEBATER *(1)*

Where is the **d** of this age? 1Co 1:20

DEBATES *(1)*

avoid foolish **d**, genealogies, Ti 3:9

DEBATING *(2)*

he heard them **d** and saw that Mk 12:28
of them were **d** in their minds Lk 3:15

DEBAUCHERY *(2)*

shame of your **d** will be exposed Ezk 23:29
desires and **d**, people who have 2Pt 2:18

DEBIR *(13)*

(AKA KIRIATH-SANNAH, KIRIATH-SEPHER, LO-DEBAR)

of Lachish, and **D** king of Eglon, Jos 10:3
turned toward **D** and attacked it. Jos 10:38
He treated **D** and its king as he Jos 10:39
country—Hebron, **D**, Anab—all Jos 11:21
the king of **D** one the king of Jos 12:13
Mahanaim to the border of **D**; Jos 13:26
ascended to **D** from the Valley Jos 15:7
inhabitants of **D** whose name used Jos 15:15
Kiriath-sannah (that is, **D**), Jos 15:49
its pasturelands, **D** with its Jos 21:15
against the residents of **D** Jdg 1:11
D was formerly named Jdg 1:11
its pasturelands, **D** and its 1Ch 6:58

DEBORAH *(10)*

D, Rebekah's nurse, died and was Gn 35:8
D, a woman who was a prophet and Jdg 4:4

the palm tree of **D** between Ramah Jdg 4:5
So **D** got up and went with Barak Jdg 4:9
him, and **D** also went with Jdg 4:10
Then **D** said to Barak, "Move on, Jdg 4:14
On that day **D** and Barak son of Jdg 5:1
Israel, until I, **D**, I arose, a Jdg 5:7
Awake! Awake, **D**! Awake! Awake, Jdg 5:12
princes of Issachar were with **D**; Jdg 5:15

DEBRIS *(2)*
the firepans from the burning **d**, Nm 16:37
and some on **d** from the ship. Ac 27:44

DEBT *(10)*
This is how to cancel **d**: Dt 15:2
millstone as security for a **d**, Dt 24:6
in the year of **d** cancellation, Dt 31:10
desperate, in **d**, or discontented 1Sm 22:2
Go sell the oil and pay your **d**; 2Kg 4:7
year and will cancel every **d**. Neh 10:31
he had be sold to pay the **d**. Mt 18:25
all that **d** because you begged Mt 18:32
forgive everyone in **d** to us. Lk 11:4
He erased the certificate of **d**, Col 2:14

DEBTOR *(2)*
and borrower, creditor and **d**. Is 24:2
returns his collateral to the **d**. Ezk 18:7

DEBTORS *(3)*
as we also have forgiven our **d**. Mt 6:12
A creditor had two **d**. Lk 7:41
each one of his master's **d**. Lk 16:5

DEBTS *(4)*
seven years you must cancel **d**. Dt 15:1
LORD's release of **d** has been Dt 15:2
year of canceling **d**, is near,' Dt 15:9
forgive us our **d**, as we also Mt 6:12

DECAPOLIS *(3)*
from Galilee, **D**, Jerusalem, Mt 4:25
proclaim in the **D** how much Jesus Mk 5:20
through the region of the **D**. Mk 7:31

DECAY *(6)*
Ephraim and like **d** to the house Hs 5:12
or allow Your Holy One to see **d**. Ac 2:27
His flesh did not experience **d**. Ac 2:31
to return to **d**, He has spoken Ac 13:34
allow Your Holy One to see **d**. Ac 13:35
whom God raised up did not **d**. Ac 13:37

DECAYED *(2)*
Lebanon is ashamed and **d**. Is 33:9
buried with his fathers, and **d**. Ac 13:36

DECEASED *(2)*
the wife of the **d** man, to Ru 4:5
perpetuate the **d** man's name on Ru 4:10

DECEIT *(34)*
and my tongue will not utter **d**. Jb 27:4
or my foot has rushed to **d**, Jb 31:5
trouble, and gives birth to **d**. Ps 7:14
Cursing, **d**, and violence fill Ps 10:7
my prayer—from lips free of **d**. Ps 17:1
and in whose spirit is no **d**! Ps 32:2
and harness your tongue for **d**. Ps 50:19
oppression and **d** never leave its Ps 55:11
Keep me from the way of **d**, Ps 119:29
statutes, for their **d** is a lie. Ps 119:118
from the wicked ⌊leads to⌋ **d**. Pr 12:5
right, but a false witness, **d**. Pr 12:17
D is in the hearts of those who Pr 12:20
his speech and harbors **d** within. Pr 26:24
with cords of **d** and ⌊pull⌋ sin Is 5:18
trusted in oppression and **d**, Is 30:12
so their houses are full of **d**. Jr 5:27
take hold of **d**; they refuse to Jr 8:5
divination, the **d** of their own Jr 14:14
prophets of the **d** of their own Jr 23:26
He will cause **d** to prosper Dn 8:25
the house of Israel, with **d**. Hs 11:12
house with violence and **d**. Zph 1:9
evil actions, **d**, lewdness, Mk 7:22
true Israelite; no **d** is in him." Jn 1:47
full of all **d** and all fraud, Ac 13:10
murder, disputes, **d**, and malice. Rm 1:29
not walking in **d** or distorting 2Co 4:2
sly as I am, I took you in by **d**! 2Co 12:16
in the techniques of **d**. Eph 4:14
and empty **d** based on human Col 2:8
wickedness, all **d**, hypocrisy, 1Pt 2:1
and no **d** was found in His mouth; 1Pt 2:22
and his lips from speaking **d**, 1Pt 3:10

DECEITFUL *(21)*
and your lips from **d** speech. Ps 34:13
Do not let my **d** enemies rejoice Ps 35:19
but contrive **d** schemes against Ps 35:20
me from the **d** and unjust man. Ps 43:1
my **d** enemies, who would destroy Ps 69:4
For wicked and **d** mouths open Ps 109:2
from lying lips and a **d** tongue." Ps 120:2
will He do to you, you **d** tongue? Ps 120:3
but one who utters lies is **d**. Pr 14:25
and one with **d** speech will fall Pr 17:20
someone who has **d** lips and is a Pr 19:1
falsehood and **d** words far from Pr 30:8
Do not trust **d** words, chanting: Jr 7:4
keep trusting in **d** words that Jr 7:8
heart is more **d** than anything Jr 17:9
tongues in their mouths are **d**. Mc 6:12
blood, totally **d**, full of Nah 3:1
a **d** tongue will not be found in Zph 3:13
false apostles, **d** workers, 2Co 11:13
that is corrupted by **d** desires; Eph 4:22
paying attention to **d** spirits 1Tm 4:1

DECEITFULLY *(12)*
brother came **d** and took your Gn 27:35
father Hamor **d** because he had Gn 34:13
They treated Abimelech **d**, Jdg 9:23
God's behalf or speak **d** for Him? Jb 13:7
false, and who has not sworn **d**. Ps 24:4
comes to visit, he speaks **d**; Ps 41:6
one who acts **d** will live in my Ps 101:7
who invoke You **d**. Ps 139:20
violence and had not spoken **d**. Is 53:9
who does the LORD's business **d**, Jr 48:10
is made with him, he will act **d**. Dn 11:23
He dealt **d** with our race and Ac 7:19

DECEIVE *(35)*
flee from me, **d** me, and not tell Gn 31:27
Why did you **d** us by telling us Jos 9:22
Why did you **d** me like this? 1Sm 19:17
asked Saul, "Why did you **d** me? 1Sm 28:12
of Ner came to **d** you and to find 2Sm 3:25
of God, do not **d** your servant." 2Kg 4:16
Didn't I say, 'Do not **d** me?' " 2Kg 4:28
'Don't let Hezekiah **d** you; 2Kg 18:29
d you by promising that 2Kg 19:10
let Hezekiah **d** you, and don't 2Ch 32:15
Could you **d** Him as you would Jb 13:9
Him as you would **d** a man? Jb 13:9
An honest witness does not **d**, Pr 14:5
Don't **d** with your lips. Pr 24:28
Don't let Hezekiah **d** you, Is 36:14
d you by saying that Jerusalem Is 37:10
every brother will certainly **d**, Jr 9:4
you and your diviners **d** you, Jr 29:8
Don't **d** yourselves by saying: Jr 37:9
with you will **d** and conquer you. Ob 7
on a hairy cloak in order to **d**. Zch 13:4
Messiah,' and they will **d** many. Mt 24:5
will rise up and **d** many. Mt 24:11
I am He,' and they will **d** many. Mk 13:6
they **d** with their tongues. Rm 3:13
words they **d** the hearts Rm 16:18
No one should **d** himself. 1Co 3:18
Let no one **d** you with empty Eph 5:6
that no one will **d** you with Col 2:4
or impurity or an intent to **d**. 1Th 2:3
let anyone **d** you in any way. 2Th 2:3
those who are trying to **d** you. 1Jn 2:26
children, let no one **d** you! 1Jn 3:7
would no longer **d** the nations Rv 20:3
will go out to **d** the nations at Rv 20:8

DECEIVED *(35)*
He **d** me, and I ate." Gn 3:13
Why have you **d** me?" Gn 29:25
And Jacob **d** Laban the Aramean, Gn 31:20
You have **d** me and taken my Gn 31:26
have stolen, **d**, and put ⌊the Jos 7:11
The old prophet **d** him, 1Kg 13:18
The **d** and the deceiver are His. Jb 12:16
they **d** Him with their mouths, Ps 78:36
the princes of Memphis are **d**. Is 19:13
⌊His⌋ **d** mind has led him astray, Is 44:20
You have certainly **d** this people Jr 4:10
You **d** me, LORD, and I was Jr 20:7
deceived me, LORD, and I was **d**. Jr 20:7
he will be **d** so that we might Jr 20:10
presumptuous heart has **d** you. Jr 49:16
if the prophet is **d** and speaks a Ezk 14:9
I, the LORD, who **d** that prophet. Ezk 14:9
presumptuous heart has **d** you, Ob 3
them, "You are **d**, because you Mt 22:29
Are you not **d** because you don't Mk 12:24
of the living. You are badly **d**." Mk 12:27
Watch out that you are not **d**. Lk 21:8
commandment, **d** me, and through Rm 7:11
kingdom? Do not be **d**: no 1Co 6:9
Do not be **d**: "Bad company 1Co 15:33
as the serpent **d** Eve by his 2Co 11:3
Don't be **d**: God is not mocked. Gl 6:7
Adam was not **d**, but the woman 1Tm 2:14
the woman was **d** and transgressed 1Tm 2:14
worse, deceiving and being **d**. 2Tm 3:13
disobedient, **d**, captives of Ti 3:3
Don't be **d**, my dearly loved Jms 1:16
nations were **d** by your sorcery Rv 18:23
by which he **d** those who accepted Rv 19:20
The Devil who **d** them was thrown Rv 20:10

DECEIVER *(4)*
The deceived and the **d** are His. Jb 12:16
The **d** is cursed who has an Mal 1:14
while this **d** was still alive Mt 27:63
is the **d** and the antichrist. 2Jn 7

DECEIVERS *(3)*
and good report; as **d** yet true; 2Co 6:8
idle talkers and **d**, especially Ti 1:10
Many **d** have gone out into the 2Jn 7

DECEIVES *(7)*
the stupidity of fools **d** ⌊them⌋. Pr 14:8
so is the man who **d** his neighbor Pr 26:19
Watch out that no one **d** you. Mt 24:4
Watch out that no one **d** you. Mk 13:5
and teaches and **d** My slaves to Rv 2:20
the one who **d** the whole world. Rv 12:9
He **d** those who live on the earth Rv 13:14

DECEIVING *(8)*
Then I will seem to be **d** him, Gn 27:12
the LORD by **d** his neighbor Lv 6:2
contrary, He's **d** the people." Jn 7:12
he is nothing, he is **d** himself. Gl 6:3
become worse, **d** and being 2Tm 3:13
not hearers only, **d** yourselves. Jms 1:22
his tongue but **d** his heart, Jms 1:26
no sin," we are **d** ourselves, 1Jn 1:8

DECENCY *(2)*
Let us walk with **d**, as in the Rm 13:13
clothing, with **d** and good sense; 1Tm 2:9

DECENTLY *(1)*
must be done **d** and in order. 1Co 14:40

DECEPTION *(11)*
their womb prepares **d**. Jb 15:35
his hatred is concealed by **d**, Pr 26:26
and **d** against the LORD Is 59:13
You live in ⌊a world⌋ of **d**. Jr 9:6
In ⌊their⌋ **d** they refuse to know Jr 9:6
deadly arrows—they speak **d**. Jr 9:8
Achzib are a **d** to the kings of Mc 1:14
Then the last **d** will be worse Mt 27:64
unrighteous **d** among those who 2Th 2:10
of you is hardened by sin's **d**. Heb 3:13
of truth and the spirit of **d**. 1Jn 4:6

DECEPTIONS *(2)*
narrows his eyes is planning **d**; Pr 16:30
in their **d** as they feast with 2Pt 2:13

DECEPTIVE *(14)*
not pay attention to **d** words." Ex 5:9
the plans of the **d** are quickly Jb 5:13
Your answers are **d**. Jb 21:34
flattering lips and **d** hearts. Ps 12:2
his mouth are malicious and **d**; Ps 36:3
lies, whose right hands are **d**. Ps 144:8
lies, whose right hands are **d**. Ps 144:11
none of them are **d** or perverse. Pr 8:8
choice food, for that food is **d**. Pr 23:3
Charm is **d** and beauty is Pr 31:30
people, **d** children, children Is 30:9
for you that were empty and **d**; Lm 2:14
scales or bags of **d** weights? Mc 6:11
will exploit you with **d** words. 2Pt 2:3

DECEPTIVELY *(5)*
must not act **d** again by refusing Ex 8:29
You must not act **d** or lie to one Lv 19:11
they acted **d**. They gathered Jos 9:4
Jehu was acting **d** in order to 2Kg 10:19
and to deal **d** with His servants Ps 105:25

DECIDE *(15)*
and let them **d** between the two Gn 31:37
I will **d** what to do with you. Ex 33:5
is⌋ the Judge **d** today between Jdg 11:27
here with you whatever you **d**." 1Sm 14:7
LORD be judge and **d** between 1Sm 24:15
think it over and **d** what answer 2Sm 24:13
Now **d** what answer I should 1Ch 21:12
that He would **d** to crush me, Jb 6:9
let us **d** together what is good. Jb 34:4
as judges and **d** the case Ezk 44:24
for them to **d** what each would Mk 15:24
sit down and **d** if he is able Lk 14:31
you rather than to God, you **d**; Ac 4:19
comes down, I will **d** your case." Ac 24:22
but instead **d** not to put a Rm 14:13

DECIDED *(30)*
I have **d** to put an end to all Gn 6:13
it had not been **d** what should be Nm 15:34
the month he had **d** on his own. 1Kg 12:33
you yourself have **d** it." 1Kg 20:40
Solomon **d** to build a temple for 2Ch 2:1
land and have **d** to seek God." 2Ch 19:3
in Jerusalem **d** to observe the 2Ch 30:2
congregation **d** to observe seven 2Ch 30:23
and what was **d** against her. Est 2:1
Haman **d** not to do away with Est 3:6
If I had **d** to say these things Ps 73:15
Darius **d** to appoint 120 satraps Dn 6:1
d to divorce her secretly. Mt 1:19
Pilate **d** to grant their demand Lk 23:24
The next day He **d** to leave for Jn 1:43
the chief priests **d** to also kill Jn 12:10
when he had **d** to release Him. Ac 3:13
he **d** to visit his brothers, Ac 7:23
d to select men from among them Ac 15:22
have unanimously **d** to select men Ac 15:25
must be **d** in a legal assembly. Ac 19:39
For Paul had **d** to sail past Ac 20:16
to the Emperor, I **d** to send him. Ac 25:25
When it was **d** that we were to Ac 27:1
the majority **d** to set sail from Ac 27:12
I have already **d** about him who 1Co 5:3
and has **d** in his heart to keep 1Co 7:37
do as he has **d** in his heart— 2Co 9:7
for I have **d** to spend the winter Ti 3:12
for You have **d** these things. Rv 16:5

DECIDES *(4)*
who brought it **d** to redeem it, Lv 27:13
the field **d** to redeem it, Lv 27:19
If a man **d** to redeem any part of Lv 27:31
Whatever my lord the king **d**, 2Sm 15:15

DECIMATION *(1)*
Desolation, **d**, devastation! Nah 2:10

DECISION *(19)*
and I make a **d** between one man Ex 18:16
until the LORD's **d** could be made Lv 24:12
for him with the **d** of the Urim. Nm 27:21
left from the **d** they declare to Dt 17:11
Israel, give us the right ⌊**d**⌋." 1Sm 14:41
Let the king's **d** regarding ⌊this Ezr 5:17
according to the **d** of the Ezr 10:8
When you make a **d**, it will be Jb 22:28
its every **d** is from the LORD. Pr 16:33
Give us counsel and make a **d**. Is 16:3
multitudes in the valley of **d**! Jl 3:14
LORD is near in the valley of **d**. Jl 3:14
For My **d** is to gather nations, Zph 3:8
What is your **d**?" They answered, Mt 26:66
What is your **d**?" And they all Mk 14:64
For it was the Holy Spirit's **d**— Ac 15:28
so a **d** was made to go back Ac 20:3
containing our **d** that they Ac 21:25
with the **d** of His will, Eph 1:11

DECISIONS *(6)*
embroidered breastpiece for **d**, Ex 28:15
heart on the breastpiece for **d**, Ex 28:29
in the breastpiece for **d**, Ex 28:30
the ⌊means of⌋ **d** for the Ex 28:30
my just **d** were like a robe and a Jb 29:14
they delivered the **d** reached by Ac 16:4

DECISIVELY *(2)*
balsam trees, act **d**, for then 2Sm 5:24
completely and **d** on the earth. Rm 9:28

DECK *(1)*
They made your **d** of cypress wood Ezk 27:6

DECKED *(1)*
who **d** your garments with gold 2Sm 1:24

DECKS *(1)*
lower, middle, and upper ⌊**d**⌋. Gn 6:16

DECLARATION *(351)*
let my **d** ⌊ring⌋ in your ears. Jb 13:17
the **d** of the LORD of Hosts— Is 14:22
and posterity"—the LORD's **d**. Is 14:22
⌊This is⌋ the **d** of the LORD of Is 14:23
⌊This is⌋ the **d** of the LORD of Is 17:3
⌊This is⌋ the **d** of the LORD, Is 17:6
⌊This is⌋ the **d** of the Lord GOD Is 19:4
the **d** of the LORD of Hosts— Is 22:25
⌊This is⌋ the LORD's **d**. Is 30:1
is⌋ the LORD's **d**—whose fire is Is 31:9
⌊This is⌋ the LORD's **d**. Is 37:34
I will help you—the LORD's **d**. Is 41:14
the LORD's **d**—"and My servant Is 43:10
the LORD's **d**—"and I am God. Is 43:12
the LORD's **d**—"you will wear Is 49:18
the LORD's **d**—"that My people Is 52:5
the LORD's **d**—"and My name is Is 52:5
⌊This is⌋ the LORD's **d**. Is 54:17
⌊This is⌋ the LORD's **d**. Is 55:8
⌊This is⌋ the **d** of the Lord GOD, Is 56:8
⌊This is⌋ the LORD's **d**. Is 59:20
⌊This is⌋ the LORD's **d**. Is 66:2
⌊This is⌋ the LORD's **d**. Is 66:17
the LORD's **d**—"so will your Is 66:22
⌊This is⌋ the LORD's **d**. Jr 1:8
⌊This is⌋ the LORD's **d**. Jr 1:15
⌊This is⌋ the LORD's **d**. Jr 1:19
⌊This is⌋ the LORD's **d**. Jr 2:3
⌊This is⌋ the LORD's **d**. Jr 2:9
⌊This is⌋ the LORD's **d**. Jr 2:12
⌊This is⌋ the **d** of the Lord GOD Jr 2:19
⌊This is⌋ the Lord GOD's **d**. Jr 2:22
⌊This is⌋ the LORD's **d**. Jr 2:29
⌊This is⌋ the LORD's **d**. Jr 3:1
⌊This is⌋ the LORD's **d**. Jr 3:10
⌊This is⌋ the LORD's **d**. Jr 3:12
⌊This is⌋ the LORD's **d**. Jr 3:12
⌊This is⌋ the LORD's **d**. Jr 3:13
the LORD's **d**—"for I am your Jr 3:14
the LORD's **d**—"no one will say Jr 3:16
⌊This is⌋ the LORD's **d**. Jr 3:20
is⌋ the LORD's **d**—⌊if⌋ you Jr 4:1
is⌋ the LORD's **d**—"the king Jr 4:9
⌊This is⌋ the LORD's **d**. Jr 4:17
⌊This is⌋ the LORD's **d**. Jr 5:9
⌊This is⌋ the LORD's **d**. Jr 5:11
⌊This is⌋ the LORD's **d**. Jr 5:15
is⌋ the LORD's **d**—"I will not Jr 5:18
⌊This is⌋ the LORD's **d**. Jr 5:22
⌊This is⌋ the LORD's **d**. Jr 5:29
⌊This is⌋ the LORD's **d**. Jr 6:12
⌊This is⌋ the LORD's **d**. Jr 7:11
is⌋ the LORD's **d**—"and because Jr 7:13
⌊This is⌋ the LORD's **d**. Jr 7:19
⌊This is⌋ the LORD's **d**. Jr 7:30
the LORD's **d**—"when ⌊this place Jr 7:32
is⌋ the LORD's **d**—"the bones Jr 8:1
⌊This is⌋ the **d** of the LORD of Jr 8:3
⌊This is⌋ the LORD's **d**. Jr 8:13
⌊This is⌋ the LORD's **d**. Jr 8:17
⌊This is⌋ the LORD's **d**. Jr 9:3
⌊This is⌋ the LORD's **d**. Jr 9:6
⌊This is⌋ the LORD's **d**. Jr 9:9
⌊This is⌋ the LORD's **d**. Jr 9:24
the LORD's **d**—"when I will Jr 9:25
⌊This is⌋ the LORD's **d**. Jr 12:17
is⌋ the LORD's **d**—"so that they Jr 13:11
and sons alike"—the LORD's **d**. Jr 13:14
is⌋ the LORD's **d**—because you Jr 13:25
is⌋ the LORD's **d**—"the sword to Jr 15:3
⌊This is⌋ the LORD's **d**. Jr 15:6
⌊This is⌋ the LORD's **d**. Jr 15:9
⌊This is⌋ the LORD's **d**. Jr 15:20
⌊this is⌋ the LORD's **d**— Jr 16:5
the LORD's **d**—"and followed Jr 16:11
the LORD's **d**—"when it will no Jr 16:14
the LORD's **d**—"and they will Jr 16:16
—⌊this is⌋ the LORD's **d**. Jr 18:6
is⌋ the LORD's **d**—"when this Jr 19:6
⌊this is⌋ the **d** of the LORD— Jr 19:12
⌊this is⌋ the LORD's **d**— Jr 21:7
⌊this is⌋ the LORD's **d**. Jr 21:10
is⌋ the LORD's **d**—you who say: Jr 21:13
done—⌊this is⌋ the LORD's **d**. Jr 21:14
is⌋ the LORD's **d**—"that this Jr 22:5
⌊This is⌋ the LORD's **d**. Jr 22:16
⌊This is⌋ the LORD's **d**. Jr 23:1
your evil acts"—the LORD's **d**. Jr 23:2
⌊This is⌋ the LORD's **d**. Jr 23:4
is⌋ the LORD's **d**—"when I will Jr 23:5
the LORD's **d**—"when it will no Jr 23:7
⌊This is⌋ the LORD's **d**. Jr 23:11
⌊This is⌋ the LORD's **d**. Jr 23:12
the LORD's **d**—"and not a God Jr 23:23
—the LORD's **d**. Jr 23:24
—the LORD's **d**. Jr 23:24
—the LORD's **d**. Jr 23:28
fire"—the LORD's **d**—"and like Jr 23:29
the LORD's **d**—"who steal My Jr 23:30
LORD's **d**—"who use their own Jr 23:31
the LORD's **d**—"telling them Jr 23:32
—⌊this is⌋ the LORD's **d**. Jr 23:32
away"—⌊this is⌋ the LORD's **d**. Jr 23:33
the LORD's **d**—'in order that Jr 25:7
is⌋ the LORD's **d**—'and ⌊send Jr 25:9
is⌋ the LORD's **d**—'the land Jr 25:12
⌊this is⌋ the **d** of the LORD of Jr 25:29
sword—⌊This is⌋ the LORD's **d**. Jr 25:31
the LORD's **d**—"until through Jr 27:8
⌊This is⌋ the LORD's **d**. Jr 27:11
is⌋ the LORD's **d**—'and they are Jr 27:15
⌊This is⌋ the LORD's **d**. Jr 27:22
is⌋ the LORD's **d**—'for I will Jr 28:4
⌊This is⌋ the LORD's **d**. Jr 29:9
is⌋ the LORD's **d**—"plans for Jr 29:11
you"—the LORD's **d**—"and I Jr 29:14
I banished you"—the LORD's **d**. Jr 29:14
is⌋ the LORD's **d**—"that I sent Jr 29:19
⌊This is⌋ the LORD's **d**. Jr 29:19
⌊This is⌋ the LORD's **d**. Jr 29:23
is⌋ the LORD's **d**—"for he has Jr 29:32
is⌋ the LORD's **d**—"when I will Jr 30:3
and Judah"—the LORD's **d**. Jr 30:3
⌊this is⌋ the **d** of the LORD of Jr 30:8
is⌋ the LORD's **d**—and do not be Jr 30:10
is⌋ the LORD's **d**—to save you! Jr 30:11
is⌋ the LORD's **d**—for they call Jr 30:17
⌊This is⌋ the LORD's **d**. Jr 30:21
the LORD's **d**—"I will be God Jr 31:1
⌊This is⌋ the LORD's **d**. Jr 31:14
is⌋ the LORD's **d**—and your Jr 31:16
is⌋ the LORD's **d**—and your Jr 31:17
⌊This is⌋ the LORD's **d**. Jr 31:20
is⌋ the LORD's **d**—"when I will Jr 31:27
is⌋ the LORD's **d**—"when I will Jr 31:31
married them"—the LORD's **d**. Jr 31:32
those days"—the LORD's **d**. Jr 31:33
of them"—the LORD's **d**. Jr 31:34
is⌋ the LORD's **d**—then also Jr 31:36
done—⌊this is⌋ the LORD's **d**. Jr 31:37
the LORD's **d**—"when the city Jr 31:38
him'—⌊this is⌋ the LORD's **d**. Jr 32:5
—⌊this is⌋ the LORD's **d**— Jr 32:30
⌊This is⌋ the LORD's **d**. Jr 32:44
is⌋ the LORD's **d**—"when I will Jr 33:14
⌊This is⌋ the LORD's **d**. Jr 34:5
the LORD's **d**—"to the sword, Jr 34:17
is⌋ the LORD's **d**—"and I will Jr 34:22
—⌊this is⌋ the LORD's **d**. Jr 35:13
is⌋ the LORD's **d**—"and you will Jr 39:17
⌊This is⌋ the LORD's **d**. Jr 39:18
is⌋ the LORD's **d**—'because I am Jr 42:11
is⌋ the LORD's **d**—'that I am Jr 44:29
is⌋ the LORD's **d**—'but I will Jr 45:5
⌊This is⌋ the LORD's **d**. Jr 46:5
I live—⌊this is⌋ the King's **d**; Jr 46:18
is⌋ the LORD's **d**—though it is Jr 46:23
⌊This is⌋ the LORD's **d**. Jr 46:26
is⌋ the LORD's **d**—for I will be Jr 46:28
is⌋ the LORD's **d**—when I will Jr 48:12
⌊This is⌋ the King's **d**; Jr 48:15
⌊This is⌋ the LORD's **d**. Jr 48:25
⌊This is⌋ the LORD's **d**. Jr 48:30
is⌋ the LORD's **d**—"the one who Jr 48:35
⌊This is⌋ the LORD's **d**. Jr 48:38
⌊This is⌋ the LORD's **d**. Jr 48:43
⌊This is⌋ the LORD's **d**. Jr 48:44
⌊This is⌋ the LORD's **d**. Jr 48:47
is⌋ the LORD's **d**—when I will Jr 49:2
⌊this is⌋ the **d** of the Lord, Jr 49:5
⌊This is⌋ the LORD's **d**. Jr 49:6

the LORD's **d**—"Bozrah will Jr 49:13
⌊This is⌋ the LORD's **d**. Jr 49:16
⌊This is⌋ the **d** of the LORD of Jr 49:26
⌊this is⌋ the LORD's **d**—for Jr 49:30
⌊This is⌋ the LORD's **d**. Jr 49:31
⌊This is⌋ the LORD's **d**. Jr 49:32
⌊This is⌋ the LORD's **d**. Jr 49:37
⌊This is⌋ the LORD's **d**. Jr 49:38
⌊This is⌋ the LORD's **d**. Jr 49:39
the LORD's **d**—the Israelites Jr 50:4
⌊This is⌋ the LORD's **d**. Jr 50:10
is⌋ the LORD's **d**—one will Jr 50:20
is⌋ the LORD's **d**—do everything Jr 50:21
⌊This is⌋ the LORD's **d**. Jr 50:30
⌊this is⌋ the **d** of the Lord GOD Jr 50:31
is⌋ the LORD's **d**—against those Jr 50:35
the LORD's **d**—so no one will Jr 50:40
⌊This is⌋ the LORD's **d**. Jr 51:24
is⌋ the LORD's **d**—you devastate Jr 51:25
⌊This is⌋ the LORD's **d**. Jr 51:26
⌊This is⌋ the LORD's **d**. Jr 51:39
⌊This is⌋ the LORD's **d**. Jr 51:48
is⌋ the LORD's **d**—when I will Jr 51:52
⌊This is⌋ the LORD's **d**. Jr 51:53
⌊This is⌋ the King's **d**; Jr 51:57
⌊this is⌋ the **d** of the Lord GOD— Ezk 5:11
⌊This is⌋ the **d** of the Lord GOD Ezk 11:8
⌊This is⌋ the **d** of the Lord GOD Ezk 11:21
⌊This is⌋ the **d** of the Lord GOD Ezk 12:25
⌊This is⌋ the **d** of the Lord GOD Ezk 12:28
is⌋ the LORD's **d**, when the LORD Ezk 13:6
is⌋ the LORD's **d**, even though I Ezk 13:7
⌊This is⌋ the **d** of the Lord GOD Ezk 13:8
⌊This is⌋ the **d** of the Lord GOD Ezk 13:16
⌊This is⌋ the **d** of the Lord GOD Ezk 14:11
⌊This is⌋ the **d** of the Lord GOD Ezk 14:14
I live"—the **d** of the Lord GOD Ezk 14:16
I live"—the **d** of the Lord GOD Ezk 14:18
I live"—the **d** of the Lord GOD Ezk 14:20
⌊This is⌋ the **d** of the Lord GOD Ezk 14:23
⌊This is⌋ the **d** of the Lord GOD Ezk 15:8
⌊This is⌋ the **d** of the Lord GOD Ezk 16:8
⌊This is⌋ the **d** of the Lord GOD Ezk 16:14
⌊This is⌋ the **d** of the Lord GOD Ezk 16:19
—the **d** of the Lord GOD— Ezk 16:23
lust⌋"—the **d** of the Lord GOD Ezk 16:30
⌊This is⌋ the **d** of the Lord GOD Ezk 16:43
I live"—the **d** of the Lord GOD Ezk 16:48
abominations"—the LORD's **d**. Ezk 16:58
⌊This is⌋ the **d** of the Lord GOD Ezk 16:63
⌊this is⌋ the **d** of the Lord GOD— Ezk 17:16
⌊this is⌋ the **d** of the Lord GOD— Ezk 18:3
⌊This is⌋ the **d** of the Lord GOD Ezk 18:9
⌊This is⌋ the **d** of the Lord GOD Ezk 18:23
⌊This is⌋ the **d** of the Lord GOD Ezk 18:30
⌊This is⌋ the **d** of the Lord GOD Ezk 18:32
⌊This is⌋ the **d** of the Lord GOD Ezk 20:3
⌊this is⌋ the **d** of the Lord GOD— Ezk 20:31
I live"—the **d** of the Lord GOD Ezk 20:33
⌊This is⌋ the **d** of the Lord GOD Ezk 20:36
mountain"—the **d** of the Lord Ezk 20:40
⌊This is⌋ the **d** of the Lord GOD Ezk 20:44
⌊This is⌋ the **d** of the Lord GOD Ezk 21:7
⌊This is⌋ the **d** of the Lord GOD. Ezk 21:13
⌊This is⌋ the **d** of the Lord GOD Ezk 22:12
⌊This is⌋ the **d** of the Lord GOD Ezk 22:31
⌊This is⌋ the **d** of the Lord GOD. Ezk 23:34
⌊This is⌋ the **d** of the Lord GOD. Ezk 24:14
⌊This is⌋ the **d** of the Lord GOD Ezk 25:14
⌊This is⌋ the **d** of the Lord GOD Ezk 26:5
⌊This is⌋ the **d** of the Lord GOD Ezk 26:14
⌊This is⌋ the **d** of the Lord GOD Ezk 26:21
⌊This is⌋ the **d** of the Lord GOD. Ezk 28:10
⌊This is⌋ the **d** of the Lord GOD Ezk 29:20
⌊This is⌋ the **d** of the Lord GOD. Ezk 30:6
hordes"—the **d** of the Lord GOD Ezk 31:18
⌊This is⌋ the **d** of the Lord GOD. Ezk 32:8
⌊This is⌋ the **d** of the Lord GOD. Ezk 32:14
⌊This is⌋ the **d** of the Lord GOD. Ezk 32:16
⌊This is⌋ the **d** of the Lord GOD. Ezk 32:31
⌊This is⌋ the **d** of the Lord GOD Ezk 32:32
I live"—the **d** of the Lord GOD Ezk 33:11
I live"—the **d** of the Lord GOD Ezk 34:8
⌊This is⌋ the **d** of the Lord GOD Ezk 34:15
⌊This is⌋ the **d** of the Lord GOD Ezk 34:30
⌊This is⌋ the **d** of the Lord GOD Ezk 34:31
⌊this is⌋ the **d** of the Lord GOD— Ezk 35:6
I live"—the **d** of the Lord GOD Ezk 35:11
⌊This is⌋ the **d** of the Lord GOD Ezk 36:14
⌊This is⌋ the **d** of the Lord GOD Ezk 36:15
Yahweh"—the **d** of the Lord GOD Ezk 36:23
will act"—the **d** of the Lord Ezk 36:32
⌊This is⌋ the **d** of the LORD. Ezk 37:14
⌊this is⌋ the **d** of the Lord GOD— Ezk 38:18
the **d** of the Lord GOD Ezk 38:21
⌊This is⌋ the **d** of the Lord GOD Ezk 39:5
⌊This is⌋ the **d** of the Lord GOD Ezk 39:8
⌊This is⌋ the **d** of the Lord GOD Ezk 39:10
⌊This is⌋ the **d** of the Lord GOD Ezk 39:13
⌊This is⌋ the **d** of the Lord GOD Ezk 39:20
⌊This is⌋ the **d** of the Lord GOD Ezk 39:29
⌊This is⌋ the **d** of the Lord GOD Ezk 43:19
⌊This is⌋ the **d** of the Lord GOD Ezk 43:27
⌊this is⌋ the **d** of the Lord GOD— Ezk 44:12
⌊This is⌋ the **d** of the Lord GOD Ezk 44:15
⌊This is⌋ the **d** of the Lord GOD Ezk 44:27
⌊This is⌋ the **d** of the Lord GOD Ezk 45:9
⌊This is⌋ the **d** of the Lord GOD Ezk 45:15
⌊This is⌋ the **d** of the Lord GOD Ezk 47:23
⌊This is⌋ the **d** of the Lord GOD Ezk 48:29
⌊This is⌋ the LORD's **d**. Hs 2:13
the LORD's **d**—you will call Hs 2:16
I will respond—the LORD's **d**. Hs 2:21
⌊This is⌋ the LORD's **d**. Hs 11:11
is⌋ the LORD's **d**—turn to Me Jl 2:12
⌊This is⌋ the LORD's **d**. Am 2:11
on that day—the LORD's **d**. Am 2:16
the LORD's **d**—those who store Am 3:10
⌊this is⌋ the **d** of the Lord GOD, Am 3:13
come to an end—the LORD's **d**. Am 3:15
⌊This is⌋ the LORD's **d**. Am 4:3
⌊This is⌋ the LORD's **d**. Am 4:5
not return to Me—the LORD's **d**. Am 4:6
not return to Me—the LORD's **d**. Am 4:8
not return to Me—the LORD's **d**. Am 4:9
not return to Me—the LORD's **d**. Am 4:10
not return to Me—the LORD's **d**. Am 4:11
Himself—the **d** of Yahweh, the Am 6:8
⌊this is⌋ the **d** of the Lord, Am 6:14
wailing"—the Lord GOD's **d**. Am 8:3
⌊this is⌋ the **d** of the Lord GOD— Am 8:9
⌊this is⌋ the **d** of the Lord GOD— Am 8:11
⌊This is⌋ the LORD's **d**. Am 9:7
house of Jacob—the LORD's **d**— Am 9:8
is⌋ the LORD's **d**—He will do Am 9:12
the LORD's **d**—when the plowman Am 9:13
⌊This is⌋ the LORD's **d**. Ob 4
day—the LORD's **d**—will I not Ob 8
is⌋ the LORD's **d**—I will Mc 4:6
the LORD's **d**—I will remove Mc 5:10
the **d** of the Lord of Hosts. Nah 2:13
the **d** of the Lord of Hosts. Nah 3:5
earth—⌊this is⌋ the LORD's **d**. Zph 1:2
of the earth—the LORD's **d**. Zph 1:3
the LORD's **d**—there will be Zph 1:10
the **d** of the LORD of Hosts, Zph 2:9
—the LORD's **d**—until the day Zph 3:8
⌊This is⌋ the **d** of the LORD of Hg 1:9
I am with you"—the LORD's **d**. Hg 1:13
Zerubbabel"—the LORD's **d**. Hg 2:4
of the land"—the LORD's **d**. Hg 2:4
the **d** of the LORD of Hosts. Hg 2:4
the **d** of the LORD of Hosts. Hg 2:8
the **d** of the LORD of Hosts. Hg 2:9
before Me"—the LORD's **d**. Hg 2:14
turn to Me"—the LORD's **d**. Hg 2:17
the **d** of the LORD of Hosts— Hg 2:23
the LORD's **d**—"and make you Hg 2:23
⌊This is⌋ the **d** of the LORD of Hg 2:23
⌊this is⌋ the **d** of the LORD of Zch 1:3
attention to Me"—the LORD's **d**. Zch 1:4
the **d** of the LORD of Hosts— Zch 1:16
The **d** of the LORD: Zch 2:5
the LORD's **d**—"for I have Zch 2:6
winds of heaven"—the LORD's **d**. Zch 2:6
dwell among you"—the LORD's **d**. Zch 2:10
the **d** of the LORD of Hosts— Zch 3:9
⌊This is⌋ the **d** of the LORD of Zch 3:10
the **d** of the LORD of Hosts— Zch 5:4
the **d** of the LORD of Hosts. Zch 8:6
the **d** of the LORD of Hosts. Zch 8:11
I hate all this"—the LORD's **d**. Zch 8:17
His name—⌊this is⌋ Yahweh's **d**. Zch 10:12
of the land"—the LORD's **d**. Zch 11:6
A **d** of the LORD, who stretched Zch 12:1
the LORD's **d**—"I will strike Zch 12:4
the **d** of the LORD of Hosts— Zch 13:2
the **d** of the LORD of Hosts. Zch 13:7
the LORD's **d**—two-thirds will Zch 13:8
⌊This is⌋ the LORD's **d**. Mal 1:2

DECLARE *(62)*

brother must **d** it to Pharaoh so Ex 7:2
have heard of Your fame will **d**, Nm 14:15
Therefore **d**: I grant him My Nm 25:12
from the decision they **d** to you. Dt 17:11
They will **d**, 'Our hands did not Dt 21:7
Then she will **d**, 'This is what Dt 25:9
D the greatness of our God! Dt 32:3
I raise My hand to heaven and **d**: Dt 32:40
yours? I hereby **d**: you and Ziba 2Sm 19:29
king who sent you and **d** to him: 2Kg 1:6
D His glory among the nations, 1Ch 16:24
I **d** to you that the LORD Himself 1Ch 17:10
my mouth would **d** me guilty. Jb 9:20
to God: Do not **d** me guilty! Let Jb 10:2
would speak and **d** His case Jb 11:5
I too will **d** what I know." Jb 32:10
silent, who can **d** ⌊Him⌋ guilty? Jb 34:29
not I! So **d** what you know. Jb 34:33
Would you **d** Me guilty to justify Jb 40:8
I will **d** the LORD's decree: Ps 2:7
I will **d** all Your wonderful Ps 9:1
that I may **d** all Your praises. Ps 9:14
The heavens **d** the glory of God, Ps 19:1
and my mouth will **d** Your praise. Ps 51:15
I will **d** wise sayings; Ps 78:2
we will **d** Your praise to Ps 79:13
the LORD will **d** peace to His Ps 85:8
For I will **d**, "Faithful love is Ps 89:2
to **d** Your faithful love in the Ps 92:2
d: "The LORD is just; He is my Ps 92:15
D His glory among the nations, Ps 96:3
so that they might **d** the name of Ps 102:21
Who can **d** the LORD's mighty acts Ps 106:2
generation will **d** Your works to Ps 145:4
and I will **d** Your greatness. Ps 145:6
kingdom and will **d** Your might, Ps 145:11
My mouth will **d** the LORD's Ps 145:21
see her and **d** her fortunate; Sg 6:9
D that His name is exalted. Is 12:4
happened. Now I **d** new events; I Is 42:9
and **d** His praise in the islands. Is 42:12
Who among them can **d** this, Is 43:9
for Myself will **d** My praise. Is 43:21
Let these gods **d** the coming Is 44:7
I **d** the end from the beginning, Is 46:10
of the LORD and **d** the God of Is 48:1
D with a shout of joy, proclaim Is 48:20
D in Judah, proclaim in Jr 4:5
D this in the house of Jacob; Jr 5:20
You must therefore **d** to them: Jr 7:28
D by the Arnon that Moab is Jr 48:20
Then **d** their abominations to Ezk 23:36
teeth into but **d** war against the Mc 3:5
today I **d** that I will restore Zch 9:12
I will **d** things kept secret from Mt 13:35
He will also **d** to you what is to Jn 16:13
what is Mine and **d** it to you. Jn 16:14
is Mine and will **d** it to you. Jn 16:15
be righteous and **d** righteous the Rm 3:26
we testify and **d** to you the 1Jn 1:2
seen and heard we also **d** to you, 1Jn 1:3
heard from Him and **d** to you: 1Jn 1:5

DECLARED *(43)*

the seventh day and **d** it holy, Gn 2:3
the Sabbath day and **d** it holy. Ex 20:11
by Yourself and **d** to them, Ex 32:13
So Moses **d** the LORD's appointed Lv 23:44
Then the Israelites **d** to Moses, Nm 17:12
He **d** His covenant to you. Dt 4:13
Israel, and He **d**, "Because this Jdg 2:20
Saul **d** to him, "May God punish 1Sm 14:44
Samuel **d**: As your sword has 1Sm 15:33
man had **d**, "Do you see this 1Sm 17:25
Then the king **d** to the man of 1Kg 13:7
before him, and **d**, "I know 2Kg 5:15
just as He had **d** through all His 2Kg 17:23
what was **d** by wise men and was Jb 15:18
For Job has **d**, "I am righteous, Jb 34:5
and who has **d**, "You have done Jb 36:23
I **d**: "You may come this far, Jb 38:11
faithful love be **d** in the grave, Ps 88:11
The LORD **d** to my Lord: Ps 110:1
A troubling vision is **d** to me: Is 21:2

have **d** to you what I have heard Is 21:10
it not been **d** to you from the Is 40:21
I alone **d**, saved, and proclaimed Is 43:12
not told you and **d** it long ago? Is 44:8
I **d** the past events long ago; Is 48:3
therefore I **d** to you long ago; Is 48:5
the idols has **d** these things? Is 48:14
iron furnace. I **d**: 'Obey Me, and Jr 11:4
has the LORD **d** all this great Jr 16:10
says: Tyre, you **d**: I am perfect Ezk 27:3
and **d**: May the name of God be Dn 2:20
to you it is **d** that the kingdom Dn 4:31
The Lord **d** to my Lord, 'Sit at Mt 22:44
The Lord **d** to my Lord, 'Sit at Mk 12:36
she **d** the reason she had touched Lk 8:47
The Lord **d** to my Lord, 'Sit at Lk 20:42
not refuse to answer, but he **d**: Jn 1:20
anyone to death," the Jews **d**. Jn 18:31
of the law will be **d** righteous. Rm 2:13
we have been **d** righteous by Rm 5:1
have now been **d** righteous by His Rm 5:9
He was **d** by God a high priest Heb 5:10
He has **d** that the first is old. Heb 8:13

DECLARES *(12)*
But if the slave **d**: Ex 21:5
as I live, **d** the LORD, I will Nm 14:28
The LORD **d** to you: 2Sm 7:11
God, the king **d**, 'Come down!'" 2Kg 1:9
not enter this city, **d** the LORD. 2Kg 19:33
have heard you—**d** the LORD. 2Kg 22:19
while the sea **d**, "I don't have Jb 28:14
The thunder **d** His presence; Jb 36:33
He **d** His word to Jacob, His Ps 147:19
the truth **d** what is right, Pr 12:17
the Mighty One of Israel, **d**: Is 1:24
believes on Him who **d** righteous Rm 4:5

DECLARING *(3)*
in the army as the sun set, **d**: 1Kg 22:36
languages and **d** the greatness of Ac 10:46
back from **d** to you the whole Ac 20:27

DECLINED *(1)*
to stay for a longer time, he **d**, Ac 18:20

DECORATE *(1)*
the prophets and **d** the monuments Mt 23:29

DECORATED *(5)*
d with palm trees and chains. 2Ch 3:5
pilaster was **d** with palm trees. Ezk 40:16
were **d** with palm trees. Ezk 40:31
pilasters were **d** with palm trees Ezk 40:34
pilasters were **d** with palm trees Ezk 40:37

DECORATES *(1)*
He **d** it with silver and gold. Jr 10:4

DECREASE *(8)*
and **d** its price in proportion to Lv 25:16
tribe⌋, and **d** it for a small one Nm 26:54
large clan and **d** it for a small Nm 33:54
does not let their livestock **d**. Ps 107:38
Multiply there; do not **d**. Jr 29:6
them, and they will not **d**; Jr 30:19
will begin to **d** in number under Hs 8:10
He must increase, but I must **d**." Jn 3:30

DECREASED *(1)*
the waters had **d** significantly. Gn 8:3

DECREE *(35)*
and confirmed to Jacob as a **d**, 1Ch 16:17
I issued a **d** and a search was Ezr 4:19
until a ⌊further⌋ **d** has been Ezr 4:21
he issued a **d** to rebuild this Ezr 5:13
is true that a **d** was issued by Ezr 5:17
he issued a **d** concerning the Ezr 6:3
hereby issue a **d** concerning what Ezr 6:8
I also issue a **d** concerning any Ezr 6:11
I, Darius, have issued the **d**. Ezr 6:12
I issue a **d** that any of the Ezr 7:13
issue a **d** to all the treasurers Ezr 7:21
personally issue a royal **d**. Est 1:19
The **d** the king issues will be Est 1:20
of the written **d** issued in Susa Est 4:8
I will declare the LORD's **d**: Ps 2:7
to Jacob as a **d** and to Israel as Ps 105:10
will obey the **d** You have spoken Ps 119:88
but the LORD's **d** will prevail. Pr 19:21
GOD of Hosts a **d** of destruction Is 28:22
has issued a **d** against Jacob Lm 1:17
He has accomplished His **d**, Lm 2:17
dream, there is one **d** for you. Dn 2:9
The **d** was issued that the wise Dn 2:13
is the **d** from the king so harsh? Dn 2:15
have issued a **d** that everyone Dn 3:10
I issue a **d** that anyone of any Dn 3:29
So I issued a **d** to bring all the Dn 4:6
This word is by **d** of the Dn 4:17
I issue a **d** that in all my royal Dn 6:26
the issuing of the **d** to restore Dn 9:25
Then he issued a **d** in Nineveh: Jnh 3:7
before the **d** takes effect and Zph 2:2
this **d** is for you priests: Mal 2:1
I sent you this **d** so My covenant Mal 2:4
In those days a **d** went out from Lk 2:1

DECREED *(17)*
the LORD had **d** that Ahithophel's 2Sm 17:14
that day David **d** for the first 1Ch 16:7
out what King Darius had **d**. Ezr 6:13
accomplish what He has **d** for me, Jb 23:14
Your God has **d** your strength. Ps 68:28
out the judgment **d** against them. Ps 149:9
forget what is **d**, and pervert Pr 31:5
Destruction has been **d**; Is 10:22
out a destruction that was **d**. Is 10:23
planted you has **d** disaster Jr 11:17
what I have **d** for you—⌊this Jr 13:25
LORD your God **d** this disaster Jr 40:2
He has done just what He **d**. Jr 40:3
weeks are **d** about your people Dn 9:24
will be war; desolations are **d**. Dn 9:26
temple until the **d** destruction Dn 9:27
what has been **d** will be Dn 11:36

DECREES *(36)*
These are the **d**, statutes, and Dt 4:45
the **d** and statutes He has Dt 6:17
'What is the meaning of the **d**, Dt 6:20
His **d**, and His statutes 2Kg 23:3
Your **d**, and Your statutes 1Ch 29:19
His **d**, and His statutes 2Ch 34:31
of Israel and the **d** of Cyrus, Ezr 6:14
and good **d** and commandments. Neh 9:13
who keep His covenant and **d**. Ps 25:10
for they did not keep His **d**. Ps 78:56
they kept His **d** and the statutes Ps 99:7
who keep His **d** and seek Him with Ps 119:2
by⌋ Your **d** as much as in all Ps 119:14
from me, for I have kept Your **d**. Ps 119:22
Your **d** are my delight and my Ps 119:24
I cling to Your **d**; LORD, do not Ps 119:31
my heart to Your **d** and not to Ps 119:36
speak of Your **d** before kings Ps 119:46
turned my steps back to Your **d**. Ps 119:59
who know Your **d**, turn to me. Ps 119:79
me, but I contemplate Your **d**. Ps 119:95
Your **d** are my meditation. Ps 119:99
I have Your **d** as a heritage Ps 119:111
therefore, I love Your **d**. Ps 119:119
so that I may know Your **d**. Ps 119:125
Your **d** are wonderful; Ps 119:129
d You issue are righteous and Ps 119:138
Your **d** are righteous forever. Ps 119:144
save me, and I will keep Your **d**. Ps 119:146
learned from Your **d** that You Ps 119:152
I have not turned from Your **d**. Ps 119:157
I obey Your **d** and love them Ps 119:167
I obey Your precepts and **d**, Ps 119:168
covenant and My **d** that I will Ps 132:12
overstepped **d**, and broken Is 24:5
acting contrary to Caesar's **d**, Ac 17:7

DEDAN *(10)*
And Raamah's sons: Sheba and **D**. Gn 10:7
Jokshan fathered Sheba and **D**. Gn 25:3
Raama's sons: Sheba and **D**. 1Ch 1:9
Jokshan's sons: Sheba and **D**. 1Ch 1:32
D, Tema, Buz, and all those who Jr 25:23
residents of **D**, for I will bring Jr 49:8
by the sword from Teman to **D**. Ezk 25:13
Men of **D** were also your Ezk 27:15
D was your merchant in Ezk 27:20
Sheba and **D** and the merchants of Ezk 38:13

DEDAN'S *(1)*
D sons were the Asshurim, Gn 25:3

DEDANITES *(1)*
the desert, you caravans of **D**. Is 21:13

DEDICATE *(7)*
Remember to **d** the Sabbath day: Ex 20:8
Be careful to **d** the Sabbath day, Dt 5:12
in battle and another man **d** it. Dt 20:5
are among you, **d** yourselves to 1Sm 7:3
God in order to **d** it to Him for 2Ch 2:4
for anyone to **d** something rashly Pr 20:25
Those who **d** and purify Is 66:17

DEDICATED *(27)*
of complete rest, **d** to the LORD. Ex 31:15
you have been **d** to the LORD, Ex 32:29
is permanently **d** ⌊to the LORD⌋ Nm 18:14
built a new house and not **d** it? Dt 20:5
are **d** to the LORD and must go Jos 6:19
King David also **d** these to the 2Sm 8:11
and gold he had **d** from all the 2Sm 8:11
the Israelites **d** the LORD's 1Kg 8:63
All the **d** money brought to the 2Kg 12:4
kings of Judah had **d** to the sun. 2Kg 23:11
King David also **d** these to the 1Ch 18:11
treasuries for what had been **d**. 1Ch 26:20
what had been **d** by King David, 1Ch 26:26
They **d** part of the plunder from 1Ch 26:27
and Joab son of Zeruiah had **d**, 1Ch 26:28
everything else that had been **d**, 1Ch 26:28
the treasuries for what is **d**. 1Ch 28:12
all the people **d** God's temple. 2Ch 7:5
tenth of the **d** things that were 2Ch 31:6
and the **d** things were brought 2Ch 31:12
They **d** it and installed its Neh 3:1
the Tower of Hananel, they **d** it. Neh 3:1
and wages will be **d** to the LORD. Is 23:18
Who is blind like ⌊My⌋ **d** one, Is 42:19
is permanently **d** ⌊to the LORD⌋ Ezk 44:29
male will be **d** to the Lord Lk 2:23
stones and gifts **d** to God, Lk 21:5

DEDICATION *(12)*
presented the **d** gift for the Nm 7:10
for the **d** of the altar." Nm 7:11
This was the **d** gift from the Nm 7:84
was the **d** gift for the altar Nm 7:88
for the **d** of the altar lasted 2Ch 7:9
celebrated the **d** of this house Ezr 6:16
For the **d** of God's house they Ezr 6:17
At the **d** of the wall of Neh 12:27
the joyous **d** with thanksgiving Neh 12:27
to attend the **d** of the statue Dn 3:2
assembled for the **d** of the Dn 3:3
the Festival of **D** took place Jn 10:22

DEED *(9)*
because you have done this **d**. 2Sm 2:6
diligent in every **d** that he 2Ch 31:21
in counsel and mighty in **d**, Jr 32:19
done a mighty **d** with His arm; Lk 1:51
about a good **d** done to a Ac 4:9
Gentiles obedient by word and **d**, Rm 15:18
in word or in **d**, do everything Col 3:17
that your good **d** might not be Phm 14
or speech, but in **d** and truth; 1Jn 3:18

DEEDS *(70)*
can perform **d** and mighty acts Dt 3:24
and terrifying **d** that Moses Dt 34:12
the righteous **d** of His warriors Jdg 5:11
Nabal's evil **d** back on his own 1Sm 25:39
told him all the **d** that the man 1Kg 13:11
His **d** among the peoples. 1Ch 16:8
and awesome **d** by driving out 1Ch 17:21
the rest of his **d** and all his 2Ch 28:26
these faithful **d**, Sennacherib 2Ch 32:1
reign⌋ and his **d** of faithful 2Ch 32:32
along with his **d** of faithful 2Ch 35:26
The rest of the **d** of Jehoiakim, 2Ch 36:8
multiplied their unfaithful **d**, 2Ch 36:14
of our evil **d** and terrible guilt Ezr 9:13
Tobiah's good **d** to me, Neh 6:19
erase the good **d** I have done for Neh 13:14
a person ⌊according to⌋ his **d**, Jb 34:11
their **d** and overthrows Jb 34:25
His **d** among the peoples. Ps 9:11
loves righteous **d**. The upright Ps 11:7
to the evil of their **d**. Ps 28:4
hand show your awe-inspiring **d**. Ps 45:4
are corrupt, and they do vile **d**. Ps 53:1
His **d** to the people of Israel. Ps 103:7
His **d** among the peoples. Ps 105:1
awe-inspiring **d** at the Red Sea. Ps 106:22
provoked the LORD with their **d**, Ps 106:29
themselves by their **d**. Ps 106:39
good man, what his ⌊**d** deserve.⌋ Pr 14:14
your evil **d** from My sight. Is 1:16
will eat the fruit of their **d**. Is 3:10

Celebrate His **d** among the Is 12:4
repay according to ⌊their⌋ **d**: Is 59:18
did awesome **d** that we did not Is 64:3
them fully for their former **d**." Is 65:7
it⌋ because of your evil **d**. Jr 4:4
their unfaithful **d** numerous. Jr 5:6
Correct your ways and your **d**, Jr 7:3
You helped me to see their **d**, Jr 11:18
correct your ways and your **d**. Jr 18:11
because of their evil **d**. Jr 21:12
evil ways and their evil **d**. Jr 23:22
of life and from your evil **d**. Jr 25:5
according to their **d** and the Jr 25:14
because of the evil of their **d**. Jr 26:3
your ways and **d** and obey the Jr 26:13
ways and the result of his **d**. Jr 32:19
bear your evil **d** and the Jr 44:22
you men fulfilled it by your **d**, Jr 44:25
Repay her according to her **d**; Jr 50:29
and all your **d** you have defiled Ezk 20:43
according to your ways and **d**. Ezk 24:14
ways and your **d** that were not Ezk 36:31
ways and repay them for their **d**. Hs 4:9
I will never forget all their **d**. Am 8:7
them wondrous **d** as in the days Mc 7:15
LORD, I stand in awe of Your **d**. Hab 3:2
your evil ways and your evil **d**. Zch 1:4
deal with us for our ways and **d**, Zch 1:6
wisdom is vindicated by her **d**." Mt 11:19
approve the **d** of your fathers Lk 11:48
light because their **d** were evil. Jn 3:19
that his **d** may not be exposed. Jn 3:20
about it—that its **d** are evil. Jn 7:7
charitable **d** for the ⌊Jewish Ac 10:2
put to death the **d** of the body, Rm 8:13
let us discard the **d** of darkness Rm 13:12
the lawless **d** he saw and heard 2Pt 2:8
foaming up their shameful **d**; Jd 13
their ungodly **d** that they have Jd 15

DEEP *(70)*

God caused a **d** sleep to come Gn 2:21
sun was setting, a **d** sleep fell Gn 15:12
We saw his **d** distress when he Gn 42:21
of the **d** that lies below Gn 49:25
springs, and **d** water sources, Dt 8:7
asleep because a **d** sleep from 1Sm 26:12
He pulled me out of **d** waters. 2Sm 22:17
and 15 feet **d** in front of the 1Kg 6:3
when **d** sleep descends on men, Jb 4:13
when **d** sleep falls on people as Jb 33:15
darkness, no **d** darkness, where Jb 34:22
think the **d** had white hair! Jb 41:32
He pulled me out of **d** waters. Ps 18:16
D calls to deep in the roar of Ps 42:7
Deep calls to **d** in the roar of Ps 42:7
You teach me wisdom **d** within. Ps 51:6
I have sunk in **d** mud, and there Ps 69:2
I have come into **d** waters, Ps 69:2
hate me, and from the **d** waters. Ps 69:14
over me or the **d** swallow me up; Ps 69:15
it with the **d** as if it were Ps 104:6
His wonderful works in the **d**. Ps 107:24
rescue me from **d** water, and set Ps 144:7
of a man's mouth are **d** waters, Pr 18:4
Laziness induces **d** sleep, and a Pr 19:15
in a man's heart is **d** water; Pr 20:5
lamp will go out in **d** darkness. Pr 20:20
the forbidden woman is a **d** pit; Pr 22:14
For a prostitute is a **d** pit, Pr 23:27
is high and the earth is **d**, Pr 25:3
is beyond ⌊reach⌋ and very **d**. Ec 7:24
and out of a **d** darkness the eyes Is 29:18
His funeral pyre is **d** and wide, Is 30:33
the waters of the great **d**, Is 51:10
ropes, and drive your pegs **d**. Is 54:2
cup, which is **d** and wide. Ezk 23:32
took revenge with **d** contempt, Ezk 25:15
I raise up the **d** against you so Ezk 26:19
over you with **d** anguish and Ezk 27:31
the underground **d** because of it: Ezk 31:15
I held back the rivers of the **d**, Ezk 31:15
it was 10 feet **d**—the first Ezk 40:6
first threshold was 10 feet **d**. Ezk 40:6
10 feet long and 10 feet **d**, Ezk 40:7
35 feet across and 21 feet **d**, Ezk 40:49
is 21 inches ⌊**d**⌋ and 21 inches Ezk 43:13
it was **d** enough to swim in, Ezk 47:5
He reveals the **d** and hidden Dn 2:22
I fell into a **d** sleep, with my Dn 8:18
them I fell into a **d** sleep, Dn 10:9
the great **d** and devoured Am 7:4
out and fallen into a **d** sleep. Jnh 1:5
The **d** roars with its voice and Hab 3:10
darkness—how **d** is that Mt 6:23
quickly since the soil wasn't **d**. Mt 13:5
since it didn't have **d** soil. Mk 4:5
Put out into **d** water and let Lk 5:4
dug **d** and laid the foundation Lk 6:48
with him were in a **d** sleep, Lk 9:32
a bucket, and the well is **d**. Jn 4:11
water flow from **d** within him." Jn 7:38
and sank into a **d** sleep as Paul Ac 20:9
and found it to be 120 feet **d**; Ac 27:28
they found it to be 90 feet **d**. Ac 27:28
even the **d** things of God. 1Co 2:10
announced to us your **d** longing, 2Co 7:7
what fear, what **d** longing, what 2Co 7:11
of joy and their **d** poverty 2Co 8:2
they will have **d** affection for 2Co 9:14
known the **d** things of Satan Rv 2:24

DEEPER *(8)*

appears to be **d** than the skin of Lv 13:3
appear to be **d** than the skin, Lv 13:4
appears to be **d** than the skin, Lv 13:25
appears to be **d** than the skin, Lv 13:30
appear to be **d** than the skin, Lv 13:31
appear to be **d** than the skin, Lv 13:32
appear to be **d** than the skin, Lv 13:34
⌊They are⌋ **d** than Sheol—what Jb 11:8

DEEPEST *(7)*

blackness like the **d** darkness, Jb 10:22
and brings the **d** darkness into Jb 12:22
he probes the **d** recesses for ore Jb 28:3
Your judgments, like the **d** sea. Ps 36:6
have covered us with **d** darkness. Ps 44:19
to Sheol into the **d** regions of Is 14:15
are set in the **d** regions of the Ezk 32:23

DEEPLY *(27)*

and were **d** grieved and angry Gn 34:7
D hurt, Hannah prayed to the 1Sm 1:10
since they were **d** humiliated. 2Sm 10:5
The king was **d** moved and went 2Sm 18:33
Solomon was **d** attached to these 1Kg 11:2
since the men were **d** humiliated. 1Ch 19:5
I am **d** depressed; therefore I Ps 42:6
drink **d** of lovemaking until Pr 7:18
breast and drink **d** and delight Is 66:11
spirit was **d** distressed within Dn 7:15
Rebels are **d** involved in Hs 5:2
They have **d** corrupted themselves Hs 9:9
you will be **d** despised. Ob 2
this, he was **d** disturbed, and Mt 2:3
And they were **d** distressed. Mt 17:23
they were **d** distressed and went Mt 18:31
D distressed, each one began to Mt 26:22
be sorrowful and **d** distressed. Mt 26:37
the king was **d** distressed, Mk 6:26
He sighed **d** and said to him, Mk 7:34
But sighing **d** in His spirit, Mk 8:12
and He began to be **d** distressed Mk 14:33
But she was **d** troubled by this Lk 1:29
angry in His spirit and **d** moved. Jn 11:33
Stephen and mourned **d** over him. Ac 8:2
Peter was **d** perplexed about Ac 10:17
how I **d** miss all of you with the Php 1:8

DEER *(14)*

as they would a gazelle or **d**, Dt 12:15
as the gazelle and **d** are eaten; Dt 12:22
d, the gazelle, the roe deer, Dt 14:5
the roe **d**, the wild goat, Dt 14:5
though it were a gazelle or **d**. Dt 15:22
the feet of⌋ a **d** and sets me 2Sm 22:34
100 sheep, besides **d**, gazelles, 1Kg 4:23
Have you watched the **d** in labor? Jb 39:1
like the feet of a **d** and sets me Ps 18:33
the LORD makes the **d** give birth Ps 29:9
As a **d** longs for streams of Ps 42:1
like a **d** bounding toward a trap Pr 7:22
the lame will leap like a **d**, Is 35:6
like those of a **d** and enables me Hab 3:19

DEFEAT *(6)*

man saw that He could not **d** him, Gn 32:25
and not the sound of a cry of **d**; Ex 32:18
may be able to **d** them and drive Nm 22:6
them over to you and you **d** them, Dt 7:2
of Babylon to **d** the land of Jr 46:13
already a total **d** for you that 1Co 6:7

DEFEATED *(63)*

with him came and **d** the Rephaim Gn 14:5
and they **d** all the territory of Gn 14:7
d Midian in the field of Moab; Gn 36:35
So Joshua **d** Amalek and his army Ex 17:13
you will be **d** by your enemies Lv 26:17
you will be **d** by your enemies Nm 14:42
Canaanites were **d**, and Israel Nm 21:3
was after he had **d** Sihon king Dt 1:4
from being **d** by your enemies. Dt 1:42
to us, and we **d** him, his sons, Dt 2:33
the Israelites **d** him after they Dt 4:46
against you to be **d** before you. Dt 28:7
cause you to be **d** before your Dt 28:25
us in battle, but we **d** them. Dt 29:7
d them in a great slaughter at Jos 10:10
Now the five ⌊**d**⌋ kings had fled Jos 10:16
attacked and **d** Israel and took Jdg 3:13
to Israel, and they **d** them. Jdg 11:21
He **d** 20 of their cities with a Jdg 11:33
They fought and **d** Ephraim, Jdg 12:4
The LORD **d** Benjamin in the Jdg 20:35
realized they had been **d**. Jdg 20:36
said, "They're **d** before us, just Jdg 20:39
Israel was **d** by the Philistines, 1Sm 4:2
did the LORD let us be **d** today 1Sm 4:3
and Israel was **d**, and each man 1Sm 4:10
bravely, **d** the Amalekites, 1Sm 14:48
David **d** the Philistine with a 1Sm 17:50
d them with such a great force 1Sm 19:8
men of Israel were **d** by David's 2Sm 2:17
Baal-perazim and **d** them there 2Sm 5:20
this, David **d** the Philistines, 2Sm 8:1
also **d** the Moabites, and after 2Sm 8:2
David also **d** Hadadezer son of 2Sm 8:3
that David had **d** the entire army 2Sm 8:9
against Hadadezer and **d** him, 2Sm 8:10
that they had been **d** by Israel, 2Sm 10:15
that they had been **d** by Israel, 2Sm 10:19
of Israel were **d** by David's 2Sm 18:7
Israel are **d** before an enemy, 1Kg 8:33
Hazael **d** the Israelites 2Kg 10:32
Jehoash **d** Ben-hadad three times 2Kg 13:25
You have indeed **d** Edom, and 2Kg 14:10
He **d** the Philistines as far as 2Kg 18:8
who **d** Midian in the country of 1Ch 1:46
who were **d** by their power. 1Ch 5:10
and David **d** the Philistines 1Ch 14:11
this, David **d** the Philistines, 1Ch 18:1
He also **d** the Moabites, and they 1Ch 18:2
David also **d** King Hadadezer of 1Ch 18:3
that David had **d** the entire army 1Ch 18:9
against Hadadezer and **d** him, 1Ch 18:10
that they had been **d** by Israel, 1Ch 19:16
that they had been **d** by Israel, 1Ch 19:19
Israel are **d** before an enemy, 2Ch 6:24
against Judah, and they were **d**. 2Ch 20:22
Look, I have **d** Edom,' and you 2Ch 25:19
of Damascus which had **d** him; 2Ch 28:23
which was **d** at Carchemish on the Jr 46:2
before Pharaoh **d** Gaza. Jr 47:1
Babylon's king, **d**, this is what Jr 49:28
When **d**, they will be helped by Dn 11:34
entangled in these things and **d**, 2Pt 2:20

DEFEATING *(4)*

returned from **d** Chedorlaomer Gn 14:17
"We are **d** them as before." Jdg 20:32
returned from **d** the Amalekites 2Sm 1:1
as he returned from **d** the kings, Heb 7:1

DEFEATS *(1)*

are enslaved to whatever **d** them. 2Pt 2:19

DEFECT *(16)*

has a physical **d** is to come near Lv 21:17
who has any **d** is to come near Lv 21:18
who has an eye **d**, a festering Lv 21:20
who has a **d** is to come near Lv 21:21
He has a **d** and is not to come Lv 21:21
he has a **d**, he must not go Lv 21:23
present anything that has a **d**, Lv 22:20
there must be no **d** in it. Lv 22:21
they are deformed and have a **d**." Lv 22:25
cow that has no **d** and has never Nm 19:2
if there is a **d** in the animal, Dt 15:21
or blind or has any serious **d**, Dt 15:21
or sheep with a **d** or any serious Dt 17:1

this is their **d**—they are not Dt 32:5
men without any physical **d**, Dn 1:4
of a lamb without **d** or blemish. 1Pt 1:19

DEFECTED *(8)*
From the day he **d** until today, 1Sm 29:3
deserters who had **d** to the king 2Kg 25:11
Some Gadites **d** to David at his 1Ch 12:8
Some Manassites **d** to David 1Ch 12:19
men from Manasseh **d** to him: 1Ch 12:20
they had **d** to him from Israel 2Ch 15:9
who had **d** to him along with Jr 39:9
deserters who had **d** to the king Jr 52:15

DEFECTIVE *(1)*
but sacrifices a **d** ⌊animal⌋ to Mal 1:14

DEFECTS *(1)*
our heads if he **d** to his master 1Ch 12:19

DEFEND *(17)*
I will **d** this city and rescue it 2Kg 19:34
I will **d** this city for My sake 2Kg 20:6
to assemble and **d** themselves, Est 8:11
gate, with no one to **d** ⌊them⌋. Jb 5:4
I will still **d** my ways before Jb 13:15
d my cause against an ungodly Ps 43:1
Arise, God, **d** Your cause! Ps 74:22
D my cause, and redeem me; Ps 119:154
and **d** the cause of the oppressed Pr 31:9
D the rights of the fatherless. Is 1:17
They do not **d** the rights of the Is 1:23
will **d** this city and rescue it, Is 37:35
of Assyria; I will **d** this city. Is 38:6
You **d** my cause, Lord; Lm 3:58
The LORD of Hosts will **d** them. Zch 9:15
the LORD will **d** the inhabitants Zch 12:8
how you should **d** yourselves or Lk 12:11

DEFENDED *(4)*
of the field, **d** it, and struck 2Sm 23:12
the middle of the plot and **d** it. 1Ch 11:14
assembled, **d** themselves, and got Est 9:16
and they have not **d** the rights Jr 5:28

DEFENDING *(1)*
that we were **d** ourselves to you 2Co 12:19

DEFENDS *(1)*
your God, who **d** His people— Is 51:22

DEFENSE *(19)*
my argument, and listen to my **d**. Jb 13:6
Him or argue the case in His **d**? Jb 13:8
and rise to my **d**, to my cause, Ps 35:23
torn down ⌊for **d**⌋ against the Jr 33:4
her **d** towers have fallen; Jr 50:15
to prepare your **d** ahead of time, Lk 21:14
to make his **d** to the people. Ac 19:33
listen now to my **d** before you." Ac 22:1
to offer my **d** in what concerns Ac 24:10
while Paul made the **d** that, Ac 25:8
to give a **d** concerning the Ac 25:16
out his hand and began his **d**: Ac 26:1
going to make a **d** before you Ac 26:2
As he was making his **d** this way, Ac 26:24
My **d** to those who examine me is 1Co 9:3
and in the **d** and establishment Php 1:7
for the **d** of the gospel; Php 1:16
At my first **d**, no one came to my 2Tm 4:16
ready to give a **d** to anyone who 1Pt 3:15

DEFENSES *(4)*
your **d** are made of clay. Jb 13:12
through my **d** again and again; Jb 16:14
He removed the **d** of Judah. Is 22:8
is the one who spied out our **d**?" Is 33:18

DEFER *(2)*
You **d** to no one, for You don't Mt 22:16
are truthful and **d** to no one, Mk 12:14

DEFIANCE *(2)*
and **d** is like wickedness and 1Sm 15:23
brag and lie in **d** of the truth. Jms 3:14

DEFIANT *(2)*
She is loud and **d**; her feet do Pr 7:11
to a disobedient and **d** people. Rm 10:21

DEFIANTLY *(3)*
But the person who acts **d**, Nm 15:30
LORD's command and **d** went up Dt 1:43
the trumpet blasts, he snorts **d**. Jb 39:25

DEFICIENT *(1)*
in the balance and found **d**. Dn 5:27

DEFIED *(4)*
for he has **d** the armies of the 1Sm 17:36
armies—you have **d** Him. 1Sm 17:45
when they **d** the Philistines 2Sm 23:9
Queen Vashti has **d** not only the Est 1:16

DEFILE *(33)*
chisel on it, you will **d** it. Ex 20:25
You must not **d** yourselves by any Lv 11:44
Do not **d** yourselves by any of Lv 18:24
If you **d** the land, it will vomit Lv 18:28
that you do not **d** yourselves by Lv 18:30
by marriage and so **d** himself. Lv 21:4
they will not **d** their camps Nm 5:3
He is not to **d** himself for his Nm 6:7
you must not **d** the Israelites' Nm 18:32
Do not **d** the land where you are, Nm 35:33
You must not **d** the land the LORD Dt 21:23
Then you will **d** your Is 30:22
D the temple and fill the courts Ezk 9:7
and no longer **d** themselves with Ezk 14:11
does not **d** his neighbor's wife Ezk 18:6
He does not **d** his neighbor's Ezk 18:15
eyes and not **d** yourselves with Ezk 20:7
d yourselves with their idols, Ezk 20:18
continue to **d** yourselves with Ezk 20:31
will no longer **d** My holy name Ezk 20:39
wisdom and will **d** your splendor. Ezk 28:7
They will not **d** themselves any Ezk 37:23
will no longer **d** My holy name Ezk 43:7
he may **d** himself for a father, Ezk 44:25
that he would not **d** himself with Dn 1:8
chief official not to **d** himself. Dn 1:8
are the things that **d** a man, Mt 15:20
hands does not **d** a man." Mt 15:20
a person from outside can **d** him, Mk 7:15
out of a person are what **d** him. Mk 7:15
man from the outside can **d** him? Mk 7:18
from within and **d** a person." Mk 7:23
dreamers likewise **d** their flesh, Jd 8

DEFILED *(81)*
that Shechem had **d** his daughter Gn 34:5
because he had **d** their sister Gn 34:13
because their sister had been **d**. Gn 34:27
your father's bed and you **d** it— Gn 49:4
by which one can become **d**— Lv 5:3
not become unclean or **d** by them. Lv 11:43
before you have **d** themselves by Lv 18:24
land has become **d**, so I am Lv 18:25
and the land has become **d**. Lv 18:27
or you will be **d** by them; Lv 19:31
marry a woman **d** by prostitution Lv 21:7
woman, or one **d** by prostitution. Lv 21:14
or anyone who is **d** because of a Nm 5:2
even though she has **d** herself, Nm 5:13
of his wife who has **d** herself— Nm 5:14
though she has not **d** herself— Nm 5:14
and become **d** while under your Nm 5:19
if you have **d** yourself and a man Nm 5:20
if she has **d** herself and been Nm 5:27
woman has not **d** herself and is Nm 5:28
his consecrated hair became **d**. Nm 6:12
because he has **d** the sanctuary Nm 19:20
of the vineyard, will be **d**. Dt 22:9
her again after she has been **d**, Dt 24:4
if the land you possess is **d**, Jos 22:19
the shield of the mighty was **d**— 2Sm 1:21
and he **d** the high places from 2Kg 23:8
He **d** Topheth, which is in the 2Kg 23:10
The king also **d** the high places 2Kg 23:13
He **d** it according to the word of 2Kg 23:16
because Reuben **d** his father's 1Ch 5:1
they **d** the LORD's temple that 2Ch 36:14
They **d** themselves by their Ps 106:39
So I **d** the officers of the Is 43:28
My own, for how can I be **d**? Is 48:11
For your hands are **d** with blood, Is 59:3
you entered, you **d** My land; Jr 2:7
protest: I am not **d**; I have not Jr 2:23
such a land become totally **d**? Jr 3:1
You have **d** the land with your Jr 3:2
she **d** the land and committed Jr 3:9
is called by My name and **d** it. Jr 7:30
called by My name and have **d** it. Jr 32:34
to the ground and **d** the kingdom Lm 2:2
in the streets, **d** by this blood, Lm 4:14
Lord GOD, I have never been **d**. Ezk 4:14
because you have **d** My sanctuary Ezk 5:11
I **d** them through their gifts in Ezk 20:26
you have **d** yourselves with, Ezk 20:43
for herself so that she is **d**! Ezk 22:3
and you are **d** from the idols you Ezk 22:4
She **d** herself with all those she Ezk 23:7
I saw that she had **d** herself; Ezk 23:13
and **d** her with their lust. Ezk 23:17
But after she was **d** by them, Ezk 23:17
they **d** My sanctuary on that same Ezk 23:38
each of you has **d** his neighbor's Ezk 33:26
they **d** it with their conduct and Ezk 36:17
because they had **d** it with their Ezk 36:18
d My temple while you offered Ezk 44:7
person so that he becomes **d**. Ezk 44:25
promiscuously; Israel is **d**. Hs 5:3
is there; Israel is **d**. Hs 6:10
all who eat it become **d**. Hs 9:4
say, "Let her be **d**, and let us Mc 4:11
city that is rebellious and **d**, Zph 3:1
If someone **d** by ⌊contact with⌋ a Hg 2:13
any of these, does it become **d**?" Hg 2:13
answered, "It becomes **d**." Hg 2:13
even what they offer there is **d**. Hg 2:14
presenting **d** food on My altar. Mal 1:7
"How have we **d** You?" Mal 1:7
Lord's table is **d**, and its Mal 1:12
they would be **d** and unable to Jn 18:28
conscience, being weak, is **d**. 1Co 8:7
those who are **d** and unbelieving Ti 1:15
their mind and conscience are **d**. Ti 1:15
sprinkling those who are **d**, Heb 9:13
even the garment **d** by the flesh. Jd 23
who have not **d** their clothes, Rv 3:4
are the ones not **d** with women, Rv 14:4

DEFILEMENT *(1)*
because **d** brings destruction— Mc 2:10

DEFILES *(11)*
a priest's daughter **d** herself by Lv 21:9
promiscuity, she **d** her father; Lv 21:9
goes astray and **d** herself while Nm 5:29
d the tabernacle of the LORD. Nm 19:13
are, for bloodshed **d** the land, Nm 35:33
shrines⌋ and **d** his neighbor's Ezk 18:11
another wickedly **d** his Ezk 22:11
into the mouth that **d** a man, Mt 15:11
out of the mouth, this **d** a man." Mt 15:11
the heart, and this **d** a man. Mt 15:18
out of a person—that **d** him. Mk 7:20

DEFILING *(11)*
do not die by **d** My tabernacle Lv 15:31
neighbor's wife, **d** yourself with Lv 18:20
any animal, **d** yourself with it Lv 18:23
d My sanctuary and profaning My Lv 20:3
d his consecrated head of hair, Nm 6:9
his sons are **d** the sanctuary, 1Sm 3:13
for **d** the priesthood as well as Neh 13:29
you **d** yourselves the way your Ezk 20:30
d yourself with their idols. Ezk 23:30
they were **d** My holy name by the Ezk 43:8
trouble and by it, **d** many. Heb 12:15

DEFINED *(1)*
be your land ⌊**d**⌋ by its borders Nm 34:12

DEFINITE *(2)*
So I gave him a **d** time, and it Neh 2:6
I have nothing **d** to write to the Ac 25:26

DEFINITELY *(1)*
and it will **d** come—then they Ezk 33:33

DEFORMED *(4)*
lame, facially disfigured, or **d**; Lv 21:18
they are **d** and have a defect. Lv 22:25
the blind, the **d**, those unable Mt 15:30
talking, the **d** restored, the Mt 15:31

DEFRAUD *(2)*
witness; do not **d**; honor your Mk 10:19
against and **d** his brother in 1Th 4:6

DEFRAUDED *(3)*
must return what he stole or **d**, Lv 6:4
so that the king would not be **d**. Dn 6:2
one, corrupted no one, **d** no one. 2Co 7:2

DEFRAUDS *(1)*
or a robbery; or **d** his neighbor; Lv 6:2

DEFY *(6)*
not **d** Him, because He will not Ex 23:21
I **d** the ranks of Israel today. 1Sm 17:10
He comes to **d** Israel. The king 1Sm 17:25
that he should **d** the armies of 1Sm 17:26

so that they **d** the king's laws. Est 3:8
for did they not **d** His commands? Ps 105:28

DEFYING *(1)*
against the LORD, **d** His glorious Is 3:8

DEGENERATE *(1)*
then could you turn into a **d**, Jr 2:21

DEGRADED *(2)*
brother will be **d** in your sight. Dt 25:3
bodies were **d** among themselves Rm 1:24

DEGRADING *(1)*
them over to **d** passions. Rm 1:26

DEGREE *(3)*
to me, but in some **d**—not to 2Co 2:5
to an extreme **d** and tried to Gl 1:13
and to that **d** He is the mediator Heb 8:6

DEITIES *(1)*
to be a preacher of foreign **d**"— Ac 17:18

DEJECTED *(2)*
through the land, **d** and hungry. Is 8:21
⌊Egypt's⌋ weavers will be **d**; Is 19:10

DELAIAH *(5)*
Akkub, Johanan, **D**, and Anani— 1Ch 3:24
the twenty-third to **D**, and the 1Ch 24:18
the house of Shemaiah son of **D**, Neh 6:10
the scribe, **D** son of Shemaiah, Jr 36:12
though Elnathan, **D**, and Gemariah Jr 36:25

DELAIAH'S *(2)*
D descendants, Tobiah's Ezr 2:60
D descendants, Tobiah's Neh 7:62

DELAY *(18)*
to them, "Do not **d** me, since the Gn 24:56
young man did not **d** doing this, Gn 34:19
Come down to me without **d**. Gn 45:9
they could not **d** and had not Ex 12:39
long will you **d** going out to Jos 18:3
my deliverer; my God, do not **d**. Ps 40:17
my deliverer; LORD, do not **d**. Ps 70:5
to God, don't **d** fulfilling it, Ec 5:4
and My salvation will not **d**. Is 46:13
I will **d** My anger for the honor Is 48:9
own sake, do not **d**, because Your Dn 9:19
Will He **d** ⌊to help⌋ them? Lk 18:7
"Don't **d** in coming with us." Ac 9:38
And now, why **d**? Get up and be Ac 22:16
had assembled here, I did not **d**. Ac 25:17
Coming One will come and not **d**. Heb 10:37
The Lord does not **d** His promise, 2Pt 3:9
understand **d**, but is patient 2Pt 3:9

DELAYED *(9)*
Laban and have been **d** until now. Gn 32:4
saw that Moses **d** in coming down Ex 32:1
of the sky and **d** its setting Jos 10:13
D hope makes the heart sick, Pr 13:12
It will no longer be **d**. Ezk 12:25
My words will be **d** any longer. Ezk 12:28
in his heart, 'My master is **d**,' Mt 24:48
the groom was **d**, they all became Mt 25:5
if I should be **d**, ⌊I have 1Tm 3:15

DELAYING *(1)*
'My master is **d** his coming,' Lk 12:45

DELAYS *(1)*
Though it **d**, wait for it, since Hab 2:3

DELEGATE *(1)*
I will **d** judgment to them, Ezk 23:24

DELEGATION *(3)*
and sent ⌊a **d**⌋ to the great king Hs 5:13
he sends a **d** and asks for terms Lk 14:32
him and sent a **d** after him, Lk 19:14

DELIBERATELY *(3)*
They **d** tested God, demanding the Ps 78:18
to rebel **d** and were beaten Ps 106:43
For if we **d** sin after receiving Heb 10:26

DELICACIES *(4)*
and he will produce royal **d**. Gn 49:20
Do not let me feast on their **d**. Ps 141:4
he filled his belly with my **d**; Jr 51:34
who used to eat **d** are destitute Lm 4:5

DELICACY *(1)*
and at our doors is every **d**— Sg 7:13

DELICATE *(2)*
Leah had **d** eyes, but Rachel was Gn 29:17
⌊Though she is⌋ beautiful and **d**, Jr 6:2

DELICIOUS *(6)*
make me the **d** food that I love Gn 27:4
and make some **d** food for me to Gn 27:7
make them into a **d** meal for your Gn 27:9
made the **d** food his father Gn 27:14
she handed the **d** food and the Gn 27:17
made some **d** food and brought Gn 27:31

DELIGHT *(70)*
my lord is old, will I have **d**?" Gn 18:12
LORD will again **d** in your Dt 30:9
say, 'I do not **d** in you,' then 2Sm 15:26
because of my **d** in the house of 1Ch 29:3
servants who **d** to revere Your Neh 1:11
Does it **d** the Almighty if you Jb 22:3
Then you will **d** in the Almighty Jb 22:26
Will he **d** in the Almighty? Jb 27:10
to God, and God will **d** in him. Jb 33:26
his **d** is in the LORD's Ps 1:2
noble ones in whom is all my **d**. Ps 16:3
I will **d** in His deliverance. Ps 35:9
Take **d** in the LORD, and He will Ps 37:4
You do not **d** in sacrifice and Ps 40:6
I **d** to do Your will, my God; Ps 40:8
By this I know that You **d** in me: Ps 41:11
its streams **d** the city of God, Ps 46:4
Then You will **d** in righteous Ps 51:19
servants take **d** in its stones Ps 102:14
he took no **d** in blessing— Ps 109:17
studied by all who **d** in them. Ps 111:2
taking great **d** in His Ps 112:1
I will **d** in Your statutes; Ps 119:16
decrees are my **d** and my Ps 119:24
I **d** in Your commands, which I Ps 119:47
but I **d** in Your instruction. Ps 119:70
for Your instruction is my **d**. Ps 119:77
instruction had not been my **d**, Ps 119:92
but Your commands are my **d**. Ps 119:143
and Your instruction is my **d**. Ps 119:174
and knowledge will **d** your heart. Pr 2:10
I was His **d** every day, always Pr 8:30
but an accurate weight is His **d**. Pr 11:1
blameless conduct are His **d**. Pr 11:20
but faithful people are His **d**. Pr 12:22
prayer of the upright is His **d**. Pr 15:8
Righteous lips are a king's **d**, Pr 16:13
A fool does not **d** in Pr 18:2
a wise son will **d** in him. Pr 23:24
he will also give you **d**. Pr 29:17
because He does not **d** in fools. Ec 5:4
will say, "I have no **d** in them"; Ec 12:1
I **d** to sit in his shade, and his Sg 2:3
His **d** will be in the fear of the Is 11:3
Chosen One; I **d** in Him. I have Is 42:1
after day and **d** to know My ways Is 58:2
they **d** in the nearness of God." Is 58:2
if you call the Sabbath a **d**, Is 58:13
then you will **d** yourself in the Is 58:14
will be called My **D** is in Her, Is 62:4
sight and chose what I did not **d** Is 65:12
a joy, and its people to be a **d**. Is 65:18
their ways and **d** in their Is 66:3
sight and chose what I didn't **d** Is 66:4
drink deeply and **d** yourselves Is 66:11
earth, for I **d** in these things Jr 9:24
words became a **d** to me and the Jr 15:16
to take the **d** of your eyes away Ezk 24:16
your power, the **d** of your eyes, Ezk 24:21
the **d** of their eyes and the Ezk 24:25
d in you with shouts of joy. Zph 3:17
My beloved Son. I take **d** in Him! Mt 3:17
Son. I take **d** in Him. Listen to Mt 17:5
My beloved Son; I take **d** in You! Mk 1:11
was listening to Him with **d**. Mk 12:37
There will be joy and **d** for you, Lk 1:14
My beloved Son. I take **d** in You! Lk 3:22
You did not **d** in whole burnt Heb 10:6
not desire or **d** in sacrifices Heb 10:8
My beloved Son. I take **d** in Him! 2Pt 1:17

DELIGHTED *(9)*
because he was **d** with Jacob's Gn 34:19
as He **d** in that of your fathers, Dt 30:9
rescued me because He **d** in me. 2Sm 22:20
He **d** in you and put you on the 1Kg 10:9
He **d** in you and put you on his 2Ch 9:8
and **d** in Your great goodness. Neh 9:25
rescued me because He **d** in me. Ps 18:19
the men of Judah, the plant He **d** Is 5:7
I am **d** over the presence of 1Co 16:17

DELIGHTFUL *(10)*
good for food and **d** to look at, Gn 3:6
loved and **d**, they were not 2Sm 1:23
praise to His name, for it is **d**. Ps 135:3
sought to find **d** sayings and to Ec 12:10
your love is more **d** than wine. Sg 1:2
my love. How **d**! Our bed is lush Sg 1:16
How **d** your love is, my sister, Sg 4:10
mourning⌋ for the **d** fields and Is 32:12
a precious son to Me, a **d** child? Jr 31:20
for you will be a **d** land," Mal 3:12

DELIGHTING *(2)*
inhabited world, **d** in the human Pr 8:31
d in their deceptions as they 2Pt 2:13

DELIGHTS *(9)*
not a God who **d** in wickedness; Ps 5:4
Who is the man who **d** in life, Ps 34:12
just as a father, the son he **d** Pr 3:12
many concubines, the **d** of men. Ec 2:8
⌊my⌋ love, with such **d**! Sg 7:6
for the LORD **d** in you, and your Is 62:4
because He **d** in faithful love. Mc 7:18
My beloved in whom My soul **d**; Mt 12:18
because your Father **d** to give Lk 12:32

DELILAH *(6)*
in love with a woman named **D**, Jdg 16:4
D said to Samson, "Please tell Jdg 16:6
Then **D** said to Samson, "You have Jdg 16:10
D took new ropes, tied him up Jdg 16:12
Then **D** said to Samson, "You have Jdg 16:13
When **D** realized that he had told Jdg 16:18

DELIVER *(104)*
birth, observe them as they **d**. Ex 1:16
and I will **d** you from the forced Ex 6:6
If You will **d** this people into Nm 21:2
land of Egypt to **d** us into the Dt 1:27
protect you and **d** your enemies Dt 23:14
on Mount Ebal to **d** the curse: Dt 27:13
LORD will **d** them over to you, Dt 31:5
you have and **d** Israel from the Jdg 6:14
Lord, how can I **d** Israel? Jdg 6:15
If You will **d** Israel by my hand, Jdg 6:36
know that You will **d** Israel by Jdg 6:37
I will **d** you with the 300 men Jdg 7:7
judge⌋ and began to **d** Israel. Jdg 10:1
I not **d** you from their power? Jdg 10:12
I will not **d** you again. Jdg 10:13
Let them **d** you in the time of Jdg 10:14
You see fit; only **d** us today!" Jdg 10:15
but you didn't **d** me from their Jdg 12:2
that you weren't going to **d** me, Jdg 12:3
Now **d** us from the power of our 1Sm 12:10
that can't profit or **d** you; 1Sm 12:21
my case and **d** me from you." 1Sm 24:15
D this one man, and I will 2Sm 20:21
and He will **d** you from the hand 2Kg 17:39
he can't **d** you from my hand. 2Kg 18:29
Certainly the LORD will **d** us! 2Kg 18:30
you, saying: The LORD will **d** us. 2Kg 18:32
is the LORD to **d** Jerusalem?' " 2Kg 18:35
is no strength to **d** ⌊them⌋. 2Kg 19:3
I will **d** you and this city from 2Kg 20:6
and You will hear and **d**." 2Ch 20:9
could not **d** their own people 2Ch 25:15
our God will **d** us from the power 2Ch 32:11
been able to **d** their land from 2Ch 32:13
was able to **d** his people from my 2Ch 32:14
has been able to **d** his people 2Ch 32:15
your gods **d** you from my power! 2Ch 32:15
that did not **d** their people 2Ch 32:17
God will not **d** His people from 2Ch 32:17
You must **d** to the God of Ezr 7:19
D me from the enemy's power or Jb 6:23
no one who can **d** from Your hand? Jb 10:7
they **d** their newborn. Jb 39:3
your own right hand can **d** you. Jb 40:14
let the LORD **d** him, since He Ps 22:8
D my life from the sword, my Ps 22:20
Guard me and **d** me; do not let me Ps 25:20
d me from the power of my Ps 31:15
to **d** them from death and to keep Ps 33:19
He will **d** them from the wicked Ps 37:40
D me from all my transgressions; Ps 39:8
LORD, be pleased to **d** me; Ps 40:13
D me from my enemies, my God; Ps 59:1
D me from those who practice sin, Ps 59:2
God, **d** me. Hurry to help me, Ps 70:1

Your justice, rescue and **d** me; Ps 71:2
D me, my God, from the hand of Ps 71:4
D us and atone for our sins, Ps 79:9
You **d** my life from the depths Ps 86:13
He Himself will **d** you from the Ps 91:3
devoted to Me, I will **d** him; Ps 91:14
d me because of the goodness of Ps 109:21
d me from lying lips and a Ps 120:2
righteousness **d** me from trouble, Ps 143:11
and faithfulness **d** a king; Pr 20:28
I will **d** Egypt into the hands of Is 19:4
by sparing ⌊it⌋, He will **d** ⌊it⌋. Is 31:5
you, for he cannot **d** you. Is 36:14
'The LORD will surely **d** us. Is 36:15
saying, 'The LORD will **d** us.' Is 36:18
the LORD should **d** Jerusalem?" Is 36:20
there is no strength to **d** them. Is 37:3
And I will **d** you and this city Is 38:6
and he cannot **d** himself, or say, Is 44:20
They cannot **d** themselves from Is 47:14
Or do I have no power to **d**? Is 50:2
collection ⌊of idols⌋ **d** you! Is 57:13
point of birth and not **d** ⌊it⌋?" Is 66:9
will I who **d**, close ⌊the womb⌋ Is 66:9
for I will be with you to **d** you. Jr 1:8
with you to save you and **d** you. Jr 15:20
I will **d** you from the power of Jr 15:21
own tongues to **d** an oracle. Jr 23:31
commanded him to **d** to all the Jr 26:8
will certainly **d** you so that you Jr 39:18
to save you and **d** you from him. Jr 42:11
off your veils and **d** My people Ezk 13:21
I will **d** My people from your Ezk 13:23
they would **d** ⌊only⌋ themselves Ezk 14:14
they could not **d** ⌊their⌋ sons or Ezk 14:16
they could not **d** ⌊their⌋ sons or Ezk 14:18
they could not **d** ⌊their⌋ son or Ezk 14:20
They would **d** ⌊only⌋ themselves Ezk 14:20
god who is able to **d** like this." Dn 3:29
effort until sundown to **d** him. Dn 6:14
and I will **d** them by the LORD Hs 1:7
I will not **d** them by bow, sword, Hs 1:7
house of Judah and **d** the house Zch 10:6
I will not **d** ⌊it⌋ from them." Zch 11:6
but **d** us from the evil one. Mt 6:13
d him into Gentile hands.' " Ac 21:11
death, and He will **d** us; 2Co 1:10
in Him that He will **d** us again. 2Co 1:10
built an ark to **d** his family. Heb 11:7

DELIVERANCE *(20)*
to keep you alive by a great **d**. Gn 45:7
'**D** will be yours tomorrow by the 1Sm 11:9
LORD has provided **d** in Israel." 1Sm 11:13
such a great **d** for Israel? 1Sm 14:45
but will grant them a little **d**. 2Ch 12:7
liberation and **d** will come to Est 4:14
result in my **d**, for no godless Jb 13:16
my heart will rejoice in Your **d**. Ps 13:5
that Israel's **d** would come from Ps 14:7
so far from my **d** and from my Ps 22:1
me with joyful shouts of **d**. Ps 32:7
and assure me: "I am your **d**." Ps 35:3
I will delight in His **d**. Ps 35:9
that Israel's **d** would come from Ps 53:6
with many counselors there is **d**. Pr 11:14
quietly for **d** from the LORD. Lm 3:26
there will be a **d** on Mount Zion, Ob 17
would give them **d** through him, Ac 7:25
will lead to my **d** through your Php 1:19
but of your **d**—and this is from Php 1:28

DELIVERED *(74)*
to face, and I have been **d**." Gn 32:30
haven't **d** Your people at all. Ex 5:23
who **d** you from the forced labor Ex 6:7
my helper and **d** me from Ex 18:4
way, and how the LORD **d** them. Ex 18:8
and you will be **d** into enemy Lv 26:25
your God and be **d** from your Nm 10:9
he **d** them from the hands of the Jos 9:26
you have **d** the Israelites from Jos 22:31
and I **d** you from his hand. Jos 24:10
He **d** Israel by striking down 600 Jdg 3:31
I **d** you from the power of Egypt Jdg 6:9
for you **d** us from the power of Jdg 8:22
their God who had **d** them from Jdg 8:34
and **d** you from the hand of Jdg 9:17
and **d** Israel from the hand of 1Sm 14:48
and I **d** you from the hand of 2Sm 12:7
that the LORD has **d** him from his 2Sm 18:19
He **d** up the men who rebelled 2Sm 18:28
the LORD has **d** you from all 2Sm 18:31
The king **d** us from the grasp of 2Sm 19:9
16 tons—and **d** it to Solomon. 1Kg 9:28
so He **d** them by the hand of 2Kg 14:27
of the nations ever **d** his land 2Kg 18:33
they **d** Samaria from my hand? 2Kg 18:34
the lands has **d** his land from my 2Kg 18:35
tons of gold, and **d** it to King 2Ch 8:18
They also **d** the king's edicts to Ezr 8:36
that was **d** by his eunuchs. Est 1:12
that was **d** by the eunuchs? Est 1:15
powerless and **d** the arm that is Jb 26:2
will not be **d** by great strength Ps 33:16
answered me and **d** me from all my Ps 34:4
For He has **d** me from every Ps 54:7
For You **d** me from death, even my Ps 56:13
but **d** their lives to the plague. Ps 78:50
and he **d** the city by his wisdom. Ec 9:15
You will be **d** by returning and Is 30:15
gods of the nations **d** his land Is 36:18
they **d** Samaria from my hand? Is 36:19
lands ⌊ever⌋ **d** his land from my Is 36:20
Your love ⌊has **d**⌋ me from the Is 38:17
captives of the righteous be **d**? Is 49:24
the prey of a tyrant will be **d**; Is 49:25
she was in pain, she **d** a boy. Is 66:7
or a nation be **d** in an instant? Is 66:8
so that you will be **d**. Jr 4:14
but he will be **d** out of it. Jr 30:7
alone would be **d**, but the land Ezk 14:16
but they alone would be **d**. Ezk 14:18
d the LORD's message to the Hg 1:13
endures to the end will be **d**. Mt 10:22
endures to the end will be **d**. Mt 24:13
endures to the end will be **d**. Mk 13:13
the demon-possessed man was **d**. Lk 8:36
Though He was **d** up according to Ac 2:23
d a public address to them. Ac 12:21
this letter to be **d** by them: Ac 15:23
the assembly, they **d** the letter. Ac 15:30
they **d** the decisions reached by Ac 16:4
Caesarea and **d** the letter to Ac 23:33
I was **d** as a prisoner from Ac 28:17
Therefore God **d** them over in the Rm 1:24
This is why God **d** them over to Rm 1:26
God **d** them over to a worthless Rm 1:28
He was **d** up for our trespasses Rm 4:25
this and safely **d** the funds to Rm 15:28
just as I **d** them to you. 1Co 11:2
He has **d** us from such a terrible 2Co 1:10
and that we may be **d** from wicked 2Th 3:2
and I have **d** them to Satan, 1Tm 1:20
Tartarus and **d** them to be kept 2Pt 2:4
the holy commandment **d** to them. 2Pt 2:21
faith that was **d** to the saints Jd 3

DELIVERER *(8)*
youngest brother as a **d** to save Jdg 3:9
Benjaminite, as a **d** for them. Jdg 3:15
my rock, my fortress, and my **d**, 2Sm 22:2
gave Israel a **d**, and they 2Kg 13:5
fortress, and my **d**, my God, my Ps 18:2
You are my help and my **d**; Ps 40:17
You are my help and my **d**; Ps 70:5
my stronghold and my **d**. Ps 144:2

DELIVERERS *(1)*
compassion You gave them **d**, Neh 9:27

DELIVERING *(2)*
LORD your God is **d** over to you Dt 7:16
the men I am **d** into your hands 2Kg 10:24

DELIVERS *(6)*
LORD your God **d** them over to you Dt 7:2
and **d** them from all their Ps 34:17
the LORD **d** him from them all. Ps 34:19
The LORD helps and **d** them; Ps 37:40
she **d** belts to the merchants. Pr 31:24
He rescues and **d**; He performs Dn 6:27

DELUGE *(10)*
that I am bringing a **d**— Gn 6:17
old when the **d** came ⌊and⌋ water Gn 7:6
because of the waters of the **d**. Gn 7:7
waters of the **d** came on the Gn 7:10
The **d** continued 40 days on the Gn 7:17
wiped out by the waters of a **d**; Gn 9:11
never again be a **d** to destroy Gn 9:11
again become a **d** to destroy all Gn 9:15
They also had sons after the **d**. Gn 10:1
two years after the **d**. Gn 11:10

DELUSION *(2)*
Look, all of them are a **d**; Is 41:29
a strong **d** so that they will 2Th 2:11

DEMAND *(12)*
considered their **d** sinful, 1Sm 8:6
Whatever you **d** from me, I will 2Kg 18:14
the LORD see and **d** an account." 2Ch 24:22
But I didn't **d** the food allotted Neh 5:18
"You will not **d** an account." Ps 10:13
you and come and **d** of you, Jr 38:25
I will **d** My flock from them and Ezk 34:10
and the judge **d** a bribe; Mc 7:3
does this generation **d** a sign? Mk 8:12
But he was stunned at this **d**, Mk 10:22
Pilate decided to grant their **d** Lk 23:24
forbid marriage and **d** abstinence 1Tm 4:3

DEMANDED *(12)*
You **d** ⌊payment⌋ from me for what Gn 31:39
If instead a ransom is **d** of him, Ex 21:30
in the full amount **d** from him. Ex 21:30
came to Absalom's house and **d**, 2Sm 14:31
trouble, for he **d** my wives, my 1Kg 20:7
'Everything you **d** of your 1Kg 20:9
the face, and **d**, "Did the Spirit 1Kg 22:24
his servants and **d** of them, 2Kg 6:11
king of Assyria **d** from King 2Kg 18:14
the face, and **d**, "Did the Spirit 2Ch 18:23
and the rulers you **d**, saying: Hs 13:10
night your life is **d** of you. Lk 12:20

DEMANDING *(4)*
tested God, **d** the food they Ps 78:18
d of Him a sign from heaven to Mk 8:11
d of Him a sign from heaven. Lk 11:16
d with loud voices that He be Lk 23:23

DEMANDS *(5)*
the woman's husband **d** from him, Ex 21:22
a man ⌊who **d**⌋ "contributions" Pr 29:4
adulterous generation **d** a sign, Mt 12:39
It **d** a sign, but no sign will be Lk 11:29
instinctively do what the law **d**, Rm 2:14

DEMAS *(3)*
physician, and **D** greet you. Col 4:14
for **D** has deserted me, because 2Tm 4:10
Aristarchus, **D**, and Luke, my Phm 24

DEMETRIUS *(3)*
a person named **D**, a silversmith Ac 19:24
if **D** and the craftsmen who are Ac 19:38
D has a ⌊good⌋ testimony from 3Jn 12

DEMISE *(2)*
Let his own eyes see his **d**; Jb 21:20
the sea are alarmed by your **d**." Ezk 26:18

DEMOLISH *(19)*
d them and smash their sacred Ex 23:24
and **d** all their high places. Nm 33:52
against the city and **d** it.' 2Sm 11:25
to destroy and **d**, to build and Jr 1:10
build them up and not **d** them; Jr 24:6
them down, to **d** and to destroy, Jr 31:28
I will rebuild and not **d** you, Jr 42:10
I have built I am about to **d**, Jr 45:4
walls of Tyre and **d** her towers. Ezk 26:4
They will also **d** your walls and Ezk 26:12
their altars and **d** their sacred Hs 10:2
will **d** the winter house and the Am 3:15
among you and **d** your cities. Mc 5:14
They may build, but I will **d**. Mal 1:4
'I can **d** God's sanctuary and Mt 26:61
One who would **d** the sanctuary Mt 27:40
I will **d** this sanctuary made by Mk 14:58
One who would **d** the sanctuary Mk 15:29
of strongholds. We **d** arguments 2Co 10:4

DEMOLISHED *(9)*
which the LORD **d** in His fierce Dt 29:23
Joab attacked Rabbah and **d** it. 1Ch 20:1
food⌋ far from their **d** homes. Ps 109:10
never be uprooted or **d** again." Jr 31:40
her walls are **d**. Since this is Jr 50:15
thick walls will be totally **d**, Jr 51:58
His wrath He has **d** the fortified Lm 2:2
He has **d** without compassion, Lm 2:17
will be **d** in a day of war, Hs 10:14

DEMOLISHES *(1)*
demands⌋ "contributions" **d** it. Pr 29:4

DEMOLITION *(1)*
God for the **d** of strongholds. 2Co 10:4

DEMON *(19)*
When the **d** had been driven out, Mt 9:33
and they say, 'He has a **d**!' Mt 11:18
is cruelly tormented by a **d**." Mt 15:22
rebuked the **d**, and it came out Mt 17:18
Him to drive the **d** out of her Mk 7:26
d has gone out of your daughter. Mk 7:29
on the bed, and the **d** was gone. Mk 7:30
the **d** came out of him without Lk 4:35
wine, and you say, 'He has a **d**!' Lk 7:33
be driven by the **d** into deserted Lk 8:29
the **d** knocked him down and threw Lk 9:42
driving out a **d** that was mute. Lk 11:14
When the **d** came out, the man who Lk 11:14
"You have a **d**!" the crowd Jn 7:20
a Samaritan and have a **d**?" Jn 8:48
I do not have a **d**," Jesus Jn 8:49
Now we know You have a **d**. Jn 8:52
He has a **d** and He's crazy! Jn 10:20
a **d** open the eyes of the blind? Jn 10:21

DEMON-POSSESSED *(13)*
pains, the **d**, the epileptics, Mt 4:24
brought to Him many who were **d**. Mt 8:16
two **d** men met Him as they came Mt 8:28
happened to those who were **d**. Mt 8:33
a **d** man who was unable to speak Mt 9:32
Then a **d** man who was blind and Mt 12:22
were sick and those who were **d**. Mk 1:32
who had been **d** by the legion, Mk 5:15
happened to the **d** man and ⌊told⌋ Mk 5:16
who had been **d** kept begging Him Mk 5:18
a **d** man from the town met Him. Lk 8:27
to them how the **d** man was Lk 8:36
aren't the words of someone **d**. Jn 10:21

DEMONIC *(2)*
with an unclean **d** spirit who Lk 4:33
but is earthly, sensual, **d**. Jms 3:15

DEMONS *(47)*
sacrificed to **d**, not God, to Dt 32:17
their sons and daughters to **d**. Ps 106:37
name, drive out **d** in Your name, Mt 7:22
us out," the **d** begged Him, "send Mt 8:31
He drives out **d** by the ruler of Mt 9:34
demons by the ruler of the **d**!" Mt 9:34
with skin diseases, drive out **d**. Mt 10:8
man drives out **d** only by Mt 12:24
Beelzebul, the ruler of the **d**." Mt 12:24
if I drive out **d** by Beelzebul, Mt 12:27
I drive out **d** by the Spirit of Mt 12:28
diseases and drove out many **d**. Mk 1:34
would not permit the **d** to speak, Mk 1:34
synagogues and driving out **d**. Mk 1:39
have authority to drive out **d**. Mk 3:15
He drives out **d** by the ruler of Mk 3:22
demons by the ruler of the **d**!" Mk 3:22
d begged Him, "Send us to the Mk 5:12
they were driving out many **d**, Mk 6:13
driving out **d** in Your name, Mk 9:38
of whom He had driven seven **d**. Mk 16:9
My name they will drive out **d**; Mk 16:17
d were coming out of many, Lk 4:41
seven **d** had come out of her Lk 8:2
because many **d** had entered him. Lk 8:30
The **d** begged Him to permit them Lk 8:32
The **d** came out of the man and Lk 8:33
found the man the **d** had departed Lk 8:35
from whom the **d** had departed Lk 8:38
and authority over all the **d**, Lk 9:1
driving out **d** in Your name, Lk 9:49
the **d** submit to us in Your name. Lk 10:17
He drives out **d** by Beelzebul, Lk 11:15
Beelzebul, the ruler of the **d**!" Lk 11:15
say I drive out **d** by Beelzebul. Lk 11:18
if I drive out **d** by Beelzebul, Lk 11:19
I drive out **d** by the finger of Lk 11:20
I'm driving out **d** and performing Lk 13:32
sacrifice to **d** and not to God. 1Co 10:20
want you to be partners with **d**! 1Co 10:20
of the Lord and the cup of **d**. 1Co 10:21
Lord's table and the table of **d**. 1Co 10:21
spirits and the teachings of **d**, 1Tm 4:1
The **d** also believe—and they Jms 2:19
stop worshiping **d** and idols of Rv 9:20
are spirits of **d** performing Rv 16:14
She has become a dwelling for **d**, Rv 18:2

DEMONSTRATE *(9)*
And I will **d** My holiness through Ezk 20:41
against her and **d** My holiness Ezk 28:22
are scattered and **d** My holiness Ezk 28:25
when I **d** My holiness through you Ezk 36:23
will **d** My holiness through them Ezk 39:27
in His blood, to **d** His Rm 3:25
presented Him to **d** His Rm 3:26
Christ Jesus might **d** the utmost 1Tm 1:16
each of you to **d** the same Heb 6:11

DEMONSTRATED *(1)*
He **d** ⌊this power⌋ in the Messiah Eph 1:20

DEMONSTRATING *(2)*
d through the Scriptures that Ac 18:28
or stealing, but **d** utter Ti 2:10

DEMONSTRATION *(1)*
but with a **d** of the Spirit and 1Co 2:4

DEMORALIZED *(1)*
all her wage earners will be **d**. Is 19:10

DEMOTE *(1)*
than to **d** you in plain view of Pr 25:7

DEN *(20)*
put his hand into a snake's **d**. Is 11:8
become a **d** of robbers in your Jr 7:11
a heap of rubble, a jackals' **d**. Jr 9:11
be made desolate, a jackals' **d**. Jr 10:22
He has left His **d** like a lion, Jr 25:38
Hazor will become a jackals' **d**, Jr 49:33
a jackals' **d**, a desolation Jr 51:37
be thrown into the lions' **d**. Dn 6:7
be thrown into the lions' **d**?" Dn 6:12
and threw him into the lions' **d**. Dn 6:16
placed over the mouth of the **d**. Dn 6:17
up and hurried to the lions' **d**. Dn 6:19
he reached the **d**, he cried out Dn 6:20
to take Daniel out of the **d**. Dn 6:23
Daniel was taken out of the **d**, Dn 6:23
and thrown into the lions' **d**— Dn 6:24
bottom of the **d** before the lions Dn 6:24
are making it a **d** of thieves!" Mt 21:13
have made it a **d** of thieves!" Mk 11:17
have made it a **d** of thieves!" Lk 19:46

DENARII *(7)*
slaves who owed him 100 **d**. Mt 18:28
go and buy 200 **d** worth of bread Mk 6:37
for more than 300 **d** and given to Mk 14:5
owed 500 **d**, and the other 50. Lk 7:41
The next day he took out two **d**, Lk 10:35
Two hundred **d** worth of bread Jn 6:7
oil sold for 300 **d** and given to Jn 12:5

DENARIUS *(9)*
workers on one **d** for the day, Mt 20:2
came, they each received one **d**. Mt 20:9
but they also received a **d** each. Mt 20:10
Didn't you agree with me on a **d**? Mt 20:13
So they brought Him a **d**. Mt 22:19
Bring Me a **d** to look at." Mk 12:15
Show Me a **d**. Whose image and Lk 20:24
A quart of wheat for a **d**, Rv 6:6
three quarts of barley for a **d**— Rv 6:6

DENIED *(21)*
Sarah **d** it. "I did not laugh," Gn 18:15
the LORD has **d** you a reward." Nm 24:11
pain that I have not **d** the words Jb 6:10
for I would have **d** God above. Jb 31:28
and have not **d** the request of Ps 21:2
We have **d** ourselves, but You Is 58:3
he **d** it in front of everyone: Mt 26:70
And again he **d** it with an oath, Mt 26:72
But he **d** it: "I don't know or Mk 14:68
again he **d** it. After a little Mk 14:70
When they all **d** it, Peter said, Lk 8:45
men will be **d** before the angels Lk 12:9
he **d** it: "Woman, I don't know Lk 22:57
until you have **d** Me three times. Jn 13:38
He **d** it and said, "I am not!" Jn 18:25
Peter then **d** it again. Jn 18:27
over and **d** in the presence Ac 3:13
But you **d** the Holy and Righteous Ac 3:14
humiliation justice was **d** Him. Ac 8:33
he has **d** the faith and is worse 1Tm 5:8
and have not **d** My name, look, I Rv 3:8

DENIES *(7)*
is the one who **d** justice to a Dt 27:19
but He **d** the wicked what they Pr 10:3
But whoever **d** Me before men, Mt 10:33
but whoever **d** Me before men will Lk 12:9
not the one who **d** that Jesus is 1Jn 2:22
the one who **d** the Father and the 1Jn 2:22
one who **d** the Son can have the 1Jn 2:23

DENOUNCE *(7)*
Jacob for me; come, **d** Israel!" Nm 23:7
How can I **d** someone the LORD has Nm 23:8
Who would **d** his behavior to his Jb 21:31
him, and tribes will **d** him; Pr 24:24
let's **d** him and pay no attention Jr 18:18
proceeded to **d** the towns where Mt 11:20
those who **d** your Christian life 1Pt 3:16

DENOUNCED *(1)*
someone the LORD has not **d**? Nm 23:8

DENS *(7)*
lairs and stay in their **d**. Jb 37:8
crouch in their **d** and lie in Jb 38:40
go back and lie down in their **d**. Ps 104:22
Hermon, from the **d** of the lions, Sg 4:8
filled up its **d** with the kill, Nah 2:12
Foxes have **d** and birds of the Mt 8:20
him, "Foxes have **d**, and birds of Lk 9:58

DENSE *(5)*
to come to you in a **d** cloud, Ex 19:9
heavens and enveloped in a **d**, Dt 4:11
Israel or a land of **d** darkness? Jr 2:31
though it is **d**, for they are Jr 46:23
a day of clouds and **d** overcast, Jl 2:2

DENSEST *(2)*
farthest outpost, its **d** forest. 2Kg 19:23
remotest heights, its **d** forest. Is 37:24

DENY *(32)*
You must not **d** justice to the Ex 23:6
sworn obligation to **d** herself. Nm 30:13
not **d** justice or show partiality Dt 16:19
Do not **d** justice to a foreign Dt 24:17
that you will not **d** your God." Jos 24:27
in order to **d** anyone access to 1Kg 15:17
in order to **d** anyone's access 2Ch 16:1
place, it will **d** ⌊knowing⌋ him, Jb 8:18
don't **d** them to me before I die: Pr 30:7
I might have too much and **d** You, Pr 30:9
eyes desired, I did not **d** them. Ec 2:10
A day for a person to **d** himself, Is 58:5
against those who **d** ⌊justice to⌋ Mal 3:5
I will also **d** him before My Mt 10:33
Me, he must **d** himself, take up Mt 16:24
you will **d** Me three times!" Mt 26:34
told Him, "I will never **d** You!" Mt 26:35
you will **d** Me three times." Mt 26:75
he must **d** himself, take up Mk 8:34
you will **d** Me three times!" Mk 14:30
with You, I will never **d** You!" Mk 14:31
you will **d** Me three times." Mk 14:72
Me, he must **d** himself, take up Lk 9:23
today until you **d** three times Lk 22:34
you will **d** Me three times." Lk 22:61
them, and we cannot **d** it! Ac 4:16
if we **d** Him, He will also deny 2Tm 2:12
we deny Him, He will also **d** us; 2Tm 2:12
for He cannot **d** Himself. 2Tm 2:13
but they **d** Him by their works. Ti 1:16
instructing us to **d** godlessness Ti 2:12
and did not **d** your faith in Me Rv 2:13

DENYING *(4)*
d justice to a man in the Lm 3:35
of religion but **d** its power. 2Tm 3:5
even **d** the Master who bought 2Pt 2:1
promiscuity and **d** our only Jd 4

DEPART *(25)*
scepter will not **d** from Judah, Gn 49:10
of flies will **d** from Pharaoh, Ex 8:29
must not **d** from your mouth; Jos 1:8
and he will **d** by the breath of Jb 15:30
D from me, all evildoers, for Ps 6:8
D from me, you evil ones, so Ps 119:115
will never **d** from his house. Pr 17:13
he is old he will not **d** from it. Pr 22:6
will not **d** from your mouth, Is 59:21
my people and **d** from them, Jr 9:2
d from the Chaldeans' land. Jr 50:8
so that I must **d** from My Ezk 8:6
of the gate and then **d**, Ezk 46:2
tear ⌊them⌋ to pieces and **d**. Hs 5:14
I will **d** and return to My place Hs 5:15
woe to them when I **d** from them! Hs 9:12

It will certainly **d** from them. Hs 10:5
D in shameful nakedness, you Mc 1:11
D from Me, you lawbreakers!' Mt 7:23
on the left, '**D** from Me, you who Mt 25:41
for a while and **d** in a time of Lk 8:13
had come to **d** from this world Jn 13:1
he was about to **d** the next day, Ac 20:7
the desire to **d** and be with Php 1:23
some will **d** from the faith, 1Tm 4:1

DEPARTED *(83)*

with Abraham, He **d**, and Abraham Gn 18:33
Lot **d** from Zoar and lived in the Gn 19:30
camels and **d** with all kinds Gn 24:10
Pharaoh and **d** from Pharaoh's Gn 47:10
community **d** from Elim and came Ex 16:1
After they **d** from Rephidim, Ex 19:2
Moab and Midian **d** with fees for Nm 22:7
They **d** from Rameses in the first Nm 33:3
Israelites **d** from Rameses and Nm 33:5
They **d** from Succoth and camped Nm 33:6
d from Etham and turned back Nm 33:7
They **d** from Pi-hahiroth and Nm 33:8
They **d** from Marah and came to Nm 33:9
They **d** from Elim and camped by Nm 33:10
They **d** from the Red Sea and Nm 33:11
They **d** from the Wilderness of Nm 33:12
They **d** from Dophkah and camped Nm 33:13
They **d** from Alush and camped at Nm 33:14
d from Rephidim and camped Nm 33:15
They **d** from the Wilderness of Nm 33:16
They **d** from Kibroth-hattaavah Nm 33:17
They **d** from Hazeroth and camped Nm 33:18
They **d** from Rithmah and camped Nm 33:19
They **d** from Rimmon-perez and Nm 33:20
They **d** from Libnah and camped Nm 33:21
They **d** from Rissah and camped at Nm 33:22
d from Kehelathah and camped Nm 33:23
They **d** from Mount Shepher and Nm 33:24
They **d** from Haradah and camped Nm 33:25
d from Makheloth and camped Nm 33:26
They **d** from Tahath and camped at Nm 33:27
They **d** from Terah and camped at Nm 33:28
They **d** from Mithkah and camped Nm 33:29
d from Hashmonah and camped Nm 33:30
d from Moseroth and camped Nm 33:31
They **d** from Bene-jaakan and Nm 33:32
They **d** from Hor-haggidgad and Nm 33:33
d from Jotbathah and camped Nm 33:34
They **d** from Abronah and camped Nm 33:35
They **d** from Ezion-geber and Nm 33:36
They **d** from Kadesh and camped Nm 33:37
d from Mount Hor and camped Nm 33:41
d from Zalmonah and camped Nm 33:42
They **d** from Punon and camped at Nm 33:43
They **d** from Oboth and camped at Nm 33:44
They **d** from Iyim and camped at Nm 33:45
d from Dibon-gad and camped Nm 33:46
They **d** from Almon-diblathaim Nm 33:47
They **d** from the Abarim ⌊range⌋ Nm 33:48
time ⌊of day⌋ you **d** from Egypt. Dt 16:6
Six hundred Danites **d** from Zorah Jdg 18:11
He got up, **d**, and arrived Jdg 19:10
"The glory has **d** from Israel," 1Sm 4:21
"The glory has **d** from Israel," 1Sm 4:22
have not **d** from the commands of Jb 23:12
d spirits tremble beneath the Jb 26:5
who drove him out, and he **d**. Ps 34:1
Do **d** spirits rise up to praise Ps 88:10
to the land of the **d** spirits. Pr 2:18
know that the **d** spirits are Pr 9:18
the assembly of the **d** spirits. Pr 21:16
the spirits of the **d** for you— Is 14:9
d spirits do not rise up. Is 26:14
will bring forth the **d** spirits. Is 26:19
sons have **d** from me and are no Jr 10:20
that the kingdom has **d** from you. Dn 4:31
⌊the more⌋ they **d** from Me. Hs 11:2
d from Galilee and went to the Mt 19:1
silver into the sanctuary and **d**. Mt 27:5
Jesus **d** with His disciples to Mk 3:7
got up and **d** from there to the Mk 7:24
temptation, he **d** from Him for a Lk 4:13
found the man the demons had **d** Lk 8:35
demons had **d** kept begging Him Lk 8:38
what Jesus said to him and **d**. Jn 4:50
So He **d** again across the Jordan Jn 10:40
the Jews but **d** from there to Jn 11:54
he **d** and went to a different Ac 12:17
Then Paul chose Silas and **d**, Ac 15:40
encouraged the brothers, and **d**. Ac 16:40
as quickly as possible, they **d**. Ac 17:15
saying good-bye, **d** to go to Ac 20:1
the Jews **d**, while engaging Ac 28:29

DEPARTING *(2)*

d quickly from the tomb with Mt 28:8
As the two men were **d** from Him, Lk 9:33

DEPARTS *(2)*

fixed order **d** from My presence Jr 31:36
that **d** from the living God. Heb 3:12

DEPARTURE *(5)*

after Israel's **d** from the land Nm 1:1
year after their **d** from the land Nm 9:1
that after my **d** savage wolves Ac 20:29
and the time for my **d** is close. 2Tm 4:6
that after my **d** you may be able 2Pt 1:15

DEPEND *(9)*

our God, for we **d** on You, and in 2Ch 14:11
Can you **d** on it because of its Jb 39:11
those who **d** on His faithful love Ps 33:18
My salvation and glory **d** on God; Ps 62:7
will no longer **d** on the one who Is 10:20
will faithfully **d** on the LORD, Is 10:20
for help and who **d** on horses! Is 31:1
and the Prophets **d** on these two Mt 22:40
then it does not **d** on human will Rm 9:16

DEPENDABLE *(1)*

you may give a **d** report to those Pr 22:21

DEPENDED *(5)*

because they **d** on the LORD, 2Ch 13:18
Because you **d** on the king of 2Ch 16:7
and have not **d** on the LORD your 2Ch 16:7
you **d** on the LORD, He handed 2Ch 16:8
and deceit, and have **d** on them, Is 30:12

DEPENDENT *(3)*

the mind ⌊that is⌋ **d** ⌊on You⌋, Is 26:3
and on all its ⌊**d**⌋ villages— Jr 19:15
and not be **d** on anyone. 1Th 4:12

DEPENDENTS *(5)*

household with food for their **d**. Gn 47:12
your households, and your **d**." Gn 47:24
livestock and cities for our **d**. Nm 32:16
our **d** will remain in the Nm 32:17
cities for your **d** and folds for Nm 32:24

DEPENDS *(2)*

he is poor and **d** on them. Dt 24:15
number of his months **d** on You, Jb 14:5

DEPICTION *(1)*

a **d** of the Babylonians in Ezk 23:15

DEPLETED *(1)*

His strength is **d**; disaster lies Jb 18:12

DEPLOY *(3)*

d ⌊the troops⌋ on Mount Tabor, Jdg 4:6
Though an army **d** against me, Ps 27:3
D small shields and large; Jr 46:3

DEPLOYED *(2)*

and his servants **d** against them Gn 14:15
like a mighty army **d** for war. Jl 2:5

DEPOPULATE *(1)*

the land and **d** it so that it Ezk 14:15

DEPORT *(5)*

and their captors **d** them to the 1Kg 8:46
their captors **d** them to a 2Ch 6:36
he will **d** them to Babylon and Jr 20:4
to death or to **d** us to Babylon!" Jr 43:3
So I will **d** you beyond Babylon! Ac 7:43

DEPORTED *(34)*

You will be **d** from the land you Dt 28:63
where they were **d** and repent 1Kg 8:47
and **d** the people to Assyria. 2Kg 15:29
He **d** its people to Kir but put 2Kg 16:9
He **d** the Israelites to Assyria 2Kg 17:6
that you have **d** and placed 2Kg 17:26
back one of the priests you **d**. 2Kg 17:27
priests they had **d** came and 2Kg 17:28
nations where they had been **d** 2Kg 17:33
king of Assyria **d** the Israelites 2Kg 18:11
Then he **d** all Jerusalem and all 2Kg 24:14
Nebuchadnezzar **d** Jehoiachin to 2Kg 24:15
d the rest of the people who 2Kg 25:11
Geba and who were **d** to Manahath: 1Ch 8:6
Gera **d** them and was the father 1Ch 8:7
where they were **d** and repent 2Ch 6:37
from the sword he **d** to Babylon, 2Ch 36:20
of Babylon had **d** to Babylon. Ezr 2:1
Ashurbanipal **d** and settled Ezr 4:10
this temple and **d** the people to Ezr 5:12
the captive exiles **d** by King Neh 7:6
in the place where they **d** him, Jr 22:12
of Babylon had **d** Jeconiah son Jr 24:1
not take when he **d** Jeconiah son Jr 27:20
had **d** from Jerusalem to Jr 29:1
the exiles I **d** from Jerusalem Jr 29:4
of the city I have **d** you to. Jr 29:7
restore you to the place I **d** you Jr 29:14
d to Babylon the rest of the Jr 39:9
who had not been **d** to Babylon, Jr 40:7
d some of the poorest of the Jr 52:15
are the people Nebuchadnezzar **d**: Jr 52:28
of the guards, **d** 745 Jews. Jr 52:30
together 4,600 people ⌊were **d**⌋. Jr 52:30

DEPOSED *(2)*

king of Egypt **d** him in Jerusalem 2Ch 36:3
he was **d** from his royal throne Dn 5:20

DEPOSIT *(7)*

his neighbor in regard to a **d**, Lv 6:2
or the **d** entrusted to him, Lv 6:4
cow's ashes and **d** them outside Nm 19:9
accountants for **d** in the royal Est 3:9
There they will **d** the most holy Ezk 42:13
what you didn't **d** and reap what Lk 19:21
what I didn't **d** and reaping what Lk 19:22

DEPOSITED *(3)*

that had been **d** in the LORD's 2Ch 34:14
having **d** the scroll in the Jr 36:20
you should have **d** my money with Mt 25:27

DEPRAVED *(5)*

are close relatives; it is **d**. Lv 18:17
a woman and her mother, it is **d**. Lv 20:14
brood of evildoers, **d** children! Is 1:4
was ⌊even⌋ more **d** in her lust Ezk 23:11
whose minds are **d** and deprived 1Tm 6:5

DEPRAVITY *(2)*

prostituted and filled with **d**. Lv 19:29
there will be no **d** among you. Lv 20:14

DEPRESSED *(5)*

Why am I so **d**? Why this turmoil Ps 42:5
I am deeply **d**; therefore I Ps 42:6
Why am I so **d**? Why this turmoil Ps 42:11
Why am I so **d**? Why this turmoil Ps 43:5
them⌋ and have become **d**. Lm 3:20

DEPRIVE *(11)*

you that will **d** you of your Lv 26:22
for a bribe and **d** the innocent Is 5:23
trial and to **d** the afflicted Is 10:2
without cause **d** the righteous Is 29:21
will no longer **d** them of ⌊their⌋ Ezk 36:12
You devour men and **d** your nation Ezk 36:13
devour men and **d** your nation Ezk 36:14
and **d** the poor of justice at the Am 5:12
They **d** a man of his home, a Mc 2:2
Do not **d** one another—except 1Co 7:5
for anyone to **d** me of my boast! 1Co 9:15

DEPRIVED *(11)*

You have **d** me of my sons. Gn 42:36
for me, if I am **d** of my sons, Gn 43:14
of my sons, then I am **d**." Gn 43:14
lives, who has **d** me of justice, Jb 27:2
yet God has **d** me of justice. Jb 34:5
For God has **d** her of wisdom; Jb 39:17
I am **d** of the rest of my years. Is 38:10
you have been **d** of will yet say Is 49:20
I was **d** of my children and Is 49:21
My soul has been **d** of peace; Lm 3:17
are depraved and **d** of the truth, 1Tm 6:5

DEPRIVES *(3)*

He **d** trusted advisers of speech Jb 12:20
He **d** the world's leaders of Jb 12:24
hungry empty and **d** the thirsty Is 32:6

DEPRIVING *(1)*

"and **d** myself from good?" Ec 4:8

DEPTH *(5)*

sea returned to its normal **d**. Ex 14:27
praying from the **d** of my anguish 1Sm 1:16
nor height, nor **d**, nor any other Rm 8:39
the **d** of the riches both of the Rm 11:33
height and **d** ⌊of God's love⌋, Eph 3:18

DEPTHS *(48)*
the surface of the watery **d**, Gn 1:2
of the watery **d** burst open, Gn 7:11
of the watery **d** and the Gn 8:2
they sank to the **d** like a stone. Ex 15:5
The watery **d** congealed in the Ex 15:8
and burns to the **d** of Sheol; Dt 32:22
and the watery **d** that lie Dt 33:13
The **d** of the sea became visible, 2Sm 22:16
pursuers into the **d** like a stone Neh 9:11
you fathom the **d** of God or Jb 11:7
ocean **d** say, "It's not in me, Jb 28:14
Him and covers the **d** of the sea. Jb 36:30
walked in the **d** of the oceans? Jb 38:16
of the watery **d** is frozen? Jb 38:30
He makes the **d** seethe like a Jb 41:31
The **d** of the sea became visible, Ps 18:15
He puts the **d** into storehouses. Ps 33:7
topple into the **d** of the seas, Ps 46:2
will go into the **d** of the earth. Ps 63:9
them⌋ back from the **d** of the sea Ps 68:22
even from the **d** of the earth. Ps 71:20
they trembled. Even the **d** shook. Ps 77:16
them drink as abundant as the **d**. Ps 78:15
my life from the **d** of Sheol. Ps 86:13
in the darkest places, in the **d**. Ps 88:6
The **d** of the earth are in His Ps 95:4
them through the **d** as through a Ps 106:9
down to the **d**, their courage Ps 107:26
Out of the **d** I call to You, Ps 130:1
in the seas and all the **d**. Ps 135:6
formed in the **d** of the earth. Ps 139:15
all sea monsters and ocean **d**, Ps 148:7
the watery **d** broke open, Pr 3:20
were no watery **d** and no springs Pr 8:24
guests are in the **d** of Sheol. Pr 9:18
from the **d** of Sheol to the Is 7:11
the city will sink into the **d**. Is 32:19
shout, **d** of the earth. Is 44:23
who says to the **d** of the sea: Is 44:27
them through the **d** like a horse Is 63:13
Yahweh, from the **d** of the Pit. Lm 3:55
the sea in the **d** of the waters; Ezk 27:34
me into the **d**, into the heart Jnh 2:3
the watery **d** overcame me; Jnh 2:5
our sins into the **d** of the sea. Mc 7:19
all the **d** of the Nile will dry Zch 10:11
drowned in the **d** of the sea! Mt 18:6
and a day in the **d** of the sea. 2Co 11:25

DEPUTIES *(7)*
of Nathan, in charge of the **d**; 1Kg 4:5
Solomon had 12 **d** for all Israel. 1Kg 4:7
Each of those **d** for a month in 1Kg 4:27
including his 3,300 **d** in charge 1Kg 5:16
These were the **d** who were over 1Kg 9:23
These were King Solomon's **d**: 2Ch 8:10
and Benaiah were **d** under the 2Ch 31:13

DEPUTY *(6)*
There was one **d** in the land of 1Kg 4:19
in Edom; a **d** served as king. 1Kg 22:47
high priest's **d** came and emptied 2Ch 24:11
Rehum the chief **d** and Shimshai Ezr 4:8
Rehum the chief **d**, Shimshai the Ezr 4:9
a reply to his chief **d** Rehum, Ezr 4:17

DERBE *(4)*
towns called Lystra and **D**, Ac 14:6
day he left with Barnabas for **D**. Ac 14:20
Then he went on to **D** and Lystra, Ac 16:1
Gaius from **D**, Timothy, and Ac 20:4

DERISION *(3)*
He drinks **d** like water. Jb 34:7
for me constant disgrace and **d**. Jr 20:8
a desolation, a **d**, and ruins Jr 25:9

DERIVED *(1)*
our prosperity is **d** from this Ac 19:25

DESCEND *(21)*
and kings will **d** from you. Gn 35:11
it will **d** on you from the sky Dt 28:24
in this scroll will **d** on him. Dt 29:20
will now **d** on me at Gilgal, 1Sm 13:12
and we will **d** on him like dew on 2Sm 17:12
his gray head to Sheol in 1Kg 2:6
the stairs that **d** from the city Neh 3:15
or will we **d** together to the Jb 17:16
D from the peak of Amana, from Sg 4:8
He made it **d**. He spread a net Lm 1:13
of the sea will **d** from their Ezk 26:16
be⌋ with those who **d** to the Pit, Ezk 26:20
with those who **d** to the Pit, Ezk 26:20
the people who **d** to the Pit. Ezk 31:14
be⌋ with those who **d** to the Pit. Ezk 31:16
be⌋ with those who **d** to the Pit: Ezk 32:18
with those who **d** to the Pit. Ezk 32:24
with those who **d** to the Pit. Ezk 32:25
with those who **d** to the Pit. Ezk 32:29
with those who **d** to the Pit. Ezk 32:30
Himself will **d** from heaven with 1Th 4:16

DESCENDANT *(17)*
No **d** of Aaron the priest who has Lv 21:21
was Jochebed, a **d** of Levi, born Nm 26:59
Jair, a **d** of Manasseh, went and Nm 32:41
Jair, a **d** of Manasseh, took over Dt 3:14
will raise up after you your **d**, 2Sm 7:12
Sheshan. Sheshan's **d**: Ahlai. 1Ch 2:31
Another **d** was named Zelophehad, 1Ch 7:15
a **d** of Perez son of Judah; 1Ch 9:4
will raise up after you your **d**, 1Ch 17:11
Sippai, a **d** of the giants, 1Ch 20:4
a **d** of Moses' son Gershom, 1Ch 26:24
He was a **d** of Perez and chief of 1Ch 27:3
a **d** of Levi son of Israel— Ezr 8:18
of Zechariah, a **d** of the Neh 11:5
I have chosen, **d** of Abraham, My Is 41:8
who was a **d** of David according Rm 1:3
am an Israelite, a **d** of Abraham, Rm 11:1

DESCENDANTS *(482)*
family records of the **d** of Adam. Gn 5:1
with you and your **d** after you, Gn 9:9
me or with my children and **d**. Gn 21:23
the land to your **d** after you. Gn 35:12
Jacob and his **d**, who went to Gn 46:8
his direct **d**, not including Gn 46:26
possession to your **d** to come.' Gn 48:4
number of Jacob's **d** was 70; Ex 1:5
as a statute for you and your **d**. Ex 12:24
Aaron and for his **d** after him. Ex 28:43
Aaron and his **d** throughout their Ex 30:21
male among Aaron's **d** may eat it. Lv 6:18
None of your **d** throughout your Lv 21:17
any of your **d** throughout your Lv 22:3
man of Aaron's **d** who has a skin Lv 22:4
The **d** of Reuben, the firstborn Nm 1:20
The **d** of Simeon: Nm 1:22
The **d** of Gad: according to their Nm 1:24
The **d** of Judah: according to Nm 1:26
The **d** of Issachar: Nm 1:28
The **d** of Zebulun: Nm 1:30
The **d** of Joseph: Nm 1:32
The **d** of Ephraim: Nm 1:32
The **d** of Manasseh: Nm 1:34
The **d** of Benjamin: Nm 1:36
The **d** of Dan: according to their Nm 1:38
The **d** of Asher: according to Nm 1:40
The **d** of Naphtali: Nm 1:42
The leader of the **d** of Judah is Nm 2:3
duties of Merari's **d** involved Nm 3:36
of you or your **d** is unclean Nm 9:10
and Talmai, the **d** of Anak, were Nm 13:22
We also saw the **d** of Anak there. Nm 13:28
and his **d** will inherit it. Nm 14:24
priesthood for him and his **d**, Nm 25:13
Israel. Reuben's **d**: the Nm 26:5
Simeon's **d** by their clans: Nm 26:12
Gad's **d** by their clans: Nm 26:15
Judah's **d** by their clans: Nm 26:20
The **d** of Perez: the Hezronite Nm 26:21
Issachar's **d** by their clans: Nm 26:23
Zebulun's **d** by their clans: Nm 26:26
Joseph's **d** by their clans ⌊from⌋ Nm 26:28
Manasseh's **d**: the Machirite clan Nm 26:29
These were Gilead's **d**: Nm 26:30
were Ephraim's **d** by their clans: Nm 26:35
These were Shuthelah's **d**: Nm 26:36
were Joseph's **d** by their clans. Nm 26:37
Benjamin's **d** by their clans: Nm 26:38
Bela's **d** ⌊from⌋ Ard and Naaman: Nm 26:40
were Dan's **d** by their clans: Nm 26:42
Asher's **d** by their clans: Nm 26:44
From Beriah's **d**: Nm 26:45
Naphtali's **d** by their clans: Nm 26:48
The **d** of Machir son of Manasseh Nm 32:39
the clan of the **d** of Gilead— Nm 36:1
of Joseph's **d** says is right. Nm 36:5
clans of the **d** of Manasseh son Nm 36:12
Jacob and their **d** after them.' Dt 1:8
We also saw the **d** of the Anakim Dt 1:28
give him and his **d** the land on Dt 1:36
brothers, the **d** of Esau, who Dt 2:4
brothers, the **d** of Esau, who Dt 2:8
possession to the **d** of Lot.'" Dt 2:9
the **d** of Esau drove them out, Dt 2:12
possession to the **d** of Lot.'" Dt 2:19
had done for the **d** of Esau who Dt 2:22
just as the **d** of Esau who live Dt 2:29
He chose their **d** after them and Dt 4:37
will bless your **d**, and the Dt 7:13
and tall, the **d** of the Anakim. Dt 9:2
He chose their **d** after them— Dt 10:15
to give them and their **d**, Dt 11:9
none of his **d**, even to the tenth Dt 23:2
none of their **d**, even to the Dt 23:3
Your **d** will be blessed, and your Dt 28:4
Your **d** will be cursed, and your Dt 28:18
against you and your **d** forever. Dt 28:46
plagues on you and your **d**, Dt 28:59
heart and the hearts of your **d**, Dt 30:6
so that you and your **d** may live, Dt 30:19
because their **d** will not have Dt 31:21
'I will give it to your **d**.' Dt 34:4
of Manasseh's **d** by their clans, Jos 13:29
are for the **d** of Machir son of Jos 13:31
half the **d** of Machir by their Jos 13:31
The **d** of Joseph became two Jos 14:4
The **d** of Judah approached Joshua Jos 14:6
for you and your **d** forever, Jos 14:9
the tribe of the **d** of Judah by Jos 15:1
boundary of the **d** of Judah Jos 15:12
among the **d** of Judah based Jos 15:13
Ahiman, and Talmai, **d** of Anak. Jos 15:14
the tribe of the **d** of Judah by Jos 15:20
tribe of the **d** of Judah toward Jos 15:21
But the **d** of Judah could not Jos 15:63
among the **d** of Judah to this Jos 15:63
for the **d** of Joseph went Jos 16:1
territory of the **d** of Ephraim by Jos 16:5
the tribe of the **d** of Ephraim by Jos 16:8
apart for the **d** of Ephraim Jos 16:9
of the **d** of Manasseh— Jos 16:9
of Manasseh's **d** by their clans, Jos 17:2
are the male **d** of Manasseh son Jos 17:2
belonged to the **d** of Ephraim. Jos 17:8
The **d** of Manasseh could not Jos 17:12
Joseph's **d** said to Joshua: Jos 17:14
But the **d** of Joseph said, Jos 17:16
of Benjamin's **d** by their clans, Jos 18:11
between Judah's **d** and Joseph's Jos 18:11
descendants and Joseph's **d**. Jos 18:11
a city of the **d** of Judah. Jos 18:14
the inheritance of Benjamin's **d**, Jos 18:20
of Benjamin's **d** by their clans: Jos 18:21
for Benjamin's **d** by their clans. Jos 18:28
tribe of his **d** by their clans, Jos 19:1
within the portion of Judah's **d**. Jos 19:1
of Simeon's **d** by their clans. Jos 19:8
of Simeon's **d** was within Jos 19:9
the territory of Judah's **d**, Jos 19:9
for Judah's **d** was too large for Jos 19:9
So Simeon's **d** received an Jos 19:9
for Zebulun's **d** by their clans. Jos 19:10
of Zebulun's **d** by their clans, Jos 19:16
of Issachar's **d** by their clans. Jos 19:17
of Issachar's **d** by their clans, Jos 19:23
of Asher's **d** by their clans. Jos 19:24
of Asher's **d** by their clans, Jos 19:31
for Naphtali's **d** by their clans. Jos 19:32
of Naphtali's **d** by their clans, Jos 19:39
who were the **d** of Aaron the Jos 21:4
The remaining **d** of Kohath Jos 21:5
Gershon's **d** received 13 cities Jos 21:6
Merari's **d** received 12 cities Jos 21:7
the tribes of the **d** of Judah and Jos 21:9
to the **d** of Aaron from the Jos 21:10
They gave to the **d** of Aaron the Jos 21:13
for the priests, the **d** of Aaron. Jos 21:19
remaining clans of Kohath's **d**, Jos 21:20
the clans of Kohath's other **d**. Jos 21:26
⌊they gave⌋ to the **d** of Gershon, Jos 21:27
to the clans of the **d** of Merari, Jos 21:34
to the clans of Merari's **d**, Jos 21:40
the future your **d** might say to Jos 22:24
might say to our **d**, Jos 22:24
us and you **d** of Reuben and Gad Jos 22:25
So your **d** may cause our Jos 22:25

may cause our **d** to stop fearing	Jos 22:25
your **d** will not be able to say	Jos 22:27
not be able to say to our **d**,	Jos 22:27
heard what the **d** of Reuben,	Jos 22:30
priest said to the **d** of Reuben,	Jos 22:31
of Canaan, and multiplied his **d**.	Jos 24:3
an inheritance for Joseph's **d**.	Jos 24:32
The **d** of the Kenite, Moses'	Jdg 1:16
not cut off my **d** or wipe out my	1Sm 24:21
of his male **d** be handed over to	2Sm 21:6
one of the **d** of the giant,	2Sm 21:16
was one of the **d** of the giant.	2Sm 21:18
to David and his **d** forever.	2Sm 22:51
on the head of his **d** forever,	1Kg 2:33
for David, his **d**, his dynasty,	1Kg 2:33
their **d** who remained in the land	1Kg 9:21
humble David's **d**, because of	1Kg 11:39
you and will sweep away your **d**:	1Kg 21:21
to you and your **d** forever."	2Kg 5:27
rejected all the **d** of Israel,	2Kg 17:20
LORD commanded the **d** of Jacob;	2Kg 17:34
'Some of your **d** who come from	2Kg 20:18
Nahshon, a leader of Judah's **d**.	1Ch 2:10
These were the **d** of Jerahmeel.	1Ch 2:33
These were Caleb's **d**.	1Ch 2:50
These were the **d** of Shobal the	1Ch 2:52
d: Pelatiah, Jeshaiah,	1Ch 3:21
22,600 **d** of Tola were recorded	1Ch 7:2
people from the **d** of Judah,	1Ch 9:3
gathered together the **d** of Aaron	1Ch 15:4
servant, Jacob's **d**—His chosen	1Ch 16:13
These were the **d** of the giant in	1Ch 20:8
along with his **d**, was set apart	1Ch 23:13
of the **d** of Aaron were as	1Ch 24:1
Eleazar's **d** than Ithamar's,	1Ch 24:4
houses were from Eleazar's **d**,	1Ch 24:4
both Eleazar's and Ithamar's **d**.	1Ch 24:5
inheritance to your **d** forever.	1Ch 28:8
their **d** who remained in the land	2Ch 8:8
to David and his **d** forever by a	2Ch 13:5
the **d** of Aaron and the Levites,	2Ch 13:9
to the LORD are **d** of Aaron,	2Ch 13:10
forever to the **d** of Abraham Your	2Ch 20:7
a Levite from Asaph's **d**),	2Ch 20:14
priests, the **d** of Aaron, have	2Ch 26:18
Then he told the **d** of Aaron,	2Ch 29:21
and to the **d** of Aaron, the	2Ch 31:19
to the tombs of David's **d**.	2Ch 32:33
priests, the **d** of Aaron, were	2Ch 35:14
for the priests, the **d** of Aaron.	2Ch 35:14
singers, the **d** of Asaph, were	2Ch 35:15
Parosh's **d** 2,172	Ezr 2:3
Shephatiah's **d** 372	Ezr 2:4
Arah's **d** 775	Ezr 2:5
Pahath-moab's **d**:	Ezr 2:6
Jeshua's and Joab's **d** 2,812	Ezr 2:6
Elam's **d** 1,254	Ezr 2:7
Zattu's **d** 945	Ezr 2:8
Zaccai's **d** 760	Ezr 2:9
Bani's **d** 642	Ezr 2:10
Bebai's **d** 623	Ezr 2:11
Azgad's **d** 1,222	Ezr 2:12
Adonikam's **d** 666	Ezr 2:13
Bigvai's **d** 2,056	Ezr 2:14
Adin's **d** 454	Ezr 2:15
Ater's **d**: Hezekiah's 98	Ezr 2:16
Bezai's **d** 323	Ezr 2:17
Jorah's **d** 112	Ezr 2:18
Hashum's **d** 223	Ezr 2:19
Gibbar's **d** 95	Ezr 2:20
Jedaiah's **d** of the house of	Ezr 2:36
Immer's **d** 1,052	Ezr 2:37
Pashhur's **d** 1,247	Ezr 2:38
and Harim's **d** 1,017	Ezr 2:39
and Kadmiel's **d** from Hodaviah's	Ezr 2:40
descendants from Hodaviah's **d** 74	Ezr 2:40
singers ⌊included⌋: Asaph's **d**	Ezr 2:41
The gatekeepers' **d** ⌊included⌋:	Ezr 2:42
Shallum's **d**, Ater's descendants,	Ezr 2:42
descendants, Ater's **d**, Talmon's	Ezr 2:42
Talmon's **d**, Akkub's descendants	Ezr 2:42
descendants, Akkub's **d**, Hatita's	Ezr 2:42
Hatita's **d**, Shobai's descendants	Ezr 2:42
Shobai's **d**, in all 139	Ezr 2:42
Ziha's **d**, Hasupha's descendants,	Ezr 2:43
Hasupha's **d**, Tabbaoth's	Ezr 2:43
descendants, Tabbaoth's **d**,	Ezr 2:43
Keros's **d**, Siaha's descendants,	Ezr 2:44
Siaha's **d**, Padon's descendants	Ezr 2:44
Siaha's descendants, Padon's **d**,	Ezr 2:44
Lebanah's **d**, Hagabah's	Ezr 2:45
Hagabah's **d**, Akkub's descendants	Ezr 2:45
descendants, Akkub's **d**,	Ezr 2:45
d, Shalmai's descendants,	Ezr 2:46
Shalmai's **d**, Hanan's descendants	Ezr 2:46
descendants, Hanan's **d**,	Ezr 2:46
Giddel's **d**, Gahar's descendants,	Ezr 2:47
descendants, Gahar's **d**, Reaiah's	Ezr 2:47
Gahar's descendants, Reaiah's **d**,	Ezr 2:47
Rezin's **d**, Nekoda's descendants,	Ezr 2:48
Nekoda's **d**, Gazzam's descendants	Ezr 2:48
descendants, Gazzam's **d**,	Ezr 2:48
Uzza's **d**, Paseah's descendants,	Ezr 2:49
Paseah's **d**, Besai's descendants	Ezr 2:49
Paseah's descendants, Besai's **d**,	Ezr 2:49
Asnah's **d**, Meunim's descendants,	Ezr 2:50
Meunim's **d**, Nephusim's	Ezr 2:50
descendants, Nephusim's **d**,	Ezr 2:50
Bakbuk's **d**, Hakupha's	Ezr 2:51
Hakupha's **d**, Harhur's	Ezr 2:51
descendants, Harhur's **d**,	Ezr 2:51
Bazluth's **d**, Mehida's	Ezr 2:52
Mehida's **d**, Harsha's descendants	Ezr 2:52
descendants, Harsha's **d**,	Ezr 2:52
d, Sisera's descendants,	Ezr 2:53
Sisera's **d**, Temah's descendants	Ezr 2:53
Sisera's descendants, Temah's **d**,	Ezr 2:53
Neziah's **d**, and Hatipha's	Ezr 2:54
descendants, and Hatipha's **d**.	Ezr 2:54
The **d** of Solomon's servants	Ezr 2:55
Sotai's **d**, Hassophereth's	Ezr 2:55
Hassophereth's **d**, Peruda's	Ezr 2:55
descendants, Peruda's **d**,	Ezr 2:55
d, Darkon's descendants,	Ezr 2:56
Darkon's **d**, Giddel's descendants	Ezr 2:56
descendants, Giddel's **d**,	Ezr 2:56
Shephatiah's **d**, Hattil's	Ezr 2:57
descendants, Hattil's **d**,	Ezr 2:57
d, and Ami's	Ezr 2:57
descendants, and Ami's **d**.	Ezr 2:57
servants and the **d** of Solomon's	Ezr 2:58
Delaiah's **d**, Tobiah's	Ezr 2:60
Tobiah's **d**, Nekoda's descendants	Ezr 2:60
descendants, Nekoda's **d** 652	Ezr 2:60
and from the **d** of the priests:	Ezr 2:61
d of Habaiah, the descendants	Ezr 2:61
of Habaiah, the **d** of Hakkoz, the	Ezr 2:61
of Hakkoz, the **d** of Barzillai—	Ezr 2:61
Gershom, from Phinehas's **d**;	Ezr 8:2
Daniel, from Ithamar's **d**;	Ezr 8:2
Hattush, from David's **d**,	Ezr 8:2
who was of Shecaniah's **d**;	Ezr 8:3
Parosh's **d**, and 150 men with	Ezr 8:3
Zerahiah from Pahath-moab's **d**,	Ezr 8:4
son of Jahaziel from Zattu's **d**,	Ezr 8:5
son of Jonathan from Adin's **d**,	Ezr 8:6
son of Athaliah from Elam's **d**,	Ezr 8:7
of Michael from Shephatiah's **d**,	Ezr 8:8
son of Jehiel from Joab's **d**,	Ezr 8:9
son of Josiphiah from Bani's **d**,	Ezr 8:10
son of Bebai from Bebai's **d**,	Ezr 8:11
son of Hakkatan from Azgad's **d**,	Ezr 8:12
from Adonikam's **d**, and their	Ezr 8:13
and Zaccur from Bigvai's **d**,	Ezr 8:14
of insight from the **d** of Mahli,	Ezr 8:18
from the **d** of Merari, and his	Ezr 8:19
women from the **d** of the priests:	Ezr 10:18
from the **d** of Jeshua son of	Ezr 10:18
and Zebadiah from Immer's **d**;	Ezr 10:20
and Uzziah from Harim's **d**;	Ezr 10:21
and Elasah from Pashhur's **d**.	Ezr 10:22
Parosh's **d**: Ramiah, Izziah,	Ezr 10:25
Elam's **d**: Mattaniah, Zechariah,	Ezr 10:26
Zattu's **d**: Elioenai, Eliashib,	Ezr 10:27
Bebai's **d**: Jehohanan, Hananiah,	Ezr 10:28
Bani's **d**: Meshullam, Malluch,	Ezr 10:29
Pahath-moab's **d**:	Ezr 10:30
Harim's **d**: Eliezer, Isshijah,	Ezr 10:31
Hashum's **d**: Mattenai, Mattattah,	Ezr 10:33
Bani's **d**: Maadai, Amram, Uel,	Ezr 10:34
Nebo's **d**: Jeiel, Mattithiah,	Ezr 10:43
Parosh's **d** 2,172	Neh 7:8
Shephatiah's **d** 372	Neh 7:9
Arah's **d** 652	Neh 7:10
Pahath-moab's **d**:	Neh 7:11
Jeshua's and Joab's **d** 2,818	Neh 7:11
Elam's **d** 1,254	Neh 7:12
Zattu's **d** 845	Neh 7:13
Zaccai's **d** 760	Neh 7:14
Binnui's **d** 648	Neh 7:15
Bebai's **d** 628	Neh 7:16
Azgad's **d** 2,322	Neh 7:17
Adonikam's **d** 667	Neh 7:18
Bigvai's **d** 2,067	Neh 7:19
Adin's **d** 655	Neh 7:20
Ater's **d**: of Hezekiah 98	Neh 7:21
Hashum's **d** 328	Neh 7:22
Bezai's **d** 324	Neh 7:23
Hariph's **d** 112	Neh 7:24
Gibeon's **d** 95	Neh 7:25
Jedaiah's **d** of the house of	Neh 7:39
Immer's **d** 1,052	Neh 7:40
Pashhur's **d** 1,247	Neh 7:41
Harim's **d** 1,017	Neh 7:42
included⌋: Jeshua's **d**: of	Neh 7:43
of Kadmiel Hodevah's **d** 74	Neh 7:43
singers ⌊included⌋: Asaph's **d**	Neh 7:44
Shallum's **d**, Ater's descendants,	Neh 7:45
descendants, Ater's **d**, Talmon's	Neh 7:45
Talmon's **d**, Akkub's descendants	Neh 7:45
descendants, Akkub's **d**, Hatita's	Neh 7:45
Hatita's **d**, Shobai's descendants	Neh 7:45
descendants, Shobai's **d** 138	Neh 7:45
Ziha's **d**, Hasupha's descendants,	Neh 7:46
Hasupha's **d**, Tabbaoth's	Neh 7:46
descendants, Tabbaoth's **d**,	Neh 7:46
Keros's **d**, Sia's descendants,	Neh 7:47
descendants, Sia's **d**, Padon's	Neh 7:47
Sia's descendants, Padon's **d**,	Neh 7:47
d, Hagaba's descendants,	Neh 7:48
Hagaba's **d**, Shalmai's	Neh 7:48
descendants, Shalmai's **d**,	Neh 7:48
Hanan's **d**, Giddel's descendants,	Neh 7:49
Giddel's **d**, Gahar's descendants	Neh 7:49
Giddel's descendants, Gahar's **d**,	Neh 7:49
Reaiah's **d**, Rezin's descendants,	Neh 7:50
descendants, Rezin's **d**, Nekoda's	Neh 7:50
Rezin's descendants, Nekoda's **d**,	Neh 7:50
Gazzam's **d**, Uzza's descendants,	Neh 7:51
descendants, Uzza's **d**, Paseah's	Neh 7:51
Uzza's descendants, Paseah's **d**,	Neh 7:51
Besai's **d**, Meunim's descendants,	Neh 7:52
Meunim's **d**, Nephishesim's	Neh 7:52
descendants, Nephishesim's **d**,	Neh 7:52
Bakbuk's **d**, Hakupha's	Neh 7:53
Hakupha's **d**, Harhur's	Neh 7:53
descendants, Harhur's **d**,	Neh 7:53
Bazlith's **d**, Mehida's	Neh 7:54
Mehida's **d**, Harsha's descendants	Neh 7:54
descendants, Harsha's **d**,	Neh 7:54
d, Sisera's descendants,	Neh 7:55
Sisera's **d**, Temah's descendants	Neh 7:55
Sisera's descendants, Temah's **d**,	Neh 7:55
Neziah's **d**, Hatipha's	Neh 7:56
descendants, Hatipha's **d**.	Neh 7:56
The **d** of Solomon's servants	Neh 7:57
Sotai's **d**, Sophereth's	Neh 7:57
Sophereth's **d**, Perida's	Neh 7:57
descendants, Perida's **d**,	Neh 7:57
Jaala's **d**, Darkon's descendants,	Neh 7:58
Darkon's **d**, Giddel's descendants	Neh 7:58
descendants, Giddel's **d**,	Neh 7:58
Shephatiah's **d**, Hattil's	Neh 7:59
descendants, Hattil's **d**,	Neh 7:59
d, Amon's descendants.	Neh 7:59
descendants, Amon's **d**.	Neh 7:59
servants and the **d** of Solomon's	Neh 7:60
Delaiah's **d**, Tobiah's	Neh 7:62
Tobiah's **d**, and Nekoda's	Neh 7:62
descendants, and Nekoda's **d** 642	Neh 7:62
d of Hobaiah, the descendants	Neh 7:63
of Hobaiah, the **d** of Hakkoz,	Neh 7:63
Hakkoz, and the **d** of Barzillai—	Neh 7:63
to give it to his **d**.	Neh 9:8
multiplied their **d** like the	Neh 9:23
So their **d** went in and possessed	Neh 9:24
and **d** of Solomon's servants—	Neh 11:3
while some of the **d** of Judah and	Neh 11:4
Judah's **d**: Athaiah son	Neh 11:4
son of Mahalalel, of Perez's **d**;	Neh 11:4
The total number of Perez's **d**,	Neh 11:6
These were Benjamin's **d**:	Neh 11:7
of Mica, of the **d** of Asaph, who	Neh 11:22
of the **d** of Zerah son of Judah,	Neh 11:24

Some of Judah's **d** lived in Neh 11:25
Benjamin's **d**: from Geba, Neh 11:31
Levi's **d**, the leaders of Neh 12:23
portions for the **d** of Aaron. Neh 12:47
themselves, their **d**, and all who Est 9:27
will not fade from their **d**. Est 9:28
and their **d** to the practices Est 9:31
many and your **d** like the grass Jb 5:25
no children or **d** among his Jb 18:19
alive, and their **d**, before their Jb 21:8
his **d** will never have enough Jb 27:14
to David and his **d** forever. Ps 18:50
will wipe their **d** from the earth Ps 21:10
All you **d** of Jacob, honor Him! Ps 22:23
All you **d** of Israel, revere Him! Ps 22:23
D will serve Him; Ps 22:30
and his **d** will inherit the land. Ps 25:13
The **d** of His servants will Ps 69:36
the **d** of Jacob and Joseph. Ps 77:15
saying, "Return, **d** of Adam." Ps 90:3
servant, Jacob's **d**—His chosen Ps 105:6
disperse their **d** among the Ps 106:27
the line of his **d** be cut off; Ps 109:13
His **d** will be powerful in the Ps 112:2
one of your **d** on your throne. Ps 132:11
d and the offshoots—all the Is 22:24
'Some of your **d** who come from Is 39:7
will bring your **d** from the east, Is 43:5
Spirit on your **d** and My blessing Is 44:3
I did not say to the **d** of Jacob: Is 45:19
All the **d** of Israel will be Is 45:25
Your **d** would have been as Is 48:19
and your **d** will dispossess Is 54:3
Their **d** will be known among the Is 61:9
I will produce **d** from Jacob, Is 65:9
by the LORD along with their **d**. Is 65:23
brothers, all the **d** of Ephraim. Jr 7:15
Why are he and his **d** hurled out Jr 22:28
None of his **d** will succeed in Jr 22:30
and led the **d** of the house Jr 23:8
the Nehelamite and his **d**. Jr 29:32
even one of his ⌊**d**⌋ living among Jr 29:32
far away, your **d**, from the land Jr 30:10
also Israel's **d** will cease to be Jr 31:36
all of Israel's **d** because of all Jr 31:37
the good of⌋ their **d** after them, Jr 32:39
I will make the **d** of My servant Jr 33:22
taking from his **d** rulers over Jr 33:26
rulers over the **d** of Abraham, Jr 33:26
punish him, his **d**, and his Jr 36:31
you from far away and your **d**, Jr 46:27
His **d** will be destroyed along Jr 49:10
oath to the **d** of Jacob's house Ezk 20:5
and your **d** will fall by the Ezk 23:25
and your **d** will be consumed by Ezk 23:25
them, from the **d** of Judah, were Dn 1:6
of heaven, but not to his **d**; Dn 11:4
I am going to rebuke your **d**, Mal 2:3
cut off any **d** from the tents Mal 2:12
you **d** of Jacob have not been Mal 3:6
to Abraham and his **d** forever. Lk 1:55
"We are **d** of Abraham," they Jn 8:33
I know you are **d** of Abraham, Jn 8:37
seat one of his **d** on his throne. Ac 2:30
and to his **d** after him, even Ac 7:5
His **d** would be strangers in a Ac 7:6
From this man's **d**, according to Ac 13:23
Abraham or to his **d** that he Rm 4:13
to guarantee it to all the **d**— Rm 4:16
So will your **d** be. Rm 4:18
because they are Abraham's **d**. Rm 9:7

DESCENDED *(32)*

and great darkness **d** on him. Gn 15:12
As Moses **d** from Mount Sinai— Ex 34:29
his hands as he **d** the mountain— Ex 34:29
Then the LORD **d** in the cloud and Nm 11:25
Then the LORD **d** in a pillar of Nm 12:5
Anak were **d** from the Nephilim. Nm 13:33
the Spirit of God **d** on him, Nm 24:2
Chesalon), **d** to Beth-shemesh, Jos 15:10
It then **d** westward to the border Jos 16:3
From Janoah it **d** to Ataroth and Jos 16:7
there the border **d** to the Brook Jos 17:9
The border **d** to the foot of the Jos 18:16
He, too, was **d** from the giant. 2Sm 21:20
These four were **d** from the giant 2Sm 21:22
10 steps it had **d** on Ahaz's 2Kg 20:11
and Eshtaolites **d** from these. 1Ch 2:53
He, too, was **d** from the giant. 1Ch 20:6
fire **d** from heaven and consumed 2Ch 7:1
when the fire **d** and the glory 2Ch 7:3
and the Levites **d** from Asaph, Ezr 3:10
went back the 10 steps it had **d**. Is 38:8
Israel and have **d** from Judah, Is 48:1
They too **d** with it to Sheol, Ezk 31:17
Levitical priests **d** from Zadok, Ezk 44:15
angel of the Lord **d** from heaven Mt 28:2
and the Holy Spirit **d** on Him in Lk 3:22
the One who **d** from heaven— Jn 3:13
all who are **d** from Israel are Rm 9:6
except that He **d** to the lower Eph 4:9
The One who **d** is the same as the Eph 4:10
from the dead, **d** from David, 2Tm 2:8
they have ⌊also⌋ **d** from Abraham. Heb 7:5

DESCENDENTS *(1)*

All your **d** will die violently. 1Sm 2:33

DESCENDING *(8)*

in my death, in my **d** to the Pit? Ps 30:9
any of those **d** into the silence Ps 115:17
d to the chambers of death. Pr 7:27
the Spirit of God **d** like a dove Mt 3:16
and the Spirit **d** to Him like a Mk 1:10
the Spirit **d** from heaven like Jn 1:32
you see the Spirit **d** and resting Jn 1:33
ascending and **d** on the Son of Jn 1:51

DESCENDS *(1)*

night, when deep sleep **d** on men, Jb 4:13

DESCENT *(10)*

striking them down on the **d**. Jos 7:5
sky along the **d** of Beth-horon Jos 10:11
Those of Israelite **d** separated Neh 9:2
of Aaronic **d** must accompany Neh 10:38
those of mixed **d** from Israel. Neh 13:3
and on the **d** to Horonaim will be Jr 48:5
my countrymen by physical **d**. Rm 9:3
by physical **d**, came the Messiah Rm 9:5
by physical **d** who are God's Rm 9:8
concerning physical **d** but based Heb 7:16

DESCRIBE *(5)*

I will **d** what I have seen, Jb 15:17
d the temple to the house of Ezk 43:10
what parable can we use to **d** it? Mk 4:30
they began to **d** what had Lk 24:35
Who will **d** His generation? Ac 8:33

DESCRIBED *(6)*

and **d** it by towns in a document Jos 18:9
He **d** trees, from the cedar in 1Kg 4:33
Then Haman **d** for them his Est 5:11
next the north ⌊is **d**⌋. Ezk 40:19
eyewitnesses **d** to them what had Mk 5:16
and not to be **d** as being in the Heb 7:11

DESCRIBING *(1)*

Barnabas and Paul **d** all the Ac 15:12

DESCRIPTION *(4)*

write a **d** of it for the purpose Jos 18:4
have written a **d** of the seven Jos 18:6
to write down a **d** of the land, Jos 18:8
land, write a **d** of it, and Jos 18:8

DESECRATE *(6)*

or he will **d** the sanctuary of Lv 21:12
He is not to **d** My sanctuaries, Lv 21:23
to **d** all ⌊its⌋ glorious beauty, Is 23:9
I am about to **d** My sanctuary, Ezk 24:21
will rise up and **d** the temple Dn 11:31
He even tried to **d** the temple, Ac 24:6

DESECRATED *(4)*

utterly **d** the dwelling place Ps 74:7
inheritance, **d** Your holy temple Ps 79:1
will lie in ruins and be **d**, Ezk 6:6
My sanctuary when it was **d**, Ezk 25:3

DESECRATING *(3)*

keeps the Sabbath without **d** it, Is 56:2
keep the Sabbath without **d** it, Is 56:6
If you keep from **d** the Sabbath, Is 58:13

DESERT *(72)*

there on the **d** surface were fine Ex 16:14
owl, the **d** owl, the osprey, Lv 11:18
the **d** owl, the osprey, the Dt 14:17
the slopes, the **d**, and the Negev Jos 12:8
on the road that leads to the **d**. 2Sm 15:23
exhausted to drink in the **d**." 2Sm 16:2
and thirsty in the **d**." 2Sm 17:29
the edge of the **d** that extends 1Ch 5:9
Bezer in the **d** and its 1Ch 6:78
at his stronghold in the **d**. 1Ch 12:8
which Moses made in the **d**, 1Ch 21:29
towers in the **d** and dug many 2Ch 26:10
swept in from the **d** and struck Jb 1:19
go up into the **d**, and perish. Jb 6:18
Like wild donkeys in the **d**, Jb 24:5
⌊on⌋ a **d** with no human life, Jb 38:26
when You marched through the **d**, Ps 68:7
d tribes kneel before him and Ps 72:9
him to the creatures of the **d**. Ps 74:14
the east, the west, or the **d**; Ps 75:6
in the **d** against the Most Ps 78:17
and grieved Him in the **d**. Ps 78:40
I am like a **d** owl, like an owl Ps 102:6
flowed like a stream in the **d**. Ps 105:41
the depths as through a **d**. Ps 106:9
and tested God in the **d**. Ps 106:14
He would make them fall in the **d** Ps 106:26
rivers into **d**, springs of water Ps 107:33
He turns a **d** into a pool of Ps 107:35
Sela in the **d** to the mountain Is 16:1
as Jazer and spread to the **d**. Is 16:8
oracle against the **d** by the sea: Is 21:1
comes from the **d**, from the land Is 21:1
in the scrublands of the **d**, Is 21:13
Then the **d** will become an Is 32:15
Sharon is like a **d**; Bashan and Is 33:9
The **d** owl and the hedgehog will Is 34:11
the **d** will rejoice and blossom Is 35:1
and streams in the **d**; Is 35:6
highway for our God in the **d**. Is 40:3
I will turn the **d** into a pool of Is 41:18
I will plant cedars in the **d**, Is 41:19
will put cypress trees in the **d**, Is 41:19
Let the **d** and its cities shout, Is 42:11
the wilderness, rivers in the **d**. Is 43:19
rivers in the **d**, to give drink Is 43:20
and her **d** like the garden of the Is 51:3
highways like a nomad in the **d**. Jr 3:2
chaff before the **d** wind. Jr 13:24
who have settled in the **d**; Jr 25:24
d creatures will live with Jr 50:39
Drunkards from the **d** were Ezk 23:42
I will leave you in the **d**, Ezk 29:5
make her like a **d** and like a Hs 2:3
the LORD rising up from the **d**. Hs 13:15
them, it is like a **d** wasteland; Jl 2:3
and Edom a **d** wasteland, because Jl 3:19
a desolate ruin, dry as the **d**. Zph 2:13
Both the **d** owl and the screech Zph 2:14
inheritance to the **d** jackals." Mal 1:3
to him in the **d** of Mount Sinai, Ac 7:30
and in the **d** for 40 years. Ac 7:36
in the **d** together with Ac 7:38
for 40 years in the **d**, Ac 7:42
of the testimony in the **d**, Ac 7:44
down from Jerusalem to **d** Gaza." Ac 8:26
He put up with them in the **d**; Ac 13:18
led 4,000 Assassins into the **d**?" Ac 21:38
they were struck down in the **d**. 1Co 10:5
on the day of testing in the **d**, Heb 3:8
whose bodies fell in the **d**? Heb 3:17
me away in the Spirit to a **d**. Rv 17:3

DESERTED *(34)*

numbers until your roads are **d**. Lv 26:22
have not **d** your brothers even Jos 22:3
main ways were **d**, because Jdg 5:6
Villages were **d**, they were Jdg 5:7
they were **d** in Israel, until I Jdg 5:7
the men of Israel **d** David and 2Sm 20:2
homes for those who are **d**. Ps 68:6
d, she will sit on the ground. Is 3:26
the fortified city will be **d**, Is 27:10
The highways are **d**; Is 33:8
like a wife **d** and wounded in Is 54:6
I **d** you for a brief moment, Is 54:7
of your being **d** and hated, Is 60:15
You will no longer be called **D**, Is 62:4
called Cared For, A City Not **D**. Is 62:12
I have **d** My inheritance. Jr 12:7
who have **d** to the Chaldeans Jr 38:19
into the mire, and they **d** you. Jr 38:22
All her gates are **d**; Lm 1:4
city like ⌊other⌋ **d** cities, Ezk 26:19
troubled him, and sleep **d** him. Dn 2:1
Isaac's high places will be **d**, Am 7:9
the disciples **d** Him and ran away Mt 26:56

and made His way to a **d** place. Mk 1:35
But He was out in **d** places, Mk 1:45
they all **d** Him and ran away. Mk 14:50
and made His way to a **d** place. Lk 4:42
withdrew to **d** places and prayed Lk 5:16
by the demon into **d** places. Lk 8:29
we are in a **d** place here." Lk 9:12
this man who had **d** them in Ac 15:38
for Demas has **d** me, because he 2Tm 4:10
assistance, but everyone **d** me. 2Tm 4:16
own position but **d** their proper Jd 6

DESERTERS *(3)*
the **d** who had defected to the 2Kg 25:11
and those **d** who had defected Jr 39:9
the **d** who had defected to the Jr 52:15

DESERTING *(5)*
and the troops were **d** him. 1Sm 13:8
the troops were **d** me and you 1Sm 13:11
"You are **d** to the Chaldeans." Jr 37:13
"I am not **d** to the Chaldeans!" Jr 37:14
of the Jews were **d** them and Jn 12:11

DESERTS *(4)*
when He led them through the **d**; Is 48:21
through a land of **d** and ravines, Jr 2:6
shepherd who **d** the flock! Zch 11:17
They wandered in **d**, mountains, Heb 11:38

DESERVE *(22)*
Yet he did not **d** to die, since Dt 19:6
all of you **d** to die since you 1Sm 26:16
Even though you **d** to die, I will 1Kg 2:26
than our sins ⌊**d**⌋ and have Ezr 9:13
give them back what they **d**. Ps 28:4
repay the proud what they **d**. Ps 94:2
us as our sins **d** or repaid us Ps 103:10
a good man, what his ⌊deeds **d**.⌋ Pr 14:14
the actions of the wicked **d**, Ec 8:14
the actions of the righteous **d**. Ec 8:14
back His enemies what they **d**! Is 66:6
It is what You **d**. For among all Jr 10:7
according to what his actions **d**. Jr 17:10
This man doesn't **d** the death Jr 26:16
who do not **d** to drink the cup Jr 49:12
will pay them back what they **d**, Lm 3:64
what you **d** will return on your Ob 15
He has done nothing to **d** death. Lk 23:15
back what we **d** for the things we Lk 23:41
practice such things **d** to die— Rm 1:32
one will **d** who has trampled Heb 10:29
them blood to drink; they **d** it! Rv 16:6

DESERVED *(2)*
yet I did not get what I **d**. Jb 33:27
Their condemnation is **d**! Rm 3:8

DESERVES *(11)*
guilty party **d** to be flogged, Dt 25:2
bring him to me—he **d** to die." 1Sm 20:31
the man who did this **d** to die! 2Sm 12:5
entire family **d** death from my 2Sm 19:28
deal with you as your folly **d**. Jb 42:8
will get what their conduct **d**, Pr 14:14
This man **d** the death sentence Jr 26:11
He will pay her what she **d**. Jr 51:6
They answered, "He **d** death!" Mt 26:66
nothing that **d** death or chains. Ac 26:31
and **d** full acceptance 1Tm 4:9

DESERVING *(9)*
an offense **d** the death penalty Dt 21:22
guilty of an offense **d** death. Dt 22:26
would be a crime **d** punishment. Jb 31:11
also be a crime **d** punishment, Jb 31:28
condemned Him to be **d** of death. Mk 14:64
and did things **d** of blows will Lk 12:48
have done anything **d** of death, Ac 25:11
not done anything **d** of death, Ac 25:25
trustworthy and **d** of full 1Tm 1:15

DESIGN *(18)*
the **d** of the tabernacle as well Ex 25:9
as well as the **d** of all its Ex 25:9
with a **d** of cherubim worked into Ex 26:1
spun linen with a **d** of cherubim Ex 26:31
to **d** artistic works in gold, Ex 31:4
to **d** artistic works in gold, Ex 35:32
of craft and **d** artistic designs Ex 35:35
with a **d** of cherubim worked into Ex 36:8
He made it with a **d** of cherubim Ex 36:35
the fine linen in a skillful **d**. Ex 39:3
This was the **d** of the carts: 1Kg 7:28
wheels' **d** was similar to that 1Kg 7:33
to execute any **d** that may be 2Ch 2:14
each with a different **d**. Est 1:7
Reveal the **d** of the temple to Ezk 43:11
complete **d** along with all its Ezk 43:11
its statutes, **d** specifications, Ezk 43:11
its complete **d** and all its Ezk 43:11

DESIGNATE *(1)*
d cities to serve as cities of Nm 35:11

DESIGNATED *(9)*
who is a slave **d** for ⌊another⌋ Lv 19:20
offerings, each on its ⌊**d**⌋ day. Lv 23:37
men who had been **d** by name, Nm 1:17
So they **d** Kedesh in the hill Jos 20:7
18,000 **d** by name to come and 1Ch 12:31
chosen and **d** by name to give 1Ch 16:41
the men who were **d** by name took 2Ch 28:15
those the king had **d** went to the 2Ch 34:22
were **d** for this judgment long Jd 4

DESIGNED *(3)*
you not heard? I **d** it long ago; 2Kg 19:25
He made skillfully **d** devices in 2Ch 26:15
you not heard? I **d** it long ago; Is 37:26

DESIGNER *(2)*
gem cutter; a **d**; an embroiderer Ex 35:35
a gem cutter, a **d**, and an Ex 38:23

DESIGNS *(1)*
of craft and design artistic **d**. Ex 35:35

DESIRABLE *(11)*
and that it was **d** for obtaining Gn 3:6
shields, and every **d** item. 2Ch 32:27
They are more **d** than gold— Ps 19:10
and nothing **d** can compare with Pr 8:11
He is absolutely **d**. Sg 5:16
day sing about a **d** vineyard: Is 27:2
My⌋ sons and give you a **d** land, Jr 3:19
They have turned My **d** plot into Jr 12:10
of them **d** young men, horsemen Ezk 23:6
steeds, all of them **d** young men. Ezk 23:12
with them—**d** young men, all Ezk 23:23

DESIRE *(81)*
Your **d** will be for your husband, Gn 3:16
Its **d** is for you, but you must Gn 4:7
My **d** will be gratified at their Ex 15:9
Do not **d** your neighbor's wife or Dt 5:21
you have a strong **d** to eat meat, Dt 12:20
wine, beer, or anything you **d**. Dt 14:26
the captives, **d** her, and want to Dt 21:11
does all Israel **d** but you and 1Sm 9:20
can do to him whatever you **d**.'" 1Sm 24:4
you will rule over all you **d**." 2Sm 3:21
whatever you **d** from me I will 2Sm 19:38
salvation and ⌊my⌋ every **d**? 2Sm 23:5
It was in the **d** of my father 1Kg 8:17
it was your **d** to build a temple 1Kg 8:18
have done well to have this **d**. 1Kg 8:18
the queen of Sheba her every **d**— 1Kg 10:13
keep this **d** forever in the 1Ch 29:18
it was your **d** to build a temple 2Ch 6:8
have done well to have this **d**. 2Ch 6:8
the queen of Sheba her every **d**, 2Ch 9:12
my people—[this is] my **d**. Est 7:3
have heard the **d** of the humble; Ps 10:17
him his heart's **d** and have not Ps 21:2
LORD; it is what I **d**: to dwell Ps 27:4
my every **d** is known to You; Ps 38:9
over to the **d** of his enemies. Ps 41:2
and the king will **d** your beauty. Ps 45:11
Surely You **d** integrity in the Ps 51:6
I **d** nothing on earth but You. Ps 73:25
they had satisfied their **d**, Ps 78:30
The **d** of the wicked will come to Ps 112:10
satisfy the **d** of every living Ps 145:16
nothing you **d** compares with her. Pr 3:15
The **d** of the righteous ⌊turns Pr 11:23
The wicked **d** what evil men have, Pr 12:12
but fulfilled **d** is a tree of Pr 13:12
D fulfilled is sweet to the Pr 13:19
A man's **d** should be loyalty to Pr 19:22
don't **d** his choice food, for Pr 23:3
and don't **d** his choice food, Pr 23:6
evil men or **d** to be with them Pr 24:1
wine or for rulers ⌊to **d**⌋ beer. Pr 31:4
the eyes see than wandering **d**. Ec 6:9
with the **d**⌋ to commit crime Ec 8:11
my **d** put me ⌊among⌋ the chariots Sg 6:12
to my love, and his **d** is for me. Sg 7:10
I have no **d** for the blood of Is 1:11
and who have no **d** for gold. Is 13:17
Our **d** is for Your name and Is 26:8
appearance that we should **d** Him. Is 53:2
the wind in the heat of her **d**. Jr 2:24
pursue their **d** for detestable Ezk 11:21
you over to the **d** of those who Ezk 16:27
eyes, and the **d** of your heart. Ezk 24:21
For I **d** loyalty and not Hs 6:6
man communicates his evil **d**, Mc 7:3
of the covenant you **d**— Mal 3:1
I **d** mercy and not sacrifice. Mt 9:13
I **d** mercy and not sacrifice, Mt 12:7
d those You have given Me to be Jn 17:24
For the **d** to do what is good is Rm 7:18
my heart's **d** and prayer to God Rm 10:1
to marry than to burn with **d**. 1Co 7:9
we will not **d** evil as they did 1Co 10:6
But **d** the greater gifts. 1Co 12:31
love and **d** spiritual gifts 1Co 14:1
what a **d** to clear yourselves, 2Co 7:11
do something but also to **d** it. 2Co 8:10
as there was eagerness to **d** it, 2Co 8:11
carry out the **d** of the flesh. Gl 5:16
impurity with a **d** for more and Eph 4:19
I have the **d** to depart and be Php 1:23
lust, evil **d**, and greed, which Col 3:5
fulfill every **d** for goodness and 2Th 1:11
are drawn away from Christ by **d**, 1Tm 5:11
You did not **d** or delight in Heb 10:8
Then after **d** has conceived, Jms 1:15
You **d** and do not have. Jms 4:2
Angels **d** to look into these 1Pt 1:12
d the unadulterated spiritual 1Pt 2:2
for and earnestly **d** the coming 2Pt 3:12

DESIRED *(16)*
and do whatever the king **d**. 2Sm 19:18
and all that Solomon **d** to do, 1Kg 9:1
and whatever Solomon **d** to build 1Kg 9:19
Whoever so **d** it, he ordained, 1Kg 13:33
everything Solomon **d** to build in 2Ch 8:6
unless he **d** her and summoned her Est 2:14
mountain God **d** for His dwelling Ps 68:16
He has **d** it for His home: Ps 132:13
home here because I have **d** it. Ps 132:14
that my eyes **d**, I did not deny Ec 2:10
of the sacred trees you **d**, Is 1:29
place where you **d** to go to live Jr 42:22
I have fervently **d** to eat this Lk 22:15
and Saul and **d** to hear God's Ac 13:7
I have strongly **d** for many years Rm 15:23
we greatly **d** and made every 1Th 2:17

DESIRES *(40)*
'The king **d** no other bride-price 1Sm 18:25
he does not escape his **d**. Jb 20:20
oppose Him? He does what He **d**. Jb 23:13
what your heart **d** and fulfill Ps 20:4
He will give you your heart's **d**. Ps 37:4
not grant the **d** of the wicked; Ps 140:8
He fulfills the **d** of those who Ps 145:19
the righteous **d** will be given to Pr 10:24
are trapped by their own **d**. Pr 11:6
himself pursues ⌊selfish⌋ **d**; Pr 18:1
A wicked person **d** evil; Pr 21:10
nothing of all he **d** for himself, Ec 6:2
back to the **d** of his heart. Is 57:17
to whom the Son **d** to reveal Him. Mt 11:27
and the **d** for other things enter Mk 4:19
whom the Son **d** to reveal Him." Lk 10:22
to carry out your father's **d**. Jn 8:44
body, so that you obey its **d**. Rm 6:12
plans to satisfy the fleshly **d**. Rm 13:14
For the flesh **d** what is against Gl 5:17
and the Spirit **d** what is against Gl 5:17
flesh with its passions and **d**. Gl 5:24
among them in our fleshly **d**, Eph 2:3
is corrupted by deceitful **d**; Eph 4:22
not with lustful **d**, like the 1Th 4:5
an overseer, he **d** a noble work." 1Tm 3:1
and many foolish and harmful **d**, 1Tm 6:9
but according to their own **d**, 2Tm 4:3
and enticed by his own evil **d**. Jms 1:14
spend it on your **d** for pleasure. Jms 4:3
conformed to the **d** of your 1Pt 1:14
from fleshly **d** that war against 1Pt 2:11
longer for human **d**, but for 1Pt 4:2
behavior, evil **d**, drunkenness, 1Pt 4:3

in the world because of evil **d**. 2Pt 1:4
the polluting **d** of the flesh 2Pt 2:10
by fleshly **d** and debauchery, 2Pt 2:18
walking according to their **d**; Jd 16
to their own ungodly **d**." Jd 18
Whoever **d** should take the living Rv 22:17

DESIRING *(1)*
d to display His wrath and to Rm 9:22

DESOLATE *(85)*
that the land won't become **d**." Gn 47:19
would become **d**, and wild animals Ex 23:29
their wrongdoings into a **d** land, Lv 16:22
So your land will become **d**, Lv 26:33
during the time it lies **d**, Lv 26:34
long as it lies **d**, it will have Lv 26:35
Sabbaths by lying **d** without the Lv 26:43
found him in a **d** land, in a Dt 32:10
a permanent ruin, **d** to this day. Jos 8:28
Tamar lived as a **d** woman in the 2Sm 13:20
the dry land, the **d** wasteland by Jb 30:3
me evil for good, making me **d**. Ps 35:12
He brought me up from a **d** pit, Ps 40:2
land that is dry, **d**, and without Ps 63:1
Make their fortification **d**; Ps 69:25
wandered in the **d** wilderness, Ps 107:4
Your land is **d**, your cities Is 1:7
many houses will become **d**, Is 5:9
the land is ruined and **d**, Is 6:11
The waters of Nimrim are **d**; Is 15:6
the earth bare and making it **d**. Is 24:1
It will be **d**, from generation to Is 34:10
them possess the **d** inheritances, Is 49:8
your waste and **d** places and your Is 49:19
and inhabit the **d** cities. Is 54:3
your land will not be called **D**; Is 62:4
the land will become a **d** waste. Jr 7:34
cities of Judah will be made **d**, Jr 10:22
him off and made his homeland **d**. Jr 10:25
plot into a **d** wasteland. Jr 12:10
It mourns, **d**, before Me. Jr 12:11
All the land is **d**, but no one Jr 12:11
make this city **d**, an object of Jr 19:8
whole land will become a **d** ruin, Jr 25:11
to make them a **d** ruin, an object Jr 25:18
In this **d** place—without man or Jr 33:12
they became the **d** ruin they are Jr 44:6
waters of Nimrim have become **d**. Jr 48:34
will become a **d** mound, and its Jr 49:2
will be made **d** because of them. Jr 49:20
it will make her land **d**. Jr 50:3
will be made **d** because of them. Jr 50:45
you will become **d** forever. Jr 51:26
it will remain **d** forever.' Jr 51:62
He made me **d**, sick all day long. Lm 1:13
My children are **d** because the Lm 1:16
tore me to pieces; He left me **d**. Lm 3:11
which lies **d** ⌊and has⌋ jackals Lm 5:18
and the high places will be **d**, Ezk 6:6
I will make the land a **d** waste, Ezk 6:14
it so that it becomes **d**, Ezk 14:15
but the land would be **d**. Ezk 14:16
make the land **d** because they Ezk 15:8
land of Egypt will be a **d** ruin. Ezk 29:9
a **d** waste from Migdol to Syene, Ezk 29:10
a desolation among **d** lands, Ezk 29:12
They will be **d** among desolate Ezk 30:7
will be desolate among **d** lands, Ezk 30:7
make Pathros **d**, set fire to Zoan Ezk 30:14
I will make the land a **d** waste, Ezk 33:28
of Israel will become **d**, Ezk 33:28
make the land a **d** waste because Ezk 33:29
you and make you a **d** waste. Ezk 35:3
Mount Seir a **d** waste and will Ezk 35:7
They are **d**. They have been Ezk 35:12
have made you **d** and have Ezk 36:3
to the **d** ruins and abandoned Ezk 36:4
The **d** land will be cultivated Ezk 36:34
instead of lying **d** in the sight Ezk 36:34
land that was **d** has become like Ezk 36:35
once ruined, **d**, and destroyed Ezk 36:35
and have replanted what was **d**. Ezk 36:36
the rebellion that makes **d**, Dn 8:13
favor to Your **d** sanctuary for Dn 9:17
banish him to a dry and **d** land, Jl 2:20
Egypt will become **d**, and Edom a Jl 3:19
will make you a **d** place and the Mc 6:16
He will make Nineveh a **d** ruin, Zph 2:13
the land was left **d** behind them, Zch 7:14
bread in this **d** place to fill Mt 15:33
your house is left to you **d**. Mt 23:38
here in this **d** place to fill Mk 8:4
Let his dwelling become **d**; Ac 1:20
the children of the **d** are many, Gl 4:27
They will make her **d** and naked, Rv 17:16

DESOLATED *(1)*
will be **d** and your incense Ezk 6:4

DESOLATION *(53)*
We caused **d** as far as Nophah, Nm 21:30
would become a **d** and a curse, 2Kg 22:19
the days of the **d** until 70 years 2Ch 36:21
How suddenly they become a **d**! Ps 73:19
a **d** overthrown by foreigners. Is 1:7
the earth a **d** and to destroy Is 13:9
the Israelites; there will be **d**. Is 17:9
Only **d** remains in the city; Is 24:12
a wilderness, Jerusalem a **d**. Is 64:10
The whole land will be a **d**, Jr 4:27
will make you a **d**, a land devoid Jr 6:8
make the cities of Judah a **d**, Jr 9:11
They have made it a **d**. Jr 12:11
destroy them and make them a **d**, Jr 25:9
land has become a **d** because of Jr 25:38
a curse and a **d**, an object of Jr 29:18
It's a **d** without man or beast; Jr 32:43
that are a **d** without man, Jr 33:10
I will make Judah's cities a **d**, Jr 34:22
a waste, a **d**, and an object Jr 44:22
For Memphis will become a **d**, Jr 46:19
her towns will become a **d**, Jr 48:9
will become a **d**, a disgrace, a Jr 49:13
Edom will become a **d**. Jr 49:17
a jackals' den, a **d** forever. Jr 49:33
will become a **d**, every bit of Jr 50:13
of Babylon an uninhabited **d**. Jr 51:29
a **d** and an object of scorn, Jr 51:37
Her cities have become a **d**, Jr 51:43
and the land will become a **d**. Ezk 12:20
with a cup of devastation and **d**, Ezk 23:33
land of Egypt a **d** among desolate Ezk 29:12
cities will be a **d** among ruined Ezk 29:12
I will bring **d** on the land and Ezk 30:12
I make the land of Egypt a **d**, Ezk 32:15
ruins, and you will become a **d**. Ezk 35:4
I will make you a perpetual **d**; Ezk 35:9
rejoices, I will make you a **d**. Ezk 35:14
of Israel because it became a **d**, Ezk 35:15
you will become a **d**, Mount Seir, Ezk 35:15
of years for the **d** of Jerusalem Dn 9:2
abomination of **d** will be on a Dn 9:27
and set up the abomination of **d**. Dn 11:31
the abomination of **d** is set up, Dn 12:11
will become a **d** on the day Hs 5:9
bringing **d** because of your sins. Mc 6:13
D, decimation, devastation! Nah 2:10
a day of destruction and **d**, Zph 1:15
What a **d** she has become, a place Zph 2:15
a pleasant land into a **d**." Zch 7:14
the abomination that causes **d**, Mt 24:15
that causes **d** standing where it Mk 13:14
that its **d** has come near. Lk 21:20

DESOLATIONS *(2)*
eyes and see our **d** and the city Dn 9:18
will be war; **d** are decreed. Dn 9:26

DESOLATOR *(1)*
is poured out on the **d**." Dn 9:27

DESPAIR *(7)*
He mocks the **d** of the innocent. Jb 9:23
broken my heart, and I am in **d**. Ps 69:20
he will gnash his teeth in **d**. Ps 112:10
myself over to **d** concerning all Ec 2:20
splendid clothes instead of **d**. Is 61:3
I will not hear their cry of **d**. Jr 14:12
we are perplexed but not in **d**; 2Co 4:8

DESPAIRED *(1)*
so that we even **d** of life. 2Co 1:8

DESPAIRING *(2)*
A **d** man should receive loyalty Jb 6:14
words or that a **d** man's words Jb 6:26

DESPERATE *(4)*
every man who was **d**, in debt, or 1Sm 22:2
He may do something **d**." 2Sm 12:18
and are **d** like a wild bear 2Sm 17:8
I suffer Your horrors; I am **d**. Ps 88:15

DESPERATELY *(2)*
while he flees **d** from its grasp. Jb 27:22
than anything else and **d** sick— Jr 17:9

DESPICABLE *(2)*
and his public speaking is **d**." 2Co 10:10
for every unclean and **d** beast. Rv 18:2

DESPISE *(36)*
My statutes and **d** My ordinances, Lv 26:15
How long will these people **d** Me? Nm 14:11
Do not **d** an Edomite, because he Dt 23:7
not **d** an Egyptian, because you Dt 23:7
all of you **d** My sacrifices and 1Sm 2:29
but those who **d** Me will be 1Sm 2:30
Why then do you **d** us? 2Sm 19:43
cause them to **d** their husbands Est 1:17
mud⌋, and my own clothes **d** me! Jb 9:31
All of my best friends **d** me, Jb 19:19
d me and keep their distance Jb 30:10
You will not **d** a broken and Ps 51:17
and does not **d** His own who are Ps 69:33
arising, You will **d** their image. Ps 73:20
and will not **d** their prayer. Ps 102:17
fools **d** wisdom and instruction. Pr 1:7
Do not **d** the LORD's instruction, Pr 3:11
People don't **d** the thief if he Pr 6:30
he will **d** the insight of your Pr 23:9
and don't **d** your mother when she Pr 23:22
offerings. I **d** ⌊your⌋ incense. Is 1:13
of Your name, don't **d** ⌊us⌋. Jr 14:21
on saying to those who **d** Me: Jr 23:17
All who honored her ⌊now⌋ **d** her, Lm 1:8
You **d** My holy things and profane Ezk 22:8
the city gate and **d** the one who Am 5:10
I hate, I **d** your feasts! Am 5:21
to you priests, who **d** My name." Mal 1:6
devoted to one and **d** the other. Mt 6:24
devoted to one and **d** the other. Lk 16:13
Or do you **d** the riches of His Rm 2:4
you did not **d** or reject me. Gl 4:14
Don't **d** prophecies, 1Th 5:20
No one should **d** your youth; 1Tm 4:12
of the flesh and **d** authority. 2Pt 2:10
defile their flesh, **d** authority, Jd 8

DESPISED *(49)*
So Esau **d** his birthright. Gn 25:34
those who have **d** Me will see it. Nm 14:23
because he has **d** the LORD's word Nm 15:31
that these men have **d** the LORD." Nm 16:30
⌊this⌋, He **d** ⌊them⌋, provoked Dt 32:19
Aren't these the people you **d**? Jdg 9:38
They **d** him and did not bring 1Sm 10:27
he **d** him because he was just a 1Sm 17:42
the blind who are **d** by David." 2Sm 5:8
and she **d** him in her heart. 2Sm 6:16
Why then have you **d** the 2Sm 12:9
house because you **d** Me and 2Sm 12:10
and she **d** him in her heart. 1Ch 15:29
they mocked and **d** us, and said, Neh 2:19
Listen, our God, for we are **d**. Neh 4:4
Why has the wicked **d** God? Ps 10:13
scorned by men and **d** by people. Ps 22:6
For He has not **d** or detested the Ps 22:24
They **d** the pleasant land and did Ps 106:24
God's commands and **d** the Ps 107:11
insignificant and **d**, but I do Ps 119:141
and how my heart **d** correction. Pr 5:12
but a twisted mind is **d**. Pr 12:8
the wisdom of the poor man is **d**, Ec 9:16
they have **d** the Holy One of Is 1:4
and they have **d** the word of the Is 5:24
has been broken, and cities **d**. Is 33:8
Holy One says to one who is **d**, Is 49:7
He was **d** and rejected by men, Is 53:3
He was **d**, and we didn't value Is 53:3
man Coniah a **d**, shattered pot, Jr 22:28
the nations, **d** among humanity. Jr 49:15
and see how I have become **d**. Lm 1:11
He has **d** king and priest in His Lm 2:6
because you were **d** on the day Ezk 16:5
who **d** her husband and children. Ezk 16:45
who **d** their husbands and Ezk 16:45
since you have **d** the oath by Ezk 16:59
whose oath he **d** and whose Ezk 17:16
He **d** the oath by breaking the Ezk 17:18
oath that he **d** and My covenant Ezk 17:19
In his place a **d** person will Dn 11:21
you will be deeply **d**. Ob 2
"How have we **d** Your name?" Mal 1:6

have made you **d** and humiliated — Mal 2:9
is The stone **d** by you builders, — Ac 4:11
Artemis may be **d** and her — Ac 19:27
insignificant and **d** things— — 1Co 1:28
endured a cross and **d** the shame, — Heb 12:2

DESPISES *(14)*

Daughter Zion, **d** you and scorns — 2Kg 19:21
and his soul ⌊**d** his⌋ favorite — Jb 33:20
is mighty, but He **d** ⌊no one⌋; — Jb 36:5
is greedy curses and **d** the LORD. — Ps 10:3
who **d** the one rejected by the — Ps 15:4
is devious in his ways **d** Him. — Pr 14:2
The one who **d** his neighbor sins, — Pr 14:21
A fool **d** his father's — Pr 15:5
but a foolish one **d** his mother. — Pr 15:20
ignores instruction **d** himself, — Pr 15:32
a father and **d** obedience to a — Pr 30:17
Daughter Zion, **d** you and scorns — Is 37:22
My son, the sword **d** every tree. — Ezk 21:10
if the sword **d** even the scepter — Ezk 21:13

DESPISING *(2)*

d Me and breaking My covenant. — Dt 31:20
God's messengers, **d** His words, — 2Ch 36:16

DESPITE *(6)*

not trust in Me **d** all the signs — Nm 14:11
His hand is heavy **d** my groaning. — Jb 23:2
But **d** ⌊his⌋ assets, man will not — Ps 49:12
D all this, they kept sinning — Ps 78:32
princes, who, **d** their strength, — Ezk 32:29
d the terror their strength — Ezk 32:30

DESPOILERS *(1)*

Your **d** will become spoil, and — Jr 30:16

DESPONDENT *(1)*

failing eyes, and a **d** spirit. — Dt 28:65

DESTINE *(2)*

I will **d** you for the sword, — Is 65:12
I will **d** you for bloodshed, — Ezk 35:6

DESTINED *(21)*

⌊**d**⌋ with you to eat their own — 2Kg 18:27
he is **d** for the sword. — Jb 15:22
houses **d** to become piles — Jb 15:28
they are **d** for the sword; — Jb 27:14
in Jerusalem who are **d** to live— — Is 4:3
against a people **d** for My rage, — Is 10:6
Assyria **d** it for wild beasts. — Is 23:13
are **d**⌋ with you to eat their — Is 36:12
bear children ⌊**d**⌋ for disaster, — Is 65:23
Those ⌊**d**⌋ for death, to death; — Jr 15:2
those ⌊**d**⌋ for the sword, to the — Jr 15:2
Those ⌊**d**⌋ for famine, to famine; — Jr 15:2
those ⌊**d**⌋ for captivity, to — Jr 15:2
Egypt—those ⌊**d**⌋ for death, to — Jr 43:11
those ⌊**d**⌋ for captivity, to — Jr 43:11
and those ⌊**d**⌋ for the sword, — Jr 43:11
You **d** them to cause punish ⌊us⌋. — Hab 1:12
child is **d** to cause the fall — Lk 2:34
was **d** before the foundation of — 1Pt 1:20
they were **d** for this. — 1Pt 2:8
If anyone is **d** for captivity, — Rv 13:10

DESTINY *(5)*

Such is the **d** of all who forget — Jb 8:13
Then I understood their **d**. — Ps 73:17
fill bowls of mixed wine for **D**, — Is 65:11
then rise to your **d** at the end — Dn 12:13
Their **d** will be according to — 2Co 11:15

DESTITUTE *(10)*

you have will become **d**." ' — Gn 45:11
brother becomes **d** and sells part — Lv 25:25
brother becomes **d** and cannot — Lv 25:35
you becomes **d** and sells himself — Lv 25:39
near him becomes **d** and sells — Lv 25:47
of the oppressed and the **d**. — Ps 82:3
the prayer of the **d** and will not — Ps 102:17
d leader who oppresses the poor — Pr 28:3
delicacies are **d** in the streets; — Lm 4:5
in goatskins, **d**, afflicted, — Heb 11:37

DESTROY *(224)*

I am going to **d** them along with — Gn 6:13
the earth to **d** all flesh under — Gn 6:17
be a deluge to **d** the earth." — Gn 9:11
become a deluge to **d** all flesh. — Gn 9:15
Will you **d** the whole city for — Gn 18:28
I will not **d** ⌊it⌋ if I find 45 — Gn 18:28
I will not **d** ⌊it⌋ on account of — Gn 18:31
I will not **d** ⌊it⌋ on account of — Gn 18:32
we are about to **d** this place — Gn 19:13
the LORD has sent us to **d** it." — Gn 19:13
LORD is about to **d** the city!" — Gn 19:14
would you **d** a nation even though — Gn 20:4
be among you to **d** ⌊you⌋ when I — Ex 12:13
my hand will **d** them." — Ex 15:9
against them and I can **d** them. — Ex 32:10
I might **d** you on the way." — Ex 33:3
a single moment, I would **d** you. — Ex 33:5
I will **d** among his people anyone — Lv 23:30
I will **d** your high places, — Lv 26:30
them so as to **d** them and break — Lv 26:44
them with a plague and **d** them. — Nm 14:12
will completely **d** their cities." — Nm 21:2
he will **d** the city's survivors. — Nm 24:19
that I did not **d** the Israelites — Nm 25:11
and you will **d** all of them." — Nm 32:15
d all their stone images and — Nm 33:52
the Amorites so they would **d** us, — Dt 1:27
not leave you, **d** you, or forget — Dt 4:31
you must completely **d** them. — Dt 7:2
and He will swiftly **d** you. — Dt 7:4
You must **d** all the peoples the — Dt 7:16
not be able to **d** them all at — Dt 7:22
LORD is about to **d** before you, — Dt 8:20
them out and **d** them swiftly, — Dt 9:3
angry enough with you to **d** you. — Dt 9:8
and I will **d** them and blot out — Dt 9:14
because He was about to **d** you. — Dt 9:19
enough with Aaron to **d** him. — Dt 9:20
LORD had threatened to **d** you. — Dt 9:25
D completely all the places — Dt 12:2
Completely **d** everyone in it as — Dt 13:15
You must completely **d** them— — Dt 20:17
you must not **d** its trees by — Dt 20:19
But you may **d** the trees that you — Dt 20:20
you to perish and to **d** you. — Dt 28:63
He will **d** these nations before — Dt 31:3
before you, and commands, "**D**!" — Dt 33:27
the land and to **d** all the — Jos 9:24
and completely **d** you, after He — Jos 24:20
Completely **d** every male, as well — Jdg 21:11
and completely **d** everything they — 1Sm 15:3
They were not willing to **d** them, — 1Sm 15:9
but they did **d** all the worthless — 1Sm 15:9
'Go and completely **d** the sinful — 1Sm 15:18
to Keilah and **d** the town because — 1Sm 23:10
Abishai, "Don't **d** him, for who — 1Sm 26:9
one of the people came to **d** him? — 1Sm 26:15
lift your hand to **d** the LORD's — 2Sm 1:14
We will **d** the heir!' — 2Sm 14:7
you're trying to **d** a city that — 2Sm 20:19
Never! I do not want to **d**! — 2Sm 20:20
I pursue my enemies and **d** them; — 2Sm 22:38
hand toward Jerusalem to **d** it, — 2Sm 24:16
and not have to **d** any cattle." — 1Kg 18:5
was unwilling to **d** Judah because — 2Kg 8:19
in order to **d** the servants of — 2Kg 10:19
He was not willing to **d** them. — 2Kg 13:23
this place to **d** it without the — 2Kg 18:25
'Attack this land and **d** it.' " — 2Kg 18:25
sent them against Judah to **d** it, — 2Kg 24:2
an angel to Jerusalem to **d** it, — 1Ch 21:15
angel was about to **d** the city, — 1Ch 21:15
I will not **d** them but will grant — 2Ch 12:7
and He did not **d** ⌊him⌋ — 2Ch 12:12
from them and did not **d** them. — 2Ch 20:10
Seir, they helped **d** each other. — 2Ch 20:23
was unwilling to **d** the house of — 2Ch 21:7
had anointed to **d** the house of — 2Ch 22:7
know that God intends to **d** you, — 2Ch 25:16
don't make Him **d** you!" — 2Ch 35:21
with us that You would **d** us, — Ezr 9:14
You did not **d** them or abandon — Neh 9:31
set out to **d** all of Mordecai's — Est 3:6
telling the officials⌋ to **d**, — Est 3:13
wrote to **d** the Jews who ⌊reside⌋ — Est 8:5
themselves, to **d**, kill, and — Est 8:11
against the Jews to **d** them. — Est 9:24
the lot) to crush and **d** them. — Est 9:24
to **d** him without just cause." — Jb 2:3
You now turn around and **d** me? — Jb 10:8
releases them, they **d** the land. — Jb 12:15
the land, so You **d** a man's hope. — Jb 14:19
it would **d** my entire harvest. — Jb 31:12
You **d** those who tell lies; — Ps 5:6
Do not **d** me along with sinners, — Ps 26:9
to harm me threaten to **d** me; — Ps 38:12
You love any words that **d**, — Ps 52:4
who seek to **d** my life will go — Ps 63:9
who would **d** me, are powerful. — Ps 69:4
You **d** all who are unfaithful to — Ps 73:27
Your right hand and **d** ⌊them⌋! — Ps 74:11
guilt and did not **d** ⌊them⌋. — Ps 78:38
over me; Your terrors **d** me. — Ps 88:16
their sins and **d** them for their — Ps 94:23
The LORD our God will **d** them. — Ps 94:23
I will **d** anyone who secretly — Ps 101:5
morning I will **d** all the wicked — Ps 101:8
They did not **d** the peoples as — Ps 106:34
The wicked hope to **d** me, but I — Ps 119:95
at Jerusalem: "**D** it! Destroy it — Ps 137:7
D it down to its foundations!" — Ps 137:7
Your faithful love **d** my enemies. — Ps 143:12
of fools will **d** them. — Pr 1:32
don't **d** his dwelling. — Pr 24:15
efforts on those who **d** kings. — Pr 31:3
words and **d** the work of your — Ec 5:6
Why should you **d** yourself? — Ec 7:16
but one sinner can **d** much good. — Ec 9:18
his intent to **d** and to cut off — Is 10:7
will completely **d** the glory of — Is 10:18
one will harm or **d** on My entire — Is 11:9
His wrath—to **d** the whole — Is 13:5
and to **d** the sinners on it — Is 13:9
⌊He⌋ will **d** the ⌊burial⌋ — Is 25:7
He will **d** death forever. — Is 25:8
hatches plots to **d** the needy — Is 32:7
this land to **d** it without the — Is 36:10
'Attack this land and **d** it.' " — Is 36:10
those who **d** and devastate you — Is 49:17
who has set himself to **d**. — Is 51:13
Don't **d** it, for there's some — Is 65:8
My servants and not **d** them all. — Is 65:8
what is evil or **d** on My entire — Is 65:25
tear down, to **d** and demolish, to — Jr 1:10
vineyard terraces and **d** them, — Jr 5:10
They will **d** with the sword your — Jr 5:17
I will **d** Daughter Zion. — Jr 6:2
Let us **d** her fortresses." — Jr 6:5
Let's **d** the tree with its fruit; — Jr 11:19
will uproot and **d** that nation." — Jr 12:17
of the land to devour and **d**. — Jr 15:3
uproot, tear down, and **d** ⌊it⌋. — Jr 18:7
the shepherds who **d** and scatter — Jr 23:1
will completely **d** them and make — Jr 25:9
demolish and to **d**, and to cause — Jr 31:28
certainly come and **d** this land — Jr 36:29
I will **d** cities with their — Jr 46:8
that is coming to **d** all the — Jr 47:4
is about to **d** the Philistines — Jr 47:4
they would **d** only what they — Jr 49:9
and **d** the people of the east! — Jr 49:28
and I will **d** the king and — Jr 49:38
completely **d** them—⌊this is⌋ — Jr 50:21
of grain and completely **d** her. — Jr 50:26
completely **d** her entire army! — Jr 51:3
is aimed at Babylon to **d** her, — Jr 51:11
LORD determined to **d** the wall of — Lm 2:8
in anger and **d** them under Your — Lm 3:66
that I will send to **d** you, — Ezk 5:16
and I will **d** your high places. — Ezk 6:3
Are You going to **d** the entire — Ezk 9:8
against him and **d** him from among — Ezk 14:9
constructed to **d** many lives. — Ezk 17:17
land so that I might not **d** it, — Ezk 22:30
I will **d** you, and you will know — Ezk 25:7
They will **d** the walls of Tyre — Ezk 26:4
be brought in to **d** the land. — Ezk 30:11
will **d** the idols and put an end — Ezk 30:13
but I will **d** the fat and the — Ezk 34:16
seen when He came to **d** the city, — Ezk 43:3
gave orders to **d** all the wise — Dn 2:12
had assigned to **d** the wise men — Dn 2:24
'Cut down the tree and **d** it, — Dn 4:23
will **d** the powerful along with — Dn 8:24
time of⌋ peace, he will **d** many; — Dn 8:25
coming prince will **d** the city — Dn 9:26
a daughter in marriage to **d** it, — Dn 11:17
eat his provisions will **d** him; — Dn 11:26
great fury to **d** and annihilate — Dn 11:44
And I will **d** your mother. — Hs 4:5
it will **d** and devour the bars of — Hs 11:6
will not turn back to **d** Ephraim. — Hs 11:9
I will **d** you, Israel; — Hs 13:9
he will **d** your strongholds and — Am 3:11
and I will **d** it from the face of — Am 9:8

will not totally **d** the house of Am 9:8
and I will **d** all her idols. Mc 1:7
will completely **d** Nineveh with Nah 1:8
I will **d** you until there is no Zph 2:5
against the north and **d** Assyria; Zph 2:13
royal thrones and **d** the power of Hg 2:22
house and **d** it along with its Zch 5:4
and I will **d** the pride of the Zch 9:6
set out to **d** all the nations Zch 12:9
search for the child to **d** Him." Mt 2:13
assume that I came to **d** the Law Mt 5:17
not come to **d** but to fulfill. Mt 5:17
and rust **d** and where thieves Mt 6:19
who is able to **d** both soul and Mt 10:28
Him, how they might **d** Him. Mt 12:14
will completely **d** those terrible Mt 21:41
Have You come to **d** us? Mk 1:24
Him, how they might **d** Him. Mk 3:6
him into fire or water to **d** him. Mk 9:22
looking for a way to **d** Him. Mk 11:18
He will come and **d** the farmers Mk 12:9
Have You come to **d** us? Lk 4:34
evil, to save life or to **d** it?" Lk 6:9
were looking for a way to **d** Him, Lk 19:47
He will come and **d** those farmers Lk 20:16
answered, "**D** this sanctuary, Jn 2:19
to steal and to kill and to **d**. Jn 10:10
will **d** this place and change the Ac 6:14
not **d** that one for whom Christ Rm 14:15
I will **d** the wisdom of the wise, 1Co 1:19
degree and tried to **d** it; Gl 1:13
the faith he once tried to **d**." Gl 1:23
Lord Jesus will **d** him with the 2Th 2:8
death He might **d** the one holding Heb 2:14
who is able to save and to **d**. Jms 4:12
to **d** the Devil's works. 1Jn 3:8
they **d** themselves with these Jd 10
time has come to **d** those who Rv 11:18
destroy those who **d** the earth. Rv 11:18

DESTROYED *(182)*

was before God **d** Sodom and Gn 13:10
when God **d** the cities of the Gn 19:29
I and my household will be **d**." Gn 34:30
the barley were **d** because the Ex 9:31
spelt were not **d** since they are Ex 9:32
completely **d** them and their Nm 21:3
You have been **d**, people of Nm 21:29
has been **d** as far as Dibon Nm 21:30
Kain will be **d** when Asshur takes Nm 24:22
The LORD **d** the Rephaim at the Dt 2:21
when He **d** the Horites before Dt 2:22
from Caphtor, **d** the Avvim, who Dt 2:23
and completely **d** the people of Dt 2:34
We completely **d** them, as we had Dt 3:6
LORD your God **d** every one of you Dt 4:3
but you will certainly be **d**. Dt 4:26
confusion until they are **d**. Dt 7:23
you, and He **d** them completely; Dt 11:4
they have been **d** before you. Dt 12:30
do until you are **d** and quickly Dt 28:20
from the sky until you are **d**. Dt 28:24
overtake you until you are **d**, Dt 28:45
on your neck until He has **d** you. Dt 28:48
soil's produce until you are **d**. Dt 28:51
of this law, until you are **d**. Dt 28:61
and their land when He **d** them. Dt 31:4
you completely **d** across the Jos 2:10
They completely **d** everything in Jos 6:21
of Ai were completely **d**. Jos 8:26
captured Ai and completely **d** it, Jos 10:1
on them until they were **d**, Jos 10:20
He completely **d** it and everyone Jos 10:28
He completely **d** it that day, Jos 10:35
He completely **d** Hebron and Jos 10:37
and completely **d** everyone in it, Jos 10:39
He completely **d** every living Jos 10:40
He completely **d** them, as Moses Jos 11:12
be completely **d** without mercy, Jos 11:20
completely **d** them with their Jos 11:21
all the nations I have **d**, Jos 23:4
and completely **d** the town. Jdg 1:17
king of Canaan until they **d** him. Jdg 4:24
against them and **d** the produce Jdg 6:4
our enemy who **d** our land and Jdg 16:24
women of Benjamin have been **d**?" Jdg 21:16
but he completely **d** all the rest 1Sm 15:8
your God, but the rest we **d**." 1Sm 15:15
I completely **d** the Amalekites. 1Sm 15:20
and I have **d** all your enemies 2Sm 7:9
d the Ammonites and besieged 2Sm 11:1
people with him will be **d**.' " 2Sm 17:16
alive until he had **d** his family 1Kg 15:29
I have not **d** Israel, but you 1Kg 18:18
They **d** the cities, and each of 2Kg 3:25
the king of Aram had **d** them, 2Kg 13:7
they **d** them completely. 2Kg 19:11
my predecessors **d** rescue them— 2Kg 19:12
So they have **d** them. 2Kg 19:18
Hezekiah had **d** and reestablished 2Kg 21:3
nations the LORD had **d** before 2Kg 21:9
nations God had **d** before them. 1Ch 5:25
and I have **d** all your enemies 1Ch 17:8
the army and **d** the Ammonites' 1Ch 20:1
had not completely **d**— 2Ch 8:8
Jerusalem and **d** all the leaders 2Ch 24:23
my fathers utterly **d** was able to 2Ch 32:14
nations the LORD had **d** before 2Ch 33:9
that Judah's Kings had **d**. 2Ch 34:11
and **d** all its valuable utensils. 2Ch 36:19
That is why this city was **d**. Ezr 4:15
who **d** this temple and deported Ezr 5:12
its gates have been **d** by fire?" Neh 2:3
gates that had been **d** by fire. Neh 2:13
your father's house will be **d**. Est 4:14
the Jews killed and **d** 500 men, Est 9:6
Jews have killed and **d** 500 men, Est 9:12
Where have the honest been **d**? Jb 4:7
Even after my skin has been **d**, Jb 19:26
Surely our opponents are **d**, Jb 22:20
Yet I am not **d** by the darkness, Jb 23:17
You have **d** the wicked; Ps 9:5
When the foundations are **d**, Ps 11:3
will be **d**, but those who Ps 37:9
those cursed by Him will be **d**. Ps 37:22
of the wicked will be **d**. Ps 37:28
watch when the wicked are **d**. Ps 37:34
future of the wicked will be **d**. Ps 37:38
so the wicked are **d** before God. Ps 68:2
the enemy has **d** in the sanctuary Ps 74:3
They were **d** at En-dor; Ps 83:10
they will be eternally **d**. Ps 92:7
the land and **d** the entire food Ps 105:16
He said He would have **d** them— Ps 106:23
the name of the LORD I **d** them. Ps 118:10
the name of the LORD I **d** them. Ps 118:11
the name of the LORD I **d** them. Ps 118:12
but foolish lips will be **d**. Pr 10:8
and foolish lips will be **d**. Pr 10:10
house of the wicked will be **d**, Pr 14:11
the rod of his fury will be **d**. Pr 22:8
when they are **d**, the righteous Pr 28:28
rebels and sinners will be **d**, Is 1:28
because you **d** your land and Is 14:20
is devastated, **d** in a night. Is 15:1
is devastated, **d** in a night. Is 15:1
and the load on it will be **d**." Is 22:25
for your haven has been **d**. Is 23:1
the Canaanite fortresses be **d**. Is 23:11
because your fortress is **d**! Is 23:14
You have visited and **d** them; Is 26:14
destroyer never **d**, you traitor Is 33:1
destroying, you will be **d**. Is 33:1
they **d** them completely. Is 37:11
my predecessors **d** rescue them— Is 37:12
So they have **d** them. Is 37:19
so that you will not be **d**. Is 48:9
sign that will not be **d**. Is 55:13
for the whole land is **d**. Jr 4:20
tents are **d**, my tent curtains, Jr 4:20
Why is the land **d** and scorched Jr 9:12
their punishment they will be **d**. Jr 10:15
My tent is **d**; all my tent cords Jr 10:20
shepherds have **d** My vineyard; Jr 12:10
my people has been **d** by a great Jr 14:17
My hand against you and **d** you. Jr 15:6
childless; I **d** My people. They Jr 15:7
until through him I have **d** it. Jr 27:8
because it is about to be **d**; Jr 48:1
he has **d** your fortresses. Jr 48:18
by the Arnon that Moab is **d**. Jr 48:20
Moab will be **d** as a people Jr 48:42
will be **d** along with his Jr 49:10
their punishment they will be **d**. Jr 51:18
its palaces and **d** its fortified Lm 2:5
He has **d** and shattered the bars Lm 2:9
My enemy has **d** those I nurtured Lm 2:22
The inhabited cities will be **d**, Ezk 12:20
and you will be **d** within it. Ezk 13:14
strongholds and **d** their cities. Ezk 19:7
and all its hordes will be **d**. Ezk 32:12
and **d** are ⌊now⌋ fortified and Ezk 36:35
rebuilt what was **d** and have Ezk 36:36
So I **d** them in My anger. Ezk 43:8
a kingdom that will never be **d**, Dn 2:44
His kingdom will never be **d**, Dn 6:26
and its body **d** and given over to Dn 7:11
is one that will not be **d**. Dn 7:14
to be completely **d** forever. Dn 7:26
My people are **d** for lack of Hs 4:6
the sin of Israel, will be **d**; Hs 10:8
of Israel will be totally **d**. Hs 10:15
The fields are **d**; the land Jl 1:10
indeed, the grain is **d**; Jl 1:10
Yet I **d** the Amorite as Israel Am 2:9
d his fruit above and his roots Am 2:9
inlaid with⌋ ivory will be **d**, Am 3:15
of Esau will be **d** by slaughter. Ob 9
with shame and **d** forever because Ob 10
and all your enemies will be **d**. Mc 5:9
their corner towers are **d**. Zph 3:6
the glorious ⌊trees⌋ are **d**! Zch 11:2
shepherds, for their glory is **d**. Zch 11:3
thickets of the Jordan are **d**. Zch 11:3
of Jacob have not been **d**. Mal 3:6
his troops, **d** those murderers Mt 22:7
the flood came and **d** them all. Lk 17:27
from heaven and **d** them all. Lk 17:29
May your silver be **d** with you, Ac 8:20
them did, and were **d** by snakes. 1Co 10:9
we are struck down but not **d**. 2Co 4:9
our outer person is being **d**, 2Co 4:16
house, a tent, is **d**, we have a 2Co 5:1
to what is **d** by being used up Col 2:22
those who draw back and are **d**, Heb 10:39
its beautiful appearance is **d**. Jms 1:11
born to be caught and **d**— 2Pt 2:12
destruction they too will be **d**, 2Pt 2:12
things are to be **d** in this way, 2Pt 3:11
later **d** those who did not Jd 5
and a third of the ships were **d**. Rv 8:9
hour such fabulous wealth was **d**! Rv 18:17
in a single hour she was **d**. Rv 18:19

DESTROYER *(16)*

and not let the **d** enter your Ex 12:23
Is that you, you **d** of Israel?" 1Kg 18:17
You **d** of nations, you have been Is 14:12
and the **d** destroys. Is 21:2
Woe, you **d** never destroyed, you Is 33:1
created the **d** to work havoc. Is 54:16
a **d** of nations has set out. Jr 4:7
suddenly the **d** will come on us Jr 6:26
mother of young men a **d** at noon. Jr 15:8
The **d** will move against every Jr 48:8
The **d** of Moab and its towns has Jr 48:15
for the **d** of Moab has come Jr 48:18
The **d** has fallen on your summer Jr 48:32
for a **d** is coming against her, Jr 51:56
did, and were killed by the **d**. 1Co 10:10
so that the **d** of the firstborn Heb 11:28

DESTROYERS *(4)*

the wilderness the **d** have come, Jr 12:12
I will appoint **d** against you, Jr 22:7
because the **d** from the north Jr 51:48
d will come against her from Me. Jr 51:53

DESTROYING *(19)*

d them completely and settling Dt 2:12
of Heshbon, **d** the men, women, Dt 3:6
the sword, completely **d** them; Jos 11:11
your mice that are **d** the land. 1Sm 6:5
the angel who was **d** the people, 2Sm 24:16
angel who was **d** ⌊the people⌋, 1Ch 21:15
the sword, killing and **d** them. Est 9:5
His wrath away from **d** ⌊them⌋. Ps 106:23
you have finished **d**, you will be Is 33:1
to keep Me⌋ from **d** them." Jr 13:14
for the LORD is **d** their pasture. Jr 25:36
a garden ⌊booth⌋, **d** His place of Lm 2:6
did not restrain Himself from **d**. Lm 2:8
and **d** lives in order to get Ezk 22:27
d ⌊because of their⌋ ancient Ezk 25:15
left, the **d** locust has eaten. Jl 1:4
the young locust, the **d** locust, Jl 2:25
was **d** those who called on this Ac 9:21
then after **d** seven nations in Ac 13:19

DESTROYS *(17)*
male or female slave and **d** it, Ex 21:26
pays back and **d** those who hate Dt 7:10
He **d** both the blameless and the Jb 9:22
nations great, then **d** them; Jb 12:23
Him, but He **d** all the wicked. Ps 145:20
whoever does so **d** himself. Pr 6:32
of the treacherous **d** them. Pr 11:3
the ungodly **d** his neighbor, Pr 11:9
The LORD **d** the house of the Pr 15:25
is a companion to a man who **d**. Pr 28:24
with prostitutes **d** his wealth. Pr 29:3
a fool, and a bribe **d** the mind. Ec 7:7
and the destroyer **d**. Is 21:2
who **d** the omens of the false Is 44:25
A fire **d** in front of them, Jl 2:3
where neither moth nor rust **d**, Mt 6:20
thief comes near and no moth **d**. Lk 12:33

DESTRUCTION *(117)*
alone, is to be set apart for **d**. Ex 22:20
set apart ⌊for **d**⌋ is to be Lv 27:29
nations, but his future is **d**. Nm 24:20
but they too will come to **d**. Nm 24:24
will be set apart for **d** like it. Dt 7:26
because it is set apart for **d**. Dt 7:26
set apart for **d** is to remain in Dt 13:17
will lead to the **d** of the Dt 29:19
are set apart to the LORD for **d**. Jos 6:17
or you will be set apart for **d**. Jos 6:18
of Israel for **d** and bring Jos 6:18
the things set apart for **d**. Jos 7:1
over to the Amorites for our **d**? Jos 7:7
they have been set apart for **d**. Jos 7:12
what was set apart for **d**, Jos 22:20
of what was set apart for **d**— 1Sm 15:21
the torrents of **d** terrified me. 2Sm 22:5
concerning the **d** and said to the 2Sm 24:16
hand the man I had devoted to **d**, 1Kg 20:42
to the south of the Mount of **D**, 2Kg 23:13
taking⌋ what was devoted to **d**. 1Ch 2:7
them apart for **d**, as they are 1Ch 4:41
the LORD bringing **d** to the whole 1Ch 21:12
relented concerning the **d**, 1Ch 21:15
death of his father, to his **d**. 2Ch 22:4
and it led to his own **d**. 2Ch 26:16
be drawn up authorizing their **d**, Est 3:9
issued in Susa ordering their **d**, Est 4:8
and I have been sold out to **d**, Est 7:4
to see the **d** of my relatives? Est 8:6
and not fear **d** when it comes. Jb 5:21
You will laugh at **d** and hunger Jb 5:22
He apportion **d** in His anger? Jb 21:17
to my **d**, without anyone Jb 30:13
d is within them; Ps 5:9
the torrents of **d** terrified me. Ps 18:4
tongue devises **d**, working Ps 52:2
d is inside it; oppression and Ps 55:11
bring them down to the pit of **d**; Ps 55:23
doomed to **d**, happy is the one Ps 137:8
the mouth of the fool hastens **d**. Pr 10:14
poverty of the poor is their **d**. Pr 10:15
but **d** awaits the malicious. Pr 10:29
comes before **d**, and an arrogant Pr 16:18
for their **d** will come suddenly; Pr 24:22
D has been decreed; Is 10:22
carrying out a **d** that was Is 10:23
My anger will turn to their **d**." Is 10:25
will come like **d** from the Is 13:6
her away with a broom of **d**." Is 14:23
raise a cry of **d** on the road to Is 15:5
oppressor has gone, **d** has ended, Is 16:4
about the **d** of my dear people. Is 22:4
a decree of **d** for the whole Is 28:22
in a sieve of **d** and to put a Is 30:28
He will set them apart for **d**, Is 34:2
people I have set apart for **d**. Is 34:5
over her for ⌊her⌋ **d** and chaos. Is 34:11
delivered⌋ me from the Pit of **d**, Is 38:17
over to total **d** and Israel to Is 43:28
devastation and **d**, famine and Is 51:19
devastation and **d** ⌊will be gone Is 60:18
from the north—a great **d**. Jr 4:6
from the north, even great **d**. Jr 6:1
Violence and **d** resound in her. Jr 6:7
shatter them with total **d**. Jr 17:18
Violence and **d**! because the word Jr 20:8
will bring **d** on all the nations Jr 30:11
I will not bring **d** on you. Jr 30:11
will bring **d** on all the nations Jr 46:28
but I will not bring **d** on you. Jr 46:28
cries of distress over the **d**: Jr 48:5
war is in the land—a great **d**. Jr 50:22
sound of great **d** from the land Jr 51:54
because of the **d** of my dear Lm 2:11
and pitfall, devastation and **d**. Lm 3:47
because of the **d** of my dear Lm 3:48
food during the **d** of my dear Lm 4:10
arrows for **d** that I will send to Ezk 5:16
spared them from **d** and did not Ezk 20:17
to brutal men, skilled at **d**. Ezk 21:31
bring about your **d** among the Ezk 32:9
cause terrible **d** and succeed Dn 8:24
until the decreed **d** is poured Dn 9:27
land with total **d** in his hand. Dn 11:16
d to them, for they rebelled Hs 7:13
for themselves for their own **d**. Hs 8:4
like Shalman's **d** of Beth-arbel. Hs 10:14
up violence and **d** in their Am 3:10
He brings **d** on the strong, Am 5:9
of Judah in the day of their **d**; Ob 12
because defilement brings **d**— Mc 2:10
destruction—a grievous **d**! Mc 2:10
will bring ⌊it⌋ to complete **d**; Nah 1:9
the **d** of animals will terrify Hab 2:17
a day of **d** and desolation, Zph 1:15
will there be a curse of **d**. Zch 14:11
road is broad that leads to **d**, Mt 7:13
against itself is headed for **d**, Mt 12:25
the **d** of that house was great! Lk 6:49
against itself is headed for **d**, Lk 11:17
except the son of **d**, so that the Jn 17:12
objects of wrath ready for **d**? Rm 9:22
to Satan for the **d** of the flesh, 1Co 5:5
This is evidence of their **d**, Php 1:28
Their end is **d**; their god is Php 3:19
then sudden **d** comes on them, 1Th 5:3
the penalty of everlasting **d**, 2Th 1:9
is revealed, the son of **d**. 2Th 2:3
plunge people into ruin and **d**. 1Tm 6:9
bring swift **d** on themselves. 2Pt 2:1
and their **d** does not sleep. 2Pt 2:3
and in their **d** they too will be 2Pt 2:12
judgment and **d** of ungodly men. 2Pt 3:7
twist them to their own **d**, 2Pt 3:16
up from the abyss and go to **d**. Rv 17:8
is of the seven and goes to **d**. Rv 17:11

DESTRUCTIVE *(8)*
refuge in his **d** behavior." Ps 52:7
hunter's net, from the **d** plague. Ps 91:3
pays attention to a **d** tongue. Pr 17:4
The scoundrel's weapons are **d**; Is 32:7
to stir up a **d** wind against Jr 51:1
with a **d** weapon in his hand. Ezk 9:1
⌊will fall⌋ in **d** fury. Ezk 13:13
secretly bring in **d** heresies, 2Pt 2:1

DETAIL *(4)*
and secured in every ⌊**d**⌋. 2Sm 23:5
in every **d** and according to 1Kg 6:38
explaining in **d** the conversion Ac 15:3
these things in **d** right now. Heb 9:5

DETAILED *(1)*
and the **d** account of Mordecai's Est 10:2

DETAILS *(3)*
David all the **d** of the battle. 2Sm 11:18
king all the **d** of the battle— 2Sm 11:19
writing, all the **d** of the plan." 1Ch 28:19

DETAINED *(2)*
girl's father, **d** him, and he Jdg 19:4
servants, **d** before the LORD 1Sm 21:7

DETECTING *(1)*
But **d** their craftiness, He said Lk 20:23

DETERMINATION *(2)*
wholehearted **d** to make David 1Ch 12:38
their faces are set in **d**. Hab 1:9

DETERMINE *(12)*
the judges to **d** whether or not Ex 22:8
two of them to **d** whether or not Ex 22:11
d when something is unclean or Lv 14:57
You are to **d** the distances and Dt 19:3
to **d** if they would keep the Jdg 3:4
the roll and **d** who has left us. 1Sm 14:17
Now **d** in your mind and heart to 1Ch 22:19
he did not **d** in his heart to 2Ch 12:14
Jerusalem to **d** its width and Zch 2:2
You are able to **d** that it is no Ac 24:11
so that you can **d** what really Php 1:10
test the spirits to **d** if they 1Jn 4:1

DETERMINED *(29)*
And Esau **d** in his heart: Gn 27:41
the matter has been **d** by God, Gn 41:32
sale will be ⌊**d**⌋ by the number Lv 25:50
Canaanites were **d** to stay in Jos 17:12
that Ruth was **d** to go with her, Ru 1:18
He has **d** to make you His 1Sm 12:22
his father was **d** to kill David. 1Sm 20:33
weight of the bronze was not **d**. 1Kg 7:47
weight of the bronze was not **d**. 2Ch 4:18
Israel who had **d** in their hearts 2Ch 11:16
had not yet **d** in their hearts 2Ch 20:33
Ezra had **d** in his heart to Ezr 7:10
man's days are **d** and the number Jb 14:5
when I **d** its boundaries and put Jb 38:10
I have **d** that my mouth will not Ps 17:3
They are **d** to throw ⌊me⌋ to the Ps 17:11
A man's steps are **d** by the LORD, Pr 20:24
The LORD **d** to destroy the wall Lm 2:8
d to hand it over to a ruler of Ezk 31:11
d that he would not defile Dn 1:8
for he is **d** to follow what is Hs 5:11
He **d** to journey to Jerusalem. Lk 9:51
because He **d** to journey to Lk 9:53
will go away as it has been **d**, Lk 22:22
up according to God's **d** plan and Ac 2:23
teaching and are **d** to bring this Ac 5:28
d to send relief to the brothers Ac 11:29
earth and has **d** their appointed Ac 17:26
I **d** to know nothing among you 1Co 2:2

DETERMINES *(2)*
way, but the LORD **d** his steps. Pr 16:9
one who walks **d** his own steps. Jr 10:23

DETEST *(9)*
the Egyptians **d** in front of them Ex 8:26
and you must **d** their carcasses. Lv 11:11
You are to **d** these birds. Lv 11:13
and we **d** this wretched food!" Nm 21:5
are to utterly **d** and abhor it, Dt 7:26
and **d** those who rebel against Ps 139:21
Do You **d** Zion? Why do You Jr 14:19
who **d** idols, do you rob their Rm 2:22
hypocrisy. **D** evil; cling to Rm 12:9

DETESTABLE *(93)*
LORD our God is **d** to the Ex 8:26
or any unclean, **d** creature, and Lv 7:21
But these are to be **d** to you: Lv 11:10
They are to remain **d** to you; Lv 11:11
and scales will be **d** to you. Lv 11:12
not be eaten because they are **d**: Lv 11:13
on all fours are to be **d** to you. Lv 11:20
four feet are to be **d** to you. Lv 11:23
that swarm on the earth are **d**; Lv 11:41
or on many feet, for they are **d**. Lv 11:42
a man as with a woman; it is **d**. Lv 18:22
do any of the **d** customs that Lv 18:30
make yourselves **d** by any land Lv 20:25
their gods every **d** thing the Dt 12:31
be true that this **d** thing has Dt 13:14
You must not eat any **d** thing. Dt 14:3
for that is **d** to the LORD your Dt 17:1
be true that this **d** thing has Dt 17:4
not imitate the **d** customs of Dt 18:9
these things is **d** to the LORD, Dt 18:12
you because of these **d** things. Dt 18:12
to do all the **d** things they do Dt 20:18
these things is **d** to the LORD Dt 22:5
both are **d** to the LORD your Dt 23:18
that would be **d** to the LORD. Dt 24:4
unfairly is **d** to the LORD your Dt 25:16
image, which is **d** to the LORD, Dt 27:15
You saw their **d** images and idols Dt 29:17
enraged Him with **d** practices. Dt 32:16
has made himself **d** to his people 1Sm 27:12
the **d** idol of the Ammonites. 1Kg 11:5
for Chemosh, the **d** idol of Moab, 1Kg 11:7
the **d** idol of the Ammonites on 1Kg 11:7
the most **d** acts by going 1Kg 21:26
the **d** idol of the Sidonians; 2Kg 23:13
for Chemosh, the **d** idol of Moab; 2Kg 23:13
and all the **d** things that were 2Kg 23:24
the king's command was **d** to him. 1Ch 21:6
and removed the **d** idols from the 2Ch 15:8
imitating the **d** practices of the 2Ch 28:3

Remove everything **d** from the 2Ch 29:5
took all the **d** things they found 2Ch 29:16
imitating the **d** practices of the 2Ch 33:2
that was **d** from all the lands 2Ch 34:33
Jehoiakim, the **d** things he did, 2Ch 36:8
imitating all the **d** practices of 2Ch 36:14
peoples whose **d** practices are Ezr 9:1
their impurity and **d** practices. Ezr 9:11
who commit these **d** practices? Ezr 9:14
the devious are **d** to the LORD, Pr 3:32
in fact, seven are **d** to Him: Pr 6:16
and wickedness is **d** to my lips. Pr 8:7
scales are **d** to the LORD, Pr 11:1
twisted minds are **d** to the LORD, Pr 11:20
Lying lips are **d** to the LORD, Pr 12:22
of the wicked is **d** to the LORD, Pr 15:8
a proud heart is **d** to the LORD; Pr 16:5
Wicked behavior is **d** to kings, Pr 16:12
just—both are **d** to the LORD. Pr 17:15
both are **d** to the LORD. Pr 20:10
weights are **d** to the LORD, Pr 20:23
of a wicked person is **d**— Pr 21:27
and a mocker is **d** to people. Pr 24:9
the law—even his prayer is **d**. Pr 28:9
unjust man is **d** to the righteous Pr 29:27
is upright is **d** to the wicked. Pr 29:27
Anyone who chooses you is **d**. Is 41:24
make something **d** with the rest Is 44:19
you made My inheritance **d**. Jr 2:7
you remove your **d** idols from My Jr 4:1
continue doing all these **d** acts! Jr 7:10
have set up their **d** things in Jr 7:30
—I have seen your **d** acts. Jr 13:27
of their **d** and abhorrent idols. Jr 16:18
have placed their **d** things in Jr 32:34
they do this **d** act causing Judah Jr 32:35
Don't do this **d** thing that I Jr 44:4
deeds and the **d** acts you have Jr 44:22
with all your **d** practices Ezk 5:11
from them, their **d** things. Ezk 7:20
wall was every form of **d** thing, Ezk 8:10
remove all its **d** things and all Ezk 11:18
their desire for **d** things and Ezk 11:21
of all your **d** idols and the Ezk 16:36
haughty and did **d** things before Ezk 16:50
throw away the **d** things that are Ezk 20:7
threw away the **d** things that Ezk 20:8
yourselves with their **d** things? Ezk 20:30
idols, their **d** things, and all Ezk 37:23
and became **d**, like the thing Hs 9:10
mouths and the **d** things from Zch 9:7
and a **d** thing has been done in Mal 2:11
They are **d**, disobedient, and Ti 1:16

DETESTED *(2)*
not despised or **d** the torment Ps 22:24
with them, and they also **d** me. Zch 11:8

DETESTING *(1)*
envy, hateful, **d** one another. Ti 3:3

DETESTS *(3)*
so that he **d** bread, and his soul Jb 33:20
LORD **d** the way of the wicked, Pr 15:9
The LORD **d** the plans of an evil Pr 15:26

DETOURED *(1)*
So they **d** there and went to the Jdg 18:15

DEUEL *(5)*
(AKA REUEL)
Eliasaph son of **D** from Gad; Nm 1:14
Gadites is Eliasaph son of **D**. Nm 2:14
the sixth day Eliasaph son of **D**, Nm 7:42
offering of Eliasaph son of **D**. Nm 7:47
and Eliasaph son of **D** was over Nm 10:20

DEVASTATE *(11)*
The famine will **d** the land. Gn 41:30
to ruins and **d** your sanctuaries. Lv 26:31
I also will **d** the land, so that Lv 26:32
He will **d** and subdue them before Dt 9:3
who destroy and **d** you will leave Is 49:17
I will **d** Elam before their Jr 49:37
you **d** the whole earth. Jr 51:25
the LORD is going to **d** Babylon; Jr 51:55
gifts in order to **d** them so they Ezk 20:26
will **d** her vines and fig trees. Hs 2:12
They will **d** the land, and I will Zch 11:6

DEVASTATED *(25)*
realize yet that Egypt is **d**?" Ex 10:7
daughter! You have **d** me! You Jdg 11:35
Assyria have **d** the nations and 2Kg 19:17
head and beard, and sat down **d**. Ezr 9:3
while I sat **d** until the evening Ezr 9:4
You have **d** my entire family. Jb 16:7
them, and frogs, which **d** them. Ps 78:45
Jacob and **d** his homeland. Ps 79:7
You have **d** the vineyard. Is 3:14
Ar in Moab is **d**, destroyed in a Is 15:1
Kir in Moab is **d**, destroyed in a Is 15:1
are completely **d**, for the raisin Is 16:7
The earth is completely **d**; Is 24:19
of Assyria have **d** all these Is 37:18
you **d** one, what are you doing Jr 4:30
from Zion: How **d** we are. We are Jr 9:19
Wail, Heshbon, for Ai is **d**; Jr 49:3
shame; Marduk is **d**; her idols Jr 50:2
her false gods, **d**. Jr 50:2
everyone will be **d** and waste Ezk 4:17
He **d** their strongholds and Ezk 19:7
It has **d** My grapevine and Jl 1:7
Nineveh is **d**; who will show Nah 3:7
Their cities lie **d**, without a Zph 3:6
We have been **d**, but we will Mal 1:4

DEVASTATING *(4)*
great and **d** signs and wonders Dt 6:22
one—like a **d** hail storm, like Is 28:2
am against you, **d** mountain— Jr 51:25
I send My four **d** judgments Ezk 14:21

DEVASTATION *(17)*
three months of **d** by your foes 1Ch 21:12
weighed and my **d** placed with it Jb 6:2
who brings **d** on the earth. Ps 46:8
of people is a ruler's **d**. Pr 14:28
mouth is his **d**, and his lips are Pr 18:7
punishment when **d** comes from far Is 10:3
D will happen to you suddenly Is 47:11
d and destruction, famine and Is 51:19
d and destruction ⌊will be gone Is 60:18
d and great disaster! Jr 48:3
and pitfall, **d** and destruction. Lm 3:47
about the **d** I have brought Ezk 14:22
with a cup of **d** and desolation, Ezk 23:33
For even if they flee from **d**, Hs 9:6
and will come as **d** from the Jl 1:15
Desolation, decimation, **d**! Nah 2:10
but **d** will be on the threshold, Zph 2:14

DEVASTATIONS *(2)*
they will restore the former **d**; Is 61:4
the **d** of many generations. Is 61:4

DEVELOP *(3)*
so that we may **d** wisdom in our Ps 90:12
d common sense, you who are Pr 8:5
or how bones ⌊**d**⌋ in the womb of Ec 11:5

DEVELOPED *(2)*
his old age he **d** a disease in 1Kg 15:23
Asa **d** a disease in his feet, 2Ch 16:12

DEVELOPS *(3)*
a skin disease **d** on a person, Lv 13:9
spot **d** where the boil was Lv 13:19
and tendons, **d** with growth from Col 2:19

DEVIANT *(1)*
rise up with **d** doctrines to lure Ac 20:30

DEVIATED *(3)*
have **d** from these and turned 1Tm 1:6
people have **d** from the faith. 1Tm 6:21
They have **d** from the truth, 2Tm 2:18

DEVIATING *(1)*
that they were **d** from the truth Gl 2:14

DEVICES *(1)*
designed **d** in Jerusalem to 2Ch 26:15

DEVIL *(30)*
to be tempted by the **D**. Mt 4:1
Then the **D** took Him to the holy Mt 4:5
the **D** took Him to a very high Mt 4:8
Then the **D** left Him, and Mt 4:11
enemy who sowed them is the **D**. Mt 13:39
for the **D** and his angels! Mt 25:41
40 days to be tempted by the **D**. Lk 4:2
The **D** said to Him, "If You are Lk 4:3
The **D** said to Him, "I will give Lk 4:6
After the **D** had finished every Lk 4:13
Then the **D** comes and takes away Lk 8:12
Yet one of you is the **D**!" Jn 6:70
You are of your father the **D**, Jn 8:44
D had already put it into the Jn 13:2
were under the tyranny of the **D**, Ac 10:38
You son of the **D**, full of all Ac 13:10
don't give the **D** an opportunity. Eph 4:27
against the tactics of the **D**. Eph 6:11
into the condemnation of the **D**. 1Tm 3:6
of death—that is, the **D**— Heb 2:14
But resist the **D**, and he will Jms 4:7
adversary the **D** is prowling 1Pt 5:8
one who commits sin is of the **D**, 1Jn 3:8
for the **D** has sinned from the 1Jn 3:8
with the **D** in a debate about Jd 9
the **D** is about to throw some of Rv 2:10
who is called the **D** and Satan, Rv 12:9
for the **D** has come down to you Rv 12:12
serpent who is the **D** and Satan, Rv 20:2
The **D** who deceived them was Rv 20:10

DEVIL'S *(4)*
into disgrace and the **D** trap. 1Tm 3:7
senses and escape the **D** trap, 2Tm 2:26
to destroy the **D** works. 1Jn 3:8
and the **D** children—are 1Jn 3:10

DEVIOUS *(7)*
His children but a **d** and crooked Dt 32:5
A **d** heart will be far from me; Ps 101:4
crooked, and whose ways are **d**. Pr 2:15
for the **d** are detestable to the Pr 3:32
but the one who is **d** in his ways Pr 14:2
a **d** tongue breaks the spirit. Pr 15:4
Their hearts are **d**; now they Hs 10:2

DEVIOUSLY *(1)*
and don't let your lips talk **d**. Pr 4:24

DEVISE *(7)*
He would **d** plans so that the one 2Sm 14:14
one who would **d** such a scheme?" Est 7:5
to harm you and **d** a wicked plan, Ps 21:11
d crimes ⌊and say,⌋ "We have Ps 64:6
They **d** clever schemes against Ps 83:3
D a plan; it will fail. Make a Is 8:10
and you will **d** an evil plan. Ezk 38:10

DEVISED *(9)*
have you **d** something similar 2Sm 14:13
his plot he had **d** against the Est 8:3
Haman had **d** against the Jews Est 9:25
in the schemes they have **d**. Ps 10:2
that they had **d** plots against me Jr 11:19
strategies He has **d** against the Jr 49:20
he has **d** a strategy against you. Jr 49:30
He has **d** against the land Jr 50:45
a plot was **d** against him by the Ac 20:3

DEVISES *(1)*
your tongue **d** destruction, Ps 52:2

DEVOID *(2)*
on earth—a creature **d** of fear! Jb 41:33
a land **d** of inhabitant. Jr 6:8

DEVOTE *(7)*
that they could **d** their energy 2Ch 31:4
Then you will **d** what they Mc 4:13
we will **d** ourselves to prayer Ac 6:4
to **d** yourselves to prayer. 1Co 7:5
D yourselves to prayer; Col 4:2
be careful to **d** themselves to Ti 3:8
also learn to **d** themselves to Ti 3:14

DEVOTED *(19)*
The LORD was **d** to you and chose Dt 7:7
the LORD was **d** to your fathers Dt 10:15
be completely **d** to the LORD our 1Kg 8:61
not completely **d** to the LORD his 1Kg 15:3
the man I had **d** to destruction, 1Kg 20:42
you because you **d** yourself to do 1Kg 21:20
d himself to do what was evil 1Kg 21:25
They **d** themselves to do what 2Kg 17:17
what was **d** to destruction. 1Ch 2:7
d myself to the construction of Neh 5:16
those who are **d** to worthless Ps 31:6
Because he is lovingly **d** to Me, Ps 91:14
or be **d** to one and despise the Mt 6:24
or he will be **d** to one and Lk 16:13
And they **d** themselves to the Ac 2:42
every day they **d** themselves ⌊to Ac 2:46
so that you may be **d** to the Lord 1Co 7:35
Achaia and have **d** themselves to 1Co 16:15
d herself to every good work. 1Tm 5:10

DEVOTION *(2)*
abandoned their **d** to the LORD. Hs 4:10
a complete and pure **d** to Christ. 2Co 11:3

DEVOUR *(45)*
land of your enemies will **d** you. Lv 26:38
of the land, for we will **d** them. Nm 14:9
This horde will **d** everything Nm 22:4
down until they **d** the prey and Nm 23:24
because locusts will **d** it. Dt 28:38
Must the sword **d** forever? 2Sm 2:26
Why would you **d** the LORD's 2Sm 20:19
His wrath, and fire will **d** them. Ps 21:9
came against me to **d** my flesh, Ps 27:2
I lie down with those who **d** men. Ps 57:4
eyes foreigners **d** your fields— Is 1:7
a sword will **d** him, but not one Is 31:8
a garment; a moth will **d** them. Is 50:9
For the moth will **d** them like a Is 51:8
They come to **d** the land and Jr 8:16
bring them to **d** ⌊her⌋. Jr 12:9
of the land to **d** and destroy. Jr 15:3
The sword will **d** and be Jr 46:10
will **d** Moab's forehead and the Jr 48:45
it will **d** Ben-hadad's citadels. Jr 49:27
and plague will **d** whoever is in Ezk 7:15
and it will **d** every green tree Ezk 20:47
they **d** people, seize wealth and Ezk 22:25
They have been given to us to **d**! Ezk 35:12
d men and deprive your nation Ezk 36:13
will no longer **d** men and deprive Ezk 36:14
It will **d** the whole earth, Dn 7:23
New Moon will **d** them along with Hs 5:7
destroy and **d** the bars of his Hs 11:6
I will **d** them there like a Hs 13:8
the sword will **d** your young Nah 2:13
Fire will **d** the bars ⌊of your Nah 3:13
The fire will **d** you there; Nah 3:15
It will **d** you like the young Nah 3:15
like an eagle, swooping to **d**. Hab 1:8
if ready to secretly **d** the weak. Hab 3:14
the rest **d** each other's flesh. Zch 11:9
he will **d** the flesh of the fat Zch 11:16
You **d** widows' houses and make Mt 23:14
They **d** widows' houses and say Mk 12:40
They **d** widows' houses and say Lk 20:47
if you bite and **d** one another, Gl 5:15
looking for anyone he can **d**. 1Pt 5:8
give birth he might **d** her child. Rv 12:4
and naked, **d** her flesh, and burn Rv 17:16

DEVOURED *(23)*
A vicious animal has **d** him. Gn 37:33
When they had **d** them, you could Gn 41:21
not tell that they had **d** them; Gn 41:21
servants, and **d** them, and I Jb 1:16
for they have **d** Jacob and Ps 79:7
They **d** all the vegetation in Ps 105:35
you will be **d** by the sword." Is 1:20
own sword has **d** your prophets Jr 2:30
all who **d** you will be devoured, Jr 30:16
all who devoured you will be **d**, Jr 30:16
All who found them **d** them. Jr 50:7
The first who **d** him was the king Jr 50:17
of Babylon has **d** me; Jr 51:34
when the fire has **d** it and it is Ezk 15:5
to tear prey, he **d** people. Ezk 19:3
to tear prey, he **d** people. Ezk 19:6
main branch and has **d** its fruit, Ezk 19:14
given to wild animals to be **d**, Ezk 33:27
d and crushed, and it trampled Dn 7:7
and flames have **d** all the trees Jl 1:19
the locust **d** your many gardens Am 4:9
the great deep and **d** the land. Am 7:4
who has **d** your assets with Lk 15:30

DEVOURER *(1)*
I will rebuke the **d** for you, Mal 3:11

DEVOURING *(5)*
D fire precedes Him, and a storm Ps 50:3
d the oppressed from the land Pr 30:14
and bronze claws, **d**, crushing, Dn 7:19
What the **d** locust has left, Jl 1:4
locust, and the **d** locust—My Jl 2:25

DEVOURS *(10)*
In the morning he **d** the prey, Gn 49:27
is one that **d** its inhabitants, Nm 13:32
it **d** the land and its produce, Dt 32:22
blood while My sword **d** flesh— Dt 32:42
because the sword **d** all alike. 2Sm 11:25
has a sword that **d** from one end Jr 12:12
for the sword **d** all around you. Jr 46:14
The fire **d** both of its ends, Ezk 15:4
and behind them a flame **d**. Jl 2:3
you, if someone **d** you, if 2Co 11:20

DEVOUT *(8)*
Live in My presence and be **d**. Gn 17:1
This man was righteous and **d**, Lk 2:25
d men from every nation under Ac 2:5
But **d** men buried Stephen and Ac 8:2
He was a **d** man and feared God Ac 10:2
slaves and a **d** soldier, Ac 10:7
of the Jews and **d** proselytes Ac 13:43
a **d** man according to the law, Ac 22:12

DEVOUTLY *(1)*
is God, of how **d**, righteously, 1Th 2:10

DEW *(35)*
from the **d** of the sky and from Gn 27:28
from the **d** of the sky above. Gn 27:39
was a layer of **d** all around the Ex 16:13
When the layer of **d** evaporated, Ex 16:14
When the **d** fell on the camp at Nm 11:9
rain and my word settle like **d**, Dt 32:2
the LORD with the **d** of heaven's Dt 33:13
even his skies drip with **d**. Dt 33:28
If **d** is only on the fleece, Jdg 6:37
fleece and wrung **d** out of it, Jdg 6:38
the **d** be all over the ground. Jdg 6:39
and **d** was all over the ground. Jdg 6:40
let no **d** or rain be on you, 2Sm 1:21
on him like **d** on the ground. 2Sm 17:12
will be no **d** or rain during 1Kg 17:1
and the **d** will rest on my Jb 29:19
speech settled on them ⌊like **d**⌋. Jb 29:22
Who fathered the drops of **d**? Jb 38:28
the **d** of Your youth belongs to Ps 110:3
It is like the **d** of Hermon Ps 133:3
and the clouds dripped with **d**. Pr 3:20
favor is like **d** on the grass. Pr 19:12
For my head is drenched with **d**, Sg 5:2
be covered with the morning **d**, Is 26:19
be drenched with **d** from the sky Dn 4:15
be drenched with **d** from the sky, Dn 4:23
drenched with **d** from the sky for Dn 4:25
drenched with **d** from the sky, Dn 4:33
was drenched with **d** from the sky Dn 5:21
like the early **d** that vanishes. Hs 6:4
like the early **d** that vanishes, Hs 13:3
I will be like the **d** to Israel; Hs 14:5
peoples like **d** from the LORD, Mc 5:7
withheld the **d** and the land its Hg 1:10
the skies will yield their **d**. Zch 8:12

DI-ZAHAB *(1)*
Tophel, Laban, Hazeroth, and **D**. Dt 1:1

DIADEM *(6)*
place the holy **d** on the turban. Ex 29:6
plate, the holy **d**, out of pure Ex 39:30
gold, the holy **d**, on the front Lv 8:9
which has a royal **d** on its head. Est 6:8
of beauty and a **d** of splendor to Is 28:5
a royal **d** in the palm of your Is 62:3

DIADEMS *(2)*
and on his heads were seven **d**. Rv 12:3
horns were 10 **d**, and on his Rv 13:1

DIAMOND *(5)*
turquoise, a sapphire, and a **d**; Ex 28:18
turquoise, a sapphire, and a **d**; Ex 39:11
With a **d** point it is engraved on Jr 17:1
made your forehead like a **d**, Ezk 3:9
topaz, and **d**, beryl, onyx, Ezk 28:13

DIBLAH *(1)*
waste, from the wilderness to **D**. Ezk 6:14

DIBLAIM *(1)*
and married Gomer daughter of **D**, Hs 1:3

DIBON *(11)*
has been destroyed as far as **D**. Nm 21:30
of⌋ Ataroth, **D**, Jazer, Nimrah, Nm 32:3
rebuilt **D**, Ataroth, Aroer Nm 32:34
the Medeba plateau as far as **D**, Jos 13:9
on the plateau—**D**, Bamoth-baal, Jos 13:17
its villages, **D** and its villages Neh 11:25
D went up to its temple to weep Is 15:2
The waters of **D** are full of Is 15:9
will bring on **D** even more ⌊than Is 15:9
resident of the daughter of **D**, Jr 48:18
D, Nebo, Beth-diblathaim, Jr 48:22

DIBON-GAD *(2)*
from Iyim and camped at **D**. Nm 33:45
departed from **D** and camped at Nm 33:46

DIBRI *(1)*
a daughter of **D** of the tribe of Lv 24:11

DICTATION *(7)*
At Jeremiah's **d**, Baruch wrote on Jr 36:4
you wrote at my **d**—the words Jr 36:6
all these words? At his **d**?" Jr 36:17
Baruch said to them, "At his **d**. Jr 36:18
had written at Jeremiah's **d**, Jr 36:27
it at Jeremiah's **d** all the words Jr 36:32
at Jeremiah's **d** in the fourth Jr 45:1

DID *(1188)*
(See pp. xi-xii.)

DIDN'T *(228)*
(See pp. xi-xii.)

DIE *(314)*
from it, you will certainly **d**." Gn 2:17
or touch it, or you will **d**.' " Gn 3:3
will not **d**," the serpent said Gn 3:4
Everything on earth will **d**. Gn 6:17
will overtake me, and I will **d**. Gn 19:19
You are about to **d** because of Gn 20:3
know that you will certainly **d**, Gn 20:7
⌊bear to⌋ watch the boy **d**!" Gn 21:16
I'm about to **d**, so what good is Gn 25:32
thought I might **d** on account of Gn 26:9
or his wife will certainly **d**." Gn 26:11
I can bless you before I **d**." Gn 27:4
the LORD's presence before I **d**.' Gn 27:7
"Give me sons, or I will **d**!" Gn 30:1
one day, the whole herd will **d**. Gn 33:13
He might **d** too, like his Gn 38:11
so that we will live and not **d**." Gn 42:2
then you won't **d**." And they Gn 42:20
live, and not **d**—neither we, Gn 43:8
have it, he must **d**, and we also Gn 44:9
to leave, his father would **d**.' Gn 44:22
boy is not with us, he will **d**. Gn 44:31
will go to see him before I **d**." Gn 45:28
At last I can **d**, now that I have Gn 46:30
Why should we **d** here in front of Gn 47:15
so that we can live and not **d**, Gn 47:19
the time drew near for him to **d**, Gn 47:29
I am about to **d**, but God will be Gn 48:21
oath, saying, 'I am about to **d**. Gn 50:5
I am about to **d**, but God will Gn 50:24
The fish in the Nile will **d**, Ex 7:18
that the Israelites own will **d**." Ex 9:4
inside will **d** when the hail Ex 9:19
you see my face, you will **d**." Ex 10:28
in the land of Egypt will **d**, Ex 11:5
said, "We're all going to **d**!" Ex 12:33
you took us to **d** in the Ex 14:11
than to **d** in the wilderness Ex 14:12
whole assembly **d** of hunger!" Ex 16:3
otherwise many of them will **d**. Ex 19:21
God speak to us, or we will **d**." Ex 20:19
man does not **d** but is confined Ex 21:18
he exits, so that he does not **d**. Ex 28:35
they do not incur guilt and **d**. Ex 28:43
water so that they will not **d**. Ex 30:20
feet so that they will not **d**; Ex 30:21
charge so that you will not **d**, Lv 8:35
or else you will **d**, and the LORD Lv 10:6
tent of meeting or you will **d**, Lv 10:7
of meeting, or else you will **d**; Lv 10:9
that they do not **d** by defiling Lv 15:31
on the ark or else he will **d**, Lv 16:2
testimony, or else he will **d**. Lv 16:13
their guilt and **d** childless. Lv 20:20
be guilty and **d** because they Lv 22:9
the holy objects or they will **d**. Nm 4:15
live and not **d** when they come Nm 4:19
for a moment, or they will **d**." Nm 4:20
when they **d**, because the hair Nm 6:7
this land to **d** by the sword? Nm 14:3
and there they will **d**." Nm 14:35
these men **d** ⌊naturally⌋ as all Nm 16:29
before Me, or else they will **d**." Nm 17:10
the LORD's tabernacle will **d**. Nm 17:13
both they and you will **d**. Nm 18:3
or they will incur guilt and **d**. Nm 18:22
so that you will not **d**." Nm 18:32
us and our livestock to **d** here? Nm 20:4
to his people⌋ and **d** there." Nm 20:26

up from Egypt to **d** in the Nm 21:5
Let me **d** the death of the Nm 23:10
of Korah, however, did not **d**. Nm 26:11
they would all **d** in the Nm 26:65
will not **d** until he stands Nm 35:12
I am going to **d** in this land. Dt 4:22
But now, why should we **d**? Dt 5:25
us and we will **d** if we hear the Dt 5:25
one condemned to **d** is to be Dt 17:6
God or to the judge, must **d**. Dt 17:12
longer, so that we will not **d**!' Dt 18:16
gods—that prophet must **d**.' Dt 18:20
Yet he did not deserve to **d**, Dt 19:6
avenger of blood and he will **d**. Dt 19:12
he may **d** in battle and another Dt 20:5
Otherwise he may **d** in battle and Dt 20:6
Otherwise he may **d** in battle and Dt 20:7
the woman and the woman must **d**. Dt 22:22
the man who raped her must **d**. Dt 22:25
sells him, the kidnapper must **d**. Dt 24:7
Then you will **d** on the mountain Dt 32:50
live and not **d** though his people Dt 33:6
flee there and not **d** at the hand Jos 20:9
be afraid, for you will not **d**." Jdg 6:23
He must **d**, because he tore down Jdg 6:30
"We're going to **d**," he said to Jdg 13:22
Must I now **d** of thirst and fall Jdg 15:18
"Let me **d** with the Philistines." Jdg 16:30
Where you **d**, I will die, and Ru 1:17
you die, I will **d**, and there I Ru 1:17
descendents will **d** violently. 1Sm 2:33
of them will **d** on the same day. 1Sm 2:34
men who did not **d** were afflicted 1Sm 5:12
your servants, so we won't **d**! 1Sm 12:19
of my son Jonathan, he must **d**!" 1Sm 14:39
was carrying. I am ready to **d**!" 1Sm 14:43
me severely if you do not **d**, 1Sm 14:44
Jonathan **d**, who accomplished 1Sm 14:45
Jonathan, and he did not **d**. 1Sm 14:45
said to him, "No, you won't **d**. 1Sm 20:2
faithful love, but if I **d**, 1Sm 20:14
him to me—he deserves to **d**." 1Sm 20:31
said, "You will **d**, Ahimelech— 1Sm 22:16
his day will come and he will **d**, 1Sm 26:10
you deserve to **d** since you 1Sm 26:16
Should Abner **d** as a fool dies? 2Sm 3:33
man who did this deserves to **d**! 2Sm 12:5
away your sin; you will not **d**. 2Sm 12:13
the son born to you will **d**." 2Sm 12:14
will certainly **d** and be like 2Sm 14:14
if half of us **d**, they will not 2Sm 18:3
to Shimei, "You will not **d**." 2Sm 19:23
so that I may **d** in my own city 2Sm 19:37
time approached for David to **d**, 1Kg 2:1
Even though you deserve to **d**, 1Kg 2:26
said, "No, for I will **d** here." 1Kg 2:30
sure that you will certainly **d**. 1Kg 2:37
sure that you will certainly **d**'? 1Kg 2:42
sons, "When I **d**, you must bury 1Kg 13:31
enter the city, the boy will **d**. 1Kg 14:12
my son so we can eat it and **d**." 1Kg 17:12
tree and prayed that he might **d**. 1Kg 19:4
you will certainly **d**.' " 2Kg 1:4
you will certainly **d**.' " 2Kg 1:6
you will certainly **d**.' " 2Kg 1:16
Why just sit here until we **d**? 2Kg 7:3
we will **d** there because the 2Kg 7:4
if we sit here, we will also **d**. 2Kg 7:4
if they kill us, we will **d**." 2Kg 7:4
of Israelites who will **d**, 2Kg 7:13
shown me that he is sure to **d**." 2Kg 8:10
so that you may live and not **d**. 2Kg 18:32
order, for you are about to **d**; 2Kg 20:1
Fathers must not **d** because of 2Ch 25:4
children must not **d** because of 2Ch 25:4
each one will **d** for his own sin. 2Ch 25:4
integrity? Curse God and **d**!" Jb 2:9
⌊why⌋ didn't I **d** as I came from Jb 3:11
up? They **d** without wisdom. Jb 4:21
their ⌊only⌋ hope will be to **d**. Jb 11:20
and wisdom will **d** with you! Jb 12:2
If so, I will be silent and **d**. Jb 13:19
and its shoots will not **d**. Jb 14:7
stump starts to **d** in the soil, Jb 14:8
maintain my integrity until I **d**. Jb 27:5
I will **d** in my own nest and Jb 29:18
They **d** suddenly in the middle of Jb 34:20
of death⌋ and **d** without Jb 36:12
d in their youth; their life Jb 36:14
up before I **d** and am gone." Ps 39:13
When will he **d** and be forgotten? Ps 41:5
For one can see that wise men **d**; Ps 49:10
have an easy time until they **d**, Ps 73:4
preserve those condemned to **d**. Ps 79:11
will **d** like men and fall like Ps 82:7
set free those condemned to **d**, Ps 102:20
they **d** and return to the dust. Ps 104:29
and caused their fish to **d**. Ps 105:29
will not **d**, but I will live and Ps 118:17
refuge in You; do not let me **d**. Ps 141:8
on that day his plans **d**. Ps 146:4
He will **d** because there is no Pr 5:23
but fools **d** for lack of sense. Pr 10:21
when the wicked **d**, there is Pr 11:10
have a refuge when they **d**. Pr 14:32
one who hates correction will **d**. Pr 15:10
who disregards his ways will **d**. Pr 19:16
him with a rod, he will not **d**. Pr 23:13
deny them to me before I **d**: Pr 30:7
to give birth and a time to **d**; Ec 3:2
Why should you **d** before your Ec 7:17
living know that they will **d**, Ec 9:5
is caught will **d** by the sword. Is 13:15
parched. Reed and rush will **d**. Is 19:6
dead did not **d** by the sword; Is 22:2
and drink, for tomorrow we **d**!" Is 22:13
There you will **d**, and there your Is 22:18
order, for you are about to **d**; Is 38:1
lack of water and **d** of thirst. Is 50:2
will **d** in like manner. Is 51:6
he will not **d** ⌊and go⌋ to the Is 51:14
Whoever eats their eggs will **d**; Is 59:5
the youth will **d** at a hundred Is 65:20
for their maggots will never **d**, Is 66:24
will certainly **d** at our hand." Jr 11:21
young men will **d** by the sword; Jr 11:22
and daughters will **d** by famine. Jr 11:22
will **d** from deadly diseases. Jr 16:4
and small will **d** in this land Jr 16:6
There you will **d**, and there you Jr 20:6
They will **d** in a great plague. Jr 21:6
this city will **d** by the sword, Jr 21:9
but he will **d** in the place where Jr 22:12
and there you will both **d**. Jr 22:26
yelling, "You must surely **d**! Jr 26:8
and your people **d** by the sword, Jr 27:13
You will **d** this year because you Jr 28:16
each will **d** for his own Jr 31:30
You will not **d** by the sword; Jr 34:4
will **d** peacefully. There will Jr 34:5
the scribe, or I will **d** there." Jr 37:20
this city will **d** by the sword, Jr 38:2
man ought to **d**, because he is Jr 38:4
where he will **d** from hunger, Jr 38:9
these things or you will **d**. Jr 38:24
of Jonathan to **d** there.' " Jr 38:26
to Egypt, and you will **d** there. Jr 42:16
for a while will **d** by the sword, Jr 42:17
plague you will **d** in the place Jr 42:22
they will **d** by the sword and by Jr 44:12
and I thought: I'm going to **d**! Lm 3:54
will surely **d**, but you do not Ezk 3:18
person will **d** for his iniquity. Ezk 3:18
he will **d** for his iniquity, Ezk 3:19
in front of him, he will **d**. Ezk 3:20
he will **d** because of his sin and Ezk 3:20
people will **d** by plague and be Ezk 5:12
who is far off will **d** by plague; Ezk 6:12
and is spared will **d** of famine. Ezk 6:12
the field will **d** by the sword. Ezk 7:15
not see it, and he will **d** there. Ezk 12:13
who should not **d** and spare those Ezk 13:19
GOD—"he will **d** in Babylon, Ezk 17:16
who sins is the one who will **d**. Ezk 18:4
he will certainly **d**. Ezk 18:13
person will not **d** for his Ezk 18:17
he will **d** for his own iniquity Ezk 18:18
who sins is the one who will **d**. Ezk 18:20
certainly live; he will not **d**. Ezk 18:21
He will **d** because of the Ezk 18:24
iniquity, he will **d** for this. Ezk 18:26
will **d** because of the iniquity Ezk 18:26
he had committed; he will not **d**. Ezk 18:28
Why should you **d**, house of Ezk 18:31
and you will **d** a violent death Ezk 28:8
You will **d** the death of the Ezk 28:10
will surely **d**, but you do not Ezk 33:8
person will **d** for his iniquity, Ezk 33:8
he will **d** for his iniquity, Ezk 33:9
Why will you **d**, house of Israel? Ezk 33:11
and he will **d** because of the Ezk 33:13
will surely **d**, but he repents Ezk 33:14
certainly live; he will not **d**. Ezk 33:15
he will **d** on account of this. Ezk 33:18
and caves will **d** by plague. Ezk 33:27
yet they will **d** by sword and Dn 11:33
and I will let her **d** of thirst. Hs 2:3
Moab will **d** with a tumult, Am 2:2
left in one house, they will **d**. Am 6:9
'Jeroboam will **d** by the sword, Am 7:11
yourself will **d** on pagan soil, Am 7:17
us, will **d** by the sword. Am 9:10
for me to **d** than to live." Jnh 4:3
fainted, and he wanted to **d**. Jnh 4:8
for me to **d** than to live." Jnh 4:8
right. I'm angry enough to **d**!" Jnh 4:9
My Holy One, You will not **d**. Hab 1:12
what is dying **d**, and let what is Zch 11:9
two-thirds will be cut off and **d**, Zch 13:8
save ⌊us⌋! We're going to **d**!" Mt 8:25
"Even if I have to **d** with You," Mt 26:35
you care that we're going to **d**?" Mk 4:38
where Their worm does not **d**, Mk 9:44
where Their worm does not **d**, Mk 9:46
where Their worm does not **d**, Mk 9:48
If I have to **d** with You, I will Mk 14:31
by him, was sick and about to **d**. Lk 7:2
Master, we're going to **d**!" Lk 8:24
For they cannot **d** anymore, Lk 20:36
his son, for he was about to **d**. Jn 4:47
anyone may eat of it and not **d**. Jn 6:50
and you will **d** in your sin. Jn 8:21
that you will **d** in your sins. Jn 8:24
He⌋, you will **d** in your sins." Jn 8:24
go so that we may **d** with Him." Jn 11:16
believes in Me will never **d**— Jn 11:26
one man should **d** for the people Jn 11:50
was going to **d** for the nation, Jn 11:51
kind of death He was about to **d**. Jn 12:33
one man should **d** for the people. Jn 18:14
sort of death He was going to **d**. Jn 18:32
according to that law He must **d**, Jn 19:7
that this disciple would not **d**. Jn 21:23
tell him that he would not **d**, Jn 21:23
but also to **d** in Jerusalem for Ac 21:13
not refuse to **d**, but if there is Ac 25:11
such things deserve to **d**— Rm 1:32
will someone **d** for a just person Rm 5:7
someone might even dare to **d**. Rm 5:7
the flesh, you are going to **d**. Rm 8:13
and if we **d**, we die to the Lord. Rm 14:8
and if we die, we **d** to the Lord. Rm 14:8
we live or **d**, we belong to Rm 14:8
place, like men condemned to **d**: 1Co 4:9
for me to **d** than for anyone 1Co 9:15
For just as in Adam all **d**, 1Co 15:22
Jesus our Lord: I **d** every day! 1Co 15:31
and drink, for tomorrow we **d**. 1Co 15:32
to **d** together and to live 2Co 7:3
men who will **d** receive tithes; Heb 7:8
is valid only when people **d**, Heb 9:17
appointed for people to **d** once— Heb 9:27
is about to **d**, for I have not Rv 3:2
will long to **d**, but death will Rv 9:6
are the dead who **d** in the Lord Rv 14:13

DIED *(246)*

lasted 930 years; then he **d**. Gn 5:5
lasted 912 years; then he **d**. Gn 5:8
lasted 905 years; then he **d**. Gn 5:11
lasted 910 years; then he **d**. Gn 5:14
lasted 895 years; then he **d**. Gn 5:17
lasted 962 years; then he **d**. Gn 5:20
lasted 969 years; then he **d**. Gn 5:27
lasted 777 years; then he **d**. Gn 5:31
everything on dry land **d**. Gn 7:22
lasted 950 years; then he **d**. Gn 9:29
Haran **d** in his native land, Gn 11:28
lived 205 years and **d** in Haran. Gn 11:32
d in Kiriath-arba (that is, Gn 23:2
last breath and **d** at a ripe old Gn 25:8
He took his last breath and **d**, Gn 25:17
had stopped up after Abraham **d**. Gn 26:18
d and was buried under the oak Gn 35:8
Rachel **d** and was buried on the Gn 35:19

He took his last breath and **d,** Gn 35:29
When Bela **d**, Jobab son of Zerah Gn 36:33
When Jobab **d**, Husham from the Gn 36:34
Husham **d**, Hadad son of Bedad Gn 36:35
When Hadad **d**, Samlah from Gn 36:36
When Samlah **d**, Shaul from Gn 36:37
When Shaul **d**, Baal-hanan son of Gn 36:38
When Baal-hanan son of Achbor **d**, Gn 36:39
wife, the daughter of Shua, **d**. Gn 38:12
but Er and Onan **d** in the land of Gn 46:12
sorrow Rachel **d** along the way, Gn 48:7
his feet into the bed and **d**. Gn 49:33
Before he **d** your father gave a Gn 50:16
Joseph **d** at the age of 110. Gn 50:26
and all that generation **d**. Ex 1:6
long time, the king of Egypt **d**. Ex 2:23
in the Nile **d**, and the river Ex 7:21
courtyards, and fields **d**. Ex 8:13
All the Egyptian livestock **d**, Ex 9:6
among the Israelite livestock **d**. Ex 9:6
If only we had **d** by the LORD's Ex 16:3
the presence of the LORD and **d**. Lv 16:1
an animal that **d** a natural death Lv 17:15
animal that **d** naturally or was Lv 22:8
Nadab and Abihu **d** in the LORD's Nm 3:4
the LORD, and the fire **d** down. Nm 11:2
If only we had **d** in the land of Nm 14:2
or if only we had **d** in this Nm 14:2
But those who **d** from the plague Nm 16:49
to those who **d** because of the Nm 16:49
a body of a person who has **d**, Nm 19:13
killed by the sword or has **d**, Nm 19:16
Miriam **d** and was buried there. Nm 20:1
Aaron **d** there on top of the Nm 20:28
them so that many Israelites **d**. Nm 21:6
but those who **d** in the plague Nm 25:9
his followers **d** and the fire Nm 26:10
they **d** in the land of Canaan. Nm 26:19
Nadab and Abihu **d** when they Nm 26:61
Our father **d** in the wilderness, Nm 27:3
he **d** because of his own sin, Nm 27:3
Hor and **d** there on the first Nm 33:38
old when he **d** on Mount Hor. Nm 33:39
men had **d** among the people Dt 2:16
Aaron **d** and was buried there, Dt 10:6
your brother Aaron **d** on Mount Dt 32:50
of the LORD **d** there in the land Dt 34:5
was 120 years old when he **d**; Dt 34:7
d in the wilderness along the Jos 5:4
of Egypt had **d** off because they Jos 5:6
the way to Azekah, and they **d**. Jos 10:11
of them **d** from the hail than Jos 10:11
son of Nun, **d** at the age of 110 Jos 24:29
And Eleazar son of Aaron **d**, Jos 24:33
to Jerusalem, and he **d** there. Jdg 1:7
the LORD, **d** at the age of 110. Jdg 2:8
the judge **d**, the Israelites Jdg 2:19
nations Joshua left when he **d**. Jdg 2:21
and Othniel son of Kenaz **d**. Jdg 3:11
of the LORD after Ehud had **d**. Jdg 4:1
it into the ground, and he **d**. Jdg 4:21
son of Joash **d** at a ripe old age Jdg 8:32
When Gideon **d**, the Israelites Jdg 8:33
Many wounded **d** as far as the Jdg 9:40
in the Tower of Shechem **d**— Jdg 9:49
thrust him through, and he **d**. Jdg 9:54
years, and when he **d**, was buried Jdg 10:2
When Jair **d**, he was buried in Jdg 10:5
time, 42,000 from Ephraim **d**. Jdg 12:6
and when he **d**, he was buried Jdg 12:7
and when he **d**, he was buried in Jdg 12:10
and when he **d**, he was buried in Jdg 12:12
and when he **d**, he was buried in Jdg 12:15
raped my concubine, and she **d**. Jdg 20:5
18,000 men who **d** from Benjamin; Jdg 20:44
Benjaminites who **d** that day were Jdg 20:46
Naomi's husband Elimelech **d**, Ru 1:3
both Mahlon and Chilion also **d**, Ru 1:5
sons, Hophni and Phinehas, **d**. 1Sm 4:11
heavy, his neck broke and he **d**. 1Sm 4:18
Samuel **d**, and all Israel 1Sm 25:1
By this time Samuel had **d**, 1Sm 28:3
on his own sword and **d** with him. 1Sm 31:5
Saul **d** together with his three 1Sm 31:6
for those who **d** by the sword— 2Sm 1:12
servant struck him, and he **d**. 2Sm 1:15
so that they all **d** together. 2Sm 2:16
and he fell and **d** right there. 2Sm 2:23
where Asahel had fallen and **d**, 2Sm 2:23
So Abner **d** in revenge for the 2Sm 3:27
that Abner had **d** in Hebron, 2Sm 4:1
and he **d** there next to the ark 2Sm 6:7
the king of the Ammonites **d**, 2Sm 10:1
of their army, who **d** there. 2Sm 10:18
Uriah the Hittite also **d**. 2Sm 11:17
top of the wall so that he **d**? 2Sm 11:21
some of the king's soldiers **d**. 2Sm 11:24
that her husband Uriah had **d**, 2Sm 11:26
On the seventh day the baby **d**. 2Sm 12:18
wept, but when he **d**, you got up 2Sm 12:21
my husband **d**," she said. 2Sm 14:5
So he **d** and was buried in his 2Sm 17:23
If only I had **d** instead of you, 2Sm 18:33
over us, has **d** in battle. 2Sm 19:10
the seven of them **d** together. 2Sm 21:9
Dan to Beer-sheba 70,000 men **d**. 2Sm 24:15
struck down Adonijah, and he **d**. 1Kg 2:25
struck Shimei down, and he **d**. 1Kg 2:46
woman's son **d** because she lay 1Kg 3:19
of the house, the boy **d**. 1Kg 14:17
royal palace over himself. He **d** 1Kg 16:18
Tibni **d** and Omri became king. 1Kg 16:22
d that evening, and blood from 1Kg 22:35
So the king **d** and was brought to 1Kg 22:37
Ahaziah **d** according to the word 2Kg 1:17
when Ahab **d**, the king of Moab 2Kg 3:5
Your servant, my husband, has **d**. 2Kg 4:1
her lap until noon and then **d**. 2Kg 4:20
He **d**, just as the man of God had 2Kg 7:17
him in the gateway, and he **d**. 2Kg 7:20
Ben-hadad **d**, and Hazael reigned 2Kg 8:15
he fled to Megiddo and **d** there. 2Kg 9:27
struck him down, and he **d**. 2Kg 12:21
sick with the illness that he **d** 2Kg 13:14
Then Elisha **d** and was buried. 2Kg 13:20
Hazael of Aram **d**, and his son 2Kg 13:24
went to Egypt, and he **d** there. 2Kg 23:34
struck down Gedaliah, and he **d**. 2Kg 25:25
When Bela **d**, Jobab son of Zerah 1Ch 1:44
When Jobab **d**, Husham from the 1Ch 1:45
When Husham **d**, Hadad son of 1Ch 1:46
When Hadad **d**, Samlah from 1Ch 1:47
When Samlah **d**, Shaul from 1Ch 1:48
When Shaul **d**, Baal-hanan son of 1Ch 1:49
When Baal-hanan **d**, Hadad ruled 1Ch 1:50
Then Hadad **d**. Edom's chiefs: 1Ch 1:51
When Azubah **d**, Caleb married 1Ch 2:19
Seled **d** without children. 1Ch 2:30
Jether **d** without children. 1Ch 2:32
fell on his own sword and **d**. 1Ch 10:5
So Saul and his three sons **d**— 1Ch 10:6
his whole house **d** together. 1Ch 10:6
Saul **d** for his unfaithfulness to 1Ch 10:13
So he **d** there in the presence of 1Ch 13:10
King Nahash of the Ammonites **d**, 1Ch 19:1
and 70,000 Israelite men **d**. 1Ch 21:14
Eleazar **d** having no sons, only 1Ch 23:22
Nadab and Abihu **d** before their 1Ch 24:2
He **d** at a good old age, full of 1Ch 29:28
the LORD struck him and he **d**. 2Ch 13:20
Asa **d** in the forty-first year of 2Ch 16:13
evening. Then he **d** at sunset. 2Ch 18:34
and he **d** from severe illnesses. 2Ch 21:19
He **d** to no one's regret and was 2Ch 21:20
Jehoiada **d** when he was old and 2Ch 24:15
after Jehoiada **d**, the rulers of 2Ch 24:17
So he **d**, and they buried him in 2Ch 24:25
Then he **d**, and they buried him 2Ch 35:24
When her father and mother **d**, Est 2:7
the young people so that they **d**, Jb 1:19
I should have **d** and never been Jb 10:18
Job **d**, old and full of days. Jb 42:17
I would have **d** in my affliction. Ps 119:92
have already **d**, more than the Ec 4:2
In the year that King Uzziah **d**, Is 6:1
In the year that King Ahaz **d**, Is 14:28
the prophet Hananiah **d** that year Jr 28:17
anything that **d** naturally or was Ezk 4:14
Pelatiah son of Benaiah **d**. Ezk 11:13
and my wife **d** in the evening. Ezk 24:18
animal that **d** naturally or was Ezk 44:31
guilt through Baal and **d**. Hs 13:1
After Herod **d**, an angel of the Mt 2:19
The first got married and **d**. Mt 22:25
Then last of all the woman **d**. Mt 22:27
took her, and he **d**, leaving no Mk 12:21
Last of all, the woman **d** too. Mk 12:22
him whether He had already **d**. Mk 15:44
the poor man **d** and was carried Lk 16:22
rich man also **d** and was buried. Lk 16:22
took a wife and **d** without Lk 20:29
seven **d** and left no children. Lk 20:31
Finally, the woman **d** too. Lk 20:32
in the wilderness, and they **d**. Jn 6:49
your fathers ate—and they **d**. Jn 6:58
Abraham **d** and so did the Jn 8:52
than our father Abraham who **d**? Jn 8:53
Even the prophets **d**. Who do You Jn 8:53
them plainly, "Lazarus has **d**. Jn 11:14
my brother wouldn't have **d**. Jn 11:21
my brother would not have **d**!" Jn 11:32
after his father **d**, God had him Ac 7:4
He and our forefathers **d** there, Ac 7:15
days she became sick and **d**. Ac 9:37
infected with worms and **d**. Ac 12:23
Christ **d** for the ungodly. Rm 5:6
still sinners Christ **d** for us! Rm 5:8
one man's trespass the many **d**, Rm 5:15
How can we who **d** to sin still Rm 6:2
a person who has **d** is freed from Rm 6:7
Now if we **d** with Christ, we Rm 6:8
For in that He **d**, He died to sin Rm 6:10
He died, He **d** to sin once for Rm 6:10
since we have **d** to what held us, Rm 7:6
I **d**. The commandment that was Rm 7:10
Christ Jesus is the One who **d**, Rm 8:34
Christ **d** and came to life for Rm 14:9
that one for whom Christ **d**. Rm 14:15
the brother for whom Christ **d**, 1Co 8:11
that Christ **d** for our sins 1Co 15:3
if One **d** for all, then all died. 2Co 5:14
if One died for all, then all **d**. 2Co 5:14
And He **d** for all so that those 2Co 5:15
for the One who **d** for them and 2Co 5:15
the law I have **d** to the law, Gl 2:19
then Christ **d** for nothing. Gl 2:21
he was so sick that he nearly **d**. Php 2:27
If you **d** with Christ to the Col 2:20
For you have **d**, and your life is Col 3:3
that Jesus **d** and rose again, 1Th 4:14
who **d** for us, so that whether we 1Th 5:10
For if we have **d** with Him, 2Tm 2:11
These all **d** in faith without Heb 11:13
in two, they **d** by the sword, Heb 11:37
so that, having **d** to sins, we 1Pt 2:24
living creatures in the sea **d**, Rv 8:9
of the people **d** from the waters, Rv 8:11
and all life in the sea **d**. Rv 16:3

DIES *(57)*

he may bless you before he **d**." Gn 27:10
so that he **d** must be put to Ex 21:12
and the slave **d** under his abuse, Ex 21:20
his neighbor's ox and it **d**, Ex 21:35
care for, but it **d**, is injured, Ex 22:10
is injured or **d** while its owner Ex 22:14
an animal that **d** naturally or is Lv 7:24
When any one of them **d** and falls Lv 11:32
animals that you use for food **d**, Lv 11:39
If someone suddenly **d** near him, Nm 6:9
law when a person **d** in a tent: Nm 19:14
When a man **d** without having a Nm 27:8
strikes another man and he **d**, Nm 35:17
of causing death and he **d**, Nm 35:18
with malicious intent and he **d**, Nm 35:20
him with his hand and he **d**, Nm 35:21
could kill a person and he **d**, Nm 35:23
his neighbor so that he **d**, Dt 19:5
away from his house or if he **d**, Dt 24:3
and one of them **d** without a son, Dt 25:5
Should Abner die as a fool **d**? 2Sm 3:33
so that he is struck down and **d**. 2Sm 11:15
is found in him, then he **d**." 1Kg 1:52
to Jeroboam and **d** in the city, 1Kg 14:11
and anyone who **d** in the field, 1Kg 14:11
to Baasha and **d** in the city, 1Kg 16:4
who is his and **d** in the field, 1Kg 16:4
to Ahab and **d** in the city, 1Kg 21:24
and he who **d** in the field, 1Kg 21:24
strong lion **d** if ⌊it catches⌋ Jb 4:11
But a man **d** and fades away; Jb 14:10
When a man **d**, will he come back Jb 14:14
person **d** in excellent health, Jb 21:23
another person **d** with a bitter Jb 21:25
For when he **d**, he will take Ps 49:17

When the wicked **d**, his Pr 11:7
a gossip, conflict **d** down. Pr 26:20
that the wise man **d** just like Ec 2:16
As one **d**, so dies the other; Ec 3:19
As one dies, so **d** the other; Ec 3:19
see what will happen after he **d**? Ec 3:22
that you should fear man who **d**, Is 51:12
from the cistern before he **d**." Jr 38:10
said, if a man **d**, having no Mt 22:24
us that if a man's brother **d**, Mk 12:19
has a wife, and **d** childless, his Lk 20:28
"come down before my boy **d**!" Jn 4:49
in Me, even if he **d**, will live. Jn 11:25
falls into the ground and **d**, Jn 12:24
But if it **d**, it produces a large Jn 12:24
from the dead, no longer **d**. Rm 6:9
her husband **d**, she is released Rm 7:2
if her husband **d**, she is free Rm 7:3
and no one **d** to himself. Rm 14:7
if her husband **d**, she is free to 1Co 7:39
not come to life unless it **d**. 1Co 15:36
Moses' law, he **d** without mercy, Heb 10:28

DIET *(1)*
and the special **d** that she Est 2:9

DIFFERENCE *(6)*
recognize ⌊the **d** between⌋ 2Ch 12:8
not explain the **d** between the Ezk 22:26
My people the **d** between the holy Ezk 44:23
to them the **d** between the clean Ezk 44:23
will again see the **d** between the Mal 3:18
really were makes no **d** to me; Gl 2:6

DIFFERENCES *(1)*
it regards **d** of bloodguilt, 2Ch 19:10

DIFFERENT *(34)*
they must take **d** stones to Lv 14:42
crossbreed two **d** kinds of your Lv 19:19
Caleb has a **d** spirit and has Nm 14:24
not have two **d** weights in your Dt 25:13
be transformed into a **d** person. 1Sm 10:6
by putting on **d** clothes and set 1Sm 28:8
goblets, each with a **d** design. Est 1:7
Their laws are **d** from everyone Est 3:8
will consist of many **d** kinds, Ezk 47:10
official gave them ⌊**d**⌋ names: Dn 1:7
the sea, each **d** from the other. Dn 7:3
It was **d** from all the beasts Dn 7:7
the one **d** from all the others, Dn 7:19
d from all the other kingdoms. Dn 7:23
Another, **d** from the previous Dn 7:24
appeared in a **d** form to two of Mk 16:12
began to speak in **d** languages, Ac 2:4
until a **d** king ruled over Egypt Ac 7:18
departed and went to a **d** place. Ac 12:17
But I see a **d** law in the parts Rm 7:23
given to us, we have **d** gifts: Rm 12:6
Now there are **d** gifts, but the 1Co 12:4
There are **d** ministries, but the 1Co 12:5
And there are **d** activities, 1Co 12:6
to another, **d** kinds of languages 1Co 12:10
doubtless many **d** kinds of 1Co 14:10
heavenly bodies is **d** from that 1Co 15:40
or you receive a **d** spirit, 2Co 11:4
received, or a **d** gospel, which 2Co 11:4
⌊and are turning⌋ to a **d** gospel— Gl 1:6
the prophets at **d** times and in Heb 1:1
different times and in **d** ways. Heb 1:1
are said belonged to a **d** tribe, Heb 7:13
and sent them out by a **d** route? Jms 2:25

DIFFERENTLY *(1)*
if you think **d** about anything, Php 3:15

DIFFERING *(3)*
must not have two **d** dry measures Dt 25:14
D weights and varying measures— Pr 20:10
D weights are detestable to the Pr 20:23

DIFFERS *(2)*
star **d** from star in splendor. 1Co 15:41
he **d** in no way from a slave, Gl 4:1

DIFFICULT *(32)*
this was a very **d** thing for Gn 21:11
give birth, and her labor was **d**. Gn 35:16
During her **d** labor, the midwife Gn 35:17
bitter with **d** labor in brick Ex 1:14
because of their **d** labor, Ex 2:23
to God because of the **d** labor. Ex 2:23
Bring me any case too **d** for you, Dt 1:17
If a case is too **d** for you— Dt 17:8
not too **d** or beyond your Dt 30:11
troops were in a **d** situation. 1Sm 13:6
was in a **d** position because 1Sm 30:6
to test him with **d** questions. 1Kg 10:1
nothing was too **d** for the king 1Kg 10:3
to Jerusalem is too **d** for you. 1Kg 12:28
You have asked for something **d**. 2Kg 2:10
test Solomon with **d** questions at 2Ch 9:1
nothing was too **d** for Solomon to 2Ch 9:2
too great or too **d** for me. Ps 131:1
how **d** Your thoughts are for me Ps 139:17
a brother is born for a **d** time. Pr 17:17
If you do nothing in a **d** time, Pr 24:10
speech is **d** to comprehend— Is 33:19
Nothing is too **d** for You! Jr 32:17
Is anything too **d** for Me? Jr 32:27
speech or **d** language but to Ezk 3:5
speech or **d** language, Ezk 3:6
asking is so **d** that no one can Dn 2:11
and a moat, but in **d** times. Dn 9:25
is the gate and **d** the road that Mt 7:14
You're a **d** man, reaping where Mt 25:24
d times will come in the last 2Tm 3:1
this, and it's **d** to explain, Heb 5:11

DIFFICULTIES *(1)*
should not cause **d** for those who Ac 15:19

DIFFICULTY *(8)*
and made them drive with **d**. Ex 14:25
redeemed my life from every **d**, 1Kg 1:29
man who also had a speech **d**, Mk 7:32
his speech **d** was removed, Mk 7:35
that whether easily or with **d**, Ac 26:29
we came with **d** as far as Cnidus. Ac 27:7
With yet more **d** we sailed along Ac 27:8
the righteous is saved with **d**, 1Pt 4:18

DIG *(9)*
wells dug that you did not **d**, Dt 6:11
d a hole with it and cover up Dt 23:13
'**D** ditch after ditch in this wadi. 2Kg 3:16
Son of man, **d** through the wall. Ezk 8:8
d through the wall and take the Ezk 12:5
They will **d** through the wall to Ezk 12:12
If they **d** down to Sheol, from Am 9:2
I **d** around it and fertilize Lk 13:8
I'm not strong enough to **d**; Lk 16:3

DIGESTIVE *(1)*
He will remove its **d** tract, Lv 1:16

DIGGING *(1)*
You must have a **d** tool in your Dt 23:13

DIGNITARIES *(5)*
chains and their **d** with iron Ps 149:8
the **d** are starving, and the Is 5:13
down go Zion's **d**, her masses, Is 5:14
Her **d** were brighter than snow, Lm 4:7
cast lots for her **d**, and all her Nah 3:10

DIGNITARY *(1)*
the commander of 50 and the **d**, Is 3:3

DIGNITY *(4)*
they chase my **d** away like the Jb 30:15
life in all godliness and **d**. 1Tm 2:2
under control with all **d**. 1Tm 3:4
integrity and **d** in your teaching Ti 2:7

DIGS *(4)*
a man uncovers a pit or **d** a pit, Ex 21:33
A worthless man **d** up evil, Pr 16:27
The one who **d** a pit will fall Pr 26:27
one who **d** a pit may fall into Ec 10:8

DIKLAH *(2)*
Hadoram, Uzal, **D**, Gn 10:27
Hadoram, Uzal, **D**, 1Ch 1:21

DILAN *(1)*
D, Mizpeh, Jokthe-el, Jos 15:38

DILIGENCE *(8)*
leading, with **d**; showing mercy, Rm 12:8
Do not lack **d**; be fervent in Rm 12:11
how much **d** this very thing 2Co 7:11
order that your **d** for us might 2Co 7:12
in all **d**, and in your love 2Co 8:7
by means of the **d** of others, 2Co 8:8
God who put the same **d** for you 2Co 8:16
the same **d** for the final Heb 6:11

DILIGENT *(11)*
So be very **d** to love the LORD Jos 23:11
He was **d** in every deed that he 2Ch 31:21
one poor, but **d** hands bring Pr 10:4
The **d** hand will rule, but Pr 12:24
game, but to a **d** man, his wealth Pr 12:27
but the **d** is fully satisfied. Pr 13:4
plans of the **d** certainly lead Pr 21:5
and, being very **d**, went out to 2Co 8:17
and found **d**—and now even more 2Co 8:22
now even more **d** because of his 2Co 8:22
d to present yourself approved 2Tm 2:15

DILIGENTLY *(13)*
your guard and **d** watch Dt 4:9
is being done **d** and succeeding Ezr 5:8
Let it be carried out **d**. Ezr 6:12
colleagues **d** carried out what Ezr 6:13
must be done **d** for the house Ezr 7:23
son of Zabbai **d** repaired another Neh 3:20
that Your precepts be **d** kept. Ps 119:4
who loves him disciplines him **d**. Pr 13:24
my spirit within me **d** seeks You, Is 26:9
If they will **d** learn the ways of Jr 12:16
d keeping the unity of the Eph 4:3
he **d** searched for me and found 2Tm 1:17
D help Zenas the lawyer and Ti 3:13

DILL *(1)*
tenth of mint, **d**, and cumin, yet Mt 23:23

DILUTED *(1)*
your beer is **d** with water. Is 1:22

DIM *(3)*
My eyes have grown **d** from grief, Jb 17:7
their eyes grow too **d** to see, Ps 69:23
of these, our eyes grow **d**: Lm 5:17

DIMENSIONS *(3)*
same casting, **d**, and shape for 1Kg 7:37
Who fixed its **d**? Certainly you Jb 38:5
corner areas had the same **d**. Ezk 46:22

DIMINISH *(1)*
sunlight and moonlight will **d**. Zch 14:6

DIMINISHED *(1)*
When they are **d** and are humbled Ps 107:39

DIMLY *(1)*
watch through the windows see **d**, Ec 12:3

DIMNAH *(1)*
(AKA RIMMON)
D with its pasturelands, and Jos 21:35

DIMONAH *(1)*
Kinah, **D**, Adadah, Jos 15:22

DINAH *(7)*
bore a daughter and named her **D**. Gn 30:21
D, Leah's daughter whom she bore Gn 34:1
He became infatuated with **D**, Gn 34:3
had defiled his daughter **D**, Gn 34:5
he had defiled their sister **D**. Gn 34:13
took **D** from Shechem's house, Gn 34:26
as well as his daughter **D**. Gn 46:15

DINAH'S *(2)*
Shechem said to **D** father and Gn 34:11
Simeon and Levi, **D** brothers, Gn 34:25

DINE *(3)*
you sit down to **d** with a ruler, Pr 23:1
d on lambs from the flock and Am 6:4
asked Him to **d** with him. Lk 11:37

DINED *(3)*
and he **d** regularly in the 2Kg 25:29
his house and **d** with him in his Jb 42:11
and he **d** regularly in the Jr 52:33

DINHABAH *(2)*
the name of his city was **D**. Gn 36:32
Bela's town was named **D**. 1Ch 1:43

DINING *(2)*
copper utensils, and **d** couches. Mk 7:4
this knowledge, **d** in an idol's 1Co 8:10

DINNER *(6)*
Invite him to eat **d**." Ex 2:20
Look, I've prepared my **d**; Mt 22:4
the ritual washing before **d**. Lk 11:38
When you give a lunch or a **d**, Lk 14:12
So they gave a **d** for Him there; Jn 12:2
in to him and have **d** with him, Rv 3:20

DIONYSIUS *(1)*
whom were **D** the Areopagite, Ac 17:34

DIOTREPHES *(1)*
the church, but **D**, who loves to 3Jn 9

DIP *(12)*
d it in the blood that is in the Ex 12:22

The priest is to **d** his finger in Lv 4:6
The priest is to **d** his finger in Lv 4:17
and **d** them all into the blood of Lv 14:6
The priest will **d** his right Lv 14:16
d them in the blood of the Lv 14:51
to take hyssop, **d** ⌊it⌋ in the Nm 19:18
his brothers and **d** his foot in Dt 33:24
some bread and **d** it in the Ru 2:14
then You **d** me in a pit ⌊of mud⌋, Jb 9:31
the winepress to **d** 50 measures Hg 2:16
send Lazarus to **d** the tip of his Lk 16:24

DIPPED *(8)*
and **d** the robe in its blood. Gn 37:31
and he **d** his finger in the blood Lv 9:9
was carrying and **d** it into the 1Sm 14:27
Naaman went down and **d** himself 2Kg 5:14
a heavy cloth, **d** it in water, 2Kg 8:15
The one who **d** his hand with Me Mt 26:23
of bread to after I have **d** it." Jn 13:26
When He had **d** the bread, Jn 13:26

DIPPING *(1)*
the one who is **d** ⌊bread⌋ with Me Mk 14:20

DIRECT *(7)*
Jacob—his **d** descendants, not Gn 46:26
LORD began to **d** him in the Camp Jdg 13:25
to **d** the music because he was 1Ch 15:22
He will **d** the blows of his Ezk 26:9
we came by a **d** route to Cos, Ac 21:1
Lord Jesus, **d** our way to you. 1Th 3:11
May the Lord **d** your hearts to 2Th 3:5

DIRECTED *(15)*
The LORD **d** Moses, "Go down and Ex 19:21
as Balaam **d**, and they offered Nm 23:2
the LORD had **d** against you, Dt 9:19
did what the LORD **d** and went to 1Sm 16:4
background, as Mordecai had **d**. Est 2:20
I **d** their course and presided as Jb 29:25
But Job has not **d** his argument Jb 32:14
has **d** the Spirit of the LORD, Is 40:13
left—wherever your blade is **d**. Ezk 21:16
and did just as Jesus **d** them. Mt 21:6
did as Jesus had **d** them and Mt 26:19
field, as the Lord **d** me. Mt 27:10
mountain where Jesus had **d** them. Mt 28:16
was divinely **d** by a holy angel Ac 10:22
and, as I **d** you, to appoint Ti 1:5

DIRECTING *(3)*
to wisdom and **d** your heart to Pr 2:2
d their rivers all around the Ezk 31:4
d that he be examined with the Ac 22:24

DIRECTION *(31)*
under the **d** of Ithamar son Ex 38:21
under the **d** of Aaron their Nm 3:4
be under the **d** of Ithamar son Nm 4:28
under the **d** of Ithamar son of Nm 4:33
registered under the **d** of Moses, Nm 4:49
under the **d** of Ithamar son of Nm 7:8
a day's journey in every **d**. Nm 11:31
in the **d** of the Red Sea." Nm 14:25
you from one **d** but flee from you Dt 28:7
them from one **d** but flee from Dt 28:25
They could not escape in any **d**, Jos 8:20
in the **d** of Zererah as far Jdg 7:22
from the **d** of the Diviners' Jdg 9:37
troops scattering in every **d**. 1Sm 14:16
all his enemies in every **d**: 1Sm 14:47
LORD in the **d** of the city You 1Kg 8:44
to You in the **d** of their land 1Kg 8:48
came from the **d** of Edom and 2Kg 3:20
to You in the **d** of this city You 2Ch 6:34
they pray in the **d** of their land 2Ch 6:38
round and round at His **d**, Jb 37:12
confuse the **d** of your paths. Is 3:12
them to the wind in every **d**, Jr 49:32
went in the **d** the Spirit was Ezk 1:20
to every **d** of the wind. Ezk 5:10
third to every **d** of the wind, Ezk 5:12
coming from the **d** of the Upper Ezk 9:2
would go in that **d**, without Ezk 10:11
troops to every **d** of the wind, Ezk 12:14
to every **d** of the wind. Ezk 17:21
law under the **d** of angels and Ac 7:53

DIRECTIONS *(5)*
but flee from you in seven **d**. Dt 28:7
but flee from them in seven **d**. Dt 28:25
they went in any of the four **d**, Ezk 1:17
would go in any of the four **d**, Ezk 10:11
having asked **d** to Simon's house, Ac 10:17

DIRECTIVE *(1)*
man who interferes with this **d**: Ezr 6:11

DIRECTLY *(18)*
your neighbor **d**, and you will Lv 19:17
its produce ⌊**d**⌋ from the field Lv 25:12
speak with him **d**, openly, and Nm 12:8
But He **d** pays back and destroys Dt 7:10
not hesitate to **d** pay back the Dt 7:10
these words **d** to them and call Dt 31:28
reported these words **d** to David, 1Sm 18:23
let your servant speak to you **d**. 1Sm 25:24
He spoke **d** to my father David, 1Kg 8:15
You spoke **d** ⌊to him⌋ and You 1Kg 8:24
him, "Do not pursue them **d**. 1Ch 14:14
He spoke **d** to my father David, 2Ch 6:4
You spoke **d** ⌊to him⌋, and You 2Ch 6:15
Go and announce **d** to Jerusalem Jr 2:2
all these things **d** to you." Jr 26:15
the LORD came **d** to Ezekiel the Ezk 1:3
He called to me **d** with a loud Ezk 9:1
able to look **d** at Moses' face 2Co 3:7

DIRECTS *(4)*
and God ⌊so⌋ **d** you, you will be Ex 18:23
you know how God **d** His clouds or Jb 37:15
He **d** it wherever He chooses. Pr 21:1
the will of the pilot **d**. Jms 3:4

DIRGE *(4)*
chanted a **d** over Josiah, 2Ch 35:25
Raise up a **d** on the barren Jr 7:29
a **d** over the wilderness grazing Jr 9:10
a lament and one another a **d**, Jr 9:20

DIRGES *(2)*
Josiah in their **d** to this very 2Ch 35:25
they are written in the **D**. 2Ch 35:25

DIRT *(10)*
Abraham, filling them with **d**. Gn 26:15
its blood and cover it with **d**. Lv 17:13
and there was **d** on his head. 1Sm 4:12
and threw stones and **d** at him. 2Sm 16:13
mule-loads of **d** be given to your 2Kg 5:17
maggots and encrusted with **d**. Jb 7:5
The **d** on his grave is sweet to Jb 21:33
the clods ⌊of **d**⌋ stick together Jb 38:38
Me will be written in the **d**, Jr 17:13
gold like the **d** of the streets. Zch 9:3

DIRTY *(2)*
my feet. How can I get them **d**? Sg 5:3
man dressed in **d** clothes also Jms 2:2

DISABILITY *(1)*
Woman, you are free of your **d**." Lk 13:12

DISABLED *(2)*
who had been **d** by a spirit for Lk 13:11
a good deed done to a **d** man— Ac 4:9

DISAGREEING *(1)*
D among themselves, they began Ac 28:25

DISAGREEMENT *(2)*
such a sharp **d** that they parted Ac 15:39
and constant **d** among men whose 1Tm 6:5

DISAGREEMENTS *(1)*
they had some **d** with him about Ac 25:19

DISAPPEAR *(9)*
until you **d** from this good land Jos 23:13
will quickly **d** from this good Jos 23:16
his name will not **d** among his Ru 4:10
they **d** from their channels in Jb 6:17
nations will **d** from their places Jb 36:20
scorner will **d**, and all those Is 29:20
even the fish of the sea **d**. Hs 4:3
Samaria's king will **d** like foam Hs 10:7
is old and aging is about to **d**. Heb 8:13

DISAPPEARED *(8)*
skin disease has **d** from the Lv 14:3
because the contamination has **d**. Lv 14:48
was busy here and there, he **d**." 1Kg 20:40
the loyal have **d** from the human Ps 12:1
and their envy have already **d**, Ec 9:6
it has **d** from their mouths. Jr 7:28
but He **d** from their sight. Lk 24:31
fled, and the mountains **d**. Rv 16:20

DISAPPEARING *(1)*
that we would be saved was **d**. Ac 27:20

DISAPPEARS *(4)*
contamination **d** from the fabric Lv 13:58
As water **d** from the sea and a Jb 14:11
fly to it, it **d**, for it makes Pr 23:5
The fortress **d** from Ephraim, Is 17:3

DISAPPOINT *(1)*
hope does not **d**, because God's Rm 5:5

DISAPPOINTED *(1)*
be ashamed and the diviners **d**. Mc 3:7

DISAPPROVED *(1)*
father Isaac **d** of the Canaanite Gn 28:8

DISARMED *(1)*
He **d** the rulers and authorities Col 2:15

DISARMS *(1)*
on nobles and **d** the strong. Jb 12:21

DISASTER *(126)*
the **d** will overtake me, and I Gn 19:19
mind about this **d** ⌊planned⌋ for Ex 32:12
about the **d** He said He would Ex 32:14
He considers no **d** for Jacob; Nm 23:21
D will come to you in the future, Dt 31:29
for their day of **d** is near, Dt 32:35
destruction and bring **d** on it. Jos 6:18
them and brought **d** ⌊on them⌋, Jdg 2:15
did not know that **d** was about to Jdg 20:34
realized that **d** had struck them. Jdg 20:41
going to bring **d** on you from 2Sm 12:11
us, heap **d** on us, and strike 2Sm 15:14
am about to bring **d** on the house 1Kg 14:10
about to bring **d** on you and will 1Kg 21:21
will not bring the **d** during his 1Kg 21:29
I will bring the **d** on his house 1Kg 21:29
good about me, but only **d**. 1Kg 22:8
good about me, but only **d**?" 1Kg 22:18
has pronounced **d** against you." 1Kg 22:23
he said, "This **d** is from the 2Kg 6:33
⌊This **d**⌋ happened because the 2Kg 17:7
to bring such **d** on Jerusalem 2Kg 21:12
about to bring **d** on this place 2Kg 22:16
not see all the **d** that I am 2Kg 22:20
good about me, but only **d**. 2Ch 18:7
good about me, but only **d**?" 2Ch 18:17
has pronounced **d** against you." 2Ch 18:22
If **d** comes on us—sword or 2Ch 20:9
about to bring **d** on this place 2Ch 34:24
not see all the **d** that I am 2Ch 34:28
brought all this **d** on us and on Neh 13:18
When **d** brings sudden death, Jb 9:23
d lies ready for him to stumble. Jb 18:12
Does **d** come on them? Jb 21:17
man is spared from the day of **d**, Jb 21:30
Doesn't **d** come to the wicked and Jb 31:3
For **d** from God terrifies me, Jb 31:23
they bring down **d** on me and Ps 55:3
their years in sudden **d**. Ps 78:33
a cruel man brings **d** on himself. Pr 11:17
No **d** ⌊overcomes⌋ the righteous, Pr 12:21
D pursues sinners, but good Pr 13:21
the wicked for the day of **d**. Pr 16:4
who rejoices over **d** will not go Pr 17:5
who sows injustice will reap **d**, Pr 22:8
who knows what **d** these two can Pr 24:22
don't know what **d** may happen on Ec 11:2
I will bring **d** on the world, Is 13:11
He also is wise and brings **d**. Is 31:2
I make success and create **d**; Is 45:7
But **d** will happen to you; Is 47:11
bear children ⌊destined⌋ for **d**, Is 65:23
D will be poured out from the Jr 1:14
guilty; **d** came on them." Jr 2:3
but in their time of **d** they beg: Jr 2:27
in your time of **d** if they can, Jr 2:28
I am bringing **d** from the north Jr 4:6
D after disaster is reported, Jr 4:20
Disaster after **d** is reported, Jr 4:20
for **d** threatens from the north, Jr 6:1
about to bring **d** on these people Jr 6:19
bring on them **d** that they cannot Jr 11:11
save them in their time of **d**. Jr 11:12
to Me at the time of their **d**. Jr 11:14
meat prevent your **d** so you can Jr 11:15
you has decreed **d** against you, Jr 11:17
for I will bring **d** on the people Jr 11:23
has been destroyed by a great **d**, Jr 14:17
all this great **d** against us? Jr 16:10
are my refuge in the day of **d**. Jr 17:17
Bring on them the day of **d**; Jr 17:18

will not bring the **d** on it I had Jr 18:8
to bring such **d** on this place Jr 19:3
all the **d** that I spoke against Jr 19:15
city to ⌊bring⌋ **d** and not good'" Jr 21:10
for I will bring **d** on them, Jr 23:12
of horror and **d** to all the Jr 24:9
and bring **d** on yourselves.' Jr 25:7
bringing **d** on the city that Jr 25:29
D goes forth from nation to Jr 25:32
concerning the **d** that I plan to Jr 26:3
concerning the **d** that He warned Jr 26:13
concerning the **d** He had Jr 26:19
prophesied war, **d**, and plague Jr 28:8
welfare, not for **d**, to give you Jr 29:11
and to cause **d**, so will I be Jr 31:28
have brought all this **d** on them. Jr 32:23
this great **d** on these people, Jr 32:42
all the **d** I have pronounced Jr 35:17
about all the **d** I am planning to Jr 36:3
on the men of Judah all the **d**, Jr 36:31
of this people, but **d**." Jr 38:4
decreed this **d** on this place, Jr 40:2
concerning the **d** that I have Jr 42:10
escapee from the **d** I will bring Jr 42:17
seen all the **d** I brought against Jr 44:2
turn against you to ⌊bring⌋ **d**, Jr 44:11
and good things and saw no **d**, Jr 44:17
this **d** has come to you, Jr 44:23
them for **d** and not for good, Jr 44:27
that My words of **d** concerning Jr 44:29
about to bring **d** on every living Jr 45:5
devastation and great **d**! Jr 48:3
his **d** is rushing swiftly. Jr 48:16
I will bring **d** on them, My Jr 49:37
from every side in the day of **d**. Jr 51:2
about all the **d** that would come Jr 51:60
because of the **d** I am bringing Jr 51:64
to bring this **d** on them without Ezk 6:10
one **d** after another is coming! Ezk 7:5
D after disaster will come, Ezk 7:26
Disaster after **d** will come, Ezk 7:26
sword in the time of their **d**, Ezk 35:5
on us so great a **d** that nothing Dn 9:12
all this **d** has come on us, Dn 9:13
the LORD kept the **d** in mind and Dn 9:14
and He relents from sending **d**. Jl 2:13
If a **d** occurs in a city, hasn't Am 3:6
D will never overtake or Am 9:10
My people in the day of their **d**. Ob 13
in the day of their **d** and do not Ob 13
in the day of their **d**. Ob 13
from the **d** He had threatened Jnh 3:10
who relents from ⌊sending⌋ **d**. Jnh 4:2
am now planning a **d** against this Mc 2:3
to escape from the reach of **d**! Hab 2:9

DISASTERS *(1)*

I will pile **d** on them; Dt 32:23

DISCARD *(2)*

Don't **d** me in my old age: Ps 71:9
let us **d** the deeds of darkness Rm 13:12

DISCARDED *(1)*

the nations like **d** pottery. Hs 8:8

DISCERN *(5)*

the king is able to **d** the good 2Sm 14:17
I **d** what is pleasant and what 2Sm 19:35
people and to **d** between good 1Kg 3:9
will be able to **d** all these Ac 24:8
so that you may **d** what is the Rm 12:2

DISCERNING *(14)*

Pharaoh look for a **d** and wise Gn 41:33
and a **d** man will obtain guidance Pr 1:5
is found on the lips of the **d**, Pr 10:13
resides in the heart of the **d**; Pr 14:33
d mind seeks knowledge, but the Pr 15:14
For the **d** the path of life leads Pr 15:24
with a wise heart is called **d**, Pr 16:21
keeps silent, **d**, when he seals Pr 17:28
The mind of the **d** acquires Pr 18:15
rebuke the **d**, and he gains Pr 19:25
but with a **d** and knowledgeable Pr 28:2
A **d** son keeps the law, but a Pr 28:7
or riches to the **d**, or favor to Ec 9:11
d what is pleasing to the Lord. Eph 5:10

DISCERNMENT *(8)*

Blessed is your **d**, and blessed 1Sm 25:33
but you asked **d** for yourself to 1Kg 3:11
also showed **d** by dispersing some 2Ch 11:23
Teach me good judgment and **d**, Ps 119:66
man who has **d** sees through him Pr 28:11
are shepherds who have no **d**; Is 56:11
People without **d** are doomed. Hs 4:14
knowledge and every kind of **d**, Php 1:9

DISCHARGE *(26)*

be clean from her **d** of blood. Lv 12:7
any man has a **d** from his body, Lv 15:2
This is uncleanness of his **d**: Lv 15:3
secretes the **d** or retains it, Lv 15:3
anything because of his **d**, Lv 15:3
man with the **d** lies on will be Lv 15:4
the man with the **d** was sitting Lv 15:6
the man with a **d** is to wash his Lv 15:7
man with the **d** spits on anyone Lv 15:8
man with the **d** rides on will be Lv 15:9
man with the **d** touches anyone Lv 15:11
man with the **d** touches must be Lv 15:12
man with the **d** has been cured Lv 15:13
the LORD because of his **d**. Lv 15:15
a woman has a **d**, and it consists Lv 15:19
If **d** is on the bed or the Lv 15:23
a woman has a **d** of her blood for Lv 15:25
or if she has a **d** beyond her Lv 15:25
all the days of her unclean **d**, Lv 15:25
the days of her **d** will be like Lv 15:26
When she is cured of her **d**, Lv 15:28
LORD because of her unclean **d**. Lv 15:30
is the law for someone with a **d**: Lv 15:32
anyone who has a **d**, whether male Lv 15:33
a skin disease or a **d** is to eat Lv 22:4
anyone who has a ⌊bodily⌋ **d**, Nm 5:2

DISCIPLE *(30)*

A **d** is not above his teacher, Mt 10:24
is enough for a **d** to become like Mt 10:25
little ones because he is a **d**— Mt 10:42
had also become a **d** of Jesus. Mt 27:57
A **d** is not above his teacher, Lk 6:40
own life—he cannot be My **d**. Lk 14:26
come after Me cannot be My **d**. Lk 14:27
his possessions cannot be My **d**. Lk 14:33
that man's **d**, but we're Moses Jn 9:28
Jesus, as was another **d**. Jn 18:15
That **d** was an acquaintance of Jn 18:15
So the other **d**, the one known to Jn 18:16
mother and the **d** He loved Jn 19:26
He said to the **d**, "Here is your Jn 19:27
that hour the **d** took her into Jn 19:27
who was a **d** of Jesus— Jn 19:38
Simon Peter and to the other **d**, Jn 20:2
Peter and the other **d** went out, Jn 20:3
but the other **d** outran Peter and Jn 20:4
The other **d**, who had reached the Jn 20:8
Therefore the **d**, the one Jesus Jn 21:7
around and saw the **d** Jesus loved Jn 21:20
⌊That **d**⌋ was the one who had Jn 21:20
that this **d** would not die. Jn 21:23
This is the **d** who testifies to Jn 21:24
there was a **d** named Ananias. Ac 9:10
they did not believe he was a **d**. Ac 9:26
there was a **d** named Tabitha, Ac 9:36
there was a **d** named Timothy, Ac 16:1
an early **d**, with whom we were Ac 21:16

DISCIPLES *(239)*

up the instruction among my **d**. Is 8:16
He sat down, His **d** came to Him. Mt 5:1
another of His **d** said, "first Mt 8:21
the boat, His **d** followed Him. Mt 8:23
So the **d** came and woke Him up, Mt 8:25
to eat with Jesus and His **d**. Mt 9:10
they asked His **d**, "Why does your Mt 9:11
Then John's **d** came to Him, Mt 9:14
often, but Your **d** do not fast?" Mt 9:14
So Jesus and His **d** got up and Mt 9:19
said to His **d**, "The harvest is Mt 9:37
Summoning His 12 **d**, He gave them Mt 10:1
giving orders to His 12 **d**, Mt 11:1
he sent ⌊a message⌋ by his **d** Mt 11:2
His **d** were hungry and began to Mt 12:1
Your **d** are doing what is not Mt 12:2
out His hand toward His **d**, Mt 12:49
the **d** came up and asked Him, Mt 13:10
His **d** approached Him and said, Mt 13:36
Then his **d** came, removed the Mt 14:12
the **d** approached Him and said, Mt 14:15
loaves and gave them to the **d**, Mt 14:19
and the **d** ⌊gave them⌋ to the Mt 14:19
He made the **d** get into the boat Mt 14:22
When the **d** saw Him walking on Mt 14:26
Why do Your **d** break the Mt 15:2
Then the **d** came up and told Him, Mt 15:12
His **d** approached Him and urged Mt 15:23
Jesus summoned His **d** and said, Mt 15:32
The **d** said to Him, "Where could Mt 15:33
kept on giving them to the **d**, Mt 15:36
and the **d** ⌊gave them⌋ to the Mt 15:36
The **d** reached the other shore, Mt 16:5
He asked His **d**, "Who do people Mt 16:13
And He gave the **d** orders to tell Mt 16:20
out to His **d** that He must go Mt 16:21
Then Jesus said to His **d**, Mt 16:24
When the **d** heard it, they fell Mt 17:6
So the **d** questioned Him, "Why Mt 17:10
Then the **d** understood that He Mt 17:13
him to Your **d**, but they couldn't Mt 17:16
Then the **d** approached Jesus Mt 17:19
At that time the **d** came to Jesus Mt 18:1
His **d** said to Him, "If the Mt 19:10
But the **d** rebuked them. Mt 19:13
Then Jesus said to His **d**, Mt 19:23
When the **d** heard this, they were Mt 19:25
took the 12 **d** aside privately Mt 20:17
When the 10 ⌊**d**⌋ heard this, Mt 20:24
Olives, Jesus then sent two **d**, Mt 21:1
The **d** went and did just as Jesus Mt 21:6
When the **d** saw it, they were Mt 21:20
They sent their **d** to Him, with Mt 22:16
to the crowds and to His **d**: Mt 23:1
His **d** came up and called His Mt 24:1
the **d** approached Him privately Mt 24:3
saying all this, He told His **d**, Mt 26:1
When the **d** saw it, they were Mt 26:8
Bread the **d** came to Jesus Mt 26:17
at your place with My **d**.'" Mt 26:18
So the **d** did as Jesus had Mt 26:19
it to the **d**, and said, "Take Mt 26:26
And all the **d** said the same Mt 26:35
and He told the **d**, "Sit here Mt 26:36
He came to the **d** and found them Mt 26:40
He came to the **d** and said to Mt 26:45
Then all the **d** deserted Him and Mt 26:56
Otherwise, His **d** may come, steal Mt 27:64
go quickly and tell His **d**, Mt 28:7
they ran to tell His **d** the news. Mt 28:8
'His **d** came during the night and Mt 28:13
The 11 **d** traveled to Galilee, Mt 28:16
and make **d** of all nations, Mt 28:19
guests with Jesus and His **d**, Mk 2:15
they asked His **d**, "Why does He Mk 2:16
Now John's **d** and the Pharisees Mk 2:18
do John's **d** and the Pharisees' Mk 2:18
and the Pharisees' **d** fast, Mk 2:18
fast, but Your **d** do not fast?" Mk 2:18
His **d** began to make their way Mk 2:23
departed with His **d** to the sea, Mk 3:7
He told His **d** to have a small Mk 3:9
explain everything to His own **d**. Mk 4:34
His **d** said to Him, "You see the Mk 5:31
and His **d** followed Him. Mk 6:1
When his **d** heard about it, Mk 6:29
His **d** approached Him and said, Mk 6:35
them to His **d** to set before Mk 6:41
He made His **d** get into the boat Mk 6:45
that some of His **d** were eating Mk 7:2
Why don't Your **d** live according Mk 7:5
the **d** asked Him about the Mk 7:17
He summoned the **d** and said to Mk 8:1
His **d** answered Him, "Where can Mk 8:4
them⌋ to His **d** to set before Mk 8:6
the boat with His **d** and went to Mk 8:10
out with His **d** to the villages Mk 8:27
And on the road He asked His **d**, Mk 8:27
around and looking at His **d**, Mk 8:33
the crowd along with His **d**, Mk 8:34
they came to the **d**, they saw a Mk 9:14
I asked Your **d** to drive it out Mk 9:18
His **d** asked Him privately, Mk 9:28
teaching His **d** and telling them Mk 9:31
the house the **d** questioned Him Mk 10:10
them, but His **d** rebuked them. Mk 10:13
looked around and said to His **d**, Mk 10:23
But the **d** were astonished at His Mk 10:24
the ⌊other⌋ 10 ⌊**d**⌋ heard this, Mk 10:41
Jericho with His **d** and a large Mk 10:46
of Olives, He sent two of His **d** Mk 11:1
And His **d** heard it. Mk 11:14

His **d**, He said to them, Mk 12:43
one of His **d** said to Him, Mk 13:1
lamb, His **d** asked Him, "Where Mk 14:12
sent two of His **d** and told them, Mk 14:13
eat the Passover with My **d**?" Mk 14:14
So the **d** went out, entered the Mk 14:16
and He told His **d**, "Sit here Mk 14:32
go, tell His **d** and Peter, 'He Mk 16:7
were complaining to His **d**, Lk 5:30
John's **d** fast often and say Lk 5:33
His **d** were picking heads of Lk 6:1
He summoned His **d**, and He chose Lk 6:13
large crowd of His **d** and a great Lk 6:17
looking up at His **d**, He said: Lk 6:20
His **d** and a large crowd were Lk 7:11
Then John's **d** told him about all Lk 7:18
So John summoned two of his **d** Lk 7:18
Then His **d** asked Him, "What does Lk 8:9
He and His **d** got into a boat, Lk 8:22
He told His **d**, "Have them sit Lk 9:14
them to the **d** to set before Lk 9:16
private and His **d** were with Him, Lk 9:18
I begged Your **d** to drive it out, Lk 9:40
He was doing, He told His **d**, Lk 9:43
When the **d** James and John saw Lk 9:54
turning to His **d** He said Lk 10:23
one of His **d** said to Him, Lk 11:1
just as John also taught his **d**." Lk 11:1
He began to say to His **d** first: Lk 12:1
Then He said to His **d**: Lk 12:22
He also said to the **d**: Lk 16:1
He said to His **d**, "Offenses will Lk 17:1
Then He told the **d**: Lk 17:22
them, but when the **d** saw it, Lk 18:15
of Olives, He sent two of the **d** Lk 19:29
crowd of the **d** began to praise Lk 19:37
Him, "Teacher, rebuke Your **d**." Lk 19:39
listening, He said to His **d**, Lk 20:45
eat the Passover with My **d**?"' Lk 22:11
Olives, and the **d** followed Him. Lk 22:39
from prayer and came to the **d**, Lk 22:45
was standing with two of his **d**. Jn 1:35
The two **d** heard him say this and Jn 1:37
Jesus and His **d** were invited to Jn 2:2
and His **d** believed in Him. Jn 2:11
and His **d**, and they stayed Jn 2:12
And His **d** remembered that it is Jn 2:17
d remembered that He had said Jn 2:22
Jesus and His **d** went to the Jn 3:22
between John's **d** and a Jew about Jn 3:25
and baptizing more **d** than John Jn 4:1
not baptizing, but His **d** were), Jn 4:2
for His **d** had gone into town to Jn 4:8
then His **d** arrived, and they Jn 4:27
meantime the **d** kept urging Him Jn 4:31
The **d** said to one another, Jn 4:33
and sat down there with His **d**. Jn 6:3
One of His **d**, Andrew, Simon Jn 6:8
full, He told His **d**, "Collect Jn 6:12
His **d** went down to the sea, Jn 6:16
not boarded the boat with His **d**, Jn 6:22
but that His **d** had gone off Jn 6:22
Jesus nor His **d** were there, Jn 6:24
when many of His **d** heard this, Jn 6:60
that His **d** were complaining Jn 6:61
many of His **d** turned back and no Jn 6:66
to Judea so Your **d** can see Your Jn 7:3
in My word, you really are My **d**. Jn 8:31
His **d** questioned Him: Jn 9:2
don't want to become His **d** too, Jn 9:27
disciple, but we're Moses' **d**. Jn 9:28
He said to the **d**, "Let's go to Jn 11:7
"Rabbi," the **d** told Him, "just Jn 11:8
Then the **d** said to Him, "Lord, Jn 11:12
to his fellow **d**, "Let's go so Jn 11:16
And He stayed there with the **d**. Jn 11:54
one of His **d**, Judas Iscariot Jn 12:4
His **d** did not understand these Jn 12:16
The **d** started looking at one Jn 13:22
One of His **d**, the one Jesus Jn 13:23
will know that you are My **d**, Jn 13:35
much fruit and prove to be My **d**. Jn 15:8
some of His **d** said to one Jn 16:17
"Ah!" His **d** said. "Now You're Jn 16:29
out with His **d** across the Kidron Jn 18:1
and He and His **d** went into it. Jn 18:1
often met there with His **d**. Jn 18:2
aren't one of this man's **d** too, Jn 18:17
Jesus about His **d** and about His Jn 18:19
You aren't one of His **d** too, Jn 18:25
Then the **d** went home again. Jn 20:10
went and announced to the **d**, Jn 20:18
the **d** were ⌊gathered together⌋ Jn 20:19
So the **d** rejoiced when they saw Jn 20:20
So the other **d** kept telling him, Jn 20:25
eight days His **d** were indoors Jn 20:26
presence of His **d** that are not Jn 20:30
Himself again to His **d** by the Jn 21:1
others of His **d** were together. Jn 21:2
the **d** did not know it was Jesus. Jn 21:4
the other **d** came in the boat, Jn 21:8
None of the **d** dared ask Him, Jn 21:12
appeared to the **d** after He was Jn 21:14
number of the **d** was multiplying Ac 6:1
whole company of the **d** and said, Ac 6:2
the number of the **d** in Jerusalem Ac 6:7
against the **d** of the Lord, Ac 9:1
was with the **d** in Damascus for Ac 9:19
but his **d** took him by night and Ac 9:25
tried to associate with the **d**, Ac 9:26
the **d** heard that Peter was there Ac 9:38
and the **d** were first called Ac 11:26
So each of the **d**, according to Ac 11:29
And the **d** were filled with joy Ac 13:52
After the **d** surrounded him, Ac 14:20
that town and made many **d**, Ac 14:21
hearts of the **d** by encouraging Ac 14:22
a considerable time with the **d**. Ac 14:28
strengthening all the **d**. Ac 18:23
wrote to the **d** urging them to Ac 18:27
came to Ephesus. He found some **d** Ac 19:1
and met separately with the **d**, Ac 19:9
people, the **d** did not let him Ac 19:30
sent for the **d**, encouraged them Ac 20:1
to lure the **d** into following Ac 20:30
we found some **d** and stayed there Ac 21:4
Some of the **d** from Caesarea also Ac 21:16

DISCIPLES' *(2)*
to wash His **d** feet and to dry Jn 13:5
putting on the **d** necks a yoke Ac 15:10

DISCIPLINE *(47)*
proceed to **d** you seven times Lv 26:18
things you do not accept My **d**, Lv 26:23
will also **d** you seven times for Lv 26:28
or saw the **d** of the LORD your Dt 11:2
to them even after they **d** him, Dt 21:18
will **d** him with a human rod and 2Sm 7:14
but I will **d** you with barbed 1Kg 12:11
I will **d** you with barbed whips. 1Kg 12:14
not reject the **d** of the Almighty Jb 5:17
do not **d** me in Your wrath. Ps 6:1
Your anger or **d** me in Your wrath Ps 38:1
You **d** a man with punishment for Ps 39:11
man knowledge—does He not **d**? Ps 94:10
is the man You **d** and teach from Ps 94:12
you turn to my **d**, then I will Pr 1:23
my son, and do not loathe His **d**; Pr 3:11
to a father's **d**, and pay Pr 4:1
How I hated **d**, and how my heart Pr 5:12
of a fool ⌊brings⌋ a rod ⌊of **d**⌋, Pr 14:3
D is harsh for the one who Pr 15:10
D your son while there is hope; Pr 19:18
the rod of **d** will drive it away Pr 22:15
D your son, and he will give you Pr 29:17
the land with **d** from His mouth, Is 11:4
because⌋ Your **d** ⌊fell⌋ on them. Is 26:16
Your own evil will **d** you; Jr 2:19
they would not accept **d**. Jr 2:30
but they refused to accept **d**. Jr 5:3
God and would not accept **d**. Jr 7:28
D me, LORD, but with justice— Jr 10:24
not listening or accepting **d**. Jr 17:23
I will **d** you justly, but I will Jr 30:11
with the **d** of someone cruel, Jr 30:14
do not listen and receive **d**. Jr 32:33
you not accept **d** by listening to Jr 35:13
I will **d** you with justice, Jr 46:28
I will **d** them in accordance with Hs 7:12
I will **d** them at my discretion; Hs 10:10
she has not accepted **d**. Zph 3:2
I **d** my body and bring it under 1Co 9:27
not take the Lord's **d** lightly, Heb 12:5
Endure it as **d**: God is dealing Heb 12:7
there whom a father does not **d**? Heb 12:7
But if you are without **d**— Heb 12:8
we had natural fathers **d** us, Heb 12:9
d seems enjoyable at the time, Heb 12:11
many as I love, I rebuke and **d**. Rv 3:19

DISCIPLINED *(14)*
and he **d** the men of Succoth with Jdg 8:16
my father **d** you with whips, 1Kg 12:11
my father **d** you with whips, 1Kg 12:14
my father **d** you with whips, 2Ch 10:11
my father **d** you with whips, 2Ch 10:14
person may be **d** on his bed with Jb 33:19
The LORD **d** me severely but did Ps 118:18
A servant cannot be **d** by words; Pr 29:19
You **d** me, and I have been Jr 31:18
and I have been **d** like an Jr 31:18
be silent, for God has **d** him. Lm 3:28
judged, we are **d** by the Lord, so 1Co 11:32
For they **d** us for a short time Heb 12:10
clear-headed and **d** for prayer. 1Pt 4:7

DISCIPLINES *(4)*
you just as a man **d** his son. Dt 8:5
for the LORD **d** the one He loves, Pr 3:12
who loves him **d** him diligently. Pr 13:24
for the Lord **d** the one He loves, Heb 12:6

DISCIPLINING *(1)*
God has been **d** you just as a man Dt 8:5

DISCLOSE *(1)*
for the day will **d** it, because 1Co 3:13

DISCLOSED *(2)*
not yet been **d** while the first Heb 9:8
and the works on it will be **d**. 2Pt 3:10

DISCLOSING *(1)*
and **d** their practices, Ac 19:18

DISCLOSURE *(1)*
At this **d**, Moses fled and became Ac 7:29

DISCOMFORT *(1)*
over Jonah's head to ease his **d**. Jnh 4:6

DISCONTENTED *(2)*
debt, or **d** rallied around him, 1Sm 22:2
These people are **d** grumblers, Jd 16

DISCOURAGE *(1)*
to frighten and **d** them in order 2Ch 32:18

DISCOURAGED *(27)*
they **d** the Israelites from Nm 32:9
Do not be afraid or **d**. Dt 1:21
Our brothers have **d** us, saying: Dt 1:28
Do not be afraid or **d**." Dt 31:8
not be afraid or **d**, for the LORD Jos 1:9
Joshua, "Do not be afraid or **d**. Jos 8:1
to them, "Do not be afraid or **d**. Jos 10:25
Don't let anyone be **d** by him; 1Sm 17:32
Don't be afraid or **d**. 1Ch 22:13
be afraid or **d**, for the LORD God 1Ch 28:20
don't be **d**, for your work has a 2Ch 15:7
be afraid or **d** because of this 2Ch 20:15
Do not be afraid or **d**. 2Ch 20:17
be afraid or **d** before the king 2Ch 32:7
in the land **d** the people of Ezr 4:4
They will become **d** in the work, Neh 6:9
grow weak or be **d** until He has Is 42:4
heard about it, and we are **d**. Jr 6:24
and do not be **d**, Israel, for Jr 46:27
their words or be **d** by ⌊the look Ezk 2:6
afraid of them or **d** by ⌊the look Ezk 3:9
spirit will be **d**, and every knee Ezk 21:7
to pray always and not become **d**: Lk 18:1
stopped ⌊walking and looked⌋ **d**. Lk 24:17
ask you not to be **d** over my Eph 3:13
so they won't become **d**. Col 3:21
comfort the **d**, help the weak, 1Th 5:14

DISCOURAGING *(1)*
are you **d** the Israelites from Nm 32:7

DISCOURSE *(2)*
Job continued his **d**, saying: Jb 27:1
Job continued his **d**, saying: Jb 29:1

DISCOVER *(13)*
test him and **d** what was in his 2Ch 32:31
books you will **d** and verify that Ezr 4:15
depths of God or **d** the limits Jb 11:7
too much⌋ to **d** and hate his sin. Ps 36:2
of the LORD and **d** the knowledge Pr 2:5
right to those who **d** knowledge. Pr 8:9
man cannot **d** the work God has Ec 3:11
that man cannot **d** anything that Ec 7:14
and very deep. Who can **d** it? Ec 7:24
is unable to **d** the work that is Ec 8:17
know it, he is unable to **d** it. Ec 8:17

so he could **d** the reason they Ac 22:24
So I **d** this principle: Rm 7:21

DISCOVERED *(26)*
will give you is **d** doing evil Dt 17:2
If a man is **d** having sexual Dt 22:22
and rapes her, and they are **d**, Dt 22:28
If a man is **d** kidnapping one of Dt 24:7
the Philistines **d** that the ark 1Sm 4:6
David and his men had been **d**. 1Sm 22:6
wilderness and **d** Saul had come 1Sm 26:3
nurse my son, I **d** he was dead. 1Kg 3:21
he **d** the boy lying dead on his 2Kg 4:32
'I have just now **d** that two 2Kg 5:22
he **d** an army with horses and 2Kg 6:15
They looked and **d** ⌊they were⌋ in 2Kg 6:20
they **d** that there was not a 2Kg 7:5
king of Assyria **d** a conspiracy 2Kg 17:4
He **d** the crown weighed 75 pounds 1Ch 20:2
turned and **d** that the battle 2Ch 13:14
It was **d** that this city has had Ezr 4:19
Then I **d** the evil that Eliashib Neh 13:7
to what their fathers **d**, Jb 8:8
this I have **d**, by adding one Ec 7:27
I have **d** that God made people Ec 7:29
he returned and **d** that the king Is 37:8
has been **d** among the men Jr 11:9
I **d** Israel like grapes in the Hs 9:10
it was **d** before they came Mt 1:18
the woman saw that she was **d**, Lk 8:47

DISCREDIT *(2)*
in order that they could **d** me. Neh 6:13
his friend or **d** his neighbor, Ps 15:3

DISCREDITED *(1)*
risk that our business may be **d**, Ac 19:27

DISCRETION *(7)*
knowledge and **d** to a young man— Pr 1:4
D will watch over you, and Pr 2:11
⌊your⌋ competence and **d**. Pr 3:21
may maintain **d** and your lips Pr 5:2
and have knowledge and **d**. Pr 8:12
with tact and **d** to Arioch, Dn 2:14
I will discipline them at my **d**; Hs 10:10

DISCRIMINATED *(1)*
haven't you **d** among yourselves Jms 2:4

DISCUSS *(2)*
it over, **d** it, and speak up! Jdg 19:30
"Come, let us **d** this," says the Is 1:18

DISCUSSED *(4)*
And they **d** among themselves, Mt 16:7
They **d** it among themselves: Lk 20:5
they **d** it among themselves and Lk 20:14
went away and **d** with the chief Lk 22:4

DISCUSSING *(7)*
Why are you **d** among yourselves Mt 16:8
were **d** among themselves that Mk 8:16
Why are you **d** that you do not Mk 8:17
d what "rising from the dead" Mk 9:10
and started **d** with one another Lk 6:11
they were **d** everything that Lk 24:14
while they were **d** and arguing, Lk 24:15

DISCUSSION *(4)*
was a lot of **d** about Him among Jn 7:12
and engaged in **d** with the Jews. Ac 18:19
engaging in **d** and trying to Ac 19:8
and turned aside to fruitless **d**. 1Tm 1:6

DISCUSSIONS *(1)*
conducting **d** every day in the Ac 19:9

DISDAIN *(1)*
Don't **d** Your glorious throne. Jr 14:21

DISEASE *(61)*
and it becomes a **d** on the skin Lv 13:2
of his body, it is a skin **d**. Lv 13:3
him unclean; he has a skin **d**. Lv 13:8
When a skin **d** develops on a Lv 13:9
it is a chronic **d** on the skin of Lv 13:11
But if the skin **d** breaks out Lv 13:12
if the skin **d** has covered his Lv 13:13
is unclean; it is a skin **d**. Lv 13:15
it is a skin **d** that has broken Lv 13:20
it is a skin **d** that has broken Lv 13:25
him unclean; it is a skin **d**. Lv 13:25
him unclean; it is a skin **d**. Lv 13:27
a skin **d** of the head or chin. Lv 13:30
it is a skin **d** breaking out on Lv 13:42
of a skin **d** on his body, Lv 13:43
man is afflicted with a skin **d**; Lv 13:44
infectious skin **d** is to have his Lv 13:45
with a skin **d** on the day of his Lv 14:2
If the skin **d** has disappeared Lv 14:3
to be cleansed from the skin **d**. Lv 14:7
who has a skin **d** and cannot Lv 14:32
law for any skin **d** or mildew, Lv 14:54
regarding skin **d** and mildew." Lv 14:57
who has a skin **d** or a discharge Lv 22:4
wasting **d** and fever that will Lv 26:16
who is afflicted with a skin **d**, Nm 5:2
in a case of infectious skin **d**, Dt 24:8
will afflict you with wasting **d**, Dt 28:22
he developed a **d** in his feet. 1Kg 15:23
warrior, but he had a skin **d**. 2Kg 5:1
would cure him of his skin **d**." 2Kg 5:3
you to cure him of his skin **d**. 2Kg 5:6
me to cure a man of his skin **d**? 2Kg 5:7
the spot and cure the skin **d**. 2Kg 5:11
Naaman's skin **d** will cling to 2Kg 5:27
a serious skin **d** until the day 2Kg 15:5
Asa developed a **d** in his feet, 2Ch 16:12
and his **d** became increasingly 2Ch 16:12
Yet even in his **d** he didn't seek 2Ch 16:12
including a **d** of the intestines, 2Ch 21:15
day after day because of the **d**." 2Ch 21:15
intestines with an incurable **d**. 2Ch 21:18
came out because of his **d**, 2Ch 21:19
a skin **d** broke out on his 2Ch 26:19
serious skin **d** and was excluded 2Ch 26:21
they said, "He has a skin **d**." 2Ch 26:23
but sent a wasting **d** among them. Ps 106:15
an emaciating **d** on the well-fed Is 10:16
on the day of **d** and incurable Is 17:11
husbands slain by deadly **d**, Jr 18:21
and healing every **d** and sickness Mt 4:23
a serious skin **d** came up and Mt 8:2
Immediately his **d** was healed. Mt 8:3
and healing every **d** and every Mt 9:35
to heal every **d** and sickness. Mt 10:1
a man who had a serious skin **d**, Mt 26:6
with a serious skin **d** came to Mk 1:40
Immediately the **d** left him, Mk 1:42
Simon who had a serious skin **d**, Mk 14:3
a serious skin **d** all over him. Lk 5:12
and immediately the **d** left him. Lk 5:13

DISEASED *(8)*
out, his hand was **d**, like snow. Ex 4:6
skin⌋ suddenly became **d**, Nm 12:10
her, he saw that she was **d** Nm 12:10
went out from his presence **d**— 2Kg 5:27
So the **d** men got up at twilight 2Kg 7:5
The **d** men went and called to the 2Kg 7:10
that he was **d** on his forehead 2Ch 26:20
King Uzziah was **d** to the time of 2Ch 26:21

DISEASES *(20)*
all the terrible **d** of Egypt that Dt 7:15
again with all the **d** of Egypt, Dt 28:60
Four men with skin **d** were at the 2Kg 7:3
He heals all your **d**. Ps 103:3
They will die from deadly **d**. Jr 16:4
various **d** and intense pains, Mt 4:24
weaknesses and carried our **d**. Mt 8:17
cleanse those with skin **d**, Mt 10:8
those with skin **d** are healed, Mt 11:5
sick with various **d** and drove Mk 1:34
all who had **d** were pressing Mk 3:10
Israel who had serious skin **d**, Lk 4:27
with various **d** brought them to Lk 4:40
Him and to be healed of their **d**; Lk 6:18
Jesus healed many people of **d**, Lk 7:21
those with skin **d** are healed, Lk 7:22
demons, and ⌊power⌋ to heal **d**. Lk 9:1
men with serious skin **d** met Him. Lk 17:12
the sick, and the **d** left them, Ac 19:12
island who had **d** also came and Ac 28:9

DISEMBARK *(1)*
handle an oar **d** from their ships Ezk 27:29

DISFIGURED *(2)*
lame, facially **d**, or deformed; Lv 21:18
was so **d** that He did not Is 52:14

DISGRACE *(72)*
uncircumcised man is a **d** to us. Gn 34:14
sexual relations, it is a **d**. Lv 20:17
she remain in **d** for seven days? Nm 12:14
away the **d** of Egypt from you. Jos 5:9
and removes this **d** from Israel? 1Sm 17:26
and to the **d** of your mother? 1Sm 20:30
could I ever go with my **d**? 2Sm 13:13
rebuke, and **d**, for children have 2Kg 19:3
are in great trouble and **d**. Neh 1:3
that we will no longer be a **d**." Neh 2:17
and would use my **d** as evidence Jb 19:5
For that would be a **d**; Jb 31:11
My **d** is before me all day long, Ps 44:15
I endure—my shame and **d**. Ps 69:19
covered with **d** and humiliation Ps 71:13
let them perish in **d**. Ps 83:17
accusers will be clothed with **d**; Ps 109:29
Turn away the **d** I dread; Ps 119:39
hate Zion be driven back in **d**. Ps 129:5
and his **d** will never be removed. Pr 6:33
pride comes, **d** follows, but with Pr 11:2
Poverty and **d** ⌊come to⌋ those Pr 13:18
but sin is a **d** to any people. Pr 14:34
and along with dishonor, **d**. Pr 18:3
is foolishness and **d** for him. Pr 18:13
the one who hears will **d** you, Pr 25:10
to himself is a **d** to his mother. Pr 29:15
by your name. Take away our **d**." Is 4:1
a **d** to the house of your lord. Is 22:18
to **d** all the honored ones of the Is 23:9
His people's **d** from the whole Is 25:8
refuge in Egypt's shadow your **d**. Is 30:3
rebuke, and **d**, ⌊as⌋ when Is 37:3
do not fear **d** by men, and do not Is 51:7
remember the **d** of your widowhood Is 54:4
cried out, "**D** is their portion, Is 61:7
let our **d** cover us. Jr 3:25
being provoked⌋ to **d**?" Jr 7:19
that I suffer **d** for Your honor. Jr 15:15
for me constant **d** and derision. Jr 20:8
of the earth, a **d**, an object of Jr 24:9
of scorn and a **d** among all the Jr 29:18
I bore the **d** of my youth. Jr 31:19
cursing, and **d**, and you will Jr 42:18
of scorn, of cursing, and of **d**. Jr 44:12
a desolation, a **d**, a ruin, and a Jr 49:13
Look, and see our **d**! Lm 5:1
you a ruin and a **d** among the Ezk 5:14
So you will be a **d** and a taunt, Ezk 5:15
You must also bear your **d**, Ezk 16:52
be ashamed and bear your **d**, Ezk 16:52
will bear your **d** and be ashamed Ezk 16:54
mouth again because of your **d**." Ezk 16:63
have made you a **d** to the nations Ezk 22:4
expelled you in **d** from the Ezk 28:16
They bear their **d** with those who Ezk 32:24
They bear their **d** with those who Ezk 32:25
They bear their **d** with those who Ezk 32:30
feel remorse for their **d** and all Ezk 39:26
will bear their **d** and the Ezk 44:13
will change their honor into **d**. Hs 4:7
leaders fervently love **d**. Hs 4:18
not make Your inheritance a **d**, Jl 2:17
make you a **d** among the nations Jl 2:19
be filled with **d** instead of Hab 2:16
and utter **d** will cover your Hab 2:16
not wanting to **d** her publicly, Mt 1:19
take away my **d** among the people. Lk 1:25
it's a **d** for him to live!" Ac 22:22
has long hair it is a **d** to him, 1Co 11:14
not fall into **d** and the Devil's 1Tm 3:7
outside the camp, bearing His **d**. Heb 13:13

DISGRACED *(26)*
those who despise Me will be **d**. 1Sm 2:30
Amnon since he **d** his sister 2Sm 13:22
day Amnon **d** his sister Tamar. 2Sm 13:32
turn back and suddenly be **d**. Ps 6:10
trusted in You and were not **d**. Ps 22:5
Do not let me be **d**; Ps 25:2
who waits for You will be **d**; Ps 25:3
without cause will be **d**. Ps 25:3
let me never be **d**. Ps 31:1
not let me be **d** when I call on Ps 31:17
Let the wicked be **d**; Ps 31:17
to kill me be **d** and humiliated; Ps 35:4
misfortune be **d** and humiliated; Ps 35:26
They will not be **d** in times of Ps 37:19
my life be **d** and confounded. Ps 40:14
and let those who hate us be **d**. Ps 44:7
hope in You be **d** because of me, Ps 69:6
my life be **d** and confounded; Ps 70:2
never let me be **d**. Ps 71:1
adversaries be **d** and confounded; Ps 71:13

harm will be **d** and confounded. Ps 71:24
be put to shame and the sun **d**, Is 24:23
you will be ashamed and **d**; Is 41:11
for you will not be **d**. Is 54:4
make those who were **d** throughout Zph 3:19
authorities and **d** them publicly; Col 2:15

DISGRACEFUL *(6)*
who sleeps during harvest is **d**. Pr 10:5
but his anger falls on a **d** one. Pr 14:35
will rule over a **d** son and share Pr 17:2
his mother is a **d** and shameful Pr 19:26
But if it is **d** for a woman to 1Co 11:6
for it is **d** for a woman to speak 1Co 14:35

DISGRACEFULLY *(1)*
wicked act disgustingly and **d**. Pr 13:5

DISGUISE *(4)*
to his wife, "Go **d** yourself, so 1Kg 14:2
I will **d** myself and go into 1Kg 22:30
I will **d** myself and go into 2Ch 18:29
his servants also **d** themselves 2Co 11:15

DISGUISED *(8)*
Saul **d** himself by putting on 1Sm 28:8
she arrives, she will be **d**." 1Kg 14:5
Why are you **d**? I have bad news 1Kg 14:6
He **d** himself with a bandage over 1Kg 20:38
of Israel **d** himself and went 1Kg 22:30
So the king of Israel **d** himself, 2Ch 18:29
to fight with him he **d** himself. 2Ch 35:22
Satan himself is **d** as an angel 2Co 11:14

DISGUISES *(1)*
hateful person **d** himself with Pr 26:24

DISGUISING *(1)*
d themselves as apostles of 2Co 11:13

DISGUST *(5)*
and feel **d** because they do Ps 119:158
she turned away from them in **d**. Ezk 23:17
from her in **d** just as I turned Ezk 23:18
those you turned away from in **d**. Ezk 23:22
those you turned away from in **d**. Ezk 23:28

DISGUSTED *(2)*
I am **d** with my life. Jb 10:1
For 40 years I was **d** with that Ps 95:10

DISGUSTING *(2)*
of Samaria I saw something **d**: Jr 23:13
You have made us **d** filth among Lm 3:45

DISGUSTINGLY *(1)*
the wicked act **d** and Pr 13:5

DISH *(17)*
was one silver **d** weighing three Nm 7:13
one silver **d** weighing three Nm 7:19
was one silver **d** weighing three Nm 7:25
was one silver **d** weighing three Nm 7:31
was one silver **d** weighing three Nm 7:37
was one silver **d** weighing three Nm 7:43
was one silver **d** weighing three Nm 7:49
was one silver **d** weighing three Nm 7:55
was one silver **d** weighing three Nm 7:61
was one silver **d** weighing three Nm 7:67
was one silver **d** weighing three Nm 7:73
was one silver **d** weighing three Nm 7:79
Each silver **d** ⌊weighed⌋ three Nm 7:85
the weight of each gold **d**; 1Ch 28:17
set me aside like an empty **d**; Jr 51:34
the outside of the cup and **d**, Mt 23:25
the outside of the cup and **d**, Lk 11:39

DISHAN *(3)*
(AKA DISHON)
Dishon, Ezer, and **D**. These are Gn 36:21
Dishon, Ezer, and **D**. These are Gn 36:30
Anah, Dishon, Ezer, and **D**. 1Ch 1:38

DISHAN'S *(2)*
These are **D** sons: Uz and Aran. Gn 36:28
and Jaakan. **D** sons: Uz and Aran 1Ch 1:42

DISHEARTENED *(1)*
Because you have **d** the righteous Ezk 13:22

DISHES *(3)*
12 silver **d**, 12 silver basins, Nm 7:84
wick trimmers, the **d**, and all 2Kg 25:14
basins, the **d**, and all the Jr 52:18

DISHEVEL *(1)*
must not **d** his hair or tear his Lv 21:10

DISHON *(5)*
(AKA DISHAN)
D, Ezer, and Dishan. These are Gn 36:21
D and Oholibamah daughter of Gn 36:25
D, Ezer, and Dishan. These are Gn 36:30
Zibeon, Anah, **D**, Ezer, and 1Ch 1:38
Anah's son: **D**. Dishon's sons: 1Ch 1:41

DISHON'S *(2)*
are **D** sons: Hemdan, Eshban, Gn 36:26
son: Dishon. **D** sons: Hamran, 1Ch 1:41

DISHONEST *(9)*
Do not give **d** testimony against Dt 5:20
they turned toward **d** gain, 1Sm 8:3
D scales are detestable to the Pr 11:1
but a **d** witness utters lies. Pr 14:5
to the LORD, and **d** scales are Pr 20:23
your iniquities in your **d** trade. Ezk 28:18
to extort with **d** scales in his Hs 12:7
price and cheat with **d** scales. Am 8:5
by teaching for **d** gain what they Ti 1:11

DISHONESTLY *(4)*
paths of all who pursue gain **d**; Pr 1:19
Don't let your mouth speak **d**, Pr 4:24
who goes around speaking **d**, Pr 6:12
one who profits **d** troubles his Pr 15:27

DISHONOR *(13)*
right for us to witness his **d**, Ezr 4:14
if they **d** My statutes and do not Ps 89:31
but He holds up fools to **d**. Pr 3:35
He will get a beating and **d**, Pr 6:33
mocker will bring **d** on himself; Pr 9:7
and along with **d**, disgrace. Pr 18:3
then lawsuits and **d** will cease. Pr 22:10
nations have heard of your **d**, Jr 46:12
I honor My Father and you **d** Me. Jn 8:49
you **d** God by breaking the law? Rm 2:23
for honor and another for **d**? Rm 9:21
sown in **d**, raised in glory; 1Co 15:43
glory and **d**, through slander 2Co 6:8

DISHONORED *(5)*
You have completely **d** his crown. Ps 89:39
Better to be **d**, yet have a Pr 12:9
counted worthy to be **d** on behalf Ac 5:41
are distinguished, but we are **d**! 1Co 4:10
Yet you **d** that poor man. Jms 2:6

DISHONORS *(3)*
is the one who **d** his father or Dt 27:16
on his head **d** his head. 1Co 11:4
her head uncovered **d** her head, 1Co 11:5

DISJOINTED *(1)*
water, and all my bones are **d**; Ps 22:14

DISLOCATED *(2)*
wrestled and **d** his hip socket. Gn 32:25
that what is lame may not be **d**, Heb 12:13

DISLODGED *(1)*
and a rock is **d** from its place, Jb 14:18

DISLOYAL *(3)*
I have seen the **d** and feel Ps 119:158
d will get what their conduct Pr 14:14
children who will not be **d**," Is 63:8

DISLOYALTY *(1)*
because of the **d** they have shown Dn 9:7

DISMAL *(1)*
to a lamp shining in a **d** place, 2Pt 1:19

DISMAY *(2)*
in his neck, and **d** dances before Jb 41:22
my heart is overcome with **d**. Ps 143:4

DISMAYED *(13)*
failed, and all Israel was **d**. 2Sm 4:1
powerless, **d**, and ashamed. 2Kg 19:26
It strikes you, and you are **d**. Jb 4:5
friends are **d** and can no longer Jb 32:15
who work with flax will be **d**; Is 19:9
boast will be **d** and ashamed. Is 20:5
perplexed to hear, too **d** to see. Is 21:3
powerless, **d**, and ashamed. Is 37:27
they will be **d** and snared. Jr 8:9
will no longer be afraid or **d**, Jr 23:4
and do not be **d**, Israel, for I Jr 30:10
will be put to shame and **d**! Jr 48:1
Moab is put to shame, indeed **d**. Jr 48:20

DISMISS *(3)*
Why did you **d** him? Now he's 2Sm 3:24
d any thought of the evil day Am 6:3
You can **d** Your slave in peace, Lk 2:29

DISMISSED *(13)*
he **d** the people who had carried Jdg 3:18
So David **d** Abner, and he went 2Sm 3:21
Hebron because David had **d** him, 2Sm 3:22
king, the king **d** him, and he 2Sm 3:23
he **d** the men, and they left. 2Kg 5:24
If I have **d** the case of my male Jb 31:13
Then He **d** the crowds and went Mt 13:36
side, while He **d** the crowds. Mt 14:22
Bethsaida, while He **d** the crowd. Mk 6:45
4,000 ⌊men⌋ were there. He **d** Mk 8:9
After the synagogue had been **d**, Ac 13:43
saying this, he **d** the assembly. Ac 19:41
the commander **d** the young man Ac 23:22

DISMISSING *(2)*
After **d** the crowds, He went up Mt 14:23
After **d** the crowds, He got into Mt 15:39

DISOBEDIENCE *(8)*
promiscuously in **d** to their God. Hs 4:12
through one man's **d** the many Rm 5:19
received mercy through their **d**, Rm 11:30
For God has imprisoned all in **d**, Rm 11:32
we are ready to punish any **d**, 2Co 10:6
and **d** received a just Heb 2:2
news did not enter because of **d**, Heb 4:6
fall into the same pattern of **d**. Heb 4:11

DISOBEDIENT *(12)*
But they were **d** and rebelled Neh 9:26
and the **d** to the understanding Lk 1:17
I was not **d** to the heavenly Ac 26:19
inventors of evil, **d** to parents, Rm 1:30
out My hands to a **d** and defiant Rm 10:21
the spirit now working in the **d**. Eph 2:2
God's wrath is coming on the **d**. Eph 5:6
God's wrath comes on the **d**, Col 3:6
blasphemers, **d** to parents, 2Tm 3:2
are detestable, **d**, and Ti 1:16
were once foolish, **d**, deceived, Ti 3:3
in the past were **d**, when God 1Pt 3:20

DISOBEY *(4)*
if you **d** the LORD and rebel 1Sm 12:15
self-seeking and **d** the truth, Rm 2:8
even if some **d** the ⌊Christian⌋ 1Pt 3:1
be for those who **d** the gospel of 1Pt 4:17

DISOBEYED *(8)*
with their fathers and **d** Me, Jdg 2:20
man of God who **d** the command 1Kg 13:26
As for those who **d** My covenant, Jr 34:18
and I have never **d** your orders, Lk 15:29
As you once **d** God, but now have Rm 11:30
they too have now **d**, ⌊resulting⌋ Rm 11:31
His rest," if not those who **d**? Heb 3:18
didn't perish with those who **d**. Heb 11:31

DISOBEYING *(2)*
are you **d** the king's command? Est 3:3
They stumble by **d** the message; 1Pt 2:8

DISORDER *(3)*
is not a God of **d** but of peace. 1Co 14:33
gossip, arrogance, and **d**. 2Co 12:20
there is **d** and every kind of Jms 3:16

DISORDERLY *(1)*
a reason for this **d** gathering." Ac 19:40

DISPATCHED *(3)*
Then Saul **d** messengers to Jesse 1Sm 16:19
and **d** him to Mordecai to learn Est 4:5
when a messenger was **d** to them. Ezk 23:40

DISPERSE *(8)*
I will **d** them throughout Jacob Gn 49:7
and would **d** their descendants Ps 106:27
the LORD when I **d** them among Ezk 12:15
that I would **d** them among the Ezk 20:23
I will **d** you among the nations Ezk 22:15
I will **d** the Egyptians among the Ezk 29:12
I will **d** the Egyptians among the Ezk 30:23
When I **d** the Egyptians among the Ezk 30:26

DISPERSED *(10)*
horn, and they **d** from the city, 2Sm 20:22
to ⌊the place⌋ where light is **d**? Jb 38:24
and gather the **d** of Israel; Is 11:12
well as those **d** in the land of Is 27:13
who gathers the **d** of Israel: Is 56:8
the nations where they were **d**. Ezk 29:13
I **d** them among the nations, Ezk 36:19
where You have **d** them because Dn 9:7
supplicants, My **d** people, will Zph 3:10
his partisans were **d** and came to Ac 5:36

DISPERSING *(1)*
discernment by **d** some of his — 2Ch 11:23
DISPERSION *(3)*
to go to the **D** among the Greeks — Jn 7:35
To the 12 tribes in the **D.** — Jms 1:1
of the **D** in the provinces — 1Pt 1:1
DISPLACE *(1)*
The wicked **d** boundary markers. — Jb 24:2
DISPLACED *(1)*
My people will be **d** from his own — Ezk 46:18
DISPLAY *(17)*
lion and again **d** Your miraculous — Jb 10:16
D the wonders of Your faithful — Ps 17:7
and He will ⌊**d** His⌋ glory in the — Is 24:23
inhabited or **d** ⌊your⌋ splendor — Ezk 26:20
I will **d** My glory within you. — Ezk 28:22
I will **d** My greatness and — Ezk 38:23
spread on the day I **d** My glory." — Ezk 39:13
I will **d** My glory among the — Ezk 39:21
and to **d** my majestic glory? — Dn 4:30
I will **d** wonders in the heavens — Jl 2:30
your face and **d** your nakedness — Nah 3:5
I will **d** wonders in the heaven — Ac 2:19
so that I may **d** My power in you, — Rm 9:17
desiring to **d** His wrath and to — Rm 9:22
always puts us on **d** in Christ, — 2Co 2:14
by an open **d** of the truth. — 2Co 4:2
ages He might **d** the immeasurable — Eph 2:7
DISPLAYED *(6)*
the bread **d** before the LORD, — Neh 10:33
He **d** the glorious wealth of his — Est 1:4
The LORD has **d** His holy arm in — Is 52:10
d His glory, and His disciples — Jn 2:11
God's works might be **d** in him. — Jn 9:3
I think God has **d** us, the — 1Co 4:9
DISPLAYING *(1)*
for ⌊**d**⌋ the rows ⌊of the bread — 2Ch 2:4
DISPLAYS *(1)*
but a fool **d** his stupidity. — Pr 13:16
DISPLEASE *(1)*
they **d** God, and are hostile to — 1Th 2:15
DISPLEASED *(5)*
Israelites, they were greatly **d.** — Neh 2:10
I was greatly **d** and threw all of — Neh 13:8
LORD will see, be **d**, and turn — Pr 24:18
king heard this, he was very **d**; — Dn 6:14
Jonah was greatly **d** and became — Jnh 4:1
DISPLEASING *(2)*
If she is **d** to her master, — Ex 21:8
but she becomes **d** to him because — Dt 24:1
DISPLEASURE *(3)*
You will know My **d.** — Nm 14:34
and abandon Your **d** with us. — Ps 85:4
A fool's **d** is known at once, — Pr 12:16
DISPOSAL *(2)*
will be at your **d** for the work, — 1Ch 28:21
was sold, wasn't it at your **d**? — Ac 5:4
DISPOSSESS *(5)*
He will certainly **d** before you — Jos 3:10
descendants will **d** nations and — Is 54:3
Israel will **d** their — Jr 49:2
house of Jacob will **d** those who — Ob 17
of My nation will **d** them. — Zph 2:9
DISPOSSESSED *(11)*
nations the LORD had **d** before — 1Kg 14:24
whom the LORD had **d** before the — 1Kg 21:26
nations the LORD had **d** before — 2Kg 16:3
that the LORD had **d** before the — 2Kg 17:8
that the LORD had **d** before the — 2Kg 21:2
nations the LORD had **d** before — 2Ch 28:3
that the LORD had **d** before the — 2Ch 33:2
the justice of all who are **d.** — Pr 31:8
then has Milcom **d** Gad and his — Jr 49:1
dispossess those who **d** them. — Ob 17
it in when they **d** the nations — Ac 7:45
DISPOSSESSORS *(1)*
Israel will dispossess their **d**, — Jr 49:2
DISPROVE *(1)*
that you can **d** ⌊my⌋ words or — Jb 6:26
DISPUTE *(20)*
they have a **d**, it comes to me, — Ex 18:16
has a **d** should go to them. — Ex 24:14
two people in the **d** must stand — Dt 19:17
ruling in every **d** and ⌊case of⌋ — Dt 21:5
If there is a **d** between men, — Dt 25:1
a grievance or **d** could come to — 2Sm 15:4
for every **d** that comes to you — 2Ch 19:10
stop the **d** before it breaks out. — Pr 17:14
for a man to resolve a **d**, — Pr 20:3
a man who incites **d** and conflict — Jr 15:10
In a **d**, they will officiate as — Ezk 44:24
But let no one **d**; let no one — Hs 4:4
LORD also has a **d** with Judah. — Hs 12:2
Then a **d** also arose among them — Lk 22:24
What is this **d** that you're — Lk 24:17
Then a **d** arose between John's — Jn 3:25
a **d** broke out between the — Ac 23:7
When the **d** became violent, — Ac 23:10
at a loss in a **d** over such — Ac 25:20
a confirming oath ends every **d.** — Heb 6:16
DISPUTED *(4)*
—cases **d** at your gates, — Dt 17:8
You **d** with her by banishing and — Is 27:8
came forward and **d** with Stephen. — Ac 6:9
were about **d** matters in their — Ac 23:29
DISPUTES *(9)*
burdens, and **d** by myself? — Dt 1:12
and that's how they settled ⌊**d**⌋. — 2Sm 20:18
⌊settling⌋ **d** of the residents — 2Ch 19:8
He will settle **d** among the — Is 2:4
He will settle **d** among many — Mc 4:3
of envy, murder, **d**, deceit, and — Rm 1:29
sick interest in **d** and arguments — 1Tm 6:4
reject foolish and ignorant **d**, — 2Tm 2:23
quarrels, and **d** about the law, — Ti 3:9
DISPUTING *(3)*
them and scribes **d** with them. — Mk 9:14
didn't find me **d** with anyone — Ac 24:12
when he was **d** with the Devil in — Jd 9
DISQUALIFIED *(4)*
so they were **d** from the — Ezr 2:62
so they were **d** from the — Neh 7:64
others, I myself will not be **d.** — 1Co 9:27
disobedient, and **d** for any good — Ti 1:16
DISQUALIFY *(1)*
Let no one **d** you, insisting on — Col 2:18
DISREGARD *(3)*
D this people's stubbornness, — Dt 9:27
They **d** My Sabbaths, and I am — Ezk 22:26
all authority. Let no one **d** you. — Ti 2:15
DISREGARDED *(6)*
He **d** his brothers and didn't — Dt 33:9
and have not **d** His statutes. — 2Sm 22:23
and have not **d** His statutes. — Ps 18:22
and human life **d.** — Is 33:8
Because they **d** the righteousness — Rm 10:3
in My covenant, I **d** them," says — Heb 8:9
DISREGARDING *(1)*
D the command of God, you keep — Mk 7:8
DISREGARDS *(2)*
one who **d** his ways will die. — Pr 19:16
If anyone **d** Moses' law, he dies — Heb 10:28
DISRESPECTFUL *(1)*
should not be **d** to them because — 1Tm 6:2
DISSENSIONS *(2)*
those who cause **d** and pitfalls — Rm 16:17
selfish ambitions, **d**, factions, — Gl 5:20
DISSIPATION *(1)*
them into the same flood of **d**— — 1Pt 4:4
DISSOLVE *(1)*
All the heavenly bodies will **d.** — Is 34:4
DISSOLVED *(3)*
Your deal with Death will be **d**, — Is 28:18
the elements will burn and be **d**, — 2Pt 3:10
will be on fire and be **d**, — 2Pt 3:12
DISTANCE *(45)*
up and saw the place in the **d.** — Gn 22:4
leave some **d** between the herds. — Gn 32:16
were still some **d** from Ephrath, — Gn 35:16
saw him in the **d**, and before he — Gn 37:18
some **d** from Ephrath in the land — Gn 48:7
stood at a **d** in order to see — Ex 2:4
must go a **d** of three days into — Ex 8:27
they trembled and stood at a **d.** — Ex 20:18
standing at a **d** as Moses — Ex 20:21
and bow in worship at a **d.** — Ex 24:1
of meeting at a **d** ⌊from it⌋. — Nm 2:2
if the **d** is too great for you — Dt 14:24
him because the **d** is great, — Dt 19:6
measure ⌊the **d**⌋ from the victim — Dt 21:2
you will view the land from a **d**, — Dt 32:52
keep a **d** of about 1,000 yards — Jos 3:4
they were some **d** from Micah's — Jdg 18:22
on top of the mountain at a **d**; — 1Sm 26:13
them from a **d** while the two — 2Kg 2:7
the man of God saw her at a **d**, — 2Kg 4:25
traveled a short **d** from Elisha, — 2Kg 5:19
When they looked from a **d**, — Jb 2:12
me and keep their **d** from me; — Jb 30:10
have looked at it from a **d.** — Jb 36:25
He smells the battle from a **d**; — Jb 39:25
its eyes penetrate the **d.** — Jb 39:29
and my relatives stand at a **d.** — Ps 38:11
friends keep their **d** from him! — Pr 19:7
flowing from a **d** ever fail? — Jr 18:14
the **d** was 43 and three-quarter — Ezk 40:13
⌊The **d**⌋ from the front of the — Ezk 40:15
he measured the **d** from the front — Ezk 40:19
He measured the **d** from gate to — Ezk 40:23
⌊The **d**⌋ from the gutter on the — Ezk 43:14
Him at a **d** right to the high — Mt 26:58
were there, looking on from a **d.** — Mt 27:55
When he saw Jesus from a **d**, — Mk 5:6
of them have come a long **d.**" — Mk 8:3
seeing in the **d** a fig tree with — Mk 11:13
Peter followed Him at a **d**, — Mk 14:54
also women looking on from a **d.** — Mk 15:40
met Him. They stood at a **d** — Lk 17:12
Peter was following at a **d.** — Lk 22:54
stood at a **d**, watching these — Lk 23:49
but they saw them from a **d**, — Heb 11:13
DISTANCED *(2)*
You have **d** my friends from me; — Ps 88:8
have **d** loved one and neighbor — Ps 88:18
DISTANCES *(1)*
determine the **d** and divide the — Dt 19:3
DISTANT *(27)*
a corpse or is on a **d** journey, — Nm 9:10
comes from a **d** country will see — Dt 29:22
We have come from a **d** land. — Jos 9:6
servant's house in the **d** future. — 2Sm 7:19
has come from a **d** land because — 1Kg 8:41
country—whether **d** or nearby— — 1Kg 8:46
They came from a **d** country, — 2Kg 20:14
servant's house in the **d** future. — 1Ch 17:17
has come from a **d** land because — 2Ch 6:32
deport them to a **d** or nearby — 2Ch 6:36
fame spread even to **d** places, — 2Ch 26:15
of the earth and of the **d** seas; — Ps 65:5
Good news from a **d** land is like — Pr 25:25
signal flag for the **d** nations — Is 5:26
pay attention, all you **d** lands; — Is 8:9
land, from the **d** horizon—the — Is 13:5
came to me from a **d** country, — Is 39:3
d peoples, pay attention. — Is 49:1
are coming from a **d** land; — Jr 4:16
or sweet cane from a **d** land? — Jr 6:20
her from the most **d** places. — Jr 50:26
he prophesies about **d** times. — Ezk 12:27
the Sabeans, to a **d** nation, for — Jl 3:8
horsemen come from **d** ⌊lands⌋. — Hab 1:8
Then all the **d** coastlands of the — Zph 2:11
will remember Me in the **d** lands; — Zch 10:9
had and traveled to a **d** country, — Lk 15:13
DISTILL *(1)*
they **d** the rain into its mist, — Jb 36:27
DISTINCTION *(9)*
will make a **d** between My people — Ex 8:23
the LORD will make a **d** between — Ex 9:4
the LORD makes a **d** between Egypt — Ex 11:7
You regard me as a man of **d**, — 1Ch 17:17
They make no **d** between the holy — Ezk 22:26
made no **d** between us and them, — Ac 15:9
believe, since there is no **d.** — Rm 3:22
there is no **d** between Jew and — Rm 10:12
don't make a **d** in the notes, — 1Co 14:7
DISTINCTLY *(2)*
on the man's eyes, and he saw **d.** — Mk 8:25
afternoon he **d** saw in a vision — Ac 10:3
DISTINGUISH *(6)*
You must **d** between the holy and — Lv 10:10
order to **d** between the unclean — Lv 11:47
you must **d** the clean animal — Lv 20:25
The people could not **d** the sound — Ezr 3:13

people who cannot **d** between Jnh 4:11
been trained to **d** between good Heb 5:14

DISTINGUISHED *(5)*
people will be **d** ⌊by this⌋ from Ex 33:16
the holy God is **d** by Is 5:16
Daniel **d** himself above the Dn 6:3
because a more **d** person than you Lk 14:8
are **d**, but we are dishonored! 1Co 4:10

DISTINGUISHING *(2)*
will be a **d** mark for you; Ex 12:13
another, **d** between spirits, to 1Co 12:10

DISTORTED *(1)*
My clothing is **d** with great Jb 30:18

DISTORTING *(1)*
in deceit or **d** God's message, 2Co 4:2

DISTORTS *(2)*
rich man who **d** right and wrong. Pr 28:6
but one who **d** right and wrong Pr 28:18

DISTRACTED *(1)*
But Martha was **d** by her many Lk 10:40

DISTRACTION *(1)*
devoted to the Lord without **d**. 1Co 7:35

DISTRAUGHT *(1)*
he saw that they looked **d**. Gn 40:6

DISTRESS *(73)*
who answered me in my day of **d**. Gn 35:3
saw his deep **d** when he pleaded Gn 42:21
When you are in **d** and all these Dt 4:30
You will see **d** ⌊in the⌋ place of 1Sm 2:32
redeemed my life from every **d**, 2Sm 4:9
I called to the LORD in my **d**; 2Sm 22:7
me in the day of my **d**, 2Sm 22:19
'Today is a day of **d**, rebuke, 2Kg 19:3
in their **d** and sought Him, 2Ch 15:4
them with every possible **d**. 2Ch 15:6
cry out to You because of our **d**, 2Ch 20:9
the time of his **d**, King Ahaz 2Ch 28:22
When he was in **d**, he sought the 2Ch 33:12
their time of **d**, they cried out Neh 9:27
they please. We are in great **d**. Neh 9:37
For **d** does not grow out of the Jb 5:6
Trouble and **d** terrify him, Jb 15:24
of his success **d** will come to Jb 20:22
his cry when **d** comes on him? Jb 27:9
him for help because of his **d**. Jb 30:24
I rejoiced over my enemy's **d**, Jb 31:29
and constant **d** in his bones, Jb 33:19
from the jaws of **d** to a spacious Jb 36:16
exertion keep ⌊you⌋ from **d**? Jb 36:19
I called to the LORD in my **d**, Ps 18:6
me in the day of my **d**, Ps 18:18
because **d** is near and there is Ps 22:11
to me, LORD, because I am in **d**; Ps 31:9
their refuge in a time of **d**. Ps 37:39
and my mouth spoke during my **d**. Ps 66:14
Your servant, for I am in **d**. Ps 69:17
called out in **d**, and I rescued Ps 81:7
call on You in the day of my **d**, Ps 86:7
cry, He took note of their **d**, Ps 106:44
He rescued them from their **d**. Ps 107:6
He saved them from their **d**. Ps 107:13
He saved them from their **d**. Ps 107:19
He brought them out of their **d**. Ps 107:28
I called to the LORD in **d**; Ps 118:5
Trouble and **d** have overtaken me Ps 119:143
In my **d** I called to the LORD, Ps 120:1
there will be darkness and **d**; Is 5:30
toward the earth and see only **d**, Is 8:22
for the humble person in his **d**, Is 25:4
they went to You in their **d**; Is 26:16
Through a land of trouble and **d**, Is 30:6
'Today is a day of **d**, rebuke, Is 37:3
D has seized us—pain like a Jr 6:24
them such **d** that they will Jr 10:18
in time of **d**, why are You like Jr 14:8
your time of **d**, with the enemy Jr 15:11
in a time of **d**, the nations will Jr 16:19
in the siege and **d** that their Jr 19:9
be heard cries of **d** over the Jr 48:5
D and labor pains have seized Jr 49:24
D has seized him—pain, like a Jr 50:43
LORD, see how I am in **d**. Lm 1:20
be a time of **d** such as never has Dn 12:1
will search for Me in their **d**. Hs 5:15
boastfully mock in the day of **d**. Ob 12
their survivors in the day of **d**. Ob 14
I called to the LORD in my **d**, Jnh 2:2
a stronghold in a day of **d**; Nah 1:7
I see the tents of Cushan in **d**; Hab 3:7
for the day of **d** to come against Hab 3:16
a day of trouble and **d**, a day of Zph 1:15
I will bring **d** on mankind, Zph 1:17
through the sea of **d** and strike Zch 10:11
there will be great **d** in the Lk 21:23
affliction and **d** for every human Rm 2:9
good because of the present **d**: 1Co 7:26
in all our **d** and persecution, 1Th 3:7
widows in their **d** and to keep Jms 1:27

DISTRESSED *(13)*
Jacob was greatly afraid and **d**; Gn 32:7
gloom of the **d** land will not be Is 9:1
spirit was deeply **d** within me, Dn 7:15
And they were deeply **d**. Mt 17:23
they were deeply **d** and went and Mt 18:31
Deeply **d**, each one began to say Mt 26:22
to be sorrowful and deeply **d**. Mt 26:37
Though the king was deeply **d**, Mk 6:26
They began to be **d** and to say to Mk 14:19
to be deeply **d** and horrified. Mk 14:33
of you and was **d** because you Php 2:26
have had to be **d** by various 1Pt 1:6
d by the unrestrained behavior 2Pt 2:7

DISTRESSES *(2)*
The **d** of my heart increase; Ps 25:17
redeem Israel, from all its **d**. Ps 25:22

DISTRESSING *(1)*
done under the sun was **d** to me. Ec 2:17

DISTRIBUTE *(9)*
the men who are to **d** the land as Nm 34:17
from each tribe to **d** the land. Nm 34:18
commanded to **d** the inheritance Nm 34:29
for you will **d** the land I swore Jos 1:6
d the land as an inheritance Jos 13:6
to God to **d** the contribution to 2Ch 31:14
to faithfully **d** ⌊it⌋ under his 2Ch 31:15
by name to **d** a portion to every 2Ch 31:19
you have and **d** it to the poor, Lk 18:22

DISTRIBUTED *(12)*
the LORD where he **d** the land to Jos 18:10
of the families **d** to the Jos 19:51
Then he **d** a loaf of bread, 2Sm 6:19
Then he **d** to each and every 1Ch 16:3
⌊they **d** it⌋ to males registered 2Ch 31:16
⌊They **d** also⌋ to those recorded 2Ch 31:17
was **d** to all the peoples so that Est 3:14
So he **d** the assets to them. Lk 15:12
giving thanks He **d** them to those Jn 6:11
property and **d** the proceeds to Ac 2:45
This was then **d** to each person Ac 4:35
as God has **d** a measure of faith Rm 12:3

DISTRIBUTES *(1)*
He **d** freely to the poor; Ps 112:9

DISTRIBUTING *(3)*
had finished **d** the land into its Jos 19:49
many and **d** land as a reward. Dn 11:39
d to each one as He wills. 1Co 12:11

DISTRIBUTION *(3)*
the **d** of the tribal household 2Ch 35:5
for the **d** to their colleagues Neh 13:13
being overlooked in the daily **d**. Ac 6:1

DISTRIBUTIONS *(1)*
and **d** ⌊of gifts⌋ from the Holy Heb 2:4

DISTRICT *(14)*
in Jerusalem in the Second **D**. 2Kg 22:14
in Jerusalem in the Second **D**. 2Ch 34:22
over half the **d** of Jerusalem, Neh 3:9
over half the **d** of Jerusalem, Neh 3:12
ruler over the **d** of Neh 3:14
ruler over the **d** of Mizpah, Neh 3:15
over half the **d** of Beth-zur, Neh 3:16
ruler over half the **d** of Keilah, Neh 3:17
Keilah, made repairs for his **d**. Neh 3:17
ruler over half the **d** of Keilah. Neh 3:18
a wailing from the Second **D**, Zph 1:10
and went to the **d** of Dalmanutha. Mk 8:10
and expelled them from their **d**. Ac 13:50
city of that **d** of Macedonia. Ac 16:12

DISTRICTS *(2)*
All the **d** of the Philistines and Jos 13:2
in all the **d** of Israel, 1Ch 13:2

DISTURB *(3)*
Don't let anyone **d** his bones." 2Kg 23:18
no cattle hooves will **d** them. Ezk 32:13
and those who **d** you wake up? Hab 2:7

DISTURBANCE *(3)*
I saw a big **d**, but I don't know 2Sm 18:29
was a major **d** about the Way. Ac 19:23
or causing a **d** among the crowd, Ac 24:12

DISTURBED *(8)*
you **d** me by bringing me up? 1Sm 28:15
live there and not be **d** again. 2Sm 7:10
live there and not be **d** again. 1Ch 17:9
spirit will be **d** within it, Is 19:3
was greatly **d** by the vision and Dn 8:27
he was deeply **d**, and all Mt 2:3
heard him he would be very **d**, Mk 6:20
not fear what they fear or be **d**, 1Pt 3:14

DISTURBING *(4)*
to perform His task, His **d** task. Is 28:21
men are seriously **d** our city. Ac 16:20
agitating and **d** the crowds. Ac 17:13
those who are **d** you might also Gl 5:12

DISTURBS *(1)*
and day so that no one **d** it. Is 27:3

DITCH *(2)*
'Dig **d** after ditch in this wadi.' 2Kg 3:16
'Dig ditch after **d** in this wadi.' 2Kg 3:16

DIVERSE *(1)*
An ethnically **d** crowd also went Ex 12:38

DIVERSIONS *(1)*
No **d** were brought to him, and he Dn 6:18

DIVERTED *(1)*
guilty acts have **d** these things Jr 5:25

DIVIDE *(22)*
and **d** it so that the Israelites Ex 14:16
overtake, I will **d** the spoil. Ex 15:9
the live ox and **d** its proceeds; Ex 21:35
must also **d** the dead animal. Ex 21:35
Then **d** the captives between the Nm 31:27
distances and **d** the land the Dt 19:3
d this land as an inheritance to Jos 13:7
Then they are to **d** it into seven Jos 18:5
you and Ziba are to **d** the land." 2Sm 19:29
innocent will **d** up his silver. Jb 27:17
bargain for him or **d** him among Jb 41:6
triumph! I will **d** up Shechem. I Ps 60:6
triumph! I will **d** up Shechem. I Ps 108:7
humble than to **d** plunder with Pr 16:19
LORD will **d** the Gulf of Suez. Is 11:15
a pair of scales and **d** the hair. Ezk 5:1
When you **d** the land by lot as an Ezk 45:1
you will ⌊use to⌋ **d** the land as Ezk 47:13
You are to **d** this land among Ezk 47:21
of the LORD to **d** the land by Mc 2:5
my brother to **d** the inheritance Lk 12:13
penetrating as far as to **d** soul, Heb 4:12

DIVIDED *(63)*
From there it **d** and became the Gn 2:10
during his days the earth was **d**; Gn 10:25
passed between the **d** ⌊animals⌋. Gn 15:17
d the people with him into two Gn 32:7
So he **d** the children among Leah, Gn 33:1
So the waters were **d**, Ex 14:21
animal with **d** hooves and that Lv 11:3
though it has **d** hooves, does not Lv 11:7
do not have a **d** hoof and do not Lv 11:26
The land is to be **d** among them Nm 26:53
The land must be **d** by lot; Nm 26:55
will be **d** by lot among Nm 26:56
that has hooves **d** in two and Dt 14:6
chew the cud or have **d** hooves, Dt 14:7
and **d** the human race, Dt 32:8
Moses, and they **d** the land. Jos 14:5
left who had not **d** up their Jos 18:2
Then he **d** the 300 men into three Jdg 7:16
d them into three companies, Jdg 9:43
They **d** the land between them in 1Kg 18:6
the earth was **d** during his 1Ch 1:19
Then David **d** them into divisions 1Ch 23:6
David **d** them according to the 1Ch 24:3
they were **d** ⌊accordingly⌋: 1Ch 24:4
They were **d** impartially by lot, 1Ch 24:5
You **d** the sea before them, Neh 9:11
They **d** my garments among Ps 22:18
d the sea with Your strength; Ps 74:13
He **d** the Red Sea His love is Ps 136:13

a young stag on the **d** mountains. Sg 2:17
whose land is **d** by rivers. Is 18:2
whose land is **d** by rivers— Is 18:7
Then abundant spoil will be **d**, Is 33:23
d the waters before them to Is 63:12
no longer be **d** into two kingdoms Ezk 37:22
it will be a **d** kingdom, though Dn 2:41
kingdom has been **d** and given to Dn 5:28
be broken up and **d** to the four Dn 11:4
countries and **d** up My land. Jl 3:2
your land will be **d** up with a Am 7:17
plunder will be **d** in your Zch 14:1
Every kingdom **d** against itself Mt 12:25
city or house **d** against itself Mt 12:25
Satan, he is **d** against himself Mt 12:26
crucifying Him they **d** His Mt 27:35
a kingdom is **d** against itself, Mk 3:24
If a house is **d** against itself, Mk 3:25
rebels against himself and is **d**, Mk 3:26
also **d** the two fish among them Mk 6:41
crucified Him and **d** His clothes, Mk 15:24
Every kingdom **d** against itself Lk 11:17
and a house **d** against itself Lk 11:17
Satan also is **d** against himself Lk 11:18
five in one household will be **d**: Lk 12:52
They will be **d**, father against Lk 12:53
And they **d** His clothes and cast Lk 23:34
His clothes and **d** them into four Jn 19:23
They **d** My clothes among Jn 19:24
like flames of fire that were **d**, Ac 2:3
the people of the city were **d**, Ac 14:4
and the assembly was **d**. Ac 23:7
Is Christ **d**? Was it Paul who was 1Co 1:13
and he is **d**. An unmarried woman 1Co 7:34

DIVIDES *(3)*
the evening he **d** the plunder." Gn 49:27
who stays at home **d** the spoil. Ps 68:12
in, and **d** up his plunder. Lk 11:22

DIVIDING *(5)*
its wings without **d** ⌊the bird⌋. Lv 1:17
So they finished **d** up the land. Jos 19:51
not finding and **d** the spoil— Jdg 5:30
as they rejoice when **d** spoils. Is 9:3
tore down the **d** wall of Eph 2:14

DIVINATION *(20)*
have learned by **d** that the LORD Gn 30:27
drinks from and uses for **d**? Gn 44:5
could uncover the truth by **d**?" Gn 44:15
not to practice **d** or sorcery. Lv 19:26
with fees for **d** in hand. Nm 22:7
Jacob and no **d** against Israel. Nm 23:23
fire, practice **d**, tell fortunes, Dt 18:10
rebellion is like the sin of **d**, 1Sm 15:23
and practiced **d** and interpreted 2Kg 17:17
practiced witchcraft and **d**, 2Kg 21:6
witchcraft, **d**, and sorcery, 2Ch 33:6
are full of ⌊**d**⌋ from the East Is 2:6
vision, worthless **d**, the deceit Jr 14:14
or flattering **d** within the house Ezk 12:24
and speak a lying **d** when you Ezk 13:7
see false visions or practice **d**. Ezk 13:23
of the two roads, to practice **d**: Ezk 21:21
seem like false **d** in the eyes of Ezk 21:23
grow dark for you—without **d**. Mc 3:6
prophets practice **d** for money. Mc 3:11

DIVINATIONS *(4)*
false visions and speak lying **d**. Ezk 13:6
false visions and speak lying **d**. Ezk 13:9
visions and lying **d** about you, Ezk 21:29
false visions and lying **d**, Ezk 22:28

DIVINE *(6)*
So a **d** fire came down from 2Kg 1:12
His place in the **d** assembly; Ps 82:1
think that the **d** nature is like Ac 17:29
His eternal power and **d** nature, Rm 1:20
For His **d** power has given us 2Pt 1:3
you may share in the **d** nature, 2Pt 1:4

DIVINELY *(1)*
was **d** directed by a holy angel Ac 10:22

DIVINER *(1)*
also killed the **d**, Balaam son of Jos 13:22

DIVINER-PRIEST *(2)*
anything like this of any **d**, Dn 2:10
man, medium, **d**, or astrologer is Dn 2:27

DIVINER-PRIESTS *(3)*
than all the **d** and mediums in Dn 1:20
gave orders to summon the **d**, Dn 2:2
When the **d**, mediums, Chaldeans, Dn 4:7

DIVINERS *(10)*
listen to fortune-tellers and **d**, Dt 18:14
priests and the **d** and pleaded, 1Sm 6:2
prophets and makes fools of **d**; Is 44:25
prophets, your **d**, your dreamers, Jr 27:9
you and your **d** deceive you, Jr 29:8
is against the **d**, and they will Jr 50:36
head of the **d**, because I know Dn 4:9
appointed him chief of the **d**, Dn 5:11
ashamed and the **d** disappointed. Mc 3:7
and the **d** see illusions; Zch 10:2

DIVINERS' *(1)*
the direction of the **D** Oak." Jdg 9:37

DIVINING *(1)*
and their **d** rods inform them. Hs 4:12

DIVISION *(57)*
His military **d** numbers 74,600. Nm 2:4
His military **d** numbers 54,400. Nm 2:6
His military **d** numbers 57,400. Nm 2:8
His military **d** numbers 46,500. Nm 2:11
His military **d** numbers 59,300. Nm 2:13
His military **d** numbers 45,650. Nm 2:15
His military **d** numbers 40,500. Nm 2:19
His military **d** numbers 32,200. Nm 2:21
His military **d** numbers 35,400. Nm 2:23
His military **d** numbers 62,700. Nm 2:26
His military **d** numbers 41,500. Nm 2:28
His military **d** numbers 53,400. Nm 2:30
to each ⌊**d**⌋ according to their Nm 7:5
was over the **d** of the Issachar Nm 10:15
was over the **d** of the Zebulun Nm 10:16
of Shedeur was over Reuben's **d**. Nm 10:18
over the **d** of Simeon's tribe, Nm 10:19
was over the **d** of the tribe Nm 10:20
Ammihud was over Ephraim's **d**. Nm 10:22
was over the **d** of the tribe Nm 10:23
was over the **d** of the tribe Nm 10:24
Ammishaddai was over Dan's **d**. Nm 10:25
was over the **d** of the tribe Nm 10:26
Enan was over the **d** of the tribe Nm 10:27
One **d** headed toward the Ophrah 1Sm 13:17
The next **d** headed toward the 1Sm 13:18
and the last **d** headed down the 1Sm 13:18
There were 24,000 in each **d**: 1Ch 27:1
was in charge of the first **d**, 1Ch 27:2
24,000 were in his **d**. 1Ch 27:2
charge of the **d** for the second 1Ch 27:4
24,000 were in his **d**. 1Ch 27:4
24,000 were in his **d**. 1Ch 27:5
was in charge of his **d**. 1Ch 27:6
24,000 were in his **d**. 1Ch 27:7
24,000 were in his **d**. 1Ch 27:8
24,000 were in his **d**. 1Ch 27:9
24,000 were in his **d**. 1Ch 27:10
24,000 were in his **d**. 1Ch 27:11
24,000 were in his **d**. 1Ch 27:12
24,000 were in his **d**. 1Ch 27:13
24,000 were in his **d**. 1Ch 27:14
24,000 were in his **d**. 1Ch 27:15
of silver I gave to Israel's **d**?" 2Ch 25:9
released the **d** that came to him 2Ch 25:10
the men of the **d** that Amaziah 2Ch 25:13
went out to war by **d** according 2Ch 26:11
each **d** corresponding to his 2Ch 31:2
and thanks, **d** by division, as Neh 12:24
division by **d**, as David the man Neh 12:24
of Abijah's **d** named Zechariah. Lk 1:5
When his **d** was on duty and he Lk 1:8
No, I tell you, but rather **d**! Lk 12:51
So a **d** occurred among the crowd Jn 7:43
And there was a **d** among them. Jn 9:16
Again a **d** took place among the Jn 10:19
there would be no **d** in the body, 1Co 12:25

DIVISIONS *(50)*
according to their **d**, in the Gn 36:30
of Egypt according to their **d**." Ex 6:26
all the **d** of the LORD went out Ex 12:41
according to their military **d**. Ex 12:51
or more by their military **d**— Nm 1:3
are to camp by their military **d**, Nm 1:52
Judah's military **d** will camp on Nm 2:3
their military **d** who belong to Nm 2:9
Reuben's military **d** will camp on Nm 2:10
their military **d** who belong to Nm 2:16
Ephraim's military **d** will camp Nm 2:18
their military **d** who belong to Nm 2:24
Dan's military **d** will camp on Nm 2:25
by their military **d** is 603,550. Nm 2:32
The military **d** of the camp of Nm 10:14
Amminadab was over Judah's **d**. Nm 10:14
The military **d** of the camp of Nm 10:18
Next the military **d** of the camp Nm 10:22
military **d** of the camp of Dan Nm 10:25
their military **d** as they set out Nm 10:28
by their military **d** under the Nm 33:1
Israelites according to their **d**. Jos 18:10
the troops into three **d**. 1Sm 11:11
the Philistine camp in three **d**. 1Sm 13:17
Your two **d** that go off duty on 2Kg 11:7
divided them into **d** according to 1Ch 23:6
d of the descendants of Aaron 1Ch 24:1
were⌋ the **d** of the gatekeepers 1Ch 26:1
These **d** of the gatekeepers, 1Ch 26:12
Those were the **d** of the 1Ch 26:19
to do with the **d** that were on 1Ch 27:1
leaders of the **d** in the king's 1Ch 28:1
plans⌋ for the **d** of the priests 1Ch 28:13
Here are the **d** of the priests 1Ch 28:21
appointed the **d** of the priests 2Ch 8:14
by their **d** with respect to each 2Ch 8:14
priest did not release the **d**. 2Ch 23:8
the **d** of the priests 2Ch 31:2
to their brothers by **d**, 2Ch 31:15
according to their **d**. 2Ch 31:16
responsibilities in their **d**; 2Ch 31:17
houses by your **d** according to 2Ch 35:4
place by the **d** of the ancestral 2Ch 35:5
Levites in their **d** according to 2Ch 35:10
be given to the **d** of the 2Ch 35:12
by their **d** and the Levites Ezr 6:18
of the Judean **d** of Levites were Neh 11:36
that there be no **d** among you, 1Co 1:10
a church there are **d** among you, 1Co 11:18
people create **d** and are merely Jd 19

DIVISIVE *(1)*
Reject a **d** person after a first Ti 3:10

DIVORCE *(13)*
he cannot **d** her as long as he Dt 22:19
He cannot **d** her as long as he Dt 22:29
may write her a **d** certificate, Dt 24:1
writes her a **d** certificate, Dt 24:3
your mother's **d** certificate that Is 50:1
given her a certificate of **d**. Jr 3:8
decided to **d** her secretly. Mt 1:19
give her a written notice of **d**. Mt 5:31
for a man to **d** his wife on any Mt 19:3
us⌋ to give **d** papers and to send Mt 19:7
permitted you to **d** your wives Mt 19:8
for a man to **d** ⌊his⌋ wife?" Mk 10:2
to write **d** papers and send her Mk 10:4

DIVORCED *(7)*
or **d** by her husband, Lv 21:7
marry a widow, a **d** woman, or one Lv 21:14
daughter becomes widowed or **d**, Lv 22:13
after he had **d** his wives Hushim 1Ch 8:8
to marry a widow or a **d** woman, Ezk 44:22
marries a **d** woman commits Mt 5:32
marries a woman **d** from her Lk 16:18

DIVORCÉE *(1)*
vow a widow or **d** put herself Nm 30:9

DIVORCES *(8)*
If a man **d** his wife and she Jr 3:1
"If he hates and **d** ⌊his wife⌋," Mal 2:16
Whoever **d** his wife must give her Mt 5:31
everyone who **d** his wife, except Mt 5:32
you, whoever **d** his wife, except Mt 19:9
Whoever **d** his wife and marries Mk 10:11
if she **d** her husband and marries Mk 10:12
Everyone who **d** his wife and Lk 16:18

DO *(1977)*
(See pp. xi-xii.)

DOCILE *(1)*
for I was like a **d** lamb led to Jr 11:19

DOCTOR *(4)*
who are well don't need a **d**, Mt 9:12
who are well don't need a **d**, Mk 2:17
to Me: '**D**, heal yourself. Lk 4:23
The healthy don't need a **d**, Lk 5:31

DOCTORS *(3)*
you are all worthless **d**. Jb 13:4

had endured much under many **d**. Mk 5:26
all she had on **d** yet could not Lk 8:43

DOCTRINE *(4)*
contrary to the **d** you have Rm 16:17
people not to teach other **d** 1Tm 1:3
teaches other **d** and does not 1Tm 6:3
they will not tolerate sound **d**, 2Tm 4:3

DOCTRINES *(4)*
as **d** the commands of men. Mt 15:9
teaching as **d** the commands of Mk 7:7
rise up with deviant **d** to lure Ac 20:30
they are human commands and **d**. Col 2:22

DOCUMENT *(11)*
it by towns in a **d** of seven Jos 18:9
on a sealed **d** ⌊containing Neh 9:38
seals were ⌊on the **d**⌋ were: Neh 10:1
A **d** written in the king's name Est 8:8
A copy of the **d** was to be issued Est 8:13
be like the words of a sealed **d**. Is 29:11
And if the **d** is given to one who Is 29:12
deaf will hear the words of a **d**, Is 29:18
edict and sign the **d** so that, Dn 6:8
So King Darius signed the **d**. Dn 6:9
that the **d** had been signed Dn 6:10

DOCUMENTS *(2)*
Let it revoke the **d** the scheming Est 8:5
He sent the **d** by mounted Est 8:10

DODAI *(1)*
(AKA DODO)
D the Ahohite was in charge of 1Ch 27:4

DODANIM *(1)*
(AKA RODANIM)
Tarshish, Kittim, and **D**. Gn 10:4

DODAVAHU *(1)*
Eliezer son of **D** of Mareshah 2Ch 20:37

DODGE *(1)*
They **d** the missiles, never Jl 2:8

DODO *(5)*
(AKA DODAI)
of **D** ⌊became judge⌋ and began Jdg 10:1
Eleazar son of **D** son of Ahohi 2Sm 23:9
Elhanan son of **D** of Bethlehem, 2Sm 23:24
Eleazar son of **D** the Ahohite was 1Ch 11:12
Elhanan son of **D** of Bethlehem, 1Ch 11:26

DOE *(3)*
Naphtali is a **d** set free that Gn 49:21
loving **d**, a graceful fawn—let Pr 5:19
Even the **d** in the field gives Jr 14:5

DOEG *(5)*
His name was **D** the Edomite, 1Sm 21:7
Then **D** the Edomite, who was in 1Sm 22:9
king said to **D**, "Go and execute 1Sm 22:18
So **D** the Edomite went and 1Sm 22:18
I knew that **D** the Edomite was 1Sm 22:22

DOER *(3)*
hearer of the word and not a **d**, Jms 1:23
hearer but a **d** who acts— Jms 1:25
you are not a **d** of the law but a Jms 4:11

DOERS *(2)*
but the **d** of the law will be Rm 2:13
But be **d** of the word and not Jms 1:22

DOES *(532)*
(See pp. xi-xii.)
and the wild **d** of the field: Sg 2:7
and the wild **d** of the field: Sg 3:5

DOESN'T *(105)*
(See pp. xi-xii.)

DOG *(12)*
not ⌊even⌋ a **d** will snarl, Ex 11:7
water with his tongue like a **d**. Jdg 7:5
Am I a **d** that you come against 1Sm 17:43
chasing after? A dead **d**? A flea? 1Sm 24:14
interest in a dead **d** like me?" 2Sm 9:8
should this dead **d** curse my lord 2Sm 16:9
servant, a mere **d**, do this 2Kg 8:13
life from the power of the **d**. Ps 22:20
As a **d** returns to its vomit, Pr 26:11
one who grabs a **d** by the ears. Pr 26:17
since a live **d** is better than a Ec 9:4
A **d** returns to its own vomit, 2Pt 2:22

DOG'S *(2)*
I a **d** head who belongs to Judah? 2Sm 3:8
a lamb, one breaks a **d** neck; Is 66:3

DOGS *(25)*
in the field; throw it to the **d**. Ex 22:31
in the city, the **d** will eat, and 1Kg 14:11
in the city, the **d** will eat, and 1Kg 16:4
where the **d** licked Naboth's 1Kg 21:19
the **d** will also lick your blood! 1Kg 21:19
The **d** will eat Jezebel in the 1Kg 21:23
the city, the **d** will eat, and he 1Kg 21:24
The **d** licked up his blood, 1Kg 22:38
The **d** will eat Jezebel in the 2Kg 9:10
the **d** will eat Jezebel's flesh. 2Kg 9:36
refused to put with my sheep **d**. Jb 30:1
For **d** have surrounded me; Ps 22:16
snarling like **d** and prowling Ps 59:6
snarling like **d** and prowling Ps 59:14
of them are mute **d**, they cannot Is 56:10
These **d** have fierce appetites; Is 56:11
to kill, the **d** to drag away, Jr 15:3
what is holy to **d** or toss your Mt 7:6
bread and throw it to their **d**." Mt 15:26
yet even the **d** eat the crumbs Mt 15:27
bread and throw it to the **d**." Mk 7:27
even the **d** under the table eat Mk 7:28
but instead the **d** would come and Lk 16:21
Watch out for "**d**," watch out for Php 3:2
are the **d**, the sorcerers, Rv 22:15

DOGS' *(1)*
blood and your **d** tongues may Ps 68:23

DOING *(167)*
(See pp. xi-xii.)

DOMAIN *(3)*
flesh like ours under sin's **d**, Rm 8:3
the ruler of the atmospheric **d**, Eph 2:2
us from the **d** of darkness Col 1:13

DOMINATE *(7)*
to **d** the day and the night, Gn 1:18
your husband, yet he will **d** you. Gn 3:16
How long will my enemy **d** me? Ps 13:2
don't let sin **d** me. Ps 119:133
rulers of the Gentiles **d** them, Mt 20:25
rulers of the Gentiles **d** them, Mk 10:42
kings of the Gentiles **d** them, Lk 22:25

DOMINATED *(1)*
of their enemies, who **d** them. Neh 9:28

DOMINATES *(1)*
you, if someone **d** you, or if 2Co 11:20

DOMINATION *(3)*
against Judah's **d** and appointed 2Ch 21:8
against Judah's **d** today. 2Ch 21:10
time against his **d** because he 2Ch 21:10

DOMINION *(25)*
light to have **d** over the day Gn 1:16
light to have **d** over the night— Gn 1:16
he had **d** over everything west 1Kg 4:24
else in the land of his **d**. 1Kg 9:19
else in the land of his **d**. 2Ch 8:6
D and dread belong to Him, Jb 25:2
His sanctuary, Israel, His **d**. Ps 114:2
The **d** will be vast, and its Is 9:7
and His **d** is from generation to Dn 4:3
and your **d** ⌊extends⌋ to the ends Dn 4:22
For His **d** is an everlasting Dn 4:34
dominion is an everlasting **d**, Dn 4:34
a decree that in all my royal **d**, Dn 6:26
destroyed, and His **d** has no end. Dn 6:26
His **d** is an everlasting dominion Dn 7:14
an everlasting **d** that will not Dn 7:14
and his **d** will be taken away, Dn 7:26
The kingdom, **d**, and greatness of Dn 7:27
His **d** will extend from sea to Zch 9:10
hour—and the **d** of darkness." Lk 22:53
order that sin's **d** over the body Rm 6:6
power and **d**, and every title Eph 1:21
To Him be the **d** forever. 1Pt 5:11
the glory and **d** forever and ever Rv 1:6
glory and **d** to the One seated Rv 5:13

DOMINIONS *(1)*
whether thrones or **d** or rulers Col 1:16

DON'T *(759)*
(See pp. xi-xii.)

DONATE *(3)*
the portion you **d** ⌊to the LORD⌋, Ezk 48:8
portion you **d** to the LORD will Ezk 48:9
And if I **d** all my goods to feed 1Co 13:3

DONATED *(3)*
Then Josiah **d** 30,000 sheep, 2Ch 35:7
officials also **d** willingly for 2Ch 35:8
d 5,000 Passover sacrifices for 2Ch 35:9

DONATION *(17)*
people for the **d** of wood by our Neh 10:34
arranged for the **d** of wood at Neh 13:31
must set aside a **d** to the LORD, Ezk 45:1
to the holy **d** ⌊of land⌋. Ezk 45:6
side of the holy **d** ⌊of land⌋ Ezk 45:7
to the holy **d** and the city's Ezk 45:7
This holy **d** will be set apart Ezk 48:10
will be a special **d** for them out Ezk 48:12
out of the ⌊holy⌋ **d** of the land, Ezk 48:12
the holy **d** will be three Ezk 48:18
will run alongside the holy **d**. Ezk 48:18
The entire **d** will be eight and Ezk 48:20
set apart the holy **d** along with Ezk 48:20
sides of the holy **d** and the city Ezk 48:21
miles⌋ of the **d** as far as the Ezk 48:21
miles of the **d**⌋ as far as the Ezk 48:21
The holy **d** and the sanctuary of Ezk 48:21

DONE *(458)*
(See pp. xi-xii.)

DONKEY *(88)*
up, saddled his **d**, and took with Gn 22:3
men, "Stay here with the **d**. Gn 22:5
his sack to get feed for his **d**, Gn 42:27
one loaded his **d** and returned to Gn 44:13
He ties his **d** to a vine, and the Gn 49:11
the colt of his **d** to the choice Gn 49:11
is a strong **d** lying down between Gn 49:14
put them on a **d**, and set out for Ex 4:20
firstborn of a **d** with a flock Ex 13:13
slave, his ox or **d**, or anything Ex 20:17
and an ox or a **d** falls into it, Ex 21:33
whether ox, **d**, or sheep—is Ex 22:4
involving an ox, a **d**, a sheep, a Ex 22:9
a man gives his neighbor a **d**, Ex 22:10
your enemy's stray ox or **d**, Ex 23:4
If you see the **d** of someone who Ex 23:5
your ox and your **d** may rest, Ex 23:12
firstborn of a **d** with a sheep, Ex 34:20
I have not taken one **d** from them Nm 16:15
saddled his **d** and went with Nm 22:21
was riding his **d**, and his two Nm 22:22
When the **d** saw the Angel of the Nm 22:23
The **d** saw the Angel of the LORD Nm 22:25
When the **d** saw the Angel of the Nm 22:27
and beat the **d** with his stick. Nm 22:27
answered the **d**, "You made me Nm 22:29
But the **d** said, "Am I not the Nm 22:30
Am I not the **d** you've ridden all Nm 22:30
you beaten your **d** these three Nm 22:32
d saw Me and turned away from Nm 22:33
slave, your ox or **d**, any of your Dt 5:14
slave, his ox or **d**, or anything Dt 5:21
the same for his **d**, his garment, Dt 22:3
your brother's **d** or ox fallen Dt 22:4
with an ox and a **d** together. Dt 22:10
Your **d** will be taken away from Dt 28:31
old, and every ox, sheep, and **d**. Jos 6:21
his ox, **d**, and sheep, his Jos 7:24
she got off her **d**, Caleb asked Jos 15:18
she got off her **d**, Caleb asked Jdg 1:14
as well as no sheep, ox or **d**. Jdg 6:4
He found a fresh jawbone of a **d**, Jdg 15:15
the jawbone of a **d** I have piled Jdg 15:16
the jawbone of a **d** I have killed Jdg 15:16
put her on his **d** and set out for Jdg 19:28
Whose ox or **d** have I taken? 1Sm 12:3
So Jesse took a **d** loaded with 1Sm 16:20
she rode the **d** down a mountain 1Sm 25:20
got off the **d** and fell with her 1Sm 25:23
rode on the **d** following David's 1Sm 25:42
he saddled his **d** and set out for 2Sm 17:23
'I'll saddle the **d** for myself so 2Sm 19:26
saddled his **d** and set out to 1Kg 2:40
his sons, "Saddle the **d** for me." 1Kg 13:13
So they saddled the **d** for him, 1Kg 13:13
saddled the **d** for the prophet he 1Kg 13:23
the **d** was standing beside it; 1Kg 13:24
his sons, "Saddle the **d** for me." 1Kg 13:27
the road with the **d** and the lion 1Kg 13:28
the corpse or mauled the **d**. 1Kg 13:28
laid it on the **d** and brought it 1Kg 13:29
saddled the **d** and said to her 2Kg 4:24
Does a wild **d** bray over fresh Jb 6:5

soon as a wild **d** is born a man! Jb 11:12
Who set the wild **d** free? Jb 39:5
the swift **d** from its harness? Jb 39:5
bridle for the **d**, and a rod for Pr 26:3
and the **d** its master's Is 1:3
who let ox and **d** range freely. Is 32:20
a wild **d** at home in the Jr 2:24
He will be buried ⌊like⌋ a **d**, Jr 22:19
like⌋ a wild **d** going off on its Hs 8:9
riding on a **d**, on a colt, the Zch 9:9
on a colt, the foal of a **d**. Zch 9:9
you will find a **d** tied there, Mt 21:2
mounted on a **d**, even on a colt Mt 21:5
They brought the **d** and the colt; Mt 21:7
will find a young **d** tied there, Mk 11:2
and found a young **d** outside in Mk 11:4
are you doing, untying the **d**?" Mk 11:5
they brought the **d** to Jesus and Mk 11:7
untie his ox or **d** from the Lk 13:15
will find a young **d** tied there, Lk 19:30
they were untying the young **d**, Lk 19:33
"Why are you untying the **d**?" Lk 19:33
throwing their robes on the **d**, Lk 19:35
found a young **d** and sat on it, Jn 12:14
speechless **d** spoke with a human 2Pt 2:16

DONKEY'S *(3)*

the LORD opened the **d** mouth, Nm 22:28
it until a **d** head ⌊sold for⌋ 80 2Kg 6:25
is coming, sitting on a **d** colt. Jn 12:15

DONKEYS *(67)*

male and female **d**, male and Gn 12:16
female slaves, and camels and **d**. Gn 24:35
female slaves, and camels and **d**. Gn 30:43
I have oxen, **d**, flocks, male and Gn 32:5
bulls, 20 female **d**, and 10 male Gn 32:15
female donkeys, and 10 male **d**. Gn 32:15
sheep, cattle, **d**, and whatever Gn 34:28
pasturing the **d** of his father Gn 36:24
grain on their **d** and left there. Gn 42:26
make us slaves, and take our **d**." Gn 43:18
feet, and got feed for their **d**. Gn 43:24
men were sent off with their **d**. Gn 44:3
10 **d** carrying the best products Gn 45:23
and 10 female **d** carrying grain, Gn 45:23
the herds of cattle, and the **d**. Gn 47:17
the horses, **d**, camels, herds, Ex 9:3
humans, cattle, **d**, sheep, and Nm 31:28
people, cattle, **d**, sheep, and Nm 31:30
61,000 **d**, Nm 31:34
from the 30,500 **d**, the tribute Nm 31:39
30,500 **d**, Nm 31:45
sacks on their **d** and old Jos 9:4
who ride on white **d**, who sit on Jdg 5:10
30 sons who rode on 30 young **d**. Jdg 10:4
30 grandsons, who rode on 70 **d**. Jdg 12:14
and a couple of **d** were with him. Jdg 19:3
his two saddled **d** and his Jdg 19:10
both straw and feed for our **d**, Jdg 19:19
him to his house and fed the **d**. Jdg 19:21
and your **d** and use them for his 1Sm 8:16
One day the **d** of Saul's father 1Sm 9:3
with you and go look for the **d**." 1Sm 9:3
about the **d** and start worrying 1Sm 9:5
As for the **d** that wandered away 1Sm 9:20
'The **d** you went looking for have 1Sm 10:2
about the **d** and is worried 1Sm 10:2
look for the **d**," Saul answered 1Sm 10:14
assured us the **d** had been found. 1Sm 10:16
and sheep, camels and **d**.'" 1Sm 15:3
and infants, oxen, **d**, and sheep. 1Sm 22:19
figs, and loaded them on **d**. 1Sm 25:18
took flocks, herds, **d**, camels, 1Sm 27:9
pair of saddled **d** loaded with 2Sm 16:1
The **d** are for the king's 2Sm 16:2
the servants and one of the **d**, 2Kg 4:22
their tents, horses, and **d**. 2Kg 7:7
but tethered horses and **d**, 2Kg 7:10
sheep, and 2,000 **d**—as well as 1Ch 5:21
came bringing food on **d**, 1Ch 12:40
was in charge of the **d**. 1Ch 27:30
and provided **d** for all the 2Ch 28:15
435 camels, and 6,720 **d**. Ezr 2:67
435 camels, and 6,720 **d**. Neh 7:69
grain and loading ⌊them⌋ on **d**, Neh 13:15
oxen, 500 female **d**, and a very Jb 1:3
and the **d** grazing nearby, Jb 1:14
They drive away the **d** ⌊owned⌋ by Jb 24:3
Like wild **d** in the desert, Jb 24:5
of oxen, and 1,000 female **d**. Jb 42:12
the wild **d** quench their thirst. Ps 104:11
riders on **d**, riders on camels Is 21:7
on the backs of **d** and their Is 30:6
The oxen and **d** that work the Is 30:24
Wild **d** stand on the barren Jr 14:6
like those of **d** and whose Ezk 23:20
the wild **d**, he was fed grass Dn 5:21
mules, camels, **d**, and all the Zch 14:15

DOOM *(6)*

and their **d** is coming quickly." Dt 32:35
their **d** would last forever. Ps 81:15
D has come on you, inhabitants Ezk 7:7
day is coming! **D** has gone out. Ezk 7:10
a time ⌊of **d**⌋ for the nations. Ezk 30:3
them on the day of Egypt's ⌊**d**⌋. Ezk 30:9

DOOMED *(2)*

Babylon, **d** to destruction, Ps 137:8
without discernment are **d**. Hs 4:14

DOOR *(79)*

sin is crouching at the **d**. Gn 4:7
You are to put a **d** in the side Gn 6:16
and shut the **d** behind him. Gn 19:6
and came up to break down the **d**. Gn 19:9
house with them, and shut the **d**. Gn 19:10
who were at the **d** of the house, Gn 19:11
they were unable to find the **d**. Gn 19:11
may go out the **d** of his house Ex 12:22
will pass over the **d** and not let Ex 12:23
bring him to the **d** or doorpost. Ex 21:6
each one at the **d** of his tent, Ex 33:8
each one at the **d** of his tent. Ex 33:10
through his ear into the **d**, Dt 15:17
woman to the **d** of her father's Dt 22:21
the house and beat on the **d**. Jdg 19:22
slept at the **d** of the palace 2Sm 11:9
out and bolt the **d** behind her!" 2Sm 13:17
out and bolted the **d** behind her. 2Sm 13:18
d for the lowest side chamber 1Kg 6:8
the first **d** had two folding 1Kg 6:34
and the second **d** had two folding 1Kg 6:34
of her feet entering the **d**, 1Kg 14:6
go in and shut the **d** behind you 2Kg 4:4
had shut the **d** behind her and 2Kg 4:5
closed the **d** behind the two of 2Kg 4:33
and stood at the **d** of Elisha's 2Kg 5:9
shut the **d** to keep him out. 2Kg 6:32
Open the **d** and escape. 2Kg 9:3
opened the **d** and escaped. 2Kg 9:10
the Angle to the **d** of the house Neh 3:20
from the **d** of Eliashib's house Neh 3:21
wife or I have lurked at his **d**, Jb 31:9
I opened my **d** to the traveler Jb 31:32
rather be at the **d** of the house Ps 84:10
keep watch at the **d** of my lips. Ps 141:3
go near the **d** of her house. Pr 5:8
A **d** turns on its hinge, and a Pr 26:14
she is a **d**, we will enclose it Sg 8:9
behind the **d** and doorpost. Is 57:8
was a chamber whose **d** ⌊opened⌋ Ezk 40:38
sanctuary each had a double **d**, Ezk 41:23
two panels for one **d** and two for Ezk 41:24
approached the **d** of the furnace Dn 3:26
room, shut your **d**, and pray to Mt 6:6
and the **d** will be opened to you. Mt 7:7
knocks, the **d** will be opened. Mt 7:8
that He is near—at the **d**! Mt 24:33
banquet, and the **d** was shut. Mt 25:10
town was assembled at the **d**, Mk 1:33
little daughter is at death's **d**. Mk 5:23
in the street, tied by a **d**. Mk 11:4
know that He is near—at the **d**! Mk 13:29
old, and she was at death's **d**. Lk 8:42
The **d** is already locked, and my Lk 11:7
and the **d** will be opened to you. Lk 11:9
knocks, the **d** will be opened. Lk 11:10
can open ⌊the **d**⌋ for him at once Lk 12:36
to enter through the narrow **d**, Lk 13:24
gets up and shuts the **d**. Lk 13:25
outside and knock on the **d**, Lk 13:25
sheep pen by the **d** but climbs in Jn 10:1
enters by the **d** is the shepherd Jn 10:2
I am the **d** of the sheep. Jn 10:7
I am the **d**. If anyone enters by Jn 10:9
standing outside by the **d**. Jn 18:16
your husband are at the **d**, Ac 5:9
in front of the **d** guarded the Ac 12:6
knocked at the **d** in the gateway, Ac 12:13
they opened the **d** and saw him, Ac 12:16
He had opened the **d** of faith to Ac 14:27
house was next **d** to the Ac 18:7
because a wide **d** for effective 1Co 16:9
d was opened to me by the Lord. 2Co 2:12
that God may open a **d** to us for Col 4:3
the judge stands at the **d**! Jms 5:9
you an open **d** that no one is Rv 3:8
I stand at the **d** and knock. Rv 3:20
hears My voice and opens the **d**, Rv 3:20
there in heaven was an open **d**. Rv 4:1

DOORKEEPER *(5)*

Maaseiah son of Shallum the **d**. Jr 35:4
and commanded the **d** to be alert. Mk 13:34
The **d** opens it for him, and the Jn 10:3
girl who was the **d** and brought Jn 18:16
who was the **d** said to Peter, Jn 18:17

DOORKEEPERS *(6)*

⌊the money⌋ the **d** have collected 2Kg 22:4
rank and the **d** to bring out 2Kg 23:4
second rank, and the three **d**. 2Kg 25:18
Levites and the **d** had collected 2Ch 34:9
singers, **d**, temple servants Ezr 7:24
second rank, and the three **d**. Jr 52:24

DOORPOST *(4)*

then bring him to the door or **d**. Ex 21:6
a chair by the **d** of the LORD's 1Sm 1:9
memorial behind the door and **d**. Is 57:8
and stand at the **d** of the gate Ezk 46:2

DOORPOSTS *(14)*

it on the two **d** and the lintel Ex 12:7
lintel and the two **d** with some Ex 12:22
on the lintel and the two **d**, Ex 12:23
them on the **d** of your house Dt 6:9
them on the **d** of your house Dt 11:20
of the **d** were five-sided. 1Kg 6:31
olive wood **d** for the sanctuary 1Kg 6:33
the doors and **d** had rectangular 1Kg 7:5
and from the **d** he had overlaid 2Kg 18:16
The **d** of the great hall were Ezk 41:21
and their **d** beside My doorposts Ezk 43:8
and their doorposts beside My **d**, Ezk 43:8
and apply ⌊it⌋ to the temple **d**, Ezk 45:19
and the **d** of the gate to the Ezk 45:19

DOORS *(60)*

goes out the **d** of your house, Jos 2:19
locking the **d** of the upstairs Jdg 3:23
and found the **d** of the upstairs Jdg 3:24
not opened the **d** of the upstairs Jdg 3:25
took the key and opened the **d**— Jdg 3:25
comes out of the **d** of my house Jdg 11:31
hold of the **d** of the city gate Jdg 16:3
opened the **d** of the house, Jdg 19:27
he opened the **d** of the LORD's 1Sm 3:15
scribbling on the **d** of the gate 1Sm 21:13
sanctuary, he made olive wood **d**. 1Kg 6:31
The two **d** were made of olive 1Kg 6:32
The two **d** were made of cypress 1Kg 6:34
All the **d** and doorposts had 1Kg 7:5
hinges for the **d** of the inner 1Kg 7:50
and for the **d** of the temple 1Kg 7:50
gold from⌋ the **d** of the LORD's 2Kg 18:16
nails for the **d** of the gateways 1Ch 22:3
its walls and **d**—with gold, and 2Ch 3:7
court, and **d** for the court. 2Ch 4:9
He overlaid the **d** with bronze. 2Ch 4:9
its inner **d** to the most holy 2Ch 4:22
the **d** of the temple sanctuary 2Ch 4:22
and towers, with **d** and bars. 2Ch 14:7
shut the **d** of the LORD's temple, 2Ch 28:24
he opened the **d** of the LORD's 2Ch 29:3
also closed the **d** of the 2Ch 29:7
it and installed its **d**. Neh 3:1
with beams and installed its **d**, Neh 3:3
with beams and installed its **d**, Neh 3:6
rebuilt it and installed its **d**, Neh 3:13
rebuilt it and installed its **d**, Neh 3:14
installed its **d**, bolts, and bars Neh 3:15
installed the **d** in the gates— Neh 6:1
shut the temple **d** because they Neh 6:10
and I had the **d** installed, Neh 7:1
and let the **d** be shut and Neh 7:3
not shut the **d** of my ⌊mother's Jb 3:10
the sea behind **d** when it burst Jb 38:8
put ⌊its⌋ bars and **d** in place, Jb 38:10
up, ancient **d**! Then the King Ps 24:7
up, ancient **d**! Then the King Ps 24:9

and opened the **d** of heaven. Ps 78:23
watching at my **d** every day, Pr 8:34
A gift opens **d** for a man and Pr 18:16
and the **d** at the street are shut Ec 12:4
and at our **d** is every delicacy— Sg 7:13
and close your **d** behind you. Is 26:20
to open the **d** before him and the Is 45:1
the bronze **d** and cut the iron Is 45:2
They have no **d**, not even a gate Jr 49:31
and each of the **d** had two Ezk 41:24
carved on the **d** of the great Ezk 41:25
you would shut the ⌊temple⌋ **d**, Mal 1:10
with the **d** locked because Jn 20:19
Even though the **d** were locked, Jn 20:26
Lord opened the **d** of the jail Ac 5:19
standing in front of the **d**; Ac 5:23
all the **d** were opened, Ac 16:26
up and saw the **d** of the prison Ac 16:27

DOORWAY *(10)*
to him at the **d** of the house. Gn 43:19
house to its **d** and quarantine Lv 14:38
assembly to the **d** of the tent Nm 20:6
collapsed at the **d** of the man's Jdg 19:26
near the **d** of the house with Jdg 19:27
her, and she stood in the **d**. 2Kg 4:15
waiting by the posts of my **d**. Pr 8:34
She sits by the **d** of her house, Pr 9:14
the wall, and there was a **d**. Ezk 8:8
not even in the **d**, and He was Mk 2:2

DOORWAYS *(2)*
of the **d** shook at the sound Is 6:4
and in the **d** of their houses Ezk 33:30

DOPHKAH *(2)*
of Sin and camped in **D**. Nm 33:12
departed from **D** and camped at Nm 33:13

DOR *(5)*
and the Slopes of **D** to the west, Jos 11:2
the king of **D** in Naphoth-dor one Jos 12:23
inhabitants of **D** with its towns; Jos 17:11
residents of **D** and its villages Jdg 1:27
villages, and **D** and its villages 1Ch 7:29

DORCAS *(2)*
(AKA TABITHA)
Tabitha, which is translated **D**. Ac 9:36
clothes that **D** had made while Ac 9:39

DOTHAN *(3)*
them say, 'Let's go to **D**.'" Gn 37:17
brothers and found them at **D**. Gn 37:17
he was told, "Elisha is in **D**," 2Kg 6:13

DOUBLE *(21)*
took this gift, **d** the amount of Gn 43:15
his possession, he must repay **d**. Ex 22:4
thief, if caught, must repay **d**. Ex 22:7
must repay **d** to his neighbor. Ex 22:9
the sixth curtain **d** at the front Ex 26:9
It must be square and folded **d**, Ex 28:16
breastpiece square and folded **d**, Ex 39:9
by giving him a **d** portion of Dt 21:17
But he gave a **d** portion to 1Sm 1:5
let there be a **d** portion of your 2Kg 2:9
penetrate his **d** layer of armor? Jb 41:13
the LORD's hand **d** for all her Is 40:2
your shame was **d**, and they cried Is 61:7
will possess **d** in their land, Is 61:7
people have committed a **d** evil: Jr 2:13
repay them **d** for their guilt Jr 16:18
the sanctuary each had a **d** door, Ezk 41:23
that I will restore **d** to you. Zch 9:12
so you could have a **d** benefit, 2Co 1:15
and **d** it according to her works. Rv 18:6
mixed, mix a **d** portion for her Rv 18:6

DOUBLE-DRACHMA *(2)*
collected the **d** tax approached Mt 17:24
your Teacher pay the **d** tax?" Mt 17:24

DOUBLE-EDGED *(2)*
made himself a **d** sword 18 inches Jdg 3:16
and as sharp as a **d** sword. Pr 5:4

DOUBLE-MINDED *(2)*
I hate the **d**, but I love Your Ps 119:113
purify your hearts, **d** people! Jms 4:8

DOUBLED *(1)*
prosperity and **d** his ⌊previous⌋ Jb 42:10

DOUBLY *(1)*
in her household are **d** clothed. Pr 31:21

DOUBT *(11)*
they will no **d** cry to Me, and I Ex 22:23
life will hang in **d** before you. Dt 28:66
No **d** you would cast ⌊lots⌋ for a Jb 6:27
No **d** you are the people, and Jb 12:2
d, if I sent you to them, they Ezk 3:6
of little faith, why did you **d**?" Mt 14:31
If you have faith and do not **d**, Mt 21:21
and does not **d** in his heart, Mk 11:23
No **d** you will quote this proverb Lk 4:23
Without a **d**, the inferior is Heb 7:7
Have mercy on some who **d**; Jd 22

DOUBTED *(1)*
Him, they worshiped, but some **d**. Mt 28:17

DOUBTER *(1)*
For the **d** is like the surging Jms 1:6

DOUBTFUL *(1)*
but don't argue about **d** issues. Rm 14:1

DOUBTING *(1)*
let him ask in faith without **d**. Jms 1:6

DOUBTLESS *(1)*
There are **d** many different kinds 1Co 14:10

DOUBTS *(4)*
And why do **d** arise in your Lk 24:38
accompany them with no **d** at all, Ac 10:20
go with them with no **d** at all. Ac 11:12
But whoever **d** stands condemned Rm 14:23

DOUGH *(11)*
people took their **d** before it Ex 12:34
baked the **d** they had brought Ex 12:39
first batch of **d** as a Nm 15:20
from the first batch of your **d**. Nm 15:21
She took **d**, kneaded it, made 2Sm 13:8
first batch of **d** to the priests Neh 10:37
the women knead **d** to make cakes Jr 7:18
first batch of **d** to the priest Ezk 44:30
the kneading of the **d** until it Hs 7:4
permeates the whole batch of **d**? 1Co 5:6
leavens the whole lump of **d**. Gl 5:9

DOVE *(18)*
he sent out a **d** to see whether Gn 8:8
but the **d** found no resting place Gn 8:9
and sent out the **d** from the ark Gn 8:10
When the **d** came to him at Gn 8:11
he sent out the **d**, but she did Gn 8:12
If only I had wings like a **d**! Ps 55:6
wings of a **d** are covered with Ps 68:13
the life of Your **d** to beasts; Ps 74:19
My **d**, in the clefts of the rock, Sg 2:14
darling, my **d**, my perfect one. Sg 5:2
But my **d**, my virtuous one, is Sg 6:9
I moan like a **d**. My eyes grow Is 38:14
like a **d** that nests inside the Jr 48:28
like a silly, senseless **d**; Hs 7:11
like a **d** and coming down Mt 3:16
descending to Him like a **d**. Mk 1:10
a physical appearance like a **d**. Lk 3:22
descending from heaven like a **d**, Jn 1:32

DOVE'S *(1)*
and a cup of **d** dung ⌊sold for⌋ 2Kg 6:25

DOVES *(13)*
very beautiful! Your eyes are **d**. Sg 1:15
your veil, your eyes are **d**. Sg 4:1
eyes are like **d** beside streams Sg 5:12
like bears and moan like **d**. Is 59:11
a cloud, like **d** to their Is 60:8
mountains like **d** of the valley, Ezk 7:16
Egypt and like **d** from the land Hs 11:11
moan like the sound of **d**, Nah 2:7
serpents and as harmless as **d**. Mt 10:16
the chairs of those selling **d**. Mt 21:12
the chairs of those selling **d**, Mk 11:15
oxen, sheep, and **d**, and ⌊He also Jn 2:14
told those who were selling **d**, Jn 2:16

DOWN *(1159)*
(See pp. xi-xii.)

DOWNCAST *(4)*
Cain was furious, and he was **d**. Gn 4:5
you furious? And why are you **d**? Gn 4:6
ate and no longer appeared **d**. 1Sm 1:18
steps; I was **d**. They dug a pit Ps 57:6

DOWNFALL *(19)*
Ahaziah's **d** was from God, 2Ch 22:7
they were the **d** of him and of 2Ch 28:23
because your **d** is certain." Est 6:13
Before his **d** a man's heart is Pr 18:12
the righteous will see their **d**. Pr 29:16
at her, laughing over her **d**. Lm 1:7
Her **d** was astonishing; Lm 1:9
quake at the sound of your **d**, Ezk 26:15
tremble on the day of your **d**; Ezk 26:18
of the sea on the day of your **d**. Ezk 27:27
quake at the sound of its **d**, Ezk 31:16
the day of your **d** each of them Ezk 32:10
causes the **d** of one of these Mt 18:6
hand or your foot causes your **d**, Mt 18:8
And if your eye causes your **d**, Mt 18:9
causes the **d** of one of these Mk 9:42
And if your hand causes your **d**, Mk 9:43
And if your foot causes your **d**, Mk 9:45
And if your eye causes your **d**, Mk 9:47

DOWNPOUR *(2)*
and wind, and there was a **d**. 1Kg 18:45
a **d** of water sweeps by. Hab 3:10

DOWNSTAIRS *(1)*
Get up, go **d**, and accompany them Ac 10:20

DOWNSTREAM *(3)*
water flowing **d** will stand up Jos 3:13
the water flowing **d** stood still, Jos 3:16
The water flowing **d** into the Sea Jos 3:16

DOWNTRODDEN *(1)*
My **d** and threshed people, I have Is 21:10

DOWNWARD *(6)*
and never **d** if you listen to Dt 28:13
slope and **d** to En-rogel. Jos 18:16
again take root **d** and bear fruit 2Kg 19:30
it smoothly **d** and westward to 2Ch 32:30
of animals goes **d** to the earth? Ec 3:21
again take root **d** and bear fruit Is 37:31

DOWRY *(1)*
gave it as a **d** to his daughter 1Kg 9:16

DRACHMAS *(4)*
tons of gold and 10,000 gold **d**, 1Ch 29:7
The governor gave 1,000 gold **d**, Neh 7:70
20,000 gold **d** and 2,200 silver Neh 7:71
the people gave 20,000 gold **d**, Neh 7:72

DRAFTED *(1)*
King Solomon **d** forced laborers 1Kg 5:13

DRAG *(9)*
and we will **d** its ⌊stones⌋ into 2Sm 17:13
not **d** me away with the wicked, Ps 28:3
to those who **d** wickedness with Is 5:18
D the wicked away like sheep to Jr 12:3
kill, the dogs to **d** away, and Jr 15:3
They **d** her and all her hordes Ezk 32:20
Then he won't **d** you before the Lk 12:58
after house, **d** off men and women Ac 8:3
oppress you and **d** you into the Jms 2:6

DRAGGED *(9)*
d off and thrown outside the Jr 22:19
lambs will certainly be **d** away, Jr 49:20
little lambs will be **d** away; Jr 50:45
was full, they **d** it ashore, sat Mt 13:48
so they came up, **d** him off, and Ac 6:12
they **d** him out of the city, Ac 14:19
Paul and Silas and **d** them into Ac 16:19
they **d** Jason and some of the Ac 17:6
d him out of the temple complex, Ac 21:30

DRAGGING *(2)*
came in the boat, **d** the net full Jn 21:8
d along Gaius and Aristarchus, Ac 19:29

DRAGNET *(2)*
them in their **d**, and gather them Hab 1:15
to their **d** and burn incense Hab 1:16

DRAGON *(12)*
a great fiery red **d** having seven Rv 12:3
And the **d** stood in front of the Rv 12:4
his angels fought against the **d**. Rv 12:7
d and his angels also fought, Rv 12:7
So the great **d** was thrown out— Rv 12:9
When the **d** saw that he had been Rv 12:13
the river that the **d** had spewed Rv 12:16
So the **d** was furious with the Rv 12:17
The **d** gave him his power, his Rv 13:2
worshiped the **d** because he gave Rv 13:4
a lamb, but he sounded like a **d**. Rv 13:11
He seized the **d**, that ancient Rv 20:2

DRAGON'S *(1)*
frogs ⌊coming⌋ from the **d** mouth, Rv 16:13

DRAGS *(3)*
But the evening **d** on endlessly, Jb 7:4
Yet God **d** away the mighty by His Jb 24:22
afflicted and **d** him in his net. Ps 10:9

DRAIN *(3)*
be eaten must **d** its blood and Lv 17:13
strangers will **d** your resources, Pr 5:10
You will drink it and **d** ⌊it⌋; Ezk 23:34

DRAINED *(3)*
blood should be **d** at the side Lv 1:15
blood is to be **d** out at the base Lv 5:9
my strength was **d** as in the Ps 32:4

DRAINING *(1)*
will drink, **d** it to the dregs. Ps 75:8

DRANK *(41)*
He **d** some of the wine, became Gn 9:21
So I **d**, and she also watered Gn 24:46
with him ate and **d** and spent the Gn 24:54
ate, **d**, got up, and went away. Gn 25:34
for them, and they ate and **d**. Gn 26:30
he brought him wine, and he **d**. Gn 27:25
They **d**, and they got drunk with Gn 43:34
saw Him, and they ate and **d**. Ex 24:11
community and their livestock **d**. Nm 20:11
you **d** wine from the finest Dt 32:14
sacrifices and **d** the wine of Dt 32:38
as they ate and **d**, they cursed Jdg 9:27
After Samson **d**, his strength Jdg 15:19
ate, **d**, and spent the nights Jdg 19:4
two of them ate and **d** together. Jdg 19:6
washed their feet and ate and **d**. Jdg 19:21
After Boaz ate, **d**, and was in Ru 3:7
after they ate and **d** at Shiloh. 1Sm 1:9
meager food and **d** from his cup; 2Sm 12:3
bread in his house, and **d** water. 1Kg 13:19
and ate bread and **d** water in the 1Kg 13:22
evening, and he **d** from the wadi. 1Kg 17:6
So he ate and **d** and lay down 1Kg 19:6
So he got up, ate, and **d**. 1Kg 19:8
in, ate and **d**, and said, "Take 2Kg 9:34
wells⌋, and I **d** foreign waters. 2Kg 19:24
They ate and **d** with great joy in 1Ch 29:22
I dug ⌊wells⌋ and **d** water. Is 37:25
The nations **d** her wine; Jr 51:7
and from the wine that he **d**. Dn 1:5
food or with the wine he **d**. Dn 1:8
his nobles and **d** wine in their Dn 5:1
and concubines **d** from them. Dn 5:3
d the wine and praised their Dn 5:4
and concubines **d** wine from them, Dn 5:23
and so they all **d** from it. Mk 14:23
'We ate and **d** in Your presence, Lk 13:26
the well and **d** from it himself Jn 4:12
who ate and **d** with Him after He Ac 10:41
and all **d** the same spiritual 1Co 10:4
For they **d** from a spiritual rock 1Co 10:4

DRAW *(50)*
the women went out to **d** water. Gn 24:11
town are coming out to **d** water. Gn 24:13
I'll also **d** water for your Gn 24:19
to the well again to **d** water. Gn 24:20
virgin who comes out to **d** water, Gn 24:43
and I'll **d** water for your camels Gn 24:44
They came to **d** water and filled Ex 2:16
expense. I will **d** my sword; my Ex 15:9
and I will **d** a sword ⌊to chase⌋ Lv 26:33
Sea **d** a line to Mount Nm 34:7
from Mount Hor **d** a line to the Nm 34:8
d a line from Hazar-enan to Nm 34:10
cut your wood and **d** your water— Dt 29:11
they **d** from the wealth of the Dt 33:19
Joshua did not **d** back his hand Jos 8:26
The youth did not **d** his sword, Jdg 8:20
D your sword and kill me, Jdg 9:54
Let's flee and **d** them away from Jdg 20:32
coming out to **d** water and asked, 1Sm 9:11
D your sword and run me through 1Sm 31:4
D your sword and run me through 1Ch 10:4
Maker can **d** the sword against Jb 40:19
D the spear and javelin against Ps 35:3
D near to me and redeem me; Ps 69:18
Better to **d** near in obedience Ec 5:1
You will joyfully **d** water from Is 12:3
together, and **d** near, you Is 45:20
and large; and **d** near for battle! Jr 46:3
and **d** the city of Jerusalem on Ezk 4:1
for I will **d** a sword ⌊to chase⌋ Ezk 5:2
and I will **d** a sword ⌊to chase⌋ Ezk 5:12
and I will **d** a sword ⌊to chase⌋ Ezk 12:14
The days **d** near, as well as the Ezk 12:23
will **d** My sword from its sheath Ezk 21:3
but it will **d** attention to Ezk 21:23
They will **d** their swords against Ezk 28:7
They will **d** their swords against Ezk 30:11
sanctuary and **d** near to My table Ezk 44:16
who **d** near to serve the LORD. Ezk 45:4
like an oven—**d** him into their Hs 7:6
D water for the siege; Nah 3:14
Now **d** some out and take it to Jn 2:8
of Samaria came to **d** water. Jn 4:7
and come here to **d** water." Jn 4:15
earth I will **d** all ⌊people⌋ to Jn 12:32
through which we **d** near to God. Heb 7:19
let us **d** near with a true heart Heb 10:22
are not those who **d** back and are Heb 10:39
D near to God, and He will draw Jms 4:8
and He will **d** near to you. Jms 4:8

DRAWING *(5)*
regular shields and **d** the bow. 2Ch 14:8
d attention to their sin of Ezk 29:16
is called Passover, was **d** near. Lk 22:1
the time was **d** near to fulfill Ac 7:17
more as you see the day **d** near. Heb 10:25

DRAWN *(24)*
the path with a **d** sword in His Nm 22:23
the path with a **d** sword in His Nm 22:31
of him with a **d** sword in His Jos 5:13
us until we have **d** them away Jos 8:6
Joshua and were **d** away from the Jos 8:16
people and were **d** away from the Jdg 20:31
of David was long and **d** out, 2Sm 3:1
with his **d** sword in his hand 1Ch 21:16
let an order be **d** up authorizing Est 3:9
The wicked have **d** the sword and Ps 37:14
than oil, but they are **d** swords. Ps 55:21
from swords, from the **d** sword, Is 21:15
the LORD has **d** up against Edom Jr 49:20
of Babylon has **d** up a plan Jr 49:30
that the LORD has **d** up against Jr 50:45
it is **d** for slaughter. Ezk 21:15
Because you have **d** attention to Ezk 21:24
⌊You are⌋ **d** for slaughter, Ezk 21:28
land of Nimrod with a **d** blade. Mc 5:6
she has not **d** near to her God. Zph 3:2
who had **d** the water knew. Jn 2:9
then everything was **d** up again Ac 11:10
when they are **d** away from Christ 1Tm 5:11
when he is **d** away and enticed Jms 1:14

DRAWS *(7)*
He **d** near the Pit, and his life Jb 33:22
a man of understanding **d** it up. Pr 20:5
and twisting a nose **d** blood, Pr 30:33
d on her strength and reveals Pr 31:17
the Father who sent Me **d** him, Jn 6:44
and if he **d** back, My soul has no Heb 10:38
for the one who **d** near to Him Heb 11:6

DREAD *(21)*
came to **d** the Israelites. Ex 1:12
and terror and **d** will fall on Ex 15:16
to put the fear and **d** of you on Dt 2:25
will put fear and **d** of you in Dt 11:25
You will be in **d** night and day, Dt 28:66
because of the **d** you will have Dt 28:67
land and that **d** of you has Jos 2:9
Would His **d** not fall on you? Jb 13:11
and sudden **d** terrifies you, Jb 22:10
Dominion and **d** belong to Him, Jb 25:2
I am an object of **d** to my Ps 31:11
There is no **d** of God before his Ps 36:1
for **d** of Israel had fallen on Ps 105:38
Turn away the disgrace I **d**; Ps 119:39
two kings you **d** will be Is 7:16
are in constant **d** all day long Is 51:13
will bring on them what they **d**, Is 66:4
hand you over to those you **d**, Jr 22:25
cry of terror, of **d**—there is Jr 30:5
weight and in **d** drink water by Ezk 4:16
and drink their water in **d**, Ezk 12:19

DREADED *(5)*
numerous, and **d** the Israelites. Nm 22:3
Egypt, which you **d**, and they Dt 28:60
was very successful, he **d** him. 1Sm 18:15
and what I **d** has happened to me. Jb 3:25
Who was it you **d** and feared, Is 57:11

DREADFUL *(4)*
see something **d**, you are afraid Jb 6:21
D sounds fill his ears; Jb 15:21
frightening and **d**, and Dn 7:7
of the LORD is terrible and **d**— Jl 2:11

DREADS *(1)*
What the wicked **d** will come to Pr 10:24

DREAM *(70)*
Abimelech in a **d** by night and Gn 20:3
Then God said to him in the **d**, Gn 20:6
I saw in a **d** that the streaked, Gn 31:10
In that **d** the Angel of God said Gn 31:11
the Aramean in a **d** at night. Gn 31:24
Joseph had a **d**. When he told it Gn 37:5
them, "Listen to this **d** I had: Gn 37:6
because of his **d** and what he had Gn 37:8
he had another **d** and told it to Gn 37:9
I had another **d**, and this time Gn 37:9
What kind of **d** is this that you Gn 37:10
in the prison, each had a **d**. Gn 40:5
Both had a **d** on the same night, Gn 40:5
and each **d** had its own meaning. Gn 40:5
cupbearer told his **d** to Joseph: Gn 40:9
In my **d** there was a vine in Gn 40:9
said to Joseph, "I also had a **d**. Gn 40:16
Two years later Pharaoh had a **d**: Gn 41:1
woke up, and it was only a **d**. Gn 41:7
each **d** had its own meaning. Gn 41:11
I have had a **d**, and no one can Gn 41:15
can hear a **d** and interpret it. Gn 41:15
In my **d** I was standing on the Gn 41:17
In my **d** I had also seen seven Gn 41:22
Because the **d** was given twice to Gn 41:32
I speak with him in a **d**. Nm 12:6
telling his friend ⌊about⌋ a **d**. Jdg 7:13
He said, "Listen, I had a **d**: Jdg 7:13
the account of the **d** and its Jdg 7:15
to Solomon in a **d** at night. 1Kg 3:5
up and realized it had been a **d**. 1Kg 3:15
fly away like a **d** and never be Jb 20:8
In a **d**, a vision in the night, Jb 33:15
one waking from a **d**, Lord, when Ps 73:20
Zion, we were like those who **d**. Ps 126:1
will then be like a **d**, a vision Is 29:7
they **d**, lie down, and love to Is 56:10
said: I had a **d**! I had a dream! Jr 23:25
said: I had a dream! I had a **d**! Jr 23:25
has ⌊only⌋ a **d** should recount Jr 23:28
a dream should recount the **d**, Jr 23:28
I have had a **d** and am anxious to Dn 2:3
servants the **d**, and we will give Dn 2:4
you don't tell me the **d** and its Dn 2:5
But if you make the **d** and its Dn 2:6
So make the **d** and its Dn 2:6
king tell the **d** to his servants Dn 2:7
If you don't tell me the **d**, Dn 2:9
So tell me the **d** and I will know Dn 2:9
to tell me the **d** I had and its Dn 2:26
d and the visions ⌊that came Dn 2:28
This was the **d**; now we will tell Dn 2:36
The **d** is true, and its Dn 2:45
I had a **d**, and it frightened me; Dn 4:5
told them the **d**, but they could Dn 4:7
before me. I told him the **d**: Dn 4:8
the visions of my **d** that I saw, Dn 4:9
This is the **d** that I, King Dn 4:18
don't let the **d** or its Dn 4:19
the **d** apply to those who hate Dn 4:19
Daniel had a **d** with visions in Dn 7:1
He wrote down the **d**, and here is Dn 7:1
Woe to those who **d** up wickedness Mc 2:1
suddenly appeared to him in a **d**, Mt 1:20
warned in a **d** not to go back to Mt 2:12
appeared to Joseph in a **d**, Mt 2:13
appeared in a **d** to Joseph in Mt 2:19
warned in a **d**, he withdrew to Mt 2:22
terribly in a **d** because of Him!" Mt 27:19
and your old men will **d** dreams. Ac 2:17

DREAM'S *(1)*
might make the **d** interpretation Dn 4:6

DREAMED *(2)*
And he **d**: A stairway was set on Gn 28:12
fell asleep and **d** a second time: Gn 41:5

DREAMER *(3)*
one another, "Here comes that **d**! Gn 37:19
prophet's words or to that **d**. Dt 13:3
That prophet or **d** must be put to Dt 13:5

DREAMERS *(2)*
your diviners, your **d**, your Jr 27:9
these **d** likewise defile their Jd 8

DREAMS *(28)*
see what becomes of his **d**!" Gn 37:20
"We had **d**," they said to him, Gn 40:8
to God? Tell me ⌊your **d**⌋." Gn 40:8
them his **d**, but no one could Gn 41:8
and I had **d** on the same night; Gn 41:11
told him our **d**, he interpreted Gn 41:12
he interpreted our **d** for us, Gn 41:12
Pharaoh's **d** mean the same thing. Gn 41:25
The **d** mean the same thing. Gn 41:26
remembered his **d** about them and Gn 42:9
someone who has **d** arises among Dt 13:1
answer him in **d** or by the Urim 1Sm 28:6
through the prophets or in **d**. 1Sm 28:15
then You frighten me with **d**, Jb 7:14
For **d** result from much work and Ec 5:3
For many **d** bring futility, Ec 5:7
a hungry one who **d** he is eating, Is 29:8
one who **d** he is drinking, Is 29:8
Through their **d** that they tell Jr 23:27
those who prophesy false **d**"— Jr 23:32
don't listen to the **d** you elicit Jr 29:8
visions and **d** of every kind. Dn 1:17
had **d** that troubled him Dn 2:1
to tell the king his **d**. Dn 2:2
and the ability to interpret **d**, Dn 5:12
men will have **d**, and your young Jl 2:28
relate empty **d** and offer empty Zch 10:2
and your old men will dream **d**. Ac 2:17

DREGS *(3)*
drink, draining it to the **d**. Ps 75:8
have drunk the goblet to the **d**— Is 51:17
settled ⌊like wine⌋ on its **d**. Jr 48:11

DRENCH *(3)*
my pillow and **d** my bed every Ps 6:6
I **d** Heshbon and Elealeh with my Is 16:9
I will **d** the land with the flow Ezk 32:6

DRENCHED *(7)*
D by mountain rains, they huddle Jb 24:8
For my head is **d** with dew, Sg 5:2
Let him be **d** with dew from the Dn 4:15
Let him be **d** with dew from the Dn 4:23
like cattle and be **d** with dew Dn 4:25
and his body was **d** with dew from Dn 4:33
and his body was **d** with dew from Dn 5:21

DRESS *(8)*
d in mourning clothes and don't 2Sm 14:2
d the heavens in black and make Is 50:3
you doing that you **d** yourself in Jr 4:30
d yourselves in sackcloth and Jr 6:26
and **d** in other clothes so that Ezk 44:19
D ⌊in sackcloth⌋ and lament, Jl 1:13
man who would **d** in purple and Lk 16:19
the women are to **d** themselves in 1Tm 2:9

DRESSED *(43)*
d for travel, your sandals on Ex 12:11
of the temple with **d** stones. 1Kg 5:17
three rows of **d** stone and a row 1Kg 6:36
three rows of **d** stone and a row 1Kg 7:12
So they **d** with sackcloth around 1Kg 20:32
David was **d** in a robe of fine 1Ch 15:27
relatives, **d** in fine linen, 2Ch 5:12
food and drink, **d** their wounds, 2Ch 28:15
d in their robes and holding Ezr 3:10
d up in her royal clothing Est 5:1
to meet him, **d** like a prostitute Pr 7:10
d in blue, governors and Ezk 23:6
splendidly **d**, horsemen riding Ezk 23:12
all splendidly **d**, a huge company Ezk 38:4
and there was a man **d** in linen, Dn 10:5
One said to the man **d** in linen, Dn 12:6
Then I heard the man **d** in linen, Dn 12:7
a young woman **d** in sackcloth, Jl 1:8
a fast and **d** in sackcloth— Jnh 3:5
valiant men are **d** in scarlet. Nah 2:3
and all who are **d** in foreign Zph 1:8
Now Joshua was **d** with filthy Zch 3:3
A man **d** in soft clothes? Mt 11:8
who was not **d** for a wedding. Mt 22:11
Him and **d** Him in a scarlet Mt 27:28
sitting there, **d** and in his Mk 5:15
They **d** Him in a purple robe, Mk 15:17
a young man **d** in a long white Mk 16:5
A man **d** in soft robes? Lk 7:25
are splendidly **d** and live in Lk 7:25
at Jesus' feet, **d** and in his Lk 8:35
d Him in a brilliant robe, Lk 23:11
"Get **d**," the angel told him, "and Ac 12:8
d in royal robes and seated on Ac 12:21
a gold ring, **d** in fine clothes, Jms 2:2
a poor man **d** in dirty clothes Jms 2:2
Son of Man, **d** in a long robe, Rv 1:13
victor will be **d** in white Rv 3:5
that you may be **d** and your Rv 3:18
24 elders **d** in white clothes, Rv 4:4
for 1,260 days, **d** in sackcloth." Rv 11:3
plagues, **d** in clean, bright Rv 15:6
The woman was **d** in purple and Rv 17:4

DREW *(24)*
She **d** water for all his camels Gn 24:20
down to the spring and **d** water. Gn 24:45
When the time **d** near for him to Gn 47:29
he **d** his feet into the bed and Gn 49:33
"I **d** him out of the water." Ex 2:10
He even **d** water for us and Ex 2:19
they **d** water and poured it out 1Sm 7:6
the Philistines **d** near to fight 1Sm 7:10
camp and **d** water from the well 2Sm 23:16
But a man **d** his bow without 1Kg 22:34
Then Jehu **d** his bow and shot 2Kg 9:24
and sword, **d** the bow, and were 1Ch 5:18
camp and **d** water from the well 1Ch 11:18
God **d** them away from him. 2Ch 18:31
But a man **d** his bow without 2Ch 18:33
foreign women **d** him into sin. Neh 13:26
streets. Our end **d** near; our Lm 4:18
When the grape harvest **d** near, Mt 21:34
out his hand and **d** his sword. Mt 26:51
those who stood by **d** his sword, Mk 14:47
He **d** near Jericho, a blind man Lk 18:35
When he **d** near, He asked him, Lk 18:40
had a sword, **d** it, struck the Jn 18:10
he **d** his sword and was going to Ac 16:27

DRIED *(27)*
the waters had **d** up from the Gn 8:7
had covered⌋ the earth was **d** up. Gn 8:13
how the LORD **d** up the waters Jos 2:10
LORD your God **d** up the waters Jos 4:23
which He **d** up before us until we Jos 4:23
how the LORD had **d** up the waters Jos 5:1
bowstrings that have not been **d**, Jdg 16:7
bowstrings that had not been **d**, Jdg 16:8
the wadi **d** up because there had 1Kg 17:7
I **d** up all the streams of Egypt 2Kg 19:24
My strength is **d** up like baked Ps 22:15
You **d** up ever-flowing rivers. Ps 74:15
the Red Sea, and it **d** up; Ps 106:9
like a wineskin ⌊**d**⌋ by smoke, Ps 119:83
I **d** up all the streams of Egypt Is 37:25
Wasn't it You who **d** up the sea, Is 51:10
in the wilderness have **d** up. Jr 23:10
waters, and they will be **d** up. Jr 50:38
bake it over **d** human excrement Ezk 4:12
the east wind **d** up its fruit. Ezk 19:12
branches were torn off and **d** up; Ezk 19:12
Our bones are **d** up, and our hope Ezk 37:11
the new wine is **d** up; and the Jl 1:10
grapevine is **d** up, and the fig Jl 1:12
Indeed, human joy has **d** up. Jl 1:12
for the river beds are **d** up, Jl 1:20
its water was **d** up to prepare Rv 16:12

DRIED-UP *(1)*
not say, "Look, I am a **d** tree." Is 56:3

DRIES *(5)*
everything **d** up, and when He Jb 12:15
by evening it withers and **d** up. Ps 90:6
a broken spirit **d** up the bones. Pr 17:22
rebukes the sea so that it **d** up, Nah 1:4
heat and **d** up the grass; Jms 1:11

DRIFT *(1)*
so that we will not **d** away. Heb 2:1

DRIFT-ANCHOR *(1)*
lowered the **d**, and in this way Ac 27:17

DRIFTING *(2)*
scatter you like **d** chaff before Jr 13:24
we were **d** in the Adriatic Sea, Ac 27:27

DRINK *(325)*
our father to **d** wine so that we Gn 19:32
father to **d** wine that night Gn 19:33
Let's get him to **d** wine again Gn 19:34
got their father to **d** wine, Gn 19:35
waterskin and gave the boy a **d**. Gn 21:19
your water jug so that I may **d**,' Gn 24:14
who responds, '**D**, and I'll water Gn 24:14
She replied, "**D**, my lord." Gn 24:18
to her hand and gave him a **d**. Gn 24:18
she had finished giving him a **d**, Gn 24:19
they have had enough to **d**." Gn 24:19
Please let me **d** a little water Gn 24:43
responds to me, '**D**, and I'll Gn 24:44
Please let me have a **d**. Gn 24:45
and said, '**D**, and I'll water Gn 24:46
where the sheep came to **d**. Gn 30:38
sheep bred when they came to **d**. Gn 30:38
He poured a **d** offering on it and Gn 35:14
be unable to **d** water from it." Ex 7:18
could not **d** water from it. Ex 7:21
Nile for water to **d** because they Ex 7:24
they could not **d** the water Ex 7:24
they could not **d** the water at Ex 15:23
Moses, "What are we going to **d**?" Ex 15:24
no water for the people to **d**. Ex 17:1
"Give us water to **d**." Ex 17:2
of it and the people will **d**." Ex 17:6
bowls for pouring **d** offerings. Ex 25:29
and a **d** offering of one quart of Ex 29:40
offering and a **d** offering with Ex 29:41
not to pour a **d** offering on it. Ex 30:9
people sat down to eat and **d**, Ex 32:6
the Israelites to **d** ⌊the water⌋. Ex 32:20
he did not eat bread or **d** water. Ex 34:28
for pouring **d** offerings. Ex 37:16
sons are not to **d** wine or beer Lv 10:9
and its **d** offering will be one Lv 23:13
grain offerings and **d** offerings, Lv 23:18
sacrifices and **d** offerings, Lv 23:37
and pitchers for the **d** offering. Nm 4:7
the woman to **d** the bitter water Nm 5:24
the woman to **d** the water. Nm 5:26
When he makes her **d** the water, Nm 5:27
He must not **d** vinegar made from Nm 6:3
He must not **d** any grape juice or Nm 6:3
grain offerings and **d** offerings, Nm 6:15
grain offering and **d** offering. Nm 6:17
that, the Nazirite may **d** wine. Nm 6:20
of wine as a **d** offering with Nm 15:5
of wine for a **d** offering as Nm 15:7
quarts of wine as a **d** offering. Nm 15:10
offering and **d** offering Nm 15:24
and there is no water to **d**!" Nm 20:5
rock and provide **d** for the Nm 20:8
or vineyard, or **d** ⌊any⌋ well Nm 20:17
if we or our herds **d** your water, Nm 20:19
We won't **d** ⌊any⌋ well water. Nm 21:22
devour the prey and **d** the blood Nm 23:24
The **d** offering is to be a quart Nm 28:7
grain offering and **d** offering as Nm 28:8
offering, and its **d** offering. Nm 28:9
offering and its **d** offering. Nm 28:10
Their **d** offerings are to be two Nm 28:14
offering with its **d** offering. Nm 28:15
be offered with its **d** offering Nm 28:24
them⌋ with their **d** offerings in Nm 28:31
grain offerings and **d** offerings. Nm 29:6
offering and **d** offerings are Nm 29:11
with its grain and **d** offerings. Nm 29:16
their grain and **d** offerings for Nm 29:18
with its grain and **d** offerings. Nm 29:19
their grain and **d** offerings for Nm 29:21
with its grain and **d** offerings. Nm 29:22
their grain and **d** offerings for Nm 29:24
with its grain and **d** offerings. Nm 29:25
their grain and **d** offerings for Nm 29:27
with its grain and **d** offerings. Nm 29:28
their grain and **d** offerings for Nm 29:30
with its grain and **d** offerings. Nm 29:31
their grain and **d** offerings for Nm 29:33
with its grain and **d** offerings. Nm 29:34
their grain and **d** offerings for Nm 29:37
with its grain and **d** offerings. Nm 29:38
burnt, grain, **d**, or fellowship Nm 29:39
no water for the people to **d**. Nm 33:14
and buy water from them to **d**. Dt 2:6
us water for silver so we may **d**. Dt 2:28
I did not eat bread or **d** water. Dt 9:9
not eat bread or **d** water because Dt 9:18
vineyards but not **d** the wine or Dt 28:39
eat bread or **d** wine or beer— Dt 29:6

the wine of their **d** offerings? Dt 32:38
little water to **d** for I am Jdg 4:19
gave him a **d**, and covered him Jdg 4:19
with everyone who kneels to **d**." Jdg 7:5
of the people knelt to **d** water. Jdg 7:6
careful not to **d** wine or other Jdg 13:4
do not **d** wine or other alcoholic Jdg 13:7
the grapevine or **d** wine or other Jdg 13:14
go and **d** from the jars the young Ru 2:9
bread to eat and water to **d**. 1Sm 30:11
house to eat and **d** and sleep 2Sm 11:11
Uriah to eat and **d** with him, 2Sm 11:13
exhausted to **d** in the desert." 2Sm 16:2
me water to **d** from the well at 2Sm 23:15
David, but he refused to **d** it. 2Sm 23:16
So he refused to **d** it. 2Sm 23:17
eat bread or **d** water in this 1Kg 13:8
eat bread or **d** water or go back 1Kg 13:9
or **d** water with you in this 1Kg 13:16
not eat bread or **d** water there 1Kg 13:17
he may eat bread and **d** water.' " 1Kg 13:18
eat bread and do not **d** water, 1Kg 13:22
You are to **d** from the wadi. 1Kg 17:4
water in a cup and let me **d**." 1Kg 17:10
Go up, eat and **d**, for there is 1Kg 18:41
So Ahab went to eat and **d**, 1Kg 18:42
and you will **d**—you and your 2Kg 3:17
can eat and **d** and go to their 2Kg 6:22
went into a tent to eat and **d**. 2Kg 7:8
poured out his **d** offering, 2Kg 16:13
offering, and their **d** offerings. 2Kg 16:15
excrement and **d** their own urine? 2Kg 18:27
every one may **d** water from his 2Kg 18:31
David, but he refused to **d** it. 1Ch 11:18
How can I **d** the blood of these 1Ch 11:19
So he would not **d** it. Such were 1Ch 11:19
along with their **d** offerings, 1Ch 29:21
food and **d**, dressed their 2Ch 28:15
and with the **d** offerings for 2Ch 29:35
and ⌊gave⌋ food, **d**, and oil to Ezr 3:7
their grain and **d** offerings, Ezr 7:17
He did not eat food or **d** water, Ezr 10:6
what is rich, **d** what is sweet, Neh 8:10
the people began to eat and **d**, Neh 8:12
king and Haman sat down to **d**, Est 3:15
Don't eat or **d** for three days, Est 4:16
sisters to eat and **d** with them. Jb 1:4
let him **d** from the Almighty's Jb 21:20
pour out their **d** offerings of Ps 16:4
You let them **d** from Your Ps 36:8
flesh of bulls or **d** the blood of Ps 50:13
given us a wine to **d** that made Ps 60:3
they gave me vinegar to **d**. Ps 69:21
turn to them and **d** in their Ps 73:10
the wicked of the earth will **d**, Ps 75:8
and gave them **d** as abundant as Ps 78:15
they could not **d** from their Ps 78:44
a full measure of tears to **d**. Ps 80:5
He will **d** from the brook by the Ps 110:7
of wickedness and **d** the wine of Pr 4:17
D water from your own cistern, Pr 5:15
let's **d** deeply of lovemaking Pr 7:18
and **d** the wine I have mixed. Pr 9:5
one who gives a **d** of water will Pr 11:25
"Eat and **d**," he says to you, but Pr 23:7
with those who **d** too much wine, Pr 23:20
I'll look for another ⌊**d**⌋." Pr 23:35
is thirsty, give him water to **d**; Pr 25:21
not for kings to **d** wine or for Pr 31:4
they will **d**, forget what is Pr 31:5
Let him **d** so that he can forget Pr 31:7
man than to eat, **d**, and to enjoy Ec 2:24
to eat, **d**, and experience Ec 5:18
except to eat, **d**, and enjoy Ec 8:15
and **d** your wine with a cheerful Ec 9:7
I **d** my wine with my milk. Sg 5:1
D, be intoxicated with love! Sg 5:1
you spiced wine to **d** from my Sg 8:2
carpet! Eat and **d**! Rise up, you Is 21:5
Let us eat and **d**, for tomorrow Is 22:13
They no longer sing and **d** wine; Is 24:9
is bitter to those who **d** it. Is 24:9
and deprives the thirsty of **d**. Is 32:6
excrement and **d** their urine?" Is 36:12
fig tree and **d** water from his Is 36:16
to give **d** to My chosen people. Is 43:20
he doesn't **d** water and is faint. Is 44:12
You will never **d** it again. Is 51:22

poured out a **d** offering to them Is 57:6
will not **d** your new wine you Is 62:8
the grapes will **d** ⌊the wine⌋ in Is 62:9
servants will **d**, but you will be Is 65:13
breast and **d** deeply and delight Is 66:11
the way to Egypt to **d** the waters Jr 2:18
way to Assyria to **d** the waters Jr 2:18
and they pour out **d** offerings to Jr 7:18
given us poisoned water to **d**, Jr 8:14
give them poisonous waters to **d**. Jr 9:15
to sit with them to eat and **d**. Jr 16:8
and poured out **d** offerings to Jr 19:13
father, did he not eat and **d**? Jr 22:15
give them poisoned water to **d**, Jr 23:15
I am sending you to **d** from it. Jr 25:15
They will **d**, stagger, and go out Jr 25:16
all the nations **d** ⌊from it⌋, Jr 25:17
of Sheshach will **d** after them. Jr 25:26
D, get drunk, and vomit. Jr 25:27
to take the cup from you and **d**, Jr 25:28
LORD of Hosts says: You must **d**! Jr 25:28
and where **d** offerings have Jr 32:29
LORD to offer them a **d** of wine." Jr 35:2
and said to them, "**D** wine!" Jr 35:5
We do not **d** wine, for Jonadab, Jr 35:6
and your sons must never **d** wine. Jr 35:6
his sons not to **d** wine, Jr 35:14
and offer **d** offerings to her Jr 44:17
and to offer her **d** offerings, Jr 44:18
and poured out **d** offerings to Jr 44:19
poured out **d** offerings to her? Jr 44:19
and to pour out **d** offerings for Jr 44:25
it will **d** its fill of their Jr 46:10
do not deserve to **d** the cup must Jr 49:12
to drink the cup must **d** it, Jr 49:12
for you must **d** ⌊it⌋ too. Jr 49:12
and the **d** offering bowls— Jr 52:19
We must pay for the water we **d**; Lm 5:4
You are also to **d** water by Ezk 4:11
⌊which⌋ you will **d** from time to Ezk 4:11
and in dread **d** water by measure. Ezk 4:16
trembling and **d** your water with Ezk 12:18
with anxiety and **d** their water Ezk 12:19
out their **d** offerings there Ezk 20:28
You will **d** your sister's cup, Ezk 23:32
You will **d** it and drain ⌊it⌋; Ezk 23:34
eat your fruit and **d** your milk. Ezk 25:4
that you **d** the clear water Ezk 34:18
and **d** what your feet have Ezk 34:19
you will eat flesh and **d** blood. Ezk 39:17
of mighty men and **d** the blood Ezk 39:18
satisfied and **d** blood until you Ezk 39:19
No priest may **d** wine before he Ezk 44:21
and **d** offerings for the Ezk 45:17
king assigned your food and **d**. Dn 1:10
to eat and water to **d**. Dn 1:12
they were to **d** and gave them Dn 1:16
concubines could **d** from them. Dn 5:2
my wool and flax, my oil and **d**. Hs 2:5
Grain and **d** offerings have been Jl 1:9
because grain and **d** offerings Jl 1:13
and sold a girl for wine to **d**. Jl 3:3
and they **d** in the house of their Am 2:8
the Nazirites **d** wine and Am 2:12
"Bring us something to **d**." Am 4:1
another city to **d** water but were Am 4:8
you will never **d** the wine from Am 5:11
They **d** wine by the bowlful and Am 6:6
vineyards and **d** their wine, Am 9:14
the nations will **d** continually. Ob 16
They will **d** and gulp down and be Ob 16
They must not eat or **d** water. Jnh 3:7
grapes but not **d** the wine. Mc 6:15
a drunkard's **d**, and like straw Nah 1:10
him who gives his neighbors **d**, Hab 2:15
You also—**d**, and expose your Hab 2:16
but never **d** their wine. Zph 1:13
You **d** but never have enough to Hg 1:6
When you eat and **d**, don't you Zch 7:6
don't you eat and **d** ⌊simply⌋ for Zch 7:6
they will **d** and be rowdy as if Zch 9:15
you will eat or what you will **d**; Mt 6:25
or 'What will we **d**?' Mt 6:31
Are you able to **d** the cup that I Mt 20:22
the cup that I am about to **d**?" Mt 20:22
You will indeed **d** My cup. Mt 20:23
and you gave Me something to **d**; Mt 25:35
and give You something to **d**? Mt 25:37

and you gave Me nothing to **d**; Mt 25:42
them and said, "**D** from it, all Mt 26:27
moment I will not **d** of this Mt 26:29
that day when I **d** it in a new Mt 26:29
this cannot pass unless I **d** it, Mt 26:42
Him wine mixed with gall to **d**. Mt 27:34
He tasted it, He would not **d** it. Mt 27:34
on a reed, and offered Him a **d**. Mt 27:48
cup of water to **d** because of My Mk 9:41
you able to **d** the cup I drink Mk 10:38
drink the cup I **d** or to be Mk 10:38
You will **d** the cup I drink, Mk 10:39
You will drink the cup I **d**, Mk 10:39
I will no longer **d** of the fruit Mk 14:25
that day when I **d** it in a new Mk 14:25
Him a **d**, and said, "Let's Mk 15:36
they should **d** anything deadly, Mk 16:18
and will never **d** wine or beer. Lk 1:15
Why do you eat and **d** with tax Lk 5:30
the same, but Yours eat and **d**." Lk 5:33
eat, **d**, and enjoy yourself." ' Lk 12:19
eat and what you should **d**, Lk 12:29
and to eat and **d** and get drunk, Lk 12:45
and serve me while I eat and **d**; Lk 17:8
later you can eat and **d**'? Lk 17:8
now on I will not **d** of the fruit Lk 22:18
you may eat and **d** at My table in Lk 22:30
"Give Me a **d**," Jesus said to her, Jn 4:7
a Jew, ask for a **d** from me, a Jn 4:9
you, 'Give Me a **d**,' you would Jn 4:10
the Son of Man and **d** His blood, Jn 6:53
food and My blood is real **d**. Jn 6:55
he should come to Me and **d**! Jn 7:37
Am I not to **d** the cup the Father Jn 18:11
days, and did not eat or **d**. Ac 9:9
to eat nor to **d** until they had Ac 23:12
not to eat or **d** until they kill Ac 23:21
give him something to **d**. Rm 12:20
not to eat meat, or **d** wine, or Rm 14:21
we have the right to eat and **d**? 1Co 9:4
a flock and does not **d** the milk 1Co 9:7
all drank the same spiritual **d**. 1Co 10:4
people sat down to eat and **d**, 1Co 10:7
You cannot **d** the cup of the Lord 1Co 10:21
you eat or **d**, or whatever you 1Co 10:31
you have houses to eat and **d** 1Co 11:22
as often as you **d** it, in 1Co 11:25
eat this bread and **d** the cup, 1Co 11:26
of the bread and **d** of the cup. 1Co 11:28
all made to **d** of one Spirit. 1Co 12:13
Let us eat and **d**, for tomorrow 1Co 15:32
I am poured out as a **d** offering Php 2:17
to food and **d** or in the matter Col 2:16
poured out as a **d** offering, 2Tm 4:6
deal with food, **d**, and various Heb 9:10
all nations **d** the wine of her Rv 14:8
he will also **d** the wine of God's Rv 14:10
You also gave them blood to **d**; Rv 16:6

DRINKABLE *(2)*

the water, the water became **d**. Ex 15:25
any **d** liquid in any container Lv 11:34

DRINKERS *(1)*

wail, all you wine **d**, because of Jl 1:5

DRINKING *(34)*

awoke from his **d** and learned Gn 9:24
After the camels had finished **d**, Gn 24:22
he has finished eating and **d**. Ru 3:3
area, eating, **d**, and celebrating 1Sm 30:16
eating and **d** in his presence, 1Kg 1:25
were⌋ eating, **d**, and rejoicing. 1Kg 4:20
Solomon's **d** cups were gold, 1Kg 10:21
was in Tirzah **d** himself drunk 1Kg 16:9
the kings were **d** in the tents, 1Kg 20:12
days, eating and **d**, for their 1Ch 12:39
King Solomon's **d** cups were gold, 2Ch 9:20
restraint was placed on the **d**. Est 1:8
While **d** the wine, the king asked Est 5:6
on the second day while **d** wine, Est 7:2
where they were **d** wine and ⌊went Est 7:7
garden to the house of wine **d**, Est 7:8
were eating and **d** wine in their Jb 1:13
were eating and **d** wine in their Jb 1:18
those who are heroes at **d** wine, Is 5:22
of meat, and **d** of wine—"Let us Is 22:13
thirsty one who dreams he is **d**, Is 29:8
When their **d** is over, they turn Hs 4:18
John did not come eating or **d**, Mt 11:18
Son of Man came eating and **d**, Mt 11:19

flood they were eating and **d**, Mt 24:38
no one, after **d** old wine, wants Lk 5:39
not come eating bread or **d** wine, Lk 7:33
of Man has come eating and **d**, Lk 7:34
eating and **d** what they offer, Lk 10:7
went on eating, **d**, marrying and Lk 17:27
went on eating, **d**, buying, Lk 17:28
of God is not eating and **d**, Rm 14:17
not **d** a lot of wine, 1Tm 3:8
Don't continue **d** only water, 1Tm 5:23

DRINKS *(16)*
that my master **d** from and uses Gn 44:5
servant taste what he eats or **d**? 2Sm 19:35
my spirit **d** their poison. Jb 6:4
who **d** injustice like water? Jb 15:16
He **d** derision like water. Jb 34:7
bread and mingle my **d** with tears Ps 102:9
off his own feet and **d** violence. Pr 26:6
anyone eats, **d**, and enjoys all Ec 3:13
and eats and **d** with drunkards, Mt 24:49
Everyone who **d** from this water Jn 4:13
whoever **d** from the water that Jn 4:14
eats My flesh and **d** My blood has Jn 6:54
My flesh and **d** My blood lives Jn 6:56
eats the bread or **d** the cup of 1Co 11:27
whoever eats and **d** without 1Co 11:29
eats and **d** judgment on himself. 1Co 11:29

DRIP *(5)*
even his skies **d** with dew. Dt 33:28
forbidden woman **d** honey and her Pr 5:3
Your lips **d** ⌊sweetness like⌋ the Sg 4:11
will **d** with sweet wine, Jl 3:18
will **d** with sweet wine, Am 9:13

DRIPPED *(2)*
and the clouds **d** with dew. Pr 3:20
hands **d** with myrrh, my fingers Sg 5:5

DRIPPING *(4)*
than honey **d** from the comb. Ps 19:10
wife's nagging is an endless **d**. Pr 19:13
An endless **d** on a rainy day and Pr 27:15
lips are lilies, **d** with flowing Sg 5:13

DRIPS *(1)*
It **d** with fat, with the blood of Is 34:6

DRIVE *(85)*
D out this slave with her son, Gn 21:10
he will **d** them out of his land Ex 6:1
he will **d** you out of here. Ex 11:1
and made them **d** with difficulty. Ex 14:25
and it will **d** the Hivites, Ex 23:28
I will not **d** them out ahead of Ex 23:29
I will **d** them out little by Ex 23:30
and you will **d** them out ahead of Ex 23:31
of you and will **d** out the Ex 33:2
I am going to **d** out before you Ex 34:11
For I will **d** out nations before Ex 34:24
to defeat them and **d** them out of Nm 22:6
against them and **d** them away.' " Nm 22:11
you must **d** out all the Nm 33:52
But if you don't **d** out the Nm 33:55
the LORD your God will **d** you. Dt 4:27
to **d** out before you nations Dt 4:38
how can I **d** them out?' Dt 7:17
your God will **d** out these Dt 7:22
Jordan to go and **d** out nations Dt 9:1
You will **d** them out and destroy Dt 9:3
LORD will **d** out these nations Dt 9:4
your God will **d** out these Dt 9:5
the LORD will **d** out all these Dt 11:23
and you will **d** out nations Dt 11:23
and you **d** them out and live in Dt 12:29
you are about to **d** out listen to Dt 18:14
so that you **d** them out and live Dt 19:1
where the LORD will **d** you. Dt 28:37
you, and you will **d** them out. Dt 31:3
I will **d** them out before the Jos 13:6
did not **d** out the Geshurites Jos 13:13
with me and I will **d** them out as Jos 14:12
Judah could not **d** out the Jos 15:63
did not **d** out the Canaanites Jos 16:10
but did not **d** them out Jos 17:13
You can also **d** out the Jos 17:18
account and **d** them out before Jos 23:5
not continue to **d** these nations Jos 23:13
they could not **d** out the people Jdg 1:19
did not **d** out the Jebusites Jdg 1:21
Ephraim failed to **d** out the Jdg 1:29
failed to **d** out the residents Jdg 1:30
Asher failed to **d** out the Jdg 1:31
they failed to **d** them out. Jdg 1:32
Naphtali did not **d** out the Jdg 1:33
I will not **d** out these people Jdg 2:3
will no longer **d** out before them Jdg 2:21
nations and did not **d** them out Jdg 2:23
you hate me and **d** me from my Jdg 11:7
Israel, but will you **d** us out? Jdg 11:23
How then can you **d** back a single 2Kg 18:24
us by coming to **d** us out of Your 2Ch 20:11
They **d** away the donkeys ⌊owned⌋ Jb 24:3
D them out because of their many Ps 5:10
hand of the wicked **d** me away. Ps 36:11
Through You we **d** back our foes; Ps 44:5
D out a mocker, and conflict Pr 22:10
discipline will **d** it away from Pr 22:15
I will **d** him, like a peg, into a Is 22:23
ropes, and **d** your pegs deep. Is 54:2
I will **d** you from My presence, Jr 7:15
you around, **d** you on, and lead Ezk 39:2
I will **d** them from My house Hs 9:15
I will **d** the northerner far from Jl 2:20
with you will **d** you to the Ob 7
d out demons in Your name, Mt 7:22
"If You **d** us out," the demons Mt 8:31
to **d** them out and to heal every Mt 10:1
skin diseases, **d** out demons. Mt 10:8
And if I **d** out demons by Mt 12:27
who is it your sons **d** them out Mt 12:27
If I **d** out demons by the Spirit Mt 12:28
"Why couldn't we **d** it out?" Mt 17:19
have authority to **d** out demons. Mk 3:15
How can Satan **d** out Satan? Mk 3:23
asking Him to **d** the demon out Mk 7:26
Your disciples to **d** it out, Mk 9:18
"Why couldn't we **d** it out?" Mk 9:28
My name they will **d** out demons; Mk 16:17
Your disciples to **d** it out, Lk 9:40
For you say I **d** out demons by Lk 11:18
And if I **d** out demons by Lk 11:19
who is it your sons **d** them out Lk 11:19
If I **d** out demons by the finger Lk 11:20

DRIVEN *(37)*
If they are **d** hard for one day, Gn 33:13
And they were **d** from Pharaoh's Ex 10:11
they had been **d** out of Egypt Ex 12:39
LORD until He has **d** His enemies Nm 32:21
You will be **d** mad by what you Dt 28:34
the LORD your God has **d** you, Dt 30:1
The LORD has **d** out great and Jos 23:9
Israel has now **d** out the Jdg 11:23
for today they have **d** me away 1Sm 26:19
which were **d** ahead of the other 1Sm 30:20
the LORD had **d** out before them. 2Kg 17:11
He is **d** from light to darkness Jb 18:18
wish me harm be **d** back and Ps 40:14
wish me harm be **d** back and Ps 70:2
hate Zion be **d** back in disgrace Ps 129:5
and they will be **d** into thick Is 8:22
d before the wind like chaff on Is 17:13
the peg that was **d** into a firm Is 22:25
a rushing stream **d** by the wind Is 59:19
will be **d** away and fall down Jr 23:12
He has **d** me away and forced ⌊me⌋ Lm 3:2
You will be **d** away from people Dn 4:25
You will be **d** away from people Dn 4:32
He was **d** away from people. Dn 4:33
He was **d** away from people, Dn 5:21
and you will be **d** along toward Am 4:3
And if they are **d** by their Am 9:4
Ashdod will be **d** out at noon, Zph 2:4
who have been **d** from the Zph 3:18
When the demon had been **d** out, Mt 9:33
of whom He had **d** seven demons. Mk 16:9
restraints and be **d** by the demon Lk 8:29
gave way to it and were **d** along. Ac 27:15
in this way they were **d** along. Ac 27:17
the surging sea, **d** and tossed Jms 1:6
large and **d** by fierce winds, Jms 3:4
water, mists **d** by a whirlwind. 2Pt 2:17

DRIVER *(1)*
never hears the shouts of a **d**. Jb 39:7

DRIVERS *(1)*
Pharaoh's slave **d** had set over Ex 5:14

DRIVES *(14)*
and He **d** out many nations before Dt 7:1
LORD your God **d** them out before Dt 9:4
He **d** out the enemy before you, Dt 33:27
your god Chemosh **d** out for you, Jdg 11:24
LORD our God **d** out before us? Jdg 11:24
of Nimshi—he **d** like a madman." 2Kg 9:20
the wicked and **d** the threshing Pr 20:26
and the LORD **d** the people far Is 6:12
He **d** out demons by the ruler of Mt 9:34
The man **d** out demons only by Mt 12:24
If Satan **d** out Satan, he is Mt 12:26
He **d** out demons by the ruler of Mk 3:22
He **d** out demons by Beelzebul, Lk 11:15
perfect love **d** out fear, because 1Jn 4:18

DRIVING *(20)*
nations I am **d** out before you Lv 18:24
nations I am **d** out before you, Lv 20:23
by **d** out all your enemies before Dt 6:19
nations you are **d** out worship Dt 12:2
your God is **d** out the nations Dt 18:12
d out nations and their gods 2Sm 7:23
the **d** is like that of Jehu son 2Kg 9:20
awesome deeds by **d** out nations 1Ch 17:21
the cold from the **d** north winds. Jb 37:9
angel of the LORD **d** them away. Ps 35:5
is like a **d** rain that leaves Pr 28:3
her by banishing and **d** her away. Is 27:8
fire, in **d** rain, a torrent, Is 30:30
synagogues and **d** out demons. Mk 1:39
And they were **d** out many demons, Mk 6:13
we saw someone **d** out demons in Mk 9:38
we saw someone **d** out demons in Lk 9:49
He was **d** out a demon that was Lk 11:14
I'm **d** out demons and performing Lk 13:32
Too much study is **d** you mad!" Ac 26:24

DROP *(7)*
because your olives will **d** off. Dt 28:40
Didn't a woman **d** an upper 2Sm 11:21
are like a **d** in a bucket; Is 40:15
your arrows **d** from your right Ezk 39:3
of a letter in the law to **d** out. Lk 16:17
the skiff and let it **d** away. Ac 27:32
swell up or suddenly **d** dead. Ac 28:6

DROPLETS *(1)*
my hair with **d** of the night. Sg 5:2

DROPPED *(10)*
it **d** ⌊them⌋ at the camp all Nm 11:31
mantle Elijah had **d** and struck 2Kg 2:14
took Jeremiah and **d** him into the Jr 38:6
They have **d** him into the cistern Jr 38:9
They **d** me alive into a pit and Lm 3:53
watched how the crowd **d** money Mk 12:41
widow came and **d** in two tiny Mk 12:42
words, Ananias **d** dead, and a Ac 5:5
she **d** dead at his feet. Ac 5:10
they **d** four anchors from the Ac 27:29

DROPPING *(2)*
saw the rich **d** their offerings Lk 21:1
saw a poor widow **d** in two tiny Lk 21:2

DROPS *(6)*
d a stone without looking that Nm 35:23
like a vine that **d** its unripe Jb 15:33
Who fathered the **d** of dew? Jb 38:28
became like **d** of blood falling Lk 22:44
withers, and the flower **d** off, 1Pt 1:24
as a fig tree **d** its unripe figs Rv 6:13

DROSS *(6)*
on earth as if they were **d**; Ps 119:119
silver has become **d**, your beer Is 1:22
burn away your **d** completely; Is 1:25
of Israel has become **d** to Me. Ezk 22:18
they are the **d** of silver. Ezk 22:18
all of you have become **d**, Ezk 22:19

DROUGHT *(7)*
burning heat, **d**, blight, and Dt 28:22
a land of **d** and darkness, Jr 2:6
to Jeremiah concerning the **d**: Jr 14:1
in a year of **d** or cease Jr 17:8
A **d** will come on her waters, Jr 50:38
wilderness, in the land of **d**. Hs 13:5
have summoned a **d** on the fields Hg 1:11

DROVE *(39)*
He **d** man out, and east of the Gn 3:24
but Abram **d** them away. Gn 15:11
and he **d** his herds to go to the Gn 31:18
arrived and **d** them away, Ex 2:17
The LORD **d** the sea ⌊back⌋ with a Ex 14:21
villages and **d** out the Amorites Nm 21:32

and **d** it through both the Nm 25:8
and **d** out the Amorites who were Nm 32:39
descendants of Esau **d** them out, Dt 2:12
so that they **d** them out and Dt 2:21
they **d** them out and have lived Dt 2:22
struck them down and **d** them out, Jos 13:12
Caleb **d** out from there the three Jos 15:14
and it **d** out the two Amorite Jos 24:12
The LORD **d** out before us all the Jos 24:18
Then Caleb **d** out the three sons Jdg 1:20
labor but never **d** them out Jdg 1:28
his temple and **d** it into the Jdg 4:21
I **d** them out before you and gave Jdg 6:9
Zebul **d** Gaal and his brothers Jdg 9:41
they **d** Jephthah out and said to Jdg 11:2
Philistines, **d** their livestock 1Sm 23:5
and who **d** out the residents 1Ch 8:13
not our God who **d** out the 2Ch 20:7
So I **d** him away from me. Neh 13:28
Abimelech, who **d** him out, and he Ps 34:1
You **d** out the nations with Your Ps 44:2
the skies and **d** the south wind Ps 78:26
He **d** out nations before them. Ps 78:55
d out the nations and planted Ps 80:8
just as I **d** out all of your Jr 7:15
He **d** out the spirits with a word Mt 8:16
complex and **d** out all those Mt 21:12
Immediately the Spirit **d** Him Mk 1:12
diseases and **d** out many demons. Mk 1:34
They got up, **d** Him out of town, Lk 4:29
He **d** everyone out of the temple Jn 2:15
nations that God **d** out before Ac 7:45
So he **d** them from the judge's Ac 18:16

DROWNED *(5)*
officers were **d** in the Red Sea. Ex 15:4
neck and he were **d** in the depths Mt 18:6
bank into the sea and **d** there. Mk 5:13
steep bank into the lake and **d**. Lk 8:33
to do this, they were **d**. Heb 11:29

DROWSY *(1)*
all became **d** and fell asleep Mt 25:5

DRUM *(3)*
lyre, harp, **d**, and every kind Dn 3:5
lyre, harp, **d**, and every kind Dn 3:10
lyre, harp, **d**, and every kind Dn 3:15

DRUNK *(43)*
wine, became **d**, and uncovered Gn 9:21
and they got **d** with Joseph. Gn 43:34
My arrows **d** with blood while Dt 32:42
When they were **d**, they said, Jdg 16:25
be heard. Eli thought she was **d** 1Sm 1:13
How long are you going to be **d**? 1Sm 1:14
was in a good mood and very **d**, 1Sm 25:36
eaten food or **d** water for three 1Sm 30:12
with him, and David got him **d**. 2Sm 11:13
eaten bread and after he had **d**, 1Kg 13:23
drinking himself **d** in the house 1Kg 16:9
him were getting **d** in the tents. 1Kg 20:16
When they had eaten and **d**, 2Kg 6:23
They are **d**, but not with wine; Is 29:9
When My sword has **d** its fill in Is 34:5
they will be **d** with their own Is 49:26
you who have **d** the cup of His Is 51:17
you who have **d** the goblet to the Is 51:17
I made them **d** with My wrath and Is 63:6
Drink, get **d**, and vomit. Jr 25:27
So we haven't **d** wine our whole Jr 35:8
they have not **d** to this very day Jr 35:14
Make him **d**, because he has Jr 48:26
hand making the whole earth **d**. Jr 51:7
I will make them **d** so that they Jr 51:39
make her princes and sages **d**, Jr 51:57
you will get **d** and expose Lm 4:21
and drink blood until you are **d**, Ezk 39:19
For as you have **d** on My holy Ob 16
You also will become **d**; Nah 3:11
wrath and even making them **d**, Hab 2:15
never have enough to become **d**. Hg 1:6
and to eat and drink and get **d**, Lk 12:45
after people have **d** freely, Jn 2:10
For these people are not **d**, Ac 2:15
is hungry while another is **d**! 1Co 11:21
And don't get **d** with wine, Eph 5:18
and those who get **d** are drunk at 1Th 5:7
who get drunk are **d** at night. 1Th 5:7
ground that has **d** the rain that Heb 6:7
the earth became **d** on the wine Rv 17:2
the woman was **d** on the blood Rv 17:6
nations have **d** the wine of her Rv 18:3

DRUNKARD *(9)*
He's a glutton and a **d**.' Dt 21:20
For the **d** and the glutton will Pr 23:21
brandished by the hand of a **d**. Pr 26:9
as a **d** staggers in his vomit. Is 19:14
staggers like a **d** and sways like Is 24:20
have become like a **d**, like a man Jr 23:9
a glutton and a **d**, a friend of Mt 11:19
a glutton and a **d**, a friend of Lk 7:34
or a reviler, a **d** or a swindler. 1Co 5:11

DRUNKARD'S *(1)*
thorns, like a **d** drink, and like Nah 1:10

DRUNKARDS *(7)*
and **d** make up songs about me. Ps 69:12
majestic crown of Ephraim's **d**, Is 28:1
of Ephraim's **d** will be trampled Is 28:3
D from the desert were brought Ezk 23:42
Wake up, you **d**, and weep; Jl 1:5
and eats and drinks with **d**, Mt 24:49
greedy people, **d**, revilers, or 1Co 6:10

DRUNKEN *(3)*
makes them stagger like **d** men. Jb 12:25
reeled and staggered like **d** men, Ps 107:27
afflicted and **d** one—but not Is 51:21

DRUNKENNESS *(7)*
for strength and not for **d**. Ec 10:17
residents of Jerusalem—with **d**. Jr 13:13
will be filled with **d** and grief, Ezk 23:33
from carousing, **d**, and worries Lk 21:34
not in carousing and **d**; Rm 13:13
envy, **d**, carousing, and anything Gl 5:21
evil desires, **d**, orgies, 1Pt 4:3

DRUSILLA *(1)*
when Felix came with his wife **D**, Ac 24:24

DRY *(82)*
and let the **d** land appear." Gn 1:9
God called the **d** land "earth," Gn 1:10
everything on **d** land died. Gn 7:22
second month, the earth was **d**. Gn 8:14
and pour it on the **d** ground. Ex 4:9
go through the sea on **d** ground. Ex 14:16
and turned the sea into **d** land. Ex 14:21
through the sea on **d** ground, Ex 14:22
through the sea on **d** ground, Ex 14:29
through the sea on **d** ground. Ex 15:19
whether **d** or mixed with oil, Lv 7:10
weights, an honest **d** measure, Lv 19:36
two differing **d** measures in your Dt 25:14
a full and honest **d** measure, Dt 25:15
land⌋ as well as the **d** ⌊land⌋. Dt 29:19
stood firmly on **d** ground in the Jos 3:17
Israel crossed on **d** ground until Jos 3:17
the Jordan on **d** ground.' Jos 4:22
of bread was **d** and crumbly. Jos 9:5
a look, it is now **d** and crumbly. Jos 9:12
the ground is **d**, I will know Jdg 6:37
Let it remain **d**, and the dew be Jdg 6:39
fleece was **d**, and dew was all Jdg 6:40
jug will not run **d** until the day 1Kg 17:14
and the oil jug did not run **d**, 1Kg 17:16
them crossed over on **d** ground. 2Kg 2:8
crossed through it on **d** ground. Neh 9:11
they would **d** up quicker than any Jb 8:12
Will You chase after **d** straw? Jb 13:25
a wadi becomes parched and **d**, Jb 14:11
His roots below **d** up, and his Jb 18:16
As **d** ground and heat snatch away Jb 24:19
they gnawed the **d** land, the Jb 30:3
for You in a land that is **d**, Ps 63:1
He turned the sea into **d** land, Ps 66:6
His hands formed the **d** land. Ps 95:5
d land into springs of water. Ps 107:35
Better a **d** crust with peace than Pr 17:1
straw and as **d** grass shrivels Is 5:24
The waters of the sea will **d** up, Is 19:5
the river will be parched and **d**. Is 19:5
heat in a **d** land, You subdue Is 25:5
its branches **d** out, they will be Is 27:11
of water in a **d** land and the Is 32:2
and the **d** land will be glad Is 35:1
of water and **d** land into springs Is 41:18
and **d** up all their vegetation. Is 42:15
into islands, and **d** up marshes. Is 42:15
and streams on the **d** ground; Is 44:3
Be **d**, and I will dry up your Is 44:27
and I will **d** up your rivers; Is 44:27
I **d** up the sea by My rebuke; Is 50:2
and like a root out of **d** ground. Is 53:2
spring whose waters never run **d**. Is 58:11
the nations—a **d** land, a Jr 50:12
I will **d** up her sea and make her Jr 51:36
sea and make her fountain run **d**. Jr 51:36
a desolation, a **d** and arid land, Jr 51:43
it has become **d** like wood. Lm 4:8
in a **d** and thirsty land Ezk 19:13
tree and every **d** tree in you. Ezk 20:47
make the streams **d** and sell the Ezk 30:12
valley, and they were very **d**. Ezk 37:2
D bones, hear the word of the Ezk 37:4
balances, an honest **d** measure, Ezk 45:10
The **d** measure and the liquid Ezk 45:11
gallons and the **d** measure Ezk 45:11
where nets are spread out to **d**. Ezk 47:10
and breasts that are **d**! Hs 9:14
and his spring will run **d**. Hs 13:15
banish him to a **d** and desolate Jl 2:20
made the sea and the **d** land." Jnh 1:9
hard to get back to **d** land, Jnh 1:13
it vomited Jonah onto **d** land. Jnh 2:10
He makes all the rivers run **d**. Nah 1:4
and like straw that is fully **d**. Nah 1:10
desolate ruin, **d** as the desert. Zph 2:13
earth, the sea and the **d** land. Hg 2:6
depths of the Nile will **d** up. Zch 10:11
what will happen when it is **d**?" Lk 23:31
and to **d** them with the towel Jn 13:5
as though they were on **d** land. Heb 11:29

DRYING *(1)*
the surface of the ground was **d**. Gn 8:13

DUE *(12)*
wages **d** a hired hand must not Lv 19:13
entire offering **d** the LORD from Nm 18:29
his gaze was fixed **d** to his age. 1Kg 14:4
with the judgment **d** the wicked; Jb 36:17
the LORD the glory **d** His name; Ps 29:2
matches the fear that is **d** You. Ps 90:11
proclaim all the praise **d** Him? Ps 106:2
give them their food in **d** time. Ps 145:15
from the one to whom it is **d**. Pr 3:27
the justice **d** the innocent. Pr 18:5
skillful work is **d** to a man's Ec 4:4
that He may exalt you in **d** time, 1Pt 5:6

DUG *(30)*
my witness that I **d** this well." Gn 21:30
slaves had **d** in the days of his Gn 26:15
that had been **d** in the days of Gn 26:18
Isaac's slaves **d** in the valley Gn 26:19
Then they **d** another well and Gn 26:21
moved from there and **d** another, Gn 26:22
slaves also **d** a well there. Gn 26:25
him about the well they had **d**, Gn 26:32
the Egyptians **d** around the Nile Ex 7:24
The princes **d** the well; The Nm 21:18
wells **d** that you did not dig, Dt 6:11
I **d** ⌊wells⌋, and I drank foreign 2Kg 19:24
in the desert and **d** many wells. 2Ch 26:10
He **d** a pit and hollowed it out, Ps 7:15
they **d** a pit for me without Ps 35:7
They **d** a pit ahead of me, but Ps 57:6
until a pit is **d** for the wicked. Ps 94:13
The arrogant have **d** pits for me; Ps 119:85
I **d** ⌊wells⌋ and drank water. Is 37:25
quarry from which you were **d**. Is 51:1
and **d** cisterns for themselves, Jr 2:13
Euphrates and **d** up the underwear Jr 13:7
Yet they have **d** a pit for me. Jr 18:20
for they have **d** a pit to capture Jr 18:22
So I **d** through the wall, Ezk 8:8
the evening I **d** through the wall Ezk 12:7
fence around it, **d** a winepress Mt 21:33
talent went off, **d** a hole in the Mt 25:18
d out a pit for a winepress, Mk 12:1
who **d** deep and laid the Lk 6:48

DULL *(4)*
skin of the body are **d** white, Lv 13:39
the axe is **d**, and one does not Ec 10:10
D the minds of these people; Is 6:10
the fine gold become **d**! Lm 4:1

DULLED *(1)*
minds are not **d** from carousing, Lk 21:34

DUMAH (4)
Mishma, **D**, Massa, Gn 25:14
Arab, **D**, Eshan, Jos 15:52
Mishma, **D**, Massa, Hadad, Tema, 1Ch 1:30
oracle against **D**: One calls to Is 21:11

DUMB (1)
you were led to **d** idols—being 1Co 12:2

DUMP (3)
into a garbage **d** because of this Ezr 6:11
houses will be made a garbage **d**. Dn 2:5
and his house made a garbage **d**. Dn 3:29

DUMPED (2)
off must be **d** in an unclean Lv 14:41
the sword and **d** into a rocky pit Is 14:19

DUNG (15)
and its **d** outside the camp; Ex 29:14
shanks, and its entrails and **d**— Lv 4:11
flesh, and **d** outside the camp Lv 8:17
hide, flesh, and **d** burned up. Lv 16:27
to be burned along with its **d**. Nm 19:5
sweeps away **d** until it is all 1Kg 14:10
cup of dove's **d** ⌊sold for⌋ five 2Kg 6:25
Serpent's Well and the **D** Gate, Neh 2:13
yards of the wall to the **D** Gate. Neh 3:13
repaired the **D** Gate. Neh 3:14
on the wall, toward the **D** Gate. Neh 12:31
vanish forever like his own **d**. Jb 20:7
straw is trampled in a **d** pile. Is 25:10
you ⌊use⌋ cow **d** instead of human Ezk 4:15
dust and their flesh like **d**. Zph 1:17

DUNGEON (6)
they should put me in the **d**." Gn 40:15
quickly brought him from the **d**. Gn 41:14
the prisoner who was in the **d**, Ex 12:29
They will be confined to a **d**; Is 24:22
bring out prisoners from the **d**, Is 42:7
a cell in the **d** and stayed there Jr 37:16

DUNGEONS (1)
in holes or imprisoned in **d**. Is 42:22

DURA (1)
the plain of **D** in the province Dn 3:1

DURING (171)
(See pp. xi-xii.)

DUSK (3)
to pieces from dawn to **d**; Jb 4:20
stumble on the mountains at **d**. Jr 13:16
From dawn to **d** he expounded and Ac 28:23

DUST (109)
man out of the **d** from the ground Gn 2:7
belly and eat **d** all the days Gn 3:14
For you are **d**, and you will Gn 3:19
and you will return to **d**." Gn 3:19
like the **d** of the earth, Gn 13:16
could count the **d** of the earth, Gn 13:16
even though I am **d** and ashes— Gn 18:27
will be like the **d** of the earth, Gn 28:14
and strike the **d** of the earth, Ex 8:16
he struck the **d** of the earth, Ex 8:17
All the **d** of the earth became Ex 8:17
become fine **d** over the entire Ex 9:9
take some of the **d** from the Nm 5:17
Who has counted the **d** of Jacob Nm 23:10
or numbered the **d** clouds of Nm 23:10
it to powder as ⌊fine as⌋ **d**. Dt 9:21
of your land into falling **d**; Dt 28:24
snakes that slither in the **d**. Dt 32:24
they all put **d** on their heads. Jos 7:6
poor from the **d** and lifts the 1Sm 2:8
clothes and **d** on his head came 2Sm 1:2
his robe torn and **d** on his head. 2Sm 15:32
them like **d** of the earth; 2Sm 22:43
you up from the **d** and made you 1Kg 16:2
stones, and the **d**, and it licked 1Kg 18:38
if Samaria's **d** amounts to a 1Kg 20:10
making them like **d** at threshing. 2Kg 13:7
beat it to **d**, and threw its 2Kg 23:6
and threw its **d** on the graves of 2Kg 23:6
threw their **d** into the Kidron 2Kg 23:12
crushed it to **d**, and burned 2Kg 23:15
numerous as the **d** of the earth. 2Ch 1:9
crushed to **d**, and scattered over 2Ch 34:4
⌊and had put⌋ **d** on their heads. Neh 9:1
robe and threw **d** into the air Jb 2:12
whose foundation is in the **d**, Jb 4:19
others will sprout from the **d**. Jb 8:19
Will You now return me to **d**? Jb 10:9
buried my strength in the **d**. Jb 16:15
we descend together to the **d**? Jb 17:16
He will stand on the **d** at last. Jb 19:25
But they both lie in the **d**, Jb 21:26
and consign your gold to the **d**, Jb 22:24
up silver like **d** and heaps up Jb 27:16
I have become like **d** and ashes. Jb 30:19
mankind would return to the **d**. Jb 34:15
when the **d** hardens like cast Jb 38:38
Hide them together in the **d**; Jb 40:13
and repent in **d** and ashes. Jb 42:6
and leave my honor in the **d**. Ps 7:5
them like **d** before the wind; Ps 18:42
You put me into the **d** of death. Ps 22:15
go down to the **d** will kneel Ps 22:29
Pit? Will the **d** praise You? Will Ps 30:9
For we have sunk down to the **d**; Ps 44:25
him and his enemies lick the **d**. Ps 72:9
He rained meat on them like **d**, Ps 78:27
You return mankind to the **d**, Ps 90:3
in its stones and favor its **d**. Ps 102:14
remembering that we are **d**. Ps 103:14
they die and return to the **d**. Ps 104:29
poor from the **d** and lifts the Ps 113:7
My life is down in the **d**; Ps 119:25
all come from **d**, and all return Ec 3:20
from dust, and all return to **d**. Ec 3:20
and the **d** returns to the earth Ec 12:7
hide in the **d** from the terror Is 2:10
blossoms will blow away like **d**, Is 5:24
For a cloud of **d** is coming from Is 14:31
thrown to the ground, to the **d**. Is 25:12
ground; He throws it to the **d**. Is 26:5
sing, you who dwell in the **d**! Is 26:19
will come from low in the **d**. Is 29:4
speech will whisper from the **d**. Is 29:4
your foes will be like fine **d**, Is 29:5
has gathered the **d** of the earth Is 40:12
as a speck of **d** on the scales; Is 40:15
up the islands like fine **d**. Is 40:15
them⌋ like **d** ⌊with⌋ his sword Is 41:2
Go down and sit in the **d**, Is 47:1
and lick the **d** at your feet. Is 49:23
up, shake the **d** off yourself! Is 52:2
the serpent's food will be **d**! Is 65:25
in sackcloth and roll in the **d**. Jr 6:26
Roll ⌊in the **d**⌋, you leaders of Jr 25:34
have thrown **d** on their heads Lm 2:10
and made me cower in the **d**. Lm 3:16
Let him put his mouth in the **d**— Lm 3:29
the ground to cover it with **d**. Ezk 24:7
that their **d** will cover you. Ezk 26:10
They throw **d** on their heads; Ezk 27:30
who sleep in the **d** of the earth Dn 12:2
the poor on the **d** of the ground Am 2:7
In Beth-leaphrah roll in the **d**. Mc 1:10
will lick the **d** like a snake; Mc 7:17
clouds are the **d** beneath His Nah 1:3
poured out like **d** and their Zph 1:17
up silver like **d** and gold like Zch 9:3
shake the **d** off your feet when Mt 10:14
shake the **d** off your feet as a Mk 6:11
shake off the **d** from your feet Lk 9:5
you even the **d** of your town that Lk 10:11
But shaking the **d** off their feet Ac 13:51
and throwing **d** into the air, Ac 22:23
from the earth and made of **d**; 1Co 15:47
the man made of **d**, so are those 1Co 15:48
so are those who are made of **d**; 1Co 15:48
the image of the man made of **d**, 1Co 15:49
They threw **d** on their heads and Rv 18:19

DUTIES (24)
They are to perform **d** for him Nm 3:7
and perform **d** for the Israelites Nm 3:8
The Gershonites' **d** at the tent Nm 3:25
for the **d** of the sanctuary. Nm 3:28
Their **d** involved the ark, the Nm 3:31
for the **d** of the sanctuary. Nm 3:32
The assigned **d** of Merari's Nm 3:36
performed the **d** of the sanctuary Nm 3:38
transportation **d** of the Nm 4:15
work and transportation **d**: Nm 4:24
transportation **d** and all their Nm 4:27
and their **d** will be under the Nm 4:28
the Levites regarding their **d**." Nm 8:26
are to perform **d** for you and for Nm 18:3
who perform the **d** of the LORD's Nm 31:30
who perform the **d** of the LORD's Nm 31:47
to the assigned **d** of their 1Ch 24:3
their assigned **d** for service 1Ch 24:19
lots impartially for their **d**, 1Ch 25:8
had **d** for ministering in the 1Ch 26:12
had the outside **d** as officers 1Ch 26:29
had assigned **d** in Israel west of 1Ch 26:30
and assigned specific **d** to each Neh 13:30
for the **d** of the temple— Ezk 44:14

DUTY (29)
Perform your **d** as her Gn 38:8
his task and transportation **d**. Nm 4:19
his work and transportation **d**, Nm 4:49
the army or be liable for any **d**. Dt 24:5
and perform the **d** of a Dt 25:5
willing to perform the **d** of a Dt 25:7
you who come on **d** on the Sabbath 2Kg 11:5
that go off **d** on the Sabbath are 2Kg 11:7
those coming on **d** on the Sabbath 2Kg 11:9
Sabbath and those going off **d**— 2Kg 11:9
of the land for military **d**; 2Kg 25:19
they had guard **d** and were in 1Ch 9:27
they were on **d** day and night. 1Ch 9:33
but their **d** will be to assist 1Ch 23:28
on rotated military **d** each month 1Ch 27:1
regardless of their tour of **d**— 2Ch 5:11
are coming on **d** on the Sabbath, 2Ch 23:4
those coming on **d** on the Sabbath 2Ch 23:8
those going off **d** on the Sabbath 2Ch 23:8
LORD's temple for their daily **d**, 2Ch 31:16
not pay tribute, **d**, or land tax, Ezr 4:13
tribute, **d**, and land tax were Ezr 4:20
that tribute, **d**, and land tax Ezr 7:24
while the guards are on **d**. Neh 7:3
of the land for military **d**; Jr 52:25
division was on **d** and he was Lk 1:8
we've only done our **d**.'" Lk 17:10
whom we can appoint to this **d**. Ac 6:3
his marital **d** to his wife, 1Co 7:3

DWARF (1)
or who is a hunchback or a **d**, Lv 21:20

DWELL (68)
he will **d** in the tents of Shem; Gn 9:27
Me so that I may **d** among them. Ex 25:8
will **d** among the Israelites and Ex 29:45
so that I might **d** among them. Ex 29:46
camps where I **d** among them." Nm 5:3
the place to have His name **d**. Dt 12:11
He chooses to have His name **d**, Dt 14:23
LORD chooses to have His name **d**. Dt 16:2
God chooses to have His name **d**. Dt 16:6
He chooses to have His name **d**— Dt 16:11
God chooses to have His name **d**. Dt 26:2
that He would **d** in thick 1Kg 8:12
the one to build Me a house to **d** 1Ch 17:4
said He would **d** in thick 2Ch 6:1
brothers who **d** in their cities 2Ch 19:10
His name to **d** there overthrow Ezr 6:12
I chose to have My name **d**." Neh 1:9
should **d** in booths during Neh 8:14
more those who **d** in clay houses, Jb 4:19
injustice to **d** in your tents— Jb 11:14
he will **d** in ruined cities, Jb 15:28
LORD, who can **d** in Your tent? Ps 15:1
and I will **d** in the house of the Ps 23:6
I love the house where You **d**, Ps 26:8
d in the house of the LORD all Ps 27:4
d in the land and live securely. Ps 37:3
is good, and **d** there forever. Ps 37:27
land and **d** in it permanently. Ps 37:29
Mount Zion where You **d**. Ps 74:2
so that glory may **d** in our land. Ps 85:9
children will **d** ⌊securely⌋, Ps 102:28
You who **d** in the gardens— Sg 8:13
My people who **d** in Zion, do not Is 10:24
Ostriches will **d** there, and wild Is 13:21
await⌋ you who **d** on the earth. Is 24:17
and sing, you who **d** in the dust! Is 26:19
will **d** in the orchard. Is 32:16
my people will **d** in a peaceful Is 32:18
among us can **d** with a consuming Is 33:14
Who among us can **d** with Is 33:14
he will **d** on the heights; Is 33:16
The people who **d** there will be Is 33:24
owl and the raven will **d** there. Is 34:11
will **d** in it from generation Is 34:17
person, to **d** in a temple. Is 44:13
and My servants will **d** there. Is 65:9
where I made My name **d** at first. Jr 7:12

and Israel will **d** securely. Jr 23:6
They will **d** once more in their Jr 23:8
and Jerusalem will **d** securely, Jr 33:16
has made me **d** in darkness like Lm 3:6
I will make you **d** in the Ezk 26:20
where I will **d** among the Ezk 43:7
and I will **d** among them forever. Ezk 43:9
quake and all who **d** in it mourn? Am 8:8
and all who **d** on it mourn; Am 9:5
I am coming to **d** among you"— Zch 2:10
I will **d** among you, and you will Zch 2:11
So Jerusalem will **d** in security. Zch 14:11
High does not **d** in sanctuaries Ac 7:48
I will **d** among them and walk 2Co 6:16
the Messiah may **d** in your hearts Eph 3:17
any praise—**d** on these things Php 4:8
have⌋ all His fullness **d** in Him, Col 1:19
the Messiah **d** richly among you Col 3:16
where righteousness will **d**. 2Pt 3:13
heavens, and you who **d** in them! Rv 12:12
—those who **d** in heaven. Rv 13:6

DWELLING *(54)*
your **d** place will be away from Gn 27:39
to Your holy **d** with Your Ex 15:13
prepared the place for Your **d**; Ex 15:17
Your **d** place is enduring; Nm 24:21
to put His name for His **d**. Dt 12:5
Look down from Your holy **d**, Dt 26:15
God of old is ⌊your⌋ **d** place, Dt 33:27
and Judah are **d** in tents, and my 2Sm 11:11
to see both it and its **d** place. 2Sm 15:25
a place for Your **d** forever. 1Kg 8:13
hear in Your **d** place in heaven 1Kg 8:30
in heaven, Your **d** place, and may 1Kg 8:39
in heaven, Your **d** place, and do 1Kg 8:43
in heaven, Your **d** place, their 1Kg 8:49
hear in Your **d** place in heaven 2Ch 6:21
in heaven, Your **d** place, and may 2Ch 6:30
hear in heaven in Your **d** place, 2Ch 6:33
heaven, in Your **d** place, their 2Ch 6:39
into His holy **d** place in heaven. 2Ch 30:27
His people and on His **d** place. 2Ch 36:15
Israel, whose **d** is in Jerusalem Ezr 7:15
such is the **d** of the wicked, Jb 18:21
and the salty wasteland its **d**. Jb 39:6
of the earth from His **d** place. Ps 33:14
holy mountain, to Your **d** place. Ps 43:3
the holy **d** place of the Most Ps 46:4
of widows is God in His holy **d**. Ps 68:5
mountain God desired for His **d**? Ps 68:16
desecrated the **d** place of Your Ps 74:7
in Salem, His **d** place in Zion. Ps 76:2
How lovely is Your **d** place, Ps 84:1
the Most High—your **d** place, Ps 91:9
d for the Mighty One of Jacob." Ps 132:5
Let us go to His **d** place; Ps 132:7
oil are in the **d** of the wise, Pr 21:20
don't destroy his **d**. Pr 24:15
She will become a **d** for jackals, Is 34:13
My **d** is plucked up and removed Is 38:12
and I will glorify My **d** place. Is 60:13
His voice from His holy **d**. Jr 25:30
My **d** place will be with them; Ezk 37:27
My people Israel are **d** securely, Ezk 38:14
whose **d** is not with mortals." Dn 2:11
Then her **d** place would not be Zph 3:7
He is coming from His holy **d**." Zch 2:13
house are many **d** places; Jn 14:2
Let his **d** become desolate; Ac 1:20
might provide a **d** place for the Ac 7:46
for God's **d** in the Spirit. Eph 2:22
d in unapproachable light, 1Tm 6:16
but deserted their proper **d**. Jd 6
blaspheme His name and His **d**— Rv 13:6
She has become a **d** for demons, Rv 18:2
God's **d** is with men, and He will Rv 21:3

DWELLINGS *(9)*
Get away from the **d** of Korah, Nm 16:24
got away from the **d** of Korah, Nm 16:27
tents, Jacob, your **d**, Israel. Nm 24:5
more than all the **d** of Jacob. Ps 87:2
and in safe and restful **d**. Is 32:18
our **d** have been torn down. Jr 9:19
and show compassion on his **d**. Jr 30:18
swallowed up all the **d** of Jacob. Lm 2:2
may welcome you into eternal **d**. Lk 16:9

DWELLS *(17)*
So Israel **d** securely; Dt 33:28
who **d** ⌊between⌋ the cherubim. 1Sm 4:4
LORD of Hosts who **d** ⌊between⌋ 2Sm 6:2
name of the LORD who **d** ⌊between⌋ 1Ch 13:6
home where your righteousness **d**. Jb 8:6
Sing to the LORD, who **d** in Zion; Ps 9:11
of the Most High **d** in the shadow Ps 91:1
from Zion; He **d** in Jerusalem. Ps 135:21
of Hosts who **d** on Mount Zion. Is 8:18
is exalted, for He **d** on high; Is 33:5
where Kedar **d** ⌊cry aloud⌋. Is 42:11
good comes but **d** in the parched Jr 17:6
darkness, and light **d** with Him. Dn 2:22
your God, who **d** in Zion, My holy Jl 3:17
for the LORD **d** in Zion. Jl 3:21
by it and by Him who **d** in it. Mt 23:21
of God's nature **d** bodily, Col 2:9

DWELT *(2)*
people of Israel **d** in their 2Kg 13:5
Righteousness once **d** in her— Is 1:21

DWINDLE *(2)*
Wealth obtained by fraud will **d**, Pr 13:11
they will **d**, and Egypt's canals Is 19:6

DYED *(7)*
ram skins **d** red and manatee Ex 25:5
the tent from ram skins **d** red, Ex 26:14
ram skins **d** red and manatee Ex 35:7
skins **d** red or manatee skins, Ex 35:23
from ram skins **d** red and a Ex 36:19
of ram skins **d** red and the Ex 39:34
of his warriors are **d** red; Nah 2:3

DYING *(14)*
for she was **d**—she named him Gn 35:18
As she was **d**, the women taking 1Sm 4:20
While he was **d**, he said, "May 2Ch 24:22
The **d** man blessed me, and I made Jb 29:13
I have seen anyone **d** for lack of Jb 31:19
Give beer to one who is **d**, Pr 31:6
him in custody until his **d** day. Jr 52:11
Let what is **d** die, and let what Zch 11:9
took a wife, and, **d**, left no Mk 12:20
and here I am **d** of hunger! Lk 15:17
also have kept this man from **d**?" Jn 11:37
as **d** and look—we live; 2Co 6:9
living is Christ and **d** is gain. Php 1:21
when he was **d**, blessed each Heb 11:21

DYNASTY *(6)*
establish a lasting **d** for him, 1Sm 2:35
to make a lasting **d** for my lord 1Sm 25:28
made me a **d** as He promised— 1Kg 2:24
his **d**, and his throne 1Kg 2:33
you a lasting **d** just as I built 1Kg 11:38
but to the **d** I am fighting. 2Ch 35:21

DYSENTERY *(1)*
bed suffering from fever and **d**. Ac 28:8

E

EACH *(615)*
(See pp. xi-xii.)

EAGER *(10)*
They are like a lion **e** to tear, Ps 17:12
schemes, feet **e** to run to evil, Pr 6:18
Sheol below is **e** to greet your Is 14:9
are well-fed, **e** stallions, each Jr 5:8
I am **e** to preach the good news Rm 1:15
my brothers, be **e** to prophesy, 1Co 14:39
e expectation and hope is that Php 1:20
I am very **e** to send him so that Php 2:28
special people, **e** to do good Ti 2:14
although I was **e** to write you Jd 3

EAGERLY *(11)*
You will **e** seek me, but I will Jb 7:21
You are my God; I **e** seek You. I Ps 63:1
the idolaters **e** seek all these Mt 6:32
Gentile world **e** seeks all these Lk 12:30
For the creation **e** waits with Rm 8:19
within ourselves, **e** waiting for Rm 8:23
we **e** wait for it with patience. Rm 8:25
spiritual gift as you **e** wait for 1Co 1:7
by the Spirit we **e** wait for the Gl 5:5
which we also **e** wait for a Php 3:20
not for the money but **e**; 1Pt 5:2

EAGERNESS *(5)*
the message with **e** and examined Ac 17:11
as there was **e** to desire it, 2Co 8:11
For if the **e** is there, it is 2Co 8:12
and to show our **e** ⌊to help⌋. 2Co 8:19
For I know your **e**, and I brag 2Co 9:2

EAGLE *(23)*
the **e**, the bearded vulture, the Lv 11:13
the **e**, the bearded vulture, the Dt 14:12
to swoop down on you like an **e**, Dt 28:49
nest like an **e** and hovers over Dt 32:11
like an **e** swooping down on ⌊its⌋ Jb 9:26
Does the **e** soar at your command Jb 39:27
youth is renewed like the **e**. Ps 103:5
and flies like an **e** to the sky. Pr 23:5
the way of an **e** in the sky, Pr 30:19
down like an **e** and spread his Jr 48:40
elevate your nest like the **e**, Jr 49:16
be like an **e** soaring upward, Jr 49:22
the left, and the face of an **e**. Ezk 1:10
and the fourth that of an **e**. Ezk 10:14
A great **e** with great wings, Ezk 17:3
another great **e** with great wings Ezk 17:7
One like an **e** comes against the Hs 8:1
to soar like an **e** and make your Ob 4
make yourselves as bald as an **e**, Mc 1:16
They fly like an **e**, swooping to Hab 1:8
creature was like a flying **e**. Rv 4:7
and I heard an **e**, flying in Rv 8:13
given two wings of a great **e**, Rv 12:14

EAGLE'S *(1)*
was like a lion but had **e** wings. Dn 7:4

EAGLES *(4)*
swifter than **e**, stronger than 2Sm 1:23
they will soar on wings like **e**; Is 40:31
His horses are swifter than **e**. Jr 4:13
were swifter than **e** in the sky; Lm 4:19

EAGLES' *(2)*
I carried you on **e** wings and Ex 19:4
hair grew like **e** ⌊feathers⌋ and Dn 4:33

EAR *(40)*
must pierce his **e** with an awl, Ex 21:6
of the right **e** of the one to be Lv 14:14
of the right **e** of the one to be Lv 14:17
through his **e** into the door, Dt 15:17
ornaments and **e** pendants, Jdg 8:26
let Your **e** be attentive to the Neh 1:11
Doesn't the **e** test words as the Jb 12:11
Doesn't the **e** test words as the Jb 34:3
I turn my **e** to a proverb; Ps 49:4
One who shaped the **e** not hear, Ps 94:9
He has turned His **e** to me, Ps 116:2
An **e** that listens to life-giving Pr 15:31
and the **e** of the wise seeks it. Pr 18:15
The hearing **e** and the seeing eye Pr 20:12
to a receptive **e** is like a gold Pr 25:12
turns his **e** away from hearing Pr 28:9
by seeing or the **e** filled with Ec 1:8
He awakens My **e** to listen like Is 50:4
The Lord GOD has opened My **e**, Is 50:5
and His **e** is not too deaf to Is 59:1
Look, their **e** is uncircumcised, Jr 6:10
a piece of an **e** from the lion's Am 3:12
slave and cut off his **e**. Mt 26:51
slave, and cut off his **e**. Mk 14:47
whispered in an **e** in private Lk 12:3
slave and cut off his right **e**. Lk 22:50
touching his **e**, He healed him. Lk 22:51
slave, and cut off his right **e**. Jn 18:10
of the man whose **e** Peter had cut Jn 18:26
eye has seen and no **e** has heard, 1Co 2:9
if the **e** should say, "Because 1Co 12:16
whole were an **e**, where would be 1Co 12:17
who has an **e** should listen to Rv 2:7
who has an **e** should listen to Rv 2:11
who has an **e** should listen to Rv 2:17
who has an **e** should listen to Rv 2:29
who has an **e** should listen to Rv 3:6
who has an **e** should listen to Rv 3:13
who has an **e** should listen to Rv 3:22
If anyone has an **e**, he should Rv 13:9

EARLIER *(13)*
ask about the **e** days that Dt 4:32
LORD's servant had commanded **e**, Jos 8:33
At an **e** period in Israel, a man Ru 4:7
who had gone **e** into the camp to 1Sm 14:21
E, when David was in Edom, 1Kg 11:15
In **e** times Phinehas son of 1Ch 9:20
of Job's life more than the **e**. Jb 42:12
one that had appeared to me **e**. Dn 8:1

the **e** prophets proclaimed to Zch 1:4
through the **e** prophets when Zch 7:7
Spirit through the **e** prophets. Zch 7:12
where John had been baptizing **e**, Jn 10:40
Remember the **e** days when, after Heb 10:32

EARLOBE *(4)*
and put it on Aaron's right **e**, Ex 29:20
and put ⌊it⌋ on Aaron's right **e**, Lv 8:23
on the right **e** of the one to be Lv 14:25
on the right **e** of the one to be Lv 14:28

EARLOBES *(2)*
his sons' right **e**, on the thumbs Ex 29:20
of the blood on their right **e**, Lv 8:24

EARLY *(71)*
you can get up **e** and go on your Gn 19:2
E in the morning Abraham went to Gn 19:27
E in the morning Abimelech got Gn 20:8
E in the morning Abraham got up, Gn 21:14
So **e** in the morning Abraham got Gn 22:3
In the **e** evening, Isaac went out Gn 24:63
They got up **e** in the morning and Gn 26:31
E in the morning Jacob took the Gn 28:18
Laban got up **e** in the morning, Gn 31:55
Get up **e** in the morning and Ex 8:20
Get up **e** in the morning and Ex 9:13
He rose **e** the next morning and Ex 24:4
E the next morning they arose, Ex 32:6
He got up **e** in the morning, Ex 34:4
They got up **e** the next morning Nm 14:40
in season, the **e** and late rains, Dt 11:14
started **e** the next morning Jos 3:1
got up **e** the next morning. Jos 6:12
E on the seventh day, they Jos 6:15
got up **e** the next morning. Jos 7:16
started **e** the next morning Jos 8:10
and went out **e** in the morning, Jos 8:14
When he got up **e** in the morning, Jdg 6:38
got up **e** and camped beside the Jdg 7:1
Then get up **e** and at sunrise, Jdg 9:33
they got up **e** in the morning and Jdg 19:5
got up **e** in the morning of the Jdg 19:8
you can get up **e** tomorrow for Jdg 19:9
E that morning, the woman made Jdg 19:26
next day the people got up **e**, Jdg 21:4
remained from **e** morning until Ru 2:7
and Hannah got up **e** to bow and 1Sm 1:19
Ashdod got up **e** the next morning 1Sm 5:3
they got up **e** the next morning 1Sm 5:4
They got up **e**, and just before 1Sm 9:26
E in the morning Samuel got up 1Sm 15:12
David got up **e** in the morning, 1Sm 17:20
So get up **e** in the morning, 1Sm 29:10
When you've all gotten up **e**, 1Sm 29:10
his men got up **e** in the morning 1Sm 29:11
He would get up **e** and stand 2Sm 15:2
they got up **e** in the morning, 2Kg 3:22
of God got up **e** and went out, 2Kg 6:15
they got up **e** and went out to 2Ch 20:20
Hezekiah got up **e**, gathered the 2Ch 29:20
rising **e** in the morning to offer Jb 1:5
vain you get up **e** and stay up Ps 127:2
a loud voice **e** in the morning, Pr 27:14
Let's go **e** to the vineyards; Sg 7:12
those who rise **e** in the morning Is 5:11
rain, both **e** and late, in its Jr 5:24
good figs, like **e** figs, but the Jr 24:2
and like the **e** dew that vanishes Hs 6:4
like the **e** dew that vanishes, Hs 13:3
to eat, no **e** fig, which I crave Mc 7:1
who went out **e** in the morning to Mt 20:1
E in the morning, as He was Mt 21:18
Very **e** in the morning, while it Mk 1:35
E in the morning, as they were Mk 11:20
the rooster or **e** in the morning. Mk 13:35
Very **e** in the morning, on the Mk 16:2
E on the first day of the week, Mk 16:9
would come **e** in the morning to Lk 21:38
the week, very **e** in the morning, Lk 24:1
They arrived **e** at the tomb, Lk 24:22
It was **e** morning. They did Jn 18:28
Magdalene came to the tomb **e**, Jn 20:1
aware that in the **e** days God Ac 15:7
a Cypriot and an **e** disciple, Ac 21:16
know that in the **e** days of the Php 4:15
it receives the **e** and the late Jms 5:7

EARN *(4)*
or anything that can **e** interest. Dt 23:19
Israel worked to **e** a wife; Hs 12:12
E your living and give ⌊your⌋ Am 7:12
the gospel should **e** their living 1Co 9:14

EARNED *(6)*
eating food **e** by hard work; Ps 127:2
them to work, and **e** five more. Mt 25:16
way the man with two **e** two more. Mt 25:17
I've **e** five more talents.' Mt 25:20
Look, I've **e** two more talents.' Mt 25:22
your mina has **e** 10 more minas.' Lk 19:16

EARNER *(2)*
The wage **e** ⌊puts his⌋ wages into Hg 1:6
and cheat the wage **e**; Mal 3:5

EARNERS *(1)*
all her wage **e** will be Is 19:10

EARNESTLY *(10)*
his God and **e** humbled himself 2Ch 33:12
if you **e** seek God and ask the Jb 8:5
everyone must call out **e** to God. Jnh 3:8
with Him **e**, saying, "He is Lk 7:4
was being made **e** to God for him Ac 12:5
attain as they **e** serve Him night Ac 26:7
we pray **e** night and day to see 1Th 3:10
he prayed **e** that it would not Jms 5:17
love one another **e** from a pure 1Pt 1:22
you wait for and **e** desire the 2Pt 3:12

EARNINGS *(4)*
prostitute's **e** into the house Dt 23:18
and your **e** will end up in a Pr 5:10
plants a vineyard with her **e**. Pr 31:16
In all my **e**, no one can find any Hs 12:8

EARNS *(2)*
The wicked man **e** an empty wage, Pr 11:18
but whoever **e** it through labor Pr 13:11

EARRING *(3)*
give me an **e** from his plunder." Jdg 8:24
threw an **e** from his plunder Jdg 8:25
him a qesitah , and a gold **e**. Jb 42:11

EARRINGS *(6)*
their foreign gods and their **e**, Gn 35:4
brooches, **e**, rings, necklaces Ex 35:22
rings, **e**, and necklaces— Nm 31:50
enemy had gold **e** because they Jdg 8:24
of the gold **e** he requested was Jdg 8:26
in your nose, **e** on your ears, Ezk 16:12

EARS *(71)*
that are on the **e** of your wives, Ex 32:2
were on their **e** and brought Ex 32:3
eyes to see, or **e** to hear. Dt 29:4
my cry for help ⌊reached⌋ His **e**. 2Sm 22:7
arrogance have reached My **e**, 2Kg 19:28
be open and Your **e** attentive to 2Ch 6:40
now be open and My **e** attentive 2Ch 7:15
open and Your **e** be attentive to Neh 1:6
my **e** caught a whisper of it. Jb 4:12
my **e** have heard and understood Jb 13:1
my declaration ⌊ring⌋ in your **e**. Jb 13:17
Dreadful sounds fill his **e**; Jb 15:21
heard news of it with our **e**." Jb 28:22
He uncovers their **e** at that time Jb 33:16
He opens their **e** to correction Jb 36:10
and my cry to Him reached His **e**. Ps 18:6
and His **e** are open to their cry Ps 34:15
You open my **e** to listen. Ps 40:6
we have heard with our **e**— Ps 44:1
deaf cobra that stops up its **e**, Ps 58:4
my **e** hear evildoers when they Ps 92:11
They have **e**, but cannot hear, Ps 115:6
Your **e** be attentive to my cry Ps 130:2
They have **e**, but cannot hear; Ps 135:17
one who shuts his **e** to the cry Pr 21:13
one who grabs a dog by the **e**. Pr 26:17
deafen their **e** and blind their Is 6:10
eyes and hear with their **e**, Is 6:10
by what He hears with His **e**, Is 11:3
your **e** will hear this command Is 30:21
and the **e** of those who hear will Is 32:3
who stops his **e** from listening Is 33:15
and the **e** of the deaf unstopped. Is 35:5
your arrogance has reached My **e**, Is 37:29
Though ⌊his⌋ **e** are open, he does Is 42:20
eyes, and are deaf, yet have **e**. Is 43:8
a long time your **e** have not been Is 48:8
have **e**, but they don't hear. Jr 5:21
you have heard with your own **e**." Jr 26:11
cry out in My **e** with a loud Ezk 8:18
and **e** to hear but do not hear, Ezk 12:2
on your **e**, and a beautiful Ezk 16:12
will cut off your nose and **e**, Ezk 23:25
listen with your **e**, and pay Ezk 40:4
with your **e** to everything I Ezk 44:5
and their **e** will become deaf. Mc 7:16
closed their **e** so they could not Zch 7:11
Anyone who has **e** should listen! Mt 11:15
Anyone who has **e** should listen!" Mt 13:9
their **e** are hard of hearing, Mt 13:15
eyes and hear with their **e**, Mt 13:15
and your **e** because they do hear! Mt 13:16
Anyone who has **e** should listen! Mt 13:43
this reaches the governor's **e**, Mt 28:14
Anyone who has **e** to hear should Mk 4:9
If anyone has **e** to hear, he Mk 4:23
If anyone has **e** to hear, he Mk 7:16
in the man's **e** and spitting, Mk 7:33
Immediately his **e** were opened, Mk 7:35
and do you have **e**, and not hear? Mk 8:18
of your greeting reached my **e**, Lk 1:44
Anyone who has **e** to hear should Lk 8:8
Anyone who has **e** to hear should Lk 14:35
with uncircumcised hearts and **e**! Ac 7:51
stopped their **e**, and rushed Ac 7:57
them reached the **e** of the church Ac 11:22
their **e** are hard of hearing, Ac 28:27
eyes and hear with their **e**, Ac 28:27
cannot see and **e** that cannot Rm 11:8
has reached the **e** of the Lord of Jms 5:4
and His **e** are open to their 1Pt 3:12

EARSHOT *(2)*
in Hebrew within **e** of the people 2Kg 18:26
in Hebrew within **e** of the people Is 36:11

EARTH *(767)*
created the heavens and the **e**. Gn 1:1
the **e** was formless and empty, Gn 1:2
God called the dry land "**e**," Gn 1:10
Let the **e** produce vegetation: Gn 1:11
trees on the **e** bearing fruit Gn 1:11
The **e** brought forth vegetation: Gn 1:12
sky to provide light on the **e**." Gn 1:15
sky to provide light on the **e**, Gn 1:17
fly above the **e** across the Gn 1:20
the birds multiply on the **e**." Gn 1:22
Let the **e** produce living Gn 1:24
wildlife of the **e** according to Gn 1:24
wildlife of the **e** according to Gn 1:25
animals, all the **e**, and the Gn 1:26
creatures that crawl on the **e**." Gn 1:26
fill the **e**, and subdue it. Gn 1:28
creature that crawls on the **e**." Gn 1:28
on the surface of the entire **e**, Gn 1:29
for all the wildlife of the **e**, Gn 1:30
creature that crawls on the **e**— Gn 1:30
heavens and the **e** and everything Gn 2:1
of the heavens and the **e**, Gn 2:4
God made the **e** and the heavens. Gn 2:4
a restless wanderer on the **e**." Gn 4:12
a restless wanderer on the **e**, Gn 4:14
multiply on the **e** and daughters Gn 6:1
were on the **e** both in those days Gn 6:4
on the **e** and that every Gn 6:5
that He had made man on the **e**, Gn 6:6
will wipe off the face of the **e**: Gn 6:7
Now the **e** was corrupt in God's Gn 6:11
and the **e** was filled with Gn 6:11
God saw how corrupt the **e** was, Gn 6:12
had corrupted its way on the **e**. Gn 6:12
the **e** is filled with violence Gn 6:13
destroy them along with the **e**. Gn 6:13
on the **e** to destroy all Gn 6:17
Everything on **e** will die. Gn 6:17
on the face of the whole **e**. Gn 7:3
it rain on the **e** 40 days and 40 Gn 7:4
the face of the **e** every living Gn 7:4
came ⌊and⌋ water covered the **e**. Gn 7:6
of the deluge came on the **e**. Gn 7:10
rain fell on the **e** 40 days and Gn 7:12
crawls on the **e** according to its Gn 7:14
continued 40 days on the **e**; Gn 7:17
ark so that it rose above the **e**. Gn 7:17
and increased greatly on the **e**, Gn 7:18
surged even higher on the **e**, Gn 7:19
creatures that crawl on the **e**, Gn 7:21
creatures that swarm on the **e**, Gn 7:21
and they were wiped off the **e**. Gn 7:23
waters surged on the **e** 150 days. Gn 7:24

a wind to pass over the e, Gn 8:1
steadily receded from the e, Gn 8:3
waters had dried up from the e. Gn 8:7
the surface of the whole e. Gn 8:9
had covered⌋ the e was dried up. Gn 8:13
the second month, the e was dry. Gn 8:14
over the e and be fruitful Gn 8:17
fruitful and multiply on the e." Gn 8:17
that crawls on the e came out of Gn 8:19
As long as the e endures, Gn 8:22
and multiply and fill the e. Gn 9:1
every living creature on the e, Gn 9:2
out over the e and multiply on Gn 9:7
wildlife of the e that are with Gn 9:10
animals of the e that came out Gn 9:10
be a deluge to destroy the e." Gn 9:11
covenant between Me and the e. Gn 9:13
clouds over the e and the bow Gn 9:14
creature of all flesh on e." Gn 9:16
between Me and all flesh on e." Gn 9:17
them the whole e was populated. Gn 9:19
was the first powerful man on e. Gn 10:8
his days the e was divided; Gn 10:25
The nations on e spread out from Gn 10:32
time the whole e had the same Gn 11:1
over the face of the whole e." Gn 11:4
over the face of the whole e, Gn 11:8
the language of the whole e, Gn 11:9
over the face of the whole e. Gn 11:9
the peoples on e will be blessed Gn 12:3
like the dust of the e, Gn 13:16
could count the dust of the e, Gn 13:16
High, Creator of heaven and e, Gn 14:19
High, Creator of heaven and e, Gn 14:22
nations of the e will be blessed Gn 18:18
of all the e do what is just? Gn 18:25
nations of the e will be blessed Gn 22:18
God of heaven and God of e, Gn 24:3
nations of the e will be blessed Gn 26:4
will be like the dust of the e, Gn 28:14
the peoples on e will be blessed Gn 28:14
was severe all over the e. Gn 41:57
and strike the dust of the e, Ex 8:16
he struck the dust of the e, Ex 8:17
the dust of the e became gnats Ex 8:17
is no one like Me in all the e. Ex 9:14
been obliterated from the e. Ex 9:15
make My name known in all the e. Ex 9:16
struck the e, and the LORD Ex 9:23
may know the e is the LORD's. Ex 9:29
hand, and the e swallowed them. Ex 15:12
although all the e is Mine, Ex 19:5
above or on the e below or in Ex 20:4
or in the waters under the e. Ex 20:4
LORD made the heavens and the e, Ex 20:11
LORD made the heavens and the e, Ex 31:17
them off the face of the e'? Ex 32:12
people on the face of the e." Ex 33:16
done in all the e or in any Ex 34:10
swarm on the e are detestable; Lv 11:41
creatures that swarm on the e, Lv 11:42
any man on the face of the e. Nm 12:3
as the whole e is filled with Nm 14:21
The e opened its mouth and Nm 16:32
The e closed over them, and they Nm 16:33
"The e may swallow us too!" Nm 16:34
The e opened its mouth and Nm 26:10
heaven or on e who can perform Dt 3:24
live on the e and may instruct Dt 4:10
the form of any beast on the e, Dt 4:17
fish in the waters under the e. Dt 4:18
I call heaven and e as witnesses Dt 4:26
man on the e and from one end Dt 4:32
showed you His great fire on e, Dt 4:36
in heaven above and on e below; Dt 4:39
above or on the e below or in Dt 5:8
or in the waters under the e. Dt 5:8
wipe you off the face of the e. Dt 6:15
peoples on the face of the e. Dt 7:6
as does the e and everything in Dt 10:14
camp⌋ the e opened its mouth Dt 11:6
as the heavens are above the e, Dt 11:21
all the days you live on the e. Dt 12:1
one end of the e to the other— Dt 13:7
peoples on the face of the e. Dt 14:2
above all the nations of the e. Dt 28:1
peoples of the e will see that Dt 28:10
and the e beneath you iron. Dt 28:23

to all the kingdoms of the e. Dt 28:25
the ends of the e, to swoop down Dt 28:49
one end of the e to the other, Dt 28:64
exiles are at the ends of the e, Dt 30:4
I call heaven and e as witnesses Dt 30:19
call heaven and e as witnesses Dt 31:28
listen, e, to the words of my Dt 32:1
with them to the ends of the e. Dt 33:17
in heaven above and on e below. Jos 2:11
Lord of all the e goes ahead of Jos 3:11
Lord of all the e, come to rest Jos 3:13
people of the e may know that Jos 4:24
wipe out our name from the e. Jos 7:9
now going the way of all the e, Jos 23:14
fields of Edom, the e trembled, Jdg 5:4
where nothing on e is lacking." Jdg 18:10
of the e are the LORD's; 1Sm 2:8
will judge the ends of the e. 1Sm 2:10
The e shook, and terror from God 1Sm 14:15
sky and the creatures of the e. 1Sm 17:46
enemies from the face of the e." 1Sm 20:15
son lives on e you and your 1Sm 20:31
form coming up out of the e," 1Sm 28:13
hands and wipe you off the e?" 2Sm 4:11
to one nation on e in order to 2Sm 7:23
name or posterity on e." 2Sm 14:7
God, knowing everything on e." 2Sm 14:20
Then the e shook and quaked; 2Sm 22:8
them like dust of the e; 2Sm 22:43
great joy that the e split open 1Kg 1:40
going the way of all of the e. 1Kg 2:2
by every king on e who had heard 1Kg 4:34
in heaven above or on e below, 1Kg 8:23
But will God indeed live on e? 1Kg 8:27
When there is famine on the e, 1Kg 8:37
the people on e will know Your 1Kg 8:43
from all the people on e, 1Kg 8:53
peoples of the e may know that 1Kg 8:60
from the face of the e. 1Kg 13:34
of all the kingdoms of the e. 2Kg 19:15
You made the heavens and the e. 2Kg 19:15
kingdoms of the e may know that 2Kg 19:19
to become a great warrior on e. 1Ch 1:10
because the e was divided during 1Ch 1:19
judgments ⌊govern⌋ the whole e. 1Ch 16:14
Sing to the LORD, all the e. 1Ch 16:23
tremble before Him, all the e. 1Ch 16:30
be glad and the e rejoice, 1Ch 16:31
for He is coming to judge the e. 1Ch 16:33
to one nation on e to redeem a 1Ch 17:21
standing between e and heaven, 1Ch 21:16
heavens and on e belongs to You. 1Ch 29:11
Our days on e are like a shadow, 1Ch 29:15
numerous as the dust of the e. 2Ch 1:9
who made the heavens and the e, 2Ch 2:12
God like You in heaven or on e, 2Ch 6:14
God indeed live on e with man? 2Ch 6:18
When there is famine on the e, 2Ch 6:28
peoples of the e will know Your 2Ch 6:33
throughout the e to show Himself 2Ch 16:9
kingdoms of the e and has 2Ch 36:23
kingdoms of the e and has Ezr 1:2
God of heaven and e and are Ezr 5:11
banished to the ends of the e, Neh 1:9
the e and all that is on it, Neh 9:6
"From roaming through the e," Jb 1:7
No one else on e is like him, Jb 1:8
"From roaming through the e," Jb 2:2
No one else on e is like him, Jb 2:3
kings and counselors of the e, Jb 3:14
rain to the e and sends water Jb 5:10
not fear the animals of the e. Jb 5:22
like the grass of the e. Jb 5:25
consigned to forced labor on e? Jb 7:1
Our days on e are but a shadow. Jb 8:9
shakes the e from its place so Jb 9:6
The e is handed over to the Jb 9:24
longer than the e and wider than Jb 11:9
Or speak to the e, and it will Jb 12:8
E, do not cover my blood; Jb 16:18
should the e be abandoned on Jb 18:4
of him perishes from the e; Jb 18:17
the time⌋ man was placed on e, Jb 20:4
and the e will rise up against Jb 20:27
He hangs the e on nothing. Jb 26:7
may come from the e, but below Jb 28:5
the surface the e is transformed Jb 28:5
to the ends of the e and sees Jb 28:24

gave Him authority over the e? Jb 34:13
animals of the e and makes us Jb 35:11
lightning to the ends of the e. Jb 37:3
snow, "Fall to the e," and the Jb 37:6
you when I established the e? Jb 38:4
the edges of the e and shake the Jb 38:13
The e is changed as clay is by a Jb 38:14
the extent of the e? Jb 38:18
wind that spreads across the e? Jb 38:24
you impose its authority on e? Jb 38:33
has no equal on e—a creature Jb 41:33
kings of the e take their stand Ps 2:2
ends of the e Your possession Ps 2:8
you judges of the e. Ps 2:10
is Your name throughout the e! Ps 8:1
is Your name throughout the e! Ps 8:9
that men of the e may terrify Ps 10:18
Then the e shook and quaked; Ps 18:7
has gone out to all the e, Ps 19:4
from the e and their offspring Ps 21:10
the ends of the e will remember Ps 22:27
prosper on e will eat and bow Ps 22:29
The e and everything in it, Ps 24:1
the e is full of the LORD's Ps 33:5
Let the whole e tremble before Ps 33:8
of the e from His dwelling Ps 33:14
all memory of them from the e. Ps 34:16
though the e trembles and the Ps 46:2
the e melts when He lifts His Ps 46:6
who brings devastation on the e. Ps 46:8
wars cease throughout the e. Ps 46:9
the nations, exalted on the e." Ps 46:10
a great King over all the e. Ps 47:2
for God is King of all the e. Ps 47:7
leaders of the e belong to God; Ps 47:9
is the joy of the whole e. Ps 48:2
reaches to the ends of the e; Ps 48:10
He summons the e from east to Ps 50:1
heaven and e in order to judge Ps 50:4
Your glory be above the whole e. Ps 57:5
Your glory be over the whole e. Ps 57:11
There is a God who judges on e!" Ps 58:11
the ends of the e that God rules Ps 59:13
the ends of the e when my heart Ps 61:2
go into the depths of the e. Ps 63:9
the ends of the e and of the Ps 65:5
You visit the e and water it Ps 65:9
You prepare the e in this way, Ps 65:9
joyfully to God, all the e! Ps 66:1
All the e will worship You and Ps 66:4
that Your way may be known on e, Ps 67:2
and lead the nations on e. Ps 67:4
The e has produced its harvest; Ps 67:6
the ends of the e will fear Him. Ps 67:7
the e trembled, and the skies Ps 68:8
to God, you kingdoms of the e; Ps 68:32
Let heaven and e praise Him, Ps 69:34
even from the depths of the e. Ps 71:20
spring showers that water the e. Ps 72:6
Euphrates to the ends of the e. Ps 72:8
the whole e is filled with His Ps 72:19
tongues strut across the e. Ps 73:9
I desire nothing on e but You. Ps 73:25
performing saving acts on the e. Ps 74:12
set all the boundaries of the e; Ps 74:17
When the e and all its Ps 75:3
the wicked of the e will drink, Ps 75:8
The e feared and grew quiet Ps 76:8
to save all the lowly of the e. Ps 76:9
is feared by the kings of the e. Ps 76:12
The e shook and quaked. Ps 77:18
like the e that He established Ps 78:69
ones to the beasts of the e. Ps 79:2
foundations of the e are shaken. Ps 82:5
up, God, judge the e, for all Ps 82:8
the Most High over all the e. Ps 83:18
Truth will spring up from the e, Ps 85:11
are Yours; the e also is Yours. Ps 89:11
greatest of the kings of the e. Ps 89:27
birth to the e and the world, Ps 90:2
Rise up, Judge of the e; Ps 94:2
depths of the e are in His hand Ps 95:4
sing to the LORD, all the e. Ps 96:1
tremble before Him, all the e. Ps 96:9
be glad and the e rejoice; Ps 96:11
for He is coming to judge the e. Ps 96:13
reigns! Let the e rejoice; let Ps 97:1
the e sees and trembles. Ps 97:4

of the Lord of all the **e**. Ps 97:5
the Most High over all the **e**; Ps 97:9
the ends of the **e** have seen our Ps 98:3
Shout to the LORD, all the **e**; Ps 98:4
for He is coming to judge the **e**. Ps 98:9
the cherubim. Let the **e** quake. Ps 99:1
to the LORD, all the **e**. Ps 100:1
the kings of the **e** Your glory, Ps 102:15
gazed out from heaven to **e**— Ps 102:19
Long ago You established the **e**, Ps 102:25
as the heavens are above the **e**, Ps 103:11
established the **e** on its Ps 104:5
will never cover the **e** again. Ps 104:9
the **e** is satisfied by the fruit Ps 104:13
producing food from the **e**, Ps 104:14
the **e** is full of Your creatures. Ps 104:24
and You renew the face of the **e**. Ps 104:30
He looks at the **e**, and it Ps 104:32
vanish from the **e** and the wicked Ps 104:35
judgments ⌊govern⌋ the whole **e**. Ps 105:7
The **e** opened up and swallowed Ps 106:17
Your glory be over the whole **e**. Ps 108:5
all⌋ memory of them from the **e**. Ps 109:15
look on the heavens and the **e**? Ps 113:6
Tremble, **e**, at the presence of Ps 114:7
the Maker of heaven and **e**. Ps 115:15
but the **e** He has given to the Ps 115:16
am a stranger on **e**; do not hide Ps 119:19
the **e** is filled with Your Ps 119:64
They almost ended my life on **e**, Ps 119:87
established the **e**, and it stands Ps 119:90
the wicked on **e** as if they were Ps 119:119
the Maker of heaven and **e**. Ps 121:2
the Maker of heaven and **e**. Ps 124:8
Maker of heaven and **e**, bless you Ps 134:3
He pleases in heaven and on **e**, Ps 135:6
to rise from the ends of the **e**. Ps 135:7
All the kings on **e** will give You Ps 138:4
formed in the depths of the **e**. Ps 139:15
the Maker of heaven and **e**, Ps 146:6
rain for the **e**, and causes grass Ps 147:8
His command throughout the **e**; Ps 147:15
Praise the LORD from the **e**, Ps 148:7
kings of the **e** and all peoples, Ps 148:11
princes and all judges of the **e**, Ps 148:11
His majesty covers heaven and **e**. Ps 148:13
The LORD founded the **e** by wisdom Pr 3:19
beginning, before the **e** began. Pr 8:23
fields, or the first soil on **e**. Pr 8:26
out the foundations of the **e**. Pr 8:29
wicked will not remain on the **e**. Pr 10:30
righteous will be repaid on **e**, Pr 11:31
eyes roam to the ends of the **e**. Pr 17:24
is high and the **e** is deep, Pr 25:3
all the ends of the **e**? Pr 30:4
e, which is never satisfied with Pr 30:16
The **e** trembles under three Pr 30:21
Four things on **e** are small, Pr 30:24
but the **e** remains forever. Ec 1:4
animals goes downward to the **e**? Ec 3:21
is in heaven and you are on **e**, Ec 5:2
man on the **e** who does good Ec 7:20
futility that is done on the **e**: Ec 8:14
activity that is done on the **e** Ec 8:16
what disaster may happen on **e**. Ec 11:2
will pour out rain on the **e**; Ec 11:3
returns to the **e** as it once was, Ec 12:7
pay attention, **e**, for the LORD Is 1:2
when He rises to terrify the **e**. Is 2:19
when He rises to terrify the **e**. Is 2:21
for them from the ends of the **e**. Is 5:26
His glory fills the whole **e**. Is 6:3
look toward the **e** and see only Is 8:22
eggs, I gathered the whole **e**. Is 10:14
from the four corners of the **e**. Is 11:12
this be known throughout the **e**. Is 12:5
make the **e** a desolation and to Is 13:9
and the **e** will shake from its Is 13:13
All the **e** is calm and at rest; Is 14:7
you—all the rulers of the **e**. Is 14:9
man who caused the **e** to tremble, Is 14:16
surface of the **e** with cities. Is 14:21
plan prepared for the whole **e**, Is 14:26
world and you who live on the **e**, Is 18:3
are the honored ones of the **e**? Is 23:8
all the honored ones of the **e**. Is 23:9
the world on the face of the **e**. Is 23:17
stripping the **e** bare and making Is 24:1
e will be stripped completely Is 24:3
The **e** mourns and withers; Is 24:4
people of the **e** waste away. Is 24:4
The **e** is polluted by its Is 24:5
a curse has consumed the **e**, Is 24:6
it will be on **e** among the Is 24:13
the ends of the **e** we hear songs: Is 24:16
await⌋ you who dwell on the **e**. Is 24:17
foundations of the **e** are shaken. Is 24:18
The **e** is completely devastated; Is 24:19
devastated; the **e** is split open; Is 24:19
the **e** is violently shaken. Is 24:19
The **e** staggers like a drunkard Is 24:20
above and kings of the **e** below. Is 24:21
disgrace from the whole **e**, Is 25:8
We have won no victories on **e**, Is 26:18
and the **e** will bring forth the Is 26:19
of the **e** for their iniquity Is 26:21
The **e** will reveal the blood shed Is 26:21
I will besiege you with **e** ramps, Is 29:3
Let the **e** hear, and all that Is 34:1
of all the kingdoms of the **e**. Is 37:16
You made the heavens and the **e**. Is 37:16
kingdoms of the **e** may know that Is 37:20
the dust of the **e** in a measure Is 40:12
the foundations of the **e**? Is 40:21
above the circle of the **e**; Is 40:22
judges of the **e** to be irrational Is 40:23
the Creator of the whole **e**. Is 40:28
the ends of the **e** tremble. Is 41:5
the ends of the **e** and called you Is 41:9
He has established justice on **e**. Is 42:4
spread out the **e** and what comes Is 42:5
praise from the ends of the **e**, Is 42:10
from the ends of the **e**— Is 43:6
shout, depths of the **e**. Is 44:23
who alone spread out the **e**; Is 44:24
Let the **e** open up that salvation Is 45:8
I made the **e**, and created man on Is 45:12
He formed the **e** and made it; Is 45:18
be saved, all the ends of the **e**. Is 45:22
My own hand founded the **e**, Is 48:13
it go out to the end of the **e**; Is 48:20
salvation to the ends of the **e**." Is 49:6
joy, you heavens! **E**, rejoice! Is 49:13
and look at the **e** beneath; Is 51:6
the **e** will wear out like a Is 51:6
laid the foundations of the **e**. Is 51:13
to found the **e**, and to say to Is 51:16
all the ends of the **e** will see Is 52:10
is called the God of all the **e**. Is 54:5
would never flood the **e** again, Is 54:9
For as heaven is higher than **e**, Is 55:9
there without saturating the **e**, Is 55:10
covers the **e**, and total darkness Is 60:2
For as the **e** brings forth its Is 61:11
Jerusalem the praise of the **e**. Is 62:7
proclaimed to the end of the **e**, Is 62:11
create a new heaven and a new **e**; Is 65:17
My throne, and **e** is My footstool Is 66:1
the new heavens and the new **e**, Is 66:22
I looked at the **e**, and it was Jr 4:23
of this, the **e** will mourn; Jr 4:28
Listen, **e**! I am about to bring Jr 6:19
the remote regions of the **e**. Jr 6:22
and righteousness on the **e**, Jr 9:24
The **e** quakes at His wrath, Jr 10:10
heavens and the **e** will perish Jr 10:11
perish from the **e** and from under Jr 10:11
He made the **e** by His power, Jr 10:12
to rise from the ends of the **e**. Jr 10:13
one end of the **e** to the other. Jr 12:12
kingdoms of the **e** because of Jr 15:4
manure on the face of the **e**. Jr 16:4
to You from the ends of the **e**, Jr 16:19
E, earth, earth, hear the word Jr 22:29
Earth, **e**, earth, hear the word Jr 22:29
Earth, earth, **e**, hear the word Jr 22:29
not fill the heavens and the **e**?" Jr 23:24
to all the kingdoms of the **e**, Jr 24:9
which are on the face of the **e**. Jr 25:26
all the inhabitants of the **e**"— Jr 25:29
all the inhabitants of the **e**. Jr 25:30
the ends of the **e** because the Jr 25:31
up from the ends of the **e**." Jr 25:32
one end of the **e** to the other. Jr 25:33
for all the nations of the **e**." Jr 26:6
I made the **e**, and the people Jr 27:5
animals on the face of the **e**. Jr 27:5
send you off the face of the **e**. Jr 28:16
to all the kingdoms of the **e**— Jr 29:18
from remote regions of the **e**— Jr 31:8
of the **e** below explored, Jr 31:37
the heavens and **e** by Your great Jr 32:17
LORD who made the **e**, the LORD Jr 33:2
before all the nations of the **e**, Jr 33:9
the fixed order of heaven and **e**, Jr 33:25
among all the nations of **e**. Jr 44:8
will go up, I will cover the **e**; Jr 46:8
and your outcry fills the **e**, Jr 46:12
of their fall the **e** will quake; Jr 49:21
hammer of the whole **e** is cut Jr 50:23
rest to the **e** but turmoil to Jr 50:34
the remote regions of the **e**. Jr 50:41
conquest the **e** will quake; Jr 50:46
hand making the whole **e** drunk. Jr 51:7
He made the **e** by His power, Jr 51:15
to rise from the ends of the **e**. Jr 51:16
you devastate the whole **e**. Jr 51:25
The **e** quakes and trembles, Jr 51:29
praise of the whole **e** seized. Jr 51:41
Heaven and **e** and everything in Jr 51:48
slain of all the **e** fell because Jr 51:49
Israel's glory from heaven to **e**. Lm 2:1
beauty, the joy of the whole **e**? Lm 2:15
The kings of the **e** and all the Lm 4:12
the creatures rose from the **e**, Ezk 1:19
the creatures rose from the **e**, Ezk 1:21
to the wicked of the **e** as spoil, Ezk 7:21
me up between **e** and heaven Ezk 8:3
their wings to rise from the **e**, Ezk 10:16
from the **e** right before my Ezk 10:19
the kings of the **e** with your Ezk 27:33
So I threw you down to the **e**; Ezk 28:17
beasts of the **e** and the birds Ezk 29:5
peoples of the **e** left its shade Ezk 31:12
of the entire **e** eat their fill Ezk 32:4
over the whole face of the **e**, Ezk 34:6
the face of the **e** will tremble Ezk 38:20
and the **e** shone with His glory. Ezk 43:2
No one on **e** can make known what Dn 2:10
mountain and filled the whole **e**. Dn 2:35
which will rule the whole **e**. Dn 2:39
language, who live in all the **e**: Dn 4:1
a tree in the middle of the **e**, Dn 4:10
visible to the ends of the **e**. Dn 4:11
plants of the **e** with the animals Dn 4:15
and was visible to all the **e**, Dn 4:20
extends⌋ to the ends of the **e**. Dn 4:22
of the **e** are counted as Dn 4:35
and the inhabitants of the **e**. Dn 4:35
language who live in all the **e**: Dn 6:25
in the heavens and on the **e**, Dn 6:27
kings who will rise from the **e**. Dn 7:17
be a fourth kingdom on the **e**, Dn 7:23
It will devour the whole **e**, Dn 7:23
of the entire **e** without touching Dn 8:5
some of the host fall to the **e**, Dn 8:10
in the dust of the **e** will awake, Dn 12:2
and it will respond to the **e**. Hs 2:21
The **e** will respond to the grain, Hs 2:22
The **e** quakes before them; Jl 2:10
in the heavens and on the **e**: Jl 2:30
heaven and **e** will shake. Jl 3:16
out of all the clans of the **e**; Am 3:2
strides on the heights of the **e**. Am 4:13
out over the face of the **e**— Am 5:8
GOD of Hosts—He touches the **e**; Am 9:5
of His vault on the **e**. Am 9:6
them out on the face of the **e**. Am 9:6
it from the face of the **e**. Am 9:8
e with its prison bars closed Jnh 2:6
pay attention, **e** and everyone in Mc 1:2
to trample the heights of the **e**. Mc 1:3
wealth to the Lord of all the **e**. Mc 4:13
extend to the ends of the **e**. Mc 5:4
enduring foundations of the **e**, Mc 6:2
Then the **e** will become a Mc 7:13
the **e** trembles at His presence— Nah 1:5
cut off your prey from the **e**, Nah 2:13
the **e** will be filled with the Hab 2:14
let everyone on **e** be silent in Hab 2:20
and the **e** is full of His praise. Hab 3:3
He stands and shakes the **e**; Hab 3:6
You split the **e** with rivers. Hab 3:9
across the **e** with indignation Hab 3:12

from the face of the **e**— Zph 1:2
mankind from the face of the **e**— Zph 1:3
The whole **e** will be consumed by Zph 1:18
of all the inhabitants of the **e**. Zph 1:18
humble of the **e**, who carry out Zph 2:3
starves all the gods of the **e**. Zph 2:11
for the whole **e** will be consumed Zph 3:8
throughout the **e** receive praise Zph 3:19
among all the peoples of the **e**, Zph 3:20
to shake the heavens and the **e**, Hg 2:6
to shake the heavens and the **e**. Hg 2:21
LORD has sent to patrol the **e**." Zch 1:10
patrolled the **e**, and right now Zch 1:11
the whole **e** is calm and quiet. Zch 1:11
scan throughout the whole **e**, Zch 4:10
by the Lord of the whole **e**." Zch 4:14
up the basket between **e** and sky. Zch 5:9
to the Lord of the whole **e**. Zch 6:5
they wanted to go patrol the **e**, Zch 6:7
LORD said, "Go, patrol the **e**." Zch 6:7
So they patrolled the **e**. Zch 6:7
River to the ends of the **e**. Zch 9:10
laid the foundation of the **e**, Zch 12:1
nations of the **e** gather against Zch 12:3
become king over all the **e**— Zch 14:9
families of the **e** not go up to Zch 14:17
because they will inherit the **e**. Mt 5:5
You are the salt of the **e**. Mt 5:13
Until heaven and **e** pass away, Mt 5:18
or by the **e**, because it is His Mt 5:35
will be done on **e** as it is in Mt 6:10
for yourselves treasures on **e**, Mt 6:19
authority on **e** to forgive sins Mt 9:6
I came to bring peace on the **e**. Mt 10:34
of heaven and **e**, because You Mt 11:25
in the heart of the **e** three days Mt 12:40
the ends of the **e** to hear the Mt 12:42
you bind on **e** is already bound Mt 16:19
you loose on **e** is already loosed Mt 16:19
you bind on **e** is already bound Mt 18:18
you loose on **e** is already loosed Mt 18:18
two of you on **e** agree about any Mt 18:19
call anyone on **e** your father, Mt 23:9
shed on the **e** will be charged Mt 23:35
the peoples of the **e** will mourn; Mt 24:30
Heaven and **e** will pass away, Mt 24:35
the **e** quaked and the rocks were Mt 27:51
given to Me in heaven and on **e**. Mt 28:18
authority on **e** to forgive sins, Mk 2:10
no launderer on **e** could whiten Mk 9:3
from the end of the **e** to the end Mk 13:27
Heaven and **e** will pass away, Mk 13:31
and peace on **e** to people He Lk 2:14
authority on **e** to forgive sins Lk 5:24
of heaven and **e**, because You Lk 10:21
the ends of the **e** to hear the Lk 11:31
I came to bring fire on the **e**, Lk 12:49
here to give peace to the **e**? Lk 12:51
appearance of the **e** and the sky, Lk 12:56
for heaven and **e** to pass away Lk 16:17
will He find that faith on **e**?" Lk 18:8
anguish on the **e** among nations Lk 21:25
Heaven and **e** will pass away, Lk 21:33
live on the face of the whole **e**. Lk 21:35
that happen on **e** and you don't Jn 3:12
one who is from the **e** is earthly Jn 3:31
up from the **e** I will draw all Jn 12:32
You on the **e** by completing Jn 17:4
and to the ends of the **e**." Ac 1:8
above and signs on the **e** below: Ac 2:19
of the **e** will be blessed Ac 3:25
the heaven, the **e**, and the sea, Ac 4:24
kings of the **e** took their stand Ac 4:26
My throne, and **e** My footstool. Ac 7:49
His life is taken from the **e**. Ac 8:33
lowered to the **e** by its four Ac 10:11
animals and reptiles of the **e**, Ac 10:12
four-footed animals of the **e**, Ac 11:6
salvation to the ends of the **e**." Ac 13:47
made the heaven, the **e**, the sea, Ac 14:15
of heaven and **e** and does not Ac 17:24
live all over the **e** and has Ac 17:26
Wipe this person off the **e**— Ac 22:22
may be proclaimed in all the **e**. Rm 9:17
and decisively on the **e**. Rm 9:28
voice has gone out to all the **e**, Rm 10:18
whether in heaven or on **e**— 1Co 8:5
e is the Lord's, and all that 1Co 10:26
was from the **e** and made of dust 1Co 15:47
heaven and things on **e** in Him. Eph 1:10
in heaven and on **e** is named. Eph 3:15
to the lower parts of the **e**? Eph 4:9
in heaven and on **e** and under the Php 2:10
and on earth and under the **e**— Php 2:10
in heaven and on **e**, the visible Col 1:16
whether things on **e** or things in Col 1:20
above, not on what is on the **e**. Col 3:2
established the **e**, and the Heb 1:10
if He were on **e**, He wouldn't be Heb 8:4
temporary residents on the **e**. Heb 11:13
Him who warned them on **e**, Heb 12:25
voice shook the **e** at that time, Heb 12:26
not only the **e** but also heaven. Heb 12:26
fruit of the **e** and is patient Jms 5:7
by heaven or by **e** or with any Jms 5:12
heavens and the **e** existed out 2Pt 3:5
heavens and **e** are held in store 2Pt 3:7
and the **e** and the works on it 2Pt 3:10
for new heavens and a new **e**, 2Pt 3:13
the ruler of the kings of the **e**. Rv 1:5
families of the **e** will mourn Rv 1:7
to test those who live on the **e**. Rv 3:10
in heaven or on **e** or under the Rv 5:3
or under the **e** was able to open Rv 5:3
of God sent into all the **e**. Rv 5:6
and they will reign on the **e**. Rv 5:10
heaven, on **e**, under the earth, Rv 5:13
earth, under the **e**, on the sea, Rv 5:13
to take peace from the **e**, Rv 6:4
to them over a fourth of the **e**, Rv 6:8
by the wild animals of the **e**. Rv 6:8
from those who live on the **e**?" Rv 6:10
fell to the **e** as a fig tree Rv 6:13
the kings of the **e**, the nobles, Rv 6:15
at the four corners of the **e**, Rv 7:1
winds of the **e** so that no wind Rv 7:1
could blow on the **e** or on the Rv 7:1
to harm the **e** and the sea: Rv 7:2
Don't harm the **e** or the sea or Rv 7:3
altar, and hurled it to the **e**; Rv 8:5
blood, were hurled to the **e**. Rv 8:7
a third of the **e** was burned up, Rv 8:7
Woe to those who live on the **e**, Rv 8:13
had fallen from heaven to **e**. Rv 9:1
the smoke locusts came to the **e**, Rv 9:3
that scorpions have on the **e**. Rv 9:3
not to harm the grass of the **e**, Rv 9:4
is in it, the **e** and what is in Rv 10:6
stand before the Lord of the **e**. Rv 11:4
to strike the **e** with any plague Rv 11:6
live on the **e** will gloat over Rv 11:10
those who live on the **e**. Rv 11:10
destroy those who destroy the **e**. Rv 11:18
heaven and hurled them to the **e**. Rv 12:4
was thrown to **e**, and his angels Rv 12:9
to the **e** and the sea, for the Rv 12:12
that he had been thrown to **e**, Rv 12:13
But the **e** helped the woman: Rv 12:16
the **e** opened its mouth and Rv 12:16
The whole **e** was amazed and Rv 13:3
who live on the **e** will worship Rv 13:8
beast coming up out of the **e**; Rv 13:11
and compels the **e** and those who Rv 13:12
from heaven to **e** before people. Rv 13:13
who live on the **e** because of the Rv 13:14
who live on the **e** to make an Rv 13:14
had been redeemed from the **e**. Rv 14:3
to the inhabitants of the **e**— Rv 14:6
the Maker of heaven and **e**, Rv 14:7
the harvest of the **e** is ripe." Rv 14:15
swung His sickle over the **e**, Rv 14:16
earth, and the **e** was harvested. Rv 14:16
his sickle toward **e** and gathered Rv 14:19
bowls of God's wrath on the **e**." Rv 16:1
poured out his bowl on the **e**, Rv 16:2
since man has been on the **e**— Rv 16:18
kings of the **e** committed sexual Rv 17:2
who live on the **e** became drunk Rv 17:2
OF THE VILE THINGS OF THE **E** Rv 17:5
who live on the **e** whose names Rv 17:8
empire over the kings of the **e**." Rv 17:18
and the **e** was illuminated by his Rv 18:1
kings of the **e** have committed Rv 18:3
merchants of the **e** have grown Rv 18:3
The kings of the **e** who have Rv 18:9
merchants of the **e** will also Rv 18:11
were the nobility of the **e**, Rv 18:23
and all those slaughtered on **e**, Rv 18:24
corrupted the **e** with her sexual Rv 19:2
the kings of the **e**, and their Rv 19:19
at the four corners of the **e**, Rv 20:8
surface of the **e** and surrounded Rv 20:9
E and heaven fled from His Rv 20:11
I saw a new heaven and a new **e**, Rv 21:1
and the first **e** had passed away, Rv 21:1
kings of the **e** will bring their Rv 21:24

EARTH'S *(12)*

water on the **e** surface had gone Gn 8:8
water on the **e** surface had gone Gn 8:11
the **e** inhabitants have been Is 24:6
e rejoicing goes into exile. Is 24:11
E rebellion weighs it down, Is 24:20
and the **e** inhabitants have not Is 26:18
a horror to all the **e** kingdoms. Jr 34:17
lay broken in all the **e** ravines. Ezk 31:12
the blood of the **e** princes: Ezk 39:18
across the **e** open spaces to Hab 1:6
of grapes from **e** vineyard, Rv 14:18
the grapes from **e** vineyard, Rv 14:19

EARTHEN *(4)*

You must make an **e** altar for Me Ex 20:24
silver refined in an **e** furnace, Ps 12:6
are like glaze on an **e** vessel. Pr 26:23
put them in an **e** storage jar so Jr 32:14

EARTHENWARE *(1)*

but also those of wood and **e**, 2Tm 2:20

EARTHLY *(12)*

of⌋ my song during my **e** life. Ps 119:54
all the **e** kingdoms under his Jr 34:1
Who do **e** kings collect tariffs Mt 17:25
from the earth is **e** and speaks Jn 3:31
earthly and speaks in **e** terms. Jn 3:31
heavenly bodies and **e** bodies, 1Co 15:40
from that of the **e** ones. 1Co 15:40
For we know that if our **e** house, 2Co 5:1
They are focused on **e** things, Php 3:19
During His **e** life, He offered Heb 5:7
for ministry and an **e** sanctuary. Heb 9:1
above, but is **e**, sensual, Jms 3:15

EARTHQUAKE *(16)*

After the wind there was an **e**, 1Kg 19:11
but the LORD was not in the **e**. 1Kg 19:11
After the **e** there was a fire, 1Kg 19:12
with thunder, **e**, and loud noise, Is 29:6
will be a great **e** in the land of Ezk 38:19
Israel, two years before the **e**. Am 1:1
you fled from the **e** in the days Zch 14:5
the **e** and the things that had Mt 27:54
Suddenly there was a violent **e**, Mt 28:2
was such a violent **e** that the Ac 16:26
A violent **e** occurred; Rv 6:12
rumblings, lightnings, and an **e**. Rv 8:5
moment a violent **e** took place, Rv 11:13
people were killed in the **e**. Rv 11:13
thunders, an **e**, and severe hail. Rv 11:19
And a severe **e** occurred like no Rv 16:18

EARTHQUAKES *(3)*

be famines and **e** in various Mt 24:7
There will be **e** in various Mk 13:8
will be violent **e**, and famines Lk 21:11

EASE *(13)*

captives are completely at **e**; Jb 3:18
my couch will **e** my complaint, Jb 7:13
one who is at **e** holds calamity Jb 12:5
I was at **e**, but He shattered me; Jb 16:12
completely secure and at **e**. Jb 21:23
are always at **e**, and they Ps 73:12
do the treacherous live at **e**? Jr 12:1
go up against a nation at **e**, Jr 49:31
enemies are at **e**, for the LORD Lm 1:5
was at **e** in my house and Dn 4:4
those who are at **e** in Zion and Am 6:1
head to **e** his discomfort. Jnh 4:6
with the nations that are at **e**, Zch 1:15

EASES *(1)*

I was like one who **e** the yoke Hs 11:4

EASIER *(7)*

For which is **e**: to say, 'Your Mt 9:5
is **e** for a camel to go through Mt 19:24
Which is **e**: to say to the Mk 2:9
is **e** for a camel to go through Mk 10:25
Which is **e**: to say, 'Your sins Lk 5:23

But it is e for heaven and earth Lk 16:17
For it is e for a camel to go Lk 18:25

EASILY *(10)*

people could e have slept with Gn 26:10
and e overtook them near Gibeah Jdg 20:43
comes⌋ e to the perceptive Pr 14:6
but a fool is e angered and is Pr 14:16
three strands is not e broken. Ec 4:12
on tablets so one may e read it. Hab 2:2
me to become a Christian so e?" Ac 26:28
that whether e or with Ac 26:29
not to be e upset in mind or 2Th 2:2
the sin that so e ensnares us, Heb 12:1

EAST *(179)*

in Eden, in the e, and there He Gn 2:8
which flows to the e of Assyria. Gn 2:14
and e of the garden of Eden He Gn 3:24
in the land of Nod, e of Eden. Gn 4:16
As people migrated from the e, Gn 11:2
to the hill country e of Bethel Gn 12:8
on the west and Ai on the e. Gn 12:8
north and south, e and west, Gn 13:14
son Isaac, to the land of the E. Gn 25:6
the west, the e, the north, Gn 28:14
thin and scorched by the e wind, Gn 41:6
and scorched by the e wind— Gn 41:23
the LORD sent an e wind over the Ex 10:13
morning the e wind had brought Ex 10:13
with a powerful e wind all that Ex 14:21
courtyard on the e side toward Ex 27:13
hangings⌋ on the e toward the Ex 38:13
throw it on the e side of the Lv 1:16
against the e side of the mercy Lv 16:14
will camp on the e side toward Nm 2:3
of the tabernacle on the e, Nm 3:38
pitched on the e are to set out. Nm 10:5
that borders Moab on the e. Nm 21:11
be across the Jordan to the e." Nm 32:19
border on the e will begin at Nm 34:3
begin at the e end of the Dead Nm 34:3
from Shepham to Riblah e of Ain. Nm 34:11
outside the city for the e side, Nm 35:5
the slopes of Pisgah on the e. Dt 3:17
north, south, and e, and see Dt 3:27
across the Jordan to the e, Dt 4:41
were across the Jordan to the e, Dt 4:47
the Arabah on the e side of the Dt 4:49
you on the e side of the Jordan. Jos 1:15
is near Beth-aven, e of Bethel, Jos 7:2
Canaanites in the e and west, Jos 11:3
to the e as far as the valley Jos 11:8
the Jordan to the e and from the Jos 12:1
the Arabah e of the Sea of Jos 12:3
from the Shihor e of Egypt to Jos 13:3
and all Lebanon e from Baal-gad Jos 13:5
them beyond the Jordan to the e, Jos 13:8
Chinnereth on the e side of the Jos 13:27
beyond the Jordan e of Jericho. Jos 13:32
the waters of Jericho on the e, Jos 16:1
on the e of Upper Beth-horon Jos 16:5
and passed it e of Janoah. Jos 16:6
the north and Issachar on the e. Jos 17:10
beyond the Jordan to the e, Jos 18:7
formed the border on the e side. Jos 18:20
and met the brook e of Jokneam. Jos 19:11
it turned e toward the sunrise Jos 19:12
it went e toward the sunrise to Jos 19:13
Judah at the Jordan on the e. Jos 19:34
Across the Jordan e of Jericho, Jos 20:8
caravan route, e of Nobah and Jdg 8:11
came to the e side of the land Jdg 11:18
them near Gibeah toward the e. Jdg 20:43
e of the highway that goes up Jdg 21:19
at Michmash, e of Beth-aven. 1Sm 13:5
of all the people of the E, 1Kg 4:30
south, and three facing e. 1Kg 7:25
said, "Open the e window." 2Kg 13:17
rooftops, blasted by the e wind. 2Kg 19:26
to the e side of the valley to 1Ch 4:39
settled in the e as far as the 1Ch 5:9
the region e of Gilead. 1Ch 5:10
Jericho, to the e of the Jordan, 1Ch 6:78
Naaran to the e, Gezer and its 1Ch 7:28
the King's Gate on the e side. 1Ch 9:18
e, west, north, and south. 1Ch 9:24
to the e and to the west. 1Ch 12:15
The lot for the e⌊gate⌋ fell to 1Ch 26:14
six Levites each day on the e, 1Ch 26:17
south, and three facing e. 2Ch 4:4
were standing e of the altar, 2Ch 5:12
keeper of the E Gate, was over 2Ch 31:14
Gate toward the e and the tower Neh 3:26
guard of the E Gate, made Neh 3:29
to the Water Gate on the e. Neh 12:37
among all the people of the e. Jb 1:3
himself with the hot e wind? Jb 15:2
those in the e tremble in horror Jb 18:20
If I go e, He is not there, and Jb 23:8
e wind picks him up, and he is Jb 27:21
source of⌋ the e wind that Jb 38:24
of Tarshish with the e wind. Ps 48:7
the earth from e to west. Ps 50:1
You make e and west shout for Ps 65:8
does not come from the e, Ps 75:6
He made the e wind blow in the Ps 78:26
far as the e is from the west, Ps 103:12
lands—from the e and the west, Ps 107:3
divination⌋ from the E and of Is 2:6
to the land e of the Jordan, Is 9:1
Aram from the e and Philistia Is 9:12
plunder the people of the e. Is 11:14
in the e honor the LORD! Is 24:15
storm on the day of the e wind. Is 27:8
rooftops, blasted by the e wind. Is 37:27
has stirred him up from the e? Is 41:2
one from the e who invokes My Is 41:25
your descendants from the e, Is 43:5
call a bird of prey from the e, Is 46:11
west, and His glory in the e; Is 59:19
the enemy like the e wind. Jr 18:17
of the Horse Gate to the e— Jr 31:40
and destroy the people of the e! Jr 49:28
their faces ⌊turned⌋ to the e. Ezk 8:16
were bowing to the e in worship Ezk 8:16
which faces e, and at the gate's Ezk 11:1
on the mountain e of the city. Ezk 11:23
when the e wind strikes it Ezk 17:10
and the e wind dried up its Ezk 19:12
people of the e as a possession Ezk 25:4
people of the e as a possession Ezk 25:10
but the e wind has shattered you Ezk 27:26
of the Travelers e of the Sea. Ezk 39:11
gate that faced e and climbed Ezk 40:6
on each side of the e gate, Ezk 40:10
This⌋ was the e; next the north Ezk 40:19
those of the gate that faced e. Ezk 40:22
gate, like the one on the e. Ezk 40:23
the inner court on the e side. Ezk 40:32
yard to the e was 175 feet. Ezk 41:14
entryway on the e side as one Ezk 42:9
as one enters on the e side, Ezk 42:12
gate that faced e and measured Ezk 42:15
He measured the e side with a Ezk 42:16
the gate, the one that faces e, Ezk 43:1
God of Israel coming from the e. Ezk 43:2
by way of the gate that faced e. Ezk 43:4
The altar's steps face e." Ezk 43:17
outer gate that faced e, Ezk 44:1
side and to the e on the east Ezk 45:7
and to the east on the e side. Ezk 45:7
that faces e must be closed Ezk 46:1
gate that faces e must be opened Ezk 46:12
of the temple toward the e, Ezk 47:1
east, for the temple faced e. Ezk 47:1
to the outer gate that faced e; Ezk 47:2
man went out e with a measuring Ezk 47:3
the e side it will run between Ezk 47:18
from the e side to the west, Ezk 48:2
from the e side to the west, Ezk 48:3
from the e side to the west, Ezk 48:4
from the e side to the west, Ezk 48:5
from the e side to the west, Ezk 48:6
from the e side to the west, Ezk 48:7
from the e side to the west, Ezk 48:8
from the e side to the west Ezk 48:8
a half ⌊miles⌋ on the e side; Ezk 48:16
feet⌋ to the e, and 425 ⌊feet⌋ Ezk 48:17
miles⌋ to the e and three and Ezk 48:18
From the e side to the west, Ezk 48:23
from the e side to the west, Ezk 48:24
from the e side to the west, Ezk 48:25
from the e side to the west, Ezk 48:26
from the e side to the west, Ezk 48:27
On the e side, which is one and Ezk 48:32
the south and the e and toward Dn 8:9
reports from the e and the north Dn 11:44
the wind and pursues the e wind. Hs 12:1
brothers, an e wind will come, Hs 13:15
to sea and roam from north to e, Am 8:12
the city and sat down e of it. Jnh 4:5
appointed a scorching e wind. Jnh 4:8
the land of the e and the land Zch 8:7
which faces Jerusalem on the e. Zch 14:4
be split in half from e to west, Zch 14:4
wise men from the e arrived Mt 2:1
His star in the e and have come Mt 2:2
the star they had seen in the e! Mt 2:9
many will come from e and west, Mt 8:11
comes from the e and flashes as Mt 24:27
They will come from e and west, Lk 13:29
angel rise up from the e, Rv 7:2
way for the kings from the e. Rv 16:12
There were three gates on the e, Rv 21:13

EASTERN *(21)*

to Sephar, the e hill country. Gn 10:30
and went to the e country. Gn 29:1
of Moab, from the e mountains: Nm 23:7
For your e border, draw a line Nm 34:10
and reach the e slope of the Sea Nm 34:11
at Gilgal on the e limits of Jos 4:19
Now the e border was along the Jos 15:5
and the e peoples came and Jdg 6:3
them in the e public square. 2Ch 29:4
If I live at the e horizon ⌊or⌋ Ps 139:9
the wise, a student of e kings." Is 19:11
entrance to the e gate of the Ezk 10:19
brought me to the e gate of the Ezk 11:1
boundary to the e boundary. Ezk 45:7
out to the e region and goes Ezk 47:8
northern⌋ border to the e sea. Ezk 47:18
This will be the e side. Ezk 47:18
from the e side to the sea, Ezk 48:1
miles⌋ wide on the e side, Ezk 48:10
as far as the e border and next Ezk 48:21
of it toward the e sea and the Zch 14:8

EASTWARD *(9)*

Then Lot journeyed e, and they Gn 13:11
was still alive he sent them e, Gn 25:6
Jericho, e toward the sunrise. Nm 34:15
including all the Arabah e: Jos 12:1
e through Beth-jeshimoth and Jos 12:3
it turned e from Taanath-shiloh Jos 16:6
It turned e to Beth-dagon, Jos 19:27
Leave here, turn e, and hide 1Kg 17:3
from the Jordan e, all the land 2Kg 10:33

EASY *(7)*

thought it would be e to go up Dt 1:41
so that they will become e prey. Dt 31:17
This is e in the LORD's sight. 2Kg 3:18
It's e for the shadow to 2Kg 20:10
They have an e time until they Ps 73:4
For My yoke is e and My burden Mt 11:30
years. Take it e; eat, drink, Lk 12:19

EAT *(534)*

You are free to e from any tree Gn 2:16
but you must not e from the tree Gn 2:17
for on the day you e from it, Gn 2:17
'You can't e from any tree in Gn 3:1
We may e the fruit from the Gn 3:2
'You must not e it or touch it, Gn 3:3
when you e it your eyes will Gn 3:5
Did you e from the tree that I Gn 3:11
I had commanded you not to e Gn 3:11
your belly and e dust all the Gn 3:14
you, 'Do not e from it': Gn 3:17
You will e from it by means of Gn 3:17
and you will e the plants of the Gn 3:18
You will e bread by the sweat of Gn 3:19
of life, and e, and live forever Gn 3:22
you must not e meat with its Gn 9:4
I will not e until I have said Gn 24:33
Let me e some of that red stuff, Gn 25:30
I love and bring it to me to e, Gn 27:4
food for me to e so that I can Gn 27:7
your father to e so that he may Gn 27:10
sit up and e some of my game Gn 27:19
and let me e some of my son's Gn 27:25
get up and e some of his son's Gn 27:31
with food to e and clothing to Gn 28:20
his relatives to e a meal. Gn 31:54
don't e the thigh muscle Gn 32:32
Then they sat down to e a meal. Gn 37:25
the birds will e the flesh from Gn 40:19

they will **e** with me at noon.”	Gn 43:16
were going to **e** a meal there,	Gn 43:25
could not **e** with Hebrews,	Gn 43:32
and you can **e** from the richness	Gn 45:18
Invite him to **e** dinner.”	Ex 2:20
They will **e** the remainder left	Ex 10:5
they will **e** every tree you have	Ex 10:5
up over it and **e** every plant	Ex 10:12
to what each person will **e**.	Ex 12:4
the houses in which they **e** them.	Ex 12:7
They are to **e** the meat that	Ex 12:8
they should **e** it, roasted over	Ex 12:8
Do not **e** any of it raw or cooked	Ex 12:9
Here is how you must **e** it:	Ex 12:11
You are to **e** it in a hurry;	Ex 12:11
You must **e** unleavened bread for	Ex 12:15
what people need to **e**—	Ex 12:16
You are to **e** unleavened bread in	Ex 12:18
Do not **e** anything leavened;	Ex 12:20
e unleavened bread in all your	Ex 12:20
Passover: no foreigner may **e** it.	Ex 12:43
a man has purchased may **e** it,	Ex 12:44
hand may not **e** the Passover.	Ex 12:45
uncircumcised person may **e** it.	Ex 12:48
you must **e** unleavened bread,	Ex 13:6
give you meat to **e** this evening	Ex 16:8
At twilight you will **e** meat,	Ex 16:12
you will **e** bread until you	Ex 16:12
the LORD has given you to **e**.	Ex 16:15
of it as each person needs to **e**.	Ex 16:16
as much as he needed to **e**.	Ex 16:18
as much as he needed to **e**,	Ex 16:21
“**E** it today,” Moses said,	Ex 16:25
Israel to **e** a meal with Moses’	Ex 18:12
You must not **e** the meat of a	Ex 22:31
among your people may **e** ⌊from	Ex 23:11
are to **e** unleavened bread for	Ex 23:15
sons are to **e** the meat of the	Ex 29:32
must **e** those things by which	Ex 29:33
person must not **e** ⌊them⌋,	Ex 29:33
people sat down to **e** and drink,	Ex 32:6
and you will **e** of their	Ex 34:15
are to **e** unleavened bread for	Ex 34:18
he did not **e** bread or drink	Ex 34:28
must not **e** any fat or any blood.	Lv 3:17
his sons may **e** the rest of it.	Lv 6:16
are to **e** it in the courtyard	Lv 6:16
Aaron’s descendants may **e** it.	Lv 6:18
it as a sin offering is to **e** it.	Lv 6:26
male among the priests may **e** it;	Lv 6:29
male among the priests may **e** it.	Lv 7:6
is clean may **e** any ⌊other⌋ meat	Lv 7:19
You are not to **e** any fat of an	Lv 7:23
purpose, but you must not **e** it.	Lv 7:24
you must not **e** the blood of any	Lv 7:26
of meeting and **e** it there with	Lv 8:31
Aaron and his sons are to **e** it.	Lv 8:31
and **e** it prepared without yeast	Lv 10:12
You must **e** it in a holy place	Lv 10:13
your daughters may **e** the breast	Lv 10:14
Why didn’t you **e** the sin	Lv 10:17
You may **e** all these ⌊kinds⌋ of	Lv 11:2
may **e** any animal with divided	Lv 11:3
hooves you are not to **e** ⌊these⌋:	Lv 11:4
Do not **e** any of their meat or	Lv 11:8
what⌋ you may **e** from all that is	Lv 11:9
may **e** everything in the water	Lv 11:9
must not **e** any of their meat,	Lv 11:11
But you may **e** these kinds of all	Lv 11:21
You may **e** these: the various	Lv 11:22
Do not **e** any of the creatures	Lv 11:42
who lives among you may **e** blood.	Lv 17:12
You must not **e** the blood of any	Lv 17:14
fifth year you may **e** its fruit.	Lv 19:25
You are not to **e** ⌊anything⌋ with	Lv 19:26
may **e** the food of his God from	Lv 21:22
discharge is to **e** from the holy	Lv 22:4
and is not to **e** from the holy	Lv 22:6
and then he may **e** from the holy	Lv 22:7
must not **e** an animal that died	Lv 22:8
is to **e** the holy offering.	Lv 22:10
hand is not to **e** the holy	Lv 22:10
that person may **e** it, and those	Lv 22:11
in his house may **e** his food.	Lv 22:11
she is not to **e** from the holy	Lv 22:12
if the people **e** their holy	Lv 22:16
you must **e** unleavened bread.	Lv 23:6
You must not **e** bread, roasted	Lv 23:14
who are to **e** it in a holy place,	Lv 24:9
you may ⌊only⌋ **e** its produce	Lv 25:12
so that you can **e**, be satisfied,	Lv 25:19
‘What will we **e** in the seventh	Lv 25:20
of food to **e** and live securely	Lv 26:5
You will **e** the old grain of the	Lv 26:10
because your enemies will **e** it.	Lv 26:16
so that you will **e** but not be	Lv 26:26
You will **e** the flesh of your	Lv 26:29
you will **e** the flesh of your	Lv 26:29
grape juice or **e** fresh grapes	Nm 6:3
He is not to **e** anything produced	Nm 6:4
They are to **e** the animal with	Nm 9:11
to me: ‘Give us meat to **e**!’	Nm 11:13
and you will **e** meat because you	Nm 11:18
give you meat and you will **e**.	Nm 11:18
You will **e**, not for one day, or	Nm 11:19
and they will **e** for a month.’	Nm 11:21
LORD when you **e** from the food	Nm 15:19
You are to **e** it as a most holy	Nm 18:10
Every male may **e** it; it is to be	Nm 18:10
person in your house may **e** it.	Nm 18:11
person in your house may **e** them.	Nm 18:13
household may **e** it anywhere.	Nm 18:31
so that you may **e**, and buy water	Dt 2:6
exchange for silver so we may **e**,	Dt 2:28
cannot see, hear, **e**, or smell.	Dt 4:28
when you **e** and are satisfied,	Dt 6:11
then He gave you manna to **e**,	Dt 8:3
where you will **e** food without	Dt 8:9
you **e** and are full, you will	Dt 8:10
When you **e** and are full, and	Dt 8:12
did not **e** bread or drink water.	Dt 9:9
I did not **e** bread or drink water	Dt 9:18
You will **e** and be satisfied.	Dt 11:15
You will **e** there in the presence	Dt 12:7
slaughter and **e** meat within any	Dt 12:15
are clean or unclean may **e** it,	Dt 12:15
but you must not **e** the blood;	Dt 12:16
Within your gates you may not **e**:	Dt 12:17
You must **e** them in the presence	Dt 12:18
‘I want to **e** meat’ because you	Dt 12:20
have a strong desire to **e** meat,	Dt 12:20
you may **e** it whenever you want.	Dt 12:20
and you may **e** it within your	Dt 12:21
you may **e** it as the gazelle and	Dt 12:22
clean and the unclean may **e** it.	Dt 12:22
But don’t **e** the blood, since the	Dt 12:23
and you must not **e** the life with	Dt 12:23
Do not **e** blood; pour it on the	Dt 12:24
not **e** it, so that you and your	Dt 12:25
God, but you may **e** the meat.	Dt 12:27
You must not **e** any detestable	Dt 14:3
These are the animals you may **e**:	Dt 14:4
You may **e** any animal that has	Dt 14:6
hooves, you are not to **e** these:	Dt 14:7
You must not **e** their meat or	Dt 14:8
You may **e** everything from the	Dt 14:9
but you may not **e** anything that	Dt 14:10
You may **e** every clean bird,	Dt 14:11
are the ones you may not **e**:	Dt 14:12
But you may **e** every clean flying	Dt 14:20
You are not to **e** any carcass;	Dt 14:21
and he may **e** it, or you may	Dt 14:21
You are to **e** a tenth of your	Dt 14:23
gates may come, **e**, and be	Dt 14:29
family are to **e** it before the	Dt 15:20
E it within your gates; both the	Dt 15:22
person and the clean ⌊may **e** it⌋,	Dt 15:22
But you must not **e** its blood;	Dt 15:23
You must not **e** leavened bread	Dt 16:3
days you are to **e** unleavened	Dt 16:3
are to cook and **e** ⌊it⌋ in the	Dt 16:7
You must **e** unleavened bread for	Dt 16:8
They will **e** the LORD’s fire	Dt 18:1
They will **e** equal portions	Dt 18:8
you may **e** as many grapes as you	Dt 23:24
so that they may **e** in your towns	Dt 26:12
offerings, **e**, and rejoice	Dt 27:7
but you will not **e** any of it.	Dt 28:31
don’t know will **e** your soil’s	Dt 28:33
because worms will **e** them.	Dt 28:39
will **e** the offspring of your	Dt 28:51
You will **e** your children,	Dt 28:53
that he will **e** because he has	Dt 28:55
will secretly **e** them for lack	Dt 28:57
did not **e** bread or drink wine	Dt 29:6
they will **e** their fill and	Dt 31:20
of the land and **e** the produce	Dt 32:13
left nothing for Israel to **e**,	Jdg 6:4
or to **e** anything unclean	Jdg 13:4
and do not **e** anything unclean,	Jdg 13:7
She must not **e** anything that	Jdg 13:14
she must not **e** anything unclean	Jdg 13:14
If I stay, I won’t **e** your food.	Jdg 13:16
the eater came something to **e**,	Jdg 14:14
something to **e** to keep up your	Jdg 19:5
Hannah wept and would not **e**.	1Sm 1:7
Why won’t you **e**? Why are you	1Sm 1:8
have a piece of bread to **e**.’ ”	1Sm 2:36
he goes to the high place to **e**.	1Sm 9:13
people won’t **e** until he comes	1Sm 9:13
after that, the guests can **e**.	1Sm 9:13
high place and **e** with me today.	1Sm 9:19
E it because it was saved for	1Sm 9:24
here and then you can **e**.	1Sm 14:34
won’t sit down to **e** until he	1Sm 16:11
to sit down and **e** with the king.	1Sm 20:5
the king sat down to **e** the meal.	1Sm 20:24
anger and did not **e** any food	1Sm 20:34
young men may **e** it only if they	1Sm 21:4
E and it will give you strength	1Sm 28:22
saying, “I won’t **e**,” but when	1Sm 28:23
him some bread to **e** and water to	1Sm 30:11
urge David to **e** bread while it	2Sm 3:35
will always **e** meals at my table.	2Sm 9:7
grandson will have food to **e**.	2Sm 9:10
is always to **e** at my table.”	2Sm 9:10
enter my house to **e** and drink	2Sm 11:11
invited Uriah to **e** and drink	2Sm 11:13
and would not **e** anything with	2Sm 12:17
and requested ⌊something to **e**⌋.	2Sm 12:20
and give me ⌊something⌋ to **e**.	2Sm 13:5
can watch and **e** from her hand.’	2Sm 13:5
so I can **e** from her hand.”	2Sm 13:6
of him, but he refused to **e**.	2Sm 13:9
“so I can **e** from your hand.”	2Sm 13:10
she brought ⌊them⌋ to him to **e**,	2Sm 13:11
are for the young men to **e**,	2Sm 16:2
and the people with him to **e**.	2Sm 17:29
among those who **e** at your table.	2Sm 19:28
among those who **e** at your table	1Kg 2:7
and I wouldn’t **e** bread or drink	1Kg 13:8
‘You must not **e** bread or drink	1Kg 13:9
Come home with me and **e** bread.	1Kg 13:15
back with you, **e** bread, or drink	1Kg 13:16
‘You must not **e** bread or drink	1Kg 13:17
so that he may **e** bread and drink	1Kg 13:18
Do not **e** bread and do not drink	1Kg 13:22
the dogs will **e**, and anyone who	1Kg 14:11
the birds of the sky will **e**,	1Kg 14:11
the dogs will **e**, and anyone who	1Kg 16:4
the birds of the sky will **e**.	1Kg 16:4
my son so we can **e** it and die.”	1Kg 17:12
of Asherah who **e** at Jezebel’s	1Kg 18:19
Ahab, “Go up, **e** and drink, for	1Kg 18:41
So Ahab went to **e** and drink,	1Kg 18:42
angel told him, “Get up and **e**.”	1Kg 19:5
Get up and **e**, or the journey	1Kg 19:7
away, and didn’t **e** any food.	1Kg 21:4
so upset that you refuse to **e**?”	1Kg 21:5
Get up, **e** some food, and be	1Kg 21:7
The dogs will **e** Jezebel in the	1Kg 21:23
the dogs will **e**, and he who dies	1Kg 21:24
the birds of the sky will **e**.’ ”	1Kg 21:24
persuaded him to **e** some food.	2Kg 4:8
by, he stopped there to **e**.	2Kg 4:8
served some for the men to **e**,	2Kg 4:40
And they were unable to **e** it.	2Kg 4:40
“Serve it for the people to **e**.”	2Kg 4:41
“Give it to the people to **e**.”	2Kg 4:42
“Give it to the people to **e**,”	2Kg 4:43
‘They will **e**, and they will have	2Kg 4:43
so they can **e** and drink and go	2Kg 6:22
son, and we will **e** him today.	2Kg 6:28
Then we will **e** my son tomorrow.’	2Kg 6:28
son, and we will **e** him,’ but	2Kg 6:29
but you won’t **e** any of it.”	2Kg 7:2
went into a tent to **e** and drink.	2Kg 7:8
but you won’t **e** any of it.”	2Kg 7:19
The dogs will **e** Jezebel in the	2Kg 9:10
the dogs will **e** Jezebel’s flesh.	2Kg 9:36
you to **e** their own excrement	2Kg 18:27
one of you may **e** from his own	2Kg 18:31
year you will **e** what grows on	2Kg 19:29
vineyards and **e** their fruit.	2Kg 19:29

we **e** and are satisfied and there 2Ch 31:10
them not to **e** the most holy Ezr 2:63
e the good things of the land, Ezr 9:12
did not **e** food or drink water, Ezr 10:6
so that we can **e** and live." Neh 5:2
them not to **e** the most holy Neh 7:65
to them, "Go and **e** what is rich, Neh 8:10
the people began to **e** and drink, Neh 8:12
Don't **e** or drink for three days, Est 4:16
three sisters to **e** and drink Jb 1:4
someone else **e** what I have sown Jb 31:8
the fatherless **e** any of it— Jb 31:17
had enough to **e** at Job's table? Jb 31:31
The humble will **e** and be Ps 22:26
on earth will **e** and bow down; Ps 22:29
Do I **e** the flesh of bulls or Ps 50:13
He rained manna for them to **e**; Ps 78:24
I even forget to **e** my food. Ps 102:4
I **e** ashes like bread and mingle Ps 102:9
will surely **e** what your hands Ps 128:2
they will **e** the fruit of their Pr 1:31
They **e** the bread of wickedness Pr 4:17
Come, **e** my bread, and drink the Pr 9:5
who love it will **e** its fruit. Pr 18:21
and you'll have enough to **e**. Pr 20:13
Don't **e** a stingy person's bread, Pr 23:6
"**E** and drink," he says to you, Pr 23:7
E honey, my son, for it is good, Pr 24:13
you find honey, **e** only what you Pr 25:16
give him food to **e**, and if he is Pr 25:21
is not good to **e** too much honey, Pr 25:27
a fig tree will **e** its fruit, Pr 27:18
it out and young vultures **e** it. Pr 30:17
better for man than to **e**, Ec 2:24
For who can **e** and who can enjoy Ec 2:25
it is appropriate to **e**, drink, Ec 5:18
man under the sun except to **e**, Ec 8:15
e your bread with pleasure, Ec 9:7
to his garden and **e** its choicest Sg 4:16
I **e** my honeycomb with my honey. Sg 5:1
with my milk. **E**, friends! Drink, Sg 5:1
will **e** the good things of the Is 1:19
for they will **e** the fruit of Is 3:10
We will **e** our own bread and Is 4:1
strangers will **e** ⌊among⌋ the Is 5:17
milk they give he will **e** butter, Is 7:22
the land will **e** butter and honey Is 7:22
the lion will **e** straw like an ox Is 11:7
out a carpet! **E** and drink! Rise Is 21:5
wine—"Let us **e** and drink, for Is 22:13
the ground will **e** salted fodder Is 30:24
with you to **e** their excrement Is 36:12
one of you will **e** from his own Is 36:16
year you will **e** what grows on Is 37:30
vineyards and **e** their fruit. Is 37:30
oppressors **e** their own flesh Is 49:26
the worm will **e** them like wool. Is 51:8
without money, come, buy, and **e**! Is 55:1
to Me, and **e** what is good, Is 55:2
seed to sow and food to **e**, Is 55:10
field and forest, come and **e**! Is 56:9
you will **e** the wealth of the Is 61:6
grain will **e** it and praise Is 62:9
servants will **e**, but you will be Is 65:13
vineyards and **e** their fruit. Is 65:21
will not plant and others **e**. Is 65:22
the lion will **e** straw like the Is 65:25
fertile land to **e** its fruit and Jr 2:7
and **e** the meat yourselves, Jr 7:21
to sit with them to **e** and drink. Jr 16:8
I will make them **e** the flesh of Jr 19:9
and they will **e** each other's Jr 19:9
father, did he not **e** and drink? Jr 22:15
gardens and **e** their produce. Jr 29:5
gardens and **e** their produce." Jr 29:28
Should women **e** their own Lm 2:20
who used to **e** delicacies are Lm 4:5
mouth and **e** what I am giving Ezk 2:8
Son of man, **e** what you find Ezk 3:1
E this scroll, then go and speak Ezk 3:1
e and fill your stomach with Ezk 3:3
are to **e** it during the number Ezk 4:9
The food you **e** each day will be Ezk 4:10
you will **e** it from time to time. Ezk 4:10
You will **e** it as ⌊you would⌋ a Ezk 4:12
Israelites will **e** their bread— Ezk 4:13
anxiously **e** bread ⌊rationed⌋ Ezk 4:16
fathers will **e** ⌊their⌋ sons Ezk 5:10
and sons will **e** their fathers. Ezk 5:10
e your bread with trembling and Ezk 12:18
They will **e** their bread with Ezk 12:19
The fathers **e** sour grapes, Ezk 18:2
He does not **e** at the mountain Ezk 18:6
He does not **e** at the mountain Ezk 18:15
live⌋ in you **e** at the mountain Ezk 22:9
your⌋ mustache or **e** the bread of Ezk 24:17
your⌋ mustache or **e** the bread of Ezk 24:22
They will **e** your fruit and drink Ezk 25:4
the entire earth **e** their fill of Ezk 32:4
You **e** ⌊meat⌋ with blood ⌊in it⌋, Ezk 33:25
e the fat, wear the wool, and Ezk 34:3
will **e** flesh and drink blood. Ezk 39:17
You will **e** the flesh of mighty Ezk 39:18
You will **e** fat until you are Ezk 39:19
My table you will **e** your fill of Ezk 39:20
the LORD will **e** the most holy Ezk 42:13
the gateway to **e** a meal before Ezk 44:3
They will **e** the grain offering, Ezk 44:29
priests may not **e** any bird or Ezk 44:31
vegetables to **e** and water to Dn 1:12
didn't **e** any rich food, no meat Dn 10:3
Those who **e** his provisions will Dn 11:26
the wild animals will **e** them. Hs 2:12
will **e** but not be satisfied; Hs 4:10
gifts and **e** the flesh, Hs 8:13
and they will **e** unclean food in Hs 9:3
all who **e** it become defiled. Hs 9:4
have plenty to **e** and be Jl 2:26
nothing to **e** in all your cities, Am 4:6
gardens and **e** their produce. Am 9:14
Those who **e** your bread will set Ob 7
They must not **e** or drink water. Jnh 3:7
You **e** the flesh of my people Mc 3:3
You will **e** but not be satisfied, Mc 6:14
⌊finds⌋ no grape cluster to **e**, Mc 7:1
You **e** but never have enough to Hg 1:6
When you **e** and drink, don't you Zch 7:6
don't you **e** and drink ⌊simply⌋ Zch 7:6
what you will **e** or what you will Mt 6:25
worry, saying, 'What will we **e**?' Mt 6:31
came as guests to **e** with Jesus Mt 9:10
does your Teacher **e** with tax Mt 9:11
began to pick and **e** some heads Mt 12:1
him or for those with him to **e**, Mt 12:4
"You give them something to **e**." Mt 14:16
wash their hands when they **e**!" Mt 15:2
even the dogs **e** the crumbs that Mt 15:27
days and have nothing to **e**. Mt 15:32
and you gave Me something to **e**; Mt 25:35
and you gave Me nothing to **e**; Mt 25:42
the Passover so You may **e** it?" Mt 26:17
and said, "Take and **e** it; Mt 26:26
Why does He **e** with tax Mk 2:16
for anyone to **e** except the Mk 2:26
they were not even able to **e**. Mk 3:20
should be given something to **e**. Mk 5:43
did not even have time to **e**. Mk 6:31
buy themselves something to **e**." Mk 6:36
"You give them something to **e**," Mk 6:37
and give them something to **e**?" Mk 6:37
not **e** unless they wash their Mk 7:3
they do not **e** unless they have Mk 7:4
under the table **e** the children's Mk 7:28
and they had nothing to **e**. Mk 8:1
days and have nothing to **e**. Mk 8:2
May no one ever **e** fruit from you Mk 11:14
the Passover so You may **e** it?" Mk 14:12
room for Me to **e** the Passover Mk 14:14
Why do you **e** and drink with tax Lk 5:30
same, but Yours **e** and drink." Lk 5:33
for any but the priests to **e**? Lk 6:4
invited Him to **e** with him. Lk 7:36
she be given something to **e**. Lk 8:55
"You give them something to **e**," Lk 9:13
e the things set before you. Lk 10:8
e, drink, and enjoy yourself." ' Lk 12:19
your life, what you will **e**; Lk 12:22
what you should **e** and what you Lk 12:29
to **e** and drink and get drunk, Lk 12:45
when He went to **e** at the house Lk 14:1
The one who will **e** bread in the Lk 14:15
He longed to **e** his fill from the Lk 15:16
'Come at once and sit down to **e**'? Lk 17:7
'Prepare something for me to **e**, Lk 17:8
serve me while I **e** and drink; Lk 17:8
later you can **e** and drink'? Lk 17:8
meal for us, so we can **e** it." Lk 22:8
room where I can **e** the Passover Lk 22:11
desired to **e** this Passover with Lk 22:15
will not **e** it again until it is Lk 22:16
that you may **e** and drink at My Lk 22:30
"Do you have anything here to **e**?" Lk 24:41
Him, "Rabbi, **e** something." Jn 4:31
I have food to **e** that you don't Jn 4:32
brought Him something to **e**?" Jn 4:33
bread so these people can **e**?" Jn 6:5
them bread from heaven to **e**." Jn 6:31
that anyone may **e** of it and not Jn 6:50
man give us His flesh to **e**?" Jn 6:52
Unless you **e** the flesh of the Jn 6:53
and unable to **e** the Passover. Jn 18:28
days, and did not **e** or drink. Ac 9:9
became hungry and wanted to **e**, Ac 10:10
"Get up, Peter; kill and **e**!" Ac 10:13
me, 'Get up, Peter; kill and **e**!' Ac 11:7
neither to **e** nor to drink until Ac 23:12
that we won't **e** anything until Ac 23:14
a curse not to **e** or drink until Ac 23:21
he had broken it, he began to **e**. Ac 27:35
believes he may **e** anything, Rm 14:2
look down on one who does not **e**; Rm 14:3
one who does not **e** must not Rm 14:3
whoever does not **e**, it is to the Rm 14:6
to the Lord that he does not **e**, Rm 14:6
brother is hurt by what you **e**, Rm 14:15
By what you **e**, do not destroy Rm 14:15
is a noble thing not to **e** meat, Rm 14:21
not even **e** with such a person. 1Co 5:11
that when they **e** food offered to 1Co 8:7
are not inferior if we don't **e**, 1Co 8:8
we are not better if we do **e**. 1Co 8:8
encouraged to **e** food offered to 1Co 8:10
I will never again **e** meat, 1Co 8:13
have the right to **e** and drink? 1Co 9:4
and does not **e** its fruit? 1Co 9:7
the temple services **e** the food 1Co 9:13
people sat down to **e** and drink, 1Co 10:7
not those who **e** the sacrifices 1Co 10:18
E everything that is sold in the 1Co 10:25
e everything that is set before 1Co 10:27
to an idol," do not **e** it, out of 1Co 10:28
whether you **e** or drink, or 1Co 10:31
is not really to **e** the Lord's 1Co 11:20
you have houses to **e** and drink 1Co 11:22
For as often as you **e** this bread 1Co 11:26
way he should **e** of the bread 1Co 11:28
when you come together to **e**, 1Co 11:33
he should **e** at home, so that 1Co 11:34
raised, Let us **e** and drink, for 1Co 15:32
For he used to **e** with the Gl 2:12
we did not **e** anyone's bread free 2Th 3:8
to work, he should not **e**." 2Th 3:10
they may **e** their own bread. 2Th 3:12
do not have a right to **e**. Heb 13:10
keep warm, and **e** well," but you Jms 2:16
you and will **e** your flesh like Jms 5:3
the right to **e** from the tree Rv 2:7
e meat sacrificed to idols and Rv 2:14
and to **e** meat sacrificed Rv 2:20
He said to me, "Take and **e** it; Rv 10:9
so that you may **e** the flesh of Rv 19:18

EATEN *(60)*

every kind of food that is **e**; Gn 6:21
except what the servants have **e**. Gn 14:24
and I have not **e** the rams from Gn 31:38
It is to be **e** in one house. Ex 12:46
Nothing leavened may be **e**. Ex 13:3
bread is to be **e** for those seven Ex 13:7
and its meat may not be **e**, Ex 21:28
It must not be **e** because it is Ex 29:34
is to be **e** as unleavened bread Lv 6:16
offering; it is not to be **e**." Lv 6:23
It must be **e** in a holy place, Lv 6:26
offering may be **e** if its blood Lv 6:30
It is to be **e** in a holy place; Lv 7:6
must be **e** on the day he Lv 7:15
it is to be **e** on the day he Lv 7:16
over may be **e** on the next day Lv 7:16
sacrifice is **e** on the third day, Lv 7:18
anything unclean must not be **e**; Lv 7:19
you should have **e** it in the Lv 10:18
if I had **e** the sin offering Lv 10:19
must not be **e** because they are Lv 11:13
detestable; they must not be **e**. Lv 11:41

that may be **e** and those that may Lv 11:47
and those that may not be **e**." Lv 11:47
bird that may be **e** must drain Lv 17:13
It is to be **e** on the day you Lv 19:6
If any is **e** on the third day, Lv 19:7
three years; it is not to be **e**. Lv 19:23
It is to be **e** on the same day. Lv 22:30
flesh is half **e** away when he Nm 12:12
bread is to be **e** for seven days. Nm 28:17
as the gazelle and deer are **e**; Dt 12:22
for you; they may not be **e**. Dt 14:19
I have not **e** any of it while in Dt 26:14
if the troops had **e** freely today 1Sm 14:30
for he hadn't **e** food or drunk 1Sm 30:12
Have we ever **e** anything of the 2Sm 19:42
after he had **e** bread and after 1Kg 13:23
The lion had not **e** the corpse or 1Kg 13:28
When they had **e** and drunk, 2Kg 6:23
yet they had **e** the Passover 2Ch 30:18
Is bland food **e** without salt? Jb 6:6
Parts of his skin are **e** away; Jb 18:13
if I have **e** my few crumbs alone Jb 31:17
hand us over to be **e** like sheep Ps 44:11
bread ⌊**e**⌋ secretly is tasty!" Pr 9:17
little you've **e** and waste your Pr 23:8
have **e** on the left, but they Is 9:20
The fathers have **e** sour grapes, Jr 31:29
now I have not **e** anything that Ezk 4:14
unleavened bread will be **e**. Ezk 45:21
you have **e** the fruit of lies. Hs 10:13
the swarming locust has **e**; Jl 1:4
left, the young locust has **e**; Jl 1:4
the destroying locust has **e**. Jl 1:4
left over by those who had **e**. Jn 6:13
When they had **e** breakfast, Jn 21:15
I have never **e** anything common Ac 10:14
without food, having **e** nothing. Ac 27:33
And having **e** enough food, they Ac 27:38

EATER *(2)*
Out of the **e** came something to Jdg 14:14
right into the mouth of the **e**! Nah 3:12

EATING *(51)*
but the birds were **e** them out of Gn 40:17
Egyptians who were **e** with him by Gn 43:32
you will be **e** from the previous Lv 25:22
You will be **e** this until the Lv 25:22
you are **e** from vineyards and Jos 24:13
he has finished **e** and drinking. Ru 3:3
against the LORD by **e** ⌊meat⌋ 1Sm 14:33
against the LORD by **e** ⌊meat⌋ 1Sm 14:34
the entire area, **e**, drinking, 1Sm 30:16
They're **e** and drinking in his 1Kg 1:25
the noise⌋ as they finished **e**. 1Kg 1:41
⌊they were⌋ **e**, drinking, and 1Kg 4:20
for three days, **e** and drinking, 1Ch 12:39
daughters were **e** and drinking Jb 1:13
daughters were **e** and drinking Jb 1:18
it⌋ down on him while he is **e**. Jb 20:23
e food earned by hard work; Ps 127:2
he will be **e** butter and honey. Is 7:15
of sheep, **e** of meat, and Is 22:13
a hungry one who dreams he is **e**, Is 29:8
secret places, **e** swine's flesh, Is 65:4
their leader, **e** meat from pigs, Is 66:17
men who are **e** the king's food, Dn 1:13
men who were **e** the king's food. Dn 1:15
finished **e** the vegetation Am 7:2
John did not come **e** or drinking, Mt 11:18
Son of Man came **e** and drinking, Mt 11:19
but **e** with unwashed hands does Mt 15:20
flood they were **e** and drinking, Mt 24:38
While they were **e**, He said, "I Mt 26:21
they were **e**, Jesus took bread, Mt 26:26
saw that He was **e** with sinners Mk 2:16
disciples were **e** their bread Mk 7:2
instead of **e** bread with ritually Mk 7:5
While they were reclining and **e**, Mk 14:18
Me—one who is **e** with Me!" Mk 14:18
As they were **e**, He took bread, Mk 14:22
them in their hands, and **e** them. Lk 6:1
did not come **e** bread or drinking Lk 7:33
of Man has come **e** and drinking, Lk 7:34
e and drinking what they offer, Lk 10:7
the carob pods the pigs were **e**, Lk 15:16
people went on **e**, drinking, Lk 17:27
people went on **e**, drinking, Lk 17:28
from **e** anything that has been Ac 15:20
from **e** anything that has been Ac 15:29

the bread, and **e**, he conversed Ac 20:11
of God is not **e** and drinking, Rm 14:17
because his **e** is not from faith, Rm 14:23
About **e** food offered to idols, 1Co 8:4
For in **e**, each one takes his own 1Co 11:21

EATS *(47)*
Whoever **e** what is leavened from Ex 12:15
If anyone **e** something leavened, Ex 12:19
The person who **e** any of it will Lv 7:18
But the one who **e** meat from the Lv 7:20
and **e** meat from the LORD's Lv 7:21
If anyone **e** animal fat from a Lv 7:25
person who **e** ⌊it⌋ must be cut Lv 7:25
Whoever **e** any blood, that person Lv 7:27
Anyone who **e** some of its carcass Lv 11:40
and whoever **e** in it is to wash Lv 14:47
live among them who **e** any blood, Lv 17:10
that person who **e** blood and cut Lv 17:10
whoever **e** it must be cut off. Lv 17:14
who **e** an animal that died a Lv 17:15
Anyone who **e** it will bear his Lv 19:8
If anyone **e** a holy offering in Lv 22:14
us like an ox **e** up the green Nm 22:4
is the man who **e** food before 1Sm 14:24
is the man who **e** food today,' 1Sm 14:28
taste what he **e** or drinks? 2Sm 19:35
with you. He **e** grass like an ox Jb 40:15
A righteous man **e** until he is Pr 13:25
she **e** and wipes her mouth and Pr 30:20
gift of God whenever anyone **e**, Ec 3:13
whether he **e** little or much; Ec 5:12
he **e** in darkness all his days, Ec 5:17
Each one **e** the flesh of his own Is 9:20
He **e** the roast and is satisfied. Is 44:16
Whoever **e** their eggs will die; Is 59:5
Anyone who **e** sour grapes— Jr 31:30
when the son **e** at the mountain Ezk 18:11
and **e** and drinks with drunkards, Mt 24:49
sinners and **e** with them!" Lk 15:2
anyone **e** of this bread he will Jn 6:51
Anyone who **e** My flesh and drinks Jn 6:54
one who **e** My flesh and drinks Jn 6:56
The one who **e** this bread will Jn 6:58
one who **e** My bread has raised Jn 13:18
who is weak **e** only vegetables Rm 14:2
One who **e** must not look down on Rm 14:3
Whoever **e**, eats to the Lord, Rm 14:6
Whoever eats, **e** to the Lord, Rm 14:6
to cause stumbling by what he **e**. Rm 14:20
doubts stands condemned if he **e**, Rm 14:23
whoever **e** the bread or drinks 1Co 11:27
For whoever **e** and drinks without 1Co 11:29
e and drinks judgment on himself. 1Co 11:29

EBAL *(8)*
(AKA OBAL)
Alvan, Manahath, **E**, Shepho, and Gn 36:23
and the curse at Mount **E**. Dt 11:29
set up these stones on Mount **E**, Dt 27:4
will stand on Mount **E** to deliver Dt 27:13
an altar on Mount **E** to the LORD, Jos 8:30
and half in front of Mount **E**, Jos 8:33
E, Abimael, Sheba, 1Ch 1:22
Alian, Manahath, **E**, Shephi, and 1Ch 1:40

EBB *(2)*
to fail and your life to **e** away. Lv 26:16
all our days **e** away under Your Ps 90:9

EBED *(6)*
Gaal son of **E** came with his Jdg 9:26
Gaal son of **E** said, "Who is Jdg 9:28
the words of Gaal son of **E**, Jdg 9:30
Look, Gaal son of **E**, with his Jdg 9:31
Gaal son of **E** went out and stood Jdg 9:35
E son of Jonathan from Adin's Ezr 8:6

EBED-MELECH *(6)*
But **E**, a Cushite court official Jr 38:7
E went from the king's palace Jr 38:8
king commanded **E**, the Cushite, Jr 38:10
So **E** took the men under his Jr 38:11
E the Cushite cried out to Jr 38:12
Go tell **E** the Cushite: Jr 39:16

EBENEZER *(3)*
battle and camped at **E** while the 1Sm 4:1
they took it from **E** to Ashdod, 1Sm 5:1
He named it **E**, explaining, "The 1Sm 7:12

EBER *(16)*
father of all the children of **E**. Gn 10:21
Shelah, and Shelah fathered **E**. Gn 10:24

E had two sons. One was named Gn 10:25
lived 30 years and fathered **E**. Gn 11:14
he fathered **E**, Shelah lived 403 Gn 11:15
E lived 34 years and fathered Gn 11:16
E lived 430 years and fathered Gn 11:17
they will afflict Asshur and **E**, Nm 24:24
Shelah, and Shelah fathered **E**. 1Ch 1:18
Two sons were born to **E**. 1Ch 1:19
E, Peleg, Reu, 1Ch 1:25
Jacan, Zia, and **E**—seven. 1Ch 5:13
E, Misham, and Shemed who built 1Ch 8:12
Ishpan, **E**, Eliel, 1Ch 8:22
Kallai of Sallai, **E** of Amok, Neh 12:20
Peleg, ⌊son⌋ of **E**, ⌊son⌋ of Lk 3:35

EBEZ *(1)*
Rabbith, Kishion, **E**, Jos 19:20

EBIASAPH *(3)*
his son **E**, his son Assir, 1Ch 6:23
Assir, son of **E**, son of Korah, 1Ch 6:37
of Kore, son of **E**, son of Korah 1Ch 9:19

EBONY *(1)*
tusks and **e** as your payment Ezk 27:15

EBRON *(1)*
(AKA ABDON)
E, Rehob, Hammon, and Kanah, as Jos 19:28

ECBATANA *(1)*
fortress of **E** in the province Ezr 6:2

ECHOES *(1)*
For their cry **e** throughout the Is 15:8

ECLIPSE *(1)*
May an **e** of the sun terrify it. Jb 3:5

EDEN *(16)*
LORD God planted a garden in **E**, Gn 2:8
went out from **E** to water the Gn 2:10
the garden of **E** to work it and Gn 2:15
the garden of **E** to work the Gn 3:23
of the garden of **E** He stationed Gn 3:24
in the land of Nod, east of **E**. Gn 4:16
son of Zimmah and **E** son of Joah 2Ch 29:12
E, Miniamin, Jeshua, Shemaiah, 2Ch 31:15
will make her wilderness like **E**, Is 51:3
Haran, Canneh, **E**, the merchants Ezk 27:23
were in **E**, the garden of God. Ezk 28:13
all the trees of **E**, which were Ezk 31:9
all the trees of **E**, all the Ezk 31:16
to be⌋ with the trees of **E**. Ezk 31:18
has become like the garden of **E**. Ezk 36:35
of them is like the Garden of **E**, Jl 2:3

EDEN'S *(1)*
and greatness among **E** trees? Ezk 31:18

EDENITES *(2)*
Rezeph, and the **E** in Telassar? 2Kg 19:12
Rezeph, and the **E** in Telassar? Is 37:12

EDER *(5)*
his tent beyond the tower at **E**. Gn 35:21
in the Negev: Kabzeel, **E**, Jagur, Jos 15:21
Zebadiah, Arad, **E**, 1Ch 8:15
Mahli, **E**, and Jeremoth—three. 1Ch 23:23
Mahli, **E**, and Jerimoth. 1Ch 24:30

EDGE *(39)*
at Etham on the **e** of the Ex 13:20
blue yarn on the **e** of the last Ex 26:4
the same on the **e** of the Ex 26:4
50 loops on the **e** of the curtain Ex 26:5
50 loops on the **e** of the one Ex 26:10
make 50 loops on the **e** of the Ex 26:10
on the **e** that is next to Ex 28:26
blue yarn on the **e** of the last Ex 36:11
the same on the **e** of the Ex 36:11
50 loops on the **e** of the curtain Ex 36:12
50 loops on the **e** of the Ex 36:17
and 50 loops on the **e** of the Ex 36:17
on the **e** that is next to Ex 39:19
reap to the very **e** of your field Lv 19:9
head or mar the **e** of your beard. Lv 19:27
shave the **e** of their beards, Lv 21:5
the way to the **e** of your field Lv 23:22
at the **e** of his territory. Nm 22:36
which is on the **e** of the Nm 33:6
Mount Hor on the **e** of the land Nm 33:37
you reach the **e** of the waters, Jos 3:8
feet touched the water at its **e** Jos 3:15
as far as the **e** of the Sea Jos 13:27
began at the **e** of Kiriath-jearim Jos 18:15
going down to the **e** of the city, 1Sm 9:27

city with the **e** of the sword." 2Sm 15:14
When they came to the camp's **e**, 2Kg 7:5
men came to the **e** of the camp, 2Kg 7:8
as far as the **e** of the desert 1Ch 5:9
and one does not sharpen its **e**, Ec 10:10
children's teeth are set on **e**. Jr 31:29
his own teeth will be set on **e**. Jr 31:30
So I spread the **e** of My garment Ezk 16:8
children's teeth are set on **e**? Ezk 18:2
rim of nine inches around its **e**. Ezk 43:13
Him to the **e** of the hill their Lk 4:29
two boats at the **e** of the lake; Lk 5:2
will fall by the **e** of the sword Lk 21:24
escaped the **e** of the sword, Heb 11:34

EDGES *(3)*
to its two **e** so that it can be Ex 28:7
joined together at its two **e**. Ex 39:4
it may seize the **e** of the earth Jb 38:13

EDIBLE *(1)*
e food coming into contact with Lv 11:34

EDICT *(12)*
command and **e** became public Est 2:8
the king's command and **e** came. Est 4:3
let ⌊a royal **e**⌋ be written. Est 8:5
⌊The **e** was written⌋ for each Est 8:9
The king's **e** gave the Jews in Est 8:11
and enforce an **e** that for 30 Dn 6:7
establish the **e** and sign the Dn 6:8
the king and asked about his **e**: Dn 6:12
you sign an **e** that for 30 days Dn 6:12
king, and the **e** you signed, for Dn 6:13
Persians that no **e** or ordinance Dn 6:15
they didn't fear the king's **e**. Heb 11:23

EDICTS *(2)*
the king's **e** to the royal Ezr 8:36
sealed ⌊the **e**⌋ with the royal Est 8:10

EDIFICATION *(2)*
speaks to people for **e**, 1Co 14:3
All things must be done for **e**. 1Co 14:26

EDOM *(91)*
(AKA ESAU, SEIR, IDUMEA)
is why he was ⌊also⌋ named **E**. Gn 25:30
land of Seir, the country of **E**. Gn 32:3
records of Esau (that is, **E**). Gn 36:1
Esau (that is, **E**) lived in the Gn 36:8
Jeush, Jalam, and Korah to **E**. Gn 36:14
of Eliphaz in the land of **E**. Gn 36:16
of Reuel in the land of **E**. Gn 36:17
Esau (that is, **E**), and these are Gn 36:19
sons of Seir, in the land of **E**. Gn 36:21
in the land of **E** before any king Gn 36:31
Bela son of Beor ruled in **E**; Gn 36:32
the chiefs of **E** will be Ex 15:15
from Kadesh to the king of **E**, Nm 20:14
E answered him, "You must not Nm 20:18
Yet **E** insisted, "You must not Nm 20:20
E refused to allow Israel to Nm 20:21
on the border of the land of **E**, Nm 20:23
Red Sea to bypass the land of **E**, Nm 21:4
E will become a possession; Nm 24:18
on the edge of the land of **E**. Nm 33:37
of Zin along the boundary of **E**. Nm 34:3
of Zin to the border of **E**. Jos 15:1
the border of **E** in the Negev: Jos 15:21
marched from the fields of **E**, Jdg 5:4
messengers to the king of **E**, Jdg 11:17
but the king of **E** would not Jdg 11:17
around the lands of **E** and Moab. Jdg 11:18
the Ammonites, **E**, the kings of 1Sm 14:47
from **E**, Moab, the Ammonites, the 2Sm 8:12
placed garrisons throughout **E**, 2Sm 8:14
of the Red Sea in the land of **E**. 1Kg 9:26
He was of the royal family in **E**. 1Kg 11:14
when David was in **E**, Joab, the 1Kg 11:15
had struck down every male in **E**. 1Kg 11:15
he had killed every male in **E**. 1Kg 11:16
There was no king in **E**; 1Kg 22:47
route of the wilderness of **E**." 2Kg 3:8
and the king of **E** set out. 2Kg 3:9
and the king of **E** went to him. 2Kg 3:12
direction of **E** and filled the 2Kg 3:20
break through to the king of **E**, 2Kg 3:26
E rebelled against Judah's 2Kg 8:20
So **E** is still in rebellion 2Kg 8:22
You have indeed defeated **E**, 2Kg 14:10
in the land of **E** before any king 1Ch 1:43
the nations—from **E**, Moab, the 1Ch 18:11
He put garrisons in **E**, and all 1Ch 18:13
the seashore in the land of **E**. 2Ch 8:17
Dead Sea and from **E** has come ⌊to 2Ch 20:2
E rebelled against Judah's 2Ch 21:8
crossed ⌊into **E**⌋ with his 2Ch 21:9
So **E** is still in rebellion 2Ch 21:10
I have defeated **E**,' and you have 2Ch 25:19
they went after the gods of **E**. 2Ch 25:20
on **E** I throw My sandal. Ps 60:8
city? Who will lead me to **E**? Ps 60:9
the tents of **E** and the Ps 83:6
on **E** I throw My sandal. Ps 108:9
city? Who will lead me to **E**? Ps 108:10
their power over **E** and Moab, Is 11:14
come down on **E** and on the people Is 34:5
slaughter in the land of **E**. Is 34:6
of paying back ⌊**E**⌋ for its Is 34:8
this coming from **E** in Is 63:1
Egypt, Judah, **E**, the Ammonites, Jr 9:26
E, Moab, and the Ammonites; Jr 25:21
Send ⌊word⌋ to the king of **E**, Jr 27:3
Ammonites and in **E** and in all Jr 40:11
About **E**, this is what the LORD Jr 49:7
E will become a desolation. Jr 49:17
I will chase **E** away from her Jr 49:19
drawn up against **E** and the Jr 49:20
glad, Daughter **E**, you resident Lm 4:21
Daughter **E**, and will expose Lm 4:22
Because **E** acted vengefully Ezk 25:12
My hand against **E** and cut off Ezk 25:13
My vengeance on **E** through My Ezk 25:14
will deal with **E** according to My Ezk 25:14
E is there, her kings and all Ezk 32:29
so will⌋ all **E** in its entirety. Ezk 35:15
of the nations and all of **E**, Ezk 36:5
E, Moab, and the prominent Dn 11:41
desolate, and **E** a desert Jl 3:19
handing them over to **E**. Am 1:6
exiles to **E** and broke a treaty Am 1:9
from punishing **E** for three Am 1:11
lime the bones of the king of **E**. Am 2:1
the remnant of **E** and all the Am 9:12
the Lord GOD has said about **E**: Ob 1
the wise ones of **E** and those who Ob 8
Though **E** says: "We have been Mal 1:4

EDOM'S *(5)*
These are **E** chiefs, according to Gn 36:43
Hadad died. **E** chiefs: Timna, 1Ch 1:51
and Iram. These were **E** chiefs. 1Ch 1:54
⌊**E**⌋ streams will be turned into Is 34:9
the hearts of **E** warriors will be Jr 49:22

EDOMITE *(7)*
not despise an **E**, because he is Dt 23:7
was Doeg the **E**, chief of Saul's 1Sm 21:7
Then Doeg the **E**, who was in 1Sm 22:9
So Doeg the **E** went and executed 1Sm 22:18
that Doeg the **E** was there that 1Sm 22:22
Moabite, Ammonite, **E**, Sidonian, 1Kg 11:1
up Hadad the **E** as an enemy 1Kg 11:14

EDOMITES *(13)*
father of the **E** in the mountains Gn 36:9
Esau was father of the **E**. Gn 36:43
down 18,000 **E** in the Valley 2Sm 8:13
and all the **E** were subject to 2Sm 8:14
along with some **E** from his 1Kg 11:17
out to attack the **E** who had 2Kg 8:21
killed 10,000 **E** in the Valley of 2Kg 14:7
down 18,000 **E** in the Valley 1Ch 18:12
and all the **E** were subject to 1Ch 18:13
out to attack the **E** who had 2Ch 21:9
came from the attack on the **E**, 2Ch 25:14
E came again, attacked Judah, 2Ch 28:17
⌊what⌋ the **E** said that day at Ps 137:7

EDREI *(8)*
whole army to do battle at **E**. Nm 21:33
who lived in Ashtaroth, at **E**. Dt 1:4
out against us for battle at **E**. Dt 3:1
Bashan as far as Salecah and **E**, Dt 3:10
lived in Ashtaroth and **E**. Jos 12:4
who reigned in Ashtaroth and **E**; Jos 13:12
Ashtaroth and **E**—are for Jos 13:31
Kedesh, **E**, En-hazor, Jos 19:37

EDUCATED *(2)*
So Moses was **e** in all the wisdom Ac 7:22
and **e** according to the strict Ac 22:3

EFFECT *(9)*
still in **e** today in the land of Gn 47:26
redeem ⌊such⌋ houses stays in **e**, Lv 25:31
law went into **e** on the Est 9:1
that reaches him will have no **e**, Jb 41:26
and the caper berry has no **e**; Ec 12:5
the **e** of righteousness will be Is 32:17
the fire had no **e** on the bodies Dn 3:27
the decree takes **e** and the day Zph 2:2
will not be emptied ⌊of its **e**⌋. 1Co 1:17

EFFECTIVE *(3)*
a wide door for **e** ministry has 1Co 16:9
may become **e** through knowing Phm 6
is living and **e** and sharper than Heb 4:12

EFFECTIVELY *(1)*
also works **e** in you believers 1Th 2:13

EFFECTS *(1)*
a warrior from the **e** of wine. Ps 78:65

EFFORT *(19)*
mighty are removed without **e**. Jb 34:20
two handfuls with **e** and pursuit Ec 4:6
It has frustrated every **e**; Ezk 24:12
and made every **e** until sundown Dn 6:14
make an **e** to settle with him on Lk 12:58
Make every **e** to enter through Lk 13:24
made every **e** to release Him. Jn 19:12
not depend on human will or **e**, Rm 9:16
which I made every **e** to do. Gl 2:10
but I make every **e** to take hold Php 3:12
and made every **e** to return and 1Th 2:17
Make every **e** to come to me soon, 2Tm 4:9
Make every **e** to come before 2Tm 4:21
make every **e** to come to me in Ti 3:12
then make every **e** to enter that Heb 4:11
make every **e** to supplement your 2Pt 1:5
make every **e** to confirm your 2Pt 1:10
also make every **e** that after my 2Pt 1:15
every **e** to be found in peace 2Pt 3:14

EFFORTS *(8)*
through the people's **e**. Ezr 5:8
on women or your **e** on those who Pr 31:3
gain for all his **e** he labors at Ec 1:3
and all his **e** that he labors Ec 2:22
drinks, and enjoys all his **e**. Ec 3:13
have a good reward for their **e**. Ec 4:9
nothing for his **e** that he can Ec 5:15
immediately made **e** to set out Ac 16:10

EGG *(3)*
Is there flavor in an **e** white? Jb 6:6
and from its **e** comes a flying Is 14:29
he asks for an **e**, will give him Lk 11:12

EGGS *(8)*
a bird's nest with chicks or **e**, Dt 22:6
is sitting on the chicks or **e**, Dt 22:6
She abandons her **e** on the ground Jb 39:14
Like one gathering abandoned **e**, Is 10:14
and hatch her **e** and will gather Is 34:15
hatch viper's **e** and weave Is 59:5
Whoever eats their **e** will die; Is 59:5
that hatches **e** it didn't lay. Jr 17:11

EGLAH *(2)*
was Ithream, by David's wife **E**. 2Sm 3:5
by David's wife **E**, was sixth. 1Ch 3:3

EGLAIM *(1)*
Their wailing reaches **E**; Is 15:8

EGLATH-SHELISHIYAH *(2)*
flee⌋ as far as Zoar, to **E**; Is 15:5
from Zoar to Horonaim ⌊and⌋ **E**— Jr 48:34

EGLON *(14)*
and Debir king of **E**, saying, Jos 10:3
Lachish, and **E**—joined forces, Jos 10:5
and **E** to Joshua out of the cave. Jos 10:23
from Lachish to **E** and all Israel Jos 10:34
him went up from **E** to Hebron Jos 10:36
as he had done at **E**, he left no Jos 10:37
the king of **E** one the king of Jos 12:12
Lachish, Bozkath, **E**, Jos 15:39
gave **E** king of Moab power over Jdg 3:12
After **E** convinced the Ammonites Jdg 3:13
served **E** king of Moab 18 Jdg 3:14
sent him to **E** king of Moab with Jdg 3:15
the tribute to **E** king of Moab, Jdg 3:17
and said, "King ⌊**E**⌋, I have a Jdg 3:19

EGLON'S *(4)*
and plunged it into **E** belly. Jdg 3:21
and **E** fat closed in over it, Jdg 3:22

And **E** insides came out. Jdg 3:22
was gone when **E** servants came Jdg 3:24

EGO *(1)*

Look, his **e** is inflated; Hab 2:4

EGYPT *(617)*

(AKA RAHAB)

Cush, **E**, Put, and Canaan. Gn 10:6
E fathered Ludim, Anamim, Gn 10:13
went down to **E** to live there for Gn 12:10
When he was about to enter **E**, Gn 12:11
Abram entered **E**, the Egyptians Gn 12:14
went up from **E** to the Negev— Gn 13:1
LORD's garden and the land of **E**. Gn 13:10
the brook of **E** to the Euphrates Gn 15:18
wife for him from the land of **E**. Gn 21:21
is opposite **E** as you go toward Gn 25:18
and said, "Do not go down to **E**. Gn 26:2
and resin, going down to **E**. Gn 37:25
who took Joseph to **E**. Gn 37:28
sold Joseph in **E** to Potiphar, Gn 37:36
Now Joseph had been taken to **E**. Gn 39:1
their master, the king of **E**. Gn 40:1
and the baker of the king of **E**, Gn 40:5
magicians of **E** and all its wise Gn 41:8
as these in all the land of **E**. Gn 41:19
coming throughout the land of **E**. Gn 41:29
in the land of **E** will be Gn 41:30
and set him over the land of **E**. Gn 41:33
the land of **E** during the seven Gn 41:34
take place in the land of **E**. Gn 41:36
you over all the land of **E**." Gn 41:41
him over all the land of **E**. Gn 41:43
or foot in all the land of **E**." Gn 41:44
went throughout the land of **E**. Gn 41:45
service of Pharaoh king of **E**. Gn 41:46
throughout the land of **E**. Gn 41:46
the land of **E** during the seven Gn 41:48
in the land of **E** came to an end, Gn 41:53
the land of **E** there was food. Gn 41:54
came to all the land of **E**, Gn 41:55
Pharaoh told all **E**, "Go to Gn 41:55
was severe in the land of **E**. Gn 41:56
to Joseph in **E** to buy grain, Gn 41:57
that there was grain in **E**, Gn 42:1
have heard there is grain in **E**. Gn 42:2
went down to buy grain from **E**. Gn 42:3
they had brought back from **E**, Gn 43:2
way down to **E** and stood before Gn 43:15
said, "the one you sold into **E**. Gn 45:4
ruler over all the land of **E**. Gn 45:8
God has made me lord of all **E**. Gn 45:9
my glory in **E** and about all you Gn 45:13
you the best of the land of **E**, Gn 45:18
the land of **E** for your young Gn 45:19
all the land of **E** is yours.' " Gn 45:20
carrying the best products of **E**, Gn 45:23
went up from **E** and came to their Gn 45:25
ruler over all the land of **E**!" Gn 45:26
not be afraid to go down to **E**, Gn 46:3
I will go down with you to **E**, Gn 46:4
his children with him went to **E**. Gn 46:6
he brought with him to **E**. Gn 46:7
his descendants, who went to **E**: Gn 46:8
born to Joseph in the land of **E**. Gn 46:20
of Jacob's sons—who came to **E**: Gn 46:26
sons who were born to him in **E**: Gn 46:27
household who had come to **E**: Gn 46:27
land of **E** is open before you; Gn 47:6
in the land of **E** and gave them Gn 47:11
The land of **E** and the land of Gn 47:13
in the land of **E** and the land Gn 47:14
from the land of **E** and the land Gn 47:15
all the land in **E** for Pharaoh, Gn 47:20
from one end of **E** to the other. Gn 47:21
effect today in the land of **E**, Gn 47:26
Israel settled in the land of **E**, Gn 47:27
lived in the land of **E** 17 years, Gn 47:28
love. Do not bury me in **E**. Gn 47:29
carry me away from **E** and bury me Gn 47:30
the land of **E** before I came to Gn 48:5
I came to you in **E** are now mine. Gn 48:5
of the land of **E** went with him, Gn 50:7
he returned to **E** with his Gn 50:14
household remained in **E**. Gn 50:22
and placed him in a coffin in **E**. Gn 50:26
Israel who came to **E** with Jacob; Ex 1:1
Joseph was already in **E**. Ex 1:5
Joseph, came to power in **E**. Ex 1:8
Then the king of **E** said to the Ex 1:15
as the king of **E** had told them; Ex 1:17
So the king of **E** summoned the Ex 1:18
a long time, the king of **E** died. Ex 2:23
the misery of My people in **E**, Ex 3:7
the Israelites, out of **E**." Ex 3:10
bring the Israelites out of **E**?" Ex 3:11
you bring the people out of **E**, Ex 3:12
what has been done to you in **E**. Ex 3:16
from the misery of **E** to the land Ex 3:17
to the king of **E** and say to him: Ex 3:18
the king of **E** will not allow Ex 3:19
My hand and strike **E** with all My Ex 3:20
relatives in **E** and see if they Ex 4:18
Return to **E**, for all the men Ex 4:19
and set out for the land of **E**. Ex 4:20
you go back to **E**, make sure you Ex 4:21
The king of **E** said to them, Ex 5:4
the land of **E** to gather stubble Ex 5:12
tell Pharaoh king of **E** to let Ex 6:11
and Pharaoh king of **E** to bring Ex 6:13
Israelites out of the land of **E**. Ex 6:13
of the land of **E** according to Ex 6:26
Pharaoh king of **E** in order to Ex 6:27
bring the Israelites out of **E**. Ex 6:27
spoke to Moses in the land of **E**, Ex 6:28
Pharaoh king of **E** everything I Ex 6:29
and wonders in the land of **E**. Ex 7:3
put My hand on **E** and bring out Ex 7:4
of the land of **E** by great acts Ex 7:4
I stretch out My hand against **E**, Ex 7:5
magicians of **E**, and they also Ex 7:11
your hand over the waters of **E**— Ex 7:19
blood throughout the land of **E**, Ex 7:19
blood throughout the land of **E**. Ex 7:21
the magicians of **E** did the same Ex 7:22
to come up onto the land of **E**." Ex 8:5
his hand over the waters of **E**, Ex 8:6
up and covered the land of **E**. Ex 8:6
frogs up onto the land of **E**. Ex 8:7
gnats throughout the land of **E**." Ex 8:16
gnats throughout the land of **E**. Ex 8:17
Throughout **E** the land was ruined Ex 8:24
Israel and the livestock of **E**, Ex 9:4
dust over the entire land of **E**. Ex 9:9
throughout the land of **E**." Ex 9:9
occurred in **E** from the day it Ex 9:18
hail throughout the land of **E**— Ex 9:22
of the field in the land of **E**." Ex 9:22
rained hail on the land of **E**. Ex 9:23
in the land of **E** since it had Ex 9:24
the land of **E**, the hail struck Ex 9:25
yet that **E** is devastated?" Ex 10:7
the land of **E** and the locusts Ex 10:12
his staff over the land of **E**, Ex 10:13
the entire land of **E** and settled Ex 10:14
on the whole territory of **E**. Ex 10:14
field throughout the land of **E**. Ex 10:15
left in all the territory of **E**. Ex 10:19
be darkness over the land of **E**, Ex 10:21
the land of **E** for three days. Ex 10:22
more plague on Pharaoh and on **E**. Ex 11:1
was feared in the land of **E**, Ex 11:3
midnight I will go throughout **E** Ex 11:4
male$_J$ in the land of **E** will die, Ex 11:5
all the land of **E** such as never Ex 11:6
between **E** and Israel. Ex 11:7
be multiplied in the land of **E**." Ex 11:9
and Aaron in the land of **E**: Ex 12:1
the land of **E** on that night Ex 12:12
male$_J$ in the land of **E**, Ex 12:12
against all the gods of **E**. Ex 12:12
when I strike the land of **E**. Ex 12:13
your ranks out of the land of **E**. Ex 12:17
through to strike **E** and sees the Ex 12:23
Israelites in **E** when He struck Ex 12:27
male$_J$ in the land of **E**, Ex 12:29
throughout **E** because there Ex 12:30
brought out of **E** into unleavened Ex 12:39
driven out of **E** they could not Ex 12:39
lived in **E** was 430 years. Ex 12:40
went out from the land of **E**. Ex 12:41
bring them out of the land of **E**. Ex 12:42
of the land of **E** according to Ex 12:51
this day when you came out of **E**, Ex 13:3
for me when I came out of **E**.' Ex 13:8
you out of **E** with a strong hand Ex 13:9
the LORD brought us out of **E**, Ex 13:14
male$_J$ in the land of **E**, Ex 13:15
us out of **E** by the strength Ex 13:16
return to **E** if they face war. Ex 13:17
left the land of **E** in battle Ex 13:18
When the king of **E** was told that Ex 14:5
the rest of the chariots of **E**, Ex 14:7
the heart of Pharaoh king of **E**, Ex 14:8
no graves in **E** that you took us Ex 14:11
to us by bringing us out of **E**? Ex 14:11
this what we told you in **E**: Ex 14:12
is fighting for them against **E**!" Ex 14:25
they had left the land of **E**. Ex 16:1
LORD's hand in the land of **E**, Ex 16:3
you out of the land of **E**; Ex 16:6
you out of the land of **E**.' " Ex 16:32
bring us out of **E** to kill us and Ex 17:3
had brought Israel out of **E**. Ex 18:1
had left the land of **E**, Ex 19:1
you out of the land of **E**, Ex 20:2
foreigners in the land of **E**. Ex 22:21
foreigners in the land of **E**. Ex 23:9
you came out of **E** in that month. Ex 23:15
them out of the land of **E**, Ex 29:46
us up from the land of **E**— Ex 32:1
you up from the land of **E**!" Ex 32:4
up from the land of **E** have acted Ex 32:7
you up from the land of **E**.' " Ex 32:8
the land of **E** with great power Ex 32:11
us up from the land of **E**— Ex 32:23
brought up from the land of **E**, Ex 33:1
you came out of **E** in the month Ex 34:18
the land of **E** to be your God, Lv 11:45
the practices of the land of **E**, Lv 18:3
foreigners in the land of **E**; Lv 19:34
you out of the land of **E**. Lv 19:36
of the land of **E** to be your God; Lv 22:33
them out of the land of **E**; Lv 23:43
out of the land of **E** to give you Lv 25:38
I brought out of the land of **E**. Lv 25:42
I brought out of the land of **E**; Lv 25:55
you out of the land of **E**, Lv 26:13
of the land of **E** in the sight Lv 26:45
departure from the land of **E**: Nm 1:1
firstborn in the land of **E**, Nm 3:13
firstborn in the land of **E**. Nm 8:17
departure from the land of **E**, Nm 9:1
the free fish we ate in **E**, Nm 11:5
We really had it good in **E**.' Nm 11:18
'Why did we ever leave **E**?' " Nm 11:20
seven years before Zoan in **E**. Nm 13:22
we had died in the land of **E**, Nm 14:2
better for us to go back to **E**?" Nm 14:3
a leader and go back to **E**." Nm 14:4
forgiven them from **E** until now." Nm 14:19
signs I performed in **E** and in Nm 14:22
of the land of **E** to be your God; Nm 15:41
led us up from **E** to bring us to Nm 20:5
Our fathers went down to **E**, Nm 20:15
and we lived in **E** many years, Nm 20:15
Angel, and brought us out of **E**. Nm 20:16
have you led us up from **E** to die Nm 21:5
a people has come out of **E**; Nm 22:5
a people has come out of **E**, Nm 22:11
God brought them out of **E**; Nm 23:22
God brought him out of **E**; Nm 24:8
who came out of the land of **E**." Nm 26:4
of Levi, born to Levi in **E**. Nm 26:59
who came up from **E** will see the Nm 32:11
of the land of **E** by their Nm 33:1
went out of the land of **E**. Nm 33:38
from Azmon to the Brook of **E**, Nm 34:5
of the land of **E** to deliver us Dt 1:27
as you saw Him do for you in **E**. Dt 1:30
did for you in **E** before your Dt 4:34
you out of **E** by His presence Dt 4:37
them after they came out of **E**, Dt 4:45
him after they came out of **E**. Dt 4:46
you out of the land of **E**, Dt 5:6
were a slave in the land of **E**, Dt 5:15
you out of the land of **E**, Dt 6:12
'We were slaves of Pharaoh in **E**, Dt 6:21
brought us out of **E** with a Dt 6:21
signs and wonders on **E**, Dt 6:22
the power of Pharaoh king of **E**. Dt 7:8
diseases of **E** that you know Dt 7:15
God did to Pharaoh and all **E**: Dt 7:18
you out of the land of **E**, Dt 8:14
left the land of **E** until you Dt 9:7

you brought out of **E** have acted Dt 9:12
brought out of **E** with a strong Dt 9:26
foreigners in the land of **E**. Dt 10:19
Your fathers went down to **E**, Dt 10:22
works He did in **E** to Pharaoh Dt 11:3
Pharaoh king of **E** and all his Dt 11:3
is not like the land of **E**, Dt 11:10
the land of **E** and redeemed you Dt 13:5
you out of the land of **E**, Dt 13:10
in the land of **E** and the LORD Dt 15:15
brought you out of **E** by night in Dt 16:1
left the land of **E** in a hurry— Dt 16:3
the day you left the land of **E**. Dt 16:3
of day⌋ you departed from **E**. Dt 16:6
that you were slaves in **E**; Dt 16:12
people back to **E** to acquire many Dt 17:16
you out of the land of **E**, Dt 20:1
journey after you came out of **E**, Dt 23:4
on the journey after you left **E**. Dt 24:9
that you were a slave in **E**, Dt 24:18
were a slave in the land of **E**. Dt 24:22
on the journey after you left **E**. Dt 25:17
He went down to **E** with a few Dt 26:5
brought us out of **E** with a Dt 26:8
afflict you with the boils of **E**, Dt 28:27
with all the diseases of **E**, Dt 28:60
in ships to **E** by a route that Dt 28:68
the LORD did in **E** to Pharaoh, Dt 29:2
in the land of **E** and passed Dt 29:16
them out of the land of **E**. Dt 29:25
to do against the land of **E**— Dt 34:11
you when you came out of **E**, Jos 2:10
who came out of **E** who were males Jos 5:4
after they had come out of **E**. Jos 5:4
after they had come out of **E**. Jos 5:5
who came out of **E** had died off Jos 5:6
the disgrace of **E** from you." Jos 5:9
fame, and all that He did in **E**, Jos 9:9
Shihor east of **E** to the border Jos 13:3
to the Brook of **E** and so the Jos 15:4
to the Brook of **E** and the Jos 15:47
and his sons went down to **E**. Jos 24:4
I plagued **E** by what I did there, Jos 24:5
fathers out of **E** and you reached Jos 24:6
own eyes saw what I did to **E**. Jos 24:7
the Euphrates River and in **E**, Jos 24:14
fathers out of the land of **E**, Jos 24:17
had brought up from **E**, Jos 24:32
brought you out of **E** and led you Jdg 2:1
who had brought them out of **E**. Jdg 2:12
brought you out of **E** and out of Jdg 6:8
the power of **E** and the power Jdg 6:9
the LORD brought us out of **E**?' Jdg 6:13
came from **E**, they seized my Jdg 11:13
But when they came from **E**, Jdg 11:16
of the land of **E** to this day. Jdg 19:30
when it was in **E** and belonged to 1Sm 2:27
them out of **E** until this day, 1Sm 8:8
'I brought Israel out of **E**, 1Sm 10:18
ancestors up from the land of **E**, 1Sm 12:6
Jacob went to **E**, your ancestors 1Sm 12:8
out of **E** and settled them 1Sm 12:8
as they were coming out of **E**. 1Sm 15:2
when they came out of **E**, 1Sm 15:6
way to Shur, which is next to **E**. 1Sm 15:7
Shur as far as the land of **E**. 1Sm 27:8
Israelites out of **E** until today 2Sm 7:6
redeemed for Yourself from **E**. 2Sm 7:23
Pharaoh king of **E** by marrying 1Kg 3:1
and as far as the border of **E**. 1Kg 4:21
than all the wisdom of **E**. 1Kg 4:30
came out from the land of **E**, 1Kg 6:1
they came out of the land of **E**. 1Kg 8:9
My people Israel out of **E**, 1Kg 8:16
them out of the land of **E**. 1Kg 8:21
You brought them out of **E**, 1Kg 8:51
their ancestors out of **E**. 1Kg 8:53
of Hamath to the Brook of **E**— 1Kg 8:65
ancestors out of the land of **E**. 1Kg 9:9
Pharaoh king of **E** had attacked 1Kg 9:16
were imported from **E** and Kue. 1Kg 10:28
imported from **E** for 15 pounds 1Kg 10:29
Hadad fled to **E**, along with some 1Kg 11:17
them from Paran and went to **E**, 1Kg 11:18
Pharaoh king of **E**, who gave 1Kg 11:18
Hadad heard in **E** that David 1Kg 11:21
he fled to **E**, to Shishak king 1Kg 11:40
Shishak king of **E**, where he 1Kg 11:40
he was still in **E** where he had 1Kg 12:2
presence, Jeroboam stayed in **E**. 1Kg 12:2
you out of the land of **E**." 1Kg 12:28
Shishak king of **E** went to war 1Kg 14:25
the kings of **E** to attack us." 2Kg 7:6
to So king of **E** and had not paid 2Kg 17:4
of the land of **E** from the power 2Kg 17:7
Pharaoh king of **E** and because 2Kg 17:7
the land of **E** with great power 2Kg 17:36
you now trust in **E**, the stalk of 2Kg 18:21
Pharaoh king of **E** is to all who 2Kg 18:21
and trust in **E** for chariots and 2Kg 18:24
the streams of **E** with the soles 2Kg 19:24
came out of **E** until today.' " 2Kg 21:15
Neco king of **E** marched up to 2Kg 23:29
took Jehoahaz and went to **E**, 2Kg 23:34
Now the king of **E** did not march 2Kg 24:7
that belonged to the king of **E**, 2Kg 24:7
the Brook of **E** to the Euphrates 2Kg 24:7
and went to **E**, for they were 2Kg 25:26
the Shihor of **E** to the entrance 1Ch 13:5
Israel out of ⌊**E**⌋ until today I 1Ch 17:5
people You redeemed from **E**. 1Ch 17:21
horses came from **E** and Kue. 2Ch 1:16
be imported from **E** for 15 pounds 2Ch 1:17
when they came out of **E**. 2Ch 5:10
Israel out of the land of **E**, 2Ch 6:5
to Hamath to the Brook of **E**— 2Ch 7:8
them out of the land of **E**. 2Ch 7:22
and as far as the border of **E**. 2Ch 9:26
for Solomon from **E** and from all 2Ch 9:28
he was in **E** where he had fled 2Ch 10:2
Jeroboam returned from **E**. 2Ch 10:2
Shishak king of **E** went to war 2Ch 12:2
who came with him from **E**— 2Ch 12:3
So King Shishak of **E** went to war 2Ch 12:9
came out of the land of **E**, 2Ch 20:10
as far as the entrance of **E**, 2Ch 26:8
Neco king of **E** marched up to 2Ch 35:20
The king of **E** deposed him in 2Ch 36:3
Neco⌋ king of **E** made Jehoahaz's 2Ch 36:4
Jehoahaz and brought him to **E**. 2Ch 36:4
ancestors in **E** and heard their Neh 9:9
to return to their slavery in **E**. Neh 9:17
God who brought you out of **E**," Neh 9:18
Ambassadors will come from **E**; Ps 68:31
in the land of **E**, the region of Ps 78:12
signs in **E** and His marvels Ps 78:43
struck all the firstborn in **E**, Ps 78:51
You uprooted a vine from **E**; Ps 80:8
went throughout the land of **E**. Ps 81:5
you up from the land of **E**. Ps 81:10
Then Israel went to **E**; Ps 105:23
E was glad when they left, Ps 105:38
Our fathers in **E** did not grasp Ps 106:7
who did great things in **E**, Ps 106:21
When Israel came out of **E**— Ps 114:1
struck down the firstborn of **E**, Ps 135:8
against you, **E**, against Pharaoh Ps 135:9
richly colored linen from **E**. Pr 7:16
over the sea as ⌊He did⌋ in **E**. Is 10:26
from Assyria, **E**, Pathros, Cush, Is 11:11
they came up from the land of **E**. Is 11:16
oracle against **E**: Look, the LORD Is 19:1
swift cloud and is coming to **E**. Is 19:1
I will provoke **E** against Egypt; Is 19:2
I will provoke Egypt against **E**; Is 19:2
I will deliver **E** into the hands Is 19:4
of Hosts has planned against **E**. Is 19:12
chieftains have led **E** astray. Is 19:13
have made **E** stagger in all she Is 19:14
be able to do anything for **E**. Is 19:15
that day **E** will be like women. Is 19:16
land of Judah will terrify **E**; Is 19:17
E will tremble because of what Is 19:17
in the land of **E** will speak Is 19:18
of the land of **E** and a pillar to Is 19:19
LORD of Hosts in the land of **E**. Is 19:20
will make Himself known to **E**, Is 19:21
and **E** will know the LORD on that Is 19:21
The LORD will strike **E**, striking Is 19:22
be a highway from **E** to Assyria. Is 19:23
will go to **E**, Egypt to Assyria Is 19:23
will go to Egypt, **E** to Assyria, Is 19:23
and **E** will worship with Assyria. Is 19:23
alliance⌋ with **E** and Assyria— Is 19:24
Blessed be **E** My people, Assyria Is 19:25
and omen against **E** and Cush, Is 20:3
the captives of **E** and the exiles Is 20:4
their hope and **E** their boast Is 20:5
the news reaches **E**, they will be Is 23:5
River as far as the Wadi of **E**, Is 27:12
dispersed in the land of **E**; Is 27:13
to go down to **E** without asking Is 30:2
go down to **E** for help and who Is 31:1
are trusting in **E**, that Is 36:6
Pharaoh king of **E** is to all who Is 36:6
and trust in **E** for chariots and Is 36:9
the streams of **E** with the soles Is 37:25
give **E** as a ransom for you, Is 43:3
The products of **E** and the Is 45:14
went down to **E** to live there, Is 52:4
brought us from the land of **E**, Jr 2:6
along the way to **E** to drink the Jr 2:18
put to shame by **E** just as you Jr 2:36
ancestors out of the land of **E**, Jr 7:22
of the land of **E** until this day, Jr 7:25
E, Judah, Edom, the Ammonites, Jr 9:26
them out of the land of **E**, Jr 11:4
of the land of **E** until today, Jr 11:7
Israelites from the land of **E**, Jr 16:14
Israelites from the land of **E**, Jr 23:7
those living in the land of **E**. Jr 24:8
Pharaoh king of **E**, his officers, Jr 25:19
he fled in fear and went to **E**. Jr 26:21
King Jehoiakim sent men to **E**: Jr 26:22
other⌋ men with him ⌊went⌋ to **E**. Jr 26:22
Uriah out of **E** and took him to Jr 26:23
them out of the land of **E**— Jr 31:32
in the land of **E** and do so to Jr 32:20
people Israel out of **E** with Jr 32:21
them out of the land of **E**, Jr 34:13
Pharaoh's army had left **E**, Jr 37:5
to return to its own land of **E**. Jr 37:7
order to make their way into **E** Jr 41:17
to the land of **E** where we will Jr 42:14
to go to **E** and live there Jr 42:15
you there in the land of **E**, Jr 42:16
follow on your heels there to **E**, Jr 42:16
resolve to go to **E** to live there Jr 42:17
pour out on you if you go to **E**. Jr 42:18
Don't go to **E**.' Know for certain Jr 42:19
must not go to **E** to live there Jr 43:2
the land of **E** because they did Jr 43:7
and strike down the land of **E**— Jr 43:11
the land of **E** as a shepherd Jr 43:12
in the land of **E** and burn down Jr 43:13
Jews living in the land of **E**— Jr 44:1
in the land of **E** where you have Jr 44:8
to the land of **E** to live there Jr 44:12
them in the land of **E** will fall Jr 44:12
in the land of **E** just as I Jr 44:13
a while there in the land of **E**— Jr 44:14
in the land of **E** at Pathros Jr 44:15
Judah who are in the land of **E**. Jr 44:24
who live in the land of **E**: Jr 44:26
of Judah in all the land of **E**, Jr 44:26
in the land of **E** will meet his Jr 44:27
from the land of **E** to the land Jr 44:28
to the land of **E** to live there Jr 44:28
About **E** and the army of Pharaoh Jr 46:2
E rises like the Nile, and its Jr 46:8
and get balm, Virgin Daughter **E**! Jr 46:11
Babylon to defeat the land of **E**: Jr 46:13
Announce it in **E**, and proclaim Jr 46:14
Pharaoh king of **E** was all noise; Jr 46:17
exile, inhabitant of Daughter **E**! Jr 46:19
E is a beautiful young cow, Jr 46:20
E will hiss like a slithering Jr 46:22
Daughter **E** will be put to shame, Jr 46:24
with Pharaoh, **E**, her gods, and Jr 46:25
a treaty with **E** and with Assyria Lm 5:6
ambassadors to **E** so they might Ezk 17:15
with hooks to the land of **E**. Ezk 19:4
known to them in the land of **E**. Ezk 20:5
of the land of **E** into a land I Ezk 20:6
yourselves with the idols of **E**. Ezk 20:7
did not forsake the idols of **E**. Ezk 20:8
them within the land of **E**. Ezk 20:8
by bringing them out of **E**. Ezk 20:9
of the land of **E** and led them Ezk 20:10
the wilderness of the land of **E**, Ezk 20:36
who acted like prostitutes in **E**, Ezk 23:3
her promiscuity that began in **E**, Ezk 23:8
a prostitute in the land of **E** Ezk 23:19
which began in the land of **E**, Ezk 23:27

at them or remember **E** any more. Ezk 23:27
fine embroidered linen from **E**, Ezk 27:7
Pharaoh king of **E** and prophesy Ezk 29:2
him and against all of **E**. Ezk 29:2
Pharaoh king of **E**, the great Ezk 29:3
inhabitants of **E** will know that Ezk 29:6
The land of **E** will be a desolate Ezk 29:9
turn the land of **E** into ruins, Ezk 29:10
make the land of **E** a desolation Ezk 29:12
the fortunes of **E** and bring them Ezk 29:14
E will be the lowliest of Ezk 29:15
give the land of **E** to Ezk 29:19
him the land of **E** as the pay he Ezk 29:20
A sword will come against **E**, Ezk 30:4
Cush when the slain fall in **E**, Ezk 30:4
Those who support **E** will fall, Ezk 30:6
I set fire to **E** and all its Ezk 30:8
to the hordes of **E** by the hand Ezk 30:10
swords against **E** and fill the Ezk 30:11
be a prince from the land of **E**. Ezk 30:13
stronghold of **E**, and will wipe Ezk 30:15
set fire to **E**; Pelusium will Ezk 30:16
break the yoke of **E** there and Ezk 30:18
execute judgments against **E**, Ezk 30:19
the arm of Pharaoh king of **E**. Ezk 30:21
I am against Pharaoh king of **E**. Ezk 30:22
wields it against the land of **E**. Ezk 30:25
Pharaoh king of **E** and to his Ezk 31:2
king of **E** and say to him: Ezk 32:2
make the land of **E** a desolation, Ezk 32:15
chant it over **E** and all its Ezk 32:16
the hordes of **E** and bring Egypt Ezk 32:18
Egypt and bring **E** and the Ezk 32:18
on to the Brook ⌊of **E**⌋ as far as Ezk 47:19
to the Brook ⌊of **E**⌋, and out to Ezk 48:28
of the land of **E** with a mighty Dn 9:15
even their gods captive to **E**, Dn 11:8
even the land of **E** will escape. Dn 11:42
and over all the riches of **E**. Dn 11:43
she came out of the land of **E**. Hs 2:15
they call to **E**, and they go to Hs 7:11
for this in the land of **E**. Hs 7:16
they will return to **E**. Hs 8:13
will return to **E**, and they will Hs 9:3
devastation, **E** will gather them Hs 9:6
and out of **E** I called My son. Hs 11:1
the land of **E** and Assyria will Hs 11:5
like birds from **E** and like doves Hs 11:11
and olive oil is carried to **E**. Hs 12:1
God ever since the land of **E**. Hs 12:9
Israel from **E** by a prophet, Hs 12:13
God ever since the land of **E**; Hs 13:4
E will become desolate, and Edom Jl 3:19
from the land of **E** and led you Am 2:10
I brought from the land of **E**: Am 3:1
the citadels in the land of **E**: Am 3:9
I sent plagues like those of **E**; Am 4:10
then subside like the Nile in **E**. Am 8:8
and subsides like the Nile of **E**. Am 9:5
bring Israel from the land of **E**, Am 9:7
the land of **E** and redeemed you Mc 6:4
Assyria and the cities of **E**, Mc 7:12
even from **E** to the Euphrates Mc 7:12
your exodus from the land of **E**. Mc 7:15
Cush and **E** were her endless Nah 3:9
to you when you came out of **E**, Hg 2:5
the land of **E** and gather them Zch 10:10
and the scepter of **E** will come Zch 10:11
the people of **E** will not go up Zch 14:18
the punishment of **E** and all the Zch 14:19
mother, flee to **E**, and stay Mt 2:13
the night, and escaped to **E**. Mt 2:14
Out of **E** I called My Son. Mt 2:15
in a dream to Joseph in **E**, Mt 2:19
E and the parts of Libya near Ac 2:10
of Joseph and sold him into **E**, Ac 7:9
Pharaoh, king of **E**, who Ac 7:10
him governor over **E** and over his Ac 7:10
came over all of **E** and Canaan, Ac 7:11
heard there was grain in **E**, Ac 7:12
and Jacob went down to **E**. Ac 7:15
flourished and multiplied in **E** Ac 7:17
king ruled over **E** who did not Ac 7:18
oppression of My people in **E**; Ac 7:34
now, come, I will send you to **E**. Ac 7:34
and signs in the land of **E**, Ac 7:36
their hearts turned back to **E**. Ac 7:39
brought us out of the land of **E**, Ac 7:40
their stay in the land of **E**, Ac 13:17
who came out of **E** under Moses? Heb 3:16
lead them out of the land of **E**. Heb 8:9
wealth than the treasures of **E**, Heb 11:26
By faith he left **E** behind, Heb 11:27
of all saved a people out of **E**, Jd 5
Sodom and **E**, where also their Rv 11:8

EGYPT'S *(17)*

the king of **E** cupbearer and his Gn 40:1
you out of **E** iron furnace to be Dt 4:20
He did to **E** army, its horses Dt 11:4
E idols will tremble before Him, Is 19:1
and **E** heart will melt within it. Is 19:1
E spirit will be disturbed Is 19:3
and **E** canals will be parched. Is 19:6
⌊**E**⌋ weavers will be dejected; Is 19:10
with bared buttocks, to **E** shame. Is 20:4
and take refuge in **E** shadow. Is 30:2
and refuge in **E** shadow your Is 30:3
E help is completely worthless; Is 30:7
a fire in the temples of **E** gods, Jr 43:12
Pharaoh Hophra, **E** king, to his Jr 44:30
Pharaoh Neco, **E** king, which was Jr 46:2
them on the day of **E** ⌊doom⌋. Ezk 30:9
They will ravage **E** pride, and Ezk 32:12

EGYPTIAN *(29)*

owned an **E** slave named Hagar. Gn 16:1
Hagar, her **E** slave, and gave Gn 16:3
the one Hagar the **E** had borne to Gn 21:9
whom Hagar the **E**, Sarah's slave, Gn 25:12
E ⌊named⌋ Potiphar, an officer Gn 39:1
the household of his **E** master. Gn 39:2
because every **E** sold his field Gn 47:20
women are not like the **E** women, Ex 1:19
He saw an **E** beating a Hebrew, Ex 2:11
he struck the **E** dead and hid him Ex 2:12
to kill me as you killed the **E**?" Ex 2:14
An **E** rescued us from the Ex 2:19
All the **E** livestock died, but Ex 9:6
came between the **E** and Israelite Ex 14:20
looked down on the **E** forces from Ex 14:24
mother and an **E** father was among Lv 24:10
not despise an **E**, because you Dt 23:7
They found an **E** in the open 1Sm 30:11
I'm an **E**, the slave of an 1Sm 30:13
He also killed an **E**, a huge man. 2Sm 23:21
Even though the **E** had a spear in 2Sm 23:21
he did have an **E** servant whose 1Ch 2:34
also killed an **E** who was seven 1Ch 11:23
Even though the **E** had a spear in 1Ch 11:23
down the temples of the **E** gods." Jr 43:13
in promiscuous acts with **E** men, Ezk 16:26
man by striking down the **E**. Ac 7:24
way you killed the **E** yesterday? Ac 7:28
Aren't you the **E** who raised a Ac 21:38

EGYPTIAN'S *(3)*

LORD blessed the **E** house because Gn 39:5
the spear out of the **E** hand, 2Sm 23:21
the spear out of the **E** hand, 1Ch 11:23

EGYPTIANS *(80)*

When the **E** see you, they will Gn 12:12
E saw that the woman was very Gn 12:14
and sold grain to the **E**, Gn 41:56
and the **E** who were eating with Gn 43:32
because **E** could not eat with Gn 43:32
so loudly that the **E** heard it, Gn 45:2
shepherds are abhorrent to **E**." Gn 46:34
all the **E** came to Joseph and Gn 47:15
and the **E** mourned for him 70 Gn 50:3
mourning on the part of the **E**." Gn 50:11
So the **E** assigned taskmasters Ex 1:11
so that the **E** came to dread Ex 1:12
the power of the **E** and to bring Ex 3:8
the way the **E** are oppressing Ex 3:9
sight of the **E** that when you go Ex 3:21
So you will plunder the **E**." Ex 3:22
whom the **E** are forcing to work Ex 6:5
labor of the **E** and free you Ex 6:6
from the forced labor of the **E**. Ex 6:7
The **E** will know that I am the Ex 7:5
the **E** will be unable to drink Ex 7:18
so bad the **E** could not drink Ex 7:21
the **E** dug around the Nile for Ex 7:24
our God is detestable to the **E**. Ex 8:26
what the **E** detest in front Ex 8:26
as well as on all the **E**. Ex 9:11
I dealt with the **E** and performed Ex 10:2
and the houses of all the **E**— Ex 10:6
favor in the sight of the **E**. Ex 11:3
He struck the **E** and spared our Ex 12:27
all his officials and all the **E**, Ex 12:30
Now the **E** pressured the people Ex 12:33
word and asked the **E** for silver Ex 12:35
this way they plundered the **E**. Ex 12:36
the **E** will know that I am the Ex 14:4
The **E**—all Pharaoh's horses and Ex 14:9
up and saw the **E** coming after Ex 14:10
so that we may serve the **E**? Ex 14:12
us to serve the **E** than to die Ex 14:12
the **E** you see today, you will Ex 14:13
hearts of the **E** so that they Ex 14:17
The **E** will know that I am the Ex 14:18
The **E** set out in pursuit— Ex 14:23
Israel," the **E** said, "because Ex 14:25
waters may come back on the **E**, Ex 14:26
the **E** were trying to escape Ex 14:27
Israel from the power of the **E**, Ex 14:30
and Israel saw the **E** dead on the Ex 14:30
the LORD used against the **E**, Ex 14:31
on you I inflicted on the **E**. Ex 15:26
Pharaoh and the **E** for Israel's Ex 18:8
when He rescued them from the **E**. Ex 18:9
Pharaoh and the power of the **E**, Ex 18:10
people from the power of the **E**. Ex 18:10
at the time the **E** acted Ex 18:11
I did to the **E** and how I carried Ex 19:4
should the **E** say, 'He brought Ex 32:12
The **E** will hear about it, Nm 14:13
but the **E** treated us and our Nm 20:15
in the sight of all the **E**. Nm 33:3
the **E** were burying every Nm 33:4
But the **E** mistreated and Dt 26:6
the **E** pursued your fathers with Jos 24:6
darkness between you and the **E**, Jos 24:7
When the **E**, Amorites, Ammonites Jdg 10:11
slaughtered the **E** with all kinds 1Sm 4:8
your hearts as the **E** and Pharaoh 1Sm 6:6
the power of the **E** and all the 1Sm 10:18
Moabites, **E**, and Amorites. Ezr 9:1
firstborn of the **E** His love is Ps 136:10
his staff over you as the **E** did. Is 10:24
E are men, not God; Is 31:3
when the **E** caressed your nipples Ezk 23:21
disperse the **E** among the nations Ezk 29:12
will gather the **E** from the Ezk 29:13
their sin of turning to the **E**. Ezk 29:16
disperse the **E** among the nations Ezk 30:23
I disperse the **E** among the Ezk 30:26
in all the wisdom of the **E**, Ac 7:22
When the **E** attempted to do this, Heb 11:29

EGYPTIANS' *(2)*

The **E** houses will swarm with Ex 8:21
favor in the **E** sight that they Ex 12:36

EHI *(1)*

Gera, Naaman, **E**, Rosh, Muppim, Gn 46:21

EHUD *(13)*

and He raised up **E** son of Gera, Jdg 3:15
E made himself a double-edged Jdg 3:16
When **E** had finished presenting Jdg 3:18
Then **E** approached him while he Jdg 3:20
E said, "I have a word from God Jdg 3:20
E reached with his left hand, Jdg 3:21
so that **E** did not withdraw the Jdg 3:22
E escaped by way of the porch, Jdg 3:23
E was gone when Eglon's servants Jdg 3:24
E escaped while the servants Jdg 3:26
After **E**, Shamgar son of Anath Jdg 3:31
of the LORD after **E** had died. Jdg 4:1
Jeush, Benjamin, **E**, Chenaanah, 1Ch 7:10

EHUD'S *(1)*

These were **E** sons, who were the 1Ch 8:6

EIGHT *(55)*

among you at **e** days old is to be Gn 17:12
his son Isaac was **e** days old, Gn 21:4
Milcah bore these **e** to Nahor, Gn 22:23
There are to be **e** planks with Ex 26:25
there were **e** planks with their Ex 36:30
four carts and **e** oxen Nm 7:8
the sixth day ⌊present⌋ **e** bulls, Nm 29:29
Israelites served him **e** years. Jdg 3:8
Abdon judged Israel **e** years, Jdg 12:14
Jesse had **e** sons, and during 1Sm 17:12
weighed about **e** pounds and who 2Sm 21:16
he reigned **e** years in Jerusalem. 2Kg 8:17

Josiah was **e** years old when he 2Kg 22:1
e ⌊heads⌋ of ancestral houses 1Ch 24:4
about **e** pounds of gold went into 2Ch 9:16
he reigned **e** years in Jerusalem. 2Ch 21:5
he reigned **e** years in Jerusalem. 2Ch 21:20
the LORD's temple for **e** days, 2Ch 29:17
Josiah was **e** years old when he 2Ch 34:1
a portion to seven or even to **e**, Ec 11:2
Johanan with **e** men and went to Jr 41:15
day will be **e** ounces by weight Ezk 4:10
was ⌊a space of⌋ **e** and Ezk 40:7
long and **e** and three-quarter Ezk 40:30
Its stairway had **e** steps. Ezk 40:31
Its stairway had **e** steps. Ezk 40:34
Its stairway had **e** steps. Ezk 40:37
e tables ⌊in all⌋ on which the Ezk 40:41
they were **e** and three-quarter Ezk 40:48
entrance were **e** and Ezk 41:2
side rooms was **e** and Ezk 41:9
free space was **e** and Ezk 41:11
the building was **e** and Ezk 41:12
e and one-third ⌊miles⌋ long and Ezk 45:1
off an area **e** and one-third Ezk 45:3
another area⌋ **e** and one-third Ezk 45:5
a mile⌋ wide and **e** and one-third Ezk 45:6
e and one-third ⌊miles⌋ wide, Ezk 48:8
the LORD will be **e** and one-third Ezk 48:9
will be **e** and one-third ⌊miles Ezk 48:10
and **e** and one-third ⌊miles⌋ long Ezk 48:10
have an area⌋ **e** and one-third Ezk 48:13
length will be **e** and one-third Ezk 48:13
a mile⌋ wide and **e** and one-third Ezk 48:15
donation will be **e** and one-third Ezk 48:20
miles⌋ by **e** and one-third ⌊miles Ezk 48:20
next to the **e** and one-third Ezk 48:21
and next to the **e** and one-third Ezk 48:21
even **e** leaders of men. Mc 5:5
When the **e** days were completed Lk 2:21
About **e** days after these words, Lk 9:28
After **e** days His disciples were Jn 20:26
had been bedridden for **e** years. Ac 9:33
not more than **e** or 10 days among Ac 25:6
a few—that is, **e** people—were 1Pt 3:20

EIGHTEENTH *(11)*
In the **e** year of ⌊Israel's⌋ King 1Kg 15:1
during the **e** year of Judah's 2Kg 3:1
In the **e** year of King Josiah, 2Kg 22:3
in the **e** year of King Josiah, 2Kg 23:23
to Hezir, the **e** to Happizzez, 1Ch 24:15
the **e** to Hanani, his sons, and 1Ch 25:25
In the **e** year of ⌊Israel's⌋ King 2Ch 13:1
In the **e** year of his reign, 2Ch 34:8
In the **e** year of Josiah's reign, 2Ch 35:19
which was the **e** year of Jr 32:1
in his **e** year, 832 people from Jr 52:29

EIGHTH *(36)*
but on the **e** day you are to give Ex 22:30
On the **e** day Moses summoned Lv 9:1
be circumcised on the **e** day. Lv 12:3
On the **e** day he must take two Lv 14:10
the **e** day he is to bring these Lv 14:23
two young pigeons on the **e** day, Lv 15:14
On the **e** day she must take two Lv 15:29
from the **e** day on, it will be Lv 22:27
On the **e** day you are to hold a Lv 23:36
and complete rest on the **e** day. Lv 23:39
When you sow in the **e** year, Lv 25:22
On the **e** day he is to bring two Nm 6:10
On the **e** day Gamaliel son of Nm 7:54
On the **e** day you are to hold a Nm 29:35
eleventh year in the **e** month, 1Kg 6:38
a festival in the **e** month on the 1Kg 12:32
fifteenth day of the **e** month, 1Kg 12:33
captive⌋ in the **e** year of his 2Kg 24:12
Johanan **e**, Elzabad ninth, 1Ch 12:12
to Hakkoz, the **e** to Abijah, 1Ch 24:10
the **e** ⌊to⌋ Jeshaiah, his sons, 1Ch 25:15
Peullethai the **e**, for God 1Ch 26:5
The **e**, for the eighth month, was 1Ch 27:11
eighth, for the **e** month, was 1Ch 27:11
On the **e** day they held a sacred 2Ch 7:9
and on the **e** day of the month 2Ch 29:17
In the **e** year of his reign, 2Ch 34:3
and on the **e** day there was an Neh 8:18
To give an **e** of an ounce of Neh 10:32
on the **e** day and afterwards, Ezk 43:27
In the **e** month, in the second Zch 1:1
the child on the **e** day, Lk 1:59
circumcised him on the **e** day; Ac 7:8
circumcised the **e** day; Php 3:5
not, is himself the **e**, yet is of Rv 17:11
chrysolite, the **e** beryl, the Rv 21:20

EIGHTIETH *(1)*
in the four hundred **e** year after 1Kg 6:1

EIGHTY *(1)*
or, if we are strong, **e** years. Ps 90:10

EITHER *(53)*
(See pp. xi-xii.)

EKER *(1)*
firstborn: Maaz, Jamin, and **E**. 1Ch 2:27

EKRON *(22)*
to the border of **E** on the north Jos 13:3
Ashkelon, Gath, and **E**, as well Jos 13:3
reached to the slope north of **E**, Jos 15:11
E, with its towns and villages; Jos 15:45
from **E** to the sea, all ⌊the Jos 15:46
Elon, Timnah, **E**, Jos 19:43
territory, and **E** and its Jdg 1:18
then sent the ark of God to **E**. 1Sm 5:10
returned to **E** that same day. 1Sm 6:16
Gaza, Ashkelon, Gath, and **E**. 1Sm 6:17
The cities from **E** to Gath, 1Sm 7:14
valley and to the gates of **E**. 1Sm 17:52
the Shaaraim road to Gath and **E**. 1Sm 17:52
the god of **E**, if I will recover 2Kg 1:2
of Baal-zebub, the god of **E**?' 2Kg 1:3
of Baal-zebub, the god of **E**? 2Kg 1:6
the god of **E**—is it because 2Kg 1:16
Ashkelon, Gaza, **E**, and the Jr 25:20
also turn My hand against **E**, Am 1:8
at noon, and **E** will be uprooted Zph 2:4
pain, as will **E**, for her hope Zch 9:5
clan in Judah and **E** like the Zch 9:7

EKRONITES *(2)*
it got there, the **E** cried out, 1Sm 5:10
The **E** called all the Philistine 1Sm 5:11

EL *(1)*
wanders with **E** and is faithful Hs 11:12

EL-BERITH *(1)*
chamber of the temple of **E**. Jdg 9:46

EL-PARAN *(1)*
as far as **E** by the wilderness. Gn 14:6

ELA *(1)*
Shimei son of **E**, in Benjamin; 1Kg 4:18

ELABORATE *(2)*
not with **e** hairstyles, gold, 1Tm 2:9
things ⌊like⌋ **e** hairstyles 1Pt 3:3

ELAH *(16)*
Oholibamah, **E**, Pinon, Gn 36:41
and camped in the Valley of **E**; 1Sm 17:2
in the Valley of **E** fighting with 1Sm 17:19
you killed in the valley of **E**, 1Sm 21:9
His son **E** became king in his 1Kg 16:6
E son of Baasha became king over 1Kg 16:8
against him while **E** was in 1Kg 16:9
went in, struck **E** down, and 1Kg 16:10
and the sins of his son **E**, 1Kg 16:13
Then Hoshea son of **E** organized a 2Kg 15:30
Hoshea son of **E** became king over 2Kg 17:1
Israel's King Hoshea son of **E**, 2Kg 18:1
Israel's King Hoshea son of **E**, 2Kg 18:9
Oholibamah, **E**, Pinon, 1Ch 1:52
Jephunneh: Iru, **E**, and Naam. 1Ch 4:15
E son of Uzzi, son of Michri; 1Ch 9:8

ELAH'S *(2)*
rest of the events of **E** ⌊reign⌋, 1Kg 16:14
Elah, and Naam. **E** son: Kenaz. 1Ch 4:15

ELAM *(21)*
Shem's sons were **E**, Asshur, Gn 10:22
king of **E**, and Tidal king Gn 14:1
against Chedorlaomer king of **E**, Gn 14:9
E, Asshur, Arpachshad, Lud, Aram, 1Ch 1:17
Hananiah, **E**, Anthothijah, 1Ch 8:24
E the fifth, Jehohanan the sixth, 1Ch 26:3
Susa (that is, the people of **E**), Ezr 4:9
Pahath-moab, **E**, Zattu, Bani, Neh 10:14
Malchijah, **E**, and Ezer. Neh 12:42
Cush, **E**, Shinar, Hamath, Is 11:11
Advance, **E**! Lay siege, you Is 21:2
E took up a quiver with chariots Is 22:6
all the kings of **E**, and all the Jr 25:25
prophet about **E** at the beginning Jr 49:34
winds against **E** from the four Jr 49:36
I will devastate **E** before their Jr 49:37
I will set My throne in **E**, Jr 49:38
will restore the fortunes of **E**. Jr 49:39
E is there with all her hordes Ezk 32:24
resting place for **E** with all her Ezk 32:25
of Susa, in the province of **E**. Dn 8:2

ELAM'S *(8)*
E descendants 1,254 Ezr 2:7
the other **E** people 1,254 Ezr 2:31
of Athaliah from **E** descendants, Ezr 8:7
E descendants: Mattaniah, Ezr 10:26
E descendants 1,254 Neh 7:12
the other **E** people 1,254 Neh 7:34
I am about to shatter **E** bow, Jr 49:35
nation to which **E** banished ones Jr 49:36

ELAMITE *(1)*
son of Jehiel, an **E**, responded Ezr 10:2

ELAMITES *(1)*
Parthians, Medes, **E**; Ac 2:9

ELASAH *(2)*
E from Pashhur's descendants. Ezr 10:22
was sent⌋ by **E** son of Shaphan Jr 29:3

ELATH *(5)*
road and from **E** and Ezion-geber. Dt 2:8
He rebuilt **E** and restored it to 2Kg 14:22
of Aram recovered **E** for Aram and 2Kg 16:6
expelled the Judahites from **E**. 2Kg 16:6
Then the Arameans came to **E**, 2Kg 16:6

ELDAAH *(2)*
Epher, Hanoch, Abida, and **E**. Gn 25:4
Epher, Hanoch, Abida, and **E**. 1Ch 1:33

ELDAD *(2)*
one named **E** and the other Medad; Nm 11:26
E and Medad are prophesying in Nm 11:27

ELDER *(9)*
the **e** of his household who Gn 24:2
Since he is my **e** brother, you 1Kg 2:22
the fortune-teller and **e**, Is 3:2
act arrogantly toward the **e**, Is 3:5
The head is the **e**, the honored Is 9:15
against an **e** unless it is 1Tm 5:19
as a fellow **e** and witness to the 1Pt 5:1
The **E**: To the elect lady and her 2Jn 1
The **E**: To my dear friend Gaius, 3Jn 1

ELDERLY *(10)*
How is your **e** father that you Gn 43:27
'We have an **e** father and a young Gn 44:20
presence of the **e** and honor the Lv 19:32
man and virgin or **e** and aged; 2Ch 36:17
Wisdom is found with the **e**, Jb 12:12
and the **e** are with us, Jb 15:10
are wise or the **e** who understand Jb 32:9
are the crown of the **e**, Pr 17:6
your yoke very heavy on the **e**. Is 47:6
as an **e** man and now also as a Phm 9

ELDERS *(190)*
the **e** of his household, Gn 50:7
and all the **e** of the land of Gn 50:7
and assemble the **e** of Israel and Ex 3:16
along with the **e** of Israel, Ex 3:18
all the **e** of the Israelites Ex 4:29
summoned all the **e** of Israel and Ex 12:21
some of the **e** of Israel with Ex 17:5
in the sight of the **e** of Israel. Ex 17:6
with all the **e** of Israel to eat Ex 18:12
He summoned the **e** of the people, Ex 19:7
and 70 of Israel's **e**, and bow in Ex 24:1
and Abihu, and 70 of Israel's **e**, Ex 24:9
He told the **e**, "Wait here for us Ex 24:14
The **e** of the assembly are to lay Lv 4:15
his sons, and the **e** of Israel. Lv 9:1
known to you as **e** and officers Nm 11:16
70 men from the **e** of the people Nm 11:24
placed ⌊the Spirit⌋ on the 70 **e**. Nm 11:25
camp along with the **e** of Israel. Nm 11:30
the **e** of Israel followed him. Nm 16:25
said to the **e** of Midian, Nm 22:4
e of Moab and Midian departed Nm 22:7
leaders and **e** when you heard Dt 5:23
the **e** of his city must send ⌊for Dt 19:12
your **e** and judges must come out Dt 21:2
The **e** of the city nearest to the Dt 21:3
e of that city will bring the Dt 21:4
All the **e** of the city nearest to Dt 21:6
bring him to the **e** of his city, Dt 21:19
will say to the **e** of his city, Dt 21:20

⌊it⌋ to the city **e** at the gate. Dt 22:15
father will say to the **e**, Dt 22:16
out the cloth before the city **e**. Dt 22:17
the **e** of that city will take Dt 22:18
must go to the **e** at the ⌊city⌋ Dt 25:7
e of his city will summon him Dt 25:8
up to him in the sight of the **e**, Dt 25:9
Moses and the **e** of Israel Dt 27:1
tribes, **e**, officials, all Dt 29:10
and to all the **e** of Israel. Dt 31:9
all your tribal **e** and officers Dt 31:28
tell you, your **e**, and they will Dt 32:7
evening, as did the **e** of Israel; Jos 7:6
Then he and the **e** of Israel led Jos 8:10
alike, with their **e**, officers, Jos 8:33
So our **e** and all the inhabitants Jos 9:11
case before the **e** of that city, Jos 20:4
its **e**, leaders, judges, Jos 23:2
Shechem and summoned Israel's **e**, Jos 24:1
lifetimes of the **e** who outlived Jos 24:31
lifetimes of the **e** who outlived Jdg 2:7
77 princes and **e** of Succoth. Jdg 8:14
So he took the **e** of the city, Jdg 8:16
the **e** of Gilead went to get Jdg 11:5
replied to the **e** of Gilead, Jdg 11:7
e of Gilead said to Jephthah, Jdg 11:10
went with the **e** of Gilead. Jdg 11:11
The **e** of the congregation said, Jdg 21:16
10 men of the city's **e** and said, Ru 4:2
presence of the **e** of my people. Ru 4:4
Boaz said to the **e** and all the Ru 4:9
e and all the people who were Ru 4:11
the camp, the **e** of Israel asked 1Sm 4:3
So all the **e** of Israel gathered 1Sm 8:4
the **e** of Jabesh said to him, 1Sm 11:3
me now before the **e** of my people 1Sm 15:30
When the **e** of the town met him, 1Sm 16:4
friends, the **e** of Judah, saying 1Sm 30:26
conferred with the **e** of Israel: 2Sm 3:17
So all the **e** of Israel came to 2Sm 5:3
The **e** of his house stood beside 2Sm 12:17
Absalom and all the **e** of Israel. 2Sm 17:4
Absalom and the **e** of Israel, 2Sm 17:15
Say to the **e** of Judah, 'Why 2Sm 19:11
assembled the **e** of Israel, 1Kg 8:1
the **e** of Israel came, and the 1Kg 8:3
with the **e** who had served his 1Kg 12:6
advice of the **e** who had advised 1Kg 12:8
the advice the **e** had given him 1Kg 12:13
called for all the **e** of the land 1Kg 20:7
the **e** and all the people said 1Kg 20:8
letters to the **e** and nobles who 1Kg 21:8
e and nobles who lived in his 1Kg 21:11
and the **e** were sitting with him. 2Kg 6:32
said to the **e**, "Do you see how 2Kg 6:32
of Jezreel, to the **e**, and to the 2Kg 10:1
of the city, the **e**, and the 2Kg 10:5
and the **e** of the priests, 2Kg 19:2
him all the **e** of Jerusalem and 2Kg 23:1
So all the **e** of Israel came to 1Ch 11:3
David, the **e** of Israel, and the 1Ch 15:25
David and the **e**, clothed in 1Ch 21:16
at Jerusalem the **e** of Israel— 2Ch 5:2
the **e** of Israel came, and the 2Ch 5:4
with the **e** who had served his 2Ch 10:6
advice of the **e** who had advised 2Ch 10:8
and gathered all the **e** of Judah 2Ch 34:29
was watching over the Jewish **e**. Ezr 5:5
we questioned the **e** and asked, Ezr 5:9
the governor and **e** of the Jews Ezr 6:7
so that the **e** of the Jews can Ezr 6:8
So the Jewish **e** continued Ezr 6:14
decision of the leaders and **e**, Ezr 10:8
together with the **e** and judges Ezr 10:14
at will and instructing his **e**. Ps 105:22
Him in the council of the **e**. Ps 107:32
more than the **e** because I obey Ps 119:100
he sits among the **e** of the land. Pr 31:23
against the **e** and leaders of His Is 3:14
glory in the presence of His **e**. Is 24:23
Take some of the **e** of the people Jr 19:1
and some of the **e** of the priests Jr 19:1
Some of the **e** of the land stood Jr 26:17
the rest of the **e** of the exiles, Jr 29:1
My priests and **e** perished in the Lm 1:19
e of Daughter Zion sit on the Lm 2:10
respected; the **e** find no favor. Lm 4:16
e are shown no respect. Lm 5:12
The **e** have left the city gate, Lm 5:14
priests and counsel from the **e**. Ezk 7:26
my house and the **e** of Judah were Ezk 8:1
Seventy **e** from the house of Ezk 8:11
you see what the **e** of the house Ezk 8:12
began with the **e** who were in Ezk 9:6
Some of the **e** of Israel came to Ezk 14:1
of Israel's **e** came to consult Ezk 20:1
speak with the **e** of Israel and Ezk 20:3
The **e** of Gebal and its wise men Ezk 27:9
Hear this, you **e**; listen, all Jl 1:2
Gather the **e** and all the Jl 1:14
break the tradition of the **e**? Mt 15:2
suffer many things from the **e**, Mt 16:21
priests and the **e** of the people Mt 21:23
priests and the **e** of the people Mt 26:3
priests and **e** of the people. Mt 26:47
scribes and the **e** had convened. Mt 26:57
priests and the **e** of the people Mt 27:1
to the chief priests and **e**. Mt 27:3
by the chief priests and **e**, Mt 27:12
The chief priests and the **e**, Mt 27:20
scribes and **e**, mocked Him and Mt 27:41
assembled with the **e** and agreed Mt 28:12
keeping the tradition of the **e**. Mk 7:3
to the tradition of the **e**, Mk 7:5
rejected by the **e**, the chief Mk 8:31
and the **e** came and asked Him, Mk 11:27
priests, the scribes, and the **e**. Mk 14:43
priests, the **e**, and the scribes Mk 14:53
had a meeting with the **e**, Mk 15:1
he sent some Jewish **e** to Him, Lk 7:3
things and be rejected by the **e**, Lk 9:22
the scribes, with the **e**, came up Lk 20:1
and the **e** who had come for Him, Lk 22:52
came, the **e** of the people, Lk 22:66
day, their rulers, **e**, and Ac 4:5
Rulers of the people and **e**: Ac 4:8
priests and the **e** had said to Ac 4:23
the people, the **e**, and the Ac 6:12
sending it to the **e** by means of Ac 11:30
had appointed **e** in every church Ac 14:23
the apostles and **e** in Jerusalem Ac 15:2
apostles, and the **e**, and they Ac 15:4
apostles and the **e** assembled to Ac 15:6
Then the apostles and the **e**, Ac 15:22
From the apostles and the **e**, Ac 15:23
apostles and **e** at Jerusalem for Ac 16:4
called for the **e** of the church. Ac 20:17
and all the **e** were present. Ac 21:18
whole council of **e** can testify Ac 22:5
chief priests and **e** and said, Ac 23:14
down with some **e** and a lawyer Ac 24:1
priests and the **e** of the Jews Ac 25:15
on of hands by the council of **e**. 1Tm 4:14
e who are good leaders should 1Tm 5:17
to appoint **e** in every town: Ti 1:5
call for the **e** of the church, Jms 5:14
I exhort the **e** among you: 1Pt 5:1
men, be subject to the **e**. 1Pt 5:5
thrones sat 24 **e** dressed in Rv 4:4
24 **e** fall down before the One Rv 4:10
Then one of the **e** said to me, Rv 5:5
creatures and among the **e**. Rv 5:6
and the 24 **e** fell down before Rv 5:8
living creatures, and of the **e**. Rv 5:11
and the **e** fell down and Rv 5:14
the throne, the **e**, and the four Rv 7:11
Then one of the **e** asked me, Rv 7:13
The 24 **e**, who were seated before Rv 11:16
four living creatures and the **e**, Rv 14:3
the 24 **e** and the four living Rv 19:4

ELDERS' *(2)*
Rehoboam rejected the **e** advice 2Ch 10:13
takes away the **e** good judgment. Jb 12:20

ELEAD *(2)*
his son Shuthelah, Ezer, and **E**. 1Ch 7:21
killed Ezer and **E** because they 1Ch 7:21

ELEADAH *(1)*
his son **E**, his son Tahath 1Ch 7:20

ELEALEH *(5)*
Nimrah, Heshbon, **E**, Sebam, Nebo, Nm 32:3
rebuilt Heshbon, **E**, Kiriathaim, Nm 32:37
Heshbon and **E** cry out; Is 15:4
Heshbon and **E** with my tears. Is 16:9
is a cry from Heshbon to **E**; Jr 48:34

ELEASAH *(4)*
Helez, and Helez fathered **E**. 1Ch 2:39
E fathered Sismai, and Sismai 1Ch 2:40
Raphah, his son **E**, and his son 1Ch 8:37
his son **E**, and his son Azel 1Ch 9:43

ELEAZAR *(72)*
Nadab and Abihu, **E** and Ithamar. Ex 6:23
Aaron's son **E** married one of the Ex 6:25
Nadab and Abihu, **E** and Ithamar. Ex 28:1
and his sons **E** and Ithamar, Lv 10:6
remaining sons, **E** and Ithamar: Lv 10:12
He was angry with **E** and Ithamar, Lv 10:16
and Abihu, **E**, and Ithamar. Nm 3:2
So **E** and Ithamar served as Nm 3:4
Levite leaders was **E** son of Nm 3:32
E, son of Aaron the priest, has Nm 4:16
Tell **E** son of Aaron the priest Nm 16:37
So **E** the priest took the bronze Nm 16:39
Give it to **E** the priest, and he Nm 19:3
E the priest is to take some of Nm 19:4
and his son **E** and bring them up Nm 20:25
and put them on his son **E**. Nm 20:26
and put them on his son **E**, Nm 20:28
Moses and **E** came down from Nm 20:28
Phinehas son of **E**, son of Aaron Nm 25:7
Phinehas son of **E**, son of Aaron Nm 25:11
said to Moses and **E** son of Aaron Nm 26:1
Moses and **E** the priest said to Nm 26:3
Nadab, Abihu, **E**, and Ithamar Nm 26:60
by Moses and **E** the priest when Nm 26:63
before Moses, **E** the priest, Nm 27:2
him stand before **E** the priest Nm 27:19
stand before **E** who will consult Nm 27:21
him stand before **E** the priest Nm 27:22
Phinehas son of **E** the priest, Nm 31:6
of war to Moses, **E** the priest, Nm 31:12
Moses, **E** the priest, and all the Nm 31:13
Then **E** the priest said to the Nm 31:21
You, **E** the priest, and the Nm 31:26
and give ⌊it⌋ to **E** the priest as Nm 31:29
So Moses and **E** the priest did as Nm 31:31
the tribute to **E** the priest as Nm 31:41
Moses and **E** the priest received Nm 31:51
Moses and **E** the priest received Nm 31:54
came to Moses, **E** the priest, Nm 32:2
about them to **E** the priest, Nm 32:28
E the priest and Joshua son of Nm 34:17
and **E** his son became priest in Dt 10:6
portions that **E** the priest, Jos 14:1
They came before **E** the priest, Jos 17:4
the portions that **E** the priest, Jos 19:51
approached **E** the priest, Jos 21:1
Phinehas son of **E** the priest to Jos 22:13
Phinehas son of **E** the priest Jos 22:31
Phinehas son of **E** the priest Jos 22:32
E son of Aaron died, and they Jos 24:33
Phinehas son of **E**, son of Aaron, Jdg 20:28
his son **E** to take care of it 1Sm 7:1
E son of Dodo son of Ahohi was 2Sm 23:9
but **E** stood ⌊his ground⌋ and 2Sm 23:10
Nadab, Abihu, **E**, and Ithamar. 1Ch 6:3
E fathered Phinehas; 1Ch 6:4
his son **E**, his son Phinehas, his 1Ch 6:50
Phinehas son of **E** had been their 1Ch 9:20
E son of Dodo the Ahohite was 1Ch 11:12
But **E** and David took their stand 1Ch 11:14
Mushi. Mahli's sons: **E** and Kish. 1Ch 23:21
E died having no sons, only 1Ch 23:22
Nadab, Abihu, **E**, and Ithamar. 1Ch 24:1
so **E** and Ithamar served as 1Ch 24:2
from the sons of **E** and Ahimelech 1Ch 24:3
ancestral house was taken for **E**, 1Ch 24:6
From Mahli: **E**, who had no sons. 1Ch 24:28
E son of Phinehas was with him. Ezr 8:33
Mijamin, **E**, Malchijah, Ezr 10:25
Shemaiah, **E**, Uzzi, Jehohanan, Neh 12:42
Eliud fathered **E**, Eleazar Mt 1:15
Eleazar, **E** fathered Matthan Mt 1:15

ELEAZAR'S *(4)*
found among **E** descendants than 1Ch 24:4
houses were from **E** descendants, 1Ch 24:4
God among both **E** and Ithamar's 1Ch 24:5
Phinehas's son, **E** son, Aaron the Ezr 7:5

ELECT *(15)*
be limited because of the **e**. Mt 24:22
astray, if possible, even the **e**. Mt 24:24
will gather His **e** from the four Mt 24:31
those days because of the **e**, Mk 13:20

lead astray, if possible, the **e**. Mk 13:22
and gather His **e** from the four Mk 13:27
justice to His **e** who cry out to Lk 18:7
an accusation against God's **e**? Rm 8:33
for, but the **e** did find it. Rm 11:7
Christ Jesus and the **e** angels, 1Tm 5:21
I endure all things for the **e**: 2Tm 2:10
faith of God's **e** and the Ti 1:1
To the **e** lady and her children, 2Jn 1
of your **e** sister send you 2Jn 13
are called and **e** and faithful." Rv 17:14

ELECTION *(4)*
according to **e** might stand, Rm 9:11
but regarding **e**, they are loved Rm 11:28
knowing your **e**, brothers loved 1Th 1:4
to confirm your calling and **e**, 2Pt 1:10

ELEMENTAL *(4)*
slavery under the **e** forces of Gl 4:3
the weak and bankrupt **e** forces? Gl 4:9
based on the **e** forces of the Col 2:8
Christ to the **e** forces of this Col 2:20

ELEMENTARY *(1)*
leaving the **e** message about the Heb 6:1

ELEMENTS *(2)*
e will burn and be dissolved, 2Pt 3:10
and the **e** will melt with the 2Pt 3:12

ELEVATE *(1)*
though you **e** your nest like the Jr 49:16

ELEVATED *(5)*
since he was **e** above everyone. Neh 8:5
yourself an **e** place in every Ezk 16:24
You built your **e** place at the Ezk 16:25
and making your **e** place in every Ezk 16:31
and tear down your **e** places. Ezk 16:39

ELEVEN *(4)*
appeared to the **E** themselves as Mk 16:14
things to the **E** and to all the Lk 24:9
They found the **E** and those with Lk 24:33
But Peter stood up with the **E**, Ac 2:14

ELEVEN-DAY *(1)*
It is an **e** journey from Horeb to Dt 1:2

ELEVENTH *(18)*
On the **e** day Pagiel son of Nm 7:72
year, in the **e** month, on the Dt 1:3
In ⌊his⌋ **e** year in the eighth 1Kg 6:38
was in the **e** year of Joram son 2Kg 9:29
until King Zedekiah's **e** year. 2Kg 25:2
tenth, and Machbannai **e**. 1Ch 12:13
the **e** to Eliashib, the twelfth 1Ch 24:12
the **e** ⌊to⌋ Azarel, his sons, and 1Ch 25:18
The **e**, for the eleventh month, 1Ch 27:14
eleventh, for the **e** month, was 1Ch 27:14
month of the **e** year of Zedekiah Jr 1:3
month of Zedekiah's **e** year, Jr 39:2
until King Zedekiah's **e** year. Jr 52:5
the **e** year, on the first ⌊day⌋ Ezk 26:1
In the **e** year, in the first Ezk 30:20
In the **e** year, in the third Ezk 31:1
twenty-fourth day of the **e** month, Zch 1:7
chrysoprase, the **e** jacinth, the Rv 21:20

ELHANAN *(4)*
and **E** son of Jaare-oregim the 2Sm 21:19
E son of Dodo of Bethlehem, 2Sm 23:24
E son of Dodo of Bethlehem, 1Ch 11:26
and **E** son of Jair killed Lahmi 1Ch 20:5

ELI *(29)*
(See also ELÍ.)
E the priest was sitting on a 1Sm 1:9
presence, **E** watched her lips 1Sm 1:12
not be heard. **E** thought she was 1Sm 1:13
E responded, "Go in peace, and 1Sm 1:17
bull and brought the boy to **E**. 1Sm 1:25
in the presence of **E** the priest. 1Sm 2:11
E would bless Elkanah and his 1Sm 2:20
Now **E** was very old. He heard 1Sm 2:22
God came to **E** and said to him, 1Sm 2:27
One day **E**, whose eyesight was 1Sm 3:2
ran to **E** and said, "Here I am; 1Sm 3:5
"I didn't call," **E** replied. 1Sm 3:5
got up, went to **E**, and said, 1Sm 3:6
got up, went to **E**, and said, 1Sm 3:8
Then **E** understood that the LORD 1Sm 3:8
out against **E** everything I said 1Sm 3:12
was afraid to tell **E** the vision, 1Sm 3:15
but **E** called him and said, 1Sm 3:16
He gave you?" **E** asked. "Don't 1Sm 3:17
E responded, "He is the LORD. 1Sm 3:18
there was **E** sitting on his chair 1Sm 4:13
E heard the outcry and asked, 1Sm 4:14
quickly came and reported to **E**. 1Sm 4:14
At that time **E** was 98 years old, 1Sm 4:15
The man said to **E**, "I'm the one 1Sm 4:16
What happened, my son?" **E** asked 1Sm 4:16
E fell backwards off the chair 1Sm 4:18
E had judged Israel 40 years. 1Sm 4:18
son of **E** the LORD's priest at 1Sm 14:3

ELÍ *(2)*
with a loud voice, "**E**, Elí, lemá Mt 27:46
voice, "Elí, **E**, lemá sabachtháni Mt 27:46

ELI'S *(9)*
Shiloh, where **E** two sons, Hophni 1Sm 1:3
E sons were wicked men; 1Sm 2:12
served the LORD in **E** presence. 1Sm 3:1
I have sworn to **E** family: 1Sm 3:14
The iniquity of **E** family will 1Sm 3:14
E two sons, Hophni and Phinehas, 1Sm 4:4
captured, and **E** two sons, Hophni 1Sm 4:11
E daughter-in-law, the wife of 1Sm 4:19
at Shiloh against **E** family. 1Kg 2:27

ELI-ZAPHAN *(1)*
E son of Parnach, a leader from Nm 34:25

ELIAB *(20)*
(AKA ELIEL, ELIHU)
E son of Helon from Zebulun; Nm 1:9
Zebulunites is **E** son of Helon. Nm 2:7
On the third day **E** son of Helon, Nm 7:24
the offering of **E** son of Helon. Nm 7:29
and **E** son of Helon was over the Nm 10:16
Abiram, sons of **E**, and On son Nm 16:1
the sons of **E**, but they said, Nm 16:12
The son of Pallu was **E**. Nm 26:8
The sons of **E** were Nemuel, Nm 26:9
the sons of **E** the Reubenite, Dt 11:6
arrived, Samuel saw **E** and said, 1Sm 16:6
names were **E**, the firstborn, 1Sm 17:13
oldest brother **E** listened as he 1Sm 17:28
Jesse fathered **E**, his firstborn; 1Ch 2:13
his son **E**, his son Jeroham, and 1Ch 6:27
chief, Obadiah second, **E** third, 1Ch 12:9
Jehiel, Unni, **E**, Benaiah, 1Ch 15:18
Jehiel, Unni, **E**, Maaseiah, and 1Ch 15:20
Mattithiah, **E**, Benaiah, 1Ch 16:5
daughter of Jesse's son **E**. 2Ch 11:18

ELIADA *(4)*
Elishama, **E**, and Eliphelet. 2Sm 5:16
up Rezon son of **E** as an enemy 1Kg 11:23
Elishama, **E**, and Eliphelet— 1Ch 3:8
from Benjamin, **E**, a brave 2Ch 17:17

ELIAHBA *(2)*
E the Shaalbonite, the sons of 2Sm 23:32
Baharumite, **E** the Shaalbonite 1Ch 11:33

ELIAKIM *(15)*
(AKA JEHOIAKIM)
the king, but **E** son of Hilkiah, 2Kg 18:18
Then **E** son of Hilkiah, Shebnah, 2Kg 18:26
Then **E** son of Hilkiah, who was 2Kg 18:37
he sent **E**, who was in charge 2Kg 19:2
Pharaoh Neco made **E** son of 2Kg 23:34
brother **E** king over Judah 2Ch 36:4
E, Maaseiah, Miniamin, Micaiah, Neh 12:41
my servant, **E** son of Hilkiah. Is 22:20
E son of Hilkiah, who was in Is 36:3
Then **E**, Shebna, and Joah said to Is 36:11
Then **E** son of Hilkiah, who was Is 36:22
he sent **E**, who was in charge Is 37:2
Abiud fathered **E**, Eliakim Mt 1:13
Eliakim, **E** fathered Azor, Mt 1:13
son⌋ of Jonam, ⌊son⌋ of **E**, Lk 3:30

ELIAKIM'S *(2)*
and changed **E** name to Jehoiakim 2Kg 23:34
and changed **E** name to Jehoiakim. 2Ch 36:4

ELIAM *(2)*
daughter of **E** and wife of Uriah 2Sm 11:3
E son of Ahithophel the Gilonite, 2Sm 23:34

ELIASAPH *(6)*
E son of Deuel from Gad; Nm 1:14
the Gadites is **E** son of Deuel. Nm 2:14
family was **E** son of Lael. Nm 3:24
On the sixth day **E** son of Deuel, Nm 7:42
the offering of **E** son of Deuel. Nm 7:47
and **E** son of Deuel was over the Nm 10:20

ELIASHIB *(16)*
Hodaviah, **E**, Pelaiah, Akkub, 1Ch 3:24
the eleventh to **E**, the twelfth 1Ch 24:12
chamber of Jehohanan son of **E**, Ezr 10:6
The singers: **E**. The gatekeepers: Ezr 10:24
E, Mattaniah, Jeremoth, Ezr 10:27
Vaniah, Meremoth, **E**, Ezr 10:36
E the high priest and his fellow Neh 3:1
men of Jericho built next to **E**, Neh 3:2
the house of **E** the high priest Neh 3:20
Joiakim fathered **E**, Eliashib Neh 12:10
Eliashib, **E** fathered Joiada, Neh 12:10
In the days of **E**, Joiada, Neh 12:22
the days of Johanan son of **E**. Neh 12:23
E the priest had been put in Neh 13:4
the evil that **E** had done on Neh 13:7
son of **E** the high priest Neh 13:28

ELIASHIB'S *(1)*
the door of **E** house to the end Neh 3:21

ELIATHAH *(2)*
Hananiah, Hanani, **E**, Giddalti, 1Ch 25:4
twentieth to **E**, his sons, and 1Ch 25:27

ELICIT *(1)*
to the dreams you **e** from them, Jr 29:8

ELIDAD *(1)*
E son of Chislon from the tribe Nm 34:21

ELIEHOENAI *(2)*
the sixth, and **E** the seventh. 1Ch 26:3
E son of Zerahiah from Ezr 8:4

ELIEL *(10)*
(AKA ELIAB, ELIHU)
Ishi, **E**, Azriel, Jeremiah, 1Ch 5:24
Jeroham, son of **E**, son of Toah, 1Ch 6:34
Elienai, Zillethai, **E**, 1Ch 8:20
Ishpan, Eber, **E**, 1Ch 8:22
E the Mahavite, Jeribai and 1Ch 11:46
E, Obed, and Jaasiel the 1Ch 11:47
Attai sixth, **E** seventh, 1Ch 12:11
E the leader and 80 of his 1Ch 15:9
Shemaiah, **E**, and Amminadab. 1Ch 15:11
Jozabad, **E**, Ismachiah, Mahath 2Ch 31:13

ELIENAI *(1)*
E, Zillethai, Eliel, 1Ch 8:20

ELIEZER *(14)*
of my house is **E** of Damascus?" Gn 15:2
and the other **E** (because ⌊he had Ex 18:4
Joash, **E**, Elioenai, Omri 1Ch 7:8
Benaiah, and **E**, were to blow 1Ch 15:24
Moses' sons: Gershom and **E**. 1Ch 23:15
E did not have any other sons, 1Ch 23:17
His relative through **E**: 1Ch 26:25
E son of Zichri was the chief 1Ch 27:16
Then **E** son of Dodavahu of 2Ch 20:37
E, Ariel, Shemaiah, Elnathan, Ezr 8:16
E, Jarib, and Gedaliah. Ezr 10:18
), Pethahiah, Judah, and **E**. Ezr 10:23
E, Isshijah, Malchijah, Shemaiah, Ezr 10:31
son⌋ of **E**, ⌊son⌋ of Jorim Lk 3:29

ELIEZER'S *(1)*
E sons were Rehabiah, first; 1Ch 23:17

ELIHOREPH *(1)*
E and Ahijah the sons of Shisha, 1Kg 4:3

ELIHU *(10)*
(AKA ELIAB, ELIEL)
Jeroham, son of **E**, son of Tohu, 1Sm 1:1
Jozabad, **E**, and Zillethai, 1Ch 12:20
brothers **E** and Semachiah were 1Ch 26:7
for Judah, **E**, one of David's 1Ch 27:18
E son of Barachel the Buzite Jb 32:2
Now **E** had waited to speak to Job Jb 32:4
So **E** son of Barachel the Buzite Jb 32:6
Then **E** continued, saying: Jb 34:1
Then **E** continued, saying: Jb 35:1
Then **E** continued, saying: Jb 36:1

ELIJAH *(110)*
Now **E** the Tishbite, from the 1Kg 17:1
E left and lived by the Wadi 1Kg 17:5
So **E** got up and went to 1Kg 17:10
E called to her and said, 1Kg 17:10
Then **E** said to her, "Don't be 1Kg 17:13
do according to the word of **E**. 1Kg 17:15
LORD He had spoken through **E**. 1Kg 17:16
She said to **E**, "Man of God, what 1Kg 17:18
But **E** said to her, "Give me your 1Kg 17:19
Then **E** took the boy, brought him 1Kg 17:23

E said, "Look, your son is alive. 1Kg 17:23
Then the woman said to **E**, 1Kg 17:24
the LORD came to **E** in the third 1Kg 18:1
So **E** went to present himself to 1Kg 18:2
along the road, **E** suddenly met 1Kg 18:7
said, "Is it you, my lord **E**?" 1Kg 18:7
tell your lord, '**E** is here!' " 1Kg 18:8
tell your lord, "**E** is here!" ' 1Kg 18:11
tell your lord, "**E** is here!" ' 1Kg 18:14
Then **E** said, "As the LORD of 1Kg 18:15
Then Ahab went to meet **E**. 1Kg 18:16
When Ahab saw **E**, Ahab said to 1Kg 18:17
Then **E** approached all the people 1Kg 18:21
Then **E** said to the people, 1Kg 18:22
Then **E** said to the prophets of 1Kg 18:25
At noon **E** mocked them. 1Kg 18:27
Then **E** said to all the people, 1Kg 18:30
E took 12 stones—according to 1Kg 18:31
E the prophet approached ⌊the 1Kg 18:36
Then **E** ordered them, "Seize the 1Kg 18:40
and **E** brought them down to the 1Kg 18:40
E said to Ahab, "Go up, eat and 1Kg 18:41
but **E** went up to the summit of 1Kg 18:42
Seven times **E** said, "Go back." 1Kg 18:43
Then **E** said, "Go and tell Ahab, 1Kg 18:44
The power of the LORD was on **E**, 1Kg 18:46
everything that **E** had done and 1Kg 19:1
Jezebel sent a messenger to **E**, 1Kg 19:2
Then **E** became afraid and 1Kg 19:3
What are you doing here, **E**?" 1Kg 19:9
When **E** heard ⌊it⌋, he wrapped 1Kg 19:13
What are you doing here, **E**?" 1Kg 19:13
E left there and found Elisha 1Kg 19:19
E walked by him and threw his 1Kg 19:19
ran to follow **E**, and said, 1Kg 19:20
left, followed **E**, and served him 1Kg 19:21
the LORD came to **E** the Tishbite: 1Kg 21:17
Ahab said to **E**, "So, you have 1Kg 21:20
the LORD came to **E** the Tishbite: 1Kg 21:28
the LORD said to **E** the Tishbite, 2Kg 1:3
certainly die.' " Then **E** left. 2Kg 1:4
He said, "It's **E** the Tishbite." 2Kg 1:8
of 50 with his 50 ⌊men⌋ to **E**. 2Kg 1:9
E responded to the captain of 2Kg 1:10
of 50 with his 50 ⌊men⌋ to **E**. 2Kg 1:11
E responded, "If I am a man of 2Kg 1:12
in front of **E** and begged him, 2Kg 1:13
The angel of the LORD said to **E**, 2Kg 1:15
Then **E** said to King Ahaziah, 2Kg 1:16
of the LORD that **E** had spoken. 2Kg 1:17
the LORD to take **E** up to heaven 2Kg 2:1
E and Elisha were traveling from 2Kg 2:1
E said to Elisha, "Stay here; 2Kg 2:2
E said to him, "Elisha, stay 2Kg 2:4
E said to him, "Stay here; 2Kg 2:6
E took his mantle, rolled it up, 2Kg 2:8
crossed over, **E** said to Elisha, 2Kg 2:9
E replied, "You have asked for 2Kg 2:10
Then **E** went up into heaven in 2Kg 2:11
Then he never saw **E** again. 2Kg 2:12
had fallen off **E** and went back 2Kg 2:13
he took the mantle **E** had dropped 2Kg 2:14
"Where is the LORD God of **E**?" 2Kg 2:14
The spirit of **E** rests on Elisha. 2Kg 2:15
His servant **E** the Tishbite: 2Kg 9:36
promised through His servant **E**." 2Kg 10:10
word of the LORD spoken to **E**. 2Kg 10:17
Jaareshiah, **E**, and Zichri were 1Ch 8:27
to Jehoram from **E** the prophet, 2Ch 21:12
Maaseiah, **E**, Shemaiah, Jehiel, Ezr 10:21
Jehiel, Abdi, Jeremoth, and **E**; Ezr 10:26
going to send you **E** the prophet Mal 4:5
he is the **E** who is to come. Mt 11:14
others, **E**; still others, Mt 16:14
Moses and **E** appeared to them, Mt 17:3
one for Moses, and one for **E**." Mt 17:4
say that **E** must come first? Mt 17:10
E is coming and will restore Mt 17:11
E has already come, and they Mt 17:12
they said, "He's calling for **E**!" Mt 27:47
see if **E** comes to save Him! Mt 27:49
But others said, "He's **E**." Mk 6:15
others, **E**; still others, Mk 8:28
E appeared to them with Moses, Mk 9:4
one for Moses, and one for **E**"— Mk 9:5
say that **E** must come first? Mk 9:11
E does come first and restores Mk 9:12
tell you that **E** really has come Mk 9:13
"Look, He's calling for **E**!" Mk 15:35
Let's see if **E** comes to take Him Mk 15:36
in the spirit and power of **E**, Lk 1:17
E was not sent to any of them Lk 4:26
some that **E** had appeared, and Lk 9:8
others, **E**; still others, Lk 9:19
talking with Him—Moses and **E**. Lk 9:30
and one for **E**"—not knowing Lk 9:33
him. "Are you **E**?" "I am not," he Jn 1:21
Messiah, or **E**, or the Prophet? Jn 1:25
says in the **E** section— Rm 11:2
E was a man with a nature like Jms 5:17

ELIJAH'S *(3)*
So the LORD listened to **E** voice, 1Kg 17:22
used to pour water on **E** hands, 2Kg 3:11
many widows in Israel in **E** days, Lk 4:25

ELIKA *(1)*
the Harodite, **E** the Harodite, 2Sm 23:25

ELIM *(6)*
they came to **E**, where there were Ex 15:27
departed from **E** and came to Ex 16:1
which is between **E** and Sinai, Ex 16:1
from Marah and came to **E**. Nm 33:9
of water and 70 date palms at **E**, Nm 33:9
They departed from **E** and camped Nm 33:10

ELIMELECH *(4)*
man's name was **E**, and his wife's Ru 1:2
Naomi's husband **E** died, and she Ru 1:3
that belonged to our brother **E**. Ru 4:3
everything that belonged to **E**, Ru 4:9

ELIMELECH'S *(2)*
noble character from **E** family. Ru 2:1
to Boaz, who was from **E** family. Ru 2:3

ELIMINATE *(13)*
to **e** them from the camp until Dt 2:15
and they will not **e** my son!" 2Sm 14:11
who would **e** both me and my 2Sm 14:16
will **e** all of Jeroboam's males, 1Kg 14:10
will **e** the house of Jeroboam. 1Kg 14:14
I will **e** all of Ahab's males, 1Kg 21:21
I will **e** all of Ahab's males, 2Kg 9:8
I am about to **e** from this place, Jr 16:9
I will **e** the sound of joy and Jr 25:10
from the peoples and **e** you from Ezk 25:7
them and **e** dangerous animals Ezk 34:25
will I not **e** the wise ones of Ob 8
will **e** the carved idol and cast Nah 1:14

ELIMINATED *(5)*
Jehu **e** Baal ⌊worship⌋ from 2Kg 10:28
But transgressors will all be **e**; Ps 37:38
be cut off or **e** from My presence Is 48:19
into the stomach and is **e**? Mt 15:17
but into the stomach and is **e**." Mk 7:19

ELIMINATING *(1)*
e all evildoers from the LORD's Ps 101:8

ELIOENAI *(6)*
E, Hizkiah, and Azrikam—three. 1Ch 3:23
E, Jaakobah, Jeshohaiah, Asaiah, 1Ch 4:36
Eliezer, **E**, Omri, Jeremoth 1Ch 7:8
E, Maaseiah, Ishmael, Nethanel, Ezr 10:22
E, Eliashib, Mattaniah, Jeremoth, Ezr 10:27
Miniamin, Micaiah, **E**, Zechariah, Neh 12:41

ELIOENAI'S *(1)*
E sons: Hodaviah, Eliashib, 1Ch 3:24

ELIPHAL *(1)*
(AKA ELIPHELET)
the Hararite, **E** son of Ur, 1Ch 11:35

ELIPHAZ *(14)*
Adah bore **E** to Esau, Basemath Gn 36:4
E son of Esau's wife Adah, Gn 36:10
The sons of **E** were Teman, Omar, Gn 36:11
a concubine of Esau's son **E**, Gn 36:12
son Eliphaz, bore Amalek to **E**. Gn 36:12
the sons of **E**, Esau's firstborn: Gn 36:15
are the chiefs of **E** in the land Gn 36:16
E, Reuel, Jeush, Jalam, and 1Ch 1:35
three friends—**E** the Temanite, Jb 2:11
Then **E** the Temanite replied: Jb 4:1
Then **E** the Temanite replied: Jb 15:1
Then **E** the Temanite replied: Jb 22:1
He said to **E** the Temanite: Jb 42:7
Then **E** the Temanite, Bildad the Jb 42:9

ELIPHAZ'S *(1)*
E sons: Teman, Omar, Zephi, 1Ch 1:36

ELIPHELEHU *(2)*
Mattithiah, **E**, Mikneiah, 1Ch 15:18
and Mattithiah, **E**, Mikneiah, 1Ch 15:21

ELIPHELET *(8)*
(AKA ELIPHAL)
Elishama, Eliada, and **E**. 2Sm 5:16
E son of Ahasbai son of the 2Sm 23:34
Ibhar, Elishua, **E**, 1Ch 3:6
Eliada, and **E**—nine sons. 1Ch 3:8
Jeush second, and **E** third. 1Ch 8:39
Elishama, Beeliada, and **E**. 1Ch 14:7
E, Jeuel, and Shemaiah, and 60 Ezr 8:13
Mattattah, Zabad, **E**, Jeremai, Ezr 10:33

ELISHA *(92)*
over Israel and **E** son of Shaphat 1Kg 19:16
and **E** will put to death whoever 1Kg 19:17
there and found **E** son of Shaphat 1Kg 19:19
E left the oxen, ran to follow 1Kg 19:20
Elijah and **E** were traveling from 2Kg 2:1
Elijah said to **E**, "Stay here; 2Kg 2:2
But **E** replied, "As the LORD 2Kg 2:2
Bethel came out to **E** and said, 2Kg 2:3
said to him, "**E**, stay here; 2Kg 2:4
But **E** said, "As the LORD lives 2Kg 2:4
Jericho came up to **E** and said, 2Kg 2:5
But **E** said, "As the LORD lives 2Kg 2:6
Elijah said to **E**, "Tell ⌊me⌋ 2Kg 2:9
So **E** answered, "Please, let 2Kg 2:9
E watched, he kept crying out, 2Kg 2:12
E picked up the mantle that had 2Kg 2:13
the left, and **E** crossed over. 2Kg 2:14
spirit of Elijah rests on **E**." 2Kg 2:15
sons of the prophets said to **E**, 2Kg 2:16
the men of the city said to **E**, 2Kg 2:19
E went out to the spring of 2Kg 2:21
to the word that **E** spoke. 2Kg 2:22
From there **E** went up to Bethel. 2Kg 2:23
From there **E** went to Mount 2Kg 2:25
answered, "**E** son of Shaphat, 2Kg 3:11
E said to King ⌊Joram⌋ of Israel, 2Kg 3:13
E responded, "As the LORD of 2Kg 3:14
the LORD's hand came on **E**. 2Kg 3:15
of the prophets cried out to **E**, 2Kg 4:1
E asked her, "What can I do for 2Kg 4:2
One day **E** went to Shunem. 2Kg 4:8
"Call her," **E** said. So Gehazi 2Kg 4:15
E said, "At this time next year 2Kg 4:16
year, as **E** had promised her. 2Kg 4:17
So **E** said to Gehazi, "Tuck your 2Kg 4:29
The boy's mother said ⌊to **E**⌋, 2Kg 4:30
back to meet **E** and told him, 2Kg 4:31
When **E** got to the house, he 2Kg 4:32
E got up, went into the house, 2Kg 4:35
E called Gehazi and said, 2Kg 4:36
Then **E** said, "Pick up your son." 2Kg 4:36
When **E** returned to Gilgal, 2Kg 4:38
Then **E** said, "Get some meal." 2Kg 4:41
E said, "Give it to the people 2Kg 4:42
people to eat," **E** said, "for 2Kg 4:43
When **E** the man of God heard that 2Kg 5:8
Then **E** sent him a messenger, 2Kg 5:10
But **E** said, "As the LORD lives, 2Kg 5:16
a short distance from **E**, 2Kg 5:19
attendant of **E** the man of God, 2Kg 5:20
go, Gehazi?" **E** asked him. "Your 2Kg 5:25
But **E** questioned him, "Wasn't my 2Kg 5:26
sons of the prophets said to **E**, 2Kg 6:1
E, the prophet in Israel, tells 2Kg 6:12
he was told, "**E** is in Dothan," 2Kg 6:13
So he asked **E**, "Oh, my master, 2Kg 6:15
E said, "Don't be afraid, for 2Kg 6:16
E prayed, "LORD, please open 2Kg 6:17
chariots of fire all around **E**. 2Kg 6:17
came against him, **E** prayed to 2Kg 6:18
Then **E** said to them, "This is 2Kg 6:19
entered Samaria, **E** said, "LORD, 2Kg 6:20
them, he said to **E**, "My father, 2Kg 6:21
E replied, "Don't kill them. 2Kg 6:22
if the head of **E** son of Shaphat 2Kg 6:31
E was sitting in his house, 2Kg 6:32
to him, **E** said to the elders, 2Kg 6:32
While **E** was still speaking with 2Kg 6:33
E said, "Hear the word of the 2Kg 7:1
E announced, "You will in fact 2Kg 7:2
E had said, "You will in fact 2Kg 7:19
E said to the woman whose son he 2Kg 8:1
the great things **E** has done." 2Kg 8:4
the king how **E** restored the dead 2Kg 8:5

is the son E restored to life. 2Kg 8:5
E came to Damascus while 2Kg 8:7
went to meet E, taking with him 2Kg 8:9
E told him, "Go say to him, 'You 2Kg 8:10
Then E stared steadily at him 2Kg 8:11
E answered, "The LORD has shown 2Kg 8:13
Hazael left E and went to his 2Kg 8:14
him, "What did E say to you?" 2Kg 8:14
The prophet E called one of the 2Kg 9:1
When E became sick with the 2Kg 13:14
E responded, "Take a bow and 2Kg 13:15
Then E said to the king of 2Kg 13:16
E put his hands on the king's 2Kg 13:16
E said, "Open the east window." 2Kg 13:17
he opened it. E said, "Shoot!" 2Kg 13:17
Then E said, "The LORD's arrow 2Kg 13:17
Then E said, "Take the arrows!" 2Kg 13:18
Then E died and was buried. 2Kg 13:20

ELISHA'S *(6)*
But E attendant asked, "What? 2Kg 4:43
stood at the door of E house. 2Kg 5:9
blindness, according to E word. 2Kg 6:18
they threw the man into E tomb. 2Kg 13:21
When he touched E bones, the 2Kg 13:21
And in the prophet E time, Lk 4:27

ELISHAH *(3)*
E, Tarshish, Kittim, and Dodanim. Gn 10:4
E, Tarshish, Kittim, and Rodanim. 1Ch 1:7
fabric from the coasts of E. Ezk 27:7

ELISHAMA *(16)*
(AKA ELISHUA)
E son of Ammihud from Ephraim, Nm 1:10
Ephraimites is E son of Ammihud. Nm 2:18
seventh day E son of Ammihud, Nm 7:48
offering of E son of Ammihud. Nm 7:53
and E son of Ammihud was over Nm 10:22
E, Eliada, and Eliphelet. 2Sm 5:16
Nethaniah, son of E, of the 2Kg 25:25
and Jekamiah fathered E. 1Ch 2:41
E, Eliada, and Eliphelet—nine 1Ch 3:8
his son Ammihud, his son E, 1Ch 7:26
E, Beeliada, and Eliphelet. 1Ch 14:7
the priests, E and Jehoram, were 2Ch 17:8
sitting there—E the scribe, Jr 36:12
in the chamber of E the scribe, Jr 36:20
the chamber of E the scribe. Jr 36:21
Nethaniah, son of E, of the Jr 41:1

ELISHAPHAT *(1)*
of Adaiah, and E son of Zichri. 2Ch 23:1

ELISHEBA *(1)*
Aaron married E, daughter of Ex 6:23

ELISHUA *(3)*
(AKA ELISHAMA)
Ibhar, E, Nepheg, Japhia, 2Sm 5:15
Ibhar, E, Eliphelet, 1Ch 3:6
Ibhar, E, Elpelet, 1Ch 14:5

ELITE *(4)*
the e of his officers were Ex 15:4
of all the e troops of Israel 2Sm 10:9
of all the e troops of Israel 1Ch 19:10
of them were the e of Assyria. Ezk 23:7

ELIUD *(2)*
Achim, Achim fathered E, Mt 1:14
E fathered Eleazar, Eleazar Mt 1:15

ELIZABETH *(9)*
of Aaron, and her name was E. Lk 1:5
children because E could not Lk 1:7
Your wife E will bear you a son, Lk 1:13
days his wife E conceived and Lk 1:24
And consider your relative E— Lk 1:36
Zechariah's house and greeted E. Lk 1:40
When E heard Mary's greeting, Lk 1:41
and E was filled with the Holy Lk 1:41
had come for E to give birth, Lk 1:57

ELIZAPHAN *(1)*
clans was E son of Uzziel. Nm 3:30

ELIZAPHANITES *(2)*
from the E, Shemaiah the leader 1Ch 15:8
Shimri and Jeuel from the E; 2Ch 29:13

ELIZUR *(5)*
E son of Shedeur from Reuben; Nm 1:5
Reubenites is E son of Shedeur. Nm 2:10
the fourth day E son of Shedeur, Nm 7:30
offering of E son of Shedeur. Nm 7:35
and E son of Shedeur was over Nm 10:18

ELKANAH *(20)*
Assir, E, and Abiasaph. Ex 6:24
His name was E son of Jeroham, 1Sm 1:1
Whenever E offered a sacrifice, 1Sm 1:4
her husband E asked. 1Sm 1:8
next morning E and Hannah got 1Sm 1:19
E was intimate with his wife 1Sm 1:19
E and all his household went 1Sm 1:21
Her husband E replied, "Do what 1Sm 1:23
E went home to Ramah, but the 1Sm 2:11
Eli would bless E and his wife: 1Sm 2:20
his son E, his son Ebiasaph, his 1Ch 6:23
his son E, his son Zophai, his 1Ch 6:26
his son Jeroham, and his son E. 1Ch 6:27
son of E, son of Jeroham, son of 1Ch 6:34
Zuph, son of E, son of Mahath, 1Ch 6:35
son of E, son of Joel, son of 1Ch 6:36
son of E who lived in the 1Ch 9:16
E, Isshiah, Azarel, Joezer, and 1Ch 12:6
Berechiah and E were to be 1Ch 15:23
E who was second to the king. 2Ch 28:7

ELKANAH'S *(1)*
E sons: Amasai and Ahimoth, 1Ch 6:25

ELKOSHITE *(1)*
of the vision of Nahum the E. Nah 1:1

ELLASAR *(2)*
Arioch king of E, Chedorlaomer Gn 14:1
Arioch king of E—four kings Gn 14:9

ELMADAM *(1)*
Cosam, ⌊son⌋ of E, ⌊son⌋ of Er, Lk 3:28

ELMS *(1)*
in the desert, e and box trees Is 41:19

ELNAAM *(1)*
the sons of E, Ithmah the 1Ch 11:46

ELNATHAN *(7)*
name was Nehushta daughter of E; 2Kg 24:8
Shemaiah, E, Jarib, Elnathan Ezr 8:16
Elnathan, Jarib, E, Nathan, Ezr 8:16
as the teachers Joiarib and E. Ezr 8:16
E son of Achbor and ⌊certain Jr 26:22
of Shemaiah, E son of Achbor, Jr 36:12
Even though E, Delaiah, and Jr 36:25

ELOI *(2)*
a loud voice, "E, Eloi, lemá Mk 15:34
voice, "Eloi, E, lemá Mk 15:34

ELON *(7)*
daughter of E the Hittite. Gn 26:34
Adah daughter of E the Hittite, Gn 36:2
sons: Sered, E, and Jahleel. Gn 46:14
the Elonite clan from E; Nm 26:26
E, Timnah, Ekron, Jos 19:43
E, who was from Zebulun, judged Jdg 12:11
After E, Abdon son of Hillel, Jdg 12:13

ELON-BETH-HANAN *(1)*
Shaalbim, Beth-shemesh, and E; 1Kg 4:9

ELONGATED *(1)*
that has an e or stunted limb, Lv 22:23

ELONITE *(1)*
the E clan from Elon; Nm 26:26

ELOQUENT *(3)*
I have never been e—either in Ex 4:10
man, a warrior, e, handsome, and 1Sm 16:18
an e man who was powerful in the Ac 18:24

ELOTH *(3)*
which is near E on the shore of 1Kg 9:26
and to E on the seashore 2Ch 8:17
He rebuilt E and restored it to 2Ch 26:2

ELPAAL *(1)*
sons by Hushim: Abitub and E. 1Ch 8:11

ELPAAL'S *(2)*
E sons: Eber, Misham, and Shemed 1Ch 8:12
Izliah, and Jobab were E sons. 1Ch 8:18

ELPELET *(1)*
Ibhar, Elishua, E, 1Ch 14:5

ELSE *(75)*
Do you have anyone e here: Gn 19:12
or anyone e in the city who Gn 19:12
Please, Lord, send someone e." Ex 4:13
e He may strike us with plague Ex 5:3
anything ⌊e⌋ lost, and someone Ex 22:9
or e they will make you sin Ex 23:33
or e when they prostitute Ex 34:15
make anything e as an offering Ex 36:6
or anything e about which he Lv 6:5
garments, or e you will die, Lv 10:6
of meeting, or e you will die; Lv 10:9
on the ark or e he will die, Lv 16:2
the testimony, or e he will die. Lv 16:13
to whatever e he can afford; Nm 6:21
you or someone e is among you Nm 15:14
before Me, or e they will die." Nm 17:10
find out what e the LORD has to Nm 22:19
or e you will be ensnared by it, Dt 7:25
and everything e you have Dt 8:13
Then everyone e will hear and be Dt 19:20
and whatever e is in the city— Dt 20:14
of anything ⌊e⌋ during the siege Dt 28:57
over to you, or e Israel might Jdg 7:2
But everyone e is to go home." Jdg 7:7
a head taller than anyone e. 1Sm 9:2
a head taller than anyone e. 1Sm 10:23
and the best of everything e. 1Sm 15:9
or e he will be grieved.'" 1Sm 20:3
or anything e before sunset!" 2Sm 3:35
leave there ⌊and go⌋ anywhere e. 1Kg 2:36
day you leave and go anywhere e, 1Kg 2:42
No one e was with us in the 1Kg 3:18
or anywhere e in the land of his 1Kg 9:19
with everything e that had been 1Ch 26:28
or anywhere e in the land of his 2Ch 8:6
pay for anything e you have to Ezr 7:20
No one e on earth is like him, Jb 1:8
No one e on earth is like him, Jb 2:3
Who ⌊e⌋ will be my sponsor? Jb 17:3
shrivel up like everything e. Jb 24:24
let someone e eat what I have Jb 31:8
or e it will not come near you. Ps 32:9
than a thousand ⌊anywhere e⌋. Ps 84:10
Your promise above everything e. Ps 138:2
And whatever e you get, get Pr 4:7
Guard your heart above all e, Pr 4:23
I, and no one e, will never be a Is 47:8
to yourself: I, and no one e. Is 47:10
Why e has he become a prey? Jr 2:14
for what e can I do because of Jr 9:7
than anything e and desperately Jr 17:9
give your rewards to someone e; Dn 5:17
or should we expect someone e?" Mt 11:3
there is no one e except Him. Mk 12:32
added this to everything e— Lk 3:20
should we look for someone e?" Lk 7:19
should we look for someone e?'" Lk 7:20
with what belongs to someone e, Lk 16:12
and looked down on everyone e: Lk 18:9
someone e saw him and said, Lk 22:58
If someone e comes in his own Jn 5:43
them that no one e has done, Jn 15:24
hands and someone e will tie you Jn 21:18
and Let someone e take his Ac 1:20
There is salvation in no one e, Ac 4:12
time on nothing e but telling Ac 17:21
But if you want something e, Ac 19:39
saying nothing e than what the Ac 26:22
Someone e considers every day to Rm 14:5
know if I baptized anyone e. 1Co 1:16
and not in respect to someone e. Gl 6:4
and to everyone e, that my Php 1:13
I have no one e like-minded who Php 2:20
anyone e thinks he has grounds Php 3:4
and for whatever e is contrary 1Tm 1:10

ELSE'S *(5)*
go and graze in someone e field, Ex 22:5
are different from everyone e, Est 3:8
neighing after someone e wife. Jr 5:8
on someone e foundation, Rm 15:20
done in someone e area ⌊of 2Co 10:16

ELSEWHERE *(3)*
not, tell me, and I will go e." Gn 24:49
whether born at home or born e. Lv 18:9
in Samaria and e in the region Ezr 4:17

ELTEKE *(1)*
E with its pasturelands, Jos 21:23

ELTEKEH *(1)*
E, Gibbethon, Baalath, Jos 19:44

ELTEKON *(1)*
Beth-anoth, and E—six cities, Jos 15:59

ELTOLAD *(2)*
(AKA TOLAD)
E, Chesil, Hormah, Jos 15:30
E, Bethul, Hormah, Jos 19:4

ELUDE *(1)*
find fortified cities and **e** us." 2Sm 20:6

ELUDED *(2)*
the wall, David **e** Saul and 1Sm 19:10
seize Him, yet He **e** their grasp. Jn 10:39

ELUL *(1)*
twenty-fifth day of the month **E**. Neh 6:15

ELUZAI *(1)*
E, Jerimoth, Bealiah, Shemariah, 1Ch 12:5

ELYMAS *(1)*
(AKA BAR-JESUS)
E, the sorcerer, which is how Ac 13:8

ELZABAD *(2)*
Johanan eighth, **E** ninth, 1Ch 12:12
Othni, Rephael, Obed, and **E**; 1Ch 26:7

ELZAPHAN *(2)*
Mishael, **E**, and Sithri. Ex 6:22
Moses summoned Mishael and **E**, Lv 10:4

EMACIATED *(3)*
E from poverty and hunger, Jb 30:3
from fasting, and my body is **e**. Ps 109:24
his healthy body will become **e**. Is 17:4

EMACIATING *(1)*
Hosts will inflict an **e** disease Is 10:16

EMBALM *(1)*
were physicians to **e** his father. Gn 50:2

EMBALMED *(2)*
his father. So they **e** Israel. Gn 50:2
They **e** him and placed him in a Gn 50:26

EMBALMING *(1)*
this, for **e** takes that long, Gn 50:3

EMBANKMENT *(1)*
will build an **e** against you, Lk 19:43

EMBARRASS *(1)*
of God and **e** those who have 1Co 11:22

EMBARRASSED *(5)*
am ashamed and **e** to lift my face Ezr 9:6
and you will be **e** because of the Is 1:29
who were **e** by your indecent Ezk 16:27
about you, I have not been **e**; 2Co 7:14
would be **e** in that situation. 2Co 9:4

EMBARRASSMENT *(1)*
urged him to the point of **e**, 2Kg 2:17

EMBEDDED *(2)*
are like firmly **e** nails. Ec 12:11
on these stones that I have **e**, Jr 43:10

EMBER *(1)*
my one remaining **e** by not 2Sm 14:7

EMBERS *(1)*
As charcoal for **e** and wood for Pr 26:21

EMBITTERED *(2)*
When I became **e** and my innermost Ps 73:21
for they **e** his spirit, and he Ps 106:33

EMBLEMS *(1)*
They set up their **e** as signs. Ps 74:4

EMBOLDENED *(1)*
were **e** by our God to speak the 1Th 2:2

EMBRACE *(7)*
or the wife you **e**, or your Dt 13:6
righteousness and peace will **e**. Ps 85:10
tree of life to those who **e** her, Pr 3:18
you **e** her, she will honor you. Pr 4:8
forbidden woman or **e** the breast Pr 5:20
Can a man **e** fire and his clothes Pr 6:27
a time to **e** and a time to avoid Ec 3:5

EMBRACED *(2)*
him, and he kissed and **e** them. Gn 48:10
himself on him, **e** him, and said, Ac 20:10

EMBRACES *(4)*
the wife he **e**, and the rest of Dt 28:54
will begrudge the husband she **e**, Dt 28:56
head, and his right hand **e** me. Sg 2:6
head, and his right hand **e** me. Sg 8:3

EMBRACING *(2)*
embrace and a time to avoid **e**; Ec 3:5
And **e** Paul, they kissed him, Ac 20:37

EMBROIDERED *(18)*
to make a screen **e** with blue, Ex 26:36
thirty-foot screen **e** with blue, Ex 27:16
finely spun linen **e** with gold, Ex 28:6
are to make an **e** breastpiece for Ex 28:15
fine linen, and make an **e** sash. Ex 28:39
He made a screen **e** with blue, Ex 36:37
the courtyard was **e** with blue, Ex 38:18
also made the **e** breastpiece with Ex 39:8
of finely spun linen of **e** blue, Ex 39:29
the spoil of an **e** garment or two Jdg 5:30
her clothing **e** with gold. Ps 45:13
I clothed you in **e** cloth and Ezk 16:10
fine linen, silk, and **e** cloth. Ezk 16:13
you took your **e** garments to Ezk 16:18
and strip off their **e** garments. Ezk 26:16
made of⌋ fine **e** linen from Egypt Ezk 27:7
purple and **e** cloth, fine linen, Ezk 27:16
cloaks of blue and **e** materials, Ezk 27:24

EMBROIDERER *(2)*
e in blue, purple, and scarlet Ex 35:35
designer, and an **e** with blue, Ex 38:23

EMEK-KEZIZ *(1)*
Jericho, Beth-hoglah, **E**, Jos 18:21

EMERALD *(5)*
row of carnelian, topaz, and **e**; Ex 28:17
row of carnelian, topaz, and **e**; Ex 39:10
sapphire, turquoise and **e**. Ezk 28:13
that looked like an **e** surrounded Rv 4:3
third chalcedony, the fourth **e**, Rv 21:19

EMERGE *(1)*
me, I will **e** as pure gold. Jb 23:10

EMERGED *(1)*
them a little horn **e** and grew Dn 8:9

EMERGES *(1)*
ineffective and justice never **e**. Hab 1:4

EMIM *(3)*
the **E** in Shaveh-kiriathaim, Gn 14:5
The **E**, a great and numerous Dt 2:10
the Moabites called them **E**. Dt 2:11

EMINENT *(1)*
and none of the **e** among them. Ezk 7:11

EMISSARIES *(6)*
David sent his **e** to console 2Sm 10:2
David sent his **e** in order to 2Sm 10:3
took David's **e**, shaved off half 2Sm 10:4
when David's **e** arrived in the 1Ch 19:2
David sent his **e** in order to 1Ch 19:3
took David's **e**, shaved them, cut 1Ch 19:4

EMISSION *(7)*
When a man has an **e** of semen, Lv 15:16
there is an **e** of semen must be Lv 15:17
a woman and has an **e** of semen, Lv 15:18
a man who has an **e** of semen, Lv 15:32
by a man who has an **e** of semen, Lv 22:4
of a bodily **e** during the night, Dt 23:10
donkeys and whose **e** was like Ezk 23:20

EMMAUS *(1)*
their way to a village called **E**, Lk 24:13

EMOTION *(1)*
overcome with **e** for his brother Gn 43:30

EMOTIONS *(1)*
thoughts and **e** is a righteous Ps 7:9

EMPEROR *(5)*
to be held for trial by the **E**, Ac 25:21
he himself appealed to the **E**, Ac 25:25
to write to the **E** about him. Ac 25:26
whether to the **E** as the supreme 1Pt 2:13
Fear God. Honor the **E**. 1Pt 2:17

EMPIRE *(2)*
that the whole **e** should be Lk 2:1
that has an **e** over the kings Rv 17:18

EMPLOYED *(2)*
capable men **e** in the ministry 1Ch 9:13
court official **e** in the king's Jr 38:7

EMPOWER *(1)*
I will **e** my two witnesses, Rv 11:3

EMPOWERED *(3)*
until you are **e** from on high." Lk 24:49
its horseman was **e** to take peace Rv 6:4
angels who were **e** to harm the Rv 7:2

EMPTIED *(7)*
She quickly **e** her jug into the Gn 24:20
servants have **e** out the money 2Kg 22:9
deputy came and **e** the chest, 2Ch 24:11
They have **e** out the money that 2Ch 34:17
so that it is **e** of everything in Ezk 32:15
will not be **e** ⌊of its effect⌋. 1Co 1:17
Instead He **e** Himself by assuming Php 2:7

EMPTINESS *(3)*
leaving great **e** in the land. Is 6:12
by Him as nothingness and **e**. Is 40:17
their images are wind and **e**. Is 41:29

EMPTY *(46)*
the earth was formless and **e**, Gn 1:2
pit. The pit was **e**; there was no Gn 37:24
one hand and an **e** pitcher with Jdg 7:16
the LORD has brought me back **e**. Ru 1:21
because your seat will be **e**. 1Sm 20:18
Saul, but David's place was **e**. 1Sm 20:25
David's place was ⌊still⌋ **e**, 1Sm 20:27
will not become **e** and the oil 1Kg 17:14
The flour jar did not become **e**, 1Kg 17:16
Go and borrow **e** containers from 2Kg 4:3
answer with **e** counsel or fill Jb 15:2
there ⌊no⌋ end to your **e** words? Jb 16:3
northern ⌊skies⌋ over **e** space; Jb 26:7
why do you keep up this **e** talk? Jb 27:12
does not listen to **e** ⌊cries⌋, Jb 35:13
The wicked man earns an **e** wage, Pr 11:18
the stomach of the wicked is **e**. Pr 13:25
is **e**, but an abundant Pr 14:4
arrogance, and his **e** boasting. Is 16:6
leaves the hungry **e** and deprives Is 32:6
He did not create it to be **e**, Is 45:18
mouth will not return to Me **e**, Is 55:11
They trust in **e** and worthless Is 59:4
and it was formless and **e**. Jr 4:23
their containers return **e**. Jr 14:3
They will **e** his containers and Jr 48:12
It is **e**. His boast is Jr 48:30
It is empty. His boast is **e**. Jr 48:30
has set me aside like an **e** dish; Jr 51:34
you that were **e** and deceptive; Lm 2:14
you that were **e** and misleading. Lm 2:14
not come off! **E** it piece by Ezk 24:6
Set the **e** pot on its coals so Ezk 24:11
Will they therefore **e** their net Hab 1:17
they relate **e** dreams and offer Zch 10:2
dreams and offer **e** comfort. Zch 10:2
things and sent the rich away **e**. Lk 1:53
faith is made **e** and the promise Rm 4:14
in the matter would not prove **e**, 2Co 9:3
deceive you with **e** arguments, Eph 5:6
philosophy and **e** deceit based on Col 2:8
These promote **e** speculations 1Tm 1:4
e speech and contradictions from 1Tm 6:20
irreverent, **e** speech, for this 2Tm 2:16
redeemed from your **e** way of life 1Pt 1:18
bombastic, **e** words, they seduce 2Pt 2:18

EMPTY-HANDED *(13)*
you would have sent me off **e**. Gn 31:42
when you go, you will not go **e**. Ex 3:21
No one is to appear before Me **e**. Ex 23:15
No one is to appear before Me **e**. Ex 34:20
free, do not send him away **e**. Dt 15:13
is to appear before the LORD **e**. Dt 16:16
back to your mother-in-law **e**.' " Ru 3:17
sent widows away **e**, and the Jb 22:9
he fathered a son, he was **e**. Ec 5:14
warrior who does not return **e**. Jr 50:9
beat him, and sent him away **e**. Mk 12:3
beat him and sent him away **e**. Lk 20:10
shamefully, and sent him away **e**. Lk 20:11

EMPTYING *(1)*
As they began **e** their sacks, Gn 42:35

EN-DOR *(2)*
inhabitants of **E** with its towns, Jos 17:11
They were destroyed at **E**; Ps 83:10

EN-EGLAIM *(1)*
beside it from En-gedi to **E**. Ezk 47:10

EN-GANNIM *(3)*
Zanoah, **E**, Tappuah, Enam, Jos 15:34
Remeth, **E**, En-haddah, Jos 19:21
and **E** with its pasturelands— Jos 21:29

EN-GEDI *(6)*
(AKA HAZAZON-TAMAR)
of Salt, and **E**—six cities, Jos 15:62
stayed in the strongholds of **E**. 1Sm 23:29
is in the wilderness near **E**." 1Sm 24:1
in Hazazon-tamar" (that is, **E**). 2Ch 20:2
to me, in the vineyards of **E**. Sg 1:14
beside it from **E** to En-eglaim. Ezk 47:10

EN-HADDAH *(1)*
En-gannim, **E**, Beth-pazzez. Jos 19:21

EN-HAKKORE *(1)*
That is why he named it **E**, Jdg 15:19

EN-HAZOR *(1)*
Kedesh, Edrei, **E**, Jos 19:37

EN-MISHPAT *(1)*
(AKA KADESH)
Then they came back to invade **E** Gn 14:7

EN-RIMMON *(1)*
in **E**, Zorah, Jarmuth, and Neh 11:29

EN-ROGEL *(4)*
of En-shemesh and ended at **E**. Jos 15:7
slope and downward to **E**. Jos 18:16
and Ahimaaz were staying at **E**, 2Sm 17:17
of Zoheleth, which is next to **E**. 1Kg 1:9

EN-SHEMESH *(2)*
to the waters of **E** and ended at Jos 15:7
went to **E** and on to Geliloth, Jos 18:17

EN-TAPPUAH *(1)*
toward the inhabitants of **E**. Jos 17:7

ENABLE *(7)*
for he will **e** Israel to inherit Dt 1:38
the people and **e** them to inherit Dt 3:28
You will **e** them to take Dt 31:7
May the LORD **e** each of you to Ru 1:9
For who can **e** him to see what Ec 3:22
and I will **e** you to speak out Ezk 29:21
the land and will **e** the people Hs 2:18

ENABLED *(7)*
of your yoke and **e** you to live Lv 26:13
with Judah and **e** them to take Jdg 1:19
the LORD **e** her to conceive, Ru 4:13
He **e** me to understand everything 1Ch 28:19
for the LORD **e** them to rejoice 2Ch 20:27
they would have **e** My people to Jr 23:22
e you to share in the saints' Col 1:12

ENABLES *(3)*
and as a garden **e** what is sown Is 61:11
those of a deer and **e** me to walk Hab 3:19
the power that **e** Him to subject Php 3:21

ENABLING *(1)*
⌊**e** you⌋ both to will and to act Php 2:13

ENACT *(1)*
reign and rulers **e** just law; Pr 8:15

ENACTED *(2)*
e in truth and uprightness. Ps 111:8
has been legally **e** on better Heb 8:6

ENACTING *(1)*
Woe to those **e** crooked statutes Is 10:1

ENAIM *(2)*
and sat at the entrance to **E**, Gn 38:14
who was beside the road at **E**?" Gn 38:21

ENAM *(1)*
Zanoah, En-gannim, Tappuah, **E**, Jos 15:34

ENAN *(5)*
Ahira son of **E** from Naphtali. Nm 1:15
Naphtalites is Ahira son of **E**. Nm 2:29
the twelfth day Ahira son of **E**, Nm 7:78
the offering of Ahira son of **E**. Nm 7:83
and Ahira son of **E** was over the Nm 10:27

ENCAMPED *(6)*
and saw Israel **e** tribe by tribe, Nm 24:2
When you are **e** against your Dt 23:9
e against them and destroyed Jdg 6:4
the troops were **e** against 1Kg 16:15
When the **e** troops heard that 1Kg 16:16
army was **e** in the Valley 1Ch 11:15

ENCAMPMENT *(6)*
each man with his **e** and under Nm 1:52
belong to Judah's **e** is 186,400; Nm 2:9
belong to Reuben's **e** is 151,450; Nm 2:16
to Ephraim's **e** number 108,100; Nm 2:24
belong to Dan's **e** is 157,600; Nm 2:31
surrounded the **e** of the saints, Rv 20:9

ENCAMPMENTS *(5)*
names by their villages and **e**: Gn 25:16
they live in **e** or fortifications Nm 13:19
lived, as well as all their **e**, Nm 31:10
so your **e** must be holy. Dt 23:14
set up their **e** and pitch their Ezk 25:4

ENCAMPS *(1)*
of the LORD **e** around those who Ps 34:7

ENCIRCLE *(3)*
strong ones of Bashan **e** me. Ps 22:12
Go around Zion, **e** it; Ps 48:12
e yourselves with firebrands; Is 50:11

ENCIRCLED *(5)*
gourds **e** it below the brim 1Kg 7:24
e by a grating and pomegranates 2Kg 25:17
You have **e** me; You have placed Ps 139:5
e by bronze latticework and Jr 52:22
after being **e** for seven days. Heb 11:30

ENCIRCLES *(2)*
which **e** the entire land of the Gn 2:11
which **e** the entire land of Cush. Gn 2:13

ENCIRCLING *(8)*
e the walls of the temple, 1Kg 6:5
pillars with two **e** rows of 1Kg 7:18
were in rows **e** each capital. 1Kg 7:20
completely **e** the reservoir. 1Kg 7:24
a band nine inches high **e** it; 1Kg 7:35
each had space, with **e** wreaths. 1Kg 7:36
it, completely **e** it, 10 every 2Ch 4:3
e me with bitterness and Lm 3:5

ENCLOSE *(2)*
we will **e** it with cedar planks. Sg 8:9
will **e** her with a wall, so that Hs 2:6

ENCLOSED *(2)*
Who **e** the sea behind doors when Jb 38:8
court there were **e** courts, Ezk 46:22

ENCLOSING *(1)*
like fire **e** it all around. Ezk 1:27

ENCOUNTER *(3)*
They **e** darkness by day, and they Jb 5:14
had made in the **e** with Baasha Jr 41:9
not knowing what I will **e** there, Ac 20:22

ENCOUNTERED *(3)*
that all those who **e** Amasa were 2Sm 20:12
I **e** trouble and sorrow. Ps 116:3
When he **e** them, he said: Jr 41:6

ENCOUNTERS *(4)*
another⌋ man **e** her in the city Dt 22:23
But if the man **e** the engaged Dt 22:25
If a man **e** a young woman, a Dt 22:28
The prophet ⌊**e**⌋ a fowler's snare Hs 9:8

ENCOURAGE *(21)*
E him, for he will enable Israel Dt 1:38
Joshua and **e** and strengthen him, Dt 3:28
city and demolish it.' **E** him." 2Sm 11:25
Go out and **e** your soldiers, 2Sm 19:7
I would **e** you with my mouth, Jb 16:5
They **e** each other in an evil Ps 64:5
how we are and to **e** your hearts. Eph 6:22
so that he may **e** your hearts. Col 4:8
strengthen and **e** you concerning 1Th 3:2
we ask and **e** you in the Lord 1Th 4:1
But we **e** you, brothers, to do so 1Th 4:10
Therefore **e** one another with 1Th 4:18
Therefore **e** one another and 1Th 5:11
e your hearts and strengthen you 2Th 2:17
Teach and **e** these things. 1Tm 6:2
and **e** with great patience and 2Tm 4:2
be able both to **e** with sound Ti 1:9
that they may **e** the young women Ti 2:4
e the young men to be sensible Ti 2:6
and **e** and rebuke with all Ti 2:15
But **e** each other daily, while it Heb 3:13

ENCOURAGED *(21)*
have comforted and **e** your slave, Ru 2:13
Horesh and **e** him in ⌊his faith 1Sm 23:16
everyone with you will be **e**." 2Sm 16:21
Then Hezekiah **e** all the Levites 2Ch 30:22
Then he **e** them, saying, 2Ch 32:6
and **e** them to serve 2Ch 35:2
and they were **e** to ⌊do⌋ this Neh 2:18
because you have **e** the wicked Ezk 13:22
and he **e** all of them to remain Ac 11:23
e the brothers and strengthened Ac 15:32
they saw and **e** the brothers, Ac 16:40
the disciples, **e** them, and after Ac 20:1
They all became **e** and took food Ac 27:36
to be mutually **e** by each other's Rm 1:12
weak conscience be **e** to eat food 1Co 8:10
may learn and everyone may be **e**. 1Co 14:31
restored, be **e**, be of the same 2Co 13:11
I also may be **e** when I hear news Php 2:19
their hearts to be **e** and joined Col 2:2
we **e**, comforted, and implored 1Th 2:12
we were **e** about you through your 1Th 3:7

ENCOURAGEMENT *(12)*
which is translated Son of **E**, Ac 4:36
Lord and in the **e** of the Holy Ac 9:31
any message of **e** for the people, Ac 13:15
they rejoiced because of its **e**. Ac 15:31
and through the **e** of the Rm 15:4
of endurance and **e** grant you Rm 15:5
edification, **e**, and consolation 1Co 14:3
I am filled with **e**; 2Co 7:4
then there is any **e** in Christ, Php 2:1
given us eternal **e** and good hope 2Th 2:16
great joy and **e** from your love, Phm 7
have strong **e** to seize the hope Heb 6:18

ENCOURAGES *(1)*
The craftsman **e** the metalworker; Is 41:7

ENCOURAGING *(3)*
disciples by **e** them to continue Ac 14:22
habitually do, but **e** each other, Heb 10:25
e you and testifying that this 1Pt 5:12

ENCROACH *(1)*
and don't **e** on the fields of the Pr 23:10

ENCRUSTED *(1)*
with maggots and **e** with dirt. Jb 7:5

END *(239)*
to put an **e** to all flesh, Gn 6:13
and by the **e** of 150 days the Gn 8:3
walk from one **e** of the land to Gn 13:17
it is at the **e** of his field. Gn 23:9
the land of Egypt came to an **e**, Gn 41:53
the cities from one **e** of Egypt Gn 47:21
At the **e** of 430 years, on that Ex 12:41
at the **e** of the year, Ex 23:16
cherub at one **e** and one cherub Ex 25:19
and one cherub at the other **e**. Ex 25:19
planks from one **e** to the other. Ex 26:28
the width 75 ⌊feet⌋ at each **e**, Ex 27:18
planks from one **e** to the other. Ex 36:33
cherub at one **e** and one cherub Ex 37:8
and one cherub at the other **e**. Ex 37:8
seat, ⌊a cherubim⌋ at each **e**. Ex 37:8
by the **e** of a full year, Lv 25:30
the **e** of 40 days they returned Nm 13:25
will come to an **e** in the Nm 14:35
you may put an **e** to their Nm 17:10
let the **e** of my ⌊life⌋ be like Nm 23:10
at the east **e** of the Dead Sea. Nm 34:3
and **e** south of Kadesh-barnea. Nm 34:4
where it will **e** at the Nm 34:5
to Ziphron and **e** at Hazar-enan. Nm 34:9
the Jordan and **e** at the Dead Sea Nm 34:12
and from one **e** of the heavens to Dt 4:32
so that in the **e** He might cause Dt 8:16
at the **e** of the 40 days and 40 Dt 9:11
beginning to the **e** of the year. Dt 11:12
from one **e** of the earth to the Dt 13:7
At the **e** of ⌊every⌋ three years, Dt 14:28
At the **e** of ⌊every⌋ seven years Dt 15:1
from one **e** of the earth to Dt 28:64
At the **e** of ⌊every⌋ seven years, Dt 31:10
mourning for Moses came to an **e**. Dt 34:8
at the northern **e** of the Valley Jos 15:8
at the northern **e** of the Valley Jos 18:16
at the southern **e** of the Jordan. Jos 18:19
At the **e** of two months, she Jdg 11:39
to lie down at the **e** of the pile Ru 3:7
his family, from beginning to **e**. 1Sm 3:12
out with the **e** of the staff he 1Sm 14:27
honey with the **e** of the staff I 1Sm 14:43
stomach with the **e** of his spear. 2Sm 2:23
this will only **e** in bitterness? 2Sm 2:26
Jerusalem at the **e** of nine 2Sm 24:8
then, at the **e** of three years, 1Kg 2:39
the **e** of 20 years during which 1Kg 9:10
on the six steps, one at each **e**. 1Kg 10:20
In the **e**, only the buildings of 2Kg 3:25
at the **e** of seven years, 2Kg 8:3
filled from one **e** to the other. 2Kg 10:21
you have put an **e** to them." 2Kg 13:17
until you had put an **e** to them, 2Kg 13:19
it at the **e** of three years. 2Kg 18:10
with it from one **e** to another. 2Kg 21:16
beginning to **e**, note that they 1Ch 29:29
the **e** of 20 years during which 2Ch 8:1
on the six steps, one at each **e**. 2Ch 9:19
from beginning to **e**, are written 2Ch 9:29

from beginning to e, are written 2Ch 12:15
from beginning to e, are written 2Ch 16:11
find them at the e of the valley 2Ch 20:16
beginning to e are written about 2Ch 20:34
from beginning to e, are written 2Ch 25:26
reign⌋, from beginning to e. 2Ch 26:22
beginning to e, they are written 2Ch 28:26
from beginning to e, are written 2Ch 35:27
filled it from e to end with Ezr 9:11
it from end to e with their Ezr 9:11
house to the e of his house. Neh 3:21
At the e of this time, the king Est 1:5
and come to an e by the breath Jb 4:9
are quickly brought to an e. Jb 5:13
they come to an e without hope. Jb 7:6
Is there ⌊no⌋ e to your empty Jb 16:3
miner puts an e to the darkness Jb 28:3
they will e their days in Jb 36:11
evil of the wicked come to an e, Ps 7:9
rises from one e of the heavens Ps 19:6
and circles to their other e; Ps 19:6
reveal to me the e of my life Ps 39:4
They come to an e, swept away by Ps 73:19
His⌋ promise at an e for all Ps 77:8
made their days e in futility, Ps 78:33
You e their life; they sleep. Ps 90:5
we e our years like a sigh. Ps 90:9
and Your years will never e. Ps 102:27
In the e he will look in triumph Ps 112:8
Your statutes to the very e. Ps 119:112
in the e she's as bitter as Pr 5:4
your earnings will e up in a Pr 5:10
At the e of your life, you will Pr 5:11
but its e is the way to death. Pr 14:12
be sad, and joy may e in grief. Pr 14:13
but in the e it is the way of Pr 16:25
In the e it bites like a snake Pr 23:32
has done from beginning to e. Ec 3:11
though there is no e to all his Ec 4:8
that is the e of all mankind, Ec 7:2
The e of a matter is better than Ec 7:8
fears God will e up with both Ec 7:18
the e of his speaking is evil Ec 10:13
there is no e to the making of Ec 12:12
Ahaz at the e of the conduit Is 7:3
and its prosperity will never e. Is 9:7
Judah's harassment will e. Is 11:13
I will put an e to the pride of Is 13:11
I have put an e to the shouting. Is 16:10
put an e to all her groaning. Is 21:2
At the e of 70 years, what the Is 23:15
And at the e of the 70 years, Is 23:17
You make an e of me from day Is 38:12
You make an e of me day and Is 38:13
I declare the e from the Is 46:10
it go out to the e of the earth; Is 48:20
to the e of the earth, Is 62:11
what will you do at the e of it? Jr 5:31
them and bring them to an e. Jr 8:13
cannot see what our e will be." Jr 12:4
from one e of the earth to Jr 12:12
prophets will meet their e. Jr 14:15
so in the e he will be a fool. Jr 17:11
and sorrow, to e my life in Jr 20:18
from one e of the earth to Jr 25:33
At the e of seven years, each of Jr 34:14
at the e of 10 days, the word Jr 42:7
will meet their e. All of them Jr 44:12
will meet their e by famine. Jr 44:12
and famine we have met our e." Jr 44:18
will meet his e by sword or Jr 44:27
treasures, your e has come, your Jr 51:13
been captured from e ⌊to end⌋. Jr 51:31
been captured from end ⌊to e⌋. Jr 51:31
The words of Jeremiah e here. Jr 51:64
She never considered her e. Lm 1:9
perish, for His mercies never e. Lm 3:22
overflow unceasingly, without e, Lm 3:49
streets. Our e drew near; our Lm 4:18
time ran out. Our e had come! Lm 4:18
Now at the e of seven days the Ezk 3:16
of Israel: An e! The end has Ezk 7:2
The e has come on the four Ezk 7:2
The e is now on you; I will send Ezk 7:3
An e has come; the end has come! Ezk 7:6
has come; the e has come! It has Ezk 7:6
I will put an e to the pride of Ezk 7:24
You bring to an e the remnant Ezk 11:13
wilderness to put an e to them. Ezk 20:13
bring them to an e in the Ezk 20:17
So I will put an e to your Ezk 23:27
So I will put an e to indecency Ezk 23:48
I will put an e to the noise of Ezk 26:13
At the e of 40 years I will Ezk 29:13
I will put an e to the hordes of Ezk 30:10
idols and put an e to the false Ezk 30:13
comes to an e in the city. Ezk 30:18
strength will come to an e. Ezk 33:28
search at the e of the seven Ezk 39:14
Put an e to your evictions of My Ezk 45:9
there at the far western e. Ezk 46:19
the northern e, along the road Ezk 48:1
and at the e of that time they Dn 1:5
At the e of 10 days they looked Dn 1:15
At the e of the time that the Dn 1:18
kingdoms and bring them to an e, Dn 2:44
At the e of 12 months, as he was Dn 4:29
But at the e of those days, Dn 4:34
kingdom and brought it to an e. Dn 5:26
and His dominion has no e. Dn 6:26
This is the e of the Dn 7:28
refers to the time of the e." Dn 8:17
to the appointed time of the e. Dn 8:19
Near the e of their kingdoms, Dn 8:23
to bring the rebellion to an e, Dn 9:24
The e will come with a flood, Dn 9:26
and until the e there will be Dn 9:26
will put an e to his taunting; Dn 11:18
for still the e will come at the Dn 11:27
until the time of the e, Dn 11:35
At the time of the e, the king Dn 11:40
will meet his e with no one to Dn 11:45
book until the time of the e. Dn 12:4
How long until the e of these Dn 12:6
sealed until the time of the e. Dn 12:9
you, go on your way to the e; Dn 12:13
destiny at the e of the days." Dn 12:13
Jehu and put an e to the kingdom Hs 1:4
I will put an e to all her Hs 2:11
great houses will come to an e— Am 3:15
sprawl out will come to an e. Am 6:7
The e has come for My people Am 8:2
There is no e to the treasure, Nah 2:9
bodies without e—they stumble Nah 3:3
about the e and will not lie. Hab 2:3
a horrifying e of all the Zph 1:18
of Egypt will come to an e. Zch 10:11
endures to the e will be Mt 10:22
The harvest is the e of the age, Mt 13:39
it will be at the e of the age. Mt 13:40
it will be at the e of the age. Mt 13:49
coming and of the e of the age?" Mt 24:3
place, but the e is not yet. Mt 24:6
endures to the e will be Mt 24:13
And then the e will come. Mt 24:14
from one e of the sky to the Mt 24:31
always, to the e of the age." Mt 28:20
place, but the e is not yet. Mk 13:7
endures to the e will be Mk 13:13
from the e of the earth to the Mk 13:27
the earth to the e of the sky. Mk 13:27
and His kingdom will have no e. Lk 1:33
the e won't come right away." Lk 21:9
will not e in death but is Jn 11:4
world, He loved them to the e. Jn 13:1
the seven days were about to e, Ac 21:27
For the e of those things is Rm 6:21
and the e is eternal life! Rm 6:22
Christ is the e of the law for Rm 10:4
will also confirm you to the e, 1Co 1:8
they will come to an e; 1Co 13:8
knowledge, it will come to an e. 1Co 13:8
the partial will come to an e. 1Co 13:10
Then comes the e, when He hands 1Co 15:24
not look at the e of what was 2Co 3:13
Their e is destruction; their Php 3:19
and Your years will never e. Heb 1:12
until the e the reality that Heb 3:14
and will be burned at the e. Heb 6:8
beginning of days nor e of life, Heb 7:3
time, at the e of the ages, for Heb 9:26
was nearing the e of his life, Heb 11:22
revealed at the e of the times 1Pt 1:20
Now the e of all things is near; 1Pt 4:7
In the e time there will be Jd 18
one who keeps My works to the e: Rv 2:26
Omega, the Beginning and the E. Rv 21:6
Last, the Beginning and the E. Rv 22:13

ENDANGER *(1)*
would e my life with the king. Dn 1:10

ENDANGERED *(1)*
splits trees may be e by them. Ec 10:9

ENDANGERS *(1)*
who provokes him e himself. Pr 20:2

ENDED *(20)*
and so the border e at the Jos 15:4
of En-shemesh and e at En-rogel. Jos 15:7
and e at the Mediterranean Sea. Jos 15:11
and e at the Mediterranean Sea. Jos 16:3
Brook of Kanah and e at the Jos 16:8
of the brook and e at the Jos 17:9
and e at the wilderness of Jos 18:12
southward, and e at Kiriath-baal Jos 18:14
Beth-hoglah and e at the Jos 18:19
to Hannathon and e at the valley Jos 19:14
and e at the Jordan— Jos 19:22
back to Hosah and e at the sea, Jos 19:29
as Lakkum, and e at the Jordan. Jos 19:33
When the time of mourning e, 2Sm 11:27
and the plague on Israel e. 2Sm 24:25
They almost e my life on earth, Ps 119:87
the rain has e and gone away. Sg 2:11
destruction has e, and marauders Is 16:4
summer has e, but we have not Jr 8:20
the days of the siege have e; Ezk 5:2

ENDING *(3)*
the oldest and e with the Gn 44:12
the last and e with the first.' Mt 20:8
raised Him up, e the pains of Ac 2:24

ENDLESS *(6)*
and aren't your iniquities e? Jb 22:5
e talk leads only to poverty. Pr 14:23
wife's nagging is an e dripping. Pr 19:13
An e dripping on a rainy day and Pr 27:15
Egypt were her e source of Nah 3:9
to myths and e genealogies. 1Tm 1:4

ENDLESSLY *(3)*
But the evening drags on e, Jb 7:4
crushed, but is not threshed e. Is 28:28
Will He be e infuriated? Jr 3:5

ENDOR *(1)*
a woman at E who is a medium." 1Sm 28:7

ENDORSING *(1)*
shuts his eyes to avoid e evil— Is 33:15

ENDOWED *(1)*
He has not e her with Jb 39:17

ENDOWS *(1)*
He e your territory with Ps 147:14

ENDS *(57)*
work at the two e of the mercy Ex 25:18
the mercy seat at its two e. Ex 25:19
the other e of the two cords Ex 28:25
work at the two e of the mercy Ex 37:7
the other e of the two cords Ex 39:18
away, from the e of the earth, Dt 28:49
are at the e of the earth, Dt 30:4
with them to the e of the earth. Dt 33:17
will judge the e of the earth. 1Sm 2:10
so long that their e were seen 1Kg 8:8
so long that their e were seen 2Ch 5:9
banished to the e of the earth, Neh 1:9
He looks to the e of the earth Jb 28:24
their life ⌊e⌋ among male cult Jb 36:14
lightning to the e of the earth. Jb 37:3
and the e of the earth Your Ps 2:8
words to the e of the inhabited Ps 19:4
All the e of the earth will Ps 22:27
reaches to the e of the earth; Ps 48:10
will know to the e of the earth Ps 59:13
to You from the e of the earth Ps 61:2
hope of all the e of the earth Ps 65:5
and all the e of the earth will Ps 67:7
Euphrates to the e of the earth. Ps 72:8
all the e of the earth have seen Ps 98:3
to rise from the e of the earth. Ps 135:7
eyes roam to the e of the earth. Pr 17:24
⌊Casting⌋ the lot e quarrels and Pr 18:18
all the e of the earth? Pr 30:4
them from the e of the earth. Is 5:26
From the e of the earth we hear Is 24:16
the e of the earth tremble. Is 41:5

you from the **e** of the earth Is 41:9
praise from the **e** of the earth, Is 42:10
from the **e** of the earth— Is 43:6
saved, all the **e** of the earth. Is 45:22
to the **e** of the earth." Is 49:6
all the **e** of the earth will see Is 52:10
to rise from the **e** of the earth. Jr 10:13
to You from the **e** of the earth, Jr 16:19
reaches to the **e** of the earth. Jr 25:31
up from the **e** of the earth." Jr 25:32
The judgment on Moab **e** here. Jr 48:47
to rise from the **e** of the earth. Jr 51:16
The fire devours both of its **e**, Ezk 15:4
visible to the **e** of the earth. Dn 4:11
extends⌋ to the **e** of the earth. Dn 4:22
extend to the **e** of the earth. Mc 5:4
River to the **e** of the earth. Zch 9:10
came from the **e** of the earth to Mt 12:42
came from the **e** of the earth to Lk 11:31
and to the **e** of the earth." Ac 1:8
to the **e** of the earth." Ac 13:47
words to the **e** of the inhabited Rm 10:18
on whom the **e** of the ages have 1Co 10:11
Love never **e**. But as for 1Co 13:8
confirming oath **e** every dispute. Heb 6:16

ENDURANCE *(27)*

By your **e** gain your lives. Lk 21:19
know that affliction produces **e**, Rm 5:3
e produces proven character, Rm 5:4
that through our **e** and through Rm 15:4
may the God of **e** and Rm 15:5
experienced in the **e** of the same 2Co 1:6
by great **e**, by afflictions, by 2Co 6:4
performed among you in all **e**— 2Co 12:12
might, for all **e** and patience, Col 1:11
and **e** of hope in our Lord Jesus 1Th 1:3
about your **e** and faith in all 2Th 1:4
to God's love and Christ's **e**. 2Th 3:5
faith, love, **e**, and gentleness. 1Tm 6:11
faith, patience, love, and **e**, 2Tm 3:10
and sound in faith, love, and **e**. Ti 2:2
you need **e**, so that after you Heb 10:36
run with **e** the race that lies Heb 12:1
of your faith produces **e**. Jms 1:3
But **e** must do its complete work, Jms 1:4
heard of Job's **e** and have seen Jms 5:11
with **e**, endurance with 2Pt 1:6
endurance, **e** with godliness, 2Pt 1:6
labor, and your **e**, and that you Rv 2:2
You also possess **e** and have Rv 2:3
faithfulness, service, and **e**. Rv 2:19
Here is the **e** and the faith of Rv 13:10
Here is the **e** of the saints, Rv 14:12

ENDURE *(38)*

will be able to **e**, and also all Ex 18:23
How long ⌊must I **e**⌋ this evil Nm 14:27
but now your reign will not **e**. 1Sm 13:14
and kingdom will **e** before Me 2Sm 7:16
his wealth will not **e**. Jb 15:29
You know the insults I **e**— Ps 69:19
May his name **e** forever; Ps 72:17
and My covenant with him will **e**. Ps 89:28
will perish, but You will **e**; Ps 102:26
the glory of the LORD **e** forever; Ps 104:31
righteous judgments **e** forever. Ps 119:160
Truthful lips **e** forever, but a Pr 12:19
A man's spirit can **e** sickness, Pr 18:14
I will make, will **e** before Me"— Is 66:22
your offspring and your name **e**. Is 66:22
the nations cannot **e** His rage. Jr 10:10
keep his covenant in order to **e**. Ezk 17:14
your courage **e** or your hands be Ezk 22:14
will no longer **e** the insults Ezk 34:29
around you will **e** their own Ezk 36:7
will not have to **e** the reproach Ezk 36:15
but will itself **e** forever. Dn 2:44
and his strength will not **e**. Dn 11:6
and dreadful—who can **e** it? Jl 2:11
The land cannot **e** all his words, Am 7:10
must **e** the LORD's rage until He Mc 7:9
Who can **e** His burning anger? Nah 1:6
But who can **e** the day of His Mal 3:2
when we are persecuted, we **e** it; 1Co 4:12
instead we **e** everything so that 1Co 9:12
and afflictions you **e**. 2Th 1:4
This is why I **e** all things for 2Tm 2:10
if we **e**, we will also reign with 2Tm 2:12
about everything, **e** hardship, do 2Tm 4:5
E it as discipline: God is Heb 12:7
is there if you **e** when you sin 1Pt 2:20
suffer, if you **e**, it brings 1Pt 2:20
you have kept My command to **e**, Rv 3:10

ENDURED *(11)*

I have **e** ⌊my punishment⌋; Jb 34:31
For I have **e** insults because of Ps 69:7
and all the hardships he **e**, Ps 132:1
because you have **e** the insults Ezk 36:6
had **e** much under many doctors. Mk 5:26
e with much patience objects of Rm 9:22
What persecutions I **e**! 2Tm 3:11
you **e** a hard struggle with Heb 10:32
that lay before Him **e** a cross Heb 12:2
Him who **e** such hostility Heb 12:3
as blessed those who have **e**. Jms 5:11

ENDURES *(38)*

As long as the earth **e**, seedtime Gn 8:22
His faithful love **e** forever. 1Ch 16:34
for His faithful love **e** forever. 1Ch 16:41
His faithful love **e** forever; 2Ch 5:13
for His faithful love **e** forever. 2Ch 7:3
His faithful love **e** forever"— 2Ch 7:6
for His faithful love **e** forever. 2Ch 20:21
love to Israel **e** forever." Ezr 3:11
for Yourself that **e** to this day. Neh 9:10
May he continue while the sun **e**, Ps 72:5
His faithfulness **e** through all Ps 100:5
fame ⌊**e**⌋ to all generations. Ps 102:12
His faithful love **e** forever. Ps 106:1
His faithful love **e** forever. Ps 107:1
His righteousness **e** forever. Ps 111:3
His praise **e** forever. Ps 111:10
and his righteousness **e** forever. Ps 112:3
his righteousness **e** forever. Ps 112:9
LORD's faithfulness **e** forever. Ps 117:2
His faithful love **e** forever. Ps 118:1
"His faithful love **e** forever." Ps 118:2
"His faithful love **e** forever." Ps 118:3
"His faithful love **e** forever." Ps 118:4
His faithful love **e** forever. Ps 118:29
LORD, Your name ⌊**e**⌋ forever, Ps 135:13
and knowledgeable person, it **e**. Pr 28:2
faithful love **e** forever as they Jr 33:11
Your throne **e** from generation to Lm 5:19
living God, and He **e** forever; Dn 6:26
the one who **e** to the end will Mt 10:22
the one who **e** to the end will Mt 24:13
the one who **e** to the end will Mk 13:13
hopes all things, **e** all things. 1Co 13:7
what **e** will be even more 2Co 3:11
His righteousness **e** forever. 2Co 9:9
Blessed is a man who **e** trials, Jms 1:12
the word of the Lord **e** forever. 1Pt 1:25
someone **e** grief from suffering 1Pt 2:19

ENDURING *(8)*

Your dwelling place is **e**; Nm 24:21
of the LORD is pure, **e** forever; Ps 19:9
an **e** barrier that it cannot Jr 5:22
you mountains and **e** foundations Mc 6:2
on to it and by **e**, bear fruit. Lk 8:15
have a better and **e** possession. Heb 10:34
here we do not have an **e** city; Heb 13:14
the living and **e** word of God. 1Pt 1:23

ENEMIES *(245)*

has handed over your **e** to you. Gn 14:20
possess the gates of their **e**. Gn 22:17
possess the gates of their **e**. Gn 24:60
will be on the necks of your **e**; Gn 49:8
may join our **e**, fight against us Ex 1:10
an enemy to your **e** and a foe to Ex 23:22
make all your **e** turn their backs Ex 23:27
would be vulnerable to their **e**. Ex 32:25
pursue your **e**, and they will Lv 26:7
your **e** will fall before you by Lv 26:8
vain because your **e** will eat it. Lv 26:16
you will be defeated by your **e**. Lv 26:17
so that your **e** who come to live Lv 26:32
you are in the land of your **e**. Lv 26:34
survive in the lands of their **e**. Lv 26:36
be able to stand against your **e**. Lv 26:37
land of your **e** will devour you Lv 26:38
lands of your **e** will waste away Lv 26:39
them into the land of their **e**— Lv 26:41
they are in the land of their **e**, Lv 26:44
and be delivered from your **e**. Nm 10:9
Let Your **e** be scattered, and Nm 10:35
you will be defeated by your **e**. Nm 14:42
I brought you to curse my **e**, Nm 23:11
you to put a curse on my **e**, Nm 24:10
become a possession of its **e**, Nm 24:18
has driven His **e** from His Nm 32:21
from being defeated by your **e**.' Dt 1:42
out all your **e** before you, Dt 6:19
rest from all the **e** around you Dt 12:10
against your **e** and see horses, Dt 20:1
to engage in battle with your **e**. Dt 20:3
you against your **e** to give you Dt 20:4
spoil of your **e** that the LORD Dt 20:14
war against your **e** and the LORD Dt 21:10
you are encamped against your **e**, Dt 23:9
you and deliver your **e** to you; Dt 23:14
rest from all the **e** around you Dt 25:19
will cause the **e** who rise up Dt 28:7
to be defeated before your **e**. Dt 28:25
flock will be given to your **e**, Dt 28:31
will serve your **e** the LORD will Dt 28:48
to your **e** as male and female Dt 28:68
these curses on your **e** who hate Dt 30:7
our Rock; even our **e** concede. Dt 32:31
loins of his adversaries and **e**, Dt 33:11
Your **e** will cringe before you, Dt 33:29
"Are You for us or for our **e**?" Jos 5:13
its back ⌊and run⌋ from its **e**? Jos 7:8
cannot stand against their **e**. Jos 7:12
backs ⌊and run⌋ from their **e**, Jos 7:12
against your **e** until you remove Jos 7:13
nation took vengeance on its **e**. Jos 10:13
Pursue your **e** and attack them Jos 10:19
do this to all the **e** you fight." Jos 10:25
None of their **e** were able to Jos 21:44
handed over all their **e** to them. Jos 21:44
the spoil of your **e** with your Jos 22:8
rest from all the **e** around them, Jos 23:1
sold them to the **e** around them, Jdg 2:14
could no longer resist their **e**. Jdg 2:14
power of their **e** while the judge Jdg 2:18
the LORD has handed over your **e**, Jdg 3:28
may all your **e** perish as Sisera Jdg 5:31
the power of the **e** around them. Jdg 8:34
brought vengeance on your **e**, Jdg 11:36
My mouth boasts over my **e**, 1Sm 2:1
save us from the hand of our **e**." 1Sm 4:3
⌊These **e**⌋ fought against them. 1Sm 12:9
us from the power of our **e**, 1Sm 12:10
the power of the **e** around you, 1Sm 12:11
I have taken vengeance on my **e**." 1Sm 14:24
plunder they took from their **e**! 1Sm 14:30
against all his **e** in every 1Sm 14:47
to take revenge on his **e**.'" 1Sm 18:25
one of David's **e** from the face 1Sm 20:15
hold David's **e** accountable." 1Sm 20:16
May your **e** and those who want 1Sm 25:26
fight against the **e** of my lord 1Sm 29:8
the plunder of the LORD's **e**." 1Sm 30:26
the power of all Israel's **e**.'" 2Sm 3:18
out against my **e** before me." 2Sm 5:20
on every side from all his **e**, 2Sm 7:1
destroyed all your **e** before you. 2Sm 7:9
give you rest from all your **e**. 2Sm 7:11
has delivered him from his **e**." 2Sm 18:19
man happen to the **e** of my lord 2Sm 18:32
You love your **e** and hate those 2Sm 19:6
us from the grasp of our **e**, 2Sm 19:9
hand of all his **e** and from the 2Sm 22:1
and I was saved from my **e**. 2Sm 22:4
I pursue my **e** and destroy them; 2Sm 22:38
have made my **e** retreat before 2Sm 22:41
He frees me from my **e**. 2Sm 22:49
death of your **e**, but you asked 1Kg 3:11
LORD put his **e** under his feet. 1Kg 5:3
go out to fight against their **e**, 1Kg 8:44
land of their **e** who took them 1Kg 8:48
from the hand of all your **e**." 2Kg 17:39
and hand them over to their **e**. 2Kg 21:14
and spoil to all their **e**, 2Kg 21:14
received help against these **e**, 1Ch 5:20
betray me to my **e** even though 1Ch 12:17
me to burst out against my **e**." 1Ch 14:11
destroyed all your **e** before you. 1Ch 17:8
I will also subdue all your **e**. 1Ch 17:10
rest from all his surrounding **e**, 1Ch 22:9
when their **e** besiege them in the 2Ch 6:28
go out to fight against their **e**, 2Ch 6:34
them to rejoice over their **e**. 2Ch 20:27

fought against the **e** of Israel.	2Ch 20:29
over to ⌊their **e**⌋ because they	2Ch 25:20
When the **e** of Judah and Benjamin	Ezr 4:1
protect us from **e** during the	Ezr 8:22
And our **e** said, "They won't know	Neh 4:11
When our **e** realized that we knew	Neh 4:15
the reproach of our foreign **e**?	Neh 5:9
the rest of our **e** heard that I	Neh 6:1
When all our **e** heard this,	Neh 6:16
You handed them over to their **e**,	Neh 9:27
them from the power of their **e**.	Neh 9:27
them to the power of their **e**,	Neh 9:28
against their **e** on that day.	Est 8:13
day when the Jews' **e** had hoped	Est 9:1
put all their **e** to the sword,	Est 9:5
and got rid of their **e**.	Est 9:16
the Jews got rid of their **e**.	Est 9:22
Your **e** will be clothed with	Jb 8:22
He regards me as ⌊one of⌋ His **e**.	Jb 19:11
strike all my **e** on the cheek;	Ps 3:7
grow old because of all my **e**.	Ps 6:7
All my **e** will be ashamed and	Ps 6:10
When my **e** retreat, they stumble	Ps 9:3
my deadly **e** who surround me.	Ps 17:9
and I was saved from my **e**.	Ps 18:3
I pursue my **e** and overtake them;	Ps 18:37
have made my **e** retreat before	Ps 18:40
He frees me from my **e**.	Ps 18:48
hand will capture all your **e**;	Ps 21:8
me in the presence of my **e**;	Ps 23:5
do not let my **e** gloat over me.	Ps 25:2
my **e**; they are numerous,	Ps 25:19
my foes and my **e** stumbled and	Ps 27:2
be high above my **e** around me;	Ps 27:6
not allowed my **e** to triumph over	Ps 30:1
the power of my **e** and from my	Ps 31:15
my deceitful **e** rejoice over me	Ps 35:19
the LORD's **e**, like the glory of	Ps 37:20
But my **e** are vigorous and	Ps 38:19
him over to the desire of his **e**.	Ps 41:2
My **e** speak maliciously about me:	Ps 41:5
Your name we trample our **e**.	Ps 44:5
the hearts of the king's **e**;	Ps 45:5
my eye has looked down on my **e**.	Ps 54:7
Then my **e** will retreat on the	Ps 56:9
Deliver me from my **e**, my God;	Ps 59:1
Your **e** will cringe before You	Ps 66:3
e scatter, and those who hate	Ps 68:1
God crushes the heads of His **e**,	Ps 68:21
have their share from the **e**."	Ps 68:23
deceitful **e**, who would destroy	Ps 69:4
ransom me because of my **e**.	Ps 69:18
my **e** talk about me, and those	Ps 71:10
him and his **e** lick the dust.	Ps 72:9
but the sea covered their **e**.	Ps 78:53
our **e** make fun of us.	Ps 80:6
subdue their **e** and turn My hand	Ps 81:14
See how Your **e** make an uproar;	Ps 83:2
e will see and be put to shame	Ps 86:17
scattered Your **e** with Your	Ps 89:10
You have made all his **e** rejoice.	Ps 89:42
how Your **e** have ridiculed,	Ps 89:51
LORD, Your **e**—indeed, Your	Ps 92:9
indeed, Your **e** will perish;	Ps 92:9
My eyes look down on my **e**;	Ps 92:11
My **e** taunt me all day long;	Ps 102:8
Their **e** oppressed them, and they	Ps 106:42
I make Your **e** Your footstool."	Ps 110:1
Rule over Your surrounding **e**.	Ps 110:2
makes me wiser than my **e**,	Ps 119:98
with ⌊their⌋ **e** at the city gate	Ps 127:5
I will clothe his **e** with shame,	Ps 132:18
my life from the anger of my **e**.	Ps 138:7
Your **e** swear ⌊by You⌋ falsely.	Ps 139:20
I consider them my **e**.	Ps 139:22
Rescue me from my **e**, LORD;	Ps 143:9
Your faithful love destroy my **e**.	Ps 143:12
makes even his **e** to be at peace	Pr 16:7
will take revenge against My **e**.	Is 1:24
him and stirred up his **e**.	Is 9:11
aloud, He prevails over His **e**.	Is 42:13
fury to His **e**, retribution to	Is 59:18
your grain to your **e** for food,	Is 62:8
⌊but⌋ our **e** have trampled down	Is 63:18
make Your name known to Your **e**,	Is 64:2
paying back His **e** what they	Is 66:6
show His wrath against His **e**.	Is 66:14
My life into the hand of her **e**.	Jr 12:7
in the presence of their **e**."	Jr 15:9
you serve your **e** in a land you	Jr 15:14
you serve your **e** in a land you	Jr 17:4
by the sword before their **e**,	Jr 19:7
siege and distress that their **e**,	Jr 19:9
sword of their **e** before your	Jr 20:4
kings of Judah over to their **e**.	Jr 20:5
to their **e**, yes, to those	Jr 21:7
will be handed over to their **e**,	Jr 34:20
his officials over to their **e**,	Jr 34:21
king, to his **e**, to those who	Jr 44:30
devastate Elam before their **e**,	Jr 49:37
they have become her **e**.	Lm 1:2
her **e** are at ease, for the LORD	Lm 1:5
All my **e** have heard of my	Lm 1:21
All your **e** open their mouths	Lm 2:16
All our **e** open their mouths	Lm 3:46
my **e** hunted me like a bird.	Lm 3:52
and handed them over to their **e**,	Ezk 39:23
from the countries of their **e**,	Ezk 39:27
its interpretation to your **e**!	Dn 4:19
by their **e** into captivity,	Am 9:4
you from the power of your **e**!	Mc 4:10
all your **e** will be destroyed.	Mc 5:9
a person's **e** are the people in	Mc 7:6
He is furious with His **e**.	Nah 1:2
will chase His **e** into darkness.	Nah 1:8
land are wide open to your **e**.	Nah 3:13
love your **e** and pray for those	Mt 5:44
a man's **e** will be the members	Mt 10:36
I put Your **e** under Your feet'	Mt 22:44
I put Your **e** under Your feet	Mk 12:36
salvation from our **e** and from	Lk 1:71
Love your **e**, do good to those	Lk 6:27
But love your **e**, do ⌊what is⌋	Lk 6:35
But bring here these **e** of mine,	Lk 19:27
on you when your **e** will build	Lk 19:43
I make Your **e** Your footstool.	Lk 20:43
I make Your **e** Your footstool.	Ac 2:35
if, while we were **e**, we were	Rm 5:10
they are **e** for your advantage,	Rm 11:28
puts all His **e** under His feet.	1Co 15:25
that many live as **e** of the cross	Php 3:18
I make Your **e** Your footstool?	Heb 1:13
waiting until His **e** are made His	Heb 10:13
mouths and consumes their **e**;	Rv 11:5
while their **e** watched them.	Rv 11:12

ENEMIES' *(2)*

fling away your **e** lives like	1Sm 25:29
rescued from our **e** clutches,	Lk 1:74

ENEMY *(105)*

Your right hand shattered the **e**.	Ex 15:6
The **e** said: "I will pursue, I	Ex 15:9
I will be an **e** to your enemies	Ex 23:22
will be delivered into **e** hands.	Lv 26:25
He will feed on **e** nations and	Nm 24:8
he was not his **e** and wasn't	Nm 35:23
hardship your **e** imposes on you.	Dt 28:53
hardship your **e** imposes on you	Dt 28:55
hardship your **e** imposes on you	Dt 28:57
not feared insult from the **e**,	Dt 32:27
the heads of the **e** leaders."	Dt 32:42
He drives out the **e** before you,	Dt 33:27
Now the **e** had gold earrings	Jdg 8:24
handed over our **e** Samson to us.	Jdg 16:23
over to us our **e** who destroyed	Jdg 16:24
Saul was David's **e** from then on.	1Sm 18:29
You sent my **e** away, and he has	1Sm 19:17
will hand your **e** over to you so	1Sm 24:4
a man finds his **e**, does he let	1Sm 24:19
has handed your **e** over to you.	1Sm 26:8
from you and has become your **e**,	1Sm 28:16
your **e** who intended to take your	2Sm 4:8
knew the best ⌊**e**⌋ soldiers were.	2Sm 11:16
my powerful **e** and from those	2Sm 22:18
there is no **e** or crisis.	1Kg 5:4
Israel are defeated before an **e**,	1Kg 8:33
when their **e** besieges them in	1Kg 8:37
and hand them over to the **e**,	1Kg 8:46
Edomite as an **e** against Solomon	1Kg 11:14
Eliada as an **e** against Solomon	1Kg 11:23
Rezon was Israel's **e** throughout	1Kg 11:25
So, you have caught me, my **e**."	1Kg 21:20
sword of your **e** overtaking you,	1Ch 21:12
Israel are defeated before an **e**,	2Ch 6:24
and hand them over to the **e**,	2Ch 6:36
make you stumble before the **e**,	2Ch 25:8
to help the king against the **e**.	2Ch 26:13
power of the **e** and from ambush	Ezr 8:31
the **e** of the Jewish people.	Est 3:10
The adversary and **e** is this evil	Est 7:6
of Haman, the **e** of the Jews.	Est 8:1
Hammedatha, the **e** of the Jews.	Est 9:10
Agagite, the **e** of all the Jews	Est 9:24
face and consider me Your **e**?	Jb 13:24
My **e** pierces me with His eyes.	Jb 16:9
May my **e** be like the wicked and	Jb 27:7
He regards me as his **e**.	Jb 33:10
may an **e** pursue and overtake me;	Ps 7:5
silence the **e** and the avenger.	Ps 8:2
The **e** has come to eternal ruin;	Ps 9:6
How long will my **e** dominate me?	Ps 13:2
my **e** will say, "I have triumphed	Ps 13:4
my powerful **e** and from those	Ps 18:17
not handed me over to the **e**.	Ps 31:8
my **e** does not shout in triumph	Ps 41:11
because of the **e** and avenger.	Ps 44:16
it is not an **e** who insults me—	Ps 55:12
tower in the face of the **e**.	Ps 61:3
life from the terror of the **e**.	Ps 64:1
to all that the **e** has destroyed	Ps 74:3
Will the **e** insult Your name	Ps 74:10
the **e** has mocked the LORD,	Ps 74:18
The **e** will not afflict him;	Ps 89:22
them from the hand of the **e**.	Ps 106:10
For the **e** has pursued me,	Ps 143:3
Don't gloat when your **e** falls,	Pr 24:17
If your **e** is hungry, give him	Pr 25:21
kisses of an **e** are excessive.	Pr 27:6
He became their **e** ⌊and⌋ fought	Is 63:10
For the **e** has a sword;	Jr 6:25
time of distress, with the **e**.	Jr 15:11
them before the **e** like the east	Jr 18:17
have struck you like an **e** would,	Jr 30:14
was his **e**, the one who wanted	Jr 44:30
for ⌊the **e**⌋ will come with an	Jr 46:22
affliction, for the **e** triumphs!	Lm 1:9
because the **e** has prevailed.	Lm 1:16
hand in the presence of the **e**.	Lm 2:3
Like an **e** He has bent His bow;	Lm 2:4
The Lord is like an **e**;	Lm 2:5
of her palaces over to the **e**.	Lm 2:7
letting the **e** gloat over you and	Lm 2:17
My **e** has destroyed those I	Lm 2:22
believe that an **e** or adversary	Lm 4:12
the **e** has said about you,	Ezk 36:2
will be handed over to his **e**.	Dn 11:11
is good; an **e** will pursue him	Hs 8:3
An **e** will surround the land;	Am 3:11
people have risen up like an **e**:	Mc 2:8
Do not rejoice over me, my **e**!	Mc 7:8
Then my **e** will see, and she will	Mc 7:10
will seek refuge from the **e**.	Nah 3:11
He has turned back your **e**.	Zph 3:15
safety from the **e** for anyone who	Zch 8:10
your neighbor and hate your **e**.	Mt 5:43
sleeping, his **e** came, sowed	Mt 13:25
'An **e** did this!' he told them.	Mt 13:28
the **e** who sowed them is the	Mt 13:39
and over all the power of the **e**;	Lk 10:19
and all fraud, **e** of all	Ac 13:10
But If your **e** is hungry, feed	Rm 12:20
The last **e** to be abolished is	1Co 15:26
now become your **e** by telling you	Gl 4:16
Yet don't treat him as an **e**,	2Th 3:15
world's friend becomes God's **e**.	Jms 4:4

ENEMY'S *(8)*

come across your **e** stray ox or	Ex 23:4
deport them to the **e** country—	1Kg 8:46
me from the **e** power or Redeem me	Jb 6:23
I rejoiced over my **e** distress,	Jb 31:29
because of the **e** oppression?"	Ps 42:9
because of the **e** oppression?	Ps 43:2
because of the **e** voice, because	Ps 55:3
will return from the **e** land.	Jr 31:16

ENERGY *(4)*

ate the honey, he had renewed **e**.	1Sm 14:27
have renewed **e** because I tasted	1Sm 14:29
could devote their **e** to the law	2Ch 31:4
spend your **e** on women or your	Pr 31:3

ENFOLDS *(1)*

He **e** the waters in His clouds,	Jb 26:8

ENFORCE *(1)*

an ordinance and **e** an edict that	Dn 6:7

ENGAGE *(17)*
of it⌋; e him in battle. Dt 2:24
you are about to e in battle, Dt 20:2
are about to e in battle with Dt 20:3
people could e Israel in battle Jos 8:14
that they would e Israel in Jos 11:20
and went to e the Philistines. 1Sm 23:28
formation to e the Arameans. 2Sm 10:9
formation to e the Ammonites. 2Sm 10:10
formation to e David in battle 2Sm 10:17
the field to e Israel in battle 2Sm 18:6
formation to e the Arameans. 1Ch 19:10
formation to e the Ammonites. 1Ch 19:11
David lined up to e the Arameans 1Ch 19:17
that you could e in prostitution Ezk 16:17
the South will e him in battle, Dn 11:40
'E in business until I come back. Lk 19:13
you may strongly e in battle, 1Tm 1:18

ENGAGED *(17)*
any man become e to a woman and Dt 20:7
who is a virgin e to a man, Dt 22:23
encounters the e woman in the Dt 22:25
the field, the e woman cried out Dt 22:27
virgin who is not e, takes hold Dt 22:28
You will become e to a woman, Dt 28:30
I was e to her for the price of 2Sm 3:14
and you e in prostitution on Ezk 16:16
You e in promiscuous acts with Ezk 16:26
Then you e in prostitution with Ezk 16:28
treachery he has e in and the Ezk 18:24
Mary had been e to Joseph, Mt 1:18
to a virgin e to a man named Lk 1:27
who was e to him and was Lk 2:5
Barnabas had e them in serious Ac 15:2
synagogue and e in discussion Ac 18:19
as the workers e in this type Ac 19:25

ENGAGING *(2)*
e in discussion and trying to Ac 19:8
while e in a prolonged debate Ac 28:29

ENGRAVE *(4)*
onyx stones and e on them the Ex 28:9
E the two stones with the names Ex 28:11
a plate of pure gold and e it, Ex 28:36
I will e an inscription on it"— Zch 3:9

ENGRAVED *(8)*
stone must be e like a seal, Ex 28:21
God's writing, e on the tablets. Ex 32:16
e with the names of Israel's Ex 39:6
stone was e like a seal with Ex 39:14
He e cherubim, lions, and palm 1Kg 7:36
point it is e on the tablet Jr 17:1
and there e all around the wall Ezk 8:10
the Chaldeans, e in vermilion, Ezk 23:14

ENGRAVES *(2)*
sons as a gem cutter e a seal. Ex 28:11
sons as a gem cutter e a seal. Ex 39:6

ENGRAVING *(5)*
it, like the e of a seal: Ex 28:36
fashioned it with an e tool, Ex 32:4
like the e on a seal: Ex 39:30
is skilled in e to work with 2Ch 2:7
do all kinds of e and to execute 2Ch 2:14

ENGRAVINGS *(1)*
temple walls with carved e— 1Kg 6:29

ENGULF *(1)*
the LORD will e them in His Ps 21:9

ENGULFED *(3)*
For the waves of death e me; 2Sm 22:5
Then the waters would have e us; Ps 124:4
The waters e me up to the neck; Jnh 2:5

ENGULFING *(1)*
the sea over them, e them. Jos 24:7

ENJOY *(42)*
rejected, and they will e it. Nm 14:31
and not begun to e its fruit? Dt 20:6
and another man e its fruit. Dt 20:6
You may e the spoil of your Dt 20:14
a vineyard but not e its fruit. Dt 28:30
stay overnight and e yourself." Jdg 19:6
the night here, e yourself, then Jdg 19:9
E your glory and stay at home. 2Kg 14:10
that they could e its fruit and Neh 9:36
with the king and e yourself." Est 5:14
so that he can e his day like Jb 14:6
He will not e the streams, Jb 20:17
doesn't e the profits from his Jb 20:18
a long life to e what is good? Ps 34:12
the land and will e abundant Ps 37:11
that I may e the prosperity of Ps 106:5
you⌋ mockers e mocking and ⌊you Pr 1:22
⌊from⌋ those who e doing evil Pr 2:14
mouth, a man will e good things, Pr 13:2
pleasure and e what is good." Ec 2:1
to let my body e life with wine Ec 2:3
eat, drink, and to e his work. Ec 2:24
and who can e life apart from Ec 2:25
to rejoice and e the good life. Ec 3:12
a person to e his activities, Ec 3:22
He has allowed him to e them, Ec 5:19
does not allow him to e them. Ec 6:2
Instead, a stranger will e them. Ec 6:2
eat, drink, and e himself, for Ec 8:15
E life with the wife you love Ec 9:9
and you will e the choicest of Is 55:2
and let you e the heritage of Is 58:14
ones will fully e the work of Is 65:22
plant and will e ⌊the fruit⌋. Jr 31:5
For He does not e bringing Lm 3:33
your nipples to e your youthful Ezk 23:21
eat, drink, and e yourself." ' Lk 12:19
invited will e my banquet!' " Lk 14:24
you were willing to e his light. Jn 5:35
Since we e great peace because Ac 24:2
us with all things to e. 1Tm 6:17
rather than to e the short-lived Heb 11:25

ENJOYABLE *(1)*
discipline seems e at the time, Heb 12:11

ENJOYED *(3)*
and the land e its Sabbath rest 2Ch 36:21
I have first e your company for Rm 15:24
the truth but e unrighteousness. 2Th 2:12

ENJOYING *(2)*
Naphtali, e approval, full of Dt 33:23
While they were e themselves, Jdg 19:22

ENJOYMENT *(1)*
So I commended e, because there Ec 8:15

ENJOYS *(1)*
drinks, and e all his efforts. Ec 3:13

ENLARGE *(5)*
before you and e your territory. Ex 34:24
E the site of your tent, and let Is 54:2
that you e your eyes with paint? Jr 4:30
in order to e their territory. Am 1:13
They e their phylacteries and Mt 23:5

ENLARGED *(2)*
You have e the nation and Is 9:3
of ministry⌋ will be greatly e, 2Co 10:15

ENLARGES *(6)*
LORD your God e your territory Dt 12:20
LORD your God e your territory Dt 19:8
The one who e Gad's ⌊territory⌋ Dt 33:20
He e nations, then leads them Jb 12:23
Therefore Sheol e its throat and Is 5:14
He e his appetite like Sheol, Hab 2:5

ENLIGHTENED *(3)*
heart may be e so you may know Eph 1:18
those who were once e, Heb 6:4
you had been e, you endured Heb 10:32

ENLISTED *(3)*
strong or brave man, he e him. 1Sm 14:52
who e the people of the land for 2Kg 25:19
who e the people of the land for Jr 52:25

ENOCH *(12)*
conceived and gave birth to E. Gn 4:17
named the city E after his son. Gn 4:17
was born to E, Irad fathered Gn 4:18
years old when he fathered E. Gn 5:18
800 years after the birth of E, Gn 5:19
E was 65 years old when he Gn 5:21
E walked with God 300 years and Gn 5:22
E walked with God, and he was Gn 5:24
E, Methuselah, Lamech, 1Ch 1:3
son⌋ of E, ⌊son⌋ of Jared, Lk 3:37
E was taken away so that he did Heb 11:5
And E, in the seventh Jd 14

ENOCH'S *(1)*
So E life lasted 365 years. Gn 5:23

ENORMOUS *(6)*
have brought such e guilt on me Gn 20:9
The work is e and spread out, Neh 4:19
and opens wide its e jaws, Is 5:14
because of your e guilt and your Jr 30:14
because of your e guilt and your Jr 30:15
E hailstones, each weighing Rv 16:21

ENOS *(1)*
⌊son⌋ of E, ⌊son⌋ of Seth, ⌊son⌋ Lk 3:38

ENOSH *(6)*
Seth also, and he named him E. Gn 4:26
years old when he fathered E. Gn 5:6
807 years after the birth of E, Gn 5:7
E was 90 years old when he Gn 5:9
E lived 815 years after the Gn 5:10
Adam, Seth, E, 1Ch 1:1

ENOSH'S *(1)*
So E life lasted 905 years; Gn 5:11

ENOUGH *(89)*
town is close e for me to run to Gn 19:20
until they have had e to drink." Gn 24:19
Isn't it e that you have taken Gn 30:15
"I have e, my brother," Esau Gn 33:9
the region is large e for them. Gn 34:21
Then Israel said, "E! Gn 45:28
has been e of God's thunder Ex 9:28
day and gather e for that day. Ex 16:4
There was more than e. Ex 36:7
and obtains e to redeem his land Lv 25:26
he cannot obtain e to repay him, Lv 25:28
for them, would they have e? Nm 11:22
for them, would they have e?" Nm 11:22
Isn't it e for you that the God Nm 16:9
Is it not e that you brought us Nm 16:13
stayed at this mountain long e. Dt 1:6
around this hill country long e; Dt 2:3
The LORD said to me, 'That's e! Dt 3:26
and He was angry e with you to Dt 9:8
LORD was angry e with Aaron to Dt 9:20
freely loan him e for whatever Dt 15:8
hill country is not e for us, Jos 17:16
community, e for us, so that Jos 22:17
But there were not e for them. Jdg 21:14
we did not get e wives for each Jdg 21:22
if that was not e, I would have 2Sm 12:8
the people, "E, withdraw your 2Sm 24:16
the altar large e to hold about 1Kg 18:32
He said, "⌊I have had⌋ e! 1Kg 19:4
the people⌋, "E, withdraw your 1Ch 21:15
God loved Israel e to establish 2Ch 9:8
since there were not e priests, 2Ch 29:34
since not e of the priests had 2Ch 30:3
consolations not e for you, Jb 15:11
you never get e of my flesh? Jb 19:22
will never have e food. Jb 27:14
has not had e to eat at Job's Jb 31:31
one is ferocious ⌊e⌋ to rouse Jb 41:10
For I have had e troubles, Ps 88:3
we've had more than e contempt. Ps 123:3
We've had more than e scorn from Ps 123:4
eyes, and you'll have e to eat. Pr 20:13
there will be e goat's milk for Pr 27:27
satisfied; four never say, "E!": Pr 30:15
and fire, which never says, "E!" Pr 30:16
I have had e of burnt offerings Is 1:11
Is it not e for you to try the Is 7:13
no fragment large e to take fire Is 30:14
Lebanon is not e for fuel, Is 40:16
or its animals e for a burnt Is 40:16
It is not e for you to be My Is 49:6
they never have e. And they are Is 56:11
is the man wise e to understand Jr 9:12
Then we had e food and good Jr 44:17
and with Assyria, to get e food. Lm 5:6
Is it not e for the house of Ezk 8:17
No one cared ⌊e⌋ about you to do Ezk 16:5
Wasn't your prostitution e? Ezk 16:20
can grow strong ⌊e⌋ to handle a Ezk 30:21
Isn't it e for you to feed on Ezk 34:18
Or ⌊isn't it e⌋ that you drink Ezk 34:18
⌊I have had⌋ e of all your Ezk 44:6
was deep e to swim in, a river Ezk 47:5
not strong e to stand against Dn 8:7
is right. I'm angry e to die!" Jnh 4:9
never have e to be satisfied. Hg 1:6
never have e to become drunk. Hg 1:6
but never have e to get warm. Hg 1:6
but it will not be e for them. Zch 10:10
Each day has e trouble of its Mt 6:34
It is e for a disciple to become Mt 10:25

and he will have more than **e**. Mt 13:12
could we get **e** bread in this Mt 15:33
there won't be **e** for us and for Mt 25:9
and he will have more than **e**. Mt 25:29
one was strong **e** to subdue him. Mk 5:4
can anyone get **e** bread here in Mk 8:4
and resting? **E**! The time has Mk 14:41
see if he has **e** to complete it? Lk 14:28
hands have more than **e** food, Lk 15:17
I'm not strong **e** to dig; Lk 16:3
two swords." "**E** of that!" He Lk 22:38
wouldn't be **e** for each of them Jn 6:7
Father, and that's **e** for us." Jn 14:8
having eaten **e** food, they began Ac 27:38
True **e**; they were broken off by Rm 11:20
might be bold **e** in Him to speak Eph 6:20
he comes soon **e**, he will be with Heb 13:23
has already been **e** time spent in 1Pt 4:3

ENRAGE *(1)*
I will **e** them with a foolish Dt 32:21

ENRAGED *(19)*
Moses became **e** and threw the Ex 32:19
"Don't be **e**, my lord," Aaron Ex 32:22
they **e** Him with detestable Dt 32:16
they have **e** Me with their Dt 32:21
were **e** with Achish and told him, 1Sm 29:4
of Aram was **e** because of this 2Kg 6:11
hand to offer incense, was **e**. 2Ch 26:19
when he became **e** with the 2Ch 26:19
e Him with their high places Ps 78:58
because He was **e** with His Ps 78:62
You have become **e** with Your Ps 89:38
they will become **e**, and, looking Is 8:21
all who are **e** against you will Is 41:11
your youth but **e** Me with all Ezk 16:43
The king was **e**, so he sent out Mt 22:7
everyone in the synagogue was **e**. Lk 4:28
they were **e** and wanted to kill Ac 5:33
they were **e** in their hearts and Ac 7:54
Being greatly **e** at them, I even Ac 26:11

ENRAGES *(1)*
For jealousy **e** a husband, and he Pr 6:34

ENRICH *(1)*
the poor to **e** oneself, Pr 22:16

ENRICHED *(3)*
A generous person will be **e**, Pr 11:25
e the kings of the earth with Ezk 27:33
you are **e** in every way for all 2Co 9:11

ENRICHES *(1)*
LORD's blessing **e**, and struggle Pr 10:22

ENRICHING *(2)*
it abundantly, **e** it greatly. Ps 65:9
as poor yet **e** many; 2Co 6:10

ENROLL *(1)*
But refuse to **e** younger widows; 1Tm 5:11

ENSLAVE *(8)*
and great kings will **e** them, Jr 25:14
and great kings will **e** him. Jr 27:7
will never again **e** him. Jr 30:8
slaves and no one **e** his Judean Jr 34:9
order not to **e** them any longer Jr 34:10
the hands of those who **e** them. Ezk 34:27
they would **e** and oppress them Ac 7:6
Christ Jesus, in order to **e** us. Gl 2:4

ENSLAVED *(9)*
they will be **e** and oppressed 400 Gn 15:13
of our daughters are already **e**, Neh 5:5
we have never been **e** to anyone. Jn 8:33
we may no longer be **e** to sin, Rm 6:6
you became **e** to righteousness. Rm 6:18
from sin and become **e** to God, Rm 6:22
you were **e** to things that by Gl 4:8
you want to be **e** to them all Gl 4:9
since people are **e** to whatever 2Pt 2:19

ENSLAVES *(1)*
put up with it if someone **e** you, 2Co 11:20

ENSNARE *(5)*
should not rule or **e** the people. Jb 34:30
let the net that he hid **e** him; Ps 35:8
height in order to **e** lives. Ezk 13:18
you **e** the lives of My people Ezk 13:18
bands that you **e** people with Ezk 13:20

ENSNARED *(4)*
or else you will be **e** by it, Dt 7:25
careful not to be **e** by their Dt 12:30
e by the words of your mouth. Pr 6:2
people you have **e** like birds. Ezk 13:20

ENSNARES *(1)*
and the sin that so easily **e** us, Heb 12:1

ENTANGLE *(1)*
learn his ways and **e** yourself in Pr 22:25

ENTANGLED *(6)*
The ropes of Sheol **e** me; 2Sm 22:6
The ropes of Sheol **e** me; Ps 18:5
he is **e** in the ropes of his own Pr 5:22
will be consumed like **e** thorns, Nah 1:10
a soldier gets **e** in the concerns 2Tm 2:4
they are again **e** in these things 2Pt 2:20

ENTER *(210)*
and you will **e** the ark with your Gn 6:18
said to Noah, "**E** the ark, you Gn 7:1
When he was about to **e** Egypt, Gn 12:11
May I never **e** their council; Gn 49:6
the destroyer **e** your houses to Ex 12:23
you **e** the land that the LORD Ex 12:25
sons whenever they **e** the tent of Ex 28:43
Whenever they **e** the tent of Ex 30:20
land that you are going to **e**; Ex 34:12
was unable to **e** the tent of Ex 40:35
or beer when you **e** the tent of Lv 10:9
Afterwards he may **e** the camp, Lv 14:8
When you **e** the land of Canaan Lv 14:34
Aaron is to **e** the ⌊most⌋ holy Lv 16:3
Then Aaron is to **e** the tent of Lv 16:23
When you **e** the land I am giving Lv 23:10
When you **e** the land I am giving Lv 25:2
brings a curse **e** your stomach, Nm 5:22
and it will **e** her and cause Nm 5:24
a curse will **e** her and cause Nm 5:27
When you **e** into battle in your Nm 10:9
none of you will **e** the land I Nm 14:30
When you **e** the land I am giving Nm 15:2
After you **e** the land where I am Nm 15:18
after that he may **e** the camp, Nm 19:7
he will not **e** the land I have Nm 20:24
After that you may **e** the camp." Nm 31:24
When you **e** the land of Canaan, Nm 34:2
E and take possession of the Dt 1:8
'You will not **e** there either. Dt 1:37
Nun, who attends you, will **e** it. Dt 1:38
good from evil, will **e** there. Dt 1:39
the kingdoms you are about to **e**. Dt 3:21
that you may live, **e**, and take Dt 4:1
the Jordan and **e** the good land Dt 4:21
you are about to **e** and possess. Dt 6:1
so that you may **e** and possess Dt 6:18
and may **e** and take possession of Dt 8:1
so that they may **e** and possess Dt 10:11
the Jordan to **e** and take Dt 11:31
When you **e** the land the LORD Dt 17:14
When you **e** the land the LORD Dt 18:9
been cut off may **e** the LORD's Dt 23:1
birth may **e** the LORD's assembly; Dt 23:2
may **e** the LORD's assembly. Dt 23:2
or Moabite may **e** the LORD's Dt 23:3
may ever **e** the LORD's assembly. Dt 23:3
generation may **e** the LORD's Dt 23:8
When you **e** your neighbor's Dt 23:24
When you **e** your neighbor's Dt 23:25
do not **e** his house to collect Dt 24:10
When you **e** the land the LORD Dt 26:1
you cross to **e** the land the LORD Dt 27:3
so that you may **e** into the Dt 29:12
so that you may **e** into His oath Dt 29:12
unless, when we **e** the land, you Jos 2:18
Don't let them **e** their cities, Jos 10:19
Arnon but did not **e** into the Jdg 11:18
her father would not let him **e**. Jdg 15:1
lame will never **e** the house." 2Sm 5:8
How can I **e** my house to eat and 2Sm 11:11
When your feet **e** the city, 1Kg 14:12
He will not **e** this city or shoot 2Kg 19:32
and he will not **e** this city, 2Kg 19:33
were not able to **e** the LORD's 2Ch 7:2
No one is to **e** the LORD's temple 2Ch 23:6
may **e** because they are holy, 2Ch 23:6
unclean could **e** for any reason. 2Ch 23:19
that he didn't **e** the LORD's 2Ch 27:2
to all who would **e** the LORD's 2Ch 31:16
and Benjamin **e** ⌊the covenant⌋. 2Ch 34:32
How can I **e** the temple and live? Neh 6:11
should ever **e** the assembly of Neh 13:1
no goods could **e** during the Neh 13:19
is not to **e** King Ahasuerus' Est 1:19
"Have him **e**," the king ordered. Est 6:5
The wild animals **e** ⌊their⌋ lairs Jb 37:8
But I **e** Your house by the Ps 5:7
swords will **e** their own hearts Ps 37:15
they **e** the king's palace. Ps 45:15
I will **e** Your house with burnt Ps 66:13
Let us **e** His presence with Ps 95:2
'They will not **e** My rest.'" Ps 95:11
an offering and **e** His courts. Ps 96:8
E His gates with thanksgiving Ps 100:4
let it **e** his body like water and Ps 109:18
I will **e** through them and give Ps 118:19
the righteous will **e** through it. Ps 118:20
I will not **e** my house or get Ps 132:3
For wisdom will **e** your mind, Pr 2:10
is inexperienced, **e** here!" Pr 9:4
is inexperienced, **e** here!" Pr 9:16
one of those who **e** agreements, Pr 22:26
e your rooms and close your Is 26:20
which will **e** and pierce the hand Is 36:6
He will not **e** this city or shoot Is 37:33
and he will not **e** this city. Is 37:34
unclean will no longer **e** you. Is 52:1
He will **e** into peace—they will Is 57:2
square, and honesty cannot **e**. Is 59:14
themselves to ⌊**e**⌋ the groves Is 66:17
They **e** the thickets and climb Jr 4:29
of Judah who **e** through these Jr 7:2
us **e** the fortified cities and Jr 8:14
I **e** the city, look—those ill Jr 14:18
Don't **e** a house where a mourning Jr 16:5
You must not **e** the house where Jr 16:8
the kings of Judah **e** and leave, Jr 17:19
of Jerusalem who **e** through these Jr 17:20
and princes will **e** through the Jr 17:25
Who can **e** our hiding places? Jr 21:13
your people who **e** these gates. Jr 22:2
throne will **e** through the gates Jr 22:4
I cannot **e** the temple of the Jr 36:5
the nations **e** her sanctuary— Lm 1:10
forbidden to **e** Your assembly. Lm 1:10
adversary could **e** Jerusalem's Lm 4:12
men will **e** it and profane Ezk 7:22
and they will not **e** the land of Ezk 13:9
the peoples and **e** into judgment Ezk 20:35
I will **e** into judgment with you. Ezk 20:36
but they will not **e** the land of Ezk 20:38
I will cause breath to **e** you, Ezk 37:5
years you will **e** a land that has Ezk 38:8
and no one will **e** through it, Ezk 44:2
He must **e** by way of the portico Ezk 44:3
and flesh, may **e** My sanctuary, Ezk 44:9
the ones who may **e** My sanctuary Ezk 44:16
When they **e** the gates of the Ezk 44:17
prince should **e** from the outside Ezk 46:2
When the people **e**, the prince Ezk 46:10
the prince will **e** with them, Ezk 46:10
and **e** the fortress of the king Dn 11:7
who will **e** the kingdom of the Dn 11:9
it will not **e** the house of the Hs 9:4
they **e** through the windows like Jl 2:9
I will **e** into judgment with them Jl 3:2
not **e** the gate of My people in Ob 13
and it will **e** the house of the Zch 5:4
of Egypt will not go up and **e**, Zch 14:18
you will never **e** the kingdom of Mt 5:20
E through the narrow gate. Mt 7:13
will **e** the kingdom of heaven, Mt 7:21
and don't **e** any Samaritan town. Mt 10:5
When you **e** any town or village, Mt 10:11
Greet a household when you **e** it, Mt 10:12
How can someone **e** a strong man's Mt 12:29
they **e** and settle down there. Mt 12:45
you will never **e** the kingdom of Mt 18:3
better for you to **e** life maimed Mt 18:8
for you to **e** life with one eye Mt 18:9
If you want to **e** into life, Mt 19:17
a rich person to **e** the kingdom Mt 19:23
rich person to **e** the kingdom of Mt 19:24
that you won't **e** into temptation Mt 26:41
could no longer **e** a town openly. Mk 1:45
one can **e** a strong man's house Mk 3:27
for other things **e** in and choke Mk 4:19
to the pigs, so we may **e** them." Mk 5:12
Whenever you **e** a house, stay Mk 6:10
of him and never **e** him again!" Mk 9:25

for you to **e** life maimed than Mk 9:43
for you to **e** life lame than to Mk 9:45
better for you to **e** the kingdom Mk 9:47
a little child will never **e** it." Mk 10:15
have wealth to **e** the kingdom of Mk 10:23
how hard it is to **e** the kingdom Mk 10:24
rich person to **e** the kingdom of Mk 10:25
As soon as you **e** it, you will Mk 11:2
that you won't **e** into temptation Mk 14:38
to **e** the sanctuary of the Lord Lk 1:9
to permit them to **e** the pigs, Lk 8:32
He let no one **e** with Him except Lk 8:51
Whatever house you **e**, stay there Lk 9:4
house you **e**, first say, 'Peace Lk 10:5
When you **e** any town, and they Lk 10:8
When you **e** any town, and they Lk 10:10
they **e** and settle down there. Lk 11:26
every effort to **e** through the Lk 13:24
many will try to **e** and won't be Lk 13:24
is strongly urged to **e** it. Lk 16:16
a little child will never **e** it." Lk 18:17
have wealth to **e** the kingdom of Lk 18:24
rich person to **e** the kingdom of Lk 18:25
As you **e** it, you will find a Lk 19:30
in the country must not **e** it, Lk 21:21
you may not **e** into temptation. Lk 22:40
you won't **e** into temptation. Lk 22:46
things and **e** into His glory? Lk 24:26
Can he **e** his mother's womb a Jn 3:4
he cannot **e** the kingdom of God. Jn 3:5
who doesn't **e** the sheep pen Jn 10:1
They did not **e** the headquarters Jn 18:28
and John about to **e** the temple Ac 3:3
he would **e** house after house, Ac 8:3
"They will not **e** My rest." Heb 3:11
that they would not **e** His rest," Heb 3:18
were unable to **e** because of Heb 3:19
we who have believed **e** the rest Heb 4:3
anger, they will not **e** My rest. Heb 4:3
They will never **e** My rest. Heb 4:5
it remains for some to **e** it, Heb 4:6
the good news did not **e** because Heb 4:6
every effort to **e** that rest, Heb 4:11
the priests **e** the first room Heb 9:6
Messiah did not **e** a sanctuary Heb 9:24
have boldness to **e** the sanctuary Heb 10:19
and no one could **e** the sanctuary Rv 15:8
Nothing profane will ever **e** it: Rv 21:27
tree of life and may **e** the city Rv 22:14

ENTERED *(150)*

sons' wives **e** the ark because Gn 7:7
male and female, **e** the ark with Gn 7:9
sons' wives **e** the ark with him Gn 7:13
⌊**e** it⌋ with all the wildlife Gn 7:14
of life in it **e** the ark with Gn 7:15
Those that **e**, male and female of Gn 7:16
e just as God had commanded him. Gn 7:16
Abram **e** Egypt, the Egyptians Gn 12:14
The two angels **e** Sodom in the Gn 19:1
left Leah's tent and **e** Rachel's. Gn 31:33
years old when he **e** the service Gn 41:46
they **e** the Wilderness of Sinai. Ex 19:1
they **e** the Wilderness of Sinai Ex 19:2
Moses **e** the cloud as he went up Ex 24:18
watch Moses until he **e** the tent. Ex 33:8
Moses **e** the tent, the pillar Ex 33:9
and Aaron then **e** the tent of Lv 9:23
wore when he **e** the ⌊most⌋ holy Lv 16:23
When Moses **e** the tent of meeting Nm 7:89
The next day Moses **e** the tent of Nm 17:8
community **e** the Wilderness Nm 20:1
God that I have **e** the land the Dt 26:3
came to you and **e** your house, Jos 2:3
They ran, **e** the city, captured Jos 8:19
and they **e** the land to waste it. Jdg 6:5
they **e** the inner chamber of the Jdg 9:46
When they **e** Micah's house and Jdg 18:18
When he **e** his house, he picked Jdg 19:29
They **e** the land of Moab and Ru 1:2
When they **e** Bethlehem, the whole Ru 1:19
So Ruth left and **e** the field to Ru 2:3
covenant of the LORD **e** the camp, 1Sm 4:5
ark of the LORD had **e** the camp, 1Sm 4:6
"The gods have **e** their camp!" 1Sm 4:7
When the man **e** the city to give 1Sm 4:13
When the troops **e** the forest, 1Sm 14:26
came to Saul and **e** his service, 1Sm 16:21
until he **e** Naioth in Ramah. 1Sm 19:23
They **e** the interior of the house 2Sm 4:6
They had **e** the house while 2Sm 4:7
before Abishai and **e** the city. 2Sm 10:14
king's sons **e** and wept loudly 2Sm 13:36
e Jerusalem just as Absalom was 2Sm 15:37
the king **e** the LORD's temple 1Kg 14:28
he **e** the citadel of the royal 1Kg 16:18
He **e** a cave there and spent the 1Kg 19:9
and angry, and he **e** Samaria. 1Kg 20:43
they **e** Samaria, Elisha said, 2Kg 6:20
came back and **e** another tent, 2Kg 7:8
As Jehu **e** the gate, she said, 2Kg 9:31
They **e** the temple of Baal, 2Kg 10:21
son of Rechab **e** the temple of 2Kg 10:23
They **e** the king's palace by way 2Kg 11:19
king of Babylon, **e** Jerusalem. 2Kg 25:8
brother Abishai and **e** the city. 1Ch 19:15
when they **e** the LORD's temple 1Ch 24:19
number was not **e** in the 1Ch 27:24
that had **e** Solomon's heart to 2Ch 7:11
the king **e** the LORD's temple 2Ch 12:11
Then they **e** into a covenant to 2Ch 15:12
They **e** the king's palace through 2Ch 23:20
They **e** Judah and Jerusalem and 2Ch 24:23
of Assyria came and **e** Judah. 2Ch 32:1
I **e** through the Valley Gate and Neh 2:15
Haman **e**, and the king asked him, Est 6:6
Mordecai **e** the king's presence Est 8:1
Have you **e** the ⌊place⌋ where the Jb 38:22
until I **e** God's sanctuary. Ps 73:17
your neighbor or **e** into an Pr 6:1
but after you **e**, you defiled My Jr 2:7
it has **e** our fortresses, cutting Jr 9:21
e and possessed it, but they Jr 32:23
and people who **e** into covenant Jr 34:10
the king of Babylon **e** and sat at Jr 39:3
foreigners have **e** the holy Jr 51:51
e Jerusalem as the Jr 52:12
the Spirit **e** me and set me on my Ezk 2:2
The Spirit **e** me and set me on my Ezk 3:24
meat has never **e** my mouth." Ezk 4:14
e into a covenant with you, Ezk 16:8
Just as I **e** into judgment with Ezk 20:36
they **e** My sanctuary to profane Ezk 23:39
the breath **e** them, and they came Ezk 37:10
priests have **e**, they must not Ezk 42:14
of the LORD **e** the temple by way Ezk 43:4
God of Israel, has **e** through it. Ezk 44:2
through the gate by which he **e**, Ezk 46:9
no meat or wine **e** my mouth, Dn 10:3
while foreigners **e** his gate and Ob 11
Rottenness **e** my bones; Hab 3:16
His mother, and **e** the land of Mt 2:21
When He **e** Capernaum, a centurion Mt 8:5
had come out, they **e** the pigs. Mt 8:32
When He **e** the house, the blind Mt 9:28
how he **e** the house of God, Mt 12:4
from there, He **e** their synagogue Mt 12:9
When He **e** Jerusalem, the whole Mt 21:10
When He **e** the temple complex, Mt 21:23
resurrection, **e** the holy city, Mt 27:53
right away He **e** the synagogue Mk 1:21
When He **e** Capernaum again after Mk 2:1
how he **e** the house of God in the Mk 2:26
Now He **e** the synagogue again, Mk 3:1
spirits came out and **e** the pigs, Mk 5:13
and **e** the place where the child Mk 5:40
He **e** a house and did not want Mk 7:24
went out, **e** the city, and found Mk 14:16
When they **e** the tomb, they saw a Mk 16:5
where she **e** Zechariah's house Lk 1:40
by the Spirit, he **e** the temple Lk 2:27
e the synagogue on the Sabbath Lk 4:16
synagogue, He **e** Simon's house. Lk 4:38
how he **e** the house of God, Lk 6:4
Sabbath He **e** the synagogue Lk 6:6
of the people, He **e** Capernaum. Lk 7:1
He **e** the Pharisee's house and Lk 7:36
this woman? I **e** your house; you Lk 7:44
because many demons had **e** him. Lk 8:30
out of the man and **e** the pigs, Lk 8:33
afraid as they **e** the cloud. Lk 9:34
and on the way they **e** a village Lk 9:52
were traveling, He **e** a village, Lk 10:38
As He **e** a village, 10 men with Lk 17:12
He **e** Jericho and was passing Lk 19:1
Then Satan **e** Judas, called Lk 22:3
when you've **e** the city, a man Lk 22:10
When they **e** Galilee, the Jn 4:45
the piece of bread, Satan **e** him. Jn 13:27
He **e** the tomb and saw the linen Jn 20:6
first, then **e** the tomb, saw, Jn 20:8
and he **e** the temple complex with Ac 3:8
they **e** the temple complex at Ac 5:21
So Ananias left and **e** the house. Ac 9:17
The following day he **e** Caesarea. Ac 10:24
When Peter **e**, Cornelius met him, Ac 10:25
or unclean has ever **e** my mouth!' Ac 11:8
they **e** the Jewish synagogue and Ac 14:1
but he himself **e** the synagogue Ac 18:19
he **e** the synagogue and spoke Ac 19:8
where we **e** the house of Philip Ac 21:8
with them, and **e** the temple, Ac 21:26
came and **e** the barracks and Ac 23:16
When these men **e** Caesarea and Ac 23:33
great pomp and **e** the auditorium Ac 25:23
And when we **e** Rome, Paul was Ac 28:16
just as sin **e** the world through Rm 5:12
person who has **e** His rest has Heb 4:10
Jesus has **e** there on our behalf Heb 6:20
He **e** the holy of holies once for Heb 9:12
breath of life from God **e** them, Rv 11:11

ENTERING *(33)*

Israelites from **e** the land the Nm 32:9
the land you are **e** to possess. Dt 4:5
the land you are **e** to possess, Dt 7:1
the land you are **e** to possess is Dt 11:10
the land you are **e** to possess is Dt 11:11
the land you are **e** to possess, Dt 11:29
which you are **e** to take Dt 12:29
the land you are **e** to possess. Dt 23:20
the land you are **e** to possess. Dt 28:21
the land you are **e** to possess. Dt 28:63
the land you are **e** to possess. Dt 30:16
the land you are **e** to possess Dt 30:18
gods of the land they are **e**. Dt 31:16
—no one leaving or **e**. Jos 6:1
woman who is **e** your house like Ru 4:11
attendant were **e** the city when 1Sm 9:14
himself by **e** a town with barred 1Sm 23:7
of the LORD was **e** the city of 2Sm 6:16
just as Absalom was **e** the city. 2Sm 15:37
dared not be seen **e** the city. 2Sm 17:17
sound of her feet **e** the door, 1Kg 14:6
of the LORD was **e** the city of 1Ch 15:29
The land you are **e** to possess is Ezr 9:11
from **e** the King's Gate. Est 4:2
Haman was just **e** the outer court Est 6:4
not catch them breaking and **e**. Jr 2:34
carrying a load while **e** the Jr 17:27
as ⌊an army⌋ **e** a breached city, Ezk 26:10
E the house, they saw the child Mt 2:11
prostitutes are **e** the kingdom of Mt 21:31
and you don't allow those **e** to Mt 23:13
beg from those **e** the temple Ac 3:2
promise remains of **e** His rest, Heb 4:1

ENTERS *(30)*

Whenever he **e** the sanctuary, Ex 28:29
be heard when he **e** the sanctuary Ex 28:35
succeeds him and **e** the tent of Ex 29:30
the house before he **e** to examine Lv 14:36
Whoever **e** the house during any Lv 14:46
from the time he **e** to make Lv 16:17
a man **e** the service in the work Nm 8:24
everyone who **e** the tent and Nm 19:14
and everyone who **e** the temple of 1Sm 5:5
Cherith where it **e** the Jordan. 1Kg 17:3
Cherith where it **e** the Jordan. 1Kg 17:5
side as one **e** the LORD's temple 2Kg 12:9
Anyone who **e** the temple is to be 2Ch 23:7
One without sense **e** an agreement Pr 17:18
He **e** into judgment with all Jr 25:31
he **e** your gates as ⌊an army⌋ Ezk 26:10
east side as one **e** them from the Ezk 42:9
wall as one **e** on the east side, Ezk 42:12
before he **e** the inner court. Ezk 44:21
When the prince **e**, he must go in Ezk 46:8
whoever **e** by way of the north Ezk 46:9
whoever **e** by way of the south Ezk 46:9
When it **e** the sea, the sea of Ezk 47:8
Wherever he **e**, tell the owner of Mk 14:14
Follow him into the house he **e**. Lk 22:10
The one who **e** by the door is the Jn 10:2
If anyone **e** by Me, he will be Jn 10:9
e the inner sanctuary behind Heb 6:19

priest alone e the second room, Heb 9:7
the high priest e the sanctuary Heb 9:25

ENTERTAIN *(2)*
"Bring Samson here to e us." Jdg 16:25
roof watching Samson e ⌊them⌋. Jdg 16:27

ENTERTAINED *(5)*
from prison, and he e them. Jdg 16:25
I never e the thought. Jr 7:31
I never e the thought. Jr 19:5
I had never e the thought that Jr 32:35
welcomed us and e us hospitably Ac 28:7

ENTHRONED *(17)*
of Israel who is e ⌊above⌋ the 2Kg 19:15
seats them forever with e kings, Jb 36:7
The One e in heaven laughs; Ps 2:4
But the LORD sits e forever; Ps 9:7
e on the praises of Israel. Ps 22:3
The LORD sat e at the flood; Ps 29:10
the LORD sits e, King forever. Ps 29:10
God, the One e from long ago, Ps 55:19
May he sit e before God forever; Ps 61:7
You who sit e ⌊on⌋ the cherubim, Ps 80:1
He is e above the cherubim. Ps 99:1
But You, LORD, are e forever; Ps 102:12
our God—the One e on high, Ps 113:5
to You, the One e in heaven. Ps 123:1
who is e above the cherubim, Is 37:16
God is e above the circle of the Is 40:22
You, LORD, are e forever; Lm 5:19

ENTHUSIASTIC *(3)*
They are e about you, but not Gl 4:17
you so you will be e about them. Gl 4:17
always good to be e about good— Gl 4:18

ENTHUSIASTICALLY *(1)*
you do, do it e, as something Col 3:23

ENTICE *(7)*
'Who will e Ahab to march up 1Kg 22:20
LORD, and said, 'I will e him.' 1Kg 22:21
certainly e him and prevail. 1Kg 22:22
'Who will e Ahab king of Israel 2Ch 18:19
LORD, and said, 'I will e him.' 2Ch 18:20
'You will e him and also prevail. 2Ch 18:21
son, if sinners e you, don't be Pr 1:10

ENTICED *(3)*
you are not e to turn aside, Dt 11:16
was secretly e and I threw them Jb 31:27
drawn away and e by his own evil Jms 1:14

ENTICES *(1)*
closest friend secretly e you, Dt 13:6

ENTIRE *(184)*
on the surface of the e earth, Gn 1:29
and water the e surface of the Gn 2:6
encircles the e land of the Gn 2:11
encircles the e land of Cush. Gn 2:13
saw that the e Jordan Valley as Gn 13:10
So Lot chose the e Jordan Valley Gn 13:11
these cities, the e plain, all Gn 19:25
lord of his e household, and Gn 45:8
was no food in that e region, Gn 47:13
dust over the e land of Egypt. Ex 9:9
went up over the e land of Egypt Ex 10:14
horsemen, the e army of Pharaoh Ex 14:28
The e Israelite community Ex 16:1
The e Israelite community Ex 16:2
Say to the e Israelite Ex 16:9
speaking to the e Israelite Ex 16:10
The e Israelite community left Ex 17:1
assembled the e Israelite Ex 35:1
Moses said to the e Israelite Ex 35:4
Then the e Israelite community Ex 35:20
visible to the e house of Israel Ex 40:38
of⌋ its fat and the e fat tail, Lv 3:9
then burned the e ram on the Lv 8:21
disease has covered his e body, Lv 13:13
Speak to the e Israelite Lv 19:2
a census of the e Israelite Nm 1:2
for him and the e community Nm 3:7
oversight of the e tabernacle Nm 4:16
will apply this e ritual to her. Nm 5:30
shave their e bodies and wash Nm 8:7
and assemble the e Israelite Nm 8:9
the e Israelite community did Nm 8:20
the e community is to gather Nm 10:3
and the e Israelite community in Nm 13:26
and said to the e Israelite Nm 14:7
the e number of you 20 years old Nm 14:29
do this to the e evil community Nm 14:35
and incited the e community to Nm 14:36
e community is to prepare one Nm 15:24
atonement for the e Israelite Nm 15:25
e Israelite community and the Nm 15:26
Aaron, and the e community. Nm 15:33
The e community is to stone him Nm 15:35
So the e community brought him Nm 15:36
Everyone in the e community is Nm 16:3
The next day the e Israelite Nm 16:41
must present the e offering due Nm 18:29
e Israelite community entered Nm 20:1
the e Israelite community came Nm 20:22
e house of Israel mourned for Nm 20:29
a census of the e Israelite Nm 26:2
and the e community at the Nm 27:2
on him so that the e Israelite Nm 27:20
him, even the e community, will Nm 27:21
the priest and the e community, Nm 27:22
out to war and the e community. Nm 31:27
38 years until the e generation Dt 2:14
cities, the e region of Argob, Dt 3:4
The e region of Argob, the whole Dt 3:13
took over the e region of Argob Dt 3:14
like this e law I set before you Dt 4:8
a loud voice to your e assembly Dt 5:22
led you on the e journey these Dt 8:2
otherwise, the e harvest, both Dt 22:9
officials, and to his e land. Dt 29:2
this song to the e assembly of Dt 31:30
came to investigate the e land." Jos 2:3
handed over the e land to us. Jos 2:24
ground until the e nation had Jos 3:17
After the e nation had finished Jos 4:1
After the e nation had been Jos 5:8
read before the e assembly of Jos 8:35
Their e provision of bread was Jos 9:5
So Joshua took the e land, Jos 11:23
The e Israelite community Jos 18:1
the e Israelite community Jos 22:12
the LORD's e community says: Jos 22:16
be angry with the e community of Jos 22:18
wrath on the e community of Jos 22:20
the man and his e family. Jdg 1:25
has handed the e Midianite camp Jdg 7:14
and the e ⌊Midianite⌋ army fled, Jdg 7:21
those left of the e army of the Jdg 8:10
of Midian and routed the e army. Jdg 8:12
against the city that e day, Jdg 9:45
possession of the e land of the Jdg 11:21
swords—the e city, the animals Jdg 20:48
a report, the e city cried out. 1Sm 4:13
him among the e population." 1Sm 10:24
the e time we were herding the 1Sm 25:16
for our master and his e family. 1Sm 25:17
spread out over the e area, 1Sm 30:16
and this e vision to David. 2Sm 7:17
had defeated the e army of 2Sm 8:9
his e household followed him. 2Sm 15:16
battle spread over the e region, 2Sm 18:8
one of the e house of Joseph 2Sm 19:20
grandfather's e family deserves 2Sm 19:28
your equal during your e life. 1Kg 3:13
the chambers along the e temple, 1Kg 6:10
overlay to the e temple until 1Kg 6:22
including the e altar that 1Kg 6:22
completed his e palace-complex 1Kg 7:1
Solomon and the e congregation 1Kg 8:5
and blessed the e congregation 1Kg 8:14
in front of the e congregation 1Kg 8:22
praying this e prayer and 1Kg 8:54
will not tear the e kingdom away 1Kg 11:13
him over the e labor force 1Kg 11:28
from the e house of Judah 1Kg 12:21
with the LORD his e life. 1Kg 15:14
struck down the e house of 1Kg 15:29
down the e house of Baasha 1Kg 16:11
the e house of Baasha 1Kg 16:12
of Aram assembled his e army. 1Kg 20:1
Do you see this e immense horde? 1Kg 20:13
hand over this e immense horde 1Kg 20:28
through the e time of the kings 2Kg 23:22
Jerusalem with his e army. 2Kg 25:1
Zedekiah's e army was scattered 2Kg 25:5
and this e vision to David. 1Ch 17:15
had defeated the e army of King 1Ch 18:9
Joab and the e army of warriors 1Ch 19:8
Solomon and the e congregation 2Ch 5:6
and blessed the e congregation 2Ch 6:3
in front of the e congregation 2Ch 6:12
in front of the e congregation 2Ch 6:13
Asa was wholehearted his e life. 2Ch 15:17
provided the e army with shields 2Ch 26:14
officials and the e congregation 2Ch 30:2
rebuilding the e broken-down 2Ch 32:5
from the e remnant of Israel, 2Ch 34:9
his e kingdom and also 2Ch 36:22
throughout his e kingdom and ⌊to Ezr 1:1
represent the e assembly. Ezr 10:14
wall until the e wall was joined Neh 4:6
The e royal staff at the King's Est 3:2
You have devastated my e family. Jb 16:7
it would destroy my e harvest. Jb 31:12
Him in charge of the e world? Jb 34:13
lets it loose beneath the e sky; Jb 37:3
and destroyed the e food supply. Ps 105:16
crush leaders over the e world. Ps 110:6
first produce of your e harvest; Pr 3:9
ruin before the e community." Pr 5:14
the e supply of bread and water, Is 3:1
night over the e site of Mount Is 4:5
streams will fill your e land, Is 8:8
destroy on My e holy mountain, Is 11:9
you the e vision will be like Is 29:11
destroy on My e holy mountain," Is 65:25
the e house of the Rechabites— Jr 35:3
fire until the e scroll was Jr 36:23
strike down the e Chaldean army Jr 37:10
with his e army and laid Jr 39:1
on behalf of this e remnant Jr 42:2
completely destroy her e army! Jr 51:3
Her e land will suffer shame, Jr 51:47
Jerusalem with his e army. Jr 52:4
Zedekiah's e army was scattered Jr 52:8
abandoned us for ⌊our⌋ e lives? Lm 5:20
to destroy the e remnant of Ezk 9:8
Their e bodies, including their Ezk 10:12
and the e house of Israel, Ezk 11:15
there the e house of Israel, Ezk 20:40
beasts of the e earth eat their Ezk 32:4
This e tract of land will be Ezk 45:1
The e donation will be eight and Ezk 48:20
and mediums in his e kingdom. Dn 1:20
him ruler over the e province of Dn 2:48
surface of the e earth without Dn 8:5
the e clan that I brought Am 3:1
and the e remnant of the people Hg 1:12
throughout the e vicinity of Mk 1:28
throughout the e vicinity. Lk 4:14
spread through the e mixture." Lk 13:21
was in charge of her e treasury. Ac 8:27
God with his e household. Ac 16:34
is obligated to keep the e law. Gl 5:3
the e law is fulfilled in one Gl 5:14
For in Him the e fullness of Col 2:9
brothers in the e region of 1Th 4:10
For whoever keeps the e law, Jms 2:10
the e moon became like blood; Rv 6:12

ENTIRELY *(6)*
of the ephod e of blue yarn. Ex 28:31
of the ephod e of blue yarn. Ex 39:22
all His ways are e just. Dt 32:4
he will be e wiped out. Nah 1:15
I made a man e well on the Jn 7:23
"You were born e in sin," they Jn 9:34

ENTIRETY *(4)*
The e of Your word is truth, Ps 119:160
will happen to you in their e, Is 47:9
and ⌊so will⌋ all Edom in its e. Ezk 35:15
whole house of Israel in its e. Ezk 36:10

ENTOURAGE *(1)*
together with her e, her father, Dn 11:6

ENTRAILS *(20)*
all the fat that covers the e, Ex 29:13
Wash its e and shanks, and place Ex 29:17
covering the e, the fatty lobe Ex 29:22
must wash its e and shanks with Lv 1:9
is to wash the e and shanks with Lv 1:13
the fat surrounding the e, Lv 3:3
all the fat that is on the e, Lv 3:3
the fat surrounding the e, Lv 3:9
entrails, all the fat on the e, Lv 3:9
the fat surrounding the e, Lv 3:14
all the fat that is on the e, Lv 3:14
the fat surrounding the e; Lv 4:8

all the fat that is on the **e**; Lv 4:8
and shanks, and its **e** and dung— Lv 4:11
the fat surrounding the **e**, Lv 7:3
all the fat that was on the **e**, Lv 8:16
he washed the **e** and shanks with Lv 8:21
all the fat that was on the **e**, Lv 8:25
He washed the **e** and the shanks Lv 9:14
the ⌊fat⌋ surrounding ⌊the **e**⌋, Lv 9:19

ENTRANCE *(147)*

sitting in the **e** of his tent Gn 18:1
he ran from the **e** of the tent to Gn 18:2
listening at the **e** of the tent Gn 18:10
to them at the **e** and shut the Gn 19:6
and sat at the **e** to Enaim, Gn 38:14
For the **e** to the tent you are to Ex 26:36
his sons to the **e** to the tent Ex 29:4
the LORD at the **e** to the tent of Ex 29:11
the basket at the **e** to the tent Ex 29:32
generations at the **e** to the tent Ex 29:42
stood at the camp's **e** and said, Ex 32:26
the camp from **e** to entrance, Ex 32:27
the camp from entrance to **e**, Ex 32:27
and remain at the **e** to the tent, Ex 33:9
remaining at the **e** to the tent, Ex 33:10
screen for the **e** to the Ex 35:15
linen for the **e** to the tent, Ex 36:37
who served at the **e** to the tent Ex 38:8
the bases for the **e** to the tent Ex 38:30
screen for the **e** to the tent; Ex 39:38
screen for the **e** to the Ex 40:5
in front of the **e** to the Ex 40:6
his sons to the **e** to the tent Ex 40:12
screen at the **e** to the Ex 40:28
offering at the **e** to the Ex 40:29
bring it to the **e** to the tent Lv 1:3
that is at the **e** to the tent Lv 1:5
slaughter it at the **e** to the Lv 3:2
the bull to the **e** to the tent Lv 4:4
that is at the **e** to the tent of Lv 4:7
that is at the **e** to the tent of Lv 4:18
community at the **e** to the tent Lv 8:3
assembled at the **e** to the tent Lv 8:4
the meat at the **e** to the tent Lv 8:31
not go outside the **e** to the tent Lv 8:33
must remain at the **e** to the tent Lv 8:35
not go outside the **e** to the tent Lv 10:7
the priest at the **e** to the tent Lv 12:6
the LORD at the **e** to the tent of Lv 14:11
the priest at the **e** to the tent Lv 14:23
the LORD at the **e** to the tent of Lv 15:14
the priest at the **e** to the tent Lv 15:29
the LORD at the **e** to the tent of Lv 16:7
bringing it to the **e** to the tent Lv 17:4
the priest at the **e** to the tent Lv 17:5
LORD's altar at the **e** to the Lv 17:6
bring it to the **e** to the tent Lv 17:9
to the LORD at the **e** to the tent Lv 19:21
the screen for the **e** to the tent Nm 3:25
for the **e** to the courtyard Nm 3:26
the screen for the **e** to the tent Nm 4:25
the screen for the **e** at the gate Nm 4:26
the priest at the **e** to the tent Nm 6:10
be brought to the **e** to the tent Nm 6:13
head at the **e** to the tent of Nm 6:18
before you at the **e** to the tent Nm 10:3
crying at the **e** of their tents. Nm 11:10
stood at the **e** to the tent, Nm 12:5
as Rehob near the **e** to Hamath. Nm 13:21
and stood at the **e** to the tent Nm 16:18
against them at the **e** to the Nm 16:19
stood at the **e** of their tents Nm 16:27
to Moses at the **e** to the tent of Nm 16:50
weeping at the **e** to the tent Nm 25:6
community at the **e** to the tent Nm 27:2
draw a line to the **e** of Hamath, Nm 34:8
stood at the **e** to the tent. Dt 31:15
down at the **e** of the city gate Jos 8:29
Hermon to the **e** of Hamath— Jos 13:5
presence at the **e** to the tent of Jos 19:51
at the **e** of the city gate, Jos 20:4
as far as the **e** to Hamath. Jdg 3:3
Stand at the **e** to the tent. Jdg 4:20
stood at the **e** of the city gate Jdg 9:35
as far as the **e** of the gate. Jdg 9:40
stand at the **e** of the city gate Jdg 9:44
approached its **e** to set it on Jdg 9:52
the way to the **e** of Minnith and Jdg 11:33
standing by the **e** of the gate, Jdg 18:16
standing by the **e** of the gate Jdg 18:17
who served at the **e** to the tent 1Sm 2:22
to the **e** of the valley 1Sm 17:52
at the **e** to the city gate 2Sm 10:8
right up to the **e** of the gate. 2Sm 11:23
the **e** of the inner sanctuary, 1Kg 6:31
doorposts for the sanctuary **e**. 1Kg 6:33
the **e** of Hamath to the Brook 1Kg 8:65
who guarded the **e** to the king's 1Kg 14:27
of Ahab to the **e** of Jezreel. 1Kg 18:46
and stood at the **e** of the cave. 1Kg 19:13
at the **e** to Samaria's gate, 1Kg 22:10
were at the **e** to the gate. 2Kg 7:3
two heaps at the **e** of the gate 2Kg 10:8
of the Horses' **E** to the king's 2Kg 11:16
the outer **e** for the king. 2Kg 16:18
the gates at the **e** of the gate 2Kg 23:8
had been⌋ at the **e** of the LORD's 2Kg 23:11
They went to the **e** of Gedor, 1Ch 4:39
camp as guardians of the **e**. 1Ch 9:19
gatekeeper at the **e** to the tent 1Ch 9:21
of Egypt to the **e** of Hamath, 1Ch 13:5
formation at the **e** of the city 1Ch 19:9
the **e** to Hamath to the Brook 2Ch 7:8
who guarded the **e** to the king's 2Ch 12:10
at the **e** to Samaria's gate, 2Ch 18:9
standing by his pillar at the **e**. 2Ch 23:13
she went by the **e** of the Horses' 2Ch 23:15
spread as far as the **e** of Egypt, 2Ch 26:8
went to the **e** of the LORD's 2Ch 29:16
valley to the **e** of the Fish Gate 2Ch 33:14
who guarded the ⌊king's⌋ **e**, Est 2:21
royal courtroom, facing its **e**. Est 5:1
who guarded the ⌊king's⌋ **e**, Est 6:2
speaks at the **e** of the city Pr 1:21
at the main **e**, she cries out: Pr 8:3
throne at the **e** to Jerusalem's Jr 1:15
near the **e** of the Potsherd Jr 19:2
sat at the **e** of the New Gate. Jr 26:10
him at the third **e** of the LORD's Jr 38:14
to the **e** of the inner gate that Ezk 8:3
of the altar gate, at the **e**. Ezk 8:5
me to the **e** of the court, Ezk 8:7
me to the **e** of the north gate Ezk 8:14
25 men at the **e** of the LORD's Ezk 8:16
it stood at the **e** to the eastern Ezk 10:19
and at the gate's **e** were 25 men. Ezk 11:1
is located at the **e** of the sea, Ezk 27:3
the width of the gate's **e**; Ezk 40:11
the gate at the **e** to the front Ezk 40:15
approaches the **e** of the north Ezk 40:40
The width of the **e** was 17 and a Ezk 41:2
sidewalls of the **e** were eight Ezk 41:2
measured the pilasters at the **e**; Ezk 41:3
The **e** was 10 and a half feet Ezk 41:3
one **e** toward the north and Ezk 41:11
reaching to the top of the **e**, Ezk 41:17
the top of the **e** and on the wall Ezk 41:20
there was an **e** on the north; Ezk 42:2
The **e** at the beginning of the Ezk 42:12
note of the **e** of the temple Ezk 44:5
the LORD at the **e** of that gate Ezk 46:3
me through the **e** that was at the Ezk 46:19
me back to the **e** of the temple Ezk 47:1
you from the **e** of Hamath to Am 6:14
stone against the **e** of the tomb. Mt 27:60
stone against the **e** to the tomb. Mk 15:46
stone from the **e** to the tomb for Mk 16:3

ENTRANCE'S *(1)*

the width of the **e** sidewalls on Ezk 41:3

ENTRANCES *(4)*

and their **e** were on the north. Ezk 42:4
and **e**, were identical. Ezk 42:11
similar to the **e** of the chambers Ezk 42:12
layout with its exits and **e**— Ezk 43:11

ENTRAP *(1)*

A wicked man's iniquities **e** him; Pr 5:22

ENTREAT *(1)*

when we are slandered, we **e**. 1Co 4:13

ENTRIES *(2)*

searched for their **e** in the Ezr 2:62
searched for their **e** in the Neh 7:64

ENTRUST *(4)*

Into Your hand I **e** my spirit; Ps 31:5
into Your hands I **e** My spirit." Lk 23:46
would not **e** Himself to them, Jn 2:24
e themselves to a faithful 1Pt 4:19

ENTRUSTED *(20)*

He **e** them to his slaves as Gn 32:16
or the deposit **e** to him, or the Lv 6:4
were **e** with the rooms and the 1Ch 9:26
was **e** with baking the bread. 1Ch 9:31
Where is the flock **e** to you, Jr 13:20
things have been **e** to Me by My Mt 11:27
things have been **e** to Me by My Lk 10:22
one who has been **e** with more. Lk 12:48
they had been **e** to the grace of Ac 14:26
were **e** with the spoken words Rm 3:2
of teaching you were **e** to, Rm 6:17
I am **e** with a stewardship. 1Co 9:17
I had been **e** with the gospel Gl 2:7
by God to be **e** with the gospel, 1Th 2:4
blessed God that was **e** to me. 1Tm 1:11
guard what has been **e** to you, 1Tm 6:20
what has been **e** to me until that 2Tm 1:12
in us, that good thing **e** to you. 2Tm 1:14
that I was **e** with by the command Ti 1:3
lording it over those **e** to you, 1Pt 5:3

ENTRUSTS *(1)*

The helpless **e** himself to You; Ps 10:14

ENTRY *(3)*

the gates at the **e** to the city, Pr 8:3
every house is closed to **e**. Is 24:10
e into the eternal kingdom of 2Pt 1:11

ENTRYWAY *(4)*

the **e** screen for the entrance to Ex 35:15
and the **e** to the temple, its 2Ch 4:22
there was an **e** on the east side Ezk 42:9
Then he went out to the **e**, Mk 14:68

ENVELOPED *(5)*

completely **e** in smoke because Ex 19:18
the heavens and **e** in a dense, Dt 4:11
The Spirit of the LORD **e** Gideon, Jdg 6:34
in righteousness, and it **e** me; Jb 29:14
LORD is robed, **e** in strength. Ps 93:1

ENVIED *(3)*

any children⌋, she **e** her sister. Gn 30:1
For I **e** the arrogant; Ps 73:3
were in God's garden, **e** it. Ezk 31:9

ENVIOUS *(3)*

the Philistines were **e** of him. Gn 26:14
camp they were **e** of Moses and Ps 106:16
will no longer be **e** of Judah, Is 11:13

ENVOY *(2)*

an **e** has been sent among the Jr 49:14
an **e** has been sent among the Ob 1

ENVOYS *(5)*

Hiram of Tyre sent **e** to David; 2Sm 5:11
had sent **e** to So king of Egypt 2Kg 17:4
Hiram of Tyre sent **e** to David, 1Ch 14:1
sends **e** by sea, in reed vessels Is 18:2
sent your **e** far away and sent Is 57:9

ENVY *(19)*

do not **e** those who do wrong. Ps 37:1
Why gaze with **e**, you mountain Ps 68:16
Don't **e** a violent man or choose Pr 3:31
Don't **e** evil men or desire to be Pr 24:1
and don't **e** the wicked. Pr 24:19
and their **e** have already Ec 9:6
Ephraim's **e** will cease; Is 11:13
handed Him over because of **e**. Mt 27:18
was because of **e** that the chief Mk 15:10
They are full of **e**, murder, Rm 1:29
there is **e** and strife among 1Co 3:3
does not **e**; is not boastful; 1Co 13:4
e, drunkenness, carousing, and Gl 5:21
Christ out of **e** and strife, Php 1:15
From these come **e**, quarreling, 1Tm 6:4
in malice and **e**, hateful, Ti 3:3
if you have bitter **e** and selfish Jms 3:14
For where **e** and selfish ambition Jms 3:16
hypocrisy, **e**, and all slander. 1Pt 2:1

ENVYING *(1)*

one another, **e** one another. Gl 5:26

EPAENETUS *(1)*

my dear friend **E**, who is the Rm 16:5

EPAPHRAS *(3)*

this from **E**, our much loved Col 1:7
E, who is one of you, a slave of Col 4:12
E, my fellow prisoner in Christ Phm 23

EPAPHRODITUS *(2)*
it necessary to send you **E**— Php 2:25
from **E** what you provided Php 4:18

EPHAH *(1)*
(See also EPHAH proper noun.)
Two quarts are a tenth of an **e**. Ex 16:36

EPHAH (proper noun) *(5)*
sons were **E**, Epher, Hanoch, Gn 25:4
E, Epher, Hanoch, Abida, and 1Ch 1:33
concubine **E** was the mother 1Ch 2:46
Geshan, Pelet, **E**, and Shaaph. 1Ch 2:47
young camels of Midian and **E**— Is 60:6

EPHAI *(1)*
the sons of **E** the Netophathite, Jr 40:8

EPHER *(4)*
were Ephah, **E**, Hanoch, Abida, Gn 25:4
Ephah, **E**, Hanoch, Abida, and 1Ch 1:33
Jether, Mered, **E**, and Jalon. 1Ch 4:17
E, Ishi, Eliel, Azriel, Jeremiah, 1Ch 5:24

EPHES-DAMMIM *(1)*
between Socoh and Azekah in **E**. 1Sm 17:1

EPHESIAN *(1)*
Trophimus the **E** in the city with Ac 21:29

EPHESIANS *(3)*
"Great is Artemis of the **E**!" Ac 19:28
"Great is Artemis of the **E**!" Ac 19:34
the city of the **E** is the temple Ac 19:35

EPHESUS *(17)*
When they reached **E** he left them Ac 18:19
Then he set sail from **E**. Ac 18:21
in the Scriptures, arrived in **E**. Ac 18:24
interior regions and came to **E**. Ac 19:1
to everyone who lived in **E**, Ac 19:17
see and hear that not only in **E**, Ac 19:26
crowd down, he said, "Men of **E**! Ac 19:35
to sail past **E** so he would not Ac 20:16
he sent to **E** and called for the Ac 20:17
animals in **E** with only human 1Co 15:32
will stay in **E** until Pentecost, 1Co 16:8
believers in Christ Jesus at **E**. Eph 1:1
remain in **E** so that you may 1Tm 1:3
how much he ministered at **E**. 2Tm 1:18
I have sent Tychicus to **E**. 2Tm 4:12
E, Smyrna, Pergamum, Thyatira, Rv 1:11
angel of the church in **E** write: Rv 2:1

EPHLAL *(2)*
Zabad fathered **E**, and Ephlal 1Ch 2:37
Ephlal, and **E** fathered Obed. 1Ch 2:37

EPHOD *(42)*
(See also EPHOD proper noun.)
on the **e** and breastpiece Ex 25:7
a breastpiece, an **e**, a robe, a Ex 28:4
are to make the **e** of finely spun Ex 28:6
that is on the **e** must be of one Ex 28:8
pieces of the **e** as memorial Ex 28:12
the same workmanship as the **e**; Ex 28:15
to the inner border of the **e**. Ex 28:26
the rings of the **e** with a cord Ex 28:28
does not come loose from the **e**. Ex 28:28
the robe of the **e** entirely of Ex 28:31
the robe for the **e**, the ephod Ex 29:5
for the ephod, the **e** itself, Ex 29:5
fasten the **e** on him with its Ex 29:5
mount on the **e** and breastpiece Ex 35:9
mount on the **e** and breastpiece Ex 35:27
Bezalel made the **e** of gold, Ex 39:2
that was on the **e** was of one Ex 39:5
was of one piece with the **e**, Ex 39:5
pieces of the **e** as memorial Ex 39:7
workmanship as the **e** of gold, Ex 39:8
to the inner border of the **e**. Ex 39:19
the rings of the **e** with a cord Ex 39:21
did not come loose from the **e**. Ex 39:21
robe of the **e** entirely of blue Ex 39:22
the robe, and put the **e** on him. Lv 8:7
woven band of the **e** around him Lv 8:7
Gideon made an **e** from all this Jdg 8:27
and he made an **e** and household Jdg 17:5
you know that there are an **e**, Jdg 18:14
with silver, the **e**, and the Jdg 18:17
with silver, the **e**, and the Jdg 18:18
was pleased and took his **e**, Jdg 18:20
presence and wore a linen **e**. 1Sm 2:18
and to wear an **e** in My presence. 1Sm 2:28
wearing an **e**, ⌊was also there⌋ 1Sm 14:3
wrapped in a cloth behind the **e**. 1Sm 21:9
and he brought an **e** with him. 1Sm 23:6
the priest, "Bring the **e**." 1Sm 23:9
of Ahimelech, "Bring me the **e**." 1Sm 30:7
the LORD wearing a linen **e** . 2Sm 6:14
David also wore a linen **e**. 1Ch 15:27
without **e** or household idols. Hs 3:4

EPHOD (proper noun) *(43)*
Hanniel son of **E**, a leader from Nm 34:23

EPHOD'S *(8)*
them⌋ to the **e** shoulder pieces Ex 28:25
the bottom of the **e** two shoulder Ex 28:27
and above the **e** woven waistband. Ex 28:27
above the **e** waistband and does Ex 28:28
them⌋ to the **e** shoulder pieces Ex 39:18
the bottom of the **e** two shoulder Ex 39:20
above the **e** woven waistband. Ex 39:20
above the **e** waistband and did Ex 39:21

EPHODS *(1)*
killed 85 men who wore linen **e**. 1Sm 22:18

EPHPHATHA *(1)*
deeply and said to him, "**E**!" Mk 7:34

EPHRAIM *(155)*
(city, AKA EPHRON)
And the second son he named **E**, Gn 41:52
Manasseh and **E** were born to Gn 46:20
his two sons, Manasseh and **E**. Gn 48:1
E and Manasseh belong to me just Gn 48:5
his right hand **E** toward Israel's Gn 48:13
and put it on the head of **E**, Gn 48:14
make you like **E** and Manasseh," Gn 48:20
putting **E** before Manasseh. Gn 48:20
Elishama son of Ammihud from **E**, Nm 1:10
The descendants of **E**: Nm 1:32
the tribe of **E** numbered 40,500 Nm 1:33
of the camp of **E** with their Nm 10:22
son of Nun from the tribe of **E**; Nm 13:8
clans ⌊from⌋ Manasseh and **E**: Nm 26:28
a leader from the tribe of **E**; Nm 34:24
Such are the ten thousands of **E**, Dt 33:17
the land of **E** and Manasseh, Dt 34:2
two tribes, Manasseh and **E**. Jos 14:4
So **E** and Manasseh, the sons of Jos 16:4
descendants of **E** by their clans: Jos 16:5
descendants of **E** by their clans, Jos 16:8
the descendants of **E** within the Jos 16:9
live in **E** to this day, Jos 16:10
to the descendants of **E**. Jos 17:8
belonged to **E** among Manasseh's Jos 17:9
that is, **E** and Manasseh), Jos 17:17
in the hill country of **E**, Jos 19:50
in the hill country of **E**, Jos 20:7
the clans of the tribes of **E**, Jos 21:5
came from the tribe of **E**. Jos 21:20
in the hill country of **E**, Jos 21:21
hill country of **E** north of Mount Jos 24:30
in the hill country of **E**. Jos 24:33
At that time **E** failed to drive Jdg 1:29
country of **E**, north of Mount Jdg 2:9
the hill country of **E**. Jdg 3:27
Bethel in the hill country of **E**, Jdg 4:5
roots in Amalek ⌊came⌋ from **E**; Jdg 5:14
hill country of **E** with this Jdg 7:24
all the men of **E** were called out Jdg 7:24
The men of **E** said to him, Jdg 8:1
the gleaning of **E** better than Jdg 8:2
Shamir in the hill country of **E**. Jdg 10:1
Benjamin, and the house of **E**. Jdg 10:9
men of **E** were called together Jdg 12:1
They fought and defeated **E**, Jdg 12:4
Ephraim, because **E** had said, "You Jdg 12:4
territories of⌋ **E** and Manasseh." Jdg 12:4
of the Jordan leading to **E**. Jdg 12:5
Whenever a fugitive from **E** said, Jdg 12:5
that time, 42,000 from **E** died. Jdg 12:6
in Pirathon in the land of **E**, Jdg 12:15
hill country of **E** named Micah. Jdg 17:1
home in the hill country of **E**. Jdg 17:8
hill country of **E** as far as the Jdg 18:2
hill country of **E** and arrived at Jdg 18:13
hill country of **E** acquired a Jdg 19:1
hill country of **E** but was Jdg 19:16
to the remote hill country of **E**, Jdg 19:18
in the hill country of **E**. 1Sm 1:1
hill country of **E** and then 1Sm 9:4
the hill country of **E** heard that 1Sm 14:22
Asher, Jezreel, **E**, Benjamin— 2Sm 2:9
were at Baal-hazor near **E**, 2Sm 13:23
took place in the forest of **E**. 2Sm 18:6
from the hill country of **E**, 2Sm 20:21
in the hill country of **E**; 1Kg 4:8
country of **E** and lived there 1Kg 12:25
me from the hill country of **E**. 2Kg 5:22
wall from the **E** Gate to the 2Kg 14:13
from the tribe of **E** for their 1Ch 6:66
in the hill country of **E**, 1Ch 6:67
Their father **E** mourned a long 1Ch 7:22
Judah, Benjamin, **E**, and Manasseh 1Ch 9:3
the Pelonite from the sons of **E**; 1Ch 27:10
Pirathonite from the sons of **E**; 1Ch 27:14
is in the hill country of **E**, 2Ch 13:4
in the hill country of **E**. 2Ch 15:8
as those from ⌊the tribes of⌋ **E**, 2Ch 15:9
the cities of **E** that his father 2Ch 17:2
hill country of **E** and brought 2Ch 19:4
came to him from **E** to go home. 2Ch 25:10
wall from the **E** Gate to the 2Ch 25:23
letters to **E** and Manasseh to 2Ch 30:1
in the land of **E** and Manasseh as 2Ch 30:10
people—many from **E**, Manasseh, 2Ch 30:18
as well as in **E** and Manasseh, 2Ch 31:1
of Manasseh, **E**, and Simeon, and 2Ch 34:6
from Manasseh, **E**, and from the 2Ch 34:9
and the square by the Gate of **E**. Neh 8:16
the Gate of **E**, and by the Old Neh 12:39
is Mine, and **E** is My helmet; Ps 60:7
did not choose the tribe of **E**. Ps 78:67
at the head of **E**, Benjamin, and Ps 80:2
is Mine, and **E** is My helmet; Ps 108:8
David that Aram had occupied **E**, Is 7:2
along with **E** and the son of Is 7:5
within 65 years **E** will be too Is 7:8
head of **E** is Samaria, and the Is 7:9
never been since **E** separated Is 7:17
E and the inhabitants of Samaria Is 9:9
Manasseh is with **E**, and Ephraim Is 9:21
Ephraim, and **E** with Manasseh; Is 9:21
E will no longer be envious of Is 11:13
and Judah will not harass **E**. Is 11:13
The fortress disappears from **E**, Is 17:3
proclaiming malice from Mount **E**. Jr 4:15
all the descendants of **E**. Jr 7:15
out in the hill country of **E**: Jr 31:6
Father, and **E** is My firstborn. Jr 31:9
I have heard **E** moaning: Jr 31:18
Isn't **E** a precious son to Me, Jr 31:20
hill country of **E** and of Gilead. Jr 50:19
the stick of **E**—and all the Ezk 37:16
which is in the hand of **E**— Ezk 37:19
west, will be **E**—one ⌊portion⌋ Ezk 48:5
Next to the territory of **E**, Ezk 48:6
E is attached to idols; Hs 4:17
I know **E**, and Israel is not Hs 5:3
For now, **E**, you have acted Hs 5:3
Israel and **E** stumble because Hs 5:5
E will become a desolation on Hs 5:9
E is oppressed, crushed in Hs 5:11
am like rot to **E** and like decay Hs 5:12
E saw his sickness and Judah Hs 5:13
E went to Assyria and sent ⌊a Hs 5:13
like a lion to **E** and like a Hs 5:14
am I going to do with you, **E**? Hs 6:4
the sins of **E** and the crimes of Hs 7:1
E has allowed himself to get Hs 7:8
E is unturned bread, baked on a Hs 7:8
So **E** has become like a silly, Hs 7:11
E has paid for love. Hs 8:9
When **E** multiplied his altars for Hs 8:11
Instead, **E** will return to Egypt, Hs 9:3
I have seen **E** like Tyre, planted Hs 9:13
so **E** will bring out his children Hs 9:13
E is blighted; their roots are Hs 9:16
E will experience shame; Hs 10:6
E is a well-trained young cow Hs 10:11
I will harness **E**; Judah will Hs 10:11
It was I who taught **E** to walk, Hs 11:3
How can I give you up, **E**? Hs 11:8
will not turn back to destroy **E**. Hs 11:9
E surrounds me with lies, the Hs 11:12
E chases the wind and pursues Hs 12:1
But **E** says: "How rich I have Hs 12:8
E has provoked bitter anger, Hs 12:14
When **E** spoke, there was Hs 13:1
E, why should I have anything Hs 14:8
territories of **E** and Samaria, Ob 19
the chariot from **E** and the horse Zch 9:10

I will fill that bow with **E**. Zch 9:13
E will be like a warrior, and Zch 10:7
wilderness, to a town called **E**. Jn 11:54

EPHRAIM'S *(17)*
placed his right hand on **E** head, Gn 48:17
to move it from **E** head to Gn 48:17
He saw **E** sons to the third Gn 50:23
E military divisions will camp Nm 2:18
belong to **E** encampment number Nm 2:24
of Ammihud was over **E** division. Nm 10:22
were **E** descendants by their Nm 26:35
E ⌊territory⌋ was to the south Jos 17:10
because **E** hill country is too Jos 17:15
E sons: Shuthelah, and his son 1Ch 7:20
E envy will cease; Is 11:13
majestic crown of **E** drunkards, Is 28:1
crown of **E** drunkards will be Is 28:3
E promiscuity is there; Hs 6:10
E watchman is with my God. Hs 9:8
E glory will fly away like a Hs 9:11
E guilt is preserved; Hs 13:12

EPHRAIMITE *(7)*
were the **E** clans ⌊numbered⌋ Nm 26:37
You Gileadites are **E** fugitives Jdg 12:4
asked him, "Are you an **E**?" Jdg 12:5
son of Tohu, son of Zuph, an **E**. 1Sm 1:1
of Nebat, was an **E** from Zeredah. 1Kg 11:26
An **E** warrior named Zichri killed 2Ch 28:7
The **E** archers turned back on the Ps 78:9

EPHRAIMITES *(6)*
leader of the **E** is Elishama son Nm 2:18
leader of the **E**, ⌊presented Nm 7:48
the **E**: 20,800 brave warriors 1Ch 12:30
the **E**, Hoshea son of Azaziah; 1Ch 27:20
is not with Israel—all the **E**. 2Ch 25:7
men who were leaders of the **E**— 2Ch 28:12

EPHRATH *(5)*
(AKA BETHLEHEM)
were still some distance from **E**, Gn 35:16
and was buried on the way to **E** Gn 35:19
some distance from **E** in the land Gn 48:7
her there along the way to **E**," Gn 48:7
Caleb married **E**, and she bore 1Ch 2:19

EPHRATHAH *(3)*
you be powerful in **E** and famous Ru 4:11
We heard of ⌊the ark⌋ in **E**; Ps 132:6
Bethlehem **E**, you are small among Mc 5:2

EPHRATHAH'S *(2)*
The sons of Hur, **E** firstborn: 1Ch 2:50
E firstborn and the father of 1Ch 4:4

EPHRATHITE *(1)*
the son of the **E** from Bethlehem 1Sm 17:12

EPHRATHITES *(1)*
They were **E** from Bethlehem in Ru 1:2

EPHRON *(13)*
(AKA EPHRAIM)
to me and ask **E** son of Zohar on Gn 23:8
E was present with the Hittites. Gn 23:10
E the Hittite answered Abraham: Gn 23:10
and said to **E** in the presence of Gn 23:13
E answered Abraham and said to Gn 23:14
agreed with **E**, and Abraham Gn 23:16
weighed out to **E** the silver that Gn 23:16
in the field of **E** son of Zohar Gn 25:9
in the field of **E** the Hittite. Gn 49:29
purchased from **E** the Hittite as Gn 49:30
burial site from **E** the Hittite. Gn 50:13
went to the cities of Mount **E**, Jos 15:9
villages, and **E** and its villages 2Ch 13:19

EPHRON'S *(1)*
So **E** field at Machpelah near Gn 23:17

EPICUREAN *(1)*
some of the **E** and Stoic Ac 17:18

EPILEPTICS *(1)*
the **e**, and the paralytics Mt 4:24

EPISTLE *(1)*
who penned this **e** in the Lord, Rm 16:22

EQUAL *(18)*
amount in silver **e** to the bridal Ex 22:17
are to be in **e** measures. Ex 30:34
They will eat **e** portions besides Dt 18:8
Who in Israel is your **e**? 1Sm 26:15
be your **e** during your entire 1Kg 3:13
has no **e** on earth—a creature Jb 41:33
compare Me to, or who is My **e**?" Is 40:25
you compare Me or make Me **e** to? Is 46:5
feet wide, with four **e** sides. Ezk 43:17
Your mina will **e** 60 shekels. Ezk 45:12
liquid measures **e** one standard Ezk 45:14
will inherit it in **e** portions, Ezk 47:14
no one was found **e** to Daniel, Dn 1:19
you made them **e** to us who bore Mt 20:12
making Himself **e** with God. Jn 5:18
and the one who waters are **e**, 1Co 3:8
a faith of **e** privilege with ours 2Pt 1:1
length, width, and height are **e**. Rv 21:16

EQUALITY *(3)*
but it is a question of **e**— 2Co 8:13
your need, that there may be **e**. 2Co 8:14
did not consider **e** with God as Php 2:6

EQUALLY *(4)*
e to all of Aaron's sons. Lv 7:10
supplies. They will share **e**." 1Sm 30:24
if both of them will be **e** good. Ec 11:6
E, a husband does not have 1Co 7:4

EQUALS *(1)*
⌊The cor **e**⌋ 10 liquid measures Ezk 45:14

EQUIP *(2)*
E some of your men for war. Nm 31:3
e you with all that is good to Heb 13:21

EQUIPMENT *(21)*
and all the **e** for the service of Ex 39:40
bases, all its **e**, and all the Nm 3:36
place all the **e** on it that they Nm 4:14
basins—all the **e** of the altar. Nm 4:14
all their **e** whenever the camp Nm 4:15
and all the **e** for their service Nm 4:26
all their **e** and all the work Nm 4:32
the sanctuary **e** or the altar; Nm 18:3
have a digging tool in your **e**; Dt 23:13
war or the **e** for his chariots. 1Sm 8:12
gave his **e** to the young man 1Sm 20:40
made all the **e** in the LORD's 1Kg 7:48
clothes and **e** the Arameans had 2Kg 7:15
or any of the **e** for its service" 1Ch 23:26
made all the **e** in God's temple: 2Ch 4:19
storing his **e** at Michmash. Is 10:28
tent curtains and all their **e**. Jr 49:29
with writing **e** at his side. Ezk 9:2
with the writing **e** at his side. Ezk 9:3
with the writing **e** at his side Ezk 9:11
Take the **e** of a foolish Zch 11:15

EQUIPPED *(9)*
in Israel—12,000 **e** for war. Nm 31:5
servants are **e** for war before Nm 32:27
About 40,000 **e** for war crossed Jos 4:13
120,000 men **e** with all the 1Ch 12:37
and 180,000 with him **e** for war. 2Ch 17:18
had an army **e** for combat that 2Ch 26:11
an army of 307,500 **e** for combat, 2Ch 26:13
be complete, **e** for every good 2Tm 3:17
was like horses **e** for battle. Rv 9:7

ER *(10)*
to a son, and he named him **E**. Gn 38:3
got a wife for **E**, his firstborn, Gn 38:6
Now **E**, Judah's firstborn, was Gn 38:7
E, Onan, Shelah, Perez, and Gn 46:12
but **E** and Onan died in the land Gn 46:12
sons included **E** and Onan, Nm 26:19
Judah's sons: **E**, Onan, and 1Ch 2:3
E, Judah's firstborn, was evil 1Ch 2:3
E the father of Lecah, Laadah 1Ch 4:21
son⌋ of Elmadam, ⌊son⌋ of **E**, Lk 3:28

ERADICATE *(1)*
to death and **e** evil from Israel. Jdg 20:13

ERAN *(1)*
the Eranite clan from **E**. Nm 26:36

ERANITE *(1)*
the **E** clan from Eran. Nm 26:36

ERASE *(6)*
please **e** me from the book You Ex 32:32
Me I will **e** from My book. Ex 32:33
don't **e** the good deeds I have Neh 13:14
to **e** all memory of them from the Ps 34:16
I will **e** the names of the idols Zch 13:2
and I will never **e** his name from Rv 3:5

ERASED *(4)*
their sin be **e** from Your sight Neh 4:5
have **e** their name forever and Ps 9:5
Let them be **e** from the book of Ps 69:28
He **e** the certificate of debt, Col 2:14

ERASTUS *(3)*
Timothy and **E**, to Macedonia, Ac 19:22
E, the city treasurer, and our Rm 16:23
E has remained at Corinth; 2Tm 4:20

ERECH *(2)*
with Babylon, **E**, Accad, and Gn 10:10
Persia, **E**, Babylon, Susa Ezr 4:9

ERECT *(1)*
he will **e** a marker next to it Ezk 39:15

ERECTED *(1)*
Absalom had **e** for himself a 2Sm 18:18

ERI *(2)*
Shuni, Ezbon, **E**, Arodi, and Gn 46:16
Ozni; the Erite clan from **E**; Nm 26:16

ERITE *(1)*
from Ozni; the **E** clan from Eri; Nm 26:16

ERODES *(1)*
opened, and the palace **e** away. Nah 2:6

ERR *(2)*
the womb; liars **e** from birth. Ps 58:3
mouth should not **e** in judgment. Pr 16:10

ERRAND *(1)*
the one who sends him ⌊on an **e**⌋. Pr 10:26

ERROR *(11)*
for the **e** he has committed Lv 5:18
eats a holy offering in **e**, Lv 22:14
the person who acts in **e** sinning Nm 15:28
for the person who acts in **e**, Nm 15:29
I've committed a grave **e**." 1Sm 26:21
e proceeding from the presence Ec 10:5
didn't come from **e** or impurity 1Th 2:3
sinner from the **e** of his way Jms 5:20
from those who live in **e**. 2Pt 2:18
led away by the **e** of the immoral 2Pt 3:17
themselves to the **e** of Balaam Jd 11

ERRS *(1)*
the whole community of Israel **e**, Lv 4:13

ESAR-HADDON *(3)*
Then his son **E** became king in 2Kg 19:37
the time King **E** of Assyria Ezr 4:2
Then his son **E** became king in Is 37:38

ESAU *(83)*
(AKA EDOM)
fur coat, and they named him **E**. Gn 25:25
E became an expert hunter, Gn 25:27
Isaac loved **E** because he had a Gn 25:28
was cooking a stew, **E** came in Gn 25:29
"Look," said **E**, "I'm about to Gn 25:32
gave bread and lentil stew to **E**; Gn 25:34
So **E** despised his birthright. Gn 25:34
When **E** was 40 years old, he took Gn 26:34
his older son **E** and said to him, Gn 27:1
to what Isaac said to his son **E**. Gn 27:5
So while **E** went to the field to Gn 27:5
talking with your brother **E**. Gn 27:6
my brother **E** is a hairy man, Gn 27:11
best clothes of her older son **E**, Gn 27:15
father, "I am **E**, your firstborn Gn 27:19
you really my son **E**, or not?" Gn 27:21
the hands are the hands of **E**." Gn 27:22
like those of his brother **E**; Gn 27:23
"Are you really my son **E**?" Gn 27:24
his brother **E** arrived from the Gn 27:30
"I am **E** your firstborn son." Gn 27:32
When **E** heard his father's words, Gn 27:34
Isaac answered **E**: "Look, I have Gn 27:37
E said to his father, "Do you Gn 27:38
my father!" And **E** wept loudly. Gn 27:38
E held a grudge against Jacob Gn 27:41
And **E** determined in his heart: Gn 27:41
her older son **E** were reported to Gn 27:42
your brother **E** is consoling Gn 27:42
the mother of Jacob and **E**. Gn 28:5
E noticed that Isaac blessed Gn 28:6
E realized that his father Isaac Gn 28:8
E went to Ishmael and married, Gn 28:9
him to his brother **E** in the land Gn 32:3
You are to say to my lord **E**, Gn 32:4
We went to your brother **E**; Gn 32:6
If **E** comes to one camp and Gn 32:8
from the hand of my brother **E**, Gn 32:11
him as a gift for his brother **E**: Gn 32:13
When my brother **E** meets you and Gn 32:17

are a gift sent to my lord **E**. Gn 32:18
same thing to **E** when you find Gn 32:19
want to appease **E** with the gift Gn 32:20
up and saw **E** coming toward him Gn 33:1
But **E** ran to meet him, hugged Gn 33:4
When **E** looked up and saw the Gn 33:5
So **E** said, "What do you mean by Gn 33:8
enough, my brother," **E** replied. Gn 33:9
Then **E** said, "Let's move on, and Gn 33:12
E said, "Let me leave some of my Gn 33:15
On that day **E** started on his way Gn 33:16
you fled from your brother **E**." Gn 35:1
His sons **E** and Jacob buried him. Gn 35:29
are the family records of **E** Gn 36:1
E took his wives from the Gn 36:2
bore Eliphaz to **E**, Basemath bore Gn 36:4
E took his wives, sons, Gn 36:6
E (that is, Edom) lived in the Gn 36:8
are the family records of **E**, Gn 36:9
the sons of **E** (that is, Edom) Gn 36:19
E was father of the Edomites. Gn 36:43
descendants of **E**, who live in Dt 2:4
I have given **E** the hill country Dt 2:5
descendants of **E**, who live in Dt 2:8
descendants of **E** drove them out, Dt 2:12
descendants of **E** who lived in Dt 2:22
descendants of **E** who live in Dt 2:29
and to Isaac I gave Jacob and **E**. Jos 24:4
of Seir to **E** as a possession, Jos 24:4
Isaac's sons: **E** and Israel. 1Ch 1:34
But I will strip **E** bare; Jr 49:10
How **E** will be pillaged, his Ob 6
from the hill country of **E**? Ob 8
hill country of **E** will be Ob 9
the house of **E** will be stubble Ob 18
will remain of the house of **E**, Ob 18
possess the hill country of **E**; Ob 19
rule over the hill country of **E**, Ob 21
"Wasn't **E** Jacob's brother?" Mal 1:2
but I hated **E**. I turned his Mal 1:3
have loved, but **E** I have hated. Rm 9:13
Jacob and **E** concerning things Heb 11:20
or irreverent person like **E**, Heb 12:16

ESAU'S *(18)*

came out grasping **E** heel with Gn 25:26
These were **E** sons, who were born Gn 36:5
These are the names of **E** sons: Gn 36:10
Eliphaz son of **E** wife Adah, Gn 36:10
Reuel son of **E** wife Basemath. Gn 36:10
a concubine of **E** son Eliphaz, Gn 36:12
were the sons of **E** wife Adah. Gn 36:12
the sons of **E** wife Basemath. Gn 36:13
the sons of **E** wife Oholibamah Gn 36:14
These are the chiefs of **E** sons: Gn 36:15
sons of Eliphaz, **E** firstborn: Gn 36:15
are the sons of Reuel, **E** son: Gn 36:17
are the sons of **E** wife Basemath. Gn 36:17
the sons of **E** wife Oholibamah Gn 36:18
the chiefs of **E** wife Oholibamah Gn 36:18
These are the names of **E** chiefs, Gn 36:40
E sons: Eliphaz, Reuel, Jeush, 1Ch 1:35
I will bring **E** calamity on him Jr 49:8

ESCALATES *(1)*

is ongoing, and conflict **e**. Hab 1:3

ESCAPE *(75)*

it, the remaining one can **e**." Gn 32:8
were trying to **e** from it, Ex 14:27
They could not **e** in any Jos 8:20
I will **e** as I did before and Jdg 16:20
If you don't **e** tonight, you will 1Sm 19:11
for me than to **e** immediately to 1Sm 27:1
in Israel, and I'll **e** from him." 1Sm 27:1
or we will not **e** from Absalom! 2Sm 15:14
Do not let even one of them **e**." 1Kg 18:40
Open the door and **e**. 2Kg 9:3
let anyone **e** from the city to 2Kg 9:15
your hands to **e** ⌊will forfeit⌋ 2Kg 10:24
that you will **e** the fate of all Est 4:13
Their way of **e** will be cut off, Jb 11:20
He will not **e** from the darkness; Jb 15:30
he does not **e** his desires. Jb 20:20
and I would **e** from my Judge Jb 23:7
E to the mountain like a bird! Ps 11:1
it provides no **e** by its great Ps 33:17
they **e** in spite of such sin? Ps 56:7
and **e** from death belongs to the Ps 68:20
Where can I go to **e** Your Spirit? Ps 139:7
E like a gazelle from a hunter, Pr 6:5
of the righteous will **e**. Pr 11:21
one who utters lies will not **e**. Pr 19:5
one who pleases God will **e** her, Ec 7:26
those who practice it to **e**. Ec 8:8
lion for those who **e** from Moab, Is 15:9
of Assyria! Now, how will we **e**?" Is 20:6
We will **e** on horses"—therefore Is 30:16
horses"—therefore you will **e**! Is 30:16
disaster that they cannot **e**. Jr 11:11
shepherds, and **e**, for the Jr 25:35
of Judah will not **e** from the Jr 32:4
you will not **e** from his hand but Jr 34:3
will not **e** from them.'" Jr 38:18
yourself will not **e** from them, Jr 38:23
who **e** the sword will return Jr 44:28
flee, and the warrior cannot **e**! Jr 46:6
one town will **e**. The valley will Jr 48:8
Run! **E** quickly! Lie low, Jr 49:30
both man and beast will **e**. Jr 50:3
E from Babylon; depart from the Jr 50:8
her; let none **e**. Repay her Jr 50:29
has walled me in so I cannot **e**; Lm 3:7
of you who will **e** the sword. Ezk 6:8
among them will **e** and live on Ezk 7:16
the one who does such things **e**? Ezk 17:15
break a covenant and ⌊still⌋ **e**? Ezk 17:15
⌊in pledge⌋. He will not **e**!" Ezk 17:18
But these will **e** from his power: Dn 11:41
even the land of Egypt will **e**. Dn 11:42
written in the book will **e**. Dn 12:1
there is no **e** from them. Jl 2:3
there will be an **e** for those on Jl 2:32
E will fail the swift, the Am 2:14
none of their fugitives will **e**. Am 9:1
to **e** from the reach of disaster! Hab 2:9
E, you who are living with Zch 2:7
they even test God and **e**." Mal 3:15
you in one town, **e** to another. Mt 10:23
How can you **e** being condemned Mt 23:33
Pray that your **e** may not be in Mt 24:20
but He could not **e** notice. Mk 7:24
strength to **e** all these things Lk 21:36
tried to **e** from the ship; Ac 27:30
no one could swim off and **e**. Ac 27:42
that you will **e** God's judgment? Rm 2:3
will be like an **e** through fire. 1Co 3:15
He will also provide a way of **e**, 1Co 10:13
woman, and they will not **e**. 1Th 5:3
senses and **e** the Devil's trap 2Tm 2:26
how will we **e** if we neglect such Heb 2:3
if they did not **e** when they Heb 12:25
don't let this one thing **e** you: 2Pt 3:8

ESCAPED *(45)*

her hand, he **e** and ran outside Gn 39:12
left to you that **e** the hail; Ex 10:5
when he has **e** from his master to Dt 23:15
Ehud **e** by way of the porch, Jdg 3:23
e while the servants waited. Jdg 3:26
men. Not one of them **e**. Jdg 3:29
600 men **e** into the wilderness Jdg 20:47
wall, David eluded Saul and **e**. 1Sm 19:10
the window, and he fled and **e**. 1Sm 19:12
my enemy away, and he has **e**!" 1Sm 19:17
So David fled and **e** and went to 1Sm 19:18
of Ahimelech son of Ahitub **e** 1Sm 22:20
that David had **e** from Keilah, 1Sm 23:13
None of them **e**, except 400 1Sm 30:17
"I've **e** from the Israelite camp." 2Sm 1:3
Rechab and his brother Baanah **e**. 2Sm 4:6
king of Aram **e** on a horse with 1Kg 20:20
prophet opened the door and **e**. 2Kg 9:10
and they **e** from the power of the 2Kg 13:5
with the sword and **e** to the land 2Kg 19:37
who had **e** and still live 1Ch 4:43
of Aram has **e** from your hand. 2Ch 16:7
on the ground; nobody had **e**. 2Ch 20:24
who have **e** from the grasp of the 2Ch 30:6
Those who **e** from the sword he 2Ch 36:20
That night sleep **e** the king, Est 6:1
and I alone have **e** to tell you!" Jb 1:15
and I alone have **e** to tell you!" Jb 1:16
and I alone have **e** to tell you!" Jb 1:17
and I alone have **e** to tell you!" Jb 1:19
have **e** by the skin of my teeth. Jb 19:20
We have **e** like a bird from the Ps 124:7
the net is torn, and we have **e**. Ps 124:7
with the sword and **e** to the land Is 37:38
son of Nethaniah **e** from Johanan Jr 41:15
You who have **e** the sword, go and Jr 51:50
anger no one **e** or survived. Lm 2:22
They may have **e** from the fire, Ezk 15:7
the night, and **e** to Egypt. Mt 2:14
he thought the prisoners had **e**. Ac 16:27
and though he has **e** the sea, Ac 28:4
in the wall and **e** his hands. 2Co 11:33
the raging of fire, **e** the edge Heb 11:34
who have barely **e** from those who 2Pt 2:18
having **e** the world's impurity 2Pt 2:20

ESCAPEE *(1)*

no survivor or **e** from the Jr 42:17

ESCAPEES *(1)*

of fugitives and **e** from the land Jr 50:28

ESCAPES *(6)*

and the matter **e** the notice of Lv 4:13
to death whoever **e** the sword of 1Kg 19:17
to death whoever **e** the sword of 1Kg 19:17
the righteous **e** from trouble. Pr 12:13
and whoever **e** from the pit will Is 24:18
of these things **e** his notice, Ac 26:26

ESCAPING *(3)*

Then Jotham fled, **e** to Beer, and Jdg 9:21
who is fleeing or her who is **e**, Jr 48:19
e the corruption that is in the 2Pt 1:4

ESCORT *(3)*

meet the king and **e** him across 2Sm 19:15
nations will **e** Israel and bring Is 14:2
come themselves and **e** us out!" Ac 16:37

ESCORTED *(6)*

and half of Israel's **e** the king. 2Sm 19:40
of Days and was **e** before Him. Dn 7:13
Then he **e** them out and said, Ac 16:30
Those who **e** Paul brought him as Ac 17:15
Then they **e** him to the ship. Ac 20:38
and children, **e** us out of the Ac 21:5

ESCORTING *(1)*

to them, and **e** them out, they Ac 16:39

ESCORTS *(4)*

of the royal **e** who guarded 1Kg 14:27
the royal **e** would carry the 1Kg 14:28
of the royal **e** who guarded 2Ch 12:10
the royal **e** would carry the 2Ch 12:11

ESCORTS' *(2)*

them back to the royal **e** armory. 1Kg 14:28
them back to the royal **e** armory. 2Ch 12:11

ESH-BAAL *(2)*

Malchishua, Abinadab, and **E**. 1Ch 8:33
Malchishua, Abinadab, and **E**. 1Ch 9:39

ESHAN *(1)*

Arab, Dumah, **E**, Jos 15:52

ESHBAN *(2)*

Hemdan, **E**, Ithran, and Cheran. Gn 36:26
Hamran, **E**, Ithran, and Cheran. 1Ch 1:41

ESHCOL *(6)*

the brother of **E** and the brother Gn 14:13
with me—Aner, **E**, and Mamre— Gn 14:24
they came to the Valley of **E**, Nm 13:23
called the Valley of **E** because Nm 13:24
up as far as **E** Valley and saw Nm 32:9
and came to the Valley of **E**, Dt 1:24

ESHEK'S *(1)*

His brother **E** sons: Ulam was his 1Ch 8:39

ESHTAOL *(7)*

foothills: **E**, Zorah, Ashnah, Jos 15:33
included Zorah, **E**, Ir-shemesh, Jos 19:41
of Dan, between Zorah and **E**. Jdg 13:25
between Zorah and **E** in the tomb Jdg 16:31
from Zorah and **E**, to spy out the Jdg 18:2
to their clans at Zorah and **E**, Jdg 18:8
from Zorah and **E** armed with Jdg 18:11

ESHTAOLITES *(1)*

The Zorathites and **E** descended 1Ch 2:53

ESHTEMOA *(5)*

(AKA ESHTEMOH)

its pasturelands, **E** with its Jos 21:14
in Aroer, in Siphmoth, and in **E**; 1Sm 30:28
and Ishbah the father of **E**. 1Ch 4:17
the father of⌋ **E** the Maacathite. 1Ch 4:19
Jattir, **E** and its pasturelands 1Ch 6:57

ESHTEMOH *(1)*

(AKA ESHTEMOA)

Anab, **E**, Anim, Jos 15:50

ESHTON *(2)*
Mehir, who was the father of E. 1Ch 4:11
E fathered Beth-rapha, Paseah, 1Ch 4:12

ESLI *(1)*
Nahum, ⌊son⌋ of E, ⌊son⌋ of Lk 3:25

ESPECIALLY *(34)*
(See pp. xi-xii.)

ESTABLISH *(51)*
But I will e My covenant with Gn 6:18
I will e My covenant between Me Gn 17:2
ahead of you to e you as a Gn 45:7
witness cannot e any wrongdoing Dt 19:15
The LORD will e you as His holy Dt 28:9
that He may e you today as His Dt 29:13
I will e a lasting dynasty for 1Sm 2:35
house of Saul and e the throne 2Sm 3:10
I will e a place for My people 2Sm 7:10
body, and I will e his kingdom. 2Sm 7:12
and I will e the throne of his 2Sm 7:13
I will e your royal throne over 1Kg 9:5
son after him and to e Jerusalem 1Kg 15:4
I will e My name forever in this 2Kg 21:7
I will e a place for My people 1Ch 17:9
sons, and I will e his kingdom. 1Ch 17:11
and I will e his throne forever. 1Ch 17:12
when he went to e his control at 1Ch 18:3
I will e the throne of his 1Ch 22:10
I will e his kingdom forever if 1Ch 28:7
I will e your royal throne, 2Ch 7:18
Israel enough to e them forever, 2Ch 9:8
I will e My name forever in this 2Ch 33:7
to an end, but e the righteous. Ps 7:9
God will e it forever. Ps 48:8
You e the mountains by Your Ps 65:6
Most High Himself will e her. Ps 87:5
You e Your faithfulness in the Ps 89:2
'I will e your offspring forever Ps 89:4
I will e his line forever, Ps 89:29
e for us the work of our hands— Ps 90:17
of our hands—e the work of our Ps 90:17
and they e a city where they can Ps 107:36
to e and sustain it with justice Is 9:7
LORD, You will e peace for us, Is 26:12
I will e a sign among them, Is 66:19
order to e the oath I swore to Jr 11:5
for yourself; e signposts! Keep Jr 31:21
the LORD who forms it to e it, Jr 33:2
and fail to e the fixed order Jr 33:25
and I will e an everlasting Ezk 16:60
I will e My covenant with you, Ezk 16:62
I will e for them a place Ezk 34:29
I will e and multiply them, Ezk 37:26
the king should e an ordinance Dn 6:7
e the edict and sign the Dn 6:8
He will e himself in the Dn 11:16
e justice in the gate. Am 5:15
God and attempted to e their own Rm 10:3
away the first to e the second. Heb 10:9
restore, e, strengthen, 1Pt 5:10

ESTABLISHED *(91)*
also e My covenant with them to Ex 6:4
Your hands have e the sanctuary. Ex 15:17
laws the LORD e between Himself Lv 26:46
burnt offering e at Mount Sinai Nm 28:6
e at the start in the Dt 19:14
fact must be e by the testimony Dt 19:15
So Joshua e peace with them and Jos 9:15
at Shechem and e a statute Jos 24:25
permanently e your reign over 1Sm 13:13
Israel will be e in your hand. 1Sm 24:20
David e ⌊this policy⌋ as a law 1Sm 30:25
the LORD had e him as king over 2Sm 5:12
throne will be e forever.' " 2Sm 7:16
e Your people Israel Your own 2Sm 7:24
David will be e before You 2Sm 7:26
For He has e an everlasting 2Sm 23:5
and his kingship was firmly e. 1Kg 2:12
the One who e me, seated me 1Kg 2:24
will remain e before the LORD 1Kg 2:45
the kingdom was e in Solomon's 1Kg 2:46
the LORD had e him as king over 1Ch 14:2
The world is firmly e; 1Ch 16:30
throne will be e forever.' " 1Ch 17:14
servant David be e before You. 1Ch 17:24
Rehoboam had e his sovereignty 2Ch 12:1
King Rehoboam e his royal power 2Ch 12:13
So the LORD e the kingdom in his 2Ch 17:5
your God, and you will be e; 2Ch 20:20
Jehoram had e himself over his 2Ch 21:4
of the LORD's temple was e. 2Ch 29:35
So the service was e; 2Ch 35:10
of the LORD was e that day for 2Ch 35:16
They e them as a statute for 2Ch 35:25
Esther had e them and just as Est 9:31
will be firmly e and unafraid. Jb 11:15
and overthrows e leaders. Jb 12:19
children are e while they are Jb 21:8
when He e a limit for the rain Jb 28:26
He e it and examined it. Jb 28:27
were you when I e the earth? Jb 38:4
You have e a stronghold from the Ps 8:2
has e His throne for judgment. Ps 9:7
on the seas and e it on the Ps 24:2
A man's steps are e by the LORD, Ps 37:23
You e the moon and the sun. Ps 74:16
e a testimony in Jacob and set Ps 78:5
the earth that He e forever. Ps 78:69
like the moon, e forever, a Ps 89:37
The world is firmly e; Ps 93:1
throne has been e from the Ps 93:2
The world is firmly e; Ps 96:10
You have e fairness; Ps 99:4
Long ago You e the earth, and Ps 102:25
offspring will be e before You." Ps 102:28
The LORD has e His throne in Ps 103:19
He e the earth on its Ps 104:5
to the place You e for them. Ps 104:8
They are e forever and ever, Ps 111:8
You e the earth, and it stands Ps 119:90
that You have e them forever. Ps 119:152
by wisdom and e the heavens Pr 3:19
and all your ways will be e. Pr 4:26
the mountains and hills were e, Pr 8:25
was there when He e the heavens, Pr 8:27
since a throne is e through Pr 16:12
and it is e by understanding; Pr 24:3
throne will be e in Pr 25:5
his throne will be e forever. Pr 29:14
Who has e all the ends of the Pr 30:4
LORD's house will be e at the Is 2:2
throne will be e by faithful Is 16:5
Salvation is e as walls and Is 26:1
until He has e justice on earth. Is 42:4
I have e an ancient people. Is 44:7
and made it; He e it; He did not Is 45:18
and you will be e on ⌊a Is 54:14
It is an e nation, an ancient Jr 5:15
e the world by His wisdom, Jr 10:12
will be e in My presence. Jr 30:20
e the world by His wisdom, Jr 51:15
as soon as he is e, his kingdom Dn 11:4
LORD's house will be e at the Mc 4:1
witnesses every fact may be e. Mt 18:16
new covenant ⌊e by⌋ My blood; Lk 22:20
and was e as the powerful Son of Rm 1:4
rooted and firmly e in love, Eph 3:17
up in Him and e in the faith, Col 2:7
Lord, You e the earth, Heb 1:10
death of the testator must be e. Heb 9:16
the heart to be e by grace and Heb 13:9
them and are e in the truth you 2Pt 1:12

ESTABLISHES *(8)*
the One who e harmony in the Jb 25:2
and His power e His rule. Is 40:10
rest until He e and makes her Is 62:7
He removes kings and e kings. Dn 2:21
the king e can be changed." Dn 6:15
my case and e justice for me. Mc 7:9
My blood ⌊that e⌋ the covenant; Mt 26:28
My blood ⌊that e⌋ the covenant; Mk 14:24

ESTABLISHMENT *(1)*
the defense and e of the gospel. Php 1:7

ESTATE *(9)*
from the sale of the family e. Dt 18:8
Queen Esther the e of Haman, Est 8:1
put him in charge of Haman's e. Est 8:2
have given Haman's e to Esther, Est 8:7
His e included 7,000 sheep, Jb 1:3
guards his e, his possessions Lk 11:21
share of the e I have coming to Lk 15:12
squandered his e in foolish Lk 15:13
that place was an e belonging to Ac 28:7

ESTATES *(1)*
they have named e after Ps 49:11

ESTEEM *(1)*
to e them very highly in love 1Th 5:13

ESTHER *(47)*
(AKA HADASSAH)
that is, E), because she Est 2:7
E was also taken to the palace Est 2:8
E did not reveal her ethnic Est 2:10
to learn how E was doing and to Est 2:11
E was the daughter of Abihail, Est 2:15
E won approval in the sight of Est 2:15
E was taken to King Ahasuerus in Est 2:16
The king loved E more than all Est 2:17
E still had not revealed her Est 2:20
he reported it to Queen E, Est 2:22
E summoned Hathach, one of the Est 4:5
that Hathach might show it to E, Est 4:8
Mordecai's response to E. Est 4:9
E spoke to Hathach and commanded Est 4:10
the messenger⌋ to reply to E, Est 4:13
E sent this reply to Mordecai: Est 4:15
everything E had ordered him. Est 4:17
E dressed up in her royal Est 5:1
as the king saw Queen E standing Est 5:2
scepter in his hand toward E, Est 5:2
"What is it, Queen E?" Est 5:3
the king," E replied, "may Est 5:4
we can do as E has requested." Est 5:5
to the banquet E had prepared. Est 5:5
the king asked E, "Whatever you Est 5:6
E answered, "⌊This is⌋ my Est 5:7
Queen E invited no one but me to Est 5:12
to the banquet E had prepared. Est 6:14
came to feast with E the queen. Est 7:1
the king asked E, "Queen Esther, Est 7:2
Esther, "Queen E, whatever you Est 7:2
Queen E answered, "If I have Est 7:3
spoke up and asked Queen E, Est 7:5
E answered, "The adversary and Est 7:6
to beg Queen E for his life Est 7:7
the couch where E was reclining. Est 7:8
awarded Queen E the estate of Est 8:1
because E had revealed her Est 8:1
and E put him in charge of Est 8:2
Then E addressed the king again. Est 8:3
the golden scepter toward E, Est 8:4
said to E the Queen and to Est 8:7
have given Haman's estate to E, Est 8:7
The king said to Queen E, Est 9:12
E answered, "If it pleases the Est 9:13
Queen E daughter of Abihail, Est 9:29
Jew and Queen E had established Est 9:31

ESTHER'S *(4)*
staff. It was E banquet. He Est 2:18
E female servants and her Est 4:4
E response was reported to Est 4:12
So E command confirmed these Est 9:32

ESTIMATION *(1)*
Do not be wise in your own e. Rm 12:16

ESTRANGED *(1)*
they are all e from Me by their Ezk 14:5

ETAM *(4)*
in the cave at the rock of E. Jdg 15:8
to the cave at the rock of E, Jdg 15:11
villages were E, Ain, Rimmon, 1Ch 4:32
He built up Bethlehem, E, Tekoa, 2Ch 11:6

ETAM'S *(1)*
These were E sons: Jezreel, 1Ch 4:3

ETERNAL *(113)*
Canaan—as an e possession, and Gn 17:8
this land as an e possession to Gn 48:4
and the bounty of the e hills. Gn 49:26
and the bounty of the e hills; Dt 33:15
the E One of Israel does not lie 1Sm 15:29
of the LORD's e love for Israel. 1Kg 10:9
The enemy has come to e ruin; Ps 9:6
Your right hand are e pleasures. Ps 16:11
Their graves are their e homes, Ps 49:11
LORD is good, and His love is e; Ps 100:5
for He is good. His love is e. Ps 136:1
the God of gods. His love is e. Ps 136:2
Lord of lords. His love is e. Ps 136:3
great wonders. His love is e. Ps 136:4
skillfully. His love is e. Ps 136:5
on the waters. His love is e. Ps 136:6
the great lights: His love is e. Ps 136:7
to rule by day, His love is e. Ps 136:8

to rule by night. His love is **e**. Ps 136:9
of the Egyptians His love is **e**. Ps 136:10
from among them His love is **e**. Ps 136:11
outstretched arm. His love is **e**. Ps 136:12
the Red Sea His love is **e**. Ps 136:13
Israel through, His love is **e**. Ps 136:14
into the Red Sea. His love is **e**. Ps 136:15
the wilderness. His love is **e**. Ps 136:16
down great kings His love is **e**. Ps 136:17
famous kings—His love is **e**. Ps 136:18
of the Amorites His love is **e**. Ps 136:19
king of Bashan—His love is **e**. Ps 136:20
an inheritance, His love is **e**. Ps 136:21
His servant. His love is **e**. Ps 136:22
our humiliation His love is **e**. Ps 136:23
us from our foes. His love is **e**. Ps 136:24
every creature. His love is **e**. Ps 136:25
God of heaven! His love is **e**. Ps 136:26
LORD, Your love is **e**; Ps 138:8
for man is headed to his **e** home, Ec 12:5
Mighty God, **E** Father, Prince Is 9:6
make you an object of **e** pride, Is 60:15
their land, and **e** joy will be Is 61:7
them to obtain **e** fame for Is 63:12
He is the living God and **e** King. Jr 10:10
His kingdom is an **e** kingdom, Dn 4:3
awake, some to **e** life, and some Dn 12:2
some to shame and **e** contempt. Dn 12:2
and be thrown into the **e** fire. Mt 18:8
good must I do to have **e** life?" Mt 19:16
more and will inherit **e** life. Mt 19:29
into the **e** fire prepared for the Mt 25:41
will go away into **e** punishment, Mt 25:46
but the righteous into **e** life." Mt 25:46
but is guilty of an **e** sin"— Mk 3:29
must I do to inherit **e** life?" Mk 10:17
and **e** life in the age to come. Mk 10:30
must I do to inherit **e** life?" Lk 10:25
welcome you into **e** dwellings. Lk 16:9
must I do to inherit **e** life?" Lk 18:18
and **e** life in the age to come." Lk 18:30
in Him will have **e** life. Jn 3:15
will not perish but have **e** life. Jn 3:16
believes in the Son has **e** life, Jn 3:36
up within him for **e** life." Jn 4:14
and gathering fruit for **e** life, Jn 4:36
who sent Me has **e** life and will Jn 5:24
think you have **e** life in them, Jn 5:39
the food that lasts for **e** life, Jn 6:27
believes in Him may have **e** life, Jn 6:40
Anyone who believes has **e** life. Jn 6:47
and drinks My blood has **e** life, Jn 6:54
You have the words of **e** life. Jn 6:68
give them **e** life, and they will Jn 10:28
world will keep it for **e** life. Jn 12:25
know that His command is **e** life. Jn 12:50
so He may give **e** life to all You Jn 17:2
This is **e** life: that they may Jn 17:3
yourselves unworthy of **e** life, Ac 13:46
appointed to **e** life believed. Ac 13:48
His **e** power and divine nature, Rm 1:20
e life to those who by patiently Rm 2:7
resulting in **e** life through Rm 5:21
and the end is **e** life! Rm 6:22
gift of God is **e** life in Christ Rm 6:23
to the command of the **e** God, Rm 16:26
incomparable **e** weight of glory. 2Co 4:17
but what is unseen is **e**. 2Co 4:18
with hands, **e** in the heavens. 2Co 5:1
Spirit will reap **e** life from the Gl 6:8
us and given us **e** encouragement 2Th 2:16
would believe in Him for **e** life. 1Tm 1:16
Now to the King **e**, immortal, 1Tm 1:17
take hold of **e** life, to which 1Tm 6:12
to whom be honor and **e** might. 1Tm 6:16
in Christ Jesus, with **e** glory. 2Tm 2:10
in the hope of **e** life that God, Ti 1:2
heirs with the hope of **e** life. Ti 3:7
the source of **e** salvation to all Heb 5:9
of the dead, and **e** judgment. Heb 6:2
having obtained **e** redemption. Heb 9:12
who through the **e** Spirit offered Heb 9:14
promise of the **e** inheritance, Heb 9:15
you to His **e** glory in Christ 1Pt 5:10
entry into the **e** kingdom of our 2Pt 1:11
to you the **e** life that was with 1Jn 1:2
He Himself made to us: **e** life. 1Jn 2:25
no murderer has **e** life residing 1Jn 3:15
has given us **e** life, and this 1Jn 5:11
may know that you have **e** life. 1Jn 5:13
He is the true God and **e** life. 1Jn 5:20
with **e** chains in darkness for Jd 6
the punishment of **e** fire. Jd 7
Lord Jesus Christ for **e** life. Jd 21
having the **e** gospel to announce Rv 14:6

ETERNALLY *(5)*
and ever—He will lead us **e**." Ps 48:14
they will be **e** destroyed. Ps 92:7
my grave, her womb **e** pregnant. Jr 20:17
Him who lives **e** that it would be Dn 12:7
The **e** blessed One, the God and 2Co 11:31

ETERNITY *(12)*
Israel, from **e** to eternity. 1Ch 29:10
Israel, from eternity to **e**. 1Ch 29:10
the world, from **e** to eternity, Ps 90:2
from eternity to **e**, You are God. Ps 90:2
the beginning; You are from **e**. Ps 93:2
from **e** to eternity the LORD's Ps 103:17
from eternity to **e** the LORD's Ps 103:17
has also put **e** in their hearts Ec 3:11
shame or humiliated for all **e**. Is 45:17
is from antiquity, from **e**. Mc 5:2
You not from **e**, Yahweh my God? Hab 1:12
both now and to the day of **e**. 2Pt 3:18

ETH-KAZIN *(1)*
sunrise to Gath-hepher and to **E**; Jos 19:13

ETHAM *(4)*
and camped at **E** on the edge Ex 13:20
from Succoth and camped at **E**, Nm 33:6
departed from **E** and turned back Nm 33:7
the Wilderness of **E** and camped Nm 33:8

ETHAN *(6)*
wiser than **E** the Ezrahite, 1Kg 4:31
Zimri, **E**, Heman, Calcol, and 1Ch 2:6
son of **E**, son of Zimmah, son of 1Ch 6:42
E son of Kishi, son of Abdi, son 1Ch 6:44
Merarites, **E** son of Kushaiah. 1Ch 15:17
and **E** were to sound the bronze 1Ch 15:19

ETHAN'S *(1)*
E son: Azariah. 1Ch 2:8

ETHANIM *(1)*
the month of **E** at the festival. 1Kg 8:2

ETHBAAL *(1)*
the daughter of **E** king of the 1Kg 16:31

ETHER *(2)*
Libnah, **E**, Ashan, Jos 15:42
Ain, Rimmon, **E**, and Ashan—four Jos 19:7

ETHIOPIAN *(1)*
(AKA CUSHITE)
There was an **E** man, a eunuch and Ac 8:27

ETHIOPIANS *(2)*
Egypt—Libyans, Sukkiim, and **E**. 2Ch 12:3
of the **E**, who was in charge Ac 8:27

ETHNAN *(1)*
Zereth, Zohar, and **E**. 1Ch 4:7

ETHNI *(1)*
son of **E**, son of Zerah, son of 1Ch 6:41

ETHNIC *(11)*
and to each **e** group in its own Est 1:22
not reveal her **e** background or Est 2:10
birthplace or her **e** background, Est 2:20
of Mordecai's **e** identity, Est 3:6
There is one **e** group, scattered Est 3:8
of each **e** group and written Est 3:12
and to each **e** group in its own Est 3:12
for each **e** group in its own Est 8:9
every **e** and provincial Est 8:11
for every **e** group so the Jews Est 8:13
many of the **e** groups of the land Est 8:17

ETHNICALLY *(1)*
An **e** diverse crowd also went up Ex 12:38

EUBULUS *(1)*
E greets you, as do Pudens, 2Tm 4:21

EUNICE *(1)*
in your mother **E**, and that I am 2Tm 1:5

EUNUCH *(8)*
the king's **e**, who is in charge Est 2:3
the king's **e** in charge of the Est 2:14
and the **e** should not say, Is 56:3
e and high official of Candace, Ac 8:27
The **e** replied to Philip, "I ask Ac 8:34
e said, "Look, there's water! Ac 8:36
both Philip and the **e** went down Ac 8:38
and the **e** did not see him any Ac 8:39

EUNUCHS *(16)*
Two or three **e** looked down at 2Kg 9:32
they will become **e** in the palace 2Kg 20:18
seven **e** who personally served Est 1:10
that was delivered by his **e**. Est 1:12
that was delivered by the **e**?" Est 1:15
two **e** who guarded the ⌊king's⌋ Est 2:21
servants and her **e** came and Est 4:4
of the king's **e** assigned to her Est 4:5
two **e** who guarded the ⌊king's⌋ Est 6:2
the **e** of the king arrived and Est 6:14
one of the royal **e**, said: Est 7:9
and they will be **e** in the palace Is 39:7
For the **e** who keep My Sabbaths, Is 56:4
For there are **e** who were born Mt 19:12
are **e** who were made by men, Mt 19:12
and there are **e** who have made Mt 19:12

EUODIA *(1)*
I urge **E** and I urge Syntyche to Php 4:2

EUPHRATES *(59)*
And the fourth river is the **E**. Gn 2:14
brook of Egypt to the **E** River: Gn 15:18
crossed the **E**, and headed for Gn 31:21
the wilderness to the **E** River. Ex 23:31
which is by the **E** in the land of Nm 22:5
Lebanon as far as the **E** River. Dt 1:7
Lebanon and from the **E** River to Dt 11:24
Lebanon to the great **E** River— Jos 1:4
lived beyond the **E** River and Jos 24:2
the region beyond the **E** River, Jos 24:3
beyond the **E** River and in Egypt Jos 24:14
worshiped beyond the **E** River, Jos 24:15
his control at the **E** River. 2Sm 8:3
who were across the **E** River, 2Sm 10:16
from the **E** River to the land 1Kg 4:21
west of the **E** from Tiphsah to 1Kg 4:24
all the kings west of the **E**. 1Kg 4:24
them beyond the **E** because they 1Kg 14:15
king of Assyria at the **E** river. 2Kg 23:29
Brook of Egypt to the **E** River. 2Kg 24:7
Rehoboth on the **E** River ruled in 1Ch 1:48
that extends to the **E** River, 1Ch 5:9
his control at the **E** River. 1Ch 18:3
were across the **E** with Shophach, 1Ch 19:16
kings from the **E** River to the 2Ch 9:26
to fight at Carchemish by the **E**, 2Ch 35:20
the region west of the **E** River. Ezr 4:10
the region west of the **E** River: Ezr 4:11
any possession west of the **E**. Ezr 4:16
the region west of the **E** River: Ezr 4:17
the region west of the **E** River, Ezr 5:3
the region west of the **E** River, Ezr 5:6
the region west of the **E** River, Ezr 6:6
the region west of the **E** River, Ezr 6:8
the region west of the **E** River, Ezr 6:13
the region west of the **E** River: Ezr 7:21
west of the **E** who know the laws Ezr 7:25
of the region west of the **E**, Ezr 8:36
the region west of the **E** River, Neh 2:7
west of the **E** and gave them Neh 2:9
the region west of the **E** River. Neh 3:7
sea and from the **E** to the ends Ps 72:8
hired from beyond the **E** River— Is 7:20
rushing waters of the **E** River— Is 8:7
hand over the **E** with His mighty Is 11:15
grain from the **E** River as far as Is 27:12
to drink the waters of the **E**? Jr 2:18
at once to the **E** River and hide Jr 13:4
So I went and hid it by the **E**, Jr 13:5
Go at once to the **E** and get the Jr 13:6
I went to the **E** and dug up the Jr 13:7
at Carchemish on the **E** River by Jr 46:2
by the bank of the **E** River, Jr 46:6
northern land by the **E** River. Jr 46:10
into the middle of the **E** River. Jr 51:63
from Egypt to the **E** River and Mc 7:12
from the **E** River to the ends of Zch 9:10
bound at the great river **E**." Rv 9:14
his bowl on the great river **E**, Rv 16:12

EUTYCHUS *(1)*
a young man named **E** was sitting Ac 20:9

EVALUATE *(4)*
counselors to **e** Judah and Ezr 7:14
however, can **e** everything, yet 1Co 2:15

In fact, I don't even **e** myself. 1Co 4:3
speak, and the others should **e**. 1Co 14:29

EVALUATED *(4)*
He considered wisdom and **e** it; Jb 28:27
it since it is **e** spiritually. 1Co 2:14
himself cannot be **e** by anyone. 1Co 2:15
that I should be **e** by you or by 1Co 4:3

EVALUATES *(3)*
but the LORD **e** the motives. Pr 21:2
She **e** a field and buys it; Pr 31:16
The One who **e** me is the Lord. 1Co 4:4

EVALUATING *(1)*
If we were properly **e** ourselves, 1Co 11:31

EVANGELIST *(2)*
the house of Philip the **e**, Ac 21:8
the work of an **e**, fulfill your 2Tm 4:5

EVANGELISTS *(1)*
prophets, some **e**, some pastors Eph 4:11

EVANGELIZE *(2)*
God had called us to **e** them. Ac 16:10
So my aim is to **e** where Christ Rm 15:20

EVANGELIZED *(1)*
After they had **e** that town and Ac 14:21

EVANGELIZING *(3)*
e many villages of the Ac 8:25
he was **e** all the towns until he Ac 8:40
And there they kept **e**. Ac 14:7

EVAPORATE *(2)*
The wadis **e** in warm weather; Jb 6:17
For He makes waterdrops **e**; Jb 36:27

EVAPORATED *(1)*
the layer of dew **e**, there on the Ex 16:14

EVE *(4)*
named his wife **E** because she was Gn 3:20
Adam knew his wife **E** intimately, Gn 4:1
deceived **E** by his cunning, 2Co 11:3
Adam was created first, then **E**. 1Tm 2:13

EVEN *(573)*
(See pp. xi-xii.)

EVENING *(137)*
E came, and then morning: Gn 1:5
E came, and then morning: Gn 1:8
E came, and then morning: Gn 1:13
E came, and then morning: Gn 1:19
E came, and then morning: Gn 1:23
E came, and then morning: Gn 1:31
at the time of the **e** breeze, Gn 3:8
When the dove came to him at **e**, Gn 8:11
in the **e** as Lot was sitting Gn 19:1
of water outside the town at **e**. Gn 24:11
the early **e**, Isaac went out to Gn 24:63
That **e**, Laban took his daughter Gn 29:23
came in from the field that **e**, Gn 30:16
in the **e** he divides the plunder. Gn 49:27
from the **e** of the fourteenth day Ex 12:18
month until the **e** of the Ex 12:18
This **e** you will know that it was Ex 16:6
meat to eat this **e** and abundant Ex 16:8
So at **e** quail came and covered Ex 16:13
Moses from morning until **e**. Ex 18:13
you from morning until **e**?" Ex 18:14
the lamp from **e** until morning Ex 27:21
the morning and half in the **e**. Lv 6:20
will be unclean until **e**, Lv 11:24
and will be unclean until **e**. Lv 11:25
will be unclean until **e**, Lv 11:27
and will be unclean until **e**. Lv 11:28
dead will be unclean until **e**. Lv 11:31
and will remain unclean until **e**; Lv 11:32
carcass will be unclean until **e**. Lv 11:39
and will be unclean until **e**. Lv 11:40
and will be unclean until **e**. Lv 11:40
it will be unclean until **e**. Lv 14:46
he will remain unclean until **e**. Lv 15:5
he will remain unclean until **e**. Lv 15:6
he will remain unclean until **e**. Lv 15:7
he will remain unclean until **e**. Lv 15:8
him will be unclean until **e**, Lv 15:10
he will remain unclean until **e**. Lv 15:10
he will remain unclean until **e**. Lv 15:11
he will remain unclean until **e**. Lv 15:16
it will remain unclean until **e**. Lv 15:17
will remain unclean until **e**. Lv 15:18
her will be unclean until **e**. Lv 15:19
he will remain unclean until **e**. Lv 15:21
he will remain unclean until **e**. Lv 15:22
it he will be unclean until **e**. Lv 15:23
he will remain unclean until **e**. Lv 15:27
he will remain unclean until **e**; Lv 17:15
unclean until **e** and is not to Lv 22:6
Sabbath from the **e** of the ninth Lv 23:32
month until the ⌊following⌋ **e**." Lv 23:32
regularly from **e** until morning Lv 24:3
tabernacle from **e** until morning. Nm 9:15
only⌋ from **e** until morning; Nm 9:21
ceremonially unclean until **e**. Nm 19:7
he will remain unclean until **e**. Nm 19:8
he will remain unclean until **e**. Nm 19:10
and he will be clean by **e**. Nm 19:19
will be unclean until **e**. Nm 19:21
it⌋ will be unclean until **e**." Nm 19:22
in the **e** of the first day Dt 16:4
this⌋ in the **e** as the sun sets Dt 16:6
When **e** approaches, he must wash Dt 23:11
will say, 'If only it were **e**!' Dt 28:67
and in the **e** you will say, Dt 28:67
Passover on the **e** of the Jos 5:10
his face to the ground until **e**, Jos 7:6
king of Ai on a tree until **e**, Jos 8:29
and they were there until **e**. Jos 10:26
the **e**, an old man came in from Jdg 19:16
wept before the LORD until **e**, Jdg 20:23
that day until **e** and offered Jdg 20:26
sat there before God until **e**. Jdg 21:2
grain⌋ in the field until **e**. Ru 2:17
This **e** he will be winnowing Ru 3:2
the man who eats food before **e**, 1Sm 14:24
Every morning and **e** for 40 days 1Sm 17:16
until the **e** of the next day. 1Sm 30:17
fasted until the **e** for those who 2Sm 1:12
One **e** David got up from his bed 2Sm 11:2
went out in the **e** to lie down on 2Sm 11:13
in the morning and in the **e**, 1Kg 17:6
the offering of the **e** sacrifice, 1Kg 18:29
for offering the ⌊**e**⌋ sacrifice, 1Kg 18:36
He died that **e**, and blood from 1Kg 22:35
offering, the **e** grain offering, 2Kg 16:15
morning and **e**, to the LORD 1Ch 16:40
the LORD, and likewise in the **e**. 1Ch 23:30
for the **e** and the morning, 2Ch 2:4
LORD every morning and every **e**, 2Ch 13:11
of the gold lampstand every **e**. 2Ch 13:11
facing the Arameans until **e**. 2Ch 18:34
morning and **e** burnt offerings, 2Ch 31:3
the morning and **e** on it to the Ezr 3:3
devastated until the **e** offering. Ezr 9:4
At the **e** offering, I got up from Ezr 9:5
would go in the **e**, and in the Est 2:14
But the **e** drags on endlessly, Jb 7:4
They return at **e**, snarling like Ps 59:6
they return at **e**, snarling like Ps 59:14
by **e** it withers and dries up. Ps 90:6
work and to his labor until **e**. Ps 104:23
of my hands as the **e** offering. Ps 141:2
twilight, in the **e**, in the dark Pr 7:9
and at **e** do not let your hand Ec 11:6
linger into the **e**, inflamed by Is 5:11
In the **e**—sudden terror! Is 17:14
the **e** shadows grow long. Jr 6:4
Then in the **e** go out in their Ezk 12:4
In the **e** I dug through the wall Ezk 12:7
and my wife died in the **e**. Ezk 24:18
had been on me the **e** before the Ezk 33:22
gate must not be closed until **e**. Ezk 46:2
the time of the **e** offering. Dn 9:21
lie down in the **e** among the Zph 2:7
but there will be light at **e**. Zch 14:7
When **e** came, they brought to Him Mt 8:16
When **e** came, the disciples Mt 14:15
When **e** came, He was there alone. Mt 14:23
When **e** comes you say, 'It will Mt 16:2
When **e** came, the owner of the Mt 20:8
When **e** came, He was reclining at Mt 26:20
When it was **e**, a rich man from Mt 27:57
When **e** came, after the sun had Mk 1:32
that day, when **e** had come, He Mk 4:35
When **e** came, the boat was in the Mk 6:47
And whenever **e** came, they would Mk 11:19
whether in the **e** or at midnight Mk 13:35
When **e** came, He arrived with the Mk 14:17
it was already **e**, because it was Mk 15:42
but in the **e** He would go out and Lk 21:37
it's almost **e**, and now the day Lk 24:29
It was about six in the **e**. Jn 4:6
When **e** came, His disciples went Jn 6:16
the **e** of that first day of the Jn 20:19
day, since it was already **e**. Ac 4:3

EVENINGS *(2)*
For 2,300 **e** and mornings; Dn 8:14
vision of the **e** and the mornings Dn 8:26

EVENLY *(1)*
gold applied **e** over the carving 1Kg 6:35

EVENT *(3)*
this great **e** ⌊ever⌋ happened Dt 4:32
for this solemn **e** at the time I 1Sm 9:24
This **e** was recorded in the court Est 2:23

EVENTS *(78)*
After these **e**, the word of the Gn 15:1
his wife told him about these **e**. 1Sm 25:37
The rest of the **e** of Solomon's 1Kg 11:41
in the Book of Solomon's **E**. 1Kg 11:41
the turn of **e** came from the LORD 1Kg 12:15
the rest of the **e** of Jeroboam's 1Kg 14:19
The rest of the **e** of Rehoboam's 1Kg 14:29
The rest of the **e** of Abijam's 1Kg 15:7
of all the **e** of Asa's ⌊reign⌋ 1Kg 15:23
The rest of the **e** of Nadab's 1Kg 15:31
The rest of the **e** of Baasha's 1Kg 16:5
The rest of the **e** of Elah's 1Kg 16:14
The rest of the **e** of Zimri's 1Kg 16:20
The rest of the **e** of Omri's 1Kg 16:27
Some time passed after these **e**. 1Kg 21:1
The rest of the **e** of Ahab's 1Kg 22:39
The rest of the **e** of 1Kg 22:45
The rest of the **e** of Ahaziah's 2Kg 1:18
The rest of the **e** of Jehoram's 2Kg 8:23
the rest of the **e** of Jehu's 2Kg 10:34
The rest of the **e** of Joash's 2Kg 12:19
The rest of the **e** of Jehoahaz's 2Kg 13:8
The rest of the **e** of Jehoash's 2Kg 13:12
The rest of the **e** of Jehoash's 2Kg 14:15
The rest of the **e** of Amaziah's 2Kg 14:18
The rest of the **e** of Jeroboam's 2Kg 14:28
The rest of the **e** of Azariah's 2Kg 15:6
the rest of the **e** of Zechariah's 2Kg 15:11
the rest of the **e** of Shallum's 2Kg 15:15
The rest of the **e** of Menahem's 2Kg 15:21
the rest of the **e** of Pekahiah's 2Kg 15:26
the rest of the **e** of Pekah's 2Kg 15:31
The rest of the **e** of Jotham's 2Kg 15:36
The rest of the **e** of Ahaz's 2Kg 16:19
The rest of the **e** of Hezekiah's 2Kg 20:20
The rest of the **e** of Manasseh's 2Kg 21:17
The rest of the **e** of Amon's 2Kg 21:25
The rest of the **e** of Josiah's 2Kg 23:28
The rest of the **e** of Jehoiakim's 2Kg 24:5
As for the **e** of King David's 1Ch 29:29
about in the **E** of Samuel the 1Ch 29:29
the **E** of Nathan the Prophet, 1Ch 29:29
and the **E** of Gad the Seer, 1Ch 29:29
The remaining **e** of Solomon's 2Ch 9:29
written about in the **E** of Nathan 2Ch 9:29
the turn of **e** came from God, 2Ch 10:15
The **e** of Rehoboam's ⌊reign⌋, 2Ch 12:15
about in the **E** of Shemaiah 2Ch 12:15
The rest of the **e** of Abijah's 2Ch 13:22
that the **e** of Asa's ⌊reign⌋, 2Ch 16:11
The rest of the **e** of 2Ch 20:34
about in the **E** of Jehu son 2Ch 20:34
this ⌊turn of **e**⌋ was from God 2Ch 25:20
The rest of the **e** of Amaziah's 2Ch 25:26
the rest of the **e** of Uzziah's 2Ch 26:22
the rest of the **e** of Jotham's 2Ch 27:7
the rest of the **e** of Hezekiah's 2Ch 32:32
The rest of the **e** of Manasseh's 2Ch 33:18
about⌋ in the **E** of Israel's 2Ch 33:18
The rest of the **e** of Josiah's 2Ch 35:26
After these **e**, during the reign Ezr 7:1
These **e** took place during the Est 1:1
records of daily **e** in the king's Est 2:23
recording daily **e** to be brought Est 6:1
recorded these **e** and sent Est 9:20
record of daily **e** of the kings Est 10:2
us the past **e**, so that we may Is 41:22
us the coming **e**, then we will Is 41:23
The past **e** have indeed happened. Is 42:9
I declare new **e**; I announce them Is 42:9
Do not remember the past **e**, Is 43:18
I declared the past **e** long ago; Is 48:3
past **e** will not be remembered Is 65:17

long will ⌊the e of⌋ this vision Dn 8:13
All these e are the beginning of Mt 24:8
about the e that have been Lk 1:1
You know the e that took place Ac 10:37
When these e were over, Paul Ac 19:21

EVER *(149)*
(See pp. xi-xii.)

EVER-BURNING *(1)*
us can dwell with e flames?" Is 33:14

EVER-FLOWING *(1)*
You dried up e rivers. Ps 74:15

EVERLASTING *(45)*
remember the e covenant between Gn 9:16
as an e covenant to be your God Gn 17:7
in your flesh as an e covenant. Gn 17:13
with him as an e covenant for Gn 17:19
worshiped the LORD, the E God. Gn 21:33
and underneath are the e arms. Dt 33:27
established an e covenant with 2Sm 23:5
and to Israel as an e covenant: 1Ch 16:17
praised from e to everlasting. 1Ch 16:36
praised from everlasting to e." 1Ch 16:36
your God from e to everlasting. Neh 9:5
your God from everlasting to e. Neh 9:5
praised from e to everlasting. Ps 41:13
praised from everlasting to e. Ps 41:13
Make Your way to the e ruins, Ps 74:3
and to Israel as an e covenant: Ps 105:10
praised from e to everlasting. Ps 106:48
praised from everlasting to e. Ps 106:48
is an e righteousness, Ps 119:142
lead me in the e way. Ps 139:24
Your kingdom is an e kingdom; Ps 145:13
and broken the e covenant. Is 24:5
in Yah, the LORD, is an e rock! Is 26:4
Yahweh is the e God, the Creator Is 40:28
by the LORD with an e salvation; Is 45:17
compassion on you with e love," Is 54:8
I will make an e covenant with Is 55:3
the LORD as an e sign that will Is 55:13
of them⌋ an e name that will Is 56:5
the LORD will be your e light, Is 60:19
the LORD will be your e light, Is 60:20
them and make an e covenant with Is 61:8
an e humiliation that will never Jr 20:11
I will bring on you e shame and Jr 23:40
I have loved you with an e love; Jr 31:3
make with them an e covenant: Jr 32:40
the LORD in an e covenant that Jr 50:5
establish an e covenant with you Ezk 16:60
it will be an e covenant with Ezk 37:26
His dominion is an e dominion, Dn 4:34
dominion is an e dominion that Dn 7:14
kingdom will be an e kingdom, Dn 7:27
to bring in e righteousness, Dn 9:24
the penalty of e destruction, 2Th 1:9
the blood of the e covenant, Heb 13:20

EVERY *(742)*
and e living creature Gn 1:21
⌊He also created⌋ e winged bird Gn 1:21
e creature that crawls on the Gn 1:28
I have given you e seed-bearing Gn 1:29
and e tree whose fruit contains Gn 1:29
the earth, for e bird of the sky Gn 1:30
and for e creature that crawls Gn 1:30
⌊I have given⌋ e green plant for Gn 1:30
of the ground e tree pleasing Gn 2:9
the sky, and to e wild animal; Gn 2:20
earth and that e scheme his mind Gn 6:5
the ark two of e living thing of Gn 6:19
and from e animal that crawls on Gn 6:20
with you e kind of food that Gn 6:21
of the earth e living thing I Gn 7:4
e creature that crawls on the Gn 7:8
e creature that crawls on the Gn 7:14
kind, all birds, e fowl, and Gn 7:14
He wiped out e living thing that Gn 7:23
Bring out e living thing of all Gn 8:17
all livestock, e bird, and every Gn 8:19
e creature that crawls on the Gn 8:19
He took some of e kind of clean Gn 8:20
clean animal and e kind of clean Gn 8:20
strike down e living thing as I Gn 8:21
you will be in e living creature Gn 9:2
on the earth, e bird of the sky, Gn 9:2
e creature that crawls on the Gn 9:2
E living creature will be food Gn 9:3
the life of e animal and every Gn 9:5
every animal and e man for your Gn 9:5
and with e living creature that Gn 9:10
Me and you and e living creature Gn 9:12
Me and you and e living creature Gn 9:15
God and e living creature Gn 9:16
E one of your males must be Gn 17:10
e male among you at eight days Gn 17:12
e male among the members of Gn 17:23
Now obey e order I give you, Gn 27:8
today and remove e sheep that is Gn 30:32
e dark-colored sheep among the Gn 30:32
e one that had any white on it— Gn 30:35
and e dark-colored sheep among Gn 30:35
city, and killed e male. Gn 34:25
placed the food in e city from Gn 41:48
There was famine in e country, Gn 41:54
because e Egyptian sold his Gn 47:20
You must throw e son born to the Ex 1:22
Nile, but let e daughter live." Ex 1:22
be remembered in e generation. Ex 3:15
E person and animal that is in Ex 9:19
man and beast and e plant of the Ex 9:22
hail beat down e plant of the Ex 9:25
and shattered e tree in the Ex 9:25
they will eat e tree you have Ex 10:5
over it and eat e plant in the Ex 10:12
and e firstborn ⌊male⌋ in the Ex 11:5
as well as e firstborn of the Ex 11:5
and strike e firstborn ⌊male Ex 12:12
LORD struck e firstborn ⌊male Ex 12:29
e firstborn of the livestock. Ex 12:29
e male in his household must be Ex 12:48
Consecrate e firstborn male to Ex 13:2
the firstborn from e womb among Ex 13:2
to the LORD e firstborn male Ex 13:12
You must redeem e firstborn of a Ex 13:13
must redeem e firstborn among Ex 13:13
LORD killed e firstborn ⌊male Ex 13:15
They gathered it e morning. Ex 16:21
can bring you e important case Ex 18:22
case but judge e minor case Ex 18:22
e minor case they would judge Ex 18:26
and bless you in e place where I Ex 20:24
tabernacle for e use and all its Ex 27:19
regularly on the altar e day: Ex 29:38
must burn it e morning when he Ex 30:7
and ability in e craft Ex 31:3
carve wood for work in e craft. Ex 31:5
within e skilled craftsman Ex 31:6
'E man fasten his sword to his Ex 32:27
male from e womb belongs to Me Ex 34:19
the tent of meeting for e use, Ex 35:21
E skilled woman spun ⌊yarn⌋ with Ex 35:25
and ability in e kind of craft Ex 35:31
for work in e kind of artistic Ex 35:33
They can do e kind of craft and Ex 35:35
and e skilled person in whose Ex 36:2
E morning the priest will burn Lv 6:12
E grain offering for a priest Lv 6:23
e kind of raven, Lv 11:15
and e bed he lies on will become Lv 15:24
the life of e creature is its Lv 17:14
the life of e creature is its Lv 17:14
E person, whether the native or Lv 17:15
before the LORD e Sabbath day as Lv 24:8
shekels for ⌊e⌋ five bushels Lv 27:16
E tenth of the land's produce, Lv 27:30
E tenth animal from the herd or Lv 27:32
the names of e male one by one. Nm 1:2
one the names of e male 20 years Nm 1:20
one the names of e male 20 years Nm 1:22
place of e firstborn Israelite Nm 3:12
because e firstborn belongs to Nm 3:13
time I struck down e firstborn Nm 3:13
I consecrated e firstborn in Nm 3:13
are to register e male one month Nm 3:15
counting e male one month old or Nm 3:22
Counting e male one month old or Nm 3:28
counting e male one month old or Nm 3:34
Register e firstborn male of the Nm 3:40
place of e firstborn among the Nm 3:41
in place of e firstborn among Nm 3:41
registered e firstborn among Nm 3:42
in place of e firstborn among Nm 3:45
E holy contribution the Nm 5:9
a cart from e two leaders and an Nm 7:3
from the womb, e Israelite Nm 8:16
For e firstborn among the Nm 8:17
day I struck down e firstborn in Nm 8:17
in place of e firstborn among Nm 8:18
a day's journey in e direction. Nm 11:31
E Israelite is to prepare these Nm 15:13
e one of their offerings that Nm 18:9
offering. E male may eat it; Nm 18:10
E ceremonially clean person in Nm 18:11
E clean person in your house may Nm 18:13
The firstborn of e living thing, Nm 18:15
the Levites e tenth in Israel Nm 18:21
to the LORD from e tenth you Nm 18:28
e male one month old or more; Nm 26:62
burnt offering for e Sabbath, Nm 28:10
her vows and e obligation she Nm 30:4
and e obligation she put herself Nm 30:11
Moses, and killed e male. Nm 31:7
"Have you let e female live?" Nm 31:15
and kill e woman who has had Nm 31:17
hair, and e article of wood. Nm 31:20
one out of ⌊e⌋ 500 humans, Nm 31:28
take one out of e 50 from the Nm 31:30
Moses took one out of ⌊e⌋ 50, Nm 31:47
and e one of your armed men Nm 32:21
e man in battle formation before Nm 32:29
were burying e firstborn male Nm 33:4
city wall 500 yards on e side. Nm 35:4
destroyed the people of e city, Dt 2:34
women, and children of e city. Dt 3:6
God destroyed e one of you who Dt 4:3
and I will tell you e command— Dt 5:31
houses full of e good thing that Dt 6:11
careful to follow e one of these Dt 6:25
carefully follow e command I am Dt 8:1
alone but on e word that comes Dt 8:3
and e living thing with them. Dt 11:6
eyes have seen e great work the Dt 11:7
Keep e command I am giving you Dt 11:8
carefully observe e one of these Dt 11:22
E place the sole of your foot Dt 11:24
and under e flourishing tree. Dt 12:2
out their names from e place. Dt 12:3
their gods e detestable thing Dt 12:31
You may eat e clean bird, Dt 14:11
e kind of raven, Dt 14:14
But you may eat e clean flying Dt 14:20
At the end of ⌊e⌋ three years, Dt 14:28
At the end of ⌊e⌋ seven years Dt 15:1
E creditor is to cancel what he Dt 15:2
careful to follow e one of these Dt 15:5
LORD your God e firstborn male Dt 15:19
provided you keep e one of these Dt 19:9
give a ruling in e dispute and Dt 21:5
Keep e command I am giving you Dt 27:1
in a loud voice to e Israelite: Dt 27:14
weary looking for them e day. Dt 28:32
inflict you with e sickness and Dt 28:61
and e curse written in this Dt 29:20
and He brought e curse written Dt 29:27
At the end of ⌊e⌋ seven years, Dt 31:10
down on a scroll e single word Dt 31:24
recited aloud e single word of Dt 31:30
I have given you e place where Jos 1:3
the sword—e man and woman, Jos 6:21
young and old, and e ox, sheep, Jos 6:21
and when e last one of them had Jos 8:24
destroyed e living being, Jos 10:40
they struck down e person with Jos 11:14
them rest on e side according to Jos 21:44
Since e good thing the LORD your Jos 23:15
bring on you e bad thing until Jos 23:15
take 10 men out of e 100 from Jdg 20:10
100 out of e 1,000, and 1,000 Jdg 20:10
and 1,000 out of e 10,000 to get Jdg 20:10
e one an experienced warrior. Jdg 20:17
Completely destroy e male, Jdg 21:11
well as e female who has slept Jdg 21:11
from his town e year to worship 1Sm 1:3
taunted her in this way e year. 1Sm 1:7
E year he would go on a circuit 1Sm 7:16
scattering in e direction. 1Sm 14:16
So e one of the troops 1Sm 14:34
all his enemies in e direction: 1Sm 14:47
E morning and evening for 40 1Sm 17:16
E time the Philistine commanders 1Sm 18:30
LORD cuts off e one of David's 1Sm 20:15
E day Jesse's son lives on earth 1Sm 20:31
In addition, e man who was 1Sm 22:2

Saul searched for him **e** day, 1Sm 23:14
May the LORD repay **e** man for 1Sm 26:23
my life from **e** distress, 2Sm 4:9
him rest on **e** side from all his 2Sm 7:1
He measured **e** two cord lengths 2Sm 8:2
son, so miserable **e** morning? 2Sm 13:4
David mourned for his son **e** day. 2Sm 13:37
he shaved ⌊it⌋ **e** year because 2Sm 14:26
and secured in **e** ⌊detail⌋. 2Sm 23:5
salvation and ⌊my⌋ **e** desire? 2Sm 23:5
my life from **e** difficulty, 1Kg 1:29
⌊sent⌋ by **e** king on earth who 1Kg 4:34
was completed in **e** detail and 1Kg 6:38
according to **e** specification. 1Kg 6:38
knowledge to do **e** kind of bronze 1Kg 7:14
below the brim, 10 **e** half yard, 1Kg 7:24
You alone know **e** human heart, 1Kg 8:39
e passerby will be appalled and 1Kg 9:8
logs and gold for his **e** wish— 1Kg 9:11
queen of Sheba her **e** desire— 1Kg 10:13
and once **e** three years the ships 1Kg 10:22
E man would bring his annual 1Kg 10:25
had struck down **e** male in Edom. 1Kg 11:15
he had killed **e** male in Edom. 1Kg 11:16
priests from **e** class of people 1Kg 12:31
priests from **e** class of people 1Kg 13:33
Asherah poles on **e** high hill and 1Kg 14:23
hill and under **e** green tree; 1Kg 14:23
land to **e** spring of water and 1Kg 18:5
spring of water and to **e** wadi. 1Kg 18:5
e knee that has not bowed to 1Kg 19:18
to Baal and **e** mouth that has 1Kg 19:18
you must attack **e** fortified city 2Kg 3:19
city and **e** choice city. 2Kg 3:19
must cut down **e** good tree and 2Kg 3:19
and stop up **e** spring of water 2Kg 3:19
You must ruin **e** good piece of 2Kg 3:19
stones to cover **e** good piece of 2Kg 3:25
stopped up **e** spring of water 2Kg 3:25
water and cut down **e** good tree. 2Kg 3:25
hills, and under **e** green tree. 2Kg 16:4
Asherah poles on **e** high hill and 2Kg 17:10
hill and under **e** green tree. 2Kg 17:10
Judah through **e** prophet and 2Kg 17:13
every prophet and **e** seer, 2Kg 17:13
Then **e** one of you may eat from 2Kg 18:31
and **e** one may drink water from 2Kg 18:31
charge of opening it **e** morning. 1Ch 9:27
of the Presence⌋ **e** Sabbath. 1Ch 9:32
to each and **e** Israelite, 1Ch 16:3
people skilled in **e** kind of work 1Ch 22:15
He given you rest on **e** side? 1Ch 22:18
also to stand **e** morning to give 1Ch 23:30
guards stationed at **e** watch. 1Ch 26:16
overseers in **e** matter relating 1Ch 26:32
the king in **e** matter to do with 1Ch 27:1
the LORD searches **e** heart and 1Ch 28:9
the intention of **e** thought. 1Ch 28:9
articles for **e** kind of service 1Ch 28:14
articles for **e** kind of service; 1Ch 28:14
E willing man of any skill will 1Ch 28:21
people are at your **e** command." 1Ch 28:21
and to **e** leader in all Israel— 2Ch 1:2
encircling it, 10 **e** half yard, 2Ch 4:3
e passerby will be appalled and 2Ch 7:21
the queen of Sheba her **e** desire, 2Ch 9:12
and once **e** three years the ships 2Ch 9:21
in each and **e** city to make them 2Ch 11:12
Those from **e** tribe of Israel who 2Ch 11:16
to the LORD **e** morning and every 2Ch 13:11
every morning and **e** evening, 2Ch 13:11
of the gold lampstand **e** evening. 2Ch 13:11
and He gave us rest on **e** side." 2Ch 14:7
them with **e** possible distress 2Ch 15:6
LORD gave them rest on **e** side. 2Ch 15:15
troops in **e** fortified city 2Ch 17:2
for **e** dispute that comes to you 2Ch 19:10
his God gave him rest on **e** side. 2Ch 20:30
hills, and under **e** green tree. 2Ch 28:4
himself altars on **e** street 2Ch 28:24
high places in **e** city of Judah 2Ch 28:25
lambs⌋ for **e** unclean person to 2Ch 30:17
cities, in each and **e** city. 2Ch 31:19
a portion to **e** male among the 2Ch 31:19
priests and to **e** Levite recorded 2Ch 31:19
was diligent in **e** deed that he 2Ch 31:21
who annihilated **e** brave warrior, 2Ch 32:21
He gave them rest on **e** side. 2Ch 32:22

shields, and **e** desirable item. 2Ch 32:27
Let **e** survivor, wherever he Ezr 1:4
given to them **e** day without fail Ezr 6:9
e one of us returned to his own Neh 4:15
wine was ⌊provided⌋ **e** 10 days. Neh 5:18
book of the law of God **e** day, Neh 8:18
year and will cancel **e** debt. Neh 10:31
our land and of **e** fruit tree to Neh 10:35
offerings, of **e** fruit tree, Neh 10:37
king's agent in **e** matter Neh 11:24
king had ordered **e** wine steward Est 1:8
peoples who are in **e** one of King Est 1:16
that **e** man should be master of Est 1:22
E day Mordecai took a walk in Est 2:11
peoples in **e** province of your Est 3:8
as law throughout **e** province, Est 3:14
Jewish people in **e** province Est 4:3
applies to **e** man or woman who Est 4:11
in each and **e** city the right Est 8:11
and annihilate **e** ethnic and Est 8:11
be issued as law in **e** province. Est 8:13
published for **e** ethnic group so Est 8:13
In **e** province and every city, Est 8:17
In every province and **e** city, Est 8:17
of them fell on **e** nationality. Est 9:2
days of the month Adar **e** year Est 9:21
days each and **e** year according Est 9:27
and celebrated by **e** generation, Est 9:28
You inspect him **e** morning, Jb 7:18
put him to the test **e** moment. Jb 7:18
The life of **e** living thing is in Jb 12:10
frighten him on **e** side and Jb 18:11
side and harass him at **e** step. Jb 18:11
tears me down on **e** side so that Jb 19:10
and his eyes spot **e** treasure. Jb 28:10
from the eyes of **e** living thing Jb 28:21
e living thing would perish Jb 34:15
look on **e** proud person and Jb 40:11
on **e** proud person and humble Jb 40:12
stand against me on **e** side. Ps 3:6
and drench my bed **e** night. Ps 6:6
God who executes justice **e** day. Ps 7:11
me, agony in my mind **e** day? Ps 13:2
terror is on **e** side. When they Ps 31:13
my **e** desire is known to You; Ps 38:9
e mortal man is only a vapor. Ps 39:5
e man is a mere vapor. Ps 39:11
for **e** animal of the forest is Ps 50:10
I know **e** bird of the mountains , Ps 50:11
has delivered me from **e** trouble, Ps 54:7
long, and punished **e** morning. Ps 73:14
burned down **e** place throughout Ps 74:8
they close in on me from **e** side. Ps 88:17
have ridiculed **e** step of Your Ps 89:51
been our refuge in **e** generation. Ps 90:1
and burns up His foes on **e** side. Ps 97:3
E morning I will destroy all the Ps 101:8
supply water for **e** wild beast; Ps 104:11
kept my feet from **e** evil path to Ps 119:101
therefore I hate **e** false way. Ps 119:104
precepts and hate **e** false way. Ps 119:128
He gives food to **e** creature. Ps 136:25
I will praise You **e** day; Ps 145:2
the desire of **e** living thing. Ps 145:16
let **e** living thing praise His Ps 145:21
and integrity—**e** good path. Pr 2:9
squares, she lurks at **e** corner. Pr 7:12
I was His delight **e** day, always Pr 8:30
watching at my doors **e** day, Pr 8:34
E sensible person acts Pr 13:16
E wise woman builds her house, Pr 14:1
but its **e** decision is from the Pr 16:33
rooms are filled with **e** precious Pr 24:4
E word of God is pure; Pr 30:5
and planted **e** kind of fruit tree Ec 2:5
and a time for **e** activity under Ec 3:1
is a time for **e** activity and Ec 3:17
for every activity and **e** work." Ec 3:17
riches and wealth to **e** man, Ec 5:19
For **e** activity there is a right Ec 8:6
will bring **e** act to judgment, Ec 12:14
including **e** hidden thing, Ec 12:14
from **e** fragrant powder Sg 3:6
and at our doors is **e** delicacy— Sg 7:13
against **e** high tower, against Is 2:15
tower, against **e** fortified wall, Is 2:15
against **e** ship of Tarshish, Is 2:16
and against **e** splendid sea Is 2:16

and from Judah **e** kind of Is 3:1
for **e** survivor in the land will Is 7:22
And on that day **e** place where Is 7:23
evildoer, and **e** mouth speaks Is 9:17
and **e** man's heart will melt. Is 13:7
and at Medeba. **E** head is shaved; Is 15:2
head is shaved; **e** beard is cut Is 15:2
let **e** one of them wail for Moab. Is 16:7
from bowls to **e** kind of jar. Is 22:24
e house is closed to entry. Is 24:10
the tears from **e** face and remove Is 25:8
E time it passes through, it Is 28:19
it will pass through **e** morning— Is 28:19
every morning—**e** day and every Is 28:19
morning—every day and **e** night. Is 28:19
the plowman plow **e** day to plant Is 28:24
will be on **e** high mountain and Is 30:25
high mountain and **e** raised hill Is 30:25
And **e** stroke of the appointed Is 30:32
for **e** joyous house in the joyful Is 32:13
Be our strength **e** morning, Is 33:2
then **e** one of you will eat from Is 36:16
E valley will be lifted up, Is 40:4
and **e** mountain and hill will be Is 40:4
forest, and **e** tree in it. Is 44:23
E knee will bow to Me, every Is 45:23
e tongue will swear allegiance. Is 45:23
lie at the head of **e** street like Is 51:20
for **e** eye will see when the LORD Is 52:8
e last one for his own gain. Is 56:11
the oaks, under **e** flourishing Is 57:5
remove ⌊**e**⌋ obstacle from My Is 57:14
free, and to tear off **e** yoke? Is 58:6
On **e** high hill and under every Jr 2:20
hill and under **e** leafy tree you Jr 2:20
She has ascended **e** high hill and Jr 3:6
and gone under **e** green tree to Jr 3:6
to strangers under **e** green tree Jr 3:13
E city flees at the sound of the Jr 4:29
among the rocks. **E** city is Jr 4:29
a sword; terror is on **e** side. Jr 6:25
You must walk in **e** way I command Jr 7:23
for **e** brother will certainly Jr 9:4
and **e** friend spread slander. Jr 9:4
E goldsmith is put to shame by Jr 10:14
and the grass of **e** field wither? Jr 12:4
E jar should be filled with wine. Jr 13:12
we know that **e** jar should be Jr 13:12
them down on **e** mountain and hill Jr 16:16
"Terror is on **e** side! Jr 20:10
Administer justice **e** morning, Jr 21:12
responsible for **e** madman who Jr 29:26
Why then do I see **e** man with his Jr 30:6
in labor and **e** face turned pale Jr 30:6
E city will be rebuilt on its Jr 30:18
e citadel will stand on its Jr 30:18
and **e** word that the LORD answers Jr 42:4
As for **e** word the LORD your God Jr 42:5
and **e** man of Judah who is in the Jr 44:27
disaster on **e** living creature' Jr 45:5
look back, terror is on **e** side! Jr 46:5
e inhabitant of the land will Jr 47:2
Tyre and Sidon **e** remaining ally. Jr 47:4
will move against **e** town; Jr 48:8
e head is bald and every beard Jr 48:37
is bald and **e** beard clipped; Jr 48:37
e hand is a gash and sackcloth Jr 48:37
to them: Terror is on **e** side! Jr 49:29
them to the wind in **e** direction, Jr 49:32
a desolation, **e** bit of her. Jr 50:13
a war cry against her on **e** side! Jr 50:15
her from **e** side in the day Jr 51:2
E goldsmith is put to shame by Jr 51:17
He has cut off **e** horn of Israel Lm 2:3
on the corner of **e** street. Lm 2:19
summoned my attackers on **e** side, Lm 2:22
They are new **e** morning; Lm 3:23
at the corner of **e** street. Lm 4:1
your survivors to **e** direction of Ezk 5:10
scatter one third to **e** direction Ezk 5:12
their abominations of **e** kind. Ezk 6:9
their altars, on **e** high hill, on Ezk 6:13
and under **e** green tree and every Ezk 6:13
green tree and **e** leafy oak— Ezk 6:13
the wall was **e** form of Ezk 8:10
all his troops to **e** direction of Ezk 12:14
passing by, and **e** vision fails? Ezk 12:22
as the fulfillment of **e** vision. Ezk 12:23

on the wrist of **e** hand and who	Ezk 13:18
of people of **e** height in order	Ezk 13:18
an elevated place in **e** square.	Ezk 16:24
at the head of **e** street and	Ezk 16:25
at the head of **e** street and	Ezk 16:31
your elevated place in **e** square.	Ezk 16:31
you with contempt from **e** side.	Ezk 16:57
will be scattered to **e** direction	Ezk 17:21
Birds of **e** kind will nest under	Ezk 17:23
Look, **e** life belongs to Me.	Ezk 18:4
When they made **e** firstborn pass	Ezk 20:26
and it will devour **e** green tree	Ezk 20:47
tree and **e** dry tree in you.	Ezk 20:47
and **e** face from the south to the	Ezk 20:47
E heart will melt, and every	Ezk 21:7
and **e** hand will become weak.	Ezk 21:7
E spirit will be discouraged,	Ezk 21:7
and **e** knee will turn to water.	Ezk 21:7
the sword despises **e** tree.	Ezk 21:10
e prince of Israel within you	Ezk 22:6
them against you from **e** side:	Ezk 23:22
against you on **e** side with	Ezk 23:24
of meat in it, **e** good piece—	Ezk 24:4
It has frustrated **e** effort;	Ezk 24:12
⌊your⌋ great wealth of **e** kind.	Ezk 27:12
and your great wealth of **e** kind,	Ezk 27:18
E kind of precious stone covered	Ezk 28:13
sword is against her on **e** side.	Ezk 28:23
E head was made bald and every	Ezk 29:18
made bald and **e** shoulder chafed	Ezk 29:18
the mountains and in **e** valley;	Ezk 31:12
will tremble **e** moment for his	Ezk 32:10
the mountains and **e** high hill.	Ezk 34:6
and⌋ food for **e** wild animal	Ezk 34:8
have trampled you from **e** side,	Ezk 36:3
e creature that crawls on the	Ezk 38:20
and **e** human being on the face of	Ezk 38:20
and **e** wall will fall to the	Ezk 38:20
and **e** man's sword will be	Ezk 38:21
you as food to **e** kind of	Ezk 39:4
Tell **e** kind of bird and all the	Ezk 39:17
On **e** wall all around, on the	Ezk 41:17
the firstfruits of **e** kind and	Ezk 44:30
contribution of **e** kind from all	Ezk 44:30
will be one percent of **e** cor.	Ezk 45:14
is one animal out of **e** 200 from	Ezk 45:15
gallon of oil for **e** half bushel.	Ezk 45:24
gallon of oil for **e** half bushel.	Ezk 46:5
gallon of oil for **e** half bushel.	Ezk 46:7
gallon of oil for **e** half bushel.	Ezk 46:11
you will offer it **e** morning.	Ezk 46:13
a grain offering **e** morning along	Ezk 46:14
and the oil **e** morning as a	Ezk 46:15
E ⌊kind of⌋ living creature that	Ezk 47:9
understanding in **e** kind of	Dn 1:17
visions and dreams of **e** kind.	Dn 1:17
In **e** matter of wisdom and	Dn 1:20
People of **e** nation and language,	Dn 3:4
harp, drum, and **e** kind of music,	Dn 3:5
lyre, harp, and **e** kind of music,	Dn 3:7
people of **e** nation and language	Dn 3:7
and **e** kind of music must fall	Dn 3:10
harp, drum, and **e** kind of music,	Dn 3:15
To those of **e** people, nation,	Dn 4:1
and **e** creature was fed from it.	Dn 4:12
Daniel and made **e** effort until	Dn 6:14
wrote to those of **e** people,	Dn 6:25
so that those of **e** people,	Dn 7:14
and magnify himself above **e** god,	Dn 11:36
prostitute on **e** grain-threshing	Hs 9:1
the treasury of **e** precious item.	Hs 13:15
out beside **e** altar on garments	Am 2:8
e last ⌊one⌋ of you with	Am 4:2
Bring your sacrifices **e** morning,	Am 4:4
your tenths **e** three days.	Am 4:4
sackcloth and **e** head to be	Am 8:10
abundance of **e** precious thing.	Nah 2:9
loins shake, **e** face grows pale!	Nah 2:10
pieces at the head of **e** street.	Nah 3:10
They laugh at **e** fortress and	Hab 1:10
this place **e** vestige of Baal	Zph 1:4
the middle of it, **e** kind of wild	Zph 2:14
And so is **e** work of their hands;	Hg 2:14
for **e** thief will be removed	Zch 5:3
from nations of **e** language will	Zch 8:23
battle bow, from them **e** ruler.	Zch 10:4
I will strike **e** horse with panic	Zch 12:4
will mourn, **e** family by itself	Zch 12:12
families, **e** family by itself,	Zch 12:14
On that day **e** prophet will be	Zch 13:4
E pot in Jerusalem and in Judah	Zch 14:21
in My name in **e** place because My	Mal 1:11
Therefore **e** tree that doesn't	Mt 3:10
alone but on **e** word that comes	Mt 4:4
and healing **e** disease and	Mt 4:23
and falsely say **e** kind of evil	Mt 5:11
e good tree produces good fruit,	Mt 7:17
E tree that doesn't produce good	Mt 7:19
and healing **e** disease and every	Mt 9:35
every disease and **e** sickness.	Mt 9:35
out and to heal **e** disease and	Mt 10:1
E kingdom divided against itself	Mt 12:25
will be forgiven **e** sin and	Mt 12:31
to account for **e** careless word	Mt 12:36
It collected **e** kind ⌊of fish⌋,	Mt 13:47
e student of Scripture	Mt 13:52
E plant that My heavenly Father	Mt 15:13
or three witnesses **e** fact may be	Mt 18:16
dead men's bones and **e** impurity.	Mt 23:27
E day I used to sit, teaching in	Mt 26:55
E day I was among you, teaching	Mk 14:49
E firstborn male will be	Lk 2:23
E year His parents traveled to	Lk 2:41
E valley will be filled, and	Lk 3:5
and **e** mountain and hill will be	Lk 3:5
Therefore **e** tree that doesn't	Lk 3:9
Devil had finished **e** temptation,	Lk 4:13
began to go out to **e** place in	Lk 4:37
who had come from **e** village of	Lk 5:17
flocking to Him from **e** town,	Lk 8:4
Him in pairs to **e** town and place	Lk 10:1
E kingdom divided against itself	Lk 11:17
mint, rue, and **e** kind of herb,	Lk 11:42
Make **e** effort to enter through	Lk 13:24
e one of you who does not say	Lk 14:33
linen, feasting lavishly **e** day.	Lk 16:19
you, and hem you in on **e** side.	Lk 19:43
E day He was teaching in the	Lk 19:47
E day while I was with you in	Lk 22:53
E branch in Me that does not	Jn 15:2
and He prunes **e** branch that	Jn 15:2
Pilate made **e** effort to release	Jn 19:12
devout men from **e** nation under	Ac 2:5
e day they devoted themselves	Ac 2:46
And **e** day the Lord added to them	Ac 2:47
there and placed **e** day at the	Ac 3:2
E day in the temple complex,	Ac 5:42
but in **e** nation the person who	Ac 10:35
that are read **e** Sabbath,	Ac 13:27
elders in **e** church and prayed	Ac 14:23
Moses has had in **e** city those	Ac 15:21
the synagogues **e** Sabbath day."	Ac 15:21
the brothers in **e** town where we	Ac 15:36
the marketplace **e** day with those	Ac 17:17
religious in **e** respect.	Ac 17:22
man He has made **e** nation of men	Ac 17:26
in the synagogue **e** Sabbath and	Ac 18:4
discussions **e** day in the lecture	Ac 19:9
In **e** way I've shown you that by	Ac 20:35
distress for **e** human being who	Rm 2:9
Considerable in **e** way.	Rm 3:2
so that **e** mouth may be shut and	Rm 3:19
through the law in **e** part of us	Rm 7:5
in me coveting of **e** kind.	Rm 7:8
else considers **e** day to be the	Rm 14:5
says the Lord, **e** knee will bow	Rm 14:11
and **e** tongue will give praise to	Rm 14:11
all those in **e** place who call	1Co 1:2
I teach everywhere in **e** church.	1Co 4:17
E sin a person can commit is	1Co 6:18
Christ is the head of **e** man,	1Co 11:3
E man who prays or prophesies	1Co 11:4
But **e** woman who prays or	1Co 11:5
Why are we in danger **e** hour?	1Co 15:30
Jesus our Lord: I die **e** day!	1Co 15:31
e ⌊action⌋ must be done with	1Co 16:14
For **e** one of God's promises is	2Co 1:20
through us in **e** place the scent	2Co 2:14
ourselves to **e** person's	2Co 4:2
are pressured in **e** way but not	2Co 4:8
ourselves clean from **e** impurity	2Co 7:1
we were afflicted in **e** way:	2Co 7:5
In **e** way you have commended	2Co 7:11
is able to make **e** grace overflow	2Co 9:8
you, so that in **e** way, always	2Co 9:8
you may excel in **e** good work.	2Co 9:8
are enriched in **e** way for all	2Co 9:11
and **e** high-minded thing that is	2Co 10:5
taking **e** thought captive to the	2Co 10:5
three witnesses **e** word will be	2Co 13:1
which I made **e** effort to do.	Gl 2:10
Again I testify to **e** man who	Gl 5:3
blessed us with **e** spiritual	Eph 1:3
far above **e** ruler and authority,	Eph 1:21
dominion, and **e** title given, not	Eph 1:21
who fills all things in **e** way.	Eph 1:23
from whom **e** family in heaven and	Eph 3:15
blown around by **e** wind of	Eph 4:14
us grow in **e** way into Him who	Eph 4:15
knit together by **e** supporting	Eph 4:16
the practice of **e** kind of	Eph 4:19
e situation take the shield of	Eph 6:16
With **e** prayer and request,	Eph 6:18
to my God for **e** remembrance of	Php 1:3
for all of you in my **e** prayer,	Php 1:4
in knowledge and **e** kind of	Php 1:9
Just that in **e** way, whether out	Php 1:18
the name that is above **e** name,	Php 2:9
name of Jesus **e** knee should bow	Php 2:10
and **e** tongue should confess that	Php 2:11
but I make **e** effort to take hold	Php 3:12
which surpasses **e** thought,	Php 4:7
Greet **e** saint in Christ Jesus.	Php 4:21
bearing fruit in **e** good work and	Col 1:10
is the head over **e** ruler and	Col 2:10
but in **e** place that your faith	1Th 1:8
and made **e** effort to return	1Th 2:17
Stay away from **e** form of evil.	1Th 5:22
and the love of **e** one of you for	2Th 1:3
fulfill **e** desire for goodness	2Th 1:11
himself above **e** so-called god	2Th 2:4
and with **e** unrighteous deception	2Th 2:10
strengthen you in **e** good work	2Th 2:17
keep away from **e** brother who	2Th 3:6
give you peace always in **e** way.	2Th 3:16
This is a sign in **e** letter;	2Th 3:17
want the men in **e** place to pray,	1Tm 2:8
is beneficial in **e** way,	1Tm 4:8
devoted herself to **e** good work.	1Tm 5:10
prepared for **e** good work.	2Tm 2:21
equipped for **e** good work.	2Tm 3:17
e effort to come to me soon,	2Tm 4:9
rescue me from **e** evil work and	2Tm 4:18
Make **e** effort to come before	2Tm 4:21
to appoint elders in **e** town:	Ti 1:5
to be ready for **e** good work,	Ti 3:1
make **e** effort to come to me in	Ti 3:12
through knowing **e** good thing	Phm 6
and **e** transgression and	Heb 2:2
be like His brothers in **e** way,	Heb 2:17
Now **e** house is built by someone,	Heb 3:4
us then make **e** effort to enter	Heb 4:11
been tested in **e** way as we are,	Heb 4:15
For **e** high priest taken from men	Heb 5:1
confirming oath ends **e** dispute.	Heb 6:16
need to offer sacrifices **e** day,	Heb 7:27
For **e** high priest is appointed	Heb 8:3
when **e** commandment had been	Heb 9:19
is a reminder of sins **e** year.	Heb 10:3
e priest stands day after day	Heb 10:11
us lay aside **e** weight and the	Heb 12:1
and punishes **e** son whom He	Heb 12:6
E generous act and every perfect	Jms 1:17
act and **e** perfect gift is	Jms 1:17
For **e** creature—animal or bird,	Jms 3:7
is disorder and **e** kind of evil.	Jms 3:16
Submit to **e** human institution	1Pt 2:13
make **e** effort to supplement your	2Pt 1:5
make **e** effort to confirm your	2Pt 1:10
I will also make **e** effort that	2Pt 1:15
make **e** effort to be found in	2Pt 3:14
not believe **e** spirit, but test	1Jn 4:1
E spirit who confesses that	1Jn 4:2
e spirit who does not confess	1Jn 4:3
may prosper in **e** way and be in	3Jn 2
the clouds, and **e** eye will see	Rv 1:7
Your blood from **e** tribe and	Rv 5:9
I heard **e** creature in heaven,	Rv 5:13
and **e** mountain and island was	Rv 6:14
and **e** slave and free person hid	Rv 6:15
sealed from **e** tribe of the sons	Rv 7:4
a vast multitude from **e** nation,	Rv 7:9
will wipe away **e** tear from their	Rv 7:17
given authority over **e** tribe,	Rv 13:7

the earth—to e nation, tribe, Rv 14:6
E island fled, and the mountains Rv 16:20
a haunt for e unclean spirit, Rv 18:2
a haunt for e unclean bird, Rv 18:2
and a haunt for e unclean and Rv 18:2
And e shipmaster, seafarer, the Rv 18:17
will wipe away e tear from their Rv 21:4
adorned with e kind of precious Rv 21:19
producing its fruit e month. Rv 22:2

EVERYBODY *(2)*
(See pp. xi-xii.)

EVERYDAY *(1)*
in the concerns of e life. 2Tm 2:4

EVERYONE *(316)*
(See pp. xi-xii.)

EVERYONE'S *(8)*
(See pp. xi-xii.)

EVERYTHING *(420)*
(See pp. xi-xii.)

EVERYTHING'S *(1)*
(See pp. xi-xii.)

EVERYWHERE *(20)*
(See pp. xi-xii.)

EVI *(2)*
kings—E, Rekem, Zur, Hur Nm 31:8
of Midian—E, Rekem, Zur, Hur, Jos 13:21

EVICTING *(1)*
e them from their property. Ezk 46:18

EVICTIONS *(1)*
an end to your e of My people." Ezk 45:9

EVICTS *(1)*
his father and e his mother is Pr 19:26

EVIDENCE *(14)*
respond to the e of the first Ex 4:8
may believe the e of the second Ex 4:8
animal⌋, he is to bring it as e; Ex 22:13
find ⌊any⌋ e of her virginity, Dt 22:14
will take the e of her virginity Dt 22:15
didn't find ⌊any⌋ e of your Dt 22:17
but here is the e of my Dt 22:17
is true and no e of the young Dt 22:20
use my disgrace as e against me, Jb 19:5
they might have e to accuse Him. Jn 8:6
him, "give e about the wrong; Jn 18:23
they provide e to you of what Ac 24:13
This is e of their destruction, Php 1:28
It is a clear e of God's 2Th 1:5

EVIDENT *(7)*
e to all who live in Jerusalem, Ac 4:16
known about God is e among them, Rm 1:19
your progress may be e to all. 1Tm 4:15
people's sins are e, going 1Tm 5:24
has now been made e through the 2Tm 1:10
Now it is e that our Lord came Heb 7:14
Devil's children—are made e. 1Jn 3:10

EVIL *(482)*
of the knowledge of good and e. Gn 2:9
of the knowledge of good and e, Gn 2:17
like God, knowing good and e." Gn 3:5
knowing good and e, he must not Gn 3:22
was nothing but e all the time, Gn 6:5
inclination is e from his youth. Gn 8:21
Now the men of Sodom were e, Gn 13:13
Don't do ⌊this⌋ e, my brothers. Gn 19:7
was e in the LORD's sight, Gn 38:7
What he did was e in the LORD's Gn 38:10
such a great e and sin against Gn 39:9
'Why have you repaid e for good? Gn 44:4
You planned e against me; Gn 50:20
Look out—you are planning e. Ex 10:10
out with an e intent to kill Ex 32:12
the people are ⌊intent⌋ on e. Ex 32:22
rashly to do what is good or e— Lv 5:4
I endure⌋ this e community that Nm 14:27
to the entire e community that Nm 14:35
to bring us to this e place? Nm 20:5
you are doing is e in My sight. Nm 22:32
now, if it is e in Your sight, I Nm 22:34
done what was e in the LORD's Nm 32:13
men in this e generation will Dt 1:35
sons who don't know good from e, Dt 1:39
and do what is e in the sight of Dt 4:25
doing what was e in the LORD's Dt 9:18
You must purge the e from you. Dt 13:5
do anything e like this among Dt 13:11
discovered doing e in the sight Dt 17:2
has done this e thing and stone Dt 17:5
You must purge the e from you. Dt 17:7
must purge the e from Israel. Dt 17:12
You must purge the e from you. Dt 19:19
do anything e like this among Dt 19:20
You must purge the e from you, Dt 21:21
You must purge the e from you. Dt 22:21
must purge the e from Israel. Dt 22:22
You must purge the e from you. Dt 22:24
You must purge the e from you. Dt 24:7
of all the e they have done Dt 31:18
will do what is e in the LORD's Dt 31:29
did what was e in the LORD's Jdg 2:11
turn from their ⌊e⌋ practices or Jdg 2:19
did what was e in the LORD's Jdg 3:7
did what was e in the LORD's Jdg 3:12
done what was e in the LORD's Jdg 3:12
did what was e in the sight Jdg 4:1
did what was e in the sight Jdg 6:1
God sent an e spirit between Jdg 9:23
the e that Abimelech had done Jdg 9:56
returned all the e of the men of Jdg 9:57
did what was e in the sight Jdg 10:6
did what was e in the LORD's Jdg 13:1
don't do ⌊this⌋ e, my brothers. Jdg 19:23
and eradicate e from Israel." Jdg 20:13
about your e actions from all 1Sm 2:23
see what a great e you committed 1Sm 12:17
all our sins the e of requesting 1Sm 12:19
you have committed all this e, 1Sm 12:20
if you continue to do what is e, 1Sm 12:25
and do what was e in the LORD's 1Sm 15:19
and an e spirit from the LORD 1Sm 16:14
see that an e spirit from God 1Sm 16:15
Whenever the e spirit from God 1Sm 16:16
the e spirit would leave him. 1Sm 16:23
arrogance and your e heart— 1Sm 17:28
next day an e spirit from God 1Sm 18:10
Now an e spirit from the LORD 1Sm 19:9
will know he has e intentions. 1Sm 20:7
out my father has e intentions 1Sm 20:9
intends to bring e on you, 1Sm 20:13
Saul was plotting e against him, 1Sm 23:9
that there is no e or rebellion 1Sm 24:11
I have done what is e to you. 1Sm 24:17
was harsh and e in ⌊his⌋ 1Sm 25:3
yet he paid me back e for good. 1Sm 25:21
may e not be found in you. 1Sm 25:28
His servant from doing e. 1Sm 25:39
brought Nabal's e deeds back on 1Sm 25:39
I done? What e is in my hand? 1Sm 26:18
evildoer according to his e!" 2Sm 3:39
what David had done to be e. 2Sm 11:27
LORD by doing what I consider e? 2Sm 12:9
up against you with e intent." 2Sm 18:32
but if e is found in him, 1Kg 1:52
know all the e that you did to 1Kg 2:44
back your e on your head, 1Kg 2:44
to discern between good and e. 1Kg 3:9
did what was e in the LORD's 1Kg 11:6
repent of his e way but again 1Kg 13:33
did what was e in the LORD's 1Kg 14:22
did what was e in the LORD's 1Kg 15:26
He did what was e in the LORD's 1Kg 15:34
because of all the e he had done 1Kg 16:7
doing what was e in the LORD's 1Kg 16:19
did what was e in the LORD's 1Kg 16:25
he did more e than all who were 1Kg 16:25
did what was e in the LORD's 1Kg 16:30
to do what is e in the LORD's 1Kg 21:20
to do what was e in the LORD's 1Kg 21:25
He did what was e in the LORD's 1Kg 22:52
He did what was e in the LORD's 2Kg 3:2
I know the e you will do to 2Kg 8:12
He did what was e in the LORD's 2Kg 8:18
and did what was e in the LORD's 2Kg 8:27
He did what was e in the LORD's 2Kg 13:2
He did what was e in the LORD's 2Kg 13:11
He did what was e in the LORD's 2Kg 14:24
He did what was e in the LORD's 2Kg 15:9
He did what was e in the LORD's 2Kg 15:18
He did what was e in the LORD's 2Kg 15:24
He did what was e in the LORD's 2Kg 15:28
He did what was e in the LORD's 2Kg 17:2
They did e things, provoking the 2Kg 17:11
Turn from your e ways and keep 2Kg 17:13
to do what was e in the LORD's 2Kg 17:17
He did what was e in the LORD's 2Kg 21:2
great amount of e in the LORD's 2Kg 21:6
did greater e than the nations 2Kg 21:9
greater e than the Amorites who 2Kg 21:11
have done what is e in My sight 2Kg 21:15
did what was e in the LORD's 2Kg 21:16
He did what was e in the LORD's 2Kg 21:20
He did what was e in the LORD's 2Kg 23:32
He did what was e in the LORD's 2Kg 23:37
He did what was e in the LORD's 2Kg 24:9
did what was e in the LORD's 2Kg 24:19
was e in the LORD's sight, 1Ch 2:3
was also e in God's sight, 1Ch 21:7
and turn from their e ways, 2Ch 7:14
did what was e, because he did 2Ch 12:14
He did what was e in the LORD's 2Ch 21:6
his mother gave him e advice. 2Ch 22:3
he did what was e in the LORD's 2Ch 22:4
and did what is e in the sight 2Ch 29:6
He did what was e in the LORD's 2Ch 33:2
a great deal of e in the LORD's 2Ch 33:6
did worse e than the nations 2Ch 33:9
He did what was e in the LORD's 2Ch 33:22
did what was e in the sight of 2Ch 36:5
He did what was e in the LORD's 2Ch 36:9
did what was e in the sight of 2Ch 36:12
that rebellious and e city, Ezr 4:12
us because of our e deeds and Ezr 9:13
did what was e in Your sight. Neh 9:28
I discovered the e that Eliashib Neh 13:7
What is this e you are doing— Neh 13:17
all this terrible e and acting Neh 13:27
and enemy is this e Haman." Est 7:6
him to revoke the e of Haman the Est 8:3
to see the e that would come Est 8:6
letter that the e plan Haman had Est 9:25
God and turned away from e. Jb 1:1
God and turns away from e." Jb 1:8
fears God and turns away from e. Jb 2:3
trouble and give birth to e; Jb 15:35
Though e tastes sweet in his Jb 20:12
the e man is spared from the day Jb 21:30
to turn from e is understanding. Jb 28:28
when I hoped for good, e came; Jb 30:26
because of the pride of e men. Jb 35:12
e cannot lodge with You. Ps 5:4
Let the e of the wicked come to Ps 7:9
is pregnant with e, conceives Ps 7:14
arm of the wicked and e person; Ps 10:15
tried me and found nothing ⌊e⌋; Ps 17:3
in whose hands are e schemes, Ps 26:10
to the e of their deeds. Ps 28:4
your tongue from e and your lips Ps 34:13
Turn away from e and do what is Ps 34:14
against those who do what is e, Ps 34:16
E brings death to the sinner, Ps 34:21
They repay me e for good, making Ps 35:12
not good and does not reject e. Ps 36:4
the man who carries out e plans. Ps 37:7
Turn away from e and do what is Ps 37:27
who repay e for good attack Ps 38:20
he stores up e in his heart; Ps 41:6
mouth for e and harness your Ps 50:19
and done this e in Your sight. Ps 51:4
Why brag about e, you hero! Ps 52:1
You love e instead of good, Ps 52:3
my adversaries for ⌊their⌋ e. Ps 54:5
because e is in their homes and Ps 55:15
thoughts are against me for e. Ps 56:5
each other in an e plan; Ps 64:5
and destroy them for their e. Ps 94:23
You who love the LORD, hate e! Ps 97:10
I will not be involved with e. Ps 101:4
They repay me e for good, and Ps 109:5
to those who speak e against me. Ps 109:20
feet from every e path to follow Ps 119:101
from me, you e ones, so that I Ps 119:115
who pursue e plans come near Ps 119:150
Rescue me, LORD, from e men. Ps 140:1
who plan e in their hearts. Ps 140:2
Let e relentlessly hunt down a Ps 140:11
turn to any e thing or wickedly Ps 141:4
is against the e acts of the Ps 141:5
rescuing you from the way of e— Pr 2:12
who enjoy doing e and celebrate Pr 2:14
the LORD and turn away from e. Pr 3:7
proceed in the way of e ones. Pr 4:14
unless they have done what is e; Pr 4:16

keep your feet away from e. Pr 4:27
who plots e with perversity in Pr 6:14
schemes, feet eager to run to e, Pr 6:18
protect you from an e woman, Pr 6:24
To fear the LORD is to hate e. Pr 8:13
hate arrogant pride, e conduct, Pr 8:13
but pursuing e ⌊leads⌋ to death. Pr 11:19
wicked desire what e men have, Pr 12:12
An e man is trapped by ⌊his⌋ Pr 12:13
the hearts of those who plot e, Pr 12:20
but fools hate to turn from e. Pr 13:19
is cautious and turns from e, Pr 14:16
The e bow before those who are Pr 14:19
those who plan e go astray? Pr 14:22
detests the plans of an e man, Pr 15:26
the wicked blurts out e things. Pr 15:28
and one turns from e by the fear Pr 16:6
highway of the upright avoids e; Pr 16:17
A worthless man digs up e, Pr 16:27
his lips brings about e. Pr 16:30
An e man seeks only rebellion; Pr 17:11
If anyone returns e for good, Pr 17:13
e will never depart from his Pr 17:13
sifts out all e with his eyes. Pr 20:8
say, "I will avenge this e!" Pr 20:22
Lashes and wounds purge away e, Pr 20:30
A wicked person desires e; Pr 21:10
Don't envy e men or desire to be Pr 24:1
one who plots e will be called Pr 24:8
For the e have no future; Pr 24:20
lips with an e heart are like Pr 26:23
his e will be revealed in the Pr 26:26
E men do not understand justice, Pr 28:5
upright into an e way will fall Pr 28:10
An e man is caught by sin, Pr 29:6
with good, not e, all the days Pr 31:12
not seen the e activity that is Ec 4:3
lives long in spite of his e. Ec 7:15
This is an e in all that is done Ec 9:3
hearts of people are full of e, Ec 9:3
people are trapped in an e time, Ec 9:12
There is an e I have seen under Ec 10:5
of his speaking is e madness. Ec 10:13
hidden thing, whether good or e. Ec 12:14
Remove your e deeds from My Is 1:16
from My sight. Stop doing e. Is 1:16
have brought e on themselves. Is 3:9
those who call e good and good Is 5:20
who call evil good and good e, Is 5:20
lie in wait with e intent will Is 29:20
his eyes to avoid endorsing e— Is 33:15
keeps his hand from doing any e. Is 56:2
away from the presence of e. Is 57:1
feet run after e, and they rush Is 59:7
turns from e is plundered. Is 59:15
you did what was e in My sight Is 65:12
not do what is e or destroy on Is 65:25
they did what is e in My sight Is 66:4
them for all the e they did when Jr 1:16
have committed a double e: Jr 2:13
Your own e will discipline you; Jr 2:19
and see how e and bitter it is Jr 2:19
⌊E⌋ generation, pay attention to Jr 2:31
also teach e women your ways. Jr 2:33
and done, the e you are capable Jr 3:5
stubbornness of their e hearts. Jr 3:17
it⌋ because of your e deeds. Jr 4:4
Wash the e from your heart, Jr 4:14
are skilled in doing what is e, Jr 4:22
have also excelled in e matters. Jr 5:28
water, so she pours forth her e. Jr 6:7
e ones are not separated out. Jr 6:29
it because of the e of My people Jr 7:12
to their own stubborn, e heart. Jr 7:24
they did more e than their Jr 7:26
done what is e in My sight." Jr 7:30
the survivors of this e family, Jr 8:3
No one regrets his e, asking: Jr 8:6
proceed from one e to another, Jr 9:3
the stubbornness of his e heart. Jr 11:8
carried out so many e schemes? Jr 11:15
Because of the e of its Jr 12:4
Concerning all My e neighbors Jr 12:14
These e people, who refuse to Jr 13:10
you who are instructed in e. Jr 13:23
pour out their own e on them." Jr 14:16
the power of e people and redeem Jr 15:21
did more e than your fathers. Jr 16:12

the stubbornness of his e heart, Jr 16:12
turns from its e, I will not Jr 18:8
it does what is e in My sight by Jr 18:10
from your e way, and correct Jr 18:11
stubbornness of his e heart." Jr 18:12
Should good be repaid with e? Jr 18:20
needy from the hand of e people. Jr 20:13
because of their e deeds. Jr 21:12
because of all your e. Jr 22:22
to you because of your e acts"— Jr 23:2
Their way of life has become e, Jr 23:10
My house I have found their e. Jr 23:11
and none turns his back on e. Jr 23:14
back from their e ways and their Jr 23:22
evil ways and their e deeds. Jr 23:22
from your e way of life and from Jr 25:5
of life and from your e deeds. Jr 25:5
each from his e way of life— Jr 26:3
because of the e of their deeds. Jr 26:3
but what is e in My sight! Jr 32:30
of all the e the Israelites Jr 32:32
city because of all their e. Jr 33:5
each one from his e way of life, Jr 35:15
them will turn from his e way. Jr 36:3
one will turn from his e way, Jr 36:7
men have been e in all they have Jr 38:9
of all the e that Ishmael son Jr 41:11
because of their e ways that Jr 44:3
from their e or stop burning Jr 44:5
can no longer bear your e deeds Jr 44:22
for all their e they have done Jr 51:24
did what was e in the LORD's Jr 52:2
of the e things they did, Ezk 6:9
out over all the e abominations Ezk 6:11
bring the most e of nations to Ezk 7:24
men who plan e and give wicked Ezk 11:2
turn from his e way to save his Ezk 13:22
after all your e—Woe, woe to Ezk 16:23
for all the e things you have Ezk 20:43
to your e ways and corrupt Ezk 20:44
land into the hands of e men. Ezk 30:12
Repent, repent of your e ways! Ezk 33:11
remember your e ways and your Ezk 36:31
and you will devise an e plan. Ezk 38:10
whose hearts are bent on e, Dn 11:27
that I remember all their e. Hs 7:2
please the king with their e, Hs 7:3
but they plot e against Me. Hs 7:15
All their e appears at Gilgal, Hs 9:15
My house because of their e, Hs 9:15
because of your extreme e. Hs 10:15
Since Gilead is full of e, Hs 12:11
such a time, for the days are e. Am 5:13
good and not e so that you may Am 5:14
Hate e and love good; establish Am 5:15
thought of the e day and bring Am 6:3
Each must turn from his e ways Jnh 3:8
had turned from their e ways— Jnh 3:10
and prepare e ⌊plans⌋ on their Mc 2:1
because it will be an e time. Mc 2:3
You hate good and love e. Mc 3:2
are good at accomplishing e: Mc 7:3
man communicates his e desire, Mc 7:3
who plots e against the LORD, Nah 1:11
eyes are too pure to look on e, Hab 1:13
The LORD will not do good or e. Zph 1:12
Turn from your e ways and your Zch 1:4
your evil ways and your e deeds. Zch 1:4
and do not plot e in your hearts Zch 7:10
Do not plot e in your hearts Zch 8:17
Everyone who does e is good in Mal 2:17
say every kind of e against you Mt 5:11
than this is from the e one. Mt 5:37
to rise on the e and the good, Mt 5:45
but deliver us from the e one. Mt 6:13
then, who are e, know how to Mt 7:11
you thinking e things in your Mt 9:4
good things when you are e? Mt 12:34
an e man produces evil things Mt 12:35
man produces e things from his Mt 12:35
things from his storeroom of e. Mt 12:35
An e and adulterous generation Mt 12:39
spirits more e than itself, Mt 12:45
also be with this e generation." Mt 12:45
e one comes and snatches away Mt 13:19
weeds are the sons of the e one, Mt 13:38
separate the e people from the Mt 13:49
The one who speaks e of father Mt 15:4

from the heart come e thoughts, Mt 15:19
An e and adulterous generation Mt 16:4
they found, both e and good. Mt 22:10
to him, 'You e, lazy slave! Mt 25:26
Sabbath to do good or to do e, Mk 3:4
Whoever speaks e of father or Mk 7:10
hearts, come e thoughts, sexual Mk 7:21
greed, e actions, deceit, Mk 7:22
All these e things come from Mk 7:23
soon afterwards speak e of Me. Mk 9:39
about all the e things Herod had Lk 3:19
Sabbath to do good or to do e, Lk 6:9
and slander your name as e, Lk 6:22
to the ungrateful and e. Lk 6:35
e man produces evil out of the Lk 6:45
man produces e out of the evil Lk 6:45
evil out of the e storeroom, Lk 6:45
plagues, and e spirits, and He Lk 7:21
had been healed of e spirits and Lk 8:2
then, who are e, know how to Lk 11:13
spirits more e than itself, Lk 11:26
generation is an e generation. Lk 11:29
you are full of greed and e. Lk 11:39
what you have said, you e slave! Lk 19:22
because their deeds were e. Jn 3:19
about it—that its deeds are e. Jn 7:7
You protect them from the e one. Jn 17:15
each of you from your e ways." Ac 3:26
matter of a crime or of moral e, Ac 18:14
and the e spirits came out of Ac 19:12
over those who had e spirits, Ac 19:13
The e spirit answered them, Ac 19:15
man who had the e spirit leaped Ac 19:16
must not speak e of a ruler of Ac 23:5
We find nothing e in this man. Ac 23:9
or spoken anything e about you. Ac 28:21
all unrighteousness, e, greed, Rm 1:29
inventors of e, disobedient to Rm 1:30
every human being who does e, Rm 2:9
us do e so that good may come" Rm 3:8
I practice the e that I do not Rm 7:19
I want to do good, e is with me. Rm 7:21
Detest e; cling to what is Rm 12:9
Do not repay anyone e for evil. Rm 12:17
Do not repay anyone evil for e. Rm 12:17
be conquered by e, but conquer Rm 12:21
evil, but conquer e with good. Rm 12:21
yet innocent about what is e. Rm 16:19
with the yeast of malice and e, 1Co 5:8
Put away the e person from among 1Co 5:13
will not desire e as they did. 1Co 10:6
be infants in e and adult in 1Co 14:20
us from this present e age, Gl 1:4
time, because the days are e. Eph 5:16
forces of e in the heavens. Eph 6:12
be able to resist in the e day, Eph 6:13
the flaming arrows of the e one. Eph 6:16
watch out for e workers, Php 3:2
mind because of your e actions. Col 1:21
impurity, lust, e desire, and Col 3:5
no one repays e for evil to 1Th 5:15
one repays evil for e to anyone, 1Th 5:15
Stay away from every form of e. 1Th 5:22
delivered from wicked and e men, 2Th 3:2
and guard you from the e one. 2Th 3:3
slanders, e suspicions, 1Tm 6:4
is a root of all kinds of e, 1Tm 6:10
E people and imposters will 2Tm 3:13
me from every e work and will 2Tm 4:18
are always liars, e beasts, lazy Ti 1:12
won't be in any of you an e, Heb 3:12
distinguish between good and e. Heb 5:14
clean⌋ from an e conscience and Heb 10:22
For God is not tempted by e, Jms 1:13
enticed by his own e desires. Jms 1:14
of all moral filth and e excess, Jms 1:21
become judges with e thoughts? Jms 2:4
is a restless e, full of deadly Jms 3:8
is disorder and every kind of e. Jms 3:16
All such boasting is e. Jms 4:16
against you as those who do e, 1Pt 2:12
those who do e and to praise 1Pt 2:14
freedom as a way to conceal e. 1Pt 2:16
not paying back e for evil or 1Pt 3:9
back evil for e or insult for 1Pt 3:9
his tongue from e and his lips 1Pt 3:10
turn away from e and do good. 1Pt 3:11
Lord is against those who do e. 1Pt 3:12

be God's will, than for doing e. 1Pt 3:17
behavior, e desires, drunkenness 1Pt 4:3
the world because of e desires. 2Pt 1:4
have had victory over the e one. 1Jn 2:13
have had victory over the e one. 1Jn 2:14
was of the e one and murdered 1Jn 3:12
his works were e, and his 1Jn 3:12
the e one does not touch him. 1Jn 5:18
is under the sway of the e one. 1Jn 5:19
to him shares in his e works. 2Jn 11
imitate what is e, but what is 3Jn 11
one who does e has not seen God 3Jn 11
and that you cannot tolerate e. Rv 2:2

EVIL-MERODACH (2)
Jehoiachin, E king of Babylon 2Kg 25:27
Jehoiachin, E king of Babylon Jr 52:31

EVILDOER (4)
LORD repay the e according to 2Sm 3:39
for everyone is a godless e, Is 9:17
I tell you, don't resist an e. Mt 5:39
a thief, an e, or as a meddler. 1Pt 4:15

EVILDOERS (32)
E will not afflict them as they 2Sm 7:10
E will not continue to oppress 1Ch 17:9
and He will not support e. Jb 8:20
the wicked and misfortune to e? Jb 31:3
company with e and walks with Jb 34:8
where e can hide themselves. Jb 34:22
Your presence; You hate all e. Ps 5:5
from me, all e, for the LORD has Ps 6:8
Will e never understand? Ps 14:4
a gang of e has closed in on me; Ps 22:16
hate a crowd of e, and I do not Ps 26:5
When e came against me to devour Ps 27:2
wicked, with the e, who speak Ps 28:3
There the e fall; they have been Ps 36:12
Do not be agitated by e; Ps 37:1
For e will be destroyed, but Ps 37:9
Will e never understand? Ps 53:4
the wicked, from the mob of e, Ps 64:2
like grass and all e flourish, Ps 92:7
all e will be scattered. Ps 92:9
my ears hear e when they attack Ps 92:11
arrogant words; all the e boast. Ps 94:4
takes a stand for me against e? Ps 94:16
eliminating all e from the Ps 101:8
will banish them with the e. Ps 125:5
me, and from the snares of e. Ps 141:9
because of e, and don't envy Pr 24:19
brood of e, depraved children Is 1:4
The offspring of e will never be Is 14:20
men and against the allies of e. Is 31:2
They strengthen the hands of e, Jr 23:14
is a city of e, tracked with Hs 6:8

EVILS (5)
forgotten the e of your fathers Jr 44:9
fathers, the e of Judah's kings Jr 44:9
kings, the e of their wives, Jr 44:9
wives, your own e, and the evils Jr 44:9
the e of your wives that were Jr 44:9

EWE (5)
had set apart seven e lambs from Gn 21:28
set apart these seven e lambs?" Gn 21:29
accept the seven e lambs from my Gn 21:30
an unblemished year-old e lamb, Lv 14:10
one small e lamb that he had 2Sm 12:3

EWES (4)
Your e and female goats have not Gn 31:38
20 male goats, 200 e, 20 rams, Gn 32:14
from tending e to be shepherd Ps 78:71
are like a flock of e coming up Sg 6:6

EXACT (6)
The e words were on them, which Dt 9:10
as well as the e amount of money Est 4:7
he reported the e words to them Jr 38:27
on the poor and e a grain tax Am 5:11
asked them the e time the star Mt 2:7
the e expression of His nature, Heb 1:3

EXACTED (2)
Then Menahem e 20 ounces of 2Kg 15:20
e the silver and the gold from 2Kg 23:35

EXACTLY (17)
"But e who will be going?" Ex 10:8
will do to you e as I heard you Nm 14:28
he is to do e as you do Nm 15:14
Shouldn't I say e what the LORD Nm 23:12
careful to do e as they instruct Dt 17:10
must do to them e as I have Dt 31:5
LORD has done e what He said 1Sm 28:17
So David did e as the LORD 2Sm 5:25
It's e like your servant said." 2Sm 13:35
Joab told her e what to say. 2Sm 14:3
told your servant e what to say. 2Sm 14:19
that is e what I will do this 1Kg 1:30
David did e as God commanded 1Ch 14:16
order was written e as Haman Est 3:12
written e as Mordecai ordered Est 8:9
e as he comes, so he will go. Ec 5:16
to find out e why Paul was being Ac 22:30

EXAGGERATE (1)
not to e—to all of you 2Co 2:5

EXALT (36)
father's God, and I will e Him. Ex 15:2
Why then do you e yourselves Nm 16:3
I will begin to e you in the Jos 3:7
You e me above my adversaries; 2Sm 22:49
by the promises of God to e him, 1Ch 25:5
You e me above my adversaries; Ps 18:48
I will e You, LORD, because You Ps 30:1
let us e His name together. Ps 34:3
I will e You among many people. Ps 35:18
let those who e themselves over Ps 35:26
and He will e you to inherit the Ps 37:34
should not e themselves. Ps 66:7
E Him who rides on the clouds— Ps 68:4
name with song and e Him with Ps 69:30
I will e him because he knows My Ps 91:14
E the LORD our God; bow in Ps 99:5
E the LORD our God; bow in Ps 99:9
Let them e Him in the assembly Ps 107:32
You are⌋ my God; I will e You. Ps 118:28
if I do not e Jerusalem as my Ps 137:6
I e You, my God the King, and Ps 145:1
E the LORD, Jerusalem; Ps 147:12
Cherish her, and she will e you; Pr 4:8
Does an ax e itself above the Is 10:15
my God; I will e You. I will Is 25:1
humble and not e itself but Ezk 17:14
e the lowly and bring down the Ezk 21:26
will never again e itself over Ezk 29:15
praise, e, and glorify the King Dn 4:37
He will e and magnify himself Dn 11:36
He will not e them at all. Hs 11:7
so that I would not e myself, 2Co 12:7
me so I would not e myself. 2Co 12:7
Messiah did not e Himself to Heb 5:5
the Lord, and He will e you. Jms 4:10
that He may e you in due time, 1Pt 5:6

EXALTATION (3)
E does not come from the east, Ps 75:6
Let the e of God be in their Ps 149:6
should boast in his e; Jms 1:9

EXALTED (76)
to the LORD, for He is highly e; Ex 15:1
to the LORD, for He is highly e; Ex 15:21
and his kingdom will be e. Nm 24:7
heart will not be e above his Dt 17:20
that day the LORD e Joshua in Jos 4:14
Israel and had e his kingdom for 2Sm 5:12
Your name will be e forever, 2Sm 7:26
the rock of my salvation, is e. 2Sm 22:47
built an e temple for You, 1Kg 8:13
Though this temple is ⌊now⌋ e, 1Kg 9:8
kingdom had been e for the sake 1Ch 14:2
and You are e as head over all. 1Ch 29:11
LORD highly e Solomon in the 1Ch 29:25
was with him and highly e him. 2Ch 1:1
have built an e temple for You, 2Ch 6:2
which was e, every passerby 2Ch 7:21
and he was e in the eyes of all 2Ch 32:23
and may it be e above all Neh 9:5
since He judges the e ones? Jb 21:22
They are e for a moment, then Jb 24:24
enthroned kings, and they are e. Jb 36:7
shows Himself e by His power. Jb 36:22
God is e beyond our knowledge; Jb 36:26
reach Him—He is e in power! Jb 37:23
How long, e men, will my honor Ps 4:2
is worthless is e by the human Ps 12:8
The God of my salvation is e. Ps 18:46
Be e, LORD, in Your strength; Ps 21:13
The LORD be e, who wants His Ps 35:27
that I am God, e among the Ps 46:10
the nations, e on the earth." Ps 46:10
belong to God; He is greatly e. Ps 47:9
God, be e above the heavens; Ps 57:5
God, be e above the heavens; Ps 57:11
only a vapor; e men, an illusion Ps 62:9
and they are e by Your Ps 89:16
by Your favor our horn is e. Ps 89:17
I have e one chosen from the Ps 89:19
My name his horn will be e. Ps 89:24
But You, LORD, are e forever. Ps 92:8
You are e above all the gods. Ps 97:9
He is e above all the peoples. Ps 99:2
God, be e above the heavens; Ps 108:5
His horn will be e in honor. Ps 112:9
The LORD is e above all the Ps 113:4
You have e Your name and Your Ps 138:2
the LORD is e, He takes note Ps 138:6
LORD, for His name alone is e. Ps 148:13
alone will be e on that day. Is 2:11
alone will be e on that day. Is 2:17
of Hosts is e by His justice, Is 5:16
Declare that His name is e. Is 12:4
the e people of the earth waste Is 24:4
The LORD is e, for He dwells on Is 33:5
lift Myself up. Now I will be e. Is 33:10
and lifted up and greatly e. Is 52:13
For the High and E One who lives Is 57:15
because he has e himself against Jr 48:26
because he has e himself against Jr 48:42
the lowly and bring down the e. Ezk 21:26
e anyone he wanted and humbled Dn 5:19
his heart was e and his spirit Dn 5:20
you have e yourself against the Dn 5:23
he was e in Israel. But he Hs 13:1
will you be e to heaven? Mt 11:23
humbles himself will be e. Mt 23:12
their thrones and e the lowly. Lk 1:52
will you be e to heaven? Lk 10:15
who humbles himself will be e." Lk 14:11
who humbles himself will be e." Lk 18:14
He has been e to the right hand Ac 2:33
God e this man to His right hand Ac 5:31
e the people during their stay Ac 13:17
myself so that you might be e, 2Co 11:7
God also highly e Him and gave Php 2:9
sinners, and e above the heavens Heb 7:26

EXALTING (3)
son of Haggith kept e himself, 1Kg 1:5
have been foolish by e yourself, Pr 30:32
over you and e the horn of your Lm 2:17

EXALTS (9)
wealth; He humbles and He e. 1Sm 2:7
Your salvation; Your help e me. 2Sm 22:36
me, and Your humility e me. Ps 18:35
brings down one and e another. Ps 75:7
Righteousness e a nation, but Pr 14:34
Whoever e himself will be Mt 23:12
everyone who e himself will be Lk 14:11
everyone who e himself will be Lk 18:14
He opposes and e himself above 2Th 2:4

EXAMINATION (3)
The priest will make an e, Lv 13:20
the priest is to make an e. Lv 13:39
so that after this e is over, Ac 25:26

EXAMINE (29)
We found this. E it. Is it your Gn 37:32
And she added, "E them. Gn 38:25
The priest will e the infection Lv 13:3
The priest will e him again on Lv 13:6
priest will e him, and if the Lv 13:8
The priest will e him. Lv 13:10
priest will e him, and if the Lv 13:17
the priest is to e it. Lv 13:25
the priest must e the infection. Lv 13:30
The priest will e the scaly Lv 13:34
the priest is to e the person. Lv 13:36
The priest is to e him, and if Lv 13:43
The priest is to e the Lv 13:50
go outside the camp and e ⌊him⌋. Lv 14:3
he enters to e the contamination Lv 14:36
priest will come to e the house. Lv 14:36
He will e it, and if the Lv 14:37
on the seventh day and e it. Lv 14:39
the priest must come and e it. Lv 14:44
not ⌊need to⌋ e a person further Jb 34:23
e my heart and mind. Ps 26:2
I, the LORD, e the mind, I test Jr 17:10

us search out and e our ways, Lm 3:40
Then e our appearance and the Dn 1:13
who were about to e him withdrew Ac 22:29
to those who e me is this: 1Co 9:3
So a man should e himself; 1Co 11:28
in the faith. E yourselves. Or 2Co 13:5
person should e his own work, Gl 6:4

EXAMINED (6)
Would it go well if He e you? Jb 13:9
He established it and e it. Jb 28:27
I e the case of the stranger. Jb 29:16
If we are being e today about a Ac 4:9
eagerness and e the Scriptures Ac 17:11
that he be e with the scourge, Ac 22:24

EXAMINES (13)
After the priest e him, he must Lv 13:3
When the priest e the raw flesh, Lv 13:15
when the priest e it, if there Lv 13:21
when the priest e it, if there Lv 13:26
When the priest e the scaly Lv 13:31
When the priest e ⌊it⌋, if the Lv 13:53
If the priest e ⌊it⌋, and the Lv 13:56
when the priest comes and e it, Lv 14:48
The One who e the thoughts and Ps 7:9
His eyes watch; He e everyone. Ps 11:4
The LORD e the righteous and the Ps 11:5
rather God, who e our hearts. 1Th 2:4
am the One who e minds and Rv 2:23

EXAMINING (3)
after e Him in your presence, Lk 23:14
By e him yourself you will be Ac 24:8
who, after e me, wanted to Ac 28:18

EXAMPLE (18)
your sons do not follow your e. 1Sm 8:5
and followed the e of his father 1Kg 15:26
and followed the e of Jeroboam 1Kg 15:34
by following the e of Jeroboam 1Kg 16:19
followed the e of Jeroboam son 1Kg 16:26
given you an e that you also Jn 13:15
e, a married woman is legally Rm 7:2
For e, I would not have known Rm 7:7
to the e you have in us. Php 3:17
you became an e to all the 1Th 1:7
ourselves an e to you so that 2Th 3:9
patience as an e to those who 1Tm 1:16
should be an e to the believers 1Tm 4:12
Set an e of good works yourself, Ti 2:7
Lord's name as an e of suffering Jms 5:10
leaving you an e, so that you 1Pt 2:21
making them an e to those who 2Pt 2:6
and serve as an e by undergoing Jd 7

EXAMPLES (3)
these things became e for us, 1Co 10:6
things happened to them as e, 1Co 10:11
you, but being e to the flock. 1Pt 5:3

EXASPERATE (1)
Fathers, do not e your children, Col 3:21

EXCEED (2)
prosperity far e the report I 1Kg 10:7
You far e the report I heard. 2Ch 9:6

EXCEEDED (1)
whose idols e those of Jerusalem Is 10:10

EXCEEDINGLY (1)
LORD must be e great and famous 1Ch 22:5

EXCEL (7)
will no longer e, because you Gn 49:4
your father e the blessings of Gn 49:26
a king because you e in cedar? Jr 22:15
seek to e in building up the 1Co 14:12
Now as you e in everything— 2Co 8:7
love for us—e also in this 2Co 8:7
you may e in every good work. 2Co 9:8

EXCELLED (1)
have also e in evil matters. Jr 5:28

EXCELLENCE (1)
is any moral e and if there is Php 4:8

EXCELLENT (5)
for you are an e man, and you 1Kg 1:42
One person dies in e health, Jb 21:23
To the most e governor Felix: Ac 23:26
places, most e Felix, with all Ac 24:3
out of my mind, most e Festus. Ac 26:25

EXCELLING (3)
of my virility, e in prominence, Gn 49:3
in prominence, e in power. Gn 49:3
always e in the Lord's work, 1Co 15:58

EXCEPT (106)
(See pp. xi-xii.)

EXCEPTION (3)
to everyone without e in Judah, 1Kg 15:22
But without e they all began to Lk 14:18
everything under Him is the e. 1Co 15:27

EXCESS (5)
gather all the ⌊e⌋ food during Gn 41:35
all the ⌊e⌋ food in the land Gn 41:48
those who are in e among the Nm 3:48
money from those in e of the Nm 3:49
of all moral filth and evil e, Jms 1:21

EXCESSIVE (6)
E speech is not appropriate on a Pr 17:7
Mocker," acts with e pride. Pr 21:24
the kisses of an enemy are e. Pr 27:6
wealth through e interest Pr 28:8
may be overwhelmed by e grief. 2Co 2:7
grown wealthy from her e luxury. Rv 18:3

EXCESSIVELY (2)
Don't be e righteous, and don't Ec 7:16
Don't be e wicked, and don't be Ec 7:17

EXCHANGE (16)
him tonight in e for your son's Gn 30:15
of Canaan in e for the grain Gn 47:14
give you food in e for your Gn 47:16
them food in e for the horses, Gn 47:17
with food in e for all their Gn 47:17
us and our land in e for food. Gn 47:19
charge, without any e of money. Ex 21:11
sell us food in e for silver so Dt 2:28
then e it for money, take the Dt 14:25
redemption or the e of property. Ru 4:7
he owns in e for his life. Jb 2:4
for what he gets in e will prove Jb 15:31
must not sell or e any of it, Ezk 48:14
a man give in e for his life? Mt 16:26
a man give in e for his life? Mk 8:37
birthright in e for one meal. Heb 12:16

EXCHANGED (15)
Gold cannot be e for it, and Jb 28:15
of fine gold cannot be e for it. Jb 28:17
They e their glory for the image Ps 106:20
Has a nation ⌊ever⌋ e its gods? Jr 2:11
My people have e their Glory for Jr 2:11
They e silver, iron, tin, and Ezk 27:12
e slaves and bronze utensils Ezk 27:13
from Beth-togarmah e horses, Ezk 27:14
They e turquoise, purple and Ezk 27:16
They e wheat from Minnith, Ezk 27:17
cane were ⌊e⌋ for your goods. Ezk 27:19
They e gold, the best of all Ezk 27:22
and e the glory of the immortal Rm 1:23
They e the truth of God for a Rm 1:25
their females e natural sexual Rm 1:26

EXCITED (2)
the whole town was e about their Ru 1:19
become e when trouble came his Jb 31:29

EXCLAIMED (13)
LORD," Jethro e, "who rescued Ex 18:10
arrival and ⌊the local women⌋ e, Ru 1:19
"Stop!" e Samuel. "Let me tell 1Sm 15:16
him⌋!" Joab e. "Why didn't you 2Sm 18:11
is blood!" they e. "The kings 2Kg 3:23
The king e, "Would he actually Est 7:8
I e, "This is my intense Jr 10:19
He e, "Look! I see four men, not Dn 3:25
Nebuchadnezzar e, "Praise to the Dn 3:28
the king e, "Is this not Babylon Dn 4:30
Then she e with a loud cry: Lk 1:42
testified concerning Him and e, Jn 1:15
Festus e in a loud voice, Ac 26:24

EXCLUDE (4)
LORD will e me from His people" Is 56:3
who hate and e you because of Me Is 66:5
when they e you, insult you, Lk 6:22
But e the courtyard outside the Rv 11:2

EXCLUDED (6)
should we be e from presenting Nm 9:7
disease and was e from access to 2Ch 26:21
and would be e from the assembly Ezr 10:8
boasting? It is e. By what kind Rm 3:27
e from the citizenship of Israel, Eph 2:12
understanding, e from the life Eph 4:18

EXCLUSIVELY (3)
they have been assigned e to him Nm 3:9
they have been e assigned to Me Nm 8:16
the Levites e to Aaron and his Nm 8:19

EXCREMENT (5)
with it and cover up your e. Dt 23:13
eat their own e and drink their 2Kg 18:27
to eat their e and drink their Is 36:12
dried human e in their sight. Ezk 4:12
cow dung instead of human e, Ezk 4:15

EXCUSE (7)
Can I e wicked scales or bags of Mc 6:11
and see it. I ask you to e me.' Lk 14:18
them out. I ask you to e me.' Lk 14:19
they have no e for their sin. Jn 15:22
a result, people are without e. Rm 1:20
of you who judges is without e. Rm 2:1
thoughts either accuse or e them Rm 2:15

EXCUSES (1)
they all began to make e. Lk 14:18

EXECRATION (2)
You will become an object of e, Jr 42:18
they will become an object of e, Jr 44:12

EXECUTE (34)
I will e judgments against all Ex 12:12
against you to e the vengeance Lv 26:25
the people and e them in broad Nm 25:4
E vengeance for the Israelites Nm 31:2
not lift a hand to e the priests 1Sm 22:17
to Doeg, "Go and e the priests!" 1Sm 22:18
in My statutes, e My ordinances, 1Kg 6:12
and to e any design that 2Ch 2:14
When will You e judgment on my Ps 119:84
He will not e justice by what He Is 11:3
righteously and e justice for Is 11:4
in My triumph, to e My wrath. Is 13:3
and is quick to e justice will Is 16:5
whirlwind—to e His anger with Is 66:15
the LORD will e judgment on all Is 66:16
I will e judgments within you Ezk 5:8
I will e judgments against you Ezk 5:10
you when I e judgments against Ezk 5:15
I will e judgments against you. Ezk 11:9
your houses and e judgments Ezk 16:41
to Babylon and e judgment on him Ezk 17:20
So I will e judgments against Ezk 25:11
I will e great vengeance against Ezk 25:17
the LORD when I e judgments Ezk 28:22
securely when I e judgments Ezk 28:26
and e judgments on Thebes. Ezk 30:14
So I will e judgments against Ezk 30:19
I will e judgment on him with Ezk 38:22
and his friends, to e them. Dn 2:13
had gone out to e the wise men Dn 2:14
appointed them to e judgment; Hab 1:12
ask for Barabbas and to e Jesus. Mt 27:20
for the Lord will e His sentence Rm 9:28
to e judgment on all, and to Jd 15

EXECUTED (24)
who does work on it must be e. Ex 35:2
the LORD had e judgment against Nm 33:4
to die is to be e on the Dt 17:6
No one is to be e on the Dt 17:6
the death penalty and is e, Dt 21:22
struck them down and e them. Jos 10:26
No one will be e this day, 1Sm 11:13
Edomite went and e the priests 1Sm 22:18
They were e in the first days of 2Sm 21:9
common people e all those who 2Kg 21:24
happened when Jehu e judgment on 2Ch 22:8
So they e judgment on Joash. 2Ch 24:24
he e his servants who had 2Ch 25:3
common people e all those who 2Ch 33:25
fair judgment be e against him, Ezr 7:26
He has e justice, striking down Ps 9:16
Justice e is a joy to the Pr 21:15
who e him with the sword and Jr 26:23
Since they e judgment against Ezk 23:10
judgment I have e and the hand I Ezk 39:21
that the wise men were to be e, Dn 2:13
against Nebuchadnezzar was e. Dn 4:33
also led away to be e with Him. Lk 23:32
because God has e your judgment Rv 18:20

with all the **e** of the sanctuary Ezk 44:5
These are the **e** of the city: Ezk 48:30

EXODUS *(2)*
the days of your **e** from the land Mc 7:15
mentioned the **e** of the sons of Heb 11:22

EXORCISTS *(1)*
itinerant Jewish **e** attempted to Ac 19:13

EXOTIC *(1)*
set out cuttings from **e** vines. Is 17:10

EXPANDED *(1)*
have **e** all the borders of the Is 26:15

EXPANSE *(15)*
Let there be an **e** between the Gn 1:6
So God made the **e** and separated Gn 1:7
water under the **e** from the water Gn 1:7
from the water above the **e**. Gn 1:7
God called the **e** "sky." Gn 1:8
be lights in the **e** of the sky to Gn 1:14
be lights in the **e** of the sky to Gn 1:15
them in the **e** of the sky to Gn 1:17
earth across the **e** of the sky." Gn 1:20
The shape of an **e**, with a gleam Ezk 1:22
And under the **e** their wings Ezk 1:23
from above the **e** over their Ezk 1:25
sapphire stone was above the **e**. Ezk 1:26
there above the **e** over the heads Ezk 10:1
the bright **e** ⌊of the heavens⌋ Dn 12:3

EXPANSES *(1)*
of God, and watery **e** are frozen. Jb 37:10

EXPECT *(9)*
whether ⌊to **e**⌋ love or hate. Ec 9:1
awesome deeds that we did not **e**, Is 64:3
or should we **e** someone else?" Mt 11:3
coming at an hour you do not **e**. Mt 24:44
day he does not **e** and at an hour Mt 24:50
from whom you **e** to receive, Lk 6:34
at an hour that you do not **e**." Lk 12:40
day he does not **e** him and at an Lk 12:46
person should not **e** to receive Jms 1:7

EXPECTANTLY *(3)*
my case to You and watch **e**. Ps 5:3
the LORD and wait **e** for Him; Ps 37:7
Now the people were waiting **e**, Lk 3:15

EXPECTATION *(6)*
Men listened to me with **e**, Jb 29:21
but the **e** of the wicked comes to Pr 10:28
dies, his **e** comes to nothing Pr 11:7
from fear and **e** of the things Lk 21:26
My eager **e** and hope is that I Php 1:20
but a terrifying **e** of judgment, Heb 10:27

EXPECTED *(9)*
I never **e** to see your face Gn 48:11
All Israel **e** me to be king, 1Kg 2:15
He **e** it to yield good grapes, Is 5:2
when I **e** a yield of good grapes, Is 5:4
You **e** much, but then it amounted Hg 1:9
more will be **e** of the one who Lk 12:48
all that the Jewish people **e**." Ac 12:11
They **e** that he would swell up or Ac 28:6
is **e** of managers that each one 1Co 4:2

EXPECTING *(7)*
good, and lend, **e** nothing in Lk 6:35
Him, for they were all **e** Him. Lk 8:40
e to get something from them. Ac 3:5
Now Cornelius was **e** them and had Ac 10:24
no charge of the sort I was **e**. Ac 25:18
I am **e** him with the brothers. 1Co 16:11
e the mercy of our Lord Jesus Jd 21

EXPECTS *(1)*
that this man **e** me to cure a man 2Kg 5:7

EXPEDITION *(1)*
Keilah, he called off the **e**. 1Sm 23:13

EXPELLED *(4)*
for Aram and **e** the Judahites 2Kg 16:6
They were **e** from human society; Jb 30:5
So I **e** you in disgrace from the Ezk 28:16
Barnabas and **e** them from their Ac 13:50

EXPELS *(1)*
want to do so and **e** them from 3Jn 10

EXPENDED *(1)*
for the labor he **e** against it. Ezk 29:18

EXPENSE *(2)*
will be gratified at their **e**. Ex 15:9
ever goes to war at his own **e**? 1Co 9:7

EXPENSIVE *(5)*
jar of very **e** fragrant oil. Mt 26:7
jar of pure and **e** fragrant oil Mk 14:3
oil—pure and **e** nard—anointed Jn 12:3
gold, pearls, or **e** apparel, 1Tm 2:9
objects of **e** wood, brass, iron, Rv 18:12

EXPERIENCE *(15)*
a youth with no **e** in leadership. 1Kg 3:7
my **e**, those who plow injustice Jb 4:8
You caused me to **e** many troubles Ps 71:20
Let me **e** Your faithful love in Ps 143:8
and **e** good in all the labor one Ec 5:18
but does not **e** happiness, do not Ec 6:6
will not **e** anything harmful Ec 8:5
I will let them **e** the abundance Jr 33:6
will no longer **e** reproach among Ezk 36:30
Ephraim will **e** shame; Hs 10:6
and His flesh did not **e** decay. Ac 2:31
that you didn't **e** any loss from 2Co 7:9
all the joy we **e** because of you 1Th 3:9
away so that he did not **e** death, Heb 11:5
whenever you **e** various trials, Jms 1:2

EXPERIENCED *(15)*
your children who **e** or saw the Dt 11:2
and who had **e** all the works the Jos 24:31
men, every one an **e** warrior. Jdg 20:17
Samuel had not yet **e** the LORD, 1Sm 3:7
father is an **e** soldier who won't 2Sm 17:8
his servants, **e** seamen, along 1Kg 9:27
ships with crews of **e** seamen. 2Ch 8:18
reign the land **e** peace for 10 2Ch 14:1
the kingdom **e** peace under him 2Ch 14:5
the land **e** peace, Asa built 2Ch 14:6
We have **e** panic and pitfall, Lm 3:47
for who has not **e** your constant Nah 3:19
which is **e** in the endurance of 2Co 1:6
and others **e** mockings and Heb 11:36
are being **e** by your brothers 1Pt 5:9

EXPERIENCES *(1)*
but soaks me with bitter **e**. Jb 9:18

EXPERIENCING *(1)*
in, never **e** the light. Jb 24:16

EXPERT *(8)*
up, Esau became an **e** hunter, an Gn 25:27
trained for battle, **e** with 1Ch 12:8
an **e** in matters of the LORD's Ezr 7:11
an **e** in the law of the God of Ezr 7:12
Ezra the priest and **e** in the law Ezr 7:21
one of them, an **e** in the law, Mt 22:35
Just then an **e** in the law stood Lk 10:25
since you are an **e** in all the Ac 26:3

EXPERTLY *(2)*
Prepare **e** blended incense from Ex 30:35
fragrant, and **e** blended incense. Ex 37:29

EXPERTS *(8)*
to confer with **e** in law and Est 1:13
The **e** in the law no longer knew Jr 2:8
Pharisees and **e** in the law had Lk 7:30
One of the **e** in the law answered Lk 11:45
Woe also to you **e** in the law! Lk 11:46
Woe to you **e** in the law! Lk 11:52
asked the law **e** and the Lk 14:3
the understanding of the **e**. 1Co 1:19

EXPLAIN *(30)*
On that day **e** to your son, Ex 13:8
of Jacob, and **e** to the Ex 19:3
Moses began to **e** this law, Dt 1:5
If you can **e** it to me during the Jdg 14:12
But if you can't **e** it to me, Jdg 14:13
were unable to **e** the riddle. Jdg 14:14
your husband to **e** the riddle to Jdg 14:15
so ⌊why⌋ should I **e** it to you?" Jdg 14:16
Then he will **e** to you what you Ru 3:4
for the king to **e** to her. 1Kg 10:3
for Solomon to **e** to her. 2Ch 9:2
show it to Esther, **e** it to her, Est 4:8
I **e** my riddle with a lyre. Ps 49:4
spoken to, that he may **e** it? Jr 9:12
e Jerusalem's abominations to Ezk 16:2
E to them the abominations of Ezk 20:4
Then **e** all her abominations to Ezk 22:2
and they do not **e** the difference Ezk 22:26
Won't you **e** to us what you mean Ezk 37:18
and **e** to them the difference Ezk 44:23
e to me the visions of my dream Dn 4:9
interpret dreams, **e** riddles, and Dn 5:12
e the vision to this man." Dn 8:16
E the parable of the weeds in Mt 13:36
to Him, "**E** this parable to Mt 15:15
He would **e** everything to His own Mk 4:34
He will **e** everything to us." Jn 4:25
Peter began to **e** to them in an Ac 11:4
if someone were to **e** it to you." Ac 13:41
difficult to **e**, since you have Heb 5:11

EXPLAINED *(18)*
just as Joseph had **e** to them. Gn 40:22
riddle, but haven't **e** it to me." Jdg 14:16
I haven't even **e** it to my father Jdg 14:16
seventh day, he **e** it to her, Jdg 14:17
Then she **e** it to her people. Jdg 14:17
to those who had **e** the riddle. Jdg 14:19
did not go and **e** to her husband, 1Sm 1:22
"Look," Absalom **e** to Joab, "I 2Sm 14:32
e the law to the people as they Neh 8:7
the words that were **e** to them. Neh 8:12
and thoroughly **e** ⌊the path to⌋ Jb 26:3
all this to heart and **e** it all: Ec 9:1
My statutes and **e** My ordinances Ezk 20:11
Then Arioch **e** the situation to Dn 2:15
among the myrtle trees **e**, Zch 1:10
the apostles and **e** to them how, Ac 9:27
he **e** to them how the Lord had Ac 12:17
him home and **e** the way of God to Ac 18:26

EXPLAINING *(6)*
it Ebenezer, **e**, "The LORD has 1Sm 7:12
on the road and **e** the Scriptures Lk 24:32
After **e** everything to them, Ac 10:8
e in detail the conversion of Ac 15:3
e and showing that the Messiah Ac 17:3
e spiritual things to spiritual 1Co 2:13

EXPLAINS *(1)*
This **e** why the rural Jews who Est 9:19

EXPLANATION *(3)*
wisdom and an **e** ⌊for things⌋, Ec 7:25
to another to find out the **e**, Ec 7:27
He gave me this **e**: Dn 9:22

EXPLICITLY *(1)*
the Spirit **e** says that in the 1Tm 4:1

EXPLOIT *(3)*
You must not **e** a foreign Ex 22:21
Don't **e** or brutalize the alien, Jr 22:3
greed they will **e** you with 2Pt 2:3

EXPLOITED *(3)*
justice for the **e** and giving Ps 146:7
resident is **e** within you. Ezk 22:7
and unlawfully **e** the foreign Ezk 22:29

EXPLOITS *(6)*
Such were the **e** of the three 2Sm 23:17
from Kabzeel, a man of many **e**. 2Sm 23:20
These were the **e** of Benaiah son 2Sm 23:22
Such were the **e** of the three 1Ch 11:19
from Kabzeel, a man of many **e**. 1Ch 11:22
These were the **e** of Benaiah son 1Ch 11:24

EXPLORE *(7)*
passed through to **e** is one that Nm 13:32
that they may **e** the land for us Dt 1:22
to spy out the land and **e** it. Jdg 18:2
told them, "Go and **e** the land." Jdg 18:2
to seek and **e** through wisdom Ec 1:13
to know, **e**, and seek wisdom Ec 7:25
a man labors hard to **e** it, Ec 8:17

EXPLORED *(4)*
through and **e** is an extremely Nm 14:7
I **e** with my mind how to let my Ec 2:3
he weighed, **e**, and arranged many Ec 12:9
of the earth below **e**, Jr 31:37

EXPORTED *(2)*
they **e** them to all the kings of 1Kg 10:29
they **e** them to all the kings of 2Ch 1:17

EXPOSE *(13)*
vulgar person would **e** himself." 2Sm 6:20
The heavens will **e** his iniquity, Jb 20:27
I will **e** your righteousness, Is 57:12
will get drunk and **e** yourself. Lm 4:21
Edom, and will **e** your sins. Lm 4:22
all around and **e** your nakedness Ezk 16:37
I am about to **e** Moab's flank Ezk 25:9
her naked and **e** her as she was Hs 2:3
Now I will **e** her shame in the Hs 2:10
valley and **e** her foundations. Mc 1:6
and **e** your uncircumcision! Hab 2:16

for He will **e** the cedar work. Zph 2:14
darkness, but instead, **e** them. Eph 5:11

EXPOSED *(22)*
God has **e** your servants' Gn 44:16
your nakedness is not **e** on it. Ex 20:26
has **e** the source of her ⌊flow⌋ Lv 20:18
leaving the city **e** while they Jos 8:17
He **e** himself today in the sight 2Sm 6:20
the world were **e** at the rebuke 2Sm 22:16
foundations of the world were **e**, Ps 18:15
and your shame will be **e**. Is 47:3
They will be **e** to the sun, Jr 8:2
thrown out ⌊to be **e**⌋ to the heat Jr 36:30
so that its foundation is **e**. Ezk 13:14
your nakedness **e** by your acts Ezk 16:36
before your wickedness was **e**? Ezk 16:57
They **e** her nakedness, seized her Ezk 23:10
promiscuity and **e** her nakedness, Ezk 23:18
of your debauchery will be **e**, Ezk 23:29
the crimes of Samaria will be **e**. Hs 7:1
so that his deeds may not be **e**. Jn 3:20
Everything **e** by the light is Eph 5:13
are naked and **e** to the eyes of Heb 4:13
were publicly **e** to taunts and Heb 10:33
shameful nakedness not be **e**, Rv 3:18

EXPOSING *(3)*
e white stripes on the branches. Gn 30:37
for it is **e** one's own blood Lv 20:19
to your guilt, **e** your Ezk 21:24

EXPOUNDED *(1)*
dawn to dusk he **e** and witnessed Ac 28:23

EXPRESS *(2)*
I will **e** my complaint and speak Jb 10:1
Although they **e** love with their Ezk 33:31

EXPRESSING *(1)*
But some were **e** indignation to Mk 14:4

EXPRESSION *(5)*
change my **e**, and smile," Jb 9:27
and the **e** on his face changed Dn 3:19
the law the full **e** of knowledge Rm 2:20
the exact **e** of His nature, Heb 1:3
Now this **e**, "Yet once more," Heb 12:27

EXPRESSLY *(1)*
if I **e** say to the young man, 1Sm 20:21

EXTEND *(22)*
will **e** Japheth; he will dwell Gn 9:27
I will **e** my hands to the LORD. Ex 9:29
are to **e** from its sides, Ex 25:32
six branches that **e** from the Ex 25:33
six branches that **e** from the Ex 25:35
they must **e** from the waist to Ex 28:42
the ravines that **e** to the site Nm 21:15
Levites ⌊will **e**⌋ from the city Nm 35:4
territory will **e** from the Dt 11:24
would bless me, **e** my border, let 1Ch 4:10
will **e** his power to the sea and Ps 89:25
The LORD will **e** Your mighty Ps 110:2
You will **e** Your hand; Ps 138:7
the Lord will ⌊**e**⌋ His hand a Is 11:11
will **e** their power over Edom Is 11:14
continued to **e** faithful love to Jr 31:3
north side it will **e** from the Ezk 47:15
The city's open space will **e**: Ezk 48:17
He will **e** his power against the Dn 11:42
His greatness will **e** to the ends Mc 5:4
dominion will **e** from sea to sea Zch 9:10
of the mountains will **e** to Azal. Zch 14:5

EXTENDED *(27)*
Their settlements **e** from Mesha Gn 10:30
Joseph and **e** kindness to him Gn 39:21
and **e** his hands to the LORD. Ex 9:33
Six branches **e** from its sides, Ex 37:18
six branches that **e** from the Ex 37:19
the six branches that **e** from it, Ex 37:21
a mass that **e** as far as Adam, Jos 3:16
and the border **e** westward; Jos 18:15
e to Rimmon, curving around to Jos 19:13
the Amorites **e** from the ascent Jdg 1:36
Angel of the LORD **e** the tip of Jdg 6:21
The battle **e** beyond Beth-aven, 1Sm 14:23
Then the angel **e** his hand toward 2Sm 24:16
His reputation **e** to all the 1Kg 4:31
father Jehoiada had **e** to him, 2Ch 24:22
He has **e** grace to us in the Ezr 9:9
The king **e** the golden scepter in Est 5:2
The king **e** the golden scepter Est 8:4
e my hand and no one paid Pr 1:24
Your tendrils have **e** to the sea; Jr 48:32
their wings **e** one toward another Ezk 1:23
So you **e** your prostitution to Ezk 16:29
for its roots **e** to abundant Ezk 31:7
gate **e** around to the pilaster Ezk 40:14
day ⌊your⌋ boundary will be **e**. Mc 7:11
he **e** his message until midnight. Ac 20:7
e through more and more people, 2Co 4:15

EXTENDING *(5)*
Gadites ⌊the area **e**⌋ from Aroer Dt 3:12
the area **e**⌋ from Gilead to Dt 3:16
was 30 feet long **e** across the 1Kg 6:3
the front **e** across the width 2Ch 3:4
Hamath and **e** from the eastern Ezk 48:1

EXTENDS *(7)*
wilderness that **e** from the Nm 21:13
the desert that **e** to the 1Ch 5:9
Only if the king **e** the golden Est 4:11
She **e** her hands to the spinning Pr 31:19
she **e** her hands to the needy. Pr 31:20
her judgment **e** to the sky and Jr 51:9
your dominion ⌊**e**⌋ to the ends Dn 4:22

EXTENSION *(2)*
there will be an **e** of your Dn 4:27
but an **e** of life was granted to Dn 7:12

EXTENSIVELY *(2)*
and he built **e** on the wall of 2Ch 27:3
and grew **e** toward the south Dn 8:9

EXTENT *(2)*
comprehended the **e** of the earth? Jb 38:18
and save to the **e** that he 1Co 16:2

EXTERIOR *(1)*
lower gate to the **e** front of the Ezk 40:19

EXTERMINATE *(2)*
Joshua proceeded to **e** the Anakim Jos 11:21
and plotted to **e** us so we would 2Sm 21:5

EXTERMINATED *(2)*
you until He has **e** you from the Dt 28:21
So Zimri **e** the entire house of 1Kg 16:12

EXTERMINATION *(1)*
to destruction, death, and **e**. Est 7:4

EXTERNAL *(1)*
had come as a man in His **e** form, Php 2:7

EXTINGUISH *(6)*
They would **e** my one remaining 2Sm 14:7
must not **e** the lamp of Israel. 2Sm 21:17
Mighty waters cannot **e** love; Sg 8:7
with no one to **e** ⌊it⌋ because Jr 4:4
with no one at Bethel to **e** it. Am 5:6
will be able to **e** the flaming Eph 6:16

EXTINGUISHED *(9)*
the vestibule, **e** the lamps, did 2Ch 29:7
My days are **e**. A graveyard Jb 17:1
the light of the wicked is **e**; Jb 18:5
they were **e** like a fire among Ps 118:12
but the lamp of the wicked is **e**. Pr 13:9
they are **e**, quenched like a wick Is 43:17
of Jerusalem and not be **e**." Jr 17:27
The blazing flame will not be **e**, Ezk 20:47
It will not be **e**." Ezk 20:48

EXTORT *(2)*
and brutally **e** your neighbors. Ezk 22:12
loves to **e** with dishonest Hs 12:7

EXTORTED *(1)*
And if I have **e** anything from Lk 19:8

EXTORTION *(5)*
the practice of **e** turns a wise Ec 7:7
gain from **e**, whose hand never Is 33:15
and committing **e** and oppression. Jr 22:17
have practiced **e** and committed Ezk 22:29
be ready as a gift and not an **e**. 2Co 9:5

EXTRA *(4)*
road, or an **e** shirt, sandals, Mt 10:10
but not put on an **e** shirt. Mk 6:9
and don't take an **e** shirt. Lk 9:3
you for whatever **e** you spend.' Lk 10:35

EXTRAORDINARY *(11)*
He will bring **e** plagues on you Dt 28:59
was a man of **e** stature with six 1Ch 20:6
⌊This⌋ **e** knowledge is beyond me. Ps 139:6
was found to have an **e** spirit, Dn 5:12
intelligence, and **e** wisdom. Dn 5:14
because he had an **e** spirit, Dn 6:3
the end of these **e** things?" Dn 12:6
was performing **e** miracles by Ac 19:11
people showed us **e** kindness, Ac 28:2
so that this **e** power may be from 2Co 4:7
because of the **e** revelations. 2Co 12:7

EXTREME *(5)*
E hunger came to all the land of Gn 41:55
I hate them with **e** hatred; Ps 139:22
came to me in my **e** weariness, Dn 9:21
Bethel, because of your **e** evil. Hs 10:15
church to an **e** degree and tried Gl 1:13

EXTREMELY *(33)*
(See pp. xi-xii.)

EXULT *(4)*
and all that is in them **e**. 1Ch 16:32
fields and everything in them **e**. Ps 96:12
warriors, who **e** in My triumph, Is 13:3
in the LORD, I **e** in my God; Is 61:10

EYE *(74)*
e for eye, tooth for tooth, hand Ex 21:24
eye for **e**, tooth for tooth, hand Ex 21:24
a man strikes the **e** of his male Ex 21:26
free in compensation for his **e**. Ex 21:26
or who has an **e** defect, a Lv 21:20
for fracture, **e** for eye, tooth Lv 24:20
eye for **e**, tooth for tooth Lv 24:20
life for life, **e** for eye, tooth Dt 19:21
life, eye for **e**, tooth for tooth Dt 19:21
him as the pupil of His **e**. Dt 32:10
everyone's right **e** and humiliate 1Sm 11:2
Keep an **e** on Shimei son of Gera, 1Kg 2:8
mouth to mouth, **e** to eye, hand 2Kg 4:34
mouth, eye to **e**, hand to hand. 2Kg 4:34
My **e** will never again see Jb 7:7
The **e** of anyone who looks on me Jb 7:8
e that saw him will see ⌊him⌋ Jb 20:9
The adulterer's **e** watches for Jb 24:15
e will see me, he covers ⌊his⌋ Jb 24:15
no falcon's **e** has seen it. Jb 28:7
Guard me as the apple of Your **e**; Ps 17:8
with My **e** on you, I will give Ps 32:8
the **e** of the LORD is on those Ps 33:18
and my **e** has looked down on my Ps 54:7
He keeps His **e** on the nations. Ps 66:7
One who formed the **e** not see? Ps 94:9
you would the pupil of your **e**. Pr 7:2
sly wink of the **e** causes grief, Pr 10:10
hearing ear and the seeing **e**— Pr 20:12
As for the **e** that ridicules a Pr 30:17
The **e** is not satisfied by seeing Ec 1:8
for every **e** will see when the Is 52:8
e has seen any God except You, Is 64:4
face to face and meet **e** to eye. Jr 32:4
face to face and meet eye to **e**. Jr 32:4
king of Babylon **e** to eye and Jr 34:3
Babylon eye to **e** and speak face Jr 34:3
you touches the pupil of His **e**. Zch 2:8
strike his arm and his right **e**! Zch 11:17
and his right **e** go completely Zch 11:17
keep a watchful **e** on the house Zch 12:4
If your right **e** causes you to Mt 5:29
An **e** for an eye and a tooth for Mt 5:38
An eye for an **e** and a tooth for Mt 5:38
The **e** is the lamp of the body. Mt 6:22
If your **e** is good, your whole Mt 6:22
But if your **e** is bad, your whole Mt 6:23
your brother's **e** but don't Mt 7:3
notice the log in your own **e**? Mt 7:3
take the speck out of your **e**,' Mt 7:4
look, there's a log in your **e**? Mt 7:4
take the log out of your **e**, Mt 7:5
speck out of your brother's **e**. Mt 7:5
And if your **e** causes your Mt 18:9
you to enter life with one **e**, Mt 18:9
go through the **e** of a needle Mt 19:24
And if your **e** causes your Mk 9:47
of God with one **e** than to have Mk 9:47
go through the **e** of a needle Mk 10:25
the speck in your brother's **e**, Lk 6:41
notice the log in your own **e**? Lk 6:41
the speck that is in your **e**,' Lk 6:42
don't see the log in your **e**? Lk 6:42
take the log out of your **e**, Lk 6:42
the speck in your brother's **e**. Lk 6:42
Your **e** is the lamp of the body. Lk 11:34
When your **e** is good, your whole Lk 11:34
go through the **e** of a needle Lk 18:25

What no **e** has seen and no ear 1Co 2:9
I'm not an **e**, I don't belong to 1Co 12:16
If the whole body were an **e**, 1Co 12:17
So the **e** cannot say to the hand, 1Co 12:21
twinkling of an **e**, at the last 1Co 15:52
and every **e** will see Him, Rv 1:7

EYEBROWS *(1)*

his beard, his **e**, and the rest Lv 14:9

EYELASHES *(1)*

her captivate you with her **e**. Pr 6:25

EYELIDS *(3)*

eyes to sleep or my **e** to slumber Ps 132:4
your eyes or slumber to your **e**. Pr 6:4
our **e** soaked with weeping. Jr 9:18

EYES *(377)*

you eat it your **e** will be opened Gn 3:5
Then the **e** of both of them were Gn 3:7
favor in the **e** of the LORD. Gn 6:8
God opened her **e**, and she saw a Gn 21:19
was old and his **e** were so weak Gn 27:1
had delicate **e**, but Rachel was Gn 29:17
night, and sleep fled from my **e**. Gn 31:40
good in the **e** of Hamor and his Gn 34:18
him favor in the **e** of the prison Gn 39:21
had him bound before their **e**. Gn 42:24
Your **e** and my brother Benjamin's Gn 45:12
Benjamin's **e** can see that it is Gn 45:12
will put his hands on your **e**." Gn 46:4
favor in our lord's **e** and will Gn 47:25
If I have found favor in your **e**, Gn 47:29
His **e** are darker than wine, Gn 49:12
do what is right in His **e**, Ex 15:26
will cause your **e** to fail and Lv 26:16
and you can serve as our **e**. Nm 10:31
your own heart and your own **e**. Nm 15:39
gouge out the **e** of these men? Nm 16:14
the LORD opened Balaam's **e**, Nm 22:31
of the man whose **e** are opened, Nm 24:3
trance⌋ with ⌊his⌋ **e** uncovered: Nm 24:4
of the man whose **e** are opened; Nm 24:15
trance⌋ with ⌊his⌋ **e** uncovered: Nm 24:16
thorns in your **e** and in your Nm 33:55
Your own **e** have seen everything Dt 3:21
and see ⌊it⌋ with your own **e**, Dt 3:27
Your **e** have seen what the LORD Dt 4:3
in the **e** of the peoples. Dt 4:6
the things your **e** have seen and Dt 4:9
for you in Egypt before your **e**? Dt 4:34
Before our **e** the LORD inflicted Dt 6:22
shattering them before your **e**. Dt 9:17
awesome works your **e** have seen. Dt 10:21
Your ⌊own⌋ **e** have seen every Dt 11:7
seems right in his own **e**. Dt 12:8
for it blinds the **e** of the wise Dt 16:19
our **e** did not see ⌊it⌋. Dt 21:7
be slaughtered before your **e**, Dt 28:31
while your **e** grow weary looking Dt 28:32
heart, failing **e**, and a Dt 28:65
seen with your own **e** everything Dt 29:2
with your own **e** the great trials Dt 29:3
to understand, **e** to see, or ears Dt 29:4
let you see it with your own **e**, Dt 34:4
his **e** were not weak, and his Dt 34:7
your sides and thorns in your **e**, Jos 23:13
Your own **e** saw what I did to Jos 24:7
these great signs before our **e**. Jos 24:17
seized him and gouged out his **e**. Jdg 16:21
the Philistines for my two **e**." Jdg 16:28
the LORD will do before your **e**. 1Sm 12:16
had beautiful **e** and a healthy, 1Sm 16:12
with your own **e** that the LORD 1Sm 24:10
to another before your very **e**, 2Sm 12:11
If I find favor in the LORD's **e**, 2Sm 15:25
but Your **e** are set against the 2Sm 22:28
the **e** of all Israel are on you 1Kg 1:20
so that Your **e** may watch over 1Kg 8:29
in the **e** of their captors 1Kg 8:50
May Your **e** be open to Your 1Kg 8:52
My **e** and My heart will be there 1Kg 9:3
I came and saw with my own **e**. 1Kg 10:7
do right in My **e** and to carry 1Kg 11:33
only what is right in My **e**. 1Kg 14:8
what was evil in the LORD's **e**. 1Kg 14:22
what was right in the LORD's **e**, 1Kg 15:5
what was right in the LORD's **e**, 1Kg 15:11
with a bandage over his **e**. 1Kg 20:38
removed the bandage from his **e**. 1Kg 20:41
seven times and opened his **e**. 2Kg 4:35
open his **e** and let him see. 2Kg 6:17
the LORD opened the servant's **e**. 2Kg 6:17
these men's **e** and let them see. 2Kg 6:20
So the LORD opened their **e**. 2Kg 6:20
in fact see it with your own **e**, 2Kg 7:2
in fact see it with your own **e**, 2Kg 7:19
she painted her **e**, adorned her 2Kg 9:30
open Your **e**, LORD, and see; 2Kg 19:16
and lifted your **e** in pride? 2Kg 19:22
Your **e** will not see all the 2Kg 22:20
Zedekiah's sons before his **e**. 2Kg 25:7
so that Your **e** watch over this 2Ch 6:20
please let Your **e** be open and 2Ch 6:40
e will now be open and My ears 2Ch 7:15
My **e** and My heart will be there 2Ch 7:16
I came and saw with my own **e**. 2Ch 9:6
For the **e** of the LORD range 2Ch 16:9
as you see with your own **e**. 2Ch 29:8
exalted in the **e** of all the 2Ch 32:23
Your **e** will not see all the 2Ch 34:28
us new life and light to our **e**. Ezr 9:8
let Your **e** be open and Your ears Neh 1:6
and hide sorrow from my **e**. Jb 3:10
a form loomed before my **e**. Jb 4:16
Your **e** will look for me, but I Jb 7:8
You have **e** of flesh, or do You Jb 10:4
Look, my **e** have seen all this; Jb 13:1
you, and why do your **e** flash Jb 15:12
My enemy pierces me with His **e**. Jb 16:9
the shadow of death covers my **e**, Jb 16:16
me and my **e** must gaze at their Jb 17:2
the **e** of his children will fail. Jb 17:5
My **e** have grown dim from grief, Jb 17:7
my **e** will look at ⌊Him⌋, and not Jb 19:27
descendants, before their **e**. Jb 21:8
Let his own **e** see his demise; Jb 21:20
but His **e** ⌊watch⌋ over their Jb 24:23
when he opens his **e**, it is gone. Jb 27:19
and his **e** spot every treasure. Jb 28:10
from the **e** of every living Jb 28:21
I was **e** to the blind and feet to Jb 29:15
is poured out before my ⌊**e**⌋, Jb 30:16
have made a covenant with my **e**. Jb 31:1
my heart has followed my **e**, Jb 31:7
or let the widow's **e** go blind, Jb 31:16
he was righteous in his own **e**. Jb 32:1
For His **e** ⌊watch⌋ over a man's Jb 34:21
its **e** penetrate the distance. Jb 39:29
while his **e** are like the rays of Jb 41:18
but now my **e** have seen You. Jb 42:5
My **e** are swollen from grief; Ps 6:7
his **e** are on the lookout for the Ps 10:8
is in heaven. His **e** watch; He Ps 11:4
Restore brightness to my **e**; Ps 13:3
You humble those with haughty **e**. Ps 18:27
radiant, making the **e** light up. Ps 19:8
My **e** are always on the LORD, Ps 25:15
faithful love is before my **e**, Ps 26:3
my **e** are worn out from angry Ps 31:9
The **e** of the LORD are on the Ps 34:15
is no dread of God before his **e**, Ps 36:1
for in his own **e** he flatters Ps 36:2
the light of my **e** has faded. Ps 38:10
My **e** fail, looking for my God. Ps 69:3
Let their **e** grow too dim to see, Ps 69:23
Their **e** bulge out from fatness; Ps 73:7
have kept me from closing my **e**; Ps 77:4
Before our **e**, let vengeance for Ps 79:10
My **e** are worn out from crying. Ps 88:9
see it with your **e** and witness Ps 91:8
My **e** look down on my enemies; Ps 92:11
anything godless before my **e**. Ps 101:3
with haughty **e** or an arrogant Ps 101:5
My **e** ⌊favor⌋ the faithful of the Ps 101:6
cannot speak, **e**, but cannot see Ps 115:5
from death, my **e** from tears, my Ps 116:8
it is wonderful in our **e**. Ps 118:23
Open my **e** so that I may see Ps 119:18
Turn my **e** from looking at what Ps 119:37
My **e** grow weary ⌊looking⌋ for Ps 119:82
My **e** grow weary ⌊looking for⌋ Ps 119:123
My **e** pour out streams of tears Ps 119:136
I raise my **e** toward the Ps 121:1
I lift my **e** to You, the One Ps 123:1
a servant's **e** on His master's Ps 123:2
a servant girl's **e** on her Ps 123:2
so our **e** are on the LORD our God Ps 123:2
not proud; my **e** are not haughty Ps 131:1
not allow my **e** to sleep or my Ps 132:4
cannot speak, **e**, but cannot see Ps 135:16
Your **e** saw me when I was Ps 139:16
my **e** ⌊look⌋ to You, Lord GOD. Ps 141:8
All **e** look to You, and You give Ps 145:15
LORD opens ⌊the **e** of⌋ the blind. Ps 146:8
Let your **e** look forward; Pr 4:25
ways are before the LORD's **e**, Pr 5:21
sleep to your **e** or slumber to Pr 6:4
winks his **e**, signals with his Pr 6:13
arrogant **e**, a lying tongue, Pr 6:17
to the teeth and smoke to the **e**, Pr 10:26
way is right in his own **e**, Pr 12:15
e of the LORD are everywhere, Pr 15:3
Bright **e** cheer the heart; Pr 15:30
ways seem right in his own **e**, Pr 16:2
who narrows his **e** is planning Pr 16:30
but a fool's **e** roam to the ends Pr 17:24
sifts out all evil with his **e**. Pr 20:8
open your **e**, and you'll have Pr 20:13
e and an arrogant heart— Pr 21:4
The LORD's **e** keep watch over Pr 22:12
As soon as your **e** fly to it, Pr 23:5
and let your **e** observe my ways. Pr 23:26
for no reason? Who has red **e**? Pr 23:29
Your **e** will see strange things, Pr 23:33
he'll become wise in his own **e**. Pr 26:5
a man who is wise in his own **e**? Pr 26:12
In his own **e**, a slacker is wiser Pr 26:16
and people's **e** are never Pr 27:20
A rich man is wise in his own **e**, Pr 28:11
who turns his **e** away will Pr 28:27
gives light to the **e** of both. Pr 29:13
that is pure in its own **e**, Pr 30:12
haughty its **e** and pretentious Pr 30:13
All that my **e** desired, I did not Ec 2:10
The wise man has **e** in his head, Ec 2:14
his **e** are still not content with Ec 4:8
to gaze at them with his **e**? Ec 5:11
Better what the **e** see than Ec 6:9
even though one's **e** do not close Ec 8:16
for the **e** to see the sun. Ec 11:7
and in the sights of your **e**; Ec 11:9
beautiful! Your **e** are doves. Sg 1:15
your veil, your **e** are doves. Sg 4:1
heart with one glance of your **e**, Sg 4:9
His **e** are like doves beside Sg 5:12
Turn your **e** away from me, for Sg 6:5
your **e** like pools in Heshbon by Sg 7:4
So in his **e** I have become like Sg 8:10
before your very **e** foreigners Is 1:7
heads held high and seductive **e**, Is 3:16
and haughty **e** are humbled. Is 5:15
⌊and⌋ because my **e** have seen the Is 6:5
their ears and blind their **e**; Is 6:10
see with their **e** and hear with Is 6:10
and the proud look in his **e**." Is 10:12
by what He sees with His **e**, Is 11:3
to death⌋ before their **e**; Is 13:16
will turn their **e** to the Holy Is 17:7
has shut your **e**—the prophets, Is 29:10
darkness the **e** of the blind will Is 29:18
Your **e** will see your Teacher, Is 30:20
Then the **e** of those who see will Is 32:3
and shuts his **e** to avoid Is 33:15
Your **e** will see the king in his Is 33:17
Your **e** will see Jerusalem, Is 33:20
Then the **e** of the blind will be Is 35:5
open Your **e**, LORD, and see; Is 37:17
and lifted your **e** in pride? Is 37:23
My **e** grow weak looking upward. Is 38:14
to open blind **e**, to bring out Is 42:7
blind, yet have **e**, and are deaf, Is 43:8
has shut their **e** so they cannot Is 44:18
we grope like those without **e**. Is 59:10
Raise your **e** and look around: Is 60:4
you enlarge your **e** with paint? Jr 4:30
don't Your **e** ⌊look for⌋ Jr 5:3
They have **e**, but they don't see. Jr 5:21
were water, my **e** a fountain of Jr 9:1
us so that our **e** may overflow Jr 9:18
My **e** will overflow with tears, Jr 13:17
Their **e** fail because there are Jr 14:6
Let my **e** overflow with tears; Jr 14:17
your very **e** and in your time Jr 16:9
enemies before your very **e**. Jr 20:4
But you have **e** and heart for Jr 22:17

I will keep My e on them for Jr 24:6
kill them before your very e. Jr 29:21
weeping and your e from tears, Jr 31:16
whose e are on all the ways of Jr 32:19
Zedekiah's sons before his e, Jr 39:6
place before your e on that day. Jr 39:16
as you can see with your own e Jr 42:2
in Zion before your very e." Jr 51:24
sons before his e and also Jr 52:10
things; my e flow with tears Lm 1:16
My e are worn out from weeping; Lm 2:11
no relief and your e no rest. Lm 2:18
My e flow with streams of tears Lm 3:48
My e overflow unceasingly, Lm 3:49
My e bring me grief because of Lm 3:51
the while our e were failing ⌊as Lm 4:17
of these, our e grow dim: Lm 5:17
rims were full of e all around. Ezk 1:18
Me and by their e that lusted Ezk 6:9
were full of e all around. Ezk 10:12
the earth right before my e; Ezk 10:19
They have e to see but do not Ezk 12:2
cannot see the land with his e. Ezk 12:12
or raise his e to the idols Ezk 18:6
he raises his e to the idols, Ezk 18:12
or raise his e to the idols Ezk 18:15
are before your e and not defile Ezk 20:7
things that were before their e, Ezk 20:8
profaned in the e of the nations Ezk 20:9
profaned in the e of the nations Ezk 20:14
profaned in the e of the nations Ezk 20:22
and their e were fixed on their Ezk 20:24
heart right before their e. Ezk 21:6
in the e of those who have Ezk 21:23
painted your e, and adorned Ezk 23:40
delight of your e away from you Ezk 24:16
delight of your e, and the Ezk 24:21
of their e and the longing Ezk 24:25
raise your e to your idols, Ezk 33:25
look with your e, listen with Ezk 40:4
look with your e and listen with Ezk 44:5
There were e in this horn like a Dn 7:8
horn that had e, and a mouth Dn 7:20
conspicuous horn between his e. Dn 8:5
horn between his e represents Dn 8:21
Open Your e and see our Dn 9:18
his e like flaming torches, Dn 10:6
Compassion is hidden from My e. Hs 13:14
food been cut off before our e, Jl 1:16
I will fix My e on them for harm Am 9:4
the e of the Lord GOD are on the Am 9:8
and let us feast our e on Zion." Mc 4:11
My e will look at her in Mc 7:10
⌊Your⌋ e are too pure to look on Hab 1:13
your fortunes before your e. Zph 3:20
on ⌊that⌋ one stone are seven e. Zch 3:9
These seven e of the LORD, Zch 4:10
for the e of men are on the LORD Zch 9:1
now I have seen with My own e. Zch 9:8
their e will rot in their Zch 14:12
Your own e will see this, and Mal 1:5
touched their e, saying, "Let it Mt 9:29
And their e were opened. Mt 9:30
and they have shut their e; Mt 13:15
see with their e and hear with Mt 13:15
But your e are blessed because Mt 13:16
than to have two e and be thrown Mt 18:9
they said to Him, "open our e!" Mt 20:33
Jesus touched their e. Mt 20:34
Lord and is wonderful in our e? Mt 21:42
could not keep their e open. Mt 26:43
Do you have e, and not see, and Mk 8:18
Spitting on his e and laying His Mk 8:23
placed His hands on the man's e, Mk 8:25
than to have two e and be thrown Mk 9:47
Lord and is wonderful in our e?" Mk 12:11
could not keep their e open. Mk 14:40
For my e have seen Your Lk 2:30
And the e of everyone in the Lk 4:20
The e that see the things you Lk 10:23
even raise his e to heaven but Lk 18:13
now it is hidden from your e. Lk 19:42
Then their e were opened, and Lk 24:31
Open your e and look at the Jn 4:35
and spread the mud on his e. Jn 9:6
"Then how were your e opened?" Jn 9:10
it on my e, and told me, Jn 9:11
and opened his e was a Sabbath. Jn 9:14
put mud on my e," he told them. Jn 9:15
Him, since He opened your e?" Jn 9:17
we don't know who opened his e. Jn 9:21
How did He open your e?" Jn 9:26
He is from, yet He opened my e! Jn 9:30
opening the e of a person born Jn 9:32
demon open the e of the blind?" Jn 10:21
the blind man's e also have kept Jn 11:37
Jesus raised His e and said, Jn 11:41
has blinded their e and hardened Jn 12:40
see with their e or understand Jn 12:40
and though his e were open, Ac 9:8
like scales fell from his e, Ac 9:18
She opened her e, saw Peter, Ac 9:40
to open their e that they may Ac 26:18
and they have shut their e; Ac 28:27
see with their e and hear with Ac 28:27
no fear of God before their e. Rm 3:18
e that cannot see and ears that Rm 11:8
Let their e be darkened so they Rm 11:10
is honorable in everyone's e. Rm 12:17
before whose e Jesus Christ was Gl 3:1
torn out your e and given them Gl 4:15
I pray⌋ that the e of your heart Eph 1:18
exposed to the e of Him to whom Heb 4:13
keeping our e on Jesus, the Heb 12:2
is very valuable in God's e. 1Pt 3:4
because the e of the Lord are on 1Pt 3:12
having e full of adultery and 2Pt 2:14
what we have seen with our e, 1Jn 1:1
the darkness has blinded his e. 1Jn 2:11
the lust of the e, and the pride 1Jn 2:16
as snow, His e like a fiery Rv 1:14
the One whose e are like a fiery Rv 2:18
spread on your e so that you may Rv 3:18
covered with e in front and in Rv 4:6
covered with e around and inside Rv 4:8
He had seven horns and seven e, Rv 5:6
away every tear from their e. Rv 7:17
His e were like a fiery flame, Rv 19:12
away every tear from their e. Rv 21:4

EYESIGHT *(2)*
Now Jacob's e was poor because Gn 48:10
Eli, whose e was failing, was 1Sm 3:2

EYEWITNESSES *(4)*
The e described to them what had Mk 5:16
as the original e and servants Lk 1:2
Meanwhile the e reported to them Lk 8:36
we were e of His majesty. 2Pt 1:16

EZBAI *(1)*
the Carmelite, Naarai son of E, 1Ch 11:37

EZBON *(2)*
Haggi, Shuni, E, Eri, Arodi, and Gn 46:16
E, Uzzi, Uzziel, Jerimoth, and 1Ch 7:7

EZEKIEL *(2)*
came directly to E the priest, Ezk 1:3
Now E will be a sign for you. Ezk 24:24

EZEL *(2)*
and stay beside the rock E. 1Sm 20:19
the south side of the stone E, 1Sm 20:41

EZEM *(3)*
Baalah, Iim, E, Jos 15:29
Hazar-shual, Balah, E, Jos 19:3
Bilhah, E, Tolad, 1Ch 4:29

EZER *(9)*
Dishon, E, and Dishan. These are Gn 36:21
Dishon, E, and Dishan. These are Gn 36:30
Anah, Dishon, E, and Dishan. 1Ch 1:38
Gedor, and E fathered Hushah. 1Ch 4:4
his son Shuthelah, E, and Elead. 1Ch 7:21
the land killed E and Elead 1Ch 7:21
E was the chief, Obadiah second, 1Ch 12:9
Next to him E son of Jeshua, Neh 3:19
Malchijah, Elam, and E. Neh 12:42

EZER'S *(2)*
are E sons: Bilhan, Zaavan, Gn 36:27
E sons: Bilhan, Zaavan, and 1Ch 1:42

EZION-GEBER *(7)*
from Abronah and camped at E. Nm 33:35
They departed from E and camped Nm 33:36
road and from Elath and E. Dt 2:8
together a fleet of ships at E, 1Kg 9:26
the ships were wrecked at E. 1Kg 22:48
Solomon went to E and to Eloth 2Ch 8:17
and they made the ships in E. 2Ch 20:36

EZRA *(26)*
of Persia, E—Seraiah's son, Ezr 7:1
E came to Jerusalem in the fifth Ezr 7:8
because E had determined in his Ezr 7:10
Artaxerxes gave to E the priest Ezr 7:11
king of kings, to E the priest, Ezr 7:12
Whatever E the priest and expert Ezr 7:21
And you, E, according to God's Ezr 7:25
While E prayed and confessed, Ezr 10:1
an Elamite, responded to E: Ezr 10:2
Then E got up and made the Ezr 10:5
E then went from the house of Ezr 10:6
Then E the priest stood up and Ezr 10:10
E the priest selected men who Ezr 10:16
They asked E the scribe to bring Neh 8:1
E the priest brought the law Neh 8:2
E the scribe stood on a high Neh 8:4
E opened the book in full view Neh 8:5
E blessed the LORD, the great Neh 8:6
the governor, E the priest and Neh 8:9
assembled before E the scribe to Neh 8:13
E read out of the book of the Neh 8:18
Jeshua: Seraiah, Jeremiah, E, Neh 12:1
Meshullam of E, Jehohanan of Neh 12:13
governor and E the priest and Neh 12:26
Azariah, E, Meshullam, Neh 12:33
E the scribe went in front of Neh 12:36

EZRAH'S *(1)*
E sons: Jether, Mered, Epher, 1Ch 4:17

EZRAHITE *(1)*
than Ethan the E, and Heman, 1Kg 4:31

EZRI *(1)*
E son of Chelub was in charge of 1Ch 27:26

F

FABRIC *(14)*
If a f is contaminated with Lv 13:47
mildew—in wool or linen f, Lv 13:47
is green or red in the f, Lv 13:49
contaminated f for seven days. Lv 13:50
If it has spread in the f, Lv 13:51
is to burn the f, the warp or Lv 13:52
has not spread in the f, Lv 13:53
spread, you must burn up the f. Lv 13:55
on the front or back ⌊of the f⌋. Lv 13:55
section out of the f, Lv 13:56
But if it reappears in the f, Lv 13:57
disappears from the f, Lv 13:58
in wool or linen f, Lv 13:59
and purple f from the coasts Ezk 27:7

FABRICS *(1)*
fine f of linen, purple, silk, Rv 18:12

FABULOUS *(1)*
a single hour such f wealth was Rv 18:17

FACE *(272)*
wipe off the f of the earth: Gn 6:7
alive on the f of the whole Gn 7:3
will wipe off the f of the earth Gn 7:4
over the f of the whole earth Gn 11:4
there over the f of the whole Gn 11:8
them over the f of the whole Gn 11:9
bowed ⌊with his⌋ f to the ground Gn 19:1
made the flocks f the streaked Gn 30:40
saw from Laban's f that his Gn 31:2
your father's f that his Gn 31:5
that, I can f him, and perhaps Gn 32:20
I have seen God f to face, Gn 32:30
I have seen God face to f, Gn 32:30
I have seen your f, ⌊and it is⌋ Gn 33:10
⌊and it is⌋ like seeing God's f, Gn 33:10
veiled ⌊her f⌋, covered herself, Gn 38:14
for she had covered her f. Gn 38:15
he washed his f and came out. Gn 43:31
have seen your f ⌊and know⌋ you Gn 46:30
expected to see your f ⌊again⌋, Gn 48:11
bowed with his f to the ground. Gn 48:12
leaning over his father's f, Gn 50:1
Moses hid his f because he was Ex 3:6
sure you never see my f again, Ex 10:28
for on the day you see my f, Ex 10:28
"I will never see your f again." Ex 10:29
return to Egypt if they f war." Ex 13:17
wings, and are to f one another. Ex 25:20
them off the f of the earth'? Ex 32:12
LORD spoke with Moses f to face, Ex 33:11
LORD spoke with Moses face to f, Ex 33:11

people on the f of the earth.”	Ex 33:16
cannot see My f, for no one can	Ex 33:20
but My f will not be seen.”	Ex 33:23
the skin of his f shone as a	Ex 34:29
Moses, the skin of his f shone!	Ex 34:30
them, he put a veil over his f.	Ex 34:33
see that Moses’ f was radiant.	Ex 34:35
veil over his f again until he	Ex 34:35
LORD make His f shine on you,	Nm 6:25
any man on the f of the earth.	Nm 12:3
father had merely spit in her f,	Nm 12:14
LORD, are seen f to face, how	Nm 14:14
seen face to f, how Your cloud	Nm 14:14
with his f ⌊to the ground⌋.	Nm 22:31
LORD spoke to you f to face from	Dt 5:4
to you face to f from the fire	Dt 5:4
wipe you off the f of the earth.	Dt 6:15
peoples on the f of the earth.	Dt 7:6
peoples on the f of the earth.	Dt 14:2
his foot, and spit in his f.	Dt 25:9
them and hide My f from them so	Dt 31:17
certainly hide My f on that day	Dt 31:18
I will hide My f from them;	Dt 32:20
whom the LORD knew f to face.	Dt 34:10
whom the LORD knew face to f.	Dt 34:10
bowed with his f to the ground	Jos 5:14
LORD with his f to the ground	Jos 7:6
Angel of the LORD f to face!”	Jdg 6:22
Angel of the LORD face to f!”	Jdg 6:22
who turned to f them, and said	Jdg 18:23
bowed with her f to the ground	Ru 2:10
fallen with his f to the ground	1Sm 5:3
fallen with his f to the ground	1Sm 5:4
formation to f the Philistines.	1Sm 17:2
he fell on his f to the ground.	1Sm 17:49
from the f of the earth.”	1Sm 20:15
fell with his f to the ground,	1Sm 20:41
fell with her f to the ground	1Sm 25:23
bowed her f to the ground and	1Sm 25:41
and he bowed his f to the ground	1Sm 28:14
your brother Joab in the f?”	2Sm 2:22
fell with her f to the ground	2Sm 14:4
fell with his f to the ground	2Sm 14:22
house, but he may not see my f.”	2Sm 14:24
down with his f to the ground	2Sm 14:33
king with his f to the ground.	2Sm 18:28
king hid his f and cried out at	2Sm 19:4
king with his f to the ground.	2Sm 24:20
to him with his f to the ground.	1Kg 1:23
bowed with her f to the ground,	1Kg 1:31
from the f of the earth.	1Kg 13:34
fell with his f ⌊to the ground⌋	1Kg 18:7
and put his f between his knees	1Kg 18:42
he wrapped his f in his mantle	1Kg 19:13
bed, turned his f away, and	1Kg 21:4
Micaiah in the f, and demanded,	1Kg 22:24
place my staff on the boy’s f.”	2Kg 4:29
placed the staff on the boy’s f,	2Kg 4:31
and spread it over the king’s f.	2Kg 8:15
Come, let us meet f to face.”	2Kg 14:8
Come, let us meet face to f.”	2Kg 14:8
Hezekiah turned his f to the	2Kg 20:2
of this, he went out to f them.	1Ch 14:8
His strength; seek His f always.	1Ch 16:11
David with his f to the ground.	1Ch 21:21
and seek My f, and turn from	2Ch 7:14
Micaiah in the f, and demanded,	2Ch 18:23
go out to f them, for the LORD	2Ch 20:17
bowed with his f to the ground,	2Ch 20:18
Come, let us meet f to face.”	2Ch 25:17
Come, let us meet face to f.”	2Ch 25:17
not turn ⌊His⌋ f away from you	2Ch 30:9
to lift my f toward You,	Ezr 9:6
mouth, Haman’s f was covered.	Est 7:8
surely curse You to Your f.”	Jb 1:11
surely curse You to Your f.”	Jb 2:5
at me; would I lie to your f?	Jb 6:28
You hide Your f and consider me	Jb 13:24
Though his f is covered with fat	Jb 15:27
me and testifies to my f.	Jb 16:8
My f has grown red with weeping,	Jb 16:16
seem⌋ near in the f of darkness.	Jb 17:12
denounce his behavior to his f?	Jb 21:31
and lift up your f to God.	Jb 22:26
thick darkness that covers my f.	Jb 23:17
will see me, he covers ⌊his⌋ f.	Jb 24:15
do not hesitate to spit in my f.	Jb 30:10
will behold His f with a shout	Jb 33:26
He hides ⌊His⌋ f, who can see	Jb 34:29
hides His f and will never see.	Ps 10:11
The upright will see His f.	Ps 11:7
will You hide Your f from me?	Ps 13:1
I will see Your f in	Ps 17:15
He did not hide His f from him,	Ps 22:24
who seek the f of the God of	Ps 24:6
my heart says, “Seek My f.”	Ps 27:8
LORD, I will seek Your f.	Ps 27:8
Do not hide Your f from me;	Ps 27:9
You hid Your f, I was terrified	Ps 30:7
The f of the LORD is set against	Ps 34:16
light of Your f, for You were	Ps 44:3
and shame has covered my f,	Ps 44:15
Turn Your f away from my sins	Ps 51:9
tower in the f of the enemy.	Ps 61:3
and shame has covered my f.	Ps 69:7
Don’t hide Your f from Your	Ps 69:17
look on the f of Your anointed	Ps 84:9
Why do You hide Your f from me?	Ps 88:14
Do not hide Your f from me in my	Ps 102:2
making his f shine with oil—	Ps 104:15
When You hide Your f, they are	Ps 104:29
You renew the f of the earth.	Ps 104:30
His strength; seek His f always.	Ps 105:4
Don’t hide Your f from me,	Ps 143:7
joyful heart makes a f cheerful,	Pr 15:13
When a king’s f lights up,	Pr 16:15
A wicked man puts on a bold f,	Pr 21:29
As the water reflects the f,	Pr 27:19
for when a f is sad, a heart may	Ec 7:3
A man’s wisdom brightens his f,	Ec 8:1
sternness of his f is changed.	Ec 8:1
let me see your f, let me hear	Sg 2:14
is sweet, and your f is lovely.	Sg 2:14
with two he covered his f,	Is 6:2
is hiding His f from the house	Is 8:17
the world on the f of the earth.	Is 23:17
tears from every f and remove	Is 25:8
ashamed and his f will no longer	Is 29:22
Hezekiah turned his f to the	Is 38:2
I did not hide My f from scorn	Is 50:6
I have set My f like flint,	Is 50:7
of anger I hid My f from you for	Is 54:8
hide ⌊His⌋ f from you so that	Is 59:2
hidden Your f from us and made	Is 64:7
continually provoke Me to My f,	Is 65:3
back to Me and not their f,	Jr 2:27
up over your f so that your	Jr 13:26
manure on the f of the earth.	Jr 16:4
back and not ⌊My⌋ f on the day	Jr 18:17
which are on the f of the earth.	Jr 25:26
animals on the f of the earth.	Jr 27:5
send you off the f of the earth.	Jr 28:16
labor and every f turned pale?	Jr 30:6
They will speak f to face and	Jr 32:4
speak face to f and meet eye to	Jr 32:4
have hidden My f from this city	Jr 33:5
eye to eye and speak f to face;	Jr 34:3
eye to eye and speak face to f;	Jr 34:3
of the four had the f of a lion	Ezk 1:10
the f of an ox on the left,	Ezk 1:10
the left, and the f of an eagle.	Ezk 1:10
have made your f as hard as	Ezk 3:8
Turn your f toward it so that it	Ezk 4:3
turn your f toward the siege	Ezk 4:7
turn your f toward the mountains	Ezk 6:2
I will turn My f from the wicked	Ezk 7:22
first f was that of a cherub,	Ezk 10:14
cover your f so that you cannot	Ezk 12:6
will cover his f so he cannot	Ezk 12:12
stumbling block before his f,	Ezk 14:4
stumbling block before his f,	Ezk 14:7
with you there f to face.	Ezk 20:35
with you there face to f.	Ezk 20:35
f the south and preach against	Ezk 20:46
every f from the south to the	Ezk 20:47
turn your f toward Jerusalem and	Ezk 21:2
turn your f toward the Ammonites	Ezk 25:2
turn your f toward Sidon and	Ezk 28:21
turn your f toward Pharaoh king	Ezk 29:2
and Memphis will f foes in broad	Ezk 30:16
over the whole f of the earth,	Ezk 34:6
turn your f toward Mount Seir	Ezk 35:2
of man, turn your f toward Gog,	Ezk 38:2
being on the f of the earth will	Ezk 38:20
I hid My f from them and handed	Ezk 39:23
and I hid My f from them.	Ezk 39:24
no longer hide My f from them,	Ezk 39:29
a human f turned toward the palm	Ezk 41:19
and a lion’s f turned toward it	Ezk 41:19
chambers that f the temple yard	Ezk 42:13
The altar’s steps f east.”	Ezk 43:17
on his f changed toward	Dn 3:19
his f turned pale, and his	Dn 5:6
terrified, his f turned pale,	Dn 5:9
terrify you or your f be pale.	Dn 5:10
greatly, and my f turned pale,	Dn 7:28
with my f ⌊to the ground⌋.	Dn 8:18
his f like the brilliance of	Dn 10:6
f grew deathly pale, and I was	Dn 10:8
sleep, with my f to the ground.	Dn 10:9
I turned my f toward the ground	Dn 10:15
look from her f and her adultery	Hs 2:2
their guilt and seek My f;	Hs 5:15
they are right in front of My f.	Hs 7:2
out over the f of the earth—	Am 5:8
them out on the f of the earth.	Am 9:6
it from the f of the earth.	Am 9:8
He will hide His f from them at	Mc 3:4
loins shake, every f grows pale!	Nah 2:10
over your f and display your	Nah 3:5
from the f of the earth—	Zph 1:2
from the f of the earth—	Zph 1:3
on your head, and wash your f,	Mt 6:17
and His f shone like the sun.	Mt 17:2
view the f of My Father	Mt 18:10
they spit in His f and beat Him;	Mt 26:67
the appearance of His f changed,	Lk 9:29
who live on the f of the whole	Lk 21:35
and with his f wrapped in a	Jn 11:44
and were slapping His f.	Jn 19:3
and saw that his f was like the	Ac 6:15
face was like the f of an angel.	Ac 6:15
will ever see my f again.	Ac 20:25
would never see his f again.	Ac 20:38
the accusers f to face and has	Ac 25:16
the accusers face to f and has	Ac 25:16
in a mirror, but then f to face.	1Co 13:12
in a mirror, but then face to f.	1Co 13:12
down on his f and worship God	1Co 14:25
directly at Moses’ f because of	2Co 3:7
of the glory from his f—	2Co 3:7
a veil over his f so that the	2Co 3:13
glory in the f of Jesus Christ.	2Co 4:6
or if someone hits you in the f.	2Co 11:20
him to his f because he stood	Gl 2:11
to return and see you f to face.	1Th 2:17
to return and see you face to f.	1Th 2:17
day to see you f to face and to	1Th 3:10
you face to f and to complete	1Th 3:10
at his own f in a mirror;	Jms 1:23
But the f of the Lord is against	1Pt 3:12
you and talk f to face so that	2Jn 12
talk face to f so that our joy	2Jn 12
and we will talk f to face.	3Jn 14
and we will talk face to f.	3Jn 14
and His f was shining like the	Rv 1:16
creature had a f like a man;	Rv 4:7
hide us from the f of the One	Rv 6:16
His f was like the sun, his legs	Rv 10:1
their lives in the f of death.	Rv 12:11
will see His f, and His name	Rv 22:4

FACECLOTHS *(1)*

so that even f or work aprons	Ac 19:12

FACED *(20)*

Amaziah of Judah f off at	2Kg 14:11
their feet and f the larger room	2Ch 3:13
Amaziah of Judah f off at	2Ch 25:21
the head f, they would go	Ezk 10:11
the gate that f east and climbed	Ezk 40:6
of the recesses f each other.	Ezk 40:13
Thirty chambers f the pavement,	Ezk 40:17
those of the gate that f east.	Ezk 40:22
Its portico f the outer court,	Ezk 40:31
Its portico f the outer court,	Ezk 40:34
Its portico f the outer court,	Ezk 40:37
building that f the temple yard	Ezk 41:12
like the chambers that f north.	Ezk 42:11
of the gate that f east and	Ezk 42:15
by way of the gate that f east.	Ezk 43:4
outer gate that f east,	Ezk 44:1
holy chambers, which f north.	Ezk 46:19
the east, for the temple f east.	Ezk 47:1
to the outer gate that f east;	Ezk 47:2
⌊I f⌋ dangers from rivers,	2Co 11:26

FACEDOWN (19)

and fell **f** ⌊on the ground⌋ Lv 9:24
Moses heard ⌊this⌋, he fell **f**. Nm 16:4
Moses and Aaron fell **f** and said, Nm 16:22
instantly." But they fell **f**. Nm 16:45
they fell **f** on the ground. Jdg 13:20
it, they fell **f** and said, 1Kg 18:39
and falling **f** before the house Ezr 10:1
I fell **f** and heard a voice Ezk 1:28
the Chebar Canal, and I fell **f**. Ezk 3:23
And I fell **f** and cried out, Ezk 9:8
Then I fell **f** and cried out with Ezk 11:13
by the Chebar Canal. I fell **f**. Ezk 43:3
filled His temple. And I fell **f**. Ezk 44:4
I was terrified and fell **f**. Dn 8:17
they fell **f** and were terrified. Mt 17:6
the slave fell **f** before him and Mt 18:26
He fell **f** and prayed, "My Mt 26:39
Jesus, fell **f**, and begged Him Lk 5:12
He fell **f** at His feet, thanking Lk 17:16

FACES (66)

Their **f** were turned away, and Gn 9:23
"Why are your **f** sad today?" Gn 40:7
him with their **f** to the ground. Gn 42:6
The **f** of the cherubim should be Ex 25:20
The **f** of the cherubim were Ex 37:9
with their **f** ⌊to the ground⌋ Nm 14:5
with their **f** ⌊to the ground⌋ Nm 20:6
which **f** Baal-zephon, Nm 33:7
top of Pisgah, which **f** Jericho, Dt 34:1
of the hill that **f** the Valley of Jos 15:8
of the hill that **f** the Valley of Jos 18:16
Their **f** were like the faces of 1Ch 12:8
faces were like the **f** of lions, 1Ch 12:8
with their **f** ⌊to the ground⌋ 1Ch 21:16
down with their **f** to the ground 2Ch 7:3
turned their **f** away from the 2Ch 29:6
LORD with their **f** to the ground. Neh 8:6
you aim your bow at their **f**. Ps 21:12
their **f** will never be ashamed. Ps 34:5
Cover their **f** with shame so that Ps 83:16
look on their **f** testifies Is 3:9
and grind the **f** of the poor?" Is 3:15
their **f** flushed with fear. Is 13:8
you with their **f** to the ground, Is 49:23
down on their **f** at your feet. Is 60:14
They made their **f** harder than Jr 5:3
backs to Me and not their **f**. Jr 32:33
⌊turning⌋ their **f** to this road. Jr 50:5
covers our **f** because foreigners Jr 51:51
them had four **f** and four wings. Ezk 1:6
four of them had **f** and wings. Ezk 1:8
each of⌋ their **f** was that of a Ezk 1:10
is what⌋ their **f** ⌊were like⌋. Ezk 1:11
each creature that had four **f**. Ezk 1:15
by ⌊the look on⌋ their **f**, Ezk 2:6
as hard as their **f** and your Ezk 3:8
by ⌊the look on⌋ their **f**, Ezk 3:9
Shame will cover all ⌊their⌋ **f**, Ezk 7:18
of the inner gate that **f** north, Ezk 8:3
temple and their **f** ⌊turned⌋ to Ezk 8:16
Gate, which **f** north, each with Ezk 9:2
one had four **f**: the first face Ezk 10:14
had four **f** and each had four Ezk 10:21
Their **f** looked like the same Ezk 10:22
looked like the same **f** I had Ezk 10:22
house, which **f** east, and at Ezk 11:1
stumbling blocks before their **f**. Ezk 14:3
turn your **f** away from all your Ezk 14:6
⌊their⌋ **f** are contorted. Ezk 27:35
This chamber that **f** south is for Ezk 40:45
The chamber that **f** north is for Ezk 40:46
Each cherub had two **f**: Ezk 41:18
the gate, the one that **f** east, Ezk 43:1
inner court that **f** east must be Ezk 46:1
the gate that **f** east must be Ezk 46:12
if he saw your **f** looking thinner Dn 1:10
before them; all **f** turn pale. Jl 2:6
f are set in determination. Hab 1:9
which **f** Jerusalem on the east. Zch 14:4
spread animal waste over your **f**, Mal 2:3
they make their **f** unattractive Mt 6:16
with unveiled **f**, are reflecting 2Co 3:18
fell on their **f** before the Rv 7:11
their **f** were like men's faces; Rv 9:7
their faces were like men's **f**; Rv 9:7
fell on their **f** and worshiped Rv 11:16

FACIALLY (1)

is blind, lame, **f** disfigured, Lv 21:18

FACING (41)

of Baal-zephon, **f** it by the sea. Ex 14:2
their wings and **f** each other. Ex 37:9
in the Abarim ⌊range⌋ **f** Nebo. Nm 33:47
in the valley **f** Beth-peor. Dt 3:29
Jordan in the valley **f** Beth-peor Dt 4:46
in the land of Moab **f** Beth-peor, Dt 34:6
at a suitable place **f** the plain Jos 8:14
LORD's covenant **f** the Levitical Jos 8:33
from the hill **f** Beth-horon on Jos 18:14
with the territory **f** Joppa. Jos 19:46
battle formation **f** each other. 1Sm 17:21
Jonathan sat **f** him and Abner 1Sm 20:25
f each other in three tiers. 1Kg 7:4
the openings **f** each other in 1Kg 7:5
on 12 oxen, three **f** north, three 1Kg 7:25
north, three **f** west, three 1Kg 7:25
west, three **f** south, and three 1Kg 7:25
facing south, and three **f** east. 1Kg 7:25
in his chariot **f** the Arameans. 1Kg 22:35
came and stood **f** them from a 2Kg 2:7
who were **f** him, saw him, 2Kg 2:15
on 12 oxen, three **f** north, three 2Ch 4:4
north, three **f** west, three 2Ch 4:4
west, three **f** south, and three 2Ch 4:4
facing south, and three **f** east. 2Ch 4:4
up in his chariot **f** the Arameans 2Ch 18:34
of the valley **f** the Wilderness 2Ch 20:16
While he was **f** the square in Neh 8:3
courtyard of the palace **f** it. Est 5:1
royal courtroom, **f** its entrance. Est 5:1
gate of the outer court **f** north, Ezk 40:20
had a gate **f** the north gate, Ezk 40:23
the north gate, **f** south, and Ezk 40:44
beside the south gate, **f** north. Ezk 40:44
the building **f** the temple yard Ezk 41:15
while those **f** the great hall Ezk 42:8
were chambers **f** the temple yard Ezk 42:10
will be three gates **f** north, Ezk 48:31
were seated there, **f** the tomb. Mt 27:61
was on the shore **f** the sea. Mk 4:1
Mary stood outside **f** the tomb, Jn 20:11

FACT (59)

In **f**, God knows that when you Gn 3:5
f, all the wealth that God has Gn 31:16
But if, in **f**, the animal was Ex 22:12
in **f**, no one must be seen Ex 34:3
A **f** must be established by the Dt 19:15
when in **f** you live among us? Jos 9:22
in **f**, his actions have been a 1Sm 19:4
In **f**, everything the king did 2Sm 3:36
In **f**, Absalom has planned this 2Sm 13:32
In **f**, today I know that if 2Sm 19:6
You will in **f** see it with your 2Kg 7:2
You will in **f** see it with your 2Kg 7:19
in **f**, seven are detestable to Pr 6:16
This will in **f** happen to them. Jr 5:13
In **f**, the lying pen of scribes Jr 8:8
In **f**, I will hand you over to Jr 22:25
In **f**, it is put into the fire as Ezk 15:4
In **f**, they are now saying: Hs 10:3
is coming; in **f**, it is near— Jl 2:1
In **f**, I have already begun to Mal 2:2
witnesses every **f** may be Mt 18:16
f, He is going ahead of you to Mt 28:7
Pharisees, in **f** all the Jews, Mk 7:3
But in **f**, after examining Him in Lk 23:14
In **f**, the water I will give him Jn 4:14
The Father, in **f**, judges no one Jn 5:22
f, He is the One speaking with Jn 9:37
In **f**, a time is coming when Jn 16:2
For, in **f**, in this city both Ac 4:27
In **f**, we run a risk of being Ac 19:40
In **f**, I myself supposed it was Ac 26:9
In **f**, it is for the hope of Ac 28:20
f, sin was in the world before Rm 5:13
In view of the **f** that I am an Rm 11:13
I did, in **f**, baptize the 1Co 1:16
In **f**, you are still not able, 1Co 3:2
In **f**, I don't even evaluate 1Co 4:3
If, in **f**, you did receive it, 1Co 4:7
In **f**, some have been so used to 1Co 8:7
man, in **f**, should not cover his 1Co 11:7
In **f**, if the trumpet makes an 1Co 14:8
raise up if in **f** the dead are 1Co 15:15
In **f**, I made up my mind about 2Co 2:1
In **f**, what had been glorious is 2Co 3:10
But if, in **f**, our gospel is 2Co 4:3
And, in **f**, we groan in this one, 2Co 5:2
In **f**, when we came into 2Co 7:5
In **f**, you put up with it if 2Co 11:20
In **f**, He was crucified in 2Co 13:4
f, we rejoice when we are weak 2Co 13:9
if in **f** it was for nothing? Gl 3:4
You were, in **f**, concerned about Php 4:10
In **f**, when we were with you, we 1Th 3:4
In **f**, you are doing this toward 1Th 4:10
f, when we were with you, this 2Th 3:10
In **f**, we labor and strive for 1Tm 4:10
In **f**, all those who want to live 2Tm 3:12
in **f**, both their mind and Ti 1:15
one man—in **f**, from one as good Heb 11:12

FACTIONS (2)

must, indeed, be **f** among you, so 1Co 11:19
ambitions, dissensions, **f**, Gl 5:20

FADE (12)

memory will not **f** from their Est 9:28
pastures, will **f** away—they Ps 37:20
they will **f** away like smoke. Ps 37:20
I **f** away because of the force of Ps 39:10
I **f** away like a lengthening Ps 109:23
and your hope will never **f**. Pr 23:18
and your hope will never **f**. Pr 24:14
the splendor of Jacob will **f**, Is 17:4
the flowers **f** when the breath of Is 40:7
the flowers **f**, but the word of Is 40:8
set, and your moon will not **f**; Is 60:20
their lives **f** away in the arms Lm 2:12

FADED (6)

the infection has **f** and has not Lv 13:6
not beneath the skin but is **f**, Lv 13:21
not beneath the skin but is **f**, Lv 13:26
not spread on the skin but is **f**, Lv 13:28
has **f** after it has been Lv 13:56
even the light of my eyes has **f**. Ps 38:10

FADES (3)

As a cloud **f** away and vanishes, Jb 7:9
But a man dies and **f** away; Jb 14:10
while the sound of the mill **f**; Ec 12:4

FADING (6)

and to the **f** flower of its Is 28:1
The **f** flower of his beautiful Is 28:4
As my life was **f** away, I Jnh 2:7
from his face—a **f** ⌊glory⌋— 2Co 3:7
For if what was **f** away was 2Co 3:11
at the end of what was **f** away. 2Co 3:13

FAIL (35)

your eyes to **f** and your life to Lv 26:16
you will never **f** to have a man 1Kg 2:4
You will never **f** to have a man 1Kg 8:25
You will never **f** to have a man 1Kg 9:5
the house of Ahab will **f**, 2Kg 10:10
You will never **f** to have a man 2Ch 6:16
You will never **f** to have a man 2Ch 7:18
to them every day without **f**, Ezr 6:9
they would not **f** to celebrate Est 9:27
the sight of the wicked will **f**. Jb 11:20
the eyes of his children will **f**. Jb 17:5
Their bulls breed without **f**; Jb 21:10
My eyes **f**, looking for my God. Ps 69:3
My flesh and my heart may **f**, Ps 73:26
f when there is no counsel, Pr 15:22
a plan; it will **f**. Make a Is 8:10
vintage will **f** and the harvest Is 32:10
Their eyes **f** because there are Jr 14:6
flowing from a distance ever **f**? Jr 18:14
I will without **f** save you from Jr 30:10
David will never **f** to have a man Jr 33:17
will never **f** to have a man Jr 33:18
the night and **f** to establish Jr 33:25
will never **f** to have a man to Jr 35:19
for without **f** I will save you Jr 46:27
and their fruit will not **f**. Ezk 47:12
a vision, but they will **f**. Dn 11:14
and the new wine will **f** them. Hs 9:2
source will **f**, and his spring Hs 13:15
Escape will **f** the swift, the Am 2:14
He does not **f** at dawn, yet the Zph 3:5
will Ekron, for her hope will **f**. Zch 9:5
you that your faith may not **f**. Lk 22:32
—unless you **f** the test. 2Co 13:5
though we ⌊may appear⌋ to **f**. 2Co 13:7

FAILED *(20)*
courage f because of you, Jos 2:11
and their courage f because Jos 5:1
made to the house of Israel f. Jos 21:45
LORD your God made to you has f. Jos 23:14
not one promise has f. Jos 23:14
time Manasseh f to take Jdg 1:27
that time Ephraim f to drive out Jdg 1:29
Zebulun f to drive out the Jdg 1:30
Asher f to drive out the Jdg 1:31
they f to drive them out. Jdg 1:32
his courage f, and all Israel 2Sm 4:1
through His servant Moses has f. 1Kg 8:56
we have f to take it from the 1Kg 22:3
because they had f to refute Jb 32:3
my strength has f because of my Ps 31:10
their spirits f within them. Ps 107:5
and you have f to remember the Is 17:10
They f to perform all You Jr 32:23
because the sun's light f. Lk 23:45
as though the word of God has f. Rm 9:6

FAILING *(6)*
LORD your God by f to keep His Dt 8:11
a trembling heart, f eyes, and a Dt 28:65
of Zin by f to treat Me as holy Dt 32:51
eyesight was f, was lying in his 1Sm 3:2
our eyes were f ⌊as we looked⌋ Lm 4:17
that we are not f the test. 2Co 13:6

FAILS *(11)*
yet f to observe the Passover Nm 9:13
The strength of the laborer f, Neh 4:10
as my strength f, do not abandon Ps 71:9
LORD; my spirit f. Don't hide Ps 143:7
grows hungry and his strength f; Is 44:12
passing by, and every vision f? Ezk 12:22
what sprouts f to yield flour. Hs 8:7
dried up; and the olive oil f. Jl 1:10
the olive crop f and the fields Hab 3:17
money so that when it f, Lk 16:9
entire law, yet f in one point, Jms 2:10

FAILURE *(1)*
and their f riches for the Rm 11:12

FAINT *(14)*
God has made my heart f; Jb 23:16
f is the word we hear of Him! Jb 26:14
I am f and severely crushed; Ps 38:8
the daughters of song grow f. Ec 12:4
He never grows f or weary; Is 40:28
Youths may f and grow weary, Is 40:30
they will walk and not f. Is 40:31
he doesn't drink water and is f. Is 44:12
The mother of seven grew f; Jr 15:9
and infants f in the streets Lm 2:11
they f like the wounded in the Lm 2:12
men also, will f from thirst. Am 8:13
People will f from fear and Lk 21:26
or f when you are reproved by Heb 12:5

FAINT-HEARTED *(2)*
Say to the f: Is 35:4
not become f and fearful when Jr 51:46

FAINTED *(3)*
Your children have f; Is 51:20
of the field f because of it. Ezk 31:15
head so that he almost f, Jnh 4:8

FAINTHEARTED *(3)*
Do not be f. Do not be afraid Dt 20:3
any man who is afraid or f? Dt 20:8
be afraid or f because of these Is 7:4

FAINTING *(1)*
children who are f from hunger Lm 2:19

FAINTS *(1)*
my body f for You in a land that Ps 63:1

FAIR *(11)*
to the king, "The sentence is f; 1Kg 2:38
said to me, 'The sentence is f; 1Kg 2:42
let a f judgment be executed Ezr 7:26
from getting a f trial and to Is 10:2
The Lord's way isn't f. Ezk 18:25
The Lord's way isn't f. Ezk 18:29
way isn't f, even though it Ezk 33:17
is their own way that isn't f. Ezk 33:17
The Lord's way isn't f. Ezk 33:20
to a place called F Havens near Ac 27:8
slaves with what is right and f, Col 4:1

FAIRLY *(7)*
judge your neighbor f. Lv 19:15
Do you judge people f? Ps 58:1
I choose a time, I will judge f. Ps 75:2
He judges the peoples f." Ps 96:10
righteously and the peoples f. Ps 98:9
and conducts his business f. Ps 112:5
that You have afflicted me f. Ps 119:75

FAIRNESS *(5)*
judgment on the peoples with f. Ps 9:8
the peoples with f and lead the Ps 67:4
You have established f; Ps 99:4
who judges the poor with f— Pr 29:14
in peace and f and turned many Mal 2:6

FAITH *(251)*
As I have kept f with you, Gn 21:23
you will keep f with me and with Gn 21:23
of⌋ you broke f with Me among Dt 32:51
him in ⌊his f in⌋ God, 1Sm 23:16
you do not stand firm in your f, Is 7:9
one will live by his f. Hab 2:4
more for you—you of little f? Mt 6:30
in Israel with so great a f! Mt 8:10
you fearful, you of little f?" Mt 8:26
Seeing their f, Jesus told the Mt 9:2
"Your f has made you well." Mt 9:22
for you according to your f!" Mt 9:29
You of little f, why did you Mt 14:31
to her, "Woman, your f is great. Mt 15:28
Jesus said, "You of little f! Mt 16:8
"Because of your little f," Mt 17:20
If you have f the size of a Mt 17:20
If you have f and do not doubt, Mt 21:21
the law—justice, mercy, and f. Mt 23:23
Seeing their f, Jesus told the Mk 2:5
Do you still have no f?" Mk 4:40
your f has made you well. Mk 5:34
"Your f has healed you." Mk 10:52
replied to them, "Have f in God. Mk 11:22
Seeing their f He said, "Friend, Lk 5:20
so great a f even in Israel! Lk 7:9
woman, "Your f has saved you. Lk 7:50
said to them, "Where is your f?" Lk 8:25
your f has made you well. Lk 8:48
He do for you—you of little f? Lk 12:28
to the Lord, "Increase our f." Lk 17:5
If you have f the size of a Lk 17:6
Your f has made you well." Lk 17:19
will He find that f on earth?" Lk 18:8
"Your f has healed you." Lk 18:42
you that your f may not fail. Lk 22:32
By f in His name, His name has Ac 3:16
So the f that comes through Him Ac 3:16
a man full of f and the Holy Ac 6:5
became obedient to the f. Ac 6:7
of the Holy Spirit and of f— Ac 11:24
the proconsul away from the f. Ac 13:8
that he had f to be healed, Ac 14:9
them to continue in the f, Ac 14:22
the door of f to the Gentiles. Ac 14:27
cleansing their hearts by f. Ac 15:9
in the f and were increased Ac 16:5
toward God and f in our Lord Ac 20:21
the subject of f in Christ Jesus Ac 24:24
who are sanctified by f in Me.' Ac 26:18
the obedience of f among all the Rm 1:5
the news of your f is being Rm 1:8
encouraged by each other's f, Rm 1:12
is revealed from f to faith, Rm 1:17
is revealed from faith to f, Rm 1:17
The righteous will live by f. Rm 1:17
through f in Jesus Christ, Rm 3:22
through f in His blood, Rm 3:25
the one who has f in Jesus. Rm 3:26
on the contrary, by a law of f. Rm 3:27
is justified by f apart from Rm 3:28
the circumcised by f and the Rm 3:30
and the uncircumcised through f. Rm 3:30
then cancel the law through f? Rm 3:31
his f is credited for Rm 4:5
F was credited to Abraham for Rm 4:9
that he had by f while still Rm 4:11
footsteps of the f our father Rm 4:12
righteousness that comes by f. Rm 4:13
f is made empty and the promise Rm 4:14
This is why the promise is by f, Rm 4:16
to those who are of Abraham's f. Rm 4:16
without weakening in the f. Rm 4:19
in his f and gave glory to Rm 4:20
been declared righteous by f, Rm 5:1
access by f into this grace Rm 5:2
righteousness that comes from f. Rm 9:30
they did not pursue it by f, Rm 9:32
that comes from f speaks like Rm 10:6
the message of f that we Rm 10:8
So f comes from what is heard, Rm 10:17
by unbelief, but you stand by f. Rm 11:20
a measure of f to each one. Rm 12:3
according to the standard of f; Rm 12:6
Accept anyone who is weak in f, Rm 14:1
Do you have f? Keep it to Rm 14:22
his eating is not from f, Rm 14:23
that is not from f is sin. Rm 14:23
the obedience of f among all Rm 16:26
that your f might not be based 1Co 2:5
another, f by the same Spirit, 1Co 12:9
if I have all f, so that I can 1Co 13:2
three remain: f, hope, and love. 1Co 13:13
foundation, and so is your f. 1Co 15:14
raised, your f is worthless; 1Co 15:17
stand firm in the f, be brave 1Co 16:13
that we have control of your f, 2Co 1:24
joy, because you stand by f. 2Co 1:24
same spirit of f in accordance 2Co 4:13
for we walk by f, not by sight— 2Co 5:7
in everything—in f, in speech, 2Co 8:7
hope that as your f increases, 2Co 10:15
to see⌋ if you are in the f. 2Co 13:5
preaches the f he once tried to Gl 1:23
the law but by f in Jesus Christ Gl 2:16
be justified by f in Christ and Gl 2:16
I live by f in the Son of God, Gl 2:20
of the law or by hearing with f? Gl 3:2
of the law or by hearing with f? Gl 3:5
those who have f are Abraham's Gl 3:7
the Gentiles by f and foretold Gl 3:8
those who have f are blessed Gl 3:9
blessed with Abraham, who had f. Gl 3:9
the righteous will live by f. Gl 3:11
But the law is not based on f; Gl 3:12
promise of the Spirit through f. Gl 3:14
the promise by f in Jesus Christ Gl 3:22
Before this f came, we were Gl 3:23
until the coming f was revealed. Gl 3:23
that we could be justified by f. Gl 3:24
But since that f has come, Gl 3:25
God through f in Christ Jesus. Gl 3:26
hope of righteousness from f. Gl 5:5
matters is f working through Gl 5:6
patience, kindness, goodness, f, Gl 5:22
belong to the household of f. Gl 6:10
heard about your f in the Lord Eph 1:15
grace you are saved through f, Eph 2:8
and confidence through f in Him. Eph 3:12
dwell in your hearts through f. Eph 3:17
one Lord, one f, one baptism, Eph 4:5
reach unity in the f and in the Eph 4:13
situation take the shield of f, Eph 6:16
and love with f, from God the Eph 6:23
advancement and joy in the f, Php 1:25
by side for the f of the gospel, Php 1:27
sacrifice and service of your f, Php 2:17
that is through f in Christ— Php 3:9
from God based on f. Php 3:9
heard of your f in Christ Jesus Col 1:4
grounded and steadfast in the f, Col 1:23
strength of your f in Christ. Col 2:5
in Him and established in the f, Col 2:7
Him through f in the working Col 2:12
your work of f, labor of love, 1Th 1:3
place that your f in God has 1Th 1:8
encourage you concerning your f, 1Th 3:2
sent to find out about your f, 1Th 3:5
good news about your f and love, 1Th 3:6
about you through your f. 1Th 3:7
what is lacking in your f? 1Th 3:10
the armor of f and love on our 1Th 5:8
since your f is flourishing, 2Th 1:3
your endurance and f in all the 2Th 1:4
for goodness and the work of f, 2Th 1:11
evil men, for not all have f. 2Th 3:2
Timothy, my true child in the f. 1Tm 1:2
God's plan, which operates by f. 1Tm 1:4
conscience, and a sincere f. 1Tm 1:5
along with the f and love that 1Tm 1:14
having f and a good conscience. 1Tm 1:19

the shipwreck of their **f**. 1Tm 1:19
of the Gentiles in **f** and truth. 1Tm 2:7
she continues in **f**, love, and 1Tm 2:15
mystery of the **f** with a clear 1Tm 3:9
boldness in the **f** that is in 1Tm 3:13
some will depart from the **f**, 1Tm 4:1
words of the **f** and of the good 1Tm 4:6
in love, in **f**, in purity. 1Tm 4:12
has denied the **f** and is worse 1Tm 5:8
away from the **f** and pierced 1Tm 6:10
godliness, **f**, love, endurance, 1Tm 6:11
Fight the good fight for the **f**; 1Tm 6:12
people have deviated from the **f**. 1Tm 6:21
your sincere **f** that first lived 2Tm 1:5
in the **f** and love that are in 2Tm 1:13
are overturning the **f** of some. 2Tm 2:18
righteousness, **f**, love, and 2Tm 2:22
worthless in regard to the **f**. 2Tm 3:8
purpose, **f**, patience, love, 2Tm 3:10
through **f** in Christ Jesus. 2Tm 3:15
the race, I have kept the **f**. 2Tm 4:7
Christ for the **f** of God's elect Ti 1:1
my true child in our common **f**. Ti 1:4
that they may be sound in the **f** Ti 1:13
and sound in **f**, love, and Ti 2:2
those who love us in the **f**. Ti 3:15
your love and **f** toward the Lord Phm 5
in the **f** may become effective Phm 6
with those who heard it in **f** Heb 4:2
from dead works, **f** in God, Heb 6:1
through **f** and perseverance Heb 6:12
heart in full assurance of **f**, Heb 10:22
My righteous one will live by **f**; Heb 10:38
who have **f** and obtain life. Heb 10:39
Now **f** is the reality of what is Heb 11:1
By **f** we understand that the Heb 11:3
f Abel offered to God a better Heb 11:4
By **f**, Enoch was taken away so Heb 11:5
Now without **f** it is impossible Heb 11:6
By **f** Noah, after being warned Heb 11:7
righteousness that comes by **f**. Heb 11:7
f Abraham, when he was called, Heb 11:8
By **f** he stayed as a foreigner in Heb 11:9
f even Sarah herself, when she Heb 11:11
all died in **f** without having Heb 11:13
f Abraham, when he was tested, Heb 11:17
f Isaac blessed Jacob and Esau Heb 11:20
By **f** Jacob, when he was dying, Heb 11:21
By **f** Joseph, as he was nearing Heb 11:22
By **f** Moses, after he was born, Heb 11:23
f Moses, when he had grown up, Heb 11:24
By **f** he left Egypt behind, Heb 11:27
By **f** he instituted the Passover Heb 11:28
By **f** they crossed the Red Sea as Heb 11:29
By **f** the walls of Jericho fell Heb 11:30
By **f** Rahab the prostitute Heb 11:31
who by **f** conquered kingdoms, Heb 11:33
were approved through their **f**, Heb 11:39
source and perfecter of our **f**, Heb 12:2
of their lives, imitate their **f**. Heb 13:7
testing of your **f** produces Jms 1:3
let him ask in **f** without Jms 1:6
hold your **f** in our glorious Lord Jms 2:1
world to be rich in **f** and heirs Jms 2:5
says he has **f**, but does not have Jms 2:14
have works? Can his **f** save him? Jms 2:14
In the same way **f**, if it doesn't Jms 2:17
say, "You have **f**, and I have Jms 2:18
Show me your **f** without works, Jms 2:18
I will show you **f** from my works. Jms 2:18
to learn that **f** without works is Jms 2:20
You see that **f** was active Jms 2:22
and by works, **f** was perfected. Jms 2:22
by works and not by **f** alone. Jms 2:24
so also **f** without works is dead. Jms 2:26
The prayer of **f** will save the Jms 5:15
power through **f** for a salvation 1Pt 1:5
that the genuineness of your **f**— 1Pt 1:7
receiving the goal of your **f**, 1Pt 1:9
so that your **f** and hope are in 1Pt 1:21
him, firm in the **f**, knowing that 1Pt 5:9
have obtained a **f** of equal 2Pt 1:1
supplement your **f** with goodness, 2Pt 1:5
has conquered the world: our **f**. 1Jn 5:4
showing your **f** by whatever you 3Jn 5
contend for the **f** that was Jd 3
in your most holy **f** and praying Jd 20
and did not deny your **f** in Me, Rv 2:13
and the **f** of the saints. Rv 13:10
of God and the **f** in Jesus." Rv 14:12

FAITHFUL (235)

you will deal with me in **f** love. Gn 47:29
have redeemed with Your **f** love; Ex 15:13
but showing **f** love to a thousand Ex 20:6
and rich in **f** love and truth, Ex 34:6
maintaining **f** love to a thousand Ex 34:7
he is **f** in all My household. Nm 12:7
to anger and rich in **f** love, Nm 14:18
the greatness of Your **f** love, Nm 14:19
have remained **f** to the LORD your Dt 4:4
but showing **f** love to a thousand Dt 5:10
the **f** God who keeps His gracious Dt 7:9
Remain **f** to Him and take oaths Dt 10:20
His ways, and remain **f** to Him— Dt 11:22
worship Him and remain **f** to Him. Dt 13:4
obey Him, and remain **f** to Him. Dt 30:20
f God, without prejudice, He is Dt 32:4
and Urim belong to Your **f** one; Dt 33:8
commands, remain **f** to Him, and Jos 22:5
remain **f** to the LORD your God, Jos 23:8
the LORD show **f** love to you as Ru 1:8
guards the steps of His **f** ones, 1Sm 2:9
will raise up a **f** priest for 1Sm 2:35
treat me with the LORD's **f** love, 1Sm 20:14
ever withdraw your **f** love from 1Sm 20:15
your servants is as **f** as David? 1Sm 22:14
But My **f** love will never leave 2Sm 7:15
person, one of the **f** in Israel, 2Sm 20:19
With the **f** You prove Yourself 2Sm 22:26
faithful You prove Yourself **f**; 2Sm 22:26
shown great and **f** love to Your 1Kg 3:6
this great and **f** love for him by 1Kg 3:6
His **f** love endures forever. 1Ch 16:34
for His **f** love endures forever. 1Ch 16:41
take away My **f** love from him as 1Ch 17:13
have shown great **f** love to my 2Ch 1:8
His **f** love endures forever; 2Ch 5:13
for His **f** love endures forever. 2Ch 7:3
"for His **f** love endures forever" 2Ch 7:6
for His **f** love endures forever. 2Ch 20:21
After these **f** deeds, Sennacherib 2Ch 32:1
reign⌋ and his deeds of **f** love, 2Ch 32:32
his deeds of **f** love according to 2Ch 35:26
f love to Israel endures forever. Ezr 3:11
because he was a **f** man who Neh 7:2
found his heart **f** in Your sight, Neh 9:8
to anger and rich in **f** love, Neh 9:17
with Your abundant, **f** love. Neh 13:22
You gave me life and **f** love, Jb 10:12
for His land, or for His **f** love. Jb 37:13
has set apart the **f** for Himself; Ps 4:3
by the abundance of Your **f** love; Ps 5:7
save me because of Your **f** love. Ps 6:4
LORD, for no **f** one remains; Ps 12:1
I have trusted in Your **f** love; Ps 13:5
not allow Your **F** One to see the Ps 16:10
the wonders of Your **f** love, Ps 17:7
With the **f** You prove Yourself Ps 18:25
faithful You prove Yourself **f**; Ps 18:25
through the **f** love of the Most Ps 21:7
goodness and **f** love will pursue Ps 23:6
Your compassion and Your **f** love, Ps 25:6
in keeping with Your **f** love, Ps 25:7
ways ⌊show⌋ **f** love and truth to Ps 25:10
For Your **f** love is before my Ps 26:3
LORD, you His **f** ones, and praise Ps 30:4
be glad in Your **f** love because Ps 31:7
save me by Your **f** love. Ps 31:16
shown His **f** love to me in a city Ps 31:21
Love the LORD, all His **f** ones. Ps 31:23
everyone who is **f** pray to You at Ps 32:6
will have **f** love surrounding Ps 32:10
those who depend on His **f** love Ps 33:18
May Your **f** love rest on us, Ps 33:22
Your **f** love ⌊reaches⌋ to heaven, Ps 36:5
Your **f** love is so valuable that Ps 36:7
Spread Your **f** love over those Ps 36:10
and will not abandon His **f** ones. Ps 37:28
will send His **f** love by day; Ps 42:8
us because of Your **f** love. Ps 44:26
we contemplate Your **f** love. Ps 48:9
Gather My **f** ones to Me, those Ps 50:5
God, according to Your **f** love; Ps 51:1
God's **f** love is constant. Ps 52:1
I trust in God's **f** love forever Ps 52:8
the presence of Your **f** people, Ps 52:9
God sends His **f** love and truth. Ps 57:3
Your **f** love is as high as the Ps 57:10
My **f** God will come to meet me; Ps 59:10
proclaim Your **f** love in the Ps 59:16
God is my stronghold—my **f** God. Ps 59:17
appoint **f** love and truth to Ps 61:7
and **f** love belongs to You, Ps 62:12
because Your **f** love is better Ps 63:3
or turned His **f** love from me. Ps 66:20
Your abundant, **f** love, God, Ps 69:13
LORD, for Your **f** love is good; Ps 69:16
Has His **f** love ceased forever? Ps 77:8
whose spirit was not **f** to God. Ps 78:8
Show us Your **f** love, LORD, and Ps 85:7
F love and truth will join Ps 85:10
Protect my life, for I am **f**. Ps 86:2
abundant in **f** love to all who Ps 86:5
For Your **f** love for me is great, Ps 86:13
abundant in **f** love and truth. Ps 86:15
Will Your **f** love be declared in Ps 88:11
about the LORD's **f** love forever; Ps 89:1
F love is built up forever; Ps 89:2
f love and truth go before You. Ps 89:14
preserve My **f** love for him, Ps 89:28
not withdraw My **f** love from him Ps 89:33
a **f** witness in the sky." Ps 89:37
acts of Your **f** love that You Ps 89:49
with Your **f** love so that we Ps 90:14
to declare Your **f** love in the Ps 92:2
Your **f** love will support me, Ps 94:18
I will sing of **f** love and Ps 101:1
eyes ⌊favor⌋ the **f** of the land Ps 101:6
He crowns you with **f** love and Ps 103:4
to anger and full of **f** love. Ps 103:8
so great is His **f** love toward Ps 103:11
the LORD's **f** love is toward Ps 103:17
His **f** love endures forever. Ps 106:1
Your many acts of **f** love; Ps 106:7
to the abundance of His **f** love. Ps 106:45
His **f** love endures forever. Ps 107:1
the LORD for His **f** love and His Ps 107:8
the LORD for His **f** love and His Ps 107:15
the LORD for His **f** love and His Ps 107:21
the LORD for His **f** love and His Ps 107:31
the LORD's acts of **f** love. Ps 107:43
For Your **f** love is higher than Ps 108:4
of the goodness of Your **f** love. Ps 109:21
save me according to Your **f** love Ps 109:26
glory because of Your **f** love, Ps 115:1
death of His **f** ones is valuable Ps 116:15
For great is His **f** love to us; Ps 117:2
His **f** love endures forever. Ps 118:1
"His **f** love endures forever." Ps 118:2
"His **f** love endures forever." Ps 118:3
"His **f** love endures forever." Ps 118:4
His **f** love endures forever. Ps 118:29
Let Your **f** love come to me, Ps 119:41
is filled with Your **f** love; Ps 119:64
May Your **f** love comfort me, Ps 119:76
in accordance with Your **f** love, Ps 119:88
servant based on Your **f** love; Ps 119:124
In keeping with Your **f** love, Ps 119:149
life, according to Your **f** love. Ps 119:159
For there is **f** love with the Ps 130:7
me—it is ⌊an act of⌋ **f** love; Ps 141:5
me experience Your **f** love in the Ps 143:8
and in Your **f** love destroy my Ps 143:12
He is my **f** love and my fortress, Ps 144:2
to anger and great in **f** love. Ps 145:8
The LORD is **f** in all His words Ps 145:13
He remains **f** forever, Ps 146:6
put their hope in His **f** love. Ps 147:11
but **f** people are His delight. Pr 12:22
and **f** love will find Pr 21:21
f man will have many blessings, Pr 28:20
The **f** city—what an adulteress Is 1:21
the Righteous City, a **F** City." Is 1:26
will be established by **f** love. Is 16:5
come in—one that remains **f**. Is 26:2
the LORD, who is **f**, the Holy One Is 49:7
f men are swept away, with no Is 57:1
known the LORD's **f** love ⌊and⌋ Is 63:7
and the abundance of His **f** love. Is 63:7
who seeks to be **f**, then I will Jr 5:1
LORD, showing **f** love, justice, Jr 9:24
⌊as well as My⌋ **f** love and Jr 16:5
to extend **f** love to you. Jr 31:3
You show **f** love to thousands but Jr 32:18

His **f** love endures forever as Jr 33:11
be a true and **f** witness against Jr 42:5
of⌋ the LORD's **f** love we do not Lm 3:22
to His abundant, **f** love. Lm 3:32
is no truth, no **f** love, and no Hs 4:1
for yourselves and reap **f** love; Hs 10:12
with El and is **f** to holy ones. Hs 11:12
to anger, rich in **f** love, and He Jl 2:13
worthless idols forsake **f** love, Jnh 2:8
angry, rich in **f** love, and One Jnh 4:2
because He delights in **f** love. Mc 7:18
to Jacob and **f** love to Abraham, Mc 7:20
Show **f** love and compassion to Zch 7:9
will be called the **F** City, Zch 8:3
be their **f** and righteous God. Zch 8:8
Who then is a **f** and sensible Mt 24:45
Well done, good and **f** slave! Mt 25:21
You were **f** over a few things; Mt 25:21
Well done, good and **f** slave! Mt 25:23
You were **f** over a few things; Mt 25:23
Who then is the **f** and sensible Lk 12:42
Whoever is **f** in very little is Lk 16:10
very little is also **f** in much, Lk 16:10
you have not been **f** with the Lk 16:11
have not been **f** with what Lk 16:12
you have been **f** in a very small Lk 19:17
grant you the **f** covenant Ac 13:34
God is **f**; by Him you were called 1Co 1:9
that each one be found **f**. 1Co 4:2
my beloved and **f** child in the 1Co 4:17
God is **f** and He will not allow 1Co 10:13
As God is **f**, our message to you 2Co 1:18
loved brother and **f** servant in Eph 6:21
To the saints and **f** brothers in Col 1:2
is a **f** minister of the Messiah Col 1:7
loved brother, a **f** servant, and Col 4:7
with Onesimus, a **f** and loved Col 4:9
calls you is **f**, who also will 1Th 5:24
But the Lord is **f**; He will 2Th 3:3
because He considered me **f**, 1Tm 1:12
self-controlled, **f** in everything. 1Tm 3:11
commit to **f** men who will be able 2Tm 2:2
He remains **f**, for He cannot deny 2Tm 2:13
having **f** children not accused of Ti 1:6
holding to the **f** message as Ti 1:9
a merciful and **f** high priest Heb 2:17
was **f** to the One who appointed Heb 3:2
Moses was **f** as a servant in all Heb 3:5
But Christ was **f** as a Son over Heb 3:6
for He who promised is **f**. Heb 10:23
the One who had promised was **f**. Heb 11:11
themselves to a **f** Creator. 1Pt 4:19
whom I consider a **f** brother, 1Pt 5:12
He is **f** and righteous to forgive 1Jn 1:9
Jesus Christ, the **f** witness, the Rv 1:5
f until death, and I will give Rv 2:10
Antipas, My **f** witness, who was Rv 2:13
The Amen, the **f** and true Rv 3:14
Him are called and elect and **f**." Rv 17:14
Its rider is called **F** and True, Rv 19:11
these words are **f** and true." Rv 21:5
These words are **f** and true. Rv 22:6

FAITHFULLY *(18)*

My statutes and **f** observe My Lv 26:3
Now if you **f** obey the LORD your Dt 28:1
if you have acted **f** and honestly Jdg 9:16
you have acted **f** and honestly Jdg 9:19
and worship Him **f** with all your 1Sm 12:24
Deal **f** with your servant, for 1Sm 20:8
careful to walk **f** before Me with 1Kg 2:4
walked before You **f** and 2Kg 20:3
dedicated things were brought **f**. 2Ch 31:12
priests were to **f** distribute 2Ch 31:15
for they had **f** consecrated 2Ch 31:18
You have acted **f**, while we have Neh 9:33
but they will **f** depend on the Is 10:20
walked before You **f** and Is 38:3
He will **f** bring justice. Is 42:3
I will **f** reward them and make an Is 61:8
will plant them **f** in this land Jr 32:41
keeps My ordinances, acting **f**. Ezk 18:9

FAITHFULNESS *(48)*

kindness and **f** from my master. Gn 24:27
kindness and **f** to my master, Gn 24:49
kindness and **f** You have shown Gn 32:10
show kindness and **f** to you when Jos 2:14
special kindness and **f** to you, 2Sm 2:6
LORD show you kindness and **f**." 2Sm 15:20
he walked before You in **f**, 1Kg 3:6
of peace and **f** to all the Jews Est 9:30
to heaven, Your **f** to the skies. Ps 36:5
about Your **f** and salvation; Ps 40:10
Because of Your **f**, annihilate Ps 54:5
Your **f** reaches to the clouds. Ps 57:10
I will praise You for Your **f**, Ps 71:22
in the grave, Your **f** in Abaddon? Ps 88:11
proclaim Your **f** to all Ps 89:1
Your **f** in the heavens." Ps 89:2
Your wonders—Your **f** also—in Ps 89:5
Your **f** surrounds You. Ps 89:8
My **f** and love will be with him, Ps 89:24
love from him or betray My **f**. Ps 89:33
You swore to David in Your **f**? Ps 89:49
His **f** will be a protective Ps 91:4
the morning and Your **f** at night, Ps 92:2
and the peoples with His **f**. Ps 96:13
His love and **f** to the house of Ps 98:3
His **f** endures through all Ps 100:5
Your **f** reaches the clouds. Ps 108:4
the LORD's **f** endures forever. Ps 117:2
Your **f** is for all generations; Ps 119:90
for Your constant love and **f**. Ps 138:2
In Your **f** listen to my plea, Ps 143:1
let loyalty and **f** leave you. Pr 3:3
plan good find loyalty and **f**. Pr 14:22
is atoned for by loyalty and **f**, Pr 16:6
Loyalty and **f** deliver a king; Pr 20:28
and **f** will be a belt Is 11:5
long ago, with perfect **f**. Is 25:1
the Pit cannot hope for Your **f**. Is 38:18
will make Your **f** known to Is 38:19
don't Your eyes ⌊look for⌋ **f**? Jr 5:3
lies and not **f** prevail in the Jr 9:3
great is Your **f**! Lm 3:23
take you to be My wife in **f**, Hs 2:20
justly, to love **f**, and to walk Mc 6:8
their unbelief cancel God's **f**? Rm 3:3
but demonstrating utter **f**, Ti 2:10
to your ⌊**f**⌋ to the truth— 3Jn 3
works—your love, **f**, service, Rv 2:19

FAITHLESS *(5)*

"Return, you **f** children"—⌊this Jr 3:14
Return, you **f** children. Jr 3:22
turn here and there, **f** daughter? Jr 31:22
flowing valley, you **f** daughter? Jr 49:4
we are **f**, He remains faithful, 2Tm 2:13

FAITHLESSLY *(1)*

sins against Me by acting **f**, Ezk 14:13

FALCON *(2)*

kite, the various kinds of **f**, Lv 11:14
kite, the various kinds of **f**, Dt 14:13

FALCON'S *(1)*

no **f** eye has seen it. Jb 28:7

FALL *(190)*

terror and dread will **f** on them. Ex 15:16
they will **f** before you by the Lv 26:7
your enemies will **f** before you Lv 26:8
and **f** though no one is pursuing Lv 26:36
no wrath will **f** on the Israelite Nm 1:53
the manna would **f** with it. Nm 11:9
Your corpses will **f** in this Nm 14:29
your corpses will **f** in this Nm 14:32
and you will **f** by the sword. Nm 14:43
wrath may not **f** on the Nm 18:5
just like the **f** of Sodom and Dt 29:23
Let my teaching **f** like rain and Dt 32:2
no wrath will **f** on us because Jos 9:20
of thirst and **f** into the hands Jdg 15:18
Then she let him **f** asleep on her Jdg 16:19
his head will **f** to the ground, 1Sm 14:45
let my blood **f** to the ground far 1Sm 26:20
your son will **f** to the ground." 2Sm 14:11
If some of our troops **f** first, 2Sm 17:9
they **f** beneath my feet. 2Sm 22:39
let us **f** into the LORD's hands 2Sm 24:14
don't let me **f** into human hands. 2Sm 24:14
of his will **f** to the ground, 1Kg 1:52
to march up and **f** at 1Kg 22:20
of God asked, "Where did it **f**?" 2Kg 6:6
do with peace? **F** in behind me." 2Kg 9:18
do with peace? **F** in behind me." 2Kg 9:19
up such trouble that you **f**— 2Kg 14:10
cause him to **f** by the sword.' 2Kg 19:7
let me **f** into the LORD's hands 1Ch 21:13
don't let me **f** into human hands. 1Ch 21:13
to march up and **f** at 2Ch 18:19
so that you **f** and Judah with you 2Ch 25:19
wrath will not **f** on the realm Ezr 7:23
shadows began to **f** on the gates Neh 13:19
before whom you have begun to **f**, Est 6:13
Would His dread not **f** on you? Jb 13:11
shoulder blade **f** from my back, Jb 31:22
to the snow, "**F** to the earth," Jb 37:6
let them **f** by their own schemes. Ps 5:10
the helpless **f** because of his Ps 10:10
they **f** beneath my feet. Ps 18:38
They collapse and **f**, but we rise Ps 20:8
let him **f** into it—to his ruin. Ps 35:8
the evildoers **f**; they have been Ps 36:12
I am about to **f**, and my pain is Ps 38:17
the peoples **f** under you. Ps 45:5
You make them **f** into ruin. Ps 73:18
He made ⌊them⌋ **f** in His camp, Ps 78:28
like men and **f** like any other Ps 82:7
Though a thousand **f** at your side Ps 91:7
would make them **f** in the desert Ps 106:26
loved cursing—let it **f** on him; Ps 109:17
You pushed me hard to make me **f**, Ps 118:13
Let hot coals **f** on them. Ps 140:10
Let the wicked **f** into their own Ps 141:10
The LORD helps all who **f**; Ps 145:14
person will **f** because of his Pr 11:5
guidance, people **f**, but with Pr 11:14
trusting in his riches will **f**, Pr 11:28
an arrogant spirit before a **f**. Pr 16:18
speech will **f** into ruin. Pr 17:20
by the LORD will **f** into it. Pr 22:14
who digs a pit will **f** into it, Pr 26:27
evil way will **f** into his own pit Pr 28:10
right and wrong will suddenly **f**. Pr 28:18
who digs a pit may **f** into it, Ec 10:8
Your men will **f** by the sword, Is 3:25
that rain should not **f** on it. Is 5:6
they will **f** and be broken; Is 8:15
prisoners or **f** among the slain Is 10:4
his burden will **f** from your Is 10:27
Lebanon with its majesty will **f**. Is 10:34
be cut off, and **f**, and the load Is 22:25
of terror will **f** into a pit, Is 24:18
slaughter when the towers **f**. Is 30:25
stumble and the helped will **f**; Is 31:3
Assyria will **f**, but not by human Is 31:8
cause him to **f** by the sword.' Is 37:7
up an idol that will not **f** over. Is 40:20
and young men stumble and **f**, Is 40:30
so that it will not **f** over. Is 41:7
And it will **f** on you, but you Is 47:11
attacks you will **f** before you. Is 54:15
as rain and snow **f** from heaven, Is 55:10
reviled you will **f** down on their Is 60:14
they will **f** among the fallen. Jr 6:15
Do ⌊people⌋ **f** and not get up Jr 8:4
they will **f** among the fallen. Jr 8:12
Human corpses will **f** like manure Jr 9:22
I will make them **f** by the sword Jr 19:7
will **f** by the sword of their Jr 20:4
I trusted watches for my **f**. Jr 20:10
be driven away and **f** down there, Jr 23:12
F down and never get up again, Jr 25:27
you will **f** and become shattered Jr 25:34
that you do not **f** by the sword. Jr 39:18
of Egypt will **f** by the sword; Jr 44:12
River, they stumble and **f**. Jr 46:6
the panic will **f** in the pit, Jr 48:44
sound of their **f** the earth will Jr 49:21
young men will **f** in her public Jr 49:26
young men will **f** in her public Jr 50:30
will stumble and **f** with no one Jr 50:32
them, and his hands **f** helpless. Jr 50:43
were slain will **f** in the land Jr 51:4
Then they will **f** asleep forever Jr 51:39
even Babylon's wall will **f**. Jr 51:44
Babylon must **f** ⌊because of⌋ the Jr 51:49
Then they will **f** asleep forever Jr 51:57
third will **f** by the sword all Ezk 5:12
The slain will **f** among you, Ezk 6:7
Israel, who will **f** by the sword, Ezk 6:11
who is near will **f** by the sword; Ezk 6:12
You will **f** by the sword, and I Ezk 11:10
who plaster ⌊it⌋ that it will **f**. Ezk 13:11
will **f**⌋ in destructive Ezk 13:13
The city will **f**, and you will be Ezk 13:14
his troops will **f** by the sword, Ezk 17:21

descendants will **f** by the sword. Ezk 23:25
left behind will **f** by the sword. Ezk 24:21
they will **f** by the sword from Ezk 25:13
pillars will **f** to the ground. Ezk 26:11
the slain will **f** within her, Ezk 28:23
will **f** on the open ground and Ezk 29:5
Cush when the slain **f** in Egypt, Ezk 30:4
land will **f** by the sword along Ezk 30:5
Those who support Egypt will **f**, Ezk 30:6
Syene they will **f** within it by Ezk 30:6
Pi-beseth will **f** by the sword, Ezk 30:17
make the sword **f** from his hand. Ezk 30:22
but Pharaoh's arms will **f**. Ezk 30:25
make your hordes **f** by the swords Ezk 32:12
They will **f** among those slain by Ezk 32:20
the ruins will **f** by the sword, Ezk 33:27
the sword will **f** on your hills, Ezk 35:8
every wall will **f** to the ground. Ezk 38:20
with you will **f** on the mountains Ezk 39:4
You will **f** on the open field, Ezk 39:5
So this land will **f** to you as an Ezk 47:14
are to **f** down and worship the Dn 3:5
does not **f** down and worship Dn 3:6
of music must **f** down and worship Dn 3:10
does not **f** down and worship Dn 3:11
f down and worship the statue I Dn 3:15
some of the host **f** to the earth, Dn 8:10
cause tens of thousands to **f**, Dn 11:12
will stumble, **f**, and be no more Dn 11:19
away, and many will **f** slain. Dn 11:26
the wise will **f** so that they may Dn 11:35
beautiful land, and many will **f**. Dn 11:41
All their kings **f**; not one of Hs 7:7
leaders will **f** by the sword Hs 7:16
and to the hills, "**F** on us!" Hs 10:8
They will **f** by the sword; Hs 13:16
be cut off and **f** to the ground. Am 3:14
daughters will **f** by the sword, Am 7:17
they will **f**, never to rise Am 8:14
a pebble will **f** to the ground. Am 9:9
when shaken, they **f**—right into Nah 3:12
Horses and their riders will **f**, Hg 2:22
Hosts, rain will not **f** on them. Zch 14:17
then rain will not **f** on them; Zch 14:18
if You will **f** down and worship Mt 4:9
blind, both will **f** into a pit." Mt 15:14
the crumbs that **f** from their Mt 15:27
the stars will **f** from the sky, Mt 24:29
to cause the **f** and rise of many Lk 2:34
Won't they both **f** into a pit? Lk 6:39
I watched Satan **f** from heaven Lk 10:18
They will **f** by the edge of the Lk 21:24
say to the mountains, '**F** on us!' Lk 23:30
shadow might **f** on some of them Ac 5:15
have sinned and **f** short of the Rm 3:23
of slavery to **f** back into fear, Rm 8:15
have they stumbled so as to **f**? Rm 11:11
if food causes my brother to **f**, 1Co 8:13
I won't cause my brother to **f**. 1Co 8:13
stands must be careful not to **f**! 1Co 10:12
result he will **f** down on his 1Co 14:25
We will not all **f** asleep, but we 1Co 15:51
become conceited and **f** into the 1Tm 3:6
that he does not **f** into disgrace 1Tm 3:7
to be rich **f** into temptation 1Tm 6:9
that no one will **f** into the same Heb 4:11
thing to **f** into the hands Heb 10:31
that you won't **f** under judgment. Jms 5:12
the immoral and **f** from your own 2Pt 3:17
the 24 elders **f** down before the Rv 4:10
F on us and hide us from the Rv 6:16

FALLEN *(74)*

bare or gather its **f** grapes. Lv 19:10
donkey or ox **f** down on the road, Dt 22:4
that dread of you has **f** on us, Jos 2:9
one of them had **f** by the sword, Jos 8:24
fields and gather **f** grain behind Ru 2:2
you let me gather **f** grain among Ru 2:7
f with his face to the ground 1Sm 5:3
f with his face to the ground 1Sm 5:4
the troops have **f** and are dead. 2Sm 1:4
that after he had **f** he couldn't 2Sm 1:10
How the mighty have **f**! 2Sm 1:19
the mighty have **f** in the thick 2Sm 1:25
mighty have **f** and the weapons 2Sm 1:27
where Asahel had **f** and died, 2Sm 2:23
leader has **f** in Israel today 2Sm 3:38
Ahaziah had **f** through the 2Kg 1:2
mantle that had **f** off Elijah and 2Kg 2:13
those who have **f** on hard times? Jb 30:25
The nations have **f** into the pit Ps 9:15
lines have **f** for me in pleasant Ps 16:6
who insult You have **f** on me. Ps 69:9
dread of Israel had **f** on them. Ps 105:38
Judah has **f** because they have Is 3:8
The bricks have **f**, but we will Is 9:10
how you have **f** from the heavens! Is 14:12
shouts have **f** silent over your Is 16:9
Babylon has **f**, has fallen. Is 21:9
Babylon has fallen, has **f**. Is 21:9
earth's inhabitants have not **f**. Is 26:18
they will fall among the **f**. Jr 6:15
they will fall among the **f**. Jr 8:12
crowns have **f** from your heads. Jr 13:18
no rain ⌊has **f**⌋ on the land. Jr 14:4
together both of them have **f**. Jr 46:12
destroyer has **f** on your summer Jr 48:32
her defense towers have **f**; Jr 50:15
her slain will lie **f** within her. Jr 51:47
gates have **f** to the ground; Lm 2:9
and women have **f** by the sword. Lm 2:21
The crown has **f** from our head. Lm 5:16
the wall has **f**, will you not be Ezk 13:12
the sky nested on its **f** trunk, Ezk 31:13
them are slain, **f** by the sword. Ezk 32:22
them are slain, **f** by the sword— Ezk 32:23
them are slain, **f** by the sword— Ezk 32:24
not lie down with the **f** warriors Ezk 32:27
She has **f**; Virgin Israel will Am 5:2
restore the **f** booth of David: Am 9:11
out and **f** into a deep sleep Jnh 1:5
I have **f**, I will stand up; Mc 7:8
cypress, for the cedar has **f**; Zch 11:2
for the stately forest has **f**! Zch 11:2
Our friend Lazarus has **f** asleep, Jn 11:11
Lord, if he has **f** asleep, he Jn 11:12
David's tent, which has **f** down. Ac 15:16
When we had all **f** to the ground, Ac 26:14
toward those who have **f**, Rm 11:22
who insult You have **f** on Me. Rm 15:3
you, and many have **f** asleep. 1Co 11:30
present, but some have **f** asleep. 1Co 15:6
who have **f** asleep in Christ 1Co 15:18
of those who have **f** asleep. 1Co 15:20
you have **f** from grace! Gl 5:4
those who have **f** asleep through 1Th 4:14
over those who have **f** asleep. 1Th 4:15
and who have **f** away, because, to Heb 6:6
the rain that has often **f** on it, Heb 6:7
then how far you have **f**; Rv 2:5
a star that had **f** from heaven to Rv 9:1
It has **f**, Babylon the Great has Rv 14:8
the Great has **f**, who made all Rv 14:8
five have **f**, one is, the other Rv 17:10
It has **f**, Babylon the Great has Rv 18:2
fallen, Babylon the Great has **f**! Rv 18:2

FALLING *(11)*

rain of your land into **f** dust; Dt 28:24
weeping and **f** facedown before Ezr 10:1
Haman was **f** on the couch where Est 7:8
dew of Hermon **f** on the mountains Ps 133:3
everyone wails, **f** down and Is 15:3
mother, and **f** to their knees, Mt 2:11
stars will be **f** from the sky, Mk 13:25
drops of blood **f** to the ground. Lk 22:44
and **f** headfirst, he burst open Ac 1:18
F to the ground, he heard a Ac 9:4
rain was **f** and it was cold. Ac 28:2

FALLS *(43)*

so that its rider **f** backwards. Gn 49:17
die when the hail **f** on them." Ex 9:19
and an ox or a donkey **f** into it, Ex 21:33
them dies and **f** on anything it Lv 11:32
If any of them **f** into any clay Lv 11:33
their carcasses **f** on will become Lv 11:35
their carcasses **f** on any seed Lv 11:37
one of their carcasses **f** on it, Lv 11:38
who **f** ⌊into a trance⌋ with ⌊his⌋ Nm 24:4
who **f** ⌊into a trance⌋ with ⌊his⌋ Nm 24:16
waging war with you, until it **f**. Dt 20:20
your house if someone **f** from it. Dt 22:8
or someone who **f** by the sword 2Sm 3:29
fell like one who **f** victim to 2Sm 3:34
when deep sleep **f** on people as Jb 33:15
and his violence **f** on the top of Ps 7:16
Though he **f**, he will not be Ps 37:24
like rain that **f** on the cut Ps 72:6
wicked messenger **f** into trouble, Pr 13:17
but his anger **f** on a disgraceful Pr 14:35
a righteous man **f** seven times, Pr 24:16
Don't gloat when your enemy **f**, Pr 24:17
his heart **f** into trouble. Pr 28:14
For if either **f**, his companion Ec 4:10
the one who **f** without another Ec 4:10
time, as it suddenly **f** on them. Ec 9:12
whether a tree **f** to the south or Ec 11:3
the place where the tree **f**, Ec 11:3
it down, and it **f**, never to rise Is 24:20
Indeed, each **f** over the other. Jr 46:16
and it **f** on the stronghold. Am 5:9
not one of them **f** to the ground Mt 10:29
He often **f** into the fire and Mt 17:15
Whoever **f** on this stone will be Mt 21:44
on whomever it **f**, it will grind Mt 21:44
house divided against itself **f**. Lk 11:17
whose son or ox **f** into a well, Lk 14:5
Everyone who **f** on that stone Lk 20:18
pieces, and if it **f** on anyone, Lk 20:18
grain of wheat **f** into the ground Jn 12:24
his own Lord he stands or **f**. Rm 14:4
to it that no one **f** short of the Heb 12:15
its flower **f** off, and its Jms 1:11

FALSE *(65)*

Do not give **f** testimony against Ex 20:16
You must not spread a **f** report. Ex 23:1
far away from a **f** accusation. Ex 23:7
and let nothing he said prove **f**. 1Sm 3:19
of ⌊capturing⌋ him proves **f**. Jb 41:9
not set his mind on what is **f**, Ps 24:4
for **f** witnesses rise up against Ps 27:12
horse is a **f** hope for safety; Ps 33:17
oppression, or **f** hope in robbery Ps 62:10
therefore I hate every **f** way. Ps 119:104
precepts and hate every **f** way. Ps 119:128
witness who gives **f** testimony, Pr 6:19
right, but a **f** witness, deceit Pr 12:17
A **f** witness will not go Pr 19:5
A **f** witness will not go Pr 19:9
A man giving **f** testimony against Pr 25:18
will sweep away the **f** refuge, Is 28:17
the omens of the **f** prophets and Is 44:25
prophesying to you a **f** vision, Jr 14:14
burn incense to **f** ⌊idols⌋ that Jr 18:15
those who prophesy **f** dreams"— Jr 23:32
her **f** gods, devastated. Jr 50:2
no longer be any **f** vision or Ezk 12:24
They see **f** visions and speak Ezk 13:6
you see a **f** vision and speak Ezk 13:7
prophets who see **f** visions and Ezk 13:9
will no longer see **f** visions or Ezk 13:23
will seem like **f** divination in Ezk 21:23
While they offer **f** visions and Ezk 21:29
them by seeing **f** visions and Ezk 22:28
an end to the **f** gods in Memphis Ezk 30:13
me something **f** or fraudulent Dn 2:9
taking **f** oaths while making Hs 10:4
Beware of **f** prophets who come to Mt 7:15
thefts, **f** testimonies, Mt 15:19
do not bear **f** witness; Mt 19:18
Many **f** prophets will rise up and Mt 24:11
F messiahs and false prophets Mt 24:24
messiahs and **f** prophets will Mt 24:24
were looking for **f** testimony Mt 26:59
though many **f** witnesses came Mt 26:60
do not bear **f** witness; Mk 10:19
f messiahs and false prophets Mk 13:22
messiahs and **f** prophets will Mk 13:22
many were giving **f** testimony Mk 14:56
and were giving **f** testimony Mk 14:57
anyone by force or **f** accusation; Lk 3:14
used to treat the **f** prophets. Lk 6:26
do not bear **f** witness; Lk 18:20
also presented **f** witnesses who Ac 6:13
a Jewish **f** prophet named Ac 13:6
found to be **f** witnesses about 1Co 15:15
For such people are **f** apostles, 2Co 11:13
and dangers among **f** brothers; 2Co 11:26
because of **f** brothers smuggled Gl 2:4
out of **f** motives or true, Php 1:18
with all kinds of **f** miracles, 2Th 2:9
they will believe what is **f**, 2Th 2:11
there were also **f** prophets among 2Pt 2:1
there will be **f** teachers among 2Pt 2:1
because many **f** prophets have 1Jn 4:1

from the mouth of the **f** prophet. Rv 16:13
along with him the **f** prophet, Rv 19:20
the beast and the **f** prophet are, Rv 20:10
one who does what is vile or **f**, Rv 21:27

FALSEHOOD *(8)*
have walked in **f** or my foot has Jb 31:5
I hate and abhor **f**, ⌊but⌋ I love Ps 119:163
Keep **f** and deceitful words far Pr 30:8
we have made **f** our refuge and Is 28:15
Surely, **f** comes from the hills, Jr 3:23
pen of scribes has produced **f**. Jr 8:8
forgotten Me and trusted in **F**. Jr 13:25
the idols speak **f**, and the Zch 10:2

FALSEHOODS *(1)*
astray with their **f** and their Jr 23:32

FALSELY *(21)*
or swears **f** about any of the Lv 6:3
else about which he swore **f**. Lv 6:5
You must not swear **f** by My name, Lv 19:12
be a liar who has **f** accused his Dt 19:18
Your enemies swear ⌊by You⌋ **f**. Ps 139:20
way and speaks **f** about the LORD. Is 32:6
lives," they are swearing **f**. Jr 5:2
prophesy **f**, and the priests Jr 5:31
to priest, everyone deals **f**. Jr 6:13
adultery, swear **f**, burn incense Jr 7:9
to priest, everyone deals **f**. Jr 8:10
that you prophesied **f** to.' " Jr 20:6
are prophesying **f** in My name; Jr 27:15
are prophesying **f** to you in My Jr 29:9
you have spoken **f** and had lying Ezk 13:8
who swears ⌊**f**⌋ will be removed Zch 5:3
the one who swears **f** by My name. Zch 5:4
you have spoken **f** in the name of Zch 13:3
against those who swear **f**; Mal 3:5
you and **f** say every kind Mt 5:11
that **f** bears that name 1Tm 6:20

FALTER *(1)*
his heart; his steps do not **f**. Ps 37:31

FALTERING *(1)*
like a rotten tooth or a **f** foot. Pr 25:19

FAME *(20)*
heard of Your **f** will declare, Nm 14:15
made in praise, **f**, and glory, Dt 26:19
and his **f** spread throughout the Jos 6:27
For we have heard of His **f**, Jos 9:9
about Solomon's **f** connected with 1Kg 10:1
Then David's **f** spread throughout 1Ch 14:17
of Sheba heard of Solomon's **f**, 2Ch 9:1
and his **f** spread as far as the 2Ch 26:8
So his **f** spread even to distant 2Ch 26:15
and his **f** spread throughout the Est 9:4
sun shines, may his **f** increase. Ps 72:17
Your **f** ⌊endures⌋ to all Ps 102:12
to obtain eternal **f** for Himself, Is 63:12
not heard of My **f** or seen My Is 66:19
might be My people for My **f**, Jr 13:11
Your **f** spread among the nations Ezk 16:14
a prostitute because of your **f**. Ezk 16:15
them⌋ and their **f** will spread Ezk 39:13
the earth receive praise and **f**. Zph 3:19
His **f** then spread throughout the Mk 1:28

FAMILIAR *(4)*
consult a medium or a **f** spirit, Dt 18:11
Surely they are **f** with the Jb 24:17
Are you **f** with the paths to its Jb 38:20
and your fathers are not **f** with. Jr 16:13

FAMILIES *(77)*
according to their **f** and their Gn 36:40
feared God, He gave them **f**. Ex 1:21
the heads of their fathers' **f**: Ex 6:14
of the Levite **f** by their clans. Ex 6:25
I ⌊ever⌋ let you and your **f** go! Ex 10:10
Even your **f** may go with you; Ex 10:24
the flock according to your **f**, Ex 12:21
on foot, besides their **f**. Ex 12:37
or from their **f** living among you Lv 25:45
who were over the Israelite **f**. Nm 36:1
clan come forward by heads of **f**, Jos 7:17
heads of the **f** of the Israelite Jos 14:1
the heads of the **f** distributed Jos 19:51
of the Levite **f** approached Jos 21:1
heads of the **f** of the Israelite Jos 21:1
heads of their **f** among the clans Jos 22:14
and the **f** of Kiriath-jearim— 1Ch 2:53
and the **f** of scribes who lived 1Ch 2:55
These were the **f** of the 1Ch 4:2
and the **f** of Aharhel son of 1Ch 4:8
the **f** of the guild of linen 1Ch 4:21
by name were leaders in their **f**. 1Ch 4:38
relatives by their **f** as they are 1Ch 5:7
heads of their patriarchal **f**. 1Ch 5:24
are the Levites' **f** according to 1Ch 6:19
13 towns in all among their **f**. 1Ch 6:60
in Bashan according to their **f**. 1Ch 6:62
Zebulun according to their **f**. 1Ch 6:63
Some of the **f** of the Kohathites 1Ch 6:66
the rest of the **f** of the 1Ch 6:70
from the heads of **f** of half the tribe 1Ch 6:71
to all the **f** of Issachar 1Ch 7:5
by heads of **f** were warriors; 1Ch 7:11
heads of the **f** living in Geba 1Ch 8:6
These were his sons, heads of **f**. 1Ch 8:10
were the heads of **f** of Aijalon's 1Ch 8:13
heads of **f**, chiefs according 1Ch 8:28
the heads of Levite **f**, stayed in 1Ch 9:33
were the heads of Levite **f**, 1Ch 9:34
are the heads of the Levite **f**. 1Ch 15:12
to the LORD, **f** of the peoples, 1Ch 16:28
the heads of the **f** of Ladan. 1Ch 23:9
the heads of **f**, according to 1Ch 23:24
the heads of **f** of the priests 1Ch 24:6
heads of the **f** of the priests 1Ch 24:31
were the heads of **f** belonging to 1Ch 26:21
by the heads of **f** who were the 1Ch 26:26
capable men who were heads of **f**. 1Ch 26:32
the heads of **f**, the commanders 1Ch 27:1
all Israel—the heads of the **f**. 2Ch 1:2
according to their ancestral **f**. 2Ch 17:14
the Israelite **f** for ⌊rendering⌋ 2Ch 19:8
the heads of the **f** of Israel, 2Ch 23:2
of heads of **f** was 2,600 brave 2Ch 26:12
ancestral **f** and the Levites 2Ch 31:17
prove that their **f** and ancestry Ezr 2:59
leaders of the **f** and said to Ezr 4:2
of Israel's **f** answered them, Ezr 4:3
the Israelite **f** in Jerusalem." Ezr 8:29
them by **f** with their swords Neh 4:13
prove that their **f** and ancestry Neh 7:61
his relatives, the leaders of **f**: Neh 11:13
leaders of the priestly **f** were: Neh 12:12
leaders of the **f** of the Levites Neh 12:22
the leaders of **f**, were recorded Neh 12:23
the **f** of the nations will bow Ps 22:27
the LORD, you **f** of the peoples, Ps 96:7
makes their **f** ⌊multiply⌋ like Ps 107:41
of Jacob and all **f** of the house Jr 2:4
You and on the **f** that don't call Jr 10:25
for all the **f** of the north' Jr 25:9
be God of all the **f** of Israel, Jr 31:1
the two **f** He had chosen. Jr 33:24
the remaining **f**, every family Zch 12:14
any of the **f** of the earth not Zch 14:17
seed all the **f** of the earth will Ac 3:25
And all the **f** of the earth will Rv 1:7

FAMILY *(170)*
These are the **f** records of the Gn 5:1
These are the **f** records of Noah. Gn 6:9
are the **f** records of Noah's Gn 10:1
according to their **f** records, Gn 10:32
These are the **f** records of Shem. Gn 11:10
are the **f** records of Terah. Gn 11:27
my land and my **f** to take a wife Gn 24:4
and to my **f** to take a wife for Gn 24:38
for my son from my **f** and from my Gn 24:40
you go to my **f** and they do not Gn 24:41
These are the **f** records of Gn 25:12
according to the **f** records are: Gn 25:13
These are the **f** records of Isaac Gn 25:19
her I too can build ⌊a **f**⌋." Gn 30:3
also do something for my own **f**?" Gn 30:30
of your fathers and to your **f**, Gn 31:3
back to your land and to your **f**, Gn 32:9
said to his **f** and all who were Gn 35:2
These are the **f** records of Esau Gn 36:1
These are the **f** records of Esau, Gn 36:9
are the **f** records of Jacob. Gn 37:2
asking about us and our **f**: Gn 43:7
each came with his **f**: Ex 1:1
a man from the **f** of Levi married Ex 2:1
because it will shame your **f**. Lv 18:10
turn against that man and his **f**, Lv 20:5
except for his immediate **f**: Lv 21:2
sister in his immediate **f**. Lv 21:3
a priest's **f** is to eat the holy Lv 22:10
to a man outside a priest's **f**, Lv 22:12
If a man has no **f** redeemer, Lv 25:26
to their **f** records by their Nm 1:20
to their **f** records by their Nm 1:22
to their **f** records by their Nm 1:24
to their **f** records by their Nm 1:26
to their **f** records by their Nm 1:28
to their **f** records by their Nm 1:30
to their **f** records by their Nm 1:32
to their **f** records by their Nm 1:34
to their **f** records by their Nm 1:36
to their **f** records by their Nm 1:38
to their **f** records by their Nm 1:40
to their **f** records by their Nm 1:42
These are the **f** records of Aaron Nm 3:1
the Gershonite **f** was Eliasaph Nm 3:24
leader of the **f** of the Kohathite Nm 3:30
leader of the **f** of the Merarite Nm 3:35
the people, **f** after family, Nm 11:10
people, family after **f**, crying Nm 11:10
These were the Levite **f** groups: Nm 26:58
and the **f** leaders of the Nm 31:26
and the **f** leaders of the Nm 32:28
The **f** leaders from the clan of Nm 36:1
God and rejoice with your **f**. Dt 14:26
because he loves you and your **f**, Dt 15:16
year you and your **f** are to eat Dt 15:20
from the sale of the **f** estate. Dt 18:8
a stranger outside ⌊the **f**⌋. Dt 25:5
And his ⌊**f**⌋ name in Israel will Dt 25:10
will also show kindness to my **f**, Jos 2:12
your father's **f** into your house Jos 2:18
out her whole **f** and settled them Jos 6:23
is to come forward **f** by family. Jos 7:14
is to come forward family by **f**. Jos 7:14
f the LORD selects is to come Jos 7:14
had Zabdi's **f** come forward man Jos 7:18
So Joshua replied to Joseph's **f** Jos 17:17
Joseph's **f** in their territory Jos 18:5
one **f** leader for each tribe of Jos 22:14
for me and my **f**, we will worship Jos 24:15
the man and his entire **f**. Jdg 1:25
of Hazor and the **f** of Heber the Jdg 4:17
my **f** is the weakest in Manasseh, Jdg 6:15
well by Jerubbaal and his **f**, Jdg 9:16
Zorah, from the **f** of Dan, whose Jdg 13:2
and his father's **f** came down, Jdg 16:31
for a tribe and **f** in Israel?" Jdg 18:19
you and your **f** will lose your Jdg 18:25
there to his own tribe and **f**. Jdg 21:24
character from Elimelech's **f**. Ru 2:1
who was from Elimelech's **f**. Ru 2:3
He is one of our **f** redeemers." Ru 2:20
for you are a **f** redeemer." Ru 3:9
is true that I am a **f** redeemer, Ru 3:12
the **f** redeemer Boaz had spoken Ru 4:1
you without a **f** redeemer today. Ru 4:14
I said your **f** and your ancestral 1Sm 2:30
strength of your ancestral **f**, 1Sm 2:31
none in your **f** will reach old 1Sm 2:31
no one in your **f** will ever again 1Sm 2:32
man from your ⌊**f**⌋ I do not cut 1Sm 2:33
is left in your **f** will come and 1Sm 2:36
everything I said about his **f**, 1Sm 3:12
to judge his **f** forever because 1Sm 3:13
I have sworn to Eli's **f**: 1Sm 3:14
iniquity of Eli's **f** will never 1Sm 3:14
you and all your father's **f**?" 1Sm 9:20
and what is my **f** or my father's 1Sm 18:18
and his father's whole **f** heard, 1Sm 22:1
father's whole **f**, who were 1Sm 22:11
you and your father's whole **f**!" 1Sm 22:16
of everyone in your father's **f**. 1Sm 22:22
out my name from my father's **f**." 1Sm 24:21
to you, to your **f**, and to all 1Sm 25:6
for our master and his entire **f**. 1Sm 25:17
Each man had his **f** with him, 1Sm 27:3
Obed-edom and his whole **f**. 2Sm 6:11
Obed-edom's **f** and all that 2Sm 6:12
and his whole **f** to appoint me 2Sm 6:21
Saul's **f** I can show kindness 2Sm 9:1
servant of Saul's **f** named Ziba. 2Sm 9:2
left of Saul's **f** I can show 2Sm 9:3
that belonged to Saul and his **f**. 2Sm 9:9
disaster on you from your own **f**: 2Sm 12:11
belonging to the **f** of the house 2Sm 16:5
entire **f** deserves death 2Sm 19:28

by Saul and his **f** when he killed 2Sm 21:1
for money from Saul or his **f**, 2Sm 21:4
bones of Saul's **f** who had been 2Sm 21:13
against me and my father's **f**." 2Sm 24:17
at Shiloh against Eli's **f**. 1Kg 2:27
He was of the royal **f** in Edom. 1Kg 11:14
had destroyed his **f** according to 1Kg 15:29
he was a son-in-law to Ahab's **f**. 2Kg 8:27
of the royal **f**, came with 10 men 2Kg 25:25
These are their **f** records: 1Ch 1:29
the father of Rechab's **f**. 1Ch 2:55
so their whole **f** did not become 1Ch 4:27
from the Kohathite **f** for their 1Ch 6:54
Obed-edom's **f** in his house for 1Ch 13:14
blessed his **f** and all that he 1Ch 13:14
me and against my father's **f**, 1Ch 21:17
the **f** heads and their younger 1Ch 24:31
Netophathite, of Othniel's **f**; 1Ch 27:15
your father's **f**, who were better 2Ch 21:13
them according to patriarchal **f**, 2Ch 25:5
So the **f** leaders of Judah and Ezr 1:5
some of the **f** leaders gave Ezr 2:68
Levites, and **f** leaders, who had Ezr 3:12
These are the **f** leaders and the Ezr 8:1
selected men who were **f** leaders, Ezr 10:16
Some of the **f** leaders gave to Neh 7:70
of the **f** leaders gave 20,000 Neh 7:71
the **f** leaders of all the people, Neh 8:13
every generation, **f**, province, Est 9:28
You have devastated my entire **f**. Jb 16:7
care about his **f** once he is dead Jb 21:21
Buzite from the **f** of Ram became Jb 32:2
from a city and two from a **f**, Jr 3:14
the survivors of this evil **f**, Jr 8:3
of the royal **f** and one of the Jr 41:1
done⌋ to me and my **f** ⌊be done⌋ Jr 51:35
one of the royal **f** and made a Ezk 17:13
from the royal **f** and from the Dn 1:3
one from her **f** will rise up, Dn 11:7
will mourn, every **f** by itself: Zch 12:12
the **f** of David's house by itself Zch 12:12
f of Nathan's house by itself Zch 12:12
the **f** of Levi's house by itself Zch 12:13
the **f** of Shimei by itself and Zch 12:13
families, every **f** by itself, and Zch 12:14
When His **f** heard this, they set Mk 3:21
the house and **f** line of David, Lk 2:4
members of the high-priestly **f**. Ac 4:6
and Joseph's **f** became known to Ac 7:13
he and all his **f** were baptized. Ac 16:33
Show **f** affection to one another Rm 12:10
from whom every **f** in heaven and Eph 3:15
toward their own **f** first and to 1Tm 5:4
built an ark to deliver his **f**. Heb 11:7

FAMINE *(99)*

There was a **f** in the land, Gn 12:10
because the **f** in the land was Gn 12:10
There was another **f** in the land Gn 26:1
of grain are seven years of **f**. Gn 41:27
years of **f** will take place, Gn 41:30
The **f** will devastate the land. Gn 41:30
of the **f** that follows it, Gn 41:31
for the **f** will be very severe. Gn 41:31
seven years of **f** that will take Gn 41:36
will not be wiped out by the **f**." Gn 41:36
before the years of **f** arrived. Gn 41:50
and the seven years of **f** began, Gn 41:54
There was **f** in every country, Gn 41:54
Because the **f** had spread across Gn 41:56
for the **f** was severe in the land Gn 41:56
the **f** was severe all over the Gn 41:57
for the **f** was in the land of Gn 42:5
the **f** in the land was severe. Gn 43:1
For the **f** has been in the land Gn 45:6
will be five more years of **f**. Gn 45:11
the **f** in the land of Canaan Gn 47:4
for the **f** was very severe. Gn 47:13
Canaan were exhausted by the **f**. Gn 47:13
field since the **f** was so severe Gn 47:20
against you, in **f**, thirst, Dt 28:48
there was a **f** in the land. Ru 1:1
reign there was a **f** for three 2Sm 21:1
three years of **f** to come on your 2Sm 24:13
When there is **f** on the earth, 1Kg 8:37
The **f** was severe in Samaria. 1Kg 18:2
there was a **f** in the land. 2Kg 4:38
there was a great **f** in Samaria, 2Kg 6:25
because the **f** is in the city, 2Kg 7:4
has announced a seven-year **f**, 2Kg 8:1
fourth⌋ month the **f** was so 2Kg 25:3
three years of **f**, three months 1Ch 21:12
When there is **f** on the earth, 2Ch 6:28
pestilence or **f**—we will stand 2Ch 20:9
to death by **f** and thirst when 2Ch 32:11
to get grain during the **f**." Neh 5:3
In **f** He will redeem you from Jb 5:20
and to keep them alive in **f**. Ps 33:19
called down **f** against the land Ps 105:16
and destruction, **f** and sword. Is 51:19
we won't see sword or **f**." Jr 5:12
and daughters will die by **f**. Jr 11:22
off by sword, **f**, and plague." Jr 14:12
'You won't see sword or suffer **f**. Jr 14:13
be sword or **f** in this land: Jr 14:15
By sword and **f** these prophets Jr 14:15
because of the **f** and the sword. Jr 14:16
city, look—those ill from **f**! Jr 14:18
destined⌋ for **f**, to famine; Jr 15:2
destined⌋ for famine, to **f**; Jr 15:2
be finished off by sword and **f**. Jr 16:4
hand their children over to **f**, Jr 18:21
sword, and the **f**—I will hand Jr 21:7
die by the sword, **f**, and plague, Jr 21:9
send the sword, **f**, and plague Jr 24:10
by sword, **f**, and plague"— Jr 27:8
die by the sword, **f**, or plague Jr 27:13
against them sword, **f**, and Jr 29:17
them with sword, **f**, and plague. Jr 29:18
of the sword, **f**, and plague, has Jr 32:24
through sword, **f**, and plague: Jr 32:36
the sword, to plague, and to **f**! Jr 34:17
die by the sword, **f**, and plague, Jr 38:2
and the **f** you are worried about Jr 42:16
die by the sword, **f**, and plague. Jr 42:17
by the sword, **f**, and plague you Jr 42:22
they will meet their end by **f**. Jr 44:12
will die by the sword and by **f**. Jr 44:12
by sword, **f**, and plague. Jr 44:13
sword and **f** we have met our Jr 44:18
end by sword or **f** until they are Jr 44:27
fourth month the **f** was so severe Jr 52:6
and be consumed by **f** within you; Ezk 5:12
deadly arrows of **f** at them, Ezk 5:16
will intensify the **f** against you Ezk 5:16
I will send **f** and dangerous Ezk 5:17
by the sword, **f**, and plague. Ezk 6:11
and is spared will die of **f**. Ezk 6:12
plague and **f** are on the inside. Ezk 7:15
and **f** and plague will devour Ezk 7:15
from the sword, **f**, and plague so Ezk 12:16
of bread, to send **f** through it, Ezk 14:13
sword, **f**, dangerous animals Ezk 14:21
be victims of **f** in the land. Ezk 34:29
and will not bring **f** on you. Ezk 36:29
the nations on account of **f**. Ezk 36:30
I will send a **f** through the land Am 8:11
not a **f** of bread or a thirst for Am 8:11
while a great **f** came over all Lk 4:25
a severe **f** struck that country, Lk 15:14
Then a **f** came over all of Egypt Ac 7:11
would be a severe **f** throughout Ac 11:28
or persecution or **f** or nakedness Rm 8:35
by the sword, by **f**, by plague, Rv 6:8
day—death, and grief, and **f**. Rv 18:8

FAMINES *(3)*

There will be **f** and earthquakes Mt 24:7
in various places, and **f**. Mk 13:8
and **f** and plagues in various Lk 21:11

FAMISHED *(3)*

and withheld food from the **f**, Jb 22:7
they are **f**, they will become Is 8:21
I send them home **f**, they will Mk 8:3

FAMOUS *(12)*

powerful men of old, the **f** men. Gn 6:4
in Ephrathah and **f** in Bethlehem. Ru 4:11
May his name be **f** in Israel. Ru 4:14
So his name became very **f**. 1Sm 18:30
Solomon more **f** than your name, 1Kg 1:47
it was the most **f** high place. 1Kg 3:4
brave warriors, **f** men, and heads 1Ch 5:24
warriors who were **f** men in their 1Ch 12:30
great and **f** and glorious in all 1Ch 22:5
Ahasuerus, **f** among the Jews, Est 10:3
and slaughtered **f** kings—His Ps 136:18
I will make you **f** and Zph 3:20

FANGS *(7)*

on them wild beasts with **f**, Dt 32:24
but the **f** of young lions are Jb 4:10
a viper's **f** will kill him. Jb 20:16
I shattered the **f** of the unjust Jb 29:17
tear out the young lions' **f**. Ps 58:6
are swords, whose **f** are knives, Pr 30:14
and it has the **f** of a lioness. Jl 1:6

FANTASIES *(2)*

whoever chases **f** lacks sense. Pr 12:11
whoever chases **f** will have his Pr 28:19

FAR *(257)*

(See pp. xi-xii.)

FARE *(1)*

He paid the **f** and went down into Jnh 1:3

FAREWELL *(2)*

send **f** gifts to Moresheth-gath; Mc 1:14
things, you will do well. **F**. Ac 15:29

FARM *(1)*

one to his own **f**, another to his Mt 22:5

FARMER *(4)*

will smash the **f** and his ox-team Jr 51:23
f will be called on to mourn, Am 5:16
the hardworking **f** who ought to 2Tm 2:6
See how the **f** waits for the Jms 5:7

FARMER'S *(1)*

wheel of ⌊the **f**⌋ cart rumbles, Is 28:28

FARMERS *(22)*

land to be vinedressers and **f**. 2Kg 25:12
he had **f** and vinedressers in the 2Ch 26:10
on the land. The **f** are ashamed; Jr 14:4
also **f** and those who move with Jr 31:24
left to be vinedressers and **f**. Jr 52:16
Be ashamed, you **f**, wail, you Jl 1:11
it to tenant **f** and went away. Mt 21:33
slaves to the **f** to collect his Mt 21:34
But the **f** took his slaves, Mt 21:35
when the tenant **f** saw the son, Mt 21:38
what will he do to those **f**?" Mt 21:40
to other **f** who will give him Mt 21:41
it to tenant **f** and went away. Mk 12:1
a slave to the **f** to collect some Mk 12:2
of the vineyard from the **f**. Mk 12:2
But those tenant **f** said among Mk 12:7
come and destroy the **f** and give Mk 12:9
it to tenant **f**, and went away Lk 20:9
a slave to the **f** so that they Lk 20:10
But the **f** beat him and sent him Lk 20:10
But when the tenant **f** saw him, Lk 20:14
and destroy those **f** and give the Lk 20:16

FARMING *(1)*

As for the **f** settlements with Neh 11:25

FARTHER *(8)*

but **f** down it became too narrow Neh 2:14
You may come this far, but no **f**; Jb 38:11
with me to Babylon, go no **f**. Jr 40:4
Going a little **f**, He fell Mt 26:39
on a little **f**, He saw James Mk 1:19
He went a little **f**, fell to the Mk 14:35
impression that He was going **f**. Lk 24:28
sailed a little **f** and sounded Ac 27:28

FARTHEST *(4)*

I came to its **f** outpost, its 2Kg 19:23
the land even to the **f** shores. Est 10:1
fly that is at the **f** streams of Is 7:18
called you from its **f** corners. Is 41:9

FASHION *(2)*

F gold filigree settings Ex 28:13
F two gold rings for the Ex 28:23

FASHIONED *(5)*

f it with an engraving tool, Ex 32:4
They also **f** two gold filigree Ex 39:16
and its rim was **f** like the brim 1Kg 7:26
and its rim was **f** like the brim 2Ch 4:5
an image **f** by human art and Ac 17:29

FAST *(47)*

Asahel was a **f** runner, like one 2Sm 2:18
that he is dead, why should I **f**? 2Sm 12:23
head was caught **f** in the tree. 2Sm 18:9
Proclaim a **f** and seat Naboth at 1Kg 21:9
proclaimed a **f** and seated Naboth 1Kg 21:12
held **f** to the LORD and did not 2Kg 18:6
he proclaimed a **f** for all Judah, 2Ch 20:3
I proclaimed a **f** by the Ahava Ezr 8:21
be found in Susa and **f** for me. Est 4:16

will also f in the same way. Est 4:16
who rode f horses bred from the Est 8:10
"We will ride on f horses"— Is 30:16
you please on the day of your f, Is 58:3
You f ⌊with⌋ contention and Is 58:4
You cannot f as ⌊you do⌋ today, Is 58:4
the f I choose be like this: Is 58:5
you call this a f and a day Is 58:5
Isn't the f I choose: To break Is 58:6
If they f, I will not hear their Jr 14:12
proclaimed a f before the LORD. Jr 36:9
All their captors hold them f; Jr 50:33
Announce a sacred f; proclaim an Jl 1:14
Announce a sacred f; proclaim an Jl 2:15
They proclaimed a f and dressed Jnh 3:5
we mourn and f in the fifth Zch 7:3
years, did you really f for Me? Zch 7:5
The f of the fourth ⌊month⌋, Zch 8:19
month⌋, the f of the fifth, Zch 8:19
the fifth, the f of the seventh, Zch 8:19
and the f of the tenth will Zch 8:19
Whenever you f, don't be Mt 6:16
But when you f, put oil on your Mt 6:17
do we and the Pharisees f often, Mt 9:14
but Your disciples do not f?" Mt 9:14
from them, and then they will f. Mt 9:15
and the Pharisees' disciples f, Mk 2:18
but Your disciples do not f?" Mk 2:18
guests cannot f while the groom Mk 2:19
groom with them, they cannot f. Mk 2:19
then they will f in that day. Mk 2:20
John's disciples f often and say Lk 5:33
wedding guests f while the groom Lk 5:34
then they will f in those days." Lk 5:35
I f twice a week; I give a tenth Lk 18:12
Since the F was already over, Ac 27:9
The bow jammed f and remained Ac 27:41
let us hold f to the confession. Heb 4:14

FASTED *(16)*

They f that day until evening Jdg 20:26
They f that day, and there they 1Sm 7:6
tree in Jabesh and f seven days. 1Sm 31:13
f until the evening for those 2Sm 1:12
He f, went ⌊home⌋, and spent the 2Sm 12:16
was alive, you f and wept, but 2Sm 12:21
f and wept because I thought, 2Sm 12:22
sackcloth over his body, and f. 1Kg 21:27
oak in Jabesh and f seven days. 1Ch 10:12
So we f and pleaded with our God Ezr 8:23
They f, wept, and lamented, and Est 4:3
I mourned and f, but it brought Ps 69:10
Why have we f, but You have not Is 58:3
When you f and lamented in the Zch 7:5
After He had f 40 days and 40 Mt 4:2
after they had f, prayed, and Ac 13:3

FASTEN *(6)*

F both stones on the shoulder Ex 28:12
F it to a cord of blue yarn so Ex 28:37
f the ephod on him with its Ex 29:5
f headbands on them, and tie Ex 29:9
'Every man f his sword to his Ex 32:27
Can you f the chains of the Jb 38:31

FASTENED *(12)*

He f them on the shoulder pieces Ex 39:7
around him and f it to him. Lv 8:7
around them, and f headbands on Lv 8:13
She f the braids with a pin and Jdg 16:14
100 pomegranates and f them into 2Ch 3:16
and securely f while the guards Neh 7:3
hangings were f with fine white Est 1:6
It is f with hammer and nails, Jr 10:4
so I f the whole house of Israel Jr 13:11
into a yoke, f together by His Lm 1:14
three-inch hooks f all around Ezk 40:43
of the heat and f itself to his Ac 28:3

FASTENS *(1)*

He f it with nails so that it Is 41:7

FASTER *(2)*

My days fly by f than a runner; Jb 9:25
those who pursue you will be f. Is 30:16

FASTING *(16)*

f and praying before the God of Neh 1:4
were f, ⌊wearing⌋ sackcloth, Neh 9:1
practices of f and lamentation Est 9:31
myself with f, and my prayer was Ps 35:13
are weak from f, and my body is Ps 109:24
of the LORD on a day of f. Jr 36:6
palace and spent the night f. Dn 6:18
petitions, with f, sackcloth, Dn 9:3
all your heart, with f, weeping, Jl 2:12
so their f is obvious to people Mt 6:16
don't show your f to people but Mt 6:18
out except by prayer and f." Mt 17:21
and the Pharisees were f. Mk 2:18
by nothing but prayer and f." Mk 9:29
ministering to the Lord and f, Ac 13:2
every church and prayed with f, Ac 14:23

FASTINGS *(1)*

and day with f and prayers. Lk 2:37

FAT *(91)*

his flock and their f portions. Gn 4:4
The f of My festival offering Ex 23:18
Take all the f that covers the Ex 29:13
two kidneys with the f on them, Ex 29:13
Take the f from the ram, the fat Ex 29:22
from the ram, the f tail, the Ex 29:22
the f covering the entrails, Ex 29:22
two kidneys and the f on them, Ex 29:22
the f surrounding the entrails, Lv 3:3
all the f that is on the Lv 3:3
kidneys with the f on them at Lv 3:4
of⌋ its f and the entire fat Lv 3:9
its fat and the entire f tail, Lv 3:9
also remove the f surrounding Lv 3:9
all the f on the entrails, Lv 3:9
kidneys with the f on them at Lv 3:10
the f surrounding the entrails, Lv 3:14
all the f that is on the Lv 3:14
kidneys with the f on them at Lv 3:15
All f belongs to the LORD. Lv 3:16
not eat any f or any blood." Lv 3:17
remove all the f from the bull Lv 4:8
the f surrounding the entrails; Lv 4:8
all the f that is on the Lv 4:8
kidneys with the f on them at Lv 4:9
just as the f is removed from Lv 4:10
remove all the f from it and Lv 4:19
burn all its f on the altar, Lv 4:26
like the f of the fellowship Lv 4:26
remove all its f just as the fat Lv 4:31
its fat just as the f is removed Lv 4:31
remove all its f just as the fat Lv 4:35
fat just as the f of the lamb is Lv 4:35
the fire and burn the f portions Lv 6:12
must present all the f from it: Lv 7:3
the f tail, the fat surrounding Lv 7:3
the f surrounding the entrails, Lv 7:3
kidneys with the f on them at Lv 7:4
are not to eat any f of an ox, Lv 7:23
The f of an animal that dies Lv 7:24
anyone eats animal f from a fire Lv 7:25
will bring the f together with Lv 7:30
is to burn the f on the altar, Lv 7:31
offering and the f will have the Lv 7:33
Moses took all the f that was on Lv 8:16
the two kidneys with their f, Lv 8:16
took the f—the fat tail, all Lv 8:25
the fat—the f tail, all the Lv 8:25
all the f that was on the Lv 8:25
the two kidneys with their f— Lv 8:25
placed ⌊them⌋ on the f portions Lv 8:26
burned the f, the kidneys, and Lv 9:10
also brought the f portions from Lv 9:19
the ram—the f tail, the ⌊fat⌋ Lv 9:19
⌊f⌋ surrounding ⌊the entrails⌋ Lv 9:19
Aaron burned the f portions on Lv 9:20
offering and the f portions on Lv 9:24
the offerings of f portions made Lv 10:15
He is to burn the f of the sin Lv 16:25
and burn the f as a pleasing Lv 17:6
and burn their f as a fire Nm 18:17
flock, with the f of lambs, rams Dt 32:14
Jeshurun became f and rebelled— Dt 32:15
you became f, bloated, and Dt 32:15
ate the f of their sacrifices Dt 32:38
who was an extremely f man. Jdg 3:17
and Eglon's f closed in over it, Jdg 3:22
Even before the f was burned, 1Sm 2:15
The f must be burned first; 1Sm 2:16
making yourselves f with the 1Sm 2:29
is better⌋ than the f of rams. 1Sm 15:22
and the f of the fellowship 1Kg 8:64
and the f of the fellowship 1Kg 8:64
and the f of the fellowship 2Ch 7:7
and the f ⌊of the fellowship 2Ch 7:7
along with the f of the 2Ch 29:35
offerings and f until night. 2Ch 35:14
is covered with f and his Jb 15:27
and rams and the f of well-fed Is 1:11
It drips with f, with the blood Is 34:6
with the f of the kidneys of Is 34:6
soil will be saturated with f. Is 34:7
with the f of your sacrifices. Is 43:24
They have become f and sleek. Jr 5:28
eat the f, wear the wool, and Ezk 34:3
destroy the f and the strong. Ezk 34:16
judge between the f sheep and Ezk 34:20
You will eat f until you are Ezk 39:19
My food—the f and the blood. Ezk 44:7
Me to offer Me f and blood." Ezk 44:15
flesh of the f ⌊sheep⌋ and tear Zch 11:16

FATAL *(4)*

I have not longed for the f day. Jr 17:16
away from you with a f blow. Ezk 24:16
but his f wound was healed. Rv 13:3
beast, whose f wound was healed Rv 13:12

FATALLY *(2)*

and strikes him f, and flees to Dt 19:11
heads appeared to be f wounded, Rv 13:3

FATE *(13)*

suffer the f of all, then the Nm 16:29
they would understand their f. Dt 32:29
escape the f of all the Jews Est 4:13
the west are appalled at his f, Jb 18:20
knew that one f comes to them Ec 2:14
For the f of people and the fate Ec 3:19
people and the f of animals is Ec 3:19
there is one f for the righteous Ec 9:2
there is one f for everyone. Ec 9:3
This is the f of those who Is 17:14
and who considered His f? Is 53:8
cities and there suffer our f, Jr 8:14
because of ⌊the f of⌋ all the Lm 3:51

FATHER *(873)*

man leaves his f and mother and Gn 2:24
he was the f of the nomadic Gn 4:20
he was the f of all who play the Gn 4:21
Ham was the f of Canaan. Gn 9:18
Ham, the f of Canaan, saw his Gn 9:22
saw his f naked and told his two Gn 9:22
they did not see their f naked. Gn 9:23
Shem was the f of all the Gn 10:21
during his f Terah's lifetime. Gn 11:28
the f of both Milcah and Iscah. Gn 11:29
become the f of many nations Gn 17:4
make you the f of many nations. Gn 17:5
He will f 12 tribal leaders, Gn 17:20
younger, "Our f is old, and Gn 19:31
let's get our f to drink wine so Gn 19:32
they got their f to drink wine Gn 19:33
came and slept with her f; Gn 19:33
I slept with my f last night. Gn 19:34
again got their f to drink wine, Gn 19:35
became pregnant by their f. Gn 19:36
He is the f of the Moabites of Gn 19:37
He is the f of the Ammonites of Gn 19:38
the daughter of my f though not Gn 20:12
spoke to his f Abraham and said Gn 22:7
father Abraham and said, "My f." Gn 22:7
Buz, Kemuel the f of Aram, Gn 22:21
that I swore to your f Abraham. Gn 26:3
in the days of his f Abraham, Gn 26:15
the days of his f Abraham and Gn 26:18
same names his f had given them. Gn 26:18
I am the God of your f Abraham. Gn 26:24
I heard your f talking with your Gn 27:6
a delicious meal for your f— Gn 27:9
take it to your f to eat so that Gn 27:10
Suppose my f touches me. Gn 27:12
the delicious food his f loved. Gn 27:14
he came to his f, he said, "My Gn 27:18
to his father, he said, "My f." Gn 27:18
replied to his f, "I am Esau, Gn 27:19
came closer to his f Isaac. Gn 27:22
Then his f Isaac said to him, Gn 27:26
the presence of his f Isaac, Gn 27:30
food and brought it to his f. Gn 27:31
he said to his f, "Let my father Gn 27:31
Let my f get up and eat some of Gn 27:31
But his f Isaac said to him, Gn 27:32
bitter cry and said to his f, Gn 27:34
Bless me—me too, my f!" Gn 27:34

Esau said to his **f**, "Do you only Gn 27:38
only have one blessing, my **f**? Gn 27:38
Bless me—me too, my **f**!" Gn 27:38
Then his **f** Isaac answered him: Gn 27:39
blessing his **f** had given him. Gn 27:41
for my **f** are approaching Gn 27:41
of Bethuel, your mother's **f**. Gn 28:2
listened to his **f** and mother and Gn 28:7
that his **f** Isaac disapproved Gn 28:8
God of your **f** Abraham and the Gn 28:13
She ran and told her **f**. Gn 29:12
from what belonged to our **f**." Gn 31:1
the God of my **f** has been with me Gn 31:5
that I've worked hard for your **f** Gn 31:6
taken from our **f** belongs to us Gn 31:16
land of his **f** Isaac in Canaan Gn 31:18
the God of your **f** said to me: Gn 31:29
because you long for your **f**— Gn 31:30
She said to her **f**, "Sir, don't Gn 31:35
If the God of my **f**, the God of Gn 31:42
the gods of their **f**—will judge Gn 31:53
by the Fear of his **f** Isaac. Gn 31:53
God of my **f** Abraham and God of Gn 32:9
Abraham and God of my **f** Isaac, Gn 32:9
Hamor, Shechem's **f**, for 100 Gn 33:19
as a wife," he told his **f** Hamor. Gn 34:4
Shechem's **f** Hamor came to speak Gn 34:6
said to Dinah's **f** and brothers, Gn 34:11
Shechem and his **f** Hamor Gn 34:13
but his **f** called him Benjamin. Gn 35:18
came to his **f** Isaac at Mamre Gn 35:27
f of the Edomites in the Gn 36:9
the donkeys of his **f** Zibeon. Gn 36:24
Esau was **f** of the Edomites. Gn 36:43
the land where his **f** had stayed, Gn 37:1
report about them to their **f**. Gn 37:2
saw that their **f** loved him more Gn 37:4
He told his **f** and brothers, Gn 37:10
brothers, but his **f** rebuked him. Gn 37:10
but his **f** kept the matter ⌊in Gn 37:11
hands and return him to his **f**. Gn 37:22
many colors to their **f** and said, Gn 37:32
His **f** recognized it. Gn 37:33
And his **f** wept for him. Gn 37:35
The youngest is now with our **f**, Gn 42:13
reached their **f** Jacob in the Gn 42:29
12 brothers, sons of the same **f**. Gn 42:32
is now with our **f** in the land of Gn 42:32
they and their **f** saw their bags Gn 42:35
Their **f** Jacob said to them, Gn 42:36
Then Reuben said to his **f**, Gn 42:37
Egypt, their **f** said to them, "Go Gn 43:2
'Is your **f** still alive? Gn 43:7
Then Judah said to his **f** Israel, Gn 43:8
their **f** Israel said to them, Gn 43:11
the God of your **f** must have put Gn 43:23
is your elderly **f** that you told Gn 43:27
Your servant our **f** is well. Gn 43:28
you can go in peace to your **f**." Gn 44:17
'Do you have a **f** or a brother?' Gn 44:19
We have an elderly **f** and a young Gn 44:20
sons left, and his **f** loves him.' Gn 44:20
'The boy cannot leave his **f**. Gn 44:22
were to leave, his **f** would die.' Gn 44:22
went back to your servant my **f**: Gn 44:24
But our **f** said, 'Go again, and Gn 44:25
Your servant my **f** said to us, Gn 44:27
your servant my **f** and the boy is Gn 44:30
your servant our **f** down to Sheol Gn 44:31
accountable to my **f** for the boy, Gn 44:32
sinning against ⌊you,⌋ my **f**.' Gn 44:32
go back to my **f** without the boy Gn 44:34
that would overwhelm my **f**." Gn 44:34
Is my **f** still living?" Gn 45:3
He has made me a **f** to Pharaoh, Gn 45:8
to my **f** and say to him, Gn 45:9
Tell my **f** all about my glory in Gn 45:13
And bring my **f** here quickly." Gn 45:13
Get your **f** and your households, Gn 45:18
wives, and bring your **f** here. Gn 45:19
He sent his **f** the following: Gn 45:23
for his **f** on the journey. Gn 45:23
came to their **f** Jacob in the Gn 45:25
spirit of their **f** Jacob revived. Gn 45:27
to the God of his **f** Isaac. Gn 46:1
I am God, the God of your **f**. Gn 46:3
Israel took their **f** Jacob in the Gn 46:5
to Goshen to meet his **f** Israel. Gn 46:29
My **f** and my brothers, with their Gn 47:1
⌊Now that⌋ your **f** and brothers Gn 47:5
settle your **f** and brothers in Gn 47:6
then brought his **f** Jacob and Gn 47:7
settled his **f** and brothers Gn 47:11
And Joseph provided his **f**, Gn 47:12
was told, "Your **f** is weaker." Gn 48:1
And Joseph said to his **f**, Gn 48:9
saw that his **f** had placed his Gn 48:17
said to his **f**, "Not that way, my Gn 48:18
his father, "Not that way, my **f**! Gn 48:18
But his **f** refused and said, Gn 48:19
listen to your **f** Israel: Gn 49:2
the God of your **f** who helps you, Gn 49:25
blessings of your **f** excel the Gn 49:26
was what their **f** said to them. Gn 49:28
were physicians to embalm his **f**. Gn 50:2
my **f** made me take an oath, Gn 50:5
Now let me go and bury my **f**. Gn 50:5
and bury your **f** in keeping with Gn 50:6
Then Joseph went to bury his **f**, Gn 50:7
mourned seven days for his **f**. Gn 50:10
After Joseph buried his **f**, Gn 50:14
had gone with him to bury his **f**. Gn 50:14
saw that their **f** was dead, Gn 50:15
he died your **f** gave a command: Gn 50:16
servants of the God of your **f**." Gn 50:17
to their **f** Reuel he asked, Ex 2:18
am the God of your **f**, the God of Ex 3:6
The God of my **f** was my helper Ex 18:4
Honor your **f** and your mother so Ex 20:12
strikes his **f** or his mother must Ex 21:15
curses his **f** or his mother must Ex 21:17
If her **f** absolutely refuses to Ex 22:17
just as you anointed their **f**, Ex 40:15
in place of his **f** will make Lv 16:32
to shame your **f** by having sex Lv 18:7
it will shame your **f**. Lv 18:8
who is adopted by your **f**; Lv 18:11
is to respect his mother and **f**. Lv 19:3
anyone curses his **f** or mother, Lv 20:9
He has cursed his **f** or mother; Lv 20:9
wife, he has shamed his **f**. Lv 20:11
his mother, **f**, son, daughter, or Lv 21:2
promiscuity, she defiles her **f**; Lv 21:9
even⌋ for his **f** or mother. Lv 21:11
and an Egyptian **f** was among Lv 24:10
the direction of Aaron their **f**. Nm 3:4
himself for his **f** or mother, Nm 6:7
If her **f** had merely spit in her Nm 12:14
Our **f** died in the wilderness, Nm 27:3
the name of our **f** be taken away Nm 27:4
If his **f** has no brothers, give Nm 27:11
and her **f** hears about her vow or Nm 30:4
if her **f** prohibits her on the Nm 30:5
her because her **f** has prohibited Nm 30:5
or between a **f** and his daughter Nm 30:16
Honor your **f** and your mother, Dt 5:16
mourn for her **f** and mother a Dt 21:13
does not obey his **f** or mother Dt 21:18
his **f** and mother must take hold Dt 21:19
young woman's **f** and mother will Dt 22:15
The young woman's **f** will say to Dt 22:16
them⌋ to the young woman's **f**, Dt 22:19
the young woman's **f** 50 silver Dt 22:29
My **f** was a wandering Aramean. Dt 26:5
who dishonors his **f** or mother.' Dt 27:16
You will **f** sons and daughters, Dt 28:41
Isn't He your **F** and Creator? Dt 32:6
your **f**, and he will tell you, Dt 32:7
He said about his **f** and mother, Dt 33:9
will spare the lives of my **f**, Jos 2:13
Bring your **f**, mother, brothers, Jos 2:18
and brought out Rahab and her **f**, Jos 6:23
Arba was the **f** of Anak). Jos 15:13
to ask her **f** for a field. Jos 15:18
of Manasseh and the **f** of Gilead, Jos 17:1
Arba was the **f** of Anak. Jos 21:11
the **f** of Abraham and Nahor, Jos 24:2
But I took your **f** Abraham from Jos 24:3
Hamor, Shechem's **f**, for 100 Jos 24:32
to ask her **f** for a field. Jdg 1:14
belongs to your **f** and cut down Jdg 6:25
Gideon's **f** called him Jerubbaal, Jdg 6:32
tomb of his **f** Joash in Ophrah Jdg 8:32
for my **f** fought for you, risked Jdg 9:17
men of Hamor, the **f** of Shechem. Jdg 9:28
had done against his **f**, Jdg 9:56
and Gilead was his **f**. Jdg 11:1
to him, "My **f**, you have given Jdg 11:36
said to her **f**, "Let me do this Jdg 11:37
returned to her **f**, and he kept Jdg 11:39
and told his **f** and his mother: Jdg 14:2
his **f** and mother said to him, Jdg 14:3
Samson told his **f**, "Get her for Jdg 14:3
his **f** and mother did not know Jdg 14:4
to Timnah with his **f** and mother Jdg 14:5
not tell his **f** or mother what Jdg 14:6
he returned to his **f** and mother, Jdg 14:9
His **f** went ⌊to visit⌋ the woman, Jdg 14:10
explained it to my **f** or mother, Jdg 14:16
But her **f** would not let him Jdg 15:1
hated her," her **f** said, "so I Jdg 15:2
to her and her **f** and burned Jdg 15:6
in the tomb of his **f** Manoah. Jdg 16:31
with me and be my **f** and priest, Jdg 17:10
us and be a **f** and a priest to Jdg 18:19
and when the girl's **f** saw him, Jdg 19:3
the girl's **f**, detained him, and Jdg 19:4
but the girl's **f** said to his Jdg 19:5
the girl's **f** said to the man Jdg 19:6
but the girl's **f** said to him, Jdg 19:8
girl's **f**, said to him, "Look, Jdg 19:9
⌊how⌋ you left your **f** and mother, Ru 2:11
was the **f** of Jesse, the father Ru 4:17
father of Jesse, the **f** of David. Ru 4:17
would not listen to their **f**, 1Sm 2:25
of Saul's **f** Kish wandered off 1Sm 9:3
or my **f** will stop ⌊worrying⌋ 1Sm 9:5
and now your **f** has stopped being 1Sm 10:2
asked, "And who is their **f**?" 1Sm 10:12
However, he did not tell his **f**. 1Sm 14:1
not heard his **f** make the troops 1Sm 14:27
Your **f** made the troops solemnly 1Sm 14:28
My **f** has brought trouble to the 1Sm 14:29
f was Kish. Abner's father 1Sm 14:51
Abner's **f** was Ner son of Abiel. 1Sm 14:51
of that man's **f** exempt from 1Sm 17:25
My **f** Saul intends to kill you. 1Sm 19:2
stand beside my **f** in the field 1Sm 19:3
well of David to his **f** Saul. 1Sm 19:4
against your **f** so that he wants 1Sm 20:1
my **f** doesn't do anything, 1Sm 20:2
Your **f** certainly knows that you 1Sm 20:3
If your **f** misses me at all, 1Sm 20:6
why take me to your **f**?" 1Sm 20:8
I ever find out my **f** has evil 1Sm 20:9
tell me if your **f** answers you 1Sm 20:10
if I sound out my **f** by this time 1Sm 20:12
If my **f** intends to bring evil on 1Sm 20:13
you, just as He was with my **f**. 1Sm 20:13
Jonathan answered his **f** back: 1Sm 20:32
knew that his **f** was determined 1Sm 20:33
Please let my **f** and mother stay 1Sm 22:3
for my **f** Saul will never lay a 1Sm 23:17
my **f** Saul knows it is true." 1Sm 23:17
See, my **f**! Look at the corner of 1Sm 24:11
to the house of your **f** Saul, 2Sm 3:8
me over your **f** and his whole 2Sm 6:21
will be a **f** to him, and he will 2Sm 7:14
because of your **f** Jonathan. 2Sm 9:7
as his **f** showed kindness to me. 2Sm 10:2
console Hanun concerning his **f**. 2Sm 10:2
he's showing respect for your **f**? 2Sm 10:3
When your **f** comes to see you, 2Sm 13:5
have become repulsive to your **f**, 2Sm 16:21
You know your **f** and his men. 2Sm 17:8
Your **f** is an experienced soldier 2Sm 17:8
that your **f** and the valiant 2Sm 17:10
the tomb of my **f** and mother. 2Sm 19:37
in the tomb of Saul's **f** Kish. 2Sm 21:14
But his **f** had never once 1Kg 1:6
on the throne of his **f** David, 1Kg 2:12
me on the throne of my **f** David, 1Kg 2:24
presence of my **f** David and you 1Kg 2:26
through all that my **f** suffered." 1Kg 2:26
without my **f** David's knowledge. 1Kg 2:32
evil that you did to my **f** David. 1Kg 2:44
in the statutes of his **f** David, 1Kg 3:3
servant, my **f** David, because 1Kg 3:6
king in my **f** David's place. 1Kg 3:7
just as your **f** David did, 1Kg 3:14
You know my **f** David was not able 1Kg 5:3
the LORD promised my **f** David: 1Kg 5:5
which I made to your **f** David. 1Kg 6:12
and his **f** was a man of Tyre, 1Kg 7:14

things of his **f** David—	1Kg 7:51
He spoke directly to my **f** David,	1Kg 8:15
desire of my **f** David to build	1Kg 8:17
But the LORD said to my **f** David,	1Kg 8:18
taken the place of my **f** David,	1Kg 8:20
to Your servant, my **f** David.	1Kg 8:24
to Your servant, my **f** David:	1Kg 8:25
to Your servant, my **f** David.	1Kg 8:26
Me as your **f** David walked,	1Kg 9:4
as I promised your **f** David:	1Kg 9:5
as his **f** David's heart had been.	1Kg 11:4
and unlike his **f** David, he did	1Kg 11:6
because of your **f** David;	1Kg 11:12
wall of the city of his **f** David.	1Kg 11:27
My judgments as his **f** David did.	1Kg 11:33
in the city of his **f** David.	1Kg 11:43
Your **f** made our yoke harsh.	1Kg 12:4
had served his **f** Solomon when he	1Kg 12:6
the yoke your **f** put on us'?"	1Kg 12:9
'Your **f** made our yoke heavy,	1Kg 12:10
Although my **f** burdened you with	1Kg 12:11
my **f** disciplined you with whips,	1Kg 12:11
My **f** made your yoke heavy,	1Kg 12:14
my **f** disciplined you with whips,	1Kg 12:14
also told their **f** the words that	1Kg 13:11
Then their **f** said to them,	1Kg 13:12
the sins his **f** had done before	1Kg 15:3
between my **f** and your father.	1Kg 15:19
between my father and your **f**.	1Kg 15:19
example of his **f** and the sin he	1Kg 15:26
let me kiss my **f** and mother,	1Kg 19:20
cities that my **f** took from your	1Kg 20:34
took from your **f** I restore to	1Kg 20:34
like my **f** set up in Samaria."	1Kg 20:34
in all the ways of his **f** Asa;	1Kg 22:43
left from the days of his **f** Asa.	1Kg 22:46
He walked in the way of his **f**,	1Kg 22:52
Israel just as his **f** had done.	1Kg 22:53
crying out, "My **f**, my father,	2Kg 2:12
My father, my **f**, the chariots	2Kg 2:12
but not like his **f** and mother,	2Kg 3:2
pillar of Baal his **f** had made.	2Kg 3:2
of your **f** and your mother!	2Kg 3:13
went out to his **f** and the	2Kg 4:18
complained to his **f**, "My head!	2Kg 4:19
His **f** told his servant,	2Kg 4:19
to him, "My **f**, if the prophet	2Kg 5:13
to Elisha, "My **f**, should I kill	2Kg 6:21
king of Judah, replacing his **f**.	2Kg 8:16
side by side behind his **f** Ahab,	2Kg 9:25
him and said, "My **f**, my father,	2Kg 13:14
My father, my **f**, the chariots	2Kg 13:14
war from Jehoash's **f** Jehoahaz.	2Kg 13:25
everything his **f** Joash had done.	2Kg 14:3
who had murdered his **f** the king.	2Kg 14:5
king in place of his **f** Amaziah.	2Kg 14:21
just as his **f** Amaziah had done	2Kg 15:3
just as his **f** Uzziah had done.	2Kg 15:34
places that his **f** Hezekiah had	2Kg 21:3
sight as his **f** Manasseh had done	2Kg 21:20
all the ways his **f** had walked;	2Kg 21:21
the idols his **f** had served,	2Kg 21:21
made him king in place of his **f**.	2Kg 23:30
in place of his **f** Josiah and	2Kg 23:34
LORD's sight as his **f** had done.	2Kg 24:9
and his **f** was Jether the	1Ch 2:17
of Machir the **f** of Gilead.	1Ch 2:21
the sons of Machir **f** of Gilead.	1Ch 2:23
bore him Ashhur the **f** of Tekoa.	1Ch 2:24
Madmannah's **f**, and of Sheva,	1Ch 2:49
the **f** of Machbenah and Gibea.	1Ch 2:49
of Shobal the **f** of	1Ch 2:52
from Hammath, the **f** of Rechab's	1Ch 2:55
and the **f** of Bethlehem:	1Ch 4:4
Mehir, who was the **f** of Eshton.	1Ch 4:11
and Tehinnah the **f** of Irnahash.	1Ch 4:12
and Ishbah the **f** of Eshtemoa.	1Ch 4:17
birth to Jered the **f** of Gedor,	1Ch 4:18
of Gedor, Heber the **f** of Soco,	1Ch 4:18
and Jekuthiel the **f** of Zanoah.	1Ch 4:18
the **f** of Keilah the Garmite and	1Ch 4:19
Garmite and ⌊the **f** of⌋ Eshtemoa	1Ch 4:19
Er the **f** of Lecah, Laadah the	1Ch 4:21
Lecah, Laadah the **f** of Mareshah,	1Ch 4:21
and Machir the **f** of Gilead.	1Ch 7:14
Their **f** Ephraim mourned a long	1Ch 7:22
them and was the **f** of Uzza and	1Ch 8:7
and he became the **f** of more sons	1Ch 14:3
will be a **f** to him, and he will	1Ch 17:13
his **f** showed kindness to me.	1Ch 19:2
to console him concerning his **f**.	1Ch 19:2
he's showing respect for your **f**?	1Ch 19:3
be My son, and I will be his **f**.	1Ch 22:10
and Abihu died before their **f**,	1Ch 24:2
authority of their **f** Jeduthun,	1Ch 25:3
f had appointed him as the first	1Ch 26:10
be My son, and I will be his **f**.	1Ch 28:6
the God of your **f**, and serve Him	1Ch 28:9
LORD God of our **f** Israel, from	1Ch 29:10
as king in place of his **f** David.	1Ch 29:23
faithful love to my **f** David,	2Ch 1:8
promise to my **f** David now come	2Ch 1:9
me⌋ what you did for my **f** David.	2Ch 2:3
appointed by my **f** David.	2Ch 2:7
His **f** is a man of Tyre.	2Ch 2:14
of my lord, your **f** David.	2Ch 2:14
census that his **f** David had	2Ch 2:17
had appeared to his **f** David,	2Ch 3:1
things of his **f** David—	2Ch 5:1
He spoke directly to my **f** David,	2Ch 6:4
the heart of my **f** David to build	2Ch 6:7
the LORD said to my **f** David,	2Ch 6:8
place of my **f** David and I sit	2Ch 6:10
to Your servant, my **f** David.	2Ch 6:15
to Your servant, my **f** David:	2Ch 6:16
Me as your **f** David walked,	2Ch 7:17
as I promised your **f** David:	2Ch 7:18
the ordinances of his **f** David,	2Ch 8:14
in the city of his **f** David.	2Ch 9:31
Your **f** made our yoke harsh.	2Ch 10:4
had served his **f** Solomon when he	2Ch 10:6
the yoke your **f** put on us'?"	2Ch 10:9
'Your **f** made our yoke heavy,	2Ch 10:10
my **f** burdened you with a heavy	2Ch 10:11
my **f** disciplined you with whips,	2Ch 10:11
My **f** made your yoke heavy,	2Ch 10:14
my **f** disciplined you with whips,	2Ch 10:14
and was the **f** of 28 sons and 60	2Ch 11:21
between my **f** and your father.	2Ch 16:3
between my father and your **f**.	2Ch 16:3
that his **f** Asa had captured	2Ch 17:2
the former ways of his **f** David.	2Ch 17:3
the God of his **f** and walked by	2Ch 17:4
walked in the way of Asa his **f**;	2Ch 20:32
f had given them many gifts	2Ch 21:3
the ways of your **f** Jehoshaphat	2Ch 21:12
after the death of his **f**,	2Ch 22:4
and he was the **f** of sons and	2Ch 24:3
that Zechariah's **f** Jehoiada had	2Ch 24:22
who had murdered his **f** the king.	2Ch 25:3
king in place of his **f** Amaziah.	2Ch 26:1
sight as his **f** Amaziah had done.	2Ch 26:4
sight as his **f** Uzziah had done,	2Ch 27:2
places that his **f** Hezekiah had	2Ch 33:3
just as his **f** Manasseh had done	2Ch 33:22
images that his **f** Manasseh had	2Ch 33:22
like his **f** Manasseh humbled	2Ch 33:23
in Jerusalem in place of his **f**.	2Ch 36:1
she didn't have a **f** or mother.	Est 2:7
When her **f** and mother died,	Est 2:7
with us, men older than your **f**.	Jb 15:10
You are my **f**, and to the worm:	Jb 17:14
I was a **f** to the needy, and I	Jb 29:16
him as ⌊his⌋ **f**, and since the	Jb 31:18
Does the rain have a **f**?	Jb 38:28
and their **f** granted them an	Jb 42:15
today I have become Your **F**.	Ps 2:7
Even if my **f** and mother abandon	Ps 27:10
A **f** of the fatherless and a	Ps 68:5
Me, 'You are my **F**, my God, the	Ps 89:26
As a **f** has compassion on his	Ps 103:13
loves, just as a **f**, the son he	Pr 3:12
When I was a son with my **f**,	Pr 4:3
A wise son brings joy to his **f**,	Pr 10:1
A wise son brings joy to his **f**,	Pr 15:20
the **f** of a fool has no joy.	Pr 17:21
is grief to his **f** and bitterness	Pr 17:25
assaults his **f** and evicts his	Pr 19:26
Whoever curses his **f** or mother—	Pr 20:20
Listen to your **f** who gave you	Pr 23:22
The **f** of a righteous son will	Pr 23:24
Let your **f** and mother have joy,	Pr 23:25
of gluttons humiliates his **f**.	Pr 28:7
one who robs his **f** or mother and	Pr 28:24
wisdom brings joy to his **f**,	Pr 29:3
that curses its **f** and does not	Pr 30:11
that ridicules a **f** and despises	Pr 30:17
A man may **f** a hundred children	Ec 6:3
house of your **f**, such a time as	Is 7:17
how to call out **f** or mother,	Is 8:4
God, Eternal **F**, Prince of Peace.	Is 9:6
he will be like a **f** to the	Is 22:21
a **f** will make Your faithfulness	Is 38:19
Your first **f** sinned, and your	Is 43:27
is the one who says to ⌊his⌋ **f**:	Is 45:10
to Abraham your **f**, and to Sarah	Is 51:2
the heritage of your **f** Jacob."	Is 58:14
Yet You are our **F**, even though	Is 63:16
You, LORD, are our **F**;	Is 63:16
Yet LORD, You are our **F**;	Is 64:8
You are my **f**, and to a stone:	Jr 2:27
My **F**, my youthful companion?	Jr 3:4
call Me, my **F**, and never turn	Jr 3:19
the fathers who **f** them in this	Jr 16:3
⌊the loss of⌋ his **f** or mother.	Jr 16:7
who brought the news to my **f**,	Jr 20:15
succeeded Josiah his **f** as king:	Jr 22:11
Your own **f**, did he not eat and	Jr 22:15
I am Israel's **F**, and Ephraim is	Jr 31:9
Your **f** was an Amorite and your	Ezk 16:3
a Hittite and your **f** an Amorite.	Ezk 16:45
The life of the **f** is like the	Ezk 18:4
though the **f** has done none of	Ezk 18:11
the sins his **f** has committed,	Ezk 18:14
As for his **f**, he will die for	Ezk 18:18
and a **f** won't suffer punishment	Ezk 18:20
F and mother are treated with	Ezk 22:7
he may defile himself for a **f**,	Ezk 44:25
entourage, her **f**, and the one	Dn 11:6
A man and his **f** have sexual	Am 2:7
a son considers his **f** a fool,	Mc 7:6
f and his mother who bore him	Zch 13:3
f and his mother who bore him	Zch 13:3
honors ⌊his⌋ **f**, and a servant	Mal 1:6
But if I am a **f**, where is My	Mal 1:6
Don't all of us have one **F**?	Mal 2:10
Judea in place of his **f** Herod,	Mt 2:22
'We have Abraham as our **f**.'	Mt 3:9
in a boat with Zebedee their **f**,	Mt 4:21
boat and their **f** and followed	Mt 4:22
give glory to your **F** in heaven.	Mt 5:16
may be sons of your **F** in heaven.	Mt 5:45
as your heavenly **F** is perfect.	Mt 5:48
no reward from your **F** in heaven.	Mt 6:1
And your **F** who sees in secret	Mt 6:4
pray to your **F** who is in secret	Mt 6:6
And your **F** who sees in secret	Mt 6:6
because your **F** knows the things	Mt 6:8
Our **F** in heaven, Your name be	Mt 6:9
your heavenly **F** will forgive you	Mt 6:14
your **F** will not forgive your	Mt 6:15
but to your **F** who is in secret.	Mt 6:18
And your **F** who sees in secret	Mt 6:18
yet your heavenly **F** feeds them.	Mt 6:26
your heavenly **F** knows that you	Mt 6:32
more will your **F** in heaven give	Mt 7:11
does the will of My **F** in heaven.	Mt 7:21
"first let me go bury my **f**."	Mt 8:21
the Spirit of your **F** is speaking	Mt 10:20
to death, and a **f** his child.	Mt 10:21
him before My **F** in heaven.	Mt 10:32
deny him before My **F** in heaven.	Mt 10:33
to turn a man against his **f**,	Mt 10:35
person who loves **f** or mother	Mt 10:37
I praise You, **F**, Lord of heaven	Mt 11:25
Yes, **F**, because this was Your	Mt 11:26
been entrusted to Me by My **F**.	Mt 11:27
one knows the Son except the **F**,	Mt 11:27
one knows the **F** except the Son	Mt 11:27
does the will of My **F** in heaven,	Mt 12:50
Honor your **f** and your mother;	Mt 15:4
speaks evil of **f** or mother must	Mt 15:4
Whoever tells his **f** or mother,	Mt 15:5
does not have to honor his **f**.'	Mt 15:6
that My heavenly **F** didn't plant	Mt 15:13
this to you, but My **F** in heaven.	Mt 16:17
angels in the glory of His **F**,	Mt 16:27
view the face of My **F** in heaven.	Mt 18:10
will of your **F** in heaven that	Mt 18:14
done for you by My **F** in heaven.	Mt 18:19
So My heavenly **F** will also do to	Mt 18:35
will leave his **f** and mother and	Mt 19:5
honor your **f** and your mother;	Mt 19:19
or sisters, **f** or mother,	Mt 19:29

it has been prepared by My **F**." Mt 20:23
not call anyone on earth your **f**, Mt 23:9
have one **F**, who is in heaven. Mt 23:9
nor the Son—except the **F** only. Mt 24:36
you who are blessed by My **F**, Mt 25:34
fell facedown and prayed, "My **F**! Mt 26:39
prayed, "My **F**, if this cannot Mt 26:42
that I cannot call on My **F**, Mt 26:53
the name of the **F** and of the Son Mt 28:19
they left their **f** Zebedee in the Mk 1:20
took the child's **f**, mother, and Mk 5:40
Honor your **f** and your mother; Mk 7:10
speaks evil of **f** or mother must Mk 7:10
'If a man tells his **f** or mother: Mk 7:11
do anything for his **f** or mother. Mk 7:12
the glory of His **F** with the holy Mk 8:38
Jesus asked his **f**. Mk 9:21
Immediately the **f** of the boy Mk 9:24
will leave his **f** and mother and Mk 10:7
honor your **f** and mother." Mk 10:19
sisters, mother or **f**, children, Mk 10:29
coming kingdom of our **f** David! Mk 11:10
so that your **F** in heaven will Mk 11:25
will your **F** in heaven forgive Mk 11:26
to death, and a **f** his child. Mk 13:12
nor the Son—except the **F**. Mk 13:32
And He said, "Abba, **F**! Mk 14:36
the **f** of Alexander and Rufus. Mk 15:21
Him the throne of His **f** David. Lk 1:32
name him Zechariah, after his **f**. Lk 1:59
motioned to his **f** to find out Lk 1:62
Then his **f** Zechariah was filled Lk 1:67
that He swore to our **f** Abraham. Lk 1:73
His **f** and mother were amazed at Lk 2:33
Your **f** and I have been anxiously Lk 2:48
'We have Abraham as our **f**,' Lk 3:8
just as your **F** also is merciful. Lk 6:36
and the child's **f** and mother. Lk 8:51
and that of the **F** and the holy Lk 9:26
and gave him back to his **f**. Lk 9:42
"first let me go bury my **f**." Lk 9:59
I praise You, **F**, Lord of heaven Lk 10:21
Yes, **F**, because this was Your Lk 10:21
been entrusted to Me by My **F**. Lk 10:22
who the Son is except the **F**, Lk 10:22
and who the **F** is except the Son, Lk 10:22
F, Your name be honored as holy. Lk 11:2
f among you, if his son asks Lk 11:11
the heavenly **F** give the Holy Lk 11:13
and your **F** knows that you need Lk 12:30
because your **F** delights to give Lk 12:32
be divided, **f** against son, son Lk 12:53
son against **f**, mother against Lk 12:53
not hate his own **f** and mother, Lk 14:26
younger of them said to his **f**, Lk 15:12
to his father, '**F**, give me the Lk 15:12
up, go to my **f**, and say to him Lk 15:18
and say to him, **F**, I have sinned Lk 15:18
So he got up and went to his **f**. Lk 15:20
f saw him and was filled with Lk 15:20
said to him, '**F**, I have sinned Lk 15:21
But the **f** told his slaves, Lk 15:22
'and your **f** has slaughtered the Lk 15:27
So his **f** came out and pleaded Lk 15:28
replied to his **f**, 'Look, I have Lk 15:29
'**F** Abraham!' he called out, Lk 16:24
'**F**,' he said, 'then I beg you Lk 16:27
'No, **f** Abraham,' he said. Lk 16:30
honor your **f** and mother." Lk 18:20
just as My **F** bestowed one on Me, Lk 22:29
F, if You are willing, take this Lk 22:42
Jesus said, "**F**, forgive them, Lk 23:34
loud voice, "**F**, into Your hands Lk 23:46
sending you what My **F** promised. Lk 24:49
the One and Only Son from the **F**, Jn 1:14
F loves the Son and has given Jn 3:35
aren't greater than our **f** Jacob, Jn 4:12
worship the **F** neither on this Jn 4:21
will worship the **F** in spirit and Jn 4:23
the **F** wants such people to Jn 4:23
The **f** realized this was the very Jn 4:53
to them, "My **F** is still working, Jn 5:17
was even calling God His own **F**, Jn 5:18
only what He sees the **F** doing. Jn 5:19
For whatever the **F** does, the Son Jn 5:19
the **F** loves the Son and shows Jn 5:20
just as the **F** raises the dead Jn 5:21
F, in fact, judges no one but Jn 5:22
Son just as they honor the **F**. Jn 5:23
not honor the **F** who sent Him. Jn 5:23
For just as the **F** has life in Jn 5:26
works that the **F** has given Me to Jn 5:36
about Me that the **F** has sent Me. Jn 5:36
The **F** who sent Me has Himself Jn 5:37
that I will accuse you to the **F**. Jn 5:45
because God the **F** has set His Jn 6:27
My **F** gives you the real bread Jn 6:32
Everyone the **F** gives Me will Jn 6:37
For this is the will of My **F**: Jn 6:40
whose **f** and mother we know? Jn 6:42
to Me unless the **F** who sent Me Jn 6:44
learned from the **F** comes to Me— Jn 6:45
has seen the **F** except the One Jn 6:46
is from God. He has seen the **F**. Jn 6:46
as the living **F** sent Me and I Jn 6:57
Me and I live because of the **F**, Jn 6:57
it is granted to him by the **F**." Jn 6:65
but I and the **F** who sent Me Jn 8:16
and the **F** who sent Me testifies Jn 8:18
asked Him, "Where is Your **F**?" Jn 8:19
"You know neither Me nor My **F**," Jn 8:19
you would also know My **F**." Jn 8:19
speaking to them about the **F**. Jn 8:27
But just as the **F** taught Me, Jn 8:28
seen in the presence of the **F**, Jn 8:38
you have heard from your **f**." Jn 8:38
"Our **f** is Abraham!" they replied. Jn 8:39
You're doing what your **f** does." Jn 8:41
"We have one **F**—God." Jn 8:41
God were your **F**, you would love Jn 8:42
You are of your **f** the Devil, Jn 8:44
he is a liar and the **f** of liars. Jn 8:44
honor My **F** and you dishonor Me. Jn 8:49
than our **f** Abraham who died Jn 8:53
My **F**—you say about Him, 'He is Jn 8:54
f Abraham was overjoyed that Jn 8:56
the **F** knows Me, and I know the Jn 10:15
knows Me, and I know the **F**. Jn 10:15
This is why the **F** loves Me, Jn 10:17
this command from My **F**." Jn 10:18
My **F**, who has given them to Me, Jn 10:29
The **F** and I are one." Jn 10:30
you many good works from the **F**. Jn 10:32
to the One the **F** set apart and Jn 10:36
that the **F** is in Me and I Jn 10:38
Father is in Me and I in the **F**." Jn 10:38
eyes and said, "**F**, I thank You Jn 11:41
serves Me, the **F** will honor him. Jn 12:26
should I say—**F**, save Me from Jn 12:27
F, glorify Your name!" Jn 12:28
the **F** Himself who sent Me has Jn 12:49
just as the **F** has told Me." Jn 12:50
depart from this world to the **F**. Jn 13:1
Jesus knew that the **F** had given Jn 13:3
comes to the **F** except through Jn 14:6
Me, you will also know My **F**. Jn 14:7
show us the **F**, and that's enough Jn 14:8
who has seen Me has seen the **F**. Jn 14:9
can you say, 'Show us the **F**'? Jn 14:9
I am in the **F** and the Father Jn 14:10
the Father and the **F** is in Me? Jn 14:10
The **F** who lives in Me does His Jn 14:10
I am in the **F** and the Father Jn 14:11
the Father and the **F** is in Me. Jn 14:11
because I am going to the **F**. Jn 14:12
it so that the **F** may be Jn 14:13
I will ask the **F**, and He will Jn 14:16
you will know that I am in My **F**, Jn 14:20
loves Me will be loved by My **F**. Jn 14:21
My **F** will love him, and We will Jn 14:23
but is from the **F** who sent Me. Jn 14:24
the **F** will send Him in My name— Jn 14:26
that I am going to the **F**, Jn 14:28
because the **F** is greater than I. Jn 14:28
may know that I love the **F**. Jn 14:31
Just as the **F** commanded Me, Jn 14:31
and My **F** is the vineyard keeper. Jn 15:1
My **F** is glorified by this: Jn 15:8
As the **F** has loved me, I have Jn 15:9
I have heard from My **F**. Jn 15:15
you ask the **F** in My name, Jn 15:16
who hates Me also hates My **F**. Jn 15:23
seen and hated both Me and My **F**. Jn 15:24
I will send to you from the **F**— Jn 15:26
truth who proceeds from the **F**— Jn 15:26
they haven't known the **F** or Me. Jn 16:3
going to the **F** and you will no Jn 16:10
Everything the **F** has is Mine. Jn 16:15
'because I am going to the **F**'?" Jn 16:17
you ask the **F** in My name, Jn 16:23
tell you plainly about the **F**. Jn 16:25
to the **F** on your behalf. Jn 16:26
For the **F** Himself loves you, Jn 16:27
I came from the **F** and have come Jn 16:28
the world and going to the **F**." Jn 16:28
alone, because the **F** is with Me. Jn 16:32
F, the hour has come. Jn 17:1
Now, **F**, glorify Me in Your Jn 17:5
F, protect them by Your name Jn 17:11
be one, as You, **F**, are in Me and Jn 17:21
F, I desire those You have given Jn 17:24
Righteous **F**! The world has not Jn 17:25
the cup the **F** has given Me?" Jn 18:11
have not yet ascended to the **F**. Jn 20:17
ascending to My **F** and your Jn 20:17
to My Father and your **F**— Jn 20:17
the **F** has sent Me, I also send Jn 20:21
periods that the **F** has set by Ac 1:7
from the **F** the promised Holy Ac 2:33
the mouth of our **f** David Your Ac 4:25
appeared to our **f** Abraham when Ac 7:2
there, after his **f** died, God had Ac 7:4
then invited his **f** Jacob and all Ac 7:14
today I have become Your **F**. Ac 13:33
woman, but his **f** was a Greek. Ac 16:1
all knew that his **f** was a Greek. Ac 16:3
that Publius' **f** was in bed Ac 28:8
from God our **F** and the Lord Rm 1:7
to make him the **f** of all who Rm 4:11
And he became the **f** of the Rm 4:12
of the faith our **f** Abraham had Rm 4:12
He is the **f** of us all Rm 4:16
made you the **f** of many nations. Rm 4:17
he became the **f** of many nations, Rm 4:18
the dead by the glory of the **F**, Rm 6:4
by whom we cry out, "Abba, **F**!" Rm 8:15
the God and **F** of our Lord Jesus Rm 15:6
from God our **F** and the Lord 1Co 1:3
is one God, the **F**, from whom are 1Co 8:6
over the kingdom to God the **F**, 1Co 15:24
from God our **F** and the Lord 2Co 1:2
be the God and **F** of our Lord 2Co 1:3
the **F** of mercies and the God of 2Co 1:3
I will be a **F** to you, and you 2Co 6:18
the God and **F** of the Lord Jesus, 2Co 11:31
and God the **F** who raised Him Gl 1:1
from God the **F** and our Lord Gl 1:3
to the will of our God and **F**, Gl 1:4
until the time set by his **f**. Gl 4:2
our hearts, crying, "Abba , **F**!" Gl 4:6
from God our **F** and the Lord Eph 1:2
be the God and **F** of our Lord Eph 1:3
the glorious **F**, would give you Eph 1:17
access by one Spirit to the **F**. Eph 2:18
I bow my knees before the **F** Eph 3:14
one God and **F** of all, who is Eph 4:6
to God the **F** in the name of our Eph 5:20
will leave his **f** and mother and Eph 5:31
Honor your **f** and mother—which Eph 6:2
God the **F** and the Lord Jesus Eph 6:23
from God our **F** and the Lord Php 1:2
to the glory of God the **F**. Php 2:11
ministry like a son with a **f**. Php 2:22
our God and **F** be glory forever Php 4:20
to you and peace from God our **F**. Col 1:2
the **F** of our Lord Jesus Christ, Col 1:3
thanks to the **F**, who has enabled Col 1:12
thanks to God the **F** through Him. Col 3:17
in God the **F** and the Lord Jesus 1Th 1:1
the presence of our God and **F**, 1Th 1:3
like a **f** with his own children, 1Th 2:11
Now may our God and **F** Himself, 1Th 3:11
our God and **F** at the coming 1Th 3:13
in God our **F** and the Lord Jesus 2Th 1:1
from God our **F** and the Lord 2Th 1:2
Christ Himself and God our **F**, 2Th 2:16
from God the **F** and Christ Jesus 1Tm 1:2
exhort him as a **f**, younger men 1Tm 5:1
from God the **F** and Christ Jesus 2Tm 1:2
from God the **F** and Christ Jesus Ti 1:4
from God our **F** and the Lord Phm 3
today I have become Your **F**, Heb 1:5
I will be His **F**, and He will be Heb 1:5
are sanctified all have one **F**. Heb 2:11

today I have become Your F, Heb 5:5
without f, mother, or genealogy, Heb 7:3
is there whom a f does not Heb 12:7
even more to the F of spirits Heb 12:9
down from the F of lights; Jms 1:17
before our God and F is this: Jms 1:27
Abraham our f justified by works Jms 2:21
With it we bless our Lord and F, Jms 3:9
of God the F and set apart 1Pt 1:2
be the God and F of our Lord 1Pt 1:3
if you address as F the One who 1Pt 1:17
honor and glory from God the F, 2Pt 1:17
was with the F and was revealed 1Jn 1:2
is with the F and with His Son 1Jn 1:3
we have an advocate with the F— 1Jn 2:1
you have come to know the F. 1Jn 2:14
love for the F is not in him. 1Jn 2:15
is not from the F, but is from 1Jn 2:16
who denies the F and the Son. 1Jn 2:22
denies the Son can have the F; 1Jn 2:23
the Son has the F as well. 1Jn 2:23
remain in the Son and in the F. 1Jn 2:24
great a love the F has given us, 1Jn 3:1
that the F has sent the Son 1Jn 4:14
us from God the F and from Jesus 2Jn 3
the Son of the F, in truth and 2Jn 3
we have received from the F. 2Jn 4
one has both the F and the Son. 2Jn 9
loved by God the F and kept by Jd 1
priests to His God and F— Rv 1:6
have received ⌊this⌋ from My F. Rv 2:27
name before My F and before His Rv 3:5
down with My F on His throne. Rv 3:21

FATHER'S *(159)*

they covered their f nakedness. Gn 9:23
your f house to the land that Gn 12:1
him and preserve our f line." Gn 19:32
and we can preserve our f line." Gn 19:34
had me wander from my f house, Gn 20:13
took me from my f house and from Gn 24:7
room in your f house for us to Gn 24:23
will go to my f household and to Gn 24:38
family and from my f household. Gn 24:40
wells that his f slaves had dug Gn 26:15
When Esau heard his f words, Gn 27:34
I return safely to my f house, Gn 28:21
Rachel came with her f sheep, Gn 29:9
that he was her f relative, Gn 29:12
all that was our f and has built Gn 31:1
see from your f face that his Gn 31:5
has taken your f herds and given Gn 31:9
inheritance in our f household? Gn 31:14
stole her f household idols Gn 31:19
important in all his f house. Gn 34:19
slept with his f concubine Gn 35:22
and Zilpah, his f wives, and he Gn 37:2
to pasture their f flocks at Gn 37:12
a widow in your f house until my Gn 38:11
went to live in her f house. Gn 38:11
all my hardship in my f house." Gn 41:51
brothers and to his f household, Gn 46:31
My brothers and my f household, Gn 46:31
all his f household with food Gn 47:12
from his ⌊f⌋ knees and bowed Gn 48:12
and took his f hand to move it Gn 48:17
you got into your f bed and you Gn 49:4
f sons will bow down to you. Gn 49:8
leaning over his f face, wept Gn 50:1
brothers, and his f household. Gn 50:8
Joseph and his f household Gn 50:22
troughs to water their f flock. Ex 2:16
married his f sister Jochebed, Ex 6:20
praise Him, my f God, and I will Ex 15:2
to have sex with your f wife; Lv 18:8
either your f daughter or your Lv 18:9
with your f wife's daughter, Lv 18:11
intercourse with your f sister; Lv 18:12
she is your f close relative. Lv 18:12
to shame your f brother by Lv 18:14
If a man sleeps with his f wife, Lv 20:11
whether his f daughter or his Lv 20:17
sister or your f sister, Lv 20:19
returns to her f house as in her Lv 22:13
youth, she may share her f food. Lv 22:13
property among our f brothers." Nm 27:4
property among their f brothers Nm 27:7
transfer their f inheritance to Nm 27:7
inheritance to his f brothers. Nm 27:10
woman in her f house during her Nm 30:3
married cousins on their f side. Nm 36:11
the tribe of their f clan. Nm 36:12
to the door of her f house, Dt 22:21
promiscuous in her f house. Dt 22:21
man is not to marry his f wife; Dt 22:30
not violate his f marriage bed. Dt 22:30
one who sleeps with his f wife, Dt 27:20
violated his f marriage bed.' Dt 27:20
whether his f daughter or his Dt 27:22
and all your f family into your Jos 2:18
prostitute, her f household, and Jos 6:25
among their f brothers, Jos 17:4
am the youngest in my f house." Jdg 6:15
Take your f young bull and a Jdg 6:25
afraid of his f household and Jdg 6:27
He went to his f house in Ophrah Jdg 9:5
have attacked my f house today, Jdg 9:18
no inheritance in our f house, Jdg 11:2
me and drive me from my f house? Jdg 11:7
burn you and your f household to Jdg 14:15
Samson returned to his f house, Jdg 14:19
and his f family came down Jdg 16:31
left him for her f house in Jdg 19:2
she brought him to her f house, Jdg 19:3
but you and all your f family?" 1Sm 9:20
Saul to tend his f flock in 1Sm 17:15
has been tending his f sheep. 1Sm 17:34
let him return to his f house. 1Sm 18:2
my family or my f clan in Israel 1Sm 18:18
because of his f shameful 1Sm 20:34
brothers and his f whole family 1Sm 22:1
Ahitub, and his f whole family, 1Sm 22:11
or any of my f household, 1Sm 22:15
you and your f whole family!" 1Sm 22:16
of everyone in your f family. 1Sm 22:22
out my name from my f family." 1Sm 24:21
to his f tomb in Bethlehem 2Sm 2:32
you sleep with my f concubine?" 2Sm 3:7
head and his f whole house, 2Sm 3:29
blame be on me and my f house, 2Sm 14:9
I was your f servant, but now I 2Sm 15:34
restore my f kingdom to me.' 2Sm 16:3
As I served in your f presence, 2Sm 16:19
Sleep with your f concubines he 2Sm 16:21
he slept with his f concubines 2Sm 16:22
and was buried in his f tomb. 2Sm 17:23
be against me and my f family." 2Sm 24:17
me and from my f house the blood 1Kg 2:31
anointed king in his f place, 1Kg 5:1
Edomites from his f servants. 1Kg 11:17
lighten your f harsh service and 1Kg 12:4
is thicker than my f loins! 1Kg 12:10
He brought his f consecrated 1Kg 15:15
but you and your f house have, 1Kg 18:18
set him on his f throne, and 2Kg 10:3
Reuben defiled his f bed. 1Ch 5:1
me and against my f family, 1Ch 21:17
out of all my f household to be 1Ch 28:4
house of Judah, my f household, 1Ch 28:4
and from my f sons, He was 1Ch 28:4
lighten your f harsh service and 2Ch 10:4
is thicker than my f loins. 2Ch 10:10
He brought his f consecrated 2Ch 15:18
himself over his f kingdom, 2Ch 21:4
brothers, your f family, who 2Ch 21:13
Both I and my f house have Neh 1:6
but you and your f house will be Est 4:14
your people and your f house, Ps 45:10
my son, to your f instruction, Pr 1:8
my⌋ sons, to a f discipline, and Pr 4:1
My son, keep your f command, and Pr 6:20
son ⌊hears his⌋ f instruction, Pr 13:1
fool despises his f instruction, Pr 15:5
A foolish son is his f ruin, Pr 19:13
your friend or your f friend, Pr 27:10
his brother in his f house, Is 3:6
throne of honor for his f house. Is 22:23
the whole burden of his f house: Is 22:24
your own f household—even Jr 12:6
will not die for his f iniquity. Ezk 18:17
punishment for the f iniquity? Ezk 18:19
punishment for the f iniquity, Ezk 18:20
intercourse with ⌊their⌋ f wife, Ezk 22:10
his sister, his f daughter. Ezk 22:11
ground without your F consent. Mt 10:29
like the sun in their F kingdom. Mt 13:43
of the two did his f will?" Mt 21:31
way in My F kingdom with you. Mt 26:29
that I had to be in my F house?" Lk 2:49
'How many of my f hired hands Lk 15:17
you to send him to my f house— Lk 16:27
the One who is at the F side— Jn 1:18
Stop turning My F house into a Jn 2:16
have come in My F name, yet you Jn 5:43
to carry out your f desires. Jn 8:44
that I do in My F name testify Jn 10:25
snatch them out of the F hand. Jn 10:29
If I am not doing My F works, Jn 10:37
In My F house are many dwelling Jn 14:2
as I have kept My F commands and Jn 15:10
but to wait for the F promise. Ac 1:4
nursed in his f home three Ac 7:20
a man is living with his f wife. 1Co 5:1
His name and His F name written Rv 14:1

FATHER-IN-LAW *(26)*

Your f is going up to Timnah to Gn 38:13
she sent her f ⌊this message⌋: Gn 38:25
the flock of his f Jethro, Ex 3:1
back to his f Jethro and said Ex 4:18
Moses' f Jethro, the priest of Ex 18:1
Now Jethro, Moses' f, had taken Ex 18:2
f Jethro, along with Moses' Ex 18:5
Moses, "I, your f Jethro, am Ex 18:6
So Moses went out to meet his f, Ex 18:7
recounted to his f all that the Ex 18:8
Jethro, Moses' f, brought a Ex 18:12
meal with Moses' f in God's Ex 18:12
When Moses' f saw everything he Ex 18:14
replied to his f, "Because the Ex 18:15
not good," Moses' f said to him. Ex 18:17
listened to his f and did Ex 18:24
Moses said goodbye to his f, Ex 18:27
son of Moses' f Reuel the Nm 10:29
Kenite, Moses' f, had gone up Jdg 1:16
Hobab, Moses' f, and pitched his Jdg 4:11
His f, the girl's father, Jdg 19:4
to go, but his f persuaded him, Jdg 19:7
servant, when his f, the girl's Jdg 19:9
deaths of her f and her husband 1Sm 4:19
of⌋ her f and her husband. 1Sm 4:21
for he was the f of Caiaphas, Jn 18:13

FATHERED *(215)*

to Enoch, Irad f Mehujael, Gn 4:18
Mehujael, Mehujael f Methushael, Gn 4:18
and Methushael f Lamech. Gn 4:18
old when he f ⌊a child⌋ in his Gn 5:3
and he f sons and daughters. Gn 5:4
105 years old when he f Enosh. Gn 5:6
and he f sons and daughters. Gn 5:7
90 years old when he f Kenan. Gn 5:9
and he f sons and daughters. Gn 5:10
years old when he f Mahalalel. Gn 5:12
and he f sons and daughters. Gn 5:13
65 years old when he f Jared. Gn 5:15
and he f sons and daughters. Gn 5:16
162 years old when he f Enoch. Gn 5:18
and he f sons and daughters. Gn 5:19
years old when he f Methuselah. Gn 5:21
God 300 years and f sons and Gn 5:22
187 years old when he f Lamech. Gn 5:25
and he f sons and daughters. Gn 5:26
182 years old when he f a son. Gn 5:28
and he f sons and daughters. Gn 5:30
years old, and he f Shem, Ham, Gn 5:32
And Noah f three sons: Gn 6:10
Cush f Nimrod, who was the first Gn 10:8
Egypt f Ludim, Anamim, Lehabim, Gn 10:13
Canaan f Sidon his firstborn, Gn 10:15
Arpachshad f Shelah, and Shelah Gn 10:24
Shelah, and Shelah f Eber. Gn 10:24
And Joktan f Almodad, Sheleph, Gn 10:26
100 years and f Arpachshad two Gn 11:10
he f Arpachshad, Shem lived Gn 11:11
500 years and f ⌊other⌋ sons Gn 11:11
lived 35 years and f Shelah. Gn 11:12
After he f Shelah, Arpachshad Gn 11:13
403 years and f ⌊other⌋ sons Gn 11:13
lived 30 years and f Eber. Gn 11:14
After he f Eber, Shelah lived Gn 11:15
403 years and f ⌊other⌋ sons Gn 11:15
Eber lived 34 years and f Peleg. Gn 11:16
After he f Peleg, Eber lived 430 Gn 11:17
430 years and f ⌊other⌋ sons Gn 11:17
Peleg lived 30 years and f Reu. Gn 11:18
After he f Reu, Peleg lived 209 Gn 11:19

209 years and f ⌊other⌋ sons Gn 11:19
Reu lived 32 years and f Serug. Gn 11:20
After he f Serug, Reu lived 207 Gn 11:21
207 years and f ⌊other⌋ sons Gn 11:21
lived 30 years and f Nahor. Gn 11:22
After he f Nahor, Serug lived Gn 11:23
200 years and f ⌊other⌋ sons Gn 11:23
lived 29 years and f Terah. Gn 11:24
After he f Terah, Nahor lived Gn 11:25
119 years and f ⌊other⌋ sons Gn 11:25
lived 70 years and f Abram, Gn 11:26
Terah f Abram, Nahor, and Haran, Gn 11:27
and Haran, and Haran f Lot. Gn 11:27
And Bethuel f Rebekah. Gn 22:23
Jokshan f Sheba and Dedan. Gn 25:3
son of Abraham. Abraham f Isaac. Gn 25:19
from Machir. Machir f Gilead; Nm 26:29
of Perez: Perez f Hezron. Ru 4:18
Hezron f Ram, who fathered Ru 4:19
fathered Ram, who f Amminadab. Ru 4:19
Amminadab f Nahshon, who Ru 4:20
fathered Nahshon, who f Salmon. Ru 4:20
f Boaz, who fathered Obed. Ru 4:21
fathered Boaz, who f Obed. Ru 4:21
And Obed f Jesse, who fathered Ru 4:22
fathered Jesse, who f David. Ru 4:22
Cush f Nimrod, who was the first 1Ch 1:10
f Ludim, Anamim, Lehabim, 1Ch 1:11
Canaan f Sidon, his firstborn, 1Ch 1:13
Arpachshad f Shelah, and Shelah 1Ch 1:18
Shelah, and Shelah f Eber. 1Ch 1:18
Joktan f Almodad, Sheleph, 1Ch 1:20
Abraham f Isaac. Isaac's sons: 1Ch 1:34
Ram f Amminadab, and 1Ch 2:10
Amminadab f Nahshon, a leader 1Ch 2:10
Nahshon f Salma, and Salma 1Ch 2:11
Salma, and Salma f Boaz. 1Ch 2:11
Boaz f Obed, and Obed fathered 1Ch 2:12
fathered Obed, and Obed f Jesse. 1Ch 2:12
Jesse f Eliab, his firstborn; 1Ch 2:13
Hur f Uri, and Uri fathered 1Ch 2:20
fathered Uri, and Uri f Bezalel. 1Ch 2:20
Segub f Jair, who possessed 23 1Ch 2:22
Attai f Nathan, and Nathan 1Ch 2:36
Nathan, and Nathan f Zabad. 1Ch 2:36
Zabad f Ephlal, and Ephlal 1Ch 2:37
Ephlal, and Ephlal f Obed. 1Ch 2:37
Obed f Jehu, and Jehu fathered 1Ch 2:38
Jehu, and Jehu f Azariah. 1Ch 2:38
Azariah f Helez, and Helez 1Ch 2:39
Helez, and Helez f Eleasah. 1Ch 2:39
Eleasah f Sismai, and Sismai 1Ch 2:40
Sismai, and Sismai f Shallum. 1Ch 2:40
Shallum f Jekamiah, and Jekamiah 1Ch 2:41
and Jekamiah f Elishama. 1Ch 2:41
his firstborn, f Ziph, and 1Ch 2:42
his second son, f Hebron. 1Ch 2:42
Shema f Raham, who fathered 1Ch 2:44
Raham, who f Jorkeam, and Rekem 1Ch 2:44
Jorkeam, and Rekem f Shammai. 1Ch 2:44
was Maon, and Maon f Beth-zur. 1Ch 2:45
Moza, and Gazez. Haran f Gazez. 1Ch 2:46
Shobal f Kiriath-jearim; 1Ch 2:50
Salma f Bethlehem, and Hareph 1Ch 2:51
and Hareph f Beth-gader. 1Ch 2:51
Reaiah son of Shobal f Jahath, 1Ch 4:2
and Jahath f Ahumai and Lahad. 1Ch 4:2
f Gedor, and Ezer fathered 1Ch 4:4
Gedor, and Ezer f Hushah. 1Ch 4:4
f Tekoa and had two wives, 1Ch 4:5
Koz f Anub, Zobebah, and the 1Ch 4:8
brother of Shuhah f Mehir, 1Ch 4:11
Eshton f Beth-rapha, Paseah, and 1Ch 4:12
Meonothai f Ophrah, and Seraiah 1Ch 4:14
and Seraiah f Joab, the ancestor 1Ch 4:14
Eleazar f Phinehas; 1Ch 6:4
Phinehas f Abishua; 1Ch 6:4
Abishua f Bukki; Bukki fathered 1Ch 6:5
fathered Bukki; Bukki f Uzzi; 1Ch 6:5
Uzzi f Zerahiah; Zerahiah 1Ch 6:6
Zerahiah f Meraioth; 1Ch 6:6
Meraioth f Amariah; 1Ch 6:7
Amariah; Amariah f Ahitub; 1Ch 6:7
Ahitub f Zadok; Zadok fathered 1Ch 6:8
fathered Zadok; Zadok f Ahimaaz; 1Ch 6:8
Ahimaaz f Azariah; Azariah 1Ch 6:9
Azariah; Azariah f Johanan; 1Ch 6:9
Johanan f Azariah, who served as 1Ch 6:10
Azariah f Amariah; Amariah 1Ch 6:11
Amariah; Amariah f Ahitub; 1Ch 6:11
Ahitub f Zadok; Zadok fathered 1Ch 6:12
fathered Zadok; Zadok f Shallum; 1Ch 6:12
Shallum f Hilkiah; Hilkiah 1Ch 6:13
Hilkiah; Hilkiah f Azariah; 1Ch 6:13
Azariah f Seraiah; and Seraiah 1Ch 6:14
and Seraiah f Jehozadak. 1Ch 6:14
and Malchiel, who f Birzaith. 1Ch 7:31
Heber f Japhlet, Shomer, and 1Ch 7:32
Benjamin f Bela, his firstborn; 1Ch 8:1
f Gibeon and lived in Gibeon. 1Ch 8:29
and Mikloth who f Shimeah. 1Ch 8:32
Ner f Kish, Kish fathered Saul, 1Ch 8:33
Kish, Kish f Saul, and Saul 1Ch 8:33
Saul, and Saul f Jonathan, 1Ch 8:33
and Merib-baal f Micah. 1Ch 8:34
Ahaz f Jehoaddah, Jehoaddah 1Ch 8:36
Jehoaddah f Alemeth, Azmaveth, 1Ch 8:36
and Zimri, and Zimri f Moza. 1Ch 8:36
f Binea. His son was Raphah, 1Ch 8:37
Jeiel f Gibeon and lived in 1Ch 9:35
Mikloth f Shimeam. These also 1Ch 9:38
Ner f Kish, Kish fathered Saul, 1Ch 9:39
Kish, Kish f Saul, and Saul 1Ch 9:39
Saul, and Saul f Jonathan, 1Ch 9:39
and Merib-baal f Micah. 1Ch 9:40
Ahaz f Jarah; Jarah fathered 1Ch 9:42
Jarah f Alemeth, Azmaveth, and 1Ch 9:42
and Zimri; Zimri f Moza. 1Ch 9:42
Moza f Binea. His son was 1Ch 9:43
and f 22 sons and 16 daughters. 2Ch 13:21
Jeshua f Joiakim, Joiakim Neh 12:10
Joiakim, Joiakim f Eliashib, Neh 12:10
Eliashib, Eliashib f Joiada, Neh 12:10
Joiada f Jonathan, and Jonathan Neh 12:11
Jonathan, and Jonathan f Jaddua. Neh 12:11
Who f the drops of dew? Jb 38:28
so when he f a son, he was Ec 5:14
Who f these for me? Is 49:21
who have f children among you. Ezk 47:22
Abraham f Isaac, Isaac fathered Mt 1:2
Isaac, Isaac f Jacob, Jacob Mt 1:2
Jacob f Judah and his brothers, Mt 1:2
f Perez and Zerah by Tamar, Mt 1:3
by Tamar, Perez f Hezron, Hezron Mt 1:3
fathered Hezron, Hezron f Aram, Mt 1:3
Aram f Aminadab, Aminadab Mt 1:4
Aminadab f Nahshon, Nahshon Mt 1:4
Nahshon, Nahshon f Salmon, Mt 1:4
Salmon f Boaz by Rahab, Boaz Mt 1:5
by Rahab, Boaz f Obed by Ruth, Mt 1:5
Obed by Ruth, Obed f Jesse, Mt 1:5
and Jesse f King David. Mt 1:6
Then David f Solomon by Uriah's Mt 1:6
Solomon f Rehoboam, Rehoboam Mt 1:7
Rehoboam f Abijah, Abijah Mt 1:7
fathered Abijah, Abijah f Asa, Mt 1:7
Asa f Jehoshaphat, Jehoshaphat Mt 1:8
Jehoshaphat f Joram, Joram Mt 1:8
fathered Joram, Joram f Uzziah, Mt 1:8
Uzziah f Jotham, Jotham fathered Mt 1:9
Jotham, Jotham f Ahaz, Ahaz Mt 1:9
fathered Ahaz, Ahaz f Hezekiah, Mt 1:9
Hezekiah f Manasseh, Manasseh Mt 1:10
Manasseh, Manasseh f Amon, Amon Mt 1:10
fathered Amon, Amon f Josiah, Mt 1:10
and Josiah f Jechoniah and his Mt 1:11
Babylon Jechoniah f Salathiel, Mt 1:12
Salathiel f Zerubbabel, Mt 1:12
Zerubbabel f Abiud, Abiud Mt 1:13
Abiud, Abiud f Eliakim, Eliakim Mt 1:13
Eliakim, Eliakim f Azor, Mt 1:13
Azor f Zadok, Zadok fathered Mt 1:14
Zadok, Zadok f Achim, Achim Mt 1:14
fathered Achim, Achim f Eliud, Mt 1:14
f Eleazar, Eleazar fathered Mt 1:15
Eleazar f Matthan, Matthan Mt 1:15
Matthan, Matthan f Jacob, Mt 1:15
and Jacob f Joseph the husband Mt 1:16
f Isaac and circumcised him on Ac 7:8
of Midian, where he f two sons. Ac 7:29
Now I have f you in Christ Jesus 1Co 4:15
whom I f while in chains— Phm 10

FATHERING *(1)*

What are you f? or to ⌊his⌋ Is 45:10

FATHERLESS *(40)*

mistreat any widow or f child. Ex 22:22
be widows and your children f. Ex 22:24
justice for the f and the widow, Dt 10:18
resident, f, and widow within Dt 14:29
resident, the f, and the widow Dt 16:11
resident, the f, and the widow Dt 16:14
a foreign resident ⌊or⌋ f child, Dt 24:17
resident, the f, and the widow, Dt 24:19
resident, the f, and the widow. Dt 24:20
resident, the f, and the widow. Dt 24:21
resident, the f, and the widow, Dt 26:12
resident, the f, and the widow, Dt 26:13
resident, a f child, or a widow. Dt 27:19
cast ⌊lots⌋ for a f child and Jb 6:27
strength of the f was crushed. Jb 22:9
owned⌋ by the f and take the Jb 24:3
f infant is snatched from the Jb 24:9
and the f child who had no one Jb 29:12
letting the f eat any of it— Jb 31:17
vote against a f child when I Jb 31:21
You are a helper of the f. Ps 10:14
justice for the f and the Ps 10:18
A father of the f and a champion Ps 68:5
justice for the needy and the f; Ps 82:3
the foreigner and murder the f. Ps 94:6
his children be f and his wife Ps 109:9
be gracious to his f children. Ps 109:12
and helps the f and the widow, Ps 146:9
encroach on the fields of the f, Pr 23:10
Defend the rights of the f. Is 1:17
not defend the rights of the f, Is 1:23
compassion on its f and widows, Is 9:17
and they can plunder the f. Is 10:2
the alien, the f, and the widow Jr 7:6
the alien, the f, or the widow. Jr 22:3
We have become orphans, f; Lm 5:3
The f and widow are oppressed in Ezk 22:7
f receives compassion in You. Hs 14:3
not oppress the widow or the f, Zch 7:10
who oppress the widow and the f, Mal 3:5

FATHERS *(280)*

will go to your f in peace and Gn 15:15
the land of your f and to your Gn 31:3
both we and our f, have raised Gn 46:34
we and our f, are shepherds. Gn 47:3
the years of my f during their Gn 47:9
When I lie down with my f, Gn 47:30
before whom my f Abraham and Gn 48:15
the names of my f Abraham and Gn 48:16
you back to the land of your f. Gn 48:21
Bury me with my f in the cave in Gn 49:29
The God of your f has sent me to Ex 3:13
the God of your f, the God of Ex 3:15
the God of your f, the God of Ex 3:16
the God of their f, the God of Ex 4:5
something your f and ancestors Ex 10:6
He swore to your f that He would Ex 13:5
as He swore to you and your f, Ex 13:11
sin and the sin of their f— Lv 26:40
the covenant with their f, Lv 26:45
You swore to ⌊give⌋ their f? Nm 11:12
land I swore to ⌊give⌋ their f. Nm 14:23
Our f went down to Egypt, and we Nm 20:15
treated us and our f badly. Nm 20:15
what your f did when I sent Nm 32:8
the inheritance of his f. Nm 36:8
swore to give to your f Abraham, Dt 1:8
the God of your f, increase you Dt 1:11
the God of your f, has told you. Dt 1:21
land I swore to give your f, Dt 1:35
God of your f, is giving you. Dt 4:1
with your f that He swore to Dt 4:31
He loved your f, He chose their Dt 4:37
make this covenant with our f, Dt 5:3
the God of your f, has promised Dt 6:3
land He swore to your f Abraham, Dt 6:10
your God swore to ⌊give⌋ your f, Dt 6:18
the land that He swore to our f. Dt 6:23
the oath He swore to your f, Dt 7:8
with you, as He swore to your f. Dt 7:12
He swore to your f that He would Dt 7:13
land the LORD swore to your f. Dt 8:1
you and your f had not known, Dt 8:3
manna that your f had not known, Dt 8:16
His covenant He swore to your f, Dt 8:18
the promise He swore to your f, Dt 9:5
land I swore to give their f.' Dt 10:11
to your f and loved them. Dt 10:15
Your f went down to Egypt, Dt 10:22

swore to your f to give them Dt 11:9
the LORD swore to give your f. Dt 11:21
the God of your f, has given you Dt 12:1
you nor your f have known, Dt 13:6
you as He swore to your f. Dt 13:17
territory as He swore to your f, Dt 19:8
F are not to be put to death for Dt 24:16
or children for ⌊their⌋ f; Dt 24:16
LORD swore to our f to give us.' Dt 26:3
the God of our f, and the LORD Dt 26:7
given us as You swore to our f, Dt 26:15
the God of your f, has promised Dt 27:3
swore to your f to give you. Dt 28:11
you nor your f have known, Dt 28:36
you nor your f have known. Dt 28:64
as He swore to your f Abraham, Dt 29:13
the God of their f, which He had Dt 29:25
into the land your f possessed, Dt 30:5
you more than ⌊He did⌋ your f. Dt 30:5
He delighted in that of your f, Dt 30:9
swore to give to your f Abraham, Dt 30:20
LORD swore to give to their f. Dt 31:7
are about to rest with your f, Dt 31:16
land I swore to ⌊give⌋ their f, Dt 31:20
which your f did not fear. Dt 32:17
swore to their f to give them as Jos 1:6
ask their f in the future, Jos 4:21
had sworn to their f to give us, Jos 5:6
the God of your f, gave you? Jos 18:3
He had sworn to give their f, Jos 21:43
to all He had sworn to their f. Jos 21:44
LORD's altar that our f made, Jos 22:28
I brought your f out of Egypt Jos 24:6
pursued your f with chariots Jos 24:6
Your f cried out to the LORD, Jos 24:7
the gods your f worshiped beyond Jos 24:15
us and our f out of the land Jos 24:17
land I had promised to your f. Jdg 2:1
God of their f, who had brought Jdg 2:12
turned from the way of their f, Jdg 2:17
They did not do as their f did. Jdg 2:17
more corruptly than their f, Jdg 2:19
made with their f and disobeyed Jdg 2:20
walking in it, as their f had." Jdg 2:22
had given their f through Moses. Jdg 3:4
that our f told us about? Jdg 6:13
When their f or brothers come to Jdg 21:22
comes and you rest with your f, 2Sm 7:12
lord the king rests with his f, 1Kg 1:21
rested with his f and was buried 1Kg 2:10
rested with his f and that Joab, 1Kg 11:21
rested with his f and was buried 1Kg 11:43
reach the grave of your f.'" 1Kg 13:22
rested with his f, and his son 1Kg 14:20
rested with his f and was buried 1Kg 14:31
buried with his f in the city 1Kg 14:31
rested with his f and was buried 1Kg 15:8
the idols that his f had made. 1Kg 15:12
rested with his f and was buried 1Kg 15:24
rested with his f and was buried 1Kg 16:6
rested with his f and was buried 1Kg 16:28
for I'm no better than my f." 1Kg 19:4
rested with his f, and his son 1Kg 22:40
rested with his f and was buried 1Kg 22:50
buried with his f in the city of 1Kg 22:50
rested with his f and was buried 2Kg 8:24
buried with his f in the city 2Kg 8:24
rested with his f, and he was 2Kg 10:35
buried him with his f in the 2Kg 12:21
Jehoahaz rested with his f, 2Kg 13:9
Jehoash rested with his f, 2Kg 13:13
F must not be put to death 2Kg 14:6
be put to death because of f; 2Kg 14:6
Jehoash rested with his f, 2Kg 14:16
Jerusalem with his f in the city 2Kg 14:20
the king rested with his f. 2Kg 14:22
Jeroboam rested with his f, 2Kg 14:29
Azariah rested with his f, 2Kg 15:7
buried with his f in the city 2Kg 15:7
LORD's sight as his f had done. 2Kg 15:9
Menahem rested with his f, 2Kg 15:22
rested with his f, and he was 2Kg 15:38
buried with his f in the city of 2Kg 15:38
rested with his f and was buried 2Kg 16:20
buried with his f in the city 2Kg 16:20
as their f did until today. 2Kg 17:41
all that your f have stored up 2Kg 20:17
Hezekiah rested with his f, 2Kg 20:21
rested with his f and was buried 2Kg 21:18
indeed gather you to your f, 2Kg 22:20
Jehoiakim rested with his f, 2Kg 24:6
families according to their f: 1Ch 6:19
time comes to be with your f, 1Ch 17:11
rested with his f and was buried 2Ch 9:31
rested with his f and was buried 2Ch 12:16
rested with his f and was buried 2Ch 14:1
his reign and rested with his f. 2Ch 16:13
rested with his f and was buried 2Ch 21:1
buried with his f in the city 2Ch 21:1
like the fire in honor of his f. 2Ch 21:19
F must not die because of 2Ch 25:4
must not die because of f, 2Ch 25:4
buried him with his f in the 2Ch 25:28
the king rested with his f. 2Ch 26:2
rested with his f, and he was 2Ch 26:23
buried with his f in the burial 2Ch 26:23
rested with his f and was buried 2Ch 27:9
rested with his f and was buried 2Ch 28:27
our f were unfaithful and did 2Ch 29:6
Our f fell by the sword, and our 2Ch 29:9
be like your f and your brothers 2Ch 30:7
obstinate now like your f did. 2Ch 30:8
what I and my f have done to all 2Ch 32:13
nations that my f utterly 2Ch 32:14
my power or the power of my f. 2Ch 32:15
rested with his f and was buried 2Ch 32:33
Manasseh rested with his f, 2Ch 33:20
us because our f have not kept 2Ch 34:21
indeed gather you to your f, 2Ch 34:28
buried him in the tomb of his f. 2Ch 35:24
But since our f angered the God Ezr 5:12
Praise the LORD God of our f, Ezr 7:27
to the LORD God of your f. Ezr 8:28
the days of our f until the Ezr 9:7
God of your f and do His will Ezr 10:11
sins and the guilt of their f. Neh 9:2
to what their f discovered, Jb 8:8
whose f I would have refused to Jb 30:1
Our f trusted in You; Ps 22:4
a sojourner like all my f. Ps 39:12
go to the generation of his f; Ps 49:19
and that our f have passed down Ps 78:3
He commanded our f to teach to Ps 78:5
they would not be like their f, Ps 78:8
wonders in the sight of their f, Ps 78:12
turned away like their f; Ps 78:57
where your f tested Me; Ps 95:9
Both we and our f have sinned; Ps 106:6
f in Egypt did not grasp ⌊the Ps 106:7
the pride of sons is their f. Pr 17:6
man f a fool to his own sorrow; Pr 17:21
and wealth are inherited from f, Pr 19:14
line that your f set up. Pr 22:28
and one who f a wise son will Pr 23:24
of the iniquity of their f. Is 14:21
all that your f have stored up Is 39:6
Kings will be your foster f, Is 49:23
where our f praised You, has Is 64:11
iniquities of your f together," Is 65:7
fault did your f find in Me that Jr 2:5
what our f have worked for Jr 3:24
both we and our f, from the time Jr 3:25
f and sons together will stumble Jr 6:21
wood, the f light the fire, Jr 7:18
Baals, as their f taught them." Jr 9:14
they and their f have not known. Jr 9:16
each other, f and sons alike"— Jr 13:14
LORD, the guilt of our f; Jr 14:20
them and the f who father them Jr 16:3
Because your f abandoned Me"— Jr 16:11
You did more evil than your f. Jr 16:12
you and your f are not familiar Jr 16:13
Our f inherited only lies, Jr 16:19
they, their f, and the kings Jr 19:4
name as their f forgot My name Jr 23:27
city that I gave you and your f. Jr 23:39
The f have eaten sour grapes, Jr 31:29
burning ceremonies for your f, Jr 34:5
you, and your f did not know. Jr 44:3
forgotten the evils of your f, Jr 44:9
just as we, our f, our kings, Jr 44:17
you, your f, your kings, your Jr 44:21
f will not turn back for their Jr 47:3
Our f sinned; they no longer Lm 5:7
f will eat ⌊their⌋ sons within Ezk 5:10
and sons will eat their f. Ezk 5:10
The f eat sour grapes, and the Ezk 18:2
the abominations of their f. Ezk 20:4
follow the statutes of your f, Ezk 20:18
way also your f blasphemed Me Ezk 20:27
yourselves the way your f did, Ezk 20:30
with your f in the wilderness Ezk 20:36
the land I swore to give your f. Ezk 20:42
in the land that I gave your f; Ezk 36:28
Jacob, where your f lived. Ezk 37:25
You, God of my f, because You Dn 2:23
kings, leaders, f, and all the Dn 9:6
and our f, because we have Dn 9:8
and the injustices of our f, Dn 9:16
and do what his f and Dn 11:24
regard for the gods of his f, Dn 11:37
a god his f did not know— Dn 11:38
saw your f like the first fruit Hs 9:10
swore to our f from days long Mc 7:20
badly when your f provoked Me to Zch 8:14
profaning the covenant of our f? Mal 2:10
Since the days of your f, Mal 3:7
turn the hearts of f to ⌊their⌋ Mal 4:6
hearts of children to their f. Mal 4:6
had lived in the days of our f, Mt 23:30
the hearts of f to their Lk 1:17
with our f and remembered His Lk 1:72
and your f killed them. Lk 11:47
you approve the deeds of your f, Lk 11:48
f worshiped on this mountain, Jn 4:20
Our f ate the manna in the Jn 6:31
Your f ate the manna in the Jn 6:49
not like the manna your f ate— Jn 6:58
from Moses but from the f— Jn 7:22
the God of our f, has glorified Ac 3:13
God of our f raised up Jesus, Ac 5:30
"Brothers and f," he said, Ac 7:2
that God drove out before our f, Ac 7:45
did your f not persecute? Ac 7:52
buried with his f, and decayed. Ac 13:36
Brothers and f, listen now to my Ac 22:1
'The God of our f has appointed Ac 22:14
promise made by God to our f, Ac 26:6
confirm the promises to the f, Rm 15:8
but you can't have many f. 1Co 4:15
that our f were all under the 1Co 10:1
And f, don't stir up anger in Eph 6:4
F, do not exasperate your Col 3:21
who kill their f and mothers, 1Tm 1:9
spoke to the f by the prophets Heb 1:1
where your f tested Me, tried Heb 3:9
made with their f on the day I Heb 8:9
we had natural f discipline us, Heb 12:9
of life inherited from the f, 1Pt 1:18
ever since the f fell asleep, 2Pt 3:4
writing to you, f, because you 1Jn 2:13
written to you, f, because you 1Jn 2:14

FATHERS' *(18)*

the heads of their f families: Ex 6:14
to ⌊their⌋ f households, Ex 12:3
the children for the f sin, Ex 20:5
consequences of the f wrongdoing Ex 34:7
of their f sins along with Lv 26:39
consequences of the f wrongdoing Nm 14:18
stand in your f place adding Nm 32:14
away from our f inheritance Nm 36:3
for the f sin to the third Dt 5:9
never give my f inheritance to 1Kg 21:3
not give you my f inheritance." 1Kg 21:4
him in his f tomb in the city 2Kg 9:28
under their own f authority for 1Ch 25:6
be made in your f record books. Ezr 4:15
lay the f sins on their sons' Jr 32:18
were fixed on their f idols. Ezk 20:24
the measure of your f sins! Mt 23:32
so I worship my f God, believing Ac 24:14

FATHOM *(1)*

Can you f the depths of God or Jb 11:7

FATLING *(1)*

and the f will be together, Is 11:6

FATLINGS *(3)*

sheep, cattle, and f, as well as 1Sm 15:9
butcher the f, but you do not Ezk 34:3
bulls, all of them f of Bashan. Ezk 39:18

FATNESS *(2)*

Their eyes bulge out from f; Ps 73:7
be broken because of ⌊his⌋ f. Is 10:27

FATTENED *(14)*
The woman had a **f** calf at her 1Sm 28:24
sacrificed an ox and a **f** calf. 2Sm 6:13
and **f** cattle near the stone of 1Kg 1:9
sacrificed oxen, **f** cattle, and 1Kg 1:19
sacrificed oxen, **f** cattle, and 1Kg 1:25
f oxen, 20 range oxen, and 100 1Kg 4:23
will offer You **f** sheep as burnt Ps 66:15
is love than a **f** calf with Pr 15:17
offerings of **f** cattle. Am 5:22
my oxen and **f** cattle have been Mt 22:4
Then bring the **f** calf and Lk 15:23
slaughtered the **f** calf because Lk 15:27
slaughtered the **f** calf for him.' Lk 15:30
You have **f** your hearts for the Jms 5:5

FATTY *(11)*
entrails, the **f** lobe of the Ex 29:13
entrails, the **f** lobe of the Ex 29:22
also remove the **f** lobe of the Lv 3:4
the **f** lobe of the liver above Lv 3:10
also remove the **f** lobe of the Lv 3:15
also remove the **f** lobe of the Lv 4:9
also remove the **f** lobe of the Lv 7:4
entrails, the **f** lobe of the Lv 8:16
entrails, the **f** lobe of the Lv 8:25
and the **f** lobe of the liver from Lv 9:10
and the **f** lobe of the liver— Lv 9:19

FAULT *(9)*
your own people who are at **f**." Ex 5:16
I've found no **f** with him." 1Sm 29:3
have found no **f** in you from the 1Sm 29:6
your head high, free from **f**. Jb 11:15
For no **f** of mine, they run and Ps 59:4
What **f** did your fathers find in Jr 2:5
Why then does He still find **f**? Rm 9:19
no one can find **f** with us 2Co 8:20
But finding **f** with His people, Heb 8:8

FAULTLESS *(3)*
of God who are **f** in a crooked Php 2:15
you holy, **f**, and blameless Col 1:22
first ⌊covenant⌋ had been **f**, Heb 8:7

FAULTS *(2)*
Pharaoh, "Today I remember my **f**. Gn 41:9
Cleanse me from my hidden **f**. Ps 19:12

FAULTY *(2)*
they became warped like a **f** bow. Ps 78:57
they are like a **f** bow. Hs 7:16

FAVOR *(124)*
found **f** in the eyes of the LORD. Gn 6:8
if I have found **f** in your sight, Gn 18:3
indeed found **f** in Your sight, Gn 19:19
If I have found **f** in your sight, Gn 30:27
in order to seek your **f**.'" Gn 32:5
"To find **f** with you, my lord," Gn 33:8
If I have found **f** with you, Gn 33:10
Grant me this **f**, and I'll give Gn 34:11
Joseph found **f** in his master's Gn 39:4
He granted him **f** in the eyes of Gn 39:21
We have found **f** in our lord's Gn 47:25
If I have found **f** in your eyes, Gn 47:29
If I have found **f** with you, Gn 50:4
this people such **f** in the sight Ex 3:21
gave the people **f** in the sight Ex 11:3
people such **f** in the Egyptians' Ex 12:36
have also found **f** in My sight.' Ex 33:12
indeed found **f** in Your sight, Ex 33:13
You and find **f** in Your sight. Ex 33:13
people have found **f** in Your Ex 33:16
you have found **f** in My sight, Ex 33:17
indeed found **f** in Your sight, Ex 34:9
LORD look with **f** on you and give Nm 6:26
we have found **f** in your sight, Nm 32:5
and with the **f** of Him who Dt 33:16
If I have found **f** in Your sight, Jdg 6:17
them, 'Show **f** to them, since Jdg 21:22
your servant find **f** with you," 1Sm 1:18
stature and in **f** with the LORD 1Sm 2:26
I haven't sought the LORD's **f**. 1Sm 13:12
my⌋ young men find **f** with you, 1Sm 25:8
If I have found **f** with you, 1Sm 27:5
his master's **f** than with the 1Sm 29:4
knows I have found **f** with you, 2Sm 14:22
If I find **f** in the LORD's eyes, 2Sm 15:25
plead for the **f** of the LORD your 1Kg 13:6
pleaded for the **f** of the LORD, 1Kg 13:6
Jehoahaz sought the LORD's **f**, 2Kg 13:4
he sought the **f** of the LORD his 2Ch 33:12
and who has shown **f** to me before Ezr 7:28
servant has found **f** with you, Neh 2:5
Remember me, my God, with **f**. Neh 13:31
him and gained his **f** so that he Est 2:9
She won more **f** and approval from Est 2:17
implore his **f**, and plead with Est 4:8
and **f** the plans of the wicked? Jb 10:3
and many will seek your **f**. Jb 11:19
and does not **f** the rich over Jb 34:19
Look on us with **f**, LORD. Ps 4:6
him with **f** like a shield. Ps 5:12
a moment, but His **f**, a lifetime. Ps 30:5
You showed Your **f**, You made me Ps 30:7
I sought **f** from my Lord: Ps 30:8
Show Your **f** to Your servant; Ps 31:16
will seek your **f** with gifts. Ps 45:12
look on us with **f** Selah Ps 67:1
to You is for a time of **f**. Ps 69:13
forever and never again show **f**? Ps 77:7
on us⌋ with **f**, and we will be Ps 80:3
on us⌋ with **f**, and we will be Ps 80:7
on us⌋ with **f**, and we will be Ps 80:19
You showed **f** to Your land; Ps 85:1
by Your **f** our horn is exalted. Ps 89:17
Let the **f** of the Lord our God be Ps 90:17
My eyes ⌊**f**⌋ the faithful of the Ps 101:6
it is time to show **f** to her— Ps 102:13
in its stones and **f** its dust. Ps 102:14
when You show **f** to Your people. Ps 106:4
have sought Your **f** with all my Ps 119:58
f to Your servant, and teach Ps 119:135
our God until He shows us **f**. Ps 123:2
Show us **f**, LORD, show us favor, Ps 123:3
LORD, show us **f**, for we've had Ps 123:3
you will find **f** and high regard Pr 3:4
and obtains **f** from the LORD, Pr 8:35
for what is good finds **f**, Pr 11:27
The good obtain **f** from the LORD, Pr 12:2
Good sense wins **f**, but the way Pr 13:15
f is like a cloud with spring Pr 16:15
and obtains **f** from the LORD. Pr 18:22
Many seek the **f** of a ruler, Pr 19:6
but his **f** is like dew on the Pr 19:12
f is better than silver and gold. Pr 22:1
later find more **f** than one who Pr 28:23
seek a ruler's **f**, but a man Pr 29:26
or **f** to the skillful; Ec 9:11
⌊But if⌋ the wicked is shown **f**, Is 26:10
He will show **f** to you at the Is 30:19
will answer you in a time of **f**, Is 49:8
show mercy to you with My **f**. Is 60:10
the year of the LORD's **f**, Is 61:2
LORD and plead for the LORD's **f**, Jr 26:19
They found **f** in the wilderness— Jr 31:2
respected; the elders find no **f**. Lm 4:16
granted Daniel **f** and compassion Dn 1:9
was given in **f** of the holy ones Dn 7:22
Show Your **f** to Your desolate Dn 9:17
he will **f** those who abandon the Dn 11:30
he wept and sought His **f**. Hs 12:4
men to plead for the LORD's **f** Zch 7:2
for the LORD's **f** and to seek the Zch 8:21
and to plead for the LORD's **f**." Zch 8:22
calling one **F** and the other Zch 11:7
my staff called **F** and cut it in Zch 11:10
pleased with you or show you **f**?" Mal 1:8
And now ask for God's **f**. Mal 1:9
will He show any of you **f**?" Mal 1:9
has looked with **f** in these days Lk 1:25
for you have found **f** with God. Lk 1:30
has looked with **f** on the humble Lk 1:48
and in **f** with God and with Lk 2:52
the year of the Lord's **f**. Lk 4:19
God and having **f** with all the Ac 2:47
He gave him **f** and wisdom in the Ac 7:10
He found **f** in God's sight and Ac 7:46
wished to do a **f** for the Jews, Ac 24:27
him to do them a **f** against Paul, Ac 25:3
wanting to do a **f** for the Jews, Ac 25:9
with pride in **f** of one person 1Co 4:6
trying to win the **f** of people, Gl 1:10
according to His **f** and will, Eph 1:5
If you look with **f** on the man Jms 2:3
For it ⌊brings⌋ **f** if, because of 1Pt 2:19
endure, it brings **f** with God. 1Pt 2:20

FAVORABLE *(5)*
will give Pharaoh a **f** answer." Gn 41:16
and they were **f** to Abimelech, Jdg 9:3
out that he is **f** toward you, 1Sm 20:12
are unanimously **f** for the king. 1Kg 22:13
are unanimously **f** for the king. 2Ch 18:12

FAVORABLY *(7)*
you have come to look **f** on me. 1Sm 20:3
May you look **f** on me, my lord 2Sm 16:4
be like theirs, and speak **f**." 1Kg 22:13
be like theirs, and speak **f**." 2Ch 18:12
Remember me **f**, my God, for all Neh 5:19
does not look **f** on any who are Jb 37:24
I will look **f** on this kind of Is 66:2

FAVORED *(3)*
he be the most **f** among his Dt 33:24
her and said, "Rejoice, **f** woman! Lk 1:28
grace that He **f** us with in the Eph 1:6

FAVORITE *(3)*
of Jacob, the **f** singer of Israel 2Sm 23:1
his soul ⌊despises his⌋ **f** food. Jb 33:20
she is the **f** of her mother, Sg 6:9

FAVORITISM *(11)*
not show **f** to a poor person in Ex 23:3
is not to show **f** to the son of Dt 21:16
that God doesn't show **f**, Ac 10:34
There is no **f** with God. Rm 2:11
God does not show **f**)—those Gl 2:6
and there is no **f** with Him. Eph 6:9
he has done, and there is no **f**. Col 3:25
doing nothing out of **f**. 1Tm 5:21
Jesus Christ without showing **f**. Jms 2:1
if you show **f**, you commit sin Jms 2:9
fruits, without **f** and hypocrisy. Jms 3:17

FAVORS *(7)*
Whoever **f** Joab and whoever is 2Sm 20:11
A king **f** a wise servant, but his Pr 14:35
scattered your **f** to strangers Jr 3:13
your sexual **f** on everyone who Ezk 16:15
all around for your sexual **f**. Ezk 16:33
offered her sexual **f** to them; Ezk 23:7
peace on earth to people He **f**! Lk 2:14

FAWN *(2)*
doe, a graceful **f**—let her Pr 5:19
abandons ⌊her **f**⌋ since there is Jr 14:5

FAWNS *(3)*
set free that bears beautiful **f**. Gn 49:21
Your breasts are like two **f**, Sg 4:5
Your breasts are like two **f**, Sg 7:3

FEAR *(262)*
The **f** and terror of you will be Gn 9:2
absolutely no **f** of God in this Gn 20:11
For now I know that you **f** God, Gn 22:12
of Abraham, the **F** of Isaac, had Gn 31:42
swore by the **F** of his father Gn 31:53
said to them, "I **f** God—do this Gn 42:18
still do not **f** the LORD God." Ex 9:30
that you will **f** Him and will not Ex 20:20
but you are to **f** your God; Lv 19:14
honor the old. **F** your God; I am Lv 19:32
another, but **f** your God, for I Lv 25:17
but **f** your God and let your Lv 25:36
them harshly but **f** your God. Lv 25:43
Moses, "Do not **f** him, for I have Nm 21:34
to put the **f** and dread of you Dt 2:25
to me, 'Do not **f** him, for I have Dt 3:2
may learn to **f** Me all the days Dt 4:10
such a heart to **f** Me and keep Dt 5:29
so that you may **f** the LORD your Dt 6:2
F the LORD your God, worship Him, Dt 6:13
statutes and to **f** the LORD our Dt 6:24
same to all the peoples you **f**. Dt 7:19
of you except to **f** the LORD your Dt 10:12
You are to **f** the LORD your God Dt 10:20
God will put **f** and dread of you Dt 11:25
the LORD your God and **f** Him. Dt 13:4
always learn to **f** the LORD your Dt 14:23
he may learn to **f** the LORD his Dt 17:19
and weary. They did not **f** God. Dt 25:18
and learn to **f** the LORD your God Dt 31:12
and learn to **f** the LORD your God Dt 31:13
which your fathers did not **f**. Dt 32:17
may always **f** the LORD your God. Jos 4:24
people's hearts to melt with **f**, Jos 14:8
f the LORD and worship Him in Jos 24:14
not **f** the gods of the Amorites Jdg 6:10
For the **f** of death pervaded the 1Sm 5:11
If you **f** the LORD, worship and 1Sm 12:14
f the LORD and worship Him 1Sm 12:24

his troops were gripped with f. 1Sm 13:7
who rules in the f of God, 2Sm 23:3
that they may f You all the days 1Kg 8:40
f You as Your people Israel do 1Kg 8:43
there, they did not f the LORD. 2Kg 17:25
them how they should f the LORD. 2Kg 17:28
None of them f the LORD or 2Kg 17:34
them, "Do not f other gods; 2Kg 17:35
Instead, f the LORD, who brought 2Kg 17:36
for you; do not f other gods. 2Kg 17:37
with you. Do not f other gods, 2Kg 17:38
but f the LORD your God, and He 2Kg 17:39
so that they may f You and walk 2Ch 6:31
f You as Your people Israel do 2Ch 6:33
saying, "In the f of the LORD, 2Ch 19:9
the teacher of the f of God. 2Ch 26:5
I was overwhelmed with f Neh 2:2
walk in the f of our God ⌊and Neh 5:9
this, because of the f of God. Neh 5:15
the queen was overcome with f. Est 4:4
or tremble in f at his presence, Est 5:9
Jews because f of the Jews had Est 8:17
Does Job f God for nothing? Jb 1:9
f and trembling came over me and Jb 4:14
by me, and I shuddered with f. Jb 4:15
slander and not f destruction Jb 5:21
and hunger and not f the animals Jb 5:22
abandons the f of the Almighty Jb 6:14
cringe in f beneath Him! Jb 9:13
I would speak and not f Him. Jb 9:35
You will lie down without f, Jb 11:19
even undermine the f ⌊of God⌋ Jb 15:4
homes are secure and free of f; Jb 21:9
The f of the Lord—that is Jb 28:28
F of me should not terrify you; Jb 33:7
Therefore, men f Him. He does Jb 37:24
no f that her labor may have Jb 39:16
He laughs at f, since he is Jb 39:22
earth—a creature devoid of f! Jb 41:33
but honors those who f the LORD, Ps 15:4
The f of the LORD is pure, Ps 19:9
You who f the LORD, praise Him! Ps 22:23
my vows before those who f You. Ps 22:25
valley, I f no danger, for Ps 23:4
the LORD is for those who f Him, Ps 25:14
my salvation—whom should I f? Ps 27:1
stored up for those who f You, Ps 31:19
the LORD is on those who f Him— Ps 33:18
encamps around those who f Him, Ps 34:7
F the LORD, you His saints, for Ps 34:9
those who f Him lack nothing. Ps 34:9
teach you the f of the LORD. Ps 34:11
will see and f, and put their Ps 40:3
They looked, and froze with f; Ps 48:5
Why should I f in times of Ps 49:5
F and trembling grip me; Ps 55:5
do not change and do not f God. Ps 55:19
I will not f. What can man do Ps 56:4
I will not f. What can man do Ps 56:11
signal flag to those who f You, Ps 60:4
to those who f Your name. Ps 61:5
everyone will f and will tell Ps 64:9
listen, all who f God, and I Ps 66:16
ends of the earth will f Him. Ps 67:7
is very near those who f Him, Ps 85:9
undivided mind to f Your name. Ps 86:11
matches the f that is due You. Ps 90:11
You will not f the terror of the Ps 91:5
the nations will f the name of Ps 102:15
love toward those who f Him. Ps 103:11
compassion on those who f Him. Ps 103:13
love is toward those who f Him, Ps 103:17
food for those who f Him; Ps 111:5
The f of the LORD is the Ps 111:10
He will not f bad news; Ps 112:7
he will not f. In the end he Ps 112:8
You who f the LORD, trust in the Ps 115:11
bless those who f the LORD— Ps 115:13
Let those who f the LORD say, Ps 118:4
I am a friend to all who f You, Ps 119:63
Those who f You will see me and Ps 119:74
Let those who f You, those who Ps 119:79
awe of You; I f Your judgments. Ps 119:120
the desires of those who f Him; Ps 145:19
The LORD values those who f Him, Ps 147:11
The f of the LORD is the Pr 1:7
didn't choose to f the LORD, Pr 1:29
be free from the f of danger." Pr 1:33
understand the f of the LORD Pr 2:5
f the LORD and turn away from Pr 3:7
Don't f sudden danger or the Pr 3:25
To f the LORD is to hate evil. Pr 8:13
The f of the LORD is the Pr 9:10
The f of the LORD prolongs life, Pr 10:27
In the f of the LORD one has Pr 14:26
The f of the LORD is a fountain Pr 14:27
little with the f of the LORD Pr 15:16
The f of the LORD is wisdom's Pr 15:33
from evil by the f of the LORD. Pr 16:6
The f of the LORD leads to life; Pr 19:23
of humility is f of the LORD, Pr 22:4
instead, always f the LORD. Pr 23:17
My son, f the LORD, as well as Pr 24:21
The f of man is a snare, but the Pr 29:25
also many words. So, f God. Ec 5:7
f God and keep His commands, Ec 12:13
for f of the thorns and briers. Is 7:25
Do not f what they fear; Is 8:12
Do not fear what they f; Is 8:12
Zion, do not f Assyria, though Is 10:24
and of the f of the LORD. Is 11:2
will be in the f of the LORD. Is 11:3
their faces flushed with f. Is 13:8
Tremble with f, all Philistia! Is 14:31
They will lie down without f. Is 17:2
She will tremble with f because Is 19:16
of violent people will f You. Is 25:3
will pass away because of f, Is 31:9
The f of the LORD is Zion's Is 33:6
strong; do not f! Here is your Is 35:4
Do not f, for I am with you; Is 41:10
Do not f, I will help you. Is 41:13
not f, you worm Jacob, you men Is 41:14
Israel—"Do not f, for I have Is 43:1
Do not f, for I am with you; Is 43:5
help you: Do not f; Jacob is My Is 44:2
do not f disgrace by men, and do Is 51:7
that you should f man who dies, Is 51:12
a long time and you do not f Me? Is 57:11
They will f the name of the LORD Is 59:19
our hearts so we do not f You. Is 63:17
your God and to have no f of Me. Jr 2:19
The priests will tremble in f, Jr 4:9
Do you not f Me? ⌊This is⌋ the Jr 5:22
Let's f the LORD our God, who Jr 5:24
Do not f them for they can do no Jr 10:5
should not f You, King of the Jr 10:7
it doesn't f when heat comes, Jr 17:8
Did he not f the LORD and plead Jr 26:19
he fled in f and went to Egypt. Jr 26:21
them, they will f Me always. Jr 32:39
and I will put f of Me in their Jr 32:40
to each other in f and said to Jr 36:16
be handed over to the men you f. Jr 39:17
king of Babylon whom you now f; Jr 42:11
the sword you f will overtake Jr 42:16
You f the sword, so I will bring Ezk 11:8
it⌋ for ⌊f of⌋ the animals, Ezk 14:15
Their kings shudder with f; Ezk 27:35
I will instill f in that land. Ezk 30:13
shudder with f because of you Ezk 32:10
must tremble in f before the God Dn 6:26
For we do not f the LORD. Hs 10:3
who will not f? The Lord GOD has Am 3:8
and it is wise to f Your name Mc 6:9
will certainly f Me and accept Zph 3:7
you need no longer f harm. Zph 3:15
Do not f; Zion, do not let Zph 3:16
master, where is ⌊your⌋ f of Me? Mal 1:6
They do not f Me," says the LORD Mal 3:5
But for you who f My name, Mal 4:2
Don't f those who kill the body Mt 10:28
f Him who is able to destroy Mt 10:28
they said, and cried out in f. Mt 14:26
shaken from f of him that they Mt 28:4
the tomb with f and great joy, Mt 28:8
came with f and trembling, Mk 5:33
startled and overcome with f. Lk 1:12
generation on those who f Him. Lk 1:50
F came on all those who lived Lk 1:65
clutches, to serve Him without f Lk 1:74
Then f came over everyone, Lk 7:16
they were gripped by great f. Lk 8:37
don't f those who kill the body, Lk 12:4
I will show you the One to f: Lk 12:5
F Him who has authority to throw Lk 12:5
to you, this is the One to f! Lk 12:5
town who didn't f God or respect Lk 18:2
though I don't f God or respect Lk 18:4
faint from f and expectation Lk 21:26
Don't you even f God, since you Lk 23:40
F no more, Daughter Zion; Jn 12:15
because of his f of the Jews— Jn 19:38
because of their f of the Jews. Jn 20:19
Then f came over everyone, Ac 2:43
and a great f came on all who Ac 5:5
Then great f came on the whole Ac 5:11
and walking in the f of the Lord Ac 9:31
and you who f God, listen! Ac 13:16
and those among you who f God, Ac 13:26
Then f fell on all of them, Ac 19:17
is no f of God before their Rm 3:18
of slavery to fall back into f, Rm 8:15
in weakness, in f, and in much 1Co 2:3
he has nothing to f from you, 1Co 16:10
then, the f of the Lord, we 2Co 5:11
complete in the f of God. 2Co 7:1
indignation, what f, what deep 2Co 7:11
him with f and trembling. 2Co 7:15
But I f that, as the serpent 2Co 11:3
For I f that perhaps when I come 2Co 12:20
I f that when I come my God will 2Co 12:21
one another in the f of Christ. Eph 5:21
masters with f and trembling, Eph 6:5
salvation with f and trembling. Php 2:12
their lives by the f of death. Heb 2:15
let us f so that none of you Heb 4:1
and they didn't f the king's Heb 11:23
the brotherhood. F God. Honor 1Pt 2:17
Do not f what they fear or be 1Pt 3:14
what they f or be disturbed, 1Pt 3:14
There is no f in love; instead, 1Jn 4:18
perfect love drives out f, 1Jn 4:18
because f involves punishment. 1Jn 4:18
only themselves without f. Jd 12
on others have mercy in f, Jd 23
So great f fell on those who saw Rv 11:11
and to those who f Your name, Rv 11:18
F God and give Him glory, Rv 14:7
who will not f and glorify Your Rv 15:4
far off in f of her torment, Rv 18:10
far off in f of her torment, Rv 18:15
you who f Him, both small Rv 19:5

FEARED *(47)*

f God and did not do as the king Ex 1:17
the midwives f God, He gave them Ex 1:21
officials who f the word of the Ex 9:20
the man Moses was f in the land Ex 11:3
the people f the LORD and Ex 14:31
if I had not f insult from the Dt 32:27
⌊or f⌋ that these foes might Dt 32:27
We greatly f for our lives Jos 9:24
people greatly f the LORD and 1Sm 12:18
of it because they f the oath. 1Sm 14:26
David f the LORD that day and 2Sm 6:9
was a man who greatly f the LORD 1Kg 18:3
have f the LORD from my youth. 1Kg 18:12
that your servant f the LORD. 2Kg 4:1
they f the LORD, but they also 2Kg 17:32
They f the LORD, but they also 2Kg 17:33
These nations f the LORD but 2Kg 17:41
David f God that day, and said, 1Ch 13:12
He is f above all gods. 1Ch 16:25
though they f the surrounding Ezr 3:3
faithful man who f God more than Neh 7:2
who f God and turned away from Jb 1:1
For the thing I f has overtaken Jb 3:25
because I greatly f the crowds, Jb 31:34
And You—You are to be f. Ps 76:7
The earth f and grew quiet Ps 76:8
He is f by the kings of the Ps 76:12
God is greatly f in the council Ps 89:7
He is f above all gods. Ps 96:4
He should be f; only He should Is 8:13
to a people f near and far, Is 18:2
a people f near and far, a Is 18:7
Who was it you dreaded and f, Is 57:11
For they f them because Ishmael Jr 41:18
they have not f or walked by My Jr 44:10
The men f the LORD even more, Jnh 1:16
So the people f the LORD. Hg 1:12
My name will be f among the Mal 1:14
time those who f the LORD spoke Mal 3:16
for those who f Yahweh and had Mal 3:16

to kill him, he f the crowd, Mt 14:5
arrest Him, they f the crowds, Mt 21:46
them, but they f the people. Lk 20:19
Him because they f the Jews. Jn 7:13
devout man and f God along with Ac 10:2
the commander f that Paul might Ac 23:10
because he f those from the Gl 2:12

FEARFUL *(8)*
'Whoever is f and trembling may Jdg 7:3
and f when the report Jr 51:46
were terrified and f of him. Dn 5:19
Why are you f, you of little Mt 8:26
He said to them, "Why are you f? Mk 4:40
They were f and amazed, asking Lk 8:25
heart must not be troubled or f. Jn 14:27
I am f for you, that perhaps my Gl 4:11

FEARFULNESS *(1)*
has not given us a spirit of f, 2Tm 1:7

FEARING *(7)*
walking in His ways and f Him. Dt 8:6
by f this glorious and awesome Dt 28:58
descendants to stop f the LORD. Jos 22:25
f they would run aground on the Ac 27:17
f we might run aground in some Ac 27:29
wholeheartedly, f the Lord. Col 3:22
f that the tempter had tempted 1Th 3:5

FEARLESS *(1)*
wine, who are f at mixing beer, Is 5:22

FEARLESSLY *(1)*
more to speak the message f. Php 1:14

FEARS *(17)*
Look, Adonijah f King Solomon, 1Kg 1:51
f God and turns away from evil. Jb 1:8
who f God and turns away from Jb 2:3
is the person who f the LORD? Ps 25:12
and delivered me from all my f. Ps 34:4
Happy is the man who f the LORD, Ps 112:1
but my heart f ⌊only⌋ Your word. Ps 119:161
is everyone who f the LORD, Ps 128:1
way the man who f the LORD will Ps 128:4
lives with integrity f the LORD, Pr 14:2
but a woman who f the LORD will Pr 31:30
For the one who f God will end Ec 7:18
so for the one who f an oath. Ec 9:2
Who among you f the LORD, Is 50:10
the person who f Him and does Ac 10:35
on the outside, f inside. 2Co 7:5
So the one who f has not reached 1Jn 4:18

FEAST *(38)*
He prepared a f and baked Gn 19:3
held a great f on the day Isaac Gn 21:8
all the men of the place to a f. Gn 29:22
gave a f for all his servants. Gn 40:20
You are to f there in the Dt 14:26
and Samson prepared a f there, Jdg 14:10
days of the f and figure it out Jdg 14:12
the whole seven days of the f, Jdg 14:17
for we have come on a f day. 1Sm 25:8
Then he held a f for all his 1Kg 3:15
he prepared a great f for them. 2Kg 6:23
the appointed f for seven days, 2Ch 30:22
celebrated the f for seven days, Neh 8:18
He held a f in the third year of Est 1:3
also gave a f for the women Est 1:9
and Haman came to f with Esther Est 7:1
full moon, on the day of our f. Ps 81:3
Do not let me f on their Ps 141:4
Let's f on each other's love! Pr 7:18
heart has a continual f. Pr 15:15
your princes f in the morning. Ec 10:16
and your princes f at the proper Ec 10:17
A f is prepared for laughter, Ec 10:19
will prepare a f for all the Is 25:6
mountain—a f of aged wine, Is 25:6
a mourning f is taking place Jr 16:5
serve them a f, and I will make Jr 51:39
to My sacrificial f that I am Ezk 39:17
a great f on the mountains of Ezk 39:17
at My sacrificial f that I have Ezk 39:19
held a great f for 1,000 of his Dn 5:1
on the day of the LORD's f? Hs 9:5
and let us f our eyes on Zion." Mc 4:11
and let's celebrate with a f, Lk 15:23
us observe the f, not with old 1Co 5:8
deceptions as they f with you, 2Pt 2:13
They f with you, nurturing only Jd 12
to the marriage f of the Lamb!" Rv 19:9

FEASTING *(11)*
was in his house, f like a king. 1Sm 25:36
became a day of f and rejoicing. Est 9:17
became a day of f and rejoicing. Est 9:18
as ⌊a time of⌋ rejoicing and f. Est 9:19
They were to be days of f, Est 9:22
a house full of f with strife. Pr 17:1
than to go to a house of f, Ec 7:2
house where f is taking place Jr 16:8
the f of those who sprawl out Am 6:7
and fine linen, f lavishly every Lk 16:19
Let their f become a snare and a Rm 11:9

FEASTS *(6)*
of the appointed f, as written 2Ch 31:3
At their f they have lyre, Is 5:12
her f, New Moons, and Sabbaths— Hs 2:11
I hate, I despise your f! Am 5:21
I will turn your f into mourning Am 8:10
dangerous reefs at your love f. Jd 12

FEATHERS *(5)*
off the tail f, and throw it Lv 1:16
but are her f and plumage like Jb 39:13
and its f with glistening gold. Ps 68:13
He will cover you with His f; Ps 91:4
like eagles' ⌊f⌋ and his nails Dn 4:33

FED *(15)*
may see the bread I f you in the Ex 16:32
He f you in the wilderness with Dt 8:16
to his house and f the donkeys. Jdg 19:21
f him to the creatures of the Ps 74:14
of flies, which f on them, and Ps 78:45
f them the bread of tears and Ps 80:5
Our cattle will be well f. Ps 144:14
of the poor will be well f, Is 14:30
mouth, and He f me the scroll. Ezk 3:2
oil, and honey that I f you. Ezk 16:19
every creature was f from it. Dn 4:12
he was f grass like cattle, Dn 5:21
I f you milk, not solid food, 1Co 3:2
to be f there for 1,260 days. Rv 12:6
where she was f for a time, Rv 12:14

FEE *(2)*
a prostitute's f is only a loaf Pr 6:26
When you paid a f instead of one Ezk 16:34

FEEBLE *(2)*
but the f are clothed with 1Sm 2:4
provided donkeys for all the f. 2Ch 28:15

FEED *(41)*
We have plenty of straw and f, Gn 24:25
Straw and f were given to the Gn 24:32
sack to get f for his donkey, Gn 42:27
and got f for their donkeys. Gn 43:24
and said, "Who will f us meat? Nm 11:4
LORD: 'Who will f us meat? We Nm 11:18
He will f on enemy nations and Nm 24:8
straw and f for our donkeys, Jdg 19:19
in prison and f him only bread 1Kg 22:27
in prison and f him only bread 2Ch 18:26
it will f on what is left in his Jb 20:26
them; worms f on them; they are Jb 24:20
creatures of the field f on it. Ps 80:13
But He would f Israel with the Ps 81:16
lips of the righteous f many, Pr 10:21
f me with the food I need. Pr 30:8
a gazelle, that f among the Sg 4:5
to f in the gardens and gather Sg 6:2
They will f along the pathways, Is 49:9
will stand and f your flocks, Is 61:5
and the lamb will f together, Is 65:25
I am about to f this people Jr 9:15
am about to f them wormwood and Jr 23:15
person and f all those who are Jr 31:25
and he will f on Carmel and Jr 50:19
themselves ⌊only to f⌋ the fire. Jr 51:58
the shepherds f their flock? Ezk 34:2
shepherds f themselves rather Ezk 34:8
will no longer f themselves, Ezk 34:10
they will f in rich pasture on Ezk 34:14
enough for you to f on the good Ezk 34:18
My flock has to f on what your Ezk 34:19
You will f on grass like cattle Dn 4:25
and you will f on grass like Dn 4:32
They f on the sin of My people; Hs 4:8
did we see You hungry and f You, Mt 25:37
him into his fields to f pigs. Lk 15:15
"F My lambs," He told him. Jn 21:15
"F My sheep," Jesus said. Jn 21:17
If your enemy is hungry, f him. Rm 12:20
all my goods to f the poor, 1Co 13:3

FEEDING *(10)*
the night by your f trough? Jb 39:9
who have been f themselves! Ezk 34:2
or the f ground of the young Nah 2:11
a large herd of pigs was f. Mt 8:30
was there, f on the hillside Mk 5:11
and laid Him in a f trough— Lk 2:7
cloth and lying in a f trough." Lk 2:12
who was lying in the f trough. Lk 2:16
was there, f on the hillside Lk 8:32
or donkey from the f trough on Lk 13:15

FEEDING-TROUGH *(2)*
are no oxen, the f is empty, Pr 14:4
and the donkey its master's f, Is 1:3

FEEDS *(7)*
mouth of fools f on foolishness. Pr 15:14
he f among the lilies. Sg 2:16
he f among the lilies. Sg 6:3
He f on ashes. ⌊His⌋ deceived Is 44:20
yet your heavenly Father f them. Mt 6:26
a barn; yet God f them. Aren't Lk 12:24
so the one who f on Me will live Jn 6:57

FEEL *(13)*
ahead of you to f terror and Ex 23:27
me where I can f the pillars Jdg 16:26
harp, and you will f better." 1Sm 16:16
then be relieved, f better, and 1Sm 16:23
Before your pots can f the heat Ps 58:9
but cannot f, feet, but cannot Ps 115:7
disloyal and f disgust because Ps 119:158
They struck me, but I f no pain! Pr 23:35
can no longer f humiliation. Jr 6:15
can no longer f humiliation. Jr 8:12
distress that they will f it. Jr 10:18
They will f remorse for their Ezk 39:26
and to those who f secure on the Am 6:1

FEELING *(4)*
if a f of jealousy comes over Nm 5:14
or if a f of jealousy comes over Nm 5:14
or when a f of jealousy comes Nm 5:30
when the king was f good from Est 1:10

FEELINGS *(2)*
and my f were stirred for him. Sg 5:4
the same f, focusing on one Php 2:2

FEELS *(2)*
know how it f to be a foreigner Ex 23:9
He f only the pain of his own Jb 14:22

FEES *(2)*
departed with f for divination Nm 22:7
never again pay f for lovers. Ezk 16:41

FEET *(450)*
The ark will be 450 f long, Gn 6:15
feet long, 75 f wide, and 45 Gn 6:15
75 feet wide, and 45 f high. Gn 6:15
above them⌋ more than 20 f. Gn 7:20
you may wash your f and rest Gn 18:4
house, wash your f, and spend Gn 19:2
to wash his f and the feet Gn 24:32
feet and the f of the men with Gn 24:32
gave them water to wash their f, Gn 43:24
or the staff from between his f, Gn 49:10
he drew his f into the bed and Gn 49:33
Take your sandals off your f, Ex 3:5
and threw it at Moses' f. Ex 4:25
sandals on your f, and your Ex 12:11
Beneath His f was something like Ex 24:10
and place ⌊them⌋ on its four f, Ex 25:12
of each curtain should be 42 f, Ex 26:2
the width of each curtain six f; Ex 26:2
should be 45 f and the width Ex 26:8
the width of each curtain six f. Ex 26:8
of each plank is to be 15 f, Ex 26:16
and a half f long, and seven Ex 27:1
and seven and a half f wide; Ex 27:1
must be four and a half f high. Ex 27:1
spun linen, 150 f long on that Ex 27:9
on the north side 150 ⌊f⌋ long. Ex 27:11
on the west side 75 f long, Ex 27:12
side toward the sunrise 75 f. Ex 27:13
of the gate⌋ 22 and a half f, Ex 27:14
other side 22 and a half ⌊f⌋, Ex 27:15

of the courtyard is to be 150 f, Ex 27:18
the width 75 ⌊f⌋ at each end, Ex 27:18
the height seven and a half f, Ex 27:18
the big toes of their right f. Ex 29:20
hands and f from the basin. Ex 30:19
their hands and f so that they Ex 30:21
length of each curtain was 42 f, Ex 36:9
the width of each curtain six f; Ex 36:9
length of each curtain was 45 f, Ex 36:15
the width of each curtain six f. Ex 36:15
length of each plank was 15 f, Ex 36:21
for it to be on its four f, Ex 37:3
and a half f long and seven Ex 38:1
and seven and a half f wide, Ex 38:1
and was four and a half f high. Ex 38:1
spun linen, 150 f in length, Ex 38:9
side were also 150 f in length, Ex 38:11
west side were 75 f in length, Ex 38:12
were also 75 f in length. Ex 38:13
the gate⌋ were 22 and a half f, Ex 38:14
hangings were 22 and a half f, Ex 38:15
It was 30 f long, and like the Ex 38:18
seven and a half f high. Ex 38:18
their hands and f from it. Ex 40:31
the big toes of their right f. Lv 8:24
legs above their f for hopping Lv 11:21
that have four f are to be Lv 11:23
walks on all fours or on many f, Lv 11:42
his head to his f so far as the Lv 13:12
around, three f off the ground, Nm 11:31
It is 13 f six inches long and Dt 3:11
long and six f wide by a Dt 3:11
and your f did not swell these Dt 8:4
sandals on your f did not wear Dt 29:5
and they assemble at Your f. Dt 33:3
When the f of the priests who Jos 3:13
their f touched the water at its Jos 3:15
the priests' f are standing, Jos 4:3
and their f stepped out on solid Jos 4:18
Remove the sandals from your f, Jos 5:15
on their f and threadbare Jos 9:5
here and put your f on the necks Jos 10:24
and put their f on their necks. Jos 10:24
he fell, he lay down at her f; Jdg 5:27
he collapsed, he fell at her f; Jdg 5:27
washed their f and ate and drank Jdg 19:21
and uncover his f, and lie down. Ru 3:4
uncovered his f, and lay down. Ru 3:7
lying at his f was a woman! Ru 3:8
lay down at his f until morning Ru 3:14
went up using his hands and f, 1Sm 14:13
He was nine f, nine inches tall 1Sm 17:4
She fell at his f and said, 1Sm 25:24
to wash the f of my lord's 1Sm 25:41
your f not placed in bronze 2Sm 3:34
had a son whose f were crippled. 2Sm 4:4
hands and f and hung ⌊their 2Sm 4:12
son who is lame in both f." 2Sm 9:3
table. He was lame in both f. 2Sm 9:13
to your house and wash your f." 2Sm 11:8
He had not taken care of his f, 2Sm 19:24
a dark cloud beneath His f. 2Sm 22:10
He makes my f like ⌊the feet of⌋ 2Sm 22:34
my feet like ⌊the f of⌋ a deer 2Sm 22:34
they fall beneath my f. 2Sm 22:39
and on the sandals of his f. 1Kg 2:5
put his enemies under his f. 1Kg 5:3
for the LORD was 90 f long, 1Kg 6:2
90 feet long, 30 f wide, and 45 1Kg 6:2
30 feet wide, and 45 f high. 1Kg 6:2
was 30 f long extending 1Kg 6:3
and 15 f deep in front of the 1Kg 6:3
was seven and a half f wide, 1Kg 6:6
the middle was nine f wide, 1Kg 6:6
third was 10 and a half f wide. 1Kg 6:6
was⌋ seven and a half f high. 1Kg 6:10
Then he lined 30 f of the rear 1Kg 6:16
most holy place, was 60 f long. 1Kg 6:17
of the sanctuary was 30 f long, 1Kg 6:20
30 feet long, 30 f wide, and 30 1Kg 6:20
30 feet wide, and 30 f high; 1Kg 6:20
two cherubim 15 f high out of 1Kg 6:23
was seven and a half f long, 1Kg 6:24
was seven and a half f long. 1Kg 6:24
was 15 f from tip to tip 1Kg 6:24
The second cherub also was 15 f; 1Kg 6:25
height was 15 f and so was the 1Kg 6:26
It was 150 f long, 75 feet wide, 1Kg 7:2
feet long, 75 f wide, and 45 1Kg 7:2
and 45 f high on four rows of 1Kg 7:2
of pillars 75 f long and 45 feet 1Kg 7:6
75 feet long and 45 f wide. 1Kg 7:6
costly stones 12 and 15 f long. 1Kg 7:10
each 27 f high and 18 feet in 1Kg 7:15
high and 18 f in circumference 1Kg 7:15
and a half f was the height 1Kg 7:16
seven and a half f was also the 1Kg 7:16
like lilies, six f ⌊high⌋. 1Kg 7:19
reservoir, 15 f from brim to 1Kg 7:23
and a half f high and 45 feet 1Kg 7:23
high and 45 f in circumference 1Kg 7:23
Each water cart was six f long, 1Kg 7:27
feet long, six f wide, and four 1Kg 7:27
and four and a half f high. 1Kg 7:27
and each was six f wide— 1Kg 7:38
the sound of her f entering the 1Kg 14:6
When your f enter the city, 1Kg 14:12
he developed a disease in his f. 1Kg 15:23
mountain, she clung to his f. 2Kg 4:27
came, fell at his f, and bowed 2Kg 4:37
prophets were sitting at his f. 2Kg 4:38
of his master's f behind him?" 2Kg 6:32
her skull, her f, and the palms 2Kg 9:35
of Egypt with the soles of my f. 2Kg 19:24
again cause the f of the 2Kg 21:8
One pillar was 27 f tall and had 2Kg 25:17
of bronze, stood five f high. 2Kg 25:17
who was seven and a half f tall. 1Ch 11:23
David rose to his f and said, 1Ch 28:2
length was 90 f, and the width 2Ch 3:3
was 90 feet, and the width 30 f. 2Ch 3:3
of the temple, was 30 f wide; 2Ch 3:4
height was 30 f; he overlaid its 2Ch 3:4
the temple, 30 f, and its width 2Ch 3:8
30 feet, and its width was 30 f. 2Ch 3:8
wings of the cherubim was 30 f: 2Ch 3:11
of one was seven and a half f, 2Ch 3:11
wing was seven and a half f, 2Ch 3:11
cherub was seven and a half f, 2Ch 3:12
wing was seven and a half f, 2Ch 3:12
of these cherubim was 30 f. 2Ch 3:13
They stood on their f and faced 2Ch 3:13
two pillars, ⌊each⌋ 27 f high. 2Ch 3:15
each was seven and half f high. 2Ch 3:15
made a bronze altar 30 f long, 2Ch 4:1
30 feet long, 30 f wide, and 15 2Ch 4:1
30 feet wide, and 15 f high. 2Ch 4:1
reservoir, 15 f from brim to 2Ch 4:2
It was seven and a half f high, 2Ch 4:2
and 45 f in circumference. 2Ch 4:2
seven and a half f long, 2Ch 6:13
seven and a half f wide, and 2Ch 6:13
four and a half f high and put 2Ch 6:13
developed a disease in his f, 2Ch 16:12
again remove the f of the 2Ch 33:8
is to be 90 f and its width 90 Ezr 6:3
be 90 feet and its width 90 f, Ezr 6:3
and their f did not swell. Neh 9:21
them build a gallows 75 f high. Est 5:14
a gallows 75 f tall at Haman's Est 7:9
She fell at his f, wept, and Est 8:3
for those whose f are slipping. Jb 12:5
You put my f in the stocks and Jb 13:27
a limit for the soles of my f. Jb 13:27
For his own f lead him into a Jb 18:8
f have followed in His tracks; Jb 23:11
when my f were bathed in cream Jb 29:6
older men stood to their f. Jb 29:8
to the blind and f to the lame. Jb 29:15
they trap my f and construct Jb 30:12
He puts my f in the stocks; Jb 33:11
You put everything under his f: Ps 8:6
Your paths; my f have not Ps 17:5
a dark cloud beneath His f. Ps 18:9
He makes my f like the feet of a Ps 18:33
my feet like the f of a deer and Ps 18:33
they fall beneath my f. Ps 18:38
they pierced my hands and my f. Ps 22:16
will pull my f out of the net. Ps 25:15
You have set my f in a spacious Ps 31:8
clay, and set my f on a rock, Ps 40:2
us and nations under our f. Ps 47:3
death, even my f from stumbling, Ps 56:13
he will wash his f in the blood Ps 58:10
does not allow our f to slip. Ps 66:9
as for me, my f almost slipped; Ps 73:2
They hurt his f with shackles; Ps 105:18
cannot feel, f, but cannot walk Ps 115:7
from tears, my f from stumbling. Ps 116:8
I have kept my f from every evil Ps 119:101
a lamp for my f and a light on Ps 119:105
Our f are standing within your Ps 122:2
because their f run toward Pr 1:16
consider the path for your f, Pr 4:26
keep your f away from evil. Pr 4:27
Her f go down to death; Pr 5:5
signals with his f, and gestures Pr 6:13
wicked schemes, f eager to run Pr 6:18
coals without scorching his f? Pr 6:28
her f do not stay at home. Pr 7:11
cuts off his own f and drinks Pr 26:6
spreads a net for his f. Pr 29:5
have washed my f. How can I get Sg 5:3
beautiful are your sandaled f, Sg 7:1
with two he covered his f, Is 6:2
remove the sandals from your f," Is 20:2
whose f have taken her to settle Is 23:7
F trample it, the feet of the Is 26:6
trample it, the f of the humble, Is 26:6
of Egypt with the soles of my f. Is 37:25
He calls righteousness to his f. Is 41:2
touching the path with his f. Is 41:3
and lick the dust at your f. Is 49:23
are the f of the herald, Is 52:7
Their f run after evil, and they Is 59:7
down on their faces at your f. Is 60:14
Keep your f from going bare and Jr 2:25
before your f stumble on the Jr 13:16
they never rest their f. Jr 14:10
and have hidden snares for my f. Jr 18:22
Your f sank into the mire, Jr 38:22
One pillar was 27 f tall, had a Jr 52:21
had a circumference of 18 f, Jr 52:21
stood seven and a half f high. Jr 52:22
a net for my f and turned me Lm 1:13
of the land beneath one's f, Lm 3:34
the soles of their f were like Ezk 1:7
up on your f and I will speak Ezk 2:1
entered me and set me on my f, Ezk 2:2
entered me and set me on my f. Ezk 3:24
stamp your f, and cry out over Ezk 6:11
strap your sandals on your f; Ezk 24:17
and your sandals on your f. Ezk 24:23
stamped ⌊your⌋ f, and rejoiced Ezk 25:6
churn up the waters with your f, Ezk 32:2
rest of the pasture with your f? Ezk 34:18
also muddy the rest with your f? Ezk 34:18
on what your f have trampled, Ezk 34:19
drink what your f have muddied. Ezk 34:19
to life and stood on their f, Ezk 37:10
was about 10 f, and its height Ezk 40:5
it was 10 f deep—the first Ezk 40:6
first threshold was 10 f deep. Ezk 40:6
was about 10 f long and 10 feet Ezk 40:7
10 feet long and 10 f deep, Ezk 40:7
and three-quarter f between the Ezk 40:7
gate's portico was about 10 f. Ezk 40:7
it was 14 f, and its pilasters Ezk 40:9
were three and a half f. Ezk 40:9
17 and a half f, while the width Ezk 40:11
was 22 and three-quarter f. Ezk 40:11
were 10 and a half f square. Ezk 40:12
was 43 and three-quarter f. Ezk 40:13
measured the pilasters—105 f. Ezk 40:14
the inside was 87 and a half f. Ezk 40:15
court; it was 175 f. ⌊This⌋ was Ezk 40:19
87 and a half f long and 43 and Ezk 40:21
and 43 and three-quarter f wide. Ezk 40:21
from gate to gate; it was 175 f. Ezk 40:23
was 87 and a half f long and 43 Ezk 40:25
and 43 and three-quarter f wide. Ezk 40:25
gate on the south; it was 175 f. Ezk 40:27
was 87 and a half f long and 43 Ezk 40:29
and 43 and three-quarter f wide. Ezk 40:29
three-quarter f long and eight Ezk 40:30
eight and three-quarter f wide. Ezk 40:30
was 87 and a half f long and 43 Ezk 40:33
and 43 and three-quarter f wide. Ezk 40:33
was 87 and a half f long and 43 Ezk 40:36
and 43 and three-quarter f wide. Ezk 40:36
175 f long and 175 feet wide. Ezk 40:47
175 feet long and 175 f wide. Ezk 40:47
three-quarter f ⌊thick⌋ on each Ezk 40:48
the gateway was 24 and a half f, Ezk 40:48

and a quarter **f** ⌊wide⌋ on each Ezk 40:48
portico was 35 **f** across and 21 Ezk 40:49
35 feet across and 21 **f** deep, Ezk 40:49
pilaster was 10 and a half **f**. Ezk 41:1
entrance was 17 and a half **f**, Ezk 41:2
three-quarter **f** ⌊wide⌋ on each Ezk 41:2
great hall, 70 **f**, and the width, Ezk 41:2
70 feet, and the width, 35 **f**. Ezk 41:2
were three and a half **f** ⌊wide⌋. Ezk 41:3
was 10 and a half **f** ⌊wide⌋, Ezk 41:3
side was 12 and a quarter **f**. Ezk 41:3
great hall, 35 **f**, and the width, Ezk 41:4
35 feet, and the width, 35 **f**. Ezk 41:4
it was 10 and a half **f** ⌊thick⌋. Ezk 41:5
around the temple was seven **f**. Ezk 41:5
rooms was 10 and a half **f** high. Ezk 41:8
was eight and three-quarter **f**. Ezk 41:9
chambers was 35 **f** wide all Ezk 41:10
three-quarter **f** wide all around Ezk 41:11
west was 122 and a half **f** wide. Ezk 41:12
and three-quarter **f** thick on all Ezk 41:12
length was 157 and a half **f**. Ezk 41:12
it was 175 **f** long. In addition Ezk 41:13
its walls, were 175 **f** long. Ezk 41:13
yard to the east was 175 **f**. Ezk 41:14
side; it was 175 **f**. The interior Ezk 41:15
and a quarter **f** high and three Ezk 41:22
and three and a half **f** long. Ezk 41:22
which was 175 **f**, there was an Ezk 42:2
the width was 87 and a half **f**. Ezk 42:2
and a half **f** wide and 175 feet Ezk 42:4
a half feet wide and 175 **f** long, Ezk 42:4
it was 87 and a half **f** long. Ezk 42:7
court were 87 and a half **f** long, Ezk 42:8
great hall were 175 **f** ⌊long⌋. Ezk 42:8
it was 875 **f** by the measuring Ezk 42:16
it was 875 **f** by the measuring Ezk 42:17
it was 875 **f** by the measuring Ezk 42:18
measured 875 **f** by the measuring Ezk 42:19
⌊**f**⌋ long and 875 ⌊feet⌋ wide, Ezk 42:20
⌊feet⌋ long and 875 ⌊**f**⌋ wide, Ezk 42:20
the place for the soles of My **f**, Ezk 43:7
ledge is three and a half **f**, Ezk 43:14
There are seven **f** from the small Ezk 43:14
altar hearth is seven **f** ⌊high⌋, Ezk 43:15
21 **f** long by 21 feet wide. Ezk 43:16
21 feet long by 21 **f** wide. Ezk 43:16
24 and a half **f** long by 24 and Ezk 43:17
long by 24 and a half **f** wide, Ezk 43:17
875 by 875 ⌊**f**⌋, with 87 and a Ezk 45:2
87 and a half **f** of open space Ezk 45:2
70 ⌊**f**⌋ long by 52 and a half Ezk 46:22
long by 52 and a half ⌊**f**⌋ wide. Ezk 46:22
425 ⌊**f**⌋ to the north, 425 ⌊feet⌋ Ezk 48:17
the north, 425 ⌊**f**⌋ to the south, Ezk 48:17
the south, 425 ⌊**f**⌋ to the east, Ezk 48:17
east, and 425 ⌊**f**⌋ to the west. Ezk 48:17
and its **f** were partly iron and Dn 2:33
statue on its **f** of iron and Dn 2:34
You saw the **f** and toes, partly Dn 2:41
the toes of the **f** were part iron Dn 2:42
90 **f** high and nine feet wide. Dn 3:1
90 feet high and nine **f** wide. Dn 3:1
ground, set on its **f** like a man, Dn 7:4
with its **f** whatever was left Dn 7:7
with its **f** whatever was left Dn 7:19
his arms and **f** like the gleam of Dn 10:6
Stand on your **f**, for I have now Dn 10:11
are the dust beneath His **f**. Nah 1:3
the **f** of one bringing good news Nah 1:15
He makes my **f** like those of a Hab 3:19
"30 **f** long and 15 feet wide." Zch 5:2
"30 feet long and 15 **f** wide." Zch 5:2
On that day His **f** will stand on Zch 14:4
rot while they stand on their **f**, Zch 14:12
soles of your **f** on the day I am Mal 4:3
will trample them with their **f**, Mt 7:6
dust off your **f** when you leave Mt 10:14
put them at His **f**, and He healed Mt 15:30
two hands or two **f** and be thrown Mt 18:8
put Your enemies under Your **f**'? Mt 22:44
hold of His **f**, and worshiped Mt 28:9
he saw Jesus, he fell at His **f** Mk 5:22
dust off your **f** as a testimony Mk 6:11
spirit came and fell at His **f**. Mk 7:25
than to have two **f** and be thrown Mk 9:45
put Your enemies under Your **f**.' Mk 12:36
to guide our **f** into the way of Lk 1:79
and stood behind Him at His **f**, Lk 7:38
to wash His **f** with her tears. Lk 7:38
She wiped His **f** with the hair of Lk 7:38
you gave Me no water for My **f**, Lk 7:44
has washed My **f** and wiped them Lk 7:44
stopped kissing My **f** since I Lk 7:45
has anointed My **f** with fragrant Lk 7:46
sitting at Jesus' **f**, dressed and Lk 8:35
at Jesus' **f** and pleaded with Lk 8:41
dust from your **f** as a testimony Lk 9:5
your town that clings to our **f**. Lk 10:11
at the Lord's **f** and was Lk 10:39
his finger and sandals on his **f**. Lk 15:22
He fell facedown at His **f**, Lk 17:16
Look at My hands and My **f**, Lk 24:39
He showed them His hands and **f**. Lk 24:40
and wiped His **f** with her hair, Jn 11:2
she fell at His **f** and told Him, Jn 11:32
anointed Jesus' **f**, and wiped His Jn 12:3
and wiped His **f** with her hair. Jn 12:3
His disciples' **f** and to dry them Jn 13:5
are You going to wash my **f**?" Jn 13:6
You will never wash my **f**— Jn 13:8
Lord, not only my **f**, but also my Jn 13:9
to wash anything except his **f**, Jn 13:10
washed their **f** and put on His Jn 13:12
washed your **f**, you also ought Jn 13:14
ought to wash one another's **f**. Jn 13:14
at the head and one at the **f**, Jn 20:12
and at once his **f** and ankles Ac 3:7
laid them at the apostles' **f**. Ac 4:35
and laid it at the apostles' **f**. Ac 4:37
and laid it at the apostles' **f**. Ac 5:2
The **f** of those who have buried Ac 5:9
she dropped dead at his **f**. Ac 5:10
Take the sandals off your **f**, Ac 7:33
robes at the **f** of a young man Ac 7:58
him, fell at his **f**, and Ac 10:25
to untie the sandals on His **f**.' Ac 13:25
dust off their **f** against them, Ac 13:51
a man without strength in his **f**, Ac 14:8
"Stand up straight on your **f**!" Ac 14:10
secured their **f** in the stocks. Ac 16:24
belt, tied his own **f** and hands, Ac 21:11
this city at the **f** of Gamaliel, Ac 22:3
But get up and stand on your **f**. Ac 26:16
and found it to be 120 **f** deep; Ac 27:28
they found it to be 90 **f** deep. Ac 27:28
Their **f** are swift to shed blood; Rm 3:15
welcome are the **f** of those who Rm 10:15
soon crush Satan under your **f**. Rm 16:20
nor again the head to the **f**, 1Co 12:21
all His enemies under His **f**. 1Co 15:25
has put everything under His **f**. 1Co 15:27
under His **f** and appointed Him as Eph 1:22
and your **f** sandaled with Eph 6:15
washed the saints' **f**, helped the 1Tm 5:10
everything under his **f**. Heb 2:8
make straight paths for your **f**, Heb 12:13
His **f** like fine bronze fired in Rv 1:15
I fell at His **f** like a dead man. Rv 1:17
and whose **f** are like fine bronze Rv 2:18
come and bow down at your **f**, Rv 3:9
and they stood on their **f**. Rv 11:11
with the moon under her **f**, Rv 12:1
a leopard, his **f** were like a Rv 13:2
I fell at his **f** to worship him, Rv 19:10
worship at the **f** of the angel Rv 22:8

FELDSPAR *(1)*

on a mosaic pavement of red **f**, Est 1:6

FELIX *(9)*

him safely to **F** the governor." Ac 23:24
the most excellent governor **F**: Ac 23:26
most excellent **F**, with all Ac 24:3
Since **F** was accurately informed Ac 24:22
when **F** came with his wife Ac 24:24
F became afraid and replied, Ac 24:25
years had passed, **F** received a Ac 24:27
for the Jews, **F** left Paul in Ac 24:27
who was left as a prisoner by **F**. Ac 25:14

FELL *(166)*

and the rain **f** on the earth 40 Gn 7:12
fled, ⌊some⌋ **f** into them, Gn 14:10
a deep sleep **f** on Abram, Gn 15:12
Then Abram **f** to the ground, Gn 17:3
f to the ground, laughed, Gn 17:17
He **f** asleep and dreamed a second Gn 41:5
They **f** to the ground before him. Gn 44:14
about 3,000 men **f** dead that day Ex 32:28
they shouted and **f** facedown ⌊on Lv 9:24
When the dew **f** on the camp at Nm 11:9
and Aaron **f** down with their Nm 14:5
heard ⌊this⌋, he **f** facedown. Nm 16:4
Moses and Aaron **f** facedown and Nm 16:22
instantly." But they **f** facedown. Nm 16:45
They **f** down with their faces ⌊to Nm 20:6
I **f** down like the first time Dt 9:18
I **f** down in the presence of the Dt 9:25
Before the men **f** asleep, she Jos 2:8
his clothes and **f** before the ark Jos 7:6
total of those who **f** that day, Jos 8:25
result, 10 tracts **f** to Manasseh, Jos 17:5
army of Sisera **f** by the sword; Jdg 4:16
collapsed, he **f**, he lay down at Jdg 5:27
he collapsed, he **f** at her feet; Jdg 5:27
he collapsed, there he **f**—dead. Jdg 5:27
camp, struck a tent, and it **f**. Jdg 7:13
they **f** facedown on the ground. Jdg 13:20
and his bonds **f** off his wrists. Jdg 15:14
he **f** in love with a woman named Jdg 16:4
and the temple **f** on the leaders Jdg 16:30
the Israelite foot soldiers **f**. 1Sm 4:10
Eli **f** backwards off the chair by 1Sm 4:18
of the LORD **f** on the people, 1Sm 11:7
and he **f** on his face to the 1Sm 17:49
f with his face to the ground, 1Sm 20:41
the donkey and **f** with her face 1Sm 25:23
She **f** at his feet and said, 1Sm 25:24
Saul **f** flat on the ground. 1Sm 28:20
Saul took his sword and **f** on it. 1Sm 31:4
he also **f** on his own sword and 1Sm 31:5
he **f** to the ground and paid 2Sm 1:2
and he **f** and died right there. 2Sm 2:23
You **f** like one who falls victim 2Sm 3:34
to flee, he **f** and became lame. 2Sm 4:4
David's soldiers **f** ⌊in battle⌋; 2Sm 11:17
f with her face to the ground 2Sm 14:4
Joab **f** with his face to the 2Sm 14:22
the Jordan, he **f** down before the 2Sm 19:18
approached, ⌊the sword⌋ **f** out. 2Sm 20:8
he **f** with his face ⌊to the 1Kg 18:7
Yahweh's fire **f** and consumed 1Kg 18:38
they **f** facedown and said, 1Kg 18:39
and the wall **f** on those 27,000 1Kg 20:30
of 50 went up and **f** on his knees 2Kg 1:13
She came, **f** at his feet, and 2Kg 4:37
iron ⌊ax head⌋ **f** into the water, 2Kg 6:5
Saul took his sword and **f** on it. 1Ch 10:4
he also **f** on his own sword and 1Ch 10:5
f down with their faces ⌊to the 1Ch 21:16
The first lot **f** to Jehoiarib, 1Ch 24:7
first lot for Asaph **f** to Joseph, 1Ch 25:9
the east ⌊gate⌋ **f** to Shelemiah. 1Ch 26:14
The Cushites **f** until they had no 2Ch 14:13
of Jerusalem **f** down before the 2Ch 20:18
Our fathers **f** by the sword, 2Ch 29:9
Then I **f** on my knees and spread Ezr 9:5
and it **f** on the twelfth month, Est 3:7
She **f** at his feet, wept, and Est 8:3
terror of them **f** on every Est 9:2
f to the ground and worshiped, Jb 1:20
but **f** into the hole he had made. Ps 7:15
and my enemies stumbled and **f**. Ps 27:2
ahead of me, but they **f** into it! Ps 57:6
His priests **f** by the sword, Ps 78:64
Your discipline ⌊**f**⌋ on them. Is 26:16
Suddenly Babylon **f** and was Jr 51:8
of all the earth **f** because of Jr 51:49
When her people **f** into the Lm 1:7
I **f** facedown and heard a voice Ezk 1:28
Chebar Canal, and I **f** facedown. Ezk 3:23
And I **f** facedown and cried out, Ezk 9:8
Then I **f** facedown and cried out Ezk 11:13
Its limbs **f** on the mountains and Ezk 31:12
so that they all **f** by the sword. Ezk 39:23
the Chebar Canal. I **f** facedown. Ezk 43:3
His temple. And I **f** facedown. Ezk 44:4
Then King Nebuchadnezzar **f** down, Dn 2:46
and language **f** down and Dn 3:7
Meshach, and Abednego **f**, bound, Dn 3:23
which three **f**—the horn that Dn 7:20
I was terrified and **f** facedown. Dn 8:17
to me, I **f** into a deep sleep Dn 8:18
but a great terror **f** on them, Dn 10:7
I heard them I **f** into a deep Dn 10:9
The rain **f**, the rivers rose, and Mt 7:25

The rain **f**, the rivers rose, the Mt 7:27
he had a sheep that **f** into a pit Mt 12:11
some seeds **f** along the path, Mt 13:4
Others **f** on rocky ground, where Mt 13:5
Others **f** among thorns, and the Mt 13:7
Still others **f** on good ground, Mt 13:8
they **f** facedown and were Mt 17:6
the slave **f** facedown before him Mt 18:26
fellow slave **f** down and began Mt 18:29
all became drowsy and **f** asleep. Mt 25:5
He **f** facedown and prayed, Mt 26:39
those possessed **f** down before Mk 3:11
Some seed **f** along the path, Mk 4:4
Other seed **f** on rocky ground Mk 4:5
Other seed **f** among thorns, Mk 4:7
Still others **f** on good ground Mk 4:8
he saw Jesus, he **f** at His feet Mk 5:22
trembling, **f** down before Him, Mk 5:33
spirit came and **f** at His feet. Mk 7:25
He **f** to the ground and rolled Mk 9:20
little farther, **f** to the ground, Mk 14:35
he **f** at Jesus' knees and said, Lk 5:8
He saw Jesus, **f** facedown, and Lk 5:12
sowing, some **f** along the path; Lk 8:5
Other seed **f** on the rock; Lk 8:6
Other seed **f** among thorns; Lk 8:7
other seed **f** on good ground; Lk 8:8
the seed that **f** among thorns, Lk 8:14
they were sailing He **f** asleep. Lk 8:23
he cried out, **f** down before Him, Lk 8:28
He **f** down at Jesus' feet and Lk 8:41
trembling and **f** down before Him. Lk 8:47
to Jericho and **f** into the hands Lk 10:30
to the man who **f** into the hands Lk 10:36
in Siloam **f** on and killed— Lk 13:4
filled with what **f** from the rich Lk 16:21
He **f** facedown at His feet, Lk 17:16
she **f** at His feet and told Him, Jn 11:32
back and **f** to the ground. Jn 18:6
and the lot **f** to Matthias. Ac 1:26
And saying this, he **f** asleep. Ac 7:60
like scales **f** from his eyes, Ac 9:18
met him, **f** at his feet, Ac 10:25
the chains **f** off his wrists. Ac 12:7
a mist and darkness **f** on him, Ac 13:11
in God's plan, **f** asleep, was Ac 13:36
the whole assembly **f** silent and Ac 15:12
and **f** down trembling before Paul Ac 16:29
Then fear **f** on all of them, Ac 19:17
of the image that **f** from heaven? Ac 19:35
by sleep he **f** down from the Ac 20:9
I **f** to the ground and heard a Ac 22:7
single day 23,000 people **f** dead. 1Co 10:8
whose bodies **f** in the desert? Heb 3:17
of Jericho **f** down after being Heb 11:30
ever since the fathers **f** asleep, 2Pt 3:4
I **f** at His feet like a dead man. Rv 1:17
and the 24 elders **f** down before Rv 5:8
and the elders **f** down and Rv 5:14
stars of heaven **f** to the earth Rv 6:13
and they **f** on their faces before Rv 7:11
like a torch, **f** from heaven. Rv 8:10
f on a third of the rivers and Rv 8:10
So great fear **f** on those who saw Rv 11:11
of the city **f**, and 7,000 people Rv 11:13
f on their faces and worshiped Rv 11:16
and the cities of the nations **f**. Rv 16:19
f from heaven on the people, Rv 16:21
living creatures **f** down and Rv 19:4
Then I **f** at his feet to worship Rv 19:10
I **f** down to worship at the feet Rv 22:8

FELLED *(2)*

which leaves a stump when **f**, Is 6:13
be cut down, the high ⌊trees⌋ **f**. Is 10:33

FELLOW *(32)*

and all your **f** Levites who are Nm 16:10
I have selected your **f** Levites Nm 18:6
If your **f** Hebrew, a man or Dt 15:12
God like all his **f** Levites who Dt 18:7
not obey their **f** Israelites. Jdg 20:13
said to his **f** prophet by the 1Kg 20:35
bread with their **f** priests. 2Kg 23:9
priest and his **f** priests before 1Ch 16:39
priest and his **f** priests began Neh 3:1
After him their **f** ⌊Levites⌋ made Neh 3:18
makes his **f** man serve without Jr 22:13
one of his **f** slaves who owed Mt 18:28
his **f** slave fell down and began Mt 18:29
have had mercy on your **f** slave, Mt 18:33
and starts to beat his **f** slaves, Mt 24:49
said to his **f** disciples, "Let's Jn 11:16
my **f** countrymen and fellow Rm 16:7
countrymen and **f** prisoners. Rm 16:7
Greet Herodion, my **f** countryman. Rm 16:11
Sosipater, my **f** countrymen, Rm 16:21
but **f** citizens with the saints, Eph 2:19
co-worker, and **f** soldier, as Php 2:25
our much loved **f** slave. Col 1:7
and a **f** slave in the Lord, Col 4:7
Aristarchus, my **f** prisoner, Col 4:10
to Archippus our **f** soldier, Phm 2
my **f** prisoner in Christ Jesus, Phm 23
will not teach his **f** citizen, Heb 8:11
as a **f** elder and witness to the 1Pt 5:1
of⌋ their **f** slaves and their Rv 6:11
I am a **f** slave with you and your Rv 19:10
I am a **f** slave with you, your Rv 22:9

FELLOWSHIP *(101)*

burnt offerings and **f** offerings, Ex 20:24
bulls as **f** offerings to Ex 24:5
from their **f** sacrifices, Ex 29:28
and presented **f** offerings. Ex 32:6
his offering is a **f** sacrifice, Lv 3:1
part of the **f** sacrifice as a Lv 3:3
his offering as a **f** sacrifice to Lv 3:6
part of the **f** sacrifice as a Lv 3:9
from the ox of the **f** sacrifice. Lv 4:10
like the fat of the **f** sacrifice. Lv 4:26
is removed from the **f** sacrifice. Lv 4:31
is removed from the **f** sacrifice. Lv 4:35
from the **f** offerings on it. Lv 6:12
the law of the **f** sacrifice that Lv 7:11
his thanksgiving sacrifice of **f**. Lv 7:13
the blood of the **f** offering; Lv 7:14
sacrifice of **f** must be eaten on Lv 7:15
the meat of his **f** sacrifice is Lv 7:18
the LORD's **f** sacrifice while Lv 7:20
from the LORD's **f** sacrifice, Lv 7:21
one who presents a **f** sacrifice Lv 7:29
from your **f** sacrifices. Lv 7:32
the blood of the **f** offering and Lv 7:33
from their **f** sacrifices, Lv 7:34
offering, and the **f** sacrifice, Lv 7:37
ox and a ram for a **f** offering to Lv 9:4
ram as the people's **f** sacrifice. Lv 9:18
offering, and the **f** offering. Lv 9:22
the Israelites' **f** sacrifices. Lv 10:14
and offer them as **f** sacrifices Lv 17:5
When you offer a **f** sacrifice to Lv 19:5
a man presents a **f** sacrifice to Lv 22:21
a year old as a **f** sacrifice. Lv 23:19
unblemished ram as a **f** offering, Nm 6:14
offer the ram as a **f** sacrifice Nm 6:17
the fire under the **f** sacrifice. Nm 6:18
a year old, for the **f** sacrifice. Nm 7:17
a year old, for the **f** sacrifice. Nm 7:23
a year old, for the **f** sacrifice. Nm 7:29
a year old, for the **f** sacrifice. Nm 7:35
a year old, for the **f** sacrifice. Nm 7:41
a year old, for the **f** sacrifice. Nm 7:47
a year old, for the **f** sacrifice. Nm 7:53
a year old, for the **f** sacrifice. Nm 7:59
a year old, for the **f** sacrifice. Nm 7:65
a year old, for the **f** sacrifice. Nm 7:71
a year old, for the **f** sacrifice. Nm 7:77
a year old, for the **f** sacrifice. Nm 7:83
for the **f** sacrifice totaled Nm 7:88
offerings and your **f** sacrifices Nm 10:10
or as a **f** offering to the LORD, Nm 15:8
grain, drink, or **f** offerings." Nm 29:39
are to sacrifice **f** offerings, Dt 27:7
sacrificed **f** offerings on it. Jos 8:31
to sacrifice **f** offerings on it Jos 22:23
sacrifices, and **f** offerings. Jos 22:27
offerings and **f** offerings to Jdg 20:26
burnt offerings and **f** offerings. Jdg 21:4
and to sacrifice **f** offerings. 1Sm 10:8
they sacrificed **f** offerings 1Sm 11:15
offering and the **f** offerings." 1Sm 13:9
burnt offerings and **f** offerings 2Sm 6:17
offering and the **f** offerings, 2Sm 6:18
burnt offerings and **f** offerings. 2Sm 24:25
burnt offerings and **f** offerings. 1Kg 3:15
sacrifice of **f** offerings to the 1Kg 8:63
the fat of the **f** offerings since 1Kg 8:64
and the fat of the **f** offerings. 1Kg 8:64
burnt offerings and **f** offerings 1Kg 9:25
the blood of his **f** offerings on 2Kg 16:13
offerings and **f** offerings in 1Ch 16:1
offerings and the **f** offerings, 1Ch 16:2
burnt offerings and **f** offerings. 1Ch 21:26
the fat of the **f** offerings since 2Ch 7:7
the fat ⌊of the **f** offerings⌋. 2Ch 7:7
the fat of the **f** offerings and 2Ch 29:35
sacrificing **f** offerings and 2Ch 30:22
burnt offerings and **f** offerings, 2Ch 31:2
LORD and offered **f** and thank 2Ch 33:16
We used to have close **f**; Ps 55:14
I've made **f** offerings; Pr 7:14
be present in the **f** of My people Ezk 13:9
burnt offerings and **f** offerings Ezk 43:27
offerings, and **f** offerings, to Ezk 45:15
f offerings to make atonement Ezk 45:17
burnt offerings and **f** offerings. Ezk 46:2
burnt offering or a **f** offering Ezk 46:12
offering or **f** offering just as Ezk 46:12
regard for your **f** offerings of Am 5:22
teaching, to **f**, to the breaking Ac 2:42
to their own **f** and reported all Ac 4:23
were called into **f** with His Son, 1Co 1:9
Or what **f** does light have with 2Co 6:14
and the **f** of the Holy Spirit be 2Co 13:13
the right hand of **f** to me and Gl 2:9
love, if any **f** with the Spirit Php 2:1
and the **f** of His sufferings, Php 3:10
you may have **f** along with us; 1Jn 1:3
and indeed our **f** is with the 1Jn 1:3
say, "We have **f** with Him," and 1Jn 1:6
we have **f** with one another, 1Jn 1:7

FELT *(7)*

wife were naked, yet **f** no shame. Gn 2:25
She **f** sorry for him and said, Ex 2:6
a darkness that can be **f**." Ex 10:21
because she **f** great compassion 1Kg 3:26
struck them, but they **f** no pain. Jr 5:3
the crowds, He **f** compassion for Mt 9:36
a huge crowd, **f** compassion for Mt 14:14

FEMALE *(104)*

He created them male and **f**. Gn 1:27
He created them male and **f**. Gn 5:2
flesh, male and **f**, to keep them Gn 6:19
a male and its **f**, of all the Gn 7:2
are not clean, a male and its **f**, Gn 7:2
pairs, male and **f**, of the birds Gn 7:3
each, male and **f**, entered the Gn 7:9
male and **f** of all flesh, Gn 7:16
herds, male and **f** donkeys, male Gn 12:16
donkeys, male and **f** slaves, and Gn 12:16
cow, a three-year-old **f** goat, a Gn 15:9
cattle and male and **f** slaves, Gn 20:14
and his **f** slaves so that they Gn 20:17
gold, male and **f** slaves, and Gn 24:35
and speckled among the **f** goats. Gn 30:32
⌊If I have⌋ any **f** goats that are Gn 30:33
speckled and spotted **f** goats— Gn 30:35
flocks, male and **f** slaves, and Gn 30:43
the tents of the two **f** slaves, Gn 31:33
Your ewes and **f** goats have not Gn 31:38
flocks, male and **f** slaves. Gn 32:5
200 **f** goats, 20 male goats, 200 Gn 32:14
10 bulls, 20 **f** donkeys, and 10 Gn 32:15
wives, his two **f** slaves, and his Gn 32:22
Rachel, and the two **f** slaves. Gn 33:1
He put the **f** slaves first, Gn 33:2
Then the **f** slaves and their Gn 33:6
and 10 **f** donkeys carrying grain, Gn 45:23
your male or **f** slave, your Ex 20:10
wife, his male or **f** slave, his Ex 20:17
his male or **f** slave with a rod, Ex 21:20
of his male or **f** slave and Ex 21:26
tooth of his male or **f** slave, Ex 21:27
the ox gores a male or **f** slave, Ex 21:32
the son of your **f** slave as well Ex 23:12
whether male or **f**, he must Lv 3:1
a male or **f** without blemish. Lv 3:6
an unblemished **f** goat as his Lv 4:28
he is to bring an unblemished **f**. Lv 4:32
a **f** lamb or goat from the flock Lv 5:6
if she gives birth to a **f** child, Lv 12:5
birth, whether to a male or **f**. Lv 12:7
a discharge, whether male or **f**; Lv 15:33
your male or **f** slave, and the Lv 25:6
Your male and **f** slaves are to be Lv 25:44
may purchase male and **f** slaves. Lv 25:44

person is a **f**, your valuation Lv 27:4
shekels and for a **f** 10 shekels. Lv 27:5
and for a **f** your valuation is Lv 27:6
a male and 10 shekels for a **f**. Lv 27:7
must send away both male or **f**; Nm 5:3
year-old **f** lamb as a sin Nm 6:14
a year-old **f** goat as a sin Nm 15:27
"Have you let every **f** live?" Nm 31:15
of any figure: a male or **f** form, Dt 4:16
your male or **f** slave, your ox Dt 5:14
your male and **f** slaves may rest Dt 5:14
his male or **f** slave, his ox Dt 5:21
male or **f** among you or your Dt 7:14
your male and **f** slaves, and the Dt 12:12
your male and **f** slave, and the Dt 12:18
Also treat your **f** slave the same Dt 15:17
male and **f** slave, the Levite Dt 16:11
your male and **f** slave, as well Dt 16:14
Do not bring a **f** prostitute's Dt 23:18
enemies as male and **f** slaves, Dt 28:68
and wine for me, your **f** servant, Jdg 19:19
as well as every **f** who has slept Jdg 21:11
like one of your **f** servants." Ru 2:13
servants, your **f** servants, your 1Sm 8:16
and with her five **f** servants 1Sm 25:42
the voice of male and **f** singers? 2Sm 19:35
Then two **f** bears came out of the 2Kg 2:24
and oxen, and male and **f** slaves? 2Kg 5:26
male and **f**, to slavery. 2Ch 28:10
their 7,337 male and **f** slaves, Ezr 2:65
their 200 male and **f** singers. Ezr 2:65
their 7,337 male and **f** slaves, Neh 7:67
as their 245 male and **f** singers. Neh 7:67
hand-picked **f** servants to her Est 2:9
Esther's **f** servants and her Est 4:4
I and my **f** servants will also Est 4:16
been sold as male and **f** slaves, Est 7:4
yoke of oxen, 500 **f** donkeys, and Jb 1:3
guests and **f** servants regard Jb 19:15
of my male or **f** servants when Jb 31:13
of oxen, and 1,000 **f** donkeys. Jb 42:12
save the son of Your **f** servant. Ps 86:16
the son of Your **f** servant. Ps 116:16
male and **f** servants and had Ec 2:7
gathered male and **f** singers for Ec 2:8
them as male and **f** slaves in the Is 14:2
servant and master, **f** servant Is 24:2
in the land—a **f** will shelter a Jr 31:22
his male and **f** Hebrew slaves Jr 34:9
free their male and **f** slaves— Jr 34:10
their male and **f** slaves they had Jr 34:11
his male and **f** slaves who had Jr 34:16
the male and **f** slaves in those Jl 2:29
beginning made them male and **f**, Mt 19:4
God made them male and **f**. Mk 10:6
to beat the male and **f** slaves, Lk 12:45
on My male and **f** slaves in those Ac 2:18
Greek, slave or free, male or **f**; Gl 3:28

FEMALES *(5)*
males were mating with the **f**. Gn 31:10
all the young **f** who have not had Nm 31:18
all the **f** who had not had sexual Nm 31:35
For even their **f** exchanged Rm 1:26
intercourse with **f** and were Rm 1:27

FENCE *(3)*
wall or a tottering stone **f**? Ps 62:3
vineyard, put a **f** around it, dug Mt 21:33
vineyard, put a **f** around it, dug Mk 12:1

FERMENT *(1)*
a perfumer's oil **f** and stink; Ec 10:1

FEROCIOUS *(1)*
No one is **f** ⌊enough⌋ to rouse Jb 41:10

FERTILE *(9)*
Is the land **f** or unproductive? Nm 13:20
in the hills and in the **f** lands. 2Ch 26:10
cities and **f** land and took Neh 9:25
the spacious and **f** land You set Neh 9:35
had a vineyard on a very **f** hill. Is 5:1
you to a **f** land to eat its Jr 2:7
the **f** field was a wilderness. Jr 4:26
are taken from the **f** field and Jr 48:33
seed and put it in a **f** field; Ezk 17:5

FERTILIZE *(1)*
until I dig around it and **f** it. Lk 13:8

FERVENT *(2)*
and being **f** in spirit, he spoke Ac 18:25
diligence; be **f** in spirit; serve Rm 12:11

FERVENTLY *(5)*
I will **f** thank the LORD with my Ps 109:30
He will **f** plead their case so Jr 50:34
leaders **f** love disgrace. Hs 4:18
I have **f** desired to eat this Lk 22:15
He prayed more **f**, and His sweat Lk 22:44

FESTERING *(7)*
It will become **f** boils on people Ex 9:9
and it became **f** boils on man and Ex 9:10
an eye defect, a **f** rash, scabs, Lv 21:20
running sore, **f** rash, or scabs; Lv 22:22
Egypt, tumors, a **f** rash, and Dt 28:27
are foul and **f** because of my Ps 38:5
welts, and **f** sores not cleansed Is 1:6

FESTIVAL *(92)*
so that they may hold a **f** for Me Ex 5:1
we must hold the LORD's **f**." Ex 10:9
celebrate it as a **f** to the LORD. Ex 12:14
to observe the ⌊**F** of⌋ Unleavened Ex 12:17
there is to be a **f** to the LORD. Ex 13:6
Celebrate a **f** in My honor three Ex 23:14
Observe the **F** of Unleavened Ex 23:15
observe⌋ the **F** of Harvest with Ex 23:16
observe⌋ the **F** of Ingathering at Ex 23:16
fat of My **f** offering must not Ex 23:18
There will be a **f** to the LORD Ex 32:5
Observe the **F** of Unleavened Ex 34:18
Observe the **F** of Weeks with the Ex 34:22
and the **F** of Ingathering at the Ex 34:22
the Passover **F** must not remain Ex 34:25
The **F** of Unleavened Bread to the Lv 23:6
The **F** of Booths to the LORD Lv 23:34
the LORD's **f** on the fifteenth Lv 23:39
it as a **f** to the LORD seven Lv 23:41
of this month there will be a **f**; Nm 28:17
the LORD at your ⌊**F** of⌋ Weeks; Nm 28:26
a seven-day **f** for the LORD. Nm 29:12
to celebrate the **F** of Weeks to Dt 16:10
to celebrate the **F** of Booths for Dt 16:13
during your **f**—you, your son Dt 16:14
hold a seven-day **f** for the LORD Dt 16:15
at the **F** of Unleavened Bread, Dt 16:16
Bread, the **F** of Weeks, Dt 16:16
of Weeks, and the **F** of Booths. Dt 16:16
during the **F** of Booths, Dt 31:10
there's an annual **f** to the LORD Jdg 21:19
the month of Ethanim at the **f**. 1Kg 8:2
observed the **f** at that time in 1Kg 8:65
Jeroboam made a **f** in the eighth 1Kg 12:32
the month, like the **f** in Judah. 1Kg 12:32
He made a **f** for the Israelites, 1Kg 12:33
in the king's presence at the **f**; 2Ch 5:3
observed the **f** at that time for 2Ch 7:8
seven days and the **f** seven days. 2Ch 7:9
the **F** of Unleavened Bread, 2Ch 8:13
Bread, the **F** of Weeks, 2Ch 8:13
of Weeks, and the **F** of Booths. 2Ch 8:13
to observe the **F** of Unleavened 2Ch 30:13
observed the **F** of Unleavened 2Ch 30:21
time and the **F** of Unleavened 2Ch 35:17
celebrated the **F** of Booths as Ezr 3:4
by ordinance for each **f** day. Ezr 3:4
observed the **F** of Unleavened Ezr 6:22
during the **f** of the seventh Neh 8:14
Bind the **f** sacrifice with cords Ps 118:27
cannot stand iniquity with a **f**. Is 1:13
that on the night of a holy **f**, Is 30:29
Zion, the city of our **f** times. Is 33:20
as on the day of an appointed **f**. Lm 2:7
as if ⌊for⌋ an appointed **f** day; Lm 2:22
a **f** of seven days ⌊during which⌋ Ezk 45:21
During the seven days of the **f**, Ezk 45:23
At the **f** ⌊that begins⌋ on the Ezk 45:25
What will you do on a **f** day, Hs 9:5
tents again, as in the **f** days. Hs 12:9
to celebrate the **F** of Booths. Zch 14:16
up to celebrate the **F** of Booths. Zch 14:18
up to celebrate the **F** of Booths. Zch 14:19
waste from your **f** sacrifices, Mal 2:3
"Not during the **f**," they said, Mt 26:5
At the **f** the governor's custom Mt 27:15
Passover and the **F** of Unleavened Mk 14:1
"Not during the **f**," they said, Mk 14:2
At the **f** it was Pilate's custom Mk 15:6
to Jerusalem for the Passover **F**. Lk 2:41
to the custom of the **f**. Lk 2:42
The **F** of Unleavened Bread, Lk 22:1
according to the **f** he had to Lk 23:17
in Jerusalem at the Passover **F**, Jn 2:23
did in Jerusalem during the **f**. Jn 4:45
For they also had gone to the **f**. Jn 4:45
this, a Jewish **f** took place, Jn 5:1
Passover, a Jewish **f**, was near. Jn 6:4
The Jewish **F** of Tabernacles was Jn 7:2
Go up to the **f** yourselves. Jn 7:8
I'm not going up to the **f** yet, Jn 7:8
brothers had gone up to the **f**, Jn 7:10
for Him at the **f** and saying, Jn 7:11
the **f** was already half over, Jn 7:14
and most important day of the **f**, Jn 7:37
Then the **F** of Dedication took Jn 10:22
won't come to the **f**, will He?" Jn 11:56
had come to the **f** heard that Jn 12:12
who went up to worship at the **f**. Jn 12:20
the Passover **F**, Jesus knew that Jn 13:1
"Buy what we need for the **f**," Jn 13:29
the matter of a **f** or a new moon Col 2:16

FESTIVALS *(20)*
serve as signs for **f** and for Gn 1:14
your appointed **f**, and the Nm 10:10
at your appointed **f**—to produce Nm 15:3
and appointed **f**, they are to do 1Ch 23:31
the appointed **f** of the LORD our 2Ch 2:4
the three annual appointed **f**: 2Ch 8:13
appointed **f**, the holy things, Neh 10:33
your New Moons and prescribed **f**. Is 1:14
after year; let the **f** recur. Is 29:1
no one comes to the appointed **f**. Lm 1:4
appointed **f** and Sabbaths Lm 2:6
during its appointed **f**. Ezk 36:38
regarding all My appointed **f**, Ezk 44:24
and drink offerings for the **f**, Ezk 45:17
At the **f** and appointed times, Ezk 46:11
to change religious **f** and laws, Dn 7:25
Moons, and Sabbaths—all her **f**. Hs 2:11
Celebrate your **f**, Judah; Nah 1:15
driven from the appointed **f**; Zph 3:18
and cheerful **f** for the house of Zch 8:19

FESTIVE *(4)*
leading the **f** procession to the Ps 42:4
f robes, capes, cloaks, purses, Is 3:22
f oil instead of mourning, Is 61:3
of angels in **f** gathering, Heb 12:22

FESTUS *(13)*
Porcius **F**, and because he Ac 24:27
Three days after **F** arrived in Ac 25:1
F answered that Paul should be Ac 25:4
Then **F**, wanting to do a favor Ac 25:9
After **F** conferred with his Ac 25:12
and paid a courtesy call on **F**. Ac 25:13
F presented Paul's case to the Ac 25:14
Agrippa said to **F**, "I would like Ac 25:22
When **F** gave the command, Paul Ac 25:23
Then **F** said: "King Agrippa and Ac 25:24
F exclaimed in a loud voice, Ac 26:24
of my mind, most excellent **F**. Ac 26:25
Agrippa said to **F**, "This man Ac 26:32

FETTERS *(4)*
I tore off your **f**. You insisted: Jr 2:20
the yoke and torn off the **f**. Jr 5:5
f and yoke bars for yourself Jr 27:2
and snap your **f** so strangers Jr 30:8

FEUDS *(2)*
me from the **f** among my people; 2Sm 22:44
me from the **f** among the people Ps 18:43

FEVER *(11)*
disease and **f** that will cause Lv 26:16
disease, **f**, inflammation, Dt 28:22
off, and my bones burn with **f**. Jb 30:30
lying in bed with a **f**. Mt 8:14
her hand, and the **f** left her. Mt 8:15
was lying in bed with a **f**, Mk 1:30
The **f** left her, and she began to Mk 1:31
was suffering from a high **f**, Lk 4:38
over her and rebuked the **f**, Lk 4:39
in the morning the **f** left him," Jn 4:52
suffering from **f** and dysentery. Ac 28:8

FEW *(63)*
with him for a **f** days until your Gn 27:44
seemed like only a **f** days to him Gn 29:20
We are **f** in number; if they Gn 34:30

My years have been f and hard, Gn 47:9
If only a f years remain until Lv 25:52
tabernacle for ⌊only⌋ a f days. Nm 9:20
are strong or weak, f or many. Nm 13:18
reduced to a f survivors among Dt 4:27
to Egypt with a f people and Dt 26:5
be left with only a f people, Dt 28:62
die though his people become f. Dt 33:6
Since the people of Ai are so f, Jos 7:3
although a f survivors ran away Jos 10:20
whether by many or by f." 1Sm 14:6
did you leave those f sheep with 1Sm 17:28
neighbors. Do not get just a f. 2Kg 4:3
When they were f in number, 1Ch 16:19
in number, very f indeed, and 1Ch 16:19
army came with only a f men, 2Ch 24:24
and ⌊took⌋ a f men with me. Neh 2:12
but there were f people in it, Neh 7:4
Are my days not f? Stop ⌊it⌋! Jb 10:20
f years are stored up for the Jb 15:20
For ⌊only⌋ a f years will pass Jb 16:22
I have eaten my f crumbs alone Jb 31:17
like a f hours of the night. Ps 90:4
When they were f in number, Ps 105:12
in number, very f indeed, and Ps 105:12
Let his days be f; let another Ps 109:8
heaven during the f days of Ec 2:3
earth, so let your words be f. Ec 5:2
during the f days of his life Ec 5:18
in the f days of his futile life Ec 6:12
a small city with f men in it. Ec 9:14
grind cease because they are f, Ec 12:3
had not left us a f survivors, Is 1:9
will be so f in number that Is 10:19
are left will be f and weak." Is 16:14
archers will be f in number." Is 21:17
burned, and only a f survive. Is 24:6
no longer live only a f days, Is 65:20
for f of us remain out of the Jr 42:2
except ⌊for a f⌋ fugitives." Jr 44:14
land of Judah only f in number, Jr 44:28
you are to take a f strands from Ezk 5:3
I will spare a f of them from Ezk 12:16
but within a f days he will be Dn 11:20
leads to life, and f find it. Mt 7:14
abundant, but the workers are f. Mt 9:37
they said, "and a f small fish." Mt 15:34
are invited, but f are chosen." Mt 22:14
were faithful over a f things; Mt 25:21
were faithful over a f things; Mt 25:23
His hands on a f sick people Mk 6:5
They also had a f small fish, Mk 8:7
abundant, but the workers are f. Lk 10:2
"are there f being saved?" Lk 13:23
they stayed there only a f days. Jn 2:12
asked him to stay for a f days. Ac 10:48
have written to you in f words. Heb 13:22
in it, a f—that is, eight 1Pt 3:20
But I have a f things against Rv 2:14
you have a f people in Sardis Rv 3:4

FEWEST *(1)*

you were the f of all peoples. Dt 7:7

FIANCÉE *(1)*

has violated his neighbor's f. Dt 22:24

FIELD *(235)*

shrub of the f had yet ⌊grown⌋ Gn 2:5
no plant of the f had yet Gn 2:5
will eat the plants of the f. Gn 3:18
Abel, "Let's go out to the f." Gn 4:8
And while they were in the f, Gn 4:8
it is at the end of his f. Gn 23:9
I give you the f, and I give you Gn 23:11
Let me pay the price of the f. Gn 23:13
So Ephron's f at Machpelah near Gn 23:17
the f with its cave and all the Gn 23:17
within the boundaries of the f— Gn 23:17
the cave of the f at Machpelah Gn 23:19
The f with its cave passed from Gn 23:20
Isaac went out to walk in the f, Gn 24:63
that man in the f coming to meet Gn 24:65
in the f of Ephron son of Zohar Gn 25:9
This was the f that Abraham Gn 25:10
came in from the f, exhausted. Gn 25:29
go out in the f to hunt some Gn 27:3
Esau went to the f to hunt some Gn 27:5
the smell of a f that the LORD Gn 27:27
He looked and saw a well in a f. Gn 29:2
found some mandrakes in the f. Gn 30:14
came in from the f that evening, Gn 30:16
called to the f ⌊where⌋ his Gn 31:4
a section of the f from the sons Gn 33:19
were with his cattle in the f, Gn 34:5
from the f when they heard Gn 34:7
was in the city and in the f. Gn 34:28
Midian in the f of Moab; Gn 36:35
sheaves of grain in the f. Gn 37:7
in the f, and asked him, Gn 37:15
sold his f since the famine Gn 47:20
seed for the f and as food for Gn 47:24
in the cave in the f of Ephron Gn 49:29
cave is in the f of Machpelah, Gn 49:30
This is the f Abraham purchased Gn 49:30
The f and the cave in it ⌊were Gn 49:32
Machpelah in the f near Mamre, Gn 50:13
your livestock in the f— Ex 9:3
you have in the f into shelters. Ex 9:19
that is in the f and not brought Ex 9:19
servants and livestock in the f. Ex 9:21
every plant of the f in the land Ex 9:22
struck down everything in the f, Ex 9:25
plant of the f and shattered Ex 9:25
shattered every tree in the f. Ex 9:25
the plants in the f throughout Ex 10:15
you won't find any in the f. Ex 16:25
a man lets a f or vineyard be Ex 22:5
and graze in someone else's f, Ex 22:5
best of his own f or vineyard. Ex 22:5
grain, or a f, the one who Ex 22:6
mauled animal ⌊found⌋ in the f; Ex 22:31
from what you sow in the f, Ex 23:16
gather your produce from the f. Ex 23:16
very edge of your f or gather Lv 19:9
to the edge of your f or gather Lv 23:22
may sow your f for six years, Lv 25:3
not to sow your f or prune your Lv 25:4
produce ⌊directly⌋ from the f. Lv 25:12
trees of the f will bear their Lv 26:4
any part of a f that he Lv 27:16
consecrates his f during the Lv 27:17
consecrates his f after the Lv 27:18
consecrated the f decides to Lv 27:19
and the f will transfer back to Lv 27:19
not redeem the f or if he has Lv 27:20
When the f is released in the Lv 27:21
LORD like a f permanently set Lv 27:21
to the LORD a f he has purchased Lv 27:22
of Jubilee the f will return to Lv 27:24
Anyone in the open f who touches Nm 19:16
through ⌊any⌋ f or vineyard, Nm 20:17
up the green plants in the f." Nm 22:4
the path and went into the f. Nm 22:23
him to Lookout F on top of Nm 23:14
house, his f, his male or female Dt 5:21
trees of the f human, to come Dt 20:19
found lying in a f in the land Dt 21:1
When he found her in the f, Dt 22:27
you reap the harvest in your f, Dt 24:19
and you forget a sheaf in the f, Dt 24:19
much seed in the f but harvest Dt 28:38
and eat the produce of the f. Dt 32:13
to ask her father for a f. Jos 15:18
to ask her father for a f. Jdg 1:14
in the f, and her husband Jdg 13:9
came in from his work in the f. Jdg 19:16
men of Israel on the f that day. Jdg 20:21
18,000 Israelites on the f; Jdg 20:25
and entered the f to gather Ru 2:3
and gather ⌊grain⌋ in another f, Ru 2:8
See which f they are harvesting, Ru 2:9
grain⌋ in the f until evening. Ru 2:17
happen to you in another f." Ru 2:22
The cart came to the f of Joshua 1Sm 6:14
was placed is in the f of Joshua 1Sm 6:18
in from the f behind his oxen. 1Sm 11:5
about 20 men in a half-acre f. 1Sm 14:14
of cheese to the f commander. 1Sm 17:18
my father in the f where you are 1Sm 19:3
hide in the f until the third 1Sm 20:5
Come on, let's go out to the f." 1Sm 20:11
both of them went out to the f. 1Sm 20:11
So David hid in the f. 1Sm 20:24
went out to the f for the 1Sm 20:35
we were in the f, we weren't 1Sm 25:15
in Gibeon, is named F of Blades. 2Sm 2:16
were in the f by themselves. 2Sm 10:8
are camping in the open f. 2Sm 11:11
came out against us in the f, 2Sm 11:23
fighting in the f with no one to 2Sm 14:6
Joab has a f right next to mine, 2Sm 14:30
servants set the f on fire. 2Sm 14:30
your servants set my f on fire?" 2Sm 14:31
into the f to engage Israel 2Sm 18:6
the highway to the f and threw a 2Sm 20:12
there was a f full of lentils. 2Sm 23:11
stand in the middle of the f, 2Sm 23:12
them were alone in the open f. 1Kg 11:29
and anyone who dies in the f, 1Kg 14:11
who is his and dies in the f, 1Kg 16:4
he who dies in the f, the birds 1Kg 21:24
out to the f to gather herbs 2Kg 4:39
to the king for her house and f. 2Kg 8:3
to the king for her house and f. 2Kg 8:5
income from the f from the day 2Kg 8:6
the surface of the f in the plot 2Kg 9:37
the highway to the Fuller's F. 2Kg 18:17
plants of the f, tender grass, 2Kg 19:26
were in the f by themselves. 1Ch 19:9
and of all the produce of the f, 2Ch 31:5
had gone back to his own f. Neh 13:10
with the stones of the f, Jb 5:23
their fodder in the f and glean Jb 24:6
and grow up in the open f. Jb 39:4
the creatures of the f are Mine. Ps 50:11
cities like the grass of the f. Ps 72:16
creatures of the f feed on it. Ps 80:13
blooms like a flower of the f; Ps 103:15
f of the poor yields abundant Pr 13:23
work, and prepare your f; Pr 24:27
I went by the f of a slacker and Pr 24:30
and goats, the price of a f; Pr 27:26
She evaluates a f and buys it; Pr 31:16
the king is served by the f. Ec 5:9
and the wild does of the f: Sg 2:7
and the wild does of the f: Sg 3:5
my love, let's go to the f; Sg 7:11
like a shack in a cucumber f, Is 1:8
house and join f to field until Is 5:8
join field to f until there is Is 5:8
by the road to the Fuller's F. Is 7:3
by the road to the Fuller's F. Is 36:2
plants of the f, tender grass, Is 37:27
is like the flower of the f. Is 40:6
animals of the f will honor Me, Is 43:20
trees of the f will clap ⌊their Is 55:12
you animals of the f and forest, Is 56:9
like those who guard a f, Jr 4:17
and the fertile f was a Jr 4:26
the tree of the f, and on the Jr 7:20
manure on the surface of the f, Jr 9:22
and the grass of every f wither? Jr 12:4
the doe in the f gives birth Jr 14:5
I go out to the f, look—those Jr 14:18
Zion will be plowed like a f, Jr 26:18
Buy my f in Anathoth for Jr 32:7
'Please buy my f in Anathoth in Jr 32:8
So I bought the f in Anathoth Jr 32:9
Buy the f with silver and call Jr 32:25
not have vineyard, f, or seed. Jr 35:9
of the armies in the f— Jr 40:7
armies in the f came to Gedaliah Jr 40:13
have hidden treasure in the f— Jr 41:8
from the fertile f and from the Jr 48:33
Whoever is in the f will die by Ezk 7:15
into the open f because you were Ezk 16:5
you thrive like plants of the f. Ezk 16:7
seed and put it in a fertile f; Ezk 17:5
planted in a good f by abundant Ezk 17:8
trees of the f will know that I Ezk 17:24
to all the trees of the f. Ezk 31:4
than all the trees of the f. Ezk 31:5
animals of the f gave birth Ezk 31:6
animals of the f were among its Ezk 31:13
trees of the f fainted because Ezk 31:15
land and hurl you on the open f. Ezk 32:4
in the open f I have given to Ezk 33:27
trees of the f will give their Ezk 34:27
the produce of the f plentiful, Ezk 36:30
animals of the f, every creature Ezk 38:20
You will fall on the open f, Ezk 39:5
in the tender grass of the f. Dn 4:15
in the tender grass of the f. Dn 4:23
weeds in the furrows of a f. Hs 10:4
of rocks on the furrows of a f. Hs 12:11
harvest of the f has perished. Jl 1:11

f received rain while a field Am 4:7
rain while a f with no rain Am 4:7
Zion will be plowed like a f, Mc 3:12
and crops in the f for everyone. Zch 10:1
your vine in your f will not be Mal 3:11
the wildflowers of the f grow: Mt 6:28
God clothes the grass of the f, Mt 6:30
who sowed good seed in his f. Mt 13:24
you sow good seed in your f? Mt 13:27
a man took and sowed in his f. Mt 13:31
of the weeds in the f to us." Mt 13:36
the f is the world; and the good Mt 13:38
buried in a f, that a man found Mt 13:44
he has and buys that f. Mt 13:44
a man in the f must not go back Mt 24:18
Then two men will be in the f: Mt 24:40
the potter's f with it as a Mt 27:7
Therefore that f has been called Mt 27:8
called "Blood F" to this day. Mt 27:8
gave them for the potter's f, Mt 27:10
a man in the f must not go back Mk 13:16
which is in the f today and is Lk 12:28
I have bought a f, and I must go Lk 14:18
99 in the open f and go after Lk 15:4
Now his older son was in the f; Lk 15:25
when he comes in from the f, Lk 17:7
who is in the f must not turn Lk 17:31
Two will be in a f: one will be Lk 17:36
this man acquired a f with his Ac 1:18
own language that f is called Ac 1:19
Hakeldama, that is, F of Blood. Ac 1:19
sold a f he owned, brought the Ac 4:37
part of the proceeds from the f? Ac 5:3
you sell the f for this price? Ac 5:8
You are God's f, God's building. 1Co 3:9
away like a flower of the f. Jms 1:10

FIELDS *(67)*
in his house and in his f. Gn 39:5
every city from the f around it. Gn 41:48
houses, courtyards, and f died. Ex 8:13
tree you have growing in the f. Ex 10:5
sow your f with two kinds of Lv 19:19
are to be classified as open f. Lv 25:31
inheritance of f and vineyards. Nm 16:14
go into the f or vineyards. Nm 21:22
grass in your f for your Dt 11:15
all the produce grown in your f. Dt 14:22
and from the f of Gomorrah. Dt 32:32
But they gave the f and villages Jos 21:12
You marched from the f of Edom, Jdg 5:4
me go into the f and gather Ru 2:2
can take your best f, vineyards, 1Sm 8:14
and the open f to all the troops 1Sm 14:15
give all of you f and vineyards? 1Sm 22:7
be on you, or f of offerings, 2Sm 1:21
all your grandfather Saul's f, 2Sm 9:7
Go to your f in Anathoth. 1Kg 2:26
Jerusalem in the f of the Kidron 2Kg 23:4
the f and villages around the 1Ch 6:56
the f and all that is in them 1Ch 16:32
worked in the f tilling the soil 1Ch 27:26
in the common f of their cities, 2Ch 31:19
are mortgaging our f, vineyards, Neh 5:3
tax on our f and vineyards. Neh 5:4
because our f and vineyards Neh 5:5
Return their f, vineyards, olive Neh 5:11
settlements with their f: Neh 11:25
Lachish with its f and Azekah Neh 11:30
and from the f of Geba and Neh 12:29
gathered from the village f, Neh 12:44
earth and sends water to the f. Jb 5:10
Let the f and everything in them Ps 96:12
They sow f and plant vineyards Ps 107:37
we found it in the f of Jaar. Ps 132:6
tens of thousands in our open f. Ps 144:13
the land, the f, or the first Pr 8:26
encroach on the f of the Pr 23:10
eyes foreigners devour your f— Is 1:7
delightful f and the fruitful Is 32:12
⌊their⌋ f and wives as well, Jr 6:12
Don't go out to the f; Jr 6:25
men, their f to new occupants Jr 8:10
hills, in the f—I have seen Jr 13:27
and all the f as far as the Jr 31:40
Houses, f, and vineyards will Jr 32:15
F will be bought in this land Jr 32:43
F will be purchased with silver, Jr 32:44
vineyards and f at that time. Jr 39:10

because the f lack produce. Lm 4:9
devour them along with their f. Hs 5:7
The f are destroyed; the land Jl 1:10
They covet f and seize them; Mc 2:2
He allots our f to traitors. Mc 2:4
the city and camp in the open f. Mc 4:10
fails and the f produce no food, Hab 3:17
drought on the f and the hills, Hg 1:11
or f because of My name will Mt 19:29
or f because of Me and the Mk 10:29
and children, and f, with Mk 10:30
leafy branches cut from the f. Mk 11:8
out in the f and keeping watch Lk 2:8
him into his f to feed pigs. Lk 15:15
your eyes and look at the f, Jn 4:35
who reaped your f cries out, Jms 5:4

FIELDWORK *(1)*
mortar, and in all kinds of f. Ex 1:14

FIERCE *(29)*
Pharaoh's presence in f anger. Ex 11:8
afraid of the f anger the LORD Dt 9:19
LORD demolished in His f anger. Dt 29:23
and the battle was f, but the Jdg 20:34
Philistines was f all of Saul's 1Sm 14:52
the table in f anger and did not 1Sm 20:34
battle that day was extremely f, 2Sm 2:17
of Zeruiah, are too f for me. 2Sm 3:39
the battle was too f for him, 2Kg 3:26
and returned home in a f rage. 2Ch 25:10
the LORD's f wrath is on you. 2Ch 28:11
and f wrath is on Israel." 2Ch 28:13
so that His f wrath may turn 2Ch 29:10
may turn His f wrath away from 2Ch 30:8
to avert the f anger of our God Ezr 10:14
may roar and the f lion growl, Jb 4:10
and a covert bribe, f rage. Pr 21:14
These dogs have f appetites; Is 56:11
So My f wrath poured forth and Jr 44:6
king and priest in His f anger. Lm 2:6
vengeance and is f in wrath. Nah 1:2
They are f and terrifying; Hab 1:7
leopards and more f than wolves Hab 1:8
A f windstorm arose, and the Mk 4:37
Then a f windstorm came down on Lk 8:23
f wind called the "northeaster" Ac 27:14
large and driven by f winds, Jms 3:4
with the wine of His f anger. Rv 16:19
winepress of the f anger of God, Rv 19:15

FIERCELY *(2)*
I am f angry with the nations Zch 1:15
began to oppose Him f and to Lk 11:53

FIERCENESS *(1)*
not turn from the f of His great 2Kg 23:26

FIERCEST *(2)*
at the front of the f fighting, 2Sm 11:15
are fiery flames—the f of all. Sg 8:6

FIERY *(21)*
a firepan full of f coals from Lv 16:12
his mouth; f sparks fly out! Jb 41:19
burn⌋ like a f furnace when you Ps 21:9
day and with a f light Ps 78:14
Love's flames are f flames— Sg 8:6
on all flesh with His f sword, Is 66:16
you walked among the f stones. Ezk 28:14
cherub, from among the f stones. Ezk 28:16
I swear in My zeal and f rage: Ezk 38:19
the sound of f flames consuming Jl 2:5
will be heaping f coals on his Rm 12:20
and His servants a f flame; Heb 1:7
when the f ordeal arises among 1Pt 4:12
snow, His eyes like a f flame, Rv 1:14
whose eyes are like a f flame, Rv 2:18
the throne were seven f torches, Rv 4:5
went out, a f red one, and its Rv 6:4
breastplates that were f red, Rv 9:17
his legs were like f pillars, Rv 10:1
was a great f red dragon having Rv 12:3
His eyes were like a f flame, Rv 19:12

FIFTEEN *(1)*
on 45 pillars, f per row. 1Kg 7:3

FIFTEENTH *(19)*
on the f day of the second month Ex 16:1
LORD is on the f day of the same Lv 23:6
LORD begins on the f day of this Lv 23:34
festival on the f day of the Lv 23:39
On the f day of this month there Nm 28:17

assembly on the f day of the Nm 29:12
on the f day of the month. Nm 33:3
On the f day he sent the people 1Kg 8:66
month on the f day of the month, 1Kg 12:32
in Bethel on the f day of the 1Kg 12:33
In the f year of Judah's King 2Kg 14:23
the f to Bilgah, the sixteenth 1Ch 24:14
the f to Jeremoth, his sons, and 1Ch 25:22
month of the f year of Asa's 2Ch 15:10
rested on the f day of the month Est 9:18
fourteenth and f days of the Est 9:21
on the f ⌊day⌋ of the month, Ezk 32:17
begins⌋ on the f day of the Ezk 45:25
In the f year of the reign of Lk 3:1

FIFTH *(53)*
and then morning: the f day. Gn 1:23
and bore Jacob a f son. Gn 30:17
are to give a f of it to Pharaoh Gn 47:24
a f ⌊of the produce⌋ belongs Gn 47:26
adding a f of its value to it, Lv 5:16
it and add a f of its value to Lv 6:5
in the f year you may eat its Lv 19:25
he must add a f to its value and Lv 22:14
must add a f to the valuation. Lv 27:13
he must add a f to the valuation Lv 27:15
he must add a f to the valuation Lv 27:19
adding a f of its value to it. Lv 27:27
add a f of its value to it, Nm 5:7
On the f day Shelumiel son of Nm 7:36
On the f day ⌊present⌋ nine Nm 29:26
first ⌊day⌋ of the f month in Nm 33:38
The f lot came out for the tribe Jos 19:24
morning of the f day to leave, Jdg 19:8
the f was Shephatiah, son of 2Sm 3:4
In the f year of King Rehoboam, 1Kg 14:25
In the f year of Israel's King 2Kg 8:16
the seventh day of the f month, 2Kg 25:8
Nethanel fourth, Raddai f, 1Ch 2:14
Shephatiah, by Abital, was f; 1Ch 3:3
Nohah fourth, and Rapha f. 1Ch 8:2
Mishmannah fourth, Jeremiah f, 1Ch 12:10
the f to Malchijah, the sixth to 1Ch 24:9
the f ⌊to⌋ Nethaniah, his sons, 1Ch 25:12
Elam the f, Jehohanan the sixth, 1Ch 26:3
the fourth, Nethanel the f, 1Ch 26:4
The f, for the fifth month, was 1Ch 27:8
The fifth, for the f month, was 1Ch 27:8
in the f year of King Rehoboam, 2Ch 12:2
to Jerusalem in the f month, Ezr 7:8
on the first day of the f month. Ezr 7:9
same message a f time by his Neh 6:5
the f month of the eleventh Jr 1:3
in the f month of the fourth Jr 28:1
the f year of Jehoiakim son of Jr 36:9
the tenth day of the f month— Jr 52:12
on the f ⌊day⌋ of the month, Ezk 1:1
On the f ⌊day⌋ of the month— Ezk 1:2
it was the f year of King Ezk 1:2
on the f ⌊day⌋ of the month, Ezk 8:1
seventh year, in the f ⌊month⌋, Ezk 20:1
on the f ⌊day⌋ of the month, Ezk 33:21
and fast in the f month as we Zch 7:3
lamented in the f and in the Zch 7:5
the fast of the f, the fast Zch 8:19
When He opened the f seal, Rv 6:9
The f angel blew his trumpet, Rv 9:1
The f poured out his bowl on the Rv 16:10
the f sardonyx, the sixth Rv 21:20

FIFTIES *(6)*
hundreds, f, and tens. Ex 18:21
hundreds, f, and tens. Ex 18:25
hundreds, f, and tens, Dt 1:15
of thousands or commanders of f, 1Sm 8:12
two captains of 50 with their f, 2Kg 1:14
down in ranks of hundreds and f. Mk 6:40

FIFTIETH *(3)*
consecrate the f year and Lv 25:10
The f year will be your Jubilee; Lv 25:11
In the f year of Judah's King 2Kg 15:23

FIFTY *(1)*
F men from the sons of the 2Kg 2:7

FIFTY-SECOND *(1)*
In the f year of Judah's King 2Kg 15:27

FIG *(42)*
so they sewed f leaves together Gn 3:7
the trees said to the f tree, Jdg 9:10
But the f tree said to them, Jdg 9:11

his own vine and his own **f** tree. 1Kg 4:25
his own vine and his own **f** tree, 2Kg 18:31
of flour, **f** cakes, raisins, wine 1Ch 12:40
their vines and **f** trees and Ps 105:33
Whoever tends a **f** tree will eat Pr 27:18
The **f** tree ripens its figs; Sg 2:13
be like a ripe **f** before the Is 28:4
and foliage on the **f** tree. Is 34:4
and his own **f** tree and drink Is 36:16
your vines and your **f** trees. Jr 5:17
no figs on the **f** tree, and even Jr 8:13
devastate her vines and **f** trees. Hs 2:12
fruit of the **f** tree in its first Hs 9:10
and splintered My **f** tree. Jl 1:7
and the **f** tree is withered; Jl 1:12
and the **f** tree and grapevine Jl 2:22
your **f** trees and olive trees, Am 4:9
and under his **f** tree with no one Mc 4:4
eat, no early **f**, which I crave. Mc 7:1
fortresses are **f** trees with figs Nah 3:12
Though the **f** tree does not bud Hab 3:17
vine, the **f**, the pomegranate, Hg 2:19
under ⌊his⌋ vine and **f** tree." Zch 3:10
a lone **f** tree by the road, Mt 21:19
At once the **f** tree withered. Mt 21:19
How did the **f** tree wither so Mt 21:20
do what was done to the **f** tree, Mt 21:21
this parable from the **f** tree: Mt 24:32
the distance a **f** tree with Mk 11:13
saw the **f** tree withered from Mk 11:20
The **f** tree that You cursed is Mk 11:21
this parable from the **f** tree: Mk 13:28
A man had a **f** tree that was Lk 13:6
fruit on this **f** tree and haven't Lk 13:7
Look at the **f** tree, and all the Lk 21:29
when you were under the **f** tree, Jn 1:48
you I saw you under the **f** tree? Jn 1:50
Can a **f** tree produce olives, Jms 3:12
the earth as a **f** tree drops its Rv 6:13

FIGHT *(122)*

join our enemies, **f** against us, Ex 1:10
The LORD will **f** for you; Ex 14:14
for us, and go **f** against Amalek. Ex 17:9
When men get in a **f**, and hit a Ex 21:22
f broke out in the camp between Lv 24:10
I may be able to **f** against them Nm 22:11
goes before you will **f** for you, Dt 1:30
will go up and **f** just as the Dt 1:41
Don't go up and **f**, for I am not Dt 1:42
Don't **f** with them, for I will Dt 2:5
to them or **f** with them, Dt 2:19
with you to **f** for you against Dt 20:4
approach a city to **f** against it, Dt 20:10
alliance to **f** against Joshua Jos 9:2
this to all the enemies you **f**." Jos 10:25
set out to **f** against Israel. Jos 24:9
be the first to **f** for us against Jdg 1:1
and let us **f** against the Jdg 1:3
Judah marched down to **f** against Jdg 1:9
Israelites ⌊how to **f** in⌋ battle, Jdg 3:2
Wadi Kishon ⌊to **f**⌋ against you, Jdg 4:7
when you went to **f** against the Jdg 8:1
despised? Now go and **f** them!" Jdg 9:38
the Jordan to **f** against Judah, Jdg 10:9
man will lead the **f** against the Jdg 10:18
let's **f** against the Ammonites. Jdg 11:6
Come with us, **f** the Ammonites, Jdg 11:8
me back to **f** the Ammonites Jdg 11:9
have come to **f** against me in my Jdg 11:12
with Israel or **f** against them? Jdg 11:25
the Ammonites to **f** against them, Jdg 11:32
crossed over to **f** against the Jdg 12:1
you come today to **f** against me?" Jdg 12:3
Gibeah to go out and **f** against Jdg 20:14
to go first to **f** for us against Jdg 20:18
went out to **f** against Benjamin Jdg 20:20
Should we again **f** against our Jdg 20:23
LORD answered: "**F** against them." Jdg 20:23
Should we again **f** against our Jdg 20:28
F, because I will hand them over Jdg 20:28
served you. Now be men and **f**!" 1Sm 4:9
drew near to **f** against Israel. 1Sm 7:10
before us, and **f** our battles." 1Sm 8:20
gathered to **f** against Israel: 1Sm 13:5
F against them until you have 1Sm 15:18
If he wins in a **f** against me and 1Sm 17:9
a man so we can **f** each other!" 1Sm 17:10
will go and **f** this Philistine!" 1Sm 17:32
You can't go **f** this Philistine. 1Sm 17:33
for me and **f** the LORD's battles 1Sm 18:17
commanders came out to **f**, 1Sm 18:30
one army to **f** against Israel. 1Sm 28:1
going along to **f** against the 1Sm 29:8
Israel or continued to **f**. 2Sm 2:28
troops advanced to **f** against the 2Sm 10:13
get so close to the city to **f**? 2Sm 11:20
Intensify your **f** against the 2Sm 11:25
people go out to **f** against their 1Kg 8:44
of Benjamin to **f** against the 1Kg 12:21
to march up and **f** against your 1Kg 12:24
we should **f** with them on the 1Kg 20:23
and let's **f** with them on the 1Kg 20:25
supplies, and went to **f** them. 1Kg 20:27
go with me to **f** Ramoth-gilead?" 1Kg 22:4
Do not **f** with anyone at all 1Kg 22:31
So they turned to **f** against him, 1Kg 22:32
go with me to **f** against Moab?" 2Kg 3:7
had come up to **f** against them. 2Kg 3:21
he is only picking a **f** with me." 2Kg 5:7
son of Ahab to **f** against Hazael 2Kg 8:28
and **f** for your master's house. 2Kg 10:3
has set out to **f** against you." 2Kg 19:9
Philistines to **f** against Saul. 1Ch 12:19
people go out to **f** against their 2Ch 6:34
to **f** against Israel to restore 2Ch 11:1
to march up and **f** against your 2Ch 11:4
don't **f** against the LORD God of 2Ch 13:12
so they didn't **f** against 2Ch 17:10
Do not **f** with anyone, small 2Ch 18:30
came ⌊to **f**⌋ against Jehoshaphat. 2Ch 20:1
has come ⌊to **f**⌋ against you; 2Ch 20:2
that comes ⌊to **f**⌋ against us. 2Ch 20:12
do not have to **f** this ⌊battle⌋. 2Ch 20:17
who came ⌊to **f**⌋ against Judah, 2Ch 20:22
King Ahab to **f** against Hazael, 2Ch 22:5
help us and to **f** our battles." 2Ch 32:8
marched up to **f** at Carchemish 2Ch 35:20
in order to **f** with him he 2Ch 35:22
to the Valley of Megiddo to **f**. 2Ch 35:22
to come and **f** against Jerusalem Neh 4:8
and **f** for your countrymen, Neh 4:14
Our God will **f** for us!" Neh 4:20
LORD; **f** those who fight Ps 35:1
LORD; fight those who **f** me. Ps 35:1
many arrogantly **f** against me. Ps 56:2
each will **f** against his brother Is 19:2
for Me, I will **f** against it, Is 27:4
He will **f** against him with Is 30:32
come down to **f** on Mount Zion Is 31:4
has set out to **f** against you." Is 37:9
will **f** against you but never Jr 1:19
They will **f** against you but will Jr 15:20
you are using to **f** the king of Jr 21:4
I will **f** against you with an Jr 21:5
'You will **f** the Chaldeans, Jr 32:5
who are going to **f** against this Jr 32:29
people coming to **f** the Chaldeans Jr 33:5
They will **f** against it, capture Jr 34:22
then return and **f** against this Jr 37:8
men and went to **f** with Ishmael Jr 41:12
return at once to **f** against the Dn 10:20
march out to **f** with the king Dn 11:11
They will **f** because the LORD is Zch 10:5
will go out to **f** against those Zch 14:3
Judah will also **f** at Jerusalem, Zch 14:14
My servants would **f**, so that I Jn 18:36
F the good fight for the faith; 1Tm 6:12
Fight the good **f** for the faith; 1Tm 6:12
before God not to **f** about words; 2Tm 2:14
fought the good **f**, I have 2Tm 4:7
obtain. You **f** and war. You do Jms 4:2
you quickly and **f** against them Rv 2:16

FIGHTING *(41)*

went out and saw two Hebrews **f**. Ex 2:13
the LORD is **f** for them against Ex 14:25
belongs to the **f** men who went Nm 31:28
a census of the **f** men under our Nm 31:49
generation of **f** men had perished Dt 2:14
When all the **f** men had died Dt 2:16
All your **f** men will cross over Dt 3:18
f against it in order to capture Dt 20:19
If two men are **f** with each other Dt 25:11
But your **f** men must cross over Jos 1:14
and its **f** men over to you. Jos 6:2
selected 30,000 **f** men and sent Jos 8:3
including all the **f** men, came Jos 10:7
LORD your God who was **f** for you. Jos 23:3
the LORD your God was **f** for you, Jos 23:10
have wronged me by **f** against me. Jdg 11:27
Philistines were **f** against each 1Sm 14:20
the Valley of Elah **f** with the 1Sm 17:19
Philistines are **f** against Keilah 1Sm 23:1
Philistines are **f** against me and 1Sm 28:15
and sent Joab and all the **f** men. 2Sm 10:7
at the front of the fiercest **f**, 2Sm 11:15
They were **f** in the field with no 2Sm 14:6
were 800,000 **f** men from Israel 2Sm 24:9
and found him **f** against Libnah. 2Kg 19:8
commanders and all the **f** men, 2Kg 24:14
Babylon all 7,000 **f** men and 2Kg 24:16
The **f** men were: Joab's brother 1Ch 11:26
They were **f** men, trained for 1Ch 12:8
officials, the **f** men, and all 1Ch 28:1
He had **f** men, brave warriors, in 2Ch 17:13
today but to the dynasty I am **f**. 2Ch 35:21
Stop ⌊your **f**⌋—and know that I Ps 46:10
of Assyria was **f** against Libnah. Is 37:8
Chaldeans who are **f** against it. Jr 32:24
nations were **f** against Jerusalem Jr 34:1
army that is **f** with you, Jr 37:10
warriors have stopped **f**; Jr 51:30
even be found **f** against God." Ac 5:39
while they were **f** and tried to Ac 7:26
one, to avoid **f**, and to be kind Ti 3:2

FIGHTS *(6)*

for the LORD your God **f** for you. Dt 3:22
He **f** for his cause with his own Dt 33:7
lord because he **f** the LORD's 1Sm 25:28
he **f** and oppresses me all day Ps 56:1
nations as He **f** on a day of Zch 14:3
of the wars and the **f** among you? Jms 4:1

FIGS *(27)*

took⌋ some pomegranates and **f**. Nm 13:23
not a place of grain, **f**, vines, Nm 20:5
barley, vines, **f**, and Dt 8:8
and 200 cakes of pressed **f**, 1Sm 25:18
some pressed **f** and two clusters 1Sm 30:12
"Bring a lump of pressed **f**." 2Kg 20:7
along with wine, grapes, and **f**. Neh 13:15
The fig tree ripens its **f**; Sg 2:13
take a lump of **f** and apply it to Is 38:21
the vine, no **f** on the fig tree Jr 8:13
two baskets of **f** placed before Jr 24:1
basket ⌊contained⌋ very good **f**, Jr 24:2
figs, like early **f**, but the Jr 24:2
basket contained very bad **f**, Jr 24:2
I said, "**F**! The good figs are Jr 24:3
good **f** are very good, but the Jr 24:3
but the bad **f** are extremely bad, Jr 24:3
Like these good **f**, so I regard Jr 24:5
for the bad **f**, so bad they are Jr 24:8
them like rotten **f** that are Jr 29:17
and I took care of sycamore **f**. Am 7:14
fig trees with **f** that ripened Nah 3:12
thornbushes or **f** from thistles? Mt 7:16
it was not the season for **f**. Mk 11:13
F aren't gathered from Lk 6:44
or a grapevine ⌊produce⌋ **f**? Jms 3:12
drops its unripe **f** when shaken Rv 6:13

FIGURATIVE *(1)*

and not using any **f** language. Jn 16:29

FIGURE *(5)*

in the shape of any **f**: Dt 4:16
were wise, they would **f** it out; Dt 32:29
days of the feast and **f** it out, Jdg 14:12
had a beautiful **f** and was Est 2:7
⌊A **f**⌋ stood there, but I could Jb 4:16

FIGUREHEAD *(1)*

with the Twin Brothers as its **f**. Ac 28:11

FIGURES *(3)*

when she saw male **f** carved on Ezk 23:14
things to you in **f** of speech. Jn 16:25
no longer speak to you in **f**, Jn 16:25

FILIGREE *(8)*

surrounded with gold **f** settings. Ex 28:11
Fashion gold **f** settings Ex 28:13
with gold **f** in their settings Ex 28:20
cords to the two **f** settings and Ex 28:25
surrounded with gold **f** settings, Ex 39:6
with gold **f** in their settings. Ex 39:13
two gold **f** settings and two Ex 39:16
two cords to the two **f** settings Ex 39:18

FILL (59)
and f the waters of the seas, Gn 1:22
fruitful, multiply, f the earth, Gn 1:28
and multiply and f the earth. Gn 9:1
orders to f their containers Gn 42:25
F the men's bags with as much Gn 44:1
will f your houses, all your Ex 10:6
that you did not f ⌊them with⌋ Dt 6:11
will eat their f and prosper. Dt 31:20
F your horn with oil and go. 1Sm 16:1
F four water pots with water and 1Kg 18:33
He will yet f your mouth with Jb 8:21
empty counsel or f himself with Jb 15:2
Dreadful sounds f his ears; Jb 15:21
before Him and f my mouth with Jb 23:4
Can you f his hide with harpoons Jb 41:7
and violence f his mouth; Ps 10:7
f their bellies with what You Ps 17:14
mouth wide, and I will f it. Ps 81:10
can't even f the hands of the Ps 129:7
property and f our houses with Pr 1:13
will have his f of poverty. Pr 28:19
streams will f your entire land, Is 8:8
and owls will f the houses. Is 13:21
possess a land or f the surface Is 14:21
and bloom and f the whole world Is 27:6
has drunk its f in the heavens Is 34:5
for Fortune and f bowls of mixed Is 65:11
I am about to f all who live in Jr 13:13
Do I not f the heavens and the Jr 23:24
priests their f with abundance, Jr 31:14
Chaldeans will f the houses with Jr 33:5
will drink its f of their blood, Jr 46:10
the arrows! F the quivers! Jr 51:11
I will f you up with men as with Jr 51:14
eat and f your stomach with this Ezk 3:3
appetites or f their stomachs, Ezk 7:19
they must also f the land with Ezk 8:17
the temple and f the courts with Ezk 9:7
F your hands with hot coals from Ezk 10:2
F it with choice bones. Ezk 24:4
against Egypt and f the land Ezk 30:11
entire earth eat their f of you. Ezk 32:4
mountains and f the valleys with Ezk 32:5
I will f its mountains with the Ezk 35:8
I will f you with people, with Ezk 36:10
I will f you with people and Ezk 36:11
will eat your f of horses and Ezk 39:20
of your camp to f your nostrils, Am 4:10
who f their master's house with Zph 1:9
I will f this house with glory, Hg 2:7
I will f that bow with Ephraim. Zch 9:13
place to f such a crowd?" Mt 15:33
F up, then, the measure of your Mt 23:32
place to f these people?" Mk 8:4
to eat his f from the carob Lk 15:16
"F the jars with water," Jesus Jn 2:7
You will f me with gladness in Ac 2:28
the God of hope f you with all Rm 15:13
that He might f all things. Eph 4:10

FILLED (158)
the earth was f with violence. Gn 6:11
for the earth is f with violence Gn 6:13
So she went and f the waterskin Gn 21:19
to the spring, f her jug, and Gn 24:16
that the land was f with them. Ex 1:7
draw water and f the troughs to Ex 2:16
whom I have f with a spirit of Ex 28:3
I have f him with God's Spirit, Ex 31:3
He has f him with God's Spirit, Ex 35:31
He has f them with skill to do Ex 35:35
of the LORD f the tabernacle. Ex 40:34
of the LORD f the tabernacle. Ex 40:35
and f with depravity. Lv 19:29
whole earth is f with the LORD's Nm 14:21
son of Nun was f with the spirit Dt 34:9
were new when we f them, Jos 9:13
the jars the young men have f." Ru 2:9
the cloud f the LORD's temple, 1Kg 8:10
glory of the LORD f the temple. 1Kg 8:11
he even f the trench with water. 1Kg 18:35
the Arameans f the landscape. 1Kg 20:27
the wadi will be f with water, 2Kg 3:17
of Edom and f the land. 2Kg 3:20
and it was f from one end to the 2Kg 10:21
blood that he f Jerusalem with 2Kg 21:16
then f their places with human 2Kg 23:14
He had f Jerusalem with innocent 2Kg 24:4
temple, was f with a cloud. 2Ch 5:13
of the LORD f God's temple. 2Ch 5:14
glory of the LORD f the temple. 2Ch 7:1
glory of the LORD f the temple 2Ch 7:2
peoples have f it from end to Ezr 9:11
They ate, were f, became Neh 9:25
him homage, he was f with rage. Est 3:5
Haman was f with rage toward Est 5:9
who f their houses with silver. Jb 3:15
who are f with much joy and are Jb 3:22
am f with shame and aware of my Jb 10:15
it was He who f their houses Jb 22:18
Then they will be f with terror, Ps 14:5
right hands are f with bribes. Ps 26:10
They are f from the abundance of Ps 36:8
right hand is f with justice. Ps 48:10
they will be f with terror— Ps 53:5
God's stream is f with water, Ps 65:9
whole earth is f with His glory. Ps 72:19
it took root and f the land. Ps 80:9
When I am f with cares, Your Ps 94:19
thirsty and f the hungry with Ps 107:9
earth is f with Your faithful Ps 119:64
Our mouths were f with laughter Ps 126:2
man who has f his quiver with Ps 127:5
your barns will be completely f, Pr 3:10
and no springs f with water. Pr 8:24
he is f with the product of his Pr 18:20
He is f with craving all day Pr 21:26
the rooms are f with every Pr 24:4
or the ear f with hearing. Ec 1:8
all his days are f with grief, Ec 2:23
of people is f ⌊with the desire Ec 8:11
and His robe f the temple. Is 6:1
and the temple was f with smoke. Is 6:4
LORD as the sea is f with water. Is 11:9
Therefore I am f with anguish. Is 21:3
town, is f with revelry. Is 22:2
He has f Zion with justice and Is 33:5
I have f your mouth with My Jr 1:9
Every jar should be f with wine. Jr 13:12
every jar should be f with wine? Jr 13:12
for You f me with indignation. Jr 15:17
They have f My inheritance with Jr 16:18
They have f this place with the Jr 19:4
them to wadis ⌊f⌋ with water Jr 31:9
I set jars f with wine and some Jr 35:5
son of Nethaniah f ⌊it⌋ with the Jr 41:9
he f his belly with my Jr 51:34
f me with bitterness, sated me Lm 3:15
let him be f with shame. Lm 3:30
them a heart f with anguish. Lm 3:65
for the land is f with crimes of Ezk 7:23
and the city is f with violence. Ezk 7:23
and the cloud f the inner court. Ezk 10:3
The temple was f with the cloud, Ezk 10:4
and the court was f with the Ezk 10:4
You will be f with drunkenness Ezk 23:33
I will be f ⌊now that⌋ she lies Ezk 26:2
trade, you were f with violence, Ezk 28:16
ravines will be f with your Ezk 32:6
cities will be f with a flock Ezk 36:38
for sacrifice is f in Jerusalem Ezk 36:38
glory of the LORD f the temple. Ezk 43:5
glory of the LORD f His temple. Ezk 44:4
mountain and f the whole earth. Dn 2:35
Nebuchadnezzar was f with rage, Dn 3:19
I am f with power by the Spirit Mc 3:8
It f up its dens with the kill, Nah 2:12
the earth will be f with the Hab 2:14
You will be f with disgrace Hab 2:16
the city will be f with boys and Zch 8:5
because they will be f. Mt 5:6
Everyone ate and was f. Mt 14:20
They all ate and were f. Mt 15:37
banquet was f with guests. Mt 22:10
got a sponge, f it with sour Mt 27:48
Everyone ate and was f. Mk 6:42
They ate and were f. Then they Mk 8:8
Someone ran and f a sponge with Mk 15:36
will be f with the Holy Spirit Lk 1:15
Elizabeth was f with the Holy Lk 1:41
Zechariah was f with the Holy Lk 1:67
became strong, f with wisdom, Lk 2:40
valley will be f, and every Lk 3:5
they came and f both boats so Lk 5:7
And they were f with awe and Lk 5:26
were f with rage and started Lk 6:11
now, because you will be f. Lk 6:21
Everyone ate and was f. Lk 9:17
so that my house may be f. Lk 14:23
him and was f with compassion Lk 15:20
He longed to be f with what fell Lk 16:21
So they f them to the brim. Jn 2:7
them and f 12 baskets with Jn 6:13
you ate the loaves and were f. Jn 6:26
So the house was f with the Jn 12:3
to you, sorrow has f your heart. Jn 16:6
and it f the whole house where Ac 2:2
they were all f with the Holy Ac 2:4
So they were f with awe and Ac 3:10
Then Peter was f with the Holy Ac 4:8
they were all f with the Holy Ac 4:31
has Satan f your heart to lie Ac 5:3
Sadducees, were f with jealousy. Ac 5:17
you have f Jerusalem with your Ac 5:28
But Stephen, f by the Holy Ac 7:55
sight and be f with the Holy Ac 9:17
called Paul—f with the Holy Ac 13:9
they were f with jealousy and Ac 13:45
disciples were f with joy and Ac 13:52
they were f with rage and began Ac 19:28
the city was f with confusion; Ac 19:29
They are f with all Rm 1:29
full of goodness, f with all Rm 15:14
instead of f with grief so that 1Co 5:2
I am f with encouragement; 2Co 7:4
so you may be f with all the Eph 3:19
but be f with the Spirit Eph 5:18
f with the fruit of Php 1:11
that you may be f with the Col 1:9
and you have been f by Him, Col 2:10
you so that I may be f with joy, 2Tm 1:4
and gold bowls f with incense, Rv 5:8
f it with fire from the altar, Rv 8:5
gold bowls f with the wrath Rv 15:7
the sanctuary was f with smoke Rv 15:8
gave her the cup f with the wine Rv 16:19
in her hand f with everything Rv 17:4
the birds were f with their Rv 19:21
the seven bowls f with the seven Rv 21:9

FILLING (4)
Abraham, f them with dirt. Gn 26:15
dew out of it, f a bowl with Jdg 6:38
love me, and f their treasuries Pr 8:21
f its streets with the dead. Ezk 11:6

FILLS (9)
When he f his stomach, God will Jb 20:23
proud snorting ⌊f one with⌋ Jb 39:20
sea and all that f it resound. Ps 96:11
Let the sea and all that f it, Ps 98:7
His glory f the whole earth. Is 6:3
and all that f it, the world Is 34:1
to the sea with all that f it, Is 42:10
and your outcry f the earth, Jr 46:12
of the One who f all things in Eph 1:23

FILTH (9)
yet is not washed from its f. Pr 30:12
washed away the f of the Is 4:4
cloths, and call them f. Is 30:22
us disgusting f among the Lm 3:45
I will throw f on you and treat Nah 3:6
like the f of all things. 1Co 4:13
all things and consider them f, Php 3:8
of all moral f and evil excess, Jms 1:21
removal of the f of the flesh, 1Pt 3:21

FILTHY (7)
gold will seem like something f. Ezk 7:19
these into something f for them. Ezk 7:20
was dressed with f clothes as he Zch 3:3
Him, "Take off his f clothes!" Zch 3:4
and f language from your mouth. Col 3:8
let the f go on being made Rv 22:11
the filthy go on being made f; Rv 22:11

FINAL (8)
your f days will be full of Jb 8:7
slipped into their ⌊f⌋ sleep. Ps 76:5
the time of f punishment, Ezk 35:5
to the Chaldeans, "My word is f: Dn 2:5
you see that my word is f. Dn 2:8
Jacob will do the f plowing. Hs 10:11
The f glory of this house will Hg 2:9
diligence for the f realization Heb 6:11

FINALIZE (1)
F plans through counsel, and Pr 20:18

FINALLY *(23)*
F, he slaughtered the ox and the Lv 9:18
F, Joshua turned toward Debir Jos 10:38
F, all the trees said to the Jdg 9:14
F, Saul son of Kish was selected. 1Sm 10:21
F, the king and all the people 2Sm 16:14
F, the LORD removed Israel from 2Kg 17:23
Judah that He f banished them 2Kg 24:20
F, the king of Babylon blinded 2Kg 25:7
F, the king of Sheshach will Jr 25:26
Judah that He f banished them Jr 52:3
F Daniel, named Belteshazzar Dn 4:8
F, he sent his son to them. Mt 21:37
F, two who came forward Mt 26:60
F he sent him to them, saying, Mk 12:6
F, the woman died too. Lk 20:32
f all hope that we would be Ac 27:20
F, brothers, rejoice. 2Co 13:11
F, be strengthened by the Lord Eph 6:10
F, my brothers, rejoice in the Php 3:1
F brothers, whatever is true, Php 4:8
F then, brothers, we ask and 1Th 4:1
F, pray for us, brothers, that 2Th 3:1
Now f, all of you should be 1Pt 3:8

FIND *(188)*
up to Me. If not, I will f out." Gn 18:21
If at Sodom I f 50 righteous Gn 18:26
destroy ⌊it⌋ if I f 45 there." Gn 18:28
not do ⌊it⌋ if I f 30 there." Gn 18:30
they were unable to f the door. Gn 19:11
did you ever f it so quickly, Gn 27:20
If you f your gods with anyone Gn 31:32
but could not f the household Gn 31:35
thing to Esau when you f him. Gn 32:19
"To f favor with you, my lord," Gn 33:8
the woman, he could not f her. Gn 38:20
saying, "I couldn't f her, and Gn 38:22
but you couldn't f ⌊her⌋." Gn 38:23
Can we f anyone like this, Gn 41:38
wherever you can f it, Ex 5:11
Today you won't f any in the Ex 16:25
gather, but they did not f any. Ex 16:27
that they may f acceptance with Ex 28:38
know You and f favor in Your Ex 33:13
that I may f out what else the Nm 22:19
and you will f ⌊Him⌋ when you Dt 4:29
but I didn't f ⌊any⌋ evidence of Dt 22:14
I didn't f ⌊any⌋ evidence of Dt 22:17
You will f no peace among those Dt 28:65
men pursuing you won't f you," Jos 2:16
the way, but did not f them. Jos 2:22
come and f refuge in my shade. Jdg 9:15
Can't you f a young woman among Jdg 14:3
wherever he could f a place. Jdg 17:8
settle wherever I can f a place. Jdg 17:9
them, "What did you f out?" Jdg 18:8
each of you to f security in the Ru 1:9
shouldn't I f security for you, Ru 3:1
until you f out how things go, Ru 3:18
your servant f favor with you, 1Sm 1:18
but they didn't f them. 1Sm 9:4
region but still didn't f them. 1Sm 9:4
—you can f him now." 1Sm 9:13
you'll f two men at Rachel's 1Sm 10:2
for him, they could not f him. 1Sm 10:21
F me someone who plays well 1Sm 16:17
F out whose son this young man 1Sm 17:56
If I ever f out my father has 1Sm 20:9
next day and I f out that he is 1Sm 20:12
and say⌋, 'Go and f the arrows!' 1Sm 20:21
Run and f the arrows I'm 1Sm 20:36
Look and f out all the places 1Sm 23:23
my⌋ young men f favor with you, 1Sm 25:8
you will f out what your servant 1Sm 28:2
F me a woman who is a medium, 1Sm 28:7
you and to f out about your 2Sm 3:25
You'll f him in Lo-debar at the 2Sm 9:4
If I f favor in the LORD's eyes, 2Sm 15:25
attack David wherever we f him, 2Sm 17:12
searched but did not f ⌊them⌋, 2Sm 17:20
he will f fortified cities and 2Sm 20:6
Perhaps we'll f grass so we can 1Kg 18:5
to Ahab and he doesn't f you, 1Kg 18:12
You'll f him in Naboth's 1Kg 21:18
three days but did not f him. 2Kg 2:17
they did not f anything but her 2Kg 9:35
and you will f them at the end 2Ch 20:16
come and f plenty of water? 2Ch 32:4
and there the weary f rest. Jb 3:17
my cry for help f no resting Jb 16:18
I will not f a wise man among Jb 17:10
my own children f me repulsive. Jb 19:17
If only I knew how to f Him, Jb 23:3
He turns south, I cannot f Him. Jb 23:9
speak so that I can f relief; Jb 32:20
I would fly away and f rest. Ps 55:6
from long ago and f comfort. Ps 119:52
until I f a place for the LORD, Ps 132:5
We'll f all kinds of valuable Pr 1:13
search for me, but won't f me. Pr 1:28
Then you will f favor and high Pr 3:4
are life to those who f them, Pr 4:22
those who search for me f me. Pr 8:17
seeks wisdom and doesn't f it, Pr 14:6
those who plan good f loyalty Pr 14:22
but who can f a trustworthy man? Pr 20:6
and faithful love will f life, Pr 21:21
If you f it, you will have a Pr 24:14
you f honey, eat only what you Pr 25:16
and renounces them will f mercy. Pr 28:13
will later f more favor than Pr 28:23
Who can f a capable wife? Pr 31:10
And I f more bitter than death Ec 7:26
to another to f out the Ec 7:27
searches for but does not f: Ec 7:28
to explore it, he cannot f it; Ec 8:17
Whatever your hands f to do, Ec 9:10
after many days you may f it. Ec 11:1
Teacher sought to f delightful Ec 12:10
I sought him, but did not f him. Sg 3:1
I sought him, but did not f him. Sg 3:2
I sought him, but did not f him. Sg 5:6
if you f my love, tell him that Sg 5:8
I would f you in public and kiss Sg 8:1
people f refuge in her. Is 14:32
there and will f a resting place Is 34:14
you, but you will not f them. Is 41:12
be justified and f glory through Is 45:25
your fathers f in Me that they Jr 2:5
they will f her in her mating Jr 2:24
If you f a single person, anyone Jr 5:1
to them—they f no pleasure in Jr 6:10
Then take it and f rest for Jr 6:16
cisterns; they f no water; their Jr 14:3
will seek Me and f Me when you Jr 29:13
⌊When⌋ Israel went to f rest, Jr 31:2
like stags that f no pasture; Lm 1:6
the elders f no favor. Lm 4:16
of man, eat what you f ⌊here⌋. Ezk 3:1
trying to f a charge against Dn 6:4
But they could f no charge or Dn 6:4
We will never f any charge Dn 6:5
Daniel unless we f something Dn 6:5
so that she cannot f her paths. Hs 2:6
will seek them but not f ⌊them⌋. Hs 2:7
the LORD but do not f ⌊Him⌋; Hs 5:6
one can f any crime in me that Hs 12:8
LORD, but they will not f it. Am 8:12
Where can I f anyone to comfort Nah 3:7
they will f pasture there. Zph 2:7
When you f Him, report back to Mt 2:8
Keep searching, and you will f. Mt 7:7
leads to life, and few f it. Mt 7:14
town or village, f out who is Mt 10:11
life because of Me will f it. Mt 10:39
and you will f rest for Mt 11:29
for rest but doesn't f any. Mt 12:43
life because of Me will f it. Mt 16:25
open its mouth you'll f a coin. Mt 17:27
At once you will f a donkey tied Mt 21:2
everyone you f to the banquet.' Mt 22:9
could not f any, even though Mt 26:60
you will f a young donkey tied Mk 11:2
He went to f out if there was Mk 11:13
suddenly and f you sleeping. Mk 13:36
to death, but they could f none. Mk 14:55
to his father to f out what he Lk 1:62
you will f a baby wrapped snugly Lk 2:12
When they did not f Him, they Lk 2:45
they could not f a way to bring Lk 5:19
that they could f a charge Lk 6:7
countryside to f food and Lk 9:12
Keep searching, and you will f. Lk 11:9
the master will f alert when he Lk 12:37
To this they could f no answer. Lk 14:6
will He f that faith on earth?" Lk 18:8
to so he could f out how much Lk 19:15
you will f a young donkey tied Lk 19:30
they could not f a way to do it, Lk 19:48
I f no grounds for charging this Lk 23:4
went in but did not f the body Lk 24:3
and when they didn't f His body, Lk 24:23
for Me, but you will not f Me; Jn 7:34
intend to go so we won't f Him? Jn 7:35
for Me, and you will not f Me; Jn 7:36
in and go out and f pasture. Jn 10:9
to him to f out who it was He Jn 13:24
I f no grounds for charging Him. Jn 18:38
let you know I f no grounds for Jn 19:4
I f no grounds for charging Him. Jn 19:6
told them, "and you'll f some." Jn 21:6
they did not f them in the jail, Ac 5:22
our forefathers could f no food. Ac 7:11
had searched and did not f him, Ac 12:19
When they did not f them, they Ac 17:6
they might reach out and f Him, Ac 17:27
he wanted to f out exactly why Ac 22:30
We f nothing evil in this man. Ac 23:9
And they didn't f me disputing Ac 24:12
but when I f time I'll call for Ac 24:25
Why then does He still f fault? Rm 9:19
Israel did not f what it was Rm 11:7
for, but the elect did f it. Rm 11:7
I did not f my brother Titus 2Co 2:13
so no one can f fault with us 2Co 8:20
with me and f you unprepared, 2Co 9:4
come I will not f you to be what 2Co 12:20
I also sent to f out about your 1Th 3:5
mercy and f grace to help us Heb 4:16
he didn't f any opportunity Heb 12:17
was very glad to f some of your 2Jn 4
seek death and will not f it; Rv 9:6
they will never f them again. Rv 18:14

FINDING *(9)*
the wilderness without f water. Ex 15:22
Are they not f and dividing the Jdg 5:30
had been confident ⌊of f water⌋. Jb 6:20
f no way to a city where they Ps 107:4
Anyone f his life will lose it, Mt 10:39
rest, and not f rest, it then Lk 11:24
F that He was under Herod's Lk 23:7
F a ship crossing over to Ac 21:2
But f fault with His people, Heb 8:8

FINDS *(36)*
whoever f me will kill me." Gn 4:14
or f something lost and lies Lv 6:3
nothing to her when he f out, Nm 30:7
he f him, he is to kill him. Nm 35:19
kill the murderer when he f him. Nm 35:21
avenger of blood f him outside Nm 35:27
to him because he f something Dt 24:1
When a man f his enemy, does he 1Sm 24:19
But He f reasons to oppose me; Jb 33:10
the king f joy in Your strength. Ps 21:1
Even a sparrow f a home, and a Ps 84:3
like one who f vast treasure. Ps 119:162
is a man who f wisdom and who Pr 3:13
For the one who f me finds life Pr 8:35
who finds me f life and obtains Pr 8:35
for what is good f favor, Pr 11:27
understands a matter f success, Pr 16:20
A man who f a wife finds a good Pr 18:22
who finds a wife f a good thing Pr 18:22
understanding f success. Pr 19:8
become like one who f peace. Sg 8:10
the nations but f no place to Lm 1:3
⌊f⌋ no grape cluster to eat, Mc 7:1
and the one who searches f, Mt 7:8
"Be sure that no one f out!" Mt 9:30
it arrives, it f ⌊the house⌋ Mt 12:44
And if he f it, I assure you: Mt 18:13
whose master f him working when Mt 24:46
and the one who searches f, Lk 11:10
f ⌊the house⌋ swept and put in Lk 11:25
near dawn, and f them alert, Lk 12:38
whose master f him working when Lk 12:43
the lost one until he f it? Lk 15:4
search carefully until she f it? Lk 15:8
When she f it, she calls her Lk 15:9
f no joy in unrighteousness, 1Co 13:6

FINE *(118)*
measures of f flour and make Gn 18:6
him with f linen garments, Gn 41:42
It will become f dust over the Ex 9:9

desert surface were **f** flakes, Ex 16:14
as **f** as frost on the ground. Ex 16:14
scarlet yarn; **f** linen and goat Ex 25:4
and scarlet yarn; and **f** linen. Ex 28:5
to weave the tunic from **f** linen, Ex 28:39
a turban of **f** linen, and make Ex 28:39
Make them out of **f** wheat flour, Ex 29:2
two quarts of **f** flour mixed with Ex 29:40
of it into a **f** powder and put Ex 30:36
scarlet yarn; **f** linen and goat Ex 35:6
or scarlet yarn, **f** linen or goat Ex 35:23
and scarlet yarn, and **f** linen. Ex 35:25
and scarlet yarn and **f** linen; Ex 35:35
and scarlet yarn, and **f** linen. Ex 38:23
and the **f** linen in a skillful Ex 39:3
the tunics of **f** woven linen for Ex 39:27
the ornate headbands of **f** linen, Ex 39:28
gift must consist of **f** flour. Lv 2:1
take a handful of **f** flour and Lv 2:2
it must be ⌊made⌋ of **f** flour, Lv 2:4
bread ⌊made⌋ of **f** flour mixed Lv 2:5
be made of **f** flour with oil. Lv 2:7
bring two quarts of **f** flour as Lv 5:11
a handful of **f** flour and olive Lv 6:15
two quarts of **f** flour as a Lv 6:20
cakes of **f** flour mixed with oil Lv 7:12
three quarts of **f** flour mixed Lv 14:10
two quarts of **f** flour mixed with Lv 14:21
four quarts of **f** flour mixed Lv 23:13
from four quarts of **f** flour, Lv 23:17
Take **f** flour and bake it into 12 Lv 24:5
cakes made from **f** flour mixed Nm 6:15
of them full of **f** flour mixed Nm 7:13
of them full of **f** flour mixed Nm 7:19
of them full of **f** flour mixed Nm 7:25
of them full of **f** flour mixed Nm 7:31
of them full of **f** flour mixed Nm 7:37
of them full of **f** flour mixed Nm 7:43
of them full of **f** flour mixed Nm 7:49
of them full of **f** flour mixed Nm 7:55
of them full of **f** flour mixed Nm 7:61
of them full of **f** flour mixed Nm 7:67
of them full of **f** flour mixed Nm 7:73
of them full of **f** flour mixed Nm 7:79
offering of **f** flour mixed with Nm 8:8
two quarts of **f** flour mixed with Nm 15:4
four quarts of **f** flour mixed Nm 15:6
six quarts of **f** flour mixed with Nm 15:9
two quarts of **f** flour for a Nm 28:5
quarts of **f** flour mixed with Nm 28:9
six quarts of **f** flour mixed with Nm 28:12
quarts of **f** flour mixed with Nm 28:12
two quarts of **f** flour mixed with Nm 28:13
is to be of **f** flour mixed with Nm 28:20
offering of **f** flour mixed with Nm 28:28
offering of **f** flour mixed with Nm 29:3
is to be of **f** flour mixed with Nm 29:9
is to be of **f** flour mixed with Nm 29:14
it to powder as ⌊**f** as⌋ dust. Dt 9:21
They will also **f** him 100 silver Dt 22:19
dead, it would be **f** with you! 2Sm 19:6
150 bushels of **f** flour and 300 1Kg 4:22
and overlaid it with **f** gold. 1Kg 10:18
six quarts of **f** meal ⌊will sell⌋ 2Kg 7:1
six quarts of **f** meal ⌊sold⌋ for 2Kg 7:16
six quarts of **f** meal ⌊will sell 2Kg 7:18
on the land a **f** of 7,500 pounds 2Kg 23:33
as well as the **f** flour, wine, 1Ch 9:29
dressed in a robe of **f** linen, 1Ch 15:27
the **f** flour for the grain 1Ch 23:29
blue, crimson yarn, and **f** linen. 2Ch 2:14
overlaid with **f** gold, and 2Ch 3:5
it with 45,000 pounds of **f** gold. 2Ch 3:8
and crimson yarn and **f** linen, 2Ch 3:14
dressed in **f** linen, with cymbals 2Ch 5:12
articles of **f** gleaming bronze Ezr 8:27
fastened with **f** white and purple Est 1:6
and a purple robe of **f** linen. Est 8:15
and articles of **f** gold cannot be Jb 28:17
gold or called **f** gold my trust, Jb 31:24
It is like **f** oil on the head, Ps 133:2
good to **f** an innocent person, Pr 17:26
her clothing is **f** linen and Pr 31:22
name is better than **f** perfume, Ec 7:1
Your mouth is like **f** wine— Sg 7:9
instead of **f** clothes, sackcloth; Is 3:24
your foes will be like **f** dust, Is 29:5
up the islands like **f** dust. Is 40:15
tarnished, the **f** gold become Lm 4:1
wrapped you in **f** linen and Ezk 16:10
clothing was ⌊made⌋ of **f** linen, Ezk 16:13
You ate **f** flour, honey, and oil. Ezk 16:13
I gave you—the **f** flour, oil, Ezk 16:19
was ⌊made of⌋ **f** embroidered Ezk 27:7
cloth, **f** linen, coral, Ezk 27:16
of oil to moisten the **f** flour— Ezk 46:14
will place a yoke on her **f** neck. Hs 10:11
merchant in search of **f** pearls. Mt 13:45
wrapped it in clean, **f** linen, Mt 27:59
After he bought some **f** linen, Mk 15:46
dress in purple and **f** linen, Lk 16:19
wrapped it in **f** linen and placed Lk 23:53
sets out the **f** wine first, Jn 2:10
have kept the **f** wine until now. Jn 2:10
it is **f** for a man to stay as he 1Co 7:26
ring, dressed in **f** clothes, and Jms 2:2
wearing the **f** clothes so that Jms 2:3
of gold ornaments or **f** clothes; 1Pt 3:3
His feet like **f** bronze fired in Rv 1:15
feet are like **f** bronze says: Rv 2:18
f fabrics of linen, purple, silk, Rv 18:12
wine, olive oil, **f** wheat flour, Rv 18:13
clothed in **f** linen, purple, Rv 18:16
was permitted to wear **f** linen, Rv 19:8
For the **f** linen represents the Rv 19:8

FINED *(2)*

hit her must be **f** as the woman's Ex 21:22
Jerusalem and **f** the land 7,500 2Ch 36:3

FINELY *(22)*

must make them of **f** spun linen, Ex 26:1
and **f** spun linen with a design Ex 26:31
scarlet yarn, and **f** spun linen. Ex 26:36
courtyard out of **f** spun linen, Ex 27:9
scarlet yarn, and **f** spun linen. Ex 27:16
⌊all of it made⌋ of **f** spun linen. Ex 27:18
make the ephod of **f** spun linen Ex 28:6
yarn, and of **f** spun linen. Ex 28:8
yarn, and of **f** spun linen. Ex 28:15
made them of **f** spun linen, Ex 36:8
scarlet yarn, and **f** spun linen. Ex 36:35
f spun linen for the entrance Ex 36:37
courtyard were of **f** spun linen, Ex 38:9
courtyard were of **f** spun linen. Ex 38:16
scarlet yarn, and **f** spun linen. Ex 38:18
yarn, and of **f** spun linen. Ex 39:2
yarn, and of **f** spun linen, just Ex 39:5
yarn, and of **f** spun linen. Ex 39:8
pomegranates of **f** spun blue, Ex 39:24
and the sash of **f** spun linen of Ex 39:29
handfuls of **f** ground fragrant Lv 16:12
wine, choice meat, **f** aged wine. Is 25:6

FINERY *(1)*

day the Lord will strip their **f**: Is 3:18

FINES *(1)*

God wine obtained through **f**. Am 2:8

FINEST *(10)*

your dead in our **f** burial place. Gn 23:6
Take for yourself the **f** spices: Ex 30:23
a pastry cooked with the **f** oil. Nm 11:8
drank wine from the **f** grapes. Dt 32:14
be your gold and your **f** silver. Jb 22:25
satisfies you with the **f** wheat. Ps 147:14
Solomon's **F** Song Sg 1:1
and planted it with the **f** vines. Is 5:2
and carried My **f** treasures to Jl 3:5
with the **f** oils but do not Am 6:6

FINGER *(29)*

"This is the **f** of God," the Ex 8:19
horns of the altar with your **f**; Ex 29:12
inscribed by the **f** of God. Ex 31:18
is to dip his **f** in the blood Lv 4:6
is to dip his **f** in the blood Lv 4:17
with his **f** and apply it to Lv 4:25
blood with his **f** and apply it to Lv 4:30
with his **f** and apply it to Lv 4:34
it with his **f** to the horns Lv 8:15
and he dipped his **f** in the blood Lv 9:9
will dip his right **f** into the Lv 14:16
the oil with his **f** seven times Lv 14:16
With his right **f** the priest will Lv 14:27
it⌋ with his **f** against the east Lv 16:14
with his **f** before the mercy Lv 16:14
on it with his **f** seven times to Lv 16:19
blood with his **f** and sprinkle it Nm 19:4
tablets, inscribed by God's **f**. Dt 9:10
'My little **f** is thicker than my 1Kg 12:10
'My little **f** is thicker than my 2Ch 10:10
did not lift a **f** to help their Neh 3:5
ring from his **f** and gave it to Est 3:10
to lift a **f** to move them. Mt 23:4
out demons by the **f** of God, Lk 11:20
put a ring on his **f** and sandals Lk 15:22
the tip of his **f** in water and Lk 16:24
on the ground with His **f**. Jn 8:6
put my **f** into the mark of the Jn 20:25
Put your **f** here and observe My Jn 20:27

FINGER-POINTING *(1)*

the **f** and malicious speaking, Is 58:9

FINGERS *(14)*

there with six **f** on each hand 2Sm 21:20
stature with six **f** ⌊on each 1Ch 20:6
the work of Your **f**, the moon and Ps 8:3
for battle and my **f** for warfare. Ps 144:1
feet, and gestures with his **f**, Pr 6:13
Tie them to your **f**; write them Pr 7:3
my **f** with flowing myrrh on the Sg 5:5
to what their **f** have made. Is 2:8
altars they made with their **f**. Is 17:8
blood, and your **f** with iniquity; Is 59:3
was hollow—four **f** thick— Jr 52:21
moment the **f** of a man's hand Dn 5:5
putting His **f** in the man's ears Mk 7:33
burdens with one of your **f**. Lk 11:46

FINISH *(16)*

F your assigned work each day, Ex 5:13
his sons are to **f** covering the Nm 4:15
temple and **f** this structure? Ezr 5:3
temple and **f** this structure? Ezr 5:9
Will they ever **f** it? Can they Neh 4:2
but I will not **f** it off. Jr 4:27
them, but do not **f** them off. Jr 5:10
I will not **f** you off. Jr 5:18
I will **f** them off by sword, Jr 14:12
after them until I **f** them off. Jr 49:37
the foundation and cannot **f** it, Lk 14:29
to build and wasn't able to **f**.' Lk 14:30
who sent Me and to **f** His work," Jn 4:34
that I may **f** my course and the Ac 20:24
But now **f** the task as well, 2Co 8:11
When they **f** their testimony, Rv 11:7

FINISHED *(104)*

When He **f** talking with him, Gn 17:22
the LORD had **f** speaking with Gn 18:33
Before he had **f** speaking, there Gn 24:15
When she had **f** giving him a Gn 24:19
After the camels had **f** drinking, Gn 24:22
Before I had **f** praying in my Gn 24:45
as Isaac had **f** blessing Jacob Gn 27:30
He **f** the week ⌊of celebration⌋, Gn 29:28
When Judah had **f** mourning, Gn 38:12
When Jacob had **f** instructing his Gn 49:33
Why haven't you **f** making your Ex 5:14
When He **f** speaking with Moses on Ex 31:18
When Moses had **f** speaking with Ex 34:33
the tent of meeting, was **f**. Ex 39:32
So Moses **f** the work. Ex 40:33
When he has **f** purifying the Lv 16:20
the day Moses **f** setting up the Nm 7:1
Just as he **f** speaking all these Nm 16:31
the officers have **f** addressing Dt 20:9
When you have **f** paying all the Dt 26:12
When Moses had **f** writing down on Dt 31:24
After Moses **f** reciting all these Dt 32:45
entire nation had **f** crossing the Jos 3:17
entire nation had **f** crossing the Jos 4:1
after everyone had **f** crossing, Jos 4:11
When Israel had **f** killing Jos 8:24
and the Israelites **f** inflicting Jos 10:20
When they had **f** distributing the Jos 19:49
So they **f** dividing up the land. Jos 19:51
When Ehud had **f** presenting the Jdg 3:18
he **f** speaking, he threw away Jdg 15:17
they have **f** all of my harvest. Ru 2:21
and the wheat harvests were **f**. Ru 2:23
there until he has **f** eating and Ru 3:3
Then Saul **f** prophesying and 1Sm 10:13
Just as he **f** offering the burnt 1Sm 13:10
followed and **f** them off. 1Sm 14:13
When David had **f** speaking with 1Sm 18:1
When David **f** saying these things 1Sm 24:16
When David had **f** offering the 2Sm 6:18
When you've **f** telling the king 2Sm 11:19

as he f speaking, the king's 2Sm 13:36
for David had f grieving over 2Sm 13:39
the people had f marching past. 2Sm 15:24
the noise⌋ as they f eating. 1Kg 1:41
of David until he f building his 1Kg 3:1
construction used f stones cut 1Kg 6:7
When he f building the temple, 1Kg 6:9
When Solomon f building the 1Kg 6:14
everything was completely f, 1Kg 6:22
So Hiram f all the work that he 1Kg 7:40
When Solomon f praying this 1Kg 8:54
When Solomon f building the 1Kg 9:1
these until they are f off.' " 1Kg 22:11
When he f offering the burnt 2Kg 10:25
When David had f offering the 1Ch 16:2
stonemasons to cut f stones for 1Ch 22:2
of the LORD's house is f. 1Ch 28:20
Huram f doing the work that he 2Ch 4:11
When Solomon f praying, fire 2Ch 7:1
So Solomon f the LORD's temple 2Ch 7:11
LORD's temple until it was f. 2Ch 8:16
these until they are f off.' " 2Ch 18:10
When they had f with the 2Ch 20:23
When they f, they presented the 2Ch 24:14
day of the first month they f. 2Ch 29:17
until the work was f and until 2Ch 29:34
and they f in the seventh month. 2Ch 31:7
is rebuilt and its walls are f, Ezr 4:13
is rebuilt and its walls are f, Ezr 4:16
king of Israel built and f. Ezr 5:11
They f the building according to Ezr 6:14
work, and it will never be f." Neh 6:9
the LORD had f speaking to Job, Jb 42:7
When you have f destroying, Is 33:1
When you have f betraying, Is 33:1
You f them off, but they refused Jr 5:3
them until I have f them off." Jr 9:16
him and f him off and made Jr 10:25
They will be f off by sword and Jr 16:4
He f the address the LORD had Jr 26:8
Jeremiah had f speaking to all Jr 43:1
or famine until they are f off. Jr 44:27
When you have f reading this Jr 51:63
until you have f the days of Ezk 4:8
When he f measuring inside the Ezk 42:15
you have f the purification, Ezk 43:23
When the locusts f eating the Am 7:2
When Jesus had f this sermon, Mt 7:28
When Jesus had f giving orders Mt 11:1
When Jesus had f these parables, Mt 13:53
When Jesus had f this Mt 19:1
Jesus had f saying all this, Mt 26:1
he cannot stand but is f! Mk 3:26
to the law of Moses were f, Lk 2:22
Devil had f every temptation, Lk 4:13
When He had f speaking, He said Lk 5:4
place, and when He f, one of His Lk 11:1
it consumes Me until it is f! Lk 12:50
sour wine, He said, "It is f!" Jn 19:30
So when I have f this and safely Rm 15:28
fight, I have f the race, I have 2Tm 4:7
His works have been f since the Heb 4:3
in the flesh has f with sin— 1Pt 4:1

FINISHES *(1)*

But when the Lord f all His work Is 10:12

FINISHING *(2)*

f⌊the sides of the ark⌋ to Gn 6:16
and evil city, f its walls, and Ezr 4:12

FINS *(5)*

the water that has f and scales, Lv 11:9
that does not have f and scales Lv 11:10
does not have f and scales will Lv 11:12
the water that has f and scales, Dt 14:9
does not have f and scales— Dt 14:10

FIR *(2)*

all ⌊kinds of⌋ f wood 2Sm 6:5
you—⌊its⌋ pine, f, and cypress Is 60:13

FIRE *(456)*

a smoking f pot and a flaming Gn 15:17
hand he took the f and the Gn 22:6
The f and the wood are here, Gn 22:7
in a flame of f within a bush. Ex 3:2
the bush was on f but was not Ex 3:2
roasted over the f along with Ex 12:8
only roasted over f—its head Ex 12:9
in a pillar of f to give them Ex 13:21
the pillar of f by night never Ex 13:22
from the pillar of f and cloud, Ex 14:24
the LORD came down on it in f. Ex 19:18
When a f gets out of control, Ex 22:6
who started the f must make full Ex 22:6
like a consuming f on the Ex 24:17
pleasing aroma, a f offering to Ex 29:18
it is a f offering to the LORD. Ex 29:25
pleasing aroma, a f offering to Ex 29:41
When I threw it into the f, Ex 32:24
Do not light a f in any of your Ex 35:3
and there was a f inside the Ex 40:38
will prepare a f on the altar Lv 1:7
altar and arrange wood on the f. Lv 1:7
a f offering of a pleasing aroma Lv 1:9
a f offering of a pleasing aroma Lv 1:13
a f offering of a pleasing aroma Lv 1:17
a f offering of a pleasing aroma Lv 2:2
part of the f offerings to Lv 2:3
a f offering of a pleasing aroma Lv 2:9
part of the f offerings to Lv 2:10
yeast or honey as a f offering Lv 2:11
roasted on the f, for your grain Lv 2:14
frankincense as a f offering to Lv 2:16
sacrifice as a f offering to the Lv 3:3
a f offering of a pleasing aroma Lv 3:5
sacrifice as a f offering to the Lv 3:9
altar as food, a f offering to Lv 3:11
his offering as a f offering to Lv 3:14
a f offering for a pleasing Lv 3:16
and must burn it on a wood f. Lv 4:12
along with the f offerings to Lv 4:35
along with the f offerings to Lv 5:12
while the f of the altar is kept Lv 6:9
offering the f has consumed Lv 6:10
The f on the altar is to be kept Lv 6:12
priest will burn wood on the f. Lv 6:12
offering on the f and burn the Lv 6:12
F must be kept burning on the Lv 6:13
portion from My f offerings. Lv 6:17
from the f offerings to Lv 6:18
on the altar as a f offering to Lv 7:5
animal fat from a f offering Lv 7:25
will bring the f offerings to Lv 7:30
portion from the f offerings to Lv 7:35
a f offering to the LORD as He Lv 8:21
pleasing aroma, a f offering to Lv 8:28
F came out from the LORD and Lv 9:24
own firepan, put f in it, placed Lv 10:1
unauthorized f before the LORD, Lv 10:1
when the LORD sent the f. Lv 10:6
left over from the f offerings Lv 10:12
sons' from the f offerings to Lv 10:13
of fat portions made by f, Lv 10:15
of one's body produced by f, Lv 13:24
on the f before the LORD, Lv 16:13
pass through ⌊the f⌋ to Molech. Lv 18:21
and they must be burned with f, Lv 20:14
they present the f offerings to Lv 21:6
to present the f offerings to Lv 21:21
on the altar as a f offering to Lv 22:22
as a gift, a f offering to the Lv 22:27
are to present a f offering to Lv 23:8
mixed with oil as a f offering Lv 23:13
a f offering of a pleasing aroma Lv 23:18
you must present a f offering to Lv 23:25
are to present a f offering to Lv 23:27
are to present a f offering to Lv 23:36
and present a f offering to the Lv 23:36
presenting f offerings to the Lv 23:37
for the bread and a f offering Lv 24:7
for him from the f offerings to Lv 24:9
unauthorized f before the LORD Nm 3:4
and put ⌊it⌋ on the f under the Nm 6:18
it appeared like f above the Nm 9:15
appearing like f at night. Nm 9:16
and the f from the LORD blazed Nm 11:1
the LORD, and the f died down. Nm 11:2
the LORD's f had blazed among Nm 11:3
and in a pillar of f by night. Nm 14:14
and you make a f offering to the Nm 15:3
It is a f offering of pleasing Nm 15:10
when he presents a f offering as Nm 15:13
wants to prepare a f offering as Nm 15:14
one made by f to the LORD, Nm 15:25
place f in them and put incense Nm 16:7
firepan, placed f in it, put Nm 16:18
F also came out from the LORD Nm 16:35
and scatter the f far away. Nm 16:37
place f from the altar in it, Nm 16:46
kept⌋ from the f will be yours; Nm 18:9
their fat as a f offering for Nm 18:17
them⌋ onto the f where the cow Nm 19:6
For f came out of Heshbon, Nm 21:28
died and the f consumed 250 men. Nm 26:10
unauthorized f before the LORD. Nm 26:61
and My food as My f offering, Nm 28:2
This is the f offering you are Nm 28:3
pleasing aroma, a f offering to Nm 28:6
It is a f offering, a pleasing Nm 28:8
pleasing aroma, a f offering to Nm 28:13
Present a f offering, a burnt Nm 28:19
for seven days as a f offering, Nm 28:24
pleasing aroma, a f offering to Nm 29:6
a f offering as a pleasing aroma Nm 29:13
a f offering as a pleasing aroma Nm 29:36
that can withstand f— Nm 31:23
put through f, and it will be Nm 31:23
that cannot withstand f, Nm 31:23
He went in the f by night and in Dt 1:33
blazing with f into the heavens Dt 4:11
LORD spoke to you from the f. Dt 4:12
to you at Horeb out of the f— Dt 4:15
LORD your God is a consuming f, Dt 4:24
speaking from the f as you have, Dt 4:33
showed you His great f on earth, Dt 4:36
you heard His words from the f. Dt 4:36
face from the f on the mountain Dt 5:4
afraid of the f and did not go Dt 5:5
your entire assembly from the f, Dt 5:22
the mountain was blazing with f. Dt 5:23
have heard His voice from the f. Dt 5:24
This great f will consume us and Dt 5:25
living God speaking from the f, Dt 5:26
ahead of you as a consuming f; Dt 9:3
you from the f on the mountain Dt 9:10
while it was blazing with f, Dt 9:15
you on the mountain from the f. Dt 10:4
in the f to their gods. Dt 12:31
will eat the LORD's f offerings; Dt 18:1
or daughter pass through the f, Dt 18:10
or see this great f any longer, Dt 18:16
For f has been kindled because Dt 32:22
taking the city, set it on f. Jos 8:8
and immediately set it on f. Jos 8:19
offerings made by f to the LORD, Jos 13:14
to the sword and set it on f. Jdg 1:8
F came up from the rock and Jdg 6:21
may f come out from the bramble Jdg 9:15
may f come from Abimelech and Jdg 9:20
and may f come from the lords of Jdg 9:20
and set it on f around the Jdg 9:49
its entrance to set it on f. Jdg 9:52
of yarn snaps when it touches f. Jdg 16:9
all the Israelite f offerings. 1Sm 2:28
there. Go and set f to it!" So 2Sm 14:30
servants set the field on f. 2Sm 14:30
servants set my field on f?" 2Sm 14:31
and consuming f ⌊came⌋ from His 2Sm 22:9
on the wood but not light the f. 1Kg 18:23
on the wood but not light the f. 1Kg 18:23
The God who answers with f, 1Kg 18:24
your god but don't light the f." 1Kg 18:25
Yahweh's f fell and consumed 1Kg 18:38
the earthquake there was a f, 1Kg 19:12
but the LORD was not in the f. 1Kg 19:12
And after the f there was a 1Kg 19:12
may f come down from heaven and 2Kg 1:10
Then f came down from heaven 2Kg 1:10
may f come down from heaven and 2Kg 1:12
So a divine f came down from 2Kg 1:12
Already f has come down from 2Kg 1:14
a chariot of f with horses of 2Kg 2:11
with horses of f suddenly 2Kg 2:11
and chariots of f all around 2Kg 6:17
will set their fortresses on f. 2Kg 8:12
made his son pass through the f, 2Kg 16:3
pass through the f and practiced 2Kg 17:17
children in the f to Adrammelech 2Kg 17:31
thrown their gods into the f, 2Kg 19:18
made his son pass through the f, 2Kg 21:6
pass through the f to Molech. 2Kg 23:10
that they be burned in the f. 1Ch 14:12
answered him with f from heaven 1Ch 21:26
f descended from heaven and 2Ch 7:1
watching when the f descended 2Ch 7:3
made a great f in his honor. 2Ch 16:14

did not hold a **f** in his honor 2Ch 21:19
honor like the **f** in honor of his 2Ch 21:19
burned his children in the **f**, 2Ch 28:3
sons through the **f** in the Valley 2Ch 33:6
lambs⌋ with **f** according to 2Ch 35:13
gates have been destroyed by **f**?" Neh 2:3
that had been destroyed by **f**. Neh 2:13
and with a pillar of **f** by night, Neh 9:12
the pillar of **f** illuminated the Neh 9:19
and **f** will consume the tents of Jb 15:34
flame of his **f** does not glow. Jb 18:5
A **f** unfanned ⌊by human hands⌋ Jb 20:26
f has consumed what they left Jb 22:20
earth is transformed as by **f**. Jb 28:5
For it is a **f** that consumes down Jb 31:12
He tips His arrows with **f**. Ps 7:13
and consuming **f** ⌊came⌋ from His Ps 18:8
His wrath, and **f** will devour Ps 21:9
of the LORD flashes flames of **f**. Ps 29:7
as I mused, a **f** burned. Ps 39:3
Devouring **f** precedes Him, and a Ps 50:3
we went through **f** and water, Ps 66:12
As wax melts before the **f**, Ps 68:2
They set Your sanctuary on **f**; Ps 74:7
then **f** broke out against Jacob, Ps 78:21
F consumed His chosen young men, Ps 78:63
jealousy keep burning like **f**? Ps 79:5
As **f** burns a forest, as a flame Ps 83:14
Your anger keep burning like **f**? Ps 89:46
F goes before Him and burns up Ps 97:3
flames of **f** His servants. Ps 104:4
and ⌊gave⌋ a **f** to light up the Ps 105:39
F blazed throughout their Ps 106:18
like a **f** among thorns; Ps 118:12
Let them be thrown into the **f**, Ps 140:10
a man embrace **f** and his clothes Pr 6:27
speech is like a scorching **f**. Pr 16:27
Without wood, **f** goes out; Pr 26:20
for embers and wood for **f**, Pr 26:21
f, which never says, "Enough! Pr 30:16
your cities burned with **f**; Is 1:7
glowing flame of **f** by night over Is 4:5
as a tongue of **f** consumes straw Is 5:24
be burned as fuel for the **f**. Is 9:5
burns like a **f** that consumes Is 9:18
people are like fuel for the **f**. Is 9:19
a burning **f** under its glory Is 10:16
Israel's Light will become a **f**, Is 10:17
The **f** for Your adversaries will Is 26:11
and a flame of consuming **f**. Is 29:6
enough to take **f** from a hearth Is 30:14
tongue is like a consuming **f**. Is 30:27
and a flame of consuming **f**, Is 30:30
with plenty of **f** and wood. Is 30:33
whose **f** is in Zion and whose Is 31:9
Your breath is **f** that will Is 33:11
cut down and burned in a **f**. Is 33:12
us can dwell with a consuming **f**? Is 33:14
thrown their gods into the **f**; Is 37:19
him with **f**, but he did not Is 42:25
when you walk through the **f**, Is 43:2
he kindles a **f** and bakes bread; Is 44:15
He burns half of it in a **f**, Is 44:16
I burned half of it in the **f**, Is 44:19
like stubble; **f** burns them up. Is 47:14
or a **f** to sit beside! Is 47:14
you who kindle a **f**, who encircle Is 50:11
the light of your **f** and in the Is 50:11
on the charcoal **f** and produces a Is 54:16
as **f** kindles the brushwood, Is 64:2
and **f** causes water to boil— Is 64:2
been burned with **f**, and all that Is 64:11
a **f** that burns all day long. Is 65:5
the LORD will come with **f**— Is 66:15
and His rebuke with flames of **f**. Is 66:15
their **f** will never go out, Is 66:24
break out like **f** and burn with Jr 4:4
My words become **f** in your mouth. Jr 5:14
and the **f** will consume them. Jr 5:14
blow, blasting the lead with **f**. Jr 6:29
light the **f**, and the women Jr 7:18
sons and daughters in the **f**, Jr 7:31
He has set **f** to it, and its Jr 11:16
will kindle a **f** that will burn Jr 15:14
for you have set My anger on **f**; Jr 17:4
I will set **f** to its gates, Jr 17:27
children in the **f** as burnt Jr 19:5
message becomes a **f** burning in Jr 20:9

will flare up like **f** and burn Jr 21:12
I will kindle a **f** in its forest Jr 21:14
and throw them into the **f**. Jr 22:7
not My word like **f**"—the LORD's Jr 23:29
of Babylon roasted in the **f**! Jr 29:22
set this city on **f**, and burn it Jr 32:29
pass through ⌊the **f**⌋ to Molech— Jr 32:35
quarters with a **f** burning in Jr 36:22
the blazing **f** until the entire Jr 36:23
by the **f** in the brazier. Jr 36:23
king, had burned in the **f**. Jr 36:32
I will kindle a **f** in the temples Jr 43:12
shadow because **f** has come out Jr 48:45
I will set **f** to the wall of Jr 49:27
I will set **f** to his cities, Jr 50:32
marshes set on **f**, and the Jr 51:32
her high gates consumed by **f**. Jr 51:58
themselves ⌊only to feed⌋ the **f**. Jr 51:58
He sent **f** from on high into my Lm 1:13
like a flaming **f** that consumes Lm 2:3
out His wrath like **f** on the tent Lm 2:4
He has ignited a **f** in Zion, Lm 4:11
great cloud with **f** flashing back Ezk 1:4
the center of the **f**, there was a Ezk 1:4
burning coals of **f** and torches. Ezk 1:13
F was moving back and forth Ezk 1:13
looked like **f** enclosing it all Ezk 1:27
I also saw what looked like **f**. Ezk 1:27
them into the **f**, and burn them Ezk 5:4
A **f** will spread from it to the Ezk 5:4
to be His waist down was **f**, Ezk 8:2
Take **f** from inside the Ezk 10:6
his hand to the **f** that was among Ezk 10:7
it is put into the **f** as fuel. Ezk 15:4
The **f** devours both of its ends, Ezk 15:4
useful when the **f** has devoured Ezk 15:5
I have given to the **f** as fuel, Ezk 15:6
may have escaped from the **f**, Ezk 15:7
through ⌊the **f**⌋ to the images. Ezk 16:21
and dried up; **f** consumed them. Ezk 19:12
F has gone out from its main Ezk 19:14
firstborn pass through ⌊the **f**⌋, Ezk 20:26
children pass through the **f**, Ezk 20:31
I am about to ignite a **f** in you, Ezk 20:47
I will blow the **f** of My fury on Ezk 21:31
You will be fuel for the **f**. Ezk 21:32
furnace to blow **f** on them and Ezk 22:20
on you with the **f** of My fury, Ezk 22:21
them with the **f** of My fury. Ezk 22:31
will be consumed by **f**. Ezk 23:25
pass through ⌊the **f**⌋ as food for Ezk 23:37
and burn their houses with **f**. Ezk 23:47
the pot on ⌊the **f**⌋—put ⌊it⌋ Ezk 24:3
on the logs and kindle the **f**! Ezk 24:10
Into the **f** with its rust! Ezk 24:12
So I sent out **f** from within you, Ezk 28:18
LORD when I set **f** to Egypt and Ezk 30:8
desolate, set **f** to Zoan, and Ezk 30:14
I will set **f** to Egypt; Pelusium Ezk 30:16
hailstones, **f**, and brimstone Ezk 38:22
I will send **f** against Magog and Ezk 39:6
into a furnace of blazing **f**." Dn 3:6
into a furnace of blazing **f**. Dn 3:11
into a furnace of blazing **f**— Dn 3:15
from the furnace of blazing **f**, Dn 3:17
into the furnace of blazing **f**. Dn 3:20
into the furnace of blazing **f**. Dn 3:21
into the furnace of blazing **f**. Dn 3:23
three men, bound, into the **f**?" Dn 3:24
around in the **f** unharmed; Dn 3:25
furnace of blazing **f** and called: Dn 3:26
and Abednego came out of the **f**. Dn 3:26
saw that the **f** had no effect Dn 3:27
there was no smell of **f** on them. Dn 3:27
His throne was flaming **f**; Dn 7:9
its wheels were blazing **f**. Dn 7:9
A river of **f** was flowing, coming Dn 7:10
and given over to the burning **f**. Dn 7:11
stirring ⌊the **f**⌋ from the Hs 7:4
it blazes like a flaming **f**. Hs 7:6
I will send **f** on their cities, Hs 8:14
for **f** has consumed the pastures Jl 1:19
and **f** has consumed the pastures Jl 1:20
A **f** destroys in front of them, Jl 2:3
blood, **f**, and columns of smoke. Jl 2:30
I will send **f** against Hazael's Am 1:4
I will send **f** against the walls Am 1:7
I will send **f** against the walls Am 1:10

I will send **f** against Teman, Am 1:12
I will set **f** to the walls of Am 1:14
I will send **f** against Moab, Am 2:2
I will send **f** against Judah, Am 2:5
burning stick snatched from a **f**, Am 4:11
will spread like **f** ⌊throughout⌋ Am 5:6
was calling for a judgment by **f**. Am 7:4
of Jacob will be a ⌊blazing⌋ **f**, Ob 18
set them on **f** and consume them Ob 18
like wax near a **f**, like water Mc 1:4
wages will be burned in the **f**, Mc 1:7
His wrath is poured out like **f**, Nah 1:6
flash like **f** on the day of its Nah 2:3
F will devour the bars ⌊of your Nah 3:13
The **f** will devour you there; Nah 3:15
to fuel the **f** and countries Hab 2:13
by the **f** of His jealousy Zph 1:18
by the **f** of My jealousy. Zph 3:8
I will be a wall of **f** around it, Zch 2:5
stick snatched from the **f**?" Zch 3:2
herself will be consumed by **f**. Zch 9:4
and **f** will consume your cedars. Zch 11:1
put this third through the **f**; Zch 13:9
a useless ⌊**f** on⌋ My altar! Mal 1:10
like a refiner's **f** and like Mal 3:2
cut down and thrown into the **f**. Mt 3:10
you with the Holy Spirit and **f**. Mt 3:11
burn up with **f** that never goes Mt 3:12
cut down and thrown into the **f**. Mt 7:19
gathered and burned in the **f**, Mt 13:40
often falls into the **f** and often Mt 17:15
be thrown into the eternal **f**. Mt 18:8
into the eternal **f** prepared for Mt 25:41
thrown him into **f** or water to Mk 9:22
go to hell—the unquenchable **f**, Mk 9:43
and the **f** is not quenched. Mk 9:44
into hell—the unquenchable **f**, Mk 9:45
and the **f** is not quenched. Mk 9:46
and the **f** is not quenched. Mk 9:48
everyone will be salted with **f**. Mk 9:49
warming himself by the **f**. Mk 14:54
cut down and thrown into the **f**." Lk 3:9
you with the Holy Spirit and **f**. Lk 3:16
burn up with a **f** that never goes Lk 3:17
us to call down **f** from heaven to Lk 9:54
I came to bring **f** on the earth, Lk 12:49
f and sulfur rained from heaven Lk 17:29
They lit a **f** in the middle of Lk 22:55
them into the **f**, and they are Jn 15:6
police had made a charcoal **f**, Jn 18:18
they saw a charcoal **f** there, Jn 21:9
like flames of **f** that were Ac 2:3
and **f** and a cloud of smoke. Ac 2:19
for they lit a **f** and took us all Ac 28:2
brushwood and put it on the **f**, Ac 28:3
off into the **f** and suffered no Ac 28:5
it will be revealed by **f**; 1Co 3:13
the **f** will test the quality of 1Co 3:13
be like an escape through **f**. 1Co 3:15
flaming **f** on those who don't 2Th 1:8
the fury of a **f** about to consume Heb 10:27
raging of **f**, escaped the edge Heb 11:34
to a blazing **f**, to darkness, Heb 12:18
for our God is a consuming **f**. Heb 12:29
a forest a small **f** ignites. Jms 3:5
the tongue is a **f**. The tongue, Jms 3:6
sets the course of life on **f**, Jms 3:6
fire, and is set on **f** by hell. Jms 3:6
and will eat your flesh like **f**. Jms 5:3
perishes though refined by **f**— 1Pt 1:7
earth are held in store for **f**, 2Pt 3:7
will be on **f** and be dissolved, 2Pt 3:12
the punishment of eternal **f**. Jd 7
by snatching ⌊them⌋ from the **f**; Jd 23
refined in the **f** so that you may Rv 3:18
filled it with **f** from the altar, Rv 8:5
hail and **f**, mixed with blood, Rv 8:7
mountain ablaze with **f** was Rv 8:8
and from their mouths came **f**, Rv 9:17
plagues—by the **f**, the smoke, Rv 9:18
f comes from their mouths and Rv 11:5
even causing **f** to come down from Rv 13:13
be tormented with **f** and sulfur Rv 14:10
had authority over **f**, came from Rv 14:18
a sea of glass mixed with **f**, Rv 15:2
the power to burn people with **f**, Rv 16:8
flesh, and burn her up with **f**. Rv 17:16
She will be burned up with **f**, Rv 18:8

the lake of f that burns with Rv 19:20
Then f came down from heaven and Rv 20:9
the lake of f and sulfur where Rv 20:10
were thrown into the lake of f. Rv 20:14
the second death, the lake of f. Rv 20:14
was thrown into the lake of f. Rv 20:15
that burns with f and sulfur, Rv 21:8

FIREBRANDS *(3)*
these two smoldering stubs of f, Is 7:4
who encircle yourselves with f; Is 50:11
fire and in the f you have lit! Is 50:11

FIRED *(8)*
partly iron and partly f clay, Dn 2:33
on its feet of iron and f clay, Dn 2:34
the iron, the f clay, the bronze Dn 2:35
of a potter's f clay and partly Dn 2:41
were part iron and part f clay— Dn 2:42
iron does not mix with f clay. Dn 2:43
iron, bronze, f clay, silver, Dn 2:45
like fine bronze f in a furnace, Rv 1:15

FIRELIGHT *(1)*
saw him sitting in the f, Lk 22:56

FIREPAN *(8)*
and Abihu each took his own f, Lv 10:1
he must take a f full of fiery Lv 16:12
Each of you is to take his f, Nm 16:17
present his f before the LORD Nm 16:17
each ⌊to present⌋ your f also." Nm 16:17
Each man took his f, placed fire Nm 16:18
Aaron, "Take your f, place fire Nm 16:46
So Aaron took his f as Moses had Nm 16:47

FIREPANS *(16)*
snuffers and f must be of pure Ex 25:38
basins, meat forks, and f; Ex 27:3
snuffers, and f of pure gold. Ex 37:23
basins, meat forks, and f; Ex 38:3
snuffers, and f, as well as its Nm 4:9
the f, meatforks, shovels, and Nm 4:14
take f, and tomorrow Nm 16:6
firepan before the LORD—250 f. Nm 16:17
to remove the f from the burning Nm 16:37
As for the f of those who sinned Nm 16:38
the LORD, and the f are holy. Nm 16:38
took the bronze f that those who Nm 16:39
basins, ladles, and f; 1Kg 7:50
took away the f and the 2Kg 25:15
ladles, and f—of purest gold; 2Ch 4:22
the bowls, the f, the sprinkling Jr 52:19

FIREPOT *(1)*
of Judah like a f in a woodpile, Zch 12:6

FIRES *(4)*
will come and make f with them, Is 27:11
will go out, kindle f, and burn Ezk 39:9
they will use them to make f. Ezk 39:9
will use the weapons to make f. Ezk 39:10

FIRM *(22)*
Stand f and see the LORD's Ex 14:13
the currents stood f like a dam. Ex 15:8
his web, but it doesn't stand f. Jb 8:15
fall, but we rise and stand f. Ps 20:8
the water stood f like a wall. Ps 78:13
the earth, and it stands f. Ps 119:90
do not stand f in your faith, Is 7:9
him, like a peg, into a f place. Is 22:23
driven into a f place will give Is 22:25
He will make a f covenant with Dn 9:27
to the Lord with a f resolve of Ac 11:23
But he who stands f in his heart 1Co 7:37
Be alert, stand f in the faith, 1Co 16:13
And our hope for you is f, 2Co 1:7
Therefore stand f and don't Gl 5:1
are standing f in one spirit, Php 1:27
and crown, stand f in the Lord, Php 4:1
if you stand f in the Lord. 1Th 3:8
stand f and hold to the 2Th 2:15
God's solid foundation stands f, 2Tm 2:19
like a sure and f anchor of the Heb 6:19
Resist him, f in the faith, 1Pt 5:9

FIRMLY *(18)*
covenant stood f on dry ground Jos 3:17
his kingship was f established. 1Kg 2:12
the kingdom was f in his grasp, 2Kg 14:5
The world is f established; 1Ch 16:30
the kingdom was f in his grasp, 2Ch 25:3
You will be f established and Jb 11:15
his thighs are woven f together. Jb 40:17
The world is f established; Ps 93:1
The world is f established; Ps 96:10
it is f fixed in heaven. Ps 119:89
are like f embedded nails. Ec 12:11
and hold f to My covenant, Is 56:4
and who hold f to My covenant— Is 56:6
If you are f resolved to go to Jr 42:15
being rooted and f established Eph 3:17
Hold f the message of life. Php 2:16
you have learned and f believed, 2Tm 3:14
if we hold f until the end Heb 3:14

FIRST *(398)*
and then morning: the f day. Gn 1:5
The name of the f is Pishon, Gn 2:11
on the f day of the month, Gn 8:5
In the six hundred and f year, Gn 8:13
first year, in the f month, on Gn 8:13
on the f day of the month, Gn 8:13
was the f to plant a vineyard. Gn 9:20
who was the f powerful man on Gn 10:8
The f one came out reddish, Gn 25:25
"F sell me your birthright." Gn 25:31
Jacob said, "Swear to me f." Gn 25:33
And he told the f one: Gn 32:17
He put the female slaves f, Gn 33:2
This one came out f." Gn 38:28
"You have broken out ⌊f⌋!" Gn 38:29
cows ate the f seven well-fed Gn 41:20
returned in our bags the f time. Gn 43:18
down here the f time only to buy Gn 43:20
to the evidence of the f sign, Ex 4:8
it is the f month of your year. Ex 12:2
On the f day you must remove Ex 12:15
leavened from the f day through Ex 12:15
assembly on the f day and Ex 12:16
bread in the f ⌊month⌋, Ex 12:18
or marital rights of the f wife. Ex 21:10
petals, on the f branch, and Ex 25:33
be under the ⌊f⌋ pair of Ex 25:35
the last curtain in the ⌊f⌋ set, Ex 26:4
the outermost in the ⌊f⌋ set, Ex 26:10
bases under the f plank for its Ex 26:19
bases under the f plank and two Ex 26:21
bases under the f plank and two Ex 26:25
their names on the f stone and Ex 28:10
The f row should be a row of Ex 28:17
With the f lamb offer two quarts Ex 29:40
stone tablets like the f ones, Ex 34:1
that were on the f tablets, Ex 34:1
stone tablets like the f ones. Ex 34:4
last curtain in the f set and Ex 36:11
curtain in the ⌊f⌋ set and 50 Ex 36:17
bases under the f plank for its Ex 36:24
bases under the f plank and two Ex 36:26
petals, on the f branch, and Ex 37:19
was under the f pair of branches Ex 37:21
f row was a row of carnelian, Ex 39:10
on the f day of the first month. Ex 40:2
on the first day of the f month. Ex 40:2
was set up in the f month of the Ex 40:17
on the f ⌊day⌋ of the month. Ex 40:17
it just as he burned the f bull. Lv 4:21
who will f present the one for Lv 5:8
anyone without ⌊f⌋ rinsing his Lv 15:11
the LORD comes in the f month, Lv 23:5
On the f day you are to hold a Lv 23:7
are to bring the f sheaf of your Lv 23:10
on the f ⌊day⌋ of the month, Lv 23:24
a sacred assembly on the f day; Lv 23:35
rest on the f day and complete Lv 23:39
On the f day you are to take the Lv 23:40
on the f ⌊day⌋ of the second Nm 1:1
community on the f day of the Nm 1:18
186,400; they will move out f. Nm 2:9
offering on the f day was Nm 7:12
of all who come f from the womb, Nm 8:16
the f month of the second year Nm 9:1
observed it in the f month on Nm 9:5
set out for the f time according Nm 10:13
with their banner set out f, Nm 10:14
season for the f ripe grapes. Nm 13:20
loaf from your f batch of dough Nm 15:20
from the f batch of your dough. Nm 15:21
of Zin in the f month, Nm 20:1
my people, but f, let me warn Nm 24:14
Amalek was f among the nations, Nm 24:20
the LORD comes in the f month, Nm 28:16
On the f day there is to be a Nm 28:18
on the f ⌊day⌋ of the month, Nm 29:1
from Rameses in the f month, Nm 33:3
died there on the f ⌊day⌋ of the Nm 33:38
month, on the f of the month, Dt 1:3
fell down like the f time in the Dt 9:18
like the f ones and come to Dt 10:1
that were on the f tablets you Dt 10:2
stone tablets like the f ones, Dt 10:3
and 40 nights like the f time. Dt 10:10
is to be the f against him to Dt 13:9
evening of the f day is to Dt 16:4
time the sickle is f ⌊put⌋ to Dt 16:9
are to be the f in putting him Dt 17:7
and the f sheared ⌊wool⌋ of your Dt 18:4
the f husband who sent her away Dt 24:4
The f son she bears will carry Dt 25:6
take some of the f of all the Dt 26:2
now brought the f of the land's Dt 26:10
on the tenth day of the f month, Jos 4:19
us as they did the f time, Jos 8:5
because they received the f lot. Jos 21:10
will be the f to fight for us Jdg 1:1
Who is to go f to fight for us Jdg 20:18
answered, "Judah will be f." Jdg 20:18
themselves on the f day. Jdg 20:22
as they were in the f battle." Jdg 20:39
f named Hannah and the second 1Sm 1:2
The fat must be burned f; 1Sm 2:16
In that f assault Jonathan and 1Sm 14:14
was the f time he had built an 1Sm 14:35
Was today the f time I inquired 1Sm 22:15
From the f day I was with you 1Sm 29:8
If some of our troops fall f, 2Sm 17:9
As the f runner came closer, 2Sm 18:25
The way the f man runs looks to 2Sm 18:27
Today I am the f one of the 2Sm 19:20
Weren't we the f to speak of 2Sm 19:43
executed in the f days of the 2Sm 21:9
King Solomon f swear to me that 1Kg 1:51
The f woman said, "No, your son 1Kg 3:22
the living baby to the f woman, 1Kg 3:27
One wing of the ⌊f⌋ cherub was 1Kg 6:24
f cherub's height was 15 feet 1Kg 6:26
the f one's wing touched ⌊one⌋ 1Kg 6:27
f door had two folding sides, 1Kg 6:34
was the height of the f capital, 1Kg 7:16
for the f capital and seven 1Kg 7:17
and became as it had been at f. 1Kg 13:6
one bull and prepare it f. 1Kg 18:25
of your servant the f time, 1Kg 20:9
leaders marched out f. 1Kg 20:17
of Israel, "F, please ask what 1Kg 22:5
and consumed the f two captains 2Kg 1:14
bread from the f bread of the 2Kg 4:42
When they f lived there, they 2Kg 17:25
who was the f to become a great 1Ch 1:10
the ⌊f⌋ lot was for them. 1Ch 6:54
The f to live in their towns on 1Ch 9:2
Whoever is the f to kill a 1Ch 11:6
Joab son of Zeruiah went up f, 1Ch 11:6
Jordan in the f month when it 1Ch 12:15
were not ⌊with⌋ us the f time, 1Ch 15:13
decreed for the f time that 1Ch 16:7
Jehiel was the f, then Zetham, 1Ch 23:8
Jahath was the f and Zizah was 1Ch 23:11
Gershom's sons: Shebuel f. 1Ch 23:16
Eliezer's sons were Rehabiah, f; 1Ch 23:17
Izhar's sons: Shelomith was f. 1Ch 23:18
Jeriah was f, Amariah second, 1Ch 23:19
Micah was f, and Isshiah second. 1Ch 23:20
The f lot fell to Jehoiarib, 1Ch 24:7
sons: Isshiah was the f. 1Ch 24:21
Jeriah ⌊the f⌋, Amariah the 1Ch 24:23
The f lot for Asaph fell to 1Ch 25:9
Shimri the f (although he was 1Ch 26:10
had appointed him as the f 1Ch 26:10
was in charge of the f division, 1Ch 27:2
first division, for the f month; 1Ch 27:2
army commanders for the f month. 1Ch 27:3
of Israel, "F, please ask what 2Ch 18:4
In the f year of his reign, 2Ch 29:3
reign, in the f month, he opened 2Ch 29:3
on the f day of the first 2Ch 29:17
on the first day of the f month, 2Ch 29:17
day of the f month they finished 2Ch 29:17
fourteenth day of the f month. 2Ch 35:1
In the f year of Cyrus king of 2Ch 36:22
In the f year of Cyrus king of Ezr 1:1

the f day of the seventh month Ezr 3:6
who had seen the f temple, Ezr 3:12
in the f year of Cyrus king of Ezr 5:13
In the f year of King Cyrus, Ezr 6:3
fourteenth day of the f month. Ezr 6:19
Babylon on the f day of the Ezr 7:9
first day of the f month and Ezr 7:9
on the f day of the fifth Ezr 7:9
day⌋ of the f month to go to Ezr 8:31
convened on the f day of the Ezr 10:16
and by the f day of the first Ezr 10:17
first day of the f month they Ezr 10:17
record of those who came back f, Neh 7:5
On the f day of the seventh Neh 8:2
from the f day to the last. Neh 8:18
loaf⌋ from our f batch of dough Neh 10:37
In the f month, the month of Est 3:7
thirteenth day of the f month, Est 3:12
trouble comes. F Series of Jb 3:26
Were you the f person ever born, Jb 15:7
He named his f ⌊daughter⌋ Jb 42:14
the f progeny of the tents of Ps 78:51
their land, all their f progeny. Ps 105:36
and with the f produce of your Pr 3:9
fields, or the f soil on earth. Pr 8:26
The f to state his case seems Pr 18:17
the LORD, am the f, and with the Is 41:4
I was the f to say to Zion: Is 41:27
Your f father sinned, and your Is 43:27
I am the f and I am the last. Is 44:6
I am the f, I am also the last. Is 48:12
At f My people went down to Is 52:4
like one bearing her f child. Jr 4:31
where I made My name dwell at f. Jr 7:12
I will f repay them double for Jr 16:18
which was the f year of Jr 25:1
from the time I ⌊f⌋ spoke to you Jr 36:2
The f who devoured him was the Jr 50:17
in the ⌊f⌋ year of his reign, Jr 52:31
from the f watch of the night. Lm 2:19
the f face was that of a cherub, Ezk 10:14
on the f ⌊day⌋ of the month, Ezk 26:1
year in the f ⌊month⌋, Ezk 29:17
on the f ⌊day⌋ of the month, Ezk 29:17
eleventh year, in the f ⌊month⌋, Ezk 30:20
on the f ⌊day⌋ of the month, Ezk 31:1
on the f ⌊day⌋ of the month, Ezk 32:1
f threshold was 10 feet deep. Ezk 40:6
same measurements as the f gate: Ezk 40:21
to give your f batch of dough Ezk 44:30
In the f ⌊month⌋, on the first Ezk 45:18
on the f ⌊day⌋ of the month, Ezk 45:18
In the f ⌊month⌋, on the Ezk 45:21
there until the f year of King Dn 1:21
At the f light of dawn the king Dn 6:19
In the f year of Belshazzar king Dn 7:1
The f was like a lion but had Dn 7:4
and three of the f horns were Dn 7:8
his eyes represents the f king. Dn 8:21
In the f year of Darius, who was Dn 9:1
in the f year of his reign, Dn 9:2
man I had seen in the f vision, Dn 9:21
twenty-fourth day of the f month, Dn 10:4
for from the f day that you Dn 10:12
the f year of Darius the Mede, Dn 11:1
a multitude larger than the f. Dn 11:13
time will not be like the f. Dn 11:29
When the LORD f spoke to Hosea, Hs 1:2
like the f fruit of the fig Hs 9:10
of the fig tree in its f season. Hs 9:10
people in this f of the nations, Am 6:1
exile as the f of the captives, Am 6:7
spring crop f began to sprout Am 7:1
set out on the f day of his walk Jnh 3:4
toward Tarshish in the f place. Jnh 4:2
pool of water from her ⌊f⌋ days, Nah 2:8
trees with figs that ripened f; Nah 3:12
on the f day of the sixth month, Hg 1:1
will be greater than the f," Hg 2:9
The f chariot had red horses, Zch 6:2
will save the tents of Judah f, Zch 12:7
Gate to the place of the F Gate, Zch 14:10
F go and be reconciled with your Mt 5:24
seek f the kingdom of God and Mt 6:33
F take the log out of your eye, Mt 7:5
"f let me go bury my father." Mt 8:21
F, Simon, who is called Peter, Mt 10:2
unless he f ties up the strong Mt 12:29

condition is worse than the f. Mt 12:45
Gather the weeds f and tie them Mt 13:30
say that Elijah must come f?" Mt 17:10
spoke to him f, "What do you Mt 17:25
and catch the f fish that comes Mt 17:27
But many who are f will be last, Mt 19:30
will be last, and the last f. Mt 19:30
the last and ending with the f.' Mt 20:8
So when the f ones came, they Mt 20:10
last will be f, and the first Mt 20:16
will be first, and the f last." Mt 20:16
wants to be f among you must be Mt 20:27
He went to the f and said, Mt 21:28
will?" "The f," they said. Jesus Mt 21:31
more than the f group, and they Mt 21:36
The f got married and died. Mt 22:25
F clean the inside of the cup, Mt 23:26
On the f day of Unleavened Bread Mt 26:17
will be worse than the f." Mt 27:64
as the f day of the week was Mt 28:1
unless he f ties up the strong Mk 3:27
by itself—f the blade, then Mk 4:28
the children to be satisfied f, Mk 7:27
say that Elijah must come f?" Mk 9:11
Elijah does come f and restores Mk 9:12
wants to be f, he must be last Mk 9:35
But many who are f will be last, Mk 10:31
will be last, and the last f." Mk 10:31
wants to be f among you must be Mk 10:44
The f took a wife, and dying, Mk 12:20
good news must f be proclaimed Mk 13:10
the f day of Unleavened Bread, Mk 14:12
on the f day of the week Mk 16:2
Early on the f day of the week, Mk 16:9
He appeared f to Mary Magdalene, Mk 16:9
everything from the very f, Lk 1:3
This f registration took place Lk 2:2
F take the log out of your eye, Lk 6:42
"f let me go bury my father." Lk 9:59
but f let me go and say good-bye Lk 9:61
house you enter, f say, 'Peace Lk 10:5
condition is worse than the f." Lk 11:26
that He did not f perform the Lk 11:38
began to say to His disciples f: Lk 12:1
some are last who will be f, Lk 13:30
some are f who will be last." Lk 13:30
The f one said to him, 'I have Lk 14:18
doesn't f sit down and calculate Lk 14:28
will not f sit down and decide Lk 14:31
my master?' he asked the f one. Lk 16:5
But f He must suffer many things Lk 17:25
The f came forward and said, Lk 19:16
The f took a wife and died Lk 20:29
these things must take place f, Lk 21:9
On the f day of the week, very Lk 24:1
He f found his own brother Simon Jn 1:41
sets out the fine wine f, Jn 2:10
performed this f sign in Cana Jn 2:11
Then the f one who got in after Jn 5:4
should be the f to throw a stone Jn 8:7
understand these things at f. Jn 12:16
F they led Him to Annas, for he Jn 18:13
the legs of the f man and of the Jn 19:32
On the f day of the week Mary Jn 20:1
Peter and got to the tomb f. Jn 20:4
who had reached the tomb f, Jn 20:8
of that f day of the week Jn 20:19
I wrote the f narrative, Ac 1:1
and sent Him f to you to bless Ac 3:26
sent our forefathers the f time. Ac 7:12
disciples were f called Ac 11:26
they passed the f and second Ac 12:10
message be spoken to you f. Ac 13:46
reported how God f intervened to Ac 15:14
On the f day of the week, we Ac 20:7
from the f day I set foot in Ac 20:18
preached to those in Damascus f, Ac 26:20
and that as the f to rise from Ac 26:23
jump overboard f and get to land Ac 27:43
F, I thank my God through Jesus Rm 1:8
who believes, f to the Jew, and Rm 1:16
who does evil, f to the Jew, and Rm 2:9
who does good, f to the Jew, and Rm 2:10
F, they were entrusted with the Rm 3:2
not understand?" F, Moses said: Rm 10:19
Or who has ever f given to Him, Rm 11:35
nearer than when we f believed. Rm 13:11
once I have f enjoyed your Rm 15:24

who is the f convert to Christ Rm 16:5
f apostles, second prophets, 1Co 12:28
the f prophet should be silent. 1Co 14:30
The f man Adam became a living 1Co 15:45
is not f, but the natural 1Co 15:46
The f man was from the earth and 1Co 15:47
the f day of the week, each of 1Co 16:2
I planned to come to you f, 2Co 1:15
which is the f commandment with Eph 6:2
gospel from the f day until now. Php 1:5
might come to have f place in Col 1:18
the dead in Christ will rise f. 1Th 4:16
the apostasy comes f and the man 2Th 2:3
F of all, then, I urge that 1Tm 2:1
Adam was created f, then Eve. 1Tm 2:13
And they must also be tested f; 1Tm 3:10
their own family f and to repay 1Tm 5:4
faith that f lived in your 2Tm 1:5
ought to be the f to get a share 2Tm 2:6
At my f defense, no one came to 2Tm 4:16
person after a f and second Ti 3:10
It was f spoken by the Lord and Heb 2:3
f, his name means "king of Heb 7:2
high priests do—f for their Heb 7:27
if that f ⌊covenant⌋ had been Heb 8:7
has declared that the f is old. Heb 8:13
Now the f ⌊covenant⌋ also had Heb 9:1
and in the f room, which is Heb 9:2
enter the f room repeatedly, Heb 9:6
while the f tabernacle was Heb 9:8
committed⌋ under the f covenant. Heb 9:15
is why even the f covenant was Heb 9:18
He takes away the f to establish Heb 10:9
the wisdom from above is f pure, Jms 3:17
F of all, you should know this: 2Pt 1:20
is worse for them than the f. 2Pt 2:20
F, be aware of this: scoffers 2Pt 3:3
We love because He f loved us. 1Jn 4:19
loves to have f place among them 3Jn 9
having f of all saved a people Jd 5
I am the F and the Last, Rv 1:17
the love ⌊you had⌋ at f. Rv 2:4
and do the works you did at f. Rv 2:5
The F and the Last, the One who Rv 2:8
works are greater than the f. Rv 2:19
The f voice that I had heard Rv 4:1
The f living creature was like a Rv 4:7
The f ⌊angel⌋ blew his trumpet, Rv 8:7
The f woe has passed. There are Rv 9:12
authority of the f beast on his Rv 13:12
on it to worship the f beast, Rv 13:12
The f went and poured out his Rv 16:2
This is the f resurrection. Rv 20:5
shares in the f resurrection! Rv 20:6
for the f heaven and the first Rv 21:1
and the f earth had passed Rv 21:1
the f foundation jasper, the Rv 21:19
the Omega, the F and the Last, Rv 22:13

FIRSTBORN *(145)*

some of the f of his flock and Gn 4:4
Canaan fathered Sidon his f, Gn 10:15
Then the f said to the younger, Gn 19:31
the f came and slept with her Gn 19:33
The next day the f said to the Gn 19:34
The f gave birth to a son and Gn 19:37
his f, his brother Buz, Kemuel Gn 22:21
Ishmael's f, then Kedar, Adbeel Gn 25:13
his father, "I am Esau, your f. Gn 27:19
"I am Esau your f son." Gn 27:32
in marriage⌋ before the f. Gn 29:26
(Jacob's f), Simeon, Levi, Gn 35:23
the sons of Eliphaz, Esau's f: Gn 36:15
wife for Er, his f, and her name Gn 38:6
Now Er, Judah's f, was evil in Gn 38:7
Joseph named the f Manasseh, Gn 41:51
from the f to the youngest. Gn 43:33
to Egypt: Jacob's f: Reuben. Gn 46:8
although Manasseh was the f. Gn 48:14
This one is the f. Gn 48:18
Reuben, you are my f, my Gn 49:3
Israel is My f son. Ex 4:22
Now I will kill your f son!" Ex 4:23
sons of Reuben, the f of Israel: Ex 6:14
and every f ⌊male⌋ in the land Ex 11:5
from the f of Pharaoh who sits Ex 11:5
throne to the f of the servant Ex 11:5
well as every f of the livestock Ex 11:5
and strike every f ⌊male⌋ in the Ex 12:12

LORD struck every **f**⌊male⌋ in Ex 12:29
from the **f** of Pharaoh who sat on Ex 12:29
throne to the **f** of the prisoner Ex 12:29
and every **f** of the livestock. Ex 12:29
Consecrate every **f** male to Me, Ex 13:2
the **f** from every womb among the Ex 13:2
the LORD every **f** male of the Ex 13:12
All **f** offspring of the livestock Ex 13:12
redeem every **f** of a donkey with Ex 13:13
redeem every **f** among your sons. Ex 13:13
LORD killed every **f**⌊male⌋ in Ex 13:15
from the **f** of man to the Ex 13:15
of man to the **f** of livestock. Ex 13:15
LORD all the **f** of the womb that Ex 13:15
I redeem all the **f** of my sons.' Ex 13:15
Give Me the **f** of your sons. Ex 22:29
The **f** male from every womb Ex 34:19
livestock, the **f** of cattle or Ex 34:19
must redeem the **f** of a donkey Ex 34:20
redeem all the **f** of your sons. Ex 34:20
consecrate a **f** of the livestock Lv 27:26
because a **f**⌊already⌋ belongs to Lv 27:26
of Reuben, the **f** of Israel: Nm 1:20
the **f**, and Abihu, Eleazar, Nm 3:2
in place of every **f** Israelite Nm 3:12
because every **f** belongs to Me. Nm 3:13
struck down every **f** in the land Nm 3:13
consecrated every **f** in Israel to Nm 3:13
Register every **f** male of the Nm 3:40
in place of every **f** among the Nm 3:41
in place of every **f** among the Nm 3:41
registered every **f** among the Nm 3:42
number of the **f** males one month Nm 3:43
in place of every **f** among the Nm 3:45
for the 273 **f** Israelites who Nm 3:46
the money from the **f** Israelites: Nm 3:50
the womb, every Israelite **f**. Nm 8:16
For every **f** among the Israelites Nm 8:17
struck down every **f** in the land Nm 8:17
in place of every **f** among the Nm 8:18
The **f** of every living thing, Nm 18:15
certainly redeem the **f** of man, Nm 18:15
and redeem the **f** of an unclean Nm 18:15
must not redeem the **f** of an ox, Nm 18:17
Reuben was the **f** of Israel. Nm 26:5
burying every **f** male the LORD Nm 33:4
and the **f** of your herds and Dt 12:6
the **f** of your herd or flock; Dt 12:17
the **f** of your herd and flock, Dt 14:23
your God every **f** male produced Dt 15:19
not to put the **f** of your oxen to Dt 15:19
or shear the **f** of your flock. Dt 15:19
the unloved wife has the **f** son, Dt 21:15
wife⌋ as his **f** over the Dt 21:16
over the **f** of the unloved Dt 21:16
He must acknowledge the **f**, Dt 21:17
he has the rights of the **f**. Dt 21:17
His **f** bull has splendor, and Dt 33:17
at the cost of⌋ his **f**; Jos 6:26
tribe of Manasseh as Joseph's **f**. Jos 17:1
the **f** of Manasseh and the father Jos 17:1
to Jether, his **f**, "Get up and Jdg 8:20
f son's name was Joel and his 1Sm 8:2
Merab, his **f**, and Michal, the 1Sm 14:49
were Eliab, the **f**, Abinadab, the 1Sm 17:13
his **f** was Amnon, by Ahinoam the 2Sm 3:2
At the cost of Abiram his **f**, 1Kg 16:34
So he took his **f** son, who was to 2Kg 3:27
fathered Sidon, his **f**, and Heth, 1Ch 1:13
Ishmael's **f**, Kedar, Adbeel, 1Ch 1:29
Er, Judah's **f**, was evil in the 1Ch 2:3
Jesse fathered Eliab, his **f**; 1Ch 2:13
sons of Jerahmeel, Hezron's **f**: 1Ch 2:25
Ram, his **f**, Bunah, Oren, Ozem, 1Ch 2:25
The sons of Ram, Jerahmeel's **f**: 1Ch 2:27
Mesha, his **f**, fathered Ziph, and 1Ch 2:42
The sons of Hur, Ephrathah's **f**: 1Ch 2:50
Amnon was the **f**, by Ahinoam of 1Ch 3:1
Johanan was the **f**, Jehoiakim 1Ch 3:15
Ephrathah's **f** and the father of 1Ch 4:4
sons of Reuben the **f** of Israel. 1Ch 5:1
He was the **f**, but his birthright 1Ch 5:1
The sons of Reuben, Israel's **f**: 1Ch 5:3
his **f** Joel, and his second son 1Ch 6:28
Benjamin fathered Bela, his **f**; 1Ch 8:1
Abdon was his **f** son, then Zur, 1Ch 8:30
Ulam was his **f**, Jeush second, 1Ch 8:39
Asaiah the **f** and his sons; 1Ch 9:5
the **f** of Shallum the Korahite, 1Ch 9:31
Abdon was his **f** son, then Zur, 1Ch 9:36
Zechariah the **f**, Jediael the 1Ch 26:2
Shemaiah the **f**, Jehozabad the 1Ch 26:4
although he was not the **f**, 1Ch 26:10
to Jehoram because he was the **f**. 2Ch 21:3
also bring⌋ the **f** of our sons Neh 10:36
will bring the **f** of our herds Neh 10:36
death's **f** consumes his limbs. Jb 18:13
He struck all the **f** in Egypt, Ps 78:51
I will also make him My **f**, Ps 89:27
struck all the **f** in their land, Ps 105:36
He struck down the **f** of Egypt, Ps 135:8
He struck the **f** of the Egyptians Ps 136:10
Then the **f** of the poor will be Is 14:30
Father, and Ephraim is My **f**. Jr 31:9
they made every **f** pass through Ezk 20:26
Should I give my **f** for my Mc 6:7
for Him as one weeps for a **f**. Zch 12:10
she gave birth to her **f** Son, Lk 2:7
Every **f** male will be dedicated Lk 2:23
He would be the **f** among many Rm 8:29
God, the **f** over all creation Col 1:15
beginning, the **f** from the dead, Col 1:18
brings His **f** into the world, Heb 1:6
of the **f** might not touch Heb 11:28
assembly of the **f** whose names Heb 12:23
f from the dead and the ruler Rv 1:5

FIRSTFRUITS *(28)*

and the **f** of my virility, Gn 49:3
with the **f** of your produce Ex 23:16
the best of the **f** of your land Ex 23:19
of Weeks with the **f** of the wheat Ex 34:22
Bring the best **f** of your land to Ex 34:26
to the LORD as an offering of **f**, Lv 2:12
grain offering of **f** to the LORD, Lv 2:14
for your grain offering of **f**. Lv 2:14
with yeast, as **f** to the LORD. Lv 23:17
the bread of **f** as a presentation Lv 23:20
give to the LORD as their **f**. Nm 18:12
The **f** of all that is in their Nm 18:13
On the day of **f**, you are to hold Nm 28:26
to give him the **f** of your grain, Dt 18:4
for he is the **f** of his virility; Dt 21:17
will⌋ bring the **f** of our land Neh 10:35
also bring the **f** of our ⌊grain⌋ Neh 10:37
contributions, **f**, and tenths. Neh 12:44
appointed times and for the **f**. Neh 13:31
the LORD, the **f** of His harvest. Jr 2:3
best of all the **f** of every kind Ezk 44:30
who have the Spirit as the **f**— Rm 8:23
if the **f** offered up are holy, Rm 11:16
the **f** of those who have fallen 1Co 15:20
Christ, the **f**; afterward, at His 1Co 15:23
are the **f** of Achaia and have 1Co 16:15
we would be the **f** of His Jms 1:18
human race as the **f** for God and Rv 14:4

FISH *(68)*

They will rule the **f** of the sea, Gn 1:26
Rule the **f** of the sea, the birds Gn 1:28
and all the **f** of the sea. Gn 9:2
The **f** in the Nile will die, Ex 7:18
The **f** in the Nile died, and the Ex 7:21
the free **f** we ate in Egypt, Nm 11:5
Or if all the **f** in the sea were Nm 11:22
or any **f** in the waters under the Dt 4:18
animals, birds, reptiles, and **f**. 1Kg 4:33
to the entrance of the **F** Gate; 2Ch 33:14
of Hassenaah built the **F** Gate. Neh 3:3
Old Gate, the **F** Gate, the Tower Neh 12:39
were importing **f** and all kinds Neh 13:16
let the **f** of the sea inform you. Jb 12:8
and **f** of the sea passing through Ps 8:8
blood and caused their **f** to die. Ps 105:29
like **f** caught in a cruel net, Ec 9:12
their **f** rot because of lack of Is 50:2
and they will **f** for them. Jr 16:16
and make the **f** of your streams Ezk 29:4
and all the **f** of your streams Ezk 29:4
and all the **f** of your streams Ezk 29:5
The **f** of the sea, the birds of Ezk 38:20
a huge number of **f** because this Ezk 47:9
Their **f** will consist of many Ezk 47:10
like the **f** of the Mediterranean Ezk 47:10
even the **f** of the sea disappear. Hs 4:3
a great **f** to swallow Jonah Jnh 1:17
Jonah was in the **f** three days Jnh 1:17
LORD his God from inside the **f**: Jnh 2:1
Then the LORD commanded the **f**, Jnh 2:10
mankind like the **f** of the sea, Hab 1:14
of the sky and the **f** of the sea, Zph 1:3
be an outcry from the **F** Gate, Zph 1:10
I will make you **f** for people!" Mt 4:19
he asks for a **f**, will give him Mt 7:10
belly of the great **f** three days Mt 12:40
It collected every kind ⌊of **f**⌋, Mt 13:47
the good ⌊**f**⌋ into containers, Mt 13:48
five loaves and two **f** here," Mt 14:17
the five loaves and the two **f**, Mt 14:19
they said, "and a few small **f**." Mt 15:34
took the seven loaves and the **f**, Mt 15:36
catch the first **f** that comes up. Mt 17:27
I will make you **f** for people!" Mk 1:17
they said, "Five, and two **f**." Mk 6:38
the five loaves and the two **f**, Mk 6:41
the two **f** among them all. Mk 6:41
full of pieces of bread and **f**. Mk 6:43
They also had a few small **f**; Mk 8:7
they caught a great number of **f**, Lk 5:6
at the catch of **f** they took, Lk 5:9
than five loaves and two **f**," Lk 9:13
the five loaves and the two **f**, Lk 9:16
son asks for a **f**, will give him Lk 11:11
give him a snake instead of a **f**? Lk 11:11
gave Him a piece of a broiled **f**, Lk 24:42
five barley loaves and two **f**— Jn 6:9
also with the **f**, as much as they Jn 6:11
you don't have any **f**, do you?" Jn 21:5
of the large number of **f**. Jn 21:6
dragging the net full of **f**. Jn 21:8
fire there, with **f** lying on it, Jn 21:9
Bring some of the **f** you've just Jn 21:10
full of large **f**—153 of them. Jn 21:11
He did the same with the **f**. Jn 21:13
for birds, and another for **f**. 1Co 15:39
bird, reptile or **f**—is tamed Jms 3:7

FISHERMEN *(6)*

Then the **f** will mourn. Is 19:8
"I am about to send for many **f**"— Jr 16:16
F will stand beside it from Ezk 47:10
into the sea, since they were **f**. Mt 4:18
into the sea, since they were **f**. Mk 1:16
the **f** had left them and were Lk 5:2

FISHHOOK *(1)*

the sea, cast in a **f**, and catch Mt 17:27

FISHHOOKS *(1)*

every last ⌊one⌋ of you with **f**. Am 4:2

FISHING *(4)*

or his head with **f** spears? Jb 41:7
and gather them in their **f** net; Hab 1:15
and burn incense to their **f** net, Hab 1:16
"I'm going **f**," Simon Peter said Jn 21:3

FISSURES *(1)*

Heal its **f**, for it shudders. Ps 60:2

FIST *(4)*

the other with a stone or **f**, Ex 21:18
shaking his **f** at the mountain of Is 10:32
strike viciously with ⌊your⌋ **f**. Is 58:4
by her jeers and shakes his **f**. Zph 2:15

FIT *(8)*

Deal with us as You see **f**; Jdg 10:15
all strong and **f** for war. 2Kg 24:16
to you to do with as you see **f**." Est 3:11
My love is **f** and strong, notable Sg 5:10
⌊**f**⌋ for the scepters of rulers; Ezk 19:11
him twice as **f** for hell as you Mt 23:15
looks back is **f** for the kingdom Lk 9:62
It isn't **f** for the soil or for Lk 14:35

FITTED *(2)*

is being **f** together in Him Eph 2:21
f and knit together by every Eph 4:16

FITTING *(3)*

husbands, as is **f** in the Lord. Col 3:18
which is **f**, since your faith 2Th 1:3
For it was **f**, in bringing many Heb 2:10

FITTINGS *(2)*

of the gateways and for the **f**, 1Ch 22:3
The **f** of the chariot flash like Nah 2:3

FIVE *(161)*

Ellasar—four kings against **f**. Gn 14:9
suppose the 50 righteous lack **f**. Gn 18:28
the whole city for lack of **f**?" Gn 18:28
portion was **f** times larger than Gn 43:34

and there will be f more years Gn 45:6
for there will be f more years Gn 45:11
of silver and f changes of Gn 45:22
He took f of his brothers and Gn 47:2
must repay f cattle for the ox Ex 22:1
F of the curtains should be Ex 26:3
the ⌊other⌋ f curtains joined Ex 26:3
Join f of the curtains by Ex 26:9
You are to make f crossbars of Ex 26:26
f crossbars for the planks on Ex 26:27
and f crossbars for the planks Ex 26:27
Make f posts of acacia wood for Ex 26:37
you are to cast f bronze bases Ex 26:37
He joined f of the curtains to Ex 36:10
and the ⌊other⌋ f curtains he Ex 36:10
He joined f of the curtains Ex 36:16
He made f crossbars of acacia Ex 36:31
f crossbars for the planks on Ex 36:32
and f crossbars for those at the Ex 36:32
with its f posts and their Ex 36:38
but their f bases were bronze. Ex 36:38
F of you will pursue 100, and Lv 26:8
is from f to 20 years old, Lv 27:5
from one month to f years old, Lv 27:6
for a male is f silver shekels, Lv 27:6
for ⌊every⌋ f bushels of barley Lv 27:16
collect f shekels for each Nm 3:47
and two bulls, f rams, five male Nm 7:17
bulls, five rams, f male Nm 7:17
and f male lambs a year old, Nm 7:17
and two bulls, f rams, five male Nm 7:23
bulls, five rams, f male Nm 7:23
and f male lambs a year old, Nm 7:23
and two bulls, f rams, five male Nm 7:29
bulls, five rams, f male Nm 7:29
and f male lambs a year old, Nm 7:29
and two bulls, f rams, five male Nm 7:35
bulls, five rams, f male Nm 7:35
and f male lambs a year old, Nm 7:35
and two bulls, f rams, five male Nm 7:41
bulls, five rams, f male Nm 7:41
and f male lambs a year old, Nm 7:41
and two bulls, f rams, five male Nm 7:47
bulls, five rams, f male Nm 7:47
and f male lambs a year old, Nm 7:47
and two bulls, f rams, five male Nm 7:53
bulls, five rams, f male Nm 7:53
and f male lambs a year old, Nm 7:53
and two bulls, f rams, five male Nm 7:59
bulls, five rams, f male Nm 7:59
and f male lambs a year old, Nm 7:59
and two bulls, f rams, five male Nm 7:65
bulls, five rams, f male Nm 7:65
and f male lambs a year old, Nm 7:65
and two bulls, f rams, five male Nm 7:71
bulls, five rams, f male Nm 7:71
and f male lambs a year old, Nm 7:71
and two bulls, f rams, five male Nm 7:77
bulls, five rams, f male Nm 7:77
and f male lambs a year old, Nm 7:77
and two bulls, f rams, five male Nm 7:83
bulls, five rams, f male Nm 7:83
and f male lambs a year old, Nm 7:83
or two days, or f days, or 10 Nm 11:19
f shekels of silver by the Nm 18:16
and Reba, the f kings of Midian. Nm 31:8
So the f Amorite kings—the Jos 10:5
Now the f ⌊defeated⌋ kings had Jos 10:16
The f kings have been found; Jos 10:17
bring those f kings to me out Jos 10:22
They brought the f kings of Jos 10:23
their bodies on f trees and they Jos 10:26
the f Philistine rulers of Gaza, Jos 13:3
the f rulers of the Philistines Jdg 3:3
and she took f pounds of silver Jdg 17:4
Danites sent out f brave men Jdg 18:2
f men left and came to Laish. Jdg 18:7
f men who had gone to spy out Jdg 18:14
Then the f men who had gone to Jdg 18:17
F gold tumors and five gold mice 1Sm 6:4
Five gold tumors and f gold mice 1Sm 6:4
When the f Philistine rulers 1Sm 6:16
cities of the f rulers, 1Sm 6:18
hand and chose f smooth stones 1Sm 17:40
Give me f loaves of bread or 1Sm 21:3
of wine, f butchered sheep, 1Sm 25:18
and with her f female servants 1Sm 25:42
He was f years old when the 2Sm 4:4
and it would be f pounds 2Sm 14:26
and the f sons whom Merab 2Sm 21:8
set f water carts on the right 1Kg 7:39
the temple and f on the left 1Kg 7:39
f on the right and five on the 1Kg 7:49
on the right and f on the left; 1Kg 7:49
⌊sold for⌋ f silver ⌊shekels⌋ 2Kg 6:25
messengers⌋ take f of the horses 2Kg 7:13
the ground f or six times. 2Kg 13:19
of bronze, stood f feet high. 2Kg 25:17
f trusted royal aides found in 2Kg 25:19
Judah had f sons in all. 1Ch 2:4
Calcol, and Dara—f in all. 1Ch 2:6
and f others—Hashubah, Ohel, 1Ch 3:20
Tochen, and Ashan—f cities, 1Ch 4:32
All f of them were chiefs. 1Ch 7:3
Uzziel, Jerimoth, and Iri—f. 1Ch 7:7
washing and he put f on the 2Ch 4:6
on the right and f on the left. 2Ch 4:6
f on the right and five on the 2Ch 4:7
on the right and f on the left. 2Ch 4:7
f on the right and five on the 2Ch 4:8
on the right and f on the left. 2Ch 4:8
four or f on its fruitful Is 17:6
On that day f cities in the land Is 19:18
the threat of f you will flee, Is 30:17
of the gate were f and a quarter Ezk 40:48
f and a quarter feet high and Ezk 41:22
containing f and a half gallons Ezk 45:11
quarts from f bushels of wheat Ezk 45:13
quarts from f bushels of barley Ezk 45:13
of silver and f bushels of Hs 3:2
we only have f loaves and two Mt 14:17
He took the f loaves and the two Mt 14:19
remember the f loaves for the Mt 16:9
Then about f he went and found Mt 20:6
who were hired about f came, Mt 20:9
F of them were foolish and five Mt 25:2
foolish and f were sensible. Mt 25:2
To one he gave f talents; Mt 25:15
who had received f talents went, Mt 25:16
them to work, and earned f more. Mt 25:16
who had received f talents Mt 25:20
presented f more talents, Mt 25:20
Master, you gave me f talents. Mt 25:20
I've earned f more talents.' Mt 25:20
they said, "F, and two fish." Mk 6:38
Then He took the f loaves and Mk 6:41
When I broke the f loaves for Mk 8:19
in seclusion for f months. Lk 1:24
no more than f loaves and two Lk 9:13
Then He took the f loaves and Lk 9:16
Aren't f sparrows sold for two Lk 12:6
f in one household will be Lk 12:52
'I have bought f yoke of oxen, Lk 14:19
because I have f brothers— Lk 16:28
your mina has made f minas.' Lk 19:18
'You will be over f towns.' Lk 19:19
For you've had f husbands, Jn 4:18
Hebrew, which has f colonnades. Jn 5:2
boy here who has f barley loaves Jn 6:9
pieces from the f barley loaves Jn 6:13
In f days we reached them at Ac 20:6
After f days Ananias the high Ac 24:1
rather speak f words with my 1Co 14:19
F times I received from the Jews 2Co 11:24
to torment ⌊them⌋ for f months; Rv 9:5
to harm people for f months. Rv 9:10
f have fallen, one is, the other Rv 17:10

FIVE-SIDED *(1)*
pillars of the doorposts were f. 1Kg 6:31

FIX *(2)*
f your gaze straight ahead. Pr 4:25
will f My eyes on them for harm Am 9:4

FIXED *(16)*
and his gaze was f because he 1Sm 4:15
his gaze was f due to his age. 1Kg 14:4
villages at f times to be with 1Ch 9:25
God f the weight of the wind Jb 28:25
Who f its dimensions? Certainly Jb 38:5
it is firmly f in heaven. Ps 119:89
to us the f weeks of the harvest Jr 5:24
f order of moon and stars for Jr 31:35
If this f order departs from My Jr 31:36
establish the f order of heaven Jr 33:25
eyes were f on their fathers' Ezk 20:24
with sour wine, f it on a reed, Mt 27:48
with sour wine, f it on a reed, Mk 15:36
in the synagogue were f on Him. Lk 4:20
chasm has been f between us and Lk 16:26
so they f a sponge full of sour Jn 19:29

FLAG *(9)*
given a signal f to those who Ps 60:4
a signal f for the distant Is 5:26
afraid because of the signal f. Is 31:9
of the mast or spread out the f. Is 33:23
Lift up a signal f toward Zion. Jr 4:6
I see the signal f and hear the Jr 4:21
and raise up a signal f; Jr 50:2
up a signal f against the walls Jr 51:12
Raise a signal f in the land; Jr 51:27

FLAGS *(1)*
beside the f of their ancestral Nm 2:2

FLAKES *(2)*
the desert surface were fine f, Ex 16:14
My skin blackens and f off, Jb 30:30

FLAME *(24)*
to him in a f of fire within Ex 3:2
a f from the city of Sihon. Nm 21:28
the f went up from the altar Jdg 13:20
of the LORD went up in its f. Jdg 13:20
the f of his fire does not glow. Jb 18:5
as a f blazes through mountains, Ps 83:14
and a glowing f of fire by night Is 4:5
as dry grass shrivels in the f, Is 5:24
a fire, and its Holy One, a f. Is 10:17
and a f of consuming fire. Is 29:6
wrath and a f of consuming fire Is 30:30
and the f will not burn you. Is 43:2
from the power of the f. Is 47:14
Heshbon and a f from within Jr 48:45
The blazing f will not be Ezk 20:47
they will die by sword and f, Dn 11:33
and behind them a f devours. Jl 2:3
house of Joseph a ⌊burning⌋ f, Ob 18
I am in agony in this f!' Lk 16:24
in the f of a burning bush. Ac 7:30
and His servants a fiery f; Heb 1:7
snow, His eyes like a fiery f, Rv 1:14
whose eyes are like a fiery f, Rv 2:18
His eyes were like a fiery f, Rv 19:12

FLAMES *(15)*
Then f leaped from the LORD's Lv 10:2
f will wither his shoots, and he Jb 15:30
and f pour out of his mouth. Jb 41:21
of the LORD flashes f of fire. Ps 29:7
His messengers, f of fire His Ps 104:4
f consumed the wicked. Ps 106:18
Love's f are fiery flames— Sg 8:6
Love's flames are fiery f— Sg 8:6
with no one to quench ⌊the f⌋. Is 1:31
can dwell with ever-burning f?" Is 33:14
and His rebuke with f of fire. Is 66:15
raging f killed those men who Dn 3:22
f have devoured all the trees Jl 1:19
sound of fiery f consuming Jl 2:5
f of fire that were divided, Ac 2:3

FLAMING *(14)*
He stationed cherubim with a f, Gn 3:24
fire pot and a f torch appeared Gn 15:17
of His presence, f coals were 2Sm 22:13
F torches shoot from his mouth; Jb 41:19
He shatters the bow's f arrows, Ps 76:3
who throws f darts and deadly Pr 26:18
her salvation like a f torch. Is 62:1
like a f fire that consumes Lm 2:3
His throne was f fire; Dn 7:9
eyes like f torches, his arms Dn 10:6
morning it blazes like a f fire. Hs 7:6
like a f torch among sheaves; Zch 12:6
extinguish the f arrows of the Eph 6:16
vengeance with f fire on those 2Th 1:8

FLANK *(3)*
on the Philistine f to the west. Is 11:14
expose Moab's f beginning with Ezk 25:9
have pushed with f and shoulder Ezk 34:21

FLANKED *(1)*
which f the gates and Ezk 40:18

FLAP *(2)*
As for the f that is left over Ex 26:12
wings of the ostrich f joyfully, Jb 39:13

FLARE *(2)*
or My anger will f up like fire Jr 21:12
Lord GOD—"My wrath will f up. Ezk 38:18

FLARED *(2)*
and anger **f** up against Israel Ps 78:21
God's anger **f** up against them, Ps 78:31

FLASH *(11)*
you, and why do your eyes **f** Jb 15:12
or makes their lightning **f**? Jb 37:15
F ⌊Your⌋ lightning and scatter Ps 144:6
away from her ⌊land⌋ in a **f**. Jr 49:19
away from her ⌊land⌋ in a **f**. Jr 50:44
polished to **f** like lightning! Ezk 21:10
It is ready to **f** like lightning; Ezk 21:15
to consume, to **f** like lightning. Ezk 21:28
the chariot **f** like fire on the Nah 2:3
at the **f** of Your flying arrows, Hab 3:11
from heaven like a lightning **f**. Lk 10:18

FLASHED *(3)*
Your arrows **f** back and forth. Ps 77:17
heaven suddenly **f** around him. Ac 9:3
heaven suddenly **f** around me. Ac 22:6

FLASHES *(6)*
His snorting **f** with light, Jb 41:18
of the LORD **f** flames of fire. Ps 29:7
and forth like **f** of lightning. Ezk 1:14
from the east and **f** as far as Mt 24:27
the lightning **f** from horizon to Lk 17:24
the throne came **f** of lightning, Rv 4:5

FLASHING *(7)*
with lightning **f** through it, Ex 9:24
when I sharpen My **f** sword, Dt 32:41
the **f** tip out of his liver. Jb 20:25
with a **f** spear and a lance. Jb 39:23
cloud with fire **f** back and forth Ezk 1:4
horseman, **f** sword, shining Nah 3:3
rays are **f** from His hand. Hab 3:4

FLASK *(4)*
Samuel took the **f** of oil, poured 1Sm 10:1
take this **f** of oil with you, 2Kg 9:1
Then, take the **f** of oil, pour it 2Kg 9:3
an alabaster **f** of fragrant oil Lk 7:37

FLASKS *(1)*
oil in their **f** with their lamps Mt 25:4

FLAT *(1)*
Saul fell **f** on the ground. 1Sm 28:20

FLATTENS *(1)*
the one who **f** with the hammer Is 41:7

FLATTER *(1)*
they **f** with their tongues. Ps 5:9

FLATTERING *(12)*
they speak with **f** lips and Ps 12:2
LORD cut off all **f** lips and the Ps 12:3
from a stranger with her **f** talk, Pr 2:16
from the **f** tongue of a stranger. Pr 6:24
a stranger with her **f** talk. Pr 7:5
she lures with her **f** talk. Pr 7:21
and a **f** mouth causes ruin. Pr 26:28
Tell us **f** things. Is 30:10
false vision or **f** divination Ezk 12:24
smooth talk and **f** words they Rm 16:18
For we never used **f** speech, 1Th 2:5
f people for their own advantage. Jd 16

FLATTERS *(3)*
his own eyes he **f** himself ⌊too Ps 36:2
than one who **f** with his tongue. Pr 28:23
A man who **f** his neighbor spreads Pr 29:5

FLATTERY *(1)*
With **f** he will corrupt those who Dn 11:32

FLAUNT *(1)*
like Sodom, they **f** their sin. Is 3:9

FLAUNTED *(1)*
When she **f** her promiscuity and Ezk 23:18

FLAVOR *(2)*
Is there **f** in an egg white? Jb 6:6
if the salt should lose its **f**, Mk 9:50

FLAW *(3)*
with a defect or any serious **f**, Dt 17:1
he did not have a single **f**. 2Sm 14:25
For my arguments are without **f**; Jb 36:4

FLAWED *(1)*
clay became **f** in the potter's Jr 18:4

FLAX *(7)*
The **f** and the barley were Ex 9:31
was ripe and the **f** was budding, Ex 9:31
the stalks of **f** that she had Jos 2:6
became like burnt **f** and his Jdg 15:14
selects wool and **f** and works Pr 31:13
work with **f** will be dismayed; Is 19:9
my wool and **f**, my oil and drink Hs 2:5

FLEA *(2)*
chasing after? A dead dog? A **f**? 1Sm 24:14
has come out to search for a **f**, 1Sm 26:20

FLECKS *(1)*
sapphire, containing **f** of gold. Jb 28:6

FLED *(117)*
kings of Sodom and Gomorrah **f**, Gn 14:10
but the rest **f** to the mountains. Gn 14:10
He **f** with all his possessions, Gn 31:21
Laban was told that Jacob had **f**. Gn 31:22
night, and sleep **f** from my eyes. Gn 31:40
to you when you **f** from your Gn 35:1
Moses **f** from Pharaoh and went Ex 2:15
was told that the people had **f**, Ex 14:5
were around them **f** because they Nm 16:34
to the city of refuge he **f** to, Nm 35:25
of the city of refuge he **f** to, Nm 35:26
but they **f** from the men of Ai. Jos 7:4
back by them and **f** toward the Jos 8:15
troops who had **f** to the Jos 8:20
they **f** before Israel, the LORD Jos 10:11
defeated⌋ kings had **f** and hidden Jos 10:16
his own city from which he **f**.' " Jos 20:6
When Adoni-bezek **f**, they pursued Jdg 1:6
left his chariot and **f** on foot. Jdg 4:15
Sisera had **f** on foot to the tent Jdg 4:17
the entire ⌊Midianite⌋ army **f**, Jdg 7:21
They **f** to Beth-shittah in the Jdg 7:22
and Zalmunna **f**, and he pursued Jdg 8:12
Then Jotham **f**, escaping to Beer, Jdg 9:21
him, and Gaal **f** before him. Jdg 9:40
and lords of the city **f** there. Jdg 9:51
So Jephthah **f** from his brothers Jdg 11:3
Benjamin turned and **f** toward the Jdg 20:45
and each man **f** to his tent. 1Sm 4:10
I **f** from there today." 1Sm 4:16
Israel has **f** from the 1Sm 4:17
that they **f** before Israel. 1Sm 7:10
force that they **f** from him. 1Sm 19:8
window, and he **f** and escaped. 1Sm 19:12
So David **f** and escaped and went 1Sm 19:18
David **f** from Naioth in Ramah and 1Sm 20:1
David **f** that day from Saul's 1Sm 21:10
was Abiathar, and he **f** to David. 1Sm 22:20
son of Ahimelech **f** to David at 1Sm 23:6
Saul that David had **f** to Gath, 1Sm 27:4
men who got on camels and **f**. 1Sm 30:17
and Israel's men **f** from them. 1Sm 31:1
they abandoned the cities and **f**. 1Sm 31:7
"The troops **f** from the battle," 2Sm 1:4
and the Beerothites **f** to Gittaim 2Sm 4:3
His nurse picked him up and **f**, 2Sm 4:4
Arameans, and they **f** before him. 2Sm 10:13
saw that the Arameans had **f**, 2Sm 10:14
they too **f** before Abishai and 2Sm 10:14
the Arameans **f** before Israel, 2Sm 10:18
got up, and each **f** on his mule. 2Sm 13:29
Meanwhile, Absalom had **f**. 2Sm 13:34
Absalom **f** and went to Talmai 2Sm 13:37
Absalom had **f** and gone to 2Sm 13:38
And all Israel **f**, each to his 2Sm 18:17
Israelite had **f** to his tent. 2Sm 19:8
but now he has **f** from the land 2Sm 19:9
The troops **f** from the 2Sm 23:11
me when I **f** from your brother 1Kg 2:7
Joab **f** to the LORD's tabernacle 1Kg 2:28
Joab has **f** to the LORD's 1Kg 2:29
Hadad **f** to Egypt, along with 1Kg 11:17
Rezon had **f** from his master 1Kg 11:23
Jeroboam, but he **f** to Egypt, to 1Kg 11:40
Egypt where he had **f** from King 1Kg 12:2
So the Arameans **f** and Israel 1Kg 20:20
who remained **f** into the city 1Kg 20:30
Ben-hadad also **f** and went into 1Kg 20:30
them, and they **f** from them. 2Kg 3:24
had gotten up and **f** at twilight 2Kg 7:7
and they had **f** for their lives. 2Kg 7:7
but his troops **f** to their tents. 2Kg 8:21
Joram turned around and **f**, 2Kg 9:23
he **f** up the road toward 2Kg 9:27
but he **f** to Megiddo and died 2Kg 9:27
Judah's men⌋ **f**, each to his own 2Kg 14:12
Jerusalem, and he **f** to Lachish. 2Kg 14:19
the warriors ⌊**f**⌋ by night by way 2Kg 25:4
and Israel's men **f** from them and 1Ch 10:1
abandoned their cities and **f**. 1Ch 10:7
the troops had **f** from the 1Ch 11:13
battle, and they **f** before him. 1Ch 19:14
saw that the Arameans had **f**, 1Ch 19:15
they likewise **f** before Joab's 1Ch 19:15
the Arameans **f** before Israel, 1Ch 19:18
Egypt where he had **f** from King 2Ch 10:2
the Israelites **f** before Judah, 2Ch 13:16
Judah, and the Cushites **f**. 2Ch 14:12
and each **f** to his own tent. 2Ch 25:22
Jerusalem, and he **f** to Lachish. 2Ch 25:27
with fear; they **f** in terror. Ps 48:5
At Your rebuke the waters **f**; Ps 104:7
sea looked and **f**; the Jordan Ps 114:3
Why was it, sea, that you **f**? Ps 114:5
those at Gibeah of Saul have **f**. Is 10:29
Madmenah has **f**. The inhabitants Is 10:31
relied on and **f** to for help to Is 20:6
For they have **f** from swords, Is 21:15
All your rulers have **f** together, Is 22:3
together; they had **f** far away. Is 22:3
all the birds of the sky had **f**. Jr 4:25
everything⌋ has **f**—they have Jr 9:10
he **f** in fear and went to Egypt. Jr 26:21
of Judah and all the soldiers **f**. Jr 39:4
into, and all the warriors **f**. Jr 52:7
Woe to them, for they **f** from Me; Hs 7:13
Jacob **f** to the land of Aram. Hs 12:12
That's why I **f** toward Tarshish Jnh 4:2
will flee as you **f** from the Zch 14:5
Then the men who tended them **f**. Mt 8:33
beat him up, and **f**, leaving him Lk 10:30
Moses **f** and became an exile in Ac 7:29
about it and **f** to the Lycaonian Ac 14:6
we who have **f** for refuge might Heb 6:18
The woman **f** into the wilderness, Rv 12:6
island **f**, and the mountains Rv 16:20
Earth and heaven **f** from His Rv 20:11

FLEE *(73)*
F at once to my brother Laban in Gn 27:43
Why did you secretly **f** from me, Gn 31:27
and livestock **f** to shelters, Ex 9:20
a place for you where he may **f**. Ex 21:13
you will **f** even though no one Lv 26:17
they will **f** as one flees from Lv 26:36
who hate You **f** from Your Nm 10:35
who kills someone may **f** there; Nm 35:6
unintentionally may **f** there. Nm 35:11
unintentionally may **f** there. Nm 35:15
where one could **f** who committed Dt 4:42
could **f** to one of these cities Dt 4:42
can **f** to these cities Dt 19:3
person may **f** to one of these Dt 19:5
direction but **f** from you in Dt 28:7
one direction but **f** from them in Dt 28:25
first time, we will **f** from them. Jos 8:5
or accidentally may **f** there. Jos 20:3
may **f** there and not die Jos 20:9
Let's **f** and draw them away from Jdg 20:32
but as she was hurrying to **f**, 2Sm 4:4
We have to **f**, or we will not 2Sm 15:14
If we have to **f**, they will not 2Sm 18:3
to **f** from your foes three months 2Sm 24:13
the chariot and **f** to Jerusalem. 1Kg 12:18
the chariot to **f** to Jerusalem. 2Ch 10:18
they **f** without seeing any good. Jb 9:25
No arrow can make him **f**; Jb 41:28
How far away I would **f**; Ps 55:7
so that they can **f** before the Ps 60:4
who hate Him **f** from His presence Ps 68:1
The kings of the armies **f**— Ps 68:12
of the armies flee—they **f**!" Ps 68:12
can I **f** from Your presence? Ps 139:7
The wicked **f** when no one is Pr 28:1
day breaks and the shadows **f**, Sg 2:17
day breaks and the shadows **f**, Sg 4:6
each one will **f** to his own land. Is 13:14
fugitives ⌊**f**⌋ as far as Zoar Is 15:5
them, and they **f** far away, Is 17:13
thousand ⌊will **f**⌋ at the threat Is 30:17
the threat of five you will **f**, Is 30:17
He will **f** from the sword, his Is 31:8
The peoples **f** at the thunderous Is 33:3
and sorrow and sighing will **f**. Is 35:10
Leave Babylon, **f** from the Is 48:20
and sorrow and sighing will **f**. Is 51:11
and let's **f** to the fortified Jr 4:5

crushed, they **f** headlong, they Jr 46:5
swift cannot **f**, and the warrior Jr 46:6
they will **f**; they will not Jr 46:21
F! Save your lives! Be like a Jr 48:6
Those who **f** will stand exhausted Jr 48:45
each will **f** to his own land. Jr 50:16
Let the animals **f** from under it, Dn 4:14
even if they **f** from devastation Hs 9:6
warriors will **f** naked on that Am 2:16
F to the land of Judah. Am 7:12
of those who **f** will get away; Am 9:1
Jonah got up to **f** to Tarshish Jnh 1:3
will **f** by My mountain valley, Zch 14:5
You will **f** as you fled from the Zch 14:5
and His mother, **f** to Egypt, and Mt 2:13
warned you to **f** from the coming Mt 3:7
Judea must **f** to the mountains! Mt 24:16
Judea must **f** to the mountains! Mk 13:14
warned you to **f** from the coming Lk 3:7
Judea must **f** to the mountains! Lk 21:21
F from sexual immorality! 1Co 6:18
dear friends, **f** from idolatry. 1Co 10:14
F from youthful passions, and 2Tm 2:22
Devil, and he will **f** from you. Jms 4:7
but death will **f** from them. Rv 9:6

FLEECE *(6)*
I will put a **f** of wool here on Jdg 6:37
is only on the **f**, and all the Jdg 6:37
he squeezed the **f** and wrung dew Jdg 6:38
make one more test with the **f**. Jdg 6:39
only the **f** was dry, and dew was Jdg 6:40
with the **f** from my sheep, Jb 31:20

FLEEING *(14)*
not telling him that he was **f**. Gn 31:20
him when he was **f** from his Gn 35:7
another as if ⌊**f**⌋ from a sword Lv 26:37
'They are **f** from us as before.' Jos 8:6
While we are **f** from them, Jos 8:6
that the Philistines were **f**, 1Sm 14:22
knew he was **f**, but they didn't 1Sm 22:17
humiliated after **f** in battle. 2Sm 19:3
His hand pierced the **f** serpent. Jb 26:13
Like a bird **f**, forced from the Is 16:2
on Leviathan, the **f** serpent— Is 27:1
Ask him who is **f** or her who is Jr 48:19
knew he was **f** from the LORD's Jnh 1:10
first⌋ days, but they are **f**. Nah 2:8

FLEES *(13)*
will flee as one **f** from a sword, Lv 26:36
for the person who **f** to his city Nm 35:32
a person and **f** there to save his Dt 19:4
and **f** to one of these cities, Dt 19:11
When someone **f** to one of these Jos 20:4
he **f** like a shadow and does not Jb 14:2
If he **f** from an iron weapon, Jb 20:24
while he **f** desperately from its Jb 27:22
do not betray the one who **f**. Is 16:3
Whoever **f** at the sound of terror Is 24:18
Every city **f** at the sound of the Jr 4:29
who **f** from the panic will fall Jr 48:44
like a man who **f** from a lion Am 5:19

FLEET *(4)*
put together a **f** of ships at 1Kg 9:26
With the **f**, Hiram sent his 1Kg 9:27
Hiram's **f** that carried gold from 1Kg 10:11
Tarshish at sea with Hiram's **f**, 1Kg 10:22

FLEETING *(4)*
is deceptive and beauty is **f**, Pr 31:30
all the days of your **f** life, Ec 9:9
under the sun, all your **f** days. Ec 9:9
and the prime of life are **f**. Ec 11:10

FLESH *(221)*
and closed the **f** at that place. Gn 2:21
of my bone, and **f** of my flesh; Gn 2:23
of my bone, and flesh of my **f**; Gn 2:23
his wife, and they become one **f**. Gn 2:24
for all **f** had corrupted its way Gn 6:12
decided to put an end to all **f**, Gn 6:13
to destroy all **f** under heaven Gn 6:17
of every living thing of all **f**, Gn 6:19
Two of all **f** that has the breath Gn 7:15
female of all **f**, entered just as Gn 7:16
All **f** perished—creatures that Gn 7:21
thing of all **f** that is with you Gn 8:17
again will all **f** be wiped out Gn 9:11
every living creature of all **f**: Gn 9:15
a deluge to destroy all **f**. Gn 9:15
creature of all **f** on earth." Gn 9:16
between Me and all **f** on earth." Gn 9:17
circumcise the **f** of your Gn 17:11
will be in your **f** as an Gn 17:13
in the **f** of his foreskin, Gn 17:14
circumcised the **f** of their Gn 17:23
old when the **f** of his foreskin Gn 17:24
old when the **f** of his foreskin Gn 17:25
you are my own **f** and blood." Gn 29:14
he is our brother, our ⌊own⌋ **f**." Gn 37:27
will eat the **f** from your body." Gn 40:19
up the bull's **f**, its hide, and Ex 29:14
and boil its **f** in a holy place. Ex 29:31
hide of the bull and all its **f**, Lv 4:11
touches its **f** will become holy Lv 6:27
with its hide, **f**, and dung Lv 8:17
He burned up the **f** and the hide Lv 9:11
The **f** of his foreskin must be Lv 12:3
a patch of raw **f** in the swelling Lv 13:10
whenever raw **f** appears on him, Lv 13:14
the priest examines the raw **f**, Lv 13:15
him unclean. Raw **f** is unclean; Lv 13:15
But if the raw **f** changes and Lv 13:16
and their hide, **f**, and dung Lv 16:27
You will eat the **f** of your sons; Lv 26:29
you will eat the **f** of your Lv 26:29
⌊baby⌋ whose **f** is half eaten Nm 12:12
God of the spirits of all **f**, Nm 16:22
Its hide, **f**, and blood, are to Nm 19:5
the God of the spirits of all **f**, Nm 27:16
the **f** of your sons and daughters Dt 28:53
children's **f** that he will eat Dt 28:55
blood while My sword devours **f**— Dt 32:42
I will trample your **f** on thorns Jdg 8:7
that I am your own **f** and blood." Jdg 9:2
I'll give your **f** to the birds 1Sm 17:44
we are, your own **f** and blood. 2Sm 5:1
own son, my own **f** and blood, 2Sm 16:11
are my brothers, my **f** and blood. 2Sm 19:12
'Aren't you my **f** and blood? 2Sm 19:13
him, the boy's **f** became warm. 2Kg 4:34
Jordan and your **f** will be 2Kg 5:10
the dogs will eat Jezebel's **f**. 2Kg 9:36
we are, your own **f** and blood. 1Ch 11:1
hand and strike his **f** and bones, Jb 2:5
stone, or my **f** made of bronze? Jb 6:12
My **f** is clothed with maggots and Jb 7:5
have eyes of **f**, or do You see Jb 10:4
You clothed me with skin and **f**, Jb 10:11
My skin and my **f** cling to my Jb 19:20
you never get enough of my **f**? Jb 19:22
yet I will see God in my **f**. Jb 19:26
His **f** wastes away to nothing, Jb 33:21
his **f** will be healthier than Jb 33:25
The folds of his **f** are joined Jb 41:23
came against me to devour my **f**, Ps 27:2
Do I eat the **f** of bulls or drink Ps 50:13
My **f** and my heart may fail, Ps 73:26
that they were ⌊only⌋ **f**, Ps 78:39
the **f** of Your godly ones to the Ps 79:2
my heart and **f** cry out for the Ps 84:2
my groaning, my **f** sticks to my Ps 102:5
his arms and consumes his own **f**. Ec 4:5
and put away pain from your **f**, Ec 11:10
one eats the **f** of his own arm. Is 9:20
their horses are **f**, not spirit. Is 31:3
your oppressors eat their own **f**, Is 49:26
Then all **f** will know that I, Is 49:26
ignore your own **f** ⌊and blood⌋? Is 58:7
eating swine's **f**, and putting Is 65:4
judgment on all **f** with His fiery Is 66:16
who makes ⌊human⌋ **f** his strength Jr 17:5
them eat the **f** of their sons Jr 19:9
eat each other's **f** in the siege Jr 19:9
enters into judgment with all **f**. Jr 25:31
I am the LORD, the God of all **f**. Jr 32:27
He has worn away my **f** and skin; Lm 3:4
and give them a heart of **f**, Ezk 11:19
I will put your **f** on the Ezk 32:5
stone and give you a heart of **f**. Ezk 36:26
on you, make **f** grow on you, Ezk 37:6
on them, **f** grew, and skin Ezk 37:8
you will eat **f** and drink blood. Ezk 39:17
You will eat the **f** of mighty men Ezk 39:18
and the **f** of the offering was to Ezk 40:43
in both heart and **f**, Ezk 44:7
uncircumcised in heart and **f**, Ezk 44:9
Get up! Gorge yourself on **f**.' Dn 7:5
sacrificial gifts and eat the **f**, Hs 8:13
strip⌋ their **f** from their bones Mc 3:2
You eat the **f** of my people after Mc 3:3
them up like **f** for the cooking Mc 3:3
like dust and their **f** like dung. Zph 1:17
the rest devour each other's **f**." Zch 11:9
will devour the **f** of the fat Zch 11:16
f will rot while they stand Zch 14:12
blessed because **f** and blood did Mt 16:17
and the two will become one **f**? Mt 19:5
are no longer two, but one **f**. Mt 19:6
is willing, but the **f** is weak." Mt 26:41
and the two will become one **f**. Mk 10:8
are no longer two, but one **f**. Mk 10:8
is willing, but the **f** is weak." Mk 14:38
does not have **f** and bones as you Lk 24:39
will of the **f**, or of the will Jn 1:13
The Word became **f** and took up Jn 1:14
is born of the **f** is flesh, Jn 3:6
is born of the flesh is **f**, Jn 3:6
the life of the world is My **f**." Jn 6:51
this man give us His **f** to eat?" Jn 6:52
you eat the **f** of the Son of Man Jn 6:53
who eats My **f** and drinks My Jn 6:54
because My **f** is real food and My Jn 6:55
one who eats My **f** and drinks My Jn 6:56
The **f** doesn't help at all. Jn 6:63
gave Him authority over all **f**; Jn 17:2
Moreover my **f** will rest in hope, Ac 2:26
and His **f** did not experience Ac 2:31
of David according to the **f** Rm 1:3
not something visible in the **f**. Rm 2:28
no **f** will be justified in His Rm 3:20
forefather according to the **f**, Rm 4:1
of the weakness of your **f**. Rm 6:19
For when we were in the **f**, Rm 7:5
am made out of **f**, sold into Rm 7:14
lives in me, that is, in my **f**. Rm 7:18
God, but with my **f**, to the law Rm 7:25
since it was limited by the **f**, Rm 8:3
sin in the **f** by sending His own Rm 8:3
His own Son in **f** like ours under Rm 8:3
to the **f** but according to Rm 8:4
according to the **f** think about Rm 8:5
think about the things of the **f**, Rm 8:5
the mind-set of the **f** is death, Rm 8:6
mind-set of the **f** is hostile to Rm 8:7
lives are in the **f** are unable to Rm 8:8
are not in the **f**, but in the Rm 8:9
obligated to the **f** to live Rm 8:12
to live according to the **f**, Rm 8:12
if you live according to the **f**, Rm 8:13
people but as people of the **f**, 1Co 3:1
for the destruction of the **f**, 1Co 5:5
The two will become one **f**. 1Co 6:16
Not all **f** is the same flesh; 1Co 15:39
Not all flesh is the same **f**; 1Co 15:39
there is one **f** for humans, 1Co 15:39
f and blood cannot inherit the 1Co 15:50
on tablets that are hearts of **f**. 2Co 3:3
be revealed in our mortal **f**. 2Co 4:11
impurity of the **f** and spirit, 2Co 7:1
we are walking in the **f**, 2Co 10:3
thorn in the **f** was given to me, 2Co 12:7
The life I now live in the **f**, Gl 2:20
to be made complete by the **f**? Gl 3:3
was born according to the **f**, Gl 4:23
according to the **f** persecuted Gl 4:29
as an opportunity for the **f**, Gl 5:13
carry out the desire of the **f**. Gl 5:16
the **f** desires what is against Gl 5:17
desires what is against the **f**; Gl 5:17
the works of the **f** are obvious: Gl 5:19
crucified the **f** with its Gl 5:24
one who sows to his **f** will reap Gl 6:8
will reap corruption from the **f**, Gl 6:8
showing in the **f** are the ones Gl 6:12
in order to boast about your **f**. Gl 6:13
of our **f** and thoughts, Eph 2:3
you were Gentiles in the **f**— Eph 2:11
done by hand in the **f**. Eph 2:11
wall of hostility. In His **f**, Eph 2:14
For no one ever hates his own **f**, Eph 5:29
and the two will become one **f**. Eph 5:31
is not against **f** and blood, Eph 6:12
Now if I live on in the **f**, Php 1:22
to remain in the **f** is more Php 1:24
for those who mutilate the **f**. Php 3:2

do not put confidence in the **f**— Php 3:3
had confidence in the **f** too. Php 3:4
grounds for confidence in the **f**, Php 3:4
in my **f** what is lacking Col 1:24
by putting off the body of **f**, Col 2:11
in the uncircumcision of your **f**, Col 2:13
He was manifested in the **f**, 1Tm 3:16
both in the **f** and in the Lord. Phm 16
the children have **f** and blood in Heb 2:14
for the purification of the **f**, Heb 9:13
the curtain (that is, His **f**); Heb 10:20
and will eat your **f** like fire. Jms 5:3
For All **f** is like grass, and all 1Pt 1:24
removal of the filth of the **f**, 1Pt 3:21
since Christ suffered in the **f**, 1Pt 4:1
suffered in the **f** has finished 1Pt 4:1
the remaining time in the **f**, 1Pt 4:2
desires of the **f** and despise 2Pt 2:10
the lust of the **f**, the lust of 1Jn 2:16
has come in the **f** is from God. 1Jn 4:2
coming of Jesus Christ in the **f**. 2Jn 7
likewise defile their **f**, Jd 8
the garment defiled by the **f**. Jd 23
devour her **f**, and burn her up Rv 17:16
that you may eat the **f** of kings, Rv 19:18
of kings, the **f** of commanders, Rv 19:18
commanders, the **f** of mighty men, Rv 19:18
the **f** of horses and of their Rv 19:18
riders, and the **f** of everyone, Rv 19:18
birds were filled with their **f**. Rv 19:21

FLESHLY *(14)*
plans to satisfy the **f** desires. Rm 13:14
because you are still **f**. 1Co 3:3
are you not **f** and living like 1Co 3:3
not by **f** wisdom but by God's 2Co 1:12
think we are walking in a **f** way. 2Co 10:2
we do not wage war in a **f** way, 2Co 10:3
of our warfare are not **f**, 2Co 10:4
among them in our **f** desires, Eph 2:3
without cause by his **f** mind. Col 2:18
any value against **f** indulgence. Col 2:23
to abstain from **f** desires that 1Pt 2:11
to death in the **f** realm but made 1Pt 3:18
be judged by men in the **f** realm, 1Pt 4:6
by **f** desires and debauchery, 2Pt 2:18

FLEW *(5)*
He rode on a cherub and **f**, 2Sm 22:11
He rode on a cherub and **f**, Ps 18:10
his feet, and with two he **f**. Is 6:2
one of the seraphim **f** to me, Is 6:6
by the wise men, **f** into a rage. Mt 2:16

FLIES *(14)*
send swarms of **f** against you, Ex 8:21
houses will swarm with **f**, Ex 8:21
are living; no **f** will be there. Ex 8:22
Thick swarms of **f** went into Ex 8:24
because of the swarms of **f**. Ex 8:24
the swarms of **f** will depart Ex 8:29
the swarms of **f** from Pharaoh, Ex 8:31
creature that **f** in the sky, Dt 4:17
but the blade **f** off the handle Dt 19:5
He sent among them swarms of **f**, Ps 78:45
night, the arrow that **f** by day, Ps 91:5
for itself and **f** like an eagle Pr 23:5
Dead **f** make a perfumer's oil Ec 10:1
strips ⌊the land⌋ and **f** away. Nah 3:16

FLIGHT *(8)*
leaf will put them to **f**, Lv 26:36
or two put ten thousand to **f**, Dt 32:30
and put to **f** all ⌊those in⌋ the 1Ch 12:15
Does the hawk take **f** by your Jb 39:26
will put them to **f** when you aim Ps 21:12
and you will not have to take **f**; Is 52:12
F will be impossible for the Jr 25:35
and put foreign armies to **f**. Heb 11:34

FLING *(1)*
He will **f** away your enemies' 1Sm 25:29

FLINGING *(1)*
were yelling and **f** aside their Ac 22:23

FLINT *(8)*
Zipporah took a **f**, cut off her Ex 4:25
Make **f** knives and circumcise the Jos 5:2
So Joshua made **f** knives and Jos 5:3
strikes the **f** and transforms Jb 28:9
the **f** into a spring of water. Ps 114:8
Their horses' hooves are like **f**; Is 5:28
I have set My face like **f**, Is 50:7
like a diamond, harder than **f**. Ezk 3:9

FLINTLIKE *(2)*
water out of the **f** rock for you. Dt 8:15
the rock and oil from **f** rock, Dt 32:13

FLITTING *(1)*
Like a **f** sparrow or a fluttering Pr 26:2

FLOAT *(3)*
it there, and made the iron **f**. 2Kg 6:6
They **f** on the surface of the Jb 24:18
you understand how the clouds **f**, Jb 37:16

FLOATED *(1)*
and the ark **f** on the surface of Gn 7:18

FLOCK *(123)*
Abel became a shepherd of a **f**, Gn 4:2
firstborn of his **f** and their fat Gn 4:4
seven ewe lambs from the **f**. Gn 21:28
Go to the **f** and bring me two Gn 27:9
Water the **f**, then go out and let Gn 29:7
to shepherd and keep your **f**. Gn 30:31
the rest of Laban's **f**. Gn 30:36
stronger of the **f** were breeding, Gn 30:41
not eaten the rams from your **f**. Gn 31:38
you any of the **f** torn by wild Gn 31:39
you a young goat from my **f**," Gn 38:17
to water their father's **f**. Ex 2:16
rescue and watered their **f**. Ex 2:17
water for us and watered the **f**." Ex 2:19
was shepherding the **f** of his Ex 3:1
He led the **f** to the far side of Ex 3:1
an animal of the **f** according to Ex 12:3
animal from the **f** according to Ex 12:21
of a donkey with a **f** animal, Ex 13:13
with your cattle and your **f**. Ex 22:30
offering from the herd or the **f**. Lv 1:2
a burnt offering is from the **f**, Lv 1:10
to the LORD is from the **f**, Lv 3:6
or goat from the **f** as a sin Lv 5:6
afford an animal from the **f**, Lv 5:7
ram from the **f** by your valuation Lv 5:15
ram from the **f** according to your Lv 5:18
an unblemished ram from the **f**, Lv 6:6
offering from the herd or **f**, Lv 22:21
from the herd or **f** that has an Lv 22:23
the herd or **f** on the same day Lv 22:28
an animal from the herd or **f**, Lv 27:26
tenth animal from the herd or **f**, Lv 27:32
to the LORD from the herd or **f**— Nm 15:3
the firstborn of your herd or **f**; Dt 12:17
of your herd or **f** He has given Dt 12:21
firstborn of your herd and **f**, Dt 14:23
generously to him from your **f**, Dt 15:14
produced by your herd and **f**. Dt 15:19
shear the firstborn of your **f**. Dt 15:19
from the herd or **f** in the place Dt 16:2
first sheared ⌊wool⌋ of your **f**. Dt 18:4
Your **f** will be given to your Dt 28:31
the herd and milk from the **f**, Dt 32:14
his father's **f** in Bethlehem. 1Sm 17:15
left the **f** with someone to keep 1Sm 17:20
carried off a lamb from the **f**, 1Sm 17:34
ram from the **f** for their guilt; Ezr 10:19
They steal a **f** and provide Jb 24:2
Your people like a **f** by the hand Ps 77:20
them like a **f** in the wilderness Ps 78:52
who guides Joseph like a **f**; Ps 80:1
well the condition of your **f**, Pr 27:23
follow the tracks of the **f**, Sg 1:8
hair is like a **f** of goats Sg 4:1
are like a **f** of newly shorn Sg 4:2
hair is like a **f** of goats Sg 6:5
are like a **f** of ewes coming Sg 6:6
protects His **f** like a shepherd Is 40:11
sea with the shepherds of His **f**? Is 63:11
put His Holy Spirit among the **f**? Is 63:11
and their whole **f** is scattered. Jr 10:21
for the LORD's **f** has been taken Jr 13:17
Where is the **f** entrusted to you, Jr 13:20
scattered My **f**, banished them, Jr 23:2
the remnant of My **f** from all the Jr 23:3
the dust⌋, you leaders of the **f**. Jr 25:34
for the leaders of the **f**. Jr 25:35
wail of the leaders of the **f**, Jr 25:36
as a shepherd ⌊guards⌋ his **f**, Jr 31:10
like the rams that lead the **f**. Jr 50:8
smash the shepherd and his **f**; Jr 51:23
choicest of the **f** and also pile Ezk 24:5
the shepherds feed their **f**? Ezk 34:2
but you do not tend the **f**. Ezk 34:3
My **f** went astray on all the Ezk 34:6
because My **f** has become ⌊prey Ezk 34:8
do not search for My **f**, Ezk 34:8
themselves rather than My **f**, Ezk 34:8
I will demand My **f** from them and Ezk 34:10
them from shepherding the **f**. Ezk 34:10
I will rescue My **f** from their Ezk 34:10
search for My **f** and look for Ezk 34:11
day he is among his scattered **f**, Ezk 34:12
flock, so I will look for My **f**. Ezk 34:12
will tend My **f** and let them lie Ezk 34:15
The Lord GOD says to you, My **f**: Ezk 34:17
My **f** has to feed on what your Ezk 34:19
I will save My **f**, and they will Ezk 34:22
My **f** will be secure in their Ezk 34:27
You are My **f**, the human flock of Ezk 34:31
the human **f** of My pasture, Ezk 34:31
them in number like a **f**. Ezk 36:37
be filled with a **f** of people, Ezk 36:38
just as the **f** of sheep for Ezk 36:38
an unblemished ram from the **f**. Ezk 43:23
young bull and a ram from the **f**, Ezk 43:25
quota⌋ from the **f** is one animal Ezk 45:15
on lambs from the **f** and calves Am 6:4
the **f** and said to me, Am 7:15
or beast, herd or **f**, is to taste Jnh 3:7
like a **f** in the middle of its Mc 2:12
for the **f**, fortified hill Mc 4:8
the **f** that is Your possession. Mc 7:14
that day as the **f** of His people; Zch 9:16
LORD of Hosts has tended His **f**, Zch 10:3
Shepherd the **f** intended for Zch 11:4
I shepherded the **f** intended for Zch 11:7
the afflicted of the **f**. Zch 11:7
Union, and I shepherded the **f**. Zch 11:7
afflicted of the **f** who were Zch 11:11
shepherd who deserts the **f**! Zch 11:17
male in his **f** and makes a vow Mal 1:14
the sheep of the **f** will be Mt 26:31
watch at night over their **f**. Lk 2:8
afraid, little **f**, because your Lk 12:32
will be one **f**, one shepherd. Jn 10:16
yourselves and for all the **f**, Ac 20:28
in among you, not sparing the **f**. Ac 20:29
who shepherds a **f** and does not 1Co 9:7
not drink the milk from the **f**? 1Co 9:7
shepherd God's **f** among you, 1Pt 5:2
but being examples to the **f**. 1Pt 5:3

FLOCK'S *(2)*
f little lambs will certainly Jr 49:20
Certainly the **f** little lambs Jr 50:45

FLOCKING *(4)*
of the Jordan were **f** to him, Mt 3:5
of Jerusalem were **f** to him, Mk 1:5
and people were **f** to Him from Lk 8:4
and everyone is **f** to Him." Jn 3:26

FLOCKS *(73)*
and Abram acquired **f** and herds, Gn 12:16
Abram, also had **f**, herds, and Gn 13:5
He had **f** of sheep, herds of Gn 26:14
f of sheep were lying there Gn 29:2
When all the **f** were gathered Gn 29:3
until all the **f** have been Gn 29:8
The **f** bred in front of the Gn 30:39
and made the **f** face the streaked Gn 30:40
dark sheep in Laban's **f**. Gn 30:40
view of the **f**, and they would Gn 30:41
As for the weaklings of the **f**, Gn 30:42
He had many **f**, male and female Gn 30:43
to the field ⌊where⌋ his **f** were. Gn 31:4
When the **f** were breeding, Gn 31:10
mating with the **f** are streaked, Gn 31:12
and six years for your **f**— Gn 31:41
and the **f**, my flocks! Gn 31:43
and the flocks, my **f**! Gn 31:43
oxen, donkeys, **f**, male and Gn 32:5
along with the **f**, cattle, and Gn 32:7
their father's **f** at Shechem. Gn 37:12
pasturing ⌊the **f**⌋ at Shechem. Gn 37:13
brothers and the **f** are doing, Gn 37:14
they are pasturing ⌊their **f**⌋?" Gn 37:16
donkeys, camels, herds, and **f**. Ex 9:3
and with our **f** and herds because Ex 10:9
only your **f** and your herds must Ex 10:24
Take even your **f** and your herds Ex 12:32
of livestock, both **f** and herds. Ex 12:38

Even the **f** and herds are not to Ex 34:3
If **f** and herds were slaughtered Nm 11:22
their cattle, **f**, and property. Nm 31:9
dependents and folds for your **f**, Nm 32:24
their herds, **f**, and all their Nm 35:3
and the newborn of your **f**, Dt 7:13
and your herds and **f** grow large, Dt 8:13
firstborn of your herds and **f**. Dt 12:6
herds and the newborn of your **f**. Dt 28:4
and the newborn of your **f**. Dt 28:18
newborn of your **f** until they Dt 28:51
the playing of pipes for the **f**? Jdg 5:16
He can take a tenth of your **f**, 1Sm 8:17
but he took **f**, herds, donkeys, 1Sm 27:9
them like two little **f** of goats, 1Kg 20:27
to seek pasture for their **f**. 1Ch 4:39
there was pasture for their **f**. 1Ch 4:41
Hagrite was in charge of the **f**. 1Ch 27:31
and the Arabs brought him **f**: 2Ch 17:11
kinds of cattle, and pens for **f**. 2Ch 32:28
of our herds and **f** to the house Neh 10:36
The pastures are clothed with **f**, Ps 65:13
families ⌊multiply⌋ like **f**. Ps 107:41
our **f** will increase by thousands Ps 144:13
many herds of cattle and **f**, Ec 2:7
beside the **f** of your companions Sg 1:7
not let ⌊their **f**⌋ rest there. Is 13:20
they will be ⌊places⌋ for **f**. Is 17:2
wild asses, and a pasture for **f**, Is 32:14
All the **f** of Kedar will be Is 60:7
will stand and feed your **f**, Is 61:5
Sharon will be a pasture for **f**, Is 65:10
for—their **f** and their herds, Jr 3:24
consume your **f** and your herds. Jr 5:17
and their **f** will come against Jr 6:3
of the young of the **f** and herds. Jr 31:12
and those who move with the **f**— Jr 31:24
land where shepherds may rest **f**. Jr 33:12
The **f** will again pass under the Jr 33:13
tents and their **f** along with Jr 49:29
go with their **f** and herds to Hs 5:6
he tended **f** for a wife. Hs 12:12
Even the **f** of sheep suffer Jl 1:18
a young lion among **f** of sheep, Mc 5:8

FLOG (4)
to sanhedrins and **f** you in their Mt 10:17
of them you will **f** in your Mt 23:34
spit on Him, **f** Him, and kill Him Mk 10:34
and after they **f** Him, they will Lk 18:33

FLOGGED (10)
guilty party deserves to be **f**, Dt 25:2
down and be **f** in his presence Dt 25:2
He may be **f** with 40 lashes, Dt 25:3
if he is **f** with more lashes than Dt 25:3
to be mocked, **f**, and crucified, Mt 20:19
having Jesus **f**, he handed Him Mt 27:26
and you will be **f** in the Mk 13:9
having Jesus **f**, he handed Him Mk 15:15
Pilate took Jesus and had Him **f**. Jn 19:1
in the apostles and had them **f**, Ac 5:40

FLOOD (27)
lived 350 years after the **f**. Gn 9:28
out from these after the **f**. Gn 10:32
Like a bursting **f**, the LORD has 2Sm 5:20
Like a bursting **f**, God has used 1Ch 14:11
and a **f** of water covers you. Jb 22:11
Terrors overtake him like a **f**; Jb 27:20
so that a **f** of water covers Jb 38:34
The LORD sat enthroned at the **f**; Ps 29:10
waters, and a **f** sweeps over me. Ps 69:2
sycamore-fig trees with a **f**. Ps 78:47
a conflict is to release a **f**; Pr 17:14
and anger is a **f**, but who can Pr 27:4
pour into Judah, **f** over it, and Is 8:8
and water will **f** your hiding Is 28:17
would never **f** the earth again Is 54:9
the wealth of nations like a **f**; Is 66:12
The end will come with a **f**, Dn 9:26
sweeping through like a **f**, Dn 11:10
A **f** of forces will be swept away Dn 11:22
and sweep through them like a **f**. Dn 11:40
Nineveh with an overwhelming **f**, Nah 1:8
days before the **f** they were Mt 24:38
know until the **f** came and swept Mt 24:39
When the **f** came, the river Lk 6:48
the **f** came and destroyed them Lk 17:27
into the same **f** of dissipation— 1Pt 4:4
when He brought a **f** on the world 2Pt 2:5

FLOODED (3)
For my sins have **f** over my head; Ps 38:4
Water **f** over my head, and I Lm 3:54
perished when it was **f** by water. 2Pt 3:6

FLOODGATES (3)
the **f** of the sky were opened, Gn 7:11
depths and the **f** of the sky were Gn 8:2
will not open the **f** of heaven Mal 3:10

FLOODING (2)
channel for the **f** rain or clears Jb 38:25
a storm with strong **f** waters. Is 28:2

FLOODS (4)
The **f** covered them; they sank to Ex 15:5
The **f** have lifted up, LORD, the Ps 93:3
f have lifted up their voice; Ps 93:3
the **f** lift up their pounding Ps 93:3

FLOODWATERS (3)
f on the earth to destroy all Gn 6:17
When great **f** come, they will not Ps 32:6
Don't let the **f** sweep over me or Ps 69:15

FLOOR (43)
reached the threshing **f** of Atad, Gn 50:10
at the threshing **f** of Atad, Gn 50:11
the tabernacle **f** and put ⌊it⌋ Nm 5:17
from the threshing **f**. Nm 15:20
from the threshing **f** or the full Nm 18:27
the threshing **f** or the winepress Nm 18:30
your threshing **f**, and your Dt 15:14
your threshing **f** and winepress. Dt 16:13
their lord lying dead on the **f**! Jdg 3:25
of wool here on the threshing **f**. Jdg 6:37
barley on the threshing **f**. Ru 3:2
Go down to the threshing **f**, Ru 3:3
to⌋ the threshing **f** and did Ru 3:6
woman came to the threshing **f**." Ru 3:14
came to Nacon's threshing **f**, 2Sm 6:6
at the threshing **f** of Araunah 2Sm 24:16
on the threshing **f** of Araunah 2Sm 24:18
the threshing **f** from you in 2Sm 24:21
the threshing **f** and the oxen for 2Sm 24:24
from the temple **f** to the surface 1Kg 6:15
also overlaid the **f** with cypress 1Kg 6:15
boards from the **f** to the surface 1Kg 6:16
the temple **f** with gold in both 1Kg 6:30
cedar from the **f** to the rafters. 1Kg 7:7
the threshing **f** at the entrance 1Kg 22:10
threshing **f** or the winepress? 2Kg 6:27
came to Chidon's threshing **f**, 1Ch 13:9
at the threshing **f** of Ornan the 1Ch 21:15
on the threshing **f** of Ornan the 1Ch 21:18
the threshing **f** and bowed to 1Ch 21:21
him at the threshing **f** of Ornan 1Ch 21:28
on the threshing **f** of Ornan the 2Ch 3:1
the threshing **f** at the entrance 2Ch 18:9
bring ⌊it⌋ to your threshing **f**? Jb 39:12
like a threshing **f** at the time Jr 51:33
on every grain-threshing **f**. Hs 9:1
Threshing **f** and wine vat will Hs 9:2
chaff blown from a threshing **f**, Hs 13:3
from My sight on the sea **f**, Am 9:3
like sheaves to the threshing **f**. Mc 4:12
His threshing **f** and gather His Mt 3:12
clear His threshing **f** and gather Lk 3:17
here on the **f** by my footstool Jms 2:3

FLOORS (3)
and raiding the threshing **f**." 1Sm 23:1
from the summer threshing **f**. Dn 2:35
The threshing **f** will be full of Jl 2:24

FLOUR (64)
of fine **f** and make bread. Gn 18:6
Make them out of fine wheat **f**, Ex 29:2
quarts of fine **f** mixed with one Ex 29:40
his gift must consist of fine **f**. Lv 2:1
of fine **f** and oil from it Lv 2:2
it must be ⌊made⌋ of fine **f**, Lv 2:4
made⌋ of fine **f** mixed with oil. Lv 2:5
must be made of fine **f** with oil. Lv 2:7
quarts of fine **f** as an offering Lv 5:11
handful of fine **f** and olive oil Lv 6:15
quarts of fine **f** as a regular Lv 6:20
cakes of fine **f** mixed with oil. Lv 7:12
quarts of fine **f** mixed with Lv 14:10
quarts of fine **f** mixed with Lv 14:21
quarts of fine **f** mixed with oil Lv 23:13
made from four quarts of fine **f**, Lv 23:17
Take fine **f** and bake it into 12 Lv 24:5
her of two quarts of barley **f**. Nm 5:15
made from fine **f** mixed with oil, Nm 6:15
full of fine **f** mixed with oil Nm 7:13
full of fine **f** mixed with oil Nm 7:19
full of fine **f** mixed with oil Nm 7:25
full of fine **f** mixed with oil Nm 7:31
full of fine **f** mixed with oil Nm 7:37
full of fine **f** mixed with oil Nm 7:43
full of fine **f** mixed with oil Nm 7:49
full of fine **f** mixed with oil Nm 7:55
full of fine **f** mixed with oil Nm 7:61
full of fine **f** mixed with oil Nm 7:67
full of fine **f** mixed with oil Nm 7:73
full of fine **f** mixed with oil Nm 7:79
of fine **f** mixed with oil, Nm 8:8
quarts of fine **f** mixed with a Nm 15:4
quarts of fine **f** mixed with a Nm 15:6
quarts of fine **f** mixed with two Nm 15:9
two quarts of fine **f** for a grain Nm 28:5
quarts of fine **f** mixed with oil Nm 28:9
quarts of fine **f** mixed with oil Nm 28:12
quarts of fine **f** mixed with oil Nm 28:12
quarts of fine **f** mixed with oil Nm 28:13
to be of fine **f** mixed with oil; Nm 28:20
of fine **f** mixed with oil, Nm 28:28
of fine **f** mixed with oil, Nm 29:3
to be of fine **f** mixed with oil, Nm 29:9
to be of fine **f** mixed with oil, Nm 29:14
bread from a half bushel of **f**. Jdg 6:19
two and one-half gallons of **f**, 1Sm 1:24
She also took **f**, kneaded it, and 1Sm 28:24
wheat, barley, **f**, roasted grain, 2Sm 17:28
of fine **f** and 300 bushels 1Kg 4:22
only a handful of **f** in the jar 1Kg 17:12
'The **f** jar will not become empty 1Kg 17:14
The **f** jar did not become empty, 1Kg 17:16
well as the fine **f**, wine, oil, 1Ch 9:29
provisions of **f**, fig cakes, 1Ch 12:40
the fine **f** for the grain 1Ch 23:29
100,000 bushels of wheat **f**, 2Ch 2:10
You ate fine **f**, honey, and oil. Ezk 16:13
you—the fine **f**, oil, and honey Ezk 16:19
of oil to moisten the fine **f**— Ezk 46:14
what sprouts fails to yield **f**. Hs 8:7
50 pounds of **f** until it spread Mt 13:33
50 pounds of **f** until it spread Lk 13:21
oil, fine wheat **f**, and grain; Rv 18:13

FLOURISH (14)
Do reeds **f** without water? Jb 8:11
and his branch will not **f**. Jb 15:32
May the righteous **f** in his days, Ps 72:7
May people **f** in the cities like Ps 72:16
like grass and all evildoers **f**, Ps 92:7
trees of the LORD **f**, the cedars Ps 104:16
righteous will **f** like foliage. Pr 11:28
are destroyed, the righteous **f**. Pr 28:28
When the righteous **f**, the people Pr 29:2
and you will **f** like grass; Is 66:14
says: Will it **f**? Will he not Ezk 17:9
though it is planted, will it **f**? Ezk 17:10
army. Will he **f**? Will the one Ezk 17:15
Grain will make the young men **f**, Zch 9:17

FLOURISHED (4)
So the preaching about God **f**, Ac 6:7
the people **f** and multiplied in Ac 7:17
God's message **f** and multiplied. Ac 12:24
Lord's message **f** and prevailed. Ac 19:20

FLOURISHES (1)
Although he **f** among ⌊his⌋ Hs 13:15

FLOURISHING (9)
hills, and under every **f** tree. Dt 12:2
well-rooted like a **f** native tree. Ps 37:35
But I am like a **f** olive tree in Ps 52:8
to irrigate a grove of **f** trees. Ec 2:6
oaks, under every **f** tree, who Is 57:5
LORD named you a **f** olive tree, Jr 11:16
in my house and **f** in my palace. Dn 4:4
I am like a **f** pine tree; Hs 14:8
your faith is **f**, and the love 2Th 1:3

FLOW (26)
exposed the source of her ⌊**f**⌋, Lv 20:18
Water will **f** from his buckets, Nm 24:7
of the Red Sea **f** over them as Dt 11:4
saw the **f** of honey, but none 1Sm 14:26
and made water **f** down like Ps 78:16
they **f** between the mountains. Ps 104:10
His winds, and the waters **f**. Ps 147:18

your springs **f** in the streets, Pr 5:16
All the streams **f** to the sea, Ec 1:7
place, and they **f** there again. Ec 1:7
mountains **f** with their blood. Is 34:3
made water **f** for them from the Is 48:21
will make peace **f** to her like a Is 66:12
have stopped the **f** of wine from Jr 48:33
things; my eyes **f** with tears. Lm 1:16
My eyes **f** with streams of tears Lm 3:48
or weep or let your tears **f**. Ezk 24:16
land with the **f** of your blood, Ezk 32:6
make their rivers **f** like oil. Ezk 32:14
and the hills will **f** with milk. Jl 3:18
of Judah will **f** with water, Jl 3:18
But let justice **f** like water, Am 5:24
all the hills will **f** ⌊with it⌋. Am 9:13
living water will **f** out from Zch 14:8
Instantly her **f** of blood ceased, Mk 5:29
of living water **f** from deep Jn 7:38

FLOWED *(6)*
from his wound **f** into the bottom 1Kg 22:35
the stream that **f** through the 2Ch 32:4
Royal wine **f** freely, according Est 1:7
it only⌋ as waters that have **f** Jb 11:16
f like a stream in the desert. Ps 105:41
and blood **f** out of the press up Rv 14:20

FLOWER *(15)*
from its base to its **f** petals. Nm 8:4
gourds and **f** blossoms. 1Kg 6:18
palm trees and **f** blossoms— 1Kg 6:29
trees and **f** blossoms on them 1Kg 6:32
trees and **f** blossoms on them 1Kg 6:35
blossoms like a **f**, then withers; Jb 14:2
he blooms like a **f** of the field; Ps 103:15
to the fading **f** of its beautiful Is 28:1
The fading **f** of his beautiful Is 28:4
is like the **f** of the field. Is 40:6
even the **f** of Lebanon withers. Nah 1:4
pass away like a **f** of the field. Jms 1:10
its **f** falls off, and its Jms 1:11
its glory like a **f** of the grass. 1Pt 1:24
withers, and the **f** drops off, 1Pt 1:24

FLOWERS *(4)*
the gold **f**, lamps, and tongs; 1Kg 7:49
the **f**, lamps, and gold tongs— 2Ch 4:21
f fade when the breath of the Is 40:7
withers, the **f** fade, but the Is 40:8

FLOWING *(43)*
a land **f** with milk and honey— Ex 3:8
a land **f** with milk and honey. Ex 3:17
a land **f** with milk and honey, Ex 13:5
up⌋ to a land **f** with milk and Ex 33:3
a land **f** with milk and honey. Lv 20:24
Indeed it is **f** with milk and Nm 13:27
a land **f** with milk and honey, Nm 14:8
up from a land **f** with milk and Nm 16:13
bring us to a land **f** with milk Nm 16:14
you a land **f** with milk and honey Dt 6:3
f in both valleys and hills; Dt 8:7
a land **f** with milk and honey. Dt 11:9
down to a continually **f** stream, Dt 21:4
a land **f** with milk and honey. Dt 26:9
a land **f** with milk and honey. Dt 26:15
a land **f** with milk and honey, Dt 27:3
⌊a land⌋ **f** with milk and honey, Dt 31:20
water **f** downstream will stand Jos 3:13
and the water **f** downstream stood Jos 3:16
The water **f** downstream into the Jos 3:16
f over all the banks as before. Jos 4:18
a land **f** with milk and honey. Jos 5:6
the rivers **f** with honey and Jb 20:17
f away on the day of God's anger. Jb 20:28
streams from **f** so that he may Jb 28:11
water **f** from your own well. Pr 5:15
deep waters, a **f** river, a Pr 18:4
The streams are **f** to the place, Ec 1:7
a well of **f** water streaming from Sg 4:15
my fingers with **f** myrrh on the Sg 5:5
lilies, dripping with **f** myrrh. Sg 5:13
f smoothly for my love gliding Sg 7:9
the slowly **f** waters of Shiloah Is 8:6
give ⌊them⌋ a land **f** with milk Jr 11:5
cold water **f** from a distance Jr 18:14
a land **f** with milk and honey. Jr 32:22
your valleys, your **f** valley, you Jr 49:4
⌊a land⌋ **f** with milk and honey, Ezk 20:6
of all lands, **f** with milk and Ezk 20:15

waists and **f** turbans on their Ezk 23:15
and there was water **f** from under Ezk 47:1
river of fire was **f**, coming out Dn 7:10
f from the throne of God and of Rv 22:1

FLOWN *(1)*
My joy has **f** away; grief has Jr 8:18

FLOWS *(6)*
which **f** to the east of Assyria. Gn 2:14
at the river that **f** to Ahava, Ezr 8:15
grace **f** from your lips. Ps 45:2
will vanish like water that **f** Ps 58:7
This water **f** out to the eastern Ezk 47:8
will live wherever the river **f**, Ezk 47:9

FLUENTLY *(1)*
tongue will speak clearly and **f**. Is 32:4

FLUID *(1)*
whose body was swollen with **f**. Lk 14:2

FLUNG *(2)*
but you have **f** Me behind your 1Kg 14:9
They **f** Your law behind their Neh 9:26

FLUSHED *(2)*
other, their faces **f** with fear. Is 13:8
While they are **f** with heat, Jr 51:39

FLUTE *(15)*
all who play the lyre and the **f**. Gn 4:21
rejoicing at the sound of the **f**. Jb 21:12
mourning and my **f** for the sound Jb 30:31
praise Him with **f** and strings. Ps 150:4
harp, tambourine, **f**, and wine. Is 5:12
who walks ⌊to the music⌋ of a **f**, Is 30:29
of the horn, **f**, zither, lyre, Dn 3:5
of the horn, **f**, zither, lyre, Dn 3:7
of the horn, **f**, zither, lyre, Dn 3:10
of the horn, **f**, zither, lyre, Dn 3:15
He saw the **f** players and a crowd Mt 9:23
We played the **f** for you, but you Mt 11:17
We played the **f** for you, but you Lk 7:32
sounds—whether **f** or harp—if 1Co 14:7
is played on the **f** or harp be 1Co 14:7

FLUTES *(4)*
tambourines, **f**, and lyres. 1Sm 10:5
playing **f** and rejoicing with 1Kg 1:40
My heart moans like **f** for Moab, Jr 48:36
moans like **f** for the people Jr 48:36

FLUTISTS *(1)*
musicians, **f**, and trumpeters Rv 18:22

FLUTTERED *(1)*
earth. No wing **f**; no beak opened Is 10:14

FLUTTERING *(1)*
flitting sparrow or a **f** swallow, Pr 26:2

FLY *(14)*
and let birds **f** above the earth Gn 1:20
as surely as sparks **f** upward. Jb 5:7
My days **f** by faster than a Jb 9:25
He will **f** away like a dream and Jb 20:8
his mouth; fiery sparks **f** out! Jb 41:19
I would **f** away and find rest. Ps 55:6
they pass quickly and we **f** away. Ps 90:10
As soon as your eyes **f** to it, Pr 23:5
will whistle to the **f** that is at Is 7:18
are these who **f** like a cloud, Is 60:8
glory will **f** away like a bird: Hs 9:11
They **f** like an eagle, swooping Hab 1:8
His arrow will **f** like lightning. Zch 9:14
so that she could **f** from the Rv 12:14

FLYING *(11)*
may eat every clean **f** creature. Dt 14:20
that crawl and **f** birds, Ps 148:10
from its egg comes a **f** serpent. Is 14:29
of viper and **f** serpent, they Is 30:6
at the flash of Your **f** arrows, Hab 3:11
up again and saw a **f** scroll. Zch 5:1
"I see a **f** scroll," I replied, Zch 5:2
creature was like a **f** eagle. Rv 4:7
heard an eagle, **f** in mid-heaven, Rv 8:13
another angel **f** in mid-heaven, Rv 14:6
all the birds **f** in mid-heaven, Rv 19:17

FOAL *(2)*
on a colt, the **f** of a donkey. Zch 9:9
the **f** of a beast of burden." Mt 21:5

FOAM *(2)*
waters roar and **f** and the Ps 46:3
disappear like **f** on the surface Hs 10:7

FOAMING *(2)*
rolled around, **f** at the mouth. Mk 9:20
f up their shameful deeds; Jd 13

FOAMS *(2)*
him down, and he **f** at the mouth, Mk 9:18
until he **f** at the mouth; Lk 9:39

FOCUS *(2)*
Wisdom is the **f** of the Pr 17:24
So we do not **f** on what is seen, 2Co 4:18

FOCUSED *(1)*
They are **f** on earthly things, Php 3:19

FOCUSING *(1)*
same feelings, **f** on one goal. Php 2:2

FODDER *(3)*
grass or an ox low over its **f**? Jb 6:5
They gather their **f** in the field Jb 24:6
will eat salted **f** scattered with Is 30:24

FOE *(10)*
enemies and a **f** to your foes. Ex 23:22
You make us retreat from the **f**, Ps 44:10
it is not a **f** who rises up Ps 55:12
Give us aid against the **f**, Ps 60:11
God, how long will the **f** mock? Ps 74:10
day He redeemed them from the **f**, Ps 78:42
His splendor to the hand of a **f**. Ps 78:61
them from the hand of the **f** Ps 107:2
Give us aid against the **f**, Ps 108:12
lightning and scatter the **f**; Ps 144:6

FOES *(30)*
enemies and a foe to your **f**. Ex 23:22
feared⌋ that these **f** might Dt 32:27
may You be a help against his **f**. Dt 33:7
to flee from your **f** three months 2Sm 24:13
by your **f** with the sword 1Ch 21:12
LORD, how my **f** increase! Ps 3:1
and my **f** will rejoice because I Ps 13:4
my **f** and my enemies stumbled and Ps 27:2
me over to the will of my **f**, Ps 27:12
Through You we drive back our **f**; Ps 44:5
victory over our **f** and let those Ps 44:7
iniquity of my **f** surrounds me. Ps 49:5
He will trample our **f**. Ps 60:12
He beat back His **f**; He gave them Ps 78:66
turn My hand against their **f**." Ps 81:14
will crush his **f** before him and Ps 89:23
high the right hand of his **f**; Ps 89:42
burns up His **f** on every side. Ps 97:3
them more numerous than their **f**, Ps 105:24
covered their **f**; not one of them Ps 106:11
He will trample our **f**. Ps 108:13
will look in triumph on his **f**. Ps 112:8
me because my **f** forget Your Ps 119:139
My persecutors and **f** are many. Ps 119:157
and rescued us from our **f**. Ps 136:24
gain satisfaction against My **f**; Is 1:24
of your **f** will be like fine Is 29:5
to His **f**, and He will repay Is 59:18
will face **f** in broad daylight Ezk 30:16
takes vengeance against His **f**; Nah 1:2

FOLD *(6)*
Then **f** the sixth curtain double Ex 26:9
them⌋ in the **f** of His ⌊garment⌋. Is 40:11
a flock in the middle of its **f**. Mc 2:12
meat in the **f** of his garment, Hg 2:12
and with his **f** touches bread, Hg 2:12
sheep that are not of this **f**; Jn 10:16

FOLDED *(3)*
It must be square and **f** double, Ex 28:16
breastpiece square and **f** double, Ex 39:9
but was **f** up in a separate Jn 20:7

FOLDING *(4)*
the first door had two **f** sides, 1Kg 6:34
second door had two **f** panels. 1Kg 6:34
a little **f** of the arms to rest, Pr 6:10
a little **f** of the arms to rest, Pr 24:33

FOLDS *(7)*
and **f** for your flocks, Nm 32:24
also shook the **f** of my robe and Neh 5:13
out like ⌊the **f** of⌋ a garment. Jb 38:14
The **f** of his flesh are joined Jb 41:23
The fool **f** his arms and consumes Ec 4:5
them in the **f** of your ⌊robe⌋. Ezk 5:3
for shepherds and **f** for sheep. Zph 2:6

FOLIAGE *(7)*
they sing among the **f**. Ps 104:12

righteous will flourish like f. Pr 11:28
Our bed is lush with f; Sg 1:16
is withered, the f is gone, Is 15:6
the vine, and f on the fig tree Is 34:4
comes, and its f remains green. Jr 17:8
beautiful branches and shady f, Ezk 31:3

FOLLOW *(163)*

unwilling to f me to this land Gn 24:5
the woman is unwilling to f you, Gn 24:8
and all the people who f you. Ex 11:8
not they will f My instructions Ex 16:4
You must not f a crowd in Ex 23:2
Do not f the practices of the Lv 18:3
f the practices of the land of Lv 18:3
You must not f their customs. Lv 18:3
both him and all who f him, Lv 20:5
You must not f the statutes of Lv 20:23
If you f My statutes and Lv 26:3
they did not f Me completely, Nm 32:11
because they did f the LORD Nm 32:12
I am teaching you to f, Dt 4:1
so that you may f them in the Dt 4:5
Carefully f ⌊them⌋, for this Dt 4:6
He commanded you to f the Ten Dt 4:13
for you to f in the land you are Dt 4:14
Learn and f them carefully. Dt 5:1
so that they may f ⌊them⌋ in the Dt 5:31
F the whole instruction the LORD Dt 5:33
so that you may f ⌊them⌋ in the Dt 6:1
and be careful to f ⌊them⌋, Dt 6:3
Do not f other gods, the gods of Dt 6:14
commanded us to f all these Dt 6:24
we are careful to f every one of Dt 6:25
that I am giving you to f today. Dt 7:11
must carefully f every command I Dt 8:1
commands I am giving you to f— Dt 11:22
be careful to f all the statutes Dt 11:32
Be careful to f these statutes Dt 12:1
he says, 'Let us f other gods,' Dt 13:2
You must f the LORD your God and Dt 13:4
are careful to f every one of Dt 15:5
carefully f these statutes. Dt 16:12
am giving you today and f them, Dt 19:9
you this day to f these statutes Dt 26:16
be careful to f them with all Dt 26:16
your God and f His commands Dt 27:10
careful to f all His commands Dt 28:1
and are careful to f ⌊them⌋. Dt 28:13
of this covenant and f them, Dt 29:9
though I f my ⌊own⌋ stubborn Dt 29:19
of your children who f you and Dt 29:22
that we may f all the words of Dt 29:29
obey Him and f all His commands Dt 30:8
it to us so that we may f it?' Dt 30:12
it to us so that we may f it?' Dt 30:13
heart, so that you may f it. Dt 30:14
be careful to f all the words Dt 31:12
to carefully f all the words of Dt 32:46
you must break camp and f it. Jos 3:3
F the LORD's command—see ⌊that Jos 8:8
He told them, "F me, because the Jdg 3:28
F your sister-in-law." Ru 1:15
you or go back and not f you. Ru 1:16
are harvesting, and f ⌊them⌋. Ru 2:9
your sons do not f your example. 1Sm 8:5
over you will f the LORD your 1Sm 12:14
turn away to f worthless things 1Sm 12:21
"F me," Jonathan told his 1Sm 14:12
to the young men who f my lord. 1Sm 25:27
among the people who f Absalom.' 2Sm 17:9
whoever is for David, f Joab!" 2Sm 20:11
seduced him ⌊to f⌋ other gods. 1Kg 11:4
did not completely f the LORD. 1Kg 11:6
that he would not f other gods, 1Kg 11:10
If Yahweh is God, f Him. 1Kg 18:21
Him. But if Baal, f him." But 1Kg 18:21
oxen, ran to f Elijah, and said 1Kg 19:20
mother, and then I will f you." 1Kg 19:20
each of the people who f me." 1Kg 20:10
F me, and I will take you to the 2Kg 6:19
not careful to f with all his 2Kg 10:31
of the LORD to f the LORD and to 2Kg 23:3
if you carefully f the statutes 1Ch 22:13
presence to f the LORD and to 2Ch 34:31
a sworn oath to f the law of God Neh 10:29
man who does not f the advice Ps 1:1
his wealth will not f him down. Ps 49:17
f close to You; Your right hand Ps 63:8
hearts to f their own plans. Ps 81:12
Me and Israel would f My ways, Ps 81:13
the upright in heart will f it. Ps 94:15
all who f His instructions have Ps 111:10
nothing wrong; they f His ways. Ps 119:3
will obey it and f it with all Ps 119:34
every evil path to f Your word. Ps 119:101
I carefully f all Your precepts Ps 119:128
do not f Your instruction. Ps 119:136
So f the way of good people, Pr 2:20
memory among those who f ⌊them⌋. Ec 1:11
under the sun f a second youth Ec 4:15
f the tracks of the flock, Sg 1:8
they will f you, they will come Is 45:14
and I will continue to f them. Jr 2:25
will cease to f the stubbornness Jr 3:17
in this place or f other gods, Jr 7:6
and f other gods that you have Jr 7:9
We will continue to f our plans, Jr 18:12
not f other gods to serve them Jr 25:6
about will f on your heels Jr 42:16
so they may f My statutes, Ezk 11:20
prophets who f their own spirit Ezk 13:3
They did not f My statutes and Ezk 20:13
and did not f My statutes. Ezk 20:16
Don't f the statutes of your Ezk 20:18
F My statutes, keep My Ezk 20:19
They did not f My statutes or Ezk 20:21
and cause you to f My statutes Ezk 36:27
They will f My ordinances, Ezk 37:24
is determined to f what is Hs 5:11
They will f the LORD; Hs 11:10
"F Me," He told them, "and I Mt 4:19
I will f You wherever You go!" Mt 8:19
Jesus told him, "F Me, and let Mt 8:22
and He said to him, "F Me!" Mt 9:9
his cross and f Me is not worthy Mt 10:38
take up his cross, and f Me. Mt 16:24
in heaven. Then come, f Me." Mt 19:21
"F Me," Jesus told them, "and I Mk 1:17
and He said to him, "F Me!" Mk 2:14
take up his cross, and f Me. Mk 8:34
in heaven. Then come, f Me." Mk 10:21
and began to f Him on the road Mk 10:52
water jug will meet you. F him. Mk 14:13
they would f Him and help Him. Mk 15:41
and He said to him, "F Me!" Lk 5:27
he got up and began to f Him. Lk 5:28
up his cross daily, and f Me. Lk 9:23
him because he does not f us." Lk 9:49
"I will f You wherever You go!" Lk 9:57
Then He said to another, "F Me." Lk 9:59
also said, "I will f You, Lord, Lk 9:61
Don't f or run after them. Lk 17:23
in heaven. Then come, f Me." Lk 18:22
he began to f Him, glorifying Lk 18:43
The time is near.' Don't f them. Lk 21:8
F him into the house he enters. Lk 22:10
Philip and told him, "F Me!" Jn 1:43
The sheep f him because they Jn 10:4
They will never f a stranger; Jn 10:5
I know them, and they f Me. Jn 10:27
anyone serves Me, he must f Me. Jn 12:26
I am going you cannot f Me now, Jn 13:36
Me now, but you will f later." Jn 13:36
asked, "why can't I f You now? Jn 13:37
this, He told him, "F Me!" Jn 21:19
that to you? As for you, f Me." Jn 21:22
you," he told him, "and f me." Ac 12:8
rest were to f, some on planks Ac 27:44
to those who f in the footsteps Rm 4:12
we must also f the Spirit. Gl 5:25
all those who f this standard, Gl 6:16
already turned away to f Satan. 1Tm 5:15
but ⌊the sins⌋ of others f them. 1Tm 5:24
and the glories that would f. 1Pt 1:11
that you should f in His steps. 1Pt 2:21
For we did not f cleverly 2Pt 1:16
Many will f their unrestrained 2Pt 2:2
those who f the polluting 2Pt 2:10
are the ones who f the Lamb Rv 14:4
labors, for their works f them!" Rv 14:13

FOLLOWED *(115)*

strongly that they f him and Gn 19:3
the camels, and f the man. Gn 24:61
and all the women f her with Ex 15:20
spirit and has f Me completely, Nm 14:24
and the elders of Israel f him. Nm 16:25
f the Israelite man into the Nm 25:8
he f the LORD completely. Dt 1:36
one of you who f Baal of Peor. Dt 4:3
of the LORD's covenant f them. Jos 6:8
So they f him, captured the Jdg 3:28
10,000 men f him, and Deborah Jdg 4:10
with this money, and they f him. Jdg 9:4
his own branch and f Abimelech. Jdg 9:49
So Manoah got up and f his wife. Jdg 13:11
his armor-bearer f and finished 1Sm 14:13
sons had f Saul to the war 1Sm 17:13
The three oldest had f Saul, 1Sm 17:14
400 men f David while 200 1Sm 25:13
of Judah, however, f David. 2Sm 2:10
Her husband f her, weeping all 2Sm 3:16
and a gift from the king f him. 2Sm 11:8
and his entire household f him. 2Sm 15:16
out, and all the people f him. 2Sm 15:17
that his advice had not been f, 2Sm 17:23
deserted David and f Sheba son 2Sm 20:2
passed by and f Joab to pursue 2Sm 20:13
Berites came together and f him. 2Sm 20:14
All the people f him, playing 1Kg 1:40
Solomon f Ashtoreth, the goddess 1Kg 11:5
No one f the house of David 1Kg 12:20
f the man of God and found him 1Kg 13:14
commandments and f Me with all 1Kg 14:8
LORD's sight and f the example 1Kg 15:26
LORD's sight and f the example 1Kg 15:34
half the people f Tibni son of 1Kg 16:21
make him king, and half f Omri. 1Kg 16:21
the people who f Omri proved 1Kg 16:22
than those who f Tibni son of 1Kg 16:22
He f the example of Jeroboam son 1Kg 16:26
commandments and f the Baals. 1Kg 18:18
Then he left, f Elijah, and 1Kg 19:21
So he got up and f her. 2Kg 4:30
So they f them as far as the 2Kg 7:15
LORD's sight and f the sins that 2Kg 13:2
LORD their God f the Levites to 2Ch 11:16
He also f their advice and went 2Ch 22:5
and half the leaders of Judah f: Neh 12:32
and I f it with half the people Neh 12:38
and he f Memucan's advice. Est 1:21
My feet have f in His tracks; Jb 23:11
way, my heart has f my eyes, or Jb 31:7
how you f Me in the wilderness, Jr 2:2
far from Me, f worthless idols Jr 2:5
by Baal and f useless idols. Jr 2:8
I have not f the Baals? Jr 2:23
have loved, served, f, pursued, Jr 8:2
they f the stubbornness of their Jr 9:14
each one f the stubbornness of Jr 11:8
words and have f other gods to Jr 11:10
and who have f other gods to Jr 13:10
and f other gods, served Jr 16:11
were closely f, so that we could Lm 4:18
you have not f and whose Ezk 11:12
You have f the path of your Ezk 23:31
their ancestors f have led them Am 2:4
you have f their policies. Mc 6:16
they left their nets and f Him. Mt 4:20
boat and their father and f Him. Mt 4:22
Large crowds f Him from Galilee, Mt 4:25
mountain, large crowds f Him. Mt 8:1
the boat, His disciples f Him. Mt 8:23
So he got up and f Him. Mt 9:9
His disciples got up and f him. Mt 9:19
two blind men f Him, shouting, Mt 9:27
Huge crowds f Him, and He healed Mt 12:15
they f Him on foot from the Mt 14:13
crowds f Him, and He healed Mt 19:2
have left everything and f You. Mt 19:27
you who have f Me will also sit Mt 19:28
Jericho, a large crowd f Him. Mt 20:29
they could see, and they f Him. Mt 20:34
and those who f kept shouting: Mt 21:9
women who had f Jesus from Mt 27:55
which f the preparation day, Mt 27:62
they left their nets and f Him. Mk 1:18
with the hired men and f Him. Mk 1:20
So he got up and f Him. Mk 2:14
great multitude f from Galilee, Mk 3:7
and His disciples f Him. Mk 6:1
have left everything and f You." Mk 10:28
but those who f Him were afraid. Mk 10:32
and those who f kept shouting: Mk 11:9
Peter f Him at a distance, Mk 14:54

left everything, and **f** Him. Lk 5:11
crowds found out, they **f** Him. Lk 9:11
left what we had and **f** You." Lk 18:28
Olives, and the disciples **f** Him. Lk 22:39
multitude of the people **f** Him, Lk 23:27
women who had **f** Him from Lk 23:49
Him from Galilee **f** along and Lk 23:55
heard him say this and **f** Jesus. Jn 1:37
two who heard John and **f** Him. Jn 1:40
they **f** her, supposing that she Jn 11:31
went out and **f**, and he did not Ac 12:9
proselytes **f** Paul and Barnabas Ac 13:43
As she **f** Paul and us she cried Ac 16:17
men should have **f** my advice not Ac 27:21
a spiritual rock that **f** them, 1Co 10:4
good teaching that you have **f**. 1Tm 4:6
But you have **f** my teaching, 2Tm 3:10
astray and have **f** the path of 2Pt 2:15
was amazed and **f** the beast. Rv 13:3
A second angel **f**, saying: Rv 14:8
a third angel **f** them and spoke Rv 14:9
were in heaven **f** Him on white Rv 19:14

FOLLOWER *(1)*
If anyone wants to be My **f**, Mk 8:34

FOLLOWERS *(11)*
he said to Korah and all his **f**, Nm 16:5
and all your **f** are to do this: Nm 16:6
you and all your **f** who have Nm 16:11
You and all your **f** are to appear Nm 16:16
and become like Korah and his **f**. Nm 16:40
and Korah's **f** fought against Nm 26:9
when his **f** died and the fire Nm 26:10
but he was not among Korah's **f**, Nm 27:3
and of their **f**, who approve of Ps 49:13
protect the way of His loyal **f**. Pr 2:8
wealth on his **f**, and he will Dn 11:24

FOLLOWING *(87)*
He sent his father the **f**: Gn 45:23
The **f** day Moses said to the Ex 32:30
each of the **f** planks for their Ex 36:24
bases under each of the **f** ones; Ex 36:26
to keep My statutes by **f** them; Lv 18:4
month until the ⌊**f**⌋ evening." Lv 23:32
you have turned from **f** Him." Nm 14:43
unfaithful by **f** your own heart Nm 15:39
If you turn back from **f** Him, Nm 32:15
you today by **f** other gods you Dt 11:28
f carefully everything the Dt 24:8
by carefully **f** all His commands Dt 28:15
struck down the **f** kings of the Jos 12:1
struck down the **f** kings of the Jos 12:7
Jephunneh ⌊the **f**⌋ portion among Jos 15:13
Tabor with 10,000 men **f** him. Jdg 4:14
to the people who are **f** me, Jdg 8:5
don't turn away from **f** the LORD. 1Sm 12:20
turned away from **f** Me and has 1Sm 15:11
went back, **f** Saul, and Saul 1Sm 15:31
The **f** day hurry down and go to 1Sm 20:19
on the donkey **f** David's 1Sm 25:42
David sang the **f** lament for Saul 2Sm 1:17
and from **f** the sheep to be 2Sm 7:8
turn away from **f** Me and do not 1Kg 9:6
sight and by **f** the example 1Kg 16:19
as if **f** the sin of Jeroboam son 1Kg 16:31
So he turned back from **f** him, 1Kg 19:21
son at the same time the **f** year, 2Kg 4:17
f the surrounding nations the 2Kg 17:15
Israel away from **f** the LORD and 2Kg 17:21
did not turn from **f** Him but kept 2Kg 18:6
The **f** were the chiefs of David's 1Ch 11:10
The **f** were the men who came to 1Ch 12:1
rulers, **f** consultation, sent 1Ch 12:19
pasture and from **f** the sheep, 1Ch 17:7
⌊The **f** were⌋ the divisions of 1Ch 26:1
⌊The **f** were⌋ in charge of the 1Ch 27:16
f day they offered sacrifices 1Ch 29:21
f the daily requirement for 2Ch 8:13
before the priests **f** the daily 2Ch 8:14
heart, you are to do the **f**: 2Ch 19:9
Amaziah turned from **f** the LORD, 2Ch 25:27
turn aside from **f** the LORD God 2Ch 34:33
The **f** are those who came from Ezr 2:59
⌊The **f**⌋ were found to have Ezr 10:18
I found ⌊the **f**⌋ written in it: Neh 7:5
The **f** are those who came from Neh 7:61
will impose ⌊the **f**⌋ commandments Neh 10:32
aside from **f** Him and did not Jb 34:27
lead the way, with musicians **f**; Ps 68:25
turning away from **f** our God, Is 59:13
the wrong path, **f** their own Is 65:2
the groves **f** their leader, Is 66:17
of you was **f** the stubbornness Jr 16:12
Stop **f** other gods to serve them. Jr 35:15
has gone into exile **f** affliction Lm 1:3
stray from **f** Me and no longer Ezk 14:11
LORD our God by **f** His Dn 9:10
LORD took me from **f** the flock Am 7:15
who turn back from **f** the LORD, Zph 1:6
amazed and said to those **f** Him, Mt 8:10
Peter was **f** Him at a distance Mt 26:58
there were many who were **f** Him. Mk 2:15
a large crowd was **f** and pressing Mk 5:24
him because he wasn't **f** us." Mk 9:38
his naked body, was **f** Him. Mk 14:51
and turning to the crowd **f** Him, Lk 7:9
Peter was **f** at a distance. Lk 22:54
turned and noticed them **f** Him, Jn 1:38
huge crowd was **f** Him because Jn 6:2
Simon Peter was **f** Jesus, Jn 18:15
Then, **f** him, Simon Peter came Jn 20:6
the disciple Jesus loved **f** them. Jn 21:20
of the census and attracted a **f**. Ac 5:37
The **f** day he entered Caesarea. Ac 10:24
presented to them the **f** Sabbath. Ac 13:42
The **f** Sabbath almost the whole Ac 13:44
The **f** day we crossed over to Ac 20:15
lure the disciples into **f** them. Ac 20:30
The **f** day Paul went in with us Ac 21:18
of people were **f** and yelling, Ac 21:36
The **f** night, the Lord stood by Ac 23:11
in giving the **f** instruction I do 1Co 11:17
must also put away all the **f**: Col 3:8
to scoff, **f** their own lusts, 2Pt 3:3
and Hades was **f** after him. Rv 6:8

FOLLOWS *(22)*
because of the famine that **f** it, Gn 41:31
planks for the tabernacle as **f**: Ex 26:18
planks for the tabernacle as **f**: Ex 36:23
put anyone who **f** her to death 2Kg 11:15
to the LORD's word, were as **f**: 1Ch 12:23
descendants of Aaron were as **f**: 1Ch 24:1
put anyone who **f** her to death 2Ch 23:14
concerning Jerusalem as **f**: Ezr 4:8
sent him a report, written as **f**: Ezr 5:7
Everyone **f** behind him, and those Jb 21:33
The one who **f** the way of Ps 101:6
He **f** her impulsively like an ox Pr 7:22
The one who **f** instruction is on Pr 10:17
comes, disgrace **f**, but with Pr 11:2
Speak as **f**: This is what the Jr 9:22
the residents of Jerusalem as **f**: Jr 25:2
He **f** My statutes and keeps My Ezk 18:9
My ordinances and **f** My statutes. Ezk 18:17
one act of bloodshed **f** another. Hs 4:2
and pestilence **f** in His steps. Hab 3:5
Anyone who **f** Me will never walk Jn 8:12
It **f** that speaking in other 1Co 14:22

FOLLY *(11)*
with you as your **f** deserves. Jb 42:8
The woman **F** is rowdy; she is Pr 9:13
but **f** is the instruction of Pr 16:22
and knowledge, madness and **f**; Ec 1:17
with wine and how to grasp **f**— Ec 2:3
madness, and **f**, for what will Ec 2:12
an advantage to wisdom over **f**, Ec 2:13
is stupidity and **f** is madness. Ec 7:25
so a little **f** outweighs wisdom Ec 10:1
of the words of his mouth is **f**, Ec 10:13
and every mouth speaks **f**. Is 9:17

FONDLED *(1)*
Their breasts were **f** there, Ezk 23:3

FOOD *(292)*
This **f** will be for you, Gn 1:29
given⌋ every green plant for **f**." Gn 1:30
in appearance and good for **f**, Gn 2:9
was good for **f** and delightful to Gn 3:6
every kind of **f** that is eaten; Gn 6:21
it as **f** for you and for them. Gn 6:21
creature will be **f** for you; Gn 9:3
Gomorrah and all their **f** and Gn 14:11
me the delicious **f** that I love Gn 27:4
some delicious **f** for me to eat Gn 27:7
the delicious **f** his father loved Gn 27:14
delicious **f** and the bread she Gn 27:17
some delicious **f** and brought it Gn 27:31
provides me with **f** to eat and Gn 28:20
anything except the **f** he ate. Gn 39:6
all the ⌊excess⌋ **f** during these Gn 41:35
authority as **f** in the cities, Gn 41:35
The **f** will be a reserve for the Gn 41:36
all the ⌊excess⌋ **f** in the land Gn 41:48
He placed the **f** in every city Gn 41:48
the land of Egypt there was **f**. Gn 41:54
cried out to Pharaoh for **f**. Gn 41:55
the land of Canaan to buy **f**," Gn 42:7
servants have come to buy **f**," Gn 42:10
take ⌊**f** to relieve⌋ the hunger Gn 42:33
"Go back and buy us some **f**." Gn 43:2
will go down and buy **f** for you. Gn 43:4
the first time only to buy **f**. Gn 43:20
money with us to buy **f**. Gn 43:22
with as much **f** as they can carry Gn 44:1
Go again, and buy us some **f**.' Gn 44:25
grain, **f**, and provisions Gn 45:23
household with **f** for their Gn 47:12
there was no **f** in that entire Gn 47:13
to Joseph and said, "Give us **f**. Gn 47:15
will give you **f** in exchange for Gn 47:16
he gave them **f** in exchange for Gn 47:17
them with **f** in exchange for Gn 47:17
and our land in exchange for **f**. Gn 47:19
field and as **f** for yourselves, Gn 47:24
Asher's **f** will be rich, and he Gn 49:20
they gathered twice as much **f**, Ex 16:22
must not reduce the **f**, clothing, Ex 21:10
will burn it on the altar as **f**, Lv 3:11
burn them on the altar as **f**, Lv 3:16
Any edible **f** coming into contact Lv 11:34
animals that you use for **f** dies, Lv 11:39
plant any kind of tree for **f**, Lv 19:23
to the LORD, the **f** of their God. Lv 21:6
he presents the **f** of your God. Lv 21:8
to present the **f** of his God. Lv 21:17
to present the **f** of his God. Lv 21:21
He may eat the **f** of his God from Lv 21:22
offerings, for that is his **f**. Lv 22:7
born in his house may eat his **f**. Lv 22:11
she may share her father's **f**. Lv 22:13
to present **f** to your God from Lv 22:25
Sabbath year can be **f** for you; Lv 25:6
may serve as **f** for your Lv 25:7
or sell ⌊him⌋ your **f** for profit. Lv 25:37
have plenty of **f** to eat and live Lv 26:5
a strong craving ⌊for other **f**⌋. Nm 11:4
you eat from the **f** of the land. Nm 15:19
and we detest this wretched **f**!" Nm 21:5
My offering and My **f** as My fire Nm 28:2
to offer the same **f** each day for Nm 28:24
may purchase **f** from them with Dt 2:6
can sell us **f** in exchange for Dt 2:28
you will eat **f** without shortage Dt 8:9
giving him **f** and clothing. Dt 10:18
because you can get **f** from them. Dt 20:19
that you know do not produce **f**. Dt 20:20
not meet you with **f** and water Dt 23:4
on money, **f**, or anything that Dt 23:19
corpses will be **f** for all the Dt 28:26
our houses as **f** on the day we Jos 9:12
If I stay, I won't eat your **f**. Jdg 13:16
need⌋ by providing them **f**. Ru 1:6
full hire themselves out for **f**, 1Sm 2:5
The **f** from our packs is gone, 1Sm 9:7
man who eats **f** before evening, 1Sm 14:24
of the troops tasted ⌊any⌋ **f**. 1Sm 14:24
is the man who eats **f** today,' 1Sm 14:28
not eat any **f** that second day 1Sm 20:34
hadn't had any **f** all day and all 1Sm 28:20
me set some **f** in front of you 1Sm 28:22
he hadn't eaten **f** or drunk water 1Sm 30:12
grandson will have **f** to eat. 2Sm 9:10
shared his meager **f** and drank 2Sm 12:3
they served him **f**, and he ate. 2Sm 12:20
he died, you got up and ate **f**." 2Sm 12:21
Let her prepare **f** in my presence 2Sm 13:5
They provided **f** for the king and 1Kg 4:7
turn provided **f** for King Solomon 1Kg 4:27
providing my household with **f**." 1Kg 5:9
of wheat as **f** for his household 1Kg 5:11
f at his table, his servants' 1Kg 10:5
ordered that he ⌊be given⌋ **f**, 1Kg 11:18
them with **f** and water when 1Kg 18:4
provided them with **f** and water. 1Kg 18:13
on the strength from that **f**, 1Kg 19:8

face away, and didn't eat any **f**. 1Kg 21:4
up, eat some **f**, and be happy. 1Kg 21:7
persuaded him to eat some **f**. 2Kg 4:8
Set **f** and water in front of them 2Kg 6:22
the people of the land had no **f**. 2Kg 25:3
came bringing **f** on donkeys, 1Ch 12:40
f at his table, his servants' 2Ch 9:4
in them with supplies of **f**, 2Ch 11:11
them sandals, **f** and drink, 2Ch 28:15
and ⌊gave⌋ **f**, drink, and oil to Ezr 3:7
He did not eat **f** or drink water, Ezr 10:6
never ate from the **f** allotted to Neh 5:14
taking **f** and wine from them, Neh 5:15
didn't demand the **f** allotted to Neh 5:18
the Israelites with **f** and water. Neh 13:2
against selling **f** on that day. Neh 13:15
sigh when **f** is ⌊put⌋ before me, Jb 3:24
Is bland **f** eaten without salt? Jb 6:6
they are like contaminated **f**. Jb 6:7
words as the palate tastes **f**? Jb 12:11
about for **f**, ⌊saying,⌋ "Where Jb 15:23
yet the **f** in his stomach turns Jb 20:14
withheld **f** from the famished, Jb 22:7
His mouth more than my daily **f**. Jb 23:12
to their task of foraging for **f**; Jb 24:5
will never have enough **f**. Jb 27:14
F may come from the earth, Jb 28:5
of the broom tree were their **f**. Jb 30:4
soul ⌊despises his⌋ favorite **f**. Jb 33:20
words as the palate tastes **f**? Jb 34:3
table was spread with choice **f**. Jb 36:16
He gives **f** in abundance. Jb 36:31
the raven's **f** when its young cry Jb 38:41
and wander about for lack of **f**? Jb 38:41
The hills yield **f** for him, Jb 40:20
lions lack **f** and go hungry, Ps 34:10
have been my **f** day and night, Ps 42:3
scavenge for **f**; they growl if Ps 59:15
You satisfy me as with rich **f**; Ps 63:5
they gave me gall for my **f**, Ps 69:21
demanding the **f** they craved. Ps 78:18
able to provide **f** in the Ps 78:19
them an abundant supply of **f**. Ps 78:25
while the **f** was still in their Ps 78:30
to the birds of the sky for **f**, Ps 79:2
I even forget to eat my **f**. Ps 102:4
producing **f** from the earth, Ps 104:14
prey and seek their **f** from God. Ps 104:21
give them their **f** at the right Ps 104:27
destroyed the entire **f** supply. Ps 105:16
They loathed all **f** and came near Ps 107:18
searching ⌊for **f**⌋ far from their Ps 109:10
He has provided **f** for those who Ps 111:5
eating **f** earned by hard work; Ps 127:2
I will abundantly bless its **f**; Ps 132:15
He gives **f** to every creature. Ps 136:25
give them their **f** in due time. Ps 145:15
and giving **f** to the hungry. Ps 146:7
the animals with their **f**, Ps 147:9
it gathers its **f** during harvest. Pr 6:8
to act important but have no **f**. Pr 12:9
his land will have plenty of **f**, Pr 12:11
of the poor yields abundant **f**, Pr 13:23
are like choice **f** that goes down Pr 18:8
F gained by fraud is sweet to a Pr 20:17
he shares his **f** with the poor. Pr 22:9
don't desire his choice **f**, Pr 23:3
food, for that **f** is deceptive. Pr 23:3
and don't desire his choice **f**, Pr 23:6
hungry, give him **f** to eat, and Pr 25:21
are like choice **f** that goes down Pr 26:22
enough goat's milk for your **f**— Pr 27:27
f for your household and Pr 27:27
a driving rain that leaves no **f**. Pr 28:3
his land will have plenty of **f**, Pr 28:19
feed me with the **f** I need. Pr 30:8
fool when he is stuffed with **f**, Pr 30:22
store up their **f** in the summer; Pr 30:25
bringing her **f** from far away. Pr 31:14
and provides **f** for her household Pr 31:15
don't even have **f** or clothing in Is 3:7
Tema meet the refugees with **f**. Is 21:14
them with ample **f** and sacred Is 23:18
ground, and the **f**, the produce Is 30:23
fortresses, his **f** provided, his Is 33:16
and his **f** will not be lacking. Is 51:14
spend money on what is not **f**, Is 55:2
seed to sow and **f** to eat, Is 55:10
grain to your enemies for **f**, Is 62:8
the serpent's **f** will be dust! Is 65:25
consume your harvest and your **f**. Jr 5:17
will become **f** for the birds Jr 7:33
will become **f** for the birds Jr 16:4
F won't be provided for the Jr 16:7
their corpses as **f** for the birds Jr 19:7
will become **f** for the birds Jr 34:20
the ram's horn or hunger for **f**, Jr 42:14
we had enough **f** and good things Jr 44:17
the people of the land had no **f**. Jr 52:6
belongings for **f** in order to Lm 1:11
searching for **f** to keep Lm 1:19
they became their **f** during the Lm 4:10
with Assyria, to get enough **f**. Lm 5:6
We secure our **f** at the risk of Lm 5:9
The **f** you eat each day will be Ezk 4:10
aroma the **f** I gave you— Ezk 16:19
them to these images as **f**. Ezk 16:20
plenty of **f**, and comfortable Ezk 16:49
the fire⌋ as **f** for the idols. Ezk 23:37
and the birds of the sky as **f**. Ezk 29:5
they became **f** for all the wild Ezk 34:5
prey and⌋ **f** for every wild Ezk 34:8
they will not be **f** for them. Ezk 34:10
will give you as **f** to every kind Ezk 39:4
temple while you offered My **f**— Ezk 44:7
providing **f** will grow along Ezk 47:12
be used for **f** and their leaves Ezk 47:12
will be **f** for the workers Ezk 48:18
from the royal **f** and from the Dn 1:5
with the king's **f** or with the Dn 1:8
king assigned your **f** and drink. Dn 1:10
men who are eating the king's **f**, Dn 1:13
who were eating the king's **f**. Dn 1:15
to remove their **f** and the wine Dn 1:16
and on it was **f** for all. Dn 4:12
and on it was **f** for all, under Dn 4:21
and share ⌊**f**⌋ with the wild Dn 4:23
eat any rich **f**, no meat or wine Dn 10:3
men who give me my **f** and water, Hs 2:5
will eat unclean **f** in Assyria. Hs 9:3
Their ⌊**f**⌋ will be like the bread Hs 9:4
I bent down to give them **f**. Hs 11:4
Hasn't the **f** been cut off before Jl 1:16
a shortage of **f** in all your Am 4:6
when they have ⌊**f**⌋ to sink their Mc 3:5
is rich and their **f** plentiful. Hab 1:16
and the fields produce no **f**, Hab 3:17
or any other **f**, does it become Hg 2:12
defiled **f** on My altar." Mal 1:7
product, its **f**, is contemptible Mal 1:12
that there may be **f** in My house. Mal 3:10
and his **f** was locusts and wild Mt 3:4
life more than **f** and the body Mt 6:25
the worker is worthy of his **f**. Mt 10:10
and buy **f** for themselves. Mt 14:15
to give them **f** at the proper Mt 24:45
one who has **f** must do the same. Lk 3:11
to find **f** and lodging, Lk 9:12
we go and buy **f** for all these Lk 9:13
is more than **f** and the body more Lk 12:23
their allotted **f** at the proper Lk 12:42
hands have more than enough **f**, Lk 15:17
had gone into town to buy **f**. Jn 4:8
I have **f** to eat that you don't Jn 4:32
My **f** is to do the will of Him Jn 4:34
work for the **f** that perishes Jn 6:27
but for the **f** that lasts for Jn 6:27
flesh is real **f** and My blood is Jn 6:55
They ate their **f** with gladness Ac 2:46
our forefathers could find no **f**. Ac 7:11
taking some **f**, he regained his Ac 9:19
supplied with **f** from the king's Ac 12:20
hearts with **f** and happiness." Ac 14:17
abstain from **f** offered to idols Ac 15:29
themselves from **f** sacrificed to Ac 21:25
Since many were going without **f**, Ac 27:21
Paul urged them all to take **f**, Ac 27:33
waiting and going without **f**, Ac 27:33
I urge you to take some **f**. Ac 27:34
and took **f** themselves. Ac 27:36
And having eaten enough **f**, Ac 27:38
down God's work because of **f**. Rm 14:20
milk, not solid **f**, because you 1Co 3:2
About **f** offered to idols: 1Co 8:1
About eating **f** offered to idols, 1Co 8:4
when they eat **f** offered to an 1Co 8:7
F will not make us acceptable to 1Co 8:8
to eat **f** offered to idols 1Co 8:10
if **f** causes my brother to fall, 1Co 8:13
eat the **f** from the temple 1Co 9:13
all ate the same spiritual **f**, 1Co 10:3
That **f** offered to idols is 1Co 10:19
"This is **f** offered to an idol," 1Co 10:28
and bread for **f** will provide 2Co 9:10
often without **f**, cold, and 2Co 11:27
you in regard to **f** and drink Col 2:16
But if we have **f** and clothing, 1Tm 6:8
You need milk, not solid **f**. Heb 5:12
But solid **f** is for the mature— Heb 5:14
and only deal with **f**, Heb 9:10
clothes and lacks daily **f**, Jms 2:15

FOODS *(6)*

will enjoy the choicest of **f**. Is 55:2
a result, He made all **f** clean. Mk 7:19
F for the stomach and the 1Co 6:13
stomach and the stomach for **f**," 1Co 6:13
abstinence from **f** that God 1Tm 4:3
by grace and not by **f**, Heb 13:9

FOOL *(73)*

You made me look like a **f**. Nm 22:29
a worthless **f** nobody can talk 1Sm 25:17
have been a **f**! I've committed a 1Sm 26:21
Should Abner die as a **f** dies? 2Sm 3:33
anger kills a **f**, and jealousy Jb 5:2
I have seen a **f** taking root, Jb 5:3
The **f** says in his heart, "God Ps 14:1
The **f** says in his heart, "God Ps 53:1
I was a **f** and didn't understand; Ps 73:22
a **f** does not understand this: Ps 92:6
the mouth of the **f** hastens Pr 10:14
whoever spreads slander is a **f**. Pr 10:18
conduct is pleasure for a **f**, Pr 10:23
and a **f** will be a slave to Pr 11:29
but a **f** displays his stupidity. Pr 13:16
speech of a **f** ⌊brings⌋ a rod Pr 14:3
but a **f** is easily angered and is Pr 14:16
A **f** despises his father's Pr 15:5
than a hundred lashes into a **f**. Pr 17:10
her cubs than a **f** in his Pr 17:12
Why does a **f** have money in his Pr 17:16
A man fathers a **f** to his own Pr 17:21
the father of a **f** has no joy. Pr 17:21
Even a **f** is considered wise when Pr 17:28
A **f** does not delight in Pr 18:2
has deceitful lips and is a **f**. Pr 19:1
is not appropriate for a **f**— Pr 19:10
but any **f** can get himself into a Pr 20:3
Don't speak to a **f**, for he will Pr 23:9
Wisdom is inaccessible to a **f**; Pr 24:7
honor is inappropriate for a **f**. Pr 26:1
Don't answer a **f** according to Pr 26:4
Answer a **f** according to his Pr 26:5
the mouth of a **f** is like lame Pr 26:7
honor to a **f** is like binding Pr 26:8
the mouth of a **f** is like a stick Pr 26:9
one who hires a **f**, or who hires Pr 26:10
so a **f** repeats his foolishness. Pr 26:11
more hope for a **f** than for him. Pr 26:12
from a **f** outweighs them Pr 27:3
you grind a **f** in a mortar with Pr 27:22
who trusts in himself is a **f**, Pr 28:26
wise man goes to court with a **f**, Pr 29:9
f gives full vent to his anger, Pr 29:11
more hope for a **f** than for him. Pr 29:20
f when he is stuffed with food, Pr 30:22
but the **f** walks in darkness. Ec 2:14
happens to the **f** will also Ec 2:15
For, just like the **f**, there is Ec 2:16
wise man dies just like the **f**? Ec 2:16
he will be a wise man or a **f**? Ec 2:19
f folds his arms and consumes Ec 4:5
the wise man have over the **f**? Ec 6:8
so is the laughter of the **f**. Ec 7:6
turns a wise person into a **f**, Ec 7:7
Even when the **f** walks along the Ec 10:3
and he shows everyone he is a **f**. Ec 10:3
The **f** is appointed to great Ec 10:6
but the lips of a **f** consume him. Ec 10:12
Yet the **f** multiplies words. Ec 10:14
A **f** will no longer be called a Is 32:5
For a **f** speaks foolishness and Is 32:6
Even the **f** will not go astray. Is 35:8
they have played the **f**. Jr 5:4
so in the end he will be a **f**. Jr 17:11

The prophet is a **f**, and the Hs 9:7
a son considers his father a **f**, Mc 7:6
says to his brother, '**F**!' Mt 5:22
But God said to him, 'You **f**! Lk 12:20
no one should consider me a **f**. 2Co 11:16
at least accept me as a **f**, 2Co 11:16
will not be a **f**, because I will 2Co 12:6
I have become a **f**; you forced it 2Co 12:11

FOOL'S *(9)*
f way is right in his own eyes, Pr 12:15
f displeasure is known at once, Pr 12:16
is not appropriate on a **f** lips; Pr 17:7
but a **f** eyes roam to the ends of Pr 17:24
A **f** lips lead to strife, and his Pr 18:6
A **f** mouth is his devastation, Pr 18:7
a message by a **f** hand cuts off Pr 26:6
work and a **f** voice from many Ec 5:3
but a **f** heart to the left. Ec 10:2

FOOLED *(1)*
to them: "Are you **f** too? Jn 7:47

FOOLISH *(54)*
you **f** and senseless people? Dt 32:6
enrage them with a **f** nation. Dt 32:21
said to Saul, "You have been **f**. 1Sm 13:13
I've been very **f**, please take 2Sm 24:10
I've been very **f**, please take 1Ch 21:8
You have been **f** in this matter, 2Ch 16:9
"You speak as a **f** woman speaks," Jb 2:10
F men, without even a name! Jb 30:8
f and the senseless also pass Ps 49:10
and a **f** people has insulted Your Ps 74:18
not let them go back to **f** ways. Ps 85:8
is **f** to spread a net where any Pr 1:17
How long, **f** ones, will you love Pr 1:22
common sense, you who are **f**. Pr 8:5
father, but a **f** son, heartache Pr 10:1
but **f** lips will be destroyed. Pr 10:8
and **f** lips will be destroyed. Pr 10:10
but a **f** heart publicizes Pr 12:23
but a **f** one tears it down with Pr 14:1
Stay away from a **f** man; Pr 14:7
but a **f** one despises his mother. Pr 15:20
A **f** son is grief to his father Pr 17:25
A **f** son is his father's ruin, Pr 19:13
but a **f** man consumes them. Pr 21:20
A **f** scheme is sin, and a mocker Pr 24:9
the **f** keep going and are Pr 27:12
If you have been **f** by exalting Pr 30:32
than an old but **f** king who no Ec 4:13
wicked, and don't be **f**. Ec 7:17
They are **f** children, without Jr 4:22
you **f** and senseless people. Jr 5:21
They are both senseless and **f**, Jr 10:8
Woe to the **f** prophets who follow Ezk 13:3
the equipment of a **f** shepherd. Zch 11:15
will be like a **f** man who built Mt 7:26
of them were **f** and five were Mt 25:2
When the **f** took their lamps, Mt 25:3
But the **f** ones said to the Mt 25:8
his estate in **f** living. Lk 15:13
both to the wise and the **f**. Rm 1:14
God made the world's wisdom **f**? 1Co 1:20
the world's **f** things to shame 1Co 1:27
he must become **f** so that he can 1Co 3:18
F one! What you sow does not 1Co 15:36
You **f** Galatians! Who has Gl 3:1
Are you so **f**? After beginning Gl 3:3
coarse and **f** talking or crude Eph 5:4
So don't be **f**, but understand Eph 5:17
and many **f** and harmful desires, 1Tm 6:9
But reject **f** and ignorant 2Tm 2:23
we too were once **f**, disobedient, Ti 3:3
avoid **f** debates, genealogies, Ti 3:9
F man! Are you willing to learn Jms 2:20
the ignorance of **f** people. 1Pt 2:15

FOOLISHLY *(6)*
my daughters. You have acted **f**. Gn 31:28
this sin we have so **f** committed. Nm 12:11
A quick-tempered man acts **f**, Pr 14:17
diviners, and they will act **f**. Jr 50:36
speak as the Lord would, but **f**. 2Co 11:17
I am talking **f**—I also dare: 2Co 11:21

FOOLISHNESS *(29)*
counsel of Ahithophel into **f**!" 2Sm 15:31
He charges His angels with **f**, Jb 4:18
and festering because of my **f**. Ps 38:5
God, You know my **f**, and my Ps 69:5
gullible inherit **f**, but the Pr 14:18
but the **f** of fools produces Pr 14:24
foolishness of fools produces **f**. Pr 14:24
a quick-tempered one promotes **f**. Pr 14:29
the mouth of fools blurts out **f**. Pr 15:2
the mouth of fools feeds on **f**. Pr 15:14
F brings joy to one without Pr 15:21
her cubs than a fool in his **f**. Pr 17:12
this is **f** and disgrace for him. Pr 18:13
A man's own **f** leads him astray, Pr 19:3
F is tangled up in the heart of Pr 22:15
a fool according to his **f**, Pr 26:4
a fool according to his **f**, Pr 26:5
vomit, so a fool repeats his **f**. Pr 26:11
not separate his **f** from him. Pr 27:22
For a fool speaks **f** and his mind Is 32:6
and makes their knowledge **f**; Is 44:25
blasphemy, pride, and **f**. Mk 7:22
the message of the cross is **f**, 1Co 1:18
through the **f** of the message 1Co 1:21
the Jews and **f** to the Gentiles 1Co 1:23
because God's **f** is wiser than 1Co 1:25
Spirit, because it is **f** to him; 1Co 2:14
of this world is **f** with God, 1Co 3:19
put up with a little **f** from me. 2Co 11:1

FOOLS *(37)*
do not make me the taunt of **f**. Ps 39:8
the insults that **f** bring against Ps 74:22
F, when will you be wise? Ps 94:8
F suffered affliction because of Ps 107:17
f despise wisdom and instruction. Pr 1:7
and ⌊you⌋ **f** hate knowledge? Pr 1:22
complacency of **f** will destroy Pr 1:32
but He holds up **f** to dishonor. Pr 3:35
but **f** die for lack of sense. Pr 10:21
but **f** hate to turn from evil. Pr 13:19
a companion of **f** will suffer Pr 13:20
stupidity of **f** deceives ⌊them⌋ Pr 14:8
F mock at making restitution, Pr 14:9
the foolishness of **f** produces Pr 14:24
she is known even among **f**. Pr 14:33
but the mouth of **f** blurts out Pr 15:2
but not so the heart of **f**. Pr 15:7
but the mouth of **f** feeds on Pr 15:14
folly is the instruction of **f**. Pr 16:22
and beatings for the backs of **f**. Pr 19:29
and a rod for the backs of **f**. Pr 26:3
to offer the sacrifice as **f** do, Ec 5:1
He does not delight in **f**. Ec 5:4
but the heart of **f** is in a house Ec 7:4
than to listen to the song of **f**. Ec 7:5
anger abides in the heart of **f**. Ec 7:9
the shouts of a ruler over **f**. Ec 9:17
The struggles of **f** weary them, Ec 10:15
princes of Zoan are complete **f**; Is 19:11
The princes of Zoan have been **f**; Is 19:13
and makes **f** of diviners; Is 44:25
My people are **f**; they do not Jr 4:22
Blind **f**! For which is greater, Mt 23:17
F! Didn't He who made the Lk 11:40
to be wise, they became **f** Rm 1:22
We are **f** for Christ, but you are 1Co 4:10
put up with **f** since you are so 2Co 11:19

FOOT *(85)*
no resting place for her **f**. Gn 8:9
his hand or **f** in all the land Gn 41:44
about 600,000 soldiers on **f**, Ex 12:37
stood at the **f** of the mountain. Ex 19:17
hand for hand, **f** for foot, Ex 21:24
hand for hand, foot for **f**, Ex 21:24
on the big toe of his right **f**. Lv 8:23
on the big toe of his right **f**. Lv 14:14
on the big toe of his right **f**, Lv 14:17
on the big toe of his right **f**. Lv 14:25
on the big toe of his right **f**, Lv 14:28
man who has a broken **f** or hand, Lv 21:19
people with 600,000 **f** soldiers, Nm 11:21
let us travel through on **f**." Nm 20:19
squeezing Balaam's **f** against it. Nm 22:25
the land on which he has set **f**, Dt 1:36
Only let us travel through on **f**, Dt 2:28
the sole of your **f** treads will Dt 11:24
in all the land where you set **f**, Dt 11:25
hand for hand, and **f** for foot. Dt 19:21
hand for hand, and foot for **f**. Dt 19:21
remove his sandal from his **f**, Dt 25:9
the sole of your **f** to the top of Dt 28:35
the sole of her **f** on the ground Dt 28:56
place for the sole of your **f**. Dt 28:65
In time their **f** will slip, Dt 32:35
and dip his **f** in ⌊olive⌋ oil. Dt 33:24
where the sole of your **f** treads, Jos 1:3
the Hivites at the **f** of Hermon Jos 11:3
Lebanon at the **f** of Mount Hermon Jos 11:17
where you have set **f** will be an Jos 14:9
to the **f** of the hill that Jos 18:16
left his chariot and fled on **f**. Jdg 4:15
Sisera had fled on **f** to the tent Jdg 4:17
400,000 armed **f** soldiers. Jdg 20:2
the Israelite **f** soldiers fell. 1Sm 4:10
200,000 **f** soldiers and 10,000 1Sm 15:4
and 20,000 **f** soldiers from him, 2Sm 8:4
hired 20,000 **f** soldiers from 2Sm 10:6
and 40,000 **f** soldiers. 2Sm 10:18
the sole of his **f** to the top of 2Sm 14:25
hand and six toes on each **f**— 2Sm 21:20
100,000 **f** soldiers in one day. 1Kg 20:29
and 10,000 **f** soldiers, because 2Kg 13:7
and 20,000 **f** soldiers from him 1Ch 18:4
and 40,000 **f** soldiers. 1Ch 19:18
hand⌋ and six toes ⌊on each **f**⌋— 1Ch 20:6
the sole of his **f** to the top of Jb 2:7
falsehood or my **f** has rushed to Jb 31:5
forgets that a **f** may crush them Jb 39:15
their **f** is caught in the net Ps 9:15
My **f** stands on level ground; Ps 26:12
Do not let the **f** of the arrogant Ps 36:11
and they crossed the river on **f**. Ps 66:6
so that your **f** may wade in blood Ps 68:23
strike your **f** against a stone Ps 91:12
If I say, "My **f** is slipping," Ps 94:18
will not allow your **f** to slip; Ps 121:3
them or set **f** on their path, Pr 1:15
your **f** will not stumble. Pr 3:23
will keep your **f** from a snare. Pr 3:26
Don't set **f** on the path of the Pr 4:14
Seldom set **f** in your neighbor's Pr 25:17
a rotten tooth or a faltering **f**. Pr 25:19
the sole of the **f** even to the Is 1:6
people walk through on **f**. Is 11:15
No human **f** will pass through it, Ezk 29:11
no animal **f** will pass through Ezk 29:11
human **f** will churn them again, Ezk 32:13
the 35 ⌊**f** space⌋ belonging Ezk 42:3
that I could not cross ⌊on **f**⌋. Ezk 47:5
could not be crossed ⌊on **f**⌋. Ezk 47:5
who is⌋ swift of **f** will not save Am 2:15
and strip ⌊him⌋ from **f** to neck. Hab 3:13
strike your **f** against a stone. Mt 4:6
Him on **f** from the towns. Mt 14:13
your hand or your **f** causes your Mt 18:8
him up hand and **f**, and throw him Mt 22:13
And if your **f** causes your Mk 9:45
strike your **f** against a stone. Lk 4:11
bound hand and **f** with linen Jn 11:44
it, not even a **f** of ground, but Ac 7:5
the first day I set **f** in Asia, Ac 20:18
the **f** should say, "Because I'm 1Co 12:15
He put his right **f** on the sea, Rv 10:2

FOOTHILLS *(17)*
in the Judean **f**, and all along Jos 9:1
the Judean **f**, and the slopes Jos 10:40
the Judean **f**, and the Slopes of Jos 11:2
Goshen, the Judean **f**, the plain, Jos 11:16
of Israel with its Judean **f**— Jos 11:16
the Judean **f**, the plain, Jos 12:8
In the Judean **f**: Eshtaol, Zorah, Jos 15:33
the Negev, and the Judean **f**. Jdg 1:9
as sycamore in the Judean **f**. 1Kg 10:27
as sycamore in the Judean **f**. 2Ch 1:15
as sycamore in the Judean **f**. 2Ch 9:27
of the Judean **f** and the Negev 2Ch 28:18
Benjamin and from the Judean **f**, Jr 17:26
the cities of the Judean **f**, Jr 32:44
the cities of the Judean **f**, Jr 33:13
from⌋ the Judean **f** will possess Ob 19
the Judean **f** were inhabited?" Zch 7:7

FOOTING *(1)*
in deep mud, and there is no **f**; Ps 69:2

FOOTPRINTS *(2)*
waters, but Your **f** were unseen. Ps 77:19
tracked with bloody **f**. Hs 6:8

FOOTSTEPS *(2)*
follow in the **f** of the faith our Rm 4:12
same spirit and in the same **f**? 2Co 12:18

FOREIGNER *(65)*

FOREIGNER'S *(2)*

FOREIGNERS *(57)*

FOREKNEW *(2)*

FOREKNOWLEDGE *(2)*

FOREMAN *(1)*

FOREMEN *(5)*

FOREMOST *(1)*

FORERUNNER *(1)*

FORESAIL *(1)*

FORESAW *(1)*

FORESIGHT *(1)*

FORESKIN *(8)*

FORESKINS *(3)*

FOREST *(50)*

FORESTED *(1)*

FORESTS *(3)*
fortresses and towers in the **f**. 2Ch 27:4
glory of its **f** and orchards as Is 10:18
or cut ⌊it⌋ down from the **f**, Ezk 39:10

FORETOLD *(2)*
by faith and **f** the good news to Gl 3:8
the words **f** by the apostles Jd 17

FOREVER *(316)*
of life, and eat, and live **f**." Gn 3:22
will not remain with mankind **f**, Gn 6:3
your offspring **f** all the land Gn 13:15
I will be guilty before you **f**. Gn 43:9
This is My name **f**; this is how I Ex 3:15
The LORD will reign **f** and ever! Ex 15:18
is a sign **f** between Me and the Ex 31:17
they will inherit ⌊it⌋ **f**.' " Ex 32:13
their children will prosper **f**. Dt 5:29
after you may prosper **f**, Dt 12:28
must remain a mound of ruins **f**; Dt 13:16
you and your descendants **f**. Dt 28:46
belong to us and our children **f**, Dt 29:29
As surely as I live **f**, Dt 32:40
for you and your descendants **f**, Jos 14:9
house would walk before Me **f**, 1Sm 2:30
to judge his family **f** because of 1Sm 3:13
a witness between you and me **f**." 1Sm 20:23
offspring and your offspring **f**." 1Sm 20:42
he will be my servant **f**." 1Sm 27:12
Must the sword devour **f**? 2Sm 2:26
my kingdom are **f** innocent before 2Sm 3:28
the throne of his kingdom **f**. 2Sm 7:13
kingdom will endure before Me **f**, 2Sm 7:16
will be established **f**.' " 2Sm 7:16
people Israel Your own people **f**, 2Sm 7:24
the promise **f** that You have made 2Sm 7:25
Your name will be exalted **f**, 2Sm 7:26
it will continue before You **f**. 2Sm 7:29
house will be blessed **f**." 2Sm 7:29
to David and his descendants **f**. 2Sm 22:51
"May my lord King David live **f**!" 1Kg 1:31
the head of his descendants **f**, 1Kg 2:33
will be peace from the LORD **f**." 1Kg 2:33
established before the LORD **f**." 1Kg 2:45
a place for Your dwelling **f**. 1Kg 8:13
built, to put My name there **f**; 1Kg 9:3
your royal throne over Israel **f**, 1Kg 9:5
unfaithfulness⌋, but not **f**.' " 1Kg 11:39
they will be your servants **f**." 1Kg 12:7
to you and your descendants **f**." 2Kg 5:27
lamp to David and to his sons **f**. 2Kg 8:19
My name **f** in this temple 2Kg 21:7
and to minister before Him **f**." 1Ch 15:2
His covenant **f**—the promise He 1Ch 16:15
His faithful love endures **f**. 1Ch 16:34
for His faithful love endures **f**. 1Ch 16:41
I will establish his throne **f**. 1Ch 17:12
My house and My kingdom **f**, 1Ch 17:14
will be established **f**.' " 1Ch 17:14
people Israel Your own people **f**, 1Ch 17:22
and his house be confirmed **f**, 1Ch 17:23
and magnified **f** in the saying, 1Ch 17:24
it may continue before You **f**. 1Ch 17:27
it, and it is blessed **f**." 1Ch 17:27
of his kingdom over Israel **f**.' 1Ch 22:10
set apart **f** to consecrate the 1Ch 23:13
blessings in His name **f**. 1Ch 23:13
has come to stay in Jerusalem **f**. 1Ch 23:25
to be king over Israel **f**. 1Ch 28:4
his kingdom **f** if he perseveres 1Ch 28:7
to your descendants **f**. 1Ch 28:8
Him, He will reject you **f**. 1Ch 28:9
this desire **f** in the thoughts 1Ch 29:18
This is ⌊ordained⌋ for Israel **f**. 2Ch 2:4
His faithful love endures **f**; 2Ch 5:13
a place for Your residence **f**. 2Ch 6:2
for His faithful love endures **f**. 2Ch 7:3
His faithful love endures **f**"— 2Ch 7:6
so that My name may be there **f**; 2Ch 7:16
enough to establish them **f**, 2Ch 9:8
they will be your servants **f**." 2Ch 10:7
his descendants **f** by a covenant 2Ch 13:5
and who gave it **f** to the 2Ch 20:7
for His faithful love endures **f**. 2Ch 20:21
lamp to David and to his sons **f**. 2Ch 21:7
that He has consecrated **f**. 2Ch 30:8
is where My name will remain **f**." 2Ch 33:4
My name **f** in this temple 2Ch 33:7
love to Israel endures **f**." Ezr 3:11
an inheritance to your sons **f**." Ezr 9:12
the king, "May the king live **f**! Neh 2:3
they perish **f** while no one Jb 4:20
will not live **f**. Leave me alone Jb 7:16
in stone **f** by an iron stylus Jb 19:24
he will vanish **f** like his own Jb 20:7
I would escape from my Judge **f**. Jb 23:7
He seats them **f** with enthroned Jb 36:7
you can take him as a slave **f**? Jb 41:4
let them shout for joy **f**. Ps 5:11
erased their name **f** and ever. Ps 9:5
But the LORD sits enthroned **f**; Ps 9:7
the afflicted will not perish **f**. Ps 9:18
The LORD is King **f** and ever; Ps 10:16
us from this generation **f**. Ps 12:7
to David and his descendants **f**. Ps 18:50
of the LORD is pure, enduring **f**; Ps 19:9
length of days **f** and ever. Ps 21:4
You give him blessings **f**; Ps 21:6
May your hearts live **f**! Ps 22:26
shepherd them, and carry them **f**. Ps 28:9
the LORD sits enthroned, King **f**. Ps 29:10
my God, I will praise You **f**. Ps 30:12
counsel of the LORD stands **f**, Ps 33:11
their inheritance will last **f**. Ps 37:18
what is good, and dwell there **f**. Ps 37:27
are kept safe **f**, but the Ps 37:28
and set me in Your presence **f**. Ps 41:12
we will praise Your name **f**. Ps 44:8
Get up! Don't reject us **f**! Ps 44:23
Therefore God has blessed you **f**. Ps 45:2
Your throne, God, is **f** and ever; Ps 45:6
will praise you **f** and ever. Ps 45:17
God will establish it **f**. Ps 48:8
This God, our God **f** and ever— Ps 48:14
one should **f** stop trying— Ps 49:8
that he may live **f** and not see Ps 49:9
why God will bring you down **f**. Ps 52:5
God's faithful love **f** and ever. Ps 52:8
will praise You **f** for what You Ps 52:9
in Your tent **f** and take refuge Ps 61:4
he sit enthroned before God **f**; Ps 61:7
He rules **f** by His might; Ps 66:7
The LORD will live ⌊there⌋ **f**! Ps 68:16
May his name endure **f**; Ps 72:17
His glorious name be praised **f**; Ps 72:19
of my heart, my portion **f**. Ps 73:26
Why have You rejected ⌊us⌋ **f**, Ps 74:1
the enemy insult Your name **f**? Ps 74:10
the lives of Your poor people **f**. Ps 74:19
for me, I will tell about Him **f**; Ps 75:9
Lord reject **f** and never again Ps 77:7
Has His faithful love ceased **f**? Ps 77:8
the earth that He established **f**. Ps 78:69
Will You be angry **f**? Ps 79:5
Your pasture, will thank You **f**; Ps 79:13
their doom would last **f**. Ps 81:15
be put to shame and terrified **f**; Ps 83:17
Will You be angry with us **f**? Ps 85:5
and will honor Your name **f**. Ps 86:12
the LORD's faithful love **f**; Ps 89:1
Faithful love is built up **f**; Ps 89:2
your offspring **f** and build up Ps 89:4
I will establish his line **f**, Ps 89:29
His offspring will continue **f**, Ps 89:36
moon, established **f**, a faithful Ps 89:37
Will You hide Yourself **f**? Ps 89:46
May the LORD be praised **f**. Ps 89:52
But You, LORD, are exalted **f**. Ps 92:8
But You, LORD, are enthroned **f**; Ps 102:12
accuse ⌊us⌋ or be angry **f**. Ps 103:9
the glory of the LORD endure **f**; Ps 104:31
He **f** remembers His covenant, Ps 105:8
His faithful love endures **f**. Ps 106:1
His faithful love endures **f**. Ps 107:1
F, You are a priest like Ps 110:4
His righteousness endures **f**. Ps 111:3
He remembers His covenant **f**. Ps 111:5
They are established **f** and ever, Ps 111:8
He has ordained His covenant **f**. Ps 111:9
His praise endures **f**. Ps 111:10
and his righteousness endures **f**. Ps 112:3
righteous will be remembered **f**. Ps 112:6
his righteousness endures **f**. Ps 112:9
LORD be praised both now and **f**. Ps 113:2
praise the LORD, both now and **f**. Ps 115:18
LORD's faithfulness endures **f**. Ps 117:2
His faithful love endures **f**. Ps 118:1
"His faithful love endures **f**." Ps 118:2
"His faithful love endures **f**." Ps 118:3
"His faithful love endures **f**." Ps 118:4
His faithful love endures **f**. Ps 118:29
keep Your law, **f** and ever. Ps 119:44
LORD, Your word is **f**; Ps 119:89
Your decrees as a heritage **f**; Ps 119:111
Your decrees are righteous **f**. Ps 119:144
You have established them **f**. Ps 119:152
righteous judgments endure **f**. Ps 119:160
coming and going both now and **f**. Ps 121:8
cannot be shaken; it remains **f**. Ps 125:1
His people, both now and **f**. Ps 125:2
in the LORD, both now and **f**. Ps 131:3
also sit on your throne, **f**." Ps 132:12
This is My resting place **f**; Ps 132:14
name ⌊endures⌋ **f**, Your Ps 135:13
and praise Your name **f** and ever. Ps 145:1
will honor Your name **f** and ever. Ps 145:2
praise His holy name **f** and ever. Ps 145:21
He remains faithful **f**, Ps 146:6
LORD reigns **f**; Zion, your God Ps 146:10
set them in position **f** and ever; Ps 148:6
be lost in her love **f**. Pr 5:19
but the righteous are secure **f**. Pr 10:25
lips endure **f**, but a lying Pr 12:19
for wealth is not **f**; Pr 27:24
throne will be established **f**. Pr 29:14
comes, but the earth remains **f**. Ec 1:4
that all God does will last **f**; Ec 3:14
righteousness from now on and **f**. Is 9:7
will sit on the throne **f**. Is 16:5
He will destroy death **f**. Is 25:8
in the LORD **f**, because in Yah, Is 26:4
be for the future, **f** and ever. Is 30:8
will become barren places **f**, Is 32:14
will be quiet confidence **f**. Is 32:17
Its smoke will go up **f**. Is 34:10
will pass through it **f** and ever. Is 34:10
They will possess it **f**; Is 34:17
the word of our God remains **f**." Is 40:8
I will be the mistress **f**. Is 47:7
But My salvation will last **f**, Is 51:6
My righteousness will last **f**, Is 51:8
and Exalted One who lives **f**, Is 57:15
For I will not accuse ⌊you⌋ **f**, Is 57:16
now on and **f**," says the LORD Is 59:21
they will possess the land **f**; Is 60:21
or remember ⌊our⌋ iniquity **f**. Is 64:9
glad and rejoice **f** in what I am Is 65:18
Will He bear a grudge **f**? Jr 3:5
I will not be angry **f**. Jr 3:12
to your ancestors **f** and ever. Jr 7:7
anger on fire; it will burn **f**. Jr 17:4
This city will be inhabited **f**. Jr 17:25
a derision, and ruins **f**. Jr 25:9
and I will make it a ruin **f**. Jr 25:12
to be a nation before Me **f**. Jr 31:36
love endures **f** as they bring Jr 33:11
her cities will become ruins **f**." Jr 49:13
a jackals' den, a desolation **f**. Jr 49:33
you will become desolate **f**. Jr 51:26
fall asleep **f** and never wake Jr 51:39
fall asleep **f** and never wake Jr 51:57
it will remain desolate **f**.' Jr 51:62
the Lord will not reject ⌊us⌋ **f**. Lm 3:31
You, LORD, are enthroned **f**; Lm 5:19
Why have You forgotten us **f**, Lm 5:20
will live in it **f** with their Ezk 37:25
David will be their prince **f**. Ezk 37:25
set My sanctuary among them **f**. Ezk 37:26
My sanctuary is among them **f**, Ezk 37:28
dwell among the Israelites **f**. Ezk 43:7
and I will dwell among them **f**. Ezk 43:9
May the king live **f**. Dn 2:4
of God be praised **f** and ever, Dn 2:20
end, but will itself endure **f**. Dn 2:44
May the king live **f**. Dn 3:9
and glorified Him who lives **f**: Dn 4:34
"May the king live **f**," she said. Dn 5:10
to him, "May King Darius live **f**. Dn 6:6
May the king live **f**. Dn 6:21
living God, and He endures **f**; Dn 6:26
the kingdom and possess it **f**, Dn 7:18
it forever, yes, **f** and ever.' Dn 7:18
to be completely destroyed **f**. Dn 7:26
like the stars **f** and ever. Dn 12:3
I will take you to be My wife **f**. Hs 2:19

But Judah will be inhabited f, Jl 3:20
and destroyed f because of Ob 10
prison bars closed behind me f! Jnh 2:6
blessing from their children f. Mc 2:9
of Yahweh our God f and ever. Mc 4:5
Zion from this time on and f. Mc 4:7
does not hold on to His anger f, Mc 7:18
And do the prophets live f? Zch 1:5
people the LORD has cursed f. Mal 1:4
and the power and the glory f. Mt 6:13
reign over the house of Jacob f, Lk 1:33
Abraham and his descendants f. Lk 1:55
of this bread he will live f. Jn 6:51
eats this bread will live f." Jn 6:58
not remain in the household f, Jn 8:35
but a son does remain f. Jn 8:35
that the Messiah will remain f. Jn 12:34
Counselor to be with you f. Jn 14:16
the Creator, who is blessed f. Rm 1:25
who is God over all, blessed f. Rm 9:5
To Him be the glory f. Rm 11:36
Christ—to Him be the glory f! Rm 16:27
His righteousness endures f. 2Co 9:9
to whom be the glory f and ever. Gl 1:5
to all generations, f and ever. Eph 3:21
and Father be glory f and ever. Php 4:20
be honor and glory f and ever. 1Tm 1:17
To Him be the glory f and ever! 2Tm 4:18
throne, O God, is f and ever, Heb 1:8
You are a priest f in the order Heb 5:6
a "high priest f in the order Heb 6:20
Son of God—remains a priest f. Heb 7:3
You are a priest f in the order Heb 7:17
His mind, You are a priest f. Heb 7:21
He remains f, He holds His Heb 7:24
a Son, who has been perfected f. Heb 7:28
one sacrifice for sins f, Heb 10:12
He has perfected f those who are Heb 10:14
same yesterday, today, and f. Heb 13:8
to whom be glory f and ever. Heb 13:21
the word of the Lord endures f. 1Pt 1:25
glory and the power f and ever. 1Pt 4:11
To Him be the dominion f. 1Pt 5:11
who does God's will remains f. 1Jn 2:17
in us and will be with us f. 2Jn 2
the blackness of darkness f! Jd 13
before all time, now, and f. Jd 25
glory and dominion f and ever. Rv 1:6
I am alive f and ever, and I Rv 1:18
the One who lives f and ever, Rv 4:9
the One who lives f and ever, Rv 4:10
and to the Lamb, f and ever! Rv 5:13
be to our God f and ever. Rv 7:12
by the One who lives f and ever, Rv 10:6
and He will reign f and ever! Rv 11:15
torment will go up f and ever. Rv 14:11
of God who lives f and ever. Rv 15:7
Her smoke ascends f and ever! Rv 19:3
day and night f and ever. Rv 20:10
And they will reign f and ever. Rv 22:5

FOREVERMORE (1)
appointed the blessing—life f. Ps 133:3

FOREWARNED (1)
you have been f, be on your 2Pt 3:17

FORFEIT (2)
to escape ⌊will f⌋ his life for 2Kg 10:24
three days would f all his Ezr 10:8

FORFEITS (1)
world, yet loses or f himself? Lk 9:25

FORGAVE (7)
You were a God who f them, Ps 99:8
him, and f him the loan. Mt 18:27
f you all that debt because you Mt 18:32
he graciously f them both. Lk 7:42
"I suppose the one he f more." Lk 7:43
as God also f you in Christ. Eph 4:32
alive with Him and f us all our Col 2:13

FORGE (1)
F the chain, for the land is Ezk 7:23

FORGET (55)
has made me f all my hardship Gn 41:51
that you don't f the things your Dt 4:9
Be careful not to f the covenant Dt 4:23
or f the covenant with your Dt 4:31
be careful not to f the LORD who Dt 6:12
that you don't f the LORD your Dt 8:11
proud and you f the LORD your Dt 8:14
If you ever f the LORD your God Dt 8:19
and do not f how you provoked Dt 9:7
Do not f the Levite within your Dt 14:27
and you f a sheaf in the field, Dt 24:19
from under heaven. Do not f. Dt 25:19
remember and not f me, and give 1Sm 1:11
not f the covenant that I have 2Kg 17:38
is the destiny of all who f God; Jb 8:13
I said, "I will f my complaint, Jb 9:27
For you will f your suffering, Jb 11:16
He does not f the cry of the Ps 9:12
all the nations that f God. Ps 9:17
Do not f the afflicted. Ps 10:12
long will You continually f me? Ps 13:1
Yourself and f our affliction Ps 44:24
f your people and your father's Ps 45:10
this, you who f God, or I will Ps 50:22
otherwise, my people will f. Ps 59:11
do not f the lives of Your poor Ps 74:19
Do not f the clamor of Your Ps 74:23
in God and not f God's works, Ps 78:7
I even f to eat my food. Ps 102:4
and do not f all His benefits. Ps 103:2
I will not f Your word. Ps 119:16
around me, I did not f Your law. Ps 119:61
smoke, I do not f Your statutes. Ps 119:83
I will never f Your precepts, Ps 119:93
yet I do not f Your instruction. Ps 119:109
because my foes f Your words. Ps 119:139
but I do not f Your precepts. Ps 119:141
for I do not f Your commands. Ps 119:176
If I f you, Jerusalem, may my Ps 137:5
may my right hand f ⌊its skill⌋. Ps 137:5
My son, don't f my teaching, but Pr 3:1
don't f or turn away from the Pr 4:5
will drink, f what is decreed Pr 31:5
so that he can f his poverty Pr 31:7
Can a woman f her nursing child, Is 49:15
Even if these f, yet I will not Is 49:15
forget, yet I will not f you. Is 49:15
For you will f the shame of your Is 54:4
LORD, who f My holy mountain, Is 65:11
Can a young woman f her jewelry Jr 2:32
My people to f My name as their Jr 23:27
I will surely f you and throw Jr 23:39
God, I will also f your sons. Hs 4:6
I will never f all their deeds. Am 8:7
He will not f your work and the Heb 6:10

FORGETFUL (1)
and is not a f hearer but a doer Jms 1:25

FORGETS (5)
from you and he f what you have Gn 27:45
The womb f them; worms feed on Jb 24:20
She f that a foot may crush them Jb 39:15
of her youth and f the covenant Pr 2:17
right away f what kind of man Jms 1:24

FORGETTING (1)
f what is behind and reaching Php 3:13

FORGIVE (67)
and perhaps he will f me." Gn 32:20
Please f your brothers' Gn 50:17
please f the transgression of Gn 50:17
Please f my sin once more and Ex 10:17
because He will not f your acts Ex 23:21
if You would only f their sin. Ex 32:32
people, f our wrongdoing Ex 34:9
made, and the LORD will f her. Nm 30:8
but you must f whatever your Dt 15:3
f Your people Israel You Dt 21:8
will not be willing to f him. Dt 29:20
please f my sin and return with 1Sm 15:25
Please f your servant's offense, 1Sm 25:28
in heaven. May You hear and f. 1Kg 8:30
in heaven and f the sin of Your 1Kg 8:34
in heaven and f the sin of Your 1Kg 8:36
and may You f, act, and repay 1Kg 8:39
May You f Your people who sinned 1Kg 8:50
blood, and the LORD would not f. 2Kg 24:4
in heaven. May You hear and f. 2Ch 6:21
in heaven and f the sin of Your 2Ch 6:25
in heaven and f the sin of Your 2Ch 6:27
and may You f and repay the man 2Ch 6:30
May You f Your people who sinned 2Ch 6:39
hear from heaven, f their sin, 2Ch 7:14
Why not f my sin and pardon my Jb 7:21
Your name, LORD, f my sin, for Ps 25:11
kind and ready to f, abundant in Ps 86:5
man is humbled. Do not f them! Is 2:9
our God, for He will freely f. Is 55:7
be faithful, then I will f her. Jr 5:1
should I f you? Your children Jr 5:7
For I will f their wrongdoing Jr 31:34
and I will f all the wrongs they Jr 33:8
Then I will f their wrongdoing Jr 36:3
for I will f those I leave as a Jr 50:20
Lord, hear! Lord, f! Lord, Dn 9:19
F all ⌊our⌋ sin and accept what Hs 14:2
I said, "Lord GOD, please f! Am 7:2
And f us our debts, as we also Mt 6:12
For if you f people their Mt 6:14
Father will f you as well. Mt 6:14
But if you don't f people, Mt 6:15
will not f your wrongdoing Mt 6:15
authority on earth to f sins"— Mt 9:6
sin against me and I f him? Mt 18:21
of you does not f his brother Mt 18:35
Who can f sins but God alone?" Mk 2:7
authority on earth to f sins," Mk 2:10
against anyone, f him, so that Mk 11:25
heaven will also f you your Mk 11:25
But if you don't f, neither will Mk 11:26
in heaven f your wrongdoing. Mk 11:26
Who can f sins but God alone?" Lk 5:21
authority on earth to f sins"— Lk 5:24
F, and you will be forgiven. Lk 6:37
And f us our sins, for we Lk 11:4
ourselves also f everyone in Lk 11:4
him, and if he repents, f him. Lk 17:3
I repent,' you must f him." Lk 17:4
said, "Father, f them, because Lk 23:34
If you f the sins of any, they Jn 20:23
now you should f and comfort him 2Co 2:7
Now to whom you f anything, 2Co 2:10
not burden you? F me this wrong! 2Co 12:13
you, so also you must ⌊f⌋. Col 3:13
and righteous to f us our sins 1Jn 1:9

FORGIVEN (44)
behalf, and they will be f. Lv 4:20
person's sin, and he will be f. Lv 4:26
on his behalf, and he will be f. Lv 4:31
has committed, and he will be f. Lv 4:35
has committed, and he will be f. Lv 5:10
these cases, and he will be f. Lv 5:13
offering, and he will be f. Lv 5:16
and he will be f. Lv 5:18
and he will be f for anything he Lv 6:7
and he will be f for the sin he Lv 19:22
as You have f them from Egypt Nm 14:19
community so that they may be f, Nm 15:25
resides among them will be f, Nm 15:26
atonement for him, he will be f. Nm 15:28
one whose transgression is f, Ps 32:1
will be f ⌊their⌋ iniquity. Is 33:24
and rebelled; You have not f. Lm 3:42
as we also have f our debtors. Mt 6:12
courage, son, your sins are f." Mt 9:2
sins are f,' or to say, 'Get Mt 9:5
people will be f every sin and Mt 12:31
the Spirit will not be f. Mt 12:31
Son of Man, it will be f him. Mt 12:32
it will not be f him, either in Mt 12:32
Son, your sins are f." Mk 2:5
sins are f,' or to say, 'Get Mk 2:9
People will be f for all sins Mk 3:28
might turn back—and be f." Mk 4:12
Friend, your sins are f you." Lk 5:20
sins are f you,' or to say, Lk 5:23
Forgive, and you will be f. Lk 6:37
her many sins have been f; Lk 7:47
But the one who is f little, Lk 7:47
said to her, "Your sins are f." Lk 7:48
the Son of Man will be f, Lk 12:10
the Holy Spirit will not be f. Lk 12:10
sins of any, they are f them; Jn 20:23
of your heart may be f you. Ac 8:22
lawless acts are f and whose Rm 4:7
For what I have f, if I have 2Co 2:10
if I have f anything, it is for 2Co 2:10
Just as the Lord has f you, Col 3:13
committed sins, he will be f. Jms 5:15
sins have been f on account of 1Jn 2:12

FORGIVENESS (17)
You there is f, so that You may Ps 130:4
Compassion and f belong to the Dn 9:9

shed for many for the **f** of sins. Mt 26:28
of repentance for the **f** of sins. Mk 1:4
the Holy Spirit never has **f**, Mk 3:29
through the **f** of their sins. Lk 1:77
of repentance for the **f** of sins, Lk 3:3
repentance for **f** of sins would Lk 24:47
Messiah for the **f** of your sins, Ac 2:38
to Israel, and **f** of sins. Ac 5:31
in Him will receive **f** of sins." Ac 10:43
this man **f** of sins is being Ac 13:38
they may receive **f** of sins and a Ac 26:18
His blood, the **f** of our Eph 1:7
have redemption, the **f** of sins. Col 1:14
shedding of blood there is no **f**. Heb 9:22
Now where there is **f** of these, Heb 10:18

FORGIVES *(2)*
He **f** all your sin; He heals all Ps 103:3
is this man who even **f** sins?" Lk 7:49

FORGIVING *(5)*
generations⌋, **f** wrongdoing, Ex 34:7
f wrongdoing and rebellion. Nm 14:18
You are a **f** God, gracious and Neh 9:17
to one another, **f** one another, Eph 4:32
one another and **f** one another if Col 3:13

FORGOT *(10)*
not remember Joseph; he **f** him. Gn 40:23
you **f** the God who brought you Dt 32:18
they **f** the LORD their God and Jdg 3:7
But they **f** the LORD their God, 1Sm 12:9
They **f** what He had done, the Ps 78:11
They soon **f** His works and would Ps 106:13
They **f** God their Savior, who did Ps 106:21
their fathers **f** My name through Jr 23:27
went after her lovers, but **f** Me. Hs 2:13
proud. Therefore they **f** Me. Hs 13:6

FORGOTTEN *(43)*
in the land of Egypt will be **f**. Gn 41:30
not violated or **f** Your commands. Dt 26:13
descendants will not have **f** it. Dt 31:21
and my close friends have **f** me. Jb 19:14
oppressed will not always be **f**; Ps 9:18
He says to himself, "God has **f**; Ps 10:11
I am **f**: gone from memory like a Ps 31:12
"When will he die and be **f**?" Ps 41:5
my rock, "Why have You **f** me? Ps 42:9
we have not **f** You or betrayed Ps 44:17
If we had **f** the name of our God Ps 44:20
Has God **f** to be gracious? Ps 77:9
for I have not **f** Your Ps 119:153
the days to come both will be **f**. Ec 2:16
because the memory of them is **f**. Ec 9:5
For you have **f** the God of your Is 17:10
Tyre will be **f** for 70 years— Is 23:15
the city, prostitute **f** ⌊by men⌋. Is 23:16
you will never be **f** by Me. Is 44:21
The Lord has **f** me!" Is 49:14
But you have **f** the LORD, your Is 51:13
troubles will be **f** and hidden Is 65:16
people have **f** Me for countless Jr 2:32
they have **f** the LORD their God. Jr 3:21
you have **f** Me and trusted Jr 13:25
Yet My people have **f** Me. Jr 18:15
that will never be **f**. Jr 20:11
that will never be **f**." Jr 23:40
All your lovers have **f** you; Jr 30:14
Have you **f** the evils of your Jr 44:9
covenant that will never be **f**. Jr 50:5
they have **f** their resting place. Jr 50:6
I have **f** what happiness is. Lm 3:17
Why have You **f** us forever, Lm 5:20
You have **f** Me." ⌊This is⌋ Ezk 22:12
Because you have **f** Me and cast Ezk 23:35
Since you have **f** the law of your Hs 4:6
Israel has **f** his Maker and built Hs 8:14
and they had **f** to take bread. Mt 16:5
They had **f** to take bread and had Mk 8:14
one of them is **f** in God's sight. Lk 12:6
And you have **f** the exhortation Heb 12:5
and has **f** the cleansing from his 2Pt 1:9

FORK *(6)*
meat **f** while the meat was 1Sm 2:13
whatever the meat **f** brought up. 1Sm 2:14
with winnowing shovel and **f**. Is 30:24
with a winnowing **f** at the gates Jr 15:7
signpost at the **f** in the road to Ezk 21:19
at the **f** of the two roads, Ezk 21:21

FORKS *(4)*
basins, meat **f**, and firepans; Ex 27:3
basins, meat **f**, and firepans; Ex 38:3
pure gold for the **f**, sprinkling 1Ch 28:17
shovels, the **f**, and all their 2Ch 4:16

FORM *(40)*
Whenever I **f** clouds over the Gn 9:14
he sees the **f** of the LORD. Nm 12:8
the words, but didn't see a **f**; Dt 4:12
did not see any **f** on the day the Dt 4:15
any figure: a male or female **f**, Dt 4:16
or the **f** of any beast on the Dt 4:17
an idol in the **f** of anything, Dt 4:25
I see a spirit **f** coming up out 1Sm 28:13
a **f** loomed before my eyes. Jb 4:16
the same God **f** us both in the Jb 31:15
my tongue will **f** words on my Jb 33:2
and their **f** will waste away in Ps 49:14
they **f** an alliance against You— Ps 83:5
day Israel will **f** a triple Is 19:24
I **f** light and create darkness, Is 45:7
and His **f** did not resemble a Is 52:14
He had no **f** or splendor that we Is 53:2
The **f** of four living creatures Ezk 1:5
appearance: They had human **f**. Ezk 1:5
The **f** of ⌊each of⌋ their faces Ezk 1:10
f of the living creatures was Ezk 1:13
and all four had the same **f**. Ezk 1:16
was a **f** with the appearance Ezk 1:26
appearance of the **f** of the Ezk 1:28
and there was a **f** that had the Ezk 8:2
wall was every **f** of detestable Ezk 8:10
to have the **f** of human hands Ezk 10:8
had the same **f**, like a wheel Ezk 10:10
with the **f** of human hands under Ezk 10:21
years they will **f** an alliance, Dn 11:6
in a different **f** to two of them Mk 16:12
and you haven't seen His **f**. Jn 5:37
down to us in the **f** of men!" Ac 14:11
its current **f** is passing away. 1Co 7:31
existing in the **f** of God, did Php 2:6
by assuming the **f** of a slave, Php 2:7
come as a man in His external **f**, Php 2:7
Stay away from every **f** of evil. 1Th 5:22
holding to the **f** of religion but 2Tm 3:5
not the actual **f** of those Heb 10:1

FORMATION *(28)*
the land of Egypt in battle **f**. Ex 13:18
man in battle **f** before the LORD, Nm 32:29
go across with you in battle **f**, Nm 32:30
over in battle **f** before the LORD Nm 32:32
over in battle **f** ahead of your Dt 3:18
over in battle **f** ahead of your Jos 1:14
went in battle **f** in front Jos 4:12
up in battle **f** against Israel, 1Sm 4:2
lined up in battle **f** to face the 1Sm 17:2
out to line up in battle **f**?" 1Sm 17:8
to its battle **f** shouting their 1Sm 17:20
up in battle **f** facing each other 1Sm 17:21
up in battle **f** at the entrance 2Sm 10:8
lined up in battle **f** to engage 2Sm 10:9
lined up in battle **f** to engage 2Sm 10:10
lined up in **f** to engage David 2Sm 10:17
assembled ⌊in **f**⌋ where there was 2Sm 23:11
up in battle **f**, came to Hebron 1Ch 12:38
up in battle **f** at the entrance 1Ch 19:9
lined up in battle **f** to engage 1Ch 19:10
lined up in battle **f** to engage 1Ch 19:11
up in battle **f** against them. 1Ch 19:17
men in battle **f** against him. 2Ch 13:3
up in battle **f** in the Valley 2Ch 14:10
men in battle **f** against you, Jr 6:23
line up in battle **f** against her; Jr 50:9
up in battle **f** around Babylon, Jr 50:14
men in battle **f** against you, Jr 50:42

FORMATIONS *(1)*
and shouted to the battle **f**: 1Sm 17:8

FORMED *(48)*
Then the LORD God **f** the man out Gn 2:7
He placed the man He had **f**. Gn 2:8
So the LORD God **f** out of the Gn 2:19
had sprouted, **f** buds, blossomed, Nm 17:8
they **f** a unified alliance to Jos 9:2
The Jordan **f** the border on the Jos 18:20
they **f** a single unit and took 2Sm 2:25
conspiracy was **f** against him in 2Kg 14:19
with the conspiracy that he **f**, 2Kg 15:15
the cherubim **f** a cover above 2Ch 5:8
Jehoshaphat **f** an alliance with 2Ch 20:36
Because you **f** an alliance with 2Ch 20:37
conspiracy was **f** against him in 2Ch 25:27
The Chaldeans **f** three bands, Jb 1:17
Your hands shaped me and **f** me. Jb 10:8
that You **f** me like clay. Jb 10:9
Ice is **f** by the breath of God, Jb 37:10
the One who **f** the eye not see? Ps 94:9
His hands **f** the dry land. Ps 95:5
which You **f** to play there. Ps 104:26
Your hands made me and **f** me; Ps 119:73
when I was **f** in the depths of Ps 139:15
I was **f** before ancient times, Pr 8:23
wonders, plans ⌊**f**⌋ long ago, Is 25:1
How can what is **f** say about the Is 29:16
say about the one who **f** it, Is 29:16
and the One who **f** you, Israel— Is 43:1
My glory. I have **f** him; indeed, Is 43:7
god was **f** before Me, and there Is 43:10
The people I **f** for Myself will Is 43:21
I **f** you, you are My servant; Is 44:21
Redeemer who **f** you from the womb Is 44:24
He **f** the earth and made it; Is 45:18
⌊but⌋ **f** it to be inhabited— Is 45:18
who **f** me from the womb to be His Is 49:5
No weapon **f** against you will Is 54:17
you before I **f** you in the womb; Jr 1:5
He is the One who **f** all things. Jr 10:16
He is the One who **f** all things. Jr 51:19
have been **f** into a yoke, Lm 1:14
breasts were **f** and your hair Ezk 16:7
and **f** the spirit of man within Zch 12:1
the marketplace and **f** a mob, Ac 17:5
Jews **f** a conspiracy and bound Ac 23:12
than 40 who had **f** this plot. Ac 23:13
Will what is **f** say to the one Rm 9:20
formed say to the one who **f** it, Rm 9:20
you until Christ is **f** in you. Gl 4:19

FORMER *(28)*
to replace the ⌊**f**⌋ ones and take Lv 14:42
fought against the **f** king of Nm 21:26
practicing the **f** customs to this 2Kg 17:34
practicing their **f** custom. 2Kg 17:40
he walked in the **f** ways of his 2Ch 17:3
and **f** acquaintances came to his Jb 42:11
where are the **f** acts of Your Ps 89:49
Why were the **f** days better than Ec 7:10
your advisers to their **f** state. Is 1:26
like that of the **f** times when He Is 9:1
this, and tell us the **f** things? Is 43:9
will restore the **f** devastations; Is 61:4
them fully for their **f** deeds." Is 65:7
For the **f** troubles will be Is 65:16
will rebuild them as in **f** times. Jr 33:7
of the land as in **f** times, Jr 33:11
the **f** kings who preceded you. Jr 34:5
renew our days as in **f** times, Lm 5:21
will return to their **f** state. Ezk 16:55
also return to your **f** state. Ezk 16:55
spoke about in **f** times through Ezk 38:17
I will go back to my **f** husband, Hs 2:7
the **f** rule will come to you, Mc 4:8
saw this house in its **f** glory? Hg 2:3
this people as in the **f** days"— Zch 8:11
heard about my **f** way of life Gl 1:13
you took off your **f** way of life, Eph 4:22
the desires of your **f** ignorance 1Pt 1:14

FORMERLY *(13)*
Ai where his tent had **f** been, Gn 13:3
Hazor had **f** been the leader Jos 11:10
Hebron was **f** named Kiriath-arba Jdg 1:10
Debir was **f** named Kiriath-sepher Jdg 1:11
the town was **f** named Luz). Jdg 1:23
The city was **f** named Laish. Jdg 18:29
F in Israel, a man who was going 1Sm 9:9
of today was **f** called the seer. 1Sm 9:9
to oppress them as they **f** have 1Ch 17:9
and those who **f** had seen him as Jn 9:8
He who **f** persecuted us now Gl 1:23
one who was **f** a blasphemer, 1Tm 1:13
those who **f** received the good Heb 4:6

FORMING *(3)*
Does clay say to the one **f** it: Is 45:9
He was **f** a swarm of locusts at Am 7:1
east to west, **f** a huge valley, Zch 14:4

FORMLESS *(3)*
Now the earth was **f** and empty, Gn 1:2
Your eyes saw me when I was **f**; Ps 139:16
earth, and it was **f** and empty. Jr 4:23

FORMS *(3)*
My skin **f** scabs and then oozes. Jb 7:5
the LORD who **f** it to establish Jr 33:2
the One who **f** the mountains, Am 4:13

FORMULA *(2)*
anything like it using its **f**. Ex 30:32
any⌋ for yourselves using its **f**. Ex 30:37

FORSAKE *(12)*
He will not leave you or **f** you." Dt 31:6
He will not leave you or **f** you. Dt 31:8
I will not leave you or **f** you. Jos 1:5
you, but if you **f** Him, He will 1Ch 28:9
leave you or **f** you until all 1Ch 28:20
If his sons **f** My instruction and Ps 89:30
The LORD will not **f** His people Ps 94:14
God of Israel, do not **f** them. Is 41:17
for them, and I will not **f** them. Is 42:16
and they did not **f** the idols of Ezk 20:8
worthless idols **f** faithful love, Jnh 2:8
I will never leave you or **f** you. Heb 13:5

FORSAKEN *(8)*
has not **f** his kindness to the Ru 2:20
God, my God, why have You **f** me? Ps 22:1
The cities of Aroer are **f**; Is 17:2
abandoned and **f** like a Is 27:10
palace will be **f**, the busy city Is 32:14
children of the **f** one will be Is 54:1
My God, why have You **f** Me?" Mt 27:46
My God, why have You **f** Me?" Mk 15:34

FORTH *(30)*
(See pp. xi-xii.)

FORTIETH *(3)*
fifth month in the **f** year after Nm 33:38
In the **f** year, in the eleventh Dt 1:3
In the **f** year of David's reign a 1Ch 26:31

FORTIFICATION *(1)*
Make their **f** desolate; Ps 69:25

FORTIFICATIONS *(6)*
they live in encampments or **f**? Nm 13:19
and come trembling from their **f**. 2Sm 22:46
their **f** and put leaders 2Ch 11:11
and come trembling from their **f**. Ps 18:45
all your **f** will be demolished Hs 10:14
you. Man the **f**! Watch the road! Nah 2:1

FORTIFIED *(63)*
and the cities are large and **f**. Nm 13:28
border, because it was **f**. Nm 21:24
remain in the **f** cities because Nm 32:17
and Beth-haran as **f** cities, Nm 32:36
are large, **f** to the heavens. Dt 1:28
these were **f** with high walls, Dt 3:5
large cities **f** to the heavens. Dt 9:1
until your high and **f** walls, Dt 28:52
Jericho was strongly **f** because Jos 6:1
ran away to the **f** cities. Jos 10:20
as well as large **f** cities. Jos 14:12
as far as the **f** city of Tyre; Jos 19:29
The **f** cities were Ziddim, Zer, Jos 19:35
the **f** cities and the outlying 1Sm 6:18
or he will find **f** cities and 2Sm 20:6
in the region of their **f** cities, 1Kg 8:37
attack every **f** city and every 2Kg 3:19
horses, a **f** city, and weaponry 2Kg 10:2
towns from watchtower to **f** city. 2Kg 17:9
from watchtower to **f** city. 2Kg 18:8
all the **f** cities of Judah 2Kg 18:13
you have crushed **f** cities into 2Kg 19:25
in the region of their **f** cities, 2Ch 6:28
Beth-horon—**f** cities with walls 2Ch 8:5
and he **f** cities in Judah. 2Ch 11:5
which are **f** cities in Judah and 2Ch 11:10
and to all the **f** cities. 2Ch 11:23
captured the **f** cities of Judah 2Ch 12:4
Asa built **f** cities in Judah. 2Ch 14:6
troops in every **f** city of Judah 2Ch 17:2
stationed in the **f** cities 2Ch 17:19
judges in all the **f** cities of 2Ch 19:5
along with **f** cities in Judah, 2Ch 21:3
corner buttress, and he **f** them. 2Ch 26:9
laid siege to the **f** cities and 2Ch 32:1
in all the **f** cities of Judah. 2Ch 33:14
They captured **f** cities and Neh 9:25
Who will bring me to the **f** city? Ps 60:9
reduced his **f** cities to ruins Ps 89:40
Who will bring me to the **f** city? Ps 108:10
rich man's wealth is his **f** city; Pr 10:15
rich man's wealth is his **f** city; Pr 18:11
harder to reach⌋ than a **f** city, Pr 18:19
tower, against every **f** wall, Is 2:15
of rubble, a **f** city, into a ruin Is 25:2
For the **f** city will be deserted, Is 27:10
her **f** cities, with thistles and Is 34:13
against all the **f** cities of Is 36:1
you have crushed **f** cities into Is 37:26
One who has made you a **f** city, Jr 1:18
and let's flee to the **f** cities. Jr 4:5
the sword your **f** cities in which Jr 5:17
us enter the **f** cities and there Jr 8:14
will make you a **f** wall of bronze Jr 15:20
left among Judah's **f** cities. Jr 34:7
demolished the **f** cities of Lm 2:2
and destroyed its **f** cities. Lm 2:5
and to Judah into **f** Jerusalem. Ezk 21:20
are ⌊now⌋ **f** and inhabited. Ezk 36:35
make plans against **f** cities, Dn 11:24
has also multiplied **f** cities. Hs 8:14
the flock, **f** hill of Daughter Mc 4:8
battle cry against the **f** cities, Zph 1:16

FORTIFY *(3)*
tear them down to **f** the wall. Is 22:10
of Babylon; **f** the watch post; Jr 51:12
to the heavens and **f** her tall Jr 51:53

FORTRESS *(36)*
and captured the royal **f**. 2Sm 12:26
is my rock, my **f**, and my 2Sm 22:2
went to the **f** of Tyre and all 2Sm 24:7
But it was in the **f** of Ecbatana Ezr 6:2
I was in the **f** city of Susa, Neh 1:1
the gates of the temple's **f**, Neh 2:8
of the **f**, because he was Neh 7:2
royal throne in the **f** at Susa. Est 1:2
were present in the **f** of Susa. Est 1:5
to the harem at the **f** of Susa. Est 2:3
man was in the **f** of Susa named Est 2:5
gathered at the **f** of Susa under Est 2:8
law was issued in the **f** of Susa. Est 3:15
also issued in the **f** of Susa. Est 8:14
In the **f** of Susa the Jews killed Est 9:6
killed in the **f** of Susa was Est 9:11
In the **f** of Susa the Jews have Est 9:12
is my rock, my **f**, and my Ps 18:2
for me, a mountain **f** to save me. Ps 31:2
For You are my rock and my **f**; Ps 31:3
for You are my rock and **f**. Ps 71:3
refuge and my **f**, my God, in whom Ps 91:2
He is my faithful love and my **f**, Ps 144:2
are like the bars of a **f**. Pr 18:19
and bring down its mighty **f**. Pr 21:22
The **f** disappears from Ephraim, Is 17:3
because your **f** is destroyed! Is 23:14
the **f** of barbarians is no longer Is 25:2
high-walled **f** will be brought Is 25:12
The **f** will be put to shame and Jr 48:1
I was in the **f** city of Susa, Dn 8:2
and enter the **f** of the king of Dn 11:7
again wage war as far as his **f**. Dn 11:10
up and desecrate the temple **f**. Dn 11:31
laugh at every **f** and build siege Hab 1:10
Tyre has built herself a **f**; Zch 9:3

FORTRESSES *(20)*
You will set their **f** on fire. 2Kg 8:12
in the villages, and in the **f**. 1Ch 27:25
He built **f** and storage cities in 2Ch 17:12
country of Judah and **f** and 2Ch 27:4
prosperity within your **f**." Ps 122:7
Hyenas will howl in the **f**, Is 13:22
the Canaanite **f** be destroyed. Is 23:11
his refuge will be the rocky **f**, Is 33:16
Let us destroy her **f**." Jr 6:5
has entered our **f**, cutting off Jr 9:21
he has destroyed your **f**. Jr 48:18
heavens and fortify her tall **f**, Jr 51:53
him into the **f** so his roar could Ezk 19:9
back to the **f** of his own land, Dn 11:19
he will honor a god of **f**— Dn 11:38
the strongest **f** with ⌊the help Dn 11:39
when it marches against our **f**, Mc 5:5
land and tear down all your **f**. Mc 5:11
All your **f** are fig trees with Nah 3:12
strengthen your **f**. Nah 3:14

FORTUNATE *(4)*
Women see her and declare her **f**; Sg 6:9
the nations will consider you **f**, Mal 3:12
consider the arrogant to be **f**. Mal 3:15
consider myself **f**, King Agrippa, Ac 26:2

FORTUNATUS *(1)*
of Stephanas, **F**, and Achaicus, 1Co 16:17

FORTUNE *(4)*
Then Leah said, "What good **f**!" Gn 30:11
a **f** through a lying tongue Pr 21:6
a table for **F** and fill bowls Is 65:11
He who makes a **f** unjustly is Jr 17:11

FORTUNE-TELLER *(1)*
and prophet, the **f** and elder, Is 3:2

FORTUNE-TELLERS *(4)*
out listen to **f** and diviners, Dt 18:14
the East and of **f** like the Is 2:6
dreamers, your **f**, or your Jr 27:9
you will not have any more **f**. Mc 5:12

FORTUNE-TELLING *(1)*
profit for her owners by **f**. Ac 16:16

FORTUNES *(25)*
tell **f**, interpret omens Dt 18:10
then He will restore your **f**, Dt 30:3
the LORD restored the **f** of Zion, Ps 126:1
Restore our **f**, LORD, like Ps 126:4
restore your **f** and gather you Jr 29:14
will restore the **f** of My people Jr 30:3
restore the **f** of Jacob's tents Jr 30:18
restore their **f**, they will once Jr 31:23
because I will restore their **f**." Jr 32:44
will restore the **f** of Judah and Jr 33:7
will restore the **f** of the land Jr 33:11
will restore their **f** and have Jr 33:26
I will restore the **f** of Moab in Jr 48:47
restore the **f** of the Ammonites Jr 49:6
I will restore the **f** of Elam. Jr 49:39
guilt and so restore your **f**. Lm 2:14
restore their **f**, the fortunes Ezk 16:53
the **f** of Sodom and her daughters Ezk 16:53
also restore your **f** among them, Ezk 16:53
will restore the **f** of Egypt and Ezk 29:14
will restore the **f** of Jacob and Ezk 39:25
when I restore the **f** of Judah Jl 3:1
will restore the **f** of My people Am 9:14
to them and restore their **f**. Zph 2:7
I restore your **f** before your Zph 3:20

FORTY-FIRST *(1)*
Asa died in the **f** year of his 2Ch 16:13

FORUM *(1)*
meet us as far as **F** of Appius Ac 28:15

FORWARD *(46)*
(See pp. xi-xii.)

FOSTER *(1)*
Kings will be your **f** fathers, Is 49:23

FOUGHT *(61)*
came and **f** against Israel. Ex 17:8
told him, and **f** against Amalek, Ex 17:10
he **f** against Israel and captured Nm 21:1
to Jahaz, he **f** against Israel. Nm 21:23
had **f** against the former king Nm 21:26
who **f** against Moses and Aaron; Nm 26:9
followers **f** against the LORD Nm 26:9
separated from the men who **f**, Nm 31:42
Gibeon, and **f** against it. Jos 10:5
because the LORD **f** for Israel. Jos 10:14
to Libnah and **f** against Libnah. Jos 10:29
the God of Israel, **f** for Israel. Jos 10:42
went up and **f** against Leshem, Jos 19:47
They **f** against you, but I handed Jos 24:8
and Jebusites—**f** against you, Jos 24:11
in Bezek, **f** against him, Jdg 1:5
The men of Judah **f** against Jdg 1:8
Israelites had **f** in any of the Jdg 3:1
those who had not **f** before. Jdg 3:2
Kings came and **f**. Then the kings Jdg 5:19
the kings of Canaan **f** at Taanach Jdg 5:19
The stars **f** from the heavens; Jdg 5:20
the stars **f** with Sisera from Jdg 5:20
for my father **f** for you, risked Jdg 9:17
of Shechem and **f** against Jdg 9:39
So Abimelech **f** against the city Jdg 9:45
the Ammonites **f** against Israel. Jdg 11:4
at Jahaz, and **f** with Israel. Jdg 11:20
They **f** and defeated Ephraim, Jdg 12:4

day the Israelites **f** against the Jdg 20:30
Philistines **f**, and Israel was 1Sm 4:10
⌊These enemies⌋ **f** against them. 1Sm 12:9
he **f** against all his enemies in 1Sm 14:47
He **f** bravely, defeated the 1Sm 14:48
David went out and **f** against the 1Sm 19:8
f against the Philistines, 1Sm 23:5
Philistines **f** against Israel, 1Sm 31:1
David had **f** against Hadadezer 2Sm 8:10
and Hadadezer had **f** many wars. 2Sm 8:10
in battle and **f** against him. 2Sm 10:17
Joab **f** against Rabbah of the 2Sm 12:26
I have **f** against Rabbah and have 2Sm 12:27
he **f** against it and captured it. 2Sm 12:29
and they **f** the Philistines, 2Sm 21:15
Samaria, and **f** against it. 1Kg 20:1
when he **f** against Aram's King 2Kg 8:29
on him when he **f** against Aram's 2Kg 9:15
marched up and **f** against Gath 2Kg 12:17
Philistines **f** against Israel, 1Ch 10:1
David had **f** against Hadadezer 1Ch 18:10
and Hadadezer had **f** many wars. 1Ch 18:10
in battle, they **f** against him. 1Ch 19:17
that the LORD had **f** against the 2Ch 20:29
when he **f** against Aram's King 2Ch 22:6
⌊They **f**⌋ on the thirteenth day Est 9:17
enemy ⌊and⌋ **f** against them. Is 63:10
because you **f** against the LORD. Jr 50:24
If I **f** wild animals in Ephesus 1Co 15:32
I have **f** the good fight, I have 2Tm 4:7
and his angels **f** against the Rv 12:7
dragon and his angels also **f**, Rv 12:7

FOUL *(2)*

My wounds are **f** and festering Ps 38:5
sea, the sea of **f** water, the Ezk 47:8

FOUND *(332)*

no helper was **f** who was like him Gn 2:20
so that whoever **f** him would not Gn 4:15
f favor in the eyes of the LORD. Gn 6:8
but the dove **f** no resting place Gn 8:9
they **f** a valley in the land of Gn 11:2
of the LORD **f** her by a spring Gn 16:7
if I have **f** favor in your sight, Gn 18:3
again, "Suppose 40 are **f** there?" Gn 18:29
Suppose 30 are **f** there?" Gn 18:30
Lord, suppose 20 are **f** there?" Gn 18:31
Suppose 10 are **f** there?" Gn 18:32
has indeed **f** favor in Your Gn 19:19
the valley and **f** a well of Gn 26:19
to him, "We have **f** water!" Gn 26:32
harvest and **f** some mandrakes Gn 30:14
If I have **f** favor in your sight, Gn 30:27
female slaves, but he **f** nothing. Gn 31:33
the whole tent but **f** nothing. Gn 31:34
Have you **f** anything of yours? Gn 31:37
If I have **f** favor with you, Gn 33:10
the Anah who **f** the hot springs Gn 36:24
A man **f** him there, wandering in Gn 37:15
brothers and **f** them at Dothan. Gn 37:17
father and said, "We **f** this. Gn 37:32
Joseph **f** favor in his master's Gn 39:4
the money we **f** at the top of our Gn 44:8
If any of us is **f** to have it, Gn 44:9
the one who is **f** to have it will Gn 44:10
and the cup was **f** in Benjamin's Gn 44:12
whose possession the cup was **f**." Gn 44:16
the cup was **f** will be my slave. Gn 44:17
the money to be **f** in the land Gn 47:14
We have **f** favor in our lord's Gn 47:25
If I have **f** favor in your eyes, Gn 47:29
If I have **f** favor with you, Gn 50:4
must not be **f** in your houses Ex 12:19
leavened may be **f** among you, Ex 13:7
no yeast may be **f** among you in Ex 13:7
or the person is **f** in his Ex 21:16
is actually **f** alive in his Ex 22:4
mauled animal ⌊**f**⌋ in the field; Ex 22:31
you have also **f** favor in My Ex 33:12
if I have indeed **f** favor in Your Ex 33:13
Your people have **f** favor in Your Ex 33:16
you have **f** favor in My sight, Ex 33:17
if I have indeed **f** favor in Your Ex 34:9
to him, or the lost item he **f**, Lv 6:4
they **f** a man gathering wood on Nm 15:32
Those who **f** him gathering wood Nm 15:33
the gold articles each man **f**— Nm 31:50
If we have **f** favor in your Nm 32:5
yeast is to be **f** anywhere in Dt 16:4
all the people **f** in it will Dt 20:11
victim is **f** lying in a field Dt 21:1
If anyone is **f** guilty of an Dt 21:22
brother has lost and you have **f**. Dt 22:3
young woman's virginity is **f**, Dt 22:20
When he **f** her in the field, Dt 22:27
He **f** him in a desolate land, Dt 32:10
the 'rock' they **f** refuge in? Dt 32:37
The five kings have been **f**; Jos 10:17
They **f** Adoni-bezek in Bezek, Jdg 1:5
They looked and **f** the doors of Jdg 3:24
If I have **f** favor in Your sight, Jdg 6:17
they **f** Baal's altar torn down, Jdg 6:28
f a fresh jawbone of a donkey, Jdg 15:15
They **f** among the inhabitants of Jdg 21:12
they **f** some young women coming 1Sm 9:11
them because they've been **f**. 1Sm 9:20
went looking for have been **f**, 1Sm 10:2
us the donkeys had been **f**." 1Sm 10:16
that you haven't **f** anything in 1Sm 12:5
The LORD has **f** a man loyal to 1Sm 13:14
could be **f** in all the land 1Sm 13:19
or spear could be **f** in the hand 1Sm 13:22
of bread or whatever can be **f**." 1Sm 21:3
life, may evil not be **f** in you. 1Sm 25:28
If I have **f** favor with you, 1Sm 27:5
I've **f** no fault with him." 1Sm 29:3
because I have **f** no fault in you 1Sm 29:6
what have you **f** against your 1Sm 29:8
the town, they **f** it burned down. 1Sm 30:3
But David **f** strength in the LORD 1Sm 30:6
They **f** an Egyptian in the open 1Sm 30:11
they **f** Saul and his three sons 1Sm 31:8
Your servant has **f** the courage 2Sm 7:27
knows I have **f** favor with you, 2Sm 14:22
even a pebble can be **f** there." 2Sm 17:13
they **f** Abishag the Shunammite 1Kg 1:3
but if evil is **f** in him, then he 1Kg 1:52
man of God and **f** him sitting 1Kg 13:14
and he went and **f** the corpse of 1Kg 13:28
something was **f** pleasing to the 1Kg 14:13
nation swear they had not **f** you. 1Kg 18:10
left there and **f** Elisha son of 1Kg 19:19
a lion **f** him and killed him. 1Kg 20:36
The prophet **f** another man and 1Kg 20:37
gather herbs and **f** a wild vine 2Kg 4:39
he **f** Jehonadab son of Rechab 2Kg 10:15
damage to the temple is **f**. 2Kg 12:5
count the money **f** there and tie 2Kg 12:10
and all the gold **f** in the 2Kg 12:18
all the utensils **f** in the LORD's 2Kg 14:14
silver and gold **f** in the LORD's 2Kg 16:8
all the silver **f** in the LORD's 2Kg 18:15
he returned and **f** him fighting 2Kg 19:8
that was **f** in his treasuries. 2Kg 20:13
I have **f** the book of the law in 2Kg 22:8
money that was **f** in the temple 2Kg 22:9
in this book that has been **f**. 2Kg 22:13
that had been **f** in the LORD's 2Kg 23:2
the priest **f** in the LORD's 2Kg 23:24
royal aides **f** in the city; 2Kg 25:19
who were **f** within the city 2Kg 25:19
They **f** rich, good pasture, and 1Ch 4:40
and the Meunim who were **f** there, 1Ch 4:41
the archers **f** him and severely 1Ch 10:3
they **f** Saul and his sons dead on 1Ch 10:8
Your servant has **f** ⌊courage⌋ to 1Ch 17:25
leaders were **f** among Eleazar's 1Ch 24:4
capable men were **f** among them 1Ch 26:31
Him, He will be **f** by you, but if 1Ch 28:9
Him, He will be **f** by you, but if 2Ch 15:2
sought Him, He was **f** by them. 2Ch 15:4
heart, and He was **f** by them. 2Ch 15:15
some good is **f** in you, for you 2Ch 19:3
They **f** among them an abundance 2Ch 20:25
the possessions **f** in the king's 2Ch 21:17
he **f** the rulers of Judah and the 2Ch 22:8
He **f** there to be 300,000 choice 2Ch 25:5
that were **f** with Obed-edom 2Ch 25:24
things they **f** in the LORD's 2Ch 29:16
Hilkiah the priest **f** the book of 2Ch 34:14
I have **f** the book of the law in 2Ch 34:15
money that was **f** in the LORD's 2Ch 34:17
words of the book that was **f**. 2Ch 34:21
that had been **f** in the LORD's 2Ch 34:30
and what was **f** against him, 2Ch 36:8
could not be **f**, so they were Ezr 2:62
a scroll was **f** with this record Ezr 6:2
priests, but **f** no Levites there Ezr 8:15
following⌋ were **f** to have Ezr 10:18
servant has **f** favor with you, Neh 2:5
I **f** the genealogical record of Neh 7:5
and I **f** ⌊the following⌋ written Neh 7:5
could not be **f**, so they were Neh 7:64
They **f** written in the law how Neh 8:14
You **f** his heart faithful in Your Neh 9:8
The command was **f** written in it Neh 13:1
I also **f** out that because the Neh 13:10
Jews who can be **f** in Susa and Est 4:16
They **f** the written report of how Est 6:2
I have **f** approval before him, Est 8:5
Since I will be **f** guilty, why Jb 9:29
Wisdom is **f** with the elderly, Jb 12:12
like a dream and never be **f**; Jb 20:8
But where can wisdom be **f**, Jb 28:12
since it cannot be **f** in the land Jb 28:13
do not claim, "We have **f** wisdom; Jb 32:13
to the Pit; I have **f** a ransom," Jb 33:24
could be **f** in all the land, Jb 42:15
tried me and **f** nothing ⌊evil⌋; Ps 17:3
You at a time that You may be **f**. Ps 32:6
for him, but he could not be **f**. Ps 37:36
wouldn't God have **f** this out, Ps 44:21
who is always **f** in times of Ps 46:1
for comforters, but **f** no one. Ps 69:20
I have **f** David My servant; Ps 89:20
let him be **f** guilty, and let Ps 109:7
we **f** it in the fields of Jaar. Ps 132:6
search for you, and I've **f** you. Pr 7:15
perverts his ways will be **f** out. Pr 10:9
Wisdom is **f** on the lips of the Pr 10:13
it is **f** in the way of Pr 16:31
sun and have **f** everything to be Ec 1:14
f everything to be futile and a Ec 2:11
people⌋ I have **f** one ⌊true⌋ man, Ec 7:28
these I have not **f** a true woman. Ec 7:28
poor wise man was **f** in the city, Ec 9:15
who go about the city **f** me. Sg 3:3
them when I **f** the one I love. Sg 3:4
who go about the city **f** me. Sg 5:7
Whoever is **f** will be stabbed, Is 13:15
of pottery will be **f** among its Is 30:14
they will not be **f** there. Is 35:9
that was **f** in his treasuries. Is 39:2
and gladness will be **f** in her, Is 51:3
the heavens, to **f** the earth, and Is 51:16
Seek the LORD while He may be **f**; Is 55:6
You **f** a renewal of your Is 57:10
was **f** by those who did not seek Is 65:1
As the new wine is **f** in a bunch Is 65:8
who ate of it **f** themselves Jr 2:3
words were **f**, and I ate them Jr 15:16
in My house I have **f** their evil. Jr 23:11
I will be **f** by you"—the LORD's Jr 29:14
They **f** favor in the wilderness— Jr 31:2
Nethaniah and **f** him by the great Jr 41:12
groaning and have **f** no rest. Jr 45:3
Was he ever **f** among thieves? Jr 48:27
All who **f** them devoured them. Jr 50:7
they will not be **f**, for I will Jr 50:20
You were **f** and captured because Jr 50:24
royal aides **f** in the city; Jr 52:25
who were **f** within the city Jr 52:25
not destroy it, but I **f** no one. Ezk 22:30
but will never be **f** again." Ezk 26:21
until wickedness was **f** in you. Ezk 28:15
no one was **f** equal to Daniel, Dn 1:19
he **f** them 10 times better than Dn 1:20
I have **f** a man among the Judean Dn 2:25
not a trace of them could be **f**. Dn 2:35
Wild animals **f** shelter under it, Dn 4:12
he was **f** to have insight, Dn 5:11
was **f** to have an extraordinary Dn 5:12
in the balance and **f** deficient. Dn 5:27
or corruption was **f** in him. Dn 6:4
as a group and **f** Daniel Dn 6:11
for I was **f** innocent before Him. Dn 6:22
people who are **f** written in the Dn 12:1
He **f** him at Bethel, and there He Hs 12:4
to Joppa and **f** a ship going to Jnh 1:3
will not be **f** in their mouths. Zph 3:13
nothing wrong was **f** on his lips. Mal 2:6
I have not **f** anyone in Israel Mt 8:10
that a man **f** and reburied. Mt 13:44
When he **f** one priceless pearl, Mt 13:46
went out and **f** one of his fellow Mt 18:28

he went and f others standing Mt 20:6
went up to it and f nothing on Mt 21:19
and gathered everyone they f, Mt 22:10
disciples and f them sleeping. Mt 26:40
came again and f them sleeping, Mt 26:43
they f a Cyrenian man named Mt 27:32
They f Him and said, "Everyone's Mk 1:37
When they f out they said, Mk 6:38
f her child lying on the bed, Mk 7:30
they went and f a young donkey Mk 11:4
He came to it, He f nothing but Mk 11:13
and f it just as He had told Mk 14:16
He came and f them sleeping. Mk 14:37
came again and f them sleeping, Mk 14:40
he f out from the centurion, Mk 15:45
for you have f favor with God. Lk 1:30
hurried off and f both Mary and Lk 2:16
they f Him in the temple complex Lk 2:46
He f the place where it was Lk 4:17
I have not f so great a faith Lk 7:9
they f the slave in good health. Lk 7:10
was a sinner f out that Jesus Lk 7:37
came to Jesus and f the man the Lk 8:35
When the crowds f out, they Lk 9:11
had spoken, only Jesus was f. Lk 9:36
for fruit on it and f none. Lk 13:6
this fig tree and haven't f any. Lk 13:7
When he has f it, he joyfully Lk 15:5
because I have f my lost sheep!' Lk 15:6
because I have f the silver coin Lk 15:9
he was lost and is f!' Lk 15:24
he was lost and is f.'" Lk 15:32
sent left and f it just as He Lk 19:32
So they went and f it just as He Lk 22:13
disciples, He f them sleeping, Lk 22:45
We f this man subverting our Lk 23:2
I have f no grounds to charge Lk 23:14
I have f in Him no grounds for Lk 23:22
f the stone rolled away from Lk 24:2
to the tomb and f it just as the Lk 24:24
They f the Eleven and those with Lk 24:33
He first f his own brother Simon Jn 1:41
him, "We have f the Messiah!" Jn 1:41
Jesus f Philip and told him, Jn 1:43
Philip f Nathanael and told him, Jn 1:45
We have f the One Moses wrote Jn 1:45
complex He f people selling Jn 2:14
and ⌊He also f⌋ the money Jn 2:14
f him in the temple complex Jn 5:14
they f Him on the other side Jn 6:25
the man out, He f him and asked, Jn 9:35
He f that Lazarus had already Jn 11:17
Jesus f a young donkey and sat Jn 12:14
They f no way to punish them, Ac 4:21
came in, they f her dead, Ac 5:10
We f the jail securely locked, Ac 5:23
them, we f no one inside!" Ac 5:23
You may even be f fighting Ac 5:39
He f favor in God's sight and Ac 7:46
so that if he f any who belonged Ac 9:2
the brothers f out, they took Ac 9:30
There he f a man named Aeneas, Ac 9:33
went on in and f that many had Ac 10:27
and when he f him he brought him Ac 11:26
'I have f David the son of Jesse, Ac 13:22
Though they f no grounds for the Ac 13:28
they f out about it and fled to Ac 14:6
Thessalonica f out that God's Ac 17:13
I even f an altar on which was Ac 17:23
where he f a Jewish man named Ac 18:2
to Ephesus. He f some disciples Ac 19:1
and f it to be 50,000 pieces of Ac 19:19
we f some disciples and stayed Ac 21:4
f out that the accusations were Ac 23:29
For we have f this man to be a Ac 24:5
province of Asia f me ritually Ac 24:18
wrongdoing they f in me when I Ac 24:20
the centurion f an Alexandrian Ac 27:6
a sounding and f it to be 120 Ac 27:28
they f it to be 90 feet deep. Ac 27:28
There we f believers and were Ac 28:14
according to the flesh, has f? Rm 4:1
I was f by those who were not Rm 10:20
that each one be f faithful. 1Co 4:2
we are f to be false witnesses 1Co 15:15
clothed, we will not be f naked. 2Co 5:3
and f diligent—and now 2Co 8:22
and I may not be f by you to be 2Co 12:20
are also f to be sinners, Gl 2:17
and be f in Him, not having a Php 3:9
searched for me and f me. 2Tm 1:17
was not to be f because God took Heb 11:5
no deceit was f in His mouth; 1Pt 2:22
effort to be f in peace without 2Pt 3:14
I f it necessary to write and Jd 3
and you have f them to be liars. Rv 2:2
for I have not f your works Rv 3:2
no one was f worthy to open Rv 5:4
No lie was f in their mouths; Rv 14:5
violently and never be f again. Rv 18:21
will ever be f in you again; Rv 18:22
on earth, was f in you. Rv 18:24
and no place was f for them. Rv 20:11
And anyone not f written in the Rv 20:15

FOUNDATION *(54)*

He will lay its f ⌊at the cost Jos 6:26
to lay the f of the temple 1Kg 5:17
The f of the LORD's temple was 1Kg 6:37
from f to coping and from the 1Kg 7:9
The f was made of large, costly 1Kg 7:10
he laid its f, and at the cost 1Kg 16:34
from the day the f ⌊was laid⌋ 2Ch 8:16
a third are to be at the F Gate, 2Ch 23:5
the altar on its f and offered Ezr 3:3
even though the f of the LORD's Ezr 3:6
had laid the f of the LORD's Ezr 3:10
LORD because the f of the LORD's Ezr 3:11
they saw the f of this house, Ezr 3:12
and laid the f of God's house Ezr 5:16
houses, whose f is in the dust, Jb 4:19
He laid its f on the seas and Ps 24:2
His f is on the holy mountains. Ps 87:1
are the f of Your throne; Ps 89:14
justice are the f of His throne. Ps 97:2
precious cornerstone, a sure f; Is 28:16
Its f will be laid. Is 44:28
on ⌊a f of⌋ righteousness Is 54:14
or a f stone from you, Jr 51:26
ground so that its f is exposed. Ezk 13:14
this f for the side rooms was 10 Ezk 41:8
and lays the f of His vault Am 9:6
from the day the f of the LORD's Hg 2:18
have laid the f of this house, Zch 4:9
laid the f of the earth, Zch 12:1
because its f was on the rock. Mt 7:25
secret from the f of the world. Mt 13:35
for you from the f of the world. Mt 25:34
deep and laid the f on the rock. Lk 6:48
house on the ground without a f. Lk 6:49
shed since the f of the world— Lk 11:50
he has laid the f and cannot Lk 14:29
loved Me before the world's f. Jn 17:24
be building on someone else's f, Rm 15:20
master builder I have laid a f, 1Co 3:10
lay any other f than what has 1Co 3:11
builds on the f with gold, 1Co 3:12
then our preaching is without f, 1Co 15:14
before the f of the world, Eph 1:4
built on the f of the apostles Eph 2:20
the pillar and f of the truth. 1Tm 3:15
a good f for the age to 1Tm 6:19
God's solid f stands firm, 2Tm 2:19
since the f of the world, Heb 4:3
laying again the f of repentance Heb 6:1
times since the f of the world. Heb 9:26
before the f of the world, 1Pt 1:20
written from the f of the world Rv 13:8
of life from the f of the world Rv 17:8
the first f jasper, the second Rv 21:19

FOUNDATIONS *(35)*

scorches the f of the mountains Dt 32:22
For the f of the earth are the 1Sm 2:8
the f of the heavens trembled; 2Sm 22:8
the f of the world were exposed 2Sm 22:16
are Solomon's f for building 2Ch 3:3
its walls, and repairing its f. Ezr 4:12
its ⌊original⌋ f be retained. Ezr 6:3
and their f were washed away by Jb 22:16
the mountains at ⌊their⌋ f. Jb 28:9
What supports its f? Jb 38:6
When the f are destroyed, what Ps 11:3
the f of the mountains trembled; Ps 18:7
the f of the world were exposed, Ps 18:15
All the f of the earth are Ps 82:5
established the earth on its f; Ps 104:5
Destroy it down to its f!" Ps 137:7
He laid out the f of the earth. Pr 8:29
The f of the doorways shook at Is 6:4
shake from its f at the wrath Is 13:13
and the f of the earth are Is 24:18
considered the f of the earth? Is 40:21
and laid the f of the earth. Is 51:13
and lay your f in sapphires. Is 54:11
restore the f laid long ago; Is 58:12
measured and the f of the earth Jr 31:37
and it has consumed her f. Lm 4:11
away, and its f are torn down. Ezk 30:4
sank to the f of the mountains; Jnh 2:6
the valley and expose her f. Mc 1:6
and enduring f of the earth, Mc 6:2
spoke when the f were laid for Zch 8:9
that the f of the jail were Ac 16:26
forward to the city that has f, Heb 11:10
city wall had 12 f, and on them Rv 21:14
The f of the city wall were Rv 21:19

FOUNDED *(5)*

from the day it was f until now. Ex 9:18
everything in it—You f them. Ps 89:11
The LORD f the earth by wisdom Pr 3:19
The LORD has f Zion, and His Is 14:32
My own hand f the earth, and My Is 48:13

FOUNDS *(1)*

with bloodshed and f a town with Hab 2:12

FOUNTAIN *(16)*

I went on to the F Gate and the Neh 2:14
of Mizpah, repaired the F Gate. Neh 3:15
At the F Gate they climbed the Neh 12:37
for with You is life's f. Ps 36:9
the LORD from the f of Israel. Ps 68:26
Let your f be blessed, and take Pr 5:18
of the righteous is a f of life, Pr 10:11
instruction is a f of life, Pr 13:14
fear of the LORD is a f of life, Pr 14:27
Insight is a f of life for its Pr 16:22
a flowing river, a f of wisdom. Pr 18:4
Me, the f of living water, Jr 2:13
water, my eyes a f of tears, I Jr 9:1
abandoned the f of living water, Jr 17:13
her sea and make her f run dry. Jr 51:36
On that day a f will be opened Zch 13:1

FOUNTAINS *(1)*

when the f of the ocean gushed Pr 8:28

FOUR *(219)*

became the source of f rivers. Gn 2:10
of Ellasar—f kings against Gn 14:9
The ⌊f kings⌋ took all the goods Gn 14:11
as much food, f quarts apiece, Ex 16:22
for the ox or f sheep for the Ex 22:1
f gold rings for it and place Ex 25:12
and place ⌊them⌋ on its f feet, Ex 25:12
Make f gold rings for it, and Ex 25:26
rings to the f corners at its Ex 25:26
the four corners at its f legs. Ex 25:26
There are to be f cups shaped Ex 25:34
Hang it on f gold-plated posts Ex 26:32
that stand⌋ on f silver bases. Ex 26:32
it must be f and a half feet Ex 27:1
horns for it on its f corners; Ex 27:2
and make f bronze rings on the Ex 27:4
on the mesh at its f corners. Ex 27:4
It is to have f posts including Ex 27:16
posts including their f bases. Ex 27:16
on it, f rows of stones: Ex 28:17
For it he made f posts of acacia Ex 36:36
And he cast f silver bases for Ex 36:36
cast f gold rings for it to be Ex 37:3
for it to be on its f feet, Ex 37:3
He cast f gold rings for it and Ex 37:13
rings to the f corners at its Ex 37:13
the four corners at its f legs. Ex 37:13
there were f cups shaped like Ex 37:20
and was f and a half feet high. Ex 38:1
horns for it on its f corners; Ex 38:2
At the f corners of the bronze Ex 38:5
grate he cast f rings as holders Ex 38:5
It had f posts, including their Ex 38:19
including their f bronze bases. Ex 38:19
They mounted f rows of gemstones Ex 39:10
that have f feet are to be Lv 11:23
is to be f quarts of fine Lv 23:13
them made from f quarts of fine Lv 23:17
is to be made with f quarts. Lv 24:5
two carts and f oxen Nm 7:7

the Merarites **f** carts and eight Nm 7:8
one gold bowl weighing **f** ounces, Nm 7:14
one gold bowl weighing **f** ounces, Nm 7:20
one gold bowl weighing **f** ounces, Nm 7:26
one gold bowl weighing **f** ounces, Nm 7:32
one gold bowl weighing **f** ounces, Nm 7:38
one gold bowl weighing **f** ounces, Nm 7:44
one gold bowl weighing **f** ounces, Nm 7:50
one gold bowl weighing **f** ounces, Nm 7:56
one gold bowl weighing **f** ounces, Nm 7:62
one gold bowl weighing **f** ounces, Nm 7:68
one gold bowl weighing **f** ounces, Nm 7:74
one gold bowl weighing **f** ounces, Nm 7:80
each ⌊weighed⌋ **f** ounces Nm 7:86
must be **f** quarts of fine flour Nm 15:6
f quarts of fine flour mixed Nm 28:9
f quarts of fine flour mixed Nm 28:12
with each bull and **f** quarts with Nm 28:20
with each bull, **f** quarts with Nm 28:28
with the bull, **f** quarts with the Nm 29:3
with the bull, **f** quarts with the Nm 29:9
f quarts with each of the two Nm 29:14
Make tassels on the **f** corners of Dt 22:12
and Ashan—**f** cities, with their Jos 19:7
its pasturelands—**f** cities. Jos 21:18
its pasturelands—**f** cities. Jos 21:22
its pasturelands—**f** cities. Jos 21:24
its pasturelands—**f** cities. Jos 21:29
its pasturelands—**f** cities. Jos 21:31
its pasturelands—**f** cities. Jos 21:35
its pasturelands—**f** cities. Jos 21:37
pasturelands—**f** cities in all. Jos 21:39
ambush for Shechem in **f** units. Jdg 9:34
⌊that⌋ **f** days each year the Jdg 11:40
I will give you **f** ounces of Jdg 17:10
there for a period of **f** months. Jdg 19:2
and stayed there **f** months. Jdg 20:47
amounted to a year and **f** months. 1Sm 27:7
must pay **f** lambs for that lamb. 2Sm 12:6
When **f** years had passed, Absalom 2Sm 15:7
These **f** were descended from the 2Sm 21:22
the LORD in the **f** hundred 1Kg 6:1
45 feet high on **f** rows of cedar 1Kg 7:2
and **f** and a half feet high. 1Kg 7:27
Each cart had **f** bronze wheels 1Kg 7:30
Underneath the **f** corners of the 1Kg 7:30
There were **f** wheels under the 1Kg 7:32
F supports were at the four 1Kg 7:34
were at the **f** corners of each 1Kg 7:34
gave the king **f** and a half tons 1Kg 10:10
about **f** pounds of gold went into 1Kg 10:17
and a horse for about **f** pounds. 1Kg 10:29
enough to hold about **f** gallons. 1Kg 18:32
Fill **f** water pots with water and 1Kg 18:33
F men with skin diseases were at 2Kg 7:3
f generations of your sons will 2Kg 10:30
F generations of your sons will 2Kg 15:12
These **f** were ⌊born to him⌋ by 1Ch 3:5
Puah, Jashub, and Shimron—**f**. 1Ch 7:1
gatekeepers were on the **f** sides: 1Ch 9:24
but the **f** chief gatekeepers, 1Ch 9:26
His **f** sons, who were with him, 1Ch 21:20
Those were Shimei's sons—**f**. 1Ch 23:10
Izhar, Hebron, and Uzziel—**f**. 1Ch 23:12
day on the east, **f** each day on 1Ch 26:17
day on the north, **f** each day on 1Ch 26:17
there were **f** at the highway and 1Ch 26:18
and a horse for about **f** pounds. 2Ch 1:17
and **f** and a half feet high and 2Ch 6:13
gave the king **f** and a half tons 2Ch 9:9
F times they sent me the same Neh 6:4
and struck the **f** corners of the Jb 1:19
never satisfied; **f** never say, Pr 30:15
are beyond me; **f** I can't Pr 30:18
it cannot bear up under **f**: Pr 30:21
F things on earth are small, Pr 30:24
f are stately in their walk: Pr 30:29
of Judah from the **f** corners of Is 11:12
f or five on its fruitful Is 17:6
I will ordain **f** kinds ⌊of Jr 15:3
would read three or **f** columns, Jr 36:23
I will bring the **f** winds against Jr 49:36
against Elam from the **f** corners Jr 49:36
was hollow—**f** fingers thick— Jr 52:21
The form of **f** living creatures Ezk 1:5
of them had **f** faces and four Ezk 1:6
them had four faces and **f** wings. Ezk 1:6
their wings on their **f** sides. Ezk 1:8
All **f** of them had faces and Ezk 1:8
and each of the **f** had the face Ezk 1:10
each creature that had **f** faces. Ezk 1:15
and all **f** had the same form. Ezk 1:16
went in any of the **f** directions, Ezk 1:17
Each of their **f** rims were full Ezk 1:18
has come on the **f** corners of the Ezk 7:2
and there were **f** wheels beside Ezk 10:9
appearance, all **f** had the same Ezk 10:10
go in any of the **f** directions, Ezk 10:11
wheels that the **f** of them had, Ezk 10:12
Each one had **f** faces: the first Ezk 10:14
Each had **f** faces and each had Ezk 10:21
four faces and each had **f** wings, Ezk 10:21
be when I send My **f** devastating Ezk 14:21
from the **f** winds and breathe Ezk 37:9
there were **f** tables inside the Ezk 40:41
inside the gate and **f** outside, Ezk 40:41
There were also **f** tables of cut Ezk 40:42
temple complex on all **f** sides. Ezk 42:20
and **f** horns project upward from Ezk 43:15
feet wide, with **f** equal sides. Ezk 43:17
apply ⌊it⌋ to the **f** horns of the Ezk 43:20
the **f** corners of the ledge, Ezk 43:20
the **f** corners of the altar's Ezk 45:19
and led me past its **f** corners. Ezk 46:21
In the **f** corners of the ⌊outer⌋ Ezk 46:22
All **f** corner areas had the same Ezk 46:22
them, around the **f** of them, with Ezk 46:23
God gave these **f** young men Dn 1:17
I see **f** men, not tied, walking Dn 3:25
suddenly the **f** winds of heaven Dn 7:2
F huge beasts came up from the Dn 7:3
a leopard with **f** wings of a bird Dn 7:6
It had **f** heads and was given Dn 7:6
huge beasts, **f** in number, are Dn 7:17
are **f** kings who will rise from Dn 7:17
F conspicuous horns came up in Dn 8:8
toward the **f** winds of heaven. Dn 8:8
The **f** horns that took the place Dn 8:22
horn represent **f** kingdoms. Dn 8:22
to the **f** winds of heaven, Dn 11:4
crimes, even **f**, because they Am 1:3
crimes, even **f**, because they Am 1:6
crimes, even **f**, because they Am 1:9
three crimes, even **f**, because he Am 1:11
crimes, even **f**, because they Am 1:13
crimes, even **f**, because he Am 2:1
crimes, even **f**, because they Am 2:4
crimes, even **f**, because they Am 2:6
I looked up and saw **f** horns. Zch 1:18
the LORD showed me **f** craftsmen. Zch 1:20
like the **f** winds of heaven"— Zch 2:6
again and saw **f** chariots coming Zch 6:1
These are the **f** spirits of Zch 6:5
His elect from the **f** winds, Mt 24:31
a paralytic, carried by **f** men. Mk 2:3
His elect from the **f** winds, Mk 13:27
I'll pay back **f** times as much!" Lk 19:8
'There are still **f** more months, Jn 4:35
rowed about three or **f** miles, Jn 6:19
already been in the tomb **f** days. Jn 11:17
stinks. It's been **f** days." Jn 11:39
and divided them into **f** parts, Jn 19:23
to the earth by its **f** corners. Ac 10:11
replied, "**F** days ago at this Ac 10:30
from heaven by its **f** corners, Ac 11:5
and assigned **f** squads of four Ac 12:4
four squads of **f** soldiers each Ac 12:4
This man had **f** virgin daughters Ac 21:9
We have **f** men who have obligated Ac 21:23
they dropped **f** anchors from the Ac 27:29
the throne were **f** living Rv 4:6
Each of the **f** living creatures Rv 4:8
and the **f** living creatures Rv 5:6
the **f** living creatures and the Rv 5:8
The **f** living creatures said, Rv 5:14
one of the **f** living creatures Rv 6:1
voice among the **f** living Rv 6:6
this I saw **f** angels standing Rv 7:1
standing at the **f** corners of the Rv 7:1
restraining the **f** winds of the Rv 7:1
voice to the **f** angels who were Rv 7:2
and the **f** living creatures, Rv 7:11
From the **f** horns of the gold Rv 9:13
Release the **f** angels bound at Rv 9:14
the **f** angels who were prepared Rv 9:15
before the **f** living creatures Rv 14:3
One of the **f** living creatures Rv 15:7
elders and the **f** living Rv 19:4
the nations at the **f** corners of Rv 20:8

FOUR-FIFTHS *(1)*

and **f** will be yours as seed for Gn 47:24

FOUR-FOOTED *(4)*

All the **f** animals that walk on Lv 11:27
In it were all the **f** animals and Ac 10:12
saw the **f** animals of the earth, Ac 11:6
mortal man, birds, **f** animals, Rm 1:23

FOUR-SIDED *(1)*

he made **f** olive wood doorposts 1Kg 6:33

FOURS *(3)*

that walk on all **f** are to be Lv 11:20
insects that walk on all **f**: Lv 11:21
walks on all **f** or on many feet Lv 11:42

FOURTEEN *(1)*

had given Heman **f** sons and three 1Ch 25:5

FOURTEENTH *(25)*

In the **f** year Chedorlaomer and Gn 14:5
it until the **f** day of this month Ex 12:6
evening of the **f** day of the Ex 12:18
twilight on the **f** day of the Lv 23:5
time on the **f** day of this month Nm 9:3
month on the **f** day at twilight Nm 9:5
month, on the **f** day at twilight. Nm 9:11
on the **f** day of the month. Nm 28:16
evening of the **f** day of the Jos 5:10
In the **f** year of King Hezekiah, 2Kg 18:13
to Huppah, the **f** to Jeshebeab, 1Ch 24:13
the **f** ⌊to⌋ Mattithiah, his sons, 1Ch 25:21
lamb on the **f** day of the second 2Ch 30:15
lambs⌋ on the **f** day of the first 2Ch 35:1
Passover on the **f** day of the Ezr 6:19
again on the **f** day of the month Est 9:15
of Adar and rested on the **f**, Est 9:17
and the **f** days of the month Est 9:18
observe the **f** day of the month Est 9:19
to celebrate the **f** and fifteenth Est 9:21
In the **f** year of King Hezekiah, Is 36:1
of the month in the **f** year after Ezk 40:1
on the **f** day of the month, Ezk 45:21
When the **f** night came, we were Ac 27:27
Today is the **f** day that you have Ac 27:33

FOURTH *(69)*

and then morning: the **f** day. Gn 1:19
the **f** river is the Euphrates. Gn 2:14
In the **f** generation they will Gn 15:16
to the third and **f** ⌊generations⌋ Ex 20:5
and the **f** row, a beryl, an onyx, Ex 28:20
to the third and **f** generation. Ex 34:7
and the **f** row, a beryl, an onyx, Ex 39:13
In the **f** year all its fruit must Lv 19:24
On the **f** day Elizur son of Nm 7:30
to the third and **f** generation. Nm 14:18
On the **f** day ⌊present⌋ 10 bulls, Nm 29:23
to the third and **f** ⌊generations⌋ Dt 5:9
The **f** lot came out for the tribe Jos 19:17
On the **f** day they said to Jdg 14:15
On the **f** day, they got up early Jdg 19:5
the **f** was Adonijah, son of 2Sm 3:4
in the **f** year of his reign over 1Kg 6:1
in ⌊Solomon's⌋ **f** year in the 1Kg 6:37
Judah in the **f** year of Israel's 1Kg 22:41
In the **f** year of King Hezekiah, 2Kg 18:9
day of the ⌊**f**⌋ month the famine 2Kg 25:3
Nethanel **f**, Raddai fifth, 1Ch 2:14
Adonijah son of Haggith was **f**; 1Ch 3:2
Zedekiah third, and Shallum **f**. 1Ch 3:15
Nohah **f**, and Rapha fifth. 1Ch 8:2
Mishmannah **f**, Jeremiah fifth, 1Ch 12:10
Jahaziel third, and Jekameam **f**. 1Ch 23:19
third to Harim, the **f** to Seorim, 1Ch 24:8
the third, and Jekameam the **f**. 1Ch 24:23
the **f** to Izri, his sons, and his 1Ch 25:11
the third, Jathniel the **f**, 1Ch 26:2
third, Sachar the **f**, Nethanel 1Ch 26:4
the third, and Zechariah the **f**. 1Ch 26:11
f ⌊commander⌋, for the fourth 1Ch 27:7
for the **f** month, was Joab's 1Ch 27:7
month in the **f** year of his reign 2Ch 3:2
Valley of Beracah on the **f** day, 2Ch 20:26
On the **f** day the silver, the Ezr 8:33
LORD their God for a **f** of the Neh 9:3
and ⌊spent⌋ another **f** of the day Neh 9:3
children to the **f** generation. Jb 42:16

He **f** his provinces from tax Est 2:18
You **f** me from affliction; Ps 4:1
You have **f** me from the feuds Ps 18:43
his hands were **f** from ⌊carrying⌋ Ps 81:6
any longer—obeyed and **f** them. Jr 34:10
slaves they had **f** and forced Jr 34:11
who had been **f** ⌊to go⌋ wherever Jr 34:16
who has died is **f** from sin's Rm 6:7

FREEDMAN *(1)*
Lord as a slave is the Lord's **f**. 1Co 7:22

FREEDMEN'S *(1)*
what is called the **F** Synagogue, Ac 6:9

FREEDOM *(22)*
been redeemed or given her **f**, Lv 19:20
and proclaim **f** in the land for Lv 25:10
and enabled you to live in **f**. Lv 26:13
captives, and **f** to the prisoners Is 61:1
Jerusalem to proclaim **f** to them, Jr 34:8
you proclaiming **f** for his Jr 34:15
not obeyed Me by proclaiming **f**, Jr 34:17
I hereby proclaim **f** for you"— Jr 34:17
servant until the year of **f**, Ezk 46:17
Me to proclaim **f** to the captives Lk 4:18
though he could have some **f**, Ac 24:23
the glorious **f** of God's children Rm 8:21
why is my **f** judged by another 1Co 10:29
of the Lord is, there is **f**. 2Co 3:17
to spy on our **f** that we have in Gl 2:4
Christ has liberated us into **f**. Gl 5:1
you are called to **f**, brothers; Gl 5:13
don't use this **f** as an Gl 5:13
perfect law of **f** and perseveres Jms 1:25
will be judged by the law of **f**. Jms 2:12
but don't use your **f** as a way to 1Pt 2:16
They promise them **f**, but they 2Pt 2:19

FREELY *(14)*
to him and **f** loan him enough Dt 15:8
because you have **f** vowed what Dt 23:23
troops had eaten **f** today from 1Sm 14:30
Royal wine flowed **f**, according Est 1:7
He distributes **f** to the poor; Ps 112:9
I will walk **f** in an open place Ps 119:45
person gives **f**, yet gains more Pr 11:24
who let ox and donkey range **f**. Is 32:20
our God, for He will **f** forgive. Is 55:7
I will **f** love them, for My anger Hs 14:4
after people have drunk **f**, Jn 2:10
are justified **f** by His grace Rm 3:24
what has been **f** given to us by 1Co 2:12
out of compulsion but **f**, 1Pt 5:2

FREES *(4)*
He **f** me from my enemies. 2Sm 22:49
He **f** me from my enemies. Ps 18:48
who **f** His servant David from the Ps 144:10
hungry. The LORD **f** prisoners. Ps 146:7

FREEWILL *(23)*
brought a **f** offering to the LORD Ex 35:29
to bring **f** offerings morning Ex 36:3
offers is a vow or a **f** offering, Lv 7:16
they present **f** gifts or payment Lv 22:18
fulfill a vow or as a **f** offering Lv 22:21
sacrifice as a **f** offering any Lv 22:23
all your **f** offerings that you Lv 23:38
a vow, or as a **f** offering, or at Nm 15:3
to your vow and **f** offerings, Nm 29:39
vow offerings and **f** offerings, Dt 12:6
you pledge; your **f** offerings; or Dt 12:17
your God with a **f** offering that Dt 16:10
was over the **f** offerings to God 2Ch 31:14
along with a **f** offering for the Ezr 1:4
that was given as a **f** offering. Ezr 1:6
leaders gave **f** offerings for Ezr 2:68
as well as the **f** offerings Ezr 3:5
with the **f** offerings given Ezr 7:16
and gold are a **f** offering to the Ezr 8:28
sacrifice a **f** offering to You Ps 54:6
the prince makes a **f** offering, Ezk 46:12
offering as a **f** offering to the Ezk 46:12
proclaim your **f** offerings, Am 4:5

FREQUENT *(2)*
On **f** journeys, ⌊I faced⌋ dangers 2Co 11:26
stomach and your **f** illnesses. 1Tm 5:23

FRESH *(24)*
then took branches of **f** poplar, Gn 30:37
must present **f** heads of grain, Lv 2:14
over **f** water in a clay Lv 14:5
slaughtered over the **f** water. Lv 14:6
a clay pot containing **f** water. Lv 14:50
bird and the **f** water, Lv 14:51
the bird, the **f** water, the live Lv 14:52
and bathe his body in **f** water; Lv 15:13
juice or eat **f** grapes or raisins Nm 6:3
all the best of the **f** olive oil, Nm 18:12
a jar, and add **f** water to them. Nm 19:17
found a **f** jawbone of a donkey, Jdg 15:15
up with seven **f** bowstrings that Jdg 16:7
her seven **f** bowstrings that Jdg 16:8
donkey bray over **f** grass or an Jb 6:5
new wine, the **f** oil, and because Jr 31:12
All its **f** leaves will wither! Ezk 17:9
water ⌊of the sea⌋ becomes **f**. Ezk 47:8
Since the water will become **f**, Ezk 47:9
they will bear **f** fruit because Ezk 47:12
put new wine into **f** wineskins, Mt 9:17
new wine is for **f** wineskins." Mk 2:22
should be put into **f** wineskins. Lk 5:38
saltwater spring yield **f** water. Jms 3:12

FRIEND *(71)*
and his **f** Hirah the Adullamite Gn 38:12
goat by his **f** the Adullamite Gn 38:20
his brother, his **f**, and his Ex 32:27
just as a man speaks with his **f**. Ex 33:11
or your closest **f** secretly Dt 13:6
telling his **f** ⌊about⌋ a dream Jdg 7:13
His **f** answered: "This is nothing Jdg 7:14
You were such a **f** to me. 2Sm 1:26
Amnon had a **f** named Jonadab, 2Sm 13:3
David's **f** Hushai the Archite 2Sm 16:16
"Is this your loyalty to your **f**?" 2Sm 16:17
"Why didn't you go with your **f**?" 2Sm 16:17
the Archite was the king's **f**. 1Ch 27:33
descendants of Abraham Your **f**? 2Ch 20:7
a price to ⌊sell⌋ your **f**. Jb 6:27
as a man ⌊pleads⌋ for his **f**. Jb 16:21
when he becomes God's **f**." Jb 34:9
not harm his **f** or discredit his Ps 15:3
as if for my **f** or brother; Ps 35:14
Even my **f** in whom I trusted, Ps 41:9
peer, my companion and good **f**! Ps 55:13
darkness is my ⌊only⌋ **f**. Ps 88:18
I am a **f** to all who fear You, Ps 119:63
but He is a **f** to the upright. Pr 3:32
A **f** loves at all times, and a Pr 17:17
and puts up security for his **f**. Pr 17:18
there is a **f** who stays closer Pr 18:24
man is separated from his **f**. Pr 19:4
everyone is a **f** of one who gives Pr 19:6
lips—the king is his **f**. Pr 22:11
wounds of a **f** are trustworthy Pr 27:6
sweetness of a **f** is better than Pr 27:9
abandon your **f** or your father's Pr 27:10
your friend or your father's **f**, Pr 27:10
to a man's jealousy of his **f**. Ec 4:4
and this is my **f**, young women Sg 5:16
brother and each against his **f**, Is 19:2
descendant of Abraham, My **f**— Is 41:8
to be on guard against his **f**. Jr 9:4
and every **f** spread slander. Jr 9:4
Each one betrays his **f**; Jr 9:5
man speaks peaceably with his **f**, Jr 9:8
is to say to his **f** and to his Jr 23:35
Do not rely on a **f**; don't trust Mc 7:5
a **f** of tax collectors and Mt 11:19
one of them, '**F**, I'm doing you Mt 20:13
said to him, '**F**, how did you get Mt 22:12
"**F**," Jesus asked him, "why have Mt 26:50
faith He said, "**F**, your sins are Lk 5:20
a **f** of tax collectors and Lk 7:34
of you has a **f** and goes to him Lk 11:5
says to him, '**F**, lend me three Lk 11:5
because a **f** of mine on a journey Lk 11:6
anything because he is his **f**, Lk 11:8
"**F**," He said to him, "who Lk 12:14
say to you, '**F**, move up higher. Lk 14:10
But the groom's **f**, who stands by Jn 3:29
Our **f** Lazarus has fallen asleep, Jn 11:11
man, you are not Caesar's **f**. Jn 19:12
a close **f** of Herod the tetrarch, Ac 13:1
Greet my dear **f** Epaenetus, Rm 16:5
my dear **f** in the Lord. Rm 16:8
Christ, and my dear **f** Stachys. Rm 16:9
Greet my dear **f** Persis, who has Rm 16:12
our dear **f** and co-worker, Phm 1
and he was called God's **f**. Jms 2:23
be the world's **f** becomes God's Jms 4:4
To my dear **f** Gaius, whom I love 3Jn 1
Dear **f**, I pray that you may 3Jn 2
Dear **f**, you are showing your 3Jn 5
Dear **f**, do not imitate what is 3Jn 11

FRIENDLY *(2)*
who speak in **f** ways with their Ps 28:3
For they do not speak in **f** ways, Ps 35:20

FRIENDS *(85)*
mountains with my **f** and mourn Jdg 11:37
left with her **f** and mourned her Jdg 11:38
some of the plunder to his **f**, 1Sm 30:26
and to his **f** and haven't handed 2Sm 3:8
had always been **f** with David. 1Kg 5:1
whether of his kinsmen or his **f**. 1Kg 16:11
men, close **f**, and priests— 2Kg 10:11
He sent for his **f** and his wife Est 5:10
Zeresh and all his **f** told him, Est 5:14
and all his **f** everything that Est 6:13
Now when Job's three **f**—Eliphaz Jb 2:11
receive loyalty from his **f**, Jb 6:14
I am a laughingstock to my **f**, Jb 12:4
f scoff at me as I weep before Jb 16:20
informs on his **f** for a price, Jb 17:5
my close **f** have forgotten me. Jb 19:14
All of my best **f** despise me, Jb 19:19
mercy on me, my **f**, have mercy, Jb 19:21
Job's three **f** because they had Jb 32:3
Job's **f** are dismayed and can no Jb 32:15
answer you and your **f** with you. Jb 35:4
angry with you and your two **f**, Jb 42:7
After Job had prayed for his **f**, Jb 42:10
My loved ones and **f** stand back Ps 38:11
thief, you make **f** with him, and Ps 50:18
You have distanced my **f** from me; Ps 88:8
Because of my brothers and **f**, Ps 122:8
and a gossip separates **f**. Pr 16:28
gossips about it separates **f**. Pr 17:9
A man with many **f** may be harmed, Pr 18:24
attracts many **f**, but a poor man Pr 19:4
much more do his **f** keep their Pr 19:7
Don't make **f** with an angry man, Pr 22:24
with my milk. Eat, **f**! Drink, be Sg 5:1
rulers are rebels, **f** of thieves. Is 1:23
f and neighbors will ⌊also⌋ Jr 6:21
appoints close **f** as leaders over Jr 13:21
you and all your **f** that you Jr 20:6
Your trusted **f** misled you and Jr 38:22
All her **f** have betrayed her; Lm 1:2
searched for Daniel and his **f**, Dn 2:13
house and told his **f** Hananiah, Dn 2:17
so Daniel and his **f** would not be Dn 2:18
I received in the house of my **f**. Zch 13:6
Him among their relatives and **f**. Lk 2:44
centurion sent **f** to tell Him, Lk 7:6
I say to you, My **f**, don't fear Lk 12:4
invite your **f**, your brothers, Lk 14:12
he calls his **f** and neighbors Lk 15:6
calls her women **f** and neighbors Lk 15:9
so I could celebrate with my **f**. Lk 15:29
make **f** for yourselves by means Lk 16:9
brothers, relatives, and **f**. Lk 21:16
day Herod and Pilate became **f**. Lk 23:12
lay down his life for his **f**. Jn 15:13
You are My **f** if you do what I Jn 15:14
called you **f**, because I have Jn 15:15
his relatives and close **f**. Ac 10:24
who were his **f**, sent word to him Ac 19:31
any of his **f** from serving him. Ac 24:23
to go to his **f** to receive their Ac 27:3
F, do not avenge yourselves; Rm 12:19
Therefore, my dear **f**, flee from 1Co 10:14
Therefore dear **f**, since we have 2Co 7:1
dear **f**, is for building 2Co 12:19
So then, my dear **f**, just as you Php 2:12
stand firm in the Lord, dear **f**. Php 4:1
this way, dear **f**, in your case Heb 6:9
Dear **f**, I urge you as aliens and 1Pt 2:11
Dear **f**, when the fiery ordeal 1Pt 4:12
Dear **f**, this is now the second 2Pt 3:1
Dear **f**, don't let this one thing 2Pt 3:8
Therefore, dear **f**, while you 2Pt 3:14
Therefore, dear **f**, since you 2Pt 3:17
Dear **f**, I am not writing you a 1Jn 2:7
Dear **f**, we are God's children 1Jn 3:2
Dear **f**, if our hearts do not 1Jn 3:21
Dear **f**, do not believe every 1Jn 4:1
Dear **f**, let us love one another, 1Jn 4:7

Dear f, if God loved us in this 1Jn 4:11
The f send you greetings. 3Jn 14
greetings. Greet the f by name. 3Jn 14
Dear f, although I was eager to Jd 3
But you, dear f, remember the Jd 17
But you, dear f, building Jd 20

FRIENDSHIP (3)
peace or f with them as long Dt 23:6
youth when God's f rested on my Jb 29:4
not know that f with the world Jms 4:4

FRIGHTEN (13)
down with nothing to f ⌊you⌋. Lv 26:6
on the wall to f and discourage 2Ch 32:18
then You f me with dreams, Jb 7:14
His terror will no longer f me. Jb 9:34
and do not let Your terror f me. Jb 13:21
Will You f a wind-driven leaf? Jb 13:25
Terrors f him on every side and Jb 18:11
and quiet with no one to f him. Jr 30:10
and quiet with no one to f him. Jr 46:27
and no one will f ⌊them⌋. Ezk 34:28
land with no one to f ⌊them⌋. Ezk 39:26
fig tree with no one to f ⌊him⌋. Mc 4:4
with nothing to f them away? Nah 2:11

FRIGHTENED (3)
I had a dream, and it f me; Dn 4:5
not being f in any way by your Php 1:28
do good and aren't f by anything 1Pt 3:6

FRIGHTENING (2)
Their rims were large and f. Ezk 1:18
beast appeared, f and dreadful, Dn 7:7

FRINGES (1)
These are but the f of His ways; Jb 26:14

FROGS (15)
all your territory with f. Ex 8:2
The Nile will swarm with f; Ex 8:3
The f will come up on you, Ex 8:4
and cause the f to come up onto Ex 8:5
the f came up and covered the Ex 8:6
and brought f up onto the land Ex 8:7
He remove the f from me and my Ex 8:8
that the f be taken away from Ex 8:9
the f will go away from you, Ex 8:11
f will remain only in the Nile. Ex 8:11
concerning the f that He had Ex 8:12
the f in the houses, courtyards, Ex 8:13
fed on them, and f, which Ps 78:45
Their land was overrun with f, Ps 105:30
unclean spirits like f ⌊coming⌋ Rv 16:13

FROLIC (1)
because you f like a young cow Jr 50:11

FROM (5527)
(See pp. xi-xii.)

FRONDS (1)
trees—palm f, boughs of leafy Lv 23:40

FRONT (197)
Rebekah is here in f of you. Gn 24:51
the troughs in f of the sheep— Gn 30:38
flocks bred in f of the branches Gn 30:39
breed in f of the branches. Gn 30:41
and camped in f of the city. Gn 33:18
there was a vine in f of me. Gn 40:9
his composure in f of all his Gn 45:1
should we die here in f of you? Gn 47:15
we perish here in f of you— Gn 47:19
sure you do in f of Pharaoh all Ex 4:21
made us reek in f of Pharaoh and Ex 5:21
Egyptians detest in f of them, Ex 8:26
its place in f of the people. Ex 13:22
and camp in f of Pi-hahiroth, Ex 14:2
must camp in f of Baal-zephon, Ex 14:2
Pi-hahiroth, in f of Baal-zephon. Ex 14:9
was going in f of the Israelite Ex 14:19
from in f of them and stood Ex 14:19
stand there in f of you on the Ex 17:6
there in f of the mountain Ex 19:2
send the hornet in f of you, Ex 23:28
illuminate the area in f of it. Ex 25:37
double at the f of the tent. Ex 26:9
veil that is in f of the Ex 27:21
shoulder pieces in the f. Ex 28:25
two shoulder pieces on its f, Ex 28:27
is to be on the f of the turban. Ex 28:37
the bull to the f of the tent Ex 29:10
place the altar in f of the veil Ex 30:6
in f of the mercy seat that is Ex 30:6
and put some in f of the Ex 30:36
sides—inscribed f and back. Ex 32:15
My goodness to pass in f of you, Ex 33:19
to graze in f of that mountain. Ex 34:3
the LORD passed in f of him and Ex 34:6
ephod's shoulder pieces in f. Ex 39:18
two shoulder pieces on its f, Ex 39:20
altar for incense in f of the Ex 40:5
offering in f of the entrance Ex 40:6
of meeting, in f of the veil, Ex 40:26
before the LORD in f of the veil Lv 4:6
the LORD in f of the veil. Lv 4:17
the LORD in f of the altar. Lv 6:14
diadem, on the f of the turban, Lv 8:9
commanded to the f of the tent Lv 9:5
from the f of the sanctuary to Lv 10:4
It is a fungus on the f or back Lv 13:55
the veil in f of the mercy seat Lv 16:2
the mercy seat and in f of it. Lv 16:15
block in f of the blind, Lv 19:14
camped in f of the tabernacle on Nm 3:38
in f of the tent of meeting Nm 3:38
them in f of the tabernacle Nm 7:3
offerings in f of the altar. Nm 7:10
light in f of the lampstand. Nm 8:2
give light⌋ in f of the Nm 8:3
to the ground⌋ in f of the whole Nm 14:5
are right in f of you, Nm 14:43
Aaron went to the f of the tent Nm 16:43
of meeting in f of the testimony Nm 17:4
rod back in f of the testimony Nm 17:10
and your sons in f of the tent Nm 18:2
times toward the f of the tent Nm 19:4
the assembly in f of the rock, Nm 20:10
were cut off in f of the ark Jos 4:7
formation in f of the Israelites Jos 4:12
man standing in f of him with a Jos 5:13
trumpets in f of the ark. Jos 6:4
seven trumpets in f of the ark Jos 6:6
troops went in f of the priests Jos 6:9
trumpets marched in f of the ark Jos 6:13
armed troops went in f of them, Jos 6:13
of them were in f of Mount Jos 8:33
and half in f of Mount Ebal, Jos 8:33
is in f of His tabernacle." Jos 22:29
and possessions in f of them. Jdg 18:21
or running in f of his chariots. 1Sm 8:11
to the north in f of Michmash 1Sm 14:5
other to the south in f of Geba. 1Sm 14:5
was walking in f of him. 1Sm 17:7
to others in f of him and asked 1Sm 17:30
the shield-bearer in f of him. 1Sm 17:41
and his men in f of the Rocks 1Sm 24:2
to the ground in f of David. 1Sm 25:23
me set some food in f of you. 1Sm 28:22
get up and compete in f of us." 2Sm 2:14
Ahio walked in f of the ark. 2Sm 6:4
a battle line in f of him and 2Sm 10:9
Uriah at the f of the fiercest 2Sm 11:15
pan and set it down in f of him, 2Sm 13:9
The portico in f of the temple 1Kg 6:3
15 feet deep in f of the temple. 1Kg 6:3
sanctuary in f of the most holy 1Kg 6:17
chains across the f of the inner 1Kg 6:21
portico was in f of the pillars 1Kg 7:6
with pillars were in f of them. 1Kg 7:6
lampstands in f of the inner 1Kg 7:49
were with him in f of the ark, 1Kg 8:5
the holy place in f of the inner 1Kg 8:8
of the LORD in f of the entire 1Kg 8:22
that was in f of the LORD's 1Kg 8:64
teams of oxen were in f of him, 1Kg 19:19
camped in f of them like two 1Kg 20:27
were prophesying in f of them. 1Kg 22:10
on his knees in f of Elijah and 2Kg 1:13
down to the ground in f of him. 2Kg 2:15
and water in f of them so they 2Kg 6:22
the LORD in f of the temple 2Kg 16:14
song in f of the tabernacle, 1Ch 6:32
a battle line in f of him and 1Ch 19:10
in f of the LORD's tabernacle. 2Ch 1:5
was in Gibeon in f of the tent 2Ch 1:13
across the f extending across 2Ch 3:4
In f of the temple he made two 2Ch 3:15
the pillars in f of the 2Ch 3:17
gold to burn in f of the inner 2Ch 4:20
around him were in f of the ark 2Ch 5:6
the holy place in f of the inner 2Ch 5:9
of the LORD in f of the entire 2Ch 6:12
knelt down in f of the entire 2Ch 6:13
that was in f of the LORD's 2Ch 7:7
had made in f of the vestibule 2Ch 8:12
So they were in f of Judah, 2Ch 13:13
the battle was in f of them and 2Ch 13:14
that was in f of the vestibule 2Ch 15:8
were prophesying in f of them. 2Ch 18:9
they went out in f of the armed 2Ch 20:21
They are in f of the altar of 2Ch 29:19
at the square in f of the Water Neh 8:1
the square in f of the Water Neh 8:3
the scribe went in f of them. Neh 12:36
you camping in f of the wall? Neh 13:21
took a walk in f of the harem's Est 2:11
city square in f of the King's Est 4:6
darkness to light in f of them, Is 42:16
your guilt is still in f of Me. Jr 2:22
law I set in f of them and did Jr 9:13
with a fire burning in f of him. Jr 36:22
the whole land is in f of you. Jr 40:4
was written on the f and back; Ezk 2:10
a stumbling block in f of him, Ezk 3:20
set it in f of you, and draw Ezk 4:1
your slain in f of your idols. Ezk 6:4
Israelites in f of their idols Ezk 6:5
Judah were sitting in f of me, Ezk 8:1
who were in f of the temple. Ezk 9:6
profane Me in f of My people for Ezk 13:19
to me and sat down in f of me. Ezk 14:1
and they sat down in f of me. Ezk 20:1
brandish My sword in f of them. Ezk 32:10
crowds, sit in f of you, and Ezk 33:31
21 inches in f of the recesses Ezk 40:12
from the f of the gate at Ezk 40:15
entrance to the f of the gate's Ezk 40:15
from the f of the lower gate Ezk 40:19
to the exterior f of the inner Ezk 40:19
altar was in f of the temple. Ezk 40:47
The width of the f of the temple Ezk 41:14
and the f of the sanctuary had Ezk 41:21
outside, in f of the portico. Ezk 41:25
In f of the chambers was a Ezk 42:4
ran in f of the chambers, Ezk 42:7
with a passageway in f of them, Ezk 42:11
way in f of the corresponding Ezk 42:12
gate to the f of the temple. Ezk 44:4
standing in f of you, and its Dn 2:31
to the one standing in f of me, Dn 10:16
they are right in f of My face. Hs 7:2
A fire destroys in f of them, Jl 2:3
land in f of them is like the Jl 2:3
his f ranks into the Dead Sea, Jl 2:20
violence are right in f of me. Hab 1:3
gift there in f of the altar. Mt 5:24
righteousness in f of people, Mt 6:1
He was transformed in f of them, Mt 17:2
the f seats in the synagogues, Mt 23:6
he denied it in f of everyone: Mt 26:70
his hands in f of the crowd, Mt 27:24
and went out in f of everyone. Mk 2:12
He was transformed in f of them, Mk 9:2
the f seats in the synagogues, Mk 12:39
You love the f seat in the Lk 11:43
in f of Him was a man whose Lk 14:2
Then those in f told him to keep Lk 18:39
the f seats in the synagogues, Lk 20:46
health in f of all of you. Ac 3:16
standing in f of the doors; Ac 5:23
the sentries in f of the door Ac 12:6
and beat him in f of the judge's Ac 18:17
the Way in f of the crowd, Ac 19:9
burned them in f of everyone. Ac 19:19
the Jews pushed him to the f. Ac 19:33
I told Cephas in f of everyone, Gl 2:14
stumbling block in f of the sons Rv 2:14
with eyes in f and in back. Rv 4:6
gold altar in f of the throne. Rv 8:3
dragon stood in f of the woman Rv 12:4

FRONTAL (2)
Israel made a f assault against Jdg 20:34
Do not make a f assault. 2Sm 5:23

FRONTIER (2)
an altar on the f of the land of Jos 22:11
beginning with its f cities, Ezk 25:9

FROST (5)
me by day and the f by night, Gn 31:40
as fine as f on the ground. Ex 16:14

gave birth to the **f** of heaven Jb 38:29
He scatters **f** like ashes; Ps 147:16
heat of day and the **f** of night. Jr 36:30

FROZE *(1)*
They looked, and **f** with fear; Ps 48:5

FROZEN *(2)*
and watery expanses are **f**. Jb 37:10
of the watery depths is **f**? Jb 38:30

FRUIT *(161)*
and **f** trees on the earth bearing Gn 1:11
earth bearing **f** with seed in it Gn 1:11
trees bearing **f** with seed in it Gn 1:12
tree whose **f** contains seed. Gn 1:29
We may eat the **f** from the trees Gn 3:2
But about the **f** of the tree in Gn 3:3
took some of its **f** and ate ⌊it⌋; Gn 3:6
gave me ⌊some **f**⌋ from the tree, Gn 3:12
and all the **f** on the trees that Ex 10:15
are to consider the **f** forbidden. Lv 19:23
year all its **f** must be Lv 19:24
fifth year you may eat its **f**. Lv 19:25
Then the land will yield its **f**, Lv 25:19
of the field will bear their **f**. Lv 26:4
the land will not bear their **f**. Lv 26:20
the soil or **f** from the trees, Lv 27:30
back some **f** from the land." Nm 13:20
showed them the **f** of the land. Nm 13:26
and here is some of its **f**. Nm 13:27
took some of the **f** from the land Dt 1:25
and not begun to enjoy its **f**? Dt 20:6
and another man enjoy its **f**. Dt 20:6
knock down the **f** from your olive Dt 24:20
a vineyard but not enjoy its **f**. Dt 28:30
bearing poisonous and bitter **f**. Dt 29:18
my sweetness and my good **f**, Jdg 9:11
100 ⌊bunches⌋ of summer **f**, 2Sm 16:1
bread and summer **f** are for the 2Sm 16:2
plant vineyards and eat their **f**. 2Kg 19:29
downward and bear **f** upward. 2Kg 19:30
olive groves, and **f** trees in Neh 9:25
could enjoy its **f** and its Neh 9:36
land and of every **f** tree to the Neh 10:35
offerings, of every **f** tree, and Neh 10:37
must return the **f** of his labor Jb 20:18
that bears its **f** in season and Ps 1:3
and the **f** of their labor to Ps 78:46
that all who pass by pick its **f**? Ps 80:12
will still bear **f** in old age, Ps 92:14
by the **f** of Your labor. Ps 104:13
and all hills, **f** trees and all Ps 148:9
they will eat the **f** of their way Pr 1:31
My **f** is better than solid gold, Pr 8:19
The **f** of the righteous is a tree Pr 11:30
of the righteous produces ⌊**f**⌋. Pr 12:12
From the **f** of his mouth a man's Pr 18:20
who love it will eat its **f**. Pr 18:21
tends a fig tree will eat its **f**, Pr 27:18
every kind of **f** tree in them. Ec 2:5
and his **f** is sweet to my taste. Sg 2:3
breasts are clusters ⌊of **f**⌋. Sg 7:7
tree and take hold of its **f**." Sg 7:8
to bring for his **f** 1,000 pieces Sg 8:11
will eat the **f** of their deeds. Is 3:10
the **f** of the land will be the Is 4:2
from his roots will bear **f**. Is 11:1
your summer ⌊**f**⌋ and your harvest Is 16:9
and fill the whole world with **f**. Is 27:6
plant vineyards and eat their **f**. Is 37:30
root downward and bear **f** upward. Is 37:31
plant vineyards and eat their **f**. Is 65:21
land to eat its **f** and bounty, Jr 2:7
the **f** of their own plotting, Jr 6:19
and on the **f** of the ground. Jr 7:20
beautiful with well-formed **f**. Jr 11:16
destroy the tree with its **f**; Jr 11:19
They have grown and produced **f**. Jr 12:2
of drought or cease producing **f**. Jr 17:8
plant and will enjoy ⌊the **f**⌋. Jr 31:5
wine, summer **f**, and oil, place Jr 40:10
amount of wine and summer **f**. Jr 40:12
on your summer **f** and grape Jr 48:32
branches, bear **f**, and become a Ezk 17:8
and strip off its **f** so that it Ezk 17:9
branches, produce **f**, and become Ezk 17:23
the east wind dried up its **f**. Ezk 19:12
branch and has devoured its **f**, Ezk 19:14
will eat your **f** and drink your Ezk 25:4
of the field will give their **f**, Ezk 34:27
and bear your **f** for My people Ezk 36:8
also make the **f** of the trees Ezk 36:30
and their **f** will not fail. Ezk 47:12
bear fresh **f** because the water Ezk 47:12
Their **f** will be used for food Ezk 47:12
beautiful, its **f** was abundant, Dn 4:12
its leaves and scatter its **f**. Dn 4:14
beautiful and its **f** abundant— Dn 4:21
like the first **f** of the fig tree Hs 9:10
they cannot bear **f**. Even if they Hs 9:16
it yields **f** for itself. Hs 10:1
The more his **f** increased, the Hs 10:1
you have eaten the **f** of lies. Hs 10:13
pine tree; your **f** comes from Me. Hs 14:8
trees bear their **f**, and the fig Jl 2:22
I destroyed his **f** above and his Am 2:9
and the **f** of righteousness Am 6:12
me this: A basket of summer **f**. Am 8:1
replied, "A basket of summer **f**." Am 8:2
when the summer **f** has been Mc 7:1
and there is no **f** on the vines, Hab 3:17
the vine will yield its **f**, Zch 8:12
produce **f** consistent with Mt 3:8
produce good **f** will be cut down Mt 3:10
recognize them by their **f**. Mt 7:16
every good tree produces good **f**, Mt 7:17
but a bad tree produces bad **f**. Mt 7:17
A good tree can't produce bad **f**; Mt 7:18
can a bad tree produce good **f**. Mt 7:18
produce good **f** is cut down Mt 7:19
recognize them by their **f**. Mt 7:20
the tree good and its **f** good, Mt 12:33
make the tree bad and its **f** bad; Mt 12:33
for a tree is known by its **f**. Mt 12:33
who does bear **f** and yields: Mt 13:23
no **f** ever come from you again! Mt 21:19
to the farmers to collect his **f**. Mt 21:34
to a nation producing its **f**. Mt 21:43
drink of this **f** of the vine Mt 26:29
one ever eat **f** from you again! Mk 11:14
some of the **f** of the vineyard Mk 12:2
drink of the **f** of the vine until Mk 14:25
produce **f** consistent with Lk 3:8
produce good **f** will be cut down Lk 3:9
good tree doesn't produce bad **f**; Lk 6:43
bad tree doesn't produce good **f**. Lk 6:43
each tree is known by its own **f**. Lk 6:44
life, and produce no mature **f**. Lk 8:14
to it and by enduring, bear **f**. Lk 8:15
looking for **f** on it and found Lk 13:6
looking for **f** on this fig tree Lk 13:7
it will bear **f** next year, Lk 13:9
give him some **f** from the Lk 20:10
not drink of the **f** of the vine Lk 22:18
and gathering **f** for eternal life Jn 4:36
does not produce **f** He removes, Jn 15:2
that produces **f** so that it will Jn 15:2
so that it will produce more **f**. Jn 15:2
to produce **f** by itself unless Jn 15:4
Me and I in him produces much **f**, Jn 15:5
produce much **f** and prove to be Jn 15:8
out and produce **f** and that your Jn 15:16
and that your **f** should remain, Jn 15:16
what **f** was produced then from Rm 6:21
you have your **f**, which results Rm 6:22
that we may bear **f** for God. Rm 7:4
part of us and bore **f** for death. Rm 7:5
vineyard and does not eat its **f**? 1Co 9:7
But the **f** of the Spirit is love, Gl 5:22
for the **f** of the light ⌊results⌋ Eph 5:9
filled with the **f** of Php 1:11
but I seek the **f** that is Php 4:17
It is bearing **f** and growing all Col 1:6
bearing **f** in every good work and Col 1:10
it yields the **f** of peace and Heb 12:11
the **f** of our lips that confess Heb 13:15
And the **f** of righteousness is Jms 3:18
for the precious **f** of the earth Jms 5:7
and the land produced its **f**. Jms 5:18
The **f** you craved has left you. Rv 18:14
of life bearing 12 kinds of **f**, Rv 22:2
producing its **f** every month. Rv 22:2

FRUITFUL *(29)*
blessed them, "Be **f**, multiply, Gn 1:22
to them, "Be **f**, multiply, fill Gn 1:28
the earth and be **f** and multiply Gn 8:17
Be **f** and multiply and fill the Gn 9:1
But you, be **f** and multiply; Gn 9:7
you extremely **f** and will make Gn 17:6
I will make him **f** and will Gn 17:20
and we will be **f** in the land." Gn 26:22
and make you **f** and multiply you Gn 28:3
God Almighty. Be **f** and multiply. Gn 35:11
God has made me **f** in the land of Gn 41:52
in it and became **f** and very Gn 47:27
'I will make you **f** and numerous; Gn 48:4
Joseph is a **f** vine, a fruitful Gn 49:22
a fruitful vine, a **f** vine beside Gn 49:22
But the Israelites were **f**, Ex 1:7
make you **f** and multiply you, Lv 26:9
The LORD made His people very **f**; Ps 105:24
and **f** land into salty wasteland, Ps 107:34
that yield a **f** harvest. Ps 107:37
be like a **f** vine within your Ps 128:3
four or five on its **f** branches. Is 17:6
fields and the **f** vines, Is 32:12
They will become **f** and numerous. Jr 23:3
it was **f** and full of branches Ezk 19:10
and they will increase and be **f**. Ezk 36:11
rain from heaven and **f** seasons, Ac 14:17
I might have a **f** ministry among Rm 1:13
flesh, this means **f** work for me; Php 1:22

FRUITLESS *(3)*
in the **f** works of darkness Eph 5:11
turned aside to **f** discussion. 1Tm 1:6
in late autumn—**f**, twice dead, Jd 12

FRUITS *(4)*
of pomegranates with choicest **f**, Sg 4:13
garden and eat its choicest **f**. Sg 4:16
200 for those who guard its **f**. Sg 8:12
of mercy and good **f**, without Jms 3:17

FRUSTRATE *(3)*
against them to **f** their plans Ezr 4:5
You ⌊sinners⌋ **f** the plans of the Ps 14:6
it, and I will **f** its plans. Is 19:3

FRUSTRATED *(4)*
Amnon was **f** to the point of 2Sm 13:2
scheme and that God had **f** it, Neh 4:15
they arrive there, they are **f**. Jb 6:20
It has **f** every effort; Ezk 24:12

FRUSTRATES *(3)*
f the schemes of the crafty so Jb 5:12
The LORD **f** the counsel of the Ps 33:10
but He **f** the ways of the wicked. Ps 146:9

FUEL *(9)*
be burned as **f** for the fire. Is 9:5
people are like **f** for the fire. Is 9:19
Lebanon is not enough for **f**, Is 40:16
It serves as **f** for man. Is 44:15
it is put into the fire as **f**. Ezk 15:4
I have given to the fire as **f**, Ezk 15:6
You will be **f** for the fire. Ezk 21:32
and also pile up the **f** under it. Ezk 24:5
labor ⌊only⌋ to **f** the fire and Hab 2:13

FUGITIVE *(7)*
until no survivor or **f** remained, Jos 8:22
Whenever a **f** from Ephraim said, Jdg 12:5
will be a **f** until death. Pr 28:17
will have no **f** or survivor to Jr 44:14
on that day a **f** will come to you Ezk 24:26
f from Jerusalem came to me and Ezk 33:21
evening before the **f** arrived, Ezk 33:22

FUGITIVES *(11)*
are Ephraimite **f** in ⌊the Jdg 12:4
whose **f** ⌊flee⌋ as far as Zoar, Is 15:5
All your **f** were captured Is 22:3
and bring all of them as **f**, Is 43:14
draw near, you **f** of the nations. Is 45:20
return except ⌊for a few⌋ **f**." Jr 44:14
with no one to gather up the **f**. Jr 49:5
is⌋ a voice of **f** and escapees Jr 50:28
All the **f** among his troops will Ezk 17:21
none of their **f** will escape. Am 9:1
crossroads to cut off their **f**, Ob 14

FULFILL *(42)*
the LORD will **f** to Abraham what Gn 18:19
to the LORD to **f** a vow or as a Lv 22:21
he must **f** whatever vow he makes Nm 6:21
his brothers to **f** Nm 8:26
a sacrifice, to **f** a vow, or as Nm 15:3
a sacrifice, to **f** a vow, or as Nm 15:8
not act, or promise and not **f**? Nm 23:19
the LORD your God to **f** any vow, Dt 23:18
f the promise forever that You 2Sm 7:25

to Hebron to **f** a vow I made to 2Sm 15:7
I will **f** My promise to you, 1Kg 6:12
you, and you will **f** your vows. Jb 22:27
heart desires and **f** your whole Ps 20:4
the LORD **f** all your requests. Ps 20:5
will **f** my vows before those who Ps 22:25
I will **f** my vows to the LORD in Ps 116:14
I will **f** my vows to the LORD, Ps 116:18
LORD will **f** ⌊His purpose⌋ for Ps 138:8
in fools. **F** what you vow. Ec 5:4
than that you vow and not **f** it. Ec 5:5
vows to the LORD and **f** them. Is 19:21
will **f** all My pleasure and say Is 44:28
when I will **f** the good promises Jr 33:14
am about to **f** My words for harm Jr 39:16
assert themselves to **f** a vision, Dn 11:14
I will **f** what I have vowed. Jnh 2:9
Judah; **f** your vows. For Nah 1:15
took place to **f** what was spoken Mt 1:22
Nazareth to **f** what was spoken Mt 2:23
way for us to **f** all Mt 3:15
This was to **f** what was spoken Mt 4:14
not come to destroy but to **f**. Mt 5:17
of vengeance to **f** all the things Lk 21:22
But this was to **f** the word of Jn 12:38
This was to **f** the words He had Jn 18:9
did this⌋ to **f** the Scripture Jn 19:24
drawing near to **f** the promise Ac 7:17
husband should **f** his marital 1Co 7:3
way you will **f** the law of Christ Gl 6:2
f my joy by thinking the same Php 2:2
f every desire for goodness and 2Th 1:11
an evangelist, **f** your ministry. 2Tm 4:5

FULFILLED *(58)*

does not come true or is not **f**, Dt 18:22
Israel failed. Everything was **f**. Jos 21:45
Everything was **f** for you; Jos 23:14
and it **f** the LORD's prophecy He 1Kg 2:27
He has **f** ⌊the promise⌋ by His 1Kg 8:15
The LORD has **f** what He promised. 1Kg 8:20
to him⌋ and You **f** ⌊Your promise⌋ 1Kg 8:24
He has **f** ⌊the promise⌋ by His 2Ch 6:4
So the LORD has **f** what He 2Ch 6:10
and You **f** ⌊Your promise⌋ by Your 2Ch 6:15
This **f** the word of the LORD 2Ch 36:21
until 70 years were **f**. 2Ch 36:21
spoken through Jeremiah was **f**. 2Ch 36:22
spoken through Jeremiah was **f**. Ezr 1:1
vows to You will be **f**. Ps 65:1
today I've **f** my vows. Pr 7:14
but **f** desire is a tree of life. Pr 13:12
Desire **f** is sweet to the taste, Pr 13:19
He has completely **f** the purposes Jr 23:20
He has completely **f** the purposes Jr 30:24
and the LORD has **f** ⌊it⌋. Jr 40:3
and you men **f** it by your deeds, Jr 44:25
The message I speak will be **f**." Ezk 12:28
through the prophet might be **f**: Mt 2:15
Jeremiah the prophet was **f**: Mt 2:17
the prophet Isaiah might be **f**: Mt 8:17
the prophet Isaiah might be **f**: Mt 12:17
Isaiah's prophecy is **f** in them, Mt 13:14
through the prophet might be **f**: Mt 13:35
through the prophet might be **f**: Mt 21:4
Scriptures be **f** that say it must Mt 26:54
Scriptures would be **f**." Mt 26:56
the prophet Jeremiah was **f**: Mt 27:9
The time is **f**, and the kingdom Mk 1:15
But the Scriptures must be **f**." Mk 14:49
the Scripture was **f** that says: Mk 15:28
that have been **f** among us, Lk 1:1
will be **f** in their proper time. Lk 1:20
to her by the Lord will be **f**!" Lk 1:45
this Scripture has been **f**." Lk 4:21
the times of the Gentiles are **f**. Lk 21:24
until it is **f** in the kingdom Lk 22:16
what is written must be **f** in Me: Lk 22:37
and the Psalms must be **f**." Lk 24:44
But the Scripture must be **f**: Jn 13:18
written in their law might be **f**: Jn 15:25
so that the Scripture may be **f**. Jn 17:12
words might be **f** signifying what Jn 18:32
that the Scripture might be **f**, Jn 19:28
that the Scripture would be **f**: Jn 19:36
had to be **f** that the Holy Ac 1:16
suffer—He has **f** in this way. Ac 3:18
have **f** their words by condemning Ac 13:27
they had **f** all that had been Ac 13:29
God has **f** this to us their Ac 13:33
who loves another has **f** the law. Rm 13:8
entire law is **f** in one statement Gl 5:14
the Scripture was **f** that says, Jms 2:23

FULFILLING *(4)*

⌊**f**⌋ all the words of the book 2Kg 22:16
⌊**f**⌋ all the curses written in 2Ch 34:24
of Your name, **f** my vows day by Ps 61:8
God, don't delay **f** it, because Ec 5:4

FULFILLMENT *(5)*

well as the **f** of every vision. Ezk 12:23
they wait for the **f** of ⌊their⌋ Ezk 13:6
about Me is coming to its **f**." Lk 22:37
therefore, is the **f** of the law. Rm 13:10
of the days of **f**— Eph 1:10

FULFILLS *(5)*

This ⌊**f**⌋ the LORD's word that He 2Kg 9:36
to God who **f** ⌊His purpose⌋ for Ps 57:2
He **f** the desires of those who Ps 145:19
His servant and **f** the counsel of Is 44:26
but who **f** the law, will judge Rm 2:27

FULL *(205)*

not yet reached its **f** measure." Gn 15:16
presence, for the **f** price, as a Gn 23:9
the troughs, in **f** view of the Gn 30:41
his people, old and **f** of days. Gn 35:29
heads of grain, **f** and good, came Gn 41:5
grain swallowed up the seven **f**, Gn 41:7
heads of grain, **f** and good, Gn 41:22
swallowed the seven **f** ones. Gn 41:24
was the **f** amount of our money, Gn 43:21
will eat bread until you are **f**. Ex 16:12
life in the **f** amount demanded Ex 21:30
A thief must make **f** restitution. Ex 22:3
fire must make **f** restitution for Ex 22:6
the man must make **f** restitution. Ex 22:14
give ⌊you⌋ the **f** number of your Ex 23:26
must make **f** restitution for it Lv 6:5
take a firepan **f** of fiery coals Lv 16:12
redeemed by the end of a **f** year, Lv 25:30
He is to pay **f** compensation, Nm 5:7
both of them **f** of fine flour Nm 7:13
four ounces, **f** of incense; Nm 7:14
both of them **f** of fine flour Nm 7:19
four ounces, **f** of incense; Nm 7:20
both of them **f** of fine flour Nm 7:25
four ounces, **f** of incense; Nm 7:26
both of them **f** of fine flour Nm 7:31
four ounces, **f** of incense; Nm 7:32
both of them **f** of fine flour Nm 7:37
four ounces, **f** of incense; Nm 7:38
both of them **f** of fine flour Nm 7:43
four ounces, **f** of incense; Nm 7:44
both of them **f** of fine flour Nm 7:49
four ounces, **f** of incense; Nm 7:50
both of them **f** of fine flour Nm 7:55
four ounces, **f** of incense; Nm 7:56
both of them **f** of fine flour Nm 7:61
four ounces, **f** of incense; Nm 7:62
both of them **f** of fine flour Nm 7:67
four ounces, **f** of incense; Nm 7:68
both of them **f** of fine flour Nm 7:73
four ounces, **f** of incense; Nm 7:74
both of them **f** of fine flour Nm 7:79
four ounces, **f** of incense; Nm 7:80
12 gold bowls **f** of incense each Nm 7:86
threshing floor or the **f** harvest Nm 18:27
give me his house **f** of silver Nm 22:18
give me his house **f** of silver Nm 24:13
houses **f** of every good thing Dt 6:11
you eat and are **f**, you will Dt 8:10
you eat and are **f**, and build Dt 8:12
her father and mother a **f** month. Dt 21:13
as you want until you are **f**, Dt 23:24
You must have a **f** and honest Dt 25:15
a **f** and honest dry measure, Dt 25:15
approval, **f** of the LORD's Dt 33:23
its setting almost a **f** day. Jos 10:13
The temple was **f** of men and Jdg 16:27
I left **f**, but the LORD has Ru 1:21
may you receive a **f** reward from Ru 2:12
Those who are **f** hire themselves 1Sm 2:5
presented them as **f** payment to 1Sm 18:27
there was a field **f** of lentils. 2Sm 23:11
Set the **f** ones to one side." 2Kg 4:4
When they were **f**, she said to 2Kg 4:6
God with his sack **f** of 20 loaves 2Kg 4:42
he reigned in Samaria a **f** month. 2Kg 15:13
A plot of ground **f** of barley was 1Ch 11:13
Give it to me for the **f** price, 1Ch 21:22
I insist on paying the **f** price, 1Ch 21:24
David was old and **f** of days, 1Ch 23:1
good old age, **f** of days, riches 1Ch 29:28
in a coffin that was **f** of spices 2Ch 16:14
day until two **f** years passed. 2Ch 21:19
it in the chest until it was **f**. 2Ch 24:10
when he was old and **f** of days; 2Ch 24:15
to be paid in **f** to these men out Ezr 6:8
opened the book in **f** view of all Neh 8:5
day Haman left **f** of joy and in Est 5:9
second letter with **f** authority Est 9:29
approach the grave in **f** vigor, Jb 5:26
days will be **f** of prosperity. Jb 8:7
short of days and **f** of trouble. Jb 14:1
His bones may be **f** of youthful Jb 20:11
f weight of misery will crush Jb 20:22
and his bones are **f** of marrow. Jb 21:24
For I am **f** of words, and my Jb 32:18
In **f** view of the public, He Jb 34:26
Job died, old and **f** of days. Jb 42:17
the earth is **f** of the LORD's Ps 33:5
my loins are **f** of burning pain Ps 38:7
mouth is **f** of praise and honor Ps 71:8
of the land are **f** of violence. Ps 74:20
f of wine blended with spices, Ps 75:8
and gave them a **f** measure of Ps 80:5
new moon and during the **f** moon, Ps 81:3
to anger and **f** of faithful love Ps 103:8
earth is **f** of Your creatures. Ps 104:24
Our storehouses will be **f**, Ps 144:13
you many days, a **f** life, and Pr 3:2
home at the time of the **f** moon." Pr 7:20
but the wicked are **f** of misery. Pr 12:21
than a house **f** of feasting with Pr 17:1
his mouth is **f** of gravel. Pr 20:17
A person who is **f** tramples on a Pr 27:7
fool gives **f** vent to his anger, Pr 29:11
the sea, yet the sea is never **f**. Ec 1:7
hearts of people are **f** of evil, Ec 9:3
the clouds are **f**, they will pour Ec 11:3
She was once **f** of justice. Is 1:21
they are **f** of ⌊divination⌋ Is 2:6
Their land is **f** of silver and Is 2:7
their land is **f** of horses, Is 2:7
Their land is **f** of idols; Is 2:8
land will be as **f** of the Is 11:9
waters of Dibon are **f** of blood, Is 15:9
best valleys were **f** of chariots, Is 22:7
His lips are **f** of fury, and His Is 30:27
They are **f** of the LORD's fury, Is 51:20
Like a cage **f** of birds, so their Jr 5:27
so their houses are **f** of deceit. Jr 5:27
But I am **f** of the LORD's wrath; Jr 6:11
For the land is **f** of adulterers; Jr 23:10
their land is **f** of guilt against Jr 51:5
four rims were **f** of eyes all Ezk 1:18
the land is **f** of bloodshed, Ezk 9:9
and the city **f** of perversity. Ezk 9:9
were **f** of eyes all around. Ezk 10:12
f plumage of many colors came Ezk 17:3
was fruitful and **f** of branches Ezk 19:10
you infamous one **f** of turmoil. Ezk 22:5
So you became **f** and heavily Ezk 27:25
f of wisdom and perfect in Ezk 28:12
the valley; it was **f** of bones. Ezk 37:1
your hand and in **f** view of the Ezk 37:20
reached the **f** measure of their Dn 8:23
was mourning for three **f** weeks. Dn 10:2
not vent the **f** fury of My anger Hs 11:9
Since Gilead is **f** of evil, Hs 12:11
floors will be **f** of grain, Jl 2:24
because the winepress is **f**; Jl 3:13
place as a wagon **f** of sheaves Am 2:13
of the city are **f** of violence, Mc 6:12
deceitful, **f** of plunder, never Nah 3:1
the earth is **f** of His praise. Hab 3:3
They will be as **f** as the Zch 9:15
Bring the **f** 10 percent into the Mal 3:10
whole body will be **f** of light. Mt 6:22
body will be **f** of darkness. Mt 6:23
and when it was **f**, they dragged Mt 13:48
up 12 baskets **f** of leftover Mt 14:20
pieces—seven large baskets **f**. Mt 15:37
but inside they are **f** of greed Mt 23:25
but inside are **f** of dead men's Mt 23:27

inside you are **f** of hypocrisy Mt 23:28
f of remorse and returned the Mt 27:3
up 12 baskets **f** of pieces of Mk 6:43
how many baskets **f** of pieces of Mk 8:19
large baskets **f** of pieces of Mk 8:20
from the Jordan, **f** of the Holy Lk 4:1
both boats so **f** that they began Lk 5:7
you who are **f** now, because you Lk 6:25
to sinners to be repaid in **f**. Lk 6:34
whole body is also **f** of light. Lk 11:34
your body is also **f** of darkness. Lk 11:34
your whole body is **f** of light, Lk 11:36
whole body will be **f** of light, Lk 11:36
inside you are **f** of greed and Lk 11:39
from the Father, **f** of grace and Jn 1:14
When they were **f**, He told His Jn 6:12
A jar **f** of sour wine was sitting Jn 19:29
fixed a sponge **f** of sour wine Jn 19:29
dragging the net **f** of fish. Jn 21:8
net ashore, **f** of large fish— Jn 21:11
said, "They're **f** of new wine!" Ac 2:13
the **f** Senate of the sons of Ac 5:21
f of the Spirit and wisdom, Ac 6:3
a man **f** of faith and the Holy Ac 6:5
Stephen, **f** of grace and power, Ac 6:8
f of the Holy Spirit and of Ac 11:24
f of all deceit and all fraud, Ac 13:10
that the city was **f** of idols. Ac 17:16
Jesus Christ with **f** boldness and Ac 28:31
They are **f** of envy, murder, Rm 1:29
they know **f** well God's just Rm 1:32
in the law the **f** expression Rm 2:20
Their mouth is **f** of cursing and Rm 3:14
more will their **f** number bring! Rm 11:12
to Israel until the **f** number of Rm 11:25
that you also are **f** of goodness, Rm 15:14
Already you are **f**! Already you 1Co 4:8
they did not make **f** use of it. 1Co 7:31
and not make **f** use of my 1Co 9:18
on the **f** armor of God so that Eph 6:11
must take up the **f** armor of God, Eph 6:13
I have received everything in **f**, Php 4:18
and deserving of **f** acceptance: 1Tm 1:15
in silence with **f** submission. 1Tm 2:11
and deserves **f** acceptance. 1Tm 4:9
a true heart in **f** assurance of Heb 10:22
restless evil, **f** of deadly Jms 3:8
f of mercy and good fruits, Jms 3:17
for one another at **f** strength, 1Pt 4:8
having eyes **f** of adultery and 2Pt 2:14
but you may receive a **f** reward. 2Jn 8
which is mixed **f** strength in the Rv 14:10

FULL-TIME *(1)*
appoint men on a **f** basis to pass Ezk 39:14

FULLER'S *(3)*
by the highway to the **F** Field. 2Kg 18:17
by the road to the **F** Field. Is 7:3
by the road to the **F** Field. Is 36:2

FULLNESS *(7)*
grace after grace from His **f**, Jn 1:16
come in the **f** of the blessing Rm 15:29
the **f** of the One who fills all Eph 1:23
be filled with all the **f** of God. Eph 3:19
stature measured by Christ's **f**. Eph 4:13
to have⌋ all His **f** dwell in Him, Col 1:19
Him the entire **f** of God's nature Col 2:9

FULLY *(27)*
You are **f** vindicated." Gn 20:16
he must compensate **f**, ox for ox; Ex 21:36
death has been **f** reported to me: Ru 2:11
but **f** repays the arrogant. Ps 31:23
but the diligent is **f** satisfied. Pr 13:4
will repay; I will repay them **f** Is 65:6
reward them **f** for their former Is 65:7
chosen ones will **f** enjoy the Is 65:22
plunderers will be **f** satisfied. Jr 50:10
and like straw that is **f** dry. Nah 1:10
happen when you **f** obey the LORD Zch 6:15
everyone who is **f** trained will Lk 6:40
and when they became **f** awake, Lk 9:32
a strong man, **f** armed, guards Lk 11:21
My time has not yet **f** come." Jn 7:8
because he was **f** convinced that Rm 4:21
one must be **f** convinced in his Rm 14:5
have **f** proclaimed the good news Rm 15:19
I will know **f**, as I am fully 1Co 13:12
know fully, as I am **f** known. 1Co 13:12
goal⌋ or am already **f** mature, Php 3:12
I am **f** supplied, having received Php 4:18
of the Lord, **f** pleasing ⌊to Him⌋ Col 1:10
to make God's message **f** known, Col 1:25
can stand mature and **f** assured Col 4:12
might be **f** made through me, 2Tm 4:17
when sin is **f** grown, it gives Jms 1:15

FUN *(5)*
man to us to make **f** of us. Gn 39:14
us came to me to make **f** of me, Gn 39:17
our enemies make **f** of us. Ps 80:6
some innocent person just for **f**! Pr 1:11
will begin to make **f** of him, Lk 14:29

FUNCTION *(1)*
parts do not have the same **f**, Rm 12:4

FUNDS *(1)*
safely delivered the **f** to them, Rm 15:28

FUNERAL *(2)*
walked behind the **f** procession. 2Sm 3:31
His **f** pyre is deep and wide, Is 30:33

FUNGUS *(1)*
It is a **f** on the front or back Lv 13:55

FUR *(2)*
covered with hair like a **f** coat, Gn 25:25
it by its **f**, strike it down, 1Sm 17:35

FURIOUS *(22)*
Cain was **f**, and he was downcast. Gn 4:5
said to Cain, "Why are you **f**? Gn 4:6
your slave did to me"—he was **f** Gn 39:19
I will act with **f** hostility Lv 26:28
So he became **f** and beat the Nm 22:27
Balak became **f** with Balaam, Nm 24:10
But Moses became **f** with the Nm 31:14
Saul was **f** and resented this 1Sm 18:8
all these things, he was **f**. 2Sm 13:21
the wall, he became **f**. Neh 4:1
being closed, they became **f**. Neh 4:7
The king became **f** and his anger Est 1:12
the LORD heard and became **f**; Ps 78:21
God heard and became **f**; Ps 78:59
the nations—**f** with all their Is 34:2
out on Jacob His **f** anger and the Is 42:25
in anger, wrath, and **f** rebukes. Ezk 5:15
against them with **f** rebukes. Ezk 25:17
Then in a **f** rage Nebuchadnezzar Dn 3:13
greatly displeased and became **f**. Jnh 4:1
He is **f** with His enemies. Nah 1:2
the dragon was **f** with the woman Rv 12:17

FURIOUSLY *(2)*
of him, and his anger burned **f**. 1Sm 11:6
Race **f**, you chariots! Jr 46:9

FURLOUGH *(1)*
there is no **f** in battle, and Ec 8:8

FURNACE *(32)*
the land like the smoke of a **f**. Gn 19:28
handfuls of **f** soot, and Moses Ex 9:8
So they took **f** soot and stood Ex 9:10
went up like the smoke of a **f**, Ex 19:18
of Egypt's iron **f** to be a people Dt 4:20
out of the middle of an iron **f**. 1Kg 8:51
silver refined in an earthen **f**, Ps 12:6
like a fiery **f** when you appear; Ps 21:9
and my bones burn like a **f**. Ps 102:3
Zion and whose **f** is in Jerusalem Is 31:9
you in the **f** of affliction. Is 48:10
of Egypt, out of the iron **f**. Jr 11:4
iron, and lead inside the **f**; Ezk 22:18
and tin into the **f** to blow fire Ezk 22:20
As silver is melted inside a **f**, Ezk 22:22
thrown into a **f** of blazing fire. Dn 3:6
thrown into a **f** of blazing fire Dn 3:11
thrown into a **f** of blazing fire Dn 3:15
us from the **f** of blazing fire, Dn 3:17
to heat the **f** seven times more Dn 3:19
them into the **f** of blazing fire. Dn 3:20
into the **f** of blazing fire Dn 3:21
urgent and the **f** extremely hot, Dn 3:22
into the **f** of blazing fire. Dn 3:23
door of the **f** of blazing fire Dn 3:26
burning like a **f**, when all the Mal 4:1
and thrown into the **f** tomorrow, Mt 6:30
the blazing **f** where there will Mt 13:42
throw them into the blazing **f**. Mt 13:50
is thrown into the **f** tomorrow, Lk 12:28
like fine bronze fired in a **f**, Rv 1:15
from a great **f** so that the sun Rv 9:2

FURNISH *(1)*
provide bread or **f** meat for His Ps 78:20

FURNISHED *(2)*
room upstairs, **f** and ready. Mk 14:15
you a large, **f** room upstairs. Lk 22:12

FURNISHINGS *(9)*
as the design of all its **f**." Ex 25:9
all the ⌊other⌋ **f** of the tent— Ex 31:7
with all its **f**, its clasps, its Ex 39:33
with all its **f** so that it will Ex 40:9
all its **f**, and everything Nm 1:50
care of all the **f** of the tent Nm 3:8
consecrated it and all its **f**, Nm 7:1
tent, all the **f**, and the people Nm 19:18
in charge of the **f** and all the 1Ch 9:29

FURNITURE *(5)*
and any **f** he sits on will be Lv 15:4
Whoever sits on **f** that the man Lv 15:6
touches any **f** she was sitting Lv 15:22
the bed or the **f** she was sitting Lv 15:23
f she sits on will be unclean Lv 15:26

FURROW *(1)*
wild ox by its harness to the **f**? Jb 39:10

FURROWS *(5)*
me and its **f** join in weeping, Jb 31:38
soaking its **f** and leveling its Ps 65:10
they made their **f** long. Ps 129:3
weeds in the **f** of a field. Hs 10:4
of rocks on the **f** of a field. Hs 12:11

FURTHER *(18)*
(See pp. xi-xii.)

FURTHERMORE *(12)*
(See pp. xi-xii.)

FURY *(34)*
and their **f**, for it is cruel Gn 49:7
in ⌊His⌋ anger, **f**, and great Dt 29:28
in more contempt and **f**. Est 1:18
up against the **f** of my Ps 7:6
f, indignation, and calamity—a Ps 78:49
You withdrew all Your **f**; Ps 85:3
A king's **f** is a messenger of Pr 16:14
the rod of his **f** will be Pr 22:8
F is cruel, and anger is a flood, Pr 27:4
are full of **f**, and His tongue Is 30:27
because of the **f** of the Is 51:13
where is the **f** of the oppressor Is 51:13
the cup of His **f** from the hand Is 51:17
They are full of the LORD's **f**, Is 51:20
that goblet, the cup of My **f**. Is 51:22
f to His enemies, retribution to Is 59:18
ground them underfoot in My **f**; Is 63:3
to execute His anger with **f**, Is 66:15
My wrath and **f** from the day it Jr 32:31
rage, and great **f**, and I will Jr 32:37
the anger and **f** that the LORD Jr 36:7
My anger and **f** were poured out Jr 42:18
so will My **f** pour out on you if Jr 42:18
will fall⌋ in destructive **f**. Ezk 13:13
it was uprooted in **f**, thrown to Ezk 19:12
blow the fire of My **f** on you. Ezk 21:31
on you with the fire of My **f**, Ezk 22:21
them with the fire of My **f**. Ezk 22:31
and rushed at him with savage **f**. Dn 8:6
go out with great **f** to destroy Dn 11:44
will pour out My **f** on them like Hs 5:10
not vent the full **f** of My anger; Hs 11:9
and the **f** of a fire about to Heb 10:27
come down to you with great **f**, Rv 12:12

FUTILE *(27)*
can you offer me such **f** comfort? Jb 21:34
futility. Everything is **f**." Ec 1:2
have found everything to be **f**, Ec 1:14
But it turned out to be **f**. Ec 2:1
everything to be **f** and a pursuit Ec 2:11
to myself that this is also **f**. Ec 2:15
everything is **f** and a pursuit Ec 2:17
under the sun. This too is **f**. Ec 2:19
This too is **f** and a great wrong. Ec 2:21
does not rest. This too is **f**. Ec 2:23
This too is **f** and a pursuit of Ec 2:26
animals, for everything is **f**. Ec 3:19
This too is **f** and a pursuit of Ec 4:4
This too is **f** and a miserable Ec 4:8
This too is **f** and a pursuit of Ec 4:16
with income. This too is **f**. Ec 5:10
This is **f** and a sickening Ec 6:2

This too is **f** and a pursuit of Ec 6:9
few days of his **f** life that he Ec 6:12
of the fool. This too is **f**. Ec 7:6
In my **f** life I have seen Ec 7:15
they did so. This too is **f**. Ec 8:10
I say that this too is **f**. Ec 8:14
be many. All that comes is **f**. Ec 11:8
the Teacher. "Everything is **f**." Ec 12:8
and the peoples plot **f** things? Ac 4:25
of the wise, that they are **f**. 1Co 3:20

FUTILITY *(13)*

made to inherit months of **f**, Jb 7:3
He made their days end in **f**, Ps 78:33
"Absolute **f**," says the Teacher. Ec 1:2
Absolute **f**. Everything is Ec 1:2
Again, I saw **f** under the sun: Ec 4:7
dreams bring **f**, also many words Ec 5:7
For he comes in **f** and he goes in Ec 6:4
are many words, they increase **f**. Ec 6:11
There is a **f** that is done on the Ec 8:14
"Absolute **f**," says the Teacher. Ec 12:8
my strength for nothing and **f**; Is 49:4
creation was subjected to **f**— Rm 8:20
in the **f** of their thoughts. Eph 4:17

FUTURE *(41)*

covenant for all **f** generations: Gn 9:12
In the **f** when you come to check Gn 30:33
In the **f**, when your son asks Ex 13:14
do to your people in the **f**." Nm 24:14
but his **f** is destruction. Nm 24:20
your son asks you in the **f**, Dt 6:20
F generations of your children Dt 29:22
will come to you in the **f**, Dt 31:29
In the **f**, when your children ask Jos 4:6
ask their fathers in the **f**, Jos 4:21
that in the **f** your descendants Jos 22:24
Then in the **f**, your descendants Jos 22:27
or to our generations in the **f**, Jos 22:28
was to teach the **f** generations Jdg 3:2
house in the distant **f**. 2Sm 7:19
house in the distant **f**. 1Ch 17:17
What is my **f**, that I should be Jb 6:11
⌊of blessing⌋; You hold my **f**. Ps 16:5
the man of peace will have a **f**. Ps 37:37
the **f** of the wicked will be Ps 37:38
you can tell a **f** generation: Ps 48:13
but must tell a **f** generation the Ps 78:4
that a **f** generation—children Ps 78:6
For then you will have a **f**, Pr 23:18
you will have a **f**, and your hope Pr 24:14
For the evil have no **f**; Pr 24:20
But in the **f** He will bring honor Is 9:1
will be for the **f**, forever and Is 30:8
the outcome. Or tell us the **f**. Is 41:22
him listen and obey in the **f**. Is 42:23
like Me, can announce ⌊the **f**⌋? Is 44:7
to give you a **f** and a hope. Jr 29:11
There is hope for your **f**— Jr 31:17
My **f** is lost, as well as my hope Lm 3:18
about what will happen in the **f**. Dn 2:29
king what will happen in the **f**. Dn 2:45
refers to many days ⌊in the **f**⌋." Dn 8:26
in the **f** you will see the Son of Mt 26:64
you are not sowing the **f** body, 1Co 15:37
In the **f**, there is reserved for 2Tm 4:8
what would be said ⌊in the **f**⌋. Heb 3:5

G

GAAL *(10)*

G son of Ebed came with his Jdg 9:26
G son of Ebed said, "Who is Jdg 9:28
the words of **G** son of Ebed, Jdg 9:30
saying, "Look, **G** son of Ebed, Jdg 9:31
G son of Ebed went out and stood Jdg 9:35
When **G** saw the people, he said Jdg 9:36
G spoke again: "Look, people Jdg 9:37
So **G** went out leading the lords Jdg 9:39
him, and **G** fled before him Jdg 9:40
and Zebul drove **G** and his Jdg 9:41

GAASH *(4)*

of Ephraim north of Mount **G**. Jos 24:30
of Ephraim, north of Mount **G**. Jdg 2:9
Hiddai from the Wadis of **G**, 2Sm 23:30
Hurai from the wadis of **G**, 1Ch 11:32

GABBAI *(1)*

and after him **G** ⌊and⌋ Sallai: Neh 11:8

GABBATHA *(1)*

Pavement (but in Hebrew **G**). Jn 19:13

GABRIEL *(4)*

G, explain the vision to this Dn 8:16
I was praying, **G**, the man I had Dn 9:21
answered him, "I am **G**, who Lk 1:19
the angel **G** was sent by God to a Lk 1:26

GAD *(41)*

fortune!" and she named him **G**. Gn 30:11
slave Zilpah were **G** and Asher. Gn 35:26
G will be attacked by Gn 49:19
Dan and Naphtali; **G** and Asher. Ex 1:4
Eliasaph son of Deuel from **G**; Nm 1:14
descendants of **G**: according to Nm 1:24
the tribe of **G** numbered 45,650 Nm 1:25
The tribe of **G** ⌊will be next⌋. Nm 2:14
the division of the tribe of **G**. Nm 10:20
of Machi from the tribe of **G**. Nm 13:15
Reuben, **G**, Asher, Zebulun, Dan, Dt 27:13
He said about **G**: The one who Dt 33:20
G, Reuben, and half the tribe of Jos 18:7
of Reuben, **G**, and Zebulun. Jos 21:7
the tribe of **G**, ⌊they gave⌋: Jos 21:38
you descendants of Reuben and **G**. Jos 22:25
Reuben, **G**, and Manasseh had to Jos 22:30
of Reuben, **G**, and Manasseh, Jos 22:31
to the land of **G** and Gilead. 1Sm 13:7
the prophet **G** said to David, 1Sm 22:5
⌊proceeded⌋ toward **G** and Jazer. 2Sm 24:5
LORD had come to the prophet **G**, 2Sm 24:11
G went to David, told him ⌊the 2Sm 24:13
David answered **G**, "I have great 2Sm 24:14
G came to David that day and 2Sm 24:18
Naphtali, **G**, and Asher. 1Ch 2:2
The sons of **G** lived next to them 1Ch 5:11
of Reuben and **G** and half the 1Ch 5:18
tribes of Reuben, **G**, and Zebulun 1Ch 6:63
the tribe of **G** ⌊they received⌋ 1Ch 6:80
Then the LORD instructed **G**, 1Ch 21:9
So **G** went to David and said to 1Ch 21:11
David answered **G**, "I have great 1Ch 21:13
LORD ordered **G** to tell David to 1Ch 21:18
and the Events of **G** the Seer, 1Ch 29:29
of David, **G** the king's seer, 2Ch 29:25
dispossessed **G** and his people Jr 49:1
west, will be **G**—one ⌊portion⌋ Ezk 48:27
territory of **G** toward the south Ezk 48:28
one, the gate of **G**; one, the Ezk 48:34
12,000 from the tribe of **G**, Rv 7:5

GAD'S *(6)*

G sons: Ziphion, Haggi, Shuni, Gn 46:16
G descendants by their clans: Nm 26:15
who enlarges **G** ⌊territory⌋ will Dt 33:20
Ramoth in Gilead from **G** tribe, Jos 20:8
up in obedience to **G** command, 2Sm 24:19
went up at **G** command spoken 1Ch 21:19

GADARENES *(1)*

the region of the **G**, two Mt 8:28

GADDI *(1)*

G son of Susi from the tribe of Nm 13:11

GADDIEL *(1)*

G son of Sodi from the tribe of Nm 13:10

GADI *(2)*

Menahem son of **G** came up from 2Kg 15:14
Menahem son of **G** became king 2Kg 15:17

GADITE *(2)*

were the **G** clans ⌊numbered⌋ Nm 26:18
Nathan from Zobah, Bani the **G**, 2Sm 23:36

GADITES *(37)*

leader of the **G** is Eliasaph son Nm 2:14
leader of the **G**, ⌊presented Nm 7:42
Reubenites and **G** had a very Nm 32:1
So the **G** and Reubenites came to Nm 32:2
asked the **G** and Reubenites, Nm 32:6
The **G** and Reubenites answered Nm 32:25
If the **G** and Reubenites cross Nm 32:29
The **G** and Reubenites replied, Nm 32:31
gave them—the **G**, Reubenites, Nm 32:33
The **G** rebuilt Dibon, Ataroth, Nm 32:34
the tribe of the **G** have received Nm 34:14
the Reubenites and **G** ⌊the area Dt 3:12
the Reubenites and **G** ⌊the area Dt 3:16
in Gilead, belonging to the **G**; Dt 4:43
Reubenites, the **G**, and half the Dt 29:8
Reubenites, the **G**, and half the Jos 1:12
The Reubenites, **G**, and half the Jos 4:12
to the Reubenites, **G**, and half Jos 12:6
Reubenites and **G** had received Jos 13:8
tribe of the **G** by their clans, Jos 13:24
of the **G** by their clans, Jos 13:28
the Reubenites, **G**, and half the Jos 22:1
The Reubenites, **G**, and half the Jos 22:9
the Reubenites, **G**, and half the Jos 22:10
the Reubenites, **G**, and half the Jos 22:11
to the Reubenites, **G**, and half Jos 22:13
to the Reubenites, **G**, and half Jos 22:15
The Reubenites, **G**, and half the Jos 22:21
the Reubenites and **G** in the land Jos 22:32
the Reubenites and **G** lived. Jos 22:33
and **G** named the altar: Jos 22:34
Gilead—the **G**, the Reubenites 2Kg 10:33
the Reubenites, **G**, and half the 1Ch 5:26
Some **G** defected to David at his 1Ch 12:8
These **G** were army commanders; 1Ch 12:14
the Reubenites, **G**, and half the 1Ch 12:37
Reubenites, the **G**, and half the 1Ch 26:32

GAHAM *(1)*

also bore Tebah, **G**, Tahash, and Gn 22:24

GAHAR'S *(2)*

descendants, **G** descendants, Ezr 2:47
descendants, **G** descendants, Neh 7:49

GAIN *(39)*

What do we **g** if we kill our Gn 37:26
gives you the power to **g** wealth, Dt 8:18
they turned toward dishonest **g**, 1Sm 8:3
stupid man will **g** understanding Jb 11:12
what will we **g** by pleading with Jb 21:15
What **g** is there in my death, Ps 30:9
decrees and not to material **g**. Ps 119:36
I **g** understanding from Your Ps 119:104
of all who pursue **g** dishonestly; Pr 1:19
so that you may **g** understanding, Pr 4:1
but violent men **g** ⌊only⌋ riches. Pr 11:16
you will **g** no knowledge from his Pr 14:7
who hates unjust **g** prolongs his Pr 28:16
a humble spirit will **g** honor. Pr 29:23
What does a man **g** for all his Ec 1:3
does the worker **g** from his Ec 3:9
What does he **g** who struggles for Ec 5:16
I will **g** satisfaction against My Is 1:24
confused will **g** understanding Is 29:24
reckless mind will **g** knowledge, Is 32:4
who refuses **g** from extortion, Is 33:15
every last one for his own **g**. Is 56:11
Now what will you **g** by traveling Jr 2:18
What will you **g** by traveling Jr 2:18
except your own unjust **g**, Jr 22:17
the unjust **g** you have made Ezk 22:13
lives in order to get unjust **g**. Ezk 22:27
their hearts pursue unjust **g**. Ezk 33:31
you are trying to **g** some time, Dn 2:8
a man to **g** the whole world Mk 8:36
By your endurance **g** your lives. Lk 21:19
do not have love, I **g** nothing. 1Co 13:3
living is Christ and dying is **g**. Php 1:21
everything that was a **g** to me, Php 3:7
filth, so that I may **g** Christ Php 3:8
is a way to material **g**. 1Tm 6:5
with contentment is a great **g**. 1Tm 6:6
for dishonest **g** what they should Ti 1:11
so that they might **g** a better Heb 11:35

GAINED *(13)*

ability have **g** this wealth for Dt 8:17
The men **g** the advantage over us 2Sm 11:23
pleased him and **g** his favor so Est 2:9
the heavens **g** their beauty; Jb 26:13
wisdom is **g** by those who take Pr 13:10
Food **g** by fraud is sweet to a Pr 20:17
inheritance **g** prematurely will Pr 20:21
I have not **g** wisdom, and I have Pr 30:3
nothing to be **g** under the sun. Ec 2:11
wealth he has **g** has perished. Jr 48:36
What have we **g** by keeping His Mal 3:14
in the Lord have **g** confidence Php 1:14
g strength after being weak, Heb 11:34

GAINING *(5)*

g a reputation among the Three. 2Sm 23:18
g a reputation among the Three. 1Ch 11:20
For **g** wisdom and being Pr 1:2
everyone is **g** profit unjustly. Jr 6:13
everyone is **g** profit unjustly. Jr 8:10

GAINS *(9)*

A man **g** nothing when he becomes Jb 34:9

Ill-gotten g do not profit Pr 10:2
A gracious woman g honor, but Pr 11:16
person gives freely, yet g more; Pr 11:24
discerning, and he g knowledge. Pr 19:25
By the power he g through his Dn 11:2
who unjustly g wealth for his Hab 2:9
a man if he g the whole world Mt 16:26
if he g the whole world Lk 9:25

GAIUS *(5)*
along G and Aristarchus, Ac 19:29
from Thessalonica, G from Derbe, Ac 20:4
G, who is host to me and to the Rm 16:23
of you except Crispus and G, 1Co 1:14
To my dear friend G, whom I love 3Jn 1

GALAL *(3)*
Heresh, G, and Mattaniah, 1Ch 9:15
son of G, son of Jeduthun 1Ch 9:16
Shammua, son of G, son of Neh 11:17

GALATIA *(4)*
of Phrygia and G and were Ac 16:6
To the churches of G. Gl 1:2
has gone to G, Titus to Dalmatia 2Tm 4:10
of Pontus, G, Cappadocia, Asia, 1Pt 1:1

GALATIAN *(2)*
after another in the G territory Ac 18:23
as I instructed the G churches. 1Co 16:1

GALATIANS *(1)*
foolish G! Who has hypnotized Gl 3:1

GALBANUM *(1)*
stacte, onycha, and g; Ex 30:34

GALE *(2)*
like dead thistles before a g. Is 17:13
and a g will scatter them. Is 41:16

GALEED *(2)*
(AKA JEGAR-SAHADUTHA, MIZPAH)
but Jacob named it G. Gn 31:47
the place was called G, Gn 31:48

GALILEAN *(5)*
"You were with Jesus the G too." Mt 26:69
of them, since you're also a G!" Mk 14:70
with Him, since he's also a G." Lk 22:59
he asked if the man was a G. Lk 23:6
Judas the G rose up in the days Ac 5:37

GALILEANS *(5)*
to Him about the G whose blood Lk 13:1
that these G were more sinful Lk 13:2
sinful than all G because they Lk 13:2
the G welcomed Him because they Jn 4:45
all these who are speaking G? Ac 2:7

GALILEE *(69)*
(AKA CHINNERETH, GENNESARET)
hill country of Naphtali in G, Jos 20:7
Kedesh in G, the city of refuge Jos 21:32
Hiram 20 towns in the land of G. 1Kg 9:11
Gilead, and G—all the land 2Kg 15:29
received⌋ Kedesh in G and its 1Ch 6:76
Jordan, and to G of the nations. Is 9:1
he withdrew to the region of G. Mt 2:22
Then Jesus came from G to John Mt 3:13
arrested, He withdrew into G. Mt 4:12
the Jordan, G of the Gentiles! Mt 4:15
was walking along the Sea of G, Mt 4:18
Jesus was going all over G, Mt 4:23
crowds followed Him from G, Mt 4:25
Jesus passed along the Sea of G. Mt 15:29
As they were meeting in G, Mt 17:22
He departed from G and went to Mt 19:1
Jesus from Nazareth in G!" Mt 21:11
I will go ahead of you to G." Mt 26:32
Jesus from G and ministered to Mt 27:55
He is going ahead of you to G; Mt 28:7
tell My brothers to leave for G, Mt 28:10
The 11 disciples traveled to G, Mt 28:16
Nazareth in G and was baptized Mk 1:9
Jesus went to G, preaching the Mk 1:14
passing along by the Sea of G, Mk 1:16
the entire vicinity of G. Mk 1:28
went into all of G, preaching in Mk 1:39
great multitude followed from G, Mk 3:7
and the leading men of G. Mk 6:21
by way of Sidon to the Sea of G, Mk 7:31
and made their way through G, Mk 9:30
I will go ahead of you to G." Mk 14:28
When He was in G, they would Mk 15:41
'He is going ahead of you to G; Mk 16:7
to a town in G called Nazareth Lk 1:26
from the town of Nazareth in G, Lk 2:4
they returned to G, to their own Lk 2:39
was tetrarch of G, his brother Lk 3:1
Jesus returned to G in the power Lk 4:14
a town in G, and was teaching Lk 4:31
in the synagogues of G. Lk 4:44
every village of G and Judea, Lk 5:17
Gerasenes, which is opposite G. Lk 8:26
He passed between Samaria and G. Lk 17:11
G where He started even to here. Lk 23:5
who had followed Him from G, Lk 23:49
with Him from G followed along Lk 23:55
to you when He was still in G, Lk 24:6
day He decided to leave for G. Jn 1:43
wedding took place in Cana of G. Jn 2:1
this first sign in Cana of G. Jn 2:11
left Judea and went again to G. Jn 4:3
two days He left there for G. Jn 4:43
they entered G, the Galileans Jn 4:45
Then He went again to Cana of G, Jn 4:46
had come from Judea into G, Jn 4:47
after He came from Judea to G. Jn 4:54
Jesus crossed the Sea of G Jn 6:1
traveled in G, since He did not Jn 7:1
these things, He stayed in G. Jn 7:9
the Messiah doesn't come from G, Jn 7:41
"You aren't from G too, are you?" Jn 7:52
that no prophet arises from G." Jn 7:52
who was from Bethsaida in G, Jn 12:21
from Cana of G, Zebedee's sons, Jn 21:2
said, "Men of G, why do you Ac 1:11
all Judea, G, and Samaria had Ac 9:31
beginning from G after the Ac 10:37
up with Him from G to Jerusalem, Ac 13:31

GALL *(2)*
they gave me g for my food, Ps 69:21
Him wine mixed with g to drink. Mt 27:34

GALLERIES *(2)*
west, with its g on each side; Ezk 41:15
because the g took away more Ezk 42:5

GALLERY *(2)*
structure rose⌋ g by gallery in Ezk 42:3
gallery by g in three tiers. Ezk 42:3

GALLIM *(2)*
son of Laish, who was from G. 1Sm 25:44
Cry aloud, daughter of G! Is 10:30

GALLIO *(3)*
While G was proconsul of Achaia, Ac 18:12
open his mouth, G said to the Ac 18:14
of these things concerned G. Ac 18:17

GALLON *(9)*
shekel), and one g of olive oil. Ex 30:24
with a third of a g of oil. Nm 15:6
a third of a g of wine for a Nm 15:7
one-sixth of a g, ⌊which⌋ you Ezk 4:11
along with a g of oil for every Ezk 45:24
as well as a g of oil for every Ezk 46:5
together with a g of oil for Ezk 46:7
along with a g of oil for every Ezk 46:11
one-third of a g of oil to Ezk 46:14

GALLONS *(13)*
two and one-half g of flour, 1Sm 1:24
and 110,000 g of beaten oil. 1Kg 5:11
lily blossom. It held 11,000 g. 1Kg 7:26
holding 220 g and each was six 1Kg 7:38
enough to hold about four g. 1Kg 18:32
barley, 110,000 g of wine, and 2Ch 2:10
of wine, and 110,000 g of oil. 2Ch 2:10
It could hold 11,000 g. 2Ch 4:5
of wheat, 550 g of wine, 550 Ezr 7:22
of wine, 550 g of oil, and salt Ezr 7:22
vineyard will yield only six g, Is 5:10
five and a half g and the dry Ezk 45:11
Each contained 20 or 30 g. Jn 2:6

GALLOP *(1)*
and they g like war horses. Jl 2:4

GALLOPING *(3)*
hammered—the g, galloping of Jdg 5:22
the galloping, g of his Jdg 5:22
g horse and jolting chariot! Nah 3:2

GALLOWS *(9)*
both men were hanged on the g. Est 2:23
them build a g 75 feet high. Est 5:14
so he had the g constructed. Est 5:14
on the g he had prepared Est 6:4
There is a g 75 feet tall at Est 7:9
Haman on the g he had prepared Est 7:10
was hanged on the g because he Est 8:7
10 sons be hung on the g." Est 9:13
hanged with his sons on the g. Est 9:25

GAMADITES *(1)*
and G were in your towers. Ezk 27:11

GAMALIEL *(7)*
G son of Pedahzur from Manasseh; Nm 1:10
Manassites is G son of Pedahzur Nm 2:20
the eighth day G son of Pedahzur Nm 7:54
offering of G son of Pedahzur Nm 7:59
G son of Pedahzur was over the Nm 10:23
A Pharisee named G, a teacher of Ac 5:34
in this city at the feet of G, Ac 22:3

GAME *(9)*
he had a taste for wild g, Gn 25:28
the field to hunt some g for me. Gn 27:3
field to hunt some g to bring Gn 27:5
'Bring me some g and make some Gn 27:7
eat some of my g so that you may Gn 27:19
some of my son's g so that I can Gn 27:25
up and eat some of his son's g, Gn 27:31
who hunted g and brought it to Gn 27:33
A lazy man doesn't roast his g, Pr 12:27

GAMUL *(1)*
Jachin, the twenty-second to G, 1Ch 24:17

GANG *(4)*
g of evildoers has closed in on Ps 22:16
a g of ruthless men seeks my Ps 86:14
on the g of young men as well. Jr 6:11
breaks in; a g pillages outside Hs 7:1

GANGED *(1)*
Citizens of Gibeah g up on me Jdg 20:5

GANGRENE *(1)*
their word will spread like g, 2Tm 2:17

GAP *(3)*
had made this g in the tribes Jdg 21:15
wall and that no g was left in Neh 6:1
and stand in the g before Me on Ezk 22:30

GAPING *(1)*
advance as through a g breach; Jb 30:14

GAPS *(3)*
that the g were being closed, Neh 4:7
go up to the g or restore the Ezk 13:5
I will repair its g, restore its Am 9:11

GARBAGE *(8)*
lifts the needy from the g pile. 1Sm 2:8
be made into a g dump because Ezr 6:11
lifts the needy from the g pile Ps 113:7
were like g in the streets. Is 5:25
garments⌋ huddle in g heaps. Lm 4:5
houses will be made a g dump. Dn 2:5
and his house made a g dump. Dn 3:29
the world's g, like the filth 1Co 4:13

GARDEN *(51)*
LORD God planted a g in Eden, Gn 2:8
of life in the midst of the g, Gn 2:9
out from Eden to water the g. Gn 2:10
him in the g of Eden to work Gn 2:15
to eat from any tree of the g, Gn 2:16
eat from any tree in the g'?" Gn 3:1
fruit from the trees in the g. Gn 3:2
the tree in the middle of the g, Gn 3:3
God walking in the g at the time Gn 3:8
God among the trees of the g. Gn 3:8
heard You in the g, and I was Gn 3:10
away from the g of Eden to work Gn 3:23
and east of the g of Eden He Gn 3:24
like the LORD's g and the land Gn 13:10
by hand as in a vegetable g. Dt 11:10
I can have it for a vegetable g, 1Kg 21:2
buried in the g of his own house 2Kg 21:18
of his own house, the g of Uzza. 2Kg 21:18
in his tomb in the g of Uzza, 2Kg 21:26
the two walls near the king's g, 2Kg 25:4
of Shelah near the king's g, Neh 3:15
banquet in the g courtyard of Est 1:5
wine and ⌊went to⌋ the palace g. Est 7:7
from the palace g to the house Est 7:8
shoots spread out over his g. Jb 8:16
are⌋ a locked g—a locked Sg 4:12
a locked g and a sealed spring. Sg 4:12
⌊You are⌋ a g spring, a well of Sg 4:15
Blow on my g, and spread the Sg 4:16

love come to his g and eat its Sg 4:16
have come to my g—my sister, Sg 5:1
My love has gone down to his g, Sg 6:2
and like a g without water. Is 1:30
desert like the g of the LORD. Is 51:3
like a watered g and like a Is 58:11
and as a g enables what is sown Is 61:11
will be like an irrigated g, Jr 31:12
of the king's g through the gate Jr 39:4
the two walls near the king's g, Jr 52:7
as if ⌊it were⌋ a g ⌊booth⌋, Lm 2:6
You were in Eden, the g of God. Ezk 28:13
cedars in God's g could not Ezk 31:8
No tree in the g of God could Ezk 31:8
were in God's g, envied it. Ezk 31:9
has become like the g of Eden. Ezk 36:35
of them is like the G of Eden, Jl 2:3
a man took and sowed in his g. Lk 13:19
there was a g, and He and His Jn 18:1
I see you with Him in the g?" Jn 18:26
There was a g in the place where Jn 19:41
A new tomb was in the g; Jn 19:41

GARDENER *(1)*
He was the g, she replied, "Sir Jn 20:15

GARDENS *(10)*
valleys, like g beside a stream, Nm 24:6
made g and parks for myself and Ec 2:5
to feed in the g and gather Sg 6:2
dwell in the g—companions are Sg 8:13
of the g you have chosen. Is 1:29
sacrificing in g, burning Is 65:3
Plant g and eat their produce. Jr 29:5
Plant g and eat their produce." Jr 29:28
your many g and vineyards, Am 4:9
make g and eat their produce. Am 9:14

GAREB *(3)*
Ira the Ithrite, G the Ithrite, 2Sm 23:38
Ira the Ithrite, G the Ithrite, 1Ch 11:40
to the hill of G and then turn Jr 31:39

GARLAND *(2)*
will be a g of grace on your Pr 1:9
will place a g of grace on your Pr 4:9

GARLANDS *(1)*
brought oxen and g to the gates. Ac 14:13

GARLIC *(1)*
melons, leeks, onions, and g. Nm 11:5

GARMENT *(54)*
grabbed him by his g and said, Gn 39:12
But leaving his g in her hand, Gn 39:12
he had left his g with her and Gn 39:13
he left his g with me and ran Gn 39:15
put Joseph's g beside her until Gn 39:16
he left his g with me and ran Gn 39:18
a sheep, a g, or anything ⌊else Ex 22:9
of its blood spatters on a g, Lv 6:27
wash that g in a holy place. Lv 6:27
or put on a g made of two kinds Lv 19:19
his donkey, his g, or anything Dt 22:3
is not to put on a woman's g, Dt 22:5
corners of the outer g you wear. Dt 22:12
sleep in ⌊the g⌋ he has given as Dt 24:12
take a widow's g as security. Dt 24:17
an embroidered g or two for my Jdg 5:30
head, and covered it with a g. 1Sm 19:13
was wearing a long-sleeved g, 2Sm 13:18
long-sleeved g she was wearing 2Sm 13:19
and threw a g over him because 2Sm 20:12
wild gourds as his g would hold. 2Kg 4:39
took his g and put it under 2Kg 9:13
bring a royal g that the king Est 6:8
the g and the horse under the Est 6:9
a g and a horse for Mordecai Est 6:10
Haman took the g and the horse. Est 6:11
rotten, like a moth-eaten g. Jb 13:28
chokes me by the neck of my g. Jb 30:18
the clouds its g and thick Jb 38:9
out like ⌊the folds of⌋ a g. Jb 38:14
violence covers them like a g. Ps 73:6
You will change them like a g, Ps 102:26
with the deep as if it were a g; Ps 104:6
Take his g, for he has put up Pr 20:16
Take his g, for he has put up Pr 27:13
them⌋ in the fold of His ⌊g⌋ Is 40:11
of them will wear out like a g; Is 50:9
earth will wear out like a g, Is 51:6
moth will devour them like a g, Is 51:8
acts are like a polluted g; Is 64:6
a shepherd picks lice off his g, Jr 43:12
the edge of My g over you and Ezk 16:8
meat in the fold of his g, Hg 2:12
"he covers his g with injustice," Mal 2:16
a camel-hair g with a leather Mt 3:4
patches an old g with unshrunk Mt 9:16
away from the g and makes the Mt 9:16
a camel-hair g with a leather Mk 1:6
of unshrunk cloth on an old g. Mk 2:21
a patch from a new g and puts it Lk 5:36
garment and puts it on an old g. Lk 5:36
from the new g will not match Lk 5:36
he tied his outer g around him Jn 21:7
hating even the g defiled by the Jd 23

GARMENTS *(76)*
and gold, and g, and gave ⌊them⌋ Gn 24:53
clothed him with fine linen g, Gn 41:42
Make holy g for your brother Ex 28:2
to make Aaron's g for Ex 28:3
These are the g that they must Ex 28:4
to make holy g for your brother Ex 28:4
Then take the g and clothe Aaron Ex 29:5
them⌋ on Aaron and his g, Ex 29:21
well as on his sons and their g. Ex 29:21
he and his g will become holy, Ex 29:21
as well as his sons and their g. Ex 29:21
The holy g that belong to Aaron Ex 29:29
specially woven g, both the holy Ex 31:10
both the holy g for Aaron the Ex 31:10
priest and the g for his sons to Ex 31:10
woven g for ministering Ex 35:19
the holy g for Aaron the priest Ex 35:19
priest and the g for his sons to Ex 35:19
use, and ⌊to make⌋ the holy g. Ex 35:21
specially woven g for ministry Ex 39:1
the holy g for Aaron from the Ex 39:1
woven g for ministering Ex 39:41
the holy g for Aaron the priest Ex 39:41
priest and the g for his sons to Ex 39:41
Clothe Aaron with the holy g, Ex 40:13
Then he must take off his g, Lv 6:11
with him, the g, the anointing Lv 8:2
them⌋ on Aaron and his g, Lv 8:30
well as on his sons and their g. Lv 8:30
he consecrated Aaron and his g, Lv 8:30
as well as his sons and their g. Lv 8:30
loose and do not tear your g, Lv 10:6
These are holy g; he must bathe Lv 16:4
off the linen g he wore when he Lv 16:23
He will put on the linen g, Lv 16:32
the linen garments, the holy g, Lv 16:32
has been ordained to wear the g, Lv 21:10
dishevel his hair or tear his g. Lv 21:10
for the corners of their g, Nm 15:38
Remove Aaron's g and put them Nm 20:26
removed Aaron's g and put them Nm 20:28
g, leather goods, things made of Nm 31:20
spoil of colored g for Sisera, Jdg 5:30
the purple g on the kings of Jdg 8:26
you 30 linen g and 30 changes Jdg 14:12
me 30 linen g and 30 changes Jdg 14:13
who decked your g with gold 2Sm 1:24
Bring out the g for all the 2Kg 10:22
So he brought out their g. 2Kg 10:22
100 priestly g to the treasury Ezr 2:69
530 priestly g to the treasury Neh 7:70
silver minas, and 67 priestly g. Neh 7:72
They divided my g among Ps 22:18
and cassia ⌊perfume⌋ all your g; Ps 45:8
In colorful g she is led to the Ps 45:14
She makes and sells linen g; Pr 31:24
fragrance of your g is like the Sg 4:11
g, linen clothes, turbans, and Is 3:23
and the bloodied g of war will Is 9:5
on your beautiful g, Jerusalem, Is 52:1
He put on g of vengeance for Is 59:17
me with the g of salvation Is 61:10
crimson-stained g from Bozrah— Is 63:1
and Your g like one who treads a Is 63:2
their blood spattered My g, Is 63:3
terrified or tear their g. Jr 36:24
beards, torn their g, and gashed Jr 41:5
reared in purple ⌊g⌋ huddle in Lm 4:5
no one dared to touch their g. Lm 4:14
some of your g and made colorful Ezk 16:16
embroidered g to cover them, Ezk 16:18
strip off their embroidered g. Ezk 26:16
were your merchants in choice g, Ezk 27:24
court they must wear linen g; Ezk 44:17
every altar on g taken as Am 2:8
clothed him in g while the Angel Zch 3:5

GARMITE *(1)*
of Keilah the G and ⌊the father 1Ch 4:19

GARRISON *(11)*
the Philistine g that was in 1Sm 13:3
has attacked the Philistine g, 1Sm 13:4
Now a Philistine g took control 1Sm 13:23
the Philistine g on the other 1Sm 14:1
cross to reach the Philistine g. 1Sm 14:4
cross over to the g of these 1Sm 14:6
be seen by the Philistine g, 1Sm 14:11
The men of the g called to 1Sm 14:12
Even the g and the raiding 1Sm 14:15
a Philistine g was at Bethlehem 2Sm 23:14
a Philistine g was at Bethlehem 1Ch 11:16

GARRISONS *(6)*
where there are Philistine g. 1Sm 10:5
Then he placed g in Aram of 2Sm 8:6
He placed g throughout Edom, 2Sm 8:14
Then he placed g in Aram of 1Ch 18:6
He put g in Edom, and all the 1Ch 18:13
Judah and set g in the land of 2Ch 17:2

GASH *(2)*
How long will you g yourself? Jr 47:5
every hand is a g and sackcloth Jr 48:37

GASHED *(2)*
they g themselves at the Jr 5:7
garments, and g themselves, and Jr 41:5

GASHES *(2)*
are not to make g on your bodies Lv 19:28
or make g on their bodies. Lv 21:5

GASPING *(2)*
woman in labor, g breathlessly. Is 42:14
of Daughter Zion g for breath, Jr 4:31

GATAM *(3)*
Omar, Zepho, G, and Kenaz. Gn 36:11
Korah, G, and Amalek. These are Gn 36:16
Omar, Zephi, G, and Kenaz; 1Ch 1:36

GATE *(262)*
as Lot was sitting at Sodom's g. Gn 19:1
who came to the g of his city, Gn 23:10
who came to the g of his city. Gn 23:18
This is the g of heaven." Gn 28:17
went to the g of their city Gn 34:20
side ⌊of the g⌋ 22 and a half Ex 27:14
g of the courtyard is to have Ex 27:16
screen for the g of the Ex 35:17
one side ⌊of the g⌋ were 22 and Ex 38:14
both sides of the courtyard g. Ex 38:15
for the g of the courtyard Ex 38:18
bases for the g of the courtyard Ex 38:31
screen for the g of the Ex 39:40
screen for the g of the Ex 40:8
screen for the g of the Ex 40:33
entrance at the g of the Nm 4:26
city, to the g of his hometown Dt 21:19
it⌋ to the city elders at the g. Dt 22:15
them out to the g of that city Dt 22:24
elders at the ⌊city⌋ g and say, Dt 25:7
the bolts of your g be iron and Dt 33:25
when the g was about to close, Jos 2:5
to pursue them, the g was shut. Jos 2:7
outside the g to the quarries Jos 7:5
of the city g and put a large Jos 8:29
at the entrance of the city g, Jos 20:4
at the entrance of the city g. Jdg 9:35
as far as the entrance of the g. Jdg 9:40
at the entrance of the city g. Jdg 9:44
all that night at the city g. Jdg 16:2
doors of the city g along with Jdg 16:3
by the entrance of the g, Jdg 18:16
entrance of the g with the 600 Jdg 18:17
Boaz went to the g ⌊of the town⌋ Ru 4:1
or from the g of his home. Ru 4:10
people who were at the g said, Ru 4:11
off the chair by the city g, 1Sm 4:18
Samuel in the g area and asked, 1Sm 9:18
the doors of the g and letting 1Sm 21:13
to the city g while the Arameans 2Sm 10:8
up to the entrance of the g. 2Sm 11:23
the road leading to the city g. 2Sm 15:2
he stood beside the g while all 2Sm 18:4
to the roof of the g and over to 2Sm 18:24

went up to the **g** chamber and 2Sm 18:33
king got up and sat in the **g**, 2Sm 19:8
the king is sitting in the **g**." 2Sm 19:8
at the city **g** of Bethlehem!" 2Sm 23:15
the well at the **g** of Bethlehem. 2Sm 23:16
When he arrived at the city **g**, 1Kg 17:10
at the entrance to Samaria's **g**, 1Kg 22:10
tomorrow at the **g** of Samaria, 2Kg 7:1
were at the entrance to the **g**. 2Kg 7:3
charge of the **g**, but the people 2Kg 7:17
a shekel at the **g** of Samaria," 2Kg 7:18
entered the **g**, she said, "⌊Do 2Kg 9:31
of the **g** until morning." 2Kg 10:8
went out and stood ⌊at the **g**⌋, 2Kg 10:9
be at the Sur **g** and a third at 2Kg 11:6
a third at the **g** behind the 2Kg 11:6
palace by way of the guards' **g**. 2Kg 11:19
from the Ephraim **G** to the Corner 2Kg 14:13
Ephraim Gate to the Corner **G**. 2Kg 14:13
built the Upper **G** of the LORD's 2Kg 15:35
the entrance of the **g** of Joshua 2Kg 23:8
(on the left at the city **g**). 2Kg 23:8
by way of the **g** between the two 2Kg 25:4
the King's **G** on the east side. 1Ch 9:18
at the city **g** of Bethlehem!" 1Ch 11:17
the well at the **g** of Bethlehem. 1Ch 11:18
Jeduthun's sons were at the **g**. 1Ch 16:42
young and old alike, for each **g**. 1Ch 26:13
lot for the east ⌊**g**⌋ fell to 1Ch 26:14
lot came out for the north ⌊**g**⌋. 1Ch 26:14
Obed-edom's was the south ⌊**g**⌋, 1Ch 26:15
it was the west ⌊**g**⌋ and the gate 1Ch 26:16
gate⌋ and the **g** of Shallecheth 1Ch 26:16
with respect to each **g**, 2Ch 8:14
at the entrance to Samaria's **g**, 2Ch 18:9
are to be at the Foundation **G**, 2Ch 23:5
of the Horses' **G** to the king's 2Ch 23:15
through the upper ⌊**g**⌋ and seated 2Ch 23:20
outside the **g** of the LORD's 2Ch 24:8
from the Ephraim **G** to the Corner 2Ch 25:23
Ephraim Gate to the Corner **G**. 2Ch 25:23
in Jerusalem at the Corner **G**, 2Ch 26:9
the Valley **G**, and the corner 2Ch 26:9
built the Upper **G** of the LORD's 2Ch 27:3
keeper of the East **G**, was over 2Ch 31:14
in the square of the city **g**. 2Ch 32:6
to the entrance of the Fish **G**; 2Ch 33:14
the gatekeepers were at each **g**. 2Ch 35:15
through the Valley **G** toward the Neh 2:13
Serpent's Well and the Dung **G**, Neh 2:13
to the Fountain **G** and the King's Neh 2:14
the Valley **G** and returned. Neh 2:15
began rebuilding the Sheep **G**. Neh 3:1
of Hassenaah built the Fish **G**. Neh 3:3
of Besodeiah repaired the Old **G**. Neh 3:6
of Zanoah repaired the Valley **G**. Neh 3:13
yards of the wall to the Dung **G**. Neh 3:13
repaired the Dung **G**. Neh 3:14
Mizpah, repaired the Fountain **G**. Neh 3:15
the Water **G** toward the east Neh 3:26
made repairs above the Horse **G**, Neh 3:28
of the East **G**, made repairs. Neh 3:29
opposite the Inspection **G**, Neh 3:31
of the corner and the Sheep **G**. Neh 3:32
square in front of the Water **G**. Neh 8:1
square in front of the Water **G**, Neh 8:3
the square by the Water **G**, Neh 8:16
the square by the **G** of Ephraim. Neh 8:16
on the wall, toward the Dung **G**. Neh 12:31
At the Fountain **G** they climbed Neh 12:37
to the Water **G** on the east. Neh 12:37
above the **G** of Ephraim, and by Neh 12:39
and by the Old **G**, the Fish Gate, Neh 12:39
Old Gate, the Fish **G**, the Tower Neh 12:39
of the Hundred, to the Sheep **G**. Neh 12:39
stopped at the **G** of the Guard. Neh 12:39
was sitting at the King's **G**. Est 2:19
was sitting at the King's **G**, Est 2:21
at the King's **G** bowed down and Est 3:2
at the King's **G** asked Mordecai, Est 3:3
went as far as the King's **G**, Est 4:2
from entering the King's **G**. Est 4:2
square in front of the King's **G**. Est 4:6
saw Mordecai at the King's **G**, Est 5:9
at the King's **G** all the time." Est 5:13
who is sitting at the King's **G**. Est 6:10
returned to the King's **G**, Est 6:12
are crushed at the ⌊city⌋ **g**, Jb 5:4
out to the city **g** and took my Jb 29:7
I had support in the ⌊city⌋ **g**, Jb 31:21
sit at the city **g** talk about me, Ps 69:12
This is the **g** of the LORD; Ps 118:20
their⌋ enemies at the city **g**. Ps 127:5
crush the oppressed at the **g**, Pr 22:22
not open his mouth at the **g**. Pr 24:7
Heshbon by the **g** of Bath-rabbim. Sg 7:4
its **g** has collapsed in ruins. Is 24:12
turn back the battle at the **g**. Is 28:6
a trap at the **g** for the mediator Is 29:21
Stand in the **g** of the house of Jr 7:2
Go and stand in the People's **G**, Jr 17:19
the entrance of the Potsherd **G**. Jr 19:2
Upper Benjamin **G** in the LORD's Jr 20:2
at the entrance of the New **G**. Jr 26:10
to the Corner **G** will be rebuilt Jr 31:38
of the Horse **G** to the east— Jr 31:40
of the New **G** of the LORD's Jr 36:10
when he was at the Benjamin **G**, Jr 37:13
was sitting at the Benjamin **G**, Jr 38:7
entered and sat at the Middle **G**: Jr 39:3
through the **g** between the two Jr 39:4
have no doors, not even a **g** bar; Jr 49:31
set ablaze, her **g** bars are Jr 51:30
by way of the **g** between the two Jr 52:7
The elders have left the city **g**, Lm 5:14
of the inner **g** that faces north, Ezk 8:3
statue north of the altar **g**, Ezk 8:5
of the north **g** of the LORD's Ezk 8:14
the direction of the Upper **G**, Ezk 9:2
to the eastern **g** of the LORD's Ezk 10:19
to the eastern **g** of the LORD's Ezk 11:1
He was standing by the **g**. Ezk 40:3
he came to the **g** that faced east Ezk 40:6
measured the threshold of the **g**; Ezk 40:6
threshold of the **g** on the temple Ezk 40:7
measured the portico of the **g**; Ezk 40:8
portico of the **g** was on the Ezk 40:9
on each side of the east **g**, Ezk 40:10
The **g** extended around to the Ezk 40:14
front of the **g** at the entrance Ezk 40:15
of the lower **g** to the exterior Ezk 40:19
He measured the **g** of the outer Ezk 40:20
measurements as the first **g**: Ezk 40:21
those of the **g** that faced east Ezk 40:22
Seven steps led up to the **g**, Ezk 40:22
court had a **g** facing the north Ezk 40:23
had a gate facing the north **g**, Ezk 40:23
the distance from **g** to gate; Ezk 40:23
the distance from gate to **g**; Ezk 40:23
there was also a **g** on the south. Ezk 40:24
Both the **g** and its portico had Ezk 40:25
court had a **g** on the south. Ezk 40:27
measured from **g** to gate on the Ezk 40:27
from gate to **g** on the south; Ezk 40:27
inner court through the south **g**. Ezk 40:28
When he measured the south **g**, Ezk 40:28
he measured the **g**, it had the Ezk 40:32
he brought me to the north **g**. Ezk 40:35
into the portico of the **g**. Ezk 40:38
portico of the **g** there were two Ezk 40:39
the entrance of the north **g**, Ezk 40:40
inside the **g** and four outside Ezk 40:41
the inner **g**, within the inner Ezk 40:44
the north **g**, facing south, Ezk 40:44
and another beside the south **g**, Ezk 40:44
the sidewalls of the **g** were five Ezk 40:48
of the north **g** into the outer Ezk 42:1
by way of the **g** that faced east Ezk 42:15
He led me to the **g**, the one that Ezk 43:1
by way of the **g** that faced east. Ezk 43:4
outer **g** that faced east, Ezk 44:1
This **g** will remain closed. Ezk 44:2
the portico of the **g** and go out Ezk 44:3
way of the north **g** to the front Ezk 44:4
doorposts of the **g** to the inner Ezk 45:19
The **g** of the inner court that Ezk 46:1
doorpost of the **g** while the Ezk 46:2
of the **g** and then depart Ezk 46:2
but the **g** must not be closed Ezk 46:2
of that **g** on the Sabbaths Ezk 46:3
of the north **g** to worship must Ezk 46:9
go out by way of the south **g**, Ezk 46:9
way of the south **g** must go out Ezk 46:9
go out by way of the north **g**. Ezk 46:9
return through the **g** by which he Ezk 46:9
must go out by the opposite **g**. Ezk 46:9
the **g** that faces east must be Ezk 46:12
and the **g** must be closed after Ezk 46:12
that was at the side of the **g**, Ezk 46:19
way of the north **g** and led me Ezk 47:2
to the outer **g** that faced east; Ezk 47:2
one, the **g** of Reuben; one, Ezk 48:31
Reuben; one, the **g** of Judah; and Ezk 48:31
and one, the **g** of Levi. Ezk 48:31
one, the **g** of Joseph; one, Ezk 48:32
one, the **g** of Benjamin; Ezk 48:32
Benjamin; and one, the **g** of Dan. Ezk 48:32
one, the **g** of Simeon; one, Ezk 48:33
one, the **g** of Issachar; Ezk 48:33
and one, the **g** of Zebulun. Ezk 48:33
gates: one, the **g** of Gad; one, Ezk 48:34
of Gad; one, the **g** of Asher; and Ezk 48:34
and one, the **g** of Naphtali. Ezk 48:34
at the city **g** and despise the Am 5:10
establish justice in the **g**. Am 5:15
entered his **g** and cast lots for Ob 11
Do not enter the **g** of My people Ob 13
approached the **g** of my people, Mc 1:9
the LORD to the **g** of Jerusalem. Mc 1:12
through the **g**, and leave by it Mc 2:13
be an outcry from the Fish **G**, Zph 1:10
from the Benjamin **G** to the place Zch 14:10
to the place of the First **G**, Zch 14:10
to the Corner **G**, and from the Zch 14:10
Enter through the narrow **g**. Mt 7:13
For the **g** is wide and the road Mt 7:13
narrow is the **g** and difficult Mt 7:14
as He neared the **g** of the town, Lk 7:12
with sores, was left at his **g**. Lk 16:20
the Sheep **G** in Jerusalem there Jn 5:2
at the temple **g** called Beautiful Ac 3:2
at the Beautiful **G** of the temple Ac 3:10
Simon's house, stood at the **g**. Ac 10:17
came to the iron **g** that leads Ac 12:10
her joy she did not open the **g**, Ac 12:14
outside the city **g** by the river, Ac 16:13
also suffered outside the **g**, Heb 13:12
each individual **g** was made of a Rv 21:21

GATE'S *(7)*

and at the **g** entrance were 25 Ezk 11:1
side next to the **g** portico was Ezk 40:7
the width of the **g** entrance; Ezk 40:11
to the front of the **g** portico on Ezk 40:15
the other side of the **g** portico. Ezk 40:40
way of the **g** portico and stand Ezk 46:2
by way of the **g** portico and go Ezk 46:8

GATEKEEPER *(2)*

He called out to the **g**, "Look! 2Sm 18:26
was the **g** at the entrance to 1Ch 9:21

GATEKEEPERS *(34)*

to the city's **g** and told them, 2Kg 7:10
The **g** called out, and ⌊the news⌋ 2Kg 7:11
The **g**: Shallum, Akkub, Talmon, 1Ch 9:17
These were the **g** from the camp 1Ch 9:18
chosen to be **g** at the thresholds 1Ch 9:22
The **g** were on the four sides: 1Ch 9:24
the four chief **g**, who were 1Ch 9:26
and the **g** Obed-edom and Jeiel. 1Ch 15:18
were to be **g** for the ark. 1Ch 15:23
were also to be **g** for the ark. 1Ch 15:24
Jeduthun and Hosah were to be **g**. 1Ch 16:38
4,000 are to be **g**, and 4,000 are 1Ch 23:5
were⌋ the divisions of the **g**: 1Ch 26:1
divisions of the **g**, under their 1Ch 26:12
divisions of the **g** from the sons 1Ch 26:19
and of the **g** by their divisions 2Ch 8:14
on the Sabbath, are to be **g**. 2Ch 23:4
He stationed **g** at the gates of 2Ch 23:19
secretaries, officers, and **g**. 2Ch 34:13
Also, the **g** were at each gate. 2Ch 35:15
The **g**' descendants ⌊included⌋: Ezr 2:42
singers, **g**, temple servants Ezr 2:70
Levites, singers, **g**, and temple Ezr 7:7
Eliashib. The **g**: Shallum, Telem, Ezr 10:24
doors installed, the **g**, singers, Neh 7:1
The **g** ⌊included⌋: Neh 7:45
Levites, **g**, temple singers, Neh 7:73
Levites, singers, **g**, and temple Neh 10:28
the priests, **g**, and singers Neh 10:39
The **g**: Akkub, Talmon, and their Neh 11:19
and Akkub were **g** who guarded Neh 12:25
along with the singers and **g**, Neh 12:45
portions for the singers and **g**. Neh 12:47
singers, and **g**, along with Neh 13:5

GATEPOSTS *(1)*
city gate along with the two **g**, Jdg 16:3

GATES *(139)*
possess the **g** of their enemies Gn 22:17
possess the **g** of their enemies. Gn 24:60
foreigner who is within your **g**. Ex 20:10
with high walls, **g**, and bars, Dt 3:5
who lives within your **g**, Dt 5:14
of your house and on your **g**. Dt 6:9
of your house and on your **g**, Dt 11:20
the Levite who is within your **g**, Dt 12:12
eat meat within any of your **g**, Dt 12:15
Within your **g** you may not eat: Dt 12:17
the Levite who is within your **g**. Dt 12:18
it within your **g** whenever you Dt 12:21
a resident alien within your **g**, Dt 14:21
forget the Levite within your **g**, Dt 14:27
and store ⌊it⌋ within your **g**. Dt 14:28
widow within your **g** may come, Dt 14:29
within any of your **g** in the land Dt 15:7
it within your **g**; both the Dt 15:22
Levite within your **g**, as well as Dt 16:11
and the widow within your **g**. Dt 16:14
out to your **g** that man or woman Dt 17:5
at your **g**, you must go up Dt 17:8
peace and opens ⌊its **g**⌋ to you, Dt 20:11
wherever he wants within your **g**. Dt 23:16
within all your **g** until your Dt 28:52
within all your **g** throughout the Dt 28:52
imposes on you within your **g**. Dt 28:57
living within your **g**— Dt 31:12
will set up its **g** ⌊at the cost Jos 6:26
new gods, then war was in the **g**. Jdg 5:8
people went down to the **g**. Jdg 5:11
valley and to the **g** of Ekron. 1Sm 17:52
entering a town with barred **g**." 1Sm 23:7
between the two **g** when the 2Sm 18:24
set up its **g**, according to the 1Kg 16:34
places of the **g** at the entrance 2Kg 23:8
assigned to the **g** of the LORD's 1Ch 9:23
cities with walls, **g**, and bars— 2Ch 8:5
at the **g** of the LORD's 2Ch 23:19
for praise in the **g** of the camp 2Ch 31:2
its **g** have been burned down." Neh 1:3
in ruins and its **g** have been Neh 2:3
to rebuild the **g** of the temple's Neh 2:8
down and its **g** that had been Neh 2:13
ruins and its **g** have been burned Neh 2:17
installed the doors in the **g**— Neh 6:1
Do not open the **g** of Jerusalem Neh 7:3
relatives, who guarded the **g**: Neh 11:19
guarded the storerooms at the **g**. Neh 12:25
the people, the **g**, and the wall. Neh 12:30
to fall on the **g** of Jerusalem Neh 13:19
orders that the **g** be closed and Neh 13:19
posted some of my men at the **g**, Neh 13:19
and guard the **g** in order to keep Neh 13:22
it go down to the **g** of Sheol, Jb 17:16
the **g** of death been revealed Jb 38:17
you seen the **g** of death's shadow Jb 38:17
Lift me up from the **g** of death, Ps 9:13
within the **g** of Daughter Zion. Ps 9:14
Lift up your heads, you **g**! Ps 24:7
Lift up your heads, you **g**! Ps 24:9
LORD loves the **g** of Zion more Ps 87:2
Enter His **g** with thanksgiving Ps 100:4
the bronze **g** and cut through Ps 107:16
and came near the **g** of death. Ps 107:18
Open the **g** of righteousness for Ps 118:19
feet are standing within your **g**, Ps 122:2
bars of your **g** and blesses your Ps 147:13
at the entrance of the city **g**: Pr 1:21
Beside the **g** at the entry to the Pr 8:3
at the **g** of the righteous. Pr 14:19
husband is known at the city **g**, Pr 31:23
works praise her at the city **g**. Pr 31:31
her **g** will lament and mourn; Is 3:26
go through the **g** of the nobles. Is 13:2
Wail, you **g**! Cry out, city! Is 14:31
were positioned at the **g**. Is 22:7
Open the **g** so a righteous nation Is 26:2
I must go to the **g** of Sheol; Is 38:10
him and the **g** will not be shut: Is 45:1
your **g** of sparkling stones, Is 54:12
Your **g** will always be open; Is 60:11
salvation, and your **g** praise. Is 60:18
Go out, go out through the **g**; Is 62:10
the entrance to Jerusalem's **g**. Jr 1:15
through these **g** to worship the Jr 7:2
mourns; her **g** languish. ⌊Her Jr 14:2
fork at the **g** of the land. Jr 15:7
and in all the **g** of Jerusalem. Jr 17:19
who enter through these **g**. Jr 17:20
it in through the **g** of Jerusalem Jr 17:21
loads through the **g** of this city Jr 17:24
through the **g** of this city. Jr 17:25
entering the **g** of Jerusalem Jr 17:27
set fire to its **g**, and it will Jr 17:27
your people who enter these **g**. Jr 22:2
through the **g** of this palace Jr 22:4
outside the **g** of Jerusalem. Jr 22:19
and her high **g** consumed by fire. Jr 51:58
All her **g** are deserted; Lm 1:4
Zion's **g** have fallen to the Lm 2:9
shattered the bars on her ⌊**g**⌋. Lm 2:9
could enter Jerusalem's **g**. Lm 4:12
for slaughter at all their **g**. Ezk 21:15
battering rams against the **g**, Ezk 21:22
he enters your **g** as ⌊an army⌋ Ezk 26:10
walls and without bars or **g**— Ezk 38:11
flanked the **g** and corresponded Ezk 40:18
to the length of the **g**; Ezk 40:18
at the temple **g** and ministering Ezk 44:11
they enter the **g** of the inner Ezk 44:17
minister at the **g** of the inner Ezk 44:17
will be three **g** facing north, Ezk 48:31
g of the city being named for Ezk 48:31
miles⌋, there will be three **g**: Ezk 48:32
miles⌋, there will be three **g**: Ezk 48:33
miles⌋, there will be three **g**: Ezk 48:34
and devour the bars of his **g**, Hs 11:6
break down the **g** of Damascus. Am 1:5
the poor of justice at the **g**. Am 5:12
The river **g** are opened, and the Nah 2:6
the **g** of your land are wide open Nah 3:13
devour the bars ⌊of your **g**⌋. Nah 3:13
peaceful judgments in your **g**. Zch 8:16
Open your **g**, Lebanon, and fire Zch 11:1
watching the **g** day and night Ac 9:24
oxen and garlands to the **g**. Ac 14:13
and at once the **g** were shut. Ac 21:30
a massive high wall, with 12 **g**. Rv 21:12
Twelve angels were at the **g**; Rv 21:12
⌊on the **g**⌋, names were inscribed, Rv 21:12
There were three **g** on the east, Rv 21:13
the east, three **g** on the north, Rv 21:13
the north, three **g** on the south, Rv 21:13
south, and three **g** on the west. Rv 21:13
the city, its **g**, and its wall. Rv 21:15
The 12 **g** are 12 pearls; Rv 21:21
Each day its **g** will never close Rv 21:25
and may enter the city by the **g**. Rv 22:14

GATEWAY *(13)*
aside to the middle of the **g**, 2Sm 3:27
people trampled him in the **g**. 2Kg 7:17
people trampled him in the **g**, 2Kg 7:20
The **g** to the peoples is Ezk 26:2
while the width of the **g** was 22 Ezk 40:11
he measured the **g** from the roof Ezk 40:13
all around the inside of the **g**. Ezk 40:16
The width of the **g** was 24 and a Ezk 40:48
will sit in the **g** to eat a meal Ezk 44:3
of Achor into a **g** of hope. Hs 2:15
When he had gone out to the **g**, Mt 26:71
He knocked at the door in the **g**, Ac 12:13
Peter was standing at the **g**. Ac 12:14

GATEWAYS *(1)*
the doors of the **g** and for the 1Ch 22:3

GATH *(35)*
in Gaza, **G**, and Ashdod. Jos 11:22
Ashkelon, **G**, and Ekron, as Jos 13:3
God should be moved to **G**," 1Sm 5:8
hand was against the city of **G**, 1Sm 5:9
Gaza, Ashkelon, **G**, and Ekron. 1Sm 6:17
The cities from Ekron to **G**, 1Sm 7:14
named Goliath, from **G**, came out 1Sm 17:4
Philistine from **G**, came forward 1Sm 17:23
Shaaraim road to **G** and Ekron. 1Sm 17:52
and went to King Achish of **G**. 1Sm 21:10
very afraid of King Achish of **G**, 1Sm 21:12
So David left **G** and took refuge 1Sm 22:1
son of Maoch, the king of **G**. 1Sm 27:2
his men stayed with Achish in **G**. 1Sm 27:3
Saul that David had fled to **G**, 1Sm 27:4
woman live to be brought to **G**, 1Sm 27:11
not tell it in **G**, don't announce 2Sm 1:20
men who came with him from **G** 2Sm 15:18
At **G** there was still another 2Sm 21:20
the giant in **G** and were killed 2Sm 21:22
Achish son of Maacah, king of **G**. 1Kg 2:39
Look, your slaves are in **G**." 1Kg 2:39
out to Achish at **G** to search for 1Kg 2:40
and brought them back from **G**. 1Kg 2:40
Jerusalem to **G** and had returned 1Kg 2:41
against **G** and captured it. 2Kg 12:17
men of **G** who were born in the 1Ch 7:21
drove out the residents of **G**, 1Ch 8:13
and took **G** and its villages from 1Ch 18:1
battle at **G** where there was 1Ch 20:6
the giant in **G** killed by David 1Ch 20:8
G, Mareshah, Ziph, 2Ch 11:8
and he tore down the wall of **G**, 2Ch 26:6
then go down to **G** of the Am 6:2
announce it in **G**, don't weep at Mc 1:10

GATH-HEPHER *(2)*
the sunrise to **G** and to Jos 19:13
Jonah son of Amittai from **G**. 2Kg 14:25

GATH-RIMMON *(4)*
(AKA BILEAM)
Jehud, Bene-berak, **G**, Jos 19:45
and **G** with its pasturelands— Jos 21:24
its pasturelands and **G** with its Jos 21:25
and **G** and its pasturelands. 1Ch 6:69

GATHER *(137)*
g it as food for you and for them. Gn 6:21
to his relatives, "**G** stones." Gn 31:46
Let them **g** all the ⌊excess⌋ food Gn 41:35
sons and said, "**G** around, and I Gn 49:1
They must go and **g** straw for Ex 5:7
land of Egypt to **g** stubble for Ex 5:12
each day and **g** enough for that Ex 16:4
much as they **g** on other days." Ex 16:5
'**G** as much of it as each person Ex 16:16
For six days you may **g** it, Ex 16:26
of the people went out to **g**, Ex 16:27
for six years and **g** its produce. Ex 23:10
when you **g** your produce from the Ex 23:16
of your field or **g** the gleanings Lv 19:9
vineyard bare or **g** its fallen Lv 19:10
of your field or **g** the gleanings Lv 23:22
vineyard and **g** its produce for Lv 25:3
we don't sow or **g** our produce?' Lv 25:20
community is to **g** before you at Nm 10:3
clans, are to **g** before you. Nm 10:4
is clean is to **g** up the cow's Nm 19:9
G the people so I may give them Nm 21:16
are to **g** all its spoil in the Dt 13:16
When you **g** the grapes of your Dt 24:21
the wine or **g** ⌊the grapes⌋, Dt 28:39
and **g** you again from all the Dt 30:3
He will **g** you and bring you back Dt 30:4
G the people—men, women, Dt 31:12
"**G** your army and come out." Jdg 9:29
the fields and **g** fallen grain Ru 2:2
the field to **g** ⌊grain⌋ behind Ru 2:3
'Will you let me **g** fallen grain Ru 2:7
go and **g** ⌊grain⌋ in another Ru 2:8
When she got up to **g** ⌊grain⌋, Ru 2:15
sure to let her **g** ⌊grain⌋ among Ru 2:15
and leave ⌊them⌋ for her to **g**. Ru 2:16
Where did you **g** ⌊barley⌋ today, Ru 2:19
Samuel said, "**G** all Israel at 1Sm 7:5
go and I will **g** all Israel to my 2Sm 3:21
the field to **g** herbs and found 2Kg 4:39
I will indeed **g** you to your 2Kg 22:20
they should **g** together with us 1Ch 13:2
g us and rescue us from the 1Ch 16:35
gave orders to **g** the foreigners 1Ch 22:2
people went to **g** the plunder. 2Ch 20:25
'I will indeed **g** you to your 2Ch 34:28
exiles should **g** at Jerusalem. Ezr 10:7
I will **g** them from there and Neh 1:9
They **g** their fodder in the field Jb 24:6
of peoples **g** around You; Ps 7:7
G My faithful ones to Me, Ps 50:5
You give it to them, they **g** it; Ps 104:28
and **g** us from the nations, Ps 106:47
righteous will **g** around me Ps 142:7
stones and a time to **g** stones; Ec 3:5
I **g** my myrrh with my spices. Sg 5:1
in the gardens and **g** lilies. Sg 6:2
the nations and **g** the dispersed Is 11:12
eggs and will **g** ⌊her brood⌋ Is 34:15
the birds of prey will **g** there, Is 34:15

He will g them by His Spirit. Is 34:16
the east, and g you from the Is 43:5
Come, g together, and draw near, Is 45:20
around. They all g together; Is 49:18
I will g to them still others Is 56:8
they all g and come to you; Is 60:4
For those who g grain will eat Is 62:9
I have come to g all nations and Is 66:18
The sons g wood, the fathers Jr 7:18
I will g them and bring them to Jr 8:13
sitting here? G together; let us Jr 8:14
reaper with no one to g ⌊it⌋. Jr 9:22
G up your belongings from the Jr 10:17
Go, g all the wild animals; Jr 12:9
I will g the remnant of My flock Jr 23:3
your fortunes and g you from all Jr 29:14
will g them from remote regions Jr 31:8
who scattered Israel will g him. Jr 31:10
am about to g them from all the Jr 32:37
for you, g wine, summer fruit, Jr 40:10
with no one to g up the Jr 49:5
will g you from the peoples and Ezk 11:17
going to g all the lovers you Ezk 16:37
I will g them against you from Ezk 16:37
from the peoples and g you from Ezk 20:34
from the peoples and g you from Ezk 20:41
I am about to g you into Ezk 22:19
I will g ⌊you⌋ in My anger and Ezk 22:20
will g you together and blow on Ezk 22:21
I g the house of Israel from Ezk 28:25
40 years I will g the Egyptians Ezk 29:13
g them from the countries, Ezk 34:13
the nations and g you from all Ezk 36:24
will g them from all around and Ezk 37:21
They will not g wood from the Ezk 39:10
G from all around to My Ezk 39:17
from the peoples and g them from Ezk 39:27
Egypt will g them, and Memphis Hs 9:6
G the elders and all the Jl 1:14
G the people; sanctify the Jl 2:16
g the children, even those Jl 2:16
will g all the nations and take Jl 3:2
nations; g yourselves. Bring Jl 3:11
I will indeed g all of you, Mc 2:12
the lame and g the scattered, Mc 4:6
no one to g ⌊them⌋ together. Nah 3:18
They g prisoners like sand. Hab 1:9
and g them in their fishing net; Hab 1:15
G yourselves together; Zph 2:1
g together, undesirable nation, Zph 2:1
For My decision is to g nations, Zph 3:8
I will g those who have been Zph 3:18
the lame and g the scattered; Zph 3:19
yes, at the time I will g you. Zph 3:20
will whistle and g them because Zch 10:8
of Egypt and g them from Assyria Zch 10:10
of the earth g against her. Zch 12:3
I will g all the nations against Zch 14:2
threshing floor and g His wheat Mt 3:12
sow or reap or g into barns, Mt 6:26
who does not g with Me scatters. Mt 12:30
want us to go and g them up?' Mt 13:28
'When you g up the weeds, you Mt 13:29
G the weeds first and tie them Mt 13:30
and they will g from His kingdom Mt 13:41
I wanted to g your children Mt 23:37
there the vultures will g. Mt 24:28
and they will g His elect from Mt 24:31
sown and g where I haven't Mt 25:26
out the angels and g His elect Mk 13:27
floor and g the wheat into His Lk 3:17
who does not g with Me scatters. Lk 11:23
I wanted to g your children Lk 13:34
They g them, throw them into the Jn 15:6
sharp sickle and g the clusters Rv 14:18
g together for the great supper Rv 19:17
and Magog, to g them for battle Rv 20:8

GATHERED *(165)*

the sky be g into one place, Gn 1:9
and he was g to his people. Gn 25:8
died, and was g to his people. Gn 25:17
all the flocks were g there, Gn 29:3
time for the animals to be g. Gn 29:7
have been g and the stone is Gn 29:8
died, and was g to his people, Gn 35:29
and your sheaves g around it and Gn 37:7
Joseph g all the ⌊excess⌋ food Gn 41:48
I am about to be g to my people. Gn 49:29
He was g to his people. Gn 49:33
Some g a lot, some a little. Ex 16:17
the person who g a lot had no Ex 16:18
the person who g a little had no Ex 16:18
Each g as much as he needed to Ex 16:18
They g it every morning. Ex 16:21
Each g as much as he needed to Ex 16:21
sixth day they g twice as much Ex 16:22
they g around Aaron and said to Ex 32:1
all the Levites g around him. Ex 32:26
after you have g the produce Lv 23:39
people walked around and g ⌊it⌋. Nm 11:8
took the least g 33 bushels— Nm 11:32
Aaron will be g to his people; Nm 20:24
Aaron will be g ⌊to his people⌋ Nm 20:26
he g his whole army and went out Nm 21:23
who g together against the LORD. Nm 27:3
will also be g to your people, Nm 27:13
you will be g to your people." Nm 31:2
when you have g in ⌊everything⌋ Dt 16:13
you will be g to your people, Dt 32:50
Hor and was g to his people. Dt 32:50
of the people g with the tribes Dt 33:5
They g provisions and took Jos 9:4
was also g to their ancestors Jdg 2:10
Qedemites g together, crossed Jdg 6:33
and of Beth-millo g together and Jdg 9:6
Tower of Shechem had g together. Jdg 9:47
Instead, Sihon g all his people, Jdg 11:20
Then Jephthah g all of the men Jdg 12:4
leaders g together to offer Jdg 16:23
men of Israel g united against Jdg 20:11
the Benjaminites g together from Jdg 20:14
So Ruth g ⌊grain⌋ in the field Ru 2:17
She beat out what she had g, Ru 2:17
young women and g ⌊grain⌋ until Ru 2:23
When they g at Mizpah, they drew 1Sm 7:6
the Israelites had g at Mizpah, 1Sm 7:7
elders of Israel g together and 1Sm 8:4
also g to fight against 1Sm 13:5
The Philistines g their forces 1Sm 17:1
the men of Israel g and camped 1Sm 17:2
So Saul g all Israel, and they 1Sm 28:4
Abner, he g all the troops. 2Sm 2:30
to David, he g all Israel, 2Sm 10:17
be g to you and that you 2Sm 17:11
They also g up the bones of 2Sm 21:13
the place they had g for battle, 2Sm 23:9
who had g around him and were 1Kg 8:5
and g men to himself. 1Kg 11:24
Israelites and g the prophets at 1Kg 18:20
mobilized, g supplies, and went 1Kg 20:27
king of Israel g the prophets, 1Kg 22:6
from which he g as many wild 2Kg 4:39
and you will be g to your grave 2Kg 22:20
and they g to him all the elders 2Kg 23:1
Philistines had g there for 1Ch 11:13
Then he g together the 1Ch 15:4
Ammonites also g from their 1Ch 19:7
he g all Israel and crossed the 1Ch 19:17
Then he g all the leaders of 1Ch 23:2
Israel who had g around him were 2Ch 5:6
of Judah who were g at Jerusalem 2Ch 12:5
and wicked men g around him to 2Ch 13:7
he g all Judah and Benjamin, 2Ch 15:9
They were g in Jerusalem in the 2Ch 15:10
king of Israel g the prophets, 2Ch 18:5
who g to seek the LORD. 2Ch 20:4
They g the Levites from all the 2Ch 23:2
So he g the priests and Levites 2Ch 24:5
did this daily and g the money 2Ch 24:11
Then Amaziah g Judah and 2Ch 25:5
Then Ahaz g up the utensils of 2Ch 28:24
and Levites and g them in the 2Ch 29:4
They g their brothers together, 2Ch 29:15
got up early, g the city 2Ch 29:20
people hadn't been g together in 2Ch 30:3
of people was g in Jerusalem to 2Ch 30:13
They g ⌊them⌋ into large piles. 2Ch 31:6
Many people g and stopped up all 2Ch 32:4
over the people and g the people 2Ch 32:6
and you will be g to your grave 2Ch 34:28
messengers⌋ and g all the elders 2Ch 34:29
and the people g together in Ezr 3:1
and I g Israelite leaders to Ezr 7:28
I g them at the river that flows Ezr 8:15
the God of Israel g around me, Ezr 9:4
and children g around him. Ezr 10:1
and Benjamin g in Jerusalem Ezr 10:9
subordinates were g there for Neh 5:16
all the people g together at the Neh 8:1
The singers g from the region Neh 12:28
Levites were g from the village Neh 12:44
I g the Levites and singers Neh 13:11
young women g at the fortress Est 2:8
of sheaves is g in its season. Jb 5:26
when I stumbled, they g in glee; Ps 35:15
in glee; they g against me. Ps 35:15
and has g them from the lands— Ps 107:3
the grain from the hills is g Pr 27:25
Who has g the wind in His hands? Pr 30:4
I g male and female singers for Ec 2:8
eggs, I g the whole earth. Is 10:14
like nations being g together! Is 13:4
if a reaper had g standing grain Is 17:5
They will be g together like Is 24:22
Israelites will be g one by one. Is 27:12
spoil will be g as locusts are Is 33:4
be gathered as locusts are g; Is 33:4
Who has g the dust of the earth Is 40:12
All the nations are g together, Is 43:9
that Israel might be g to Him; Is 49:5
others besides those already g." Is 56:8
of Kedar will be g to you; Is 60:7
all the nations will be g to it, Jr 3:17
not be mourned, g, or buried. Jr 25:33
Judah that has g to you so that Jr 40:15
be taken away or g ⌊for burial⌋. Ezk 29:5
a people g from the nations Ezk 38:12
the king's advisers g around, Dn 3:27
Israelites will be g together. Hs 1:11
nations will be g against them Hs 10:10
that He has g them like sheaves Mc 4:12
fruit has been g after the Mc 7:1
Are grapes g from thornbushes or Mt 7:16
large crowds g around Him that Mt 13:2
as the weeds are g and burned Mt 13:40
and g the good ⌊fish⌋ into Mt 13:48
two or three are g together in Mt 18:20
on the roads and g everyone they Mt 22:10
nations will be g before Him, Mt 25:32
So when they had g together, Mt 27:17
headquarters and g the whole Mt 27:27
the Pharisees g before Pilate Mt 27:62
So many people g together that Mk 2:2
and the crowd g again so that Mk 3:20
a very large crowd g around Him. Mk 4:1
a large crowd g around Him while Mk 5:21
The apostles g around Jesus and Mk 6:30
from Jerusalem g around Him. Mk 7:1
Figs aren't g from thornbushes, Lk 6:44
the younger son g together all Lk 15:13
also the vultures will be g." Lk 17:37
crowds that had g for this Lk 23:48
and those with them g together, Lk 24:33
disciples were ⌊g together⌋ with Jn 20:19
they arrived and g the church Ac 14:27
and spoke to the women g there. Ac 16:13
As Paul g a bundle of brushwood Ac 28:3
when they had g he said to them Ac 28:17
The person who g much did not 2Co 8:15
the person who g little did not 2Co 8:15
Christ and our being g to Him: 2Th 2:1
toward earth and g the grapes Rv 14:19
their armies g together to wage Rv 19:19

GATHERER *(1)*

like a grape g over the branches Jr 6:9

GATHERING *(19)*

and He called the g of the water Gn 1:10
It is a solemn g; you are not to Lv 23:36
all the next day g the quail— Nm 11:32
they found a man g wood on the Nm 15:32
who found him g wood brought Nm 15:33
Philistines were g at Michmash, 1Sm 13:11
a g of water and thick clouds. 2Sm 22:12
was a widow woman g wood. 1Kg 17:10
I am g a couple of sticks in 1Kg 17:12
were g the plunder for three 2Ch 20:25
g possessions without knowing Ps 39:6
the task of g and accumulating Ec 2:26
Like one g abandoned eggs, Is 10:14
haven't sown and g where you Mt 25:24
large crowd was g, and people Lk 8:4
pay and g fruit for eternal Jn 4:36
and after g the assembly, they Ac 15:30

a reason for this disorderly g." Ac 19:40
myriads of angels in festive g, Heb 12:22

GATHERS (11)

Then the one who g up the cow's Nm 19:10
He g the waters of the sea into Ps 33:7
He g Israel's exiled people. Ps 147:2
it g its food during harvest. Pr 6:8
The son who g during summer is Pr 10:5
He g the lambs in His arms and Is 40:11
who g the dispersed of Israel: Is 56:8
Just as one g silver, copper, Ezk 22:20
He g all the nations to himself; Hab 2:5
as a hen g her chicks under her Mt 23:37
as a hen g her chicks under her Lk 13:34

GATHITES (1)

The G then sent the ark of God 1Sm 5:10

GAVE (607)

The man g names to all the Gn 2:20
also g ⌊some⌋ to her husband, Gn 3:6
The woman You g to be with me— Gn 3:12
she g me ⌊some fruit⌋ from the Gn 3:12
conceived and g birth to Cain. Gn 4:1
Then she also g birth to his Gn 4:2
conceived and g birth to Enoch. Gn 4:17
and she g birth to a son and Gn 4:25
as ⌊I g⌋ the green plants, Gn 9:3
Then Pharaoh g ⌊his⌋ men orders Gn 12:20
And Abram g him a tenth of Gn 14:20
and g her to her husband Abram Gn 16:3
So Hagar g birth to Abram's son, Gn 16:15
and Abram g the name Ishmael to Gn 16:15
He g it to a young man, who Gn 18:7
The firstborn g birth to a son Gn 19:37
younger also g birth to a son, Gn 19:38
slaves, g them to Abraham, Gn 20:14
waterskin and g the boy a drink Gn 21:19
and cattle and g them to Gn 21:27
to her hand and g him a drink. Gn 24:18
garments, and g ⌊them⌋ to Gn 24:53
He also g precious gifts to her Gn 24:53
Abraham g everything he owned to Gn 25:5
And Abraham g gifts to the sons Gn 25:6
Then Jacob g bread and lentil Gn 25:34
He g them the same names his Gn 26:18
the land God g to Abraham." Gn 28:4
Leah and g her to Jacob, Gn 29:23
And Laban g his slave Zilpah to Gn 29:24
and Laban g him his daughter Gn 29:28
And Laban g his slave Bilhah to Gn 29:29
conceived, g birth to a son, Gn 29:32
again, g birth to a son, Gn 29:33
again, g birth to a son, Gn 29:34
again, g birth to a son, Gn 29:35
So Rachel g her slave Bilhah to Gn 30:4
Zilpah and g her to Jacob as Gn 30:9
After Rachel g birth to Joseph, Gn 30:25
Then they g Jacob all their Gn 35:4
The land that I g to Abraham and Gn 35:12
conceived and g birth to a son, Gn 38:3
again, g birth to a son, Gn 38:4
She g birth to another son and Gn 38:5
Chezib that she g birth to him. Gn 38:5
So he g them to her and slept Gn 38:18
he g a feast for all his Gn 40:20
Pharaoh g Joseph the name Gn 41:45
and g him a wife, Gn 41:45
Joseph then g orders to fill Gn 42:25
g them water to wash their feet, Gn 43:24
Joseph g them wagons as Pharaoh Gn 45:21
and he g them provisions for the Gn 45:21
g each of the brothers changes Gn 45:22
but he g Benjamin 300 pieces of Gn 45:22
Laban g to his daughter Leah Gn 46:18
whom Laban g to his daughter Gn 46:25
of Egypt and g them property Gn 47:11
and he g them food in exchange Gn 47:17
he died your father g a command: Gn 50:16
feared God, He g them families. Ex 1:21
pregnant and g birth to a son; Ex 2:2
and he g his daughter Zipporah Ex 2:21
She g birth to a son whom he Ex 2:22
and Aaron and g them commands Ex 6:13
The LORD g the people favor in Ex 11:3
And the LORD g the people such Ex 12:36
sight that they g them what they Ex 12:36
He g him the two tablets of the Ex 31:18
it off,' and they g ⌊it⌋ to me. Ex 32:24
After Moses g an order, they Ex 36:6
because he g his offspring to Lv 20:3
commands the LORD g Moses for Lv 27:34
He g the redemption money to Nm 3:51
carts and oxen and g them to the Nm 7:6
He g the Gershonites two carts Nm 7:7
and g the Merarites four carts Nm 7:8
So they g a negative report to Nm 13:32
of their leaders g him a staff, Nm 17:6
He g up his sons as refugees, Nm 21:29
Moses g the tribute to Eleazar Nm 31:41
He g them to the Levites who Nm 31:47
So Moses g orders about them to Nm 32:28
So Moses g them—the Gadites, Nm 32:33
They g names to the cities they Nm 32:38
So Moses g Gilead to ⌊the clan Nm 32:40
its possession the LORD g them. Dt 2:12
LORD our God g everything to us Dt 2:36
g to the Reubenites and Gadites Dt 3:12
g to half the tribe of Manasseh Dt 3:13
I g Gilead to Machir, Dt 3:15
and I g to the Reubenites and Dt 3:16
the law Moses g the Israelites. Dt 4:44
stone tablets and g them to me. Dt 5:22
then He g you manna to eat, Dt 8:3
the LORD g me the two stone Dt 9:10
The LORD g me the two stone Dt 9:11
the fire. The LORD g them to me, Dt 10:4
'I g my daughter to this man as Dt 22:16
because that man g an Israelite Dt 22:19
this place and g us this land, Dt 26:9
to all the commands You g me. Dt 26:13
commands and statutes He g you. Dt 28:45
took their land and g it as an Dt 29:8
this law and g it to the priests Dt 31:9
the Most High g the nations Dt 32:8
the Rock who g you birth; Dt 32:18
g the Israelites before his Dt 33:1
Moses g us instruction, a Dt 33:4
the land Moses g you on this Jos 1:14
LORD's servant g you on the east Jos 1:15
the people g a great shout, Jos 6:20
the day the LORD g the Amorites Jos 10:12
Joshua then g it as an Jos 11:23
LORD's servant g their land as Jos 12:6
Joshua g their land as an Jos 12:7
inheritance Moses g them beyond Jos 13:8
by their clans, Moses g Jos 13:15
Gadites by their clans, Moses g Jos 13:24
by their clans, Moses g Jos 13:29
the portions Moses g ⌊them⌋ on Jos 13:32
tribes g them in the land Jos 14:1
But he g no inheritance among Jos 14:3
of Jephunneh and g him Hebron as Jos 14:13
He g Caleb son of Jephunneh ⌊the Jos 15:13
and Caleb g his daughter Achsah Jos 15:17
So he g her the upper and lower Jos 15:19
So they g them an inheritance Jos 17:4
the God of your fathers, g you? Jos 18:3
the LORD's servant g them." Jos 18:7
the Israelites g Joshua son of Jos 19:49
g him the city Timnath-serah Jos 19:50
g the Levites these cities with Jos 21:3
The Israelites g these cities Jos 21:8
The Israelites g these cities by Jos 21:9
They g them Kiriath-arba (that Jos 21:11
But they g the fields and Jos 21:12
They g to the descendants of Jos 21:13
the tribe of Benjamin ⌊they g⌋: Jos 21:17
The Israelites g them: Shechem, Jos 21:21
From the tribe of Dan ⌊they g⌋: Jos 21:23
the tribe of Manasseh ⌊they g⌋: Jos 21:25
⌊they g⌋ to the descendants of Jos 21:27
the tribe of Issachar ⌊they g⌋: Jos 21:28
the tribe of Asher ⌊they g⌋: Jos 21:30
the tribe of Naphtali ⌊they g⌋: Jos 21:32
⌊they g⌋ to the clans of the Jos 21:34
the tribe of Reuben, ⌊they g⌋: Jos 21:36
From the tribe of Gad, ⌊they g⌋: Jos 21:38
the LORD g Israel all the land Jos 21:43
The LORD g them rest on every Jos 21:44
the LORD's servant g you across Jos 22:4
Moses the LORD's servant g you: Jos 22:5
his descendants. I g him Isaac, Jos 24:3
and to Isaac I g Jacob and Esau. Jos 24:4
I g the hill country of Seir to Jos 24:4
I g you a land you did not labor Jos 24:13
and Caleb g his daughter Achsah Jdg 1:13
So Caleb g her both the upper Jdg 1:15
Judah g Hebron to Caleb, just as Jdg 1:20
g their own daughters to their Jdg 3:6
He g Eglon king of Moab power Jdg 3:12
of milk, g him a drink, Jdg 4:19
for water; she g him milk. She Jdg 5:25
before you and g you their land. Jdg 6:9
companies and g each of the men Jdg 7:16
they g him 70 pieces of silver Jdg 9:4
g his 30 daughters in marriage Jdg 12:9
the woman g birth to a son and Jdg 13:24
he g ⌊some⌋ to them and they ate Jdg 14:9
them and g their clothes to Jdg 14:19
so I g her to one of the men who Jdg 15:2
of silver and g it to a Jdg 17:4
and Israel g them the women they Jdg 21:14
from her meal and g ⌊it⌋ to her. Ru 2:18
He g me these six ⌊measures⌋ of Ru 3:17
his sandal and g ⌊it⌋ to the Ru 4:7
and she g birth to a son. Ru 4:13
he always g portions of the meat 1Sm 1:4
But he g a double portion to 1Sm 1:5
conceived and g birth to a son. 1Sm 1:20
since the LORD g me what I asked 1Sm 1:27
conceived and g birth to three 1Sm 2:21
I also g your house all the 1Sm 2:28
What was the message He g you? 1Sm 3:17
collapsed and g birth because 1Sm 4:19
and g them a place at the head 1Sm 9:22
meat that I g you and told you 1Sm 9:23
which the LORD your God g you. 1Sm 13:13
Then Saul g up the pursuit of 1Sm 14:46
on the mission the LORD g me: 1Sm 15:20
people g him the same answer 1Sm 17:30
was wearing and g it to David, 1Sm 18:4
Then Saul g his daughter Michal 1Sm 18:27
Then Jonathan g his equipment to 1Sm 20:40
"The king g me a mission, 1Sm 21:2
the priest g him the consecrated 1Sm 21:6
for him and g him provisions. 1Sm 22:10
He also g him the sword of 1Sm 22:10
You g him bread and a sword and 1Sm 22:13
But Saul g his daughter Michal, 1Sm 25:44
That day Achish g Ziklag to him, 1Sm 27:6
They g him some bread to eat and 1Sm 30:11
they g him some pressed figs 1Sm 30:12
So David g orders to the young 2Sm 4:12
I g your master's house to you 2Sm 12:8
and I g you the house of Israel 2Sm 12:8
She g birth to a son and named 2Sm 12:24
is the one who g orders to me; 2Sm 14:19
Ahithophel g in those days was 2Sm 16:23
So he g the pillar his name. 2Sm 18:18
Then the king g him his oath. 2Sm 19:23
Joab g the king the total of the 2Sm 24:9
for the LORD g it to him. 1Kg 2:15
Then King Solomon g the order to 1Kg 2:25
and the command that I g you?" 1Kg 2:43
the third day after I g birth, 1Kg 3:18
was not the son I g birth to." 1Kg 3:21
God g Solomon wisdom, very great 1Kg 4:29
The LORD g Solomon wisdom, 1Kg 5:12
the land You g their ancestors 1Kg 8:34
land that You g Your people for 1Kg 8:36
on the land You g our ancestors. 1Kg 8:40
land that You g their ancestors, 1Kg 8:48
Israel from the land I g them, 1Kg 9:7
King Solomon g Hiram 20 towns in 1Kg 9:11
and g it as a dowry to his 1Kg 9:16
Then she g the king four and a 1Kg 10:10
of Sheba g to King Solomon. 1Kg 10:10
Solomon g the queen of Sheba 1Kg 10:13
of Egypt, who g Hadad a house, 1Kg 11:18
be given⌋ food, and g him land. 1Kg 11:18
so much that he g him a wife, 1Kg 11:19
sister g birth to Hadad's 1Kg 11:20
He g a sign that day. He said, 1Kg 13:3
house of David, and g it to you. 1Kg 14:8
good soil that He g to their 1Kg 14:15
the LORD his God g him a lamp in 1Kg 15:4
Then King Asa g a command to 1Kg 15:22
the house, and g him to his 1Kg 17:23
took the bull that he g them, 1Kg 18:26
the meat and g it to the people, 1Kg 19:21
conceived and g birth to a son 2Kg 4:17
So he g it to them, and as the 2Kg 4:44
Naaman g them to two of his 2Kg 5:23
So he g him his hand, and Jehu 2Kg 10:15
The priest g to the commanders 2Kg 11:10

crown on him, **g** him the 2Kg 11:12
the LORD **g** Israel a deliverer, 2Kg 13:5
Menahem **g** Pul 75,000 pounds of 2Kg 15:19
So Hezekiah **g** ⌊him⌋ all the 2Kg 18:15
overlaid and **g** it to the king 2Kg 18:16
Hezekiah **g** them a hearing and 2Kg 20:13
from the land I **g** to their 2Kg 21:8
and he **g** the book to Shaphan, 2Kg 22:8
Jehoiakim **g** the silver and the 2Kg 23:35
Sheshan **g** his daughter in 1Ch 2:35
"I **g** birth to him in pain." 1Ch 4:9
wife Bithiah **g** birth to Miriam, 1Ch 4:17
His Judean wife **g** birth to Jered 1Ch 4:18
So the Israelites **g** these towns 1Ch 6:64
wife Maacah **g** birth to a son, 1Ch 7:16
Hammolecheth **g** birth to Ishhod, 1Ch 7:18
conceived and **g** birth to a son. 1Ch 7:23
and the LORD **g** them a great 1Ch 11:14
Joab **g** David the total of the 1Ch 21:5
I the one who **g** the order to 1Ch 21:17
So David **g** Ornan 15 pounds of 1Ch 21:25
So David **g** orders to gather the 1Ch 22:2
Then David **g** his son Solomon the 1Ch 28:11
of the king's work **g** willingly. 1Ch 29:6
house they **g** 185 tons of gold 1Ch 29:7
precious⌋ stones **g** them to the 1Ch 29:8
He **g** King David a wise son with 2Ch 2:12
to the land You **g** them and their 2Ch 6:25
land that You **g** Your people for 2Ch 6:27
on the land You **g** our ancestors. 2Ch 6:31
land that You **g** their ancestors, 2Ch 6:38
from the soil that I **g** them, 2Ch 7:20
cities Hiram **g** him and having 2Ch 8:2
Then she **g** the king four and a 2Ch 9:9
of Sheba **g** to King Solomon. 2Ch 9:9
Solomon **g** the queen of Sheba 2Ch 9:12
He **g** them plenty of provisions 2Ch 11:23
God of Israel **g** the kingship 2Ch 13:5
because the LORD **g** him rest. 2Ch 14:6
Him and He **g** us rest on every 2Ch 14:7
So the LORD **g** them rest on every 2Ch 15:15
Israel and who **g** it forever to 2Ch 20:7
possession that You **g** us as an 2Ch 20:11
for his God **g** him rest on every 2Ch 20:30
but he **g** the kingdom to Jehoram 2Ch 21:3
his mother **g** him evil advice. 2Ch 22:3
the priest **g** to the commanders 2Ch 23:9
crown on him, **g** him the 2Ch 23:11
king and Jehoiada **g** it to those 2Ch 24:12
pounds of silver I **g** to Israel's 2Ch 25:9
the LORD, God **g** him success. 2Ch 26:5
The Ammonites **g** Uzziah tribute 2Ch 26:8
year they **g** him 7,500 pounds 2Ch 27:5
clothed them, **g** them sandals, 2Ch 28:15
the rulers and **g** the plunder to 2Ch 28:21
Israelites **g** liberally of the 2Ch 31:5
He **g** them rest on every side. 2Ch 32:22
to him and **g** him a miraculous 2Ch 32:24
for God **g** him abundant 2Ch 32:29
and **g** him the money brought into 2Ch 34:9
They ⌊in turn⌋ **g** it to the 2Ch 34:10
they **g** it to the carpenters and 2Ch 34:11
and he **g** the book to Shaphan. 2Ch 34:15
"Hilkiah the priest **g** me a book," 2Ch 34:18
g 2,600 Passover sacrifices and 2Ch 35:8
family leaders **g** freewill Ezr 2:68
could give, they **g** 61,000 gold Ezr 2:69
They **g** money to the stonecutters Ezr 3:7
artisans, and ⌊**g**⌋ food, drink, Ezr 3:7
all the people **g** a great shout Ezr 3:11
Who **g** you the order to rebuild Ezr 5:3
Who **g** you the order to rebuild Ezr 5:9
This is the reply they **g** us: Ezr 5:11
Darius **g** the order, and they Ezr 6:1
King Artaxerxes **g** to Ezra the Ezr 7:11
You **g** through Your servants the Ezr 9:11
ordinances You **g** Your servant Neh 1:7
the wine and **g** it to the king. Neh 2:1
So I **g** him a definite time, Neh 2:6
Euphrates and **g** them the king's Neh 2:9
I **g** them this reply, "The God of Neh 2:20
and I **g** them the same reply. Neh 6:4
family leaders **g** to the project. Neh 7:70
The governor **g** 1,000 gold Neh 7:70
the family leaders **g** 20,000 gold Neh 7:71
rest of the people **g** 20,000 gold Neh 7:72
You **g** them impartial ordinances, Neh 9:13
them, and **g** them commandments, Neh 9:14

and You **g** them water for their Neh 9:20
You **g** them kingdoms and peoples Neh 9:22
You **g** them deliverers, Neh 9:27
and warnings You **g** them. Neh 9:34
abundant goodness You **g** them, Neh 9:35
in the land You **g** our ancestors Neh 9:36
opposite them—**g** praise and Neh 12:24
large processions that **g** thanks. Neh 12:31
I **g** orders that the gates be Neh 13:19
Queen Vashti also **g** a feast for Est 1:9
tax payments and **g** gifts worthy Est 2:18
him in rank and **g** him a higher Est 3:1
his finger and **g** it to Haman son Est 3:10
Mordecai also **g** him a copy of Est 4:8
⌊**g**⌋ the report that saved the Est 7:9
from Haman and **g** it to Mordecai, Est 8:2
king's edict **g** the Jews in each Est 8:11
The king **g** the orders for this Est 9:14
He **g** them over to their Jb 8:4
You **g** me life and faithful love, Jb 10:12
g no water to the thirsty and Jb 22:7
Who **g** Him authority over the Jb 34:13
the spirit and breath He ⌊**g**⌋, Jb 34:14
Who **g** birth to the frost of Jb 38:29
in the heart or **g** the mind Jb 38:36
Each one **g** him a qesitah , Jb 42:11
for life, and You **g** it to him— Ps 21:4
The Lord **g** the command; Ps 68:11
they **g** me gall for my food, Ps 69:21
my thirst they **g** me vinegar to Ps 69:21
wilderness and **g** them drink as Ps 78:15
He **g** a command to the clouds Ps 78:23
He **g** them grain from heaven. Ps 78:24
for He **g** them what they craved. Ps 78:29
He **g** their crops to the Ps 78:46
g up His strength to captivity Ps 78:61
He **g** them lasting shame. Ps 78:66
They **g** the corpses of Your Ps 79:2
bread of tears and **g** them a full Ps 80:5
So I **g** them over to their Ps 81:12
before You **g** birth to the earth Ps 90:2
and the statutes He **g** them. Ps 99:7
He **g** them hail for rain, and Ps 105:32
a covering and ⌊**g**⌋ a fire to Ps 105:39
He **g** them the lands of the Ps 105:44
He **g** them what they asked for, Ps 106:15
He **g** their land as an Ps 135:12
and **g** their land as an Ps 136:21
He **g** an order that will never Ps 148:6
to your father who **g** you life, Pr 23:22
and let her who **g** birth to you Pr 23:25
spirit returns to God who **g** it. Ec 12:7
to the one who **g** her birth. Sg 6:9
she conceived and **g** you birth. Sg 8:5
conceived and **g** birth to a son. Is 8:3
in pain; we **g** birth to wind. We Is 26:18
LORD, or who **g** Him His counsel Is 40:13
Who **g** Him understanding and Is 40:14
and I **g** a herald of good news to Is 41:27
Who **g** Jacob to the robber, Is 42:24
and **g** Jacob over to total Is 43:28
g My back to those who beat Me, Is 50:6
and to Sarah who **g** birth to you Is 51:2
Spirit of the LORD **g** them rest. Is 63:14
Zion was in labor, she **g** birth; Is 66:7
in labor, she **g** birth to her Is 66:8
to a stone: You **g** birth to me. Jr 2:27
the land I **g** to your ancestors Jr 7:7
the place that I **g** you and your Jr 7:14
mother, that you **g** birth to me, Jr 15:10
their land that I **g** to their Jr 16:15
your inheritance that I **g** you. Jr 17:4
the mother who **g** birth to you Jr 22:26
the city that I **g** you and your Jr 23:39
from the land I **g** to them and Jr 24:10
land the LORD **g** to you and your Jr 25:5
to the land I **g** to their Jr 30:3
and **g** the purchase agreement to Jr 32:12
You **g** them this land You swore Jr 32:22
the land that I **g** you and your Jr 35:15
ancestor's command he **g** them, Jr 35:16
scroll and **g** it to Baruch son Jr 36:32
So King Zedekiah **g** orders, Jr 37:21
and he **g** them vineyards and Jr 39:10
of Babylon **g** orders concerning Jr 39:11
of the guard **g** him a ration Jr 40:5
aroma the food I **g** you— Ezk 16:19
My children and **g** them up when Ezk 16:21

I **g** you over to the desire of Ezk 16:27
but you **g** gifts to all your Ezk 16:33
children that you **g** to them, Ezk 16:36
even though he **g** his hand ⌊in Ezk 17:18
Then I **g** them My statutes and Ezk 20:11
I also **g** them My Sabbaths to Ezk 20:12
I also **g** them statutes that were Ezk 20:25
became Mine and **g** birth to sons Ezk 23:4
in you; they **g** you splendor. Ezk 27:10
which I **g** to My servant Jacob. Ezk 28:25
of the field **g** birth beneath its Ezk 31:6
the land that I **g** your fathers; Ezk 36:28
the land that I **g** to My servant Ezk 37:25
official **g** them ⌊different⌋ Dn 1:7
he **g** the name Belteshazzar; Dn 1:7
to drink and **g** them vegetables. Dn 1:16
God **g** these four young men Dn 1:17
So the king **g** orders to summon Dn 2:2
angry and **g** orders to destroy Dn 2:12
and **g** orders to present an Dn 2:46
Daniel and **g** him many generous Dn 2:48
Nebuchadnezzar **g** orders to bring Dn 3:13
He **g** orders to heat the furnace Dn 3:19
Belshazzar **g** orders to bring in Dn 5:2
the Most High God **g** sovereignty, Dn 5:18
of the greatness He **g** him, Dn 5:19
Then Belshazzar **g** an order, Dn 5:29
prayed, and **g** thanks to his God Dn 6:10
the king **g** the order, and they Dn 6:16
overjoyed and **g** orders to take Dn 6:23
The king then **g** the command, Dn 6:24
He **g** me this explanation: Dn 9:22
again and **g** birth to a daughter Hs 1:6
conceived and **g** birth to a son. Hs 1:8
it is I who **g** her the grain, Hs 2:8
they **g** birth to illegitimate Hs 5:7
I **g** parables through the Hs 12:10
g you absolutely nothing to eat Am 4:6
and ⌊**g**⌋ his inheritance to the Mal 1:3
and peace, and I **g** these to him; Mal 2:5
who **g** birth to Jesus who is Mt 1:16
until she **g** birth to a son. Mt 1:25
He **g** orders to massacre all the Mt 2:16
g the order to go to the other Mt 8:18
awestruck and **g** glory to God who Mt 9:8
He **g** them authority over unclean Mt 10:1
broke the loaves and **g** them to the Mt 14:19
the disciples ⌊**g** them⌋ to the Mt 14:19
And they **g** glory to the God of Mt 15:31
the fish, and He **g** thanks, broke Mt 15:36
the disciples ⌊**g** them⌋ to the Mt 15:36
And He **g** the disciples orders to Mt 16:20
last man the same as I **g** you. Mt 20:14
Who **g** You this authority?" Mt 21:23
a king who **g** a wedding banquet Mt 22:2
To one he **g** five talents; Mt 25:15
Master, you **g** me five talents. Mt 25:20
Master, you **g** me two talents. Mt 25:22
hungry and you **g** Me something to Mt 25:35
thirsty and you **g** Me something Mt 25:35
hungry and you **g** Me nothing to Mt 25:42
thirsty and you **g** Me nothing to Mt 25:42
and broke it, **g** it to the Mt 26:26
He **g** it to them and said, Mt 26:27
and they **g** them for the potter's Mt 27:10
they **g** Him wine mixed with gall Mt 27:34
loud voice and **g** up His spirit. Mt 27:50
they **g** the soldiers a large sum Mt 28:12
astounded and **g** glory to God, Mk 2:12
also **g** some to his companions? Mk 2:26
To Simon, He **g** the name Peter; Mk 3:16
He **g** the name "Boanerges" Mk 3:17
And He **g** them permission. Mk 5:13
He **g** them strict orders that Mk 5:43
in pairs and **g** them authority Mk 6:7
when Herod **g** a banquet for his Mk 6:21
a platter, and **g** it to the girl. Mk 6:28
the girl **g** it to her mother. Mk 6:28
seven loaves, He **g** thanks, broke Mk 8:6
Who **g** You this authority to do Mk 11:28
For they all **g** out of their Mk 12:44
g authority to his slaves, Mk 13:34
to his slaves, **g** each one his Mk 13:34
and broke it, **g** it to them, and Mk 14:22
giving thanks, He **g** it to them, Mk 14:23
he **g** the corpse to Joseph. Mk 15:45
she **g** birth to her firstborn Lk 2:7
g it back to the attendant, Lk 4:20

He even **g** some to those who were Lk 6:4
and Jesus **g** him to his mother. Lk 7:15
you **g** Me no water for My feet, Lk 7:44
You **g** Me no kiss, but she hasn't Lk 7:45
pigs, and He **g** them permission Lk 8:32
Then He **g** orders that she be Lk 8:55
He **g** them power and authority Lk 9:1
and **g** him back to his father. Lk 9:42
out two denarii, **g** them to the Lk 10:35
yet you never **g** me a young goat Lk 15:29
a loud voice, **g** glory to God. Lk 17:15
they saw it, **g** praise to God. Lk 18:43
of his slaves, **g** them 10 minas, Lk 19:13
is it who **g** You this authority? Lk 20:2
He took bread, **g** thanks, broke Lk 22:19
thanks, broke it, **g** it to them, Lk 22:19
and He **g** the impression that He Lk 24:28
and broke it, and **g** it to them. Lk 24:30
So they **g** Him a piece of a Lk 24:42
He **g** them the right to be Jn 1:12
He **g** His One and Only Son, Jn 3:16
He **g** us the well and drank from Jn 4:12
bread after the Lord **g** thanks. Jn 6:23
g them bread from heaven to eat. Jn 6:31
Jesus **g** them this illustration, Jn 10:6
they **g** a dinner for Him there; Jn 12:2
the bread, He **g** it to Judas, Jn 13:26
for You **g** Him authority over all Jn 17:2
the work You **g** Me to do. Jn 17:4
to the men You **g** Me from the Jn 17:6
were Yours, You **g** them to Me, Jn 17:6
because the words that You **g** Me, Jn 17:8
His head, He **g** up His spirit. Jn 19:30
Pilate **g** him permission, so he Jn 19:38
the bread, and **g** it to them. Jn 21:13
as the Spirit **g** them ability for Ac 2:4
Then He **g** him the covenant of Ac 7:8
He **g** him favor and wisdom in the Ac 7:10
turned away and **g** them up to Ac 7:42
He **g** her his hand and helped her Ac 9:41
them in and **g** them lodging. Ac 10:23
if God **g** them the same gift that Ac 11:17
gift that He also **g** to us when Ac 11:17
He **g** their land to them as an Ac 13:19
g them judges until Samuel the Ac 13:20
so God **g** them Saul the son of Ac 13:21
some to whom we **g** no Ac 15:24
of the crowd **g** Alexander advice Ac 19:33
When Festus **g** the command, Ac 25:23
already over, Paul **g** his advice Ac 27:9
we **g** way to it and were driven Ac 27:15
he **g** thanks to God in the Ac 27:35
we sailed, they **g** us what we Ac 28:10
in his faith and **g** glory to God, Rm 4:20
God **g** them a spirit of stupor, Rm 11:8
watered, but God **g** the growth. 1Co 3:6
g thanks, broke it, and said, 1Co 11:24
who **g** us the Spirit as a down 2Co 5:5
Christ and **g** us the ministry 2Co 5:18
they **g** themselves especially to 2Co 8:5
which the Lord **g** for building 2Co 10:8
g warning, and I give warning— 2Co 13:2
the Lord **g** me for building up 2Co 13:10
who **g** Himself for our sins to Gl 1:4
they **g** the right hand of Gl 2:9
loved me and **g** Himself for me. Gl 2:20
grace that He **g** to me for you? Eph 3:2
captivity; He **g** gifts to people. Eph 4:8
And He personally **g** some to be Eph 4:11
callous and **g** themselves over to Eph 4:19
loved us and **g** Himself for us, Eph 5:2
church and **g** Himself for her, Eph 5:25
exalted Him and **g** Him the name Php 2:9
what commands we **g** you through 1Th 4:2
g Himself—a ransom for all, 1Tm 2:6
who **g** a good confession before 1Tm 6:13
He **g** Himself for us to redeem us Ti 2:14
I am with the children God **g** Me. Heb 2:13
and Abraham **g** him a tenth of Heb 7:2
Abraham the patriarch **g** a tenth Heb 7:4
of Israel and **g** instructions Heb 11:22
He **g** us a new birth by the Jms 1:18
and the sky **g** rain and the land Jms 5:18
from the dead and **g** Him glory, 1Pt 1:21
Christ that God **g** Him to show Rv 1:1
I **g** her time to repent, but she Rv 2:21
terrified and **g** glory to the God Rv 11:13
But she **g** birth to a Son— Rv 12:5
the woman who **g** birth to the Rv 12:13
The dragon **g** him his power, Rv 13:2
dragon because he **g** authority to Rv 13:4
creatures **g** the seven angels Rv 15:7
You also **g** them blood to drink; Rv 16:6
He **g** her the cup filled with the Rv 16:19
Then the sea **g** up its dead, Rv 20:13
Death and Hades **g** up their dead; Rv 20:13

GAZA *(22)*

going toward Gerar as far as **G**, Gn 10:19
lived in villages as far as **G**, Dt 2:23
from Kadesh-barnea to **G**, Jos 10:41
except for some remaining in **G**, Jos 11:22
the five Philistine rulers of **G**, Jos 13:3
G, with its towns and villages, Jos 15:47
Judah captured **G** and its Jdg 1:18
of the land, even as far as **G**. Jdg 6:4
Samson went to **G**, where he saw a Jdg 16:1
down to **G** and bound him with Jdg 16:21
Ashdod, **G**, Ashkelon, Gath, and 1Sm 6:17
from Tiphsah to **G** and over all 1Kg 4:24
as far as **G** and its borders, 2Kg 18:8
Ashkelon, **G**, Ekron, and the Jr 25:20
before Pharaoh defeated **G**. Jr 47:1
Baldness is coming to **G**. Jr 47:5
from punishing **G** for three Am 1:6
fire against the walls of **G**, Am 1:7
For **G** will be abandoned, and Zph 2:4
G too, and will writhe in great Zch 9:5
will cease to be a king in **G**, Zch 9:5
from Jerusalem to desert **G**." Ac 8:26

GAZE *(13)*

and his **g** was fixed because he 1Sm 4:15
his **g** was fixed due to his age. 1Kg 14:4
and my eyes must **g** at their Jb 17:2
g at the clouds high above you. Jb 35:5
not remove His **g** from the Jb 36:7
Your angry **g** from me so that Ps 39:13
I **g** on You in the sanctuary to Ps 63:2
Why **g** with envy, you mountain Ps 68:16
fix your **g** straight ahead. Pr 4:25
Don't **g** at wine when it is red, Pr 23:31
except to **g** at them with his Ec 5:11
of Zion, and **g** at King Solomon, Sg 3:11
My **g** takes in all their ways. Jr 16:17

GAZED *(5)*

if I have **g** at the sun when it Jb 31:26
the LORD **g** out from heaven to Ps 102:19
dark, for the sun has **g** on me. Sg 1:6
you have **g** on their genitals. Is 57:8
the Holy Spirit, **g** into heaven. Ac 7:55

GAZELLE *(10)*

as they would a **g** or deer, Dt 12:15
may eat it as the **g** and deer are Dt 12:22
the deer, the **g**, the roe deer, Dt 14:5
as though it were a **g** or deer. Dt 15:22
Escape like a **g** from a hunter, Pr 6:5
love is like a **g** or a young stag Sg 2:9
and be like a **g** or a young stag Sg 2:17
twins of a **g**, that feed among Sg 4:5
like two fawns, twins of a **g**. Sg 7:3
and be like a **g** or a young stag Sg 8:14

GAZELLES *(6)*

runner, like one of the wild **g**. 2Sm 2:18
besides deer, **g**, roebucks, 1Kg 4:23
as swift as **g** on the mountains 1Ch 12:8
the **g** and the wild does of the Sg 2:7
the **g** and the wild does of the Sg 3:5
Like wandering **g** and like sheep Is 13:14

GAZES *(1)*

He **g** on all the inhabitants of Ps 33:14

GAZEZ *(2)*

mother of Haran, Moza, and **G**. 1Ch 2:46
and Gazez. Haran fathered **G**. 1Ch 2:46

GAZING *(3)*

g on the beauty of the LORD and Ps 27:4
behind our wall, **g** through the Sg 2:9
going, they were **g** into heaven, Ac 1:10

GAZITES *(1)*

When the **G** ⌊heard⌋ that Samson Jdg 16:2

GAZZAM'S *(2)*

descendants, **G** descendants, Ezr 2:48
G descendants, Uzza's Neh 7:51

GEAR *(2)*

your ⌊hunting⌋ **g**, your quiver Gn 27:3
threw the ship's **g** overboard Ac 27:19

GEBA *(16)*

Ophni, and **G**—12 cities, with Jos 18:24
its pasturelands, **G** with its Jos 21:17
out of their places west of **G**. Jdg 20:33
garrison that was in **G**, 1Sm 13:3
were staying in **G** of Benjamin, 1Sm 13:16
to the south in front of **G**. 1Sm 14:5
all the way from **G** to Gezer. 2Sm 5:25
King Asa built **G** of Benjamin 1Kg 15:22
places from **G** to Beer-sheba, 2Kg 23:8
they were given⌋ **G** and its 1Ch 6:60
families living in **G** and who 1Ch 8:6
Then he built **G** and Mizpah with 2Ch 16:6
from **G**, Michmash, Aija, and Neh 11:31
the fields of **G** and Azmaveth, Neh 12:29
"We will spend the night at **G**." Is 10:29
the land from **G** to Rimmon south Zch 14:10

GEBA'S *(2)*

Ramah's and **G** people 621 Ezr 2:26
Ramah's and **G** men 621 Neh 7:30

GEBAL *(2)*

G, Ammon, and Amalek, Philistia Ps 83:7
The elders of **G** and its wise men Ezk 27:9

GEBALITES *(2)*

the land of the **G**; Jos 13:5
along with the **G**, quarried ⌊the 1Kg 5:18

GEBER *(1)*

G son of Uri, in the land of 1Kg 4:19

GEBIM *(1)*

inhabitants of **G** have sought Is 10:31

GECKO *(1)*

the **g**, the monitor lizard, the Lv 11:30

GEDALIAH *(31)*

appointed **G** son of Ahikam, 2Kg 25:22
king of Babylon had appointed **G**, 2Kg 25:23
they came to **G** at Mizpah. 2Kg 25:23
G swore an oath to them and 2Kg 25:24
with 10 men and struck down **G**, 2Kg 25:25
G, Zeri, Jeshaiah, Shimei, 1Ch 25:3
—12⌋⌊to⌋ **G** the second: 1Ch 25:9
Maaseiah, Eliezer, Jarib, and **G**. Ezr 10:18
son of Mattan, **G** son of Pashhur, Jr 38:1
him over to **G** son of Ahikam, Jr 39:14
Return to **G** son of Ahikam, Jr 40:5
went to **G** son of Ahikam at Jr 40:6
had appointed **G** son of Ahikam Jr 40:7
they came to **G** at Mizpah. Jr 40:8
G son of Ahikam, son of Shaphan, Jr 40:9
had appointed **G** son of Ahikam, Jr 40:11
land of Judah, to **G** at Mizpah, Jr 40:12
in the field came to **G** at Mizpah Jr 40:13
But **G** son of Ahikam would not Jr 40:14
suggested to **G** in private at Jr 40:15
But **G** son of Ahikam responded to Jr 40:16
with 10 men to **G** son of Ahikam Jr 41:1
and struck down **G** son of Ahikam, Jr 41:2
who were with **G** at Mizpah, Jr 41:3
day after he had killed **G**, Jr 41:4
"Come to **G** son of Ahikam!" Jr 41:6
had appointed **G** son of Ahikam. Jr 41:10
had killed **G** son of Ahikam— Jr 41:16
had struck down **G** son of Ahikam, Jr 41:18
to remain with **G** son of Ahikam Jr 43:6
Cushi, son of **G**, son of Amariah Zph 1:1

GEDER *(1)*

of Debir one the king of **G** one Jos 12:13

GEDERAH *(2)*

Adithaim, **G**, and Gederothaim— Jos 15:36
and residents of Netaim and **G**. 1Ch 4:23

GEDERATHITE *(1)*

Johanan, Jozabad the **G**; 1Ch 12:4

GEDERITE *(1)*

Baal-hanan the **G** was in charge 1Ch 27:28

GEDEROTH *(2)*

G, Beth-dagon, Naamah, and Jos 15:41
Aijalon, **G**, Soco and its 2Ch 28:18

GEDEROTHAIM *(1)*

Gederah, and **G**—14 cities, with Jos 15:36

GEDOR *(7)*

Halhul, Beth-zur, **G**, Jos 15:58
Penuel fathered **G**, and Ezer 1Ch 4:4

birth to Jered the father of G, 1Ch 4:18
They went to the entrance of G, 1Ch 4:39
G, Ahio, Zecher, 1Ch 8:31
G, Ahio, Zechariah, and Mikloth. 1Ch 9:37
the sons of Jeroham from G. 1Ch 12:7

GEHAZI *(20)*
He ordered his attendant G, 2Kg 4:12
Then he said to G, "Say to her, 2Kg 4:13
G answered, "Well, she has no 2Kg 4:14
G called her, and she stood in 2Kg 4:15
he said to his attendant G, 2Kg 4:25
G came to push her away, but the 2Kg 4:27
So Elisha said to G, "Tuck your 2Kg 4:29
G went ahead of them and placed 2Kg 4:31
Elisha called G and said, 2Kg 4:36
G, the attendant of Elisha the 2Kg 5:20
So G pursued Naaman. 2Kg 5:21
G said, "It's all right. 2Kg 5:22
He urged G and then packed 150 2Kg 5:23
men who carried them ahead of G. 2Kg 5:23
When G came to the hill, he took 2Kg 5:24
G came and stood by his master. 2Kg 5:25
"Where did you go, G?" 2Kg 5:25
So G went out from his presence 2Kg 5:27
The king had been speaking to G, 2Kg 8:4
So G said, "My lord the king, 2Kg 8:5

GELILOTH *(1)*
went to En-shemesh and on to G, Jos 18:17

GEM *(4)*
sons as a g cutter engraves Ex 28:11
do all the work of a g cutter; Ex 35:35
tribe of Dan, a g cutter, a Ex 38:23
sons as a g cutter engraves Ex 39:6

GEMALLI *(1)*
Ammiel son of G from the tribe Nm 13:12

GEMARIAH *(5)*
of Shaphan and G son of Hilkiah Jr 29:3
the chamber of G son of Shaphan Jr 36:10
son of G, son of Shaphan, Jr 36:11
son of Achbor, G son of Shaphan, Jr 36:12
and G had urged the king not to Jr 36:25

GEMSTONES *(7)*
with ⌊other⌋ g for mounting Ex 25:7
Place a setting of g on it, Ex 28:17
to cut g for mounting, and to Ex 31:5
and onyx with g to mount on the Ex 35:9
brought onyx and g to mount on Ex 35:27
to cut g for mounting, and to Ex 35:33
mounted four rows of g on it. Ex 39:10

GENEALOGICAL *(8)*
and they kept a g record for 1Ch 4:33
to the g records of their 1Ch 7:4
according to their g records. 1Ch 9:9
according to the g records of 1Ch 26:31
their entries in the g records, Ezr 2:62
leaders and the g records of Ezr 8:1
found the g record of those who Neh 7:5
their entries in the g records, Neh 7:64

GENEALOGIES *(12)*
in the g during the reigns 1Ch 5:17
recorded as warriors in their g. 1Ch 7:2
totalled 87,000 in their g. 1Ch 7:5
22,034 were listed in their g. 1Ch 7:7
Their g were recorded according 1Ch 7:9
listed in their g for military 1Ch 7:40
chiefs according to their g, 1Ch 8:28
in the g that are written 1Ch 9:1
chiefs according to their g, 1Ch 9:34
of Iddo the Seer concerning g. 2Ch 12:15
to myths and endless g. 1Tm 1:4
foolish debates, g, quarrels, Ti 3:9

GENEALOGY *(13)*
of Levi according to their g: Ex 6:16
Levites according to their g. Ex 6:19
Now this is the g of Perez: Ru 4:18
not listed in the g according to 1Ch 5:1
as they are recorded in their g: 1Ch 5:7
registered by g in their 1Ch 9:22
registered by g three years old 2Ch 31:16
recorded by g of the priests 2Ch 31:17
to those registered by g— 2Ch 31:18
to every Levite recorded by g. 2Ch 31:19
him who were registered by g; Ezr 8:3
people to be registered by g. Neh 7:5
mother, or g, having neither Heb 7:3

GENERAL *(1)*
son of Ner, the g of his army, 1Sm 26:5

GENERATION *(102)*
righteous before Me in this g. Gn 7:1
In the fourth g they will return Gn 15:16
Ephraim's sons to the third g; Gn 50:23
brothers and all that g died. Ex 1:6
am to be remembered in every g. Ex 3:15
Amalek from g to generation." Ex 17:16
Amalek from generation to g." Ex 17:16
to the third and fourth g. Ex 34:7
to the third and fourth g. Nm 14:18
until the whole g that had done Nm 32:13
men in this evil g will see the Dt 1:35
the entire g of fighting men Dt 2:14
even to the tenth g, may enter Dt 23:2
to the tenth g, may ever enter Dt 23:3
them in the third g may enter Dt 23:8
but a devious and crooked g. Dt 32:5
for they are a perverse g— Dt 32:20
That whole g was also gathered Jdg 2:10
them another g rose up who did Jdg 2:10
and celebrated by every g, Est 9:28
ask the previous g, and pay Jb 8:8
their children to the fourth g. Jb 42:16
from g to generation without Ps 10:6
to g without calamity. Ps 10:6
protect us from this g forever. Ps 12:7
next g will be told about the Ps 22:30
Such is the g of those who seek Ps 24:6
His heart from g to generation. Ps 33:11
His heart from generation to g. Ps 33:11
so that you can tell a future g: Ps 48:13
homes from g to generation, Ps 49:11
homes from generation to g, Ps 49:11
will go to the g of his fathers; Ps 49:19
Your power to ⌊another⌋ g, Ps 71:18
must tell a future g the praises Ps 78:4
that a future g—children yet Ps 78:6
a stubborn and rebellious g, Ps 78:8
g whose heart was not loyal and Ps 78:8
Your praise to g after Ps 79:13
praise to generation after g. Ps 79:13
have been our refuge in every g. Ps 90:1
I was disgusted with that g; Ps 95:10
will be written for a later g, Ps 102:18
be blotted out in the next g. Ps 109:13
the g of the upright will be Ps 112:2
One g will declare Your works to Ps 145:4
There is a g that curses its Pr 30:11
There is a g that is pure in its Pr 30:12
There is a g—how haughty its Pr 30:13
There is a g whose teeth are Pr 30:14
A g goes and a generation comes, Ec 1:4
A generation goes and a g comes, Ec 1:4
lived in from g to generation; Is 13:20
lived in from generation to g; Is 13:20
desolate, from g to generation; Is 34:10
desolate, from generation to g; Is 34:10
in it from g to generation. Is 34:17
in it from generation to g. Is 34:17
⌊Evil⌋ g, pay attention to the Jr 2:31
abandoned the g under His wrath Jr 7:29
endures from g to generation. Lm 5:19
endures from generation to g. Lm 5:19
is from g to generation. Dn 4:3
is from generation to g. Dn 4:3
kingdom is from g to generation. Dn 4:34
kingdom is from generation to g. Dn 4:34
and their children the next g. Jl 1:3
Jerusalem from g to generation. Jl 3:20
Jerusalem from generation to g. Jl 3:20
To what should I compare this g? Mt 11:16
and adulterous g demands a sign, Mt 12:39
with this g and condemn it, Mt 12:41
with this g and condemn it, Mt 12:42
will also be with this evil g." Mt 12:45
and adulterous g wants a sign, Mt 16:4
unbelieving and rebellious g! Mt 17:17
things will come on this g! Mt 23:36
This g will certainly not pass Mt 24:34
Why does this g demand a sign? Mk 8:12
sign will be given to this g!" Mk 8:12
in this adulterous and sinful g, Mk 8:38
to them, "You unbelieving g! Mk 9:19
This g will certainly not pass Mk 13:30
mercy is from g to generation Lk 1:50
generation to g on those who Lk 1:50
I compare the people of this g, Lk 7:31
unbelieving and rebellious g! Lk 9:41
This g is an evil generation. Lk 11:29
This generation is an evil g. Lk 11:29
Son of Man will be to this g. Lk 11:30
the men of this g and condemn Lk 11:31
with this g and condemn it, Lk 11:32
so that this g may be held Lk 11:50
this g will be held responsible. Lk 11:51
and be rejected by this g. Lk 17:25
This g will certainly not pass Lk 21:32
"Be saved from this corrupt g!" Ac 2:40
Who will describe His g? Ac 8:33
serving his own g in God's plan, Ac 13:36
in a crooked and perverted g, Php 2:15
provoked with this g and said, Heb 3:10
in the seventh ⌊g⌋ from Adam, Jd 14

GENERATIONS *(84)*
a covenant for all future g: Gn 9:12
after you throughout their g, Gn 17:7
throughout their g are to keep Gn 17:9
Throughout your g, every male Gn 17:12
throughout your g as a permanent Ex 12:14
throughout your g as a permanent Ex 12:17
Israelites throughout their g. Ex 12:42
be preserved throughout your g, Ex 16:32
be preserved throughout your g." Ex 16:33
third and fourth ⌊g⌋ of those Ex 20:5
to a thousand ⌊g⌋ of those who Ex 20:6
Israelites throughout their g. Ex 27:21
throughout your g at the Ex 29:42
the LORD throughout your g. Ex 30:8
Throughout your g he is to Ex 30:10
descendants throughout their g." Ex 30:21
anointing oil throughout your g. Ex 30:31
Me and you throughout your g, Ex 31:13
throughout their g as a Ex 31:16
faithful love to a thousand ⌊g⌋, Ex 34:7
for them throughout their g." Ex 40:15
statute throughout your g, Lv 3:17
throughout your g from the fire Lv 6:18
portion throughout their g. Lv 7:36
statute throughout your g. Lv 10:9
for them throughout their g. Lv 17:7
throughout your g who has a Lv 21:17
throughout your g is in a state Lv 22:3
throughout your g wherever you Lv 23:14
you live throughout your g. Lv 23:21
throughout your g wherever you Lv 23:31
for you throughout your g; Lv 23:41
so that your g may know that I Lv 23:43
statute throughout your g. Lv 24:3
its purchaser throughout his g. Lv 25:30
statute throughout your g. Nm 10:8
as you do throughout your g. Nm 15:14
statute throughout your g. Nm 15:15
Throughout your g, you are to Nm 15:21
and onward throughout your g— Nm 15:23
their g they are to make Nm 15:38
statute throughout your g. Nm 18:23
throughout your g wherever you Nm 35:29
third and fourth ⌊g⌋ of those Dt 5:9
to a thousand ⌊g⌋ of those who Dt 5:10
for a thousand g with those who Dt 7:9
Future g of your children who Dt 29:22
and between the g after us, Jos 22:27
to us or to our g in the future, Jos 22:28
teach the future g of the Jdg 3:2
four g of your sons will sit on 2Kg 10:30
Four g of your sons will sit on 2Kg 15:12
He ordained for a thousand g, 1Ch 16:15
name to be remembered for all g; Ps 45:17
may his years span many g. Ps 61:6
as the moon, throughout all g. Ps 72:5
promise at an end for all g? Ps 77:8
prolong Your anger for all g? Ps 85:5
Your faithfulness to all g. Ps 89:1
up your throne for all g.' " Ps 89:4
endures through all g. Ps 100:5
Your fame ⌊endures⌋ to all g. Ps 102:12
years continue through all g. Ps 102:24
He ordained for a thousand g— Ps 105:8
throughout all g to come. Ps 106:31
Your faithfulness is for all g; Ps 119:90
reputation, LORD, through all g. Ps 135:13
Your rule is for all g. Ps 145:13
your God ⌊reigns⌋ for all g. Ps 146:10
the g from the beginning? Is 41:4

and My salvation for all **g**. Is 51:8
days past, as in **g** of long ago. Is 51:9
the devastations of many **g**. Is 61:4
or lived in through all **g**. Jr 50:39
will again in all the **g** to come. Jl 2:2
So all the **g** from Abraham to Mt 1:17
from Abraham to David were 14 **g**; Mt 1:17
the exile to Babylon, 14 **g**; Mt 1:17
Babylon until the Messiah, 14 **g**. Mt 1:17
from now on all **g** will call me Lk 1:48
In past **g** He allowed all the Ac 14:16
people in other **g** as it is now Eph 3:5
and in Christ Jesus to all **g**, Eph 3:21
for ages and **g** but now revealed Col 1:26

GENEROSITY *(4)*
giving, with **g**; leading, with Rm 12:8
into the wealth of their **g**. 2Co 8:2
enriched in every way for all **g**, 2Co 9:11
and for your **g** in sharing with 2Co 9:13

GENEROUS *(9)*
He is always **g**, always lending, Ps 37:26
A **g** person will be enriched, Pr 11:25
A **g** person will be blessed, Pr 22:9
and a **g** blessing will come to Pr 24:25
and gave him many **g** gifts. Dn 2:48
Are you jealous because I'm **g**?' Mt 20:15
in advance the **g** gift you 2Co 9:5
works, to be **g**, willing to share 1Tm 6:18
Every **g** act and every perfect Jms 1:17

GENEROUSLY *(9)*
Give **g** to him from your flock, Dt 15:14
be able to give as **g** as this? 1Ch 29:14
because He has treated me **g**. Ps 13:6
a man who lends **g** and conducts Ps 112:5
Deal **g** with Your servant so that Ps 119:17
me because You deal **g** with me. Ps 142:7
person who sows **g** will also reap 2Co 9:6
generously will also reap **g**. 2Co 9:6
who gives to all **g** and without Jms 1:5

GENITALS *(2)*
out her hand and grabs his **g**, Dt 25:11
you have gazed on their **g**. Is 57:8

GENNESARET *(3)*
(AKA GALILEE, CHINNERETH)
over, they came to land at **G**. Mt 14:34
came to land at **G** and beached Mk 6:53
He was standing by Lake **G**. Lk 5:1

GENTILE *(6)*
the power of the **G** kingdoms. Hg 2:22
the **G** world eagerly seeks all Lk 12:30
deliver him into **G** hands.' " Ac 21:11
but so do all the **G** churches. Rm 16:4
like a **G** and not like a Jew, Gl 2:14
by birth and not "**G** sinners"; Gl 2:15

GENTILES *(86)*
uncleanness of the **G** of the land Ezr 6:21
the Jordan, Galilee of the **G**! Mt 4:15
Don't even the **G** do the same? Mt 5:47
Him over to the **G** to be mocked, Mt 20:19
rulers of the **G** dominate them, Mt 20:25
will hand Him over to the **G**, Mk 10:33
rulers of the **G** dominate them, Mk 10:42
to the **G** and glory to Your Lk 2:32
He will be handed over to the **G**, Lk 18:32
trampled by the **G** until the Lk 21:24
times of the **G** are fulfilled. Lk 21:24
kings of the **G** dominate them, Lk 22:25
Why did the **G** rage, and the Ac 4:25
with the **G** and the peoples of Ac 4:27
to carry My name before **G**, Ac 9:15
been poured out on the **G** also. Ac 10:45
heard that the **G** had welcomed Ac 11:1
in life to even the **G**!" Ac 11:18
life, we now turn to the **G**! Ac 13:46
you as a light for the **G**, Ac 13:47
When the **G** heard this, they Ac 13:48
the minds of the **G** against the Ac 14:2
was made by both the **G** and Jews, Ac 14:5
the door of faith to the **G**. Ac 14:27
detail the conversion of the **G**, Ac 15:3
by my mouth the **G** would hear Ac 15:7
done through them among the **G**. Ac 15:12
take from the **G** a people for His Ac 15:14
even all the **G** who are called by Ac 15:17
turn to God from among the **G**, Ac 15:19
from among the **G** in Antioch, Ac 15:23
From now on I will go to the **G**." Ac 18:6
God did among the **G** through his Ac 21:19
are among the **G** to abandon Moses Ac 21:21
regard to the **G** who have Ac 21:25
send you far away to the **G**.' " Ac 22:21
from the people and from the **G**, Ac 26:17
and to the **G**, that they should Ac 26:20
to our people and to the **G**." Ac 26:23
of God has been sent to the **G**; Ac 28:28
just as among the rest of the **G**. Rm 1:13
So, when **G**, who do not have the Rm 2:14
among the **G** because of you. Rm 2:24
both Jews and **G** are all under Rm 3:9
Is He not also for **G**? Rm 3:29
for Gentiles? Yes, for **G** too, Rm 3:29
the Jews but also from the **G**? Rm 9:24
G, who did not pursue Rm 9:30
has come to the **G** to make Israel Rm 11:11
their failure riches for the **G**, Rm 11:12
Now I am speaking to you **G**. Rm 11:13
that I am an apostle to the **G**, Rm 11:13
full number of the **G** has come Rm 11:25
so that **G** may glorify God for Rm 15:9
I will praise You among the **G**, Rm 15:9
Rejoice, you **G**, with His people! Rm 15:10
Praise the Lord, all you **G**; Rm 15:11
the One who rises to rule the **G**; Rm 15:12
in Him the **G** will hope. Rm 15:12
of Christ Jesus to the **G**, Rm 15:16
offering of the **G** may be Rm 15:16
to make the **G** obedient by word Rm 15:18
if the **G** have shared in their Rm 15:27
Jews and foolishness to the **G**. 1Co 1:23
not even condoned among the **G**— 1Co 5:1
dangers from the **G**, dangers in 2Co 11:26
I could preach Him among the **G**, Gl 1:16
gospel I preach among the **G**— Gl 2:2
at work with me among the **G**. Gl 2:8
should go to the **G** and they to Gl 2:9
to eat with the **G** before certain Gl 2:12
can you compel **G** to live like Gl 2:14
would justify the **G** by faith and Gl 3:8
come to the **G** in Christ Jesus, Gl 3:14
time you were **G** in the flesh— Eph 2:11
Jesus on behalf of you **G**— Eph 3:1
the **G** are co-heirs, members of Eph 3:6
proclaim to the **G** the Eph 3:8
no longer walk as the **G** walk, Eph 4:17
those among the **G** the glorious Col 1:27
speaking to the **G** so that they 1Th 2:16
like the **G** who don't know God. 1Th 4:5
a teacher of the **G** in faith and 1Tm 2:7
preached among the **G**, believed 1Tm 3:16
me, and all the **G** might hear. 2Tm 4:17
honorably among the **G**, 1Pt 2:12

GENTLE *(14)*
like **g** rain on new grass and Dt 32:2
A **g** answer turns away anger, Pr 15:1
and a **g** tongue can break a bone. Pr 25:15
Blessed are the **g**, because they Mt 5:5
because I am **g** and humble in Mt 11:29
is coming to you, **g**, and mounted Mt 21:5
When a **g** south wind sprang up, Ac 27:13
such a person with a **g** spirit, Gl 6:1
instead we were **g** among you, 1Th 2:7
not a bully but **g**, not 1Tm 3:3
but must be **g** to everyone, 2Tm 2:24
peace-loving, **g**, compliant, full Jms 3:17
to the good and **g** but also to 1Pt 2:18
quality of a **g** and quiet spirit, 1Pt 3:4

GENTLENESS *(10)*
or in love and a spirit of **g**? 1Co 4:21
to you by the **g** and graciousness 2Co 10:1
g, self-control. Against such Gl 5:23
humility and **g**, with patience, Eph 4:2
humility, **g**, and patience, Col 3:12
faith, love, endurance, and **g**. 1Tm 6:11
his opponents with **g**. 2Tm 2:25
always showing **g** to all people. Ti 3:2
by good conduct with wisdom's **g**. Jms 3:13
do this with **g** and respect, 1Pt 3:16

GENTLY *(4)*
man Absalom **g** for my sake." 2Sm 18:5
words that ⌊deal⌋ **g** with you? Jb 15:11
He **g** leads those that are Is 40:11
is able to deal **g** with those who Heb 5:2

GENUBATH *(2)*
gave birth to Hadad's son **G**. 1Kg 11:20
and **G** ⌊lived⌋ there along with 1Kg 11:20

GENUINE *(4)*
fasting, and my prayer was **g**. Ps 35:13
G righteousness ⌊leads⌋ to life, Pr 11:19
that John was a **g** prophet. Mk 11:32
will trust you with what is **g**? Lk 16:11

GENUINELY *(3)*
who will **g** care about your Php 2:20
Support widows who are **g** widows. 1Tm 5:3
can help those who are **g** widows. 1Tm 5:16

GENUINENESS *(2)*
I am testing the **g** of your love. 2Co 8:8
so that the **g** of your faith— 1Pt 1:7

GERA *(10)*
Becher, Ashbel, **G**, Naaman, Ehi, Gn 46:21
and He raised up Ehud son of **G**, Jdg 3:15
His name was Shimei son of **G**, 2Sm 16:5
Shimei son of **G**, a Benjaminite 2Sm 19:16
Shimei son of **G** crossed the 2Sm 19:18
Keep an eye on Shimei son of **G**, 1Kg 2:8
Bela's sons: Addar, **G**, Abihud, 1Ch 8:3
G, Shephuphan, and Huram. 1Ch 8:5
Ahijah, and **G**. Gera deported 1Ch 8:7
G deported them and was the 1Ch 8:7

GERAHS *(5)*
shekel (20 **g** to the shekel). Ex 30:13
shekel, 20 **g** to the shekel. Lv 27:25
shekel—20 **g** to the shekel. Nm 3:47
sanctuary shekel, which is 20 **g**. Nm 18:16
The shekel will weigh 20 **g**. Ezk 45:12

GERAR *(10)*
going toward **G** as far as Gaza, Gn 10:19
and Shur. While he lived in **G**, Gn 20:1
king of **G** had Sarah brought Gn 20:2
king of the Philistines, at **G**. Gn 26:1
So Isaac settled in **G**. Gn 26:6
camped in the valley of **G**, Gn 26:17
the herdsmen of **G** quarreled with Gn 26:20
came to him from **G** with Ahuzzath Gn 26:26
him pursued them as far as **G**. 2Ch 14:13
the cities around **G** because the 2Ch 14:14

GERASENE *(1)*
people of the **G** region asked Him Lk 8:37

GERASENES *(2)*
the sea, to the region of the **G**. Mk 5:1
sailed to the region of the **G**, Lk 8:26

GERIZIM *(4)*
at Mount **G** and the curse at Dt 11:29
stand on Mount **G** to bless the Dt 27:12
front of Mount **G** and half in Jos 8:33
climbed to the top of Mount **G**, Jdg 9:7

GERMINATE *(1)*
and making it **g** and sprout, Is 55:10

GERSHOM *(11)*
birth to a son whom he named **G**, Ex 2:22
whom was named **G** (because Moses Ex 18:3
Jonathan son of **G**, son of Moses, Jdg 18:30
G, Kohath, and Merari. 1Ch 6:1
G, Kohath, and Merari. 1Ch 6:16
Of **G**: his son Libni, his son 1Ch 6:20
Jahath, son of **G**, son of Levi. 1Ch 6:43
G, Kohath, and Merari. 1Ch 23:6
Moses' sons: **G** and Eliezer. 1Ch 23:15
a descendant of Moses' son **G**, 1Ch 26:24
G, from Phinehas's descendants; Ezr 8:2

GERSHOM'S *(2)*
These are the names of **G** sons: 1Ch 6:17
G sons: Shebuel first. 1Ch 23:16

GERSHOMITES *(4)*
The **G** ⌊were assigned⌋ 13 towns 1Ch 6:62
The **G** ⌊received⌋: 1Ch 6:71
from the **G**, Joel the leader and 1Ch 15:7
The **G**: Ladan and Shimei. 1Ch 23:7

GERSHON *(7)*
G, Kohath, and Merari. Gn 46:11
G, Kohath, and Merari. Ex 6:16
The sons of **G**: Libni and Shimei, Ex 6:17
G, Kohath, and Merari. Nm 3:17
the Shimeite clan came from **G**; Nm 3:21
the Gershonite clan from **G**; Nm 26:57
gave⌋ to the descendants of **G**, Jos 21:27

or trying to **g** even with Me? Jl 3:4
of those who flee will **g** away; Am 9:1
G up! Go to the great city of Jnh 1:2
sound asleep? **G** up! Call to your Jnh 1:6
rowed hard to **g** back to dry land Jnh 1:13
G up! Go to the great city of Jnh 3:2
G up and leave, for this is not Mc 2:10
is what they **g** for their pride, Zph 2:10
but never have enough to **g** warm. Hg 1:6
G up! Leave the land of the Zch 2:6
in a dream, saying, "**G** up! Mt 2:13
saying, "**G** up! Take the child Mt 2:20
You will never **g** out of there Mt 5:26
or to say, '**G** up and walk'? Mt 9:5
the paralytic, "**G** up, pick up Mt 9:6
does He **g** all these things? Mt 13:56
the disciples **g** into the boat Mt 14:22
Where could we **g** enough bread in Mt 15:33
told Peter, "**G** behind Me, Satan Mt 16:23
touched them, and said, "**G** up; Mt 17:7
they assumed they would **g** more, Mt 20:10
how did you **g** in here without Mt 22:12
not come down to **g** things out of Mt 24:17
not go back to **g** his clothes. Mt 24:18
G up; let's go! See—My Mt 26:46
or to say, '**G** up, pick up your Mk 2:9
g up, pick up your stretcher, Mk 2:11
her so she can **g** well and live." Mk 5:23
girl, I say to you, **g** up!" Mk 5:41
did this man **g** these things?" Mk 6:2
His disciples **g** into the boat Mk 6:45
Where can anyone **g** enough bread Mk 8:4
and said, "**G** behind Me, Satan Mk 8:33
Have courage! **G** up; He's calling Mk 10:49
down or go in to **g** anything out Mk 13:15
not go back to **g** his clothes. Mk 13:16
G up; let's go! See—My Mk 14:42
to decide what each would **g**. Mk 15:24
the sick, and they will **g** well." Mk 16:18
or to say, '**G** up and walk'? Lk 5:23
g up, pick up your stretcher, Lk 5:24
hand, "**G** up and stand here. Lk 6:8
Young man, I tell you, **g** up!" Lk 7:14
and called out, "Child, **g** up!" Lk 8:54
can't **g** up to give you anything. Lk 11:7
though he won't **g** up and give Lk 11:8
will **g** up and give him as much Lk 11:8
He will **g** ready, have them Lk 12:37
to eat and drink and **g** drunk, Lk 12:45
you will never **g** out of there Lk 12:59
G away from Me, all you workers Lk 13:27
told Him, "Go, **g** out of here! Lk 13:31
I'll **g** up, go to my father, and Lk 15:18
me to eat, **g** ready, and serve Lk 17:8
He told him, "**G** up and go on Lk 17:19
must not come down to **g** them. Lk 17:31
give a tenth of everything I **g**.' Lk 18:12
they helped Jesus **g** on it. Lk 19:35
for a way to **g** their hands on Lk 20:19
G up and pray, so that you won't Lk 22:46
G these things out of here! Jn 2:16
So where do you **g** this 'living Jn 4:11
this water will **g** thirsty again. Jn 4:13
him will never **g** thirsty again— Jn 4:14
so I won't **g** thirsty and come Jn 4:15
to him, "Do you want to **g** well?" Jn 5:6
"**G** up," Jesus told him, "pick up Jn 5:8
Rabbi, when did You **g** here?" Jn 6:25
fallen asleep, he will **g** well." Jn 11:12
Me, so I do. "**G** up; let's leave Jn 14:31
expecting to **g** something from Ac 3:5
the Nazarene, **g** up and walk!" Ac 3:6
G out of your country and away Ac 7:3
G up and go south to the road Ac 8:26
But **g** up and go into the city, Ac 9:6
G up and go to the street called Ac 9:11
G up and make your own bed," Ac 9:34
the body said, "Tabitha, **g** up!" Ac 9:40
voice said to him, "**G** up, Peter; Ac 10:13
G up, go downstairs, and Ac 10:20
voice telling me, '**G** up, Peter; Ac 11:7
him up and said, "Quick, **g** up!" Ac 12:7
"**G** dressed," the angel told him, Ac 12:8
pay for them to **g** their heads Ac 21:24
he was not able to **g** reliable Ac 21:34
'**G** up and go into Damascus, Ac 22:10
G up and be baptized, and wash Ac 22:16
'Hurry and **g** out of Jerusalem Ac 22:18
G 200 soldiers ready with 70 Ac 23:23
your accusers **g** here too." Ac 23:35
But **g** up and stand on your feet. Ac 26:16
were barely able to **g** control of Ac 27:16
overboard first and **g** to land. Ac 27:43
He should not **g** circumcised. 1Co 7:18
if you do **g** married, you have 1Co 7:28
not sinning; they can **g** married. 1Co 7:36
Jerusalem to **g** to know Cephas, Gl 1:18
you that if you **g** circumcised, Gl 5:2
you might also **g** themselves Gl 5:12
So we must not **g** tired of doing Gl 6:9
G up, sleeper, and rise up from Eph 5:14
And don't **g** drunk with wine, Eph 5:18
and those who **g** drunk are drunk 1Th 5:7
to be the first to **g** a share of 2Tm 2:6
so that you might **g** him back Phm 15
g your minds ready for action, 1Pt 1:13

GETHER *(2)*
Uz, Hul, **G**, and Mash. Gn 10:23
Aram, Uz, Hul, **G**, and Meshech. 1Ch 1:17

GETHSEMANE *(2)*
with them to a place called **G**, Mt 26:36
they came to a place named **G**, Mk 14:32

GETS *(11)*
When a fire **g** out of control, Ex 22:6
from⌊ her menstruation **g** on him, Lv 15:24
down to eat until he **g** here." 1Sm 16:11
king's anger **g** stirred up and 2Sm 11:20
for what he **g** in exchange will Jb 15:31
not be afraid when a man **g** rich, Ps 49:16
the homeowner **g** up and shuts Lk 13:25
toss for it, to see who **g** it." Jn 19:24
before he **g** near, we are ready Ac 23:15
every man who **g** circumcised that Gl 5:3
serving as a soldier **g** entangled 2Tm 2:4

GETTING *(17)*
were old and **g** on in years. Gn 18:11
was now old, **g** on in years, Gn 24:1
rich and kept **g** richer until he Gn 26:13
Joshua was old, **g** on in years. Jos 23:1
them, "I am old, **g** on in years, Jos 23:2
back, and as it was **g** light, she Jdg 19:26
dismiss him? Now he's **g** away. 2Sm 3:24
David was old and **g** on in years. 1Kg 1:1
because he was **g** things done. 1Kg 11:28
helping him were **g** drunk in the 1Kg 20:16
the poor from **g** a fair trial Is 10:2
the sea was **g** worse and worse Jnh 1:11
saw that he was **g** nowhere, Mt 27:24
As He was **g** into the boat, Mk 5:18
G down on their knees, they were Mk 15:19
So **g** into the boat, He returned. Lk 8:37
because we're **g** back what we Lk 23:41

GEUEL *(1)*
G son of Machi from the tribe of Nm 13:15

GEZER *(15)*
Horam king of **G** went to help Jos 10:33
of Eglon one the king of **G** one Jos 12:12
then to **G**, and ended at Jos 16:3
the Canaanites who lived in **G**. Jos 16:10
country of Ephraim, **G** with its Jos 21:21
Canaanites who were living in **G**, Jdg 1:29
have lived among them in **G**. Jdg 1:29
all the way from Geba to **G**. 2Sm 5:25
and Hazor, Megiddo, and **G**. 1Kg 9:15
had attacked and captured **G**. 1Kg 9:16
Solomon rebuilt **G**, Lower 1Kg 9:17
country of Ephraim, **G** and its 1Ch 6:67
G and its villages to the west, 1Ch 7:28
army from Gibeon to **G**. 1Ch 14:16
out with the Philistines at **G**. 1Ch 20:4

GHOST *(4)*
"It's a **g**!" they said, Mt 14:26
it was a **g** and cried out; Mk 6:49
thought they were seeing a **g**. Lk 24:37
because a **g** does not have flesh Lk 24:39

GHOSTS *(1)*
will seek idols, **g**, spirits of Is 19:3

GIAH *(1)*
which is opposite **G** on the way 2Sm 2:24

GIANT *(6)*
one of the descendants of the **g**, 2Sm 21:16
one of the descendants of the **g**. 2Sm 21:18
too, was descended from the **g**. 2Sm 21:20
from the **g** in Gath and were 2Sm 21:22
too, was descended from the **g**. 1Ch 20:6
of the **g** in Gath killed 1Ch 20:8

GIANTS *(1)*
a descendant of the **g**, and the 1Ch 20:4

GIBBAR'S *(1)*
(AKA GIBEON'S)
G descendants 95 Ezr 2:20

GIBBETHON *(6)*
Eltekeh, **G**, Baalath, Jos 19:44
its pasturelands, **G** with its Jos 21:23
him down at **G** of the Philistines 1Kg 15:27
and all Israel were besieging **G**. 1Kg 15:27
encamped against **G** of the 1Kg 16:15
marched up from **G** and besieged 1Kg 16:17

GIBEA *(1)*
the father of Machbenah and **G**. 1Ch 2:49

GIBEAH *(46)*
Kain, **G**, and Timnah—10 cities, Jos 15:57
is, Jerusalem), **G**, and Kiriath— Jos 18:28
buried him at **G**, which had been Jos 24:33
Israelites. Let's move on to **G**." Jdg 19:12
spend the night in **G** or Ramah." Jdg 19:13
as they neared **G** in Benjamin. Jdg 19:14
go in and spend the night in **G**. Jdg 19:15
Ephraim but was residing in **G**, Jdg 19:16
I went to **G** in Benjamin with my Jdg 20:4
Citizens of **G** ganged up on me Jdg 20:5
this is what we will do to **G**: Jdg 20:9
when they go to **G** in Benjamin to Jdg 20:10
perverted men in **G** so we can put Jdg 20:13
their cities to **G** to go out and Jdg 20:14
rallied by the inhabitants of **G**. Jdg 20:15
set out and camped near **G**. Jdg 20:19
battle positions against **G**. Jdg 20:20
came out of **G** and slaughtered Jdg 20:21
came out from **G** to meet them Jdg 20:25
set up an ambush around **G**. Jdg 20:29
positions against **G** as before. Jdg 20:30
the other to **G** through the open Jdg 20:31
a frontal assault against **G**, Jdg 20:34
ambush they had set against **G**. Jdg 20:36
had rushed quickly against **G**; Jdg 20:37
them near **G** toward the east. Jdg 20:43
and his attendant arrived at **G**, 1Sm 10:10
Saul also went to his home in **G**, 1Sm 10:26
When the messengers came to **G**, 1Sm 11:4
with Jonathan in **G** of Benjamin. 1Sm 13:2
from Gilgal to **G** in Benjamin. 1Sm 13:15
in Migron on the outskirts of **G**. 1Sm 14:2
watchmen in **G** of Benjamin 1Sm 14:16
up to his home in **G** of Saul. 1Sm 15:34
At that time Saul was in **G**, 1Sm 22:6
came up to Saul at **G** and said, 1Sm 23:19
came to Saul at **G** saying, 1Sm 26:1
of the LORD at **G** of Saul, 2Sm 21:6
son of Ribai from **G** of the 2Sm 23:29
son of Ribai from **G** of the 1Ch 11:31
she was⌊ from **G**. There was war 2Ch 13:2
those at **G** of Saul have fled. Is 10:29
Blow the horn in **G**, the trumpet Hs 5:8
themselves as in the days of **G**. Hs 9:9
have sinned since the days of **G**; Hs 10:9
the unjust overtake them in **G**? Hs 10:9

GIBEATH-HAARALOTH *(1)*
the Israelite men at **G**. Jos 5:3

GIBEATHITE *(1)*
Ahiezer son of Shemaah the **G**. 1Ch 12:3

GIBEON *(36)*
inhabitants of **G** heard what Jos 9:3
their cities were **G**, Chephirah, Jos 9:17
inhabitants of **G** had made peace Jos 10:1
alarmed because **G** was a large Jos 10:2
We will attack **G**, because they Jos 10:4
armies, besieged **G**, and fought Jos 10:5
Then the men of **G** sent⌊word⌋ to Jos 10:6
them in a great slaughter at **G**, Jos 10:10
still over **G**, and moon, over Jos 10:12
the land of Goshen as far as **G**. Jos 10:41
the Hivites who inhabited **G**; Jos 11:19
G, Ramah, Beeroth, Jos 18:25
G with its pasturelands, Geba Jos 21:17
marched out from Mahanaim to **G**. 2Sm 2:12
and met them by the pool of **G**. 2Sm 2:13
which is in **G**, is named Field 2Sm 2:16
the way to the wilderness of **G**. 2Sm 2:24
to death in the battle at **G**. 2Sm 3:30

great stone in **G** when Amasa 2Sm 20:8
The king went to **G** to sacrifice 1Kg 3:4
G the LORD appeared to Solomon 1Kg 3:5
as He had appeared to him at **G**. 1Kg 9:2
fathered **G** and lived in Gibeon. 1Ch 8:29
fathered Gibeon and lived in **G**. 1Ch 8:29
Jeiel fathered **G** and lived in 1Ch 9:35
fathered Gibeon and lived in **G**. 1Ch 9:35
Philistine army from **G** to Gezer. 1Ch 14:16
the LORD at the high place in **G** 1Ch 16:39
were at the high place in **G**, 1Ch 21:29
that was in **G** because God's 2Ch 1:3
place that was in **G** in front of 2Ch 1:13
and the men of **G** and Mizpah, Neh 3:7
the valley of **G**, to do His work Is 28:21
son of Azzur from **G** said to me Jr 28:1
him by the great pool in **G**. Jr 41:12
whom he brought back from **G**. Jr 41:16

GIBEON'S *(1)*
(AKA GIBBAR'S)
G descendants 95 Neh 7:25

GIBEONITE *(3)*
and reached the **G** cities on the Jos 9:17
Ishmaiah the **G**, a warrior among 1Ch 12:4
Next to them Melatiah the **G**, Neh 3:7

GIBEONITES *(10)*
they heard that the **G** were their Jos 9:16
So the **G** became woodcutters and Jos 9:21
summoned the **G** and said to them, Jos 9:22
The **G** answered him, "It was Jos 9:24
family when he killed the **G**." 2Sm 21:1
The **G** were not Israelites but 2Sm 21:2
summoned the **G** and spoke to 2Sm 21:2
asked the **G**, "What should I do 2Sm 21:3
The **G** said to him, "We are not 2Sm 21:4
and handed them over to the **G**. 2Sm 21:9

GIDDALTI *(2)*
Eliathah, **G**, Romamti-ezer, 1Ch 25:4
twenty-second to **G**, his sons, 1Ch 25:29

GIDDEL'S *(4)*
G descendants, Gahar's Ezr 2:47
descendants, **G** descendants, Ezr 2:56
descendants, **G** descendants, Neh 7:49
descendants, **G** descendants, Neh 7:58

GIDEON *(41)*
(AKA JERUBBAAL, JERUBBESHETH)
His son **G** was threshing wheat in Jdg 6:11
G said to Him, "Please Sir, if Jdg 6:13
So **G** went and prepared a young Jdg 6:19
When **G** realized that He was the Jdg 6:22
So **G** built an altar to the LORD Jdg 6:24
G took 10 of his male servants Jdg 6:27
said, "**G** son of Joash did it. Jdg 6:29
Spirit of the LORD enveloped **G**, Jdg 6:34
Then **G** said to God, "If You will Jdg 6:36
G then said to God, "Don't be Jdg 6:39
night God did ⌊as **G** requested⌋: Jdg 6:40
that is, **G**) and everyone who Jdg 7:1
LORD said to **G**, "You have too Jdg 7:2
the LORD said to **G**, "There are Jdg 7:4
the LORD said to **G**, "Separate Jdg 7:5
LORD said to **G**, "I will deliver Jdg 7:7
So **G** sent all the Israelites to Jdg 7:8
When **G** arrived, there was a man Jdg 7:13
the sword of **G** son of Joash, Jdg 7:14
When **G** heard the account of the Jdg 7:15
sword of the LORD and of **G**!'" Jdg 7:18
G and the 100 men who were with Jdg 7:19
"The sword of the LORD and of **G**!" Jdg 7:20
G sent messengers throughout the Jdg 7:24
Oreb and Zeeb to **G** across the Jdg 7:25
G and the 300 men came to the Jdg 8:4
G replied, "Very well, when the Jdg 8:7
G traveled on the caravan route, Jdg 8:11
G son of Joash returned from the Jdg 8:13
So **G** got up, killed Zebah and Jdg 8:21
Then the Israelites said to **G**, Jdg 8:22
But **G** said to them, "I will not Jdg 8:23
G made an ephod from all this Jdg 8:27
a snare to **G** and his household Jdg 8:27
40 years during the days of **G**. Jdg 8:28
that is, **G**)⌋ son of Joash went Jdg 8:29
G had 70 sons, his own offspring, Jdg 8:30
Then **G** son of Joash died at a Jdg 8:32
When **G** died, the Israelites Jdg 8:33
that is,⌋ **G**) for all the good he Jdg 8:35
short for me to tell about **G**, Heb 11:32

GIDEON'S *(2)*
G father called him Jerubbaal, Jdg 6:32
When **G** men blew their 300 Jdg 7:22

GIDEONI *(5)*
Abidan son of **G** from Benjamin; Nm 1:11
Benjaminites is Abidan son of **G**. Nm 2:22
the ninth day Abidan son of **G**, Nm 7:60
the offering of Abidan son of **G**. Nm 7:65
and Abidan son of **G** was over the Nm 10:24

GIDOM *(1)*
them at **G** and struck 2,000 Jdg 20:45

GIFT *(92)*
"God has given me a good **g**," Gn 30:20
with him as a **g** for his brother Gn 32:13
They are a **g** sent to my lord Gn 32:18
Esau with the **g** that is going Gn 32:20
the **g** was sent on ahead of him Gn 32:21
you, take this **g** from my hand. Gn 33:10
me the compensation and the **g**; Gn 34:12
them down to the man as a **g**— Gn 43:11
The men took this **g**, double the Gn 43:15
prepared their **g** for Joseph's Gn 43:25
brought him the **g** they had Gn 43:26
If his **g** is a burnt offering Lv 1:3
But if his **g** for a burnt Lv 1:10
If his **g** to the LORD is a burnt Lv 1:14
offering as a **g** to the LORD, Lv 2:1
g must consist of fine flour. Lv 2:1
If your **g** is a grain offering Lv 2:5
If your **g** is a grain offering Lv 2:7
it will be acceptable as a **g**, Lv 22:27
the dedication **g** for the altar Nm 7:10
dedication **g** from the leaders Nm 7:84
the dedication **g** for the altar Nm 7:88
the Israelites as a **g** for you, Nm 18:6
work of the priesthood as a **g**, Nm 18:7
appear⌋ with a **g** suited to his Dt 16:17
Let me bring my **g** and set it Jdg 6:18
goat ⌊as a **g**⌋ and visited his Jdg 15:1
and there's no **g** to take to the 1Sm 9:7
him and did not bring him a **g**, 1Sm 10:27
Accept this **g** your servant has 1Sm 25:27
Here is a **g** for you from the 1Sm 30:26
and a **g** from the king followed 2Sm 11:8
have sent you a **g** of silver and 1Kg 15:19
accept a **g** from your servant. 2Kg 5:15
Take a **g** with you and go meet 2Kg 8:8
Elisha, taking with him a **g**: 2Kg 8:9
to the king of Assyria as a **g**. 2Kg 16:8
letters and a **g** to Hezekiah 2Kg 20:12
of them would bring his own **g**— 2Ch 9:24
A **g** opens doors for a man and Pr 18:16
A secret **g** soothes anger, and a Pr 21:14
boasts about a **g** that does not Pr 25:14
It is also the **g** of God whenever Ec 3:13
his labor. This is a **g** of God, Ec 5:19
At that time a **g** will be brought Is 18:7
letters and a **g** to Hezekiah Is 39:1
the nations as a **g** to the LORD Is 66:20
a ration and a **g** and released Jr 40:5
prince gives a **g** to each of his Ezk 46:16
But if he gives a **g** from his Ezk 46:17
offering your **g** on the altar, Mt 5:23
leave your **g** there in front of Mt 5:24
and then come and offer your **g**. Mt 5:24
and offer the **g** that Moses Mt 8:4
from me is a **g** ⌊committed to Mt 15:5
oath by the **g** that is on it is Mt 23:18
the **g** or the altar that Mt 23:19
the altar that sanctifies the **g**? Mt 23:19
a **g** ⌊committed to the temple⌋ Mk 7:11
If you knew the **g** of God, Jn 4:10
will receive the **g** of the Holy Ac 2:38
you thought the **g** of God could Ac 8:20
because the **g** of the Holy Spirit Ac 10:45
them the same **g** that He also Ac 11:17
some spiritual **g** to strengthen Rm 1:11
pay is not considered as a **g**, Rm 4:4
But the **g** is not like the Rm 5:15
of God and the **g** overflowed to Rm 5:15
And the **g** is not like the one Rm 5:16
from many trespasses came the **g**, Rm 5:16
grace and the **g** of righteousness Rm 5:17
but the **g** of God is eternal life Rm 6:23
any spiritual **g** as you eagerly 1Co 1:7
But each has his own **g** from God, 1Co 7:7
If I have ⌊the **g** of⌋ prophecy, 1Co 13:2
your gracious **g** to Jerusalem. 1Co 16:3
behalf for the **g** that came to us 2Co 1:11
us with this **g** that is being 2Co 8:19
the generous **g** you promised, 2Co 9:5
will be ready as a **g** and not an 2Co 9:5
to God for His indescribable **g**. 2Co 9:15
from yourselves; it is God's **g**— Eph 2:8
gospel⌋ by the **g** of God's grace Eph 3:7
the measure of the Messiah's **g**. Eph 4:7
that I seek the **g**, but I seek Php 4:17
neglect the **g** that is in you; 1Tm 4:14
keep ablaze the **g** of God that is 2Tm 1:6
who tasted the heavenly **g**, Heb 6:4
every perfect **g** is from above, Jms 1:17
Based on the **g** they have 1Pt 4:10
spring of living water as a **g**. Rv 21:6
take the living water as a **g**. Rv 22:17

GIFTS *(61)*
gave precious **g** to her brother Gn 24:53
And Abraham gave **g** to the sons Gn 25:6
consecrate as all their holy **g**. Ex 28:38
present freewill **g** or payment of Lv 22:18
Sabbaths, your **g**, all your vow Lv 23:38
of their **g** also belongs to you. Nm 18:11
due the LORD from all your **g**. Nm 18:29
with the choice **g** of the land Dt 33:16
⌊He sent **g**⌋ to those in Bethel, 1Sm 30:27
consecrated **g** and his own 1Kg 15:15
consecrated **g** into the LORD's 1Kg 15:15
he took the **g** from them and 2Kg 5:24
consecrated **g** and his own 2Ch 15:18
own consecrated **g** into God's 2Ch 15:18
also brought **g** and silver as 2Ch 17:11
had given them many **g** of silver, 2Ch 21:3
and valuable **g** to King Hezekiah 2Ch 32:23
payments and gave **g** worthy of Est 2:18
when they send **g** to one another. Est 9:19
and of sending **g** to one another Est 9:22
will seek your favor with **g**. Ps 45:12
You received **g** from people, Ps 68:18
kings of Sheba and Seba offer **g**. Ps 72:10
or be persuaded by lavish **g**. Pr 6:35
is a friend of one who gives **g**. Pr 19:6
Him, and His **g** accompany Him. Is 40:10
Men give **g** to all prostitutes, Ezk 16:33
but you gave **g** to all your Ezk 16:33
them through their **g** in order to Ezk 20:26
you offer your **g**, making your Ezk 20:31
holy name with your **g** and idols. Ezk 20:39
contributions and choicest **g**, Ezk 20:40
from all your **g** will belong to Ezk 44:30
me, you'll receive **g**, a reward, Dn 2:6
and gave him many generous **g**. Dn 2:48
may keep your **g**, and give your Dn 5:17
sacrificial **g** and eat the flesh Hs 8:13
send farewell **g** to Mc 1:14
and presented Him with **g**: Mt 2:11
to give good **g** to your children Mt 7:11
to give good **g** to your children Lk 11:13
people have put in **g** out of Lk 21:4
stones and **g** dedicated to God, Lk 21:5
charitable **g** and offerings to Ac 24:17
God's gracious **g** and calling are Rm 11:29
to us, we have different **g**: Rm 12:6
Now there are different **g**, 1Co 12:4
g of healing by the one Spirit, 1Co 12:9
miracles, then **g** of healing, 1Co 12:28
Do all have **g** of healing? 1Co 12:30
But desire the greater **g**. 1Co 12:31
love and desire spiritual **g**, 1Co 14:1
captivity; He gave **g** to people. Eph 4:8
you sent ⌊**g**⌋ for my need several Php 4:16
of **g**⌋ from the Holy Heb 2:4
to offer both **g** and sacrifices Heb 5:1
to offer **g** and sacrifices; Heb 8:3
those offering the **g** prescribed Heb 8:4
during which **g** and sacrifices Heb 9:9
because God approved his **g**, Heb 11:4
and send **g** to one another, Rv 11:10

GIHON *(6)*
name of the second river is **G**, Gn 2:13
mule, and take him down to **G**. 1Kg 1:33
David's mule, and took him to **G**. 1Kg 1:38
have anointed him king in **G**. 1Kg 1:45
of the Upper **G** and channeled it 2Ch 32:30
from west of **G** in the valley to 2Ch 33:14

GILALAI *(1)*
Milalai, **G**, Maai, Nethanel Neh 12:36

GILBOA *(8)*
Israel, and they camped at **G**. 1Sm 28:4
Many were killed on Mount **G**. 1Sm 31:1
his three sons dead on Mount **G**. 1Sm 31:8
"I happened to be on Mount **G**," 2Sm 1:6
Mountains of **G**, let no dew or 2Sm 1:21
Philistines killed Saul at **G**. 2Sm 21:12
them and were killed on Mount **G**. 1Ch 10:1
and his sons dead on Mount **G**. 1Ch 10:8

GILEAD *(94)*
for the hill country of **G**. Gn 31:21
and overtook him at Mount **G**. Gn 31:23
tents⌋ in the hill country of **G**. Gn 31:25
of Ishmaelites coming from **G**. Gn 37:25
Machir fathered **G**; the Gileadite Nm 26:29
the Gileadite clan from **G**. Nm 26:29
Hepher, son of **G**, son of Machir, Nm 27:1
the lands of Jazer and **G**, Nm 32:1
remain here in the cities of **G**, Nm 32:26
the land of **G** as a possession Nm 32:29
son of Manasseh went to **G**, Nm 32:39
So Moses gave **G** to ⌊the clan of⌋ Nm 32:40
clan of the descendants of **G**— Nm 36:1
in the valley, even as far as **G**. Dt 2:36
of the plateau, **G**, and Bashan as Dt 3:10
hill country of **G** along with its Dt 3:12
the rest of **G** and all Bashan, Dt 3:13
I gave **G** to Machir, Dt 3:15
extending⌋ from **G** to the Arnon Dt 3:16
Ramoth in **G**, belonging to the Dt 4:43
all the land: **G** as far as Dan, Dt 34:1
and half of **G** up to the Jabbok Jos 12:2
and half of **G** to the border of Jos 12:5
also **G** and the territory of the Jos 13:11
Jazer and all the cities of **G**, Jos 13:25
But half of **G**, and Og's royal Jos 13:31
G and Bashan came to Machir, Jos 17:1
of Manasseh and the father of **G**, Jos 17:1
Hepher, son of **G**, son of Machir, Jos 17:3
the land of **G** and Bashan, Jos 17:5
The land of **G** belonged to the Jos 17:6
Ramoth in **G** from Gad's tribe, Jos 20:8
Ramoth in **G**, the city of refuge Jos 21:38
to go to their own land of **G**, Jos 22:9
of Manasseh, in the land of **G**. Jos 22:13
in the land of **G**, and told them, Jos 22:15
in the land of **G** to the Jos 22:32
G remained beyond the Jordan. Jdg 5:17
turn back and leave Mount **G**.' " Jdg 7:3
had 30 towns in **G**, which are Jdg 10:4
the land of the Amorites in **G**. Jdg 10:8
together, and they camped in **G**. Jdg 10:17
The rulers of **G** said to one Jdg 10:18
of all the inhabitants of **G**." Jdg 10:18
and **G** was his father. Jdg 11:1
the elders of **G** went to get Jdg 11:5
replied to the elders of **G**, Jdg 11:7
of all the inhabitants of **G**." Jdg 11:8
elders of **G** said to Jephthah, Jdg 11:10
went with the elders of **G**. Jdg 11:11
traveled through **G** and Manasseh, Jdg 11:29
and then through Mizpah of **G**. Jdg 11:29
the Ammonites from Mizpah of **G**. Jdg 11:29
gathered all of the men of **G**. Jdg 12:4
in one of the cities of **G**. Jdg 12:7
and from the land of **G** came out, Jdg 20:1
Jordan to the land of Gad and **G**. 1Sm 13:7
him king over **G**, Asher, Jezreel, 2Sm 2:9
Absalom camped in the land of **G** 2Sm 17:26
They went to **G** and to the land 2Sm 24:6
which are in **G**, and he had the 1Kg 4:13
in the land of **G**, the country 1Kg 4:19
from the **G** settlers, said to 1Kg 17:1
all the land of **G**—the Gadites, 2Kg 10:33
Valley through **G** to Bashan. 2Kg 10:33
Kedesh, Hazor, **G**, and Galilee— 2Kg 15:29
of Machir the father of **G**. 1Ch 2:21
23 towns in the land of **G**. 1Ch 2:22
the sons of Machir father of **G**. 1Ch 2:23
had increased in the land of **G**. 1Ch 5:9
throughout the region east of **G**. 1Ch 5:10
Jaroah, son of **G**, son of Michael 1Ch 5:14
They lived in **G**, in Bashan and 1Ch 5:16
received⌋ Ramoth in **G** and its 1Ch 6:80
and Machir the father of **G**. 1Ch 7:14
the sons of **G** son of Machir, 1Ch 7:17
found among them at Jazer in **G**. 1Ch 26:31
half the tribe of Manasseh in **G**, 1Ch 27:21
G is Mine, Manasseh is Mine, and Ps 60:7
G is Mine, Manasseh is Mine, and Ps 108:8
of goats streaming down Mount **G**. Sg 4:1
of goats streaming down from **G**. Sg 6:5
Is there no balm in **G**? Jr 8:22
You are like **G** to Me, ⌊or⌋ the Jr 22:6
Go up to **G** and get balm, Virgin Jr 46:11
country of Ephraim and of **G**. Jr 50:19
Jordan between **G** and the land Ezk 47:18
G is a city of evildoers, Hs 6:8
Since **G** is full of evil, they Hs 12:11
they threshed **G** with iron Am 1:3
pregnant women of **G** in order to Am 1:13
while Benjamin will possess **G**. Ob 19
in Bashan and **G** as in ancient Mc 7:14
to the land of **G** and to Lebanon, Zch 10:10

GILEAD'S *(2)*
These were **G** descendants: Nm 26:30
G wife bore him sons, and when Jdg 11:2

GILEADITE *(10)*
the **G** clan from Gilead. Nm 26:29
After him came Jair the **G**, Jdg 10:3
Jephthah the **G** was a great Jdg 11:1
the daughter of Jephthah the **G**. Jdg 11:40
and Barzillai the **G** from Rogelim 2Sm 17:27
Barzillai the **G** had come down 2Sm 19:31
Barzillai the **G** and let them be 1Kg 2:7
were 50 **G** men with Pekah. 2Kg 15:25
Barzillai the **G** and was called Ezr 2:61
Barzillai the **G** and was called Neh 7:63

GILEADITES *(3)*
You **G** are Ephraimite fugitives Jdg 12:4
The **G** captured the fords of the Jdg 12:5
over," the **G** asked him, "Are Jdg 12:5

GILGAL *(39)*
Arabah, opposite **G**, near the Dt 11:30
and camped at **G** on the eastern Jos 4:19
Joshua set up in **G** the 12 stones Jos 4:20
has been called **G** to this day. Jos 5:9
camped at **G** on the plains Jos 5:10
in the camp at **G** and said to him Jos 9:6
to Joshua in the camp at **G**: Jos 10:6
the fighting men, came from **G**. Jos 10:7
after marching all night from **G**. Jos 10:9
him returned to the camp at **G**. Jos 10:15
all Israel to the camp at **G**. Jos 10:43
one the king of Goiim in **G** one Jos 12:23
of Judah approached Joshua at **G**, Jos 14:6
north to the **G** that is opposite Jos 15:7
LORD went up from **G** to Bochim Jdg 2:1
carved images near **G** he returned Jdg 3:19
circuit to Bethel, **G**, and Mizpah 1Sm 7:16
Afterwards, go ahead of me to **G**. 1Sm 10:8
let's go to **G**, so we can renew 1Sm 11:14
So all the people went to **G**, 1Sm 11:15
were summoned to join Saul at **G**. 1Sm 13:4
was still at **G**, and all his 1Sm 13:7
but Samuel didn't come to **G**, 1Sm 13:8
will now descend on me at **G**, 1Sm 13:12
Samuel went from **G** to Gibeah in 1Sm 13:15
around and went down to **G**." 1Sm 15:12
to the LORD your God at **G**." 1Sm 15:21
to pieces before the LORD at **G**. 1Sm 15:33
Judah came to **G** to meet the king 2Sm 19:15
king went on to **G**, and Chimham 2Sm 19:40
Elisha were traveling from **G**, 2Kg 2:1
When Elisha returned to **G**, 2Kg 4:38
Do not go to **G** or make a Hs 4:15
All their evil appears at **G**, Hs 9:15
They sacrifice bulls in **G**; Hs 12:11
rebel even more at **G**! Am 4:4
Bethel or go to **G** or journey to Am 5:5
for **G** will certainly go into Am 5:5
from Acacia Grove to **G**, Mc 6:5

GILOH *(2)*
Holon, and **G**—11 cities, with Jos 15:51
Gilonite, from his city of **G**. 2Sm 15:12

GILONITE *(2)*
adviser Ahithophel the **G**, 2Sm 15:12
Eliam son of Ahithophel the **G**, 2Sm 23:34

GIMZO *(1)*
its villages, **G** and its villages 2Ch 28:18

GINATH *(2)*
people followed Tibni son of **G**, 1Kg 16:21
who followed Tibni son of **G**. 1Kg 16:22

GINNETHOI *(1)*
Iddo, **G**, Abijah, Neh 12:4

GINNETHON *(2)*
Daniel, **G**, Baruch, Neh 10:6
of Iddo, Meshullam of **G**, Neh 12:16

GIRDED *(1)*
ropes and tackle and **g** the ship. Ac 27:17

GIRGASHITES *(7)*
Jebusites, the Amorites, the **G**, Gn 10:16
Canaanites, **G**, and Jebusites." Gn 15:21
you—the Hittites, **G**, Amorites, Dt 7:1
Perizzites, **G**, Amorites, Jos 3:10
Hittites, **G**, Hivites, Jos 24:11
the Jebusites, Amorites, **G**, 1Ch 1:14
Jebusites, and **G**—to give it to Neh 9:8

GIRL *(31)*
Let the **g** to whom I say, 'Please Gn 24:14
Now the **g** was very beautiful, Gn 24:16
The **g** ran and told her mother's Gn 24:28
Let the **g** stay with us for about Gn 24:55
Let's call the **g** and ask her Gn 24:57
loved the young **g** and spoke Gn 34:3
"Get me this **g** as a wife," Gn 34:4
Just give the **g** to be my wife!" Gn 34:12
she sent her slave **g** to get it. Ex 2:5
So the **g** went and called the Ex 2:8
of the servant **g** who is behind Ex 11:5
a **g** or two for each warrior, Jdg 5:30
where a servant **g** would come 2Sm 17:17
for a beautiful **g** throughout the 1Kg 1:3
The **g** was of unsurpassed beauty, 1Kg 1:4
of Israel a young **g** who served 2Kg 5:2
master what the **g** from the land 2Kg 5:4
and a serving **g** when she ousts Pr 30:23
and sold a **g** for wine to drink. Jl 3:3
relations with the same **g**, Am 2:7
because the **g** isn't dead, Mt 9:24
by the hand, and the **g** got up. Mt 9:25
on a platter and given to the **g**, Mt 14:11
Little **g**, I say to you, get Mk 5:41
Immediately the **g** got up and Mk 5:42
king said to the **g**, "Ask me Mk 6:22
a platter, and gave it to the **g**. Mk 6:28
the **g** gave it to her mother. Mk 6:28
out and spoke to the **g** who was Jn 18:16
Then the slave **g** who was the Jn 18:17
slave **g** met us who had a spirit Ac 16:16

GIRL'S *(7)*
and when the **g** father saw him, Jdg 19:3
the **g** father, detained Jdg 19:4
but the **g** father said to his Jdg 19:5
Then the **g** father said to the Jdg 19:6
but the **g** father said to him, Jdg 19:8
the **g** father, said to Jdg 19:9
like a servant **g** eyes on her Ps 123:2

GIRLS *(5)*
while her servant **g** walked along Ex 2:5
of the slave **g** of his subjects 2Sm 6:20
by the slave **g** you spoke about." 2Sm 6:22
put him on a leash for your **g**? Jb 41:5
boys and **g** playing in them." Zch 8:5

GIRZITES *(1)*
Geshurites, the **G**, and the 1Sm 27:8

GISHPA *(1)*
Ziha and **G** supervised the temple Neh 11:21

GITTAIM *(2)*
fled to **G** and still live 2Sm 4:3
Hazor, Ramah, **G**, Neh 11:33

GITTITE *(7)*
to the house of Obed-edom the **G**. 2Sm 6:10
The king said to Ittai the **G**, 2Sm 15:19
So Ittai the **G** marched past with 2Sm 15:22
and one third under Ittai the **G**. 2Sm 18:2
killed Goliath the **G**. 2Sm 21:19
to the house of Obed-edom the **G**. 1Ch 13:13
the brother of Goliath the **G**. 1Ch 20:5

GITTITES *(1)*
and the **G**—600 men who came 2Sm 15:18

GIVE *(818)*
never again **g** you its yield. Gn 4:12
I will **g** this land to your Gn 12:7
for I will **g** you and your Gn 13:15
other, for I will **g** it to you." Gn 13:17
g praise to God Most High who Gn 14:20
said to Abram, "**G** me the people, Gn 14:21

what can You g me, since I am Gn 15:2
Chaldeans to g you this land to Gn 15:7
I g this land to your offspring, Gn 15:18
you I will g the land where Gn 17:8
I will g you a son by her. Gn 17:16
ninety-year-old woman, g birth?" Gn 17:17
G me a burial site among you so Gn 23:4
to g me the cave of Machpelah Gn 23:9
Let him g it to me in your Gn 23:9
g you the field, and I give you Gn 23:11
and I g you the cave that is in Gn 23:11
I g it to you in the presence of Gn 23:11
'I will g this land to your Gn 24:7
and they do not g ⌊her⌋ to you— Gn 24:41
When her time came to g birth, Gn 25:24
For I will g all these lands to Gn 26:3
will g your offspring all these Gn 26:4
Now obey every order I g you, Gn 27:8
May God g to you—from the dew Gn 27:28
May God g you and your offspring Gn 28:4
I will g you and your offspring Gn 28:13
and I will g to You a tenth of Gn 28:22
a tenth of all that You g me." Gn 28:22
Better that I g her to you than Gn 29:19
said to Laban, "G me my wife, Gn 29:21
in this place to g the younger Gn 29:26
and we will also g you this Gn 29:27
"G me sons, or I will die!" Gn 30:1
Please g me some of your son's Gn 30:14
G me my wives and my children Gn 30:26
asked, "What should I g you?" Gn 30:31
You don't need to g me anything. Gn 30:31
Please g her to him as a wife. Gn 34:8
g your daughters to us, and take Gn 34:9
and I'll g you whatever you say. Gn 34:11
I'll g you whatever you ask me. Gn 34:12
Just g the girl to be my wife!" Gn 34:12
we will g you our daughters, Gn 34:16
our wives and g our daughters to Gn 34:21
and Isaac I will g to you. Gn 35:12
And I will g the land to your Gn 35:12
Rachel began to g birth, and her Gn 35:16
What will you g me for sleeping Gn 38:16
"What should I g you?" he asked. Gn 38:18
since I did not g her to my son Gn 38:26
time came for her to g birth, Gn 38:27
It is God who will g Pharaoh a Gn 41:16
and g them provisions for their Gn 42:25
I will then g your brother back Gn 42:34
will g you the best of the land Gn 45:18
to Joseph and said, "G us food. Gn 47:15
Joseph said, "G me your Gn 47:16
will g you food in exchange for Gn 47:16
G us seed so that we can live Gn 47:19
you are to g a fifth of it to Gn 47:24
and I will g this land as an Gn 48:4
help the Hebrew women g birth, Ex 1:16
are vigorous and g birth before Ex 1:19
And I will g this people such Ex 3:21
with them to g them the land Ex 6:4
that I swore to g to Abraham, Ex 6:8
and I will g it to you as a Ex 6:8
that day I will g special Ex 8:22
Therefore g orders to bring your Ex 9:19
the LORD will g you as He Ex 12:25
fathers that He would g you, Ex 13:5
pillar of fire to g them light Ex 13:21
The LORD will g you meat to eat Ex 16:8
day He will g you two days' Ex 16:29
"G us water to drink." Ex 17:2
will g you some advice, and God Ex 18:19
Do not g false testimony against Ex 20:16
then you must g life for life, Ex 21:23
must g 30 shekels of silver to Ex 21:32
of the pit must g compensation; Ex 21:34
refuses to g her to him, Ex 22:17
G Me the firstborn of your sons. Ex 22:29
day you are to g them to Me. Ex 22:30
will g ⌊you⌋ the full number of Ex 23:26
so that I may g you the stone Ex 24:12
whose heart stirs him ⌊to g⌋. Ex 25:2
that I will g you into the ark. Ex 25:16
that I will g you into the ark. Ex 25:21
Aaron's sons to ⌊g them⌋ glory Ex 28:40
must g this contribution to the Ex 30:14
The wealthy may not g more, Ex 30:15
and the poor may not g less, Ex 30:15
sky and will g your offspring Ex 32:13

I will g it to your offspring. Ex 33:1
you⌋, and I will g you rest." Ex 33:14
to it, and g it to the priest Lv 5:16
You are to g the right thigh to Lv 7:32
of meeting, and g them to the Lv 15:14
to the poor or g preference to Lv 19:15
since I will g it to you to Lv 20:24
to its value and g the holy Lv 22:14
the Israelites g to the LORD Lv 22:15
that you g to the LORD. Lv 23:38
land of Egypt to g you the land Lv 25:38
I will g you rain at the right Lv 26:4
I will g peace to the land, Lv 26:6
G the money to Aaron and his Nm 3:48
and g ⌊it⌋ to the individual he Nm 5:7
holy contribution is his ⌊to g⌋; Nm 5:10
favor on you and g you peace. Nm 6:26
and g this offering to the Nm 7:5
But he did not g ⌊any⌋ to the Nm 7:9
lamps are to g light in front Nm 8:2
its lamps ⌊to g light⌋ in front Nm 8:3
I will g it to you.' Come Nm 10:29
Did I g them birth so You should Nm 11:12
You swore to ⌊g⌋ their fathers? Nm 11:12
I get meat to g all these people Nm 11:13
to me: 'G us meat to eat!' Nm 11:13
The LORD will g you meat and Nm 11:18
say, 'I will g them meat, and Nm 11:21
milk and honey, and g it to us. Nm 14:8
the land He swore to ⌊g⌋ them, Nm 14:16
I swore to ⌊g⌋ their fathers. Nm 14:23
you are to g the LORD a Nm 15:21
and honey or g us an inheritance Nm 16:14
their offerings that they g Me, Nm 18:9
the Israelites g to the LORD as Nm 18:12
I g to you and to your sons and Nm 18:19
G some of it to Aaron the priest Nm 18:28
G it to Eleazar the priest, Nm 19:3
people so I may g them water." Nm 21:16
and I will g you the answer the Nm 22:8
If Balak were to g me his house Nm 22:18
If Balak were to g me his house Nm 24:13
g us property among our father's Nm 27:4
You are to g them hereditary Nm 27:7
g his inheritance to his Nm 27:9
g his inheritance to his Nm 27:10
g his inheritance to the nearest Nm 27:11
their half and g ⌊it⌋ to Eleazar Nm 31:29
and g them to the Levites who Nm 31:30
the land I swore ⌊to g⌋ Abraham, Nm 32:11
you are to g them the land of Nm 32:29
the Israelites to g cities out Nm 35:2
you are to g the Levites ⌊will Nm 35:4
The cities you g the Levites Nm 35:6
to these, g 42 ⌊other⌋ cities Nm 35:6
of cities you g the Levites will Nm 35:7
the cities that you g from the Nm 35:8
tribe⌋ is to g some of its Nm 35:8
my lord to g the land as Nm 36:2
by the LORD to g our brother Nm 36:2
LORD swore to g to your fathers Dt 1:8
land I swore to g your fathers, Dt 1:35
and I will g him and his Dt 1:36
I will g them the land, and they Dt 1:39
I will not g you any of their Dt 2:5
I will not g you any of their Dt 2:9
for I will not g you any of the Dt 2:19
and g us water for silver so we Dt 2:28
I have begun to g Sihon and his Dt 2:31
bring you in and g you their Dt 4:38
Do not g dishonest testimony Dt 5:20
and Jacob that He would g you— Dt 6:10
God swore to ⌊g⌋ your fathers, Dt 6:18
lead us in and g us the land Dt 6:23
Do not g your daughters to their Dt 7:3
fathers that He would g you. Dt 7:13
your God will g them over to you Dt 7:23
land I swore to g their fathers. Dt 10:11
your fathers to g them and their Dt 11:9
LORD swore to g your fathers. Dt 11:21
you may g it to a resident alien Dt 14:21
brother and g him ⌊nothing⌋. Dt 15:9
G to him, and don't have a Dt 15:10
have a stingy heart when you g, Dt 15:10
G generously to him from your Dt 15:14
You are to g him whatever the Dt 15:14
that you g in proportion to Dt 16:10
your God will g you is Dt 17:2

and they will g you a verdict in Dt 17:9
verdict they g you at the place Dt 17:10
instruction they g you and the Dt 17:11
You are to g him the firstfruits Dt 18:4
the land He promised to g them— Dt 19:8
your enemies to g you victory.' Dt 20:4
and they are to g a ruling in Dt 21:5
shekels⌋ and g ⌊them⌋ to the Dt 22:19
raped her must g the young Dt 22:29
swore to our fathers to g us.' Dt 26:3
you are to g ⌊it⌋ to the Levite, Dt 26:12
swore to your fathers to g you. Dt 28:11
g your land rain in its season Dt 28:12
the LORD will g you a trembling Dt 28:65
command that I g you today is Dt 30:11
LORD swore to g to your fathers Dt 30:20
LORD swore to g to their fathers Dt 31:7
I swore to ⌊g⌋ their fathers, Dt 31:20
the land I swore ⌊to g them⌋." Dt 31:21
I bring death and I g life; Dt 32:39
'I will g it to your descendants. Dt 34:4
to their fathers to g them as an Jos 1:6
LORD your God will g you rest, Jos 1:13
and He will g you this land.' Jos 1:13
kindness to you. G me a sure Jos 2:12
⌊We will g⌋ our lives for yours. Jos 2:14
sworn to their fathers to g us, Jos 5:6
all the people g a mighty shout. Jos 6:5
Achan, "My son, g glory to the Jos 7:19
Moses to g you all the land Jos 9:24
He did not g any inheritance to Jos 13:14
But Moses did not g a portion to Jos 13:33
Now g me this hill country the Jos 14:12
I will g my daughter Achsah as a Jos 15:16
She replied, "G me a blessing. Jos 15:19
g me the springs of water also." Jos 15:19
Moses to g us an inheritance Jos 17:4
Why did you g us only one tribal Jos 17:14
the city and g him a place to Jos 20:4
He had sworn to g their fathers, Jos 21:43
I will g my daughter Achsah to Jdg 1:12
answered him, "G me a blessing. Jdg 1:15
g me springs of water also." Jdg 1:15
Please g me a little water to Jdg 4:19
travel on the road, g praise! Jdg 5:10
g me a sign that You are Jdg 6:17
Please g some loaves of bread to Jdg 8:5
we should g bread to your army? Jdg 8:6
that we should g bread to your Jdg 8:15
Everyone g me an earring from Jdg 8:24
They said, "We agree to g them." Jdg 8:25
conceive and g birth to a son. Jdg 13:3
conceive and g birth to a son. Jdg 13:5
conceive and g a birth to a son Jdg 13:7
I will g you 30 linen garments Jdg 14:12
you must g me 30 linen garments Jdg 14:13
of us will then g you 1,100 Jdg 16:5
and I will g you four ounces of Jdg 17:10
G your judgment and verdict here Jdg 20:7
of us will g his daughter to Jdg 21:1
LORD not to g them any of our Jdg 21:7
we can't g them our daughters Jdg 21:18
didn't actually g ⌊the women⌋ to Jdg 21:22
LORD will g you by this young Ru 4:12
forget me, and g Your servant a 1Sm 1:11
I will g him to the LORD all the 1Sm 1:11
I now g the boy to the LORD. 1Sm 1:28
He will g power to His king; 1Sm 2:10
G the priest ⌊some⌋ meat to 1Sm 2:15
May the LORD g you children by 1Sm 2:20
entered the city to g a report, 1Sm 4:13
pregnant and about to g birth. 1Sm 4:19
G glory to Israel's God, and 1Sm 6:5
"G us a king to judge us," 1Sm 8:6
olive orchards and g them to his 1Sm 8:14
your vineyards and g them to his 1Sm 8:15
I'll g it to the man of God, 1Sm 9:8
you are and g you two ⌊loaves 1Sm 10:4
G us those men so we can kill 1Sm 11:12
g us the right ⌊decision⌋." 1Sm 14:41
rich and will g him his daughter 1Sm 17:25
and I'll g your flesh to the 1Sm 17:44
and g the corpses of the 1Sm 17:46
I'll g her to you as a wife, 1Sm 18:17
it was time to g Saul's daughter 1Sm 18:19
"I'll g her to him," Saul 1Sm 18:21
G me five loaves of bread or 1Sm 21:3
it!" David said. "G it to me." 1Sm 21:9

son going to **g** all of you fields 1Sm 22:7
Please **g** whatever you can afford 1Sm 25:8
shearers and **g** them to men who 1Sm 25:11
Eat and it will **g** you strength 1Sm 28:22
we will not **g** any of the plunder 1Sm 30:22
son of Saul, "**G** me back my wife, 2Sm 3:14
I will **g** you rest from all your 2Sm 7:11
your wives and **g** them to another 2Sm 12:11
Tamar come and **g** me ⌊something⌋ 2Sm 13:5
to Ahithophel, "**G** ⌊me⌋ your 2Sm 16:20
and my ankles do not **g** way. 2Sm 22:37
Let him **g** me Abishag the 1Kg 2:17
"Ask. What should I **g** you?" 1Kg 3:5
So **g** Your servant an obedient 1Kg 3:9
I will **g** you a wise and 1Kg 3:12
will **g** you what you did not ask 1Kg 3:13
I will **g** you a long life." 1Kg 3:14
boy in two and **g** half to one and 1Kg 3:25
"My lord, **g** her the living baby," 1Kg 3:26
G the living baby to the first 1Kg 3:27
and may You **g** them compassion in 1Kg 8:50
away from you and **g** it to your 1Kg 11:11
I will **g** one tribe to your son 1Kg 11:13
I will **g** you 10 tribes, 1Kg 11:31
son's hand and **g** them to you. 1Kg 11:35
I will **g** one tribe to his son, 1Kg 11:36
David, and I will **g** you Israel. 1Kg 11:38
and I'll **g** you a reward." 1Kg 13:7
If you were to **g** me half your 1Kg 13:8
He will **g** up Israel, because of 1Kg 14:16
said to her, "**G** me your son." 1Kg 17:19
children you are to **g** to me. 1Kg 20:5
G me your vineyard so I can have 1Kg 21:2
will **g** you a better vineyard in 1Kg 21:2
will **g** you its value in silver. 1Kg 21:2
I will never **g** my fathers' 1Kg 21:3
I will not **g** you my fathers' 1Kg 21:4
G me your vineyard for silver, 1Kg 21:6
I will **g** you a vineyard in its 1Kg 21:6
'I won't **g** you my vineyard!' " 1Kg 21:6
⌊For⌋ I will **g** you the vineyard 1Kg 21:7
who refused to **g** it to you for 1Kg 21:15
"**G** it to the people to eat." 2Kg 4:42
"**G** it to the people to eat," 2Kg 4:43
g them 75 pounds of silver 2Kg 5:22
said to me, '**G** up your son, 2Kg 6:28
the next day, '**G** up your son, 2Kg 6:29
promised to **g** a lamp to David 2Kg 8:19
"If it is, **g** me your hand." 2Kg 10:15
G your daughter to my son as a 2Kg 14:9
men of Israel to **g** to the king 2Kg 15:20
g you 2,000 horses if you're 2Kg 18:23
in turn⌋ are to **g** it to the 2Kg 22:5
⌊They are to **g** it⌋ to the 2Kg 22:6
taxed the land to **g** the money. 2Kg 23:35
valuation, to **g** it to Pharaoh 2Kg 23:35
and to **g** thanks and praise to 1Ch 16:4
G thanks to the LORD; call on 1Ch 16:8
I will **g** the land of Canaan to 1Ch 16:18
G thanks to the LORD, for He is 1Ch 16:34
so that we may **g** thanks to Your 1Ch 16:35
by name to **g** thanks to the LORD 1Ch 16:41
G me this threshing-floor plot 1Ch 21:22
G it to me for the full price, 1Ch 21:22
I **g** the oxen for the burnt 1Ch 21:23
grain offering—I **g** it all." 1Ch 21:23
I will **g** him rest from all his 1Ch 22:9
and I will **g** peace and quiet to 1Ch 22:9
may the LORD **g** you insight and 1Ch 22:12
every morning to **g** thanks and 1Ch 23:30
I now **g** my personal treasures of 1Ch 29:3
their leaders' willingness to **g**, 1Ch 29:9
great and to **g** strength to all. 1Ch 29:12
we **g** You thanks and praise Your 1Ch 29:13
be able to **g** as generously as 1Ch 29:14
G my son Solomon a whole heart 1Ch 29:19
him: "Ask. What should I **g** you?" 2Ch 1:7
will also **g** you riches, wealth, 2Ch 1:12
I will **g** your servants, the 2Ch 2:10
G thanks to the LORD, for His 2Ch 20:21
promised to **g** a lamp to David 2Ch 21:7
LORD is able to **g** you much more 2Ch 25:9
G your daughter to my son as a 2Ch 25:18
him and did not **g** him support. 2Ch 28:20
G your allegiance to the LORD, 2Ch 30:8
was in Judah to **g** them one heart 2Ch 30:12
in Jerusalem to **g** a contribution 2Ch 31:4
you to **g** you over to death 2Ch 32:11

Based on what they could **g**, Ezr 2:69
for us and **g** us a stake in His Ezr 9:8
to **g** us a wall in Judah and Ezr 9:9
So do not **g** your daughters to Ezr 9:12
G Your servant success today, Neh 1:11
so that he will **g** me timber to Neh 2:8
You **g** life to all of them, Neh 9:6
covenant with him to **g** the land Neh 9:8
to **g** it to his descendants. Neh 9:8
land You had sworn to **g** them. Neh 9:15
We will not **g** our daughters in Neh 10:30
To **g** an eighth of an ounce of Neh 10:32
You must not **g** your daughters in Neh 13:25
and **g** them the required beauty Est 2:3
A man will **g** up everything he Jb 2:4
G me ⌊something⌋ or Pay a bribe Jb 6:22
I **g** up! I will not live forever. Jb 7:16
trouble and **g** birth to evil; Jb 15:35
hands must **g** back his wealth. Jb 20:10
I would **g** Him an account of all Jb 31:37
Almighty that **g** him Jb 32:8
and I will not **g** anyone an Jb 32:21
not know how to **g** ⌊such⌋ titles; Jb 32:22
what do you **g** Him, or what does Jb 35:7
when mountain goats **g** birth? Jb 39:1
can know the time they **g** birth? Jb 39:2
crouch down to **g** birth to their Jb 39:3
Do you **g** strength to the horse? Jb 39:19
who argues with God **g** an answer. Jb 40:2
and my ankles do not **g** way. Ps 18:36
May He **g** you what your heart Ps 20:4
LORD, **g** victory to the king! Ps 20:9
You **g** him blessings forever; Ps 21:6
I will **g** praise in the great Ps 22:25
Do not **g** me over to the will of Ps 27:12
g them back what they deserve. Ps 28:4
G the LORD—you heavenly beings Ps 29:1
g the LORD glory and strength. Ps 29:1
G the LORD the glory due His Ps 29:2
the deer **g** birth and strips Ps 29:9
My eye on you, I will **g** counsel. Ps 32:8
and He will **g** you your heart's Ps 37:4
from anger and **g** up ⌊your⌋ rage; Ps 37:8
You will not **g** him over to the Ps 41:2
But You **g** us victory over our Ps 44:7
and **g** me a willing spirit. Ps 51:12
a sacrifice, or I would **g** it; Ps 51:16
G us aid against the foe, for Ps 60:11
G the command to save me, for Ps 71:3
g Your justice to the king and Ps 72:1
not **g** the life of Your dove to Ps 74:19
We **g** thanks to You, God; Ps 75:1
g thanks to You, for Your name Ps 75:1
love, LORD, and **g** us Your Ps 85:7
G me an undivided mind to fear Ps 86:11
G Your strength to Your servant; Ps 86:16
For He will **g** His angels orders Ps 91:11
will rescue him and **g** him honor. Ps 91:15
to **g** him relief from troubled Ps 94:13
G thanks to Him and praise His Ps 100:4
for You to **g** them their food Ps 104:27
When You **g** it to them, they Ps 104:28
G thanks to the LORD, call on Ps 105:1
I will **g** the land of Canaan to Ps 105:11
G thanks to the LORD, for He is Ps 106:1
so that we may **g** thanks to Your Ps 106:47
G thanks to the LORD, for He is Ps 107:1
them **g** thanks to the LORD for Ps 107:8
them **g** thanks to the LORD for Ps 107:15
them **g** thanks to the LORD for Ps 107:21
them **g** thanks to the LORD for Ps 107:31
G us aid against the foe, for Ps 108:12
G praise, servants of the LORD; Ps 113:1
but to Your name **g** glory because Ps 115:1
G thanks to the LORD, for He is Ps 118:1
but did not **g** me over to death. Ps 118:18
through them and **g** thanks to the Ps 118:19
I will **g** thanks to You because Ps 118:21
my God, and I will **g** You thanks. Ps 118:28
G thanks to the LORD, for He is Ps 118:29
g me life through Your word. Ps 119:25
and graciously **g** me Your Ps 119:29
g me life in Your ways. Ps 119:37
G me life through Your Ps 119:40
g me understanding so that I can Ps 119:73
G me life in accordance with Ps 119:88
g me life through Your word. Ps 119:107
g me understanding so that I may Ps 119:125

G me understanding, and I will Ps 119:144
LORD, **g** me life, in keeping with Ps 119:149
g me life, as You promised. Ps 119:154
g me life, according to Your Ps 119:156
LORD, **g** me life, according to Ps 119:159
g me understanding according to Ps 119:169
will He **g** you, and what will Ps 120:3
go up to **g** thanks to the name of Ps 122:4
G praise, you servants of the Ps 135:1
G thanks to the LORD, for He is Ps 136:1
G thanks to the God of gods. Ps 136:2
G thanks to the Lord of lords. Ps 136:3
G thanks to the God of heaven! Ps 136:26
I will **g** You thanks with all my Ps 138:1
holy temple and **g** thanks to Your Ps 138:2
on earth will **g** You thanks, Ps 138:4
They will **g** a testimony of Your Ps 145:7
and You **g** them their food in due Ps 145:15
I'll **g** it tomorrow"—when it is Pr 3:28
will **g** you a crown of beauty. Pr 4:9
you will **g** up your vitality to Pr 5:9
Don't **g** sleep to your eyes or Pr 6:4
he must **g** up all the wealth in Pr 6:31
and He will **g** a reward to the Pr 19:17
the righteous **g** and don't hold Pr 21:26
so that you may **g** a dependable Pr 22:21
My son, **g** me your heart, and let Pr 23:26
is hungry, **g** him food to eat Pr 25:21
if he is thirsty, **g** him water to Pr 25:21
and he will **g** you comfort; Pr 29:17
he will also **g** you delight. Pr 29:17
G me neither poverty nor wealth; Pr 30:8
two daughters: **G**, Give. Three Pr 30:15
daughters: Give, **G**. Three things Pr 30:15
G beer to one who is dying, Pr 31:6
G her the reward of her labor, Pr 31:31
So I began to **g** myself over to Ec 2:20
but he must **g** his portion to a Ec 2:21
in order to **g** to the one who is Ec 2:26
a time to **g** birth and a time to Ec 3:2
G a portion to seven or even to Ec 11:2
blossoming vines **g** off their Sg 2:13
that you would **g** us this charge? Sg 5:9
There I will **g** you my love. Sg 7:12
The mandrakes **g** off a fragrance, Sg 7:13
I would **g** you spiced wine to Sg 8:2
a man were to **g** all his wealth Sg 8:7
I will also **g** orders to the Is 5:6
Lord Himself will **g** you a sign: Is 7:14
milk they **g** he will eat butter Is 7:22
you will say: "**G** thanks to the Is 12:4
will not **g** their light. Is 13:10
G us counsel and make a decision. Is 16:3
wisest advisers **g** stupid advice! Is 19:11
into a firm place will **g** way, Is 22:25
woman about to **g** birth writhes Is 26:17
The Lord will **g** you meager bread Is 30:20
you will **g** birth to stubble. Is 33:11
I'll **g** you 2,000 horses if you Is 36:8
will not **g** My glory to another, Is 42:8
Let them **g** glory to the LORD, Is 42:12
no one saying "**G** ⌊it⌋ back!" Is 42:22
g Egypt as a ransom for you, Is 43:3
I will **g** human beings in your Is 43:4
to the north: **G** ⌊them⌋ up! and Is 43:6
to **g** drink to My chosen people. Is 43:20
I will **g** you the treasures of Is 45:3
I **g** a name to you, though you do Is 45:4
will not **g** My glory to another. Is 48:11
I will **g** Him the many as Is 53:12
barren one, who did not **g** birth; Is 54:1
I will **g** them, in My house and Is 56:5
I will **g** each ⌊of them⌋ an Is 56:5
but⌋ you did not say, "I **g** up!" Is 57:10
trouble and **g** birth to iniquity. Is 59:4
to **g** them a crown of beauty Is 61:3
Do not **g** Him rest until He Is 62:7
I will no longer **g** your grain to Is 62:8
but He will **g** His servants Is 65:15
I will **g** you shepherds who are Jr 3:15
My⌋ sons and **g** you a desirable Jr 3:19
I speak to and **g** such a warning Jr 6:10
I did **g** them this command: Jr 7:23
I will **g** their wives to other Jr 8:10
wormwood and **g** them poisonous Jr 9:15
to **g** ⌊them⌋ a land flowing with Jr 11:5
G glory to the LORD your God Jr 13:16
will certainly **g** you true peace Jr 14:13

can the skies alone g showers? Jr 14:22
of them I will g over to the Jr 15:9
treasures I will g as plunder, Jr 15:13
treasures I will g up as plunder Jr 17:3
the heart to g to each according Jr 17:10
I will g away all the wealth of Jr 20:5
and will not g him his wages, Jr 22:13
wormwood and g them poisoned Jr 23:15
will g them a heart to know Me, Jr 24:7
I g it to anyone I please. Jr 27:5
your sons and g your daughters Jr 29:6
to g you a future and a hope. Jr 29:11
see whether a male can g birth. Jr 30:6
and those about to g birth. Jr 31:8
into joy, g them consolation, Jr 31:13
I will g the priests their fill Jr 31:14
men in order to g to each person Jr 32:19
land You swore ⌊to g⌋ to their Jr 32:22
I will g them one heart and one Jr 32:39
I am about to g the command"— Jr 34:22
Besides, if I g you advice, you Jr 38:15
God had sent him to g them— Jr 43:1
G yourself no relief and your Lm 2:18
You will g them a heart filled Lm 3:65
from My mouth, g them a warning Ezk 3:17
plan evil and g wicked advice Ezk 11:2
and I will g you the land of Ezk 11:17
And I will g them one heart and Ezk 11:19
their bodies and g them a heart Ezk 11:19
so I will g up the residents of Ezk 15:6
Men g gifts to all prostitutes, Ezk 16:33
I will g them to you as Ezk 16:61
Egypt so they might g him horses Ezk 17:15
that I swore to g them and they Ezk 20:28
land I swore to g your fathers, Ezk 20:42
battering rams, g the order to Ezk 21:22
She didn't g up her promiscuity Ezk 23:8
am about to g you to the people Ezk 25:4
against you and g you as plunder Ezk 25:7
I will g it along with Ammon to Ezk 25:10
am going to g the land of Egypt Ezk 29:19
the moon will not g its light. Ezk 32:7
from My mouth, g them a warning Ezk 33:7
of the field will g their fruit, Ezk 34:27
I will g you a new heart and put Ezk 36:26
heart of stone and g you a heart Ezk 36:26
I will g you as food to every Ezk 39:4
that day I will g Gog a burial Ezk 39:11
are to g a bull from the herd Ezk 43:19
You are to g them no possession Ezk 44:28
You are to g your first batch of Ezk 44:30
oppress My people but g the Ezk 45:8
will be whatever he wants to g, Ezk 46:5
he wants to g with the lambs, Ezk 46:11
since I swore to g it to your Ezk 47:14
we will g the interpretation. Dn 2:4
we will g the interpretation. Dn 2:7
I will know you can g me its Dn 2:9
the king to g him some time, Dn 2:16
so that he could g the king the Dn 2:16
I will g him the interpretation. Dn 2:24
don't need to g you an answer to Dn 3:16
he will g the interpretation. Dn 5:12
they could not g its Dn 5:15
that you can g interpretations Dn 5:16
this inscription and g me its Dn 5:16
and g your rewards to someone Dn 5:17
I've come now to g you Dn 9:22
I have come to g it, for you are Dn 9:23
He will g him a daughter in Dn 11:17
the people will g understanding Dn 11:33
the men who g me my food and Hs 2:5
There I will g her vineyards Hs 2:15
G them, LORD—What should You Hs 9:14
them, LORD—What should You g? Hs 9:14
G them a womb that miscarries Hs 9:14
I bent down to g them food. Hs 11:4
How can I g you up, Ephraim? Hs 11:8
G me a king and leaders? Hs 13:10
I g you a king in My anger and Hs 13:11
your living and g ⌊your⌋ Am 7:12
for I am about to g the command, Am 9:9
Should I g my firstborn for my Mc 6:7
do save, I will g to the sword. Mc 6:14
I will g the remnant of this Zch 8:12
and He will g them showers of Zch 10:1
right to you, g me my wages; Zch 11:12
She will g birth to a son, Mt 1:21

pregnant and g birth to a son, Mt 1:23
He will g His angels orders Mt 4:6
I will g You all these things if Mt 4:9
good works and g glory to your Mt 5:16
his wife must g her a written Mt 5:31
G to the one who asks you, Mt 5:42
So whenever you g to the poor, Mt 6:2
But when you g to the poor, Mt 6:3
G us today our daily bread. Mt 6:11
Don't g what is holy to dogs or Mt 7:6
for bread, will g him a stone? Mt 7:9
for a fish, will g him a snake? Mt 7:10
know how to g good gifts to your Mt 7:11
Father in heaven g good things Mt 7:11
of charge; g free of charge. Mt 10:8
burdened, and I will g you rest. Mt 11:28
with an oath to g her whatever Mt 14:7
G me John the Baptist's head Mt 14:8
"You g them something to eat." Mt 14:16
I will g you the keys of the Mt 16:19
what will a man g in exchange Mt 16:26
Take it and g it to them for Me Mt 17:27
command ⌊us⌋ to g divorce papers Mt 19:7
belongings and g to the poor, Mt 19:21
I'll g you whatever is right. Mt 20:4
workers and g them their pay, Mt 20:8
I want to g this last man the Mt 20:14
right and left is not Mine to g; Mt 20:23
to serve, and to g His life—a Mt 20:28
who will g him his produce Mt 21:41
g back to Caesar the things that Mt 22:21
to g them food at the proper Mt 24:45
sensible ones, 'G us some of Mt 25:8
from him and g it to the one who Mt 25:28
thirsty and g You something to Mt 25:37
willing to g me if I hand Him Mt 26:15
Therefore g orders that the tomb Mt 27:64
you want, and I'll g it to you." Mk 6:22
you ask me I will g you, Mk 6:23
I want you to g me John the Mk 6:25
"You g them something to eat," Mk 6:37
of bread and g them something to Mk 6:37
What can a man g in exchange for Mk 8:37
all you have and g to the poor, Mk 10:21
right or left is not Mine to g; Mk 10:40
to serve, and to g His life—a Mk 10:45
the farmers and g the vineyard Mk 12:9
G back to Caesar the things that Mk 12:17
and promised to g him silver. Mk 14:11
They tried to g Him wine mixed Mk 15:23
conceive and g birth to a son, Lk 1:31
Lord God will g Him the throne Lk 1:32
come for Elizabeth to g birth, Lk 1:57
to g His people knowledge of Lk 1:77
time came for her to g birth. Lk 2:6
I will g You their splendor and Lk 4:6
and I can g it to anyone I want. Lk 4:6
He will g His angels orders Lk 4:10
G to everyone who asks from you, Lk 6:30
G, and it will be given to you; Lk 6:38
"You g them something to eat," Lk 9:13
So tell her to g me a hand." Lk 10:40
G us each day our daily bread. Lk 11:3
can't get up to g you anything.' Lk 11:7
won't get up and g him anything Lk 11:8
will get up and g him as much as Lk 11:8
will g him a snake instead of a Lk 11:11
an egg, will g him a scorpion? Lk 11:12
know how to g good gifts to your Lk 11:13
heavenly Father g the Holy Lk 11:13
But g to charity what is within, Lk 11:41
You g a tenth of mint, rue, and Lk 11:42
delights to g you the kingdom. Lk 12:32
possessions and g to the poor. Lk 12:33
to g them their allotted Lk 12:42
I came here to g peace to the Lk 12:51
'G your place to this man,' Lk 14:9
When you g a lunch or a dinner, Lk 14:12
g me the share of the estate I Lk 15:12
but no one would g him any. Lk 15:16
G an account of your management, Lk 16:2
who will g you what is your own? Lk 16:12
any return to g glory to God Lk 17:18
G me justice against my adversary. Lk 18:3
me, I will g her justice, so she Lk 18:5
g a tenth of everything I get.' Lk 18:12
I'll g half of my possessions to Lk 19:8
from him and g it to the one who Lk 19:24

that they might g him some fruit Lk 20:10
farmers and g the vineyard to Lk 20:16
g back to Caesar the things that Lk 20:25
for I will g you such words and Lk 21:15
glad and agreed to g him silver. Lk 22:5
We need to g an answer to those Jn 1:22
"G Me a drink," Jesus said to Jn 4:7
saying to you, 'G Me a drink,' Jn 4:10
He would g you living water." Jn 4:10
that I will g him will never Jn 4:14
water I will g him will become Jn 4:14
g me this water so I won't get Jn 4:15
which the Son of Man will g you, Jn 6:27
Moses didn't g you the bread Jn 6:32
they said, "Sir, g us this bread Jn 6:34
bread that I will g for the life Jn 6:51
can this man g us His flesh to Jn 6:52
Didn't Moses g you the law? Jn 7:19
and told him, "G glory to God. Jn 9:24
I g them eternal life, and they Jn 10:28
ask from God, God will g You." Jn 11:22
He's the one I g the piece of Jn 13:26
or that he should g something to Jn 13:29
I g you a new commandment: Jn 13:34
and He will g you another Jn 14:16
you. My peace I g to you. I do Jn 14:27
I do not g to you as the world Jn 14:27
in My name, He will g you. Jn 15:16
in My name, He will g you. Jn 16:23
so He may g eternal life to all Jn 17:2
g evidence about the wrong; Jn 18:23
Jesus did not g him an answer. Jn 19:9
but what I have, I g to you: Ac 3:6
right for us to g up preaching Ac 6:2
didn't g him an inheritance in Ac 7:5
but He promised to g it to him Ac 7:5
God would g them deliverance Ac 7:25
living oracles to g to us. Ac 7:38
saying, "G me this power too, so Ac 8:19
he did not g the glory to God, Ac 12:23
that we can g as a reason for Ac 19:40
you up and to g you an Ac 20:32
blessed to g than to receive. Ac 20:35
I will g you a hearing whenever Ac 23:35
graciousness to g us a brief Ac 24:4
no one can g me up to them. Ac 25:11
custom to g any man up before Ac 25:16
an opportunity to g a defense Ac 25:16
he is thirsty, g him something Rm 12:20
tongue will g praise to God. Rm 14:11
each of us will g an account of Rm 14:12
G my greetings to Prisca and Rm 16:3
but I do g an opinion as one who 1Co 7:25
something for which I g thanks? 1Co 10:30
G no offense to the Jews or the 1Co 10:32
And I will g instructions about 1Co 11:34
and if I g my body to be burned, 1Co 13:3
those who ought to g me joy, 2Co 2:3
received mercy, we do not g up. 2Co 4:1
in our hearts to g the light 2Co 4:6
Therefore we do not g up; 2Co 4:16
g no opportunity for stumbling 2Co 6:3
warning, and I g warning—as 2Co 13:2
given that was able to g life, Gl 3:21
woman who does not g birth. Gl 4:27
proper time if we don't g up. Gl 6:9
would g you a spirit of wisdom Eph 1:17
and don't g the Devil an Eph 4:27
in order to g grace to those who Eph 4:29
I g thanks to my God for every Php 1:3
G my greetings to the brothers Col 4:15
to g recognition to those who 1Th 5:12
G thanks in everything, for this 1Th 5:18
peace Himself g you peace always 2Th 3:16
I g thanks to Christ Jesus our 1Tm 1:12
g your attention to public 1Tm 4:13
and g the adversary no 1Tm 5:14
the Lord will g you 2Tm 2:7
Judge, will g me on that day, 2Tm 4:8
to whom we must g an account. Heb 4:13
as those who will g an account, Heb 13:17
but you don't g them what the Jms 2:16
always be ready to g a defense 1Pt 3:15
They will g an account to the 1Pt 4:5
and God will g life to him— 1Jn 5:16
I will g the victor the right to Rv 2:7
and I will g you the crown of Rv 2:10
I will g the victor some of the Rv 2:17

I will also g him a white stone, Rv 2:17
and I will g to each of you Rv 2:23
I will g him authority over the Rv 2:26
I will also g him the morning Rv 2:28
I will g him the right to sit Rv 3:21
the living creatures g glory, Rv 4:9
and asked him to g me the little Rv 10:9
and to g the reward to Your Rv 11:18
in labor and agony to g birth. Rv 12:2
woman who was about to g birth, Rv 12:4
when she did g birth he might Rv 12:4
was permitted to g a spirit to Rv 13:15
Fear God and g Him glory, Rv 14:7
did not repent and g Him glory. Rv 16:9
and they g their power and Rv 17:13
and to g their kingdom to the Rv 17:17
g her that much torment and Rv 18:7
rejoice, and g Him glory, Rv 19:7
I will g to the thirsty from the Rv 21:6
the Lord God will g them light. Rv 22:5

GIVEN *(397)*

I have g you every seed-bearing Gn 1:29
⌊I have g⌋ every green plant for Gn 1:30
God has g me another child in Gn 4:25
plants, I have g you everything. Gn 9:3
You have g me no offspring, Gn 15:3
and feed were g to the camels, Gn 24:32
He has g him sheep and cattle, Gn 24:35
and he has g him everything he Gn 24:36
names his father had g them. Gn 26:18
have g him all of his relatives Gn 27:37
blessing his father had g him. Gn 27:41
unloved and has g me this ⌊son⌋ Gn 29:33
He has heard me and g me a son," Gn 30:6
"God has g me a good gift," Gn 30:20
father's herds and g them to me. Gn 31:9
has graciously g your servant." Gn 33:5
had not been g to him as a wife Gn 38:14
dream was g twice to Pharaoh, Gn 41:32
allotment Pharaoh had g them; Gn 47:22
are my sons God has g me here." Gn 48:9
straw has been g to your Ex 5:16
No straw will be g to you, Ex 5:18
bread the LORD has g you to eat. Ex 16:15
the LORD has g you the Sabbath; Ex 16:29
He has also g both him and Ex 35:34
The LORD has g them wisdom and Ex 36:1
commanded this to be g to them Lv 7:36
the LORD has g to them through Lv 10:11
been redeemed or g her freedom, Lv 19:20
I have g the Levites exclusively Nm 8:19
I have g them to you and your Nm 18:8
I have g all the Israelites' Nm 18:11
I have g the Levites every tenth Nm 18:21
For I have g them the tenth that Nm 18:24
tenth that I have g you as your Nm 18:26
into the land I have g them." Nm 20:12
land I have g the Israelites, Nm 20:24
Each is to be g its inheritance Nm 26:54
inheritance was g to them among Nm 26:62
that I have g the Israelites. Nm 27:12
this land be g to your servants Nm 32:5
the land the LORD has g them? Nm 32:7
the land the LORD had g them. Nm 32:9
because I have g you the land to Nm 33:53
commanded to be g to the nine Nm 34:13
because I have g Esau the hill Dt 2:5
I have g Ar as a possession Dt 2:9
I have g it as a possession to Dt 2:19
your God has g you this land to Dt 3:18
remain in the cities I have g Dt 3:19
possession that I have g you. Dt 3:20
for the good land He has g you. Dt 8:10
possess the land I have g you'; Dt 9:23
g you to possess all the days Dt 12:1
the LORD your God has g you. Dt 12:15
your herd or flock He has g you, Dt 12:21
the LORD your God has g you. Dt 16:17
are to be g the shoulder, Dt 18:3
the LORD your God has g you. Dt 20:14
garment⌋ he has g as security. Dt 24:12
that You, LORD, have g me. Dt 26:10
LORD your God has g you and your Dt 26:11
I have also g it to the Levite, Dt 26:13
land You have g us as You swore Dt 26:15
flock will be g to your enemies, Dt 28:31
will be g to another people Dt 28:32
the LORD your God has g you. Dt 28:52
LORD your God has g you during Dt 28:53
the LORD has not g you a mind to Dt 29:4
unless the LORD had g them up? Dt 32:30
I have g you every place where Jos 1:3
rest, as ⌊He has g⌋ you, and Jos 1:15
the LORD has g you this land Jos 2:9
For the LORD has g you the city. Jos 6:16
command that He had g Joshua. Jos 8:27
the LORD's servant had g them: Jos 13:8
Moses had g the inheritance Jos 14:3
of the land was g to the Levites Jos 14:4
Since you have g me land in the Jos 15:19
Moses that we be g cities to Jos 21:2
Now that He has g your brothers Jos 22:4
Moses had g ⌊territory⌋ to half Jos 22:7
but Joshua had g ⌊territory⌋ to Jos 22:7
after the LORD had g Israel rest Jos 23:1
the LORD your God has g you. Jos 23:13
the LORD your God has g you. Jos 23:15
this good land He has g you." Jos 23:16
which had been g to his son Jos 24:33
Since you have g me land in the Jdg 1:15
commands He had g their fathers Jdg 3:4
for I have g it into your hand. Jdg 7:9
I have g my word to the LORD and Jdg 11:35
have g your word to the LORD. Jdg 11:36
and his wife was g to one of the Jdg 14:20
wife and g her to another Jdg 15:6
seven sons, has g birth to him." Ru 4:15
he lives, he is g to the LORD." 1Sm 1:28
the one she has g to the LORD." 1Sm 2:20
You've g birth to a son!" 1Sm 4:20
you today and has g it to your 1Sm 15:28
she was g to Adriel the 1Sm 18:19
and let it be g to the young men 1Sm 25:27
me be g a place in one of the 1Sm 27:5
of your hand and g it to your 1Sm 28:17
with what the LORD has g us. 1Sm 30:23
and the LORD had g him rest on 2Sm 7:1
I have g to your master's 2Sm 9:9
I would have g you even more. 2Sm 12:8
Ahithophel has g this time is 2Sm 17:7
for Ahithophel has g this advice 2Sm 17:21
I would have g you 10 silver 2Sm 18:11
You have g me the shield of Your 2Sm 22:36
Shunammite be g to your brother 1Kg 2:21
the judgment the king had g, 1Kg 3:28
my God has now g me rest all 1Kg 5:4
He has g David a wise son to be 1Kg 5:7
He has g rest to His people 1Kg 8:56
towns that Solomon had g him, 1Kg 9:12
are these towns you've g me, 1Kg 9:13
what he had g her out of his 1Kg 10:13
ordered that he ⌊be g⌋ food, 1Kg 11:18
the advice the elders had g him 1Kg 12:13
the man of God had g by the word 1Kg 13:5
The LORD has g him to the lion, 1Kg 13:26
Let two bulls be g to us. 1Kg 18:23
the LORD had g victory to Aram. 2Kg 5:1
of dirt be g to your servant, 2Kg 5:17
voluntarily g for the LORD's 2Kg 12:4
was g to those doing the work, 2Kg 12:14
and the warnings He had g them. 2Kg 17:15
the priest has g me a book," 2Kg 22:10
allowance was g to him by the 2Kg 25:30
his birthright was g to the sons 1Ch 5:1
the birthright was g to Joseph. 1Ch 5:2
to the regulations ⌊g⌋ to them. 1Ch 6:32
They were g Hebron in the land 1Ch 6:55
the city were g to Caleb son 1Ch 6:56
sons were g: Hebron (a city 1Ch 6:57
they were g⌋ Geba and its 1Ch 6:60
the Kohathites were g towns from 1Ch 6:66
pasturelands ⌊were g⌋ to the 1Ch 6:70
that thanks be g to the LORD 1Ch 16:7
hasn't He g you rest on every 1Ch 22:18
God of Israel has g rest to His 1Ch 23:25
were ⌊g⌋ by the promises of God 1Ch 25:5
God had g Heman fourteen sons 1Ch 25:5
the LORD has g me many sons— 1Ch 28:5
for they had g to the LORD with 1Ch 29:9
we have g You only what comes 1Ch 29:14
have willingly g all these 1Ch 29:17
and knowledge are g to you. 2Ch 1:12
any design that may be g him. 2Ch 2:14
father had g them many gifts 2Ch 21:3
the blood they had been g. 2Ch 35:11
they might be g to the divisions 2Ch 35:12
has g me all the kingdoms of the 2Ch 36:23
has g me all the kingdoms of the Ezr 1:2
to all that was g as a freewill Ezr 1:6
authorization ⌊g⌋ them by King Ezr 3:7
let it be g to them every day Ezr 6:9
LORD, the God of Israel, had g. Ezr 7:6
have willingly g to the God of Ezr 7:15
offerings g by the people Ezr 7:16
the articles g to you for the Ezr 7:19
God has g us new life and light Ezr 9:8
that the LORD had g Israel. Neh 8:1
the law of God g through God's Neh 10:29
God had g them great joy. Neh 12:43
for the Levites had not been g, Neh 13:10
is to be g to another woman Est 1:19
she was g whatever she requested Est 2:13
and people are g to you to do Est 3:11
the kingdom, will be g to you." Est 5:3
you ask will be g to you. Est 5:6
him in rank and g him a high Est 5:11
have been g to Mordecai for this Est 6:3
you ask will be g to you. Est 7:2
I have g Haman's estate to Est 8:7
you ask will be g to you. Est 9:12
Why is light g to one burdened Jb 3:20
⌊Why is life g⌋ to a man whose Jb 3:23
land was g to them alone when Jb 15:19
You have g me the shield of Your Ps 18:35
have g him his heart's desire Ps 21:2
I was g over to You at birth; Ps 22:10
You have g us a wine to drink Ps 60:3
have g a signal flag to those Ps 60:4
You have g a heritage to those Ps 61:5
They will be g over to the power Ps 63:10
May gold from Sheba be g to him. Ps 72:15
the earth He has g to the human Ps 115:16
LORD is God and has g us light. Ps 118:27
You have g me hope through it. Ps 119:49
Your promise has g me life. Ps 119:50
for You have g me life through Ps 119:93
desires will be g to him. Pr 10:24
God has g people this miserable Ec 1:13
that God has g people to keep Ec 3:10
days of his life God has g him, Ec 5:18
God has also g riches and wealth Ec 5:19
exists was g its name long ago, Ec 6:10
which has been g to you under Ec 9:9
sayings are g by one Shepherd Ec 12:11
the LORD has g me to be signs Is 8:18
for us, a son will be g to us, Is 9:6
answer will be g to the Is 14:32
not been in labor or g birth. Is 23:4
If it is g to one who can read Is 29:11
the document is g to one who Is 29:12
of Lebanon will be g to it, Is 35:2
The Lord GOD has g Me the tongue Is 50:4
of man who is g up like grass? Is 51:12
her away and had g her a Jr 3:8
the land I have g your ancestors Jr 3:18
Whatever I have g them will be Jr 8:13
He has g us poisoned water to Jr 8:14
have g the love of My life into Jr 12:7
won't be g him because Jr 16:7
I have even g him the wild Jr 27:6
After I had g the purchase Jr 32:16
was g a loaf of bread each day Jr 37:21
lives, who has g us this life, I Jr 38:16
the LORD has g it a command? Jr 47:7
allowance was g to him by the Jr 52:34
this land has been g to us as a Ezk 11:15
which I have g to the fire as Ezk 15:6
the gold and silver I had g you, Ezk 16:17
into the land I had g ⌊them⌋— Ezk 20:15
The sword is g to be polished, Ezk 21:11
are g over to the sword with Ezk 21:12
I have g the judgment to Him. Ezk 21:27
have g you to the beasts of the Ezk 29:5
have g him the land of Egypt as Ezk 29:20
the land has been g to us as a Ezk 33:24
field I have g to wild animals Ezk 33:27
have been g to us to devour! Ezk 35:12
us be g vegetables to eat and Dn 1:12
because You have g me wisdom and Dn 2:23
of heaven has g you sovereignty Dn 2:37
and let him be g the mind of an Dn 4:16
been divided and g to the Medes Dn 5:28
like a man, and g a human mind. Dn 7:4
heads and was g authority to Dn 7:6

body destroyed and **g** over to the Dn 7:11
He was **g** authority to rule, Dn 7:14
and a judgment was **g** in favor of Dn 7:22
heaven will be **g** to the people, Dn 7:27
daily sacrifice, will be **g** over. Dn 8:12
She will be **g** up, together with Dn 11:6
honors will not be **g** to him, Dn 11:21
that her lovers have **g** her. Hs 2:12
from the land I have **g** them. Am 9:15
she who is in labor has **g** birth; Mc 5:3
asking, and it will be **g** to you. Mt 7:7
to God who had **g** such authority Mt 9:8
For you will be **g** what to say at Mt 10:19
no sign will be **g** to it except Mt 12:39
have been **g** for you to know Mt 13:11
but it has not been **g** to them. Mt 13:11
more⌋ will be **g** to him, and he Mt 13:12
on a platter and **g** to the girl, Mt 14:11
no sign will be **g** to it except Mt 16:4
but only those it has been **g** to. Mt 19:11
away from you and **g** to a nation Mt 21:43
marry nor are **g** in marriage but Mt 22:30
more will be **g**, and he will have Mt 25:29
a great deal and **g** to the poor." Mt 26:9
His betrayer had **g** them a sign: Mt 26:48
has been **g** to Me in heaven Mt 28:18
has, it will be **g**, and from the Mk 4:25
she should be **g** something to eat Mk 5:43
What is this wisdom **g** to Him, Mk 6:2
himself had **g** orders to arrest Mk 6:17
will be **g** to this generation! Mk 8:12
marry nor are **g** in marriage but Mk 12:25
whatever is **g** to you in that Mk 13:11
300 denarii and **g** to the poor." Mk 14:5
betrayer had **g** them a signal. Mk 14:44
He has **g** us the privilege, Lk 1:73
the name **g** by the angel before Lk 2:21
it has been **g** over to me, Lk 4:6
the prophet Isaiah was **g** to Him, Lk 4:17
Give, and it will be **g** to you; Lk 6:38
God have been **g** for you to know Lk 8:10
has, more will be **g** to him; Lk 8:18
that she be **g** something to eat. Lk 8:55
I have **g** you the authority to Lk 10:19
asking, and it will be **g** to you. Lk 11:9
no sign will be **g** to it except Lk 11:29
of everyone who has been **g** much. Lk 12:48
slaves he had **g** the money to so Lk 19:15
who has, more will be **g**; Lk 19:26
age marry and are **g** in marriage. Lk 20:34
marry nor are **g** in marriage. Lk 20:35
is My body, which is **g** for you. Lk 22:19
the law was **g** through Moses; Jn 1:17
thing unless it's **g** to him from Jn 3:27
Son and has **g** all things into Jn 3:35
that Jacob had **g** his son Joseph. Jn 4:5
no one but has **g** all judgment to Jn 5:22
the Father has **g** Me to Jn 5:36
of those He has **g** Me but should Jn 6:39
Moses has **g** you circumcision— Jn 7:22
Father, who has **g** them to Me, is Jn 10:29
Pharisees had **g** orders that if Jn 11:57
300 denarii and **g** to the poor?" Jn 12:5
who sent Me has **g** Me a command Jn 12:49
the Father had **g** everything into Jn 13:3
For I have **g** you an example that Jn 13:15
when she has **g** birth to a child Jn 16:21
life to all You have **g** Him. Jn 17:2
things You have **g** to Me are from Jn 17:7
that You gave Me, I have **g** them. Jn 17:8
but for those You have **g** Me, Jn 17:9
by Your name that You have **g** Me, Jn 17:11
by Your name that You have **g** Me. Jn 17:12
I have **g** them Your word. Jn 17:14
I have **g** them the glory You have Jn 17:22
them the glory You have **g** Me. Jn 17:22
those You have **g** Me to be with Jn 17:24
which You have **g** Me because You Jn 17:24
one of those You have **g** Me." Jn 18:9
the cup the Father has **g** Me?" Jn 18:11
it hadn't been **g** you from above. Jn 19:11
after He had **g** orders through Ac 1:2
to have a murderer **g** to you. Ac 3:14
through Him has **g** him this Ac 3:16
name under heaven **g** to people by Ac 4:12
whom God has **g** to those who obey Ac 5:32
Holy Spirit was **g** through the Ac 8:18
After he had **g** permission, Ac 21:40
money would be **g** to him by Paul. Ac 24:26
has graciously **g** you all those Ac 27:24
the Holy Spirit who was **g** to us. Rm 5:5
Or who has ever first **g** to Him, Rm 11:35
For by the grace **g** to me, I tell Rm 12:3
According to the grace **g** to us, Rm 12:6
because of the grace **g** me by God Rm 15:15
God's grace **g** to you in Christ 1Co 1:4
has been freely **g** to us by God. 1Co 2:12
has the role the Lord has **g**. 1Co 3:5
to God's grace that was **g** to me, 1Co 3:10
For her hair is **g** to her as a 1Co 11:15
the Spirit is **g** to each person 1Co 12:7
to one is **g** a message of wisdom 1Co 12:8
thanks may be **g** by many on our 2Co 1:11
Macedonia and be **g** a start by 2Co 1:16
sealed us and **g** us the Spirit as 2Co 1:22
live are always **g** over to death 2Co 4:11
He has **g** to the poor; His 2Co 9:9
thorn in the flesh was **g** to me, 2Co 12:7
the grace that had been **g** to me, Gl 2:9
a law had been **g** that was able Gl 3:21
Christ might be **g** to those who Gl 3:22
out your eyes and **g** them to me. Gl 4:15
and every title **g**, not only in Eph 1:21
grace that was **g** to me by the Eph 3:7
This grace was **g** to me—the Eph 3:8
Now grace was **g** to each one of Eph 4:7
message may be **g** to me when I Eph 6:19
For it has been **g** to you on Php 1:29
that was **g** to me for you, Col 1:25
has loved us and **g** us eternal 2Th 2:16
was **g** to you through prophecy, 1Tm 4:14
For God has not **g** us a spirit of 2Tm 1:7
was **g** to us in Christ Jesus 2Tm 1:9
For if Joshua had **g** them rest, Heb 4:8
and it will be **g** to him. Jms 1:5
He has **g** us a new birth into a 1Pt 1:3
divine power has **g** us everything 2Pt 1:3
By these He has **g** us very great 2Pt 1:4
Lord and Savior ⌊**g**⌋ through your 2Pt 3:2
to the wisdom **g** to him, 2Pt 3:15
a love the Father has **g** us, 1Jn 3:1
is from the Spirit He has **g** us. 1Jn 3:24
He has **g** to us from His Spirit. 1Jn 4:13
that He has **g** about His Son. 1Jn 5:9
that God has **g** about His Son. 1Jn 5:10
God has **g** us eternal life, 1Jn 5:11
come and has **g** us understanding 1Jn 5:20
crown was **g** to him, and he went Rv 6:2
And a large sword was **g** to him. Rv 6:4
Authority was **g** to them over a Rv 6:8
white robe was **g** to each of them Rv 6:11
seven trumpets were **g** to them. Rv 8:2
He was **g** a large amount of Rv 8:3
shaft of the abyss was **g** to him. Rv 9:1
and power was **g** to them like the Rv 9:3
Then I was **g** a measuring reed Rv 11:1
because it is **g** to the nations, Rv 11:2
The woman was **g** two wings of a Rv 12:14
A mouth was **g** to him to speak Rv 13:5
He was also **g** authority to act Rv 13:5
He was also **g** authority over Rv 13:7
to be **g** a mark on his right hand Rv 13:16
was **g** the power to burn people Rv 16:8
on them who were **g** authority to Rv 20:4

GIVER *(1)*

for God loves a cheerful **g**. 2Co 9:7

GIVES *(115)*

your fathers, and **g** it to you, Ex 13:11
If his master **g** him a wife and Ex 21:4
When a man **g** his neighbor money Ex 22:7
When a man **g** his neighbor a Ex 22:10
pregnant and **g** birth to a male Lv 12:2
But if she **g** birth to a female Lv 12:5
in Israel who **g** any of his Lv 20:2
way when that man **g** any of his Lv 20:4
any of these he **g** to the LORD Lv 27:9
what each one **g** to the priest Nm 5:10
until the LORD **g** rest to your Dt 3:20
LORD your God **g** you the power to Dt 8:18
and He **g** you rest from all the Dt 12:10
and **g** you all the land He Dt 19:8
when that man **g** what he has to Dt 21:16
conduct, and **g** her a bad name, Dt 22:14
LORD your God **g** you rest from Dt 25:19
until the LORD **g** our brothers Jos 1:15
when the LORD **g** us the land." Jos 2:14
and the LORD **g** them to me, Jdg 11:9
Anyone who **g** a wife to a Jdg 21:18
barren woman **g** birth to seven, 1Sm 2:5
LORD brings death and **g** life; 1Sm 2:6
brings poverty and **g** wealth; 1Sm 2:7
noblemen and **g** them a throne 1Sm 2:8
g me vengeance and casts down 2Sm 22:48
Araunah **g** everything here to the 2Sm 24:23
The LORD **g**, and the LORD takes Jb 1:21
He **g** rain to the earth and sends Jb 5:10
He **g** them a sense of security, Jb 24:23
of the Almighty **g** me life. Jb 33:4
who **g** us more understanding than Jb 35:11
but He **g** justice to the Jb 36:6
He **g** food in abundance. Jb 36:31
trouble, and **g** birth to deceit. Ps 7:14
He **g** me vengeance and subdues Ps 18:47
g great victories to His king; Ps 18:50
that the LORD **g** victory to His Ps 20:6
The LORD **g** His people strength; Ps 29:11
The God of Israel **g** power and Ps 68:35
The LORD **g** grace and glory; Ps 84:11
He **g** the childless woman a Ps 113:9
light and **g** understanding to Ps 119:130
certainly He **g** sleep to the one Ps 127:2
He **g** food to every creature. Ps 136:25
the One who **g** victory to kings, Ps 144:10
He **g** names to all of them. Ps 147:4
For the LORD **g** wisdom; Pr 2:6
but **g** grace to the humble. Pr 3:34
witness who **g** false testimony, Pr 6:19
One person **g** freely, yet gains Pr 11:24
and the one who **g** a drink of Pr 11:25
The one who **g** an answer before Pr 18:13
is a friend of one who **g** gifts. Pr 19:6
person's insight **g** him patience, Pr 19:11
He who **g** an honest answer gives Pr 24:26
an honest answer **g** a kiss on the Pr 24:26
The one who **g** to the poor will Pr 28:27
A fool **g** full vent to his anger, Pr 29:11
the LORD **g** light to the eyes of Pr 29:13
in His sight, He **g** wisdom, Ec 2:26
but to the sinner He **g** the task Ec 2:26
God **g** a man riches, wealth, and Ec 6:2
days that God **g** him under the Ec 8:15
When the LORD **g** you rest from Is 14:3
He **g** wonderful advice; Is 28:29
advice; He **g** great wisdom. Is 28:29
He **g** strength to the weary and Is 40:29
who **g** breath to the people on it Is 42:5
our God, who **g** the rain, both Jr 5:24
doe in the field **g** birth and Jr 14:5
The One who **g** the sun for light Jr 31:35
bread, but no one **g** them ⌊any⌋. Lm 4:4
g his bread to the hungry and Ezk 18:7
He **g** his bread to the hungry and Ezk 18:16
the prince **g** a gift to each of Ezk 46:16
But if he **g** a gift from his Ezk 46:17
He **g** wisdom to the wise and Dn 2:21
He **g** it to anyone He wants and Dn 4:17
and He **g** it to anyone He wants. Dn 4:25
and He **g** it to anyone He wants." Dn 4:32
this inscription and **g** me its Dn 5:7
because He **g** you the autumn rain Jl 2:23
He **g** orders to his officers; Nah 2:5
Woe to him who **g** his neighbors Hab 2:15
and it **g** light for all who are Mt 5:15
And whoever **g** just a cup of cold Mt 10:42
even your accent **g** you away." Mt 26:73
And whoever **g** you a cup of water Mk 9:41
true light, who **g** light to Jn 1:9
since He **g** the Spirit without Jn 3:34
raises the dead and **g** them life, Jn 5:21
so the Son also **g** life to anyone Jn 5:21
the testimony He **g** about Me is Jn 5:32
but My Father **g** you the real Jn 6:32
heaven and **g** life to the world. Jn 6:33
the Father **g** Me will come to Me Jn 6:37
Spirit is the One who **g** life. Jn 6:63
not give to you as the world **g**. Jn 14:27
since He Himself **g** everyone life Ac 17:25
who **g** life to the dead and calls Rm 4:17
if she **g** herself to another man Rm 7:3
if she **g** herself to another man, Rm 7:3
Lord, since he **g** thanks to God; Rm 14:6
but only God who **g** the growth. 1Co 3:7
But God **g** it a body as He wants, 1Co 15:38
who **g** us the victory through our 1Co 15:57

was like the g of beryl, Ezk 1:16
with a g like awe-inspiring Ezk 1:22
up, I saw a g like amber, with Ezk 1:27
bright, like the g of amber. Ezk 8:2
wheels was like the g of beryl. Ezk 10:9
and feet like the g of polished Dn 10:6

GLEAMING *(1)*
two articles of fine g bronze, Ezr 8:27

GLEAMS *(1)*
when it g in the cup and goes Pr 23:31

GLEAN *(3)*
you must not g what is left. Dt 24:21
in the field and g the vineyards Jb 24:6
G as thoroughly as a vine the Jr 6:9

GLEANED *(2)*
mother-in-law saw what she had g. Ru 2:18
as if one had g heads of grain Is 17:5

GLEANING *(3)*
Is not the g of Ephraim better Jdg 8:2
like a g after a grape harvest. Is 24:13
gathered after the g of the Mc 7:1

GLEANINGS *(4)*
or gather the g of your harvest. Lv 19:9
or gather the g of your harvest. Lv 23:22
Only g will be left in Israel, Is 17:6
wouldn't they leave some g? Jr 49:9

GLEE *(1)*
I stumbled, they gathered in g; Ps 35:15

GLIDING *(1)*
for my love g past my lips Sg 7:9

GLIMMER *(1)*
turned my last g of hope into Is 21:4

GLISTEN *(1)*
g of rain on sprouting grass. 2Sm 23:4

GLISTENING *(1)*
and its feathers with g gold. Ps 68:13

GLOAT *(8)*
of the uncircumcised will g. 2Sm 1:20
do not let my enemies g over me. Ps 25:2
how long will the wicked g? Ps 94:3
Don't g when your enemy falls, Pr 24:17
letting the enemy g over you and Lm 2:17
not g over your brother in the Ob 12
not g over their misery in the Ob 13
on the earth will g over them Rv 11:10

GLOATING *(1)*
g as if ready to secretly devour Hab 3:14

GLOATS *(1)*
after he is on his way, he g. Pr 20:14

GLOOM *(14)*
May darkness and g reclaim it, Jb 3:5
go to a land of darkness and g, Jb 10:21
Others sat in darkness and g— Ps 107:10
darkness and g and broke their Ps 107:14
wicked is like the darkest g; Pr 4:19
and the g of affliction, Is 8:22
g of the distressed land will Is 9:1
brings darkest g and makes thick Jr 13:16
like slippery paths in the g. Jr 23:12
of darkness and g, a day of Jl 2:2
even g without any brightness in Am 5:20
of darkness and g, a day of Zph 1:15
fire, to darkness, g, and storm, Heb 12:18
The g of darkness has been 2Pt 2:17

GLOOMY *(2)*
deepest darkness, g and chaotic, Jb 10:22
for ore in the g darkness. Jb 28:3

GLORIES *(1)*
and the g that would follow 1Pt 1:11

GLORIFIED *(32)*
I will be g in him." Is 49:3
Holy One of Israel, has g you." Is 55:5
One of Israel, who has g you. Is 60:9
of My hands, so that I may be g. Is 60:21
the LORD be g, so that we can Is 66:5
and honored and g Him who lives Dn 4:34
But you have not g the God who Dn 5:23
be pleased with it and be g," Hg 1:8
and they g God, saying, Lk 7:16
Jesus had not yet been g. Jn 7:39
Son of God may be g through it." Jn 11:4
when Jesus was g, then they Jn 12:16
come for the Son of Man to be g. Jn 12:23
I have g it, and I will glorify Jn 12:28
the Son of Man is g, and God is Jn 13:31
glorified, and God is g in Him. Jn 13:31
God is g in Him, God will also Jn 13:32
the Father may be g in the Son. Jn 14:13
My Father is g by this: Jn 15:8
I have g You on the earth by Jn 17:4
and I have been g in them. Jn 17:10
our fathers, has g His Servant Ac 3:13
Then they g God, saying, "So God Ac 11:18
they rejoiced and g the message Ac 13:48
heard it, they g God and said, Ac 21:20
that we may also be g with Him. Rm 8:17
those He justified, He also g. Rm 8:30
And they g God because of me. Gl 1:24
He comes to be g by His saints 2Th 1:10
our Lord Jesus will be g by you, 2Th 1:12
God may be g through Jesus 1Pt 4:11
As much as she g herself and Rv 18:7

GLORIFIES *(2)*
and g Himself through Israel. Is 44:23
—He is the One who g Me. Jn 8:54

GLORIFY *(27)*
the king's mind to g the house Ezr 7:27
My lips will g You because Your Ps 63:3
all nations! G Him, all peoples Ps 117:1
I will g My beautiful house. Is 60:7
and I will g My dwelling place. Is 60:13
planted by the LORD, to g Him. Is 61:3
exalt, and g the King of heaven Dn 4:37
was restored and began to g God. Lk 13:13
he began to g God, saying, "This Lk 23:47
"If I g Myself," Jesus answered, Jn 8:54
Father, g Your name!" Jn 12:28
it, and I will g it again!" Jn 12:28
God will also g Him in Himself Jn 13:32
Himself and will g Him at once. Jn 13:32
He will g Me, because He will Jn 16:14
G Your Son so that the Son may Jn 17:1
Son so that the Son may g You, Jn 17:1
g Me in Your presence with that Jn 17:5
kind of death he would g God. Jn 21:19
did not g Him as God or show Rm 1:21
so that you may g the God and Rm 15:6
Gentiles may g God for His mercy Rm 15:9
therefore g God in your body. 1Co 6:20
they will g God for your 2Co 9:13
g God in a day of visitation. 1Pt 2:12
but should g God with that name. 1Pt 4:16
will not fear and g Your name? Rv 15:4

GLORIFYING *(3)*
g and praising God for all they Lk 2:20
lying on, and went home g God. Lk 5:25
he began to follow Him, g God. Lk 18:43

GLORIOUS *(51)*
Your right hand is g in power. Ex 15:6
Who is like You, g in holiness, Ex 15:11
by fearing this g and awesome Dt 28:58
and famous and g in all the 1Ch 22:5
thanks and praise Your g name. 1Ch 29:13
Praise Your g name, and may it Neh 9:5
He displayed the g wealth of his Est 1:4
for them his g wealth and his Est 5:11
the royal daughter is all g, Ps 45:13
of His name; make His praise g. Ps 66:2
May His g name be praised Ps 72:19
G things are said about you, Ps 87:3
the crown he wears will be g." Ps 132:18
speak of Your g splendor and Ps 145:5
acts and of the g splendor of Ps 145:12
Gray hair is a g crown; Pr 16:31
LORD, defying His g presence. Is 3:8
LORD will be beautiful and g, Is 4:2
and His resting place will be g. Is 11:10
LORD, for He has done g things. Is 12:5
and there your g chariots will Is 22:18
to desecrate all ⌊its⌋ g beauty, Is 23:9
His⌋ instruction and make it g. Is 42:21
You will be a g crown in the Is 62:3
sent His g arm at Moses' right Is 63:12
way to make a g name for Is 63:14
yourselves from her g breasts. Is 66:11
for your g crowns have fallen Jr 13:18
Don't disdain Your g throne. Jr 14:21
is shattered, the g staff! Jr 48:17
the g ⌊trees⌋ are destroyed! Zch 11:2
Son of Man sits on His g throne, Mt 19:28
over all the g things He was Lk 13:17
into the g freedom of God's Rm 8:21
of the Spirit not be more g? 2Co 3:8
what had been g is not glorious 2Co 3:10
glorious is not g in this case 2Co 3:10
if what was fading away was g, 2Co 3:11
endures will be even more g. 2Co 3:11
the praise of His g grace that Eph 1:6
Christ, the g Father, would Eph 1:17
what are the g riches of His Eph 1:18
into the likeness of His g body, Php 3:21
according to His g might, for Col 1:11
Gentiles the g wealth of this Col 1:27
and from His g strength, 2Th 1:9
based on the g gospel of the 1Tm 1:11
faith in our g Lord Jesus Christ Jms 2:1
with inexpressible and g joy, 1Pt 1:8
when they blaspheme the g ones; 2Pt 2:10
and blaspheme g beings. Jd 8

GLORY *(308)*
all about my g in Egypt and Gn 45:13
I will receive g by means of Ex 14:4
and I will receive g by means of Ex 14:17
I receive g through Pharaoh, Ex 14:18
see the LORD's g because He has Ex 16:7
a cloud, the LORD's g appeared. Ex 16:10
The g of the LORD settled on Ex 24:16
the LORD's g to the Israelites Ex 24:17
brother Aaron, for g and beauty. Ex 28:2
to ⌊give them⌋ g and beauty. Ex 28:40
will be consecrated by My g. Ex 29:43
Please, let me see Your g." Ex 33:18
and when My g passes by, I will Ex 33:22
and the g of the LORD filled the Ex 40:34
and the g of the LORD filled the Ex 40:35
the g of the LORD may appear Lv 9:6
and the g of the LORD appeared Lv 9:23
I will reveal My g before all Lv 10:3
g of the LORD appeared to all Nm 14:10
is filled with the LORD's g, Nm 14:21
have seen My g and the signs I Nm 14:22
g of the LORD appeared to the Nm 16:19
and the LORD's g appeared. Nm 16:42
and the g of the LORD appeared Nm 20:6
shown us His g and greatness, Dt 5:24
praise, fame, and g, and that Dt 26:19
My son, give g to the LORD, the Jos 7:19
"The g has departed from Israel," 1Sm 4:21
"The g has departed from Israel," 1Sm 4:22
Give g to Israel's God, and 1Sm 6:5
for the g of the LORD filled the 1Kg 8:11
Enjoy your g and stay at home. 2Kg 14:10
Declare His g among the nations, 1Ch 16:24
to the LORD g and strength. 1Ch 16:28
to the LORD the g of His name; 1Ch 16:29
power and the g and the splendor 1Ch 29:11
wealth, or g, or for the life 2Ch 1:11
wealth, and g, such that it was 2Ch 1:12
for the g of the LORD filled 2Ch 5:14
and the g of the LORD filled the 2Ch 7:1
because the g of the LORD filled 2Ch 7:2
and the g of the LORD came 2Ch 7:3
that you will get g. 2Ch 25:19
had abundant riches and g, 2Ch 32:27
yourself with honor and g. Jb 40:10
around me, my g, and the One who Ps 3:3
crowned him with g and honor. Ps 8:5
heavens declare the g of God, Ps 19:1
His g is great through Your Ps 21:5
Then the King of g will come in. Ps 24:7
Who is this King of g? Ps 24:8
Then the King of g will come in. Ps 24:9
Who is He, this King of g? Ps 24:10
of Hosts, He is the King of g. Ps 24:10
the place where Your g resides. Ps 26:8
give the LORD g and strength. Ps 29:1
the LORD the g due His name; Ps 29:2
God of g thunders—the LORD, Ps 29:3
In His temple all cry, "G!" Ps 29:9
like the g of the pastures, Ps 37:20
let Your g be above the whole Ps 57:5
let Your g be over the whole Ps 57:11
salvation and g depend on God; Ps 62:7
to see Your strength and Your g. Ps 63:2
Sing the g of His name; Ps 66:2
earth is filled with His g. Ps 72:19
You will take me up in g. Ps 73:24
us—for the g of Your name. Ps 79:9
The LORD gives grace and g; Ps 84:11

so that **g** may dwell in our land. Ps 85:9
Declare His **g** among the nations, Ps 96:3
to the LORD **g** and strength. Ps 96:7
to the LORD the **g** of His name; Ps 96:8
all the peoples see His **g**. Ps 97:6
the kings of the earth Your **g**, Ps 102:15
He will appear in His **g**. Ps 102:16
May the **g** of the LORD endure Ps 104:31
exchanged their **g** for the image Ps 106:20
let Your **g** be over the whole Ps 108:5
the nations, His **g** above the Ps 113:4
Your name give **g** because of Your Ps 115:1
for the LORD's **g** is great. Ps 138:5
speak of the **g** of Your kingdom Ps 145:11
godly celebrate in triumphal **g**; Ps 149:5
The **g** of young men is their Pr 20:29
It is the **g** of God to conceal a Pr 25:2
a matter and the **g** of kings to Pr 25:2
honey, or to seek **g** after glory. Pr 25:27
honey, or to seek glory after **g**. Pr 25:27
be the pride and **g** of Israel's Is 4:2
will be a canopy over all the **g**, Is 4:5
His **g** fills the whole earth. Is 6:3
king of Assyria and all his **g**. Is 8:7
a burning fire under its **g**. Is 10:16
destroy the **g** of its forests Is 10:18
the **g** of the pride of the Is 13:19
all the **g** of Kedar will be gone. Is 21:16
display His⌋ **g** in the presence Is 24:23
The **g** of Lebanon will be given Is 35:2
They will see the **g** of the LORD, Is 35:2
And the **g** of the LORD will Is 40:5
I will not give My **g** to another, Is 42:8
Let them give **g** to the LORD, Is 42:12
by My name and created for My **g**. Is 43:7
and find **g** through the LORD. Is 45:25
I will not give My **g** to another. Is 48:11
and the LORD's **g** will be your Is 58:8
the west, and His **g** in the east; Is 59:19
the **g** of the LORD shines over Is 60:1
and His **g** will appear over you. Is 60:2
g of Lebanon will come to you Is 60:13
and all kings your **g**. Is 62:2
they will come and see My **g**. Is 66:18
heard of My fame or seen My **g**. Is 66:19
will proclaim My **g** among the Is 66:19
exchanged their **G** for useless Jr 2:11
praise, and **g**, but they would Jr 13:11
Give **g** to the LORD your God Jr 13:16
A throne of **g** on high from the Jr 17:12
and **g** before all the nations of Jr 33:9
Come down from **g**; sit on parched Jr 48:18
down Israel's **g** from heaven to Lm 2:1
of the form of the LORD's **g**. Ezk 1:28
praise the **g** of the LORD in His Ezk 3:12
The LORD's **g** was present there, Ezk 3:23
like the **g** I had seen by the Ezk 3:23
I saw the **g** of the God of Israel Ezk 8:4
Then the **g** of the God of Israel Ezk 9:3
Then the **g** of the LORD rose from Ezk 10:4
the brightness of the LORD's **g**. Ezk 10:4
the **g** of the LORD moved away Ezk 10:18
The **g** of the God of Israel was Ezk 10:19
and the **g** of the God of Israel Ezk 11:22
The **g** of the LORD rose up from Ezk 11:23
I will display My **g** within you. Ezk 28:22
are you like in **g** and greatness Ezk 31:18
on the day I display My **g**." Ezk 39:13
will display My **g** among the Ezk 39:21
and I saw the **g** of the God of Ezk 43:2
and the earth shone with His **g**. Ezk 43:2
The **g** of the LORD entered the Ezk 43:4
and the **g** of the LORD filled the Ezk 43:5
and the **g** of the LORD filled His Ezk 44:4
power, strength, and **g**. Dn 2:37
and to display my majestic **g**?" Dn 4:30
to me for the **g** of my kingdom. Dn 4:36
greatness, **g**, and majesty to Dn 5:18
throne and his **g** was taken from Dn 5:20
to rule, and **g**, and a kingdom; Dn 7:14
for the **g** of the kingdom; Dn 11:20
Ephraim's **g** will fly away like a Hs 9:11
will mourn over it, over its **g**. Hs 10:5
the knowledge of the LORD's **g**, Hab 2:14
with disgrace instead of **g**. Hab 2:16
disgrace will cover your **g**. Hab 2:16
saw this house in its former **g**? Hg 2:3
I will fill this house with **g**," Hg 2:7
The final **g** of this house will Hg 2:9
and I will be the **g** within it." Zch 2:5
sent Me for ⌊His⌋ **g** against the Zch 2:8
for their **g** is destroyed. Zch 11:3
so that the **g** of David's house Zch 12:7
house and the **g** of Jerusalem's Zch 12:7
works and give **g** to your Father Mt 5:16
and the power and the **g** forever. Mt 6:13
and gave **g** to God who had Mt 9:8
And they gave **g** to the God of Mt 15:31
angels in the **g** of His Father, Mt 16:27
heaven with power and great **g**. Mt 24:30
the Son of Man comes in His **g**, Mt 25:31
will sit on the throne of His **g**. Mt 25:31
all astounded and gave **g** to God, Mk 2:12
He comes in the **g** of His Father Mk 8:38
and at Your left in Your **g**." Mk 10:37
clouds with great power and **g**. Mk 13:26
and the **g** of the Lord shone Lk 2:9
G to God in the highest heaven, Lk 2:14
Gentiles and **g** to Your people Lk 2:32
and they were giving **g** to God. Lk 5:26
when He comes in His **g** and that Lk 9:26
They appeared in **g** and were Lk 9:31
they saw His **g** and the two men Lk 9:32
a loud voice, gave **g** to God. Lk 17:15
return to give **g** to God except Lk 17:18
in heaven and **g** in the highest Lk 19:38
a cloud with power and great **g**. Lk 21:27
things and enter into His **g**?" Lk 24:26
We observed His **g**, the glory as Jn 1:14
the **g** as the One and Only Son Jn 1:14
He displayed His **g**, and His Jn 2:11
I do not accept **g** from men, Jn 5:41
While accepting **g** from one Jn 5:44
you don't seek the **g** that comes Jn 5:44
for himself seeks his own **g**. Jn 7:18
who seeks the **g** of the One who Jn 7:18
I do not seek My **g**; the One who Jn 8:50
answered, "My **g** is nothing. Jn 8:54
and told him, "Give **g** to God. Jn 9:24
death but is for the **g** of God, Jn 11:4
you would see the **g** of God?" Jn 11:40
he saw His **g** and spoke about Jn 12:41
with that **g** I had with You Jn 17:5
given them the **g** You have given Jn 17:22
will see My **g**, which You have Jn 17:24
were all giving **g** to God over Ac 4:21
The God of **g** appeared to our Ac 7:2
He saw God's **g**, with Jesus Ac 7:55
he did not give the **g** to God, Ac 12:23
exchanged the **g** of the immortal Rm 1:23
patiently doing good seek for **g**, Rm 2:7
but **g**, honor, and peace for Rm 2:10
truth is amplified to His **g**, Rm 3:7
and fall short of the **g** of God. Rm 3:23
in his faith and gave **g** to God, Rm 4:20
in the hope of the **g** of God. Rm 5:2
the dead by the **g** of the Father, Rm 6:4
with the **g** that is going to Rm 8:18
adoption, the **g**, the covenants, Rm 9:4
the riches of His **g** on objects Rm 9:23
He prepared beforehand for **g**— Rm 9:23
To Him be the **g** forever. Rm 11:36
accepted you, to the **g** of God. Rm 15:7
—to Him be the **g** forever! Rm 16:27
before the ages for our **g**. 1Co 2:7
have crucified the Lord of **g**. 1Co 2:8
do everything for God's **g**. 1Co 10:31
because he is God's image and **g**, 1Co 11:7
and glory, but woman is man's **g**. 1Co 11:7
has long hair, it is her **g**? 1Co 11:15
sown in dishonor, raised in **g**; 1Co 15:43
Him for God's **g** through us. 2Co 1:20
came with **g**, so that the sons 2Co 3:7
because of the **g** from his face— 2Co 3:7
from his face—a fading ⌊**g**⌋— 2Co 3:7
ministry of condemnation had **g**, 2Co 3:9
overflows with even more **g**. 2Co 3:9
because of the **g** that surpasses 2Co 3:10
are reflecting the **g** of the Lord 2Co 3:18
the same image from **g** to glory; 2Co 3:18
the same image from glory to **g**; 2Co 3:18
the gospel of the **g** of Christ, 2Co 4:4
knowledge of God's **g** in the face 2Co 4:6
to overflow to God's **g**. 2Co 4:15
eternal weight of **g**. 2Co 4:17
through **g** and dishonor, through 2Co 6:8
by us for the **g** of the Lord 2Co 8:19
the churches, the **g** of Christ. 2Co 8:23
to whom be the **g** forever and Gl 1:5
might bring praise to His **g**. Eph 1:12
to the praise of His **g**. Eph 1:14
behalf, for they are your **g**. Eph 3:13
to the riches of His **g**, Eph 3:16
to Him be **g** in the church and in Eph 3:21
to the **g** and praise of God. Php 1:11
to the **g** of God the Father. Php 2:11
their **g** is in their shame. Php 3:19
His riches in **g** in Christ Jesus Php 4:19
and Father be **g** forever and ever Php 4:20
is Christ in you, the hope of **g**. Col 1:27
will be revealed with Him in **g**. Col 3:4
we didn't seek **g** from people, 1Th 2:6
you into His own kingdom and **g**. 1Th 2:12
For you are our **g** and joy! 1Th 2:20
might obtain the **g** of our Lord 2Th 2:14
be honor and **g** forever and ever. 1Tm 1:17
on in the world, taken up in **g**. 1Tm 3:16
in Christ Jesus, with eternal **g**. 2Tm 2:10
Him be the **g** forever and ever! 2Tm 4:18
of the **g** of our great God Ti 2:13
is in us for ⌊the **g** of⌋ Christ. Phm 6
He is the radiance of His **g**, Heb 1:3
You crowned him with **g** and honor Heb 2:7
crowned with **g** and honor because Heb 2:9
in bringing many sons to **g**, Heb 2:10
worthy of more **g** than Moses, Heb 3:3
The cherubim of **g** were above it Heb 9:5
to whom be **g** forever and ever. Heb 13:21
result in praise, **g**, and honor 1Pt 1:7
from the dead and gave Him **g**, 1Pt 1:21
and all its **g** like a flower of 1Pt 1:24
Him belong the **g** and the power 1Pt 4:11
joy at the revelation of His **g**. 1Pt 4:13
the Spirit of **g** and of God rests 1Pt 4:14
participant in the **g** about to be 1Pt 5:1
receive the unfading crown of **g**. 1Pt 5:4
His eternal **g** in Christ Jesus, 1Pt 5:10
us by His own **g** and goodness. 2Pt 1:3
received honor and **g** from God 2Pt 1:17
came to Him from the Majestic **G**: 2Pt 1:17
To Him be the **g** both now and to 2Pt 3:18
stand in the presence of His **g**, Jd 24
our Lord, be **g**, majesty, power, Jd 25
to Him be the **g** and dominion Rv 1:6
the living creatures give **g**, Rv 4:9
worthy to receive **g** and honor Rv 4:11
and honor and **g** and blessing! Rv 5:12
and honor and **g** and dominion to Rv 5:13
Blessing and **g** and wisdom and Rv 7:12
terrified and gave **g** to the God Rv 11:13
God and give Him **g**, because the Rv 14:7
smoke from God's **g** and from His Rv 15:8
did not repent and give Him **g**. Rv 16:9
Salvation, **g**, and power belong Rv 19:1
and give Him **g**, because the Rv 19:7
with God's **g**. Her radiance was Rv 21:11
because God's **g** illuminates it, Rv 21:23
will bring their **g** into it. Rv 21:24
They will bring the **g** and honor Rv 21:26

GLOW *(2)*

flame of his fire does not **g**. Jb 18:5
⌊shrouded⌋ in a golden ⌊**g**⌋; Jb 37:22

GLOWING *(2)*

by day and a **g** flame of fire Is 4:5
his hand was a **g** coal that he Is 6:6

GLOWS *(1)*

it becomes hot and its copper **g**. Ezk 24:11

GLUTTED *(1)*

their way and be **g** with their Pr 1:31

GLUTTON *(4)*

He's a **g** and a drunkard.' Dt 21:20
and the **g** will become poor Pr 23:21
say, 'Look, a **g** and a drunkard, Mt 11:19
say, 'Look, a **g** and a drunkard, Lk 7:34

GLUTTONS *(2)*

a companion of **g** humiliates his Pr 28:7
liars, evil beasts, lazy **g**. Ti 1:12

GNASH *(2)*

he will **g** his teeth in despair. Ps 112:10
They hiss and **g** ⌊their⌋ teeth, Lm 2:16

G completed His work that He had Gn 2:2
G blessed the seventh day and Gn 2:3
that the LORD **G** made the earth Gn 2:4
for the LORD **G** had not made it Gn 2:5
Then the LORD **G** formed the man Gn 2:7
The LORD **G** planted a garden in Gn 2:8
The LORD **G** caused to grow out of Gn 2:9
The LORD **G** took the man and Gn 2:15
the LORD **G** commanded the man, Gn 2:16
Then the LORD **G** said, "It is not Gn 2:18
So the LORD **G** formed out of the Gn 2:19
the LORD **G** caused a deep sleep Gn 2:21
G took one of his ribs and Gn 2:21
Then the LORD **G** made the rib He Gn 2:22
that the LORD **G** had made. Gn 3:1
the woman, "Did **G** really say, Gn 3:1
of the garden, **G** said, 'You must Gn 3:3
G knows that when you eat it Gn 3:5
opened and you will be like **G**, Gn 3:5
sound of the LORD **G** walking in Gn 3:8
from the LORD **G** among the trees Gn 3:8
So the LORD **G** called out to the Gn 3:9
So the LORD **G** asked the woman, Gn 3:13
Then the LORD **G** said to the Gn 3:14
The LORD **G** made clothing out of Gn 3:21
The LORD **G** said, "Since man has Gn 3:22
So the LORD **G** sent him away from Gn 3:23
G has given me another child Gn 4:25
On the day that **G** created man, Gn 5:1
made him in the likeness of **G**; Gn 5:1
Enoch walked with **G** 300 years Gn 5:22
walked with **G**, and he was not Gn 5:24
not there, because **G** took him. Gn 5:24
the sons of **G** saw that the Gn 6:2
when the sons of **G** came to the Gn 6:4
Noah walked with **G**. Gn 6:9
G saw how corrupt the earth was, Gn 6:12
Then **G** said to Noah, "I have Gn 6:13
everything that **G** had commanded Gn 6:22
just as **G** had commanded him. Gn 7:9
entered just as **G** had commanded Gn 7:16
G remembered Noah, as well as Gn 8:1
G caused a wind to pass over the Gn 8:1
Then **G** spoke to Noah, Gn 8:15
G blessed Noah and his sons and Gn 9:1
for **G** made man in His image. Gn 9:6
Then **G** said to Noah and his sons Gn 9:8
And **G** said, "This is the sign of Gn 9:12
between **G** and every living Gn 9:16
G said to Noah, "This is the Gn 9:17
Praise the LORD, the **G** of Shem; Gn 9:26
G will extend Japheth; he will Gn 9:27
was before **G** destroyed Sodom Gn 13:10
he was a priest to **G** Most High. Gn 14:18
Abram is blessed by **G** Most High, Gn 14:19
give praise to **G** Most High who Gn 14:20
oath to the LORD, **G** Most High, Gn 14:22
Abram said, "Lord **G**, what can Gn 15:2
he said, "Lord **G**, how can I know Gn 15:8
The **G** Who Sees, for she said, Gn 16:13
him, saying, "I am **G** Almighty. Gn 17:1
ground, and **G** spoke with him: Gn 17:3
to be your **G** and the ⌊God⌋ Gn 17:7
your God and the ⌊**G**⌋ of your Gn 17:7
and I will be their **G**." Gn 17:8
G also said to Abraham, "As for Gn 17:9
G said to Abraham, "As for your Gn 17:15
Abraham said to **G**, "If only Gn 17:18
But **G** said, "No. Your wife Sarah Gn 17:19
talking with him, **G** withdrew Gn 17:22
just as **G** had said to him. Gn 17:23
when **G** destroyed the cities of Gn 19:29
But **G** came to Abimelech in a Gn 20:3
Then **G** said to him in the dream, Gn 20:6
no fear of **G** in this place. Gn 20:11
when **G** had me wander from my Gn 20:13
prayed to **G**, and God healed Gn 20:17
to God, and **G** healed Abimelech, Gn 20:17
appointed time **G** had told him. Gn 21:2
him, as **G** had commanded him. Gn 21:4
said, "**G** has made me laugh, Gn 21:6
But **G** said to Abraham, "Do not Gn 21:12
G heard the voice of the boy, Gn 21:17
the angel of **G** called to Hagar Gn 21:17
for **G** has heard the voice of the Gn 21:17
Then **G** opened her eyes, and she Gn 21:19
G was with the boy, and he grew; Gn 21:20
G is with you in everything you Gn 21:22
me here by **G** that you will not Gn 21:23
the LORD, the Everlasting **G**. Gn 21:33
these things **G** tested Abraham Gn 22:1
go to the place **G** had told him Gn 22:3
G Himself will provide the lamb Gn 22:8
at the place that **G** had told him Gn 22:9
For now I know that you fear **G**, Gn 22:12
G of heaven and God of earth, Gn 24:3
God of heaven and **G** of earth, Gn 24:3
The LORD, the **G** of heaven, who Gn 24:7
"LORD, **G** of my master Abraham," Gn 24:12
the **G** of my master Abraham, Gn 24:27
LORD, **G** of my master Abraham, if Gn 24:42
the **G** of my master Abraham, Gn 24:48
death, **G** blessed his son Gn 25:11
I am the **G** of your father Gn 26:24
LORD your **G** worked it out for Gn 27:20
May **G** give to you—from the dew Gn 27:28
G Almighty bless you and make Gn 28:3
G give you and your offspring Gn 28:4
the land **G** gave to Abraham." Gn 28:4
the **G** of your father Abraham and Gn 28:13
Abraham and the **G** of Isaac. Gn 28:13
none other than the house of **G**. Gn 28:17
If **G** will be with me and watch Gn 28:20
then the LORD will be my **G**. Gn 28:21
Rachel said, "**G** has vindicated Gn 30:6
In ⌊my⌋ wrestlings with **G**, Gn 30:8
G listened to Leah, and she Gn 30:17
G has rewarded me for giving my Gn 30:18
"**G** has given me a good gift," Gn 30:20
Then **G** remembered Rachel. Gn 30:22
"**G** has taken away my shame." Gn 30:23
but the **G** of my father has been Gn 31:5
But **G** has not let him harm me. Gn 31:7
G has taken your father's herds Gn 31:9
the Angel of **G** said to me, Gn 31:11
I am the **G** of Bethel, where you Gn 31:13
the wealth that **G** has taken from Gn 31:16
do whatever **G** has said to you. Gn 31:16
But **G** came to Laban the Aramean Gn 31:24
Watch yourself!" **G** warned him. Gn 31:24
last night the **G** of your father Gn 31:29
the **G** of my father, the God of Gn 31:42
of my father, the **G** of Abraham, Gn 31:42
But **G** has seen my affliction and Gn 31:42
understand that **G** will be a Gn 31:50
The **G** of Abraham, and the gods Gn 31:53
G of my father Abraham and God Gn 32:9
Abraham and **G** of my father Isaac Gn 32:9
struggled with **G** and with men Gn 32:28
I have seen **G** face to face, Gn 32:30
The children **G** has graciously Gn 33:5
because **G** has been gracious to Gn 33:11
an altar there and called it "**G**, Gn 33:20
it "God, the **G** of Israel." Gn 33:20
G said to Jacob, "Get up! Gn 35:1
there to the **G** who appeared to Gn 35:1
there to the **G** who answered me Gn 35:3
a terror from **G** came over the Gn 35:5
called the place **G** of Bethel Gn 35:7
it was there that **G** had revealed Gn 35:7
G appeared to Jacob again after Gn 35:9
G said to him: Your name is Gn 35:10
G also said to him: I am God Gn 35:11
said to him: I am **G** Almighty. Be Gn 35:11
Then **G** withdrew from him at the Gn 35:13
place where **G** had spoken with Gn 35:15
a great evil and sin against **G**?" Gn 39:9
interpretations belong to **G**? Gn 40:8
It is **G** who will give Pharaoh a Gn 41:16
G has revealed to Pharaoh what Gn 41:25
G has shown Pharaoh what He is Gn 41:28
matter has been determined by **G**, Gn 41:32
who has the spirit of **G** in him?" Gn 41:38
Since **G** has made all this known Gn 41:39
G has made me forget all my Gn 41:51
G has made me fruitful in the Gn 41:52
to them, "I fear **G**—do this and Gn 42:18
is this that **G** has done to us?" Gn 42:28
May **G** Almighty cause the man to Gn 43:14
G and the God of your father Gn 43:23
God and the **G** of your father Gn 43:23
May **G** be gracious to you, Gn 43:29
G has exposed your servants' Gn 44:16
because **G** sent me ahead of you Gn 45:5
G sent me ahead of you to Gn 45:7
not you who sent me here, but **G**. Gn 45:8
G has made me lord of all Egypt. Gn 45:9
sacrifices to the **G** of his Gn 46:1
That night **G** spoke to Israel in Gn 46:2
G said, "I am God, the God of Gn 46:3
God said, "I am **G**, the God of Gn 46:3
I am God, the **G** of your father. Gn 46:3
G Almighty appeared to me at Luz Gn 48:3
They are my sons **G** has given me Gn 48:9
but now **G** has even let me see Gn 48:11
The **G** before whom my fathers Gn 48:15
the **G** who has been my shepherd Gn 48:15
May **G** make you like Ephraim and Gn 48:20
but **G** will be with you and will Gn 48:21
the **G** of your father who helps Gn 49:25
of the **G** of your father. Gn 50:17
afraid. Am I in the place of **G**? Gn 50:19
G planned it for good to bring Gn 50:20
G will certainly come to your Gn 50:24
When **G** comes to your aid, Gn 50:25
feared **G** and did not do as the Ex 1:17
So **G** was good to the midwives, Ex 1:20
Since the midwives feared **G**, Ex 1:21
for help ascended to **G** because Ex 2:23
So **G** heard their groaning, Ex 2:24
G saw the Israelites, and He Ex 2:25
to Horeb, the mountain of **G**. Ex 3:1
G called out to him from the Ex 3:4
I am the **G** of your father, Ex 3:6
your father, the **G** of Abraham, Ex 3:6
God of Abraham, the **G** of Isaac, Ex 3:6
of Isaac, and the **G** of Jacob." Ex 3:6
he was afraid to look at **G**. Ex 3:6
Moses asked **G**, "Who am I that Ex 3:11
all worship **G** at this mountain. Ex 3:12
Then Moses asked **G**, "If I go to Ex 3:13
The **G** of your fathers has sent Ex 3:13
G replied to Moses, "I AM WHO I Ex 3:14
G also said to Moses, "Say this Ex 3:15
Yahweh, the **G** of your fathers, Ex 3:15
your fathers, the **G** of Abraham, Ex 3:15
God of Abraham, the **G** of Isaac, Ex 3:15
Isaac, and the **G** of Jacob, has Ex 3:15
Yahweh, the **G** of your fathers, Ex 3:16
fathers, the **G** of Abraham, Isaac Ex 3:16
The LORD, the **G** of the Hebrews, Ex 3:18
may sacrifice to the LORD our **G**. Ex 3:18
the LORD, the **G** of their fathers Ex 4:5
their fathers, the **G** of Abraham, Ex 4:5
God of Abraham, the **G** of Isaac, Ex 4:5
Isaac, and the **G** of Jacob, has Ex 4:5
and you will serve as **G** to him. Ex 4:16
mountain of **G** and kissed him. Ex 4:27
the LORD, the **G** of Israel, says: Ex 5:1
The **G** of the Hebrews has met Ex 5:3
may sacrifice to the LORD our **G**, Ex 5:3
us go and sacrifice to our **G**.' Ex 5:8
Then **G** spoke to Moses, telling Ex 6:2
and Jacob as **G** Almighty, but I Ex 6:3
My people, and I will be your **G**. Ex 6:7
know that I am Yahweh your **G**, Ex 6:7
have made you like **G** to Pharaoh, Ex 7:1
The LORD, the **G** of the Hebrews, Ex 7:16
is no one like the LORD our **G**, Ex 8:10
"This is the finger of **G**," Ex 8:19
sacrifice to your **G** within the Ex 8:25
to the LORD our **G** is detestable Ex 8:26
LORD our **G** as He instructs us. Ex 8:27
to the LORD your **G** in the Ex 8:28
the LORD, the **G** of the Hebrews, Ex 9:1
the **G** of the Hebrews says: Ex 9:13
still do not fear the LORD **G**." Ex 9:30
the LORD, the **G** of the Hebrews, Ex 10:3
may worship the LORD their **G**. Ex 10:7
the LORD your **G**," Pharaoh said. Ex 10:8
the LORD your **G** and against you. Ex 10:16
an appeal to the LORD your **G**, Ex 10:17
to prepare for the LORD our **G**. Ex 10:25
them to worship the LORD our **G**. Ex 10:26
G did not lead them along the Ex 13:17
for **G** said, "The people will Ex 13:17
G will certainly come to your Ex 13:19
the Angel of **G**, who was going Ex 14:19
This is my **G**, and I will praise Ex 15:2
Him, my father's **G**, and I will Ex 15:2
carefully obey the LORD your **G**, Ex 15:26
know that I am the LORD your **G**." Ex 16:12
everything that **G** had done for Ex 18:1
The **G** of my father was my Ex 18:4

was camped at the mountain of **G**. Ex 18:5
offering and sacrifices to **G**, Ex 18:12
come to me to inquire of **G**. Ex 18:15
some advice, and **G** be with you. Ex 18:19
people before **G** and bring their Ex 18:19
do this, and **G** ⌊so⌋ directs you Ex 18:23
went up ⌊the mountain⌋ to **G**, Ex 19:3
out of the camp to meet **G**, Ex 19:17
Moses spoke and **G** answered him Ex 19:19
Then **G** spoke all these words: Ex 20:1
the LORD your **G**, who brought you Ex 20:2
I, the LORD your **G**, am a jealous Ex 20:5
God, am a jealous **G**, punishing Ex 20:5
the name of the LORD your **G**, Ex 20:7
is a Sabbath to the LORD your **G**. Ex 20:10
the LORD your **G** is giving you. Ex 20:12
but don't let **G** speak to us, Ex 20:19
for **G** has come to test you, Ex 20:20
the thick darkness where **G** was. Ex 20:21
and yet **G** caused it to happen by Ex 21:13
not blaspheme **G** or curse a Ex 22:28
are to appear before the Lord **G**. Ex 23:17
to the house of the LORD your **G**. Ex 23:19
the LORD your **G**, and He will Ex 23:25
and they saw the **G** of Israel. Ex 24:10
G did not harm the Israelite Ex 24:11
and went up the mountain of **G**. Ex 24:13
the Israelites and be their **G**. Ex 29:45
know that I am the LORD their **G**, Ex 29:46
them. I am the LORD their **G**. Ex 29:46
inscribed by the finger of **G**. Ex 31:18
make us a **g** who will go before Ex 32:1
this is your **G**, who brought you Ex 32:4
this is your **G**, who brought you Ex 32:8
interceded with the LORD his **G**: Ex 32:11
The tablets were the work of **G**, Ex 32:16
'Make us a **g** who will go before Ex 32:23
the LORD, the **G** of Israel, says, Ex 32:27
made for themselves a **g** of gold. Ex 32:31
a compassionate and gracious **G**, Ex 34:6
down to another **g** because the Ex 34:14
by nature, is a jealous **G**. Ex 34:14
are to appear before the Lord **G**, Ex 34:23
the Lord GOD, the **G** of Israel. Ex 34:23
appear before the LORD your **G**. Ex 34:24
to the house of the LORD your **G**. Ex 34:26
of the covenant with your **G**. Lv 2:13
of the LORD his **G** by doing what Lv 4:22
am the LORD your **G**, so you must Lv 11:44
the land of Egypt to be your **G**, Lv 11:45
tell them: I am the LORD your **G**. Lv 18:2
them; I am the LORD your **G**. Lv 18:4
not profane the name of your **G**; Lv 18:21
by them; I am the LORD your **G**." Lv 18:30
I, the LORD your **G**, am holy. Lv 19:2
Sabbaths; I am the LORD your **G**. Lv 19:3
I am the LORD your **G**. Lv 19:4
resident; I am the LORD your **G**. Lv 19:10
profaning the name of your **G**; Lv 19:12
but you are to fear your **G**; Lv 19:14
for you; I am the LORD your **G**. Lv 19:25
by them; I am the LORD your **G**. Lv 19:31
old. Fear your **G**; I am the LORD. Lv 19:32
of Egypt; I am the LORD your **G**. Lv 19:34
the LORD your **G**, who brought you Lv 19:36
holy, for I am the LORD your **G**. Lv 20:7
am the LORD your **G** who set you Lv 20:24
holy to their **G** and not profane Lv 21:6
not profane the name of their **G**, Lv 21:6
the LORD, the food of their **G**. Lv 21:6
for the priest is holy to his **G**. Lv 21:7
he presents the food of your **G**. Lv 21:8
the sanctuary of his **G**, Lv 21:12
oil of his **G** is on him; Lv 21:12
to present the food of his **G**. Lv 21:17
to present the food of his **G**. Lv 21:21
the food of his **G** from what is Lv 21:22
food to your **G** from any of these Lv 22:25
the land of Egypt to be your **G**; Lv 22:33
brought the offering of your **G**. Lv 23:14
resident; I am the LORD your **G**." Lv 23:22
before the LORD your **G**. Lv 23:28
the LORD your **G** for seven days. Lv 23:40
of Egypt; I am the LORD your **G**." Lv 23:43
anyone curses his **G**, he will Lv 24:15
because I am the LORD your **G**." Lv 24:22
but fear your **G**, for I am the Lv 25:17
God, for I am the LORD your **G**. Lv 25:17
but fear your **G** and let your Lv 25:36
the LORD your **G**, who brought you Lv 25:38
land of Canaan and to be your **G**. Lv 25:38
them harshly but fear your **G**. Lv 25:43
of Egypt; I am the LORD your **G**. Lv 25:55
to it, for I am the LORD your **G**. Lv 26:1
walk among you and be your **G**, Lv 26:12
the LORD your **G**, who brought you Lv 26:13
since I am the LORD their **G**. Lv 26:44
of the nations to be their **G**; Lv 26:45
to his **G** is on his head. Nm 6:7
the LORD your **G** and be delivered Nm 10:9
reminder for you before your **G**: Nm 10:10
your God: I am the LORD your **G**." Nm 10:10
to the LORD, "**G**, please heal her Nm 12:13
commands and be holy to your **G**. Nm 15:40
the LORD your **G** who brought you Nm 15:41
the land of Egypt to be your **G**; Nm 15:41
your God; I am the LORD your **G**." Nm 15:41
for you that the **G** of Israel has Nm 16:9
and said, "**G**, God of the spirits Nm 16:22
G of the spirits of all flesh, Nm 16:22
spoke against **G** and Moses: Nm 21:5
Then **G** came to Balaam and asked, Nm 22:9
Balaam replied to **G**, "Balak son Nm 22:10
Then **G** said to Balaam, "You are Nm 22:12
the LORD my **G** to do ⌊anything⌋ Nm 22:18
G came to Balaam at night and Nm 22:20
But **G** was incensed that Balaam Nm 22:22
the message **G** puts in my mouth. Nm 22:38
G met with him and Balaam said Nm 23:4
curse someone **G** has not cursed? Nm 23:8
G is not a man who lies, or a Nm 23:19
The LORD their **G** is with them, Nm 23:21
G brought them out of Egypt; Nm 23:22
"What ⌊great things⌋ **G** has done!" Nm 23:23
be agreeable to **G** that you can Nm 23:27
Spirit of **G** descended on him, Nm 24:2
one who hears the sayings of **G**, Nm 24:4
G brought him out of Egypt; Nm 24:8
the sayings of **G** and has Nm 24:16
who can live when **G** does this? Nm 24:23
zealous for his **G** and made Nm 25:13
the **G** of the spirits of all Nm 27:16
The LORD our **G** spoke to us at Dt 1:6
LORD your **G** has so multiplied Dt 1:10
the LORD, the **G** of your fathers Dt 1:11
for judgment belongs to **G**. Dt 1:17
as the LORD our **G** had commanded Dt 1:19
the LORD our **G** is giving us. Dt 1:20
the LORD your **G** has set the land Dt 1:21
the LORD, the **G** of your fathers Dt 1:21
the LORD our **G** is giving us is Dt 1:25
the command of the LORD your **G**. Dt 1:26
The LORD your **G** who goes before Dt 1:30
the LORD your **G** carried you as Dt 1:31
did not trust the LORD your **G**, Dt 1:32
as the LORD our **G** commanded us.' Dt 1:41
the LORD your **G** has blessed you Dt 2:7
LORD your **G** has been with you Dt 2:7
the LORD our **G** is giving us.' Dt 2:29
the LORD your **G** made his spirit Dt 2:30
The LORD our **G** handed him over Dt 2:33
The LORD our **G** gave everything Dt 2:36
the LORD our **G** had commanded. Dt 2:37
So the LORD our **G** also handed Dt 3:3
The LORD your **G** has given you Dt 3:18
the LORD your **G** is giving them Dt 3:20
LORD your **G** has done to these Dt 3:21
the LORD your **G** fights for you. Dt 3:22
Lord **G**, You have begun to show Dt 3:24
for what **g** is there in heaven or Dt 3:24
the LORD, the **G** of your fathers, Dt 4:1
the LORD your **G** I am giving you Dt 4:2
the LORD your **G** destroyed every Dt 4:3
to the LORD your **G** are all alive Dt 4:4
as the LORD my **G** has commanded Dt 4:5
there that has a **g** near to it as Dt 4:7
it as the LORD our **G** is ⌊to us⌋ Dt 4:7
before the LORD your **G** at Horeb, Dt 4:10
LORD your **G** has provided them Dt 4:19
the LORD your **G** is giving you as Dt 4:21
of the LORD your **G** that He made Dt 4:23
the LORD your **G** is a consuming Dt 4:24
a consuming fire, a jealous **G**. Dt 4:24
in the sight of the LORD your **G**, Dt 4:25
the LORD your **G** will drive you. Dt 4:27
will search for the LORD your **G**, Dt 4:29
to the LORD your **G** in later days Dt 4:30
the LORD your **G** is a Dt 4:31
your God is a compassionate **G**. Dt 4:31
from the day **G** created man on Dt 4:32
has a **g** ⌊ever⌋ attempted to go Dt 4:34
the LORD your **G** did for you in Dt 4:34
would know that the LORD is **G**; Dt 4:35
the LORD is **G** in heaven above Dt 4:39
the LORD your **G** is giving you Dt 4:40
The LORD our **G** made a covenant Dt 5:2
the LORD your **G**, who brought you Dt 5:6
I, the LORD your **G**, am a jealous Dt 5:9
God, am a jealous **G**, punishing Dt 5:9
the name of the LORD your **G**, Dt 5:11
as the LORD your **G** has commanded Dt 5:12
is a Sabbath to the LORD your **G**. Dt 5:14
the LORD your **G** brought you out Dt 5:15
the LORD your **G** has commanded Dt 5:15
as the LORD your **G** has commanded Dt 5:16
the LORD your **G** is giving you. Dt 5:16
the LORD our **G** has shown us His Dt 5:24
we have seen that **G** speaks with Dt 5:24
of the LORD our **G** any longer. Dt 5:25
voice of the living **G** speaking Dt 5:26
everything the LORD our **G** says. Dt 5:27
the LORD our **G** tells you; Dt 5:27
as the LORD your **G** has commanded Dt 5:32
the LORD your **G** has commanded Dt 5:33
the LORD your **G** has instructed Dt 6:1
the LORD your **G** all the days Dt 6:2
the LORD, the **G** of your fathers, Dt 6:3
The LORD our **G**, the LORD is One. Dt 6:4
the LORD your **G** with all your Dt 6:5
When the LORD your **G** brings you Dt 6:10
the LORD your **G**, worship Him, Dt 6:13
the LORD your **G**, who is among Dt 6:15
is among you, is a jealous **G**. Dt 6:15
LORD your **G** will become angry Dt 6:15
the LORD your **G** as you tested Dt 6:16
the commands of the LORD your **G**, Dt 6:17
the LORD your **G** swore to ⌊give⌋ Dt 6:18
the LORD our **G** has commanded you Dt 6:20
fear the LORD our **G** for our Dt 6:24
commands before the LORD our **G**, Dt 6:25
When the LORD your **G** brings you Dt 7:1
the LORD your **G** delivers them Dt 7:2
belonging to the LORD your **G**. Dt 7:6
The LORD your **G** has chosen you Dt 7:6
Know that Yahweh your **G** is God, Dt 7:9
Know that Yahweh your God is **G**, Dt 7:9
the faithful **G** who keeps His Dt 7:9
the LORD your **G** will keep His Dt 7:12
the LORD your **G** is delivering Dt 7:16
the LORD your **G** did to Pharaoh Dt 7:18
the LORD your **G** brought you out. Dt 7:19
The LORD your **G** will do the same Dt 7:19
The LORD your **G** will also send Dt 7:20
for the LORD your **G**, a great and Dt 7:21
and awesome **G**, is among you. Dt 7:21
The LORD your **G** will drive out Dt 7:22
The LORD your **G** will give them Dt 7:23
is abhorrent to the LORD your **G**. Dt 7:25
that the LORD your **G** led you on Dt 8:2
that the LORD your **G** has been Dt 8:5
of the LORD your **G** by walking in Dt 8:6
the LORD your **G** is bringing you Dt 8:7
LORD your **G** for the good land Dt 8:10
the LORD your **G** by failing to Dt 8:11
the LORD your **G** who brought you Dt 8:14
that the LORD your **G** gives you Dt 8:18
the LORD your **G** and go after Dt 8:19
you do not obey the LORD your **G**. Dt 8:20
the LORD your **G** will cross over Dt 9:3
the LORD your **G** drives them out Dt 9:4
the LORD your **G** will drive out Dt 9:5
the LORD your **G** is not giving Dt 9:6
the LORD your **G** in the Dt 9:7
sinned against the LORD your **G**; Dt 9:16
the command of the LORD your **G**. Dt 9:23
Lord **G**, do not annihilate Your Dt 9:26
as the LORD your **G** told him. Dt 10:9
the LORD your **G** ask of you Dt 10:12
the LORD your **G** by walking in Dt 10:12
the LORD your **G** with all your Dt 10:12
belong to the LORD your **G**, Dt 10:14
For the LORD your **G** is the God Dt 10:17
your God is the **G** of gods and Dt 10:17
mighty, and awesome **G**, showing Dt 10:17

the LORD your **G** and worship Him.	Dt 10:20
is your praise and He is your **G**,	Dt 10:21
the LORD your **G** has made you as	Dt 10:22
the LORD your **G** and always keep	Dt 11:1
discipline of the LORD your **G**:	Dt 11:2
land the LORD your **G** cares for.	Dt 11:12
the LORD your **G** and worship Him	Dt 11:13
the LORD your **G**, walk in all His	Dt 11:22
LORD your **G** will put fear and	Dt 11:25
the LORD your **G** I am giving you	Dt 11:27
the commands of the LORD your **G**,	Dt 11:28
When the LORD your **G** brings you	Dt 11:29
the LORD your **G** is giving you.	Dt 11:31
the LORD, the **G** of your fathers,	Dt 12:1
the LORD your **G** this way.	Dt 12:4
the LORD your **G** chooses from all	Dt 12:5
the LORD your **G** and rejoice with	Dt 12:7
the LORD your **G** has blessed you.	Dt 12:7
the LORD your **G** is giving you.	Dt 12:9
the LORD your **G** is giving you to	Dt 12:10
then the LORD your **G** will choose	Dt 12:11
rejoice before the LORD your **G**—	Dt 12:12
the LORD your **G** has given you.	Dt 12:15
of the LORD your **G** at the place	Dt 12:18
place the LORD your **G** chooses—	Dt 12:18
LORD your **G** in everything you	Dt 12:18
the LORD your **G** enlarges your	Dt 12:20
the LORD your **G** chooses to put	Dt 12:21
on the altar of the LORD your **G**.	Dt 12:27
the altar of the LORD your **G**,	Dt 12:27
in the sight of the LORD your **G**.	Dt 12:28
When the LORD your **G** annihilates	Dt 12:29
do the same to the LORD your **G**,	Dt 12:31
the LORD your **G** is testing you	Dt 13:3
the LORD your **G** with all your	Dt 13:3
the LORD your **G** and fear Him.	Dt 13:4
the LORD your **G** who brought you	Dt 13:5
the LORD your **G** has commanded	Dt 13:5
the LORD your **G** who brought you	Dt 13:10
the LORD your **G** is giving you to	Dt 13:12
its spoil for the LORD your **G**.	Dt 13:16
if you obey the LORD your **G**,	Dt 13:18
in the sight of the LORD your **G**.	Dt 13:18
You are sons of the LORD your **G**;	Dt 14:1
belonging to the LORD your **G**.	Dt 14:2
belonging to the LORD your **G**.	Dt 14:21
of the LORD your **G** at the place	Dt 14:23
learn to fear the LORD your **G**.	Dt 14:23
the LORD your **G** chooses to put	Dt 14:24
the LORD your **G** has blessed you,	Dt 14:24
place the LORD your **G** chooses.	Dt 14:25
the LORD your **G** and rejoice with	Dt 14:26
the LORD your **G** will bless you	Dt 14:29
the LORD your **G** is giving you to	Dt 15:4
the LORD your **G** and are careful	Dt 15:5
the LORD your **G** blesses you as	Dt 15:6
the LORD your **G** is giving you,	Dt 15:7
the LORD your **G** will bless you	Dt 15:10
the LORD your **G** has blessed you	Dt 15:14
the LORD your **G** redeemed you;	Dt 15:15
the LORD your **G** will bless you	Dt 15:18
the LORD your **G** every firstborn	Dt 15:19
the LORD your **G** in the place	Dt 15:20
sacrifice it to the LORD your **G**.	Dt 15:21
the Passover to the LORD your **G**,	Dt 16:1
the LORD your **G** brought you out	Dt 16:1
to the LORD your **G** a Passover	Dt 16:2
the LORD your **G** is giving you.	Dt 16:5
the LORD your **G** chooses to have	Dt 16:6
place the LORD your **G** chooses,	Dt 16:7
assembly to the LORD your **G**,	Dt 16:8
the LORD your **G** with a freewill	Dt 16:10
the LORD your **G** has blessed you	Dt 16:10
the LORD your **G** in the place	Dt 16:11
the LORD your **G** in the place He	Dt 16:15
the LORD your **G** will bless you	Dt 16:15
the LORD your **G** in the place He	Dt 16:16
the LORD your **G** has given you.	Dt 16:17
the LORD your **G** is giving you.	Dt 16:18
the LORD your **G** is giving you.	Dt 16:20
will build for the LORD your **G**,	Dt 16:21
the LORD your **G** hates them.	Dt 16:22
the LORD your **G** an ox or sheep	Dt 17:1
detestable to the LORD your **G**.	Dt 17:1
the LORD your **G** will give you is	Dt 17:2
of the LORD your **G** and violating	Dt 17:2
place the LORD your **G** chooses.	Dt 17:8
the LORD your **G** or to the judge,	Dt 17:12
the LORD your **G** is giving you,	Dt 17:14
king the LORD your **G** chooses.	Dt 17:15
learn to fear the LORD his **G**,	Dt 17:19
the LORD your **G** has chosen him	Dt 18:5
of the LORD his **G** like all his	Dt 18:7
the LORD your **G** is giving you,	Dt 18:9
the LORD your **G** is driving out	Dt 18:12
before the LORD your **G**.	Dt 18:13
LORD your **G** has not permitted	Dt 18:14
The LORD your **G** will raise up	Dt 18:15
from the LORD your **G** at Horeb on	Dt 18:16
of the LORD our **G** or see this	Dt 18:16
When the LORD your **G** annihilates	Dt 19:1
the LORD your **G** is giving you to	Dt 19:2
the LORD your **G** is granting you	Dt 19:3
If the LORD your **G** enlarges your	Dt 19:8
the LORD your **G** and walking in	Dt 19:9
the LORD your **G** is giving you as	Dt 19:10
the LORD your **G** is giving you to	Dt 19:14
the LORD your **G**, who brought you	Dt 20:1
the LORD your **G** is the One who	Dt 20:4
the LORD your **G** hands it over to	Dt 20:13
the LORD your **G** has given you.	Dt 20:14
the LORD your **G** is giving you as	Dt 20:16
the LORD your **G** has commanded	Dt 20:17
you sin against the LORD your **G**.	Dt 20:18
the LORD your **G** is giving you to	Dt 21:1
the LORD your **G** has chosen them	Dt 21:5
the LORD your **G** hands them over	Dt 21:10
the LORD your **G** is giving you as	Dt 21:23
detestable to the LORD your **G**.	Dt 22:5
the LORD your **G** would not listen	Dt 23:5
the LORD your **G** loves you.	Dt 23:5
the LORD your **G** walks throughout	Dt 23:14
the LORD your **G** to fulfill any	Dt 23:18
detestable to the LORD your **G**.	Dt 23:18
the LORD your **G** may bless you	Dt 23:20
make a vow to the LORD your **G**,	Dt 23:21
you promised to the LORD your **G**.	Dt 23:23
the LORD your **G** is giving you as	Dt 24:4
the LORD your **G** did to Miriam	Dt 24:9
to you before the LORD your **G**.	Dt 24:13
and the LORD your **G** redeemed you	Dt 24:18
the LORD your **G** may bless you	Dt 24:19
the LORD your **G** is giving you.	Dt 25:15
detestable to the LORD your **G**.	Dt 25:16
and weary. They did not fear **G**.	Dt 25:18
the LORD your **G** gives you rest	Dt 25:19
the LORD your **G** is giving you to	Dt 25:19
the LORD your **G** is giving you as	Dt 26:1
the LORD your **G** is giving you	Dt 26:2
the LORD your **G** chooses to have	Dt 26:2
to the LORD your **G** that I have	Dt 26:3
the altar of the LORD your **G**.	Dt 26:4
the presence of the LORD your **G**:	Dt 26:5
the LORD, the **G** of our fathers,	Dt 26:7
the LORD your **G** and bow down to	Dt 26:10
the LORD your **G** has given you	Dt 26:11
the presence of the LORD your **G**:	Dt 26:13
I have obeyed the LORD my **G**;	Dt 26:14
The LORD your **G** is commanding	Dt 26:16
the LORD is your **G** and that you	Dt 26:17
the LORD your **G** as He promised.	Dt 26:19
the LORD your **G** is giving you,	Dt 27:2
the LORD your **G** is giving you,	Dt 27:3
the LORD, the **G** of your fathers	Dt 27:3
there to the LORD your **G**—	Dt 27:5
the LORD your **G** and offer burnt	Dt 27:6
to the LORD your **G** on it.	Dt 27:6
the presence of the LORD your **G**.	Dt 27:7
the people of the LORD your **G**.	Dt 27:9
the LORD your **G** and follow His	Dt 27:10
the LORD your **G** and are careful	Dt 28:1
the LORD your **G** will put you far	Dt 28:1
you obey the LORD your **G**:	Dt 28:2
the LORD your **G** is giving you.	Dt 28:8
the LORD your **G** and walk in His	Dt 28:9
the LORD your **G** by carefully	Dt 28:15
obey the LORD your **G** and keep	Dt 28:45
serve the LORD your **G** with joy	Dt 28:47
the LORD your **G** has given you.	Dt 28:52
the LORD your **G** has given you	Dt 28:53
awesome name—Yahweh, your **G**	Dt 28:58
did not obey the LORD your **G**.	Dt 28:62
know that I am the LORD your **G**.	Dt 29:6
today before the LORD your **G**—	Dt 29:10
the covenant of the LORD your **G**,	Dt 29:12
He may be your **G** as He promised	Dt 29:13
of the LORD our **G** and with those	Dt 29:15
the LORD our **G** to go and worship	Dt 29:18
the LORD, the **G** of their fathers	Dt 29:25
things belong to the LORD our **G**,	Dt 29:29
the LORD your **G** has driven you,	Dt 30:1
to the LORD your **G** and obey Him	Dt 30:2
the LORD your **G** has scattered	Dt 30:3
The LORD your **G** will bring you	Dt 30:5
The LORD your **G** will circumcise	Dt 30:6
The LORD your **G** will put all	Dt 30:7
The LORD your **G** will make you	Dt 30:9
the LORD your **G** by keeping His	Dt 30:10
today to love the LORD your **G**,	Dt 30:16
the LORD your **G** may bless you	Dt 30:16
love the LORD your **G**, obey Him,	Dt 30:20
The LORD your **G** is the One who	Dt 31:3
is the LORD your **G** who goes with	Dt 31:6
the LORD your **G** at the place He	Dt 31:11
the LORD your **G** and be careful	Dt 31:12
the LORD your **G** as long as you	Dt 31:13
us because our **G** is no longer	Dt 31:17
the covenant of the LORD your **G**,	Dt 31:26
Declare the greatness of our **G**!	Dt 32:3
A faithful **G**, without prejudice,	Dt 32:4
with no help from a foreign **g**.	Dt 32:12
He abandoned the **G** who made him	Dt 32:15
to demons, not **G**, to gods they	Dt 32:17
you forgot the **G** who brought you	Dt 32:18
He; there is no **G** but Me. I	Dt 32:39
Moses, the man of **G**, gave the	Dt 33:1
is none like the **G** of Jeshurun,	Dt 33:26
The **G** of old is ⌊your⌋ dwelling	Dt 33:27
for the LORD your **G** is with you	Jos 1:9
the LORD your **G** is giving you to	Jos 1:11
'The LORD your **G** will give you	Jos 1:13
the LORD your **G** is giving them.	Jos 1:15
may the LORD your **G** be with you,	Jos 1:17
the LORD your **G** is God in heaven	Jos 2:11
your God is **G** in heaven above	Jos 2:11
the LORD your **G** carried by the	Jos 3:3
the words of the LORD your **G**."	Jos 3:9
that the living **G** is among you	Jos 3:10
of the LORD your **G** in the middle	Jos 4:5
For the LORD your **G** dried up the	Jos 4:23
the LORD your **G** did to the Red	Jos 4:23
always fear the LORD your **G**."	Jos 4:24
"Oh, Lord **G**," Joshua said, "why	Jos 7:7
the LORD, the **G** of Israel, says,	Jos 7:13
the LORD, the **G** of Israel, and	Jos 7:19
the LORD, the **G** of Israel.	Jos 7:20
for the LORD your **G** has handed	Jos 8:7
to the LORD, the **G** of Israel,	Jos 8:30
reputation of the LORD your **G**.	Jos 9:9
by the LORD, the **G** of Israel.	Jos 9:18
the LORD, the **G** of Israel, and	Jos 9:19
carriers for the house of my **G**."	Jos 9:23
the LORD your **G** had commanded	Jos 9:24
the LORD your **G** has handed them	Jos 10:19
the LORD, the **G** of Israel, had	Jos 10:40
LORD, the **G** of Israel, fought	Jos 10:42
to the LORD, the **G** of Israel.	Jos 13:14
The LORD, the **G** of Israel, was	Jos 13:33
the man of **G** at Kadesh-barnea	Jos 14:6
remained loyal to the LORD my **G**.	Jos 14:8
loyal to the LORD my **G**.'	Jos 14:9
to the LORD, the **G** of Israel.	Jos 14:14
the LORD, the **G** of your fathers,	Jos 18:3
the presence of the LORD our **G**.	Jos 18:6
the command of the LORD your **G**.	Jos 22:3
the LORD your **G**, walk in all His	Jos 22:5
today against the **G** of Israel by	Jos 22:16
the altar of the LORD our **G**.	Jos 22:19
The LORD is the **G** of gods!	Jos 22:22
The LORD is the **G** of gods!	Jos 22:22
with the LORD, the **G** of Israel?	Jos 22:24
the altar of the LORD our **G**,	Jos 22:29
the report, and they praised **G**.	Jos 22:33
between us that the LORD is **G**.	Jos 22:34
the LORD your **G** did to all these	Jos 23:3
the LORD your **G** who was fighting	Jos 23:3
The LORD your **G** will force them	Jos 23:5
as the LORD your **G** promised you.	Jos 23:5
faithful to the LORD your **G**,	Jos 23:8
the LORD your **G** was fighting for	Jos 23:10
love the LORD your **G** for your	Jos 23:11
the LORD your **G** will not	Jos 23:13
the LORD your **G** has given you.	Jos 23:13
the LORD your **G** made to you has	Jos 23:14

the LORD your **G** promised you has Jos 23:15
the LORD your **G** has given you. Jos 23:15
the covenant of the LORD your **G**, Jos 23:16
presented themselves before **G**. Jos 24:1
the LORD, the **G** of Israel, says: Jos 24:2
the LORD our **G** brought us and Jos 24:17
the LORD, because He is our **G**." Jos 24:18
LORD, because He is a holy **G**. Jos 24:19
He is a jealous **G**; He will not Jos 24:19
to the LORD, the **G** of Israel." Jos 24:23
the LORD our **G** and obey Him." Jos 24:24
in the book of the law of **G**; Jos 24:26
that you will not deny your **G**." Jos 24:27
G has repaid me for what I have Jdg 1:7
LORD, the **G** of their fathers, Jdg 2:12
the LORD their **G** and worshiped Jdg 3:7
"I have a word from **G** for you," Jdg 3:20
the LORD, the **G** of Israel, Jdg 4:6
That day **G** subdued Jabin king of Jdg 4:23
praise to the LORD **G** of Israel. Jdg 5:3
the LORD, the **G** of Israel. Jdg 5:5
what the LORD **G** of Israel says: Jdg 6:8
am the LORD your **G**. Do not fear Jdg 6:10
The Angel of **G** said to him, Jdg 6:20
LORD, he said, "Oh no, Lord **G**! Jdg 6:22
to the LORD your **G** on the top of Jdg 6:26
If he is a **g**, let him plead his Jdg 6:31
Gideon said to **G**, "If You will Jdg 6:36
then said to **G**, "Don't be angry Jdg 6:39
That night **G** did ⌊as Gideon Jdg 6:40
G has handed the entire Jdg 7:14
G handed over to you Oreb and Jdg 8:3
and made Baal-berith their **g**. Jdg 8:33
the LORD their **G** who had Jdg 8:34
and may **G** listen to you: Jdg 9:7
oil that honors both **G** and man, Jdg 9:9
wine that cheers both **G** and man, Jdg 9:13
G sent an evil spirit between Jdg 9:23
went to the house of their **g**, Jdg 9:27
his 70 brothers, **G** turned back Jdg 9:56
And **G** also returned all the evil Jdg 9:57
abandoned our **G** and worshiped Jdg 10:10
Then the LORD **G** of Israel handed Jdg 11:21
The LORD **G** of Israel has now Jdg 11:23
whatever your **g** Chemosh drives Jdg 11:24
the LORD our **G** drives out before Jdg 11:24
be a Nazirite to **G** from birth, Jdg 13:5
husband, "A man of **G** came to me. Jdg 13:6
the awe-inspiring Angel of **G**. Jdg 13:6
a Nazirite to **G** from birth until Jdg 13:7
let the man of **G** you sent come Jdg 13:8
G listened to Manoah, and the Jdg 13:9
and the Angel of **G** came again to Jdg 13:9
wife, "because we have seen **G**!" Jdg 13:22
G split a hollow place ⌊in the Jdg 15:19
I am a Nazirite to **G** from birth. Jdg 16:17
sacrifice to their **g** Dagon. Jdg 16:23
Our **g** has handed over our enemy Jdg 16:23
they praised their **g** and said: Jdg 16:24
Our **g** has handed over to us our Jdg 16:24
Lord **G**, please remember me. Jdg 16:28
me, **G**, just once more. Jdg 16:28
inquire of **G** so we will know Jdg 18:5
for **G** has handed it over to you. Jdg 18:10
as the house of **G** was in Shiloh. Jdg 18:31
to Bethel, and inquired of **G**. Jdg 20:18
of the covenant of **G** was there, Jdg 20:27
there before **G** until evening. Jdg 21:2
out, "Why, LORD **G** of Israel, has Jdg 21:3
back to her people and to her **g**. Ru 1:15
and your **G** will be my God. Ru 1:16
and your God will be my **G**. Ru 1:16
from the LORD **G** of Israel, Ru 2:12
may the **G** of Israel grant the 1Sm 1:17
And there is no rock like our **G**. 1Sm 2:2
the LORD is a **G** of knowledge, 1Sm 2:3
another man, **G** can intercede for 1Sm 2:25
A man of **G** came to Eli and said 1Sm 2:27
LORD, the **G** of Israel, says: 1Sm 2:30
the lamp of **G** had gone out, 1Sm 3:3
where the ark of **G** was located. 1Sm 3:3
May **G** punish you and do so 1Sm 3:17
the ark of the covenant of **G**. 1Sm 4:4
The ark of **G** was captured, 1Sm 4:11
was anxious about the ark of **G**. 1Sm 4:13
the ark of **G** has been captured. 1Sm 4:17
When he mentioned the ark of **G**, 1Sm 4:18
of the ark of **G** and to ⌊the 1Sm 4:21
the ark of **G** has been captured. 1Sm 4:22
had captured the ark of **G**, 1Sm 5:1
ark of Israel's **G** must not stay 1Sm 5:7
against us and our **g** Dagon." 1Sm 5:7
do with the ark of Israel's **G**?" 1Sm 5:8
of Israel's **G** should be moved 1Sm 5:8
then sent the ark of **G** to Ekron, 1Sm 5:10
ark of Israel's **G** to us to kill 1Sm 5:10
Send the ark of Israel's **G** away. 1Sm 5:11
send the ark of Israel's **G** away, 1Sm 6:3
to Israel's **G**, and perhaps He 1Sm 6:5
G struck down the men of 1Sm 6:19
presence of this holy LORD **G**? 1Sm 6:20
out to the LORD our **G** for us, 1Sm 7:8
a man of **G** in this city who 1Sm 9:6
no gift to take to the man of **G**. 1Sm 9:7
I'll give it to the man of **G**, 1Sm 9:8
going to inquire of **G** would say, 1Sm 9:9
the city where the man of **G** was. 1Sm 9:10
reveal the word of **G** to you." 1Sm 9:27
men going up to **G** at Bethel will 1Sm 10:3
to the Hill of **G** where there are 1Sm 10:5
require because **G** is with you. 1Sm 10:7
to leave Samuel, **G** changed his 1Sm 10:9
the Spirit of **G** took control 1Sm 10:10
the LORD, the **G** of Israel, says: 1Sm 10:18
today you have rejected your **G**, 1Sm 10:19
whose hearts **G** had touched went 1Sm 10:26
the Spirit of **G** suddenly took 1Sm 11:6
they forgot the LORD their **G**, 1Sm 12:9
the LORD your **G** is your king. 1Sm 12:12
you will follow the LORD your **G**. 1Sm 12:14
to the LORD your **G** for your 1Sm 12:19
which the LORD your **G** gave you 1Sm 13:13
shook, and terror from **G** spread. 1Sm 14:15
Bring the ark of **G**," for it was 1Sm 14:18
said, "We must consult **G** here." 1Sm 14:36
Saul inquired of **G**, "Should I go 1Sm 14:37
But **G** did not answer him that 1Sm 14:37
to the LORD, "**G** of Israel, give 1Sm 14:41
May **G** punish me severely if you 1Sm 14:44
a sacrifice to the LORD your **G**, 1Sm 15:15
to the LORD your **G** at Gilgal." 1Sm 15:21
and worship the LORD your **G**." 1Sm 15:30
evil spirit from **G** is tormenting 1Sm 16:15
spirit from **G** ⌊troubles⌋ you, 1Sm 16:16
spirit from **G** ⌊troubled⌋ Saul 1Sm 16:23
the armies of the living **G**?" 1Sm 17:26
the armies of the living **G**." 1Sm 17:36
the **G** of Israel's armies— 1Sm 17:45
will know that Israel has a **G**, 1Sm 17:46
evil spirit from **G** took control 1Sm 18:10
the Spirit of **G** came on Saul's 1Sm 19:20
Spirit of **G** also came on him, 1Sm 19:23
the LORD, the **G** of Israel, if I 1Sm 20:12
then may **G** punish Jonathan and 1Sm 20:13
I know what **G** will do for me." 1Sm 22:3
sword and inquired of **G** for him, 1Sm 22:13
time I inquired of **G** for him? 1Sm 22:15
G has handed him over to me, 1Sm 23:7
said, "LORD **G** of Israel, Your 1Sm 23:10
LORD **G** of Israel, please tell 1Sm 23:11
but **G** did not hand David over to 1Sm 23:14
him in ⌊his faith in⌋ **G**, 1Sm 23:16
May **G** punish me, and even more 1Sm 25:22
the LORD your **G** protects the 1Sm 25:29
Praise to the LORD **G** of Israel, 1Sm 25:32
as the LORD **G** of Israel lives, 1Sm 25:34
Today **G** has handed your enemy 1Sm 26:8
against me and **G** has turned 1Sm 28:15
as reliable as an angel of **G**. 1Sm 29:9
strength in the LORD his **G**. 1Sm 30:6
Swear to me by **G** that you won't 1Sm 30:15
"As **G** lives," Joab replied, "if 2Sm 2:27
May **G** punish Abner and do so 2Sm 3:9
May **G** punish me and do so 2Sm 3:35
and the LORD **G** of Hosts was with 2Sm 5:10
the ark of **G** from Baale-judah 2Sm 6:2
set the ark of **G** on a new cart 2Sm 6:3
the ark of **G** from Abinadab's 2Sm 6:4
to the ark of **G** and took hold 2Sm 6:6
G struck him dead on the spot 2Sm 6:7
died there next to the ark of **G**. 2Sm 6:7
to him because of the ark of **G**." 2Sm 6:12
and had the ark of **G** brought up 2Sm 6:12
the ark of **G** sits inside tent 2Sm 7:2
Who am I, Lord **G**, and what is my 2Sm 7:18
to You, Lord **G**, for You have 2Sm 7:19
revelation for mankind, Lord **G**. 2Sm 7:19
You know Your servant, Lord **G**. 2Sm 7:20
is why You are great, Lord **G**. 2Sm 7:22
and there is no **G** besides You, 2Sm 7:22
G came to one nation on earth in 2Sm 7:23
You, LORD, have become their **G**. 2Sm 7:24
Now, LORD **G**, fulfill the promise 2Sm 7:25
LORD of Hosts is **G** over Israel.' 2Sm 7:26
LORD of Hosts, **G** of Israel, have 2Sm 7:27
Lord **G**, You are God; Your words 2Sm 7:28
GOD, You are **G**; Your words are 2Sm 7:28
You, Lord **G**, have spoken, and 2Sm 7:29
can show the kindness of **G** to?" 2Sm 9:3
and for the cities of our **G**. 2Sm 10:12
what the LORD **G** of Israel says: 2Sm 12:7
pleaded with **G** for the boy. 2Sm 12:16
the king invoke the LORD your **G**, 2Sm 14:11
similar against the people of **G**? 2Sm 14:13
G would not take away a life; 2Sm 14:14
and the bad like the Angel of **G**. 2Sm 14:17
the LORD your **G** be with you." 2Sm 14:17
the wisdom of the Angel of **G**, 2Sm 14:20
the ark of the covenant of **G**. 2Sm 15:24
They set the ark of **G** down, 2Sm 15:24
Return the ark of **G** to the city. 2Sm 15:25
the ark of **G** to Jerusalem 2Sm 15:29
where he used to worship **G**, 2Sm 15:32
asking about a word from **G**— 2Sm 16:23
May the LORD your **G** be praised! 2Sm 18:28
May **G** punish me and do so 2Sm 19:13
the king is like the Angel of **G**, 2Sm 19:27
G answered prayer for the land. 2Sm 21:14
my **G**, my mountain where I seek 2Sm 22:3
called to my **G**. From His temple 2Sm 22:7
turned from my **G** to wickedness. 2Sm 22:22
and with my **G** I can leap over a 2Sm 22:30
G—His way is perfect; the word 2Sm 22:31
For who is **G** besides the LORD? 2Sm 22:32
And who is a rock? Only our **G**. 2Sm 22:32
G is my strong refuge; He makes 2Sm 22:33
G, the rock of my salvation, is 2Sm 22:47
G—He gives me vengeance and 2Sm 22:48
one anointed by the **G** of Jacob, 2Sm 23:1
The **G** of Israel spoke; the Rock 2Sm 23:3
who rules in the fear of **G**, 2Sm 23:3
it not true my house is with **G**? 2Sm 23:5
May the LORD your **G** multiply the 2Sm 24:3
May the LORD your **G** accept you 2Sm 24:23
to the LORD my **G** burnt offerings 2Sm 24:24
servant by the LORD your **G**, 1Kg 1:17
to you by the LORD **G** of Israel: 1Kg 1:30
the **G** of my lord the king, 1Kg 1:36
'May your **G** make the name of 1Kg 1:47
'May the LORD **G** of Israel be 1Kg 1:48
the LORD your **G** to walk in His 1Kg 2:3
May **G** punish me and do so 1Kg 2:23
of the Lord **G** in the presence 1Kg 2:26
dream at night. **G** said, "Ask. 1Kg 3:5
LORD my **G**, You have now made 1Kg 3:7
So **G** said to him, "Because you 1Kg 3:11
G gave Solomon wisdom, very 1Kg 4:29
for the name of the LORD his **G**. 1Kg 5:3
The LORD my **G** has now given me 1Kg 5:4
for the name of the LORD my **G**, 1Kg 5:5
May the LORD **G** of Israel be 1Kg 8:15
name of the LORD **G** of Israel. 1Kg 8:17
name of the LORD **G** of Israel. 1Kg 8:20
LORD **G** of Israel, there is no 1Kg 8:23
there is no **G** like You in heaven 1Kg 8:23
Therefore, LORD **G** of Israel, 1Kg 8:25
Now LORD **G** of Israel, please 1Kg 8:26
But will **G** indeed live on earth? 1Kg 8:27
LORD my **G**, so that You may 1Kg 8:28
For You, Lord **G**, have set them 1Kg 8:53
the LORD our **G** be with us as He 1Kg 8:57
the LORD our **G** day and night, 1Kg 8:59
may know that the LORD is **G**. 1Kg 8:60
to the LORD our **G** to walk in His 1Kg 8:61
the presence of the LORD our **G**, 1Kg 8:65
the LORD their **G** who brought 1Kg 9:9
May the LORD your **G** be praised! 1Kg 10:9
the wisdom that **G** had put in his 1Kg 10:24
completely with the LORD his **G**, 1Kg 11:4
away from the LORD **G** of Israel, 1Kg 11:9
G raised up Rezon son of Eliada 1Kg 11:23
what the LORD **G** of Israel says: 1Kg 11:31
Chemosh, the **g** of Moab, and to 1Kg 11:33
to Milcom, the **g** of the 1Kg 11:33

revelation from **G** came to 1Kg 12:22
came to Shemaiah, the man of **G**: 1Kg 12:22
here is your **G** who brought you 1Kg 12:28
A man of **G** came from Judah to 1Kg 13:1
The man of **G** cried out against 1Kg 13:2
that the man of **G** had cried out 1Kg 13:4
sign that the man of **G** had given 1Kg 13:5
king responded to the man of **G**, 1Kg 13:6
the LORD your **G** and pray for me 1Kg 13:6
So the man of **G** pleaded for the 1Kg 13:6
king declared to the man of **G**, 1Kg 13:7
But the man of **G** replied, 1Kg 13:8
that the man of **G** had done that 1Kg 13:11
by the man of **G** who had come 1Kg 13:12
the man of **G** and found him 1Kg 13:14
Are you the man of **G** who came 1Kg 13:14
and the man of **G** went back with 1Kg 13:19
to the man of **G** who had come 1Kg 13:21
LORD your **G** commanded you, 1Kg 13:21
is the man of **G** who disobeyed 1Kg 13:26
of the man of **G** thrown on the 1Kg 13:28
of the man of **G** and laid it 1Kg 13:29
where the man of **G** is buried; 1Kg 13:31
what the LORD **G** of Israel says: 1Kg 14:7
to the LORD **G** of Israel. 1Kg 14:13
the LORD his **G** as his ancestor 1Kg 15:3
the LORD his **G** gave him a lamp 1Kg 15:4
the LORD **G** of Israel with. 1Kg 15:30
the LORD **G** of Israel with 1Kg 16:13
the LORD **G** of Israel with 1Kg 16:26
provoke the LORD **G** of Israel 1Kg 16:33
As the LORD **G** of Israel lives, 1Kg 17:1
As the LORD your **G** lives, 1Kg 17:12
what the LORD **G** of Israel says: 1Kg 17:14
Elijah, "Man of **G**, what do we 1Kg 17:18
said, "My LORD **G**, have You also 1Kg 17:20
said, "My LORD **G**, please let 1Kg 17:21
are a man of **G** and the LORD's 1Kg 17:24
the LORD your **G** lives, there is 1Kg 18:10
If Yahweh is **G**, follow Him. 1Kg 18:21
you call on the name of your **g**, 1Kg 18:24
The **G** who answers with fire, 1Kg 18:24
who answers with fire, He is **G**." 1Kg 18:24
name of your **g** but don't light 1Kg 18:25
Shout loudly, for he's a **g**! 1Kg 18:27
and said, "LORD **G** of Abraham, 1Kg 18:36
that You are **G** in Israel and I 1Kg 18:36
are **G** and that You have turned 1Kg 18:37
and said, "Yahweh, He is **G**! 1Kg 18:39
He is God! Yahweh, He is **G**!" 1Kg 18:39
to Horeb, the mountain of **G**. 1Kg 19:8
zealous for the LORD **G** of Hosts, 1Kg 19:10
for the LORD **G** of Hosts," 1Kg 19:14
Then the man of **G** approached 1Kg 20:28
The LORD is a **g** of the mountains 1Kg 20:28
and not a **g** of the valleys, 1Kg 20:28
"You have cursed **G** and king!" 1Kg 21:10
"Naboth has cursed **G** and king!" 1Kg 21:13
the LORD **G** of Israel just as 1Kg 22:53
Baal-zebub, the **g** of Ekron, if I 2Kg 1:2
there is no **G** in Israel that you 2Kg 1:3
of Baal-zebub, the **g** of Ekron?' 2Kg 1:3
there is no **G** in Israel that 2Kg 1:6
of Baal-zebub, the **g** of Ekron? 2Kg 1:6
Man of **G**, the king declares 2Kg 1:9
I am a man of **G**, may fire come 2Kg 1:10
Man of **G**, this is what 2Kg 1:11
I am a man of **G**, may fire come 2Kg 1:12
him, "Man of **G**, please let my 2Kg 1:13
Baal-zebub, the **g** of Ekron—is 2Kg 1:16
there is no **G** in Israel for you 2Kg 1:16
"Where is the LORD **G** of Elijah?" 2Kg 2:14
She went and told the man of **G**, 2Kg 4:7
by here is a holy man of **G**, 2Kg 4:9
Man of **G**, do not deceive your 2Kg 4:16
him on the bed of the man of **G**, 2Kg 4:21
to the man of **G** and then come 2Kg 4:22
to the man of **G** at Mount Carmel. 2Kg 4:25
When the man of **G** saw her at a 2Kg 4:25
to the man of **G** at the mountain 2Kg 4:27
the man of **G** said, "Leave her 2Kg 4:27
death in the pot, man of **G**!" 2Kg 4:40
to the man of **G** with his sack 2Kg 4:42
and asked, "Am I **G**, killing and 2Kg 5:7
Elisha the man of **G** heard that 2Kg 5:8
on the name of Yahweh his **G**, 2Kg 5:11
to the command of the man of **G**. 2Kg 5:14
went back to the man of **G**, 2Kg 5:15

I know there's no **G** in the whole 2Kg 5:15
to any other **g** but Yahweh. 2Kg 5:17
of Elisha the man of **G**, 2Kg 5:20
Then the man of **G** asked, "Where 2Kg 6:6
place, the man of **G** cut a stick, 2Kg 6:6
But the man of **G** sent ⌊word⌋ to 2Kg 6:9
place the man of **G** had told him 2Kg 6:10
The man of **G** repeatedly warned 2Kg 6:10
of the man of **G** got up early and 2Kg 6:15
May **G** punish me and do so 2Kg 6:31
responded to the man of **G**, 2Kg 7:2
as the man of **G** had predicted 2Kg 7:17
When the man of **G** had said to 2Kg 7:18
had answered the man of **G**, 2Kg 7:19
and did what the man of **G** said. 2Kg 8:2
the servant of the man of **G**, 2Kg 8:4
"The man of **G** has come here." 2Kg 8:7
you and go meet the man of **G**. 2Kg 8:8
was ashamed. The man of **G** wept, 2Kg 8:11
what the LORD **G** of Israel says: 2Kg 9:6
the law of the LORD **G** of Israel. 2Kg 10:31
man of **G** was angry with him 2Kg 13:19
the LORD, the **G** of Israel, had 2Kg 14:25
of the LORD his **G** like his 2Kg 16:2
the LORD their **G** who had brought 2Kg 17:7
right against the LORD their **G**. 2Kg 17:9
not believe the LORD their **G**. 2Kg 17:14
of the LORD their **G**. 2Kg 17:16
of the LORD their **G** but lived 2Kg 17:19
the custom of the **G** of the land. 2Kg 17:26
custom of the **G** of the land." 2Kg 17:26
custom of the **G** of the land." 2Kg 17:27
the LORD your **G**, and He will 2Kg 17:39
trusted in the LORD **G** of Israel; 2Kg 18:5
the LORD their **G** but violated 2Kg 18:12
We trust in the LORD our **G**. 2Kg 18:22
the LORD your **G** will hear all 2Kg 19:4
sent to mock the living **G**, 2Kg 19:4
that the LORD your **G** has heard. 2Kg 19:4
Don't let your **G**, whom you trust 2Kg 19:10
G of Israel who is enthroned 2Kg 19:15
You are **G**—You alone— 2Kg 19:15
has sent to mock the living **G**. 2Kg 19:16
Now, LORD our **G**, please save us 2Kg 19:19
know that You are the LORD **G**— 2Kg 19:19
The LORD, the **G** of Israel says: 2Kg 19:20
in the temple of his **g** Nisroch, 2Kg 19:37
what the LORD **G** of your ancestor 2Kg 20:5
what the LORD **G** of Israel says: 2Kg 21:12
the LORD **G** of his ancestors 2Kg 21:22
what the LORD **G** of Israel says, 2Kg 22:15
what the LORD **G** of Israel says: 2Kg 22:18
by the man of **G** who proclaimed 2Kg 23:16
tomb of the man of **G** who came 2Kg 23:17
of the LORD your **G** as written in 2Kg 23:21
just as **G** had predicted. 2Kg 24:13
called out to the **G** of Israel: 1Ch 4:10
And **G** granted his request. 1Ch 4:10
they cried out to **G** in battle. 1Ch 5:20
unfaithful to the **G** of their 1Ch 5:25
of the nations **G** had destroyed 1Ch 5:25
So the **G** of Israel put it into 1Ch 5:26
the servant of **G** had commanded. 1Ch 6:49
LORD your **G** also said to you, 1Ch 11:2
a thing in the presence of **G**! 1Ch 11:19
may the **G** of our ancestors look 1Ch 12:17
helps you, for your **G** helps you. 1Ch 12:18
a great army, like an army of **G**. 1Ch 12:22
if this is from the LORD our **G**, 1Ch 13:2
us bring back the ark of our **G**, 1Ch 13:3
bring the ark of **G** from 1Ch 13:5
to take from there the ark of **G**, 1Ch 13:6
set the ark of **G** on a new cart. 1Ch 13:7
their might before **G** with songs 1Ch 13:8
died there in the presence of **G**. 1Ch 13:10
David feared **G** that day, and 1Ch 13:12
ever bring the ark of **G** to me?" 1Ch 13:12
move the ark of **G** home to the 1Ch 13:13
The ark of **G** remained with 1Ch 13:14
inquired of **G**, "Should I go to 1Ch 14:10
G has used me to burst out 1Ch 14:11
So David again inquired of **G**, 1Ch 14:14
of God, and **G** answered him, "Do 1Ch 14:14
G will have marched out ahead 1Ch 14:15
did exactly as **G** commanded him, 1Ch 14:16
for the ark of **G** and pitched a 1Ch 15:1
Levites may carry the ark of **G**, 1Ch 15:2
ark of the LORD **G** of Israel to 1Ch 15:12

For the LORD our **G** burst out ⌊in 1Ch 15:13
the ark of the LORD **G** of Israel. 1Ch 15:14
the ark of **G** the way Moses had 1Ch 15:15
trumpets before the ark of **G**. 1Ch 15:24
And because **G** helped the Levites 1Ch 15:26
the ark of **G** and placed it 1Ch 16:1
celebrate the LORD **G** of Israel, 1Ch 16:4
the ark of the covenant of **G**. 1Ch 16:6
is the LORD our **G**; His judgments 1Ch 16:14
Save us, **G** of our salvation; 1Ch 16:35
May the LORD, the **G** of Israel, 1Ch 16:36
and musical instruments of **G**. 1Ch 16:42
your heart, for **G** is with you." 1Ch 17:2
the word of **G** came to Nathan: 1Ch 17:3
Who am I, LORD **G**, and what is 1Ch 17:16
thing to You, **G**, for You have 1Ch 17:17
as a man of distinction, LORD **G**. 1Ch 17:17
and there is no **G** besides You, 1Ch 17:20
G, You came to one nation on 1Ch 17:21
You, LORD, have become their **G**. 1Ch 17:22
of Hosts, the **G** of Israel, is 1Ch 17:24
of Israel, is **G** over Israel.' 1Ch 17:24
Since You, my **G**, have revealed 1Ch 17:25
You indeed are **G**, and You have 1Ch 17:26
and for the cities of our **G**. 1Ch 19:13
David said to **G**, "I have sinned 1Ch 21:8
G sent an angel to Jerusalem 1Ch 21:15
David said to **G**, "Wasn't I the 1Ch 21:17
My LORD **G**, please let Your hand 1Ch 21:17
go before it to inquire of **G**, 1Ch 21:30
This is the house of the LORD **G**, 1Ch 22:1
house for the LORD **G** of Israel. 1Ch 22:6
for the name of the LORD my **G**, 1Ch 22:7
the house of the LORD your **G**, 1Ch 22:11
keep the law of the LORD your **G**. 1Ch 22:12
The LORD your **G** is with you, 1Ch 22:18
heart to seek the LORD your **G**. 1Ch 22:19
holy articles of **G** to the temple 1Ch 22:19
As for Moses the man of **G**, 1Ch 23:14
The LORD **G** of Israel has given 1Ch 23:25
and officers of **G** among both 1Ch 24:5
as the LORD **G** of Israel had 1Ch 24:19
the promises of **G** to exalt him, 1Ch 25:5
for **G** had given Heman fourteen 1Ch 25:5
the eighth, for **G** blessed him. 1Ch 26:5
relating to **G** and the king. 1Ch 26:32
and as a footstool for our **G**. 1Ch 28:2
but **G** said to me, 'You are not 1Ch 28:3
Yet the LORD **G** of Israel chose 1Ch 28:4
and in the hearing of our **G**, 1Ch 28:8
the LORD your **G** so that you may 1Ch 28:8
know the **G** of your father, 1Ch 28:9
for the LORD **G**, my God, is with 1Ch 28:20
the LORD God, my **G**, is with you. 1Ch 28:20
son Solomon—**G** has chosen him 1Ch 29:1
be for man, but for the LORD **G**. 1Ch 29:1
provision for the house of my **G**: 1Ch 29:2
my delight in the house of my **G**, 1Ch 29:3
the house of my **G** over and above 1Ch 29:3
LORD **G** of our father Israel, 1Ch 29:10
therefore, our **G**, we give You 1Ch 29:13
LORD our **G**, all this wealth that 1Ch 29:16
I know, my **G**, that You test the 1Ch 29:17
LORD **G** of Abraham, Isaac, and 1Ch 29:18
Praise the LORD your **G**." 1Ch 29:20
praised the LORD **G** of their 1Ch 29:20
The LORD his **G** was with him and 2Ch 1:1
brought the ark of **G** from 2Ch 1:4
That night **G** appeared to Solomon 2Ch 1:7
Solomon said to **G**: "You have 2Ch 1:8
LORD **G**, let Your promise to my 2Ch 1:9
G said to Solomon, "Because this 2Ch 1:11
name of the LORD my **G** in order 2Ch 2:4
festivals of the LORD our **G**. 2Ch 2:4
for our **G** is greater than any of 2Ch 2:5
May the LORD **G** of Israel, who 2Ch 2:12
May the LORD **G** of Israel be 2Ch 6:4
name of the LORD **G** of Israel. 2Ch 6:7
name of the LORD **G** of Israel. 2Ch 6:10
LORD **G** of Israel, there is no 2Ch 6:14
there is no **G** like You in heaven 2Ch 6:14
Therefore, LORD **G** of Israel, 2Ch 6:16
Now, LORD **G** of Israel, please 2Ch 6:17
But will **G** indeed live on earth 2Ch 6:18
LORD my **G**, so that You may 2Ch 6:19
Now, my **G**, please let Your eyes 2Ch 6:40
Arise, LORD **G**, ⌊come⌋ to Your 2Ch 6:41

priests, LORD **G**, be clothed with	2Ch 6:41
LORD **G**, do not reject Your	2Ch 6:42
the LORD **G** of their ancestors	2Ch 7:22
command of David, the man of **G**.	2Ch 8:14
May the LORD your **G** be praised!	2Ch 9:8
as king for the LORD your **G**.	2Ch 9:8
Because Your **G** loved Israel	2Ch 9:8
hear the wisdom **G** had put in his	2Ch 9:23
the turn of events came from **G**,	2Ch 10:15
came to Shemaiah, the man of **G**:	2Ch 11:2
seek the LORD their **G** followed	2Ch 11:16
the LORD **G** of their ancestors.	2Ch 11:16
that the LORD **G** of Israel gave	2Ch 13:5
as for us, the LORD is our **G**.	2Ch 13:10
requirements of the LORD our **G**,	2Ch 13:11
G and His priests are with us at	2Ch 13:12
against the LORD **G** of your	2Ch 13:12
G routed Jeroboam and all Israel	2Ch 13:15
and **G** handed them over to them.	2Ch 13:16
on the LORD, the **G** of their	2Ch 13:18
in the sight of the LORD his **G**.	2Ch 14:2
to seek the LORD **G** of their	2Ch 14:4
we sought the LORD our **G**.	2Ch 14:7
Asa cried out to the LORD his **G**:	2Ch 14:11
us, LORD our **G**, for we depend	2Ch 14:11
LORD, You are our **G**. Do not let	2Ch 14:11
The Spirit of **G** came on Azariah	2Ch 15:1
has been without the true **G**,	2Ch 15:3
to the LORD **G** of Israel in their	2Ch 15:4
for **G** troubled them with every	2Ch 15:6
the LORD his **G** was with him.	2Ch 15:9
to seek the LORD **G** of their	2Ch 15:12
seek the LORD **G** of Israel would	2Ch 15:13
not depended on the LORD your **G**,	2Ch 16:7
but sought the **G** of his father	2Ch 17:4
G will hand it over to the king.	2Ch 18:5
I will say whatever my **G** says."	2Ch 18:13
G drew them away from him.	2Ch 18:31
and have decided to seek **G**."	2Ch 19:3
back to the LORD **G** of their	2Ch 19:4
bribes with the LORD our **G**."	2Ch 19:7
LORD **G** of our ancestors, are You	2Ch 20:6
are You not the **G** who is in	2Ch 20:6
Are You not our **G** who drove out	2Ch 20:7
Our **G**, will You not judge them?	2Ch 20:12
praise the LORD **G** of Israel	2Ch 20:19
Believe in the LORD your **G**,	2Ch 20:20
The terror of **G** was on all the	2Ch 20:29
for his **G** gave him rest on every	2Ch 20:30
to worship⌋ the **G** of their	2Ch 20:33
the LORD **G** of his ancestors.	2Ch 21:10
what the LORD **G** of your ancestor	2Ch 21:12
Ahaziah's downfall was from **G**,	2Ch 22:7
temple of your **G** as needed year	2Ch 24:5
respect to **G** and His temple.	2Ch 24:16
of the LORD **G** of their ancestors	2Ch 24:18
The Spirit of **G** took control of	2Ch 24:20
to them, "This is what **G** says:	2Ch 24:20
the LORD **G** of their ancestors	2Ch 24:24
a man of **G** came to him and said,	2Ch 25:7
⌊But⌋ **G** will make you stumble	2Ch 25:8
for **G** has the power to help or	2Ch 25:8
Amaziah said to the man of **G**,	2Ch 25:9
The man of **G** replied, "The LORD	2Ch 25:9
I know that **G** intends to destroy	2Ch 25:16
was from **G** in order to hand	2Ch 25:20
He sought **G** throughout the	2Ch 26:5
the teacher of the fear of **G**.	2Ch 26:5
the LORD, **G** gave him success	2Ch 26:5
G helped him against the	2Ch 26:7
⌊**G**⌋ made ⌊him⌋ very powerful.	2Ch 26:8
against the LORD his **G** by going	2Ch 26:16
receive honor from the LORD **G**."	2Ch 26:18
waver in obeying the LORD his **G**.	2Ch 27:6
So the LORD his **G** handed Ahaz	2Ch 28:5
the LORD **G** of their ancestors	2Ch 28:6
the LORD **G** of your ancestors	2Ch 28:9
guilty before the LORD your **G**?	2Ch 28:10
he provoked the **G** of his	2Ch 28:25
of the LORD **G** of your ancestors	2Ch 29:5
in the sight of the LORD our **G**.	2Ch 29:6
holy place of the **G** of Israel.	2Ch 29:7
the LORD **G** of Israel so that	2Ch 29:10
rejoiced over how **G** had prepared	2Ch 29:36
of the LORD **G** of Israel.	2Ch 30:1
Passover of the LORD **G** of Israel	2Ch 30:5
return to the LORD **G** of Abraham,	2Ch 30:6
to the LORD **G** of their ancestors	2Ch 30:7
the LORD your **G** so that He may	2Ch 30:8
For the LORD your **G** is gracious	2Ch 30:9
the hand of **G** was in Judah to	2Ch 30:12
the law of Moses the man of **G**.	2Ch 30:16
his whole heart on seeking **G**,	2Ch 30:19
the LORD **G** of his ancestors,	2Ch 30:19
to the LORD **G** of their ancestors	2Ch 30:22
the people, and **G** heard their	2Ch 30:27
consecrated to the LORD their **G**.	2Ch 31:6
offerings to **G** to distribute	2Ch 31:14
and true before the LORD his **G**.	2Ch 31:20
to seek his **G**, and he prospered	2Ch 31:21
the LORD our **G** to help us and to	2Ch 32:8
The LORD our **G** will deliver us	2Ch 32:11
that your **G** should be able to do	2Ch 32:14
no **g** of any nation or kingdom	2Ch 32:15
the LORD **G** and against His	2Ch 32:16
to mock the LORD **G** of Israel,	2Ch 32:17
so Hezekiah's **G** will not deliver	2Ch 32:17
against the **G** of Jerusalem like	2Ch 32:19
He went to the temple of his **g**,	2Ch 32:21
for **G** gave him abundant	2Ch 32:29
G left him to test him and	2Ch 32:31
about which **G** had said to David	2Ch 33:7
of the LORD his **G** and earnestly	2Ch 33:12
before the **G** of his ancestors.	2Ch 33:12
came to know that the LORD is **G**.	2Ch 33:13
to serve the LORD **G** of Israel.	2Ch 33:16
but only to the LORD their **G**.	2Ch 33:17
prayer to his **G** and the words	2Ch 33:18
name of the LORD **G** of Israel,	2Ch 33:18
His prayer and how **G** granted his	2Ch 33:19
to seek the **G** of his ancestor	2Ch 34:3
the temple of the LORD his **G**.	2Ch 34:8
what the LORD **G** of Israel says:	2Ch 34:23
what the LORD **G** of Israel says:	2Ch 34:26
yourself before **G** when you heard	2Ch 34:27
carried out the covenant of **G**,	2Ch 34:32
of God, the **G** of their ancestors	2Ch 34:32
to serve the LORD their **G**.	2Ch 34:33
the LORD **G** of their ancestors	2Ch 34:33
the LORD your **G** and His people	2Ch 35:3
I am fighting. **G** told me to	2Ch 35:21
Stop opposing **G** who is with me;	2Ch 35:21
words from the mouth of **G**,	2Ch 35:22
in the sight of the LORD his **G**.	2Ch 36:5
of the LORD his **G** and did not	2Ch 36:12
made him swear allegiance by **G**.	2Ch 36:13
to the LORD **G** of Israel.	2Ch 36:13
the LORD **G** of their ancestors	2Ch 36:15
The LORD, the **G** of heaven, has	2Ch 36:23
may the LORD his **G** be with him.	2Ch 36:23
The LORD, the **G** of heaven, has	Ezr 1:2
people, may his **G** be with him,	Ezr 1:3
the LORD, the **G** of Israel, the	Ezr 1:3
the **G** who is in Jerusalem.	Ezr 1:3
the house of **G** in Jerusalem."	Ezr 1:4
everyone **G** had motivated—	Ezr 1:5
the house of **G** in order to have	Ezr 2:68
of Israel's **G** in order to offer	Ezr 3:2
the law of Moses the man of **G**.	Ezr 3:2
those working on the house of **G**.	Ezr 3:9
for the LORD, the **G** of Israel,	Ezr 4:1
worship your **G** and have been	Ezr 4:2
in building a house for our **G**,	Ezr 4:3
for the LORD, the **G** of Israel,	Ezr 4:3
the name of the **G** of Israel who	Ezr 5:1
prophets of **G** were with them,	Ezr 5:2
But **G** was watching over the	Ezr 5:5
of the great **G** in the province	Ezr 5:8
servants of the **G** of heaven and	Ezr 5:11
fathers angered the **G** of heaven,	Ezr 5:12
to rebuild this house of **G**.	Ezr 5:13
let the house of **G** be rebuilt on	Ezr 5:15
this house of **G** in Jerusalem.	Ezr 5:17
the house of **G** in Jerusalem:	Ezr 6:3
and put into the house of **G**.	Ezr 6:5
of this house of **G** alone.	Ezr 6:7
house of **G** on its ⌊original⌋	Ezr 6:7
can rebuild this house of **G**:	Ezr 6:8
offerings to the **G** of heaven,	Ezr 6:9
aroma to the **G** of heaven and	Ezr 6:10
May the **G** who caused His name to	Ezr 6:12
this house of **G** in Jerusalem.	Ezr 6:12
the command of the **G** of Israel	Ezr 6:14
of this house of **G** with joy.	Ezr 6:16
the service of **G** in Jerusalem,	Ezr 6:18
the LORD, the **G** of Israel.	Ezr 6:21
on the house of the **G** of Israel.	Ezr 6:22
the LORD, the **G** of Israel, had	Ezr 7:6
of the LORD his **G** was on him.	Ezr 7:6
hand of his **G** was on him,	Ezr 7:9
in the law of the **G** of heaven:	Ezr 7:12
according to the law of your **G**,	Ezr 7:14
given to the **G** of Israel,	Ezr 7:15
house of their **G** in Jerusalem.	Ezr 7:16
house of your **G** in Jerusalem.	Ezr 7:17
according to the will of your **G**.	Ezr 7:18
deliver to the **G** of Jerusalem	Ezr 7:19
service of the house of your **G**.	Ezr 7:19
needs of the house of your **G**.	Ezr 7:20
the law of the **G** of heaven asks	Ezr 7:21
commanded by the **G** of heaven	Ezr 7:23
the house of the **G** of heaven,	Ezr 7:23
servants of this house of **G**.	Ezr 7:24
the laws of your **G** and to teach	Ezr 7:25
the law of your **G** and the law	Ezr 7:26
the LORD **G** of our fathers,	Ezr 7:27
strengthened by the LORD my **G**,	Ezr 7:28
for the house of our **G**.	Ezr 8:17
hand of our **G** was on us,	Ezr 8:18
before our **G** and ask Him for	Ezr 8:21
The hand of our **G** is gracious to	Ezr 8:22
pleaded with our **G** about this,	Ezr 8:23
house of our **G** that the king,	Ezr 8:25
to the LORD **G** of your fathers.	Ezr 8:28
the house of our **G** in Jerusalem.	Ezr 8:30
We were strengthened by our **G**,	Ezr 8:31
the house of our **G** into the care	Ezr 8:33
offerings to the **G** of Israel:	Ezr 8:35
the people and the house of **G**.	Ezr 8:36
the words of the **G** of Israel	Ezr 9:4
out my hands to the LORD my **G**.	Ezr 9:5
My **G**, I am ashamed and	Ezr 9:6
toward You, my **G**, because our	Ezr 9:6
from the LORD our **G** to preserve	Ezr 9:8
G has given us new life and	Ezr 9:8
G has not abandoned us in our	Ezr 9:9
house of our **G** and repair its	Ezr 9:9
Now, our **G**, what can we say in	Ezr 9:10
though You, our **G**, have punished	Ezr 9:13
LORD **G** of Israel, You are	Ezr 9:15
facedown before the house of **G**,	Ezr 10:1
unfaithful to our **G** by marrying	Ezr 10:2
before our **G** to send away all	Ezr 10:3
at the commandment of our **G**.	Ezr 10:3
then went from the house of **G**,	Ezr 10:6
in the square at the house of **G**,	Ezr 10:9
the LORD **G** of your fathers and	Ezr 10:11
anger of our **G** concerning this	Ezr 10:14
praying before the **G** of heaven.	Neh 1:4
I said, LORD **G** of heaven, the	Neh 1:5
awe-inspiring **G** who keeps His	Neh 1:5
So I prayed to the **G** of heaven	Neh 2:4
graciously strengthened by my **G**.	Neh 2:8
anyone what my **G** had laid on my	Neh 2:12
hand of my **G** had been on me,	Neh 2:18
The **G** of heaven is the One who	Neh 2:20
Listen, our **G**, for we are	Neh 4:4
we prayed to our **G** and stationed	Neh 4:9
scheme and that **G** had frustrated	Neh 4:15
Our **G** will fight for us!"	Neh 4:20
fear of our **G** ⌊and not invite	Neh 5:9
May **G** likewise shake from his	Neh 5:13
this, because of the fear of **G**.	Neh 5:15
favorably, my **G**, for all that I	Neh 5:19
But now, ⌊my **G**,⌋ strengthen me.	Neh 6:9
at the house of **G** inside the	Neh 6:10
I realized that **G** had not sent	Neh 6:12
My **G**, remember Tobiah and	Neh 6:14
had been accomplished by our **G**.	Neh 6:16
man who feared **G** more than most.	Neh 7:2
Then my **G** put it into my mind to	Neh 7:5
LORD, the great **G**, and with	Neh 8:6
read the book of the law of **G**,	Neh 8:8
day is holy to the LORD your **G**.	Neh 8:9
the court of the house of **G**,	Neh 8:16
book of the law of **G** every day,	Neh 8:18
of the LORD their **G** for a fourth	Neh 9:3
and worship of the LORD their **G**.	Neh 9:3
out loudly to the LORD their **G**.	Neh 9:4
the LORD your **G** from everlasting	Neh 9:5
are the LORD **G** who chose Abram	Neh 9:7
But You are a forgiving **G**,	Neh 9:17
This is your **G** who brought you	Neh 9:18
a gracious and compassionate **G**.	Neh 9:31

So now, our **G**—the great, Neh 9:32
awe-inspiring **G** who keeps His Neh 9:32
peoples to ⌊obey⌋ the law of **G**— Neh 10:28
the law of **G** given through Neh 10:29
service of the house of our **G**: Neh 10:32
the work of the house of our **G**. Neh 10:33
on the altar of the LORD our **G**, Neh 10:34
flocks to the house of our **G**, Neh 10:36
of the house of our **G**. Neh 10:37
treasury in the house of our **G**. Neh 10:38
not neglect the house of our **G**. Neh 10:39
the work outside the house of **G**; Neh 11:16
the man of **G** had prescribed. Neh 12:24
of David, the man of **G**. Neh 12:36
stood in the house of **G**. Neh 12:40
rejoiced because **G** had given Neh 12:43
of their **G** and the service Neh 12:45
of praise and thanksgiving to **G**. Neh 12:46
ever enter the assembly of **G**, Neh 13:1
but our **G** turned the curse into Neh 13:2
of the house of our **G**. Neh 13:4
the house of **G** restored there, Neh 13:9
the house of **G** been neglected? Neh 13:11
me for this, my **G**, and don't Neh 13:14
the house of my **G** and for its Neh 13:14
so that our **G** brought all this Neh 13:18
this also, my **G**, and look on me Neh 13:22
take an oath before **G** and said: Neh 13:25
loved by his **G** and God made him Neh 13:26
by his God and **G** made him king Neh 13:26
our **G** by marrying foreign Neh 13:27
them, my **G**, for defiling Neh 13:29
Remember me, my **G**, with favor. Neh 13:31
feared **G** and turned away from Jb 1:1
having cursed **G** in their hearts. Jb 1:5
the sons of **G** came to present Jb 1:6
G and turns away from evil. Jb 1:8
Does Job fear **G** for nothing? Jb 1:9
not sin or blame **G** for anything. Jb 1:22
day the sons of **G** came again to Jb 2:1
who fears **G** and turns away from Jb 2:3
integrity? Curse **G** and die!" Jb 2:9
good from **G** and not adversity? Jb 2:10
May **G** above not care about it, Jb 3:4
is hidden, whom **G** has hedged Jb 3:23
blast from **G** and come to an end Jb 4:9
person be more righteous than **G**, Jb 4:17
If **G** puts no trust in His Jb 4:18
would appeal to **G** and would Jb 5:8
how happy the man is **G** corrects; Jb 5:17
be granted and **G** would provide Jb 6:8
Does **G** pervert justice? Does the Jb 8:3
you earnestly seek **G** and ask the Jb 8:5
the destiny of all who forget **G**; Jb 8:13
G does not reject a person of Jb 8:20
a person be justified before **G**? Jb 9:2
could not answer **G** once in a Jb 9:3
G is wise and all-powerful. Jb 9:4
G does not hold back His anger; Jb 9:13
I will say to **G**: Do not declare Jb 10:2
But if only **G** would speak and Jb 11:5
Know then that **G** has chosen to Jb 11:6
the depths of **G** or discover Jb 11:7
by calling on **G**, who answers me. Jb 12:4
those who provoke **G** are secure; Jb 12:6
Wisdom and strength belong to **G**; Jb 12:13
and argue my case before **G**. Jb 13:3
things to me, ⌊**G**⌋, so that I Jb 13:20
the fear ⌊of **G**⌋ and hinder Jb 15:4
listen in on the council of **G**, Jb 15:8
anger against **G** and allow such Jb 15:13
If **G** puts no trust in His holy Jb 15:15
his hand against **G** and has Jb 15:25
G hands me over to unjust men; Jb 16:11
scoff at me as I weep before **G**. Jb 16:20
a man and **G** just as a man Jb 16:21
of the one who does not know **G**. Jb 18:21
that it is **G** who has wronged me Jb 19:6
do you persecute me as **G** ⌊does⌋? Jb 19:22
yet I will see **G** in my flesh. Jb 19:26
G will force it from his stomach. Jb 20:15
G will send His burning anger Jb 20:23
is the wicked man's lot from **G**, Jb 20:29
the inheritance **G** ordained for Jb 20:29
no rod from **G** ⌊strikes⌋ them. Jb 21:9
Yet they say to **G**: "Leave us Jb 21:14
G reserves a person's punishment Jb 21:19
Let **G** repay the person himself, Jb 21:19
Can anyone teach **G** knowledge, Jb 21:22
Can a man be of ⌊any⌋ use to **G**? Jb 22:2
Isn't **G** as high as the heavens? Jb 22:12
say: "What does **G** know? Can He Jb 22:13
were the ones who said to **G**, Jb 22:17
to terms with **G** and be at peace; Jb 22:21
and lift up your face to **G**. Jb 22:26
Lift ⌊them⌋ up," **G** will save the Jb 22:29
G has made my heart faint; Jb 23:16
yet **G** pays no attention to this Jb 24:12
Yet **G** drags away the mighty by Jb 24:22
a person be justified before **G**? Jb 25:4
is naked before **G**, and Abaddon Jb 26:6
As **G** lives, who has deprived me Jb 27:2
the breath from **G** remains in my Jb 27:3
when **G** takes away his life? Jb 27:8
G hear his cry when distress Jb 27:9
Will he call on **G** at all times? Jb 27:10
is a wicked man's lot from **G**, Jb 27:13
But **G** understands the way to Jb 28:23
When **G** fixed the weight of the Jb 28:25
the days when **G** watched over me Jb 29:2
Because **G** has loosened my Jb 30:11
would I have⌋ from **G** above, Jb 31:2
let **G** weigh me with an accurate Jb 31:6
could I do when **G** stands up ⌊to Jb 31:14
Did not the same **G** form us both Jb 31:15
disaster from **G** terrifies me, Jb 31:23
for I would have denied **G** above. Jb 31:28
justified himself rather than **G**. Jb 32:2
let **G** deal with him, not man." Jb 32:13
The Spirit of **G** has made me, Jb 33:4
I am just like you before **G**; Jb 33:6
since **G** is greater than man. Jb 33:12
For **G** speaks time and again, Jb 33:14
G spares his soul from the Pit, Jb 33:18
He will pray to **G**, and God will Jb 33:26
and **G** will delight in him. Jb 33:26
and **G** will restore his Jb 33:26
G certainly does all these Jb 33:29
G has deprived me of justice. Jb 34:5
impossible for **G** ⌊to do⌋ wrong, Jb 34:10
it is true that **G** does not act Jb 34:12
G is not partial to princes and Jb 34:19
G does not ⌊need to⌋ examine a Jb 34:23
But when **G** is silent, who can Jb 34:29
Suppose someone says to **G**, Jb 34:31
Should **G** repay ⌊you⌋ on your Jb 34:33
multiplying his words against **G**. Jb 34:37
"I am righteous before **G**"? Jb 35:2
you sin, how does it affect **G**? Jb 35:6
asks, "Where is **G** my Maker, who Jb 35:10
G does not listen to empty Jb 35:13
Yes, **G** is mighty, but He Jb 36:5
G tells them what they have done Jb 36:9
even when **G** binds them, they do Jb 36:13
G rescues the afflicted by Jb 36:15
G shows Himself exalted by His Jb 36:22
G is exalted beyond our Jb 36:26
G thunders with His majestic Jb 37:4
G thunders marvelously with His Jb 37:5
is formed by the breath of **G**, Jb 37:10
Do you know how **G** directs His Jb 37:15
can you help **G** spread out the Jb 37:18
the sons of **G** shouted for joy Jb 38:7
cry out to **G** and wander about Jb 38:41
G has deprived her of wisdom; Jb 39:17
argues with **G** give an answer. Jb 40:2
"There is no help for him in **G**." Ps 3:2
Save me, my **G**! You strike all Ps 3:7
when I call, **G**, who vindicates Ps 4:1
my King and my **G**, for I pray to Ps 5:2
For You are not a **G** who delights Ps 5:4
Punish them, **G**; let them fall by Ps 5:10
LORD my **G**, I seek refuge in You; Ps 7:1
LORD my **G**, if I have done this, Ps 7:3
and emotions is a righteous **G**. Ps 7:9
My shield is with **G**, who saves Ps 7:10
G is a righteous judge, and a Ps 7:11
and a **G** who executes justice Ps 7:11
not repent, **G** will sharpen His Ps 7:12
less than **G** and crowned him Ps 8:5
all the nations that forget **G**. Ps 9:17
⌊since⌋ **G** does not exist." Ps 10:4
to himself, "**G** has forgotten; Ps 10:11
Rise up, LORD **G**! Lift up Your Ps 10:12
Why has the wicked despised **G**? Ps 10:13
me and answer, LORD, my **G**. Ps 13:3
his heart, "**G** does not exist." Ps 14:1
who is wise, one who seeks **G**. Ps 14:2
for **G** is with those who are Ps 14:5
Protect me, **G**, for I take refuge Ps 16:1
take another ⌊**g**⌋ for themselves Ps 16:4
I call on You, **G**, because You Ps 17:6
my deliverer, my **G**, my mountain Ps 18:2
and I cried to my **G** for help. Ps 18:6
turned from my **G** to wickedness. Ps 18:21
my **G** illuminates my darkness. Ps 18:28
and with my **G** I can leap over a Ps 18:29
G—His way is perfect; the word Ps 18:30
For who is **G** besides the LORD? Ps 18:31
And who is a rock? Only our **G**. Ps 18:31
G—He clothes me with strength Ps 18:32
G of my salvation is exalted. Ps 18:46
G—He gives me vengeance and Ps 18:47
heavens declare the glory of **G**, Ps 19:1
name of Jacob's **G** protect you. Ps 20:1
the banner in the name of our **G**. Ps 20:5
in the name of the LORD our **G**. Ps 20:7
My **G**, my God, why have You Ps 22:1
My God, my **G**, why have You Ps 22:1
My **G**, I cry by day, but You do Ps 22:2
have been my **G** from my mother's Ps 22:10
from the **G** of his salvation. Ps 24:5
seek the face of the **G** of Jacob. Ps 24:6
My **G**, I trust in You. Do not let Ps 25:2
You are the **G** of my salvation Ps 25:5
G, redeem Israel, from all its Ps 25:22
or abandon me, **G** of my salvation Ps 27:9
The **G** of glory thunders—the Ps 29:3
LORD my **G**, I cried to You for Ps 30:2
LORD my **G**, I will praise You Ps 30:12
You redeem me, LORD, **G** of truth. Ps 31:5
LORD; I say, "You are my **G**." Ps 31:14
the nation whose **G** is the LORD— Ps 33:12
to my cause, my **G** and my LORD! Ps 35:23
me, LORD, my **G**, in keeping with Ps 35:24
no dread of **G** before his eyes, Ps 36:1
G, Your faithful love is so Ps 36:7
of his **G** is in his heart; Ps 37:31
You will answer, Lord my **G**. Ps 38:15
my **G**, do not be far from me. Ps 38:21
a hymn of praise to our **G**. Ps 40:3
LORD my **G**, You have done many Ps 40:5
I delight to do Your will, my **G**; Ps 40:8
deliverer; my **G**, do not delay. Ps 40:17
May the LORD, the **G** of Israel, Ps 41:13
of water, so I long for You, **G**. Ps 42:1
I thirst for **G**, the living God. Ps 42:2
I thirst for God, the living **G**. Ps 42:2
can I come and appear before **G**? Ps 42:2
say to me, "Where is your **G**?" Ps 42:3
procession to the house of **G**, Ps 42:4
Put your hope in **G**, for I will Ps 42:5
praise Him, my Savior and my **G**. Ps 42:5
a prayer to the **G** of my life. Ps 42:8
I will say to **G**, my rock, "Why Ps 42:9
say to me, "Where is your **G**?" Ps 42:10
Put your hope in **G**, for I will Ps 42:11
praise Him, my Savior and my **G**. Ps 42:11
Vindicate me, **G**, and defend my Ps 43:1
For You are the **G** of my refuge. Ps 43:2
I will come to the altar of **G**, Ps 43:4
of God, to **G**, my greatest joy Ps 43:4
You with the lyre, **G**, my God. Ps 43:4
You with the lyre, God, my **G**. Ps 43:4
Put your hope in **G**, for I will Ps 43:5
praise Him, my Savior and my **G**. Ps 43:5
G, we have heard with our ears— Ps 44:1
are my King, my **G**, who ordains Ps 44:4
We boast in **G** all day long; Ps 44:8
the name of our **G** and spread out Ps 44:20
out our hands to a foreign **g**, Ps 44:20
wouldn't **G** have found this out, Ps 44:21
Therefore **G** has blessed you Ps 45:2
Your throne, **G**, is forever and Ps 45:6
therefore **G**, your God, has Ps 45:7
God, your **G**, has anointed you, Ps 45:7
G is our refuge and strength, Ps 46:1
streams delight the city of **G**, Ps 46:4
G is within her; she will not be Ps 46:5
G will help her when the morning Ps 46:5
G of Jacob is our stronghold. Ps 46:7
know that I am **G**, exalted among Ps 46:10
G of Jacob is our stronghold. Ps 46:11
shout to **G** with a jubilant cry. Ps 47:1

G ascends amid shouts of joy, Ps 47:5
Sing praise to **G**, sing praise; Ps 47:6
for **G** is King of all the earth. Ps 47:7
G reigns over the nations; Ps 47:8
G is seated on His holy throne. Ps 47:8
the people of the **G** of Abraham. Ps 47:9
of the earth belong to **G**; Ps 47:9
praised in the city of our **G**. Ps 48:1
G is known as a stronghold in Ps 48:3
of Hosts, in the city of our **G**; Ps 48:8
G will establish it forever. Ps 48:8
G, within Your temple, we Ps 48:9
Your name, **G**, like Your praise, Ps 48:10
This **G**, our God forever and ever Ps 48:14
This God, our **G** forever and ever Ps 48:14
person or pay his ransom to **G**— Ps 49:7
But **G** will redeem my life from Ps 49:15
G, the LORD God speaks; He Ps 50:1
God, the LORD **G** speaks; He Ps 50:1
of beauty, **G** appears in radiance Ps 50:2
Our **G** is coming; He will not be Ps 50:3
for **G** is the judge. Ps 50:6
you, Israel. I am **G**, your God. Ps 50:7
you, Israel. I am God, your **G**. Ps 50:7
Sacrifice a thank offering to **G**, Ps 50:14
But **G** says to the wicked: Ps 50:16
you who forget **G**, or I will tear Ps 50:22
show him the salvation of **G**." Ps 50:23
gracious to me, **G**, according to Ps 51:1
G, create a clean heart for me Ps 51:10
of bloodshed, **G**, the God of my Ps 51:14
God, the **G** of my salvation, Ps 51:14
to **G** is a broken spirit. Ps 51:17
G, You will not despise a broken Ps 51:17
is why **G** will bring you down Ps 52:5
who would not make **G** his refuge, Ps 52:7
olive tree in the house of **G**; Ps 52:8
his heart, "**G** does not exist." Ps 53:1
G looks down from heaven on the Ps 53:2
one who is wise and who seeks **G**. Ps 53:2
bread; they do not call on **G**. Ps 53:4
because **G** will scatter the bones Ps 53:5
to shame, for **G** has rejected Ps 53:5
When **G** restores His captive Ps 53:6
G, save me by Your name, and Ps 54:1
G, hear my prayer; listen to the Ps 54:2
They have no regard for **G**. Ps 54:3
G is my helper; the Lord is the Ps 54:4
G, listen to my prayer and do Ps 55:1
the crowd into the house of **G**. Ps 55:14
But I call to **G**, and the LORD Ps 55:16
G, the One enthroned from long Ps 55:19
do not change and do not fear **G**. Ps 55:19
You, **G**, will bring them down to Ps 55:23
gracious to me, **G**, for man Ps 56:1
G, whose word I praise, in God Ps 56:4
word I praise, in **G** I trust; Ps 56:4
G, bring down the nations in Ps 56:7
call. This I know: **G** is for me. Ps 56:9
G, whose word I praise, in the Ps 56:10
in **G** I trust; I will not fear. Ps 56:11
am obligated by vows to You, **G**; Ps 56:12
to walk before **G** in the light of Ps 56:13
gracious to me, **G**, be gracious Ps 57:1
call to **G** Most High, to God who Ps 57:2
to **G** who fulfills ⌊His purpose⌋ Ps 57:2
Selah **G** sends His faithful love Ps 57:3
G, be exalted above the heavens; Ps 57:5
is confident, **G**, my heart is Ps 57:7
G, be exalted above the heavens; Ps 57:11
G, knock the teeth out of their Ps 58:6
is a **G** who judges on earth! Ps 58:11
me from my enemies, my **G**; Ps 59:1
You, LORD **G** of Hosts, God of Ps 59:5
God of Hosts, **G** of Israel, rise Ps 59:5
because **G** is my stronghold. Ps 59:9
My faithful **G** will come to meet Ps 59:10
G will let me look down on my Ps 59:10
the earth that **G** rules over Ps 59:13
because **G** is my stronghold— Ps 59:17
my stronghold—my faithful **G**. Ps 59:17
G, You have rejected us; Ps 60:1
G has spoken in His sanctuary: Ps 60:6
Is it not You, **G**, who have Ps 60:10
G, You do not march out with our Ps 60:10
G we will perform valiantly; Ps 60:12
G, hear my cry; pay attention to Ps 61:1
G, You have heard my vows; Ps 61:5
sit enthroned before **G** forever; Ps 61:7
I am at rest in **G** alone; Ps 62:1
Rest in **G** alone, my soul, for my Ps 62:5
salvation and glory depend on **G**; Ps 62:7
strong rock, my refuge, is in **G**. Ps 62:7
before Him. **G** is our refuge. Ps 62:8
G has spoken once; I have heard Ps 62:11
twice: strength belongs to **G**, Ps 62:11
G, You are my God; I eagerly Ps 63:1
God, You are my **G**; I eagerly Ps 63:1
But the king will rejoice in **G**; Ps 63:11
G, hear my voice when I complain. Ps 64:1
But **G** will shoot them with Ps 64:7
is rightfully Yours, **G**, in Zion; Ps 65:1
works, **G** of our salvation, Ps 65:5
joyfully to **G**, all the earth! Ps 66:1
Say to **G**, "How awe-inspiring are Ps 66:3
Come and see the works of **G**; Ps 66:5
Praise our **G**, you peoples; Ps 66:8
For You, **G**, tested us; You Ps 66:10
all who fear **G**, and I will tell Ps 66:16
However, **G** has listened; Ps 66:19
May **G** be praised! He has not Ps 66:20
G be gracious to us and bless Ps 67:1
Let the peoples praise You, **G**; Ps 67:3
peoples praise You, **G**, let all Ps 67:5
its harvest; **G**, our God, blesses Ps 67:6
harvest; God, our **G**, blesses us. Ps 67:6
G will bless us, and all the Ps 67:7
G arises. His enemies scatter, Ps 68:1
wicked are destroyed before **G**. Ps 68:2
rejoice before **G** and celebrate Ps 68:3
Sing to **G**! Sing praises to His Ps 68:4
of widows is **G** in His holy Ps 68:5
G provides homes for those who Ps 68:6
G, when You went out before Your Ps 68:7
poured down ⌊rain⌋ before **G**, Ps 68:8
before God, the **G** of Sinai, Ps 68:8
of Sinai, before **G**, the God of Ps 68:8
before God, the **G** of Israel. Ps 68:8
You, **G**, showered abundant rain; Ps 68:9
You provided for the poor, **G**. Ps 68:10
the mountain **G** desired for His Ps 68:16
so that the LORD **G** might live Ps 68:18
our burdens; **G** is our salvation Ps 68:19
Our **G** is a God of salvation, Ps 68:20
Our God is a **G** of salvation, Ps 68:20
death belongs to the Lord **G**. Ps 68:20
Surely **G** crushes the heads of Ps 68:21
procession, **G**, the procession Ps 68:24
the procession of my **G**, my King, Ps 68:24
Praise **G** in the assemblies; Ps 68:26
G has decreed your strength. Ps 68:28
Your strength, **G**, You who have Ps 68:28
will stretch out its hands to **G**. Ps 68:31
Sing to **G**, you kingdoms of the Ps 68:32
power to **G**. His majesty is Ps 68:34
G, You are awe-inspiring in Your Ps 68:35
The **G** of Israel gives power and Ps 68:35
to His people. May **G** be praised! Ps 68:35
Save me, **G**, for the water has Ps 69:1
My eyes fail, looking for my **G**. Ps 69:3
G, You know my foolishness, and Ps 69:5
because of me, Lord **G** of Hosts; Ps 69:6
because of me, **G** of Israel. Ps 69:6
faithful love, **G**, answer me with Ps 69:13
Your salvation protect me, **G**. Ps 69:29
You who seek **G**, take heart! Ps 69:32
for **G** will save Zion and build Ps 69:35
G, deliver me. Hurry to help me, Ps 70:1
continually say, "**G** is great!" Ps 70:4
hurry to me, **G**. You are my help Ps 70:5
Deliver me, my **G**, from the hand Ps 71:4
my hope, Lord **G**, my confidence Ps 71:5
saying, "**G** has abandoned him; Ps 71:11
G, do not be far from me; Ps 71:12
far from me; my **G**, hurry to help Ps 71:12
the mighty acts of the Lord **G**; Ps 71:16
G, You have taught me from my Ps 71:17
old and gray, **G**, do not abandon Ps 71:18
reaches heaven, **G**, You who have Ps 71:19
great things; **G**, who is like You Ps 71:19
You for Your faithfulness, my **G**; Ps 71:22
G, give Your justice to the king Ps 72:1
May the LORD **G**, the God of Ps 72:18
the LORD God, the **G** of Israel, Ps 72:18
G is indeed good to Israel, Ps 73:1
They say, "How can **G** know? Ps 73:11
but **G** is the strength of my Ps 73:26
have made the Lord **G** my refuge, Ps 73:28
You rejected ⌊us⌋ forever, **G**? Ps 74:1
the land where **G** met with us. Ps 74:8
G, how long will the foe mock? Ps 74:10
G my king is from ancient times, Ps 74:12
Arise, **G**, defend Your cause! Ps 74:22
We give thanks to You, **G**; Ps 75:1
for **G** is the judge: He brings Ps 75:7
sing praise to the **G** of Jacob. Ps 75:9
G is known in Judah; His name is Ps 76:1
At Your rebuke, **G** of Jacob, both Ps 76:6
when **G** rose up to judge and to Ps 76:9
your vows to the LORD your **G**; Ps 76:11
I cry aloud to **G**, aloud to God, Ps 77:1
to God, aloud to **G**, and He will Ps 77:1
I think of **G**; I groan; I Ps 77:3
Has **G** forgotten to be gracious? Ps 77:9
G, Your way is holy. What god is Ps 77:13
What **g** is great like God? Ps 77:13
What god is great like **G**? Ps 77:13
You are the **G** who works wonders; Ps 77:14
waters saw You, **G**. The waters Ps 77:16
confidence in **G** and not forget Ps 78:7
spirit was not faithful to **G**. Ps 78:8
They deliberately tested **G**, Ps 78:18
spoke against **G**, saying, "Is God Ps 78:19
Is **G** able to provide food in the Ps 78:19
did not believe **G** or rely on His Ps 78:22
repented and searched for **G**. Ps 78:34
that **G** was their rock, Ps 78:35
the Most High **G**, their Redeemer. Ps 78:35
constantly tested **G** and provoked Ps 78:41
tested the Most High **G**, Ps 78:56
G heard and became furious; Ps 78:59
G, the nations have invaded Your Ps 79:1
G of our salvation, help us— Ps 79:9
nations ask, "Where is their **G**?" Ps 79:10
Restore us, **G**; look ⌊on us⌋ with Ps 80:3
LORD **G** of Hosts, how long will Ps 80:4
Restore us, **G** of Hosts; look ⌊on Ps 80:7
Return, **G** of Hosts. Look down Ps 80:14
Restore us, LORD **G** of Hosts; Ps 80:19
Sing for joy to **G** our strength; Ps 81:1
in triumph to the **G** of Jacob. Ps 81:1
a judgment of the **G** of Jacob. Ps 81:4
not be a strange **g** among you; Ps 81:9
not bow down to a foreign **g**. Ps 81:9
am Yahweh your **G**, who brought Ps 81:10
G has taken His place in the Ps 82:1
Rise up, **G**, judge the earth, for Ps 82:8
G, do not keep silent. Do not be Ps 83:1
not be deaf, **G**; do not be idle Ps 83:1
tumbleweed, my **G**, like straw Ps 83:13
flesh cry out for the living **G**. Ps 84:2
LORD of Hosts, my King and my **G**. Ps 84:3
each appears before **G** in Zion. Ps 84:7
LORD **G** of Hosts, hear my prayer; Ps 84:8
prayer; listen, **G** of Jacob. Ps 84:8
our shield, **G**; look on the face Ps 84:9
the house of my **G** than to live Ps 84:10
For the LORD **G** is a sun and Ps 84:11
to us, **G** of our salvation, Ps 85:4
will listen to what **G** will say; Ps 85:8
You are my **G**; save Your servant Ps 86:2
wonders; You alone are **G**. Ps 86:10
heart, Lord my **G**, and will honor Ps 86:12
G, arrogant people have attacked Ps 86:14
a compassionate and gracious **G**, Ps 86:15
are said about you, city of **G**. Ps 87:3
LORD, **G** of my salvation, I cry Ps 88:1
G is greatly feared in the Ps 89:7
LORD **G** of Hosts, who is strong Ps 89:8
my Father, my **G**, the rock of my Ps 89:26
eternity to eternity, You are **G**. Ps 90:2
of the Lord our **G** be on us; Ps 90:17
my fortress, my **G**, in whom I Ps 91:2
in the courtyards of our **G**. Ps 92:13
LORD, **G** of vengeance—God of Ps 94:1
of vengeance—**G** of vengeance, Ps 94:1
The **G** of Jacob doesn't pay Ps 94:7
my **G** is the rock of my Ps 94:22
LORD our **G** will destroy them. Ps 94:23
For the LORD is a great **G**, Ps 95:3
For He is our **G**, and we are the Ps 95:7
the LORD our **G**; bow in worship Ps 99:5
LORD our **G**, You answered them. Ps 99:8
You were a **G** who forgave them, Ps 99:8

the LORD our **G**; bow in worship Ps 99:9
for the LORD our **G** is holy. Ps 99:9
Acknowledge that the LORD is **G**. Ps 100:3
My **G**, do not take me in the Ps 102:24
LORD my **G**, You are very great; Ps 104:1
prey and seek their food from **G**. Ps 104:21
praise to my **G** while I live. Ps 104:33
is the LORD our **G**; His judgments Ps 105:7
and tested **G** in the desert. Ps 106:14
They forgot **G** their Savior, Ps 106:21
us, LORD our **G**, and gather us Ps 106:47
May the LORD, the **G** of Israel, Ps 106:48
My heart is confident, **G**; Ps 108:1
G, be exalted above the heavens; Ps 108:5
G has spoken in His sanctuary: Ps 108:7
Have You not rejected us, **G**? Ps 108:11
G, You do not march out with our Ps 108:11
G we will perform valiantly; Ps 108:13
G of my praise, do not be silent. Ps 109:1
You, **G** my Lord, deal ⌊kindly⌋ Ps 109:21
Help me, LORD my **G**; save me Ps 109:26
Who is like the LORD our **G**— Ps 113:5
the presence of the **G** of Jacob, Ps 114:7
nations say, "Where is their **G**?" Ps 115:2
Our **G** is in heaven and does Ps 115:3
righteous; our **G** is Ps 116:5
The LORD is **G** and has given us Ps 118:27
are my **G**, and I will give You Ps 118:28
You are⌋ my **G**; I will exalt You. Ps 118:28
of the house of the LORD our **G**, Ps 122:9
on the LORD our **G** until He shows Ps 123:2
courts of the house of our **G**. Ps 135:2
Give thanks to the **G** of gods. Ps 136:2
Give thanks to the **G** of heaven! Ps 136:26
G, how difficult Your thoughts Ps 139:17
G, if only You would kill the Ps 139:19
Search me, **G**, and know my heart; Ps 139:23
say to the LORD, "You are my **G**." Ps 140:6
Lord **G**, my strong Savior, You Ps 140:7
my eyes ⌊look⌋ to You, Lord **G**. Ps 141:8
do Your will, for You are my **G**. Ps 143:10
G, I will sing a new song to You; Ps 144:9
the people whose **G** is the LORD. Ps 144:15
I exalt You, my **G** the King, and Ps 145:1
whose help is the **G** of Jacob, Ps 146:5
whose hope is in the LORD his **G**, Ps 146:5
your **G** ⌊reigns⌋ for all Ps 146:10
How good it is to sing to our **G**, Ps 147:1
play the lyre to our **G**, Ps 147:7
Jerusalem; praise your **G**, Zion! Ps 147:12
the exaltation of **G** be in their Ps 149:6
Praise **G** in His sanctuary. Ps 150:1
and discover the knowledge of **G**. Pr 2:5
forgets the covenant of her **G**; Pr 2:17
in the sight of **G** and man. Pr 3:4
It is the glory of **G** to conceal Pr 25:2
Every word of **G** is pure; Pr 30:5
profaning the name of my **G**. Pr 30:9
G has given people this Ec 1:13
the task that **G** has given people Ec 3:10
discover the work **G** has done Ec 3:11
the gift of **G** whenever anyone Ec 3:13
I know that all **G** does will last Ec 3:14
G works so that people will be Ec 3:14
G repeats what has passed. Ec 3:15
G will judge the righteous and Ec 3:17
so that **G** may test them and they Ec 3:18
when you go to the house of **G**. Ec 5:1
to make a speech before **G**. Ec 5:2
G is in heaven and you are on Ec 5:2
you make a vow to **G**, don't delay Ec 5:4
Why should **G** be angry with your Ec 5:6
also many words. So, fear **G**. Ec 5:7
of his life **G** has given him, Ec 5:18
G has also given riches and Ec 5:19
his labor. This is a gift of **G**, Ec 5:19
his life because **G** keeps him Ec 5:20
G gives a man riches, wealth, Ec 6:2
G does not allow him to enjoy Ec 6:2
the work of **G**; for who can Ec 7:13
G has made the one as well as Ec 7:14
one who fears **G** will end up with Ec 7:18
who pleases **G** will escape her Ec 7:26
discovered that **G** made people Ec 7:29
Concerning an oath by **G**, Ec 8:2
they are not reverent before **G**. Ec 8:13
his days that **G** gives him under Ec 8:15
the work of **G** ⌊and concluded⌋ Ec 8:17

for **G** has already accepted your Ec 9:7
know the work of **G** who makes Ec 11:5
of these things **G** will bring you Ec 11:9
spirit returns to **G** who gave it. Ec 12:7
fear **G** and keep His commands, Ec 12:13
For **G** will bring every act to Ec 12:14
to the instruction of our **G**, Is 1:10
Therefore the Lord **G** of Hosts, Is 1:24
to the house of the **G** of Jacob. Is 2:3
The Lord **G** of Hosts is about to Is 3:1
says the Lord **G** of Hosts. Is 3:15
and the holy **G** is distinguished Is 5:16
This is what the Lord **G** says: Is 7:7
a sign from the LORD your **G**— Is 7:11
also try the patience of my **G**? Is 7:13
not happen. For **G** is with us. Is 8:10
a people consult their **G**? Is 8:19
curse their king and their **G**. Is 8:21
Mighty **G**, Eternal Father, Is 9:6
the Lord **G** of Hosts will Is 10:16
of Jacob, to the Mighty **G**. Is 10:21
the land the Lord **G** of Hosts is Is 10:23
the Lord **G** of Hosts says this: Is 10:24
Lord **G** of Hosts will chop off Is 10:33
Indeed, **G** is my salvation. Is 12:2
Gomorrah when **G** overthrew them. Is 13:19
my throne above the stars of **G**. Is 14:13
of the LORD, the **G** of Israel. Is 17:6
forgotten the **G** of your Is 17:10
of the Lord **G** of Hosts. Is 19:4
LORD of Hosts, the **G** of Israel. Is 21:10
the LORD, the **G** of Israel, has Is 21:17
the Lord **G** of Hosts had a day Is 22:5
day the Lord **G** of Hosts called Is 22:12
The Lord **G** of Hosts has spoken. Is 22:14
The Lord **G** of Hosts said: Is 22:15
of the LORD, the **G** of Israel. Is 24:15
LORD, You are my **G**; I will exalt Is 25:1
The Lord **G** will wipe away the Is 25:8
be said, "Look, this is our **G**; Is 25:9
LORD, our **G**, other lords than Is 26:13
Therefore the Lord **G** said: Is 28:16
the Lord **G** of Hosts a decree Is 28:22
His **G** teaches him order; Is 28:26
stand in awe of the **G** of Israel. Is 29:23
For the Lord **G**, the Holy One of Is 30:15
for the LORD is a just **G**. Is 30:18
Egyptians are men, not **G**; Is 31:3
the LORD, the splendor of our **G**. Is 35:2
Here is your **G**; vengeance is Is 35:4
We trust in the LORD our **G**. Is 36:7
the LORD your **G** will hear the Is 37:4
sent to mock the living **G**, Is 37:4
that the LORD your **G** has heard. Is 37:4
Don't let your **G**, whom you trust Is 37:10
LORD of Hosts, **G** of Israel, who Is 37:16
You are **G**—You alone— Is 37:16
has sent to mock the living **G**. Is 37:17
Now, LORD our **G**, save us from Is 37:20
The LORD, the **G** of Israel, says: Is 37:21
in the temple of his **g** Nisroch, Is 37:38
what the LORD **G** of your ancestor Is 38:5
comfort My people," says your **G**. Is 40:1
highway for our **G** in the desert. Is 40:3
word of our **G** remains forever. Is 40:8
of Judah, "Here is your **G**!" Is 40:9
the Lord **G** comes with strength, Is 40:10
Who will you compare **G** with? Is 40:18
G is enthroned above the circle Is 40:22
my claim is ignored by my **G**"? Is 40:27
Yahweh is the everlasting **G**, Is 40:28
not be afraid, for I am your **G**. Is 41:10
the LORD your **G**, hold your right Is 41:13
I, the **G** of Israel, do not Is 41:17
This is what **G** the LORD says— Is 42:5
I the LORD your **G**, the Holy One Is 43:3
No **g** was formed before Me, Is 43:10
not some foreign **g** among you. Is 43:12
declaration—"and I am **G**. Is 43:12
the last. There is no **G** but Me. Is 44:6
Is there any **G** but Me? There is Is 44:8
Who makes a **g** or casts a metal Is 44:10
it into a **g** and worships it Is 44:15
makes a **g** or his idol with the Is 44:17
it, "Save me, for you are my **g**." Is 44:17
the **G** of Israel call you by your Is 45:3
there is no **G** but Me. I will Is 45:5
G is indeed with you, and there Is 45:14

no other; there is no other **G**. Is 45:14
You are a **G** who hides Himself, Is 45:15
hides Himself, **G** of Israel, Is 45:15
G is the Creator of the heavens. Is 45:18
and pray to a **g** who cannot save, Is 45:20
There is no other **G** but Me, Is 45:21
Me, a righteous **G** and Savior; Is 45:21
For I am **G**, and there is no Is 45:22
and he makes it into a **g**. Is 46:6
ago, for I am **G**, and there is no Is 46:9
[I am]**G**, and no one is like Me. Is 46:9
and declare the **G** of Israel, Is 48:1
and lean on the **G** of Israel; Is 48:2
And now the Lord **G** has sent me Is 48:16
the LORD your **G**, who teaches you Is 48:17
and my reward is with my **G**. Is 49:4
LORD, and my **G** is my strength Is 49:5
This is what the Lord **G** says: Is 49:22
The Lord **G** has given Me the Is 50:4
The Lord **G** has opened My ear, Is 50:5
The Lord **G** will help Me; Is 50:7
truth, the Lord **G** will help Me; Is 50:9
the LORD; let him lean on his **G**. Is 50:10
am the LORD your **G** who stirs up Is 51:15
fury, the rebuke of your **G**. Is 51:20
even your **G**, who defends His Is 51:22
this is what the Lord **G** says: Is 52:4
says to Zion, "Your **G** reigns!" Is 52:7
will see the salvation of our **G**. Is 52:10
and the **G** of Israel is your rear Is 52:12
struck down by **G**, and afflicted. Is 53:4
is called the **G** of all the earth Is 54:5
she is rejected," says your **G**. Is 54:6
the LORD your **G**, even the Holy Is 55:5
him, and to our **G**, for He will Is 55:7
the declaration of the Lord **G**, Is 56:8
for the wicked," says my **G**. Is 57:21
abandon the justice of their **G**. Is 58:2
delight in the nearness of **G**." Is 58:2
barriers between you and your **G**, Is 59:2
away from following our **G**, Is 59:13
the honor of the LORD your **G**, Is 60:9
your **G** will be your splendor. Is 60:19
Spirit of the Lord **G** is on Me, Is 61:1
of you as ministers of our **G**; Is 61:6
in the LORD, I exult in my **G**; Is 61:10
so the Lord **G** will cause Is 61:11
diadem in the palm of your **G**. Is 62:3
so your **G** will rejoice over you. Is 62:5
eye has seen any **G** except You, Is 64:4
this is what the Lord **G** says: Is 65:13
and the Lord **G** will kill you; Is 65:15
be blessed by the **G** of truth, Is 65:16
will swear by the **G** of truth. Is 65:16
close ⌊the womb⌋?" says your **G**. Is 66:9
But I protested, "Oh no, Lord **G**! Jr 1:6
the LORD your **G** while He was Jr 2:17
the LORD your **G** and to have no Jr 2:19
of the Lord **G** of Hosts. Jr 2:19
against the LORD your **G**. Jr 3:13
have forgotten the LORD their **G**. Jr 3:21
for You are the LORD our **G**. Jr 3:22
is only in the LORD our **G**. Jr 3:23
sinned against the LORD our **G**, Jr 3:25
the voice of the LORD our **G**." Jr 3:25
said, "Oh no, Lord **G**, You have Jr 4:10
LORD, the justice of their **G**. Jr 5:4
LORD, the justice of their **G**. Jr 5:5
what the Lord **G** of Hosts says: Jr 5:14
the LORD our **G** done all these Jr 5:19
Let's fear the LORD our **G**, Jr 5:24
of Hosts, the **G** of Israel, says: Jr 7:3
this is what the Lord **G** says: Jr 7:20
of Hosts, the **G** of Israel, says: Jr 7:21
and then I will be your **G**, Jr 7:23
the LORD their **G** and would not Jr 7:28
the LORD our **G** has condemned us Jr 8:14
of Hosts, the **G** of Israel, says: Jr 9:15
But the LORD is the true **G**; Jr 10:10
is the living **G** and eternal King Jr 10:10
the LORD, the **G** of Israel, says: Jr 11:3
people, and I will be your **G**,' Jr 11:4
the LORD, the **G** of Israel, says: Jr 13:12
the LORD your **G** before He brings Jr 13:16
And I replied, "Oh no, Lord **G**! Jr 14:13
Are You not the LORD our **G**? Jr 14:22
by Your name, LORD **G** of Hosts. Jr 15:16
of Hosts, the **G** of Israel, says: Jr 16:9

against the LORD our **G**?	Jr 16:10
of Hosts, the **G** of Israel, says:	Jr 19:3
of Hosts, the **G** of Israel, says:	Jr 19:15
the LORD, the **G** of Israel, says:	Jr 21:4
the LORD their **G** and worshiped	Jr 22:9
the LORD, the **G** of Israel, says	Jr 23:2
"Am I a **G** who is only near"—	Jr 23:23
and not a **G** who is far away?	Jr 23:23
the words of the living **G**,	Jr 23:36
God, the LORD of Hosts, our **G**.	Jr 23:36
the LORD, the **G** of Israel, says:	Jr 24:5
I will be their **G** because they	Jr 24:7
the LORD, the **G** of Israel, said	Jr 25:15
of Hosts, the **G** of Israel, says:	Jr 25:27
the LORD your **G** so that He might	Jr 26:13
in the name of the LORD our **G**!"	Jr 26:16
of Hosts, the **G** of Israel, says:	Jr 27:4
of Hosts, the **G** of Israel, says	Jr 27:21
of Hosts, the **G** of Israel, says:	Jr 28:2
of Hosts, the **G** of Israel, says:	Jr 28:14
of Hosts, the **G** of Israel, says	Jr 29:4
of Hosts, the **G** of Israel, says:	Jr 29:8
of Hosts, the **G** of Israel, says	Jr 29:21
of Hosts, the **G** of Israel, says:	Jr 29:25
the LORD, the **G** of Israel, says:	Jr 30:2
LORD their **G** and I will raise	Jr 30:9
My people, and I will be your **G**.	Jr 30:22
I will be **G** of all the families	Jr 31:1
up to Zion, to the LORD our **G**!	Jr 31:6
return, for you, LORD, are my **G**.	Jr 31:18
of Hosts, the **G** of Israel, says:	Jr 31:23
I will be their **G**, and they will	Jr 31:33
of Hosts, the **G** of Israel, says:	Jr 32:14
of Hosts, the **G** of Israel, says:	Jr 32:15
Ah, Lord **G**! You Yourself made	Jr 32:17
great and mighty **G** whose name is	Jr 32:18
You, Lord **G**, have said to me:	Jr 32:25
am the LORD, the **G** of all flesh.	Jr 32:27
the LORD, the **G** of Israel, says	Jr 32:36
people, and I will be their **G**.	Jr 32:38
the LORD, the **G** of Israel, says	Jr 33:4
the LORD, the **G** of Israel, says:	Jr 34:2
the LORD, the **G** of Israel, says:	Jr 34:13
a man of **G**, who had a chamber	Jr 35:4
of Hosts, the **G** of Israel, says:	Jr 35:13
the LORD, the **G** of Hosts, the	Jr 35:17
of Hosts, the **G** of Israel, says	Jr 35:17
of Hosts, the **G** of Israel, says:	Jr 35:18
of Hosts, the **G** of Israel, says:	Jr 35:19
pray to the LORD our **G** for us!"	Jr 37:3
the LORD, the **G** of Israel, says:	Jr 37:7
the LORD, the **G** of Hosts, the	Jr 38:17
of Hosts, the **G** of Israel, says	Jr 38:17
of Hosts, the **G** of Israel, says:	Jr 39:16
The LORD your **G** decreed this	Jr 40:2
the LORD your **G** on our behalf,	Jr 42:2
that the LORD your **G** may tell us	Jr 42:3
to the LORD your **G** according to	Jr 42:4
the LORD your **G** sends you to	Jr 42:5
of the LORD our **G** to whom we are	Jr 42:6
the voice of the LORD our **G**!"	Jr 42:6
the **G** of Israel to whom you sent	Jr 42:9
the voice of the LORD your **G**,	Jr 42:13
of Hosts, the **G** of Israel, says:	Jr 42:15
of Hosts, the **G** of Israel, says:	Jr 42:18
who sent me to the LORD your **G**,	Jr 42:20
to the LORD our **G** on our behalf,	Jr 42:20
all that the LORD our **G** says,	Jr 42:20
the LORD your **G** in everything He	Jr 42:21
the words of the LORD their **G**—	Jr 43:1
the LORD their **G** had sent him to	Jr 43:1
The LORD our **G** has not sent you	Jr 43:2
of Hosts, the **G** of Israel, says:	Jr 43:10
of Hosts, the **G** of Israel, says:	Jr 44:2
the LORD, the **G** of Hosts, the	Jr 44:7
of Hosts, the **G** of Israel, says	Jr 44:7
of Hosts, the **G** of Israel, says:	Jr 44:11
of Hosts, the **G** of Israel, says:	Jr 44:25
saying, As the Lord **G** lives.	Jr 44:26
the LORD, the **G** of Israel, says	Jr 45:2
the Lord, the **G** of Hosts, a day	Jr 46:10
to the Lord, the **G** of Hosts, in	Jr 46:10
of Hosts, the **G** of Israel, says:	Jr 46:25
to punish Amon, ⌊**g**⌋ of Thebes,	Jr 46:25
of Hosts, the **G** of Israel, says:	Jr 48:1
of the Lord, the **G** of Hosts—	Jr 49:5
and will seek the LORD their **G**.	Jr 50:4
of Hosts, the **G** of Israel, says:	Jr 50:18
a task of the Lord **G** of Hosts in	Jr 50:25
the vengeance of the LORD our **G**,	Jr 50:28
of the Lord **G** of Hosts—	Jr 50:31
Just as when **G** overthrew Sodom	Jr 50:40
are not left widowed by their **G**,	Jr 51:5
the LORD our **G** has accomplished	Jr 51:10
of Hosts, the **G** of Israel, says:	Jr 51:33
the LORD is a **G** of retribution;	Jr 51:56
for **G** has disciplined him.	Lm 3:28
and ⌊our⌋ hands to **G** in heaven:	Lm 3:41
opened and I saw visions of **G**.	Ezk 1:1
This is what the Lord **G** says.	Ezk 2:4
This is what the Lord **G** says,	Ezk 3:11
This is what the Lord **G** says.	Ezk 3:27
said, "Ah, Lord **G**, I have never	Ezk 4:14
This is what the Lord **G** says:	Ezk 5:5
this is what the Lord **G** says:	Ezk 5:7
this is what the Lord **G** says:	Ezk 5:8
the declaration of the Lord **G**—	Ezk 5:11
hear the word of the Lord **G**!	Ezk 6:3
is what the Lord **G** says to the	Ezk 6:3
This is what the Lord **G** says:	Ezk 6:11
what the Lord **G** says to the land	Ezk 7:2
This is what the Lord **G** says:	Ezk 7:5
of the Lord **G** came down on me	Ezk 8:1
me in visions of **G** to Jerusalem,	Ezk 8:3
glory of the **G** of Israel there	Ezk 8:4
glory of the **G** of Israel rose	Ezk 9:3
and cried out, "Ah, Lord **G**!	Ezk 9:8
the voice of **G** Almighty when He	Ezk 10:5
The glory of the **G** of Israel was	Ezk 10:19
had seen beneath the **G** of Israel	Ezk 10:20
this is what the Lord **G** says:	Ezk 11:7
the declaration of the Lord **G**.	Ezk 11:8
Ah, Lord **G**! Will You bring	Ezk 11:13
This is what the Lord **G** says:	Ezk 11:16
This is what the Lord **G** says:	Ezk 11:17
people, and I will be their **G**.	Ezk 11:20
the declaration of the Lord **G**.	Ezk 11:21
the glory of the **G** of Israel was	Ezk 11:22
a vision from the Spirit of **G**.	Ezk 11:24
This is what the Lord **G** says:	Ezk 12:10
is what the Lord **G** says about	Ezk 12:19
This is what the Lord **G** says:	Ezk 12:23
the declaration of the Lord **G**.	Ezk 12:25
This is what the Lord **G** says:	Ezk 12:28
the declaration of the Lord **G**.	Ezk 12:28
This is what the Lord **G** says:	Ezk 13:3
this is what the Lord **G** says:	Ezk 13:8
the declaration of the Lord **G**.	Ezk 13:8
will know that I am the Lord **G**.	Ezk 13:9
So this is what the Lord **G** says:	Ezk 13:13
the declaration of the Lord **G**.	Ezk 13:16
This is what the Lord **G** says:	Ezk 13:18
this is what the Lord **G** says:	Ezk 13:20
This is what the Lord **G** says:	Ezk 14:4
This is what the Lord **G** says:	Ezk 14:6
people and I will be their **G**."	Ezk 14:11
the declaration of the Lord **G**.	Ezk 14:11
the declaration of the Lord **G**.	Ezk 14:14
the declaration of the Lord **G**—	Ezk 14:16
the declaration of the Lord **G**—	Ezk 14:18
the declaration of the Lord **G**—	Ezk 14:20
this is what the Lord **G** says:	Ezk 14:21
the declaration of the Lord **G**.	Ezk 14:23
this is what the Lord **G** says:	Ezk 15:6
the declaration of the Lord **G**.	Ezk 15:8
is what the Lord **G** says to	Ezk 16:3
the declaration of the Lord **G**.	Ezk 16:8
the declaration of the Lord **G**.	Ezk 16:14
the declaration of the Lord **G**.	Ezk 16:19
the declaration of the Lord **G**—	Ezk 16:23
the declaration of the Lord **G**—	Ezk 16:30
This is what the Lord **G** says:	Ezk 16:36
the declaration of the Lord **G**.	Ezk 16:43
the declaration of the Lord **G**—	Ezk 16:48
this is what the Lord **G** says:	Ezk 16:59
the declaration of the Lord **G**.	Ezk 16:63
This is what the Lord **G** says:	Ezk 17:3
This is what the Lord **G** says:	Ezk 17:9
the declaration of the Lord **G**—	Ezk 17:16
this is what the Lord **G** says:	Ezk 17:19
This is what the Lord **G** says:	Ezk 17:22
the declaration of the Lord **G**—	Ezk 18:3
the declaration of the Lord **G**.	Ezk 18:9
the declaration of the Lord **G**.	Ezk 18:23
the declaration of the Lord **G**.	Ezk 18:30
the declaration of the Lord **G**.	Ezk 18:32
This is what the Lord **G** says:	Ezk 20:3
the declaration of the Lord **G**.	Ezk 20:3
This is what the Lord **G** says:	Ezk 20:5
saying: I am the LORD your **G**.	Ezk 20:5
of Egypt. I am the LORD your **G**.	Ezk 20:7
I am the LORD your **G**. Follow My	Ezk 20:19
know that I am the LORD your **G**.	Ezk 20:20
This is what the Lord **G** says:	Ezk 20:27
This is what the Lord **G** says:	Ezk 20:30
the declaration of the Lord **G**—	Ezk 20:31
the declaration of the Lord **G**—	Ezk 20:33
the declaration of the Lord **G**.	Ezk 20:36
this is what the Lord **G** says:	Ezk 20:39
the declaration of the Lord **G**—	Ezk 20:40
the declaration of the Lord **G**.	Ezk 20:44
This is what the Lord **G** says:	Ezk 20:47
said, "Ah, Lord **G**, they are	Ezk 20:49
the declaration of the Lord **G**.	Ezk 21:7
the declaration of the Lord **G**.	Ezk 21:13
this is what the Lord **G** says:	Ezk 21:24
This is what the Lord **G** says:	Ezk 21:26
what the Lord **G** says concerning	Ezk 21:28
This is what the Lord **G** says:	Ezk 22:3
the declaration of the Lord **G**.	Ezk 22:12
this is what the Lord **G** says:	Ezk 22:19
This is what the Lord **G** says,	Ezk 22:28
the declaration of the Lord **G**.	Ezk 22:31
this is what the Lord **G** says:	Ezk 23:22
this is what the Lord **G** says:	Ezk 23:28
This is what the Lord **G** says:	Ezk 23:32
the declaration of the Lord **G**.	Ezk 23:34
this is what the Lord **G** says:	Ezk 23:35
This is what the Lord **G** says:	Ezk 23:46
will know that I am the Lord **G**."	Ezk 23:49
This is what the Lord **G** says:	Ezk 24:3
this is what the Lord **G** says:	Ezk 24:6
this is what the Lord **G** says:	Ezk 24:9
the declaration of the Lord **G**.	Ezk 24:14
This is what the Lord **G** says:	Ezk 24:21
will know that I am the Lord **G**.	Ezk 24:24
Hear the word of the Lord **G**:	Ezk 25:3
This is what the Lord **G** says:	Ezk 25:3
this is what the Lord **G** says:	Ezk 25:6
This is what the Lord **G** says:	Ezk 25:8
This is what the Lord **G** says:	Ezk 25:12
this is what the Lord **G** says:	Ezk 25:13
the declaration of the Lord **G**.	Ezk 25:14
This is what the Lord **G** says:	Ezk 25:15
this is what the Lord **G** says:	Ezk 25:16
this is what the Lord **G** says:	Ezk 26:3
the declaration of the Lord **G**.	Ezk 26:5
this is what the Lord **G** says:	Ezk 26:7
the declaration of the Lord **G**.	Ezk 26:14
is what the Lord **G** says to Tyre:	Ezk 26:15
this is what the Lord **G** says:	Ezk 26:19
the declaration of the Lord **G**.	Ezk 26:21
This is what the Lord **G** says:	Ezk 27:3
This is what the Lord **G** says:	Ezk 28:2
have said: I am a **g**; I sit in	Ezk 28:2
Yet you are a man and not a **g**,	Ezk 28:2
your heart as that of a **g**.	Ezk 28:2
this is what the Lord **G** says:	Ezk 28:6
your heart as that of a **g**,	Ezk 28:6
I am a **g**, in the presence of	Ezk 28:9
be⌋ a man, not a **g**, in the hands	Ezk 28:9
the declaration of the Lord **G**.	Ezk 28:10
This is what the Lord **G** says:	Ezk 28:12
were in Eden, the garden of **G**.	Ezk 28:13
were on the holy mountain of **G**;	Ezk 28:14
disgrace from the mountain of **G**,	Ezk 28:16
This is what the Lord **G** says:	Ezk 28:22
will know that I am the Lord **G**.	Ezk 28:24
This is what the Lord **G** says:	Ezk 28:25
that I am the LORD their **G**."	Ezk 28:26
This is what the Lord **G** says:	Ezk 29:3
this is what the Lord **G** says:	Ezk 29:8
this is what the Lord **G** says:	Ezk 29:13
will know that I am the Lord **G**."	Ezk 29:16
this is what the Lord **G** says:	Ezk 29:19
the declaration of the Lord **G**.	Ezk 29:20
This is what the Lord **G** says:	Ezk 30:2
the declaration of the Lord **G**.	Ezk 30:6
This is what the Lord **G** says:	Ezk 30:10
This is what the Lord **G** says:	Ezk 30:13
this is what the Lord **G** says:	Ezk 30:22
in the garden of **G** could compare	Ezk 31:8
this is what the Lord **G** says:	Ezk 31:10
This is what the Lord **G** says:	Ezk 31:15

the declaration of the Lord **G**. Ezk 31:18
This is what the Lord **G** says: Ezk 32:3
the declaration of the Lord **G**. Ezk 32:8
this is what the Lord **G** says: Ezk 32:11
the declaration of the Lord **G**. Ezk 32:14
the declaration of the Lord **G**. Ezk 32:16
the declaration of the Lord **G**. Ezk 32:31
the declaration of the Lord **G**. Ezk 32:32
the declaration of the Lord **G**— Ezk 33:11
This is what the Lord **G** says: Ezk 33:25
This is what the Lord **G** says: Ezk 33:27
is what the Lord **G** says to the Ezk 34:2
the declaration of the Lord **G**— Ezk 34:8
This is what the Lord **G** says: Ezk 34:10
this is what the Lord **G** says: Ezk 34:11
the declaration of the Lord **G**. Ezk 34:15
The Lord **G** says to you, My Ezk 34:17
is what the Lord **G** says to them: Ezk 34:20
will be their **G**, and My servant Ezk 34:24
the LORD their **G**, am with them, Ezk 34:30
the declaration of the Lord **G**. Ezk 34:30
of My pasture, and I am your **G**." Ezk 34:31
the declaration of the Lord **G**. Ezk 34:31
This is what the Lord **G** says: Ezk 35:3
the declaration of the Lord **G**— Ezk 35:6
the declaration of the Lord **G**— Ezk 35:11
This is what the Lord **G** says: Ezk 35:14
This is what the Lord **G** says: Ezk 36:2
This is what the Lord **G** says: Ezk 36:3
hear the word of the Lord **G**. Ezk 36:4
is what the Lord **G** says to the Ezk 36:4
This is what the Lord **G** says: Ezk 36:5
This is what the Lord **G** says: Ezk 36:6
this is what the Lord **G** says: Ezk 36:7
This is what the Lord **G** says: Ezk 36:13
the declaration of the Lord **G**. Ezk 36:14
the declaration of the Lord **G**. Ezk 36:15
This is what the Lord **G** says: Ezk 36:22
the declaration of the Lord **G**— Ezk 36:23
My people, and I will be your **G**. Ezk 36:28
the declaration of the Lord **G**— Ezk 36:32
This is what the Lord **G** says: Ezk 36:33
This is what the Lord **G** says: Ezk 36:37
replied, "Lord **G**, ⌊only⌋ You Ezk 37:3
is what the Lord **G** says to these Ezk 37:5
This is what the Lord **G** says: Ezk 37:9
This is what the Lord **G** says: Ezk 37:12
This is what the Lord **G** says: Ezk 37:19
This is what the Lord **G** says: Ezk 37:21
people, and I will be their **G**. Ezk 37:23
I will be their **G**, and they will Ezk 37:27
This is what the Lord **G** says: Ezk 38:3
This is what the Lord **G** says: Ezk 38:10
This is what the Lord **G** says: Ezk 38:14
This is what the Lord **G** says: Ezk 38:17
the declaration of the Lord **G**— Ezk 38:18
the declaration of the Lord **G**— Ezk 38:21
This is what the Lord **G** says: Ezk 39:1
the declaration of the Lord **G**. Ezk 39:5
the declaration of the Lord **G**. Ezk 39:8
the declaration of the Lord **G**. Ezk 39:10
the declaration of the Lord **G**. Ezk 39:13
this is what the Lord **G** says: Ezk 39:17
the declaration of the Lord **G**. Ezk 39:20
know that I am the LORD their **G**. Ezk 39:22
So this is what the Lord **G** says: Ezk 39:25
the LORD their **G** when I regather Ezk 39:28
the declaration of the Lord **G**. Ezk 39:29
visions of **G** He took me to the Ezk 40:2
glory of the **G** of Israel coming Ezk 43:2
this is what the Lord **G** says: Ezk 43:18
the declaration of the Lord **G**. Ezk 43:19
the declaration of the Lord **G**. Ezk 43:27
the LORD, the **G** of Israel, has Ezk 44:2
This is what the Lord **G** says: Ezk 44:6
This is what the Lord **G** says: Ezk 44:9
the declaration of the Lord **G**— Ezk 44:12
the declaration of the Lord **G**. Ezk 44:15
the declaration of the Lord **G**. Ezk 44:27
This is what the Lord **G** says: Ezk 45:9
the declaration of the Lord **G**. Ezk 45:9
the declaration of the Lord **G**. Ezk 45:15
This is what the Lord **G** says: Ezk 45:18
This is what the Lord **G** says: Ezk 46:1
This is what the Lord **G** says: Ezk 46:16
This is what the Lord **G** says: Ezk 47:13
the declaration of the Lord **G**. Ezk 47:23
the declaration of the Lord **G**. Ezk 48:29

the vessels from the house of **G**. Dn 1:2
to the house of his **g**, and put Dn 1:2
in the treasury of his **g**. Dn 1:2
G had granted Daniel favor and Dn 1:9
G gave these four young men Dn 1:17
them to ask the **G** of heaven for Dn 2:18
Daniel praised the **G** of heaven Dn 2:19
May the name of **G** be praised Dn 2:20
praise to You, **G** of my fathers, Dn 2:23
But there is a **G** in heaven who Dn 2:28
The **G** of heaven has given you Dn 2:37
the **G** of heaven will set up a Dn 2:44
The great **G** has told the king Dn 2:45
Your **G** is indeed God of gods, Dn 2:47
Your God is indeed **G** of gods, Dn 2:47
and who is the **g** who can rescue Dn 3:15
the **G** we serve exists, then He Dn 3:17
servants of the Most High **G**— Dn 3:26
Praise to the **G** of Shadrach, Dn 3:28
worship any **g** except their own Dn 3:28
any god except their own **G**. Dn 3:28
against the **G** of Shadrach, Dn 3:29
is no other **g** who is able to Dn 3:29
the Most High **G** has done for me. Dn 4:2
after the name of my **g**— Dn 4:8
the house of **G** in Jerusalem, Dn 5:3
Most High **G** gave sovereignty, Dn 5:18
the Most High **G** is ruler over Dn 5:21
glorified the **G** who holds your Dn 5:23
MENE ⌊means that⌋ **G** has numbered Dn 5:26
concerning the law of his **G**." Dn 6:5
petitions any **g** or man except Dn 6:7
thanks to his **G**, just as he had Dn 6:10
petitioning and imploring his **G**. Dn 6:11
petitions any **g** or man except Dn 6:12
May your **G**, whom you serve Dn 6:16
of the living **G**," the king said, Dn 6:20
has your **G** whom you serve Dn 6:20
My **G** sent His angel and shut the Dn 6:22
for he trusted in his **G**. Dn 6:23
in fear before the **G** of Daniel: Dn 6:26
is the living **G**, and He endures Dn 6:26
to the Lord **G** to seek Him by Dn 9:3
to the LORD my **G** and confessed: Dn 9:4
awe-inspiring **G** who keeps His Dn 9:4
belong to the Lord our **G**, Dn 9:9
of the LORD our **G** by following Dn 9:10
servant of **G**, has been poured Dn 9:11
the LORD our **G** by turning from Dn 9:13
for the LORD our **G** is righteous Dn 9:14
Now, Lord our **G**, who brought Dn 9:15
Therefore, our **G**, hear the Dn 9:17
Listen, my **G**, and hear. Open Dn 9:18
My **G**, for Your own sake, do not Dn 9:19
before Yahweh my **G** concerning Dn 9:20
the holy mountain of my **G**— Dn 9:20
for you are treasured ⌊by **G**⌋. Dn 9:23
you are a man treasured ⌊by **G**⌋. Dn 10:11
humble yourself before your **G**, Dn 10:12
you who are treasured ⌊by **G**⌋. Dn 10:19
who know their **G** will be strong Dn 11:32
magnify himself above every **g**, Dn 11:36
things against the **G** of gods. Dn 11:36
the **g** longed for by women, Dn 11:37
for any other **g**, because he will Dn 11:37
will honor a **g** of fortresses— Dn 11:38
a **g** his fathers did not know— Dn 11:38
with ⌊the help of⌋ a foreign **g**. Dn 11:39
them by the LORD their **G**. Hs 1:7
and I will not be your **G**. Hs 1:9
be called: Sons of the living **G**. Hs 1:10
and he will say: ⌊You are⌋ My **G**. Hs 2:23
the LORD their **G** and David their Hs 3:5
no knowledge of **G** in the land! Hs 4:1
forgotten the law of your **G**, Hs 4:6
in disobedience to their **G**. Hs 4:12
them⌋ to return to their **G**, Hs 5:4
the knowledge of **G** rather than Hs 6:6
not return to the LORD their **G**, Hs 7:10
out to Me: My **G**, we know You! Hs 8:2
made it, and it is not **G**. Hs 8:6
promiscuously, leaving your **G**. Hs 9:1
Ephraim's watchman is with my **G**. Hs 9:8
is in the house of his **G**! Hs 9:8
My **G** will reject them because Hs 9:17
For I am **G** and not man, the Holy Hs 11:9
as an adult he wrestled with **G**. Hs 12:3
Yahweh is the **G** of Hosts; Hs 12:5

But you must return to your **G**. Hs 12:6
and always put your hope in **G**. Hs 12:6
been the LORD your **G** ever since Hs 12:9
been the LORD your **G** ever since Hs 13:4
you know no **G** but Me, and no Hs 13:4
she has rebelled against her **G**. Hs 13:16
return to the LORD your **G**, Hs 14:1
ministers of my **G**, because grain Jl 1:13
from the house of your **G**. Jl 1:13
at the house of the LORD your **G**, Jl 1:14
from the house of our **G**? Jl 1:16
and return to the LORD your **G**. Jl 2:13
and wine to the LORD your **G**. Jl 2:14
peoples, 'Where is their **G**?' " Jl 2:17
and be glad in the LORD your **G**, Jl 2:23
the name of Yahweh your **G**, Jl 2:26
and that I am the LORD your **G**, Jl 2:27
know that I am the LORD your **G**, Jl 3:17
perish. The Lord **G** has spoken. Am 1:8
house of their **G** wine obtained Am 2:8
the Lord **G** does nothing without Am 3:7
fear? The Lord **G** has spoken; who Am 3:8
Therefore, the Lord **G** says: Am 3:11
the declaration of the Lord **G**, Am 3:13
of the Lord GOD, the **G** of Hosts. Am 3:13
The Lord **G** has sworn by His Am 4:2
Israel, prepare to meet your **G**! Am 4:12
Yahweh, the **G** of Hosts, is His Am 4:13
For the Lord **G** says: The city Am 5:3
the LORD, the **G** of Hosts, will Am 5:14
the LORD, the **G** of Hosts, will Am 5:15
the **G** of Hosts, the Lord, Am 5:16
king and Kaiwan your star **g**, Am 5:26
Yahweh, the **G** of Hosts, is His Am 5:27
Lord **G** has sworn by Himself— Am 6:8
of Yahweh, the **G** of Hosts: Am 6:8
the Lord, the **G** of Hosts—and Am 6:14
The Lord **G** showed me this: Am 7:1
I said, "Lord **G**, please forgive! Am 7:2
The Lord **G** showed me this: Am 7:4
The Lord **G** was calling for a Am 7:4
I said, "Lord **G**, please stop! Am 7:5
happen either," said the Lord **G**. Am 7:6
The Lord **G** showed me this: Am 8:1
the declaration of the Lord **G**— Am 8:9
the declaration of the Lord **G**— Am 8:11
and say, "As your **g** lives, Dan," Am 8:14
The Lord, the **G** of Hosts—He Am 9:5
eyes of the Lord **G** are on the Am 9:8
Yahweh your **G** has spoken. Am 9:15
what the Lord **G** has said about Ob 1
and each cried out to his **g**. Jnh 1:5
Call to your **g**. Maybe this god Jnh 1:6
Maybe this **g** will consider us, Jnh 1:6
Yahweh, the **G** of the heavens, Jnh 1:9
the LORD his **G** from inside the Jnh 2:1
my life from the Pit, LORD my **G**! Jnh 2:6
men of Nineveh believed in **G**. Jnh 3:5
must call out earnestly to **G**. Jnh 3:8
knows? **G** may turn and relent; Jnh 3:9
Then **G** saw their actions— Jnh 3:10
so **G** relented from the disaster Jnh 3:10
a merciful and compassionate **G**, Jnh 4:2
Then the LORD **G** appointed a Jnh 4:6
G appointed a worm that attacked Jnh 4:7
G appointed a scorching east Jnh 4:8
Then **G** asked Jonah, "Is it right Jnh 4:9
The Lord **G** will be a witness Mc 1:2
there will be no answer from **G**. Mc 3:7
to the house of the **G** of Jacob. Mc 4:2
of Yahweh our **G** forever and ever Mc 4:5
majestic name of Yahweh His **G**. Mc 5:4
I come to bow before **G** on high? Mc 6:6
and to walk humbly with your **G**. Mc 6:8
wait for the **G** of my salvation. Mc 7:7
my salvation. My **G** will hear me. Mc 7:7
"Where is the LORD your **G**?" Mc 7:10
tremble before the LORD our **G**; Mc 7:17
Who is a **G** like You, removing Mc 7:18
is a jealous and avenging **G**; Nah 1:2
their strength is their **g**. Hab 1:11
not from eternity, Yahweh my **G**? Hab 1:12
G comes from Teman, the Holy One Hab 3:3
in the **G** of my salvation! Hab 3:18
in the presence of the Lord **G**, Zph 1:7
the LORD their **G** will return to Zph 2:7
of Hosts, the **G** of Israel—Moab Zph 2:9
she has not drawn near to her **G**. Zph 3:2

The LORD your **G** is among you,	Zph 3:17
the LORD their **G** and the words	Hg 1:12
the LORD their **G** had sent him.	Hg 1:12
of Yahweh of Hosts, their **G**,	Hg 1:14
you fully obey the LORD your **G**."	Zch 6:15
their faithful and righteous **G**."	Zch 8:8
have heard that **G** is with you."	Zch 8:23
will become a remnant for our **G**;	Zch 9:7
Lord **G** will sound the trumpet	Zch 9:14
The LORD their **G** will save them	Zch 9:16
For I am the LORD their **G**,	Zch 10:6
The LORD my **G** says this:	Zch 11:4
the LORD of Hosts, their **G**.	Zch 12:5
house of David will be like **G**,	Zch 12:8
will say: The LORD is our **G**."	Zch 13:9
Then the LORD my **G** will come	Zch 14:5
Didn't one **G** create us? Why	Mal 2:10
the daughter of a foreign **g**.	Mal 2:11
Didn't the one ⌊**G**⌋ make ⌊us⌋	Mal 2:15
says the LORD **G** of Israel,	Mal 2:16
or "Where is the **G** of justice?"	Mal 2:17
Will a man rob **G**? Yet you are	Mal 3:8
It is useless to serve **G**.	Mal 3:14
they even test **G** and escape."	Mal 3:15
who serves **G** and one who does	Mal 3:18
is translated "**G** is with us."	Mt 1:23
I tell you that **G** is able to	Mt 3:9
the Spirit of **G** descending like	Mt 3:16
are the Son of **G**, tell these	Mt 4:3
that comes from the mouth of **G**."	Mt 4:4
are the Son of **G**, throw Yourself	Mt 4:6
Do not test the Lord your **G**."	Mt 4:7
the Lord your **G**, and serve only	Mt 4:10
heart, because they will see **G**.	Mt 5:8
they will be called sons of **G**.	Mt 5:9
be slaves of **G** and of money.	Mt 6:24
that's how **G** clothes the grass	Mt 6:30
first the kingdom of **G** and His	Mt 6:33
have to do with us, Son of **G**?	Mt 8:29
gave glory to **G** who had given	Mt 9:8
how he entered the house of **G**,	Mt 12:4
out demons by the Spirit of **G**,	Mt 12:28
kingdom of **G** has come to you.	Mt 12:28
"Truly You are the Son of **G**!"	Mt 14:33
G said: Honor your father and	Mt 15:4
gave glory to the **G** of Israel.	Mt 15:31
the Son of the living **G**!"	Mt 16:16
Therefore what **G** has joined	Mt 19:6
to enter the kingdom of **G**."	Mt 19:24
with **G** all things are possible.	Mt 19:26
the kingdom of **G** before you!	Mt 21:31
the kingdom of **G** will be taken	Mt 21:43
teach truthfully the way of **G**.	Mt 22:16
and to **G** the things that are	Mt 22:21
Scriptures or the power of **G**.	Mt 22:29
what was spoken to you by **G**:	Mt 22:31
am the **G** of Abraham and the God	Mt 22:32
Abraham and the **G** of Isaac and	Mt 22:32
God of Isaac and the **G** of Jacob?	Mt 22:32
He is not the **G** of the dead,	Mt 22:32
the Lord your **G** with all your	Mt 22:37
By the living **G** I place You	Mt 26:63
are the Messiah, the Son of **G**!"	Mt 26:63
You are the Son of **G**, come down	Mt 27:40
He has put His trust in **G**;	Mt 27:43
let **G** rescue Him now—if He	Mt 27:43
that is, "My **G**, My God, why	Mt 27:46
is, "My God, My **G**, why have You	Mt 27:46
of Jesus Christ, the Son of **G**.	Mk 1:1
preaching the good news of **G**:	Mk 1:14
the kingdom of **G** has come near.	Mk 1:15
You are—the Holy One of **G**!"	Mk 1:24
can forgive sins but **G** alone?"	Mk 2:7
astounded and gave glory to **G**,	Mk 2:12
the house of **G** in the time	Mk 2:26
out, "You are the Son of **G**!"	Mk 3:11
does the will of **G** is My brother	Mk 3:35
the kingdom of **G** has been	Mk 4:11
"The kingdom of **G** is like this,"	Mk 4:26
we illustrate the kingdom of **G**,	Mk 4:30
Jesus, Son of the Most High **G**?	Mk 5:7
beg You before **G**, don't torment	Mk 5:7
Disregarding the command of **G**,	Mk 7:8
the kingdom of **G** come in power."	Mk 9:1
the kingdom of **G** with one eye	Mk 9:47
of creation **G** made them male	Mk 10:6
Therefore what **G** has joined	Mk 10:9
the kingdom of **G** belongs to such	Mk 10:14
the kingdom of **G** like a little	Mk 10:15
No one is good but One—**G**.	Mk 10:18
to enter the kingdom of **G**!"	Mk 10:23
it is to enter the kingdom of **G**!	Mk 10:24
to enter the kingdom of **G**."	Mk 10:25
but not with **G**, because all	Mk 10:27
all things are possible with **G**."	Mk 10:27
to them, "Have faith in **G**.	Mk 11:22
teach truthfully the way of **G**.	Mk 12:14
and to **G** the things that are	Mk 12:17
Scriptures or the power of **G**?	Mk 12:24
bush, how **G** spoke to him:	Mk 12:26
am the **G** of Abraham and the God	Mk 12:26
Abraham and the **G** of Isaac and	Mk 12:26
God of Isaac and the **G** of Jacob?	Mk 12:26
He is not **G** of the dead but of	Mk 12:27
The Lord our **G**, The Lord is One.	Mk 12:29
the Lord your **G** with all your	Mk 12:30
not far from the kingdom of **G**."	Mk 12:34
world, which **G** created, until	Mk 13:19
a new way in the kingdom of **G**."	Mk 14:25
translated, "My **G**, My God, why	Mk 15:34
My God, My **G**, why have You	Mk 15:34
forward to the kingdom of **G**,	Mk 15:43
sat down at the right hand of **G**.	Mk 16:19
was serving as priest before **G**,	Lk 1:8
of Israel to the Lord their **G**.	Lk 1:16
who stands in the presence of **G**,	Lk 1:19
Gabriel was sent by **G** to a town	Lk 1:26
for you have found favor with **G**.	Lk 1:30
and the Lord **G** will give Him the	Lk 1:32
will be called the Son of **G**.	Lk 1:35
will be impossible with **G**."	Lk 1:37
has rejoiced in **G** my Savior,	Lk 1:47
he began to speak, praising **G**.	Lk 1:64
the Lord, the **G** of Israel,	Lk 1:68
angel, praising **G** and saying:	Lk 2:13
to **G** in the highest heaven,	Lk 2:14
and praising **G** for all they had	Lk 2:20
his arms, praised **G**, and said:	Lk 2:28
serving **G** night and day with	Lk 2:37
began to thank **G** and to speak	Lk 2:38
in favor with **G** and with people	Lk 2:52
will see the salvation of **G**."	Lk 3:6
I tell you that **G** is able to	Lk 3:8
Seth, ⌊son⌋ of Adam, ⌊son⌋ of **G**.	Lk 3:38
the Son of **G**, tell this stone	Lk 4:3
the Lord your **G**, and serve Him	Lk 4:8
are the Son of **G**, throw Yourself	Lk 4:9
Do not test the Lord your **G**."	Lk 4:12
You are—the Holy One of **G**!"	Lk 4:34
saying, "You are the Son of **G**!"	Lk 4:41
the kingdom of **G** to the other	Lk 4:43
can forgive sins but **G** alone?"	Lk 5:21
and went home glorifying **G**.	Lk 5:25
and they were giving glory to **G**.	Lk 5:26
how he entered the house of **G**,	Lk 6:4
spent all night in prayer to **G**.	Lk 6:12
the kingdom of **G** is yours.	Lk 6:20
they glorified **G**, saying, "A	Lk 7:16
and "**G** has visited His people."	Lk 7:16
the kingdom of **G** is greater than	Lk 7:28
the plan of **G** for themselves.	Lk 7:30
good news of the kingdom of **G**.	Lk 8:1
the kingdom of **G** have been given	Lk 8:10
The seed is the word of **G**.	Lk 8:11
who hear and do the word of **G**."	Lk 8:21
You Son of the Most High **G**?	Lk 8:28
tell all that **G** has done for you	Lk 8:39
the kingdom of **G** and to heal the	Lk 9:2
to them about the kingdom of **G**,	Lk 9:11
they see the kingdom of **G**."	Lk 9:27
at the greatness of **G**.	Lk 9:43
the news of the kingdom of **G**."	Lk 9:60
is fit for the kingdom of **G**."	Lk 9:62
kingdom of **G** has come near you.	Lk 10:9
the kingdom of **G** has come near.'	Lk 10:11
the Lord your **G** with all your	Lk 10:27
out demons by the finger of **G**,	Lk 11:20
kingdom of **G** has come to you.	Lk 11:20
the word of **G** and keep it are	Lk 11:28
bypass justice and love for **G**.	Lk 11:42
the wisdom of **G** said, 'I will	Lk 11:49
him before the angels of **G**,	Lk 12:8
denied before the angels of **G**.	Lk 12:9
But **G** said to him, 'You fool!	Lk 12:20
and is not rich toward **G**."	Lk 12:21
or a barn; yet **G** feeds them.	Lk 12:24
If that's how **G** clothes the	Lk 12:28
restored and began to glorify **G**.	Lk 13:13
What is the kingdom of **G** like,	Lk 13:18
I compare the kingdom of **G** to?	Lk 13:20
the kingdom of **G** but yourselves	Lk 13:28
the table in the kingdom of **G**.	Lk 13:29
in the kingdom of **G** is blessed!"	Lk 14:15
be slaves to both **G** and money."	Lk 16:13
of others, but **G** knows your	Lk 16:15
of the kingdom of **G** has been	Lk 16:16
a loud voice, gave glory to **G**.	Lk 17:15
to give glory to **G** except this	Lk 17:18
when the kingdom of **G** will come,	Lk 17:20
The kingdom of **G** is not coming	Lk 17:20
the kingdom of **G** is among you."	Lk 17:21
didn't fear **G** or respect man.	Lk 18:2
I don't fear **G** or respect man,	Lk 18:4
Will not **G** grant justice to His	Lk 18:7
'**G**, I thank You that I'm not	Lk 18:11
and saying, '**G**, turn Your wrath	Lk 18:13
the kingdom of **G** belongs to such	Lk 18:16
the kingdom of **G** like a little	Lk 18:17
No one is good but One—**G**.	Lk 18:19
to enter the kingdom of **G**!	Lk 18:24
to enter the kingdom of **G**."	Lk 18:25
with men is possible with **G**."	Lk 18:27
because of the kingdom of **G**,	Lk 18:29
to follow Him, glorifying **G**.	Lk 18:43
they saw it, gave praise to **G**.	Lk 18:43
the kingdom of **G** was going to	Lk 19:11
began to praise **G** joyfully with	Lk 19:37
teach truthfully the way of **G**.	Lk 20:21
Caesar's and to **G** the things	Lk 20:25
like angels and are sons of **G**,	Lk 20:36
calls the Lord the **G** of Abraham	Lk 20:37
Abraham and the **G** of Isaac and	Lk 20:37
God of Isaac and the **G** of Jacob.	Lk 20:37
He is not **G** of the dead but of	Lk 20:38
stones and gifts dedicated to **G**,	Lk 21:5
that the kingdom of **G** is near.	Lk 21:31
fulfilled in the kingdom of **G**."	Lk 22:16
until the kingdom of **G** comes."	Lk 22:18
right hand of the Power of **G**."	Lk 22:69
Are You, then, the Son of **G**?"	Lk 22:70
you even fear **G**, since you are	Lk 23:40
to glorify **G**, saying, "This	Lk 23:47
forward to the kingdom of **G**.	Lk 23:51
and speech before **G** and all the	Lk 24:19
the temple complex blessing **G**.	Lk 24:53
Word was with **G**, and the Word	Jn 1:1
with God, and the Word was **G**.	Jn 1:1
He was with **G** in the beginning.	Jn 1:2
named John who was sent from **G**.	Jn 1:6
the right to be children of **G**,	Jn 1:12
or of the will of man, but of **G**.	Jn 1:13
has ever seen **G**. The One and	Jn 1:18
is the Lamb of **G**, who takes away	Jn 1:29
that He is the Son of **G**!"	Jn 1:34
he said, "Look! The Lamb of **G**!"	Jn 1:36
replied, "You are the Son of **G**!	Jn 1:49
the angels of **G** ascending and	Jn 1:51
have come from **G** as a teacher,	Jn 3:2
You do unless **G** were with him."	Jn 3:2
he cannot see the kingdom of **G**."	Jn 3:3
cannot enter the kingdom of **G**.	Jn 3:5
For **G** loved the world in this	Jn 3:16
For **G** did not send His Son into	Jn 3:17
of the One and Only Son of **G**.	Jn 3:18
shown to be accomplished by **G**."	Jn 3:21
has affirmed that **G** is true.	Jn 3:33
For **G** sent Him, and He speaks	Jn 3:34
the wrath of **G** remains on him.	Jn 3:36
If you knew the gift of **G**,	Jn 4:10
G is spirit, and those who	Jn 4:24
even calling **G** His own Father,	Jn 5:18
making Himself equal with **G**.	Jn 5:18
hear the voice of the Son of **G**,	Jn 5:25
have no love for **G** within you.	Jn 5:42
that comes from the only **G**.	Jn 5:44
because **G** the Father has set His	Jn 6:27
do to perform the works of **G**?"	Jn 6:28
replied, "This is the work of **G**:	Jn 6:29
the bread of **G** is the One who	Jn 6:33
they will all be taught by **G**.	Jn 6:45
except the One who is from **G**.	Jn 6:46
that You are the Holy One of **G**!"	Jn 6:69
teaching is from **G** or if I am	Jn 7:17
the truth that I heard from **G**.	Jn 8:40

"We have one Father—**G**." Jn 8:41
to them, "If **G** were your Father Jn 8:42
I came from **G** and I am here. Jn 8:42
one who is from **G** listens to Jn 8:47
because you are not from **G**." Jn 8:47
say about Him, 'He is our **G**.' Jn 8:54
is not from **G**, for He doesn't Jn 9:16
and told him, "Give glory to **G**. Jn 9:24
We know that **G** has spoken to Jn 9:29
We know that **G** doesn't listen to Jn 9:31
If this man were not from **G**, Jn 9:33
being a man—make Yourself **G**." Jn 10:33
the word of **G** came to 'gods' Jn 10:35
I said: I am the Son of **G**? Jn 10:36
death but is for the glory of **G**, Jn 11:4
that the Son of **G** may be Jn 11:4
that whatever You ask from **G**, Jn 11:22
ask from God, **G** will give You." Jn 11:22
the Son of **G**, who was to come Jn 11:27
you would see the glory of **G**?" Jn 11:40
the scattered children of **G**. Jn 11:52
men more than praise from **G**. Jn 12:43
had come from **G**, and that He was Jn 13:3
and that He was going back to **G**. Jn 13:3
and **G** is glorified in Him. Jn 13:31
If **G** is glorified in Him, God Jn 13:32
G will also glorify Him in Jn 13:32
Believe in **G**; believe also in Me Jn 14:1
he is offering service to **G**. Jn 16:2
believed that I came from **G**. Jn 16:27
believe that You came from **G**." Jn 16:30
the only true **G**, and the One You Jn 17:3
He made Himself the Son of **G**." Jn 19:7
Father—to My **G** and your God." Jn 20:17
Father—to My God and your **G**." Jn 20:17
to Him, "My Lord and my **G**!" Jn 20:28
the Son of **G**, and by believing Jn 20:31
of death he would glorify **G**. Jn 21:19
speaking about the kingdom of **G**. Ac 1:3
the magnificent acts of **G**." Ac 2:11
last days, says **G**, that I will Ac 2:17
out to you by **G** with miracles, Ac 2:22
and signs that **G** did among you Ac 2:22
G raised Him up, ending the Ac 2:24
he knew that **G** had sworn an oath Ac 2:30
G has resurrected this Jesus. Ac 2:32
right hand of **G** and has received Ac 2:33
certainty that **G** has made this Ac 2:36
as the Lord our **G** will call." Ac 2:39
praising **G** and having favor with Ac 2:47
leaping, and praising **G**. Ac 3:8
saw him walking and praising **G**, Ac 3:9
The **G** of Abraham, Isaac, and Ac 3:13
and Jacob, the **G** of our fathers, Ac 3:13
whom **G** raised from the dead; Ac 3:15
But what **G** predicted through the Ac 3:18
which **G** spoke about by the mouth Ac 3:21
Lord your **G** will raise up for Ac 3:22
covenant that **G** made with your Ac 3:25
G raised up His Servant and sent Ac 3:26
crucified and whom **G** raised from Ac 4:10
in the sight of **G** ⌊for us⌋ to Ac 4:19
listen to you rather than to **G**, Ac 4:19
giving glory to **G** over what had Ac 4:21
their voices to **G** unanimously Ac 4:24
have not lied to men but to **G**!" Ac 5:4
We must obey **G** rather than men. Ac 5:29
The **G** of our fathers raised up Ac 5:30
G exalted this man to His right Ac 5:31
Holy Spirit whom **G** has given to Ac 5:32
but if it is of **G**, you will not Ac 5:39
be found fighting against **G**." Ac 5:39
preaching about **G** to wait on Ac 6:2
preaching about **G** flourished, Ac 6:7
words against Moses and **G**!" Ac 6:11
The **G** of glory appeared to our Ac 7:2
G had him move to this land in Ac 7:4
G spoke in this way: His Ac 7:6
will serve as slaves, **G** said. Ac 7:7
into Egypt, but **G** was with him Ac 7:9
the promise that **G** had made to Ac 7:17
and he was beautiful before **G**. Ac 7:20
understand that **G** would give Ac 7:25
I am the **G** of your forefathers— Ac 7:32
forefathers—the **G** of Abraham, Ac 7:32
this one **G** sent as a ruler and a Ac 7:35
G will raise up for you a Ac 7:37
Then **G** turned away and gave them Ac 7:42
and the star of your **g** Rephan, Ac 7:43
nations that **G** drove out before Ac 7:45
place for the **G** of Jacob. Ac 7:46
standing at the right hand of **G**, Ac 7:55
at the right hand of **G**!" Ac 7:56
is called the Great Power of **G**!" Ac 8:10
the kingdom of **G** and the name Ac 8:12
the gift of **G** could be obtained Ac 8:20
heart is not right before **G**. Ac 8:21
Jesus Christ is the Son of **G**." Ac 8:37
"He is the Son of **G**." Ac 9:20
man and feared **G** along with his Ac 10:2
people and always prayed to **G**. Ac 10:2
vision an angel of **G** who came in Ac 10:3
as a memorial offering before **G**. Ac 10:4
to him, "What **G** has made clean, Ac 10:15
But **G** has shown me that I must Ac 10:28
So we are all present before **G**, Ac 10:33
I understand that **G** doesn't show Ac 10:34
how **G** anointed Jesus of Nazareth Ac 10:38
Devil, because **G** was with Him. Ac 10:38
G raised up this man on the Ac 10:40
appointed beforehand by **G**, Ac 10:41
appointed by **G** to be the Judge Ac 10:42
declaring the greatness of **G**. Ac 10:46
time, 'What **G** has made clean, Ac 11:9
G gave them the same gift that Ac 11:17
how could I possibly hinder **G**?" Ac 11:17
they glorified **G**, saying, "So Ac 11:18
So **G** has granted repentance Ac 11:18
arrived and saw the grace of **G**, Ac 11:23
made earnestly to **G** for him by Ac 12:5
voice of a **g** and not of a man! Ac 12:22
he did not give the glory to **G**, Ac 12:23
and you who fear **G**, listen! Ac 13:16
G of this people Israel chose Ac 13:17
so **G** gave them Saul the son of Ac 13:21
to the promise, **G** brought the Ac 13:23
and those among you who fear **G**, Ac 13:26
But **G** raised Him from the dead, Ac 13:30
G has fulfilled this to us their Ac 13:33
But the One whom **G** raised up did Ac 13:37
to continue in the grace of **G**. Ac 13:43
things to the living **G**, Ac 14:15
our way into the kingdom of **G**." Ac 14:22
to the grace of **G** for the work Ac 14:26
everything **G** had done with them Ac 14:27
reported all that **G** had done Ac 15:4
the early days **G** made a choice Ac 15:7
And **G**, who knows the heart, Ac 15:8
are you now testing **G** by putting Ac 15:10
and wonders **G** had done through Ac 15:12
reported how **G** first intervened Ac 15:14
those who turn to **G** from among Ac 15:19
concluding that **G** had called us Ac 16:10
who worshiped **G**, was listening. Ac 16:14
the slaves of the Most High **G**, Ac 16:17
praying and singing hymns to **G**, Ac 16:25
had believed **G** with his entire Ac 16:34
and with those who worshiped **G**, Ac 17:17
TO AN UNKNOWN **G** Therefore, Ac 17:23
The **G** who made the world and Ac 17:24
so that they might seek **G**, Ac 17:27
G now commands all people Ac 17:30
worshiper of **G**, whose house was Ac 18:7
the word of **G** among them. Ac 18:11
people to worship **G** contrary to Ac 18:13
back to you again, if **G** wills." Ac 18:21
the way of **G** to him more Ac 18:26
related to the kingdom of **G**. Ac 19:8
G was performing extraordinary Ac 19:11
toward **G** and faith in our Ac 20:21
to you the whole plan of **G**. Ac 20:27
to shepherd the church of **G**, Ac 20:28
I commit you to **G** and to the Ac 20:32
one by one what **G** did among the Ac 21:19
they glorified **G** and said, Ac 21:20
Being zealous for **G**, just as all Ac 22:3
'The **G** of our fathers has Ac 22:14
my life before **G** in all good Ac 23:1
G is going to strike you, Ac 23:3
so I worship my fathers' **G**, Ac 24:14
have a hope in **G**, which these Ac 24:15
conscience toward **G** and men. Ac 24:16
made by **G** to our fathers, Ac 26:6
of you that **G** raises the dead Ac 26:8
from the power of Satan to **G**, Ac 26:18
should repent and turn to **G**, Ac 26:20
obtained help that comes from **G**, Ac 26:22
"I wish before **G**," replied Paul, Ac 26:29
angel of the **G** I belong to and Ac 27:23
G has graciously given you all Ac 27:24
I believe **G** that it will be Ac 27:25
gave thanks to **G** in the presence Ac 27:35
their minds and said he was a **g**. Ac 28:6
he thanked **G** and took courage. Ac 28:15
about the kingdom of **G**. Ac 28:23
saving work of **G** has been sent Ac 28:28
kingdom of **G** and teaching the Ac 28:31
powerful Son of **G** by the Rm 1:4
Rome, loved by **G**, called as Rm 1:7
you and peace from **G** our Father Rm 1:7
thank my **G** through Jesus Christ Rm 1:8
For **G**, whom I serve with my Rm 1:9
known about **G** is evident among Rm 1:19
because **G** has shown it to them. Rm 1:19
though they knew **G**, they did not Rm 1:21
glorify Him as **G** or show Rm 1:21
of the immortal **G** for images Rm 1:23
Therefore **G** delivered them over Rm 1:24
the truth of **G** for a lie, Rm 1:25
is why **G** delivered them over Rm 1:26
to have **G** in their knowledge Rm 1:28
G delivered them over to a Rm 1:28
There is no favoritism with **G**. Rm 2:11
law are not righteous before **G**, Rm 2:13
on the day when **G** judges what Rm 2:16
rest in the law, and boast in **G**, Rm 2:17
you dishonor **G** by breaking the Rm 2:23
name of **G** is blasphemed among Rm 2:24
is not from men but from **G**. Rm 2:29
with the spoken words of **G**. Rm 3:2
G must be true, but everyone is Rm 3:4
Is **G** unrighteous to inflict Rm 3:5
how will **G** judge the world? Rm 3:6
there is no one who seeks **G**. Rm 3:11
is no fear of **G** before their Rm 3:18
fall short of the glory of **G**. Rm 3:23
G presented Him as a Rm 3:25
in His restraint **G** passed over Rm 3:25
Or is **G** for Jews only? Is He not Rm 3:29
there is one **G** who will justify Rm 3:30
brag about—but not before **G**. Rm 4:2
Abraham believed **G**, and it was Rm 4:3
of the man to whom **G** credits Rm 4:6
He believed in **G**, who gives life Rm 4:17
his faith and gave glory to **G**, Rm 4:20
have peace with **G** through our Rm 5:1
in the hope of the glory of **G**. Rm 5:2
But **G** proves His own love for us Rm 5:8
reconciled to **G** through the Rm 5:10
also rejoice in **G** through our Rm 5:11
have the grace of **G** and the gift Rm 5:15
in that He lives, He lives to **G**. Rm 6:10
but alive to **G** in Christ Jesus. Rm 6:11
yourselves to **G**, and all the Rm 6:13
yourselves to **G** as weapons for Rm 6:13
But thank **G** that, although you Rm 6:17
sin and become enslaved to **G**, Rm 6:22
the gift of **G** is eternal life Rm 6:23
that we may bear fruit for **G**. Rm 7:4
I thank **G** through Jesus Christ Rm 7:25
am a slave to the law of **G**, Rm 7:25
was limited by the flesh, **G** did. Rm 8:3
is hostile to **G** because it does Rm 8:7
flesh are unable to please **G**. Rm 8:8
the Spirit of **G** lives in you. Rm 8:9
heirs of **G** and co-heirs with Rm 8:17
according to the will of **G**. Rm 8:27
the good of those who love **G**: Rm 8:28
If **G** is for us, who is against Rm 8:31
G is the One who justifies. Rm 8:33
right hand of **G** and intercedes Rm 8:34
from the love of **G** that is in Rm 8:39
Messiah, who is **G** over all, Rm 9:5
though the word of **G** has failed. Rm 9:6
Is there injustice with **G**? Rm 9:14
effort, but on **G** who shows mercy Rm 9:16
anyone who talks back to **G**? Rm 9:20
And what if **G**, desiring to Rm 9:22
be called sons of the living **G**. Rm 9:26
and prayer to **G** concerning them Rm 10:1
them that they have zeal for **G**, Rm 10:2
from **G** and attempted to Rm 10:3
in your heart that **G** raised Him Rm 10:9
has **G** rejected His people? Rm 11:1

G has not rejected His people Rm 11:2
he pleads with **G** against Israel? Rm 11:2
G gave them a spirit of stupor, Rm 11:8
For if **G** did not spare the Rm 11:21
because **G** has the power to graft Rm 11:23
once disobeyed **G**, but now have Rm 11:30
For **G** has imprisoned all in Rm 11:32
wisdom and the knowledge of **G**! Rm 11:33
the mercies of **G**, I urge you to Rm 12:1
holy and pleasing to **G**; Rm 12:1
pleasing, and perfect will of **G**. Rm 12:2
G has distributed a measure of Rm 12:3
is no authority except from **G**, Rm 13:1
that exist are instituted by **G**. Rm 13:1
because **G** has accepted him. Rm 14:3
since he gives thanks to **G**; Rm 14:6
does not eat, yet he thanks **G**. Rm 14:6
before the judgment seat of **G**. Rm 14:10
tongue will give praise to **G**. Rm 14:11
give an account of himself to **G**. Rm 14:12
the kingdom of **G** is not eating Rm 14:17
is acceptable to **G** and approved Rm 14:18
Keep it to yourself before **G**. Rm 14:22
Now may the **G** of endurance and Rm 15:5
may glorify the **G** and Father of Rm 15:6
accepted you, to the glory of **G**. Rm 15:7
on behalf of the truth of **G**, Rm 15:8
may glorify **G** for His mercy. Rm 15:9
Now may the **G** of hope fill you Rm 15:13
of the grace given me by **G** Rm 15:15
regarding what pertains to **G**. Rm 15:17
your prayers to **G** on my behalf: Rm 15:30
The **G** of peace be with all of Rm 15:33
The **G** of peace will soon crush Rm 16:20
to the command of the eternal **G**, Rm 16:26
the only wise **G**, through Jesus Rm 16:27
you and peace from **G** our Father 1Co 1:3
thank my **G** for you because 1Co 1:4
G is faithful; by Him you were 1Co 1:9
thank **G** that I baptized none of 1Co 1:14
Hasn't **G** made the world's wisdom 1Co 1:20
did not know **G** through wisdom, 1Co 1:21
G was pleased to save those who 1Co 1:21
G has chosen the world's foolish 1Co 1:27
G has chosen the world's weak 1Co 1:27
G has chosen the world's 1Co 1:28
for us became wisdom from **G**, 1Co 1:30
the testimony of **G** to you, 1Co 2:1
which **G** predestined before the 1Co 2:7
is what **G** has prepared for those 1Co 2:9
Now **G** has revealed them to us by 1Co 2:10
even the deep things of **G**. 1Co 2:10
the concerns of **G** except the 1Co 2:11
of God except the Spirit of **G**. 1Co 2:11
but the Spirit who is from **G**, 1Co 2:12
been freely given to us by **G**. 1Co 2:12
watered, but **G** gave the growth. 1Co 3:6
but only **G** who gives the growth. 1Co 3:7
the Spirit of **G** lives in you? 1Co 3:16
sanctuary, **G** will ruin him; 1Co 3:17
world is foolishness with **G**, 1Co 3:19
to Christ, and Christ to **G**. 1Co 3:23
will come to each one from **G**. 1Co 4:5
For I think **G** has displayed us, 1Co 4:9
the kingdom of **G** is not in talk 1Co 4:20
But **G** judges outsiders. Put away 1Co 5:13
and by the Spirit of our **G**. 1Co 6:11
but **G** will do away with both of 1Co 6:13
G raised up the Lord and will 1Co 6:14
is in you, whom you have from **G**? 1Co 6:19
glorify **G** in your body. 1Co 6:20
each has his own gift from **G**, 1Co 7:7
G has called you to peace. 1Co 7:15
Lord assigned when **G** called him. 1Co 7:17
should remain with **G** in whatever 1Co 7:24
I also have the Spirit of **G**. 1Co 7:40
anyone loves **G**, he is known by 1Co 8:3
that "there is no **G** but one." 1Co 8:4
yet for us there is one **G**, 1Co 8:6
not make us acceptable to **G**. 1Co 8:8
Is **G** really concerned with oxen? 1Co 9:9
But **G** was not pleased with most 1Co 10:5
G is faithful and He will not 1Co 10:13
to demons and not to **G**. 1Co 10:20
the Greeks or the church of **G**, 1Co 10:32
and **G** is the head of Christ. 1Co 11:3
and all things come from **G**. 1Co 11:12
woman to pray to **G** with her head 1Co 11:13
nor do the churches of **G**. 1Co 11:16
on the church of **G** and embarrass 1Co 11:22
by the Spirit of **G** says, 1Co 12:3
but the same **G** is active in 1Co 12:6
But now **G** has placed the parts, 1Co 12:18
G has put the body together, 1Co 12:24
And **G** has placed these in the 1Co 12:28
is not speaking to men but to **G**, 1Co 14:2
thank **G** that I speak in ⌊other⌋ 1Co 14:18
down on his face and worship **G**, 1Co 14:25
proclaiming, "**G** is really among 1Co 14:25
and speak to himself and to **G**. 1Co 14:28
since **G** is not a God of disorder 1Co 14:33
since God is not a **G** of disorder 1Co 14:33
Did the word of **G** originate from 1Co 14:36
I persecuted the church of **G**. 1Co 15:9
to be false witnesses about **G**, 1Co 15:15
testified about **G** that He raised 1Co 15:15
the kingdom to **G** the Father, 1Co 15:24
so that **G** may be all in all. 1Co 15:28
people are ignorant about **G**. 1Co 15:34
But **G** gives it a body as He 1Co 15:38
cannot inherit the kingdom of **G**, 1Co 15:50
But thanks be to **G**, who gives us 1Co 15:57
you and peace from **G** our Father 2Co 1:2
Blessed be the **G** and Father of 2Co 1:3
and the **G** of all comfort. 2Co 1:3
we ourselves receive from **G**. 2Co 1:4
but in **G** who raises the dead. 2Co 1:9
As **G** is faithful, our message to 2Co 1:18
For the Son of **G**, Jesus Christ, 2Co 1:19
and has anointed us, is **G**; 2Co 1:21
I call on **G** as a witness against 2Co 1:23
thanks be to **G**, who always puts 2Co 2:14
For to **G** we are the fragrance of 2Co 2:15
as from **G** and before God. 2Co 2:17
as from God and before **G**. 2Co 2:17
with the Spirit of the living **G**; 2Co 3:3
toward **G** through Christ: 2Co 3:4
but our competence is from **G**. 2Co 3:5
g of this age has blinded the 2Co 4:4
Christ, who is the image of **G**. 2Co 4:4
For **G**, who said, "Light shall 2Co 4:6
may be from **G** and not from us. 2Co 4:7
we have a building from **G**, 2Co 5:1
us for this very thing is **G**, 2Co 5:5
We are completely open before **G**, 2Co 5:11
out of our mind, it is for **G**; 2Co 5:13
is from **G**, who reconciled us 2Co 5:18
G was reconciling the world to 2Co 5:19
certain that **G** is appealing 2Co 5:20
behalf, "Be reconciled to **G**." 2Co 5:20
the righteousness of **G** in Him. 2Co 5:21
of truth, by the power of **G**; 2Co 6:7
the sanctuary of the living **G**, 2Co 6:16
of the living God, as **G** said: 2Co 6:16
I will be their **G**, and they will 2Co 6:16
complete in the fear of **G**. 2Co 7:1
But **G**, who comforts the humble, 2Co 7:6
you were grieved as **G** willed, 2Co 7:9
this grieving as **G** wills— 2Co 7:11
plain to you in the sight of **G**. 2Co 7:12
about the grace of **G** granted to 2Co 8:1
Thanks be to **G** who put the same 2Co 8:16
for **G** loves a cheerful giver. 2Co 9:7
G is able to make every grace 2Co 9:8
thanksgiving to **G** through us. 2Co 9:11
many acts of thanksgiving to **G**. 2Co 9:12
they will glorify **G** for your 2Co 9:13
surpassing grace of **G** on you. 2Co 9:14
Thanks be to **G** for His 2Co 9:15
powerful through **G** for the 2Co 10:4
up against the knowledge of **G**, 2Co 10:5
ministry⌋ that **G** has assigned to 2Co 10:13
the gospel of **G** to you free of 2Co 11:7
I don't love you? **G** knows I do! 2Co 11:11
the **G** and Father of the Lord 2Co 11:31
the body, I don't know; **G** knows. 2Co 12:2
body I do not know, **G** knows— 2Co 12:3
the sight of **G** we are speaking 2Co 12:19
that when I come my **G** will again 2Co 12:21
Now we pray to **G** that you do 2Co 13:7
and the **G** of love and peace will 2Co 13:11
and the love of **G**, and the 2Co 13:13
Jesus Christ and **G** the Father Gl 1:1
and peace from **G** the Father and Gl 1:3
to the will of our **G** and Father, Gl 1:4
win the favor of people, or **G**? Gl 1:10
But when **G**, who from my mother's Gl 1:15
I'm not lying. **G** is my witness. Gl 1:20
they glorified **G** because of me. Gl 1:24
G does not show favoritism Gl 2:6
the law, that I might live to **G**. Gl 2:19
I live by faith in the Son of **G**, Gl 2:20
do not set aside the grace of **G**; Gl 2:21
G supply you with the Spirit Gl 3:5
Just as Abraham believed **G**, Gl 3:6
foresaw that **G** would justify Gl 3:8
justified before **G** by the law, Gl 3:11
was previously ratified by **G**, Gl 3:17
but **G** granted it to Abraham Gl 3:18
just one person, but **G** is one. Gl 3:20
are all sons of **G** through faith Gl 3:26
the time came, **G** sent His Son, Gl 4:4
G has sent the Spirit of His Son Gl 4:6
a son, then an heir through **G**. Gl 4:7
you didn't know **G**, you were Gl 4:8
since you know **G**, or rather have Gl 4:9
rather have become known by **G**, Gl 4:9
received me as an angel of **G**, Gl 4:14
not inherit the kingdom of **G**. Gl 5:21
be deceived: **G** is not mocked. Gl 6:7
also be on the Israel of **G**! Gl 6:16
you and peace from **G** our Father Eph 1:2
Blessed be the **G** and Father of Eph 1:3
I pray⌋ that the **G** of our Lord Eph 1:17
But **G**, who is abundant in mercy, Eph 2:4
which **G** prepared ahead of time Eph 2:10
hope and without **G** in the world. Eph 2:12
reconcile both to **G** in one body Eph 2:16
for ages in **G** who created all Eph 3:9
with all the fullness of **G**. Eph 3:19
one **G** and Father of all, who is Eph 4:6
excluded from the life of **G**, Eph 4:18
just as **G** also forgave you in Eph 4:32
be imitators of **G**, as dearly Eph 5:1
and fragrant offering to **G**. Eph 5:2
kingdom of the Messiah and of **G**. Eph 5:5
for everything to **G** the Father Eph 5:20
full armor of **G** so that you can Eph 6:11
take up the full armor of **G**, Eph 6:13
from **G** the Father and the Lord Eph 6:23
you and peace from **G** our Father Php 1:2
I give thanks to my **G** for every Php 1:3
G is my witness, how I deeply Php 1:8
to the glory and praise of **G**. Php 1:11
—and this is from **G**. Php 1:28
existing in the form of **G**, Php 2:6
equality with **G** as something to Php 2:6
For this reason **G** also highly Php 2:9
to the glory of **G** the Father. Php 2:11
For it is **G** who is working in Php 2:13
children of **G** who are faultless Php 2:15
However, **G** had mercy on him, and Php 2:27
who serve by the Spirit of **G**, Php 3:3
from **G** based on faith. Php 3:9
G will reveal this to you also. Php 3:15
their **g** is their stomach; Php 3:19
requests be made known to **G**. Php 4:6
the peace of **G**, which surpasses Php 4:7
and the **G** of peace will be with Php 4:9
sacrifice, pleasing to **G**. Php 4:18
And my **G** will supply all your Php 4:19
Now to our **G** and Father be glory Php 4:20
you and peace from **G** our Father. Col 1:2
We always thank **G**, the Father of Col 1:3
growing in the knowledge of **G**. Col 1:10
is the image of the invisible **G**, Col 1:15
For **G** was pleased ⌊to have⌋ all Col 1:19
G wanted to make known to those Col 1:27
faith in the working of **G**, Col 2:12
develops with growth from **G**. Col 2:19
seated at the right hand of **G**. Col 3:1
is hidden with the Messiah in **G**. Col 3:3
gratitude in your hearts to **G**. Col 3:16
giving thanks to **G** the Father Col 3:17
for us that **G** may open a door Col 4:3
co-workers for the kingdom of **G**, Col 4:11
assured in everything **G** wills. Col 4:12
Thessalonians in **G** the Father 1Th 1:1
always thank **G** for all of you, 1Th 1:2
presence of our **G** and Father, 1Th 1:3
election, brothers loved by **G**. 1Th 1:4
your faith in **G** has gone out, 1Th 1:8
how you turned to **G** from idols 1Th 1:9
to serve the living and true **G**, 1Th 1:9

emboldened by our **G** to speak the 1Th 2:2
the gospel of **G** to you in spite 1Th 2:2
approved by **G** to be entrusted 1Th 2:4
men, but rather **G**, who examines 1Th 2:4
motives—**G** is our witness 1Th 2:5
the gospel of **G** but also our own 1Th 2:8
and so is **G**, of how devoutly, 1Th 2:10
one of you to walk worthy of **G**, 1Th 2:12
is why we constantly thank **G**, 1Th 2:13
message about **G** that you heard 1Th 2:13
the message of **G**, which also 1Th 2:13
displease **G**, and are hostile 1Th 2:15
How can we thank **G** for you in 1Th 3:9
because of you before our **G**, 1Th 3:9
may our **G** and Father Himself, 1Th 3:11
before our **G** and Father at 1Th 3:13
how you must walk and please **G**— 1Th 4:1
the Gentiles who don't know **G**. 1Th 4:5
For **G** has not called us to 1Th 4:7
reject man, but **G**, who also 1Th 4:8
are taught by **G** to love one 1Th 4:9
the same way **G** will bring with 1Th 4:14
and with the trumpet of **G**, 1Th 4:16
For **G** did not appoint us to 1Th 5:9
Now may the **G** of peace Himself 1Th 5:23
Thessalonians in **G** our Father 2Th 1:1
you and peace from **G** our Father 2Th 1:2
We must always thank **G** for you, 2Th 1:3
is righteous for **G** to repay with 2Th 1:6
don't know **G** and on those who 2Th 1:8
for you that our **G** will consider 2Th 1:11
the grace of our **G** and the Lord 2Th 1:12
every so-called **g** or object of 2Th 2:4
that he himself is **G**. 2Th 2:4
For this reason **G** sends them a 2Th 2:11
we must always thank **G** for you, 2Th 2:13
the beginning **G** has chosen you 2Th 2:13
Christ Himself and **G** our Father, 2Th 2:16
to the command of **G** our Savior 1Tm 1:1
and peace from **G** the Father and 1Tm 1:2
of the blessed **G** that was 1Tm 1:11
the only **G**, be honor and glory 1Tm 1:17
and it pleases **G** our Savior, 1Tm 2:3
there is one **G** and one mediator 1Tm 2:5
one mediator between **G** and man, 1Tm 2:5
who affirm that they worship **G**. 1Tm 2:10
is the church of the living **G**, 1Tm 3:15
from foods that **G** created to be 1Tm 4:3
everything created by **G** is good, 1Tm 4:4
by the word of **G** and by prayer. 1Tm 4:5
put our hope in the living **G**, 1Tm 4:10
parents, for this pleases **G**. 1Tm 5:4
put her hope in **G** and continues 1Tm 5:5
before **G** and Christ Jesus and 1Tm 5:21
you, man of **G**, run from these 1Tm 6:11
presence of **G**, who gives life 1Tm 6:13
which **G** will bring about in His 1Tm 6:15
of wealth, but on **G**, who richly 1Tm 6:17
and peace from **G** the Father and 2Tm 1:2
I thank **G**, whom I serve with a 2Tm 1:3
the gift of **G** that is in you 2Tm 1:6
For **G** has not given us a spirit 2Tm 1:7
relying on the power of **G**, 2Tm 1:8
them before **G** not to fight about 2Tm 2:14
present yourself approved to **G**, 2Tm 2:15
Perhaps **G** will grant them 2Tm 2:25
rather than lovers of **G**, 2Tm 3:4
is inspired by **G** and is 2Tm 3:16
the man of **G** may be complete 2Tm 3:17
Before **G** and Christ Jesus, 2Tm 4:1
a slave of **G**, and an apostle Ti 1:1
the hope of eternal life that **G**, Ti 1:2
by the command of **G** our Savior: Ti 1:3
and peace from **G** the Father Ti 1:4
profess to know **G**, but they deny Ti 1:16
the teaching of **G** our Savior Ti 2:10
For the grace of **G** has appeared, Ti 2:11
glory of our great **G** and Savior, Ti 2:13
man appeared from **G** our Savior, Ti 3:4
have believed **G** might be careful Ti 3:8
you and peace from **G** our Father Phm 3
always thank my **G** when I mention Phm 4
Long ago **G** spoke to the fathers Heb 1:1
Your throne, O **G**, is forever and Heb 1:8
this is why **G**, Your God, has Heb 1:9
is why God, Your **G**, has anointed Heb 1:9
G also testified by signs and Heb 2:4
am with the children **G** gave Me. Heb 2:13

high priest in service to **G**, Heb 2:17
One who built everything is **G**. Heb 3:4
that departs from the living **G**. Heb 3:12
seventh day **G** rested from all Heb 4:4
works, just as **G** did from His. Heb 4:10
For the word of **G** is living and Heb 4:12
Jesus the Son of **G**—let us hold Heb 4:14
in service to **G** for the people, Heb 5:1
is called by **G**, just as Aaron Heb 5:4
was declared by **G** a high priest Heb 5:10
from dead works, faith in **G**, Heb 6:1
we will do this if **G** permits. Heb 6:3
the Son of **G** and holding Him up Heb 6:6
receives a blessing from **G**. Heb 6:7
For **G** is not unjust; He will not Heb 6:10
For when **G** made a promise to Heb 6:13
Because **G** wanted to show His Heb 6:17
it is impossible for **G** to lie, Heb 6:18
priest of the Most High **G**, Heb 7:1
but resembling the Son of **G**— Heb 7:3
through which we draw near to **G**. Heb 7:19
those who come to **G** through Him, Heb 7:25
I will be their **G**, and they will Heb 8:10
Himself without blemish to **G**, Heb 9:14
works to serve the living **G**? Heb 9:14
covenant that **G** has commanded Heb 9:20
in the presence of **G** for us. Heb 9:24
scroll—to do Your will, O **G**!" Heb 10:7
sat down at the right hand of **G**. Heb 10:12
high priest over the house of **G**, Heb 10:21
has trampled on the Son of **G**, Heb 10:29
into the hands of the living **G**! Heb 10:31
was created by the word of **G**, Heb 11:3
Abel offered to **G** a better Heb 11:4
because **G** approved his gifts, Heb 11:4
found because **G** took him away. Heb 11:5
was approved, having pleased **G**. Heb 11:5
it is impossible to please **G**, Heb 11:6
architect and builder is **G**. Heb 11:10
Therefore **G** is not ashamed to be Heb 11:16
ashamed to be called their **G**, Heb 11:16
He considered **G** to be able even Heb 11:19
the people of **G** rather than to Heb 11:25
since **G** had provided something Heb 11:40
G is dealing with you as sons. Heb 12:7
of the grace of **G** and that no Heb 12:15
to the city of the living **G** Heb 12:22
to **G** who is the judge of all, Heb 12:23
we may serve **G** acceptably, Heb 12:28
for our **G** is a consuming fire. Heb 12:29
because **G** will judge immoral Heb 13:4
offer up to **G** a sacrifice of Heb 13:15
for **G** is pleased with such Heb 13:16
Now may the **G** of peace, who Heb 13:20
a slave of **G** and of the Lord Jms 1:1
should ask **G**, who gives to all Jms 1:5
"I am being tempted by **G**." Jms 1:13
For **G** is not tempted by evil, Jms 1:13
before our **G** and Father is this Jms 1:27
Didn't **G** choose the poor in this Jms 2:5
You believe that **G** is one; Jms 2:19
Abraham believed **G**, and it was Jms 2:23
the world is hostility toward **G**? Jms 4:4
G resists the proud, but gives Jms 4:6
submit to **G**. But resist Jms 4:7
Draw near to **G**, and He will draw Jms 4:8
foreknowledge of **G** the Father 1Pt 1:2
Blessed be the **G** and Father of 1Pt 1:3
through Him are believers in **G**, 1Pt 1:21
your faith and hope are in **G**. 1Pt 1:21
living and enduring word of **G**. 1Pt 1:23
but chosen and valuable to **G**— 1Pt 2:4
acceptable to **G** through Jesus 1Pt 2:5
G in a day of visitation. 1Pt 2:12
brotherhood. Fear **G**. Honor the 1Pt 2:17
because of conscience toward **G**, 1Pt 2:19
endure, it brings favor with **G**. 1Pt 2:20
who hoped in **G** also beautified 1Pt 3:5
that He might bring you to **G**, 1Pt 3:18
when **G** patiently waited in the 1Pt 3:20
of a good conscience toward **G** 1Pt 3:21
might live by **G** in the spiritual 1Pt 4:6
of the varied grace of **G**. 1Pt 4:10
be⌋ like the oracles of **G**; 1Pt 4:11
from the strength **G** provides, 1Pt 4:11
in everything **G** may be glorified 1Pt 4:11
of glory and of **G** rests on you. 1Pt 4:14
should glorify **G** with that name. 1Pt 4:16

who disobey the gospel of **G**? 1Pt 4:17
because **G** resists the proud, 1Pt 5:5
under the mighty hand of **G**, 1Pt 5:6
Now the **G** of all grace, who 1Pt 5:10
this is the true grace of **G**. 1Pt 5:12
of our **G** and Savior Jesus 2Pt 1:1
knowledge of **G** and of Jesus our 2Pt 1:2
and glory from **G** the Father, 2Pt 1:17
Holy Spirit, men spoke from **G**. 2Pt 1:21
For if **G** didn't spare the angels 2Pt 2:4
through water by the word of **G**. 2Pt 3:5
the coming of the day of **G**, 2Pt 3:12
G is light, and there is 1Jn 1:5
him the love of **G** is perfected. 1Jn 2:5
The Son of **G** was revealed for 1Jn 3:8
has been born of **G** does not sin, 1Jn 3:9
because he has been born of **G**. 1Jn 3:9
do what is right is not of **G**, 1Jn 3:10
G is greater than our hearts and 1Jn 3:20
us⌋ we have confidence before **G**, 1Jn 3:21
to determine if they are from **G**, 1Jn 4:1
is how you know the Spirit of **G**: 1Jn 4:2
has come in the flesh is from **G**. 1Jn 4:2
not confess Jesus is not from **G**. 1Jn 4:3
You are from **G**, little children, 1Jn 4:4
We are from **G**. Anyone who knows 1Jn 4:6
who knows **G** listens to us; 1Jn 4:6
is not from **G** does not listen 1Jn 4:6
love is from **G**, and everyone who 1Jn 4:7
been born of **G** and knows God. 1Jn 4:7
been born of God and knows **G**. 1Jn 4:7
does not love does not know **G**, 1Jn 4:8
not know God, because **G** is love. 1Jn 4:8
G sent His One and Only Son into 1Jn 4:9
not that we loved **G**, but that He 1Jn 4:10
if **G** loved us in this way, 1Jn 4:11
has ever seen **G**. If we love one 1Jn 4:12
G remains in us and His love is 1Jn 4:12
that Jesus is the Son of **G**— 1Jn 4:15
G remains in him and he in God. 1Jn 4:15
God remains in him and he in **G**. 1Jn 4:15
the love that **G** has for us. 1Jn 4:16
G is love, and the one who 1Jn 4:16
remains in love remains in **G**, 1Jn 4:16
in God, and **G** remains in him. 1Jn 4:16
says, "I love **G**," yet hates his 1Jn 4:20
cannot love **G** whom he has not 1Jn 4:20
one who loves **G** must also love 1Jn 4:21
the Messiah has been born of **G**, 1Jn 5:1
when we love **G** and obey His 1Jn 5:2
For this is what love for **G** is: 1Jn 5:3
has been born of **G** conquers the 1Jn 5:4
that Jesus is the Son of **G**? 1Jn 5:5
the Son of **G** has the testimony 1Jn 5:10
does not believe **G** has made Him 1Jn 5:10
testimony that **G** has given about 1Jn 5:10
G has given us eternal life, 1Jn 5:11
have the Son of **G** does not have 1Jn 5:12
in the name of the Son of **G**, 1Jn 5:13
and **G** will give life to him— 1Jn 5:16
has been born of **G** does not sin, 1Jn 5:18
One who is born of **G** keeps him, 1Jn 5:18
that we are of **G**, and the whole 1Jn 5:19
that the Son of **G** has come and 1Jn 5:20
He is the true **G** and eternal 1Jn 5:20
be with us from **G** the Father 2Jn 3
goes beyond it, does not have **G**. 2Jn 9
journey in a manner worthy of **G**, 3Jn 6
The one who does good is of **G**; 3Jn 11
who does evil has not seen **G**. 3Jn 11
loved by **G** the Father and kept Jd 1
grace of our **G** into promiscuity Jd 4
yourselves in the love of **G**, Jd 21
the only **G** our Savior, through Jd 25
Christ that **G** gave Him to show Rv 1:1
priests to His **G** and Father— Rv 1:6
the Lord **G**, "the One who is, Rv 1:8
which is in the paradise of **G**. Rv 2:7
The Son of **G**, the One whose eyes Rv 2:18
seven spirits of **G** and the seven Rv 3:1
your works complete before My **G**. Rv 3:2
pillar in the sanctuary of My **G**, Rv 3:12
write on him the name of My **G**, Rv 3:12
the name of the city of My **G**— Rv 3:12
down out of heaven from My **G**— Rv 3:12
are the seven spirits of **G**. Rv 4:5
holy, Lord **G**, the Almighty, Rv 4:8
Our Lord and **G**, You are worthy Rv 4:11

seven spirits of **G** sent into all Rv 5:6
people⌋ for **G** by Your blood Rv 5:9
a kingdom and priests to our **G**, Rv 5:10
had the seal of the living **G**. Rv 7:2
the slaves of our **G** on their Rv 7:3
Salvation belongs to our **G**, Rv 7:10
the throne and worshiped **G**, Rv 7:11
be to our **G** forever and ever. Rv 7:12
they are before the throne of **G**, Rv 7:15
and **G** will wipe away every tear Rv 7:17
who stand in the presence of **G**; Rv 8:2
the presence of **G** from the Rv 8:4
the gold altar that is before **G**, Rv 9:13
of life from **G** entered them, Rv 11:11
gave glory to the **G** of heaven. Rv 11:13
seated before **G** on their thrones Rv 11:16
on their faces and worshiped **G**, Rv 11:16
thank You, Lord **G**, the Almighty, Rv 11:17
was caught up to **G** and to His Rv 12:5
she had a place prepared by **G**, Rv 12:6
kingdom of our **G** and the Rv 12:10
them before our **G** day and night. Rv 12:10
the commandments of **G** and have Rv 12:17
to speak blasphemies against **G**: Rv 13:6
firstfruits for **G** and the Lamb. Rv 14:4
Fear **G** and give Him glory, Rv 14:7
commandments of **G** and the faith Rv 14:12
sea of glass with harps from **G**. Rv 15:2
works, Lord **G**, the Almighty; Rv 15:3
the wrath of **G** who lives forever Rv 15:7
Yes, Lord **G**, the Almighty, true Rv 16:7
the name of **G** who had the power Rv 16:9
blasphemed the **G** of heaven Rv 16:11
battle of the great day of **G**, Rv 16:14
they blasphemed **G** for the plague Rv 16:21
For **G** has put it into their Rv 17:17
and **G** has remembered her crimes. Rv 18:5
because the Lord **G** who judges Rv 18:8
because **G** has executed your Rv 18:20
and power belong to our **G**, Rv 19:1
fell down and worshiped **G**, Rv 19:4
Praise our **G**, all you His Rv 19:5
our Lord **G**, the Almighty, Rv 19:6
"These words of **G** are true." Rv 19:9
Worship **G**, because the testimony Rv 19:10
name is called the Word of **G**. Rv 19:13
of the fierce anger of **G**, Rv 19:15
for the great supper of **G**, Rv 19:17
be priests of **G** and the Messiah, Rv 20:6
down out of heaven from **G**, Rv 21:2
and **G** Himself will be with them Rv 21:3
be with them and be their **G**. Rv 21:3
I will be his **G**, and he will be Rv 21:7
down out of heaven from **G**, Rv 21:10
because the Lord **G** the Almighty Rv 21:22
the throne of **G** and of the Lamb Rv 22:1
The throne of **G** and of the Lamb Rv 22:3
because the Lord **G** will give Rv 22:5
the **G** of the spirits of the Rv 22:6
words of this book. Worship **G**." Rv 22:9
G will add to him the plagues Rv 22:18
G will take away his share of Rv 22:19

GOD'S *(357)*

earth was corrupt in **G** sight, Gn 6:11
You are **G** chosen one among us. Gn 23:6
and **G** angels were going up and Gn 28:12
up as a marker will be **G** house, Gn 28:22
said, "Am I in **G** place, who has Gn 30:2
his way, and **G** angels met him. Gn 32:1
Jacob said, "This is **G** camp." Gn 32:2
⌊and it is⌋ like seeing **G** face, Gn 33:10
And Moses took **G** staff in his Ex 4:20
been enough of **G** thunder and Ex 9:28
hilltop with **G** staff in my hand. Ex 17:9
father-in-law in **G** presence. Ex 18:12
⌊them⌋ **G** statutes and laws. Ex 18:16
I have filled him with **G** Spirit, Ex 31:3
and the writing was **G** writing, Ex 32:16
He has filled him with **G** Spirit, Ex 35:31
ever heard **G** voice speaking Dt 4:33
tablets, inscribed by **G** finger. Dt 9:10
on a tree⌋ is under **G** curse. Dt 21:23
the LORD your **G** commands I am Dt 28:13
in the assembly of **G** people: Jdg 20:2
the capture of **G** ark and the 1Sm 4:19
G hand was very heavy there. 1Sm 5:11
he worked with **G** help today." 1Sm 14:45
and my son from **G** inheritance. 2Sm 14:16

they saw that **G** wisdom was in 1Kg 3:28
killed because it was **G** battle. 1Ch 5:22
of the tabernacle, **G** temple. 1Ch 6:48
the chief official of **G** temple; 1Ch 9:11
in the ministry of **G** temple. 1Ch 9:13
and the treasuries of **G** temple. 1Ch 9:26
in the vicinity of **G** temple, 1Ch 9:27
offerings in **G** presence. 1Ch 16:1
was also evil in **G** sight, 1Ch 21:7
stones for building **G** house. 1Ch 22:2
the LORD **G** sanctuary so that 1Ch 22:19
of the service of **G** temple— 1Ch 23:28
for the service of **G** temple. 1Ch 25:6
the treasuries of **G** temple and 1Ch 26:20
the treasuries of **G** house, 1Ch 28:12
for all the service of **G** house. 1Ch 28:21
the service of **G** house they gave 1Ch 29:7
Gibeon because **G** tent of meeting 2Ch 1:3
for building **G** temple: 2Ch 3:3
for King Solomon in **G** temple: 2Ch 4:11
all the equipment in **G** temple: 2Ch 4:19
in the treasuries of **G** temple. 2Ch 5:1
of the LORD filled **G** temple. 2Ch 5:14
the people dedicated **G** temple. 2Ch 7:5
consecrated gifts into **G** temple: 2Ch 15:18
the battle is not yours, but **G**. 2Ch 20:15
with them in **G** temple six years. 2Ch 22:12
with the king in **G** temple. 2Ch 23:3
quivers that were in **G** temple. 2Ch 23:9
that the tax **G** servant Moses 2Ch 24:9
They restored **G** temple to its 2Ch 24:13
with Obed-edom in **G** temple, 2Ch 25:24
up the utensils of **G** temple, 2Ch 28:24
Azariah the ruler of **G** temple. 2Ch 31:13
in the service of **G** temple, 2Ch 31:21
he had made, in **G** temple, about 2Ch 33:7
the money brought into **G** temple. 2Ch 34:9
leaders of **G** temple, gave 2,600 2Ch 35:8
kept ridiculing **G** messengers, 2Ch 36:16
all the articles of **G** temple, 2Ch 36:18
the Chaldeans burned **G** temple. 2Ch 36:19
they arrived at **G** house in Ezr 3:8
construction of **G** house in Ezr 4:24
began to rebuild **G** house in Ezr 5:2
silver articles of **G** house that Ezr 5:14
the foundation of **G** house in Ezr 5:16
silver articles of **G** house that Ezr 6:5
the dedication of **G** house they Ezr 6:17
according to **G** wisdom that you Ezr 7:25
given through **G** servant Moses Neh 10:29
the wood⌋ to our **G** house to burn Neh 10:34
who serve in our **G** house. Neh 10:36
the chief official of **G** house, Neh 11:11
for the service of **G** house. Neh 11:22
a room in the courts of **G** house. Neh 13:7
G terrors are arrayed against me. Jb 6:4
G power provides this. Jb 12:6
unjustly on **G** behalf or speak Jb 13:7
Would **G** majesty not terrify you? Jb 13:11
G consolations not enough for Jb 15:11
depart by the breath of **G** mouth. Jb 15:30
mercy, for **G** hand has struck Jb 19:21
away on the day of **G** anger. Jb 20:28
I will teach you about **G** power. Jb 27:11
of my youth when **G** friendship Jb 29:4
when he becomes **G** friend." Jb 34:9
because **G** anger does not punish Jb 35:15
more to be said on **G** behalf. Jb 36:2
thunder roars from **G** pavilion? Jb 36:29
Stop and consider **G** wonders. Jb 37:14
Do you have an arm like **G**? Jb 40:9
He is the foremost of **G** works; Jb 40:19
G faithful love is constant. Ps 52:1
I trust in **G** faithful love Ps 52:8
fear and will tell about **G** work, Ps 64:9
G stream is filled with water, Ps 65:9
Mount Bashan is **G** towering Ps 68:15
G chariots are tens of thousands, Ps 68:17
I will praise **G** name with song Ps 69:30
until I entered **G** sanctuary. Ps 73:17
But as for me, **G** presence is my Ps 73:28
in God and not forget **G** works, Ps 78:7
They did not keep **G** covenant and Ps 78:10
G anger flared up against them, Ps 78:31
Let us seize **G** pastures for Ps 83:12
earth have seen our **G** victory. Ps 98:3
rebelled against **G** commands and Ps 107:11
that I may obey my **G** commands. Ps 119:115

G verdict is on the lips of a Pr 16:10
that even this is from **G** hand. Ec 2:24
one who is pleasing in **G** sight. Ec 2:26
and their works are in **G** hands. Ec 9:1
G retribution is coming; Is 35:4
and the day of our **G** vengeance; Is 61:2
⌊This is⌋ the Lord **G** declaration. Jr 2:22
under the rod of **G** wrath. Lm 3:1
The cedars in **G** garden could not Ezk 31:8
which were in **G** garden, envied Ezk 31:9
the Lord **G** declaration. Am 8:3
And now ask for **G** favor. Mal 1:9
heaven, because it is **G** throne; Mt 5:34
why do you break **G** commandment Mt 15:3
you have revoked **G** word because Mt 15:6
not thinking about **G** concerns, Mt 16:23
to God the things that are **G**." Mt 22:21
takes an oath by **G** throne and by Mt 23:22
'I can demolish **G** sanctuary and Mt 26:61
For He said, 'I am **G** Son.'" Mt 27:43
"This man really was **G** Son!" Mt 27:54
invalidate **G** command in order to Mk 7:9
You revoke **G** word by your Mk 7:13
not thinking about **G** concerns, Mk 8:33
to God the things that are **G**." Mk 12:17
"This man really was **G** Son!" Mk 15:39
Both were righteous in **G** sight, Lk 1:6
Because of our **G** merciful Lk 1:78
wisdom, and **G** grace was on Him Lk 2:40
G word came to John the son of Lk 3:2
in on Jesus to hear **G** word, Lk 5:1
they acknowledged **G** way of Lk 7:29
Peter answered, "**G** Messiah!" Lk 9:20
of them is forgotten in **G** sight. Lk 12:6
presence of **G** angels over one Lk 15:10
people is revolting in **G** sight. Lk 16:15
to God the things that are **G**." Lk 20:25
Himself if this is **G** Messiah, Lk 23:35
and He speaks **G** words, since He Jn 3:34
is from God listens to **G** words. Jn 8:47
about⌋ so that **G** works might be Jn 9:3
according to **G** determined plan Ac 2:23
began to speak **G** message with Ac 4:31
found favor in **G** sight and asked Ac 7:46
He saw **G** glory, with Jesus Ac 7:55
Samaria had welcomed **G** message, Ac 8:14
have been remembered in **G** sight. Ac 10:31
had welcomed **G** message also. Ac 11:1
Then **G** message flourished and Ac 12:24
they proclaimed **G** message in the Ac 13:5
and desired to hear **G** message. Ac 13:7
his own generation in **G** plan, Ac 13:36
necessary that **G** message be Ac 13:46
found out that **G** message had Ac 17:13
Being **G** offspring, then, we Ac 17:29
to the gospel of **G** grace. Ac 20:24
you dare revile **G** high priest?" Ac 23:4
singled out for **G** good news— Rm 1:1
that if it is somehow in **G** will, Rm 1:10
because it is **G** power for Rm 1:16
For in it **G** righteousness is Rm 1:17
For **G** wrath is revealed from Rm 1:18
know full well **G** just sentence— Rm 1:32
We know that **G** judgment on those Rm 2:2
that you will escape **G** judgment? Rm 2:3
recognizing that **G** kindness is Rm 2:4
when **G** righteous judgment is Rm 2:5
unbelief cancel **G** faithfulness? Rm 3:3
highlights **G** righteousness, Rm 3:5
But if by my lie **G** truth is Rm 3:7
become subject to **G** judgment. Rm 3:19
G righteousness has been Rm 3:21
G righteousness through faith in Rm 3:22
in **G** sight. As it is written: I Rm 4:17
waver in unbelief at **G** promise, Rm 4:20
because **G** love has been poured Rm 5:5
I joyfully agree with **G** law. Rm 7:22
does not submit itself to **G** law, Rm 8:7
those led by **G** Spirit are God's Rm 8:14
led by God's Spirit are **G** sons. Rm 8:14
spirit that we are **G** children, Rm 8:16
anticipation for **G** sons to be Rm 8:19
glorious freedom of **G** children. Rm 8:21
an accusation against **G** elect? Rm 8:33
descent who are **G** children, Rm 9:8
so that **G** purpose according to Rm 9:11
submitted to **G** righteousness. Rm 10:3
But what was **G** reply to him? Rm 11:4

GOD-FEARING *(5)*

GOD-GIVEN *(1)*

GOD-HATERS *(1)*

GODDESS *(4)*

GODLESS *(13)*

GODLESSNESS *(4)*

GODLINESS *(14)*

GODLY *(18)*

GODS *(241)*

driving out worship their g— Dt 12:2
the carved images of their g, Dt 12:3
Do not inquire about their g, Dt 12:30
these nations worship their g? Dt 12:30
for their g every detestable Dt 12:31
in the fire to their g. Dt 12:31
us follow other g,' which you Dt 13:2
'Let us go and worship other g'— Dt 13:6
any of the g of the peoples Dt 13:7
'Let us go and worship other g,' Dt 13:13
worship other g by bowing down Dt 17:3
speaks in the name of other g— Dt 18:20
things they do for their g, Dt 20:18
after other g to worship them. Dt 28:14
there you will worship other g, Dt 28:36
worship other g of wood and Dt 28:64
and worship the g of those Dt 29:18
They began to worship other g, Dt 29:26
bowing down to g they had not Dt 29:26
g that the LORD had not Dt 29:26
down to other g and worship them Dt 30:17
the foreign g of the land they Dt 31:16
have done by turning to other g. Dt 31:18
turn to other g and worship them Dt 31:20
His jealousy with foreign g; Dt 32:16
not God, to g they had not known Dt 32:17
new g that had just arrived, Dt 32:17
with ⌊their⌋ so-called g; Dt 32:21
Where are their g, the 'rock' Dt 32:37
The LORD is the God of g! Jos 22:22
The LORD is the God of g! Jos 22:22
names of their g or make an oath Jos 23:7
and go and worship other g, Jos 23:16
River and worshiped other g. Jos 24:2
Get rid of the g your ancestors Jos 24:14
the g your fathers worshiped Jos 24:15
the g of the Amorites in whose Jos 24:15
the LORD to worship other g! Jos 24:16
the LORD and worship foreign g, Jos 24:20
of the foreign g that are among Jos 24:23
their g will be a trap to you. Jdg 2:3
went after other g from the Jdg 2:12
themselves with other g, Jdg 2:17
going after other g to worship Jdg 2:19
sons, and worshiped their g. Jdg 3:6
Israel chose new g, then war was Jdg 5:8
not fear the g of the Amorites Jdg 6:10
the g of Aram, Sidon, Jdg 10:6
and the g of the Ammonites and Jdg 10:6
Me and worshiped other g. Jdg 10:13
out to the g you have chosen. Jdg 10:14
rid of the foreign g among them Jdg 10:16
ephod, household g, and a carved Jdg 18:14
You took the g I had made and Jdg 18:24
had taken the g Micah had made Jdg 18:27
"The g have entered their camp!" 1Sm 4:7
the hand of these magnificent g? 1Sm 4:8
These are the g that slaughtered 1Sm 4:8
you, your g, and your land. 1Sm 6:5
of the foreign g and the 1Sm 7:3
Me and worshiping other g. 1Sm 8:8
Then he cursed David by his g. 1Sm 17:43
'Go and worship other g.' 1Sm 26:19
nations and their g before Your 2Sm 7:23
and serve other g and worship 1Kg 9:6
clung to other g and worshiped 1Kg 9:9
you away ⌊from Me⌋ to their g." 1Kg 11:2
seduced him ⌊to follow⌋ other g. 1Kg 11:4
offering sacrifices to their g. 1Kg 11:8
he would not follow other g, 1Kg 11:10
other g and cast images, 1Kg 14:9
May the g punish me and do so 1Kg 19:2
May the g punish me and do so 1Kg 20:10
Their g are gods of the hill 1Kg 20:23
Their gods are g of the hill 1Kg 20:23
they had worshiped other g. 2Kg 17:7
their own g and putting them 2Kg 17:29
Anammelech, the g of the 2Kg 17:31
their own g according to 2Kg 17:33
them, "Do not fear other g; 2Kg 17:35
for you; do not fear other g. 2Kg 17:37
with you. Do not fear other g, 2Kg 17:38
Has any of the g of the nations 2Kg 18:33
Where are the g of Hamath and 2Kg 18:34
Where are the g of Sepharvaim, 2Kg 18:34
among all the g of the lands has 2Kg 18:35
Did the g of the nations that my 2Kg 19:12
thrown their g into the fire, 2Kg 19:18
they were not g but made by 2Kg 19:18
incense to other g in order to 2Kg 22:17
with the g of the nations God 1Ch 5:25
temple of their g and hung his 1Ch 10:10
He is feared above all g. 1Ch 16:25
For all the g of the peoples are 1Ch 16:26
is greater than any of the g. 2Ch 2:5
and serve other g and worship 2Ch 7:19
clung to other g and worshiped 2Ch 7:22
that Jeroboam made for you as g. 2Ch 13:8
a priest of what are not g. 2Ch 13:9
he brought the g of the Seirites 2Ch 25:14
and set them up as his g. 2Ch 25:14
a people's g that could not 2Ch 25:15
they went after the g of Edom. 2Ch 25:20
to the g of Damascus which 2Ch 28:23
Since the g of the kings of Aram 2Ch 28:23
to offer incense to other g, 2Ch 28:25
of the national g of the lands 2Ch 32:13
among all the g of these nations 2Ch 32:14
will your g deliver you from 2Ch 32:15
the national g of the lands that 2Ch 32:17
against the g of the peoples 2Ch 32:19
the foreign g and the idol 2Ch 33:15
incense to other g in order to 2Ch 34:25
placed in the house of his g. Ezr 1:7
assembly; He judges among the g: Ps 82:1
I said, "You are g; you are all Ps 82:6
is no one like You among the g, Ps 86:8
God, a great King above all g. Ps 95:3
He is feared above all g. Ps 96:4
For all the g of the peoples are Ps 96:5
All the g must worship Him. Ps 97:7
You are exalted above all the g. Ps 97:9
offered to lifeless g. Ps 106:28
our Lord is greater than all g. Ps 135:5
Give thanks to the God of g. Ps 136:2
the idols of her g have been Is 21:9
any one of the g of the nations Is 36:18
Where are the g of Hamath and Is 36:19
Where are the g of Sepharvaim? Is 36:19
Who of all the g of these lands Is 36:20
Did the g of the nations that my Is 37:12
thrown their g into the fire; Is 37:19
they were not g but made by Is 37:19
we will know that you are g. Is 41:23
images: You are our g! Is 42:17
Let these g declare the coming Is 44:7
The g cower; they crouch Is 46:2
to other g and to worship Jr 1:16
a nation ⌊ever⌋ exchanged its g? Jr 2:11
they were not g!) Yet My people Jr 2:11
where are your g you made for Jr 2:28
for your g are as numerous as Jr 2:28
sworn by those who are not g. Jr 5:7
served foreign g in your land, Jr 5:19
in this place or follow other g, Jr 7:6
and follow other g that you have Jr 7:9
offerings to other g so that Jr 7:18
The g that did not make the Jr 10:11
other g to worship them. Jr 11:10
cry out to the g they have been Jr 11:12
Your g are indeed as numerous as Jr 11:13
have followed other g to serve Jr 13:10
followed other g, served them, Jr 16:11
worship other g both day and Jr 16:13
Can one make g for himself? Jr 16:20
for himself? But they are not g. Jr 16:20
in it to other g that they, Jr 19:4
out drink offerings to other g." Jr 19:13
worshiped and served other g." Jr 22:9
not follow other g to serve them Jr 25:6
out to other g to provoke Me to Jr 32:29
following other g to serve them. Jr 35:15
in the temples of Egypt's g, Jr 43:12
the temples of the Egyptian g." Jr 43:13
incense to serve other g they, Jr 44:3
stop burning incense to other g. Jr 44:5
incense to other g in the land Jr 44:8
were burning incense to other g, Jr 44:15
Egypt, her g, and her kings— Jr 46:25
and burns incense to his g. Jr 48:35
her false g, devastated. Jr 50:2
in the seat of g in the heart Ezk 28:2
end to the false g in Memphis. Ezk 30:13
it known to him except the g, Dn 2:11
Your God is indeed God of g, Dn 2:47
do not serve your g or worship Dn 3:12
you don't serve my g or worship Dn 3:14
not serve your g or worship the Dn 3:18
looks like a son of the g." Dn 3:25
spirit of the holy g is in him— Dn 4:8
spirit of the holy g and that no Dn 4:9
have the spirit of the holy g. Dn 4:18
and praised their g made of gold Dn 5:4
the spirit of the holy g in him. Dn 5:11
wisdom like the wisdom of the g. Dn 5:11
have the spirit of the g in you, Dn 5:14
you praised the g made of silver Dn 5:23
take even their g captive to Dn 11:8
things against the God of g. Dn 11:36
regard for the g of his fathers, Dn 11:37
turn to other g and love raisin Hs 3:1
proclaim: Our g! to the work of Hs 14:3
walk in the name of their g, Mc 4:5
image from the house of your g; Nah 1:14
starves all the g of the earth. Zph 2:11
in your law, I said, you are g? Jn 10:34
the word of God came to 'g'— Jn 10:35
Make us g who will go before us. Ac 7:40
The g have come down to us in Ac 14:11
saying that g made by hand are Ac 19:26
gods made by hand are not g! Ac 19:26
even if there are so-called g, 1Co 8:5
there are many "g" and many 1Co 8:5
things that by nature are not g. Gl 4:8

GODS' *(1)*
the mount of the ⌊g⌋ assembly, Is 14:13

GOES *(84)*
(See pp. xi-xii.)

GOFER *(1)*
Make yourself an ark of g wood. Gn 6:14

GOG *(11)*
his son G, his son Shimei, 1Ch 5:4
your face toward G, of the land Ezk 38:2
am against you, G, chief prince Ezk 38:3
son of man, and say to G: Ezk 38:14
in the last days, G, that I will Ezk 38:16
the day when G comes against the Ezk 38:18
prophesy against G and say: Ezk 39:1
am against you, G, chief prince Ezk 39:1
day I will give G a burial place Ezk 39:11
for G and all his hordes will be Ezk 39:11
of the earth, G and Magog, to Rv 20:8

GOIIM *(3)*
of Elam, and Tidal king of G Gn 14:1
Tidal king of G, Amraphel king Gn 14:9
one the king of G in Gilgal one Jos 12:23

GOING *(296)*
(See pp. xi-xii.)

GOLAN *(4)*
or G in Bashan, belonging to the Dt 4:43
and G in Bashan from Manasseh's Jos 20:8
G, the city of refuge for the Jos 21:27
G in Bashan and its pasturelands, 1Ch 6:71

GOLD *(469)*
the Havilah, where there is g. Gn 2:11
G from that land is pure; Gn 2:12
in livestock, silver, and g. Gn 13:2
the man took a g ring weighing Gn 24:22
weighing 10 shekels of g. Gn 24:22
silver and g, male and female Gn 24:35
out objects of silver and g, Gn 24:53
and placed a g chain around his Gn 41:42
How could we steal g and silver Gn 44:8
house for silver and g jewelry, Ex 3:22
neighbors for g and silver Ex 11:2
for silver and g jewelry and for Ex 12:35
make ⌊gods of g⌋ for yourselves Ex 20:23
receive from them: g, silver, Ex 25:3
Overlay it with pure g; Ex 25:11
Also make a g molding all around Ex 25:11
four g rings for it and place Ex 25:12
wood and overlay them with g. Ex 25:13
Make a mercy seat of pure g, Ex 25:17
Make two cherubim of g; Ex 25:18
it with pure g and make a gold Ex 25:24
gold and make a g molding all Ex 25:24
it and make a g molding for it Ex 25:25
Make four g rings for it, and Ex 25:26
them with g so that the table Ex 25:28
Make them out of pure g. Ex 25:29
out of pure, hammered g. Ex 25:31
single hammered piece of pure g. Ex 25:36

and firepans must be of pure g.	Ex 25:38
made from 75 pounds of pure g.	Ex 25:39
Also make 50 g clasps and join	Ex 26:6
Then overlay the planks with g,	Ex 26:29
their rings of g as the holders	Ex 26:29
overlay the crossbars with g.	Ex 26:29
wood that have g hooks ⌊and that	Ex 26:32
screen and overlay them with g;	Ex 26:37
hooks are to be g, and you are	Ex 26:37
They should use g; blue, purple,	Ex 28:5
spun linen embroidered with g,	Ex 28:6
to the same workmanship of g,	Ex 28:8
surrounded with g filigree	Ex 28:11
Fashion g filigree settings	Ex 28:13
and two chains of pure g;	Ex 28:14
make it of g, of blue, purple,	Ex 28:15
be adorned with g filigree in	Ex 28:20
chains of pure g cord work for	Ex 28:22
Fashion two g rings for the	Ex 28:23
attach the two g cords to the	Ex 28:24
cords to the two g rings at the	Ex 28:24
Make two ⌊other⌋ g rings and put	Ex 28:26
Make two ⌊more⌋ g rings and	Ex 28:27
Put g bells between them all the	Ex 28:33
⌊so that⌋ g bells and	Ex 28:34
plate of pure g and engrave it,	Ex 28:36
and its horns with pure g;	Ex 30:3
make a g molding all around it.	Ex 30:3
Make two g rings for it under	Ex 30:4
wood and overlay them with g.	Ex 30:5
to design artistic works in g,	Ex 31:4
the pure ⌊g⌋ lampstand with all	Ex 31:8
Take off the g rings that are on	Ex 32:2
took off the g rings that were	Ex 32:3
took ⌊the g⌋ from their hands,	Ex 32:4
Whoever has g, take it off,'	Ex 32:24
made for themselves a god of g.	Ex 32:31
LORD's offering: g, silver, and	Ex 35:5
and all kinds of g jewelry—	Ex 35:22
offering of g to the LORD.	Ex 35:22
to design artistic works in g,	Ex 35:32
He also made 50 g clasps and	Ex 36:13
them with g and made their	Ex 36:34
for the crossbars out of g.	Ex 36:34
overlaid the crossbars with g.	Ex 36:34
wood and overlaid them with g;	Ex 36:36
hooks were of g. And he cast	Ex 36:36
posts and their bands with g,	Ex 36:38
it with pure g inside and out	Ex 37:2
out and made a g molding all	Ex 37:2
cast four g rings for it to be	Ex 37:3
wood and overlaid them with g.	Ex 37:4
He made a mercy seat of pure g,	Ex 37:6
He made two cherubim of g;	Ex 37:7
it with pure g and made a gold	Ex 37:11
gold and made a g molding all	Ex 37:11
it and made a g molding all	Ex 37:12
He cast four g rings for it and	Ex 37:13
wood and overlaid them with g.	Ex 37:15
be on the table out of pure g:	Ex 37:16
out of pure hammered g.	Ex 37:17
single hammered piece of pure g.	Ex 37:22
and firepans of pure g.	Ex 37:23
utensils of 75 pounds of pure g.	Ex 37:24
and its horns with pure g.	Ex 37:26
Then he made a g molding all	Ex 37:26
He made two g rings for it under	Ex 37:27
wood and overlaid them with g.	Ex 37:28
All the g of the presentation	Ex 38:24
Bezalel made the ephod of g,	Ex 39:2
hammered out thin sheets of g,	Ex 39:3
to the same workmanship of g,	Ex 39:5
surrounded with g filigree	Ex 39:6
workmanship as the ephod of g,	Ex 39:8
surrounded with g filigree in	Ex 39:13
braided chains of pure g cord	Ex 39:15
fashioned two g filigree	Ex 39:16
settings and two g rings and	Ex 39:16
the two g cords to the two	Ex 39:17
cords to the two g rings on the	Ex 39:17
made two ⌊other⌋ g rings and put	Ex 39:19
made two ⌊more⌋ g rings and	Ex 39:20
bells of pure g and attached	Ex 39:25
out of pure g, and wrote on it	Ex 39:30
the pure ⌊g⌋ lampstand, with its	Ex 39:37
the g altar; the anointing oil;	Ex 39:38
Place the g altar for incense in	Ex 40:5
installed the g altar in the	Ex 40:26
head and placed the plate of g,	Lv 8:9
lamps on the pure ⌊g⌋ lampstand	Lv 24:4
on the pure ⌊g⌋ table before the	Lv 24:6
a blue cloth over the g altar,	Nm 4:11
one g bowl weighing four ounces,	Nm 7:14
one g bowl weighing four ounces,	Nm 7:20
one g bowl weighing four ounces,	Nm 7:26
one g bowl weighing four ounces,	Nm 7:32
one g bowl weighing four ounces,	Nm 7:38
one g bowl weighing four ounces,	Nm 7:44
one g bowl weighing four ounces,	Nm 7:50
one g bowl weighing four ounces,	Nm 7:56
one g bowl weighing four ounces,	Nm 7:62
one g bowl weighing four ounces,	Nm 7:68
one g bowl weighing four ounces,	Nm 7:74
one g bowl weighing four ounces,	Nm 7:80
silver basins, and 12 g bowls.	Nm 7:84
12 g bowls full of incense each	Nm 7:86
weight⌋ of the g bowls was three	Nm 7:86
it was a hammered work of g,	Nm 8:4
his house full of silver and g,	Nm 22:18
his house full of silver and g,	Nm 24:13
the g, silver, bronze, iron,	Nm 31:22
offering of the g articles each	Nm 31:50
all the articles made out of g.	Nm 31:51
All the g of the contribution	Nm 31:52
received the g from the	Nm 31:54
the silver and g on the images	Dt 7:25
and your silver and g multiply,	Dt 8:13
of silver and g for himself.	Dt 17:17
silver, and g, which were among	Dt 29:17
the silver and g, and the	Jos 6:19
silver and g and the articles	Jos 6:24
and a bar of g weighing 50	Jos 7:21
cloak, and the bar of g, his	Jos 7:24
and silver, g, bronze, iron,	Jos 22:8
the enemy had g earrings because	Jdg 8:24
The weight of the g earrings he	Jdg 8:26
was about 43 pounds of g,	Jdg 8:26
Five g tumors and five gold mice	1Sm 6:4
tumors and five g mice	1Sm 6:4
and put the g objects in a box	1Sm 6:8
containing⌋ the g mice and the	1Sm 6:11
box containing the g objects,	1Sm 6:15
sent back one g tumor for each	1Sm 6:17
The number of g mice also	1Sm 6:18
your garments with g ornaments.	2Sm 1:24
David took the g shields of	2Sm 8:7
of silver, g, and bronze with	2Sm 8:10
silver and g he had dedicated	2Sm 8:11
crown weighed 75 pounds of g,	2Sm 12:30
he overlaid it with pure g.	1Kg 6:20
of the temple with pure g,	1Kg 6:21
and he hung g chains across the	1Kg 6:21
and overlaid it with g.	1Kg 6:21
So he added the g overlay to the	1Kg 6:22
overlaid the cherubim with g.	1Kg 6:28
floor with g in both the inner	1Kg 6:30
them and overlaid them with g,	1Kg 6:32
hammering g over the cherubim	1Kg 6:32
them with g applied evenly	1Kg 6:35
temple: the g altar; the gold	1Kg 7:48
g table that the bread of the	1Kg 7:48
the pure g lampstands in front	1Kg 7:49
the g flowers, lamps, and tongs;	1Kg 7:49
the pure g ceremonial bowls,	1Kg 7:50
and the g hinges for the doors	1Kg 7:50
the silver, the g, and the	1Kg 7:51
cypress logs and g for his every	1Kg 9:11
sent the king 9,000 pounds of g.	1Kg 9:14
to Ophir and acquired g there—	1Kg 9:28
bearing spices, g in great	1Kg 10:2
king four and a half tons of g,	1Kg 10:10
that carried g from Ophir	1Kg 10:11
The weight of g that came to	1Kg 10:14
200 large shields of hammered g;	1Kg 10:16
15 pounds of g went into each	1Kg 10:16
300 small shields of hammered g;	1Kg 10:17
four pounds of g went into each	1Kg 10:17
and overlaid it with fine g.	1Kg 10:18
Solomon's drinking cups were g,	1Kg 10:21
Forest of Lebanon were pure g.	1Kg 10:21
Tarshish would arrive bearing g,	1Kg 10:22
of silver and g, clothing,	1Kg 10:25
Then he made two g calves,	1Kg 12:28
He took all the g shields that	1Kg 14:26
silver, g, and utensils.	1Kg 15:15
the silver and g that remained	1Kg 15:18
sent you a gift of silver and g.	1Kg 15:19
'Your silver and your g are mine!	1Kg 20:3
Your silver, your g, your wives,	1Kg 20:5
silver, and my g, and I didn't	1Kg 20:7
Tarshish to go to Ophir for g,	1Kg 22:48
150 pounds of g, and 10 changes	2Kg 5:5
up the silver, g, and clothing	2Kg 7:8
any articles of g or silver were	2Kg 12:13
items and all the g found in the	2Kg 12:18
He took all the g and silver and	2Kg 14:14
the silver and g found in the	2Kg 16:8
tons of silver and one ton of g.	2Kg 18:14
stripped ⌊the g from⌋ the doors	2Kg 18:16
the silver, the g, the spices,	2Kg 20:13
of silver and 75 pounds of g.	2Kg 23:33
the silver and the g to Pharaoh,	2Kg 23:35
silver and the g from the people	2Kg 23:35
pieces all the g articles that	2Kg 24:13
whatever was g or silver.	2Kg 25:15
David took the g shields carried	1Ch 18:7
all kinds of items of g,	1Ch 18:10
the silver and g he had carried	1Ch 18:11
crown weighed 75 pounds of g,	1Ch 20:2
15 pounds of g for the plot.	1Ch 21:25
3,775 tons of g, 37,750 tons	1Ch 22:14
in g, silver, bronze, and iron—	1Ch 22:16
the weight of g for all the	1Ch 28:14
the weight of the g lampstands	1Ch 28:15
lampstands and their g lamps,	1Ch 28:15
the weight of g for each table	1Ch 28:16
the pure g for the forks,	1Ch 28:17
the weight of each g dish;	1Ch 28:17
weight of refined g for the	1Ch 28:18
chariot of the g cherubim that	1Ch 28:18
g for the gold ⌊articles⌋,	1Ch 29:2
gold for the g ⌊articles⌋,	1Ch 29:2
treasures of g and silver for	1Ch 29:3
100 tons of g (gold of Ophir)	1Ch 29:4
100 tons of gold (g of Ophir)	1Ch 29:4
g for the gold ⌊work⌋ and the	1Ch 29:5
gold for the g ⌊work⌋ and the	1Ch 29:5
185 tons of g and 10,000 gold	1Ch 29:7
of gold and 10,000 g drachmas,	1Ch 29:7
king made silver and g as common	2Ch 1:15
in engraving to work with g,	2Ch 2:7
He knows how to work with g,	2Ch 2:14
its inner surface with pure g.	2Ch 3:4
with fine g, and decorated	2Ch 3:5
and the g was the gold of	2Ch 3:6
the gold was the g of Parvaim.	2Ch 3:6
doors—with g, and he carved	2Ch 3:7
it with 45,000 pounds of fine g.	2Ch 3:8
of the nails was 20 ounces of g,	2Ch 3:9
he overlaid the ceiling with g.	2Ch 3:9
and he overlaid them with g.	2Ch 3:10
He made the 10 g lampstands	2Ch 4:7
He also made 100 g bowls.	2Ch 4:8
temple: the g altar; the tables	2Ch 4:19
lamps of pure g to burn in front	2Ch 4:20
lamps, and g tongs—of purest	2Ch 4:21
and gold tongs—of purest g;	2Ch 4:21
and firepans—of purest g;	2Ch 4:22
of the temple sanctuary—of g.	2Ch 4:22
the silver, the g, and all the	2Ch 5:1
took from there 17 tons of g,	2Ch 8:18
bearing spices, g in abundance,	2Ch 9:1
king four and a half tons of g,	2Ch 9:9
who brought g from Ophir also	2Ch 9:10
The weight of g that came to	2Ch 9:13
land also brought g and silver	2Ch 9:14
200 large shields of hammered g;	2Ch 9:15
of hammered g went into each	2Ch 9:15
300 small shields of hammered g;	2Ch 9:16
eight pounds of g went into each	2Ch 9:16
and overlaid it with pure g.	2Ch 9:17
covered in g for the throne,	2Ch 9:18
Solomon's drinking cups were g,	2Ch 9:20
Forest of Lebanon were pure g.	2Ch 9:20
Tarshish would arrive bearing g,	2Ch 9:21
of silver and g, clothing,	2Ch 9:24
and the ⌊g⌋ calves he had made.	2Ch 11:15
He took the g shields that	2Ch 12:9
lamps of the g lampstand every	2Ch 13:11
silver, g, and utensils.	2Ch 15:18
out the silver and g from the	2Ch 16:2
I have sent you silver and g.	2Ch 16:3
gifts of silver, g, and valuable	2Ch 21:3
and articles of g and silver.	2Ch 24:14

He took all the **g**, silver, all 2Ch 25:24
for silver, **g**, precious stones, 2Ch 32:27
of silver and 75 pounds of **g**. 2Ch 36:3
region with silver, **g**, goods, Ezr 1:4
silver articles, **g**, goods, Ezr 1:6
g basins, 1,000 silver basins, Ezr 1:9
30 **g** bowls, 410 various silver Ezr 1:10
g and silver articles totaled Ezr 1:11
they gave 61,000 **g** coins, 6,250 Ezr 2:69
in Babylon the **g** and silver Ezr 5:14
The **g** and silver articles of Ezr 6:5
silver and **g** the king and his Ezr 7:15
all the silver and **g** you receive Ezr 7:16
the rest of the silver and **g**, Ezr 7:18
the silver, the **g**, and the Ezr 8:25
7,500 pounds, 7,500 pounds of **g**, Ezr 8:26
20 **g** bowls worth 1,000 gold Ezr 8:27
gold bowls worth 1,000 **g** coins, Ezr 8:27
bronze, as valuable as **g**. Ezr 8:27
The silver and **g** are a freewill Ezr 8:28
the silver, the **g**, and the Ezr 8:30
the silver, the **g**, and the Ezr 8:33
governor gave 1,000 **g** drachmas, Neh 7:70
gave 20,000 **g** drachmas and 2,200 Neh 7:71
people gave 20,000 **g** drachmas, Neh 7:72
G and silver couches ⌊were Est 1:6
served in an array of **g** goblets, Est 1:7
or with princes who had **g**, Jb 3:15
and consign your **g** to the dust, Jb 22:24
⌊the **g** of⌋ Ophir to the stones Jb 22:24
will be your **g** and your finest Jb 22:25
me, I will emerge as pure **g**. Jb 23:10
and a place where **g** is refined. Jb 28:1
containing flecks of **g**. Jb 28:6
G cannot be exchanged for it, Jb 28:15
be valued in the **g** of Ophir, Jb 28:16
G and glass do not compare with Jb 28:17
articles of fine **g** cannot be Jb 28:17
it cannot be valued in pure **g**. Jb 28:19
confidence in **g** or called fine Jb 31:24
gold or called fine **g** my trust, Jb 31:24
him a qesitah , and a **g** earring. Jb 42:11
They are more desirable than **g**— Ps 19:10
than an abundance of pure **g**; Ps 19:10
a crown of pure **g** on his head. Ps 21:3
adorned with **g** from Ophir, Ps 45:9
her clothing embroidered with **g**. Ps 45:13
its feathers with glistening **g**. Ps 68:13
g from Sheba be given to him. Ps 72:15
Israel out with silver and **g**, Ps 105:37
Their idols are silver and **g**, Ps 115:4
thousands of **g** and silver pieces Ps 119:72
commandments more than **g**, Ps 119:127
than gold, even the purest **g**, Ps 119:127
the nations are of silver and **g**, Ps 135:15
your head and a ⌊**g**⌋ chain around Pr 1:9
her revenue is better than **g**. Pr 3:14
knowledge rather than pure **g**. Pr 8:10
My fruit is better than solid **g**, Pr 8:19
is like a **g** ring in a pig's Pr 11:22
how much better it is than **g**! Pr 16:16
for silver and a smelter for **g**, Pr 17:3
There is **g** and a multitude of Pr 20:15
is better than silver and **g**. Pr 22:1
ear is like a **g** ring or an Pr 25:12
a gold ring or an ornament of **g**. Pr 25:12
in a crucible, **g** in a smelter, Pr 27:21
amassed silver and **g** for myself, Ec 2:8
We will make **g** jewelry for you, Sg 1:11
its back of **g**, and its seat Sg 3:10
head is purest **g**. His hair is Sg 5:11
are rods of **g** set with topaz. Sg 5:14
set on pedestals of pure **g**. Sg 5:15
land is full of silver and **g**, Is 2:7
throw their silver and **g** idols, Is 2:20
I will make man scarcer than **g**, Is 13:12
more rare than the **g** of Ophir. Is 13:12
and who have no desire for **g**. Is 13:17
the silver and **g** idols that your Is 31:7
the silver, the **g**, the spices, Is 39:2
plates with **g** and makes silver Is 40:19
their bags of **g** and weigh out Is 46:6
They will carry **g** and Is 60:6
their silver and **g** with them, Is 60:9
will bring **g** instead of bronze; Is 60:17
adorn yourself with **g** jewelry, Jr 4:30
decorates it with silver and **g**. Jr 10:4
and **g** from Uphaz from the hands Jr 10:9
—whatever was **g** or silver. Jr 52:19
How the **g** has become tarnished, Lm 4:1
the fine **g** become dull! Lm 4:1
worth their weight in pure **g**— Lm 4:2
and their **g** will seem like Ezk 7:19
silver and **g** will be unable Ezk 7:19
were adorned with **g** and silver, Ezk 16:13
made from the **g** and silver I had Ezk 16:17
They exchanged **g**, the best of Ezk 27:22
have acquired **g** and silver for Ezk 28:4
and settings were crafted in **g**; Ezk 28:13
to make off with silver and **g**, Ezk 38:13
head of the statue was pure **g**, Dn 2:32
and the **g** were shattered and Dn 2:35
them all. You are the head of **g**. Dn 2:38
fired clay, silver, and **g**. Dn 2:45
Nebuchadnezzar made a **g** statue, Dn 3:1
and worship the **g** statue that Dn 3:5
worshiped the **g** statue that King Dn 3:7
down and worship the **g** statue. Dn 3:10
or worship the **g** statue you have Dn 3:12
or worship the **g** statue I have Dn 3:14
worship the **g** statue you set up. Dn 3:18
to bring in the **g** and silver Dn 5:2
brought in the **g** vessels that Dn 5:3
their gods made of **g** and silver, Dn 5:4
have a **g** chain around his neck, Dn 5:7
have a **g** chain around your neck, Dn 5:16
the gods made of silver and **g**, Dn 5:23
⌊placed⌋ a **g** chain around his Dn 5:29
with a belt of **g** from Uphaz Dn 10:5
articles of silver and **g**. Dn 11:8
not know—with **g**, silver, Dn 11:38
treasures of **g** and silver and Dn 11:43
I lavished silver and **g** on her, Hs 2:8
their silver and **g** into idols Hs 8:4
My silver and **g** and carried My Jl 3:5
Plunder the **g**!" There is no end Nah 2:9
may be plated with **g** and silver, Hab 2:19
and their **g** will not be able Zph 1:18
"The silver and **g** belong to Me"— Hg 2:8
I see a solid **g** lampstand there Zch 4:2
beside the two **g** conduits, Zch 4:12
Take silver and **g**, make crowns Zch 6:11
like dust and **g** like the dirt Zch 9:3
and test them as **g** is tested. Zch 13:9
g, silver, and clothing in great Zch 14:14
refine them like **g** and silver. Mal 3:3
g, frankincense, and myrrh. Mt 2:11
Don't take along **g**, silver, or Mt 10:9
oath by the **g** of the sanctuary Mt 23:16
the **g** or the sanctuary that Mt 23:17
sanctuary that sanctified the **g**? Mt 23:17
I have neither silver nor **g**, Ac 3:6
nature is like **g** or silver or Ac 17:29
silver or **g** or clothing. Ac 20:33
builds on the foundation with **g**, 1Co 3:12
hairstyles, **g**, pearls, or 1Tm 2:9
are not only **g** and silver bowls 2Tm 2:20
contained the **g** altar of incense Heb 9:4
covered with **g** on all sides, Heb 9:4
there was a **g** jar containing Heb 9:4
your meeting wearing a **g** ring, Jms 2:2
your silver and **g** are corroded, Jms 5:3
valuable than **g**, which perishes 1Pt 1:7
things, like silver or **g**, 1Pt 1:18
the wearing of **g** ornaments or 1Pt 3:3
turned I saw seven **g** lampstands, Rv 1:12
and with a **g** sash wrapped around Rv 1:13
and of the seven **g** lampstands, Rv 1:20
the seven **g** lampstands says Rv 2:1
you to buy from Me **g** refined in Rv 3:18
with **g** crowns on their heads. Rv 4:4
had a harp and **g** bowls filled Rv 5:8
angel, with a **g** incense burner, Rv 8:3
saints on the **g** altar in front Rv 8:3
were something like **g** crowns; Rv 9:7
four horns of the **g** altar that Rv 9:13
demons and idols of **g**, Rv 9:20
with a **g** crown on His head and a Rv 14:14
with **g** sashes wrapped around Rv 15:6
angels seven **g** bowls filled with Rv 15:7
adorned with **g**, precious stones, Rv 17:4
She had a **g** cup in her hand Rv 17:4
merchandise of **g**, silver, Rv 18:12
adorned with **g**, precious stones, Rv 18:16
with me had a **g** measuring rod to Rv 21:15
city was pure **g** like clear glass Rv 21:18
street of the city was pure **g**, Rv 21:21

GOLD-PLATED *(2)*
it on four **g** posts of acacia Ex 26:32
idols and your **g** images. Is 30:22

GOLDEN *(11)*
worshiping⌋ the **g** calves that 2Kg 10:29
have with you the **g** calves that 2Ch 13:8
king extends the **g** scepter will Est 4:11
extended the **g** scepter in his Est 5:2
extended the **g** scepter toward Est 8:4
a great **g** crown and a purple Est 8:15
comes, ⌊shrouded⌋ in a **g** ⌊glow⌋; Jb 37:22
time is like **g** apples on a Pr 25:11
and the **g** bowl is broken, Ec 12:6
Babylon was a **g** cup in the Jr 51:7
from which **g** ⌊oil⌋ pours out?" Zch 4:12

GOLDSMITH *(5)*
Harhaiah, the **g**, made repairs, Neh 3:8
they hire a **g** and he makes it Is 46:6
Uphaz from the hands of a **g**, Jr 10:9
Every **g** is put to shame by ⌊his⌋ Jr 10:14
Every **g** is put to shame by ⌊his⌋ Jr 51:17

GOLDSMITHS *(2)*
one of the **g**, made repairs to Neh 3:31
The **g** and merchants made repairs Neh 3:32

GOLGOTHA *(3)*
they came to a place called **G** Mt 27:33
Jesus to the place called **G** Mk 15:22
which in Hebrew is called **G**. Jn 19:17

GOLIATH *(7)*
champion named **G**, from Gath, 1Sm 17:4
suddenly the champion named **G**, 1Sm 17:23
all the Israelite men saw **G**, 1Sm 17:24
The sword of **G** the Philistine, 1Sm 21:9
the sword of **G** the Philistine. 1Sm 22:10
killed **G** the Gittite. 2Sm 21:19
the brother of **G** the Gittite. 1Ch 20:5

GOLIATH'S *(2)*
David took **G** head and brought it 1Sm 17:54
he put **G** weapons in his ⌊own⌋ 1Sm 17:54

GOMER *(5)*
G, Magog, Madai, Javan, Tubal, Gn 10:2
G, Magog, Madai, Javan, Tubal, 1Ch 1:5
G with all its troops; Ezk 38:6
went and married **G** daughter of Hs 1:3
G had weaned No Compassion, Hs 1:8

GOMER'S *(2)*
G sons: Ashkenaz, Riphath, and Gn 10:3
G sons: Ashkenaz, Riphath, and 1Ch 1:6

GOMORRAH *(23)*
toward Sodom, **G**, Admah, and Gn 10:19
God destroyed Sodom and **G**. Gn 13:10
Birsha king of **G**, Shinab king of Gn 14:2
the king of **G**, the king of Admah Gn 14:8
the kings of Sodom and **G** fled, Gn 14:10
of Sodom and **G** and all their Gn 14:11
against Sodom and **G** is immense, Gn 18:20
on Sodom and **G** from the LORD Gn 19:24
Sodom and **G** and all the land Gn 19:28
like the fall of Sodom and **G**, Dt 29:23
Sodom and from the fields of **G**. Dt 32:32
like Sodom, we would resemble **G**. Is 1:9
of our God, you people of **G**! Is 1:10
be like Sodom and **G** when God Is 13:19
residents are like **G**. Jr 23:14
Sodom and **G** were overthrown Jr 49:18
overthrew Sodom and **G** and their Jr 50:40
you as I overthrew Sodom and **G**, Am 4:11
Sodom and the Ammonites like **G**— Zph 2:9
of Sodom and **G** than for that Mt 10:15
we would have been made like **G**. Rm 9:29
cities of Sodom and **G** to ashes 2Pt 2:6
and **G** and the cities around Jd 7

GONE *(156)*
(See pp. xi-xii.)

GONG *(1)*
I am a sounding **g** or a clanging 1Co 13:1

GOOD *(636)*
God saw that the light was **g**, Gn 1:4
And God saw that it was **g**. Gn 1:10
And God saw that it was **g**. Gn 1:12
And God saw that it was **g**. Gn 1:18
And God saw that it was **g**. Gn 1:21
And God saw that it was **g**. Gn 1:25

He had made, and it was very g. Gn 1:31
in appearance and g for food, Gn 2:9
of the knowledge of g and evil. Gn 2:9
of the knowledge of g and evil, Gn 2:17
It is not g for the man to be Gn 2:18
like God, knowing g and evil." Gn 3:5
saw that the tree was g for food Gn 3:6
of Us, knowing g and evil, he Gn 3:22
what g is a birthright to me?" Gn 25:32
only done what was g to you, Gn 26:29
one of them, what g is my life?" Gn 27:46
Leah said, "What g fortune!" Gn 30:11
"God has given me a g gift," Gn 30:20
"G," said Laban. "Let it be as Gn 30:34
to Jacob, either g or bad." Gn 31:24
to Jacob, either g or bad.' Gn 31:29
Their words seemed g in the eyes Gn 34:18
grain, full and g, came up on Gn 41:5
up the seven full, g ones. Gn 41:7
grain, full and g, coming up on Gn 41:22
seven g cows are seven years, Gn 41:26
and the seven g heads are seven Gn 41:26
during these g years that are Gn 41:35
'Why have you repaid evil for g? Gn 44:4
place was g and that the land Gn 49:15
planned it for g to bring about Gn 50:20
So God was g to the midwives, Ex 1:20
that land to a g and spacious Ex 3:8
over all the g things the LORD Ex 18:9
"What you're doing is not g," Ex 18:17
rashly to do what is g or evil— Lv 5:4
for it, either g for bad, or bad Lv 27:10
good for bad, or bad for g. Lv 27:10
inspect whether it is g or bad, Lv 27:33
has promised g things to Israel. Nm 10:29
whatever g the LORD does for us Nm 10:32
We really had it g in Egypt.' Nm 11:18
the land they live in g or bad? Nm 13:19
explored is an extremely g land. Nm 14:7
do ⌊anything⌋ g or bad of my own Nm 24:13
the region was a ⌊g⌋ one for Nm 32:1
is ⌊g⌋ land for livestock, Nm 32:4
'What you propose to do is g.' Dt 1:14
The plan seemed g to me, so I Dt 1:23
our God is giving us is g.' Dt 1:25
will see the g land I swore to Dt 1:35
sons who don't know g from evil, Dt 1:39
that g hill country and Lebanon. Dt 3:25
careful for your own g— Dt 4:15
and enter the g land the LORD Dt 4:21
take possession of this g land. Dt 4:22
full of every g thing that you Dt 6:11
is right and g in the LORD's Dt 6:18
and possess the g land the LORD Dt 6:18
is bringing you into a g land, Dt 8:7
your God for the g land He has Dt 8:10
you this g land to possess Dt 9:6
you today, for your own g. Dt 10:13
from the g land the LORD is Dt 11:17
be doing what is g and right Dt 12:28
in all the g things the LORD Dt 26:11
None of the g promises the LORD Jos 21:45
from this g land the LORD your Jos 23:13
that none of the g promises the Jos 23:14
Since every g thing the LORD Jos 23:15
you from this g land the LORD Jos 23:15
from this g land He has given Jos 23:16
after He has been g to you." Jos 24:20
for all the g he had done for Jdg 8:35
my sweetness and my g fruit, Jdg 9:11
that the LORD will be g to me, Jdg 17:13
seen the land, and it is very g. Jdg 18:9
it is g for you to work with his Ru 2:22
and was in g spirits, he went Ru 3:7
wants to redeem you, ⌊that's⌋ g. Ru 3:13
from the LORD's people is not g. 1Sm 2:24
of all that is g in Israel, 1Sm 2:32
He will do what He thinks is g." 1Sm 3:18
"G," Saul replied to his 1Sm 9:10
teach you the g and right way. 1Sm 12:23
If he says, 'G,' then your 1Sm 20:7
done what is g to me though I 1Sm 24:17
me today what g you did for me: 1Sm 24:18
repay you with g for what you've 1Sm 24:19
yet he paid me back evil for g. 1Sm 25:21
my lord all the g He promised 1Sm 25:30
the LORD does g things for my 1Sm 25:31
Nabal was in a g mood and very 1Sm 25:36

What you have done is not g. 1Sm 26:16
to Achish, "G, you will find out 1Sm 28:2
I think it is g to have you 1Sm 29:6
to spread the g news in the 1Sm 31:9
David replied, "G, I will make a 2Sm 3:13
he was a bearer of g news, 2Sm 4:10
Amnon, either g or bad, because 2Sm 13:22
until he is in a g mood from the 2Sm 13:28
discern the g and the bad like 2Sm 14:17
your claims are g and right, 2Sm 15:3
proposal seemed g to Absalom and 2Sm 17:4
has given this time is not g." 2Sm 17:7
that Ahithophel's g advice be 2Sm 17:14
tell the king the g news that 2Sm 18:19
the man to take g news today. 2Sm 18:20
today you aren't taking g news, 2Sm 18:20
If he's alone, he bears g news." 2Sm 18:25
one is also bringing g news," 2Sm 18:26
runs." "This is a g man; he 2Sm 18:27
he comes with g news," the king 2Sm 18:27
lord the king hear the g news: 2Sm 18:31
Do for him what seems g to you." 2Sm 19:37
do for him what seems g to you, 2Sm 19:38
you must be bringing g news." 1Kg 1:42
to discern between g and evil. 1Kg 3:9
teach them the g way they should 1Kg 8:36
of all the g promises He made 1Kg 8:56
Israel from this g soil that He 1Kg 14:15
answered, "That ⌊sounds⌋ g." 1Kg 18:24
he never prophesies g about me, 1Kg 22:8
he never prophesies g about me, 1Kg 22:18
that the city's location is g, 2Kg 2:19
cut down every g tree and stop 2Kg 3:19
must ruin every g piece of land 2Kg 3:19
to cover every g piece of land. 2Kg 3:25
water and cut down every g tree. 2Kg 3:25
Today is a day of g news. 2Kg 7:9
done what is g in Your sight." 2Kg 20:3
LORD that you have spoken is g," 2Kg 20:19
They found rich, g pasture, and 1Ch 4:40
to spread the g news to their 1Ch 10:9
If it seems g to you, and if 1Ch 13:2
thanks to the LORD, for He is g; 1Ch 16:34
promised this g thing to Your 1Ch 17:26
possess this g land and leave 1Ch 28:8
He died at a g old age, full of 1Ch 29:28
LORD: For He is g; His faithful 2Ch 5:13
teach them the g way they should 2Ch 6:27
For He is g, for His faithful 2Ch 7:3
conditions were g in Judah. 2Ch 12:12
Asa did what was g and right in 2Ch 14:2
he never prophesies g about me, 2Ch 18:7
he never prophesies g about me, 2Ch 18:17
However, some g is found in you, 2Ch 19:3
be with those who do what is g." 2Ch 19:11
done ⌊what was⌋ g in Israel with 2Ch 24:16
the g LORD provide atonement 2Ch 30:18
did what was g and upright and 2Ch 31:20
LORD: "For He is g; His faithful Ezr 3:11
eat the g things of the land, Ezr 9:12
encouraged to ⌊do⌋ this g work. Neh 2:18
Tobiah's g deeds to me, Neh 6:19
and g decrees and commandments. Neh 9:13
You sent Your g Spirit to Neh 9:20
don't erase the g deeds I have Neh 13:14
was feeling g from the wine, Est 1:10
full of joy and in g spirits. Est 5:9
to seek g for his people Est 10:3
accept only g from God and not Jb 2:10
will never again see anything g. Jb 7:7
they flee without seeing any g. Jb 9:25
Is it g for You to oppress, Jb 10:3
away the elders' g judgment. Jb 12:20
words that serve no g purpose? Jb 15:3
their houses with g things. Jb 22:18
in this way g will come to you. Jb 22:21
when I hoped for g, evil came; Jb 30:26
us decide together what is g. Jb 34:4
"Who can show us anything g?" Ps 4:6
There is no one who does g. Ps 14:1
There is no one who does g, Ps 14:3
I have no g besides You." Ps 16:2
The LORD is g and upright; Ps 25:8
He will live a g life, and his Ps 25:13
and see that the LORD is g. Ps 34:8
LORD will not lack any g thing. Ps 34:10
a long life to enjoy what is g? Ps 34:12
away from evil and do what is g; Ps 34:14

repay me evil for g, making me Ps 35:12
acting wisely and doing g. Ps 36:3
path that is not g and does not Ps 36:4
in the LORD and do what is g; Ps 37:3
away from evil and do what is g, Ps 37:27
repay evil for g attack me for Ps 38:20
good attack me for pursuing g. Ps 38:20
from ⌊speaking⌋ g, and my pain Ps 39:2
Your g pleasure, cause Zion to Ps 51:18
You love evil instead of g, Ps 52:3
hope in Your name, for it is g. Ps 52:9
There is no one who does g. Ps 53:1
There is no one who does g, Ps 53:3
name, LORD, because it is g. Ps 54:6
my companion and g friend! Ps 55:13
of women brought the g news: Ps 68:11
for Your faithful love is g; Ps 69:16
God is indeed g to Israel, Ps 73:1
for me, God's presence is my g. Ps 73:28
withhold the g from those who Ps 84:11
the LORD will provide what is g, Ps 85:12
It is g to praise the LORD, Ps 92:1
For the LORD is g, and His love Ps 100:5
are satisfied with g things. Ps 104:28
thanks to the LORD, for He is g; Ps 106:1
thanks to the LORD, for He is g; Ps 107:1
filled the hungry with g things. Ps 107:9
me evil for g, and hatred for Ps 109:5
His instructions have g insight. Ps 111:10
G will come to a man who lends Ps 112:5
for the LORD has been g to you. Ps 116:7
LORD all the g He has done for Ps 116:12
thanks to the LORD, for He is g; Ps 118:1
thanks to the LORD, for He is g; Ps 118:29
indeed, Your judgments are g. Ps 119:39
Teach me g judgment and Ps 119:66
You are g, and You do what is Ps 119:68
are good, and You do what is g; Ps 119:68
It was g for me to be afflicted Ps 119:71
our God, I will seek your g. Ps 122:9
Do what is g, LORD, to the good, Ps 125:4
LORD, to the g, to those whose Ps 125:4
How g and pleasant it is when Ps 133:1
the LORD, for the LORD is g; Ps 135:3
thanks to the LORD, for He is g. Ps 136:1
The LORD is g to everyone; Ps 145:9
How g it is to sing to our God, Ps 147:1
and integrity—every g path. Pr 2:9
So follow the way of g people, Pr 2:20
don't withhold g from the one to Pr 3:27
I am giving you g instruction. Pr 4:2
I possess g advice and Pr 8:14
woman who rejects g sense is Pr 11:22
for what is g finds favor, Pr 11:27
g obtain favor from the LORD, Pr 12:2
be satisfied with g by the words Pr 12:14
but a g word cheers it up. Pr 12:25
a man will enjoy g things, Pr 13:2
G sense wins favor, but the way Pr 13:15
but g rewards the righteous. Pr 13:21
A g man leaves an inheritance to Pr 13:22
deserves, and a g man, what his Pr 14:14
evil bow before those who are g, Pr 14:19
those who plan g find loyalty Pr 14:22
observing the wicked and the g. Pr 15:3
a timely word—how g that is! Pr 15:23
g news strengthens the bones. Pr 15:30
to correction acquires g sense. Pr 15:32
him in a way that is not g. Pr 16:29
If anyone returns evil for g, Pr 17:13
A joyful heart is g medicine, Pr 17:22
is certainly not g to fine an Pr 17:26
is not g to show partiality to Pr 18:5
a wife finds a g thing and Pr 18:22
Even zeal is not g without Pr 19:2
one who acquires g sense loves Pr 19:8
A g name is to be chosen over Pr 22:1
my son, for it is g, and the Pr 24:13
is not g to show partiality in Pr 24:23
G news from a distant land is Pr 25:25
It is not g to eat too much Pr 25:27
will inherit what is g. Pr 28:10
It is not g to show partiality— Pr 28:21
and he will not lack anything g. Pr 31:11
rewards him with g, not evil, Pr 31:12
She sees that her profits are g, Pr 31:18
pleasure and enjoy what is g." Ec 2:1
see what is g for people to do Ec 2:3

to rejoice and enjoy the g life. Ec 3:12
"and depriving myself from g?" Ec 4:8
they have a g reward for their Ec 4:9
When g things increase, the ones Ec 5:11
is what I have seen to be g: Ec 5:18
experience g in all the labor Ec 5:18
satisfied by g things and does Ec 6:3
knows what is g for man in life Ec 6:12
A g name is better than fine Ec 7:1
is as g as an inheritance, Ec 7:11
It is g that you grasp the one Ec 7:18
earth who does g and never sins. Ec 7:20
wicked, for the g and the bad, Ec 9:2
As it is for the g, so it is for Ec 9:2
one sinner can destroy much g. Ec 9:18
both of them will be equally g. Ec 11:6
hidden thing, whether g or evil. Ec 12:14
to do what is g. Seek justice. Is 1:17
you will eat the g things of the Is 1:19
expected it to yield g grapes, Is 5:2
I expected a yield of g grapes, Is 5:4
who call evil g and good evil, Is 5:20
who call evil good and g evil, Is 5:20
is bad and choose what is g, Is 7:15
is bad and choose what is g, Is 7:16
to pray, it will do him no g. Is 16:12
they are g for nothing but shame Is 30:5
done what is g in Your sight." Is 38:3
LORD that you have spoken is g." Is 39:8
Zion, herald of g news, go up on Is 40:9
herald of g news, raise your Is 40:9
of the soldering, "It is g." Is 41:7
do ⌊something⌋ g or bad, then we Is 41:23
gave a herald of g news to Is 41:27
who brings news of g things, Is 52:7
and eat what is g, and you will Is 55:2
Me to bring g news to the poor. Is 61:1
even the many g things ⌊He has Is 63:7
there's some g in it, so I will Is 65:8
do not know how to do what is g. Jr 4:22
Which is the way to what is g? Jr 6:16
peace, but there was nothing g; Jr 8:15
harm—and they cannot do any g. Jr 10:5
might be able to do what is g, Jr 13:23
peace, but there was nothing g; Jr 14:19
cannot see when g comes but Jr 17:6
not bring the g I had said I Jr 18:10
Should g be repaid with evil? Jr 18:20
You to speak g on their behalf, Jr 18:20
bring⌋ disaster and not g'"— Jr 21:10
basket ⌊contained⌋ very g figs, Jr 24:2
g figs are very good, but the Jr 24:3
figs are very g, but the bad Jr 24:3
Like these g figs, so I regard Jr 24:5
so I regard as g the exiles from Jr 24:5
them for their g and will return Jr 24:6
what you think is g and right. Jr 26:14
any ever see the g that I will Jr 29:32
that for their g and for ⌊the Jr 32:39
good and for ⌊the g of⌋ their Jr 32:39
turn away from doing g to them, Jr 32:40
them to do what is g to them, Jr 32:41
on them all the g I am promising Jr 32:42
hear of all the g I will do for Jr 33:9
of all the g and all the peace Jr 33:9
of Hosts, for the LORD is g; Jr 33:11
fulfill the g promises that I Jr 33:14
Chaldeans will leave us for g, Jr 37:9
harm and not for g against this Jr 39:16
it seems g and right for you Jr 40:4
enough food and g things and saw Jr 44:17
them for disaster and not for g, Jr 44:27
The LORD is g to those who wait Lm 3:25
It is g to wait quietly for Lm 3:26
It is g for a man to bear the Lm 3:27
both adversity and g come from Lm 3:38
planted in a g field by abundant Ezk 17:8
that were not g and ordinances Ezk 20:25
in it, every g piece—thigh Ezk 24:4
Because you said: G! about My Ezk 25:3
Jerusalem: G! The gateway to Ezk 26:2
I will tend them with g pasture, Ezk 34:14
lie down in a g grazing place; Ezk 34:14
you to feed on the g pasture? Ezk 34:18
enemy has said about you, 'G! Ezk 36:2
and your deeds that were not g, Ezk 36:31
my advice seem g to you my king. Dn 4:27
Israel has rejected what is g; Hs 8:3

our⌋ sin and accept what is g, Hs 14:2
Seek g and not evil so that you Am 5:14
evil and love g; establish Am 5:15
on them for harm and not for g. Am 9:4
anxiously wait for something g, Mc 1:12
My words bring g to the one who Mc 2:7
You hate g and love evil. Mc 3:2
you men what is g and what it is Mc 6:8
hands are g at accomplishing Mc 7:3
The LORD is g, a stronghold in a Nah 1:7
of one bringing g news and Nah 1:15
The LORD will not do g or evil. Zph 1:12
to do what is g to Jerusalem Zch 8:15
who does evil is g in the LORD's Mal 2:17
doesn't produce g fruit will be Mt 3:10
preaching the g news of the Mt 4:23
It's no longer g for anything Mt 5:13
may see your g works and give Mt 5:16
to rise on the evil and the g, Mt 5:45
your eye is g, your whole body Mt 6:22
know how to give g gifts to your Mt 7:11
in heaven give g things to those Mt 7:11
g tree produces good fruit, Mt 7:17
good tree produces g fruit, Mt 7:17
g tree can't produce bad fruit; Mt 7:18
can a bad tree produce g fruit. Mt 7:18
doesn't produce g fruit is cut Mt 7:19
preaching the g news of the Mt 9:35
the poor are told the g news. Mt 11:5
this was Your g pleasure. Mt 11:26
lawful to do g on the Sabbath. Mt 12:12
was restored, as g as the other. Mt 12:13
make the tree g and its fruit Mt 12:33
the tree good and its fruit g, Mt 12:33
can you speak g things when you Mt 12:34
g man produces good things from Mt 12:35
man produces g things from his Mt 12:35
things from his storeroom of g, Mt 12:35
Still others fell on g ground, Mt 13:8
the one sown on the g ground— Mt 13:23
a man who sowed g seed in his Mt 13:24
didn't you sow g seed in your Mt 13:27
who sows the g seed is the Son Mt 13:37
and the g seed—these are the Mt 13:38
and gathered the g ⌊fish⌋ into Mt 13:48
'It will be g weather because Mt 16:2
Lord, it's g for us to be here Mt 17:4
what g must I do to have eternal Mt 19:16
do you ask Me about what is g?" Mt 19:17
There is only One who is g. Mt 19:17
they found, both evil and g. Mt 22:10
This g news of the kingdom will Mt 24:14
him, 'Well done, g and faithful Mt 25:21
him, 'Well done, g and faithful Mt 25:23
looking for a g opportunity to Mt 26:16
met them and said, "G morning!" Mt 28:9
preaching the g news of God: Mk 1:14
and believe in the g news!" Mk 1:15
Sabbath to do g or to do evil, Mk 3:4
others fell on g ground and Mk 4:8
ones sown on g ground are those Mk 4:20
it is g for us to be here! Mk 9:5
is g, but if the salt should Mk 9:50
and asked Him, "G Teacher, what Mk 10:17
"Why do you call Me g?" Mk 10:18
No one is g but One—God. Mk 10:18
And the g news must first be Mk 13:10
and you can do g for them Mk 14:7
looking for a g opportunity to Mk 14:11
It also seemed g to me, since I Lk 1:3
to you and tell you this g news. Lk 1:19
hungry with g things and sent Lk 1:53
proclaim to you g news of great Lk 2:10
doesn't produce g fruit will be Lk 3:9
he proclaimed g news to the Lk 3:18
Me to preach g news to the poor. Lk 4:18
I must proclaim the g news about Lk 4:43
Sabbath to do g or to do evil, Lk 6:9
do g to those who hate you, Lk 6:27
do ⌊what is⌋ g to those who are Lk 6:33
good to those who are g to you, Lk 6:33
do ⌊what is⌋ g, and lend, Lk 6:35
a g measure—pressed down, Lk 6:38
A g tree doesn't produce bad Lk 6:43
tree doesn't produce g fruit. Lk 6:43
A g man produces good out of the Lk 6:45
man produces g out of the good Lk 6:45
good out of the g storeroom of Lk 6:45

found the slave in g health. Lk 7:10
poor have the g news preached to Lk 7:22
and telling the g news of the Lk 8:1
other seed fell on g ground; Lk 8:8
But the seed in the g ground— Lk 8:15
word with an honest and g heart, Lk 8:15
proclaiming the g news and Lk 9:6
it's g for us to be here! Lk 9:33
this was Your g pleasure. Lk 10:21
know how to give g gifts to your Lk 11:13
your eye is g, your whole body Lk 11:34
Now, salt is g, but if salt Lk 14:34
the g news of the kingdom of God Lk 16:16
life you received your g things, Lk 16:25
ruler asked Him, "G Teacher, Lk 18:18
"Why do you call Me g?" Lk 18:19
No one is g but One—God. Lk 18:19
'Well done, g slave!' Lk 19:17
and proclaiming the g news, Lk 20:1
looking for a g opportunity to Lk 22:6
There was a g and righteous man Lk 23:50
anything g come out of Nazareth? Jn 1:46
those who have done g things, Jn 5:29
were saying, "He's a g man." Jn 7:12
I am the g shepherd. The good Jn 10:11
g shepherd lays down his life Jn 10:11
I am the g shepherd. I know My Jn 10:14
have shown you many g works from Jn 10:32
stoning You for a g work," Jn 10:33
today about a g deed done to Ac 4:9
and proclaiming the g news that Ac 5:42
you seven men of g reputation, Ac 6:3
the message of g news. Ac 8:4
he proclaimed the g news about Ac 8:12
to tell him the g news about Ac 8:35
always doing g works and acts Ac 9:36
who has a g reputation with the Ac 10:22
proclaiming the g news of peace Ac 10:36
went about doing g and curing Ac 10:38
proclaiming the g news about the Ac 11:20
for he was a g man, full of the Ac 11:24
to you the g news of the promise Ac 13:32
are proclaiming g news to you, Ac 14:15
a witness, since He did g: Ac 14:17
was telling the g news about Ac 17:18
having a g reputation with all Ac 22:12
God in all g conscience until Ac 23:1
words of truth and g judgment. Ac 26:25
singled out for God's g news— Rm 1:1
⌊telling⌋ the g news about His Rm 1:9
to preach the g news to you also Rm 1:15
doing g seek for glory, Rm 2:7
peace for everyone who does g, Rm 2:10
us do evil so that g may come"? Rm 3:8
there is no one who does g, Rm 3:12
though for a g person perhaps Rm 5:7
is holy and just and g. Rm 7:12
did what is g cause my death? Rm 7:13
death in me through what is g, Rm 7:13
agree with the law that it is g. Rm 7:16
know that nothing g lives in me, Rm 7:18
to do what is g is with me, Rm 7:18
I do not do the g that I want to Rm 7:19
I want to do g, evil is with me Rm 7:21
together for the g of those who Rm 8:28
yet or done anything g or bad, Rm 9:11
announce the gospel of g things! Rm 10:15
you may discern what is the g, Rm 12:2
Detest evil; cling to what is g. Rm 12:9
evil, but conquer evil with g. Rm 12:21
are not a terror to g conduct, Rm 13:3
Do g and you will have its Rm 13:3
is God's servant to you for g. Rm 13:4
do not let your g be slandered, Rm 14:16
please his neighbor for his g, Rm 15:2
as a priest of God's g news. Rm 15:16
proclaimed the g news about Rm 15:19
you to be wise about what is g, Rm 16:19
Your boasting is not g. 1Co 5:6
It is g for a man not to have 1Co 7:1
It is g for them if they remain 1Co 7:8
I consider this to be g because 1Co 7:26
No one should seek his own ⌊g⌋, 1Co 10:24
but ⌊the g⌋ of the other person. 1Co 10:24
hope, what g does that do me 1Co 15:32
Bad company corrupts g morals. 1Co 15:33
in the body, whether g or bad. 2Co 5:10
through slander and g report; 2Co 6:8

you may excel in every g work. 2Co 9:8
foretold the g news to Abraham Gl 3:8
about you, but not for any g. Gl 4:17
Now it is always g to be Gl 4:18
to be enthusiastic about g— Gl 4:18
must not get tired of doing g, Gl 6:9
we must work for the g of all, Gl 6:10
who want to make a g showing in Gl 6:12
to His g pleasure that He Eph 1:9
in Christ Jesus for g works, Eph 2:10
proclaimed the g news of peace Eph 2:17
only what is g for the building Eph 4:29
service with a g attitude, Eph 6:7
that whatever g each one does, Eph 6:8
who started a g work in you will Php 1:6
but others out of g will. Php 1:15
and to act for His g purpose. Php 2:13
in every g work and growing Col 1:10
rejoicing to see your g order Col 2:5
and brought us g news about your 1Th 3:6
always have g memories of us, 1Th 3:6
pursue what is g for one another 1Th 5:15
things. Hold on to what is g. 1Th 5:21
and g hope by grace, 2Th 2:16
you in every g work and word. 2Th 2:17
do not grow weary in doing g. 2Th 3:13
a pure heart, a g conscience, 1Tm 1:5
Now we know that the law is g, 1Tm 1:8
having faith and a g conscience. 1Tm 1:19
This is g, and it pleases God 1Tm 2:3
with decency and g sense; 1Tm 2:9
but with g works, as is proper 1Tm 2:10
and holiness, with g sense. 1Tm 2:15
must have a g reputation among 1Tm 3:7
deacons acquire a g standing for 1Tm 3:13
everything created by God is g, 1Tm 4:4
will be a g servant of Christ 1Tm 4:6
faith and of the g teaching that 1Tm 4:6
and is well known for g works— 1Tm 5:10
devoted herself to every g work. 1Tm 5:10
elders who are g leaders should 1Tm 5:17
Likewise, g works are obvious, 1Tm 5:25
Fight the g fight for the faith; 1Tm 6:12
and have made a g confession 1Tm 6:12
who gave a g confession before 1Tm 6:13
them⌋ to do g, to be rich in 1Tm 6:18
to be rich in g works, to be 1Tm 6:18
themselves a g foundation for 1Tm 6:19
that g thing entrusted to you. 2Tm 1:14
suffering as a g soldier of 2Tm 2:3
prepared for every g work. 2Tm 2:21
without love for what is g, 2Tm 3:3
equipped for every g work. 2Tm 3:17
I have fought the g fight, 2Tm 4:7
loving what is g, sensible, Ti 1:8
and disqualified for any g work. Ti 1:16
⌊They are⌋ to teach what is g, Ti 2:3
be sensible, pure, g homemakers, Ti 2:5
an example of g works yourself, Ti 2:7
people, eager to do g works. Ti 2:14
to be ready for every g work, Ti 3:1
to devote themselves to g works. Ti 3:8
These are g and profitable for Ti 3:8
themselves to g works for cases Ti 3:14
knowing every g thing that is in Phm 6
so that your g deed might not be Phm 14
received the g news just as they Heb 4:2
received the g news did not Heb 4:6
distinguish between g and evil. Heb 5:14
tasted God's g word and the Heb 6:5
priest of the g things that have Heb 9:11
shadow of the g things to come, Heb 10:1
to promote love and g works, Heb 10:24
from one as g as dead—came Heb 11:12
based on what seemed g to them, Heb 12:10
for it is g for the heart to be Heb 13:9
neglect to do g and to share, Heb 13:16
all that is g to do His will, Heb 13:21
Sit here in a g place," and yet Jms 2:3
What g is it, my brothers, if Jms 2:14
the body needs, what g is it? Jms 2:16
show his works by g conduct with Jms 3:13
full of mercy and g fruits, Jms 3:17
who knows to do g and doesn't do Jms 4:17
have tasted that the Lord is g. 1Pt 2:3
by observing your g works, 1Pt 2:12
and to praise those who do g. 1Pt 2:14
that you, by doing g, silence 1Pt 2:15
not only to the g and gentle but 1Pt 2:18
But when you do g and suffer, 1Pt 2:20
children when you do g and 1Pt 3:6
life and to see g days must keep 1Pt 3:10
turn away from evil and do g. 1Pt 3:11
are passionate for what is g? 1Pt 3:13
is better to suffer for doing g, 1Pt 3:17
the pledge of a g conscience 1Pt 3:21
g managers of the varied grace 1Pt 4:10
should, in doing g, entrust 1Pt 4:19
in every way and be in g health, 3Jn 2
what is evil, but what is g. 3Jn 11
The one who does g is of God; 3Jn 11
Demetrius has a ⌊g⌋ testimony 3Jn 12

GOOD-BYE *(8)*

After He said g to them, He went Mk 6:46
me go and say g to those at my Lk 9:61
who does not say g to all his Lk 14:33
g to the brothers and sailed Ac 18:18
said g and stated, "I'll come Ac 18:21
after saying g, departed to go Ac 20:1
we said g to one another. Ac 21:6
I said g to them and left for 2Co 2:13

GOOD-FOR-NOTHING *(2)*

And throw this g slave into the Mt 25:30
should say, 'We are g slaves; Lk 17:10

GOOD-LOOKING *(2)*

figure and was extremely g. Est 2:7
physical defect, g, suitable for Dn 1:4

GOODBYE *(1)*

Then Moses said g to his Ex 18:27

GOODNESS *(32)*

cause all My g to pass in front Ex 33:19
show the same g to you because 2Sm 2:6
and restore g to me instead 2Sm 16:12
for all the g that the LORD had 1Kg 8:66
Your godly people rejoice in g. 2Ch 6:41
hearts for the g the LORD had 2Ch 7:10
and delighted in Your great g. Neh 9:25
Your abundant g You gave them, Neh 9:35
could enjoy its fruit and its g. Neh 9:36
Only g and faithful love will Ps 23:6
remember me because of Your g, Ps 25:7
see the LORD's g in the land Ps 27:13
great is Your g that You have Ps 31:19
with the g of Your house, Ps 65:4
You crown the year with Your g; Ps 65:11
by Your g You provided for the Ps 68:10
Show me a sign of Your g; Ps 86:17
He satisfies you with g; Ps 103:5
because of the g of Your Ps 109:21
Your great g and will joyfully Ps 145:7
and all its g is like the flower Is 40:6
joy because of the LORD's g, Jr 31:12
will be satisfied with My g. Jr 31:14
LORD and to His g in the last Hs 3:5
you that you also are full of g, Rm 15:14
patience, kindness, g, faith, Gl 5:22
of the light ⌊results⌋ in all g, Eph 5:9
every desire for g and the work 2Th 1:11
But when the g and love for man Ti 3:4
us by His own glory and g. 2Pt 1:3
to supplement your faith with g, 2Pt 1:5
with goodness, g with knowledge, 2Pt 1:5

GOODS *(31)*

kings⌋ took all the g of Sodom Gn 14:11
back all the g and also his Gn 14:16
also his relative Lot and his g, Gn 14:16
kinds of his master's g in hand. Gn 24:10
sorts of baked g for Pharaoh, Gn 40:17
his neighbor money or g to keep, Ex 22:7
garments, leather g, things made Nm 31:20
amount of plundered g with them. 2Sm 3:22
of all kinds of g from Damascus. 2Kg 8:9
an abundance of g on the bodies 2Ch 20:25
silver, gold, g, and livestock, Ezr 1:4
articles, gold, g, livestock, Ezr 1:6
kinds of g were being brought Neh 13:15
so that no g could enter during Neh 13:19
all kinds of g camped outside Neh 13:20
to you to barter for your g. Ezk 27:9
and bronze utensils for your g. Ezk 27:13
honey, oil, and balm for your g. Ezk 27:17
were ⌊exchanged⌋ for your g. Ezk 27:19
were the carriers for your g. Ezk 27:25
merchandise, and g, your sailors Ezk 27:27
those who barter for your g, Ezk 27:27
with your abundant wealth and g. Ezk 27:33
your g and the people within you Ezk 27:34
himself with g taken in pledge. Hab 2:6
anyone to carry g through the Mk 11:16
all my grain and my g there. Lk 12:18
You have many g stored up for Lk 12:19
I donate all my g to feed the 1Co 13:3
must share his g with the Gl 6:6
has this world's g and sees his 1Jn 3:17

GOODWILL *(1)*

there is g among the upright. Pr 14:9

GORE *(3)*

'You will g the Arameans with 1Kg 22:11
'You will g the Arameans with 2Ch 18:10
will be filled with your ⌊g⌋. Ezk 32:6

GORES *(4)*

When an ox g a man or a woman to Ex 21:28
If it g a son or a daughter, Ex 21:31
If the ox g a male or female Ex 21:32
g all the peoples with them to Dt 33:17

GORGE *(2)*

with those who g themselves on Pr 23:20
told, 'Get up! G yourself on Dn 7:5

GORGED *(1)*

you became fat, bloated, and g. Dt 32:15

GORING *(2)*

if the ox was in the habit of g, Ex 21:29
the ox was in the habit of g, Ex 21:36

GOSHEN *(15)*

the land of G and be near me— Gn 45:10
to prepare for his arrival at G. Gn 46:28
When they came to the land of G, Gn 46:28
and went up to G to meet his Gn 46:29
to settle in the land of G, Gn 46:34
and are now in the land of G." Gn 47:1
settle in the land of G." Gn 47:4
They can live in the land of G. Gn 47:6
of Egypt, in the region of G. Gn 47:27
were left in the land of G. Gn 50:8
treatment to the land of G, Ex 8:22
was in the land of G where the Ex 9:26
all the land of G as far as Jos 10:41
all the land of G, the Judean Jos 11:16
G, Holon, and Giloh—11 cities, Jos 15:51

GOSPEL *(81)*

Wherever this g is proclaimed in Mt 26:13
of the g of Jesus Christ Mk 1:1
of Me and the g will save it. Mk 8:35
fields because of Me and the g, Mk 10:29
Wherever the g is proclaimed in Mk 14:9
and preach the g to the whole Mk 16:15
would hear the g message and Ac 15:7
testify to the g of God's grace. Ac 20:24
For I am not ashamed of the g, Rm 1:16
according to my g through Christ Rm 2:16
announce the g of good things! Rm 10:15
But all did not obey the g. Rm 10:16
Regarding the g, they are Rm 11:28
you according to my g and the Rm 16:25
to preach the g—not with 1Co 1:17
in Christ Jesus through the g. 1Co 4:15
will not hinder the g of Christ. 1Co 9:12
who preach the g should earn 1Co 9:14
earn their living by the g. 1Co 9:14
if I preach the g, I have no 1Co 9:16
to me if I do not preach the g! 1Co 9:16
preach the g and offer it free 1Co 9:18
use of my authority in the g. 1Co 9:18
I do all this because of the g, 1Co 9:23
for you the g I proclaimed to 1Co 15:1
to Troas for the g of Christ, 2Co 2:12
in fact, our g is veiled, it is 2Co 4:3
the light of the g of the glory 2Co 4:4
the churches for his g ministry. 2Co 8:18
confession of the g of Christ, 2Co 9:13
to you with the g of Christ. 2Co 10:14
may preach the g to the regions 2Co 10:16
or a different g, which you had 2Co 11:4
I preached the g of God to you 2Co 11:7
are turning⌋ to a different g— Gl 1:6
not that there is another ⌊g⌋, Gl 1:7
want to change the g of Christ. Gl 1:7
preach to you a g other than Gl 1:8
to you a g contrary to what Gl 1:9
that the g preached by me is not Gl 1:11
to them the g I preach among Gl 2:2

truth of the **g** would remain for Gl 2:5
entrusted with the **g** for the Gl 2:7
from the truth of the **g**, Gl 2:14
I preached the **g** to you in Gl 4:13
of truth, the **g** of your Eph 1:13
in Christ Jesus through the **g**. Eph 3:6
servant of this ⌊**g**⌋ by the gift Eph 3:7
readiness for the **g** of peace. Eph 6:15
boldness the mystery of the **g**. Eph 6:19
in the **g** from the first day Php 1:5
and establishment of the **g**. Php 1:7
in the advancement of the **g**, Php 1:12
for the defense of the **g**; Php 1:16
worthy of the **g** of Christ. Php 1:27
by side for the faith of the **g**, Php 1:27
with me in the **g** ministry like a Php 2:22
contended for the **g** at my side, Php 4:3
that in the early days of the **g**, Php 4:15
the **g** that has come to you. Col 1:6
hope of the **g** that you heard. Col 1:23
⌊This **g**⌋ has been proclaimed in Col 1:23
For our **g** did not come to you in 1Th 1:5
God to speak the **g** of God to you 1Th 2:2
God to be entrusted with the **g**, 1Th 2:4
not only the **g** of God but also 1Th 2:8
we preached God's **g** to you. 1Th 2:9
co-worker in the **g** of Christ, 1Th 3:2
don't obey the **g** of our Lord 2Th 1:8
you to this through our **g**, 2Th 2:14
on the glorious **g** of the blessed 1Tm 1:11
share in suffering for the **g**, 2Tm 1:8
to light through the **g**. 2Tm 1:10
For this ⌊**g**⌋ I was appointed a 2Tm 1:11
from David, according to my **g**. 2Tm 2:8
for the **g** he might serve me Phm 13
who preached the **g** to you by the 1Pt 1:12
was preached as the **g** to you. 1Pt 1:25
this reason the **g** was also 1Pt 4:6
those who disobey the **g** of God? 1Pt 4:17
the eternal **g** to announce to Rv 14:6

GOSSIP *(8)*

I have heard the **g** of many; Ps 31:13
A **g** goes around revealing a Pr 11:13
and a **g** separates friends. Pr 16:28
reveals secrets is a constant **g**; Pr 20:19
without a **g**, conflict dies down. Pr 26:20
I have heard the **g** of the Jr 20:10
of people's **g** and slander, Ezk 36:3
slander, **g**, arrogance, 2Co 12:20

GOSSIP'S *(2)*

A **g** words are like choice food Pr 18:8
A **g** words are like choice food Pr 26:22

GOSSIPS *(3)*

but whoever **g** about it separates Pr 17:9
deceit, and malice. They are **g**, Rm 1:29
but are also **g** and busybodies, 1Tm 5:13

GOT *(231)*

ran to the herd and **g** a tender, Gn 18:7
The men **g** up from there and Gn 18:16
⌊them⌋, he **g** up to meet them. Gn 19:1
I've **g** two daughters who haven't Gn 19:8
as the angels **g** them outside, Gn 19:17
So they **g** their father to drink Gn 19:33
she lay down or when she **g** up. Gn 19:33
they again **g** their father to Gn 19:35
she lay down or when she **g** up. Gn 19:35
in the morning Abimelech **g** up, Gn 20:8
in the morning Abraham **g** up, Gn 21:14
and his mother **g** a wife for him Gn 21:21
in the morning Abraham **g** up, Gn 22:3
and they **g** up and went together Gn 22:19
Then Abraham **g** up from beside Gn 23:3
When they **g** up in the morning, Gn 24:54
and her young women **g** up, Gn 24:61
saw Isaac, she **g** down from her Gn 24:64
he ate, drank, **g** up, and went Gn 25:34
They **g** up early in the morning Gn 26:31
he went and **g** them and brought Gn 27:14
Then Jacob **g** up and put his Gn 31:17
Laban **g** up early in the morning, Gn 31:55
night Jacob **g** up and took his Gn 32:22
Judah **g** a wife for Er, his Gn 38:6
and she **g** pregnant by him. Gn 38:18
She **g** up and left, then removed Gn 38:19
and **g** feed for their donkeys. Gn 43:24
and they **g** drunk with Joseph. Gn 43:34
because you **g** into your father's Gn 49:4
defiled it—he **g** into my bed. Gn 49:4
she **g** a papyrus basket for him Ex 2:3
During the night Pharaoh **g** up, Ex 12:30
So he **g** his chariot ready and Ex 14:6
and drink, then **g** up to revel. Ex 32:6
He **g** up early in the morning, Ex 34:4
They **g** up early the next morning Nm 14:40
Moses **g** up and went to Dathan Nm 16:25
they **g** away from the dwellings Nm 16:27
So Balaam **g** up the next morning Nm 22:13
When he **g** up in the morning, Nm 22:21
he **g** up from the assembly, Nm 25:7
Joshua **g** up early the next Jos 6:12
Joshua **g** up early the next Jos 7:16
As she **g** off her donkey, Caleb Jos 15:18
As she **g** off her donkey, Caleb Jdg 1:14
of Joseph **g** the upper hand, Jdg 1:35
So Deborah **g** up and went with Jdg 4:9
men of the city **g** up in the Jdg 6:28
When he **g** up early in the Jdg 6:38
g up early and camped beside the Jdg 7:1
So Gideon **g** up, killed Zebah Jdg 8:21
people with him **g** up at night Jdg 9:34
were with him **g** up from their Jdg 9:35
they **g** rid of the foreign gods Jdg 10:16
So Manoah **g** up and followed his Jdg 13:11
bed until midnight when he **g** up, Jdg 16:3
Then her husband **g** up and went Jdg 19:3
they **g** up early in the morning Jdg 19:5
The man **g** up to go, but his Jdg 19:7
He **g** up early in the morning of Jdg 19:8
The man **g** up to go with his Jdg 19:9
He **g** up, departed, and arrived Jdg 19:10
When her master **g** up in the Jdg 19:27
men of Israel **g** up from their Jdg 20:33
next day the people **g** up early, Jdg 21:4
When she **g** up to gather ⌊grain⌋, Ru 2:15
morning but **g** up while it was Ru 3:14
Hannah **g** up after they ate and 1Sm 1:9
and Hannah **g** up early to bow 1Sm 1:19
Samuel **g** up, went to Eli, and 1Sm 3:6
He **g** up, went to Eli, and said, 1Sm 3:8
people of Ashdod **g** up early the 1Sm 5:3
when they **g** up early the next 1Sm 5:4
Ekron, but when it **g** there, the 1Sm 5:10
They **g** up early, and just before 1Sm 9:26
Saul **g** up, and both he and 1Sm 9:26
They ran and **g** him from there. 1Sm 10:23
morning Samuel **g** up to confront 1Sm 15:12
So David **g** up early in the 1Sm 17:20
But David **g** away from him 1Sm 18:11
He **g** up from the table in fierce 1Sm 20:34
David **g** up from the south side 1Sm 20:41
Then David **g** up and secretly 1Sm 24:4
After that, David **g** up, went out 1Sm 24:8
she quickly **g** off the donkey and 1Sm 25:23
Then Abigail **g** up quickly, 1Sm 25:42
g up off the ground and sat on 1Sm 28:23
they **g** up and left that night. 1Sm 28:25
So David and his men **g** up early 1Sm 29:11
me when I **g** sick three days ago 1Sm 30:13
young men who **g** on camels and 1Sm 30:17
David **g** everything back. 1Sm 30:19
they **g** up and were counted off 2Sm 2:15
evening David **g** up from his bed 2Sm 11:2
with him, and David **g** him drunk. 2Sm 11:13
David **g** up from the ground. 2Sm 12:20
he died, you **g** up and ate food. 2Sm 12:21
rest of⌋ the king's sons **g** up, 2Sm 13:29
Joab **g** up, went to Geshur, and 2Sm 14:23
his hair⌋ **g** so heavy for him 2Sm 14:26
Absalom **g** himself a chariot, 2Sm 15:1
When King David **g** to Bahurim, 2Sm 16:5
people with him **g** up and crossed 2Sm 17:22
So the king **g** up and sat in the 2Sm 19:8
he went and **g** the bones of Saul 2Sm 21:12
When David **g** up in the morning, 2Sm 24:11
Adonijah's guests **g** up trembling 1Kg 1:49
so he **g** up and went to take hold 1Kg 1:50
She **g** up in the middle of the 1Kg 3:20
When I **g** up in the morning to 1Kg 3:21
he **g** up from kneeling before the 1Kg 8:54
donkey for him, and he **g** on it. 1Kg 13:13
Jeroboam's wife **g** up and left 1Kg 14:17
So Elijah **g** up and went to 1Kg 17:10
So Ahab **g** in ⌊his chariot⌋ and 1Kg 18:45
So he **g** up, ate, and drank. 1Kg 19:8
he **g** up to go down to the 1Kg 21:16
So he **g** up and went down with 2Kg 1:15
When they **g** up early in the 2Kg 3:22
So he **g** up and followed her. 2Kg 4:30
When Elisha **g** to the house, 2Kg 4:32
g up, went into the house, 2Kg 4:35
But Naaman **g** angry and left, 2Kg 5:11
he **g** down from the chariot to 2Kg 5:21
when the man **g** down from his 2Kg 5:26
the man of God **g** up early and 2Kg 6:15
before the messenger **g** to him, 2Kg 6:32
diseased men **g** up at twilight 2Kg 7:5
the king **g** up in the night and 2Kg 7:12
the woman **g** ready and did what 2Kg 8:2
So Jehu **g** up and went into the 2Kg 9:6
Jehu **g** into his chariot and went 2Kg 9:16
So he **g** a bow and arrows. 2Kg 13:15
When the people **g** up the ⌊next⌋ 2Kg 19:35
the morning they **g** up early and 2Ch 20:20
But they **g** very angry with Judah 2Ch 25:10
King Hezekiah **g** up early, 2Ch 29:20
I **g** up from my humiliation, Ezr 9:5
Then Ezra **g** up and made the Ezr 10:5
I **g** up at night and ⌊took⌋ a few Neh 2:12
so she **g** up and stood before the Est 8:4
and **g** rid of their enemies. Est 9:16
days the Jews **g** rid of their Est 9:22
When the people **g** up the ⌊next⌋ Is 37:36
underwear and **g** it from the Jr 13:7
were with him **g** up and struck Jr 41:2
So I **g** up and went out to the Ezk 3:23
times a day he **g** down on his Dn 6:10
dawn the king **g** up and hurried Dn 6:19
Then I **g** up and went about the Dn 8:27
Jonah **g** up to flee to Tarshish Jnh 1:3
Jonah **g** up and went to Nineveh Jnh 3:3
of Nineveh, he **g** up from his Jnh 3:6
In one month I **g** rid of three Zch 11:8
When Joseph **g** up from sleeping, Mt 1:24
So he **g** up, took the child and Mt 2:14
So he **g** up, took the child and Mt 2:21
you: They've **g** their reward! Mt 6:2
you: They've **g** their reward! Mt 6:5
you: They've **g** their reward! Mt 6:16
Then she **g** up and began to serve Mt 8:15
As He **g** into the boat, His Mt 8:23
Then He **g** up and rebuked the Mt 8:26
So He **g** into a boat, crossed Mt 9:1
And he **g** up and went home. Mt 9:7
So he **g** up and followed Him. Mt 9:9
His disciples **g** up and followed Mt 9:19
by the hand, and the girl **g** up. Mt 9:25
around Him that He **g** into a boat Mt 13:2
When they **g** into the boat, Mt 14:32
He **g** into the boat and went to Mt 15:39
his master **g** angry and handed Mt 18:34
The first **g** married and died. Mt 22:25
those virgins **g** up and trimmed Mt 25:7
one of them ran and **g** a sponge, Mt 27:48
still dark, He **g** up, went out, Mk 1:35
Immediately he **g** up, picked up Mk 2:12
So he **g** up and followed Him. Mk 2:14
So He **g** into a boat on the sea Mk 4:1
He **g** up, rebuked the wind, and Mk 4:39
As soon as He **g** out of the boat, Mk 5:2
the girl **g** up and began to walk Mk 5:42
Then He **g** into the boat with Mk 6:51
As they **g** out of the boat, Mk 6:54
He **g** up and departed from there Mk 7:24
and immediately **g** into the boat Mk 8:10
g on board ⌊the boat⌋ again, Mk 8:13
g up, drove Him out of town, Lk 4:29
She **g** up immediately and began Lk 4:39
He **g** into one of the boats, Lk 5:3
Immediately he **g** up before them, Lk 5:25
he **g** up and began to follow Him. Lk 5:28
So he **g** up and stood there. Lk 6:8
and His disciples **g** into a boat, Lk 8:22
Then He **g** up and rebuked the Lk 8:24
When He **g** out on land, a Lk 8:27
returned, and she **g** up at once. Lk 8:55
another said, 'I just **g** married, Lk 14:20
So he **g** up and went to his Lk 15:20
He **g** up from prayer and came Lk 22:45
Peter, however, **g** up and ran to Lk 24:12
very hour they **g** up and returned Lk 24:33
them at what time he **g** better. Jn 4:52
the first one who **g** in after the Jn 5:4
the man **g** well, picked up Jn 5:9

g into a boat, and started Jn 6:17
they g into the boats and went Jn 6:24
g up quickly and went to Him. Jn 11:29
her saw that Mary g up quickly Jn 11:31
So He g up from supper, laid Jn 13:4
outran Peter and g to the tomb Jn 20:4
went out and g into the boat, Jn 21:3
When they g out on land, they Jn 21:9
So Simon Peter g up and hauled Jn 21:11
The young men g up, wrapped ⌊his Ac 5:6
when the temple police g there, Ac 5:22
he g up and went. There was an Ac 8:27
Then Saul g up from the ground, Ac 9:8
Then he g up and was baptized. Ac 9:18
and immediately he g up. Ac 9:34
Peter g up and went with them. Ac 9:39
The next day he g up and set out Ac 10:23
he g up and went into the town. Ac 14:20
these days we g ready and went Ac 21:15
When Paul g to the steps, he had Ac 21:35
Pharisees' party g up and Ac 23:9
those sitting with them g up, Ac 26:30
this way, all g safely to land. Ac 27:44
eat and drink, and g up to play. 1Co 10:7
from which he also g him back as Heb 11:19

GOTTEN (2)

When you've all g up early, 1Sm 29:10
So they had g up and fled at 2Kg 7:7

GOUGE (5)

Will you g out the eyes of these Nm 16:14
that I g out everyone's right 1Sm 11:2
g it out and throw it away. Mt 5:29
g it out and throw it away. Mt 18:9
causes your downfall, g it out. Mk 9:47

GOUGED (1)

seized him and g out his eyes. Jdg 16:21

GOURDS (4)

with ⌊ornamental⌋ g and flower 1Kg 6:18
⌊Ornamental⌋ g encircled it 1Kg 7:24
The g were cast in two rows when 1Kg 7:24
as many wild g as his garment 2Kg 4:39

GOVERN (4)

His judgments ⌊g⌋ the whole 1Ch 16:14
who hates justice g ⌊the world⌋? Jb 34:17
His judgments ⌊g⌋ the whole Ps 105:7
and the unstable will g them." Is 3:4

GOVERNING (4)

over the household g the people 2Kg 15:5
king's household g the people 2Ch 26:21
while Quirinius was g Syria. Lk 2:2
submit to the g authorities, Rm 13:1

GOVERNMENT (3)

and the g will be on His Is 9:6
g is God's servant to you for Rm 13:4
For g is God's servant, an Rm 13:4

GOVERNOR (41)

him to Amon, the g of the city, 1Kg 22:26
gate of Joshua the g of the city 2Kg 23:8
him to Amon, the g of the city, 2Ch 18:25
Azrikam g of the palace, 2Ch 28:7
with Maaseiah the g of the city 2Ch 34:8
g ordered them not to eat the Ezr 2:63
Tattenai the g of the region Ezr 5:3
Tattenai the g of the region Ezr 5:6
the g by the appointment of King Ezr 5:14
Tattenai g of the region west of Ezr 6:6
Let the g and elders of the Jews Ezr 6:7
Then Tattenai g of the region Ezr 6:13
authority of the g of the region Neh 3:7
me to be their g in the land of Neh 5:14
from the food allotted to the g. Neh 5:14
the food allotted to the g, Neh 5:18
g ordered them not to eat the Neh 7:65
The g gave 1,000 gold drachmas, Neh 7:70
Nehemiah the g, Ezra the priest Neh 8:9
Nehemiah the g, son of Hacaliah, Neh 10:1
of Nehemiah the g and Ezra the Neh 12:26
and chief g over all the wise Dn 2:48
Shealtiel, the g of Judah, and Hg 1:1
of Shealtiel, g of Judah, the Hg 1:14
son of Shealtiel, g of Judah, to Hg 2:2
Speak to Zerubbabel, g of Judah: Hg 2:21
Bring it to your g! Mal 1:8
Him over to Pilate, the g. Mt 27:2
Now Jesus stood before the g. Mt 27:11
the Jews?" the g asked Him. Mt 27:11
that the g was greatly amazed. Mt 27:14
The g asked them, "Which of the Mt 27:21
Pontius Pilate was g of Judea, Lk 3:1
who appointed him g over Egypt Ac 7:10
him safely to Felix the g." Ac 23:24
To the most excellent g Felix: Ac 23:26
delivered the letter to the g, Ac 23:33
case against Paul to the g. Ac 24:1
When the g motioned to him to Ac 24:10
So the king, the g, Bernice, and Ac 26:30
the g under King Aretas guarded 2Co 11:32

GOVERNOR'S (5)

the festival the g custom was to Mt 27:15
Then the g soldiers took Jesus Mt 27:27
If this reaches the g ears, Mt 28:14
Him over to the g rule and Lk 20:20
Caiaphas to the g headquarters. Jn 18:28

GOVERNORS (24)

Arabian kings and g of the land. 1Kg 10:15
kings and g of the land also 2Ch 9:14
the nobles, the g of the people, 2Ch 23:20
satraps and g of the region Ezr 8:36
written⌋ to the g of the region Neh 2:7
I went to the g of the region Neh 2:9
g who preceded me had heavily Neh 5:15
the g of each of the provinces, Est 3:12
the satraps, the g, and the Est 8:9
satraps, the g, and the royal Est 9:3
I will smash g and officials. Jr 51:23
her g and all her officials, Jr 51:28
along with her g, officials, Jr 51:57
dressed in blue, g and prefects, Ezk 23:6
g and prefects, warriors Ezk 23:12
all of them g and prefects, Ezk 23:23
satraps, prefects, g, advisers, Dn 3:2
satraps, prefects, g, advisers, Dn 3:3
prefects, g, and the king's Dn 3:27
and g have agreed that the king Dn 6:7
brought before g and kings Mt 10:18
stand before g and kings because Mk 13:9
before kings and g because of My Lk 21:12
or to g as those sent out by him 1Pt 2:14

GOZAN (2)

such as⌋ G, Haran, Rezeph, 2Kg 19:12
rescue them—G, Haran, Rezeph, Is 37:12

GOZAN'S (3)

Halah and by the Habor, G river, 2Kg 17:6
Halah and by the Habor, G river, 2Kg 18:11
Habor, Hara, and G river, ⌊where 1Ch 5:26

GRAB (3)

your hand and g it by the tail. Ex 4:4
me, I would g it by its fur, 1Sm 17:35
every language will g the robe Zch 8:23

GRABBED (9)

for him, the men g his hand, his Gn 19:16
She g him by his garment and Gn 39:12
took a tent peg, g a hammer, and Jdg 4:21
Saul g the hem of his robe, 1Sm 15:27
He g the Philistine's sword, 1Sm 17:51
Then each man g his opponent by 2Sm 2:16
him to eat, he g her and said, 2Sm 13:11
right hand Joab g Amasa by the 2Sm 20:9
He g him, started choking him, Mt 18:28

GRABS (4)

out her hand and g his genitals, Dt 25:11
g it, but it does not hold up. Jb 8:15
She g him and kisses him; Pr 7:13
is like one who g a dog by the Pr 26:17

GRACE (138)

promised this g to Your servant. 2Sm 7:28
g has come from the LORD our God Ezr 9:8
He has extended g to us in the Ezr 9:9
g flows from your lips. Ps 45:2
do not show g to any wicked Ps 59:5
The LORD gives g and glory; Ps 84:11
be a garland of g on your head Pr 1:9
but gives g to the humble. Pr 3:34
a garland of g on your head; Pr 4:9
for I will not grant you g. Jr 16:13
by shouts of: G, grace to it!'" Zch 4:7
by shouts of: Grace, g to it!'" Zch 4:7
out a spirit of g and prayer Zch 12:10
wisdom, and God's g was on Him. Lk 2:40
the Father, full of g and truth. Jn 1:14
have all received g after grace Jn 1:16
grace after g from His fullness, Jn 1:16
g and truth came through Jesus Jn 1:17
and great g was on all of them. Ac 4:33
Stephen, full of g and power, Ac 6:8
he arrived and saw the g of God, Ac 11:23
to continue in the g of God. Ac 13:43
message of His g by granting Ac 14:3
entrusted to the g of God for Ac 14:26
through the g of the Lord Jesus Ac 15:11
commended to the g of the Lord Ac 15:40
who had believed through g. Ac 18:27
to the gospel of God's g. Ac 20:24
God and to the message of His g, Ac 20:32
have received g and apostleship Rm 1:5
G to you and peace from God our Rm 1:7
freely by His g through the Rm 3:24
that it may be according to g, Rm 4:16
faith into this g in which we Rm 5:2
much more have the g of God and Rm 5:15
many by the g of the one man, Rm 5:15
the overflow of g and the gift Rm 5:17
multiplied, g multiplied even Rm 5:20
so also g will reign through Rm 5:21
in order that g may multiply? Rm 6:1
are not under law but under g. Rm 6:14
are not under law but under g? Rm 6:15
time a remnant chosen by g. Rm 11:5
Now if by g, then it is not by Rm 11:6
otherwise g ceases to be grace. Rm 11:6
otherwise grace ceases to be g. Rm 11:6
For by the g given to me, I tell Rm 12:3
According to the g given to us, Rm 12:6
because of the g given me by God Rm 15:15
The g of our Lord Jesus be with Rm 16:20
The g of our Lord Jesus Christ Rm 16:24
G to you and peace from God our 1Co 1:3
because of God's g given to you 1Co 1:4
to God's g that was given to 1Co 3:10
But by God's g I am what I am, 1Co 15:10
and His g toward me was not 1Co 15:10
but God's g that was with me. 1Co 15:10
The g of our Lord Jesus be with 1Co 16:23
G to you and peace from God our 2Co 1:2
fleshly wisdom but by God's g. 2Co 1:12
of you, so that g, extended 2Co 4:15
"Don't receive God's g in vain." 2Co 6:1
about the g of God granted to 2Co 8:1
also complete this g to you. 2Co 8:6
for us—excel also in this g. 2Co 8:7
For you know the g of our Lord 2Co 8:9
to make every g overflow to you, 2Co 9:8
the surpassing g of God on you. 2Co 9:14
My g is sufficient for you, 2Co 12:9
The g of the Lord Jesus Christ, 2Co 13:13
G to you and peace from God the Gl 1:3
called you by the g of Christ, Gl 1:6
me apart and called me by His g, Gl 1:15
acknowledged the g that had been Gl 2:9
I do not set aside the g of God; Gl 2:21
you have fallen from g! Gl 5:4
the g of our Lord Jesus Christ Gl 6:18
G to you and peace from God our Eph 1:2
His glorious g that He favored Eph 1:6
according to the riches of His g Eph 1:7
trespasses. By g you are saved! Eph 2:5
of His g in ⌊His⌋ kindness Eph 2:7
For by g you are saved through Eph 2:8
of God's g that He gave to me Eph 3:2
gift of God's g that was given Eph 3:7
This g was given to me—the Eph 3:8
Now g was given to each one of Eph 4:7
in order to give g to those who Eph 4:29
G be with all who have undying Eph 6:24
G to you and peace from God our Php 1:2
are all partners with me in g, Php 1:7
The g of the Lord Jesus Christ Php 4:23
G to you and peace from God our Col 1:2
recognized God's g in the truth. Col 1:6
my imprisonment. G be with you. Col 4:18
Jesus Christ. G to you and peace 1Th 1:1
May the g of our Lord Jesus 1Th 5:28
G to you and peace from God our 2Th 1:2
according to the g of our God 2Th 1:12
and good hope by g, 2Th 2:16
The g of our Lord Jesus Christ 2Th 3:18
G, mercy, and peace from God the 1Tm 1:2
the g of our Lord overflowed, 1Tm 1:14
the faith. G be with all of you. 1Tm 6:21
G, mercy, and peace from God the 2Tm 1:2

to His own purpose and g, 2Tm 1:9
be strong in the g that is in 2Tm 2:1
with your spirit. G be with you! 2Tm 4:22
G and peace from God the Father Ti 1:4
For the g of God has appeared, Ti 2:11
having been justified by His g, Ti 3:7
in the faith. G be with all of Ti 3:15
G to you and peace from God our Phm 3
The g of the Lord Jesus Christ Phm 25
that by God's g He might taste Heb 2:9
the throne of g with boldness, Heb 4:16
mercy and find g to help us at Heb 4:16
and insulted the Spirit of g? Heb 10:29
short of the g of God and that Heb 12:15
be shaken, let us hold on to g. Heb 12:28
established by g and not by Heb 13:9
G be with all of you. Heb 13:25
But He gives greater g. Jms 4:6
but gives g to the humble. Jms 4:6
May g and peace be multiplied to 1Pt 1:2
about the g that would come to 1Pt 1:10
on the g to be brought to 1Pt 1:13
as co-heirs of the g of life, 1Pt 3:7
managers of the varied g of God. 1Pt 4:10
but gives g to the humble. 1Pt 5:5
the God of all g, who called you 1Pt 5:10
that this is the true g of God. 1Pt 5:12
May g and peace be multiplied to 2Pt 1:2
But grow in the g and knowledge 2Pt 3:18
G, mercy, and peace will be with 2Jn 3
turning the g of our God into Jd 4
G and peace to you from the One Rv 1:4
The g of the Lord Jesus be with Rv 22:21

GRACEFUL *(2)*
power, and his g proportions. Jb 41:12
A loving doe, a g fawn—let her Pr 5:19

GRACIOUS *(66)*
God has been g to me and I have Gn 33:11
May God be g to you, my son." Gn 43:29
I will be g to whom I will be Ex 33:19
be gracious to whom I will be g, Ex 33:19
is a compassionate and g God, Ex 34:6
shine on you, and be g to you; Nm 6:25
who keeps His g covenant loyalty Dt 7:9
The LORD may be g to me and let 2Sm 12:22
keeping the g covenant with Your 1Kg 8:23
the LORD was g to them and had 2Kg 13:23
keeping His g covenant with Your 2Ch 6:14
LORD your God is g and merciful; 2Ch 30:9
g hand of his God was on him, Ezr 7:9
Since the g hand of our God was Ezr 8:18
of our God is g to all who seek Ezr 8:22
who keeps His g covenant with Neh 1:5
them how the g hand of my God Neh 2:18
a forgiving God, g and Neh 9:17
You are a g and compassionate Neh 9:31
God who keeps His g covenant— Neh 9:32
and to be g to him and say, Jb 33:24
be g to me and hear my prayer. Ps 4:1
Be g to me, LORD, for I am weak; Ps 6:2
Be g to me, LORD; consider my Ps 9:13
Turn to me and be g to me, Ps 25:16
redeem me and be g to me. Ps 26:11
be g to me and answer me. Ps 27:7
LORD, listen and be g to me; Ps 30:10
g to me, LORD, because I am in Ps 31:9
the righteous is g and giving. Ps 37:21
I said, "LORD, be g to me; Ps 41:4
be g to me and raise me up; Ps 41:10
Be g to me, God, according to Ps 51:1
g to me, God, for man tramples Ps 56:1
Be g to me, God, be gracious to Ps 57:1
to me, God, be g to me, for I Ps 57:1
May God be g to us and bless us; Ps 67:1
Has God forgotten to be g? Ps 77:9
Be g to me, Lord, for I call to Ps 86:3
are a compassionate and g God, Ps 86:15
Turn to me and be g to me. Ps 86:16
The LORD is compassionate and g, Ps 103:8
let no one be g to his Ps 109:12
The LORD is g and compassionate. Ps 111:4
He is g, compassionate, and Ps 112:4
The LORD is g and righteous; Ps 116:5
be g to me according to Your Ps 119:58
Turn to me and be g to me, Ps 119:132
May Your g Spirit lead me on Ps 143:10
The LORD is g and compassionate, Ps 145:8
all His words and g in all His Ps 145:13
His ways and g in all His acts Ps 145:17
A g woman gains honor, but Pr 11:16
loves a pure heart and g lips— Pr 22:11
the mouth of a wise man are g, Ec 10:12
Creator will not be g to them. Is 27:11
LORD, be g to us! We wait for Is 33:2
who keeps His g covenant with Dn 9:4
For He is g and compassionate, Jl 2:13
will be g to the remnant of Am 5:15
Will He be g to us? Mal 1:9
amazed by the g words that came Lk 4:22
He is g to the ungrateful and Lk 6:35
since God's g gifts and calling Rm 11:29
to carry your g gift to 1Co 16:3
Your speech should always be g, Col 4:6

GRACIOUSLY *(7)*
children God has g given your Gn 33:5
for I was g strengthened by my Neh 2:8
and g give me Your instruction. Ps 119:29
When he speaks g, don't believe Pr 26:25
I have g returned to Jerusalem; Zch 1:16
pay it back, he g forgave them Lk 7:42
has g given you all those who Ac 27:24

GRACIOUSNESS *(3)*
I beg you in your g to give us a Ac 24:4
the gentleness and g of Christ— 2Co 10:1
Let your g be known to everyone. Php 4:5

GRAFT *(2)*
They all love g and chase after Is 1:23
the power to g them in again. Rm 11:23

GRAFTED *(5)*
branch, were g in among them, Rm 11:17
broken off so that I might be g Rm 11:19
will be g in, because God Rm 11:23
nature were g into a cultivated Rm 11:24
be g into their own olive tree? Rm 11:24

GRAIN *(280)*
an abundance of g and new wine. Gn 27:28
him with g and new wine. Gn 27:37
sheaves of g in the field. Gn 37:7
Seven heads of g, full and good, Gn 41:5
seven heads of g, thin and Gn 41:6
The thin heads of g swallowed up Gn 41:7
had also seen seven heads of g, Gn 41:22
seven heads of g—withered, Gn 41:23
thin heads of g swallowed the Gn 41:24
heads of g are seven years Gn 41:27
store the g under Pharaoh's Gn 41:35
Joseph stored up g in such Gn 41:49
and sold g to the Egyptians, Gn 41:56
to Joseph in Egypt to buy g, Gn 41:57
that there was g in Egypt, Gn 42:1
have heard there is g in Egypt. Gn 42:2
went down to buy g from Egypt. Gn 42:3
among those who came to buy g, Gn 42:5
he sold g to all its people. Gn 42:6
you go and take g ⌊to relieve⌋ Gn 42:19
to fill their containers with g, Gn 42:25
They loaded the g on their Gn 42:26
had used up the g they had Gn 43:2
night and opened our bags of g, Gn 43:21
bag, along with his g money." Gn 44:2
10 female donkeys carrying g, Gn 45:23
in exchange for the g they were Gn 47:14
and consumes stacks of cut g, Ex 22:6
grain, standing g, or a field, Ex 22:6
Offer a g offering and a drink Ex 29:41
on it, or a burnt or g offering; Ex 30:9
and the g offering on it, Ex 40:29
anyone presents a g offering as Lv 2:1
the rest of the g offering will Lv 2:3
you present a g offering baked Lv 2:4
your gift is a g offering Lv 2:5
oil on it; it is a g offering. Lv 2:6
If your gift is a g offering Lv 2:7
to the LORD the g offering made Lv 2:8
portion from the g offering and Lv 2:9
the rest of the g offering will Lv 2:10
No g offering that you present Lv 2:11
each of your g offerings with Lv 2:13
omit from your g offering the Lv 2:13
If you present a g offering of Lv 2:14
must present fresh heads of g, Lv 2:14
for your g offering of Lv 2:14
on it; it is a g offering. Lv 2:15
priest, like the g offering." Lv 5:13
is the law of the g offering: Lv 6:14
olive oil from the g offering, Lv 6:15
flour as a regular g offering, Lv 6:20
present it as a g offering of Lv 6:21
Every g offering for a priest Lv 6:23
Any g offering that is baked in Lv 7:9
But any g offering, whether dry Lv 7:10
offering, the g offering, the Lv 7:37
and a g offering mixed with oil. Lv 9:4
he presented the g offering, Lv 9:17
Take the g offering that is left Lv 10:12
a g offering of three quarts of Lv 14:10
offering and the g offering on Lv 14:20
with olive oil for a g offering, Lv 14:21
together with the g offering. Lv 14:31
Its g offering is to be four Lv 23:13
bread, roasted g, or ⌊any⌋ new Lv 23:14
or ⌊any⌋ new g until this very Lv 23:14
offering of new g to the LORD. Lv 23:16
with their g offerings and drink Lv 23:18
burnt offerings and g offerings, Lv 23:37
eat the old g of the previous Lv 26:10
g from the soil or fruit from Lv 27:30
incense, the daily g offering, Nm 4:16
it because it is a g offering of Nm 5:15
g offering for remembrance that Nm 5:15
in her hands the g offering for Nm 5:18
which is the g offering of Nm 5:18
is to take the g offering of Nm 5:25
a handful of the g offering as Nm 5:26
along with their g offerings and Nm 6:15
the accompanying g offering and Nm 6:17
mixed with oil for a g offering; Nm 7:13
mixed with oil for a g offering; Nm 7:19
mixed with oil for a g offering; Nm 7:25
mixed with oil for a g offering; Nm 7:31
mixed with oil for a g offering; Nm 7:37
mixed with oil for a g offering; Nm 7:43
mixed with oil for a g offering; Nm 7:49
mixed with oil for a g offering; Nm 7:55
mixed with oil for a g offering; Nm 7:61
mixed with oil for a g offering; Nm 7:67
mixed with oil for a g offering; Nm 7:73
mixed with oil for a g offering; Nm 7:79
old, with their g offerings, and Nm 7:87
bull and its g offering of fine Nm 8:8
also present a g offering of two Nm 15:4
If you prepare a g offering with Nm 15:6
a g offering of six quarts of Nm 15:9
with its g offering and drink Nm 15:24
Me, whether the g offering, sin Nm 18:9
oil, new wine, and g, which the Nm 18:12
if ⌊it were your⌋ g from the Nm 18:27
not a place of g, figs, vines, Nm 20:5
flour for a g offering mixed Nm 28:5
the same kind of g offering and Nm 28:8
mixed with oil as a g offering, Nm 28:9
oil as a g offering for each Nm 28:12
with oil as a g offering for Nm 28:12
oil as a g offering for each Nm 28:13
The g offering with them is to Nm 28:20
offering of new g to the LORD at Nm 28:26
with their g offering of fine Nm 28:28
offering and its g offering. Nm 28:31
with their g offering of fine Nm 29:3
with their g offerings and drink Nm 29:6
Their g offering is to be of Nm 29:9
offering with its g offering and Nm 29:11
Their g offering is to be of Nm 29:14
offering with its g and drink Nm 29:16
with their g and drink offerings Nm 29:18
offering with its g and drink Nm 29:19
with their g and drink offerings Nm 29:21
offering with its g and drink Nm 29:22
with their g and drink offerings Nm 29:24
offering with its g and drink Nm 29:25
with their g and drink offerings Nm 29:27
offering with its g and drink Nm 29:28
with their g and drink offerings Nm 29:30
offering with its g and drink Nm 29:31
with their g and drink offerings Nm 29:33
offering with its g and drink Nm 29:34
with their g and drink offerings Nm 29:37
offering with its g and drink Nm 29:38
whether burnt, g, drink, or Nm 29:39
your soil—your g, new wine, Dt 7:13
and you will harvest your g, Dt 11:14
tenth of your g, new wine, or Dt 12:17
are to eat a tenth of your g, Dt 14:23

first ⌊put⌋ to the standing **g**. Dt 16:9
him the firstfruits of your **g**, Dt 18:4
your neighbor's standing **g**, Dt 23:25
pluck heads of **g** with your hand, Dt 23:25
a sickle to your neighbor's **g**. Dt 23:25
an ox while it treads out **g**. Dt 25:4
leave you no **g**, new wine, oil, Dt 28:51
in a land of **g** and new wine; Dt 33:28
and roasted **g** from the produce Jos 5:11
offerings and **g** offerings on it, Jos 22:23
for burnt offering, **g** offering, Jos 22:29
young goat and a **g** offering and Jdg 13:19
and the **g** offering from us Jdg 13:23
into the standing **g** of the Jdg 15:5
up the piles of **g** and the Jdg 15:5
and the standing **g** as well as Jdg 15:5
forced to grind **g** in the prison. Jdg 16:21
gather fallen **g** behind someone Ru 2:2
the field to gather ⌊**g**⌋ behind Ru 2:3
me gather fallen **g** among the Ru 2:7
go and gather ⌊**g**⌋ in another Ru 2:8
and he offered her roasted **g**. Ru 2:14
When she got up to gather ⌊**g**⌋, Ru 2:15
let her gather ⌊**g**⌋ among the Ru 2:15
Ruth gathered ⌊**g**⌋ in the field Ru 2:17
She picked up ⌊the **g**⌋ and went Ru 2:18
gathered ⌊**g**⌋ until the barley Ru 2:23
a tenth of your **g** and your 1Sm 8:15
of roasted **g** along with these 1Sm 17:17
of roasted **g**, 100 clusters 1Sm 25:18
and scattered **g** on it so nobody 2Sm 17:19
roasted **g**, beans, lentils, 2Sm 17:28
burnt offering, the **g** offering, 1Kg 8:64
offerings, the **g** offerings, 1Kg 8:64
the time for the **g** offering the 2Kg 3:20
offering and his **g** offering, 2Kg 16:13
the evening **g** offering, 2Kg 16:15
offering and his **g** offering. 2Kg 16:15
of the land, their **g** offering, 2Kg 16:15
land—a land of **g** and new wine, 2Kg 18:32
the wheat for the **g** offering— 1Ch 21:23
fine flour for the **g** offering, 1Ch 23:29
burnt offering, the **g** offering, 2Ch 7:7
liberally of the best of the **g**, 2Ch 31:5
warehouses for the harvest of **g**, 2Ch 32:28
along with their **g** and drink Ezr 7:17
Let us get **g** so that we can eat Neh 5:2
to get **g** during the famine. Neh 5:3
been lending them money and **g**. Neh 5:10
of the money, **g**, new wine, and Neh 5:11
or any kind of **g** to sell on the Neh 10:31
the LORD, the daily **g** offering, Neh 10:33
of our ⌊**g**⌋ offerings, Neh 10:37
to bring the contributions of **g**, Neh 10:39
stored the **g** offerings, Neh 13:5
and the tenths of **g**, new wine, Neh 13:5
along with the **g** offering and Neh 13:9
Judah brought a tenth of the **g**, Neh 13:12
stores of **g** and loading ⌊them⌋ Neh 13:15
They wither like heads of **g**. Jb 24:24
own wife grind ⌊**g**⌋ for another Jb 31:10
to harvest your **g** and bring ⌊it⌋ Jb 39:12
have when their **g** and new wine Ps 4:7
providing ⌊people⌋ with **g**. Ps 65:9
and the valleys covered with **g**. Ps 65:13
be plenty of **g** in the land; Ps 72:16
He gave them **g** from heaven. Ps 78:24
will curse anyone who hoards **g**, Pr 11:26
with a pestle along with **g**, Pr 27:22
appears and the **g** from the hills Pr 27:25
reaper had gathered standing **g**— Is 17:5
arm harvesting the heads of **g**— Is 17:5
gleaned heads of **g** in the valley Is 17:5
revenue was the **g** from Shihor— Is 23:3
LORD will thresh **g** from the Is 27:12
Bread **g** is crushed, but is not Is 28:28
land, a land of **g** and new wine, Is 36:17
you have offered a **g** offering; Is 57:6
give your **g** to your enemies Is 62:8
those who gather **g** will eat it Is 62:9
one offers a **g** offering, one Is 66:3
newly cut **g** after the reaper Jr 9:22
burnt offering and **g** offering, Jr 14:12
g offerings and frankincense, Jr 17:26
what is straw ⌊compared⌋ to **g**?" Jr 23:28
because of the **g**, the new wine, Jr 31:12
to burn **g** offerings, and to Jr 33:18
who were carrying **g** and incense Jr 41:5
cow treading **g** and neigh like Jr 50:11
like mounds of **g** and completely Jr 50:26
Where is the **g** and wine? Lm 2:12
I will summon the **g** and make it Ezk 36:29
offerings—the **g** offerings, sin Ezk 42:13
They will eat the **g** offering, Ezk 44:29
⌊These are⌋ for the **g** offerings, Ezk 45:15
burnt offerings, **g** offerings, Ezk 45:17
offerings, **g** offerings, burnt Ezk 45:17
provide a **g** offering of half Ezk 45:24
burnt offerings, **g** offerings, Ezk 45:25
The **g** offering will be half a Ezk 46:5
the **g** offering with the lambs Ezk 46:5
will provide a **g** offering of Ezk 46:7
the **g** offering will be half a Ezk 46:11
also prepare a **g** offering every Ezk 46:14
a **g** offering to the LORD. Ezk 46:14
offer the lamb, the **g** offering, Ezk 46:15
they will bake the **g** offering, Ezk 46:20
that it is I who gave her the **g**, Hs 2:8
will take back My **g** in its time Hs 2:9
The earth will respond to the **g**, Hs 2:22
slash themselves for **g** and wine; Hs 7:14
There is no standing **g**; Hs 8:7
will grow **g** and blossom like Hs 14:7
G and drink offerings have been Jl 1:9
indeed, the **g** is destroyed; Jl 1:10
because **g** and drink offerings Jl 1:13
because the **g** has withered away. Jl 1:17
⌊so you can⌋ offer **g** and wine to Jl 2:14
about to send you **g**, new wine, Jl 2:19
floors will be full of **g**, Jl 2:24
full of sheaves crushes ⌊**g**⌋. Am 2:13
poor and exact a **g** tax from him, Am 5:11
burnt offerings and **g** offerings, Am 5:22
sacrifices and **g** offerings that Am 5:25
Moon be over so we may sell **g**, Am 8:5
hills, on the **g**, new wine, olive Hg 1:11
someone came to a ⌊**g**⌋ heap of 20 Hg 2:16
G will make the young men Zch 9:17
to pick and eat some heads of **g**. Mt 12:1
plants sprouted and produced **g**, Mt 13:26
way picking some heads of **g**. Mk 2:23
and then the ripe **g** on the head. Mk 4:28
were picking heads of **g**, Lk 6:1
and store all my **g** and my goods Lk 12:18
will be grinding **g** together: Lk 17:35
Unless a **g** of wheat falls into Jn 12:24
heard there was **g** in Egypt, Ac 7:12
ship by throwing the **g** overboard Ac 27:38
an ox while it treads out the **g**. 1Co 9:9
perhaps of wheat or another **g**. 1Co 15:37
an ox that is threshing **g**, 1Tm 5:18
oil, fine wheat flour, and **g**; Rv 18:13

GRAIN-THRESHING *(1)*
a prostitute on every **g** floor. Hs 9:1

GRAINFIELDS *(3)*
through the **g** on the Sabbath. Mt 12:1
He was going through the **g**, Mk 2:23
He passed through the **g**. Lk 6:1

GRAINS *(4)*
with the choicest **g** of wheat; Dt 32:14
would outnumber the **g** of sand; Ps 139:18
of your body like its **g**; Is 48:19
as innumerable as the **g** of sand Heb 11:12

GRANARIES *(2)*
places. Open her **g**; pile her up Jr 50:26
and the **g** are broken down, Jl 1:17

GRANARY *(1)*
there still seed left in the **g**? Hg 2:19

GRAND *(2)*
g and lovely ones without Is 5:9
Levi hosted a **g** banquet for Him Lk 5:29

GRANDCHILDREN *(11)*
let me kiss my **g** and my Gn 31:28
children, and **g**, your sheep, Gn 45:10
the children and **g** to the third Ex 34:7
to your children and your **g**. Dt 4:9
children and **g** and have been Dt 4:25
children and **g** continue doing as 2Kg 17:41
His righteousness toward the **g** Ps 103:17
leaves an inheritance to his **g**, Pr 13:22
G are the crown of the elderly, Pr 17:6
with their children and **g**, Ezk 37:25
if any widow has children or **g**, 1Tm 5:4

GRANDDAUGHTER *(4)*
of Anah and **g** of Zibeon the Gn 36:2
of Anah and **g** of Zibeon: Gn 36:14
was Athaliah, **g** of Israel's King 2Kg 8:26
name was Athaliah, **g** of Omri. 2Ch 22:2

GRANDDAUGHTERS *(1)*
daughters and **g**, indeed all his Gn 46:7

GRANDFATHER *(1)*
to you all your **g** Saul's fields, 2Sm 9:7

GRANDFATHER'S *(2)*
and to all his maternal **g** clan, Jdg 9:1
For my **g** entire family deserves 2Sm 19:28

GRANDMOTHER *(3)*
also removed his **g** Maacah from 1Kg 15:13
Maacah, his **g**, from being queen 2Ch 15:16
that first lived in your **g** Lois, 2Tm 1:5

GRANDMOTHER'S *(1)*
His **g** name was Maacah daughter 1Kg 15:10

GRANDSON *(9)*
Abram, his **g** Lot (Haran's son) Gn 11:31
your son and **g** how severely I Ex 10:2
son, and your **g**, and so that you Dt 6:2
to your master's **g** all that 2Sm 9:9
your master's **g** will have food 2Sm 9:10
your master's **g**, is always to 2Sm 9:10
Saul's **g**, also went down to 2Sm 19:24
He is the **g** of Jehoshaphat who 2Ch 22:9
and his **g** until the time for his Jr 27:7

GRANDSONS *(5)*
kissed his **g** and daughters, Gn 31:55
sons and **g**, his daughters and Gn 46:7
as well as your sons and your **g**, Jdg 8:22
40 sons and 30 **g**, who rode on 70 Jdg 12:14
They had many sons and **g**— 1Ch 8:40

GRANT *(34)*
I'll **g** your request about this Gn 19:21
he prayed, "**g** me success today, Gn 24:12
and brothers, "**G** me this favor, Gn 34:11
I **g** him My covenant of peace. Nm 25:12
burning anger and **g** you mercy, Dt 13:17
The LORD will **g** you a blessing Dt 28:8
the God of Israel **g** the petition 1Sm 1:17
the king will **g** his servant's 2Sm 14:15
Joab, "I hereby **g** this request. 2Sm 14:21
g me wisdom and knowledge so 2Ch 1:10
them but will **g** them a little 2Ch 12:7
that they will **g** me ⌊safe⌋ Neh 2:7
the One who will **g** us success. Neh 2:20
the king to **g** my petition Est 5:8
Only **g** ⌊these⌋ two things to me, Jb 13:20
LORD, please **g** us success! Ps 118:25
do not **g** the desires of the Ps 140:8
for I will not **g** you grace. Jr 16:13
I will **g** you compassion, and he Jr 42:12
'but I will **g** you your life like Jr 45:5
I will also **g** you access among Zch 3:7
He is worthy for You to **g** this, Lk 7:4
Will not God **g** justice to His Lk 18:7
He will swiftly **g** them justice. Lk 18:8
Pilate decided to **g** their demand Lk 23:24
and **g** that Your slaves may speak Ac 4:29
to **g** repentance to Israel, Ac 5:31
I will **g** you the faithful Ac 13:34
also with Him **g** us everything? Rm 8:32
encouragement **g** you agreement Rm 15:5
⌊I pray⌋ that He may **g** you, Eph 3:16
May the Lord **g** mercy to the 2Tm 1:16
May the Lord **g** that he obtain 2Tm 1:18
God will **g** them repentance 2Tm 2:25

GRANTED *(27)*
g him favor in the eyes of the Gn 39:21
said and have **g** your request." 1Sm 25:35
the LORD has **g** vengeance to my 2Sm 4:8
the king has **g** the request of 2Sm 14:22
And God **g** his request. 1Ch 4:10
He **g** their request because they 1Ch 5:20
his petition and **g** his request, 2Ch 33:13
and how God **g** his request, 2Ch 33:19
The king had **g** him everything he Ezr 7:6
this, and He **g** our request. Ezr 8:23
The king **g** my ⌊requests⌋, Neh 2:8
request would be **g** and God would Jb 6:8
and their father **g** them an Jb 42:15
I have **g** help to a warrior; Ps 89:19
God had **g** Daniel favor and Dn 1:9
of life was **g** to them for a Dn 7:12

the prophets and g many visions; Hs 12:10
that it be g because of his Mt 14:9
of God has been g to you, Mk 4:11
and He g sight to many blind Lk 7:21
so also He has g to the Son to Jn 5:26
And He has g Him the right to Jn 5:27
to Me unless it is g to him by Jn 6:65
So God has g repentance Ac 11:18
grace of God g to the churches 2Co 8:1
Now g, I have not burdened you; 2Co 12:16
but God g it to Abraham through Gl 3:18

GRANTING *(2)*
the LORD your God is g you as an Dt 19:3
of His grace by g that signs and Ac 14:3

GRAPE *(12)*
will continue until g harvest, Lv 26:5
and the g harvest will continue Lv 26:5
not drink any g juice or eat Nm 6:3
blossom becomes a ripening g, Is 18:5
a gleaning after a g harvest. Is 24:13
once more like a g gatherer over Jr 6:9
your summer fruit and g harvest. Jr 48:32
If g harvesters came to you, Jr 49:9
If g pickers came to you, Ob 5
the gleaning of the g harvest— Mc 7:1
⌊finds⌋ no g cluster to eat, Mc 7:1
When the g harvest drew near, Mt 21:34

GRAPES *(42)*
and its clusters ripened into g. Gn 40:10
and I took the g, squeezed them Gn 40:11
and his robes in the blood of g. Gn 49:11
bare or gather its fallen g. Lv 19:10
harvest the g of your untended Lv 25:5
juice or eat fresh g or raisins. Nm 6:3
the season for the first ripe g. Nm 13:20
with a single cluster of g, Nm 13:23
cluster ⌊of g⌋ the Israelites Nm 13:24
may eat as many g as you want Dt 23:24
you gather the g of your Dt 24:21
the wine or gather ⌊the g⌋, Dt 28:39
drank wine from the finest g. Dt 32:14
Their g are poisonous; Dt 32:32
and harvested g from their Jdg 9:27
They trod the g and held a Jdg 9:27
along with wine, g, and figs. Neh 13:15
drops its unripe g and like an Jb 15:33
breasts be like clusters of g, Sg 7:8
He expected it to yield good g, Is 5:2
but it yielded worthless g. Is 5:2
I expected a yield of good g, Is 5:4
did it yield worthless g? Is 5:4
No one tramples g in the Is 16:10
harvest the g will drink ⌊the Is 62:9
wine is found in a bunch of g, Is 65:8
There will be no g on the vine, Jr 8:13
those who tread ⌊g⌋, against all Jr 25:30
The fathers have eaten sour g, Jr 31:29
who eats sour g—his own teeth Jr 31:30
Judah ⌊like g⌋ in a winepress. Lm 1:15
fathers eat sour g, and the Ezk 18:2
Israel like g in the wilderness. Hs 9:10
Come and trample ⌊the g⌋ because Jl 3:13
reaper and the one who treads g, Am 9:13
wouldn't they leave some g? Ob 5
you will tread⌋ g but not drink Mc 6:15
Are g gathered from thornbushes Mt 7:16
or g picked from a bramble bush. Lk 6:44
the clusters of g from earth's Rv 14:18
because its g have ripened." Rv 14:18
and gathered the g from earth's Rv 14:19

GRAPEVINE *(9)*
eat anything produced by the g, Nm 6:4
said to the g, "Come and reign Jdg 9:12
But the g said to them, "Should Jdg 9:13
comes from the g or drink wine Jdg 13:14
devastated My g and splintered Jl 1:7
The g is dried up, and the fig Jl 1:12
the fig tree and g yield their Jl 2:22
sit under his g and under his Mc 4:4
brothers, or a g ⌊produce⌋ figs? Jms 3:12

GRAPEVINES *(1)*
and the g of Sibmah have Is 16:8

GRASP *(19)*
us from the g of our enemies, 2Sm 19:9
us from the g of the Philistines 2Sm 19:9
the kingdom was firmly in his g, 2Kg 14:5
the kingdom was firmly in his g, 2Ch 25:3
escaped from the g of the kings 2Ch 30:6
me from the g of the ruthless? Jb 6:23
he flees desperately from its g. Jb 27:22
from the g of the unjust and Ps 71:4
in Egypt did not g ⌊the Ps 106:7
me free from the g of foreigners Ps 144:7
me from the g of foreigners Ps 144:11
with wine and how to g folly— Ec 2:3
good that you g the one and do Ec 7:18
They g bow and javelin. Jr 6:23
They g bow and javelin. Jr 50:42
so that they could not g it, Lk 9:45
they did not g what was said. Lk 18:34
Him, yet He eluded their g. Jn 10:39
me from Herod's g and from all Ac 12:11

GRASPED *(5)*
mind has thoroughly g wisdom and Ec 1:16
hand I have g to subdue nations Is 45:1
polished, to be g in the hand. Ezk 21:11
When Israel g you by the hand, Ezk 29:7
In the womb he g his brother's Hs 12:3

GRASPING *(1)*
came out g Esau's heel with Gn 25:26

GRASPS *(1)*
wind and g oil with his right Pr 27:16

GRASS *(54)*
I will provide g in your fields Dt 11:15
gentle rain on new g and showers Dt 32:2
glisten of rain on sprouting g." 2Sm 23:4
we'll find g so we can keep 1Kg 18:5
of the field, tender g, grass on 2Kg 19:26
tender grass, g on the rooftops, 2Kg 19:26
like the g of the earth. Jb 5:25
bray over fresh g or an ox low Jb 6:5
and cause the g to sprout? Jb 38:27
with you. He eats g like an ox. Jb 40:15
quickly like g and wilt like Ps 37:2
rain that falls on the cut g, Ps 72:6
cities like the g of the field. Ps 72:16
They are like g that grows in Ps 90:5
sprout like g and all evildoers Ps 92:7
is afflicted, withered like g; Ps 102:4
and I wither away like g. Ps 102:11
days are like g—he blooms like Ps 103:15
He causes g to grow for the Ps 104:14
them be like g on the rooftops Ps 129:6
and causes g to grow on the Ps 147:8
his favor is like dew on the g. Pr 19:12
straw and as dry g shrivels in Is 5:24
the g is withered, the foliage Is 15:6
there will be g, reeds, and Is 35:7
of the field, tender g, grass on Is 37:27
tender grass, g on the rooftops, Is 37:27
All humanity is g, and all its Is 40:6
The g withers, the flowers fade Is 40:7
indeed, the people are g. Is 40:7
The g withers, the flowers fade, Is 40:8
sprout among the g like poplars Is 44:4
of man who is given up like g? Is 51:12
and you will flourish like g; Is 66:14
mourn and the g of every field Jr 12:4
her fawn⌋ since there is no g. Jr 14:5
in the tender g of the field. Dn 4:15
in the tender g of the field. Dn 4:23
You will feed on g like cattle Dn 4:25
will feed on g like cattle for Dn 4:32
He ate g like cattle, and his Dn 4:33
he was fed g like cattle, Dn 5:21
showers on the g, which do not Mc 5:7
God clothes the g of the field, Mt 6:30
the crowds to sit down on the g. Mt 14:19
down in groups on the green g. Mk 6:39
If that's how God clothes the g, Lk 12:28
was plenty of g in that place, Jn 6:10
heat and dries up the g; Jms 1:11
All flesh is like g, and all its 1Pt 1:24
glory like a flower of the g. 1Pt 1:24
The g withers, and the flower 1Pt 1:24
all the green g was burned up. Rv 8:7
not to harm the g of the earth, Rv 9:4

GRASS-EATING *(1)*
glory for the image of a g ox. Ps 106:20

GRASSHOPPER *(5)*
and the various kinds of g. Lv 11:22
locust, or g, when their enemy 1Kg 8:37
mildew, locust, or g, when their 2Ch 6:28
I command the g to consume the 2Ch 7:13
blossoms, the g loses its spring Ec 12:5

GRASSHOPPERS *(2)*
To ourselves we seemed like g, Nm 13:33
its inhabitants are like g. Is 40:22

GRATE *(6)*
Construct a g for it of bronze Ex 27:4
offering with its bronze g, Ex 35:16
for the altar a g of bronze mesh Ex 38:4
of the bronze g he cast four Ex 38:5
bronze altar and its bronze g, Ex 38:30
bronze altar with its bronze g, Ex 39:39

GRATEFUL *(1)*
Judah was g to the priests Neh 12:44

GRATEFULLY *(1)*
we g receive them always and in Ac 24:3

GRATIFIED *(1)*
desire will be g at their Ex 15:9

GRATIFY *(1)*
Then, willing to g the crowd, Mk 15:15

GRATING *(6)*
the one g to cover the capital 1Kg 7:18
rounded surface next to the g, 1Kg 7:20
for each g covering both 1Kg 7:42
by a g and pomegranates 2Kg 25:17
was the same, with its own g. 2Kg 25:17
for each g covering both 2Ch 4:13

GRATINGS *(5)*
pillars had g of latticework, 1Kg 7:17
two g for covering both bowls 1Kg 7:41
400 pomegranates for the two g 1Kg 7:42
two g for covering both bowls 2Ch 4:12
400 pomegranates for the two g 2Ch 4:13

GRATITUDE *(3)*
glorify Him as God or show g. Rm 1:21
with g in your hearts to God. Col 3:16
be received with g by those who 1Tm 4:3

GRAVE *(32)*
Jacob set up a marker on her g; Gn 35:20
at Rachel's g to this day. Gn 35:20
led them into ⌊such⌋ a g sin?" Ex 32:21
bone, or a g, will be unclean Nm 19:16
touched a bone, a g, a corpse, Nm 19:18
this day knows where his g is. Dt 34:6
two men at Rachel's G at Zelzah 1Sm 10:2
I've committed a g error." 1Sm 26:21
reach the g of your fathers 1Kg 13:22
he laid the corpse in his own g, 1Kg 13:30
bury me in the g where the man 1Kg 13:31
sons⌋ will come to the g, 1Kg 14:13
be gathered to your g in peace. 2Kg 22:20
be gathered to your g in peace. 2Ch 34:28
are glad when they reach the g? Jb 3:22
approach the g in full vigor, Jb 5:26
soon I will lie down in the g. Jb 7:21
carried from the womb to the g. Jb 10:19
will lie down with him in the g. Jb 20:11
is carried to the g, and someone Jb 21:32
dirt on his g is sweet to him Jb 21:33
imprison them in the g. Jb 40:13
their throat is an open g; Ps 5:9
like the slain lying in the g, Ps 88:5
love be declared in the g, Ps 88:11
you are thrown out without a g, Is 14:19
They made His g with the wicked, Is 53:9
Their quiver is like an open g; Jr 5:16
my mother might have been my g, Jr 20:17
all her hordes around her g. Ezk 32:24
will prepare your g, for you are Nah 1:14
Their throat is an open g; Rm 3:13

GRAVEL *(2)*
his mouth is full of g. Pr 20:17
my teeth on g and made me cower Lm 3:16

GRAVEN *(1)*
Me to anger with their g images, Jr 8:19

GRAVES *(14)*
there are no g in Egypt that you Ex 14:11
its dust on the g of the common 2Kg 23:6
over the g of those who had 2Ch 34:4
Their g are their eternal homes, Ps 49:11
among the g, spending nights Is 65:4
will be brought out of their g. Jr 8:1
her g are all around her. Ezk 32:22
Her g are set in the deepest Ezk 32:23
Her g are all around her. Ezk 32:25

Their **g** are all around them. Ezk 32:26
to open your **g** and bring you up Ezk 37:12
I open your **g** and bring you up Ezk 37:13
You are like unmarked **g**; Lk 11:44
who are in the **g** will hear His Jn 5:28

GRAVEYARD *(1)*
are extinguished. A **g** awaits me. Jb 17:1

GRAY *(11)*
you will bring my **g** hairs down Gn 42:38
you will bring my **g** hairs down Gn 44:29
have brought the **g** hairs of your Gn 44:31
me, I'm old and **g**, and my sons 1Sm 12:2
do not let his **g** head descend to 1Kg 2:6
him to bring his **g** head down to 1Kg 2:9
when I am old and **g**, God, do not Ps 71:18
G hair is a glorious crown; Pr 16:31
splendor of old men is **g** hair. Pr 20:29
bear ⌊you⌋ up when you turn **g**. Is 46:4
his hair is streaked with **g**, Hs 7:9

GRAY-HAIRED *(2)*
the infant and the **g** man. Dt 32:25
Both the **g** and the elderly are Jb 15:10

GRAZE *(11)*
then go out and let them **g**." Gn 29:7
and began to **g** among the reeds. Gn 41:2
and began to **g** among the reeds. Gn 41:18
to go and **g** in someone else's Ex 22:5
are not to **g** in front of that Ex 34:3
Lambs will **g** as ⌊if in⌋ their Is 5:17
for oxen to **g** and for sheep to Is 7:25
The cow and the bear will **g**, Is 11:7
Calves will **g** there, and there Is 27:10
cattle will **g** in open pastures Is 30:23
Let them **g** in Bashan and Gilead Mc 7:14

GRAZED *(2)*
lets a field or vineyard be **g** Ex 22:5
of the herds that **g** in Sharon, 1Ch 27:29

GRAZING *(16)*
there is no **g** land for your Gn 47:4
and the donkeys **g** nearby, Jb 1:14
over the wilderness **g** land, Jr 9:10
return them to their **g** land. Jr 23:3
the **g** lands in the wilderness Jr 23:10
He roars loudly over His **g** land; Jr 25:30
Peaceful **g** land will become Jr 25:37
will once more be a **g** land where Jr 33:12
the perennially watered **g** land. Jr 49:19
and their **g** land will be made Jr 49:20
their righteous **g** land, the hope Jr 50:7
return Israel to his **g** land, Jr 50:19
the perennially watered **g** land. Jr 50:44
certainly the **g** land will be Jr 50:45
and their **g** place will be on Ezk 34:14
will lie down in a good **g** place; Ezk 34:14

GREAT *(587)*
God made the two **g** lights— Gn 1:16
My punishment is too **g** to bear! Gn 4:13
Nineveh and the **g** city Calah. Gn 10:12
I will make you into a **g** nation, Gn 12:2
make your name **g**, and you will Gn 12:2
your reward will be very **g**. Gn 15:1
terror and **g** darkness descended Gn 15:12
I will make him into a **g** nation. Gn 17:20
is to become a **g** and powerful Gn 18:18
its people is **g** before the LORD, Gn 19:13
You have shown me **g** kindness by Gn 19:19
Abraham held a **g** feast on the Gn 21:8
for I will make him a **g** nation." Gn 21:18
I could do you **g** harm, but last Gn 31:29
could I do such a **g** evil and sin Gn 39:9
Seven years of **g** abundance are Gn 41:29
you alive by a **g** deliverance. Gn 45:7
will make you a **g** nation there. Gn 46:3
a tribe, and he too will be **g**; Gn 48:19
arm and **g** acts of judgment. Ex 6:6
of Egypt by **g** acts of judgment Ex 7:4
there will be a **g** cry of anguish Ex 11:6
Israel saw the **g** power that the Ex 14:31
adversaries by Your **g** majesty. Ex 15:7
will make you into a **g** nation." Ex 32:10
of Egypt with **g** power and a Ex 32:11
from Your **g** anger and change Ex 32:12
You have committed a **g** sin. Ex 32:30
people has committed a **g** sin; Ex 32:31
we saw in it are men of **g** size. Nm 13:32
so that a **g** amount of water Nm 20:11
God to do ⌊anything⌋ small or **g**. Nm 22:18
"What ⌊**g** things⌋ God has done!" Nm 23:23
listen to small and **g** alike. Dt 1:17
across all the **g** and terrible Dt 1:19
a **g** and numerous people as tall Dt 2:10
a **g** and numerous people, tall as Dt 2:21
'This **g** nation is indeed a wise Dt 4:6
For what **g** nation is there that Dt 4:7
And what **g** nation has righteous Dt 4:8
anything like this **g** event Dt 4:32
arm, by **g** terrors, as the LORD Dt 4:34
showed you His **g** fire on earth, Dt 4:36
by His presence and **g** power, Dt 4:37
This **g** fire will consume us and Dt 5:25
LORD inflicted **g** and devastating Dt 6:22
the **g** trials that you saw, Dt 7:19
your God, a **g** and awesome God Dt 7:21
them into **g** confusion until Dt 7:23
you through the **g** and terrible Dt 8:15
brought out by Your **g** power and Dt 9:29
Lord of lords, the **g**, mighty, Dt 10:17
for you these **g** and awesome Dt 10:21
have seen every **g** work the LORD Dt 11:7
distance is too **g** for you to Dt 14:24
or see this **g** fire any longer Dt 18:16
him because the distance is **g**, Dt 19:6
There he became a **g**, powerful, Dt 26:5
own eyes the **g** trials and those Dt 29:3
trials and those **g** signs and Dt 29:3
Why this **g** outburst of anger?' Dt 29:24
fury, and **g** wrath, and threw Dt 29:28
Lebanon to the **g** Euphrates River Jos 1:4
the people gave a **g** shout, Jos 6:20
will You do about Your **g** name?" Jos 7:9
defeated them in a **g** slaughter Jos 10:10
pursuing them as far as **G** Sidon Jos 11:8
but a **g** deal of the land remains Jos 13:1
have many people and **g** strength. Jos 17:17
and Kanah, as far as **G** Sidon. Jos 19:28
to your homes with **g** wealth: Jos 22:8
has driven out **g** and powerful Jos 23:9
performed these **g** signs before Jos 24:17
all the LORD's **g** works He had Jdg 2:7
There was **g** searching of heart Jdg 5:15
There was **g** searching of heart Jdg 5:16
tents like a **g** swarm of locusts Jdg 6:5
the Gileadite was a **g** warrior, Jdg 11:1
their cities with a **g** slaughter Jdg 11:33
You have brought **g** misery on me. Jdg 11:35
from limb with a **g** slaughter, Jdg 15:8
this **g** victory through Jdg 15:18
you where his **g** strength comes Jdg 16:5
where does your **g** strength ⌊come Jdg 16:6
what makes your strength so **g**!" Jdg 16:15
to offer a **g** sacrifice to their Jdg 16:23
they sent up a **g** cloud of smoke Jdg 20:38
For a **g** oath had been taken Jdg 21:5
there was a **g** slaughter among 1Sm 4:17
city of Gath, causing a **g** panic. 1Sm 5:9
struck them with a **g** slaughter. 1Sm 6:19
and see this **g** thing that the 1Sm 12:16
and see what a **g** evil you 1Sm 12:17
of His **g** name and because 1Sm 12:22
considering the **g** things He has 1Sm 12:24
each other in **g** confusion! 1Sm 14:20
such a **g** deliverance for 1Sm 14:45
have been a **g** advantage to you. 1Sm 19:4
brought about a **g** victory for 1Sm 19:5
with such a **g** force that they 1Sm 19:8
do anything, **g** or small, without 1Sm 20:2
certainly do **g** things and will 1Sm 26:25
because of the **g** amount of 1Sm 30:16
must know that a **g** leader has 2Sm 3:38
all these **g** things to Your 2Sm 7:21
This is why You are **g**, Lord GOD. 2Sm 7:22
for them **g** and awesome acts 2Sm 7:23
worse than the **g** wrong you've 2Sm 13:16
were at the **g** stone in Gibeon 2Sm 20:8
brought about a **g** victory that 2Sm 23:10
LORD brought about a **g** victory. 2Sm 23:12
answered Gad, "I have **g** anxiety. 2Sm 24:14
hands because His mercies are **g**, 2Sm 24:14
with such a **g** joy that the earth 1Kg 1:40
You have shown **g** and faithful 1Kg 3:6
continued this **g** and faithful 1Kg 3:6
to judge this **g** people of Yours? 1Kg 3:9
because she felt **g** compassion 1Kg 3:26
g cities with walls and bronze 1Kg 4:13
Solomon wisdom, very **g** insight, 1Kg 4:29
son to be over this **g** people!" 1Kg 5:7
the outside to the **g** courtyard. 1Kg 7:9
Around the **g** courtyard, as well 1Kg 7:12
had **g** skill, understanding, 1Kg 7:14
they will hear of Your **g** name, 1Kg 8:42
Israel with him—a **g** assembly, 1Kg 8:65
spices, gold in **g** abundance, and 1Kg 10:2
tons of gold, a **g** quantity of 1Kg 10:10
A **g** and mighty wind was tearing 1Kg 19:11
He inflicted a **g** slaughter on 1Kg 20:21
G wrath was on the Israelites, 2Kg 3:27
a **g** man in his master's sight 2Kg 5:1
had told you to do some **g** thing, 2Kg 5:13
he prepared a **g** feast for them. 2Kg 6:23
So there was a **g** famine in 2Kg 6:25
chariots, horses, and a **g** army. 2Kg 7:6
Tell me all the **g** things Elisha 2Kg 8:4
Jezreel—all his **g** men, close 2Kg 10:11
for I have a **g** sacrifice for 2Kg 10:19
Offer on the **g** altar the morning 2Kg 16:15
and caused them to commit **g** sin. 2Kg 17:21
the land of Egypt with **g** power 2Kg 17:36
this is what the **g** king, 2Kg 18:19
Hear the word of the **g** king, 2Kg 18:28
He did a **g** amount of evil in the 2Kg 21:6
For **g** is the LORD's wrath that 2Kg 22:13
of His **g** wrath and anger, 2Kg 23:26
he burned down all the **g** houses. 2Kg 25:9
to become a **g** warrior on earth 1Ch 1:10
the LORD gave them a **g** victory. 1Ch 11:14
David until there was a **g** army, 1Ch 12:22
For the LORD is **g** and is highly 1Ch 16:25
known all these **g** ⌊promises⌋ 1Ch 17:19
Yourself through **g** and awesome 1Ch 17:21
answered Gad, "I have **g** anxiety. 1Ch 21:13
because His mercies are very **g**, 1Ch 21:13
supplied a **g** deal of iron to 1Ch 22:3
must be exceedingly **g** and famous 1Ch 22:5
much blood and waged **g** wars. 1Ch 22:8
I have taken **g** pains to provide 1Ch 22:14
The task is **g**, for the temple 1Ch 29:1
and a **g** quantity of marble. 1Ch 29:2
Your hand to make **g** and to give 1Ch 29:12
and drank with **g** joy in the 1Ch 29:22
You have shown **g** faithful love 2Ch 1:8
judge this **g** people of Yours? 2Ch 1:10
that I am building will be **g**, 2Ch 2:5
will be **g** and wonderful. 2Ch 2:9
utensils in such **g** abundance 2Ch 4:18
because of Your **g** name and Your 2Ch 6:32
with him—a very **g** assembly, 2Ch 7:8
even told half of your **g** wisdom! 2Ch 9:6
tons of gold, a **g** quantity of 2Ch 9:9
carried off a **g** supply of loot. 2Ch 14:13
there was a **g** deal of plunder 2Ch 14:14
from Israel in **g** numbers when 2Ch 15:9
then they made a **g** fire in his 2Ch 16:14
and carried out **g** works in the 2Ch 17:13
small or **g**, except the king 2Ch 18:30
and took a **g** deal of plunder. 2Ch 25:13
who struck him with **g** force: 2Ch 28:5
also took a **g** deal of plunder 2Ch 28:8
Bread seven days with **g** joy, 2Ch 30:21
He did a **g** deal of evil in the 2Ch 33:6
For **g** is the LORD's wrath that 2Ch 34:21
all the people from **g** to small. 2Ch 34:30
people gave a **g** shout of praise Ezr 3:11
whom the **g** and illustrious Ezr 4:10
the house of the **g** God in the Ezr 5:8
which a **g** king of Israel built Ezr 5:11
but His **g** anger is against all Ezr 8:22
are in **g** trouble and disgrace. Neh 1:3
the **g** and awe-inspiring God who Neh 1:5
them⌋ by Your **g** power and strong Neh 1:10
opposite the **g** tower that juts Neh 3:27
Remember the **g** and awe-inspiring Neh 4:14
I am doing a **g** work and cannot Neh 6:3
the LORD, the **g** God, and with Neh 8:6
and have a **g** celebration, Neh 8:12
because of Your **g** compassion. Neh 9:19
delighted in Your **g** goodness. Neh 9:25
So now, our God—the **g**, mighty, Neh 9:32
please. We are in **g** distress. Neh 9:37
day they offered **g** sacrifices Neh 12:43
God had given them **g** joy. Neh 12:43
king held a **g** banquet for all Est 2:18
There was **g** mourning among the Est 4:3

with a g golden crown and a Est 8:15
exercised⌋ g power in the palace Est 9:4
of Mordecai's g rank to which Est 10:2
the small and the g are there, Jb 3:19
He does g and unsearchable Jb 5:9
He performs g and unsearchable Jb 9:10
makes nations g, then destroys Jb 12:23
is distorted with g force; Jb 30:18
my wealth is g or because my own Jb 31:25
He does g things that we cannot Jb 37:5
gives g victories to His king; Ps 18:50
there is g reward in keeping Ps 19:11
His glory is g through Your Ps 21:5
praise in the g congregation Ps 22:25
forgive my sin, for it is g. Ps 25:11
How g is Your goodness that You Ps 31:19
When g floodwaters come, they Ps 32:6
not be delivered by g strength. Ps 33:16
no escape by its g power. Ps 33:17
You in the g congregation; Ps 35:18
righteousness in the g assembly; Ps 40:9
and truth from the g assembly. Ps 40:10
continually say, The LORD is g!" Ps 40:16
a g King over all the earth. Ps 47:2
The LORD is g and is highly Ps 48:1
north is the city of the g King. Ps 48:2
You because of Your g strength. Ps 66:3
a g company of women brought the Ps 68:11
keeping with Your g compassion, Ps 69:16
continually say, "God is g!" Ps 70:4
You who have done g things; Ps 71:19
His name is g in Israel. Ps 76:1
What god is g like God? Ps 77:13
Your path through the g waters, Ps 77:19
according to Your g power, Ps 79:11
For You are g and perform Ps 86:10
Your faithful love for me is g, Ps 86:13
the LORD is a g God, a great Ps 95:3
a great God, a g King above all Ps 95:3
For the LORD is g and is highly Ps 96:4
The LORD is g in Zion; Ps 99:2
them praise Your g and Ps 99:3
so g is His faithful love toward Ps 103:11
⌊all⌋ His angels of g strength, Ps 103:20
LORD my God, You are very g; Ps 104:1
who did g things in Egypt, Ps 106:21
works are g, studied by all Ps 111:2
taking g delight in His Ps 112:1
the LORD—small and g alike. Ps 115:13
g is His faithful love to us; Ps 117:2
LORD has done g things for them. Ps 126:2
LORD had done g things for us; Ps 126:3
with things too g or too Ps 131:1
For I know that the LORD is g; Ps 135:5
He alone does g wonders. Ps 136:4
made the g lights: His love is Ps 136:7
He struck down g kings His love Ps 136:17
for the LORD's glory is g. Ps 138:5
Yahweh is g and is highly Ps 145:3
of Your g goodness and will Ps 145:7
to anger and g in faithful love Ps 145:8
Our Lord is g, vast in power; Ps 147:5
lost because of his g stupidity. Pr 5:23
to be poor but has g wealth. Pr 13:7
person ⌊shows⌋ g understanding, Pr 14:29
of the righteous has g wealth, Pr 15:6
of the LORD than g treasure with Pr 15:16
righteousness than g income with Pr 16:8
man and brings him before the g. Pr 18:16
A person with g anger bears the Pr 19:19
is to be chosen over g wealth; Pr 22:1
stand in the place of the g; Pr 25:6
triumph, there is g rejoicing, Pr 28:12
I became g and surpassed all who Ec 2:9
too is futile and a g wrong. Ec 2:21
A g king came against it, Ec 9:14
calmness puts g offenses to rest Ec 10:4
fool is appointed to g heights, Ec 10:6
leaving g emptiness in the land. Is 6:12
LORD said to me with g power, Is 8:11
in darkness have seen a g light; Is 9:2
with His harsh, g, and strong Is 27:1
On that day a g trumpet will be Is 27:13
advice; He gives g wisdom. Is 28:29
those who go to g lengths to Is 29:15
on the day of g slaughter when Is 30:25
chariots and in the g strength Is 31:1
a g slaughter in the land of Is 34:6
and the g owl and the raven will Is 34:11
The g king, the king of Assyria, Is 36:4
to the words of the g king, Is 36:13
that I had such g bitterness; Is 38:17
Because of His g power and Is 40:26
waters of the g deep, who made Is 51:10
take you back with g compassion. Is 54:7
their prosperity will be g, Is 54:13
up proudly in His g might? Is 63:1
lye and use a g amount of soap, Jr 2:22
the north—a g destruction. Jr 4:6
the north, even g destruction. Jr 6:1
a g nation will be awakened from Jr 6:22
like You. You are g; Your name Jr 10:6
Your name is g in power. Jr 10:6
a g commotion from the land to Jr 10:22
consumed with a g roaring sound. Jr 11:16
I will ruin the g pride of both Jr 13:9
because of your g guilt that Jr 13:22
been destroyed by a g disaster, Jr 14:17
g and small will die in this Jr 16:6
all this g disaster against Jr 16:10
to you," bringing him g joy. Jr 20:15
with anger, rage, and g wrath. Jr 21:5
They will die in a g plague. Jr 21:6
do such a thing to this g city? Jr 22:8
many nations and g kings will Jr 25:14
A g storm is stirred up from the Jr 25:32
about to bring g harm on Jr 26:19
My g strength and outstretched Jr 27:5
many nations and g kings will Jr 27:7
many lands and g kingdoms. Jr 28:8
return here as a g assembly! Jr 31:8
earth by Your g power and with Jr 32:17
g and mighty God whose name is Jr 32:18
the One g in counsel and mighty Jr 32:19
arm, and with g terror. Jr 32:21
rage, and g fury, and I will Jr 32:37
brought all this g disaster on Jr 32:42
you and tell you g and wondrous Jr 33:3
against this people are g." Jr 36:7
and harvested a g amount of wine Jr 40:12
him by the g pool in Gibeon. Jr 41:12
you doing such g harm to Jr 44:7
standing by—a g assembly—and Jr 44:15
'I have sworn by My g name, Jr 44:26
do you seek g things for Jr 45:5
devastation and g disaster! Jr 48:3
Moab's pride, g pride, indeed— Jr 48:29
assembly of g nations from the Jr 50:9
in the land—a g destruction. Jr 50:22
g nation and many kings will be Jr 50:41
The sound of g destruction from Jr 51:54
She who was g among the nations Lm 1:1
g is Your faithfulness! Lm 3:23
g cloud with fire flashing back Ezk 1:4
and I heard a g rumbling sound Ezk 3:12
beside them, a g rumbling sound. Ezk 3:13
g abominations that the house Ezk 8:6
Israel and Judah is extremely g; Ezk 9:9
A g eagle with great wings, Ezk 17:3
A great eagle with g wings, Ezk 17:3
was another g eagle with great Ezk 17:7
eagle with g wings and thick Ezk 17:7
G strength and many people will Ezk 17:9
him with ⌊his⌋ g army and vast Ezk 17:17
a sword for g massacre—it Ezk 21:14
I will execute g vengeance Ezk 25:17
of ⌊your⌋ g wealth of every Ezk 27:12
and your g wealth of every Ezk 27:18
By your g skill in trading you Ezk 28:5
g monster lying in the middle Ezk 29:3
all the g nations lived in its Ezk 31:6
Since it became g in height and Ezk 31:10
would become g in height and set Ezk 31:14
honor the holiness of My g name, Ezk 36:23
There were a g many of them on Ezk 37:2
possessions, to seize g spoil? Ezk 38:13
day there will be a g earthquake Ezk 38:19
a g feast on the mountains of Ezk 39:17
me into the g hall and measured Ezk 41:1
the length of the g hall, Ezk 41:2
the room adjacent to the g hall, Ezk 41:4
The interior of the g hall and Ezk 41:15
and on the wall of the g hall. Ezk 41:20
of the g hall were square Ezk 41:21
g hall and the sanctuary each Ezk 41:23
doors of the g hall like those Ezk 41:25
those facing the g hall were 175 Ezk 42:8
a reward, and g honor from me. Dn 2:6
no king, however g and powerful, Dn 2:10
statue became a g mountain and Dn 2:35
The g God has told the king what Dn 2:45
How g are His miracles, and how Dn 4:3
the earth, and its height was g. Dn 4:10
you have become g and strong: Dn 4:22
not Babylon the G that I have Dn 4:30
held a g feast for 1,000 Dn 5:1
of heaven stirred up the g sea. Dn 7:2
whatever he wanted and became g. Dn 8:4
the male goat became very g, Dn 8:8
It made itself g, even up to the Dn 8:11
power will be g, but it will not Dn 8:24
own mind he will make himself g. Dn 8:25
the g and awe-inspiring God who Dn 9:4
on us so g a disaster that Dn 9:12
true and was about a g conflict. Dn 10:1
on the bank of the g river, Dn 10:4
but a g terror fell on them, Dn 10:7
alone, looking at this g vision. Dn 10:8
who will raise a g multitude, Dn 11:11
advance with a g army and many Dn 11:13
to his land with g wealth, Dn 11:28
go out with g fury to destroy Dn 11:44
time Michael the g prince who Dn 12:1
the day of Jezreel will be g. Hs 1:11
a delegation⌋ to the g king. Hs 5:13
as an offering to the g king. Hs 10:6
a g and strong people ⌊appears⌋, Jl 2:2
for the LORD has done g things. Jl 2:21
My g army that I sent against Jl 2:25
blood before the g and Jl 2:31
wickedness of the nations is g. Jl 3:13
and see the g turmoil in the Am 3:9
and the g houses will come to an Am 3:15
go from there to g Hamath; Am 6:2
It consumed the g deep and Am 7:4
Go to the g city of Nineveh and Jnh 1:2
appointed a g fish to swallow Jnh 1:17
Go to the g city of Nineveh and Jnh 3:2
about the g city of Nineveh, Jnh 4:11
is slow to anger but g in power; Nah 1:3
stirring up the g waters. Hab 3:15
The g Day of the LORD is near, Zph 1:14
'What are you, g mountain? Zch 4:7
Therefore g anger came from the Zch 7:12
jealous for her with g wrath." Zch 8:2
and will writhe in g pain, Zch 9:5
will be as g as the mourning Zch 12:11
On that day a g panic from the Zch 14:13
and clothing in g abundance. Zch 14:14
The LORD is g, ⌊even⌋ beyond the Mal 1:5
My name will be g among the Mal 1:11
will be g among the nations, Mal 1:11
I am a g King," says the LORD Mal 1:14
before the g and awesome Day Mal 4:5
weeping, and g mourning, Rachel Mt 2:18
in darkness have seen a g light, Mt 4:16
your reward is g in heaven. Mt 5:12
will be called g in the kingdom Mt 5:19
it is the city of the g King. Mt 5:35
And its collapse was g!" Mt 7:27
in Israel with so g a faith! Mt 8:10
And there was a g calm. Mt 8:26
belly of the g fish three days Mt 12:40
to her, "Woman, your faith is g. Mt 15:28
wants to become g among you Mt 20:26
there will be g tribulation, Mt 24:21
and perform g signs and wonders Mt 24:24
heaven with power and g glory. Mt 24:30
been sold for a g deal and given Mt 26:9
after rolling a g stone against Mt 27:60
the tomb with fear and g joy, Mt 28:8
and a g multitude followed from Mk 3:7
The g multitude came to Him Mk 3:8
ceased, and there was a g calm. Mk 4:39
wants to become g among you Mk 10:43
Do you see these g buildings? Mk 13:2
clouds with g power and glory. Mk 13:26
For he will be g in the sight of Lk 1:15
He will be g and will be called Lk 1:32
One has done g things for me, Lk 1:49
Lord had shown her His g mercy, Lk 1:58
good news of g joy that will be Lk 2:10
months while a g famine came Lk 4:25
they caught a g number of fish, Lk 5:6

disciples and a **g** multitude of Lk 6:17
your reward is **g** in heaven, Lk 6:23
Then your reward will be **g**, Lk 6:35
of that house was **g**!" Lk 6:49
have not found so **g** a faith even Lk 7:9
"A **g** prophet has risen among us," Lk 7:16
they were gripped by **g** fear. Lk 8:37
among you—this one is **g**." Lk 9:48
Now **g** crowds were traveling with Lk 14:25
a **g** chasm has been fixed between Lk 16:26
sights and **g** signs from heaven. Lk 21:11
for there will be **g** distress in Lk 21:23
a cloud with power and **g** glory. Lk 21:27
A **g** multitude of the people Lk 23:27
to Jerusalem with **g** joy. Lk 24:52
before the **g** and remarkable day Ac 2:20
And with **g** power the apostles Ac 4:33
and **g** grace was on all of them. Ac 4:33
and a **g** fear came on all who Ac 5:5
Then **g** fear came on the whole Ac 5:11
was performing **g** wonders and Ac 6:8
Canaan, with **g** suffering, and Ac 7:11
So there was **g** joy in that city. Ac 8:8
while claiming to be somebody **g**. Ac 8:9
is called the **G** Power of God!" Ac 8:10
the signs and **g** miracles that Ac 8:13
there was a **g** commotion among Ac 12:18
a way that a **g** number of both Ac 14:1
and they created **g** joy among all Ac 15:3
including a **g** number of Ac 17:4
provided a **g** deal of business Ac 19:24
temple of the **g** goddess Artemis Ac 19:27
"**G** is Artemis of the Ephesians!" Ac 19:28
"**G** is Artemis of the Ephesians!" Ac 19:34
guardian of the **g** Artemis, Ac 19:35
There was a **g** deal of weeping by Ac 20:37
When there was a **g** hush, he Ac 21:40
Since we enjoy **g** peace because Ac 24:2
came with **g** pomp and entered Ac 25:23
and testify to both small and **g**, Ac 26:22
such a hope, we use **g** boldness— 2Co 3:12
by **g** endurance, by afflictions, 2Co 6:4
I have **g** confidence in you; 2Co 7:4
I have **g** pride in you. 2Co 7:4
because of his **g** confidence in 2Co 8:22
So it is no **g** thing if his 2Co 11:15
because of His **g** love that He Eph 2:4
you to know how **g** a struggle I Col 2:1
to you in spite of **g** opposition. 1Th 2:2
and **g** boldness in the faith that 1Tm 3:13
the mystery of godliness is **g**: 1Tm 3:16
with contentment is a **g** gain. 1Tm 6:6
encourage with **g** patience and 2Tm 4:2
coppersmith did **g** harm to me. 2Tm 4:14
glory of our **g** God and Savior, Ti 2:13
For I have **g** joy and Phm 7
although I have **g** boldness in Phm 8
we neglect such a **g** salvation? Heb 2:3
since we have a **g** high priest Heb 4:14
We have a **g** deal to say about Heb 5:11
Now consider how **g** this man was, Heb 7:4
since we have a **g** high priest Heb 10:21
which has a **g** reward. Heb 10:35
the **g** Shepherd of the sheep— Heb 13:20
it a **g** joy, my brothers, Jms 1:2
the body⌋, it boasts **g** things. Jms 3:5
According to His **g** mercy, He has 1Pt 1:3
also rejoice with **g** joy at the 1Pt 4:13
has given us very **g** and precious 2Pt 1:4
Look at how **g** a love the Father 1Jn 3:1
for the judgment of the **g** day, Jd 6
glory, blameless and with **g** joy, Jd 24
with her into **g** tribulation, Rv 2:22
because the **g** day of Their wrath Rv 6:17
coming out of the **g** tribulation. Rv 7:14
like a **g** mountain ablaze Rv 8:8
trumpet, and a **g** star, blazing Rv 8:10
smoke from a **g** furnace so that Rv 9:2
bound at the **g** river Euphrates." Rv 9:14
the public square of the **g** city, Rv 11:8
So **g** fear fell on those who saw Rv 11:11
have taken Your **g** power and have Rv 11:17
both small and **g**, and the time Rv 11:18
A **g** sign appeared in heaven: Rv 12:1
There was a **g** fiery red dragon Rv 12:3
So the **g** dragon was thrown out— Rv 12:9
come down to you with **g** fury, Rv 12:12
given two wings of a **g** eagle, Rv 12:14
his throne, and **g** authority. Rv 13:2
He also performs **g** signs, even Rv 13:13
small and **g**, rich and poor, free Rv 13:16
Babylon the **G** has fallen, who Rv 14:8
them into the **g** winepress of Rv 14:19
I saw another **g** and Rv 15:1
G and awe-inspiring are Your Rv 15:3
bowl on the **g** river Euphrates Rv 16:12
the battle of the **g** day of God, Rv 16:14
the earth—so **g** was the quake. Rv 16:18
The **g** city split into three Rv 16:19
Babylon the **G** was remembered in Rv 16:19
BABYLON THE **G** THE MOTHER Rv 17:5
you saw is the **g** city that has Rv 17:18
angel with **g** authority coming Rv 18:1
Babylon the **G** has fallen! Rv 18:2
Woe, woe, the **g** city, Babylon, Rv 18:10
Woe, woe, the **g** city, clothed in Rv 18:16
"Who is like the **g** city?" Rv 18:18
Woe, woe, the **g** city, where all Rv 18:19
Babylon the **g** city will be Rv 18:21
who fear Him, both small and **g**! Rv 19:5
for the **g** supper of God, Rv 19:17
free and slave, small and **g**." Rv 19:18
the abyss and a **g** chain in his Rv 20:1
Then I saw a **g** white throne and Rv 20:11
the dead, the **g** and the small, Rv 20:12
the Spirit to a **g** and high Rv 21:10

GREATER *(80)*

g light to have dominion over Gn 1:16
in this house is **g** than I am. Gn 39:9
throne will I be **g** than you." Gn 41:40
brother will be **g** than he, Gn 48:19
the LORD is **g** than all gods, Ex 18:11
to a **g** amount of years Lv 25:16
make you into a **g** and mightier Nm 14:12
His king will be **g** than Agag, Nm 24:7
you nations **g** and stronger than Dt 4:38
'These nations are **g** than I; Dt 7:17
out nations **g** and stronger than Dt 9:1
out nations **g** and stronger than Dt 11:23
would have been much **g**." 1Sm 14:30
her with was **g** than the love he 2Sm 13:15
so we have a **g** ⌊claim⌋ to David 2Sm 19:43
his throne **g** than the throne 1Kg 1:37
make his throne **g** than your 1Kg 1:47
wisdom was **g** than the wisdom 1Kg 4:30
g than all the wisdom of Egypt. 1Kg 4:30
so that they did **g** evil than the 2Kg 21:9
g evil than the Amorites who 2Kg 21:11
for our God is **g** than any of the 2Ch 2:5
since God is **g** than man. Jb 33:12
G than the roar of many waters— Ps 93:4
our Lord is **g** than all gods. Ps 135:5
my dear people is **g** than that of Lm 4:6
will see even **g** abominations." Ezk 8:6
will see even **g** abominations, Ezk 8:13
will see even **g** abominations Ezk 8:15
cedar became **g** in height than Ezk 31:5
will rule a kingdom **g** than his. Dn 11:5
house will be **g** than the first," Hg 2:9
may not be **g** than that of Judah Zch 12:7
born of women no one **g** than John Mt 11:11
kingdom of heaven is **g** than he. Mt 11:11
that something **g** than the temple Mt 12:6
something **g** than Jonah is here! Mt 12:41
g than Solomon is here! Mt 12:42
For which is **g**, the gold or the Mt 23:17
For which is **g**, the gift or the Mt 23:19
other commandment **g** than these." Mk 12:31
of women no one is **g** than John, Lk 7:28
kingdom of God is **g** than he." Lk 7:28
g than Solomon is here! Lk 11:31
something **g** than Jonah is here! Lk 11:32
will receive **g** punishment." Lk 20:47
For who is **g**, the one at the Lk 22:27
will see **g** things than this." Jn 1:50
You aren't **g** than our father Jn 4:12
will show Him **g** works than these Jn 5:20
But I have a **g** testimony than Jn 5:36
You **g** than our father Abraham Jn 8:53
given them to Me, is **g** than all. Jn 10:29
slave is not **g** than his master, Jn 13:16
is not **g** than the one who Jn 13:16
he will do even **g** works than Jn 14:12
because the Father is **g** than I. Jn 14:28
No one has **g** love than this, Jn 15:13
A slave is not **g** than his master Jn 15:20
Me over to you has the **g** sin." Jn 19:11
to put no **g** burden on you than Ac 15:28
to **g** and greater lawlessness, Rm 6:19
to greater and **g** lawlessness, Rm 6:19
we clothe these with **g** honor, 1Co 12:23
giving **g** honor to the less 1Co 12:24
But desire the **g** gifts. 1Co 12:31
prophesies is **g** than the person 1Co 14:5
you is even **g** as he remembers 2Co 7:15
will produce an even **g** measure 2Tm 2:16
since He had no one **g** to swear Heb 6:13
by something **g** than themselves, Heb 6:16
In the **g** and more perfect Heb 9:11
the Messiah to be **g** wealth than Heb 11:26
But He gives **g** grace. Jms 4:6
who are **g** in might and power, 2Pt 2:11
God is **g** than our hearts and 1Jn 3:20
is in you is **g** than the one who 1Jn 4:4
testimony is **g**, because it is 1Jn 5:9
I have no **g** joy than this: 3Jn 4
last works are **g** than the first. Rv 2:19

GREATEST *(29)*

Arba was the **g** man among the Jos 14:15
like that of the **g** in the land. 2Sm 7:9
the **g** of them for a thousand. 1Ch 12:14
like that of the **g** in the land. 1Ch 17:8
people, from the **g** to the least, Est 1:5
from the least to the **g**." Est 1:20
Job was the **g** man among all the Jb 1:3
altar of God, to God, my **g** joy. Ps 43:4
g of the kings of the earth. Ps 89:27
not exalt Jerusalem as my **g** joy! Ps 137:6
from the least to the **g** of them, Jr 6:13
for from the least to the **g**, Jr 8:10
the least to the **g** of them"— Jr 31:34
people from the least to the one **g**, Jr 42:1
people from the least to the **g**. Jr 42:8
least to the **g**, they will die Jr 44:12
from the **g** of them to the least. Jnh 3:5
is **g** in the kingdom of heaven? Mt 18:1
this one is the **g** in the kingdom Mt 18:4
in the law is the **g**?" Mt 22:36
This is the **g** and most important Mt 22:38
The **g** among you will be your Mt 23:11
one another about who was the **g**. Mk 9:34
who would be the **g** of them. Lk 9:46
who should be considered the **g**. Lk 22:24
whoever is **g** among you must Lk 22:26
from the least of them to the **g**, Ac 8:10
But the **g** of these is love. 1Co 13:13
from the least to the **g** of them. Heb 8:11

GREATLY *(56)*

(See pp. xi-xii.)

GREATNESS *(28)*

with the **g** of Your faithful Nm 14:19
to show Your **g** and power to Your Dt 3:24
has shown us His glory and **g**, Dt 5:24
through Your **g** and brought out Dt 9:26
His **g**, strong hand, and Dt 11:2
Declare the **g** of our God! Dt 32:3
done all this **g**, making known 1Ch 17:19
is the **g** and the power and the 1Ch 29:11
splendor of his **g** for a total of Est 1:4
Proclaim with me the LORD's **g**; Ps 34:3
His **g** is unsearchable. Ps 145:3
and I will declare Your **g**. Ps 145:6
praise Him for His abundant **g**. Ps 150:2
Israel is among you in ⌊His⌋ **g**." Is 12:6
Who are you like in your **g**? Ezk 31:2
It was beautiful in its **g**, Ezk 31:7
like in glory and **g** among Eden's Ezk 31:18
will display My **g** and holiness, Ezk 38:23
g has grown and even reaches Dn 4:22
and even more **g** came to me. Dn 4:36
gave sovereignty, **g**, glory, and Dn 5:18
Because of the **g** He gave him, Dn 5:19
and **g** of the kingdoms under all Dn 7:27
then His **g** will extend to the Mc 5:4
proclaims the **g** of the Lord, Lk 1:46
all astonished at the **g** of God. Lk 9:43
and declaring the **g** of God. Ac 10:46
immeasurable **g** of His power to Eph 1:19

GREECE *(5)*

goat represents the king of **G**, Dn 8:21
the prince of **G** will come. Dn 10:20
against the kingdom of **G**. Dn 11:2

Zion, against your sons, **G**. Zch 9:13
them at length, he came to **G** Ac 20:2

GREED *(10)*

of his sinful **g** I was angry, Is 57:17
they are full of **g** and Mt 23:25
adulteries, **g**, evil actions, Mk 7:22
you are full of **g** and evil. Lk 11:39
against all **g** because one's Lk 12:15
evil, **g**, and wickedness. Rm 1:29
impurity or **g** should not even Eph 5:3
evil desire, and **g**, which is Col 3:5
In their **g** they will exploit you 2Pt 2:3
and with hearts trained in **g**. 2Pt 2:14

GREEDY *(12)*

the one who is **g** curses and Ps 10:3
g man is in a hurry for wealth; Pr 28:22
A **g** person provokes conflict, Pr 28:25
other people—**g**, unrighteous, Lk 18:11
or to the **g** and swindlers, 1Co 5:10
who is sexually immoral or **g**, 1Co 5:11
thieves, **g** people, drunkards, 1Co 6:10
immoral or impure or **g** person, Eph 5:5
know, or had **g** motives—God is 1Th 2:5
gentle, not quarrelsome, not **g**— 1Tm 3:3
a lot of wine, not **g** for money, 1Tm 3:8
not a bully, not **g** for money, Ti 1:7

GREEK *(14)*

the woman was **G**, a Mk 7:26
written in Hebrew, Latin, and **G**. Jn 19:20
woman, but his father was a **G**. Ac 16:1
knew that his father was a **G**. Ac 16:3
the prominent **G** women as well as Ac 17:12
He replied, "Do you know **G**? Ac 21:37
to the Jew, and also to the **G**. Rm 1:16
to the Jew, and also to the **G**; Rm 2:9
to the Jew, and also to the **G**. Rm 2:10
distinction between Jew and **G**, Rm 10:12
though he was a **G**, was compelled Gl 2:3
is no Jew or **G**, slave or free, Gl 3:28
Here there is not **G** and Jew, Col 3:11
and in **G** he has the name Rv 9:11

GREEKS *(16)*

Jerusalem to the **G** to remove Jl 3:6
among the **G** and teach the Greeks Jn 7:35
the Greeks and teach the **G**, Jn 7:35
some **G** were among those who Jn 12:20
of both Jews and **G** believed. Ac 14:1
a great number of God-fearing **G**, Ac 17:4
to persuade both Jews and **G**. Ac 18:4
both Jews and **G**, heard the word Ac 19:10
in Ephesus, both Jews and **G**. Ac 19:17
both Jews and **G** about repentance Ac 20:21
also brought **G** into the temple Ac 21:28
both to **G** and barbarians, Rm 1:14
for signs and the **G** seek wisdom, 1Co 1:22
both Jews and **G**, Christ is God's 1Co 1:24
the Jews or the **G** or the church 1Co 10:32
whether Jews or **G**, whether 1Co 12:13

GREEN *(29)*

given⌋ every **g** plant for food." Gn 1:30
as ⌊I gave⌋ the **g** plants, I have Gn 9:3
Nothing **g** was left on the trees Ex 10:15
contamination is **g** or red in the Lv 13:49
house consists of **g** or red Lv 14:37
ox eats up the **g** plants in the Nm 22:4
hill and under every **g** tree; 1Kg 14:23
hills, and under every **g** tree. 2Kg 16:4
hill and under every **g** tree. 2Kg 17:10
hills, and under every **g** tree. 2Ch 28:4
searching for anything **g**. Jb 39:8
lets me lie down in **g** pastures; Ps 23:2
and wilt like tender **g** plants. Ps 37:2
whether **g** or burning—He Ps 58:9
fruit in old age, healthy and **g**, Ps 92:14
gone under every **g** tree to Jr 3:6
under every **g** tree and have not Jr 3:13
because there are no **g** plants. Jr 14:6
by the **g** trees on the high hills Jr 17:2
and its foliage remains **g**. Jr 17:8
and under every **g** tree and every Ezk 6:13
I cause the **g** tree to wither and Ezk 17:24
devour every **g** tree and every Ezk 20:47
pastures have turned **g**, Jl 2:22
down in groups on the **g** grass. Mk 6:39
these things when the wood is **g**, Lk 23:31
and there was a pale **g** horse. Rv 6:8
and all the **g** grass was burned Rv 8:7
earth, or any **g** plant, or any Rv 9:4

GREET *(53)*

went out to **g** Sisera and said Jdg 4:18
went out to **g** him and said to Jdg 4:22
my house to **g** me when I return Jdg 11:31
So Saul went out to **g** him, 1Sm 13:10
come to Nabal, **g** him in my name. 1Sm 25:5
the wilderness to **g** our master, 1Sm 25:14
to King David to **g** him and to 2Sm 8:10
The king stood up to **g** her, 1Kg 2:19
don't ⌊stop to⌋ **g** him, and if a 2Kg 4:29
come down to **g** the king's sons 2Kg 10:13
to King David to **g** him and to 1Ch 18:10
below is eager to **g** your coming. Is 14:9
And if you **g** only your brothers, Mt 5:47
G a household when you enter it, Mt 10:12
were amazed and ran to **g** Him. Mk 9:15
don't **g** anyone along the road. Lk 10:4
G also the church that meets in Rm 16:5
G my dear friend Epaenetus, Rm 16:5
G Mary, who has worked very hard Rm 16:6
G Andronicus and Junia, my Rm 16:7
G Ampliatus, my dear friend in Rm 16:8
G Urbanus, our co-worker in Rm 16:9
G Apelles, who is approved in Rm 16:10
G those who belong to the Rm 16:10
G Herodion, my fellow Rm 16:11
G those who belong to the Rm 16:11
G Tryphaena and Tryphosa, who Rm 16:12
G my dear friend Persis, who has Rm 16:12
G Rufus, chosen in the Lord; Rm 16:13
G Asyncritus, Phlegon, Hermes, Rm 16:14
G Philologus and Julia, Nereus Rm 16:15
G one another with a holy kiss. Rm 16:16
my fellow countrymen, **g** you. Rm 16:21
this epistle in the Lord, **g** you. Rm 16:22
and our brother Quartus **g** you. Rm 16:23
of the Asian province **g** you. 1Co 16:19
and Priscilla **g** you heartily 1Co 16:19
All the brothers **g** you. 1Co 16:20
G one another with a holy kiss. 1Co 16:20
G one another with a holy kiss. 2Co 13:12
holy kiss. All the saints **g** you. 2Co 13:12
G every saint in Christ Jesus. Php 4:21
brothers who are with me **g** you. Php 4:21
All the saints **g** you, but Php 4:22
physician, and Demas **g** you. Col 4:14
G all the brothers with a holy 1Th 5:26
G Prisca and Aquila, and the 2Tm 4:19
All those who are with me **g** you. Ti 3:15
G those who love us in the faith. Ti 3:15
G all your leaders and all the Heb 13:24
Those who are from Italy **g** you. Heb 13:24
G one another with a kiss of 1Pt 5:14
you greetings. **G** the friends by 3Jn 14

GREETED *(7)*

at the home of Micah and **g** him. Jdg 18:15
approached the men, he **g** them, 1Sm 30:21
g him and then asked, "Is your 2Kg 10:15
house and **g** Elizabeth. Lk 1:40
he went up and **g** the church, Ac 18:22
where we **g** the brothers and Ac 21:7
from a distance, **g** them, and Heb 11:13

GREETING *(7)*

what kind of **g** this could be. Lk 1:29
When Elizabeth heard Mary's **g**, Lk 1:41
sound of your **g** reached my ears Lk 1:44
After **g** them, he related one by Ac 21:19
This **g** is in my own hand— 1Co 16:21
This **g** is in my own hand— Col 4:18
This **g** is in my own hand— 2Th 3:17

GREETINGS *(17)*

west of the Euphrates River: **G**. Ezr 4:17
follows: To King Darius: All **g**. Ezr 5:7
the God of heaven: **G** ⌊to you⌋. Ezr 7:12
g in the marketplaces, and to be Mt 23:7
to Jesus and said, "**G**, Rabbi!" Mt 26:49
and who want **g** in the Mk 12:38
the synagogues and **g** in the Lk 11:43
robes and who love **g** in the Lk 20:46
Antioch, Syria, and Cilicia: **G**. Ac 15:23
excellent governor Felix: **G**. Ac 23:26
Give my **g** to Prisca and Aquila, Rm 16:3
churches of Christ send you **g**. Rm 16:16
Give my **g** to the brothers in Col 4:15
12 tribes in the Dispersion. **G**. Jms 1:1
sends you **g**, as does Mark, my 1Pt 5:13
of your elect sister send you **g**. 2Jn 13
The friends send you **g**. 3Jn 14

GREETS *(6)*

and if a man **g** you, don't answer 2Kg 4:29
and to the whole church, **g** you. Rm 16:23
fellow prisoner, **g** you, as does Col 4:10
a slave of Christ Jesus, **g** you. Col 4:12
Eubulus **g** you, as do Pudens, 2Tm 4:21
Christ Jesus, **g** you, and so do Phm 23

GREW *(47)*

and whatever **g** on the ground. Gn 19:25
The child **g** and was weaned, Gn 21:8
God was with the boy, and he **g**; Gn 21:20
When the boys **g** up, Esau became Gn 25:27
When the child **g** older, she Ex 2:10
when the sun **g** hot, it melted. Ex 16:21
When Moses' hands **g** heavy, Ex 17:12
of the trumpet **g** louder and Ex 19:19
He **g** angry and swore an oath: Dt 1:34
when the Israelites **g** stronger, Jos 17:13
and when they **g** up, they drove Jdg 11:2
The boy **g**, and the LORD blessed Jdg 13:24
the boy Samuel **g** up in the 1Sm 2:21
the boy Samuel **g** in stature and 1Sm 2:26
Samuel **g**, and the LORD was with 1Sm 3:19
When Samuel **g** old, he appointed 1Sm 8:1
It lived and **g** up with him and 2Sm 12:3
So the conspiracy **g** strong, 2Sm 15:12
the sky **g** dark with clouds and 1Kg 18:45
The child **g** and one day went out 2Kg 4:18
David steadily **g** more powerful, 1Ch 11:9
However, Abijah **g** strong, 2Ch 13:21
Jehoshaphat **g** stronger and 2Ch 17:12
he **g** arrogant and it led to his 2Ch 26:16
so I **g** silent and would not go Jb 31:34
My heart **g** hot within me; Ps 39:3
The earth feared and **g** quiet Ps 76:8
rejoiced when the waves **g** quiet. Ps 107:30
He **g** up before Him like a young Is 53:2
The mother of seven **g** faint; Jr 15:9
You **g** up and matured and became Ezk 16:7
were formed and your hair **g**, Ezk 16:7
its boughs **g** long as it spread Ezk 31:5
and it **g** proud on account of its Ezk 31:10
on them, flesh **g**, and skin Ezk 37:8
The tree **g** large and strong; Dn 4:11
you saw, which **g** large and Dn 4:20
until his hair **g** like eagles' Dn 4:33
horn emerged and **g** extensively Dn 8:9
It **g** as high as the heavenly Dn 8:10
face **g** deathly pale, and I was Dn 10:8
it **g** up to provide shade over Jnh 4:6
The child **g** up and became Lk 1:80
The boy **g** up and became strong, Lk 2:40
It **g** and became a tree, and the Lk 13:19
Saul **g** more capable, and kept Ac 9:22
The shouting **g** loud, and some of Ac 23:9

GRIDDLE *(4)*

offering prepared on the **g**, Lv 2:5
to be prepared with oil on a **g**; Lv 6:21
or prepared in a pan or on a **g**, Lv 7:9
is unturned bread, baked on a **g**. Hs 7:8

GRIEF *(41)*

not bear to see the **g** that would Gn 44:34
the people were overcome with **g**. Nm 14:39
altar will bring **g** and sadness 1Sm 2:33
given to one burdened with **g**, Jb 3:20
only my **g** could be weighed and Jb 6:2
My eyes have grown dim from **g**, Jb 17:7
My eyes are swollen from **g**; Ps 6:7
have seen trouble and **g**, Ps 10:14
my life is consumed with **g**, Ps 31:10
bowed down with **g**, like one Ps 35:14
I am weary from **g**; strengthen me Ps 119:28
A sly wink of the eye causes **g**, Pr 10:10
be sad, and joy may end in **g**. Pr 14:13
A foolish son is **g** to his father Pr 17:25
increases, **g** increases. Ec 1:18
all his days are filled with **g**, Ec 2:23
G is better than laughter, Ec 7:3
has flown away; **g** has settled on Jr 8:18
and ⌊bring⌋ happiness out of **g**. Jr 31:13
I struck my thigh ⌊in **g**⌋. Jr 31:19
heart is poured out in **g** because Lm 2:11
My eyes bring me **g** because of Lm 3:51
the prince will be clothed in **g**; Ezk 7:27

though I have not caused him g, Ezk 13:22
strike ⌊your⌋ thigh ⌊in g⌋. Ezk 21:12
filled with drunkenness and g, Ezk 23:33
I will make that g like mourning Am 8:10
you slash yourself ⌊in g⌋; Mc 5:1
exhausted from their g. Lk 22:45
of filled with g so that he who 1Co 5:2
be overwhelmed by excessive g. 2Co 2:7
but because your g led to 2Co 7:9
godly g produces a repentance 2Co 7:10
but worldly g produces death. 2Co 7:10
not have one g on top of another Php 2:27
do this with joy and not with g, Heb 13:17
someone endures g from suffering 1Pt 2:19
her that much torment and g. Rv 18:7
widow, and I will never see g,' Rv 18:7
day—death, and g, and famine. Rv 18:8
g, crying, and pain will exist Rv 21:4

GRIEVANCE *(2)*
anyone had a g to bring before 2Sm 15:2
who had a g or dispute could 2Sm 15:4

GRIEVE *(11)*
g for you, Jonathan my brother. 2Sm 1:26
Do not g, because your strength Neh 8:10
since today is holy. Do not g." Neh 8:11
sword. Who will g for you? How Is 51:19
her young women g, and she Lm 1:4
made the ramparts and walls g; Lm 2:8
G like a young woman dressed in Jl 1:8
oils but do not g over the ruin Am 6:6
and I will g for many who sinned 2Co 12:21
And don't g God's Holy Spirit, Eph 4:30
you will not g like the rest, 1Th 4:13

GRIEVED *(12)*
and He was g in His heart. Gn 6:6
and were deeply g and angry. Gn 34:7
this, or else he will be g.' " 1Sm 20:3
for he was g because of his 1Sm 20:34
Has my soul not g for the needy? Jb 30:25
wilderness and g Him in the Ps 78:40
rebelled, and g His Holy Spirit. Is 63:10
Peter was g that He asked him Jn 21:17
For although I g you with my 2Co 7:8
I saw that the letter g you, 2Co 7:8
because you were g, but because 2Co 7:9
For you were g as God willed, 2Co 7:9

GRIEVES *(1)*
the land g; indeed, the grain Jl 1:10

GRIEVING *(9)*
had finished g over Amnon's 2Sm 13:39
"The king is g over his son." 2Sm 19:2
I went about ⌊g⌋ as if for my Ps 35:14
I caused g on the day the cedar Ezk 31:15
he went away g, because he had Mt 19:22
he went away g, because he had Mk 10:22
g most of all over his statement Ac 20:38
as g yet always rejoicing; 2Co 6:10
thing—this g as God wills— 2Co 7:11

GRIEVOUS *(2)*
and incurred g guilt by taking Ezk 25:12
destruction—a g destruction! Mc 2:10

GRIEVOUSLY *(1)*
Jerusalem has sinned g; Lm 1:8

GRIND *(9)*
G some of it into a fine powder Ex 30:36
he was forced to g grain in the Jdg 16:21
let my own wife g ⌊grain⌋ for Jb 31:10
Though you g a fool in a mortar Pr 27:22
the women who g cease because Ec 12:3
crush My people and g the faces Is 3:15
Take millstones and g meal; Is 47:2
falls, it will g him to powder!" Mt 21:44
it will g him to powder!" Lk 20:18

GRINDING *(4)*
it⌋ on a pair of g stones or Nm 11:8
thoroughly g it to powder as Dt 9:21
Two women will be g at the mill: Mt 24:41
women will be g grain together: Lk 17:35

GRINDS *(1)*
foams at the mouth, g his teeth, Mk 9:18

GRIP *(2)*
strengthen his g on the kingdom. 2Kg 15:19
Fear and trembling g me; Ps 55:5

GRIPPED *(3)*
all his troops were g with fear. 1Sm 13:7
run; panic has g her. Distress Jr 49:24
they were g by great fear. Lk 8:37

GRIPS *(2)*
Pain g me, like the pain of a Is 21:3
so that anguish g you like a Mc 4:9

GROAN *(22)*
the city, men g; the mortally Jb 24:12
I g because of the anguish of my Ps 38:8
I complain and g morning, noon, Ps 55:17
think of God; I g; I meditate; Ps 77:3
when the wicked rule, people g. Pr 29:2
All the carousers now g. Is 24:7
I will g like a woman in labor, Is 42:14
how you will g when labor pains Jr 22:23
wounded will g throughout her Jr 51:52
her priests g, her young women Lm 1:4
All her people g while they Lm 1:11
the men who sigh and g over all Ezk 9:4
But you, son of man, g! Ezk 21:6
G bitterly with a broken heart Ezk 21:6
G quietly; do not observe Ezk 24:17
sins and will g to one another. Ezk 24:23
when the wounded g and slaughter Ezk 26:15
and he will g before him as a Ezk 30:24
How the animals g! The herds of Jl 1:18
we also g within ourselves, Rm 8:23
And, in fact, we g in this one, 2Co 5:2
we who are in this tent g, 2Co 5:4

GROANED *(2)*
Israelites g because of their Ex 2:23
whenever they g because of those Jdg 2:18

GROANING *(17)*
God heard their g, and He Ex 2:24
I have heard the g of the Ex 6:5
His hand is heavy despite my g. Jb 23:2
I am weary from my g; Ps 6:6
afflicted and the g of the poor, Ps 12:5
and from my words of g? Ps 22:1
with grief, and my years with g; Ps 31:10
brittle from my g all day long. Ps 32:3
Because of the sound of my g, Ps 102:5
hear a prisoner's g, to set free Ps 102:20
I will put an end to all her g." Is 21:2
worn out with g and have found Jr 45:3
have heard me g, but there is no Lm 1:21
you: Why are you g? then say: Ezk 21:7
with weeping and g, because He Mal 2:13
have heard their g and have come Ac 7:34
creation has been g together Rm 8:22

GROANINGS *(1)*
for us with unspoken g. Rm 8:26

GROANS *(4)*
and my g pour out like water. Jb 3:24
Let the g of the prisoners reach Ps 79:11
She herself g and turns away. Lm 1:8
For my g are many, and I am sick Lm 1:22

GROGGINESS *(1)*
g will clothe ⌊them⌋ in rags. Pr 23:21

GROOM *(15)*
It is like a g coming from the Ps 19:5
be sad while the g is with them? Mt 9:15
come when the g will be taken Mt 9:15
and went out to meet the g. Mt 25:1
Since the g was delayed, they Mt 25:5
Here's the g! Come out to meet Mt 25:6
gone to buy some, the g arrived. Mt 25:10
fast while the g is with them, Mk 2:19
as they have the g with them, Mk 2:19
come when the g is taken away Mk 2:20
fast while the g is with them, Lk 5:34
come when the g will be taken Lk 5:35
the water knew. He called the g Jn 2:9
He who has the bride is the g. Jn 3:29
the voice of a g and bride will Rv 18:23

GROOM'S *(2)*
But the g friend, who stands by Jn 3:29
rejoices greatly at the g voice. Jn 3:29

GROPE *(5)*
noon you will g as a blind man Dt 28:29
and they g at noon as if it were Jb 5:14
g around in darkness without Jb 12:25
g along a wall like the blind; Is 59:10
we g like those without eyes. Is 59:10

GROPES *(1)*
as a blind man g in the dark. Dt 28:29

GROUND *(276)*
that crawl on the g according to Gn 1:25
there was no man to work the g. Gn 2:5
come out of the g and water the Gn 2:6
the dust from the g and breathed Gn 2:7
to grow out of the g every tree Gn 2:9
out of the g each wild animal Gn 2:19
The g is cursed because of you. Gn 3:17
brow until you return to the g, Gn 3:19
Eden to work the g from which he Gn 3:23
cries out to Me from the g! Gn 4:10
from the g that opened its Gn 4:11
by the g the LORD has cursed. Gn 5:29
crawls on the g according to its Gn 6:20
creature that crawls on the g, Gn 7:8
was on the surface of the g, Gn 7:23
the surface of the g was drying. Gn 8:13
creatures that crawl on the g— Gn 8:17
curse the g because of man, Gn 8:21
creature that crawls on the g, Gn 9:2
fell to the g, and God spoke Gn 17:3
Abraham fell to the g, laughed, Gn 17:17
to meet them and bowed to the g. Gn 18:2
bowed ⌊with his⌋ face to the g Gn 19:1
and whatever grew on the g. Gn 19:25
bowed to the g before the LORD Gn 24:52
was set on the g with its top Gn 28:12
and bowed to the g seven times Gn 33:3
bow down to the g before you?" Gn 37:10
semen on the g so that he would Gn 38:9
him with their faces to the g. Gn 42:6
they bowed to the g before him. Gn 43:26
his sack to the g and opened it. Gn 44:11
They fell to the g before him. Gn 44:14
bowed with his face to the g. Gn 48:12
you are standing is holy g." Ex 3:5
He said, "Throw it on the g." Ex 4:3
threw it on the g, and it became Ex 4:3
Nile and pour it on the dry g. Ex 4:9
will become blood on the g." Ex 4:9
plants on the g and all the Ex 10:15
can go through the sea on dry g. Ex 14:16
went through the sea on dry g, Ex 14:22
walked through the sea on dry g, Ex 14:29
walked through the sea on dry g. Ex 15:19
as fine as frost on the g. Ex 16:14
it⌋ up, and g ⌊it⌋ to powder. Ex 32:20
down to the g and worshiped. Ex 34:8
and fell facedown ⌊on the g⌋. Lv 9:24
their feet for hopping on the g. Lv 11:21
swarm on the g are unclean for Lv 11:29
creature that crawls on the g. Lv 11:44
creatures that swarm on the g, Lv 11:46
of finely g fragrant incense, Lv 16:12
or whatever crawls on the g; Lv 20:25
g ⌊it⌋ on a pair of grinding Nm 11:8
feet off the g, about a day's Nm 11:31
their faces ⌊to the g⌋ in front Nm 14:5
and the g opens its mouth and Nm 16:30
the g beneath them split open. Nm 16:31
with their faces ⌊to the g⌋, Nm 20:6
bowed with his face ⌊to the g⌋. Nm 22:31
creature that crawls on the g, Dt 4:18
pour it on the g like water. Dt 12:16
pour it on the g like water. Dt 12:24
pour it on the g like water. Dt 15:23
tree or on the g along the road Dt 22:6
her foot on the g because of her Dt 28:56
firmly on dry g in the middle Jos 3:17
crossed on dry g until the Jos 3:17
feet stepped out on solid g, Jos 4:18
crossed the Jordan on dry g.' Jos 4:22
his face to the g in worship and Jos 5:14
his face to the g until evening, Jos 7:6
Why are you on the g? Jos 7:10
in the g inside my tent, Jos 7:21
temple and drove it into the g, Jdg 4:21
and all the g is dry, I will Jdg 6:37
and the dew be all over the g." Jdg 6:39
and dew was all over the g. Jdg 6:40
they fell facedown on the g. Jdg 13:20
hollow place ⌊in the g⌋ at Lehi, Jdg 15:19
face to the g and said to him Ru 2:10
a loud shout that the g shook. 1Sm 4:5
his face to the g before the ark 1Sm 5:3
his face to the g before the ark 1Sm 5:4
to plow his g or reap his 1Sm 8:12
and there was honey on the g. 1Sm 14:25

slaughtered them on the **g**, 1Sm 14:32
of his head will fall to the **g**, 1Sm 14:45
he fell on his face to the **g**. 1Sm 17:49
fell with his face to the **g**, 1Sm 20:41
David bowed to the **g** in homage. 1Sm 24:8
her face to the **g** in front of 1Sm 25:23
her face to the **g** and said, 1Sm 25:41
stuck in the **g** by his head. 1Sm 26:7
him into the **g** just once. 1Sm 26:8
blood fall to the **g** far from the 1Sm 26:20
face to the **g** and paid homage 1Sm 28:14
Saul fell flat on the **g**. 1Sm 28:20
He got up off the **g** and sat on 1Sm 28:23
fell to the **g** and paid homage. 2Sm 1:2
should I strike you to the **g**? 2Sm 2:22
making them lie down on the **g**, 2Sm 8:2
down to the **g** and paid homage. 2Sm 9:6
are to work the **g** for him, 2Sm 9:10
spent the night lying on the **g**. 2Sm 12:16
him to get him up from the **g**, 2Sm 12:17
Then David got up from the **g**. 2Sm 12:20
lay down on the **g**, and all his 2Sm 13:31
her face to the **g** in homage and 2Sm 14:4
of your son will fall to the **g**." 2Sm 14:11
like water poured out on the **g**, 2Sm 14:14
with his face to the **g** in homage 2Sm 14:22
face to the **g** before the king 2Sm 14:33
on him like dew on the **g**. 2Sm 17:12
strike him to the **g** right there? 2Sm 18:11
the king with his face to the **g**. 2Sm 18:28
his intestines out on the **g**. 2Sm 20:10
stood ⌊his **g**⌋ and attacked 2Sm 23:10
the king with his face to the **g**. 2Sm 24:20
to him with his face to the **g**. 1Kg 1:23
bowed with her face to the **g**, 1Kg 1:31
hair of his will fall to the **g**, 1Kg 1:52
his face ⌊to the **g**⌋ and said, 1Kg 18:7
down to the **g** and put his face 1Kg 18:42
of them crossed over on dry **g**. 2Kg 2:8
down to the **g** in front of him. 2Kg 2:15
at his feet, and bowed to the **g**; 2Kg 4:37
him on the plot of **g** belonging 2Kg 9:25
king of Israel, "Strike the **g**!" 2Kg 13:18
So he struck the **g** three times 2Kg 13:18
have struck the **g** five or six 2Kg 13:19
A plot of **g** full of barley was 1Ch 11:13
with their faces ⌊to the **g**⌋. 1Ch 21:16
to David with his face to the **g**. 1Ch 21:21
much blood on the **g** before Me. 1Ch 22:8
faces to the **g** on the pavement. 2Ch 7:3
bowed with his face to the **g**, 2Ch 20:18
were corpses lying on the **g**; 2Ch 20:24
in the burial **g** of the kings' 2Ch 26:23
LORD with their faces to the **g**. Neh 8:6
crossed through it on dry **g**. Neh 9:11
He fell to the **g** and worshiped, Jb 1:20
they sat on the **g** with him seven Jb 2:13
does not sprout from the **g**. Jb 5:6
grow old in the **g** and its stump Jb 14:8
and pours my bile on the **g**. Jb 16:13
lies hidden for him on the **g**, Jb 18:10
dry **g** and heat snatch away the Jb 24:19
taken from the **g**, and copper is Jb 28:2
to those who walk above **g**. Jb 28:4
the rocks and in holes in the **g**. Jb 30:6
her eggs on the **g** and lets them Jb 39:14
trample me to the **g** and leave my Ps 7:5
to throw ⌊me⌋ to the **g**. Ps 17:11
My foot stands on level **g**; Ps 26:12
our bodies cling to the **g**. Ps 44:25
they became manure for the **g**. Ps 83:10
springs of water into thirsty **g**, Ps 107:33
me to the **g**, making me live Ps 143:3
Spirit lead me on level **g**. Ps 143:10
leaves him, he returns to the **g**; Ps 146:4
but brings the wicked to the **g**. Ps 147:6
covered the **g**, and the stone Pr 24:31
walking on the **g** like slaves. Ec 10:7
in the rocks and holes in the **g**, Is 2:19
deserted, she will sit on the **g**. Is 3:26
you have been cut down to the **g**. Is 14:12
have been shattered on the **g**." Is 21:9
thrown to the **g**, to the dust. Is 25:12
He brings it down to the **g**; Is 26:5
it, and burn it to the **g**. Is 27:4
you will speak from the **g**, Is 29:4
that of a spirit from the **g**; Is 29:4
that you have sown in the **g**, Is 30:23
produce of the **g**, will be rich Is 30:23
that work the **g** will eat salted Is 30:24
for the **g** of my people growing Is 32:13
the parched **g** will become a pool Is 35:7
the uneven **g** will become smooth, Is 40:4
root in the **g** when He blows Is 40:24
and rough places into level **g**. Is 42:16
land, and streams on the dry **g**; Is 44:3
Sit on the **g** without a throne, Is 47:1
you with their faces to the **g**, Is 49:23
You made your back like the **g**, Is 51:23
and like a root out of dry **g**. Is 53:2
in My anger and **g** them underfoot Is 63:3
poured out their blood on the **g**. Is 63:6
Break up the unplowed **g**; Jr 4:3
and on the fruit of the **g**. Jr 7:20
up your belongings from the **g**, Jr 10:17
are on the **g** in mourning; Jr 14:2
The **g** is cracked since no rain Jr 14:4
manure on the surface of the **g**. Jr 25:33
on parched **g**, resident of the Jr 48:18
them⌋ to the **g** and defiled Lm 2:2
gates have fallen to the **g**; Lm 2:9
Zion sit on the **g** in silence. Lm 2:10
have bowed their heads to the **g**. Lm 2:10
lying on the **g** in the streets. Lm 2:21
He **g** my teeth on gravel and made Lm 3:16
one wheel on the **g** beside each Ezk 1:15
knock it to the **g** so that its Ezk 13:14
thrown to the **g**, and the east Ezk 19:12
it on the **g** to cover it with Ezk 24:7
pillars will fall to the **g**. Ezk 26:11
will sit on the **g**, tremble Ezk 26:16
to ashes on the **g** in the sight Ezk 28:18
on the open **g** and will not be Ezk 29:5
creature that crawls on the **g**, Ezk 38:20
every wall will fall to the **g**. Ezk 38:20
remain on the surface of the **g**, Ezk 39:14
from the **g** to the windows Ezk 41:16
were carved from the **g** to the Ezk 41:20
back from the **g** more than the Ezk 42:6
the gutter on the **g** to the lower Ezk 43:14
stump with its roots in the **g**, Dn 4:15
roots in the **g** and with a band Dn 4:23
It was lifted up from the **g**, Dn 7:4
earth without touching the **g**. Dn 8:5
him to the **g** and trampled him Dn 8:7
throw truth to the **g** and will be Dn 8:12
sleep, with my face ⌊to the **g**⌋. Dn 8:18
sleep, with my face to the **g**. Dn 10:9
face toward the **g** and was Dn 10:15
creatures that crawl on the **g**. Hs 2:18
break up your untilled **g**. Hs 10:12
the dust of the **g** and block the Am 2:7
archer will not stand ⌊his **g**⌋, Am 2:15
a trap on the **g** if there is no Am 3:5
spring from the **g** when it has Am 3:5
be cut off and fall to the **g**. Am 3:14
throw righteousness to the **g**. Am 5:7
not a pebble will fall to the **g**. Am 9:9
Who can bring me down to the **g**? Ob 3
reptiles slithering on the **g**. Mc 7:17
or the feeding **g** of the young Nah 2:11
and whatever the **g** yields, Hg 1:11
not ruin the produce of your **g**, Mal 3:11
them falls to the **g** without your Mt 10:29
fell on rocky **g**, where there Mt 13:5
Still others fell on good **g**, Mt 13:8
And the one sown on rocky **g**— Mt 13:20
But the one sown on the good **g**— Mt 13:23
the crowd to sit down on the **g**, Mt 15:35
dug a hole in the **g**, and hid his Mt 25:18
and hid your talent in the **g**. Mt 25:25
fell on rocky **g** where it didn't Mk 4:5
fell on good **g** and produced a Mk 4:8
are the ones sown on rocky **g**: Mk 4:16
ones sown on good **g** are those Mk 4:20
A man scatters seed on the **g**; Mk 4:26
than all the seeds on the **g**. Mk 4:31
the crowd to sit down on the **g**. Mk 8:6
He fell to the **g** and rolled Mk 9:20
fell to the **g**, and began to pray Mk 14:35
a house on the **g** without a Lk 6:49
Still other seed fell on good **g**; Lk 8:8
But the seed in the good **g**— Lk 8:15
children within you to the **g**, Lk 19:44
drops of blood falling to the **g**. Lk 22:44
and bowed down to the **g**. Lk 24:5
on the **g** with His finger. Jn 8:6
and continued writing on the **g**. Jn 8:8
these things He spit on the **g**, Jn 9:6
wheat falls into the **g** and dies, Jn 12:24
stepped back and fell to the **g**. Jn 18:6
a foot of **g**, but He promised Ac 7:5
you are standing is holy **g**. Ac 7:33
Falling to the **g**, he heard a Ac 9:4
Then Saul got up from the **g**, Ac 9:8
fell to the **g** and heard a voice Ac 22:7
When we had all fallen to the **g**, Ac 26:14
For **g** that has drunk the rain Heb 6:7
caves, and holes in the **g**. Heb 11:38

GROUNDED *(1)*

you remain **g** and steadfast Col 1:23

GROUNDS *(9)*

to divorce his wife on any **g**?" Mt 19:3
find no **g** for charging this man. Lk 23:4
I have found no **g** to charge this Lk 23:14
found in Him no **g** for the death Lk 23:22
I find no **g** for charging Him. Jn 18:38
I find no **g** for charging Him. Jn 19:4
I find no **g** for charging Him. Jn 19:6
they found no **g** for the death Ac 13:28
thinks he has **g** for confidence Php 3:4

GROUP *(20)*

Each ⌊**g**⌋ had its own language. Gn 10:5
So neither **g** came near the other Ex 14:20
over to the registered **g**, Ex 38:26
you will meet a **g** of prophets 1Sm 10:5
at Gibeah, a **g** of prophets met 1Sm 10:10
when they saw the **g** of prophets 1Sm 19:20
and sent a third **g** of agents, 1Sm 19:21
and to each ethnic **g** in its own Est 1:22
There is one ethnic **g**, scattered Est 3:8
of each ethnic **g** and written for Est 3:12
and to each ethnic **g** in its own Est 3:12
for each ethnic **g** in its own Est 8:9
for every ethnic **g** so the Jews Est 8:13
sinners, or join a **g** of mockers! Ps 1:1
brought me to the **g** of chambers Ezk 42:1
men went as a **g** and found Daniel Dn 6:11
than the first **g**, and they did Mt 21:36
women from our **g** astounded us. Lk 24:22
and a **g** of about 400 men rallied Ac 5:36
and a large **g** of priests became Ac 6:7

GROUPS *(8)*

came out of the ark by their **g**. Gn 8:19
These were the Levite family **g**: Nm 26:58
The two **g** took up positions on 2Sm 2:13
by their **g** to the service Ezr 6:18
many of the ethnic **g** of the land Est 8:17
sit down in **g** on the green grass Mk 6:39
sit down in **g** of about 50 each. Lk 9:14
made both **g** one and tore down Eph 2:14

GROVE *(8)*

your vineyard and your olive **g**. Ex 23:11
Israel was staying in Acacia **G**, Nm 25:1
two men as spies from Acacia **G**, Jos 2:1
and left Acacia **G** with all the Jos 3:1
to irrigate a **g** of flourishing Ec 2:6
down to the walnut **g** to see the Sg 6:11
from Acacia **G** to Gilgal, Mc 6:5
from the mount called Olive **G**, Ac 1:12

GROVES *(6)*

and olive **g** that you did not Dt 6:11
and olive **g** you did not plant. Jos 24:13
as the vineyards and olive **g**. Jdg 15:5
vineyards, olive **g**, and houses Neh 5:11
olive **g**, and fruit trees Neh 9:25
to ⌊enter⌋ the **g** following their Is 66:17

GROW *(67)*

God caused to **g** out of the Gn 2:9
and may they **g** to be numerous Gn 48:16
let the hair of his head **g** long. Nm 6:5
your herds and flocks **g** large, Dt 8:13
while your eyes **g** weary looking Dt 28:32
hair began to **g** back after it Jdg 16:22
to wait for them to **g** up? Ru 1:13
until your beards **g** back; 2Sm 10:5
until your beards **g** back; 1Ch 19:5
May its morning stars **g** dark. Jb 3:9
does not **g** out of the soil, Jb 5:6
Does papyrus **g** where there is no Jb 8:11
If its roots **g** old in the ground Jb 14:8
hands are clean will **g** stronger. Jb 17:9

then let thorns g instead of Jb 31:40
are healthy and g up in the open Jb 39:4
they g old because of all my Ps 6:7
Let their eyes g too dim to see, Ps 69:23
a palm tree and g like a cedar Ps 92:12
causes grass to g for the Ps 104:14
My eyes g weary ⌊looking⌋ for Ps 119:82
My eyes g weary ⌊looking for⌋ Ps 119:123
I will make a horn g for David; Ps 132:17
causes grass to g on the hills. Ps 147:8
the daughters of song g faint. Ec 12:4
thorns and briers will g up. Is 5:6
a shoot will g from the stump Is 11:1
will help them to g, and in the Is 17:11
My eyes g weak looking upward. Is 38:14
Youths may faint and g weary, Is 40:30
they will run and not g weary; Is 40:31
He will not g weak or be Is 42:4
He lets it g strong among the Is 44:14
laurel, and the rain makes it g. Is 44:14
therefore you did not g weak. Is 57:10
spirit would g weak before Me, Is 57:16
the skies above will g dark. Jr 4:28
the evening shadows g long. Jr 6:4
will no longer g weak ⌊from Jr 31:12
her. They will g weary.' " The Jr 51:64
of these, our eyes g dim: Lm 5:17
so that it can g strong ⌊enough⌋ Ezk 30:21
The waters caused it to g; Ezk 31:4
you, make flesh g on you, and Ezk 37:6
heads or let their hair g long, Ezk 44:20
food will g along both banks Ezk 47:12
of the South will g powerful, Dn 11:5
commanders will g more powerful Dn 11:5
thistles will g over their Hs 10:8
They will g grain and blossom Hs 14:7
The sun and moon g dark, and the Jl 2:10
The sun and moon will g dark, Jl 3:15
not labor over and did not g. Jnh 4:10
it will g dark for you—without Mc 3:6
do not let your hands g weak. Zph 3:16
the wildflowers of the field g: Mt 6:28
Let both g together until the Mt 13:30
the love of many will g cold. Mt 24:12
Consider how the wildflowers g: Lk 12:27
for yourselves that won't g old, Lk 12:33
But when you g old, you will Jn 21:18
let us g in every way into Him Eph 4:15
confidence may g in Christ Jesus Php 1:26
do not g weary in doing good. 2Th 3:13
that you won't g weary and lose Heb 12:3
that you may g by it in ⌊your⌋ 1Pt 2:2
But g in the grace and knowledge 2Pt 3:18

GROWING *(11)*

tree you have g in the fields. Ex 10:5
with no plant g on it, just like Dt 29:23
with David g stronger and the 2Sm 3:1
to the hyssop g out of the wall. 1Kg 4:33
g old and becoming powerful? Jb 21:7
of my people g thorns and briers Is 32:13
in Him and is g into a holy Eph 2:21
⌊g⌋ into a mature man with a Eph 4:13
love will keep on g in knowledge Php 1:9
bearing fruit and g all over the Col 1:6
good work and g in the knowledge Col 1:10

GROWL *(6)*

may roar and the fierce lion g, Jb 4:10
g if they are not satisfied. Ps 59:15
they g and seize their prey and Is 5:29
all g like bears and moan like Is 59:11
they will g like lion cubs. Jr 51:38
a young lion g from its lair Am 3:4

GROWLS *(1)*

or young lion g over its prey Is 31:4

GROWN *(22)*

field had yet ⌊g⌋ on the land, Gn 2:5
Shelah had g up, she had not Gn 38:14
after Moses had g up, he went Ex 2:11
and black hair has g in it, Lv 13:37
the produce g in your fields. Dt 14:22
young men who had g up with him 1Kg 12:8
men who had g up with him told 1Kg 12:10
young men who had g up with him, 2Ch 10:8
men who had g up with him told 2Ch 10:10
My face has g red with weeping, Jb 16:16
My eyes have g dim from grief, Jb 17:7
they have g powerful and rich. Jr 5:27
They have g and produced fruit. Jr 12:2
Violence has g into a rod of Ezk 7:11
greatness has g and even reaches Dn 4:22
people's heart has g callous; Mt 13:15
seeds, but when g, it's taller Mt 13:32
people's heart has g callous, Ac 28:27
when he had g up, refused to be Heb 11:24
sin is fully g, it gives birth Jms 1:15
My name, and have not g weary. Rv 2:3
the earth have g wealthy from Rv 18:3

GROWS *(18)*

house until my son Shelah g up." Gn 38:11
to reap what g by itself from Lv 25:5
sow, reap what g by itself, or Lv 25:11
you will eat what g on its own, 2Kg 19:29
second year what g from that. 2Kg 19:29
The light in his tent g dark, Jb 18:6
like grass that g in the morning Ps 90:5
in the morning it sprouts and g; Ps 90:6
which withers before it g up Ps 129:6
of them g weary or stumbles; Is 5:27
wine. All joy g dark; earth's Is 24:11
you will eat what g on its own, Is 37:30
second year what g from that. Is 37:30
He never g faint or weary; Is 40:28
he g hungry and his strength Is 44:12
loins shake, every face g pale! Nah 2:10
and the seed sprouts and g— Mk 4:27
comes up and g taller than all Mk 4:32

GROWTH *(8)*

All of its g may serve as food Lv 25:7
it with showers and bless its g, Ps 65:10
is removed and new g appears and Pr 27:25
as the earth brings forth its g, Is 61:11
watered, but God gave the g. 1Co 3:6
but only God who gives the g. 1Co 3:7
promotes the g of the body for Eph 4:16
develops with g from God. Col 2:19

GRUDGE *(5)*

Esau held a g against Jacob Gn 27:41
is holding a g against us, Gn 50:15
or bear a g against members Lv 19:18
Will He bear a g forever? Jr 3:5
So Herodias held a g against him Mk 6:19

GRUDGINGLY *(3)*

you will look g at his brother, Dt 28:54
Foreigners submit to me g; 2Sm 22:45
Foreigners submit to me g; Ps 18:44

GRUMBLE *(1)*

and those who g will accept Is 29:24

GRUMBLED *(6)*

The people g to Moses, "What are Ex 15:24
community g against Moses Ex 16:2
for water, and g against Moses. Ex 17:3
You g in your tents and said, Dt 1:27
whole community g against the Jos 9:18
They g in their tents and did Ps 106:25

GRUMBLERS *(1)*

These people are discontented g, Jd 16

GRUMBLING *(1)*

without g and arguing, Php 2:14

GUARANTEE *(3)*

G Your servant's well-being; Ps 119:122
to g it to all the descendants— Rm 4:16
also become the g of a better Heb 7:22

GUARANTEED *(1)*

promise, He g it with an oath Heb 6:17

GUARANTEES *(1)*

who g to us the fixed weeks of Jr 5:24

GUARD *(92)*

whirling sword to g the way to Gn 3:24
and the captain of the g. Gn 37:36
and the captain of the g, Gn 39:1
house of the captain of the g, Gn 40:3
captain of the g assigned Joseph Gn 40:4
custody of the captain of the g. Gn 41:10
to join you and g the tent of Nm 18:4
You are to g the sanctuary and Nm 18:5
Only be on your g and diligently Dt 4:9
and the rear g went behind the Jos 6:9
and the rear g went behind the Jos 6:13
city and its rear g to the west Jos 8:13
men by it to g the kings. Jos 10:18
Be on your g in the morning and 1Sm 19:2
palace and placed them under g. 2Sm 20:3
Amasa was not on g against the 2Sm 20:10
only your sons g their walk 1Kg 8:25
to me and said, 'G this man! 1Kg 20:39
so the king would be on his g. 2Kg 6:10
Ramoth-gilead on g against 2Kg 9:14
from the g ⌊and⌋ the crowd, 2Kg 11:13
assigned to g the thresholds 1Ch 9:19
because they had g duty and were 1Ch 9:27
only your sons g their way to 2Ch 6:16
G ⌊them⌋ carefully until you Ezr 8:29
by the courtyard of the g. Neh 3:25
of Shecaniah, g of the East Gate Neh 3:29
stationed a g because of them Neh 4:9
they can stand g by night and Neh 4:22
stopped at the Gate of the G. Neh 12:39
themselves and g the gates in Neh 13:22
that You keep me under g? Jb 7:12
You, LORD, will g us; You will Ps 12:7
G me as the apple of Your eye; Ps 17:8
G me and deliver me; do not let Ps 25:20
I will g my ways so that I may Ps 39:1
I will g my mouth with a muzzle Ps 39:1
love and truth will always g me. Ps 40:11
love and truth to g him. Ps 61:7
LORD, set up a g for my mouth; Ps 141:3
so that He may g the paths of Pr 2:8
and understanding will g you, Pr 2:11
love her, and she will g you. Pr 4:6
G it, for it is your life. Pr 4:13
G your heart above all else, Pr 4:23
G your step when you go to the Ec 5:1
at his side ⌊to g⌋ against the Sg 3:8
200 for those who g its fruits. Sg 8:12
I g it night and day so that no Is 27:3
God of Israel is your rear g. Is 52:12
glory will be your rear g. Is 58:8
as your g and righteousness Is 60:17
like those who g a field, Jr 4:17
has to be on g against his Jr 9:4
an officer of the g was there, Jr 37:13
captain of the g, King Jr 39:11
captain of the g, Nebushazban Jr 39:13
captain of the g, released him Jr 40:1
captain of the g took Jeremiah Jr 40:2
captain of the g gave him a Jr 40:5
captain of the g, had appointed Jr 41:10
captain of the g, had allowed to Jr 43:6
around you; you will be their g. Ezk 38:7
said to the g whom the chief Dn 1:11
So the g continued to remove Dn 1:16
the commander of the king's g, Dn 2:14
and his rear g into the Jl 2:20
stand at my g post and station Hab 2:1
of a priest should g knowledge, Mal 2:7
"You have a g ⌊of soldiers⌋," Mt 27:65
the stone and setting the g. Mt 27:66
some of the g came into the city Mt 28:11
But you, be on your g! Mk 13:9
Him and take Him away under g." Mk 14:44
Be on your g against the yeast Lk 12:1
and be on g against all greed Lk 12:15
Be on your g. If your brother Lk 17:3
Be on your g, so that your minds Lk 21:34
the commander of the temple g, Ac 4:1
of four soldiers each to g him, Ac 12:4
the first and second g posts, Ac 12:10
Be on g for yourselves and for Ac 20:28
he be kept under g in Herod's Ac 23:35
the centurion keep Paul under g, Ac 24:23
throughout the whole imperial g, Php 1:13
g your hearts and your minds Php 4:7
strengthen and g you from the 2Th 3:3
g what has been entrusted to you, 1Tm 6:20
He is able to g what has been 2Tm 1:12
G, through the Holy Spirit who 2Tm 1:14
on your g, so that you are not 2Pt 3:17
Little children, g yourselves 1Jn 5:21

GUARD'S *(11)*

imprisoned in the g courtyard Jr 32:2
came⌋ to the g courtyard as the Jr 32:8
sitting in the g courtyard. Jr 32:12
confined in the g courtyard, Jr 33:1
was placed in the g courtyard. Jr 37:21
remained in the g courtyard. Jr 37:21
which was in the g courtyard, Jr 38:6
to stay in the g courtyard. Jr 38:13
remained in the g courtyard Jr 38:28

brought from the **g** courtyard and Jr 39:14
was confined in the **g** courtyard: Jr 39:15

GUARDED *(17)*
and **g** him as the pupil of His Dt 32:10
I **g** everything that belonged to 1Sm 25:21
escorts who **g** the entrance to 1Kg 14:27
the priests who **g** the threshold 2Kg 12:9
escorts who **g** the entrance to 2Ch 12:10
relatives, who **g** the gates: Neh 11:19
gatekeepers who **g** the storerooms Neh 12:25
two eunuchs who **g** the ⌊king's⌋ Est 2:21
two eunuchs who **g** the ⌊king's⌋ Est 6:2
and Your care has **g** my life. Jb 10:12
although he was **g**, bound by Lk 8:29
I **g** them and not one of them is Jn 17:12
front of the door **g** the prison. Ac 12:6
jailer to keep them securely **g**. Ac 16:23
and I **g** the clothes of those who Ac 22:20
with the soldier who **g** him. Ac 28:16
under King Aretas **g** the city of 2Co 11:32

GUARDHOUSE *(1)*
one of you be confined to the **g**, Gn 42:19

GUARDIAN *(8)*
"Am I my brother's **g**?" Gn 4:9
was the legal **g** of his cousin Est 2:7
You were an anointed **g** cherub, Ezk 28:14
and banished you, **g** cherub, from Ezk 28:16
is the temple **g** of the great Ac 19:35
then, was our **g** until Christ, so Gl 3:24
we are no longer under a **g**, Gl 3:25
shepherd and **g** of your souls. 1Pt 2:25

GUARDIANS *(6)*
and to the **g** of Ahab's sons, 2Kg 10:1
and the **g** sent ⌊a message⌋ to 2Kg 10:5
camp as **g** of the entrance. 1Ch 9:19
the day when the **g** of the house Ec 12:3
from me—the **g** of the walls. Sg 5:7
he is under **g** and stewards until Gl 4:2

GUARDING *(2)*
sat down and were **g** Him there. Mt 27:36
with him, who were **g** Jesus, saw Mt 27:54

GUARDS *(47)*
a slave of the captain of the **g**, Gn 41:12
He **g** the steps of His faithful 1Sm 2:9
ordered the **g** standing by him 1Sm 22:17
Jehu said to the **g** and officers, 2Kg 10:25
Then the **g** and officers threw 2Kg 10:25
the Carites, and the **g**. 2Kg 11:4
third at the gate behind the **g**. 2Kg 11:6
Then the **g** stood with their 2Kg 11:11
appointed **g** for the LORD's 2Kg 11:18
the Carites, the **g**, and all the 2Kg 11:19
commander of the **g**, a servant 2Kg 25:8
commander of the **g** tore down the 2Kg 25:10
commander of the **g**, deported the 2Kg 25:11
the commander of the **g** left some 2Kg 25:12
commander of the **g** took away 2Kg 25:15
commander of the **g** also took 2Kg 25:18
commander of the **g**, took them 2Kg 25:20
There were **g** stationed at every 1Ch 26:16
the troops, the **g**, and those 2Ch 23:12
and the **g** with me never took off Neh 4:23
while the **g** are on duty. Neh 7:3
the citizens of Jerusalem as **g**, Neh 7:3
The LORD **g** the inexperienced; Ps 116:6
The LORD **g** all those who love Ps 145:20
The one who **g** his mouth protects Pr 13:3
Righteousness **g** people of Pr 13:6
the one who **g** his way protects Pr 16:17
The one who **g** his mouth and Pr 21:23
the one who **g** himself stays far Pr 22:5
g who go about the city found Sg 3:3
g who go about the city found Sg 5:7
him as a shepherd ⌊**g**⌋ his flock, Jr 31:10
commander of the **g**, deported to Jr 39:9
commander of the **g**, left in the Jr 39:10
commander of the **g**, entered Jr 52:12
commander of the **g** tore down all Jr 52:14
commander of the **g**, deported Jr 52:15
commander of the **g**, left to be Jr 52:16
commander of the **g** took away the Jr 52:19
commander of the **g** also took Jr 52:24
commander of the **g**, took them Jr 52:26
commander of the **g**, deported 745 Jr 52:30
serving as **g** at the temple gates Ezk 44:11
The **g** were so shaken from fear Mt 28:4
fully armed, **g** his estate, his Lk 11:21
with the **g** standing in front of Ac 5:23
interrogated the **g** and ordered Ac 12:19

GUARDS' *(1)*
palace by way of the **g** gate. 2Kg 11:19

GUDGODAH *(2)*
They traveled from there to **G**, Dt 10:7
and from **G** to Jotbathah, Dt 10:7

GUESSED *(1)*
he **g** that the baby was dead. 2Sm 12:19

GUEST *(4)*
lamb and prepared it for his **g**. 2Sm 12:4
Where is the **g** room for Me to Mk 14:14
Where is the **g** room where I can Lk 22:11
also prepare a **g** room for me, Phm 22

GUESTS *(21)*
after that, the **g** can eat. 1Sm 9:13
all the invited **g** who were with 1Kg 1:41
of Adonijah's **g** got up trembling 1Kg 1:49
well as **g** from the surrounding Neh 5:17
My house **g** and female servants Jb 19:15
that her **g** are in the depths of Pr 9:18
He has consecrated His **g**. Zph 1:7
sinners came as **g** to eat with Mt 9:10
Can the wedding **g** be sad while Mt 9:15
because of his oaths and his **g**. Mt 14:9
banquet was filled with **g**. Mt 22:10
the king came in to view the **g**, Mt 22:11
sinners were also **g** with Jesus Mk 2:15
The wedding **g** cannot fast while Mk 2:19
she pleased Herod and his **g**. Mk 6:22
oaths and the **g** he did not want Mk 6:26
and others who were **g** with them. Lk 5:29
make the wedding **g** fast while Lk 5:34
the presence of all the other **g**. Lk 14:10
Jason has received them as **g**! Ac 17:7
angels as **g** without knowing it Heb 13:2

GUIDANCE *(7)*
altar will be for me to seek **g**." 2Kg 16:15
even consulted a medium for **g**, 1Ch 10:13
a discerning man will obtain **g**— Pr 1:5
Without **g**, people fall, but with Pr 11:14
but **g** from the wicked ⌊leads to⌋ Pr 12:5
and wage war with sound **g**. Pr 20:18
should wage war with sound **g**— Pr 24:6

GUIDE *(18)*
You will **g** ⌊them⌋ to Your holy Ex 15:13
cloud by day to **g** you on the Dt 1:33
G me in Your truth and teach me, Ps 25:5
lead and **g** me because of Your Ps 31:3
You **g** me with Your counsel, Ps 73:24
and He will **g** you on the right Pr 3:6
here and there, they will **g** you; Pr 6:22
I will **g** them on paths they have Is 42:16
compassionate One will **g** them, Is 49:10
is no one to **g** her among all Is 51:18
And if the blind **g** the blind, Mt 15:14
to **g** our feet into the way of Lk 1:79
Can the blind **g** the blind? Lk 6:39
will **g** you into all the truth. Jn 16:13
who became a **g** to those who Ac 1:16
that you are a **g** for the blind, Rm 2:19
we also **g** the whole animal. Jms 3:3
He will **g** them to springs of Rv 7:17

GUIDED *(8)*
g me on the right way to take Gn 24:48
day I was born I **g** the widow— Jb 31:18
like sheep and **g** them like a Ps 78:52
a pure heart and **g** them with his Ps 78:72
He **g** them to the harbor they Ps 107:30
with joy and be peacefully **g**; Is 55:12
G by the Spirit, he entered the Lk 2:27
are **g** by a very small rudder Jms 3:4

GUIDES *(7)*
who **g** Joseph like a flock; Ps 80:1
integrity of the upright **g** them, Pr 11:3
The lamp that **g** the wicked— Pr 21:4
They are blind **g**. And if the Mt 15:14
Woe to you, blind **g**, who say, Mt 23:16
Blind **g**! You strain out a gnat, Mt 23:24
he said, "unless someone **g** me?" Ac 8:31

GUIDING *(6)*
of Abinadab, were **g** the cart 2Sm 6:3
Uzzah and Ahio were **g** the cart. 1Ch 13:7
away from them, **g** them on their Neh 9:19
I am **g** you on straight paths. Pr 4:11
my mind still **g** me with wisdom— Ec 2:3
g them the wrong way in the Jr 50:6

GUILD *(1)*
families of the **g** of linen 1Ch 4:21

GUILT *(98)*
such enormous **g** on me and on my Gn 20:9
you would have brought **g** on us." Gn 26:10
always bear the **g** for sinning Gn 44:32
there is **g** of bloodshed. Ex 22:3
may bear the **g** connected with Ex 28:38
they do not incur **g** and die. Ex 28:43
sins, bringing **g** on the people, Lv 4:3
and incur **g** by doing what is Lv 4:13
is prohibited, and incurs **g**, Lv 4:22
is prohibited, and incurs **g**, Lv 4:27
he incurs **g** in such an instance. Lv 5:4
someone incurs **g** in one of these Lv 5:5
bears the consequences of his **g**. Lv 5:17
and acknowledged ⌊his⌋ **g**— Lv 6:4
the day he acknowledges ⌊his⌋ **g**. Lv 6:5
he may have done to incur **g**." Lv 6:7
take away the **g** of the community Lv 10:17
will not incur **g** because of him. Lv 19:17
will bear their **g** and die Lv 20:20
The husband will be free of **g**, Nm 5:31
bear the consequences of her **g**." Nm 5:31
his **g** remains on him." Nm 15:31
or they will incur **g** and die. Nm 18:22
will not incur **g** because of it Nm 18:32
from Israel the **g** of shedding Dt 19:13
yourselves the **g** of shedding Dt 21:9
You must not bring **g** on the land Dt 24:4
return it with a **g** offering, 1Sm 6:3
What **g** offering should we send 1Sm 6:4
sending Him as a **g** offering. 1Sm 6:8
As a **g** offering to the LORD, 1Sm 6:17
and said, "The **g** is mine, my 1Sm 25:24
he has pronounced his own **g**. 2Sm 14:13
I wipe out this **g** so that you 2Sm 21:3
take away Your servant's **g**." 2Sm 24:10
remind me of my **g** and to kill my 1Kg 17:18
should he bring **g** on Israel?" 1Ch 21:3
take away Your servant's **g**." 1Ch 21:8
will not incur **g** before the LORD 2Ch 19:10
this, and you will not incur **g**. 2Ch 19:10
Jerusalem for this **g** of theirs. 2Ch 24:18
you plan to bring **g** on us from 2Ch 28:13
to add to our sins and our **g**. 2Ch 28:13
For we have much **g**, and fierce 2Ch 28:13
instead, Amon increased ⌊his⌋ **g**. 2Ch 33:23
heads and our **g** is as high as Ezr 9:6
Our **g** has been terrible from the Ezr 9:7
our evil deeds and terrible **g**— Ezr 9:13
we are before You with our **g**, Ezr 9:15
women, adding to Israel's **g**. Ezr 10:10
ram from the flock for their **g**; Ezr 10:19
not cover their **g** or let their Neh 4:5
sins and the **g** of their fathers Neh 9:2
do by hiding my **g** in my heart, Jb 31:33
I am clean and have no **g**. Jb 33:9
You took away the **g** of my sin. Ps 32:5
So I confess my **g**; I am anxious Ps 38:18
Wash away my **g**, and cleanse me Ps 51:2
my sins and blot out all my **g**. Ps 51:9
Save me from the **g** of bloodshed, Ps 51:14
Add **g** to their guilt; do not let Ps 69:27
guilt to their **g**; do not let Ps 69:27
atoned for ⌊their⌋ **g** and did not Ps 78:38
You took away Your people's **g**; Ps 85:2
his forefathers' **g** be remembered Ps 109:14
let your mouth bring **g** on you, Ec 5:6
stain of your **g** is still in Jr 2:22
acknowledge your **g**—you have Jr 3:13
of your great **g** that your skirts Jr 13:22
Though our **g** testifies against Jr 14:7
remember their **g** and punish Jr 14:10
LORD, the **g** of our fathers; Jr 14:20
us? What is our **g**? What is our Jr 16:10
and their **g** is not hidden from Jr 16:17
for their **g** and sin because Jr 16:18
Do not wipe out their **g**; Jr 18:23
for their **g**, and I will make it Jr 25:12
of your enormous **g** and your Jr 30:14
of your enormous **g** and your Jr 30:15
one will search for Israel's **g**, Jr 50:20
land is full of **g** against the Jr 51:5
Don't be silenced by her **g**. Jr 51:6
not reveal your **g** and so restore Lm 2:14

and the **g** of her priests, Lm 4:13
to ⌊their⌋ **g** so that they will Ezk 21:23
have drawn attention to your **g**, Ezk 21:24
grievous **g** by taking revenge Ezk 25:12
recognize their **g** and seek My Hs 5:15
remember their **g** and punish Hs 8:13
of your **g** and hostility. Hs 9:7
He will remember their **g**; Hs 9:9
now they must bear their **g**. Hs 10:2
But he incurred **g** through Baal Hs 13:1
Ephraim's **g** is preserved; Hs 13:12
will bear her **g** because she has Hs 13:16
swear by the **g** of Samaria and Am 8:14
I have removed your **g** from you, Zch 3:4
take away the **g** of this land Zch 3:9

GUILTY *(59)*
I will be **g** before you forever. Gn 43:9
I and my people are the **g** ones. Ex 9:27
death, no one is **g** of bloodshed. Ex 22:2
I will not justify the **g**. Ex 23:7
not leave ⌊the **g**⌋ unpunished, Ex 34:7
public call to testify, he is **g**. Lv 5:1
of it, he is unclean and **g**. Lv 5:2
later⌋ recognizes ⌊it⌋, he is **g**. Lv 5:3
he is indeed **g** before the LORD." Lv 5:19
who eats any of it will be **g**. Lv 7:18
they will be **g** and die because Lv 22:9
toward the LORD and is **g**. Nm 5:6
atonement for the ⌊**g**⌋ person. Nm 5:8
not leave ⌊the **g**⌋ unpunished, Nm 14:18
will not be **g** of bloodshed, Nm 35:27
a murderer who is **g** of killing Nm 35:31
against you, and you will be **g**. Dt 15:9
will not become **g** of bloodshed Dt 19:10
anyone is found **g** of an offense Dt 21:22
she is not **g** of an offense Dt 22:26
you, and you will be held **g**. Dt 24:15
the innocent and condemn the **g**. Dt 25:1
If the **g** party deserves to be Dt 25:2
so you are not **g** ⌊of breaking Jdg 21:22
If I am **g**, let him kill me." 2Sm 14:32
don't hold me **g**, and don't 2Sm 19:19
who was **g** of wrongdoing. 2Ch 20:35
you not also **g** before the LORD 2Ch 28:10
away, and being **g**, ⌊they Ezr 10:19
my mouth would declare me **g**. Jb 9:20
I will be found **g**, why should I Jb 9:29
not declare me **g**! Let me know Jb 10:2
He will ⌊even⌋ rescue the **g** one, Jb 22:30
silent, who can declare ⌊Him⌋ **g**? Jb 34:29
you declare Me **g** to justify Jb 40:8
I was **g** ⌊when I⌋ was born; Ps 51:5
one who goes on in his **g** acts. Ps 68:21
my **g** acts are not hidden from Ps 69:5
let him be found **g**, and let his Ps 109:7
Acquitting the **g** and condemning Pr 17:15
to the **g** by perverting Pr 18:5
A **g** man's conduct is crooked, Pr 21:8
says to the **g**, "You are innocent Pr 24:24
with those who convict the **g**, Pr 24:25
you, and you will become **g**. Pr 30:10
who acquit the **g** for a bribe and Is 5:23
its inhabitants have become **g**; Is 24:6
ate of it found themselves **g**; Jr 2:3
Your **g** acts have diverted these Jr 5:25
said: We're not **g**; instead, they Jr 50:7
You are **g** of the blood you have Ezk 22:4
don't let Judah become **g**! Hs 4:15
convicts ⌊the **g**⌋ at the city Am 5:10
never leave ⌊the **g**⌋ unpunished. Nah 1:3
They are **g**; their strength Hab 1:11
sin and those **g** of lawlessness. Mt 13:41
but is **g** of an eternal sin"— Mk 3:29
way will be **g** of sin against 1Co 11:27
is **g** of ⌊breaking it⌋ all. Jms 2:10

GULF *(1)*
LORD will divide the **G** of Suez. Is 11:15

GULL *(2)*
owl, the **g**, the various kinds Lv 11:16
owl, the **g**, the various kinds Dt 14:15

GULLIBLE *(3)*
fool, and jealousy slays the **g**. Jb 5:2
she is **g** and knows nothing. Pr 9:13
The **g** inherit foolishness, Pr 14:18

GULP *(2)*
will drink and **g** down and be as Ob 16
out a gnat, yet **g** down a camel! Mt 23:24

GULPS *(1)*
Its brood **g** down blood, and Jb 39:30

GUM *(2)*
camels were carrying aromatic **g**, Gn 37:25
honey, aromatic **g** and resin, Gn 43:11

GUNI *(4)*
Jahzeel, **G**, Jezer, and Shillem. Gn 46:24
the Gunite clan from **G**; Nm 26:48
of Abdiel, son of **G**, was head of 1Ch 5:15
Jahziel, **G**, Jezer, and Shallum— 1Ch 7:13

GUNITE *(1)*
the **G** clan from Guni; Nm 26:48

GUR *(1)*
his chariot at **G** Pass near 2Kg 9:27

GUR-BAAL *(1)*
that live in **G**, and the Meunites 2Ch 26:7

GUSH *(2)*
the springs to **g** into the Ps 104:10
for water will **g** in the Is 35:6

GUSHED *(6)*
a great amount of water **g** out, Nm 20:11
until blood **g** out on them. 1Kg 18:28
struck the rock and water **g** out; Ps 78:20
opened a rock, and water **g** out; Ps 105:41
fountains of the ocean **g** forth, Pr 8:28
split the rock, and water **g** out. Is 48:21

GUSHES *(1)*
As a well **g** out its water, Jr 6:7

GUSTING *(1)*
G to the south, turning to the Ec 1:6

GUTTER *(3)*
the **g** is 21 inches ⌊deep⌋ and 21 Ezk 43:13
from the **g** on the ground to Ezk 43:14
its **g** is 21 inches all around Ezk 43:17

GUY *(3)*
said, "How can this **g** save us?" 1Sm 10:27
this **g** in prison and feed him 1Kg 22:27
this **g** in prison and feed him 2Ch 18:26

GUZZLE *(1)*
some⌋ wine, let's **g** ⌊some⌋ beer; Is 56:12

H

HA *(1)*
their heads, and saying, "**H**! Mk 15:29

HAAHASHTARI *(1)*
Ahuzzam, Hepher, Temeni, and **H**. 1Ch 4:6

HABAIAH *(1)*
of **H**, the descendants Ezr 2:61

HABAKKUK *(2)*
oracle that **H** the prophet saw Hab 1:1
A prayer of **H** the prophet. Hab 3:1

HABAZZINIAH *(1)*
Jeremiah, son of **H**, and his Jr 35:3

HABIT *(2)*
the ox was in the **h** of goring, Ex 21:29
the ox was in the **h** of goring, Ex 21:36

HABITATION *(1)*
cuts a shaft far from human **h**, Jb 28:4

HABITUALLY *(1)*
meetings, as some **h** do, but Heb 10:25

HABOR *(3)*
them in Halah and by the **H**, 2Kg 17:6
put them in Halah and by the **H**, 2Kg 18:11
them to Halah, **H**, Hara, and 1Ch 5:26

HACALIAH *(2)*
The words of Nehemiah son of **H**: Neh 1:1
son of **H**, and Zedekiah, Neh 10:1

HACHILAH *(3)*
on the hill of **H** south of 1Sm 23:19
the hill of **H** opposite Jeshimon. 1Sm 26:1
at the hill of **H** opposite 1Sm 26:3

HACHMONI *(2)*
Jashobeam son of **H** was chief of 1Ch 11:11
Jehiel son of **H** attended the 1Ch 27:32

HACKED *(2)*
Then he **h** Agag to pieces before 1Sm 15:33
it You who **h** Rahab to pieces, Is 51:9

HAD *(2450)*
(See pp. xi-xii.)

HADAD *(17)*
(AKA HADAR, RIMMON)
H, Tema, Jetur, Naphish, and Gn 25:15
H son of Bedad ruled in his Gn 36:35
H died, Samlah from Masrekah Gn 36:36
LORD raised up **H** the Edomite as 1Kg 11:14
H fled to Egypt, along with some 1Kg 11:17
At the time **H** was a small boy. 1Kg 11:17
H and his men set out from 1Kg 11:18
Egypt, who gave **H** a house, 1Kg 11:18
Pharaoh liked **H** so much that he 1Kg 11:19
H heard in Egypt that David 1Kg 11:21
was dead, **H** said to Pharaoh 1Kg 11:21
to the trouble **H** ⌊had caused⌋. 1Kg 11:25
Mishma, Dumah, Massa, **H**, Tema, 1Ch 1:30
Husham died, **H** son of Bedad, who 1Ch 1:46
H died, Samlah from Masrekah 1Ch 1:47
Baal-hanan died, **H** ruled in his 1Ch 1:50
Then **H** died. Edom's chiefs: 1Ch 1:51

HADAD'S *(3)*
gave birth to **H** son Genubath. 1Kg 11:20
H town was named Avith. 1Ch 1:46
H city was named Pai, and his 1Ch 1:50

HADAD-RIMMON *(1)*
the mourning of **H** in the plain Zch 12:11

HADADEZER *(13)*
also defeated **H** son of Rehob, 2Sm 8:3
came to assist King **H** of Zobah, 2Sm 8:5
defeated the entire army of **H**, 2Sm 8:9
fought against **H** and defeated 2Sm 8:10
for Toi and **H** had fought many 2Sm 8:10
and the spoil of **H** son of Rehob, 2Sm 8:12
H sent ⌊messengers⌋ to bring the 2Sm 10:16
from his master **H** king of Zobah 1Kg 11:23
defeated King **H** of Zobah at 1Ch 18:3
came to assist King **H** of Zobah, 1Ch 18:5
entire army of King **H** of Zobah, 1Ch 18:9
fought against **H** and defeated 1Ch 18:10
for Tou and **H** had fought many 1Ch 18:10

HADADEZER'S *(8)*
the gold shields of **H** officers 2Sm 8:7
Betah and Berothai, **H** cities. 2Sm 8:8
commander of **H** army, leading 2Sm 10:16
kings who were **H** subjects saw 2Sm 10:19
shields carried by **H** officers 1Ch 18:7
Tibhath and Cun, **H** cities, David 1Ch 18:8
commander of **H** army, leading 1Ch 19:16
When **H** subjects saw that they 1Ch 19:19

HADAR *(1)*
(AKA HADAD)
of Achbor died, **H** ruled in his Gn 36:39

HADASHAH *(1)*
Zenan, **H**, Migdal-gad, Jos 15:37

HADASSAH *(1)*
(AKA ESTHER)
legal guardian of his cousin **H** Est 2:7

HADES *(10)*
You will go down to **H**. Mt 11:23
and the forces of **H** will not Mt 16:18
No, you will go down to **H**! Lk 10:15
And being in torment in **H**, Lk 16:23
You will not leave my soul in **H**, Ac 2:27
was not left in **H**, and His flesh Ac 2:31
I hold the keys of death and **H**. Rv 1:18
and **H** was following after him. Rv 6:8
and Death and **H** gave up their Rv 20:13
Death and **H** were thrown into the Rv 20:14

HADID *(1)*
H, Zeboim, Neballat, Neh 11:34

HADID'S *(2)*
Lod's, **H**, and Ono's people 725 Ezr 2:33
Lod's, **H**, and Ono's people 721 Neh 7:37

HADLAI *(1)*
and Amasa son of **H**—stood in 2Ch 28:12

HADN'T *(8)*
(See pp. xi-xii.)

HADORAM *(5)*
H, Uzal, Diklah, Gn 10:27
H, Uzal, Diklah, 1Ch 1:21
he sent his son **H** to King David 1Ch 18:10
⌊**H** brought⌋ all kinds of items 1Ch 18:10
Then King Rehoboam sent **H**, 2Ch 10:18

HADRACH *(1)*
LORD is against the land of **H**, Zch 9:1

HAELEPH *(1)*
Zela, **H**, Jebus (that is, Jos 18:28

HAGAB'S *(1)*
H descendants, Shalmai's Ezr 2:46

HAGABA'S *(1)*
descendants, **H** descendants, Neh 7:48

HAGABAH'S *(1)*
descendants, **H** descendants, Ezr 2:45

HAGAR *(13)*
owned an Egyptian slave named **H**. Gn 16:1
So Abram's wife Sarai took **H**, Gn 16:3
He slept with **H**, and she became Gn 16:4
He said, "**H**, slave of Sarai, Gn 16:8
So **H** gave birth to Abram's son, Gn 16:15
name Ishmael to the son **H** had. Gn 16:15
years old when **H** bore Ishmael to Gn 16:16
the one **H** the Egyptian had borne Gn 21:9
of God called to **H** from heaven Gn 21:17
said to her, "What's wrong, **H**? Gn 21:17
Ishmael, whom **H** the Egyptian, Gn 25:12
into slavery—this is **H**. Gl 4:24
Now **H** is Mount Sinai in Arabia Gl 4:25

HAGAR'S *(1)*
⌊put them⌋ on **H** shoulders, Gn 21:14

HAGGAI *(11)*
the prophets **H** and Zechariah son Ezr 5:1
the prophesying of **H** the prophet Ezr 6:14
came through **H** the prophet to Hg 1:1
LORD came through **H** the prophet: Hg 1:3
and the words of the prophet **H**, Hg 1:12
H, the LORD's messenger, Hg 1:13
LORD came through **H** the prophet: Hg 2:1
the LORD came to **H** the prophet: Hg 2:10
H asked, "If someone defiled Hg 2:13
Then **H** replied, "So is this Hg 2:14
the LORD came to **H** a second time Hg 2:20

HAGGEDOLIM *(1)*
Zabdiel son of **H**, was their Neh 11:14

HAGGI *(2)*
Ziphion, **H**, Shuni, Ezbon, Eri, Gn 46:16
the Haggite clan from **H**; Nm 26:15

HAGGIAH *(1)*
Shimea, his son **H**, and his son 1Ch 6:30

HAGGITE *(1)*
the **H** clan from Haggi; Nm 26:15

HAGGITH *(5)*
fourth was Adonijah, son of **H**; 2Sm 3:4
Adonijah son of **H** kept exalting 1Kg 1:5
Adonijah son of **H** has become 1Kg 1:11
Adonijah son of **H** came to 1Kg 2:13
Adonijah son of **H** was fourth; 1Ch 3:2

HAGRI *(1)*
of Nathan, Mibhar son of **H**, 1Ch 11:38

HAGRITE *(1)*
Jaziz the **H** was in charge of the 1Ch 27:31

HAGRITES *(5)*
they waged war against the **H**, 1Ch 5:10
They waged war against the **H**, 1Ch 5:19
and the **H** and all their allies 1Ch 5:20
of the **H** were killed because 1Ch 5:22
the Ishmaelites, Moab and the **H**, Ps 83:6

HAGRITES' *(2)*
They captured the **H** livestock— 1Ch 5:21
lived there in the **H** place until 1Ch 5:22

HAIL *(33)*
down the worst **h** that has ever Ex 9:18
die when the **h** falls on them." Ex 9:19
let there be **h** throughout the Ex 9:22
and the LORD sent thunder and **h**. Ex 9:23
the LORD rained **h** on the land Ex 9:23
The **h**, with lightning flashing Ex 9:24
the **h** struck down everything in Ex 9:25
The **h** beat down every plant of Ex 9:25
place it didn't **h** was in the Ex 9:26
enough of God's thunder and **h**. Ex 9:28
and there will be no more **h**, Ex 9:29
Then the thunder and **h** ceased, Ex 9:33
that the rain, **h**, and thunder Ex 9:34
left to you that escaped the **h**; Ex 10:5
everything that the **h** left." Ex 10:12
the trees that the **h** had left. Ex 10:15
them died from the **h** than the Jos 10:11
you seen the storehouses of **h**, Jb 38:22
onward with **h** and blazing coals Ps 18:12
their vines with **h** and their Ps 78:47
livestock to **h** and their cattle Ps 78:48
He gave them **h** for rain, and Ps 105:32
lightning and **h**, snow and cloud, Ps 148:8
like a devastating **h** storm, Is 28:2
H will sweep away the false Is 28:17
But **h** will level the forest, Is 32:19
mildew, and **h**, but you didn't Hg 2:17
and mocked Him: "**H**, King of the Mt 27:29
to salute Him, "**H**, King of the Mk 15:18
Him and said, "**H**, King of the Jn 19:3
trumpet, and **h** and fire, mixed Rv 8:7
an earthquake, and severe **h**. Rv 11:19
for the plague of **h** because that Rv 16:21

HAILSTONES *(7)*
LORD threw large **h** on them from Jos 10:11
He throws His **h** like crumbs. Ps 147:17
driving rain, a torrent, and **h**. Is 30:30
and I will send **h** plunging down, Ezk 13:11
and **h** ⌊will fall⌋ in destructive Ezk 13:13
torrential rain, **h**, fire, and Ezk 38:22
Enormous **h**, each weighing about Rv 16:21

HAIR *(89)*
covered with **h** like a fur coat, Gn 25:25
yarn; fine linen and goat **h**; Ex 25:4
of goat **h** for a tent over Ex 26:7
yarn; fine linen and goat **h**; Ex 35:6
linen or goat **h**, ram skins dyed Ex 35:23
spun the goat **h** by virtue of Ex 35:26
of goat **h** for a tent over Ex 36:14
Do not let your **h** hang loose and Lv 10:6
If the **h** in the infection has Lv 13:3
and the **h** in it has not turned Lv 13:4
that has turned the **h** white, Lv 13:10
skin and the **h** in it has turned Lv 13:20
if there is no white **h** in it, Lv 13:21
If the **h** in the spot has turned Lv 13:25
there is no white **h** in the spot Lv 13:26
and the **h** in it is yellow and Lv 13:30
and there is no black **h** in it, Lv 13:31
is no yellow **h** in it and it does Lv 13:32
not need to look for yellow **h**; Lv 13:36
and black **h** has grown in it, Lv 13:37
a man loses the **h** of his head, Lv 13:40
he loses the **h** at his hairline Lv 13:41
torn and his **h** hanging loose, Lv 13:45
off all his **h**, and bathe with Lv 14:8
shave off all his **h** ⌊again⌋ on Lv 14:9
eyebrows, and the rest of his **h**. Lv 14:9
to cut off the **h** at the sides Lv 19:27
not dishevel his **h** or tear his Lv 21:10
to let down her **h** and place in Nm 5:18
must not cut his **h** throughout Nm 6:5
is to let the **h** of his head grow Nm 6:5
because the **h** consecrated to his Nm 6:7
his consecrated head of **h**, Nm 6:9
consecrated **h** became defiled. Nm 6:12
take the **h** from his head, Nm 6:18
made of goat **h**, and every Nm 31:20
never cut his **h**, because the boy Jdg 13:5
to her, "My **h** has never been Jdg 16:17
But his **h** began to grow back Jdg 16:22
a stone at a **h** and not miss. Jdg 20:16
and his **h** will never be cut." 1Sm 1:11
not a **h** of his head will fall to 1Sm 14:45
some goats' **h** on its head, 1Sm 19:13
with some goats' **h** on its head. 1Sm 19:16
not a **h** of your son will fall to 2Sm 14:11
because ⌊his **h**⌋ got so heavy for 2Sm 14:26
would weigh the **h** from his head 2Sm 14:26
not a single **h** of his will fall 1Kg 1:52
out some of the **h** from my head Ezr 9:3
men, and pulled out their **h**. Neh 13:25
think the deep had white **h**! Jb 41:32
Gray **h** is a glorious crown; Pr 16:31
splendor of old men is gray **h**. Pr 20:29
Your **h** is like a flock of goats Sg 4:1
my **h** with droplets of the night. Sg 5:2
His **h** is wavy and black as a Sg 5:11
Your **h** is like a flock of goats Sg 6:5
the **h** of your head like purple Sg 7:5
instead of beautifully styled **h**, Is 3:24
the head, the **h** on the legs, and Is 7:20
Cut off the **h** of your sacred vow Jr 7:29
who clip the **h** on their temples Jr 9:26
pair of scales and divide the **h**. Ezk 5:1
from the **h** and secure them Ezk 5:3
and took me by the **h** of my head. Ezk 8:3
were formed and your **h** grew, Ezk 16:7
heads or let their **h** grow long, Ezk 44:20
but must carefully trim their **h**. Ezk 44:20
not a **h** of their heads was Dn 3:27
until his **h** grew like eagles' Dn 4:33
and the **h** of His head like Dn 7:9
his **h** is streaked with gray, Hs 7:9
and cut off your **h** in sorrow for Mc 1:16
make a single **h** white or black. Mt 5:36
His feet with the **h** of her head, Lk 7:38
feet and wiped them with her **h**. Lk 7:44
but not a **h** of your head will be Lk 21:18
and wiped His feet with her **h**, Jn 11:2
and wiped His feet with her **h**. Jn 12:3
since not a **h** will be lost from Ac 27:34
not covered, her **h** should be cut 1Co 11:6
to have her **h** cut off or her 1Co 11:6
a man has long **h** it is a 1Co 11:14
but that if a woman has long **h**, 1Co 11:15
For her **h** is given to her as a 1Co 11:15
His head and **h** were white like Rv 1:14
like sackcloth made of goat **h**; Rv 6:12
they had **h** like women's hair; Rv 9:8
they had hair like women's **h**; Rv 9:8

HAIRLINE *(1)*
if he loses the hair at his **h**, Lv 13:41

HAIRS *(7)*
bring my gray **h** down to Sheol Gn 42:38
bring my gray **h** down to Sheol Gn 44:29
the gray **h** of your servant Gn 44:31
are more than the **h** of my head, Ps 40:12
numerous than the **h** of my head; Ps 69:4
But even the **h** of your head have Mt 10:30
the **h** of your head are all Lk 12:7

HAIRSTYLES *(2)*
with elaborate **h**, gold, pearls, 1Tm 2:9
elaborate **h** and the wearing 1Pt 3:3

HAIRY *(5)*
my brother Esau is a **h** man, Gn 27:11
his hands were **h** like those of Gn 27:23
A **h** man with a leather belt 2Kg 1:8
the **h** head of one who goes on in Ps 68:21
not put on a **h** cloak in order to Zch 13:4

HAKELDAMA *(1)*
language that field is called **H**, Ac 1:19

HAKKATAN *(1)*
Johanan son of **H** from Azgad's Ezr 8:12

HAKKOZ *(5)*
the seventh to **H**, the eighth to 1Ch 24:10
of **H**, the descendants Ezr 2:61
Uriah, son of **H**, made repairs. Neh 3:4
Uriah, son of **H**, made repairs to Neh 3:21
the descendants of **H**, and the Neh 7:63

HAKUPHA'S *(2)*
descendants, **H** descendants, Ezr 2:51
descendants, **H** descendants, Neh 7:53

HALAH *(4)*
settled them in **H** and by the 2Kg 17:6
and put them in **H** and by the 2Kg 18:11
He took them to **H**, Habor, Hara, 1Ch 5:26
who are in **H** who are among Ob 20

HALAK *(2)*
from Mount **H**, which ascends to Jos 11:17
valley of Lebanon to Mount **H**, Jos 12:7

HALF *(212)*
a gold ring weighing **h** a shekel, Gn 24:22
Moses took **h** the blood and set Ex 24:6
the ⌊other⌋ **h** of the blood he Ex 24:6
leftover **h** curtain is to hang Ex 26:12
The **h** yard on one side and the Ex 26:13
one side and the **h** yard on the Ex 26:13
square, seven and a **h** feet long, Ex 27:1
and seven and a **h** feet wide; Ex 27:1
must be four and a **h** feet high. Ex 27:1
of the gate⌋ 22 and a **h** feet, Ex 27:14
other side 22 and a **h** ⌊feet⌋, Ex 27:15
the height seven and a **h** feet, Ex 27:18
must pay **h** a shekel according Ex 30:13
This **h** shekel is a contribution Ex 30:13
than **h** a shekel when giving the Ex 30:15
12 and a **h** pounds of liquid Ex 30:23
of liquid myrrh, **h** as much (six Ex 30:23
12 and a **h** pounds of cassia Ex 30:24
and a **h** feet long and seven Ex 38:1
and seven and a **h** feet wide, Ex 38:1
and was four and a **h** feet high. Ex 38:1
the gate⌋ were 22 and a **h** feet, Ex 38:14

hangings were 22 and a **h** feet, Ex 38:15
seven and a **h** feet high. Ex 38:18
h a shekel according to the Ex 38:26
h of it in the morning and half Lv 6:20
morning and **h** in the evening. Lv 6:20
whose flesh is **h** eaten away when Nm 12:12
from their **h** and give ⌊it⌋ to Nm 31:29
the Israelites' **h**, take one out Nm 31:30
The **h** portion for those who went Nm 31:36
the Israelites' **h**, which Moses Nm 31:42
the community's **h** was: 337,500 Nm 31:43
from the Israelites' **h**. Nm 31:47
and **h** the tribe of Manasseh son Nm 32:33
to the nine and a **h** tribes. Nm 34:13
and **h** the tribe of Manasseh has Nm 34:14
The two and a **h** tribes have Nm 34:15
and **h** the hill country of Gilead Dt 3:12
gave to **h** the tribe of Manasseh Dt 3:13
and **h** the tribe of Manasseh. Dt 29:8
and **h** the tribe of Manasseh: Jos 1:12
and **h** the tribe of Manasseh went Jos 4:12
h of them were in front of Mount Jos 8:33
Gerizim and **h** in front of Mount Jos 8:33
and **h** of Gilead up to the Jabbok Jos 12:2
and **h** of Gilead to the border of Jos 12:5
and **h** the tribe of Manasseh. Jos 12:6
the nine tribes and **h** the tribe Jos 13:7
With the other **h** of the tribe, Jos 13:8
and **h** the land of the Ammonites Jos 13:25
And to **h** the tribe of Manasseh, Jos 13:29
to **h** the tribe of Manasseh's Jos 13:29
But **h** of Gilead, and Og's royal Jos 13:31
h the descendants of Machir by Jos 13:31
for the nine and a **h** tribes, Jos 14:2
to the two and a **h** tribes beyond Jos 14:3
and **h** the tribe of Manasseh have Jos 18:7
and **h** the tribe of Manasseh. Jos 21:5
and **h** the tribe of Manasseh in Jos 21:6
From **h** the tribe of Manasseh Jos 21:25
From **h** the tribe of Manasseh, Jos 21:27
and **h** the tribe of Manasseh, Jos 22:1
given ⌊territory⌋ to **h** the tribe Jos 22:7
⌊territory⌋ to the other **h**, Jos 22:7
and **h** the tribe of Manasseh left Jos 22:9
h the tribe of Manasseh built Jos 22:10
and **h** the tribe of Manasseh have Jos 22:11
and **h** the tribe of Manasseh, Jos 22:13
and **h** the tribe of Manasseh, Jos 22:15
and **h** the tribe of Manasseh Jos 22:21
bread from a **h** bushel of flour. Jdg 6:19
shaved off **h** their beards, 2Sm 10:4
their clothes in **h** at the hips, 2Sm 10:4
Even if **h** of us die, they will 2Sm 18:3
of Judah and **h** of Israel's 2Sm 19:40
two and give **h** to one and half 1Kg 3:25
half to one and **h** to the other." 1Kg 3:25
was seven and a **h** feet wide, 1Kg 6:6
third was 10 and a **h** feet wide. 1Kg 6:6
was⌋ seven and a **h** feet high. 1Kg 6:10
was seven and a **h** feet long, 1Kg 6:24
was seven and a **h** feet long. 1Kg 6:24
and a **h** feet was the height 1Kg 7:16
and seven and a **h** feet was also 1Kg 7:16
was seven and a **h** feet high and 1Kg 7:23
brim, 10 every **h** yard, 1Kg 7:24
and four and a **h** feet high. 1Kg 7:27
Indeed, I was not even told **h**. 1Kg 10:7
king four and a **h** tons of gold, 1Kg 10:10
were to give me **h** your house, 1Kg 13:8
commander of **h** his chariots, 1Kg 16:9
of Israel were split in **h**: 1Kg 16:21
h the people followed Tibni son 1Kg 16:21
him king, and **h** followed Omri. 1Kg 16:21
Haroeh, **h** of the Manahathites, 1Ch 2:52
and **h** of the Manahathites, 1Ch 2:54
Reuben and Gad and **h** the tribe 1Ch 5:18
The sons of **h** the tribe of 1Ch 5:23
and **h** the tribe of Manasseh into 1Ch 5:26
towns from the **h** tribe of 1Ch 6:61
From **h** the tribe of Manasseh, 1Ch 6:70
from the families of **h** the tribe 1Ch 6:71
who was seven and a **h** feet tall. 1Ch 11:23
From **h** the tribe of Manasseh: 1Ch 12:31
and **h** the tribe of Manasseh: 1Ch 12:37
their clothes in **h** at the hips, 1Ch 19:4
and **h** the tribe of Manasseh as 1Ch 26:32
for **h** the tribe of Manasseh, 1Ch 27:20
for **h** the tribe of Manasseh in 1Ch 27:21
of one was seven and a **h** feet, 2Ch 3:11
wing was seven and a **h** feet, 2Ch 3:11
cherub was seven and a **h** feet, 2Ch 3:12
wing was seven and a **h** feet, 2Ch 3:12
each was seven and **h** feet high. 2Ch 3:15
It was seven and a **h** feet high, 2Ch 4:2
it, 10 every **h** yard, completely 2Ch 4:3
seven and a **h** feet long, 2Ch 6:13
long, seven and a **h** feet wide, 2Ch 6:13
and four and a **h** feet high and 2Ch 6:13
not even told **h** of your great 2Ch 9:6
king four and a **h** tons of gold, 2Ch 9:9
ruler over **h** the district of Neh 3:9
ruler over **h** the district of Neh 3:12
ruler over **h** the district of Neh 3:16
ruler over **h** the district of Neh 3:17
ruler over **h** the district of Neh 3:18
together up to **h** its ⌊height⌋, Neh 4:6
h of my men did the work while Neh 4:16
while the other **h** held spears, Neh 4:16
while **h** of the men were holding Neh 4:21
Hoshaiah and **h** the leaders of Neh 12:32
it with **h** the people along Neh 12:38
⌊did⌋ I and **h** of the officials Neh 12:40
H of their children spoke the Neh 13:24
want, even to **h** the kingdom, Est 5:3
want, even to **h** the kingdom, Est 5:6
seek, even to **h** the kingdom, Est 7:2
will not live out **h** their days. Ps 55:23
He burns **h** of it in a fire, Is 44:16
and he roasts meat on that **h**. Is 44:16
I burned **h** of it in the fire, Is 44:19
stood seven and a **h** feet high. Jr 52:22
not commit ⌊even⌋ **h** your sins. Ezk 16:51
were three and a **h** feet. Ezk 40:9
was 17 and a **h** feet, while the Ezk 40:11
were 10 and a **h** feet square. Ezk 40:12
the inside was 87 and a **h** feet. Ezk 40:15
87 and a **h** feet long and 43 and Ezk 40:21
It was 87 and a **h** feet long and Ezk 40:25
It was 87 and a **h** feet long and Ezk 40:29
It was 87 and a **h** feet long and Ezk 40:33
It was 87 and a **h** feet long and Ezk 40:36
⌊each⌋ 31 and a **h** inches long, Ezk 40:42
long, 31 and a **h** inches wide, Ezk 40:42
the gateway was 24 and a **h** feet, Ezk 40:48
pilaster was 10 and a **h** feet. Ezk 41:1
entrance was 17 and a **h** feet, Ezk 41:2
were three and a **h** feet ⌊wide⌋. Ezk 41:3
was 10 and a **h** feet ⌊wide⌋, Ezk 41:3
it was 10 and a **h** feet ⌊thick⌋. Ezk 41:5
rooms was 10 and a **h** feet high. Ezk 41:8
west was 122 and a **h** feet wide. Ezk 41:12
length was 157 and a **h** feet. Ezk 41:12
and three and a **h** feet long. Ezk 41:22
the width was 87 and a **h** feet. Ezk 42:2
and a **h** feet wide and 175 feet Ezk 42:4
it was 87 and a **h** feet long. Ezk 42:7
court were 87 and a **h** feet long, Ezk 42:8
ledge is three and a **h** feet, Ezk 43:14
is 24 and a **h** feet long by 24 Ezk 43:17
long by 24 and a **h** feet wide, Ezk 43:17
around it is 10 and a **h** inches, Ezk 43:17
with 87 and a **h** feet of open Ezk 45:2
five and a **h** gallons and the dry Ezk 45:11
measure ⌊holding⌋ **h** a bushel. Ezk 45:11
offering of **h** a bushel per bull Ezk 45:24
per bull and **h** a bushel per ram, Ezk 45:24
of oil for every **h** bushel. Ezk 45:24
offering will be **h** a bushel with Ezk 46:5
of oil for every **h** bushel. Ezk 46:5
grain offering of **h** a bushel Ezk 46:7
with the bull, **h** a bushel with Ezk 46:7
of oil for every **h** bushel. Ezk 46:7
offering will be **h** a bushel with Ezk 46:11
with the bull, **h** a bushel with Ezk 46:11
of oil for every **h** bushel. Ezk 46:11
long by 52 and a **h** ⌊feet⌋ wide. Ezk 46:22
one and a **h** ⌊miles⌋ on the north Ezk 48:16
one and a **h** ⌊miles⌋ on the south Ezk 48:16
one and a **h** ⌊miles⌋ on the east Ezk 48:16
and one and a **h** ⌊miles⌋ on the Ezk 48:16
measures one and a **h** ⌊miles⌋, Ezk 48:30
which is one and a **h** ⌊miles⌋, Ezk 48:32
measures one and a **h** ⌊miles⌋, Ezk 48:33
which is one and a **h** ⌊miles⌋, Ezk 48:34
for a time, times, and **h** a time. Dn 7:25
a time, times, and **h** ⌊a time⌋. Dn 12:7
H the city will go into exile, Zch 14:2
will be split in **h** from east to Zch 14:4
so that **h** the mountain will move Zch 14:4
to the north and **h** to the south. Zch 14:4
h of it toward the eastern sea Zch 14:8
sea and the other **h** toward the Zch 14:8
give you, up to **h** my kingdom." Mk 6:23
and fled, leaving him **h** dead. Lk 10:30
I'll give **h** of my possessions to Lk 19:8
the festival was already **h** over, Jn 7:14
in heaven for about **h** an hour. Rv 8:1
for three and a **h** days and not Rv 11:9
after the three and a **h** days, Rv 11:11
for a time, times, and **h** a time. Rv 12:14

HALF-ACRE *(1)*
down about 20 men in a **h** field. 1Sm 14:14

HALF-BUSHEL *(1)*
Take this **h** of roasted grain 1Sm 17:17

HALFWAY *(2)*
the mesh comes **h** up the altar. Ex 27:5
under its ledge, **h** up from the Ex 38:4

HALHUL *(1)*
H, Beth-zur, Gedor, Jos 15:58

HALI *(1)*
Helkath, **H**, Beten, Achshaph Jos 19:25

HALL *(18)*
brought them to the banquet **h**, 1Sm 9:22
He made the **h** of pillars 75 feet 1Kg 7:6
made the **H** of the Throne where 1Kg 7:7
would judge—the **H** of Judgment. 1Kg 7:7
other courtyard behind the **h**, 1Kg 7:8
house like this **h** for Pharaoh's 1Kg 7:8
He brought me to the banquet **h**, Sg 2:4
me into the great **h** and measured Ezk 41:1
the length of the great **h**, Ezk 41:2
room adjacent to the great **h**, Ezk 41:4
of the great **h** and the porticoes Ezk 41:15
and on the wall of the great **h**. Ezk 41:20
of the great **h** were square, Ezk 41:21
The great **h** and the sanctuary Ezk 41:23
of the great **h** like those carved Ezk 41:25
facing the great **h** were 175 feet Ezk 42:8
the queen came to the banquet **h**. Dn 5:10
in the lecture **h** of Tyrannus. Ac 19:9

HALLELUJAH *(27)*
My soul, praise the LORD! **H**! Ps 104:35
statutes and obey His laws. **H**! Ps 105:45
H! Give thanks to the LORD, for Ps 106:1
all the people say, "Amen!" **H**! Ps 106:48
H! I will praise the LORD with Ps 111:1
H! Happy is the man who fears Ps 112:1
H! Give praise, servants of the Ps 113:1
joyful mother of children. **H**! Ps 113:9
LORD, both now and forever. **H**! Ps 115:18
—within you, Jerusalem. **H**! Ps 116:19
faithfulness endures forever. **H**! Ps 117:2
H! Praise the name of the LORD. Ps 135:1
Zion; He dwells in Jerusalem. **H**! Ps 135:21
H! My soul, praise the LORD. Ps 146:1
reigns⌋ for all generations. **H**! Ps 146:10
H! How good it is to sing to our Ps 147:1
do not know ⌊His⌋ judgments. **H**! Ps 147:20
H! Praise the LORD from the Ps 148:1
the people close to Him. **H**! Ps 148:14
H! Sing to the LORD a new song, Ps 149:1
is for all His godly people. **H**! Ps 149:9
H! Praise God in His sanctuary. Ps 150:1
breathes praise the LORD. **H**! Ps 150:6
heaven, saying: **H**! Salvation, Rv 19:1
time they said: **H**! Her smoke Rv 19:3
on the throne, saying: Amen! **H**! Rv 19:4
H—because our Lord God, the Rv 19:6

HALLOHESH *(2)*
Beside him Shallum son of **H**, Neh 3:12
H, Pilha, Shobek, Neh 10:24

HALTED *(4)*
living, and the plague was **h**. Nm 16:48
since the plague had been **h**. Nm 16:50
plague on the people may be **h**." 2Sm 24:21
plague on the people may be **h**." 1Ch 21:22

HAM *(13)*
fathered Shem, **H**, and Japheth. Gn 5:32
sons: Shem, **H**, and Japheth. Gn 6:10
his sons Shem, **H**, and Japheth, Gn 7:13
ark were Shem, **H**, and Japheth. Gn 9:18
H was the father of Canaan. Gn 9:18

H, the father of Canaan, saw his Gn 9:22
sons, Shem, **H**, and Japheth. Gn 10:1
the Zuzim in **H**, the Emim in Gn 14:5
sons: Shem, **H**, and Japheth. 1Ch 1:4
first progeny of the tents of **H**. Ps 78:51
as a foreigner in the land of **H**. Ps 105:23
and wonders in the land of **H**. Ps 105:27
works in the land of **H**, Ps 106:22

HAM'S *(3)*
H sons: Cush, Egypt, Put, and Gn 10:6
are **H** sons, by their clans, Gn 10:20
H sons: Cush, Mizraim, Put, and 1Ch 1:8

HAMAN *(46)*
Ahasuerus honored **H**, son of Est 3:1
bowed down and paid homage to **H**, Est 3:2
they told **H** to see if Mordecai's Est 3:4
When **H** saw that Mordecai was not Est 3:5
H decided not to do away with Est 3:6
was cast before **H** for each day Est 3:7
Then **H** informed King Ahasuerus, Est 3:8
and gave it to **H** son of Est 3:10
Then the king told **H**, "The money Est 3:11
written exactly as **H** commanded. Est 3:12
king and **H** sat down to drink, Est 3:15
amount of money **H** had promised Est 4:7
may the king and **H** come today to Est 5:4
and get **H** so we can do as Esther Est 5:5
So the king and **H** went to the Est 5:5
may the king and **H** come to the Est 5:8
That day **H** left full of joy and Est 5:9
But when **H** saw Mordecai at the Est 5:9
H was filled with rage toward Est 5:9
H controlled himself and went Est 5:10
Then **H** described for them his Est 5:11
"What's more," **H** added, "Queen Est 5:12
The advice pleased **H**, so he had Est 5:14
Now **H** was just entering the Est 6:4
H is standing in the court." Est 6:5
H entered, and the king asked Est 6:6
H thought to himself, "Who is Est 6:6
H told the king, "For the man Est 6:7
The king told **H**, "Hurry, and do Est 6:10
So **H** took the garment and the Est 6:11
King's Gate, but **H**, overwhelmed, Est 6:12
H told his wife Zeresh and all Est 6:13
and rushed **H** to the banquet Est 6:14
king and **H** came to feast with Est 7:1
and enemy is this evil **H**." Est 7:6
H stood terrified before the Est 7:6
H remained to beg Queen Esther Est 7:7
H was falling on the couch where Est 7:8
They hanged **H** on the gallows he Est 7:10
Queen Esther the estate of **H**, Est 8:1
recovered from **H** and gave it to Est 8:2
the evil of **H** the Agagite, Est 8:3
the scheming **H** son of Hammedatha Est 8:5
these 10 sons of **H** son of Est 9:10
For **H** son of Hammedatha the Est 9:24
that the evil plan **H** had devised Est 9:25

HAMAN'S *(7)*
king's mouth, **H** face was covered Est 7:8
75 feet tall at **H** house that he Est 7:9
put him in charge of **H** estate. Est 8:2
I have given **H** estate to Esther, Est 8:7
500 men, including **H** 10 sons. Est 9:12
the bodies of⌋ **H** 10 sons be hung Est 9:13
hung ⌊the bodies of⌋ **H** 10 sons. Est 9:14

HAMATH *(32)*
as Rehob near the entrance to **H**. Nm 13:21
a line to the entrance of **H**, Nm 34:8
Hermon to the entrance of **H**— Jos 13:5
as far as the entrance to **H**. Jdg 3:3
King Toi of **H** heard that David 2Sm 8:9
the entrance of **H** to the Brook 1Kg 8:65
for Israel Damascus and **H**, 2Kg 14:28
Cuthah, Avva, **H**, and Sepharvaim 2Kg 17:24
the men of **H** made Ashima, 2Kg 17:30
are the gods of **H** and Arpad? 2Kg 18:34
is the king of **H**, the king of 2Kg 19:13
in the land of **H** to keep him 2Kg 23:33
at Riblah in the land of **H**. 2Kg 25:21
of Egypt to the entrance of **H**, 1Ch 13:5
of Zobah at **H** when he went to 1Ch 18:3
King Tou of **H** heard that David 1Ch 18:9
the entrance to **H** to the Brook 2Ch 7:8
cities that he built in **H**. 2Ch 8:4
Isn't **H** like Arpad? Isn't Is 10:9
Elam, Shinar, **H**, and the coasts Is 11:11
are the gods of **H** and Arpad? Is 36:19
is the king of **H**, the king of Is 37:13
at Riblah in the land of **H**. Jr 39:5
H and Arpad are put to shame, Jr 49:23
at Riblah in the land of **H**, Jr 52:9
at Riblah in the land of **H**. Jr 52:27
of Damascus and the border of **H** Ezk 47:16
the territory of **H** to the north. Ezk 47:17
alongside **H** and extending from Ezk 48:1
go from there to great **H**; Am 6:2
the entrance of **H** to the Brook Am 6:14
also against **H**, which borders Zch 9:2

HAMATH-ZOBAH *(1)*
Solomon went to **H** and seized it. 2Ch 8:3

HAMATHITES *(2)*
the Zemarites, and the **H**. Gn 10:18
Arvadites, Zemarites, and **H**. 1Ch 1:16

HAMITES *(1)*
for some **H** had lived there 1Ch 4:40

HAMITES' *(1)*
attacked the **H** tents and the 1Ch 4:41

HAMMATH *(2)*
were Ziddim, Zer, **H**, Rakkath, Jos 19:35
are the Kenites who came from **H**, 1Ch 2:55

HAMMEDATHA *(5)*
Haman, son of **H** the Agagite. Est 3:1
to Haman son of **H** the Agagite, Est 3:10
Haman son of **H** the Agagite, Est 8:5
these 10 sons of Haman son of **H**, Est 9:10
For Haman son of **H** the Agagite, Est 9:24

HAMMER *(6)*
peg, grabbed a **h**, and went Jdg 4:21
cut at the quarry so that no **h**, 1Kg 6:7
flattens with the **h** ⌊supports⌋ Is 41:7
It is fastened with **h** and nails, Jr 10:4
How the **h** of the whole earth is Jr 50:23
H your plowshares into swords Jl 3:10

HAMMERED *(20)*
make them of **h** work at the two Ex 25:18
a lampstand out of pure, **h** gold. Ex 25:31
to be a single **h** piece of pure Ex 25:36
made them of **h** work at the two Ex 37:7
lampstand out of pure **h** gold. Ex 37:17
it was a single **h** piece of pure Ex 37:22
They **h** out thin sheets of gold, Ex 39:3
was a **h** work of gold, hammered Nm 8:4
h from its base to its flower Nm 8:4
two trumpets of **h** silver to Nm 10:2
make them into **h** sheets as Nm 16:38
and they were **h** into plating for Nm 16:39
h the peg into his temple and Jdg 4:21
The horses' hooves then **h**— Jdg 5:22
Then she **h** Sisera—she crushed Jdg 5:26
200 large shields of **h** gold; 1Kg 10:16
300 small shields of **h** gold; 1Kg 10:17
200 large shields of **h** gold; 2Ch 9:15
15 pounds of **h** gold went into 2Ch 9:15
300 small shields of **h** gold; 2Ch 9:16

HAMMERING *(1)*
h gold over the cherubim and 1Kg 6:32

HAMMERS *(1)*
the idol with **h**, and works it Is 44:12

HAMMOLECHETH *(1)*
His sister **H** gave birth to 1Ch 7:18

HAMMON *(2)*
Ebron, Rehob, **H**, and Kanah, as Jos 19:28
its pasturelands, **H** and its 1Ch 6:76

HAMMOTH-DOR *(1)*
its pasturelands, **H** with its Jos 21:32

HAMMUEL *(1)*
his son **H**, his son Zaccur, and 1Ch 4:26

HAMON-GOG *(2)*
will be called the Valley of **H**. Ezk 39:11
buried it in the Valley of **H**. Ezk 39:15

HAMONAH *(1)*
even be a city named **H** ⌊there⌋. Ezk 39:16

HAMOR *(13)*
of the field from the sons of **H**, Gn 33:19
Shechem son of **H** the Hivite, Gn 34:2
a wife," he told his father **H**. Gn 34:4
Shechem's father **H** came to speak Gn 34:6
H said to Jacob's sons, "My son Gn 34:8
and his father **H** deceitfully Gn 34:13
in the eyes of **H** and his son Gn 34:18
So **H** and his son Shechem went to Gn 34:20
men listened to **H** and his son Gn 34:24
killed **H** and his son Shechem Gn 34:26
purchased from the sons of **H**, Jos 24:32
You are to serve the men of **H**, Jdg 9:28
from the sons of **H** in Shechem. Ac 7:16

HAMRAN *(1)*
(AKA HEMDAN)
H, Eshban, Ithran, and Cheran. 1Ch 1:41

HAMSTRING *(2)*
and on a whim they **h** oxen. Gn 49:6
You are to **h** their horses and Jos 11:6

HAMSTRUNG *(3)*
he **h** their horses and burned up Jos 11:9
him, and he **h** all the horses, 2Sm 8:4
from him and **h** all the horses, 1Ch 18:4

HAMUL *(3)*
Perez's sons: Hezron and **H**. Gn 46:12
the Hamulite clan from **H**. Nm 26:21
Perez's sons: Hezron and **H**. 1Ch 2:5

HAMULITE *(1)*
the **H** clan from Hamul. Nm 26:21

HAMUTAL *(3)*
mother's name was **H** daughter of 2Kg 23:31
mother's name was **H** daughter of 2Kg 24:18
mother's name was **H** daughter of Jr 52:1

HANAMEL *(4)*
H, the son of your uncle Shallum, Jr 32:7
Then my cousin **H** ⌊came⌋ to the Jr 32:8
in Anathoth from my cousin **H**, Jr 32:9
in the sight of my cousin **H**, Jr 32:12

HANAN *(10)*
Abdon, Zichri, **H**, 1Ch 8:23
Sheariah, Obadiah, and **H**. 1Ch 8:38
Sheariah, Obadiah, and **H**. 1Ch 9:44
H son of Maacah, Joshaphat the 1Ch 11:43
Jozabad, **H**, and Pelaiah, who Neh 8:7
Hodiah, Kelita, Pelaiah, **H**, Neh 10:10
Pelatiah, **H**, Anaiah, Neh 10:22
Ahiah, **H**, Anan, Neh 10:26
Levites, with **H** son of Zaccur, Neh 13:13
the sons of **H** son of Igdaliah Jr 35:4

HANAN'S *(2)*
descendants, **H** descendants, Ezr 2:46
H descendants, Giddel's Neh 7:49

HANANEL *(4)*
the Hundred and the Tower of **H**, Neh 3:1
the Tower of **H**, and the Tower Neh 12:39
the Tower of **H** to the Corner Jr 31:38
from the Tower of **H** to the royal Zch 14:10

HANANI *(11)*
to Jehu son of **H** against Baasha: 1Kg 16:1
prophet Jehu son of **H** the word 1Kg 16:7
Hananiah, **H**, Eliathah, Giddalti 1Ch 25:4
the eighteenth to **H**, his sons, 1Ch 25:25
H the seer came to King Asa of 2Ch 16:7
Then Jehu son of **H** the seer went 2Ch 19:2
in the Events of Jehu son of **H**, 2Ch 20:34
H and Zebadiah from Immer's Ezr 10:20
H, one of my brothers, arrived Neh 1:2
I put my brother **H** in charge Neh 7:2
Judah, and **H**, with the musical Neh 12:36

HANANIAH *(28)*
(AKA SHADRACH)
Meshullam and **H**, with their 1Ch 3:19
H, Elam, Anthothijah, 1Ch 8:24
Jerimoth, **H**, Hanani, Eliathah 1Ch 25:4
sixteenth to **H**, his sons, and 1Ch 25:23
under the authority of **H**, 2Ch 26:11
H, Zabbai, and Athlai; Ezr 10:28
and next to him **H** son of the Neh 3:8
Next to him **H** son of Shelemiah Neh 3:30
along with **H**, commander Neh 7:2
Hoshea, **H**, Hasshub, Neh 10:23
of Seraiah, **H** of Jeremiah, Neh 12:12
Zechariah, and **H**, with trumpets; Neh 12:41
the prophet **H** son of Azzur from Jr 28:1
to the prophet **H** in the presence Jr 28:5
The prophet **H** then took the yoke Jr 28:10
of all the people **H** proclaimed, Jr 28:11
Jeremiah after **H** the prophet had Jr 28:12
Go say to **H**: This is what the Jr 28:13
Jeremiah said to the prophet **H**, Jr 28:15
prophet Hananiah, "Listen, **H**! Jr 28:15

And the prophet **H** died that year Jr 28:17
Zedekiah son of **H**, and all the Jr 36:12
Shelemiah, son of **H**, and he Jr 37:13
Judah, were Daniel, **H**, Mishael, Dn 1:6
Belteshazzar; to **H**, Shadrach; to Dn 1:7
assigned to Daniel, **H**, Mishael, Dn 1:11
equal to Daniel, **H**, Mishael, and Dn 1:19
house and told his friends **H**, Dn 2:17

HANANIAH'S *(1)*
H descendants: Pelatiah, 1Ch 3:21

HAND *(820)*
I have raised my **h** in an oath to Gn 14:22
His **h** will be against everyone, Gn 16:12
and everyone's **h** will be against Gn 16:12
men grabbed his **h**, his wife's Gn 19:16
hand, his wife's **h**, and the Gn 19:16
lambs from my **h** so that this act Gn 21:30
his **h** he took the fire and the Gn 22:6
Do not lay a **h** on the boy or do Gn 22:12
Place your **h** under my thigh, Gn 24:2
placed his **h** under his master Gn 24:9
of his master's goods in **h**. Gn 24:10
her jug to her **h** and gave him a Gn 24:18
grasping Esau's heel with his **h**. Gn 25:26
me from the **h** of my brother Esau Gn 32:11
you, take this gift from my **h**. Gn 33:10
but don't lay a **h** on him"— Gn 37:22
and not lay a **h** on him, Gn 37:27
cord, and the staff in your **h**." Gn 38:18
one of them put out his **h**, Gn 38:28
But then he pulled his **h** back, Gn 38:29
scarlet ⌊thread⌋ tied to his **h**, Gn 38:30
leaving his garment in her **h**, Gn 39:12
Pharaoh's cup was in my **h**, Gn 40:11
placed the cup in Pharaoh's **h**." Gn 40:11
cup in his **h** the way you used to Gn 40:13
placed the cup in Pharaoh's **h**; Gn 40:21
signet ring from his **h** and put Gn 41:42
hand and put it on Joseph's **h**, Gn 41:42
to raise his **h** or foot in all Gn 41:44
put your **h** under my thigh ⌊and Gn 47:29
with his right **h** Ephraim toward Gn 48:13
with his left **h** Manasseh toward Gn 48:13
his right **h** and put it on the Gn 48:14
placed his right **h** on Ephraim's Gn 48:17
took his father's **h** to move it Gn 48:17
Put your right **h** on his head." Gn 48:18
took from the **h** of the Amorites Gn 48:22
Your **h** will be on the necks of Gn 49:8
he is forced⌋ by a strong **h**. Ex 3:19
stretch out My **h** and strike Ex 3:20
"What is that in your **h**?" Ex 4:2
Stretch out your **h** and grab it Ex 4:4
out his **h** and caught it, Ex 4:4
and it became a staff in his **h**. Ex 4:4
"Put your **h** inside your cloak." Ex 4:6
So he put his **h** inside his Ex 4:6
took it out, his **h** was diseased, Ex 4:6
your **h** back inside your cloak. Ex 4:7
He put his **h** back inside his Ex 4:7
staff in your **h** that you will Ex 4:17
Moses took God's staff in his **h**. Ex 4:20
a sword in their **h** to kill us!" Ex 5:21
them go because of My strong **h**; Ex 6:1
land because of My strong **h**." Ex 6:1
but I will put My **h** on Egypt and Ex 7:4
stretch out My **h** against Egypt, Ex 7:5
Take in your **h** the staff that Ex 7:15
the Nile with the staff in my **h**, Ex 7:17
out your **h** over the waters Ex 7:19
out your **h** with your staff Ex 8:5
out his **h** over the waters Ex 8:6
out his **h** with his staff, Ex 8:17
then the LORD's **h** will bring a Ex 9:3
stretched out My **h** and struck Ex 9:15
Stretch out your **h** toward heaven Ex 9:22
Stretch out your **h** over the land Ex 10:12
out your **h** toward heaven, Ex 10:21
out his **h** toward heaven, Ex 10:22
feet, and your staff in your **h**. Ex 12:11
resident or hired **h** may not eat Ex 12:45
here by the strength of ⌊His⌋ **h**. Ex 13:3
for you on your **h** and as a Ex 13:9
out of Egypt with a strong **h**. Ex 13:9
of ⌊His⌋ **h** the LORD brought Ex 13:14
be a sign on your **h** and a symbol Ex 13:16
Egypt by the strength of His **h**." Ex 13:16
stretch out your **h** over the sea, Ex 14:16
out his **h** over the sea. Ex 14:21
out your **h** over the sea so Ex 14:26
out his **h** over the sea, Ex 14:27
Your right **h** is glorious in Ex 15:6
right **h** shattered the enemy. Ex 15:6
my **h** will destroy them." Ex 15:9
You stretched out Your right **h**, Ex 15:12
took a tambourine in her **h**, Ex 15:20
died by the LORD's **h** in the land Ex 16:3
the Nile with in your **h** and go. Ex 17:5
with God's staff in my **h**." Ex 17:9
While Moses held up his **h**, Ex 17:11
but whenever he put his **h** down, Ex 17:11
⌊my⌋ **h** is ⌊lifted up⌋ toward the Ex 17:16
No **h** may touch him; instead he Ex 19:13
caused it to happen by his **h**, Ex 21:13
tooth for tooth, **h** for hand, Ex 21:24
hand for **h**, foot for foot, Ex 21:24
with great power and a strong **h**? Ex 32:11
cover you with My **h** until I have Ex 33:22
Then I will take My **h** away, Ex 33:23
the two stone tablets in his **h**, Ex 34:4
is to lay his **h** on the head of Lv 1:4
is to lay his **h** on the head of Lv 3:2
He must lay his **h** on the head of Lv 3:8
must lay his **h** on its head and Lv 3:13
lay his **h** on the bull's head, Lv 4:4
is to lay his **h** on the head of Lv 4:24
is to lay his **h** on the head of Lv 4:29
is to lay his **h** on the head of Lv 4:33
on the thumb of his right **h**, Lv 8:23
on the thumb of his right **h**, Lv 14:14
on the thumb of his right **h**, Lv 14:17
on the thumb of his right **h**, Lv 14:25
on the thumb of his right **h**, Lv 14:28
due a hired **h** must not remain Lv 19:13
man who has a broken foot or **h**, Lv 21:19
priest or a hired **h** is not to Lv 22:10
and the hired **h** or foreigner who Lv 25:6
you as a hired **h** or temporary Lv 25:40
the daily wages of a hired **h**. Lv 25:50
of jealousy from the woman's **h**, Nm 5:25
Moses raised his **h** and struck Nm 20:11
with fees for divination in **h**. Nm 22:7
with a drawn sword in His **h**, Nm 22:23
a sword in my **h**, I'd kill you Nm 22:29
with a drawn sword in His **h**. Nm 22:31
assembly, took a spear in his **h**, Nm 25:7
man has in his **h** a stone capable Nm 35:17
man has in his **h** a wooden object Nm 35:18
him with his **h** and he dies, Nm 35:21
from the **h** of the avenger Nm 35:25
the LORD's **h** was against them, Dt 2:15
in order to **h** him over to you, Dt 2:30
a strong **h** and an outstretched Dt 4:34
with a strong **h** and an Dt 5:15
a sign on your **h** and let them be Dt 6:8
us out of Egypt with a strong **h**. Dt 6:21
with a strong **h** and redeemed you Dt 7:8
the strong **h** and outstretched Dt 7:19
He will **h** their kings over to Dt 7:24
out of Egypt with a strong **h**. Dt 9:26
with the two tablets in my **h**. Dt 10:3
strong **h**, and outstretched Dt 11:2
and irrigated by **h** as in a Dt 11:10
h is to be the first against Dt 13:9
is to remain in your **h**, Dt 13:17
the money in your **h**, and go to Dt 14:25
are to open your **h** to him and Dt 15:8
open your **h** to your afflicted Dt 15:11
twice the wages of a hired **h**. Dt 15:18
and his **h** swings the ax to chop Dt 19:5
and **h** him over to the avenger of Dt 19:12
tooth for tooth, **h** for hand, and Dt 19:21
tooth, hand for **h**, and foot for Dt 19:21
heads of grain with your **h**, Dt 23:25
certificate, **h** it to her, and Dt 24:1
oppress a hired **h** who is poor Dt 24:14
she puts out her **h** and grabs his Dt 25:11
you are to cut off her **h**. Dt 25:12
from your **h** and place it before Dt 26:4
with a strong **h** and an Dt 26:8
Our own **h** has prevailed; Dt 32:27
can rescue ⌊anyone⌋ from My **h**. Dt 32:39
I raise My **h** to heaven and Dt 32:40
and My **h** takes hold of judgment, Dt 32:41
from His right **h** for them. Dt 33:2
Your holy ones are in Your **h**, Dt 33:3
that the LORD's **h** is mighty, Jos 4:24
him with a drawn sword in His **h**. Jos 5:13
across the Jordan to **h** us over Jos 7:7
the sword in your **h** toward Ai, Jos 8:18
I will **h** the city over to you. Jos 8:18
he held out his **h**, the men in Jos 8:19
draw back his **h** that was holding Jos 8:26
tomorrow I will **h** all of them Jos 11:6
they must not **h** the one who Jos 20:5
not die at the **h** of the avenger Jos 20:9
and I delivered you from his **h**. Jos 24:10
house of Joseph got the upper **h**, Jdg 1:35
did not **h** them over to Joshua. Jdg 2:23
Ehud reached with his left **h**, Jdg 3:21
them into the **h** of Jabin king Jdg 4:2
I will **h** him over to you.'" Jdg 4:7
sell Sisera into a woman's **h**." Jdg 4:9
peg, her right **h**, for a Jdg 5:26
that was in His **h** and touched Jdg 6:21
You will deliver Israel by my **h**, Jdg 6:36
for Me to **h** the Midianites Jdg 7:2
who lapped and **h** the Midianites Jdg 7:7
for I have given it into your **h**. Jdg 7:9
a trumpet in one **h** and an empty Jdg 7:16
you from the **h** of Midian, Jdg 9:17
his ax in his **h** and cut a branch Jdg 9:48
If You will **h** over the Ammonites Jdg 11:30
to arrest you and **h** you over to Jdg 15:12
securely and **h** you over to them. Jdg 15:13
reached out his **h**, took it, and Jdg 15:15
who was leading him by the **h**, Jdg 16:26
one on his right **h** and the other Jdg 16:29
H over the perverted men in Jdg 20:13
because I will **h** them over to Jdg 20:28
the LORD's **h** has turned against Ru 1:13
insist that you **h** it over right 1Sm 2:16
us from the **h** of our enemies. 1Sm 4:3
rescue us from the **h** of these 1Sm 4:8
because His **h** is severe against 1Sm 5:7
LORD's **h** was against the city 1Sm 5:9
God's **h** was very heavy there. 1Sm 5:11
the reason His **h** hasn't been 1Sm 6:3
was not His **h** that punished us 1Sm 6:9
you from the **h** of the 1Sm 7:3
save us from the **h** of the 1Sm 7:8
The LORD's **h** was against the 1Sm 7:13
them from the **h** of the 1Sm 9:16
whose **h** have I taken a bribe 1Sm 12:3
taken anything from anyone's **h**," 1Sm 12:4
found anything in my **h**." 1Sm 12:5
the LORD's **h** will be against you 1Sm 12:15
be found in the **h** of any of the 1Sm 13:22
Will You **h** them over to Israel?" 1Sm 14:37
Israel from the **h** of those who 1Sm 14:48
me from the **h** of this Philistine 1Sm 17:37
staff in his **h** and chose five 1Sm 17:40
sling in his **h**, he approached 1Sm 17:40
the LORD will **h** you over to me. 1Sm 17:46
He will **h** you over to us." 1Sm 17:47
David put his **h** in the bag, 1Sm 17:49
head still in his **h**. 1Sm 17:57
My **h** doesn't need to be against 1Sm 18:17
let the **h** of the Philistines be 1Sm 18:17
the **h** of the Philistines will 1Sm 18:21
Now what do you have on **h**? 1Sm 21:3
There is no ordinary bread on **h**. 1Sm 21:4
you have a spear or sword on **h**? 1Sm 21:8
spear was in his **h**, and all his 1Sm 22:6
would not lift a **h** to execute 1Sm 22:17
I will **h** the Philistines over 1Sm 23:4
of Keilah **h** me over to him? 1Sm 23:11
of Keilah **h** me and my men over 1Sm 23:12
but God did not **h** David over to 1Sm 23:14
Saul will never lay a **h** on you. 1Sm 23:17
Our part will be to **h** him over 1Sm 23:20
'I will **h** your enemy over to you 1Sm 24:4
never⌋ lift my **h** against him, 1Sm 24:6
won't lift my **h** against my lord 1Sm 24:10
the corner of your robe in my **h**, 1Sm 24:11
but my **h** will never be against 1Sm 24:12
My **h** will never be against you. 1Sm 24:13
will be established in your **h**. 1Sm 24:20
avenging yourself by your own **h**. 1Sm 25:26
avenging myself by my own **h**. 1Sm 25:33
who can lift a **h** against the 1Sm 26:9
never lift my **h** against the 1Sm 26:11
I done? What evil is in my **h**? 1Sm 26:18
to lift my **h** against the LORD's 1Sm 26:23

out of your **h** and given it to 1Sm 28:17
LORD will also **h** Israel over to 1Sm 28:19
the LORD will **h** Israel's army 1Sm 28:19
afraid to lift your **h** to destroy 2Sm 1:14
your side to **h** all Israel over 2Sm 3:12
Will you **h** them over to me?" 2Sm 5:19
will certainly **h** the Philistines 2Sm 5:19
you from the **h** of Saul. 2Sm 12:7
can watch and eat from her **h**.' " 2Sm 13:5
so I can eat from her **h**." 2Sm 13:6
"so I can eat from your **h**." 2Sm 13:10
She put her **h** on her head and 2Sm 13:19
'**H** over the one who killed his 2Sm 14:7
from the **h** of this man who 2Sm 14:16
Absalom reached out his **h**, 2Sm 15:5
1,000 pieces of silver in my **h**, 2Sm 18:12
not raise my **h** against the 2Sm 18:12
spears in his **h** and thrust them 2Sm 18:14
with his right **h** Joab grabbed 2Sm 20:9
against the sword in Joab's **h**, 2Sm 20:10
answered, "I will **h** them over." 2Sm 21:6
fingers on each **h** and six toes 2Sm 21:20
from the **h** of all his enemies 2Sm 22:1
enemies and from the **h** of Saul. 2Sm 22:1
can never be picked up by **h**. 2Sm 23:6
until his **h** was tired and stuck 2Sm 23:10
Egyptian had a spear in his **h**, 2Sm 23:21
spear out of the Egyptian's **h**, 2Sm 23:21
extended his **h** toward Jerusalem 2Sm 24:16
Enough, withdraw your **h** now!" 2Sm 24:16
let Your **h** be against me and my 2Sm 24:17
So she sat down at his right **h**. 1Kg 2:19
was established in Solomon's **h**. 1Kg 2:46
name, mighty **h**, and outstretched 1Kg 8:42
with them and **h** them over to 1Kg 8:46
tear it out of your son's **h**. 1Kg 11:12
the kingdom out of Solomon's **h**. 1Kg 11:31
from his **h** but will let him 1Kg 11:34
from his son's **h** and give them 1Kg 11:35
out his **h** from the altar 1Kg 13:4
But the **h** he stretched out 1Kg 13:4
me so that my **h** may be restored 1Kg 13:6
and the king's **h** was restored to 1Kg 13:6
me a piece of bread in your **h**." 1Kg 17:11
small as a man's **h** coming from 1Kg 18:44
will **h** over this entire immense 1Kg 20:28
from your **h** the man I had 1Kg 20:42
take it from the **h** of the king 1Kg 22:3
and the Lord will **h** it over to 1Kg 22:6
for the LORD will **h** it over to 1Kg 22:12
LORD will **h** it over to the king. 1Kg 22:15
at His right **h** and at His left 1Kg 22:19
right hand and at His left **h**. 1Kg 22:19
only to **h** us over to Moab." 2Kg 3:10
kings to **h** us over to Moab. 2Kg 3:13
the LORD's **h** came on Elisha. 2Kg 3:15
He will also **h** Moab over to you. 2Kg 3:18
to mouth, eye to eye, **h** to hand. 2Kg 4:34
to mouth, eye to eye, hand to **h**. 2Kg 4:34
will wave his **h** over the spot 2Kg 5:11
blood shed by the **h** of Jezebel— 2Kg 9:7
"If it is, give me your **h**." 2Kg 10:15
he gave him his **h**, and Jehu 2Kg 10:15
the king with weapons in **h**. 2Kg 11:8
their weapons in **h** surrounding 2Kg 11:11
h it over for the repair of the 2Kg 12:7
Israel, "Put your **h** on the bow." 2Kg 13:16
So the king put his **h** on it, 2Kg 13:16
them by the **h** of Jeroboam son 2Kg 14:27
you from the **h** of all your 2Kg 17:39
he can't deliver you from my **h**. 2Kg 18:29
delivered Samaria from my **h**? 2Kg 18:34
letter from the **h** of the 2Kg 19:14
save us from his **h** so that all 2Kg 19:19
this city from the **h** of the king 2Kg 20:6
inheritance and **h** them over to 2Kg 21:14
put it into the **h** of those doing 2Kg 22:9
border, let Your **h** be with me, 1Ch 4:10
Asaph, who stood at his right **h**: 1Ch 6:39
a spear in his **h** like a weaver's 1Ch 11:23
spear out of the Egyptian's **h**, 1Ch 11:23
either their right or left **h**, 1Ch 12:2
Will You **h** them over to me?" 1Ch 14:10
and I will **h** them over to you." 1Ch 14:10
fingers ⌊on each **h**⌋ and six toes 1Ch 20:6
Enough, withdraw your **h** now!" 1Ch 21:15
sword in his **h** stretched out 1Ch 21:16
please let Your **h** be against me 1Ch 21:17

the LORD's **h** on me, He enabled 1Ch 28:19
In Your **h** are power and might, 1Ch 29:12
it is in Your **h** to make great 1Ch 29:12
what comes from Your own **h**. 1Ch 29:14
holy name comes from Your **h**; 1Ch 29:16
and Your mighty **h** and 2Ch 6:32
with them and **h** them over to 2Ch 6:36
you into the **h** of Shishak.' " 2Ch 12:5
kingdom in the **h** of ⌊one of⌋ 2Ch 13:8
of Aram has escaped from your **h**. 2Ch 16:7
the kingdom in his **h**. 2Ch 17:5
God will **h** it over to the king. 2Ch 18:5
for the LORD will **h** it over to 2Ch 18:11
at His right **h** and at His left 2Ch 18:18
right hand and at His left **h**. 2Ch 18:18
Power and might are in Your **h**, 2Ch 20:6
the king with weapons in **h**. 2Ch 23:7
their weapons in **h** surrounding 2Ch 23:10
their own people from your **h**?" 2Ch 25:15
God in order to **h** them over to 2Ch 25:20
a censer in his **h** to offer 2Ch 26:19
letters from the **h** of the king 2Ch 30:6
h of God was in Judah to give 2Ch 30:12
from the **h** of the Levites, 2Ch 30:16
⌊written⌋ by the **h** of Moses. 2Ch 34:14
put it into the **h** of the 2Ch 34:17
and the **h** of those doing 2Ch 34:17
them by the **h** of his messengers 2Ch 36:15
because the **h** of the LORD his Ezr 7:6
The gracious **h** of his God was on Ezr 7:9
the gracious **h** of our God was Ezr 8:18
The **h** of our God is gracious to Ezr 8:22
Your great power and strong **h**. Neh 1:10
how the gracious **h** of my God had Neh 2:18
worked with one **h** and held a Neh 4:17
who had an open letter in his **h**. Neh 6:5
scepter in his **h** toward Esther, Est 5:2
stretch out Your **h** and strike Jb 1:11
not lay a **h** on Job ⌊himself⌋. Jb 1:12
stretch out Your **h** and strike Jb 2:5
days like those of a hired **h**? Jb 7:1
to lay his **h** on both of us. Jb 9:33
one who can deliver from Your **h**? Jb 10:7
if there is iniquity in your **h**, Jb 11:14
know that the **h** of the LORD has Jb 12:9
every living thing is in His **h**, Jb 12:10
remove Your **h** from me, and do Jb 13:21
enjoy his day like a hired **h**. Jb 14:6
the day of darkness is at **h**. Jb 15:23
stretched out his **h** against God Jb 15:25
for God's **h** has struck me. Jb 19:21
put ⌊your⌋ **h** over ⌊your⌋ mouth. Jb 21:5
His **h** is heavy despite my Jb 23:2
His **h** pierced the fleeing Jb 26:13
my bow will be renewed in my **h**. Jb 29:20
harass me with Your strong **h**. Jb 30:21
out ⌊his⌋ **h** against a ruined Jb 30:24
because my own **h** has acquired Jb 31:25
does He receive from your **h**? Jb 35:7
I place my **h** over my mouth. Jb 40:4
own right **h** can deliver you. Jb 40:14
a **h** on him. You will remember Jb 41:8
Lift up Your **h**. Do not forget Ps 10:12
Because He is at my right **h**, Ps 16:8
in Your right **h** are eternal Ps 16:11
who rebel against Your right **h**. Ps 17:7
Your **h**, LORD, ⌊save me⌋ from Ps 17:14
right **h** upholds me, and Your Ps 18:35
victories from His right **h**. Ps 20:6
Your **h** will capture all your Ps 21:8
your right **h** will seize those Ps 21:8
Into Your **h** I entrust my spirit; Ps 31:5
night Your **h** was heavy on me; Ps 32:4
near me or the **h** of the wicked Ps 36:11
because the LORD holds his **h**. Ps 37:24
him in his **h** or allow him to Ps 37:33
and Your **h** has pressed down on Ps 38:2
because of the force of Your **h**. Ps 39:10
out the nations with Your **h**; Ps 44:2
but by Your right **h**, Your arm, Ps 44:3
You **h** us over to be eaten like Ps 44:11
May your right **h** show your Ps 45:4
Ophir, stands at your right **h**. Ps 45:9
Your right **h** is filled with Ps 48:10
Your right **h**, and answer me, Ps 60:5
Your right **h** holds on to me. Ps 63:8
God, from the **h** of the wicked, Ps 71:4
with You; You hold my right **h**. Ps 73:23

Why do You hold back Your **h**? Ps 74:11
out Your right **h** and destroy Ps 74:11
there is a cup in the LORD's **h**, Ps 75:8
warriors was able to lift a **h**. Ps 76:5
the right **h** of the Most High Ps 77:10
a flock by the **h** of Moses and Ps 77:20
mountain His right **h** acquired. Ps 78:54
His splendor to the **h** of a foe. Ps 78:61
root Your right **h** has planted, Ps 80:15
Let Your **h** be with the man at Ps 80:17
be with the man at Your right **h**, Ps 80:17
and turn My **h** against their foes Ps 81:14
them from the **h** of the wicked." Ps 82:4
mighty arm; Your **h** is powerful; Ps 89:13
Your right **h** is lifted high. Ps 89:13
My **h** will always be with him, Ps 89:21
and his right **h** to the rivers. Ps 89:25
high the right **h** of his foes; Ps 89:42
ten thousand at your right **h**, Ps 91:7
of the earth are in His **h**, Ps 95:4
them from the **h** of the wicked. Ps 97:10
right **h** and holy arm have won Ps 98:1
when You open Your **h**, they are Ps 104:28
from the **h** of the adversary; Ps 106:10
them from the **h** of the enemy. Ps 106:10
So He raised His **h** against them Ps 106:26
them from the **h** of the foe Ps 107:2
with Your right **h** and answer me Ps 108:6
an accuser stand at his right **h**. Ps 109:6
this is Your **h** and that You, Ps 109:27
at the right **h** of the needy, Ps 109:31
Sit at My right **h** until I make Ps 110:1
The Lord is at Your right **h**; Ps 110:5
The LORD's right **h** strikes with Ps 118:15
The LORD's right **h** is raised! Ps 118:16
The LORD's right **h** strikes with Ps 118:16
May Your **h** be ready to help me, Ps 119:173
eyes on His master's **h**, Ps 123:2
girl's eyes on her mistress's **h**, Ps 123:2
arrows in the **h** of a warrior are Ps 127:4
with a strong **h** and outstretched Ps 136:12
my right **h** forget ⌊its skill⌋ Ps 137:5
You will extend Your **h**; Ps 138:7
Your right **h** will save me. Ps 138:7
You have placed Your **h** on me. Ps 139:5
even there Your **h** will lead me; Ps 139:10
Your right **h** will hold on to me. Ps 139:10
You open Your **h** and satisfy the Ps 145:16
extended my **h** and no one paid Pr 1:24
Long life is in her right **h**; Pr 3:16
The diligent **h** will rule, but Pr 12:24
money in his **h** with no intention Pr 17:16
buries his **h** in the bowl; Pr 19:24
a water channel in the LORD's **h**: Pr 21:1
by a fool's **h** cuts off his own Pr 26:6
by the **h** of a drunkard. Pr 26:9
buries his **h** in the bowl; Pr 26:15
and grasps oil with his right **h**. Pr 27:16
put your **h** over your mouth. Pr 30:32
that even this is from God's **h**. Ec 2:24
let the other slip from your **h**. Ec 7:18
evening do not let your **h** rest, Ec 11:6
His left **h** is under my head, Sg 2:6
and his right **h** embraces me. Sg 2:6
My love thrust his **h** through the Sg 5:4
His left **h** is under my head, Sg 8:3
and his right **h** embraces me. Sg 8:3
I will turn My **h** against you and Is 1:25
He raised His **h** against them and Is 5:25
and His **h** is still raised ⌊to Is 5:25
and in his **h** was a glowing coal Is 6:6
and His **h** is still raised ⌊to Is 9:12
and His **h** is still raised ⌊to Is 9:17
and His **h** is still raised ⌊to Is 9:21
and His **h** is still raised ⌊to Is 10:4
As my **h** seized the idolatrous Is 10:10
My **h** has reached out, as if into Is 10:14
will put his **h** into a snake's Is 11:8
extend⌋ His **h** a second time to Is 11:11
He will wave His **h** over the Is 11:15
Wave your **h**, and they will go Is 13:2
and this is the **h** stretched out Is 14:26
is His **h** that is outstretched, Is 14:27
of the threatening **h** of the LORD Is 19:16
put your authority into his **h**, Is 22:21
out His **h** over the sea; Is 23:11
Your **h** is lifted up ⌊to take Is 26:11
it across the land with ⌊His⌋ **h**. Is 28:2

it while it is still in his **h**. Is 28:4
LORD raises His **h** ⌊to strike⌋, Is 31:3
whose **h** never takes a bribe, Is 33:15
h allotted their portion with Is 34:17
and pierce the **h** of anyone who Is 36:6
his land from the **h** of the king Is 36:18
delivered Samaria from my **h**? Is 36:19
delivered his land from my **h**, Is 36:20
save us from his **h** so that all Is 37:20
this city from the **h** of the king Is 38:6
from the LORD's **h** double for all Is 40:2
hollow of his **h** or marked off Is 40:12
with the span ⌊of his **h**⌋? Is 40:12
you with My righteous right **h**. Is 41:10
your right **h** and say to you: Is 41:13
that the **h** of the LORD has done Is 41:20
and I will hold you by your **h**. Is 42:6
can take ⌊anything⌋ from My **h**. Is 43:13
another will write on his **h**: Is 44:5
there a lie in my right **h**?" Is 44:20
whose right **h** I have grasped to Is 45:1
My own **h** founded the earth, Is 48:13
and My right **h** spread out the Is 48:13
hid me in the shadow of His **h**. Is 49:2
lift up My **h** to the nations, Is 49:22
Is My **h** too short to redeem? Is 50:2
is what you'll get from My **h**: Is 50:11
you in the shadow of My **h**, Is 51:16
His fury from the **h** of the LORD; Is 51:17
to take hold of her **h** among all Is 51:18
cup of staggering from your **h**; Is 51:22
the LORD will succeed by His **h**. Is 53:10
and keeps his **h** from doing any Is 56:2
the LORD's **h** is not too short to Is 59:1
glorious crown in the LORD's **h**, Is 62:3
with His right **h** and His strong Is 62:8
glorious arm at Moses' right **h**, Is 63:12
My **h** made all these things, Is 66:2
Then the LORD reached out His **h**, Jr 1:9
Pass your **h** once more like a Jr 6:9
will stretch out My **h** against Jr 6:12
will certainly die at our **h**." Jr 11:21
life into the **h** of her enemies. Jr 12:7
stretched out My **h** against you Jr 15:6
Because Your **h** was ⌊on me⌋, Jr 15:17
became flawed in the potter's **h**, Jr 18:4
like clay in the potter's **h**, Jr 18:6
are you in My **h**, house of Israel Jr 18:6
h their children over to famine, Jr 18:21
by the **h** of those who want to Jr 19:7
I will **h** Judah over to the king Jr 20:4
will **h** all the treasures of the Jr 20:5
needy from the **h** of evil people. Jr 20:13
an outstretched **h** and a mighty Jr 21:5
I will **h** over to King Jr 21:7
from the **h** of his oppressor Jr 21:12
from the **h** of his oppressor Jr 22:3
a signet ring on My right **h**, Jr 22:24
I will **h** you over to those you Jr 22:25
of wrath from My **h** and make all Jr 25:15
from the LORD's **h** and made all Jr 25:17
I am about to **h** them over to Jr 29:21
took them by the **h** to bring them Jr 31:32
am about to **h** this city over to Jr 32:3
with a strong **h** and an Jr 32:21
am about to **h** this city over to Jr 32:28
am about to **h** this city over to Jr 34:2
from his **h** but are certain Jr 34:3
I will **h** Zedekiah king of Judah Jr 34:21
not kill you or **h** you over to Jr 38:16
They may **h** me over to them to Jr 38:19
"They will not **h** you over," Jr 38:20
you against us to **h** us over to Jr 43:3
I am about to **h** over Pharaoh Jr 44:30
I will **h** them over to those who Jr 46:26
Moab's calamity is near at **h**; Jr 48:16
on every **h** is a gash and Jr 48:37
in the LORD's **h** making the whole Jr 51:7
stretch out My **h** against you, Jr 51:25
fell into the adversary's **h**, Lm 1:7
fastened together by His **h**; Lm 1:14
His right **h** in the presence Lm 2:3
His right **h** is positioned like Lm 2:4
turns His **h** against me all day Lm 3:3
instant without a **h** laid on it. Lm 4:6
And the LORD's **h** was on him Ezk 1:3
and saw a **h** reaching out to Ezk 2:9
and the LORD's **h** was on me Ezk 3:14
Then the **h** of the LORD was on me Ezk 3:22
stretch out My **h** against them, Ezk 6:14
I will **h** these things over to Ezk 7:21
and there the **h** of the Lord GOD Ezk 8:1
appeared to be a **h** and took me Ezk 8:3
had an incense burner in his **h**, Ezk 8:11
a destructive weapon in his **h**." Ezk 9:1
each with a war club in his **h**. Ezk 9:2
reached out his **h** to the fire Ezk 10:7
out of the city and **h** you over Ezk 11:9
I dug through the wall by **h**; Ezk 12:7
My **h** will be against the Ezk 13:9
wrist of every **h** and who make Ezk 13:18
will stretch out My **h** against Ezk 14:9
I stretch out My **h** against it to Ezk 14:13
I stretched out My **h** against you Ezk 16:27
I will **h** you over to them, Ezk 16:39
he gave his **h** ⌊in pledge⌋. Ezk 17:18
but keeps his **h** from wrongdoing Ezk 18:8
keeps his **h** from ⌊harming⌋ the Ezk 18:17
I withheld My **h** and acted Ezk 20:22
rule over you with a strong **h**, Ezk 20:33
with a strong **h**, an outstretched Ezk 20:34
and every **h** will become weak. Ezk 21:7
to be grasped in the **h**. Ezk 21:11
be put in the **h** of the slayer. Ezk 21:11
appears in his right **h**, Ezk 21:22
I will **h** you over to brutal men, Ezk 21:31
am going to **h** you over to those Ezk 23:28
I will put her cup in your **h**." Ezk 23:31
to stretch out My **h** against you Ezk 25:7
stretch out My **h** against Edom Ezk 25:13
to stretch out My **h** against the Ezk 25:16
Israel grasped you by the **h**, Ezk 29:7
of Egypt by the **h** of Ezk 30:10
make the sword fall from his **h**. Ezk 30:22
and place My sword in his **h**. Ezk 30:24
My sword in the **h** of Babylon's Ezk 30:25
I determined to **h** it over to a Ezk 31:11
Now the **h** of the LORD had been Ezk 33:22
will stretch out My **h** against Ezk 35:3
The **h** of the LORD was on me, Ezk 37:1
that they become one in your **h**. Ezk 37:17
which is in the **h** of Ephraim— Ezk 37:19
so that they become one in My **h**. Ezk 37:19
are in your **h** and in full view Ezk 37:20
to turn your **h** against ruins now Ezk 38:12
from your left **h** and make your Ezk 39:3
arrows drop from your right **h**. Ezk 39:3
executed and the **h** I have laid Ezk 39:21
very day the LORD's **h** was on me, Ezk 40:1
and a measuring rod in his **h**. Ezk 40:3
rod in the man's **h** was six units Ezk 40:5
with a measuring line in his **h**, Ezk 47:3
off without a **h** touching it, Dn 2:34
without a **h** touching it, Dn 2:45
hold back His **h** or say to Him, Dn 4:35
of a man's **h** appeared and began Dn 5:5
watched the **h** that was writing Dn 5:5
in His **h** and who controls Dn 5:23
He sent the **h**, and this writing Dn 5:24
with a mighty **h** and made Your Dn 9:15
a **h** touched me and raised me to Dn 10:10
with total destruction in his **h**. Dn 11:16
also turn My **h** against Ekron, Am 1:8
and rests his **h** against the wall Am 5:19
so I will **h** over the city and Am 6:8
wall with a plumb line in His **h**. Am 7:7
from there My **h** will take them; Am 9:2
do not **h** over their survivors Ob 14
Your **h** will be lifted up against Mc 5:9
LORD's right **h** will come around Hab 2:16
rays are flashing from His **h**. Hab 3:4
stretch out My **h** against Judah Zph 1:4
stretch out His **h** against the Zph 2:13
with a measuring line in his **h**. Zch 2:1
plumb line in Zerubbabel's **h**." Zch 4:10
with a staff in **h** because of Zch 8:4
will also turn My **h** against the Zch 13:7
will seize the **h** of another, Zch 14:13
and the **h** of one will rise Zch 14:13
You, on the other **h**, have turned Mal 2:8
winnowing shovel is in His **h**, Mt 3:12
your adversary will **h** you over Mt 5:25
if your right **h** causes you to Mt 5:30
let your left **h** know what your Mt 6:3
know what your right **h** is doing, Mt 6:3
out His **h** He touched him, Mt 8:3
He touched her **h**, and the fever Mt 8:15
but come and lay Your **h** on her, Mt 9:18
went in and took her by the **h**, Mt 9:25
Because people will **h** you over Mt 10:17
But when they **h** you over, don't Mt 10:19
saw a man who had a paralyzed **h**. Mt 12:10
the man, "Stretch out your **h**." Mt 12:13
stretching out His **h** toward His Mt 12:49
Jesus reached out His **h**, Mt 14:31
If your **h** or your foot causes Mt 18:8
Then they will **h** Him over to the Mt 20:19
Tie him up **h** and foot, and throw Mt 22:13
Sit at My right **h** until I put Mt 22:44
Then they will **h** you over for Mt 24:9
give me if I **h** Him over to you? Mt 26:15
one who dipped his **h** with Me in Mt 26:23
reached out his **h** and drew his Mt 26:51
at the right **h** of the Power Mt 26:64
placed a reed in His right **h**. Mt 27:29
took her by the **h**, and raised Mk 1:31
out His **h** and touched him Mk 1:41
was there who had a paralyzed **h**. Mk 3:1
the man with the paralyzed **h**, Mk 3:3
the man, "Stretch out your **h**." Mk 3:5
it out, and his **h** was restored. Mk 3:5
On the other **h**, no one can enter Mk 3:27
child by the **h** and said to her Mk 5:41
Jesus to lay His **h** on him. Mk 7:32
man by the **h** and brought him Mk 8:23
taking him by the **h**, raised him, Mk 9:27
And if your **h** causes your Mk 9:43
Then they will **h** Him over to the Mk 10:33
Sit at My right **h** until I put Mk 12:36
They will **h** you over to Mk 13:9
they arrest you and **h** you over, Mk 13:11
priests to **h** Him over to them Mk 14:10
at the right **h** of the Power Mk 14:62
sat down at the right **h** of God. Mk 16:19
the Lord's **h** was with him. Lk 1:66
shovel is in His **h** to clear His Lk 3:17
out His **h**, He touched him Lk 5:13
whose right **h** was paralyzed. Lk 6:6
the man with the paralyzed **h**, Lk 6:8
told him, "Stretch out your **h**." Lk 6:10
did so, and his **h** was restored. Lk 6:10
on the other **h**, a bad tree Lk 6:43
her by the **h** and called out, Lk 8:54
one who puts his **h** to the plow Lk 9:62
So tell her to give me a **h**." Lk 10:40
the judge **h** you over to the Lk 12:58
to **h** Him over to the governor's Lk 20:20
to my Lord, 'Sit at My right **h** Lk 20:42
They will **h** you over to the Lk 21:12
how he could **h** Him over to them. Lk 22:4
the **h** of the one betraying Me is Lk 22:21
you never laid a **h** on Me. Lk 22:53
at the right **h** of the Power of Lk 22:69
but your time is always at **h**. Jn 7:6
no one laid a **h** on Him because Jn 7:30
will snatch them out of My **h**. Jn 10:28
them out of the Father's **h**. Jn 10:29
came out bound **h** and foot with Jn 11:44
and put my **h** into His side, Jn 20:25
Reach out your **h** and put it into Jn 20:27
because He is at my right **h**, Ac 2:25
to the right **h** of God and has Ac 2:33
to my Lord, 'Sit at My right **h** Ac 2:34
by the right **h** he raised him up Ac 3:7
do whatever Your **h** and Your plan Ac 4:28
stretch out Your **h** for healing, Ac 4:30
man to His right **h** as ruler and Ac 5:31
Did not My **h** make all these Ac 7:50
standing at the right **h** of God, Ac 7:55
standing at the right **h** of God!" Ac 7:56
took him by the **h** and led him Ac 9:8
He gave her his **h** and helped her Ac 9:41
The Lord's **h** was with them, Ac 11:21
to them with his **h** to be silent, Ac 12:17
The Lord's **h** is against you: Ac 13:11
someone to lead him by the **h**. Ac 13:11
motioned with his **h** and spoke: Ac 13:16
one will lay a **h** on you to hurt Ac 18:10
gods made by **h** are not gods! Ac 19:26
with his **h**, Alexander wanted Ac 19:33
with his **h** to the people. Ac 21:40
I was led by the **h** by those who Ac 22:11
the commander took him by the **h**, Ac 23:19
stretched out his **h** and began Ac 26:1

and fastened itself to his **h**. Ac 28:3
the creature hanging from his **h**, Ac 28:4
also is at the right **h** of God Rm 8:34
I'm not a **h**, I don't belong 1Co 12:15
So the eye cannot say to the **h**, 1Co 12:21
This greeting is in my own **h**— 1Co 16:21
on the right **h** and the left, 2Co 6:7
gave the right **h** of fellowship Gl 2:9
at His right **h** in the heavens Eph 1:20
done by **h** in the flesh. Eph 2:11
seated at the right **h** of God. Col 3:1
This greeting is in my own **h**— Col 4:18
This greeting is in my own **h**— 2Th 3:17
Paul, write this with my own **h**: Phm 19
at the right **h** of the Majesty Heb 1:3
Sit at My right **h** until I make Heb 1:13
at the right **h** of the throne Heb 8:1
them by their **h** to lead them out Heb 8:9
sat down at the right **h** of God. Heb 10:12
at the right **h** of God's throne. Heb 12:2
at God's right **h**, with angels, 1Pt 3:22
under the mighty **h** of God, 1Pt 5:6
In His right **h** He had seven Rv 1:16
He laid His right **h** on me, Rv 1:17
stars you saw in My right **h**, Rv 1:20
in His right **h** and who walks Rv 2:1
saw in the right **h** of the One Rv 5:1
out of the right **h** of the One Rv 5:7
it had a balance scale in his **h**. Rv 6:5
of God from the angel's **h**. Rv 8:4
a little scroll opened in his **h**. Rv 10:2
raised his right **h** to heaven. Rv 10:5
open in the **h** of the angel who Rv 10:8
from the angel's **h** and ate it. Rv 10:10
mark on his right **h** or on his Rv 13:16
on his forehead or on his **h**, Rv 14:9
and a sharp sickle in His **h**. Rv 14:14
a gold cup in her **h** filled with Rv 17:4
and a great chain in his **h**. Rv 20:1

HAND-PICKED *(1)*

assigned seven **h** female servants Est 2:9

HANDED *(123)*

High who has **h** over your enemies Gn 14:20
Then she **h** the delicious food Gn 27:17
for I have **h** him over to you Nm 21:34
I have **h** Sihon the Amorite, Dt 2:24
LORD our God **h** him over to us, Dt 2:33
for I have **h** him over to you, Dt 3:2
LORD our God also **h** over Og king Dt 3:3
The LORD has **h** over the entire Jos 2:24
I have **h** Jericho, its king, Jos 6:2
I have **h** over to you the king of Jos 8:1
your God has **h** it over to you. Jos 8:7
for I have **h** them over to you. Jos 10:8
your God has **h** them over to you. Jos 10:19
The LORD also **h** it and its king Jos 10:30
The LORD **h** Lachish over to Jos 10:32
The LORD **h** them over to Israel, Jos 11:8
for the LORD **h** over all their Jos 21:44
you, but I **h** them over to you. Jos 24:8
you, but I **h** them over to you. Jos 24:11
I have **h** the land over to him." Jdg 1:2
the LORD **h** the Canaanites and Jdg 1:4
and He **h** them over to marauders Jdg 2:14
and the LORD **h** over Jdg 3:10
LORD has **h** over your enemies, Jdg 3:28
day the LORD has **h** Sisera over Jdg 4:14
the LORD **h** them over to Midian Jdg 6:1
us and **h** us over to Midian. Jdg 6:13
God has **h** the entire Midianite Jdg 7:14
for the LORD has **h** the Midianite Jdg 7:15
God **h** over to you Oreb and Zeeb, Jdg 8:3
when the LORD has **h** Zebah and Jdg 8:7
God of Israel **h** over Sihon and Jdg 11:21
and the LORD **h** them over to him. Jdg 11:32
and the LORD **h** them over to me. Jdg 12:3
so the LORD **h** them over to the Jdg 13:1
Our god has **h** over our enemy Jdg 16:23
Our god has **h** over to us our Jdg 16:24
for God has **h** it over to you. Jdg 18:10
so He **h** them over to Sisera 1Sm 12:9
the LORD has **h** them over to us— 1Sm 14:10
for the LORD has **h** them over to 1Sm 14:12
God has **h** him over to me, 1Sm 23:7
that the LORD **h** you over to me 1Sm 24:10
when the LORD **h** me over to you, 1Sm 24:18
Today God has **h** your enemy over 1Sm 26:8
the LORD **h** you over to me 1Sm 26:23
He protected us and **h** over to us 1Sm 30:23
and haven't **h** you over to David 2Sm 3:8
the LORD has **h** the kingdom over 2Sm 16:8
descendants be **h** over to us so 2Sm 21:6
and **h** them over to the 2Sm 21:9
and **h** them over to plunderers 2Kg 17:20
will not be **h** over to the king 2Kg 18:30
will not be **h** over to the king 2Kg 19:10
allies were **h** over to them, 1Ch 5:20
For He has **h** the land's 1Ch 22:18
and God **h** them over to them. 2Ch 13:16
on the LORD, He **h** them over to 2Ch 16:8
for they will be **h** over to you." 2Ch 18:14
the LORD **h** over a vast army to 2Ch 24:24
the LORD his God **h** Ahaz over to 2Ch 28:5
Ahaz was also **h** over to the king 2Ch 28:5
your ancestors **h** them over to 2Ch 28:9
He **h** them all over to him. 2Ch 36:17
He **h** them over to King Ezr 5:12
iniquities we have been **h** over, Ezr 9:7
before them and **h** their kings Neh 9:24
So You **h** them over to their Neh 9:27
You **h** them over to the Neh 9:30
The earth is **h** over to the Jb 9:24
and have not **h** me over to the Ps 31:8
h over their livestock to hail Ps 78:48
He **h** them over to the nations; Ps 106:41
will not be **h** over to the king Is 36:15
won't be **h** over to the king Is 37:10
It will be **h** over to the king Jr 21:10
so he was not **h** over to the Jr 26:24
certainly be **h** over to Babylon's Jr 32:4
has been **h** over to the Chaldeans Jr 32:24
the city has been **h** over to the Jr 32:25
It has been **h** over to Babylon's Jr 32:36
it has been **h** over to the Jr 32:43
be captured and **h** over to him. Jr 34:3
will be **h** over to their enemies, Jr 34:20
You will be **h** over to the king Jr 37:17
certainly be **h** over to the king Jr 38:3
this city will be **h** over to the Jr 38:18
will not be **h** over to the men Jr 39:17
just as I **h** over Judah's King Jr 44:30
h over to a northern people. Jr 46:24
He has **h** me over to those I Lm 1:14
has **h** the walls of her palaces Lm 2:7
I **h** her over to her lovers, Ezk 23:9
ancient hatred and **h** over the Ezk 35:5
from them and **h** them over to Ezk 39:23
The Lord **h** Jehoiakim king of Dn 1:2
He has **h** them over to you and Dn 2:38
ones will be **h** over to him for Dn 7:25
will be **h** over to his enemy Dn 11:11
because they **h** over a whole Am 1:9
got angry and **h** him over to Mt 18:34
of Man will be **h** over to the Mt 20:18
Son of Man will be **h** over to be Mt 26:2
led Him away and **h** Him over to Mt 27:2
knew they had **h** Him over because Mt 27:18
he **h** Him over to be crucified. Mt 27:26
tradition that you have **h** down. Mk 7:13
of Man will be **h** over to the Mk 10:33
led Him away and **h** Him over to Mk 15:1
chief priests had **h** Him over. Mk 15:10
he **h** Him over to be crucified. Mk 15:15
of the word **h** them down to us. Lk 1:2
For He will be **h** over to the Lk 18:32
But he **h** Jesus over to their Lk 23:25
and leaders **h** Him over to be Lk 24:20
wouldn't have **h** Him over to you. Jn 18:30
chief priests **h** You over to me. Jn 18:35
I wouldn't be **h** over to the Jews Jn 18:36
why the one who **h** Me over to you Jn 19:11
he **h** Him over to be crucified. Jn 19:16
whom you **h** over and denied in Ac 3:13
that Moses **h** down to us." Ac 6:14
they **h** over Paul and some other Ac 27:1

HANDFUL *(8)*

will take a **h** of fine flour Lv 2:2
who will take a **h** from it as its Lv 5:12
is to remove a **h** of fine flour Lv 6:15
offering, took a **h** of it, and Lv 9:17
is to take a **h** of the grain Nm 5:26
only a **h** of flour in the jar and 1Kg 17:12
dust amounts to a **h** for each of 1Kg 20:10
Better one **h** with rest, than two Ec 4:6

HANDFULS *(4)*

Aaron, "Take **h** of furnace soot Ex 9:8
LORD and two **h** of finely ground Lv 16:12
than two **h** with effort and Ec 4:6
of My people for **h** of barley and Ezk 13:19

HANDING *(3)*

that you are **h** your servant over 1Kg 18:9
I am **h** it over to you today so 1Kg 20:13
whole community, **h** them over to Am 1:6

HANDIWORK *(2)*

like jewelry, the **h** of a master. Sg 7:1
Assyria My **h**, and Israel My Is 19:25

HANDLE *(7)*

flies off the **h** and strikes his Dt 19:5
Even the **h** went in after the Jdg 3:22
who are able to **h** shields, Jr 46:9
who are able to **h** and string the Jr 46:9
All those who **h** an oar disembark Ezk 27:29
strong ⌊enough⌋ to **h** a sword. Ezk 30:21
Don't **h**, don't taste, don't Col 2:21

HANDLES *(1)*

myrrh on the **h** of the bolt. Sg 5:5

HANDS *(431)*

the agonizing labor of our **h**, Gn 5:29
Here, your slave is in your **h**; Gn 16:6
and the **h** of his two daughters. Gn 19:16
a clear conscience and clean **h**." Gn 20:5
goatskins on his **h** and the Gn 27:16
the **h** are the hands of Esau." Gn 27:22
the hands are the **h** of Esau." Gn 27:22
because his **h** were hairy like Gn 27:23
him from their **h** and return him Gn 37:22
will put his **h** on your eyes." Gn 46:4
and crossing his **h**, put his left Gn 48:14
agile by the **h** of the Mighty One Gn 49:24
I will extend my **h** to the LORD. Ex 9:29
and extended his **h** to the LORD. Ex 9:33
Your **h** have established the Ex 15:17
When Moses' **h** grew heavy, they Ex 17:12
Aaron and Hur supported his **h**, Ex 17:12
so that his **h** remained steady Ex 17:12
must lay their **h** on the bull's Ex 29:10
are to lay their **h** on the ram's Ex 29:15
must lay their **h** on the ram's Ex 29:19
on the thumbs of their right **h**, Ex 29:20
them in the **h** of Aaron and his Ex 29:24
from their **h** and burn ⌊them⌋ Ex 29:25
sons must wash their **h** and feet Ex 30:19
must wash their **h** and feet so Ex 30:21
He took ⌊the gold⌋ from their **h**, Ex 32:4
of the testimony in his **h**. Ex 32:15
threw the tablets out of his **h**, Ex 32:19
in his **h** as he descended Ex 34:29
yarn⌋ with her **h** and brought it: Ex 35:25
washed their **h** and feet from it Ex 40:31
are to lay their **h** on the bull's Lv 4:15
His own **h** will bring the fire Lv 7:30
sons laid their **h** on the head Lv 8:14
sons laid their **h** on the head Lv 8:18
sons laid their **h** on the head Lv 8:22
on the thumbs of their right **h**, Lv 8:24
these⌋ in the **h** of Aaron and his Lv 8:27
them from their **h** and burned Lv 8:28
up his **h** toward the people Lv 9:22
first⌋ rinsing his **h** in water, Lv 15:11
will lay both his **h** on the head Lv 16:21
his blood is on his own **h**. Lv 20:9
their blood is on their own **h**. Lv 20:11
their blood is on their own **h**. Lv 20:12
their blood is on their own **h**. Lv 20:13
their blood is on their own **h**." Lv 20:27
him⌋ lay their **h** on his head; Lv 24:14
will be delivered into enemy **h**. Lv 26:25
and place in her **h** the grain Nm 5:18
them⌋ into the **h** of the Nazirite Nm 6:19
Israelites lay their **h** on them. Nm 8:10
are to lay their **h** on the heads Nm 8:12
deliver this people into our **h**, Nm 21:2
struck his **h** together, and said Nm 24:10
in him, and lay your **h** on him. Nm 27:18
laid his **h** on him, and Nm 27:23
fruit from the land in their **h**, Dt 1:25
us into the **h** of the Amorites so Dt 1:27
you in all the work of your **h**. Dt 2:7
of the covenant were in my **h**. Dt 9:15
and threw them from my **h**, Dt 9:17
bind them as a sign on your **h**, Dt 11:18
then the **h** of all the people. Dt 13:9
the work of your **h** that you do. Dt 14:29

and in all the work of your **h**, Dt 16:15
The witnesses' **h** are to be the Dt 17:7
after that, the **h** of all the Dt 17:7
LORD your God **h** it over to you, Dt 20:13
will wash their **h** by the stream Dt 21:6
'Our **h** did not shed this blood; Dt 21:7
LORD your God **h** them over to you Dt 21:10
certificate, **h** it to her, and Dt 24:3
you in all the work of your **h**. Dt 24:19
to bless all the work of your **h**. Dt 28:12
work of your **h** with children, Dt 30:9
Him with what your **h** have made." Dt 31:29
for his cause with his own **h**, Dt 33:7
and accept the work of his **h**. Dt 33:11
Moses had laid his **h** on him. Dt 34:9
we are in your **h**. Do to us Jos 9:25
them from the **h** of the Jos 9:26
with their **h** to their mouths Jdg 7:6
pitchers that were in their **h**. Jdg 7:19
their torches in their left **h**, Jdg 7:20
their trumpets in their right **h**, Jdg 7:20
now in your **h** that we should Jdg 8:6
life in my own **h** and crossed Jdg 12:3
with his bare **h** as he might have Jdg 14:6
honey⌋ into his **h** and ate ⌊it⌋ Jdg 14:9
and fall into the **h** of the Jdg 15:18
house with her **h** on the Jdg 19:27
palms of his **h** were broken off 1Sm 5:4
went up using his **h** and feet, 1Sm 14:13
death at the **h** of the 1Sm 18:25
his life in his **h** when he struck 1Sm 19:5
my life in my **h** and did what you 1Sm 28:21
Your **h** were not bound, your feet 2Sm 3:34
blood from your **h** and wipe you 2Sm 4:11
cut off their **h** and feet and 2Sm 4:12
to the cleanness of my **h**. 2Sm 22:21
He trains my **h** for war; 2Sm 22:35
into the LORD's **h** because His 2Sm 24:14
don't let me fall into human **h**." 2Sm 24:14
spread out his **h** toward heaven. 1Kg 8:22
spreading out his **h** toward this 1Kg 8:38
with his **h** spread out toward 1Kg 8:54
it into the **h** of his servants 1Kg 15:18
the work of his **h** and being like 1Kg 16:7
lay their **h** on and take away. 1Kg 20:6
to pour water on Elijah's **h**, 2Kg 3:11
feet, and the palms of her **h**. 2Kg 9:35
into your **h** to escape ⌊will 2Kg 10:24
and clapped their **h** and cried, 2Kg 11:12
money into the **h** of those doing 2Kg 12:11
Elisha put his **h** on the king's 2Kg 13:16
put his hands on the king's **h**. 2Kg 13:16
not gods but made by human **h**— 2Kg 19:18
be put into the **h** of those doing 2Kg 22:5
put into their **h** since they work 2Kg 22:7
Me with all the work of their **h**. 2Kg 22:17
exile at the **h** of Nebuchadnezzar 1Ch 6:15
even though my **h** have done no 1Ch 12:17
into the LORD's **h** because His 1Ch 21:13
don't let me fall into human **h**." 1Ch 21:13
of Israel and spread out his **h**. 2Ch 6:12
spread out his **h** toward heaven. 2Ch 6:13
spreading out his **h** toward this 2Ch 6:29
temple into the **h** of the 2Ch 23:18
who laid their **h** on them. 2Ch 29:23
which were made by human **h**. 2Ch 32:19
put it into the **h** of those doing 2Ch 34:10
all that was placed in their **h**. 2Ch 34:16
with all the works of their **h**. 2Ch 34:25
spread out my **h** to the LORD my Ezr 9:5
with their **h** uplifted all the Neh 8:6
have blessed the work of his **h**, Jb 1:10
and have strengthened weak **h**. Jb 4:3
He strikes, but His **h** also heal. Jb 5:18
and cleanse my **h** with lye, Jb 9:30
to reject the work of Your **h**, Jb 10:3
Your **h** shaped me and formed me. Jb 10:8
and lift up your **h** to Him ⌊in Jb 11:13
and take my life in my own **h**? Jb 13:14
long for the work of Your **h**. Jb 14:15
God **h** me over to unjust men; Jb 16:11
me into the **h** of the wicked. Jb 16:11
although my **h** are free from Jb 16:17
the one whose **h** are clean will Jb 17:9
for his own **h** must give back his Jb 20:10
by human **h**⌋ will consume him Jb 20:26
rescued by the purity of your **h**. Jb 22:30
It claps its **h** at him and scorns Jb 27:23

their mouths with ⌊their⌋ **h**. Jb 29:9
me was the strength of their **h**? Jb 30:2
or impurity has stained my **h**, Jb 31:7
they are all the work of His **h**. Jb 34:19
He covers ⌊His⌋ **h** with lightning Jb 36:32
if there is injustice on my **h**, Ps 7:3
lord over the works of Your **h**; Ps 8:6
at the **h** of those who hate Ps 9:13
wicked by the work of their **h**. Ps 9:16
to take the matter into Your **h**. Ps 10:14
to the cleanness of my **h**. Ps 18:20
cleanness of my **h** in His sight. Ps 18:24
He trains my **h** for war; Ps 18:34
sky proclaims the work of His **h**. Ps 19:1
they pierced my **h** and my feet. Ps 22:16
who has clean **h** and a pure heart Ps 24:4
I wash my **h** in innocence and go Ps 26:6
in whose **h** are evil schemes, Ps 26:10
whose right **h** are filled with Ps 26:10
I lift up my **h** toward Your holy Ps 28:2
to the work of their **h**; Ps 28:4
has done or the work of His **h**, Ps 28:5
spread out our **h** to a foreign Ps 44:20
Clap your **h**, all you peoples; Ps 47:1
with your **h** you weigh out Ps 58:2
Your name, I will lift up my **h**. Ps 63:4
will stretch out its **h** to God. Ps 68:31
and wash my **h** in innocence for Ps 73:13
My **h** were lifted up all night Ps 77:2
guided them with his skillful **h**. Ps 78:72
his **h** were freed from ⌊carrying⌋ Ps 81:6
I spread out my **h** to You. Ps 88:9
for us the work of our **h**— Ps 90:17
establish the work of our **h**! Ps 90:17
with their **h** so that you will Ps 91:12
because of the works of Your **h**. Ps 92:4
His **h** formed the dry land. Ps 95:5
Let the rivers clap their **h**; Ps 98:8
heavens are the work of Your **h**. Ps 102:25
The works of His **h** are truth and Ps 111:7
and gold, made by human **h**. Ps 115:4
They have **h**, but cannot feel, Ps 115:7
will lift up my **h** to Your Ps 119:48
Your **h** made me and formed me; Ps 119:73
not apply their **h** to injustice. Ps 125:3
eat what your **h** have worked for. Ps 128:2
even fill the **h** of the reaper Ps 129:7
up your **h** in the holy place, Ps 134:2
and gold, made by human **h**. Ps 135:15
not abandon the work of Your **h**. Ps 138:8
raising of my **h** as the evening Ps 141:2
I reflect on the work of Your **h**. Ps 143:5
I spread out my **h** to You; Ps 143:6
who trains my **h** for battle and Ps 144:1
whose right **h** are deceptive. Ps 144:8
whose right **h** are deceptive. Ps 144:11
a two-edged sword in their **h**, Ps 149:6
h that shed innocent blood, Pr 6:17
Idle **h** make one poor, but Pr 10:4
but diligent **h** bring riches. Pr 10:4
of a man's **h** will reward him Pr 12:14
tears it down with her own **h**. Pr 14:1
because his **h** refuse to work. Pr 21:25
has gathered the wind in His **h**? Pr 30:4
lizard can be caught in your **h**, Pr 30:28
flax and works with willing **h**. Pr 31:13
extends her **h** to the spinning Pr 31:19
and her **h** hold the spindle. Pr 31:19
Her **h** reach out to the poor, Pr 31:20
she extends her **h** to the needy. Pr 31:20
and destroy the work of your **h**? Ec 5:6
that he can carry in his **h**. Ec 5:15
heart a net, and her **h** chains. Ec 7:26
and their works are in God's **h**. Ec 9:1
Whatever your **h** find to do, Ec 9:10
of negligent **h** the house leaks. Ec 10:18
My **h** dripped with myrrh, my Sg 5:5
you lift up your **h** ⌊in prayer⌋, Is 1:15
Your **h** are covered with blood. Is 1:15
bow down to the work of their **h**, Is 2:8
do not see the work of His **h**. Is 5:12
staff in their **h** is My wrath. Is 10:5
everyone's **h** will become weak, Is 13:7
made with their **h** or to the Is 17:8
Egypt into the **h** of harsh Is 19:4
with the trickery of his **h**. Is 25:11
the work of My **h** within his Is 29:23
that your own **h** have sinfully Is 31:7

the weak **h**, steady the shaking Is 35:3
not gods but made by human **h**— Is 37:19
The LORD **h** nations over to him, Is 41:2
your work ⌊say⌋: He has no **h**? Is 45:9
Me about the work of My **h**. Is 45:11
It was My **h** that stretched out Is 45:12
you on the palms of My **h**; Is 49:16
put it into the **h** of your Is 51:23
the field will clap ⌊their⌋ **h**. Is 55:12
For your **h** are defiled with Is 59:3
and violent acts are in their **h**. Is 59:6
the work of My **h**, so that I may Is 60:21
we all are the work of Your **h**. Is 64:8
spread out My **h** all day long to Is 65:2
fully enjoy the work of their **h**. Is 65:22
the works of their own **h**. Jr 1:16
here with your **h** on your head Jr 2:37
breath, stretching out her **h**: Jr 4:31
worked by the **h** of a craftsman Jr 10:3
Uphaz from the **h** of a goldsmith, Jr 10:9
the weapons of war in your **h**, Jr 21:4
strengthen the **h** of evildoers, Jr 23:14
to anger by the work of your **h**. Jr 25:6
the work of your **h** and bring Jr 25:7
and the work of their **h**.'" Jr 25:14
He **h** them over to the sword— Jr 25:31
As for me, here I am in your **h**; Jr 26:14
man with his **h** on his stomach Jr 30:6
anger by the work of their **h**"— Jr 32:30
pass under the **h** of the one who Jr 33:13
he's in your **h** since the king Jr 38:5
the chains that were on your **h**. Jr 40:4
to anger by the work of your **h**. Jr 44:8
thrown up her **h** ⌊in surrender⌋; Jr 50:15
them, and his **h** fall helpless. Jr 50:43
Zion stretches out her **h**; Lm 1:17
scornfully⌋ clap their **h** at you. Lm 2:15
Lift up your **h** to Him for the Lm 2:19
and ⌊our⌋ **h** to God in heaven Lm 3:41
to the work of their **h**. Lm 3:64
jars, the work of a potter's **h**! Lm 4:2
h of compassionate women have Lm 4:10
one rescues ⌊us⌋ from their **h**. Lm 5:8
Princes are hung up by their **h**; Lm 5:12
⌊They had⌋ human **h** under their Ezk 1:8
Clap your **h**, stamp your feet, Ezk 6:11
All their **h** will become weak, Ezk 7:17
and the **h** of the people of the Ezk 7:27
Fill your **h** with hot coals from Ezk 10:2
put ⌊it⌋ into the **h** of the man Ezk 10:7
form of human **h** under their Ezk 10:8
their backs, **h**, wings, and the Ezk 10:12
form of human **h** under their Ezk 10:21
deliver My people from your **h**, Ezk 13:21
no longer be prey in your **h**. Ezk 13:21
deliver My people from your **h**. Ezk 13:23
and clap ⌊your⌋ **h** together. Ezk 21:14
I also will clap My **h** together, Ezk 21:17
I clap My **h** together against the Ezk 22:13
endure or your **h** be strong in Ezk 22:14
and blood is on their **h**; Ezk 23:37
on the women's **h** and beautiful Ezk 23:42
and blood is on their **h**. Ezk 23:45
Because you clapped ⌊your⌋ **h**, Ezk 25:6
in the **h** of those who kill you. Ezk 28:9
at the **h** of strangers. Ezk 28:10
the land into the **h** of evil men. Ezk 30:12
in it by the **h** of foreigners. Ezk 30:12
his blood is on his own **h**. Ezk 33:5
them from the **h** of those who Ezk 34:27
be shattered, not by human **h**. Dn 8:25
and raised me to my **h** and knees. Dn 10:10
raised both his **h** toward heaven Dn 12:7
one will rescue her from My **h**. Hs 2:10
with dishonest scales in his **h**. Hs 12:7
to the work of our **h**. For the Hs 14:3
into the **h** of the people Jl 3:8
because the power is in their **h**. Mc 2:1
remove sorceries from your **h**, Mc 5:12
again to the work of your **h**. Mc 5:13
Both **h** are good at accomplishing Mc 7:3
will put ⌊their⌋ **h** over ⌊their⌋ Mc 7:16
clap their **h** because of you, Nah 3:19
do not let your **h** grow weak. Zph 3:16
and on all that your **h** produce." Hg 1:11
And so is every work of their **h**; Hg 2:14
work of your **h**—with blight, Hg 2:17
Zerubbabel's **h** have laid the Zch 4:9

and his **h** will complete it. Zch 4:9
Let your **h** be strong, you who Zch 8:9
let your **h** be strong." Zch 8:13
this has come from your **h**, Mal 1:9
accept no offering from your **h**. Mal 1:10
I to accept that from your **h**?" Mal 1:13
them⌋ gladly from your **h**. Mal 2:13
with their **h** so that you will Mt 4:6
wash their **h** when they eat!" Mt 15:2
with unwashed **h** does not defile Mt 15:20
is going to suffer at their **h**." Mt 17:12
be betrayed into the **h** of men. Mt 17:22
than to have two **h** or two feet Mt 18:8
might put His **h** on them and pray Mt 19:13
After putting His **h** on them, Mt 19:15
betrayed into the **h** of sinners. Mt 26:45
washed his **h** in front of the Mt 27:24
and lay Your **h** on her so she can Mk 5:23
miracles performed by His **h**? Mk 6:2
that He laid His **h** on a few sick Mk 6:5
unclean—that is, unwashed—**h**. Mk 7:2
they wash their **h** ritually, Mk 7:3
bread with ritually unclean **h**?" Mk 7:5
eyes and laying His **h** on him, Mk 8:23
Jesus placed His **h** on the man's Mk 8:25
betrayed into the **h** of men. Mk 9:31
to have two **h** and go to hell Mk 9:43
laid His **h** on them and blessed Mk 10:16
betrayed into the **h** of sinners. Mk 14:41
sanctuary made by ⌊human⌋ **h**, Mk 14:58
build another not made by **h**.' " Mk 14:58
they will lay **h** on the sick, Mk 16:18
will support you with their **h**, Lk 4:11
As He laid His **h** on each one of Lk 4:40
in their **h**, and eating them. Lk 6:1
be betrayed into the **h** of men." Lk 9:44
and fell into the **h** of robbers. Lk 10:30
fell into the **h** of the robbers? Lk 10:36
Then He laid His **h** on her, Lk 13:13
father's hired **h** have more than Lk 15:17
me like one of your hired **h**.' Lk 15:19
to get their **h** on Him that very Lk 20:19
they will lay their **h** on you and Lk 21:12
Your **h** I entrust My spirit." Lk 23:46
into the **h** of sinful men, Lk 24:7
Look at My **h** and My feet, that Lk 24:39
He showed them His **h** and feet. Lk 24:40
up His **h** He blessed them. Lk 24:50
has given all things into His **h**. Jn 3:35
Him, but no one laid **h** on Him. Jn 7:44
had given everything into His **h**, Jn 13:3
but also my **h** and my head." Jn 13:9
showed them His **h** and His side. Jn 20:20
the mark of the nails in His **h**, Jn 20:25
finger here and observe My **h**. Jn 20:27
out your **h** and someone else Jn 21:18
through the **h** of the apostles. Ac 5:12
prayed and laid their **h** on them. Ac 6:6
what their **h** had made. Ac 7:41
in sanctuaries made with **h**, Ac 7:48
and John laid their **h** on them, Ac 8:17
laying on of the apostles' **h**, Ac 8:18
anyone I lay **h** on may receive Ac 8:19
and placing his **h** on him so he Ac 9:12
he placed his **h** on him and said, Ac 9:17
prayed, and laid **h** on them, they Ac 13:3
not live in shrines made by **h**. Ac 17:24
Neither is He served by human **h**, Ac 17:25
Paul had laid his **h** on them, Ac 19:6
miracles by Paul's **h**, Ac 19:11
know that these **h** have provided Ac 20:34
own feet and **h**, and said, "This Ac 21:11
deliver him into Gentile **h**.' " Ac 21:11
came and took him from our **h**, Ac 24:7
gear overboard with their own **h**. Ac 27:19
praying and laying his **h** on him, Ac 28:8
into the **h** of the Romans Ac 28:17
spread out My **h** to a disobedient Rm 10:21
labor, working with our own **h**. 1Co 4:12
when He **h** over the kingdom to 1Co 15:24
a house not made with **h**, eternal 2Co 5:1
in the wall and escaped his **h**. 2Co 11:33
do honest work with his own **h**, Eph 4:28
a circumcision not done with **h**, Col 2:11
and to work with your own **h**, 1Th 4:11
lifting up holy **h** without anger 1Tm 2:8
laying on of **h** by the council 1Tm 4:14
be too quick to lay **h** on anyone, 1Tm 5:22
through the laying on of my **h**. 2Tm 1:6
heavens are the works of Your **h**; Heb 1:10
laying on of **h**, the resurrection Heb 6:2
tabernacle not made with **h** Heb 9:11
enter a sanctuary made with **h** Heb 9:24
to fall into the **h** of the living Heb 10:31
your tired **h** and weakened knees, Heb 12:12
Cleanse your **h**, sinners, and Jms 4:8
and have touched with our **h**, 1Jn 1:1
with palm branches in their **h**. Rv 7:9
works of their **h** to stop Rv 9:20
His servants that was on her **h**. Rv 19:2
on their foreheads or their **h**. Rv 20:4

HANDSOME *(8)*

Now Joseph was well-built and **h**. Gn 39:6
and a healthy, **h** appearance. 1Sm 16:12
eloquent, **h**, and the LORD is 1Sm 16:18
was just a youth, healthy and **h**. 1Sm 17:42
all Israel was as **h** and highly 2Sm 14:25
was quite **h** and was born after 1Kg 1:6
You are the most **h** of men; Ps 45:2
How **h** you are, my love. Sg 1:16

HANDWRITING *(1)*

have written to you in my own **h**. Gl 6:11

HANES *(1)*

messengers reach as far as **H**, Is 30:4

HANG *(17)*

off you—and **h** you on a tree. Gn 40:19
curtain is to **h** down over the Ex 26:12
H it on four gold-plated posts Ex 26:32
H the veil under the clasps and Ex 26:33
courtyard and **h** the screen for Ex 40:8
let your hair **h** loose and do not Lv 10:6
and you **h** his body on a tree, Dt 21:22
Your life will **h** in doubt before Dt 28:66
it **h** over Joab's head and his 2Sm 3:29
to us so we may **h** them in the 2Sm 21:6
the morning to **h** Mordecai on it. Est 5:14
to ask the king to **h** Mordecai on Est 6:4
king commanded, "**H** him on it." Est 7:9
is like lame legs that **h** limp. Pr 26:7
They will **h** on him the whole Is 22:24
again or to **h** up my curtains. Jr 10:20
make a peg from it to **h** things Ezk 15:3

HANGED *(9)*

but he **h** the chief baker, just Gn 40:22
and the other man was **h**." Gn 41:13
affairs in order and **h** himself. 2Sm 17:23
They **h** them on the hill in the 2Sm 21:9
both men were **h** on the gallows. Est 2:23
They **h** Haman on the gallows he Est 7:10
and he was **h** on the gallows Est 8:7
he should be **h** with his sons Est 9:25
Then he went and **h** himself. Mt 27:5

HANGING *(8)*

curtains should be **h** down over Ex 26:13
torn and his hair **h** loose, Lv 13:45
saw Absalom **h** in an oak tree! 2Sm 18:10
and oxen were wreaths of **h** work. 1Kg 7:29
the criminals **h** there began to Lk 23:39
had murdered by **h** Him on a tree. Ac 5:30
killed Him by **h** Him on a tree. Ac 10:39
the creature **h** from his hand, Ac 28:4

HANGINGS *(19)*

⌊Make the **h**⌋ on the south of the Ex 27:9
Then ⌊make the **h**⌋ on the north Ex 27:11
⌊Make⌋ the **h** of the courtyard on Ex 27:12
Make the **h** of the courtyard on Ex 27:13
⌊Make⌋ the **h** on one side ⌊of the Ex 27:14
And make the **h** on the other side Ex 27:15
h of the courtyard, its posts Ex 35:17
The **h** on the south side of the Ex 38:9
⌊The **h**⌋ on the north side were Ex 38:11
The **h** on the west side were 75 Ex 38:12
⌊The **h**⌋ on the east toward the Ex 38:13
The **h** on one side ⌊of the gate⌋ Ex 38:14
The **h** were 22 and a half feet, Ex 38:15
All the **h** around the courtyard Ex 38:16
and like the **h** of the courtyard, Ex 38:18
h of the courtyard, its posts Ex 39:40
the **h** of the courtyard, the Nm 3:26
the **h** of the courtyard, the Nm 4:26
and violet linen **h** were fastened Est 1:6

HANGS *(1)*

He **h** the earth on nothing. Jb 26:7

HANNAH *(17)*

the first named **H** and the second 1Sm 1:2
children, but **H** was childless. 1Sm 1:2
he gave a double portion to **H**, 1Sm 1:5
LORD had kept **H** from conceiving 1Sm 1:6
H wept and would not eat. 1Sm 1:7
"**H**, why are you crying?" 1Sm 1:8
H got up after they ate and 1Sm 1:9
H prayed to the LORD and wept 1Sm 1:10
H was speaking to herself, 1Sm 1:13
"No, my lord," **H** replied. 1Sm 1:15
Then **H** went on her way; 1Sm 1:18
Elkanah and **H** got up early to 1Sm 1:19
was intimate with his wife **H**, 1Sm 1:19
H conceived and gave birth to a 1Sm 1:20
H did not go and explained to 1Sm 1:22
So **H** stayed there and nursed 1Sm 1:23
H prayed: My heart rejoices in 1Sm 2:1

HANNAH'S *(1)*

LORD paid attention to **H** ⌊need⌋, 1Sm 2:21

HANNATHON *(1)*

on the north to **H** and ended at Jos 19:14

HANNIEL *(2)*

H son of Ephod, a leader from Nm 34:23
Ulla's sons: Arah, **H**, and Rizia. 1Ch 7:39

HANOCH *(6)*

Ephah, Epher, **H**, Abida, and Gn 25:4
H, Pallu, Hezron, and Carmi. Gn 46:9
H and Pallu, Hezron and Carmi. Ex 6:14
the Hanochite clan ⌊from⌋ **H**; Nm 26:5
Ephah, Epher, **H**, Abida, and 1Ch 1:33
H, Pallu, Hezron, and Carmi. 1Ch 5:3

HANOCHITE *(1)*

the **H** clan ⌊from⌋ Hanoch; Nm 26:5

HANUN *(11)*

and his son **H** became king in his 2Sm 10:1
kindness to **H** son of Nahash, 2Sm 10:2
to console **H** concerning his 2Sm 10:2
leaders said to **H** their lord, 2Sm 10:3
So **H** took David's emissaries, 2Sm 10:4
kindness to **H** son of Nahash, 1Ch 19:2
the Ammonite leaders said to **H**, 1Ch 19:3
So **H** took David's emissaries, 1Ch 19:4
H and the Ammonites sent 38 tons 1Ch 19:6
H and the inhabitants of Zanoah Neh 3:13
of Shelemiah and **H** the sixth son Neh 3:30

HAPHARAIM *(1)*

H, Shion, Anaharath, Jos 19:19

HAPPEN *(76)*

"Something might **h** to him." Gn 42:4
you what will **h** to you in the Gn 49:1
to see what would **h** to him. Ex 2:4
God caused it to **h** by his hand, Ex 21:13
I have promised will **h** to you." Nm 11:23
When all these things **h** to you— Dt 30:1
nothing will **h** to you in another Ru 2:22
bad will **h** to you because 1Sm 28:10
the young man **h** to the enemies 2Sm 18:32
have let this **h** without letting 1Kg 1:27
of Samaria is certain to **h**." 1Kg 13:32
you what will **h** to the boy." 1Kg 14:3
in heaven, could this really **h**?" 2Kg 7:2
in heaven, could this really **h**?" 2Kg 7:19
Let whatever comes **h** to me. Jb 13:13
causes this to **h** for punishment, Jb 37:13
to the fool will also **h** to me. Ec 2:15
see what will **h** after he dies? Ec 3:22
man what will **h** after him under Ec 6:12
Yet no one knows what will **h**, Ec 8:7
who can tell him what will **h**? Ec 8:7
and chance **h** to all of them. Ec 9:11
knows what will **h**, and who can Ec 10:14
anyone what will **h** after him? Ec 10:14
what disaster may **h** on earth. Ec 11:2
says: It will not **h**; it will not Is 7:7
it will not **h**. For God is with Is 8:10
have purposed it, so it will **h**. Is 14:24
the prostitute will **h** to Tyre: Is 23:15
come and tell us what will **h**. Is 41:22
Ask Me what is to **h** to My sons, Is 45:11
things will **h** to you suddenly Is 47:9
They will **h** to you in their Is 47:9
But disaster will **h** to you; Is 47:11
will **h** to you suddenly Is 47:11
monthly what will **h** to you. Is 47:13
LORD and insisted, "It won't **h**. Jr 5:12

This will in fact **h** to them. Jr 5:13
you have in mind will never **h**. Ezk 20:32
it is coming and it will **h**." Ezk 21:7
this will not **h** until He comes; Ezk 21:27
It will **h** in the last days, Ezk 38:16
it is coming, and it will **h**." Ezk 39:8
of what would **h**⌋ if he saw your Dn 1:10
know what will **h** in the last Dn 2:28
about what will **h** in the future. Dn 2:29
has let you know what will **h**. Dn 2:29
king what will **h** in the future. Dn 2:45
you what will **h** at the Dn 8:19
what will **h** to your people Dn 10:14
judgment⌋ will **h** to both people Hs 4:9
"It will not **h**," He said. Am 7:3
"This will not **h** either," said Am 7:6
to see what would **h** to the city. Jnh 4:5
All this will **h** because of Mc 1:5
This will **h** when you fully obey Zch 6:15
This will never **h** to You!" Mt 16:22
us, when will these things **h**? Mt 24:3
that say it must **h** this way?" Mt 26:54
the things that would **h** to Him. Mk 10:32
that what he says will **h**, Mk 11:23
us, when will these things **h**? Mk 13:4
Pray it won't **h** in winter. Mk 13:18
How could this **h** to me, that the Lk 1:43
Him saw what was going to **h**, Lk 22:49
what will **h** when it is dry?" Lk 23:31
things that **h** on earth and you Jn 3:12
worse doesn't **h** to you." Jn 5:14
when it does **h** you will believe Jn 13:19
when it does **h** you may believe. Jn 14:29
that was about to **h** to Him, Jn 18:4
you have said may **h** to me." Ac 8:24
the prophets does not **h** to you: Ac 13:40
saw nothing unusual **h** to him, Ac 28:6
to make it **h** that way for me 1Co 9:15
⌊All this will **h**⌋ because your Rv 18:23

HAPPENED *(98)*

⌊This **h**⌋ after Abram had lived Gn 16:3
Jacob told him all that had **h**. Gn 29:13
told him all that had **h** to them: Gn 42:29
This is what **h** when we went back Gn 44:24
h that the LORD confronted him Ex 4:24
don't know what has **h** to him!" Ex 32:1
don't know what has **h** to him!' Ex 32:23
Since these things have **h** to me, Lv 10:19
since it **h** to all the people Nm 15:26
all these things have **h** to you, Dt 4:30
like this great event ⌊ever⌋ **h**, Dt 4:32
thing has **h** among you, Dt 13:14
thing has **h** in Israel, Dt 17:4
everything that had **h** to them. Jos 2:23
is with us, why has all this **h**? Jdg 6:13
And that is what **h**. Jdg 6:38
this has ever **h** or been seen Jdg 19:30
She **h** to be in the portion of Ru 2:3
nothing like this has **h** before. 1Sm 4:7
"What **h**, my son?" 1Sm 4:16
that **h** to us by chance. 1Sm 6:9
When these signs have **h** to you, 1Sm 10:7
What has **h** to the son of Kish? 1Sm 10:11
Something unexpected has **h**; 1Sm 20:26
"I **h** to be on Mount Gilboa," 2Sm 1:6
mule when he **h** to meet David's 2Sm 18:9
son of Bichri, **h** to be there. 2Sm 20:1
⌊This **h**⌋ in the second year of 2Kg 1:17
This is what **h** to him: 2Kg 7:20
⌊This disaster⌋ **h** because the 2Kg 17:7
This **h** to Israel only at the 2Kg 24:3
So it **h** when Jehu executed 2Ch 22:8
sign that **h** in the land, 2Ch 32:31
all that has **h** to us because Ezr 9:13
everything that had **h** as well as Est 4:7
friends everything that had **h**. Est 6:13
them, just the opposite **h**. Est 9:1
and what had **h** to them, Est 9:26
adversity that had **h** to him, Jb 2:11
and what I dreaded has **h** to me. Jb 3:25
But now that this has **h** to you, Jb 4:5
this has **h** to us, but we have Ps 44:17
⌊All this **h**⌋ so that they might Ps 105:45
this is what has **h** to those we Is 20:6
The past events have indeed **h**. Is 42:9
Remember what **h** long ago, for I Is 46:9
These two things have **h** to you: Is 51:19
Why have these things **h** to me? Jr 13:22
What You have spoken has **h**. Jr 32:24
and he was ⌊there⌋ when it **h**. Jr 38:28
obeyed Him, this thing has **h**. Jr 40:3
or her who is escaping, What **h**? Jr 48:19
⌊Yet it **h**⌋ because of the sins Lm 4:13
remember what has **h** to us. Lm 5:1
and this should never have **h**! Ezk 16:16
you. That is what **h**." ⌊This is⌋ Ezk 16:19
⌊This **h**⌋ so that no trees Ezk 31:14
All this **h** to King Dn 4:28
like this ever **h** in your days Jl 1:2
and ⌊what **h**⌋ from Acacia Grove Mc 6:5
what had **h** to those who were Mt 8:33
master everything that had **h**. Mt 18:31
The same **h** to the second also, Mt 22:26
But all this has **h** so that the Mt 26:56
and the things that had **h**, Mt 27:54
priests everything that had **h**. Mt 28:11
people went to see what had **h**. Mk 5:14
to them what had **h** to the Mk 5:16
knowing what had **h** to her, Mk 5:33
it **h** that he was chosen by lot, Lk 1:9
to Bethlehem and see what has **h**, Lk 2:15
who tended them saw what had **h**, Lk 8:34
went out to see what had **h**. Lk 8:35
them to tell no one what had **h**. Lk 8:56
A priest **h** to be going down that Lk 10:31
When the centurion saw what **h**, Lk 23:47
went home, amazed at what had **h**. Lk 24:12
the things that **h** there in these Lk 24:18
third day since these things **h**. Lk 24:21
describe what had **h** on the road Lk 24:35
All this **h** in Bethany across the Jn 1:28
But ⌊this **h**⌋ so that the Jn 15:25
For these things **h** so that the Jn 19:36
at what had **h** to him. Ac 3:10
came in, not knowing what had **h**. Ac 5:7
This **h** three times, and then the Ac 10:16
Now this **h** three times, and then Ac 11:10
seeing what **h**, believed and was Ac 13:12
The same thing **h** in Iconium; Ac 14:1
with those who **h** to be there. Ac 17:17
with rioting for what **h** today, Ac 19:40
It **h** that Publius' father was in Ac 28:8
Now these things **h** to them as 1Co 10:11
What **h** to this blessedness of Gl 4:15
that what has **h** to me has Php 1:12
and as you know, it **h**. 1Th 3:4
of this ⌊**h**⌋ without an oath. Heb 7:20
has **h** to them according to the 2Pt 2:22

HAPPENING *(9)*

she said, "Why is this **h** to me?" Gn 25:22
men of Ashdod saw what was **h**, 1Sm 5:7
of Judah saw ⌊what was **h**⌋, 2Kg 9:27
While all this was **h**, I was not Neh 13:6
and to see what was **h** to her. Est 2:11
long has this been **h** to him?" Mk 9:21
when you see these things **h**, Mk 13:29
when you see these things **h**, Lk 21:31
something unusual were **h** to you. 1Pt 4:12

HAPPENS *(12)*

Everything **h** to me!" Gn 42:36
If anything **h** to him on your Gn 42:38
from me and anything **h** to him, Gn 44:29
But if this **h** after sunrise, Ex 22:3
What **h** to the fool will also Ec 2:15
This **h** concerning people, Ec 3:18
Based on ⌊what **h** to⌋ them, Jr 29:22
is there who speaks and it **h**, Lm 3:37
When this **h**, you will know that Ezk 24:24
⌊This **h**⌋ because he is a hired Jn 10:13
am telling you now before it **h**, Jn 13:19
now before it **h** so that when it Jn 14:29

HAPPIER *(1)*

But she is **h** if she remains as 1Co 7:40

HAPPINESS *(6)*

brief and the **h** of the godless Jb 20:5
prosperity and their years in **h**. Jb 36:11
but does not experience **h**, Ec 6:6
and ⌊bring⌋ **h** out of grief. Jr 31:13
I have forgotten what **h** is. Lm 3:17
your hearts with food and **h**." Ac 14:17

HAPPIZZEZ *(1)*

to Hezir, the eighteenth to **H**, 1Ch 24:15

HAPPY *(51)*

h that the women call me happy, Gn 30:13
happy that the women call me **h**," Gn 30:13
How **h** you are, Israel! Dt 33:29
h are your men. How happy are 1Kg 10:8
How **h** are these servants of 1Kg 10:8
Get up, eat some food, and be **h**. 1Kg 21:7
rejoicing and with **h** hearts for 2Ch 7:10
h are your men. How happy are 2Ch 9:7
How **h** are these servants of 2Ch 9:7
See how **h** the man is God Jb 5:17
How **h** is the man who does not Ps 1:1
who take refuge in Him are **h**. Ps 2:12
How **h** is the one whose Ps 32:1
How **h** is the man the LORD does Ps 32:2
H is the nation whose God is the Ps 33:12
h is the man who takes refuge Ps 34:8
How **h** is the man who has put his Ps 40:4
H is one who cares for the poor; Ps 41:1
How **h** is the one You choose and Ps 65:4
How **h** are those who reside in Ps 84:4
H are the people whose strength Ps 84:5
h is the person who trusts in Ps 84:12
H are the people who know the Ps 89:15
h is the man You discipline and Ps 94:12
How **h** are those who uphold Ps 106:3
H is the man who fears the LORD, Ps 112:1
How **h** are those whose way is Ps 119:1
H are those who keep His decrees Ps 119:2
H is the man who has filled his Ps 127:5
How **h** is everyone who fears the Ps 128:1
You will be **h**, and it will go Ps 128:2
h is the one who pays you back Ps 137:8
H is he who takes your little Ps 137:9
H are the people with such Ps 144:15
H are the people whose God is Ps 144:15
H is the one whose help is the Ps 146:5
H is a man who finds wisdom and Pr 3:13
those who hold on to her are **h**. Pr 3:18
those who keep my ways are **h**. Pr 8:32
Anyone who listens to me is **h**, Pr 8:34
kindness to the poor will be **h**. Pr 14:21
trusts in the LORD will be **h**. Pr 16:20
who come after him will be **h**. Pr 20:7
H is the one who is always Pr 28:14
one who keeps the law will be **h**. Pr 29:18
wine makes life **h**, and money is Ec 10:19
H are all who wait patiently for Is 30:18
H are you who sow seed beside Is 32:20
H is the man who does this, Is 56:2
How **h** those whose lawless acts Rm 4:7
How **h** the man whom the Lord will Rm 4:8

HAR-HERES *(1)*

The Amorites refused to leave **H**, Jdg 1:35

HARA *(1)*

to Halah, Habor, **H**, and Gozan's 1Ch 5:26

HARADAH *(2)*

Mount Shepher and camped at **H**. Nm 33:24
departed from **H** and camped at Nm 33:25

HARAN *(20)*

fathered Abram, Nahor, and **H**. Gn 11:26
Abram, Nahor, and **H**, and Haran Gn 11:27
and Haran, and **H** fathered Lot. Gn 11:27
H died in his native land, Gn 11:28
She was the daughter of **H**, Gn 11:29
they came to **H**, they settled Gn 11:31
lived 205 years and died in **H**. Gn 11:32
was 75 years old when he left **H**. Gn 12:4
the people he had acquired in **H**, Gn 12:5
once to my brother Laban in **H**, Gn 27:43
Beer-sheba and went toward **H**. Gn 28:10
"We're from **H**," they answered. Gn 29:4
such as⌋ Gozan, **H**, Rezeph, 2Kg 19:12
Ephah was the mother of **H**, 1Ch 2:46
and Gazez. **H** fathered Gazez. 1Ch 2:46
Haziel, and **H**—three. 1Ch 23:9
rescue them—Gozan, **H**, Rezeph, Is 37:12
H, Canneh, Eden, the merchants Ezk 27:23
before he settled in **H**, Ac 7:2
the Chaldeans and settled in **H**. Ac 7:4

HARAN'S *(1)*

grandson Lot (**H** son), and his Gn 11:31

HARARITE *(5)*

was Shammah son of Agee the **H**. 2Sm 23:11
Shammah the **H**, Ahiam son of 2Sm 23:33
Ahiam son of Sharar the **H**, 2Sm 23:33
Jonathan son of Shagee the **H**, 1Ch 11:34
Ahiam son of Sachar the **H**, 1Ch 11:35

HARASS *(6)*
will **h** you in the land where Nm 33:55
us, we did not **h** them, and 1Sm 25:7
every side and **h** him at every Jb 18:11
You **h** me with Your strong hand. Jb 30:21
on me and **h** me in anger. Ps 55:3
and Judah will not **h** Ephraim. Is 11:13

HARASSED *(2)*
we weren't **h** and nothing of ours 1Sm 25:15
came out of the city and **h** him, 2Kg 2:23

HARASSES *(1)*
tears ⌊at me⌋, and He **h** me. Jb 16:9

HARASSMENT *(1)*
Judah's **h** will end. Is 11:13

HARBONA *(2)*
Biztha, **H**, Bigtha, Abagtha Est 1:10
H, one of the royal eunuchs, Est 7:9

HARBOR *(6)*
and will be a **h** for ships, Gn 49:13
have a godless heart **h** anger; Jb 36:13
them to the **h** they longed for. Ps 107:30
How long will you **h** malicious Jr 4:14
Since the **h** was unsuitable to Ac 27:12
a **h** on Crete open to the Ac 27:12

HARBORED *(1)*
and he **h** his rage incessantly. Am 1:11

HARBORS *(2)*
seashore and stayed in his **h**. Jdg 5:17
his speech and **h** deceit within. Pr 26:24

HARD *(42)*
how **h** I have worked for you. Gn 30:26
I've worked **h** for your father Gn 31:6
my affliction and my **h** work, Gn 31:42
they are driven **h** for one day, Gn 33:13
My years have been few and **h**, Gn 47:9
their broken spirit and **h** labor. Ex 6:9
the **h** cases they would bring to Ex 18:26
and forced us to do **h** labor. Dt 26:6
who have fallen on **h** times? Jb 30:25
the skies as **h** as a cast metal Jb 37:18
water becomes as **h** as stone, Jb 38:30
you leave it to do your **h** work? Jb 39:11
His heart is as **h** as a rock, Jb 41:24
as **h** as a lower millstone! Jb 41:24
their spirits with **h** labor; Ps 107:12
You pushed me **h** to make me fall, Ps 118:13
hearts are **h** and insensitive Ps 119:70
eating food earned by **h** work; Ps 127:2
There is profit in all **h** work, Pr 14:23
a man labors **h** to explore it, Ec 8:17
and the **h** labor you were forced Is 14:3
your face as **h** as their faces Ezk 3:8
your forehead as **h** as their Ezk 3:8
the men rowed **h** to get back to Jnh 1:13
their ears are **h** of hearing, Mt 13:15
will be **h** for a rich person to Mt 19:23
loads that are **h** to carry and Mt 23:4
How **h** it is for those who have Mk 10:23
how **h** it is to enter the kingdom Mk 10:24
we've worked **h** all night long Lk 5:5
burdens that are **h** to carry, Lk 11:46
How **h** it is for those who have Lk 18:24
they said, "This teaching is **h**! Jn 6:60
It is **h** for you to kick against Ac 26:14
their ears are **h** of hearing, Ac 28:27
who has worked very **h** for you. Rm 16:6
who have worked **h** in the Lord. Rm 16:12
has worked very **h** in the Lord. Rm 16:12
him that he works **h** for you, Col 4:13
those who work **h** at preaching 1Tm 5:17
you endured a **h** struggle with Heb 10:32
that are **h** to understand. 2Pt 3:16

HARDEN *(11)*
But I will **h** his heart so that Ex 4:21
But I will **h** Pharaoh's heart and Ex 7:3
I will **h** Pharaoh's heart so that Ex 14:4
am going to **h** the hearts of the Ex 14:17
intention to **h** their hearts, Jos 11:20
Why **h** your hearts as the 1Sm 6:6
Do not **h** your hearts as at Ps 95:8
You **h** our hearts so we do not Is 63:17
do not **h** your hearts as in the Heb 3:8
do not **h** your hearts as in the Heb 3:15
His voice, do not **h** your hearts. Heb 4:7

HARDENED *(23)*
Pharaoh's heart **h**, and he did Ex 7:13
Pharaoh's heart **h**, and he would Ex 7:22
he **h** his heart and would not Ex 8:15
Pharaoh's heart **h**, and he would Ex 8:19
Pharaoh **h** his heart this time Ex 8:32
But Pharaoh's heart was **h**, Ex 9:7
But the LORD **h** Pharaoh's heart Ex 9:12
he sinned again and **h** his heart, Ex 9:34
Pharaoh's heart **h**, and he did Ex 9:35
for I have **h** his heart and the Ex 10:1
But the LORD **h** Pharaoh's heart, Ex 10:20
But the LORD **h** Pharaoh's heart, Ex 10:27
but the LORD **h** Pharaoh's heart, Ex 11:10
The LORD **h** the heart of Pharaoh Ex 14:8
Egyptians and Pharaoh **h** theirs? 1Sm 6:6
obstinate and **h** his heart 2Ch 36:13
They have become **h**; Ps 17:10
Instead, their hearts were **h**. Mk 6:52
or comprehend? Is your heart **h**? Mk 8:17
their eyes and **h** their hearts, Jn 12:40
when some became **h** and would not Ac 19:9
did find it. The rest were **h**, Rm 11:7
none of you is **h** by sin's Heb 3:13

HARDENING *(1)*
a partial **h** has come to Israel Rm 11:25

HARDENS *(3)*
when the dust **h** like cast metal Jb 38:38
but one who **h** his heart falls Pr 28:14
wills, and He **h** whom He wills. Rm 9:18

HARDER *(3)*
brother is ⌊**h** to reach⌋ than Pr 18:19
made their faces **h** than rock, Jr 5:3
like a diamond, **h** than flint. Ezk 3:9

HARDHEADED *(1)*
of Israel is **h** and hardhearted. Ezk 3:7

HARDHEARTED *(4)*
you must not be **h** or tightfisted Dt 15:7
Listen to me, you **h**, far removed Is 46:12
children are obstinate and **h**. Ezk 2:4
of Israel is hardheaded and **h**. Ezk 3:7

HARDLY *(4)*
old age; he could **h** see. Joseph Gn 48:10
their stem **h** takes root in the Is 40:24
h touching the path with his Is 41:3
him, it **h** ever leaves him Lk 9:39

HARDNESS *(6)*
because of the **h** of your hearts. Mt 19:8
sorrow at the **h** of their hearts Mk 3:5
because of the **h** of your hearts. Mk 10:5
their unbelief and **h** of heart, Mk 16:14
of your **h** and unrepentant Rm 2:5
of the **h** of their hearts. Eph 4:18

HARDSHIP *(16)*
forget all my **h** in my father's Gn 41:51
openly before the LORD about **h**. Nm 11:1
regard it as a **h** when you set Dt 15:18
it, the bread of **h**—because you Dt 16:3
our misery, **h**, and oppression Dt 26:7
the siege and **h** your enemy Dt 28:53
the siege and **h** your enemy Dt 28:55
the siege and **h** your enemy Dt 28:57
have made Your people suffer **h**; Ps 60:3
me with bitterness and **h**. Lm 3:5
afflictions, by **h**, by pressures, 2Co 6:4
relief for others and **h** for you, 2Co 8:13
labor and **h**, many sleepless 2Co 11:27
well by sharing with me in my **h**. Php 4:14
you remember our labor and **h**, 1Th 2:9
everything, endure **h**, do the 2Tm 4:5

HARDSHIPS *(5)*
all the **h** that confronted them Ex 18:8
'You know all the **h** that have Nm 20:14
lightly all the **h** that have Neh 9:32
H assault me, wave after wave. Jb 10:17
David and all the **h** he endured, Ps 132:1

HARDWORKING *(1)*
It is the **h** farmer who ought to 2Tm 2:6

HARE *(2)*
the **h**, though it chews the cud, Lv 11:6
the camel, the **h**, and the hyrax, Dt 14:7

HAREM *(5)*
virgins to the **h** at the fortress Est 2:3
the **h** regulation required her to Est 2:12
her from the **h** to the palace. Est 2:13
return to a second **h** under the Est 2:14
official in charge of the **h**, Est 2:15

HAREM'S *(2)*
servants to the **h** best quarters. Est 2:9
in front of the **h** courtyard to Est 2:11

HAREPH *(1)*
and **H** fathered Beth-gader. 1Ch 2:51

HARHAIAH *(1)*
After him Uzziel son of **H**, Neh 3:8

HARHAS *(1)*
(AKA HASRAH)
son of Tikvah, son of **H**, keeper 2Kg 22:14

HARHUR'S *(2)*
descendants, **H** descendants, Ezr 2:51
descendants, **H** descendants, Neh 7:53

HARIM *(5)*
the third to **H**, the fourth to 1Ch 24:8
son of **H** and Hasshub son Neh 3:11
H, Meremoth, Obadiah, Neh 10:5
Malluch, **H**, Baanah. Neh 10:27
Adna of **H**, Helkai of Meraioth, Neh 12:15

HARIM'S *(6)*
H people 320 Ezr 2:32
and **H** descendants 1,017 Ezr 2:39
and Uzziah from **H** descendants; Ezr 10:21
H descendants: Eliezer, Isshijah, Ezr 10:31
H people 320 Neh 7:35
H descendants 1,017 Neh 7:42

HARIPH *(1)*
H, Anathoth, Nebai, Neh 10:19

HARIPH'S *(1)*
H descendants 112 Neh 7:24

HARM *(73)*
we'll do more **h** to you than to Gn 19:9
You will not **h** us, just as we Gn 26:29
But God has not let him **h** me. Gn 31:7
do you great **h**, but last night Gn 31:29
and this marker to do me **h**. Gn 31:52
I tell you not to **h** the boy? Gn 42:22
who has redeemed me from all **h**— Gn 48:16
But if he didn't intend any **h**, Ex 21:13
God did not **h** the Israelite Ex 24:11
and wasn't trying to **h** him, Nm 35:23
single him out for **h** from all Dt 29:21
against ⌊you⌋, **h** you, and Jos 24:20
when I **h** the Philistines." Jdg 15:3
Look, David intends to **h** you'? 1Sm 24:9
I will never **h** you again because 1Sm 26:21
will do more **h** to us than 2Sm 20:6
keep me from **h**, so that I will 1Ch 4:10
anointed ones or **h** My prophets." 1Ch 16:22
who dares to **h** or interfere with Ezr 6:12
But they were planning to **h** me. Neh 6:2
those who intended to **h** them. Est 9:2
no **h** will touch you in seven. Jb 5:19
if I have done **h** to one at peace Ps 7:4
who does not **h** his friend or Ps 15:3
they intend to **h** you and devise Ps 21:11
who plan to **h** me be turned back Ps 35:4
agitated—it can only bring **h**. Ps 37:8
who want to **h** me threaten to Ps 38:12
who wish me **h** be driven back Ps 40:14
about me; they plan to **h** me. Ps 41:7
who wish me **h** be driven back Ps 70:2
who seek my **h** be covered with Ps 71:13
who seek my **h** will be disgraced Ps 71:24
no **h** will come to you; no plague Ps 91:10
ones, or **h** My prophets." Ps 105:15
will protect you from all **h**; Ps 121:7
Don't plan any **h** against your Pr 3:29
when he has done you no **h**. Pr 3:30
of fools will suffer **h**. Pr 13:20
kept by its owner to his **h**. Ec 5:13
authority over another to his **h**. Ec 8:9
has plotted **h** against you. Is 7:5
No one will **h** or destroy on My Is 11:9
won't happen. **H** won't come to us Jr 5:12
gods, bringing **h** on yourselves, Jr 7:6
fear them for they can do no **h**— Jr 10:5
because of the **h** the house of Jr 11:17
about to bring **h** to you and make Jr 18:11
said, No **h** will come to you. Jr 23:17
Then I will do you no **h**. Jr 25:6
to bring great **h** on ourselves!" Jr 26:19
and don't let any **h** come to him; Jr 39:12
My words for **h** and not for good Jr 39:16
such great **h** to yourselves? Jr 44:7
they plan **h** against her in Jr 48:2

on them for **h** and not for good Am 9:4
you need no longer fear **h**. Zph 3:15
deadly, it will never **h** them; Mk 16:18
nothing will ever **h** you. Lk 10:19
how much **h** he has done to Your Ac 9:13
voice, "Don't **h** yourself, Ac 16:28
into the fire and suffered no **h**. Ac 28:5
coppersmith did great **h** to me. 2Tm 4:14
because, to their own **h**, they Heb 6:6
And who will **h** you if you are 1Pt 3:13
suffering **h** as the payment for 2Pt 2:13
but do not **h** the olive oil and Rv 6:6
were empowered to **h** the earth Rv 7:2
Don't **h** the earth or the sea or Rv 7:3
were told not to **h** the grass Rv 9:4
the power to **h** people for five Rv 9:10
If anyone wants to **h** them, Rv 11:5
if anyone wants to **h** them, Rv 11:5

HARMED *(4)*
as we have not **h** you but have Gn 26:29
you in the house should be **h**, Jos 2:19
man with many friends may be **h**, Pr 18:24
will never be **h** by the second Rv 2:11

HARMFUL *(6)*
the contamination is **h** mildew; Lv 13:51
Since it is **h** mildew it must be Lv 13:52
in the house, it is **h** mildew; Lv 14:44
is a rebellious city, **h** to kings Ezr 4:15
will not experience anything **h**, Ec 8:5
and many foolish and **h** desires, 1Tm 6:9

HARMING *(2)*
who prevented me from **h** you, 1Sm 25:34
his hand from ⌊**h**⌋ the poor, Ezk 18:17

HARMLESS *(1)*
as serpents and as **h** as doves. Mt 10:16

HARMON *(1)*
will be driven along toward **H**. Am 4:3

HARMONY *(1)*
establishes **h** in the heavens. Jb 25:2

HARMS *(2)*
Whoever **h** this man or his wife Gn 26:11
who sins against me **h** himself; Pr 8:36

HARNEPHER *(1)*
Suah, **H**, Shual, Beri, Imrah, 1Ch 7:36

HARNESS *(7)*
"**H**!" Joram shouted, and they 2Kg 9:21
the swift donkey from its **h**? Jb 39:5
wild ox by its **h** to the furrow? Jb 39:10
for evil and **h** your tongue for Ps 50:19
H the horses; mount the steeds; Jr 46:4
neck. I will **h** Ephraim; Judah Hs 10:11
H the horses to the chariot, Mc 1:13

HARNESSED *(1)*
shouted, and they **h** his chariot. 2Kg 9:21

HAROD *(1)*
camped beside the spring of **H**. Jdg 7:1

HARODITE *(2)*
Shammah the **H**, Elika the 2Sm 23:25
the Harodite, Elika the **H**, 2Sm 23:25

HAROEH *(1)*
H, half of the Manahathites, 1Ch 2:52

HARORITE *(1)*
Shammoth the **H**, Helez the 1Ch 11:27

HAROSHETH *(3)*
who lived in **H** of the Nations. Jdg 4:2
with him from **H** of the Nations Jdg 4:13
army as far as **H** of the Nations, Jdg 4:16

HARP *(24)*
who knows how to play the **h**. 1Sm 16:16
that person can play the **h**, 1Sm 16:16
who knows how to play ⌊the **h**⌋. 1Sm 16:18
would pick up his **h** and play, 1Sm 16:23
was playing ⌊the **h**⌋ as usual, 1Sm 18:10
David was playing ⌊the **h**⌋. 1Sm 19:9
to Him with a ten-stringed **h**. Ps 33:2
soul! Wake up, **h** and lyre! I Ps 57:8
I will sing to You with a **h**, Ps 71:22
the melodious lyre, and the **h**. Ps 81:2
a ten-stringed **h** and the music Ps 92:3
Wake up, **h** and lyre! I will wake Ps 108:2
on a ten-stringed **h** for You— Ps 144:9
praise Him with **h** and lyre. Ps 150:3
they have lyre, **h**, tambourine, Is 5:12
Pick up ⌊your⌋ **h**, stroll through Is 23:16
zither, lyre, **h**, drum, and every Dn 3:5
zither, lyre, **h**, and every kind Dn 3:7
zither, lyre, **h**, drum, and every Dn 3:10
zither, lyre, **h**, drum, and every Dn 3:15
sound of the **h** and invent their Am 6:5
flute or **h**—if they don't 1Co 14:7
on the flute or **h** be recognized? 1Co 14:7
Each one had a **h** and gold bowls Rv 5:8

HARPISTS *(2)*
was also like **h** playing on their Rv 14:2
The sound of **h**, musicians, Rv 18:22

HARPOONS *(1)*
his hide with **h** or his head with Jb 41:7

HARPS *(20)*
They will be preceded by **h**, 1Sm 10:5
lyres, **h**, tambourines, 2Sm 6:5
palace and into **h** and lyres for 1Kg 10:12
and with lyres, **h**, tambourines, 1Ch 13:8
instruments—**h**, lyres, and 1Ch 15:16
were to play **h** according to 1Ch 15:20
and the playing of **h** and lyres. 1Ch 15:28
Jeiel played the **h** and lyres, 1Ch 16:5
by lyres, **h**, and cymbals. 1Ch 25:1
with cymbals, **h**, and lyres for 1Ch 25:6
with cymbals, **h** and lyres, were 2Ch 5:12
palace and into **h** and lyres for 2Ch 9:11
to the LORD's temple with **h**, 2Ch 20:28
with cymbals, **h**, and lyres 2Ch 29:25
by cymbals, **h**, and lyres. Neh 12:27
ivory palaces **h** bring you joy. Ps 45:8
⌊along with⌋ the music of your **h**. Is 14:11
listen to the music of your **h**. Am 5:23
harpists playing on their **h**. Rv 14:2
sea of glass with **h** from God. Rv 15:2

HARSH *(13)*
h and evil in ⌊his⌋ dealings. 1Sm 25:3
Your father made our yoke **h**. 1Kg 12:4
your father's **h** service and the 1Kg 12:4
Your father made our yoke **h**. 2Ch 10:4
your father's **h** service and the 2Ch 10:4
but a **h** word stirs up wrath. Pr 15:1
Discipline is **h** for the one who Pr 15:10
into the hands of **h** masters, Is 19:4
On that day the LORD with His **h**, Is 27:1
affliction and **h** slavery; Lm 1:3
the decree from the king so **h**?" Dn 2:15
"Your words against Me are **h**," Mal 3:13
and of all the **h** things ungodly Jd 15

HARSHA'S *(2)*
descendants, **H** descendants, Ezr 2:52
descendants, **H** descendants, Neh 7:54

HARSHER *(3)*
men of Judah were **h** than those 2Sm 19:43
you will receive a **h** punishment. Mt 23:14
will receive **h** punishment." Mk 12:40

HARSHLY *(10)*
strangers and spoke **h** to them. Gn 42:7
country spoke **h** to us and Gn 42:30
rule over them **h** but fear your Lv 25:43
not rule over one another **h**. Lv 25:46
rule over him **h** in your sight. Lv 25:53
he **h** oppressed them 20 years. Jdg 4:3
if your father answers you **h**?" 1Sm 20:10
the king answered the people **h**. 1Kg 12:13
Then the king answered them **h**. 2Ch 10:13
treats her young **h**, as if ⌊they⌋ Jb 39:16

HARUM *(1)*
families of Aharhel son of **H**. 1Ch 4:8

HARUMAPH *(1)*
Jedaiah son of **H** made repairs Neh 3:10

HARUPHITE *(1)*
Shemariah, Shephatiah the **H**; 1Ch 12:5

HARUZ *(1)*
was Meshullemeth daughter of **H**; 2Kg 21:19

HARVEST *(94)*
(Festival of, AKA PENTECOST, Festival of WEEKS)
seedtime and **h**, cold and heat, Gn 8:22
during the wheat **h** and found Gn 30:14
one-fifth ⌊of the **h**⌋ of the land Gn 41:34
At **h**, you are to give a fifth of Gn 47:24
from⌋ your **h** or your vats. Ex 22:29
the Festival of **H** with the Ex 23:16
the firstfruits of the wheat **h**, Ex 34:22
you reap the **h** of your land, Lv 19:9
gather the gleanings of your **h**. Lv 19:9
I am giving you and reap its **h**, Lv 23:10
sheaf of your **h** to the priest. Lv 23:10
you reap the **h** of your land, Lv 23:22
gather the gleanings of your **h**. Lv 23:22
or **h** the grapes of your untended Lv 25:5
by itself, or **h** its untended Lv 25:11
number of ⌊remaining⌋ **h** years. Lv 25:15
be eating from the previous **h**. Lv 25:22
the ninth year when its **h** comes Lv 25:22
will continue until grape **h**, Lv 26:5
and the grape **h** will continue Lv 26:5
floor or the full **h** from the Nm 18:27
and you will **h** your grain, Dt 11:14
the entire **h**, both the crop you Dt 22:9
you reap the **h** in your field, Dt 24:19
produce that you **h** from the land Dt 26:2
seed in the field but **h** little, Dt 28:38
with the bountiful **h** from the Dt 33:14
banks throughout the **h** season. Jos 3:15
the wheat **h**, Samson ⌊took⌋ Jdg 15:1
the beginning of the barley **h**. Ru 1:22
have finished all of my **h**.' " Ru 2:21
plow his ground or reap his **h**, 1Sm 8:12
Isn't the wheat **h** today? 1Sm 12:17
days of the **h** at the beginning 2Sm 21:9
the beginning of the barley **h**. 2Sm 21:9
beginning of the **h** until the 2Sm 21:10
went down at **h** time and came to 2Sm 23:13
from the first bread of the **h**. 2Kg 4:42
warehouses for the **h** of grain, 2Ch 32:28
Its abundant **h** goes to the kings Neh 9:37
consume his **h**, even taking it Jb 5:5
it would destroy my entire **h**. Jb 31:12
the wild ox to **h** your grain and Jb 39:12
The earth has produced its **h**; Ps 67:6
that yield a fruitful **h**. Ps 107:37
first produce of your entire **h**; Pr 3:9
it gathers its food during **h**. Pr 6:8
and my **h** than pure silver. Pr 8:19
sleeps during **h** is disgraceful. Pr 10:5
an abundant **h** ⌊comes⌋ through Pr 14:4
at **h** time he looks, and there is Pr 20:4
the coolness of snow on a **h** day; Pr 25:13
snow in summer and rain at **h**, Pr 26:1
they rejoice at **h** time and as Is 9:3
your summer ⌊fruit⌋ and your **h**. Is 16:9
⌊but⌋ the **h** will vanish on the Is 17:11
like a rain cloud in **h** heat. Is 18:4
For before the **h**, when the Is 18:5
from Shihor—the **h** of the Nile. Is 23:3
like a gleaning after a grape **h**. Is 24:13
a ripe fig before the summer **h**. Is 28:4
fail and the **h** will not come. Is 32:10
and those who **h** the grapes will Is 62:9
LORD, the firstfruits of His **h**. Jr 2:3
consume your **h** and your food. Jr 5:17
to us the fixed weeks of the **h**. Jr 5:24
H has passed, summer has ended, Jr 8:20
your summer fruit and grape **h**. Jr 48:32
who wields the sickle at **h** time. Jr 50:16
while her **h** time will come. Jr 51:33
A **h** is also appointed for you, Hs 6:11
because the **h** of the field has Jl 1:11
sickle because the **h** is ripe. Jl 3:13
were still three months until **h**. Am 4:7
the gleaning of the grape **h**— Mc 7:1
brought ⌊the **h**⌋ to your house, Hg 1:9
disciples, "The **h** is abundant, Mt 9:37
to the Lord of the **h** to send out Mt 9:38
to send out workers into His **h**." Mt 9:38
both grow together until the **h**. Mt 13:30
At **h** time I'll tell the reapers: Mt 13:30
The **h** is the end of the age, Mt 13:39
When the grape **h** drew near, Mt 21:34
give him his produce at the **h**." Mt 21:41
the sickle, because **h** has come." Mk 4:29
At **h** time he sent a slave to the Mk 12:2
The **h** is abundant, but the Lk 10:2
to the Lord of the **h** to send out Lk 10:2
to send out workers into His **h**. Lk 10:2
At **h** time he sent a slave to the Lk 20:10
more months, then comes the **h**'? Jn 4:35
for they are ready for **h**. Jn 4:35
and increase the **h** of your 2Co 9:10
the **h** of the earth is ripe. Rv 14:15

HARVESTED *(6)*
countryside and **h** grapes from Jdg 9:27

like a **h** olive tree, like a Is 24:13
have sown wheat but **h** thorns. Jr 12:13
and **h** a great amount of wine and Jr 40:12
have planted much but **h** little. Hg 1:6
the earth, and the earth was **h**. Rv 14:16

HARVESTERS *(9)*
to gather ⌊grain⌋ behind the **h**. Ru 2:3
he said to the **h**, "The LORD be Ru 2:4
who was in charge of the **h**, Ru 2:5
among the bundles behind the **h**?' Ru 2:7
So she sat beside the **h**, Ru 2:14
out to his father and the **h**. 2Kg 4:18
If grape **h** came to you, wouldn't Jr 49:9
the age, and the **h** are angels. Mt 13:39
the outcry of the **h** has reached Jms 5:4

HARVESTING *(5)*
more years without plowing or **h**. Gn 45:6
rest during plowing and **h** times. Ex 34:21
See which field they are **h**, Ru 2:9
Beth-shemesh were **h** wheat in the 1Sm 6:13
his arm **h** the heads of grain— Is 17:5

HARVESTS *(4)*
the land produced outstanding **h**. Gn 41:47
selling to you is a number of **h**. Lv 25:16
and the wheat **h** were finished. Ru 2:23
put to shame by your **h** because Jr 12:13

HAS *(2350)*
(See pp. xi-xii.)

HASADIAH *(1)*
Ohel, Berechiah, **H**, and 1Ch 3:20

HASH-BADDANAH *(1)*
Malchijah, Hashum, **H**, Zechariah, Neh 8:4

HASHABIAH *(15)*
son of **H**, son of Amaziah, son of 1Ch 6:45
son of **H** of the Merarites; 1Ch 9:14
Shimei, **H**, and Mattithiah 1Ch 25:3
the twelfth to **H**, his sons, and 1Ch 25:19
H and his relatives, 1,700 1Ch 26:30
the Levites, **H** son of Kemuel; 1Ch 27:17
and Nethanel, and **H**, Jeiel, and 2Ch 35:9
H, along with Jeshaiah, from Ezr 8:19
with Sherebiah, **H**, and 10 of Ezr 8:24
Beside him **H**, ruler over half Neh 3:17
Mica, Rehob, **H**, Neh 10:11
Azrikam, son of **H**, son of Bunni; Neh 11:15
of Bani, son of **H**, son of Neh 11:22
H of Hilkiah, and Nethanel of Neh 12:21
of the Levites—**H**, Sherebiah, Neh 12:24

HASHABNAH *(1)*
Rehum, **H**, Maaseiah, Neh 10:25

HASHABNEIAH *(2)*
the son of **H** made repairs. Neh 3:10
Kadmiel, Bani, **H**, Sherebiah, Neh 9:5

HASHEM *(1)*
(AKA JASHEN)
the sons of **H** the Gizonite, 1Ch 11:34

HASHMONAH *(2)*
from Mithkah and camped at **H**. Nm 33:29
departed from **H** and camped at Nm 33:30

HASHUBAH *(1)*
five others—**H**, Ohel, Berechiah 1Ch 3:20

HASHUM *(3)*
(AKA HUSHIM)
Dan's son: **H**. Gn 46:23
Malchijah, **H**, Hash-baddanah, Neh 8:4
Hodiah, **H**, Bezai, Neh 10:18

HASHUM'S *(3)*
H descendants 223 Ezr 2:19
H descendants: Mattenai, Ezr 10:33
H descendants 328 Neh 7:22

HASN'T *(27)*
(See pp. xi-xii.)

HASRAH *(1)*
(AKA HARHAS)
son of Tokhath, son of **H**, keeper 2Ch 34:22

HASSENAAH *(1)*
(AKA SENAAH'S)
The sons of **H** built the Fish Neh 3:3

HASSENUAH *(2)*
son of Hodaviah, son of **H**; 1Ch 9:7
and Judah son of **H** was second in Neh 11:9

HASSHUB *(5)*
son of **H**, son of Azrikam 1Ch 9:14
son of Harim and **H** son of Neh 3:11
them Benjamin and **H** made repairs Neh 3:23
Hoshea, Hananiah, **H**, Neh 10:23
son of **H**, son of Azrikam Neh 11:15

HASSOPHERETH'S *(1)*
(AKA SOPHERETH'S)
descendants, **H** descendants, Ezr 2:55

HASTE *(2)*
had thrown off in their **h**. 2Kg 7:15
the couriers rode out in **h**, Est 8:14

HASTENS *(1)*
mouth of the fool **h** destruction. Pr 10:14

HASTILY *(2)*
and the one who acts **h** sins. Pr 19:2
Don't take a matter to court **h**. Pr 25:8

HASTY *(1)*
Do not be **h** to speak, and do not Ec 5:2

HASUPHA'S *(2)*
descendants, **H** descendants, Ezr 2:43
descendants, **H** descendants, Neh 7:46

HATCH *(2)*
she will lay and **h** her eggs and Is 34:15
They **h** viper's eggs and weave Is 59:5

HATCHED *(1)*
one open, and a viper is **h**. Is 59:5

HATCHES *(2)*
he **h** plots to destroy the needy Is 32:7
partridge that **h** eggs it didn't Jr 17:11

HATCHETS *(1)*
the carvings with **h** and picks. Ps 74:6

HATE *(98)*
generations⌋ of those who **h** Me, Ex 20:5
You must not **h** your brother in Lv 19:17
Those who **h** you will rule over Lv 26:17
and those who **h** You flee from Nm 10:35
generations⌋ of those who **h** Me, Dt 5:9
and destroys those who **h** Him. Dt 7:10
inflict them on all who **h** you. Dt 7:15
not previously **h** his neighbor. Dt 19:6
with her, and comes to **h** her, Dt 22:13
your enemies who **h** and persecute Dt 30:7
and repay those who **h** Me. Dt 32:41
and did not **h** him beforehand. Jos 20:5
Didn't you **h** me and drive me Jdg 11:7
You **h** me and don't love me! Jdg 14:16
enemies and **h** those who love 2Sm 19:6
but I **h** him because he never 1Kg 22:8
for the life of those who **h** you, 2Ch 1:11
but I **h** him because he never 2Ch 18:7
and love those who **h** the LORD? 2Ch 19:2
presence; You **h** all evildoers. Ps 5:5
at the hands of those who **h** me. Ps 9:13
I annihilate those who **h** me. Ps 18:40
hand will seize those who **h** you. Ps 21:8
and they **h** me violently. Ps 25:19
I **h** a crowd of evildoers, and I Ps 26:5
I **h** those who are devoted to Ps 31:6
and those who **h** the righteous Ps 34:21
let those who **h** me without cause Ps 35:19
much⌋ to discover and **h** his sin. Ps 36:2
many **h** me for no reason. Ps 38:19
All who **h** me whisper together Ps 41:7
let those who **h** us be disgraced Ps 44:7
and those who **h** us have taken Ps 44:10
righteousness and **h** wickedness; Ps 45:7
You **h** instruction and turn your Ps 50:17
those who **h** Him flee from His Ps 68:1
Those who **h** me without cause are Ps 69:4
be rescued from those who **h** me, Ps 69:14
Those who **h** the LORD would Ps 81:15
those who **h** You have acted Ps 83:2
him and strike those who **h** him. Ps 89:23
You who love the LORD, **h** evil! Ps 97:10
I **h** the doing of transgression; Ps 101:3
He turned to **h** His people and to Ps 105:25
in triumph on those who **h** me. Ps 118:7
therefore I **h** every false way. Ps 119:104
h the double-minded, but I love Ps 119:113
precepts and **h** every false way. Ps 119:128
I **h** and abhor falsehood, ⌊but⌋ I Ps 119:163
too long with those who **h** peace. Ps 120:6
all who **h** Zion be driven back Ps 129:5
don't I **h** those who hate You, Ps 139:21
don't I hate those who **h** You, Ps 139:21
I **h** them with extreme hatred; Ps 139:22
and ⌊you⌋ fools **h** knowledge? Pr 1:22
To fear the LORD is to **h** evil. Pr 8:13
h arrogant pride, evil conduct, Pr 8:13
all who **h** me love death." Pr 8:36
a mocker, or he will **h** you; Pr 9:8
The righteous **h** lying, but the Pr 13:5
but fools **h** to turn from evil. Pr 13:19
brothers of a poor man **h** him; Pr 19:7
he'll get sick of you and **h** you. Pr 25:17
men **h** an honest person Pr 29:10
thief's partner is to **h** oneself; Pr 29:24
a time to love and a time to **h**; Ec 3:8
whether ⌊to expect⌋ love or **h**. Ec 9:1
love, their **h**, and their envy Ec 9:6
h your New Moons and prescribed Is 1:14
I **h** robbery and injustice; Is 61:8
brothers who **h** and exclude you Is 66:5
against Me. Therefore, I **h** her. Jr 12:8
this detestable thing that I **h**. Jr 44:4
the desire of those who **h** you, Ezk 16:27
to hand you over to those you **h**, Ezk 23:28
Since you did not **h** bloodshed, Ezk 35:6
dream apply to those who **h** you, Dn 4:19
for there I came to **h** them. Hs 9:15
They **h** the one who convicts ⌊the Am 5:10
H evil and love good; establish Am 5:15
I **h**, I despise your feasts! Am 5:21
pride and **h** his citadels, Am 6:8
You **h** good and love evil. Mc 3:2
perjury, for I **h** all this"— Zch 8:17
your neighbor and **h** your enemy. Mt 5:43
either he will **h** one and love Mt 6:24
one another and **h** one another. Mt 24:10
the clutches of those who **h** us. Lk 1:71
are you when people **h** you, Lk 6:22
do good to those who **h** you, Lk 6:27
Me and does not **h** his own father Lk 14:26
either he will **h** one and love Lk 16:13
world cannot **h** you, but it does Jn 7:7
but it does **h** Me because I Jn 7:7
I want to do, but I do what I **h**. Rm 7:15
you **h** the practices of the Rv 2:6
the Nicolaitans, which I also **h**. Rv 2:6
beast, will **h** the prostitute. Rv 17:16

HATED *(38)*
h me and sent me away from you. Gn 26:27
they **h** him and could not bring Gn 37:4
brothers, they **h** him even more. Gn 37:5
So they **h** him even more because Gn 37:8
destroy us, because He **h** us. Dt 1:27
because He **h** them, He brought Dt 9:28
"I was sure you **h** her," her Jdg 15:2
h Tamar with such intensity 2Sm 13:15
that the hatred he **h** her with 2Sm 13:15
because he **h** Amnon since he 2Sm 13:22
enemy and from those who **h** me, 2Sm 22:18
I annihilate those who **h** me. 2Sm 22:41
overpowered those who **h** them. Est 9:1
pleased to those who **h** them. Est 9:5
75,000 of those who **h** them, Est 9:16
enemy and from those who **h** me, Ps 18:17
those who **h** them ruled them. Ps 106:41
Because they **h** knowledge, didn't Pr 1:29
will say, "How I **h** discipline, Pr 5:12
and a man who schemes is **h**. Pr 14:17
A poor man is **h** even by his Pr 14:20
I **h** life because the work that Ec 2:17
I **h** all my work at which I Ec 2:18
of your being deserted and **h**, Is 60:15
as well as all those you **h**. Ezk 16:37
but I **h** Esau. I turned his Mal 1:3
will be **h** by everyone because Mt 10:22
You will be **h** by all nations Mt 24:9
And you will be **h** by everyone Mk 13:13
But his subjects **h** him and sent Lk 19:14
will be **h** by everyone because Lk 21:17
that it **h** Me before it hated Jn 15:18
it hated Me before it **h** you. Jn 15:18
have seen and **h** both Me and My Jn 15:24
They **h** Me for no reason. Jn 15:25
world **h** them because they are Jn 17:14
I have loved, but Esau I have **h**. Rm 9:13
righteousness and **h** lawlessness; Heb 1:9

HATEFUL *(3)*
me with **h** words and attack Ps 109:3
h person disguises himself with Pr 26:24
malice and envy, **h**, detesting Ti 3:3

HATES *(30)*
of someone who **h** you lying Ex 23:5
pay back the one who **h** Him. Dt 7:10
detestable thing the LORD **h**. Dt 12:31
the LORD your God **h** them. Dt 16:22
But if someone **h** his neighbor, Dt 19:11
man as a wife, but he **h** her. Dt 22:16
the second man **h** her, writes her Dt 24:3
Could one who **h** justice govern Jb 34:17
He **h** the lover of violence. Ps 11:5
Six things the LORD **h**; Pr 6:16
the one who **h** such agreements Pr 11:15
but one who **h** correction is Pr 12:1
will not use the rod **h** his son, Pr 13:24
the one who **h** correction will Pr 15:10
but the one who **h** bribes will Pr 15:27
A lying tongue **h** those it Pr 26:28
but one who **h** unjust gain Pr 28:16
If he **h** and divorces ⌊his wife⌋, Mal 2:16
wicked things **h** the light and Jn 3:20
and the one who **h** his life in Jn 12:25
If the world **h** you, understand Jn 15:18
you out of it, the world **h** you. Jn 15:19
The one who **h** Me also hates My Jn 15:23
who hates Me also **h** My Father. Jn 15:23
For no one ever **h** his own flesh, Eph 5:29
the light but **h** his brother is 1Jn 2:9
But the one who **h** his brother is 1Jn 2:11
brothers, if the world **h** you. 1Jn 3:13
Everyone who **h** his brother is a 1Jn 3:15
love God," yet **h** his brother, he 1Jn 4:20

HATHACH *(5)*
Esther summoned **H**, one of the Est 4:5
So **H** went out to Mordecai in the Est 4:6
so that **H** might show it to Est 4:8
H came and repeated Mordecai's Est 4:9
Esther spoke to **H** and commanded Est 4:10

HATHATH *(1)*
Othniel's sons: **H** and Meonothai. 1Ch 4:13

HATING *(4)*
trustworthy, and **h** bribes. Ex 18:21
without previously **h** him. Dt 4:42
without previously **h** him: Dt 19:4
h even the garment defiled by Jd 23

HATIPHA'S *(2)*
descendants, and **H** descendants. Ezr 2:54
descendants, **H** descendants. Neh 7:56

HATITA'S *(2)*
descendants, **H** descendants, Ezr 2:42
descendants, **H** descendants, Neh 7:45

HATRED *(12)*
anyone in **h** pushes a person or Nm 35:20
that the **h** he hated her with 2Sm 13:15
for good, and **h** for my love. Ps 109:5
I hate them with extreme **h**; Ps 139:22
H stirs up conflicts, but love Pr 10:12
who conceals **h** has lying lips, Pr 10:18
than a fattened calf with **h**. Pr 15:17
Though his **h** is concealed by Pr 26:26
They will treat you with **h**, Ezk 23:29
because of their⌋ ancient **h**, Ezk 25:15
an ancient **h** and handed over Ezk 35:5
you showed in your **h** of them. Ezk 35:11

HATREDS *(1)*
sorcery, **h**, strife, jealousy Gl 5:20

HATTIL'S *(2)*
descendants, **H** descendants, Ezr 2:57
descendants, **H** descendants, Neh 7:59

HATTUSH *(5)*
H, Igal, Bariah, Neariah, and 1Ch 3:22
H, from David's descendants, Ezr 8:2
Next to him **H** the son of Neh 3:10
H, Shebaniah, Malluch, Neh 10:4
Amariah, Malluch, **H**, Neh 12:2

HAUGHTINESS *(1)*
he is—his **h**, his pride, his Is 16:6

HAUGHTY *(12)*
He surveys everything that is **h**; Jb 41:34
You humble those with **h** eyes. Ps 18:27
anyone with **h** eyes or an Ps 101:5
my eyes are not **h**. I do not get Ps 131:1
but He knows the **h** from afar. Ps 138:6
h eyes and an arrogant heart— Pr 21:4
how **h** its eyes and pretentious Pr 30:13
the daughters of Zion are **h**, Is 3:16
is humbled, and **h** eyes are Is 5:15
arrogance, pride, and **h** heart. Jr 48:29
They were **h** and did detestable Ezk 16:50
never again be **h** on My holy Zph 3:11

HAUL *(3)*
I will **h** you up from the middle Ezk 29:4
they will **h** you up in My net. Ezk 32:3
were unable to **h** it in because Jn 21:6

HAULED *(1)*
got up and **h** the net ashore, Jn 21:11

HAUNT *(5)*
crushed us in a **h** of jackals and Ps 44:19
In the **h** of jackals, in their Is 35:7
a **h** for every unclean spirit, Rv 18:2
a **h** for every unclean bird, Rv 18:2
and a **h** for every unclean and Rv 18:2

HAURAN *(2)*
which is on the border of **H**. Ezk 47:16
run between **H** and Damascus, Ezk 47:18

HAVE *(4077)*
(See pp. xi-xii.)

HAVEN *(1)*
for your **h** has been destroyed. Is 23:1

HAVEN'T *(55)*
(See pp. xi-xii.)

HAVENS *(1)*
place called Fair **H** near the Ac 27:8

HAVILAH *(7)*
the entire land of the **H**, Gn 2:11
Seba, **H**, Sabtah, Raamah, and Gn 10:7
Ophir, **H**, and Jobab. Gn 10:29
And they settled from **H** to Shur, Gn 25:18
Amalekites from **H** all the way to 1Sm 15:7
Seba, **H**, Sabta, Raama, and 1Ch 1:9
Ophir, **H**, and Jobab. 1Ch 1:23

HAVING *(95)*
(See pp. xi-xii.)

HAVOC *(2)*
Wherever he turned, he caused **h**. 1Sm 14:47
created the destroyer to work **h**. Is 54:16

HAWK *(3)*
gull, the various kinds of **h**, Lv 11:16
gull, the various kinds of **h**, Dt 14:15
Does the **h** take flight by your Jb 39:26

HAY *(3)*
When **h** is removed and new growth Pr 27:25
the cutting of the king's **h**. Am 7:1
stones, wood, **h**, or straw, 1Co 3:12

HAZAEL *(25)*
are to anoint **H** as king over 1Kg 19:15
whoever escapes the sword of **H**, 1Kg 19:17
the king said to **H**, "Take a gift 2Kg 8:8
H went to meet Elisha, taking 2Kg 8:9
at him until **H** was ashamed. 2Kg 8:11
and **H** asked, "Why is my lord 2Kg 8:12
H said, "How could your servant, 2Kg 8:13
H left Elisha and went to his 2Kg 8:14
The next day **H** took a heavy 2Kg 8:15
and **H** reigned instead of him. 2Kg 8:15
to fight against **H** king of Aram 2Kg 8:28
he fought against Aram's King **H**. 2Kg 8:29
on guard against **H** king of Aram. 2Kg 9:14
he fought against Aram's King **H**. 2Kg 9:15
H defeated the Israelites 2Kg 10:32
At that time **H** king of Aram 2Kg 12:17
sent ⌊them⌋ to **H** king of Aram. 2Kg 12:18
Then **H** withdrew from Jerusalem. 2Kg 12:18
to the power of **H** king of Aram 2Kg 13:3
H king of Aram oppressed Israel 2Kg 13:22
King **H** of Aram died, and his son 2Kg 13:24
son of **H** the cities that 2Kg 13:25
the cities that **H** had taken in 2Kg 13:25
King Ahab to fight against **H**, 2Ch 22:5
he fought against Aram's King **H**. 2Ch 22:6

HAZAEL'S *(1)*
will send fire against **H** palace, Am 1:4

HAZAIAH *(1)*
son of **H**, son of Adaiah, Neh 11:5

HAZAR-ADDAR *(1)*
(AKA ADDAR)
It will go to **H** and proceed to Nm 34:4

HAZAR-ENAN *(2)*
(AKA HAZAR-ENON)
will go to Ziphron and end at **H**. Nm 34:9
draw a line from **H** to Shepham. Nm 34:10

HAZAR-ENON *(2)*
(AKA HAZAR-ENAN)
from the sea to **H** at the border Ezk 47:17
to Lebo-hamath as far as **H**, Ezk 48:1

HAZAR-GADDAH *(1)*
H, Heshmon, Beth-pelet, Jos 15:27

HAZAR-SHUAL *(4)*
H, Beer-sheba, Biziothiah, Jos 15:28
H, Balah, Ezem, Jos 19:3
lived in Beer-sheba, Moladah, **H**, 1Ch 4:28
H, and Beer-sheba and its Neh 11:27

HAZAR-SUSAH *(1)*
Ziklag, Beth-marcaboth, **H**, Jos 19:5

HAZAR-SUSIM *(1)*
Beth-marcaboth, **H**, Beth-biri, 1Ch 4:31

HAZARMAVETH *(2)*
Almodad, Sheleph, **H**, Jerah, Gn 10:26
Almodad, Sheleph, **H**, Jerah, 1Ch 1:20

HAZAZON-TAMAR *(2)*
(AKA EN-GEDI)
as the Amorites who lived in **H**. Gn 14:7
are already in **H**" (that is, 2Ch 20:2

HAZER-HATTICON *(1)*
Hamath), ⌊as far as⌋ **H**, which is Ezk 47:16

HAZEROTH *(5)*
moved on to **H** and remained there Nm 11:35
people set out from **H** and camped Nm 12:16
and camped at **H**. Nm 33:17
departed from **H** and camped at Nm 33:18
Tophel, Laban, **H**, and Di-zahab. Dt 1:1

HAZIEL *(1)*
Shelomoth, **H**, and Haran—three. 1Ch 23:9

HAZO *(1)*
Chesed, **H**, Pildash, Jidlaph, and Gn 22:22

HAZOR *(18)*
(AKA KERIOTH-HEZRON)
king of **H** heard ⌊this news⌋ Jos 11:1
back, captured **H**, and struck Jos 11:10
because **H** had formerly been the Jos 11:10
Then he burned down **H**. Jos 11:11
stood on their mounds except **H**, Jos 11:13
of Madon one the king of **H** one Jos 12:19
Kedesh, **H**, Ithnan, Jos 15:23
Kerioth-hezron (that is, **H**), Jos 15:25
Adamah, Ramah, **H**, Jos 19:36
of Canaan, who reigned in **H**. Jdg 4:2
Jabin king of **H** and the family Jdg 4:17
commander of the army of **H**, 1Sm 12:9
Jerusalem, and **H**, Megiddo, and 1Kg 9:15
Janoah, Kedesh, **H**, Gilead, and 2Kg 15:29
H, Ramah, Gittaim, Neh 11:33
Kedar and the kingdoms of **H**, Jr 49:28
low, residents of **H**—⌊this is⌋ Jr 49:30
H will become a jackals' den, Jr 49:33

HAZOR-HADATTAH *(1)*
H, Kerioth-hezron (that is, Hazor) Jos 15:25

HAZZELELPONI *(1)*
and their sister was named **H**. 1Ch 4:3

HE *(9551)*
(See pp. xi-xii.)

HE'LL *(4)*
(See pp. xi-xii.)

HE'S *(54)*
(See pp. xi-xii.)

HEAD *(317)*
will strike your **h**, and you will Gn 3:15
it there at his **h**, and lay down Gn 28:11
was near his **h** and set it up as Gn 28:18
lift up your **h** and restore you Gn 40:13
of white bread were on my **h**. Gn 40:16
them out of the basket on my **h**." Gn 40:17
Pharaoh will lift up your **h**— Gn 40:19
in thanks⌋ at the **h** of his bed. Gn 47:31
and put it on the **h** of Ephraim, Gn 48:14
put his left on Manasseh's **h**, Gn 48:14
his right hand on Ephraim's **h**, Gn 48:17
from Ephraim's **h** to Manasseh's. Gn 48:17
Put your right hand on his **h**." Gn 48:18
they rest on the **h** of Joseph, Gn 49:26
its **h** as well as its legs and Ex 12:9

turban on his **h** and place the Ex 29:6
it⌋ on his **h**, and anoint him Ex 29:7
lay their hands on the bull's **h**. Ex 29:10
lay their hands on the ram's **h**. Ex 29:15
them⌋ with its **h** and its pieces Ex 29:17
lay their hands on the ram's **h**. Ex 29:19
his hand on the **h** of the burnt Lv 1:4
the pieces, the **h**, and the suet Lv 1:8
pieces with its **h** and its suet, Lv 1:12
twist off its **h** and burn ⌊it⌋ Lv 1:15
hand on the **h** of his offering Lv 3:2
hand on the **h** of his offering Lv 3:8
his hand on its **h** and slaughter Lv 3:13
lay his hand on the bull's **h**, Lv 4:4
flesh, with its **h** and shanks, Lv 4:11
on the bull's **h** before the LORD Lv 4:15
his hand on the **h** of the goat Lv 4:24
his hand on the **h** of the sin Lv 4:29
his hand on the **h** of the sin Lv 4:33
He must twist its **h** at the back Lv 5:8
the turban on his **h** and placed Lv 8:9
oil on Aaron's **h** and anointed Lv 8:12
hands on the **h** of the bull for Lv 8:14
their hands on the **h** of the ram. Lv 8:18
into pieces and burned the **h**, Lv 8:20
their hands on the **h** of the ram. Lv 8:22
along with the **h**, and he burned Lv 9:13
person from his **h** to his feet so Lv 13:12
an infection on the **h** or chin, Lv 13:29
a skin disease of the **h** or chin. Lv 13:30
a man loses the hair of his **h**, Lv 13:40
on the bald **h** or forehead, Lv 13:42
out on his **h** or forehead. Lv 13:42
on his bald **h** or forehead is Lv 13:43
the infection is on his **h**. Lv 13:44
his **h**, his beard, his eyebrows, Lv 14:9
to put on the **h** of the one to be Lv 14:18
to put on the **h** of the one to be Lv 14:29
him⌋ and wrap his **h** with a linen Lv 16:4
hands on the **h** of the live goat Lv 16:21
on the goat's **h** and send ⌊it⌋ Lv 16:21
sides of your **h** or mar the edge Lv 19:27
oil poured on his **h** and has been Lv 21:10
him⌋ lay their hands on his **h**; Lv 24:14
each one the **h** of his ancestral Nm 1:4
let the hair of his **h** grow long. Nm 6:5
to his God is on his **h**. Nm 6:7
his consecrated **h** of hair, Nm 6:9
must shave his **h** on the day of Nm 6:9
must consecrate his **h** ⌊again⌋. Nm 6:11
consecrated **h** at the entrance Nm 6:18
hair from his **h**, and put ⌊it⌋ Nm 6:18
he has shaved his consecrated **h**. Nm 6:19
back tomorrow and **h** for the Nm 14:25
staff for the **h** of each Nm 17:3
a tribal **h** of an ancestral house Nm 25:15
to turn back and **h** for the Dt 1:40
a bald spot on your **h** on behalf Dt 14:1
shave her **h**, trim her nails, Dt 21:12
make you the **h** and not the tail Dt 28:13
your foot to the top of your **h**. Dt 28:35
will be the **h**, and you will be Dt 28:44
these rest on the **h** of Joseph, Dt 33:16
tears off an arm or even a **h**. Dt 33:20
his blood will be on his own **h**, Jos 2:19
Sisera—she crushed his **h**; Jdg 5:26
on Abimelech's **h** and fractured Jdg 9:53
seven braids on my **h** with the Jdg 16:13
off the seven braids on his **h**. Jdg 16:19
and there was dirt on his **h**. 1Sm 4:12
both Dagon's **h** and the palms of 1Sm 5:4
He stood a **h** taller than anyone 1Sm 9:2
a place at the **h** of the 30 or so 1Sm 9:22
poured it out on Saul's **h**, 1Sm 10:1
he stood a **h** taller than anyone 1Sm 10:23
not a hair of his **h** will fall to 1Sm 14:45
on David's **h** and had him put 1Sm 17:38
down, cut your **h** off, and give 1Sm 17:46
Then he cut off his **h**. When the 1Sm 17:51
took Goliath's **h** and brought it 1Sm 17:54
the Philistine's **h** still in his 1Sm 17:57
some goats' hair on its **h**, 1Sm 19:13
with some goats' hair on its **h**. 1Sm 19:16
evil deeds back on his own **h**." 1Sm 25:39
stuck in the ground by his **h**. 1Sm 26:7
and the water jug by his **h**, 1Sm 26:11
and the water jug by Saul's **h**, 1Sm 26:12
water jug that were by his **h**?" 1Sm 26:16

cut off Saul's **h**, stripped off 1Sm 31:9
and dust on his **h** came from 2Sm 1:2
was on his **h** and the armband 2Sm 1:10
on your own **h** because your own 2Sm 1:16
opponent by the **h** and ⌊thrust⌋ 2Sm 2:16
a dog's **h** who belongs to Judah? 2Sm 3:8
over Joab's **h** and his father's 2Sm 3:29
him, took his **h**, and traveled by 2Sm 4:7
Ish-bosheth's **h** to David at 2Sm 4:8
Here's the **h** of Ish-bosheth son 2Sm 4:8
Ish-bosheth's **h** and buried it 2Sm 4:12
crown from the **h** of their king, 2Sm 12:30
it was ⌊placed⌋ on David's **h**. 2Sm 12:30
Tamar put ashes on her **h** and 2Sm 13:19
her hand on her **h** and went away 2Sm 13:19
of his foot to the top of his **h**, 2Sm 14:25
he shaved his **h**—he shaved ⌊it⌋ 2Sm 14:26
hair from his **h** and it would be 2Sm 14:26
His **h** was covered, and he was 2Sm 15:30
his robe torn and dust on his **h**. 2Sm 15:32
me go over and cut his **h** off!" 2Sm 16:9
Absalom's **h** was caught fast in 2Sm 18:9
His **h** will be thrown over the 2Sm 20:21
they cut off the **h** of Sheba son 2Sm 20:22
appointed me the **h** of nations; 2Sm 22:44
let his gray **h** descend to Sheol 1Kg 2:6
bring his gray **h** down to Sheol 1Kg 2:9
blood on his own **h** because he 1Kg 2:32
back on Joab's **h** and on the head 1Kg 2:33
head and on the **h** of his 1Kg 2:33
blood will be on your own **h**." 1Kg 2:37
back your evil on your **h**, 1Kg 2:44
done on his own **h** and providing 1Kg 8:32
and there at his **h** was a loaf of 1Kg 19:6
Naboth at the **h** of the people. 1Kg 21:9
Naboth at the **h** of the people. 1Kg 21:12
complained to his father, "My **h**! 2Kg 4:19
My head! My **h**!" His father told 2Kg 4:19
the iron ⌊ax **h**⌋ fell into the 2Kg 6:5
until a donkey's **h** ⌊sold for⌋ 80 2Kg 6:25
severely if the **h** of Elisha son 2Kg 6:31
sent ⌊someone⌋ to cut off my **h**? 2Kg 6:32
pour it on his **h**, and say, 'This 2Kg 9:3
the oil on his **h** and said, 2Kg 9:6
adorned her **h**, and looked down 2Kg 9:30
shakes ⌊her⌋ **h** behind your back. 2Kg 19:21
was **h** of their ancestral houses. 1Ch 5:15
cut off his **h**, took his armor, 1Ch 10:9
crown from the **h** of their king, 1Ch 20:2
it was ⌊placed⌋ on David's **h**. 1Ch 20:2
Jerijah was the **h** of the 1Ch 26:31
You are exalted as **h** over all. 1Ch 29:11
done on his own **h** and providing 2Ch 6:23
priests are with us at our **h**. 2Ch 13:12
with Jehoshaphat at their **h**, 2Ch 20:27
of the hair from my **h** and beard, Ezr 9:3
crown on her **h** and made her Est 2:17
has a royal diadem on its **h**. Est 6:8
off for home with his **h** covered. Est 6:12
return on his own **h** and that he Est 9:25
tore his robe and shaved his **h**. Jb 1:20
of his foot to the top of his **h**. Jb 2:7
dust into the air and on his **h**. Jb 2:12
I cannot lift up my **h**. Jb 10:15
then you will hold your **h** high, Jb 11:15
you and shake my **h** at you, Jb 16:4
and removed the crown from my **h**. Jb 19:9
and his **h** touches the clouds, Jb 20:6
when His lamp shone above my **h**, Jb 29:3
harpoons or his **h** with fishing Jb 41:7
and the One who lifts up my **h**. Ps 3:3
trouble comes back on his own **h**, Ps 7:16
falls on the top of his **h**. Ps 7:16
appointed me the **h** of nations; Ps 18:43
a crown of pure gold on his **h**. Ps 21:3
You anoint my **h** with oil; Ps 23:5
Then my **h** will be high above my Ps 27:6
my sins have flooded over my **h**; Ps 38:4
are more than the hairs of my **h**, Ps 40:12
the hairy **h** of one who goes on Ps 68:21
numerous than the hairs of my **h**; Ps 69:4
at the **h** of Ephraim, Benjamin, Ps 80:2
He will lift up His **h**. Ps 110:7
It is like fine oil on the **h**, Ps 133:2
You shield my **h** on the day of Ps 140:7
rebuke me—it is oil for my **h**; Ps 141:5
of grace on your **h** and a ⌊gold⌋ Pr 1:9
a garland of grace on your **h**; Pr 4:9

her steps **h** straight for Sheol. Pr 5:5
are on the **h** of the righteous, Pr 10:6
one who keeps a cool **h** is a man Pr 17:27
you will heap coals on his **h**, Pr 25:22
and a king at the **h** of his army. Pr 30:31
The wise man has eyes in his **h**, Ec 2:14
let oil be lacking on your **h**. Ec 9:8
His left hand is under my **h**, Sg 2:6
For my **h** is drenched with dew, Sg 5:2
His **h** is purest gold. His hair Sg 5:11
Your **h** crowns you like Mount Sg 7:5
the hair of your **h** like purple Sg 7:5
His left hand is under my **h**, Sg 8:3
The whole **h** is hurt, and the Is 1:5
sole of the foot even to the **h**, Is 1:6
The **h** of Aram is Damascus, Is 7:8
the **h** of Damascus is Rezin Is 7:8
the **h** of Ephraim is Samaria, Is 7:9
and the **h** of Samaria is the son Is 7:9
to shave the **h**, the hair on the Is 7:20
cut off Israel's **h** and tail, Is 9:14
The **h** is the elder, the honored Is 9:15
Medeba. Every **h** is shaved; every Is 15:2
No **h** or tail, palm or reed, will Is 19:15
shakes ⌊her⌋ **h** behind your back. Is 37:22
lie at the **h** of every street Is 51:20
to bow his **h** like a reed, and to Is 58:5
a helmet of salvation on His **h**; Is 59:17
hands on your **h** since the LORD Jr 2:37
If my **h** were water, my eyes a Jr 9:1
himself or shave his **h** for them. Jr 16:6
be horrified and shake his **h**. Jr 18:16
whirl about the **h** of the wicked. Jr 23:19
whirl about the **h** of the wicked. Jr 30:23
of him you shake ⌊your **h**⌋." Jr 48:27
every **h** is bald and every beard Jr 48:37
over my **h**, and I thought: Lm 3:54
The crown has fallen from our **h**. Lm 5:16
and shave your **h** and beard. Ezk 5:1
and took me by the hair of my **h**. Ezk 8:3
But wherever the **h** faced, they Ezk 10:11
and a beautiful tiara on your **h**. Ezk 16:12
place at the **h** of every street Ezk 16:25
mound at the **h** of every street Ezk 16:31
actions down on your own **h**." Ezk 16:43
down on his **h** My oath that he Ezk 17:19
Every **h** was made bald and every Ezk 29:18
his blood will be on his own **h**. Ezk 33:4
The **h** of the statue was pure Dn 2:32
them all. You are the **h** of gold. Dn 2:38
trousers, robes, **h** coverings, Dn 3:21
Belteshazzar, **h** of the diviners, Dn 4:9
the hair of His **h** like whitest Dn 7:9
10 horns on its **h** and about the Dn 7:20
and every **h** to be shaved. Am 8:10
will return on your own **h**. Ob 15
seaweed was wrapped around my **h**. Jnh 2:5
shade over Jonah's **h** to ease his Jnh 4:6
down on Jonah's **h** so that he Jnh 4:8
pieces at the **h** of every street Nah 3:10
You pierce his **h** with his own Hab 3:14
so no one could raise his **h**. Zch 1:21
put a clean turban on his **h**." Zch 3:5
turban was placed on his **h**, Zch 3:5
place them on the **h** of Joshua Zch 6:11
should you swear by your **h**, Mt 5:36
put oil on your **h**, and wash your Mt 6:17
Man has no place to lay His **h**." Mt 8:20
they called the **h** of the house Mt 10:25
hairs of your **h** have all been Mt 10:30
the Baptist's **h** here on a Mt 14:8
His **h** was brought on a platter Mt 14:11
poured it on His **h** as He was Mt 26:7
put it on His **h**, and placed a Mt 27:29
and kept hitting Him on the **h**. Mt 27:30
Above His **h** they put up the Mt 27:37
blade, then the **h**, and then the Mk 4:28
then the ripe grain on the **h**. Mk 4:28
"John the Baptist's **h**!" Mk 6:24
the Baptist's **h** on a platter— Mk 6:25
commanded him to bring John's **h**. Mk 6:27
brought his **h** on a platter, Mk 6:28
hit him on the **h** and treated him Mk 12:4
the jar and poured it on His **h**. Mk 14:3
hitting Him on the **h** with a reed Mk 15:19
His feet with the hair of her **h**, Lk 7:38
You didn't anoint My **h** with oil, Lk 7:46
Man has no place to lay His **h**." Lk 9:58

hairs of your **h** are all counted Lk 12:7
a hair of your **h** will be lost. Lk 21:18
but also my hands and my **h**." Jn 13:9
put it on His **h**, and threw a Jn 19:2
Then bowing His **h**, He gave up Jn 19:30
had been on His **h** was not lying Jn 20:7
at the **h** and one at the feet, Jn 20:12
He shaved his **h** at Cenchreae, Ac 18:18
was unable to **h** into the wind, Ac 27:15
lost from the **h** of any of you." Ac 27:34
be heaping fiery coals on his **h**. Rm 12:20
Christ is the **h** of every man, 1Co 11:3
the man is the **h** of the woman, 1Co 11:3
and God is the **h** of Christ. 1Co 11:3
something on his **h** dishonors his 1Co 11:4
on his head dishonors his **h**. 1Co 11:4
with her **h** uncovered dishonors 1Co 11:5
head uncovered dishonors her **h**, 1Co 11:5
the same as having her **h** shaved. 1Co 11:5
if a woman's **h** is not covered, 1Co 11:6
hair cut off or her **h** shaved, 1Co 11:6
not cover his **h**, because he is 1Co 11:7
a symbol of⌊ authority on her **h**: 1Co 11:10
to God with her **h** uncovered? 1Co 11:13
nor again the **h** to the feet, 1Co 12:21
Him as **h** over everything Eph 1:22
way into Him who is the **h**— Eph 4:15
the husband is **h** of the wife as Eph 5:23
also Christ is **h** of the church. Eph 5:23
He is also the **h** of the body, Col 1:18
is the **h** over every ruler and Col 2:10
He doesn't hold on to the **h**, Col 2:19
keep a clear **h** about everything, 2Tm 4:5
His **h** and hair were white like Rv 1:14
with a rainbow over his **h**. Rv 10:1
a crown of 12 stars on her **h**. Rv 12:1
gold crown on His **h** and a sharp Rv 14:14
and on His **h** were many crowns. Rv 19:12

HEADBANDS *(5)*

and **h** for Aaron's sons to ⌊give Ex 28:40
fasten **h** on them, and tie sashes Ex 29:9
and the ornate **h** of fine linen, Ex 39:28
them, and fastened **h** on them, as Lv 8:13
ankle bracelets, **h**, crescents, Is 3:18

HEADCOUNT *(2)*

number of men was 38,000 by **h**. 1Ch 23:3
registration by name in the **h**— 1Ch 23:24

HEADDRESSES *(1)*

h, ankle jewelry, sashes, Is 3:20

HEADED *(11)*

and **h** for the hill country of Gn 31:21
turned back and **h** for the Dt 2:1
One division **h** toward the Ophrah 1Sm 13:17
The next division **h** toward the 1Sm 13:18
last division **h** down the border 1Sm 13:18
Like sheep they are **h** for Sheol; Ps 49:14
man is **h** to his eternal home, Ec 12:5
itself is **h** for destruction, Mt 12:25
itself is **h** for destruction, Lk 11:17
this voyage is **h** toward damage Ac 27:10
to the wind and **h** for the beach. Ac 27:40

HEADFIRST *(1)*

and falling **h**, he burst open in Ac 1:18

HEADING *(3)*

Then **h** back, I entered through Neh 2:15
at the shore where they were **h**. Jn 6:21
went out, **h** for the tomb. Jn 20:3

HEADLONG *(3)*

He rushes **h** at Him with his Jb 15:26
they flee **h**, they never look Jr 46:5
each man **h**, with no one to Jr 49:5

HEADQUARTERS *(6)*

took Jesus into **h** and gathered Mt 27:27
that is, **h**) and called Mk 15:16
Caiaphas to the governor's **h**. Jn 18:28
did not enter the **h** themselves; Jn 18:28
Pilate went back into the **h**, Jn 18:33
back into the **h** and asked Jesus, Jn 19:9

HEADS *(143)*

He lifted up the **h** of the chief Gn 40:20
Seven **h** of grain, full and good, Gn 41:5
them, seven **h** of grain, thin Gn 41:6
The thin **h** of grain swallowed up Gn 41:7
had also seen seven **h** of grain, Gn 41:22
After them, seven **h** of grain— Gn 41:23
thin **h** of grain swallowed the Gn 41:24
seven good **h** are seven years. Gn 41:26
scorched **h** of grain are seven Gn 41:27
are the **h** of their fathers' Ex 6:14
These are the **h** of the Levite Ex 6:25
must present fresh **h** of grain, Lv 2:14
not make bald spots on their **h**, Lv 21:5
the **h** of Israel's clans." Nm 1:16
the **h** of their ancestral houses, Nm 7:2
hands on the **h** of the bulls. Nm 8:12
the leaders, the **h** of Israel's Nm 10:4
you may pluck **h** of grain with Dt 23:25
the **h** of the enemy leaders." Dt 32:42
his blood will be on our **h**. Jos 2:19
they all put dust on their **h**. Jos 7:6
come forward by **h** of families, Jos 7:17
and the **h** of the families of the Jos 14:1
and the **h** of the families Jos 19:51
The **h** of the Levite families Jos 21:1
and the **h** of the families of the Jos 21:1
All of them were **h** of their Jos 22:14
the **h** of Israel's clans who were Jos 22:30
brought the **h** of Oreb and Zeeb Jdg 7:25
the men of Shechem on their **h**. Jdg 9:57
than with the **h** of our men? 1Sm 29:4
him covered their **h** and went up, 2Sm 15:30
all the tribal **h** and the 1Kg 8:1
waists and ropes around our **h**, 1Kg 20:31
waists and ropes around their **h**, 1Kg 20:32
bring me the **h** of your master's 2Kg 10:6
all 70, put their **h** in baskets, 2Kg 10:7
have brought the **h** of the king's 2Kg 10:8
These were the **h** of their 1Ch 5:24
and **h** of their patriarchal 1Ch 5:24
the **h** of their ancestral houses. 1Ch 7:2
were warriors and **h** of their 1Ch 7:7
according to the **h** of their 1Ch 7:9
listed by **h** of families were 1Ch 7:11
They were the **h** of their 1Ch 7:40
who were the **h** of the families 1Ch 8:6
were his sons, **h** of families. 1Ch 8:10
who were the **h** of families of 1Ch 8:13
These were **h** of families, chiefs 1Ch 8:28
these men were **h** of their 1Ch 9:9
relatives, the **h** of households. 1Ch 9:13
The singers, the **h** of Levite 1Ch 9:33
These were the **h** of Levite 1Ch 9:34
It will be our **h** if he defects 1Ch 12:19
You are the **h** of the Levite 1Ch 15:12
Those were the **h** of the families 1Ch 23:9
houses—the **h** of families, 1Ch 23:24
16 **h** of ancestral houses were 1Ch 24:4
eight ⌊**h**⌋ of ancestral houses 1Ch 24:4
and the **h** of families of the 1Ch 24:6
and the **h** of the families of the 1Ch 24:31
the family **h** and their younger 1Ch 24:31
Ladan and were the **h** of families 1Ch 26:21
the **h** of families who were the 1Ch 26:26
men who were **h** of families. 1Ch 26:32
Israelites, the **h** of families, 1Ch 27:1
Israel—the **h** of the families 2Ch 1:2
all the tribal **h**, the ancestral 2Ch 5:2
and some of the **h** of the 2Ch 19:8
Judah and the **h** of the families 2Ch 23:2
total number of **h** of families 2Ch 26:12
and **h** of the Israelite families Ezr 8:29
than ⌊our⌋ **h** and our guilt is Ezr 9:6
on their own **h** and let them be Neh 4:4
⌊and had put⌋ dust on their **h**. Neh 9:1
These are the **h** of the province Neh 11:3
They wither like **h** of grain. Jb 24:24
they sneer and shake their **h**: Ps 22:7
Lift up your **h**, you gates! Ps 24:7
Lift up your **h**, you gates! Ps 24:9
who see them will shake their **h**. Ps 64:8
You let men ride over our **h**; Ps 66:12
crushes the **h** of His enemies, Ps 68:21
You smashed the **h** of the sea Ps 74:13
You crushed the **h** of Leviathan; Ps 74:14
they shake their **h** ⌊in scorn⌋. Ps 109:25
As for the **h** of those who Ps 140:9
walking with **h** held high and Is 3:16
scabs on the **h** of the daughters Is 3:17
arm harvesting the **h** of grain— Is 17:5
as if one had gleaned **h** of grain Is 17:5
wailing, for shaven **h**, and for Is 22:12
and covered your **h**—the seers. Is 29:10
crowns have fallen from your **h**. Jr 13:18
humiliated; they cover their **h**. Jr 14:3
are ashamed; they cover their **h**. Jr 14:4
dust on their **h** and put on Lm 2:10
bowed their **h** to the ground. Lm 2:10
and shake their **h** at Daughter Lm 2:15
out over the **h** of the living Ezk 1:22
above the expanse over their **h**; Ezk 1:25
and all their **h** will be bald. Ezk 7:18
actions down on their own **h**." Ezk 9:10
over the **h** of the cherubim Ezk 10:1
actions down on their own **h**." Ezk 11:21
veils for the **h** of people of Ezk 13:18
actions down on their own **h**." Ezk 22:31
and flowing turbans on their **h**; Ezk 23:15
and beautiful crowns on their **h**. Ezk 23:42
on your **h** and your sandals Ezk 24:23
They throw dust on their **h**; Ezk 27:30
They shave their **h** because of Ezk 27:31
were placed under their **h**. Ezk 32:27
turbans on their **h** and linen Ezk 44:18
not shave their **h** or let their Ezk 44:20
a hair of their **h** was singed, Dn 3:27
It had four **h** and was given Dn 7:6
bring retribution on your **h**. Jl 3:4
bring retribution on your **h**. Jl 3:7
They trample the **h** of the poor Am 2:7
them down on the **h** of all the Am 9:1
to pick and eat some **h** of grain. Mt 12:1
insults at Him, shaking their **h** Mt 27:39
way picking some **h** of grain. Mk 2:23
shaking their **h**, and saying, "Ha Mk 15:29
were picking **h** of grain, Lk 6:1
stand up and lift up your **h**, Lk 21:28
Your blood is on your own **h**! Ac 18:6
for them to get their **h** shaved. Ac 21:24
with gold crowns on their **h**. Rv 4:4
On their **h** were something like Rv 9:7
h of the horses were like lions' Rv 9:17
the horses were like lions' **h**, Rv 9:17
snakes, have **h**, and they inflict Rv 9:19
having seven **h** and 10 horns, Rv 12:3
and on his **h** were seven diadems. Rv 12:3
He had 10 horns and seven **h**. Rv 13:1
and on his **h** were blasphemous Rv 13:1
One of his **h** appeared to be Rv 13:3
having seven **h** and 10 horns. Rv 17:3
with the seven **h** and the 10 Rv 17:7
the seven **h** are seven mountains Rv 17:9
dust on their **h** and kept crying Rv 18:19

HEAL *(44)*

the LORD, "God, please **h** her!" Nm 12:13
I wound and I **h**. No one can Dt 32:39
Look, I will **h** you. On the third 2Kg 20:5
the LORD will **h** me and that I 2Kg 20:8
their sin, and **h** their land. 2Ch 7:14
strikes, but His hands also **h**. Jb 5:18
h me, LORD, for my bones are Ps 6:2
You will **h** him on the bed where Ps 41:3
h me, for I have sinned against Ps 41:4
H its fissures, for it shudders. Ps 60:2
a time to kill and a time to **h**; Ec 3:3
hear their prayers and **h** them. Is 19:22
seen his ways, but I will **h** him; Is 57:18
far or near, and I will **h** him. Is 57:19
has sent Me to **h** the Is 61:1
I will **h** your unfaithfulness. Jr 3:22
H me, LORD, and I will be healed; Jr 17:14
You have nothing that can **h** you. Jr 30:13
health and will **h** you of your Jr 30:17
to it and will indeed **h** them. Jr 33:6
We tried to **h** Babylon, but she Jr 51:9
vast as the sea. Who can **h** you? Lm 2:13
cannot cure you or **h** your wound. Hs 5:13
has torn ⌊us⌋, and He will **h** us; Hs 6:1
when I **h** Israel, the sins of Hs 7:1
I will **h** their apostasy; Hs 14:4
seek the lost or **h** the broken. Zch 11:16
"I will come and **h** him," He told Mt 8:7
them out and to **h** every disease Mt 10:1
H the sick, raise the dead, Mt 10:8
it lawful to **h** on the Sabbath? Mt 12:10
but they couldn't **h** him." Mt 17:16
whether He would **h** him on the Mk 3:2
Me: 'Doctor, **h** yourself.' 'All Lk 4:23
one of them, He would **h** them. Lk 4:40
Lord's power to **h** was in Him. Lk 5:17
if He would **h** on the Sabbath, Lk 6:7
and ⌊power⌋ to **h** diseases. Lk 9:1
of God and to **h** the sick. Lk 9:2

H the sick who are there, and Lk 10:9
Is it lawful to **h** on the Sabbath Lk 14:3
Him to come down and **h** his son, Jn 4:47
converted, and I would **h** them. Jn 12:40
—and I would **h** them.' Ac 28:27

HEALED *(58)*
to God, and God **h** Abimelech, his Gn 20:17
has grown in it, then it has **h**; Lv 13:37
offering, and you will be **h**. 1Sm 6:3
'I have **h** this water. 2Kg 2:21
heard Hezekiah and **h** the people. 2Ch 30:20
to You for help, and You **h** me. Ps 30:2
He sent His word and **h** them; Ps 107:20
minds, turn back, and be **h**. Is 6:10
and we are **h** by His wounds. Is 53:5
incurable, refusing to be **h**? Jr 15:18
Heal me, LORD, and I will be **h**; Jr 17:14
wound—perhaps she can be **h**. Jr 51:8
Babylon, but she could not be **h**. Jr 51:9
the weak, **h** the sick, bandaged Ezk 34:4
and marshes will not be **h**; Ezk 47:11
they never knew that I **h** them. Hs 11:3
the paralytics. And He **h** them. Mt 4:24
Immediately his disease was **h**. Mt 8:3
with a word and **h** all who were Mt 8:16
those with skin diseases are **h**, Mt 11:5
followed Him, and He **h** them all. Mt 12:15
He **h** him, so that the man could Mt 12:22
for them, and **h** their sick. Mt 14:14
them at His feet, and He **h** them. Mt 15:30
from that moment the boy was **h**. Mt 17:18
Him, and He **h** them there. Mt 19:2
temple complex, and He **h** them. Mt 21:14
and He **h** many who were sick with Mk 1:34
disease left him, and he was **h**. Mk 1:42
Since He had **h** many, all who had Mk 3:10
on a few sick people and **h** them. Mk 6:5
"Your faith has **h** you." Mk 10:52
yet not one of them was **h**— Lk 4:27
hear Him and to be **h** of their Lk 5:15
Him and to be **h** of their Lk 6:18
At that time Jesus **h** many people Lk 7:21
those with skin diseases are **h**, Lk 7:22
who had been **h** of evil spirits Lk 8:2
yet could not be **h** by any, Lk 8:43
Jesus had **h** on the Sabbath, Lk 13:14
those days and be **h** and not on Lk 13:14
He took the man, **h** him, and sent Lk 14:4
they were going, they were **h**. Lk 17:14
seeing that he was **h**, returned Lk 17:15
"Your faith has **h** you." Lk 18:42
And touching his ear, He **h** him. Lk 22:51
said to the man who had been **h**, Jn 5:10
man—by what means he was **h**— Ac 4:9
man who had been **h** standing with Ac 4:14
spirits, and they were all **h**. Ac 5:16
were paralyzed and lame were **h**. Ac 8:7
that he had faith to be **h**, Ac 14:9
his hands on him, he **h** him. Ac 28:8
be dislocated, but **h** instead. Heb 12:13
another, so that you may be **h**. Jms 5:16
by His wounding you have been **h**. 1Pt 2:24
but his fatal wound was **h**. Rv 13:3
beast, whose fatal wound was **h**. Rv 13:12

HEALER *(1)*
I'm not a **h**. I don't even have Is 3:7

HEALING *(23)*
This will be **h** for your body and Pr 3:8
tongue of the wise ⌊brings⌋ **h**. Pr 12:18
trustworthy courier ⌊brings⌋ **h**. Pr 13:17
strike Egypt, striking and **h**. Is 19:22
for a time of **h**, but there was Jr 8:15
So why has the **h** of my dear Jr 8:22
us with no hope of **h** for us? Jr 14:19
for a time of **h**, but there was Jr 14:19
bring health and **h** to it and Jr 33:6
there is no **h** for you. Jr 46:11
will rise with **h** in its wings, Mal 4:2
and **h** every disease and sickness Mt 4:23
and **h** every disease and every Mt 9:35
sick people with oil, and **h**. Mk 6:13
out from Him and **h** them all. Lk 6:19
the good news and **h** everywhere. Lk 9:6
and cured those who needed **h**. Lk 9:11
whom this sign of **h** had been Ac 4:22
You stretch out Your hand for **h**, Ac 4:30
gifts of **h** by the one Spirit, 1Co 12:9
then gifts of **h**, helping, 1Co 12:28
Do all have gifts of **h**? 1Co 12:30
the tree are for **h** the nations, Rv 22:2

HEALINGS *(1)*
and performing **h** today and Lk 13:32

HEALS *(7)*
For I am the LORD who **h** you." Ex 15:26
the skin of one's body and it **h**, Lv 13:18
He **h** all your diseases. Ps 103:3
He **h** the brokenhearted and binds Ps 147:3
The tongue that **h** is a tree of Pr 15:4
injuries and **h** the wounds He Is 30:26
"Aeneas, Jesus Christ **h** you. Ac 9:34

HEALTH *(12)*
One person dies in excellent **h**, Jb 21:23
is no **h** in my bones because Ps 38:3
and there is no **h** in my body. Ps 38:7
and **h** to one's whole body. Pr 4:22
man cares about his animal's **h**, Pr 12:10
to the taste and **h** to the body. Pr 16:24
me to **h** and let me live. Is 38:16
I will bring you **h** and will heal Jr 30:17
certainly bring **h** and healing to Jr 33:6
they found the slave in good **h**. Lk 7:10
this perfect **h** in front of all Ac 3:16
in every way and be in good **h**, 3Jn 2

HEALTHIER *(2)*
flesh will be **h** than in his Jb 33:25
looked better and **h** than all the Dn 1:15

HEALTHY *(12)*
cows ate the **h**, well-fed cows. Gn 41:4
He had beautiful eyes and a **h**, 1Sm 16:12
just a youth, **h** and handsome. 1Sm 17:42
water remains **h** to this very day 2Kg 2:22
Their offspring are **h** and grow Jb 39:4
fruit in old age, **h** and green, Ps 92:14
still **h** as they go down to the Pr 1:12
and his **h** body will become Is 17:4
the dead among those who are **h**. Is 59:10
He will not sustain the **h**, Zch 11:16
The **h** don't need a doctor, Lk 5:31
is standing here before you **h**. Ac 4:10

HEALTHY-LOOKING *(2)*
when seven **h**, well-fed cows came Gn 41:2
h cows came up from the Nile and Gn 41:18

HEAP *(14)*
outside the camp to the ash **h**, Lv 4:12
It is to be burned at the ash **h**. Lv 4:12
and **h** your dead bodies on the Lv 26:30
donkey I have piled them in a **h**. Jdg 15:16
overtake us, **h** disaster on us, 2Sm 15:14
he may **h** ⌊it⌋ up, but the Jb 27:17
the waters of the sea into a **h**; Ps 33:7
you will **h** coals on his head, Pr 25:22
This **h** of rubble will be under Is 3:6
It has become a ruined **h**. Is 17:1
make Jerusalem a **h** of rubble, Jr 9:11
will become a **h** of rubble, Jr 51:37
I will make Samaria a **h** of ruins Mc 1:6
to a ⌊grain⌋ **h** of 20 measures, Hg 2:16

HEAPED *(3)*
The waters **h** up at the blast of Ex 15:8
has **h** up silver like dust and Zch 9:3
So they **h** many honors on us, Ac 28:10

HEAPING *(2)*
judge the nations, **h** up corpses; Ps 110:6
doing you will be **h** fiery coals Rm 12:20

HEAPS *(6)*
They piled them in countless **h**, Ex 8:14
them in two **h** at the entrance 2Kg 10:8
like dust and **h** up a wardrobe Jb 27:16
garments⌋ huddle in garbage **h**. Lm 4:5
altars will be like **h** of rocks Hs 12:11
h of slain, mounds of corpses, Nah 3:3

HEAR *(323)*
Adah and Zillah, **h** my voice; Gn 4:23
you that you can **h** a dream and Gn 41:15
When the peoples **h**, they will Ex 15:14
the people will **h** when I speak Ex 19:9
I will certainly **h** their cry. Ex 22:23
I **h** the sound of singing! Ex 32:18
here until I **h** what the LORD Nm 9:8
The Egyptians will **h** about it, Nm 14:13
H ⌊the cases⌋ between your Dt 1:16
for you, and I will **h** it. Dt 1:17
will **h** the report about you, Dt 2:25
When they **h** about all these Dt 4:6
and I will let them **h** My words, Dt 4:10
cannot see, **h**, eat, or smell. Dt 4:28
He let you **h** His voice from Dt 4:36
proclaiming as you **h** them today. Dt 5:1
we will die if we **h** the voice of Dt 5:25
All Israel will **h** and be afraid, Dt 13:11
If you **h** it said about one of Dt 13:12
if you are told or **h** ⌊about it⌋, Dt 17:4
the people will **h** ⌊about it⌋, Dt 17:13
not continue to **h** the voice of Dt 18:16
else will **h** and be afraid, Dt 19:20
all Israel will **h** and be afraid. Dt 21:21
the judges will **h** their case. Dt 25:1
eyes to see, or ears to **h**. Dt 29:4
h Judah's cry and bring him to Dt 33:7
of the horn and you **h** its sound, Jos 6:5
live in the land **h** about this, Jos 7:9
Why don't I **h** the hoofbeats of Jdg 5:28
they replied. "Let's **h** it." Jdg 14:13
the report I **h** from the LORD's 1Sm 2:24
saying, "Let the Hebrews **h**!" 1Sm 13:3
sound of sheep and cattle I **h**?" 1Sm 15:14
Saul will **h** ⌊about it⌋ and kill 1Sm 16:2
I **h** that you are shearing. 1Sm 25:7
the king please **h** the words of 1Sm 26:19
When you **h** the sound of marching 2Sm 5:24
When you **h** the sound of the 2Sm 15:10
everything you **h** from the king's 2Sm 15:35
everything you **h** through them." 2Sm 15:36
h what he has to say as well. 2Sm 17:5
someone is sure to **h** and say, 2Sm 17:9
lord the king **h** the good news: 2Sm 18:31
Can I still **h** the voice of male 2Sm 19:35
as soon as they **h**, they obey me. 2Sm 22:45
that You may **h** the cry and the 1Kg 8:28
that You may **h** the prayer that 1Kg 8:29
H the petition of Your servant 1Kg 8:30
May You **h** in Your dwelling place 1Kg 8:30
heaven. May You **h** and forgive. 1Kg 8:30
may You **h** in heaven and act. 1Kg 8:32
may You **h** in heaven and forgive 1Kg 8:34
may You **h** in heaven and forgive 1Kg 8:36
may You **h** in heaven, Your 1Kg 8:39
for they will **h** of Your great 1Kg 8:42
may You **h** in heaven, Your 1Kg 8:43
may You **h** their prayer and 1Kg 8:45
may You **h** in heaven, Your 1Kg 8:49
Solomon to **h** the wisdom that 1Kg 10:24
said, "Therefore, **h** the word of 1Kg 22:19
Elisha said, "**H** the word of the 2Kg 7:1
the Aramean camp to **h** the sound 2Kg 7:6
H the word of the great king, 2Kg 18:28
your God will **h** all the words 2Kg 19:4
and he will **h** a rumor and return 2Kg 19:7
Listen closely, LORD, and **h**; 2Kg 19:16
h the words that Sennacherib has 2Kg 19:16
said to Hezekiah, "**H** the word of 2Kg 20:16
you **h** the sound of marching 1Ch 14:15
that You may **h** the cry and the 2Ch 6:19
that You may **h** the prayer Your 2Ch 6:20
H the petitions of Your servant 2Ch 6:21
May You **h** in Your dwelling place 2Ch 6:21
heaven. May You **h** and forgive. 2Ch 6:21
may You **h** in heaven and act. 2Ch 6:23
may You **h** in heaven and forgive 2Ch 6:25
may You **h** in heaven and forgive 2Ch 6:27
may You **h** in heaven, Your 2Ch 6:30
may You **h** in heaven in Your 2Ch 6:33
may You **h** their prayer and 2Ch 6:35
may You **h** in heaven, in Your 2Ch 6:39
then I will **h** from heaven, 2Ch 7:14
with Solomon to **h** the wisdom God 2Ch 9:23
Jeroboam and all Israel, **h** me. 2Ch 13:4
all Judah and Benjamin, **h** me. 2Ch 15:2
said, "Therefore, **h** the word of 2Ch 18:18
and You will **h** and deliver." 2Ch 20:9
stood and said, "**H** me, Judah and 2Ch 20:20
He said to them, "**H** me, Levites. 2Ch 29:5
be attentive to **h** Your servant's Neh 1:6
you **h** the trumpet sound, Neh 4:20
then should we **h** about you doing Neh 13:27
Media who **h** about the queen's Est 1:18
they do not **h** the voice of Jb 3:18
H it and understand ⌊it⌋ for Jb 5:27
H now my argument, and listen to Jb 13:6
Him, and He will **h** you, and you Jb 22:27
faint is the word we **h** of Him! Jb 26:14

Will God **h** his cry when distress Jb 27:9
I had someone to **h** my ⌊case⌋! Jb 31:35
H my words, you wise men, and Jb 34:2
⌊have⌋ understanding, **h** this; Jb 34:16
with the wise men who **h** me, Jb 34:34
gracious to me and **h** my prayer. Ps 4:1
the LORD will **h** when I call to Ps 4:3
daybreak, LORD, You **h** my voice; Ps 5:3
LORD, **h** a just cause; pay Ps 17:1
closely to me; **h** what I say. Ps 17:6
as soon as they **h**, they obey me. Ps 18:44
LORD, **h** my voice when I call; Ps 27:7
the humble will **h** and be glad. Ps 34:2
person; I do not **h**. I am like Ps 38:13
a man who does not **h** and has no Ps 38:14
H my prayer, LORD, and listen to Ps 39:12
H this, all you peoples; Ps 49:1
Let me **h** joy and gladness; Ps 51:8
God, **h** my prayer; listen to the Ps 54:2
long ago, will **h**, and will Ps 55:19
"For who," ⌊they say,⌋ "will **h**?" Ps 59:7
God, **h** my cry; pay attention to Ps 61:1
h my voice when I complain. Ps 64:1
aloud to God, and He will **h** me. Ps 77:1
My people, **h** my instruction; Ps 78:1
LORD God of Hosts, **h** my prayer; Ps 84:8
LORD, **h** my prayer; listen to my Ps 86:6
my ears **h** evildoers when they Ps 92:11
One who shaped the ear not **h**, Ps 94:9
Today, if you **h** His voice: Ps 95:7
LORD, **h** my prayer; let my cry Ps 102:1
to **h** a prisoner's groaning, Ps 102:20
ears, but cannot **h**, noses, but Ps 115:6
Your faithful love, **h** my voice. Ps 119:149
They have ears, but cannot **h**; Ps 135:17
when they **h** what You have Ps 138:4
LORD, **h** my prayer. In Your Ps 143:1
you may **h** your servant cursing Ec 7:21
your face, let me **h** your voice; Sg 2:14
for your voice—let me **h** you! Sg 8:13
H the word of the LORD, you Is 1:10
eyes and **h** with their ears, Is 6:10
LORD and He will **h** their prayers Is 19:22
perplexed to **h**, too dismayed to Is 21:3
ends of the earth we **h** songs: Is 24:16
h the word of the LORD, Is 28:14
Listen and **h** my voice. Pay Is 28:23
Pay attention and **h** what I say. Is 28:23
day the deaf will **h** the words Is 29:18
your ears will **h** this command Is 30:21
ears of those who **h** will listen. Is 32:3
are far off, **h** what I have done Is 33:13
Let the earth **h**, and all that Is 34:1
LORD your God will **h** the words Is 37:4
him and he will **h** a rumor and Is 37:7
Listen closely, LORD, and **h**; Is 37:17
h all the words that Sennacherib Is 37:17
H the word of the LORD of Hosts: Is 39:5
so that people may **h** and say, Is 43:9
So now **h** this, lover of luxury, Is 47:8
His ear is not too deaf to **h**. Is 59:1
I spoke and you did not **h**; Is 65:12
are still speaking, I will **h**. Is 65:24
I spoke and they didn't **h**; Is 66:4
at His word, **h** the word of the Is 66:5
H the word of the LORD, house of Jr 2:4
the signal flag and **h** the sound Jr 4:21
I **h** a cry like a woman in labor, Jr 4:31
H this, you foolish and Jr 5:21
have ears, but they don't **h**. Jr 5:21
H the word of the LORD, all ⌊you Jr 7:2
Now **h** the word of the LORD, Jr 9:20
H the word that the LORD has Jr 10:1
to Me, but I will not **h** them. Jr 11:11
I will not **h** their cry of Jr 14:12
H how they keep challenging me, Jr 17:15
H the word of the LORD, kings of Jr 17:20
H what my opponents are saying! Jr 18:19
H the word of the LORD, kings of Jr 19:3
Let him **h** an outcry in the Jr 20:16
'**H** the word of the LORD! Jr 21:11
H the word of the LORD, king of Jr 22:2
earth, earth, **h** the word of the Jr 22:29
the LORD to see and **h** His word? Jr 23:18
people to **h** My words and would Jr 23:22
⌊**H**⌋ the sound of the shepherds' Jr 25:36
H the word of the LORD, all you Jr 29:20
Nations, **h** the word of the LORD, Jr 31:10

will **h** of all the good I will Jr 33:9
Yet **h** the LORD's word, Zedekiah, Jr 34:4
If the officials **h** that I have Jr 38:25
will not see war or **h** the sound Jr 42:14
then **h** the word of the LORD, Jr 42:15
the women, "**H** the word of the Jr 44:24
Therefore, **h** the word of the Jr 44:26
h the plans that the LORD has Jr 49:20
h the plans that the LORD has Jr 50:45
You **h** my plea: Do not ignore my Lm 3:56
LORD, You **h** their insults, all Lm 3:61
you **h** a word from My mouth, Ezk 3:17
h the word of the Lord GOD! Ezk 6:3
and ears to **h** but do not hear, Ezk 12:2
and ears to hear but do not **h**, Ezk 12:2
H the word of the LORD! Ezk 13:2
prostitute, **h** the word of the Ezk 16:35
H the word of the LORD! Ezk 20:47
H the word of the Lord GOD: Ezk 25:3
you **h** a word from My mouth, Ezk 33:7
Come and **h** what the message is Ezk 33:30
front of you, and **h** your words, Ezk 33:31
h your words, but they don't Ezk 33:32
you shepherds, **h** the word of the Ezk 34:7
you shepherds, **h** the word of the Ezk 34:9
of Israel, **h** the word of the Ezk 36:1
h the word of the Lord GOD. Ezk 36:4
Dry bones, **h** the word of the Ezk 37:4
you **h** the sound of the horn, Dn 3:5
you **h** the sound of the horn, Dn 3:15
do not see or **h** or understand. Dn 5:23
h the prayer and the petitions Dn 9:17
my God, and **h**. Open Your eyes Dn 9:18
Lord, **h**! Lord, forgive! Lord, Dn 9:19
H the word of the LORD, people Hs 4:1
H this, priests! Pay attention, Hs 5:1
H this, you elders; listen, all Jl 1:2
Now **h** the word of the LORD. Am 7:16
H this, you who trample on the Am 8:4
H this! The days are coming— Am 8:11
H this! The days are coming— Am 9:13
and let the hills **h** your voice. Mc 6:1
my salvation. My God will **h** me. Mc 7:7
who **h** the news about you will Nah 3:19
not believe when you **h** about it. Hab 1:5
their ears so they could not **h**. Zch 7:11
you who now **h** these words that Zch 8:9
you **h** in a whisper, proclaim Mt 10:27
to John what you **h** and see: Mt 11:4
healed, the deaf **h**, the dead are Mt 11:5
and no one will **h** His voice in Mt 12:19
of the earth to **h** the wisdom Mt 12:42
eyes and **h** with their ears, Mt 13:15
and your ears because they do **h**! Mt 13:16
to **h** the things you hear yet Mt 13:17
the things you **h** yet didn't hear Mt 13:17
you hear yet didn't **h** them. Mt 13:17
Do You **h** what these ⌊children⌋ Mt 21:16
You are going to **h** of wars and Mt 24:6
Don't You **h** how much they are Mt 27:13
has ears to **h** should listen!" Mk 4:9
when they **h**, immediately Satan Mk 4:15
they **h** the word, immediately Mk 4:16
are the ones who **h** the word, Mk 4:18
ground are those who **h** the word, Mk 4:20
has ears to **h**, he should listen! Mk 4:23
Pay attention to what you **h**. Mk 4:24
yet would **h** him gladly. Mk 6:20
has ears to **h**, he should listen! Mk 7:16
He even makes deaf people **h**, Mk 7:37
and do you have ears, and not **h**? Mk 8:18
When you **h** of wars and rumors of Mk 13:7
in on Jesus to **h** God's word, Lk 5:1
come together to **h** Him and to be Lk 5:15
They came to **h** Him and to be Lk 6:18
healed, the deaf **h**, the dead are Lk 7:22
has ears to **h** should listen!" Lk 8:8
who, when they **h**, welcome the Lk 8:13
are those who **h** and do the word Lk 8:21
who is this I **h** such things Lk 9:9
to **h** the things you hear yet Lk 10:24
the things you **h** yet didn't hear Lk 10:24
you hear yet didn't **h** them." Lk 10:24
those who **h** the word of God and Lk 11:28
of the earth to **h** the wisdom Lk 11:31
has ears to **h** should listen!" Lk 14:35
'What is this I **h** about you? Lk 16:2
When you **h** of wars and Lk 21:9

the morning to **h** Him in the Lk 21:38
pleases, and you **h** its sound, Jn 3:8
when the dead will **h** the voice Jn 5:25
and those who **h** will live. Jn 5:25
in the graves will **h** His voice Jn 5:28
judge only as I **h**, and My Jn 5:30
Why do you want to **h** it again? Jn 9:27
and the sheep **h** his voice. Jn 10:3
sheep **h** My voice, I know them, Jn 10:27
I know that You always **h** Me, Jn 11:42
The word that you **h** is not Mine Jn 14:24
How is it that we **h**, each of us, Ac 2:8
we **h** them speaking in our own Ac 2:11
out what you both see and **h**. Ac 2:33
house and to **h** a message from Ac 10:22
to **h** everything you have been Ac 10:33
and desired to **h** God's message. Ac 13:7
town assembled to **h** the message Ac 13:44
Gentiles would **h** the gospel Ac 15:7
"We will **h** you about this again." Ac 17:32
You both see and **h** that not only Ac 19:26
will certainly **h** that you've Ac 21:22
but they did not **h** the voice of Ac 22:9
and to **h** the sound of His voice. Ac 22:14
would like to **h** the man myself. Ac 25:22
he said, "you will **h** him." Ac 25:22
it suitable to **h** from you what Ac 28:22
eyes and **h** with their ears, Ac 28:27
And how can they **h** without a Rm 10:14
But I ask, "Did they not **h**?" Rm 10:18
see and ears that cannot **h**, Rm 11:8
I **h** that when you come together 1Co 11:18
the law, don't you **h** the law? Gl 4:21
to give grace to those who **h**. Eph 4:29
I will **h** about you that you are Php 1:27
saw I had and now **h** about me. Php 1:30
when I **h** news about you. Php 2:19
For we **h** that there are some 2Th 3:11
have an itch to **h** something new. 2Tm 4:3
and all the Gentiles might **h**. 2Tm 4:17
because I **h** of your love and Phm 5
Today, if you **h** His voice, Heb 3:7
Today, if you **h** His voice, do Heb 3:15
Today if you **h** His voice, do not Heb 4:7
everyone must be quick to **h**, Jms 1:19
h that my children are walking 3Jn 4
those who **h** the words of this Rv 1:3
are not able to see, **h**, or walk. Rv 9:20

HEARD *(598)*

the man and his wife **h** the sound Gn 3:8
And he said, "I **h** You in the Gn 3:10
When Abram **h** that his relative Gn 14:14
for the LORD has **h** your ⌊cry of⌋ Gn 16:11
As for Ishmael, I have **h** you. Gn 17:20
God **h** the voice of the boy, Gn 21:17
for God has **h** the voice of the Gn 21:17
I hadn't **h** about it until today. Gn 21:26
and when he had **h** his sister Gn 24:30
Abraham's servant **h** their words, Gn 24:52
The LORD **h** his prayer, and his Gn 25:21
h your father talking with your Gn 27:6
When Esau **h** his father's words, Gn 27:34
When Laban **h** the news about his Gn 29:13
The LORD **h** that I am unloved and Gn 29:33
He has **h** me and given me a son," Gn 30:6
Now Jacob **h** what Laban's sons Gn 31:1
Jacob **h** that Shechem had defiled Gn 34:5
field when they **h** ⌊about the Gn 34:7
Bilhah, and Israel **h** about it. Gn 35:22
I **h** them say, 'Let's go to Gn 37:17
When Reuben **h** this, he tried to Gn 37:21
When he **h** me screaming for help, Gn 39:15
When his master **h** the story his Gn 39:19
But I have **h** it said about you Gn 41:15
I have **h** there is grain in Gn 42:2
the men had **h** that they were Gn 43:25
loudly that the Egyptians **h** it, Gn 45:2
also Pharaoh's household **h** it. Gn 45:2
When Pharaoh **h** about this, Ex 2:15
So God **h** their groaning, and He Ex 2:24
and have **h** them crying out Ex 3:7
when they **h** that the LORD had Ex 4:31
I have **h** the groaning of the Ex 6:5
because He has **h** your complaints Ex 16:7
for He has **h** the complaints that Ex 16:8
for He has **h** your complaints.'" Ex 16:9
I have **h** the complaints of the Ex 16:12
h about everything that God had Ex 18:1

they must not be **h** on your lips. Ex 23:13
sound will be **h** when he enters Ex 28:35
When Joshua **h** the sound of the Ex 32:17
When the people **h** this bad news, Ex 33:4
he has seen, **h**, or known about Lv 5:1
When Moses **h** this, it was Lv 10:20
have all who **h** ⌊him⌋ lay their Lv 24:14
he **h** the voice speaking to him Nm 7:89
When the LORD **h**, His anger Nm 11:1
Moses **h** the people, family after Nm 11:10
And the LORD **h** ⌊it⌋. Nm 12:2
They have **h** that You, LORD, are Nm 14:14
that have **h** of Your fame will Nm 14:15
I have **h** the Israelites' Nm 14:27
to you exactly as I **h** you say. Nm 14:28
When Moses **h** ⌊this⌋, he fell Nm 16:4
the LORD, He **h** our voice, sent Nm 20:16
h that Israel was coming on the Nm 21:1
When Balak **h** that Balaam was Nm 22:36
to her when he **h** ⌊about them⌋. Nm 30:14
h the Israelites were coming. Nm 33:40
When the LORD **h** your words, Dt 1:34
or has anything like it been **h** Dt 4:32
Has a people ever **h** God's voice Dt 4:33
and you **h** His words from the Dt 4:36
and elders when you **h** the voice Dt 5:23
and we have **h** His voice from the Dt 5:24
of all mankind has **h** the voice Dt 5:26
The LORD **h** your words when you Dt 5:28
'I have **h** the words that these Dt 5:28
and you have **h** it said about Dt 9:2
and the LORD **h** our cry and saw Dt 26:7
For we have **h** how the LORD dried Jos 2:10
When we **h** this, we lost heart, Jos 2:11
near the sea **h** how the LORD had Jos 5:1
shout or let your voice be **h**. Jos 6:10
When they **h** the blast of the Jos 6:20
all the kings **h** ⌊about Jericho Jos 9:1
of Gibeon **h** what Joshua had done Jos 9:3
For we have **h** of His fame, Jos 9:9
they **h** that the Gibeonites were Jos 9:16
of Jerusalem **h** that Joshua had Jos 10:1
king of Hazor **h** ⌊this news⌋, Jos 11:1
because you **h** then that the Jos 14:12
Then the Israelites **h** ⌊it⌋ said, Jos 22:11
When the Israelites **h** ⌊this⌋, Jos 22:12
h what the descendants of Reuben, Jos 22:30
for it has **h** all the words the Jos 24:27
When Gideon **h** the account of the Jdg 7:15
h the words of Gaal son of Ebed, Jdg 9:30
lords of the Tower of Shechem **h**, Jdg 9:46
the Gazites ⌊**h**⌋ that Samson was Jdg 16:2
and that I **h** you utter a curse Jdg 17:2
The Benjaminites **h** that the Jdg 20:3
because she had **h** in Moab that Ru 1:6
her voice could not be **h**. 1Sm 1:13
He **h** about everything his sons 1Sm 2:22
I have **h** about your evil actions 1Sm 2:23
The Philistines **h** the sound of 1Sm 4:6
Eli **h** the outcry and asked, 1Sm 4:14
When she **h** the news about the 1Sm 4:19
the Philistines **h** that the 1Sm 7:7
the Israelites **h** ⌊about it⌋, 1Sm 7:7
When Saul **h** these words, the 1Sm 11:6
and the Philistines **h** about it. 1Sm 13:3
And all Israel **h** the news, 1Sm 13:4
country of Ephraim **h** that the 1Sm 14:22
had not **h** his father make 1Sm 14:27
and all Israel **h** these words 1Sm 17:11
his usual words, which David **h**. 1Sm 17:23
and his father's whole family **h**, 1Sm 22:1
Saul **h** that David and his men 1Sm 22:6
Your servant has **h** that Saul 1Sm 23:10
down as Your servant has **h**? 1Sm 23:11
Saul **h** of this and pursued David 1Sm 23:25
he **h** that Nabal was shearing 1Sm 25:4
I have **h** what you said and have 1Sm 25:35
David **h** that Nabal was dead, 1Sm 25:39
of Jabesh-gilead **h** what the 1Sm 31:11
David **h** ⌊about it⌋ later and 2Sm 3:28
Ish-bosheth⌋ **h** that Abner had 2Sm 4:1
the Philistines **h** that David had 2Sm 5:17
but he **h** about it and went down 2Sm 5:17
as all we have **h** confirms. 2Sm 7:22
Toi of Hamath **h** that David had 2Sm 8:9
David **h** about it and sent Joab 2Sm 10:7
Uriah's wife **h** that her husband 2Sm 11:26
King David **h** about all these 2Sm 13:21

All the people **h** the king's 2Sm 18:5
For we **h** the king command you, 2Sm 18:12
on that day the troops **h**, 2Sm 19:2
From His temple He **h** my voice, 2Sm 22:7
Have you not **h** that Adonijah son 1Kg 1:11
were with him **h** ⌊the noise⌋ as 1Kg 1:41
Joab **h** the sound of the ram's 1Kg 1:41
that's the noise you **h**. 1Kg 1:45
All Israel **h** about the judgment 1Kg 3:28
earth who had **h** of his wisdom, 1Kg 4:34
Solomon when he **h** that he had 1Kg 5:1
When Hiram **h** Solomon's words, 1Kg 5:7
saying, "I have **h** your message; 1Kg 5:8
iron tool was **h** in the temple 1Kg 6:7
have **h** your prayer and petition 1Kg 9:3
queen of Sheba **h** about Solomon's 1Kg 10:1
The report I **h** in my own country 1Kg 10:6
far exceed the report I **h**. 1Kg 10:7
Hadad **h** in Egypt that David 1Kg 11:21
son of Nebat **h** ⌊about it⌋, 1Kg 12:2
When all Israel **h** that Jeroboam 1Kg 12:20
When the king **h** the word that 1Kg 13:4
back from his way **h** ⌊about it⌋, 1Kg 13:26
When Ahijah **h** the sound of her 1Kg 14:6
Baasha **h** ⌊about it⌋, he quit 1Kg 15:21
encamped troops **h** that Zimri had 1Kg 16:16
When Elijah **h** ⌊it⌋, he wrapped 1Kg 19:13
When Ben-hadad **h** this response, 1Kg 20:12
we have **h** that the kings of the 1Kg 20:31
When Jezebel **h** that Naboth had 1Kg 21:15
Ahab **h** that Naboth was dead, 1Kg 21:16
When Ahab **h** these words, he tore 1Kg 21:27
Moab had **h** that the kings had 2Kg 3:21
the man of God **h** that the king 2Kg 5:8
When the king **h** the woman's 2Kg 6:30
Jezebel **h** about it, so she 2Kg 9:30
When Athaliah **h** the noise from 2Kg 11:13
and the LORD **h** him, for He saw 2Kg 13:4
King Hezekiah **h** ⌊their report⌋, 2Kg 19:1
that the LORD your God has **h**. 2Kg 19:4
because of the words you have **h**, 2Kg 19:6
the Rabshakeh **h** that the king 2Kg 19:8
The king had **h** this about 2Kg 19:9
you have **h** what the kings of 2Kg 19:11
'I have **h** your prayer to Me 2Kg 19:20
Have you not **h**? I designed it 2Kg 19:25
says: I have **h** your prayer; I 2Kg 20:5
since he **h** that Hezekiah had 2Kg 20:12
When the king **h** the words of the 2Kg 22:11
As for the words that you **h**, 2Kg 22:18
LORD when you **h** what I spoke 2Kg 22:19
I Myself have **h** you—declares 2Kg 22:19
h that the king of Babylon had 2Kg 25:23
Jabesh-gilead **h** of everything 1Ch 10:11
the Philistines **h** that David had 1Ch 14:8
when David **h** of this, he went 1Ch 14:8
as all we have **h** confirms. 1Ch 17:20
Tou of Hamath **h** that David had 1Ch 18:9
David **h** about this and sent Joab 1Ch 19:8
I have **h** your prayer and have 2Ch 7:12
queen of Sheba **h** of Solomon's 2Ch 9:1
The report I **h** in my own country 2Ch 9:5
You far exceed the report I **h**. 2Ch 9:6
son of Nebat **h** ⌊about it⌋— 2Ch 10:2
When Asa **h** these words and the 2Ch 15:8
Baasha **h** ⌊about it⌋, he quit 2Ch 16:5
lands when they **h** that the LORD 2Ch 20:29
When Athaliah **h** the noise from 2Ch 23:12
the LORD **h** Hezekiah and healed 2Ch 30:20
people, and God **h** their voice, 2Ch 30:27
so He **h** his petition and granted 2Ch 33:13
When the king **h** the words of the 2Ch 34:19
As for the words that you **h**, 2Ch 34:26
when you **h** His words against 2Ch 34:27
Me, I Myself have **h**'—this is 2Ch 34:27
And the sound was **h** far away. Ezr 3:13
and Benjamin **h** that the returned Ezr 4:1
When I **h** this report, I tore my Ezr 9:3
When I **h** these words, I sat down Neh 1:4
official **h** that someone had Neh 2:10
Geshem the Arab **h** ⌊about this⌋, Neh 2:19
When Sanballat **h** that we were Neh 4:1
and Ashdodites **h** that the repair Neh 4:7
angry when I **h** their outcry and Neh 5:6
of our enemies **h** that I had Neh 6:1
rumors will be **h** by the king. Neh 6:7
When all our enemies **h** this, Neh 6:16
weeping as they **h** the words of Neh 8:9

in Egypt and **h** their cry at the Neh 9:9
to You, and You **h** from heaven. Neh 9:27
You **h** from heaven and rescued Neh 9:28
rejoicing was **h** far away. Neh 12:43
When they **h** the law, they Neh 13:3
issues will be **h** throughout his Est 1:20
h about all this adversity that Jb 2:11
may no joyful shout be **h** in it. Jb 3:7
my eyes. I **h** a quiet voice: Jb 4:16
ears have **h** and understood it. Jb 13:1
I have **h** many things like these. Jb 16:2
I have **h** a rebuke that insults Jb 20:3
have **h** news of it with our ears. Jb 28:22
When they **h** me, they blessed me, Jb 29:11
and I have **h** these very words: Jb 33:8
and He **h** the outcry of the Jb 34:28
when His ⌊rumbling⌋ voice is **h**. Jb 37:4
had **h** rumors about You, but now Jb 42:5
the LORD has **h** the sound of my Ps 6:8
The LORD has **h** my plea for help; Ps 6:9
You have **h** the desire of the Ps 10:17
From His temple He **h** my voice, Ps 18:6
no words; their voice is not **h**. Ps 19:3
for He has **h** the sound of my Ps 28:6
I have **h** the gossip of many; Ps 31:13
But You **h** the sound of my Ps 31:22
and the LORD **h** ⌊him⌋ and saved Ps 34:6
to me and **h** my cry for help Ps 40:1
God, we have **h** with our ears— Ps 44:1
Just as we **h**, so we have seen in Ps 48:8
God, You have **h** my vows; Ps 61:5
once; I have **h** this twice: Ps 62:11
the sound of His praise be **h**. Ps 66:8
things we have **h** and known and Ps 78:3
the LORD **h** and became furious; Ps 78:21
God **h** and became furious; Ps 78:59
I **h** an unfamiliar language: Ps 81:5
He **h** their cry, He took note Ps 106:44
because He has **h** my appeal for Ps 116:1
We **h** of ⌊the ark⌋ in Ephrathah; Ps 132:6
Understanding make her voice **h**? Pr 8:1
all has been **h**, the conclusion Ec 12:13
cooing is **h** in our land. Sg 2:12
but **h** cries of wretchedness. Is 5:7
Then I **h** the voice of the Lord Is 6:8
their voices are **h** as far away Is 15:4
We have **h** of Moab's pride— Is 16:6
you what I have **h** from the LORD Is 21:10
I have **h** from the Lord GOD of Is 28:22
His voice **h** and reveal His arm Is 30:30
King Hezekiah **h** ⌊their report⌋, Is 37:1
that the LORD your God has **h**. Is 37:4
because of the words you have **h**, Is 37:6
the Rabshakeh **h** that the king Is 37:8
The king had **h** this about Is 37:9
So when he **h** this, he sent Is 37:9
you have **h** what the kings of Is 37:11
Have you not **h**? I designed it Is 37:26
says: I have **h** your prayer; I Is 38:5
since he **h** that he had been Is 39:1
Have you not **h**? Has it not been Is 40:21
know? Have you not **h**? Yahweh is Is 40:28
told it, no one **h** your words. Is 41:26
make His voice **h** in the streets. Is 42:2
You have **h** it. Observe it all. Is 48:6
you have not **h** of them before Is 48:7
You have never **h**; you have never Is 48:8
understand what they had not **h**. Is 52:15
Who has believed what we have **h**? Is 53:1
to make your voice **h** on high. Is 58:4
again be **h** of in your land; Is 60:18
From ancient times no one has **h**, Is 64:4
will no longer be **h** in her. Is 65:19
Who has **h** of such a thing? Is 66:8
have not **h** of My fame or seen Is 66:19
A sound is **h** on the barren Jr 3:21
have **h** the sound of the ram's Jr 4:19
We have **h** about it, and we are Jr 6:24
From Dan is **h** the snorting of Jr 8:16
sound of cattle is no longer **h**. Jr 9:10
of lamentation is **h** from Zion: Jr 9:19
Who has **h** ⌊things⌋ like these? Jr 18:13
Let a cry be **h** from their houses Jr 18:22
h Jeremiah prophesying these Jr 20:1
For I have **h** the gossip of the Jr 20:10
I have **h** what the prophets who Jr 23:25
all the people **h** Jeremiah Jr 26:7
of Judah **h** these things, Jr 26:10

you have **h** with your own ears. Jr 26:11
that you have **h** against this Jr 26:12
all the officials **h** his words, Jr 26:21
When Uriah **h**, he fled in fear Jr 26:21
We have **h** a cry of terror, Jr 30:5
A voice was **h** in Ramah, a lament Jr 31:15
I have **h** Ephraim moaning: Jr 31:18
beast—there will be **h** again Jr 33:10
h all the words of the LORD from Jr 36:11
words he had **h** when Baruch read Jr 36:13
When they had **h** all the words, Jr 36:16
As they **h** all these words, Jr 36:24
Jerusalem, **h** the report, they Jr 37:5
son of Malchijah **h** the words Jr 38:1
h Jeremiah had been put into the Jr 38:7
him because nothing had been **h**. Jr 38:27
h that the king of Babylon had Jr 40:7
other lands also **h** that the king Jr 40:11
armies with him **h** of all the Jr 41:11
prophet said to them, "I have **h**. Jr 42:4
nations have **h** of your dishonor Jr 46:12
Horonaim will be **h** cries of Jr 48:5
We have **h** of Moab's pride, Jr 48:29
shout of battle **h** against Rabbah Jr 49:2
have **h** a message from the LORD; Jr 49:14
cry will be **h** at the Red Sea. Jr 49:21
for they have **h** a bad report and Jr 49:23
of Babylon has **h** reports about Jr 50:43
a cry will be **h** among the Jr 50:46
because we have **h** insults. Jr 51:51
People have **h** me groaning, Lm 1:21
my enemies have **h** of my Lm 1:21
h the sound of their wings like Ezk 1:24
facedown and **h** a voice speaking Ezk 1:28
and I **h** a great rumbling sound Ezk 3:12
wings could be **h** as far as the Ezk 10:5
When the nations **h** about him, Ezk 19:4
no longer be **h** on the mountains Ezk 19:9
your lyres will no longer be **h**. Ezk 26:13
⌊Since⌋ he **h** the sound of the Ezk 33:5
have **h** all the blasphemies you Ezk 35:12
against Me. I **h** ⌊it⌋ Myself! Ezk 35:13
the nations to be **h** against you, Ezk 36:15
I **h** someone speaking to me from Ezk 43:6
when all the people **h** the sound Dn 3:7
I've **h** that you have the spirit Dn 5:14
I have **h** about you that you can Dn 5:16
As soon as the king **h** this, Dn 6:14
Then I **h** a holy one speaking, Dn 8:13
I **h** a human voice calling from Dn 8:16
h the words he said, and when I Dn 10:9
and when I **h** them I fell into a Dn 10:9
your God, your prayers were **h**. Dn 10:12
Then I **h** the man dressed in Dn 12:7
I **h** but did not understand. Dn 12:8
We have **h** a message from the Ob 1
belly of Sheol; You **h** my voice. Jnh 2:2
will never be **h** again. Nah 2:13
I have **h** the report about You; Hab 3:2
I **h**, and I trembled within; Hab 3:16
have **h** the taunting of Moab and Zph 2:8
we have **h** that God is with you. Zch 8:23
When King Herod **h** this, he was Mt 2:3
A voice was **h** in Ramah, weeping, Mt 2:18
But when he **h** that Archelaus was Mt 2:22
When He **h** that John had been Mt 4:12
You have **h** that it was said to Mt 5:21
You have **h** that it was said, Mt 5:27
you have **h** that it was said to Mt 5:33
You have **h** that it was said, Mt 5:38
You have **h** that it was said, Mt 5:43
they'll be **h** for their many Mt 6:7
But when He **h** this, He said, Mt 9:12
When John **h** in prison what the Mt 11:2
When the Pharisees **h** this, Mt 12:24
the tetrarch **h** the report about Mt 14:1
When Jesus **h** about it, He Mt 14:13
When the crowds **h** this, they Mt 14:13
when they **h** this statement?" Mt 15:12
the disciples **h** it, they fell Mt 17:6
the young man **h** that command, Mt 19:22
When the disciples **h** this, Mt 19:25
When the 10 ⌊disciples⌋ **h** this, Mt 20:24
When they **h** that Jesus was Mt 20:30
the Pharisees **h** His parables, Mt 21:45
When they **h** this, they were Mt 22:22
And when the crowds **h** this, Mt 22:33
When the Pharisees **h** that He had Mt 22:34

now you've **h** the blasphemy! Mt 26:65
of those standing there **h** this, Mt 27:47
When Jesus **h** this, He told them, Mk 2:17
because they **h** about everything Mk 3:8
When His family **h** this, they set Mk 3:21
Having **h** about Jesus, she came Mk 5:27
and many who **h** Him were Mk 6:2
King Herod **h** of this, because Mk 6:14
When Herod **h** of it, he said, Mk 6:16
Herod **h** him he would be very Mk 6:20
When his disciples **h** about it, Mk 6:29
to wherever they **h** He was. Mk 6:55
other⌋ 10 ⌊disciples⌋ **h** this, Mk 10:41
When he **h** that it was Jesus the Mk 10:47
And His disciples **h** it. Mk 11:14
and the scribes **h** it and started Mk 11:18
When he **h** them debating and saw Mk 12:28
And when they **h** this, they were Mk 14:11
We **h** Him say, 'I will demolish Mk 14:58
You have **h** the blasphemy! Mk 14:64
of those standing there **h** this, Mk 15:35
when they **h** that He was alive Mk 16:11
because your prayer has been **h**. Lk 1:13
Elizabeth **h** Mary's greeting, Lk 1:41
relatives **h** that the Lord had Lk 1:58
All who **h** about ⌊him⌋ took ⌊it⌋ Lk 1:66
and all who **h** it were amazed at Lk 2:18
God for all they had seen and **h**, Lk 2:20
And all those who **h** Him were Lk 2:47
All we've **h** that took place Lk 4:23
When they **h** this, everyone in Lk 4:28
the centurion **h** about Jesus, Lk 7:3
Jesus **h** this and was amazed at Lk 7:9
the things you have seen and **h**: Lk 7:22
the tax collectors, **h** this, they Lk 7:29
the path are those who have **h**. Lk 8:12
when they have **h**, go on their Lk 8:14
having **h** the word with an honest Lk 8:15
Jesus **h** it, He answered him, Lk 8:50
the tetrarch **h** about everything Lk 9:7
the dark will be **h** in the light, Lk 12:3
table with Him **h** these things, Lk 14:15
the house, he **h** music and Lk 15:25
When Jesus **h** this, He told him, Lk 18:22
After he **h** this, he became Lk 18:23
Those who **h** this asked, "Then Lk 18:26
were captivated by what they **h**. Lk 19:48
But when they **h** this they said, Lk 20:16
since we've **h** it ourselves from Lk 22:71
When Pilate **h** this, he asked if Lk 23:6
because he had **h** about Him and Lk 23:8
The two disciples **h** him say this Jn 1:37
of the two who **h** John and Jn 1:40
to what He has seen and **h**, Jn 3:32
the Pharisees **h** He was making Jn 4:1
for we have **h** for ourselves and Jn 4:42
When this man **h** that Jesus had Jn 4:47
You have not **h** His voice at any Jn 5:37
many of His disciples **h** this, Jn 6:60
The Pharisees **h** the crowd Jn 7:32
from the crowd **h** these words, Jn 7:40
When they **h** this, they left one Jn 8:9
and what I have **h** from Him— Jn 8:26
you have **h** from your father. Jn 8:38
you the truth that I **h** from God. Jn 8:40
no one has ever **h** of someone Jn 9:32
Jesus **h** that they had thrown Jn 9:35
who were with Him **h** these things Jn 9:40
When Jesus **h** it, He said, "This Jn 11:4
So when He **h** that he was sick, Jn 11:6
soon as Martha **h** that Jesus was Jn 11:20
soon as she **h** this, she got up Jn 11:29
I thank You that You **h** Me. Jn 11:41
to the festival **h** that Jesus was Jn 12:12
because they **h** He had done this Jn 12:18
standing there **h** it and said it Jn 12:29
We have **h** from the law that the Jn 12:34
You have **h** Me tell you, 'I am Jn 14:28
I have **h** from My Father. Jn 15:15
those who **h** what I told them. Jn 18:21
When Pilate **h** this statement, Jn 19:8
When Pilate **h** these words, Jn 19:13
When Simon Peter **h** that it was Jn 21:7
said, "is what⌋ you **h** from Me; Ac 1:4
because each one **h** them speaking Ac 2:6
When they **h** this, they were Ac 2:37
many of those who **h** the message Ac 4:4
about what we have seen and **h**." Ac 4:20

When they **h** this, they raised Ac 4:24
When he **h** these words, Ananias Ac 5:5
a great fear came on all who **h**. Ac 5:5
and on all who **h** these things. Ac 5:11
chief priests **h** these things, Ac 5:24
When they **h** this, they were Ac 5:33
We **h** him speaking blasphemous Ac 6:11
For we **h** him say that Jesus, Ac 6:14
When Jacob **h** there was grain in Ac 7:12
I have **h** their groaning and have Ac 7:34
When they **h** these things, they Ac 7:54
as they **h** and saw the signs he Ac 8:6
at Jerusalem **h** that Samaria had Ac 8:14
he **h** him reading the prophet Ac 8:30
he **h** a voice saying to him, Ac 9:4
I have **h** from many people about Ac 9:13
But all who **h** him were astounded Ac 9:21
the disciples **h** that Peter was Ac 9:38
prayer has been **h**, and your acts Ac 10:31
on all those who **h** the message. Ac 10:44
For they **h** them speaking in Ac 10:46
throughout Judea **h** that the Ac 11:1
I also **h** a voice telling me, Ac 11:7
When they **h** this they became Ac 11:18
When the Gentiles **h** this, they Ac 13:48
and **h** Paul speaking. After Ac 14:9
when they **h** this and rushed Ac 14:14
Because we have **h** that some to Ac 15:24
afraid when they **h** that Paul and Ac 16:38
officials who **h** these things. Ac 17:8
When they **h** about resurrection Ac 17:32
when they **h**, believed and were Ac 18:8
Priscilla and Aquila **h** him, Ac 18:26
we haven't even **h** that there is Ac 19:2
Jews and Greeks, **h** the word of Ac 19:10
When they had **h** this, they were Ac 19:28
When we **h** this, both we and the Ac 21:12
When they **h** it, they glorified Ac 21:20
When they **h** that he was Ac 22:2
the ground and **h** a voice saying Ac 22:7
of what you have seen and **h**. Ac 22:15
When the centurion **h** this, Ac 22:26
h a voice speaking to me in the Ac 26:14
from there had **h** the news about Ac 28:15
So faith comes from what is **h**, Rm 10:17
and what is **h** comes through the Rm 10:17
who have not **h** will understand. Rm 15:21
eye has seen and no ear has **h**, 1Co 2:9
acceptable time, I **h** you, and in 2Co 6:2
He **h** inexpressible words, which 2Co 12:4
For you have **h** about my former Gl 1:13
when you **h** the word of truth, Eph 1:13
since I **h** about your faith in Eph 1:15
you have **h**, haven't you, about Eph 3:2
assuming you **h** Him and were Eph 4:21
not even be **h** of among you, Eph 5:3
because you **h** that he was sick. Php 2:26
received and **h** and seen in me, Php 4:9
for we have **h** of your faith in Col 1:4
have already **h** about ⌊this hope Col 1:5
the day you **h** it and recognized Col 1:6
the day we **h** this, we haven't Col 1:9
hope of the gospel that you **h**. Col 1:23
about God that you **h** from us, 1Th 2:13
that you have **h** from me, 2Tm 1:13
And what you have **h** from me in 2Tm 2:2
attention to what we have **h**, Heb 2:1
to us by those who **h** Him. Heb 2:3
For who **h** and rebelled? Heb 3:16
message they **h** did not benefit Heb 4:2
with those who **h** it in faith Heb 4:2
and He was **h** because of His Heb 5:7
Those who **h** it begged that not Heb 12:19
have **h** of Job's endurance and Jms 5:11
And we **h** this voice when it came 2Pt 1:18
the lawless deeds he saw and **h** 2Pt 2:8
we have **h**, what we have seen 1Jn 1:1
have seen and **h** we also declare 1Jn 1:3
the message we have **h** from Him 1Jn 1:5
is the message you have **h**. 1Jn 2:7
And as you have **h**, "Antichrist 1Jn 2:18
What you have **h** from the 1Jn 2:24
If what you have **h** from the 1Jn 2:24
message you have **h** from the 1Jn 3:11
you have **h** that he is coming, 1Jn 4:3
command as you have **h** it from 2Jn 6
and I **h** behind me a loud voice Rv 1:10
what you have received and **h**; Rv 3:3

voice that I had **h** speaking to Rv 4:1
and **h** the voice of many angels Rv 5:11
I **h** every creature in heaven, Rv 5:13
and I **h** one of the four living Rv 6:1
I **h** the second living creature Rv 6:3
I **h** the third living creature Rv 6:5
Then I **h** something like a voice Rv 6:6
I **h** the voice of the fourth Rv 6:7
And I **h** the number of those who Rv 7:4
I looked, and I **h** an eagle, Rv 8:13
that is before God, I **h** a voice Rv 9:13
200 million; I **h** their number. Rv 9:16
Then I **h** a voice from heaven, Rv 10:4
the voice that I **h** from heaven Rv 10:8
Then they **h** a loud voice from Rv 11:12
Then I **h** a loud voice in heaven Rv 12:10
I **h** a sound from heaven like the Rv 14:2
The sound I **h** was also like Rv 14:2
Then I **h** a voice from heaven Rv 14:13
Then I **h** a loud voice from the Rv 16:1
I **h** the angel of the waters say: Rv 16:5
Then I **h** someone from the altar Rv 16:7
Then I **h** another voice from Rv 18:4
will never be **h** in you again; Rv 18:22
will never be **h** in you again; Rv 18:22
will never be **h** in you again. Rv 18:23
After this I **h** something like Rv 19:1
I **h** something like the voice Rv 19:6
Then I **h** a loud voice from the Rv 21:3
am the one who **h** and saw these Rv 22:8
When I **h** and saw them, I fell Rv 22:8

HEARER *(2)*

if anyone is a **h** of the word and Jms 1:23
not a forgetful **h** but a doer who Jms 1:25

HEARERS *(4)*

For the **h** of the law are not Rm 2:13
save both yourself and your **h**. 1Tm 4:16
and leads to the ruin of the **h**. 2Tm 2:14
of the word and not **h** only, Jms 1:22

HEARING *(50)*

to in the **h** of the Hittites Gn 23:16
You kept **h** the sound of the Dt 4:12
in your presence **h** your wisdom. 1Kg 10:8
gave them a **h** and showed them 2Kg 20:13
LORD, and in the **h** of our God, 1Ch 28:8
in your presence **h** your wisdom. 2Ch 9:7
He read in their **h** all the words 2Ch 34:30
Surely you have spoken in my **h**, Jb 33:8
The **h** ear and the seeing eye— Pr 20:12
his ear away from **h** the law— Pr 28:9
seeing or the ear filled with **h**. Ec 1:8
In my **h** the LORD of Hosts ⌊has Is 5:9
has revealed ⌊this⌋ in my **h**: Is 22:14
of will yet say in your **h**: Is 49:20
speaking in your **h** and in the Jr 28:7
and in the **h** of all the people Jr 28:7
this letter in the **h** of Jeremiah Jr 29:29
the LORD in the **h** of the people Jr 36:6
read them in the **h** of all the Jr 36:6
in the **h** of all the people, Jr 36:10
scroll in the **h** of the people. Jr 36:13
you read in the **h** of the people, Jr 36:14
down and read ⌊it⌋ in our **h**." Jr 36:15
So Baruch read ⌊it⌋ in their **h**. Jr 36:15
everything in the **h** of the king. Jr 36:20
read it in the **h** of the king and Jr 36:21
To the others He said in my **h**, Ezk 9:5
but of **h** the words of the LORD. Am 8:11
After **h** the king, they went on Mt 2:9
H this, Jesus was amazed and Mt 8:10
and **h** they do not listen or Mt 13:13
are hard of **h**, and they have Mt 13:15
immediately after **h** about Him, Mk 7:25
sayings in the **h** of the people, Lk 7:1
and **h** they may not understand. Lk 8:10
H a crowd passing by, he Lk 18:36
h the sound but seeing no one. Ac 9:7
but telling or **h** something new. Ac 17:21
On **h** this, they were baptized in Ac 19:5
of Paul's sister, **h** about their Ac 23:16
will give you a **h** whenever your Ac 23:35
to give us a brief **h**. Ac 24:4
adjourned the **h**, saying, "When Ac 24:22
are hard of **h**, and they have Ac 28:27
believe without **h** about Him? Rm 10:14
an eye, where would the **h** be? 1Co 12:17
they simply kept **h**: Gl 1:23
of the law or by **h** with faith? Gl 3:2
of the law or by **h** with faith? Gl 3:5
turn away from **h** the truth and 2Tm 4:4

HEARS *(50)*

everyone who **h** will laugh with Gn 21:6
oracle of one who **h** the sayings Nm 24:4
oracle of one who **h** the sayings Nm 24:16
and her father **h** about her vow Nm 30:4
her on the day he **h** ⌊about it⌋, Nm 30:5
and her husband **h** ⌊about it⌋ and Nm 30:7
her when he **h** ⌊about it⌋, Nm 30:8
and her husband **h** ⌊about it⌋, Nm 30:11
them on the day he **h** ⌊about it⌋, Nm 30:12
them after he **h** ⌊about them⌋, Nm 30:15
When someone **h** the words of this Dt 29:19
everyone who **h** about it will 1Sm 3:11
When all Israel **h** that you have 2Sm 16:21
everyone who **h** about it will 2Kg 21:12
village and never **h** the shouts Jb 39:7
h the officers' shouts and the Jb 39:25
out, and the LORD **h**, and Ps 34:17
and night, and He **h** my voice. Ps 55:17
to You, the One who **h** prayer. Ps 65:2
h and is glad, and the towns Ps 97:8
h their cry for help and saves Ps 145:19
A wise son ⌊**h** his⌋ father's Pr 13:1
but a poor man **h** no threat. Pr 13:8
but He **h** the prayer of the Pr 15:29
the one who **h** will disgrace you, Pr 25:10
he **h** the curse but will not Pr 29:24
by what He **h** with His ears, Is 11:3
when He **h**, He will answer you. Is 30:19
everyone who **h** about it will Jr 19:3
the house of Judah **h** about all Jr 36:3
if anyone **h** the sound of the Ezk 33:4
that everyone who **h** the sound of Dn 3:10
everyone who **h** these words of Mt 7:24
But everyone who **h** these words Mt 7:26
When anyone **h** the word about the Mt 13:19
this is one who **h** the word and Mt 13:20
this is one who **h** the word, Mt 13:22
is one who **h** and understands Mt 13:23
who comes to Me, **h** My words, and Lk 6:47
But the one who **h** and does not Lk 6:49
who **h** My word and believes Jn 5:24
a man before it **h** from him and Jn 7:51
If anyone **h** My words and doesn't Jn 12:47
but He will speak whatever He **h**. Jn 16:13
what he sees in me or **h** from me, 2Co 12:6
according to His will, He **h** us. 1Jn 5:14
know that He **h** whatever we ask 1Jn 5:15
If anyone **h** My voice and opens Rv 3:20
Anyone who **h** should say, Rv 22:17
to everyone who **h** the prophetic Rv 22:18

HEART *(527)*

and He was grieved in His **h**. Gn 6:6
thought in his **h**, "Can a child Gn 17:17
I had finished praying in my **h**, Gn 24:45
And Esau determined in his **h**: Gn 27:41
he sees you, his **h** will rejoice. Ex 4:14
will harden his **h** so that he Ex 4:21
Pharaoh's **h** and multiply My Ex 7:3
Pharaoh's **h** hardened, and he Ex 7:13
So Pharaoh's **h** hardened, and he Ex 7:22
and didn't even take this to **h**. Ex 7:23
he hardened his **h** and would not Ex 8:15
But Pharaoh's **h** hardened, and he Ex 8:19
hardened his **h** this time also Ex 8:32
But Pharaoh's **h** was hardened, Ex 9:7
Pharaoh's **h** and he did not Ex 9:12
sinned again and hardened his **h**, Ex 9:34
So Pharaoh's **h** hardened, and he Ex 9:35
hardened his **h** and the hearts Ex 10:1
the LORD hardened Pharaoh's **h**, Ex 10:20
the LORD hardened Pharaoh's **h**, Ex 10:27
the LORD hardened Pharaoh's **h**, Ex 11:10
Pharaoh's **h** so that he will Ex 14:4
hardened the **h** of Pharaoh king Ex 14:8
congealed in the **h** of the sea. Ex 15:8
everyone whose **h** stirs him ⌊to Ex 25:2
sons over his **h** on the Ex 28:29
be over Aaron's **h** whenever he Ex 28:30
over his **h** before the LORD. Ex 28:30
everyone whose **h** is willing Ex 35:5
Everyone whose **h** was moved and Ex 35:21
person in whose **h** the LORD had Ex 36:2
everyone whose **h** moved him, Ex 36:2
not hate your brother in your **h**. Lv 19:17
your own **h** and your own eyes Nm 15:39
stubborn and his **h** obstinate in Dt 2:30
with all your **h** and all your Dt 4:29
they had such a **h** to fear Me and Dt 5:29
LORD your God with all your **h**, Dt 6:5
you today are to be in your **h**. Dt 6:6
you to know what was in your **h**, Dt 8:2
that your **h** doesn't become Dt 8:14
with all your **h** and all your Dt 10:12
with all your **h** and all your Dt 11:13
with all your **h** and all your Dt 13:3
this wicked thought in your **h**, Dt 15:9
have a stingy **h** when you give, Dt 15:10
so that his **h** won't go astray. Dt 17:17
Then his **h** will not be exalted Dt 17:20
with all your **h** and all your Dt 26:16
God with joy and a cheerful **h**, Dt 28:47
will give you a trembling **h**, Dt 28:65
will have in your **h** and because Dt 28:67
you today whose **h** turns away Dt 29:18
I follow my ⌊own⌋ stubborn **h**.' Dt 29:19
with all your **h** and all your Dt 30:2
circumcise your **h** and the hearts Dt 30:6
with all your **h** and all your Dt 30:6
with all your **h** and all your Dt 30:10
in your mouth and in your **h**, Dt 30:14
But if your **h** turns away and you Dt 30:17
Take to **h** all these words I am Dt 32:46
this, we lost **h**, and everyone's Jos 2:11
they lost **h** and their courage Jos 5:1
with all your **h** and all your Jos 22:5
with all your **h** and all your Jos 23:14
My **h** is with the leaders of Jdg 5:9
searching of **h** among the clans Jdg 5:15
searching of **h** among the clans Jdg 5:16
when your **h** is not with me? Jdg 16:15
I am a woman with a broken **h**. 1Sm 1:15
out my **h** before the LORD. 1Sm 1:15
My **h** rejoices in the LORD; 1Sm 2:1
do whatever is in My **h** and mind. 1Sm 2:35
to the LORD with all your **h**, 1Sm 7:3
you everything that's in your **h**. 1Sm 9:19
God changed his **h**, and all the 1Sm 10:9
the LORD with all your **h**. 1Sm 12:20
Him faithfully with all your **h**, 1Sm 12:24
"Do what is in your **h**. 1Sm 14:7
but the LORD sees the **h**." 1Sm 16:7
your arrogance and your evil **h**— 1Sm 17:28
took this to **h** and became very 1Sm 21:12
and she despised him in her **h**. 2Sm 6:16
Go and do all that is on your **h**, 2Sm 7:3
Don't take this thing to **h**." 2Sm 13:20
man with the **h** of a lion will 2Sm 17:10
into Absalom's **h** while he was 2Sm 18:14
May the king not take it to **h**. 2Sm 19:19
Foreigners lose **h** and come 2Sm 22:46
Me with their whole mind and **h**, 1Kg 2:4
an obedient **h** to judge Your 1Kg 3:9
you a wise and understanding **h**, 1Kg 3:12
before You with their whole **h**. 1Kg 8:23
You know his **h**, for You alone 1Kg 8:39
You alone know every human **h**, 1Kg 8:39
whole mind and **h** in the land of 1Kg 8:48
Let your **h** be completely devoted 1Kg 8:61
eyes and My **h** will be there at 1Kg 9:3
integrity of **h** and uprightness, 1Kg 9:4
that God had put in his **h**. 1Kg 10:24
they turned his **h** away ⌊from the 1Kg 11:3
h was not completely with the 1Kg 11:4
his father David's **h** had been. 1Kg 11:4
because his **h** had turned away 1Kg 11:9
h of these people will return 1Kg 12:27
followed Me with all of his **h**, 1Kg 14:8
but Asa's **h** was completely with 1Kg 15:14
The arrow went through his **h**, 2Kg 9:24
"Is your **h** one with mine?" 2Kg 10:15
of Ahab all that was in My **h**, 2Kg 10:30
with all his **h** the law of the 2Kg 10:31
because your **h** was tender and 2Kg 22:19
all his mind and with all his **h**, 2Kg 23:3
with all his **h** and with all his 2Kg 23:25
my **h** will be united with you, 1Ch 12:17
and she despised him in her **h**. 1Ch 15:29
Do all that is on your **h**, 1Ch 17:2
It was in my **h** to build a house 1Ch 22:7
your mind and **h** to seek the LORD 1Ch 22:19
It was in my **h** to build a house 1Ch 28:2
Him with a whole **h** and a willing 1Ch 28:9
searches every **h** and understands 1Ch 28:9

to the LORD with a whole **h**. 1Ch 29:9
You test the **h** and that You are 1Ch 29:17
these things with an upright **h**, 1Ch 29:17
Solomon a whole **h** to keep and to 1Ch 29:19
Because this was in your **h**, 2Ch 1:11
Now it was in the **h** of my father 2Ch 6:7
before You with their whole **h**. 2Ch 6:14
You know his **h**, for You alone 2Ch 6:30
for You alone know the human **h**, 2Ch 6:30
whole mind and **h** in the land of 2Ch 6:38
entered Solomon's **h** to do for 2Ch 7:11
eyes and My **h** will be there at 2Ch 7:16
the wisdom God had put in his **h**. 2Ch 9:23
in his **h** to seek the LORD 2Ch 12:14
all their mind and all their **h**. 2Ch 15:12
had sought Him with all their **h**, 2Ch 15:15
and with a whole **h**, you are to 2Ch 19:9
sought the LORD with all his **h**." 2Ch 22:9
Joash took it to **h** to renovate 2Ch 24:4
It is in my **h** now to make a 2Ch 29:10
to give them one **h** to carry out 2Ch 30:12
sets his whole **h** on seeking God, 2Ch 30:19
because his **h** was proud, 2Ch 32:25
himself for the pride of his **h**— 2Ch 32:26
and discover what was in his **h**. 2Ch 32:31
because your **h** was tender and 2Ch 34:27
with all his **h** and with all his 2Ch 34:31
and hardened his **h** against 2Ch 36:13
in his **h** to study the law Ezr 7:10
is nothing but sadness of **h**." Neh 2:2
God had laid on my **h** to do for Neh 2:12
You found his **h** faithful in Your Neh 9:8
these ⌊thoughts⌋ in Your **h**; Jb 10:13
redirect your **h** and lift up your Jb 11:13
Why has your **h** misled you, Jb 15:12
even the things dear to my **h**. Jb 17:11
a stranger. My **h** longs within me Jb 19:27
and place His sayings in your **h**. Jb 22:22
God has made my **h** faint; Jb 23:16
I made the widow's **h** rejoice. Jb 29:13
my **h** has followed my eyes, Jb 31:7
If my **h** has been seduced by ⌊my Jb 31:9
that my **h** was secretly enticed Jb 31:27
do by hiding my guilt in my **h**, Jb 31:33
My **h** is like unvented wine; Jb 32:19
words ⌊come from⌋ my upright **h**, Jb 33:3
have a godless **h** harbor anger; Jb 36:13
My **h** pounds at this and leaps Jb 37:1
on any who are wise in **h**. Jb 37:24
wisdom in the **h** or gave the mind Jb 38:36
His **h** is as hard as a rock, Jb 41:24
reflect in your **h** and be still. Ps 4:4
more joy in my **h** than they have Ps 4:7
who saves the upright in **h**. Ps 7:10
thank the LORD with all my **h**; Ps 9:1
the shadows at the upright in **h**. Ps 11:2
my **h** will rejoice in Your Ps 13:5
fool says in his **h**, "God does Ps 14:1
the truth in his **h**— Ps 15:2
Therefore my **h** is glad, and my Ps 16:9
have tested my **h**; You have Ps 17:3
Foreigners lose **h** and come Ps 18:45
are right, making the **h** glad; Ps 19:8
of my **h** be acceptable to Ps 19:14
give you what your **h** desires and Ps 20:4
my **h** is like wax, melting within Ps 22:14
has clean hands and a pure **h**, Ps 24:4
The distresses of my **h** increase; Ps 25:17
examine my **h** and mind. Ps 26:2
against me, my **h** is not afraid; Ps 27:3
In Your behalf my **h** says, Ps 27:8
and let your **h** be strong. Ps 27:14
my **h** trusts in Him, and I am Ps 28:7
Therefore my **h** rejoices, and I Ps 28:7
for joy, all you upright in **h**. Ps 32:11
plans of His **h** from generation Ps 33:11
An oracle within my **h** concerning Ps 36:1
over the upright in **h**. Ps 36:10
of his God is in his **h**; Ps 37:31
because of the anguish of my **h**. Ps 38:8
My **h** races, my strength leaves Ps 38:10
My **h** grew hot within me; Ps 39:3
hide Your righteousness in my **h**; Ps 40:10
he stores up evil in his **h**; Ps 41:6
this as I pour out my **h**: Ps 42:4
He knows the secrets of the **h**? Ps 44:21
h is moved by a noble theme as Ps 45:1
create a clean **h** for me and Ps 51:10

despise a broken and humbled **h**. Ps 51:17
fool says in his **h**, "God does Ps 53:1
My **h** shudders within me; Ps 55:4
are smooth, but war is in his **h**. Ps 55:21
My **h** is confident, God, my heart Ps 57:7
God, my **h** is confident. Ps 57:7
the earth when my **h** is without Ps 61:2
man and the **h** are mysterious. Ps 64:6
the upright in **h** offer praise. Ps 64:10
been aware of malice in my **h**, Ps 66:18
have broken my **h**, and I am in Ps 69:20
You who seek God, take **h**! Ps 69:32
to Israel, to the pure in **h**. Ps 73:1
Did I purify my **h** and wash my Ps 73:13
My flesh and my **h** may fail, Ps 73:26
but God is the strength of my **h**, Ps 73:26
meditate in my **h**, and my spirit Ps 77:6
generation whose **h** was not loyal Ps 78:8
with a pure **h** and guided them Ps 78:72
my **h** and flesh cry out for the Ps 84:2
I will praise You with all my **h**, Ps 86:12
in my **h** I carry ⌊abuse⌋ from all Ps 89:50
the upright in **h** will follow it. Ps 94:15
gladness for the upright in **h**. Ps 97:11
with integrity of **h** in my house. Ps 101:2
A devious **h** will be far from me; Ps 101:4
haughty eyes or an arrogant **h**. Ps 101:5
My **h** is afflicted, withered like Ps 102:4
wine that makes man's **h** glad— Ps 104:15
and bread that sustains man's **h**. Ps 104:15
My **h** is confident, God; Ps 108:1
my **h** is wounded within me. Ps 109:22
with all my **h** in the assembly Ps 111:1
his **h** is confident, trusting in Ps 112:7
His **h** is assured; he will not Ps 112:8
and seek Him with all their **h**. Ps 119:2
with a sincere **h** when I learn Ps 119:7
I have sought You with all my **h**; Ps 119:10
Your word in my **h** so that I may Ps 119:11
it and follow it with all my **h**. Ps 119:34
Turn my **h** to Your decrees and Ps 119:36
sought Your favor with all my **h**; Ps 119:58
Your precepts with all my **h**. Ps 119:69
May my **h** be blameless regarding Ps 119:80
they are the joy of my **h**. Ps 119:111
with all my **h**; answer me, LORD Ps 119:145
but my **h** fears ⌊only⌋ Your word. Ps 119:161
LORD, my **h** is not proud; Ps 131:1
give You thanks with all my **h**; Ps 138:1
Search me, God, and know my **h**; Ps 139:23
Do not let my **h** turn to any evil Ps 141:4
my **h** is overcome with dismay. Ps 143:4
directing your **h** to Pr 2:2
knowledge will delight your **h**. Pr 2:10
but let your **h** keep my commands; Pr 3:1
them on the tablet of your **h**. Pr 3:3
in the LORD with all your **h**, Pr 3:5
Your **h** must hold on to my words. Pr 4:4
keep them within your **h**. Pr 4:21
Guard your **h** above all else, Pr 4:23
how my **h** despised correction. Pr 5:12
evil with perversity in his **h**— Pr 6:14
a **h** that plots wicked schemes, Pr 6:18
Always bind them to your **h**; Pr 6:21
lust in your **h** for her beauty Pr 6:25
them on the tablet of your **h**. Pr 7:3
Don't let your **h** turn aside to Pr 7:25
A wise **h** accepts commands, Pr 10:8
the **h** of the wicked is of little Pr 10:20
to someone whose **h** is wise. Pr 11:29
but a foolish **h** publicizes Pr 12:23
in a man's **h** weighs it down, Pr 12:25
Delayed hope makes the **h** sick, Pr 13:12
The **h** knows its own bitterness, Pr 14:10
Even in laughter a **h** may be sad, Pr 14:13
tranquil **h** is life to the body, Pr 14:30
resides in the **h** of the Pr 14:33
but not so the **h** of fools. Pr 15:7
joyful **h** makes a face cheerful, Pr 15:13
but a sad **h** ⌊produces⌋ a broken Pr 15:13
but a cheerful **h** has a continual Pr 15:15
Bright eyes cheer the **h**; Pr 15:30
of the **h** belong to man, Pr 16:1
with a proud **h** is detestable to Pr 16:5
A man's **h** plans his way, but the Pr 16:9
Anyone with a wise **h** is called Pr 16:21
A wise **h** instructs its mouth and Pr 16:23
A joyful **h** is good medicine, Pr 17:22

his downfall a man's **h** is proud, Pr 18:12
his **h** rages against the LORD. Pr 19:3
Many plans are in a man's **h**, Pr 19:21
in a man's **h** is deep water; Pr 20:5
can say, "I have kept my **h** pure; Pr 20:9
A king's **h** is a water channel in Pr 21:1
haughty eyes and an arrogant **h**— Pr 21:4
who loves a pure **h** and gracious Pr 22:11
tangled up in the **h** of a youth; Pr 22:15
but his **h** is not with you. Pr 23:7
My son, if your **h** is wise, my Pr 23:15
heart is wise, my **h** will indeed Pr 23:15
son, give me your **h**, and let Pr 23:26
don't let your **h** rejoice when he Pr 24:17
I saw, and took it to **h**; Pr 24:32
to a troubled **h** is like taking Pr 25:20
with an evil **h** are like glaze Pr 26:23
are seven abominations in his **h**. Pr 26:25
and incense bring joy to the **h**, Pr 27:9
and bring my **h** joy, so that I Pr 27:11
so the **h** reflects the person. Pr 27:19
who hardens his **h** falls into Pr 28:14
The **h** of her husband trusts in Pr 31:11
occupied with the joy of his **h**. Ec 5:20
the living should take it to **h**. Ec 7:2
a face is sad, a **h** may be glad. Ec 7:3
The **h** of the wise is in a house Ec 7:4
but the **h** of fools is in a house Ec 7:4
anger abides in the **h** of fools. Ec 7:9
is a trap, her **h** a net, and her Ec 7:26
a wise **h** knows the right time Ec 8:5
the **h** of people is filled Ec 8:11
all this to **h** and explained it Ec 9:1
your wine with a cheerful **h**, Ec 9:7
A wise man's **h** ⌊goes⌋ to the Ec 10:2
but a fool's **h** to the left. Ec 10:2
the road, his **h** lacks sense, and Ec 10:3
and let your **h** be glad in the Ec 11:9
the ways of your **h** and in the Ec 11:9
Remove sorrow from your **h**, Ec 11:10
have captured my **h**, my sister, Sg 4:9
captured my **h** with one glance Sg 4:9
I sleep, but my **h** is awake. Sg 5:2
Set me as a seal on your **h**, Sg 8:6
hurt, and the whole **h** is sick. Is 1:5
from the **h** of Jerusalem Is 4:4
the **h** of Ahaz and the hearts of Is 7:2
and every man's **h** will melt. Is 13:7
My **h** cries out over Moab, whose Is 15:5
and Egypt's **h** will melt within Is 19:1
My **h** staggers; horror terrifies Is 21:4
And ⌊your⌋ **h** will rejoice like Is 30:29
take it to **h**, you transgressors! Is 46:8
these things to **h** or think about Is 47:7
people in whose **h** is My Is 51:7
and no one takes it to **h**; Is 57:1
remember Me or take it to **h**? Is 57:11
and revive the **h** of the Is 57:15
back to the desires of his **h**. Is 57:17
uttering lying words from the **h**. Is 59:13
and your **h** will tremble and Is 60:5
shout for joy from a glad **h**, Is 65:14
cry out from an anguished **h**, Is 65:14
return to Me with all her **h**— Jr 3:10
Wash the evil from your **h**, Jr 4:14
because it has reached your **h**! Jr 4:18
the pain in my **h**! My heart Jr 4:19
in my heart! My **h** pounds; I Jr 4:19
to their own stubborn, evil **h**. Jr 7:24
has settled on me. My **h** is sick. Jr 8:18
Israel is uncircumcised in **h**." Jr 9:26
the stubbornness of his evil **h**. Jr 11:8
who tests **h** and mind, let me see Jr 11:20
test whether my **h** is with You. Jr 12:3
but no one takes it to **h**. Jr 12:11
to me and the joy of my **h**, Jr 15:16
the stubbornness of his evil **h**, Jr 16:12
and turns his **h** from the LORD. Jr 17:5
The **h** is more deceitful than Jr 17:9
I test the **h** to give to each Jr 17:10
the stubbornness of his evil **h**." Jr 18:12
becomes a fire burning in my **h**, Jr 20:9
and seeing the **h** and mind, Jr 20:12
you have eyes and **h** for nothing Jr 22:17
h is broken within me, and all Jr 23:9
of his **h** they have said, Jr 23:17
fulfilled the purposes of His **h**. Jr 23:20
I will give them a **h** to know Me, Jr 24:7

return to Me with all their **h**. Jr 24:7
search for Me with all your **h**. Jr 29:13
fulfilled the purposes of His **h**. Jr 30:24
give them one **h** and one way so Jr 32:39
land with all My mind and **h**. Jr 32:41
arrogance, pride, and haughty **h**. Jr 48:29
My **h** moans like flutes for Moab, Jr 48:36
and My **h** moans like flutes for Jr 48:36
In that day the **h** of Moab's Jr 48:41
be like the **h** of a woman with Jr 48:41
presumptuous **h** has deceived you Jr 49:16
be like the **h** of a woman with Jr 49:22
my **h** is broken, for I have been Lm 1:20
are many, and I am sick at **h**. Lm 1:22
My **h** is poured out in grief Lm 2:11
out your **h** like water before Lm 2:19
will give them a **h** filled with Lm 3:65
Because of this, our **h** is sick; Lm 5:17
to you and take ⌊them⌋ to **h**. Ezk 3:10
give them one **h** and put a new Ezk 11:19
remove their **h** of stone from Ezk 11:19
and give them a **h** of flesh, Ezk 11:19
Israel sets up idols in his **h**, Ezk 14:4
up idols in his **h** and putting a Ezk 14:7
How your **h** was inflamed ⌊with Ezk 16:30
a new **h** and a new spirit Ezk 18:31
with a broken **h** right before Ezk 21:6
Every **h** will melt, and every Ezk 21:7
eyes, and the desire of your **h**. Ezk 24:21
realm was in the **h** of the sea; Ezk 27:4
loaded in the **h** of the sea. Ezk 27:25
you in the **h** of the sea. Ezk 27:26
sink into the **h** of the sea on Ezk 27:27
Your **h** is proud, and you have Ezk 28:2
of gods in the **h** of the sea. Ezk 28:2
regarded your **h** as that of a god Ezk 28:2
but your **h** has become proud Ezk 28:5
you regard your **h** as that of a Ezk 28:6
death in the **h** of the sea. Ezk 28:8
Your **h** became proud because of Ezk 28:17
give you a new **h** and put a new Ezk 36:26
will remove your **h** of stone and Ezk 36:26
stone and give you a **h** of flesh. Ezk 36:26
in both **h** and flesh, Ezk 44:7
uncircumcised in **h** and flesh, Ezk 44:9
But when his **h** was exalted and Dn 5:20
humbled your **h**, even though you Dn 5:22
his **h** will be set against the Dn 11:28
I have had a change of **h**; Hs 11:8
turn to Me with all your **h**, Jl 2:12
presumptuous **h** has deceived you Ob 3
depths, into the **h** of the seas, Jnh 2:3
and rejoice with all ⌊your⌋ **h**, Zph 3:14
take it to **h** to honor My name, Mal 2:2
you are not taking it to **h**. Mal 2:2
Blessed are the pure in **h**, Mt 5:8
adultery with her in his **h**. Mt 5:28
there your **h** will be also. Mt 6:21
I am gentle and humble in **h**, Mt 11:29
from the overflow of the **h**. Mt 12:34
will be in the **h** of the earth Mt 12:40
this people's **h** has grown Mt 13:15
away what was sown in his **h**. Mt 13:19
but their **h** is far from Me. Mt 15:8
of the mouth comes from the **h**, Mt 15:18
For from the **h** come evil Mt 15:19
forgive his brother from his **h**." Mt 18:35
Lord your God with all your **h**, Mt 22:37
wicked slave says in his **h**, Mt 24:48
but their **h** is far from Me. Mk 7:6
doesn't go into his **h** but into Mk 7:19
comprehend? Is your **h** hardened? Mk 8:17
and does not doubt in his **h**, Mk 11:23
Lord your God with all your **h**, Mk 12:30
And to love Him with all your **h**, Mk 12:33
unbelief and hardness of **h**, Mk 16:14
about ⌊him⌋ took ⌊it⌋ to **h**, Lk 1:66
things in her **h** and meditating Lk 2:19
kept all these things in her **h**. Lk 2:51
of the good storeroom of his **h**. Lk 6:45
from the overflow of the **h**. Lk 6:45
word with an honest and good **h**, Lk 8:15
Lord your God with all your **h**, Lk 10:27
there your **h** will be also. Lk 12:34
if that slave says in his **h**, Lk 12:45
put it into the **h** of Judas, Jn 13:2
Your **h** must not be troubled. Jn 14:1
Your **h** must not be troubled or Jn 14:27
you, sorrow has filled your **h**. Jn 16:6
Therefore my **h** was glad, and my Ac 2:26
pierced to the **h** and said to Ac 2:37
gladness and simplicity of **h**, Ac 2:46
believed were of one **h** and soul, Ac 4:32
Satan filled your **h** to lie to Ac 5:3
planned this thing in your **h**? Ac 5:4
because your **h** is not right Ac 8:21
intent of your **h** may be forgiven Ac 8:22
with all your **h** you may." Ac 8:37
with a firm resolve of the **h**— Ac 11:23
a man after My **h**, who will carry Ac 13:22
who knows the **h**, testified to Ac 15:8
Lord opened her **h** to pay Ac 16:14
weeping and breaking my **h**? Ac 21:13
this people's **h** has grown Ac 28:27
with their **h**, and be converted— Ac 28:27
unrepentant **h** you are storing Rm 2:5
and circumcision is of the **h**— Rm 2:29
obeyed from the **h** that pattern Rm 6:17
and continual anguish in my **h**. Rm 9:2
not say in your **h**, "Who will go Rm 10:6
in your mouth and in your **h**. Rm 10:8
believe in your **h** that God Rm 10:9
With the **h** one believes, Rm 10:10
has never come into a man's **h**, 1Co 2:9
But he who stands firm in his **h** 1Co 7:37
decided in his **h** to keep his own 1Co 7:37
secrets of his **h** will be 1Co 14:25
and anguished **h** I wrote to you 2Co 2:4
appearance rather than in the **h**. 2Co 5:12
our **h** has been opened wide. 2Co 6:11
for you into the **h** of Titus. 2Co 8:16
do as he has decided in his **h**— 2Co 9:7
the eyes of your **h** may be Eph 1:18
music to the Lord in your **h**, Eph 5:19
in the sincerity of your **h**, Eph 6:5
do God's will from your **h**. Eph 6:6
because I have you in my **h**, Php 1:7
person, not in **h**), we greatly 1Th 2:17
is love from a pure **h**, 1Tm 1:5
call on the Lord from a pure **h**. 2Tm 2:22
refresh my **h** in Christ. Phm 20
unbelieving **h** that departs from Heb 3:12
the ideas and thoughts of the **h**. Heb 4:12
near with a true **h** in full Heb 10:22
you won't grow weary and lose **h**. Heb 12:3
is good for the **h** to be Heb 13:9
his tongue but deceiving his **h**, Jms 1:26
and selfish ambition in your **h**, Jms 3:14
another earnestly from a pure **h**, 1Pt 1:22
hidden person of the **h** with the 1Pt 3:4
Because she says in her **h**, Rv 18:7

HEART'S *(5)*

given him his **h** desire and have Ps 21:2
He will give you your **h** desires. Ps 37:4
my **h** meditation ⌊brings⌋ Ps 49:3
the day of his **h** rejoicing. Sg 3:11
my **h** desire and prayer to God Rm 10:1

HEARTACHE *(1)*

a foolish son, **h** to his mother. Pr 10:1

HEARTFELT *(1)*

and loved, put on **h** compassion, Col 3:12

HEARTH *(5)*

on the altar's **h** all night until Lv 6:9
fire from a **h** or scoop water Is 30:14
altar **h** is seven feet ⌊high⌋, Ezk 43:15
horns project upward from the **h**. Ezk 43:15
The **h** is square, 21 feet long by Ezk 43:16

HEARTILY *(1)*

greet you **h** in the Lord, 1Co 16:19

HEARTS *(180)*

my bag." Their **h** sank. Trembling Gn 42:28
heart and the **h** of his officials Ex 10:1
to harden the **h** of the Egyptians Ex 14:17
who had willing **h** brought Ex 35:22
women whose **h** were moved spun Ex 35:26
women whose **h** prompted them Ex 35:29
anxiety in the **h** of those of you Lv 26:36
uncircumcised **h** will be humbled, Lv 26:41
circumcise your **h** and don't be Dt 10:16
of Mine on your **h** and souls, Dt 11:18
his brothers' **h** won't melt like Dt 20:8
your heart and the **h** of your Dt 30:6
the people's **h** melted and became Jos 7:5
intention to harden their **h**, Jos 11:20
the people's **h** to melt with fear Jos 14:8
and offer your **h** to the LORD, Jos 24:23
Why harden your **h** as the 1Sm 6:6
men whose **h** God had touched 1Sm 10:26
Absalom stole the **h** of the men 2Sm 15:6
The **h** of the men of Israel are 2Sm 15:13
He incline our **h** toward Him to 1Kg 8:58
and with joyful **h** for all the 1Kg 8:66
You have turned their **h** back." 1Kg 18:37
let the **h** of those who seek the 1Ch 16:10
of the **h** of Your people, 1Ch 29:18
and confirm their **h** toward You. 1Ch 29:18
with happy **h** for the goodness 2Ch 7:10
in their **h** to seek the LORD 2Ch 11:16
for those whose **h** are completely 2Ch 16:9
in their **h** ⌊to worship⌋ 2Ch 20:33
with willing **h** brought burnt 2Ch 29:31
having cursed God in their **h**. Jb 1:5
You will strengthen their **h**. Ps 10:17
flattering lips and deceptive **h**. Ps 12:2
May your **h** live forever! Ps 22:26
while malice is in their **h**. Ps 28:3
He alone crafts their **h**; Ps 33:15
our **h** rejoice in Him, because Ps 33:21
Do not let them say in their **h**, Ps 35:25
swords will enter their own **h**, Ps 37:15
Our **h** have not turned back; Ps 44:18
pierce the **h** of the king's Ps 45:5
practice injustice in your **h**; Ps 58:2
pour out your **h** before Him. Ps 62:8
of their **h** run wild. Ps 73:7
said in their **h**, "Let us oppress Ps 74:8
their **h** were insincere toward Ps 78:37
their stubborn **h** to follow their Ps 81:12
whose **h** are set on pilgrimage. Ps 84:5
we may develop wisdom in our **h**. Ps 90:12
not harden your **h** as at Meribah, Ps 95:8
are a people whose **h** go astray; Ps 95:10
let the **h** of those who seek the Ps 105:3
whose **h** He turned to hate His Ps 105:25
h are hard and insensitive, Ps 119:70
to those whose **h** are upright. Ps 125:4
who plan evil in their **h**. Ps 140:2
Deceit is in the **h** of those who Pr 12:20
LORD—how much more, human **h**. Pr 15:11
but the LORD is a tester of **h**. Pr 17:3
for their **h** plan violence, Pr 24:2
He who weighs **h** consider it? Pr 24:12
so the **h** of kings cannot be Pr 25:3
also put eternity in their **h**, Ec 3:11
h of people are full of evil, Ec 9:3
is in their **h** while they live— Ec 9:3
of Ahaz and the **h** of his people Is 7:2
yet their **h** are far from Me, Is 29:13
You harden our **h** so we do not Is 63:17
stubbornness of their evil **h**. Jr 3:17
remove the foreskin of your **h**, Jr 4:4
have stubborn and rebellious **h**. Jr 5:23
of their **h** and the Baals, Jr 9:14
the stubbornness of their own **h**, Jr 13:10
tablet of their **h** and on the Jr 17:1
them and write it on their **h**. Jr 31:33
of Me in their **h** so they will Jr 32:40
In that day the **h** of Edom's Jr 49:22
The **h** of the people cry out to Lm 2:18
us lift up our **h** and ⌊our⌋ hands Lm 3:41
has left our **h**; our dancing has Lm 5:15
promiscuous **h** that turned away Ezk 6:9
for those whose **h** pursue their Ezk 11:21
up idols in their **h** and have put Ezk 14:3
the house of Israel by their **h**, Ezk 14:5
For their **h** went after their Ezk 20:16
that their **h** may melt and many Ezk 21:15
eyes and the longing of their **h**, Ezk 24:25
trouble the **h** of many peoples Ezk 32:9
their **h** pursue unjust gain. Ezk 33:31
kings, whose **h** are bent on evil Dn 11:27
they—their **h** like an oven— Hs 7:6
do not cry to Me from their **h**; Hs 7:14
Their **h** are devious; now they Hs 10:2
and their **h** became proud. Hs 13:6
open the rib cage over their **h**. Hs 13:8
Tear your **h**, not just your Jl 2:13
H melt, knees tremble, loins Nah 2:10
plot evil in your **h** against one Zch 7:10
They made their **h** like a rock so Zch 7:12
plot evil in your **h** against your Zch 8:17
and their **h** will be glad as if Zch 10:7
h will rejoice in the LORD. Zch 10:7

he will turn the **h** of fathers to Mal 4:6
children and the **h** of children Mal 4:6
thinking evil things in your **h**? Mt 9:4
with their **h** and turn back— Mt 13:15
of the hardness of your **h**. Mt 19:8
these things in your **h**? Mk 2:8
at the hardness of their **h**, Mk 3:5
Instead, their **h** were hardened. Mk 6:52
out of people's **h**, come evil Mk 7:21
of the hardness of your **h**. Mk 10:5
turn the **h** of fathers to their Lk 1:17
of the thoughts of their **h**; Lk 1:51
of many **h** may be revealed. Lk 2:35
you reasoning this in your **h**? Lk 5:22
away the word from their **h**, Lk 8:12
knowing the thoughts of their **h**, Lk 9:47
of others, but God knows your **h**. Lk 16:15
believe in your **h** all that the Lk 24:25
Weren't our **h** ablaze within us Lk 24:32
why do doubts arise in your **h**? Lk 24:38
their eyes and hardened their **h**, Jn 12:40
eyes or understand with their **h**, Jn 12:40
Your **h** will rejoice, and no one Jn 16:22
You, Lord, know the **h** of all; Ac 1:24
and in their **h** turned back to Ac 7:39
with uncircumcised **h** and ears! Ac 7:51
enraged in their **h** and gnashed Ac 7:54
and satisfying your **h** with food Ac 14:17
the **h** of the disciples Ac 14:22
cleansing their **h** by faith. Ac 15:9
words and unsettled your **h**, Ac 15:24
cravings of their **h** to sexual Rm 1:24
the law is written on their **h**. Rm 2:15
out in our **h** through the Holy Rm 5:5
who searches the **h** knows the Rm 8:27
they deceive the **h** of the Rm 16:18
reveal the intentions of the **h**. 1Co 4:5
as a down payment in our **h**. 2Co 1:22
written on our **h**, recognized and 2Co 3:2
on tablets that are **h** of flesh. 2Co 3:3
read, a veil lies over their **h**, 2Co 3:15
has shone in our **h** to give the 2Co 4:6
us into your **h**. We have wronged 2Co 7:2
said that you are in our **h**, 2Co 7:3
Spirit of His Son into our **h**, Gl 4:6
dwell in your **h** through faith. Eph 3:17
of the hardness of their **h**. Eph 4:18
we are and to encourage your **h**. Eph 6:22
will guard your **h** and your minds Php 4:7
want⌋ their **h** to be encouraged Col 2:2
in one body, control your **h**. Col 3:15
with gratitude in your **h** to God. Col 3:16
so that he may encourage your **h**. Col 4:8
rather God, who examines our **h**. 1Th 2:4
May He make your **h** blameless in 1Th 3:13
encourage your **h** and strengthen 2Th 2:17
Lord direct your **h** to God's love 2Th 3:5
because the **h** of the saints have Phm 7
do not harden your **h** as in the Heb 3:8
always go astray in their **h**, Heb 3:10
do not harden your **h** as in the Heb 3:15
His voice, do not harden your **h**. Heb 4:7
I will write them on their **h**, Heb 8:10
I will put My laws on their **h**, Heb 10:16
our **h** sprinkled ⌊clean⌋ from an Heb 10:22
and purify your **h**, double-minded Jms 4:8
have fattened your **h** for the day Jms 5:5
Strengthen your **h**, because the Jms 5:8
the Messiah as Lord in your **h**, 1Pt 3:15
morning star arises in your **h**. 2Pt 1:19
and with **h** trained in greed. 2Pt 2:14
convince our **h** in His presence, 1Jn 3:19
because if our **h** condemn us, 1Jn 3:20
greater than our **h** and knows all 1Jn 3:20
if our **h** do not condemn ⌊us⌋ we 1Jn 3:21
One who examines minds and **h**, Rv 2:23
it into their **h** to carry out His Rv 17:17

HEAT *(30)*

harvest, cold and **h**, summer and Gn 8:22
tent during the **h** of the day. Gn 18:1
the **h** consumed me by day and the Gn 31:40
of blood in the **h** of his anger Dt 19:6
burning **h**, drought, blight, Dt 28:22
them until the **h** of the day. 1Sm 11:11
during the **h** of the day while 2Sm 4:5
As dry ground and **h** snatch away Jb 24:19
nothing is hidden from its **h**. Ps 19:6
drained as in the summer's **h**. Ps 32:4
can feel the **h** of the thorns— Ps 58:9
a booth for shade from **h** by day, Is 4:6
like shimmering **h** in sunshine, Is 18:4
like a rain cloud in harvest **h**. Is 18:4
the rain, a shade from the **h**. Is 25:4
like **h** in a dry land, You subdue Is 25:5
cloud ⌊cools⌋ the **h** of the day, Is 25:5
the scorching **h** or sun will not Is 49:10
the wind in the **h** of her desire. Jr 2:24
it doesn't fear when **h** comes, Jr 17:8
be exposed⌋ to the **h** of day and Jr 36:30
While they are flushed with **h**, Jr 51:39
gave orders to **h** the furnace Dn 3:19
are sick with the **h** of wine— Hs 7:5
of the day and the burning **h**!' Mt 20:12
because of the **h** and fastened Ac 28:3
with its scorching **h** and dries Jms 1:11
elements will melt with the **h**. 2Pt 3:12
the sun strike them, or any **h**. Rv 7:16
were burned by the intense **h**. Rv 16:9

HEATED *(1)*

like an oven **h** by a baker who Hs 7:4

HEAVEN *(437)*

flesh under **h** with the breath Gn 6:17
High, Creator of **h** and earth, Gn 14:19
High, Creator of **h** and earth, Gn 14:22
to Hagar from **h** and said to her, Gn 21:17
called to him from **h** and said, Gn 22:11
to Abraham a second time from **h** Gn 22:15
God of **h** and God of earth, Gn 24:3
LORD, the God of **h**, who took me Gn 24:7
ground with its top reaching **h**, Gn 28:12
This is the gate of **h**." Gn 28:17
throw it toward **h** in the sight Ex 9:8
threw it toward **h**, and it became Ex 9:10
hand toward **h** and let there be Ex 9:22
out his staff toward **h**, Ex 9:23
Stretch out your hand toward **h**, Ex 10:21
stretched out his hand toward **h**, Ex 10:22
to rain bread from **h** for you. Ex 16:4
the memory of Amalek under **h**." Ex 17:14
I have spoken to you from **h**. Ex 20:22
the peoples everywhere under **h**. Dt 2:25
is there in **h** or on earth who Dt 3:24
the array of **h**—do not be led Dt 4:19
all people everywhere under **h**. Dt 4:19
I call **h** and earth as witnesses Dt 4:26
voice from **h** to instruct you. Dt 4:36
LORD is God in **h** above and on Dt 4:39
wipe out their names under **h**. Dt 7:24
and blot out their name under **h**. Dt 9:14
memory of Amalek from under **h**. Dt 25:19
dwelling, from **h**, and bless Your Dt 26:15
will blot out his name under **h**, Dt 29:20
It is not in **h**, so that you have Dt 30:12
will go up to **h**, get it for us, Dt 30:12
I call **h** and earth as witnesses Dt 30:19
to them and call **h** and earth as Dt 31:28
raise My hand to **h** and declare: Dt 32:40
God is God in **h** above and on Jos 2:11
outcry of the city went up to **h**. 1Sm 5:12
down from **h** on the bodies. 2Sm 21:10
The LORD thundered from **h**; 2Sm 22:14
spread out his hands toward **h**. 1Kg 8:22
God like You in **h** above or on 1Kg 8:23
Even **h**, the highest heaven, 1Kg 8:27
the highest **h**, cannot contain 1Kg 8:27
in Your dwelling place in **h**. 1Kg 8:30
may You hear in **h** and act. 1Kg 8:32
You hear in **h** and forgive the 1Kg 8:34
You hear in **h** and forgive the 1Kg 8:36
may You hear in **h**, Your dwelling 1Kg 8:39
may You hear in **h**, Your dwelling 1Kg 8:43
and petition in **h** and uphold 1Kg 8:45
may You hear in **h**, Your dwelling 1Kg 8:49
his hands spread out toward **h**, 1Kg 8:54
down from **h** and consume you 2Kg 1:10
came down from **h** and consumed 2Kg 1:10
down from **h** and consume you 2Kg 1:12
came down from **h** and consumed 2Kg 1:12
come down from **h** and consumed 2Kg 1:14
Elijah up to **h** in a whirlwind. 2Kg 2:1
went up into **h** in the whirlwind. 2Kg 2:11
LORD were to make windows in **h**, 2Kg 7:2
LORD were to make windows in **h**, 2Kg 7:19
the name of Israel from under **h**, 2Kg 14:27
standing between earth and **h**, 1Ch 21:16
with fire from **h** on the altar 1Ch 21:26
as numerous as the stars of **h**. 1Ch 27:23
since even **h** and the highest 2Ch 2:6
and the highest **h** cannot contain 2Ch 2:6
spread out his hands toward **h**. 2Ch 6:13
God like You in **h** or on earth, 2Ch 6:14
Even **h**, the highest heaven, 2Ch 6:18
the highest **h**, cannot contain 2Ch 6:18
in Your dwelling place in **h**. 2Ch 6:21
may You hear in **h** and act. 2Ch 6:23
You hear in **h** and forgive the 2Ch 6:25
You hear in **h** and forgive the 2Ch 6:27
may You hear in **h**, Your dwelling 2Ch 6:30
may You hear in **h** in Your 2Ch 6:33
and petition in **h** and uphold 2Ch 6:35
may You hear in **h**, in Your 2Ch 6:39
descended from **h** and consumed 2Ch 7:1
will hear from **h**, forgive their 2Ch 7:14
are You not the God who is in **h**, 2Ch 20:6
in a rage that has reached **h**. 2Ch 28:9
His holy dwelling place in **h**. 2Ch 30:27
about this and cried out to **h**, 2Ch 32:20
LORD, the God of **h**, has given me 2Ch 36:23
LORD, the God of **h**, has given me Ezr 1:2
the God of **h** and earth and are Ezr 5:11
fathers angered the God of **h**, Ezr 5:12
burnt offerings to the God of **h**, Ezr 6:9
to the God of **h** and pray for Ezr 6:10
in the law of the God of **h**: Ezr 7:12
of the God of **h** asks of you must Ezr 7:21
by the God of **h** must be done Ezr 7:23
for the house of the God of **h**, Ezr 7:23
and praying before the God of **h**. Neh 1:4
I said, LORD God of **h**, the great Neh 1:5
So I prayed to the God of **h** Neh 2:4
The God of **h** is the One who will Neh 2:20
Sinai, and spoke to them from **h**. Neh 9:13
bread from **h** for their hunger; Neh 9:15
the stars of **h** and brought them Neh 9:23
to You, and You heard from **h** Neh 9:27
heard from **h** and rescued them Neh 9:28
A lightning storm struck from **h**. Jb 1:16
Even now my witness is in **h**, Jb 16:19
Though his arrogance reaches **h**, Jb 20:6
Who gave birth to the frost of **h** Jb 38:29
Do you know the laws of **h**? Jb 38:33
who can tilt the water jars of **h** Jb 38:37
under **h** belongs to Me. Jb 41:11
The One enthroned in **h** laughs; Ps 2:4
the LORD's throne is in **h**. Ps 11:4
looks down from **h** on the human Ps 14:2
The LORD thundered from **h**; Ps 18:13
him from His holy **h** with mighty Ps 20:6
The LORD looks down from **h**; Ps 33:13
faithful love ⌊reaches⌋ to **h**, Ps 36:5
He summons **h** and earth in order Ps 50:4
looks down from **h** on the human Ps 53:2
down from **h** and saves me, Ps 57:3
Let **h** and earth praise Him, Ps 69:34
Your righteousness reaches **h**, Ps 71:19
They set their mouths against **h**, Ps 73:9
Whom do I have in **h** but You? Ps 73:25
your horn against **h** or speak Ps 75:5
From **h** You pronounced judgment. Ps 76:8
above and opened the doors of **h**. Ps 78:23
He gave them grain from **h**. Ps 78:24
Look down from **h** and see; Ps 80:14
will look down from **h**. Ps 85:11
his throne as long as **h** lasts. Ps 89:29
LORD gazed out from **h** to earth— Ps 102:19
has established His throne in **h**, Ps 103:19
them with bread from **h**. Ps 105:40
God is in **h** and does whatever Ps 115:3
LORD, the Maker of **h** and earth. Ps 115:15
it is firmly fixed in **h**. Ps 119:89
LORD, the Maker of **h** and earth. Ps 121:2
to You, the One enthroned in **h**. Ps 123:1
LORD, the Maker of **h** and earth. Ps 124:8
LORD, Maker of **h** and earth, Ps 134:3
He pleases in **h** and on earth, Ps 135:6
Give thanks to the God of **h**! Ps 136:26
If I go up to **h**, You are there; Ps 139:8
Maker of **h** and earth, the sea Ps 146:6
His majesty covers **h** and earth. Ps 148:13
the **h** is high and the earth is Pr 25:3
has gone up to **h** and come down? Pr 30:4
wisdom all that is done under **h**. Ec 1:13
to do under **h** during the few Ec 2:3
time for every activity under **h**: Ec 3:1

is in **h** and you are on earth, Ec 5:2
of Sheol to the heights of **h**." Is 7:11
the host of **h** above and kings Is 24:21
the Spirit from **h** is poured out Is 32:15
For as **h** is higher than earth, Is 55:9
as rain and snow fall from **h**, Is 55:10
Look down from **h** and see from Is 63:15
create a new **h** and a new earth; Is 65:17
H is My throne, and earth is My Is 66:1
make cakes for the queen of **h**, Jr 7:18
hosts of **h** cannot be counted; Jr 33:22
the fixed order of **h** and earth, Jr 33:25
the queen of **h** and offer drink Jr 44:17
to the queen of **h** and to offer Jr 44:18
to the queen of **h** and poured out Jr 44:19
the queen of **h** and to pour out Jr 44:25
H and earth and everything in Jr 51:48
Israel's glory from **h** to earth. Lm 2:1
and ⌊our⌋ hands to God in **h**: Lm 3:41
LORD looks down from **h** and sees. Lm 3:50
earth and **h** and carried me Ezk 8:3
to ask the God of **h** for mercy Dn 2:18
and Daniel praised the God of **h** Dn 2:19
there is a God in **h** who reveals Dn 2:28
The God of **h** has given you Dn 2:37
the God of **h** will set up a Dn 2:44
a holy one, coming down from **h**. Dn 4:13
coming down from **h** and saying, Dn 4:23
as you acknowledge that **H** rules. Dn 4:26
mouth, a voice came from **h**: Dn 4:31
looked up to **h**, and my sanity Dn 4:34
with the army of **h** and the Dn 4:35
and glorify the King of **h**, Dn 4:37
yourself against the Lord of **h**. Dn 5:23
the four winds of **h** stirred up Dn 7:2
man coming with the clouds of **h**. Dn 7:13
under all of **h** will be given to Dn 7:27
toward the four winds of **h**. Dn 8:8
ever been done under all of **h**. Dn 9:12
divided to the four winds of **h**, Dn 11:4
hands toward **h** and swore by Him Dn 12:7
h and earth will shake. Jl 3:16
they climb up to **h**, from there I Am 9:2
you like the four winds of **h**"— Zch 2:6
spirits of **h** going out after Zch 6:5
the floodgates of **h** and pour out Mal 3:10
the kingdom of **h** has come near!" Mt 3:2
And there came a voice from **h**: Mt 3:17
the kingdom of **h** has come near!" Mt 4:17
the kingdom of **h** is theirs. Mt 5:3
the kingdom of **h** is theirs. Mt 5:10
your reward is great in **h**. Mt 5:12
give glory to your Father in **h**. Mt 5:16
Until **h** and earth pass away, Mt 5:18
least in the kingdom of **h**. Mt 5:19
great in the kingdom of **h**. Mt 5:19
never enter the kingdom of **h**. Mt 5:20
either by **h**, because it is God's Mt 5:34
may be sons of your Father in **h**. Mt 5:45
no reward from your Father in **h**. Mt 6:1
Our Father in **h**, Your name be Mt 6:9
be done on earth as it is in **h**. Mt 6:10
for yourselves treasures in **h**, Mt 6:20
Father in **h** give good things Mt 7:11
will enter the kingdom of **h**, Mt 7:21
does the will of My Father in **h**. Mt 7:21
and Jacob in the kingdom of **h**. Mt 8:11
'The kingdom of **h** has come near. Mt 10:7
him before My Father in **h**. Mt 10:32
deny him before My Father in **h**. Mt 10:33
the kingdom of **h** is greater than Mt 11:11
the kingdom of **h** has been Mt 11:12
will you be exalted to **h**? Mt 11:23
Father, Lord of **h** and earth, Mt 11:25
does the will of My Father in **h**, Mt 12:50
the kingdom of **h** have been given Mt 13:11
kingdom of **h** may be compared Mt 13:24
The kingdom of **h** is like a Mt 13:31
The kingdom of **h** is like yeast Mt 13:33
The kingdom of **h** is like Mt 13:44
the kingdom of **h** is like a Mt 13:45
the kingdom of **h** is like a large Mt 13:47
in the kingdom of **h** is like a Mt 13:52
looking up to **h**, He blessed them Mt 14:19
Him to show them a sign from **h**. Mt 16:1
this to you, but My Father in **h**. Mt 16:17
the keys of the kingdom of **h**, Mt 16:19
on earth is already bound in **h**, Mt 16:19

earth is already loosed in **h**." Mt 16:19
greatest in the kingdom of **h**?" Mt 18:1
never enter the kingdom of **h**. Mt 18:3
greatest in the kingdom of **h**. Mt 18:4
tell you that in **h** their angels Mt 18:10
view the face of My Father in **h**. Mt 18:10
your Father in **h** that one of Mt 18:14
on earth is already bound in **h**, Mt 18:18
on earth is already loosed in **h**. Mt 18:18
done for you by My Father in **h**. Mt 18:19
the kingdom of **h** can be compared Mt 18:23
way because of the kingdom of **h**. Mt 19:12
the kingdom of **h** is made up of Mt 19:14
and you will have treasure in **h**. Mt 19:21
to enter the kingdom of **h**! Mt 19:23
For the kingdom of **h** is like a Mt 20:1
Hosanna in the highest **h**! Mt 21:9
come from? From **h** or from men?" Mt 21:25
we say, 'From **h**,' He will say to Mt 21:25
The kingdom of **h** may be compared Mt 22:2
but are like angels in **h**. Mt 22:30
have one Father, who is in **h**. Mt 23:9
up the kingdom of **h** from people. Mt 23:13
takes an oath by **h** takes an oath Mt 23:22
the clouds of **h** with power and Mt 24:30
H and earth will pass away, Mt 24:35
the angels in **h**, nor the Son— Mt 24:36
the kingdom of **h** will be like 10 Mt 25:1
and coming on the clouds of **h**." Mt 26:64
descended from **h** and approached Mt 28:2
given to Me in **h** and on earth. Mt 28:18
And a voice came from **h**: Mk 1:11
and looking up to **h**, He blessed Mk 6:41
looking up to **h**, He sighed Mk 7:34
Him a sign from **h** to test Him. Mk 8:11
and you will have treasure in **h**. Mk 10:21
Hosanna in the highest **h**! Mk 11:10
your Father in **h** will also Mk 11:25
your Father in **h** forgive your Mk 11:26
baptism from **h** or from men? Mk 11:30
we say, 'From **h**,' He will say, Mk 11:31
but are like angels in **h**. Mk 12:25
H and earth will pass away, Mk 13:31
the angels in **h** nor the Son— Mk 13:32
coming with the clouds of **h**." Mk 14:62
taken up into **h** and sat down at Mk 16:19
Glory to God in the highest **h**, Lk 2:14
had left them and returned to **h**, Lk 2:15
As He was praying, **h** opened, Lk 3:21
And a voice came from **h**: Lk 3:22
your reward is great in **h**, Lk 6:23
and looking up to **h**, He blessed Lk 9:16
fire from **h** to consume them? Lk 9:54
will you be exalted to **h**? Lk 10:15
Satan fall from **h** like a Lk 10:18
your names are written in **h**." Lk 10:20
Father, Lord of **h** and earth, Lk 10:21
demanding of Him a sign from **h**. Lk 11:16
an inexhaustible treasure in **h**, Lk 12:33
be more joy in **h** over one sinner Lk 15:7
sinned against **h** and in your Lk 15:18
sinned against **h** and in your Lk 15:21
it is easier for **h** and earth to Lk 16:17
rained from **h** and destroyed them Lk 17:29
his eyes to **h** but kept striking Lk 18:13
and you will have treasure in **h**. Lk 18:22
Peace in **h** and glory in the Lk 19:38
and glory in the highest **h**! Lk 19:38
of John from **h** or from men?" Lk 20:4
we say, 'From **h**,' He will say, Lk 20:5
sights and great signs from **h**. Lk 21:11
H and earth will pass away, Lk 21:33
an angel from **h** appeared to Him, Lk 22:43
them and was carried up into **h**. Lk 24:51
descending from **h** like a dove, Jn 1:32
You will see **h** opened and the Jn 1:51
if I tell you about things of **h**? Jn 3:12
ascended into **h** except the One Jn 3:13
the One who descended from **h**— Jn 3:13
unless it's given to him from **h**. Jn 3:27
who comes from **h** is above all. Jn 3:31
gave them bread from **h** to eat." Jn 6:31
give you the bread from **h**, Jn 6:32
gives you the real bread from **h**. Jn 6:32
comes down from **h** and gives life Jn 6:33
For I have come down from **h**, Jn 6:38
bread that came down from **h**." Jn 6:41
I have come down from **h**'?" Jn 6:42

comes down from **h** so that anyone Jn 6:50
bread that came down from **h**. Jn 6:51
the bread that came down from **h**; Jn 6:58
Then a voice came from **h**: Jn 12:28
looked up to **h**, and said: Jn 17:1
were gazing into **h**, and suddenly Ac 1:10
do you stand looking up into **h**? Ac 1:11
has been taken from you into **h**, Ac 1:11
you have seen Him going into **h**." Ac 1:11
rushing wind came from **h**, Ac 2:2
men from every nation under **h**. Ac 2:5
wonders in the **h** above and signs Ac 2:19
H must welcome Him until the Ac 3:21
name under **h** given to people Ac 4:12
You are the One who made the **h**, Ac 4:24
up to worship the host of **h**, Ac 7:42
H is My throne, and earth My Ac 7:49
the Holy Spirit, gazed into **h**. Ac 7:55
a light from **h** suddenly flashed Ac 9:3
He saw **h** opened and an object Ac 10:11
the object was taken up into **h**. Ac 10:16
being lowered from **h** by its four Ac 11:5
answered from **h** a second time, Ac 11:9
was drawn up again into **h**. Ac 11:10
God, who made the **h**, the earth, Ac 14:15
you rain from **h** and fruitful Ac 14:17
He is Lord of **h** and earth and Ac 17:24
of the image that fell from **h**? Ac 19:35
light from **h** suddenly flashed Ac 22:6
saw a light from **h** brighter than Ac 26:13
is revealed from **h** against all Rm 1:18
heart, "Who will go up to **h**?" Rm 10:6
whether in **h** or on earth— 1Co 8:5
the second man is from **h**. 1Co 15:47
to put on our house from **h**, 2Co 5:2
into the third **h** 14 years ago. 2Co 12:2
an angel from **h** should preach to Gl 1:8
both things in **h** and things on Eph 1:10
every family in **h** and on earth Eph 3:15
their and your Master is in **h**, Eph 6:9
those who are in **h** and on earth Php 2:10
but our citizenship is in **h**, Php 3:20
the hope reserved for you in **h**. Col 1:5
was created, in **h** and on earth, Col 1:16
things on earth or things in **h**. Col 1:20
in all creation under **h**, Col 1:23
that you too have a Master in **h**. Col 4:1
and to wait for His Son from **h**, 1Th 1:10
descend from **h** with a shout, 1Th 4:16
Lord Jesus from **h** with His 2Th 1:7
one) but into **h** itself, that He Heb 9:24
as the stars of **h** and as Heb 11:12
names have been written in **h**, Heb 12:23
from Him who warns us from **h**. Heb 12:25
not only the earth but also **h**. Heb 12:26
either by **h** or by earth or with Jms 5:12
and unfading, kept in **h** for you, 1Pt 1:4
by the Holy Spirit sent from **h**. 1Pt 1:12
Now that He has gone into **h**, 1Pt 3:22
it came from **h** while we were 2Pt 1:18
down out of **h** from My God— Rv 3:12
and there in **h** was an open door. Rv 4:1
and there in **h** a throne was set. Rv 4:2
But no one in **h** or on earth or Rv 5:3
I heard every creature in **h**, Rv 5:13
the stars of **h** fell to the earth Rv 6:13
was silence in **h** for about half Rv 8:1
like a torch, fell from **h**. Rv 8:10
that had fallen from **h** to earth. Rv 9:1
mighty angel coming down from **h**, Rv 10:1
Then I heard a voice from **h**, Rv 10:4
land raised his right hand to **h**. Rv 10:5
who created **h** and what is in it, Rv 10:6
I heard from **h** spoke to me again Rv 10:8
voice from **h** saying to them, Rv 11:12
They went up to **h** in a cloud, Rv 11:12
and gave glory to the God of **h**. Rv 11:13
were loud voices in **h** saying: Rv 11:15
God's sanctuary in **h** was opened, Rv 11:19
A great sign appeared in **h**: Rv 12:1
Then another sign appeared in **h**: Rv 12:3
the stars in **h** and hurled them Rv 12:4
Then war broke out in **h**: Rv 12:7
place for them in **h** any longer. Rv 12:8
I heard a loud voice in **h** say: Rv 12:10
dwelling—those who dwell in **h**. Rv 13:6
come down from **h** to earth before Rv 13:13
a sound from **h** like the sound Rv 14:2

the Maker of **h** and earth, Rv 14:7
I heard a voice from **h** saying, Rv 14:13
came out of the sanctuary in **h**. Rv 14:17
and awe-inspiring sign in **h**: Rv 15:1
the God of **h** because of their Rv 16:11
fell from **h** on the people, Rv 16:21
authority coming down from **h**, Rv 18:1
I heard another voice from **h**: Rv 18:4
For her sins are piled up to **h**, Rv 18:5
over her, **h**, and you saints, Rv 18:20
voice of a vast multitude in **h**, Rv 19:1
Then I saw **h** opened, and there Rv 19:11
that were in **h** followed Him Rv 19:14
down from **h** with the key to Rv 20:1
came down from **h** and consumed Rv 20:9
Earth and **h** fled from His Rv 20:11
I saw a new **h** and a new earth Rv 21:1
for the first **h** and the first Rv 21:1
coming down out of **h** from God, Rv 21:2
coming down out of **h** from God, Rv 21:10

HEAVEN'S *(1)*

LORD with the dew of **h** bounty Dt 33:13

HEAVENLY *(41)*

the whole **h** host was standing 1Kg 22:19
the whole **h** host and served 2Kg 17:16
the whole **h** host and served 2Kg 21:3
to the whole **h** host in both 2Kg 21:5
Asherah, and the whole **h** host. 2Kg 23:4
and the whole **h** host. 2Kg 23:5
the whole **h** host was standing 2Ch 18:18
the whole **h** host and served 2Ch 33:3
to the whole **h** host in both 2Ch 33:5
and the **h** host worships You. Neh 9:6
the LORD—you **h** beings—give Ps 29:1
Who among the **h** beings is like Ps 89:6
Your praise before the **h** beings. Ps 138:1
All the **h** bodies will dissolve. Is 34:4
and the whole **h** host, which they Jr 8:2
to the whole **h** host and poured Jr 19:13
It grew as high as the **h** host, Dn 8:10
on the rooftops to the **h** host; Zph 1:5
as your **h** Father is perfect. Mt 5:48
your **h** Father will forgive you Mt 6:14
yet your **h** Father feeds them. Mt 6:26
and your **h** Father knows that you Mt 6:32
plant that My **h** Father didn't Mt 15:13
So My **h** Father will also do to Mt 18:35
a multitude of the **h** host with Lk 2:13
much more will the **h** Father give Lk 11:13
not disobedient to the **h** vision. Ac 26:19
There are **h** bodies and earthly 1Co 15:40
splendor of the **h** bodies is 1Co 15:40
like the **h** man, so are those who 1Co 15:48
man, so are those who are **h**. 1Co 15:48
bear the image of the **h** man. 1Co 15:49
by God's **h** call in Christ Php 3:14
me safely into His **h** kingdom. 2Tm 4:18
and companions in a **h** calling, Heb 3:1
who tasted the **h** gift, became Heb 6:4
copy and shadow of the **h** things, Heb 8:5
but the **h** things themselves ⌊to Heb 9:23
to a better land—a **h** one. Heb 11:16
living God (the **h** Jerusalem), to Heb 12:22
I looked, and the **h** sanctuary— Rv 15:5

HEAVENS *(147)*

God created the **h** and the earth. Gn 1:1
So the **h** and the earth and Gn 2:1
records of the **h** and the earth, Gn 2:4
God made the earth and the **h**. Gn 2:4
with blessings of the **h** above, Gn 49:25
of anything in the **h** above or on Ex 20:4
LORD made the **h** and the earth, Ex 20:11
LORD made the **h** and the earth, Ex 31:17
are large, fortified to the **h**. Dt 1:28
fire into the **h** and enveloped Dt 4:11
look to the **h** and see the sun Dt 4:19
one end of the **h** to the other: Dt 4:32
of anything in the **h** above or on Dt 5:8
large cities fortified to the **h**. Dt 9:1
The **h**, indeed the highest Dt 10:14
indeed the highest **h**, belong to Dt 10:14
as long as the **h** are above the Dt 11:21
Pay attention, **h**, and I will Dt 32:1
who rides the **h** to your aid on Dt 33:26
trembled, the **h** poured ⌊rain⌋, Jdg 5:4
The stars fought from the **h**; Jdg 5:20
thunder in the **h** against them. 1Sm 2:10
foundations of the **h** trembled; 2Sm 22:8
He parted the **h** and came down, 2Sm 22:10
You made the **h** and the earth. 2Kg 19:15
idols, but the LORD made the **h**. 1Ch 16:26
Let the **h** be glad and the earth 1Ch 16:31
everything in the **h** and on earth 1Ch 29:11
who made the **h** and the earth, 2Ch 2:12
our guilt is as high as the **h**. Ezr 9:6
You created the **h**, the highest Neh 9:6
the highest **h** with all their Neh 9:6
stretches out the **h** and treads Jb 9:8
⌊They are⌋ higher than the **h**— Jb 11:8
wake up until the **h** are no more; Jb 14:12
holy ones and the **h** are not pure Jb 15:15
The **h** will expose his iniquity, Jb 20:27
Isn't God as high as the **h**? Jb 22:12
establishes harmony in the **h**. Jb 25:2
By His breath the **h** gained their Jb 26:13
and sees everything under the **h**. Jb 28:24
Look at the **h** and see; Jb 35:5
have covered the **h** with Your Ps 8:1
I observe Your **h**, the work of Ps 8:3
He parted the **h** and came down, Ps 18:9
The **h** declare the glory of God, Ps 19:1
In the **h** He has pitched a tent Ps 19:4
one end of the **h** and circles to Ps 19:6
The **h** were made by the word of Ps 33:6
h proclaim His righteousness, Ps 50:6
God, be exalted above the **h**; Ps 57:5
love is as high as the **h**; Ps 57:10
God, be exalted above the **h**; Ps 57:11
rides in the ancient, highest **h**. Ps 68:33
Your faithfulness in the **h**." Ps 89:2
the **h** praise Your wonders— Ps 89:5
The **h** are Yours; the earth also Ps 89:11
idols, but the LORD made the **h**. Ps 96:5
Let the **h** be glad and the earth Ps 96:11
h proclaim His righteousness; Ps 97:6
and the **h** are the work of Your Ps 102:25
For as high as the **h** are above Ps 103:11
love is higher than the **h**; Ps 108:4
God, be exalted above the **h**; Ps 108:5
nations, His glory above the **h**. Ps 113:4
to look on the **h** and the earth? Ps 113:6
The **h** are the LORD's, but the Ps 115:16
He made the **h** skillfully. Ps 136:5
part Your **h** and come down. Ps 144:5
Praise the LORD from the **h**; Ps 148:1
Him, highest **h**, and you waters Ps 148:4
and you waters above the **h**. Ps 148:4
Praise Him in His mighty **h**. Ps 150:1
established the **h** by Pr 3:19
there when He established the **h**, Pr 8:27
Listen, **h**, and pay attention, Is 1:2
I will make the **h** tremble, Is 13:13
how you have fallen from the **h**! Is 14:12
I will ascend to the **h**; Is 14:13
its fill in the **h** it will then Is 34:5
You made the **h** and the earth. Is 37:16
marked off the **h** with the span Is 40:12
out the **h** like thin cloth Is 40:22
who created the **h** and stretched Is 42:5
Rejoice, **h**, for the LORD has Is 44:23
stretched out the **h** by Myself; Is 44:24
H, sprinkle from above, and let Is 45:8
hands that stretched out the **h**, Is 45:12
God is the Creator of the **h**. Is 45:18
My right hand spread out the **h**; Is 48:13
Shout for joy, you **h**! Is 49:13
I dress the **h** in black and make Is 50:3
Look up to the **h**, and look at Is 51:6
the **h** will vanish like smoke, Is 51:6
who stretched out the **h** and laid Is 51:13
order to plant the **h**, to found Is 51:16
would tear the **h** open ⌊and⌋ come Is 64:1
just as the new **h** and the new Is 66:22
Be horrified at this, **h**; Jr 2:12
looked⌋ to the **h**, and their Jr 4:23
be terrified by signs in the **h**, Jr 10:2
did not make the **h** and the earth Jr 10:11
earth and from under these **h**. Jr 10:11
and spread out the **h** by His Jr 10:12
waters in the **h** are in turmoil, Jr 10:13
I not fill the **h** and the earth?" Jr 23:24
If the **h** above can be measured Jr 31:37
made the **h** and earth by Your Jr 32:17
from the four corners of the **h**, Jr 49:36
and spread out the **h** by His Jr 51:15
waters in the **h** are in turmoil, Jr 51:16
ascend to the **h** and fortify her Jr 51:53
and destroy them under Your **h**. Lm 3:66
the **h** opened and I saw visions Ezk 1:1
will cover the **h** and darken Ezk 32:7
lights in the **h** over you, Ezk 32:8
wonders in the **h** and on the Dn 6:27
the bright expanse ⌊of the **h**⌋, Dn 12:3
wonders in the **h** and on the Jl 2:30
upper chambers in the **h** and lays Am 9:6
the God of the **h**, who made the Jnh 1:9
Selah His splendor covers the **h**, Hab 3:3
to shake the **h** and the earth, Hg 2:6
to shake the **h** and the earth. Hg 2:21
stretched out the **h**, laid the Zch 12:1
The **h** suddenly opened for Him, Mt 3:16
He saw the **h** being torn open and Mk 1:10
David who ascended into the **h**, Ac 2:34
see the **h** opened and the Son of Ac 7:56
with hands, eternal in the **h**. 2Co 5:1
spiritual blessing in the **h**, Eph 1:3
Him at His right hand in the **h**— Eph 1:20
and seated us with Him in the **h**, Eph 2:6
rulers and authorities in the **h**. Eph 3:10
ascended far above all the **h**, Eph 4:10
forces of evil in the **h**. Eph 6:12
and the **h** are the works of Your Heb 1:10
who has passed through the **h**— Heb 4:14
and exalted above the **h**. Heb 7:26
throne of the Majesty in the **h**, Heb 8:1
things in the **h** to be purified Heb 9:23
long ago the **h** and the earth 2Pt 3:5
word the present **h** and earth are 2Pt 3:7
that ⌊day⌋ the **h** will pass away 2Pt 3:10
of which the **h** will be on fire 2Pt 3:12
wait for new **h** and a new earth 2Pt 3:13
rejoice, O **h**, and you who dwell Rv 12:12

HEAVIER *(1)*

Impose **h** work on the men. Ex 5:9

HEAVILY *(4)*

preceded me had **h** burdened the Neh 5:15
Your wrath weighs **h** on me; Ps 88:7
and it weighs **h** on humanity: Ec 6:1
became full and **h** loaded in the Ezk 27:25

HEAVILY-ARMED *(1)*

with a large force of **h** people. Nm 20:20

HEAVY *(31)*

Moses' hands grew **h**, they took a Ex 17:12
the task is too **h** for you. Ex 18:18
your bag, one **h** and one light. Dt 25:13
and since he was old and **h**, 1Sm 4:18
God's hand was very **h** there. 1Sm 5:11
and inflicted **h** losses on them. 1Sm 23:5
hair⌋ got so **h** for him that he 2Sm 14:26
service and the **h** yoke he put on 1Kg 12:4
'Your father made our yoke **h**, 1Kg 12:10
burdened you with a **h** yoke, 1Kg 12:11
My father made your yoke **h**, 1Kg 12:14
next day Hazael took a **h** cloth, 2Kg 8:15
service and the **h** yoke he put on 2Ch 10:4
'Your father made our yoke **h**, 2Ch 10:10
burdened you with a **h** yoke, 2Ch 10:11
My father made your yoke **h**, 2Ch 10:14
and because of the **h** rain. Ezr 10:9
burden on the people was so **h**. Neh 5:18
His hand is **h** despite my Jb 23:2
and night Your hand was **h** on me; Ps 32:4
a burden too **h** for me to bear. Ps 38:4
A stone is **h** and sand, a burden, Pr 27:3
man's troubles are **h** on him. Ec 8:6
anger burning and **h** with smoke. Is 30:27
your yoke very **h** on the elderly. Is 47:6
and our sins are ⌊**h**⌋ on us, Ezk 33:10
make Jerusalem a **h** stone for all Zch 12:3
for him if a **h** millstone were Mt 18:6
tie up **h** loads that are hard Mt 23:4
for him if a **h** millstone were Mk 9:42
headed toward damage and **h** loss, Ac 27:10

HEBER *(10)*

sons were **H** and Malchiel. Gn 46:17
the Heberite clan from **H**; Nm 26:45
Now **H** the Kenite had moved away Jdg 4:11
Jael, the wife of **H** the Kenite, Jdg 4:17
and the family of **H** the Kenite. Jdg 4:17
women, the wife of **H** the Kenite; Jdg 5:24
father of Gedor, **H** the father of 1Ch 4:18
H, and Malchiel, who fathered 1Ch 7:31

H fathered Japhlet, Shomer, and 1Ch 7:32
Zebadiah, Meshullam, Hizki, **H**, 1Ch 8:17

HEBER'S *(1)*
H wife Jael took a tent peg, Jdg 4:21

HEBERITE *(1)*
the **H** clan from Heber; Nm 26:45

HEBRAIC *(1)*
against the **H** Jews that their Ac 6:1

HEBREW *(32)*
came and told Abram the **H**, Gn 14:13
brought a **H** man to us to make Gn 39:14
The **H** slave you brought to us Gn 39:17
Now a young **H**, a slave of the Gn 41:12
of Egypt said to the **H** midwives, Ex 1:15
you help the **H** women give birth Ex 1:16
The **H** midwives, however, feared Ex 1:17
The **H** women are not like the Ex 1:19
"This is one of the **H** boys." Ex 2:6
He saw an Egyptian beating a **H**, Ex 2:11
When you buy a **H** slave, he is to Ex 21:2
If your fellow **H**, a man or woman Dt 15:12
with us in **H** within earshot 2Kg 18:26
and called out loudly in **H**. 2Kg 18:28
out loudly in **H** to the people 2Ch 32:18
peoples but could not speak **H**. Neh 13:24
speak to us in **H** within earshot Is 36:11
and called out loudly in **H**: Is 36:13
male and female **H** slaves and no Jr 34:9
must free his **H** brother who sold Jr 34:14
He answered them, "I am a **H**. Jnh 1:9
Bethesda in **H**, which has five Jn 5:2
Pavement (but in **H** Gabbatha). Jn 19:13
which in **H** is called Golgotha. Jn 19:17
was written in **H**, Latin, and Jn 19:20
said to Him in **H**, "Rabbouni!" Jn 20:16
them in the **H** language: Ac 21:40
them in the **H** language, Ac 22:2
to me in the **H** language, Ac 26:14
Benjamin, a **H** born of Hebrews; Php 3:5
his name in **H** is Abaddon, and in Rv 9:11
the place called in **H** Armagedon. Rv 16:16

HEBREWS *(20)*
from the land of the **H**, Gn 40:15
Egyptians could not eat with **H**, Gn 43:32
son born to the **H** into the Nile, Ex 1:22
woman from the **H** to nurse the Ex 2:7
went out and saw two **H** fighting. Ex 2:13
the God of the **H**, has met with Ex 3:18
The God of the **H** has met with us Ex 5:3
the God of the **H**, has sent me to Ex 7:16
LORD, the God of the **H**, says: Ex 9:1
the LORD, the God of the **H** says: Ex 9:13
LORD, the God of the **H**, says: Ex 10:3
you'll serve the **H** just like 1Sm 4:9
land saying, "Let the **H** hear!" 1Sm 13:3
Some **H** even crossed the Jordan 1Sm 13:7
H will make swords or spears. 1Sm 13:19
H are coming out of the holes 1Sm 14:11
There were **H** from the area who 1Sm 14:21
"What are these **H** ⌊doing here⌋?" 1Sm 29:3
Are they **H**? So am I. Are they 2Co 11:22
of Benjamin, a Hebrew born of **H**; Php 3:5

HEBREWS' *(1)*
this loud shout in the **H** camp?" 1Sm 4:6

HEBRON *(69)*
(AKA KIRIATH-ARBA, MAMRE)
beside the oaks of Mamre at **H**, Gn 13:18
that is, **H**) in the land Gn 23:2
Mamre (that is, **H**) in the land Gn 23:19
that is, **H**), where Abraham Gn 35:27
sent him from the valley of **H**, Gn 37:14
Amram, Izhar, **H**, and Uzziel. Ex 6:18
Amram, Izhar, **H**, and Uzziel. Nm 3:19
through the Negev and came to **H**, Nm 13:22
H was built seven years before Nm 13:22
sent ⌊word⌋ to Hoham king of **H**, Jos 10:3
of Jerusalem, **H**, Jarmuth, Jos 10:5
of Jerusalem, **H**, Jarmuth, Jos 10:23
from Eglon to **H** and attacked it Jos 10:36
destroyed **H** and everyone in it. Jos 10:37
he had treated **H** and as he had Jos 10:39
hill country—**H**, Debir, Anab— Jos 11:21
Jerusalem one the king of **H** one Jos 12:10
gave him **H** as an inheritance. Jos 14:13
H has belonged to Caleb son of Jos 14:14
Kiriath-arba (that is, **H**; Jos 15:13
that is, **H**), and Zior—nine Jos 15:54
that is, **H**) in the hill country Jos 20:7
that is, **H**) with its surrounding Jos 21:11
H, the city of refuge for the Jos 21:13
Canaanites who were living in **H** Jdg 1:10
H was formerly named Jdg 1:10
Judah gave **H** to Caleb, just as Jdg 1:20
of the mountain overlooking **H**. Jdg 16:3
to those in **H**, and to ⌊those in⌋ 1Sm 30:31
"To **H**," the LORD replied. 2Sm 2:1
settled in the towns near **H**. 2Sm 2:3
was king in **H** over the house 2Sm 2:11
all night and reached **H** at dawn. 2Sm 2:32
Sons were born to David in **H**: 2Sm 3:2
These were born to David in **H**. 2Sm 3:5
and went to **H** to inform David 2Sm 3:19
and 20 men came to David at **H**, 2Sm 3:20
with David in **H** because David 2Sm 3:22
returned to **H**, Joab pulled him 2Sm 3:27
When they buried Abner in **H**, 2Sm 3:32
heard that Abner had died in **H**, 2Sm 4:1
head to David at **H** and said to 2Sm 4:8
their bodies⌋ by the pool in **H**, 2Sm 4:12
buried it in Abner's tomb in **H**. 2Sm 4:12
came to David at **H** and said, 2Sm 5:1
of Israel came to the king at **H**. 2Sm 5:3
with them at **H** in the LORD's 2Sm 5:3
In **H** he reigned over Judah seven 2Sm 5:5
he arrived from **H**, David took 2Sm 5:13
let me go to **H** to fulfill a vow 2Sm 15:7
I will worship the LORD in **H**." 2Sm 15:8
said to him. So he went to **H**. 2Sm 15:9
has become king in **H**!' " 2Sm 15:10
seven years in **H** and 33 years 1Kg 2:11
his second son, fathered **H**. 1Ch 2:42
sons who were born to him in **H**: 1Ch 3:1
sons were born to David in **H**, 1Ch 3:4
Amram, Izhar, **H**, and Uzziel. 1Ch 6:2
Amram, Izhar, **H** and Uzziel. 1Ch 6:18
They were given **H** in the land of 1Ch 6:55
H (a city of refuge), Libnah and 1Ch 6:57
together to David at **H** and said, 1Ch 11:1
of Israel came to the king at **H**. 1Ch 11:3
with them at **H** in the LORD's 1Ch 11:3
to David at **H** to turn Saul's 1Ch 12:23
came to **H** with wholehearted 1Ch 12:38
Amram, Izhar, **H**, and Uzziel— 1Ch 23:12
he reigned in **H** for seven years 1Ch 29:27
Zorah, Aijalon, and **H**, which are 2Ch 11:10

HEBRON'S *(4)*
H name used to be Kiriath-arba; Jos 14:15
H sons: Korah, Tappuah, Rekem, 1Ch 2:43
H sons: Jeriah was first, 1Ch 23:19
H sons: Jeriah ⌊the first⌋, 1Ch 24:23

HEBRONITE *(2)*
the Izharite clan, the **H** clan, Nm 3:27
clan, the **H** clan, the Mahlite Nm 26:58

HEBRONITES *(5)*
from the **H**, Eliel the leader and 1Ch 15:9
the Izharites, the **H**, and the 1Ch 26:23
From the **H**: Hashabiah and his 1Ch 26:30
From the **H**: Jerijah was the head 1Ch 26:31
Jerijah was the head of the **H**, 1Ch 26:31

HEDGE *(4)*
You placed a **h** around him, Jb 1:10
way is like a thorny **h**, Pr 15:19
will remove its **h**, and it will Is 5:5
is worse than a **h** of thorns. Mc 7:4

HEDGED *(1)*
path is hidden, whom God has **h** Jb 3:23

HEDGEHOG *(1)*
owl and the **h** will possess it, Is 34:11

HEEDED *(2)*
and his words are not **h**." Ec 9:16
of the wise are **h** more than the Ec 9:17

HEEDS *(1)*
but a person who **h** correction is Pr 15:5

HEEL *(6)*
and you will strike his **h**. Gn 3:15
grasping Esau's **h** with his hand. Gn 25:26
A trap catches ⌊him⌋ by the **h**; Jb 18:9
has lifted up his **h** against me. Ps 41:9
womb he grasped his brother's **h**, Hs 12:3
has raised his **h** against Me. Jn 13:18

HEELS *(4)*
the horses' **h** so that its rider Gn 49:17
but he will attack their **h**. Gn 49:19
set out at his **h** in the valley. Jdg 5:15
follow on your **h** there to Egypt, Jr 42:16

HEGAI *(3)*
⌊Put them⌋ under the care of **H**, Est 2:3
and placed under the care of **H**, Est 2:8
ask for anything except what **H**, Est 2:15

HEGAI'S *(1)*
fortress of Susa under **H** care. Est 2:8

HEIFER *(2)*
stream over the **h** whose neck has Dt 21:6
ashes of a **h** sprinkling those Heb 9:13

HEIGHT *(27)*
and the **h** seven and a half feet, Ex 27:18
first cherub's **h** was 15 feet and 1Kg 6:26
half feet was the **h** of the first 1Kg 7:16
was also the **h** of the second 1Kg 7:16
feet wide; its **h** was 30 feet; he 2Ch 3:4
Its **h** is to be 90 feet and its Ezr 6:3
together up to half its ⌊**h**⌋, Neh 4:6
At the **h** of his success distress Jb 20:22
your tomb on the **h** and cutting a Is 22:16
of people of every **h** in order to Ezk 13:18
in **h** with its branches turned Ezk 17:6
its **h** towered among the clouds. Ezk 19:11
for its **h** as well as its many Ezk 19:11
shady foliage, and of lofty **h**. Ezk 31:3
became greater in **h** than all the Ezk 31:5
became great in **h** and set its Ezk 31:10
grew proud on account of its **h**, Ezk 31:10
become great in **h** and set their Ezk 31:14
trees would reach them in **h**. Ezk 31:14
10 feet, and its **h** was the same. Ezk 40:5
the earth, and its **h** was great. Dn 4:10
his **h** was like the cedars, Am 2:9
cubit to his **h** by worrying? Mt 6:27
a cubit to his **h** by worrying? Lk 12:25
nor **h**, nor depth, nor any other Rm 8:39
h and depth ⌊of God's love⌋, Eph 3:18
length, width, and **h** are equal. Rv 21:16

HEIGHTENED *(1)*
Ophel, and he **h** it considerably 2Ch 33:14

HEIGHTENING *(1)*
broken-down wall and **h** the 2Ch 32:5

HEIGHTS *(35)*
of Moab, the lords of Arnon's **h**. Nm 21:28
ride on the **h** of the land and Dt 32:13
on the **h** of the battlefield. Jdg 5:18
of Israel lies slain on your **h**. 2Sm 1:19
Jonathan ⌊lies⌋ slain on your **h**. 2Sm 1:25
and sets me securely on the **h**. 2Sm 22:34
gone up to the **h** of the 2Kg 19:23
and my advocate is in the **h**! Jb 16:19
and sets me securely on the **h**. Ps 18:33
ascended to the **h**, taking away Ps 68:18
built His sanctuary like the **h**, Ps 78:69
He looked down from His holy **h** Ps 102:19
praise Him in the **h**. Ps 148:1
At the **h** overlooking the road, Pr 8:2
fool is appointed to great **h**, Ec 10:6
they are afraid of **h** and dangers Ec 12:5
of Sheol to the **h** of heaven." Is 7:11
he will dwell on the **h**; Is 33:16
gone up to the **h** of the Is 37:24
to its remotest **h**, its densest Is 37:24
open rivers on the barren **h**, Is 41:18
will be on all the barren **h**. Is 49:9
you ride over the **h** of the land, Is 58:14
Look to the barren **h** and see. Jr 3:2
sound is heard on the barren **h**, Jr 3:21
from the barren **h** in the Jr 4:11
up a dirge on the barren **h**, Jr 7:29
all the barren **h** in the Jr 12:12
on the barren **h** panting for air Jr 14:6
shout for joy on the **h** of Zion; Jr 31:12
The ancient **h** have become our Ezk 36:2
strides on the **h** of the earth. Am 4:13
the rock in your home on the **h**, Ob 3
to trample the **h** of the earth. Mc 1:3
me to walk on mountain **h**! Hab 3:19

HEINOUS *(1)*
h prostitution on the hills, Jr 13:27

HEIR *(13)*
and the **h** of my house is Gn 15:2
born in my house will be my **h**." Gn 15:3
This one will not be your **h**; Gn 15:4
your own body will be your **h**." Gn 15:4

We will destroy the **h**!' 2Sm 14:7
Is he without an **h**? Why then has Jr 49:1
themselves, 'This is the **h**. Mt 21:38
themselves, 'This is the **h**. Mk 12:7
and said, 'This is the **h**. Lk 20:14
as long as the **h** is a child, Gl 4:1
if a son, then an **h** through God. Gl 4:7
He has appointed **h** of all things Heb 1:2
world and became an **h** of the Heb 11:7

HEIRS *(11)*
There must be **h** for the Jdg 21:17
to annihilate all the royal **h**. 2Kg 11:1
all the royal **h** of the house of 2Ch 22:10
h to My mountains from Judah; Is 65:9
those who are of the law are **h**, Rm 4:14
children, also **h**—heirs of God Rm 8:17
h of God and co-heirs with Rm 8:17
h according to the promise. Gl 3:29
we may become **h** with the hope of Ti 3:7
clearly to the **h** of the promise, Heb 6:17
in faith and **h** of the kingdom Jms 2:5

HELAH *(1)*
and had two wives, **H** and Naarah. 1Ch 4:5

HELAH'S *(1)*
H sons: Zereth, Zohar, and 1Ch 4:7

HELAM *(2)*
they came to **H** with Shobach, 2Sm 10:16
the Jordan, and went to **H**. 2Sm 10:17

HELBAH *(1)*
Ahlab, Achzib, **H**, Aphik, or Jdg 1:31

HELBON *(1)*
in wine from **H** and white wool. Ezk 27:18

HELD *(40)*
and Abraham **h** a great feast on Gn 21:8
Esau **h** a grudge against Jacob Gn 27:41
While Moses **h** up his hand, Ex 17:11
you, and you will be **h** guilty. Dt 24:15
So Joshua **h** out his sword Jos 8:18
When he **h** out his hand, the men Jos 8:19
They **h** their torches in their Jdg 7:20
the grapes and **h** a celebration. Jdg 9:27
When she **h** it out, he shoveled Ru 3:15
David **h** a banquet for him and 2Sm 3:20
Then he **h** a feast for all his 1Kg 3:15
blossom. It **h** 11,000 gallons. 1Kg 7:26
h fast to the LORD and did not 2Kg 18:6
eighth day they **h** a sacred 2Ch 7:9
while the other half **h** spears, Neh 4:16
one hand and **h** a weapon with Neh 4:17
h a feast in the third year of Est 1:3
the king **h** a week-long banquet Est 1:5
The king **h** a great banquet for Est 2:18
I **h** on to him and would not let Sg 3:4
king could be **h** captive in your Sg 7:5
with heads **h** high and seductive Is 3:16
only He should be **h** in awe. Is 8:13
committed will be **h** against him. Ezk 18:22
I **h** back the rivers of the deep, Ezk 31:15
committed will be **h** against him. Ezk 33:16
King Belshazzar **h** a great feast Dn 5:1
So Herodias **h** a grudge against Mk 6:19
may be **h** responsible for Lk 11:50
will be **h** responsible. Lk 11:51
on hyssop and **h** it up to His Jn 19:29
possible for Him to be **h** by it. Ac 2:24
but instead they **h** everything in Ac 4:32
Paul appealed to be **h** for trial Ac 25:21
the ropes that **h** the rudders. Ac 27:40
since we have died to what **h** us, Rm 7:6
nourished and **h** together by its Col 2:19
those who were **h** in slavery all Heb 2:15
and earth are **h** in store for 2Pt 3:7
who had **h** the seven bowls filled Rv 21:9

HELDAI *(3)*
(AKA HELEB, HELED, HELEM)
month, was **H** the Netophathite, 1Ch 27:15
the exiles, from **H**, Tobijah, and Zch 6:10
temple as a memorial to **H**, Zch 6:14

HELEB *(1)*
(AKA HELDAI, HELED)
H son of Baanah the Netophahite, 2Sm 23:29

HELECH *(1)*
of Arvad and **H** were ⌊stationed Ezk 27:11

HELED *(1)*
(AKA HELEB, HELDAI)
H son of Baanah the Netophathite, 1Ch 11:30

HELEK *(2)*
the Helekite clan from **H**; Nm 26:30
of Abiezer, **H**, Asriel, Shechem Jos 17:2

HELEKITE *(1)*
the **H** clan from Helek; Nm 26:30

HELEM'S *(1)*
(AKA HELDAI)
brother **H** sons: Zophah, Imna, 1Ch 7:35

HELEPH *(1)*
went from **H** and from the oak Jos 19:33

HELEZ *(5)*
H the Paltite, Ira son of Ikkesh 2Sm 23:26
Azariah fathered **H**, and Helez 1Ch 2:39
Helez, and **H** fathered Eleasah. 1Ch 2:39
the Harorite, **H** the Pelonite, 1Ch 11:27
was **H** the Pelonite from the sons 1Ch 27:10

HELI *(1)*
the son of Joseph, ⌊son⌋ of **H**, Lk 3:23

HELKAI *(1)*
Adna of Harim, **H** of Meraioth, Neh 12:15

HELKATH *(2)*
(AKA HUKOK)
Their boundary included **H**, Jos 19:25
H with its pasturelands, and Jos 21:31

HELL *(10)*
whole body to be thrown into **h**. Mt 5:29
your whole body to go into **h**! Mt 5:30
destroy both soul and body in **h**. Mt 10:28
twice as fit for **h** as you are! Mt 23:15
you escape being condemned to **h**? Mt 23:33
to have two hands and go to **h**— Mk 9:43
two feet and be thrown into **h**— Mk 9:45
two eyes and be thrown into **h**, Mk 9:47
people⌋ into **h** after death. Lk 12:5
fire, and is set on fire by **h**. Jms 3:6

HELLENISTIC *(2)*
complaint by the **H** Jews against Ac 6:1
and debated with the **H** Jews, Ac 9:29

HELLENISTS *(1)*
and began speaking to the **H**, Ac 11:20

HELLFIRE *(2)*
will be subject to **h**. Mt 5:22
two eyes and be thrown into **h**! Mt 18:9

HELMET *(7)*
wore a bronze **h** and bronze scale 1Sm 17:5
put a bronze **h** on David's head 1Sm 17:38
is Mine, and Ephraim is My **h**; Ps 60:7
is Mine, and Ephraim is My **h**; Ps 108:8
a **h** of salvation on His head; Is 59:17
Take the **h** of salvation, and the Eph 6:17
and put on a **h** of the hope of 1Th 5:8

HELMETS *(5)*
shields, spears, **h**, armor, bows 2Ch 26:14
take your positions with **h** on! Jr 46:4
with shields, bucklers, and **h**. Ezk 23:24
They hung shields and **h** in you; Ezk 27:10
all of them with shields and **h**; Ezk 38:5

HELMSMEN *(3)*
you, Tyre; they were your **h**. Ezk 27:8
your sailors and **h**, those who Ezk 27:27
and all the **h** of the sea stand Ezk 27:29

HELON *(5)*
Eliab son of **H** from Zebulun; Nm 1:9
Zebulunites is Eliab son of **H**. Nm 2:7
On the third day Eliab son of **H**, Nm 7:24
the offering of Eliab son of **H**. Nm 7:29
and Eliab son of **H** was over the Nm 10:16

HELP *(187)*
a male child with the LORD's **h**." Gn 4:1
up, **h** the boy up, and sustain Gn 21:18
he heard me screaming for **h**, Gn 39:15
but when I screamed for **h**, Gn 39:18
When you **h** the Hebrew women Ex 1:16
their cry for **h** ascended to God Ex 2:23
cry for **h** has come to Me, Ex 3:9
I will **h** you speak and I will Ex 4:12
I will **h** both you and him ⌊to Ex 4:15
in and cried for **h** to Pharaoh: Ex 5:15
out to the LORD for **h** concerning Ex 8:12
and cried out to the LORD for **h**. Ex 14:10
helping it, you must **h** with it. Ex 23:5
They will **h** you bear the burden Nm 11:17
you must **h** him lift it up. Dt 22:4
and no one will **h** ⌊you⌋. Dt 28:29
enemies, and no one will **h** you. Dt 28:31
with no **h** from a foreign god. Dt 32:12
Let them rise up and **h** you; Dt 32:38
may You be a **h** against his foes Dt 33:7
ahead of your brothers and **h** Jos 1:14
Come up and **h** me. We will attack Jos 10:4
H us, for all the Amorite kings Jos 10:6
king of Gezer went to **h** Lachish, Jos 10:33
they did not come to **h** the LORD, Jdg 5:23
to **h** the LORD against the mighty Jdg 5:23
Perhaps the LORD will **h** us. 1Sm 14:6
he worked with God's **h** today." 1Sm 14:45
said, "then you will be my **h**. 2Sm 10:11
for you, I'll come to **h** you. 2Sm 10:11
afraid to ever **h** the Ammonites 2Sm 10:19
and said, "**H** me, my king!" 2Sm 14:4
and my cry for **h** ⌊reached⌋ His 2Sm 22:7
salvation; Your **h** exalts me. 2Sm 22:36
to him, "My lord the king, **h**!" 2Kg 6:26
If the LORD doesn't **h** you, 2Kg 6:27
where can I get **h** for you? 2Kg 6:27
There was no one to **h** Israel, 2Kg 14:26
They received **h** against these 1Ch 5:20
you have come in peace to **h** me, 1Ch 12:17
they did not **h** the Philistines 1Ch 12:19
day after day to **h** David until 1Ch 12:22
of purpose to **h** David. 1Ch 12:33
Joab said, "then you'll be my **h**. 1Ch 19:12
too strong for you, I'll **h** you. 1Ch 19:12
never willing to **h** the Ammonites 1Ch 19:19
of Israel to **h** his son Solomon: 1Ch 22:17
one besides You to **h** the mighty 2Ch 14:11
H us, LORD our God, for we 2Ch 14:11
Do you **h** the wicked and love 2Ch 19:2
the power to **h** or to make one 2Ch 25:8
force to **h** the king against 2Ch 26:13
asked the king of Assyria for **h**. 2Ch 28:16
of Assyria, it did not **h** him. 2Ch 28:21
to them so that they will **h** me." 2Ch 28:23
our God to **h** us and to fight 2Ch 32:8
lift a finger to **h** their Neh 3:5
Since I cannot **h** myself, ⌊the Jb 6:13
H me understand what I did wrong. Jb 6:24
may my cry for **h** find no resting Jb 16:18
I call for **h**, but there is no Jb 19:7
the mortally wounded cry for **h**, Jb 24:12
poor man who cried out for **h**, Jb 29:12
without anyone to **h** them. Jb 30:13
out to You for **h**, but You do not Jb 30:20
out to him for **h** because of his Jb 30:24
assembly and cried out for **h**. Jb 30:28
they shout for **h** from the arm of Jb 35:9
them, they do not cry for **h**. Jb 36:13
can you **h** God spread out the Jb 37:18
"There is no **h** for him in God." Ps 3:2
LORD has heard my plea for **h**; Ps 6:9
H, LORD, for no faithful one Ps 12:1
and I cried to my God for **h**. Ps 18:6
They cry for **h**, but there is no Ps 18:41
May He send you **h** from the Ps 20:2
near and there is no one to **h**. Ps 22:11
strength, come quickly to **h** me. Ps 22:19
when he cried to Him for **h**. Ps 22:24
have been my **h**; do not leave me Ps 27:9
when I cry to You for **h**, Ps 28:2
to You for **h**, and You healed Ps 30:2
when I cried to You for **h**. Ps 31:22
He is our **h** and shield. Ps 33:20
are open to their cry for **h**. Ps 34:15
Hurry to **h** me, Lord, my Savior. Ps 38:22
and listen to my cry for **h**; Ps 39:12
to me and heard my cry for **h**. Ps 40:1
deliver me; hurry to **h** me, LORD. Ps 40:13
You are my **h** and my deliverer; Ps 40:17
Rise up! **H** us! Redeem us because Ps 44:26
God will **h** her when the morning Ps 46:5
and do not ignore my plea for **h**. Ps 55:1
Awake to **h** me, and take notice. Ps 59:4
foe, for human **h** is worthless. Ps 60:11
You are my **h**; I will rejoice Ps 63:7
deliver me. Hurry to **h** me, LORD! Ps 70:1
You are my **h** and my deliverer; Ps 70:5
from me; my God, hurry to **h** me. Ps 71:12
among the people, **h** the poor, Ps 72:4

of our salvation, **h** us—for the Ps 79:9
But I call to You for **h**, LORD; Ps 88:13
I have granted **h** to a warrior; Ps 89:19
If the LORD had not been my **h**, Ps 94:17
my cry for **h** come before You. Ps 102:1
and there was no one to **h**. Ps 107:12
foe, for human **h** is worthless. Ps 108:12
H me, LORD my God; save me Ps 109:26
He is their **h** and shield. Ps 115:9
He is their **h** and shield. Ps 115:10
He is their **h** and shield. Ps 115:11
H me understand the meaning of Ps 119:27
H me understand Your instruction, Ps 119:34
H me stay on the path of Your Ps 119:35
persecute me with lies—**h** me! Ps 119:86
before dawn and cry out for **h**; Ps 119:147
May Your hand be ready to **h** me, Ps 119:173
may Your judgments **h** me. Ps 119:175
Where will my **h** come from? Ps 121:1
My **h** comes from the LORD, the Ps 121:2
h is in the name of the LORD, Ps 124:8
be attentive to my cry for **h**. Ps 130:2
Listen, LORD, to my cry for **h**. Ps 140:6
You; hurry to ⌊**h**⌋ me. Listen to Ps 141:1
their cry for **h** and saves them. Ps 145:19
is the one whose **h** is the God of Ps 146:5
until death. Let no one **h** him. Pr 28:17
Who will you run to for **h**? Is 10:3
plant, you will **h** them to grow, Is 17:11
morning you will **h** your seed to Is 17:11
and fled to for **h** to rescue ⌊us⌋ Is 20:6
because of a people who can't **h**. Is 30:5
of no benefit, they are no **h**; Is 30:5
to a people who will not **h** them. Is 30:6
Egypt's **h** is completely Is 30:7
to Egypt for **h** and who depend Is 31:1
they do not seek the LORD's **h**. Is 31:1
you; I will **h** you; I will hold Is 41:10
Do not fear, I will **h** you. Is 41:13
I will **h** you—the LORD's Is 41:14
birth; He will **h** you: Do not Is 44:2
and I will **h** you in the day of Is 49:8
The Lord GOD will **h** Me; Is 50:7
truth, the Lord GOD will **h** Me; Is 50:9
but there was no one to **h**, Is 63:5
not succeed even with their **h**. Jr 2:37
deceitful words that cannot **h**. Jr 7:8
siege; no one can **h** ⌊them⌋. All Jr 13:19
which has come out to **h** you, Jr 37:7
hand, she had no one to **h**. Lm 1:7
when I cry out and plead for **h**, Lm 3:8
for a nation that refused to **h**. Lm 4:17
Pharaoh will not **h** him with Ezk 17:17
came to **h** me after I had been Dn 10:13
I have come to **h** you understand Dn 10:14
with ⌊the **h** of⌋ a foreign god. Dn 11:39
his end with no one to **h** him. Dn 11:45
Israel; you have no **h** but Me. Hs 13:9
cried out for **h** in the belly of Jnh 2:2
must I call for **h** and You do not Hab 1:2
Him, and said, "Lord, **h** me!" Mt 15:25
or in prison, and not **h** You?" Mt 25:44
have compassion on us and **h** us." Mk 9:22
I do believe! **H** my unbelief." Mk 9:24
they would follow Him and **h** Him. Mk 15:41
other boat to come and **h** them; Lk 5:7
Will He delay ⌊to **h**⌋ them? Lk 18:7
The flesh doesn't **h** at all. Jn 6:63
temple complex, he asked for **h**. Ac 3:3
over to Macedonia and **h** us!" Ac 16:9
necessary to **h** the weak and to Ac 20:35
shouting, "Men of Israel, **h**! Ac 21:28
have obtained **h** that comes from Ac 26:22
also joins to **h** in our weakness, Rm 8:26
matter she may require your **h**. Rm 16:2
go on to Macedonia with your **h**, 2Co 1:16
to show our eagerness ⌊to **h**⌋. 2Co 8:19
prayers and **h** from the Spirit Php 1:19
to **h** these women who have Php 4:3
the discouraged, **h** the weak, be 1Th 5:14
widows, she should **h** them, and 1Tm 5:16
so that it can **h** those who are 1Tm 5:16
Diligently **h** Zenas the lawyer Ti 3:13
does not reach out to **h** angels, Heb 2:16
but to **h** Abraham's offspring. Heb 2:16
He is able to **h** those who are Heb 2:18
find grace to **h** us at the proper Heb 4:16

HELPED *(28)*
who had **h** him kill his brothers. Jdg 9:24
The LORD has **h** us to this point. 1Sm 7:12
warriors who **h** him in battle. 1Ch 12:1
They **h** David against the 1Ch 12:21
because God **h** the Levites who 1Ch 15:26
cried out and the LORD **h** him. 2Ch 18:31
they **h** destroy each other. 2Ch 20:23
God **h** him against the 2Ch 26:7
marvelously **h** until he became 2Ch 26:15
Levite brothers **h** them until the 2Ch 29:34
the city, and they **h** him. 2Ch 32:3
How you have **h** the powerless and Jb 26:2
heart trusts in Him, and I am **h**. Ps 28:7
You, LORD, have **h** and comforted Ps 86:17
make me fall, but the LORD **h** me. Ps 118:13
lives with integrity will be **h**, Pr 28:18
stumble and the **h** will fall; Is 31:3
You **h** me to see their deeds, Jr 11:18
they will be **h** by some, but many Dn 11:34
she had and was not **h** at all. Mk 5:26
He has **h** His servant Israel, Lk 1:54
donkey, they **h** Jesus get on it Lk 19:35
her his hand and **h** her stand up. Ac 9:41
But Peter **h** him up and said, Ac 10:26
he greatly **h** those who had Ac 18:27
the day of salvation, I **h** you. 2Co 6:2
saints' feet, **h** the afflicted, 1Tm 5:10
But the earth **h** the woman: Rv 12:16

HELPER *(11)*
will make a **h** who is like him." Gn 2:18
for the man no **h** was found who Gn 2:20
father was my **h** and delivered me Ex 18:4
You are a **h** of the fatherless. Ps 10:14
gracious to me; LORD, be my **h**." Ps 30:10
a **h** who is always found in times Ps 46:1
God is my **h**; the Lord is the Ps 54:4
and the afflicted who have no **h**. Ps 72:12
With the LORD for me as my **h**, Ps 118:7
h will stumble and the helped Is 31:3
The Lord is my **h**; I will not be Heb 13:6

HELPFUL *(3)*
but not everything is **h**. 1Co 6:12
but not everything is **h**. 1Co 10:23
it is not **h**, but I will move on 2Co 12:1

HELPING *(6)*
you want to refrain from **h** it, Ex 23:5
kings who were **h** him were 1Kg 20:16
of the kings of Aram are **h** them, 2Ch 28:23
of God were with them, **h** them. Ezr 5:2
gifts of healing, **h**, managing, 1Co 12:28
can join in **h** with prayer for 2Co 1:11

HELPLESS *(14)*
you lying ⌊**h**⌋ under its load Ex 23:5
him, tie him up, and make him **h**. Jdg 16:5
tie you up and make you **h**?" Jdg 16:6
she rendered him **h**, and his Jdg 16:19
are on the lookout for the **h**. Ps 10:8
the **h** fall because of his Ps 10:10
The **h** entrusts himself to You; Ps 10:14
on the poor and **h** and save the Ps 72:13
I was **h**, and He saved me. Ps 116:6
ruler over a **h** people is like Pr 28:15
Why are You like a **h** man, like a Jr 14:9
because they will be utterly **h** Jr 47:3
them, and his hands fall **h**. Jr 50:43
For while we were still **h**, Rm 5:6

HELPS *(8)*
God of your father who **h** you, Gn 49:25
and peace to him who **h** you, 1Ch 12:18
helps you, for your God **h** you. 1Ch 12:18
The LORD **h** and delivers them; Ps 37:40
The LORD **h** all who fall; Ps 145:14
foreigners and **h** the fatherless Ps 146:9
The LORD **h** the afflicted but Ps 147:6
Each one **h** the other, and says Is 41:6

HEM *(7)*
on its lower **h** and all around it Ex 28:33
around the lower **h** of the robe. Ex 28:34
yarn on the lower **h** of the robe. Ex 39:24
all around the **h** of the robe Ex 39:25
around the lower **h** of the robe. Ex 39:26
Saul grabbed the **h** of his robe, 1Sm 15:27
and **h** you in on every side. Lk 19:43

HEMAN *(15)*
(AKA HOMAM)
sons of Lotan were Hori and **H**. Gn 36:22
the Ezrahite, and **H**, Calcol, and 1Kg 4:31
Zimri, Ethan, **H**, Calcol, and 1Ch 2:6
H the singer, son of Joel, son 1Ch 6:33
Levites appointed **H** son of Joel; 1Ch 15:17
The singers **H**, Asaph, and Ethan 1Ch 15:19
With them were **H**, Jeduthun, and 1Ch 16:41
H and Jeduthun had with them 1Ch 16:42
sons of Asaph, **H**, and Jeduthun, 1Ch 25:1
From **H**: Heman's sons: Bukkiah, 1Ch 25:4
these sons of **H**, the king's seer 1Ch 25:5
God had given **H** fourteen sons 1Ch 25:5
and **H** were under the king's 1Ch 25:6
of Asaph, of **H**, of Jeduthun, 2Ch 5:12
of David, Asaph, **H**, and Jeduthun 2Ch 35:15

HEMAN'S *(2)*
H relative was Asaph, who stood 1Ch 6:39
From Heman: **H** sons: Bukkiah, 1Ch 25:4

HEMANITES *(1)*
Jehiel and Shimei from the **H**; 2Ch 29:14

HEMDAN *(1)*
(AKA HAMRAN)
H, Eshban, Ithran, and Cheran. Gn 36:26

HEMMING *(1)*
the crowds are **h** You in and Lk 8:45

HEN *(2)*
(See also HEN proper noun.)
as a **h** gathers her chicks under Mt 23:37
as a **h** gathers her chicks under Lk 13:34

HEN (proper noun) *(1)*
Jedaiah, and **H** son of Zephaniah. Zch 6:14

HENA *(3)*
of Sepharvaim, **H**, and Ivvah? 2Kg 18:34
of Sepharvaim, **H**, or Ivvah?'" 2Kg 19:13
of Sepharvaim, **H**, or Ivvah?'" Is 37:13

HENADAD *(4)*
and the sons of Judah and of **H**, Ezr 3:9
repairs ⌊under⌋ Binnui son of **H**, Neh 3:18
Binnui son of **H** made repairs to Neh 3:24
of the sons of **H**, Kadmiel, Neh 10:9

HENNA *(3)*
a cluster of **h** blossoms to me, Sg 1:14
choicest fruits, **h** with nard— Sg 4:13
the night among the **h** blossoms. Sg 7:11

HEPHER *(9)*
the Hepherite clan ⌊from⌋ **H**; Nm 26:32
son of **H** had no sons— Nm 26:33
⌊Zelophehad was the⌋ son of **H**, Nm 27:1
of Tappuah one the king of **H** one Jos 12:17
Asriel, Shechem, **H**, and Shemida. Jos 17:2
son of **H**, son of Gilead, Jos 17:3
Socoh and the whole land of **H** 1Kg 4:10
bore him Ahuzzam, **H**, Temeni, and 1Ch 4:6
H the Mecherathite, Ahijah the 1Ch 11:36

HEPHERITE *(1)*
the **H** clan ⌊from⌋ Hepher; Nm 26:32

HEPHZIBAH *(1)*
His mother's name was **H**. 2Kg 21:1

HER *(1611)*
(See pp. xi-xii.)

HERALD *(9)*
Zion, **h** of good news, go up on a Is 40:9
Jerusalem, **h** of good news, raise Is 40:9
and I gave a **h** of good news to Is 41:27
mountains are the feet of the **h**, Is 52:7
messenger, and **h** to meet herald, Jr 51:31
herald to meet **h**, to announce to Jr 51:31
h loudly proclaimed, "People of Dn 3:4
For this I was appointed a **h**, 1Tm 2:7
gospel⌋ I was appointed a **h**, 2Tm 1:11

HERB *(1)*
every kind of **h**, and you bypass Lk 11:42

HERBS *(3)*
unleavened bread and bitter **h**. Ex 12:8
unleavened bread and bitter **h**; Nm 9:11
field to gather **h** and found a 2Kg 4:39

HERD *(28)*
ran to the **h** and got a tender, Gn 18:7
one day, the whole **h** will die. Gn 33:13
from the **h** or the flock. Lv 1:2
is a burnt offering from the **h**, Lv 1:3
an animal⌋ from the **h**, Lv 3:1
offering from the **h** or flock, Lv 22:21
animal from the **h** or flock that Lv 22:23

an animal from the **h** or flock on Lv 22:28
an animal from the **h** or flock, Lv 27:26
animal from the **h** or flock, Lv 27:32
the LORD from the **h** or flock— Nm 15:3
firstborn of your **h** or flock; Dt 12:17
any of your **h** or flock He has Dt 12:21
firstborn of your **h** and flock, Dt 14:23
produced by your **h** and flock. Dt 15:19
animal from the **h** or flock in Dt 16:2
cream from the **h** and milk from Dt 32:14
and cheese from the **h** for David 2Sm 17:29
the **h** of bulls with the calves Ps 68:30
a bull from the **h** as a sin Ezk 43:19
man or beast, **h** or flock, is to Jnh 3:7
a large **h** of pigs was feeding. Mt 8:30
"send us into the **h** of pigs." Mt 8:31
suddenly the whole **h** rushed down Mt 8:32
Now a large **h** of pigs was there, Mk 5:11
and the **h** of about 2,000 rushed Mk 5:13
A large **h** of pigs was there, Lk 8:32
and the **h** rushed down the steep Lk 8:33

HERDING *(1)*
entire time we were **h** the sheep. 1Sm 25:16

HERDS *(43)*
and Abram acquired flocks and **h**, Gn 12:16
also had flocks, **h**, and tents. Gn 13:5
flocks of sheep, **h** of cattle, Gn 26:14
I have done for you and your **h**. Gn 30:29
your father's **h** and given them Gn 31:9
and he drove his **h** to go to the Gn 31:18
as separate **h** and said to them, Gn 32:16
some distance between the **h**." Gn 32:16
their **h**, their possessions, Gn 34:23
as well as his **h**, all his Gn 36:6
of their **h**, the land where Gn 36:7
the horses, the **h** of sheep, the Gn 47:17
herds of sheep, the **h** of cattle, Gn 47:17
donkeys, camels, **h**, and flocks. Ex 9:3
our flocks and **h** because we must Ex 10:9
and your **h** must stay behind. Ex 10:24
flocks and your **h** as you asked, Ex 12:32
of livestock, both flocks and **h**. Ex 12:38
flocks and **h** are not to graze Ex 34:3
If flocks and **h** were slaughtered Nm 11:22
if we or our **h** drink your water Nm 20:19
will be for their **h**, Nm 35:3
young of your **h**, and the newborn Dt 7:13
your **h** and flocks grow large, Dt 8:13
firstborn of your **h** and flocks. Dt 12:6
young of your **h** and the newborn Dt 28:4
young of your **h**, and the newborn Dt 28:18
oil, young of your **h**, or newborn Dt 28:51
he took flocks, **h**, donkeys, 1Sm 27:9
because their **h** had increased in 1Ch 5:9
in charge of the **h** that grazed 1Ch 27:29
charge of the **h** in the valleys. 1Ch 27:29
and he acquired **h** of sheep and 2Ch 32:29
firstborn of our **h** and flocks to Neh 10:36
and pay attention to your **h**, Pr 27:23
also owned many **h** of cattle and Ec 2:7
flocks and their **h**, their sons Jr 3:24
consume your flocks and your **h**. Jr 5:17
the young of the flocks and **h**. Jr 31:12
their massive **h** of cattle will Jr 49:32
flocks and **h** to seek the LORD Hs 5:6
The **h** of cattle wander in Jl 1:18
H will lie down in the middle of Zph 2:14

HERDSMAN *(1)*
rather, I was a **h**, and I took Am 7:14

HERDSMEN *(8)*
was the father of the nomadic **h**. Gn 4:20
between the **h** of Abram's Gn 13:7
livestock and the **h** of Lot's Gn 13:7
between your **h** and my herdsmen Gn 13:8
between your herdsmen and my **h**, Gn 13:8
the **h** of Gerar quarreled with Gn 26:20
with Isaac's **h** and said, Gn 26:20
the tents of the **h** and captured 2Ch 14:15

HERE *(360)*
(See pp. xi-xii.)

HERE'S *(3)*
(See pp. xi-xii.)

HEREBY *(4)*
said to Joab, "I **h** grant this 2Sm 14:21
of yours? I **h** declare: you 2Sm 19:29
I **h** issue a decree concerning Ezr 6:8
I **h** proclaim freedom for you"— Jr 34:17

HEREDITARY *(3)*
to give them **h** property among Nm 27:7
we will keep our **h** possession Nm 32:32
out of their **h** property for Nm 35:2

HERES *(1)*
the battle by the ascent of **H**. Jdg 8:13

HERESH *(1)*
Bakbakkar, **H**, Galal, and 1Ch 9:15

HERESIES *(1)*
secretly bring in destructive **h**, 2Pt 2:1

HERETH *(1)*
and went to the forest of **H**. 1Sm 22:5

HERITAGE *(10)*
You have given a **h** to those who Ps 61:5
He was enraged with His **h**. Ps 78:62
they afflict Your **h**. Ps 94:5
His people or abandon His **h**, Ps 94:14
nation, and boast about Your **h**. Ps 106:5
Your decrees as a **h** forever; Ps 119:111
are indeed a **h** from the LORD, Ps 127:3
This is the **h** of the LORD's Is 54:17
you enjoy the **h** of your father Is 58:14
servants, the tribes of Your **h**. Is 63:17

HERMAS *(1)*
Patrobas, **H**, and the brothers Rm 16:14

HERMES *(2)*
Zeus, and Paul, **H**, because he Ac 14:12
Phlegon, **H**, Patrobas, Hermas, Rm 16:14

HERMOGENES *(1)*
me, including Phygelus and **H**. 2Tm 1:15

HERMON *(13)*
(AKA BAAL-HERMON, SENIR, SION, SIRION)
Arnon Valley as far as Mount **H**, Dt 3:8
far as Mount Sion (that is, **H**) Dt 4:48
at the foot of **H** in the land of Jos 11:3
Lebanon at the foot of Mount **H**. Jos 11:17
the Arnon Valley to Mount **H**, Jos 12:1
ruled over Mount **H**, Salecah, all Jos 12:5
below Mount **H** to the entrance Jos 13:5
all Mount **H**, and all Bashan to Jos 13:11
that is, Senir or Mount **H**). 1Ch 5:23
of Jordan and the peaks of **H**, Ps 42:6
Tabor and **H** shout for joy at Ps 89:12
It is like the dew of **H** falling Ps 133:3
from the summit of Senir and **H**, Sg 4:8

HERO *(3)*
saw that their **h** was dead, 1Sm 17:51
Why brag about evil, you **h**! Ps 52:1
the **h** and warrior, the judge and Is 3:2

HEROD *(39)*
(See also AGRIPPA, ARCHELAUS, PHILIP.)
of Judea in the days of King **H**, Mt 2:1
When King **H** heard this, he was Mt 2:3
H secretly summoned the wise Mt 2:7
in a dream not to go back to **H**, Mt 2:12
For **H** is about to search for the Mt 2:13
Then **H**, when he saw that he had Mt 2:16
After **H** died, an angel of the Mt 2:19
Judea in place of his father **H**, Mt 2:22
that time **H** the tetrarch heard Mt 14:1
For **H** had arrested John, chained Mt 14:3
before them and pleased **H**. Mt 14:6
King **H** heard of this, because Mk 6:14
When **H** heard of it, he said, Mk 6:16
For **H** himself had given orders Mk 6:17
had been telling **H**, "It is not Mk 6:18
because **H** was in awe of John and Mk 6:20
H heard him he would be very Mk 6:20
when **H** gave a banquet for his Mk 6:21
she pleased **H** and his guests. Mk 6:22
Pharisees and the yeast of **H**." Mk 8:15
In the days of King **H** of Judea, Lk 1:5
H was tetrarch of Galilee, Lk 3:1
H the tetrarch, being rebuked Lk 3:19
all the evil things **H** had done, Lk 3:19
H the tetrarch heard about Lk 9:7
beheaded John," **H** said, "but who Lk 9:9
of here! **H** wants to kill You! Lk 13:31
sent Him to **H**, who was also in Lk 23:7
H was very glad to see Jesus; Lk 23:8
Then **H**, with his soldiers, Lk 23:11
very day **H** and Pilate became Lk 23:12
Neither has **H**, because he sent Lk 23:15
in this city both **H** and Pontius Ac 4:27
time King **H** cruelly attacked Ac 12:1
night before **H** was to bring him Ac 12:6
After **H** had searched and did not Ac 12:19
Then **H** went down from Judea to Ac 12:19
H delivered a public address to Ac 12:21
close friend of **H** the tetrarch, Ac 13:1

HEROD'S *(6)*
He stayed there until **H** death, Mt 2:15
But when **H** birthday celebration Mt 14:6
the wife of Chuza, **H** steward; Lk 8:3
He was under **H** jurisdiction, Lk 23:7
rescued me from **H** grasp and from Ac 12:11
be kept under guard in **H** palace. Ac 23:35

HERODIANS *(3)*
disciples to Him, with the **H**. Mt 22:16
plotting with the **H** against Him, Mk 3:6
and the **H** to Him to trap Mk 12:13

HERODIAS *(4)*
him in prison on account of **H**, Mt 14:3
him in prison on account of **H**, Mk 6:17
So **H** held a grudge against him Mk 6:19
being rebuked by him about **H**, Lk 3:19

HERODIAS' *(2)*
H daughter danced before them Mt 14:6
When **H** own daughter came in and Mk 6:22

HERODION *(1)*
Greet **H**, my fellow countryman. Rm 16:11

HEROES *(1)*
those who are **h** at drinking wine Is 5:22

HEROIC *(1)*
sword is against her **h** warriors, Jr 50:36

HERON *(2)*
various kinds of **h**, the hoopoe, Lv 11:19
various kinds of **h**, the hoopoe, Dt 14:18

HERS *(2)*
(See pp. xi-xii.)

HERSELF *(56)*
(See pp. xi-xii.)

HESHBON *(36)*
H and all its villages. Nm 21:25
H was the city of Sihon king of Nm 21:26
Come to **H**, let it be rebuilt; Nm 21:27
For fire came out of **H**, a flame Nm 21:28
H has been destroyed as far as Nm 21:30
the Amorites, who lived in **H**." Nm 21:34
Nimrah, **H**, Elealeh, Sebam, Nm 32:3
Reubenites rebuilt **H**, Elealeh, Nm 32:37
who lived in **H**, and Og king of Dt 1:4
Amorite, king of **H**, and his land Dt 2:24
to Sihon king of **H** from the Dt 2:26
Sihon king of **H** would not let us Dt 2:30
the Amorites, who lived in **H**.' Dt 3:2
we had done to Sihon king of **H**, Dt 3:6
He lived in **H**, and Moses and the Dt 4:46
Sihon king of **H** and Og king of Dt 29:7
Sihon king of **H** and Og king of Jos 9:10
king of the Amorites lived in **H**. Jos 12:2
the border of Sihon, king of **H**. Jos 12:5
who reigned in **H**, to the border Jos 13:10
with **H** and all its cities on the Jos 13:17
the Amorites, who reigned in **H**. Jos 13:21
from **H** to Ramath-mizpeh and Jos 13:26
the kingdom of Sihon king of **H**. Jos 13:27
H with its pasturelands, and Jos 21:39
king of the Amorites, king of **H**. Jdg 11:19
300 years in **H** and its villages Jdg 11:26
H and its pasturelands, and 1Ch 6:81
Sihon king of **H** and of the land Neh 9:22
eyes like pools in **H** by the gate Sg 7:4
H and Elealeh cry out; Is 15:4
I drench **H** and Elealeh with my Is 16:9
they plan harm against her in **H**: Jr 48:2
is a cry from **H** to Elealeh; Jr 48:34
has come out from **H** and a flame Jr 48:45
Wail, **H**, for Ai is devastated; Jr 49:3

HESHBON'S *(2)*
For **H** terraced vineyards and the Is 16:8
exhausted in **H** shadow because Jr 48:45

HESHMON *(1)*
Hazar-gaddah, **H**, Beth-pelet, Jos 15:27

HESITANT *(1)*
I am slow and **h** in speech." Ex 4:10

HESITATE *(4)*
He will not **h** to directly pay Dt 7:10
Don't **h** to go and invade and Jdg 18:9
How long will you **h** between two 1Kg 18:21
do not **h** to spit in my face. Jb 30:10

HESITATED *(1)*
But he **h**, so because of the Gn 19:16

HESITATING *(1)*
not **h** to keep Your commands. Ps 119:60

HETH *(1)*
Sidon, his firstborn, and **H**, 1Ch 1:13

HETHLON *(2)*
by way of **H** and Lebo-hamath Ezk 47:15
the road of **H**, to Lebo-hamath Ezk 48:1

HEWED *(2)*
the tomb that I **h** out for myself Gn 50:5
of it and even **h** out a winepress Is 5:2

HEWN *(1)*
that he had **h** out for himself 2Ch 16:14

HEZEKIAH *(126)*
(AKA HIZKIAH)
and his son **H** became king in his 2Kg 16:20
H son of Ahaz became king of 2Kg 18:1
H trusted in the LORD God of 2Kg 18:5
In the fourth year of King **H**, 2Kg 18:9
the sixth year of **H**, which was 2Kg 18:10
the fourteenth year of King **H**, 2Kg 18:13
So **H** king of Judah sent word to 2Kg 18:14
from King **H** of Judah 11 tons 2Kg 18:14
So **H** gave ⌊him⌋ all the silver 2Kg 18:15
that time **H** stripped ⌊the gold 2Kg 18:16
Lachish to King **H** at Jerusalem. 2Kg 18:17
Tell **H** this is what the great 2Kg 18:19
places and altars **H** has removed, 2Kg 18:22
'Don't let **H** deceive you; 2Kg 18:29
let **H** persuade you to trust 2Kg 18:30
Don't listen to **H**, for this is 2Kg 18:31
don't listen to **H** when he 2Kg 18:32
to **H** with their clothes torn 2Kg 18:37
King **H** heard ⌊their report⌋, 2Kg 19:1
to him, "This is what **H** says: 2Kg 19:3
of King **H** went to Isaiah, 2Kg 19:5
he again sent messengers to **H**, 2Kg 19:9
Say this to **H** king of Judah: 2Kg 19:10
H took the letter from the hand 2Kg 19:14
Then **H** prayed before the LORD: 2Kg 19:15
of Amoz sent ⌊a message⌋ to **H**: 2Kg 19:20
those days **H** became terminally 2Kg 20:1
Then **H** turned his face to the 2Kg 20:2
And **H** wept bitterly. 2Kg 20:3
back and tell **H**, the leader of 2Kg 20:5
H had asked Isaiah, "What is the 2Kg 20:8
Then **H** answered, "It's easy for 2Kg 20:10
and a gift to **H** since he heard 2Kg 20:12
he heard that **H** had been sick. 2Kg 20:12
H gave them a hearing and 2Kg 20:13
his realm that **H** did not show 2Kg 20:13
came to King **H** and asked him, 2Kg 20:14
H replied, "They came from a 2Kg 20:14
H answered, "They have seen 2Kg 20:15
Isaiah said to **H**, "Hear the word 2Kg 20:16
Then **H** said to Isaiah, "The word 2Kg 20:19
H rested with his fathers, 2Kg 20:21
that his father **H** had destroyed 2Kg 21:3
Ahaz, his son **H**, his son 1Ch 3:13
in the days of King **H** of Judah, 1Ch 4:41
and his son **H** became king in his 2Ch 28:27
H was 25 years old when he 2Ch 29:1
went inside to King **H** and said, 2Ch 29:18
King **H** got up early, gathered 2Ch 29:20
H stationed the Levites in the 2Ch 29:25
Then **H** ordered that the burnt 2Ch 29:27
Then King **H** and the officials 2Ch 29:30
H concluded, "Now you are 2Ch 29:31
Then **H** and all the people 2Ch 29:36
Then **H** sent ⌊word⌋ throughout 2Ch 30:1
But **H** had interceded for them, 2Ch 30:18
So the LORD heard **H** and healed 2Ch 30:20
H encouraged all the Levites 2Ch 30:22
for **H** king of Judah contributed 2Ch 30:24
H reestablished the divisions of 2Ch 31:2
When **H** and his officials came 2Ch 31:8
H asked the priests and Levites 2Ch 31:9
H told them to prepare chambers 2Ch 31:11
of King **H** and of Azariah 2Ch 31:13
H did this throughout all Judah. 2Ch 31:20
H saw that Sennacherib had come 2Ch 32:2
Then **H** strengthened his position 2Ch 32:5
on the words of King **H** of Judah. 2Ch 32:8
against King **H** of Judah and 2Ch 32:9
Isn't **H** misleading you to give 2Ch 32:11
Didn't **H** himself remove His high 2Ch 32:12
So now, don't let **H** deceive you, 2Ch 32:15
God and against His servant **H**. 2Ch 32:16
King **H** and the prophet Isaiah 2Ch 32:20
So the LORD saved **H** and the 2Ch 32:22
gifts to King **H** of Judah, 2Ch 32:23
In those days **H** became sick to 2Ch 32:24
H didn't respond according to 2Ch 32:25
Then **H** humbled himself for the 2Ch 32:26
H had abundant riches and glory, 2Ch 32:27
This same **H** blocked the outlet 2Ch 32:30
H succeeded in everything he did. 2Ch 32:30
H rested with his fathers and 2Ch 32:33
that his father **H** had torn down 2Ch 33:3
Ater's descendants: of **H** 98 Neh 7:21
Ater, **H**, Azzur, Neh 10:17
the men of **H**, king of Judah, Pr 25:1
Ahaz, and **H**, kings of Judah. Is 1:1
the fourteenth year of King **H**, Is 36:1
Lachish to King **H** at Jerusalem. Is 36:2
Rabshakeh said to them, "Tell **H**: Is 36:4
places and altars **H** has removed, Is 36:7
Don't let **H** deceive you, for he Is 36:14
let **H** persuade you to trust Is 36:15
Don't listen to **H**. For the king Is 36:16
⌊Beware⌋ that **H** does not mislead Is 36:18
came to **H** with their clothes Is 36:22
King **H** heard ⌊their report⌋, Is 37:1
They said to him, "**H** says: Is 37:3
he sent messengers to **H**, saying, Is 37:9
Say this to **H** king of Judah: Is 37:10
H took the letter from the Is 37:14
H prayed to the LORD: Is 37:15
of Amoz sent ⌊a message⌋ to **H**: Is 37:21
those days **H** became terminally Is 38:1
Then **H** turned his face to the Is 38:2
And **H** wept bitterly. Is 38:3
Go and tell **H** that this is what Is 38:5
A poem by **H** king of Judah after Is 38:9
And **H** had asked, "What is the Is 38:22
and a gift to **H** since he heard Is 39:1
H was pleased with them, and Is 39:2
his realm that **H** did not show Is 39:2
came to King **H** and asked him, Is 39:3
H replied, "They came to me Is 39:3
H answered, "They have seen Is 39:4
Isaiah said to **H**, "Hear the word Is 39:5
Then **H** said to Isaiah, "The word Is 39:8
because of Manasseh son of **H**, Jr 15:4
in the days of **H** king of Judah Jr 26:18
Did **H** king of Judah and all ⌊the Jr 26:19
Ahaz, and **H**, kings of Judah, Hs 1:1
Ahaz, and **H**, kings of Judah. Mc 1:1
Amariah, son of **H**, in the days Zph 1:1
fathered Ahaz, Ahaz fathered **H**, Mt 1:9
H fathered Manasseh, Manasseh Mt 1:10

HEZEKIAH'S *(6)*
rest of the events of **H** ⌊reign⌋, 2Kg 20:20
so **H** God will not deliver His 2Ch 32:17
come on them during **H** lifetime. 2Ch 32:26
the events of **H** ⌊reign⌋ and his 2Ch 32:32
Ater's descendants: **H** 98 Ezr 2:16
When King **H** servants came to Is 37:5

HEZION *(1)*
son of **H** king of Aram who 1Kg 15:18

HEZIR *(2)*
seventeenth to **H**, the eighteenth 1Ch 24:15
Magpiash, Meshullam, **H**, Neh 10:20

HEZRO *(2)*
H the Carmelite, Paarai the 2Sm 23:35
H the Carmelite, Naarai son of 1Ch 11:37

HEZRON *(17)*
Hanoch, Pallu, **H**, and Carmi. Gn 46:9
Perez's sons: **H** and Hamul. Gn 46:12
Hanoch and Pallu, **H** and Carmi. Ex 6:14
the Hezronite clan from **H**; Nm 26:6
the Hezronite clan from **H**; Nm 26:21
passed **H**, ascended to Addar, Jos 15:3
of Perez: Perez fathered **H**. Ru 4:18
H fathered Ram, who fathered Ru 4:19
Perez's sons: **H** and Hamul. 1Ch 2:5
Caleb son of **H** had children by 1Ch 2:18
H slept with the daughter of 1Ch 2:21
H had married her when he was 60 1Ch 2:21
H, Carmi, Hur, and Shobal. 1Ch 4:1
Hanoch, Pallu, **H**, and Carmi. 1Ch 5:3
fathered **H**, Hezron fathered Mt 1:3
Hezron, **H** fathered Aram, Mt 1:3
Ram, ⌊son⌋ of **H**, ⌊son⌋ of Perez Lk 3:33

HEZRON'S *(3)*
H sons, who were born to him: 1Ch 2:9
H death in Caleb-ephrathah, 1Ch 2:24
sons of Jerahmeel, **H** firstborn: 1Ch 2:25

HEZRONITE *(2)*
the **H** clan from Hezron; Nm 26:6
the **H** clan from Hezron; Nm 26:21

HID *(34)*
and they **h** themselves from the Gn 3:8
because I was naked, so I **h**." Gn 3:10
and Jacob **h** them under the oak Gn 35:4
she **h** him for three months. Ex 2:2
dead and **h** him in the sand. Ex 2:12
Moses **h** his face because he was Ex 3:6
because she **h** the men we sent. Jos 6:17
because she **h** the men Joshua had Jos 6:25
survived, because he **h** himself. Jdg 9:5
They **h** in caves, thickets, among 1Sm 13:6
place where you **h** on the day 1Sm 20:19
So David **h** in the field. 1Sm 20:24
the king **h** his face and cried 2Sm 19:4
took 100 prophets and **h** them, 1Kg 18:4
I **h** 100 of the prophets of the 1Kg 18:13
and went off and **h** them. 2Kg 7:8
picked ⌊things⌋ up, and **h** them. 2Kg 7:8
who were with him, **h** themselves. 1Ch 21:20
h Joash from Athaliah so that 2Ch 22:11
when You **h** Your face, I was Ps 30:7
They **h** their net for me without Ps 35:7
the net that he **h** ensnare him; Ps 35:8
He **h** me in the shadow of His Is 49:2
arrow; He **h** me in His quiver. Is 49:2
of anger I **h** My face from you Is 54:8
I was angry and **h**; but he went Is 57:17
So I went and **h** it by the Jr 13:5
I **h** My face from them and handed Ezk 39:23
and I **h** My face from them. Ezk 39:24
on them, and they ran and **h**. Dn 10:7
the ground, and **h** his master's Mt 25:18
and went off and **h** your talent Mt 25:25
then went away and **h** from them. Jn 12:36
and free person **h** in the caves Rv 6:15

HIDDAI *(1)*
(AKA HURAI)
H from the Wadis of Gaash, 2Sm 23:30

HIDDEN *(70)*
The **h** things belong to the LORD Dt 29:29
of the seas and the **h** treasures Dt 33:19
taken the two men and **h** them. Jos 2:4
up to the roof and **h** them among Jos 2:6
kings had fled and **h** themselves Jos 10:16
into the cave where they had **h**. Jos 10:27
he is, **h** among the supplies. 1Sm 10:22
a mountain pass **h** from view, 1Sm 25:20
and nothing is **h** from the king— 2Sm 18:13
and the LORD has **h** it from me. 2Kg 4:27
him,' but she has **h** her son." 2Kg 6:29
he was **h** from Athaliah and was 2Kg 11:2
why⌋ was I not **h** like a Jb 3:16
for it more than for **h** treasure, Jb 3:21
given⌋ to a man whose path is **h**, Jb 3:23
know that this was Your **h** plan: Jb 10:13
A rope lies **h** for him on the Jb 18:10
he may bring to light what is **h**. Jb 28:11
It is **h** from the eyes of every Jb 28:21
nothing is **h** from its heat. Ps 19:6
Cleanse me from my **h** faults. Ps 19:12
my sighing is not **h** from You. Ps 38:9
guilty acts are not **h** from You. Ps 69:5
bones were not **h** from You when I Ps 139:15
they have **h** a trap for me. Ps 142:3
search for it like **h** treasure, Pr 2:4
a prostitute, having a **h** agenda. Pr 7:10
including every **h** thing, whether Ec 12:14
and have **h** behind treachery. Is 28:15
of the perceptive will be **h**. Is 29:14
My way is **h** from the LORD, Is 40:27
h things that you have not known. Is 48:6
For You have **h** Your face from us Is 64:7
forgotten and **h** from My sight. Is 65:16

from the place where I had **h** it, Jr 13:7
guilt is not **h** from My sight. Jr 16:17
me and have **h** snares for my feet Jr 18:22
I have **h** My face from this city Jr 33:5
but the LORD had **h** them. Jr 36:26
for we have **h** treasure in the Jr 41:8
no secret is **h** from you! Ezk 28:3
reveals the deep and **h** things; Dn 2:22
control over the **h** treasures of Dn 11:43
and Israel is not **h** from Me. Hs 5:3
Compassion is **h** from My eyes. Hs 13:14
his **h** treasures searched out! Ob 6
This is where His power is **h**. Hab 3:4
situated on a hill cannot be **h**. Mt 5:14
and nothing **h** that won't be made Mt 10:26
because You have **h** these things Mt 11:25
and nothing **h** except to come to Mk 4:22
and nothing **h** that won't be made Lk 8:17
because You have **h** these things Lk 10:21
nothing **h** that won't be made Lk 12:2
This saying was **h** from them, Lk 18:34
I have kept it **h** away in a cloth Lk 19:20
but now it is **h** from your eyes. Lk 19:42
But Jesus was **h** and went out of Jn 8:59
we speak God's **h** wisdom in a 1Co 2:7
to light what is **h** in darkness 1Co 4:5
of the mystery **h** for ages in God Eph 3:9
the mystery **h** for ages and Col 1:26
of wisdom and knowledge are **h**. Col 2:3
your life is **h** with the Messiah Col 3:3
not ⌊obvious⌋ cannot remain **h**. 1Tm 5:25
No creature is **h** from Him, Heb 4:13
was **h** by his parents for three Heb 11:23
consist of⌋ the **h** person of the 1Pt 3:4
the victor some of the **h** manna. Rv 2:17
then God's **h** plan will be Rv 10:7

HIDE *(78)*

and I must **h** myself from Your Gn 4:14
Should I **h** from Abraham what I Gn 18:17
We cannot **h** from our lord that Gn 47:18
when she could no longer **h** him, Ex 2:3
bull's flesh, its **h**, and its Ex 29:14
the **h** of the bull and all its Lv 4:11
the **h** of the burnt offering he Lv 7:8
burned up the bull with its **h**, Lv 8:17
flesh and the **h** outside the camp Lv 9:11
outside the camp and their **h**, Lv 16:27
Its **h**, flesh, and blood, are to Nm 19:5
abandon them and **h** My face from Dt 31:17
will certainly **h** My face on that Dt 31:18
I will **h** My face from them; Dt 32:20
H yourselves there for three Jos 2:16
Don't **h** anything from me." Jos 7:19
wine vat in order to **h** it from Jdg 6:11
Go and **h** in the vineyards. Jdg 21:20
asked. "Don't **h** it from me. May 1Sm 3:17
severely if you **h** anything from 1Sm 3:17
and did not **h** anything from him. 1Sm 3:18
the morning and **h** in a secret 1Sm 19:2
So why would he **h** this matter 1Sm 20:2
I'll **h** in the field until the 1Sm 20:5
and **h** yourself at the Wadi 1Kg 17:3
see when you go to **h** yourself in 1Kg 22:25
left the camp to **h** in the open 2Kg 7:12
see when you go to **h** yourself in 2Ch 18:24
and **h** sorrow from my eyes. Jb 3:10
will not have to **h** from Your Jb 13:20
Why do You **h** Your face and Jb 13:24
If only You would **h** me in Sheol Jb 14:13
evildoers can **h** themselves. Jb 34:22
H them together in the dust; Jb 40:13
Can you fill his **h** with harpoons Jb 41:7
do You **h** in times of trouble? Ps 10:1
long will You **h** Your face from Ps 13:1
h me in the shadow of Your wings Ps 17:8
He did not **h** His face from him, Ps 22:24
He will **h** me under the cover of Ps 27:5
Do not **h** Your face from me; Ps 27:9
You **h** them in the protection of Ps 31:20
did not **h** Your righteousness in Ps 40:10
Why do You **h** Yourself and forget Ps 44:24
otherwise I could **h** from him. Ps 55:12
H me from the scheming of the Ps 64:2
Don't **h** Your face from Your Ps 69:17
We must not **h** them from their Ps 78:4
Why do You **h** Your face from me? Ps 88:14
Will You **h** Yourself forever? Ps 89:46
Do not **h** Your face from me in my Ps 102:2
When You **h** Your face, they are Ps 104:29
do not **h** Your commands from me. Ps 119:19
Surely the darkness will **h** me, Ps 139:11
proud **h** a trap with ropes for Ps 140:5
Don't **h** Your face from me, Ps 143:7
to power, people **h** themselves. Pr 28:12
power, people **h**, but when they Pr 28:28
into the rocks and **h** in the dust Is 2:10
dark as night. **H** the refugee; do Is 16:3
H for a little while until the Is 26:20
great lengths to **h** their plans Is 29:15
Teacher will not **h** Himself any Is 30:20
I did not **h** My face from scorn Is 50:6
sins have made Him **h** ⌊His⌋ face Is 59:2
River and **h** it in a rocky Jr 13:4
I commanded you to **h** there." Jr 13:6
Can a man **h** himself in secret Jr 23:24
and Jeremiah must **h** yourselves Jr 36:19
don't **h** anything from me." Jr 38:14
don't **h** anything from us and we Jr 38:25
He will try to **h** himself, but he Jr 49:10
proclaim, and **h** nothing. Jr 50:2
I will no longer **h** My face from Ezk 39:29
If they **h** themselves on the top Am 9:3
He will **h** His face from them at Mc 3:4
drunk; you will **h** yourself. You Nah 3:11
Fall on us and **h** us from the Rv 6:16

HIDES *(4)*

out all the places where he **h**. 1Sm 23:23
When He **h** ⌊His⌋ face, who can Jb 34:29
h His face and will never see. Ps 10:11
You are a God who **h** Himself, Is 45:15

HIDING *(22)*

and those **h** from you perish. Dt 7:20
are **h** in the cave at Makkedah. Jos 10:17
the Israelites made **h** places for Jdg 6:2
the holes where they've been **h**!" 1Sm 14:11
men who had been **h** in the hill 1Sm 14:22
David is **h** among us in the 1Sm 23:19
David is **h** on the hill of 1Sm 26:1
probably already **h** in one of the 2Sm 17:9
Joash was in **h** with Jehosheba in 2Kg 11:3
him (he was **h** in Samaria). 2Ch 22:9
he was **h** with them in God's 2Ch 22:12
of the land are forced into **h**. Jb 24:4
as others do by **h** my guilt in my Jb 31:33
h in the protection of marshy Jb 40:21
He made darkness His **h** place, Ps 18:11
You are my **h** place; You protect Ps 32:7
they talk about **h** traps and say, Ps 64:5
who is **h** His face from the house Is 8:17
water will flood your **h** place. Is 28:17
Who can enter our **h** places? Jr 21:13
waiting in ambush, a lion in **h**; Lm 3:10
out of their **h** places like Mc 7:17

HIEL *(1)*

H the Bethelite built Jericho. 1Kg 16:34

HIERAPOLIS *(1)*

in Laodicea, and for those in **H**. Col 4:13

HIGGAION *(1)*

work of their hands. **H**. Selah Ps 9:16

HIGH *(346)*

75 feet wide, and 45 feet **h**. Gn 6:15
all the **h** mountains under the Gn 7:19
he was a priest to God Most **H**. Gn 14:18
Abram is blessed by God Most **H**, Gn 14:19
to God Most **H** who has handed Gn 14:20
LORD, God Most **H**, Creator of Gn 14:22
27 inches wide, and 27 inches **h**. Ex 25:10
18 inches wide, and 27 inches **h**. Ex 25:23
must be four and a half feet **h**. Ex 27:1
it must be 36 inches **h**. Ex 30:2
27 inches wide, and 27 inches **h**. Ex 37:1
18 inches wide, and 27 inches **h**. Ex 37:10
was 36 inches **h**. Its horns were Ex 37:25
and was four and a half feet **h**. Ex 38:1
seven and a half feet **h**. Ex 38:18
to serve as ⌊**h**⌋ priest in place Lv 16:32
I will destroy your **h** places, Lv 26:30
set its value, whether **h** or low; Lv 27:12
its value, whether **h** or low. Lv 27:14
has knowledge from the Most **H**, Nm 24:16
and demolish all their **h** places. Nm 33:52
death of the **h** priest who was Nm 35:25
until the death of the **h** priest. Nm 35:28
death of the **h** priest may the Nm 35:28
the death of the ⌊**h**⌋ priest. Nm 35:32
were fortified with **h** walls, Dt 3:5
their gods—on the **h** mountains, Dt 12:2
gates until your **h** and fortified Dt 28:52
When the Most **H** gave the nations Dt 32:8
death of the **h** priest serving Jos 20:6
the people at the **h** place today. 1Sm 9:12
he goes to the **h** place to eat. 1Sm 9:13
them on his way to the **h** place. 1Sm 9:14
of me to the **h** place and eat 1Sm 9:19
down from the **h** place to the 1Sm 9:25
down from the **h** place 1Sm 10:5
and went to the **h** place. 1Sm 10:13
tamarisk tree at the **h** place. 1Sm 22:6
the Most **H** projected His voice. 2Sm 22:14
down from on **h** and took hold of 2Sm 22:17
of the man raised on **h**, 2Sm 23:1
sacrificing on the **h** places, 1Kg 3:2
burned incense on the **h** places. 1Kg 3:3
it was the most famous **h** place. 1Kg 3:4
30 feet wide, and 45 feet **h**. 1Kg 6:2
was⌋ seven and a half feet **h**. 1Kg 6:10
30 feet wide, and 30 feet **h**; 1Kg 6:20
cherubim 15 feet **h** out of olive 1Kg 6:23
and 45 feet **h** on four rows of 1Kg 7:2
each 27 feet **h** and 18 feet in 1Kg 7:15
like lilies, six feet ⌊**h**⌋. 1Kg 7:19
and a half feet **h** and 45 feet 1Kg 7:23
and four and a half feet **h**. 1Kg 7:27
nine inches **h** encircling it; 1Kg 7:35
Solomon built a **h** place for 1Kg 11:7
shrines on the **h** places and set 1Kg 12:31
priests for the **h** places he had 1Kg 12:32
priests of the **h** places who are 1Kg 13:2
the shrines of the **h** places in 1Kg 13:32
of people for the **h** places. 1Kg 13:33
became priests of the **h** places. 1Kg 13:33
built for themselves **h** places, 1Kg 14:23
poles on every **h** hill and under 1Kg 14:23
h places were not taken away; 1Kg 15:14
h places were not taken away; 1Kg 22:43
burned incense on the **h** places. 1Kg 22:43
Yet the **h** places were not taken 2Kg 12:3
burning incense on the **h** places. 2Kg 12:3
and the **h** priest would go 2Kg 12:10
h places were not taken away, 2Kg 14:4
burning incense on the **h** places. 2Kg 14:4
h places were not taken away; 2Kg 15:4
burning incense on the **h** places. 2Kg 15:4
h places were not taken away; 2Kg 15:35
burning incense on the **h** places. 2Kg 15:35
burned incense on the **h** places, 2Kg 16:4
They built **h** places in all their 2Kg 17:9
poles on every **h** hill and under 2Kg 17:10
on all the **h** places just like 2Kg 17:11
the shrines of the **h** places that 2Kg 17:29
in the shrines of the **h** places. 2Kg 17:32
He removed the **h** places and 2Kg 18:4
He the One whose **h** places and 2Kg 18:22
He rebuilt the **h** places that his 2Kg 21:3
to Hilkiah the **h** priest so that 2Kg 22:4
the **h** priest told Shaphan 2Kg 22:8
commanded Hilkiah the **h** priest 2Kg 23:4
burn incense at the **h** places in 2Kg 23:5
defiled the **h** places from Geba 2Kg 23:8
He tore down the **h** places of the 2Kg 23:8
The priests of the **h** places, 2Kg 23:9
defiled the **h** places that were 2Kg 23:13
at Bethel and the **h** place that 2Kg 23:15
Then he burned the **h** place, 2Kg 23:15
shrines of the **h** places that 2Kg 23:19
priests of the **h** places who were 2Kg 23:20
of bronze, stood five feet **h**. 2Kg 25:17
LORD at the **h** place in Gibeon 1Ch 16:39
were at the **h** place in Gibeon, 1Ch 21:29
him went to the **h** place that was 2Ch 1:3
from the **h** place that was 2Ch 1:13
two pillars, ⌊each⌋ 27 feet **h**. 2Ch 3:15
each was seven and half feet **h**. 2Ch 3:15
30 feet wide, and 15 feet **h**. 2Ch 4:1
It was seven and a half feet **h**, 2Ch 4:2
four and a half feet **h** and put 2Ch 6:13
own priests for the **h** places, 2Ch 11:15
pagan altars and the **h** places. 2Ch 14:3
He also removed the **h** places and 2Ch 14:5
The **h** places were not taken away 2Ch 15:17
again removed the **h** places and 2Ch 17:6
h places were not taken away; 2Ch 20:33
Jehoram also built **h** places in 2Ch 21:11

Jehoiada the **h** ⌊priest⌋ and said 2Ch 24:6
and the **h** priest's deputy 2Ch 24:11
burned incense on the **h** places, 2Ch 28:4
made **h** places in every city of 2Ch 28:25
tore down the **h** places and 2Ch 31:1
remove His **h** places and His 2Ch 32:12
He rebuilt the **h** places that his 2Ch 33:3
sacrificed at the **h** places, 2Ch 33:17
where he built **h** places and set 2Ch 33:19
and Jerusalem of the **h** places, 2Ch 34:3
went to Hilkiah the **h** priest, 2Ch 34:9
guilt is as **h** as the heavens. Ezr 9:6
Eliashib the **h** priest and his Neh 3:1
house of Eliashib the **h** priest. Neh 3:20
stood on a **h** wooden platform Neh 8:4
son of Eliashib the **h** priest, Neh 13:28
and given him a **h** position over Est 5:11
them build a gallows 75 feet **h**. Est 5:14
the lowly on **h**, and mourners are Jb 5:11
then you will hold your head **h**, Jb 11:15
Isn't God as **h** as the heavens? Jb 22:12
from the Almighty on **h**? Jb 31:2
gaze at the clouds **h** above you. Jb 35:5
command and make its nest on **h**? Jb 39:27
take Your seat on **h** over it. Ps 7:7
name of the LORD, the Most **H**. Ps 7:17
sing about Your name, Most **H**. Ps 9:2
the Most **H** projected His voice. Ps 18:13
down from on **h** and took hold of Ps 18:16
of the Most **H** he is not shaken Ps 21:7
He will set me **h** on a rock. Ps 27:5
my head will be **h** above my Ps 27:6
dwelling place of the Most **H**. Ps 46:4
the LORD Most **H** is awe-inspiring Ps 47:2
both low and **h**, rich and poor Ps 49:2
h, He summons heaven and earth Ps 50:4
and pay your vows to the Most **H**. Ps 50:14
I call to God Most **H**, to God who Ps 57:2
love is as **h** as the heavens; Ps 57:10
me to a rock that is **h** above me, Ps 61:2
him down from his **h** position. Ps 62:4
the Most **H** know everything?" Ps 73:11
hand of the Most **H** has changed." Ps 77:10
the desert against the Most **H**. Ps 78:17
rock, the Most **H** God, their Ps 78:35
tested the Most **H** God, Ps 78:56
Him with their **h** places and Ps 78:58
you are all sons of the Most **H**. Ps 82:6
are the Most **H** over all the Ps 83:18
The Most **H** Himself will Ps 87:5
Your right hand is lifted **h**. Ps 89:13
You have lifted **h** the right hand Ps 89:42
of the Most **H** dwells in the Ps 91:1
the Most **H**—your dwelling Ps 91:9
praise to Your name, Most **H**, Ps 92:1
the LORD on **h** is majestic. Ps 93:4
are the Most **H** over all the Ps 97:9
as **h** as the heavens are above Ps 103:11
The **h** mountains are for the wild Ps 104:18
the counsel of the Most **H**. Ps 107:11
God—the One enthroned on **h**, Ps 113:5
Reach down from on **h**; rescue me Ps 144:7
find favor and **h** regard in the Pr 3:4
one who builds a **h** threshold Pr 17:19
imagination it is like a **h** wall. Pr 18:11
the heaven is **h** and the earth is Pr 25:3
against all the **h** mountains, Is 2:14
against every **h** tower, against Is 2:15
with heads held **h** and seductive Is 3:16
seated on a **h** and lofty throne Is 6:1
cut down, the **h** ⌊trees⌋ felled. Is 10:33
make myself like the Most **H**." Is 14:14
temple to weep at its **h** places. Is 15:2
Moab appears on the **h** place, Is 16:12
a bulge in a **h** wall whose Is 30:13
will be on every **h** mountain and Is 30:25
is exalted, for He dwells on **h**; Is 33:5
He the One whose **h** places and Is 36:7
news, go up on a **h** mountain. Is 40:9
your bed on a **h** and lofty Is 57:7
For the **H** and Exalted One who Is 57:15
I live in a **h** and holy place, Is 57:15
to make your voice heard on **h**. Is 58:4
On every **h** hill and under every Jr 2:20
ascended every **h** hill and gone Jr 3:6
have built the **h** places of Jr 7:31
the green trees on the **h** hills— Jr 17:2
the sin of your **h** places within Jr 17:3
of glory on **h** from the beginning Jr 17:12
They have built **h** places to Baal Jr 19:5
The LORD roars from on **h**; Jr 25:30
have built the **h** places of Baal Jr 32:35
on the **h** place and burns Jr 48:35
her **h** gates consumed by fire. Jr 51:58
stood seven and a half feet **h**. Jr 52:22
fire from on **h** into my bones; Lm 1:13
in the presence of the Most **H**, Lm 3:35
from the mouth of the Most **H**? Lm 3:38
a human on the throne **h** above. Ezk 1:26
I will destroy your **h** places. Ezk 6:3
ruins and the **h** places will be Ezk 6:6
altars, on every **h** hill, on all Ezk 6:13
and made colorful **h** places for Ezk 16:16
plant ⌊it⌋ on a **h** towering Ezk 17:22
on Israel's **h** mountain so that Ezk 17:23
and they saw any **h** hill or leafy Ezk 20:28
What is this **h** place you are Ezk 20:29
And it is called **H** Place to this Ezk 20:29
mountain, Israel's **h** mountain"— Ezk 20:40
brought you onto the **h** seas, Ezk 27:26
the mountains and every **h** hill. Ezk 34:6
me down on a very **h** mountain. Ezk 40:2
inches wide, and 21 inches **h**. Ezk 40:42
rooms was 10 and a half feet **h**. Ezk 41:8
and a quarter feet **h** and three Ezk 41:22
their kings at their **h** places. Ezk 43:7
altar hearth is seven feet ⌊**h**⌋, Ezk 43:15
90 feet **h** and nine feet wide. Dn 3:1
you servants of the Most **H** God— Dn 3:26
the Most **H** God has done for Dn 4:2
that the Most **H** is ruler over Dn 4:17
of the Most **H** that has been Dn 4:24
that the Most **H** is ruler over Dn 4:25
that the Most **H** is ruler over Dn 4:32
I praised the Most **H** and honored Dn 4:34
the Most **H** God gave sovereignty, Dn 5:18
the Most **H** God is ruler over Dn 5:21
ones of the Most **H** will receive Dn 7:18
of the holy ones of the Most **H**, Dn 7:22
against the Most **H** and oppress Dn 7:25
the holy ones of the Most **H**. Dn 7:25
the holy ones of the Most **H**. Dn 7:27
It grew as **h** as the heavenly Dn 8:10
The **h** places of Aven, the sin of Hs 10:8
Though they call to Him on **h**, Hs 11:7
Isaac's **h** places will be Am 7:9
what is the **h** place of Judah? Mc 1:5
I come to bow before God on **h**? Mc 6:6
house to place his nest on **h**, Hab 2:9
its voice and lifts its waves **h**. Hab 3:10
and against the **h** corner towers. Zph 1:16
son of Jehozadak, the **h** priest: Hg 1:1
the **h** priest Joshua son of Hg 1:12
spirit of the **h** priest Joshua Hg 1:14
to the **h** priest Joshua son of Hg 2:2
son of Jehozadak, **h** priest. Hg 2:4
me Joshua the **h** priest standing Zch 3:1
Listen, Joshua the **h** priest, you Zch 3:8
son of Jehozadak, the **h** priest. Zch 6:11
Yahweh and had **h** regard for His Mal 3:16
took Him to a very **h** mountain Mt 4:8
and led them up on a **h** mountain Mt 17:1
and the men of **h** position Mt 20:25
in the palace of the **h** priest, Mt 26:3
He struck the **h** priest's slave Mt 26:51
away to Caiaphas the **h** priest, Mt 26:57
right to the **h** priest's Mt 26:58
The **h** priest then stood up and Mt 26:62
Then the **h** priest said to Him, Mt 26:63
Then the **h** priest tore his robes Mt 26:65
of Abiathar the **h** priest and ate Mk 2:26
Jesus, Son of the Most **H** God? Mk 5:7
and led them up on a **h** mountain Mk 9:2
and their men of **h** positions Mk 10:42
struck the **h** priest's slave, Mk 14:47
led Jesus away to the **h** priest, Mk 14:53
right into the **h** priest's Mk 14:54
the **h** priest stood up before Mk 14:60
Again the **h** priest questioned Mk 14:61
Then the **h** priest tore his robes Mk 14:63
one of the **h** priest's servants Mk 14:66
be called the Son of the Most **H**, Lk 1:32
of the Most **H** will overshadow Lk 1:35
called a prophet of the Most **H**, Lk 1:76
the Dawn from on **h** will visit us Lk 1:78
during the **h** priesthood of Annas Lk 3:2
was suffering from a **h** fever, Lk 4:38
you will be sons of the Most **H**. Lk 6:35
You Son of the Most **H** God? Lk 8:28
them struck the **h** priest's slave Lk 22:50
Him into the **h** priest's house. Lk 22:54
you are empowered from on **h**." Lk 24:49
Then a **h** wind arose, and the sea Jn 6:18
who was **h** priest that year, Jn 11:49
but being **h** priest that year he Jn 11:51
struck the **h** priest's slave, Jn 18:10
who was **h** priest that year. Jn 18:13
an acquaintance of the **h** priest; Jn 18:15
Jesus into the **h** priest's Jn 18:15
the one known to the **h** priest, Jn 18:16
The **h** priest questioned Jesus Jn 18:19
way you answer the **h** priest?" Jn 18:22
bound to Caiaphas the **h** priest. Jn 18:24
One of the **h** priest's slaves, Jn 18:26
with Annas the **h** priest, Ac 4:6
Then the **h** priest took action. Ac 5:17
When the **h** priest and those who Ac 5:21
and the **h** priest asked, Ac 5:27
this true?" the **h** priest asked. Ac 7:1
the Most **H** does not dwell in Ac 7:48
a eunuch and **h** official of Ac 8:27
the Lord, went to the **h** priest Ac 9:1
religious women of **h** standing Ac 13:50
the slaves of the Most **H** God, Ac 16:17
as both the **h** priest and the Ac 22:5
But the **h** priest Ananias ordered Ac 23:2
you dare revile God's **h** priest?" Ac 23:4
that it was the **h** priest. Ac 23:5
Ananias the **h** priest came down Ac 24:1
He ascended on **h**, He took Eph 4:8
right hand of the Majesty on **h**. Heb 1:3
and faithful **h** priest in service Heb 2:17
the apostle and **h** priest of our Heb 3:1
we have a great **h** priest who has Heb 4:14
we do not have a **h** priest who is Heb 4:15
every **h** priest taken from men Heb 5:1
Himself to become a **h** priest, Heb 5:5
declared by God a **h** priest "in Heb 5:10
has become a "**h** priest forever Heb 6:20
priest of the Most **H** God, who Heb 7:1
is the kind of **h** priest we need: Heb 7:26
every day, as **h** priests do— Heb 7:27
appoints as **h** priests men who Heb 7:28
we have this kind of **h** priest, Heb 8:1
For every **h** priest is appointed Heb 8:3
the **h** priest alone enters the Heb 9:7
h priest of the good things that Heb 9:11
as the **h** priest enters the Heb 9:25
have a great **h** priest over the Heb 10:21
holies by the **h** priest as a sin Heb 13:11
figs when shaken by a **h** wind; Rv 6:13
to a great and **h** mountain and Rv 21:10
⌊The city⌋ had a massive **h** wall, Rv 21:12

HIGH-MINDED *(1)*

and every **h** thing that is raised 2Co 10:5

HIGH-PRIESTLY *(1)*

all the members of the **h** family. Ac 4:6

HIGH-WALLED *(1)*

The **h** fortress will be brought Is 25:12

HIGHER *(13)*

surged even **h** on the earth, Gn 7:19
more numerous and **h** in rank than Nm 22:15
you will rise **h** and higher above Dt 28:43
rise higher and **h** above you, Dt 28:43
iniquities are **h** than ⌊our⌋ Ezr 9:6
and gave him a **h** position than Est 3:1
⌊They are⌋ **h** than the heavens— Jb 11:8
love is **h** than the heavens Ps 108:4
and **h** officials ⌊protect⌋ them. Ec 5:8
For as heaven is **h** than earth, Is 55:9
so My ways are **h** than your ways, Is 55:9
say to you, 'Friend, move up **h**.' Lk 14:10
So He became **h** in rank than the Heb 1:4

HIGHEST *(21)*

The priest who is **h** among his Lv 21:10
indeed the **h** heavens, belong to Dt 10:14
heaven, the **h** heaven, cannot 1Kg 8:27
heaven and the **h** heaven cannot 2Ch 2:6
heaven, the **h** heaven, cannot 2Ch 6:18
the **h** heavens with all their Neh 9:6
and occupied the **h** positions Est 1:14
And look at the **h** stars—how Jb 22:12
is like the **h** mountain; Ps 36:6

rides in the ancient, **h** heavens. Ps 68:33
Praise Him, **h** heavens, and you Ps 148:4
out from the **h** points of the Pr 9:3
on a seat at the **h** point of the Pr 9:14
will ascend above the **h** clouds; Is 14:14
lowest story to the **h** by means Ezk 41:7
and have the third **h** position in Dn 5:7
and have the third **h** position in Dn 5:16
Hosanna in the **h** heaven! Mt 21:9
Hosanna in the **h** heaven! Mk 11:10
Glory to God in the **h** heaven, Lk 2:14
and glory in the **h** heaven! Lk 19:38

HIGHLAND (1)

Lebanon ever leave the **h** crags? Jr 18:14

HIGHLANDS (1)

near the Pisgah **h** that overlook Nm 21:20

HIGHLIGHTS (1)

unrighteousness **h** God's Rm 3:5

HIGHLY (21)

the LORD, for He is **h** exalted; Ex 15:1
the LORD, for He is **h** exalted; Ex 15:21
in this city who is **h** respected; 1Sm 9:6
as handsome and **h** praised as 2Sm 14:25
sight and **h** regarded because 2Kg 5:1
LORD is great and is **h** praised; 1Ch 16:25
LORD **h** exalted Solomon in the 1Ch 29:25
was with him and **h** exalted him. 2Ch 1:1
and **h** popular with many of his Est 10:3
You think so **h** of him and pay so Jb 7:17
is great and is **h** praised in the Ps 48:1
LORD is great and is **h** praised; Ps 96:4
is great and is **h** praised; Ps 145:3
slave, who was **h** valued by him, Lk 7:2
For what is **h** admired by people Lk 16:15
but the people praised them **h**. Ac 5:13
and Iconium spoke **h** of him. Ac 16:2
of himself more **h** than he should Rm 12:3
Christ will be **h** honored in my Php 1:20
reason God also **h** exalted Him Php 2:9
them very **h** in love because 1Th 5:13

HIGHWAY (20)

We will travel the King's **H**; Nm 20:17
travel the King's **H** until we Nm 21:22
we will keep strictly to the **h**. Dt 2:27
east of the **h** that goes up from Jdg 21:19
They stayed on that one **h**, 1Sm 6:12
blood in the middle of the **h**, 2Sm 20:12
Amasa from the **h** to the field 2Sm 20:12
he was removed from the **h**, 2Sm 20:13
is by the **h** to the Fuller's 2Kg 18:17
Shallecheth on the ascending **h**. 1Ch 26:16
were four at the **h** and two at 1Ch 26:18
the path of the upright is a **h**. Pr 15:19
h of the upright avoids evil; Pr 16:17
will be a **h** for the remnant Is 11:16
there will be a **h** from Egypt to Is 19:23
make a straight **h** for our God in Is 40:3
Build it up, build up the **h**; Is 62:10
walk on ⌊new⌋ paths, not the **h**. Jr 18:15
Keep the **h** in mind, the way you Jr 31:21
by the **h** and look, resident Jr 48:19

HIGHWAYS (7)

about 30 men of Israel on the **h**, Jdg 20:31
away from the city to the **h**." Jdg 20:32
killed 5,000 men on the **h**. Jdg 20:45
The **h** are deserted; Is 33:8
and My **h** will be raised up. Is 49:11
them beside the **h** like a nomad Jr 3:2
'Go out into the **h** and lanes and Lk 14:23

HILEN (1)

H and its pasturelands, Debir 1Ch 6:58

HILKIAH (31)

Eliakim son of **H**, who was in 2Kg 18:18
Eliakim son of **H**, Shebnah, and 2Kg 18:26
Eliakim son of **H**, who was in 2Kg 18:37
Go up to **H** the high priest so 2Kg 22:4
H the high priest told Shaphan 2Kg 22:8
H the priest has given me a book, 2Kg 22:10
Then he commanded **H** the priest, 2Kg 22:12
So **H** the priest, Ahikam, Achbor, 2Kg 22:14
king commanded **H** the high priest 2Kg 23:4
the book that **H** the priest found 2Kg 23:24
Shallum fathered **H**; Hilkiah 1Ch 6:13
Hilkiah; **H** fathered Azariah 1Ch 6:13
son of Amaziah, son of **H**, 1Ch 6:45
Azariah son of **H**, son of 1Ch 9:11
H the second, Tebaliah the third, 1Ch 26:11
they went to **H** the high priest 2Ch 34:9
H the priest found the book of 2Ch 34:14
H told Shaphan the court 2Ch 34:15
"**H** the priest gave me a book," 2Ch 34:18
Then he commanded **H**, Ahikam 2Ch 34:20
So **H** and those the king had 2Ch 34:22
H, Zechariah, and Jehiel, 2Ch 35:8
Anaiah, Uriah, **H**, and Maaseiah Neh 8:4
Seraiah son of **H**, son of Neh 11:11
Sallu, Amok, **H**, Jedaiah. Neh 12:7
Hashabiah of **H**, and Nethanel of Neh 12:21
my servant, Eliakim son of **H**. Is 22:20
Eliakim son of **H**, who was in Is 36:3
Eliakim son of **H**, who was in Is 36:22
the son of **H**, one of the priests Jr 1:1
Gemariah son of **H** whom Zedekiah Jr 29:3

HILKIAH'S (1)

son, Azariah's son, **H** son, Ezr 7:1

HILL (153)

Sephar, the eastern **h** country. Gn 10:30
moved on to the **h** country east Gn 12:8
headed for the **h** country of Gn 31:21
his tent in the **h** country, Gn 31:25
tents⌋ in the **h** country of Gn 31:25
Hur went up to the top of the **h**. Ex 17:10
then go up into the **h** country. Nm 13:17
Amorites live in the **h** country; Nm 13:29
up the ridge of the **h** country, Nm 14:40
up the ridge of the **h** country, Nm 14:44
part of the⌋ **h** country came down Nm 14:45
So he went to a barren **h**. Nm 23:3
journey and go to the **h** country Dt 1:7
the Arabah, the **h** country, the Dt 1:7
saw on the way to the **h** country Dt 1:19
You have reached the **h** country Dt 1:20
up into the **h** country and came Dt 1:24
to go up into the **h** country. Dt 1:41
went up into the **h** country. Dt 1:43
around the **h** country of Seir for Dt 2:1
around this **h** country long Dt 2:3
given Esau the **h** country of Seir Dt 2:5
and the cities of the **h** country, Dt 2:37
and half the **h** country of Gilead Dt 3:12
that good **h** country and Lebanon. Dt 3:25
Go to the **h** country so that the Jos 2:16
men went into the **h** country and Jos 2:22
came down from the **h** country, Jos 2:23
of the Jordan in the **h** country, Jos 9:1
living in the **h** country have Jos 10:6
region—the **h** country, the Jos 10:40
of the north in the **h** country, Jos 11:2
and Jebusites in the **h** country, Jos 11:3
this land—the **h** country, all Jos 11:16
and the **h** country of Israel with Jos 11:16
the Anakim from the **h** country— Jos 11:21
all the **h** country of Judah and Jos 11:21
the **h** country, the Judean Jos 12:8
inhabitants of the **h** country Jos 13:6
on the **h** in the valley, Jos 13:19
give me this **h** country the LORD Jos 14:12
to the top of the **h** that faces Jos 15:8
the top of the **h** the border Jos 15:9
the **h** country: Shamir, Jattir, Jos 15:48
Jericho into the **h** country of Jos 16:1
Ephraim's **h** country is too Jos 17:15
The **h** country is not enough for Jos 17:16
because the **h** country will be Jos 17:18
through the **h** country westward, Jos 18:12
over the **h** south of Lower Jos 18:13
from the **h** facing Beth-horon on Jos 18:14
to the foot of the **h** that faces Jos 18:16
in the **h** country of Ephraim, Jos 19:50
Kedesh in the **h** country of Jos 20:7
Shechem in the **h** country of Jos 20:7
in the **h** country of Judah. Jos 20:7
in the **h** country of Judah. Jos 21:11
in the **h** country of Ephraim Jos 21:21
I gave the **h** country of Seir to Jos 24:4
the **h** country of Ephraim north Jos 24:30
Phinehas in the **h** country of Jos 24:33
were living in the **h** country, Jdg 1:9
possession of the **h** country, Jdg 1:19
into the **h** country and did Jdg 1:34
in the **h** country of Ephraim, Jdg 2:9
throughout the **h** country of Jdg 3:27
with him from the **h** country, Jdg 3:27
and Bethel in the **h** country of Jdg 4:5
them, below the **h** of Moreh, in Jdg 7:1
throughout the **h** country of Jdg 7:24
in Shamir in the **h** country of Jdg 10:1
in the **h** country of the Jdg 12:15
a man from the **h** country of Jdg 17:1
home in the **h** country of Ephraim Jdg 17:8
They came to the **h** country of Jdg 18:2
traveled to the **h** country of Jdg 18:13
part of the **h** country of Ephraim Jdg 19:1
He was from the **h** country of Jdg 19:16
to the remote **h** country of Jdg 19:18
in the **h** country of Ephraim. 1Sm 1:1
it to Abinadab's house on the **h**. 1Sm 7:1
went through the **h** country of 1Sm 9:4
were climbing the **h** to the city, 1Sm 9:11
will come to the **H** of God where 1Sm 10:5
and in Bethel's **h** country, 1Sm 13:2
hiding in the **h** country of 1Sm 14:22
were standing on one **h**, 1Sm 17:3
on another **h** with a ravine 1Sm 17:3
strongholds and in the **h** country 1Sm 23:14
in Horesh on the **h** of Hachilah 1Sm 23:19
is hiding on the **h** of Hachilah 1Sm 26:1
the road at the **h** of Hachilah 1Sm 26:3
gone as far as the **h** of Ammah, 2Sm 2:24
took their stand on top of a **h**. 2Sm 2:25
house, which was on the **h**. 2Sm 6:3
from Abinadab's house on the **h**. 2Sm 6:4
the ridge of the **h** opposite him. 2Sm 16:13
from the **h** country of Ephraim, 2Sm 20:21
them on the **h** in the presence 2Sm 21:9
in the **h** country of Ephraim; 1Kg 4:8
the Ammonites on the **h** across 1Kg 11:7
Shechem in the **h** country of 1Kg 12:25
on every high **h** and under every 1Kg 14:23
then he bought the **h** of Samaria 1Kg 16:24
silver, and he built up the **h**. 1Kg 16:24
name Shemer, the owner of the **h**. 1Kg 16:24
gods are gods of the **h** country. 1Kg 20:23
he was sitting on top of the **h**. 2Kg 1:9
to me from the **h** country of 2Kg 5:22
When Gehazi came to the **h**, 2Kg 5:24
on every high **h** and under every 2Kg 17:10
in the **h** country of Ephraim 1Ch 6:67
which is in the **h** country of 2Ch 13:4
captured in the **h** country of 2Ch 15:8
Beer-sheba to the **h** country of 2Ch 19:4
cities in the **h** country of Judah 2Ch 27:4
Go out to the **h** country and Neh 8:15
myrrh and the **h** of frankincense Sg 4:6
a vineyard on a very fertile **h**. Is 5:1
Zion, the **h** of Jerusalem. Is 10:32
mountaintop or a banner on a **h**. Is 30:17
and every raised **h** on the day of Is 30:25
on Mount Zion and on its **h**. Is 31:4
The **h** and the watchtower will Is 32:14
mountain and **h** will be leveled; Is 40:4
On every high **h** and under every Jr 2:20
every high **h** and gone under Jr 3:6
every mountain and **h** and out of Jr 16:16
from the **h** country and from the Jr 17:26
the temple mount a forested **h**.' Jr 26:18
call out in the **h** country of Jr 31:6
straight to the **h** of Gareb and Jr 31:39
the cities of the **h** country, Jr 32:44
in the cities of the **h** country, Jr 33:13
wandered from mountain to **h**; Jr 50:6
satisfied in the **h** country of Jr 50:19
altars, on every high **h**, on all Ezk 6:13
saw any high **h** or leafy tree, Ezk 20:28
the mountains and every high **h**. Ezk 34:6
the area around My **h** a blessing: Ezk 34:26
who are on the **h** of Samaria, Am 4:1
secure on the **h** of Samaria— Am 6:1
from the **h** country of Esau? Ob 8
from the **h** country of Esau Ob 9
possess the **h** country of Esau Ob 19
rule over the **h** country of Esau Ob 21
and the **h** of the temple mount Mc 3:12
fortified **h** of Daughter Zion, Mc 4:8
situated on a **h** cannot be hidden Mt 5:14
a town in the **h** country of Judah Lk 1:39
throughout the **h** country of Lk 1:65
mountain and **h** will be made low Lk 3:5
the edge of the **h** their town was Lk 4:29

HILLEL (1)

Elon, Abdon son of **H**, who was Jdg 12:13

HILLS *(57)*
and the bounty of the eternal **h**. Gn 49:26
and I watch them from the **h**. Nm 23:9
flowing in both valleys and **h**; Dt 8:7
and from whose **h** you will mine Dt 8:9
on the **h**, and under every Dt 12:2
and the bounty of the eternal **h**; Dt 33:15
scattered on the **h** like sheep 1Kg 22:17
places, on the **h**, and under 2Kg 16:4
scattered on the **h** like sheep 2Ch 18:16
high places in the **h** of Judah, 2Ch 21:11
in the **h** and in the fertile 2Ch 26:10
places, on the **h**, and under 2Ch 28:4
you brought forth before the **h**? Jb 15:7
h⌋ stand out like ⌊the folds Jb 38:14
The **h** yield food for him, while Jb 40:20
the cattle on a thousand **h**. Ps 50:10
and the **h** are robed with joy. Ps 65:12
and the **h**, righteousness. Ps 72:3
like rams, the **h**, like lambs. Ps 114:4
like rams? **H**, like lambs? Ps 114:6
causes grass to grow on the **h**. Ps 147:8
mountains and all **h**, fruit trees Ps 148:9
mountains and **h** were established Pr 8:25
the grain from the **h** is gathered Pr 27:25
mountains, bounding over the **h**. Sg 2:8
and will be raised above the **h**. Is 2:2
against all the lofty **h**, Is 2:14
go to all the **h** that were once Is 7:25
⌊Those **h**⌋ will be places for Is 7:25
chaff on the **h** and like dead Is 17:13
prey on the **h** and for the wild Is 18:6
a balance and the **h** in scales? Is 40:12
them⌋, and make **h** like chaff. Is 41:15
will lay waste mountains and **h**, Is 42:15
mountains move and the **h** shake, Is 54:10
mountains and the **h** will break Is 55:12
and reproached Me on the **h**, Is 65:7
falsehood comes from the **h**, Jr 3:23
were quaking; all the **h** shook. Jr 4:24
heinous prostitution on the **h**, Jr 13:27
the green trees on the high **h**— Jr 17:2
says to the mountains and the **h**, Ezk 6:3
the sword will fall on your **h**, Ezk 35:8
GOD says to the mountains and **h**, Ezk 36:4
and say to the mountains and **h**, Ezk 36:6
they burn offerings on the **h**, Hs 4:13
and to the **h**, "Fall on us!" Hs 10:8
and the **h** will flow with milk. Jl 3:18
all the **h** will flow ⌊with it⌋ Am 9:13
and will be raised above the **h**. Mc 4:1
and let the **h** hear your voice. Mc 6:1
before Him, and the **h** melt; Nah 1:5
the ancient **h** sink down. Hab 3:6
and a loud crashing from the **h**. Zph 1:10
Go up into the **h**, bring down Hg 1:8
drought on the fields and the **h**, Hg 1:11
and to the **h**, 'Cover us!' Lk 23:30

HILLSIDE *(3)*
99 on the **h** and go and search Mt 18:12
was there, feeding on the **h**. Mk 5:11
was there, feeding on the **h**. Lk 8:32

HILLTOP *(1)*
stand on the **h** with God's staff Ex 17:9

HIM *(5595)*
(See pp. xi-xii.)

HIMSELF *(416)*
(See pp. xi-xii.)

HINDER *(4)*
Do not let a mere mortal **h** You." 2Ch 14:11
of God⌋ and **h** meditation before Jb 15:4
how could I possibly **h** God?" Ac 11:17
so that we will not **h** the gospel 1Co 9:12

HINDERED *(4)*
walk, your steps will not be **h**; Pr 4:12
you **h** those who were going in. Lk 11:52
time and again—but Satan **h** us. 1Th 2:18
that your prayers will not be **h**. 1Pt 3:7

HINDERING *(1)*
h us from speaking to the 1Th 2:16

HINDQUARTERS *(2)*
them and all their **h** were toward 1Kg 7:25
them and all their **h** were toward 2Ch 4:4

HINDRANCE *(1)*
full boldness and without **h**. Ac 28:31

HINGE *(1)*
turns on its **h**, and a slacker, Pr 26:14

HINGES *(1)*
and the gold **h** for the doors of 1Kg 7:50

HINNOM *(13)*
the Valley of **H** to the southern Jos 15:8
the Valley of **H** on the west, Jos 15:8
the Valley of **H** at the northern Jos 18:16
the Valley of **H** toward the south Jos 18:16
which is in the Valley of **H**, 2Kg 23:10
the Valley of **H** and burned his 2Ch 28:3
the fire in the Valley of **H**. 2Ch 33:6
Beer-sheba to the Valley of **H**. Neh 11:30
the Valley of **H** in order to burn Jr 7:31
Topheth and the Valley of **H**, Jr 7:32
to the Valley of **H** near the Jr 19:2
Topheth and the Valley of **H**, Jr 19:6
in the Valley of **H** to make their Jr 32:35

HINT *(1)*
latched onto the **h** and said, 1Kg 20:33

HIP *(8)*
struck Jacob's **h** as they Gn 32:25
and dislocated his **h** socket. Gn 32:25
by Penuel—limping on his **h**. Gn 32:31
muscle that is at the **h** socket: Gn 32:32
struck Jacob's **h** socket at the Gn 32:32
will be carried on the **h**. Is 60:4
nurse and be carried on ⌊her⌋ **h**, Is 66:12
him that his **h** joints shook and Dn 5:6

HIPS *(3)*
their clothes in half at the **h**, 2Sm 10:4
their clothes in half at the **h**, 1Ch 19:4
and made all their **h** unsteady. Ezk 29:7

HIRAH *(2)*
near an Adullamite named **H**. Gn 38:1
and his friend **H** the Adullamite Gn 38:12

HIRAM *(26)*
(AKA HURAM, HURAM-ABI)
King **H** of Tyre sent envoys to 2Sm 5:11
H king of Tyre sent his servants 1Kg 5:1
for **H** had always been friends 1Kg 5:1
sent ⌊this message⌋ to **H**: 1Kg 5:2
When **H** heard Solomon's words, 1Kg 5:7
H sent ⌊a reply⌋ to Solomon, 1Kg 5:8
So **H** provided Solomon with all 1Kg 5:10
Solomon provided **H** with 100,000 1Kg 5:11
did this for **H** year after year. 1Kg 5:11
peace between **H** and Solomon, 1Kg 5:12
King Solomon had **H** brought from 1Kg 7:13
H had great skill, understanding, 1Kg 7:14
Then **H** made the basins, the 1Kg 7:40
So **H** finished all the work that 1Kg 7:40
utensils that **H** made for King 1Kg 7:45
H king of Tyre having supplied 1Kg 9:11
King Solomon gave **H** 20 towns in 1Kg 9:11
So **H** went out from Tyre to look 1Kg 9:12
Now **H** had sent the king 9,000 1Kg 9:14
With the fleet, **H** sent his 1Kg 9:27
King **H** of Tyre sent envoys to 1Ch 14:1
sent ⌊word⌋ to King **H** of Tyre: 2Ch 2:3
Then King **H** of Tyre wrote a 2Ch 2:11
H also said: May the LORD God of 2Ch 2:12
rebuilt the cities **H** gave him 2Ch 8:2
H sent him ships with crews of 2Ch 8:18

HIRAM'S *(5)*
builders and **H** builders, 1Kg 5:18
H fleet that carried gold from 1Kg 10:11
of Tarshish at sea with **H** fleet, 1Kg 10:22
H servants and Solomon's 2Ch 9:10
to Tarshish with **H** servants, 2Ch 9:21

HIRE *(5)*
who are full **h** themselves out 1Sm 2:5
38 tons of silver to **h** chariots 1Ch 19:6
they **h** a goldsmith and he makes Is 46:6
though they **h** ⌊lovers⌋ among Hs 8:10
the morning to **h** workers for his Mt 20:1

HIRED *(34)*
for I have **h** you with my son's Gn 30:16
resident or **h** hand may not eat Ex 12:45
The wages due a **h** hand must not Lv 19:13
a priest or a **h** hand is not to Lv 22:10
and the **h** hand or foreigner who Lv 25:6
with you as a **h** hand or Lv 25:40
the daily wages of a **h** hand. Lv 25:50
him like a man **h** year by year. Lv 25:53
twice the wages of a **h** hand. Dt 15:18
was **h** to curse you. Dt 23:4
not oppress a **h** hand who is poor Dt 24:14
Abimelech **h** worthless and Jdg 9:4
and that he had **h** him as his Jdg 18:4
they **h** 20,000 foot soldiers from 2Sm 10:6
has just **h** sheepshearers. 2Sm 13:24
of Israel must have **h** the kings 2Kg 7:6
They **h** 32,000 chariots and the 1Ch 19:7
of silver he **h** 100,000 brave 2Ch 25:6
Tobiah and Sanballat had **h** him. Neh 6:12
He was **h**, so that I would be Neh 6:13
they **h** Balaam against them to Neh 13:2
his days like those of a **h** hand? Jb 7:1
like a **h** man he waits for his Jb 7:2
can enjoy his day like a **h** hand. Jb 14:6
will use a razor **h** from beyond Is 7:20
as a **h** worker counts years, Is 16:14
as a **h** worker counts years, Is 21:16
Because no one **h** us,' they said Mt 20:7
who were **h** about five came, Mt 20:9
boat with the **h** men and followed Mk 1:20
of my father's **h** hands have more Lk 15:17
me like one of your **h** hands.' Lk 15:19
The **h** man, since he is not the Jn 10:12
he is a **h** man and doesn't Jn 10:13

HIRES *(2)*
The one who **h** a fool, or who Pr 26:10
or who **h** those passing by, Pr 26:10

HIRING *(1)*
were **h** masons and carpenters 2Ch 24:12

HIS *(7326)*
(See pp. xi-xii.)

HISS *(5)*
will be appalled and will **h**. 1Kg 9:8
Egypt will **h** like a slithering Jr 46:22
They **h** and shake their heads at Lm 2:15
They **h** and gnash ⌊their⌋ teeth, Lm 2:16
among the peoples **h** at you; Ezk 27:36

HISSING *(1)*
horror, and **h**, as you see with 2Ch 29:8

HISTORIAN *(6)*
son of Ahilud was court **h**; 2Sm 8:16
son of Ahilud was court **h**; 2Sm 20:24
Jehoshaphat son of Ahilud, **h**; 1Kg 4:3
Asaph, the court **h**, came out to 2Kg 18:18
Asaph, the court **h**, came to 2Kg 18:37
son of Ahilud was court **h**; 1Ch 18:15

HISTORIC *(1)*
share, right, or **h** claim in Neh 2:20

HISTORICAL *(36)*
in the **H** Record of Israel's 1Kg 14:19
about in the **H** Record of Judah's 1Kg 14:29
about in the **H** Record of Judah's 1Kg 15:7
about in the **H** Record of Judah's 1Kg 15:23
in the **H** Record of Israel's 1Kg 15:31
in the **H** Record of Israel's 1Kg 16:5
in the **H** Record of Israel's 1Kg 16:14
in the **H** Record of Israel's 1Kg 16:20
in the **H** Record of Israel's 1Kg 16:27
in the **H** Record of Israel's 1Kg 22:39
about in the **H** Record of Judah's 1Kg 22:45
in the **H** Record of Israel's 2Kg 1:18
in the **H** Record of Israel's 2Kg 8:23
in the **H** Record of Israel's 2Kg 10:34
about in the **H** Record of Judah's 2Kg 12:19
in the **H** Record of Israel's 2Kg 13:8
in the **H** Record of Israel's 2Kg 13:12
in the **H** Record of Israel's 2Kg 14:15
about in the **H** Record of Judah's 2Kg 14:18
in the **H** Record of Israel's 2Kg 14:28
about in the **H** Record of Judah's 2Kg 15:6
in the **H** Record of Israel's 2Kg 15:11
in the **H** Record of Israel's 2Kg 15:15
in the **H** Record of Israel's 2Kg 15:21
in the **H** Record of Israel's 2Kg 15:26
in the **H** Record of Israel's 2Kg 15:31
about in the **H** Record of Judah's 2Kg 15:36
about in the **H** Record of Judah's 2Kg 16:19
about in the **H** Record of Judah's 2Kg 20:20
about in the **H** Record of Judah's 2Kg 21:17
about in the **H** Record of Judah's 2Kg 21:25
about in the **H** Record of Judah's 2Kg 23:28
about in the **H** Record of Judah's 2Kg 24:5
entered in the **H** Record of King 1Ch 27:24
the Book of the **H** Records during Neh 12:23
The **h** record of Jesus Christ, Mt 1:1

HISTORY *(1)*
Throughout **h** no one has ever Jn 9:32

HIT *(14)*
when you **h** the rock, water will Ex 17:6
and **h** a pregnant woman so that Ex 21:22
the one who **h** her must be fined Ex 21:22
So Balaam **h** her to return her to Nm 22:23
it. So he **h** her once again. Nm 22:25
and **h** the Philistine on his 1Sm 17:49
so Abner **h** him in the stomach 2Sm 2:23
Chenaanah came up, **h** Micaiah in 1Kg 22:24
Chenaanah came up, **h** Micaiah in 2Ch 18:23
and commands it to **h** its mark. Jb 36:32
to us, Messiah! Who **h** You?" Mt 26:68
and they **h** him on the head and Mk 12:4
asking, "Prophesy! Who **h** You?" Lk 22:64
if rightly, why do you **h** Me?" Jn 18:23

HITCH *(1)*
H the cows to the cart, but take 1Sm 6:7

HITCHED *(2)*
Joseph **h** ⌊the horses to⌋ his Gn 46:29
two milk cows, **h** them to the 1Sm 6:10

HITS *(2)*
If anyone **h** you on the cheek, Lk 6:29
or if someone **h** you in the face. 2Co 11:20

HITTING *(2)*
and kept **h** Him on the head. Mt 27:30
They kept **h** Him on the head with Mk 15:19

HITTITE *(25)*
Ephron the **H** answered Abraham: Gn 23:10
of Ephron son of Zohar the **H**. Gn 25:9
Judith daughter of Beeri the **H**, Gn 26:34
Basemath daughter of Elon the **H**. Gn 26:34
life because of these **H** women. Gn 27:46
Jacob marries a **H** woman like one Gn 27:46
Adah daughter of Elon the **H**, Gn 36:2
in the field of Ephron the **H**. Gn 49:29
from Ephron the **H** as a burial Gn 49:30
a burial site from Ephron the **H**. Gn 50:13
destroy them—the **H**, Amorite, Dt 20:17
Ahimelech the **H** and Joab's 1Sm 26:6
Eliam and wife of Uriah the **H**." 2Sm 11:3
"Send me Uriah the **H**." 2Sm 11:6
Uriah the **H** also died. 2Sm 11:17
Uriah the **H** is dead also.' " 2Sm 11:21
Uriah the **H** is also dead." 2Sm 11:24
down Uriah the **H** with the sword 2Sm 12:9
of Uriah the **H** to be your own 2Sm 12:10
and Uriah the **H**. There were 37 2Sm 23:39
Edomite, Sidonian, and **H** women 1Kg 11:1
in the matter of Uriah the **H**. 1Kg 15:5
Uriah the **H**, Zabad son of Ahlai, 1Ch 11:41
an Amorite and your mother a **H**. Ezk 16:3
mother was a **H** and your father Ezk 16:45

HITTITES *(37)*
Sidon his firstborn, and the **H**, Gn 10:15
H, Perizzites, Rephaim, Gn 15:20
dead ⌊wife⌋ and spoke to the **H**: Gn 23:3
The **H** replied to Abraham, Gn 23:5
rose and bowed down to the **H**, Gn 23:7
Ephron was present with the **H**. Gn 23:10
presence of all the **H** who came Gn 23:10
to in the hearing of the **H**: Gn 23:16
presence of all the **H** who came Gn 23:18
passed from the **H** to Abraham as Gn 23:20
that Abraham bought from the **H**. Gn 25:10
it ⌊were purchased⌋ from the **H**." Gn 49:32
of the Canaanites, **H**, Amorites, Ex 3:8
of the Canaanites, **H**, Amorites, Ex 3:17
the Canaanites, **H**, Amorites, Ex 13:5
of⌋ the Amorites, **H**, Perizzites, Ex 23:23
Canaanites, and **H** away from you. Ex 23:28
Amorites, **H**, Perizzites, Hivites Ex 33:2
Canaanites, **H**, Perizzites, Ex 34:11
the **H**, Jebusites, and Amorites Nm 13:29
before you—the **H**, Girgashites, Dt 7:1
the land of the **H**—and west to Jos 1:4
you the Canaanites, **H**, Hivites, Jos 3:10
Lebanon—the **H**, Amorites, Jos 9:1
the Amorites, **H**, Perizzites, Jos 11:3
the Negev of the **H**, Amorites, Jos 12:8
Canaanites, **H**, Girgashites, Jos 24:11
man went to the land of the **H**, Jdg 1:26
the Canaanites, **H**, Amorites, Jdg 3:5
the land of the **H** and continued 2Sm 24:6
of the Amorites, **H**, Perizzites, 1Kg 9:20
kings of the **H** and to the kings 1Kg 10:29
the kings of the **H** and the kings 2Kg 7:6
kings of the **H** and to the kings 2Ch 1:17
peoples who remained of the **H**, 2Ch 8:7
the Canaanites, **H**, Perizzites, Ezr 9:1
of the Canaanites, **H**, Amorites, Neh 9:8

HIVITE *(3)*
When Shechem son of Hamor the **H**, Gn 34:2
granddaughter of Zibeon the **H**; Gn 36:2
Perizzite, **H**, and Jebusite—as Dt 20:17

HIVITES *(22)*
the **H**, the Arkites, the Sinites, Gn 10:17
Perizzites, **H**, and Jebusites. Ex 3:8
Perizzites, **H**, and Jebusites— Ex 3:17
Amorites, **H**, and Jebusites, Ex 13:5
Canaanites, **H**, and Jebusites, Ex 23:23
it will drive the **H**, Canaanites, Ex 23:28
Perizzites, **H**, and Jebusites. Ex 33:2
Perizzites, **H**, and Jebusites. Ex 34:11
Perizzites, **H** and Jebusites, Dt 7:1
Hittites, **H**, Perizzites, Jos 3:10
Perizzites, **H**, and Jebusites— Jos 9:1
men of Israel replied to the **H**, Jos 9:7
and the **H** at the foot of Hermon Jos 11:3
except the **H** who inhabited Jos 11:19
Perizzites, **H**, and Jebusites): Jos 12:8
Girgashites, **H**, and Jebusites— Jos 24:11
and the **H** who lived in the Jdg 3:3
Perizzites, **H**, and Jebusites. Jdg 3:5
cities of the **H** and Canaanites. 2Sm 24:7
Perizzites, **H**, and Jebusites, 1Kg 9:20
H, Arkites, Sinites, 1Ch 1:15
Perizzites, **H**, and Jebusites, 2Ch 8:7

HIZKI *(1)*
Zebadiah, Meshullam, **H**, Heber, 1Ch 8:17

HIZKIAH *(1)*
(AKA HEZEKIAH)
H, and Azrikam—three. 1Ch 3:23

HOARDS *(1)*
will curse anyone who **h** grain, Pr 11:26

HOBAB *(2)*
(AKA JETHRO, REUEL)
Moses said to **H**, son of Moses' Nm 10:29
Kenites, the sons of **H**, Moses' Jdg 4:11

HOBAH *(1)*
them as far as **H** to the north Gn 14:15

HOBAIAH *(1)*
of **H**, the descendants Neh 7:63

HOD *(1)*
Bezer, **H**, Shamma, Shilshah, 1Ch 7:37

HODAVIAH *(3)*
H, Eliashib, Pelaiah, Akkub, 1Ch 3:24
Jeremiah, **H**, and Jahdiel. 1Ch 5:24
son of **H**, son of Hassenuah 1Ch 9:7

HODAVIAH'S *(1)*
descendants from **H** descendants Ezr 2:40

HODESH *(1)*
His sons by his wife **H**: 1Ch 8:9

HODEVAH'S *(1)*
of Kadmiel **H** descendants 74 Neh 7:43

HODIAH *(5)*
Shabbethai, **H**, Maaseiah, Kelita Neh 8:7
Sherebiah, **H**, Shebaniah, Neh 9:5
Shebaniah, **H**, Kelita, Pelaiah, Neh 10:10
H, Bani, and Beninu. Neh 10:13
H, Hashum, Bezai, Neh 10:18

HODIAH'S *(1)*
The sons of **H** wife, the sister 1Ch 4:19

HOE *(1)*
that were once tilled with a **h**, Is 7:25

HOGLAH *(4)*
were Mahlah, Noah, **H**, Milcah, Nm 26:33
Mahlah, Noah, **H**, Milcah, and Nm 27:1
Mahlah, Tirzah, **H**, Milcah, and Nm 36:11
Mahlah, Noah, **H**, Milcah, and Jos 17:3

HOHAM *(1)*
sent ⌊word⌋ to **H** king of Hebron, Jos 10:3

HOISTED *(1)*
Then they **h** the foresail to the Ac 27:40

HOISTING *(1)*
After **h** it up, they used ropes Ac 27:17

HOLD *(132)*
You can **h** me personally Gn 43:9
that they may **h** a festival for Ex 5:1
because we must **h** the LORD's Ex 10:9
You are to **h** a sacred assembly Ex 12:16
You must not **h** back ⌊offerings Ex 22:29
I will **h** them accountable for Ex 32:34
day you are to **h** a sacred Lv 23:7
proclamation and **h** a sacred Lv 23:21
You are to **h** a sacred assembly Lv 23:27
day you are to **h** a sacred Lv 23:36
priest is to **h** the bitter water Nm 5:18
please don't **h** against us this Nm 12:11
day you are to **h** a sacred Nm 28:25
you are to **h** a sacred assembly Nm 28:26
You are to **h** a sacred assembly Nm 29:1
You are to **h** a sacred assembly Nm 29:7
You are to **h** a sacred assembly Nm 29:12
day you are to **h** a solemn Nm 29:35
So I took **h** of the tablets and Dt 9:17
are to **h** a seven-day festival Dt 16:15
will **h** accountable whoever does Dt 18:19
and do not **h** the shedding of Dt 21:8
must take **h** of him and bring Dt 21:19
takes **h** of her and rapes her, Dt 22:28
and My hand takes **h** of judgment, Dt 32:41
H out the sword in your hand Jos 8:18
LORD Himself **h** us accountable Jos 22:23
and take **h** of your captives, Jdg 5:12
took **h** of the doors of the city Jdg 16:3
Samson took **h** of the two middle Jdg 16:29
a knife, took **h** of his concubine Jdg 19:29
you're wearing and **h** it out." Ru 3:15
May the LORD **h** David's enemies 1Sm 20:16
Then David took **h** of his clothes 2Sm 1:11
the ark of God and took **h** of it, 2Sm 6:6
his hand, took **h** of him, and 2Sm 15:5
My lord, don't **h** me guilty, and 2Sm 19:19
from on high and took **h** of me; 2Sm 22:17
and went to take **h** of the horns 1Kg 1:50
and he has taken **h** of the horns 1Kg 1:51
and took **h** of the horns 1Kg 2:28
Ahijah took **h** of the new cloak 1Kg 11:30
large enough to **h** about four 1Kg 18:32
He took **h** of his own clothes and 2Kg 2:12
gourds as his garment would **h**. 2Kg 4:39
Uzzah reached out to **h** the ark, 1Ch 13:9
his **h** on his kingdom. 2Ch 1:1
It could **h** 11,000 gallons. 2Ch 4:5
people did not **h** a fire in his 2Ch 21:19
grabs it, but it does not **h** up. Jb 8:15
God does not **h** back His anger; Jb 9:13
then you will **h** your head high, Jb 11:15
and if I **h** back, what have I Jb 16:6
person will **h** to his way, Jb 17:9
The pillars ⌊that **h** up⌋ the sky Jb 26:11
which I **h** in reserve for times Jb 38:23
Can you **h** the wild ox by its Jb 39:10
of blessing⌋; You **h** my future. Ps 16:5
from on high and took **h** of me; Ps 18:16
with You; You **h** my right hand. Ps 73:23
Why do You **h** back Your hand? Ps 74:11
Do not **h** past sins against us; Ps 79:8
Your right hand will **h** on to me. Ps 139:10
and those who **h** on to her are Pr 3:18
Your heart must **h** on to my words Pr 4:4
H on to instruction; don't let Pr 4:13
righteous give and don't **h** back. Pr 21:26
and her hands **h** the spindle. Pr 31:19
tree and take **h** of its fruit." Sg 7:8
He will take **h** of you, Is 22:17
Or let it take **h** of My strength; Is 27:5
they cannot **h** the base of the Is 33:23
I will **h** on to you with My Is 41:10
h your right hand and say to you: Is 41:13
and I will **h** you by your hand. Is 42:6
the south: Do not **h** ⌊them⌋ back! Is 43:6
no one to take **h** of her hand Is 51:18
out; do not **h** back; lengthen Is 54:2
and **h** firmly to My covenant, Is 56:4
who **h** firmly to My covenant— Is 56:6
Cry out loudly, don't **h** back! Is 58:1
striving to take **h** of You. Is 64:7
cisterns that cannot **h** water. Jr 2:13
away? They take **h** of deceit; Jr 8:5
horror has taken **h** of me. Jr 8:21
there. Do not **h** back a word. Jr 26:2
all the people took **h** of him, Jr 26:8
All their captors **h** them fast; Jr 50:33
Yet I will **h** you responsible for Ezk 3:18

Yet I will **h** you responsible for Ezk 3:20
that I may take **h** of the house Ezk 14:5
oppress anyone, **h** collateral, or Ezk 18:16
but I will **h** the watchman Ezk 33:6
yet I will **h** you responsible for Ezk 33:8
another but will not **h** together, Dn 2:43
no one who can **h** back His hand Dn 4:35
He does not **h** on to His anger Mc 7:18
take **h** of the brick-mold! Nah 3:14
wouldn't take **h** of it and lift Mt 12:11
hand, caught **h** of him, and said Mt 14:31
they came up, took **h** of Jesus, Mt 26:50
came up, took **h** of His feet, Mt 28:9
Then they took **h** of Him and Mk 14:46
Him. They caught **h** of him, Mk 14:51
don't **h** back your shirt either. Lk 6:29
h on to it and by enduring, Lk 8:15
are going to **h** a somewhat more Ac 23:20
if you **h** to the message I 1Co 15:2
H firmly the message of life. Php 2:16
with all joy and **h** men like him Php 2:29
effort to take **h** of it because I Php 3:12
have been taken **h** of by Christ Php 3:12
myself to have taken **h** of it. Php 3:13
by Him all things **h** together. Col 1:17
He doesn't **h** on to the head, Col 2:19
test all things. **H** on to what is 1Th 5:21
stand firm and **h** to the 2Th 2:15
take **h** of eternal life, to which 1Tm 6:12
they may take **h** of life that is 1Tm 6:19
H on to the pattern of sound 2Tm 1:13
we are if we **h** on to the courage Heb 3:6
the Messiah if we **h** firmly until Heb 3:14
let us **h** fast to the confession. Heb 4:14
Let us **h** on to the confession of Heb 10:23
be shaken, let us **h** on to grace. Heb 12:28
h your faith in our glorious Jms 2:1
and I **h** the keys of death and Rv 1:18
some there who **h** to the teaching Rv 2:14
have those who **h** to the teaching Rv 2:15
who do not **h** this teaching, Rv 2:24
But **h** on to what you have until Rv 2:25
H on to what you have, so that Rv 3:11

HOLDERS *(7)*
to the frame as **h** for the poles Ex 25:27
of gold as the **h** for the Ex 26:29
of it to be **h** for the poles to Ex 30:4
their rings and **h** for the Ex 36:34
to the frame as **h** for the poles Ex 37:14
of it to be **h** for the poles to Ex 37:27
four rings as **h** for the poles. Ex 38:5

HOLDING *(22)*
If Joseph is **h** a grudge against Gn 50:15
let ⌊them⌋ go and keep **h** them, Ex 9:2
hand that was **h** the sword until Jos 8:26
usual, but Saul was **h** a spear, 1Sm 18:10
sitting in his palace **h** a spear. 1Sm 19:9
our clan is **h** a sacrifice 1Sm 20:29
basin **h** 220 gallons and each 1Kg 7:38
in their robes and **h** trumpets, Ezr 3:10
Asaph, **h** cymbals, took their Ezr 3:10
of the men were **h** spears from Neh 4:21
I am tired of **h** it back. Jr 6:11
I become tired of **h** it in, Jr 20:9
dry measure ⌊**h**⌋ half a bushel. Ezk 45:11
The men who were **h** Jesus started Lk 22:63
While he was **h** on to Peter and Ac 3:11
the ropes **h** the skiff and let Ac 27:32
h the mystery of the faith with 1Tm 3:9
h to the form of religion but 2Tm 3:5
h to the faithful message as Ti 1:9
destroy the one **h** the power of Heb 2:14
Son of God and **h** Him up to Heb 6:6
And you are **h** on to My name and Rv 2:13

HOLDINGS *(1)*
Their **h** and settlements were 1Ch 7:28

HOLDS *(10)*
one who is at ease **h** calamity in Jb 12:5
because the LORD **h** his hand. Ps 37:24
Your right hand **h** on to me. Ps 63:8
but He **h** up fools to dishonor. Pr 3:35
but a wise man **h** it in check. Pr 29:11
and scorn, for it **h** ⌊so⌋ much. Ezk 23:32
the God who **h** your life-breath Dn 5:23
since it **h** promise for the 1Tm 4:8
He **h** His priesthood permanently. Heb 7:24
The One who **h** the seven stars in Rv 2:1

HOLE *(6)*
a **h** with it and cover up your Dt 23:13
a chest, bored a **h** in its lid, 2Kg 12:9
but fell into the **h** he had made. Ps 7:15
there was a **h** in the wall. Ezk 8:7
into a bag with a **h** in it." Hg 1:6
went off, dug a **h** in the ground, Mt 25:18

HOLES *(7)*
rocks, and in **h** and cisterns. 1Sm 13:6
out of the **h** where they've 1Sm 14:11
rocks and in **h** in the ground. Jb 30:6
the rocks and **h** in the ground, Is 2:19
and in all the water **h**. Is 7:19
them trapped in **h** or imprisoned Is 42:22
caves, and **h** in the ground. Heb 11:38

HOLIDAY *(3)*
There was a celebration and a **h**. Est 8:17
is a **h** when they send gifts to Est 9:19
and their mourning into a **h**. Est 9:22

HOLIES *(4)*
was called "the holy of **h**." Heb 9:3
the holy of **h** had not yet been Heb 9:8
the holy of **h** once for all, Heb 9:12
into the holy of **h** by the high Heb 13:11

HOLIEST *(4)*
the **h** part of the fire offerings Lv 2:3
the **h** part of the fire offerings Lv 2:10
for it is the **h** portion for him Lv 24:9
portion of the **h** offerings ⌊kept Nm 18:9

HOLINESS *(28)*
You, glorious in **h**, revered with Ex 15:11
will show My **h** to those who are Lv 10:3
Me to show My **h** in the sight Nm 20:12
and He showed His **h** to them. Nm 20:13
to show My **h** in their sight at Nm 27:14
LORD in the splendor of ⌊His⌋ **h**; 1Ch 16:29
praise the splendor of ⌊His⌋ **h**. 2Ch 20:21
LORD in the splendor of ⌊His⌋ **h**. Ps 29:2
house, the **h** of Your temple. Ps 65:4
I have sworn an oath by My **h**; Ps 89:35
h is the beauty of Your house Ps 93:5
LORD in the splendor of ⌊His⌋ **h**; Ps 96:9
will demonstrate My **h** through Ezk 20:41
demonstrate My **h** through her. Ezk 28:22
demonstrate My **h** through them Ezk 28:25
will honor the **h** of My great Ezk 36:23
demonstrate My **h** through you in Ezk 36:23
will display My greatness and **h**, Ezk 38:23
demonstrate My **h** through them Ezk 39:27
do not transmit **h** to the people Ezk 44:19
and transmit **h** to the people." Ezk 46:20
The Lord GOD has sworn by His **h**: Am 4:2
in **h** and righteousness in His Lk 1:75
according to the Spirit of **h**. Rm 1:4
blameless in **h** before our God 1Th 3:13
love, and **h**, with good sense 1Tm 2:15
so that we can share His **h**. Heb 12:10
everyone, and **h**—without it no Heb 12:14

HOLLOW *(7)*
with boards so that it is **h**. Ex 27:8
with boards so that it was **h**. Ex 38:7
So God split a **h** place ⌊in the Jdg 15:19
He cast two ⌊**h**⌋ bronze pillars: 1Kg 7:15
the waters in the **h** of his hand Is 40:12
of 18 feet, was **h**—four fingers Jr 52:21
you residents of the **H**, for all Zph 1:11

HOLLOWED *(2)*
of the people **h** it out with Nm 21:18
He dug a pit and **h** it out, Ps 7:15

HOLON *(3)*
H, and Giloh—11 cities, Jos 15:51
H with its pasturelands, Debir Jos 21:15
the plateau—to **H**, Jahzah, Jr 48:21

HOLY *(617)*
seventh day and declared it **h**, Gn 2:3
you are standing is **h** ground." Ex 3:5
them⌋ to Your **h** dwelling with Ex 15:13
complete rest, a **h** Sabbath to Ex 16:23
of priests and My **h** nation. Ex 19:6
the mountain and consider it **h**." Ex 19:23
Sabbath day and declared it **h**. Ex 20:11
Be My **h** people. You must not eat Ex 22:31
you between the **h** place and the Ex 26:33
holy place and the most **h** place. Ex 26:33
testimony in the most **h** place. Ex 26:34
Make **h** garments for your brother Ex 28:2
They are to make **h** garments for Ex 28:4
of a seal: **H** TO THE LORD Ex 28:36
with the **h** offerings that Ex 28:38
consecrate as all their **h** gifts. Ex 28:38
head and place the **h** diadem on Ex 29:6
and his garments will become **h**, Ex 29:21
The **h** garments that belong to Ex 29:29
and boil its flesh in a **h** place. Ex 29:31
them⌋, for these things are **h**. Ex 29:33
not be eaten because it is **h**. Ex 29:34
altar will become especially **h**; Ex 29:37
touches the altar will become **h**. Ex 29:37
is especially **h** to the LORD." Ex 30:10
from these a **h** anointing oil, Ex 30:25
it will be **h** anointing oil. Ex 30:25
and they will be especially **h**. Ex 30:29
This will be My **h** anointing oil Ex 30:31
It is **h**, and it must be holy to Ex 30:32
holy, and it must be **h** to you. Ex 30:32
seasoned with salt, pure and **h**. Ex 30:35
It must be especially **h** to you. Ex 30:36
both the **h** garments for Aaron Ex 31:10
the Sabbath, for it is **h** to you. Ex 31:14
day you are to have a **h** day, Ex 35:2
the **h** garments for Aaron the Ex 35:19
and ⌊to make⌋ the **h** garments. Ex 35:21
He also made the **h** anointing oil Ex 37:29
the **h** garments for Aaron from Ex 39:1
made a plate, the **h** diadem, out Ex 39:30
on a seal: **H** TO THE LORD Ex 39:30
the **h** garments for Aaron the Ex 39:41
so that it will be **h**. Ex 40:9
so that it will be especially **h**. Ex 40:10
Aaron with the **h** garments, Ex 40:13
to any of the LORD's **h** things, Lv 5:15
his sin regarding any **h** thing, Lv 5:16
unleavened bread in a **h** place; Lv 6:16
It is especially **h**, like the sin Lv 6:17
the offerings will become **h**." Lv 6:18
offering is most **h** and must be Lv 6:25
It must be eaten in a **h** place, Lv 6:26
touches its flesh will become **h**, Lv 6:27
wash that garment in a **h** place. Lv 6:27
may eat it; it is especially **h**. Lv 6:29
make atonement in the **h** place; Lv 6:30
offering; it is especially **h**. Lv 7:1
It is to be eaten in a **h** place; Lv 7:6
holy place; it is especially **h**. Lv 7:6
plate of gold, the **h** diadem, on Lv 8:9
between the **h** and the common, Lv 10:10
because it is especially **h**. Lv 10:12
eat it in a **h** place because it Lv 10:13
it is especially **h**, and He has Lv 10:17
and be **h** because I am holy Lv 11:44
and be holy because I am **h**. Lv 11:44
so you must be **h** because I am Lv 11:45
you must be holy because I am **h**. Lv 11:45
must not touch any **h** thing or go Lv 12:4
the priest; it is especially **h**. Lv 14:13
he wants into the **h** place behind Lv 16:2
enter the ⌊most⌋ **h** place in this Lv 16:3
He is to wear a **h** linen tunic, Lv 16:4
These are **h** garments; he must Lv 16:4
the ⌊most⌋ **h** place in this way Lv 16:16
in the ⌊most⌋ **h** place until he Lv 16:17
purifying the ⌊most⌋ **h** place, Lv 16:20
he entered the ⌊most⌋ **h** place, Lv 16:23
with water in a **h** place and put Lv 16:24
into the ⌊most⌋ **h** place to make Lv 16:27
linen garments, the **h** garments, Lv 16:32
and purify the most **h** place. Lv 16:33
Be **h** because I, the LORD your Lv 19:2
I, the LORD your God, am **h**. Lv 19:2
profaned what is **h** to the LORD. Lv 19:8
and profaning My **h** name. Lv 20:3
Consecrate yourselves and be **h**, Lv 20:7
You are to be **h** to Me because I, Lv 20:26
I, the LORD, am **h**, and I have Lv 20:26
They are to be **h** to their God Lv 21:6
of their God. They must be **h**. Lv 21:6
for the priest is **h** to his God. Lv 21:7
to consider him **h** since he Lv 21:8
He will be **h** to you because I, Lv 21:8
LORD who sets you apart, am **h**. Lv 21:8
what is especially **h** as well as Lv 21:22
holy as well as from what is **h**. Lv 21:22
respectfully with the **h** Lv 22:2
they do not profane My **h** name; Lv 22:2

approaches the **h** offerings that	Lv 22:3
eat from the **h** offerings until	Lv 22:4
to eat from the **h** offerings	Lv 22:6
he may eat from the **h** offerings,	Lv 22:7
family is to eat the **h** offering.	Lv 22:10
is not to eat the **h** offering.	Lv 22:10
to eat from the **h** contributions.	Lv 22:12
If anyone eats a **h** offering in	Lv 22:14
value and give the **h** offering to	Lv 22:14
must not profane the **h** offerings	Lv 22:15
people eat their **h** offerings.	Lv 22:16
You must not profane My **h** name;	Lv 22:32
must be treated as **h** among the	Lv 22:32
lambs will be **h** to the LORD for	Lv 23:20
who are to eat it in a **h** place,	Lv 24:9
It is to be **h** to you because it	Lv 25:12
he gives to the LORD will be **h**.	Lv 27:9
and its substitute will be **h**.	Lv 27:10
his house as **h** to the LORD,	Lv 27:14
it will be **h** to the LORD like a	Lv 27:21
on that day as a **h** offering to	Lv 27:23
is especially **h** to the LORD.	Lv 27:28
the LORD; it is **h** to the LORD.	Lv 27:30
rod, will be **h** to the LORD.	Lv 27:32
and its substitute will be **h**;	Lv 27:33
concerns the most **h** objects.	Nm 4:4
covering the **h** objects and all	Nm 4:15
to touch the **h** objects or they	Nm 4:15
h objects and their utensils.	Nm 4:16
come near the most **h** objects:	Nm 4:19
go in and look at the **h** objects,	Nm 4:20
Every **h** contribution the	Nm 5:9
Each one's **h** contribution is his	Nm 5:10
is to take **h** water in a clay	Nm 5:17
He must be **h** until the time is	Nm 6:5
He is **h** to the LORD during the	Nm 6:8
is a **h** portion for the priest,	Nm 6:20
related to the **h** objects carried	Nm 7:9
transporting the **h** objects;	Nm 10:21
commands and be **h** to your God.	Nm 15:40
in the entire community is **h**,	Nm 16:3
because they are **h**, and scatter	Nm 16:37
LORD, and the firepans are **h**.	Nm 16:38
for all the **h** offerings of the	Nm 18:8
will be most **h** for you and your	Nm 18:9
to eat it as a most **h** offering.	Nm 18:10
eat it; it is to be **h** to you.	Nm 18:10
a goat; they are **h**. You are to	Nm 18:17
all the **h** contributions	Nm 18:19
the Israelites' **h** offerings,	Nm 18:32
care were the **h** objects and	Nm 31:6
who was anointed with the **h** oil.	Nm 35:25
For you are a **h** people belonging	Dt 7:6
are to take the **h** offerings you	Dt 12:26
for you are a **h** people belonging	Dt 14:2
For you are a **h** people belonging	Dt 14:21
so your encampments must be **h**.	Dt 23:14
Look down from Your **h** dwelling,	Dt 26:15
you will be a **h** people to the	Dt 26:19
establish you as His **h** people,	Dt 28:9
to treat Me as **h** in their	Dt 32:51
came with ten thousand **h** ones,	Dt 33:2
Your **h** ones are in Your hand,	Dt 33:3
where you are standing is **h**."	Jos 5:15
the LORD, because He is a **h** God.	Jos 24:19
There is no one **h** like the LORD.	1Sm 2:2
the presence of this **h** LORD God?	1Sm 6:20
sanctuary, the most **h** place.	1Kg 6:16
in front of the most **h** place,	1Kg 6:17
is, the most **h** place) and for	1Kg 7:50
and the **h** utensils that were in	1Kg 8:4
to the most **h** place beneath the	1Kg 8:6
seen from the **h** place in front	1Kg 8:8
priests came out of the **h** place,	1Kg 8:10
by here is a **h** man of God,	2Kg 4:9
Against the **H** One of Israel!	2Kg 19:22
the work of the most **h** place.	1Ch 6:49
Honor His **h** name; let the hearts	1Ch 16:10
to Your **h** name and rejoice	1Ch 16:35
and the **h** articles of God	1Ch 22:19
to consecrate the most **h** things,	1Ch 23:13
of all the **h** things,	1Ch 23:28
meeting, to the **h** place, and to	1Ch 23:32
I've provided for the **h** house:	1Ch 29:3
a house for Your **h** name comes	1Ch 29:16
Then he made the most **h** place;	2Ch 3:8
for the most **h** place, and he	2Ch 3:10
inner doors to the most **h** place,	2Ch 4:22
and the **h** utensils that were in	2Ch 5:5
to the most **h** place, beneath	2Ch 5:7
seen from the **h** place in front	2Ch 5:9
came out of the **h** place—	2Ch 5:11
ark of the LORD has come are **h**."	2Ch 8:11
may enter because they are **h**,	2Ch 23:6
detestable from the **h** place.	2Ch 29:5
in the **h** place of the God	2Ch 29:7
came into His **h** dwelling place	2Ch 30:27
consecrated themselves as **h**	2Ch 31:18
all Israel the **h** things of the	2Ch 35:3
Put the **h** ark in the temple	2Ch 35:3
Serve in the **h** place by the	2Ch 35:5
They boiled the **h** ⌊sacrifices⌋	2Ch 35:13
to eat the most **h** things until	Ezr 2:63
LORD's appointed **h** occasions,	Ezr 3:5
to them, "You are **h** to the LORD,	Ezr 8:28
LORD, and the articles are **h**.	Ezr 8:28
so that the **h** people has become	Ezr 9:2
give us a stake in His **h** place.	Ezr 9:8
to eat the most **h** things until	Neh 7:65
This day is **h** to the LORD your	Neh 8:9
since today is **h** to our Lord.	Neh 8:10
Be still, since today is **h**.	Neh 8:11
revealed Your **h** Sabbath to them	Neh 9:14
them on the Sabbath or a **h** day.	Neh 10:31
festivals, the **h** things, the sin	Neh 10:33
in Jerusalem, the **h** city, while	Neh 11:1
All the Levites in the **h** city:	Neh 11:18
order to keep the Sabbath day **h**.	Neh 13:22
Which of the **h** ones will you	Jb 5:1
denied the words of the **H** One.	Jb 6:10
no trust in His **h** ones and the	Jb 15:15
My King on Zion, My **h** mountain."	Ps 2:6
answers me from His **h** mountain.	Ps 3:4
bow down toward Your **h** temple in	Ps 5:7
The LORD is in His **h** temple;	Ps 11:4
Who can live on Your **h** mountain?	Ps 15:1
As for the **h** people who are in	Ps 16:3
him from His **h** heaven with	Ps 20:6
But You are **h**, enthroned on the	Ps 22:3
Who may stand in His **h** place?	Ps 24:3
hands toward Your **h** sanctuary.	Ps 28:2
ones, and praise His **h** name.	Ps 30:4
because we trust in His **h** name.	Ps 33:21
bring me to Your **h** mountain,	Ps 43:3
the **h** dwelling place of the Most	Ps 46:4
God is seated on His **h** throne.	Ps 47:8
city of our God. His **h** mountain,	Ps 48:1
or take Your **H** Spirit from me.	Ps 51:11
widows is God in His **h** dwelling.	Ps 68:5
with a harp, **H** One of Israel.	Ps 71:22
God, Your way is **h**. What god is	Ps 77:13
provoked the **H** One of Israel.	Ps 78:41
He brought them to His **h** land,	Ps 78:54
desecrated Your **h** temple, and	Ps 79:1
is on the **h** mountains.	Ps 87:1
in the assembly of the **h** ones.	Ps 89:5
in the council of the **h** ones,	Ps 89:7
our king to the **H** One of Israel.	Ps 89:18
ones, and praise His **h** name.	Ps 97:12
right hand and **h** arm have won	Ps 98:1
and awe-inspiring name. He is **h**.	Ps 99:3
at His footstool. He is **h**.	Ps 99:5
in worship at His **h** mountain,	Ps 99:9
for the LORD our God is **h**.	Ps 99:9
looked down from His **h** heights—	Ps 102:19
is within me, praise His **h** name.	Ps 103:1
Honor His **h** name; let the hearts	Ps 105:3
He remembered His **h** promise to	Ps 105:42
and of Aaron, the LORD's **h** one.	Ps 106:16
to Your **h** name and rejoice	Ps 106:47
In **h** splendor, from the womb of	Ps 110:3
His name is **h** and awe-inspiring.	Ps 111:9
up your hands in the **h** place,	Ps 134:2
toward Your **h** temple and give	Ps 138:2
thing praise His **h** name forever	Ps 145:21
knowledge of the **H** One is	Pr 9:10
have no knowledge of the **H** One.	Pr 30:3
came and went from the **h** place,	Ec 8:10
despised the **H** One of Israel;	Is 1:4
in Jerusalem will be called **h**—	Is 4:3
and the **h** God is distinguished	Is 5:16
the plan of the **H** One of Israel	Is 5:19
the word of the **H** One of Israel.	Is 5:24
H, holy, holy is the LORD of	Is 6:3
Holy, **h**, holy is the LORD of	Is 6:3
Holy, holy, **h** is the LORD of	Is 6:3
when felled, the **h** seed is the	Is 6:13
only the LORD of Hosts as **h**.	Is 8:13
a fire, and its **H** One, a flame.	Is 10:17
the LORD, the **H** One of Israel.	Is 10:20
destroy on My entire **h** mountain,	Is 11:9
for the **H** One of Israel is among	Is 12:6
eyes to the **H** One of Israel.	Is 17:7
at Jerusalem on the **h** mountain.	Is 27:13
rejoice in the **H** One of Israel.	Is 29:19
will honor the **H** One of Jacob	Is 29:23
Rid us of the **H** One of Israel."	Is 30:11
Therefore the **H** One of Israel	Is 30:12
Lord GOD, the **H** One of Israel,	Is 30:15
on the night of a **h** festival,	Is 30:29
not look to the **H** One of Israel	Is 31:1
it will be called the **H** Way.	Is 35:8
Against the **H** One of Israel!	Is 37:23
is My equal?" asks the **H** One.	Is 40:25
Redeemer is the **H** One of Israel.	Is 41:14
boast in the **H** One of Israel.	Is 41:16
the **H** One of Israel has created	Is 41:20
your God, the **H** One of Israel,	Is 43:3
Redeemer, the **H** One of Israel	Is 43:14
the LORD, your **H** One, the	Is 43:15
the **H** One of Israel and its	Is 45:11
The **H** One of Israel is our	Is 47:4
they are named after the **H** City,	Is 48:2
Redeemer, the **H** One of Israel	Is 48:17
his **H** One says to one who is	Is 49:7
faithful, the **H** One of Israel—	Is 49:7
garments, Jerusalem, the **H** City!	Is 52:1
displayed His **h** arm in the sight	Is 52:10
and the **H** One of Israel is your	Is 54:5
God, even the **H** One of Israel,	Is 55:5
them to My **h** mountain and let	Is 56:7
land and possess My **h** mountain.	Is 57:13
whose name is **H** says this:	Is 57:15
I live in a high and **h** place,	Is 57:15
whatever you want on My **h** day;	Is 58:13
and the **h** ⌊day⌋ of the LORD	Is 58:13
your God, the **H** One of Israel,	Is 60:9
Zion of the **H** One of Israel.	Is 60:14
drink ⌊the wine⌋ in My **h** courts.	Is 62:9
will be called the **H** People,	Is 62:12
and grieved His **H** Spirit.	Is 63:10
is He who put His **H** Spirit among	Is 63:11
lofty home—**h** and beautiful.	Is 63:15
Your **h** people had a possession	Is 63:18
Your **h** cities have become a	Is 64:10
Our **h** and beautiful temple,	Is 64:11
near me, for I am too **h** for you!	Is 65:5
who forget My **h** mountain, who	Is 65:11
on My entire **h** mountain,"	Is 65:25
to My **h** mountain Jerusalem,	Is 66:20
Israel was **h** to the LORD, the	Jr 2:3
Can **h** meat prevent your disaster	Jr 11:15
LORD, because of His **h** words.	Jr 23:9
His voice from His **h** dwelling.	Jr 25:30
settlement, **h** mountain.	Jr 31:23
east—will be **h** to the LORD.	Jr 31:40
against the **H** One of Israel.	Jr 50:29
against the **H** One of Israel.	Jr 51:5
have entered the **h** places of the	Jr 51:51
LORD who sets them apart as **h**.	Ezk 20:12
My Sabbaths **h**, and they will	Ezk 20:20
longer defile My **h** name with	Ezk 20:39
For on My **h** mountain, Israel's	Ezk 20:40
gifts, all your **h** offerings.	Ezk 20:40
You despise My **h** things and	Ezk 22:8
My law and profane My **h** things.	Ezk 22:26
between the **h** and the common,	Ezk 22:26
were on the **h** mountain of God	Ezk 28:14
profaned My **h** name, because it	Ezk 36:20
I had concern for My **h** name,	Ezk 36:21
but for My **h** name, which you	Ezk 36:22
when I show Myself **h** through	Ezk 38:16
I will make My **h** name known	Ezk 39:7
the LORD, the **H** One in Israel.	Ezk 39:7
I will be jealous for My **h** name.	Ezk 39:25
"This is the most **h** place."	Ezk 41:4
yard are the **h** chambers where	Ezk 42:13
will eat the most **h** offerings.	Ezk 42:13
deposit the most **h** offerings—	Ezk 42:13
offerings—for the place is **h**.	Ezk 42:13
go out from the **h** area to the	Ezk 42:14
minister in, for these are **h**.	Ezk 42:14
separate the **h** from the common	Ezk 42:20
longer defile My **h** name by their	Ezk 43:7

they were defiling My **h** name by Ezk 43:8
mountain will be especially **h**. Ezk 43:12
charge of My **h** things but have Ezk 44:8
near any of My **h** things or the Ezk 44:13
things or the most **h** things. Ezk 44:13
leave them in the **h** chambers, Ezk 44:19
between the **h** and the common, Ezk 44:23
and keep My Sabbaths **h**. Ezk 44:24
to the LORD, a **h** portion of the Ezk 45:1
entire tract of land will be **h**. Ezk 45:1
From this **h** portion, you will Ezk 45:3
the most **h** place, will stand. Ezk 45:3
It will be a **h** area of the land Ezk 45:4
as well as a **h** area for the Ezk 45:4
adjacent to the **h** donation ⌊of Ezk 45:6
each side of the **h** donation ⌊of Ezk 45:7
adjacent to the **h** donation and Ezk 45:7
into the priests' **h** chambers, Ezk 46:19
h donation will be set apart Ezk 48:10
for them out of the ⌊**h**⌋ donation Ezk 48:12
a most **h** place adjacent to the Ezk 48:12
land, for it is **h** to the LORD. Ezk 48:14
alongside the **h** donation will be Ezk 48:18
run alongside the **h** donation. Ezk 48:18
set apart the **h** donation along Ezk 48:20
on both sides of the **h** donation Ezk 48:21
The **h** donation and the sanctuary Ezk 48:21
spirit of the **h** gods is in him Dn 4:8
a spirit of the **h** gods and that Dn 4:9
observer, a **h** one, coming down Dn 4:13
is a command from the **h** ones. Dn 4:17
have the spirit of the **h** gods. Dn 4:18
observer, a **h** one, coming down Dn 4:23
the spirit of the **h** gods in him. Dn 5:11
But the **h** ones of the Most High Dn 7:18
made war with the **h** ones and was Dn 7:21
in favor of the **h** ones of the Dn 7:22
and the **h** ones took possession Dn 7:22
and oppress the **h** ones of the Dn 7:25
and the **h** ones will be handed Dn 7:25
the **h** ones of the Most High. Dn 7:27
Then I heard a **h** one speaking, Dn 8:13
and another **h** one said to the Dn 8:13
along with the **h** people. Dn 8:24
city Jerusalem, Your **h** mountain; Dn 9:16
concerning the **h** mountain of my Dn 9:20
your people and your **h** city— Dn 9:24
and to anoint the most **h** place. Dn 9:24
be set against the **h** covenant; Dn 11:28
rage against the **h** covenant and Dn 11:30
who abandon the **h** covenant. Dn 11:30
and the beautiful **h** mountain, Dn 11:45
the power of the **h** people is Dn 12:7
not man, the **H** One among you; Hs 11:9
El and is faithful to **h** ones. Hs 11:12
the alarm on My **h** mountain! Jl 2:1
nations: Prepare for **h** war; Jl 3:9
dwells in Zion, My **h** mountain. Jl 3:17
will be **h**, and foreigners Jl 3:17
same girl, profaning My **h** name. Am 2:7
you have drunk on My **h** mountain, Ob 16
on Mount Zion, and it will be **h**; Ob 17
once more toward Your **h** temple. Jnh 2:4
came to You, to Your **h** temple. Jnh 2:7
the Lord, from His **h** temple. Mc 1:2
My **H** One, You will not die. Hab 1:12
But the LORD is in His **h** temple; Hab 2:20
the **H** One from Mount Paran. Hab 3:3
be haughty on My **h** mountain. Zph 3:11
other food, does it become **h**?" Hg 2:12
as His portion in the **H** Land, Zch 2:12
is coming from His **h** dwelling." Zch 2:13
of Hosts, and the **H** Mountain." Zch 8:3
and all the **h** ones with Him. Zch 14:5
⌊the words⌋ **H** TO THE LORD will Zch 14:20
Judah will be **h** to the LORD of Zch 14:21
was pregnant by the **H** Spirit. Mt 1:18
in her is by the **H** Spirit. Mt 1:20
you with the **H** Spirit and fire. Mt 3:11
Devil took Him to the **h** city, Mt 4:5
Your name be honored as **h**. Mt 6:9
give what is **h** to dogs or toss Mt 7:6
speaks against the **H** Spirit, Mt 12:32
standing in the **h** place" (let Mt 24:15
entered the **h** city, and appeared Mt 27:53
of the Son and of the **H** Spirit, Mt 28:19
baptize you with the **H** Spirit." Mk 1:8
who You are—the **H** One of God!" Mk 1:24
against the **H** Spirit never has Mk 3:29
he was a righteous and **h** man. Mk 6:20
His Father with the **h** angels." Mk 8:38
himself says by the **H** Spirit: Mk 12:36
you speaking, but the **H** Spirit. Mk 13:11
filled with the **H** Spirit while Lk 1:15
The **H** Spirit will come upon you, Lk 1:35
Therefore the **h** One to be born Lk 1:35
was filled with the **H** Spirit. Lk 1:41
for me, and His name is **h**. Lk 1:49
was filled with the **H** Spirit and Lk 1:67
the mouth of His **h** prophets in Lk 1:70
and remembered His **h** covenant— Lk 1:72
and the **H** Spirit was on him. Lk 2:25
to him by the **H** Spirit that he Lk 2:26
you with the **H** Spirit and fire. Lk 3:16
the **H** Spirit descended on Him Lk 3:22
full of the **H** Spirit, and was Lk 4:1
who You are—the **H** One of God!" Lk 4:34
of the Father and the **h** angels. Lk 9:26
in the **H** Spirit and said Lk 10:21
Your name be honored as **h**. Lk 11:2
Father give the **H** Spirit to Lk 11:13
against the **H** Spirit will not be Lk 12:10
For the **H** Spirit will teach you Lk 12:12
baptizes with the **H** Spirit.' Jn 1:33
that You are the **H** One of God!" Jn 6:69
Counselor, the **H** Spirit—the Jn 14:26
H Father, protect them by Your Jn 17:11
and said, "Receive the **H** Spirit. Jn 20:22
orders through the **H** Spirit to Ac 1:2
with the **H** Spirit not many Ac 1:5
power when the **H** Spirit has come Ac 1:8
that the **H** Spirit through Ac 1:16
filled with the **H** Spirit and Ac 2:4
allow Your **H** One to see decay. Ac 2:27
Father the promised **H** Spirit, Ac 2:33
the gift of the **H** Spirit. Ac 2:38
you denied the **H** and Righteous Ac 3:14
by the mouth of His **h** prophets Ac 3:21
filled with the **H** Spirit and Ac 4:8
You said through the **H** Spirit, Ac 4:25
against Your **h** Servant Jesus, Ac 4:27
name of Your **h** Servant Jesus." Ac 4:30
filled with the **H** Spirit and Ac 4:31
to lie to the **H** Spirit and keep Ac 5:3
and so is the **H** Spirit whom God Ac 5:32
full of faith and the **H** Spirit, Ac 6:5
against this **h** place and the law Ac 6:13
you are standing is **h** ground. Ac 7:33
always resisting the **H** Spirit; Ac 7:51
filled by the **H** Spirit, gazed Ac 7:55
they might receive the **H** Spirit. Ac 8:15
and they received the **H** Spirit. Ac 8:17
saw that the **H** Spirit was given Ac 8:18
on may receive the **H** Spirit." Ac 8:19
be filled with the **H** Spirit." Ac 9:17
encouragement of the **H** Spirit, Ac 9:31
directed by a **h** angel to call Ac 10:22
with the **H** Spirit and with Ac 10:38
the **H** Spirit came down on all Ac 10:44
gift of the **H** Spirit had been Ac 10:45
received the **H** Spirit just as we Ac 10:47
the **H** Spirit came down on them, Ac 11:15
be baptized with the **H** Spirit.' Ac 11:16
of the **H** Spirit and of faith Ac 11:24
and fasting, the **H** Spirit said, Ac 13:2
Being sent out by the **H** Spirit, Ac 13:4
filled with the **H** Spirit, stared Ac 13:9
not allow Your **H** One to see Ac 13:35
with joy and the **H** Spirit. Ac 13:52
to them by giving the **H** Spirit, Ac 15:8
For it was the **H** Spirit's Ac 15:28
prevented by the **H** Spirit from Ac 16:6
receive the **H** Spirit when you Ac 19:2
heard that there is a **H** Spirit." Ac 19:2
the **H** Spirit came on them, Ac 19:6
town the **H** Spirit testifies Ac 20:23
among whom the **H** Spirit has Ac 20:28
This is what the **H** Spirit says: Ac 21:11
and has profaned this **h** place." Ac 21:28
The **H** Spirit correctly spoke Ac 28:25
prophets in the **H** Scriptures— Rm 1:2
through the **H** Spirit who was Rm 5:5
So then, the law is **h**, and the Rm 7:12
commandment is **h** and just and Rm 7:12
to me with the **H** Spirit— Rm 9:1
firstfruits offered up are **h**, Rm 11:16
And if the root is **h**, so are the Rm 11:16
sacrifice, **h** and pleasing to Rm 12:1
peace, and joy in the **H** Spirit. Rm 14:17
by the power of the **H** Spirit. Rm 15:13
sanctified by the **H** Spirit. Rm 15:16
Greet one another with a **h** kiss. Rm 16:16
sanctuary is **h**, and that is what 1Co 3:17
sanctuary of the **H** Spirit who is 1Co 6:19
be unclean, but now they are **h**. 1Co 7:14
that she may be **h** both in body 1Co 7:34
Lord," except by the **H** Spirit. 1Co 12:3
Greet one another with a **h** kiss. 1Co 16:20
kindness, by the **H** Spirit, by 2Co 6:6
Greet one another with a **h** kiss. 2Co 13:12
of the **H** Spirit be with 2Co 13:13
to be **h** and blameless in His Eph 1:4
with the promised **H** Spirit. Eph 1:13
is growing into a **h** sanctuary in Eph 2:21
now revealed to His **h** apostles Eph 3:5
And don't grieve God's **H** Spirit, Eph 4:30
to make her **h**, cleansing her in Eph 5:26
such thing, but **h** and blameless. Eph 5:27
to present you **h**, faultless, Col 1:22
chosen ones, **h** and loved, put Col 3:12
power, in the **H** Spirit, and with 1Th 1:5
with the joy from the **H** Spirit. 1Th 1:6
who also gives you His **H** Spirit. 1Th 4:8
all the brothers with a **h** kiss. 1Th 5:26
lifting up **h** hands without anger 1Tm 2:8
and called us with a **h** calling, 2Tm 1:9
through the **H** Spirit who lives 2Tm 1:14
righteous, **h**, self-controlled, Ti 1:8
and renewal by the **H** Spirit. Ti 3:5
gifts⌋ from the **H** Spirit Heb 2:4
h brothers and companions in a Heb 3:1
Therefore, as the **H** Spirit says: Heb 3:7
companions with the **H** Spirit, Heb 6:4
h, innocent, undefiled, Heb 7:26
which is called "the **h** place," Heb 9:2
was called "the **h** of holies." Heb 9:3
The **H** Spirit was making it clear Heb 9:8
the way into the **h** of holies had Heb 9:8
He entered the **h** of holies once Heb 9:12
The **H** Spirit also testifies to Heb 10:15
is brought into the **h** of holies Heb 13:11
to you by the **H** Spirit sent 1Pt 1:12
as the One who called you is **h**, 1Pt 1:15
you also are to be **h** in all your 1Pt 1:15
is written, Be **h**, because I am 1Pt 1:16
Be holy, because I am **h**. 1Pt 1:16
for a **h** priesthood to offer 1Pt 2:5
priesthood, a **h** nation, a people 1Pt 2:9
h women who hoped in God also 1Pt 3:5
were with Him on the **h** mountain. 2Pt 1:18
moved by the **H** Spirit, men spoke 2Pt 1:21
turn back from the **h** commandment 2Pt 2:21
spoken by the **h** prophets, 2Pt 3:2
you should be in **h** conduct and 2Pt 3:11
an anointing from the **H** One, 1Jn 2:20
with thousands of His **h** ones Jd 14
up in your most **h** faith and Jd 20
and praying in the **H** Spirit, Jd 20
The **H** One, the True One, the One Rv 3:7
H, holy, holy, Lord God, the Rv 4:8
Holy, **h**, holy, Lord God, the Rv 4:8
Holy, holy, **h**, Lord God, the Rv 4:8
O Lord, **h** and true, how long Rv 6:10
will trample the **h** city for 42 Rv 11:2
in the sight of the **h** angels and Rv 14:10
You alone are **h**, because all Rv 15:4
and who was, the **H** One, for You Rv 16:5
Blessed and **h** is the one who Rv 20:6
I also saw the **H** City, new Rv 21:2
and showed me the **h** city, Rv 21:10
let the **h** go on being made holy. Rv 22:11
the holy go on being made **h**." Rv 22:11
the tree of life and the **h** city, Rv 22:19

HOMAGE *(17)*

David bowed to the ground in **h**. 1Sm 24:8
face to the ground and paid **h**. 1Sm 28:14
fell to the ground and paid **h**. 2Sm 1:2
down to the ground and paid **h**. 2Sm 9:6
to the ground in **h** and said, 2Sm 14:4
to the ground in **h** and praised 2Sm 14:22
down and paid **h** to the king, 1Kg 1:16
ground, paying **h** to the king, 1Kg 1:31
came and paid **h** to King Solomon 1Kg 1:53
bowed down and paid **h** to the 1Ch 29:20

came and paid **h** to the king. 2Ch 24:17
bowed down and paid **h** to Haman, Est 3:2
would not bow down or pay **h**. Est 3:2
not bowing down or paying him **h**, Est 3:5
Pay **h** to the Son, or He will be Ps 2:12
fell down, paid **h** to Daniel, and Dn 2:46
knees, they were paying Him **h**. Mk 15:19

HOMAM *(1)*
(AKA HEMAN)
sons: Hori and **H**. Timna was 1Ch 1:39

HOME *(145)*
was a quiet man who stayed at **h**. Gn 25:27
Then Laban left to return **h**. Gn 31:55
her until his master came **h**. Gn 39:16
When Joseph came **h**, they brought Gn 43:26
will be able to go **h** satisfied." Ex 18:23
whether born at **h** or born Lv 18:9
Now go to your **h**! I said I would Nm 24:11
Let him leave and return **h**. Dt 20:5
Let him leave and return **h**. Dt 20:6
Let him leave and return **h**. Dt 20:7
Let him leave and return **h**, Dt 20:8
animal to your **h** to remain with Dt 22:2
⌊to stay⌋ at **h** for one year, Dt 24:5
may return **h** to his own city Jos 20:6
But everyone else is to go **h**." Jdg 7:7
was dead, they all went **h**. Jdg 9:55
went to his **h** in Mizpah, Jdg 11:34
he came to Micah's **h** in the hill Jdg 17:8
as far as the **h** of Micah and Jdg 18:2
While they were near Micah's **h**, Jdg 18:3
young Levite at the **h** of Micah Jdg 18:15
and Micah turned to go back **h**, Jdg 18:26
for your journey and go **h**." Jdg 19:9
them into their **h** to spend the Jdg 19:15
No one has taken me into his **h**, Jdg 19:18
on his donkey and set out for **h**. Jdg 19:28
you go back to your mother's **h**. Ru 1:8
"Return **h**, my daughters. Ru 1:11
Return **h**, my daughters. Ru 1:12
or from the gate of his **h**. Ru 4:10
they returned **h** to Ramah. 1Sm 1:19
Elkanah went **h** to Ramah, but the 1Sm 2:11
Then they would go **h**. 1Sm 2:20
Ramah because his **h** was there, 1Sm 7:17
the people away, each to his **h**. 1Sm 10:25
also went to his **h** in Gibeah, 1Sm 10:26
went up to his **h** in Gibeah of 1Sm 15:34
Horesh, while Jonathan went **h**. 1Sm 23:18
Saul went back **h**, and David and 1Sm 24:22
buried him by his **h** in Ramah. 1Sm 25:1
him and said, "Go **h** in peace. 1Sm 25:35
on his way, and Saul returned **h**. 1Sm 26:25
people left, each to his own **h**. 2Sm 6:19
David returned ⌊**h**⌋ to bless his 2Sm 6:20
Afterwards, she returned **h**. 2Sm 11:4
Uriah didn't go **h**," David 2Sm 11:10
a journey? Why didn't you go **h**?" 2Sm 11:10
servants, but he did not go **h**. 2Sm 11:13
Nathan went **h**. The LORD struck 2Sm 12:15
He fasted, went ⌊**h**⌋, and spent 2Sm 12:16
Then he went **h** and requested 2Sm 12:20
The king told the woman, "Go **h**. 2Sm 14:8
and Barzillai returned to his **h**. 2Sm 19:39
said to him, "Go to your **h**." 1Kg 1:53
two months they were at **h**. 1Kg 5:14
king and went **h** to their tents 1Kg 8:66
Go **h** for three days and then 1Kg 12:5
Each of you must return **h**, 1Kg 12:24
of God, "Come **h** with me, refresh 1Kg 13:7
"Come **h** with me and eat bread." 1Kg 13:15
of Israel left for **h** resentful 1Kg 20:43
everyone return **h** in peace.' 1Kg 22:17
Enjoy your glory and stay at **h**. 2Kg 14:10
He returned ⌊**h**⌋ and lived in 2Kg 19:36
had been misfortune in his **h**. 1Ch 7:23
the ark of God **h** to the city 1Ch 13:13
David returned ⌊**h**⌋ to bless his 1Ch 16:43
Each of you must return **h**, 2Ch 11:4
let each return **h** in peace.' 2Ch 18:16
returned to his **h** in Jerusalem 2Ch 19:1
to him from Ephraim to go **h**. 2Ch 25:10
and returned **h** in a fierce rage 2Ch 25:10
Now stay at **h**. Why stir up such 2Ch 25:19
and the **h** where I will live." Neh 2:8
controlled himself and went **h**. Est 5:10
hurried off for **h** with his head Est 6:12
each of them came from his **h**. Jb 2:11
pronounced a curse on his **h**. Jb 5:3
missing when you inspect your **h**. Jb 5:24
and restore the **h** where your Jb 8:6
He looks for a **h** among the Jb 8:17
Sheol as my **h**, spread out my Jb 17:13
sulfur is scattered over his **h**. Jb 18:15
is the road to the **h** of light? Jb 38:19
with the paths to its **h**? Jb 38:20
I made the wilderness its **h**, Jb 39:6
She who stays at **h** divides the Ps 68:12
finds a **h**, and a swallow, Ps 84:3
stork makes its **h** in the pine Ps 104:17
He has desired it for His **h**: Ps 132:13
I will make My **h** here because I Ps 132:14
He blesses the **h** of the Pr 3:33
her feet do not stay at **h**. Pr 7:11
My husband isn't **h**; he went on a Pr 7:19
him and will come **h** at the time Pr 7:20
share a **h** with shrewdness and Pr 8:12
will be at **h** among the wise. Pr 15:31
from his **h** is like a bird Pr 27:8
man is headed to his eternal **h**, Ec 12:5
the prisoners to return **h**?" Is 14:17
He returned ⌊**h**⌋ and lived in Is 37:37
and see from Your lofty **h**— Is 63:15
And what place could be My **h**? Is 66:1
a wild donkey at **h** in the Jr 2:24
son of Shaphan, to take him **h**. Jr 39:14
He goes **h** and rests his hand Am 5:19
rock in your **h** on the heights, Ob 3
They deprive a man of his **h**, Mc 2:2
are the people in his own **h**. Mc 7:6
servant is lying at **h** paralyzed, Mt 8:6
up your stretcher, and go **h**." Mt 9:6
And he got up and went **h**. Mt 9:7
was reported that He was at **h**. Mk 2:1
up your stretcher, and go **h**." Mk 2:11
Then He went **h**, and the crowd Mk 3:20
Go back **h** to your own people, Mk 5:19
When she went back to her **h**, Mk 7:30
If I send them **h** famished, Mk 8:3
He sent him **h**, saying, "Don't Mk 8:26
were completed, he went back **h**. Lk 1:23
then she returned to her **h**. Lk 1:56
up your stretcher, and go **h**." Lk 5:24
and went **h** glorifying God. Lk 5:25
Go back to your **h**, and tell all Lk 8:39
Martha welcomed Him into her **h**. Lk 10:38
and coming **h**, he calls his Lk 15:6
place, went **h**, striking their Lk 23:48
So he went **h**, amazed at what had Lk 24:12
to him and make Our **h** with him. Jn 14:23
will be scattered to his own **h**, Jn 16:32
disciple took her into his **h**. Jn 19:27
Then the disciples went **h** again. Jn 20:10
in his father's **h** three months, Ac 7:20
in his chariot on his way **h**, Ac 8:28
they took him **h** and explained Ac 18:26
brought the boy **h** alive and were Ac 20:12
the ship, and they returned **h**. Ac 21:6
church that meets in their **h**. Rm 16:5
should eat at **h**, so that you can 1Co 11:34
ask their own husbands at **h**, 1Co 14:35
church that meets in their **h**. 1Co 16:19
while we are at **h** in the body we 2Co 5:6
the body and at **h** with the Lord. 2Co 5:8
whether we are at **h** or away, 2Co 5:9
do not receive him into your **h**, 2Jn 10

HOMELAND *(11)*
so that I can return to my **h**. Gn 30:25
arose and went back to his **h**, Nm 24:25
up the road to its **h** toward 1Sm 6:9
and an exile from your **h**. 2Sm 15:19
from their **h** until today. 2Kg 17:23
Jacob and devastated his **h**. Ps 79:7
Israel and bring it to its **h**. Is 14:2
him off and made his **h** desolate. Jr 10:25
go into exile from its **h**.' " Am 7:11
go into exile from its **h**. Am 7:17
clear that they are seeking a **h**. Heb 11:14

HOMELESS *(3)*
make them **h** wanderers and bring Ps 59:11
the poor and **h** into your house, Is 58:7
clothed, roughly treated, **h**; 1Co 4:11

HOMELESSNESS *(2)*
her affliction and **h** Jerusalem Lm 1:7
Remember my affliction and my **h**, Lm 3:19

HOMEMAKERS *(1)*
pure, good **h**, and submissive to Ti 2:5

HOMEOWNER *(3)*
If the **h** had known what time the Mt 24:43
if the **h** had known at what hour Lk 12:39
once the **h** gets up and shuts the Lk 13:25

HOMES *(26)*
unleavened bread in all your **h**." Ex 12:20
Egyptians and spared our **h**.' " Ex 12:27
in any of your **h** on the Sabbath Ex 35:3
not return to our **h** until each Nm 32:18
return to your **h** in your own Jos 22:4
way, and they went to their **h**. Jos 22:6
them to their **h** and blessed them Jos 22:7
Return to your **h** with great Jos 22:8
all the people left for their **h**, 1Ch 16:43
daughters, your wives and **h**." Neh 4:14
h to get grain during the famine. Neh 5:3
posts and some at their **h**." Neh 7:3
Their **h** are secure and free of Jb 21:9
graves are their eternal **h**, Ps 49:11
their **h** from generation to Ps 49:11
is in their **h** and within them Ps 55:15
God provides **h** for those who are Ps 68:6
far from their demolished **h**. Ps 109:10
they make their **h** in the cliffs; Pr 30:26
h have been set ablaze, Jr 51:30
and tear down your beautiful **h**. Ezk 26:12
a blessing may rest on your **h**. Ezk 44:30
I will settle them in their **h**. Hs 11:11
out of their comfortable **h**, Mc 2:9
will welcome me into their **h**.' Lk 16:4
and in various **h**, they continued Ac 5:42

HOMETOWN *(13)*
his city, to the gate of his **h**. Dt 21:19
and put it in Ophrah, his **h**. Jdg 8:27
to Gibeah, Saul's ⌊**h**⌋, and told 1Sm 11:4
set out for his house in his **h**. 2Sm 17:23
returned to his **h** Jerusalem and Ezr 2:1
his **h** will no longer remember Jb 7:10
He went to His **h** and began to Mt 13:54
honor except in his **h** and in his Mt 13:57
from there and came to His **h**, Mk 6:1
without honor except in his **h**, Mk 6:4
do here in Your **h** also.' " Lk 4:23
No prophet is accepted in his **h**. Lk 4:24
the **h** of Andrew and Peter. Jn 1:44

HOMOSEXUALS *(2)*
adulterers, male prostitutes, **h**, 1Co 6:9
for the sexually immoral and **h**, 1Tm 1:10

HONEST *(24)*
one man. We are **h**; your servants Gn 42:11
If you are **h** men, let one of you Gn 42:19
We are **h** men and not spies. Gn 42:31
I will know if you are **h** men: Gn 42:33
you are not spies but **h** men. Gn 42:34
You are to have **h** balances, Lv 19:36
honest balances, **h** weights, an Lv 19:36
weights, an **h** dry measure, Lv 19:36
and an **h** liquid measure; Lv 19:36
must have a full and **h** weight, Dt 25:15
a full and **h** dry measure, so Dt 25:15
and I brought back an **h** report. Jos 14:7
Where have the **h** been destroyed? Jb 4:7
How painful **h** words can be! Jb 6:25
An **h** witness does not deceive, Pr 14:5
H balances and scales are the Pr 16:11
He who gives an **h** answer gives a Pr 24:26
men hate an **h** person, Pr 29:10
You must have **h** balances, Ezk 45:10
balances, an **h** dry measure, Ezk 45:10
and an **h** liquid measure. Ezk 45:10
render **h** and peaceful judgments Zch 8:16
word with an **h** and good heart, Lk 8:15
he must do **h** work with his own Eph 4:28

HONESTLY *(5)*
faithfully and **h** in making Jdg 9:16
faithfully and **h** with Jerubbaal Jdg 9:19
The one who lives **h**, practices Ps 15:2
and he loves one who speaks **h**. Pr 16:13
no one pleads **h**. They trust in Is 59:4

HONESTY *(3)*
my **h** will testify for me. Gn 30:33
or to beat a noble for his **h**. Pr 17:26
square, and **h** cannot enter. Is 59:14

HONEY *(60)*
balsam and some **h**, aromatic gum Gn 43:11
a land flowing with milk and **h**— Ex 3:8
a land flowing with milk and **h**. Ex 3:17
a land flowing with milk and **h**, Ex 13:5
like wafers ⌊made⌋ with **h**. Ex 16:31
a land flowing with milk and **h**. Ex 33:3
burn any yeast or **h** as a fire Lv 2:11
a land flowing with milk and **h**. Lv 20:24
it is flowing with milk and **h**, Nm 13:27
a land flowing with milk and **h**, Nm 14:8
with milk and **h** to kill us Nm 16:13
with milk and **h** or give us Nm 16:14
a land flowing with milk and **h**. Dt 6:3
a land of olive oil and **h**; Dt 8:8
a land flowing with milk and **h**. Dt 11:9
a land flowing with milk and **h**. Dt 26:9
a land flowing with milk and **h**. Dt 26:15
a land flowing with milk and **h**, Dt 27:3
⌊a land⌋ flowing with milk and **h**, Dt 31:20
him with **h** from the rock Dt 32:13
a land flowing with milk and **h**. Jos 5:6
of bees with **h** in the carcass. Jdg 14:8
scooped ⌊some **h**⌋ into his hands Jdg 14:9
scooped the **h** from the lion's Jdg 14:9
What is sweeter than **h**? Jdg 14:18
and there was **h** on the ground. 1Sm 14:25
saw the flow of **h**, but none of 1Sm 14:26
he ate the **h**, he had renewed 1Sm 14:27
because I tasted a little **h**. 1Sm 14:29
I tasted a little **h** with the end 1Sm 14:43
h, curds, sheep, and cheese from 2Sm 17:29
and a jar of **h**, and go to him. 1Kg 14:3
a land of olive trees and **h**— 2Kg 18:32
grain, wine, oil, **h**, and of all 2Ch 31:5
rivers flowing with **h** and cream. Jb 20:17
and sweeter than **h**—than honey Ps 19:10
than **h** dripping from the comb. Ps 19:10
you with **h** from the rock." Ps 81:16
⌊sweeter⌋ than **h** to my mouth. Ps 119:103
woman drip **h** and her words are Pr 5:3
Eat **h**, my son, for it is good, Pr 24:13
If you find **h**, eat only what you Pr 25:16
is not good to eat too much **h**, Pr 25:27
H and milk are under your tongue. Sg 4:11
I eat my honeycomb with my **h**. Sg 5:1
he will be eating butter and **h**. Is 7:15
the land will eat butter and **h**. Is 7:22
a land flowing with milk and **h**, Jr 11:5
a land flowing with milk and **h**. Jr 32:22
wheat, barley, oil, and **h**!" Jr 41:8
was as sweet as **h** in my mouth. Ezk 3:3
You ate fine flour, **h**, and oil. Ezk 16:13
oil, and **h** that I fed you. Ezk 16:19
⌊a land⌋ flowing with milk and **h**, Ezk 20:6
lands, flowing with milk and **h**— Ezk 20:15
Minnith, meal, **h**, oil, and balm Ezk 27:17
his food was locusts and wild **h**. Mt 3:4
and ate locusts and wild **h**. Mk 1:6
be as sweet as **h** in your mouth." Rv 10:9
was as sweet as **h** in my mouth, Rv 10:10

HONEYCOMB *(6)*
and dipped it into the **h**. 1Sm 14:27
Pleasant words are a **h**: Pr 16:24
and the **h** is sweet to your Pr 24:13
who is full tramples on a **h**, Pr 27:7
drip ⌊sweetness like⌋ the **h**, Sg 4:11
I eat my **h** with my honey. Sg 5:1

HONEYMOON *(1)*
and the bride her **h** chamber. Jl 2:16

HONOR *(141)*
of your **h** to all who are with Gn 20:16
my husband will **h** me because I Gn 30:20
And they bowed down to **h** him. Gn 43:28
night of vigil in **h** of the LORD, Ex 12:42
same night is in **h** of the LORD, Ex 12:42
H your father and your mother so Ex 20:12
a festival in My **h** three times a Ex 23:14
of the elderly and **h** the old. Lv 19:32
My Sabbaths and **h** My sanctuary; Lv 26:2
for I will greatly **h** you and do Nm 22:17
H your father and your mother, Dt 5:16
will receive no **h** on the road Jdg 4:9
so that we may **h** You when Your Jdg 13:17
and gives them a throne of **h**. 1Sm 2:8
I will **h** those who honor Me, 1Sm 2:30
I will honor those who **h** Me, 1Sm 2:30
h me now before the elders 1Sm 15:30
both riches and **h**, so that no 1Kg 3:13
H His holy name; let the hearts 1Ch 16:10
Riches and **h** come from You, 1Ch 29:12
days, riches, and **h**, and his son 1Ch 29:28
they made a great fire in his **h**. 2Ch 16:14
had riches and **h** in abundance. 2Ch 17:5
had riches and **h** in abundance, 2Ch 18:1
a fire in his **h** like the fire 2Ch 21:19
the fire in **h** of his fathers. 2Ch 21:19
not receive **h** from the LORD God. 2Ch 26:18
paid him **h** at his death. 2Ch 32:33
all women will **h** their husbands, Est 1:20
What **h** and special recognition Est 6:3
the man the king wants to **h**?" Est 6:6
would want to **h** more than me?" Est 6:6
For the man the king wants to **h**: Est 6:7
the man the king wants to **h**, Est 6:9
the man the king wants to **h**.' " Est 6:9
the man the king wants to **h**." Est 6:11
with gladness, joy and **h**. Est 8:16
his sons receive **h**, he does not Jb 14:21
therefore You will not **h** ⌊them⌋. Jb 17:4
stripped me of my **h** and removed Jb 19:9
yourself with **h** and glory. Jb 40:10
men, will my **h** be insulted? Ps 4:2
and leave my **h** in the dust. Ps 7:5
crowned him with glory and **h**. Ps 8:5
you descendants of Jacob, **h** Him! Ps 22:23
rescue you, and you will **h** Me." Ps 50:15
of praise and **h** to You all day Ps 71:8
will increase my **h** and comfort Ps 71:21
You, Lord, and will **h** Your name. Ps 86:9
and will **h** Your name forever. Ps 86:12
will rescue him and give him **h**. Ps 91:15
H His holy name; let the hearts Ps 105:3
His horn will be exalted in **h**. Ps 112:9
I will **h** Your name forever and Ps 145:2
This **h** is for all His godly Ps 149:9
H the LORD with your possessions Pr 3:9
in her left, riches and **h**. Pr 3:16
will inherit **h**, but He holds up Pr 3:35
you embrace her, she will **h** you. Pr 4:8
are riches and **h**, lasting wealth Pr 8:18
woman gains **h**, but violent men Pr 11:16
and humility comes before **h**. Pr 15:33
but before **h** comes humility. Pr 18:12
find life, righteousness, and **h**. Pr 21:21
along with wealth, **h**, and life. Pr 22:4
h is inappropriate for a fool. Pr 26:1
Giving **h** to a fool is like Pr 26:8
but a humble spirit will gain **h**. Pr 29:23
Strength and **h** are her clothing, Pr 31:25
and **h** so that he lacks nothing Ec 6:2
folly outweighs wisdom and **h**. Ec 10:1
future He will bring **h** to the Is 9:1
a throne of **h** for his father's Is 22:23
in the east **h** the LORD! Is 24:15
islands of the west ⌊**h**⌋ the name Is 24:15
a strong people will **h** You. Is 25:3
their mouths to **h** Me with Is 29:13
they will **h** My name, they will Is 29:23
will **h** the Holy One of Jacob Is 29:23
animals of the field will **h** Me, Is 43:20
My anger for the **h** of My name, Is 48:9
if you **h** it, not going your own Is 58:13
for the **h** of the LORD your God, Is 60:9
I suffer disgrace for Your **h**. Jr 15:15
I will **h** them, and they will not Jr 30:19
will **h** the holiness of My great Ezk 36:23
a reward, and great **h** from me. Dn 2:6
he will **h** a god of fortresses— Dn 11:38
He will greatly **h** those who Dn 11:39
change their **h** into disgrace. Hs 4:7
if I am a father, where is My **h**? Mal 1:6
take it to heart to **h** My name," Mal 2:2
is not without **h** except in his Mt 13:57
H your father and your mother; Mt 15:4
does not have to **h** his father.' Mt 15:6
These people **h** Me with their Mt 15:8
h your father and your mother; Mt 19:19
love the place of **h** at banquets, Mt 23:6
is not without **h** except in his Mk 6:4
These people **h** Me with their Mk 7:6
H your father and your mother; Mk 7:10
h your father and mother." Mk 10:19
and the places of **h** at banquets. Mk 12:39
h your father and mother." Lk 18:20
and the places of **h** at banquets. Lk 20:46
a prophet has no **h** in his own Jn 4:44
all people will **h** the Son just Jn 5:23
Son just as they **h** the Father. Jn 5:23
who does not **h** the Son does not Jn 5:23
Son does not **h** the Father who Jn 5:23
I **h** My Father and you dishonor Jn 8:49
Me, the Father will **h** him. Jn 12:26
seek for glory, **h**, and Rm 2:7
but glory, **h**, and peace for Rm 2:10
of pottery for **h** and another for Rm 9:21
Outdo one another in showing **h**. Rm 12:10
and **h** to those you owe honor. Rm 13:7
and honor to those you owe **h**. Rm 13:7
we clothe these with greater **h**, 1Co 12:23
giving greater **h** to the less 1Co 12:24
H your father and mother— Eph 6:2
joy and hold men like him in **h**, Php 2:29
vessel in sanctification and **h**, 1Th 4:4
be **h** and glory forever and ever. 1Tm 1:17
to whom be **h** and eternal might. 1Tm 6:16
You crowned him with glory and **h** Heb 2:7
crowned with glory and **h** because Heb 2:9
has more **h** than the house. Heb 3:3
No one takes this **h** on himself; Heb 5:4
and **h** at the revelation of Jesus 1Pt 1:7
So the **h** is for you who believe; 1Pt 2:7
H everyone. Love the brotherhood. 1Pt 2:17
Fear God. **H** the Emperor. 1Pt 2:17
yet showing them **h** as co-heirs 1Pt 3:7
He received **h** and glory from 2Pt 1:17
give glory, **h**, and thanks to Rv 4:9
receive glory and **h** and power, Rv 4:11
and strength and **h** and glory and Rv 5:12
Blessing and **h** and glory and Rv 5:13
and thanksgiving and **h** and power Rv 7:12
the glory and **h** of the nations Rv 21:26

HONORABLE *(12)*
LORD lives, you are an **h** man. 1Sm 29:6
Jabez was more **h** than his 1Ch 4:9
LORD is a stronghold for the **h**, Pr 10:29
It is **h** for a man to resolve a Pr 20:3
and the worthless toward the **h**. Is 3:5
the holy ⌊day⌋ of the LORD **h**; Is 58:13
sequence, most **h** Theophilus, Lk 1:3
to do what is **h** in everyone's Rm 12:17
body that we think to be less **h**, 1Co 12:23
greater honor to the less **h**, 1Co 12:24
making provision for what is **h**, 2Co 8:21
whatever is **h**, whatever is just Php 4:8

HONORABLY *(2)*
ourselves **h** in everything. Heb 13:18
yourselves **h** among the Gentiles 1Pt 2:12

HONORARIUM *(1)*
considered worthy of an ample **h**, 1Tm 5:17

HONORED *(28)*
You have **h** your sons more than 1Sm 2:29
bodyguard, and **h** in your house. 1Sm 22:14
king of Israel **h** himself today!" 2Sm 6:20
I will be **h** by the slave girls 2Sm 6:22
of the king's or been **h** at all?" 2Sm 19:42
he not the most **h** of the Three? 2Sm 23:19
He was the most **h** of the Thirty, 2Sm 23:23
He was the most **h** of the Three 1Ch 11:21
He was the most **h** of the Thirty, 1Ch 11:25
King Ahasuerus **h** Haman, son Est 3:1
are among your **h** women; Ps 45:9
who accepts rebuke will be **h**. Pr 13:18
after his master will be **h**. Pr 27:18
head is the elder, the **h** one; Is 9:15
are the **h** ones of the earth Is 23:8
disgrace all the **h** ones of the Is 23:9
nation; You are **h**. You have Is 26:15
are precious in My sight and **h**, Is 43:4
burnt offerings or **h** Me with Is 43:23
for I am **h** in the sight of the Is 49:5
All who **h** her ⌊now⌋ despise her, Lm 1:8
Most High and **h** and glorified Dn 4:34
heaven, Your name be **h** as holy. Mt 6:9
Father, Your name be **h** as holy. Lk 11:2
will then be **h** in the presence Lk 14:10
one member is **h**, all the members 1Co 12:26
will be highly **h** in my body, Php 1:20
may spread rapidly and be **h**, 2Th 3:1

HONORING *(1)*
say to You for **h** Your servant? 1Ch 17:18

HONORS *(7)*
my oil that **h** both God and man, Jdg 9:9

but **h** those who fear the LORD, Ps 15:4
a thank offering **h** Me, Ps 50:23
who is kind to the needy **h** Him. Pr 14:31
h will not be given to him, Dn 11:21
A son **h** ⌊his⌋ father, and a Mal 1:6
So they heaped many **h** on us, Ac 28:10

HOOF *(2)*
not a **h** will be left behind Ex 10:26
have a divided **h** and do not chew Lv 11:26

HOOFBEATS *(1)*
I hear the **h** of his horses?" Jdg 5:28

HOOK *(5)*
I will put My **h** in your nose and 2Kg 19:28
Leviathan with a **h** or tie his Jb 41:1
nose or pierce his jaw with a **h**? Jb 41:2
I will put My **h** in your nose and Is 37:29
pull them all up with a **h**, Hab 1:15

HOOKS *(21)*
have gold **h** ⌊and that stand⌋ Ex 26:32
their **h** are to be gold, and you Ex 26:37
h and bands of the posts must Ex 27:10
h and bands of the posts must Ex 27:11
and have silver **h** and bronze Ex 27:17
with gold; their **h** were of gold. Ex 36:36
with its five posts and their **h**. Ex 36:38
h and bands of the posts were Ex 38:10
h and bands of the posts were Ex 38:11
h and bands of the posts were Ex 38:12
h and bands of the posts were Ex 38:17
Their **h** were silver, and the Ex 38:19
he made the **h** for the posts, Ex 38:28
They captured Manasseh with **h**, 2Ch 33:11
those who cast **h** into the Nile Is 19:8
led him away with **h** to the land Ezk 19:4
on him with **h** and led him away Ezk 19:9
I will put **h** in your jaws and Ezk 29:4
you around, put **h** in your jaws, Ezk 38:4
were three-inch **h** fastened all Ezk 40:43
you will be taken away with **h**, Am 4:2

HOOPOE *(2)*
of heron, the **h**, and the bat. Lv 11:19
of heron, the **h**, and the bat. Dt 14:18

HOOVES *(20)*
with divided **h** and that chews Lv 11:3
the cud or have **h** you are not to Lv 11:4
does not have **h**—it is unclean Lv 11:4
does not have **h**—it is unclean Lv 11:5
does not have **h**—it is unclean Lv 11:6
it has divided **h**, does not chew Lv 11:7
that have **h** but do not have Lv 11:26
animal that has **h** divided in two Dt 14:6
chew the cud or have divided **h**, Dt 14:7
they do not have **h**—they are Dt 14:7
though it has **h**, it does not Dt 14:8
The horses' **h** then hammered— Jdg 5:22
than a bull with horns and **h**. Ps 69:31
Their horses' **h** are like flint; Is 5:28
of the stomping **h** of his Jr 47:3
feet were like the **h** of a calf, Ezk 1:7
with the **h** of his horses. Ezk 26:11
and no cattle **h** will disturb Ezk 32:13
horns iron and your **h** bronze, Mc 4:13
⌊sheep⌋ and tear off their **h**. Zch 11:16

HOPE *(167)*
was ⌊still⌋ **h** for me to have Ru 1:12
were looking for a sign of **h**, 1Kg 20:33
are like a shadow, without **h**. 1Ch 29:15
but there is still **h** for Israel Ezr 10:2
integrity of your life your **h**? Jb 4:6
the poor have **h**, and injustice Jb 5:16
God would provide what I **h** for: Jb 6:8
that I should continue to **h**? Jb 6:11
⌊the **h** for⌋ success has been Jb 6:13
merchants of Sheba **h** for them. Jb 6:19
they come to an end without **h**. Jb 7:6
h of the godless will perish. Jb 8:13
confident, because there is **h**. Jb 11:18
their ⌊only⌋ **h** will be to die. Jb 11:20
if He kills me, I will **h** in Him. Jb 13:15
There is **h** for a tree: If it is Jb 14:7
land, so You destroy a man's **h**. Jb 14:19
where then is my **h**? Who can see Jb 17:15
Who can see ⌊any⌋ **h** for me? Jb 17:15
He uproots my **h** like a tree. Jb 19:10
For what **h** does the godless man Jb 27:8
Any **h** of ⌊capturing⌋ him proves Jb 41:9
the **h** of the afflicted will not Ps 9:18
LORD, I turn my **h** to You. Ps 25:1
you who put your **h** in the LORD. Ps 31:24
horse is a false **h** for safety; Ps 33:17
LORD, for we put our **h** in You. Ps 33:22
who put their **h** in the LORD will Ps 37:9
I put my **h** in You, LORD; Ps 38:15
do I wait for? My **h** is in You. Ps 39:7
Put your **h** in God, for I will Ps 42:5
Put your **h** in God, for I will Ps 42:11
Put your **h** in God, for I will Ps 43:5
I will put my **h** in Your name, Ps 52:9
soul, for my **h** comes from Him. Ps 62:5
or false **h** in robbery. Ps 62:10
the **h** of all the ends of the Ps 65:5
who put their **h** in You be Ps 69:6
For You are my **h**, Lord GOD, my Ps 71:5
I will **h** continually and will Ps 71:14
since I set my **h** on You, Lord. Ps 86:4
for I **h** in Your judgments. Ps 119:43
You have given me **h** through it. Ps 119:49
for I put my **h** in Your word. Ps 119:74
I put my **h** in Your word. Ps 119:81
The wicked **h** to destroy me, Ps 119:95
I put my **h** in Your word. Ps 119:114
not let me be ashamed of my **h**. Ps 119:116
I put my **h** in Your word. Ps 119:147
I **h** for Your salvation and carry Ps 119:166
wait, and put my **h** in His word. Ps 130:5
Israel, put your **h** in the LORD. Ps 130:7
Israel, put your **h** in the LORD, Ps 131:3
whose **h** is in the LORD his God, Ps 146:5
who put their **h** in His faithful Ps 147:11
The **h** of the righteous is joy, Pr 10:28
and **h** placed in wealth vanishes. Pr 11:7
but the **h** of the wicked ⌊leads Pr 11:23
Delayed **h** makes the heart sick, Pr 13:12
your son while there is **h**; Pr 19:18
and your **h** will never fade. Pr 23:18
and your **h** will never fade. Pr 24:14
There is more **h** for a fool than Pr 26:12
There is more **h** for a fool than Pr 29:20
But there is **h** for whoever is Ec 9:4
Cush their **h** and Egypt their Is 20:5
last glimmer of **h** into sheer Is 21:4
to the Pit cannot **h** for Your Is 38:18
who put their **h** in Me will not Is 49:23
will put their **h** in Me, Is 51:5
We **h** for light, but there is Is 59:9
We **h** for justice, but there is Is 59:11
H of Israel, its Savior in time Jr 14:8
us with no **h** of healing for us Jr 14:19
We therefore put our **h** in You, Jr 14:22
LORD, the **h** of Israel, all who Jr 17:13
to give you a future and a **h**. Jr 29:11
There is **h** for your future— Jr 31:17
grazing land, the **h** of their Jr 50:7
as well as my **h** from the LORD. Lm 3:18
to mind, and therefore I have **h**: Lm 3:21
I will put my **h** in Him. Lm 3:24
perhaps there is ⌊still⌋ **h**. Lm 3:29
vain⌋, that her **h** was lost, she Ezk 19:5
up, and our **h** has perished; Ezk 37:11
of Achor into a gateway of **h**. Hs 2:15
and always put your **h** in God. Hs 12:6
will Ekron, for her **h** will fail. Zch 9:5
you prisoners who have **h**; Zch 9:12
will put their **h** in His name. Mt 12:21
on whom you have set your **h**. Jn 5:45
my flesh will rest in **h**, Ac 2:26
saw that their **h** of profit was Ac 16:19
because of the **h** of the Ac 23:6
And I have a **h** in God, which Ac 24:15
trial for the **h** of the promise Ac 26:6
12 tribes **h** to attain as they Ac 26:7
Because of this **h** I am being Ac 26:7
finally all **h** that we would be Ac 27:20
it is for the **h** of Israel that Ac 28:20
h, with hope he believed, Rm 4:18
hope, with **h** he believed, so Rm 4:18
we rejoice in the **h** of the glory Rm 5:2
and proven character produces **h**. Rm 5:4
This **h** does not disappoint, Rm 5:5
Him who subjected it—in the **h** Rm 8:20
Now in this **h** we were saved, Rm 8:24
yet **h** that is seen is not hope, Rm 8:24
yet hope that is seen is not **h**, Rm 8:24
But if we **h** for what we do not Rm 8:25
Rejoice in **h**; be patient in Rm 12:12
of the Scriptures we may have **h**. Rm 15:4
in Him the Gentiles will **h**. Rm 15:12
may the God of **h** fill you with Rm 15:13
may overflow with **h** by the power Rm 15:13
I do **h** to see you when I pass Rm 15:24
he who plows ought to plow in **h**, 1Co 9:10
should do so in **h** of sharing the 1Co 9:10
remain: faith, **h**, and love. 1Co 13:13
have placed our **h** in Christ for 1Co 15:19
in Ephesus with only human **h**, 1Co 15:32
for I **h** to spend some time with 1Co 16:7
And our **h** for you is firm, 2Co 1:7
have placed our **h** in Him that He 2Co 1:10
I **h** you will understand 2Co 1:13
Therefore having such a **h**, 2Co 3:12
and I **h** we are completely open 2Co 5:11
But we have the **h** that as your 2Co 10:15
And I **h** you will recognize that 2Co 13:6
wait for the **h** of righteousness Gl 5:5
already put our **h** in the Messiah Eph 1:12
what is the **h** of His calling, Eph 1:18
with no **h** and without God in the Eph 2:12
called to one **h** at your calling; Eph 4:4
expectation and **h** is that I will Php 1:20
I **h** in the Lord Jesus to send Php 2:19
I **h** to send him as soon as I see Php 2:23
because of the **h** reserved for Col 1:5
about ⌊this **h**⌋ in the message Col 1:5
away from the **h** of the gospel Col 1:23
Christ in you, the **h** of glory. Col 1:27
and endurance of **h** in our Lord 1Th 1:3
For who is our **h**, or joy, or 1Th 2:19
like the rest, who have no **h**. 1Th 4:13
a helmet of the **h** of salvation. 1Th 5:8
and good **h** by grace, 2Th 2:16
and of Christ Jesus, our **h**: 1Tm 1:1
we have put our **h** in the living 1Tm 4:10
has put her **h** in God and 1Tm 5:5
or to set their **h** on the 1Tm 6:17
in the **h** of eternal life that Ti 1:2
for the blessed **h** and the Ti 2:13
with the **h** of eternal life. Ti 3:7
I **h** that through your prayers Phm 22
and the confidence of our **h**. Heb 3:6
the final realization of your **h**, Heb 6:11
to seize the **h** set before us. Heb 6:18
We have this ⌊**h**⌋—like a sure Heb 6:19
but a better **h** is introduced, Heb 7:19
of our **h** without wavering Heb 10:23
birth into a living **h** through 1Pt 1:3
and set your **h** completely on the 1Pt 1:13
your faith and **h** are in God. 1Pt 1:21
reason for the **h** that is in you 1Pt 3:15
who has this **h** in Him purifies 1Jn 3:3
I **h** to be with you and talk face 2Jn 12
I **h** to see you soon, and we will 3Jn 14

HOPED *(7)*
enemies had **h** to overpower them Est 9:1
when I **h** for good, evil came; Jb 30:26
We **h** for peace, but there was Jr 8:15
We **h** for peace, but there was Jr 14:19
and not just as we had **h**. 2Co 8:5
is the reality of what is **h** for, Heb 11:1
the holy women who **h** in God also 1Pt 3:5

HOPELESS *(3)*
understand all this, it seemed **h** Ps 73:16
you say: It's **h**; I love Jr 2:25
will say: It's **h**. We will Jr 18:12

HOPES *(2)*
because who **h** for what he sees? Rm 8:24
all things, **h** all things, 1Co 13:7

HOPHNI *(5)*
Eli's two sons, **H** and Phinehas, 1Sm 1:3
your two sons **H** and Phinehas: 1Sm 2:34
Eli's two sons, **H** and Phinehas, 1Sm 4:4
Eli's two sons, **H** and Phinehas, 1Sm 4:11
Your two sons, **H** and Phinehas, 1Sm 4:17

HOPHRA *(1)*
am about to hand over Pharaoh **H**, Jr 44:30

HOPING *(6)*
⌊**h**⌋ to make your voice heard on Is 58:4
about Him and was **h** to see some Lk 23:8
we were **h** that He was the One Lk 24:21
he was also **h** that money would Ac 24:26
h somehow to reach Phoenix, Ac 27:12
things to you, **h** to come to you 1Tm 3:14

HOPPING *(1)*
their feet for **h** on the ground. Lv 11:21

HOR *(12)*
community came to Mount **H**. Nm 20:22
Aaron at Mount **H** on the border Nm 20:23
and bring them up Mount **H**. Nm 20:25
climbed Mount **H** in the sight Nm 20:27
out from Mount **H** by way of the Nm 21:4
camped at Mount **H** on the edge Nm 33:37
climbed Mount **H** and died there Nm 33:38
old when he died on Mount **H**. Nm 33:39
from Mount **H** and camped at Nm 33:41
Sea draw a line to Mount **H**; Nm 34:7
from Mount **H** draw a line to the Nm 34:8
died on Mount **H** and was gathered Dt 32:50

HOR-HAGGIDGAD *(2)*
Bene-jaakan and camped at **H**. Nm 33:32
departed from **H** and camped at Nm 33:33

HORAM *(1)*
that time **H** king of Gezer went Jos 10:33

HORDE *(5)*
This **h** will devour everything Nm 22:4
you see this entire immense **h**? 1Kg 20:13
this entire immense **h** to you. 1Kg 20:28
great army and vast **h** in battle, Ezk 17:17
—a mighty **h**, a huge army? Ezk 38:15

HORDES *(15)*
put an end to the **h** of Egypt by Ezk 30:10
king of Egypt and to his **h**: Ezk 31:2
This is Pharaoh and all his **h**"— Ezk 31:18
I will make your **h** fall by the Ezk 32:12
and all its **h** will be destroyed. Ezk 32:12
it over Egypt and all its **h**." Ezk 32:16
wail over the **h** of Egypt and Ezk 32:18
drag her and all her **h** away. Ezk 32:20
with all her **h** around her grave Ezk 32:24
place for Elam with all her **h**. Ezk 32:25
are there, with all their **h**. Ezk 32:26
be comforted over all his **h**— Ezk 32:31
and all his **h** will be laid to Ezk 32:32
assembled your **h** to carry off Ezk 38:13
Gog and all his **h** will be buried Ezk 39:11

HOREB *(17)*
(AKA SINAI)
of the wilderness and came to **H**, Ex 3:1
front of you on the rock at **H**; Ex 17:6
jewelry from Mount **H** ⌊onward⌋. Ex 33:6
journey from **H** to Kadesh-barnea Dt 1:2
LORD our God spoke to us at **H**, Dt 1:6
set out from **H** and went across Dt 1:19
before the LORD your God at **H**, Dt 4:10
spoke to you at **H** out of the Dt 4:15
made a covenant with us at **H**. Dt 5:2
You provoked the LORD at **H**, Dt 9:8
LORD your God at **H** on the day Dt 18:16
He had made with them at **H**. Dt 29:1
that Moses had put there at **H**, 1Kg 8:9
40 days and 40 nights to **H**, 1Kg 19:8
that Moses had put ⌊in it⌋ at **H**, 2Ch 5:10
At **H** they made a calf and Ps 106:19
him at **H** for all Israel. Mal 4:4

HOREM *(1)*
Iron, Migdal-el, **H**, Beth-anath, Jos 19:38

HORESH *(4)*
of Ziph in **H** when he saw that 1Sm 23:15
to David in **H** and encouraged 1Sm 23:16
remained in **H**, while Jonathan 1Sm 23:18
the strongholds in **H** on the hill 1Sm 23:19

HORI *(3)*
sons of Lotan were **H** and Heman. Gn 36:22
Shaphat son of **H** from the tribe Nm 13:5
Lotan's sons: **H** and Homam. 1Ch 1:39

HORITE *(1)*
are the sons of Seir the **H**, Gn 36:20

HORITES *(6)*
and the **H** in the mountains of Gn 14:6
These are the chiefs of the **H**, Gn 36:21
These are the chiefs of the **H**: Gn 36:29
These are the chiefs of the **H**, Gn 36:30
The **H** had previously lived in Dt 2:12
He destroyed the **H** before them; Dt 2:22

HORIZON *(6)*
He laid out the **h** on the surface Jb 26:10
at the eastern **h** ⌊or⌋ settle at Ps 139:9
He laid out the **h** on the surface Pr 8:27
from the distant **h**—the LORD Is 13:5
flashes from **h** to horizon and Lk 17:24
from horizon to **h** and lights up Lk 17:24

HORMAH *(9)*
(AKA ZEPHATH)
and routed them as far as **H**. Nm 14:45
So they named the place **H**. Nm 21:3
you from Seir as far as **H**. Dt 1:44
the king of **H** one the king of Jos 12:14
Eltolad, Chesil, **H**, Jos 15:30
Eltolad, Bethul, **H**, Jos 19:4
So they named the town **H**. Jdg 1:17
to those in **H**, in Bor-ashan, and 1Sm 30:30
Bethuel, **H**, Ziklag, 1Ch 4:30

HORN *(67)*
When the ram's **h** sounds a long Ex 19:13
blast of the **h** and you hear its Jos 6:5
sounded the ram's **h** throughout Jdg 3:27
he blew the ram's **h** and the Jdg 6:34
my **h** is lifted up by the LORD. 1Sm 2:1
lift up the **h** of His anointed 1Sm 2:10
blew the ram's **h** throughout the 1Sm 13:3
Fill your **h** with oil and go. 1Sm 16:1
So Samuel took the **h** of oil, 1Sm 16:13
Then Joab blew the ram's **h**, 2Sm 2:28
and the sound of the ram's **h**. 2Sm 6:15
hear the sound of the ram's **h**, 2Sm 15:10
blew the ram's **h**, and the troops 2Sm 18:16
He blew the ram's **h** and shouted: 2Sm 20:1
he blew the ram's **h**, and they 2Sm 20:22
shield, the **h** of my salvation, 2Sm 22:3
to blow the ram's **h** and say, 1Kg 1:34
the priest took the **h** of oil 1Kg 1:39
Then they blew the ram's **h**, 1Kg 1:39
sound of the ram's **h** and said, 1Kg 1:41
blew the ram's **h** and proclaimed, 2Kg 9:13
sound of the ram's **h**, trumpets, 1Ch 15:28
shield and the **h** of my salvation Ps 18:2
wicked, 'Do not lift up your **h**. Ps 75:4
lift up your **h** against heaven Ps 75:5
Blow the **h** during the new moon Ps 81:3
by Your favor our **h** is exalted. Ps 89:17
My name his **h** will be exalted. Ps 89:24
have lifted up my **h** like that of Ps 92:10
of the ram's **h** shout Ps 98:6
His **h** will be exalted in honor. Ps 112:9
I will make a **h** grow for David; Ps 132:17
raised up a **h** for His people, Ps 148:14
Blow the ram's **h** throughout the Jr 4:5
heard the sound of the ram's **h**— Jr 4:19
hear the sound of the ram's **h**? Jr 4:21
Sound the ram's **h** in Tekoa; Jr 6:1
for the sound of the ram's **h**. Jr 6:17
of the ram's **h** or hunger for Jr 42:14
Moab's **h** is chopped off; Jr 48:25
a ram's **h** among the nations; Jr 51:27
cut off every **h** of Israel in His Lm 2:3
and exalting the **h** of your Lm 2:17
I will cause a **h** to sprout for Ezk 29:21
you hear the sound of the **h**, Dn 3:5
people heard the sound of the **h**, Dn 3:7
who hears the sound of the **h**, Dn 3:10
you hear the sound of the **h**, Dn 3:15
another **h**, a little one, Dn 7:8
eyes in this **h** like a man's, Dn 7:8
words the **h** was speaking. Dn 7:11
about the other **h** that came up, Dn 7:20
fell—the **h** that had eyes, Dn 7:20
this **h** made war with the holy Dn 7:21
a conspicuous **h** between his eyes Dn 8:5
the large **h** was shattered. Dn 8:8
them a little **h** emerged and grew Dn 8:9
The **h** will throw truth to the Dn 8:12
and the large **h** between his eyes Dn 8:21
the shattered **h** represent four Dn 8:22
the **h** in Gibeah, the trumpet Hs 5:8
⌊Put⌋ the **h** to your mouth! Hs 8:1
Blow the **h** in Zion; sound the Jl 2:1
Blow the **h** in Zion! Announce a Jl 2:15
and the sound of the ram's **h**. Am 2:2
If a ram's **h** is blown in a city, Am 3:6
has raised up a **h** of salvation Lk 1:69

HORNET *(3)*
will send the **h** in front of you Ex 23:28
also send the **h** against them Dt 7:20
I sent the **h** ahead of you, Jos 24:12

HORNS *(64)*
caught by its **h** in the thicket. Gn 22:13
Make **h** for it on its four Ex 27:2
the **h** are to be of one piece. Ex 27:2
it⌋ to the **h** of the altar with Ex 29:12
Its **h** must be of one piece. Ex 30:2
sides, and its **h** with pure gold; Ex 30:3
rite on the **h** of the altar. Ex 30:10
Its **h** were of one piece. Ex 37:25
sides, and its **h** with pure gold. Ex 37:26
He made **h** for it on its four Ex 38:2
the **h** were of one piece. Ex 38:2
the blood to the **h** of the altar Lv 4:7
the blood to the **h** of the altar Lv 4:18
apply it to the **h** of the altar Lv 4:25
apply it to the **h** of the altar Lv 4:30
apply it to the **h** of the altar Lv 4:34
his finger to the **h** of the altar Lv 8:15
it to the **h** of the altar. Lv 9:9
put ⌊it⌋ on the **h** on all sides Lv 16:18
is like the **h** of a wild ox for Nm 23:22
is like the **h** of a wild ox for Nm 24:8
and **h** like those of a wild ox; Dt 33:17
take hold of the **h** of the altar. 1Kg 1:50
hold of the **h** of the altar, 1Kg 1:51
took hold of the **h** of the altar. 1Kg 2:28
Chenaanah made iron **h** and said, 1Kg 22:11
with trumpets, and with rams' **h**. 2Ch 15:14
Chenaanah made iron **h** and said, 2Ch 18:10
me from the **h** of the wild oxen. Ps 22:21
than a bull with **h** and hooves. Ps 69:31
cut off all the **h** of the wicked, Ps 75:10
but the **h** of the righteous will Ps 75:10
cords to the **h** of the altar. Ps 118:27
and on the **h** of their altars, Jr 17:1
ones with your **h** until you Ezk 34:21
and four **h** project upward from Ezk 43:15
it⌋ to the four **h** of the altar, Ezk 43:20
before it, and it had 10 **h**. Dn 7:7
While I was considering the **h**, Dn 7:8
of the first **h** were uprooted Dn 7:8
know⌋ about the 10 **h** on its head Dn 7:20
The 10 **h** are 10 kings who will Dn 7:24
He had two **h**. The two horns Dn 8:3
The two **h** were long, but one was Dn 8:3
his two **h**, and the ram was Dn 8:7
Four conspicuous **h** came up in Dn 8:8
The four **h** that took the place Dn 8:22
the **h** of the altar will be cut Am 3:14
I will make your **h** iron and your Mc 4:13
Then I looked up and saw four **h**. Zch 1:18
These are the **h** that scattered Zch 1:19
These are the **h** that scattered Zch 1:21
to cut off the **h** of the nations Zch 1:21
raised ⌊their⌋ **h** against the Zch 1:21
He had seven **h** and seven eyes, Rv 5:6
the four **h** of the gold altar Rv 9:13
having seven heads and 10 **h**, Rv 12:3
He had 10 **h** and seven heads. Rv 13:1
On his **h** were 10 diadems, and on Rv 13:1
he had two **h** like a lamb, but he Rv 13:11
having seven heads and 10 **h**. Rv 17:3
the seven heads and the 10 **h**, Rv 17:7
10 **h** you saw are 10 kings who Rv 17:12
The 10 **h** you saw, and the beast, Rv 17:16

HORONAIM *(4)*
of destruction on the road to **H**. Is 15:5
A voice cries out from **H**: Jr 48:3
the descent to **H** will be heard Jr 48:5
from Zoar to **H** ⌊and⌋ Jr 48:34

HORONITE *(3)*
When Sanballat the **H** and Tobiah Neh 2:10
When Sanballat the **H**, Tobiah the Neh 2:19
a son-in-law to Sanballat the **H**. Neh 13:28

HORRIBLE *(8)*
Don't do this **h** thing. Jdg 19:23
don't do this **h** thing to this Jdg 19:24
committed a **h** shame in Israel Jdg 20:6
Don't do this **h** thing! 2Sm 13:12
possessions with a **h** affliction. 2Ch 21:14
A **h**, terrible thing has taken Jr 5:30
Jerusalem also I saw a **h** thing: Jr 23:14
seen something **h** in the house Hs 6:10

HORRIFIED *(8)*
be **h** because of their shame. Ps 40:15
They will be **h**; pain and agony Is 13:8
Be **h** at this, heavens; Jr 2:12

by it will be **h** and shake his Jr 18:16
it will be **h** and scoff because Jr 19:8
by her will be **h** and scoff Jr 49:17
Babylon will be **h** and scoff Jr 50:13
to be deeply distressed and **h**. Mk 14:33

HORRIFYING *(1)*
h end of all the inhabitants of Zph 1:18

HORROR *(24)*
be an object of **h** to all the Dt 28:25
You will become an object of **h**, Dt 28:37
them for all the **h** they did in Jdg 20:10
of terror, **h**, and hissing, as 2Ch 29:8
an object of **h** as you yourselves 2Ch 30:7
those in the east tremble in **h**. Jb 18:20
and my body trembles in **h**. Jb 21:6
h has overwhelmed me. Ps 55:5
heart staggers; **h** terrifies me. Is 21:4
will be a **h** to all mankind." Is 66:24
h has taken hold of me. Jr 8:21
I will make them a **h** to all the Jr 15:4
They have made their land a **h**, Jr 18:16
an object of **h** and disaster to Jr 24:9
I will make them a **h** to all the Jr 29:18
I will make you a **h** to all the Jr 34:17
a **h** Babylon has become among Jr 50:23
a **h** Babylon has become among Jr 51:41
warning and a **h**, to the nations Ezk 5:15
and **h** will overwhelm them. Ezk 7:18
I will make you an object of **h**, Ezk 26:21
an object of **h** and will never Ezk 27:36
an object of **h** and will never Ezk 28:19
Nations writhe in **h** before them; Jl 2:6

HORRORS *(1)*
I suffer Your **h**; I am desperate. Ps 88:15

HORSE *(38)*
has thrown the **h** and its rider Ex 15:1
has thrown the **h** and its rider Ex 15:21
and a **h** for about four pounds. 1Kg 10:29
escaped on a **h** with the cavalry 1Kg 20:20
army you lost—**h** for horse, 1Kg 20:25
lost—horse for **h**, chariot for 1Kg 20:25
silver⌋ and a **h** for about four 2Ch 1:17
made repairs above the **H** Gate, Neh 3:28
worn and a **h** the king himself Est 6:8
garment and the **h** under the Est 6:9
him on the **h** through the city Est 6:9
a garment and a **h** for Mordecai Est 6:10
took the garment and the **h**. Est 6:11
laughs at the **h** and its rider. Jb 39:18
Do you give strength to the **h**? Jb 39:19
Do not be like a **h** or mule, Ps 32:9
h is a false hope for safety; Ps 33:17
both chariot and **h** lay still. Ps 76:6
by the strength of a **h**; Ps 147:10
A **h** is prepared for the day of Pr 21:31
A whip for the **h**, a bridle for Pr 26:3
brings out the chariot and **h**, Is 43:17
depths like a **h** in the Is 63:13
his course like a **h** rushing into Jr 8:6
corner of the **H** Gate to the east Jr 31:40
will smash the **h** and its rider; Jr 51:21
the one riding a **h** will not save Am 2:15
galloping **h** and jolting chariot! Nah 3:2
and saw a man riding on a red **h**. Zch 1:8
and the **h** from Jerusalem. Zch 9:10
will strike every **h** with panic Zch 12:4
looked, and there was a white **h**. Rv 6:2
Then another **h** went out, a fiery Rv 6:4
looked, and there was a black **h**. Rv 6:5
and there was a pale green **h**. Rv 6:8
opened, and there was a white **h**! Rv 19:11
rider on the **h** and against His Rv 19:19
the mouth of the rider on the **h**, Rv 19:21

HORSEFLY *(1)*
but a **h** from the north is coming Jr 46:20

HORSEMAN *(8)*
So a **h** went to meet Jehu and 2Kg 9:18
So he sent out a second **h**, 2Kg 9:19
sound of the **h** and the archer. Jr 4:29
Charging **h**, flashing sword, Nah 3:3
The **h** on it had a bow; Rv 6:2
and its **h** was empowered to take Rv 6:4
The **h** on it had a balance scale Rv 6:5
The **h** on it was named Death, Rv 6:8

HORSEMEN *(33)*
chariots, his **h**, and his army— Ex 14:9
army, and his chariots and **h**. Ex 14:17
his chariots, and his **h**." Ex 14:18
chariots, and his **h**—and went Ex 14:23
on their chariots and **h**." Ex 14:26
and covered the chariots and **h**, Ex 14:28
his chariots and **h** went into the Ex 15:19
chariots and **h** as far as the sea Jos 24:6
chariots, 6,000 **h**, and troops as 1Sm 13:5
captured 1,700 **h** and 20,000 foot 2Sm 8:4
for his chariots, and 12,000 **h**. 1Kg 4:26
and 12,000 **h** and stationed them 1Kg 10:26
the chariots and **h** of Israel!" 2Kg 2:12
except for 50 **h**, 10 chariots, 2Kg 13:7
the chariots and **h** of Israel!" 2Kg 13:14
in Egypt for chariots and for **h**? 2Kg 18:24
chariots, 7,000 **h**, and 20,000 1Ch 18:4
hire chariots and **h** from 1Ch 19:6
1,400 chariots and 12,000 **h**, 2Ch 1:14
and chariots, and 12,000 **h**. 2Ch 9:25
with very many chariots and **h**? 2Ch 16:8
riders—pairs of **h**, riders on Is 21:7
Look, riders come—**h** in pairs." Is 21:9
up a quiver with chariots and **h**, Is 22:6
and **h** were positioned at the Is 22:7
in Egypt for chariots and **h**? Is 36:9
young men, **h** riding on steeds. Ezk 23:6
dressed, **h** riding on steeds, Ezk 23:12
chariots, **h**, and many ships. Dn 11:40
Their **h** charge ahead; Hab 1:8
h come from distant ⌊lands⌋ Hab 1:8
and they will put **h** to shame. Zch 10:5
The **h** had breastplates that were Rv 9:17

HORSES *(117)*
hitched ⌊the **h** to⌋ his chariot Gn 46:29
them food in exchange for the **h**, Gn 47:17
H and chariots went up with him; Gn 50:9
the field—the **h**, donkeys, Ex 9:3
all Pharaoh's **h** and chariots, Ex 14:9
all Pharaoh's **h**, his chariots, Ex 14:23
When Pharaoh's **h** with his Ex 15:19
army, its **h** and chariots, Dt 11:4
not acquire many **h** for himself Dt 17:16
back to Egypt to acquire many **h**, Dt 17:16
against your enemies and see **h**, Dt 20:1
a vast number of **h** and chariots. Jos 11:4
hamstring their **h** and burn up Jos 11:6
hamstrung their **h** and burned up Jos 11:9
I hear the hoofbeats of his **h**?" Jdg 5:28
chariots, on his **h**, or running 1Sm 8:11
and he hamstrung all the **h**, 2Sm 8:4
a chariot, **h**, and 50 men to run 2Sm 15:1
stalls of **h** for his chariots 1Kg 4:26
and the other **h** to the required 1Kg 4:28
spices, and **h** and mules. 1Kg 10:25
Solomon's **h** were imported from 1Kg 10:28
can keep the **h** and mules alive 1Kg 18:5
along with **h** and chariotry, 1Kg 20:1
people, my **h** as your horses, 1Kg 22:4
people, my horses as your **h**." 1Kg 22:4
of fire with **h** of fire suddenly 2Kg 2:11
people, my **h** as your horses. 2Kg 3:7
people, my horses as your **h**." 2Kg 3:7
came with his **h** and chariots 2Kg 5:9
he sent **h**, chariots, and a 2Kg 6:14
an army with **h** and chariots 2Kg 6:15
was covered with **h** and chariots 2Kg 6:17
of chariots, **h**, and a great army 2Kg 7:6
their tents, **h**, and donkeys. 2Kg 7:7
but tethered **h** and donkeys, 2Kg 7:10
take five of the **h** that are left 2Kg 7:13
took two chariots with **h**, 2Kg 7:14
on the wall and on the **h**, 2Kg 9:33
have chariots, **h**, a fortified 2Kg 10:2
They carried him back on **h**, 2Kg 14:20
give you 2,000 **h** if you're able 2Kg 18:23
away with the **h** that the kings 2Kg 23:11
him and hamstrung all the **h**, 1Ch 18:4
Solomon's **h** came from Egypt and 2Ch 1:16
spices, and **h** and mules—as 2Ch 9:24
4,000 stalls for **h** and chariots, 2Ch 9:25
They were bringing **h** for Solomon 2Ch 9:28
him back on **h** and buried him 2Ch 25:28
They had 736 **h**, 245 mules, Ezr 2:66
They had 736 **h**, 245 mules, Neh 7:68
who rode fast **h** bred from the Est 8:10
On their royal **h**, the couriers Est 8:14
and others in **h**, but we take Ps 20:7
seen slaves on **h**, but princes Ec 10:7
land is full of **h**, and there is Is 2:7
rumbles, his **h** do not crush it. Is 28:28
will escape on **h**"—therefore Is 30:16
"We will ride on fast **h**"— Is 30:16
for help and who depend on **h**! Is 31:1
their **h** are flesh, not spirit. Is 31:3
give you 2,000 **h** if you can put Is 36:8
to the LORD on **h** and chariots, Is 66:20
His **h** are swifter than eagles. Jr 4:13
they ride on **h**, lined up like Jr 6:23
Dan is heard the snorting of **h**. Jr 8:16
how can you compete with **h**? Jr 12:5
in chariots and on **h** with their Jr 17:25
riding on chariots and **h**— Jr 22:4
Harness the **h**; mount the steeds; Jr 46:4
is against his **h** and chariots Jr 50:37
they ride on **h**, lined up like Jr 50:42
bring up **h** like a swarm of Jr 51:27
might give him **h** and a large Ezk 17:15
all of them riding on **h**. Ezk 23:23
Tyre from the north with **h**, Ezk 26:7
His **h** will be so numerous that Ezk 26:10
with the hooves of his **h**. Ezk 26:11
from Beth-togarmah exchanged **h**, Ezk 27:14
horses, war **h**, and mules for Ezk 27:14
army, including **h** and riders, Ezk 38:4
are all riding **h**—a mighty Ezk 38:15
eat your fill of **h** and riders, Ezk 39:20
or war, or by **h** and cavalry. Hs 1:7
not ride on **h**, and we will no Hs 14:3
appearance is like that of **h**, Jl 2:4
and they gallop like war **h**. Jl 2:4
along with your captured **h**. Am 4:10
h run on rock, or does someone Am 6:12
Harness the **h** to the chariot, Mc 1:13
will remove your **h** from you and Mc 5:10
h are swifter than leopards Hab 1:8
the sea when You ride on Your **h**, Hab 3:8
You tread the sea with Your **h**, Hab 3:15
H and their riders will fall, Hg 2:22
were red, sorrel, and white **h**. Zch 1:8
The first chariot had red **h**, Zch 6:2
the second chariot black **h**, Zch 6:2
the third chariot white **h**, Zch 6:3
the fourth chariot dappled **h**— Zch 6:3
dappled horses—⌊all⌋ strong **h**. Zch 6:3
one with the black **h** is going to Zch 6:6
white **h** are going after them, Zch 6:6
but the dappled **h** are going to Zch 6:6
As the strong **h** went out, they Zch 6:7
strike all the **h** of the nations Zch 12:4
previous one will strike the **h**, Zch 14:15
will be on the bells of the **h**. Zch 14:20
the mouths of **h** to make them Jms 3:3
locusts was like **h** equipped for Rv 9:7
chariots with many **h** rushing Rv 9:9
is how I saw the **h** in my vision: Rv 9:17
heads of the **h** were like lions' Rv 9:17
the power of the **h** is in their Rv 9:19
and sheep; **h** and carriages; Rv 18:13
heaven followed Him on white **h**, Rv 19:14
the flesh of **h** and of their Rv 19:18

HORSES' *(6)*
that bites the **h** heels so that Gn 49:17
The **h** hooves then hammered— Jdg 5:22
out by way of the **H** Entrance to 2Kg 11:16
entrance of the **H** Gate to the 2Ch 23:15
Their **h** hooves are like flint; Is 5:28
press up to the **h** bridles for Rv 14:20

HOSAH *(5)*
it turned back to **H** and ended at Jos 19:29
son of Jeduthun and **H** were to be 1Ch 16:38
H, from the Merarites, also had 1Ch 26:10
brothers of **H** were 13 in all. 1Ch 26:11
Shuppim and **H** it was the west 1Ch 26:16

HOSANNA *(6)*
H to the Son of David! Mt 21:9
H in the highest heaven! Mt 21:9
complex cheering, "**H** to the Son Mt 21:15
kept shouting: **H**! Blessed is He Mk 11:9
H in the highest heaven! Mk 11:10
kept shouting: "**H** ! Blessed is Jn 12:13

HOSEA *(3)*
LORD that came to **H** son of Beeri Hs 1:1
When the LORD first spoke to **H**, Hs 1:2
He also says in **H**: I will call Rm 9:25

of the Lord GOD of **H** in the land Jr 50:25
of the Lord GOD of **H**— Jr 50:31
This is what the LORD of **H** says: Jr 50:33
the LORD of **H** is His name. Jr 50:34
God, the LORD of **H**, though their Jr 51:5
The LORD of **H** has sworn by Jr 51:14
the LORD of **H** is His name. Jr 51:19
For this is what the LORD of **H**, Jr 51:33
the LORD of **H** is His name. Jr 51:57
This is what the LORD of **H** says: Jr 51:58
Yahweh is the God of **H**; Hs 12:5
of the Lord GOD, the God of **H**. Am 3:13
the God of **H**, is His name. Am 4:13
LORD, the God of **H**, will be with Am 5:14
LORD, the God of **H**, will be Am 5:15
the God of **H**, the Lord, says: Am 5:16
the God of **H**, is His name. Am 5:27
of Yahweh, the God of **H**: Am 6:8
the GOD of **H**—and they will Am 6:14
Lord, the GOD of **H**—He touches Am 9:5
of the LORD of **H** has promised Mc 4:4
declaration of the Lord of **H**. Nah 2:13
declaration of the Lord of **H**. Nah 3:5
Is it not from the LORD of **H**, Hab 2:13
declaration of the LORD of **H**, Zph 2:9
the people of the LORD of **H**. Zph 2:10
The LORD of **H** says this: Hg 1:2
Now, the LORD of **H** says this: Hg 1:5
The LORD of **H** says this: Hg 1:7
declaration of the LORD of **H**. Hg 1:9
on the house of Yahweh of **H**, Hg 1:14
declaration of the LORD of **H**. Hg 2:4
For the LORD of **H** says this: Hg 2:6
with glory," says the LORD of **H**. Hg 2:7
declaration of the LORD of **H**. Hg 2:8
the first," says the LORD of **H**. Hg 2:9
declaration of the LORD of **H**. Hg 2:9
This is what the LORD of **H** says: Hg 2:11
declaration of the LORD of **H**— Hg 2:23
declaration of the LORD of **H**. Hg 2:23
This is what the LORD of **H** says: Zch 1:3
declaration of the LORD of **H**— Zch 1:3
to you, says the LORD of **H**. Zch 1:3
This is what the LORD of **H** says: Zch 1:4
the LORD of **H** purposed to deal Zch 1:6
How long, LORD of **H**, will You Zch 1:12
The LORD of **H** says: I am Zch 1:14
declaration of the LORD of **H**— Zch 1:16
This is what the LORD of **H** says: Zch 1:17
For the LORD of **H** says this: Zch 2:8
that the LORD of **H** has sent Me. Zch 2:9
that the LORD of **H** has sent Me Zch 2:11
This is what the LORD of **H** says: Zch 3:7
declaration of the LORD of **H**— Zch 3:9
declaration of the LORD of **H**. Zch 3:10
My Spirit,' says the LORD of **H**. Zch 4:6
that the LORD of **H** has sent me Zch 4:9
declaration of the LORD of **H**— Zch 5:4
This is what the LORD of **H** says: Zch 6:12
that the LORD of **H** has sent Me Zch 6:15
house of the LORD of **H** as well Zch 7:3
of the LORD of **H** came to me: Zch 7:4
The LORD of **H** says this: Zch 7:9
the LORD of **H** had sent by His Zch 7:12
anger came from the LORD of **H**. Zch 7:12
not listen," says the LORD of **H**. Zch 7:13
The word of the LORD of **H** came: Zch 8:1
The LORD of **H** says this: Zch 8:2
the mountain of the LORD of **H**, Zch 8:3
The LORD of **H** says this: Zch 8:4
The LORD of **H** says this: Zch 8:6
declaration of the LORD of **H**. Zch 8:6
The LORD of **H** says this: Zch 8:7
The LORD of **H** says this: Zch 8:9
the house of the LORD of **H**. Zch 8:9
declaration of the LORD of **H**. Zch 8:11
For the LORD of **H** says this: Zch 8:14
not relent," says the LORD of **H**, Zch 8:14
of the LORD of **H** came to me: Zch 8:18
The LORD of **H** says this: Zch 8:19
The LORD of **H** says this: Zch 8:20
favor and to seek the LORD of **H**. Zch 8:21
seek the LORD of **H** in Jerusalem Zch 8:22
The LORD of **H** says this: Zch 8:23
The LORD of **H** will defend them. Zch 9:15
For the LORD of **H** has tended His Zch 10:3
strength through the LORD of **H**, Zch 12:5
declaration of the LORD of **H**— Zch 13:2
declaration of the LORD of **H**. Zch 13:7
the LORD of **H**, and to celebrate Zch 14:16
the LORD of **H**, rain will not Zch 14:17
will be holy to the LORD of **H**. Zch 14:21
in the house of the LORD of **H**. Zch 14:21
the LORD of **H** says this: Mal 1:4
the LORD of **H** to you priests, Mal 1:6
you favor?" asks the LORD of **H**. Mal 1:8
you favor?" asks the LORD of **H**. Mal 1:9
says the LORD of **H**, "and I will Mal 1:10
nations," says the LORD of **H**. Mal 1:11
scorn it," says the LORD of **H**. Mal 1:13
says the LORD of **H**, "and My name Mal 1:14
says the LORD of **H**, "I will send Mal 2:2
continue," says the LORD of **H**. Mal 2:4
the messenger of the LORD of **H**. Mal 2:7
of Levi," says the LORD of **H**. Mal 2:8
an offering to the LORD of **H**. Mal 2:12
injustice," says the LORD of **H**. Mal 2:16
is coming," says the LORD of **H**. Mal 3:1
fear Me," says the LORD of **H**. Mal 3:5
to you," says the LORD of **H**. Mal 3:7
this way," says the LORD of **H**. Mal 3:10
be barren," says the LORD of **H**. Mal 3:11
land," says the LORD of **H**. Mal 3:12
mournfully before the LORD of **H**? Mal 3:14
says the LORD of **H**, "a special Mal 3:17
says the LORD of **H**, "not leaving Mal 4:1
preparing," says the LORD of **H**. Mal 4:3
If the Lord of **H** had not left us Rm 9:29
the ears of the Lord of **H**. Jms 5:4

HOT *(18)*

the Anah who found the **h** springs Gn 36:24
when the sun grew **h**, it melted. Ex 16:21
by the time the sun is **h**.' " 1Sm 11:9
baked over **h** stones and a jug 1Kg 19:6
of Jerusalem until the sun is **h**, Neh 7:3
their channels in **h** weather. Jb 6:17
himself with the **h** east wind? Jb 15:2
clothes get **h** when the south Jb 37:17
My heart grew **h** within me; Ps 39:3
Let **h** coals fall on them. Ps 140:10
Our skin is as **h** as an oven from Lm 5:10
your hands with **h** coals from Ezk 10:2
that it becomes **h** and its copper Ezk 24:11
and the furnace extremely **h**, Dn 3:22
All of them are as **h** as an oven, Hs 7:7
that you are neither cold nor **h**. Rv 3:15
I wish that you were cold or **h**. Rv 3:15
and neither **h** nor cold, I am Rv 3:16

HOT-TEMPERED *(4)*

A **h** man stirs up conflict, Pr 15:18
than with a nagging and **h** wife. Pr 21:19
don't be a companion of a **h** man, Pr 22:24
and a **h** man increases rebellion. Pr 29:22

HOTHAM *(2)*

Shomer, and **H**, with their sister 1Ch 7:32
the sons of **H** the Aroerite, 1Ch 11:44

HOTHIR *(2)*

Mallothi, **H**, and Mahazioth. 1Ch 25:4
twenty-first to **H**, his sons, and 1Ch 25:28

HOUND *(1)*

synagogues and **h** from town to Mt 23:34

HOUR *(55)*

be given what to say at that **h**, Mt 10:19
'These last men put in one **h**, Mt 20:12
that day and **h** no one knows— Mt 24:36
is coming at an **h** you do not Mt 24:44
and at an **h** he does not know Mt 24:50
know either the day or the **h**. Mt 25:13
you stay awake with Me one **h**? Mt 26:40
is given to you in that **h**— Mk 13:11
that day or **h** no one knows— Mk 13:32
the **h** might pass from Him. Mk 14:35
Couldn't you stay awake one **h**? Mk 14:37
At the **h** of incense the whole Lk 1:10
that same **h** He rejoiced in the Lk 10:21
that very **h** what must be said. Lk 12:12
known at what **h** the thief was Lk 12:39
coming at an **h** that you do not Lk 12:40
and at an **h** he does not know. Lk 12:46
their hands on Him that very **h**, Lk 20:19
When the **h** came, He reclined at Lk 22:14
But this is your **h**—and the Lk 22:53
About an **h** later, another kept Lk 22:59
That very **h** they got up and Lk 24:33
"My **h** has not yet come." Jn 2:4
an **h** is coming when you will Jn 4:21
But an **h** is coming, and is now Jn 4:23
was the very **h** at which Jesus Jn 4:53
An **h** is coming, and is now here, Jn 5:25
Him because His **h** had not yet Jn 7:30
because His **h** had not come. Jn 8:20
The **h** has come for the Son of Jn 12:23
Father, save Me from this **h**? Jn 12:27
that is why I came to this **h**. Jn 12:27
knew that His **h** had come to Jn 13:1
An **h** is coming, and has come, Jn 16:32
Father, the **h** has come. Jn 17:1
And from that **h** the disciple Jn 19:27
complex at the **h** of prayer at Ac 3:1
days ago at this **h**, at three Ac 10:30
them the same **h** of the night Ac 16:33
And in that very **h** I looked up Ac 22:13
is already the **h** for you to wake Rm 13:11
Up to the present **h** we are both 1Co 4:11
Why are we in danger every **h**? 1Co 15:30
to these people for even an **h**, Gl 2:5
Children, it is the last **h**. 1Jn 2:18
from this that it is the last **h**. 1Jn 2:18
no idea at what **h** I will come Rv 3:3
you from the **h** of testing that Rv 3:10
in heaven for about half an **h**. Rv 8:1
who were prepared for the **h**, Rv 9:15
because the **h** of His judgment Rv 14:7
kings with the beast for one **h**. Rv 17:12
For in a single **h** your judgment Rv 18:10
in a single **h** such fabulous Rv 18:17
in a single **h** she was destroyed Rv 18:19

HOURS *(4)*

like a few **h** of the night. Ps 90:4
"Aren't there 12 **h** in a day?" Jn 11:9
an interval of about three **h**; Ac 5:7
all of them for about two **h**: Ac 19:34

HOUSE *(1104)*

your father's **h** to the land that Gn 12:1
woman was taken to Pharaoh's **h**. Gn 12:15
Pharaoh and his **h** with severe Gn 12:17
and the heir of my **h** is Eliezer Gn 15:2
born in my **h** will be my heir. Gn 15:3
born in your **h** and one purchased Gn 17:12
born in your **h**, as well as one Gn 17:13
born in his **h** or purchased with Gn 17:23
slaves born in his **h** and those Gn 17:27
children and his **h** after him to Gn 18:19
turn aside to your servant's **h**, Gn 19:2
him and went into his **h**. Gn 19:3
population, surrounded the **h**. Gn 19:4
Lot into the **h** with them, Gn 19:10
who were at the door of the **h**, Gn 19:11
me wander from my father's **h**, Gn 20:13
from my father's **h** and from my Gn 24:7
your father's **h** for us to spend Gn 24:23
journey to the **h** of my master's Gn 24:27
prepared the **h** and a place for Gn 24:31
came to the **h**, and the camels Gn 24:32
which were there at the **h**, Gn 27:15
to the **h** of Bethuel, your Gn 28:2
is none other than the **h** of God. Gn 28:17
return safely to my father's **h**, Gn 28:21
up as a marker will be God's **h**, Gn 28:22
Then he took him to his **h**, Gn 29:13
He built a **h** for himself and Gn 33:17
important in all his father's **h**. Gn 34:19
took Dinah from Shechem's **h**, Gn 34:26
in your father's **h** until my son Gn 38:11
went to live in her father's **h**. Gn 38:11
the Egyptian's **h** because of Gn 39:5
in his **h** and in his fields. Gn 39:5
himself with anything in his **h**, Gn 39:8
No one in this **h** is greater than Gn 39:9
went into the **h** to do his work, Gn 39:11
custody in the **h** of the captain Gn 40:3
with him in his master's **h**, Gn 40:7
will be over my **h**, and all my Gn 41:40
my hardship in my father's **h**." Gn 41:51
"Take the men to ⌊my⌋ **h**. Gn 43:16
and brought them to Joseph's **h**. Gn 43:17
they were taken to Joseph's **h**. Gn 43:18
to him at the doorway of the **h**. Gn 43:19
brought the men into Joseph's **h**, Gn 43:24
they had carried into the **h**, Gn 43:26
and silver from your master's **h**? Gn 44:8
his brothers reached Joseph's **h**, Gn 44:14
the news reached Pharaoh's **h**, Gn 45:16

the money to Pharaoh's **h**.	Gn 47:14
staying in her **h** for silver and	Ex 3:22
nearest his **h** are to select one	Ex 12:4
the door of his **h** until morning.	Ex 12:22
there wasn't a **h** without someone	Ex 12:30
It is to be eaten in one **h**.	Ex 12:46
any of the meat outside the **h**,	Ex 12:46
The **h** of Israel named the	Ex 16:31
you must say to the **h** of Jacob,	Ex 19:3
Do not covet your neighbor's **h**.	Ex 20:17
are stolen from that person's **h**,	Ex 22:7
the owner of the **h** must present	Ex 22:8
land to the **h** of the LORD your	Ex 23:19
land to the **h** of the LORD your	Ex 34:26
to the entire **h** of Israel	Ex 40:38
the whole **h** of Israel, may	Lv 10:6
in a **h** in the land you	Lv 14:34
owner of the **h** is to come and	Lv 14:35
has appeared in my **h**.	Lv 14:35
to clear the **h** before he enters	Lv 14:36
in the **h** becomes unclean.	Lv 14:36
will come to examine the **h**.	Lv 14:36
the walls of the **h** consists of	Lv 14:37
go outside the **h** to its doorway	Lv 14:38
quarantine the **h** for seven days.	Lv 14:38
spread on the walls of the **h**,	Lv 14:39
the inside of the **h** completely	Lv 14:41
plaster to replaster the **h**.	Lv 14:42
in the **h** after the stones	Lv 14:43
and after the **h** has been scraped	Lv 14:43
has spread in the **h**,	Lv 14:44
mildew; the **h** is unclean.	Lv 14:44
Whoever enters the **h** during any	Lv 14:46
lies down in the **h** is to wash	Lv 14:47
not spread in the **h** after it was	Lv 14:48
to pronounce the **h** clean because	Lv 14:48
and hyssop to purify the **h**,	Lv 14:49
and sprinkle the **h** seven times.	Lv 14:51
will purify the **h** with the blood	Lv 14:52
will make atonement for the **h**,	Lv 14:53
mildew in clothing or on a **h**,	Lv 14:55
Anyone from the **h** of Israel who	Lv 17:3
Anyone from the **h** of Israel or	Lv 17:8
Anyone from the **h** of Israel or	Lv 17:10
born in his **h** may eat his food	Lv 22:11
her father's **h** as in her youth	Lv 22:13
Any man of the **h** of Israel or of	Lv 22:18
then the **h** in the walled city is	Lv 25:30
h sold in a city they possess—	Lv 25:33
consecrates his **h** as holy to the	Lv 27:14
consecrated his **h** redeems ⌊it⌋,	Lv 27:15
one the head of his ancestral **h**.	Nm 1:4
represented his ancestral **h**.	Nm 1:44
his clan and by his ancestral **h**.	Nm 2:34
from them for each ancestral **h**,	Nm 17:2
the head of each ancestral **h**.	Nm 17:3
representing the **h** of Levi,	Nm 17:8
and your ancestral **h** will be	Nm 18:1
person in your **h** may eat it.	Nm 18:11
person in your **h** may eat them.	Nm 18:13
the entire **h** of Israel mourned	Nm 20:29
to give me his **h** full of silver	Nm 22:18
to give me his **h** full of silver	Nm 24:13
of a Simeonite ancestral **h**.	Nm 25:14
of an ancestral **h** in Midian.	Nm 25:15
in her father's **h** during her	Nm 30:3
her husband's **h** has made a vow	Nm 30:10
daughter in his **h** during her	Nm 30:16
wife or covet your neighbor's **h**,	Dt 5:21
you sit in your **h** and when you	Dt 6:7
of your **h** and on your gates	Dt 6:9
any abhorrent thing into your **h**,	Dt 7:26
you sit in your **h** and when you	Dt 11:19
of your **h** and on your gates	Dt 11:20
man built a new **h** and not	Dt 20:5
are to bring her into your **h**.	Dt 21:12
live in your **h**, and mourn for	Dt 21:13
build a new **h**, make a railing	Dt 22:8
on your **h** if someone falls	Dt 22:8
to the door of her father's **h**,	Dt 22:21
promiscuous in her father's **h**.	Dt 22:21
into the **h** of the LORD your	Dt 23:18
and send her away from his **h**.	Dt 24:1
after leaving his **h** she goes and	Dt 24:2
away from his **h** or if he dies,	Dt 24:3
not enter his **h** to collect what	Dt 24:10
not build up his brother's **h**.'	Dt 25:9
called 'The **h** of the man whose	Dt 25:10
dry measures in your **h**,	Dt 25:14
consecrated portion out of my **h**;	Dt 26:13
You will build a **h** but not live	Dt 28:30
they came to the **h** of a woman,	Jos 2:1
came to you and entered your **h**,	Jos 2:3
lived in a **h** that was ⌊built⌋	Jos 2:15
father's family into your **h**.	Jos 2:18
goes out the doors of your **h**,	Jos 2:19
with you in the **h** should be	Jos 2:19
with her in the **h** will live,	Jos 6:17
the prostitute's **h** and bring the	Jos 6:22
the treasury of the LORD's **h**.	Jos 6:24
carriers for the **h** of my God."	Jos 9:23
had made to the **h** of Israel	Jos 21:45
The **h** of Joseph also attacked	Jdg 1:22
When the **h** of Joseph got the	Jdg 1:35
the youngest in my father's **h**."	Jdg 6:15
went back to live at his **h**.	Jdg 8:29
kindness to the **h** of Jerubbaal	Jdg 8:35
to his father's **h** in Ophrah and	Jdg 9:5
attacked my father's **h** today,	Jdg 9:18
Jerubbaal and his **h** this day,	Jdg 9:19
they went to the **h** of their god,	Jdg 9:27
Benjamin, and the **h** of Ephraim.	Jdg 10:9
inheritance in our father's **h**,	Jdg 11:2
and drive me from my father's **h**?	Jdg 11:7
the doors of my **h** to greet me	Jdg 11:31
will burn your **h** down with you	Jdg 12:1
returned to his father's **h**,	Jdg 14:19
silver, and it was in Micah's **h**.	Jdg 17:4
priest and lived in Micah's **h**.	Jdg 17:12
and arrived at Micah's **h**.	Jdg 18:13
and went to the **h** of the young	Jdg 18:15
entered Micah's **h** and took the	Jdg 18:18
a priest for the **h** of one person	Jdg 18:19
some distance from Micah's **h**,	Jdg 18:22
as long as the **h** of God was in	Jdg 18:31
for her father's **h** in Bethlehem	Jdg 19:2
brought him to her father's **h**,	Jdg 19:3
I'm going to the **h** of the LORD.	Jdg 19:18
brought him to his **h** and fed the	Jdg 19:21
city surrounded the **h** and beat	Jdg 19:22
man who was the owner of the **h**,	Jdg 19:22
came to your **h** so we can have	Jdg 19:22
The owner of the **h** went out and	Jdg 19:23
this man has come into my **h**.	Jdg 19:23
of the man's **h** where her master	Jdg 19:26
opened the doors of the **h**,	Jdg 19:27
doorway of the **h** with her hands	Jdg 19:27
he entered his **h**, he picked up	Jdg 19:29
and surrounded the **h** at night.	Jdg 20:5
to his tent or return to his **h**.	Jdg 20:8
security in the **h** of your ⌊new⌋	Ru 1:9
is entering your **h** like Rachel	Ru 4:11
together built the **h** of Israel.	Ru 4:11
May your **h** become like the house	Ru 4:12
become like the **h** of Perez,	Ru 4:12
she went up to the LORD's **h**,	1Sm 1:7
him to the LORD's **h** at Shiloh.	1Sm 1:24
to your ancestral **h** when it was	1Sm 2:27
selected your **h** from the tribes	1Sm 2:28
I also gave your **h** all the	1Sm 2:28
your ancestral **h** would walk	1Sm 2:30
the doors of the LORD's **h**.	1Sm 3:15
it to Abinadab's **h** on the hill.	1Sm 7:1
Then the whole **h** of Israel began	1Sm 7:2
tell me where the seer's **h** is?"	1Sm 9:18
him return to his father's **h**.	1Sm 18:2
to David's **h** to watch for him	1Sm 19:11
a covenant with the **h** of David,	1Sm 20:16
one going to come into my **h**?"	1Sm 21:15
and honored in your **h**.	1Sm 22:14
and there he was in his **h**,	1Sm 25:36
had a fattened calf at her **h**,	1Sm 28:24
people, and the **h** of Israel.	2Sm 1:12
David king over the **h** of Judah.	2Sm 2:4
the **h** of Judah has anointed me	2Sm 2:7
h of Judah, however, followed	2Sm 2:10
Hebron over the **h** of Judah was	2Sm 2:11
war between the **h** of Saul and	2Sm 3:1
of Saul and the **h** of David was	2Sm 3:1
and the **h** of Saul becoming	2Sm 3:1
war between the **h** of Saul and	2Sm 3:6
of Saul and the **h** of David,	2Sm 3:6
more power in the **h** of Saul.	2Sm 3:6
loyal to the **h** of your father	2Sm 3:8
the kingdom from the **h** of Saul	2Sm 3:10
and the whole **h** of Benjamin.	2Sm 3:19
head and his father's whole **h**,	2Sm 3:29
and may the **h** of Joab never be	2Sm 3:29
Ish-bosheth's **h** during the heat	2Sm 4:5
interior of the **h** as if to get	2Sm 4:6
had entered the **h** while	2Sm 4:7
man in his own **h** on his own bed!	2Sm 4:11
lame will never enter the **h**."	2Sm 5:8
it from Abinadab's **h**,	2Sm 6:3
from Abinadab's **h** on the hill.	2Sm 6:4
and the whole **h** of Israel were	2Sm 6:5
he took it to the **h** of Obed-edom	2Sm 6:10
remained in his **h** three months,	2Sm 6:11
from Obed-edom's **h** to the city	2Sm 6:12
and the whole **h** of Israel were	2Sm 6:15
living in a cedar **h** while the	2Sm 7:2
you to build a **h** for Me to live	2Sm 7:5
today I have not lived in a **h**;	2Sm 7:6
you built Me a **h** of cedar?'	2Sm 7:7
Himself will make a **h** for you.	2Sm 7:11
He will build a **h** for My name,	2Sm 7:13
Your **h** and kingdom will endure	2Sm 7:16
and what is my **h** that You have	2Sm 7:18
Your servant's **h** in the distant	2Sm 7:19
made to Your servant and his **h**.	2Sm 7:25
The **h** of Your servant David	2Sm 7:26
'I will build a **h** for you.'	2Sm 7:27
Your servant's **h** so that it will	2Sm 7:29
Your servant's **h** will be blessed	2Sm 7:29
Lo-debar at the **h** of Machir son	2Sm 9:4
brought from the **h** of Machir son	2Sm 9:5
living in Ziba's **h** were	2Sm 9:12
Go down to your **h** and wash your	2Sm 11:8
he did not go down to his **h**.	2Sm 11:9
I enter my **h** to eat and drink	2Sm 11:11
David had her brought to his **h**.	2Sm 11:27
your master's **h** to you and your	2Sm 12:8
and I gave you the **h** of Israel	2Sm 12:8
never leave your **h** because you	2Sm 12:10
elders of his **h** stood beside him	2Sm 12:17
to the LORD's **h**, and worshiped.	2Sm 12:20
brother Amnon's **h** and prepare a	2Sm 13:7
went to his **h** while Amnon was	2Sm 13:8
woman in the **h** of her brother	2Sm 13:20
be on me and my father's **h**,	2Sm 14:9
return to his **h**, but he may not	2Sm 14:24
So Absalom returned to his **h**,	2Sm 14:24
to Absalom's **h** and demanded,	2Sm 14:31
They stopped at the last **h**	2Sm 15:17
the **h** of Israel will restore my	2Sm 16:3
family of the **h** of Saul was just	2Sm 16:5
blood of the **h** of Saul in whose	2Sm 16:8
and came to the **h** of a man in	2Sm 17:18
to the woman at the **h** and asked,	2Sm 17:20
out for his **h** in his hometown	2Sm 17:23
Joab went into the **h** to the king	2Sm 19:5
has reached the king at his **h**.	2Sm 19:11
an attendant from the **h** of Saul,	2Sm 19:17
of the entire **h** of Joseph to	2Sm 19:20
Is it not true my **h** is with God?	2Sm 23:5
my father's **h** the blood that	1Kg 2:31
buried at his **h** in the	1Kg 2:34
Build a **h** for yourself in	1Kg 2:36
woman and I live in the same **h**,	1Kg 3:17
a baby while she was in the **h**.	1Kg 3:17
one else was with us in the **h**;	1Kg 3:18
He built the **H** of the Forest of	1Kg 7:2
And he made a **h** like this hall	1Kg 7:8
of David to the **h** that Solomon	1Kg 9:24
put them in the **H** of the Forest	1Kg 10:17
utensils of the **H** of the Forest	1Kg 10:21
gave Hadad a **h**, ordered that he	1Kg 11:18
labor force of the **h** of Joseph.	1Kg 11:28
now look after your own **h**!	1Kg 12:16
against the **h** of David until	1Kg 12:19
followed the **h** of David except	1Kg 12:20
from the entire **h** of Judah and	1Kg 12:21
fight against the **h** of Israel to	1Kg 12:21
to the whole **h** of Judah and	1Kg 12:23
might return to the **h** of David.	1Kg 12:26
will be born to the **h** of David,	1Kg 13:2
you were to give me half your **h**,	1Kg 13:8
with you to your **h** so that he	1Kg 13:18
bread in his **h**, and drank water	1Kg 13:19
For the **h** of Jeroboam, this was	1Kg 13:34
and arrived at Ahijah's **h**.	1Kg 14:4
away from the **h** of David,	1Kg 14:8
disaster on the **h** of Jeroboam:	1Kg 14:10
sweep away the **h** of Jeroboam as	1Kg 14:10

you, get up and go to your **h**.	1Kg 14:12
alone⌋ out of the **h** of Jeroboam	1Kg 14:13
eliminate the **h** of Jeroboam.	1Kg 14:14
crossing the threshold of the **h**,	1Kg 14:17
of Ahijah of the **h** of Issachar	1Kg 15:27
down the entire **h** of Jeroboam.	1Kg 15:29
sweep away Baasha and his **h**,	1Kg 16:3
will make your **h** like the house	1Kg 16:3
house like the **h** of Jeroboam son	1Kg 16:3
and against his **h** because of all	1Kg 16:7
being like the **h** of Jeroboam,	1Kg 16:7
struck down the **h** of Jeroboam.	1Kg 16:7
himself drunk in the **h** of Arza,	1Kg 16:9
down the entire **h** of Baasha.	1Kg 16:11
the entire **h** of Baasha,	1Kg 16:12
who owned the **h** became ill.	1Kg 17:17
from the upper room into the **h**,	1Kg 17:23
you and your father's **h** have,	1Kg 18:18
the kings of the **h** of Israel are	1Kg 20:31
will make your **h** like the house	1Kg 21:22
house like the **h** of Jeroboam son	1Kg 21:22
and like the **h** of Baasha son	1Kg 21:22
disaster on his **h** during his	1Kg 21:29
what do you have in the **h**?"	2Kg 4:2
nothing in the **h** except a jar	2Kg 4:2
got to the **h**, he discovered	2Kg 4:32
went into the **h**, and paced back	2Kg 4:35
stood at the door of Elisha's **h**.	2Kg 5:9
them and stored them in the **h**.	2Kg 5:24
Elisha was sitting in his **h**,	2Kg 6:32
to the king for her **h** and field.	2Kg 8:3
to the king for her **h** and field.	2Kg 8:5
as the **h** of Ahab had done,	2Kg 8:18
the way of the **h** of Ahab and did	2Kg 8:27
LORD's sight like the **h** of Ahab,	2Kg 8:27
Jehu got up and went into the **h**.	2Kg 9:6
strike down the **h** of your master	2Kg 9:7
The whole **h** of Ahab will perish,	2Kg 9:8
I will make the **h** of Ahab like	2Kg 9:9
Ahab like the **h** of Jeroboam son	2Kg 9:9
and like the **h** of Baasha son	2Kg 9:9
and fight for your master's **h**.	2Kg 10:3
against the **h** of Ahab will fail	2Kg 10:10
remained of the **h** of Ahab in	2Kg 10:11
remained from ⌊the **h** of⌋ Ahab in	2Kg 10:17
until he had annihilated his **h**,	2Kg 10:17
done to the **h** of Ahab all that	2Kg 10:30
sins that the **h** of Jeroboam had	2Kg 13:6
in a separate **h**, while Jotham,	2Kg 15:5
tore Israel from the **h** of David,	2Kg 17:21
remnant of the **h** of Israel will	2Kg 19:30
them his whole treasure **h**—	2Kg 20:13
level ⌊used on⌋ the **h** of Ahab,	2Kg 21:13
in the garden of his own **h**,	2Kg 21:18
and killed him in his own **h**.	2Kg 21:23
to the gates of the LORD's **h**,	1Ch 9:23
LORD's house, the **h** of the tent.	1Ch 9:23
his whole **h** died together.	1Ch 10:6
leader of the **h** of Aaron, with	1Ch 12:27
from his own ancestral **h**.	1Ch 12:28
their allegiance to the **h** of	1Ch 12:29
Abinadab's **h**, they set the ark	1Ch 13:7
he took it to the **h** of Obed-edom	1Ch 13:13
in his **h** for three months,	1Ch 13:14
LORD from the **h** of Obed-edom.	1Ch 15:25
living in a cedar **h** while the	1Ch 17:1
the one to build Me a **h** to dwell	1Ch 17:4
today I have not lived in a **h**;	1Ch 17:5
you built Me a **h** of cedar?'	1Ch 17:6
Himself will build a **h** for you.	1Ch 17:10
He will build a **h** for Me, and I	1Ch 17:12
him over My **h** and My kingdom	1Ch 17:14
and what is my **h** that You have	1Ch 17:16
Your servant's **h** in the distant	1Ch 17:17
servant and his **h** be confirmed	1Ch 17:23
May the **h** of Your servant	1Ch 17:24
that You will build him a **h**,	1Ch 17:25
Your servant's **h** that it may	1Ch 17:27
This is the **h** of the LORD God,	1Ch 22:1
stones for building God's **h**.	1Ch 22:2
the **h** that is to be built for	1Ch 22:5
to build a **h** for the LORD God	1Ch 22:6
heart to build a **h** for the name	1Ch 22:7
are not to build a **h** for My name	1Ch 22:8
who will build a **h** for My name.	1Ch 22:10
in building the **h** of the LORD	1Ch 22:11
provide for the **h** of the LORD—	1Ch 22:14
an ancestral **h** ⌊and received⌋	1Ch 23:11

One ancestral **h** was taken for	1Ch 24:6
heart to build a **h** as a resting	1Ch 28:2
are not to build a **h** for My name	1Ch 28:3
and from the **h** of Judah, my	1Ch 28:4
is to build My **h** and My courts,	1Ch 28:6
you to build a **h** for the	1Ch 28:10
for the courts of the LORD's **h**,	1Ch 28:12
the treasuries of God's **h**,	1Ch 28:12
work of service in the LORD's **h**;	1Ch 28:13
of service of the LORD's **h**;	1Ch 28:13
of the LORD's **h** is finished.	1Ch 28:20
for all the service of God's **h**.	1Ch 28:21
provision for the **h** of my God:	1Ch 29:2
my delight in the **h** of my God,	1Ch 29:3
silver for the **h** of my God over	1Ch 29:3
I've provided for the holy **h**:	1Ch 29:3
service of God's **h** they gave 185	1Ch 29:7
of the LORD's **h** under the care	1Ch 29:8
building You a **h** for Your holy	1Ch 29:16
cedars to build him a **h** to live	2Ch 2:3
should build a **h** for Him except	2Ch 2:6
of David to the **h** he had built	2Ch 8:11
not live in the **h** of David king	2Ch 8:11
put them in the **H** of the Forest	2Ch 9:16
utensils of the **H** of the Forest	2Ch 9:20
look after your own **h** now!	2Ch 10:16
against the **h** of David until	2Ch 10:19
he mobilized the **h** of Judah and	2Ch 11:1
the ruler of the **h** of Judah,	2Ch 19:11
as the **h** of Ahab had done,	2Ch 21:6
to destroy the **h** of David since	2Ch 21:7
like the **h** of Ahab prostituted	2Ch 21:13
in the ways of the **h** of Ahab,	2Ch 22:3
LORD's sight like the **h** of Ahab,	2Ch 22:4
to destroy the **h** of Ahab.	2Ch 22:7
judgment on the **h** of Ahab,	2Ch 22:8
So the **h** of Ahaziah had no one	2Ch 22:9
royal heirs of the **h** of Judah.	2Ch 22:10
and he was buried in his own **h**.	2Ch 33:20
put him to death in his own **h**.	2Ch 33:24
the sword in the **h** of their	2Ch 36:17
me to build Him a **h** at Jerusalem	Ezr 1:2
and build the **h** of the LORD,	Ezr 1:3
offering for the **h** of God in	Ezr 1:4
the LORD's **h** in Jerusalem.	Ezr 1:5
of the LORD's **h** that	Ezr 1:7
had placed in the **h** of his gods.	Ezr 1:7
of the **h** of Jeshua 973	Ezr 2:36
at the LORD's **h** in Jerusalem,	Ezr 2:68
for the **h** of God in order	Ezr 2:68
arrived at God's **h** in Jerusalem,	Ezr 3:8
the work on the LORD's **h**.	Ezr 3:8
those working on the **h** of God.	Ezr 3:9
of the LORD's **h** had been laid.	Ezr 3:11
saw the foundation of this **h**,	Ezr 3:12
us in building a **h** for our God,	Ezr 4:3
of God's **h** in Jerusalem had	Ezr 4:24
to rebuild God's **h** in Jerusalem.	Ezr 5:2
went to the **h** of the great God	Ezr 5:8
decree to rebuild this **h** of God.	Ezr 5:13
articles of God's **h** that	Ezr 5:14
and let the **h** of God be rebuilt	Ezr 5:15
of God's **h** in Jerusalem.	Ezr 5:16
to rebuild this **h** of God in	Ezr 5:17
concerning the **h** of God in	Ezr 6:3
Let the **h** be rebuilt as a place	Ezr 6:3
articles of God's **h** that	Ezr 6:5
and put into the **h** of God.	Ezr 6:5
of this **h** of God alone.	Ezr 6:7
rebuild this **h** of God on its	Ezr 6:7
Jews can rebuild this **h** of God:	Ezr 6:8
torn from his **h** and raised up;	Ezr 6:11
and his **h** will be made into a	Ezr 6:11
with this **h** of God in Jerusalem	Ezr 6:12
h was completed on the third	Ezr 6:15
of this **h** of God with joy.	Ezr 6:16
of God's **h** they offered 100	Ezr 6:17
in the work on the **h** of the God	Ezr 6:22
priests to the **h** of their God	Ezr 7:16
the altar at the **h** of your God	Ezr 7:17
service of the **h** of your God.	Ezr 7:19
the needs of the **h** of your God.	Ezr 7:20
diligently for the **h** of the God	Ezr 7:23
servants of this **h** of God.	Ezr 7:24
to glorify the **h** of the LORD	Ezr 7:27
ministers for the **h** of our God.	Ezr 8:17
for the **h** of our God that	Ezr 8:25
of the LORD's **h** before the	Ezr 8:29

bring ⌊them⌋ to the **h** of our God	Ezr 8:30
weighed out in the **h** of our God	Ezr 8:33
the people and the **h** of God.	Ezr 8:36
we can rebuild the **h** of our God	Ezr 9:9
facedown before the **h** of God,	Ezr 10:1
then went from the **h** of God,	Ezr 10:6
in the square at the **h** of God,	Ezr 10:9
I and my father's **h** have sinned.	Neh 1:6
made repairs across from his **h**.	Neh 3:10
pool and the **H** of the Warriors.	Neh 3:16
to the door of the **h** of Eliashib	Neh 3:20
of Eliashib's **h** to the end of	Neh 3:21
house to the end of his **h**.	Neh 3:21
made repairs opposite their **h**.	Neh 3:23
made repairs beside his **h**.	Neh 3:23
from the **h** of Azariah to the	Neh 3:24
Gate, each opposite his own **h**.	Neh 3:28
made repairs opposite his **h**.	Neh 3:29
repairs to the **h** of the temple	Neh 3:31
shake from his **h** and property	Neh 5:13
I went to the **h** of Shemaiah son	Neh 6:10
who was restricted ⌊to his **h**⌋.	Neh 6:10
us meet at the **h** of God inside	Neh 6:10
of the **h** of Jeshua 973	Neh 7:39
the court of the **h** of God,	Neh 8:16
the service of the **h** of our God:	Neh 10:32
the work of the **h** of our God.	Neh 10:33
wood⌋ to our God's **h** to burn on	Neh 10:34
to the LORD's **h** year by year.	Neh 10:35
and flocks to the **h** of our God,	Neh 10:36
who serve in our God's **h**.	Neh 10:36
storerooms of the **h** of our God.	Neh 10:37
treasury in the **h** of our God.	Neh 10:38
not neglect the **h** of our God.	Neh 10:39
the chief official of God's **h**,	Neh 11:11
the work outside the **h** of God;	Neh 11:16
for the service of God's **h**.	Neh 11:22
and went⌋ above the **h** of David	Neh 12:37
stood in the **h** of God.	Neh 12:40
storerooms of the **h** of our God.	Neh 13:4
a room in the courts of God's **h**.	Neh 13:7
of the **h** of God restored	Neh 13:9
has the **h** of God been neglected?	Neh 13:11
done for the **h** of my God and for	Neh 13:14
be master of his own **h** and speak	Est 1:22
your father's **h** will be	Est 4:14
to the **h** of wine drinking,	Est 7:8
tall at Haman's **h** that he made	Est 7:9
banquets, each at his **h** in turn.	Jb 1:4
in their oldest brother's **h**,	Jb 1:13
in their oldest brother's **h**.	Jb 1:18
the four corners of the **h**.	Jb 1:19
He will never return to his **h**;	Jb 7:10
My **h** guests and female servants	Jb 19:15
he seized a **h** he did not build.	Jb 20:19
in his **h** will be removed,	Jb 20:28
"Where now is the nobleman's **h**?"	Jb 21:28
The **h** he built is like a moth's	Jb 27:18
came to his **h** and dined with him	Jb 42:11
and dined with him in his **h**.	Jb 42:11
I enter Your **h** by the abundance	Ps 5:7
dwell in the **h** of the LORD as	Ps 23:6
I love the **h** where You dwell,	Ps 26:8
dwell in the **h** of the LORD all	Ps 27:4
from the abundance of Your **h**;	Ps 36:8
procession to the **h** of God,	Ps 42:4
your people and your father's **h**,	Ps 45:10
the wealth of his **h** increases.	Ps 49:16
olive tree in the **h** of God;	Ps 52:8
the crowd into the **h** of God.	Ps 55:14
with the goodness of Your **h**,	Ps 65:4
I will enter Your **h** with burnt	Ps 66:13
zeal for Your **h** has consumed me,	Ps 69:9
are those who reside in Your **h**,	Ps 84:4
the door of the **h** of my God than	Ps 84:10
Planted in the **h** of the LORD,	Ps 92:13
beauty of Your **h** for all the	Ps 93:5
faithfulness to the **h** of Israel;	Ps 98:3
with integrity of heart in my **h**.	Ps 101:2
Wealth and riches are in his **h**,	Ps 112:3
the **h** of Jacob from a people who	Ps 114:1
H of Aaron, trust in the LORD!	Ps 115:10
He will bless the **h** of Israel;	Ps 115:12
He will bless the **h** of Aaron;	Ps 115:12
in the courts of the LORD's **h**—	Ps 116:19
Let the **h** of Aaron say, "His	Ps 118:3
From the **h** of the LORD we bless	Ps 118:26
"Let us go to the **h** of the LORD."	Ps 122:1

thrones of the **h** of David.	Ps 122:5
Because of the **h** of the LORD our	Ps 122:9
Unless the LORD builds a **h**,	Ps 127:1
a fruitful vine within your **h**,	Ps 128:3
not enter my **h** or get into my	Ps 132:3
stand in the LORD's **h** at night!	Ps 134:1
who stand in the **h** of the LORD,	Ps 135:2
the courts of the **h** of our God.	Ps 135:2
H of Israel, praise the LORD!	Ps 135:19
H of Aaron, praise the LORD!	Ps 135:19
H of Levi, praise the LORD!	Ps 135:20
her **h** sinks down to death and	Pr 2:18
Don't go near the door of her **h**.	Pr 5:8
will end up in a foreigner's **h**.	Pr 5:10
give up all the wealth in his **h**.	Pr 6:31
window of my **h** I looked through	Pr 7:6
strolled down the road to her **h**	Pr 7:8
Her **h** is the road to Sheol,	Pr 7:27
Wisdom has built her **h**;	Pr 9:1
sits by the doorway of her **h**,	Pr 9:14
but the **h** of the righteous will	Pr 12:7
Every wise woman builds her **h**,	Pr 14:1
The **h** of the wicked will be	Pr 14:11
The **h** of the righteous has great	Pr 15:6
destroys the **h** of the proud,	Pr 15:25
peace than a **h** full of feasting	Pr 17:1
will never depart from his **h**.	Pr 17:13
h and wealth are inherited from	Pr 19:14
than to share a **h** with a nagging	Pr 21:9
considers the **h** of the wicked;	Pr 21:12
h is built by wisdom, and it is	Pr 24:3
afterwards, build your **h**.	Pr 24:27
set foot in your neighbor's **h**;	Pr 25:17
a roof than in a **h** shared with	Pr 25:24
to your brother's **h** in your time	Pr 27:10
slaves who were born in my **h**.	Ec 2:7
when you go to the **h** of God.	Ec 5:1
to go to a **h** of mourning than	Ec 7:2
than to go to a **h** of feasting,	Ec 7:2
the wise is in a **h** of mourning,	Ec 7:4
of fools is in a **h** of pleasure.	Ec 7:4
of negligent hands the **h** leaks.	Ec 10:18
the guardians of the **h** tremble,	Ec 12:3
the beams of our **h** are cedars,	Sg 1:17
I brought him to my mother's **h**—	Sg 3:4
to the **h** of my mother who taught	Sg 8:2
of the LORD's **h** will be	Is 2:2
to the **h** of the God of Jacob.	Is 2:3
H of Jacob, come and let us walk	Is 2:5
Your people, the **h** of Jacob,	Is 2:6
his brother in his father's **h**,	Is 3:6
have food or clothing in my **h**.	Is 3:7
of Hosts is the **h** of Israel,	Is 5:7
to those who add **h** to house and	Is 5:8
add house to **h** and join field	Is 5:8
known to the **h** of David that	Is 7:2
said, "Listen, **h** of David!	Is 7:13
and the **h** of your father,	Is 7:17
His face from the **h** of Jacob.	Is 8:17
of the **h** of Jacob will no	Is 10:20
be united with the **h** of Jacob.	Is 14:1
the **h** of Israel will possess	Is 14:2
weapons in the **H** of the Forest.	Is 22:8
disgrace to the **h** of your lord.	Is 22:18
Jerusalem and to the **H** of Judah.	Is 22:21
the key of the **H** of David on his	Is 22:22
of honor for his father's **h**.	Is 22:23
whole burden of his father's **h**:	Is 22:24
every **h** is closed to entry.	Is 24:10
says this about the **h** of Jacob:	Is 29:22
up against the **h** of wicked men	Is 31:2
for every joyous **h** in the joyful	Is 32:13
and went to the **h** of the LORD.	Is 37:1
up to the LORD's **h** and spread it	Is 37:14
remnant of the **h** of Judah will	Is 37:31
our lives at the **h** of the LORD.	Is 38:20
and showed them his treasure **h**—	Is 39:2
in darkness from the prison **h**.	Is 42:7
Listen to Me, **h** of Jacob, all	Is 46:3
the remnant of the **h** of Israel,	Is 46:3
Listen to this, **h** of Jacob—	Is 48:1
in My **h** and within My walls,	Is 56:5
them rejoice in My **h** of prayer.	Is 56:7
for My **h** will be called a house	Is 56:7
will be called a **h** of prayer for	Is 56:7
and the **h** of Jacob their sins.	Is 58:1
poor and homeless into your **h**,	Is 58:7
I will glorify My beautiful **h**.	Is 60:7
done$_J$ for the **h** of Israel and	Is 63:7
What **h** could you possibly build	Is 66:1
vessel to the **h** of the LORD.	Is 66:20
h of Jacob and all families of	Jr 2:4
all families of the **h** of Israel.	Jr 2:4
so the **h** of Israel has been put	Jr 2:26
those days the **h** of Judah will	Jr 3:18
will join with the **h** of Israel,	Jr 3:18
have betrayed Me, **h** of Israel.	Jr 3:20
at the prostitute's **h**.	Jr 5:7
the **h** of Israel and the house of	Jr 5:11
of Israel and the **h** of Judah,	Jr 5:11
away against you, **h** of Israel.	Jr 5:15
Declare this in the **h** of Jacob;	Jr 5:20
in the gate of the **h** of the LORD	Jr 7:2
Me in this **h** called by My name	Jr 7:10
Has this **h**, which is called by	Jr 7:11
will do to the **h** that is called	Jr 7:14
the **h** in which you trust—	Jr 7:14
things in the **h** that is called	Jr 7:30
and the whole **h** of Israel is	Jr 9:26
has spoken to you, **h** of Israel.	Jr 10:1
The **h** of Israel and the house of	Jr 11:10
Israel and the **h** of Judah broke	Jr 11:10
My beloved have to be in My **h**,	Jr 11:15
of the harm the **h** of Israel and	Jr 11:17
Israel and the **h** of Judah	Jr 11:17
I have abandoned My **h**;	Jr 12:7
will uproot the **h** of Judah from	Jr 12:14
I fastened the whole **h** of Israel	Jr 13:11
Don't enter a **h** where a mourning	Jr 16:5
not enter the **h** where feasting	Jr 16:8
offerings to the **h** of the LORD.	Jr 17:26
down at once to the potter's **h**;	Jr 18:2
I went down to the potter's **h**,	Jr 18:3
H of Israel, can I not treat you	Jr 18:6
are you in My hand, **h** of Israel.	Jr 18:6
officer in the **h** of the LORD,	Jr 20:1
and all who live in your **h**,	Jr 20:6
to the **h** of the king of Judah	Jr 21:11
H of David, this is what the	Jr 21:12
"that this **h** will become a ruin."	Jr 22:5
concerning the **h** of the king	Jr 22:6
descendants of the **h** of Israel	Jr 23:8
even in My **h** I have found their	Jr 23:11
when I will sow the **h** of Israel	Jr 31:27
Israel and the **h** of Judah with	Jr 31:27
covenant with the **h** of Israel	Jr 31:31
Israel and with the **h** of Judah.	Jr 31:31
make with the **h** of Israel after	Jr 31:33
things in the **h** that is called	Jr 32:34
concerning the **h** of Israel	Jr 33:14
of Israel and the **h** of Judah.	Jr 33:14
the throne of the **h** of Israel.	Jr 33:17
Go to the **h** of the Rechabites,	Jr 35:2
the entire **h** of the Rechabites—	Jr 35:3
the sons of the **h** of the	Jr 35:5
must not build a **h** or sow seed	Jr 35:7
said to the **h** of the Rechabites:	Jr 35:18
when the **h** of Judah hears about	Jr 36:3
him in jail in the **h** of Jonathan	Jr 37:15
in his **h** privately asked him,	Jr 37:17
me back to the **h** of Jonathan	Jr 37:20
return me to the **h** of Jonathan	Jr 38:26
just as the **h** of Israel was put	Jr 48:13
a shout in the **h** of the LORD as	Lm 2:7
for they are a rebellious **h**—	Ezk 2:5
for they are a rebellious **h**.	Ezk 2:6
like that rebellious **h**.	Ezk 2:8
and speak to the **h** of Israel."	Ezk 3:1
go to the **h** of Israel and speak	Ezk 3:4
language but to the **h** of Israel.	Ezk 3:5
the **h** of Israel will not want	Ezk 3:7
For the whole **h** of Israel is	Ezk 3:7
though they are a rebellious **h**."	Ezk 3:9
a watchman over the **h** of Israel.	Ezk 3:17
shut yourself inside your **h**.	Ezk 3:24
for they are a rebellious **h**.	Ezk 3:26
for they are a rebellious **h**.	Ezk 3:27
be a sign for the **h** of Israel.	Ezk 4:3
of the **h** of Israel on it	Ezk 4:4
the iniquity of the **h** of Israel.	Ezk 4:5
the iniquity of the **h** of Judah.	Ezk 4:6
it to the whole **h** of Israel.	Ezk 5:4
abominations of the **h** of Israel,	Ezk 6:11
sitting in my **h** and the elders	Ezk 8:1
that the **h** of Israel is	Ezk 8:6
the idols of the **h** of Israel.	Ezk 8:10
elders from the **h** of Israel were	Ezk 8:11
elders of the **h** of Israel are	Ezk 8:12
the north gate of the LORD's **h**,	Ezk 8:14
the inner court of the LORD's **h**,	Ezk 8:16
enough for the **h** of Judah to	Ezk 8:17
iniquity of the **h** of Israel and	Ezk 9:9
eastern gate of the LORD's **h**.	Ezk 10:19
eastern gate of the LORD's **h**,	Ezk 11:1
you are thinking, **h** of Israel;	Ezk 11:5
and the entire **h** of Israel,	Ezk 11:15
are living among a rebellious **h**.	Ezk 12:2
for they are a rebellious **h**.	Ezk 12:2
though they are a rebellious **h**.	Ezk 12:3
you a sign to the **h** of Israel."	Ezk 12:6
man, hasn't the **h** of Israel,	Ezk 12:9
that rebellious **h**, asked you:	Ezk 12:9
and all the **h** of Israel who are	Ezk 12:10
within the **h** of Israel.	Ezk 12:24
days, rebellious **h**, I will speak	Ezk 12:25
notice that the **h** of Israel is	Ezk 12:27
wall around the **h** of Israel so	Ezk 13:5
the register of the **h** of Israel,	Ezk 13:9
anyone from the **h** of Israel sets	Ezk 14:4
take hold of the **h** of Israel by	Ezk 14:5
say to the **h** of Israel:	Ezk 14:6
when anyone from the **h** of Israel	Ezk 14:7
order that the **h** of Israel may	Ezk 14:11
a parable to the **h** of Israel.	Ezk 17:2
Now say to that rebellious **h**:	Ezk 17:12
to the idols of the **h** of Israel.	Ezk 18:6
to the idols of the **h** of Israel.	Ezk 18:15
Now listen, **h** of Israel:	Ezk 18:25
But the **h** of Israel says:	Ezk 18:29
that are unfair, **h** of Israel?	Ezk 18:29
Therefore, **h** of Israel, I will	Ezk 18:30
Why should you die, **h** of Israel?	Ezk 18:31
of Jacob's **h** and made Myself	Ezk 20:5
But the **h** of Israel rebelled	Ezk 20:13
man, speak to the **h** of Israel,	Ezk 20:27
say to the **h** of Israel:	Ezk 20:30
consulted by you, **h** of Israel?	Ezk 20:31
As for you, **h** of Israel, this is	Ezk 20:39
there the entire **h** of Israel,	Ezk 20:40
I am the LORD, **h** of Israel, when	Ezk 20:44
the **h** of Israel has become dross	Ezk 22:18
is what they did inside My **h**.	Ezk 23:39
a parable to the rebellious **h**.	Ezk 24:3
'Say to the **h** of Israel:	Ezk 24:21
and about the **h** of Judah when	Ezk 25:3
the **h** of Judah is like all the	Ezk 25:8
against the **h** of Judah and	Ezk 25:12
The **h** of Israel will no longer	Ezk 28:24
When I gather the **h** of Israel	Ezk 28:25
of reed to the **h** of Israel.	Ezk 29:6
of trust for the **h** of Israel,	Ezk 29:16
to sprout for the **h** of Israel,	Ezk 29:21
a watchman for the **h** of Israel.	Ezk 33:7
of man, say to the **h** of Israel:	Ezk 33:10
Why will you die, **h** of Israel?	Ezk 33:11
to his ways, **h** of Israel."	Ezk 33:20
that they, the **h** of Israel, are	Ezk 34:30
of the **h** of Israel because	Ezk 35:15
with the whole **h** of Israel in	Ezk 36:10
while the **h** of Israel lived in	Ezk 36:17
which the **h** of Israel profaned	Ezk 36:21
say to the **h** of Israel:	Ezk 36:22
that I will act, **h** of Israel,	Ezk 36:22
of your ways, **h** of Israel!	Ezk 36:32
respond to the **h** of Israel and	Ezk 36:37
bones are the whole **h** of Israel.	Ezk 37:11
and all the **h** of Israel	Ezk 37:16
The **h** of Israel will spend seven	Ezk 39:12
day forward the **h** of Israel will	Ezk 39:22
know that the **h** of Israel went	Ezk 39:23
on the whole **h** of Israel,	Ezk 39:25
My Spirit on the **h** of Israel."	Ezk 39:29
you see to the **h** of Israel."	Ezk 40:4
h of$_J$ Israel and their kings	Ezk 43:7
the temple to the **h** of Israel,	Ezk 43:10
people, the **h** of Israel:	Ezk 44:6
your abominations, **h** of Israel.	Ezk 44:6
to the **h** of Israel before	Ezk 44:12
offspring of the **h** of Israel,	Ezk 44:22
be for the whole **h** of Israel.	Ezk 45:6
the$_J$ land to the **h** of Israel	Ezk 45:8
times of the **h** of Israel—	Ezk 45:17
on behalf of the **h** of Israel.	Ezk 45:17
the vessels from the **h** of God.	Dn 1:2

of Babylon, to the **h** of his god, Dn 1:2
Daniel went to his **h** and told Dn 2:17
limb and his **h** made a garbage Dn 3:29
at ease in my **h** and flourishing Dn 4:4
the **h** of God in Jerusalem, Dn 5:3
from His **h** were brought to Dn 5:23
been signed, he went into his **h**. Dn 6:10
Jezreel on the **h** of Jehu and put Hs 1:4
the kingdom of the **h** of Israel. Hs 1:4
compassion on the **h** of Israel. Hs 1:6
compassion on the **h** of Judah, Hs 1:7
Pay attention, **h** of Israel! Hs 5:1
Listen, royal **h**! For the Hs 5:1
like decay to the **h** of Judah. Hs 5:12
a young lion to the **h** of Judah. Hs 5:14
horrible in the **h** of Israel: Hs 6:10
comes against the **h** of the LORD, Hs 8:1
not enter the **h** of the LORD. Hs 9:4
is in the **h** of his God! Hs 9:8
them from My **h** because of their Hs 9:15
with lies, the **h** of Israel, with Hs 11:12
cut off from the **h** of the LORD; Jl 1:9
withheld from the **h** of your God. Jl 1:13
the land at the **h** of the LORD Jl 1:14
gladness from the **h** of our God? Jl 1:16
will issue from the LORD's **h**, Jl 3:18
drink in the **h** of their God wine Am 2:8
testify against the **h** of Jacob— Am 3:13
the winter **h** and the summer Am 3:15
winter house and the summer **h**; Am 3:15
for you, a lament, **h** of Israel: Am 5:1
ten left in the **h** of Israel. Am 5:3
LORD says to the **h** of Israel: Am 5:4
throughout⌋ the **h** of Joseph; Am 5:6
H of Israel, was it sacrifices Am 5:25
those the **h** of Israel comes to. Am 6:1
there are 10 men left in one **h**, Am 6:9
remove his corpse from the **h**. Am 6:10
in the inner recesses of the **h**, Am 6:10
The large **h** will be smashed to Am 6:11
and the small **h** to rubble. Am 6:11
against you, **h** of Israel—⌊this Am 6:14
against the **h** of Jeroboam with Am 7:9
right here⌋ in the **h** of Israel. Am 7:10
preach against the **h** of Isaac. Am 7:16
totally destroy the **h** of Jacob— Am 9:8
will shake the **h** of Israel among Am 9:9
the **h** of Jacob will dispossess Ob 17
Then the **h** of Jacob will be a Ob 18
and the **h** of Joseph a ⌊burning⌋ Ob 18
but the **h** of Esau will be Ob 18
will remain of the **h** of Esau, Ob 18
and the sins of the **h** of Israel. Mc 1:5
H of Jacob, should it be asked: Mc 2:7
you rulers of the **h** of Israel. Mc 3:1
leaders of the **h** of Jacob, Mc 3:9
you rulers of the **h** of Israel, Mc 3:9
of the LORD's **h** will be Mc 4:1
to the **h** of the God of Jacob. Mc 4:2
measure in the **h** of the wicked? Mc 6:10
of Ahab's **h** have been observed Mc 6:16
image from the **h** of your gods; Nah 1:14
wealth for his **h** to place his Hab 2:9
shame for your **h** by wiping out Hab 2:10
leader of the **h** of the wicked Hab 3:13
their master's **h** with violence Zph 1:9
the remnant of the **h** of Judah; Zph 2:7
not come for the **h** of the LORD Hg 1:2
while this **h** lies in ruins?" Hg 1:4
down lumber, and build the **h**. Hg 1:8
brought ⌊the harvest⌋ to your **h**, Hg 1:9
Because My **h** still lies in Hg 1:9
of you is busy with his own **h**. Hg 1:9
began work on the **h** of Yahweh of Hg 1:14
you who saw this **h** in its former Hg 2:3
I will fill this **h** with glory," Hg 2:7
glory of this **h** will be greater Hg 2:9
h will be rebuilt within it"— Zch 1:16
both rule My **h** and take care Zch 3:7
laid the foundation of this **h**, Zch 4:9
it will enter the **h** of the thief Zch 5:4
thief and the **h** of the one who Zch 5:4
stay inside his **h** and destroy it Zch 5:4
same day to the **h** of Josiah son Zch 6:10
who were at the **h** of the LORD of Zch 7:3
the **h** of the LORD of Hosts. Zch 8:9
h of Judah and house of Israel, Zch 8:13
house of Judah and **h** of Israel, Zch 8:13
to Jerusalem and the **h** of Judah. Zch 8:15
festivals for the **h** of Judah. Zch 8:19
up camp at My **h** against an army Zch 9:8
His flock, the **h** of Judah; Zch 10:3
will strengthen the **h** of Judah Zch 10:6
and deliver the **h** of Joseph. Zch 10:6
threw it into the **h** of the LORD, Zch 11:13
eye on the **h** of Judah but strike Zch 12:4
glory of David's **h** and the glory Zch 12:7
and the **h** of David will be like Zch 12:8
and prayer on the **h** of David Zch 12:10
family of David's **h** by itself Zch 12:12
family of Nathan's **h** by itself Zch 12:12
family of Levi's **h** by itself and Zch 12:13
opened for the **h** of David and Zch 13:1
received in the **h** of my friends. Zch 13:6
The pots in the **h** of the LORD Zch 14:20
a Canaanite in the **h** of the LORD Zch 14:21
that there may be food in My **h**. Mal 3:10
Entering the **h**, they saw the Mt 2:11
light for all who are in the **h**. Mt 5:15
man who built his **h** on the rock. Mt 7:24
winds blew and pounded that **h**. Mt 7:25
man who built his **h** on the sand. Mt 7:26
winds blew and pounded that **h**, Mt 7:27
When Jesus went into Peter's **h**, Mt 8:14
reclining at the table in the **h**, Mt 9:10
Jesus came to the leader's **h**, Mt 9:23
He entered the **h**, the blind men Mt 9:28
lost sheep of the **h** of Israel. Mt 10:6
when you leave that **h** or town. Mt 10:14
the head of the **h** 'Beelzebul,' Mt 10:25
how he entered the **h** of God, Mt 12:4
and no city or **h** divided against Mt 12:25
a strong man's **h** and steal his Mt 12:29
Then he can rob his **h**. Mt 12:29
'I'll go back to my **h** that I Mt 12:44
it finds ⌊the **h**⌋ vacant, swept, Mt 12:44
out of the **h** and was sitting Mt 13:1
the crowds and went into the **h**. Mt 13:36
lost sheep of the **h** of Israel." Mt 15:24
went into the **h**, Jesus spoke to Mt 17:25
My **h** will be called a house of Mt 21:13
will be called a **h** of prayer. Mt 21:13
your **h** is left to you desolate. Mt 23:38
down to get things out of his **h**. Mt 24:17
and not let his **h** be broken Mt 24:43
in Bethany at the **h** of Simon, Mt 26:6
Simon and Andrew's **h** with James Mk 1:29
at the table in Levi's **h**, Mk 2:15
he entered the **h** of God in the Mk 2:26
a **h** is divided against itself, Mk 3:25
itself, that **h** cannot stand. Mk 3:25
a strong man's **h** and rob his Mk 3:27
Then he will rob his **h**. Mk 3:27
synagogue leader's **h** and said, Mk 5:35
They came to the leader's **h**, Mk 5:38
you enter a **h**, stay there until Mk 6:10
He went into the **h** away from the Mk 7:17
He entered a **h** and did not want Mk 7:24
He went into a **h**, His disciples Mk 9:28
He was in the **h**, He asked them, Mk 9:33
Now in the **h** the disciples Mk 10:10
there is no one who has left **h**, Mk 10:29
My **h** will be called a house of Mk 11:17
will be called a **h** of prayer for Mk 11:17
in to get anything out of his **h**. Mk 13:15
who left his **h**, gave authority Mk 13:34
the master of the **h** is coming— Mk 13:35
Bethany at the **h** of Simon who Mk 14:3
the owner of the **h**, 'The Teacher Mk 14:14
named Joseph, of the **h** of David. Lk 1:27
reign over the **h** of Jacob Lk 1:33
Zechariah's **h** and greeted Lk 1:40
for us in the **h** of His servant Lk 1:69
he was of the **h** and family line Lk 2:4
I had to be in my Father's **h**?" Lk 2:49
synagogue, He entered Simon's **h**. Lk 4:38
grand banquet for Him at his **h**. Lk 5:29
how he entered the **h** of God, Lk 6:4
He is like a man building a **h**, Lk 6:48
against that **h** and couldn't Lk 6:48
man who built a **h** on the ground Lk 6:49
of that **h** was great!" Lk 6:49
when He was not far from the **h**, Lk 7:6
had been sent returned to the **h**, Lk 7:10
the Pharisee's **h** and reclined at Lk 7:36
the table in the Pharisee's **h**. Lk 7:37
I entered your **h**; you gave Me no Lk 7:44
not stay in a **h** but in the tombs Lk 8:27
with Him to come to his **h**, Lk 8:41
from the synagogue leader's ⌊**h**⌋, Lk 8:49
He came to the **h**, He let no one Lk 8:51
Whatever **h** you enter, stay there Lk 9:4
say good-bye to those at my **h**." Lk 9:61
h you enter, first say, Lk 10:5
Remain in the same **h**, eating and Lk 10:7
Don't be moving from **h** to house. Lk 10:7
Don't be moving from house to **h**. Lk 10:7
and a **h** divided against itself Lk 11:17
go back to my **h** where I came Lk 11:24
finds ⌊the **h**⌋ swept and put in Lk 11:25
not have let his **h** be broken Lk 12:39
your **h** is abandoned to you. Lk 13:35
went to eat at the **h** of one of Lk 14:1
master of the **h** told his slave, Lk 14:21
so that my **h** may be filled. Lk 14:23
a lamp, sweep the **h**, and search Lk 15:8
came near the **h**, he heard music Lk 15:25
to send him to my father's **h**— Lk 16:27
whose belongings are in the **h**, Lk 17:31
down to his **h** justified rather Lk 18:14
is no one who has left a **h**, Lk 18:29
today I must stay at your **h**." Lk 19:5
salvation has come to this **h**," Lk 19:9
My **h** will be a house of prayer, Lk 19:46
My house will be a **h** of prayer, Lk 19:46
Follow him into the **h** he enters. Lk 22:10
the owner of the **h**, 'The Teacher Lk 22:11
Him into the high priest's **h**. Lk 22:54
My Father's **h** into a marketplace Jn 2:16
Zeal for Your **h** will consume Me. Jn 2:17
So each one went to his **h**. Jn 7:53
Mary remained seated in the **h**. Jn 11:20
with her in the **h** consoling her Jn 11:31
So the **h** was filled with the Jn 12:3
In My Father's **h** are many Jn 14:2
the whole **h** where they were Ac 2:2
all the **h** of Israel know with Ac 2:36
and broke bread from **h** to house. Ac 2:46
and broke bread from house to **h**. Ac 2:46
in the desert, O **h** of Israel? Ac 7:42
was Solomon who built Him a **h**. Ac 7:47
What sort of **h** will you build Ac 7:49
he would enter **h** after house, Ac 8:3
he would enter house after **h**, Ac 8:3
to him, "to the **h** of Judas, and Ac 9:11
Ananias left and entered the **h**. Ac 9:17
tanner, whose **h** is by the sea." Ac 10:6
asked directions to Simon's **h**, Ac 10:17
to call you to his **h** and to hear Ac 10:22
I was praying in my **h**. Ac 10:30
the tanner's **h** by the sea.' Ac 10:32
arrived at the **h** where we were. Ac 11:11
and we went into the man's **h**. Ac 11:12
standing in his **h** and saying, Ac 11:13
he went to the **h** of Mary, the Ac 12:12
Lord, come and stay at my **h**." Ac 16:15
along with everyone in his **h**. Ac 16:32
He brought them up into his **h**, Ac 16:34
came to Lydia's **h** where they saw Ac 16:40
Jason's **h**, they searched Ac 17:5
and went to the **h** of a man named Ac 18:7
whose **h** was next door to the Ac 18:7
ran out of that **h** naked and Ac 19:16
in public and from **h** to house. Ac 20:20
in public and from house to **h**. Ac 20:20
where we entered the **h** of Philip Ac 21:8
whole years in his own rented **h**. Ac 28:30
we know that if our earthly **h**, 2Co 5:1
from God, a **h** not made with 2Co 5:1
to put on our **h** from heaven, 2Co 5:2
Nympha and the church in her **h**. Col 4:15
be idle, going from **h** to house; 1Tm 5:13
be idle, going from house to **h**; 1Tm 5:13
Now in a large **h** there are not 2Tm 2:20
the church that meets in your **h**. Phm 2
has more honor than the **h**. Heb 3:3
Now every **h** is built by someone, Heb 3:4
covenant with the **h** of Israel Heb 8:8
Israel and with the **h** of Judah— Heb 8:8
make with the **h** of Israel after Heb 8:10
high priest over the **h** of God, Heb 10:21
into a spiritual **h** for a holy 1Pt 2:5

HOUSED *(1)*

the rooms ⌊that **h**⌋ the supplies, Neh 12:44

HOUSEHOLD *(146)*

and all your **h**, for I have seen Gn 7:1
men, born in his **h**, and they Gn 14:14
the members of Abraham's **h**— Gn 17:23
And all the men of his **h**— Gn 17:27
in Abimelech's **h** on account of Gn 20:18
elder of his **h** who managed all Gn 24:2
told her mother's **h** about these Gn 24:28
to my father's **h** and to my Gn 24:38
family and from my father's **h**. Gn 24:40
inheritance in our father's **h**? Gn 31:14
stole her father's **h** idols. Gn 31:19
had taken Laban's **h** idols, Gn 31:34
but could not find the **h** idols. Gn 31:35
years I have worked in your **h**— Gn 31:41
I and my **h** will be destroyed." Gn 34:30
and all the people of his **h**, Gn 36:6
serving in the **h** of his Egyptian Gn 39:2
charge of his **h** and placed all Gn 39:4
charge of his **h** and of all that Gn 39:5
and none of the **h** servants was Gn 39:11
she called the **h** servants. Gn 39:14
and also Pharaoh's **h** heard it. Gn 45:2
of his entire **h**, and ruler over Gn 45:8
you, your **h**, and everything you Gn 45:11
of Jacob's **h** who had come to Gn 46:27
brothers and to his father's **h**, Gn 46:31
My brothers and my father's **h**, Gn 46:31
all his father's **h** with food for Gn 47:12
Joseph said to Pharaoh's **h**, Gn 50:4
the elders of his **h**, and all the Gn 50:7
along with all Joseph's **h**, Gn 50:8
brothers, and his father's **h**. Gn 50:8
and his father's **h** remained in Gn 50:22
households, one animal per **h**. Ex 12:3
If the **h** is too small for a Ex 12:4
every male in his **h** must be Ex 12:48
atonement for himself and his **h**. Lv 16:6
atonement for himself and his **h**, Lv 16:11
himself, his **h**, and the whole Lv 16:17
he is faithful in all My **h**. Nm 12:7
then you and your **h** may eat it Nm 18:31
Egypt, on Pharaoh and all his **h**, Dt 6:22
with your **h** in everything you Dt 12:7
God has given you and your **h**. Dt 26:11
her father's **h**, and all who Jos 6:25
of his father's **h** and the men Jdg 6:27
a snare to Gideon and his **h**. Jdg 8:27
and your father's **h** to death. Jdg 14:15
he made an ephod and **h** idols, Jdg 17:5
are an ephod, **h** gods, and a Jdg 18:14
ephod, and the **h** idols, while Jdg 18:17
ephod, and the **h** idols, the Jdg 18:18
took his ephod, **h** idols, and Jdg 18:20
and all his **h** went up to make 1Sm 1:21
also make the **h** of that man's 1Sm 17:25
Michal took the **h** idol and put 1Sm 19:13
the **h** idol was on the bed with 1Sm 19:16
your faithful love from my **h**— 1Sm 20:15
servant or any of my father's **h**, 1Sm 22:15
one with his **h**, and they settled 2Sm 2:3
returned ⌊home⌋ to bless his **h**, 2Sm 6:20
and his entire **h** followed him. 2Sm 15:16
are for the king's **h** to ride, 2Sm 16:2
bring the king's **h** across and do 2Sm 19:18
the king and his **h** across the 2Sm 19:41
food for the king and his **h**; 1Kg 4:7
by providing my **h** with food." 1Kg 5:9
as food for his **h** and 110,000 1Kg 5:11
in charge of the **h** at Tirzah. 1Kg 16:9
and he and her **h** ate for many 1Kg 17:15
Let's go tell the king's **h**." 2Kg 7:9
was reported to the king's **h**. 2Kg 7:11
you and your **h**, and go and live 2Kg 8:1
and her **h** lived as foreigners 2Kg 8:2
was over the **h** governing the 2Kg 15:5
the spiritists, **h** idols, images, 2Kg 23:24
and his relatives from his **h**, 1Ch 9:19
returned ⌊home⌋ to bless his **h**. 1Ch 16:43
my father's **h** to be king over 1Ch 28:4
Judah, my father's **h**, and from 1Ch 28:4
was over the king's **h** governing 2Ch 26:21
chief priest of the **h** of Zadok, 2Ch 31:10
of the tribal **h** of the Levites. 2Ch 35:5
of Tobiah's **h** possessions out Neh 13:8
steward in his **h** to serve as Est 1:8
him, his **h**, and everything Jb 1:10
his **h** will no longer see him. Jb 20:9
the members of my **h** said, Jb 31:31
a bull from your **h** or male goats Ps 50:9
He made him master of his **h**, Ps 105:21
gives the childless woman a **h**, Ps 113:9
curse is on the **h** of the wicked, Pr 3:33
ruin on his **h** will inherit Pr 11:29
dishonestly troubles his **h**, Pr 15:27
food for your **h** and nourishment Pr 27:27
food for her **h** and portions for Pr 31:15
afraid for her **h** when it snows, Pr 31:21
for all in her **h** are doubly Pr 31:21
of her **h** and is never idle Pr 31:27
when your king is a **h** servant, Ec 10:16
own father's **h**—even they were Jr 12:6
will punish that man and his **h**. Jr 23:34
and you and your **h** will survive. Jr 38:17
and without ephod or **h** idols. Hs 3:4
Greet a **h** when you enter it, Mt 10:12
and if the **h** is worthy, let your Mt 10:13
much more the members of his **h**! Mt 10:25
will be the members of his **h**. Mt 10:36
in his hometown and in his **h**." Mt 13:57
has put in charge of his **h**, Mt 24:45
his relatives, and in his **h**." Mk 6:4
first say, 'Peace to this **h**.' Lk 10:5
charge of his **h** servants to give Lk 12:42
five in one **h** will be divided: Lk 12:52
No **h** slave can be the slave of Lk 16:13
along with his whole **h**. Jn 4:53
not remain in the **h** forever, Jn 8:35
over Egypt and over his whole **h**. Ac 7:10
God along with his whole **h**. Ac 10:2
called two of his **h** slaves and a Ac 10:7
and all your **h** will be saved.' Ac 11:14
she and her **h** were baptized, Ac 16:15
will be saved—you and your **h**." Ac 16:31
believed God with his entire **h**. Ac 16:34
Lord, along with his whole **h**; Ac 18:8
to criticize another's **h** slave? Rm 14:4
belong to the **h** of Aristobulus. Rm 16:10
belong to the **h** of Narcissus who Rm 16:11
of Chloe's **h**, that there are 1Co 1:11
baptize the **h** of Stephanas; 1Co 1:16
you know the **h** of Stephanas: 1Co 16:15
who belong to the **h** of faith. Gl 6:10
saints, and members of God's **h**, Eph 2:19
those from Caesar's **h**. Php 4:22
manages his own **h** competently, 1Tm 3:4
know how to manage his own **h**, 1Tm 3:5
people ought to act in God's **h**, 1Tm 3:15
for his **h**, he has denied 1Tm 5:8
mercy to the **h** of Onesiphorus, 2Tm 1:16
and the **h** of Onesiphorus. 2Tm 4:19
as Moses was in all God's **h**. Heb 3:2
as a servant in all God's **h**, Heb 3:5
faithful as a Son over His **h**, Heb 3:6
whose **h** we are if we hold on to Heb 3:6
H slaves, submit yourselves to 1Pt 2:18
judgment to begin with God's **h**; 1Pt 4:17

HOUSEHOLDS *(13)*

relieve⌋ the hunger of your **h**. Gn 42:19
relieve⌋ the hunger of your **h**, Gn 42:33
Get your father and your **h**, Gn 45:18
yourselves, your **h**, and your Gn 47:24
according to ⌊their⌋ fathers' **h**, Ex 12:3
and swallowed them and their **h**, Nm 16:32
them, their **h**, their tents, Dt 11:6
their relatives, the heads of **h**. 1Ch 9:13
Then the leaders of the **h**, 1Ch 29:6
and their own **h** competently. 1Tm 3:12
manage their **h**, and give 1Tm 5:14
their way into **h** and capture 2Tm 3:6
overthrow whole **h** by teaching Ti 1:11

HOUSES *(149)*

plundered everything in the **h**. Gn 34:29
into the **h** of your officials and Ex 8:3
taken away from you and your **h**, Ex 8:9
you, your **h**, your officials, Ex 8:11
the frogs in the **h**, courtyards, Ex 8:13
your people, and your **h**. Ex 8:21
The Egyptians' **h** will swarm with Ex 8:21
palace and his officials' **h**. Ex 8:24
They will fill your **h**, all your Ex 10:6
officials' **h**, and the houses Ex 10:6
and the **h** of all the Egyptians— Ex 10:6
lintel of the **h** in which they Ex 12:7
The blood on the **h** where you are Ex 12:13
must remove yeast from your **h**. Ex 12:15
found in your **h** for seven days. Ex 12:19
enter your **h** to strike ⌊you⌋. Ex 12:23
passed over the **h** of the Ex 12:27
But **h** in villages that have no Lv 25:31
redeem ⌊such⌋ **h** stays in effect Lv 25:31
right to redeem **h** in the cities Lv 25:32
because the **h** in the Levitical Lv 25:33
clans and their ancestral **h**, Nm 1:2
clans and their ancestral **h**, Nm 1:18
clans and their ancestral **h**, Nm 1:20
clans and their ancestral **h**, Nm 1:22
clans and their ancestral **h**, Nm 1:24
clans and their ancestral **h**, Nm 1:26
clans and their ancestral **h**, Nm 1:28
clans and their ancestral **h**, Nm 1:30
clans and their ancestral **h**, Nm 1:32
clans and their ancestral **h**, Nm 1:34
clans and their ancestral **h**, Nm 1:36
clans and their ancestral **h**, Nm 1:38
clans and their ancestral **h**, Nm 1:40
clans and their ancestral **h**, Nm 1:42
registered by their ancestral **h**. Nm 1:45
the flags of their ancestral **h**. Nm 2:2
registered by their ancestral **h**. Nm 2:32
ancestral **h** and their clans Nm 3:15
clans by their ancestral **h**. Nm 3:20
clans and their ancestral **h**, Nm 4:2
ancestral **h** and their clans Nm 4:22
clans and their ancestral **h**. Nm 4:29
clans and their ancestral **h**, Nm 4:34
clans and their ancestral **h**, Nm 4:38
ancestral **h** numbered 2,630. Nm 4:40
clans and their ancestral **h**, Nm 4:42
clans and their ancestral **h**, Nm 4:46
the heads of their ancestral **h**, Nm 7:2
leaders of their ancestral **h**. Nm 17:2
leaders of their ancestral **h**. Nm 17:6
their ancestral **h** of those 20 Nm 26:2
according to their ancestral **h**, Nm 34:14
h full of every good thing that Dt 6:11
build beautiful **h** to live in, Dt 8:12
and live in their cities and **h**, Dt 19:1
took it from our **h** as food on Jos 9:12
overlaid with silver in these **h**? Jdg 18:14
who were in the **h** near it Jdg 18:22
Solomon had built the two **h**, 1Kg 9:10
palace and your servants' **h**. 1Kg 20:6
tore down the **h** of the male 2Kg 23:7
and all the **h** of Jerusalem; 2Kg 25:9
he burned down all the great **h**. 2Kg 25:9
Their ancestral **h** increased 1Ch 4:38
according to their ancestral **h**: 1Ch 5:13
was head of their ancestral **h**. 1Ch 5:15
the heads of their ancestral **h**: 1Ch 5:24
the heads of their ancestral **h**. 1Ch 7:2
records of their ancestral **h**, 1Ch 7:4
and heads of their ancestral **h**; 1Ch 7:7
the heads of their ancestral **h**— 1Ch 7:9
the heads of their ancestral **h**, 1Ch 7:40
were heads of their ancestral **h**. 1Ch 9:9
famous men in their ancestral **h**. 1Ch 12:30
David built **h** for himself in the 1Ch 15:1
of Levi by their ancestral **h**— 1Ch 23:24
heads of ancestral **h** were from 1Ch 24:4
of ancestral **h** were from 1Ch 24:4
according to their ancestral **h**. 1Ch 24:30
their ancestral **h** because they 1Ch 26:6
according to their ancestral **h**, 1Ch 26:13
your ancestral **h** by your 2Ch 35:4
of the ancestral **h** for your 2Ch 35:5
of the ancestral **h** of the lay 2Ch 35:12
to represent their ancestral **h**. Ezr 10:16
and **h** to them immediately, Neh 5:11
and no **h** had been built yet. Neh 7:4
possession of well-supplied **h**, Neh 9:25
our ancestral **h** at the appointed Neh 10:34
who filled their **h** with silver. Jb 3:15
more those who dwell in clay **h**, Jb 4:19
abandoned **h** destined to become Jb 15:28
filled their **h** with good things Jb 22:18
In the dark they break into **h**; Jb 24:16
and fill our **h** with plunder. Pr 1:13
I built **h** and planted vineyards Ec 2:4
from the poor is in your **h**. Is 3:14
many **h** will become desolate, Is 5:9
inhabitants, **h** are without Is 6:11
but for the two **h** of Israel, Is 8:14
h will be looted, and their Is 13:16

there, and owls will fill the **h**. Is 13:21
You counted the **h** of Jerusalem Is 22:10
will build **h** and live ⌊in them Is 65:21
so their **h** are full of deceit. Jr 5:27
Their **h** will be turned over to Jr 6:12
out of your **h** on the Sabbath Jr 17:22
heard from their **h** when You Jr 18:22
h of Jerusalem and the houses Jr 19:13
Jerusalem and the **h** of the kings Jr 19:13
all the **h** on whose rooftops they Jr 19:13
Build **h** and live ⌊in them⌋. Jr 29:5
Build **h** and settle down. Jr 29:28
H, fields, and vineyards will Jr 32:15
along with the **h** where incense Jr 32:29
concerning the **h** of this city Jr 33:4
will fill the **h** with the corpses Jr 33:5
have not built **h** to live in and Jr 35:9
and the people's **h** and tore down Jr 39:8
palace, all the **h** of Jerusalem, Jr 52:13
and all the **h** of the nobles. Jr 52:13
strangers, our **h** to foreigners. Lm 5:2
to take possession of their **h**. Ezk 7:24
Isn't the time near to build **h**? Ezk 11:3
burn down your **h** and execute Ezk 16:41
and burn their **h** with fire. Ezk 23:47
securely, build **h**, and plant Ezk 28:26
and in the doorways of their **h**. Ezk 33:30
It will be a place for their **h**, Ezk 45:4
your **h** will be made a garbage Dn 2:5
they climb into the **h**; Jl 2:9
the **h** ⌊inlaid with⌋ ivory will Am 3:15
and the great **h** will come to an Am 3:15
live in the **h** of cut stone you Am 5:11
the **h** of Achzib are a deception Mc 1:14
they also take **h**. They deprive a Mc 2:2
plunder and their **h** a ruin. Zph 1:13
They will build **h** but never live Zph 1:13
evening among the **h** of Ashkelon, Zph 2:7
to live in your paneled **h**, Hg 1:4
be captured, the **h** looted, and Zch 14:2
And everyone who has left **h**, Mt 19:29
devour widows' **h** and make long Mt 23:14
now at this time—**h**, brothers Mk 10:30
devour widows' **h** and say long Mk 12:40
devour widows' **h** and say long Lk 20:47
who owned lands or **h** sold them, Ac 4:34
you have **h** to eat and drink 1Co 11:22

HOUSETOP *(4)*
man on the **h** must not come down Mt 24:17
man on the **h** must not come down Mk 13:15
a man on the **h**, whose belongings Lk 17:31
to pray on the **h** at about noon. Ac 10:9

HOUSETOPS *(2)*
in a whisper, proclaim on the **h**. Mt 10:27
will be proclaimed on the **h**. Lk 12:3

HOVERING *(2)*
of God was **h** over the surface Gn 1:2
Like **h** birds, so the LORD of Is 31:5

HOVERS *(1)*
an eagle and **h** over His young; Dt 32:11

HOW *(627)*

HOWEVER *(181)*
(See pp. xi-xii.)

HOWL *(2)*
Hyenas will **h** in the fortresses, Is 13:22
I will **h** like the jackals and Mc 1:8

HOWLING *(1)*
land, in a barren, **h** wilderness; Dt 32:10

HOZAI *(1)*
about in the Records of **H**. 2Ch 33:19

HUBBAH *(1)*
Ahi, Rohgah, **H**, and Aram. 1Ch 7:34

HUBS *(1)*
and **h** were all of cast metal. 1Kg 7:33

HUDDLE *(3)*
rains, they **h** against the rocks, Jb 24:8
they **h** beneath the thistles. Jb 30:7
garments⌋ **h** in garbage heaps Lm 4:5

HUGE *(18)*
along with a **h** number of Ex 12:38
h number of cattle, and silver, Jos 22:8
David also took **h** quantities of 2Sm 8:8
and piled a **h** mound of stones 2Sm 18:17
A **h** man was there with six 2Sm 21:20
killed an Egyptian, a **h** man. 2Sm 23:21
David also took **h** quantities of 1Ch 18:8
a **h** company armed with shields Ezk 38:4
a mighty horde, a **h** army? Ezk 38:15
there will be a **h** number of fish Ezk 47:9
Four **h** beasts came up from the Dn 7:3
'These **h** beasts, four in number, Dn 7:17
west, forming a **h** valley, so Zch 14:4
H crowds followed Him, and He Mt 12:15
ashore, He saw a **h** crowd, felt Mt 14:14
He saw a **h** crowd and had Mk 6:34
And a **h** crowd was following Him Jn 6:2
up and noticed a **h** crowd coming Jn 6:5

HUGGED *(2)*
to meet him, **h** him, and kissed Gn 29:13
to meet him, **h** him, threw his Gn 33:4

HUKKOK *(1)*
and went from there to **H**, Jos 19:34

HUKOK *(1)*
(AKA HELKATH)
H and its pasturelands, and 1Ch 6:75

HUL *(2)*
Uz, **H**, Gether, and Mash. Gn 10:23
Lud, Aram, Uz, **H**, Gether, and 1Ch 1:17

HULDAH *(2)*
Asaiah went to the prophetess **H**, 2Kg 22:14
went to the prophetess **H**, 2Ch 34:22

HUMAN *(122)*
to him, "Who made the **h** mouth? Ex 4:11
if⌋ he touches **h** uncleanness— Lv 5:3
unclean, whether **h** uncleanness, Lv 7:21
unclean because of a **h** corpse, Nm 9:6
unclean because of a **h** corpse. Nm 9:7
who touches any **h** corpse will be Nm 19:11
has died, or a **h** bone, or a Nm 19:16
the captives, both **h** and animal. Nm 31:11
what was captured, **h** and animal. Nm 31:26
of the field **h**, to come under Dt 20:19
and divided the **h** race, Dt 32:8
him with a **h** rod and with blows 2Sm 7:14
don't let me fall into **h** hands." 2Sm 24:14
You alone know every **h** heart, 1Kg 8:39
H bones will be burned on you.' 1Kg 13:2
no one was there—no **h** sounds. 2Kg 7:10
not gods but made by **h** hands— 2Kg 19:18
their places with **h** bones. 2Kg 23:14
and he burned **h** bones on the 2Kg 23:20
don't let me fall into **h** hands." 1Ch 21:13
for You alone know the **h** heart, 2Ch 6:30
He has only **h** strength, but we 2Ch 32:8
which were made by **h** hands. 2Ch 32:19
or do You see as a **h** sees? Jb 10:4
Are Your days like those of a **h**, Jb 10:5
fire unfanned ⌊by **h** hands⌋ will Jb 20:26
a shaft far from **h** habitation, Jb 28:4
were expelled from **h** society; Jb 30:5
righteousness ⌊another⌋ **h** being. Jb 35:8
⌊on⌋ a desert with no **h** life, Jb 38:26
disappeared from the **h** race. Ps 12:1
is exalted by the **h** race. Ps 12:8
heaven on the **h** race to see if Ps 14:2
their offspring from the **h** race. Ps 21:10
heaven on the **h** race to see if Ps 53:2
foe, for **h** help is worthless. Ps 60:11
Even **h** wrath will praise You; Ps 76:10
wonderful works for the **h** race. Ps 107:8
wonderful works for the **h** race. Ps 107:15
wonderful works for the **h** race. Ps 107:21
wonderful works for the **h** race. Ps 107:31
foe, for **h** help is worthless. Ps 108:12
and gold, made by **h** hands. Ps 115:4
He has given to the **h** race. Ps 115:16
Redeem me from **h** oppression, Ps 119:134
and gold, made by **h** hands. Ps 135:15
world, delighting in the **h** race. Pr 8:31
LORD—how much more, **h** hearts. Pr 15:11
H pride will be humbled, and the Is 2:11
So **h** pride will be brought low, Is 2:17
will fall, but not by **h** sword; Is 31:8
and **h** life disregarded. Is 33:8
not gods but made by **h** hands— Is 37:19
I will give **h** beings in your Is 43:4
it according to a **h** likeness, Is 44:13
did not resemble a **h** being— Is 52:14
H corpses will fall like manure Jr 9:22
who makes ⌊**h**⌋ flesh his strength Jr 17:5
no **h** being will even stay in it Jr 49:18
no **h** being will even stay in it Jr 49:33
no **h** being will even stay in it Jr 50:40
where no **h** being passes through. Jr 51:43
appearance: They had **h** form, Ezk 1:5
⌊They had⌋ **h** hands under their Ezk 1:8
appearance of a **h** on the throne Ezk 1:26
it over dried **h** excrement in Ezk 4:12
cow dung instead of **h** excrement, Ezk 4:15
have the form of **h** hands under Ezk 10:8
with the form of **h** hands under Ezk 10:21
No **h** foot will pass through it, Ezk 29:11
No **h** foot will churn them again, Ezk 32:13
the **h** flock of My pasture, Ezk 34:31
and every **h** being on the face of Ezk 38:20
and one of them sees a **h** bone, Ezk 39:15
a **h** face turned toward the palm Ezk 41:19
like a man, and given a **h** mind. Dn 7:4
I heard a **h** voice calling from Dn 8:16
be shattered, not by **h** hands. Dn 8:25
one with **h** likeness touched Dn 10:16
the one with **h** likeness touched Dn 10:18
I led them with **h** cords, with Hs 11:4
Indeed, **h** joy has dried up. Jl 1:12
because of **h** bloodshed and Hab 2:8
because of ⌊your⌋ **h** bloodshed Hab 2:17
sanctuary made by ⌊**h**⌋ hands, Mk 14:58
You judge by **h** standards. Jn 8:15
Neither is He served by **h** hands, Ac 17:25
image fashioned by **h** art and Ac 17:29
for every **h** being who does Rm 2:9
to say? I use a **h** argument: Is Rm 3:5
am using a **h** analogy because of Rm 6:19
not depend on **h** will or effort, Rm 9:16
is wiser than **h** wisdom, 1Co 1:25
is stronger than **h** strength. 1Co 1:25
are wise from a **h** perspective, 1Co 1:26
not in words taught by **h** wisdom, 1Co 2:13
by you or by a **h** court. 1Co 4:3
this from a **h** perspective? 1Co 9:8
in Ephesus with only **h** hope, 1Co 15:32
plan in a purely **h** way so that I 2Co 1:17
know anyone in a purely **h** way. 2Co 5:16
known Christ in a purely **h** way, 2Co 5:16
many boast from a **h** perspective, 2Co 11:18
not based on a **h** point of view. Gl 1:11
it from a **h** source and I was Gl 1:12
of the law no **h** being will be Gl 2:16
I'm using a **h** illustration. Gl 3:15
aside even a **h** covenant that has Gl 3:15
by **h** cunning with cleverness in Eph 4:14
obey your **h** masters with fear Eph 6:5
deceit based on **h** tradition, Col 2:8
they are **h** commands and Col 2:22
obey your **h** masters in Col 3:22
welcomed it not as a **h** message, 1Th 2:13
Submit to every **h** institution 1Pt 2:13
no longer for **h** desires, but for 1Pt 4:2
donkey spoke with a **h** voice and 2Pt 2:16
to kill a third of the **h** race. Rv 9:15
A third of the **h** race was killed Rv 9:18
were redeemed from the **h** race as Rv 14:4
and **h** bodies and souls. Rv 18:13
according to **h** measurement, Rv 21:17

HUMANITY *(12)*
All **h** will come to You, the One Ps 65:2
and it weighs heavily on **h**: Ec 6:1
because this ⌊is for⌋ all **h**. Ec 12:13
So **h** is brought low, and man is Is 2:9
H is brought low, man is humbled, Is 5:15
not look on **h** any longer with Is 38:11
all **h** will see ⌊it⌋ together, Is 40:5
All **h** is grass, and all its Is 40:6
the nations, despised among **h**. Jr 49:15
pour out My Spirit on all **h**; Jl 2:28
pour out My Spirit on all **h**; Ac 2:17
you except what is common to **h**. 1Co 10:13

HUMANS *(3)*
of ⌊every⌋ 500 **h**, cattle, Nm 31:28
shame, and the craftsmen are **h**. Is 44:11
is one flesh for **h**, another for 1Co 15:39

HUMBLE *(51)*
you refuse to **h** yourself before Ex 10:3
Moses was a very **h** man, more so Nm 12:3
that He might **h** you and test you Dt 8:2
in order to **h** and test you, Dt 8:16
I will **h** myself even more and 2Sm 6:22
against the proud—You **h** them. 2Sm 22:28
I will **h** David's descendants, 1Kg 11:39
called by My name **h** themselves, 2Ch 7:14

But he did not **h** himself before 2Ch 33:23
God and did not **h** himself before 2Ch 36:12
that we might **h** ourselves before Ezr 8:21
them⌋ up," God will save the **h**. Jb 22:29
on every proud person and **h** him; Jb 40:12
have heard the desire of the **h**; Ps 10:17
but You **h** those with haughty Ps 18:27
The **h** will eat and be satisfied; Ps 22:26
He leads the **h** in what is right Ps 25:9
the **h** will hear and be glad. Ps 34:2
But the **h** will inherit the land Ps 37:11
The **h** will see it and rejoice. Ps 69:32
exalted, He takes note of the **h**; Ps 138:6
He adorns the **h** with salvation. Ps 149:4
mock, but gives grace to the **h**. Pr 3:34
Go, **h** yourself, and plead with Pr 6:3
spirit with the **h** than to divide Pr 16:19
A person's pride will **h** him, Pr 29:23
but a **h** spirit will gain honor. Pr 29:23
for the **h** person in his Is 25:4
it, the feet of the **h**, the steps Is 26:6
The **h** will have joy after joy in Is 29:19
one who is **h**, submissive in Is 66:2
Take a **h** seat, for your glorious Jr 13:18
have not become **h** to this day, Jr 44:10
kingdom might be **h** and not exalt Ezk 17:14
He is able to **h** those who walk Dn 4:37
and to **h** yourself before Dn 10:12
LORD, all you **h** of the earth, Zph 2:3
a meek and **h** people among you Zph 3:12
and victorious, **h** and riding on Zch 9:9
I am gentle and **h** in heart, Mt 11:29
favor on the **h** condition of His Lk 1:48
instead, associate with the **h**. Rm 12:16
who comforts the **h**, comforted us 2Co 7:6
I who am **h** among you in person, 2Co 10:1
the body of our **h** condition Php 3:21
The brother of **h** circumstances Jms 1:9
proud, but gives grace to the **h**. Jms 4:6
H yourselves before the Lord, Jms 4:10
and be compassionate and **h**, 1Pt 3:8
proud, but gives grace to the **h**. 1Pt 5:5
H yourselves therefore under the 1Pt 5:6

HUMBLED *(35)*

uncircumcised hearts will be **h**, Lv 26:41
He **h** you by letting you go Dt 8:3
Ahab has **h** himself before Me 1Kg 21:29
because he has **h** himself before 1Kg 21:29
tender and you **h** yourself before 2Kg 22:19
and the king **h** themselves and 2Ch 12:6
saw that they had **h** themselves, 2Ch 12:7
They have **h** themselves; 2Ch 12:7
When Rehoboam **h** himself, the 2Ch 12:12
For the LORD **h** Judah because of 2Ch 28:19
Zebulun **h** themselves and came 2Ch 30:11
Then Hezekiah **h** himself for the 2Ch 32:26
and earnestly **h** himself before 2Ch 33:12
images before he **h** himself, 2Ch 33:19
his father Manasseh **h** himself; 2Ch 33:23
tender and you **h** yourself before 2Ch 34:27
because you **h** yourself before 2Ch 34:27
I **h** myself with fasting, and my Ps 35:13
despise a broken and **h** heart. Ps 51:17
as many days as You have **h** us, Ps 90:15
diminished and are **h** by cruel Ps 107:39
is brought low, and man is **h**. Is 2:9
pride will be **h**, and the Is 2:11
is lifted up—it will be **h**— Is 2:12
the loftiness of men will be **h**; Is 2:17
low, man is **h**, and haughty eyes Is 5:15
humbled, and haughty eyes are **h**. Is 5:15
times when He **h** the land of Is 9:1
For He has **h** those who live in Is 26:5
wanted and **h** anyone he wanted. Dn 5:19
have not **h** your heart, even Dn 5:22
exalts himself will be **h**, Mt 23:12
who exalts himself will be **h**, Lk 14:11
who exalts himself will be **h**, Lk 18:14
h Himself by becoming obedient Php 2:8

HUMBLES *(6)*

wealth; He **h** and He exalts. 1Sm 2:7
He **h** the spirit of leaders; Ps 76:12
whoever **h** himself like this Mt 18:4
and whoever **h** himself will be Mt 23:12
and the one who **h** himself will Lk 14:11
but the one who **h** himself will Lk 18:14

HUMBLING *(1)*

commit a sin by **h** myself so that 2Co 11:7

HUMBLY *(2)*

and to walk **h** with your God. Mc 6:8
h receive the implanted word, Jms 1:21

HUMILIATE *(9)*

the bundles, and don't **h** her. Ru 2:15
right eye and **h** all Israel." 1Sm 11:2
myself even more and **h** myself. 2Sm 6:22
Don't **h** me, for such a thing 2Sm 13:12
ridiculing with no one to **h** you? Jb 11:3
on every proud person and **h** him. Jb 40:11
and will **h** them Selah because Ps 55:19
the arrogant and **h** the insolence Is 13:11
my God will again **h** me in your 2Co 12:21

HUMILIATED *(24)*

because you have **h** her. Dt 21:14
them, since they were deeply **h**. 2Sm 10:5
in when they are **h** after fleeing 2Sm 19:3
since the men were deeply **h**. 1Ch 19:5
You have **h** me ten times now, Jb 19:3
When others are **h** and you say, Jb 22:29
to kill me be disgraced and **h**; Ps 35:4
misfortune be disgraced and **h**; Ps 35:26
me harm be driven back and **h**. Ps 40:14
But You have rejected and **h** us; Ps 44:9
who seek You be **h** because of me, Ps 69:6
me harm be driven back and **h**. Ps 70:2
them are put to shame, even **h**; Is 45:16
put to shame or **h** for all Is 45:17
therefore I have not been **h**; Is 50:7
don't be **h**, for you will not be Is 54:4
They are ashamed and **h**; Jr 14:3
she was ashamed and **h**. Jr 15:9
be ashamed and **h** because of all Jr 22:22
was ashamed and **h** because I bore Jr 31:19
your mother will be utterly **h**; Jr 50:12
Be ashamed and **h** because of your Ezk 36:32
despised and **h** before all the Mal 2:9
all His adversaries were **h**, Lk 13:17

HUMILIATES *(2)*

if your opponent **h** you? Pr 25:8
of gluttons **h** his father. Pr 28:7

HUMILIATION *(12)*

got up from my **h**, with my tunic Ezr 9:5
be covered with disgrace and **h**. Ps 71:13
us in our **h** His love is eternal Ps 136:23
of idols go in **h** together. Is 45:16
They can no longer feel **h**. Jr 6:15
They can no longer feel **h**. Jr 8:12
an everlasting **h** that will never Jr 20:11
shame and **h** that will never be Jr 23:40
H covers our faces because Jr 51:51
and then in **h**, you will proceed Lk 14:9
In His **h** justice was denied Him. Ac 8:33
is rich ⌊should boast⌋ in his **h**, Jms 1:10

HUMILITY *(13)*

me, and Your **h** exalts me. Ps 18:35
cause of truth, **h**, and justice. Ps 45:4
but with **h** comes wisdom. Pr 11:2
instruction, and **h** comes before Pr 15:33
proud, but before honor comes **h**. Pr 18:12
The result of **h** is fear of the Pr 22:4
Seek righteousness, seek **h**; Zph 2:3
serving the Lord with all **h**, Ac 20:19
with all **h** and gentleness, Eph 4:2
but in **h** consider others as more Php 2:3
ascetic practices, **h**, and severe Col 2:23
kindness, **h**, gentleness, Col 3:12
yourselves with **h** toward one 1Pt 5:5

HUMPS *(1)*

treasures on the **h** of camels, Is 30:6

HUMTAH *(1)*

H, Kiriath-arba (that is, Hebron) Jos 15:54

HUNCHBACK *(1)*

or who is a **h** or a dwarf, or who Lv 21:20

HUNDRED *(21)*

In the six **h** and first year, Gn 8:13
he reaped a **h** times ⌊what was Gn 26:12
h Danites departed from Zorah Jdg 18:11
Two **h** men from Jerusalem went 2Sm 15:11
in the four **h** eightieth year 1Kg 6:1
of them was a match for a **h**, 1Ch 12:14
of His people a **h** times over! 1Ch 21:3
Six **h** bulls and 3,000 sheep were 2Ch 29:33
the Tower of the **H** and the Tower Neh 3:1
the Tower of the **H**, to the Sheep Neh 12:39
more than a **h** lashes into a fool Pr 17:10
man may father a **h** children and Ec 6:3
commits crime a **h** times and Ec 8:12
the youth will die at a **h** years, Is 65:20
one who misses a **h** years will be Is 65:20
will have ⌊only⌋ a **h** left, Am 5:3
marches out a **h** ⌊strong⌋ will Am 5:3
'A **h** measures of oil,' he said. Lk 16:6
'A **h** measures of wheat,' Lk 16:7
Two **h** denarii worth of bread Jn 6:7
since he was about a **h** years old Rm 4:19

HUNDRED-YEAR-OLD *(1)*

Can a child be born to a **h** man? Gn 17:17

HUNDREDS *(29)*

of thousands, **h**, fifties, and Ex 18:21
of thousands, **h**, fifties, and Ex 18:25
thousands and commanders of **h**, Nm 31:14
of thousands and of **h**, Nm 31:48
of thousands and of **h**, Nm 31:52
thousands and of **h** and brought Nm 31:54
for thousands, **h**, fifties, and Dt 1:15
thousands and commanders of **h**? 1Sm 22:7
their units of⌋ **h** and thousands, 1Sm 29:2
commanders of **h** and of thousands 2Sm 18:1
marched out by **h** and thousands. 2Sm 18:4
brought in the commanders of **h**, 2Kg 11:4
commanders of **h** did everything 2Kg 11:9
commanders of **h** King David's 2Kg 11:10
the commanders of **h** in charge of 2Kg 11:15
with him⌋ the commanders of **h**, 2Kg 11:19
commanders of **h** and of thousands 1Ch 13:1
of the thousands and of the **h**, 1Ch 26:26
and the commanders of **h**, 1Ch 27:1
and the commanders of **h**, 1Ch 28:1
of thousands and of **h**, 1Ch 29:6
of thousands and of **h**, 2Ch 1:2
commanders of **h** into a covenant 2Ch 23:1
commanders of **h** did everything 2Ch 23:8
the commanders of **h** King David's 2Ch 23:9
sent out the commanders of **h**, 2Ch 23:14
with him⌋ the commanders of **h**, 2Ch 23:20
according to commanders of **h**. 2Ch 25:5
down in ranks of **h** and fifties. Mk 6:40

HUNDREDTH *(1)*

the six **h** year of Noah's life, Gn 7:11

HUNG *(21)*

and the altar and **h** a screen for Ex 40:33
anyone **h** ⌊on a tree⌋ is under Dt 21:23
h ⌊the body of⌋ the king of Ai Jos 8:29
He **h** their bodies on five trees Jos 10:26
the Ashtoreths and **h** his body on 1Sm 31:10
and feet and **h** ⌊their bodies⌋ 2Sm 4:12
Philistines had **h** them the day 2Sm 21:12
of Saul's family who had been **h**. 2Sm 21:13
and he **h** gold chains across the 1Kg 6:21
of their gods and **h** his skull in 1Ch 10:10
10 sons be **h** on the gallows." Est 9:13
and they **h** ⌊the bodies of⌋ Est 9:14
There we **h** up our lyres on the Ps 137:2
thousand bucklers are **h** on it— Sg 4:4
Princes are **h** up by their hands; Lm 5:12
They **h** shields and helmets in Ezk 27:10
They **h** their shields all around Ezk 27:11
millstone were **h** around his neck Mt 18:6
millstone were **h** around his neck Mk 9:42
millstone were **h** around his neck Lk 17:2
is everyone who is **h** on a tree. Gl 3:13

HUNGER *(25)*

Extreme **h** came to all the land Gn 41:55
to relieve⌋ the **h** of your Gn 42:19
to relieve⌋ the **h** of your Gn 42:33
this whole assembly die of **h**!" Ex 16:3
will be weak from **h**, ravaged by Dt 32:24
who are starving ⌊**h**⌋ no more. 1Sm 2:5
bread from heaven for their **h**; Neh 9:15
destruction and **h** and not fear Jb 5:22
Emaciated from poverty and **h**, Jb 30:3
will be satisfied in days of **h**. Ps 37:19
for him because his **h** urges him Pr 16:26
I will kill your root with **h**, Is 14:30
They will not **h** or thirst, Is 49:10
no longer grow weak ⌊from **h**⌋. Jr 31:12
where he will die from **h**, Jr 38:9
of the ram's horn or **h** for food, Jr 42:14
fainting from **h** on the corner Lm 2:19
off than those slain by **h**, Lm 4:9
an oven from the ravages of **h**. Lm 5:10
for there will be **h** within you. Mc 6:14

are those who **h** and thirst for Mt 5:6
food, and here I am dying of **h**! Lk 15:17
sleepless nights, by times of **h**, 2Co 6:5
nights, **h** and thirst, often 2Co 11:27
no longer will they **h**; Rv 7:16

HUNGRY *(49)*
humbled you by letting you go **h**; Dt 8:3
The people must be **h**, exhausted, 2Sm 17:29
The **h** consume his harvest, Jb 5:5
They carry sheaves but go **h**. Jb 24:10
Young lions lack food and go **h**, Ps 34:10
If I were **h**, I would not tell Ps 50:12
They were **h** and thirsty; Ps 107:5
and filled the **h** with good Ps 107:9
He causes the **h** to settle there, Ps 107:36
and giving food to the **h**. Ps 146:7
to satisfy himself when he is **h**. Pr 6:30
will not let the righteous go **h**, Pr 10:3
and a lazy person will go **h**. Pr 19:15
your enemy is **h**, give him food Pr 25:21
but to a **h** person, any bitter Pr 27:7
the land, dejected and **h**. Is 8:21
right, but they are ⌊still⌋ **h**; Is 9:20
will be like a **h** one who dreams Is 29:8
then wakes and is still **h**; Is 29:8
He leaves the **h** empty and Is 32:6
Also he grows **h** and his strength Is 44:12
to share your bread with the **h**, Is 58:7
if you offer yourself to the **h**, Is 58:10
will eat, but you will be **h**; Is 65:13
bread to the **h** and covers the Ezk 18:7
bread to the **h** and covers the Ezk 18:16
40 days and 40 nights, He was **h**. Mt 4:2
disciples were **h** and began to Mt 12:1
those who were with him were **h**— Mt 12:3
don't want to send them away **h**; Mt 15:32
returning to the city, He was **h**. Mt 21:18
For I was **h** and you gave Me Mt 25:35
did we see You **h** and feed You, Mt 25:37
For I was **h** and you gave Me Mt 25:42
did we see You **h**, or thirsty, Mt 25:44
did when he was in need and **h**— Mk 2:25
came out from Bethany, He was **h**. Mk 11:12
satisfied the **h** with good things Lk 1:53
when they were over, He was **h**. Lk 4:2
with him did when he was **h**— Lk 6:3
Blessed are you who are **h** now, Lk 6:21
full now, because you will be **h**. Lk 6:25
who comes to Me will ever be **h**, Jn 6:35
Then he became **h** and wanted to Ac 10:10
If your enemy is **h**, feed him. Rm 12:20
hour we are both **h** and thirsty; 1Co 4:11
one person is **h** while another is 1Co 11:21
If anyone is **h**, he should eat at 1Co 11:34
whether well-fed or **h**, whether Php 4:12

HUNT *(8)*
in the field to **h** some game for Gn 27:3
to the field to **h** some game to Gn 27:5
brother Esau arrived from the **h**. Gn 27:30
You **h** me like a lion and again Jb 10:16
Can you **h** prey for a lioness or Jb 38:39
relentlessly **h** down a violent Ps 140:11
and they will **h** them down on Jr 16:16
they **h** each other with a net. Mc 7:2

HUNTED *(2)*
who **h** game and brought it to me? Gn 27:33
my enemies **h** me like a bird. Lm 3:52

HUNTER *(5)*
He was a powerful **h** in the sight Gn 10:9
a powerful **h** in the sight of the Gn 10:9
an expert **h**, an outdoorsman Gn 25:27
Escape like a gazelle from a **h**, Pr 6:5
away exhausted before the **h**. Lm 1:6

HUNTER'S *(2)*
will deliver you from the **h** net, Ps 91:3
like a bird from the **h** net; Ps 124:7

HUNTERS *(1)*
Then I will send for many **h**, Jr 16:16

HUNTING *(2)*
Take your ⌊**h**⌋ gear, your quiver Gn 27:3
though you are **h** me down to take 1Sm 24:11

HUNTS *(1)*
who **h** down a wild animal or bird Lv 17:13

HUPHAM *(1)*
the Huphamite clan from **H**. Nm 26:39

HUPHAMITE *(1)*
the **H** clan from Hupham. Nm 26:39

HUPPAH *(1)*
thirteenth to **H**, the fourteenth 1Ch 24:13

HUPPIM *(3)*
Ehi, Rosh, Muppim, **H**, and Ard. Gn 46:21
Shuppim and **H** were sons of Ir, 1Ch 7:12
took wives from **H** and Shuppim. 1Ch 7:15

HUR *(15)*
and **H** went up to the top of the Ex 17:10
Then Aaron and **H** supported his Ex 17:12
Aaron and **H** are here with you. Ex 24:14
of Uri, son of **H**, of the tribe Ex 31:2
of Uri, son of **H**, of the tribe Ex 35:30
of Uri, son of **H**, of the tribe Ex 38:22
Evi, Rekem, Zur, **H**, and Reba, Nm 31:8
Evi, Rekem, Zur, **H**, and Reba— Jos 13:21
Ephrath, and she bore him **H**. 1Ch 2:19
H fathered Uri, and Uri fathered 1Ch 2:20
The sons of **H**, Ephrathah's 1Ch 2:50
Hezron, Carmi, **H**, and Shobal. 1Ch 4:1
were the sons of **H**, Ephrathah's 1Ch 4:4
son of Uri, son of **H**, had made, 2Ch 1:5
Next to them Rephaiah son of **H**, Neh 3:9

HURAI *(1)*
(AKA HIDDAI)
H from the wadis of Gaash, 1Ch 11:32

HURAM *(3)*
(AKA HIRAM)
Gera, Shephuphan, and **H**. 1Ch 8:5
Then **H** made the pots, the 2Ch 4:11
H finished doing the work that 2Ch 4:11

HURAM-ABI *(2)*
(AKA HIRAM, HURAM)
have now sent **H**, a skillful man 2Ch 2:13
H made them for King Solomon 2Ch 4:16

HURI *(1)*
the sons of Abihail son of **H**, 1Ch 5:14

HURL *(4)*
So I will **h** you from this land Jr 16:13
I will **h** you and the mother who Jr 22:26
the land and **h** you on the open Ezk 32:4
intending to **h** Him over the Lk 4:29

HURLED *(11)*
h⌋ lightning bolts and routed 2Sm 22:15
You **h** their pursuers into the Neh 9:11
He **h** lightning bolts and routed Ps 18:14
the reproach they have **h** at You, Ps 79:12
but **h** Pharaoh and his army into Ps 136:15
his descendants **h** out and cast Jr 22:28
Then the LORD **h** a violent wind Jnh 1:4
altar, and **h** it to the earth; Rv 8:5
with blood, were **h** to the earth. Rv 8:7
with fire was **h** into the sea. Rv 8:8
in heaven and **h** them to the Rv 12:4

HURRIED *(17)*
So Abraham **h** into the tent and Gn 18:6
young man, who **h** to prepare it. Gn 18:7
the trough and **h** to the well Gn 24:20
Joseph **h** out because he was Gn 43:30
The people **h** across, Jos 4:10
men of the city **h** and went out Jos 8:14
Abigail **h**, taking 200 loaves of 1Sm 25:18
h down with the men of Judah to 2Sm 19:16
He himself also **h** to get out 2Ch 26:20
h off for home with his head Est 6:12
of Your thunder they **h** away— Ps 104:7
I **h**, not hesitating to keep Your Ps 119:60
king got up and **h** to the lions' Dn 6:19
Immediately she **h** to the king Mk 6:25
They **h** throughout that vicinity Mk 6:55
Mary set out and **h** to a town in Lk 1:39
They **h** off and found both Mary Lk 2:16

HURRY *(34)*
H up! Run there, for I cannot do Gn 19:22
You are to eat it in a **h**; Ex 12:11
left the land of Egypt in a **h**— Dt 16:3
H and do what you have seen me Jdg 9:48
H, he just now came to the city, 1Sm 9:12
brothers and **h** to their camp. 1Sm 17:17
following day **h** down and go to 1Sm 20:19
called to him, "**H** up and don't 1Sm 20:38
H ⌊and get⌋ Micaiah son of Imlah! 1Kg 22:9
so I can **h** to the man of God and 2Kg 4:22
to her servant, "**H**, don't slow 2Kg 4:24
H ⌊and get⌋ Micaiah son of Imlah! 2Ch 18:8
However, the Levites did not **h**. 2Ch 24:5
God told me to **h**. Stop opposing 2Ch 35:21
commanded, "**H**, and get Haman Est 5:5
told Haman, "**H**, and do just as Est 6:10
H to help me, Lord, my Savior. Ps 38:22
to deliver me; **h** to help me, Ps 40:13
I would **h** to my shelter from the Ps 55:8
deliver me. **H** to help me, LORD Ps 70:1
and needy; **h** to me, God. You are Ps 70:5
from me; my God, **h** to help me. Ps 71:12
I call on You; **h** to ⌊help⌋ me. Ps 141:1
and they **h** to commit murder Pr 1:16
but one in a **h** to get rich will Pr 28:20
greedy man is in a **h** for wealth; Pr 28:22
do not be in a **h**. Leave his Ec 8:3
Take me with you—let us **h**. Sg 1:4
H ⌊to me⌋, my love, and be like Sg 8:14
Let Him **h** up and do His work Is 5:19
Your builders **h**; those who Is 49:17
For you will not leave in a **h**, Is 52:12
"Zacchaeus, **h** and come down, Lk 19:5
'**H** and get out of Jerusalem Ac 22:18

HURRYING *(3)*
though David was **h** to get away 1Sm 23:26
as she was **h** to flee, he fell 2Sm 4:4
because he was **h** to be in Ac 20:16

HURT *(11)*
Deeply **h**, Hannah prayed to the 1Sm 1:10
They **h** his feet with shackles; Ps 105:18
rebukes a wicked man will get **h**. Pr 9:7
stones may be **h** by them; Ec 10:9
whole head is **h**, and the whole Is 1:5
will no longer be **h** by prickling Ezk 28:24
They haven't **h** me, for I was Dn 6:22
will lay a hand on you to **h** you, Ac 18:10
brother is **h** by what you eat Rm 14:15
cheer me other than the one **h**? 2Co 2:2
you should be **h**, but that you 2Co 2:4

HURTING *(1)*
out of him without **h** him at all. Lk 4:35

HUSBAND *(109)*
she also gave ⌊some⌋ to her **h**, Gn 3:6
Your desire will be for your **h**, Gn 3:16
her to her **h** Abram as a wife Gn 16:3
surely my **h** will love me now." Gn 29:32
my **h** will become attached to me Gn 29:34
enough that you have taken my **h**? Gn 30:15
me for giving my slave to my **h**," Gn 30:18
This time my **h** will honor me Gn 30:20
my **h** brought a Hebrew man to us Gn 39:14
as the woman's **h** demands from Ex 21:22
or divorced by her **h**, Lv 21:7
but it is concealed from her **h**, Nm 5:13
comes over the **h** and he becomes Nm 5:14
other than your **h** has slept with Nm 5:20
and been unfaithful to her **h**, Nm 5:27
comes over a **h** and he becomes Nm 5:30
The **h** will be free of guilt, Nm 5:31
and her **h** hears ⌊about it⌋ and Nm 30:7
But if her **h** prohibits her when Nm 30:8
and her **h** hears ⌊about it⌋, Nm 30:11
But if her **h** cancels them on the Nm 30:12
Her **h** has canceled them, and the Nm 30:12
Her **h** may confirm or cancel any Nm 30:13
If her **h** says nothing at all to Nm 30:14
relations with her and be her **h**, Dt 21:13
first **h** who sent her away may Dt 24:4
in to rescue her **h** from the one Dt 25:11
begrudge the **h** she embraces, Dt 28:56
the woman went and told her **h**, Jdg 13:6
and her **h** Manoah was not with Jdg 13:9
quickly to her **h** and told him, Jdg 13:10
Persuade your **h** to explain the Jdg 14:15
Then her **h** got up and went after Jdg 19:3
the **h** of the murdered woman, Jdg 20:4
Naomi's **h** Elimelech died, and Ru 1:3
two children and without her **h**. Ru 1:5
in the house of your ⌊new⌋ **h**." Ru 1:9
I am too old to have another **h**. Ru 1:12
for me to have a **h** tonight and Ru 1:12
her **h** Elkanah asked. 1Sm 1:8
not go and explained to her **h**, 1Sm 1:22
Her **h** Elkanah replied, "Do what 1Sm 1:23
she went with her **h** to offer the 1Sm 2:19
of her father-in-law and her **h**, 1Sm 4:19
of⌋ her father-in-law and her **h**. 1Sm 4:21

I

I is formed by the breath of God, Jb 37:10
Whose womb did the i come from? Jb 38:29

ICHABOD *(2)*
named the boy I, saying, "The 1Sm 4:21
brother of I son of Phinehas, 1Sm 14:3

ICONIUM *(6)*
them, they proceeded to I. Ac 13:51
The same thing happened in I; Ac 14:1
Jews came from Antioch and I, Ac 14:19
to Lystra, to I, and to Antioch, Ac 14:21
at Lystra and I spoke highly of Ac 16:2
to me in Antioch, I, and Lystra. 2Tm 3:11

IDALAH *(1)*
Shimron, I, and Bethlehem— Jos 19:15

IDBASH *(1)*
Ishma, and I, and their sister 1Ch 4:3

IDDO *(13)*
son of I, ⌊in⌋ Mahanaim; 1Kg 4:14
Joah, his son I, his son Zerah, 1Ch 6:21
in Gilead, I son of Zechariah; 1Ch 27:21
and the Visions of I the Seer 2Ch 9:29
the Prophet and of I the Seer 2Ch 12:15
in the Writing of the Prophet I. 2Ch 13:22
Zechariah son of I prophesied to Ezr 5:1
prophet and Zechariah son of I. Ezr 6:14
I sent them to I, the leader at Ezr 8:17
I, Ginnethoi, Abijah, Neh 12:4
Zechariah of I, Meshullam of Neh 12:16
son of Berechiah, son of I: Zch 1:1
son of Berechiah, son of I: Zch 1:7

IDEA *(2)*
have any i about all this. 1Sm 22:15
and you have no i at what hour I Rv 3:3

IDEAS *(2)*
want to know what these i mean." Ac 17:20
is a judge of the i and thoughts Heb 4:12

IDENTICAL *(1)*
and entrances, were i. Ezk 42:11

IDENTIFIED *(2)*
All were i by name. Ezr 8:20
leaders, all ⌊i⌋ by name, to Ezr 10:16

IDENTITY *(2)*
revealed his i to his brothers Gn 45:1
learned of Mordecai's ethnic i, Est 3:6

IDLE *(8)*
not be deaf, God; do not be i. Ps 83:1
I hands make one poor, but Pr 10:4
of her household and is never i. Pr 31:27
also learn to be i, going from 1Tm 5:13
are not only i, but are also 1Tm 5:13
capture i women burdened down 2Tm 3:6
rebellious people, i talkers and Ti 1:10
long ago, is not i, and their 2Pt 2:3

IDOL *(31)*
Do not make an i for yourself, Ex 20:4
and make an i for yourselves Dt 4:16
and make an i for yourselves in Dt 4:23
make an i in the form of Dt 4:25
Do not make an i for yourself in Dt 5:8
makes a carved i or cast image, Dt 27:15
took the household i and put it 1Sm 19:13
the household i was on the bed 1Sm 19:16
the detestable i of the 1Kg 11:5
detestable i of Moab, and for 1Kg 11:7
detestable i of the Ammonites 1Kg 11:7
the detestable i of the 2Kg 23:13
the detestable i of Moab; 2Kg 23:13
image of the i he had made, 2Ch 33:7
gods and the i from the LORD's 2Ch 33:15
To an i?—⌊something that⌋ a Is 40:19
set up an i that will not fall Is 40:20
shapes the i with hammers, Is 44:12
makes it an i and bows down to Is 44:15
a god or his i with the rest Is 44:17
not claim: My i caused them; my Is 48:5
image and cast i control them. Is 48:5
praises an i—all these have Is 66:3
each at the shrine of his i? Ezk 8:12
the carved i and cast image Nah 1:14
use is a carved i after its Hab 2:18
offered sacrifice to the i, Ac 7:41
we know that "an i is nothing in 1Co 8:4
they eat food offered to an i, 1Co 8:7
or that an i is anything? 1Co 10:19
"This is food offered to an i," 1Co 10:28

IDOL'S *(1)*
dining in an i temple, won't his 1Co 8:10

IDOLATER *(2)*
or greedy, an i or a reviler, 1Co 5:11
person, who is an i, has an Eph 5:5

IDOLATERS *(7)*
babble like the i, since they Mt 6:7
For the i eagerly seek all these Mt 6:32
greedy and swindlers, or to i; 1Co 5:10
immoral people, i, adulterers, 1Co 6:9
Don't become i as some of them 1Co 10:7
sorcerers, i, and all liars— Rv 21:8
murderers, the i, and everyone Rv 22:15

IDOLATROUS *(3)*
away with the i priests the 2Kg 23:5
my hand seized the i kingdoms, Is 10:10
its i priests rejoiced over it; Hs 10:5

IDOLATRY *(7)*
is like wickedness and i. 1Sm 15:23
consequences for your sins of i. Ezk 23:49
been so used to i up until now, 1Co 8:7
my dear friends, flee from i. 1Co 10:14
i, sorcery, hatreds, strife, Gl 5:20
desire, and greed, which is i. Col 3:5
carousing, and lawless i. 1Pt 4:3

IDOLS *(136)*
stole her father's household i. Gn 31:19
that Rachel had stolen ⌊the i⌋. Gn 31:32
had taken Laban's household i Gn 31:34
could not find the household i. Gn 31:35
Do not turn to i or make cast Lv 19:4
Do not make i for yourselves, Lv 26:1
the lifeless bodies of your i; Lv 26:30
images and i ⌊made⌋ of wood, Dt 29:17
Me with their worthless i. Dt 32:21
made an ephod and household i, Jdg 17:5
the household i, while the Jdg 18:17
the household i, the priest said Jdg 18:18
ephod, household i, and carved Jdg 18:20
temples of their i and among the 1Sm 31:9
abandoned their i there, 2Sm 5:21
all of the i that his fathers 1Kg 15:12
Israel with their worthless i. 1Kg 16:13
Israel with their worthless i. 1Kg 16:26
by going after i as the Amorites 1Kg 21:26
They served i, although the LORD 2Kg 17:12
pursued worthless i and became 2Kg 17:15
LORD but also served their i. 2Kg 17:41
means of his i has also caused 2Kg 21:11
he served the i his father had 2Kg 21:21
household i, images, and all 2Kg 23:24
news to their i and their people 1Ch 10:9
abandoned their i there, 1Ch 14:12
the gods of the peoples are i, 1Ch 16:26
the detestable i from the whole 2Ch 15:8
the Asherah poles and the i. 2Ch 24:18
who are devoted to worthless i, Ps 31:6
the gods of the peoples are i, Ps 96:5
who boast in i, will be put to Ps 97:7
served their i, which became Ps 106:36
sacrificed to the i of Canaan; Ps 106:38
Their i are silver and gold, Ps 115:4
The i of the nations are of Ps 135:15
Their land is full of i; Is 2:8
The i will vanish completely. Is 2:18
throw their silver and gold i, Is 2:20
whose i exceeded those of Is 10:10
Samaria and its i will I not Is 10:11
also do to Jerusalem and its i? Is 10:11
Egypt's i will tremble before Is 19:1
will seek i, ghosts, spirits Is 19:3
All the i of her gods have been Is 21:9
your silver-plated i and your Is 30:22
silver and gold i that your own Is 31:7
to another, or My praise to i. Is 42:8
those who trust in i and say to Is 42:17
All who make i are nothing, Is 44:9
makers of i go in humiliation Is 45:16
Those who carry their wooden i, Is 45:20
Their i are consigned to beasts Is 46:1
Who among the i has declared Is 48:14
collection ⌊of i⌋ deliver you! Is 57:13
followed worthless i, and became Jr 2:5
by Baal and followed useless i. Jr 2:8
their Glory for useless i. Jr 2:11
your detestable i from My Jr 4:1
with their worthless foreign i? Jr 8:19
patch, their i cannot speak. Jr 10:5
by worthless i ⌊made of⌋ wood! Jr 10:8
the worthless i of the nations Jr 14:22
detestable and abhorrent i." Jr 16:18
i of no benefit at all. Jr 16:19
to false ⌊i⌋ that make them Jr 18:15
her i are put to shame; Jr 50:2
your slain in front of your i. Ezk 6:4
front of their i and scatter Ezk 6:5
your i smashed and obliterated, Ezk 6:6
eyes that lusted after their i. Ezk 6:9
lie among their i around their Ezk 6:13
pleasing aromas to all their i. Ezk 6:13
well as all the i of the house Ezk 8:10
have set up i in their hearts Ezk 14:3
Israel sets up i in his heart, Ezk 14:4
him⌋ according to his many i, Ezk 14:4
estranged from Me by their i. Ezk 14:5
and turn away from your i; Ezk 14:6
setting up i in his heart and Ezk 14:7
your detestable i and the blood Ezk 16:36
his eyes to the i of the house Ezk 18:6
he raises his eyes to the i, Ezk 18:12
his eyes to the i of the house Ezk 18:15
yourselves with the i of Egypt. Ezk 20:7
did not forsake the i of Egypt. Ezk 20:8
their hearts went after their i. Ezk 20:16
defile yourselves with their i, Ezk 20:18
were fixed on their fathers' i. Ezk 20:24
with all your i to this day. Ezk 20:31
and serve your i, each of you. Ezk 20:39
holy name with your gifts and i. Ezk 20:39
consults the i, and observes Ezk 21:21
and who makes i for herself so Ezk 22:3
from the i you have made. Ezk 22:4
after and with all their i. Ezk 23:7
defiling yourself with their i. Ezk 23:30
committed adultery with their i. Ezk 23:37
the fire⌋ as food for the i. Ezk 23:37
their children for their i, Ezk 23:39
will destroy the i and put an Ezk 30:13
raise your eyes to your i, Ezk 33:25
had defiled it with their i. Ezk 36:18
your impurities and all your i. Ezk 36:25
any more with their i, Ezk 37:23
strayed from Me after their i, Ezk 44:10
before their i and became a Ezk 44:12
without ephod or household i. Hs 3:4
people consult their wooden ⌊i⌋, Hs 4:12
Ephraim is attached to i; Hs 4:17
and gold into i for themselves Hs 8:4
and burning offerings to i. Hs 11:2
i skillfully made from their Hs 13:2
have anything more to do with i? Hs 14:8
to worthless i forsake faithful Jnh 2:8
and I will destroy all her i. Mc 1:7
in it and makes i that cannot Hab 2:18
For the i speak falsehood, Zch 10:2
names of the i from the land, Zch 13:2
from things polluted by i, Ac 15:20
abstain from food offered to i, Ac 15:29
saw that the city was full of i. Ac 17:16
from food sacrificed to i, Ac 21:25
You who detest i, do you rob Rm 2:22
About food offered to i: 1Co 8:1
About eating food offered to i, 1Co 8:4
to eat food offered to i? 1Co 8:10
food offered to i is anything, 1Co 10:19
were led to dumb i—being led 1Co 12:2
God's sanctuary have with i? 2Co 6:16
turned to God from i to serve 1Th 1:9
guard yourselves from i. 1Jn 5:21
sacrificed to i and to commit Rv 2:14
and to eat meat sacrificed to i. Rv 2:20
worshiping demons and i of gold, Rv 9:20

IDUMEA *(1)*
(AKA EDOM, SEIR)
Jerusalem, I, beyond the Jordan, Mk 3:8

IEZER *(1)*
the Iezerite clan ⌊from⌋ I; Nm 26:30

IEZERITE *(1)*
the I clan ⌊from⌋ Iezer; Nm 26:30

IF *(1769)*
(See pp. xi-xii.)

IGAL *(3)*
(AKA JOEL)
I son of Joseph from the tribe Nm 13:7

I son of Nathan from Zobah, 2Sm 23:36
Hattush, **I**, Bariah, Neariah, and 1Ch 3:22

IGDALIAH *(1)*
by⌋ the sons of Hanan son of **I**, Jr 35:4

IGNITE *(2)*
His anger may **i** at any moment. Ps 2:12
I am about to **i** a fire in you, Ezk 20:47

IGNITED *(3)*
Then he **i** the torches and Jdg 15:5
presence, flaming coals were **i**. 2Sm 22:13
He has **i** a fire in Zion, and it Lm 4:11

IGNITES *(1)*
large a forest a small fire **i**. Jms 3:5

IGNORANCE *(11)*
conceals ⌊My⌋ counsel with **i**?" Jb 42:3
foolish ones, will you love **i**? Pr 1:22
unintentionally or through **i**. Ezk 45:20
I know that you did it in **i**, Ac 3:17
worship in **i**, this I proclaim Ac 17:23
overlooked the times of **i**, Ac 17:30
because of the **i** that is in them Eph 4:18
it was out of **i** that I had acted 1Tm 1:13
of the people committed in **i**. Heb 9:7
to the desires of your former **i** 1Pt 1:14
silence the **i** of foolish people. 1Pt 2:15

IGNORANT *(9)*
My⌋ counsel with **i** words? Jb 38:2
for they are **i** and do wrong. Ec 5:1
Everyone is stupid and **i**. Jr 10:14
Everyone is stupid and **i**. Jr 51:17
instructor of the **i**, a teacher Rm 2:20
some people are **i** about God. 1Co 15:34
for we are not **i** of his 2Co 2:11
reject foolish and **i** disputes, 2Tm 2:23
those who are **i** and are going Heb 5:2

IGNORE *(9)*
straying, you must not **i** it; Dt 22:1
have found. You must not **i** ⌊it⌋. Dt 22:3
on the road, you must not **i** it; Dt 22:4
and do not **i** my plea for help Ps 55:1
and be wise; don't **i** it. Pr 8:33
to⌋ those who **i** instruction, Pr 13:18
and to not **i** your own flesh ⌊and Is 58:7
Do not **i** my cry for relief. Lm 3:56
They willfully **i** this: 2Pt 3:5

IGNORED *(6)*
You **i** the Rock who gave you Dt 32:18
and my claim is **i** by my God"? Is 40:27
the trumpet but **i** the warning, Ezk 33:5
These men have **i** you, the king; Dn 3:12
exiles, has **i** you, the king, Dn 6:13
ignores this, he will be **i**. 1Co 14:38

IGNORES *(4)*
but whoever **i** an insult is Pr 12:16
who **i** instruction despises Pr 15:32
the trumpet but **i** the warning, Ezk 33:4
But if anyone **i** this, he will be 1Co 14:38

IIM *(1)*
Baalah, **I**, Ezem, Jos 15:29

IJON *(3)*
He attacked **I**, Dan, 1Kg 15:20
of Assyria came and captured **I**, 2Kg 15:29
They attacked **I**, Dan, Abel-maim, 2Ch 16:4

IKKESH *(3)*
Ira son of **I** the Tekoite, 2Sm 23:26
son of **I** the Tekoite, Abiezer 1Ch 11:28
was Ira son of **I** the Tekoite; 1Ch 27:9

ILAI *(1)*
(AKA ZALMON)
the Hushathite, **I** the Ahohite, 1Ch 11:29

ILL *(9)*
borne to David, and he became **i**. 2Sm 12:15
who owned the house became **i**. 1Kg 17:17
son of Ahab since Joram was **i**. 2Kg 8:29
Hezekiah became terminally **i**. 2Kg 20:1
son of Ahab since Joram was **i**. 2Ch 22:6
Hezekiah became terminally **i**. Is 38:1
look—those **i** from famine! Jr 14:18
whose son was **i** at Capernaum. Jn 4:46
many are sick and **i** among you, 1Co 11:30

ILL-GOTTEN *(1)*
I gains do not profit anyone, Pr 10:2

ILLEGAL *(1)*
It's **i** for you to pick up your Jn 5:10

ILLEGITIMATE *(3)*
No one of **i** birth may enter the Dt 23:2
they gave birth to **i** children. Hs 5:7
then you are **i** children and not Heb 12:8

ILLICIT *(1)*
they now have **i** sex with her, Ezk 23:43

ILLNESS *(6)*
not inflict any **i** on you I Ex 15:26
⌊when there is⌋ any plague or **i**, 1Kg 8:37
His **i** became very severe until 1Kg 17:17
sick with the **i** that he died 2Kg 13:14
⌊when there is⌋ any plague or **i**, 2Ch 6:28
and had recovered from his **i**: Is 38:9

ILLNESSES *(4)*
I will take away your **i**. Ex 23:25
will be struck⌋ with many **i**, 2Ch 21:15
and he died from severe **i**. 2Ch 21:19
stomach and your frequent **i**. 1Tm 5:23

ILLUMINATE *(2)*
set up so they **i** the area in Ex 25:37
to **i** the way they should go. Neh 9:12

ILLUMINATED *(2)*
pillar of fire **i** the way they Neh 9:19
the earth was **i** by his splendor Rv 18:1

ILLUMINATES *(3)*
the LORD **i** my darkness. 2Sm 22:29
my God **i** my darkness. Ps 18:28
God's glory **i** it, and its lamp Rv 21:23

ILLUSION *(1)*
exalted men, an **i**. On a balance Ps 62:9

ILLUSIONS *(2)*
flattering things. Prophesy **i**. Is 30:10
and the diviners see **i**; Zch 10:2

ILLUSTRATE *(1)*
How can we **i** the kingdom of God, Mk 4:30

ILLUSTRATION *(3)*
gave them this **i**, but they did Jn 10:6
Brothers, I'm using a human **i**. Gl 3:15
he also got him back as an **i**. Heb 11:19

ILLUSTRATIONS *(1)*
things are **i**, for the women Gl 4:24

ILLUSTRIOUS *(1)*
the great and **i** Ashurbanipal Ezr 4:10

ILLYRICUM *(1)*
all the way around to **I**. Rm 15:19

IMAGE *(61)*
Let Us make man in Our **i**, Gn 1:26
So God created man in His own **i**; Gn 1:27
He created him in the **i** of God; Gn 1:27
according to his **i**, and named Gn 5:3
for God made man in His **i**. Gn 9:6
and made it into an **i** of a calf. Ex 32:4
for themselves an **i** of a calf. Ex 32:8
set up a carved **i** or sacred Lv 26:1
Make a snake ⌊**i**⌋ and mount it on Nm 21:8
made a cast **i** for themselves. Dt 9:12
made a calf **i** for yourselves. Dt 9:16
makes a carved idol or cast **i**, Dt 27:15
to make a carved **i** overlaid with Jdg 17:3
it into a carved **i** overlaid with Jdg 17:4
and a carved **i** overlaid with Jdg 18:14
took the carved **i** overlaid with Jdg 18:17
took the carved **i** overlaid with Jdg 18:18
and carved **i**, and went with Jdg 18:20
up the carved **i** for themselves. Jdg 18:30
Micah's carved **i** that he had Jdg 18:31
made an obscene **i** of Asherah. 1Kg 15:13
down her obscene **i** and burned it 1Kg 15:13
set up the carved **i** of Asherah 2Kg 21:7
made an obscene **i** of Asherah. 2Ch 15:16
Asa chopped down her obscene **i**, 2Ch 15:16
set up a carved **i** of the idol he 2Ch 33:7
they had cast an **i** of a calf for Neh 9:18
You will despise their **i**. Ps 73:20
and worshiped the cast metal **i**. Ps 106:19
for the **i** of a grass-eating Ps 106:20
casts a metal **i** for no profit? Is 44:10
carved **i** and cast idol control Is 48:5
put to shame by ⌊his⌋ carved **i**, Jr 10:14
cakes in her **i** and poured out Jr 44:19
put to shame by ⌊his⌋ carved **i**, Jr 51:17
and make themselves a cast **i**, Hs 13:2
idol and cast **i** from the house Nah 1:14
is ⌊only⌋ a cast **i**, a teacher of Hab 2:18
Whose **i** and inscription is this? Mt 22:20
Whose **i** and inscription is this? Mk 12:16
i and inscription does it have? Lk 20:24
an **i** fashioned by human art and Ac 17:29
and of the **i** that fell from Ac 19:35
conformed to the **i** of His Son, Rm 8:29
because he is God's **i** and glory, 1Co 11:7
have borne the **i** of the man made 1Co 15:49
also bear the **i** of the heavenly 1Co 15:49
into the same **i** from glory to 2Co 3:18
of Christ, who is the **i** of God. 2Co 4:4
is the **i** of the invisible God, Col 1:15
to the **i** of his Creator. Col 3:10
to make an **i** of the beast who Rv 13:14
a spirit to the **i** of the beast, Rv 13:15
so that the **i** of the beast could Rv 13:15
not worship the **i** of the beast Rv 13:15
the beast and his **i** and receives Rv 14:9
who worship the beast and his **i**, Rv 14:11
the beast, his **i**, and the number Rv 15:2
beast and who worshiped his **i**. Rv 16:2
and those who worshiped his **i**. Rv 19:20
worshiped the beast or his **i**, Rv 20:4

IMAGES *(50)*
Do not make cast **i** of gods for Ex 34:17
idols or make cast **i** of gods for Lv 19:4
their stone **i** and cast images Nm 33:52
their stone images and cast **i**, Nm 33:52
and burn up their carved **i**. Dt 7:5
up the carved **i** of their gods. Dt 7:25
gold on the **i** and take it for Dt 7:25
down the carved **i** of their gods, Dt 12:3
detestable **i** and idols ⌊made Dt 29:17
At the carved **i** near Gilgal he Jdg 3:19
near the carved **i** and reached Jdg 3:26
i of your tumors and of your 1Sm 6:5
mice and the **i** of the tumors. 1Sm 6:11
yourself other gods and cast **i**, 1Kg 14:9
its altars and **i** into pieces, 2Kg 11:18
made for themselves molded **i**— 2Kg 17:16
household idols, **i**, and all the 2Kg 23:24
its altars and **i** into pieces 2Ch 23:17
and made cast **i** of the Baals. 2Ch 28:2
poles and carved **i** before he 2Ch 33:19
all the carved **i** that his father 2Ch 33:22
poles, the carved **i**, and the 2Ch 34:3
carved images, and the cast **i**. 2Ch 34:3
poles, the carved **i**, and the 2Ch 34:4
and the cast **i** he shattered, 2Ch 34:4
and the carved **i** to powder. 2Ch 34:7
jealousy with their carved **i**. Ps 78:58
serve carved **i**, those who boast Ps 97:7
idols and your gold-plated **i**. Is 30:22
their **i** are wind and emptiness. Is 41:29
idols and say to metal-plated **i**: Is 42:17
The ⌊**i**⌋ you carry are loaded, Is 46:1
Me to anger with their graven **i**, Jr 8:19
image, for his cast **i** are a lie; Jr 10:14
For it is a land of carved **i**, Jr 50:38
image, for his cast **i** are a lie; Jr 51:17
will punish Babylon's carved **i**. Jr 51:47
when I will punish her carved **i**, Jr 51:52
their abhorrent **i** from them, Ezk 7:20
you made male **i** so that you Ezk 16:17
them to these **i** as food. Ezk 16:20
through ⌊the fire⌋ to the **i**. Ezk 16:21
on the wall, **i** of the Chaldeans, Ezk 23:14
the **i** and visions in my mind Dn 4:5
with their metal **i** and their Dn 11:8
i you have made for yourselves. Am 5:26
All her carved **i** will be smashed Mc 1:7
your carved **i** and sacred pillars Mc 5:13
the **i** that you made to worship. Ac 7:43
immortal God for **i** resembling Rm 1:23

IMAGINATION *(4)*
in his **i** it is like a high wall. Pr 18:11
who prophesy out of their own **i**: Ezk 13:2
who prophesy out of their own **i**. Ezk 13:17
fashioned by human art and **i**. Ac 17:29

IMAGINATIONS *(1)*
the **i** of their hearts run wild. Ps 73:7

IMAGINE *(2)*
since they **i** they'll be heard Mt 6:7
who **i** that godliness is a way to 1Tm 6:5

IMITATE *(8)*
Do not **i** their practices. Ex 23:24
do not **i** the detestable customs Dt 18:9
had commanded them not to **i**. 2Kg 17:15

admonished not to i your Ezk 23:48
know how you must i us: 2Th 3:7
to you so that you would i us. 2Th 3:9
of their lives, i their faith. Heb 13:7
friend, do not i what is evil, 3Jn 11

IMITATED *(1)*
They i all the abominations of 1Kg 14:24

IMITATING *(6)*
i the abominations of the 2Kg 16:3
i the abominations of the 2Kg 21:2
i the detestable practices of 2Ch 28:3
i the detestable practices of 2Ch 33:2
i all the detestable practices 2Ch 36:14
Join in i me, brothers, and Php 3:17

IMITATORS *(6)*
I urge you, be i of me. 1Co 4:16
Be i of me, as I also am of 1Co 11:1
Therefore, be i of God, as Eph 5:1
you became i of us and of the 1Th 1:6
became i of God's churches in 1Th 2:14
but i of those who inherit the Heb 6:12

IMLAH *(4)*
He is Micaiah son of I." 1Kg 22:8
and get Micaiah son of I!" 1Kg 22:9
He is Micaiah son of I." 2Ch 18:7
and get Micaiah son of I!" 2Ch 18:8

IMMANUEL *(3)*
have a son, and name him I. Is 7:14
will fill your entire land, I! Is 8:8
they will name Him I, which is Mt 1:23

IMMATURE *(1)*
teacher of the i, having in the Rm 2:20

IMMEASURABLE *(3)*
together with an i quantity of 1Ch 22:3
and what is the i greatness of Eph 1:19
might display the i riches of Eph 2:7

IMMEDIATE *(2)*
except for his i family: Lv 21:2
sister in his i family. Lv 21:3

IMMEDIATELY *(74)*
Moses i bowed down to the ground Ex 34:8
'Get up and go down i from here. Dt 9:12
it, and i set it on fire. Jos 8:19
and did not drive them out i. Jdg 2:23
Go up i—you can find him now." 1Sm 9:13
I, David went to the place where 1Sm 26:5
me than to escape i to the land 1Sm 27:1
I, Saul fell flat on the ground. 1Sm 28:20
Get up and i ford the river, 2Sm 17:21
were also i above the rounded 1Kg 7:20
afraid and i ran for his life 1Kg 19:3
'Come down i!'" 2Kg 1:11
they i went to the Jews in Ezr 4:23
and houses to them i, along with Neh 5:11
I i pronounced a curse on his Jb 5:3
and worship will i be thrown Dn 3:6
you will i be thrown into a Dn 3:15
He went up i from the water. Mt 3:16
and i angels came and began to Mt 4:11
I they left their nets and Mt 4:20
I they left the boat and their Mt 4:22
I his disease was healed. Mt 8:3
the word and i receives it with Mt 13:20
of the word, i he stumbles. Mt 13:21
I He made the disciples get into Mt 14:22
I Jesus spoke to them. Mt 14:27
I Jesus reached out His hand, Mt 14:31
I they could see, and they Mt 20:34
them, and i he will send them. Mt 21:3
I after the tribulation of those Mt 24:29
Then he went on a journey. I Mt 25:15
I a rooster crowed, Mt 26:74
I one of them ran and got a Mt 27:48
I the Spirit drove Him into the Mk 1:12
I they left their nets and Mk 1:18
I He called them, and they left Mk 1:20
I the disease left him, and he Mk 1:42
I he got up, picked up the Mk 2:12
I the Pharisees went out and Mk 3:6
i Satan comes and takes away the Mk 4:15
i they receive it with joy. Mk 4:16
of the word, they i stumble. Mk 4:17
I the girl got up and began to Mk 5:42
I she hurried to the king and Mk 6:25
The king i sent for an Mk 6:27
I He made His disciples get into Mk 6:45
I He spoke with them and said, Mk 6:50
boat, people i recognized Him. Mk 6:54
i after hearing about Him, Mk 7:25
I his ears were opened, his Mk 7:35
and i got into the boat with His Mk 8:10
saw Him, it i convulsed the boy Mk 9:20
I the father of the boy cried Mk 9:24
I he could see and began to Mk 10:52
I a rooster crowed a second time, Mk 14:72
I his mouth was opened and his Lk 1:64
She got up i and began to serve Lk 4:39
and i the disease left him. Lk 5:13
I he got up before them, picked Lk 5:25
against it, and i it collapsed. Lk 6:49
will not i pull him out on the Lk 14:5
I, while he was still speaking, Lk 22:60
piece of bread, he went out i. Jn 13:30
I a rooster crowed. Jn 18:27
I he began proclaiming Jesus in Ac 9:20
your own bed," and i he got up. Ac 9:34
Therefore I i sent for you, Ac 10:33
one street, and i the angel left Ac 12:10
we i made efforts to set out for Ac 16:10
and i all the doors were opened, Ac 16:26
the brothers i sent Paul away to Ac 17:14
centurions, he i ran down to Ac 21:32
I did not i consult with anyone. Gl 1:16
I I was in the Spirit, and there Rv 4:2

IMMENSE *(4)*
against Sodom and Gomorrah is i, Gn 18:20
through this i wilderness. Dt 2:7
'Do you see this entire i horde? 1Kg 20:13
over this entire i horde to you. 1Kg 20:28

IMMER *(7)*
son of Meshillemith, son of I; 1Ch 9:12
to Bilgah, the sixteenth to I, 1Ch 24:14
and I but were unable to prove Ezr 2:59
them Zadok son of I made repairs Neh 3:29
Addon, and I, but were unable Neh 7:61
son of Meshillemoth, son of I, Neh 11:13
the son of I and chief officer Jr 20:1

IMMER'S *(3)*
I descendants 1,052 Ezr 2:37
and Zebadiah from I descendants; Ezr 10:20
I descendants 1,052 Neh 7:40

IMMORAL *(17)*
like one of the i men in Israel! 2Sm 13:13
Where have you not been i? Jr 3:2
you committed i acts in addition Ezk 16:43
they commit i acts within you. Ezk 22:9
with sexually i people— 1Co 5:9
to this world's i people, 1Co 5:10
who is sexually i or greedy, 1Co 5:11
no sexually i people, idolaters, 1Co 6:9
who is sexually i sins against 1Co 6:18
sexually i or impure or greedy Eph 5:5
the sexually i and homosexuals 1Tm 1:10
there isn't any i or irreverent Heb 12:16
God will judge i people and Heb 13:4
unrestrained behavior of the i 2Pt 2:7
the error of the i and fall from 2Pt 3:17
sexually i, sorcerers, Rv 21:8
the sexually i, the murderers, Rv 22:15

IMMORALITIES *(2)*
sexual i, thefts, false Mt 15:19
sexual i, thefts, murders Mk 7:21

IMMORALITY *(30)*
to your indecency and sexual i, Ezk 23:27
except in a case of sexual i, Mt 5:32
except for sexual i, and marries Mt 19:9
"We weren't born of sexual i," Jn 8:41
idols, from sexual i, from Ac 15:20
strangled, and from sexual i. Ac 15:29
strangled, and from sexual i." Ac 21:25
there is sexual i among you, 1Co 5:1
of sexual i that is not even 1Co 5:1
not for sexual i but for the 1Co 6:13
Flee from sexual i! 1Co 6:18
of sexual i, each man should 1Co 7:2
commit sexual i as some of them 1Co 10:8
sexual i, and promiscuity 2Co 12:21
sexual i, moral impurity, Gl 5:19
But sexual i and any impurity or Eph 5:3
sexual i, impurity, lust, evil Col 3:5
that you abstain from sexual i, 1Th 4:3
committed sexual i and practiced Jd 7
to idols and to commit sexual i. Rv 2:14
commit sexual i and to eat meat Rv 2:20
want to repent of her sexual i. Rv 2:21
their sexual i, or their thefts. Rv 9:21
drink the wine of her sexual i, Rv 14:8
committed sexual i with her, Rv 17:2
on the wine of her sexual i." Rv 17:2
drunk the wine of her sexual i, Rv 18:3
committed sexual i with her, Rv 18:3
committed sexual i and lived Rv 18:9
the earth with her sexual i; Rv 19:2

IMMORTAL *(2)*
glory of the i God for images Rm 1:23
the King eternal, i, invisible, 1Tm 1:17

IMMORTALITY *(5)*
seek for glory, honor, and i; Rm 2:7
mortal must be clothed with i. 1Co 15:53
this mortal is clothed with i, 1Co 15:54
the only One who has i, dwelling 1Tm 6:16
life and i to light through 2Tm 1:10

IMMOVABLE *(4)*
together, solid as metal and i. Jb 41:23
the root of the righteous is i. Pr 12:3
bow jammed fast and remained i, Ac 27:41
steadfast, i, always excelling 1Co 15:58

IMNA *(1)*
Zophah, I, Shelesh, and Amal. 1Ch 7:35

IMNAH *(4)*
I, Ishvah, Ishvi, Beriah, and Gn 46:17
the Imnite clan from I; Nm 26:44
I, Ishvah, Ishvi, and Beriah, 1Ch 7:30
Kore son of I the Levite, the 2Ch 31:14

IMNITE *(1)*
the I clan from Imnah; Nm 26:44

IMPALED *(1)*
will be i on it, and his house Ezr 6:11

IMPART *(1)*
that I may i to you some Rm 1:11

IMPARTIAL *(1)*
You gave them i ordinances, Neh 9:13

IMPARTIALLY *(3)*
They were divided i by lot, 1Ch 24:5
They cast lots i for their 1Ch 25:8
One who judges i based on each 1Pt 1:17

IMPARTS *(1)*
A rod of correction i wisdom, Pr 29:15

IMPATIENT *(4)*
but the people became i because Nm 21:4
Then why shouldn't I be i? Jb 21:4
Is the Spirit of the LORD i? Mc 2:7
I became i with them, and they Zch 11:8

IMPERFECTION *(1)*
my darling, with no i in you. Sg 4:7

IMPERIAL *(2)*
named Julius, of the I Regiment. Ac 27:1
throughout the whole i guard, Php 1:13

IMPERISHABLE *(4)*
crown, but we an i one. 1Co 9:25
into an inheritance that is i, 1Pt 1:4
of perishable seed but of i— 1Pt 1:23
the heart with the i quality of 1Pt 3:4

IMPETUOUS *(1)*
i nation that marches across the Hab 1:6

IMPLANTED *(1)*
humbly receive the i word, Jms 1:21

IMPLEMENT *(1)*
or any i used for work. Lv 11:32

IMPLORE *(3)*
approach the king, i his favor, Est 4:8
Now I i you, brothers, through Rm 15:30
Now I i you, brothers, watch out Rm 16:17

IMPLORED *(1)*
and i each one of you to walk 1Th 2:12

IMPLORING *(1)*
petitioning and i his God. Dn 6:11

IMPORTANCE *(1)*
It is of little i that I should 1Co 4:3

IMPORTANT *(16)*
he was the most i in all his Gn 34:19
bring you every i case but judge Ex 18:22
clan the least i of all the 1Sm 9:21
than to act i but have no food. Pr 12:9
nor a scoundrel said to be i. Is 32:5

greatest and most **i** commandment. Mt 22:38
the more **i** matters of the law Mt 23:23
is the most **i** of all?" Mk 12:28
is the most **i**," Jesus answered Mk 12:29
is far more ⌊**i**⌋ than all the Mk 12:33
the last and most **i** day of the Jn 7:37
Cilicia, a citizen of an **i** city. Ac 21:39
on to you as most **i** what I also 1Co 15:3
But from those recognized as **i** Gl 2:6
recognized as **i** added nothing to Gl 2:6
as more **i** than yourselves. Php 2:3

IMPORTED *(3)*
were **i** from Egypt and Kue. 1Kg 10:28
chariot was **i** from Egypt for 15 1Kg 10:29
chariot could be **i** from Egypt 2Ch 1:17

IMPORTING *(1)*
living there were **i** fish and all Neh 13:16

IMPOSE *(3)*
I heavier work on the men. Ex 5:9
We will **i** ⌊the following⌋ Neh 10:32
you **i** its authority on earth? Jb 38:33

IMPOSED *(12)*
They ruthlessly **i** all this work Ex 1:14
that time Joshua **i** this curse: Jos 6:26
they **i** forced labor on the Jos 17:13
King Solomon had **i** to build the 1Kg 9:15
Solomon **i** forced labor on them; 1Kg 9:21
and he **i** on the land a fine of 2Kg 23:33
Solomon **i** forced labor on them; 2Ch 8:8
the tax ⌊**i** by⌋ the LORD's 2Ch 24:6
servant Moses ⌊**i**⌋ on Israel 2Ch 24:9
must not be **i** on any priests, Ezr 7:24
Ahasuerus **i** a tax throughout Est 10:1
various washings **i** until the Heb 9:10

IMPOSES *(3)*
hardship your enemy **i** on you. Dt 28:53
your enemy **i** on you in all your Dt 28:55
your enemy **i** on you within your Dt 28:57

IMPOSSIBLE *(14)*
plan to do will be **i** for them. Gn 11:6
Is anything **i** for the LORD? Gn 18:14
but it seemed **i** to do anything 2Sm 13:2
It is **i** for God ⌊to do⌋ wrong, Jb 34:10
Flight will be **i** for the Jr 25:35
Nothing will be **i** for you. Mt 17:20
With men this is **i**, but with God Mt 19:26
With men it is **i**, but not with Mk 10:27
For nothing will be **i** with God." Lk 1:37
What is **i** with men is possible Lk 18:27
For it is **i** to renew to Heb 6:4
in which it is **i** for God to lie, Heb 6:18
For it is **i** for the blood of Heb 10:4
faith it is **i** to please God, Heb 11:6

IMPOSTERS *(1)*
Evil people and **i** will become 2Tm 3:13

IMPOVERISH *(1)*
The Lord will **i** her and cast her Zch 9:4

IMPOVERISHED *(1)*
and the **i** will lie down in Is 14:30

IMPRESS *(1)*
I these words of Mine on your Dt 11:18

IMPRESSED *(1)*
He is not **i** by the strength of a Ps 147:10

IMPRESSION *(1)*
and He gave the **i** that He was Lk 24:28

IMPRESSIVE *(5)*
it was a very **i** procession. Gn 50:9
i altar there by the Jordan. Jos 22:10
son named Saul, an **i** young man. 1Sm 9:2
was no one more **i** among the 1Sm 9:2
What **i** buildings!" Mk 13:1

IMPRISON *(1)*
i them in the grave. Jb 40:13

IMPRISONED *(10)*
of you will be **i** so that your Gn 42:16
So Joseph **i** them together for Gn 42:17
Pharaoh Neco **i** him at Riblah in 2Kg 23:33
in holes or **i** in dungeons. Is 42:22
the prophet was **i** in the guard's Jr 32:2
king of Judah had **i** him, Jr 32:3
believed in You **i** and beaten. Ac 22:19
For God has **i** all in Rm 11:32
Scripture has **i** everything under Gl 3:22
i until the coming faith was Gl 3:23

IMPRISONMENT *(8)*
confiscation of property, or **i**. Ezr 7:26
both in my **i** and in the defense Php 1:7
else, that my **i** is for Christ. Php 1:13
from my **i** and dare even more Php 1:14
to cause ⌊me⌋ trouble in my **i**. Php 1:17
Remember my **i**. Grace be with Col 4:18
that in my **i** for the gospel he Phm 13
as well as bonds and **i**. Heb 11:36

IMPRISONMENTS *(2)*
by beatings, by **i**, by riots, by 2Co 6:5
labors, many more **i**, far worse 2Co 11:23

IMPRISONS *(1)*
whoever He **i** cannot be released. Jb 12:14

IMPROPER *(2)*
see anything **i** among you or He Dt 23:14
he finds something **i** about her, Dt 24:1

IMPROPERLY *(2)*
he is acting **i** toward his virgin 1Co 7:36
does not act **i**; is not selfish; 1Co 13:5

IMPROVISE *(1)*
They **i** songs to the sound of the Am 6:5

IMPULSIVE *(1)*
and do not be **i** to make a speech Ec 5:2

IMPULSIVELY *(1)*
follows her **i** like an ox going Pr 7:22

IMPURE *(6)*
to possess is an **i** land. Ezr 9:11
something pure from what is **i**? Jb 14:4
will become **i** like that place Jr 19:13
become something **i** among them. Lm 1:17
And **i** meat has never entered my Ezk 4:14
immoral or **i** or greedy person, Eph 5:5

IMPURITIES *(7)*
the Israelites' **i** and rebellious Lv 16:16
it is surrounded by their **i**. Lv 16:16
it apart from the Israelites' **i**. Lv 16:19
Remove **i** from silver, and a Pr 25:4
I will remove all your **i**. Is 1:25
you from all your **i** and all your Ezk 36:25
vile and with the **i** of her Rv 17:4

IMPURITY *(29)*
the days of her menstrual **i**. Lv 12:2
is⌋ during her ⌊menstrual⌋ **i**. Lv 12:5
like her bed during menstrual **i**; Lv 15:26
her menstrual **i** to have sexual Lv 18:19
his brother's wife, it is **i**. Lv 20:21
the water ⌊to remove⌋ **i**; Nm 19:9
the water for **i** has not been Nm 19:13
The water for **i** has not been Nm 19:20
the water for **i** is to wash his Nm 19:21
the water for **i** will be unclean Nm 19:21
by their **i** and detestable Ezr 9:11
or **i** has stained my hands, Jb 31:7
a woman during her menstrual **i**. Ezk 18:6
women during their menstrual **i**. Ezk 22:10
Then its **i** will melt inside it; Ezk 24:11
before Me was like menstrual **i**. Ezk 36:17
to wash away⌋ sin and **i**. Zch 13:1
of dead men's bones and every **i**. Mt 23:27
of their hearts to sexual **i**, Rm 1:24
yourselves as slaves to moral **i**, Rm 6:19
not in sexual **i** and promiscuity; Rm 13:13
clean from every **i** of the flesh 2Co 7:1
moral **i**, promiscuity, Gl 5:19
of every kind of **i** with a desire Eph 4:19
and any **i** or greed should Eph 5:3
immorality, **i**, lust, evil desire Col 3:5
from error or **i** or an intent to 1Th 2:3
For God has not called us to **i**, 1Th 4:7
escaped the world's **i** through 2Pt 2:20

IMRAH *(1)*
Suah, Harnepher, Shual, Beri, **I**, 1Ch 7:36

IMRI *(2)*
of Omri, son of **I**, son of Bani, 1Ch 9:4
to them Zaccur son of **I** built. Neh 3:2

IN *(10,892)*
(See pp. xi-xii.)

INACCESSIBLE *(3)*
was no city that was **i** to us, Dt 2:36
Wisdom is **i** to a fool; Pr 24:7
in lofty places—an **i** city. Is 26:5

INANIMATE *(1)*
Even **i** things producing sounds— 1Co 14:7

INAPPROPRIATE *(1)*
harvest, honor is **i** for a fool. Pr 26:1

INAUGURATE *(1)*
will serve to **i** a permanent Ex 40:15

INAUGURATED *(2)*
first covenant was **i** with blood. Heb 9:18
living way that He has **i** for us, Heb 10:20

INCALCULABLE *(1)*
to the Gentiles the **i** riches of Eph 3:8

INCAPABLE *(2)*
will they be **i** of innocence? Hs 8:5
people are **i** of doing right— Am 3:10

INCENSE *(142)*
oil and for the fragrant **i**; Ex 25:6
an altar for the burning of **i**; Ex 30:1
must burn fragrant **i** on it; Ex 30:7
at twilight, he must burn **i**. Ex 30:8
is to be an **i** ⌊offering⌋ before Ex 30:8
not offer unauthorized **i** on it, Ex 30:9
its utensils, the altar of **i**, Ex 30:27
expertly blended **i** from these; Ex 30:35
As for the **i** you are making, Ex 30:37
its utensils, the altar of **i**, Ex 31:8
and the fragrant **i** for the Ex 31:11
oil and for the fragrant **i**; Ex 35:8
the altar of **i** with its poles; Ex 35:15
oil and the fragrant **i**; Ex 35:15
oil, and for the fragrant **i**. Ex 35:28
the altar of **i** out of acacia Ex 37:25
and expertly blended **i**. Ex 37:29
the fragrant **i**; the screen for Ex 39:38
the gold altar for **i** in front of Ex 40:5
and burned fragrant **i** on it, Ex 40:27
of fragrant **i** that is before Lv 4:7
fire in it, placed **i** on it, and Lv 10:1
of finely ground fragrant **i**, Lv 16:12
He is to put the **i** on the fire Lv 16:13
the cloud of **i** covers the mercy Lv 16:13
cut down your **i** altars, and heap Lv 26:30
the fragrant **i**, the daily grain Nm 4:16
weighing four ounces, full of **i**; Nm 7:14
weighing four ounces, full of **i**; Nm 7:20
weighing four ounces, full of **i**; Nm 7:26
weighing four ounces, full of **i**; Nm 7:32
weighing four ounces, full of **i**; Nm 7:38
weighing four ounces, full of **i**; Nm 7:44
weighing four ounces, full of **i**; Nm 7:50
weighing four ounces, full of **i**; Nm 7:56
weighing four ounces, full of **i**; Nm 7:62
weighing four ounces, full of **i**; Nm 7:68
weighing four ounces, full of **i**; Nm 7:74
weighing four ounces, full of **i**; Nm 7:80
bowls full of **i** each ⌊weighed⌋ Nm 7:86
in them and put **i** on them before Nm 16:7
firepan, place **i** on it, and Nm 16:17
fire in it, put **i** on it, and Nm 16:18
men who were presenting the **i**. Nm 16:35
to offer **i** before the LORD Nm 16:40
from the altar in it, and add **i**. Nm 16:46
After he added **i**, he made Nm 16:47
they will set **i** before You and Dt 33:10
My altar, to burn **i**, and to wear 1Sm 2:28
and burned **i** on the high places. 1Kg 3:3
and he burned **i** with them in the 1Kg 9:25
who were burning **i** and offering 1Kg 11:8
on the altar, and burned **i**. 1Kg 12:33
beside the altar to burn **i**. 1Kg 13:1
places who are burning **i** on you. 1Kg 13:2
and burned **i** on the high places. 1Kg 22:43
burning **i** on the high places. 2Kg 12:3
burning **i** on the high places. 2Kg 14:4
burning **i** on the high places. 2Kg 15:4
burning **i** on the high places. 2Kg 15:35
and burned **i** on the high places, 2Kg 16:4
They burned **i** on all the high 2Kg 17:11
burned **i** to it up to that 2Kg 18:4
Me and burned **i** to other gods in 2Kg 22:17
appointed to burn **i** at the high 2Kg 23:5
They had burned **i** to Baal, 2Kg 23:5
where the priests had burned **i**. 2Kg 23:8
on the altar of **i** to make 1Ch 6:49
flour, wine, oil, **i**, and spices. 1Ch 9:29
to burn **i** in the presence of the 1Ch 23:13
refined gold for the altar of **i**; 1Ch 28:18
for burning sweet **i** before Him, 2Ch 2:4
as a place to burn **i** before Him? 2Ch 2:6
and fragrant **i** to the LORD every 2Ch 13:11

places and the **i** altars from all 2Ch 14:5
them and burned **i** to them. 2Ch 25:14
to burn **i** on the incense 2Ch 26:16
to burn incense on the **i** altar. 2Ch 26:16
right to offer **i** to the LORD— 2Ch 26:18
have the right to offer **i**. 2Ch 26:18
a censer in his hand to offer **i**, 2Ch 26:19
temple beside the altar of **i**, 2Ch 26:19
He burned **i** in the Valley of 2Ch 28:3
and burned **i** on the high places, 2Ch 28:4
Judah to offer **i** to other gods, 2Ch 28:25
did not burn **i**, and did not 2Ch 29:7
His ministers and burners of **i**." 2Ch 29:11
took away the **i** altars and threw 2Ch 30:14
and you must burn **i** on it"? 2Ch 32:12
and the **i** altars that were above 2Ch 34:4
down all the **i** altars throughout 2Ch 34:7
Me and burned **i** to other gods in 2Ch 34:25
prayer be set before You as **i**, Ps 141:2
and **i** bring joy to the heart, Pr 27:9
despise ⌊your⌋ **i**. New Moons and Is 1:13
Asherahs and **i** altars they made Is 17:8
Asherah poles or **i** altars will Is 27:9
offerings or wearied you with **i**. Is 43:23
in gardens, burning **i** on bricks, Is 65:3
they burned **i** on the mountains Is 65:7
offers **i**, one praises an idol Is 66:3
Me to burn **i** to other gods and Jr 1:16
falsely, burn **i** to Baal, and Jr 7:9
they have been burning **i** to, Jr 11:12
altars to burn **i** to Baal— Jr 11:13
to anger by burning **i** to Baal." Jr 11:17
burn **i** to false ⌊idols⌋ that Jr 18:15
have burned **i** in it to other Jr 19:4
they have burned **i** to the whole Jr 19:13
houses where **i** has been burned Jr 32:29
grain and **i** offerings to bring Jr 41:5
and burning **i** to serve other Jr 44:3
or stop burning **i** to other gods. Jr 44:5
You are burning **i** to other gods Jr 44:8
were burning **i** to other gods, Jr 44:15
burn **i** to the queen of heaven Jr 44:17
we ceased to burn **i** to the queen Jr 44:18
When we burned **i** to the queen of Jr 44:19
As for the **i** you burned in Jr 44:21
you burned **i** and sinned against Jr 44:23
have made to burn **i** to the queen Jr 44:25
place and burns **i** to his gods. Jr 48:35
and your **i** altars smashed. Ezk 6:4
your **i** altars cut down, Ezk 6:6
had an **i** burner in his hand, Ezk 8:11
cloud of **i** was rising up. Ezk 8:11
set My oil and **i** before them. Ezk 16:18
which you had set My **i** and oil. Ezk 23:41
an offering and **i** to him. Dn 2:46
Baals when she burned **i** to them, Hs 2:13
and burn **i** to their fishing Hab 1:16
I and pure offerings will be Mal 1:11
of the Lord and burn **i**. Lk 1:9
At the hour of **i** the whole Lk 1:10
to the right of the altar of **i**. Lk 1:11
the gold altar of **i** and the ark Heb 9:4
and gold bowls filled with **i**, Rv 5:8
angel, with a gold **i** burner, Rv 8:3
large amount of **i** to offer with Rv 8:3
The smoke of the **i**, with the Rv 8:4
The angel took the **i** burner, Rv 8:5
cinnamon, spice, **i**, myrrh, and Rv 18:13

INCENSED *(3)*

Then Jacob became **i** and brought Gn 31:36
But God was **i** that Balaam was Nm 22:22
All who are **i** against Him will Is 45:24

INCESSANTLY *(1)*

and he harbored his rage **i**. Am 1:11

INCH *(1)*

not even an **i** of it, because I Dt 2:5

INCHES *(52)*

to within 18 **i** ⌊of the roof.⌋ Gn 6:16
wood, 45 **i** long, 27 inches Ex 25:10
inches long, 27 **i** wide, and 27 Ex 25:10
27 inches wide, and 27 **i** high. Ex 25:10
45 **i** long and 27 inches wide. Ex 25:17
45 inches long and 27 **i** wide. Ex 25:17
wood, 36 **i** long, 18 inches Ex 25:23
inches long, 18 **i** wide, and 27 Ex 25:23
18 inches wide, and 27 **i** high. Ex 25:23
the width of each plank 27 **i**. Ex 26:16
i long and nine inches wide. Ex 28:16
inches long and nine **i** wide. Ex 28:16
18 **i** long and 18 inches wide; Ex 30:2
18 inches long and 18 **i** wide; Ex 30:2
it must be 36 **i** high. Ex 30:2
and the width of each was 27 **i**. Ex 36:21
wood, 45 **i** long, 27 inches Ex 37:1
inches long, 27 **i** wide, and 27 Ex 37:1
27 inches wide, and 27 **i** high. Ex 37:1
45 **i** long and 27 inches wide. Ex 37:6
45 inches long and 27 **i** wide. Ex 37:6
wood, 36 **i** long, 18 inches Ex 37:10
inches long, 18 **i** wide, and 27 Ex 37:10
18 inches wide, and 27 **i** high. Ex 37:10
18 **i** long and 18 inches wide; Ex 37:25
18 inches long and 18 **i** wide; Ex 37:25
wide; it was 36 **i** high. Its Ex 37:25
i long and nine inches wide. Ex 39:9
inches long and nine **i** wide. Ex 39:9
is 13 feet six **i** long and six Dt 3:11
a double-edged sword 18 **i** long. Jdg 3:16
He was nine feet, nine **i** tall 1Sm 17:4
The reservoir was three **i** thick, 1Kg 7:26
the crown on top was 18 **i** wide. 1Kg 7:31
made as a pedestal 27 **i** wide. 1Kg 7:31
each wheel was 27 **i** tall. 1Kg 7:32
a band nine **i** high encircling 1Kg 7:35
The reservoir was three **i** thick, 2Ch 4:5
hand was six units of 21 **i**; Ezk 40:5
standard length plus three **i**. Ezk 40:5
was a barrier of 21 **i** in front Ezk 40:12
⌊each⌋ 31 and a half **i** long, Ezk 40:42
31 and a half **i** wide, and 21 Ezk 40:42
half inches wide, and 21 **i** high. Ezk 40:42
the standard length plus three **i** Ezk 43:13
the gutter is 21 **i** ⌊deep⌋ and 21 Ezk 43:13
21 inches ⌊deep⌋ and 21 **i** wide, Ezk 43:13
a rim of nine **i** around its edge. Ezk 43:13
width ⌊of the ledge⌋ is 21 **i**. Ezk 43:14
⌊whose⌋ width is also 21 **i**. Ezk 43:14
around it is 10 and a half **i**, Ezk 43:17
gutter is 21 **i** all around it. Ezk 43:17

INCIDENT *(6)*

about the **i**⌋ and were deeply Gn 34:7
who died because of the Korah **i**. Nm 16:49
used against you in the Peor **i**. Nm 25:18
against the LORD in the Peor **i**, Nm 31:16
on the day this **i** began and stay 1Sm 20:19
for this **i** has come from Me.' " 2Ch 11:4

INCIDENTS *(1)*

and the **i** that affected him and 1Ch 29:30

INCITE *(1)*

I am going to **i** your lovers Ezk 23:22

INCITED *(7)*

who returned and **i** the entire Nm 14:36
i the Israelites to Nm 31:16
LORD who has **i** you against me, 1Sm 26:19
because his wife Jezebel **i** him. 1Kg 21:25
Israel and **i** David to count 1Ch 21:1
though you **i** Me against him, Jb 2:3
But the Jews **i** the religious Ac 13:50

INCITES *(1)*

a man who **i** dispute and conflict Jr 15:10

INCITING *(1)*

son of Neriah is **i** you against Jr 43:3

INCLINATION *(1)*

though man's **i** is evil from his Gn 8:21

INCLINATIONS *(1)*

carrying out the **i** of our flesh Eph 2:3

INCLINE *(1)*

May He **i** our hearts toward Him 1Kg 8:58

INCLUDE *(2)*

the Levites will **i** six cities of Nm 35:6
But he did not **i** Levi and 1Ch 21:6

INCLUDED *(27)*

Judah's sons **i** Er and Onan, Nm 26:19
⌊Their land also **i**⌋ the Jordan Jos 13:27
Their inheritance **i**: Jos 19:2
to Jezreel, and ⌊**i**⌋ Chesulloth, Jos 19:18
Their boundary **i** Helkath, Hali, Jos 19:25
of their inheritance **i** Zorah, Jos 19:41
⌊These nations **i**:⌋ the five Jdg 3:3
⌊The commanders **i**⌋ Ishmael son 2Kg 25:23
⌊Also **i** were plans⌋ for the 1Ch 28:13
number of the Israelite men ⌊**i**⌋: Ezr 2:2
The priests ⌊**i**⌋: Jedaiah's Ezr 2:36
The Levites ⌊**i**⌋: Jeshua's and Ezr 2:40
The singers ⌊**i**⌋: Asaph's Ezr 2:41
gatekeepers' descendants ⌊**i**⌋: Ezr 2:42
The temple servants ⌊**i**⌋: Ezr 2:43
of Solomon's servants ⌊**i**⌋: Ezr 2:55
number of the Israelite men ⌊**i**⌋: Neh 7:7
The priests ⌊**i**⌋: Jedaiah's Neh 7:39
The Levites ⌊**i**⌋: Jeshua's Neh 7:43
The singers ⌊**i**⌋: Asaph's Neh 7:44
The gatekeepers ⌊**i**⌋: Neh 7:45
The temple servants ⌊**i**⌋: Neh 7:46
of Solomon's servants ⌊**i**⌋: Neh 7:57
⌊This **i**⌋ Mattaniah, Bakbukiah, Neh 12:25
His estate **i** 7,000 sheep, 3,000 Jb 1:3
⌊These **i**:⌋ Jerusalem and the Jr 25:18
⌊The commanders **i**⌋ Ishmael son Jr 40:8

INCLUDES *(1)*

i a slave born in your house Gn 17:12

INCLUDING *(61)*

(See pp. xi-xii.)

INCOME *(4)*

with all the **i** from the field 2Kg 8:6
accompanies the **i** of the wicked. Pr 15:6
than great **i** with injustice. Pr 16:8
is⌋ never ⌊satisfied⌋ with **i**. Ec 5:10

INCOMPARABLE *(1)*

an absolutely **i** eternal weight 2Co 4:17

INCORRUPTIBILITY *(2)*

must be clothed with **i**, 1Co 15:53
corruptible is clothed with **i**, 1Co 15:54

INCORRUPTIBLE *(1)*

and the dead will be raised **i**, 1Co 15:52

INCORRUPTION *(2)*

Sown in corruption, raised in **i**; 1Co 15:42
and corruption cannot inherit **i**. 1Co 15:50

INCREASE *(29)*

way its yield will **i** for you; Lv 19:25
You are to **i** its price in Lv 25:16
I the inheritance for a large Nm 26:54
I the inheritance for a large Nm 33:54
i you a thousand times more, Dt 1:11
so that you may live and **i**, Dt 8:1
continued to **i** against Jabin Jdg 4:24
of blood will not **i** the loss, 2Sm 14:11
Absalom continued to **i**. 2Sm 15:12
the damage will **i** and the royal Ezr 4:22
if his children **i**, they are Jb 27:14
LORD, how my foes **i**! Ps 3:1
The distresses of my heart **i**; Ps 25:17
You will **i** my honor and comfort Ps 71:21
the sun shines, may his fame **i**. Ps 72:17
ease, and they **i** their wealth. Ps 73:12
our flocks will **i** by thousands Ps 144:13
will listen and **i** his learning, Pr 1:5
When the wicked **i**, rebellion Pr 29:16
When good things **i**, the ones who Ec 5:11
are many words, they **i** futility. Ec 6:11
you multiply and **i** in the land, Jr 3:16
and they will **i** and be fruitful. Ezk 36:11
May your prosperity **i**. Dn 4:1
about, and knowledge will **i**." Dn 12:4
said to the Lord, "**I** our faith." Lk 17:5
He must **i**, but I must decrease." Jn 3:30
your seed and **i** the harvest of 2Co 9:10
cause you to **i** and overflow with 1Th 3:12

INCREASED *(21)*

the waters **i** and lifted up the Gn 7:17
waters surged and **i** greatly on Gn 7:18
but now your wealth has **i**. Gn 30:30
were fruitful, **i** rapidly, Ex 1:7
Philistine camp **i** in intensity. 1Sm 14:19
ancestral houses **i** greatly. 1Ch 4:38
their herds had **i** in the land of 1Ch 5:9
instead, Amon **i** ⌊his⌋ guilt. 2Ch 33:23
You **i** strength within me. Ps 138:3
I **i** my achievements. Ec 2:4
the nation and **i** its joy. Is 9:3
passed by and **i** your Ezk 16:25
and **i** your prostitution to Ezk 16:26
But she **i** her promiscuity when Ezk 23:14
trading you have **i** your wealth, Ezk 28:5
The more his fruit **i**, the more Hs 10:1
the more he **i** the altars. Hs 10:1
and produced a crop that **i** 30, Mk 4:8
And Jesus **i** in wisdom and Lk 2:52

Spirit, and it **i** in numbers. Ac 9:31
and were **i** in number daily. Ac 16:5

INCREASES *(12)*
and everything else you have **i**, Dt 8:13
when the wealth of his house **i**. Ps 49:16
If wealth **i**, pay no attention to Ps 62:10
and pleasant speech **i** learning. Pr 16:21
mouth and **i** learning with its Pr 16:23
a robber and **i** those among men Pr 23:28
Whoever **i** his wealth through Pr 28:8
rebellion **i**, but the righteous Pr 29:16
a hot-tempered man **i** rebellion. Pr 29:22
as knowledge **i**, grief increases. Ec 1:18
as knowledge increases, grief **i**. Ec 1:18
the hope that as your faith **i**, 2Co 10:15

INCREASING *(6)*
measure while **i** the price and Am 8:5
the crowds were **i**, He began Lk 11:29
added to the Lord in **i** numbers— Ac 5:14
fruit that is **i** to your account Php 4:17
one of you for one another is **i**. 2Th 1:3
qualities are yours and are **i**, 2Pt 1:8

INCREASINGLY *(1)*
and his disease became **i** severe. 2Ch 16:12

INCREDIBLE *(4)*
it may seem **i** to the remnant Zch 8:6
should it also seem **i** to Me?" Zch 8:6
"We have seen **i** things today!" Lk 5:26
is it considered **i** by any of you Ac 26:8

INCREDIBLY *(1)*
and dreadful, and **i** strong, with Dn 7:7

INCUR *(8)*
they do not **i** guilt and die. Ex 28:43
commands and **i** guilt by doing Lv 4:13
he may have done to **i** guilt." Lv 6:7
and you will not **i** guilt because Lv 19:17
or they will **i** guilt and die. Nm 18:22
You will not **i** guilt because of Nm 18:32
so they will not **i** guilt before 2Ch 19:10
this, and you will not **i** guilt. 2Ch 19:10

INCURABLE *(8)*
with painful and **i** boils from Dt 28:35
intestines with an **i** disease. 2Ch 21:18
infected Job with **i** boils from Jb 2:7
My wound is **i**, though I am Jb 34:6
the day of disease and **i** pain. Is 17:11
my wound **i**, refusing to be Jr 15:18
injury is **i**; your wound most Jr 30:12
her wound is **i** and has reached Mc 1:9

INCURRED *(2)*
of Judah and **i** grievous guilt Ezk 25:12
But he **i** guilt through Baal and Hs 13:1

INCURS *(4)*
what is prohibited, and **i** guilt, Lv 4:22
what is prohibited, and **i** guilt, Lv 4:27
he **i** guilt in such an instance. Lv 5:4
If someone **i** guilt in one of Lv 5:5

INDEBTED *(1)*
pleased, and they are **i** to them. Rm 15:27

INDECENCY *(8)*
of your **i** and abominations"— Ezk 16:58
revisited the **i** of your youth, Ezk 23:21
put an end to your **i** and sexual Ezk 23:27
both your **i** and promiscuity. Ezk 23:29
of your **i** and promiscuity." Ezk 23:35
put an end to **i** in the land, Ezk 23:48
They will repay you for your **i**, Ezk 23:49
Because of the **i** of your Ezk 24:13

INDECENT *(2)*
embarrassed by your **i** behavior. Ezk 16:27
not to imitate your **i** behavior. Ezk 23:48

INDECISIVE *(1)*
An **i** man is unstable in all his Jms 1:8

INDEED *(160)*
(See pp. xi-xii.)

INDENTATIONS *(1)*
of green or red **i** that appear to Lv 14:37

INDEPENDENT *(2)*
woman is not **i** of man, and man 1Co 11:11
and man is not **i** of woman. 1Co 11:11

INDESCRIBABLE *(1)*
Thanks be to God for His **i** gift. 2Co 9:15

INDESTRUCTIBLE *(1)*
based on the power of an **i** life. Heb 7:16

INDIA *(2)*
127 provinces from **I** to Cush. Est 1:1
127 provinces from **I** to Cush. Est 8:9

INDICATE *(3)*
for Me the one I **i** to you." 1Sm 16:3
to go by sea to the place you **i**. 1Kg 5:9
and not to **i** the charges against Ac 25:27

INDICATED *(1)*
Moses even **i** ⌊in the passage⌋ Lk 20:37

INDICATES *(2)*
place the lot **i** for someone will Nm 33:54
i the removal of what can be Heb 12:27

INDICATING *(2)*
⌊**i**⌋ that he should set up Ezk 21:22
within them was **i** when He 1Pt 1:11

INDICT *(1)*
Can anyone **i** me? If so, I will Jb 13:19

INDICTMENT *(1)*
Let my Opponent compose ⌊His⌋ **i**. Jb 31:35

INDIFFERENT *(1)*
I to her prostitution, she Jr 3:9

INDIGNANT *(6)*
they became **i** with the two Mt 20:24
the Son of David!" they were **i** Mt 21:15
disciples saw it, they were **i**. Mt 26:8
He was **i** and said to them, Mk 10:14
they began to be **i** with James Mk 10:41
i because Jesus had healed on Lk 13:14

INDIGNATION *(14)*
in my body because of Your **i**; Ps 38:3
fury, **i**, and calamity—a band Ps 78:49
because of Your **i** and wrath; Ps 102:10
alone, for You filled me with **i**. Jr 15:17
I will pour out My **i** on you; Ezk 21:31
received rain in the day of **i**. Ezk 22:24
have poured out My **i** on them and Ezk 22:31
Who can withstand His **i**? Nah 1:6
march across the earth with **i**; Hab 3:12
order to pour out My **i** on them, Zph 3:8
expressing **i** to one another: Mk 14:4
but wrath and **i** to those who are Rm 2:8
what **i**, what fear, what 2Co 7:11
and I do not burn with **i**? 2Co 11:29

INDIRECT *(1)*
traveled their **i** route for seven 2Kg 3:9

INDIRECTLY *(1)*
this to address the issue **i**, 2Sm 14:20

INDISTINCTLY *(1)*
now we see **i**, as in a mirror, 1Co 13:12

INDIVIDUAL *(6)*
You may take two quarts per **i**, Ex 16:16
it⌋ to the **i** he has wronged. Nm 5:7
But if that **i** has no relative to Nm 5:8
of Christ, and **i** members of it. 1Co 12:27
proper working of each **i** part. Eph 4:16
each **i** gate was made of a single Rv 21:21

INDIVIDUALLY *(1)*
in Christ and **i** members of one Rm 12:5

INDIVIDUALS *(1)*
over both **i** and nations, Jb 34:29

INDOORS *(1)*
days His disciples were **i** again, Jn 20:26

INDUCED *(1)*
they **i** men to say, "We heard Ac 6:11

INDUCES *(1)*
Laziness **i** deep sleep, and a Pr 19:15

INDULGE *(1)*
Please **i** me, my lord." Gn 33:15

INDULGED *(1)*
the land and have **i** yourselves. Jms 5:5

INDULGENCE *(1)*
of any value against fleshly **i**. Col 2:23

INEDIBLE *(4)*
bad figs, so bad they were **i**. Jr 24:2
bad, so bad they are **i**." Jr 24:3
so bad they are **i**, this is what Jr 24:8
figs that are **i** because they are Jr 29:17

INEFFECTIVE *(2)*
why the law is **i** and justice Hab 1:4
His grace toward me was not **i**. 1Co 15:10

INEXHAUSTIBLE *(1)*
grow old, an **i** treasure in Lk 12:33

INEXPERIENCE *(1)*
Leave **i** behind, and you will Pr 9:6

INEXPERIENCED *(17)*
My son Solomon is young and **i**, 1Ch 22:5
him alone—is young and **i**. 1Ch 29:1
was young, **i**, and unable to 2Ch 13:7
trustworthy, making the **i** wise. Ps 19:7
The LORD guards the **i**; Ps 116:6
gives understanding to the **i**. Ps 119:130
teaching shrewdness to the **i**, Pr 1:4
of the **i** will kill them, Pr 1:32
I saw among the **i**, I noticed Pr 7:7
to be shrewd, you who are **i**; Pr 8:5
"Whoever is **i**, enter here!" Pr 9:4
"Whoever is **i**, enter here!" Pr 9:16
The **i** believe anything, but the Pr 14:15
and the **i** learn a lesson; Pr 19:25
is punished, the **i** become wiser; Pr 21:11
but the **i** keep going and are Pr 22:3
on milk is **i** with the message Heb 5:13

INEXPRESSIBLE *(2)*
He heard **i** words, which a man is 2Co 12:4
rejoice with **i** and glorious joy 1Pt 1:8

INFAMOUS *(1)*
you **i** one full of turmoil. Ezk 22:5

INFANT *(6)*
the **i** and the gray-haired man. Dt 32:25
fatherless **i** is snatched from Jb 24:9
i will play beside the cobra's Is 11:8
a nursing **i** will no longer live Is 65:20
woman, child and **i** from Judah, Jr 44:7
because he is an **i**. Heb 5:13

INFANT'S *(1)*
The nursing **i** tongue clings to Lm 4:4

INFANTRY *(2)*
ask the king for **i** and cavalry Ezr 8:22
officers of the **i** and cavalry Neh 2:9

INFANTS *(17)*
their wives, children, and **i**. Nm 16:27
children and **i**, oxen and sheep, 1Sm 15:3
children and **i**, oxen, donkeys, 1Sm 22:19
before the LORD with their **i**, 2Ch 20:13
with all their **i**, wives, sons, 2Ch 31:18
like **i** who never see daylight? Jb 3:16
of children and nursing **i**, Ps 8:2
I ⌊just⌋ weaned from milk? Is 28:9
children and **i** faint in the Lm 2:11
own children, the **i** they have Lm 2:20
learned and revealed them to **i**. Mt 11:25
of children and nursing **i**?" Mt 21:16
and have revealed them to **i**. Lk 10:21
even bringing **i** to Him so He Lk 18:15
leave their **i** outside so they Ac 7:19
but be **i** in evil and adult in 1Co 14:20
Like newborn **i**, desire the 1Pt 2:2

INFATUATED *(3)*
He became **i** with Dinah, daughter Gn 34:3
son Amnon was **i** with her. 2Sm 13:1
would you be **i** with a forbidden Pr 5:20

INFECTED *(8)*
quarantine the **i** person for Lv 13:4
skin of the **i** person from his Lv 13:12
to pronounce the **i** person clean. Lv 13:13
pronounce the **i** person clean; Lv 13:17
it and applied it to his **i** skin, 2Kg 20:7
presence and **i** Job with Jb 2:7
figs and apply it to his **i** skin, Is 38:21
and he became **i** with worms and Ac 12:23

INFECTION *(17)*
will examine the **i** on the skin Lv 13:3
the hair in the **i** has turned Lv 13:3
white and the **i** appears to be Lv 13:3
the **i** remains unchanged in his Lv 13:5
If the **i** has faded and has not Lv 13:6
and if the **i** has turned white, Lv 13:17
him unclean; it is an **i**. Lv 13:22
or woman has an **i** on the head or Lv 13:29
the priest must examine the **i**. Lv 13:30
the priest examines the scaly **i**, Lv 13:31
with the scaly **i** for seven days. Lv 13:31
reexamine the **i** on the seventh Lv 13:32
a reddish-white **i** on the bald Lv 13:42
swelling of the **i** on his bald Lv 13:43
the **i** is on his head. Lv 13:44
unclean as long as he has the **i**; Lv 13:46
someone who has an **i** or leprosy 2Sm 3:29

INFECTIOUS *(2)*
with an **i** skin disease is Lv 13:45
in a case of **i** skin disease, Dt 24:8

INFERIOR *(9)*
their jealousy with an **i** people; Dt 32:21
a mind; I am not **i** to you. Who Jb 12:3
I also know; I am not **i** to you. Jb 13:2
another kingdom, **i** to yours, and Dn 2:39
people have drunk freely, the **i**. Jn 2:10
We are not **i** if we don't eat, 1Co 8:8
myself in no way **i** to the 2Co 11:5
since I am in no way **i** to the 2Co 12:11
i is blessed by the superior. Heb 7:7

INFERTILE *(1)*
will be no **i** male or female Dt 7:14

INFESTATION *(1)*
over it like an **i** of locusts. Is 33:4

INFINITE *(1)*
His understanding is **i**. Ps 147:5

INFLAME *(1)*
Mockers **i** a city, but the wise Pr 29:8

INFLAMED *(3)*
into the evening, **i** by wine. Is 5:11
your heart was **i** ⌊with lust⌋"— Ezk 16:30
females and were **i** in their lust Rm 1:27

INFLAMMATION *(1)*
disease, fever, **i**, burning heat, Dt 28:22

INFLATED *(6)*
Look, his ego is **i**; Hab 2:4
of you will be **i** with pride in 1Co 4:6
Now some are **i** with pride, 1Co 4:18
of those who are **i** with pride. 1Co 4:19
you are **i** with pride, instead 1Co 5:2
realm and **i** without cause Col 2:18

INFLATES *(1)*
Knowledge **i** with pride, but 1Co 8:1

INFLICT *(8)*
will not **i** any illness on you I Ex 15:26
against Midian to **i** the LORD's Nm 31:3
but He will **i** them on all who Dt 7:15
LORD will also **i** you with every Dt 28:61
of Hosts will **i** an emaciating Is 10:16
to take their life, **i** on them. Jr 19:9
Is God unrighteous to **i** wrath? Rm 3:5
and they **i** injury with them. Rv 9:19

INFLICTED *(15)*
on you I **i** on the Egyptians Ex 15:26
And the LORD **i** a plague on the Ex 32:35
injury he **i** on the person, Lv 24:20
the same is to be **i** on him. Lv 24:20
our eyes the LORD **i** great and Dt 6:22
sicknesses the LORD has **i** on it. Dt 29:22
and **i** heavy losses on them. 1Sm 23:5
He **i** a great slaughter on Aram. 1Kg 20:21
that the Arameans had **i** on him 2Kg 8:29
the Arameans had **i** on him when 2Kg 9:15
the king of Aram **i** on Israel. 2Kg 13:4
from the wounds they **i** on him in 2Ch 22:6
and heals the wounds He **i**. Is 30:26
her inhabitants **i** their terror. Ezk 26:17
After they had **i** many blows on Ac 16:23

INFLICTING *(3)*
Israelites finished **i** a terrible Jos 10:20
the man struck him, **i** a wound. 1Kg 20:37
i vengeance on the nations and Ps 149:7

INFLICTS *(2)*
If any man **i** a permanent injury Lv 24:19
plague the LORD **i** on the nations Zch 14:18

INFLUENCE *(3)*
and stumble under the **i** of beer: Is 28:7
Under the **i** of the wine, Dn 5:2
his cunning and by his **i**, Dn 8:25

INFLUENTIAL *(2)*
There was an **i** man of Benjamin 1Sm 9:1
man and an **i** man lived on it. Jb 22:8

INFORM *(17)*
⌊this message⌋ to **i** my lord, Gn 32:5
I will go up and **i** Pharaoh, Gn 46:31
I thought I should **i** you: Ru 4:4
Or they will **i** on us and say, 1Sm 27:11
to Hebron to **i** David about all 2Sm 3:19
and sent word to **i** David: 2Sm 11:5
word comes from you to **i** me." 2Sm 15:28
turn would go and **i** King David, 2Sm 17:17
we have sent to **i** the king Ezr 4:14
let the fish of the sea **i** you. Jb 12:8
Listen to me and I will **i** you. Jb 15:17
and I will **i** you, for there is Jb 36:2
I question you, you will **i** Me. Jb 38:3
I question you, you will **i** Me. Jb 40:7
I question you, you will **i** Me." Jb 42:4
I am about to **i** them, and this Jr 16:21
and their divining rods **i** them. Hs 4:12

INFORMATION *(4)*
come back to me with accurate **i**, 1Sm 23:23
come and pass along **i** to them. 2Sm 17:17
of their leaders for your **i**. Ezr 5:10
able to get reliable **i** because Ac 21:34

INFORMED *(15)*
So Joseph went and **i** Pharaoh: Gn 47:1
arrival, the LORD had **i** Samuel, 1Sm 9:15
of Nabal's young men **i** Abigail, 1Sm 25:14
Abner also **i** the Benjaminites 2Sm 3:19
arrived, Joab was **i**, "Abner son 2Sm 3:23
man did see them and **i** Absalom. 2Sm 17:18
well and went and **i** King David. 2Sm 17:21
of the men saw ⌊him⌋ and **i** Joab. 2Sm 18:10
Shimei was **i**, "Look, your slaves 1Kg 2:39
Then Haman **i** King Ahasuerus, Est 3:8
how Mordecai had **i** on Bigthana Est 6:2
The LORD **i** me, so I knew. Jr 11:18
that you have **i** me about this." Ac 23:22
When I was **i** that there was a Ac 23:30
was accurately **i** about the Way, Ac 24:22

INFORMER *(1)*
Then an **i** came to David and 2Sm 15:13

INFORMING *(2)*
i ⌊all⌋ people of Your mighty Ps 145:12
Therefore I am **i** you that no one 1Co 12:3

INFORMS *(3)*
someone **i** him about the sin he Lv 4:23
if someone **i** him about the sin Lv 4:28
If a man **i** on his friends for a Jb 17:5

INFURIATED *(6)*
down to them. They **i** the LORD, Jdg 2:12
David was **i** with the man and 2Sm 12:5
i and tried to assassinate Est 2:21
Will He be endlessly **i**? Jr 3:5
the ram, and **i** with him, he Dn 8:7
I, the king of the South will Dn 11:11

INFURIATING *(1)*
i Him with what your hands have Dt 31:29

INGATHERING *(2)*
(Festival of, AKA Festival of BOOTHS, Festival of TABERNACLES)
the Festival of **I** at the end of Ex 23:16
the Festival of **I** at the turn Ex 34:22

INHABIT *(6)*
Canaanites who **i** the valley area Jos 17:16
waters and ⌊all⌋ that **i** them. Jb 26:5
listen, all who **i** the world, Ps 49:1
For the upright will **i** the land, Pr 2:21
justice will **i** the wilderness, Is 32:16
nations and **i** the desolate Is 54:3

INHABITANT *(12)*
city is abandoned; no **i** is left. Jr 4:29
desolation, a land devoid of **i**. Jr 6:8
man, without **i**, and without Jr 33:10
cities a desolation, without **i**." Jr 34:22
ruin today without an **i** in them Jr 44:2
cursing, without **i**, as ⌊you see⌋ Jr 44:22
bags for exile, **i** of Daughter Jr 46:19
and every **i** of the land will Jr 47:2
become a desolation, without **i**. Jr 48:9
says the **i** of Zion; Jr 51:35
an object of scorn, without **i**. Jr 51:37
without a person, without an **i**. Zph 3:6

INHABITANTS *(125)*
plain, all the **i** of the cities, Gn 19:25
me odious to the **i** of the land, Gn 34:30
the Horite, the **i** of the land: Gn 36:20
the Canaanite **i** of the land saw Gn 50:11
will seize the **i** of Philistia. Ex 15:14
the **i** of Canaan will panic; Ex 15:15
I will place the **i** of the land Ex 23:31
treaty with the **i** of the land Ex 34:12
a treaty with the **i** of the land, Ex 34:15
the land will vomit out its **i**. Lv 18:25
in the land for all its **i**. Lv 25:10
is one that devours its **i**, Nm 13:32
tell ⌊it to⌋ the **i** of this land. Nm 14:14
because of the **i** of the land. Nm 32:17
drive out all the **i** of the land Nm 33:52
drive out the **i** of the land Nm 33:55
led the **i** of their city astray, Dt 13:13
strike down the **i** of that city Dt 13:15
sword until all the **i** of Ai were Jos 8:26
When the **i** of Gibeon heard what Jos 9:3
and all the **i** of our land told Jos 9:11
destroy all the **i** of the land Jos 9:24
that the **i** of Gibeon had made Jos 10:1
all the **i** of the hill country Jos 13:6
against the **i** of Debir whose Jos 15:15
toward the **i** of En-tappuah. Jos 17:7
and the **i** of Dor with its towns; Jos 17:11
the **i** of En-dor with its towns, Jos 17:11
the **i** of Taanach with its towns, Jos 17:11
and the **i** of Megiddo with its Jos 17:11
curse her **i**, for they did not Jdg 5:23
leader of all the **i** of Gilead." Jdg 10:18
leader of all the **i** of Gilead." Jdg 11:8
men rallied by the **i** of Gibeah. Jdg 20:15
there from the **i** of Jdg 21:9
Go and kill the **i** of Jdg 21:10
found among the **i** of Jdg 21:12
David rescued the **i** of Keilah. 1Sm 23:5
had been the **i** of the region 1Sm 27:8
Their **i** have become powerless, 2Kg 19:26
on this place and on its **i**, 2Kg 22:16
this place and against its **i**, 2Kg 22:19
and all the **i** of Jerusalem, 2Kg 23:2
The **i** of Jebus said to David, 1Ch 11:5
handed the land's **i** over to me, 1Ch 22:18
who drove out the **i** of this land 2Ch 20:7
and ⌊the **i** of⌋ Mount Seir. 2Ch 20:10
Judah and you **i** of Jerusalem, 2Ch 20:15
Judah and the **i** of Jerusalem 2Ch 20:18
Judah and you **i** of Jerusalem. 2Ch 20:20
and ⌊the **i** of⌋ Mount Seir who 2Ch 20:22
against the **i** of Mount Seir 2Ch 20:23
had finished with the **i** of Seir, 2Ch 20:23
he caused the **i** of Jerusalem to 2Ch 21:11
Judah and the **i** of Jerusalem to 2Ch 21:13
Then the **i** of Jerusalem made 2Ch 22:1
but the **i** laughed at them and 2Ch 30:10
Hezekiah and the **i** of Jerusalem 2Ch 32:22
he and the **i** of Jerusalem— 2Ch 32:26
Judah and the **i** of Jerusalem 2Ch 32:33
Judah and the **i** of Jerusalem to 2Ch 33:9
and the **i** of Jerusalem. 2Ch 34:9
on this place and on its **i**, 2Ch 34:24
this place and against its **i**, 2Ch 34:27
on this place and on its **i**.' " 2Ch 34:28
of Judah and the **i** of Jerusalem, 2Ch 34:30
all the **i** of Jerusalem carried 2Ch 34:32
Judah⌋, and the **i** of Jerusalem. 2Ch 35:18
Hanun and the **i** of Zanoah Neh 3:13
the world and its **i**, belong to Ps 24:1
let all the **i** of the world stand Ps 33:8
gazes on all the **i** of the earth Ps 33:14
the earth and all its **i** shake, Ps 75:3
Philistia with the **i** of Tyre. Ps 83:7
of the wickedness of its **i**. Ps 107:34
grand and lovely ones without **i**. Is 5:9
cities lie in ruins without **i**, Is 6:11
a snare to the **i** of Jerusalem. Is 8:14
Ephraim and the **i** of Samaria— Is 9:9
warrior, I subjugated the **i**. Is 10:13
The **i** of Gebim have sought Is 10:31
All you **i** of the world and you Is 18:3
And the **i** of this coastland will Is 20:6
The **i** of the land of Tema meet Is 21:14
a father to the **i** of Jerusalem Is 22:21
Mourn, **i** of the coastland, you Is 23:2
wail, **i** of the coastland! Is 23:6
its surface and scatter its **i**: Is 24:1
The earth is polluted by its **i**, Is 24:5
and its **i** have become guilty; Is 24:6
the earth's **i** have been burned, Is 24:6
the **i** of the world will learn Is 26:9
the earth's **i** have not fallen Is 26:18
to punish the **i** of the earth for Is 26:21
Their **i** have become powerless, Is 37:27
longer with the **i** of what is Is 38:11
its **i** are like grasshoppers. Is 40:22
it, you islands with your **i**. Is 42:10
Let the **i** of Sela sing for joy; Is 42:11

be indeed too small for the **i**, Is 49:19
and its **i** will die in like Is 51:6
cities are in ruins, without **i**. Jr 2:15
all the **i** of the earth"— Jr 25:29
against all the **i** of the earth. Jr 25:30
in it, the cities and their **i**. Jr 47:2
blood be on the **i** of Chaldea," Jr 51:35
the world's **i** did not believe Lm 4:12
destroy you, ⌊**i** of Jerusalem⌋, I Ezk 5:16
has come on you, **i** of the land. Ezk 7:7
and all of her **i** inflicted their Ezk 26:17
The **i** of Sidon and Arvad were Ezk 27:8
All the **i** of the coasts and Ezk 27:35
all the **i** of Egypt will know Ezk 29:6
Then the **i** of Israel's cities Ezk 39:9
All the **i** of the earth are Dn 4:35
heaven and the **i** of the earth. Dn 4:35
case against the **i** of the land: Hs 4:1
listen, all you **i** of the land. Jl 1:2
a wasteland because of its **i**, Mc 7:13
end of all the **i** of the earth. Zph 1:18
Woe, **i** of the seacoast, nation Zph 2:5
on the **i** of the land"— Zch 11:6
will defend the **i** of Jerusalem, Zch 12:8
that all the **i** of the province Ac 19:10
announce to the **i** of the earth— Rv 14:6

INHABITED *(31)*

until they came to an **i** land. Ex 16:35
except the Hivites who **i** Gibeon; Jos 11:19
the Jebusites who **i** the land. 2Sm 5:6
Jebusites who **i** the land were 1Ch 11:4
Canaanites who **i** the land before Neh 9:24
and chased from the **i** world. Jb 18:18
over the surface of the **i** world. Jb 37:12
to the ends of the **i** world. Ps 19:4
I was rejoicing in His **i** world, Pr 8:31
It will never be **i** or lived in Is 13:20
She will be **i**, and to the cities Is 44:26
⌊but⌋ formed it to be **i**— Is 45:18
This city will be **i** forever. Jr 17:25
it will be **i** again as in ancient Jr 46:26
LORD's wrath, she will not be **i**; Jr 50:13
never again be **i** or lived in Jr 50:39
The **i** cities will be destroyed, Ezk 12:20
no longer be **i** or display ⌊your Ezk 26:20
and in all the **i** places of the Ezk 34:13
your cities will not be **i**. Ezk 35:9
cities will be **i** and the ruins Ezk 36:10
I will make you **i** as you once Ezk 36:11
I will cause the cities to be **i**, Ezk 36:33
are ⌊now⌋ fortified and **i**. Ezk 36:35
against ruins now **i** and against Ezk 38:12
But Judah will be **i** forever, Jl 3:20
Jerusalem will be **i** without Zch 2:4
when Jerusalem was **i** and secure, Zch 7:7
the Judean foothills were **i**?" Zch 7:7
continues to be **i** on its site, Zch 12:6
to the ends of the **i** world. Rm 10:18

INHERIT *(43)*

they will **i** ⌊it⌋ forever.' " Ex 32:13
You will **i** their land, since I Lv 20:24
sons after you to **i** as property; Lv 25:46
and his descendants will **i** it. Nm 14:24
he will enable Israel to **i** it. Dt 1:38
enable them to **i** this land that Dt 3:28
possess the land you are to **i**, Dt 11:8
your God is giving you to **i**, Dt 12:10
your God is giving you to **i**.' " Jos 1:11
have been made to **i** months of Jb 7:3
me and make me **i** the iniquities Jb 13:26
his descendants will **i** the land. Ps 25:13
in the LORD will **i** the land. Ps 37:9
the humble will **i** the land and Ps 37:11
blessed by Him will **i** the land, Ps 37:22
righteous will **i** the land and Ps 37:29
He will exalt you to **i** the land. Ps 37:34
of His servants will **i** it, Ps 69:36
The wise will **i** honor, but He Pr 3:35
his household will **i** the wind, Pr 11:29
The gullible **i** foolishness, Pr 14:18
blameless will **i** what is good. Pr 28:10
refuge in Me will **i** the land and Is 57:13
have given your ancestors to **i**." Jr 3:18
You will **i** it in equal portions, Ezk 47:14
because they will **i** the earth. Mt 5:5
more and will **i** eternal life. Mt 19:29
i the kingdom prepared for you Mt 25:34
must I do to **i** eternal life?" Mk 10:17
must I do to **i** eternal life?" Lk 10:25
must I do to **i** eternal life?" Lk 18:18
that he would **i** the world was Rm 4:13
unjust will not **i** God's kingdom? 1Co 6:9
swindlers will **i** God's kingdom. 1Co 6:10
and blood cannot **i** the kingdom 1Co 15:50
cannot **i** incorruption. 1Co 15:50
slave will never **i** with the son Gl 4:30
things will not **i** the kingdom of Gl 5:21
who are going to **i** salvation? Heb 1:14
of those who **i** the promises Heb 6:12
he wanted to **i** the blessing, Heb 12:17
so that you can **i** a blessing. 1Pt 3:9
The victor will **i** these things, Rv 21:7

INHERITANCE *(231)*

any portion or **i** in our father's Gn 31:14
brothers with regard to their **i**. Gn 48:6
honey or give us an **i** of fields Nm 16:14
not have an **i** in their land; Nm 18:20
portion and your **i** among the Nm 18:20
in Israel as an **i** in return for Nm 18:21
will not receive an **i** among the Nm 18:23
as a contribution for ⌊their⌋ **i**. Nm 18:24
not receive an **i** among the Nm 18:24
that I have given you as your **i**, Nm 18:26
among them as an **i** based on the Nm 26:53
Increase the **i** for a large Nm 26:54
to be given its **i** according to Nm 26:54
will receive an **i** according to Nm 26:55
Each **i** will be divided by lot Nm 26:56
because no **i** was given to them Nm 26:62
their father's **i** to them. Nm 27:7
transfer his **i** to his daughter. Nm 27:8
give his **i** to his brothers. Nm 27:9
give his **i** to his father's Nm 27:10
give his **i** to the nearest Nm 27:11
has taken possession of his **i**. Nm 32:18
not have an **i** with them across Nm 32:19
because our **i** will be across the Nm 32:19
land as an **i** by lot according Nm 33:54
Increase the **i** for a large clan Nm 33:54
will receive an **i** according to Nm 33:54
to you as an **i** with these Nm 34:2
are to receive by lot as an **i**, Nm 34:13
received ⌊their **i**⌋ according to Nm 34:14
of Manasseh has received its **i**. Nm 34:14
received their **i** across the Nm 34:15
the land as an **i** for you: Nm 34:17
distribute the **i** to the Nm 34:29
to the **i** it receives." Nm 35:8
give the land as an **i** by lot to Nm 36:2
Zelophehad's **i** to his daughters. Nm 36:2
their **i** will be taken away from Nm 36:3
our fathers' **i** and added to that Nm 36:3
of our allotted **i** would be taken Nm 36:3
their **i** will be added to that of Nm 36:4
and their **i** will be taken away Nm 36:4
away from the **i** of our ancestral Nm 36:4
An **i** belonging to the Israelites Nm 36:7
to retain the **i** of his ancestral Nm 36:7
who possesses an **i** from an Nm 36:8
possess the **i** of his fathers. Nm 36:8
No **i** is to transfer from one Nm 36:9
tribes is to retain its **i**." Nm 36:9
and their **i** remained within the Nm 36:12
to be a people for His **i**, Dt 4:20
your God is giving you as an **i**. Dt 4:21
and give you their land as an **i**, Dt 4:38
Your people, Your **i**, whom You Dt 9:26
people, Your **i**, whom You brought Dt 9:29
a portion or **i** like his brothers Dt 10:9
the LORD is his **i**, as the LORD Dt 10:9
place and the **i** the LORD your Dt 12:9
has no portion or **i** among you. Dt 12:12
has no portion or **i** among you. Dt 14:27
has no portion or **i** among you, Dt 14:29
giving you to possess as an **i**— Dt 15:4
no portion or **i** with Israel. Dt 18:1
that is their **i**. Dt 18:1
Levi has no **i** among his brothers Dt 18:2
LORD is his **i**, as He promised Dt 18:2
you as an **i** into three regions Dt 19:3
your God is giving you as an **i**. Dt 19:10
start in the **i** you will receive Dt 19:14
your God is giving you as an **i**. Dt 20:16
what he has to his sons as an **i**, Dt 21:16
your God is giving you as an **i**. Dt 21:23
your God is giving you as an **i**. Dt 24:4
giving you to possess as an **i**, Dt 25:19
your God is giving you as an **i**, Dt 26:1
gave it as an **i** to the Dt 29:8
the nations their **i** and divided Dt 32:8
is His people, Jacob, His own **i**. Dt 32:9
fathers to give them as an **i**. Jos 1:6
the land of your **i** and take Jos 1:15
then gave it as an **i** to Israel Jos 11:23
their land as an **i** to the Jos 12:6
their land as an **i** to the tribes Jos 12:7
the land as an **i** for Israel, Jos 13:6
this land as an **i** to the nine Jos 13:7
received the **i** Moses gave them Jos 13:8
did not give any **i** to the tribe Jos 13:14
This was its **i**, just as He had Jos 13:14
This was the **i** of the Reubenites Jos 13:23
This was the **i** of the Gadites by Jos 13:28
was their **i**, just as He had Jos 13:33
Their **i** was by lot as the LORD Jos 14:2
Moses had given the **i** to the two Jos 14:3
But he gave no **i** among them to Jos 14:3
foot will be an **i** for you and Jos 14:9
and gave him Hebron as an **i**. Jos 14:13
Kenizzite as an **i** to this day, Jos 14:14
This was the **i** of the tribe of Jos 15:20
of Joseph, received their **i**. Jos 16:4
The border of their **i** went from Jos 16:5
This was the **i** of the tribe of Jos 16:8
within the **i** of the descendants Jos 16:9
to give us an **i** among our male Jos 17:4
they gave them an **i** among their Jos 17:4
received an **i** among his sons. Jos 17:6
one tribal allotment as an **i**? Jos 17:14
who had not divided up their **i**. Jos 18:2
it for the purpose of their **i**, Jos 18:4
their **i** is the priesthood Jos 18:7
have taken their **i** beyond the Jos 18:7
This was the **i** of Benjamin's Jos 18:20
This was the **i** for Benjamin's Jos 18:28
but their **i** was within the Jos 19:1
Their **i** included: Jos 19:2
This was the **i** of the tribe of Jos 19:8
i of Simeon's descendants was Jos 19:9
received an **i** within Judah's Jos 19:9
of their **i** stretched as far Jos 19:10
This was the **i** of Zebulun's Jos 19:16
This was the **i** of the tribe of Jos 19:23
This was the **i** of the tribe of Jos 19:31
This was the **i** of the tribe of Jos 19:39
of their **i** included Zorah, Jos 19:41
This was the **i** of the Danite Jos 19:48
son of Nun an **i** among them. Jos 19:49
their pasturelands from their **i**. Jos 21:3
to you as an **i** for your tribes, Jos 23:4
people away, each to his own **i**. Jos 24:28
It was an **i** for Joseph's Jos 24:32
of the land, each to his own **i**. Jdg 2:6
him in the territory of his **i**, Jdg 2:9
will have no **i** in our father's Jdg 11:2
They went back to their own **i**, Jdg 21:23
from there to his own **i**. Jdg 21:24
or I will ruin my ⌊own⌋ **i**. Ru 4:6
anointed you ruler over His **i**? 1Sm 10:1
sharing in the **i** of the LORD 1Sm 26:19
me and my son from God's **i**. 2Sm 14:16
in David, no **i** in Jesse's son. 2Sm 20:1
would you devour the LORD's **i**? 2Sm 20:19
a blessing on the LORD's **i**?" 2Sm 21:3
You gave Your people for an **i**. 1Kg 8:36
they are Your people and Your **i**; 1Kg 8:51
them apart as Your **i** from all 1Kg 8:53
have no **i** in the son of Jesse. 1Kg 12:16
give my fathers' **i** to you." 1Kg 21:3
not give you my fathers' **i**." 1Kg 21:4
remnant of My **i** and hand them 2Kg 21:14
and leave it as an **i** to your 1Ch 28:8
You gave Your people for an **i**. 2Ch 6:27
have no **i** in the son of Jesse. 2Ch 10:16
that You gave us as an **i**. 2Ch 20:11
leave ⌊it⌋ as an **i** to your sons Ezr 9:12
the **i** God ordained for him. Jb 20:29
the **i** the ruthless receive from Jb 27:13
or ⌊what⌋ **i** from the Almighty on Jb 31:2
granted them an **i** with their Jb 42:15
the nations Your **i** and the ends Ps 2:8
indeed, I have a beautiful **i**. Ps 16:6
and their **i** will last forever. Ps 37:18
chooses for us our **i**—the pride Ps 47:4

You revived Your **i** when it Ps 68:9
apportioned their **i** by lot and Ps 78:55
Jacob—over Israel, His **i**. Ps 78:71
the nations have invaded Your **i**, Ps 79:1
and He abhorred His own **i**. Ps 106:40
them the **i** of the nations. Ps 111:6
He gave their land as an **i**, Ps 135:12
an **i** to His people Israel. Ps 135:12
and gave their land as an **i**, Ps 136:21
an **i** to Israel His servant. Ps 136:22
wealth as an **i** to those who love Pr 8:21
good man leaves an **i** to his Pr 13:22
and share an **i** among brothers. Pr 17:2
An **i** gained prematurely will not Pr 20:21
Wisdom is as good as an **i**, Ec 7:11
My handiwork, and Israel My **i**." Is 19:25
you made My **i** detestable. Jr 2:7
most beautiful **i** of all the Jr 3:19
Israel is the tribe of His **i**; Jr 10:16
I have deserted My **i**. Jr 12:7
My **i** has acted toward Me like a Jr 12:8
Is My **i** like a hyena to Me? Jr 12:9
who attack the **i** that I Jr 12:14
one to his **i** and to his land Jr 12:15
They have filled My **i** with the Jr 16:18
your **i** that I gave you Jr 17:4
the right of **i** and redemption. Jr 32:8
who plundered My **i**—because you Jr 50:11
⌊Israel is⌋ the tribe of His **i**; Jr 51:19
Our **i** has been turned over to Lm 5:2
rejoiced over the **i** of the house Ezk 35:15
you, and you will be their **i**. Ezk 36:12
This will be their **i**: Ezk 44:28
I am their **i**. You are to give Ezk 44:28
divide the land by lot as an **i**, Ezk 45:1
to each of his sons as their **i**, Ezk 46:16
will become their property by **i**. Ezk 46:16
a gift from his **i** to one of his Ezk 46:17
His **i** belongs only to his sons; Ezk 46:17
not take any of the people's **i**, Ezk 46:18
is to provide an **i** for his sons Ezk 46:18
the land as an **i** for the 12 Ezk 47:13
land will fall to you as an **i**. Ezk 47:14
allot it as an **i** for yourselves Ezk 47:22
allotted an **i** among the tribes Ezk 47:22
you will assign his **i** there." Ezk 47:23
to allot as an **i** to Israel's Ezk 48:29
do not make Your **i** a disgrace, Jl 2:17
of My people, My **i** Israel. Jl 3:2
of his home, a person of his **i**. Mc 2:2
for the remnant of His **i**? Mc 7:18
people all these things as an **i**. Zch 8:12
and ⌊gave⌋ his **i** to the desert Mal 1:3
let's kill him and take his **i**!' Mt 21:38
him, and the **i** will be ours!' Mk 12:7
to divide the **i** with me." Lk 12:13
him, so the **i** will be ours!' Lk 20:14
He didn't give him an **i** in it, Ac 7:5
gave their land to them as an **i**. Ac 13:19
to give you an **i** among all who Ac 20:32
For if the **i** is from the law, Gl 3:18
In Him we were also made His **i**, Eph 1:11
He is the down payment of our **i**, Eph 1:14
of His **i** among the saints, Eph 1:18
has an **i** in the kingdom of the Eph 5:5
in the saints' **i** in the light. Col 1:12
reward of an **i** from the Lord— Col 3:24
the promise of the eternal **i**, Heb 9:15
he was going to receive as an **i**; Heb 11:8
and into an **i** that is 1Pt 1:4

INHERITANCES *(1)*
them possess the desolate **i**, Is 49:8

INHERITED *(10)*
not part of his **i** landholding, Lv 27:22
animal, or his **i** landholding, Lv 27:28
to you as your **i** portion." 1Ch 16:18
each on his own **i** property. Neh 11:20
to you as your **i** portion." Ps 105:11
they **i** what other peoples had Ps 105:44
and wealth are **i** from fathers, Pr 19:14
say, "Our fathers **i** only lies, Jr 16:19
as the name He **i** is superior to Heb 1:4
way of life **i** from the fathers 1Pt 1:18

INIQUITIES *(22)*
because our **i** are higher than Ezr 9:6
Because of our **i** we have been Ezr 9:7
How many **i** and sins have I Jb 13:23
me inherit the **i** of my youth. Jb 13:26
and aren't your **i** endless? Jb 22:5
I overwhelm me; only You can Ps 65:3
A wicked man's **i** entrap him; Pr 5:22
you have wearied Me with your **i**. Is 43:24
sold for your **i**, and your mother Is 50:1
crushed because of our **i**; Is 53:5
and He will carry their **i**. Is 53:11
But your **i** have built barriers Is 59:2
are with us, and we know our **i**: Is 59:12
and our **i** carry us away like the Is 64:6
⌊for⌋ your **i** and the iniquities Is 65:7
and the **i** of your fathers Is 65:7
of your **i** in your dishonest Ezk 28:18
for your **i** and abominations. Ezk 36:31
I cleanse you from all your **i**, Ezk 36:33
they may be ashamed of their **i**. Ezk 43:10
will punish you for all your **i**. Am 3:2
He will vanquish our **i**. Mc 7:19

INIQUITY *(64)*
the **i** of the Amorites has not Gn 15:16
has exposed your servants' **i**. Gn 44:16
because of the **i** he knows about: 1Sm 3:13
The **i** of Eli's family will never 1Sm 3:14
If He sees **i**, will He not take Jb 11:11
if there is **i** in your hand, Jb 11:14
and You would cover over my **i**. Jb 14:17
Your **i** teaches you what to say, Jb 15:5
The heavens will expose his **i**, Jb 20:27
and insists they repent from **i**. Jb 36:10
that you do not turn to **i**, Jb 36:21
to You and did not conceal my **i**. Ps 32:5
The **i** of my foes surrounds me. Ps 49:5
and a wicked mouth swallows **i**. Pr 19:28
terror to those who practice **i**. Pr 21:15
people weighed down with **i**, Is 1:4
cannot stand **i** with a festival. Is 1:13
their ⌊own⌋ **i**, on the wicked. Is 13:11
because of the **i** of their Is 14:21
of the earth for their **i**. Is 26:21
Jacob's **i** will be purged Is 27:9
this **i** of yours will be like a Is 30:13
and his mind plots **i**. Is 32:6
will be forgiven ⌊their⌋ **i**. Is 33:24
over, her **i** has been pardoned, Is 40:2
Him for the **i** of us all. Is 53:6
blood, and your fingers with **i**; Is 59:3
trouble and give birth to **i**. Is 59:4
made us melt because of our **i**. Is 64:7
or remember ⌊our⌋ **i** forever. Is 64:9
But He will punish your **i**, Lm 4:22
person will die for his **i**. Ezk 3:18
will die for his **i**, but you will Ezk 3:19
righteousness and practices **i**, Ezk 3:20
and place the **i** of the house Ezk 4:4
will bear their **i** for the number Ezk 4:4
the years of their **i** according Ezk 4:5
you will bear the **i** of the house Ezk 4:5
and bear the **i** of the house of Ezk 4:6
waste away because of their **i**. Ezk 4:17
his life because of his **i**. Ezk 7:13
moaning, each over his own **i**. Ezk 7:16
that brought about their **i**. Ezk 7:19
The **i** of the house of Israel and Ezk 9:9
this was the **i** of your sister Ezk 16:49
will not die for his father's **i**. Ezk 18:17
die for his own **i** because he Ezk 18:18
punishment for the father's **i**? Ezk 18:19
punishment for the father's **i**, Ezk 18:20
punishment for the son's **i**. Ezk 18:20
righteousness and practices **i**, Ezk 18:24
righteousness and practices **i**, Ezk 18:26
because of the **i** he has Ezk 18:26
taken away because of their **i**, Ezk 33:6
person will die for his **i**, Ezk 33:8
will die for his **i**, but you will Ezk 33:9
his righteousness and commits **i**, Ezk 33:13
because of the **i** he has Ezk 33:13
of life without practicing **i**— Ezk 33:15
his righteousness and commits **i**, Ezk 33:18
exile on account of their **i**, Ezk 39:23
removing **i** and passing over Mc 7:18
This is their **i** in all the land. Zch 5:6
by bitterness and bound by **i**." Ac 8:23

INJURE *(1)*
to lift it will **i** themselves Zch 12:3

INJURED *(8)*
and the **i** man does not die but Ex 21:18
but it dies, is **i**, or is stolen, Ex 22:10
and it is **i** or dies while its Ex 22:14
that is blind, **i**, maimed, or has Lv 22:22
upper room in Samaria and was **i**. 2Kg 1:2
bandaged the **i**, brought back Ezk 34:4
bandage the **i**, and strengthen Ezk 34:16
the scattered, those I have **i**. Mc 4:6

INJURES *(1)*
When a man's ox **i** his neighbor's Ex 21:35

INJURIES *(1)*
His people's **i** and heals the Is 30:26

INJURY *(10)*
but there is no **i**, the one who Ex 21:22
If there is an **i**, then you must Ex 21:23
a permanent **i** on his neighbor, Lv 24:19
Whatever **i** he inflicted on the Lv 24:20
if I will recover from this **i**." 2Kg 1:2
a high threshold invites **i**. Pr 17:19
LORD says: Your **i** is incurable; Jr 30:12
Why do you cry out about your **i**? Jr 30:15
There is no remedy for your **i**; Nah 3:19
and they inflict **i** with them. Rv 9:19

INJUSTICE *(26)*
for there is no **i** or partiality 2Ch 19:7
those who plow **i** and those who Jb 4:8
hope, and **i** shuts its mouth. Jb 5:16
and don't allow **i** to dwell in Jb 11:14
who drinks **i** like water? Jb 15:16
If you banish **i** from your tent Jb 22:23
So **i** is broken like a tree. Jb 24:20
if there is **i** on my hands, Ps 7:3
you practice **i** in your hearts; Ps 58:2
and all **i** shuts its mouth. Ps 107:42
will not apply their hands to **i**. Ps 125:3
than great income with **i**. Pr 16:8
The one who sows **i** will reap Pr 22:8
He looked for justice but saw **i**, Is 5:7
spoken lies, and you mutter **i**. Is 59:3
I hate robbery and **i**; Is 61:8
his upper rooms through **i**, Jr 22:13
by turning from our **i** and paying Dn 9:13
to sin, to wipe away **i**, to bring Dn 9:24
plowed wickedness and reaped **i**; Hs 10:13
bloodshed and Jerusalem with **i**. Mc 3:10
do You force me to look at **i**? Hab 1:3
and founds a town with **i**! Hab 2:12
"he covers his garment with **i**," Mal 2:16
Is there **i** with God? Rm 9:14
Why not rather put up with **i**? 1Co 6:7

INJUSTICES *(2)*
and from your **i** by showing mercy Dn 4:27
sins and the **i** of our fathers, Dn 9:16

INK *(4)*
was writing on the scroll in **i**." Jr 36:18
not written with **i** but with the 2Co 3:3
want to do so with paper and **i**. 2Jn 12
to write to you with pen and **i**. 3Jn 13

INLAID *(4)*
Its interior is **i** with love by Sg 3:10
of Cyprus, ⌊**i**⌋ with ivory. Ezk 27:6
the houses ⌊**i** with⌋ ivory will Am 3:15
They lie on beds ⌊**i** with⌋ ivory, Am 6:4

INN *(2)*
was no room for them at the **i**. Lk 2:7
him to an **i**, and took care Lk 10:34

INNER *(70)*
He went into an **i** room to weep. Gn 43:30
well as its legs and **i** organs. Ex 12:9
is next to the **i** border of the Ex 28:26
is next to the **i** border of the Ex 39:19
they entered the **i** chamber of Jdg 9:46
against the **i** chamber and set it Jdg 9:49
lying inside the **i** circle of the 1Sm 26:5
asleep in the **i** circle of the 1Sm 26:7
sanctuary and the **i** sanctuary. 1Kg 6:5
the interior as an **i** sanctuary, 1Kg 6:16
He prepared the **i** sanctuary 1Kg 6:19
the front of the **i** sanctuary and 1Kg 6:21
that belongs in the **i** sanctuary. 1Kg 6:22
In the **i** sanctuary he made two 1Kg 6:23
cherubim inside the **i** temple. 1Kg 6:27
in both the **i** and outer 1Kg 6:29
gold in both the **i** and outer 1Kg 6:30
the entrance of the **i** sanctuary, 1Kg 6:31
He built the **i** courtyard with 1Kg 6:36
with saws on the **i** and outer 1Kg 7:9
well as the **i** courtyard of the 1Kg 7:12

in front of the **i** sanctuary, 1Kg 7:49
for the doors of the **i** temple 1Kg 7:50
into the **i** sanctuary of the 1Kg 8:6
in front of the **i** sanctuary, 1Kg 8:8
went into an **i** room in the city 1Kg 20:30
yourself in an **i** chamber on that 1Kg 22:25
and take him to an **i** room. 2Kg 9:2
and went into the **i** room of the 2Kg 10:25
gone out of the **i** courtyard when 2Kg 20:4
upper rooms, **i** rooms, and the 1Ch 28:11
he overlaid its **i** surface with 2Ch 3:4
chainwork in the **i** sanctuary and 2Ch 3:16
in front of the **i** sanctuary 2Ch 4:20
its **i** doors to the most holy 2Ch 4:22
into the **i** sanctuary of the 2Ch 5:7
in front of the **i** sanctuary, 2Ch 5:9
yourself in an **i** chamber on that 2Ch 18:24
the king in the **i** courtyard and Est 4:11
and stood in the **i** courtyard of Est 5:1
desire integrity in the **i** self, Ps 51:6
The **i** man and the heart are Ps 64:6
My **i** being yearns for him; Jr 31:20
entrance of the **i** gate that Ezk 8:3
brought me to the **i** court of the Ezk 8:16
the cloud filled the **i** court. Ezk 10:3
The ⌊**i**⌋ threshold of the gate on Ezk 40:7
exterior front of the **i** court; Ezk 40:19
i court had a gate facing the Ezk 40:23
The **i** court had a gate on the Ezk 40:27
me to the **i** court through Ezk 40:28
me to the **i** court on the east Ezk 40:32
Outside the **i** gate, within the Ezk 40:44
gate, within the **i** court, there Ezk 40:44
and as far as the **i** temple and Ezk 41:17
belonging to the **i** court and Ezk 42:3
and brought me to the **i** court, Ezk 43:5
gates of the **i** court they must Ezk 44:17
gates of the **i** court and within Ezk 44:17
before he enters the **i** court. Ezk 44:21
into the **i** court to minister in Ezk 44:27
of the gate to the **i** court. Ezk 45:19
The gate of the **i** court that Ezk 46:1
to someone in the **i** recesses of Am 6:10
'Look, he's in the **i** rooms!' Mt 24:26
put them into the **i** prison and Ac 16:24
in my **i** self I joyfully agree Rm 7:22
i person is being renewed day 2Co 4:16
through His Spirit in the **i** man, Eph 3:16
that enters the **i** sanctuary Heb 6:19

INNERMOST *(8)*

and my **i** being was wounded Ps 73:21
that goes down to one's **i** being. Pr 18:8
the LORD, searching the **i** parts. Pr 20:27
beatings cleanse the **i** parts. Pr 20:30
My **i** being will cheer when your Pr 23:16
that goes down to one's **i** being. Pr 26:22
⌊as does⌋ my **i** being for Is 16:11
my **i** being will weep in secret Jr 13:17

INNKEEPER *(1)*

them to the **i**, and said, 'Take Lk 10:35

INNOCENCE *(3)*

wash my hands in **i** and go around Ps 26:6
wash my hands in **i** for nothing? Ps 73:13
will they be incapable of **i**? Hs 8:5

INNOCENT *(53)*

a nation even though it is **i**? Gn 20:4
eaten, but the ox's owner is **i**. Ex 21:28
Do not kill the **i** and the just, Ex 23:7
In this way, **i** blood will not be Dt 19:10
the guilt of shedding **i** blood, Dt 19:13
of **i** blood against them. Dt 21:8
the guilt of shedding **i** blood, Dt 21:9
will clear the **i** and condemn Dt 25:1
a bribe to kill an **i** person.' Dt 27:25
his own head, and we will be **i**. Jos 2:19
you sin against **i** blood by 1Sm 19:5
are forever **i** before the LORD 2Sm 3:28
the king and his throne be **i**." 2Sm 14:9
to all the people, "You are **i**. 2Kg 10:9
also shed so much **i** blood that 2Kg 21:16
of all the **i** blood he had shed 2Kg 24:4
filled Jerusalem with **i** blood, 2Kg 24:4
who has perished when he was **i**? Jb 4:7
He mocks the despair of the **i**. Jb 9:23
and the **i** are roused against the Jb 17:8
the **i** mock them, ⌊saying⌋, Jb 22:19
and the **i** will divide up his Jb 27:17
he kills the **i** in secret places; Ps 10:8
or take a bribe against the **i**— Ps 15:5
Then I will be **i**, and cleansed Ps 19:13
from concealed places at the **i**. Ps 64:4
and condemn the **i** to death. Ps 94:21
They shed **i** blood—the blood of Ps 106:38
attack some **i** person just for Pr 1:11
tongue, hands that shed **i** blood, Pr 6:17
not good to fine an **i** person, Pr 17:26
the justice due the **i**. Pr 18:5
behavior of the **i** is upright. Pr 21:8
guilty, "You are **i**"—people Pr 24:24
and deprive the **i** of justice. Is 5:23
and they rush to shed **i** blood. Is 59:7
with the blood of the **i** poor. Jr 2:34
you claim: I am **i**. His anger is Jr 2:35
no longer shed **i** blood in this Jr 7:6
place with the blood of the **i**. Jr 19:4
shed **i** blood in this place. Jr 22:3
shedding **i** blood and committing Jr 22:17
you will bring **i** blood on Jr 26:15
for I was found **i** before Him. Dn 6:22
in whose land they shed **i** blood. Jl 3:19
don't charge us with **i** blood! Jnh 1:14
violate the Sabbath and are **i**? Mt 12:5
would not have condemned the **i**. Mt 12:7
sinned by betraying **i** blood," Mt 27:4
I am **i** of this man's blood. Mt 27:24
day that I am **i** of everyone's Ac 20:26
what is good, yet **i** about what Rm 16:19
holy, **i**, undefiled, separated Heb 7:26

INNOCENTLY *(1)*

been invited and were going **i**, 2Sm 15:11

INNUMERABLE *(7)*

camels were as **i** as the sand Jdg 7:12
and **i** cedar logs, because the 1Ch 22:4
enormous guilt and your **i** sins. Jr 30:14
enormous guilt and your **i** sins. Jr 30:15
Levites who minister to Me **i**." Jr 33:22
crimes are many and your sins **i**. Am 5:12
of heaven and as **i** as the grains Heb 11:12

INQUIRE *(27)*

So she went to **i** of the LORD. Gn 25:22
people come to me to **i** of God. Ex 18:15
Do not **i** about their gods, Dt 12:30
you are to **i**, investigate, and Dt 13:14
spirit, or **i** of the dead. Dt 18:11
Please **i** of God so we will know Jdg 18:5
was going to **i** of God would say 1Sm 9:9
sent someone to **i** about her, 2Sm 11:3
Go **i** of Baal-zebub, the god of 2Kg 1:2
are going to **i** of Baal-zebub, 2Kg 1:3
these men⌋ to **i** of Baal-zebub, 2Kg 1:6
messengers to **i** of Baal-zebub, 2Kg 1:16
Israel for you to **i** of His will? 2Kg 1:16
i of the LORD through him." 2Kg 3:11
I of the LORD through him, 2Kg 8:8
Go and **i** of the LORD for me, 2Kg 22:13
who sent you to **i** of the LORD: 2Kg 22:18
but he did not **i** of the LORD. 1Ch 10:14
we did not **i** of Him in Saul's 1Ch 13:3
for we didn't **i** of Him about the 1Ch 15:13
not go before it to **i** of God, 1Ch 21:30
were sent to him to **i** about the 2Ch 32:31
I of the LORD for me and for 2Ch 34:21
who sent you to **i** of the LORD: 2Ch 34:26
who is sending you to **i** of Me: Jr 37:7
comes to the prophet to **i** of Me, Ezk 14:7
not seek the LORD or **i** of Him. Zph 1:6

INQUIRED *(29)*

Moses **i** about the male goat of Lv 10:16
the Israelites **i** of the LORD, Jdg 1:1
went to Bethel, and **i** of God. Jdg 20:18
until evening, and **i** of Him: Jdg 20:23
the Israelites **i** of the LORD. Jdg 20:27
They again **i** of the LORD, 1Sm 10:22
Saul **i**, and they repeated to 1Sm 11:5
So Saul **i** of God, "Should I go 1Sm 14:37
Ahimelech **i** of the LORD for him 1Sm 22:10
a sword and **i** of God for him, 1Sm 22:13
first time I **i** of God for him? 1Sm 22:15
So David **i** of the LORD: 1Sm 23:2
Once again, David **i** of the LORD, 1Sm 23:4
i, "Where did you raid today? 1Sm 27:10
He **i** of the LORD, but the LORD 1Sm 28:6
David **i** of the young man who had 2Sm 1:13
time later, David **i** of the LORD: 2Sm 2:1
Then David **i** of the LORD: 2Sm 5:19
So David **i** of the LORD, and He 2Sm 5:23
years, so David **i** of the LORD. 2Sm 21:1
so David **i** of God, "Should I go 1Ch 14:10
So David again **i** of God, and God 1Ch 14:14
the assembly **i** of Him ⌊there⌋. 2Ch 1:5
The king **i**, "What honor and Est 6:3
Then he **i** of me, "Don't you know Zch 4:13
So I **i** of the angel who was Zch 6:4
by, he **i** what this meant. Lk 18:36
aside, and **i** privately, "What Ac 23:19
They **i** into what time or what 1Pt 1:11

INQUIRES *(1)*

the one who **i** will be the same Ezk 14:10

INQUIRING *(1)*

word of the LORD came to me **i**, Jr 1:13

INQUIRY *(1)*

more careful **i** about him. Ac 23:20

INSANE *(3)*

pretended to be **i** in their 1Sm 21:13
pretended to be **i** in the Ps 34:1
and the inspired man is **i**, Hs 9:7

INSCRIBE *(2)*

presence and **i** it on a scroll; Is 30:8
clearly **i** it on tablets so one Hab 2:2

INSCRIBED *(11)*

stone tablets **i** by the finger of Ex 31:18
They were **i** on both sides— Ex 32:15
both sides—**i** front and back. Ex 32:15
tablets, **i** by God's finger. Dt 9:10
or were **i** in stone forever by an Jb 19:24
I have **i** you on the palms of My Is 49:16
hand, and this writing was **i**. Dn 5:24
This is the writing that was **i**: Dn 5:25
found an altar on which was **i**: Ac 17:23
new name is **i** that no one knows Rv 2:17
gates⌋, names were **i**, the names Rv 21:12

INSCRIPTION *(14)*

wrote on it an **i** like the Ex 39:30
reads this **i** and gives me its Dn 5:7
could read the **i** or make known Dn 5:8
me to read this **i** and make its Dn 5:15
can read this **i** and give me its Dn 5:16
I will read the **i** for the king Dn 5:17
I will engrave an **i** on it"— Zch 3:9
"Whose image and **i** is this?" Mt 22:20
"Whose image and **i** is this?" Mk 12:16
The **i** of the charge written Mk 15:26
Whose image and **i** does it have?" Lk 20:24
An **i** was above Him: Lk 23:38
on the cross. The **i** was: JESUS Jn 19:19
stands firm, having this **i**: 2Tm 2:19

INSECT *(1)*

land of buzzing **i** wings beyond Is 18:1

INSECTS *(6)*

All winged **i** that walk on all Lv 11:20
all the winged **i** that walk on Lv 11:21
other⌋ winged **i** that have four Lv 11:23
winged **i** are unclean for you; Dt 14:19
Whirring **i** will take possession Dt 28:42
He spoke, and **i** came—gnats Ps 105:31

INSENSITIVE *(1)*

Their hearts are hard and **i**, Ps 119:70

INSERT *(5)*

I the poles into the rings on Ex 25:14
cloth on top, and **i** its poles. Nm 4:6
and **i** the poles ⌊in the table⌋. Nm 4:8
manatee skin, and **i** its poles. Nm 4:11
skin over it and **i** its poles. Nm 4:14

INSERTED *(5)*

are to be **i** into the rings, Ex 27:7
He **i** the poles into the rings on Ex 37:5
Then he **i** the poles into the Ex 38:7
its planks, **i** its crossbars, and Ex 40:18
would be **i** into the temple 1Kg 6:6

INSIDE *(82)*

(See pp. xi-xii.)

INSIDES *(2)*

And Eglon's **i** came out. Jdg 3:22
and all his **i** spilled out. Ac 1:18

INSIGHT *(16)*

very great **i**, and understanding 1Kg 4:29
LORD give you **i** and 1Ch 22:12
a wise son with **i** and 2Ch 2:12

a man of **i** from the descendants Ezr 8:18
his words are without **i**." Jb 34:35
His instructions have good **i**. Ps 111:10
I have more **i** than all my Ps 119:99
you call out to **i** and lift your Pr 2:3
A man is praised for his **i**, Pr 12:8
I is a fountain of life for its Pr 16:22
A person's **i** gives him patience, Pr 19:11
despise the **i** of your words. Pr 23:9
has the perception or **i** to say, Is 44:19
he was found to have **i**, Dn 5:11
that you have **i**, intelligence, Dn 5:14
to understand my **i** about the Eph 3:4

INSIGHTFUL *(3)*
son Zechariah, an **i** counselor, 1Ch 26:14
for understanding **i** sayings; Pr 1:2
and whoever is **i** recognize them. Hs 14:9

INSIGHTS *(1)*
listened to your **i** as you sought Jb 32:11

INSIGNIFICANT *(7)*
if they become **i**, he is unaware Jb 14:21
I am so **i**. How can I answer You? Jb 40:4
am **i** and despised, but I do not Ps 119:141
them, and they will not be **i**. Jr 30:19
make you **i** among the nations Jr 49:15
I will make you **i** among the Ob 2
the world's **i** and despised 1Co 1:28

INSINCERE *(1)*
their hearts were **i** toward Him, Ps 78:37

INSINCERELY *(1)*
many others will join them **i**. Dn 11:34

INSIST *(5)*
I **i** that you hand it over right 1Sm 2:16
I **i** on buying it from you for a 2Sm 24:24
I **i** on paying the full price, 1Ch 21:24
house called by My name and **i**: Jr 7:10
I want you to **i** on these things, Ti 3:8

INSISTED *(5)*
The overseers **i**, "Finish your Ex 5:13
Yet Edom **i**, "You must not travel Nm 20:20
Naaman **i**, "Please, accept 150 2Kg 5:23
fetters. You **i**: I will not serve Jr 2:20
contradicted the LORD and **i**, Jr 5:12

INSISTENTLY *(1)*
they begged us **i** for the 2Co 8:4

INSISTING *(6)*
But he kept **i**, "If I have to die Mk 14:31
another kept **i**, "This man was Lk 22:59
they kept **i**, "He stirs up the Lk 23:5
But she kept **i** that it was true. Ac 12:15
i on ascetic practices and the Col 2:18
are saying or what they are **i** 1Tm 1:7

INSISTS *(1)*
to correction and **i** they repent Jb 36:10

INSOLENCE *(2)*
and humiliate the **i** of tyrants. Is 13:11
indeed—his **i**, arrogance, pride Jr 48:29

INSOLENT *(1)*
of their sin, an **i** king, skilled Dn 8:23

INSPECT *(3)*
is not to **i** whether it is good Lv 27:33
be missing when you **i** your home. Jb 5:24
You **i** him every morning, and put Jb 7:18

INSPECTED *(3)*
Moses **i** all the work they had Ex 39:43
and I **i** the walls of Jerusalem Neh 2:13
of the valley and **i** the wall. Neh 2:15

INSPECTION *(2)*
opposite the **I** Gate, and as far Neh 3:31
After I made an **i**, I stood up Neh 4:14

INSPIRE *(1)*
perhaps you will **i** terror! Is 47:12

INSPIRED *(4)*
the terror their strength **i**. Ezk 32:30
a fool, and the **i** man is insane, Hs 9:7
that David, **i** by the Spirit, Mt 22:43
All Scripture is **i** by God and is 2Tm 3:16

INSTALL *(1)*
Then we can **i** Tabeel's son as Is 7:6

INSTALLED *(12)*
Moses also **i** the gold altar in Ex 40:26
and **i** one of his sons to be his Jdg 17:5
i his son Solomon as king over 1Ch 23:1
dedicated it and **i** its doors. Neh 3:1
it with beams and **i** its doors, Neh 3:3
it with beams and **i** its doors, Neh 3:6
They rebuilt it and **i** its doors, Neh 3:13
He rebuilt it and **i** its doors, Neh 3:14
Then he **i** its doors, bolts, and Neh 3:15
that time I had not **i** the doors Neh 6:1
rebuilt and I had the doors **i**, Neh 7:1
They have **i** kings, but not Hs 8:4

INSTANCE *(1)*
he incurs guilt in such an **i**. Lv 5:4

INSTANT *(4)*
Maker would remove me in an **i**. Jb 32:22
Then suddenly, in an **i**, Is 29:5
a nation be delivered in an **i**? Is 66:8
overthrown in an **i** without a Lm 4:6

INSTANTLY *(10)*
so I may consume them **i**. Nm 16:21
so that I may consume them **i**." Nm 16:45
be shattered **i**—beyond recovery Pr 6:15
I her flow of blood ceased, Mk 5:29
I her bleeding stopped. Lk 8:44
Him and how she was **i** cured. Lk 8:47
and **i** she was restored and began Lk 13:13
I he could see, and he began to Lk 18:43
I the man got well, picked up Jn 5:9
I she dropped dead at his feet. Ac 5:10

INSTEAD *(176)*
(See pp. xi-xii.)

INSTIGATED *(1)*
with the conspiracy that he **i**, 1Kg 16:20

INSTILL *(1)*
So I will **i** fear in that land. Ezk 30:13

INSTINCT *(2)*
creatures of **i** born to be caught 2Pt 2:12
they know by **i**, like unreasoning Jd 10

INSTINCTIVELY *(1)*
i do what the law demands, Rm 2:14

INSTITUTED *(2)*
those that exist are **i** by God. Rm 13:1
By faith he **i** the Passover and Heb 11:28

INSTITUTION *(1)*
to every human **i** because of the 1Pt 2:13

INSTRUCT *(20)*
I them about the statutes and Ex 18:20
You are to **i** all the skilled Ex 28:3
I the Israelites to bring you an Nm 19:2
earth and may **i** their children. Dt 4:10
His voice from heaven to **i** you. Dt 4:36
to do exactly as they **i** you. Dt 17:10
Levitical priests **i** you to do. Dt 24:8
sent Your good Spirit to **i** them. Neh 9:20
and **i** her to approach the king, Est 4:8
animals, and they will **i** you; Jb 12:7
to the earth, and it will **i** you; Jb 12:8
will **i** you and show you the way Ps 32:8
I a wise man, and he will be Pr 9:9
Who is he trying to **i**? Is 28:9
and **i** Me about the work of My Is 45:11
and able to **i** one another. Rm 15:14
Lord's mind, that he may **i** Him? 1Co 2:16
I those who are rich in the 1Tm 6:17
⌊**I** them⌋ to do good, to be rich 1Tm 6:18
are able to **i** you for salvation 2Tm 3:15

INSTRUCTED *(46)*
The LORD **i** Moses, "When you go Ex 4:21
The LORD **i** Moses: Nm 5:1
did as the LORD **i** Moses. Nm 5:4
The LORD **i** Moses: Nm 6:1
The LORD **i** Moses: Nm 15:1
The LORD **i** Moses: Nm 15:17
The LORD **i** Moses: Nm 17:1
The LORD **i** Moses, Nm 18:25
your God has **i** ⌊me⌋ to teach you Dt 6:1
Israelites, as Moses had **i** them. Jos 4:12
of refuge, as I **i** you through Jos 20:2
her mother-in-law had **i** her. Ru 3:6
and set out as Jesse had **i** him. 1Sm 17:20
Then the king **i** Zadok, "Return 2Sm 15:25
to die, he **i** his son Solomon 1Kg 2:1
Then the old prophet **i** his sons, 1Kg 13:27
who went to call Micaiah **i** him, 1Kg 22:13
time Jehoiada the priest **i** him, 2Kg 12:2
Then the LORD **i** Gad, David's 1Ch 21:9
son Solomon and **i** him to build 1Ch 22:6
who went to call Micaiah **i** him, 2Ch 18:12
as King David of Israel had **i**. Ezr 3:10
Then I **i** the Levites to purify Neh 13:22
You have **i** many and have Jb 4:3
for You Yourself have **i** me. Ps 119:102
For gaining wisdom and being **i**; Pr 1:2
I have **i** you today—even you— Pr 22:19
those who are **i** to know how to Is 50:4
to listen like those being **i**. Is 50:4
i by worthless idols ⌊made of⌋ Jr 10:8
as the LORD **i** me and put it Jr 13:2
is good, you who are **i** in evil. Jr 13:23
After I was **i**, I struck my thigh Jr 31:19
I **i** Baruch in their sight, Jr 32:13
of Scripture **i** in the kingdom Mt 13:52
money and did as they were **i**. Mt 28:15
i them to take nothing for the Mk 6:8
Then He **i** them to have all the Mk 6:39
about which you have been **i**. Lk 1:4
He **i** them to tell no one what Lk 8:56
warned and **i** them to tell this Lk 9:21
This man had been **i** in the way Ac 18:25
released him and **i** the chief Ac 22:30
the young man and **i** him, Ac 23:22
superior, being **i** from the law, Rm 2:18
do the same as I **i** the Galatian 1Co 16:1

INSTRUCTING *(7)*
Jacob had finished **i** his sons, Gn 49:33
David sent 10 young men **i** them, 1Sm 25:5
So he sent messengers **i** them: 2Kg 1:2
who were **i** the people said Neh 8:9
at will and **i** his elders. Ps 105:22
i his opponents with gentleness. 2Tm 2:25
i us to deny godlessness and Ti 2:12

INSTRUCTION *(99)*
I have written for their **i**." Ex 24:12
You must keep My **i** to not do any Lv 18:30
must keep My **i**, or they will be Lv 22:9
Follow the whole **i** the LORD your Dt 5:33
must abide by the **i** they give Dt 17:11
a copy of this **i** for himself Dt 17:18
observe all the words of this **i**, Dt 17:19
Moses gave us **i**, a possession Dt 33:4
to Jacob and Your **i** to Israel; Dt 33:10
the whole **i** My servant Moses Jos 1:7
This book of **i** must not depart Jos 1:8
based on the LORD's **i** to Joshua: Jos 15:13
in keeping with the LORD's **i**. Jos 17:4
the command and **i** that Moses Jos 22:5
Judah about the **i** in this book 2Kg 22:13
carry out the **i** and the command 2Ch 14:4
book of the LORD's **i** with them. 2Ch 17:9
the written **i** of David king of 2Ch 35:4
Receive **i** from His mouth, and Jb 22:22
his delight is in the LORD's **i**, Ps 1:2
receive **i**, you judges of the Ps 2:10
The **i** of the LORD is perfect, Ps 19:7
i of his God is in his heart; Ps 37:31
Your **i** resides within me." Ps 40:8
a song of **i**, for God is King Ps 47:7
You hate **i** and turn your back on Ps 50:17
My people, hear my **i**; Ps 78:1
forsake My **i** and do not live Ps 89:30
and graciously give me Your **i**. Ps 119:29
Help me understand Your **i**, Ps 119:34
I do not turn away from Your **i**. Ps 119:51
of the wicked who reject Your **i**. Ps 119:53
but I delight in Your **i**. Ps 119:70
I from Your lips is better for Ps 119:72
live, for Your **i** is my delight. Ps 119:77
they violate Your **i**. Ps 119:85
If Your **i** had not been my Ps 119:92
yet I do not forget Your **i**. Ps 119:109
but I love Your **i**. Ps 119:113
people do not follow Your **i**. Ps 119:136
and Your **i** is true. Ps 119:142
they are far from Your **i**. Ps 119:150
for I have not forgotten Your **i**. Ps 119:153
falsehood, ⌊but⌋ I love Your **i**. Ps 119:163
to those who love Your **i**; Ps 119:165
LORD, and Your **i** is my delight. Ps 119:174
receiving wise **i** ⌊in⌋ Pr 1:3
fools despise wisdom and **i**. Pr 1:7
to your father's **i**, and don't Pr 1:8
Do not despise the LORD's **i**, Pr 3:11
for I am giving you good **i**. Pr 4:2
on to **i**; don't let go. Guard Pr 4:13
will die because there is no **i**, Pr 5:23

Accept my **i** instead of silver, Pr 8:10
Listen to **i** and be wise; Pr 8:33
one who follows **i** is on the path Pr 10:17
Whoever loves **i** loves knowledge, Pr 12:1
wise son ⌊hears his⌋ father's **i**, Pr 13:1
has contempt for **i** will pay the Pr 13:13
A wise man's **i** is a fountain of Pr 13:14
come to⌋ those who ignore **i**, Pr 13:18
A fool despises his father's **i**, Pr 15:5
who ignores **i** despises himself, Pr 15:32
fear of the LORD is wisdom's **i**, Pr 15:33
but folly is the **i** of fools. Pr 16:22
and receive **i** so that you may be Pr 19:20
If you stop listening to **i**, Pr 19:27
Apply yourself to **i** and listen Pr 23:12
truth, wisdom, **i**, and Pr 23:23
I looked, and received **i**: Pr 24:32
and loving **i** is on her tongue. Pr 31:26
Listen to the **i** of our God, Is 1:10
For **i** will go out of Zion and Is 2:3
have rejected the **i** of the LORD Is 5:24
up the **i** among my disciples. Is 8:16
those who grumble will accept **i**. Is 29:24
who do not obey the LORD's **i**. Is 30:9
islands will wait for His **i**." Is 42:4
to magnify ⌊His⌋ **i** and make it Is 42:21
they would not listen to His **i**. Is 42:24
for **i** will come from Me, and My Is 51:4
people in whose heart is My **i**: Is 51:7
among the nations, **i** is no more, Lm 2:9
but **i** will perish from the Ezk 7:26
suitable for **i** in all wisdom, Dn 1:4
For **i** will go out of Zion and Mc 4:2
they do violence to **i**. Zph 3:4
True **i** was in his mouth, and Mal 2:6
should seek **i** from his mouth, Mal 2:7
many to stumble by your **i**. Mal 2:8
showing partiality in ⌊your⌋ **i**." Mal 2:9
Remember the **i** of Moses My Mal 4:4
When Jesus had finished this **i**, Mt 19:1
before was written for our **i**, Rm 15:4
the following **i** I do not praise 1Co 11:17
the training and **i** of the Lord. Eph 6:4
not obey our **i** in this letter, 2Th 3:14
the goal of our **i** is love from a 1Tm 1:5
giving you this **i** in keeping 1Tm 1:18

INSTRUCTIONS *(23)*
My statutes, and My **i**." Gn 26:5
or not they will follow My **i**. Ex 16:4
to keep My commands and **i**? Ex 16:28
These ⌊**i**⌋ will be a statutory Nm 35:29
and has not carried out My **i**." 1Sm 15:11
have carried out the LORD's **i**." 1Sm 15:13
to all ⌊the **i**⌋ King Ahaz sent 2Kg 16:11
receive written **i** about this Ezr 5:5
reliable **i**, and good decrees Neh 9:13
of all the **i** in this letter as Est 9:26
the written **i** and according to Est 9:27
who remember to observe His **i**. Ps 103:18
all His **i** are trustworthy. Ps 111:7
who follow His **i** have good Ps 111:10
and corrective **i** are the way to Pr 6:23
by following His **i** that He set Dn 9:10
walk in My ways and keep My **i**, Zch 3:7
these 12 after giving them **i**: Mt 10:5
and after receiving **i** for Silas Ac 17:15
these were his **i**, since he Ac 20:13
I will give **i** about the other 1Co 11:34
whom you have received **i**: Col 4:10
Israel and gave **i** concerning his Heb 11:22

INSTRUCTOR *(1)*
an **i** of the ignorant, a teacher Rm 2:20

INSTRUCTORS *(1)*
you can have 10,000 **i** in Christ, 1Co 4:15

INSTRUCTS *(6)*
to the LORD our God as He **i** us." Ex 8:27
He **i** them by means of their Jb 36:15
at night my conscience **i** me. Ps 16:7
The One who **i** nations, the One Ps 94:10
A wise heart **i** its mouth and Pr 16:23
God teaches him order; He **i** him. Is 28:26

INSTRUMENT *(3)*
and plays skillfully on an **i**. Ezk 33:32
is My chosen **i** to carry My name Ac 9:15
will be a special **i**, set apart, 2Tm 2:21

INSTRUMENTS *(15)*
and with three-stringed **i**. 1Sm 18:6
all ⌊kinds of⌋ fir wood ⌊**i**⌋, 2Sm 6:5
joy accompanied by musical **i**— 1Ch 15:16
to play and musical **i** of God. 1Ch 16:42
LORD with the **i** that I have made 1Ch 23:5
and musical **i**, in praise to 2Ch 5:13
with the musical **i** of the LORD, 2Ch 7:6
with musical **i** were leading 2Ch 23:13
stood with the **i** of David, 2Ch 29:26
by the **i** of David king 2Ch 29:27
LORD day after day with loud **i**. 2Ch 30:21
were all skilled on musical **i**. 2Ch 34:12
with the musical **i** of David, Neh 12:36
play stringed **i** all the days Is 38:20
their own musical **i** like David. Am 6:5

INSUBORDINATE *(1)*
been more **i** than the nations Ezk 5:7

INSULT *(13)*
had not feared **i** from the enemy Dt 32:27
of those who **i** You have fallen Ps 69:9
Will the enemy **i** Your name Ps 74:10
i and contempt away from me, Ps 119:22
ignores an **i** is sensible. Pr 12:16
of cursing and **i** among all the Jr 44:8
you when they **i** you and Mt 5:11
exclude you, **i** you, and slander Lk 6:22
say these things You **i** us too." Lk 11:45
of those who **i** You have fallen Rm 15:3
i and slander must be removed Eph 4:31
evil for evil or **i** for insult 1Pt 3:9
evil for evil or insult for **i** 1Pt 3:9

INSULTED *(4)*
exalted men, will my honor be **i**? Ps 4:2
foolish people has **i** Your name. Ps 74:18
and He will be mocked, **i**, spit Lk 18:32
and **i** the Spirit of grace? Heb 10:29

INSULTING *(1)*
what Paul was saying by **i** him. Ac 13:45

INSULTS *(24)*
against Nabal's **i** and restrained 1Sm 25:39
Make their **i** return on their own Neh 4:4
I have heard a rebuke that **i** me, Jb 20:3
it is not an enemy who **i** me— Ps 55:12
I have endured **i** because of You, Ps 69:7
the **i** of those who insult You Ps 69:9
and fasted, but it brought me **i**. Ps 69:10
You know the **i** I endure—my Ps 69:19
I have broken my heart, and I am Ps 69:20
Remember the **i** that fools bring Ps 74:22
the poor **i** their Maker, Pr 14:31
who mocks the poor **i** his Maker, Pr 17:5
ashamed because we have heard **i**. Jr 51:51
hear their **i**, all their plots Lm 3:61
endure the **i** of the nations. Ezk 34:29
endured the **i** of the nations. Ezk 36:6
you will endure their own **i**. Ezk 36:7
allow the **i** of the nations Ezk 36:15
of Moab and the **i** of the Zph 2:8
passed by were yelling **i** at Him, Mt 27:39
passed by were yelling **i** at Him, Mk 15:29
there began to yell **i** at Him: Lk 23:39
The **i** of those who insult You Rm 15:3
weaknesses, in **i**, in 2Co 12:10

INTACT *(2)*
camp was **i**, and they had fled 2Kg 7:7
donkeys, and the tents were **i**." 2Kg 7:10

INTEGRITY *(42)*
of your righteousness or your **i**. Dt 9:5
righteousness, and **i**. 1Kg 3:6
with **i** of heart and uprightness, 1Kg 9:4
work, since they worked with **i**. 2Kg 12:15
hands since they work with **i**." 2Kg 22:7
the LORD, with **i**, and with a 2Ch 19:9
men were doing the work with **i**. 2Ch 34:12
He was a man of perfect **i**, Jb 1:1
man of perfect **i**, who fears God Jb 1:8
man of perfect **i**, who fears God Jb 2:3
retains his **i**, even though you Jb 2:3
Do you still retain your **i**? Jb 2:9
the **i** of your life your hope? Jb 4:6
does not reject a person of **i**, Jb 8:20
will maintain my **i** until I die. Jb 27:5
and He will recognize my **i**. Jb 31:6
to my righteousness and my **i**. Ps 7:8
May **i** and uprightness keep me, Ps 25:21
have lived with **i** and have Ps 26:1
But I live with **i**; Ps 26:11
me because of my **i** and set me in Ps 41:12
You desire **i** in the inner self Ps 51:6
good from those who live with **i**. Ps 84:11
pay attention to the way of **i**. Ps 101:2
will live with **i** of heart in my Ps 101:2
the way of **i** may serve me. Ps 101:6
all who call out to Him with **i**. Ps 145:18
righteousness, justice, and **i**; Pr 1:3
shield for those who live with **i** Pr 2:7
and **i**—every good path. Pr 2:9
those of **i** will remain in it; Pr 2:21
who lives with **i** lives securely, Pr 10:9
i of the upright guides them, Pr 11:3
guards people of **i**, Pr 13:6
lives with **i** fears the LORD, Pr 14:2
who walks in **i** than someone who Pr 19:1
who lives with **i** is righteous; Pr 20:7
who lives with **i** than a rich man Pr 28:6
who lives with **i** will be helped, Pr 28:18
the one who speaks with **i**. Am 5:10
he is without **i**. But the Hab 2:4
with **i** and dignity in your Ti 2:7

INTELLIGENCE *(2)*
have insight, **i**, and wisdom like Dn 5:11
you have insight, **i**, and Dn 5:14

INTELLIGENT *(5)*
is no one as **i** and wise as you. Gn 41:39
The woman was **i** and beautiful, 1Sm 25:3
i person restrains his words, Pr 17:27
I am the least **i** of men, and I Pr 30:2
Sergius Paulus, an **i** man. Ac 13:7

INTELLIGENTLY *(1)*
Jesus saw that he answered **i**, Mk 12:34

INTELLIGIBLE *(1)*
use your tongue for **i** speech, 1Co 14:9

INTEND *(8)*
What did you **i** when you did this Gn 20:10
i to overpower us, seize us, Gn 43:18
But if he didn't **i** any harm, Ex 21:13
since I **i** to show you kindness 2Sm 9:7
Though they **i** to harm you and Ps 21:11
He will **i** to change religious Dn 7:25
Where does He **i** to go so we Jn 7:35
He doesn't **i** to go to the Jn 7:35

INTENDED *(17)*
do to him as he **i** to do to his Dt 19:19
if ⌊we **i**⌋ to offer burnt Jos 22:23
If the LORD had **i** to kill us, Jdg 13:23
i to kill me, but they raped Jdg 20:5
since the LORD **i** to kill them. 1Sm 2:25
that Jonathan **i** to cross to 1Sm 14:4
Saul **i** to cause David's death at 1Sm 18:25
your enemy who **i** to take your 2Sm 4:8
wore new armor, **i** to kill David. 2Sm 21:16
cities and **i** to break into them 2Ch 32:1
⌊It was **i** for⌋ the royal satraps, Est 3:12
attack those who **i** to harm them. Est 9:2
the flock **i** for slaughter. Zch 11:4
the flock **i** for slaughter, Zch 11:7
with the crowds, **i** to offer Ac 14:13
kindness is **i** to lead you to Rm 2:4
other languages is **i** as a sign, 1Co 14:22

INTENDING *(7)*
i to rescue him from their hands Gn 37:22
brothers, **i** to make him king. 2Ch 11:22
i to hurl Him over the cliff. Lk 4:29
day and night **i** to kill him, Ac 9:24
i to bring him out to the people Ac 12:4
from there **i** to take Paul on Ac 20:13
i to sail to ports along the Ac 27:2

INTENDS *(7)*
My father Saul **i** to kill you. 1Sm 19:2
If my father **i** to bring evil on 1Sm 20:13
heard that Saul **i** to come to 1Sm 23:10
'Look, David **i** to harm you'? 1Sm 24:9
and blood, **i** to take my life 2Sm 16:11
I know that God **i** to destroy you 2Ch 25:16
But this is not what he **i**; Is 10:7

INTENSE *(7)*
that his suffering was very **i**. Jb 2:13
This is my **i** suffering, but I Jr 10:19
various diseases and **i** pains, Mt 4:24
noon an **i** light from heaven Ac 22:6
that I have **i** sorrow and Rm 9:2
The **i** prayer of the righteous is Jms 5:16
were burned by the **i** heat. Rv 16:9

INTENSELY *(1)*
us and are **i** angry with us. Lm 5:22

INTENSIFIED *(4)*
and as the battle **i**, Israel was 1Sm 4:2
When the battle **i** against Saul, 1Sm 31:3
When the battle **i** against Saul, 1Ch 10:3
speaking⌋ good, and my pain **i**. Ps 39:2

INTENSIFY *(3)*
I will **i** your labor pains; Gn 3:16
I your fight against the city 2Sm 11:25
I will **i** the famine against you Ezk 5:16

INTENSITY *(2)*
Philistine camp increased in **i**. 1Sm 14:19
with such **i** that the hatred 2Sm 13:15

INTENT *(10)*
out with an evil **i** to kill them Ex 32:12
that the people are ⌊**i**⌋ on evil. Ex 32:22
with malicious **i** and he dies, Nm 35:20
at him without malicious **i** Nm 35:22
up against you with evil **i**." 2Sm 18:32
don't be **i** on killing him. Pr 19:18
is his **i** to destroy and to cut Is 10:7
wait with evil **i** will be killed Is 29:20
Lord that the **i** of your heart Ac 8:22
or impurity or an **i** to deceive. 1Th 2:3

INTENTION *(4)*
was the LORD's **i** to harden their Jos 11:20
That is not ⌊my⌋ **i**. 2Sm 20:21
understands the **i** of every 1Ch 28:9
hand with no **i** of buying wisdom Pr 17:16

INTENTIONS *(5)*
you will know he has evil **i**. 1Sm 20:7
father has evil **i** against you, 1Sm 20:9
know the LORD's **i** or understand Mc 4:12
and reveal the **i** of the hearts. 1Co 4:5
we are not ignorant of his **i**. 2Co 2:11

INTENTLY *(5)*
looked at him **i** and said, Ac 3:4
Sanhedrin looked **i** at him and Ac 6:15
Looking **i** at him, he became Ac 10:4
Paul looked **i** at the Sanhedrin Ac 23:1
one who looks **i** into the perfect Jms 1:25

INTERCEDE *(6)*
I with the LORD so that He will Nm 21:7
man, God can **i** for him, but if 1Sm 2:25
the LORD, who can **i** for him?" 1Sm 2:25
I will **i** for you in a time of Jr 15:11
them **i** with the LORD of Hosts Jr 27:18
He always lives to **i** for them. Heb 7:25

INTERCEDED *(4)*
But Moses **i** with the LORD his Ex 32:11
And Moses **i** for the people. Nm 21:7
But Hezekiah had **i** for them, 2Ch 30:18
of many and **i** for the rebels. Is 53:12

INTERCEDES *(3)*
the Spirit Himself **i** for us with Rm 8:26
because He **i** for the saints Rm 8:27
right hand of God and **i** for us. Rm 8:34

INTERCEDING *(1)*
amazed that there was no one **i**; Is 59:16

INTERCEPT *(1)*
Come down to **i** the Midianites Jdg 7:24

INTERCESSION *(1)*
perseverance and **i** for all the Eph 6:18

INTERCESSIONS *(1)*
prayers, **i**, and thanksgivings 1Tm 2:1

INTERCOURSE *(25)*
has sexual **i** with an animal Ex 22:19
any close relative for sexual **i**; Lv 18:6
must not have sexual **i** with her. Lv 18:7
to have sexual **i** with your Lv 18:9
to have sexual **i** with your son's Lv 18:10
to have sexual **i** with your Lv 18:11
to have sexual **i** with your Lv 18:12
to have sexual **i** with your Lv 18:13
near his wife to have sexual **i**; Lv 18:14
not to have sexual **i** with your Lv 18:15
not to have sexual **i** with your Lv 18:16
to have sexual **i** with a woman Lv 18:17
have sexual **i** with her during Lv 18:18
to have sexual **i** with her. Lv 18:19
not to have sexual **i** with your Lv 18:20
have sexual **i** with any animal, Lv 18:23
man has sexual **i** with a woman Lv 19:20
man has sexual **i** with an animal Lv 20:15
has had sexual **i** with his sister Lv 20:17
woman and has sexual **i** with her, Lv 20:18
not have sexual **i** with your Lv 20:19
has sexual **i** with any animal. Dt 27:21
you have sexual **i** with ⌊their⌋ Ezk 22:10
natural sexual **i** for what is Rm 1:26
natural sexual **i** with females Rm 1:27

INTEREST *(20)*
you must not charge him **i**. Ex 22:25
not profit or take **i** from him, Lv 25:36
your silver with **i** or sell ⌊him⌋ Lv 25:37
charge your brother **i** on money, Dt 23:19
or anything that can earn **i**. Dt 23:19
You may charge a foreigner **i**, Dt 23:20
must not charge your brother **i**, Dt 23:20
that you take an **i** in a dead dog 2Sm 9:8
is charging his countrymen **i**." Neh 5:7
let us stop charging this **i**. Neh 5:10
the king's best **i** to tolerate Est 3:8
his money at **i** or take a bribe Ps 15:5
excessive **i** collects it for Pr 28:8
doesn't lend at **i** or for profit Ezk 18:8
and lends at **i** or for profit, Ezk 18:13
taking **i** or profit ⌊on a loan⌋ Ezk 18:17
take **i** and profit ⌊on a loan⌋ Ezk 22:12
received my money back with **i**. Mt 25:27
would have collected it with **i**!' Lk 19:23
but having a sick **i** in disputes 1Tm 6:4

INTERESTED *(1)*
were not **i** in my counsel, and Pr 1:30

INTERESTS *(5)*
and the royal **i** will suffer. Ezr 4:22
out not ⌊only⌋ for his own **i**, Php 2:4
but also for the **i** of others. Php 2:4
genuinely care about your **i**; Php 2:20
all seek their own **i**, not those Php 2:21

INTERFERE *(1)*
to harm or **i** with this house Ezr 6:12

INTERFERES *(1)*
any man who **i** with this Ezr 6:11

INTERFERING *(1)*
but **i** with the work ⌊of others⌋. 2Th 3:11

INTERIOR *(9)*
entered the **i** of the house as 2Sm 4:6
he paneled the **i** temple walls 1Kg 6:15
he overlaid the **i** with wood. 1Kg 6:15
and he built the **i** as an inner 1Kg 6:16
The **i** of the sanctuary was 30 1Kg 6:20
overlaid the **i** of the temple 1Kg 6:21
Its **i** is inlaid with love by the Sg 3:10
The **i** of the great hall and the Ezk 41:15
through the **i** regions and came Ac 19:1

INTERMARRY *(6)*
I with us; give your daughters Gn 34:9
Do not **i** with them. Dt 7:3
and if you **i** or associate with Jos 23:12
about, "Do not **i** with them, and 1Kg 11:2
and they must not **i** with you, 1Kg 11:2
again and **i** with the peoples who Ezr 9:14

INTERPRET *(11)*
"but there is no one to **i** them." Gn 40:8
but no one could **i** them for him. Gn 41:8
a dream, and no one can **i** it. Gn 41:15
you can hear a dream and **i** it." Gn 41:15
tell fortunes, **i** omens, practice Dt 18:10
and the ability to **i** dreams, Dn 5:12
You know how to **i** the appearance Lk 12:56
you know how to **i** this time? Lk 12:56
speak in languages? Do all **i**? 1Co 12:30
should pray that he can **i**. 1Co 14:13
in turn, and someone must **i**. 1Co 14:27

INTERPRETATION *(40)*
"This is its **i**," Joseph said to Gn 40:12
saw that the **i** was positive, Gn 40:16
"This is its **i**," Joseph replied. Gn 40:18
for us, and each had its own **i**. Gn 41:12
account of the dream and its **i**, Jdg 7:15
and who knows the **i** of a matter? Ec 8:1
dream, and we will give the **i**." Dn 2:4
tell me the dream and its **i**, Dn 2:5
the dream and its **i** known to me, Dn 2:6
dream and its **i** known to me." Dn 2:6
and we will give the **i**." Dn 2:7
know you can give me its **i**." Dn 2:9
he could give the king the **i**. Dn 2:16
and I will give him the **i**." Dn 2:24
can let the king know the **i**." Dn 2:25
me the dream I had and its **i**?" Dn 2:26
order that the **i** might be made Dn 2:30
now we will tell the king its **i**. Dn 2:36
is true, and its **i** certain." Dn 2:45
make the dream's **i** known to me. Dn 4:6
not make its **i** known to me. Dn 4:7
my dream that I saw, and its **i**. Dn 4:9
tell me the **i**, because none of Dn 4:18
can make the **i** known to me. Dn 4:18
the dream or its **i** alarm you." Dn 4:19
and its **i** to your enemies! Dn 4:19
This is the **i**, Your Majesty, and Dn 4:24
gives me its **i** will be clothed Dn 5:7
or make known its **i** to him. Dn 5:8
Daniel, and he will give the **i**." Dn 5:12
and make its **i** known to me, Dn 5:15
but they could not give its **i**. Dn 5:15
inscription and give me its **i**, Dn 5:16
and make the **i** known to him. Dn 5:17
This is the **i** of the message: Dn 5:26
me know the **i** of these things Dn 7:16
This is the end of the **i**. Dn 7:28
to another, **i** of languages. 1Co 12:10
another⌋ language, or an **i**. 1Co 14:26
comes from one's own **i**, 2Pt 1:20

INTERPRETATIONS *(2)*
to them, "Don't **i** belong to God? Gn 40:8
that you can give **i** and solve Dn 5:16

INTERPRETED *(4)*
our dreams, he **i** our dreams for Gn 41:12
just the way he **i** them to us: Gn 41:13
divination and **i** omens. 2Kg 17:17
He **i** for them the things Lk 24:27

INTERPRETER *(2)*
there was an **i** between them. Gn 42:23
if there is no **i**, that person 1Co 14:28

INTERPRETS *(1)*
unless he **i** so that the church 1Co 14:5

INTERROGATE *(1)*
investigate, and **i** thoroughly. Dt 13:14

INTERROGATED *(2)*
the men of Succoth and **i** him. Jdg 8:14
i the guards and ordered their Ac 12:19

INTERTWINED *(1)*
His roots are **i** around a pile of Jb 8:17

INTERVAL *(2)*
There was an **i** of about three Ac 5:7
will no longer be an **i** of time, Rv 10:6

INTERVENED *(2)*
But Phinehas stood up and **i**, Ps 106:30
reported how God first **i** to take Ac 15:14

INTERVIEWED *(1)*
The king **i** them, and among all Dn 1:19

INTERWEAVE *(1)*
from them⌋ to **i** with the blue, Ex 39:3

INTESTINES *(5)*
and spilled his **i** out on the 2Sm 20:10
including a disease of the **i**, 2Ch 21:15
until your **i** come out day after 2Ch 21:15
him in his **i** with an incurable 2Ch 21:18
Then his **i** came out because of 2Ch 21:19

INTIMATE *(8)*
this woman and was **i** with her, Dt 22:14
she had never been **i** with a man. Jdg 11:39
When he was **i** with her, the LORD Ru 4:13
Then Elkanah was **i** with his wife 1Sm 1:19
but he was not **i** with them. 2Sm 20:3
but he was not **i** with her. 1Kg 1:4
was then **i** with the prophetess, Is 8:3
I have not been **i** with a man?" Lk 1:34

INTIMATELY *(6)*
knew his wife Eve **i**, and she Gn 4:1
knew his wife **i**, and she Gn 4:17
Adam knew his wife **i** again, Gn 4:25
who had not known a man **i**. Gn 24:16
And he did not know her **i** again. Gn 38:26
not know her **i** until she gave Mt 1:25

INTIMIDATE *(3)*
they were all trying to **i** us, Neh 6:9
prophets who wanted to **i** me. Neh 6:14
And Tobiah sent letters to **i** me. Neh 6:19

INTIMIDATED *(5)*
Do not be i by anyone, for Dt 1:17
so that I would be i, do as he Neh 6:13
nations were i and lost their Neh 6:16
Do not be i by them or I will Jr 1:17
him, and being i, he will Dn 11:30

INTO *(1072)*
(See pp. xi-xii.)

INTOXICATED *(1)*
Drink, be i with love! Sg 5:1

INTOXICATING *(1)*
fragrance of your perfume is i; Sg 1:3

INTRIGUE *(2)*
king, skilled in i, will come to Dn 8:23
and seize the kingdom by i. Dn 11:21

INTRODUCED *(3)*
the kings of Israel had i. 2Kg 17:8
to the customs Israel had i. 2Kg 17:19
better hope is i, through which Heb 7:19

INVADE *(7)*
they came back to i En-mishpat Gn 14:7
hesitate to go and i and take Jdg 18:9
and did not i Israel's territory 1Sm 7:13
let Israel i them when Israel 2Ch 20:10
He will i countries and sweep Dn 11:40
He will also i the beautiful Dn 11:41
thorns will i their tents. Hs 9:6

INVADED *(6)*
they i the Ammonite camp and 1Sm 11:11
Pul king of Assyria i the land, 2Kg 15:19
of Assyria i the whole land, 2Kg 17:5
to war against Judah and i it. 2Ch 21:17
nations have i Your inheritance Ps 79:1
For a nation has i My land, Jl 1:6

INVADER'S *(1)*
one missing from ⌊the i⌋ ranks. Is 14:31

INVADERS *(1)*
land and bury the i who remain Ezk 39:14

INVADES *(2)*
When Assyria i our land, when it Mc 5:5
from Assyria when it i our land, Mc 5:6

INVADING *(1)*
to come against the people i us. Hab 3:16

INVALIDATE *(1)*
You completely i God's command Mk 7:9

INVENT *(1)*
of the harp and i their own Am 6:5

INVENTING *(1)*
are i them in your own mind." Neh 6:8

INVENTORS *(1)*
proud, boastful, i of evil, Rm 1:30

INVENTORY *(2)*
is the i for the tabernacle, Ex 38:21
This was the i: 30 gold basins, Ezr 1:9

INVENTS *(1)*
man of spirit comes and i lies: Mc 2:11

INVESTIGATE *(10)*
are to inquire, i, and Dt 13:14
it⌋, you must i it thoroughly. Dt 17:4
here tonight to i the land." Jos 2:2
they came to i the entire land. Jos 2:3
Let us i how this sin has 1Sm 14:38
I and watch carefully where he 1Sm 23:22
the tenth month to i the matter, Ezr 10:16
glory of kings to i a matter. Pr 25:2
I and you will see that no Jn 7:52
were going to i his case more Ac 23:15

INVESTIGATED *(5)*
the report was i and verified, Est 2:23
We have i this, and it is true! Jb 5:27
the hearts of kings cannot be i. Pr 25:3
I have carefully i everything Lk 1:3
to you searched and carefully i. 1Pt 1:10

INVESTIGATION *(3)*
judges are to make a careful i, Dt 19:18
After they made a thorough i, Jdg 6:29
without an i and sets others Jb 34:24

INVISIBLE *(5)*
of the world His i attributes, Rm 1:20
He is the image of the i God, Col 1:15
visible and the i, whether Col 1:16
immortal, i, the only God, be 1Tm 1:17
as one who sees Him who is i. Heb 11:27

INVITATION *(1)*
would send an i to their three Jb 1:4

INVITE *(15)*
I him to eat dinner." Ex 2:20
gods, they will i you, and you Ex 34:15
Did you i us here to rob us?" Jdg 14:15
Then i Jesse to the sacrifice, 1Sm 16:3
but he did not i Nathan the 1Kg 1:10
but he did not i your servant 1Kg 1:19
But he did not i me—me, your 1Kg 1:26
our God ⌊and not i⌋ the reproach Neh 5:9
I will i him to Me, and he will Jr 30:21
of you will i his neighbor to Zch 3:10
the city and i everyone you find Mt 22:9
a dinner, don't i your friends, Lk 14:12
because they might i you back, Lk 14:12
host a banquet, i those who are Lk 14:13
to Joppa and i Simon here, Ac 10:32

INVITED *(38)*
So Laban i all the men of the Gn 29:22
mountain and i his relatives to Gn 31:54
The women i them to the Nm 25:2
the 30 or so men who had been i. 1Sm 9:22
I said, 'I've i the people.'" 1Sm 9:24
and his sons and i them to the 1Sm 16:5
Then David i Uriah to eat and 2Sm 11:13
and Absalom i all the king's 2Sm 13:23
They had been i and were going 2Sm 15:11
He i all his royal brothers and 1Kg 1:9
He i all the king's sons, 1Kg 1:19
He i all the sons of the king, 1Kg 1:25
and all the i guests who were 1Kg 1:41
Queen Esther i no one but me to Est 5:12
am i again tomorrow to join her Est 5:12
summon those i to the banquet, Mt 22:3
and said, 'Tell those who are i: Mt 22:4
who were i were not worthy. Mt 22:8
For many are i, but few are Mt 22:14
the Pharisees i Him to eat with Lk 7:36
Pharisee who had i Him saw this, Lk 7:39
a parable to those who were i, Lk 14:7
When you are i by someone to a Lk 14:8
may have been i by your host. Lk 14:8
The one who i both of you may Lk 14:9
when you are i, go and recline Lk 14:10
when the one who i you comes, Lk 14:10
said to the one who had i Him, Lk 14:12
a large banquet and i many. Lk 14:16
to tell those who were i, Lk 14:17
men who were i will enjoy my Lk 14:24
Jesus, however, i them: Lk 18:16
disciples were i to the wedding Jn 2:2
Joseph then i his father Jacob Ac 7:14
So he i Philip to come up and Ac 8:31
Peter then i them in and gave Ac 10:23
and were i to stay with them Ac 28:14
are those i to the marriage Rv 19:9

INVITES *(3)*
opens his lips i his own ruin. Pr 13:3
a high threshold i injury. Pr 17:19
the unbelievers i you over and 1Co 10:27

INVOICE *(2)*
'Take your i,' he told him, Lk 16:6
'Take your i,' he told him, Lk 16:7

INVOKE *(4)*
Israel will i blessings by you, Gn 48:20
must not i the names of other Ex 23:13
the king i the LORD your God, 2Sm 14:11
who i You deceitfully. Ps 139:20

INVOKED *(2)*
never again be i by anyone of Jr 44:26
Yahweh's name must not be i." Am 6:10

INVOKES *(1)*
one from the east who i My name. Is 41:25

INVOLVE *(1)*
Jerusalem will also i Judah. Zch 12:2

INVOLVED *(7)*
of meeting i the tabernacle, Nm 3:25
Their duties i the ark, the Nm 3:31
descendants i the tabernacle's Nm 3:36
I will not be i with evil. Ps 101:4
I do not get i with things too Ps 131:1
are deeply i in slaughter; Hs 5:2
since those i in them have not Heb 13:9

INVOLVES *(4)*
to the LORD that i the valuation Lv 27:2
If the vow i one of the animals Lv 27:9
If the vow i any of the unclean Lv 27:11
because fear i punishment. 1Jn 4:18

INVOLVING *(4)*
any case of wrongdoing i an ox, Ex 22:9
for sin i your priesthood. Nm 18:1
same in the case i their sister Nm 25:18
there i the whole clan. 1Sm 20:6

INWARD *(2)*
from the supporting terraces i. 2Sm 5:9
was You who created my i parts; Ps 139:13

INWARDLY *(4)*
their mouths, but they curse i. Ps 62:4
but i he sets up an ambush. Jr 9:8
clothing but i are ravaging Mt 7:15
a person is a Jew who is one i, Rm 2:29

IPHDEIAH *(1)*
I, and Penuel were Shashak's 1Ch 8:25

IPHTAH *(1)*
I, Ashnah, Nezib, Jos 15:43

IPHTAH-EL *(2)*
and ended at the valley of I, Jos 19:14
Zebulun and the valley of I, Jos 19:27

IR *(1)*
(AKA IRI)
and Huppim were sons of I, 1Ch 7:12

IR-SHEMESH *(1)*
included Zorah, Eshtaol, I, Jos 19:41

IRA *(6)*
I the Jairite was David's priest. 2Sm 20:26
I son of Ikkesh the Tekoite, 2Sm 23:26
I the Ithrite, Gareb the Ithrite, 2Sm 23:38
I son of Ikkesh the Tekoite, 1Ch 11:28
I the Ithrite, Gareb the Ithrite, 1Ch 11:40
was I son of Ikkesh the Tekoite; 1Ch 27:9

IRAD *(2)*
I was born to Enoch, Irad Gn 4:18
born to Enoch, I fathered Gn 4:18

IRAM *(2)*
Magdiel, and I. These are Edom's Gn 36:43
Magdiel, and I. These were 1Ch 1:54

IRI *(1)*
(AKA IR)
Uzziel, Jerimoth, and I—five. 1Ch 7:7

IRIJAH *(2)*
whose name was I son of Jr 37:13
I would not listen to him but Jr 37:14

IRNAHASH *(1)*
and Tehinnah the father of I. 1Ch 4:12

IRON *(98)*
(See also IRON proper noun.)
all kinds of bronze and i tools. Gn 4:22
your sky like i and your land Lv 26:19
silver, bronze, i, tin, and lead Nm 31:22
person with an i object and Nm 35:16
bed was made of i. Isn't it in Dt 3:11
out of Egypt's i furnace to be Dt 4:20
whose rocks are i and from whose Dt 8:9
must not use any i tool on them. Dt 27:5
and the earth beneath you i. Dt 28:23
He will place an i yoke on your Dt 28:48
of your gate be i and bronze, Dt 33:25
the articles of bronze and i, Jos 6:19
bronze and i into the treasury Jos 6:24
on which no i tool has been used Jos 8:31
the valley area have i chariots, Jos 17:16
they have i chariots and are Jos 17:18
gold, bronze, i, and a large Jos 22:8
those people had i chariots. Jdg 1:19
Jabin had 900 i chariots, Jdg 4:3
all his 900 i chariots and all Jdg 4:13
and the i point of his spear 1Sm 17:7
with saws, i picks, and iron 2Sm 12:31
iron picks, and i axes, and to 2Sm 12:31
be armed with i and the shaft 2Sm 23:7
or any i tool was heard in the 1Kg 6:7
of the middle of an i furnace. 1Kg 8:51
Chenaanah made i horns and said, 1Kg 22:11
the i ⌊ax head⌋ fell into the 2Kg 6:5
it there, and made the i float. 2Kg 6:6
with saws, i picks, and axes 1Ch 20:3
a great deal of i to make the 1Ch 22:3
and bronze and i that can't be 1Ch 22:14
bronze, and i—beyond number. 1Ch 22:16

for the bronze, **i** for the iron, 1Ch 29:2
iron for the **i**, and wood for 1Ch 29:2
of bronze, and 4,000 tons of **i**. 1Ch 29:7
bronze, and **i**, and with purple, 2Ch 2:7
silver, bronze, **i**, stone, and 2Ch 2:14
Chenaanah made **i** horns and said, 2Ch 18:10
forever by an **i** stylus and lead! Jb 19:24
If he flees from an **i** weapon, Jb 20:24
I is taken from the ground, Jb 28:2
his limbs are like **i** rods. Jb 40:18
regards **i** as straw, and bronze Jb 41:27
will break them with a rod of **i**; Ps 2:9
his neck was put in an **i** collar. Ps 105:18
and cut through the **i** bars. Ps 107:16
dignitaries with **i** shackles, Ps 149:8
I sharpens iron, and one man Pr 27:17
Iron sharpens **i**, and one man Pr 27:17
doors and cut the **i** bars in two. Is 45:2
and your neck is **i** and your Is 48:4
will bring silver instead of **i**, Is 60:17
wood, and **i** instead of stones. Is 60:17
city, an **i** pillar, and bronze Jr 1:18
⌊They are⌋ bronze and **i**; Jr 6:28
of Egypt, out of the **i** furnace. Jr 11:4
anyone smash **i**, iron from the Jr 15:12
smash iron, **i** from the north, Jr 15:12
is written with an **i** stylus. Jr 17:1
you will make an **i** yoke bar. Jr 28:13
I have put an **i** yoke on the neck Jr 28:14
him in stocks and an **i** collar. Jr 29:26
Take an **i** plate and set it up as Ezk 4:3
set it up as an **i** wall between Ezk 4:3
copper, tin, **i**, and lead inside Ezk 22:18
silver, copper, **i**, lead, and tin Ezk 22:20
your towers with his **i** tools. Ezk 26:9
silver, **i**, tin, and lead Ezk 27:12
wrought **i**, cassia, and aromatic Ezk 27:19
its legs were **i**, and its feet Dn 2:33
were partly **i** and partly fired Dn 2:33
on its feet of **i** and fired clay, Dn 2:34
Then the **i**, the fired clay, the Dn 2:35
kingdom will be as strong as **i**; Dn 2:40
for **i** crushes and shatters Dn 2:40
and like **i** that smashes, it Dn 2:40
fired clay and partly of **i**— Dn 2:41
the strength of **i** will be in it. Dn 2:41
You saw the **i** mixed with clay, Dn 2:41
feet were part **i** and part fired Dn 2:42
You saw the **i** mixed with clay— Dn 2:43
as **i** does not mix with fired Dn 2:43
it crushed the **i**, bronze, fired Dn 2:45
with a band of **i** and bronze Dn 4:15
with a band of **i** and bronze Dn 4:23
silver, bronze, **i**, wood, and Dn 5:4
gold, bronze, **i**, wood, and stone Dn 5:23
strong, with large **i** teeth. Dn 7:7
with **i** teeth and bronze claws, Dn 7:19
threshed Gilead with **i** sledges. Am 1:3
your horns **i** and your hooves Mc 4:13
came to the **i** gate that leads Ac 12:10
shepherd them with an **i** scepter; Rv 2:27
had chests like **i** breastplates; Rv 9:9
all nations with an **i** scepter— Rv 12:5
wood, brass, **i**, and marble; Rv 18:12
shepherd them with an **i** scepter. Rv 19:15

IRON (proper noun) *(1)*
I, Migdal-el, Horem, Beth-anath, Jos 19:38

IRONWORKER *(1)*
The **i** labors over the coals, Is 44:12

IRPEEL *(1)*
Rekem, **I**, Taralah, Jos 18:27

IRRATIONAL *(2)*
the judges of the earth to be **i**. Is 40:23
these people, like **i** animals— 2Pt 2:12

IRRECONCILABLE *(1)*
unloving, **i**, slanderers, without 2Tm 3:3

IRRESPONSIBLE *(2)*
So when I planned this, was I **i**? 2Co 1:17
we were not **i** among you; 2Th 3:7

IRRESPONSIBLY *(2)*
who walks **i** and not according 2Th 3:6
are some among you who walk **i**, 2Th 3:11

IRREVERENCE *(1)*
him dead on the spot for his **i**, 2Sm 6:7

IRREVERENT *(5)*
the unholy and **i**, for those who 1Tm 1:9
to do with **i** and silly myths. 1Tm 4:7
to you, avoiding **i**, empty speech 1Tm 6:20
But avoid **i**, empty speech, for 2Tm 2:16
any immoral or **i** person like Heb 12:16

IRREVOCABLE *(3)*
it is **i** and cannot be changed." Dn 6:8
the order stands and is **i**." Dn 6:12
gifts and calling are **i**. Rm 11:29

IRRIGATE *(1)*
myself from which to **i** a grove Ec 2:6

IRRIGATED *(2)*
sowed your seed and **i** by hand as Dt 11:10
life will be like an **i** garden, Jr 31:12

IRU *(1)*
of Jephunneh: **I**, Elah, and Naam 1Ch 4:15

IS *(7538)*
(See pp. xi-xii.)

ISAAC *(128)*
a son, and you will name him **I**. Gn 17:19
will confirm My covenant with **I**, Gn 17:21
the one Sarah bore to him—**I**. Gn 21:3
When his son **I** was eight days Gn 21:4
when his son **I** was born to him Gn 21:5
feast on the day **I** was weaned. Gn 21:8
not be a co-heir with my son **I**!" Gn 21:10
will be traced through **I**. Gn 21:12
only ⌊son⌋ **I**, whom you love, Gn 22:2
of his young men and his son **I**. Gn 22:3
and laid it on his son **I**. Gn 22:6
Then **I** spoke to his father Gn 22:7
I said, "The fire and the wood Gn 22:7
bound his son **I** and placed him Gn 22:9
to take a wife for my son **I**." Gn 24:4
appointed for Your servant **I**. Gn 24:14
Now **I** was returning from Gn 24:62
I went out to walk in the field, Gn 24:63
and when she saw **I**, she got down Gn 24:64
the servant told **I** everything he Gn 24:66
And **I** brought her into the tent Gn 24:67
I loved her, and he was Gn 24:67
gave everything he owned to **I**. Gn 25:5
away from his son **I**, to the land Gn 25:6
sons **I** and Ishmael buried him Gn 25:9
blessed his son **I**, who lived Gn 25:11
records of **I** son of Abraham. Gn 25:19
of Abraham. Abraham fathered **I**. Gn 25:19
I was 40 years old when he took Gn 25:20
I prayed to the LORD on behalf Gn 25:21
I was 60 years old when they Gn 25:26
I loved Esau because he had a Gn 25:28
And **I** went to Abimelech, king of Gn 26:1
So **I** settled in Gerar. Gn 26:6
When **I** had been there for some Gn 26:8
surprised to see **I** caressing his Gn 26:8
Abimelech sent for **I** and said, Gn 26:9
I answered him, "Because I Gn 26:9
I sowed seed in that land, Gn 26:12
said to **I**, "Leave us, for Gn 26:16
So **I** left there, camped in the Gn 26:17
I reopened the water wells that Gn 26:18
I said to them, "Why have you Gn 26:27
Then **I** sent them on their way, Gn 26:31
life bitter for **I** and Rebekah. Gn 26:35
When **I** was old and his eyes were Gn 27:1
to what **I** said to his son Gn 27:5
But **I** said to his son, "How did Gn 27:20
Then **I** said to Jacob, "Please Gn 27:21
came closer to his father **I**. Gn 27:22
Then his father **I** said to him, Gn 27:26
When **I** smelled his clothes, Gn 27:27
As soon as **I** had finished Gn 27:30
the presence of his father **I**, Gn 27:30
But his father **I** said to him, Gn 27:32
I began to tremble Gn 27:33
But **I** answered Esau: "Look, I Gn 27:37
Then his father **I** answered him: Gn 27:39
Rebekah said to **I**, "I'm sick of Gn 27:46
I summoned Jacob, blessed him, Gn 28:1
So **I** sent Jacob to Paddan-aram, Gn 28:5
noticed that **I** blessed Jacob Gn 28:6
I commanded Jacob not to marry a Gn 28:6
that his father **I** disapproved Gn 28:8
father Abraham and the God of **I**. Gn 28:13
land of his father **I** in Canaan. Gn 31:18
the Fear of **I**, had not been with Gn 31:42
by the Fear of his father **I**. Gn 31:53
Abraham and God of my father **I**, Gn 32:9
to Abraham and **I** I will give to Gn 35:12
came to his father **I** at Mamre in Gn 35:27
where Abraham and **I** had stayed. Gn 35:27
I lived 180 years. Gn 35:28
to the God of his father **I**. Gn 46:1
my fathers Abraham and **I** walked, Gn 48:15
of my fathers Abraham and **I**, Gn 48:16
I and his wife Rebekah are Gn 49:31
promised Abraham, **I**, and Jacob." Gn 50:24
with Abraham, **I**, and Jacob. Ex 2:24
the God of **I**, and the God Ex 3:6
the God of **I**, and the God Ex 3:15
of Abraham, **I**, and Jacob, has Ex 3:16
the God of **I**, and the God Ex 4:5
to Abraham, **I**, and Jacob as God Ex 6:3
give to Abraham, **I**, and Jacob, Ex 6:8
servants Abraham, **I**, and Israel Ex 32:13
to Abraham, **I**, and Jacob, saying Ex 33:1
covenant with **I** and My covenant Lv 26:42
to give⌋ Abraham, **I**, and Jacob— Nm 32:11
fathers Abraham, **I**, and Jacob Dt 1:8
Abraham, **I**, and Jacob that Dt 6:10
fathers, Abraham, **I**, and Jacob. Dt 9:5
servants Abraham, **I**, and Jacob. Dt 9:27
fathers Abraham, **I**, and Jacob. Dt 29:13
fathers Abraham, **I**, and Jacob." Dt 30:20
Abraham, **I**, and Jacob, 'I Dt 34:4
his descendants. I gave him **I**, Jos 24:3
and to **I** I gave Jacob and Esau. Jos 24:4
God of Abraham, **I**, and Israel, 1Kg 18:36
with Abraham, **I**, and Jacob. 2Kg 13:23
Abraham's sons: **I** and Ishmael. 1Ch 1:28
fathered **I**. Isaac's sons: 1Ch 1:34
made with Abraham, swore to **I**, 1Ch 16:16
God of Abraham, **I**, and Israel, 1Ch 29:18
God of Abraham, **I**, and Israel so 2Ch 30:6
made with Abraham, swore to **I**, Ps 105:9
of Abraham, **I**, and Jacob. Jr 33:26
preach against the house of **I**. Am 7:16
fathered **I**, Isaac fathered Mt 1:2
Isaac, **I** fathered Jacob, Mt 1:2
table with Abraham, **I**, and Jacob Mt 8:11
and the God of **I** and the God of Mt 22:32
and the God of **I** and the God of Mk 12:26
Jacob, ⌊son⌋ of **I**, ⌊son⌋ of Lk 3:34
see Abraham, **I**, Jacob, and all Lk 13:28
and the God of **I** and the God of Lk 20:37
of Abraham, **I**, and Jacob, the Ac 3:13
fathered **I** and circumcised him Ac 7:8
I did the same with Jacob, Ac 7:8
of Abraham, of **I**, and of Jacob. Ac 7:32
in **I** your seed will be called. Rm 9:7
pregnant by **I** our forefather Rm 9:10
brothers, like **I**, are children Gl 4:28
in tents with **I** and Jacob, Heb 11:9
he was tested, offered up **I**; Heb 11:17
In **I** your seed will be called. Heb 11:18
faith **I** blessed Jacob and Esau Heb 11:20
when he offered **I** his son on the Jms 2:21

ISAAC'S *(6)*
I slaves dug in the valley and Gn 26:19
quarreled with **I** herdsmen and Gn 26:20
I slaves also dug a well there. Gn 26:25
that same day **I** slaves came to Gn 26:32
fathered Isaac. **I** sons: Esau and 1Ch 1:34
I high places will be deserted, Am 7:9

ISAIAH *(54)*
to the prophet **I** son of Amoz. 2Kg 19:2
of King Hezekiah went to **I**, 2Kg 19:5
Then **I** son of Amoz sent ⌊a 2Kg 19:20
The prophet **I** son of Amoz came 2Kg 20:1
I had not yet gone out of the 2Kg 20:4
Then **I** said, "Bring a lump of 2Kg 20:7
had asked **I**, "What is the sign 2Kg 20:8
I said, "This is the sign to you 2Kg 20:9
So **I** the prophet called out to 2Kg 20:11
Then the prophet **I** came to King 2Kg 20:14
I asked, "What have they seen in 2Kg 20:15
Then **I** said to Hezekiah, "Hear 2Kg 20:16
Hezekiah said to **I**, "The word 2Kg 20:19
Now the prophet **I** son of Amoz 2Ch 26:22
and the prophet **I** son of Amoz 2Ch 32:20
of the Prophet **I** son of Amoz, 2Ch 32:32
Jerusalem that **I** son of Amoz saw Is 1:1
vision that **I** son of Amoz saw Is 2:1
the LORD said to **I**, "Go out with Is 7:3
I said, "Listen, house of David! Is 7:13
Babylon that **I** son of Amoz saw: Is 13:1

distinction between Egypt and I.	Ex 11:7
community of I that on the tenth	Ex 12:3
community of I will slaughter	Ex 12:6
day must be cut off from I.	Ex 12:15
cut off from the community of I.	Ex 12:19
the elders of I and said to them	Ex 12:21
community of I must celebrate it	Ex 12:47
have released I from serving us.	Ex 14:5
get away from I," the Egyptians	Ex 14:25
the LORD saved I from the power	Ex 14:30
and I saw the Egyptians dead on	Ex 14:30
When I saw the great power that	Ex 14:31
Then Moses led I on from the Red	Ex 15:22
The house of I named the	Ex 16:31
of the elders of I with you.	Ex 17:5
in the sight of the elders of I.	Ex 17:6
came and fought against I.	Ex 17:8
held up his hand, I prevailed,	Ex 17:11
done for Moses and His people I,	Ex 18:1
LORD had brought I out of Egypt.	Ex 18:1
had done for I when He rescued	Ex 18:9
acted arrogantly against I."	Ex 18:11
the elders of I to eat a meal	Ex 18:12
men from all I and made them	Ex 18:25
and I camped there in front of	Ex 19:2
the 12 tribes of I at the base	Ex 24:4
and they saw the God of I.	Ex 24:10
Then they said, "I, this is your	Ex 32:4
it, and said, 'I, this is your	Ex 32:8
and I by Yourself and declared	Ex 32:13
LORD, the God of I, says, 'Every	Ex 32:27
the Lord GOD, the God of I.	Ex 34:23
you and with I based on these	Ex 34:27
entire house of I throughout all	Ex 40:38
the whole community of I errs,	Lv 4:13
his sons, and the elders of I.	Lv 9:1
whole house of I, may mourn over	Lv 10:6
and the whole assembly of I.	Lv 16:17
the house of I who slaughters	Lv 17:3
from the house of I or from the	Lv 17:8
from the house of I or from the	Lv 17:10
living in I who gives any	Lv 20:2
of the house of I or of the	Lv 22:18
residents in I who presents his	Lv 22:18
the native-born of I must live	Lv 23:42
of Reuben, the firstborn of I:	Nm 1:20
of⌋ the 12 leaders of I;	Nm 1:44
every firstborn in I to Myself,	Nm 3:13
the leaders of I registered all	Nm 4:46
the leaders of I, the heads of	Nm 7:2
the leaders of I for the altar	Nm 7:84
has promised good things to I."	Nm 10:29
to the countless thousands of I.	Nm 10:36
70 men from I known to you as	Nm 11:16
camp along with the elders of I.	Nm 11:30
All the men were leaders in I.	Nm 13:3
that the God of I has separated	Nm 16:9
the elders of I followed him.	Nm 16:25
the people of I⌋ who were around	Nm 16:34
Everything in I that is	Nm 18:14
every tenth in I as an	Nm 18:21
person will be cut off from I.	Nm 19:13
is what your brother I says,	Nm 20:14
refused to allow I to travel	Nm 20:21
and I turned away from them.	Nm 20:21
entire house of I mourned for	Nm 20:29
heard that I was coming on the	Nm 21:1
fought against I and captured	Nm 21:1
Then I made a vow to the LORD,	Nm 21:2
and I completely destroyed them	Nm 21:3
Then I sang this song:	Nm 21:17
I sent messengers to say to	Nm 21:21
would not let I travel through	Nm 21:23
out to confront I in the	Nm 21:23
to Jahaz, he fought against I.	Nm 21:23
I struck him with the sword and	Nm 21:24
I took all the cities and lived	Nm 21:25
I lived in the Amorites' land.	Nm 21:31
I captured its villages and	Nm 21:32
Zippor saw all that I had done	Nm 22:2
Jacob for me; come, denounce I!"	Nm 23:7
numbered the dust clouds of I?	Nm 23:10
He sees no trouble for I.	Nm 23:21
and no divination against I.	Nm 23:23
now be said about Jacob and I,	Nm 23:23
it pleased the LORD to bless I,	Nm 24:1
up and saw I encamped tribe	Nm 24:2
tents, Jacob, your dwellings, I.	Nm 24:5
and a scepter will arise from I.	Nm 24:17
its enemies, but I will be	Nm 24:18
While I was staying in Acacia	Nm 25:1
So I aligned itself with Baal of	Nm 25:3
LORD's anger burned against I.	Nm 25:3
anger may turn away from I."	Nm 25:4
Reuben was the firstborn of I.	Nm 26:5
out of the thousands in I—	Nm 31:5
down before the community of I,	Nm 32:4
LORD'S anger burned against I,	Nm 32:13
LORD's burning anger against I.	Nm 32:14
obligation to the LORD and to I.	Nm 32:22
spoke to all I across the Jordan	Dt 1:1
he will enable I to inherit it.	Dt 1:38
just as I did in the land of its	Dt 2:12
Now, I, listen to the statutes	Dt 4:1
summoned all I and said to them	Dt 5:1
and said to them, "I, listen to	Dt 5:1
Listen, I, and be careful to	Dt 6:3
Listen, I: The LORD our God, the	Dt 6:4
Listen, I: Today you are about	Dt 9:1
And now, I, what does the LORD	Dt 10:12
All I will hear and be afraid,	Dt 13:11
thing has happened in I,	Dt 17:4
You must purge the evil from I.	Dt 17:12
ruling many years over I.	Dt 17:20
portion or inheritance with I.	Dt 18:1
he lives in I and wants to go	Dt 18:6
pity but purge from I the guilt	Dt 19:13
them: 'Listen, I: Today you are	Dt 20:3
Your people I You redeemed,	Dt 21:8
and all I will hear and be	Dt 21:21
an outrage in I by being	Dt 22:21
You must purge the evil from I.	Dt 22:22
will not be blotted out from I.	Dt 25:6
his brother's name in I.	Dt 25:7
family⌋ name in I will be called	Dt 25:10
Your people I and the land You	Dt 26:15
the elders of I commanded the	Dt 27:1
priests spoke to all I,	Dt 27:9
Be silent, I, and listen!	Dt 27:9
summoned all I and said to them	Dt 29:2
officials, all the men of I,	Dt 29:10
harm from all the tribes of I,	Dt 29:21
to speak these words to all I,	Dt 31:1
to him in the sight of all I,	Dt 31:7
and to all the elders of I.	Dt 31:9
when all I assembles in the	Dt 31:11
this law aloud before all I.	Dt 31:11
to the entire assembly of I:	Dt 31:30
the number of the people of I.	Dt 32:8
I is a nation lacking sense with	Dt 32:28
all these words to all I,	Dt 32:45
gathered with the tribes of I.	Dt 33:5
Jacob and Your instruction to I;	Dt 33:10
and His ordinances for I.	Dt 33:21
So I dwells securely;	Dt 33:28
How happy you are, I!	Dt 33:29
arisen again in I like Moses,	Dt 34:10
performed in the sight of all I.	Dt 34:12
exalt you in the sight of all I,	Jos 3:7
12 men from the tribes of I,	Jos 3:12
all I crossed on dry ground	Jos 3:17
Joshua in the sight of all I,	Jos 4:14
'I crossed the Jordan on dry	Jos 4:22
the camp of I for destruction	Jos 6:18
them outside the camp of I.	Jos 6:23
and she lives in I to this day.	Jos 6:25
evening, as did the elders of I;	Jos 7:6
now that I has turned its back	Jos 7:8
I has sinned. They have violated	Jos 7:11
LORD, the God of I, says, 'There	Jos 7:13
are among you, I, things set	Jos 7:13
committed an outrage in I.'"	Jos 7:15
He had I come forward tribe by	Jos 7:16
the LORD, the God of I, and make	Jos 7:19
against the LORD, the God of I.	Jos 7:20
Joshua and all I with him took	Jos 7:24
So all I stoned him to death.	Jos 7:25
the elders of I led the troops	Jos 8:10
could engage I in battle at	Jos 8:14
Joshua and all I pretended to be	Jos 8:15
who did not go out after I,	Jos 8:17
exposed while they pursued I.	Jos 8:17
Joshua and all I saw that the	Jos 8:21
When I had finished killing	Jos 8:24
all I returned to Ai and struck	Jos 8:24
I plundered only the cattle and	Jos 8:27
Ebal to the LORD, the God of I,	Jos 8:30
All I, foreigner and citizen	Jos 8:33
Ebal, to bless the people of I.	Jos 8:33
before the entire assembly of I,	Jos 8:35
to fight against Joshua and I.	Jos 9:2
said to him and the men of I,	Jos 9:6
The men of I replied to the	Jos 9:7
Then the men ⌊of I⌋ took some of	Jos 9:14
them by the LORD, the God of I.	Jos 9:18
LORD, the God of I, and now we	Jos 9:19
made peace with I and were	Jos 10:1
them into confusion before I.	Jos 10:10
fled before I, the LORD threw	Jos 10:11
the LORD in the presence of I:	Jos 10:12
because the LORD fought for I.	Jos 10:14
Joshua and all I with him	Jos 10:15
all the men of I and said to	Jos 10:24
and all I with him crossed	Jos 10:29
it and its king over to I.	Jos 10:30
and all I with him crossed	Jos 10:31
LORD handed Lachish over to I,	Jos 10:32
to Eglon and all I with him.	Jos 10:34
Joshua and all I with him went	Jos 10:36
And all I was with him.	Jos 10:38
the God of I, had commanded.	Jos 10:40
LORD, the God of I, fought for	Jos 10:42
the God of Israel, fought for I.	Jos 10:42
with all I to the camp at	Jos 10:43
the waters of Merom to attack I.	Jos 11:5
hand all of them over dead to I.	Jos 11:6
The LORD handed them over to I,	Jos 11:8
I did not burn any of the cities	Jos 11:13
country of I with its Judean	Jos 11:16
they would engage I in battle,	Jos 11:20
hill country of Judah and of I.	Jos 11:21
an inheritance to I according to	Jos 11:23
to the tribes of I according to	Jos 12:7
land as an inheritance for I,	Jos 13:6
Maacath live in I to this day.	Jos 13:13
fire to the LORD, the God of I.	Jos 13:14
LORD, the God of I, was their	Jos 13:33
to Moses while I was journeying	Jos 14:10
loyal to the LORD, the God of I.	Jos 14:14
the LORD gave I all the land He	Jos 21:43
made to the house of I failed.	Jos 21:45
leader for each tribe of I.	Jos 22:14
families among the clans of I.	Jos 22:14
the God of I by turning away	Jos 22:16
with the entire community of I.	Jos 22:18
on the entire community of I?	Jos 22:20
He knows, and may I also know.	Jos 22:22
with the LORD, the God of I?	Jos 22:24
LORD had given I rest from all	Jos 23:1
summoned all I, including its	Jos 23:2
all the tribes of I at Shechem	Jos 24:1
the LORD, the God of I, says:	Jos 24:2
set out to fight against I.	Jos 24:9
to the LORD, the God of I."	Jos 24:23
I worshiped the LORD throughout	Jos 24:31
works the LORD had done for I.	Jos 24:31
I became stronger, they made	Jdg 1:28
great works He had done for I.	Jdg 2:7
or the works He had done for I.	Jdg 2:10
LORD's anger burned against I,	Jdg 2:14
LORD'S anger burned against I,	Jdg 2:20
did this⌋ to test I and to see	Jdg 2:22
LORD left in order to test I,	Jdg 3:1
The LORD left them to test I,	Jdg 3:4
LORD's anger burned against I,	Jdg 3:8
was on him, and he judged I.	Jdg 3:10
Eglon king of Moab power over I,	Jdg 3:12
and defeated I and took	Jdg 3:13
became subject to I that day,	Jdg 3:30
He delivered I by striking down	Jdg 3:31
was judging I at that time.	Jdg 4:4
the God of I, commanded ⌊you⌋	Jdg 4:6
When the leaders lead in I,	Jdg 5:2
praise to the LORD God of I.	Jdg 5:3
before the LORD, the God of I.	Jdg 5:5
were deserted in I, until I,	Jdg 5:7
Deborah, I arose, a mother in I.	Jdg 5:7
I chose new gods, then war was	Jdg 5:8
was seen among 40,000 in I.	Jdg 5:8
heart is with the leaders of I,	Jdg 5:9
deeds of His warriors in I,	Jdg 5:11
and they oppressed I.	Jdg 6:2
They left nothing for I to eat,	Jdg 6:4
So I became poverty stricken	Jdg 6:6

what the LORD God of I says:	Jdg 6:8
and deliver I from the power	Jdg 6:14
Lord, how can I deliver I?	Jdg 6:15
You will deliver I by my hand,	Jdg 6:36
will deliver I by my strength,	Jdg 6:37
to you, or else I might brag:	Jdg 7:2
Then the men of I were called	Jdg 7:23
all I prostituted themselves	Jdg 8:27
all the good he had done for I.	Jdg 8:35
had ruled over I three years,	Jdg 9:22
judge⌋ and began to deliver I.	Jdg 10:1
Tola judged I 23 years, and when	Jdg 10:2
who judged I 22 years.	Jdg 10:3
LORD's anger burned against I,	Jdg 10:7
I was greatly oppressed,	Jdg 10:9
the Ammonites fought against I.	Jdg 11:4
the Ammonites made war with I,	Jdg 11:5
When I came from Egypt,	Jdg 11:13
I did not take away the land of	Jdg 11:15
I traveled through the	Jdg 11:16
I sent messengers to the king of	Jdg 11:17
So I stayed in Kadesh.	Jdg 11:17
Then I sent messengers to Sihon	Jdg 11:19
I said to him, 'Please let us	Jdg 11:19
but Sihon did not trust I.	Jdg 11:20
at Jahaz, and fought with I.	Jdg 11:20
the LORD God of I handed over	Jdg 11:21
Sihon and all his people to I,	Jdg 11:21
So I took possession of the	Jdg 11:21
The LORD God of I has now driven	Jdg 11:23
Amorites before His people I,	Jdg 11:23
contend with I or fight against	Jdg 11:25
While I lived 300 years in	Jdg 11:26
Now it became a custom in I	Jdg 11:39
young women of I would	Jdg 11:40
Jephthah judged I six years,	Jdg 12:7
judged I after Jephthah	Jdg 12:8
Ibzan judged I seven years,	Jdg 12:9
Zebulun, judged I after Ibzan.	Jdg 12:11
He judged I 10 years,	Jdg 12:11
who was from Pirathon, judged I.	Jdg 12:13
Abdon judged I eight years,	Jdg 12:14
begin to save I from the power	Jdg 13:5
Philistines were ruling over I.	Jdg 14:4
And he judged I 20 years in the	Jdg 15:20
So he judged I 20 years.	Jdg 16:31
days there was no king in I;	Jdg 17:6
was no king in I, and the Danite	Jdg 18:1
by them⌋ among the tribes of I.	Jdg 18:1
for a tribe and family in I?"	Jdg 18:19
ancestor Dan, who was born to I.	Jdg 18:29
when there was no king in I,	Jdg 19:1
throughout the territory of I.	Jdg 19:29
all the tribes of I presented	Jdg 20:2
committed a horrible shame in I.	Jdg 20:6
100 from all the tribes of I,	Jdg 20:10
all the horror they did in I."	Jdg 20:10
all the men of I gathered united	Jdg 20:11
Then the tribes of I sent men	Jdg 20:12
and eradicate evil from I."	Jdg 20:13
The men of I went out to fight	Jdg 20:20
22,000 men of I on the field	Jdg 20:21
So I set up an ambush around	Jdg 20:29
30 men of I on the highways	Jdg 20:31
all the men of I got up from	Jdg 20:33
men from all I made a frontal	Jdg 20:34
Benjamin in the presence of I,	Jdg 20:35
men of I had retreated before	Jdg 20:36
The men of I had a prearranged	Jdg 20:38
the men of I would return to the	Jdg 20:39
killing about 30 men of I,	Jdg 20:39
Then the men of I returned,	Jdg 20:41
before the men of I toward the	Jdg 20:42
and I killed 5,000 men on the	Jdg 20:45
The men of I turned back against	Jdg 20:48
The men of I had sworn an oath	Jdg 21:1
LORD God of I, has it occurred	Jdg 21:3
tribe is ⌊missing⌋ in I today?"	Jdg 21:3
the tribes of I didn't come to	Jdg 21:5
a tribe has been cut off from I.	Jdg 21:6
the tribes of I didn't come to	Jdg 21:8
and I gave them the women they	Jdg 21:14
this gap in the tribes of I.	Jdg 21:15
that a tribe of I will not be	Jdg 21:17
days there was no king in I;	Jdg 21:25
reward from the LORD God of I,	Ru 2:12
At an earlier period in I,	Ru 4:7
binding a transaction in I.	Ru 4:7
together built the house of I.	Ru 4:11
May his name be famous in I.	Ru 4:14
may the God of I grant the	1Sm 1:17
doing to all I and how they were	1Sm 2:22
the tribes of I to be priests,	1Sm 2:28
the offerings of My people I.'	1Sm 2:29
the LORD, the God of I, says:	1Sm 2:30
spite of all that is good in I,	1Sm 2:32
do something in I that everyone	1Sm 3:11
I from Dan to Beer-sheba knew	1Sm 3:20
Samuel's words came to all I.	1Sm 4:1
I went out to meet the	1Sm 4:1
in battle formation against I,	1Sm 4:2
I was defeated by the	1Sm 4:2
the elders of I asked, "Why did	1Sm 4:3
fought, and I was defeated, and	1Sm 4:10
I has fled from the Philistines,	1Sm 4:17
Eli had judged I 40 years.	1Sm 4:18
"The glory has departed from I,"	1Sm 4:21
"The glory has departed from I,"	1Sm 4:22
they send I away, and Israel	1Sm 6:6
send Israel away, and I left?	1Sm 6:6
whole house of I began to seek	1Sm 7:2
Gather all I at Mizpah, and I	1Sm 7:5
rulers marched up toward I.	1Sm 7:7
out to the LORD on behalf of I,	1Sm 7:9
drew near to fight against I.	1Sm 7:10
that they fled before I.	1Sm 7:10
Then the men of I charged out of	1Sm 7:11
which they had taken from I,	1Sm 7:14
I even rescued their surrounding	1Sm 7:14
peace between I and the Amorites	1Sm 7:14
Samuel judged I throughout his	1Sm 7:15
and would judge I at all these	1Sm 7:16
there, he judged I there, and he	1Sm 7:17
his sons as judges over I.	1Sm 8:1
the elders of I gathered	1Sm 8:4
Then Samuel told the men of I,	1Sm 8:22
Formerly in I, a man who was	1Sm 9:9
him ruler over My people I.	1Sm 9:16
who does all I desire but you	1Sm 9:20
the LORD, the God of I, says:	1Sm 10:18
'I brought I out of Egypt,	1Sm 10:18
the tribes of I come forward,	1Sm 10:20
right eye and humiliate all I."	1Sm 11:2
throughout the territory of I.	1Sm 11:3
the land of I by messengers who	1Sm 11:7
has provided deliverance in I."	1Sm 11:13
all the men of I greatly	1Sm 11:15
Then Samuel said to all I,	1Sm 12:1
and he reigned 42 years over I.	1Sm 13:1
3,000 men from I for himself:	1Sm 13:2
And all I heard the news,	1Sm 13:4
and I is now repulsive to the	1Sm 13:4
gathered to fight against I:	1Sm 13:5
The men of I saw that they were	1Sm 13:6
established your reign over I,	1Sm 13:13
be found in all the land of I,	1Sm 13:19
LORD has handed them over to I."	1Sm 14:12
So the LORD saved I that day.	1Sm 14:23
and the men of I were worn out	1Sm 14:24
Will You hand them over to I?"	1Sm 14:37
as the LORD lives who saves I,	1Sm 14:39
he said to all I, "You will be	1Sm 14:40
the LORD, "God of I, give us the	1Sm 14:41
such a great deliverance for I?	1Sm 14:45
assumed the kingship over I,	1Sm 14:47
and delivered I from the hand of	1Sm 14:48
you as king over His people I.	1Sm 15:1
the leader of the tribes of I?	1Sm 15:17
LORD anointed you king over I	1Sm 15:17
you from being king over I."	1Sm 15:26
the kingship of I away from you	1Sm 15:28
Eternal One of I does not lie	1Sm 15:29
of my people and before I.	1Sm 15:30
He had made Saul king over I.	1Sm 15:35
rejected him as king over I?	1Sm 16:1
and the men of I gathered and	1Sm 17:2
I defy the ranks of I today.	1Sm 17:10
Saul and all I heard these words	1Sm 17:11
all the men of I are in the	1Sm 17:19
I and the Philistines lined up	1Sm 17:21
comes to defy I. The king will	1Sm 17:25
exempt from paying taxes in I."	1Sm 17:25
removes this disgrace from I?	1Sm 17:26
will know that I has a God,	1Sm 17:46
The men of I and Judah rallied,	1Sm 17:52
the cities of I to meet King	1Sm 18:6
But all I and Judah loved David	1Sm 18:16
father's clan in I that I should	1Sm 18:18
about a great victory for all I.	1Sm 19:5
the God of I, if I sound out	1Sm 20:12
LORD God of I, Your servant has	1Sm 23:10
LORD God of I, please tell Your	1Sm 23:11
yourself will be king over I,	1Sm 23:17
has the king of I come after?	1Sm 24:14
and the kingdom of I will be	1Sm 24:20
and all I assembled to mourn for	1Sm 25:1
and appoints you ruler over I,	1Sm 25:30
Praise to the LORD God of I,	1Sm 25:32
as the LORD God of I lives,	1Sm 25:34
by 3,000 of the choice men of I,	1Sm 26:2
Who in I is your equal?	1Sm 26:15
for the king of I has come out	1Sm 26:20
for me everywhere in I,	1Sm 27:1
detestable to his people I,	1Sm 27:12
one army to fight against I.	1Sm 28:1
all I had mourned for him and	1Sm 28:3
gathered all I, and they camped	1Sm 28:4
LORD will also hand I over to	1Sm 28:19
at Aphek while I was camped	1Sm 29:1
servant of King Saul of I.	1Sm 29:3
an ordinance for I ⌊and it	1Sm 30:25
Philistines fought against I,	1Sm 31:1
When the men of I on the other	1Sm 31:7
people, and the house of I.	2Sm 1:12
The splendor of I lies slain on	2Sm 1:19
Daughters of I, weep for Saul,	2Sm 1:24
Ephraim, Benjamin—over all I.	2Sm 2:9
when he began his reign over I;	2Sm 2:10
and the men of I were defeated	2Sm 2:17
longer pursued I or continued to	2Sm 2:28
of David over I and Judah from	2Sm 3:10
side to hand all I over to you."	2Sm 3:12
conferred with the elders of I:	2Sm 3:17
save My people I from the power	2Sm 3:18
was agreed on by I and the whole	2Sm 3:19
I will gather all I to my lord	2Sm 3:21
troops and all I were convinced	2Sm 3:37
leader has fallen in I today.	2Sm 3:38
failed, and all I was dismayed.	2Sm 4:1
the tribes of I came to David at	2Sm 5:1
My people I and be ruler over	2Sm 5:2
Israel and be ruler over I.'"	2Sm 5:2
the elders of I came to the king	2Sm 5:3
they anointed David king over I.	2Sm 5:3
33 years over all I and Judah.	2Sm 5:5
as king over I and had exalted	2Sm 5:12
for the sake of His people I.	2Sm 5:12
had been anointed king over I,	2Sm 5:17
all the choice men in I,	2Sm 6:1
house of I were celebrating	2Sm 6:5
whole house of I were bringing	2Sm 6:15
multitude of the people of I,	2Sm 6:19
the king of I honored himself	2Sm 6:20
ruler over the LORD's people I.	2Sm 6:21
anyone among the tribes of I,	2Sm 7:7
to shepherd My people I:	2Sm 7:7
to be ruler over My people I.	2Sm 7:8
for My people I and plant them,	2Sm 7:10
judges to be over My people I.	2Sm 7:11
And who is like Your people I?	2Sm 7:23
Your people I Your own people	2Sm 7:24
LORD of Hosts is God over I.'	2Sm 7:26
Hosts, God of I, have revealed	2Sm 7:27
So David reigned over all I,	2Sm 8:15
elite troops of I and lined up	2Sm 10:9
they had been defeated by I,	2Sm 10:15
he gathered all I, crossed the	2Sm 10:17
But the Arameans fled before I,	2Sm 10:18
they had been defeated by I,	2Sm 10:19
made peace with I and became	2Sm 10:19
with his officers and all I.	2Sm 11:1
David, "The ark, I, and Judah	2Sm 11:11
what the LORD God of I says:	2Sm 12:7
'I anointed you king over I,	2Sm 12:7
you the house of I and Judah,	2Sm 12:8
this before all I and in broad	2Sm 12:12
thing should never be done in I.	2Sm 13:12
one of the immoral men in I!	2Sm 13:13
No man in all I was as handsome	2Sm 14:25
is from one of the tribes of I,"	2Sm 15:2
the hearts of the men of I.	2Sm 15:6
the tribes of I with this	2Sm 15:10
the men of I are with Absalom.	2Sm 15:13
the house of I will restore my	2Sm 16:3

all the men of **I** have chosen. 2Sm 16:18
When all **I** hears that you have 2Sm 16:21
in the sight of all **I**. 2Sm 16:22
Absalom and all the elders of **I**. 2Sm 17:4
because all **I** knows that your 2Sm 17:10
I advise that all **I** from Dan to 2Sm 17:11
all **I** will bring ropes to that 2Sm 17:13
and all the men of **I** said, 2Sm 17:14
Absalom and the elders of **I**, 2Sm 17:15
Jordan with all the men of **I**. 2Sm 17:24
And **I** and Absalom camped in 2Sm 17:26
the field to engage **I** in battle, 2Sm 18:6
The people of **I** were defeated by 2Sm 18:7
their pursuit of **I** because Joab 2Sm 18:16
all **I** fled, each to his tent. 2Sm 18:17
the tribes of **I** were arguing: 2Sm 19:9
talk of all **I** has reached the 2Sm 19:11
any man be killed in **I** today? 2Sm 19:22
that today I'm king over **I**?" 2Sm 19:22
all the men of **I** came to the 2Sm 19:41
Judah responded to the men of **I**, 2Sm 19:42
The men of **I** answered the men 2Sm 19:43
than those of the men of **I**. 2Sm 19:43
Each man to his tent, **I**! 2Sm 20:1
all the men of **I** deserted David 2Sm 20:2
all the tribes of **I** to Abel of 2Sm 20:14
the faithful in **I**, but you're 2Sm 20:19
city that is like a mother in **I**. 2Sm 20:19
commanded the whole army of **I**; 2Sm 20:23
put anyone to death in **I**." 2Sm 21:4
within the whole territory of **I**, 2Sm 21:5
again waged war against **I**. 2Sm 21:15
not extinguish the lamp of **I**." 2Sm 21:17
When he taunted **I**, Jonathan, son 2Sm 21:21
Jacob, the favorite singer of **I**: 2Sm 23:1
The God of **I** spoke; the Rock of 2Sm 23:3
the Rock of **I** said to me, 2Sm 23:3
The men of **I** retreated in the 2Sm 23:9
anger burned against **I** again, 2Sm 24:1
the people of⌋ **I** and Judah." 2Sm 24:1
all the tribes of **I** from Dan to 2Sm 24:2
to register the troops of **I**. 2Sm 24:4
men from **I** and 500,000 men 2Sm 24:9
sent a plague on **I** from that 2Sm 24:15
land, and the plague on **I** ended. 2Sm 24:25
throughout the territory of **I**; 1Kg 1:3
the eyes of all **I** are on you to 1Kg 1:20
to you by the LORD God of **I**: 1Kg 1:30
to anoint him as king over **I**. 1Kg 1:34
to be ruler over **I** and Judah." 1Kg 1:35
the LORD God of **I** be praised! 1Kg 1:48
have a man on the throne of **I**.' 1Kg 2:4
reigned over **I** was 40 years: 1Kg 2:11
All **I** expected me to be king, 1Kg 2:15
All **I** heard about the judgment 1Kg 3:28
King Solomon ruled over **I**, 1Kg 4:1
had 12 deputies for all **I**. 1Kg 4:7
Judah and **I** were as numerous as 1Kg 4:20
Judah and **I** lived in safety from 1Kg 4:25
forced laborers from all **I**; 1Kg 5:13
fourth year of his reign over **I**, 1Kg 6:1
and not abandon My people **I**." 1Kg 6:13
assembled the elders of **I**, 1Kg 8:1
all the men of **I** were assembled 1Kg 8:2
the elders of **I** came, and the 1Kg 8:3
the entire congregation of **I**, 1Kg 8:5
congregation of **I** while they 1Kg 8:14
the LORD God of **I** be praised! 1Kg 8:15
My people **I** out of Egypt, 1Kg 8:16
in among any of the tribes of **I**, 1Kg 8:16
David to rule My people **I**." 1Kg 8:16
the name of the LORD God of **I**. 1Kg 8:17
and I sit on the throne of **I**, 1Kg 8:20
the name of the LORD God of **I**. 1Kg 8:20
congregation of **I** and spread out 1Kg 8:22
LORD God of **I**, there is no God 1Kg 8:23
LORD God of **I**, keep what You 1Kg 8:25
before Me on the throne of **I**, 1Kg 8:25
LORD God of **I**, please confirm 1Kg 8:26
Your servant and Your people **I**, 1Kg 8:30
When Your people **I** are defeated 1Kg 8:33
the sin of Your people **I**. 1Kg 8:34
Your servants and Your people **I**, 1Kg 8:36
from Your people **I** might have— 1Kg 8:38
of Your people **I** but has come 1Kg 8:41
Your people **I** do and know that 1Kg 8:43
the petition of Your people **I**, 1Kg 8:52
congregation of **I** with a loud 1Kg 8:55
to His people **I** according to all 1Kg 8:56
and the cause of His people **I**, 1Kg 8:59
The king and all **I** with him were 1Kg 8:62
Solomon and all **I** with him— 1Kg 8:65
David and for His people **I**. 1Kg 8:66
royal throne over **I** forever, 1Kg 9:5
have a man on the throne of **I**. 1Kg 9:5
I will cut off **I** from the land I 1Kg 9:7
I will become an object of scorn 1Kg 9:7
and put you on the throne of **I**, 1Kg 10:9
the LORD's eternal love for **I**. 1Kg 10:9
away from the LORD God of **I**, 1Kg 11:9
For Joab and all **I** had remained 1Kg 11:16
over Aram, but he loathed **I**. 1Kg 11:25
what the LORD God of **I** says: 1Kg 11:31
out of all the tribes of **I**. 1Kg 11:32
and you will be king over **I**. 1Kg 11:37
David, and I will give you **I**. 1Kg 11:38
over all **I** totaled 40 years. 1Kg 11:42
for all **I** had gone to Shechem to 1Kg 12:1
assembly of **I** came and spoke to 1Kg 12:3
When all **I** saw that the king had 1Kg 12:16
I, return to your tents; 1Kg 12:16
So **I** went to their tents, 1Kg 12:16
but all **I** stoned him to death. 1Kg 12:18
I is in rebellion against the 1Kg 12:19
When all **I** heard that Jeroboam 1Kg 12:20
and made him king over all **I**. 1Kg 12:20
the house of **I** to restore 1Kg 12:21
I, here is your God who brought 1Kg 12:28
is what the LORD God of **I** says: 1Kg 14:7
you ruler over My people **I**, 1Kg 14:7
both slave and free, in **I**; 1Kg 14:10
I will mourn for him and bury 1Kg 14:13
pleasing to the LORD God of **I**. 1Kg 14:13
up for Himself a king over **I**, 1Kg 14:14
will strike **I** ⌊and the people 1Kg 14:15
He will uproot **I** from this good 1Kg 14:15
He will give up **I**, because of 1Kg 14:16
and caused **I** to commit." 1Kg 14:16
and all **I** mourned for him, 1Kg 14:18
the tribes of **I** to put His name 1Kg 14:21
Baasha king of **I** throughout 1Kg 15:16
Baasha king of **I** so that he will 1Kg 15:19
armies against the cities of **I**. 1Kg 15:20
became king over **I** in the second 1Kg 15:25
he reigned over **I** two years. 1Kg 15:25
sin he had caused **I** to commit. 1Kg 15:26
Nadab and all **I** were besieging 1Kg 15:27
and had caused **I** to commit 1Kg 15:30
provoked the LORD God of **I** with. 1Kg 15:30
Baasha king of **I** throughout 1Kg 15:32
king over all **I** at Tirzah; 1Kg 15:33
sin he had caused **I** to commit. 1Kg 15:34
made you ruler over My people **I**, 1Kg 16:2
have caused My people **I** to sin, 1Kg 16:2
became king over **I** in Tirzah; 1Kg 16:8
and caused **I** to commit, 1Kg 16:13
the LORD God of **I** with their 1Kg 16:13
the king, then all **I** made Omri, 1Kg 16:16
king over **I** that very day in the 1Kg 16:16
Omri along with all **I** marched up 1Kg 16:17
the sin he caused **I** to commit. 1Kg 16:19
the people of **I** were split in 1Kg 16:21
Asa, Omri became king over **I**; 1Kg 16:23
the sins he caused **I** to commit, 1Kg 16:26
the LORD God of **I** with their 1Kg 16:26
became king over **I** in the 1Kg 16:29
Omri reigned over **I** in Samaria 1Kg 16:29
the LORD God of **I** than all the 1Kg 16:33
the kings of **I** who were before 1Kg 16:33
As the LORD God of **I** lives, 1Kg 17:1
what the LORD God of **I** says: 1Kg 17:14
that you, you destroyer of **I**?" 1Kg 18:17
not destroyed **I**, but you and 1Kg 18:18
Now summon all **I** to meet me at 1Kg 18:19
come, saying, "**I** will be your 1Kg 18:31
Isaac, and **I**, today let it be 1Kg 18:36
You are God in **I** and I am Your 1Kg 18:36
as king over **I** and Elisha son 1Kg 19:16
But I will leave 7,000 in **I**— 1Kg 19:18
Ahab king of **I** and said to him 1Kg 20:2
Then the king of **I** answered, 1Kg 20:4
Then the king of **I** called for 1Kg 20:7
The king of **I** answered, "Say 1Kg 20:11
came to Ahab king of **I** and said, 1Kg 20:13
fled and **I** pursued them, 1Kg 20:20
Then the king of **I** marched out 1Kg 20:21
the king of **I** and said to him, 1Kg 20:22
went up to Aphek to battle **I**. 1Kg 20:26
and said to the king of **I**, 1Kg 20:28
of the house of **I** are kings ⌊who 1Kg 20:31
let's go out to the king of **I**. 1Kg 20:31
the king of **I**, and said, "Your 1Kg 20:32
The king of **I** said to him, 1Kg 20:40
The king of **I** recognized that he 1Kg 20:41
The king of **I** left for home 1Kg 20:43
your royal power over **I**. 1Kg 21:7
and go to meet Ahab king of **I**, 1Kg 21:18
both slave and free, in **I**; 1Kg 21:21
My⌋ anger and caused **I** to sin. 1Kg 21:22
without war between Aram and **I**. 1Kg 22:1
went to visit the king of **I**. 1Kg 22:2
The king of **I** had said to his 1Kg 22:3
replied to the king of **I**, 1Kg 22:4
said to the king of **I**, 1Kg 22:5
So the king of **I** gathered the 1Kg 22:6
The king of **I** said to 1Kg 22:8
So the king of **I** called an 1Kg 22:9
the king of **I** and Jehoshaphat 1Kg 22:10
I saw all **I** scattered on the 1Kg 22:17
So the king of **I** said to 1Kg 22:18
Then the king of **I** ordered, 1Kg 22:26
the king of **I** and Judah's King 1Kg 22:29
But the king of **I** said to 1Kg 22:30
So the king of **I** disguised 1Kg 22:30
at all except the king of **I**." 1Kg 22:31
"He must be the king of **I**!" 1Kg 22:32
that he was not the king of **I**, 1Kg 22:33
the king of **I** through the joints 1Kg 22:34
made peace with the king of **I**. 1Kg 22:44
became king over **I** in Samaria 1Kg 22:51
he reigned over **I** two years. 1Kg 22:51
Nebat, who had caused **I** to sin. 1Kg 22:52
the LORD God of **I** just as his 1Kg 22:53
Ahab, Moab rebelled against **I**. 2Kg 1:1
is no God in **I** that you are 2Kg 1:3
there is no God in **I** that you're 2Kg 1:6
is no God in **I** for you to 2Kg 1:16
the chariots and horsemen of **I**!" 2Kg 2:12
became king over **I** in Samaria 2Kg 3:1
of Nebat had caused **I** to commit. 2Kg 3:3
pay the king of **I** 100,000 lambs 2Kg 3:4
rebelled against the king of **I**. 2Kg 3:5
that time and mobilized all **I**. 2Kg 3:6
So the king of **I**, the king of 2Kg 3:9
Then the king of **I** said, "Oh no, 2Kg 3:10
of the king of **I** answered, 2Kg 3:11
So the king of **I** and Jehoshaphat 2Kg 3:12
said to King ⌊Joram⌋ of **I**, 2Kg 3:13
But the king of **I** replied, 2Kg 3:13
So **I** went into the land and 2Kg 3:24
the land of **I** a young girl who 2Kg 5:2
from the land of **I** had said. 2Kg 5:4
with you⌋ to the king of **I**." 2Kg 5:5
the letter to the king of **I**, 2Kg 5:6
the king of **I** read the letter 2Kg 5:7
the king of **I** tore his clothes 2Kg 5:8
know there is a prophet in **I**." 2Kg 5:8
better than all the waters of **I**? 2Kg 5:12
in the whole world except in **I**. 2Kg 5:15
Aram was waging war against **I**, 2Kg 6:8
sent ⌊word⌋ to the king of **I**: 2Kg 6:9
the king of **I** sent ⌊word⌋ to the 2Kg 6:10
one of us is for the king of **I**?" 2Kg 6:11
the prophet in **I**, tells the king 2Kg 6:12
the king of **I** even the words 2Kg 6:12
When the king of **I** saw them, 2Kg 6:21
As the king of **I** was passing by 2Kg 6:26
The king of **I** must have hired 2Kg 7:6
you will do to the people of **I**. 2Kg 8:12
in the way of the kings of **I**, 2Kg 8:18
"I anoint you king over **I**." 2Kg 9:3
what the LORD God of **I** says: 2Kg 9:6
king over the LORD's people, **I**. 2Kg 9:6
both slave and free, in **I**. 2Kg 9:8
I anoint you king over **I**.'" 2Kg 9:12
Joram and all **I** had been at 2Kg 9:14
Joram king of **I** and Ahaziah king 2Kg 9:21
messengers⌋ throughout all **I**, 2Kg 10:21
Baal ⌊worship⌋ from **I**, 2Kg 10:28
Nebat had caused **I** to commit— 2Kg 10:29
will sit on the throne of **I**." 2Kg 10:30
the law of the LORD God of **I**. 2Kg 10:31
Jeroboam had caused **I** to commit. 2Kg 10:31
began to reduce the size of **I**. 2Kg 10:32

reign over I in Samaria was 28	2Kg 10:36
became king over I in Samaria;	2Kg 13:1
of Nebat had caused I to commit;	2Kg 13:2
LORD's anger burned against I,	2Kg 13:3
the king of Aram inflicted on I.	2Kg 13:4
the LORD gave I a deliverer,	2Kg 13:5
the people of I dwelt in their	2Kg 13:5
Jeroboam had caused I to commit.	2Kg 13:6
became king over I in Samaria;	2Kg 13:10
of Nebat had caused I to commit,	2Kg 13:11
in Samaria with the kings of I.	2Kg 13:13
Jehoash king of I went down and	2Kg 13:14
the chariots and horsemen of I!"	2Kg 13:14
Elisha said to the king of I,	2Kg 13:16
and he said to the king of I,	2Kg 13:18
of Aram oppressed I throughout	2Kg 13:22
and recovered the cities of I.	2Kg 13:25
Jehu, king of I, saying, "Come,	2Kg 14:8
King Jehoash of I sent ⌊word⌋ to	2Kg 14:9
so King Jehoash of I advanced.	2Kg 14:11
Judah was routed before I,	2Kg 14:12
King Jehoash of I captured	2Kg 14:13
in Samaria with the kings of I.	2Kg 14:16
became king of I in Samaria;	2Kg 14:23
of Nebat had caused I to commit.	2Kg 14:24
LORD, the God of I, had spoken	2Kg 14:25
affliction of I was very bitter	2Kg 14:26
There was no one to help I,	2Kg 14:26
out the name of I from under	2Kg 14:27
he recovered for I Damascus and	2Kg 14:28
his fathers, the kings of I.	2Kg 14:29
became king over I in Samaria	2Kg 15:8
of Nebat had caused I to commit.	2Kg 15:9
will sit on the throne of I."	2Kg 15:12
son of Gadi became king over I;	2Kg 15:17
of Nebat had caused I to commit.	2Kg 15:18
the wealthy men of I to give to	2Kg 15:20
became king over I in Samaria;	2Kg 15:23
of Nebat had caused I to commit.	2Kg 15:24
became king over I in Samaria;	2Kg 15:27
of Nebat had caused I to commit.	2Kg 15:28
In the days of Pekah king of I,	2Kg 15:29
in the way of the kings of I.	2Kg 16:3
of Aram and of the king of I,	2Kg 16:7
became king over I in Samaria;	2Kg 17:1
the kings of I who preceded him	2Kg 17:2
the people of I had sinned	2Kg 17:7
the kings of I had introduced.	2Kg 17:8
the LORD warned I and Judah	2Kg 17:13
the LORD was very angry with I,	2Kg 17:18
to the customs I had introduced.	2Kg 17:19
all the descendants of I,	2Kg 17:20
the LORD tore I from the house	2Kg 17:21
I made Jeroboam son of Nebat	2Kg 17:21
Then Jeroboam led I away from	2Kg 17:21
the LORD removed I from His	2Kg 17:23
So I has been exiled to Assyria	2Kg 17:23
of Jacob; He renamed him I.	2Kg 17:34
trusted in the LORD God of I;	2Kg 18:5
LORD God of I who is enthroned	2Kg 19:15
The LORD, the God of I says:	2Kg 19:20
Against the Holy One of I!	2Kg 19:22
the house of I will again take	2Kg 19:30
as King Ahab of I had done;	2Kg 21:3
out of all the tribes of I.	2Kg 21:7
what the LORD God of I says:	2Kg 21:12
what the LORD God of I says,	2Kg 22:15
is what the LORD God of I says:	2Kg 22:18
Solomon king of I had built for	2Kg 23:13
who caused I to sin, had made	2Kg 23:15
which the kings of I had made to	2Kg 23:19
judges who judged I through the	2Kg 23:22
of the kings of I and Judah.	2Kg 23:22
sight just as I have removed I.	2Kg 23:27
This happened to I only at the	2Kg 24:3
Solomon king of I had made for	2Kg 24:13
Isaac. Isaac's sons: Esau and I.	1Ch 1:34
brought trouble on I when he was	1Ch 2:7
called out to the God of I:	1Ch 4:10
of Reuben the firstborn of I.	1Ch 5:1
to the sons of Joseph son of I,	1Ch 5:1
So the God of I put it into the	1Ch 5:26
Kohath, son of Levi, son of I.	1Ch 6:38
atonement for I according to all	1Ch 6:49
Joseph son of I lived in these	1Ch 7:29
All I was registered in the	1Ch 9:1
in the Book of the Kings of I.	1Ch 9:1
Philistines fought against I,	1Ch 10:1
all the men of I in the valley	1Ch 10:7
All I came together to David at	1Ch 11:1
My people I and be ruler over	1Ch 11:2
be ruler over My people I.'"	1Ch 11:2
the elders of I came to the king	1Ch 11:3
they anointed David king over I,	1Ch 11:3
David and all I marched to	1Ch 11:4
together with all I, strongly	1Ch 11:10
to the LORD's word about I.	1Ch 11:10
times and knew what I should do:	1Ch 12:32
to make David king over all I.	1Ch 12:38
the rest of I was also of one	1Ch 12:38
Indeed, there was joy in I.	1Ch 12:40
said to the whole assembly of I,	1Ch 13:2
in all the districts of I,	1Ch 13:2
assembled all I, from the Shihor	1Ch 13:5
David and all I went to Baalah	1Ch 13:6
David and all I were celebrating	1Ch 13:8
him as king over I and that his	1Ch 14:2
for the sake of His people I.	1Ch 14:2
been anointed king over all I,	1Ch 14:8
assembled all I at Jerusalem to	1Ch 15:3
the LORD God of I to ⌊the place⌋	1Ch 15:12
up the ark of the LORD God of I.	1Ch 15:14
the elders of I, and the	1Ch 15:25
So all I was bringing the ark of	1Ch 15:28
to celebrate the LORD God of I,	1Ch 16:4
you offspring of I His servant,	1Ch 16:13
and to I as an everlasting	1Ch 16:17
LORD, the God of I, be praised	1Ch 16:36
He had commanded I to keep.	1Ch 16:40
time I brought I out of ⌊Egypt⌋	1Ch 17:5
In all My travels throughout I,	1Ch 17:6
to even one of the judges of I,	1Ch 17:6
to be ruler over My people I.	1Ch 17:7
for My people I and plant them,	1Ch 17:9
judges to be over My people I.	1Ch 17:10
And who is like Your people I?	1Ch 17:21
Your people I Your own people	1Ch 17:22
Hosts, the God of I, is God over	1Ch 17:24
God of Israel, is God over I.'	1Ch 17:24
So David reigned over all I,	1Ch 18:14
elite troops of I and lined up	1Ch 19:10
they had been defeated by I,	1Ch 19:16
gathered all I and crossed the	1Ch 19:17
But the Arameans fled before I,	1Ch 19:18
they had been defeated by I,	1Ch 19:19
When he taunted I, Jonathan, son	1Ch 20:7
stood up against I and incited	1Ch 21:1
to count ⌊the people of⌋ I.	1Ch 21:1
Go and count I from Beer-sheba	1Ch 21:2
Why should he bring guilt on I?"	1Ch 21:3
throughout I and then returned	1Ch 21:4
In all I there were 1,100,000	1Ch 21:5
God's sight, so He afflicted I.	1Ch 21:7
to the whole territory of I.'	1Ch 21:12
So the LORD sent a plague on I,	1Ch 21:14
altar of burnt offering for I."	1Ch 22:1
that were in the land of I,	1Ch 22:2
a house for the LORD God of I.	1Ch 22:6
and quiet to I during his reign	1Ch 22:9
of his kingdom over I forever.'	1Ch 22:10
in charge of I so that you may	1Ch 22:12
LORD commanded Moses for I.	1Ch 22:13
the leaders of I to help his son	1Ch 22:17
his son Solomon as king over I.	1Ch 23:1
gathered all the leaders of I,	1Ch 23:2
The LORD God of I has given rest	1Ch 23:25
the LORD God of I had commanded	1Ch 24:19
as officers and judges over I.	1Ch 26:29
duties in I west of the Jordan	1Ch 26:30
in charge of the tribes of I:	1Ch 27:16
the leaders of the tribes of I.	1Ch 27:22
He would make I as numerous as	1Ch 27:23
wrath against I because of this	1Ch 27:24
Jerusalem all the leaders of I:	1Ch 28:1
the LORD God of I chose me out	1Ch 28:4
to be king over I forever.	1Ch 28:4
to make me king over all I.	1Ch 28:4
of the LORD's kingdom over I.	1Ch 28:5
So now in the sight of all I,	1Ch 28:8
the leaders of the tribes of I,	1Ch 29:6
of our father I, from eternity	1Ch 29:10
Isaac, and I, our ancestors,	1Ch 29:18
in abundance for all I.	1Ch 29:21
prospered, and all I obeyed him.	1Ch 29:23
the sight of all I and bestowed	1Ch 29:25
on any king over I before him.	1Ch 29:25
of Jesse was king over all I.	1Ch 29:26
his reign over I was 40 years;	1Ch 29:27
affected him and I and all the	1Ch 29:30
Then Solomon spoke to all I,	2Ch 1:2
and to every leader in all I—	2Ch 1:2
meeting, and he reigned over I.	2Ch 1:13
is ⌊ordained⌋ for I forever.	2Ch 2:4
May the LORD God of I, who made	2Ch 2:12
foreign men in the land of I,	2Ch 2:17
at Jerusalem the elders of I—	2Ch 5:2
all the men of I were assembled	2Ch 5:3
the elders of I came, and the	2Ch 5:4
congregation of I who had	2Ch 5:6
congregation of I while they	2Ch 6:3
the LORD God of I be praised!	2Ch 6:4
My people I out of the land	2Ch 6:5
in among any of the tribes of I,	2Ch 6:5
to be ruler over My people I.	2Ch 6:5
David to be over My people I."	2Ch 6:6
the name of the LORD God of I.	2Ch 6:7
and I sit on the throne of I,	2Ch 6:10
the name of the LORD God of I.	2Ch 6:10
congregation of I and spread out	2Ch 6:12
of the entire congregation of I,	2Ch 6:13
LORD God of I, there is no God	2Ch 6:14
LORD God of I, keep what You	2Ch 6:16
before Me on the throne of I,	2Ch 6:16
LORD God of I, please confirm	2Ch 6:17
Your servant and Your people I,	2Ch 6:21
If Your people I are defeated	2Ch 6:24
the sin of Your people I.	2Ch 6:25
Your servants and Your people I,	2Ch 6:27
from your people I might have—	2Ch 6:29
of Your people I but has come	2Ch 6:32
Your people I do and know that	2Ch 6:33
So Solomon and all I with him—	2Ch 7:8
Solomon, and for His people I.	2Ch 7:10
have a man on the throne of I.	2Ch 7:18
I will uproot I from the soil	2Ch 7:20
Jebusites, who were not from I—	2Ch 8:7
of David king of I because the	2Ch 8:11
Your God loved I enough to	2Ch 9:8
over all I for 40 years.	2Ch 9:30
for all I had gone to Shechem to	2Ch 10:1
Jeroboam and all I came and	2Ch 10:3
When all I saw that the king had	2Ch 10:16
I, each man to your tent;	2Ch 10:16
So all I went to their tents.	2Ch 10:16
I is in rebellion against the	2Ch 10:19
fight against I to restore the	2Ch 11:1
to all I in Judah and Benjamin,	2Ch 11:3
throughout I took their stand	2Ch 11:13
every tribe of I who had	2Ch 11:16
LORD—he and all I with him.	2Ch 12:1
So the leaders of I and the king	2Ch 12:6
the tribes of I to put His name	2Ch 12:13
Jeroboam and all I, hear me.	2Ch 13:4
the LORD God of I gave the	2Ch 13:5
kingship over I to David and his	2Ch 13:5
Jeroboam and all I before Abijah	2Ch 13:15
choice men of I were killed.	2Ch 13:17
many years I has been without	2Ch 15:3
the LORD God of I in their	2Ch 15:4
to him from I in great numbers	2Ch 15:9
the LORD God of I would be put	2Ch 15:13
were not taken away from I;	2Ch 15:17
his armies to the cities of I.	2Ch 16:4
of the Kings of Judah and I.	2Ch 16:11
strengthened himself against I.	2Ch 17:1
according to the practices of I.	2Ch 17:4
said to the king of I,	2Ch 18:4
So the king of I gathered the	2Ch 18:5
The king of I said to	2Ch 18:7
So the king of I called an	2Ch 18:8
Now the king of I and King	2Ch 18:9
I saw all I scattered on the	2Ch 18:16
So the king of I said to	2Ch 18:17
entice Ahab king of I to march	2Ch 18:19
Then the king of I ordered,	2Ch 18:25
the king of I and Judah's King	2Ch 18:28
But the king of I said to	2Ch 18:29
So the king of I disguised	2Ch 18:29
or great, except the king of I."	2Ch 18:30
"He must be the king of I!"	2Ch 18:31
that he was not the king of I,	2Ch 18:32
the king of I through the joints	2Ch 18:33
the king of I propped himself	2Ch 18:34
Your people I and who gave it	2Ch 20:7

You did not let I invade them 2Ch 20:10
invade them when I came out of 2Ch 20:10
but I turned away from them and 2Ch 20:10
the LORD God of I shouting in a 2Ch 20:19
fought against the enemies of I. 2Ch 20:29
as some of the princes of I. 2Ch 21:4
in the way of the kings of I, 2Ch 21:6
in the way of the kings of I, 2Ch 21:13
the heads of the families of I, 2Ch 23:2
money from all I to repair the 2Ch 24:5
the assembly of I for the tent 2Ch 24:6
imposed⌋ on I in the wilderness 2Ch 24:9
was⌋ good in I with respect to 2Ch 24:16
100,000 brave warriors from I. 2Ch 25:6
for the LORD is not with I— 2Ch 25:7
Jehu, king of I, saying, "Come, 2Ch 25:17
King Jehoash of I sent ⌊word⌋ to 2Ch 25:18
So King Jehoash of I advanced. 2Ch 25:21
Judah was routed before I, 2Ch 25:22
King Jehoash of I captured 2Ch 25:23
of the Kings of Judah and I. 2Ch 25:26
of the Kings of I and Judah. 2Ch 27:7
of the kings of I and made cast 2Ch 28:2
handed over to the king of I, 2Ch 28:5
and fierce wrath is on I." 2Ch 28:13
downfall of him and of all I. 2Ch 28:23
of the Kings of Judah and I. 2Ch 28:26
the holy place of the God of I. 2Ch 29:7
the LORD God of I so that His 2Ch 29:10
to make atonement for all I, 2Ch 29:24
and sin offering were for all I. 2Ch 29:24
instruments of David king of I. 2Ch 29:27
throughout all I and Judah, 2Ch 30:1
Passover of the LORD God of I. 2Ch 30:1
the message throughout all I, 2Ch 30:5
the LORD God of I in Jerusalem, 2Ch 30:5
went throughout I and Judah with 2Ch 30:6
and I so that He may return to 2Ch 30:6
whole assembly that came from I, 2Ch 30:25
who came from the land of I, 2Ch 30:25
son of David, the king of I. 2Ch 30:26
all I who had attended went out 2Ch 31:1
the LORD and His people I. 2Ch 31:8
to mock the LORD God of I, 2Ch 32:17
of the Kings of Judah and I. 2Ch 32:32
out of all the tribes of I. 2Ch 33:7
to serve the LORD God of I. 2Ch 33:16
the name of the LORD God of I, 2Ch 33:18
the land of I and returned to 2Ch 34:7
from the entire remnant of I, 2Ch 34:9
those remaining in I and Judah, 2Ch 34:21
is what the LORD God of I says: 2Ch 34:23
is what the LORD God of I says: 2Ch 34:26
were present in I to serve the 2Ch 34:33
who taught all I the holy things 2Ch 35:3
Solomon son of David king of I. 2Ch 35:3
LORD your God and His people I. 2Ch 35:3
David king of I and that of his 2Ch 35:4
like it in I since the days 2Ch 35:18
of the kings of I ever observed 2Ch 35:18
them as a statute for I, 2Ch 35:25
of the Kings of I and Judah. 2Ch 35:27
returning to the LORD God of I. 2Ch 36:13
the God of I, the God who is Ezr 1:3
and ⌊the rest of⌋ I ⌊settled⌋ in Ezr 2:70
King David of I had instructed. Ezr 3:10
love to I endures forever. Ezr 3:11
for the LORD, the God of I, Ezr 4:1
the God of I, as King Cyrus, Ezr 4:3
of the God of I who was over Ezr 5:1
a great king of I built and Ezr 5:11
of the God of I and the decrees Ezr 6:14
as a sin offering for all I— Ezr 6:17
worship the LORD, the God of I. Ezr 6:21
on the house of the God of I. Ezr 6:22
LORD, the God of I, had given. Ezr 7:6
statutes and ordinances in I. Ezr 7:10
commandments and statutes for I: Ezr 7:11
willingly given to the God of I, Ezr 7:15
a descendant of Levi son of I— Ezr 8:18
burnt offerings to the God of I: Ezr 8:35
bulls for all I, 96 rams, and 77 Ezr 8:35
The people of I, the priests, Ezr 9:1
of the God of I gathered around Ezr 9:4
God of I, You are righteous, Ezr 9:15
still hope for I in spite of Ezr 10:2
all I take an oath to do what Ezr 10:5
all I settled in their towns. Neh 7:73

Moses that the LORD had given I. Neh 8:1
sin offerings to atone for I, Neh 10:33
The rest of I, the priests, and Neh 11:20
all I contributed the daily Neh 12:47
those of mixed descent from I. Neh 13:3
anger against I by profaning Neh 13:18
King Solomon of I sin in matters Neh 13:26
God made him king over all I, Neh 13:26
will rejoice; I will be glad. Ps 14:7
enthroned on the praises of I. Ps 22:3
descendants of I, revere Him! Ps 22:23
God, redeem I, from all its Ps 25:22
LORD, the God of I, be praised Ps 41:13
I will testify against you, I. Ps 50:7
will rejoice; I will be glad. Ps 53:6
of Hosts, God of I, rise up to Ps 59:5
Sinai, before God, the God of I. Ps 68:8
the LORD from the fountain of I. Ps 68:26
majesty is over I, His power Ps 68:34
The God of I gives power and Ps 68:35
because of me, God of I. Ps 69:6
You with a harp, Holy One of I. Ps 71:22
God, the God of I, be praised, Ps 72:18
is indeed good to I, to the pure Ps 73:1
His name is great in I. Ps 76:1
in Jacob and set up a law in I, Ps 78:5
and anger flared up against I Ps 78:21
and provoked the Holy One of I. Ps 78:41
the tribes of I in their tents. Ps 78:55
He completely rejected I. Ps 78:59
Jacob—over I, His inheritance. Ps 78:71
Shepherd of I, who guides Joseph Ps 80:1
For this is a statute for I, Ps 81:4
I, if you would only listen to Ps 81:8
listen to Me; I did not obey Me Ps 81:11
to Me and I would follow My Ps 81:13
He would feed I with the best Ps 81:16
our king to the Holy One of I. Ps 89:18
faithfulness to the house of I; Ps 98:3
His deeds to the people of I. Ps 103:7
a decree and to I as an Ps 105:10
Then I went to Egypt; Ps 105:23
He brought I out with silver Ps 105:37
for dread of I had fallen on Ps 105:38
LORD, the God of I, be praised Ps 106:48
When I came out of Egypt— Ps 114:1
His sanctuary, I, His dominion. Ps 114:2
I, trust in the LORD! Ps 115:9
He will bless the house of I; Ps 115:12
Let I say, "His faithful love Ps 118:2
Protector of I does not slumber Ps 121:4
This is an ordinance for I. Ps 122:4
been on our side—let I say— Ps 124:1
the evildoers. Peace be with I. Ps 125:5
children! Peace be with I. Ps 128:6
often attacked me—let I say— Ps 129:1
I, put your hope in the LORD. Ps 130:7
He will redeem I from all its Ps 130:8
I, put your hope in the LORD, Ps 131:3
I as His treasured possession. Ps 135:4
an inheritance to His people I. Ps 135:12
House of I, praise the LORD! Ps 135:19
brought I out from among them Ps 136:11
and led I through, His love is Ps 136:14
an inheritance to I His servant. Ps 136:22
His statutes and judgments to I. Ps 147:19
Let I celebrate its Maker; Ps 149:2
Solomon son of David, king of I: Pr 1:1
been king over I in Jerusalem. Ec 1:12
warriors from the mighty of I. Sg 3:7
but⌋ I does not know; Is 1:3
have despised the Holy One of I; Is 1:4
the Mighty One of I, declares: Is 1:24
LORD of Hosts is the house of I, Is 5:7
the Holy One of I take place so Is 5:19
the word of the Holy One of I. Is 5:24
Remaliah, king of I, waged war Is 7:1
but for the two houses of I, Is 8:14
and wonders in I from the LORD Is 8:18
Jacob; it came against I. Is 9:8
have consumed I with open mouths Is 9:12
the remnant of I and the Is 10:20
on the LORD, the Holy One of I. Is 10:20
I, even if your people were as Is 10:22
and gather the dispersed of I; Is 11:12
there was for I when they came Is 11:16
the Holy One of I is among you Is 12:6
Jacob and will choose I again. Is 14:1

will escort I and bring it to Is 14:2
the house of I will possess them Is 14:2
gleanings will be left in I, Is 17:6
of the LORD, the God of I. Is 17:6
their eyes to the Holy One of I. Is 17:7
On that day I will form a triple Is 19:24
handiwork, and I My inheritance. Is 19:25
the LORD of Hosts, the God of I. Is 21:10
LORD, the God of I, has spoken. Is 21:17
name of the LORD, the God of I. Is 24:15
I will blossom and bloom and Is 27:6
the LORD strike I as He struck Is 27:7
He struck the one who struck I? Is 27:7
rejoice in the Holy One of I. Is 29:19
stand in awe of the God of I. Is 29:23
Rid us of the Holy One of I." Is 30:11
the Holy One of I says: Is 30:12
the Holy One of I, has said: Is 30:15
of the LORD, to the Rock of I. Is 30:29
Holy One of I and they do not Is 31:1
of Hosts, God of I, who is Is 37:16
The LORD, the God of I, says: Is 37:21
Against the Holy One of I! Is 37:23
do you say, and I, why do you Is 40:27
But you, I, My servant, Jacob, Is 41:8
you worm Jacob, you men of I: Is 41:14
Redeemer is the Holy One of I. Is 41:14
will boast in the Holy One of I. Is 41:16
I, the God of I, do not forsake Is 41:17
Holy One of I has created it. Is 41:20
the robber, and I to the Is 42:24
formed you, I—"Do not fear, Is 43:1
the Holy One of I, and your Is 43:3
the Holy One of I says: Is 43:14
the Creator of I, your King. Is 43:15
on Me, because, I, you have Is 43:22
destruction and I to abuse. Is 43:28
Jacob My servant, I whom I have Is 44:1
⌊himself⌋ by the name of I." Is 44:5
the King of I and its Redeemer, Is 44:6
Jacob, and I, for you are My Is 44:21
I, you will never be forgotten Is 44:21
and glorifies Himself through I. Is 44:23
the God of I call you by your Is 45:3
My servant and I My chosen one. Is 45:4
the Holy One of I and its Maker, Is 45:11
hides Himself, God of I, Savior. Is 45:15
I will be saved by the LORD with Is 45:17
descendants of I will be Is 45:25
the remnant of the house of I, Is 46:3
in Zion, My splendor in I. Is 46:13
Holy One of I is our Redeemer Is 47:4
by the name I and have descended Is 48:1
LORD and declare the God of I, Is 48:1
City, and lean on the God of I; Is 48:2
Me, Jacob, and I, the one called Is 48:12
the Holy One of I says: Is 48:17
to me, "You are My servant, I; Is 49:3
to Him so that I might be Is 49:5
the protected ones of I. Is 49:6
the Redeemer of I, his Holy One Is 49:7
the Holy One of I—and He has Is 49:7
and the God of I is your rear Is 52:12
the Holy One of I is your Is 54:5
the Holy One of I, has glorified Is 55:5
who gathers the dispersed of I: Is 56:8
the Holy One of I, who has Is 60:9
Zion of the Holy One of I. Is 60:14
the house of I and has done for Is 63:7
not know us and I doesn't Is 63:16
I was holy to the LORD, the Jr 2:3
all families of the house of I. Jr 2:4
Is I a slave? Was he born into Jr 2:14
the house of I has been put to Jr 2:26
a wilderness to I or a land of Jr 2:31
seen what unfaithful I has done? Jr 3:6
unfaithful I had committed Jr 3:8
Unfaithful I has shown herself Jr 3:11
Return, unfaithful I. Jr 3:12
will join with the house of I, Jr 3:18
have betrayed Me, house of I. Jr 3:20
the children of I weeping and Jr 3:21
salvation of I is only in the Jr 3:23
If you return, I—⌊this is⌋ the Jr 4:1
the house of I and the house of Jr 5:11
away against you, house of I. Jr 5:15
as a vine the remnant of I. Jr 6:9
of Hosts, the God of I, says: Jr 7:3

of the evil of My people I. Jr 7:12
of Hosts, the God of I, says: Jr 7:21
of Hosts, the God of I, says: Jr 9:15
house of I is uncircumcised Jr 9:26
has spoken to you, house of I. Jr 10:1
I is the tribe of His Jr 10:16
the LORD, the God of I, says: Jr 11:3
The house of I and the house of Jr 11:10
the house of I and the house Jr 11:17
to My people, I, I am about to Jr 12:14
whole house of I and of Judah to Jr 13:11
the LORD, the God of I, says: Jr 13:12
Hope of I, its Savior in time of Jr 14:8
of Hosts, the God of I, says: Jr 16:9
the hope of I, all who abandon Jr 17:13
House of I, can I not treat you Jr 18:6
are you in My hand, house of I. Jr 18:6
I has done a most terrible Jr 18:13
of Hosts, the God of I, says: Jr 19:3
of Hosts, the God of I, says: Jr 19:15
the LORD, the God of I, says: Jr 21:4
LORD, the God of I, says about Jr 23:2
and I will dwell securely. Jr 23:6
of the house of I from the land Jr 23:8
Baal and led My people I astray. Jr 23:13
the LORD, the God of I, says: Jr 24:5
LORD, the God of I, said to me: Jr 25:15
of Hosts, the God of I, says: Jr 25:27
of Hosts, the God of I, says: Jr 27:4
Hosts, the God of I, says about Jr 27:21
of Hosts, the God of I, says: Jr 28:2
of Hosts, the God of I, says: Jr 28:14
Hosts, the God of I, says to all Jr 29:4
of Hosts, the God of I, says: Jr 29:8
the God of I, says to Ahab son Jr 29:21
an outrage in I by committing Jr 29:23
of Hosts, the God of I, says: Jr 29:25
the LORD, the God of I, says: Jr 30:2
of My people I and Judah"— Jr 30:3
the LORD spoke to I and Judah. Jr 30:4
not be dismayed, I, for I will Jr 30:10
be God of all the families of I, Jr 31:1
⌊When⌋ I went to find rest, Jr 31:2
you will be rebuilt, Virgin I. Jr 31:4
Your people, the remnant of I! Jr 31:7
who scattered I will gather him Jr 31:10
Return, Virgin I! Return to Jr 31:21
of Hosts, the God of I, says: Jr 31:23
sow the house of I and the house Jr 31:27
with the house of I and with the Jr 31:31
the house of I after those days Jr 31:33
of Hosts, the God of I, says: Jr 32:14
of Hosts, the God of I, says: Jr 32:15
very day both in I and among Jr 32:20
Your people I out of Egypt with Jr 32:21
LORD, the God of I, says to this Jr 32:36
the God of I, says concerning Jr 33:4
of Judah and of I and will Jr 33:7
the house of I and the house of Jr 33:14
on the throne of the house of I. Jr 33:17
the LORD, the God of I, says: Jr 34:2
the LORD, the God of I, says: Jr 34:13
of Hosts, the God of I, says: Jr 35:13
of Hosts, the God of I, says: Jr 35:17
of Hosts, the God of I, says: Jr 35:18
of Hosts, the God of I, says: Jr 35:19
have spoken to you concerning I, Jr 36:2
the LORD, the God of I, says: Jr 37:7
of Hosts, the God of I, says: Jr 38:17
of Hosts, the God of I, says: Jr 39:16
encounter with Baasha king of I. Jr 41:9
the God of I to whom you sent me Jr 42:9
of Hosts, the God of I, says: Jr 42:15
of Hosts, the God of I, says: Jr 42:18
of Hosts, the God of I, says: Jr 43:10
of Hosts, the God of I, says: Jr 44:2
of Hosts, the God of I, says: Jr 44:7
of Hosts, the God of I, says: Jr 44:11
of Hosts, the God of I, says: Jr 44:25
LORD, the God of I, says to you, Jr 45:2
of Hosts, the God of I, says: Jr 46:25
be discouraged, I, for without Jr 46:27
of Hosts, the God of I, says: Jr 48:1
as the house of I was put to Jr 48:13
Wasn't I a laughingstock to you? Jr 48:27
LORD says: Does I have no sons? Jr 49:1
I will dispossess their Jr 49:2
I is a stray lamb, chased by Jr 50:17
of Hosts, the God of I, says: Jr 50:18
I will return I to his grazing Jr 50:19
against the Holy One of I. Jr 50:29
For I and Judah are not left Jr 51:5
guilt against the Holy One of I. Jr 51:5
⌊I is⌋ the tribe of His Jr 51:19
of Hosts, the God of I, says: Jr 51:33
⌊because of⌋ the slain of I, Jr 51:49
every horn of I in His burning Lm 2:3
He has swallowed up I. Lm 2:5
go and speak to the house of I." Ezk 3:1
to the house of I and speak My Ezk 3:4
language but to the house of I. Ezk 3:5
the house of I will not want to Ezk 3:7
whole house of I is hardheaded Ezk 3:7
a watchman over the house of I. Ezk 3:17
be a sign for the house of I. Ezk 4:3
of the house of I on it. Ezk 4:4
the iniquity of the house of I. Ezk 4:5
from it to the whole house of I. Ezk 5:4
the mountains of I and prophesy Ezk 6:2
Mountains of I, hear the word of Ezk 6:3
abominations of the house of I, Ezk 6:11
Lord GOD says to the land of I: Ezk 7:2
the glory of the God of I there, Ezk 8:4
the house of I is committing Ezk 8:6
all the idols of the house of I. Ezk 8:10
the house of I were standing Ezk 8:11
of the house of I are doing Ezk 8:12
of the God of I rose from above Ezk 9:3
remnant of I when You pour out Ezk 9:8
of the house of I and Judah is Ezk 9:9
of the God of I was above them, Ezk 10:19
the God of I by the Chebar Ezk 10:20
you are thinking, house of I; Ezk 11:5
judge you at the border of I. Ezk 11:10
judge you at the border of I, Ezk 11:11
to an end the remnant of I?" Ezk 11:13
and the entire house of I, Ezk 11:15
I will give you the land of I. Ezk 11:17
of the God of I was above them. Ezk 11:22
you a sign to the house of I." Ezk 12:6
the house of I, that rebellious Ezk 12:9
the house of I who are living Ezk 12:10
of Jerusalem in the land of I: Ezk 12:19
have about the land of I, Ezk 12:22
they will not use it again in I. Ezk 12:23
within the house of I. Ezk 12:24
that the house of I is saying: Ezk 12:27
the prophets of I who are Ezk 13:2
Your prophets, I, are like Ezk 13:4
the house of I so that it might Ezk 13:5
the register of the house of I, Ezk 13:9
will not enter the land of I. Ezk 13:9
prophets of I who prophesied to Ezk 13:16
the elders of I came to me and Ezk 14:1
the house of I sets up idols Ezk 14:4
the house of I by their hearts Ezk 14:5
say to the house of I: Ezk 14:6
from the house of I or from the Ezk 14:7
reside in I separates himself Ezk 14:7
him from among My people I. Ezk 14:9
the house of I may no longer Ezk 14:11
a parable to the house of I. Ezk 17:2
concerning the land of I: Ezk 18:2
no longer use this proverb in I. Ezk 18:3
to the idols of the house of I. Ezk 18:6
to the idols of the house of I. Ezk 18:15
Now listen, house of I: Ezk 18:25
But the house of I says: Ezk 18:29
that are unfair, house of I? Ezk 18:29
house of I, I will judge each Ezk 18:30
Why should you die, house of I? Ezk 18:31
lament for the princes of I Ezk 19:1
be heard on the mountains of I. Ezk 19:9
the elders of I and tell them: Ezk 20:3
the day I chose I, I swore an Ezk 20:5
Myself known to I by bringing Ezk 20:9
the house of I rebelled against Ezk 20:13
the house of I, and tell them: Ezk 20:27
Therefore say to the house of I: Ezk 20:30
be consulted by you, house of I? Ezk 20:31
will not enter the land of I. Ezk 20:38
you, house of I, this is what Ezk 20:39
there the entire house of I, Ezk 20:40
I lead you into the land of I, Ezk 20:42
LORD, house of I, when I have Ezk 20:44
Prophesy against the land of I, Ezk 21:2
is against all the princes of I! Ezk 21:12
profane and wicked prince of I, Ezk 21:25
every prince of I within you has Ezk 22:6
the house of I has become dross Ezk 22:18
'Say to the house of I: Ezk 24:21
the land of I when it was laid Ezk 25:3
over the land of I with Ezk 25:6
on Edom through My people I, Ezk 25:14
and the land of I were your Ezk 27:17
The house of I will no longer be Ezk 28:24
the house of I from the peoples Ezk 28:25
made⌋ of reed to the house of I. Ezk 29:6
When I grasped you by the hand, Ezk 29:7
of trust for the house of I, Ezk 29:16
to sprout for the house of I, Ezk 29:21
a watchman for the house of I. Ezk 33:7
of man, say to the house of I: Ezk 33:10
Why will you die, house of I? Ezk 33:11
to his ways, house of I." Ezk 33:20
in the land of I are saying: Ezk 33:24
The mountains of I will become Ezk 33:28
against the shepherds of I. Ezk 34:2
Woe to the shepherds of I, Ezk 34:2
them on the mountains of I, Ezk 34:13
pasture on the mountains of I. Ezk 34:14
the house of I, are My people." Ezk 34:30
against the mountains of I, Ezk 35:12
of the house of I because it Ezk 35:15
to the mountains of I and say: Ezk 36:1
Mountains of I, hear the word of Ezk 36:1
mountains of I, hear the word Ezk 36:4
the land of I and say to Ezk 36:6
mountains of I, will put forth Ezk 36:8
bear your fruit for My people I, Ezk 36:8
house of I in its entirety. Ezk 36:10
My people I, to walk on you; Ezk 36:12
the house of I lived in their Ezk 36:17
the house of I profaned among Ezk 36:21
say to the house of I: Ezk 36:22
act, house of I, but for My holy Ezk 36:22
of your ways, house of I! Ezk 36:32
the house of I and do this for Ezk 36:37
bones are the whole house of I. Ezk 37:11
and lead you into the land of I. Ezk 37:12
the house of I associated with Ezk 37:16
the tribes of I associated with Ezk 37:19
the mountains of I, and one king Ezk 37:22
that I, the LORD, sanctify I." Ezk 37:28
peoples to the mountains of I, Ezk 38:8
when My people I are dwelling Ezk 38:14
against My people I like a cloud Ezk 38:16
the prophets of I, who for years Ezk 38:17
comes against the land of I"— Ezk 38:18
earthquake in the land of I. Ezk 38:19
you against the mountains of I. Ezk 39:2
will fall on the mountains of I. Ezk 39:4
among My people I and will no Ezk 39:7
am the LORD, the Holy One in I. Ezk 39:7
Gog a burial place there in I— Ezk 39:11
The house of I will spend seven Ezk 39:12
feast on the mountains of I; Ezk 39:17
the house of I will know that I Ezk 39:22
the house of I went into exile Ezk 39:23
on the whole house of I, Ezk 39:25
My Spirit on the house of I." Ezk 39:29
to the land of I and set me down Ezk 40:2
you see to the house of I." Ezk 40:4
glory of the God of I coming Ezk 43:2
⌊The house of⌋ I and their kings Ezk 43:7
the temple to the house of I, Ezk 43:10
LORD, the God of I, has entered Ezk 44:2
people, the house of I: Ezk 44:6
your abominations, house of I. Ezk 44:6
away from Me when I went astray, Ezk 44:10
to the house of I before their Ezk 44:12
the offspring of the house of I, Ezk 44:22
to give them no possession in I: Ezk 44:28
Everything in I that is Ezk 44:29
be for the whole house of I. Ezk 45:6
his land as a possession in I. Ezk 45:8
to the house of I according to Ezk 45:8
have gone too far, princes of I! Ezk 45:9
the well-watered pastures of I. Ezk 45:15
for the prince in I. Ezk 45:16
times of the house of I— Ezk 45:17
on behalf of the house of I. Ezk 45:17
for the 12 tribes of I. Ezk 47:13
Gilead and the land of I; Ezk 47:18

according to the tribes of **I**. Ezk 47:21
among the tribes of **I**. Ezk 47:22
the tribes of **I** will cultivate Ezk 48:19
being named for the tribes of **I**: Ezk 48:31
and all **I**—those who are Dn 9:7
All **I** has broken Your law and Dn 9:11
sin and the sin of my people **I**, Dn 9:20
son of Joash, king of **I**. Hs 1:1
the kingdom of the house of **I**. Hs 1:4
break the bow of **I** in the valley Hs 1:5
compassion on the house of **I**. Hs 1:6
the people of **I** will return and Hs 3:5
LORD, people of **I**, for the LORD Hs 4:1
I, if you act promiscuously, Hs 4:15
For **I** is as obstinate as a Hs 4:16
Pay attention, house of **I**! Hs 5:1
and **I** is not hidden from Me. Hs 5:3
promiscuously; **I** is defiled. Hs 5:3
Both **I** and Ephraim stumble Hs 5:5
certain among the tribes of **I**. Hs 5:9
horrible in the house of **I**: Hs 6:10
is there; **I** is defiled. Hs 6:10
when I heal **I**, the sins of Hs 7:1
I cries out to Me: My God, we Hs 8:2
I has rejected what is good; Hs 8:3
For this thing is from **I**— Hs 8:6
I is swallowed up! Now they are Hs 8:8
I has forgotten his Maker and Hs 8:14
I, do not rejoice jubilantly as Hs 9:1
have come. Let **I** recognize it! Hs 9:7
discovered **I** like grapes in the Hs 9:10
I is a lush vine; it yields Hs 10:1
I will be ashamed of its counsel. Hs 10:6
Aven, the sin of **I**, will be Hs 10:8
I, you have sinned since the Hs 10:9
the king of **I** will be totally Hs 10:15
When **I** was a child, I loved him, Hs 11:1
I will not return to the land of Hs 11:5
How can I surrender you, **I**? Hs 11:8
the house of **I**, with deceit. Hs 11:12
I worked to earn a wife; Hs 12:12
The LORD brought **I** from Egypt by Hs 12:13
and **I** was tended by a prophet. Hs 12:13
was exalted in **I**. But he Hs 13:1
I will destroy you, **I**; Hs 13:9
I, return to the LORD your God, Hs 14:1
I will be like the dew to **I**; Hs 14:5
I am present in **I** and that I am Jl 2:27
of My people, My inheritance **I**. Jl 3:2
saw regarding **I** in the days of Am 1:1
Joash, king of **I**, two years Am 1:1
from punishing **I** for three Am 2:6
the Amorite as **I** advanced; Am 2:9
day I punish **I** for its crimes; Am 3:14
Therefore, **I**, that is what I Am 4:12
do that to you, **I**, prepare to Am 4:12
for you, a lament, house of **I**: Am 5:1
Virgin **I** will never rise again. Am 5:2
ten left in the house of **I**. Am 5:3
the LORD says to the house of **I**: Am 5:4
House of **I**, was it sacrifices Am 5:25
those the house of **I** comes to. Am 6:1
you, house of **I**—⌊this is⌋ Am 6:14
a plumb line among My people **I**; Am 7:8
word⌋ to Jeroboam king of **I**, Am 7:10
right here⌋ in the house of **I**. Am 7:10
and **I** will certainly go into Am 7:11
prophesy to My people **I**.'" Am 7:15
Do not prophesy against **I**; Am 7:16
and **I** will certainly go into Am 7:17
end has come for My people **I**; Am 8:2
Didn't I bring **I** from the land Am 9:7
shake the house of **I** among all Am 9:9
the fortunes of My people **I**. Am 9:14
and the sins of the house of **I**. Mc 1:5
a deception to the kings of **I**. Mc 1:14
The nobility of **I** will come to Mc 1:15
I will collect the remnant of **I**. Mc 2:12
you rulers of the house of **I**. Mc 3:1
his rebellion and to **I** his sin. Mc 3:8
you rulers of the house of **I**, Mc 3:9
the judge of **I** on the cheek with Mc 5:1
you to be ruler over **I** for Me. Mc 5:2
will return to the people of **I**. Mc 5:3
and He will argue it against **I**. Mc 6:2
majesty of **I**, though ravagers Nah 2:2
the God of **I**—Moab will be Zph 2:9
The remnant of **I** will no longer Zph 3:13

Zion; shout loudly, **I**! Be glad Zph 3:14
King of **I**, the LORD, is among Zph 3:15
Judah, **I**, and Jerusalem. Zch 1:19
house of Judah and house of **I**, Zch 8:13
against all the tribes of **I** Zch 9:1
brotherhood between Judah and **I**. Zch 11:14
word of the LORD concerning **I**. Zch 12:1
the LORD to **I** through Malachi. Mal 1:1
⌊even⌋ beyond the borders of **I**. Mal 1:5
been done in **I** and in Jerusalem Mal 2:11
says the LORD God of **I**, Mal 2:16
him at Horeb for all **I**. Mal 4:4
who will shepherd My people **I**." Mt 2:6
mother and go to the land of **I**, Mt 2:20
and entered the land of **I**. Mt 2:21
found anyone in **I** with so great Mt 8:10
this has ever been seen in **I**!" Mt 9:33
lost sheep of the house of **I**. Mt 10:6
the towns of **I** before the Son Mt 10:23
lost sheep of the house of **I**." Mt 15:24
they gave glory to the God of **I**. Mt 15:31
judging the 12 tribes of **I**. Mt 19:28
price was set by the sons of **I**, Mt 27:9
is the King of **I**! Let Him come Mt 27:42
Listen, **I**! The Lord our God Mk 12:29
the King of **I**, come down now Mk 15:32
of the sons of **I** to the Lord Lk 1:16
He has helped His servant **I**, Lk 1:54
the God of **I**, because He has Lk 1:68
of his public appearance to **I**. Lk 1:80
and glory to Your people **I**. Lk 2:32
rise of many in **I** and to be a Lk 2:34
many widows in **I** in Elijah's Lk 4:25
were many in **I** who had serious Lk 4:27
so great a faith even in **I**!" Lk 7:9
judging the 12 tribes of **I**. Lk 22:30
One who was about to redeem **I**. Lk 24:21
so He might be revealed to **I**." Jn 1:31
You are the King of **I**!" Jn 1:49
a teacher of **I** and don't know Jn 3:10
of the Lord—the King of **I**!" Jn 12:13
You restoring the kingdom to **I**?" Ac 1:6
Men of **I**, listen to these words: Ac 2:22
all the house of **I** know with Ac 2:36
Men of **I**, why are you amazed at Ac 3:12
you and to all the people of **I**, Ac 4:10
Gentiles and the peoples of **I**, Ac 4:27
full Senate of the sons of **I**— Ac 5:21
repentance to **I**, and forgiveness Ac 5:31
to them, "Men of **I**, be careful Ac 5:35
his brothers, the sons of **I**. Ac 7:23
Moses who said to the sons of **I**, Ac 7:37
in the desert, O house of **I**? Ac 7:42
kings, and the sons of **I**. Ac 9:15
the message to the sons of **I**, Ac 10:36
Men of **I**, and you who fear God, Ac 13:16
God of this people **I** chose our Ac 13:17
brought the Savior, Jesus, to **I**. Ac 13:23
to all the people of **I**. Ac 13:24
shouting, "Men of **I**, help! Ac 21:28
for the hope of **I** that I'm Ac 28:20
are descended from **I** are Israel. Rm 9:6
are descended from Israel are **I**. Rm 9:6
Isaiah cries out concerning **I**: Rm 9:27
But **I**, pursuing the law for Rm 9:31
I ask, "Did **I** not understand? Rm 10:19
But to **I** he says: All day long I Rm 10:21
he pleads with God against **I**? Rm 11:2
I did not find what it was Rm 11:7
the Gentiles to make **I** jealous. Rm 11:11
has come to **I** until the full Rm 11:25
in this way all **I** will be saved, Rm 11:26
Look at the people of **I**. 1Co 10:18
the sons of **I** were not able to 2Co 3:7
the sons of **I** could not look 2Co 3:13
mercy also be on the **I** of God! Gl 6:16
from the citizenship of **I**, Eph 2:12
of the nation of **I**, of the tribe Php 3:5
with the house of **I** and with the Heb 8:8
the house of **I** after those days, Heb 8:10
of the sons of **I** and gave Heb 11:22
block in front of the sons of **I**: Rv 2:14
every tribe of the sons of **I**: Rv 7:4
the 12 tribes of the sons of **I**. Rv 21:12

ISRAEL'S *(127)*

hand Ephraim toward **I** left, Gn 48:13
hand Manasseh toward **I** right— Gn 48:13
and the Egyptians for **I** sake, Ex 18:8
and 70 of **I** elders, and bow Ex 24:1
and Abihu, and 70 of **I** elders, Ex 24:9
on them the names of **I** sons: Ex 28:9
with the names of **I** sons as a Ex 28:11
to the names of **I** sons. Ex 28:21
the names of **I** sons over his Ex 28:29
with the names of **I** sons as a Ex 39:6
to the names of **I** sons. Ex 39:14
second year after **I** departure Nm 1:1
who can serve in **I** army. Nm 1:3
tribes, the heads of **I** clans." Nm 1:16
who could serve in **I** army, Nm 1:45
the heads of **I** clans, are to Nm 10:4
The LORD listened to **I** request, Nm 21:3
So Moses told **I** judges, "Kill Nm 25:5
more who can serve in **I** army." Nm 26:2
the heads of **I** clans who were Jos 22:30
Shechem and summoned **I** elders, Jos 24:1
He returned to **I** camp and said, Jdg 7:15
but He became weary of **I** misery. Jdg 10:16
sent her throughout **I** territory, Jdg 20:6
The ark of **I** God must not stay 1Sm 5:7
we do with the ark of **I** God?" 1Sm 5:8
The ark of **I** God should be 1Sm 5:8
moved the ark of **I** God to us to 1Sm 5:10
Send the ark of **I** God away. 1Sm 5:11
you send the ark of **I** God away, 1Sm 6:3
Give glory to **I** God, and perhaps 1Sm 6:5
not invade **I** territory again. 1Sm 7:13
the smallest of **I** tribes and 1Sm 9:21
the God of **I** armies—you have 1Sm 17:45
Saul took 3,000 of **I** choice men 1Sm 24:2
the LORD will hand **I** army over 1Sm 28:19
Israel, and **I** men fled from them 1Sm 31:1
Jordan saw that **I** men had run 1Sm 31:7
the power of all **I** enemies.'" 2Sm 3:18
and half of **I** escorted the king 2Sm 19:40
to the two commanders of **I** army, 1Kg 2:5
commander of **I** army, and Amasa 1Kg 2:32
Rezon was **I** enemy throughout 1Kg 11:25
Historical Record of **I** Kings. 1Kg 14:19
year of ⌊**I**⌋ King Jeroboam son 1Kg 15:1
year of **I** King Jeroboam, 1Kg 15:9
I King Baasha went to war 1Kg 15:17
Historical Record of **I** Kings. 1Kg 15:31
Historical Record of **I** Kings. 1Kg 16:5
Historical Record of **I** Kings. 1Kg 16:14
Historical Record of **I** Kings. 1Kg 16:20
Historical Record of **I** Kings. 1Kg 16:27
Historical Record of **I** Kings. 1Kg 22:39
the fourth year of **I** King Ahab. 1Kg 22:41
Historical Record of **I** Kings. 2Kg 1:18
the Moabites came to **I** camp, 2Kg 3:24
did not come into **I** land again. 2Kg 6:23
fifth year of **I** King Joram son 2Kg 8:16
Historical Record of **I** Kings. 2Kg 8:23
twelfth year of **I** King Joram son 2Kg 8:25
granddaughter of **I** King Omri. 2Kg 8:26
Historical Record of **I** Kings. 2Kg 10:34
Historical Record of **I** Kings. 2Kg 13:8
Historical Record of **I** Kings. 2Kg 13:12
second year of **I** King Jehoash 2Kg 14:1
Historical Record of **I** Kings. 2Kg 14:15
the death of **I** King Jehoash son 2Kg 14:17
It was he who restored **I** border 2Kg 14:25
Historical Record of **I** Kings. 2Kg 14:28
year of **I** King Jeroboam, 2Kg 15:1
Historical Record of **I** Kings. 2Kg 15:11
Historical Record of **I** Kings. 2Kg 15:15
Historical Record of **I** Kings. 2Kg 15:21
Historical Record of **I** Kings. 2Kg 15:26
Historical Record of **I** Kings. 2Kg 15:31
second year of **I** King Pekah son 2Kg 15:32
King Rezin and **I** King Pekah son 2Kg 16:5
third year of **I** King Hoshea son 2Kg 18:1
seventh year of **I** King Hoshea 2Kg 18:9
the ninth year of **I** King Hoshea, 2Kg 18:10
These were **I** sons: Reuben, 1Ch 2:1
The sons of Reuben, **I** firstborn: 1Ch 5:3
King Jotham and **I** King Jeroboam. 1Ch 5:17
I men fled from them and were 1Ch 10:1
year of ⌊**I**⌋ King Jeroboam, 2Ch 13:1
I King Baasha went to war 2Ch 16:1
your treaty with **I** King Baasha 2Ch 16:3
for **I** King Ahab asked Judah's 2Ch 18:3
recorded in the Book of **I** Kings. 2Ch 20:34
an alliance with **I** King Ahaziah, 2Ch 20:35
with Joram son of **I** King Ahab to 2Ch 22:5

do not let **I** army go with you, 2Ch 25:7
of silver I gave to **I** division?" 2Ch 25:9
the death of **I** King Jehoash son 2Ch 25:25
about⌋ in the Events of **I** Kings. 2Ch 33:18
about in the Book of **I** Kings. 2Ch 36:8
the altar of **I** God in order to Ezr 3:2
other leaders of **I** families Ezr 4:3
women, adding to **I** guilt. Ezr 10:10
that **I** deliverance would come Ps 14:7
that **I** deliverance would come Ps 53:6
He struck down **I** choice young Ps 78:31
a nation so that **I** name will no Ps 83:4
He gathers **I** exiled people. Ps 147:2
pride and glory of **I** survivors. Is 4:2
LORD cut off **I** head and tail, Is 9:14
not rejoice over **I** young men and Is 9:17
I Light will become a fire, Is 10:17
I watchmen are blind, all of Is 56:10
stumble, for I am **I** Father, and Jr 31:9
then also **I** descendants will Jr 31:36
will reject all of **I** descendants Jr 31:37
one will search for **I** guilt, Jr 50:20
has thrown down **I** glory from Lm 2:1
plant it on **I** high mountain so Ezk 17:23
some of **I** elders came to consult Ezk 20:1
holy mountain, **I** high mountain" Ezk 20:40
will be on **I** lofty mountains Ezk 34:14
inhabitants of **I** cities will go Ezk 39:9
as an inheritance to **I** tribes, Ezk 48:29
I leaders fervently love Hs 4:18
I arrogance testifies against Hs 5:5
I arrogance testifies against Hs 7:10
and **I** sanctuaries will be in Am 7:9
because **I** acts of rebellion can Mc 1:13
forward to **I** consolation, Lk 2:25
the number of **I** sons is like Rm 9:27

ISRAELITE *(108)*

the **I** people are more numerous Ex 1:9
Then the **I** foremen, whom Ex 5:14
So the **I** foremen went in and Ex 5:15
The **I** foremen saw that they were Ex 5:19
none among the **I** livestock died. Ex 9:6
single one of the **I** livestock Ex 9:7
going in front of the **I** forces, Ex 14:19
the Egyptian and **I** forces. Ex 14:20
The entire **I** community departed Ex 16:1
The entire **I** community grumbled Ex 16:2
Say to the entire **I** community, Ex 16:9
to the entire **I** community, Ex 16:10
The entire **I** community left the Ex 17:1
Then he sent out young **I** men, Ex 24:5
God did not harm the **I** nobles; Ex 24:11
the entire **I** community and said Ex 35:1
said to the entire **I** community, Ex 35:4
Then the entire **I** community left Ex 35:20
to take from the **I** community two Lv 16:5
Any **I** or foreigner living among Lv 17:13
to the entire **I** community and Lv 19:2
Any **I** or foreigner living in Lv 20:2
Now the son of an **I** mother and Lv 24:10
camp between the **I** woman's son Lv 24:10
woman's son and an **I** man. Lv 24:10
of the entire **I** community by Nm 1:2
will fall on the **I** community." Nm 1:53
every firstborn **I** from the womb. Nm 3:12
assemble the entire **I** community. Nm 8:9
the womb, every **I** firstborn. Nm 8:16
and the entire **I** community did Nm 8:20
the entire **I** community in the Nm 13:26
assembly of the **I** community. Nm 14:5
said to the entire **I** community: Nm 14:7
Every **I** is to prepare these Nm 15:13
for the entire **I** community so Nm 15:25
The entire **I** community and the Nm 15:26
he is an **I** or a foreigner Nm 15:29
250 prominent **I** men who were Nm 16:2
from the **I** community to bring Nm 16:9
next day the entire **I** community Nm 16:41
be kept by the **I** community for Nm 19:9
The entire **I** community entered Nm 20:1
the entire **I** community came to Nm 20:22
An **I** man came bringing a Nm 25:6
and the whole **I** community while Nm 25:6
the **I** man into the tent, Nm 25:8
through both the **I** man and the Nm 25:8
The name of the slain **I** man, Nm 25:14
of the entire **I** community by Nm 26:2
These registered **I** men numbered Nm 26:51
that the entire **I** community will Nm 27:20
the leaders of the **I** tribes, Nm 30:1
men to war from each **I** tribe." Nm 31:4
recruited from each **I** tribe out Nm 31:5
and the **I** community at the camp Nm 31:12
family leaders of the **I** tribes. Nm 32:28
who were over the **I** families. Nm 36:1
men from the ⌊other⌋ **I** tribes, Nm 36:3
from an **I** tribe must marry Nm 36:8
each of the **I** tribes is to Nm 36:9
of the whole **I** ⌊camp⌋ the earth Dt 11:6
that man gave an **I** virgin a bad Dt 22:19
No **I** woman is to be a cult Dt 23:17
and no **I** man is to be a cult Dt 23:17
one of his **I** brothers, Dt 24:7
in a loud voice to every **I**: Dt 27:14
some of the **I** men have come here Jos 2:2
one for each of the **I** tribes, Jos 4:5
one for each of the **I** tribes, Jos 4:8
and circumcise the **I** men again." Jos 5:2
and circumcised the **I** men at Jos 5:3
trapped⌋ between the **I** forces, Jos 8:22
families of the **I** tribes gave Jos 14:1
The entire **I** community assembled Jos 18:1
to the **I** tribes by lot at Jos 19:51
of the families of the **I** tribes. Jos 21:1
Within the **I** possession there Jos 21:41
of the Jordan, on the **I** side." Jos 22:11
the entire **I** community assembled Jos 22:12
the leaders of the **I** clans, Jos 22:21
of Gideon son of Joash, the **I**. Jdg 7:14
Each **I** took his position around Jdg 7:21
But the **I** army rallied and again Jdg 20:22
The whole **I** army went to Bethel Jdg 20:26
house all the **I** fire offerings. 1Sm 2:28
30,000 of the **I** foot soldiers 1Sm 4:10
When all the **I** men who had been 1Sm 14:22
When all the **I** men saw Goliath, 1Sm 17:24
Previously, an **I** man had 1Sm 17:25
"I've escaped from the **I** camp." 2Sm 1:3
son of a man named Ithra the **I**; 2Sm 17:25
each **I** had fled to his tent. 2Sm 19:8
he counted all the **I** troops: 1Kg 20:15
distributed to each and every **I**, 1Ch 16:3
Israel, and 70,000 **I** men died. 1Ch 21:14
the heads of the **I** families for 2Ch 19:8
number of the **I** men ⌊included⌋: Ezr 2:2
families and ancestry were **I**: Ezr 2:59
Israel—one for each **I** tribe. Ezr 6:17
and I gathered **I** leaders to Ezr 7:28
and heads of the **I** families in Ezr 8:29
large assembly of **I** men, Ezr 10:1
number of the **I** men ⌊included⌋: Neh 7:7
families and ancestry were **I**: Neh 7:61
Those of **I** descent separated Neh 9:2
about him, "Here is a true **I**; Jn 1:47
For I too am an **I**, a descendant Rm 11:1

ISRAELITES *(572)*

the **I** don't eat the thigh muscle Gn 32:32
any king ruled over the **I**: Gn 36:31
These are the names of the **I**, Gn 46:8
Joseph made the **I** take an oath: Gn 50:25
But the **I** were fruitful, Ex 1:7
over the **I** to oppress them with Ex 1:11
Egyptians came to dread the **I**. Ex 1:12
They worked the **I** ruthlessly Ex 1:13
The **I** groaned because of their Ex 2:23
God saw the **I**, and He took Ex 2:25
My people, the **I**, out of Egypt." Ex 3:10
bring the **I** out of Egypt?" Ex 3:11
If I go to the **I** and say to them Ex 3:13
is what you are to say to the **I**: Ex 3:14
to Moses, "Say this to the **I**: Ex 3:15
all the elders of the **I**. Ex 4:29
heard the groaning of the **I**, Ex 6:5
Therefore tell the **I**: Ex 6:6
told this to the **I**, but they did Ex 6:9
to let the **I** go from his land. Ex 6:11
If the **I** will not listen to me, Ex 6:12
both the **I** and Pharaoh king Ex 6:13
to bring the **I** out of the land Ex 6:13
Bring the **I** out of the land of Ex 6:26
to bring the **I** out of Egypt. Ex 6:27
he will let the **I** go from his Ex 7:2
the ranks of My people the **I**, Ex 7:4
bring out the **I** from among them. Ex 7:5
of all that the **I** own will die." Ex 9:4
land of Goshen where the **I** were. Ex 9:26
and he did not let the **I** go, Ex 9:35
and he did not let the **I** go. Ex 10:20
Yet all the **I** had light where Ex 10:23
against all the **I**, whether man Ex 11:7
would not let the **I** go out of Ex 11:10
houses of the **I** in Egypt when He Ex 12:27
Then the **I** went and did ⌊this⌋; Ex 12:28
you and the **I**, and go, worship Ex 12:31
The **I** acted on Moses' word and Ex 12:35
The **I** traveled from Rameses to Ex 12:37
time that the **I** lived in Egypt Ex 12:40
for all the **I** throughout their Ex 12:42
Then all the **I** did ⌊this⌋; Ex 12:50
brought the **I** out of the land Ex 12:51
from every womb among the **I**, Ex 13:2
And the **I** left the land of Egypt Ex 13:18
had made the **I** swear a solemn Ex 13:19
Tell the **I** to turn back and camp Ex 14:2
Pharaoh will say of the **I**: Ex 14:3
So the **I** did this. Ex 14:4
he pursued the **I**, who were going Ex 14:8
the **I** looked up and saw the Ex 14:10
Then the **I** were terrified and Ex 14:10
Tell the **I** to break camp. Ex 14:15
it so that the **I** can go through Ex 14:16
and the **I** went through the sea Ex 14:22
But the **I** had walked through the Ex 14:29
Moses and the **I** sang this song Ex 15:1
But the **I** walked through the sea Ex 15:19
The **I** said to them, "If only we Ex 16:3
and Aaron said to all the **I**: Ex 16:6
heard the complaints of the **I**. Ex 16:12
When the **I** saw it, they asked Ex 16:15
So the **I** did this. Ex 16:17
The **I** ate manna for 40 years, Ex 16:35
because the **I** complained, Ex 17:7
month⌋ that the **I** had left the Ex 19:1
of Jacob, and explain to the **I**: Ex 19:3
that you are to say to the **I**." Ex 19:6
is what you are to say to the **I**: Ex 20:22
LORD's glory to the **I** was like a Ex 24:17
Tell the **I** to take an offering Ex 25:2
I command you regarding the **I**. Ex 25:22
to command the **I** to bring you Ex 27:20
statute for the **I** throughout Ex 27:21
to you from the **I** to serve Me as Ex 28:1
as memorial stones for the **I**. Ex 28:12
for the **I** over his heart Ex 28:30
that the **I** consecrate as all Ex 28:38
as a regular portion from the **I**, Ex 29:28
will also meet with the **I** there, Ex 29:43
dwell among the **I** and be their Ex 29:45
a census of the **I** to register Ex 30:12
money from the **I** and use it for Ex 30:16
for the **I** before the LORD Ex 30:16
Tell the **I**: This will be My holy Ex 30:31
Tell the **I**: You must observe My Ex 31:13
The **I** must observe the Sabbath, Ex 31:16
forever between Me and the **I**, Ex 31:17
and forced the **I** to drink ⌊the Ex 32:20
to Moses: "Tell the **I**: You are a Ex 33:5
So the **I** ⌊remained⌋ stripped of Ex 33:6
Aaron and all the **I** saw Moses, Ex 34:30
Afterwards all the **I** came near, Ex 34:32
would tell the **I** what he had Ex 34:34
and the **I** would see that Moses' Ex 34:35
So the **I** brought a freewill Ex 35:29
Moses then said to the **I**: Ex 35:30
that the **I** had brought for Ex 36:3
as memorial stones for the **I**, Ex 39:7
The **I** did everything just as the Ex 39:32
The **I** had done all the work Ex 39:42
The **I** set out whenever the cloud Ex 40:36
Speak to the **I** and tell them: Lv 1:2
Tell the **I**: When someone sins Lv 4:2
Tell the **I**: You are not to eat Lv 7:23
Tell the **I**: The one who presents Lv 7:29
have taken from the **I** the breast Lv 7:34
a permanent portion from the **I**." Lv 7:34
to them by the **I** on the day He Lv 7:36
commanded the **I** to present their Lv 7:38
tell the **I**: 'Take a male goat Lv 9:3
and teach the **I** all the statutes Lv 10:11
Tell the **I**: You may eat all Lv 11:2
Tell the **I**: When a woman becomes Lv 12:2
Speak to the **I** and tell them: Lv 15:2
You must keep the **I** from their Lv 15:31
atonement for the **I** once a year Lv 16:34

and all the **I** and tell them: Lv 17:2
This is so the **I** will bring to Lv 17:5
Therefore I say to the **I**: Lv 17:12
is its blood, I have told the **I**: Lv 17:14
Speak to the **I** and tell them: Lv 18:2
Say to the **I**: Any Israelite or Lv 20:2
and his sons and to all the **I**. Lv 21:24
offerings of the **I** that they Lv 22:2
that the **I** consecrate to Lv 22:3
offerings the **I** give to the LORD Lv 22:15
and all the **I** and tell them: Lv 22:18
be treated as holy among the **I**. Lv 22:32
Speak to the **I** and tell them: Lv 23:2
Speak to the **I** and tell them: Lv 23:10
Tell the **I**: In the seventh Lv 23:24
Tell the **I**: The Festival of Lv 23:34
that I made the **I** live in booths Lv 23:43
LORD's appointed times to the **I**. Lv 23:44
Command the **I** to bring you pure Lv 24:2
obligation on the part of the **I**. Lv 24:8
Egyptian father was among the **I**. Lv 24:10
And tell the **I**: If anyone curses Lv 24:15
After Moses spoke to the **I**, Lv 24:23
So the **I** did as the LORD had Lv 24:23
Speak to the **I** and tell them: Lv 25:2
their possession among the **I**. Lv 25:33
brothers, the **I**, you must not Lv 25:46
For the **I** are My slaves. Lv 25:55
Himself and the **I** through Moses Lv 26:46
Speak to the **I** and tell them: Lv 27:2
Moses for the **I** on Mount Sinai. Lv 27:34
So all the **I** 20 years old or Nm 1:45
of Levi with the ⌊other⌋ **I**. Nm 1:49
The **I** are to camp by their Nm 1:52
The **I** did everything just as the Nm 1:54
The **I** are to camp under their Nm 2:2
These are the **I** registered by Nm 2:32
were not registered among the **I**, Nm 2:33
The **I** did everything the LORD Nm 2:34
duties for the **I** by attending to Nm 3:8
exclusively to him from the **I**. Nm 3:9
Levites from the **I** in place of Nm 3:12
as a service on behalf of the **I**, Nm 3:38
male of the **I** one month old or Nm 3:40
of every firstborn among the **I**, Nm 3:41
every firstborn among the **I**, Nm 3:42
of every firstborn among the **I**, Nm 3:45
273 firstborn **I** who outnumber Nm 3:46
who are in excess among the **I**." Nm 3:48
the money from the firstborn **I**: Nm 3:50
Command the **I** to send away Nm 5:2
The **I** did this, sending them Nm 5:4
The **I** did as the LORD instructed Nm 5:4
Tell the **I**: When a man or woman Nm 5:6
contribution the **I** present to Nm 5:9
Speak to the **I** and tell them: Nm 5:12
Speak to the **I** and tell them: Nm 6:2
sons how you are to bless the **I**. Nm 6:23
they will put My name on the **I**, Nm 6:27
among the **I** and ceremonially Nm 8:6
and have the **I** lay their hands Nm 8:10
offering from the **I**, Nm 8:11
the rest of the **I** so that the Nm 8:14
assigned to Me from the **I**. Nm 8:16
firstborn among the **I** is Mine, Nm 8:17
of every firstborn among the **I**. Nm 8:18
From the **I**, I have given the Nm 8:19
the work for the **I** at the tent Nm 8:19
come against the **I** when they Nm 8:19
The **I** did everything to them the Nm 8:20
The **I** are to observe the Nm 9:2
So Moses told the **I** to observe Nm 9:4
The **I** did everything as the LORD Nm 9:5
time with the ⌊other⌋ **I**?" Nm 9:7
Tell the **I**: When any one of you Nm 9:10
the tent, the **I** would set out; Nm 9:17
stopped, there the **I** camped. Nm 9:17
LORD's command the **I** set out, Nm 9:18
the **I** carried out the LORD's Nm 9:19
the **I** camped and did not set out Nm 9:22
The **I** traveled on from the Nm 10:12
of march for the **I** by their Nm 10:28
The **I** cried again and said, Nm 11:4
of Canaan I am giving to the **I**. Nm 13:2
of grapes⌋ the **I** cut there. Nm 13:24
report to the **I** about the land Nm 13:32
All the **I** complained about Moses Nm 14:2
appeared to all the **I** at the Nm 14:10

these words to all the **I**, Nm 14:39
Speak to the **I** and tell them: Nm 15:2
Speak to the **I** and tell them: Nm 15:18
While the **I** were in the Nm 15:32
Speak to the **I** and tell them Nm 15:38
They will be a sign to the **I**." Nm 16:38
a reminder for the **I** that no Nm 16:40
Speak to the **I** and take one Nm 17:2
spoke to the **I**, and each of Nm 17:6
LORD's presence to all the **I**. Nm 17:9
Then the **I** declared to Moses, Nm 17:12
may not fall on the **I** again. Nm 18:5
Levites from the **I** as a gift for Nm 18:6
all the holy offerings of the **I**, Nm 18:8
which the **I** give to the LORD as Nm 18:12
that the **I** present to the LORD Nm 18:19
your inheritance among the **I**. Nm 18:20
The **I** must never again come near Nm 18:22
an inheritance among the **I**; Nm 18:23
the tenth that the **I** present to Nm 18:24
an inheritance among the **I**." Nm 18:24
from the **I** the tenth that I Nm 18:26
tenth you receive from the **I**. Nm 18:28
Instruct the **I** to bring you an Nm 19:2
statute for the **I** and for the Nm 19:10
holiness in the sight of the **I**, Nm 20:12
where the **I** quarreled with the Nm 20:13
road," the **I** replied to them Nm 20:19
the land I have given the **I**, Nm 20:24
bit them so that many **I** died. Nm 21:6
The **I** set out and camped at Nm 21:10
The **I** traveled on and camped in Nm 22:1
numerous, and dreaded the **I**. Nm 22:3
the plague on the **I** was stopped, Nm 25:8
wrath from the **I** because he was Nm 25:11
not destroy the **I** in My zeal. Nm 25:11
and made atonement for the **I**." Nm 25:13
Moses and the **I** who came out Nm 26:4
registered among the ⌊other⌋ **I**, Nm 26:62
was given to them among the **I**. Nm 26:62
registered the **I** on the plains Nm 26:63
registered the **I** in the Nm 26:64
Tell the **I**: When a man dies Nm 27:8
ordinance for the **I** as the LORD Nm 27:11
land that I have given the **I**. Nm 27:12
He and all the **I** with him, Nm 27:21
Command the **I** and say to them: Nm 28:2
So Moses told the **I** everything Nm 29:40
vengeance for the **I** against the Nm 31:2
The **I** took the Midianite women Nm 31:9
incited the **I** to unfaithfulness Nm 31:16
for the **I** before the LORD Nm 31:54
discouraging the **I** from crossing Nm 32:7
discouraged the **I** from entering Nm 32:9
go⌋ ahead of the **I** until we have Nm 32:17
until each of the **I** has taken Nm 32:18
the Passover the **I** went out Nm 33:3
The **I** departed from Rameses and Nm 33:5
year after the **I** went out of the Nm 33:38
Canaan, heard the **I** were coming. Nm 33:40
Tell the **I**: When you cross the Nm 33:51
Command the **I** and say to them: Nm 34:2
So Moses commanded the **I**, Nm 34:13
inheritance to the **I** in the land Nm 34:29
Command the **I** to give cities out Nm 35:2
Speak to the **I** and tell them: Nm 35:10
a refuge for the **I** and for the Nm 35:15
the LORD, reside among the **I**." Nm 35:34
an inheritance by lot to the **I**. Nm 36:2
the Jubilee comes for the **I**, Nm 36:4
Moses commanded the **I** at the Nm 36:5
belonging to the **I** must not Nm 36:7
each of the **I** is to retain Nm 36:7
that each of the **I** will possess Nm 36:8
commanded the **I** through Moses Nm 36:13
Moses told the **I** everything the Dt 1:3
ahead of your brothers the **I**. Dt 3:18
is the law Moses gave the **I**. Dt 4:44
and Moses and the **I** defeated him Dt 4:46
The **I** traveled from Beeroth Dt 10:6
make with the **I** in the land of Dt 29:1
and teach it to the **I**; Dt 31:19
a witness for Me against the **I**. Dt 31:19
that day and taught it to the **I**. Dt 31:22
will bring the **I** into the land I Dt 31:23
am giving the **I** as a possession Dt 32:49
Me among the **I** at the waters Dt 32:51
I am giving the **I**, you will not Dt 32:52

gave the **I** before his death. Dt 33:1
The **I** wept for Moses in the Dt 34:8
So the **I** obeyed him and did as Dt 34:9
to the land I am giving the **I**. Jos 1:2
Acacia Grove with all the **I**. Jos 3:1
Joshua told the **I**, "Come closer Jos 3:9
the 12 men selected from the **I**, Jos 4:4
always be a memorial for the **I**." Jos 4:7
The **I** did just as Joshua had Jos 4:8
formation in front of the **I**, Jos 4:12
and he said to the **I**, "When your Jos 4:21
before the **I** until they had Jos 5:1
courage failed because of the **I**. Jos 5:1
For the **I** wandered in the Jos 5:6
While the **I** camped at Gilgal on Jos 5:10
was no more manna for the **I**, Jos 5:12
fortified because of the **I**— Jos 6:1
The **I**, however, were unfaithful Jos 7:1
anger burned against the **I**. Jos 7:1
This is why the **I** cannot stand Jos 7:12
them to Joshua and all the **I**, Jos 7:23
When the king of Ai saw ⌊the **I**⌋, Jos 8:14
servant had commanded the **I**. Jos 8:31
in the presence of the **I**. Jos 8:32
So the **I** set out and reached the Jos 9:17
But the **I** did not attack them, Jos 9:18
them from the hands of the **I**, Jos 9:26
peace with Joshua and the **I**." Jos 10:4
the hail than the **I** killed with Jos 10:11
gave the Amorites over to the **I**, Jos 10:12
So Joshua and the **I** finished Jos 10:20
could say a thing against the **I**. Jos 10:21
The **I** plundered all the spoils Jos 11:14
peace with the **I** except the Jos 11:19
were left in the land of the **I**, Jos 11:22
The **I** struck down the following Jos 12:1
servant and the **I** struck them Jos 12:6
Joshua and the **I** struck down the Jos 12:7
drive them out before the **I**, Jos 13:6
but the **I** did not drive out the Jos 13:13
with those the **I** put to death, Jos 13:22
The **I** received these portions Jos 14:1
So the **I** did as the LORD Jos 14:5
when the **I** grew stronger, Jos 17:13
tribes among the **I** were left who Jos 18:2
said to the **I**, "How long will Jos 18:3
the land to the **I** according to Jos 18:10
the **I** gave Joshua son of Nun an Jos 19:49
Tell the **I**: 'Select your cities Jos 20:2
for all the **I** and foreigners Jos 20:9
So the **I**, by the LORD's command, Jos 21:3
The **I** gave these cities with Jos 21:8
The **I** gave these cities by name Jos 21:9
The **I** gave them: Shechem, the Jos 21:21
of Manasseh left the **I** at Shiloh Jos 22:9
Then the **I** heard ⌊it⌋ said, Jos 22:11
When the **I** heard ⌊this⌋, the Jos 22:12
The **I** sent Phinehas son of Jos 22:13
delivered the **I** from the LORD's Jos 22:31
Gilead to the **I** in the land of Jos 22:32
The **I** were pleased with the Jos 22:33
which the **I** had brought up from Jos 24:32
the **I** inquired of the LORD, Jdg 1:1
spoken these words to all the **I**, Jdg 2:4
the **I** went to take possession Jdg 2:6
The **I** did what was evil in the Jdg 2:11
Whenever the **I** went out, the Jdg 2:15
raised up a judge for the **I**, Jdg 2:18
the **I** would act even more Jdg 2:19
none of these **I** had fought in Jdg 3:1
of the **I** ⌊how to fight Jdg 3:2
The **I** took their daughters as Jdg 3:6
The **I** did what was evil in the Jdg 3:7
the **I** served him eight years. Jdg 3:8
The **I** cried out to the LORD. Jdg 3:9
as a deliverer to save the **I**. Jdg 3:9
The **I** again did what was evil in Jdg 3:12
The **I** served Eglon king of Moab Jdg 3:14
the **I** cried out to the LORD, Jdg 3:15
The **I** sent him to Eglon king of Jdg 3:15
I came down with him from the Jdg 3:27
The **I** again did what was evil in Jdg 4:1
the **I** cried out to the LORD, Jdg 4:3
and the **I** went up to her for Jdg 4:5
king of Canaan before the **I**. Jdg 4:23
The power of the **I** continued to Jdg 4:24
The **I** did what was evil in the Jdg 6:1
the **I** made hiding places for Jdg 6:2

Whenever the I planted crops, Jdg 6:3
and the I cried out to the LORD. Jdg 6:6
When the I cried out to Him Jdg 6:7
sent all the I to their tents, Jdg 7:8
Then the I said to Gideon, Jdg 8:22
Midian was subdued before the I, Jdg 8:28
the I turned and prostituted Jdg 8:33
The I did not remember the LORD Jdg 8:34
When the I saw that Abimelech Jdg 9:55
Then the I again did what was Jdg 10:6
and crushed the I that year, Jdg 10:8
the same to⌋ all the I who were Jdg 10:8
LORD said to the I, "When the Jdg 10:11
But the I said, "We have sinned. Jdg 10:15
So the I assembled and camped at Jdg 10:17
between the I and the Ammonites Jdg 11:27
were subdued before the I. Jdg 11:33
The I again did what was evil in Jdg 13:1
city where there are no I. Jdg 19:12
since the day the I came out of Jdg 19:30
All the I from Dan to Beer-sheba Jdg 20:1
heard that the I had gone up to Jdg 20:3
The I asked, "Tell us, how did Jdg 20:3
Look, all of you are I. Jdg 20:7
would not obey their fellow I. Jdg 20:13
go out and fight against the I. Jdg 20:14
The I, apart from Benjamin, Jdg 20:17
The I asked, "Who is to go first Jdg 20:18
the I set out and camped near Jdg 20:19
day the I advanced against Jdg 20:24
18,000 I on the field; Jdg 20:25
Then the I inquired of the LORD. Jdg 20:27
before it. The I asked: "Should Jdg 20:28
third day the I fought against Jdg 20:30
But the I said, "Let's flee and Jdg 20:32
while the I in ambush charged Jdg 20:33
on that day the I slaughtered Jdg 20:35
The I asked, "Who of all the Jdg 21:5
the I had compassion on their Jdg 21:6
For the I had sworn: Jdg 21:18
of the I returned from there Jdg 21:24
treated all the I who came there 1Sm 2:14
all the I raised such a loud 1Sm 4:5
So the I removed the Baals and 1Sm 7:4
to lead⌋ the I at Mizpah as 1Sm 7:6
heard that the I had gathered at 1Sm 7:7
When the I heard ⌊about it⌋, 1Sm 7:7
I said to Samuel, "Don't stop 1Sm 7:8
impressive among the I than he. 1Sm 9:2
and said to the I, "This is what 1Sm 10:18
were 300,000 I and 30,000 men 1Sm 11:8
So all the I went to the 1Sm 13:20
it was with the I at that time. 1Sm 14:18
they joined the I who were with 1Sm 14:21
I struck down the Philistines 1Sm 14:31
Since the I were completely 1Sm 14:31
did to the I when they opposed 1Sm 15:2
to all the I when they came out 1Sm 15:6
and the I were standing on 1Sm 17:3
When the I returned from the 1Sm 17:53
I brought the I out of Egypt 2Sm 7:6
all My journeys with all the I, 2Sm 7:7
did this to all the I who came 2Sm 15:6
and all the I came to Jerusalem 2Sm 16:15
Gibeonites were not I but rather 2Sm 21:2
The I had taken an oath 2Sm 21:2
in his zeal for the I and Judah. 2Sm 21:2
year after the I came out from 1Kg 6:1
live among the I and not abandon 1Kg 6:13
leaders of the I before him at 1Kg 8:1
with the I when they came 1Kg 8:9
king and all the I dedicated the 1Kg 8:63
and Jebusites, who were not I— 1Kg 9:20
those whom the I were unable to 1Kg 9:21
not consign the I to slavery; 1Kg 9:22
the LORD had told the I about, 1Kg 11:2
reigned over the I living in the 1Kg 12:17
against your brothers, the I. 1Kg 12:24
He made a festival for the I, 1Kg 12:33
had dispossessed before the I. 1Kg 14:24
summoned all the I and gathered 1Kg 18:20
but the I have abandoned Your 1Kg 19:10
but the I have abandoned Your 1Kg 19:14
The I mobilized, gathered 1Kg 20:27
The I camped in front of them 1Kg 20:27
and the I struck down the 1Kg 20:29
had dispossessed before the I. 1Kg 21:26
camp, the I attacked them, 2Kg 3:24
wrath was on the I, and they 2Kg 3:27
multitude of I who will die, 2Kg 7:13
defeated the I throughout their 2Kg 10:32
as the I were burying a man, 2Kg 13:21
had dispossessed before the I. 2Kg 16:3
He deported the I to Assyria and 2Kg 17:6
before the I and the customs 2Kg 17:8
The I secretly did what was not 2Kg 17:9
The I persisted in all the sins 2Kg 17:22
in place of the I in the cities 2Kg 17:24
for the I burned incense to it 2Kg 18:4
deported the I to Assyria and 2Kg 18:11
had dispossessed before the I. 2Kg 21:2
the feet of the I to wander 2Kg 21:8
LORD had destroyed before the I. 2Kg 21:9
any king ruled over the I: 1Ch 1:43
So the I gave these towns and 1Ch 6:64
their own property again were I, 1Ch 9:2
the I went up to Baal-perazim, 1Ch 14:11
This is the list of the I, 1Ch 27:1
the ancestral chiefs of the I— 2Ch 5:2
with the I when they came 2Ch 5:10
is that He made with the I. 2Ch 6:11
All the I were watching when the 2Ch 7:3
and having settled the I there— 2Ch 8:2
those whom the I had not 2Ch 8:8
not consign the I to be slaves 2Ch 8:9
But as for the I living in the 2Ch 10:17
but the I stoned him to death. 2Ch 10:18
I, don't fight against the LORD 2Ch 13:12
So the I fled before Judah, 2Ch 13:16
The I were subdued at that time. 2Ch 13:18
had dispossessed before the I. 2Ch 28:3
Then the I took 200,000 captives 2Ch 28:8
The I brought them to Jericho, 2Ch 28:15
command, saying, "I, return to 2Ch 30:6
The I who were present in 2Ch 30:21
Then all the I returned to their 2Ch 31:1
the I gave liberally of the best 2Ch 31:5
As for the I and Judahites who 2Ch 31:6
had dispossessed before the I. 2Ch 33:2
the feet of the I from upon the 2Ch 33:8
LORD had destroyed before the I. 2Ch 33:9
the lands belonging to the I, 2Ch 34:33
I who were present ⌊in Judah⌋ 2Ch 35:17
I who were present ⌊in Judah⌋ 2Ch 35:18
I had settled in their towns, Ezr 3:1
Then the I, including the Ezr 6:16
I who had returned from exile Ezr 6:21
Some of the I, priests, Levites, Ezr 7:7
that any of the I in my kingdom, Ezr 7:13
and all the I who were present Ezr 8:25
The I: Parosh's descendants: Ezr 10:25
night for Your servants, the I. Neh 1:6
to seek the well-being of the I, Neh 2:10
month came and the I had settled Neh 8:1
Moses that the I should dwell in Neh 8:14
The I celebrated the feast for Neh 8:18
of this month the I assembled; Neh 9:1
For the I and the Levites are to Neh 10:39
towns—the I, priests, Levites Neh 11:3
did not meet the I with food and Neh 13:2
ones, from the I, the people Ps 148:14
be like the splendor of the I. Is 17:3
were abandoned because of the I; Is 17:9
and you I will be gathered one Is 27:12
to the One the I have greatly Is 31:6
just as the I bring an offering Is 66:20
who brought the I from the land Jr 16:14
who brought the I from the land Jr 16:15
who brought the I from the land Jr 23:7
the I and Judeans have done Jr 32:30
the evil the I and Judeans have Jr 32:32
the I and Judeans will come Jr 50:4
I and Judeans alike have been Jr 50:33
am sending you to the I ⌊and⌋ to Ezk 2:3
The I and their ancestors have Ezk 2:3
This is how the I will eat their Ezk 4:13
corpses of the I in front of Ezk 6:5
handed over the I to the power Ezk 35:5
Judah and the I associated with Ezk 37:16
going to take the I out of the Ezk 37:21
will dwell among the I forever. Ezk 43:7
a foreigner who is among the I. Ezk 44:9
sanctuary when the I went astray Ezk 44:15
treat them like native-born I; Ezk 47:22
did when the I went astray. Ezk 48:11
some of the I from the royal Dn 1:3
the number of the I will be like Hs 1:10
Judeans and the I will be Hs 1:11
loves the I though they turn Hs 3:1
For the I must live many days Hs 3:4
have scattered the I in foreign Jl 3:2
people, a stronghold for the I. Jl 3:16
Is this not the case, I? Am 2:11
against you, I, against the Am 3:1
the I who live in Samaria will Am 3:12
that is what you I love ⌊to do⌋! Am 4:5
I, are you not like the Cushites Am 9:7
exiles of the I who are in Halah Ob 20
They are I, and to them belong Rm 9:4
am I. Are they I? So am I. Are 2Co 11:22

ISRAELITES' (16)

The I cry for help has come to Ex 3:9
It will be the I contribution Ex 29:28
children from the I fellowship Lv 10:14
sins because of the I impurities Lv 16:16
it apart from the I impurities. Lv 16:19
over it all the I wrongdoings Lv 16:21
firstborn among the I cattle." Nm 3:41
have heard the I complaints that Nm 14:27
Myself of the I complaints that Nm 17:5
given all the I presentation Nm 18:11
not defile the I holy offerings, Nm 18:32
From the I half, take one out of Nm 31:30
From the I half, which Moses Nm 31:42
the livestock from the I half. Nm 31:47
stages of the I journey when Nm 33:1
you give from the I territory, Nm 35:8

ISSACHAR (35)

husband," and she named him I. Gn 30:18
Levi, Judah, I, and Zebulun. Gn 35:23
I is a strong donkey lying down Gn 49:14
I, Zebulun, and Benjamin; Ex 1:3
Nethanel son of Zuar from I; Nm 1:8
The descendants of I: Nm 1:28
the tribe of I numbered 54,400 Nm 1:29
The tribe of I will camp next to Nm 2:5
of Zuar, leader of I, presented Nm 7:18
the division of the I tribe, Nm 10:15
of Joseph from the tribe of I; Nm 13:7
a leader from the tribe of I; Nm 34:26
Simeon, Levi, Judah, I, Joseph, Dt 27:12
journeys, and I, in your tents. Dt 33:18
on the north and I on the east. Jos 17:10
Within I and Asher, Manasseh had Jos 17:11
the clans of the tribes of I, Jos 21:6
From the tribe of I ⌊they gave⌋: Jos 21:28
The princes of I were with Jdg 5:15
with Deborah; I was with Barak. Jdg 5:15
was from I and lived in Shamir Jdg 10:1
Jehoshaphat son of Paruah, in I; 1Kg 4:17
of the house of I conspired 1Kg 15:27
Simeon, Levi, Judah, I, Zebulun, 1Ch 2:1
13 towns from the tribes of I, 1Ch 6:62
the tribe of I ⌊they received⌋ 1Ch 6:72
families of I totalled 87,000 1Ch 7:5
neighbors from as far away as I, 1Ch 12:40
Ammiel the sixth, I the seventh, 1Ch 26:5
for I, Omri son of Michael; 1Ch 27:18
Manasseh, I, and Zebulun— 2Ch 30:18
west, will be I—one ⌊portion⌋ Ezk 48:25
Next to the territory of I, Ezk 48:26
one, the gate of I; Ezk 48:33
12,000 from the tribe of I, Rv 7:7

ISSACHAR'S (6)

I sons: Tola, Puvah, Jashub, and Gn 46:13
I descendants by their clans: Nm 26:23
These were I clans ⌊numbered⌋ by Nm 26:25
for the tribe of I descendants Jos 19:17
of the tribe of I descendants by Jos 19:23
I sons: Tola, Puah, Jashub, and 1Ch 7:1

ISSACHARITES (2)

leader of the I is Nethanel son Nm 2:5
From the I, who understood the 1Ch 12:32

ISSHIAH (5)

Michael, Obadiah, Joel, I. 1Ch 7:3
Elkanah, I, Azarel, Joezer, and 1Ch 12:6
Micah was first, and I second. 1Ch 23:20
sons: I was the first. 1Ch 24:21
brother: I; from Isshiah's 1Ch 24:25

ISSHIAH'S (1)

Isshiah; from I sons: Zechariah. 1Ch 24:25

ISSHIJAH *(1)*
Eliezer, **I**, Malchijah, Shemaiah, Ezr 10:31

ISSUE *(19)*
will **i** a command on your behalf. 2Sm 14:8
to address the **i** indirectly, 2Sm 14:20
What is ⌊the **i**⌋ between you and 2Ch 35:21
of Persia to **i** a proclamation 2Ch 36:22
King Cyrus to **i** a proclamation Ezr 1:1
i an order for these men to stop, Ezr 4:21
I hereby **i** a decree concerning Ezr 6:8
I also **i** a decree concerning any Ezr 6:11
I **i** a decree that any of the Ezr 7:13
i a decree to all the treasurers Ezr 7:21
personally **i** a royal decree. Est 1:19
my righteousness is still the **i**. Jb 6:29
The decrees You **i** are righteous Ps 119:138
his ruler will **i** from him. Jr 30:21
Therefore I **i** a decree that Dn 3:29
i a decree that in all my royal Dn 6:26
a spring will **i** from the LORD's Jl 3:18
Her leaders **i** rulings for a Mc 3:11
⌊This **i** arose⌋ because of false Gl 2:4

ISSUED *(21)*
He **i** His verdict last night." Gn 31:42
the day the LORD **i** the commands Nm 15:23
the king of Assyria **i** a command: 2Kg 17:27
proclamation was **i** in Judah and 2Ch 24:9
I **i** a decree and a search was Ezr 4:19
he **i** a decree to rebuild this Ezr 5:13
a decree was **i** by King Cyrus to Ezr 5:17
he **i** a decree concerning the Ezr 6:3
I, Darius, have **i** the decree. Ezr 6:12
i as law throughout every Est 3:14
the law was **i** in the fortress Est 3:15
decree **i** in Susa ordering Est 4:8
was to be **i** as law in every Est 8:13
law was also **i** in the fortress Est 8:14
The LORD has **i** a decree against Lm 1:17
The decree was **i** that the wise Dn 2:13
You as king have **i** a decree that Dn 3:10
So I **i** a decree to bring all the Dn 4:6
and **i** a proclamation concerning Dn 5:29
Then he **i** a decree in Nineveh: Jnh 3:7
The LORD has **i** an order Nah 1:14

ISSUES *(2)*
decree the king **i** will be heard Est 1:20
don't argue about doubtful **i**. Rm 14:1

ISSUING *(1)*
From the **i** of the decree to Dn 9:25

IT *(5030)*
(See pp. xi-xii.)

IT'S *(52)*
(See pp. xi-xii.)

ITALIAN *(1)*
what was called the **I** Regiment. Ac 10:1

ITALY *(4)*
come from **I** with his wife Ac 18:2
that we were to sail to **I**, Ac 27:1
ship sailing for **I** and put us on Ac 27:6
Those who are from **I** greet you. Heb 13:24

ITCH *(1)*
they have an **i** to hear something 2Tm 4:3

ITEM *(4)*
to him, or the lost **i** he found, Lv 6:4
unclean—any **i** of wood, Lv 11:32
shields, and every desirable **i**. 2Ch 32:27
treasury of every precious **i**. Hs 13:15

ITEMS *(13)*
to get back the **i** he had left Gn 38:20
her keep ⌊the **i**⌋ for herself; Gn 38:23
the man to whom these **i** belong." Gn 38:25
needs to be done with these **i**. Nm 4:26
by name the **i** that they are Nm 4:32
Joram had **i** of silver, gold, and 2Sm 8:10
beds, basins, and pottery **i**. 2Sm 17:28
i of silver and gold, clothing, 1Kg 10:25
the consecrated **i** that his 2Kg 12:18
own consecrated **i** and all the 2Kg 12:18
brought⌋ all kinds of **i** of gold, 1Ch 18:10
his own gift—**i** of silver and 2Ch 9:24
on the bodies and valuable **i**. 2Ch 20:25

ITHAI *(1)*
(AKA ITTAI)
I son of Ribai from Gibeah of 1Ch 11:31

ITHAMAR *(17)*
Nadab and Abihu, Eleazar and **I**. Ex 6:23
Nadab and Abihu, Eleazar and **I**. Ex 28:1
the direction of **I** son of Aaron Ex 38:21
and his sons Eleazar and **I**, Lv 10:6
remaining sons, Eleazar and **I**: Lv 10:12
He was angry with Eleazar and **I**, Lv 10:16
and Abihu, Eleazar, and **I**. Nm 3:2
So Eleazar and **I** served as Nm 3:4
the direction of **I** son of Aaron Nm 4:28
the direction of **I** son of Aaron Nm 4:33
the direction of **I** son of Aaron Nm 7:8
Eleazar, and **I** were born to Nm 26:60
Nadab, Abihu, Eleazar, and **I**. 1Ch 6:3
Nadab, Abihu, Eleazar, and **I**. 1Ch 24:1
so Eleazar and **I** served as 1Ch 24:2
Ahimelech from the sons of **I**, 1Ch 24:3
for Eleazar, and then one for **I**. 1Ch 24:6

ITHAMAR'S *(4)*
Eleazar's descendants than **I**, 1Ch 24:4
of ancestral houses were from **I**. 1Ch 24:4
Eleazar's and **I** descendants. 1Ch 24:5
Daniel, from **I** descendants; Ezr 8:2

ITHIEL *(3)*
son of **I**, son of Jeshaiah Neh 11:7
man's oration to **I**, to Ithiel Pr 30:1
to Ithiel, to **I** and Ucal: Pr 30:1

ITHLAH *(1)*
Shaalabbin, Aijalon, **I**, Jos 19:42

ITHMAH *(1)*
sons of Elnaam, **I** the Moabite, 1Ch 11:46

ITHNAN *(1)*
Kedesh, Hazor, **I**, Jos 15:23

ITHRA *(2)*
(AKA JETHER)
of a man named **I** the Israelite; 2Sm 17:25
I had married Abigail daughter 2Sm 17:25

ITHRAN *(3)*
Hemdan, Eshban, **I**, and Cheran. Gn 36:26
Hamran, Eshban, **I**, and Cheran. 1Ch 1:41
Shamma, Shilshah, **I**, and Beera. 1Ch 7:37

ITHREAM *(2)*
the sixth was **I**, by David's wife 2Sm 3:5
I, by David's wife Eglah, was 1Ch 3:3

ITHRITE *(4)*
Ira the **I**, Gareb the Ithrite, 2Sm 23:38
Ira the Ithrite, Gareb the **I**, 2Sm 23:38
Ira the **I**, Gareb the Ithrite, 1Ch 11:40
Ira the Ithrite, Gareb the **I**, 1Ch 11:40

ITHRITES *(1)*
Kiriath-jearim—the **I**, Puthites, 1Ch 2:53

ITINERANT *(1)*
some of the **i** Jewish exorcists Ac 19:13

ITS *(1281)*
(See pp. xi-xii.)

ITSELF *(53)*
(See pp. xi-xii.)

ITTAI *(8)*
(AKA ITHAI)
The king said to **I** the Gittite, 2Sm 15:19
But in response, **I** vowed to the 2Sm 15:21
"March on," David replied to **I**. 2Sm 15:22
So **I** the Gittite marched past 2Sm 15:22
one third under **I** the Gittite. 2Sm 18:2
Abishai, and **I**, "Treat the young 2Sm 18:5
you, Abishai, and **I**, 'Protect 2Sm 18:12
I son of Ribai from Gibeah of 2Sm 23:29

ITUREA *(1)*
the region of **I** and Trachonitis Lk 3:1

IVORY *(13)*
also made a large **i** throne and 1Kg 10:18
gold, silver, **i**, apes, and 1Kg 10:22
the **i** palace he built, 1Kg 22:39
also made a large **i** throne and 2Ch 9:17
gold, silver, **i**, apes, and 2Ch 9:21
from **i** palaces harps bring you Ps 45:8
His body is an **i** panel covered Sg 5:14
Your neck is like a tower of **i**, Sg 7:4
of Cyprus, ⌊inlaid⌋ with **i**. Ezk 27:6
brought back **i** tusks and ebony Ezk 27:15
with⌋ **i** will be destroyed, Am 3:15
lie on beds ⌊inlaid with⌋ **i**, Am 6:4
products; objects of **i**; objects Rv 18:12

IVVAH *(3)*
(AKA AVVA)
gods of Sepharvaim, Hena, and **I**? 2Kg 18:34
of Sepharvaim, Hena, or **I**?'" 2Kg 19:13
of Sepharvaim, Hena, or **I**?'" Is 37:13

IYE-ABARIM *(2)*
camped at **I** in the wilderness Nm 21:11
and camped at **I** on the border Nm 33:44

IYIM *(1)*
departed from **I** and camped at Nm 33:45

IZHAR *(8)*
(AKA ZOHAR)
Amram, **I**, Hebron, and Uzziel. Ex 6:18
sons of **I**: Korah, Nepheg, and Ex 6:21
clans were Amram, **I**, Hebron, and Nm 3:19
Korah son of **I**, son of Kohath, Nm 16:1
Amram, **I**, Hebron, and Uzziel. 1Ch 6:2
Amram, **I**, Hebron and Uzziel. 1Ch 6:18
son of **I**, son of Kohath, son of 1Ch 6:38
Amram, **I**, Hebron, and Uzziel— 1Ch 23:12

IZHAR'S *(1)*
I sons: Shelomith was first. 1Ch 23:18

IZHARITE *(1)*
Amramite clan, the **I** clan, the Nm 3:27

IZHARITES *(2)*
From the **I**: Shelomoth; from 1Ch 24:22
the **I**, the Hebronites, 1Ch 26:23

IZLIAH *(1)*
Ishmerai, **I**, and Jobab were 1Ch 8:18

IZRAHIAH *(1)*
Uzzi's son: **I**. Izrahiah's sons: 1Ch 7:3

IZRAHIAH'S *(1)*
son: Izrahiah. **I** sons: Michael, 1Ch 7:3

IZRAHITE *(1)*
the commander Shamhuth the **I**; 1Ch 27:8

IZRAHITES *(1)*
From the **I**: Chenaniah and his 1Ch 26:29

IZRI *(1)*
the fourth to **I**, his sons, and 1Ch 25:11

IZZIAH *(1)*
Ramiah, **I**, Malchijah, Mijamin, Ezr 10:25

J

JAAKAN *(1)*
(AKA AKAN)
Bilhan, Zaavan, and **J**. 1Ch 1:42

JAAKOBAH *(1)*
Elioenai, **J**, Jeshohaiah, Asaiah, 1Ch 4:36

JAALA'S *(1)*
J descendants, Darkon's Neh 7:58

JAALAH'S *(1)*
J descendants, Darkon's Ezr 2:56

JAAR *(1)*
we found it in the fields of **J**. Ps 132:6

JAARE-OREGIM *(1)*
(AKA JAIR)
son of **J** the Bethlehemite 2Sm 21:19

JAARESHIAH *(1)*
J, Elijah, and Zichri were 1Ch 8:27

JAASIEL *(2)*
Obed, and **J** the Mezobaite. 1Ch 11:47
for Benjamin, **J** son of Abner; 1Ch 27:21

JAASU *(1)*
Mattaniah, Mattenai, **J**, Ezr 10:37

JAAZANIAH *(4)*
(AKA AZARIAH, JEZANIAH)
and **J** son of the Maacathite— 2Kg 25:23
So I took **J** son of Jeremiah, Jr 35:3
with **J** son of Shaphan standing Ezk 8:11
Among them I saw **J** son of Azzur, Ezk 11:1

JAAZIAH *(2)*
and from⌋ his sons, **J** his son. 1Ch 24:26
Merari's sons, by his son **J**: 1Ch 24:27

JAAZIEL *(1)*
(AKA AZIEL)
Zechariah, **J**, Shemiramoth, 1Ch 15:18

JABAL *(1)*
Adah bore **J**; he was the father Gn 4:20

JABBOK *(7)*
and crossed the ford of **J**. Gn 32:22
land from the Arnon to the **J**, Nm 21:24

the bank of the **J** River and the Dt 2:37
up to the **J** River, the border Dt 3:16
half of Gilead up to the **J** River Jos 12:2
Arnon to the **J** and the Jordan. Jdg 11:13
from the Arnon to the **J** and from Jdg 11:22

JABESH *(12)*

All the men of **J** said to him, 1Sm 11:1
the elders of **J** said to him, 1Sm 11:3
him the words of the men from **J**. 1Sm 11:5
messengers told the men of **J**, 1Sm 11:9
the men of **J** said to ⌊Nahash⌋ 1Sm 11:10
they arrived at **J**, they burned 1Sm 31:12
tree in **J** and fasted seven 1Sm 31:13
Shallum son of **J** conspired 2Kg 15:10
Shallum son of **J** became king; 2Kg 15:13
down Shallum son of **J** there. 2Kg 15:14
his sons and brought them to **J**. 1Ch 10:12
the oak in **J** and fasted seven 1Ch 10:12

JABESH-GILEAD *(12)*

that no one from **J** had come to Jdg 21:8
there from the inhabitants of **J**. Jdg 21:9
inhabitants of **J** with the sword, Jdg 21:10
inhabitants of **J** 400 young Jdg 21:12
they had kept alive from **J**. Jdg 21:14
came up and laid siege to **J**. 1Sm 11:1
Tell this to the men of **J**: 1Sm 11:9
the residents of **J** heard what 1Sm 31:11
the men of **J** who buried Saul. 2Sm 2:4
the men of **J** and said to them, 2Sm 2:5
Jonathan from the leaders of **J**. 2Sm 21:12
When all **J** heard of everything 1Ch 10:11

JABEZ *(4)*

of scribes who lived in **J**— 1Ch 2:55
J was more honorable than his 1Ch 4:9
His mother named him **J** and said, 1Ch 4:9
J called out to the God of 1Ch 4:10

JABIN *(7)*

When **J** king of Hazor heard ⌊this 1Jos 11:1
the hand of **J** king of Canaan, Jdg 4:2
because **J** had 900 iron chariots, Jdg 4:3
peace between **J** king of Hazor Jdg 4:17
day God subdued **J** king of Canaan Jdg 4:23
increase against **J** king of Jdg 4:24
with Sisera and **J** at the Kishon Ps 83:9

JABIN'S *(1)*

Sisera commander of **J** forces, Jdg 4:7

JABNEEL *(2)*
(AKA JABNEH)

Baalah, went to **J**, and ended at Jos 15:11
including Adami-nekeb and **J**, Jos 19:33

JABNEH *(1)*
(AKA JABNEEL)

Gath, the wall of **J**, and the 2Ch 26:6

JACAN *(1)*

Sheba, Jorai, **J**, Zia, and Eber— 1Ch 5:13

JACHIN *(8)*
(AKA JARIB)

Ohad, **J**, Zohar, and Shaul, Gn 46:10
Ohad, **J**, Zohar, and Shaul, Ex 6:15
the Jachinite clan from **J**; Nm 26:12
the right pillar and named it **J**; 1Kg 7:21
priests: Jedaiah; Jehoiarib; **J**; 1Ch 9:10
twenty-first to **J**, the 1Ch 24:17
one on the right **J** and the one 2Ch 3:17
Jedaiah son of Joiarib, **J**, and Neh 11:10

JACHINITE *(1)*

the **J** clan from Jachin; Nm 26:12

JACINTH *(3)*

third row, a **j**, an agate, and Ex 28:19
third row, a **j**, an agate, and Ex 39:12
the eleventh **j**, the twelfth Rv 21:20

JACKALS *(13)*

a brother to **j** and a companion Jb 30:29
in a haunt of **j** and have covered Ps 44:19
fortresses, and **j**, in the Is 13:22
will become a dwelling for **j**, Is 34:13
the haunt of **j**, in their lairs Is 35:7
will honor Me, **j** and ostriches, Is 43:20
heights panting for air like **j**. Jr 14:6
creatures will live with **j**, Jr 50:39
Even **j** offer ⌊their⌋ breasts to Lm 4:3
and has⌋ **j** prowling in it. Lm 5:18
Israel, are like **j** among ruins. Ezk 13:4
howl like the **j** and mourn like Mc 1:8
inheritance to the desert **j**." Mal 1:3

JACKALS' *(5)*

they will become the **j** prey. Ps 63:10
a heap of rubble, a **j** den. Jr 9:11
will be made desolate, a **j** den. Jr 10:22
Hazor will become a **j** den, Jr 49:33
of rubble, a **j** den, a desolation Jr 51:37

JACOB *(367)*
(AKA ISRAEL)

So he was named **J**. Isaac was 60 Gn 25:26
but **J** was a quiet man who stayed Gn 25:27
wild game, but Rebekah loved **J**. Gn 25:28
Once when **J** was cooking a stew, Gn 25:29
said to **J**, "Let me eat some of Gn 25:30
J replied, "First sell me your Gn 25:31
J said, "Swear to me first." Gn 25:33
So he swore to **J** and sold his Gn 25:33
J gave bread and lentil stew Gn 25:34
Rebekah said to her son **J**, Gn 27:6
J answered Rebekah his mother, Gn 27:11
had her younger son **J** wear them. Gn 27:15
bread she had made to her son **J**. Gn 27:17
J replied to his father, "I am Gn 27:19
Isaac said to **J**, "Please come Gn 27:21
So **J** came closer to his father Gn 27:22
The voice is the voice of **J**, Gn 27:22
J brought it to him, and he Gn 27:25
finished blessing **J** and Jacob Gn 27:30
blessing Jacob and **J** had left Gn 27:30
Isn't he rightly named **J**? Gn 27:36
held a grudge against **J** because Gn 27:41
then I will kill my brother **J**." Gn 27:41
younger son **J** and said to him Gn 27:42
J marries a Hittite woman like Gn 27:46
Isaac summoned **J**, blessed him, Gn 28:1
So Isaac sent **J** to Paddan-aram, Gn 28:5
the mother of **J** and Esau. Gn 28:5
Isaac blessed **J** and sent him to Gn 28:6
Isaac commanded **J** not to marry a Gn 28:6
And **J** listened to his father and Gn 28:7
J left Beer-sheba and went Gn 28:10
When **J** awoke from his sleep, Gn 28:16
in the morning **J** took the stone Gn 28:18
Then **J** made a vow: "If God will Gn 28:20
J resumed his journey and went Gn 29:1
J asked the men at the well, Gn 29:4
of Nahor?" **J** asked them. They Gn 29:5
"Is he well?" **J** asked. "Yes," Gn 29:6
Then **J** said, "Look, it is still Gn 29:7
As soon as **J** saw his uncle Gn 29:10
Then **J** kissed Rachel and wept Gn 29:11
news about his sister's son **J**, Gn 29:13
and **J** told him all that had Gn 29:13
After **J** had stayed with him a Gn 29:14
J loved Rachel, so he answered Gn 29:18
So **J** worked seven years for Gn 29:20
Then **J** said to Laban, "Give me Gn 29:21
daughter Leah and gave her to **J**, Gn 29:23
And **J** did just that. He finished Gn 29:28
J slept with Rachel also, and Gn 29:30
not bearing **J** ⌊any children⌋, Gn 30:1
or I will die!" she said to **J**. Gn 30:1
J became angry with Rachel and Gn 30:2
her slave Bilhah to **J** as a wife, Gn 30:4
conceived and bore **J** a son. Gn 30:5
again and bore **J** a second son. Gn 30:7
and gave her to **J** as a wife. Gn 30:9
slave Zilpah bore **J** a son. Gn 30:10
Zilpah bore **J** a second son, Gn 30:12
When **J** came in from the field Gn 30:16
So **J** slept with her that night. Gn 30:16
and bore **J** a fifth son. Gn 30:17
again and bore **J** a sixth son. Gn 30:19
to Joseph, **J** said to Laban, Gn 30:25
So **J** said to him, "You know what Gn 30:29
And **J** said, "You don't need to Gn 30:31
journey between himself and **J**. Gn 30:36
J, meanwhile, was shepherding Gn 30:36
J then took branches of fresh Gn 30:37
J separated the lambs and made Gn 30:40
J placed the branches in the Gn 30:41
and the stronger ones to **J**. Gn 30:42
Now **J** heard what Laban's sons Gn 31:1
J has taken all that was our Gn 31:1
And **J** saw from Laban's face that Gn 31:2
J had Rachel and Leah called to Gn 31:4
Angel of God said to me, '**J**!' Gn 31:11
Then **J** got up and put his Gn 31:17
J deceived Laban the Aramean, Gn 31:20
Laban was told that **J** had fled. Gn 31:22
him, pursued **J** for seven days, Gn 31:23
say anything to **J**, either good Gn 31:24
Laban overtook **J**, Jacob had Gn 31:25
J had pitched his tent in the Gn 31:25
Laban said to **J**, "What have you Gn 31:26
say anything to **J**, either good Gn 31:29
J answered, "I was afraid, for I Gn 31:31
J did not know that Rachel had Gn 31:32
Then **J** became incensed and Gn 31:36
Laban answered **J**, "The daughters Gn 31:43
So **J** picked out a stone and set Gn 31:45
Then **J** said to his relatives, Gn 31:46
but **J** named it Galeed. Gn 31:47
also said to **J**, "Look at this Gn 31:51
And **J** swore by the Fear of his Gn 31:53
Then **J** offered a sacrifice on Gn 31:54
J went on his way, and God's Gn 32:1
he saw them, **J** said, "This is Gn 32:2
J sent messengers ahead of him Gn 32:3
is what your servant **J** says. Gn 32:4
the messengers returned to **J**, Gn 32:6
J was greatly afraid and Gn 32:7
Then **J** said, "God of my father Gn 32:9
'They belong to your servant **J**. Gn 32:18
servant **J** is right behind us. Gn 32:20
the night **J** got up and took Gn 32:22
J was left alone, and a man Gn 32:24
Then He said to **J**, "Let Me go, Gn 32:26
But **J** said, "I will not let You Gn 32:26
the man asked. "**J**!" he replied. Gn 32:27
"Your name will no longer be **J**," Gn 32:28
Then **J** asked Him, "Please tell Gn 32:29
J then named the place Peniel, Gn 32:30
Now **J** looked up and saw Esau Gn 33:1
But **J** said, "No, please! Gn 33:10
So **J** urged him until he Gn 33:11
J replied, "My lord knows that Gn 33:13
but **J** went on to Succoth. Gn 33:17
After **J** came from Paddan-aram, Gn 33:18
daughter whom she bore to **J**, Gn 34:1
with Dinah, daughter of **J**. Gn 34:3
J heard that Shechem had defiled Gn 34:5
Hamor came to speak with **J**. Gn 34:6
Then **J** said to Simeon and Levi, Gn 34:30
God said to **J**, "Get up! Gn 35:1
So **J** said to his family and all Gn 35:2
Then they gave **J** all their Gn 35:4
J hid them under the oak near Gn 35:4
So **J** and all who were with him Gn 35:6
J built an altar there and Gn 35:7
So **J** named it Oak of Weeping. Gn 35:8
God appeared to **J** again after he Gn 35:9
him: Your name is **J**; you will no Gn 35:10
you will no longer be named **J**, Gn 35:10
J set up a marker at the place Gn 35:14
J named the place where God had Gn 35:15
J set up a marker on her grave; Gn 35:20
heard about it. **J** had 12 sons: Gn 35:22
are the sons of **J**, who were born Gn 35:26
J came to his father Isaac at Gn 35:27
His sons Esau and **J** buried him. Gn 35:29
a land away from his brother **J**. Gn 36:6
J lived in the land where his Gn 37:1
are the family records of **J**. Gn 37:2
Then **J** tore his clothes, put Gn 37:34
When **J** learned that there was Gn 42:1
But **J** did not send Joseph's Gn 42:4
their father **J** in the land Gn 42:29
Their father **J** said to them, Gn 42:36
But **J** answered, "My son will not Gn 42:38
to their father **J** in the land Gn 45:25
J was stunned, for he did not Gn 45:26
when they told **J** all that Joseph Gn 45:27
of their father **J** revived. Gn 45:27
a vision: "**J**, Jacob!" He said. Gn 46:2
a vision: "Jacob, **J**!" He said. Gn 46:2
And **J** replied, "Here I am." Gn 46:2
J left Beer-sheba. The sons of Gn 46:5
their father **J** in the wagons Gn 46:5
Then **J** and all his children with Gn 46:6
of the Israelites, **J** and his Gn 46:8
sons born to **J** in Paddan-aram, Gn 46:15
Leah—that she bore to **J**: Gn 46:18
sons who were born to **J**: Gn 46:22
She bore to **J**: seven persons. Gn 46:25
of persons belonging to **J**— Gn 46:26
J had sent Judah ahead of him Gn 46:28

his father J and presented him	Gn 47:7
Pharaoh, and J blessed Pharaoh.	Gn 47:7
Pharaoh said to J, "How many	Gn 47:8
J said to Pharaoh, "My	Gn 47:9
J blessed Pharaoh and departed	Gn 47:10
Now J lived in the land of Egypt	Gn 47:28
And J said, "Swear to me."	Gn 47:31
J was told, "Your son Joseph	Gn 48:2
J said to Joseph, "God Almighty	Gn 48:3
So J said, "Bring them to me	Gn 48:9
Then J called his sons and said,	Gn 49:1
together and listen, sons of J;	Gn 49:2
them throughout J and scatter	Gn 49:7
hands of the Mighty One of J,	Gn 49:24
When J had finished instructing	Gn 49:33
promised Abraham, Isaac, and J."	Gn 50:24
Israel who came to Egypt with J;	Ex 1:1
with Abraham, Isaac, and J.	Ex 2:24
God of Isaac, and the God of J."	Ex 3:6
and the God of J, has sent me to	Ex 3:15
Isaac, and J, has appeared to me	Ex 3:16
and the God of J, has appeared	Ex 4:5
Isaac, and J as God Almighty,	Ex 6:3
Isaac, and J, and I will give it	Ex 6:8
you must say to the house of J,	Ex 19:3
Abraham, Isaac, and J, saying:	Ex 33:1
remember My covenant with J.	Lv 26:42
Come, put a curse on J for me;	Nm 23:7
the dust of J or numbered	Nm 23:10
He considers no disaster for J;	Nm 23:21
against J and no divination	Nm 23:23
now be said about J and Israel,	Nm 23:23
your tents, J, your dwellings	Nm 24:5
will come from J, and a scepter	Nm 24:17
One who comes from J will rule;	Nm 24:19
to give⌋ Abraham, Isaac, and J—	Nm 32:11
J and their descendants after	Dt 1:8
and J that He would give you—	Dt 6:10
fathers, Abraham, Isaac, and J.	Dt 9:5
servants Abraham, Isaac, and J.	Dt 9:27
fathers Abraham, Isaac, and J.	Dt 29:13
fathers Abraham, Isaac, and J."	Dt 30:20
is His people, J, His own	Dt 32:9
for the assembly of J.	Dt 33:4
Your ordinances to J and Your	Dt 33:10
J lives untroubled in a land of	Dt 33:28
Isaac, and J, 'I will give it to	Dt 34:4
and to Isaac I gave J and Esau.	Jos 24:4
but J and his sons went down to	Jos 24:4
parcel of land J had purchased	Jos 24:32
When J went to Egypt, your	1Sm 12:8
one anointed by the God of J,	2Sm 23:1
of the tribes of the sons of J,	1Kg 18:31
with Abraham, Isaac, and J.	2Kg 13:23
commanded the descendants of J;	2Kg 17:34
and confirmed to J as a decree,	1Ch 16:17
captive people, J will rejoice;	Ps 14:7
you descendants of J, honor Him!	Ps 22:23
seek the face of the God of J.	Ps 24:6
who ordains victories for J.	Ps 44:4
the God of J is our stronghold.	Ps 46:7
the God of J is our stronghold.	Ps 46:11
the pride of J, whom He loves.	Ps 47:4
captive people, J will rejoice;	Ps 53:6
the earth that God rules over J.	Ps 59:13
sing praise to the God of J.	Ps 75:9
rebuke, God of J, both chariot	Ps 76:6
the descendants of J and Joseph.	Ps 77:15
testimony in J and set up a law	Ps 78:5
then fire broke out against J,	Ps 78:21
be shepherd over His people J—	Ps 78:71
have devoured J and devastated	Ps 79:7
in triumph to the God of J.	Ps 81:1
a judgment of the God of J.	Ps 81:4
prayer; listen, God of J. Selah	Ps 84:8
than all the dwellings of J.	Ps 87:2
The God of J doesn't pay	Ps 94:7
justice and righteousness in J.	Ps 99:4
and confirmed to J as a decree	Ps 105:10
J lived as a foreigner in the	Ps 105:23
the house of J from a people who	Ps 114:1
at the presence of the God of J,	Ps 114:7
a vow to the Mighty One of J:	Ps 132:2
for the Mighty One of J."	Ps 132:5
LORD has chosen J for Himself,	Ps 135:4
one whose help is the God of J,	Ps 146:5
He declares His word to J,	Ps 147:19
to the house of the God of J.	Is 2:3
House of J, come and let us walk	Is 2:5
the house of J, because they are	Is 2:6
His face from the house of J.	Is 8:17
Lord sent a message against J;	Is 9:8
of the house of J will no longer	Is 10:20
the remnant of J, to the Mighty	Is 10:21
compassion on J and will choose	Is 14:1
be united with the house of J.	Is 14:1
day the splendor of J will fade,	Is 17:4
days to come, J will take root.	Is 27:6
says this about the house of J:	Is 29:22
J will no longer be ashamed and	Is 29:22
the Holy One of J and stand in	Is 29:23
J, why do you say, and Israel,	Is 40:27
My servant, J, whom I have	Is 41:8
fear, you worm J, you men of	Is 41:14
Who gave J to the robber, and	Is 42:24
He poured out on J His furious	Is 42:25
created you, J, and the One who	Is 43:1
But J, you have not called on	Is 43:22
and gave J over to total	Is 43:28
And now listen, J My servant,	Is 44:1
Do not fear; J is My servant; I	Is 44:2
call ⌊himself⌋ by the name of J;	Is 44:5
these things, J, and Israel, for	Is 44:21
For the LORD has redeemed J,	Is 44:23
because of J My servant and	Is 45:4
not say to the descendants of J:	Is 45:19
to Me, house of J, all the	Is 46:3
this, house of J—those who are	Is 48:1
Listen to Me, J, and Israel, the	Is 48:12
has redeemed His servant J!"	Is 48:20
to bring J back to Him so that	Is 49:5
up the tribes of J and restoring	Is 49:6
Redeemer, the Mighty One of J."	Is 49:26
and the house of J their sins.	Is 58:1
the heritage of your father J."	Is 58:14
and to those in J who turn from	Is 59:20
Redeemer, the Mighty One of J.	Is 60:16
will produce descendants from J,	Is 65:9
house of J and all families of	Jr 2:4
Declare this in the house of J;	Jr 5:20
name, for they have consumed J;	Jr 10:25
will be a time of trouble for J,	Jr 30:7
you, My servant J, do not be	Jr 30:10
J will return and have calm and	Jr 30:10
Sing with joy for J; shout for	Jr 31:7
has ransomed J and redeemed him	Jr 31:11
the seed of J and of My servant	Jr 33:26
of Abraham, Isaac, and J.	Jr 33:26
you, My servant J, do not be	Jr 46:27
J will return and have calm and	Jr 46:27
you, My servant J, do not be	Jr 46:28
a decree against J that his	Lm 1:17
up all the dwellings of J.	Lm 2:2
blazed against J like a flaming	Lm 2:3
which I gave to My servant J.	Ezk 28:25
that I gave to My servant J,	Ezk 37:25
the fortunes of J and have	Ezk 39:25
J will do the final plowing.	Hs 10:11
about to punish J according to	Hs 12:2
J struggled with the Angel and	Hs 12:4
J fled to the land of Aram.	Hs 12:12
testify against the house of J—	Am 3:13
How will J survive since he is	Am 7:2
How will J survive since he is	Am 7:5
has sworn by the Pride of J:	Am 8:7
totally destroy the house of J—	Am 9:8
violence done to your brother J.	Ob 10
the house of J will dispossess	Ob 17
Then the house of J will be a	Ob 18
What is the rebellion of J?	Mc 1:5
House of J, should it be asked:	Mc 2:7
indeed gather all of you, J;	Mc 2:12
listen, leaders of J, you rulers	Mc 3:1
to proclaim to J his rebellion	Mc 3:8
leaders of the house of J,	Mc 3:9
to the house of the God of J.	Mc 4:2
the remnant of J will be among	Mc 5:7
the remnant of J will be among	Mc 5:8
show loyalty to J and faithful	Mc 7:20
will restore the majesty of J,	Nah 2:2
"Even so, I loved J,	Mal 1:2
descendants from the tents of J,	Mal 2:12
descendants of J have not been	Mal 3:6
Isaac fathered J, Jacob fathered	Mt 1:2
J fathered Judah and his	Mt 1:2
Matthan, Matthan fathered J,	Mt 1:15
J fathered Joseph the husband	Mt 1:16
and J in the kingdom of heaven.	Mt 8:11
God of Isaac and the God of J?	Mt 22:32
God of Isaac and the God of J?	Mk 12:26
over the house of J forever,	Lk 1:33
of J, ⌊son⌋ of Isaac, ⌊son⌋	Lk 3:34
see Abraham, Isaac, J, and all	Lk 13:28
God of Isaac and the God of J.	Lk 20:37
property that J had given his	Jn 4:5
greater than our father J,	Jn 4:12
Isaac, and J, the God of our	Ac 3:13
Isaac did the same with J,	Ac 7:8
and J with the 12 patriarchs.	Ac 7:8
When J heard there was grain in	Ac 7:12
invited his father J and all his	Ac 7:14
and J went down to Egypt.	Ac 7:15
of Abraham, of Isaac, and of J.	Ac 7:32
dwelling place for the God of J.	Ac 7:46
J I have loved, but Esau I have	Rm 9:13
turn away godlessness from J.	Rm 11:26
in tents with Isaac and J,	Heb 11:9
Isaac blessed J and Esau	Heb 11:20
By faith J, when he was dying,	Heb 11:21

JACOB'S *(34)*

So Laban went into J tent,	Gn 31:33
He struck J hip as they wrestled	Gn 32:25
because He struck J hip socket	Gn 32:32
J sons returned from the field	Gn 34:7
by sleeping with J daughter,	Gn 34:7
Hamor said to J sons, "My son	Gn 34:8
But J sons answered Shechem and	Gn 34:13
was delighted with J daughter.	Gn 34:19
in pain, two of J sons, Simeon	Gn 34:25
J ⌊other⌋ sons came to the	Gn 34:27
and they did not pursue J sons.	Gn 35:5
sons were Reuben (J firstborn),	Gn 35:23
went to Egypt: J firstborn:	Gn 46:8
The sons of J wife Rachel:	Gn 46:19
including the wives of J sons—	Gn 46:26
All those of J household who had	Gn 46:27
Now J eyesight was poor because	Gn 48:10
J sons did for him what he had	Gn 50:12
total number of J descendants	Ex 1:5
His servant, J descendants—His	1Ch 16:13
the name of J God protect you	Ps 20:1
You restored J prosperity.	Ps 85:1
His servant, J descendants—His	Ps 105:6
Therefore J iniquity will be	Is 27:9
your arguments," says J King.	Is 41:21
J Portion is not like these	Jr 10:16
the fortunes of J tents and show	Jr 30:18
J leader will be one of them;	Jr 30:21
J Portion is not like these	Jr 51:19
descendants of J house and made	Ezk 20:5
I loathe J pride and hate his	Am 6:8
happen because of J rebellion	Mc 1:5
"Wasn't Esau J brother?"	Mal 1:2
J well was there, and Jesus,	Jn 4:6

JADA *(2)*

Shammai and J. Shammai's sons:	1Ch 2:28
sons of J brother of Shammai:	1Ch 2:32

JADDAI *(1)*

Zabad, Zebina, J, Joel, and	Ezr 10:43

JADDUA *(3)*

Meshezabel, Zadok, J,	Neh 10:21
and Jonathan fathered J.	Neh 12:11
Johanan, and J, the leaders	Neh 12:22

JADON *(1)*

Gibeonite, J the Meronothite,	Neh 3:7

JAEL *(6)*

fled on foot to the tent of J,	Jdg 4:17
J went out to greet Sisera and	Jdg 4:18
Heber's wife J took a tent peg,	Jdg 4:21
J went out to greet him and said	Jdg 4:22
in the days of J, the main ways	Jdg 5:6
J is most blessed of women,	Jdg 5:24

JAGGED *(1)*

His undersides are j potsherds,	Jb 41:30

JAGUR *(1)*

in the Negev: Kabzeel, Eder, J,	Jos 15:21

JAHATH *(8)*

Reaiah son of Shobal fathered J,	1Ch 4:2
and J fathered Ahumai and Lahad.	1Ch 4:2
his son J, his son Zimmah,	1Ch 6:20
son of J, son of Gershom, son of	1Ch 6:43
J, Zizah, Jeush, and Beriah.	1Ch 23:10

J was the first and Zizah was 1Ch 23:11
from Shelomoth's sons: **J**. 1Ch 24:22
overseers were **J** and Obadiah 2Ch 34:12

JAHAZ *(6)*
(AKA JAHZAH)
When he came to **J**, he fought Nm 21:23
out against us for battle at **J**. Dt 2:32
J, Kedemoth, Mephaath, Jos 13:18
camped at **J**, and fought with Jdg 11:20
are heard as far away as **J**. Is 15:4
raise their voices as far as **J**— Jr 48:34

JAHAZIEL *(6)*
Jeremiah, **J**, Johanan, Jozabad 1Ch 12:4
Benaiah and **J** ⌊blew⌋ the 1Ch 16:6
Amariah second, **J** third, and 1Ch 23:19
Amariah the second, **J** the third, 1Ch 24:23
the Spirit of the LORD came on **J** 2Ch 20:14
Shecaniah son of **J** from Zattu's Ezr 8:5

JAHDAI'S *(1)*
J sons: Regem, Jotham, Geshan, 1Ch 2:47

JAHDIEL *(1)*
Jeremiah, Hodaviah, and **J**. 1Ch 5:24

JAHDO *(1)*
Jeshishai, son of **J**, son of Buz. 1Ch 5:14

JAHLEEL *(2)*
sons: Sered, Elon, and **J**. Gn 46:14
the Jahleelite clan from **J**. Nm 26:26

JAHLEELITE *(1)*
the **J** clan from Jahleel. Nm 26:26

JAHMAI *(1)*
Rephaiah, Jeriel, **J**, Ibsam, and 1Ch 7:2

JAHZAH *(3)*
(AKA JAHAZ)
its pasturelands, **J** with its Jos 21:36
its pasturelands, **J** and its 1Ch 6:78
plateau—to Holon, **J**, Mephaath, Jr 48:21

JAHZEEL *(2)*
(AKA JAHZIEL)
J, Guni, Jezer, and Shillem. Gn 46:24
the Jahzeelite clan from **J**; Nm 26:48

JAHZEELITE *(1)*
the **J** clan from Jahzeel; Nm 26:48

JAHZEIAH *(1)*
of Asahel and **J** son of Tikvah Ezr 10:15

JAHZERAH *(1)*
of Adiel, son of **J**, son of 1Ch 9:12

JAHZIEL *(1)*
(AKA JAHZEEL)
J, Guni, Jezer, and Shallum— 1Ch 7:13

JAIL *(12)*
and placed him in **j** in the house Jr 37:15
and put them in the city **j**. Ac 5:18
doors of the **j** during the night Ac 5:19
orders⌋ to the **j** to have them Ac 5:21
they did not find them in the **j**, Ac 5:22
We found the **j** securely locked, Ac 5:23
men you put in **j** are standing Ac 5:25
they threw them in **j**, ordering Ac 16:23
of the **j** were shaken, Ac 16:26
citizens, and threw us in **j**. Ac 16:37
After leaving the **j**, they came Ac 16:40
putting both men and women in **j**, Ac 22:4

JAILER *(4)*
ordering the **j** to keep them Ac 16:23
When the **j** woke up and saw the Ac 16:27
Then the **j** called for lights, Ac 16:29
The **j** reported these words to Ac 16:36

JAILERS *(1)*
him over to the **j** until he could Mt 18:34

JAIR *(8)*
(AKA JAARE-OREGIM)
J, a descendant of Manasseh, Nm 32:41
J, a descendant of Manasseh, Dt 3:14
After him came **J** the Gileadite, Jdg 10:3
When **J** died, he was buried in Jdg 10:5
villages of **J** son of Manasseh 1Kg 4:13
Segub fathered **J**, who possessed 1Ch 2:22
Elhanan son of **J** killed Lahmi 1Ch 20:5
of Susa named Mordecai son of **J**, Est 2:5

JAIR'S *(5)*
which he renamed **J** Villages. Nm 32:41
his own name, **J** Villages, as it Dt 3:14
including all of **J** Villages that Jos 13:30
are called **J** Villages to this Jdg 10:4
Aram captured **J** Villages along 1Ch 2:23

JAIRITE *(1)*
Ira the **J** was David's priest. 2Sm 20:26

JAIRUS *(2)*
leaders, named **J**, came, and when Mk 5:22
Just then, a man named **J** came. Lk 8:41

JAKEH *(1)*
The words of Agur son of **J**. Pr 30:1

JAKIM *(2)*
J, Zichri, Zabdi, 1Ch 8:19
to Eliashib, the twelfth to **J**, 1Ch 24:12

JALAM *(4)*
bore Jeush, **J**, and Korah. Gn 36:5
She bore Jeush, **J**, and Korah to Gn 36:14
Chiefs Jeush, **J**, and Korah. Gn 36:18
Reuel, Jeush, **J**, and Korah. 1Ch 1:35

JALON *(1)*
Jether, Mered, Epher, and **J**. 1Ch 4:17

JAMBRES *(1)*
as Jannes and **J** resisted Moses, 2Tm 3:8

JAMES *(40)*
other brothers, **J** the son of Mt 4:21
J the son of Zebedee, and John Mt 10:2
J the son of Alphaeus, and Mt 10:3
His brothers **J**, Joseph, Simon, Mt 13:55
took Peter, **J**, and his brother Mt 17:1
Mary the mother of **J** and Joseph, Mt 27:56
He saw **J** the son of Zebedee and Mk 1:19
Andrew's house with **J** and John. Mk 1:29
and to **J** the son of Zebedee, Mk 3:17
J the son of Alphaeus, and Mk 3:18
except Peter, **J**, and John, Mk 5:37
the brother of **J**, Joses, Judas, Mk 6:3
took Peter, **J**, and John and led Mk 9:2
Then **J** and John, the sons of Mk 10:35
to be indignant with **J** and John. Mk 10:41
complex, Peter, **J**, John, and Mk 13:3
He took Peter, **J**, and John with Mk 14:33
Mary the mother of **J** the younger Mk 15:40
the mother of **J**, and Salome Mk 16:1
so were **J** and John, Zebedee's Lk 5:10
his brother; **J** and John; Philip Lk 6:14
J the son of Alphaeus, and Simon Lk 6:15
Judas the son of **J**, and Judas Lk 6:16
Peter, John, **J**, and the child's Lk 8:51
Peter, John, and **J**, and went up Lk 9:28
the disciples **J** and John saw Lk 9:54
the mother of **J**, and the other Lk 24:10
Peter, John, **J**, Andrew, Philip, Ac 1:13
Matthew, **J** the son of Alphaeus, Ac 1:13
Zealot, and Judas the son of **J**. Ac 1:13
and he killed **J**, John's brother, Ac 12:2
things to **J** and the brothers, Ac 12:17
stopped speaking, **J** responded: Ac 15:13
day Paul went in with us to **J**, Ac 21:18
He appeared to **J**, then to all 1Co 15:7
of the other apostles except **J**, Gl 1:19
When **J**, Cephas, and John, Gl 2:9
before certain men came from **J**. Gl 2:12
J, a slave of God and of the Jms 1:1
Christ, and a brother of **J**: Jd 1

JAMES' *(1)*
James, and John, **J** brother. Mk 5:37

JAMIN *(6)*
Jemuel, **J**, Ohad, Jachin, Zohar, Gn 46:10
Jemuel, **J**, Ohad, Jachin, Zohar, Ex 6:15
the Jaminite clan from **J**; Nm 26:12
firstborn: Maaz, **J**, and Eker. 1Ch 2:27
Nemuel, **J**, Jarib, Zerah, and 1Ch 4:24
Bani, Sherebiah, **J**, Akkub, Neh 8:7

JAMINITE *(1)*
the **J** clan from Jamin; Nm 26:12

JAMLECH *(1)*
Meshobab, **J**, Joshah son of 1Ch 4:34

JAMMED *(1)*
The bow **j** fast and remained Ac 27:41

JANAI *(1)*
in command⌋, **J**, and Shaphat 1Ch 5:12

JANIM *(1)*
J, Beth-tappuah, Aphekah, Jos 15:53

JANNAI *(1)*
son⌋ of **J**, ⌊son⌋ of Joseph Lk 3:24

JANNES *(1)*
Just as **J** and Jambres resisted 2Tm 3:8

JANOAH *(3)*
and passed it east of **J**. Jos 16:6
From **J** it descended to Ataroth Jos 16:7
J, Kedesh, Hazor, 2Kg 15:29

JAPHETH *(8)*
he fathered Shem, Ham, and **J**. Gn 5:32
three sons: Shem, Ham, and **J**. Gn 6:10
Shem, Ham, and **J**, Noah's wife, Gn 7:13
the ark were Shem, Ham, and **J**. Gn 9:18
Then Shem and **J** took a cloak and Gn 9:23
God will extend **J**; he will dwell Gn 9:27
Noah's sons, Shem, Ham, and **J**. Gn 10:1
Noah's sons: Shem, Ham, and **J**. 1Ch 1:4

JAPHETH'S *(4)*
J sons: Gomer, Magog, Madai, Gn 10:2
These are ⌊**J** sons⌋ by their Gn 10:5
And Shem, **J** older brother, also Gn 10:21
J sons: Gomer, Magog, Madai, 1Ch 1:5

JAPHIA *(5)*
of Jarmuth, **J** king of Lachish Jos 10:3
to Daberath, and went up to **J**. Jos 19:12
Ibhar, Elishua, Nepheg, **J**, 2Sm 5:15
Nogah, Nepheg, **J**, 1Ch 3:7
Nogah, Nepheg, **J**, 1Ch 14:6

JAPHLET *(1)*
Heber fathered **J**, Shomer, and 1Ch 7:32

JAPHLET'S *(2)*
J sons: Pasach, Bimhal, and 1Ch 7:33
These were **J** sons. 1Ch 7:33

JAPHLETITES *(1)*
border of the **J** as far as the Jos 16:3

JAR *(25)*
put them⌋ in a **j**, and add fresh Nm 19:17
of flour, and a **j** of wine. 1Sm 1:24
cakes, and a **j** of honey, and go 1Kg 14:3
of flour in the **j** and a bit of 1Kg 17:12
'The flour **j** will not become 1Kg 17:14
flour **j** did not become empty, 1Kg 17:16
in the house except a **j** of oil." 2Kg 4:2
the sea like an ointment **j**. Jb 41:31
and the **j** is shattered at the Ec 12:6
from bowls to every kind of **j**. Is 22:24
the shattering of a potter's **j**, Is 30:14
Every **j** should be filled with Jr 13:12
know that every **j** should be Jr 13:12
the **j** that he was making from Jr 18:4
so he made it into another **j**, Jr 18:4
a potter's **j** that can never Jr 19:11
shattered pot, a **j** no one wants? Jr 22:28
earthen storage **j** so they will Jr 32:14
Moab like a **j** no one wants." Jr 48:38
an alabaster **j** of very expensive Mt 26:7
with an alabaster **j** of pure and Mk 14:3
She broke the **j** and poured it on Mk 14:3
Then the woman left her water **j**, Jn 4:28
j full of sour wine was sitting Jn 19:29
there was a gold **j** containing Heb 9:4

JARAH *(2)*
(AKA JEHOADDAH)
Ahaz fathered **J**; Jarah fathered 1Ch 9:42
J fathered Alemeth, Azmaveth, 1Ch 9:42

JARED *(6)*
65 years old when he fathered **J**. Gn 5:15
830 years after the birth of **J**, Gn 5:16
J was 162 years old when he Gn 5:18
J lived 800 years after the Gn 5:19
Kenan, Mahalalel, **J**, 1Ch 1:2
of Enoch, ⌊son⌋ of **J**, ⌊son⌋ of Lk 3:37

JARED'S *(1)*
So **J** life lasted 962 years; Gn 5:20

JARHA *(2)*
servant whose name was **J**. 1Ch 2:34
in marriage to his servant **J**, 1Ch 2:35

JARIB *(3)*
(AKA JACHIN)
Nemuel, Jamin, **J**, Zerah, and 1Ch 4:24
Elnathan, **J**, Elnathan, Nathan, Ezr 8:16
Eliezer, **J**, and Gedaliah. Ezr 10:18

JARMUTH *(7)*
Piram king of **J**, Japhia king Jos 10:3
Jerusalem, Hebron, **J**, Lachish, Jos 10:5
Jerusalem, Hebron, **J**, Lachish, Jos 10:23
the king of **J** one the king of Jos 12:11

J, Adullam, Socoh, Azekah, Jos 15:35
J with its pasturelands, and Jos 21:29
in En-rimmon, Zorah, **J**, and Neh 11:29

JAROAH *(1)*
Huri, son of **J**, son of Gilead, 1Ch 5:14

JARS *(10)*
as well as its **j** of oil by which Nm 4:9
drink from the **j** the young men Ru 2:9
can tilt the water **j** of heaven Jb 38:37
set **j** filled with wine and some Jr 35:5
place them in your ⌊storage⌋ **j**, Jr 40:10
his containers and smash his **j**. Jr 48:12
how they are regarded as clay **j**, Lm 4:2
six stone water **j** had been set Jn 2:6
"Fill the **j** with water," Jesus Jn 2:7
we have this treasure in clay **j**, 2Co 4:7

JASHAR *(2)*
this written in the Book of **J**? Jos 10:13
It is written in the Book of **J**: 2Sm 1:18

JASHEN *(1)*
(AKA HASHEM)
the sons of **J**, Jonathan son 2Sm 23:32

JASHOBEAM *(3)*
J son of Hachmoni was chief of 1Ch 11:11
Joezer, and **J**, the Korahites; 1Ch 12:6
J son of Zabdiel was in charge 1Ch 27:2

JASHUB *(4)*
Tola, Puvah, **J**, and Shimron. Gn 46:13
the Jashubite clan from **J**; Nm 26:24
Tola, Puah, **J**, and Shimron— 1Ch 7:1
Malluch, Adaiah, **J**, Sheal, and Ezr 10:29

JASHUBITE *(1)*
the **J** clan from Jashub; Nm 26:24

JASON *(4)*
they dragged **J** and some of the Ac 17:6
and **J** has received them as Ac 17:7
bond from **J** and the others, Ac 17:9
and Lucius, **J**, and Sosipater, my Rm 16:21

JASON'S *(1)*
Attacking **J** house, they searched Ac 17:5

JASPER *(7)*
row, a beryl, an onyx, and a **j**. Ex 28:20
row, a beryl, an onyx, and a **j**. Ex 39:13
beryl, onyx, and **j**, sapphire, Ezk 28:13
looked like **j** and carnelian Rv 4:3
stone, like a **j** stone, bright as Rv 21:11
material of its wall was **j**, Rv 21:18
first foundation **j**, the second Rv 21:19

JATHNIEL *(1)*
the third, **J** the fourth, 1Ch 26:2

JATTIR *(4)*
hill country: Shamir, **J**, Socoh, Jos 15:48
J with its pasturelands, Jos 21:14
Ramoth of the Negev, and in **J**; 1Sm 30:27
pasturelands, **J**, Eshtemoa and 1Ch 6:57

JAVAN *(5)*
Magog, Madai, **J**, Tubal, Meshech, Gn 10:2
Magog, Madai, **J**, Tubal, Meshech, 1Ch 1:5
Tubal, **J**, and the islands Is 66:19
J, Tubal, and Meshech were your Ezk 27:13
Vedan and **J** from Uzal dealt in Ezk 27:19

JAVAN'S *(2)*
And **J** sons: Elishah, Tarshish, Gn 10:4
J sons: Elishah, Tarshish, 1Ch 1:7

JAVELIN *(4)*
laughs at the whirring of a **j**. Jb 41:29
Draw the spear and **j** against my Ps 35:3
They grasp bow and **j**. Jr 6:23
They grasp bow and **j**. Jr 50:42

JAW *(1)*
or pierce his **j** with a hook? Jb 41:2

JAWBONE *(4)*
He found a fresh **j** of a donkey, Jdg 15:15
With the **j** of a donkey I have Jdg 15:16
With the **j** of a donkey I have Jdg 15:16
threw away the **j** and named that Jdg 15:17

JAWS *(8)*
the shoulder, **j**, and stomach. Dt 18:3
you from the **j** of distress to Jb 36:16
Who can open his **j**, surrounded Jb 41:14
and opens wide its enormous **j**, Is 5:14
a bridle on the **j** of the peoples Is 30:28
hooks in your **j** and make the Ezk 29:4
hooks in your **j**, and bring you Ezk 38:4
who eases the yoke from their **j**; Hs 11:4

JAZANIAH *(1)*
of Kareah, **J** son of Hoshaiah, Jr 42:1

JAZER *(13)*
After Moses sent spies to **J**, Nm 21:32
the lands of **J** and Gilead, Nm 32:1
Ataroth, Dibon, **J**, Nimrah, Nm 32:3
Atroth-shophan, **J**, Jogbehah, Nm 32:35
J and all the cities of Gilead, Jos 13:25
and **J** with its pasturelands— Jos 21:39
proceeded⌋ toward Gad and **J**. 2Sm 24:5
and **J** and its pasturelands. 1Ch 6:81
found among them at **J** in Gilead. 1Ch 26:31
reached as far as **J** and spread Is 16:8
So I join with **J** to weep for the Is 16:9
more than the weeping for **J**. Jr 48:32
reached to the sea ⌊and to⌋ **J**. Jr 48:32

JAZIZ *(1)*
J the Hagrite was in charge of 1Ch 27:31

JEALOUS *(28)*
His brothers were **j** of him, Gn 37:11
your God, am a **j** God, punishing Ex 20:5
the LORD, being **j** by nature, is Ex 34:14
jealous by nature, is a **j** God. Ex 34:14
and he becomes **j** because of his Nm 5:14
and he becomes **j** of her though Nm 5:14
and he becomes **j** of his wife. Nm 5:30
him, "Are you **j** on my account? Nm 11:29
is a consuming fire, a **j** God. Dt 4:24
your God, am a **j** God, punishing Dt 5:9
who is among you, is a **j** God. Dt 6:15
God. He is a **j** God; He will not Jos 24:19
provoked Him to **j** anger more 1Kg 14:22
Don't be **j** of sinners; Pr 23:17
When I vent My **j** rage on you, Ezk 23:25
I will be **j** for My holy name. Ezk 39:25
the LORD became **j** for His land Jl 2:18
LORD is a **j** and avenging God; Nah 1:2
I am extremely **j** for Jerusalem Zch 1:14
I am extremely **j** for Zion; Zch 8:2
am **j** for her with great wrath." Zch 8:2
you **j** because I'm generous?' Mt 20:15
patriarchs became **j** of Joseph Ac 7:9
the Jews became **j**, and when they Ac 17:5
I will make you **j** of those who Rm 10:19
the Gentiles to make Israel **j**. Rm 11:11
my own people **j** and save some Rm 11:14
For I am **j** over you with a godly 2Co 11:2

JEALOUSLY *(2)*
watched David **j** from that day 1Sm 18:9
caused to live in us yearns **j**? Jms 4:5

JEALOUSY *(32)*
and if a feeling of **j** comes over Nm 5:14
if a feeling of **j** comes over him Nm 5:14
it is a grain offering of **j**, Nm 5:15
is the grain offering of **j**. Nm 5:18
offering of **j** from the woman's Nm 5:25
law regarding **j** when a wife goes Nm 5:29
when a feeling of **j** comes over a Nm 5:30
anger and **j** will burn against Dt 29:20
provoked His **j** with foreign gods Dt 32:16
have provoked My **j** with ⌊their⌋ Dt 32:21
provoke their **j** with an inferior Dt 32:21
kills a fool, and **j** slays the Jb 5:2
and provoked His **j** with their Ps 78:58
Will Your **j** keep burning like Ps 79:5
For **j** enrages a husband, and he Pr 6:34
j is rottenness to the bones. Pr 14:30
flood, but who can withstand **j**? Pr 27:4
due to a man's **j** of his friend. Ec 4:4
the LORD, have spoken in My **j**. Ezk 5:13
that provokes **j** was located. Ezk 8:3
your bloodshed in wrath and **j**. Ezk 16:38
My **j** will turn away from you. Ezk 16:42
to the anger and **j** you showed in Ezk 35:11
consumed by the fire of His **j**. Zph 1:18
be consumed by the fire of My **j**. Zph 3:8
Sadducees, were filled with **j**. Ac 5:17
were filled with **j** and began to Ac 13:45
not in quarreling and **j**. Rm 13:13
are we provoking the Lord to **j**? 1Co 10:22
jealous over you with a godly **j**, 2Co 11:2
may be quarreling, **j**, outbursts 2Co 12:20
hatreds, strife, **j**, outbursts of Gl 5:20

JEARIM *(1)*
(AKA CHESALON)
to the northern slope of Mount **J** Jos 15:10

JEATHERAI *(1)*
his son Zerah, and his son **J**. 1Ch 6:21

JEBERECHIAH *(1)*
priest and Zechariah son of **J**." Is 8:2

JEBUS *(5)*
(AKA JERUSALEM, ZION)
Zela, Haeleph, **J** (that is, Jos 18:28
arrived opposite **J** (that is, Jdg 19:10
they were near **J** and the day was Jdg 19:11
to Jerusalem (that is, **J**); 1Ch 11:4
inhabitants of **J** said to David, 1Ch 11:5

JEBUSITE *(11)*
Hivite, and **J**—as the LORD your Dt 20:17
Hinnom to the southern **J** slope Jos 15:8
toward the south **J** slope and Jos 18:16
us stop at this **J** city and spend Jdg 19:11
floor of Araunah the **J**. 2Sm 24:16
floor of Araunah the **J**." 2Sm 24:18
first to kill a **J** will become 1Ch 11:6
threshing floor of Ornan the **J**. 1Ch 21:15
threshing floor of Ornan the **J**. 1Ch 21:18
threshing floor of Ornan the **J**, 1Ch 21:28
threshing floor of Ornan the **J**. 2Ch 3:1

JEBUSITES *(30)*
the **J**, the Amorites, the Gn 10:16
Canaanites, Girgashites, and **J**." Gn 15:21
Perizzites, Hivites, and **J**. Ex 3:8
Hivites, and **J**—a land flowing Ex 3:17
Hivites, and **J**, which He swore Ex 13:5
Hivites, and **J**, and I will wipe Ex 23:23
Perizzites, Hivites, and **J**. Ex 33:2
Perizzites, Hivites, and **J**. Ex 34:11
the Hittites, **J**, and Amorites Nm 13:29
Hivites and **J**, seven nations Dt 7:1
Girgashites, Amorites, and **J** Jos 3:10
Perizzites, Hivites, and **J**— Jos 9:1
and **J** in the hill country, Jos 11:3
Perizzites, Hivites, and **J**): Jos 12:8
not drive out the **J** who lived in Jos 15:63
So the **J** live in Jerusalem among Jos 15:63
Hivites, and **J**—fought against Jos 24:11
drive out the **J** who were living Jdg 1:21
The **J** have lived among the Jdg 1:21
Perizzites, Hivites, and **J**. Jdg 3:5
against the **J** who inhabited 2Sm 5:6
The **J** had said to David: 2Sm 5:6
attacks the **J** must go through 2Sm 5:8
Hivites, and **J**, who were not 1Kg 9:20
the **J**, Amorites, Girgashites, 1Ch 1:14
J who inhabited the land were 1Ch 11:4
Hivites, and **J**, who were not 2Ch 8:7
Perizzites, **J**, Ammonites, Ezr 9:1
Perizzites, **J**, and Girgashites— Neh 9:8
in Judah and Ekron like the **J**. Zch 9:7

JECHONIAH *(2)*
(AKA CONIAH, JEHOIACHIN)
Josiah fathered **J** and his Mt 1:11
exile to Babylon **J** fathered Mt 1:12

JECOLIAH *(2)*
His mother's name was **J**; 2Kg 15:2
His mother's name was **J**; 2Ch 26:3

JECONIAH *(7)*
his sons **J** and Zedekiah. 1Ch 3:16
The sons of **J** the captive: 1Ch 3:17
Babylon took King **J** of Judah Est 2:6
had deported **J** son of Jehoiakim Jr 24:1
he deported **J** son of Jehoiakim Jr 27:20
this place **J** son of Jehoiakim, Jr 28:4
was⌋ after King **J**, the queen Jr 29:2

JEDAIAH *(11)*
Allon, son of **J**, son of Shimri, 1Ch 4:37
The priests: **J**; Jehoiarib; 1Ch 9:10
to Jehoiarib, the second to **J**, 1Ch 24:7
After them **J** son of Harumaph Neh 3:10
J son of Joiarib, Jachin, and Neh 11:10
Shemaiah, Joiarib, **J**, Neh 12:6
Sallu, Amok, Hilkiah, **J**. Neh 12:7
Mattenai of Joiarib, Uzzi of **J**, Neh 12:19
of Hilkiah, and Nethanel of **J**. Neh 12:21
Tobijah, and **J**, who have arrived Zch 6:10
Heldai, Tobijah, **J**, and Hen son Zch 6:14

JEDAIAH'S *(2)*
J descendants of the house of Ezr 2:36
J descendants of the house of Neh 7:39

JEDIAEL *(5)*
Bela, Becher, and **J**. 1Ch 7:6
these sons of **J** listed by heads 1Ch 7:11
J son of Shimri and his brother 1Ch 11:45
Adnah, Jozabad, **J**, Michael, 1Ch 12:20
the firstborn, **J** the second, 1Ch 26:2

JEDIAEL'S *(1)*
J son: Bilhan. Bilhan's sons: 1Ch 7:10

JEDIDAH *(1)*
mother's name was **J** the daughter 2Kg 22:1

JEDIDIAH *(1)*
(AKA SOLOMON)
who named him **J**, because of the 2Sm 12:25

JEDUTHUN *(11)*
son of Galal, son of **J**; 1Ch 9:16
Obed-edom son of **J** and Hosah 1Ch 16:38
them were Heman, **J**, and the rest 1Ch 16:41
Heman and **J** had with them 1Ch 16:42
Asaph, Heman, and **J**, who were to 1Ch 25:1
From **J**: Jeduthun's sons: 1Ch 25:3
the authority of their father **J**, 1Ch 25:3
Asaph, **J**, and Heman were under 1Ch 25:6
of Heman, of **J**, and of their 2Ch 5:12
Heman, and **J** the king's seer. 2Ch 35:15
Shammua, son of Galal, son of **J**. Neh 11:17

JEDUTHUN'S *(2)*
J sons were at the gate. 1Ch 16:42
From Jeduthun: **J** sons: Gedaliah, 1Ch 25:3

JEDUTHUNITES *(1)*
Shemaiah and Uzziel from the **J**. 2Ch 29:14

JEERS *(1)*
passes by her **j** and shakes his Zph 2:15

JEGAR-SAHADUTHA *(1)*
(AKA GALEED, MIZPAH)
named the mound **J**, but Jacob Gn 31:47

JEHALLELEL *(1)*
Azariah son of **J** from the 2Ch 29:12

JEHALLELEL'S *(1)*
J sons: Ziph, Ziphah, Tiria, and 1Ch 4:16

JEHDEIAH *(2)*
Shubael; from Shubael's sons: **J**. 1Ch 24:20
J the Meronothite was in charge 1Ch 27:30

JEHEZKEL *(1)*
Pethahiah, the twentieth to **J**, 1Ch 24:16

JEHIAH *(1)*
(AKA JEHIEL)
Obed-edom and **J** were also to be 1Ch 15:24

JEHIEL *(14)*
(AKA JEHIAH)
Shemiramoth, **J**, Unni, Eliab, 1Ch 15:18
Shemiramoth, **J**, Unni, Eliab, 1Ch 15:20
Shemiramoth, **J**, Mattithiah, 1Ch 16:5
J was the first, then Zetham, 1Ch 23:8
J son of Hachmoni attended the 1Ch 27:32
the care of **J** the Gershonite. 1Ch 29:8
Azariah, **J**, Zechariah, Azariah, 2Ch 21:2
J and Shimei from the Hemanites; 2Ch 29:14
J, Azaziah, Nahath, Asahel, 2Ch 31:13
Zechariah, and **J**, leaders of 2Ch 35:8
Obadiah son of **J** from Joab's Ezr 8:9
Shecaniah son of **J**, an Elamite, Ezr 10:2
Elijah, Shemaiah, **J**, and Uzziah Ezr 10:21
Zechariah, **J**, Abdi, Jeremoth, Ezr 10:26

JEHIELI *(2)*
to Ladan the Gershonite: **J**. 1Ch 26:21
The sons of **J**, Zetham and his 1Ch 26:22

JEHIZKIAH *(1)*
Meshillemoth, **J** son of Shallum, 2Ch 28:12

JEHOADDAH *(2)*
(AKA JARAH)
Ahaz fathered **J**, Jehoaddah 1Ch 8:36
Jehoaddah, **J** fathered Alemeth, 1Ch 8:36

JEHOADDAN *(2)*
His mother's name was **J** and was 2Kg 14:2
His mother's name was **J**; 2Ch 25:1

JEHOAHAZ *(23)*
(AKA SHALLUM)
His son **J** became king in his 2Kg 10:35
J son of Jehu became king over 2Kg 13:1
Then **J** sought the LORD's favor, 2Kg 13:4
J walked in them, and the 2Kg 13:6
J did not have an army left, 2Kg 13:7
J rested with his fathers, 2Kg 13:9
Jehoash son of **J** became king 2Kg 13:10
throughout the reign of **J**, 2Kg 13:22
Then Jehoash son of **J** took back 2Kg 13:25
in war from Jehoash's father **J**. 2Kg 13:25
Israel's King Jehoash son of **J**, 2Kg 14:1
messengers to Jehoash son of **J**, 2Kg 14:8
Israel's King Jehoash son of **J**. 2Kg 14:17
people took **J** son of Josiah, 2Kg 23:30
J was 23 years old when he 2Kg 23:31
But Neco took **J** and went to 2Kg 23:34
a son was left to him except **J**, 2Ch 21:17
sent ⌊word⌋ to Jehoash son of **J**, 2Ch 25:17
Joash, son of **J**, at Beth-shemesh 2Ch 25:23
Israel's King Jehoash son of **J**. 2Ch 25:25
people took **J** son of Josiah 2Ch 36:1
J was 23 years old when he 2Ch 36:2
his brother **J** and brought him 2Ch 36:4

JEHOAHAZ'S *(2)*
rest of the events of **J** ⌊reign⌋, 2Kg 13:8
of Egypt made **J** brother Eliakim 2Ch 36:4

JEHOASH *(23)*
(AKA JOASH)
His son **J** became king in his 2Kg 13:9
J son of Jehoahaz became king 2Kg 13:10
J rested with his fathers, 2Kg 13:13
J was buried in Samaria with the 2Kg 13:13
J king of Israel went down and 2Kg 13:14
Then **J** son of Jehoahaz took back 2Kg 13:25
J defeated Ben-hadad three times 2Kg 13:25
Israel's King **J** son of Jehoahaz 2Kg 14:1
messengers to **J** son of Jehoahaz, 2Kg 14:8
King **J** of Israel sent ⌊word⌋ to 2Kg 14:9
so King **J** of Israel advanced. 2Kg 14:11
J of Israel captured Judah's 2Kg 14:13
Then **J** went to Jerusalem and 2Kg 14:13
J rested with his fathers, 2Kg 14:16
Israel's King **J** son of Jehoahaz 2Kg 14:17
Jeroboam son of **J** became king 2Kg 14:23
the hand of Jeroboam son of **J**. 2Kg 14:27
⌊word⌋ to **J** son of Jehoahaz, 2Ch 25:17
King **J** of Israel sent ⌊word⌋ to 2Ch 25:18
So King **J** of Israel advanced. 2Ch 25:21
J of Israel captured Judah's 2Ch 25:23
Then **J** took him to Jerusalem and 2Ch 25:23
Israel's King **J** son of Jehoahaz 2Ch 25:25

JEHOASH'S *(3)*
rest of the events of **J** ⌊reign⌋, 2Kg 13:12
in war from **J** father Jehoahaz. 2Kg 13:25
rest of the events of **J** ⌊reign⌋, 2Kg 14:15

JEHOHANAN *(8)*
Elam the fifth, **J** the sixth, and 1Ch 26:3
J the commander and 280,000 2Ch 17:15
Ishmael son of **J**, Azariah son of 2Ch 23:1
the chamber of **J** son of Eliashib Ezr 10:6
J, Hananiah, Zabbai, and Athlai; Ezr 10:28
and his son **J** had married the Neh 6:18
Meshullam of Ezra, **J** of Amariah, Neh 12:13
Eleazar, Uzzi, **J**, Malchijah, Neh 12:42

JEHOIACHIN *(13)*
(AKA CONIAH, JECHONIAH)
and his son **J** became king in his 2Kg 24:6
J was 18 years old when he 2Kg 24:8
J king of Judah, along with his 2Kg 24:12
deported **J** to Babylon. 2Kg 24:15
of the exile of Judah's King **J**, 2Kg 25:27
pardoned King **J** of Judah ⌊and 2Kg 25:27
So **J** changed his prison clothes, 2Kg 25:29
His brother **J** became king in his 2Ch 36:8
J was 18 years old when he 2Ch 36:9
in place of **J** son of Jehoiakim Jr 37:1
of the exile of Judah's King **J**, Jr 52:31
pardoned King **J** of Judah and Jr 52:31
So **J** changed his prison clothes, Jr 52:33

JEHOIACHIN'S *(3)*
made Mattaniah, **J** uncle, king in 2Kg 24:17
Then he made **J** brother Zedekiah 2Ch 36:10
the fifth year of King **J** exile— Ezk 1:2

JEHOIADA *(53)*
Benaiah son of **J** ⌊was over⌋ the 2Sm 8:18
Benaiah son of **J** was over the 2Sm 20:23
Benaiah son of **J** was the son of 2Sm 23:20
exploits of Benaiah son of **J**, 2Sm 23:22
Benaiah son of **J**, Nathan the 1Kg 1:8
Benaiah son of **J** or your servant 1Kg 1:26
and Benaiah son of **J** for me." 1Kg 1:32
Benaiah son of **J** replied to the 1Kg 1:36
Benaiah son of **J**, the 1Kg 1:38
Benaiah son of **J**, the 1Kg 1:44
the order to Benaiah son of **J**, 1Kg 2:25
Benaiah son of **J** and told ⌊him⌋, 1Kg 2:29
Benaiah son of **J** went up, struck 1Kg 2:34
Benaiah son of **J** in Joab's place 1Kg 2:35
king commanded Benaiah son of **J**, 1Kg 2:46
Benaiah son of **J**, in charge of 1Kg 4:4
J sent ⌊messengers⌋ and brought 2Kg 11:4
did everything **J** the priest 2Kg 11:9
duty—and went to **J** the priest. 2Kg 11:9
Then **J** the priest ordered the 2Kg 11:15
Then **J** made a covenant between 2Kg 11:17
Then ⌊**J**⌋ the priest appointed 2Kg 11:18
Throughout the time **J** the priest 2Kg 12:2
King Joash called **J** the priest 2Kg 12:7
Then **J** the priest took a chest, 2Kg 12:9
Benaiah son of **J** was the son of 1Ch 11:22
exploits of Benaiah son of **J**, 1Ch 11:24
in addition to **J**, leader of the 1Ch 12:27
Benaiah son of **J** was over the 1Ch 18:17
was Benaiah son of **J** the priest; 1Ch 27:5
came **J** son of Benaiah, 1Ch 27:34
and the wife of **J** the priest. 2Ch 22:11
J summoned his courage and took 2Ch 23:1
J said to them, "Here is the 2Ch 23:3
did everything **J** the priest 2Ch 23:8
for **J** the priest did not release 2Ch 23:8
J the priest gave to the 2Ch 23:9
J and his sons anointed him and 2Ch 23:11
Then **J** the priest sent out the 2Ch 23:14
Then **J** made a covenant between 2Ch 23:16
Then **J** put the oversight of the 2Ch 23:18
the time of **J** the priest, 2Ch 24:2
J acquired two wives for him, 2Ch 24:3
the king called **J** the high 2Ch 24:6
the king and **J** gave it to those 2Ch 24:12
of the money to the king and **J**, 2Ch 24:14
J died when he was old and full 2Ch 24:15
However, after **J** died, the 2Ch 24:17
Zechariah son of **J** the priest. 2Ch 24:20
father **J** had extended to 2Ch 24:22
of the sons of **J** the priest. 2Ch 24:25
Even one of the sons of **J**, Neh 13:28
in place of **J** the priest to be Jr 29:26

JEHOIADA'S *(1)*
LORD's temple throughout **J** life. 2Ch 24:14

JEHOIAKIM *(36)*
(AKA ELIAKIM)
and changed Eliakim's name to **J**. 2Kg 23:34
J gave the silver and the gold 2Kg 23:35
J was 25 years old when he 2Kg 23:36
J became his vassal for three 2Kg 24:1
and Ammonite raiders against **J**. 2Kg 24:2
J rested with his fathers, 2Kg 24:6
LORD's sight just as **J** had done. 2Kg 24:19
firstborn, **J** second, Zedekiah 1Ch 3:15
and changed Eliakim's name to **J**. 2Ch 36:4
J was 25 years old when he 2Ch 36:5
The rest of the deeds of **J**, 2Ch 36:8
the days of **J** son of Josiah, Jr 1:3
says concerning **J** son of Josiah, Jr 22:18
Coniah son of **J**, the king of Jr 22:24
Jeconiah son of **J** king of Judah, Jr 24:1
fourth year of **J** son of Josiah, Jr 25:1
of the reign of **J** son of Josiah, Jr 26:1
King **J**, all his warriors, and Jr 26:21
But King **J** sent men to Egypt: Jr 26:22
of Egypt and took him to King **J**, Jr 26:23
he deported Jeconiah son of **J**, Jr 27:20
to this place Jeconiah son of **J**, Jr 28:4
in the days of **J** son of Josiah, Jr 35:1
fourth year of **J** son of Josiah, Jr 36:1
fifth year of **J** son of Josiah, Jr 36:9
J would cut the scroll with a Jr 36:23
scroll that **J** king of Judah Jr 36:28
concerning **J** king of Judah: Jr 36:29
says concerning **J** king of Judah: Jr 36:30
the words of the scroll that **J**, Jr 36:32
in place of Jehoiachin son of **J**, Jr 37:1
fourth year of **J** son of Josiah, Jr 45:1
of Judah's King **J** son of Josiah: Jr 46:2
LORD's sight just as **J** had done. Jr 52:2
of the reign of **J** king of Judah, Dn 1:1
The Lord handed **J** king of Judah Dn 1:2

JEHOIAKIM'S *(2)*
rest of the events of J ⌊reign⌋, 2Kg 24:5
J sons: his sons Jeconiah and 1Ch 3:16

JEHOIARIB *(2)*
(AKA JOIARIB)
The priests: Jedaiah; J; Jachin; 1Ch 9:10
lot fell to J, the second to 1Ch 24:7

JEHONADAB *(3)*
found J son of Rechab ⌊coming⌋ 2Kg 10:15
"It is," J replied. 2Kg 10:15
Then Jehu and J son of Rechab 2Kg 10:23

JEHONATHAN *(2)*
Shemiramoth, J, Adonijah, 2Ch 17:8
of Bilgah, J of Shemaiah, Neh 12:18

JEHORAM *(22)*
(AKA JORAM)
His son J became king in his 1Kg 22:50
of Judah's King J son of 2Kg 1:17
J son of Jehoshaphat became king 2Kg 8:16
So J crossed over to Zair with 2Kg 8:21
J rested with his fathers and 2Kg 8:24
Ahaziah son of J became king of 2Kg 8:25
Ahaziah son of J went down to 2Kg 8:29
Jehoshaphat, J, and Ahaziah— 2Kg 12:18
his son J, his son Ahaziah, his 1Ch 3:11
Elishama and J, were with these 2Ch 17:8
His son J became king in his 2Ch 21:1
the kingdom to J because he was 2Ch 21:3
When J had established himself 2Ch 21:4
J was 32 years old when he 2Ch 21:5
J crossed ⌊into Edom⌋ with his 2Ch 21:9
J also built high places in the 2Ch 21:11
a letter came to J from Elijah 2Ch 21:12
near the Cushites to attack J. 2Ch 21:16
J was 32 years old when he 2Ch 21:20
So Ahaziah son of J became king 2Ch 22:1
Ahaziah son of J went down to 2Ch 22:6
daughter of King J and the wife 2Ch 22:11

JEHORAM'S *(4)*
During J reign, Edom rebelled 2Kg 8:20
rest of the events of J ⌊reign⌋, 2Kg 8:23
⌊who was⌋ King J daughter and 2Kg 11:2
During J reign, Edom rebelled 2Ch 21:8

JEHOSHABEATH *(2)*
(AKA JEHOSHEBA)
J, the king's daughter, rescued 2Ch 22:11
Now J was the daughter of King 2Ch 22:11

JEHOSHAPHAT *(84)*
J son of Ahilud was court 2Sm 8:16
J son of Ahilud was court 2Sm 20:24
J son of Ahilud, historian; 1Kg 4:3
J son of Paruah, in Issachar; 1Kg 4:17
His son J became king in his 1Kg 15:24
J king of Judah went to visit 1Kg 22:2
So he asked J, "Will you go with 1Kg 22:4
J replied to the king of 1Kg 22:4
J said to the king of Israel, 1Kg 22:5
But J asked, "Isn't there a 1Kg 22:7
The king of Israel said to J, 1Kg 22:8
shouldn't say that!" J replied. 1Kg 22:8
of Israel and J king of Judah, 1Kg 22:10
So the king of Israel said to J, 1Kg 22:18
and Judah's King J went up to 1Kg 22:29
the king of Israel said to J, 1Kg 22:30
the chariot commanders saw J, 1Kg 22:32
against him, but J cried out. 1Kg 22:32
J son of Asa became king over 1Kg 22:41
J was 35 years old when he 1Kg 22:42
J also made peace with the king 1Kg 22:44
J made ships of Tarshish to go 1Kg 22:48
Ahaziah son of Ahab said to J, 1Kg 22:49
ships," but J was not willing 1Kg 22:49
J rested with his fathers and 1Kg 22:50
year of Judah's King J; 1Kg 22:51
Judah's King Jehoram son of J. 2Kg 1:17
year of Judah's King J; 2Kg 3:1
a message⌋ to King J of Judah: 2Kg 3:7
J said, "I will go. 2Kg 3:7
But J said, "Isn't there a 2Kg 3:11
J affirmed, "The LORD's words 2Kg 3:12
of Israel and J and the king 2Kg 3:12
respect for King J of Judah, 2Kg 3:14
Jehoram son of J became king of 2Kg 8:16
Jehu son of J, son of Nimshi. 2Kg 9:2
Jehu son of J, son of Nimshi, 2Kg 9:14
Judah's kings J, Jehoram, and 2Kg 12:18
Abijah, his son Asa, his son J, 1Ch 3:10
J son of Ahilud was court 1Ch 18:15
His son J became king in his 2Ch 17:1
LORD was with J because he 2Ch 17:3
of his reign, J sent his 2Ch 17:7
so they didn't fight against J. 2Ch 17:10
and silver as tribute to J, 2Ch 17:11
J grew stronger and stronger. 2Ch 17:12
Now J had riches and honor in 2Ch 18:1
King Ahab asked Judah's King J, 2Ch 18:3
J said to the king of Israel, 2Ch 18:4
But J asked, "Isn't there a 2Ch 18:6
The king of Israel said to J, 2Ch 18:7
shouldn't say that," J replied. 2Ch 18:7
of Israel and King J of Judah, 2Ch 18:9
So the king of Israel said to J, 2Ch 18:17
and Judah's King J went up to 2Ch 18:28
the king of Israel said to J, 2Ch 18:29
the chariot commanders saw J, 2Ch 18:31
but J cried out and the LORD 2Ch 18:31
J king of Judah returned to his 2Ch 19:1
confront him and said to King J, 2Ch 19:2
J lived in Jerusalem, and once 2Ch 19:4
J also appointed in Jerusalem 2Ch 19:8
came ⌊to fight⌋ against J. 2Ch 20:1
came and told J, "A vast 2Ch 20:2
J was afraid, so he resolved to 2Ch 20:3
Then J stood in the assembly of 2Ch 20:5
of Jerusalem, and King J. 2Ch 20:15
Then J bowed with his face to 2Ch 20:18
to go out, J stood and said, 2Ch 20:20
Then J and his people went to 2Ch 20:25
back with J at their head, 2Ch 20:27
J became king over Judah. 2Ch 20:31
Judah's King J made an alliance 2Ch 20:35
J formed an alliance with him to 2Ch 20:36
Mareshah prophesied against J, 2Ch 20:37
J rested with his fathers and 2Ch 21:1
He had brothers, sons of J: 2Ch 21:2
all these were the sons of J, 2Ch 21:2
of your father J or in the ways 2Ch 21:12
is the grandson of J who sought 2Ch 22:9
take them to the Valley of J. Jl 3:2
and come to the Valley of J, Jl 3:12
Asa fathered J, Jehoshaphat Mt 1:8
Jehoshaphat, J fathered Joram, Mt 1:8

JEHOSHAPHAT'S *(3)*
rest of the events of J ⌊reign⌋, 1Kg 22:45
Then J kingdom was quiet, for 2Ch 20:30
rest of the events of J ⌊reign⌋ 2Ch 20:34

JEHOSHEBA *(2)*
(AKA JEHOSHABEATH)
J, ⌊who was⌋ King Jehoram's 2Kg 11:2
in hiding with J in the LORD's 2Kg 11:3

JEHOZABAD *(4)*
of Shimeath and J son of Shomer 2Kg 12:21
firstborn, J the second, Joah 1Ch 26:4
J and 180,000 with him equipped 2Ch 17:18
Shimeath, and J, son of the 2Ch 24:26

JEHOZADAK *(8)*
and Seraiah fathered J. 1Ch 6:14
J went into exile when the LORD 1Ch 6:15
Joshua son of J, the high priest Hg 1:1
the high priest Joshua son of J, Hg 1:12
the high priest Joshua son of J, Hg 1:14
the high priest Joshua son of J, Hg 2:2
Joshua son of J, high priest. Hg 2:4
on the head of Joshua son of J, Zch 6:11

JEHU *(68)*
the LORD came to J son of Hanani 1Kg 16:1
the prophet J son of Hanani 1Kg 16:7
Baasha through J the prophet, 1Kg 16:12
are to anoint J son of Nimshi as 1Kg 19:16
Then J will put to death whoever 1Kg 19:17
whoever escapes the sword of J. 1Kg 19:17
look for J son of Jehoshaphat, 2Kg 9:2
J asked, "For which one of us?" 2Kg 9:5
So J got up and went into the 2Kg 9:6
When J came out to his master's 2Kg 9:11
So J said, "He talked to me 2Kg 9:12
and put it under J on the bare 2Kg 9:13
and proclaimed, "J is king!" 2Kg 9:13
Then J son of Jehoshaphat, 2Kg 9:14
J said, "If you ⌊commanders⌋ 2Kg 9:15
J got into his chariot and went 2Kg 9:16
went to meet J and said, 2Kg 9:18
J replied, "What do you have 2Kg 9:18
J answered, "What do you have 2Kg 9:19
like that of J son of Nimshi— 2Kg 9:20
and met J at the plot of land of 2Kg 9:21
When Joram saw J he asked, 2Kg 9:22
Do you come in⌋ peace, J?" 2Kg 9:22
Then J drew his bow and shot 2Kg 9:24
J said to Bidkar his aide, 2Kg 9:25
J pursued him, shouting, "Shoot 2Kg 9:27
When J came to Jezreel, Jezebel 2Kg 9:30
As J entered the gate, she said, 2Kg 9:31
the horses, and J rode over her. 2Kg 9:33
J wrote letters and sent them to 2Kg 10:1
guardians sent ⌊a message⌋ to J: 2Kg 10:5
Then J wrote them a second 2Kg 10:6
and sent them to J at Jezreel. 2Kg 10:7
So J killed all who remained of 2Kg 10:11
J met the relatives of Ahaziah 2Kg 10:13
J ordered, "Take them alive. 2Kg 10:14
J said, "If it is, give me your 2Kg 10:15
and J pulled him up into the 2Kg 10:15
J came to Samaria, he struck 2Kg 10:17
Then J brought all the people 2Kg 10:18
but J will serve him a lot. 2Kg 10:18
J was acting deceptively in 2Kg 10:19
J commanded, "Consecrate a 2Kg 10:20
Then J sent ⌊messengers⌋ 2Kg 10:21
Then J and Jehonadab son of 2Kg 10:23
and J said to the servants of 2Kg 10:23
Now J had stationed 80 men 2Kg 10:24
J said to the guards and 2Kg 10:25
J eliminated Baal ⌊worship⌋ from 2Kg 10:28
the LORD said to J, "Because you 2Kg 10:30
J was not careful to follow with 2Kg 10:31
J rested with his fathers, 2Kg 10:35
seventh year of J, Joash became 2Kg 12:1
Jehoahaz son of J became king 2Kg 13:1
son of J, king of Israel 2Kg 14:8
the LORD that He spoke to J was, 2Kg 15:12
Obed fathered J, and Jehu 1Ch 2:38
Jehu, and J fathered Azariah. 1Ch 2:38
Joel, J son of Joshibiah, son of 1Ch 4:35
Beracah, J the Anathothite; 1Ch 12:3
Then J son of Hanani the seer 2Ch 19:2
the Events of J son of Hanani, 2Ch 20:34
Joram to meet J son of Nimshi, 2Ch 22:7
it happened when J executed 2Ch 22:8
Then J looked for Ahaziah, 2Ch 22:9
Then they brought him to J, 2Ch 22:9
son of J, king of Israel 2Ch 25:17
on the house of J and put an end Hs 1:4

JEHU'S *(4)*
He saw J troops approaching and 2Kg 9:17
rest of the events of J ⌊reign⌋, 2Kg 10:34
length of J reign over Israel 2Kg 10:36
and J soldiers captured him 2Ch 22:9

JEHUCAL *(1)*
Zedekiah sent J son of Shelemiah Jr 37:3

JEHUD *(1)*
J, Bene-berak, Gath-rimmon, Jos 19:45

JEHUDI *(4)*
Baruch through J son of Jr 36:14
The king sent J to get the Jr 36:21
J then read it in the hearing of Jr 36:21
As soon as J would read three or Jr 36:23

JEIEL *(12)*
J the chief, Zechariah, 1Ch 5:7
⌊J⌋, fathered Gibeon and lived 1Ch 8:29
J fathered Gibeon and lived in 1Ch 9:35
Shama and J the sons of Hotham 1Ch 11:44
gatekeepers Obed-edom and J. 1Ch 15:18
Obed-edom, J, and Azaziah were 1Ch 15:21
J, Shemiramoth, Jehiel, 1Ch 16:5
J played the harps and lyres, 1Ch 16:5
Benaiah, son of J, son of 2Ch 20:14
as recorded by J the court 2Ch 26:11
and Hashabiah, J, and Jozabad, 2Ch 35:9
J, Mattithiah, Zabad, Zebina, Ezr 10:43

JEKABZEEL *(1)*
(AKA KABZEEL)
villages, and J and its villages Neh 11:25

JEKAMEAM *(2)*
Jahaziel third, and J fourth. 1Ch 23:19
the third, and J the fourth. 1Ch 24:23

JEKAMIAH *(3)*
Shallum fathered J, and Jekamiah 1Ch 2:41
Jekamiah, and J fathered 1Ch 2:41
Pedaiah, Shenazzar, J, Hoshama, 1Ch 3:18

JEKUTHIEL *(1)*
and J the father of Zanoah. 1Ch 4:18

JEMIMAH *(1)*
He named his first ⌊daughter⌋ J, Jb 42:14

JEMUEL *(2)*
(AKA NEMUEL)
J, Jamin, Ohad, Jachin, Zohar, Gn 46:10
J, Jamin, Ohad, Jachin, Zohar, Ex 6:15

JEOPARDIZE *(1)*
you must not j your neighbor's Lv 19:16

JEOPARDIZED *(1)*
If I had j my own life—and 2Sm 18:13

JEPHTHAH *(26)*
J the Gileadite was a great Jdg 11:1
drove J out and said to him, Jdg 11:2
So J fled from his brothers and Jdg 11:3
men joined J and traveled with Jdg 11:3
went to get J from the land Jdg 11:5
J replied to the elders of Jdg 11:7
They answered J, "Since that's Jdg 11:8
So J said to them, "If you are Jdg 11:9
The elders of Gilead said to J, Jdg 11:10
So J went with the elders of Jdg 11:11
and J repeated all his terms in Jdg 11:11
J sent messengers to the king of Jdg 11:12
J again sent messengers to the Jdg 11:14
tell him, "This is what J says: Jdg 11:15
Spirit of the LORD came on J, Jdg 11:29
J made this vow to the LORD: Jdg 11:30
J crossed over to the Ammonites Jdg 11:32
When J went to his home in Jdg 11:34
the daughter of J the Gileadite. Jdg 11:40
They said to J, "Why have you Jdg 12:1
Then J said to them, "My people Jdg 12:2
Then J gathered all of the men Jdg 12:4
J judged Israel six years, Jdg 12:7
Bethlehem, judged Israel after J Jdg 12:8
Jerubbaal, Barak, J, and Samuel. 1Sm 12:11
Barak, Samson, J, of David and Heb 11:32

JEPHTHAH'S *(2)*
Ammonites said to J messengers, Jdg 11:13
not listen to J message that he Jdg 11:28

JEPHUNNEH *(16)*
Caleb son of J from the tribe of Nm 13:6
son of Nun and Caleb son of J, Nm 14:6
Caleb son of J and Joshua son Nm 14:30
Caleb son of J remained alive Nm 14:38
Caleb son of J and Joshua son Nm 26:65
Caleb son of J the Kenizzite Nm 32:12
Caleb son of J from the tribe of Nm 34:19
except Caleb the son of J. Dt 1:36
and Caleb son of J the Kenizzite Jos 14:6
Caleb son of J and gave him Jos 14:13
to Caleb son of J the Kenizzite Jos 14:14
Caleb son of J ⌊the following⌋ Jos 15:13
to Caleb son of J as his Jos 21:12
The sons of Caleb son of J: 1Ch 4:15
were given to Caleb son of J. 1Ch 6:56
J, Pispa, and Ara. 1Ch 7:38

JERAH *(2)*
Sheleph, Hazarmaveth, J, Gn 10:26
Sheleph, Hazarmaveth, J, 1Ch 1:20

JERAHMEEL *(7)*
J, Ram, and Chelubai. 1Ch 2:9
The sons of J, Hezron's 1Ch 2:25
J had another wife named Atarah, 1Ch 2:26
These were the descendants of J. 1Ch 2:33
The sons of Caleb brother of J: 1Ch 2:42
Kish, ⌊from⌋ Kish's sons: J. 1Ch 24:29
king commanded J the king's son, Jr 36:26

JERAHMEEL'S *(1)*
The sons of Ram, J firstborn: 1Ch 2:27

JERAHMEELITES *(2)*
"The south country of the J," 1Sm 27:10
the towns of the J, and in the 1Sm 30:29

JERED *(1)*
wife gave birth to J the father 1Ch 4:18

JEREMAI *(1)*
Zabad, Eliphelet, J, Manasseh, Ezr 10:33

JEREMIAH *(144)*
name was Hamutal daughter of J; 2Kg 23:31
name was Hamutal daughter of J; 2Kg 24:18
Eliel, Azriel, J, Hodaviah, 1Ch 5:24
J, Jahaziel, Johanan, Jozabad 1Ch 12:4
Mishmannah fourth, J fifth, 1Ch 12:10
J tenth, and Machbannai eleventh. 1Ch 12:13
J chanted a dirge over Josiah, 2Ch 35:25
himself before J the prophet at 2Ch 36:12
the LORD through J and the land 2Ch 36:21
spoken through J was fulfilled. 2Ch 36:22
spoken through J was fulfilled. Ezr 1:1
Seraiah, Azariah, J, Neh 10:2
with Jeshua: Seraiah, J, Ezra, Neh 12:1
of Seraiah, Hananiah of J, Neh 12:12
Benjamin, Shemaiah, and J. Neh 12:34
The words of J, the son of Jr 1:1
asking, "What do you see, J?" Jr 1:11
that came to J from the LORD: Jr 7:1
that came to J from the LORD: Jr 11:1
LORD that came to J concerning Jr 14:1
that came to J from the LORD: Jr 18:1
let's make plans against J, Jr 18:18
J came back from Topheth, where Jr 19:14
J prophesying these things. Jr 20:1
So Pashhur had J the prophet Jr 20:2
released J from the stocks Jr 20:3
from the stocks, J said to him, Jr 20:3
that came to J from the LORD Jr 21:1
Zephaniah son of Maaseiah to J, Jr 21:1
J answered, "This is what you Jr 21:3
to me, "What do you see, J?" Jr 24:3
that came to J concerning all Jr 25:1
The prophet J spoke concerning Jr 25:2
in this book that J prophesied Jr 25:13
people heard J speaking these Jr 26:7
assembled against J at the Jr 26:9
Then J said to all the officials Jr 26:12
in words like all those of J. Jr 26:20
son of Shaphan supported J, Jr 26:24
word came to J from the LORD: Jr 27:1
The prophet J replied to the Jr 28:5
The prophet J said, "Amen! Jr 28:6
from the neck of J the prophet Jr 28:10
J the prophet then went on Jr 28:11
LORD came to J after Hananiah Jr 28:12
from the neck of J the prophet: Jr 28:12
prophet J said to the prophet Jr 28:15
the letter that J the prophet Jr 29:1
not rebuked J of Anathoth who Jr 29:27
in the hearing of J the prophet. Jr 29:29
the word of the LORD came to J: Jr 29:30
that came to J from the LORD. Jr 30:1
that came to J from the LORD Jr 32:1
and J the prophet was imprisoned Jr 32:2
J replied, "The word of the LORD Jr 32:6
the word of the LORD came to J: Jr 32:26
LORD came to J a second time: Jr 33:1
The word of the LORD came to J: Jr 33:19
The word of the LORD came to J: Jr 33:23
that came to J from the LORD Jr 34:1
So J the prophet related all Jr 34:6
that came to J from the LORD Jr 34:8
LORD came to J from the LORD: Jr 34:12
that came to J from the LORD Jr 35:1
So I took Jaazaniah son of J, Jr 35:3
the word of the LORD came to J: Jr 35:12
J said to the house of the Jr 35:18
word came to J from the LORD: Jr 36:1
So J summoned Baruch son of Jr 36:4
words the LORD had spoken to J. Jr 36:4
Then J commanded Baruch, "I am Jr 36:5
did everything J the prophet had Jr 36:8
You and J must hide yourselves Jr 36:19
the scribe and J the prophet, Jr 36:26
the word of the LORD came to J: Jr 36:27
Then J took another scroll and Jr 36:32
He spoke through J the prophet. Jr 37:2
the priest, to J the prophet, Jr 37:3
J was going about his daily Jr 37:4
the LORD came to J the prophet: Jr 37:6
J ⌊started to⌋ leave Jerusalem Jr 37:12
he apprehended J the prophet, Jr 37:13
"⌊That's⌋ a lie," J replied. Jr 37:14
but apprehended J and took him Jr 37:14
were angry at J and beat him and Jr 37:15
So J went into a cell in the Jr 37:16
"There is," J responded, and he Jr 37:17
Then J said to King Zedekiah, Jr 37:18
and J was placed in the guard's Jr 37:21
So J remained in the guard's Jr 37:21
heard the words J was speaking Jr 38:1
So they took J and dropped him Jr 38:6
lowering J with ropes. Jr 38:6
only mud, and J sank in the mud. Jr 38:6
heard J had been put into the Jr 38:7
they have done to J the prophet. Jr 38:9
and pull J the prophet up Jr 38:10
by ropes to J in the cistern. Jr 38:11
the Cushite cried out to J, Jr 38:12
and the ropes." J did so, Jr 38:12
Zedekiah sent for J the prophet Jr 38:14
king said to J, "I am going to Jr 38:14
J replied to Zedekiah, "If I Jr 38:15
Zedekiah swore to J in private, Jr 38:16
J therefore said to Zedekiah, Jr 38:17
But King Zedekiah said to J, Jr 38:19
not hand you over," J replied. Jr 38:20
Zedekiah warned J, "Don't let Jr 38:24
came to J and questioned Jr 38:27
J remained in the guard's Jr 38:28
gave orders concerning J, Jr 39:11
had J brought from the guard's Jr 39:14
LORD had come to J when he was Jr 39:15
that came to J from the LORD Jr 40:1
the guard took J and said to him Jr 40:2
J had not yet turned ⌊to go, Jr 40:5
J therefore went to Gedaliah son Jr 40:6
J the prophet and said, "May our Jr 42:2
So J the prophet said to them, Jr 42:4
they said to J, "As for every Jr 42:5
the word of the LORD came to J, Jr 42:7
When J had finished speaking to Jr 43:1
arrogant men responded to J, Jr 43:2
along with J the prophet and Jr 43:6
the LORD came to J at Tahpanhes: Jr 43:8
that came to J for all the Jews Jr 44:1
of Egypt at Pathros answered J, Jr 44:15
J responded to all the people Jr 44:20
Then J said to all the people, Jr 44:24
the word that J the prophet Jr 45:1
that came to J the prophet about Jr 46:1
LORD spoke to J the prophet Jr 46:13
that came to J the prophet about Jr 47:1
that came to J the prophet about Jr 49:34
through J the prophet: Jr 50:1
⌊This is⌋ what J the prophet Jr 51:59
J wrote on one scroll about all Jr 51:60
J told Seraiah, "When you get to Jr 51:61
The words of J end here. Jr 51:64
name was Hamutal daughter of J; Jr 52:1
the LORD to J the prophet that Dn 9:2
spoken through J the prophet was Mt 2:17
J or one of the prophets." Mt 16:14
the prophet J was fulfilled: Mt 27:9

JEREMIAH'S *(5)*
At J dictation, Baruch wrote on Jr 36:4
Baruch read J words from the Jr 36:10
had written at J dictation, Jr 36:27
wrote on it at J dictation all Jr 36:32
words on a scroll at J dictation Jr 45:1

JEREMOTH *(7)*
(AKA JERIMOTH)
Elioenai, Omri, J, Abijah, 1Ch 7:8
Ahio, Shashak, and J. 1Ch 8:14
Mahli, Eder, and J—three. 1Ch 23:23
fifteenth to J, his sons, and 1Ch 25:22
Jehiel, Abdi, J, and Elijah; Ezr 10:26
Mattaniah, J, Zabad, and Aziza; Ezr 10:27
Adaiah, Jashub, Sheal, and J; Ezr 10:29

JERIAH *(2)*
J was first, Amariah second, 1Ch 23:19
J ⌊the first⌋, Amariah the 1Ch 24:23

JERIBAI *(1)*
the Mahavite, J and Joshaviah, 1Ch 11:46

JERICHO *(63)*
near the Jordan across from J. Nm 22:1
by the Jordan ⌊across from⌋ J, Nm 26:3
by the Jordan ⌊across from⌋ J. Nm 26:63
by the Jordan ⌊across from⌋ J. Nm 31:12
by the Jordan ⌊across from⌋ J. Nm 33:48
by the Jordan ⌊across from⌋ J. Nm 33:50
across the Jordan from J, Nm 34:15
by the Jordan ⌊across from⌋ J: Nm 35:1
by the Jordan ⌊across from⌋ J. Nm 36:13
Moab, across from J, and view Dt 32:49
which faces J, and the LORD Dt 34:1
the region from the Valley of J, Dt 34:3
scout the land, especially J." Jos 2:1
The king of J was told, "Look, Jos 2:2
Then the king of J sent ⌊word⌋ Jos 2:3

the people crossed opposite **J**. Jos 3:16
to the plains of **J** in the LORD's Jos 4:13
on the eastern limits of **J**. Jos 4:19
at Gilgal on the plains of **J**, Jos 5:10
Joshua was near **J**, he looked up Jos 5:13
Now **J** was strongly fortified Jos 6:1
I have handed **J**, its king, and Jos 6:2
men Joshua had sent to spy on **J**, Jos 6:25
the rebuilding of this city, **J**. Jos 6:26
Joshua sent men from **J** to Ai, Jos 7:2
king as you did **J** and its king; Jos 8:2
kings heard ⌊about **J** and Ai⌋, Jos 9:1
Joshua had done to **J** and Ai, Jos 9:3
he had done to **J** and its king, Jos 10:1
as he had the king of **J**. Jos 10:28
king as he had the king of **J**. Jos 10:30
king of **J** one the king of Ai, Jos 12:9
beyond the Jordan east of **J**. Jos 13:32
the Jordan at **J** to the waters Jos 16:1
to the waters of **J** on the east, Jos 16:1
ascending from **J** into the hill Jos 16:1
and then reached **J** and went to Jos 16:7
to the slope of **J** on the north, Jos 18:12
J, Beth-hoglah, Emek-keziz, Jos 18:21
Across the Jordan east of **J**, Jos 20:8
the Jordan and came to **J**. Jos 24:11
The people of **J**—as well as the Jos 24:11
Stay in **J** until your beards grow 2Sm 10:5
Hiel the Bethelite built **J**. 1Kg 16:34
the LORD is sending me to **J**." 2Kg 2:4
So they went to **J**. 2Kg 2:4
who were in **J** came up to Elisha 2Kg 2:5
the sons of the prophets from **J**, 2Kg 2:15
returned to him in **J** where he 2Kg 2:18
overtook him in the plains of **J**. 2Kg 25:5
Reuben across the Jordan at **J**, 1Ch 6:78
Stay in **J** until your beards grow 1Ch 19:5
Israelites brought them to **J**, 2Ch 28:15
The men of **J** built next to Neh 3:2
Zedekiah in the plains of **J**, Jr 39:5
Zedekiah in the plains of **J**. Jr 52:8
were leaving **J**, a large crowd Mt 20:29
They came to **J**. And as He was Mk 10:46
as He was leaving **J** with His Mk 10:46
from Jerusalem to **J** and fell Lk 10:30
As He drew near **J**, a blind man Lk 18:35
He entered **J** and was passing Lk 19:1
the walls of **J** fell down after Heb 11:30

JERICHO'S *(2)*
J people 345 Ezr 2:34
J people 345 Neh 7:36

JERIEL *(1)*
Rephaiah, **J**, Jahmai, Ibsam, 1Ch 7:2

JERIJAH *(1)*
J was the head of the Hebronites, 1Ch 26:31

JERIJAH'S *(1)*
There were among **J** relatives, 1Ch 26:32

JERIMOTH *(7)*
(AKA JEREMOTH)
Uzzi, Uzziel, **J**, and Iri—five. 1Ch 7:7
Eluzai, **J**, Bealiah, Shemariah, 1Ch 12:5
Mahli, Eder, and **J**. 1Ch 24:30
Uzziel, Shebuel, **J**, Hananiah, 1Ch 25:4
for Naphtali, **J** son of Azriel; 1Ch 27:19
of David's son **J** and of Abihail 2Ch 11:18
Asahel, **J**, Jozabad, Eliel 2Ch 31:13

JERIOTH *(1)*
by ⌊his⌋ wife Azubah and by **J**. 1Ch 2:18

JEROBOAM *(97)*
servant, **J** son of Nebat, was 1Kg 11:26
J rebelled against Solomon, 1Kg 11:26
Now the man **J** was capable, 1Kg 11:28
Shilonite met **J** on the road as 1Kg 11:29
on the road as **J** came out of 1Kg 11:29
and said to **J**, "Take 10 pieces 1Kg 11:31
tried to kill **J**, but he fled to 1Kg 11:40
When **J** son of Nebat heard ⌊about 1Kg 12:2
presence, **J** stayed in Egypt. 1Kg 12:2
and **J** and the whole assembly of 1Kg 12:3
So **J** and all the people came to 1Kg 12:12
the Shilonite to **J** son of Nebat. 1Kg 12:15
heard that **J** had come back, 1Kg 12:20
J built Shechem in the hill 1Kg 12:25
J said to himself, "⌊The way 1Kg 12:26
J also built shrines on the high 1Kg 12:31
J made a festival in the eighth 1Kg 12:32
the LORD while **J** was standing 1Kg 13:1
J stretched out his hand from 1Kg 13:4
After all this **J** did not repent 1Kg 13:33
For the house of **J**, this was the 1Kg 13:34
Abijah son of **J** became sick. 1Kg 14:1
J said to his wife, "Go disguise 1Kg 14:2
he said, "Come in, wife of **J**! 1Kg 14:6
tell **J**, 'This is what the LORD 1Kg 14:7
disaster on the house of **J**: 1Kg 14:10
the house of **J** as one sweeps 1Kg 14:10
who belongs to **J** and dies in the 1Kg 14:11
of the house of **J** something was 1Kg 14:13
will eliminate the house of **J**. 1Kg 14:14
Rehoboam and **J** throughout their 1Kg 14:30
Israel's⌋ King **J** son of Nebat, 1Kg 15:1
Rehoboam and **J** all the days 1Kg 15:6
also war between Abijam and **J**. 1Kg 15:7
year of Israel's King **J**, 1Kg 15:9
Nadab son of **J** became king over 1Kg 15:25
down the entire house of **J**. 1Kg 15:29
He did not leave **J** anyone alive 1Kg 15:29
the example of **J** and the sin he 1Kg 15:34
in the way of **J** and have caused 1Kg 16:2
the house of **J** son of Nebat: 1Kg 16:3
and being like the house of **J**, 1Kg 16:7
had struck down the house of **J**. 1Kg 16:7
the example of **J** and the sin he 1Kg 16:19
the example of **J** son of Nebat 1Kg 16:26
the sin of **J** son of Nebat were 1Kg 16:31
like the house of **J** son of Nebat 1Kg 21:22
in the way of **J** son of Nebat, 1Kg 22:52
the sins that **J** son of Nebat had 2Kg 3:3
like the house of **J** son of Nebat 2Kg 9:9
the sins that **J** son of Nebat had 2Kg 10:29
the sins that **J** had caused 2Kg 10:31
the sins that **J** son of Nebat had 2Kg 13:2
the house of **J** had caused Israel 2Kg 13:6
the sins that **J** son of Nebat had 2Kg 13:11
his fathers, and **J** sat on his 2Kg 13:13
His son **J** became king in his 2Kg 14:16
J son of Jehoash became king of 2Kg 14:23
all the sins **J** son of Nebat had 2Kg 14:24
by the hand of **J** son of Jehoash. 2Kg 14:27
J rested with his fathers, 2Kg 14:29
year of Israel's King **J**, 2Kg 15:1
son of **J** became king over 2Kg 15:8
from the sins **J** son of Nebat had 2Kg 15:9
from the sins **J** son of Nebat had 2Kg 15:18
from the sins **J** son of Nebat had 2Kg 15:24
from the sins **J** son of Nebat had 2Kg 15:28
Israel made **J** son of Nebat king. 2Kg 17:21
Then **J** led Israel away from 2Kg 17:21
the sins that **J** committed and 2Kg 17:22
high place that **J** son of Nebat, 2Kg 23:15
King Jotham and Israel's King **J**. 1Ch 5:17
Seer concerning **J** son of Nebat. 2Ch 9:29
When **J** son of Nebat heard ⌊about 2Ch 10:2
presence—**J** returned from Egypt 2Ch 10:2
Then **J** and all Israel came and 2Ch 10:3
So **J** and all the people came to 2Ch 10:12
the Shilonite to **J** son of Nebat. 2Ch 10:15
back from going against **J**. 2Ch 11:4
because **J** and his sons refused 2Ch 11:14
J appointed his own priests for 2Ch 11:15
Rehoboam and **J** throughout their 2Ch 12:15
year of ⌊Israel's⌋ King **J**, 2Ch 13:1
was war between Abijah and **J**. 2Ch 13:2
J arranged his mighty army of 2Ch 13:3
and said, "**J** and all Israel, 2Ch 13:4
But **J** son of Nebat, a servant of 2Ch 13:6
calves that **J** made for you as 2Ch 13:8
Now **J** had sent an ambush around 2Ch 13:13
God routed **J** and all Israel 2Ch 13:15
Abijah pursued **J** and captured 2Ch 13:19
J no longer retained his power 2Ch 13:20
of Judah, and of **J** son of Joash, Hs 1:1
of Judah, and **J** son of Joash, Am 1:1
the house of **J** with a sword." Am 7:9
sent ⌊word⌋ to **J** king of Israel, Am 7:10
'**J** will die by the sword, and Am 7:11

JEROBOAM'S *(11)*
won't know that you're **J** wife, 1Kg 14:2
J wife did that: she went to 1Kg 14:4
J wife is coming soon to ask you 1Kg 14:5
I will eliminate all of **J** males, 1Kg 14:10
alone out of **J** ⌊sons⌋ will come 1Kg 14:13
because of **J** sins that he 1Kg 14:16
Then **J** wife got up and left and 1Kg 14:17
rest of the events of **J** ⌊reign⌋, 1Kg 14:19
The length of **J** reign was 22 1Kg 14:20
This was because of **J** sins he 1Kg 15:30
of the events of **J** ⌊reign⌋— 2Kg 14:28

JEROHAM *(9)*
His name was Elkanah son of **J**, 1Sm 1:1
Eliab, his son **J**, and his son 1Ch 6:27
Elkanah, son of **J**, son of Eliel, 1Ch 6:34
Ibneiah son of **J**; Elah son of 1Ch 9:8
Adaiah son of **J**, son of Pashhur, 1Ch 9:12
the sons of **J** from Gedor. 1Ch 12:7
for Dan, Azarel son of **J**. 1Ch 27:22
Azariah son of **J**, Ishmael son of 2Ch 23:1
son of **J**, son of Pelaliah, Neh 11:12

JEROHAM'S *(1)*
Elijah, and Zichri were **J** sons. 1Ch 8:27

JERUBBAAL *(14)*
(AKA GIDEON, JERUBBESHETH)
Gideon's father called him **J**, Jdg 6:32
J (that is, Gideon) and everyone Jdg 7:1
J ⌊(that is, Gideon)⌋ son of Jdg 8:29
show kindness to the house of **J** Jdg 8:35
Abimelech son of **J** went to his Jdg 9:1
all the sons of **J**, rule over you Jdg 9:2
the sons of **J**, on top of a large Jdg 9:5
youngest son of **J**, survived, Jdg 9:5
done well by **J** and his family, Jdg 9:16
honestly with **J** and his house Jdg 9:19
the 70 sons of **J** might come to Jdg 9:24
he the son of **J**, and isn't Zebul Jdg 9:28
of Jotham son of **J** came on them. Jdg 9:57
the LORD sent **J**, Barak, Jephthah 1Sm 12:11

JERUBBESHETH *(1)*
(AKA GIDEON, JERUBBAAL)
who struck Abimelech son of **J**? 2Sm 11:21

JERUEL *(1)*
facing the Wilderness of **J**. 2Ch 20:16

JERUSALEM *(798)*
(AKA ARIEL, JEBUS, SALEM, ZION)
king of **J** heard that Joshua Jos 10:1
king of **J** sent ⌊word⌋ to Jos 10:3
the kings of **J**, Hebron, Jarmuth, Jos 10:5
brought the five kings of **J**, Jos 10:23
the king of **J** one the king of Jos 12:10
slope (that is, **J**) and ascended Jos 15:8
the Jebusites who lived in **J**. Jos 15:63
Jebusites live in **J** among the Jos 15:63
Jebus (that is, **J**), Gibeah, and Jos 18:28
brought him to **J**, and he died Jdg 1:7
against **J** and captured it. Jdg 1:8
Jebusites who were living in **J**. Jdg 1:21
Benjaminites in **J** to this day. Jdg 1:21
opposite Jebus (that is, **J**). Jdg 19:10
head and brought it to **J**, 1Sm 17:54
in **J** he reigned 33 years over 2Sm 5:5
his men marched to **J** against the 2Sm 5:6
more concubines and wives in **J**, 2Sm 5:13
names of those born to him in **J**: 2Sm 5:14
officers and brought them to **J**. 2Sm 8:7
lived in **J** because he always ate 2Sm 9:13
the Ammonites and went to **J**. 2Sm 10:14
Rabbah, but David remained in **J**. 2Sm 11:1
So Uriah stayed in **J** that day 2Sm 11:12
all his troops returned to **J**. 2Sm 12:31
and brought Absalom to **J**. 2Sm 14:23
Absalom resided in **J** two years 2Sm 14:28
LORD really brings me back to **J**, 2Sm 15:8
hundred men from **J** went with 2Sm 15:11
all the servants with him in **J**, 2Sm 15:14
ark of God to **J** and stayed there 2Sm 15:29
entered **J** just as Absalom was 2Sm 15:37
he's staying in **J**," Ziba replied 2Sm 16:3
all the Israelites came to **J**. 2Sm 16:15
them⌋, so they returned to **J**. 2Sm 17:20
the day my lord the king left **J**. 2Sm 19:19
he came from **J** to meet the king 2Sm 19:25
for you at my side in **J**." 2Sm 19:33
should go up to **J** with the king? 2Sm 19:34
all the way to **J** remained loyal 2Sm 20:2
David came to his palace in **J**, 2Sm 20:3
they left **J** to pursue Sheba son 2Sm 20:7
Joab returned to the king in **J**. 2Sm 20:22
they returned to **J** at the end of 2Sm 24:8
his hand toward **J** to destroy it, 2Sm 24:16
in Hebron and 33 years in **J**. 1Kg 2:11
yourself in **J** and live there, 1Kg 2:36
lived in **J** for a long time 1Kg 2:38
had gone from **J** to Gath and had 1Kg 2:41

and the wall surrounding J. 1Kg 3:1
He went to J, stood before the 1Kg 3:15
before him at J in order to 1Kg 8:1
the wall of J, and Hazor, 1Kg 9:15
Solomon desired to build in J, 1Kg 9:19
She came to J with a very large 1Kg 10:2
cities and with the king in J. 1Kg 10:26
silver as common in J as stones, 1Kg 10:27
on the hill across from J. 1Kg 11:7
and because of J that I chose." 1Kg 11:13
road as Jeroboam came out of J. 1Kg 11:29
servant David and because of J, 1Kg 11:32
have a lamp before Me in J, 1Kg 11:36
reign in J over all Israel 1Kg 11:42
into the chariot and flee to J. 1Kg 12:18
When Rehoboam arrived in J, 1Kg 12:21
in the LORD's temple in J, 1Kg 12:27
Going to J is too difficult for 1Kg 12:28
17 years in J, the city the LORD 1Kg 14:21
of Egypt went to war against J. 1Kg 14:25
he reigned three years in J. 1Kg 15:2
him a lamp in J to raise up his 1Kg 15:4
son after him and to establish J 1Kg 15:4
he reigned 41 years in J. 1Kg 15:10
he reigned 25 years in J. 1Kg 22:42
he reigned eight years in J. 2Kg 8:17
he reigned one year in J. 2Kg 8:26
carried him to J in a chariot 2Kg 9:28
he reigned 40 years in J. 2Kg 12:1
Then he planned to attack J. 2Kg 12:17
Then Hazael withdrew from J. 2Kg 12:18
he reigned 29 years in J. 2Kg 14:2
was Jehoaddan and was from J. 2Kg 14:2
Jehoash went to J and broke 2Kg 14:13
was formed against him in J, 2Kg 14:19
was buried in J with his fathers 2Kg 14:20
he reigned 52 years in J. 2Kg 15:2
was Jecoliah; ⌊she was⌋ from J. 2Kg 15:2
he reigned 16 years in J. 2Kg 15:33
he reigned 16 years in J. 2Kg 16:2
came to wage war against J. 2Kg 16:5
he reigned 29 years in J. 2Kg 18:2
Lachish to King Hezekiah at J. 2Kg 18:17
They advanced and came to J, 2Kg 18:17
saying to Judah and to J: 2Kg 18:22
worship at this altar in J?' 2Kg 18:22
is the LORD to deliver J?' " 2Kg 18:35
by promising that J will not be 2Kg 19:10
Daughter J shakes ⌊her⌋ head 2Kg 19:21
a remnant will go out from J, 2Kg 19:31
he reigned 55 years in J. 2Kg 21:1
"J is where I will put My name." 2Kg 21:4
forever in this temple and in J, 2Kg 21:7
disaster on J and Judah that 2Kg 21:12
stretch over J the measuring 2Kg 21:13
and I will wipe J clean as one 2Kg 21:13
that he filled J with it from 2Kg 21:16
he reigned two years in J. 2Kg 21:19
he reigned 31 years in J. 2Kg 22:1
She lived in J in the Second 2Kg 22:14
all the elders of J and Judah. 2Kg 23:1
and all the inhabitants of J, 2Kg 23:2
them outside J in the fields 2Kg 23:4
and in the areas surrounding J. 2Kg 23:5
to the Kidron Valley outside J. 2Kg 23:6
to the altar of the LORD in J; 2Kg 23:9
places that were across from J, 2Kg 23:13
Then he returned to J. 2Kg 23:20
was observed to the LORD in J. 2Kg 23:23
in the land of Judah and in J. 2Kg 23:24
I will reject this city J, 2Kg 23:27
him into J, and buried him 2Kg 23:30
he reigned three months in J. 2Kg 23:31
to keep him from reigning in J, 2Kg 23:33
he reigned 11 years in J. 2Kg 23:36
He had filled J with innocent 2Kg 24:4
he reigned three months in J. 2Kg 24:8
of Elnathan; ⌊she was⌋ from J. 2Kg 24:8
king of Babylon marched up to J, 2Kg 24:10
Then he deported all J and all 2Kg 24:14
into exile from J to Babylon. 2Kg 24:15
he reigned 11 years in J. 2Kg 24:18
to the point in J and Judah that 2Kg 24:20
against J with his entire 2Kg 25:1
the king of Babylon, entered J. 2Kg 25:8
palace, and all the houses of J; 2Kg 25:9
down the walls surrounding J. 2Kg 25:10
and he ruled in J 33 years. 1Ch 3:4

sons⌋ were born to him in J: 1Ch 3:5
temple that Solomon built in J; 1Ch 6:10
sent Judah and J into exile at 1Ch 6:15
built the LORD's temple in J, 1Ch 6:32
genealogies, and lived in J. 1Ch 8:28
opposite their relatives in J, 1Ch 8:32
and Manasseh settled in J: 1Ch 9:3
genealogies, and lived in J. 1Ch 9:34
relatives in J with their ⌊other 1Ch 9:38
and all Israel marched to J 1Ch 11:4
David took more wives in J, 1Ch 14:3
the children born to him in J: 1Ch 14:4
all Israel at J to bring the ark 1Ch 15:3
officers and brought them to J. 1Ch 18:7
Then Joab went to J. 1Ch 19:15
it, but David remained in J. 1Ch 20:1
all his troops returned to J. 1Ch 20:3
Israel and then returned to J. 1Ch 21:4
an angel to J to destroy it, 1Ch 21:15
his hand stretched out over J, 1Ch 21:16
has come to stay in J forever. 1Ch 23:25
assembled in J all the leaders 1Ch 28:1
for seven years and in J for 33. 1Ch 29:27
had pitched a tent for it in J, 2Ch 1:4
Solomon went to J from the high 2Ch 1:13
cities and with the king in J. 2Ch 1:14
gold as common in J as stones, 2Ch 1:15
who are with me in Judah and J, 2Ch 2:7
You can then take them up to J. 2Ch 2:16
temple in J on Mount Moriah 2Ch 3:1
assembled at J the elders of 2Ch 5:2
I have chosen J so that My name 2Ch 6:6
Solomon desired to build in J, 2Ch 8:6
questions at J with a very large 2Ch 9:1
cities and with the king in J. 2Ch 9:25
silver as common in J as stones, 2Ch 9:27
reigned in J over all Israel 2Ch 9:30
into the chariot to flee to J. 2Ch 10:18
When Rehoboam arrived in J, 2Ch 11:1
stayed in J, and he fortified 2Ch 11:5
and went to Judah and J, 2Ch 11:14
the Levites to J to sacrifice to 2Ch 11:16
of Egypt went to war against J 2Ch 12:2
of Judah and came as far as J. 2Ch 12:4
were gathered at J because of 2Ch 12:5
poured out on J through Shishak 2Ch 12:7
of Egypt went to war against J. 2Ch 12:9
his royal power in J. 2Ch 12:13
17 years in J, the city the LORD 2Ch 12:13
he reigned three years in J. 2Ch 13:2
Then they returned to J. 2Ch 14:15
were gathered in J in the third 2Ch 15:10
men, brave warriors, in J. 2Ch 17:13
to his home in J in peace. 2Ch 19:1
lived in J, and once again he 2Ch 19:4
also appointed in J some of the 2Ch 19:8
disputes of the residents of J. 2Ch 19:8
of Judah and J in the LORD's 2Ch 20:5
Judah and you inhabitants of J, 2Ch 20:15
⌊He is⌋ with you, Judah and J. 2Ch 20:17
inhabitants of J fell down 2Ch 20:18
Judah and you inhabitants of J, 2Ch 20:20
of Judah and J turned back with 2Ch 20:27
joyfully to J, for the LORD 2Ch 20:27
they came into J to the LORD's 2Ch 20:28
he reigned 25 years in J. 2Ch 20:31
he reigned eight years in J. 2Ch 21:5
inhabitants of J to prostitute 2Ch 21:11
inhabitants of J to prostitute 2Ch 21:13
he reigned eight years in J. 2Ch 21:20
inhabitants of J made Ahaziah, 2Ch 22:1
he reigned one year in J. 2Ch 22:2
of Israel, and they came to J. 2Ch 23:2
he reigned 40 years in J. 2Ch 24:1
Judah and J the tax ⌊imposed 2Ch 24:6
in Judah and J that the tax 2Ch 24:9
Judah and J for this guilt 2Ch 24:18
Judah and J and destroyed all 2Ch 24:23
he reigned 29 years in J. 2Ch 25:1
was Jehoaddan; ⌊she was⌋ from J. 2Ch 25:1
took him to J and broke down 200 2Ch 25:23
was formed against him in J, 2Ch 25:27
he reigned 52 years in J. 2Ch 26:3
was Jecoliah; ⌊she was⌋ from J. 2Ch 26:3
built towers in J at the Corner 2Ch 26:9
devices in J to shoot arrows 2Ch 26:15
he reigned 16 years in J. 2Ch 27:1
he reigned 16 years in J. 2Ch 27:8

he reigned 16 years in J. 2Ch 28:1
the people of Judah and J, 2Ch 28:10
on every street corner in J. 2Ch 28:24
in the city, in J, and his son 2Ch 28:27
he reigned 29 years in J. 2Ch 29:1
of the LORD was on Judah and J, 2Ch 29:8
LORD's temple in J to observe 2Ch 30:1
congregation in J decided to 2Ch 30:2
been gathered together in J. 2Ch 30:3
of the LORD God of Israel in J, 2Ch 30:5
themselves and came to J. 2Ch 30:11
was gathered in J to observe 2Ch 30:13
away the altars that were in J, 2Ch 30:14
who were present in J observed 2Ch 30:21
been seen in J since the days 2Ch 30:26
people who lived in J to give a 2Ch 31:4
and that he planned war on J, 2Ch 32:2
his servants to J against King 2Ch 32:9
those of Judah who were in J, 2Ch 32:9
who remain under the siege of J? 2Ch 32:10
altars and say to Judah and J: 2Ch 32:12
to the people of J who were on 2Ch 32:18
the God of J like they had 2Ch 32:19
inhabitants of J from the power 2Ch 32:22
to the LORD to J and valuable 2Ch 32:23
him, upon Judah, and upon J. 2Ch 32:25
he and the inhabitants of J— 2Ch 32:26
inhabitants of J paid him honor 2Ch 32:33
he reigned 55 years in J. 2Ch 33:1
J is where My name will remain 2Ch 33:4
forever in this temple and in J, 2Ch 33:7
inhabitants of J to stray so 2Ch 33:9
and brought him back to J, 2Ch 33:13
of the LORD's temple and in J, 2Ch 33:15
he reigned two years in J. 2Ch 33:21
he reigned 31 years in J. 2Ch 34:1
cleanse Judah and J of the high 2Ch 34:3
So he cleansed Judah and J. 2Ch 34:5
of Israel and returned to J. 2Ch 34:7
and the inhabitants of J. 2Ch 34:9
She lived in J in the Second 2Ch 34:22
all the elders of Judah and J. 2Ch 34:29
Judah and the inhabitants of J, 2Ch 34:30
those present in J and Benjamin 2Ch 34:32
the inhabitants of J carried out 2Ch 34:32
and the inhabitants of J. 2Ch 35:18
chariot, and brought him to J. 2Ch 35:24
All Judah and J mourned for 2Ch 35:24
him king in J in place of his 2Ch 36:1
he reigned three months in J. 2Ch 36:2
deposed him in J and fined the 2Ch 36:3
over Judah and J and changed 2Ch 36:4
he reigned 11 years in J. 2Ch 36:5
three months and 10 days in J. 2Ch 36:9
Zedekiah king over Judah and J. 2Ch 36:10
he reigned 11 years in J. 2Ch 36:11
that He had consecrated in J. 2Ch 36:14
Him a temple at J in Judah. 2Ch 36:23
build Him a house at J in Judah. Ezr 1:2
and may he go to J in Judah and Ezr 1:3
of Israel, the God who is in J. Ezr 1:3
for the house of God in J." Ezr 1:4
rebuild the LORD's house in J. Ezr 1:5
had taken from J and had placed Ezr 1:7
went up from Babylon to J. Ezr 1:11
to his hometown J and Judah. Ezr 2:1
at the LORD's house in J, Ezr 2:68
people gathered together in J. Ezr 3:1
arrived at God's house in J, Ezr 3:8
had returned to J from the Ezr 3:8
the residents of Judah and J. Ezr 4:6
concerning J as follows: Ezr 4:8
you have returned to us at J. Ezr 4:12
also ruled over J and exercised Ezr 4:20
to the Jews in J and forcibly Ezr 4:23
of God's house in J had stopped Ezr 4:24
Jews who were in Judah and J, Ezr 5:1
to rebuild God's house in J. Ezr 5:2
the temple in J and carried Ezr 5:14
put them in the temple in J, Ezr 5:15
foundation of God's house in J. Ezr 5:16
rebuild this house of God in J. Ezr 5:17
the house of God in J: Ezr 6:3
the temple in J and carried to Ezr 6:5
be brought to the temple in J, Ezr 6:5
requested by the priests in J— Ezr 6:9
with this house of God in J. Ezr 6:12
to the service of God in J, Ezr 6:18

him⌋ to **J** in the seventh year Ezr 7:7
Ezra came to **J** in the fifth Ezr 7:8
arrived in **J** on the first day Ezr 7:9
want to go to **J**, may go with you Ezr 7:13
evaluate Judah and **J** according Ezr 7:14
Israel, whose dwelling is in **J**, Ezr 7:15
to the house of their God in **J**. Ezr 7:16
at the house of your God in **J**. Ezr 7:17
to the God of **J** all the articles Ezr 7:19
the house of the LORD in **J**, Ezr 7:27
of the Israelite families in **J**." Ezr 8:29
to the house of our God in **J**. Ezr 8:30
of the first month to go to **J**. Ezr 8:31
we arrived at **J** and rested there Ezr 8:32
give us a wall in Judah and **J**. Ezr 9:9
Judah and **J** that all the exiles Ezr 10:7
the exiles should gather at **J**. Ezr 10:7
gathered in **J** within the three Ezr 10:9
them about **J** and the Jewish Neh 1:2
I arrived in **J** and had been Neh 2:11
laid on my heart to do for **J**. Neh 2:12
the walls of **J** that had been Neh 2:13
J lies in ruins and its gates Neh 2:17
right, or historic claim in **J**." Neh 2:20
They restored **J** as far as the Neh 3:8
over half the district of **J**, Neh 3:9
over half the district of **J**, Neh 3:12
the walls of **J** was progressing Neh 4:7
and fight against **J** and throw it Neh 4:8
spend the night inside **J**, Neh 4:22
up the prophets in **J** to proclaim Neh 6:7
brother Hanani in charge of **J**, Neh 7:2
the gates of **J** until the sun is Neh 7:3
the citizens of **J** as guards, Neh 7:3
to his own town in **J** and Judah. Neh 7:6
all their towns and in **J**, Neh 8:15
of the people stayed in **J**, Neh 11:1
of ten to come and live in **J**, Neh 11:1
who volunteered to live in **J**. Neh 11:2
of the province who stayed in **J** Neh 11:3
Judah and Benjamin settled in **J** Neh 11:4
settled in **J**, was 468 capable Neh 11:6
of the Levites in **J** was Uzzi son Neh 11:22
the dedication of the wall of **J**, Neh 12:27
brought them to **J** to celebrate Neh 12:27
from the region around **J**, Neh 12:28
for themselves around **J**. Neh 12:29
I was not in **J**, because I had Neh 13:6
so I could return to **J**. Neh 13:7
brought to **J** on the Sabbath Neh 13:15
to the people of Judah in **J**. Neh 13:16
on the gates of **J** just before Neh 13:19
kinds of goods camped outside **J**, Neh 13:20
into exile from **J** with the other Est 2:6
build the walls of **J**. Ps 51:18
Because of Your temple at **J**, Ps 68:29
temple, and turned **J** into ruins. Ps 79:1
blood like water all around **J**, Ps 79:3
in Zion and His praise in **J**, Ps 102:21
LORD's house—within you, **J**. Ps 116:19
standing within your gates, **J**— Ps 122:2
J, built as a city ⌊should be⌋, Ps 122:3
Pray for the peace of **J**: Ps 122:6
J—the mountains surround her. Ps 125:2
the prosperity of **J** all the days Ps 128:5
He dwells in **J**. Hallelujah! Ps 135:21
If I forget you, **J**, may my right Ps 137:5
I do not exalt **J** as my greatest Ps 137:6
the Edomites said that day at **J**: Ps 137:7
The LORD rebuilds **J**; Ps 147:2
Exalt the LORD, **J**; Ps 147:12
son of David, king in **J**. Ec 1:1
have been king over Israel in **J**. Ec 1:12
those who were over **J** before me, Ec 1:16
all who were before me in **J**. Ec 2:7
all who were before me in **J**; Ec 2:9
Daughters of **J**, I am dark like Sg 1:5
Young women of **J**, I charge you, Sg 2:7
Young women of **J**, I charge you, Sg 3:5
love by the young women of **J**. Sg 3:10
Young women of **J**, I charge you: Sg 5:8
is my friend, young women of **J**. Sg 5:16
lovely as **J**, awe-inspiring as Sg 6:4
Young women of **J**, I charge you: Sg 8:4
Judah and **J** that Isaiah son Is 1:1
Amoz saw concerning Judah and **J**: Is 2:1
and the word of the LORD from **J**. Is 2:3
to remove from **J** and from Judah Is 3:1
For **J** has stumbled and Judah has Is 3:8
is left in **J** will be called Is 4:3
in **J** who are destined to live Is 4:3
from the heart of **J** by a spirit Is 4:4
residents of **J** and men of Judah, Is 5:3
war against **J**, but he could not Is 7:1
a snare to the inhabitants of **J**. Is 8:14
exceeded those of **J** and Samaria, Is 10:10
not also do to **J** and its idols? Is 10:11
work against Mount Zion and **J**, Is 10:12
of Daughter Zion, the hill of **J**. Is 10:32
houses of **J** so that you could Is 22:10
inhabitants of **J** and to the Is 22:21
as king on Mount Zion in **J**, Is 24:23
worship the LORD at **J** on the Is 27:13
who rule this people in **J**. Is 28:14
live on Zion in **J** and will never Is 30:19
LORD of Hosts will protect **J**— Is 31:5
Zion and whose furnace is in **J**. Is 31:9
Your eyes will see **J**, a peaceful Is 33:20
Lachish to King Hezekiah at **J**. Is 36:2
removed, saying to Judah and **J**: Is 36:7
that the LORD should deliver **J**?" Is 36:20
by saying that **J** won't be handed Is 37:10
Daughter **J** shakes ⌊her⌋ head Is 37:22
a remnant will go out from **J**, Is 37:32
tenderly to **J**, and announce to Is 40:2
J, herald of good news, raise Is 40:9
gave a herald of good news to **J**. Is 41:27
who says to **J**: She will be Is 44:26
all My pleasure and say to **J**: Is 44:28
Stand up, **J**, you who have drunk Is 51:17
garments, **J**, the Holy City! Is 52:1
Take your seat, **J**. Is 52:2
together, you ruins of **J**! Is 52:9
He has redeemed **J**. Is 52:9
Poor ⌊**J**⌋, storm-tossed, and not Is 54:11
keep still because of **J** until Is 62:1
J, I have appointed watchmen on Is 62:6
makes her **J** the praise of the Is 62:7
a wilderness, **J** a desolation. Is 64:10
for I will create **J** to be a joy, Is 65:18
will rejoice in **J** and be glad in Is 65:19
Be glad for **J** and rejoice over Is 66:10
and you will be comforted in **J**. Is 66:13
holy mountain **J**, says the LORD, Is 66:20
the people of **J** went into exile. Jr 1:3
directly to **J** that this is what Jr 2:2
At that time **J** will be called, Jr 3:17
to the name of the LORD in **J**. Jr 3:17
says to the men of Judah and **J**: Jr 4:3
men of Judah and residents of **J**. Jr 4:4
Judah, proclaim in **J**, and say: Jr 4:5
deceived this people and **J**, Jr 4:10
be said to this people and to **J**, Jr 4:11
from your heart, **J**, so that you Jr 4:14
Look! Proclaim to **J**: Those who Jr 4:16
Roam through the streets of **J**. Jr 5:1
cover, Benjaminites, out of **J**! Jr 6:1
raise a siege ramp against **J**. Jr 6:6
Be warned, **J**, or I will be torn Jr 6:8
Judah and in the streets of **J**? Jr 7:17
streets of **J** the sound of joy Jr 7:34
residents of **J** will be brought Jr 8:1
Why is **J** always turning away? Jr 8:5
I will make **J** a heap of rubble, Jr 9:11
of Judah and the residents of **J**. Jr 11:2
Judah and in the streets of **J**: Jr 11:6
of Judah and the residents of **J**. Jr 11:9
residents of **J** will go and cry Jr 11:12
as numerous as the streets of **J**. Jr 11:13
great pride of both Judah and **J**. Jr 13:9
and all the residents of **J**— Jr 13:13
Woe to you, **J**! You are unclean Jr 13:27
into the streets of **J** because of Jr 14:16
of Judah, for what he did in **J**. Jr 15:4
Who will have pity on you, **J**? Jr 15:5
and in all the gates of **J**. Jr 17:19
the residents of **J** who enter Jr 17:20
the gates of **J** on the Sabbath Jr 17:21
Judah, and the residents of **J**. Jr 17:25
and from the area around **J**, Jr 17:26
the gates of **J** on the Sabbath Jr 17:27
the citadels of **J** and not be Jr 17:27
Judah and to the residents of **J**: Jr 18:11
of Judah and residents of **J**. Jr 19:3
of Judah and **J** in this place. Jr 19:7
The houses of **J** and the houses Jr 19:13
thrown outside the gates of **J**. Jr 22:19
the prophets of **J** also I saw a Jr 23:14
prophets of **J** ungodliness has Jr 23:15
from **J** and had brought Jr 24:1
the remnant of **J**—those Jr 24:8
the residents of **J** as follows: Jr 25:2
J and the ⌊other⌋ cities of Jr 25:18
like a field, **J** will become Jr 26:18
to Zedekiah king of Judah in **J**. Jr 27:3
Judah, and in **J** go to Babylon.' Jr 27:18
from **J** to Babylon along with all Jr 27:20
all the nobles of Judah and **J**. Jr 27:20
of the king of Judah, and in **J**: Jr 27:21
prophet sent from **J** to the rest Jr 29:1
had deported from **J** to Babylon. Jr 29:1
the officials of Judah and **J**, Jr 29:2
and the metalsmiths had left **J**. Jr 29:2
I deported from **J** to Babylon: Jr 29:4
I have sent from **J** to Babylon. Jr 29:20
letters to all the people of **J**, Jr 29:25
king of Babylon was besieging **J**, Jr 32:2
Judah, and the residents of **J**. Jr 32:32
in the areas surrounding **J**, Jr 32:44
surrounding **J** and Judah's cities Jr 33:13
and **J** will dwell securely, Jr 33:16
fighting against **J** and all its Jr 34:1
to Zedekiah king of Judah in **J** Jr 34:6
was attacking **J** and all of Jr 34:7
people who were in **J** to proclaim Jr 34:8
The officials of Judah and **J**, Jr 34:19
let's go into **J** to get away from Jr 35:11
So we have been living in **J**." Jr 35:11
of Judah and the residents of **J**: Jr 35:13
residents of **J** all the disaster Jr 35:17
the people of **J** and all those Jr 36:9
cities into **J** proclaimed a fast Jr 36:9
residents of **J**, and on the men Jr 36:31
were besieging **J**, heard the Jr 37:5
report, they withdrew from **J**. Jr 37:5
army withdrew from **J** because of Jr 37:11
to⌋ leave **J** to go to the land Jr 37:12
until the day **J** was captured, Jr 38:28
against **J** with his entire Jr 39:1
and tore down the walls of **J**. Jr 39:8
the exiles of **J** and Judah who Jr 40:1
against **J** and all Judah's Jr 44:2
Judah and in the streets of **J**? Jr 44:9
just as I punished **J** by sword, Jr 44:13
inhabitants of Chaldea," says **J**. Jr 51:35
and let **J** come to your mind. Jr 51:50
he reigned 11 years in **J**. Jr 52:1
to the point in **J** and Judah that Jr 52:3
against **J** with his entire Jr 52:4
entered **J** as the representative Jr 52:12
all the houses of **J**, and all the Jr 52:13
all the walls surrounding **J**. Jr 52:14
year, 832 people from **J**; Jr 52:29
and homelessness **J** remembers all Lm 1:7
J has sinned grievously; Lm 1:8
J has become something impure Lm 1:17
women of **J** have bowed their Lm 2:10
can I compare you, Daughter **J**? Lm 2:13
shake their heads at Daughter **J**: Lm 2:15
and draw the city of **J** on it. Ezk 4:1
the siege of **J** with your arm Ezk 4:7
off the supply of bread in **J**. Ezk 4:16
I have set this **J** in the center Ezk 5:5
am against you, ⌊**J**⌋, and I will Ezk 5:8
will eat ⌊their⌋ sons within **J**, Ezk 5:10
inhabitants of ⌊**J**⌋, I will Ezk 5:16
will leave you childless, ⌊**J**⌋. Ezk 5:17
me in visions of God to **J**, Ezk 8:3
"Pass throughout the city of **J**," Ezk 9:4
You pour out Your wrath on **J**?" Ezk 9:8
residents of **J** have said this Ezk 11:15
prince in **J** and all the house Ezk 12:10
the residents of **J** in the land Ezk 12:19
prophesied to **J** and saw a vision Ezk 13:16
judgments against **J**— Ezk 14:21
devastation I have brought on **J**, Ezk 14:22
will give up the residents of **J**. Ezk 15:6
is what the Lord GOD says to **J**: Ezk 16:3
The king of Babylon came to **J**, Ezk 17:12
your face toward **J** and preach Ezk 21:2
and to Judah into fortified **J**. Ezk 21:20
answer marked **J** appears in his Ezk 21:22
I am about to gather you into **J**. Ezk 22:19
and Oholibah represents **J**. Ezk 23:4

laid siege to **J** this very day. Ezk 24:2
because Tyre said about **J**: Ezk 26:2
a fugitive from **J** came to me and Ezk 33:21
is filled in **J** during its Ezk 36:38
year after **J** had been captured, Ezk 40:1
Babylon came to **J** and laid siege Dn 1:1
had taken from the temple in **J**, Dn 5:2
house of God in **J**, and the king Dn 5:3
its upper room opened toward **J**, Dn 6:10
the desolation of **J** would be 70. Dn 9:2
residents of **J**, and all Israel Dn 9:7
has been done to **J** has ever been Dn 9:12
turn away from Your city **J**, Dn 9:16
J and Your people have become an Dn 9:16
and rebuild **J** until Messiah Dn 9:25
those on Mount Zion and in **J**, Jl 2:32
the fortunes of Judah and **J**, Jl 3:1
of Judah and **J** to the Greeks to Jl 3:6
Zion and raise His voice from **J**; Jl 3:16
J will be holy, and foreigners Jl 3:17
and **J** from generation to Jl 3:20
and raises His voice from **J**; Am 1:2
will consume the citadels of **J**. Am 2:5
his gate and cast lots for **J**, Ob 11
and the exiles of **J** who are in Ob 20
Samaria and **J** in the days of Mc 1:1
high place of Judah? Isn't it **J**? Mc 1:5
gate of my people, as far as **J**. Mc 1:9
from the LORD to the gate of **J**. Mc 1:12
bloodshed and **J** with injustice. Mc 3:10
like a field, **J** will become Mc 3:12
and the word of the LORD from **J**. Mc 4:2
will come to Daughter **J**. Mc 4:8
against all the residents of **J**. Zph 1:4
time I will search **J** with lamps Zph 1:12
all ⌊your⌋ heart, Daughter **J**! Zph 3:14
that day it will be said to **J**: Zph 3:16
mercy from **J** and the cities Zch 1:12
jealous for **J** and Zion. Zch 1:14
I have graciously returned to **J**; Zch 1:16
will be stretched out over **J**. Zch 1:16
Zion and again choose **J**." Zch 1:17
scattered Judah, Israel, and **J**." Zch 1:19
To measure **J** to determine its Zch 2:2
J will be inhabited without Zch 2:4
and He will once again choose **J**. Zch 2:12
who has chosen **J** rebuke you! Zch 3:2
prophets when **J** was inhabited Zch 7:7
return to Zion and live in **J**. Zch 8:3
Then **J** will be called the Zch 8:3
sit along the streets of **J**, Zch 8:4
bring them ⌊back⌋ to live in **J**. Zch 8:8
what is good to **J** and the house Zch 8:15
of Hosts in **J** and to plead for Zch 8:22
Shout in triumph, Daughter **J**! Zch 9:9
Ephraim and the horse from **J**. Zch 9:10
I will make **J** a cup that causes Zch 12:2
siege against **J** will also Zch 12:2
day I will make **J** a heavy stone Zch 12:3
residents of **J** are my strength Zch 12:5
J continues to be inhabited Zch 12:6
be inhabited on its site, in **J**. Zch 12:6
defend the inhabitants of **J**, Zch 12:8
the nations that come against **J**. Zch 12:9
of David and the residents of **J**, Zch 12:10
the mourning in **J** will be as Zch 12:11
and for the residents of **J**, Zch 13:1
nations against **J** for battle. Zch 14:2
which faces **J** on the east. Zch 14:4
water will flow out from **J**, Zch 14:8
south of **J** will be changed Zch 14:10
But ⌊**J**⌋ will be raised up and Zch 14:10
So **J** will dwell in security. Zch 14:11
who have warred against **J**: Zch 14:12
Judah will also fight at **J**, Zch 14:14
came against **J** will go up year Zch 14:16
earth not go up to **J** to worship Zch 14:17
Every pot in **J** and in Judah will Zch 14:21
been done in Israel and in **J**. Mal 2:11
of Judah and **J** will please the Mal 3:4
east arrived unexpectedly in **J**, Mt 2:1
disturbed, and all **J** with him. Mt 2:3
Then ⌊people from⌋ **J**, all Judea, Mt 3:5
Decapolis, **J**, Judea, and beyond Mt 4:25
or by **J**, because it is the city Mt 5:35
scribes came from **J** to Jesus and Mt 15:1
He must go to **J** and suffer many Mt 16:21
While going up to **J**, Jesus took Mt 20:17
We are going up to **J**. Mt 20:18
they approached **J** and came to Mt 21:1
He entered **J**, the whole city Mt 21:10
J, Jerusalem! The city who kills Mt 23:37
Jerusalem, **J**! The city who kills Mt 23:37
the people of **J** were flocking to Mk 1:5
J, Idumea, beyond the Jordan, Mk 3:8
who had come down from **J** said, Mk 3:22
had come from **J** gathered around Mk 7:1
going up to **J**, and Jesus was Mk 10:32
We are going up to **J**. Mk 10:33
they approached **J**, at Bethphage Mk 11:1
And He went into **J** and into the Mk 11:11
They came to **J**, and He went into Mk 11:15
They came again to **J**. Mk 11:27
had come up with Him to **J**. Mk 15:41
Him up to **J** to present Him to Lk 2:22
was a man in **J** whose name was Lk 2:25
forward to the redemption of **J**. Lk 2:38
traveled to **J** for the Passover Lk 2:41
boy Jesus stayed behind in **J**, Lk 2:43
they returned to **J** to search for Lk 2:45
he took Him to **J**, had Him stand Lk 4:9
and Judea, and also from **J**. Lk 5:17
from all Judea and **J** and from Lk 6:17
He was about to accomplish in **J**. Lk 9:31
He determined to journey to **J**. Lk 9:51
He determined to journey to **J**. Lk 9:53
going down from **J** to Jericho and Lk 10:30
all the people who live in **J**? Lk 13:4
and making His way to **J**. Lk 13:22
prophet to perish outside of **J**! Lk 13:33
J, Jerusalem! The city who kills Lk 13:34
Jerusalem, **J**! The city who kills Lk 13:34
traveling to **J**, He passed Lk 17:11
We are going up to **J**. Lk 18:31
a parable because He was near **J**, Lk 19:11
He went on ahead, going up to **J**. Lk 19:28
When you see **J** surrounded by Lk 21:20
and **J** will be trampled by the Lk 21:24
who was also in **J** during those Lk 23:7
Daughters of **J**, do not weep for Lk 23:28
was about seven miles from **J**. Lk 24:13
only visitor in **J** who doesn't Lk 24:18
they got up and returned to **J**. Lk 24:33
all the nations, beginning at **J**. Lk 24:47
returned to **J** with great joy. Lk 24:52
the Jews from **J** sent priests Jn 1:19
was near, so Jesus went up to **J**. Jn 2:13
He was in **J** at the Passover Jn 2:23
the place to worship is in **J**." Jn 4:20
on this mountain nor in **J**. Jn 4:21
He did in **J** during the festival Jn 4:45
place, and Jesus went up to **J**. Jn 5:1
Sheep Gate in **J** there is a pool Jn 5:2
of the people of **J** were saying, Jn 7:25
of Dedication took place in **J**, Jn 10:22
was near **J** (about two miles Jn 11:18
many went up to **J** from the Jn 11:55
that Jesus was coming to **J**, Jn 12:12
commanded them not to leave **J**, Ac 1:4
you will be My witnesses in **J**, Ac 1:8
returned to **J** from the mount Ac 1:12
is near **J**—a Sabbath day's Ac 1:12
known to all the residents of **J**, Ac 1:19
There were Jews living in **J**, Ac 2:5
men and all you residents of **J**, Ac 2:14
and scribes assembled in **J** Ac 4:5
evident to all who live in **J**, Ac 4:16
from the towns surrounding **J**, Ac 5:16
you have filled **J** with your Ac 5:28
the disciples in **J** multiplied Ac 6:7
out against the church in **J**, Ac 8:1
who were at **J** heard that Samaria Ac 8:14
traveled back to **J**, evangelizing Ac 8:25
down from **J** to desert Gaza." Ac 8:26
He had come to worship in **J** Ac 8:27
bring them as prisoners to **J**. Ac 9:2
he has done to Your saints in **J**. Ac 9:13
man who, in **J**, was destroying Ac 9:21
When he arrived in **J**, he tried Ac 9:26
coming and going with them in **J**, Ac 9:28
the Judean country and in **J**; Ac 10:39
Peter went up to **J**, those who Ac 11:2
the ears of the church in **J**, Ac 11:22
came down from **J** to Antioch. Ac 11:27
Saul returned to **J** after they Ac 12:25
left them and went back to **J**. Ac 13:13
residents of **J** and their rulers Ac 13:27
up with Him from Galilee to **J**, Ac 13:31
and elders in **J** concerning this Ac 15:2
they arrived at **J**, they were Ac 15:4
and elders at **J** for them to Ac 16:4
and Achaia and go to **J**. Ac 19:21
he was hurrying to be in **J**, Ac 20:16
And now I am on my way to **J**, Ac 20:22
the Spirit not to go to **J**. Ac 21:4
way the Jews in **J** will bind the Ac 21:11
begged him not to go up to **J**. Ac 21:12
also to die in **J** for the name Ac 21:13
we got ready and went up to **J**. Ac 21:15
When we reached **J**, the brothers Ac 21:17
that all **J** was in chaos. Ac 21:31
there to be punished in **J**. Ac 22:5
I came back to **J** and was praying Ac 22:17
'Hurry and get out of **J** quickly, Ac 22:18
have testified about Me in **J**, Ac 23:11
since I went up to worship in **J**. Ac 24:11
he went up to **J** from Caesarea. Ac 25:1
that he might summon him to **J**. Ac 25:3
come down from **J** stood around Ac 25:7
Are you willing to go up to **J**, Ac 25:9
When I was in **J**, the chief Ac 25:15
wished to go to **J** and be tried Ac 25:20
to me, both in **J** and here, Ac 25:24
among my own nation and in **J**. Ac 26:4
actually did in **J**, and I locked Ac 26:10
and to those in **J** and in all the Ac 26:20
a prisoner from **J** into the hands Ac 28:17
the Messiah from **J** all the way Rm 15:19
I am traveling to **J** to serve the Rm 15:25
the poor among the saints in **J**. Rm 15:26
my service for **J** may be Rm 15:31
carry your gracious gift to **J**. 1Co 16:3
not go up to **J** to those who had Gl 1:17
I did go up to **J** to get to know Gl 1:18
up again to **J** with Barnabas, Gl 2:1
corresponds to the present **J**, Gl 4:25
But the **J** above is free, and she Gl 4:26
God (the heavenly **J**), to myriads Heb 12:22
My God—the new **J**, which comes Rv 3:12
Holy City, new **J**, coming down Rv 21:2
the holy city, **J**, coming down Rv 21:10

JERUSALEM'S *(17)*

down 200 yards of **J** wall from 2Kg 14:13
down 200 yards of **J** wall from 2Ch 25:23
They tore down **J** wall, burned 2Ch 36:19
J wall has been broken down, Neh 1:3
let's rebuild **J** wall, so that we Neh 2:17
and **J** rejoicing was heard far Neh 12:43
at the entrance to **J** gates. Jr 1:15
in mourning; **J** cry rises up. Jr 14:2
J residents are like Gomorrah. Jr 23:14
cities and **J** streets that are Jr 33:10
were poured out on **J** residents, Jr 42:18
cities and **J** streets so that Jr 44:6
Judah's cities and in **J** streets. Jr 44:17
cities and in **J** streets— Jr 44:21
adversary could enter **J** gates. Lm 4:12
explain **J** abominations to her. Ezk 16:2
and the glory of **J** residents may Zch 12:7

JERUSHA *(1)*
(AKA JERUSHAH)

name was **J** daughter of Zadok 2Kg 15:33

JERUSHAH *(1)*
(AKA JERUSHA)

name was **J** daughter of Zadok 2Ch 27:1

JESARELAH *(1)*
(AKA ASARELAH)

seventh ⌊to⌋ **J**, his sons, and 1Ch 25:14

JESHAIAH *(7)*

Pelatiah, **J**, and the sons of 1Ch 3:21
Gedaliah, Zeri, **J**, Shimei, 1Ch 25:3
the eighth ⌊to⌋ **J**, his sons, and 1Ch 25:15
his son **J**, his son Joram, 1Ch 26:25
J son of Athaliah from Elam's Ezr 8:7
along with **J**, from the Ezr 8:19
son of Ithiel, son of **J**, Neh 11:7

JESHANAH *(1)*

its villages, **J** and its villages 2Ch 13:19

JESHEBEAB *(1)*

to Huppah, the fourteenth to **J**, 1Ch 24:13

JESHER *(1)*

J, Shobab, and Ardon. 1Ch 2:18

JESHIMON *(4)*
the hill of Hachilah south of J. 1Sm 23:19
Maon in the Arabah south of J, 1Sm 23:24
hill of Hachilah opposite J." 1Sm 26:1
the hill of Hachilah opposite J. 1Sm 26:3

JESHISHAI *(1)*
Michael, son of J, son of Jahdo, 1Ch 5:14

JESHOHAIAH *(1)*
Jaakobah, J, Asaiah, Adiel, 1Ch 4:36

JESHUA *(25)*
(AKA JOSHUA)
the ninth to J, the tenth to 1Ch 24:11
Eden, Miniamin, J, Shemaiah, 2Ch 31:15
with Zerubbabel, J, Nehemiah, Ezr 2:2
descendants of the house of J Ezr 2:36
J son of Jozadak and his Ezr 3:2
of Shealtiel, J son of Jozadak, Ezr 3:8
J with his sons and brothers, Ezr 3:9
But Zerubbabel, J, and the other Ezr 4:3
Shealtiel and J son of Jozadak Ezr 5:2
Jozabad son of J and Noadiah son Ezr 8:33
descendants of J son of Jozadak Ezr 10:18
Next to him Ezer son of J, Neh 3:19
with Zerubbabel, J, Nehemiah, Neh 7:7
descendants of the house of J Neh 7:39
J, Bani, Sherebiah, Jamin, Akkub, Neh 8:7
J, Bani, Kadmiel, Shebaniah, Neh 9:4
the Levites—J, Kadmiel, Bani, Neh 9:5
J son of Azaniah, Binnui of the Neh 10:9
in J, Moladah, Beth-pelet, Neh 11:26
son of Shealtiel and with J: Neh 12:1
relatives in the days of J. Neh 12:7
J, Binnui, Kadmiel, Sherebiah, Neh 12:8
J fathered Joiakim, Joiakim Neh 12:10
Sherebiah, and J son of Kadmiel, Neh 12:24
in the days of Joiakim son of J, Neh 12:26

JESHUA'S *(4)*
J and Joab's descendants 2,812 Ezr 2:6
J and Kadmiel's descendants from Ezr 2:40
J and Joab's descendants 2,818 Neh 7:11
included: J descendants: Neh 7:43

JESHURUN *(4)*
Then J became fat and rebelled— Dt 32:15
became King in J when the Dt 33:5
There is none like the God of J, Dt 33:26
is My servant; I have chosen J. Is 44:2

JESIMIEL *(1)*
Asaiah, Adiel, J, Benaiah, 1Ch 4:36

JESSE *(36)*
was the father of J, the father Ru 4:17
Obed fathered J, who fathered Ru 4:22
am sending you to J of Bethlehem 1Sm 16:1
Then invite J to the sacrifice, 1Sm 16:3
he consecrated J and his sons 1Sm 16:5
J called Abinadab and presented 1Sm 16:8
Then J presented Shammah, but 1Sm 16:9
After J presented seven of his 1Sm 16:10
him, Samuel told J, "The LORD 1Sm 16:10
Samuel told J, "Send for him. 1Sm 16:11
So J sent for him. He had 1Sm 16:12
seen a son of J of Bethlehem who 1Sm 16:18
messengers to J and said, 1Sm 16:19
So J took a donkey loaded with 1Sm 16:20
Then Saul sent word to J: 1Sm 16:22
Bethlehem of Judah named J. 1Sm 17:12
J had eight sons, and during 1Sm 17:12
J had told his son David, 1Sm 17:17
and set out as J had instructed 1Sm 17:20
of your servant J of Bethlehem," 1Sm 17:58
proclamation of David son of J, 2Sm 23:1
no inheritance in the son of J. 1Kg 12:16
Obed, and Obed fathered J, 1Ch 2:12
J fathered Eliab, his firstborn; 1Ch 2:13
kingdom over to David son of J. 1Ch 10:14
we are with you, son of J! 1Ch 12:18
David son of J was king over all 1Ch 29:26
no inheritance in the son of J. 2Ch 10:16
of David son of J are concluded. Ps 72:20
will grow from the stump of J, Is 11:1
day the root of J will stand as Is 11:10
Obed by Ruth, Obed fathered J, Mt 1:5
and J fathered King David. Mt 1:6
son of J, son of Obed, son Lk 3:32
'I have found David the son of J, Ac 13:22
The root of J will appear, Rm 15:12

JESSE'S *(11)*
J three oldest sons had followed 1Sm 17:13
Why didn't J son come to the 1Sm 20:27
siding with J son to your own 1Sm 20:30
Every day J son lives on earth 1Sm 20:31
J son going to give all of you 1Sm 22:7
son makes a covenant with J son. 1Sm 22:8
I saw J son come to Ahimelech 1Sm 22:9
Why did you and J son conspire 1Sm 22:13
Who is J son? Many slaves 1Sm 25:10
David, no inheritance in J son. 2Sm 20:1
Abihail daughter of J son Eliab. 2Ch 11:18

JESUS *(927)*
historical record of J Christ, Mt 1:1
gave birth to J who is called Mt 1:16
The birth of J Christ came about Mt 1:18
and you are to name Him J, Mt 1:21
to a son. And he named Him J. Mt 1:25
After J was born in Bethlehem of Mt 2:1
Then J came from Galilee to John Mt 3:13
J answered him, "Allow it for Mt 3:15
After J was baptized, He went up Mt 3:16
Then J was led up by the Spirit Mt 4:1
J told him, "It is also written: Mt 4:7
J told him, "Go away, Satan! Mt 4:10
From then on J began to preach, Mt 4:17
J was going all over Galilee, Mt 4:23
When J had finished this sermon, Mt 7:28
Then J told him, "See that you Mt 8:4
J was amazed and said to those Mt 8:10
Then J told the centurion, Mt 8:13
When J went into Peter's house, Mt 8:14
When J saw large crowds around Mt 8:18
J told him, "Foxes have dens and Mt 8:20
But J told him, "Follow Me, and Mt 8:22
whole town went out to meet J. Mt 8:34
their faith, J told the Mt 9:2
their thoughts, J said, "Why are Mt 9:4
As J went on from there, He saw Mt 9:9
to eat with J and His disciples Mt 9:10
J said to them, "Can the wedding Mt 9:15
J and His disciples got up and Mt 9:19
But J turned and saw her. Mt 9:22
When J came to the leader's Mt 9:23
As J went on from there, two Mt 9:27
Him, and J said to them, "Do Mt 9:28
Then J warned them sternly, Mt 9:30
Then J went to all the towns and Mt 9:35
J sent out these 12 after giving Mt 10:5
J had finished giving orders Mt 11:1
J replied to them, "Go and Mt 11:4
J began to speak to the crowds Mt 11:7
At that time J said, "I praise Mt 11:25
that time J passed through the Mt 12:1
When J became aware of this, Mt 12:15
On that day J went out of the Mt 13:1
J told the crowds all these Mt 13:34
When J had finished these Mt 13:53
But J said to them, "A prophet Mt 13:57
heard the report about J. Mt 14:1
and went and reported to J. Mt 14:12
When J heard about it, He Mt 14:13
need to go away," J told them. Mt 14:16
Immediately J spoke to them. Mt 14:27
on the water and came toward J. Mt 14:29
Immediately J reached out His Mt 14:31
from Jerusalem to J and asked, Mt 15:1
When J left there, He withdrew Mt 15:21
Then J replied to her, "Woman, Mt 15:28
J passed along the Sea of Mt 15:29
Now J summoned His disciples Mt 15:32
do you have?" J asked them. Mt 15:34
Then J told them, "Watch out and Mt 16:6
Aware of this, J said, "You of Mt 16:8
When J came to the region of Mt 16:13
And J responded, "Simon son of Mt 16:17
From then on J began to point Mt 16:21
Then J said to His disciples, Mt 16:24
After six days J took Peter, Mt 17:1
Peter said to J, "Lord, it's Mt 17:4
Then J came up, touched them, Mt 17:7
saw no one except Him—J alone. Mt 17:8
the mountain, J commanded them, Mt 17:9
J replied, "You unbelieving and Mt 17:17
Then J rebuked the demon, and it Mt 17:18
approached J privately and said Mt 17:19
in Galilee, J told them, "The Mt 17:22
into the house, J spoke to him Mt 17:25
the sons are free," J told him. Mt 17:26
disciples came to J and said, Mt 18:1
many as seven," J said to him, Mt 18:22
When J had finished this Mt 19:1
Then J said, "Leave the children Mt 19:14
J answered, Do not murder; Mt 19:18
to be perfect," J said to him, Mt 19:21
Then J said to His disciples, Mt 19:23
But J looked at them and said, Mt 19:26
J said to them, "I assure you: Mt 19:28
J took the 12 disciples aside Mt 20:17
But J answered, "You don't know Mt 20:22
But J called them over and said, Mt 20:25
they heard that J was passing Mt 20:30
J stopped, called them, and said, Mt 20:32
with compassion, J touched their Mt 20:34
J then sent two disciples, Mt 21:1
and did just as J directed them. Mt 21:6
is the prophet J from Nazareth Mt 21:11
J went into the temple complex Mt 21:12
"Yes," J told them. Mt 21:16
J answered them, "I assure you: Mt 21:21
J answered them, "I will also Mt 21:24
they answered J, "We don't know. Mt 21:27
J said to them, "I assure you: Mt 21:31
J said to them, "Have you never Mt 21:42
Once more J spoke to them in Mt 22:1
their malice, J said, "Why are Mt 22:18
J answered them, "You are Mt 22:29
together, J questioned them, Mt 22:41
Then J spoke to the crowds and Mt 23:1
As J left and was going out of Mt 24:1
Then J replied to them: Mt 24:4
When J had finished saying all Mt 26:1
to arrest J in a treacherous Mt 26:4
While J was in Bethany at the Mt 26:6
But J, aware of this, said to Mt 26:10
disciples came to J and asked, Mt 26:17
disciples did as J had directed Mt 26:19
they were eating, J took bread, Mt 26:26
Then J said to them, "Tonight Mt 26:31
"I assure you," J said to him, Mt 26:34
Then J came with them to a place Mt 26:36
he went right up to J and said, Mt 26:49
"Friend," J asked him, "why have Mt 26:50
up, took hold of J, and arrested Mt 26:50
of those with J reached out his Mt 26:51
Then J told him, "Put your sword Mt 26:52
At that time J said to the Mt 26:55
had arrested J led Him away to Mt 26:57
against J so they could put Mt 26:59
But J kept silent. Then the high Mt 26:63
"You have said it," J told him. Mt 26:64
were with J the Galilean too. Mt 26:69
man was with J the Nazarene!" Mt 26:71
the words J had spoken, Mt 26:75
plotted against J to put Him to Mt 27:1
Now J stood before the governor. Mt 27:11
J answered, "You have said it." Mt 27:11
or J who is called Messiah?" Mt 27:17
for Barabbas and to execute J. Mt 27:20
What should I do then with J, Mt 27:22
But after having J flogged, Mt 27:26
took J into headquarters Mt 27:27
IS J THE KING OF THE JEWS Mt 27:37
the afternoon J cried out with Mt 27:46
J shouted again with a loud Mt 27:50
who were guarding J, saw the Mt 27:54
who had followed J from Galilee Mt 27:55
had also become a disciple of J. Mt 27:57
are looking for J who was Mt 28:5
Just then J met them and said, Mt 28:9
Then J told them, "Do not be Mt 28:10
mountain where J had directed Mt 28:16
Then J came near and said to Mt 28:18
of the gospel of J Christ, Mk 1:1
In those days J came from Mk 1:9
was arrested, J went to Galilee, Mk 1:14
"Follow Me," J told them, "and I Mk 1:17
to do with us, J—Nazarene? Mk 1:24
But J rebuked him and said, Mk 1:25
J reached out His hand and Mk 1:41
result that J could no longer Mk 1:45
to bring him to J because of the Mk 2:4
their faith, J told the Mk 2:5
Right away J understood in His Mk 2:8
Then J went out again beside the Mk 2:13
also guests with J and His Mk 2:15

When **J** heard this, He told them, Mk 2:17
J said to them, "The wedding Mk 2:19
J departed with His disciples to Mk 3:7
When he saw **J** from a distance, Mk 5:6
do with me, **J**, Son of the Most Mk 5:7
They came to **J** and saw the man Mk 5:15
how much **J** had done for him, Mk 5:20
When **J** had crossed over again by Mk 5:21
when he saw **J**, he fell at His Mk 5:22
So **J** went with him, and a large Mk 5:24
heard about **J**, she came behind Mk 5:27
At once **J** realized in Himself Mk 5:30
But when **J** overheard what was Mk 5:36
Then **J** said to them, "A prophet Mk 6:4
gathered around **J** and reported Mk 6:30
and begged **J** to lay His hand on Mk 7:32
Again **J** placed His hands on the Mk 8:25
J went out with His disciples to Mk 8:27
After six days **J** took Peter, Mk 9:2
and they were talking with **J**. Mk 9:4
Peter said to **J**, "Rabbi, it is Mk 9:5
anyone with them except **J** alone. Mk 9:8
J asked his father. Mk 9:21
J said to him, " 'If You can? Mk 9:23
When **J** saw that a crowd was Mk 9:25
But **J**, taking him by the hand, Mk 9:27
him," said **J**, "because there Mk 9:39
But **J** told them, "He wrote this Mk 10:5
When **J** saw it, He was indignant Mk 10:14
call Me good?" **J** asked him. "No Mk 10:18
J loved him and said to him, Mk 10:21
J looked around and said to His Mk 10:23
Again **J** said to them, "Children, Mk 10:24
at them, **J** said, "With men Mk 10:27
"I assure you," **J** said, "there Mk 10:29
and **J** was walking ahead of them. Mk 10:32
But **J** said to them, "You don't Mk 10:38
J said to them, "You will drink Mk 10:39
J called them over and said to Mk 10:42
that it was **J** the Nazarene, Mk 10:47
of David, **J**, have mercy on me! Mk 10:47
J stopped and said, "Call him." Mk 10:49
coat, jumped up, and came to **J**. Mk 10:50
Then **J** answered him, "What do Mk 10:51
"Go your way," **J** told him. Mk 10:52
them just as **J** had said, Mk 11:6
the donkey to **J** and threw their Mk 11:7
J replied to them, "Have faith Mk 11:22
J said to them, "I will ask you Mk 11:29
they answered **J**, "We don't know. Mk 11:33
And **J** said to them, "Neither Mk 11:33
Then **J** told them, "Give back to Mk 12:17
J told them, "Are you not Mk 12:24
and saw that **J** answered them Mk 12:28
the most important," **J** answered: Mk 12:29
When **J** saw that he answered Mk 12:34
So **J** asked this question as He Mk 12:35
J said to him, "Do you see these Mk 13:2
Then **J** began by telling them: Mk 13:5
Then **J** said, "Leave her alone. Mk 14:6
and eating, **J** said, "I assure Mk 14:18
Then **J** said to them, "All of you Mk 14:27
"I assure you," **J** said to him, Mk 14:30
But **J** said to them, "Have you Mk 14:48
They led **J** away to the high Mk 14:53
testimony against **J** to put Him Mk 14:55
them all and questioned **J**, Mk 14:60
"I am," said **J**, "and all of you Mk 14:62
were with that Nazarene, **J**." Mk 14:67
remembered when **J** had spoken Mk 14:72
After tying **J** up, they led Him Mk 15:1
But **J** still did not answer Mk 15:5
And after having **J** flogged, Mk 15:15
And they brought **J** to the place Mk 15:22
And at three **J** cried out with a Mk 15:34
But **J** let out a loud cry and Mk 15:37
are looking for **J** the Nazarene, Mk 16:6
the Lord **J** was taken up into Mk 16:19
and you will call His name **J**. Lk 1:31
He was named **J**—the name given Lk 2:21
the child **J** to perform for Him Lk 2:27
the boy **J** stayed behind in Lk 2:43
And **J** increased in wisdom and Lk 2:52
were baptized, **J** also was Lk 3:21
J was about 30 years old and was Lk 3:23
Then **J** returned from the Jordan, Lk 4:1
But **J** answered him, "It is Lk 4:4
And **J** answered him, "It is Lk 4:8
And **J** answered him, "It is said: Lk 4:12
Then **J** returned to Galilee in Lk 4:14
to do with us, **J**—Nazarene? Lk 4:34
But **J** rebuked him and said, Lk 4:35
pressing in on **J** to hear God's Lk 5:1
"Don't be afraid," **J** told Simon. Lk 5:10
He saw **J**, fell facedown, and Lk 5:12
middle of the crowd before **J**. Lk 5:19
thoughts, **J** replied to them Lk 5:22
J went out and saw a tax Lk 5:27
J replied to them, "The healthy Lk 5:31
J said to them, "You can't make Lk 5:34
J answered them, "Haven't you Lk 6:3
Then **J** said to them, "I ask you: Lk 6:9
another what they might do to **J**. Lk 6:11
the centurion heard about **J**, Lk 7:3
they reached **J**, they pleaded Lk 7:4
J went with them, and when He Lk 7:6
J heard this and was amazed at Lk 7:9
and **J** gave him to his mother. Lk 7:15
that time **J** healed many people Lk 7:21
found out that **J** was reclining Lk 7:37
J replied to him, "Simon, I have Lk 7:40
he saw **J**, he cried out, fell Lk 8:28
have to do with me, **J**, You Son Lk 8:28
is your name?" **J** asked him. Lk 8:30
They came to **J** and found the man Lk 8:35
town all that **J** had done for him Lk 8:39
When **J** returned, the crowd Lk 8:40
touched Me?" **J** asked. When they Lk 8:45
"Somebody did touch Me," said **J**. Lk 8:46
J heard it, He answered him, Lk 8:50
they reported to **J** all that they Lk 9:10
Peter said to **J**, "Master, it's Lk 9:33
had spoken, only **J** was found. Lk 9:36
J replied, "You unbelieving and Lk 9:41
J rebuked the unclean spirit, Lk 9:42
But **J**, knowing the thoughts of Lk 9:47
"Don't stop him," **J** told him, Lk 9:50
J told him, "Foxes have dens, Lk 9:58
But **J** said to him, "No one who Lk 9:62
he asked **J**, "And who is my Lk 10:29
J took up ⌊the question⌋ and Lk 10:30
Then **J** told him, "Go and do the Lk 10:37
When **J** saw her, He called out to Lk 13:12
indignant because **J** had healed Lk 13:14
J asked the law experts and the Lk 14:3
voices, saying, "**J**, Master, have Lk 17:13
Then **J** said, "Were not 10 Lk 17:17
J, however, invited them: Lk 18:16
call Me good?" **J** asked him. "No Lk 18:19
When **J** heard this, He told him, Lk 18:22
he became sad, **J** said, "How hard Lk 18:24
"**J** the Nazarene is passing by," Lk 18:37
he called out, "**J**, Son of David, Lk 18:38
J stopped and commanded that he Lk 18:40
your sight!" **J** told him. "Your Lk 18:42
He was trying to see who **J** was, Lk 19:3
up a sycamore tree to see **J**, Lk 19:4
When **J** came to the place, He Lk 19:5
to this house," **J** told him, Lk 19:9
Then they brought it to **J**, Lk 19:35
donkey, they helped **J** get on it. Lk 19:35
J said to them, "Neither will Lk 20:8
J told them, "The sons of this Lk 20:34
J sent Peter and John, saying, Lk 22:8
He came near **J** to kiss Him, Lk 22:47
but **J** said to him, "Judas, are Lk 22:48
J responded, "No more of this! Lk 22:51
J said to the chief priests, Lk 22:52
were holding **J** started mocking Lk 22:63
Herod was very glad to see **J**; Lk 23:8
questions, but **J** did not answer Lk 23:9
to release **J**, addressed them Lk 23:20
But he handed **J** over to their Lk 23:25
cross on him to carry behind **J**. Lk 23:26
to them, **J** said, "Daughters Lk 23:28
Then **J** said, "Father, forgive Lk 23:34
Then he said, "**J**, remember me Lk 23:42
And **J** called out with a loud Lk 23:46
not find the body of the Lord **J**. Lk 24:3
J Himself came near and began to Lk 24:15
concerning **J** the Nazarene, Lk 24:19
and truth came through **J** Christ. Jn 1:17
day John saw **J** coming toward him Jn 1:29
When he saw **J** passing by, he Jn 1:36
him say this and followed **J**. Jn 1:37
When **J** turned and noticed them Jn 1:38
and he brought ⌊Simon⌋ to **J**. Jn 1:42
When **J** saw him, He said, "You Jn 1:42
J found Philip and told him, Jn 1:43
J the son of Joseph, from Jn 1:45
Then **J** saw Nathanael coming Jn 1:47
tree, I saw you," **J** answered. Jn 1:48
J responded to him, "Do you Jn 1:50
J and His disciples were invited Jn 2:2
Me, woman?" **J** asked. "My hour Jn 2:4
jars with water," **J** told them. Jn 2:7
J performed this first sign in Jn 2:11
so **J** went up to Jerusalem. Jn 2:13
J answered, "Destroy this Jn 2:19
and the statement **J** had made. Jn 2:22
J, however, would not entrust Jn 2:24
J replied, "I assure you: Jn 3:3
J answered, "I assure you: Jn 3:5
know these things?" **J** replied. Jn 3:10
J and His disciples went to the Jn 3:22
When **J** knew that the Pharisees Jn 4:1
though **J** Himself was not Jn 4:2
was there, and **J**, worn out from Jn 4:6
"Give Me a drink," **J** said to her, Jn 4:7
J answered, "If you knew the Jn 4:10
J said, "Everyone who drinks Jn 4:13
don't have a husband,' " **J** said. Jn 4:17
J told her, "Believe Me, woman, Jn 4:21
"I am ⌊He⌋," **J** told her, "the Jn 4:26
finish His work," **J** told them. Jn 4:34
J Himself testified that a Jn 4:44
man heard that **J** had come from Jn 4:47
J told him, "Unless you ⌊people⌋ Jn 4:48
"Go," **J** told him, "your son will Jn 4:50
man believed what **J** said to him Jn 4:50
hour at which **J** had told him, Jn 4:53
second sign **J** performed after Jn 4:54
and **J** went up to Jerusalem. Jn 5:1
When **J** saw him lying there and Jn 5:6
"Get up," **J** told him, "pick up Jn 5:8
because **J** had slipped away into Jn 5:13
J found him in the temple Jn 5:14
that it was **J** who had made him Jn 5:15
persecuting **J** because He was Jn 5:16
But **J** responded to them, "My Jn 5:17
Then **J** replied, "I assure you: Jn 5:19
J crossed the Sea of Galilee Jn 6:1
So **J** went up a mountain and sat Jn 6:3
when **J** looked up and noticed a Jn 6:5
Then **J** said, "Have the people Jn 6:10
J took the loaves, and after Jn 6:11
when **J** knew that they were about Jn 6:15
but **J** had not yet come to them. Jn 6:17
they saw **J** walking on the sea. Jn 6:19
knew⌋ that **J** had not boarded Jn 6:22
saw that neither **J** nor His Jn 6:24
went to Capernaum looking for **J**. Jn 6:24
J answered, "I assure you: Jn 6:26
J replied, "This is the work of Jn 6:29
J said to them, "I assure you: Jn 6:32
the bread of life," **J** told them. Jn 6:35
Isn't this **J** the son of Joseph, Jn 6:42
J answered them, "Stop Jn 6:43
J said to them, "I assure you: Jn 6:53
J, knowing in Himself that His Jn 6:61
For **J** knew from the beginning Jn 6:64
Therefore **J** said to the Twelve, Jn 6:67
J replied to them, "Didn't I Jn 6:70
After this, **J** traveled in Jn 7:1
J told them, "My time has not Jn 7:6
J went up into the temple Jn 7:14
J answered them, "My teaching Jn 7:16
you are all amazed," **J** answered. Jn 7:21
complex, **J** cried out, "You Jn 7:28
Then **J** said, "I am only with you Jn 7:33
J stood up and cried out, Jn 7:37
because **J** had not yet been Jn 7:39
But **J** went to the Mount of Jn 8:1
J stooped down and started Jn 8:6
When **J** stood up, He said to her, Jn 8:10
do I condemn you," said **J**. Jn 8:11
Then **J** spoke to them again: Jn 8:12
about Myself," **J** replied, "My Jn 8:14
Me nor My Father," **J** answered. Jn 8:19
very beginning," **J** told them. Jn 8:25
J said to them, "When you lift Jn 8:28
So **J** said to the Jews who had Jn 8:31
J responded, "I assure you: Jn 8:34
children," **J** told them, "you Jn 8:39

J said to them, "If God were	Jn 8:42
not have a demon," **J** answered.	Jn 8:49
glorify Myself," **J** answered, "My	Jn 8:54
J said to them, "I assure you:	Jn 8:58
But **J** was hidden and went out of	Jn 8:59
parents sinned," **J** answered.	Jn 9:3
The man called **J** made mud,	Jn 9:11
The day that **J** made the mud and	Jn 9:14
J heard that they had thrown	Jn 9:35
J answered, "You have seen Him;	Jn 9:37
J said, "I came into this world	Jn 9:39
were blind," **J** told them, "you	Jn 9:41
J gave them this illustration,	Jn 10:6
So **J** said again, "I assure you:	Jn 10:7
J was walking in the temple	Jn 10:23
don't believe," **J** answered them.	Jn 10:25
J replied, "I have shown you	Jn 10:32
J answered them, "Isn't it	Jn 10:34
When **J** heard it, He said, "This	Jn 11:4
J loved Martha, her sister, and	Jn 11:5
hours in a day?" **J** answered. "If	Jn 11:9
J, however, was speaking about	Jn 11:13
So **J** then told them plainly,	Jn 11:14
When **J** arrived, He found that	Jn 11:17
Martha heard that **J** was coming,	Jn 11:20
Martha said to **J**, "Lord, if You	Jn 11:21
will rise again," **J** told her.	Jn 11:23
J said to her, "I am the	Jn 11:25
J had not yet come into the	Jn 11:30
came to where **J** was and saw Him,	Jn 11:32
When **J** saw her crying, and the	Jn 11:33
J wept.	Jn 11:35
Then **J**, angry in Himself again,	Jn 11:38
"Remove the stone," **J** said.	Jn 11:39
J said to her, "Didn't I tell	Jn 11:40
Then **J** raised His eyes and said,	Jn 11:41
J said to them, "Loose him and	Jn 11:44
and told them what **J** had done.	Jn 11:46
prophesied that **J** was going to	Jn 11:51
Therefore **J** no longer walked	Jn 11:54
were looking for **J** and asking	Jn 11:56
J came to Bethany where Lazarus	Jn 12:1
the one **J** had raised from the	Jn 12:1
J answered, "Leave her alone;	Jn 12:7
They came not only because of **J**,	Jn 12:9
them and believing in **J**.	Jn 12:11
heard that **J** was coming to	Jn 12:12
J found a young donkey and sat	Jn 12:14
However, when **J** was glorified,	Jn 12:16
of him, "Sir, we want to see **J**."	Jn 12:21
and Philip went and told **J**.	Jn 12:22
J replied to them, "The hour has	Jn 12:23
J responded, "This voice came,	Jn 12:30
J answered, "The light will be	Jn 12:35
J said this, then went away and	Jn 12:36
Then **J** cried out, "The one who	Jn 12:44
J knew that His hour had come to	Jn 13:1
J knew that the Father had given	Jn 13:3
J answered him, "What I'm doing	Jn 13:7
J replied, "If I don't wash you,	Jn 13:8
who has bathed," **J** told him,	Jn 13:10
When **J** had washed their feet and	Jn 13:12
When **J** had said this, He was	Jn 13:21
disciples, the one **J** loved, was	Jn 13:23
was reclining close beside **J**.	Jn 13:23
back against **J** and asked Him,	Jn 13:25
J replied, "He's the one I give	Jn 13:26
Therefore **J** told him, "What	Jn 13:27
thought that **J** was telling him,	Jn 13:29
had gone out, **J** said, "Now the	Jn 13:31
J answered, "Where I am going	Jn 13:36
J replied, "Will you lay down	Jn 13:38
J told him, "I am the way, the	Jn 14:6
J said to him, "Have I been	Jn 14:9
J answered, "If anyone loves Me,	Jn 14:23
J knew they wanted to question	Jn 16:19
J responded to them, "Do you now	Jn 16:31
J spoke these things, looked up	Jn 17:1
One You have sent—**J** Christ.	Jn 17:3
After **J** had said these things,	Jn 18:1
because **J** often met there with	Jn 18:2
Then **J**, knowing everything that	Jn 18:4
"**J** the Nazarene," they answered.	Jn 18:5
"I am He," **J** told them.	Jn 18:5
"**J** the Nazarene," they said.	Jn 18:7
told you I am ⌊He⌋," **J** replied.	Jn 18:8
At that, **J** said to Peter,	Jn 18:11
arrested **J** and tied Him up	Jn 18:12
Simon Peter was following **J**,	Jn 18:15
so he went with **J** into the high	Jn 18:15
priest questioned **J** about His	Jn 18:19
to the world," **J** answered him.	Jn 18:20
police standing by slapped **J**,	Jn 18:22
spoken wrongly," **J** answered him,	Jn 18:23
Then they took **J** from Caiaphas	Jn 18:28
summoned **J**, and said to Him,	Jn 18:33
J answered, "Are you asking this	Jn 18:34
is not of this world," said **J**.	Jn 18:36
say that I'm a king," **J** replied.	Jn 18:37
Then Pilate took **J** and had Him	Jn 19:1
J came out wearing the crown	Jn 19:5
the headquarters and asked **J**,	Jn 19:9
But **J** did not give him an	Jn 19:9
over Me at all," **J** answered him,	Jn 19:11
words, he brought **J** outside.	Jn 19:13
Therefore they took **J** away.	Jn 19:16
side, with **J** in the middle.	Jn 19:18
J THE NAZARENE THE KING	Jn 19:19
the place where **J** was crucified	Jn 19:20
When the soldiers crucified **J**,	Jn 19:23
the cross of **J** were His mother	Jn 19:25
When **J** saw His mother and the	Jn 19:26
when **J** knew that everything was	Jn 19:28
When **J** had received the sour	Jn 19:30
When they came to **J**, they did	Jn 19:33
a disciple of **J**—but secretly	Jn 19:38
They place **J** there because of	Jn 19:42
the one **J** loved, and said	Jn 20:2
around and saw **J** standing there,	Jn 20:14
she did not know it was **J**.	Jn 20:14
"Woman," **J** said to her, "why are	Jn 20:15
J said, "Mary." Turning around,	Jn 20:16
cling to Me," **J** told her, "for I	Jn 20:17
Then **J** came, stood among them,	Jn 20:19
J said to them again, "Peace to	Jn 20:21
was not with them when **J** came.	Jn 20:24
J came and stood among them.	Jn 20:26
J said, "Because you have seen	Jn 20:29
J performed many other signs in	Jn 20:30
may believe **J** is the Messiah,	Jn 20:31
J revealed Himself again to His	Jn 21:1
daybreak came, **J** stood on the	Jn 21:4
disciples did not know it was **J**.	Jn 21:4
"Men," **J** called to them, "you	Jn 21:5
the one **J** loved, said to	Jn 21:7
just caught," **J** told them.	Jn 21:10
have breakfast," **J** told them.	Jn 21:12
J came, took the bread, and gave	Jn 21:13
now the third time **J** appeared to	Jn 21:14
eaten breakfast, **J** asked Simon	Jn 21:15
"Feed My sheep," **J** said.	Jn 21:17
the disciple **J** loved following	Jn 21:20
back against **J** at the supper	Jn 21:20
him, he said to **J**, "Lord—what	Jn 21:21
until I come," **J** answered, "what	Jn 21:22
Yet **J** did not tell him that he	Jn 21:23
many other things that **J** did,	Jn 21:25
about all that **J** began to do and	Ac 1:1
This **J**, who has been taken from	Ac 1:11
including Mary the mother of **J**,	Ac 1:14
a guide to those who arrested **J**.	Ac 1:16
time the Lord **J** went in and out	Ac 1:21
This **J** the Nazarene was a man	Ac 2:22
God has resurrected this **J**.	Ac 2:32
that God has made this **J**,	Ac 2:36
in the name of **J** the Messiah for	Ac 2:38
In the name of **J** Christ the	Ac 3:6
has glorified His Servant **J**,	Ac 3:13
and He may send **J**, who has been	Ac 3:20
the person of **J** the resurrection	Ac 4:2
by the name of **J** Christ the	Ac 4:10
This ⌊**J**⌋ is The stone despised	Ac 4:11
knew that they had been with **J**.	Ac 4:13
teach at all in the name of **J**.	Ac 4:18
against Your holy Servant **J**,	Ac 4:27
name of Your holy Servant **J**."	Ac 4:30
the resurrection of the Lord **J**,	Ac 4:33
God of our fathers raised up **J**,	Ac 5:30
in the name of **J** and released	Ac 5:40
good news that the Messiah is **J**.	Ac 5:42
For we heard him say that **J**,	Ac 6:14
J standing at the right hand	Ac 7:55
"Lord **J**, receive my spirit!"	Ac 7:59
of God and the name of **J** Christ,	Ac 8:12
in the name of the Lord **J**.	Ac 8:16
tell him the good news about **J**,	Ac 8:35
I believe that **J** Christ is the	Ac 8:37
am **J**, whom you are persecuting,	Ac 9:5
Saul, the Lord **J**, who appeared	Ac 9:17
proclaiming **J** in the synagogues	Ac 9:20
spoken boldly in the name of **J**.	Ac 9:27
him, "Aeneas, **J** Christ heals you	Ac 9:34
news of peace through **J** Christ—	Ac 10:36
God anointed **J** of Nazareth with	Ac 10:38
in the name of **J** Christ.	Ac 10:48
believed on the Lord **J** Christ,	Ac 11:17
the good news about the Lord **J**.	Ac 11:20
the Savior, **J**, to Israel.	Ac 13:23
their children by raising up **J**,	Ac 13:33
through the grace of the Lord **J**,	Ac 15:11
the name of our Lord **J** Christ.	Ac 15:26
the Spirit of **J** did not allow	Ac 16:7
in the name of **J** Christ to come	Ac 16:18
on the Lord **J**, and you will be	Ac 16:31
This is the Messiah, **J**, whom I	Ac 17:3
that there is another king—**J**!"	Ac 17:7
the good news about **J** and the	Ac 17:18
the Jews that the Messiah is **J**.	Ac 18:5
the things about **J** accurately,	Ac 18:25
that **J** is the Messiah.	Ac 18:28
come after him, that is, in **J**."	Ac 19:4
in the name of the Lord **J**.	Ac 19:5
name of the Lord **J** over those	Ac 19:13
you by the **J** whom Paul preaches	Ac 19:13
answered them, "**J** I know, and	Ac 19:15
of the Lord **J** was magnified.	Ac 19:17
God and faith in our Lord **J**.	Ac 20:21
I received from the Lord **J**,	Ac 20:24
in mind the words of the Lord **J**,	Ac 20:35
for the name of the Lord **J**."	Ac 21:13
to me, 'I am **J** the Nazarene,	Ac 22:8
subject of faith in Christ **J**.	Ac 24:24
religion and about a certain **J**,	Ac 25:19
to the name of **J** the Nazarene.	Ac 26:9
'I am **J**, whom you are	Ac 26:15
them concerning **J** from both the	Ac 28:23
the Lord **J** Christ with full	Ac 28:31
slave of Christ **J**, called as an	Rm 1:1
His Son, **J** Christ our Lord,	Rm 1:3
who are also **J** Christ's by	Rm 1:6
Father and the Lord **J** Christ.	Rm 1:7
my God through **J** Christ for all	Rm 1:8
to my gospel through Christ **J**.	Rm 2:16
through faith in **J** Christ,	Rm 3:22
redemption that is in Christ **J**.	Rm 3:24
the one who has faith in **J**.	Rm 3:26
Him who raised **J** our Lord from	Rm 4:24
God through our Lord **J** Christ.	Rm 5:1
God through our Lord **J** Christ,	Rm 5:11
grace of the one man, **J** Christ.	Rm 5:15
through the one man, **J** Christ.	Rm 5:17
life through **J** Christ our Lord.	Rm 5:21
into Christ **J** were baptized	Rm 6:3
but alive to God in Christ **J**.	Rm 6:11
life in Christ **J** our Lord.	Rm 6:23
God through **J** Christ our Lord!	Rm 7:25
exists for those in Christ **J**,	Rm 8:1
life in Christ **J** has set you	Rm 8:2
Him who raised **J** from the dead	Rm 8:11
Christ **J** is the One who died,	Rm 8:34
that is in Christ **J** our Lord!	Rm 8:39
with your mouth, "**J** is Lord,"	Rm 10:9
But put on the Lord **J** Christ,	Rm 13:14
by the Lord **J** that nothing is	Rm 14:14
another, according to Christ **J**,	Rm 15:5
Father of our Lord **J** Christ with	Rm 15:6
of Christ **J** to the Gentiles,	Rm 15:16
boast in Christ **J** regarding what	Rm 15:17
through the Lord **J** Christ and	Rm 15:30
my co-workers in Christ **J**,	Rm 16:3
grace of our Lord **J** be with you.	Rm 16:20
of our Lord **J** Christ be with	Rm 16:24
the proclamation of **J** Christ,	Rm 16:25
God, through **J** Christ—to Him	Rm 16:27
of Christ **J** by God's will,	1Co 1:1
in Christ **J** and called as saints	1Co 1:2
on the name of **J** Christ our Lord	1Co 1:2
Father and the Lord **J** Christ.	1Co 1:3
grace given to you in Christ **J**,	1Co 1:4
revelation of our Lord **J** Christ.	1Co 1:7
in the day of our Lord **J** Christ.	1Co 1:8
with His Son, **J** Christ our Lord.	1Co 1:9
the name of our Lord **J** Christ,	1Co 1:10
from Him you are in Christ **J**,	1Co 1:30

among you except **J** Christ and 1Co 2:2
been laid—that is, **J** Christ. 1Co 3:11
you in Christ **J** through the 1Co 4:15
you about my ways in Christ **J**, 1Co 4:17
In the name of our Lord **J**, 1Co 5:4
with the power of our Lord **J**, 1Co 5:4
in the name of the Lord **J** Christ 1Co 6:11
and one Lord, **J** Christ, through 1Co 8:6
Have I not seen **J** our Lord? 1Co 9:1
betrayed, the Lord **J** took bread, 1Co 11:23
of God says, "**J** is cursed," and 1Co 12:3
one can say, "**J** is Lord," except 1Co 12:3
I have in Christ **J** our Lord: 1Co 15:31
through our Lord **J** Christ! 1Co 15:57
grace of our Lord **J** be with you. 1Co 16:23
be with all of you in Christ **J**. 1Co 16:24
of Christ **J** by God's will, 2Co 1:1
Father and the Lord **J** Christ. 2Co 1:2
and Father of our Lord **J** Christ, 2Co 1:3
ours, in the day of our Lord **J**. 2Co 1:14
Son of God, **J** Christ, who was 2Co 1:19
ourselves but **J** Christ as Lord, 2Co 4:5
as your slaves because of **J**. 2Co 4:5
glory in the face of **J** Christ. 2Co 4:6
the death of **J** in our body, 2Co 4:10
that the life of **J** may also be 2Co 4:10
over to death because of **J**, 2Co 4:11
raised the Lord **J** will raise us 2Co 4:14
Jesus will raise us also with **J**, 2Co 4:14
the grace of our Lord **J** Christ: 2Co 8:9
comes and preaches another **J**, 2Co 11:4
God and Father of the Lord **J**, 2Co 11:31
yourselves that **J** Christ is in 2Co 13:5
The grace of the Lord **J** Christ, 2Co 13:13
but by **J** Christ and God the Gl 1:1
Father and our Lord **J** Christ, Gl 1:3
by a revelation from **J** Christ. Gl 1:12
that we have in Christ **J**, Gl 2:4
law but by faith in **J** Christ. Gl 2:16
we have believed in Christ **J**, Gl 2:16
before whose eyes **J** Christ was Gl 3:1
to the Gentiles in Christ **J**, Gl 3:14
by faith in **J** Christ might be Gl 3:22
God through faith in Christ **J**. Gl 3:26
for you are all one in Christ **J**. Gl 3:28
of God, as Christ **J** ⌊Himself⌋. Gl 4:14
For in Christ **J** neither Gl 5:6
to Christ **J** have crucified Gl 5:24
the cross of our Lord **J** Christ, Gl 6:14
carry the marks of **J** on my body. Gl 6:17
of our Lord **J** Christ be with Gl 6:18
of Christ **J** by God's will: Eph 1:1
in Christ **J** at Ephesus. Eph 1:1
Father and the Lord **J** Christ. Eph 1:2
and Father of our Lord **J** Christ, Eph 1:3
adopted through **J** Christ for Eph 1:5
in the Lord **J** and your love for Eph 1:15
the God of our Lord **J** Christ, Eph 1:17
Him in the heavens, in Christ **J**, Eph 2:6
His⌋ kindness to us in Christ **J**. Eph 2:7
in Christ **J** for good works, Eph 2:10
now in Christ **J**, you who were Eph 2:13
with Christ **J** Himself as the Eph 2:20
of Christ **J** on behalf of you Eph 3:1
promise in Christ **J** through the Eph 3:6
made in the Messiah, **J** our Lord, Eph 3:11
and in Christ **J** to all Eph 3:21
because the truth is in **J**: Eph 4:21
the name of our Lord **J** Christ, Eph 5:20
Father and the Lord **J** Christ. Eph 6:23
love for our Lord **J** Christ. Eph 6:24
and Timothy, slaves of Christ **J**: Php 1:1
saints in Christ **J** who are in Php 1:1
Father and the Lord **J** Christ. Php 1:2
until the day of Christ **J**. Php 1:6
with the affection of Christ **J**. Php 1:8
that ⌊comes⌋ through **J** Christ, Php 1:11
from the Spirit of **J** Christ. Php 1:19
grow in Christ **J** when I come to Php 1:26
own attitude that of Christ **J**, Php 2:5
at the name of **J** every knee Php 2:10
confess that **J** Christ is Lord, Php 2:11
in the Lord **J** to send Timothy Php 2:19
not those of **J** Christ. Php 2:21
boast in Christ **J**, and do not Php 3:3
of knowing Christ **J** my Lord. Php 3:8
been taken hold of by Christ **J**. Php 3:12
God's heavenly call in Christ **J**. Php 3:14
for a Savior, the Lord **J** Christ. Php 3:20
and your minds in Christ **J**. Php 4:7
His riches in glory in Christ **J**. Php 4:19
Greet every saint in Christ **J**. Php 4:21
of the Lord **J** Christ be with Php 4:23
of Christ **J** by God's will, Col 1:1
the Father of our Lord **J** Christ, Col 1:3
faith in Christ **J** and of the Col 1:4
have received Christ **J** the Lord, Col 2:6
in the name of the Lord **J**, Col 3:17
and so does **J** who is called Col 4:11
a slave of Christ **J**, greets you. Col 4:12
Father and the Lord **J** Christ. 1Th 1:1
of hope in our Lord **J** Christ, 1Th 1:3
from the dead—**J**, who rescues 1Th 1:10
in Christ **J** that are in Judea 1Th 2:14
the Lord **J** and the prophets, 1Th 2:15
of our Lord **J** at His coming? 1Th 2:19
and our Lord **J**, direct our way 1Th 3:11
coming of our Lord **J** with all 1Th 3:13
and encourage you in the Lord **J**, 1Th 4:1
we gave you through the Lord **J**. 1Th 4:2
we believe that **J** died and rose 1Th 4:14
have fallen asleep through **J**. 1Th 4:14
through our Lord **J** Christ, 1Th 5:9
God's will for you in Christ **J**. 1Th 5:18
the coming of our Lord **J** Christ. 1Th 5:23
of our Lord **J** Christ be with 1Th 5:28
Father and the Lord **J** Christ. 2Th 1:1
Father and the Lord **J** Christ. 2Th 1:2
of the Lord **J** from heaven with 2Th 1:7
obey the gospel of our Lord **J**. 2Th 1:8
name of our Lord **J** will be 2Th 1:12
our God and the Lord **J** Christ. 2Th 1:12
of our Lord **J** Christ and our 2Th 2:1
The Lord **J** will destroy him with 2Th 2:8
the glory of our Lord **J** Christ. 2Th 2:14
our Lord **J** Christ Himself and 2Th 2:16
the name of our Lord **J** Christ, 2Th 3:6
by the Lord **J** Christ, that 2Th 3:12
of our Lord **J** Christ be with 2Th 3:18
apostle of Christ **J** according to 1Tm 1:1
God our Savior and of Christ **J**, 1Tm 1:1
Father and Christ **J** our Lord. 1Tm 1:2
thanks to Christ **J** our Lord, 1Tm 1:12
and love that are in Christ **J**. 1Tm 1:14
Christ **J** came into the world to 1Tm 1:15
Christ **J** might demonstrate the 1Tm 1:16
God and man, a man, Christ **J**, 1Tm 2:5
the faith that is in Christ **J**. 1Tm 3:13
be a good servant of Christ **J**, 1Tm 4:6
God and Christ **J** and the elect 1Tm 5:21
of our Lord **J** Christ and with 1Tm 6:3
before Christ **J**, who gave a good 1Tm 6:13
appearing of our Lord **J** Christ, 1Tm 6:14
of Christ **J** by God's will, 2Tm 1:1
the promise of life in Christ **J**: 2Tm 1:1
Father and Christ **J** our Lord. 2Tm 1:2
to us in Christ **J** before time 2Tm 1:9
of our Savior Christ **J**, 2Tm 1:10
and love that are in Christ **J**. 2Tm 1:13
the grace that is in Christ **J**. 2Tm 2:1
as a good soldier of Christ **J**. 2Tm 2:3
in mind **J** Christ, risen from 2Tm 2:8
is in Christ **J**, with eternal 2Tm 2:10
life in Christ **J** will be 2Tm 3:12
through faith in Christ **J**. 2Tm 3:15
God and Christ **J**, who is going 2Tm 4:1
and an apostle of **J** Christ for Ti 1:1
Father and Christ **J** our Savior. Ti 1:4
great God and Savior, **J** Christ. Ti 2:13
through **J** Christ our Savior Ti 3:6
of Christ **J**, and Timothy, our Phm 1
Father and the Lord **J** Christ. Phm 3
toward the Lord **J** and for all Phm 5
also as a prisoner of Christ **J**, Phm 9
my fellow prisoner in Christ **J**, Phm 23
of the Lord **J** Christ be with Phm 25
we do see **J**—made lower than Heb 2:9
calling, consider **J**, the apostle Heb 3:1
For **J** is considered worthy of Heb 3:3
the heavens—**J** the Son of God— Heb 4:14
J has entered there on our Heb 6:20
So **J** has also become the Heb 7:22
J has now obtained a superior Heb 8:6
of the body of **J** Christ once and Heb 10:10
through the blood of **J**, Heb 10:19
keeping our eyes on **J**, the Heb 12:2
J (mediator of a new covenant) Heb 12:24
J Christ is the same yesterday, Heb 13:8
Therefore **J** also suffered Heb 13:12
up from the dead our Lord **J**— Heb 13:20
sight, through **J** Christ, to whom Heb 13:21
of God and of the Lord **J** Christ: Jms 1:1
glorious Lord **J** Christ without Jms 2:1
Peter, an apostle of **J** Christ: 1Pt 1:1
with the blood of **J** Christ. 1Pt 1:2
and Father of our Lord **J** Christ. 1Pt 1:3
resurrection of **J** Christ from 1Pt 1:3
at the revelation of **J** Christ. 1Pt 1:7
at the revelation of **J** Christ. 1Pt 1:13
to God through **J** Christ. 1Pt 2:5
the resurrection of **J** Christ. 1Pt 3:21
be glorified through **J** Christ. 1Pt 4:11
His eternal glory in Christ **J**, 1Pt 5:10
and an apostle of **J** Christ: 2Pt 1:1
of our God and Savior **J** Christ. 2Pt 1:1
of God and of **J** our Lord. 2Pt 1:2
knowledge of our Lord **J** Christ. 2Pt 1:8
Lord and Savior **J** Christ will be 2Pt 1:11
as our Lord **J** Christ has also 2Pt 1:14
and coming of our Lord **J** Christ; 2Pt 1:16
of our Lord and Savior **J** Christ, 2Pt 2:20
of our Lord and Savior **J** Christ. 2Pt 3:18
and with His Son **J** Christ. 1Jn 1:3
the blood of **J** His Son cleanses 1Jn 1:7
J Christ the righteous One. 1Jn 2:1
denies that **J** is the Messiah? 1Jn 2:22
in the name of His Son **J** Christ, 1Jn 3:23
confesses that **J** Christ has come 1Jn 4:2
not confess **J** is not from God 1Jn 4:3
confesses that **J** is the Son of 1Jn 4:15
believes that **J** is the Messiah 1Jn 5:1
believes that **J** is the Son of 1Jn 5:5
J Christ—He is the One who 1Jn 5:6
that is, in His Son **J** Christ. 1Jn 5:20
the Father and from **J** Christ, 2Jn 3
the coming of **J** Christ in the 2Jn 7
Jude, a slave of **J** Christ, and a Jd 1
the Father and kept by **J** Christ. Jd 1
only Master and Lord, **J** Christ. Jd 4
apostles of our Lord **J** Christ; Jd 17
mercy of our Lord **J** Christ for Jd 21
through **J** Christ our Lord, Jd 25
revelation of **J** Christ that God Rv 1:1
to the testimony about **J** Christ, Rv 1:2
and from **J** Christ, the faithful Rv 1:5
perseverance in **J**, was on the Rv 1:9
word and the testimony about **J**. Rv 1:9
and have the testimony about **J**. Rv 12:17
of God and the faith in **J**." Rv 14:12
the blood of the witnesses to **J**. Rv 17:6
who have the testimony about **J**. Rv 19:10
testimony about **J** is the spirit Rv 19:10
testimony about **J** and because of Rv 20:4
I, **J**, have sent My angel to Rv 22:16
quickly." Amen! Come, Lord **J**! Rv 22:20
grace of the Lord **J** be with all Rv 22:21

JESUS' *(16)*

Pilate and asked for **J** body. Mt 27:58
because **J** name had become well Mk 6:14
passing by, to carry **J** cross. Mk 15:21
to Pilate and asked for **J** body. Mk 15:43
he fell at **J** knees and said, Lk 5:8
from, sitting at **J** feet, dressed Lk 8:35
He fell down at **J** feet and Lk 8:41
Pilate and asked for **J** body. Lk 23:52
J mother was there, and Jn 2:1
wine ran out, **J** mother told Him Jn 2:3
—anointed **J** feet, and wiped Jn 12:3
this so that **J** words might be Jn 18:32
that he might remove **J** body. Jn 19:38
they took **J** body and wrapped Jn 19:40
where **J** body had been lying. Jn 20:12
so that **J** life may also be 2Co 4:11

JETHER *(7)*

(AKA ITHRA)
he said to **J**, his firstborn, Jdg 8:20
son of Ner and Amasa son of **J**. 1Kg 2:5
and Amasa son of **J**, commander of 1Kg 2:32
his father was **J** the Ishmaelite. 1Ch 2:17
of Shammai: **J** and Jonathan. 1Ch 2:32
J died without children. 1Ch 2:32
J, Mered, Epher, and Jalon. 1Ch 4:17

JETHER'S *(1)*

J sons: Jephunneh, Pispa, and 1Ch 7:38

JETHETH *(2)*
Chiefs Timna, Alvah, J, Gn 36:40
Edom's chiefs: Timna, Alvah, J, 1Ch 1:51

JETHRO *(10)*
(AKA HOBAB, REUEL)
flock of his father-in-law J, Ex 3:1
father-in-law J and said to him Ex 4:18
J said to Moses, "Go in peace." Ex 4:18
father-in-law J, the priest Ex 18:1
Now J, Moses' father-in-law, had Ex 18:2
father-in-law J, along with Ex 18:5
father-in-law J, am coming to Ex 18:6
J rejoiced over all the good Ex 18:9
is the LORD," J exclaimed, "who Ex 18:10
Then J, Moses' father-in-law, Ex 18:12

JETTISON *(1)*
they began to j the cargo the Ac 27:18

JETUR *(3)*
Hadad, Tema, J, Naphish, and Gn 25:15
J, Naphish, and Kedemah. 1Ch 1:31
the Hagrites, J, Naphish, and 1Ch 5:19

JEUEL *(3)*
J and 690 of their relatives. 1Ch 9:6
Shimri and J from the 2Ch 29:13
Eliphelet, J, and Shemaiah, and Ezr 8:13

JEUSH *(9)*
Oholibamah bore J, Jalam, and Gn 36:5
She bore J, Jalam, and Korah to Gn 36:14
Chiefs J, Jalam, and Korah. Gn 36:18
Eliphaz, Reuel, J, Jalam, and 1Ch 1:35
J, Benjamin, Ehud, Chenaanah, 1Ch 7:10
was his firstborn, J second, and 1Ch 8:39
Jahath, Zizah, J, and Beriah. 1Ch 23:10
J and Beriah did not have many 1Ch 23:11
J, Shemariah, and Zaham. 2Ch 11:19

JEUZ *(1)*
J, Sachia, and Mirmah. These 1Ch 8:10

JEW *(25)*
he had told them he was a J. Est 3:4
I see Mordecai the J sitting at Est 5:13
and a horse for Mordecai the J, Est 6:10
the Queen and to Mordecai the J, Est 8:7
along with Mordecai the J, Est 9:29
as Mordecai the J and Queen Est 9:31
Mordecai the J was second only Est 10:3
disciples and a J about Jn 3:25
it that You, a J, ask for a Jn 4:9
"I'm not a J, am I?" Pilate Jn 18:35
A J named Apollos, a native Ac 18:24
they recognized that he was a J, Ac 19:34
first to the J, and also to the Rm 1:16
evil, first to the J, and also Rm 2:9
good, first to the J, and also Rm 2:10
Now if you call yourself a J, Rm 2:17
a person is not a J who is one Rm 2:28
a person is a J who is one Rm 2:29
what advantage does the J have? Rm 3:1
distinction between J and Greek, Rm 10:12
To the Jews I became like a J, 1Co 9:20
If you, who are a J, live like a Gl 2:14
like a Gentile and not like a J, Gl 2:14
There is no J or Greek, slave or Gl 3:28
Here there is not Greek and J, Col 3:11

JEWEL *(2)*
with one j of your necklace. Sg 4:9
Babylon, the j of the kingdoms Is 13:19

JEWELRY *(20)*
her house for silver and gold j, Ex 3:22
for gold and silver j." Ex 11:2
silver and gold j and for Ex 12:35
and didn't put on their j. Ex 33:4
Now take off your j, and I will Ex 33:5
of their j from Mount Horeb Ex 33:6
kinds of gold j—everyone who Ex 35:22
cheeks are beautiful with j, Sg 1:10
We will make gold j for you, Sg 1:11
of your thighs are like j, Sg 7:1
ankle j, sashes, perfume Is 3:20
wear all your children as j, Is 49:18
woman forget her j or a bride Jr 2:32
you adorn yourself with gold j, Jr 4:30
adorned you with j, putting Ezk 16:11
your beautiful j made from the Ezk 16:17
your beautiful j, and leave you Ezk 16:39
and take your beautiful j. Ezk 23:26
yourself with j for them. Ezk 23:40
her rings and j, and went after Hs 2:13

JEWELS *(6)*
She is more precious than j; Pr 3:15
is gold and a multitude of j, Pr 20:15
She is far more precious than j. Pr 31:10
washed in milk and set like j. Sg 5:12
bride adorns herself with her j. Is 61:10
for they are like j in a crown, Zch 9:16

JEWISH *(43)*
was watching over the J elders. Ezr 5:5
So the J elders continued Ezr 6:14
and the J remnant that had Neh 1:2
against their J countrymen. Neh 5:1
to buy back our J countrymen who Neh 5:8
A J man was in the fortress of Est 2:5
the enemy of the J people. Est 3:10
annihilate all the J people— Est 3:13
among the J people in every Est 4:3
will come to the J people from Est 4:14
begun to fall, is J, you won't Est 6:13
significance in J life and their Est 9:28
the robe of a J man tightly, Zch 8:23
spread among J people to this Mt 28:15
he sent some J elders to Him, Lk 7:3
set there for J purification. Jn 2:6
J Passover was near, so Jesus Jn 2:13
After this, a J festival took Jn 5:1
the Passover, a J festival, was Jn 6:4
J Festival of Tabernacles was Jn 7:2
J Passover was near, and many Jn 11:55
and the J temple police arrested Jn 18:12
because of the J preparation Jn 19:42
J men and all you residents of Ac 2:14
deeds for the ⌊J⌋ people and Ac 10:2
with the whole J nation, Ac 10:22
forbidden for a J man to Ac 10:28
all that the J people expected. Ac 12:11
message in the J synagogues. Ac 13:5
a J false prophet named Ac 13:6
they entered the J synagogue and Ac 14:1
the son of a believing J woman, Ac 16:1
where there was a J synagogue. Ac 17:1
he found a J man named Aquila Ac 18:2
of the itinerant J exorcists Ac 19:13
sons of Sceva, a J chief priest, Ac 19:14
I am a J man from Tarsus of Ac 21:39
continued, "I am a J man, born Ac 22:3
who was J, he sent for Paul Ac 24:24
Neither against the J law, Ac 25:8
whom the whole J community has Ac 25:24
an expert in all the J customs Ac 26:3
may not pay attention to J myths Ti 1:14

JEWS *(211)*
they killed⌋ the J and the 2Kg 25:25
king that the J who came from Ezr 4:12
went to the J in Jerusalem Ezr 4:23
to the J who were in Judah Ezr 5:1
came to the J and asked, Ezr 5:3
and elders of the J rebuild this Ezr 6:7
elders of the J can rebuild this Ezr 6:8
for I had not yet told the J, Neh 2:16
became furious. He mocked the J Neh 4:1
What are these pathetic J doing? Neh 4:2
When the J who lived nearby Neh 4:12
There were 150 J and officials, Neh 5:17
you and the J plan to rebel. Neh 6:6
I also saw J who had married Neh 13:23
people, the J, throughout Est 3:6
for the slaughter of the J. Est 4:7
fate of all the J because you Est 4:13
all the J who can be found Est 4:16
of Haman, the enemy of the J. Est 8:1
he had devised against the J. Est 8:3
to destroy the J who ⌊reside⌋ in Est 8:5
because he attacked the J. Est 8:7
pleases you concerning the J, Est 8:8
as Mordecai ordered for the J, Est 8:9
and to the J in their own script Est 8:9
edict gave the J in each and Est 8:11
group so the J could be ready to Est 8:13
and the J celebrated with Est 8:16
took place among the J. Est 8:17
themselves to be J because fear Est 8:17
fear of the J had overcome them Est 8:17
J overpowered those who hated Est 9:1
provinces the J assembled in Est 9:2
aided the J because they were Est 9:3
The J put all their enemies to Est 9:5
of Susa the J killed and Est 9:6
Hammedatha, the enemy of the J. Est 9:10
of Susa the J have killed Est 9:12
may the J who are in Susa also Est 9:13
The J in Susa assembled again on Est 9:15
The rest of the J in the royal Est 9:16
But the J in Susa had assembled Est 9:18
why the rural J who live in Est 9:19
to all the J in all of King Est 9:20
days the J got rid of their Est 9:22
So the J agreed to continue the Est 9:23
enemy of all the J, had plotted Est 9:24
against the J to destroy them. Est 9:24
against the J return on his own Est 9:25
the J bound themselves, their Est 9:27
to all the J who were in the 127 Est 9:30
famous among the J, and highly Est 10:3
for all the J living in the land Jr 44:1
in the seventh year, 3,023 J; Jr 52:28
of the guards, deported 745 J. Jr 52:30
and maliciously accuse the J. Dn 3:8
There are some J you have Dn 3:12
who has been born King of the J? Mt 2:2
"Are You the King of the J?" Mt 27:11
Him: "Hail, King of the J!" Mt 27:29
IS JESUS THE KING OF THE J Mt 27:37
in fact all the J, will not eat Mk 7:3
"Are You the King of the J?" Mk 15:2
the King of the J for you?" Mk 15:9
One you call the King of the J?" Mk 15:12
Him, "Hail, King of the J!" Mk 15:18
Him was THE KING OF THE J. Mk 15:26
"Are You the King of the J?" Lk 23:3
If You are the King of the J, Lk 23:37
THIS IS THE KING OF THE J Lk 23:38
when the J from Jerusalem Jn 1:19
So the J replied to Him, "What Jn 2:18
Therefore the J said, "This Jn 2:20
Nicodemus, a ruler of the J. Jn 3:1
For J do not associate with Jn 4:9
yet you ⌊J⌋ say that the place Jn 4:20
because salvation is from the J. Jn 4:22
so the J said to the man who had Jn 5:10
reported to the J that it was Jn 5:15
the J began persecuting Jesus Jn 5:16
This is why the J began trying Jn 5:18
Therefore the J started Jn 6:41
the J argued among themselves, Jn 6:52
because the J were trying to Jn 7:1
J were looking for Him at the Jn 7:11
Him because they feared the J. Jn 7:13
Then the J were amazed and said, Jn 7:15
Then the J said to one another, Jn 7:35
So the J said again, "He won't Jn 8:22
said to the J who had believed Jn 8:31
The J responded to Him, "Aren't Jn 8:48
Then the J said, "Now we know Jn 8:52
The J replied, "You aren't 50 Jn 8:57
The J did not believe this about Jn 9:18
they were afraid of the J, Jn 9:22
since the J had already agreed Jn 9:22
place among the J because of Jn 10:19
Then the J surrounded Him and Jn 10:24
Again the J picked up rocks to Jn 10:31
a good work," the J answered, Jn 10:33
just now the J tried to stone Jn 11:8
Many of the J had come to Martha Jn 11:19
The J who were with her in the Jn 11:31
and the J who had come with her Jn 11:33
So the J said, "See how He loved Jn 11:36
many of the J who came to Mary Jn 11:45
openly among the J but departed Jn 11:54
crowd of the J learned He was Jn 12:9
many of the J were deserting Jn 12:11
and just as I told the J, Jn 13:33
had advised the J that it was Jn 18:14
where all the J congregate, Jn 18:20
to death," the J declared. Jn 18:31
"Are You the King of the J?" Jn 18:33
be handed over to the J. Jn 18:36
went out to the J again and told Jn 18:38
to you the King of the J?" Jn 18:39
and said, "Hail, King of the J!" Jn 19:3
a law," the J replied to him, Jn 19:7
But the J shouted, "If you Jn 19:12
he told the J, "Here is your Jn 19:14
THE KING OF THE J Jn 19:19

Many of the **J** read this sign, Jn 19:20
priests of the **J** said to Pilate, Jn 19:21
The King of the **J**,' but that He Jn 19:21
'I am the King of the **J**.' " Jn 19:21
the **J** did not want the bodies to Jn 19:31
because of his fear of the **J**— Jn 19:38
to the burial custom of the **J**. Jn 19:40
because of their fear of the **J**. Jn 20:19
were **J** living in Jerusalem, Ac 2:5
Rome, both **J** and proselytes, Ac 2:10
by the Hellenistic **J** against the Ac 6:1
the Hebraic **J** that their widows Ac 6:1
kept confounding the **J** who lived Ac 9:22
the **J** conspired to kill him, Ac 9:23
debated with the Hellenistic **J**, Ac 9:29
the message to no one except **J**. Ac 11:19
he saw that it pleased the **J**, Ac 12:3
many of the **J** and devout Ac 13:43
But when the **J** saw the crowds, Ac 13:45
But the **J** incited the religious Ac 13:50
number of both **J** and Greeks Ac 14:1
But the **J** who refused to believe Ac 14:2
siding with the **J** and some with Ac 14:4
made by both the Gentiles and **J**, Ac 14:5
Then some **J** came from Antioch Ac 14:19
because of the **J** who were in Ac 16:3
disturbing our city. They are **J**, Ac 16:20
But the **J** became jealous, and Ac 17:5
The **J** stirred up the crowd and Ac 17:8
into the synagogue of the **J**. Ac 17:10
But when the **J** from Thessalonica Ac 17:13
with the **J** and with those who Ac 17:17
ordered all the **J** to leave Rome. Ac 18:2
to persuade both **J** and Greeks. Ac 18:4
to the **J** that the Messiah Ac 18:5
the **J** made a united attack Ac 18:12
Gallio said to the **J**, "If it Ac 18:14
for me to put up with you **J**. Ac 18:14
in discussion with the **J**. Ac 18:19
refuted the **J** in public, Ac 18:28
Asia, both **J** and Greeks, heard Ac 19:10
in Ephesus, both **J** and Greeks. Ac 19:17
advice when the **J** pushed him to Ac 19:33
devised against him by the **J**, Ac 20:3
me through the plots of the **J**— Ac 20:19
to both **J** and Greeks about Ac 20:21
'In this way the **J** in Jerusalem Ac 21:11
many thousands of **J** there are Ac 21:20
teach all the **J** who are among Ac 21:21
the **J** from the province of Asia Ac 21:27
with all the **J** residing there, Ac 22:12
Paul was being accused by the **J**, Ac 22:30
the **J** formed a conspiracy and Ac 23:12
"The **J**," he said, "have agreed Ac 23:20
seized by the **J** and was about to Ac 23:27
among all the **J** throughout the Ac 24:5
The **J** also joined in the attack, Ac 24:9
some **J** from the province of Asia Ac 24:18
wished to do a favor for the **J**, Ac 24:27
leaders of the **J** presented their Ac 25:2
the **J** who had come down from Ac 25:7
wanting to do a favor for the **J**, Ac 25:9
I have done no wrong to the **J**, Ac 25:10
elders of the **J** presented their Ac 25:15
I am accused of by the **J**, Ac 26:2
All the **J** know my way of life Ac 26:4
I am being accused by the **J**, Ac 26:7
For this reason the **J** seized me Ac 26:21
together the leaders of the **J**. Ac 28:17
Because the **J** objected, I was Ac 28:19
things, the **J** departed, while Ac 28:29
that both **J** and Gentiles are Rm 3:9
Or is God for **J** only? Is He not Rm 3:29
only from the **J** but also from Rm 9:24
to minister to **J** in material Rm 15:27
For the **J** ask for signs and the 1Co 1:22
block to the **J** and foolishness 1Co 1:23
are called, both **J** and Greeks, 1Co 1:24
To the **J** I became like a Jew, 1Co 9:20
I became like a Jew, to win **J**; 1Co 9:20
offense to the **J** or the Greeks 1Co 10:32
body—whether **J** or Greeks, 1Co 12:13
from the **J** 40 lashes minus 2Co 11:24
the rest of the **J** joined his Gl 2:13
compel Gentiles to live like **J**?" Gl 2:14
We are **J** by birth and not Gl 2:15
just as they did from the **J**. 1Th 2:14
who say they are **J** and are not, Rv 2:9
who claim to be **J** and are not, Rv 3:9

JEWS' *(1)*

the day when the **J** enemies had Est 9:1

JEZANIAH *(1)*

(AKA AZARIAH, JAAZANIAH)
and **J** son of the Maacathite— Jr 40:8

JEZEBEL *(19)*

he married **J**, the daughter 1Kg 16:31
and water when **J** slaughtered 1Kg 18:4
what I did when **J** slaughtered 1Kg 18:13
Ahab told **J** everything that 1Kg 19:1
So **J** sent a messenger to Elijah, 1Kg 19:2
Then his wife **J** came to him and 1Kg 21:5
Then his wife **J** said to him, 1Kg 21:7
did as **J** had commanded them, 1Kg 21:11
Then they sent ⌊word⌋ to **J**, 1Kg 21:14
J heard that Naboth had been 1Kg 21:15
The LORD also speaks of **J**: 1Kg 21:23
The dogs will eat **J** in the plot 1Kg 21:23
because his wife **J** incited him. 1Kg 21:25
blood shed by the hand of **J**— 2Kg 9:7
The dogs will eat **J** in the plot 2Kg 9:10
witchcraft from your mother **J**?" 2Kg 9:22
to Jezreel, **J** heard about it, 2Kg 9:30
be able⌋ to say: This is **J**.' " 2Kg 9:37
the woman **J**, who calls herself Rv 2:20

JEZEBEL'S *(3)*

of Asherah who eat at **J** table." 1Kg 18:19
the dogs will eat **J** flesh. 2Kg 9:36
J corpse will be like manure on 2Kg 9:37

JEZER *(3)*

Jahzeel, Guni, **J**, and Shillem. Gn 46:24
the Jezerite clan from **J**; Nm 26:49
Jahziel, Guni, **J**, and Shallum— 1Ch 7:13

JEZERITE *(1)*

the **J** clan from Jezer; Nm 26:49

JEZIEL *(1)*

J and Pelet sons of Azmaveth; 1Ch 12:3

JEZRAHIAH *(1)*

sang, with **J** as the leader. Neh 12:42

JEZREEL *(38)*

J, Jokdeam, Zanoah, Jos 15:56
its towns and in the **J** Valley." Jos 17:16
Their territory went to **J**, Jos 19:18
and camped in the Valley of **J**. Jdg 6:33
David also married Ahinoam of **J**, 1Sm 25:43
Ahinoam of **J** and Abigail of 1Sm 27:3
was camped by the spring in **J**. 1Sm 29:1
the Philistines went up to **J**. 1Sm 29:11
Gilead, Asher, **J**, Ephraim, 2Sm 2:9
Saul and Jonathan came from **J**. 2Sm 4:4
is beside Zarethan below **J**, 1Kg 4:12
in ⌊his chariot⌋ and went to **J**. 1Kg 18:45
of Ahab to the entrance of **J**. 1Kg 18:46
was in **J** next to the palace of 1Kg 21:1
in the plot of land at **J**: 1Kg 21:23
Joram returned to **J** to recover 2Kg 8:29
went down to **J** to visit Joram 2Kg 8:29
in the plot of land at **J**— 2Kg 9:10
had returned to **J** to recover 2Kg 9:15
city to go tell about it in **J**." 2Kg 9:15
and went to **J** since Joram was 2Kg 9:16
was standing on the tower in **J**. 2Kg 9:17
Jehu came to **J**, Jezebel heard 2Kg 9:30
'In the plot of land at **J**, 2Kg 9:36
plot of land at **J** so that no one 2Kg 9:37
to Samaria to the rulers of **J**, 2Kg 10:1
sons at this time tomorrow at **J**. 2Kg 10:6
and sent them to Jehu at **J**. 2Kg 10:7
of the house of Ahab in **J**— 2Kg 10:11
the firstborn, by Ahinoam of **J**; 1Ch 3:1
J, Ishma, and Idbash, and their 1Ch 4:3
so he returned to **J** to recover 2Ch 22:6
went down to **J** to visit Joram 2Ch 22:6
him **J**, for in a little while Hs 1:4
the bloodshed of **J** on the house Hs 1:4
of Israel in the valley of **J**. Hs 1:5
For the day of **J** will be great. Hs 1:11
and they will respond to **J**. Hs 2:22

JEZREELITE *(11)*

Ahinoam the **J** and Abigail the 1Sm 30:5
Ahinoam the **J** and Abigail, 2Sm 2:2
was Amnon, by Ahinoam the **J**; 2Sm 3:2
Naboth the **J** had a vineyard; 1Kg 21:1
what Naboth the **J** had told him. 1Kg 21:4
I spoke to Naboth the **J**," 1Kg 21:6
the vineyard of Naboth the **J**." 1Kg 21:7
of Naboth the **J** who refused to 1Kg 21:15
of Naboth the **J** to take 1Kg 21:16
plot of land of Naboth the **J**. 2Kg 9:21
belonging to Naboth the **J**. 2Kg 9:25

JIDLAPH *(1)*

Hazo, Pildash, **J**, and Bethuel." Gn 22:22

JINGLING *(1)*

prancing steps, **j** their ankle Is 3:16

JOAB *(135)*

So **J** son of Zeruiah and David's 2Sm 2:13
Abner said to **J**, "Let's have 2Sm 2:14
"Let them get up," **J** replied. 2Sm 2:14
J, Abishai, and Asahel. 2Sm 2:18
your brother **J** in the face?" 2Sm 2:22
but **J** and Abishai pursued Abner. 2Sm 2:24
Then Abner called out to **J**: 2Sm 2:26
"As God lives," **J** replied, "if 2Sm 2:27
Then **J** blew the ram's horn, 2Sm 2:28
When **J** had turned back from 2Sm 2:30
Then **J** and his men marched all 2Sm 2:32
soldiers and **J** returned from a 2Sm 3:22
When **J** and all his army arrived, 2Sm 3:23
army arrived, **J** was informed, 2Sm 3:23
J went to the king and said, 2Sm 3:24
Then **J** left David and sent 2Sm 3:26
J pulled him aside to the middle 2Sm 3:27
and there **J** stabbed him in the 2Sm 3:27
the house of **J** never be without 2Sm 3:29
J and his brother Abishai killed 2Sm 3:30
then ordered **J** and all the 2Sm 3:31
J son of Zeruiah was over the 2Sm 8:16
about it and sent **J** and all the 2Sm 10:7
When **J** saw that there was a 2Sm 10:9
strong for me," **J** said, "then 2Sm 10:11
J and his troops advanced to 2Sm 10:13
So **J** withdrew from the attack 2Sm 10:14
David sent **J** with his officers 2Sm 11:1
David sent orders to **J**: 2Sm 11:6
So **J** sent Uriah to David. 2Sm 11:6
David asked how **J** and the troops 2Sm 11:7
and my master **J** and his soldiers 2Sm 11:11
a letter to **J** and sent it with 2Sm 11:14
When **J** was besieging the city, 2Sm 11:16
city came out and attacked **J**, 2Sm 11:17
J sent someone to report to 2Sm 11:18
David all that **J** had sent him 2Sm 11:22
the messenger, "Say this to **J**: 2Sm 11:25
J fought against Rabbah of the 2Sm 12:26
Then **J** sent messengers to David 2Sm 12:27
J son of Zeruiah observed that 2Sm 14:1
So **J** sent someone to Tekoa to 2Sm 14:2
Then **J** told her exactly what to 2Sm 14:3
"Did **J** put you up to all this?" 2Sm 14:19
your servant **J** is the one who 2Sm 14:19
J your servant has done this to 2Sm 14:20
king said to **J**, "I hereby grant 2Sm 14:21
J fell with his face to the 2Sm 14:22
"Today," **J** said, "your servant 2Sm 14:22
So **J** got up, went to Geshur, and 2Sm 14:23
sent for **J** in order to send 2Sm 14:29
but **J** was unwilling to come. 2Sm 14:29
J has a field right next to mine, 2Sm 14:30
Then **J** came to Absalom's house 2Sm 14:31
Absalom explained to **J**, 2Sm 14:32
J went to the king and told him. 2Sm 14:33
one third under **J**, one third 2Sm 18:2
The king commanded **J**, Abishai, 2Sm 18:5
men saw ⌊him⌋ and informed **J**. 2Sm 18:10
saw ⌊him⌋!" **J** exclaimed. "Why 2Sm 18:11
man replied to **J**, "Even if I had 2Sm 18:12
J said, "I'm not going to waste 2Sm 18:14
Afterwards, **J** blew the ram's 2Sm 18:16
Israel because **J** restrained them 2Sm 18:16
J replied to him, "You are not 2Sm 18:20
J then said to the Cushite, 2Sm 18:21
Cushite bowed to **J** and took off 2Sm 18:21
Zadok persisted and said to **J**, 2Sm 18:22
J replied, "My son, why do you 2Sm 18:22
Then run!" **J** said to him. So 2Sm 18:23
When **J** sent the king's servant 2Sm 18:29
was reported to **J**, "The king is 2Sm 19:1
Then **J** went into the house to 2Sm 19:5
from now on instead of **J**!' " 2Sm 19:13
J was wearing his uniform and 2Sm 20:8
J asked Amasa, "Are you well, my 2Sm 20:9
his right hand **J** grabbed Amasa 2Sm 20:9

and J stabbed him in the stomach 2Sm 20:10
J did not stab him again for 2Sm 20:10
J and his brother Abishai 2Sm 20:10
Whoever favors J and whoever is 2Sm 20:11
whoever is for David, follow J!" 2Sm 20:11
and followed J to pursue Sheba 2Sm 20:13
the troops with J were battering 2Sm 20:15
Please tell J to come here and 2Sm 20:16
the woman asked, "Are you J?" 2Sm 20:17
J protested: "Never! I do not 2Sm 20:20
The woman replied to J, 2Sm 20:21
son of Bichri and threw it to J. 2Sm 20:22
J returned to the king in 2Sm 20:22
J commanded the whole army of 2Sm 20:23
for J son of Zeruiah, 2Sm 23:37
king said to J, the commander 2Sm 24:2
J replied to the king, "May the 2Sm 24:3
prevailed over J and the 2Sm 24:4
So J and the commanders of the 2Sm 24:4
J gave the king the total of the 2Sm 24:9
conspired with J son of Zeruiah 1Kg 1:7
and J the commander of the army, 1Kg 1:19
J heard the sound of the ram's 1Kg 1:41
also know what J son of Zeruiah 1Kg 2:5
and for J son of Zeruiah." 1Kg 2:22
The news reached J. Since he had 1Kg 2:28
J fled to the LORD's tabernacle 1Kg 2:28
J has fled to the LORD's 1Kg 2:29
to the tabernacle and said to J, 1Kg 2:30
But J said, "No, for I will 1Kg 2:30
This is what J said, and this is 1Kg 2:30
the blood that J shed without 1Kg 2:31
J murdered Abner son of Ner, 1Kg 2:32
up, struck down J, and put him 1Kg 2:34
was in Edom, J, the commander 1Kg 11:15
J and all Israel had remained 1Kg 11:16
with his fathers and that J, 1Kg 11:21
Abishai, J, and Asahel. 1Ch 2:16
Seraiah fathered J, the ancestor 1Ch 4:14
J son of Zeruiah went up first, 1Ch 11:6
and J restored the rest of the 1Ch 11:8
for J son of Zeruiah, 1Ch 11:39
J son of Zeruiah was over the 1Ch 18:15
this and sent J and the entire 1Ch 19:8
When J saw that there was a 1Ch 19:10
strong for me," J said, "then 1Ch 19:12
J and the people with him 1Ch 19:14
Then J went to Jerusalem. 1Ch 19:15
J led the army and destroyed the 1Ch 20:1
J attacked Rabbah and demolished 1Ch 20:1
So David said to J and the 1Ch 21:2
J replied, "May the LORD 1Ch 21:3
king's order prevailed over J. 1Ch 21:4
J left and traveled throughout 1Ch 21:4
J gave David the total of the 1Ch 21:5
and J son of Zeruiah had 1Ch 26:28
J son of Zeruiah began to count 1Ch 27:24
J was the commander of the 1Ch 27:34

JOAB'S *(22)*

Hittite and J brother Abishai 1Sm 26:6
the death of Asahel, J brother. 2Sm 3:27
May it hang over J head and his 2Sm 3:29
Amasa over the army in J place. 2Sm 17:25
a sister to Zeruiah, J mother. 2Sm 17:25
third under J brother Abishai 2Sm 18:2
men who were J armor-bearers 2Sm 18:15
So J men, the Cherethites, the 2Sm 20:7
against the sword in J hand, 2Sm 20:10
of J young men had stood over 2Sm 20:11
J troops came and besieged 2Sm 20:15
J brother and son of Zeruiah, 2Sm 23:18
J brother Asahel, Elhanan son of 2Sm 23:24
will come back on J head and on 1Kg 2:33
son of Jehoiada in J place over 1Kg 2:35
Abishai, J brother, was the 1Ch 11:20
J brother Asahel, Elhanan son of 1Ch 11:26
fled before J brother Abishai 1Ch 19:15
month, was J brother Asahel, 1Ch 27:7
Jeshua's and J descendants 2,812 Ezr 2:6
of Jehiel from J descendants, Ezr 8:9
Jeshua's and J descendants 2,818 Neh 7:11

JOAH *(11)*

secretary, and J son of Asaph, 2Kg 18:18
and J said to the Rabshakeh, 2Kg 18:26
secretary, and J son of Asaph, 2Kg 18:37
his son J, his son Iddo, his son 1Ch 6:21
the second, J the third, Sachar 1Ch 26:4
J son of Zimmah and Eden son of 2Ch 29:12
and Eden son of J from the 2Ch 29:12
the recorder J son of Joahaz, 2Ch 34:8
the scribe, and J son of Asaph, Is 36:3
and J said to the Rabshakeh, Is 36:11
the scribe, and J son of Asaph, Is 36:22

JOAHAZ *(1)*

and the recorder Joah son of J, 2Ch 34:8

JOANAN *(1)*

of J, ⌊son⌋ of Rhesa, ⌊son⌋ Lk 3:27

JOANNA *(2)*

J the wife of Chuza, Herod's Lk 8:3
Mary Magdalene, J, Mary the Lk 24:10

JOASH *(46)*
(AKA JEHOASH)

belonged to J, the Abiezrite. Jdg 6:11
said, "Gideon son of J did it." Jdg 6:29
the men of the city said to J, Jdg 6:30
But J said to all who stood Jdg 6:31
the sword of Gideon son of J, Jdg 7:14
Gideon son of J returned from Jdg 8:13
son of J went back to live at Jdg 8:29
Gideon son of J died at a ripe Jdg 8:32
tomb of his father J in Ophrah Jdg 8:32
city, and to J, the king's son 1Kg 22:26
secretly rescued J son of 2Kg 11:2
J was in hiding with Jehosheba 2Kg 11:3
Then J sat on the throne of the 2Kg 11:19
J was seven years old when he 2Kg 12:21
year of Jehu, J became king; 2Kg 12:1
J did what was right in the 2Kg 12:2
Then J said to the priests, 2Kg 12:4
year ⌊of the reign⌋ of King J, 2Kg 12:6
So King J called Jehoiada the 2Kg 12:7
So King J of Judah took all the 2Kg 12:18
Judah's King J son of Ahaziah, 2Kg 13:1
year of Judah's King J, 2Kg 13:10
Amaziah son of J became king of 2Kg 14:1
his father J had done. 2Kg 14:3
Judah's King Amaziah son of J, 2Kg 14:13
Amaziah son of J lived 15 years 2Kg 14:17
Judah's King Amaziah son of J, 2Kg 14:23
his son Ahaziah, his son J, 1Ch 3:11
and J and Saraph, who married 1Ch 4:22
Zemirah, J, Eliezer, Elioenai, 1Ch 7:8
Then there was his brother J; 1Ch 12:3
J was in charge of the stores of 1Ch 27:28
city, and to J, the king's son 2Ch 18:25
rescued J son of Ahaziah from 2Ch 22:11
she hid J from Athaliah so that 2Ch 22:11
J was seven years old when he 2Ch 24:1
J did what was right in the 2Ch 24:2
J took it to heart to renovate 2Ch 24:4
King J didn't remember the 2Ch 24:22
army went to war against J. 2Ch 24:23
So they executed judgment on J. 2Ch 24:24
saw that J had many wounds, 2Ch 24:25
Judah's King Amaziah son of J, 2Ch 25:23
Amaziah son of J lived 15 years 2Ch 25:25
son of J, king of Israel Hs 1:1
son of J, king of Israel Am 1:1

JOASH'S *(2)*

rest of the events of J⌊reign⌋, 2Kg 12:19
J servants conspired against him 2Kg 12:20

JOB *(55)*

in the country of Uz named J. Jb 1:1
J was the greatest man among all Jb 1:3
J would send ⌊for his children⌋ Jb 1:5
of them. For J thought: Perhaps Jb 1:5
you considered My servant J? Jb 1:8
Does J fear God for nothing? Jb 1:9
not lay a hand on J ⌊himself⌋." Jb 1:12
came to J and reported: Jb 1:14
Then J stood up, tore his robe Jb 1:20
Throughout all this J did not Jb 1:22
you considered My servant J? Jb 2:3
and infected J with incurable Jb 2:7
Then J took a piece of broken Jb 2:8
all this J did not sin in what Jb 2:10
After this J began to speak and Jb 3:1
Then J answered: Jb 6:1
Then J answered: Jb 9:1
Then J answered: Jb 12:1
Then J answered: Jb 16:1
Then J answered: Jb 19:1
Then J answered: Jb 21:1
Then J answered: Jb 23:1
Then J answered: Jb 26:1
J continued his discourse, Jb 27:1
J continued his discourse, Jb 29:1
The words of J are concluded. Jb 31:40
three men quit answering J, Jb 32:1
He was angry at J because he had Jb 32:2
to speak to J because they were Jb 32:4
three men could not answer J, Jb 32:5
Yet no one proved J wrong; Jb 32:12
But J has not directed his Jb 32:14
But now, J, pay attention to my Jb 33:1
Pay attention, J, and listen to Jb 33:31
For J has declared, "I am Jb 34:5
What man is like J? He drinks Jb 34:7
J speaks without knowledge; Jb 34:35
If only J were tested to the Jb 34:36
J opens his mouth in vain and Jb 35:16
Listen to this, J. Stop and Jb 37:14
the LORD answered J from the Jb 38:1
The LORD answered J: Jb 40:1
Then J answered the LORD: Jb 40:3
the LORD answered J from the Jb 40:6
Then J replied to the LORD: Jb 42:1
LORD had finished speaking to J, Jb 42:7
about Me, as My servant J has. Jb 42:7
go to My servant J, and offer a Jb 42:8
Then My servant J will pray for Jb 42:8
about Me, as My servant J has." Jb 42:8
After J had prayed for his Jb 42:10
J lived 140 years after this and Jb 42:16
J died, old and full of days. Jb 42:17
Daniel, and J—were in it, Ezk 14:14
Daniel, and J were in it, as I Ezk 14:20

JOB'S *(10)*

This was J regular practice. Jb 1:5
day when J sons and daughters Jb 1:13
Now when J three friends— Jb 2:11
had enough to eat at J table?" Jb 31:31
also angry at J three friends Jb 32:3
J friends are dismayed and can Jb 32:15
the LORD accepted J ⌊prayer⌋. Jb 42:9
latter part of J life more than Jb 42:12
beautiful as J daughters could Jb 42:15
have heard of J endurance and Jms 5:11

JOBAB *(9)*

Ophir, Havilah, and J. Gn 10:29
J son of Zerah from Bozrah ruled Gn 36:33
J died, Husham from the land Gn 36:34
J king of Madon, the kings of Jos 11:1
Ophir, Havilah, and J. 1Ch 1:23
J son of Zerah from Bozrah ruled 1Ch 1:44
J died, Husham from the land 1Ch 1:45
J, Zibia, Mesha, Malcam, 1Ch 8:9
and J were Elpaal's sons. 1Ch 8:18

JOCHEBED *(2)*

married his father's sister J, Ex 6:20
The name of Amram's wife was J, Nm 26:59

JODA *(1)*

son⌋ of Josech, ⌊son⌋ of J, Lk 3:26

JOED *(1)*

son of J, son of Pedaiah, Neh 11:7

JOEL *(20)*
(AKA IGAL)

son's name was J and his second 1Sm 8:2
J, Jehu son of Joshibiah, son of 1Ch 4:35
of Azaz, son of Shema, son of J. 1Ch 5:8
J the chief, Shapham the second 1Ch 5:12
his firstborn J, and his second 1Ch 6:28
singer, son of J, son of Samuel, 1Ch 6:33
son of J, son of Azariah 1Ch 6:36
Michael, Obadiah, J, Isshiah. 1Ch 7:3
J the brother of Nathan, Mibhar 1Ch 11:38
J the leader and 130 of his 1Ch 15:7
Uriel, Asaiah, J, Shemaiah, 1Ch 15:11
appointed Heman son of J; 1Ch 15:17
then Zetham, and J—three. 1Ch 23:8
his brother J, were in charge 1Ch 26:22
of Manasseh, J son of Pedaiah; 1Ch 27:20
of Amasai and J son of Azariah 2Ch 29:12
Zebina, Jaddai, J, and Benaiah. Ezr 10:43
J son of Zichri was the officer Neh 11:9
that came to J son of Pethuel: Jl 1:1
spoken through the prophet J: Ac 2:16

JOEL'S *(1)*

J sons: his son Shemaiah, his 1Ch 5:4

JOELAH *(1)*

and J and Zebadiah, the sons of 1Ch 12:7

JOEZER *(1)*
Azarel, **J**, and Jashobeam, 1Ch 12:6

JOGBEHAH *(2)*
Atroth-shophan, Jazer, **J**, Nm 32:35
of Nobah and **J**, and attacked Jdg 8:11

JOGLI *(1)*
Bukki son of **J**, a leader from Nm 34:22

JOHA *(2)*
Ishpah, and **J** were Beriah's sons 1Ch 8:16
and his brother **J** the Tizite, 1Ch 11:45

JOHANAN *(25)*
(AKA JONATHAN)
of Nethaniah, **J** son of Kareah, 2Kg 25:23
J was the firstborn, Jehoiakim 1Ch 3:15
Pelaiah, Akkub, **J**, Delaiah, and 1Ch 3:24
Azariah; Azariah fathered **J**; 1Ch 6:9
J fathered Azariah, who served 1Ch 6:10
Jeremiah, Jahaziel, **J**, Jozabad 1Ch 12:4
J eighth, Elzabad ninth, 1Ch 12:12
Azariah son of **J**, Berechiah son 2Ch 28:12
J son of Hakkatan from Azgad's Ezr 8:12
Eliashib, Joiada, **J**, and Jaddua, Neh 12:22
the days of **J** son of Eliashib. Neh 12:23
J and Jonathan the sons of Jr 40:8
J son of Kareah and all the Jr 40:13
Then **J** son of Kareah suggested Jr 40:15
responded to **J** son of Kareah, Jr 40:16
When **J** son of Kareah and all the Jr 41:11
with Ishmael saw **J** son of Kareah Jr 41:13
and rejoined **J** son of Kareah. Jr 41:14
escaped from **J** with eight men Jr 41:15
J son of Kareah and all the Jr 41:16
along with **J** son of Kareah, Jr 42:1
and he summoned **J** son of Kareah, Jr 42:8
of Hoshaiah, **J** son of Kareah, Jr 43:2
So **J** son of Kareah and all the Jr 43:4
J son of Kareah and all the Jr 43:5

JOHN *(124)*
those days **J** the Baptist came, Mt 3:1
J himself had a camel-hair Mt 3:4
from Galilee to **J** at the Jordan, Mt 3:13
But **J** tried to stop Him, saying, Mt 3:14
He heard that **J** had been Mt 4:12
of Zebedee, and his brother **J**. Mt 4:21
of Zebedee, and **J** his brother; Mt 10:2
When **J** heard in prison what the Mt 11:2
Go and report to **J** what you hear Mt 11:4
to speak to the crowds about **J**: Mt 11:7
greater than **J** the Baptist has Mt 11:11
From the days of **J** the Baptist Mt 11:12
and the law prophesied until **J**; Mt 11:13
For **J** did not come eating or Mt 11:18
"This is **J** the Baptist!" Mt 14:2
had arrested **J**, chained him, Mt 14:3
since **J** had been telling him, Mt 14:4
Give me **J** the Baptist's head Mt 14:8
sent orders and had **J** beheaded Mt 14:10
said, "Some say **J** the Baptist; Mt 16:14
and his brother **J**, and led them Mt 17:1
to them about **J** the Baptist. Mt 17:13
thought **J** was a prophet." Mt 21:26
For **J** came to you in the way of Mt 21:32
J came baptizing in the Mk 1:4
J wore a camel-hair garment with Mk 1:6
was baptized in the Jordan by **J**. Mk 1:9
After **J** was arrested, Jesus went Mk 1:14
of Zebedee and his brother **J**. Mk 1:19
Andrew's house with James and **J**. Mk 1:29
to his brother **J**, He gave the Mk 3:17
James, and **J**, James' brother. Mk 5:37
J the Baptist has been raised Mk 6:14
of it, he said, "**J**, the one I Mk 6:16
to arrest **J** and to chain him Mk 6:17
J had been telling Herod, Mk 6:18
was in awe of **J** and was Mk 6:20
"**J** the Baptist's head!" Mk 6:24
you to give me **J** the Baptist's Mk 6:25
answered Him, "**J** the Baptist; Mk 8:28
and **J** and led them up on a high Mk 9:2
J said to Him, "Teacher, we saw Mk 9:38
Then James and **J**, the sons of Mk 10:35
be indignant with James and **J**. Mk 10:41
thought that **J** was a genuine Mk 11:32
Peter, James, **J**, and Andrew Mk 13:3
James, and **J** with Him, and He Mk 14:33
a son, and you will name him **J**. Lk 1:13
No! He will be called **J**." Lk 1:60
HIS NAME IS **J** And they were all Lk 1:63
God's word came to **J** the son of Lk 3:2
their minds whether **J** might be Lk 3:15
J answered them all, "I baptize Lk 3:16
else—he locked **J** up in prison. Lk 3:20
were James and **J**, Zebedee's sons Lk 5:10
his brother; James and **J**; Philip Lk 6:14
So **J** summoned two of his Lk 7:18
J the Baptist sent us to ask Lk 7:20
and report to **J** the things you Lk 7:22
to speak to the crowds about **J**: Lk 7:24
women no one is greater than **J**, Lk 7:28
For **J** the Baptist did not come Lk 7:33
with Him except Peter, **J**, James, Lk 8:51
some said that **J** had been raised Lk 9:7
"I beheaded **J**," Herod said, "but Lk 9:9
They answered, "**J** the Baptist; Lk 9:19
took along Peter, **J**, and James, Lk 9:28
J responded, "Master, we saw Lk 9:49
disciples James and **J** saw this, Lk 9:54
as **J** also taught his disciples. Lk 11:1
and the Prophets were until **J**; Lk 16:16
was the baptism of **J** from heaven Lk 20:4
convinced that **J** was a prophet." Lk 20:6
sent Peter and **J**, saying, "Go Lk 22:8
was a man named **J** who was sent Jn 1:6
J testified concerning Him and Jn 1:15
with water," **J** answered them. Jn 1:26
Jordan, where **J** was baptizing. Jn 1:28
The next day **J** saw Jesus coming Jn 1:29
And **J** testified, "I watched the Jn 1:32
J was standing with two of his Jn 1:35
two who heard **J** and followed Him Jn 1:40
said, "You are Simon, son of **J**. Jn 1:42
J also was baptizing in Aenon Jn 3:23
since **J** had not yet been thrown Jn 3:24
So they came to **J** and told him, Jn 3:26
J responded, "No one can receive Jn 3:27
baptizing more disciples than **J** Jn 4:1
You have sent ⌊messengers⌋ to **J**, Jn 5:33
J was a burning and shining lamp, Jn 5:35
the place where **J** had been Jn 10:40
Him and said, "**J** never did a Jn 10:41
but everything **J** said about this Jn 10:41
Simon, son of **J**, do you love Me Jn 21:15
son of **J**, do you love Me?" Jn 21:16
son of **J**, do you love Me?" Jn 21:17
for **J** baptized with water, Ac 1:5
Peter, **J**, James, Andrew, Philip, Ac 1:13
the baptism of **J** until the day Ac 1:22
Now Peter and **J** were going up Ac 3:1
saw Peter and **J** about to enter Ac 3:3
along with **J**, looked at him Ac 3:4
was holding on to Peter and **J**, Ac 3:11
Caiaphas, **J** and Alexander, Ac 4:6
had Peter and **J** stand before Ac 4:7
of Peter and **J** and realized that Ac 4:13
But Peter and **J** answered them, Ac 4:19
they sent Peter and **J** to them. Ac 8:14
Peter and **J** laid their hands Ac 8:17
the baptism that **J** preached: Ac 10:37
how He said, '**J** baptized with Ac 11:16
the mother of **J** Mark, where many Ac 12:12
on which they took **J** Mark. Ac 12:25
They also had **J** as their Ac 13:5
J, however, left them and went Ac 13:13
J had previously proclaimed a Ac 13:24
as **J** was completing his life Ac 13:25
wanted to take along **J** Mark. Ac 15:37
J baptized with a baptism of Ac 19:4
Cephas, and **J**, recognized as Gl 2:9
His angel to His slave **J**, Rv 1:1
J: To the seven churches in the Rv 1:4
I, **J**, your brother and partner Rv 1:9
I, **J**, am the one who heard and Rv 22:8

JOHN'S *(16)*
Then **J** disciples came to Him, Mt 9:14
Where did **J** baptism come from? Mt 21:25
J disciples and the Pharisees Mk 2:18
Why do **J** disciples and the Mk 2:18
commanded him to bring **J** head. Mk 6:27
J baptism from heaven or from Mk 11:30
J disciples fast often and say Lk 5:33
Then **J** disciples told him about Lk 7:18
J messengers left, He began Lk 7:24
been baptized with **J** baptism. Lk 7:29
is **J** testimony when the Jews Jn 1:19
arose between **J** disciples and a Jn 3:25
testimony than **J** because of the Jn 5:36
he killed James, **J** brother, with Ac 12:2
although he knew only **J** baptism. Ac 18:25
"With **J** baptism," they replied. Ac 19:3

JOIADA *(4)*
J son of Paseah and Meshullam Neh 3:6
Eliashib, Eliashib fathered **J**, Neh 12:10
J fathered Jonathan, and Neh 12:11
days of Eliashib, **J**, Johanan, Neh 12:22

JOIAKIM *(4)*
Jeshua fathered **J**, Joiakim Neh 12:10
Joiakim, **J** fathered Eliashib Neh 12:10
In the days of **J**, the leaders of Neh 12:12
in the days of **J** son of Jeshua, Neh 12:26

JOIARIB *(5)*
(AKA JEHOIARIB)
as the teachers **J** and Elnathan. Ezr 8:16
Adaiah, son of **J**, son of Neh 11:5
Jedaiah son of **J**, Jachin, and Neh 11:10
Shemaiah, **J**, Jedaiah, Neh 12:6
Mattenai of **J**, Uzzi of Jedaiah, Neh 12:19

JOIN *(33)*
may I never **j** their assembly. Gn 49:6
out, they may **j** our enemies, Ex 1:10
Do not **j** the wicked to be a Ex 23:1
gold clasps and **j** the curtains Ex 26:6
J five of the curtains by Ex 26:9
loops and **j** the tent together Ex 26:11
bronze clasps to **j** the tent Ex 36:18
so they may **j** you and serve with Nm 18:2
They are to **j** you and guard the Nm 18:4
Amalekites to **j** forces with him Jdg 3:13
summoned to **j** Saul at Gilgal. 1Sm 13:4
the camp to **j** the Philistines 1Sm 14:21
j with their noble brothers and Neh 10:29
and his wife Zeresh to **j** him. Est 5:10
no one but me to **j** the king at Est 5:12
tomorrow to **j** her with the king Est 5:12
they **j** themselves together Jb 16:10
me and its furrows **j** in weeping, Jb 31:38
of sinners, or **j** a group of Ps 1:1
love and truth will **j** together; Ps 85:10
to house and **j** field to field Is 5:8
foreigner will **j** them and be Is 14:1
You will not **j** them in burial, Is 14:20
I **j** with Jazer to weep for the Is 16:9
of Judah will **j** with the house Jr 3:18
will come and **j** themselves to Jr 50:5
Then **j** them together into a Ezk 37:17
others will **j** them insincerely Dn 11:34
Many nations will **j** themselves Zch 2:11
of the rest dared to **j** them, Ac 5:13
Philip, "Go and **j** that chariot." Ac 8:29
And you can **j** in helping with 2Co 1:11
J in imitating me, brothers, and Php 3:17

JOINED *(42)*
curtains should be **j** together, Ex 26:3
other⌋ five curtains **j** together. Ex 26:3
and **j** together at the top in a Ex 26:24
so that it can be **j** together. Ex 28:7
j five of the curtains to each Ex 36:10
curtains he **j** to each other. Ex 36:10
gold clasps and **j** the curtains Ex 36:13
He **j** five of the curtains Ex 36:16
at the bottom and **j** together at Ex 36:29
it was **j** together at its two Ex 39:4
and Eglon—**j** forces, advanced Jos 10:5
country have **j** forces against us Jos 10:6
All these kings **j** forces; Jos 11:5
some lawless men **j** Jephthah and Jdg 11:3
but even they **j** the Israelites 1Sm 14:21
they also **j** Saul and Jonathan in 1Sm 14:22
they went down and **j** him there. 1Sm 22:1
in Gibeon when Amasa **j** them. 2Sm 20:8
j to the temple with cedar beams; 1Kg 6:10
and singers **j** together to praise 2Ch 5:13
j together to supervise those Ezr 3:9
entire wall was **j** together up to Neh 4:6
and all who **j** with them ⌊to a Est 9:27
They are **j** to one another, Jb 41:17
of his flesh are **j** together, Jb 41:23
Even Assyria has **j** them; Ps 83:8
should be⌋, solidly **j** together, Ps 122:3
for whoever is **j** with all the Ec 9:4
and mother and be **j** to his wife, Mt 19:5
what God has **j** together, Mt 19:6
and mother and be **j** to his wife, Mk 10:7

what God has **j** together, Mk 10:9
Then the mob **j** in the attack Ac 16:22
persuaded and **j** Paul and Silas, Ac 17:4
some men **j** him and believed, Ac 17:34
The Jews also **j** in the attack, Ac 24:9
For if we have been **j** with Him Rm 6:5
that anyone **j** to a prostitute 1Co 6:16
But anyone **j** to the Lord is one 1Co 6:17
of the Jews **j** his hypocrisy, Gl 2:13
and mother and be **j** to his wife, Eph 5:31
encouraged and **j** together in Col 2:2

JOINING *(1)*
timbers—for **j** and to make 2Ch 34:11

JOINS *(1)*
the Spirit also **j** to help in our Rm 8:26

JOINTED *(1)*
those that have **j** legs above Lv 11:21

JOINTS *(4)*
through the **j** of his armor. 1Kg 22:34
through the **j** of his armor. 2Ch 18:33
him that his hip **j** shook and his Dn 5:6
soul, spirit, **j**, and marrow; Heb 4:12

JOKDEAM *(1)*
Jezreel, **J**, Zanoah, Jos 15:56

JOKE *(4)*
You make us a **j** among the Ps 44:14
clothing, and I was a **j** to them. Ps 69:11
he has become a **j** to his Ps 89:41
and rulers are a **j** to them. Hab 1:10

JOKIM *(1)*
J, the men of Cozeba; and Joash 1Ch 4:22

JOKING *(3)*
sons-in-law thought he was **j**. Gn 19:14
and says, "I was only **j**!" Pr 26:19
or crude **j** are not suitable Eph 5:4

JOKMEAM *(2)*
as far as the other side of **J**; 1Kg 4:12
J and its pasturelands, 1Ch 6:68

JOKNEAM *(3)*
one the king of **J** in Carmel one Jos 12:22
and met the brook east of **J**. Jos 19:11
J with its pasturelands, Kartah Jos 21:34

JOKSHAN *(3)*
him Zimran, **J**, Medan, Midian, Gn 25:2
J fathered Sheba and Dedan. Gn 25:3
J, Medan, Midian, Ishbak, 1Ch 1:32

JOKSHAN'S *(1)*
Ishbak, and Shuah. **J** sons: Sheba 1Ch 1:32

JOKTAN *(4)*
his brother was named **J**. Gn 10:25
And **J** fathered Almodad, Sheleph, Gn 10:26
the name of his brother was **J**. 1Ch 1:19
J fathered Almodad, Sheleph, 1Ch 1:20

JOKTAN'S *(2)*
All these were **J** sons. Gn 10:29
All of these were **J** sons. 1Ch 1:23

JOKTHE-EL *(1)*
Dilan, Mizpeh, **J**, Jos 15:38

JOKTHEEL *(1)*
Sela in battle and called it **J**, 2Kg 14:7

JOLTING *(1)*
galloping horse and **j** chariot! Nah 3:2

JONADAB *(12)*
Amnon had a friend named **J**, 2Sm 13:3
J was a very shrewd man, 2Sm 13:3
J said to him, "Lie down on your 2Sm 13:5
But **J**, son of David's brother 2Sm 13:32
J said to the king, "Look, the 2Sm 13:35
drink wine, for **J**, son of our Jr 35:6
We have obeyed the voice of **J**, Jr 35:8
as our ancestor **J** commanded us. Jr 35:10
The words of **J**, son of Rechab, Jr 35:14
the sons of **J** son of Rechab Jr 35:16
of your ancestor **J** and have kept Jr 35:18
J son of Rechab will never fail Jr 35:19

JONAH *(25)*
prophet **J** son of Amittai from 2Kg 14:25
LORD came to **J** son of Amittai: Jnh 1:1
J got up to flee to Tarshish Jnh 1:3
J had gone down to the lowest Jnh 1:5
and the lot singled out **J**. Jnh 1:7
they picked up **J** and threw him Jnh 1:15
a great fish to swallow **J**, Jnh 1:17
and **J** was in the fish three days Jnh 1:17
J prayed to the LORD his God Jnh 2:1
and it vomited **J** onto dry land. Jnh 2:10
LORD came to **J** a second time: Jnh 3:1
So **J** got up and went to Nineveh Jnh 3:3
J set out on the first day of Jnh 3:4
But **J** was greatly displeased and Jnh 4:1
J left the city and sat down Jnh 4:5
J was greatly pleased with the Jnh 4:6
Then God asked **J**, "Is it right Jnh 4:9
the sign of the prophet **J**. Mt 12:39
For as **J** was in the belly of the Mt 12:40
greater than **J** is here! Mt 12:41
to it except the sign of **J**." Mt 16:4
Simon son of **J**, you are blessed Mt 16:17
to it except the sign of **J**. Lk 11:29
For just as **J** became a sign to Lk 11:30
greater than **J** is here! Lk 11:32

JONAH'S *(4)*
shade over **J** head to ease his Jnh 4:6
beat down on **J** head so that he Jnh 4:8
they repented at **J** proclamation; Mt 12:41
they repented at **J** proclamation, Lk 11:32

JONAM *(1)*
Joseph, ⌊son⌋ of **J**, ⌊son⌋ of Lk 3:30

JONATHAN *(111)*
(AKA JOHANAN)
J son of Gershom, son of Moses, Jdg 18:30
and 1,000 were with **J** in Gibeah 1Sm 13:2
J attacked the Philistine 1Sm 13:3
Saul, his son **J**, and the troops 1Sm 13:16
troops who were with Saul and **J**; 1Sm 13:22
and his son **J** had ⌊weapons⌋. 1Sm 13:22
same day Saul's son **J** said to 1Sm 14:1
did not know that **J** had left. 1Sm 14:3
of the pass that **J** intended to 1Sm 14:4
J said to the attendant who 1Sm 14:6
"All right," **J** replied, "we'll 1Sm 14:8
garrison called to **J** and his 1Sm 14:12
J told his armor-bearer, 1Sm 14:12
J went up using his hands and 1Sm 14:13
J cut them down, and his 1Sm 14:13
that first assault **J** and his 1Sm 14:14
roll and saw that **J** and his 1Sm 14:17
who were with Saul and **J**. 1Sm 14:21
joined Saul and **J** in the battle. 1Sm 14:22
J had not heard his father make 1Sm 14:27
J replied, "My father has 1Sm 14:29
if it is because of my son **J**, 1Sm 14:39
I and my son **J** will be on the 1Sm 14:40
J and Saul were selected, 1Sm 14:41
lot⌋ between me and my son **J**," 1Sm 14:42
Jonathan," and **J** was selected. 1Sm 14:42
J told him, "I tasted a little 1Sm 14:43
severely if you do not die, **J**!" 1Sm 14:44
said to Saul, "Must **J** die, who 1Sm 14:45
So the people rescued **J**, 1Sm 14:45
Saul's sons were **J**, Ishvi, and 1Sm 14:49
J committed himself to David, 1Sm 18:1
J made a covenant with David 1Sm 18:3
Then **J** removed the robe he was 1Sm 18:4
ordered his son **J** and all his 1Sm 19:1
Saul's son **J** liked David very 1Sm 19:1
J spoke well of David to his 1Sm 19:4
So **J** summoned David and told 1Sm 19:7
Then **J** brought David to Saul, 1Sm 19:7
Ramah and came to **J** and asked, 1Sm 20:1
J said to him, "No, you won't 1Sm 20:2
He has said, '**J** must not know of 1Sm 20:3
J said to David, "Whatever you 1Sm 20:4
"No!" **J** responded. "If I ever 1Sm 20:9
So David asked **J**, "Who will tell 1Sm 20:10
may God punish **J** and do so 1Sm 20:13
Then **J** made a covenant with the 1Sm 20:16
J once again swore to David in 1Sm 20:17
Then **J** said to him, "Tomorrow is 1Sm 20:18
J sat facing him and Abner took 1Sm 20:25
and Saul asked his son **J**, 1Sm 20:27
J answered, "David asked for my 1Sm 20:28
became angry with **J** and shouted, 1Sm 20:30
J answered his father back: 1Sm 20:32
his spear at **J** to kill him, 1Sm 20:33
In the morning **J** went out to the 1Sm 20:35
J shot an arrow beyond him. 1Sm 20:36
of the arrow that **J** had shot, 1Sm 20:37
but **J** called to him and said, 1Sm 20:37
Then **J** called to him, "Hurry up 1Sm 20:38
only **J** and David knew the 1Sm 20:39
Then **J** gave his equipment to the 1Sm 20:40
Then he and **J** kissed each other 1Sm 20:41
J then said to David, "Go in the 1Sm 20:42
David left, and **J** went into the 1Sm 20:42
Then Saul's son **J** came to David 1Sm 23:16
in Horesh, while **J** went home. 1Sm 23:18
killed his sons, **J**, Abinadab, 1Sm 31:2
Saul and his son **J** are dead." 2Sm 1:4
Saul and his son **J** are dead?" 2Sm 1:5
for Saul, his son **J**, the LORD's 2Sm 1:12
lament for Saul and his son **J**, 2Sm 1:17
and **J**, loved and delightful, 2Sm 1:23
J ⌊lies⌋ slain on your heights. 2Sm 1:25
I grieve for you, **J** my brother. 2Sm 1:26
Saul's son **J** had a son whose 2Sm 4:4
about Saul and **J** came from 2Sm 4:4
show kindness to because of **J**?" 2Sm 9:1
son of **J** son of Saul came to 2Sm 9:6
because of your father **J**. 2Sm 9:7
Ahimaaz and Abiathar's son **J**. 2Sm 15:27
Ahimaaz and Abiathar's son **J**, 2Sm 15:36
J and Ahimaaz were staying at 2Sm 17:17
"Where are Ahimaaz and **J**?" 2Sm 17:20
Ahimaaz and **J** climbed out of the 2Sm 17:21
son of Saul's son **J**, because of 2Sm 21:7
that was between David and **J**, 2Sm 21:7
and his son **J** from the leaders 2Sm 21:12
Saul and his son **J** at Zela in 2Sm 21:14
Israel, **J**, son of David's 2Sm 21:21
the sons of Jashen, **J** son 2Sm 23:32
speaking when **J** son of Abiathar 1Kg 1:42
not," **J** answered him. 1Kg 1:43
Jether and **J**. Jether died 1Ch 2:32
and Saul fathered **J**, Malchishua, 1Ch 8:33
and Saul fathered **J**, Malchishua, 1Ch 9:39
sons and killed Saul's sons **J**, 1Ch 10:2
J son of Shagee the Hararite, 1Ch 11:34
Israel, **J**, son of David's 1Ch 20:7
J son of Uzziah was in charge of 1Ch 27:25
David's uncle **J** was a counselor; 1Ch 27:32
Ebed son of **J** from Adin's Ezr 8:6
J son of Asahel and Jahzeiah Ezr 10:15
Joiada fathered **J**, and Jonathan Neh 12:11
Jonathan, and **J** fathered Jaddua. Neh 12:11
J of Malluchi, Joseph of Neh 12:14
son of **J**, son of Shemaiah Neh 12:35
in the house of **J** the scribe, Jr 37:15
to the house of **J** the scribe, Jr 37:20
the house of **J** to die there.' Jr 38:26
and **J** the sons of Kareah, Jr 40:8

JONATHAN'S *(7)*
listened to **J** advice and swore 1Sm 19:6
J young man picked up the arrow 1Sm 20:38
J bow never retreated, Saul's 2Sm 1:22
There is still **J** son who is lame 2Sm 9:3
J sons: Peleth and Zaza. These 1Ch 2:33
J son was Merib-baal, and 1Ch 8:34
J son was Merib-baal, and 1Ch 9:40

JOPPA *(14)*
with the territory facing **J**. Jos 19:46
to you as rafts by sea to **J**. 2Ch 2:16
wood from Lebanon to **J** by sea, Ezr 3:7
He went down to **J** and found a Jnh 1:3
In **J** there was a disciple named Ac 9:36
Lydda was near **J**, the disciples Ac 9:38
became known throughout all **J**, Ac 9:42
on many days in **J** with Simon, Ac 9:43
Now send men to **J** and call for Ac 10:5
to them, he sent them to **J**. Ac 10:8
brothers from **J** went with him. Ac 10:23
send someone to **J** and invite Ac 10:32
I was in the town of **J** praying, Ac 11:5
saying, 'Send to **J**, and call for Ac 11:13

JORAH'S *(1)*
J descendants 112 Ezr 2:18

JORAI *(1)*
Meshullam, Sheba, **J**, Jacan, Zia, 1Ch 5:13

JORAM *(36)*
(AKA JEHORAM)
he sent his son **J** to King David 2Sm 8:10
J had items of silver, gold, and 2Sm 8:10
J became king in his place. 2Kg 1:17
J son of Ahab became king over 2Kg 3:1
J clung to the sins that 2Kg 3:3
So King **J** marched out from 2Kg 3:6
J replied, "The route of the 2Kg 3:8
said to King ⌊**J**⌋ of Israel, 2Kg 3:13

of Israel's King **J** son of Ahab, 2Kg 8:16
of Israel's King **J** son of Ahab, 2Kg 8:25
went with **J** son of Ahab to 2Kg 8:28
and the Arameans wounded **J**. 2Kg 8:28
So King **J** returned to Jezreel to 2Kg 8:29
Jezreel to visit **J** son of Ahab 2Kg 8:29
son of Ahab since **J** was ill. 2Kg 8:29
of Nimshi, conspired against **J**. 2Kg 9:14
J and all Israel had been at 2Kg 9:14
But King **J** had returned to 2Kg 9:15
to Jezreel since **J** was laid up 2Kg 9:16
Judah had gone down to visit **J**. 2Kg 9:16
J responded, "Choose a rider 2Kg 9:17
J shouted, and they harnessed 2Kg 9:21
J king of Israel and Ahaziah 2Kg 9:21
When **J** saw Jehu he asked, 2Kg 9:22
J turned around and fled, 2Kg 9:23
his bow and shot **J** between the 2Kg 9:24
year of **J** son of Ahab that 2Kg 9:29
his son **J**, his son Zichri, 1Ch 26:25
and went with **J** son of Israel's 2Ch 22:5
The Arameans wounded **J**, 2Ch 22:5
Jezreel to visit **J** son of Ahab 2Ch 22:6
son of Ahab since **J** was ill. 2Ch 22:6
With his going to **J**, Ahaziah's 2Ch 22:7
went out with **J** to meet Jehu son 2Ch 22:7
fathered **J**, Joram fathered Mt 1:8
Joram, **J** fathered Uzziah Mt 1:8

JORDAN *(201)*

that the entire **J** Valley as far Gn 13:10
chose the entire **J** Valley for Gn 13:11
over this **J** with my staff, Gn 32:10
is across the **J**, they lamented Gn 50:10
Abel-mizraim. It is across the **J**. Gn 50:11
by the sea and along the **J**." Nm 13:29
of Moab near the **J** across from Nm 22:1
of Moab by the **J** ⌊across from⌋ Nm 26:3
of Moab by the **J** ⌊across from⌋ Nm 26:63
of Moab by the **J** ⌊across from⌋ Nm 31:12
Don't make us cross the **J**." Nm 32:5
them across the **J** and beyond, Nm 32:19
be across the **J** to the east." Nm 32:19
crosses the **J** before the LORD Nm 32:21
Reubenites cross the **J** with you, Nm 32:29
possession across the **J**." Nm 32:32
of Moab by the **J** ⌊across from⌋ Nm 33:48
They camped by the **J** from Nm 33:49
of Moab by the **J** ⌊across from⌋ Nm 33:50
you cross the **J** into the land Nm 33:51
go down to the **J** and end at the Nm 34:12
across the **J** from Jericho, Nm 34:15
of Moab by the **J** ⌊across from⌋ Nm 35:1
you cross the **J** into the land Nm 35:10
across the **J** and three cities Nm 35:14
of Moab by the **J** ⌊across from⌋ Nm 36:13
across the **J** in the wilderness Dt 1:1
the **J** in the land of Moab, Dt 1:5
we cross the **J** into the land Dt 2:29
two Amorite kings across the **J**, Dt 3:8
Arabah and **J** are also borders Dt 3:17
God is giving them across the **J**. Dt 3:20
land on the other side of the **J**, Dt 3:25
for you will not cross this **J**. Dt 3:27
not cross the **J** and enter the Dt 4:21
be crossing the **J** because I am Dt 4:22
about to cross the **J** to possess. Dt 4:26
cities across the **J** to the east, Dt 4:41
the **J** in the valley facing Dt 4:46
were across the **J** to the east, Dt 4:47
east side of the **J** as far as the Dt 4:49
to cross the **J** to go and drive Dt 9:1
these mountains across the **J**, Dt 11:30
to cross the **J** to enter and take Dt 11:31
When you cross the **J** and live in Dt 12:10
you cross the **J** into the land Dt 27:2
When you have crossed the **J**, Dt 27:4
When you have crossed the **J**, Dt 27:12
to possess across the **J**. Dt 30:18
'You will not cross this **J**.' Dt 31:2
are crossing the **J** to possess." Dt 31:13
are crossing the **J** to possess." Dt 32:47
cross over the **J** to the land I Jos 1:2
be crossing the **J** to go in and Jos 1:11
gave you on this side of the **J**. Jos 1:14
you on the east side of the **J**." Jos 1:15
the road to the fords of the **J**, Jos 2:7
destroyed across the **J**. Jos 2:10
country, and crossed ⌊the **J**⌋. Jos 2:23
as far as the **J** and stayed there Jos 3:1
the waters, stand in the **J**.' " Jos 3:8
goes ahead of you into the **J**. Jos 3:11
broke camp to cross the **J**, Jos 3:14
Now the **J** overflows its banks Jos 3:15
carrying the ark reached the **J**, Jos 3:15
ground in the middle of the **J**, Jos 3:17
had finished crossing the **J**. Jos 3:17
had finished crossing the **J**, Jos 4:1
the middle of the **J** where the Jos 4:3
your God in the middle of the **J**. Jos 4:5
'The waters of the **J** were cut Jos 4:7
it crossed the **J**, the Jordan's Jos 4:7
stones from the middle of the **J**, Jos 4:8
middle of the **J** where the Jos 4:9
middle of the **J** until everything Jos 4:10
to come up from the **J**." Jos 4:16
priests, "Come up from the **J**." Jos 4:17
up from the middle of the **J**, Jos 4:18
waters of the **J** resumed their Jos 4:18
up from the **J** on the tenth day Jos 4:19
they had taken from the **J**, Jos 4:20
crossed the **J** on dry ground.' Jos 4:22
waters of the **J** before you until Jos 4:23
kings across the **J** to the west Jos 5:1
the waters of the **J** before the Jos 5:1
across the **J** to hand us over Jos 7:7
on the other side of the **J**! Jos 7:7
facing the plain ⌊of the **J**⌋. Jos 8:14
were west of the **J** in the hill Jos 9:1
two Amorite kings beyond the **J**— Jos 9:10
land beyond the **J** to the east Jos 12:1
land beyond the **J** to the west, Jos 12:7
them beyond the **J** to the east, Jos 13:8
was the **J** and its plain. Jos 13:23
included⌋ the **J** and its Jos 13:27
on the east side of the **J**. Jos 13:27
beyond the **J** east of Jericho Jos 13:32
and a half tribes beyond the **J**. Jos 14:3
Dead Sea to the mouth of the **J**. Jos 15:5
the sea at the mouth of the **J**. Jos 15:5
went from the **J** at Jericho to Jos 16:1
Jericho and went to the **J**. Jos 16:7
Bashan, which are beyond the **J**, Jos 17:5
beyond the **J** to the east, Jos 18:7
the north side began at the **J**, Jos 18:12
slope opposite the **J** Valley and Jos 18:18
at the southern end of the **J**. Jos 18:19
The **J** formed the border on the Jos 18:20
and ended at the **J**—16 cities, Jos 19:22
as Lakkum, and ended at the **J**. Jos 19:33
and Judah at the **J** on the east. Jos 19:34
Across the **J** east of Jericho, Jos 20:8
servant gave you across the **J**. Jos 22:4
on the west side of the **J**. Jos 22:7
the region of the **J** in the land Jos 22:10
impressive altar there by the **J**. Jos 22:10
Canaan at the region of the **J**, Jos 22:11
has made the **J** a border between Jos 22:25
from the **J** westward to the Jos 23:4
Amorites who lived beyond the **J**. Jos 24:8
then crossed the **J** and came to Jos 24:11
over ⌊the **J**⌋ near the carved Jdg 3:26
fords of the **J** leading to Moab Jdg 3:28
Gilead remained beyond the **J**. Jdg 5:17
crossed over ⌊the **J**⌋, and camped Jdg 6:33
as far as Beth-barah and the **J**." Jdg 7:24
as far as Beth-barah and the **J**. Jdg 7:24
and Zeeb to Gideon across the **J**. Jdg 7:25
came to the **J** and crossed it. Jdg 8:4
other side of the **J** in the land Jdg 10:8
crossed the **J** to fight against Jdg 10:9
Arnon to the Jabbok and the **J**. Jdg 11:13
from the wilderness to the **J**. Jdg 11:22
and crossed ⌊the **J**⌋ to Zaphon. Jdg 12:1
the fords of the **J** leading to Jdg 12:5
him at the fords of the **J**. Jdg 12:6
even crossed the **J** to the land 1Sm 13:7
side of the **J** saw that Israel's 1Sm 31:7
They crossed the **J**, marched all 2Sm 2:29
crossed the **J**, and went to Helam 2Sm 10:17
the wilderness ford ⌊of the **J**⌋, 2Sm 17:16
him got up and crossed the **J**. 2Sm 17:22
one who had not crossed the **J**. 2Sm 17:22
crossed the **J** with all the men 2Sm 17:24
arrived at the **J**, Judah came to 2Sm 19:15
and escort him across the **J**. 2Sm 19:15
down to the **J** ahead of the king 2Sm 19:17
They forded the **J** to bring the 2Sm 19:18
son of Gera crossed the **J**, 2Sm 19:18
the king to the **J** River to see 2Sm 19:31
River to see him off at the **J**. 2Sm 19:31
king a little way across the **J**, 2Sm 19:36
So all the people crossed the **J**, 2Sm 19:39
and his household across the **J**, 2Sm 19:41
Judah from the **J** all the way to 2Sm 20:2
They crossed the **J** and camped in 2Sm 24:5
down to meet me at the **J** River, 1Kg 2:8
molds in the **J** Valley between 1Kg 7:46
Cherith where it enters the **J**. 1Kg 17:3
Cherith where it enters the **J**. 1Kg 17:5
LORD is sending me to the **J**." 2Kg 2:6
the two of them stood by the **J**. 2Kg 2:7
and stood on the bank of the **J**. 2Kg 2:13
times in the **J** and your flesh 2Kg 5:10
himself in the **J** seven times, 2Kg 5:14
let us go to the **J** where we can 2Kg 6:2
and when they came to the **J**, 2Kg 6:4
followed them as far as the **J**. 2Kg 7:15
the **J** eastward, all the land 2Kg 10:33
Reuben across the **J** at Jericho, 1Ch 6:78
east of the **J**, ⌊they received 1Ch 6:78
who crossed the **J** in the first 1Ch 12:15
From across the **J**—from the 1Ch 12:37
all Israel and crossed the **J**. 1Ch 19:17
west of the **J** for all the work 1Ch 26:30
molds in the **J** Valley between 2Ch 4:17
even if the **J** surges up to his Jb 40:23
from the land of **J** and the peaks Ps 42:6
and fled; the **J** turned back. Ps 114:3
J, that you turned back? Ps 114:5
to the land east of the **J**, Is 9:1
you do in the thickets of the **J**? Jr 12:5
thickets of the **J** to the Jr 49:19
thickets of the **J** to the Jr 50:44
along the **J** between Gilead and Ezk 47:18
thickets of the **J** are destroyed. Zch 11:3
vicinity of the **J** were flocking Mt 3:5
by him in the **J** River as they Mt 3:6
from Galilee to John at the **J**, Mt 3:13
sea road, beyond the **J**, Galilee Mt 4:15
Judea, and beyond the **J**. Mt 4:25
region of Judea across the **J**. Mt 19:1
by him in the **J** River as they Mk 1:5
was baptized in the **J** by John. Mk 1:9
beyond the **J**, and around Tyre Mk 3:8
of Judea and across the **J**. Mk 10:1
into all the vicinity of the **J**, Lk 3:3
Then Jesus returned from the **J**, Lk 4:1
in Bethany across the **J**, Jn 1:28
who was with you across the **J**, Jn 3:26
again across the **J** to the place Jn 10:40

JORDAN'S *(2)*

come to rest in the **J** waters, Jos 3:13
the **J** waters were cut off.' Jos 4:7

JORIM *(1)*

son⌋ of **J**, ⌊son⌋ of Matthat Lk 3:29

JORKEAM *(1)*

who fathered **J**, and Rekem 1Ch 2:44

JOSECH *(1)*

son⌋ of **J**, ⌊son⌋ of Joda, Lk 3:26

JOSEPH *(231)*
(AKA BARNABAS, BARSABBAS, JOSES, JUDAS, JUSTUS, ZAPHENATH-PANEAH)

She named him **J**: "May the LORD Gn 30:24
After Rachel gave birth to **J**, Gn 30:25
next, and Rachel and **J** last. Gn 33:2
and then **J** and Rachel approached Gn 33:7
sons were **J** and Benjamin. Gn 35:24
J tended sheep with his brothers. Gn 37:2
Now Israel loved **J** more than his Gn 37:3
sons because **J** was a son ⌊born Gn 37:3
Then **J** had a dream. When he told Gn 37:5
said to **J**, "Your brothers, Gn 37:13
"I'm ready," **J** replied. Gn 37:13
for my brothers," **J** said. Gn 37:16
So **J** set out after his Gn 37:17
When **J** came to his brothers, Gn 37:23
they pulled **J** out of the pit and Gn 37:28
who took **J** to Egypt. Gn 37:28
and saw that **J** was not there, Gn 37:29
J has been torn to pieces!" Gn 37:33
the Midianites sold **J** in Egypt Gn 37:36
Now **J** had been taken to Egypt. Gn 39:1

LORD was with **J**, and he became Gn 39:2
J found favor in his master's Gn 39:4
Egyptian's house because of **J**. Gn 39:5
Now **J** was well-built and Gn 39:6
looked longingly at **J** and said, Gn 39:7
she spoke to **J** day after day, Gn 39:10
So **J** was there in prison. Gn 39:20
the LORD was with **J** and extended Gn 39:21
the prison where **J** was confined. Gn 40:3
of the guard assigned **J** to them, Gn 40:4
When **J** came to them in the Gn 40:6
Then **J** said to them, "Don't Gn 40:8
cupbearer told his dream to **J**: Gn 40:9
interpretation," **J** said to him. Gn 40:12
he said to **J**, "I also had a Gn 40:16
its interpretation," **J** replied. Gn 40:18
just as **J** had explained to them. Gn 40:22
cupbearer did not remember **J**; Gn 40:23
Pharaoh sent for **J**, and they Gn 41:14
Pharaoh said to **J**, "I have had a Gn 41:15
not able to," **J** answered Pharaoh Gn 41:16
So Pharaoh said to **J**: Gn 41:17
Then **J** said to Pharaoh, Gn 41:25
Pharaoh said to **J**, "Since God Gn 41:39
also said to **J**, "See, I am Gn 41:41
He had **J** ride in his second Gn 41:43
said to **J**, "I am Pharaoh, Gn 41:44
Pharaoh gave **J** the name Gn 41:45
And **J** went throughout the land Gn 41:45
J was 30 years old when he Gn 41:46
J left Pharaoh's presence and Gn 41:46
J gathered all the ⌊excess⌋ food Gn 41:48
So **J** stored up grain in such Gn 41:49
were born to **J** before the years Gn 41:50
J named the firstborn Manasseh, Gn 41:51
began, just as **J** had said. Gn 41:54
Go to **J** and do whatever he tells Gn 41:55
J opened up ⌊all the Gn 41:56
world came to **J** in Egypt to buy Gn 41:57
J was in charge of the country; Gn 42:6
When **J** saw his brothers, he Gn 42:7
Although **J** recognized his Gn 42:8
J remembered his dreams about Gn 42:9
Then **J** said to them, "I have Gn 42:14
J imprisoned them together for Gn 42:17
On the third day **J** said to them, Gn 42:18
realize that **J** understood them Gn 42:23
J then gave orders to fill their Gn 42:25
J is gone and Simeon is gone. Gn 42:36
to Egypt and stood before **J**. Gn 43:15
When **J** saw Benjamin with them, Gn 43:16
The man did as **J** had said and Gn 43:17
When **J** came home, they brought Gn 43:26
J hurried out because he was Gn 43:30
and they got drunk with **J**. Gn 43:34
Then **J** commanded his steward: Gn 44:1
So he did as **J** told him. Gn 44:2
from the city when **J** said to his Gn 44:4
you have done?" **J** said to them. Gn 44:15
J said, "I swear that I will Gn 44:17
J could no longer keep his Gn 45:1
J said to his brothers, "I am Gn 45:3
said to his brothers, "I am **J**! Gn 45:3
Then **J** said to his brothers, Gn 45:4
"I am **J**, your brother," he said, Gn 45:4
This is what your son **J** says: Gn 45:9
that it is I ⌊, **J**,⌋ who am Gn 45:12
Then **J** threw his arms around Gn 45:14
J kissed each of his brothers as Gn 45:15
Pharaoh said to **J**, "Tell your Gn 45:17
J gave them wagons as Pharaoh Gn 45:21
So **J** sent his brothers on their Gn 45:24
They said, "**J** is still alive, Gn 45:26
Jacob all that **J** had said to Gn 45:27
saw the wagons that **J** had sent Gn 45:27
My son **J** is still alive. Gn 45:28
J will put his hands on your eyes. Gn 46:4
wife Rachel: **J** and Benjamin. Gn 46:19
were born to **J** in the land of Gn 46:20
ahead of him to **J** to prepare for Gn 46:28
J hitched ⌊the horses to⌋ his Gn 46:29
J presented himself to him, Gn 46:29
Israel said to **J**, "At last I can Gn 46:30
J said to his brothers and to Gn 46:31
So **J** went and informed Pharaoh: Gn 47:1
Pharaoh said to **J**, "⌊Now that⌋ Gn 47:5
J then brought his father Jacob Gn 47:7
Then **J** settled his father and Gn 47:11
And **J** provided his father, Gn 47:12
J collected all the money to be Gn 47:14
Egyptians came to **J** and said, Gn 47:15
But **J** said, "Give me your Gn 47:16
brought their livestock to **J**, Gn 47:17
J acquired all the land in Egypt Gn 47:20
and **J** moved the people to the Gn 47:21
Then **J** said to the people, Gn 47:23
So **J** made it a law, still in Gn 47:26
called his son **J** and said to him Gn 47:29
J answered, "I will do what you Gn 47:30
Swear to me." So **J** swore to him. Gn 47:31
after this, **J** was told, "Your Gn 48:1
"Your son **J** has come to you," Gn 48:2
Jacob said to **J**, "God Almighty Gn 48:3
And **J** said to his father, Gn 48:9
J brought them to him, and he Gn 48:10
Israel said to **J**, "I never Gn 48:11
Then **J** took them from his Gn 48:12
Then **J** took them both—with his Gn 48:13
Then he blessed **J** and said: Gn 48:15
When **J** saw that his father had Gn 48:17
J said to his father, "Not that Gn 48:18
Then Israel said to **J**, "Look! Gn 48:21
J is a fruitful vine, a fruitful Gn 49:22
May they rest on the head of **J**, Gn 49:26
J, leaning over his father's Gn 50:1
J said to Pharaoh's household, Gn 50:4
Then **J** went to bury his father, Gn 50:7
and **J** mourned seven days for his Gn 50:10
After **J** buried his father, Gn 50:14
If **J** is holding a grudge against Gn 50:15
So they sent this message to **J**, Gn 50:16
'Say this to **J**: Please forgive Gn 50:17
J wept when their message came Gn 50:17
But **J** said to them, "Don't be Gn 50:19
J and his father's household Gn 50:22
in Egypt. **J** lived 110 years. Gn 50:22
son Machir were recognized by **J**. Gn 50:23
J said to his brothers, "I am Gn 50:24
So **J** made the Israelites take an Gn 50:25
J died at the age of 110. Gn 50:26
J was already in Egypt. Ex 1:5
Then **J** and all his brothers and Ex 1:6
had not known **J**, came to power Ex 1:8
took the bones of **J** with him, Ex 13:19
J had made the Israelites Ex 13:19
from the sons of **J**: Elishama son Nm 1:10
The descendants of **J**: Nm 1:32
Igal son of **J** from the tribe of Nm 13:7
Manasseh (from the tribe of **J**); Nm 13:11
clans of Manasseh, the son of **J**. Nm 27:1
the tribe of Manasseh son of **J**— Nm 32:33
from the sons of **J**: Hanniel son Nm 34:23
of the sons of **J** approached Nm 36:1
of Manasseh son of **J**, Nm 36:12
Issachar, **J**, and Benjamin. Dt 27:12
He said about **J**: May his land be Dt 33:13
May these rest on the head of **J**, Dt 33:16
descendants of **J** became two Jos 14:4
the descendants of **J** went from Jos 16:1
the sons of **J**, received their Jos 16:4
of Manasseh son of **J**, Jos 17:2
But the descendants of **J** said, Jos 17:16
The house of **J** also attacked Jdg 1:22
the house of **J** got the upper Jdg 1:35
entire house of **J** to come down 2Sm 19:20
labor force of the house of **J**. 1Kg 11:28
Dan, **J**, Benjamin, Naphtali, Gad, 1Ch 2:2
to the sons of **J** son of Israel, 1Ch 5:1
the birthright was given to **J**. 1Ch 5:2
sons of **J** son of Israel lived 1Ch 7:29
Zaccur, **J**, Nethaniah, and 1Ch 25:2
first lot for Asaph fell to **J**, 1Ch 25:9
Shallum, Amariah, and **J**; Ezr 10:42
of Malluchi, **J** of Shebaniah, Neh 12:14
the descendants of Jacob and **J**. Ps 77:15
the tent of **J** and did not choose Ps 78:67
who guides **J** like a flock; Ps 80:1
an ordinance for **J** when He went Ps 81:5
ahead of them—**J**, who was sold Ps 105:17
Belonging to **J**—the stick of Ezk 37:16
going to take the stick of **J**— Ezk 37:19
J will receive two shares. Ezk 47:13
one, the gate of **J**; one, the Ezk 48:32
⌊throughout⌋ the house of **J**; Am 5:6
be gracious to the remnant of **J**. Am 5:15
not grieve over the ruin of **J**. Am 6:6
and the house of **J** a ⌊burning⌋ Ob 18
and deliver the house of **J**. Zch 10:6
and Jacob fathered **J** the husband Mt 1:16
Mary had been engaged to **J**, Mt 1:18
So her husband **J**, being a Mt 1:19
dream, saying, "**J**, son of David, Mt 1:20
When **J** got up from sleeping, Mt 1:24
appeared to **J** in a dream, Mt 2:13
in a dream to **J** in Egypt, Mt 2:19
brothers James, **J**, Simon, and Mt 13:55
Mary the mother of James and **J**, Mt 27:56
from Arimathea named **J** came, Mt 27:57
J took the body, wrapped it in Mt 27:59
J of Arimathea, a prominent Mk 15:43
he gave the corpse to **J**. Mk 15:45
virgin engaged to a man named **J**, Lk 1:27
And **J** also went up from the town Lk 2:4
off and found both Mary and **J**, Lk 2:16
was thought to be the son of **J**, Lk 3:23
son⌋ of Jannai, ⌊son⌋ of **J**, Lk 3:24
son⌋ of **J**, ⌊son⌋ of Jonam Lk 3:30
good and righteous man named **J**, Lk 23:50
the son of **J**, from Nazareth! Jn 1:45
that Jacob had given his son **J**. Jn 4:5
Isn't this Jesus the son of **J**, Jn 6:42
After this, **J** of Arimathea, who Jn 19:38
J, called Barsabbas, who was Ac 1:23
J, a Levite and a Cypriot by Ac 4:36
became jealous of **J** and sold him Ac 7:9
J was revealed to his brothers, Ac 7:13
J then invited his father Jacob Ac 7:14
over Egypt who did not know **J**. Ac 7:18
blessed each of the sons of **J**, Heb 11:21
faith **J**, as he was nearing the Heb 11:22
12,000 from the tribe of **J**, Rv 7:8

JOSEPH'S *(32)*

So they took **J** robe, slaughtered Gn 37:31
that he owned under **J** authority; Gn 39:6
She put **J** garment beside her Gn 39:16
in the prison under **J** authority, Gn 39:22
with anything under **J** authority, Gn 39:23
his hand and put it on **J** hand, Gn 41:42
So 10 of **J** brothers went down to Gn 42:3
did not send **J** brother Benjamin Gn 42:4
and brought them to **J** house. Gn 43:17
they were taken to **J** house. Gn 43:18
they approached **J** steward and Gn 43:19
brought the men into **J** house, Gn 43:24
gift for **J** arrival at noon. Gn 43:25
served to them from **J** table, Gn 43:34
his brothers reached **J** house, Gn 44:14
Pharaoh's house, "**J** brothers Gn 45:16
And **J** sons who were born to him Gn 46:27
When Israel saw **J** sons, he said, Gn 48:8
along with all **J** household, Gn 50:8
When **J** brothers saw that their Gn 50:15
J descendants by their clans Nm 26:28
were **J** descendants by their Nm 26:37
the tribe of **J** descendants says Nm 36:5
of Manasseh as **J** firstborn. Jos 17:1
J descendants said to Joshua: Jos 17:14
So Joshua replied to **J** family Jos 17:17
and **J** family in their territory Jos 18:5
descendants and **J** descendants. Jos 18:11
J bones, which the Israelites Jos 24:32
inheritance for **J** descendants. Jos 24:32
they said, "Isn't this **J** son?" Lk 4:22
and **J** family became known to Ac 7:13

JOSES *(3)*

(AKA JOSEPH)
of James, **J**, Judas, and Simon Mk 6:3
of James the younger and of **J**, Mk 15:40
the mother of **J** were watching Mk 15:47

JOSHAH *(1)*

Jamlech, **J** son of Amaziah, 1Ch 4:34

JOSHAPHAT *(2)*

son of Maacah, **J** the Mithnite, 1Ch 11:43
Shebaniah, **J**, Nethanel, Amasai, 1Ch 15:24

JOSHAVIAH *(1)*

Jeribai and **J**, the sons of 1Ch 11:46

JOSHBEKASHAH *(2)*

Romamti-ezer, **J**, Mallothi, 1Ch 25:4
seventeenth to **J**, his sons, and 1Ch 25:24

JOSHEB-BASSHEBETH *(1)*

J the Tahchemonite was chief of 2Sm 23:8

JOSHIBIAH *(1)*
Jehu son of **J**, son of Seraiah, 1Ch 4:35

JOSHUA *(219)*
(AKA HOSHEA, JESHUA)
Moses said to **J**, "Select some Ex 17:9
J did as Moses had told him, Ex 17:10
J defeated Amalek and his army Ex 17:13
a reminder and recite it to **J**: Ex 17:14
arose with his assistant **J**, Ex 24:13
When **J** heard the sound of the Ex 32:17
the young man **J** son of Nun, Ex 33:11
J son of Nun, assistant to Moses Nm 11:28
renamed Hoshea son of Nun, **J**. Nm 13:16
J son of Nun and Caleb son of Nm 14:6
of Jephunneh and **J** son of Nun. Nm 14:30
Only **J** son of Nun and Caleb son Nm 14:38
of Jephunneh and **J** son of Nun. Nm 26:65
to Moses, "Take **J** son of Nun, a Nm 27:18
He took **J**, had him stand before Nm 27:22
the Kenizzite and **J** son of Nun, Nm 32:12
the priest, **J** son of Nun, Nm 32:28
the priest and **J** son of Nun. Nm 34:17
J son of Nun, who attends you, Dt 1:38
I commanded **J** at that time: Dt 3:21
But commission **J** and encourage Dt 3:28
J is the one who will cross Dt 31:3
then summoned **J** and said to him Dt 31:7
Call **J** and present yourselves at Dt 31:14
When Moses and **J** went and Dt 31:14
LORD commissioned **J** son of Nun, Dt 31:23
Moses came with **J** son of Nun and Dt 32:44
J son of Nun was filled with the Dt 34:9
the LORD spoke to **J** son of Nun, Jos 1:1
Then **J** commanded the officers of Jos 1:10
J said to the Reubenites, the Jos 1:12
They answered **J**, "Everything you Jos 1:16
J son of Nun secretly sent two Jos 2:1
They went to **J** son of Nun and Jos 2:23
told **J**, "The LORD has handed Jos 2:24
J started early the next morning Jos 3:1
J told the people, "Consecrate Jos 3:5
The LORD spoke to **J**: Jos 3:7
Then **J** told the Israelites, Jos 3:9
the Jordan, the LORD spoke to **J**, Jos 4:1
J summoned the 12 men selected Jos 4:4
just as **J** had commanded them. Jos 4:8
just as the LORD had told **J**. Jos 4:8
J also set up 12 stones in the Jos 4:9
had commanded **J** to tell the Jos 4:10
all that Moses had commanded **J**. Jos 4:10
the LORD exalted **J** in the sight Jos 4:14
The LORD told **J**, Jos 4:15
So **J** commanded the priests, Jos 4:17
Then **J** set up in Gilgal the 12 Jos 4:20
At that time the LORD said to **J**, Jos 5:2
So **J** made flint knives and Jos 5:3
is the reason **J** circumcised Jos 5:4
J raised up their sons in their Jos 5:7
then said to **J**, "Today I have Jos 5:9
When **J** was near Jericho, he Jos 5:13
J approached Him and asked, Jos 5:13
Then **J** bowed with his face to Jos 5:14
of the Lord's army said to **J**, Jos 5:15
standing is holy." And **J** did so. Jos 5:15
LORD said to **J**, "Look, I have Jos 6:2
So **J** son of Nun summoned the Jos 6:6
J had spoken to the people, Jos 6:8
But **J** had commanded the people: Jos 6:10
J got up early the next morning. Jos 6:12
and **J** said to the people, Jos 6:16
J said to the two men who had Jos 6:22
But **J** spared Rahab the Jos 6:25
hid the men **J** had sent to spy Jos 6:25
At that time **J** imposed this Jos 6:26
LORD was with **J**, and his fame Jos 6:27
J sent men from Jericho to Ai, Jos 7:2
returning to **J** they reported to Jos 7:3
Then **J** tore his clothes and fell Jos 7:6
"Oh, Lord GOD," **J** said, "why did Jos 7:7
LORD then said to **J**, "Stand up! Jos 7:10
J got up early the next morning. Jos 7:16
J said to Achan, "My son, give Jos 7:19
Achan replied to **J**, "It is true. Jos 7:20
So **J** sent messengers who ran to Jos 7:22
brought them to **J** and all the Jos 7:23
Then **J** and all Israel with him Jos 7:24
J said, "Why have you troubled Jos 7:25
The LORD said to **J**, "Do not be Jos 8:1
J and the whole military force Jos 8:3
J selected 30,000 fighting men Jos 8:3
J sent them out, and they went Jos 8:9
J started early the next morning Jos 8:10
Now **J** had taken about 5,000 men Jos 8:12
And that night **J** went into the Jos 8:13
J and all Israel pretended to be Jos 8:15
they pursued **J** and were drawn Jos 8:16
LORD said to **J**, "Hold out the Jos 8:18
So **J** held out his sword toward Jos 8:18
When **J** and all Israel saw that Jos 8:21
Ai alive and brought him to **J**. Jos 8:23
J did not draw back his hand Jos 8:26
command that He had given **J**. Jos 8:27
J burned Ai and left it a Jos 8:28
and at sunset **J** commanded that Jos 8:29
At that time **J** built an altar on Jos 8:30
J copied the law of Moses, Jos 8:32
J read aloud all the words of Jos 8:34
commanded that **J** did not read Jos 8:35
to fight against **J** and Israel. Jos 9:2
Gibeon heard what **J** had done to Jos 9:3
They went to **J** in the camp at Jos 9:6
They said to **J**, "We are your Jos 9:8
Then **J** asked them, "Who are you Jos 9:8
So **J** established peace with them Jos 9:15
J summoned the Gibeonites and Jos 9:22
This is what **J** did to them: Jos 9:26
heard that **J** had captured Ai Jos 10:1
peace with **J** and the Israelites. Jos 10:4
sent ⌊word⌋ to **J** in the camp at Jos 10:6
So **J** and his whole military Jos 10:7
The LORD said to **J**, "Do not be Jos 10:8
So **J** caught them by surprise, Jos 10:9
J spoke to the LORD in the Jos 10:12
Then **J** and all Israel with him Jos 10:15
It was reported to **J**: Jos 10:17
J said, "Roll large stones Jos 10:18
So **J** and the Israelites finished Jos 10:20
safely to **J** in the camp at Jos 10:21
Then **J** said, "Open the mouth of Jos 10:22
and Eglon to **J** out of the cave. Jos 10:23
J summoned all the men of Israel Jos 10:24
J said to them, "Do not be Jos 10:25
J struck them down and executed Jos 10:26
At sunset **J** commanded that they Jos 10:27
On that day **J** captured Makkedah Jos 10:28
J and all Israel with him Jos 10:29
J and all Israel with him Jos 10:31
and **J** captured it on the second Jos 10:32
but **J** struck him down along with Jos 10:33
Then **J** crossed from Lachish to Jos 10:34
J and all Israel with him went Jos 10:36
J turned toward Debir and Jos 10:38
J conquered the whole region— Jos 10:40
J conquered everyone from Jos 10:41
J captured all these kings and Jos 10:42
Then **J** returned with all Israel Jos 10:43
The LORD said to **J**, "Do not be Jos 11:6
J and his whole military force Jos 11:7
J treated them as the LORD had Jos 11:9
At that time **J** turned back, Jos 11:10
J captured all these kings and Jos 11:12
except Hazor, which **J** burned. Jos 11:13
Moses, Moses commanded **J**. Jos 11:15
That is what **J** did, leaving Jos 11:15
So **J** took all this land—the Jos 11:16
J waged war with all these kings Jos 11:18
At that time **J** proceeded to Jos 11:21
J completely destroyed them with Jos 11:21
So **J** took the entire land, Jos 11:23
J then gave it as an inheritance Jos 11:23
J and the Israelites struck down Jos 12:7
J gave their land as an Jos 12:7
J was now old, advanced in years, Jos 13:1
the priest, **J** son of Nun, Jos 14:1
of Judah approached **J** at Gilgal, Jos 14:6
Then **J** blessed Caleb son of Jos 14:13
on the LORD's instruction to **J**: Jos 15:13
the priest, **J** son of Nun, Jos 17:4
Joseph's descendants said to **J**: Jos 17:14
many people," **J** replied to them Jos 17:15
So **J** replied to Joseph's family Jos 17:17
So **J** said to the Israelites, Jos 18:3
J commanded them to write down a Jos 18:8
They returned to **J** at the camp Jos 18:9
J cast lots for them at Shiloh Jos 18:10
the Israelites gave **J** son of Nun Jos 19:49
the priest, **J** son of Nun, Jos 19:51
Then the LORD spoke to **J**, Jos 20:1
the priest, **J** son of Nun, Jos 21:1
J summoned the Reubenites, Jos 22:1
J blessed them and sent them on Jos 22:6
but **J** had given ⌊territory⌋ to Jos 22:7
When **J** sent them to their homes Jos 22:7
around them, **J** was old, getting Jos 23:1
So **J** summoned all Israel, Jos 23:2
J assembled all the tribes of Jos 24:1
J said to all the people, Jos 24:2
But **J** told the people, "You will Jos 24:19
the people answered **J**. Jos 24:21
J then told the people, "You are Jos 24:22
people said to **J**, "We will Jos 24:24
that day **J** made a covenant for Jos 24:25
J recorded these things in the Jos 24:26
And **J** said to all the people, Jos 24:27
Then **J** sent the people away, Jos 24:28
LORD's servant, **J** son of Nun, Jos 24:29
of the elders who outlived **J**, Jos 24:31
the death of **J**, the Israelites Jdg 1:1
J sent the people away, and the Jdg 2:6
of the elders who outlived **J**. Jdg 2:7
J son of Nun, the servant of the Jdg 2:8
of the nations **J** left when he Jdg 2:21
He did not hand them over to **J**. Jdg 2:23
the field of **J** of Beth-shemesh 1Sm 6:14
the field of **J** of Beth-shemesh 1Sm 6:18
had spoken through **J** son of Nun. 1Kg 16:34
of the gate of **J** the governor 2Kg 23:8
his son Nun, and his son **J**. 1Ch 7:27
the days of **J** son of Nun until Neh 8:17
and to **J** son of Jehozadak, Hg 1:1
the high priest **J** son of Hg 1:12
the high priest **J** son of Hg 1:14
the high priest **J** son of Hg 2:2
Be strong, **J** son of Jehozadak, Hg 2:4
he showed me **J** the high priest Zch 3:1
Now **J** was dressed with filthy Zch 3:3
the Angel of the LORD charged **J**: Zch 3:6
Listen, **J** the high priest, you Zch 3:8
the stone I have set before **J**; Zch 3:9
on the head of **J** son of Zch 6:11
⌊son⌋ of **J**, ⌊son⌋ of Eliezer, Lk 3:29
it and with **J** brought it in when Ac 7:45
For if **J** had given them rest, Heb 4:8

JOSHUA'S *(2)*
LORD throughout **J** lifetime and Jos 24:31
LORD throughout **J** lifetime and Jdg 2:7

JOSIAH *(54)*
of David, named **J**, and he will 1Kg 13:2
and made his son **J** king in his 2Kg 21:24
and his son **J** became king in his 2Kg 21:26
J was eight years old when he 2Kg 22:1
the eighteenth year of King **J**, 2Kg 22:3
Then **J** brought all the priests 2Kg 23:8
As **J** turned, he saw the tombs 2Kg 23:16
J also removed all the shrines 2Kg 23:19
J did the same things to them 2Kg 23:19
the eighteenth year of King **J**, 2Kg 23:23
In addition, **J** removed the 2Kg 23:24
King **J** went to confront him, 2Kg 23:29
people took Jehoahaz son of **J**, 2Kg 23:30
Eliakim son of **J** king in place 2Kg 23:34
of his father **J** and changed 2Kg 23:34
his son Amon, and his son **J**. 1Ch 3:14
and made his son **J** king in his 2Ch 33:25
J was eight years old when he 2Ch 34:1
J began to seek the God of his 2Ch 34:3
J sent Shaphan son of Azaliah, 2Ch 34:8
So **J** removed everything that was 2Ch 34:33
J observed the LORD's Passover 2Ch 35:1
Then **J** donated 30,000 sheep, 2Ch 35:7
to the command of King **J**. 2Ch 35:16
the one that **J** observed with 2Ch 35:18
all this that **J** had prepared for 2Ch 35:20
and **J** went out to confront him. 2Ch 35:20
J did not turn away from him; 2Ch 35:22
shot King **J**, and he said to 2Ch 35:23
and Jerusalem mourned for **J**. 2Ch 35:24
Jeremiah chanted a dirge over **J**, 2Ch 35:25
still speak of **J** in their dirges 2Ch 35:25
Jehoahaz son of **J** and made him 2Ch 36:1
of the reign of **J** son of Amon, Jr 1:2
the days of Jehoiakim son of **J**, Jr 1:3
year of Zedekiah son of **J**, Jr 1:3
days of King **J** the LORD asked Jr 3:6

concerning Shallum son of **J**, Jr 22:11
who succeeded **J** his father as Jr 22:11
concerning Jehoiakim son of **J**, Jr 22:18
year of Jehoiakim son of **J**, Jr 25:1
year of **J** son of Amon, Jr 25:3
the reign of Jehoiakim son of **J**, Jr 26:1
the reign of Zedekiah son of **J**, Jr 27:1
the days of Jehoiakim son of **J**, Jr 35:1
year of Jehoiakim son of **J**, Jr 36:1
year of Jehoiakim son of **J**, Jr 36:9
Zedekiah son of **J** reigned as Jr 37:1
year of Jehoiakim son of **J**, Jr 45:1
Judah's King Jehoiakim son of **J**: Jr 46:2
in the days of **J** son of Amon, Zph 1:1
to the house of **J** son of Zch 6:10
fathered Amon, Amon fathered **J**, Mt 1:10
and **J** fathered Jechoniah and his Mt 1:11

JOSIAH'S *(5)*

rest of the events of **J** ⌊reign⌋, 2Kg 23:28
J sons: Johanan was the 1Ch 3:15
the eighteenth year of **J** reign, 2Ch 35:19
rest of the events of **J** ⌊reign⌋, 2Ch 35:26
to you during **J** reign until Jr 36:2

JOSIPHIAH *(1)*

Shelomith son of **J** from Bani's Ezr 8:10

JOTBAH *(1)*

of Haruz; ⌊she was⌋ from **J**. 2Kg 21:19

JOTBATHAH *(3)*

Hor-haggidgad and camped at **J**. Nm 33:33
departed from **J** and camped at Nm 33:34
from Gudgodah to **J**, a land with Dt 10:7

JOTHAM *(26)*

But **J**, the youngest son of Jdg 9:5
When they told **J**, he climbed to Jdg 9:7
Then **J** fled, escaping to Beer, Jdg 9:21
So the curse of **J** son of Jdg 9:57
house, while **J**, the king's son, 2Kg 15:5
His son **J** became king in his 2Kg 15:7
year of **J** son of Uzziah. 2Kg 15:30
J son of Uzziah became king of 2Kg 15:32
was **J** who built the Upper Gate 2Kg 15:35
J rested with his fathers, 2Kg 15:38
Ahaz son of **J** became king of 2Kg 16:1
Regem, **J**, Geshan, Pelet, Ephah, 1Ch 2:47
his son Azariah, his son **J**, 1Ch 3:12
of Judah's King **J** and Israel's 1Ch 5:17
while his son **J** was over the 2Ch 26:21
His son **J** became king in his 2Ch 26:23
J was 25 years old when he 2Ch 27:1
J built the Upper Gate of the 2Ch 27:3
J strengthened himself because 2Ch 27:6
J rested with his fathers and 2Ch 27:9
reigns of Uzziah, **J**, Ahaz, and Is 1:1
of Ahaz, son of **J**, son of Uzziah Is 7:1
reigns of Uzziah, **J**, Ahaz, and Hs 1:1
and Jerusalem in the days of **J**, Mc 1:1
Uzziah fathered **J**, Jotham Mt 1:9
Jotham, **J** fathered Ahaz, Mt 1:9

JOTHAM'S *(2)*

rest of the events of **J** ⌊reign⌋, 2Kg 15:36
rest of the events of **J** ⌊reign⌋, 2Ch 27:7

JOURNEY *(64)*

LORD had made his **j** a success. Gn 24:21
has led me on the **j** to the house Gn 24:27
you and make your **j** a success, Gn 24:40
You will make my **j** successful! Gn 24:42
LORD has made my **j** a success. Gn 24:56
me and watch over me on this **j**, Gn 28:20
Jacob resumed his **j** and went to Gn 29:1
a three-day **j** between himself Gn 30:36
them provisions for their **j**. Gn 42:25
happens to him on your **j**, Gn 42:38
gave them provisions for the **j**. Gn 45:21
for his father on the **j**. Gn 45:23
all the stages of their **j**. Ex 40:36
all the stages of their **j**. Ex 40:38
a corpse or is on a distant **j**, Nm 9:10
is not on a **j**, and yet fails to Nm 9:13
on a three-day **j** to seek a Nm 10:33
about a day's **j** in every Nm 11:31
impatient because of the **j**. Nm 21:4
the Israelites' **j** when they went Nm 33:1
for the stages of their **j**; Nm 33:2
took a three-day **j** into the Nm 33:8
is an eleven-day **j** from Horeb to Dt 1:2
Resume your **j** and go to the hill Dt 1:7
before you on the **j** to seek out Dt 1:33
watched over your **j** through this Dt 2:7
on the entire **j** these 40 years Dt 8:2
Continue your **j** ahead of the Dt 10:11
water on the **j** after you came Dt 23:4
Miriam on the **j** after you left Dt 24:9
to you on the **j** after you left Dt 25:17
provisions with you for the **j**; Jos 9:11
out from the extremely long **j**." Jos 9:13
if we will have a successful **j**." Jdg 18:5
watching over the **j** you are Jdg 18:6
for your **j** and go home." Jdg 19:9
So they continued on their **j**, Jdg 19:14
and went out to leave on his **j**, Jdg 19:27
Haven't you just come from a **j**? 2Sm 11:10
he went on a day's **j** into the 1Kg 19:4
the **j** will be too much for you. 1Kg 19:7
He began the **j** from Babylon on Ezr 7:9
and ask Him for a safe **j** for us, Ezr 8:21
us from enemies during the **j**, Ezr 8:22
How long will your **j** take, Neh 2:6
them, guiding them on their **j**. Neh 9:19
he went on a long **j**. Pr 7:19
go to Gilgal or **j** to Beer-sheba, Am 5:5
is just like a man going on a **j**. Mt 25:14
Then he went on a **j**. Mt 25:15
As He was setting out on a **j**, Mk 10:17
like a man on a **j**, who left his Mk 13:34
party, they went a day's **j**. Lk 2:44
He determined to **j** to Jerusalem. Lk 9:51
He determined to **j** to Jerusalem. Lk 9:53
on his **j** came up to him, Lk 10:33
of mine on a **j** has come to me, Lk 11:6
worn out from His **j**, sat down at Jn 4:6
a Sabbath day's **j** away. Ac 1:12
continued their **j** from Perga Ac 13:14
we left to continue our **j**, Ac 21:5
a start by you on my **j** to Judea. 2Co 1:16
lawyer and Apollos on their **j**, Ti 3:13
them on their **j** in a manner 3Jn 6

JOURNEYED *(5)*

Then Abram **j** by stages to the Gn 12:9
Then Lot **j** eastward, and they Gn 13:11
They **j** for three days in the Ex 15:22
and he **j** to his own land. Ex 18:27
brave men set out, **j** all night, 1Sm 31:12

JOURNEYING *(1)*

while Israel was **j** in the Jos 14:10

JOURNEYS *(4)*

in your **j**, and Issachar, Dt 33:18
In all My **j** with all the 2Sm 7:7
You became weary on your many **j**, Is 57:10
On frequent **j**, ⌊I faced⌋ dangers 2Co 11:26

JOY *(202)*

you away with **j** and singing, Gn 31:27
and you will have abundant **j**. Dt 16:15
he can bring **j** to the wife he Dt 24:5
your God with **j** and a cheerful Dt 28:47
with shouts of **j**, and with 1Sm 18:6
such a great **j** that the earth 1Kg 1:40
Indeed, there was **j** in Israel. 1Ch 12:40
their voices with **j** accompanied 1Ch 15:16
strength and **j** are in His place. 1Ch 16:27
shout for **j** before the LORD, 1Ch 16:33
drank with great **j** in the LORD's 1Ch 29:22
Bread seven days with great **j**, 2Ch 30:21
they observed seven days with **j**, 2Ch 30:23
of this house of God with **j**. Ezr 6:16
Bread for seven days with **j**, Ezr 6:22
And there was tremendous **j**. Neh 8:17
God had given them great **j**. Neh 12:43
Haman left full of **j** and in good Est 5:9
with gladness, **j** and honor. Est 8:16
filled with much **j** and are glad Jb 3:22
would leap for **j** in unrelenting Jb 6:10
this is the **j** of his way of life Jb 8:19
and your lips with a shout of **j**. Jb 8:21
the **j** of the wicked has been Jb 20:5
His face with a shout of **j**, Jb 33:26
the sons of God shouted for **j**? Jb 38:7
have put more **j** in my heart than Ps 4:7
let them shout for **j** forever. Ps 5:11
in Your presence is abundant **j**; Ps 16:11
us shout for **j** at your victory Ps 20:5
the king finds **j** in Your Ps 21:1
cheer him with **j** in Your Ps 21:6
in His tent with shouts of **j**. Ps 27:6
but there is **j** in the morning. Ps 30:5
shout for **j**, all you upright in Ps 32:11
look to Him are radiant with **j**; Ps 34:5
shout for **j** and be glad; Ps 35:27
of God, to God, my greatest **j**. Ps 43:4
companions, with the oil of **j**. Ps 45:7
ivory palaces harps bring you **j**. Ps 45:8
God ascends amid shouts of **j**, Ps 47:5
is the **j** of the whole earth. Ps 48:2
Let me hear **j** and gladness; Ps 51:8
Restore the **j** of Your salvation Ps 51:12
make east and west shout for **j**. Ps 65:8
and the hills are robed with **j**. Ps 65:12
nations rejoice and shout for **j**, Ps 67:4
before God and celebrate with **j**. Ps 68:3
will shout for **j** when I sing Ps 71:23
Sing for **j** to God our strength; Ps 81:1
Bring **j** to Your servant's life, Ps 86:4
Hermon shout for **j** at Your name. Ps 89:12
may shout with **j** and be glad all Ps 90:14
will shout for **j** because of the Ps 92:4
cares, Your comfort brings me **j**. Ps 94:19
of the forest will shout for **j** Ps 96:12
jubilant, shout for **j**, and sing. Ps 98:4
mountains shout together for **j** Ps 98:8
chosen ones with shouts of **j**. Ps 105:43
rejoice in the **j** of Your nation, Ps 106:5
His works with shouts of **j**. Ps 107:22
are shouts of **j** and victory Ps 118:15
they are the **j** of my heart. Ps 119:111
our tongues with shouts of **j**. Ps 126:2
will reap with shouts of **j**. Ps 126:5
come back with shouts of **j**, Ps 126:6
Your godly people shout for **j**. Ps 132:9
godly people will shout for **j**. Ps 132:16
Jerusalem as my greatest **j**! Ps 137:6
them shout for **j** on their beds. Ps 149:5
wise son brings **j** to his father, Pr 10:1
The hope of the righteous is **j**, Pr 10:28
those who promote peace have **j**. Pr 12:20
and no outsider shares in its **j**. Pr 14:10
may be sad, and **j** may end in Pr 14:13
wise son brings **j** to his father, Pr 15:20
brings **j** to one without Pr 15:21
A man takes **j** in giving an Pr 15:23
the father of a fool has no **j**. Pr 17:21
executed is a **j** to the righteous Pr 21:15
your father and mother have **j**, Pr 23:25
incense bring **j** to the heart, Pr 27:9
bring my heart **j**, so that I can Pr 27:11
wisdom brings **j** to his father, Pr 29:3
knowledge, and **j**, but to the Ec 2:26
with the **j** of his heart. Ec 5:20
the nation and increased its **j**. Is 9:3
J and rejoicing have been Is 16:10
or shouting for **j** in the Is 16:10
j and gladness, butchering of Is 22:13
cry for wine. All **j** grows dark; Is 24:11
The humble will have **j** after joy Is 29:19
have joy after **j** in the LORD, Is 29:19
forever, the **j** of wild asses, Is 32:14
also rejoice with **j** and singing. Is 35:2
of the mute will sing for **j**, Is 35:6
crowned with unending **j**. Is 35:10
J and gladness will overtake Is 35:10
inhabitants of Sela sing for **j**; Is 42:11
Declare with a shout of **j**, Is 48:20
Shout for **j**, you heavens! Is 49:13
J and gladness will be found in Is 51:3
crowned with unending **j**. Is 51:11
J and gladness will overtake Is 51:11
voices, shouting for **j** together; Is 52:8
go out with **j** and be peacefully Is 55:12
pride, a **j** from age to age Is 60:15
and eternal **j** will be theirs. Is 61:7
will shout for **j** from a glad Is 65:14
will create Jerusalem to be a **j**, Is 65:18
so that we can see your **j**! Is 66:5
the sound of **j** and gladness Jr 7:34
My **j** has flown away; grief has Jr 8:18
to me and the **j** of my heart, Jr 15:16
the sound of **j** and gladness, Jr 16:9
to you," bringing him great **j**. Jr 20:15
the sound of **j** and gladness from Jr 25:10
says: Sing with **j** for Jacob; Jr 31:7
and shout for **j** on the heights Jr 31:12
will be radiant with **j** because Jr 31:12
will turn their mourning into **j**, Jr 31:13

bear on My behalf a name of **j**, Jr 33:9
a sound of **j** and gladness, Jr 33:11
J and celebration are taken from Jr 48:33
one will tread with shouts of **j**. Jr 48:33
shouting is not a shout of **j**. Jr 48:33
the town that brings Me **j**? Jr 49:25
will shout for **j** over Babylon Jr 51:48
of beauty, the **j** of the whole Lm 2:15
J has left our hearts; our Lm 5:15
their pride and **j**, the delight Ezk 24:25
Indeed, human **j** has dried up. Jl 1:12
j and gladness from the house of Jl 1:16
Sing for **j**, Daughter Zion; Zph 3:14
in you with shouts of **j**." Zph 3:17
Zion, shout for **j** and be glad, Zch 2:10
tenth will become times of **j**, Zch 8:19
immediately receives it with **j**. Mt 13:20
Then in his **j** he goes and sells Mt 13:44
Share your master's **j**!' Mt 25:21
things. Share your master's **j**!' Mt 25:23
the tomb with fear and great **j**, Mt 28:8
they receive it with **j**. Mk 4:16
There will be **j** and delight for Lk 1:14
the baby leaped for **j** inside me! Lk 1:44
news of great **j** that will be for Lk 2:10
in that day and leap for **j**! Lk 6:23
hear, welcome the word with **j**. Lk 8:13
The Seventy returned with **j**, Lk 10:17
will be more **j** in heaven over Lk 15:7
there is **j** in the presence of Lk 15:10
of ⌊their⌋ **j** and were amazed, Lk 24:41
to Jerusalem with great **j**. Lk 24:52
So this **j** of mine is complete. Jn 3:29
you so that My **j** may be in you Jn 15:11
you and your **j** may be complete Jn 15:11
but your sorrow will turn to **j**. Jn 16:20
because of the **j** that a person Jn 16:21
no one will rob you of your **j**. Jn 16:22
that your **j** may be complete. Jn 16:24
they may have My **j** completed in Jn 17:13
there was great **j** in that city. Ac 8:8
because of her **j** she did not Ac 12:14
were filled with **j** and the Holy Ac 13:52
they created great **j** among all Ac 15:3
peace, and **j** in the Holy Spirit. Rm 14:17
fill you with all **j** and peace in Rm 15:13
to you with **j** and be refreshed Rm 15:32
finds no **j** in unrighteousness, 1Co 13:6
are workers with you for your **j**, 2Co 1:24
those who ought to give me **j**, 2Co 2:3
all of you that my **j** is yours. 2Co 2:3
I am overcome with **j** in all our 2Co 7:4
even more over the **j** Titus had, 2Co 7:13
abundance of **j** and their deep 2Co 8:2
Spirit is love, **j**, peace, Gl 5:22
praying with **j** for all of you Php 1:4
advancement and **j** in the faith, Php 1:25
fulfill my **j** by thinking the Php 2:2
and share your **j** with me. Php 2:18
Lord with all **j** and hold men Php 2:29
brothers, my **j** and crown, stand Php 4:1
endurance and patience, with **j** Col 1:11
message with the **j** from the Holy 1Th 1:6
who is our hope, or **j**, or crown 1Th 2:19
For you are our glory and **j**! 1Th 2:20
for all the **j** we experience 1Th 3:9
so that I may be filled with **j**, 2Tm 1:4
For I have great **j** and Phm 7
may I have **j** from you in the Phm 20
companions, with the oil of **j**. Heb 1:9
accepted with **j** the confiscation Heb 10:34
for the **j** that lay before Him Heb 12:2
can do this with **j** and not with Heb 13:17
it a great **j**, my brothers, Jms 1:2
mourning and your **j** to sorrow. Jms 4:9
inexpressible and glorious **j**, 1Pt 1:8
with great **j** at the revelation 1Pt 4:13
so that our **j** may be complete. 1Jn 1:4
so that our **j** may be complete 2Jn 12
I have no greater **j** than this: 3Jn 4
blameless and with great **j**, Jd 24

JOYFUL *(22)*

and with **j** hearts for all 1Kg 8:66
the sound of the **j** shouting from Ezr 3:13
the LORD had made them **j**, Ezr 6:22
may no **j** shout be heard in it. Jb 3:7
You surround me with **j** shouts of Ps 32:7
on the strings, with a **j** shout. Ps 33:3
with **j** and thankful shouts. Ps 42:4
will praise You with **j** lips. Ps 63:5
the people who know the **j** shout; Ps 89:15
come before Him with **j** songs. Ps 100:2
⌊making her⌋ the **j** mother of Ps 113:9
great things for us; we were **j**. Ps 126:3
wicked die, there is **j** shouting. Pr 11:10
A **j** heart makes a face cheerful, Pr 15:13
A **j** heart is good medicine, Pr 17:22
In the day of prosperity be **j**, Ec 7:14
The **j** tambourines have ceased. Is 24:8
The **j** lyre has ceased. Is 24:8
joyous house in the **j** city. Is 32:13
Mountains break into **j** shouts! Is 49:13
j, rejoice together, you ruins Is 52:9
again and go forth in **j** dancing. Jr 31:4

JOYFULLY *(14)*

here giving **j** and willingly to 1Ch 29:17
head, returning **j** to Jerusalem, 2Ch 20:27
but many ⌊others⌋ shouted **j**. Ezr 3:12
The wings of the ostrich flap **j**, Jb 39:13
strength and will **j** proclaim Ps 59:16
Shout **j** to God, all the earth! Ps 66:1
let us shout **j** to the LORD, Ps 95:1
goodness and will **j** sing of Your Ps 145:7
You will **j** draw water from the Is 12:3
the one who **j** does what is right Is 64:5
he **j** puts it on his shoulders, Lk 15:5
came down and welcomed Him **j**. Lk 19:6
praise God **j** with a loud voice Lk 19:37
my inner self I **j** agree with Rm 7:22

JOYOUS *(3)*

and on your **j** occasions, Nm 10:10
celebrate the **j** dedication with Neh 12:27
for every **j** house in the joyful Is 32:13

JOZABAD *(11)*
(AKA ZABAD)

His servants **J** son of Shimeath 2Kg 12:21
Johanan, **J** the Gederathite; 1Ch 12:4
Adnah, **J**, Jediael, Michael, 1Ch 12:20
Jediael, Michael, **J**, Elihu, and 1Ch 12:20
Jerimoth, **J**, Eliel, Ismachiah 2Ch 31:13
Hashabiah, Jeiel, and **J**, 2Ch 35:9
The Levites **J** son of Jeshua and Ezr 8:33
Ishmael, Nethanel, **J**, and Elasah Ezr 10:22
J, Shimei, Kelaiah (that is Ezr 10:23
Kelita, Azariah, **J**, Hanan, and Neh 8:7
Shabbethai and **J**, from the Neh 11:16

JOZADAK *(5)*

Jeshua son of **J** and his brothers Ezr 3:2
Jeshua son of **J**, and the rest of Ezr 3:8
Jeshua son of **J** began to rebuild Ezr 5:2
Jeshua son of **J** and his brothers Ezr 10:18
Jeshua, son of **J**, and in the Neh 12:26

JUBAL *(1)*

His brother was named **J**; Gn 4:21

JUBILANT *(5)*

shout to God with a **j** cry. Ps 47:1
be **j**, shout for joy, and sing. Ps 98:4
city, the **j** town, is filled Is 22:2
Is this your **j** ⌊city⌋, whose Is 23:7
The noise of the **j** has stopped. Is 24:8

JUBILANTLY *(1)*

do not rejoice **j** as the nations Hs 9:1

JUBILATION *(3)*

commemoration and **j**—a sacred Lv 23:24
This will be a day of **j** for you. Nm 29:1
rejoicing and **j** took place among Est 8:17

JUBILEE *(21)*

It will be your **J**, when each of Lv 25:10
fiftieth year will be your **J**; Lv 25:11
holy to you because it is the **J**; Lv 25:12
In this Year of **J**, each of you Lv 25:13
of years since the last **J**. Lv 25:15
purchaser until the Year of **J**. Lv 25:28
It is to be released at the **J**, Lv 25:28
is not to be released on the **J**. Lv 25:30
are to be released at the **J**. Lv 25:31
must be released at the **J**, Lv 25:33
for you until the Year of **J**. Lv 25:40
to him until the Year of **J**. Lv 25:50
remain until the Year of **J**, Lv 25:52
to be released at the Year of **J**. Lv 25:54
his field during the Year of **J**, Lv 27:17
his field after the **J**, Lv 27:18
left until the ⌊next⌋ Year of **J**, Lv 27:18
the field is released in the **J**, Lv 27:21
valuation up to the Year of **J**, Lv 27:23
In the Year of **J** the field will Lv 27:24
When the **J** comes for the Nm 36:4

JUCAL *(1)*

son of Pashhur, **J** son of Jr 38:1

JUDAH *(720)*
(AKA JUDEA)

Therefore she named him **J**. Gn 29:35
Simeon, Levi, **J**, Issachar, and Gn 35:23
Then **J** said to his brothers, Gn 37:26
At that time **J** left his brothers Gn 38:1
There **J** saw the daughter of a Gn 38:2
J got a wife for Er, his Gn 38:6
Then **J** said to Onan, "Sleep with Gn 38:8
Then **J** said to his Gn 38:11
When **J** had finished mourning, Gn 38:12
When **J** saw her, he thought she Gn 38:15
When **J** sent the young goat by Gn 38:20
So the Adullamite returned to **J**, Gn 38:22
J replied, "Let her keep ⌊the Gn 38:23
three months later **J** was told, Gn 38:24
Bring her out!" **J** said. "Let her Gn 38:24
J recognized ⌊them⌋ and said, Gn 38:26
But **J** said to him, "The man Gn 43:3
J said to his father Israel, Gn 43:8
When **J** and his brothers reached Gn 44:14
say to my lord?" **J** replied. "How Gn 44:16
But **J** approached him and said, Gn 44:18
Jacob had sent **J** ahead of him to Gn 46:28
J, your brothers will praise you. Gn 49:8
J is a young lion—my son, you Gn 49:9
scepter will not depart from **J**, Gn 49:10
Reuben, Simeon, Levi, and **J**; Ex 1:2
son of Hur, of the tribe of **J**. Ex 31:2
son of Hur, of the tribe of **J**. Ex 35:30
of the tribe of **J**, made Ex 38:22
Nahshon son of Amminadab from **J**; Nm 1:7
descendants of **J**: according to Nm 1:26
the tribe of **J** numbered 74,600 Nm 1:27
descendants of **J** is Nahshon son Nm 2:3
Amminadab from the tribe of **J**. Nm 7:12
of the camp of **J** with their Nm 10:14
Jephunneh from the tribe of **J**; Nm 13:6
Jephunneh from the tribe of **J**; Nm 34:19
Simeon, Levi, **J**, Issachar, Dt 27:12
He said this about **J**: LORD, hear Dt 33:7
all the land of **J** as far as the Dt 34:2
of the tribe of **J**, took some of Jos 7:1
and the tribe of **J** was selected. Jos 7:16
had the clans of **J** come forward, Jos 7:17
of the tribe of **J**, was selected. Jos 7:18
hill country of **J** and of Israel. Jos 11:21
descendants of **J** approached Jos 14:6
descendants of **J** by their clans Jos 15:1
descendants of **J** around their Jos 15:12
descendants of **J** based on the Jos 15:13
descendants of **J** by their clans. Jos 15:20
descendants of **J** toward the Jos 15:21
descendants of **J** could not drive Jos 15:63
descendants of **J** to this day. Jos 15:63
J is to remain in its territory Jos 18:5
a city of the descendants of **J**. Jos 18:14
and **J** at the Jordan on the east. Jos 19:34
) in the hill country of **J**. Jos 20:7
by lot from the tribes of **J**, Jos 21:4
the descendants of **J** and Simeon Jos 21:9
in the hill country of **J**. Jos 21:11
The LORD answered, "**J** is to go. Jdg 1:2
J said to his brother Simeon, Jdg 1:3
When **J** attacked, the LORD handed Jdg 1:4
The men of **J** fought against Jdg 1:8
the men of **J** marched down to Jdg 1:9
J also marched against the Jdg 1:10
with the men of **J** from the City Jdg 1:16
of Palms to the Wilderness of **J**, Jdg 1:16
J went with his brother Simeon, Jdg 1:17
J captured Gaza and its Jdg 1:18
LORD was with **J** and enabled them Jdg 1:19
J gave Hebron to Caleb, just as Jdg 1:20
the Jordan to fight against **J**, Jdg 10:9
up, camped in **J**, and raided Lehi Jdg 15:9
So the men of **J** said, "Why have Jdg 15:10
3,000 men of **J** went to the cave Jdg 15:11
from Bethlehem in **J**, who resided Jdg 17:7
resided within the clan of **J**. Jdg 17:7
of Bethlehem in **J** to settle Jdg 17:8
am a Levite from Bethlehem in **J**, Jdg 17:9

camped at Kiriath-jearim in **J**. Jdg 18:12
Bethlehem in **J** as his concubine Jdg 19:1
house in Bethlehem in **J**. Jdg 19:2
Bethlehem in **J** to the remote Jdg 19:18
to Bethlehem in **J**, and now I'm Jdg 19:18
answered, "**J** will be first." Jdg 20:18
Bethlehem in **J** with his wife Ru 1:1
Ephrathites from Bethlehem in **J**. Ru 1:2
leading back to the land of **J**. Ru 1:7
the son Tamar bore to **J**, because Ru 4:12
and 30,000 men from **J**. 1Sm 11:8
soldiers and 10,000 men from **J**. 1Sm 15:4
war at Socoh in **J** and camped 1Sm 17:1
Bethlehem of **J** named Jesse. 1Sm 17:12
The men of Israel and **J** rallied, 1Sm 17:52
But all Israel and **J** loved David 1Sm 18:16
and return to the land of **J**." 1Sm 22:5
Look, we're afraid here in **J**; 1Sm 23:3
him among all the clans of **J**." 1Sm 23:23
belongs to the kings of **J** today. 1Sm 27:6
"The south country of **J**," 1Sm 27:10
territory⌋ of **J**, and the south 1Sm 30:14
Philistines and the land of **J**. 1Sm 30:16
the elders of **J**, saying, "Here 1Sm 30:26
I go to one of the towns of **J**?" 2Sm 2:1
the men of **J** came, and there 2Sm 2:4
David king over the house of **J**. 2Sm 2:4
the house of **J** has anointed me 2Sm 2:7
house of **J**, however, followed 2Sm 2:10
the house of **J** was seven years 2Sm 2:11
a dog's head who belongs to **J**?" 2Sm 3:8
over Israel and **J** from Dan to 2Sm 3:10
reigned over **J** seven years and 2Sm 5:5
33 years over all Israel and **J**. 2Sm 5:5
and **J** are dwelling in tents, 2Sm 11:11
you the house of Israel and **J**, 2Sm 12:8
the elders of **J**, 'Why should you 2Sm 19:11
So he won over all the men of **J**, 2Sm 19:14
J came to Gilgal to meet the 2Sm 19:15
with the men of **J** to meet King 2Sm 19:16
All the troops of **J** and half of 2Sm 19:40
the men of **J**, take you away 2Sm 19:41
the men of **J** responded to the 2Sm 19:42
of Israel answered the men of **J**: 2Sm 19:43
the men of **J** were harsher than 2Sm 19:43
but the men of **J** from the Jordan 2Sm 20:2
Summon the men of **J** to me 2Sm 20:4
went to summon **J**, but he took 2Sm 20:5
zeal for the Israelites and **J**. 2Sm 21:2
the people of⌋ Israel and **J**." 2Sm 24:1
to the Negev of **J** at Beer-sheba. 2Sm 24:7
Israel and 500,000 men from **J**. 2Sm 24:9
brothers and all the men of **J**, 1Kg 1:9
to be ruler over Israel and **J**." 1Kg 1:35
was one deputy in the land of **J**. 1Kg 4:19
J and Israel were as numerous as 1Kg 4:20
J and Israel lived in safety 1Kg 4:25
Tamar in the Wilderness of **J**, 1Kg 9:18
living in the cities of **J**. 1Kg 12:17
except the tribe of **J** alone. 1Kg 12:20
entire house of **J** and the tribe 1Kg 12:21
Solomon, king of **J**, to the whole 1Kg 12:23
whole house of **J** and Benjamin, 1Kg 12:23
their lord, Rehoboam king of **J**. 1Kg 12:27
and go back to the king of **J**." 1Kg 12:27
month, like the festival in **J**. 1Kg 12:32
man of God came from **J** to Bethel 1Kg 13:1
of God who had come from **J**. 1Kg 13:12
man of God who came from **J**?" 1Kg 13:14
of God who had come from **J**, 1Kg 13:21
Solomon's son, reigned in **J**. 1Kg 14:21
J did what was evil in the 1Kg 14:22
Abijam became king over **J**; 1Kg 15:1
Jeroboam, Asa became king of **J**; 1Kg 15:9
Baasha went to war against **J**. 1Kg 15:17
everyone without exception in **J**, 1Kg 15:22
Beer-sheba that belonged to **J**, 1Kg 19:3
king of **J** went to visit 1Kg 22:2
and Jehoshaphat king of **J**, 1Kg 22:10
became king over **J** in the fourth 1Kg 22:41
to King Jehoshaphat of **J**: 2Kg 3:7
the king of **J**, and the king 2Kg 3:9
for King Jehoshaphat of **J**, 2Kg 3:14
of Jehoshaphat became king of **J**, 2Kg 8:16
to destroy **J** because of His 2Kg 8:19
son of Jehoram became king of **J**. 2Kg 8:25
Ahaziah king of **J** had gone down 2Kg 9:16
and Ahaziah king of **J** set out, 2Kg 9:21

King Ahaziah of **J** saw ⌊what was 2Kg 9:27
Ahaziah had become king over **J**. 2Kg 9:29
of Ahaziah king of **J** and asked, 2Kg 10:13
So King Joash of **J** took all the 2Kg 12:18
son of Joash became king of **J**. 2Kg 14:1
⌊word⌋ to Amaziah king of **J**, 2Kg 14:9
you fall—you and **J** with you?" 2Kg 14:10
King Amaziah of **J** faced off at 2Kg 14:11
Beth-shemesh that belongs to **J**. 2Kg 14:11
J was routed before Israel, 2Kg 14:12
war against Amaziah king of **J**, 2Kg 14:15
the people of **J** took Azariah, 2Kg 14:21
restored it to **J** after ⌊Amaziah⌋ 2Kg 14:22
had belonged to **J**—are written 2Kg 14:28
son of Amaziah became king of **J**. 2Kg 15:1
son of Uzziah became king of **J**. 2Kg 15:32
Pekah son of Remaliah against **J**. 2Kg 15:37
son of Jotham became king of **J**. 2Kg 16:1
warned Israel and **J** through 2Kg 17:13
Only the tribe of **J** remained. 2Kg 17:18
Even **J** did not keep the 2Kg 17:19
son of Ahaz became king of **J**. 2Kg 18:1
of the kings of **J** was like him, 2Kg 18:5
cities of **J** and captured them. 2Kg 18:13
Hezekiah king of **J** sent word to 2Kg 18:14
King Hezekiah of **J** 11 tons of 2Kg 18:14
saying to **J** and to Jerusalem: 2Kg 18:22
Say this to Hezekiah king of **J**: 2Kg 19:10
Manasseh king of **J** has 2Kg 21:11
idols has also caused **J** to sin, 2Kg 21:11
on Jerusalem and **J** that everyone 2Kg 21:12
sin he caused **J** to commit so 2Kg 21:16
and all **J** about the instruction 2Kg 22:13
that the king of **J** has read, 2Kg 22:16
to the king of **J** who sent you to 2Kg 22:18
the elders of Jerusalem and **J**. 2Kg 23:1
with all the men of **J** and all 2Kg 23:2
the kings of **J** had appointed to 2Kg 23:5
the cities of **J** and in the areas 2Kg 23:5
priests from the cities of **J**, 2Kg 23:8
the kings of **J** had dedicated to 2Kg 23:11
that the kings of **J** had made— 2Kg 23:12
who came from **J** and proclaimed 2Kg 23:17
of the kings of Israel and **J**. 2Kg 23:22
in the land of **J** and in 2Kg 23:24
burned against **J** because of all 2Kg 23:26
will also remove **J** from My sight 2Kg 23:27
them against **J** to destroy it, 2Kg 24:2
king of **J**, along with his 2Kg 24:12
Jerusalem and **J** that He finally 2Kg 24:20
So **J** went into exile from its 2Kg 25:21
people he left in the land of **J**. 2Kg 25:22
Jehoiachin of **J** ⌊and released 2Kg 25:27
Simeon, Levi, **J**, Issachar, 1Ch 2:1
J had five sons in all. 1Ch 2:4
The sons of Shelah son of **J**: 1Ch 4:21
the days of King Hezekiah of **J**, 1Ch 4:41
Although **J** became strong among 1Ch 5:2
the LORD sent **J** and Jerusalem 1Ch 6:15
in the land of **J** and its 1Ch 6:55
But **J** was exiled to Babylon 1Ch 9:1
from the descendants of **J**, 1Ch 9:3
a descendant of Perez son of **J**; 1Ch 9:4
men from **J** also went to David 1Ch 12:16
which belongs to **J**, to take from 1Ch 13:6
swordsmen and in **J** itself 1Ch 21:5
for **J**, Elihu, one of David's 1Ch 27:18
For He chose **J** as leader, and 1Ch 28:4
from the house of **J**, my father's 1Ch 28:4
are with me in **J** and Jerusalem, 2Ch 2:7
them been seen in the land of **J**. 2Ch 9:11
living in the cities of **J**, 2Ch 10:17
the house of **J** and Benjamin— 2Ch 11:1
Solomon, king of **J**, to all 2Ch 11:3
to all Israel in **J** and Benjamin, 2Ch 11:3
and he fortified cities in **J**. 2Ch 11:5
cities in **J** and in Benjamin. 2Ch 11:10
So **J** and Benjamin were his. 2Ch 11:12
and went to **J** and Jerusalem, 2Ch 11:14
the kingdom of **J** and supported 2Ch 11:17
the regions of **J** and Benjamin 2Ch 11:23
cities of **J** and came as far as 2Ch 12:4
the leaders of **J** who were 2Ch 12:5
conditions were good in **J**. 2Ch 12:12
Abijah became king over **J**; 2Ch 13:1
So they were in front of **J**, 2Ch 13:13
J turned and discovered that the 2Ch 13:14
and the men of **J** raised the 2Ch 13:15

When the men of **J** raised the 2Ch 13:15
all Israel before Abijah and **J**. 2Ch 13:15
So the Israelites fled before **J**, 2Ch 13:16
people of⌋ **J** to seek the LORD 2Ch 14:4
altars from all the cities of **J**, 2Ch 14:5
Asa built fortified cities in **J**. 2Ch 14:6
So he said to ⌊the people of⌋ **J**, 2Ch 14:7
of 300,000 from **J** bearing large 2Ch 14:8
before Asa and before **J**, 2Ch 14:12
So the people of **J** carried off a 2Ch 14:13
Asa and all **J** and Benjamin, 2Ch 15:2
the whole land of **J** and Benjamin 2Ch 15:8
he gathered all **J** and Benjamin, 2Ch 15:9
All **J** rejoiced over the oath, 2Ch 15:15
Baasha went to war against **J**. 2Ch 16:1
Then King Asa brought all **J**, 2Ch 16:6
King Asa of **J** and said to him, 2Ch 16:7
of the Kings of **J** and Israel. 2Ch 16:11
city of **J** and set garrisons 2Ch 17:2
in the land of **J** and in the 2Ch 17:2
Then all **J** brought him tribute, 2Ch 17:5
places and Asherah poles from **J**. 2Ch 17:6
to teach in the cities of **J**. 2Ch 17:7
They taught throughout **J**, 2Ch 17:9
the towns of **J** and taught the 2Ch 17:9
of the lands that surrounded **J**, 2Ch 17:10
and storage cities in **J** 2Ch 17:12
great works in the towns of **J**. 2Ch 17:13
For **J**, the commanders of 2Ch 17:14
cities throughout all **J**. 2Ch 17:19
and King Jehoshaphat of **J**, 2Ch 18:9
king of **J** returned to his 2Ch 19:1
cities of the land of **J**, 2Ch 19:5
the ruler of the house of **J**, 2Ch 19:11
he proclaimed a fast for all **J**, 2Ch 20:3
all the cities of **J** to seek Him. 2Ch 20:4
the assembly of **J** and Jerusalem 2Ch 20:5
All **J** was standing before the 2Ch 20:13
all **J** and you inhabitants of 2Ch 20:15
is⌋ with you, **J** and Jerusalem. 2Ch 20:17
and all **J** and the inhabitants of 2Ch 20:18
J and you inhabitants of 2Ch 20:20
who came ⌊to fight⌋ against **J**, 2Ch 20:22
When **J** came to a place 2Ch 20:24
all the men of **J** and Jerusalem 2Ch 20:27
Jehoshaphat became king over **J**. 2Ch 20:31
sons of Jehoshaphat, king of **J**. 2Ch 21:2
with fortified cities in **J**, 2Ch 21:3
high places in the hills of **J**, 2Ch 21:11
themselves, and he led **J** astray. 2Ch 21:11
or in the ways of Asa king of **J** 2Ch 21:12
caused **J** and the inhabitants 2Ch 21:13
to war against **J** and invaded it. 2Ch 21:17
son of Jehoram became king of **J**. 2Ch 22:1
the rulers of **J** and the sons 2Ch 22:8
royal heirs of the house of **J**. 2Ch 22:10
made a circuit throughout **J**. 2Ch 23:2
the cities of **J** and the heads 2Ch 23:2
to the cities of **J** and collect 2Ch 24:5
bring from **J** and Jerusalem the 2Ch 24:6
was issued in **J** and Jerusalem 2Ch 24:9
the rulers of **J** came and paid 2Ch 24:17
wrath against **J** and Jerusalem 2Ch 24:18
They entered **J** and Jerusalem 2Ch 24:23
the people of **J** had abandoned 2Ch 24:24
Amaziah gathered **J** and assembled 2Ch 25:5
or more for all **J** and Benjamin. 2Ch 25:5
very angry with **J** and returned 2Ch 25:10
the cities of **J** from Samaria to 2Ch 25:13
King Amaziah of **J** took counsel 2Ch 25:17
⌊word⌋ to King Amaziah of **J**, 2Ch 25:18
that you fall and **J** with you?" 2Ch 25:19
King Amaziah of **J** faced off at 2Ch 25:21
faced off at Beth-shemesh in **J**. 2Ch 25:21
J was routed before Israel, 2Ch 25:22
of the Kings of **J** and Israel. 2Ch 25:26
his fathers in the city of **J**. 2Ch 25:28
All the people of **J** took Uzziah, 2Ch 26:1
restored it to **J** after ⌊Amaziah⌋ 2Ch 26:2
hill country of **J** and fortresses 2Ch 27:4
of the Kings of Israel and **J**. 2Ch 27:7
killed 120,000 in **J** in one day— 2Ch 28:6
because of His wrath against **J**, 2Ch 28:9
the people of **J** and Jerusalem, 2Ch 28:10
again, attacked **J**, and took 2Ch 28:17
and the Negev of **J** and captured 2Ch 28:18
LORD humbled **J** because of King 2Ch 28:19
Judah because of King Ahaz of **J**, 2Ch 28:19

off restraint in J and was 2Ch 28:19
every city of J to offer incense 2Ch 28:25
of the Kings of J and Israel. 2Ch 28:26
the LORD was on J and Jerusalem, 2Ch 29:8
for the sanctuary, and for J. 2Ch 29:21
throughout all Israel and J, 2Ch 30:1
Israel and J with letters 2Ch 30:6
of God was in J to give them one 2Ch 30:12
Hezekiah king of J contributed 2Ch 30:24
assembly of J with the priests 2Ch 30:25
and those who were living in J, 2Ch 30:25
to the cities of J and broke up 2Ch 31:1
throughout J and Benjamin, 2Ch 31:1
who lived in the cities of J, 2Ch 31:6
did this throughout all J. 2Ch 31:20
of Assyria came and entered J. 2Ch 32:1
the words of King Hezekiah of J. 2Ch 32:8
Hezekiah of J and against all 2Ch 32:9
against all those of J who were 2Ch 32:9
and say to J and Jerusalem: 2Ch 32:12
gifts to King Hezekiah of J, 2Ch 32:23
upon him, upon J, and upon 2Ch 32:25
of the Kings of J and Israel. 2Ch 32:32
All J and the inhabitants of 2Ch 32:33
So Manasseh caused J and the 2Ch 33:9
all the fortified cities of J. 2Ch 33:14
Then he told J to serve the LORD 2Ch 33:16
began to cleanse J and Jerusalem 2Ch 34:3
So he cleansed J and Jerusalem. 2Ch 34:5
and from all J, Benjamin, 2Ch 34:9
those remaining in Israel and J, 2Ch 34:21
the presence of the king of J, 2Ch 34:24
to the king of J who sent you to 2Ch 34:26
the elders of J and Jerusalem. 2Ch 34:29
all the men of J and the 2Ch 34:30
present ⌊in J⌋ also observed 2Ch 35:17
Levites, all J, the Israelites 2Ch 35:18
who were present ⌊in J⌋, 2Ch 35:18
between you and me, king of J? 2Ch 35:21
All J and Jerusalem mourned for 2Ch 35:24
of the Kings of Israel and J. 2Ch 35:27
king over J and Jerusalem 2Ch 36:4
king over J and Jerusalem. 2Ch 36:10
Him a temple at Jerusalem in J. 2Ch 36:23
Him a house at Jerusalem in J. Ezr 1:2
go to Jerusalem in J and build Ezr 1:3
leaders of J and Benjamin, Ezr 1:5
to Sheshbazzar the prince of J. Ezr 1:8
to his hometown Jerusalem and J. Ezr 2:1
the sons of J and of Henadad, Ezr 3:9
the enemies of J and Benjamin Ezr 4:1
the people of J and made them Ezr 4:4
residents of J and Jerusalem. Ezr 4:6
who were in J and Jerusalem, Ezr 5:1
great God in the province of J. Ezr 5:8
to evaluate J and Jerusalem Ezr 7:14
us a wall in J and Jerusalem. Ezr 9:9
throughout J and Jerusalem that Ezr 10:7
So all the men of J and Benjamin Ezr 10:9
Pethahiah, J, and Eliezer. Ezr 10:23
men from J, and I questioned Neh 1:2
send me to J and to the city Neh 2:5
safe⌋ passage until I reach J. Neh 2:7
In J, it was said: The strength Neh 4:10
supported all the people of J, Neh 4:16
governor in the land of J— Neh 5:14
"There is a king in J." Neh 6:7
nobles of J sent many letters Neh 6:17
For many in J were bound by oath Neh 6:18
his own town in Jerusalem and J. Neh 7:6
the villages of J each lived on Neh 11:3
descendants of J and Benjamin Neh 11:4
J son of Hassenuah was second Neh 11:9
were in all the villages of J, Neh 11:20
descendants of Zerah son of J, Neh 11:24
Sherebiah, J, and Mattaniah—he Neh 12:8
leaders of J up on top of the Neh 12:31
half the leaders of J followed: Neh 12:32
J, Benjamin, Shemaiah, and Neh 12:34
Maai, Nethanel, J, and Hanani, Neh 12:36
because J was grateful to the Neh 12:44
Then all J brought a tenth of Neh 13:12
I saw people in J treading wine Neh 13:15
to the people of J in Jerusalem. Neh 13:16
nobles of J and said to them: Neh 13:17
King Jeconiah of J into exile. Est 2:6
The towns of J rejoice because Ps 48:11
is My helmet; J is My scepter. Ps 60:7

the rulers of J in their Ps 68:27
and build up the cities of J. Ps 69:35
God is known in J; His name is Ps 76:1
He chose instead the tribe of J, Ps 78:68
the towns of J rejoice because Ps 97:8
is My helmet; J is My scepter. Ps 108:8
J became His sanctuary, Israel, Ps 114:2
of Hezekiah, king of J, copied. Pr 25:1
concerning J and Jerusalem Is 1:1
Ahaz, and Hezekiah, kings of J. Is 1:1
saw concerning J and Jerusalem: Is 2:1
Jerusalem and from J every kind Is 3:1
has stumbled and J has fallen Is 3:8
of Jerusalem and men of J, Is 5:3
and the men of J, the plant He Is 5:7
Jotham, son of Uzziah king of J: Is 7:1
go up against J, terrorize it, Is 7:6
since Ephraim separated from J— Is 7:17
will pour into J, flood over it, Is 8:8
together, both are against J. Is 9:21
the scattered of J from the four Is 11:12
will no longer be envious of J, Is 11:13
and J will not harass Ephraim. Is 11:13
land of J will terrify Egypt; Is 19:17
whenever J is mentioned, Egypt Is 19:17
He removed the defenses of J. Is 22:8
Jerusalem and to the House of J. Is 22:21
will be sung in the land of J: Is 26:1
cities of J and captured them. Is 36:1
saying to J and Jerusalem: Is 36:7
Say this to Hezekiah king of J: Is 37:10
the house of J will again take Is 37:31
Hezekiah king of J after he had Is 38:9
the cities of J, "Here is your Is 40:9
and to the cities of J: Is 44:26
and have descended from J, Is 48:1
heirs to My mountains from J; Is 65:9
Josiah son of Amon, king of J. Jr 1:2
Josiah, king of J, until the Jr 1:3
Josiah, king of J, when the Jr 1:3
and all the other cities of J. Jr 1:15
the kings of J, its officials, Jr 1:18
as numerous as your cities, J. Jr 2:28
her treacherous sister J saw it. Jr 3:7
sister J was not afraid Jr 3:8
sister J didn't return to Jr 3:10
righteous than treacherous J. Jr 3:11
the house of J will join with Jr 3:18
to the men of J and Jerusalem: Jr 4:3
men of J and residents of Jr 4:4
Declare in J, proclaim in Jr 4:5
voices against the cities of J. Jr 4:16
of Israel and the house of J, Jr 5:11
proclaim it in J, saying: Jr 5:20
you people⌋ of J who enter Jr 7:2
in the cities of J and in the Jr 7:17
the cities of J and the streets Jr 7:34
the bones of the kings of J, Jr 8:1
the cities of J a desolation, Jr 9:11
Egypt, J, Edom, the Ammonites, Jr 9:26
The cities of J will be made Jr 10:22
to the men of J and the Jr 11:2
in the cities of J and in the Jr 11:6
among the men of J and the Jr 11:9
and the house of J broke My Jr 11:10
the cities of J and the Jr 11:12
your cities, J, and the altars Jr 11:13
and the house of J brought on Jr 11:17
the house of J from among them. Jr 12:14
pride of both J and Jerusalem. Jr 13:9
of Israel and of J to Me"— Jr 13:11
All of J has been taken into Jr 13:19
J mourns; her gates languish. Jr 14:2
Have You completely rejected J? Jr 14:19
the king of J, for what he did Jr 15:4
The sin of J is written with an Jr 17:1
the kings of J enter and leave, Jr 17:19
the LORD, kings of J, all Judah, Jr 17:20
kings of Judah, all J, and all Jr 17:20
the men of J, and the residents Jr 17:25
the cities of J and from the Jr 17:26
say to the men of J and to the Jr 18:11
kings of J and residents of Jr 19:3
the kings of J have never known Jr 19:4
the plans of J and Jerusalem Jr 19:7
of the kings of J will become Jr 19:13
will hand J over to the king of Jr 20:4
of the kings of J over to their Jr 20:5

Zedekiah of J, his officers, Jr 21:7
of the king of J ⌊say this⌋: Jr 21:11
of the king of J and announce Jr 22:1
the LORD, king of J, you who sit Jr 22:2
the house of the king of J: Jr 22:6
Josiah, king of J, who succeeded Jr 22:11
son of Josiah, king of J: Jr 22:18
king of J, were a signet ring Jr 22:24
of David or ruling again in J. Jr 22:30
In His days J will be saved, Jr 23:6
son of Jehoiakim king of J, Jr 24:1
the officials of J, and the Jr 24:1
the exiles from J I sent away Jr 24:5
deal with Zedekiah king of J, Jr 24:8
the people of J in the fourth Jr 25:1
of Josiah, king of J (which was Jr 25:1
all the people of J and all the Jr 25:2
Amon, king of J, until this very Jr 25:3
and the ⌊other⌋ cities of J, Jr 25:18
Josiah, king of J, this word Jr 26:1
the officials of J heard these Jr 26:10
king of J and said to all Jr 26:18
said to all the people of J, Jr 26:18
Hezekiah king of J and all ⌊the Jr 26:19
the people of⌋ J put him to Jr 26:19
Josiah, king of J, this word Jr 27:1
Zedekiah king of J in Jerusalem. Jr 27:3
king of J in the same way Jr 27:12
in the palace of the king of J, Jr 27:18
king of J, from Jerusalem to Jr 27:20
the nobles of J and Jerusalem. Jr 27:20
in the palace of the king of J, Jr 27:21
the reign of Zedekiah king of J, Jr 28:1
Jehoiakim, king of J, and all Jr 28:4
all the exiles from J who went Jr 28:4
officials of J and Jerusalem, Jr 29:2
Zedekiah king of J had sent to Jr 29:3
all the exiles of J who are in Jr 29:22
of My people Israel and J"— Jr 30:3
the LORD spoke to Israel and J. Jr 30:4
in the land of J and in its Jr 31:23
J and all its cities will live Jr 31:24
and the house of J with the seed Jr 31:27
Israel and with the house of J. Jr 31:31
year of Zedekiah king of J, Jr 32:1
in the palace of the king of J. Jr 32:2
king of J had imprisoned Jr 32:3
king of J will not escape Jr 32:4
the men of J, and the residents Jr 32:32
detestable act causing J to sin! Jr 32:35
the fortunes of J and of Israel Jr 33:7
of Israel and the house of J. Jr 33:14
In those days J will be saved, Jr 33:16
king of J, and tell him: Jr 34:2
word, Zedekiah, king of J. Jr 34:4
Zedekiah king of J in Jerusalem Jr 34:6
officials of J and Jerusalem, Jr 34:19
Zedekiah king of J and his Jr 34:21
son of Josiah, king of J: Jr 35:1
to the men of J and the Jr 35:13
certainly bring to J and to all Jr 35:17
Josiah, king of J, this word Jr 36:1
concerning Israel, J, and all Jr 36:2
the house of J hears about all Jr 36:3
Josiah, king of J, in the ninth Jr 36:9
that Jehoiakim king of J burned. Jr 36:28
concerning Jehoiakim king of J: Jr 36:29
concerning Jehoiakim king of J: Jr 36:30
on the men of J all the disaster Jr 36:31
king in the land of J in place Jr 37:1
year of Zedekiah king of J, Jr 39:1
Zedekiah king of J and all the Jr 39:4
the land of J some of the poor Jr 39:10
Jerusalem and J who were being Jr 40:1
appointed over the cities of J, Jr 40:5
a remnant in J and had appointed Jr 40:11
and came to the land of J, Jr 40:12
scatter all of J that has Jr 40:15
the remnant of J would perish?" Jr 40:15
word of the LORD, remnant of J! Jr 42:15
concerning you, remnant of J: Jr 42:19
LORD to stay in the land of J. Jr 43:4
took the whole remnant of J, Jr 43:5
in the land of J for a while— Jr 43:5
and infant from J, leaving Jr 44:7
in the land of J and in the Jr 44:9
disaster, to cut off all J. Jr 44:11
will take away the remnant of J, Jr 44:12

the remnant of J—those going Jr 44:14
to the land of J where they are Jr 44:14
all J who are in the land of Jr 44:24
by anyone of J in all the land Jr 44:26
and every man of J who is in the Jr 44:27
to the land of J only few in Jr 44:28
and the whole remnant of J, Jr 44:28
son of Josiah, king of J: Jr 45:1
the reign of Zedekiah king of J. Jr 49:34
For Israel and J are not left Jr 51:5
Zedekiah king of J in the fourth Jr 51:59
Jerusalem and J that He finally Jr 52:3
Thus J went into exile from its Jr 52:27
Jehoiachin of J and released him Jr 52:31
J has gone into exile following Lm 1:3
Virgin Daughter J ⌊like grapes⌋ Lm 1:15
fortified cities of Daughter J. Lm 2:2
lamentation within Daughter J. Lm 2:5
virgins in the cities of J. Lm 5:11
the iniquity of the house of J. Ezk 4:6
and the elders of J were sitting Ezk 8:1
for the house of J to commit Ezk 8:17
of Israel and J is extremely Ezk 9:9
and to J into fortified Ezk 21:20
the house of J when they went Ezk 25:3
the house of J is like all the Ezk 25:8
the house of J and incurred Ezk 25:12
J and the land of Israel were Ezk 27:17
to J and the Israelites Ezk 37:16
together with the stick of J. Ezk 37:19
west, will be J—one ⌊portion⌋ Ezk 48:7
Next to the territory of J, Ezk 48:8
the territory of J and that of Ezk 48:22
one, the gate of J; and one, the Ezk 48:31
reign of Jehoiakim king of J, Dn 1:1
Jehoiakim king of J over to him, Dn 1:2
from the descendants of J, Dn 1:6
the king brought from J? Dn 5:13
the men of J, the residents of Dn 9:7
kings of J, and of Jeroboam Hs 1:1
compassion on the house of J, Hs 1:7
don't let J become guilty! Hs 4:15
even J will stumble with them. Hs 5:5
The princes of J are like those Hs 5:10
like decay to the house of J. Hs 5:12
his sickness and J his wound, Hs 5:13
a young lion to the house of J. Hs 5:14
am I going to do with you, J? Hs 6:4
is also appointed for you, J. Hs 6:11
J has also multiplied fortified Hs 8:14
Ephraim; J will plow; Jacob Hs 10:11
J still wanders with El and is Hs 11:12
LORD also has a dispute with J. Hs 12:2
the fortunes of J and Jerusalem, Jl 3:1
the people of J and Jerusalem to Jl 3:6
the hands of the people of J, Jl 3:8
the streams of J will flow with Jl 3:18
to the people of J in whose land Jl 3:19
But J will be inhabited forever, Jl 3:20
Uzziah, king of J, and Jeroboam Am 1:1
from punishing J for three Am 2:4
I will send fire against J, Am 2:5
Flee to the land of J. Am 7:12
over the people of J in the day Ob 12
Ahaz, and Hezekiah, kings of J. Mc 1:1
And what is the high place of J? Mc 1:5
and has reached even J; Mc 1:9
are small among the clans of J; Mc 5:2
Celebrate your festivals, J; Nah 1:15
Josiah son of Amon, king of J. Zph 1:1
hand against J and against all Zph 1:4
the remnant of the house of J; Zph 2:7
the governor of J, and to Joshua Hg 1:1
governor of J, the spirit Hg 1:14
governor of J, to the high Hg 2:2
to Zerubbabel, governor of J: Hg 2:21
the cities of J that You have Zch 1:12
are the horns that scattered J, Zch 1:19
that scattered J so no one could Zch 1:21
the land of J to scatter it." Zch 1:21
possession of J as His portion Zch 2:12
house of J and house of Israel, Zch 8:13
to Jerusalem and the house of J. Zch 8:15
festivals for the house of J. Zch 8:19
like a clan in J and Ekron like Zch 9:7
For I will bend J ⌊as My bow⌋; Zch 9:13
His flock, the house of J; Zch 10:3
the house of J and deliver the Zch 10:6
between J and Israel. Zch 11:14
Jerusalem will also involve J. Zch 12:2
on the house of J but strike all Zch 12:4
the leaders of J will think to Zch 12:5
the leaders of J like a firepot Zch 12:6
will save the tents of J first, Zch 12:7
not be greater than that of J. Zch 12:7
in the days of Uzziah king of J. Zch 14:5
J will also fight at Jerusalem, Zch 14:14
and in J will be holy to Zch 14:21
J has acted treacherously, Mal 2:11
For J has profaned the LORD's Mal 2:11
the offerings of J and Jerusalem Mal 3:4
Jacob fathered J and his Mt 1:2
J fathered Perez and Zerah by Mt 1:3
the land of J, are by no means Mt 2:6
least among the leaders of J: Mt 2:6
a town in the hill country of J Lk 1:39
son⌋ of J, ⌊son⌋ of Joseph Lk 3:30
son⌋ of Perez, ⌊son⌋ of J, Lk 3:33
that our Lord came from J, Heb 7:14
Israel and with the house of J— Heb 8:8
The Lion from the tribe of J, Rv 5:5
sealed from the tribe of J, Rv 7:5

JUDAH'S *(102)*

Now Er, J firstborn, was evil in Gn 38:7
After a long time J wife, the Gn 38:12
J sons: Er, Onan, Shelah, Perez, Gn 46:12
J military divisions will camp Nm 2:3
who belong to J encampment is Nm 2:9
Amminadab was over J divisions. Nm 10:14
J sons included Er and Onan, Nm 26:19
J descendants by their clans: Nm 26:20
These were J clans ⌊numbered⌋ by Nm 26:22
hear J cry and bring him to his Dt 33:7
lay between J descendants Jos 18:11
the portion of J descendants. Jos 19:1
the territory of J descendants, Jos 19:9
the share for J descendants was Jos 19:9
an inheritance within J portion. Jos 19:9
of Jether, commander of J army. 1Kg 2:32
Historical Record of J Kings. 1Kg 14:29
Historical Record of J Kings. 1Kg 15:7
anyone access to J King Asa. 1Kg 15:17
Historical Record of J Kings. 1Kg 15:23
the second year of J King Asa; 1Kg 15:25
In the third year of J King Asa, 1Kg 15:28
In the third year of J King Asa, 1Kg 15:33
twenty-sixth year of J King Asa, 1Kg 16:8
year of J King Asa, 1Kg 16:10
year of J King Asa, 1Kg 16:15
thirty-first year of J King Asa, 1Kg 16:23
thirty-eighth year of J King Asa; 1Kg 16:29
of Israel and J King Jehoshaphat 1Kg 22:29
Historical Record of J Kings. 1Kg 22:45
year of J King Jehoshaphat; 1Kg 22:51
second year of J King Jehoram 2Kg 1:17
year of J King Jehoshaphat; 2Kg 3:1
rebelled against J control and 2Kg 8:20
against J control today. 2Kg 8:22
Then J King Ahaziah son of 2Kg 8:29
his ancestors—J kings 2Kg 12:18
Historical Record of J Kings. 2Kg 12:19
year of J King Joash son 2Kg 13:1
year of J King Joash, 2Kg 13:10
war against J King Amaziah, 2Kg 13:12
Israel, and ⌊J men⌋ fled, each 2Kg 14:12
Israel captured J King Amaziah 2Kg 14:13
J King Amaziah son of Joash 2Kg 14:17
Historical Record of J Kings. 2Kg 14:18
year of J King Amaziah son 2Kg 14:23
Historical Record of J Kings. 2Kg 15:6
year of J King Azariah, 2Kg 15:8
year of J King Uzziah, 2Kg 15:13
year of J King Azariah, 2Kg 15:17
fiftieth year of J King Azariah, 2Kg 15:23
year of J King Azariah, 2Kg 15:27
Historical Record of J Kings. 2Kg 15:36
Historical Record of J Kings. 2Kg 16:19
the twelfth year of J King Ahaz, 2Kg 17:1
Historical Record of J Kings. 2Kg 20:20
Historical Record of J Kings. 2Kg 21:17
Historical Record of J Kings. 2Kg 21:25
Historical Record of J Kings. 2Kg 23:28
Historical Record of J Kings. 2Kg 24:5
the exile of J King Jehoiachin 2Kg 25:27
J sons: Er, Onan, and Shelah. 1Ch 2:3
Er, J firstborn, was evil in the 1Ch 2:3
J daughter-in-law Tamar bore him 1Ch 2:4
a leader of J descendants. 1Ch 2:10
J sons: Perez, Hezron, Carmi, 1Ch 4:1
the reigns of J King Jotham 1Ch 5:17
going or coming—to J King Asa. 2Ch 16:1
King Ahab asked J King 2Ch 18:3
of Israel and J King Jehoshaphat 2Ch 18:28
J King Jehoshaphat made an 2Ch 20:35
rebelled against J domination 2Ch 21:8
against J domination today 2Ch 21:10
Then J King Ahaziah son of 2Ch 22:6
Israel captured J King Amaziah 2Ch 25:23
J King Amaziah son of Joash 2Ch 25:25
the buildings that J Kings had 2Ch 34:11
in Jerusalem): J descendants: Neh 11:4
Some of J descendants lived in Neh 11:25
J harassment will end. Is 11:13
speak to all J cities that are Jr 26:2
Jerusalem, and in J cities—the Jr 32:44
city and the palaces of J kings, Jr 33:4
in J cities and Jerusalem's Jr 33:10
Jerusalem and J cities, Jr 33:13
and all of J remaining cities— Jr 34:7
were left among J fortified Jr 34:7
I will make J cities a Jr 34:22
those coming in from J cities Jr 36:9
that Jehoiakim, J king, had Jr 36:32
is what you will say to J king, Jr 37:7
in the palace of J king will be Jr 38:22
also⌋ slaughtered all J nobles. Jr 39:6
Jerusalem and all J cities; Jr 44:2
forth and burned in J cities and Jr 44:6
the evils of J kings, the evils Jr 44:9
our officials did in J cities Jr 44:17
incense you burned in J cities Jr 44:21
I handed over J King Zedekiah to Jr 44:30
fourth year of J King Jehoiakim Jr 46:2
none, and for J sins, but they Jr 50:20
the exile of J King Jehoiachin Jr 52:31

JUDAHITES *(7)*

ordered that the J be taught 2Sm 1:18
and expelled the J from Elath. 2Kg 16:6
above from the tribes of the J, 1Ch 6:65
From the J: 6,800 armed troops 1Ch 12:24
The J succeeded because they 2Ch 13:18
and the J captured 10,000 alive. 2Ch 25:12
the Israelites and J who lived 2Ch 31:6

JUDAISM *(3)*

my former way of life in J: Gl 1:13
and I advanced in J beyond many Gl 1:14
especially those from J. Ti 1:10

JUDAS *(33)*

(AKA BARSABBAS, JOSEPH, JUDE, JUSTUS, THADDAEUS)

the Zealot, and J Iscariot, who Mt 10:4
James, Joseph, Simon, and J? Mt 13:55
the man called J Iscariot— Mt 26:14
Then J, His betrayer, replied, Mt 26:25
still speaking, J, one of the Mt 26:47
J, His betrayer, seeing that Mt 27:3
J Iscariot, who also betrayed Mk 3:19
of James, Joses, J, and Simon? Mk 6:3
Then J Iscariot, one of the Mk 14:10
still speaking, J, one of the Mk 14:43
J the son of James, and Judas Lk 6:16
of James, and J Iscariot, who Lk 6:16
Satan entered J, called Iscariot Lk 22:3
Twelve named J was leading them Lk 22:47
said to him, "J, are you Lk 22:48
was referring to J, Simon Jn 6:71
His disciples, J Iscariot (who Jn 12:4
put it into the heart of J, Jn 13:2
gave it to J, Simon Iscariot's Jn 13:26
⌊J ate⌋ the piece of bread, Jn 13:27
Since J kept the money-bag, Jn 13:29
J (not Iscariot) said to Him, Jn 14:22
J, who betrayed Him, also knew Jn 18:2
So J took a company of soldiers Jn 18:3
J, who betrayed Him, was also Jn 18:5
the Zealot, and J the son of Ac 1:13
David spoke in advance about J, Ac 1:16
service that J left to go to his Ac 1:25
J the Galilean rose up in the Ac 5:37
to the house of J, and ask for a Ac 9:11
J, called Barsabbas, and Silas, Ac 15:22
we have sent J and Silas, Ac 15:27
Both J and Silas, who were also Ac 15:32

JUDE *(1)*
(AKA JUDAS)
J, a slave of Jesus Christ, and Jd 1

JUDEA *(41)*
(AKA JUDAH)
in Bethlehem of **J** in the days of Mt 2:1
Bethlehem of **J**," they told him Mt 2:5
ruling over **J** in place of his Mt 2:22
preaching in the Wilderness of **J** Mt 3:1
from⌋ Jerusalem, all **J**, and all Mt 3:5
Jerusalem, **J**, and beyond Mt 4:25
to the region of **J** across the Mt 19:1
then those in **J** must flee to the Mt 24:16
followed from Galilee, **J**, Mk 3:7
the region of **J** and across the Mk 10:1
then those in **J** must flee to the Mk 13:14
In the days of King Herod of **J**, Lk 1:5
the hill country of **J**. Lk 1:65
in Galilee, to **J**, to the city of Lk 2:4
Pilate was governor of **J**, Lk 3:1
every village of Galilee and **J**, Lk 5:17
people from all **J** and Jerusalem Lk 6:17
went throughout **J** and all the Lk 7:17
Then those in **J** must flee to the Lk 21:21
teaching throughout all **J**, Lk 23:5
He left **J** and went again to Jn 4:3
had come from **J** into Galilee, Jn 4:47
after He came from **J** to Galilee. Jn 4:54
to travel in **J** because the Jews Jn 7:1
here and go to **J** so Your Jn 7:3
"Let's go to **J** again." Jn 11:7
Jerusalem, in all **J** and Samaria, Ac 1:8
in **J** and Cappadocia, Ac 2:9
the land of **J** and Samaria. Ac 8:1
So the church throughout all **J**, Ac 9:31
took place throughout all **J**, Ac 10:37
who were throughout **J** heard that Ac 11:1
to the brothers who lived in **J**. Ac 11:29
went down from **J** to Caesarea Ac 12:19
came down from **J** and began to Ac 15:1
named Agabus came down from **J**. Ac 21:10
and in all the region of **J**, Ac 26:20
any letters about you from **J**; Ac 28:21
from the unbelievers in **J**, Rm 15:31
start by you on my journey to **J**. 2Co 1:16
in Christ Jesus that are in **J**, 1Th 2:14

JUDEAN *(30)*
country, in the **J** foothills, and Jos 9:1
the Negev, the **J** foothills, Jos 10:40
of Chinnereth, the **J** foothills, Jos 11:2
land of Goshen, the **J** foothills, Jos 11:16
of Israel with its **J** foothills— Jos 11:16
hill country, the **J** foothills, Jos 12:8
In the **J** foothills: Eshtaol, Jos 15:33
the Negev, and the **J** foothills. Jdg 1:9
as sycamore in the **J** foothills. 1Kg 10:27
His **J** wife gave birth to Jered 1Ch 4:18
as sycamore in the **J** foothills. 2Ch 1:15
as sycamore in the **J** foothills. 2Ch 9:27
cities of the **J** foothills and 2Ch 28:18
Some of the **J** divisions of Neh 11:36
and from the **J** foothills, Jr 17:26
the cities of the **J** foothills, Jr 32:44
the cities of the **J** foothills, Jr 33:13
no one enslave his **J** brother. Jr 34:9
this⌋ in the sight of the **J** men Jr 43:9
slaughtered the **J** commanders. Jr 52:10
a man among the **J** exiles who can Dn 2:25
one of the **J** exiles that my Dn 5:13
Daniel, one of the **J** exiles, has Dn 6:13
⌊those from⌋ the **J** foothills Ob 19
region and the **J** foothills were Zch 7:7
The whole **J** countryside and all Mk 1:5
from Arimathea, a **J** town, and Lk 23:51
went to the **J** countryside, Jn 3:22
He did in both the **J** country and Ac 10:39
unknown to the **J** churches in Gl 1:22

JUDEANS *(13)*
not become as numerous as the **J**. 1Ch 4:27
For the **J** have done what is evil Jr 7:30
and all the **J** sitting in the Jr 32:12
Israelites and **J** have done Jr 32:30
the Israelites and **J** have done Jr 32:32
of all the **J** who are coming Jr 36:6
about the **J** who have deserted Jr 38:19
When all the **J** in Moab and among Jr 40:11
down all the **J** who were with Jr 41:3
all you **J** who live in the land Jr 44:26
Israelites and **J** will come Jr 50:4
Israelites and **J** alike have been Jr 50:33
the **J** and the Israelites will Hs 1:11

JUDGE *(170)*
I will **j** the nation they serve, Gn 15:14
the LORD **j** between me and you. Gn 16:5
Won't the **J** of all the earth do Gn 18:25
but he's acting like a **j**! Gn 19:9
father—will **j** between us." Gn 31:53
Dan will **j** his people as one of Gn 49:16
you a leader and **j** over us?" Ex 2:14
LORD take note of you and **j**," Ex 5:21
Moses sat down to **j** the people, Ex 18:13
Why are you alone sitting as **j**, Ex 18:14
They should **j** the people at all Ex 18:22
case but **j** every minor case Ex 18:22
case they would **j** themselves. Ex 18:26
j your neighbor fairly. Lv 19:15
assembly is to **j** between the Nm 35:24
and **j** rightly between a man and Dt 1:16
They are to **j** the people with Dt 16:18
and to the **j** who presides at Dt 17:9
the LORD your God or to the **j**, Dt 17:12
the **j** will make him lie down and Dt 25:2
LORD raised up a **j** for the Jdg 2:18
while the **j** was still alive. Jdg 2:18
Whenever the **j** died, the Jdg 2:19
Shamgar son of Anath ⌊became **j**⌋. Jdg 3:31
of Dodo ⌊became **j**⌋ and began to Jdg 10:1
LORD ⌊who is⌋ the **J** decide today Jdg 11:27
The LORD will **j** the ends of the 1Sm 2:10
I am going to **j** his family 1Sm 3:13
at Mizpah as ⌊their⌋ **j**. 1Sm 7:6
Mizpah and would **j** Israel at all 1Sm 7:16
a king to **j** us the same as 1Sm 8:5
Give us a king to **j** us," Samuel 1Sm 8:6
king will **j** us, go out before 1Sm 8:20
so I may **j** you before the LORD 1Sm 12:7
May the LORD **j** between you and 1Sm 24:12
May the LORD be **j** and decide 1Sm 24:15
would appoint me **j** in the land. 2Sm 15:4
obedient heart to **j** Your people 1Kg 3:9
who is able to **j** this great 1Kg 3:9
of the Throne where he would **j**— 1Kg 7:7
May You **j** Your servants, 1Kg 8:32
our ancestors look on it and **j**." 1Ch 12:17
for He is coming to **j** the earth. 1Ch 16:33
for who can **j** this great people 2Ch 1:10
that you may **j** My people over 2Ch 1:11
May You **j** Your servants, 2Ch 6:23
you do not **j** for man, but for 2Ch 19:6
Our God, will You not **j** them? 2Ch 20:12
and judges to **j** all the people Ezr 7:25
I could only beg my **j** for mercy. Jb 9:15
There is no one to **j** between us, Jb 9:33
Can He **j** through thick darkness? Jb 22:13
would escape from my **J** forever. Jb 23:7
I do when God stands up ⌊to **j**⌋? Jb 31:14
elderly who understand how to **j**. Jb 32:9
Let us **j** for ourselves what is Jb 34:4
is a righteous **j**, and a God who Ps 7:11
on Your throne as a righteous **j**. Ps 9:4
earth in order to **j** His people. Ps 50:4
righteousness, for God is the **j**. Ps 50:6
You are blameless when You **j**. Ps 51:4
Do you **j** people fairly? Ps 58:1
for You **j** the peoples with Ps 67:4
He will **j** Your people with Ps 72:2
choose a time, I will **j** fairly. Ps 75:2
for God is the **j**: He brings down Ps 75:7
God rose up to **j** and to save all Ps 76:9
long will you **j** unjustly and Ps 82:2
Rise up, God, **j** the earth, for Ps 82:8
Rise up, **J** of the earth; Ps 94:2
for He is coming to **j** the earth. Ps 96:13
He will **j** the world with Ps 96:13
for He is coming to **j** the earth. Ps 98:9
He will **j** the world righteously Ps 98:9
will **j** the nations, heaping up Ps 110:6
For the LORD will **j** His people Ps 135:14
on a throne to **j** sifts out all Pr 20:8
Speak up, **j** righteously, and Pr 31:9
God will **j** the righteous and the Ec 3:17
and warrior, the **j** and prophet, Is 3:2
case and stands to **j** the people. Is 3:13
please **j** between Me and My Is 5:3
He will not **j** by what He sees Is 11:3
but He will **j** the poor Is 11:4
A **j** who seeks what is right and Is 16:5
the LORD is our **J**, the LORD is Is 33:22
will certainly **j** you because you Jr 2:35
the wrong done to me; **j** my case. Lm 3:59
against you and **j** you according Ezk 7:3
against you and **j** you according Ezk 7:8
and I will **j** them by their own Ezk 7:27
and I will **j** you at the border Ezk 11:10
I will **j** you at the border of Ezk 11:11
will **j** you the way adulteresses Ezk 16:38
I will **j** each one of you Ezk 18:30
I will **j** you in the place where Ezk 21:30
and they will **j** you by their own Ezk 23:24
righteous men will **j** them the Ezk 23:45
I will **j** you according to your Ezk 24:14
will **j** each of you according to Ezk 33:20
am going to **j** between one sheep Ezk 34:17
I Myself will **j** between the fat Ezk 34:20
I will **j** between one sheep and Ezk 34:22
known among them when I **j** you. Ezk 35:11
I will sit down to **j** all the Jl 3:12
will cut off the **j** from the land Am 2:3
are striking the **j** of Israel Mc 5:1
and the **j** demand a bribe; Mc 7:3
will hand you over to the **j**, Mt 5:25
the judge, the **j** to the officer, Mt 5:25
Do not **j**, so that you won't be Mt 7:1
Do not **j**, and you will not be Lk 6:37
appointed Me a **j** or arbitrator Lk 12:14
Why don't you **j** for yourselves Lk 12:57
he won't drag you before the **j**, Lk 12:58
the **j** hand you over to the Lk 12:58
There was a **j** in one town who Lk 18:2
to what the unjust **j** says. Lk 18:6
'I will **j** you by what you have Lk 19:22
world that He might **j** the world, Jn 3:17
I **j** only as I hear, and My Jn 5:30
rather **j** according to righteous Jn 7:24
law doesn't **j** a man before it Jn 7:51
You **j** by human standards. Jn 8:15
by human standards. I **j** no one. Jn 8:15
And if I do **j**, My judgment is Jn 8:16
Father who sent Me ⌊**j** together⌋. Jn 8:16
to say and to **j** about you, Jn 8:26
keep them, I do not **j** him; Jn 12:47
did not come to **j** the world but Jn 12:47
My sayings has this as his **j**: Jn 12:48
spoken will **j** him on the last Jn 12:48
yourselves and **j** Him according Jn 18:31
I will **j** the nation that they Ac 7:7
you a ruler and a **j** over us? Ac 7:27
appointed you a ruler and a **j**? Ac 7:35
by God to be the **J** of the living Ac 10:42
which He is going to **j** the world Ac 17:31
want to be a **j** of such things." Ac 18:15
and wanted to **j** him according to Ac 24:6
you have been a **j** of this nation Ac 24:10
For when you **j** another, you Rm 2:1
since you, the **j**, do the same Rm 2:1
will **j** you who are a lawbreaker Rm 2:27
words and triumph when You **j**. Rm 3:4
how will God **j** the world? Rm 3:6
Therefore don't **j** anything 1Co 4:5
what is it to me to **j** outsiders? 1Co 5:12
Do you not **j** those who are 1Co 5:12
the saints will **j** the world? 1Co 6:2
you unworthy to **j** the smallest 1Co 6:2
not know that we will **j** angels— 1Co 6:3
no standing in the church to **j**? 1Co 6:4
J for yourselves what I say. 1Co 10:15
J for yourselves: Is it proper 1Co 11:13
let anyone **j** you in regard to Col 2:16
who is going to **j** the living and 2Tm 4:1
the righteous **J**, will give me 2Tm 4:8
it is a **j** of the ideas and Heb 4:12
The Lord will **j** His people. Heb 10:30
to God who is the **j** of all, Heb 12:23
because God will **j** immoral Heb 13:4
if you **j** the law, you are not Jms 4:11
not a doer of the law but a **j**. Jms 4:11
one lawgiver and **j** who is able Jms 4:12
who are you to **j** your neighbor? Jms 4:12
Look, the **j** stands at the door! Jms 5:9
who stands ready to **j** the living 1Pt 4:5
long until You **j** and avenge our Rv 6:10
who were given authority to **j**. Rv 20:4

JUDGE'S *(7)*
he was sitting on the **j** bench, Mt 27:19

sat down on the **j** bench in a Jn 19:13
and brought him to the **j** bench. Ac 18:12
he drove them from the **j** bench. Ac 18:16
him in front of the **j** bench. Ac 18:17
day, seated at the **j** bench, he Ac 25:6
day I sat at the **j** bench and Ac 25:17

JUDGED *(47)*

They **j** the people at all times; Ex 18:26
was on him, and he **j** Israel. Jdg 3:10
for a man is **j** by his strength." Jdg 8:21
Tola **j** Israel 23 years, and when Jdg 10:2
who **j** Israel 22 years. Jdg 10:3
Jephthah **j** Israel six years, Jdg 12:7
from Bethlehem, **j** Israel after Jdg 12:8
Ibzan **j** Israel seven years, Jdg 12:9
was from Zebulun, **j** Israel after Jdg 12:11
He **j** Israel 10 years, Jdg 12:11
who was from Pirathon, **j** Israel. Jdg 12:13
Abdon **j** Israel eight years, Jdg 12:14
And he **j** Israel 20 years in the Jdg 15:20
So he **j** Israel 20 years. Jdg 16:31
Eli had **j** Israel 40 years. 1Sm 4:18
Samuel **j** Israel throughout his 1Sm 7:15
was there, he **j** Israel there, 1Sm 7:17
the judges who **j** Israel through 2Kg 23:22
the nations be **j** in Your Ps 9:19
to be condemned when he is **j**. Ps 37:33
When he is **j**, let him be found Ps 109:7
and those who shed blood are **j**. Ezk 16:38
and those who shed blood are **j**, Ezk 23:45
I **j** them according to their Ezk 36:19
judge, so that you won't be **j**. Mt 7:1
you use, you will be **j**, and with Mt 7:2
judge, and you will not be **j**. Lk 6:37
"You have **j** correctly," He told Lk 7:43
who believes in Him is not **j**, Jn 3:18
does not believe is already **j**, Jn 3:18
ruler of this world has been **j**. Jn 16:11
I am being **j** because of the hope Ac 23:6
'Today I am being **j** before you Ac 24:21
the law will be **j** by the law. Rm 2:12
am I also still **j** as a sinner? Rm 3:7
And if the world is **j** by you, 1Co 6:2
why is my freedom **j** by another 1Co 10:29
ourselves, we would not be **j**, 1Co 11:31
but when we are **j**, we are 1Co 11:32
by all and is **j** by all. 1Co 14:24
those who will be **j** by the law Jms 2:12
so that you will not be **j**. Jms 5:9
they might be **j** by men in the 1Pt 4:6
has come for the dead to be **j**, Rv 11:18
because He has **j** the notorious Rv 19:2
and the dead were **j** according to Rv 20:12
all were **j** according to their Rv 20:13

JUDGES *(67)*

him to the **j** and then bring Ex 21:6
himself to the **j** to determine Ex 22:8
parties is to come before the **j**. Ex 22:9
The one the **j** condemn must repay Ex 22:9
So Moses told Israel's **j**, Nm 25:5
I commanded your **j** at that time: Dt 1:16
Appoint **j** and officials for your Dt 16:18
the priests and **j** in authority Dt 19:17
The **j** are to make a careful Dt 19:18
your elders and **j** must come out Dt 21:2
and the **j** will hear their case. Dt 25:1
officers, and **j**, stood on either Jos 8:33
leaders, **j**, and officers, Jos 23:2
leaders, **j**, and officers, Jos 24:1
LORD raised up **j**, who saved them Jdg 2:16
they did not listen to their **j**. Jdg 2:17
the time of the **j**, there was a Ru 1:1
his sons as **j** over Israel. 1Sm 8:1
They were **j** in Beer-sheba. 1Sm 8:2
the day I ordered **j** to be over 2Sm 7:11
the time of the **j** who judged 2Kg 23:22
to even one of the **j** of Israel, 1Ch 17:6
the day I ordered **j** to be over 1Ch 17:10
6,000 are to be officers and **j**, 1Ch 23:4
as officers and **j** over Israel. 1Ch 26:29
hundreds, to the **j**, and to every 2Ch 1:2
He appointed **j** in all the 2Ch 19:5
he said to the **j**, "Consider what 2Ch 19:6
the **j** and magistrates from Ezr 4:9
magistrates and **j** to judge all Ezr 7:25
the elders and **j** of each town, Ezr 10:14
blindfolds its **j**. If it isn't He Jb 9:24
barefoot and makes **j** go mad. Jb 12:17
since He **j** the exalted ones? Jb 21:22
For He **j** the nations with these; Jb 36:31
instruction, you **j** of the earth. Ps 2:10
The LORD **j** the peoples; Ps 7:8
He **j** the world with Ps 9:8
There is a God who **j** on earth!" Ps 58:11
assembly; He **j** among the gods: Ps 82:1
He **j** the peoples fairly." Ps 96:10
princes and all **j** of the earth, Ps 148:11
do nobles ⌊and⌋ all righteous **j**. Pr 8:16
A king who **j** the poor with Pr 29:14
restore your **j** to what they once Is 1:26
and makes the **j** of the earth to Is 40:23
of Hosts, who **j** righteously, who Jr 11:20
will officiate as **j** and decide Ezk 44:24
treasurers, **j**, magistrates, and Dn 3:2
treasurers, **j**, magistrates, and Dn 3:3
her **j** are wolves of the night, Zph 3:3
this reason they will be your **j**. Mt 12:27
this reason they will be your **j**. Lk 11:19
j no one but has given all Jn 5:22
the One who seeks it also **j**. Jn 8:50
He gave them **j** until Samuel the Ac 13:20
of you who **j** is without excuse Rm 2:1
of you who **j** those who do such Rm 2:3
day when God **j** what people have Rm 2:16
God **j** outsiders. Put away the 1Co 5:13
and become **j** with evil thoughts? Jms 2:4
a brother or **j** his brother Jms 4:11
the law and **j** the law. Jms 4:11
the One who **j** impartially based 1Pt 1:17
Himself to the One who **j** justly. 1Pt 2:23
Lord God who **j** her is mighty. Rv 18:8
He **j** and makes war. Rv 19:11

JUDGING *(5)*

was **j** Israel at that time. Jdg 4:4
j the 12 tribes of Israel. Mt 19:28
sit on thrones **j** the 12 tribes Lk 22:30
Stop **j** according to outward Jn 7:24
sitting there **j** me according to Ac 23:3

JUDGMENT *(137)*

arm and great acts of **j**. Ex 6:6
of Egypt by great acts of **j**. Ex 7:4
act unjustly when rendering **j**. Lv 19:15
had executed **j** against their Nm 33:4
partiality when rendering **j**; Dt 1:17
by anyone, for **j** belongs to God. Dt 1:17
the people with righteous **j**. Dt 16:18
and My hand takes hold of **j**, Dt 32:41
Israelites went up to her for **j**. Jdg 4:5
your **j** and verdict here ⌊and Jdg 20:7
LORD has pronounced ⌊**j**⌋ on me, Ru 1:21
heard about the **j** the king had 1Kg 3:28
he would judge—the Hall of **J**. 1Kg 7:7
is with you in the matter of **j**. 2Ch 19:6
us—sword or **j**, pestilence or 2Ch 20:9
Jehu executed **j** on the house 2Ch 22:8
So they executed **j** on Joash. 2Ch 24:24
let a fair **j** be executed against Ezr 7:26
takes away the elders' good **j**. Jb 12:20
You bring me into **j** against You? Jb 14:3
that you may know there is a **j**. Jb 19:29
not reserve times for **j**? Jb 24:1
with the **j** due the wicked; Jb 36:17
j and justice have seized you. Jb 36:17
wicked will not survive the **j**, Ps 1:5
You have ordained a **j**. Ps 7:6
established His throne for **j**. Ps 9:7
executes **j** on the peoples with Ps 9:8
From heaven You pronounced **j**. Ps 76:8
for Israel, a **j** of the God of Ps 81:4
Teach me good **j** and discernment, Ps 119:66
will You execute **j** on my Ps 119:84
There, thrones for **j** are placed, Ps 122:5
not bring Your servant into **j**, Ps 143:2
out the **j** decreed against Ps 149:9
his mouth should not err in **j**. Pr 16:10
he rebels against all sound **j**. Pr 18:1
good to show partiality in **j**. Pr 24:23
at the place of **j** and there is Ec 3:16
things God will bring you to **j**. Ec 11:9
God will bring every act to **j**, Ec 12:14
by a spirit of **j** and a spirit of Is 4:4
will bring **j** on Leviathan, Is 27:1
to the one who sits in **j**, Is 28:6
by charging the poor during a **j**. Is 32:7
because of oppression and **j**; Is 53:8
will execute **j** on all flesh with Is 66:16
four kinds ⌊of **j**⌋ for them"— Jr 15:3
He enters into **j** with all flesh. Jr 25:31
J has come to the land of the Jr 48:21
The **j** on Moab ends here. Jr 48:47
for her **j** extends to the sky and Jr 51:9
and execute **j** on him there for Ezk 17:20
Will you pass **j** against them, Ezk 20:4
will you pass **j**, son of man? Ezk 20:4
and enter into **j** with you there Ezk 20:35
I entered into **j** with your Ezk 20:36
I will enter into **j** with you." Ezk 20:36
I have given the **j** to Him. Ezk 21:27
son of man, will you pass **j**? Ezk 22:2
Will you pass **j** against the city Ezk 22:2
her time of **j** has come and who Ezk 22:3
have brought your ⌊**j**⌋ days near Ezk 22:4
they executed **j** against her, Ezk 23:10
I will delegate **j** to them, Ezk 23:24
will you pass **j** against Oholah Ezk 23:36
I will execute **j** on him with Ezk 38:22
will see the **j** I have executed Ezk 39:21
arrived and a **j** was given in Dn 7:22
⌊The same **j**⌋ will happen to both Hs 4:9
For the **j** applies to you because Hs 5:1
crushed in **j**, for he is Hs 5:11
My **j** strikes like lightning. Hs 6:5
enter into **j** with them there Jl 3:2
GOD was calling for a **j** by fire. Am 7:4
You appointed them to execute **j**; Hab 1:12
come to you in **j**, and I will be Mal 3:5
murders will be subject to **j**. Mt 5:21
brother will be subject to **j**. Mt 5:22
For with the **j** you use, you will Mt 7:2
on the day of **j** for the land of Mt 10:15
on the day of **j** than for you. Mt 11:22
on the day of **j** than for you." Mt 11:24
on the day of **j** people will have Mt 12:36
stand up at the **j** with this Mt 12:41
will rise up at the **j** with this Mt 12:42
and Sidon at the **j** than for you. Lk 10:14
rise up at the **j** with the men Lk 11:31
will rise up at the **j** with this Lk 11:32
This, then, is the **j**: Jn 3:19
but has given all **j** to the Son, Jn 5:22
not come under **j** but has passed Jn 5:24
granted Him the right to pass **j**, Jn 5:27
to the resurrection of **j**. Jn 5:29
I hear, and My **j** is righteous, Jn 5:30
judge according to righteous **j**." Jn 7:24
I do judge, My **j** is true, Jn 8:16
I came into this world for **j**, Jn 9:39
Now is the **j** of this world. Jn 12:31
about sin, righteousness, and **j**: Jn 16:8
and about **j**, because the ruler Jn 16:11
Therefore, in my **j**, we should Ac 15:19
and the **j** to come, Felix became Ac 24:25
and asked for a **j** against him. Ac 25:15
words of truth and good **j**. Ac 26:25
know that God's **j** on those who Rm 2:2
that you will escape God's **j**? Rm 2:3
God's righteous **j** is revealed. Rm 2:5
may become subject to God's **j**. Rm 3:19
because from one sin came the **j**, Rm 5:16
it will bring **j** on themselves. Rm 13:2
stand before the **j** seat of God. Rm 14:10
eats and drinks **j** on himself. 1Co 11:29
come together and not cause **j**. 1Co 11:34
before the **j** seat of Christ, 2Co 5:10
God's righteous **j** that you will 2Th 1:5
before them to **j**, but ⌊the sins⌋ 1Tm 5:24
one of power, love, and sound **j**. 2Tm 1:7
of the dead, and eternal **j**. Heb 6:2
die once—and after this, **j**— Heb 9:27
a terrifying expectation of **j**, Heb 10:27
j is without mercy to the one Jms 2:13
Mercy triumphs over **j**. Jms 2:13
we will receive a stricter **j**; Jms 3:1
so that you won't fall under **j**. Jms 5:12
has come for **j** to begin with 1Pt 4:17
in chains of darkness until **j**; 2Pt 2:4
punishment until the day of **j**, 2Pt 2:9
the day of **j** and destruction 2Pt 3:7
have confidence in the day of **j**; 1Jn 4:17
designated for this **j** long ago, Jd 4
for the **j** of the great day Jd 6
to execute **j** on all, and to Jd 15
the hour of His **j** has come. Rv 14:7
show you the **j** of the notorious Rv 17:1

a single hour your **j** has come. Rv 18:10
God has executed your **j** on her! Rv 18:20

JUDGMENTS *(57)*
I will execute **j** against all the Ex 12:12
j, and testimonies. 1Kg 2:3
ordinances, and **j**, which He 1Kg 8:58
statutes and My **j** as his father 1Kg 11:33
and the **j** He has pronounced, 1Ch 16:12
His **j** ⌊govern⌋ the whole earth. 1Ch 16:14
the LORD's **j** and for ⌊settling⌋ 2Ch 19:8
statutes, or **j**—you are to warn 2Ch 19:10
all the law, statutes, and **j**." 2Ch 33:8
Your lofty **j** are beyond his Ps 10:5
Your **j**, like the deepest sea. Ps 36:6
Judah rejoice because of Your **j**. Ps 48:11
Judah rejoice because of Your **j**, Ps 97:8
and the **j** He has pronounced, Ps 105:5
His **j** ⌊govern⌋ the whole earth. Ps 105:7
when I learn Your righteous **j**. Ps 119:7
all the **j** from Your mouth Ps 119:13
overcome by longing for Your **j**. Ps 119:20
indeed, Your **j** are good. Ps 119:39
my mouth, for I hope in Your **j**. Ps 119:43
I remember Your **j** from long ago Ps 119:52
thank You for Your righteous **j**. Ps 119:62
that Your **j** are just and that Ps 119:75
today in accordance with Your **j**, Ps 119:91
I have not turned from Your **j**, Ps 119:102
sworn to keep Your righteous **j**. Ps 119:106
of praise, and teach me Your **j**. Ps 119:108
in awe of You; I fear Your **j**. Ps 119:120
LORD, and Your **j** are just. Ps 119:137
me life, according to Your **j**. Ps 119:156
Your righteous **j** endure forever. Ps 119:160
a day for Your righteous **j**. Ps 119:164
may Your **j** help me. Ps 119:175
His statutes and **j** to Israel. Ps 147:19
they do not know ⌊His⌋ **j**. Ps 147:20
J are prepared for mockers, Pr 19:29
for You in the path of Your **j**. Is 26:8
for when Your **j** are ⌊in⌋ the Is 26:9
they stumble in ⌊their⌋ **j**. Is 28:7
They ask Me for righteous **j**; Is 58:2
pronounce My **j** against them for Jr 1:16
also pronounce **j** against them." Jr 4:12
and I will execute **j** within you Ezk 5:8
I will execute **j** against you and Ezk 5:10
you when I execute **j** against you Ezk 5:15
I will execute **j** against you. Ezk 11:9
four devastating **j** against Ezk 14:21
houses and execute **j** against you Ezk 16:41
I will execute **j** against Moab, Ezk 25:11
LORD when I execute **j** against Ezk 28:22
when I execute **j** against all Ezk 28:26
Zoan, and execute **j** on Thebes. Ezk 30:14
I will execute **j** against Egypt, Ezk 30:19
and peaceful **j** in your gates. Zch 8:16
His **j** and untraceable Rm 11:33
true and righteous are Your **j**. Rv 16:7
because His **j** are true and Rv 19:2

JUDICIAL *(1)*
pay according to **j** assessment. Ex 21:22

JUDITH *(1)*
as his wives **J** daughter of Beeri Gn 26:34

JUG *(20)*
lower your water **j** so that I may Gn 24:14
coming with a **j** on her shoulder. Gn 24:15
filled her **j**, and came up. Gn 24:16
a little water from your **j**." Gn 24:17
quickly lowered her **j** to her Gn 24:18
emptied her **j** into the trough Gn 24:20
a little water from your **j**, Gn 24:43
with her **j** on her shoulder Gn 24:45
lowered her **j** from her ⌊shoulder Gn 24:46
and the water **j** by his head, 1Sm 26:11
and the water **j** by Saul's head, 1Sm 26:12
spear and water **j** that were by 1Sm 26:16
jar and a bit of oil in the **j**. 1Kg 17:12
and the oil **j** will not run dry 1Kg 17:14
and the oil **j** did not run dry, 1Kg 17:16
hot stones and a **j** of water. 1Kg 19:6
Go, buy a potter's clay **j**. Jr 19:1
to shatter the **j** in the presence Jr 19:10
a water **j** will meet you. Mk 14:13
a water **j** will meet you. Lk 22:10

JUGS *(1)*
of cups, **j**, copper utensils Mk 7:4

JUICE *(2)*
drink any grape **j** or eat fresh Nm 6:3
to drink from my pomegranate **j**. Sg 8:2

JULIA *(1)*
Philologus and **J**, Nereus and his Rm 16:15

JULIUS *(2)*
to a centurion named **J**, Ac 27:1
and **J** treated Paul kindly and Ac 27:3

JUMP *(2)*
out and playfully **j** like calves Mal 4:2
could swim to **j** overboard first Ac 27:43

JUMPED *(4)*
Nebuchadnezzar **j** up in alarm. Dn 3:24
off his coat, **j** up, and came to Mk 10:50
he **j** up, stood, and started to Ac 3:8
And he **j** up and started to walk Ac 14:10

JUNIA *(1)*
Andronicus and **J**, my fellow Rm 16:7

JUNIPER *(2)*
will be like a **j** in the Arabah; Jr 17:6
Be like a **j** bush in the Jr 48:6

JURISDICTION *(1)*
that He was under Herod's **j**, Lk 23:7

JUSHAB-HESED *(1)*
Berechiah, Hasadiah, and **J**. 1Ch 3:20

JUST *(426)*
j as God had commanded him. Gn 7:9
entered **j** as God had commanded Gn 7:16
that very day, **j** as God had said Gn 17:23
by doing what is right and **j**. Gn 18:19
of all the earth do what is **j**?" Gn 18:25
j as the LORD has spoken." Gn 24:51
j as we have not harmed you but Gn 26:29
J obey me and go get them for me. Gn 27:13
J because you're my relative, Gn 29:15
Jacob did **j** that. He finished Gn 29:28
J give the girl to be my wife!" Gn 34:12
j three days Pharaoh will lift Gn 40:13
j three days Pharaoh will lift Gn 40:19
j as Joseph had explained to Gn 40:22
It turned out **j** the way he Gn 41:13
It is **j** as I told Pharaoh: Gn 41:28
of famine began, **j** as Joseph had Gn 41:54
belong to me **j** as Reuben and Gn 48:5
j as ⌊you did⌋ when straw was Ex 5:13
they did **j** as the LORD commanded Ex 7:6
Pharaoh and did **j** as the LORD Ex 7:10
and Aaron did **j** as the LORD had Ex 7:20
they did **j** as the LORD had Ex 12:28
they did **j** as the LORD had Ex 12:50
not kill the innocent and the **j**, Ex 23:7
are to make it **j** as it was shown Ex 27:8
j as a man speaks with his Ex 33:11
j as the LORD had commanded him. Ex 34:4
j as the LORD had commanded Ex 39:1
j as the LORD had commanded Ex 39:5
j as the LORD had commanded Ex 39:7
⌊They did⌋ **j** as the LORD had Ex 39:21
j as the LORD had commanded Ex 39:26
⌊They did⌋ **j** as the LORD had Ex 39:29
j as the LORD had commanded Ex 39:31
did everything **j** as the LORD had Ex 39:32
They had done **j** as the LORD Ex 39:43
Anoint them **j** as you anointed Ex 40:15
did everything **j** as the LORD had Ex 40:16
j as the LORD had commanded Ex 40:19
j as the LORD had commanded him. Ex 40:21
j as the LORD had commanded him. Ex 40:23
j as the LORD had commanded him. Ex 40:25
j as the LORD had commanded him. Ex 40:27
j as the LORD had commanded him. Ex 40:29
j as the LORD had commanded Ex 40:32
j as the fat is removed from the Lv 4:10
offer this bull **j** as he did with Lv 4:20
camp and burn it **j** as he burned Lv 4:21
all its fat **j** as the fat is Lv 4:31
remove all its fat **j** as the fat Lv 4:35
price will stand **j** as the priest Lv 27:14
j as the LORD commanded Moses. Nm 1:19
did everything **j** as the LORD had Nm 1:54
are to move out **j** as they camp, Nm 2:17
j as the LORD had commanded Nm 2:33
j as the LORD commanded Moses. Nm 3:51
the lampstand **j** as the LORD had Nm 8:3
be magnified **j** as You have Nm 14:17
j as You have forgiven them from Nm 14:19
offer it **j** like a contribution Nm 15:20
J as he finished speaking all Nm 16:31
j as the LORD commanded him Nm 16:40
LORD's presence **j** as He had Nm 20:9
servants will do **j** as my lord Nm 32:25
j as the LORD our God had Dt 1:19
j as you saw Him do for you in Dt 1:30
up and fight **j** as the LORD our Dt 1:41
j as Israel did in the land of Dt 2:12
This was **j** as He had done for Dt 2:22
j as the descendants of Esau who Dt 2:29
disciplining you **j** as a man Dt 8:5
This case is **j** like one in which Dt 22:26
J as the LORD was glad to cause Dt 28:63
j like the fall of Sodom and Dt 29:23
all His ways are entirely **j**. Dt 32:4
new gods that had **j** arrived, Dt 32:17
j as your brother Aaron died on Dt 32:50
foot treads, **j** as I promised Jos 1:3
be with you, **j** as I was with Jos 1:5
j as we obeyed Moses in Jos 1:17
will be with you **j** as I was with Jos 3:7
Israelites did **j** as Joshua had Jos 4:8
j as the LORD had told Joshua. Jos 4:8
j as the LORD your God did to Jos 4:23
are with her, **j** as you promised Jos 6:22
j as Moses the LORD's servant Jos 8:31
j as he had done to Libnah. Jos 10:32
j as he had done to Lachish. Jos 10:35
J as he had done at Eglon, Jos 10:37
J as the LORD had commanded His Jos 11:15
j as the LORD had commanded Jos 11:20
j as Moses the LORD's servant Jos 13:8
its inheritance, **j** as He had Jos 13:14
j as He had promised them. Jos 13:33
You will not have **j** one lot, Jos 17:17
brothers rest, **j** as He promised Jos 22:4
Hebron to Caleb, **j** as Moses had Jdg 1:20
j as He had promised and sworn Jdg 2:15
of Penuel answered **j** as the men Jdg 8:8
to me today has **j** come back!" Jdg 13:10
Strengthen me, God, **j** once more. Jdg 16:28
j as they were in the first Jdg 20:39
her severely **j** to provoke her, 1Sm 1:6
the Hebrews **j** like they served 1Sm 4:9
it was **j** something that happened 1Sm 6:9
he **j** now came to the city, 1Sm 9:12
got up early, and **j** before dawn, 1Sm 9:26
J then Saul was coming in from 1Sm 11:5
J as he finished offering the 1Sm 13:10
J look at how I have renewed 1Sm 14:29
J who is this uncircumcised 1Sm 17:26
David. "It was **j** a question." 1Sm 17:29
You're **j** a youth, and he's been 1Sm 17:33
him because he was **j** a youth, 1Sm 17:42
j as He was with my father. 1Sm 20:13
David had **j** said, "I guarded 1Sm 25:21
him into the ground **j** once. 1Sm 26:8
J as I considered your life 1Sm 26:24
J then David's soldiers and Joab 2Sm 3:22
ate at David's table **j** like one 2Sm 9:11
j as his father showed kindness 2Sm 10:2
J because David has sent men 2Sm 10:3
Now she had **j** been purifying 2Sm 11:4
Haven't you **j** come from a 2Sm 11:10
asked him, "What did you **j** do? 2Sm 12:21
Your servant has **j** hired 2Sm 13:24
did to Amnon **j** as Absalom had 2Sm 13:29
J as he finished speaking, 2Sm 13:36
Jerusalem **j** as Absalom was 2Sm 15:37
house of Saul was **j** coming out. 2Sm 16:5
I **j** saw Absalom hanging in an 2Sm 18:10
"You **j** saw ⌊him⌋!" Joab 2Sm 18:11
J then the Cushite came and said, 2Sm 18:31
j as the LORD had commanded. 2Sm 24:19
j as I swore to you by the LORD 1Kg 1:30
J as the LORD was with my lord 1Kg 1:37
So now I have **j** one request of 1Kg 2:16
I have **j** one small request of 1Kg 2:20
said to him, "Do **j** as he says. 1Kg 2:31
that Joab shed without **j** cause. 1Kg 2:31
Yet I am **j** a youth with no 1Kg 3:7
commandments **j** as your father 1Kg 3:14
j the two of us were there. 1Kg 3:18
a second time **j** as He had 1Kg 9:2
lasting dynasty **j** as I built for 1Kg 11:38
J now, I am gathering a couple 1Kg 17:12
answered, "**J** as you say, my 1Kg 20:4

God of Israel **j** as his father 1Kg 22:53
neighbors. Do not get **j** a few. 2Kg 4:3
'I have **j** now discovered that 2Kg 5:22
Why **j** sit here until we die? 2Kg 7:3
j as the man of God had 2Kg 7:17
the LORD's sight **j** as his father 2Kg 15:3
the LORD's sight **j** as his father 2Kg 15:34
the high places **j** like those 2Kg 17:11
from His presence **j** as He had 2Kg 17:23
LORD's sight **j** as his ancestor 2Kg 18:3
My sight **j** as I have removed 2Kg 23:27
LORD's sight **j** as his ancestors 2Kg 23:32
LORD's sight **j** as his ancestors 2Kg 23:37
LORD's sanctuary, **j** as God had 2Kg 24:13
LORD's sight **j** as Jehoiakim had 2Kg 24:19
J because David has sent men 1Ch 19:3
LORD's temple, **j** as their 1Ch 26:12
j as the king had ordered, 2Ch 10:12
j as the LORD promised 2Ch 23:3
LORD's sight **j** as his ancestor 2Ch 29:2
J like the national gods of the 2Ch 32:17
the LORD's sight **j** as his father 2Ch 33:22
our children are ⌊**j**⌋ like our Neh 5:5
make booths, **j** as it is written. Neh 8:15
of Jerusalem **j** before the Neh 13:19
Now Haman was **j** entering the Est 6:4
Hurry, and do **j** as you proposed. Est 6:10
J as the king returned from the Est 7:8
overpower them, **j** the opposite Est 9:1
their proper time **j** as Mordecai Est 9:31
them and **j** as they had Est 9:31
to destroy him without **j** cause." Jb 2:3
man and God **j** as a man ⌊pleads⌋ Jb 16:21
my **j** decisions were like a robe Jb 29:14
I am **j** like you before God; Jb 33:6
you think it is **j** when you say, Jb 35:2
J listen to His thunderous voice Jb 37:2
For You have upheld my **j** cause; Ps 9:4
LORD, hear a **j** cause; pay Ps 17:1
hearts, "Aha! **J** what we wanted." Ps 35:25
his tongue speaks what is **j**. Ps 37:30
J as we heard, so we have seen Ps 48:8
you thought I was **j** like you. Ps 50:21
The LORD is **j**; He is my rock, Ps 92:15
who make them are **j** like them, Ps 115:8
servant well, **j** as You promised. Ps 119:65
judgments are **j** and that You Ps 119:75
I have done what is **j** and right; Ps 119:121
LORD, and Your judgments are **j**. Ps 119:137
who make them are **j** like them, Ps 135:18
LORD upholds the **j** cause of the Ps 140:12
some innocent person **j** for fun! Pr 1:11
the one He loves, **j** as a father, Pr 3:12
reign and rulers enact **j** law; Pr 8:15
of the righteous ⌊are⌋ **j**, Pr 12:5
guilty and condemning the **j**— Pr 17:15
is righteous and **j** is more Pr 21:3
For, **j** like the fool, there is Ec 2:16
wise man dies **j** like the fool? Ec 2:16
J as you don't know the path of Ec 11:5
I had **j** passed them when I found Sg 3:4
J let us be called by your name. Is 4:1
j as ⌊You did⌋ on the day of Is 9:4
j a little while My wrath will Is 10:25
Infants ⌊**j**⌋ weaned from milk? Is 28:9
true that⌋ in **j** a little while Is 29:17
I call her: Rahab Who **J** Sits. Is 30:7
for the LORD is a **j** God. Is 30:18
J as many were appalled at You— Is 52:14
For **j** as rain and snow fall from Is 55:10
j as the Israelites bring an Is 66:20
For **j** as the new heavens and the Is 66:22
shame by Egypt **j** as you were put Jr 2:36
They are **j** the poor; they Jr 5:4
J as you abandoned Me and served Jr 5:19
j as I drove out all of your Jr 7:15
Why are we **j** sitting here? Jr 8:14
j as they taught My people to Jr 12:16
J like this I will ruin the Jr 13:9
J as underwear clings to one's Jr 13:11
j as I commanded your ancestors. Jr 17:22
J like clay in the potter's Jr 18:6
J as I watched over them to Jr 31:28
J as I have brought all this Jr 32:42
for you **j** like the burning Jr 34:5
He has done **j** what He decreed. Jr 40:3
'**J** as My anger and fury were Jr 42:18
land of Egypt **j** as I punished Jr 44:13

drink offerings to her **j** as we, Jr 44:17
j as I handed over Judah's King Jr 44:30
j as the house of Israel was put Jr 48:13
and his land **j** as I punished Jr 50:18
j as she has done, do the same Jr 50:29
J as when God overthrew Sodom Jr 50:40
In **j** a little while her harvest Jr 51:33
LORD's sight **j** as Jehoiakim had Jr 52:2
So I did **j** as I was commanded. Ezk 12:7
J as I have done, so it will be Ezk 12:11
and does what is **j** and right: Ezk 18:5
has done what is **j** and right, Ezk 18:19
and does what is **j** and right, Ezk 18:21
and does what is **j** and right, Ezk 18:27
J as I entered into judgment Ezk 20:36
Isn't he ⌊**j**⌋ posing riddles?" Ezk 20:49
J as one gathers silver, copper, Ezk 22:20
in disgust **j** as I turned away Ezk 23:18
morning I did **j** as I was Ezk 24:18
you will do **j** as I have done: Ezk 24:22
j as the sea raises its waves. Ezk 26:3
and does what is **j** and right— Ezk 33:14
He has done what is **j** and right; Ezk 33:16
and does what is **j** and right, Ezk 33:19
J as you rejoiced over the Ezk 35:15
j as the flock of sheep for Ezk 36:38
j like the chambers that faced Ezk 42:11
the altar **j** as they did with Ezk 43:22
and do what is **j** and right. Ezk 45:9
fellowship offering **j** as he does Ezk 46:12
j as iron does not mix with Dn 2:43
are true and His ways are **j**. Dn 4:37
to his God, **j** as he had done Dn 6:10
J as it is written in the law of Dn 9:13
j as the LORD loves the Hs 3:1
your hearts, not **j** your clothes, Jl 2:13
you were **j** like one of them. Ob 11
have done **j** as You pleased." Jnh 1:14
he would be **j** the preacher for Mc 2:11
you supposed to know what is **j**? Mc 3:1
J as He had called, and they Zch 7:13
J then some men brought to Him a Mt 9:2
J then, a woman who had suffered Mt 9:20
If I can **j** touch His robe, Mt 9:21
J as they were going out, a Mt 9:32
whoever gives **j** a cup of cold Mt 10:42
Therefore **j** as the weeds are Mt 13:40
J then a Canaanite woman from Mt 15:22
J then someone came up and asked Mt 19:16
j as the Son of Man did not come Mt 20:28
went and did **j** as Jesus directed Mt 21:6
make long prayers **j** for show. Mt 23:14
For it is **j** like a man going on Mt 25:14
j as a shepherd separates the Mt 25:32
Man will go **j** as it is written Mt 26:24
been resurrected, **j** as He said. Mt 28:6
J then Jesus met them and said, Mt 28:9
J then a man with an unclean Mk 1:23
If I can **j** touch His robes, Mk 5:28
they might touch **j** the tassel of Mk 6:56
j as it is written about him." Mk 9:13
answered them **j** as Jesus had Mk 11:6
and say long prayers **j** for show. Mk 12:40
and found it **j** as He had told Mk 14:16
Man will go **j** as it is written Mk 14:21
see Him there **j** as He told you.' Mk 16:7
j as the original eyewitnesses Lk 1:2
j as He spoke to our ancestors, Lk 1:55
j as He spoke by the mouth of Lk 1:70
seen and heard, **j** as they had Lk 2:20
j as it is written in the law of Lk 2:23
J then some men came, carrying Lk 5:18
J as you want others to do for Lk 6:31
j as your Father also is Lk 6:36
J as He neared the gate of the Lk 7:12
J then, a man named Jairus came. Lk 8:41
J then a man from the crowd Lk 9:38
J then an expert in the law Lk 10:25
j as John also taught his Lk 11:1
For **j** as Jonah became a sign to Lk 11:30
another said, 'I **j** got married, Lk 14:20
j as Lazarus received bad things, Lk 16:25
J as it was in the days of Noah, Lk 17:26
and found it **j** as He had told Lk 19:32
and say long prayers **j** for show. Lk 20:47
and found it **j** as He had told Lk 22:13
j as My Father bestowed one on Lk 22:29
and found it **j** as the women had Lk 24:24

j as Isaiah the prophet said." Jn 1:23
J as Moses lifted up the snake Jn 3:14
J then His disciples arrived, Jn 4:27
And **j** as the Father raises the Jn 5:21
honor the Son **j** as they honor Jn 5:23
For **j** as the Father has life in Jn 5:26
the wilderness, **j** as it is Jn 6:31
J as the living Father sent Me Jn 6:57
But **j** as the Father taught Me, Jn 8:28
j now the Jews tried to stone Jn 11:8
and sat on it, **j** as it is Jn 12:14
j as the Father has told Me. Jn 12:50
also should do **j** as I have done Jn 13:15
and **j** as I told the Jews, Jn 13:33
J as I have loved you, you must Jn 13:34
J as the Father commanded Me, Jn 14:31
J as a branch is unable to Jn 15:4
j as I have kept My Father's Jn 15:10
of the fish you've **j** caught," Jn 21:10
you through Him, **j** as you Ac 2:22
j as your leaders also did. Ac 3:17
j as He who spoke to Moses Ac 7:44
J then a man in a dazzling robe Ac 10:30
the Holy Spirit **j** as we have?" Ac 10:47
j as on us at the beginning. Ac 11:15
temple was **j** outside the town Ac 14:13
Holy Spirit, **j** as He also did Ac 15:8
j as all of you are today, Ac 22:3
that it will be **j** the way it was Ac 27:25
When it was **j** about daylight, Ac 27:33
j as among the rest of the Rm 1:13
faith to faith, **j** as it is Rm 1:17
full well God's **j** sentence— Rm 1:32
j as some people slanderously Rm 3:8
someone die for a **j** person— Rm 5:7
j as sin entered the world Rm 5:12
For **j** as through one man's Rm 5:19
j as sin reigned in death, Rm 5:21
j as Christ was raised from the Rm 6:4
For **j** as you offered the parts Rm 6:19
is holy and **j** and good. Rm 7:12
And **j** as Isaiah predicted: Rm 9:29
j as the Messiah also accepted Rm 15:7
j as I teach everywhere in every 1Co 4:17
that all people were **j** like me. 1Co 7:7
j as I also try to please all 1Co 10:33
the traditions **j** as I delivered 1Co 11:2
For **j** as woman came from man, 1Co 11:12
in the body **j** as He wanted. 1Co 12:18
j as in Adam all die, so also 1Co 15:22
And **j** as we have borne the image 1Co 15:49
to see you now **j** in passing, 1Co 16:7
the Lord's work, **j** as I am. 1Co 16:10
and not **j** as we had hoped. 2Co 8:5
Titus that, **j** as he had begun, 2Co 8:6
that **j** as there was eagerness to 2Co 8:11
would be prepared **j** as I said. 2Co 9:3
j as he belongs to Christ, 2Co 10:7
to be regarded **j** as we are in 2Co 11:12
j as Peter was for the Gl 2:7
J as Abraham believed God, Gl 3:6
is not for **j** one person, Gl 3:20
and not **j** when I am with you. Gl 4:18
But **j** as then the child born Gl 4:29
j as you were called to one hope Eph 4:4
j as God also forgave you in Eph 4:32
j as also Christ loved the Eph 5:25
j as Christ does for the church, Eph 5:29
J that in every way, whether out Php 1:18
J one thing: live your life in a Php 1:27
j as you have always obeyed, Php 2:12
whatever is **j**, whatever is pure, Php 4:8
j as it has among you since the Col 1:6
in the faith, **j** as you were Col 2:7
J as the Lord has forgiven you, Col 3:13
j as we have been approved by 1Th 2:4
j as they did from the Jews. 1Th 2:14
for everyone, **j** as we also do 1Th 3:12
Lord will come **j** like a thief 1Th 5:2
and be honored, **j** as it was with 2Th 3:1
J as Jannes and Jambres resisted 2Tm 3:8
j as the name He inherited is Heb 1:4
received a **j** punishment, Heb 2:2
j as Moses was in all God's Heb 3:2
j as the builder has more honor Heb 3:3
the good news **j** as they did; Heb 4:2
his own works, **j** as God did from Heb 4:10
called by God, **j** as Aaron was. Heb 5:4

And **j** as it is appointed for Heb 9:27
For **j** as the body without the Jms 2:26
j as Sarah obeyed Abraham, 1Pt 3:6
j as there will be false 2Pt 2:1
j as our dear brother Paul, 2Pt 3:15
Him should walk **j** as He walked. 1Jn 2:6
j as it has taught you, remain 1Jn 2:27
himself **j** as He is pure. 1Jn 3:3
is righteous, **j** as He is 1Jn 3:7
in good health, **j** as your soul 3Jn 2
perversions, **j** as they did, and Jd 7
j as I have received ⌊this⌋ from Rv 2:27
j as I also won the victory and Rv 3:21
to be killed **j** as they had been Rv 6:11

JUSTICE *(150)*

with a crowd to pervert ⌊**j**⌋. Ex 23:2
must not deny **j** to the poor Ex 23:6
He executes **j** for the fatherless Dt 10:18
Do not deny **j** or show partiality Dt 16:19
Pursue **j** and justice alone, Dt 16:20
Pursue justice and **j** alone, Dt 16:20
not deny **j** to a foreign resident Dt 24:17
one who denies **j** to a foreign Dt 27:19
out the LORD's **j** and His Dt 33:21
might come to **j** and their blood Jdg 9:24
took bribes, and perverted **j**. 1Sm 8:3
j and righteousness 2Sm 8:15
would make sure he received **j**." 2Sm 15:4
one who rules the people with **j**, 2Sm 23:3
for yourself to understand **j**, 1Kg 3:11
was in him to carry out **j**. 1Kg 3:28
and providing **j** for the 1Kg 8:32
to carry out **j** and righteousness 1Kg 10:9
j and righteousness 1Ch 18:14
and providing **j** for the 2Ch 6:23
to carry out **j** and righteousness 2Ch 9:8
with experts in law and **j**. Est 1:13
Does God pervert **j**? Does the Jb 8:3
is a matter of **j**, who can summon Jb 9:19
for help, but there is no **j**. Jb 19:7
deprived me of **j**, and the Jb 27:2
yet God has deprived me of **j**. Jb 34:5
the Almighty does not pervert **j**. Jb 34:12
who hates **j** govern ⌊the world⌋ Jb 34:17
but He gives **j** to the afflicted. Jb 36:6
judgment and **j** have seized you. Jb 36:17
In His **j** and righteousness, Jb 37:23
Would you really challenge My **j**? Jb 40:8
a God who executes **j** every day. Ps 7:11
He has executed **j**, striking down Ps 9:16
doing **j** for the fatherless and Ps 10:18
He loves righteousness and **j**; Ps 33:5
the dawn, your **j** like the Ps 37:6
the LORD loves **j** and will not Ps 37:28
cause of truth, humility, and **j**. Ps 45:4
Your kingdom is a scepter of **j**. Ps 45:6
right hand is filled with **j**. Ps 48:10
Your **j**, rescue and deliver me; Ps 71:2
give Your **j** to the king and Your Ps 72:1
and Your afflicted ones with **j**. Ps 72:2
Provide **j** for the needy and the Ps 82:3
Righteousness and **j** are the Ps 89:14
for **j** will again be righteous, Ps 94:15
righteousness and **j** are the Ps 97:2
The mighty King loves **j**. Ps 99:4
administered **j** and righteousness Ps 99:4
sing of faithful love and **j**; Ps 101:1
of righteousness and **j** for all Ps 103:6
happy are those who uphold **j**, Ps 106:3
of His hands are truth and **j**; Ps 111:7
me life, in keeping with Your **j**. Ps 119:149
of the poor, **j** for the needy. Ps 140:12
executing **j** for the exploited Ps 146:7
righteousness, **j**, and integrity; Pr 1:3
guard the paths of **j** and protect Pr 2:8
j, and integrity— Pr 2:9
along the paths of **j**, Pr 8:20
but without **j**, it is swept away Pr 13:23
to subvert the course of **j**. Pr 17:23
perverting the **j** due the Pr 18:5
A worthless witness mocks **j**, Pr 19:28
J executed is a joy to the Pr 21:15
Evil men do not understand **j**, Pr 28:5
By **j** a king brings stability to Pr 29:4
a man receives **j** from the LORD. Pr 29:26
and pervert **j** for all the Pr 31:5
for the **j** of all who are Pr 31:8
perversion of **j** and Ec 5:8
do what is good. Seek **j**. Correct Is 1:17
She was once full of **j**. Is 1:21
Zion will be redeemed by **j**, Is 1:27
He looked for **j** but saw Is 5:7
of Hosts is exalted by His **j**, Is 5:16
and deprive the innocent of **j**. Is 5:23
sustain it with **j** and Is 9:7
afflicted among my people of **j**, Is 10:2
has been decreed; **j** overflows. Is 10:22
not execute **j** by what He hears Is 11:3
and execute **j** for the oppressed Is 11:4
quick to execute **j** will sit on Is 16:5
spirit of **j** to the one who sits Is 28:6
And I will make **j** the measuring Is 28:17
deprive the righteous of **j**. Is 29:21
Then **j** will inhabit the Is 32:16
filled Zion with **j** and Is 33:5
and taught Him the paths of **j**? Is 40:14
He will bring **j** to the nations. Is 42:1
He will faithfully bring **j**. Is 42:3
He has established **j** on earth. Is 42:4
hardhearted, far removed from **j**: Is 46:12
I am bringing My **j** near; Is 46:13
and My **j** for a light to the Is 51:4
will bring **j** to the nations. Is 51:5
Preserve **j** and do what is right, Is 56:1
not abandon the **j** of their God. Is 58:2
and there is no **j** in their ways. Is 59:8
Therefore **j** is far from us, Is 59:9
hope for **j**, but there is none; Is 59:11
J is turned back, and Is 59:14
LORD saw that there was no **j**, Is 59:15
For I the LORD love **j**; Is 61:8
lives, in truth, in **j**, and in Jr 4:2
of the LORD, the **j** of their God. Jr 5:4
of the LORD, the **j** of their God. Jr 5:5
faithful love, **j**, and Jr 9:24
LORD, but with **j**—not in Your Jr 10:24
Administer **j** every morning, Jr 21:12
Administer **j** and righteousness. Jr 22:3
He administered **j** and Jr 22:15
and administer **j** and Jr 23:5
will administer **j** and Jr 33:15
I will discipline you with **j**, Jr 46:28
denying **j** to a man in the Lm 3:35
carries out true **j** between men. Ezk 18:8
I will shepherd them with **j**. Ezk 34:16
in righteousness, **j**, love, and Hs 2:19
love and **j**, and always put Hs 12:6
Those who turn **j** into wormwood Am 5:7
the poor of **j** at the gates. Am 5:12
establish **j** in the gate. Am 5:15
But let **j** flow like water, Am 5:24
you have turned **j** into poison Am 6:12
the LORD, with **j** and courage, to Mc 3:8
who abhor **j** and pervert Mc 3:9
case and establishes **j** for me. Mc 7:9
ineffective and **j** never emerges. Hab 1:4
j comes out perverted. Hab 1:4
their views of **j** and sovereignty Hab 1:7
He applies His **j** morning by Zph 3:5
Render true **j**. Show faithful Zch 7:9
or "Where is the God of **j**?" Mal 2:17
those who deny ⌊**j** to⌋ the Mal 3:5
will proclaim **j** to the nations. Mt 12:18
until He has led **j** to victory. Mt 12:20
the law—**j**, mercy, and faith. Mt 23:23
and you bypass **j** and love for Lk 11:42
'Give me **j** against my adversary.' Lk 18:3
will give her **j**, so she doesn't Lk 18:5
not God grant **j** to His elect who Lk 18:7
He will swiftly grant them **j**. Lk 18:8
humiliation **j** was denied Him. Ac 8:33
J does not allow him to live!" Ac 28:4
deep longing, what zeal, what **j**! 2Co 7:11
Your kingdom is a scepter of **j**. Heb 1:8
administered **j**, obtained Heb 11:33

JUSTIFICATION *(4)*

there is no **j** that we can give Ac 19:40
trespasses and raised for our **j**. Rm 4:25
came the gift, resulting in **j**. Rm 5:16
is life-giving **j** for everyone. Rm 5:18

JUSTIFIED *(28)*

can a person be **j** before God? Jb 9:2
can a person be **j** before God? Jb 25:4
because he had **j** himself rather Jb 32:2
Israel will be **j** and find glory Is 45:25
down to his house **j** rather than Lk 18:14
in Him is **j** from everything, Ac 13:39
you could not be **j** from through Ac 13:39
That You may be **j** in Your words Rm 3:4
no flesh will be **j** in His sight Rm 3:20
They are **j** freely by His grace Rm 3:24
that a man is **j** by faith apart Rm 3:28
If Abraham was **j** by works, Rm 4:2
and those He called, He also **j**; Rm 8:30
and those He **j**, He also Rm 8:30
myself, but I am not **j** by this. 1Co 4:4
you were **j** in the name of the 1Co 6:11
that no one is **j** by the works Gl 2:16
that we might be **j** by faith in Gl 2:16
law no human being will be **j**. Gl 2:16
while seeking to be **j** by Christ, Gl 2:17
clear that no one is **j** before Gl 3:11
so that we could be **j** by faith. Gl 3:24
trying to be **j** by the law are Gl 5:4
in the flesh, **j** in the Spirit, 1Tm 3:16
that having been **j** by His grace, Ti 3:7
our father **j** by works when he Jms 2:21
that a man is **j** by works and not Jms 2:24
prostitute also **j** by works when Jms 2:25

JUSTIFIES *(3)*

they have done **j** the cry that Gn 18:21
The One who **j** Me is near; Is 50:8
God is the One who **j**. Rm 8:33

JUSTIFY *(9)*

How can we **j** ourselves? Gn 44:16
because I will not **j** the guilty. Ex 23:7
for I would like to **j** you. Jb 33:32
declare Me guilty to **j** yourself? Jb 40:8
righteous servant will **j** many, Is 53:11
But wanting to **j** himself, he Lk 10:29
are the ones who **j** yourselves Lk 16:15
God who will **j** the circumcised Rm 3:30
that God would **j** the Gentiles by Gl 3:8

JUSTLY *(9)*

because they refuse to act **j**. Pr 21:7
and rulers will rule **j**. Is 32:1
No one makes claims **j**; Is 59:4
anyone who acts **j**, who seeks to Jr 5:1
if you act **j** toward one another, Jr 7:5
discipline you **j**, but I will by Jr 30:11
Only to act **j**, to love Mc 6:8
We are punished **j**, because we're Lk 23:41
Himself to the One who judges **j**. 1Pt 2:23

JUSTUS *(3)*

(AKA BARSABBAS, JOSEPH, JUDAS)

also known as **J**, and Matthias. Ac 1:23
house of a man named Titius **J**, Ac 18:7
so does Jesus who is called **J**. Col 4:11

JUTS *(3)*

and tower that **j** out from the Neh 3:25
east and the tower that **j** out. Neh 3:26
the great tower that **j** out, Neh 3:27

JUTTAH *(2)*

Maon, Carmel, Ziph, **J**, Jos 15:55
its pasturelands, **J** with its Jos 21:16

K

KABZEEL *(3)*
(AKA JEKABZEEL)
in the Negev: **K**, Eder, Jagur, Jos 15:21
the son of a brave man from **K**, 2Sm 23:20
the son of a brave man from **K**, 1Ch 11:22

KADESH *(15)*
(AKA EN-MISHPAT, ZIN)
that is, **K**), and they defeated Gn 14:7
is located between **K** and Bered. Gn 16:14
and settled between **K** and Shur. Gn 20:1
in the Wilderness of Paran at **K**. Nm 13:26
month, and they settled in **K**. Nm 20:1
messengers from **K** to the king of Nm 20:14
Now look, we are in **K**, a city on Nm 20:16
After they set out from **K**, Nm 20:22
Meribah of **K** in the Wilderness Nm 27:14
Wilderness of Zin (that is, **K**). Nm 33:36
departed from **K** and camped at Nm 33:37
you stayed in **K** as long as you Dt 1:46
to the Red Sea and came to **K**. Jdg 11:16
So Israel stayed in **K**. Jdg 11:17
LORD shakes the wilderness of **K**. Ps 29:8

KADESH-BARNEA *(10)*
sent them from **K** to see the land Nm 32:8
to Zin, and end south of **K**. Nm 34:4
from Horeb to **K** by way of Mount Dt 1:2
When we reached **K**, Dt 1:19
traveling from **K** until we Dt 2:14
When the LORD sent you from **K**, Dt 9:23
everyone from **K** to Gaza, Jos 10:41
man of God at **K** about you and me Jos 14:6
me from **K** to scout the land, Jos 14:7
ascended to the south of **K**, Jos 15:3

KADMIEL *(7)*
and brothers, **K** with his sons, Ezr 3:9
of **K** Hodevah's descendants 74 Neh 7:43
Jeshua, Bani, **K**, Shebaniah, Neh 9:4
Levites—Jeshua, **K**, Bani, Neh 9:5
of the sons of Henadad, **K**, Neh 10:9
Jeshua, Binnui, **K**, Sherebiah, Neh 12:8
Jeshua son of **K**, along with Neh 12:24

KADMIEL'S *(1)*
Jeshua's and **K** descendants from Ezr 2:40

KADMONITES *(1)*
of⌋ the Kenites, Kenizzites, **K**, Gn 15:19

KAIN *(2)*
K will be destroyed when Asshur Nm 24:22
K, Gibeah, and Timnah—10 Jos 15:57

KAIWAN *(1)*
(AKA REPHAN)
your king and **K** your star god, Am 5:26

KALLAI *(1)*
K of Sallai, Eber of Amok, Neh 12:20

KAMON *(1)*
Jair died, he was buried in **K**. Jdg 10:5

KANAH *(3)*
along the Brook of **K** and ended Jos 16:8
descended to the Brook of **K**; Jos 17:9
Hammon, and **K**, as far as Great Jos 19:28

KAREAH *(14)*
Johanan son of **K**, Seraiah son of 2Kg 25:23
and Jonathan the sons of **K**, Jr 40:8
Johanan son of **K** and all the Jr 40:13
Johanan son of **K** suggested to Jr 40:15
responded to Johanan son of **K**, Jr 40:16
When Johanan son of **K** and all Jr 41:11
saw Johanan son of **K** and all the Jr 41:13
and rejoined Johanan son of **K**. Jr 41:14
Johanan son of **K** and all the Jr 41:16
along with Johanan son of **K**, Jr 42:1
he summoned Johanan son of **K**, Jr 42:8
Johanan son of **K**, and all the Jr 43:2
So Johanan son of **K** and all the Jr 43:4
Johanan son of **K** and all the Jr 43:5

KARKA *(1)*
to Addar, and turned to **K**. Jos 15:3

KARKOR *(1)*
Zebah and Zalmunna were in **K**, Jdg 8:10

KARNAIM *(1)*
(AKA ASHTAROTH, ASHTEROTH-KARNAIM, BEESHTERAH)
we capture **K** for ourselves Am 6:13

KARTAH *(1)*
its pasturelands, **K** with its Jos 21:34

KARTAN *(1)*
(AKA KIRIATHAIM)
and **K** with its pasturelands— Jos 21:32

KATTATH *(1)*
along with **K**, Nahalal, Shimron, Jos 19:15

KATYDID *(1)*
various kinds of **k**, the various Lv 11:22

KEDAR *(11)*
then K, Adbeel, Mibsam Gn 25:13
firstborn, **K**, Adbeel, Mibsam, 1Ch 1:29
have lived among the tents of **K**! Ps 120:5
I am dark like the tents of **K**, Sg 1:5
all the glory of **K** will be gone. Is 21:16
where **K** dwells ⌊cry aloud Is 42:11
the flocks of **K** will be gathered Is 60:7
Send ⌊someone⌋ to **K** and consider Jr 2:10
About **K** and the kingdoms of Jr 49:28
up, go against **K**, and destroy Jr 49:28
the princes of **K** were your Ezk 27:21

KEDARITE *(1)*
The remaining **K** archers will be Is 21:17

KEDEMAH *(2)*
Tema, Jetur, Naphish, and **K**. Gn 25:15
Jetur, Naphish, and **K**. 1Ch 1:31

KEDEMOTH *(4)*
from the Wilderness of **K**, Dt 2:26
Jahaz, **K**, Mephaath, Jos 13:18
K with its pasturelands, and Jos 21:37
K and its pasturelands, and 1Ch 6:79

KEDESH *(12)*
(AKA KISHION)
the king of **K** one the king of Jos 12:22
K, Hazor, Ithnan, Jos 15:23
K, Edrei, En-hazor, Jos 19:37
So they designated **K** in the hill Jos 20:7
K in Galilee, the city of refuge Jos 21:32
of Abinoam from **K** in Naphtali Jdg 4:6
got up and went with Barak to **K**. Jdg 4:9
Zebulun and Naphtali to **K**; Jdg 4:10
of Zaanannim, which was near **K**. Jdg 4:11
Janoah, **K**, Hazor, Gilead, 2Kg 15:29
they received⌋ **K** and its 1Ch 6:72
they received⌋ **K** in Galilee and 1Ch 6:76

KEEP *(320)*
and female, to k them alive with Gn 6:19
so that you can **k** them alive. Gn 6:20
in order to **k** offspring alive on Gn 7:3
I will **k** My covenant between Me Gn 17:7
are to **k** My covenant. Gn 17:9
which you are to **k**, between Me Gn 17:10
house after him to **k** the way of Gn 18:19
so you will **k** faith with me and Gn 21:23
to shepherd and **k** your flock. Gn 30:31
Esau replied. "**K** what you have." Gn 33:9
Let her **k** ⌊the items⌋ for Gn 38:23
Why do you **k** looking at each Gn 42:1
could no longer **k** his composure Gn 45:1
the land and to **k** you alive by a Gn 45:7
⌊them⌋ go and **k** holding them, Ex 9:2
You are to **k** it until the Ex 12:6
K this command permanently as a Ex 12:24
K this statute at its appointed Ex 13:10
commands, and **k** all His statutes Ex 15:26
will you refuse to **k** My commands Ex 16:28
Me and carefully **k** My covenant, Ex 19:5
who love Me and **k** My commands. Ex 20:6
neighbor money or goods to **k**, Ex 22:7
in order to **k** the lamp burning Ex 27:20
seven days and **k** the LORD's Lv 8:35
You must **k** the Israelites from Lv 15:31
and you are to **k** My statutes by Lv 18:4
K My statutes and ordinances; Lv 18:5
But you are to **k** My statutes and Lv 18:26
You must **k** My instruction to not Lv 18:30
You are to **k** My Sabbaths; Lv 19:3
You are to **k** My statutes. Lv 19:19
must **k** My Sabbaths and revere Lv 19:30
You must **k** all My statutes and Lv 19:37
K My statutes and do them; Lv 20:8
You are to **k** all My statutes and Lv 20:22
They must **k** My instruction, Lv 22:9
You are to **k** My commands and do Lv 22:31
You must **k** My Sabbaths and honor Lv 26:2
'Let nothing **k** you from coming Nm 22:16
but **k** alive for yourselves all Nm 31:18
but we will **k** our hereditary Nm 32:32
not with you to **k** you from being Dt 1:42
we will **k** strictly to the Dt 2:27
that you may **k** the commands of Dt 4:2
recognize and **k** in mind that the Dt 4:39
K His statutes and commands, Dt 4:40
who love Me and **k** My commands. Dt 5:10
you to **k** the Sabbath day Dt 5:15
fear Me and **k** all My commands, Dt 5:29
who love Him and **k** His commands. Dt 7:9
So **k** the command—the statutes Dt 7:11
are careful to **k** these Dt 7:12
your God will **k** His covenant Dt 7:12
or not you would **k** His commands. Dt 8:2
K in mind that the LORD your God Dt 8:5
So **k** the commands of the LORD Dt 8:6
by failing to **k** His command— Dt 8:11
in order to **k** the promise He Dt 9:5
K the LORD's commands and Dt 10:13
God and always **k** His mandate and Dt 11:1
K every command I am giving you Dt 11:8
You must **k** His commands and Dt 13:4
provided you **k** every one of Dt 19:9
not be slow to **k** it, because He Dt 23:21
in His ways, **k** His statutes, Dt 26:17
that you are to **k** all His Dt 26:18
K every command I am giving you Dt 27:1
your God and **k** the commands Dt 28:45
His ways, and to **k** His commands, Dt 30:16
But **k** a distance of about 1,000 Jos 3:4
But **k** yourselves from the things Jos 6:18
in all His ways, **k** His commands, Jos 22:5
they would **k** the LORD's way Jdg 2:22
if they would **k** the LORD's Jdg 3:4
Be quiet. **K** your mouth shut Jdg 18:19
to eat to **k** up your strength Jdg 19:5
"Please **k** up your strength." Jdg 19:8
Nothing can **k** the LORD from 1Sm 14:6
the flock with someone to **k** it, 1Sm 17:20
your servant to **k** me from going 1Sm 29:8
for he won't **k** me from you." 2Sm 13:13
do I have to **k** on making appeals 2Sm 19:28
Why **k** on speaking about ⌊these⌋ 2Sm 19:29
k your obligation to the LORD 1Kg 2:3
His ways and to **k** His statutes, 1Kg 2:3
K an eye on Shimei son of Gera, 1Kg 2:8
in My ways and **k** My statutes 1Kg 3:14
and **k** all My commandments by 1Kg 6:12
k what You promised to Your 1Kg 8:25
His ways and to **k** His commands, 1Kg 8:58
and to **k** His commands, 1Kg 8:61
and if you **k** My statutes and 1Kg 9:4
Me and do not **k** My commands— 1Kg 9:6
this and did not **k** My covenant 1Kg 11:11
sight in order to **k** My statutes 1Kg 11:38
and did not **k** the commandment 1Kg 13:21
grass so we can **k** the horses and 1Kg 18:5
shut the door to **k** him out. 2Kg 6:32
ways and **k** My commandments 2Kg 17:13
did not **k** the commandments 2Kg 17:19
the LORD and to **k** His 2Kg 23:3
K the Passover of the LORD your 2Kg 23:21
of Hamath to **k** him from reigning 2Kg 23:33
be with me, and **k** me from harm, 1Ch 4:10
he did not **k** the LORD's word. 1Ch 10:13
He had commanded Israel to **k**. 1Ch 16:40
so that you may **k** the law of the 1Ch 22:12
k this desire forever in the 1Ch 29:18
whole heart to **k** and to carry 1Ch 29:19
k what You promised to Your 2Ch 6:16
and if you **k** My statutes and 2Ch 7:17
the LORD and to **k** His 2Ch 34:31
who does not **k** the law of your Ezr 7:26
who love Him and **k** His commands, Neh 1:5
had the will to **k** working. Neh 4:6
who doesn't **k** this promise. Neh 5:13
in order to **k** the Sabbath day Neh 13:22
If you **k** silent at this time, Est 4:14
Yet who can **k** from speaking? Jb 4:2
that You **k** me under guard? Jb 7:12
so that you can **k** on ridiculing Jb 11:3
why do you **k** up this empty talk? Jb 27:12

despise me and **k** their distance Jb 30:10
they **k** rolling in through the Jb 30:14
He does not **k** the wicked alive, Jb 36:6
physical exertion **k** ⌊you⌋ from Jb 36:19
I **k** the LORD in mind always. Ps 16:8
k Your servant from willful sins; Ps 19:13
to those who **k** His covenant Ps 25:10
integrity and uprightness **k** me, Ps 25:21
from death and to **k** them alive Ps 33:19
K your tongue from evil and your Ps 34:13
Wait for the LORD and **k** His way, Ps 37:34
I do not **k** my mouth closed— Ps 40:9
The LORD will **k** him and preserve Ps 41:2
I will **k** watch for You, my Ps 59:9
Make and **k** your vows to the LORD Ps 76:11
works, but **k** His commandments Ps 78:7
They did not **k** God's covenant Ps 78:10
for they did not **k** His decrees. Ps 78:56
Your jealousy **k** burning like Ps 79:5
God, do not **k** silent. Do not be Ps 83:1
and do not **k** My commandments, Ps 89:31
Will Your anger **k** burning like Ps 89:46
of those who **k** His covenant, Ps 103:18
that they might **k** His statutes Ps 105:45
are those who **k** His decrees Ps 119:2
I will **k** Your statutes; Ps 119:8
can a young man **k** his way pure? Ps 119:9
then I will **k** Your word. Ps 119:17
K me from the way of deceit, Ps 119:29
and I will always **k** them. Ps 119:33
will always **k** Your law, forever Ps 119:44
night, LORD, and I **k** Your law. Ps 119:55
I have promised to **k** Your words. Ps 119:57
hesitating to **k** Your commands. Ps 119:60
to those who **k** Your precepts. Ps 119:63
astray, but now I **k** Your word. Ps 119:67
sworn to **k** Your righteous Ps 119:106
and I will **k** Your precepts. Ps 119:134
and I will **k** Your decrees. Ps 119:146
because they do not **k** Your word. Ps 119:158
your sons **k** My covenant and My Ps 132:12
K me safe from violent men Ps 140:1
K me safe from violent men who Ps 140:4
k watch at the door of my lips. Ps 141:3
and **k** to the paths of the Pr 2:20
let your heart **k** my commands; Pr 3:1
confidence and will **k** your foot Pr 3:26
K my commands and live. Pr 4:4
k them within your heart. Pr 4:21
k your feet away from evil. Pr 4:27
K your way far from her. Pr 5:8
My son, **k** your father's command, Pr 6:20
K my commands and live; Pr 7:2
She will **k** you from a forbidden Pr 7:5
those who **k** my ways are happy. Pr 8:32
do his friends **k** their distance Pr 19:7
inexperienced **k** going and are Pr 22:3
The LORD's eyes **k** watch over Pr 22:12
pleasing if you **k** them within Pr 22:18
k your mind on the right course. Pr 23:19
the foolish **k** going and are Pr 27:12
but those who **k** the law battle Pr 28:4
K falsehood and deceitful words Pr 30:8
task to **k** them occupied. Ec 1:13
a time to **k** and a time to throw Ec 3:6
given people to **k** them occupied. Ec 3:10
down together, they can **k** warm; Ec 4:11
how can one person alone **k** warm? Ec 4:11
K the king's command. Concerning Ec 8:2
fear God and **k** His commands, Ec 12:13
Why do you **k** on rebelling? Is 1:5
K listening, but do not Is 6:9
k looking, but do not perceive. Is 6:9
to **k** me from going the way of Is 8:11
k the poor from getting a fair Is 10:2
You will **k** in perfect peace the Is 26:3
I will **k** you, and I make you a Is 42:6
I will **k** you, and I will appoint Is 49:8
the eunuchs who **k** My Sabbaths, Is 56:4
all who **k** the Sabbath without Is 56:6
If you **k** from desecrating the Is 58:13
I will not **k** silent because of Is 62:1
and I will not **k** still because Is 62:1
Will You **k** silent and afflict Is 64:12
K to yourself, don't come near Is 65:5
I will not **k** silent, but I will Is 65:6
K your feet from going bare and Jr 2:25
and wounds **k** coming to My Jr 6:7

k trusting in deceitful words Jr 7:8
or compassion ⌊to **k** Me⌋ from Jr 13:14
Me and did not **k** My law. Jr 16:11
Hear how they **k** challenging me, Jr 17:15
They **k** on saying to those who Jr 23:17
I will **k** My eyes on them for Jr 24:6
K your voice from weeping and Jr 31:16
K the highway in mind, the way Jr 31:21
If I do not ⌊**k**⌋ My covenant with Jr 33:25
will **k** his life like the spoils Jr 38:2
you will **k** your life like the Jr 39:18
We will **k** our vows we have made Jr 44:25
me⌋, no one to **k** me alive. Lm 1:16
for food to **k** themselves alive. Lm 1:19
My statutes, **k** My ordinances, Ezk 11:20
The days **k** passing by, and every Ezk 12:22
itself but might **k** his covenant Ezk 17:14
their idols, or **k** their Ezk 20:18
My statutes, **k** My ordinances, Ezk 20:19
K My Sabbaths holy, and they Ezk 20:20
or carefully **k** My ordinances— Ezk 20:21
and **k** My statutes and obey them. Ezk 37:24
for the priests who **k** charge of Ezk 40:45
the priests who **k** charge of the Ezk 40:46
others⌋ to **k** charge of My Ezk 44:8
They will **k** My mandate. Ezk 44:16
festivals, and **k** My Sabbaths Ezk 44:24
the king, "You may **k** your gifts, Dn 5:17
love Him and **k** His commandments Dn 9:4
k these words secret and seal Dn 12:4
person will **k** silent at such Am 5:13
My ways and **k** My instructions, Zch 3:7
but if not, **k** ⌊them⌋." So they Zch 11:12
I will **k** a watchful eye on the Zch 12:4
but you must **k** your oaths to the Mt 5:33
K asking, and it will be given Mt 7:7
K searching, and you will find. Mt 7:7
K knocking, and the door will be Mt 7:7
don't try to **k** them from coming Mt 19:14
into life, **k** the commandments. Mt 19:17
The crowd told them to **k** quiet, Mt 20:31
could not **k** their eyes open. Mt 26:43
deal with him and **k** you out of Mt 28:14
they have received and **k**, Mk 7:4
you **k** the tradition of men." Mk 7:8
Many people told him to **k** quiet, Mk 10:48
could not **k** their eyes open. Mk 14:40
and tried to **k** Him from leaving Lk 4:42
I say to you, **k** asking, and it Lk 11:9
K searching, and you will find. Lk 11:9
K knocking, and the door will be Lk 11:9
of God and **k** it are blessed! Lk 11:28
Don't **k** striving for what you Lk 12:29
in front told him to **k** quiet, Lk 18:39
if they were to **k** silent, the Lk 19:40
I do know Him, and I **k** His word. Jn 8:55
for He doesn't **k** the Sabbath!" Jn 9:16
You going to **k** us in suspense? Jn 10:24
this world will **k** it for eternal Jn 12:25
My words and doesn't **k** them, Jn 12:47
you will **k** My commandments. Jn 14:15
loves Me, he will **k** My word. Jn 14:23
love Me will not **k** My words. Jn 14:24
If you **k** My commands you will Jn 15:10
My word, they will also **k** yours. Jn 15:20
these things to **k** you from Jn 16:1
the Holy Spirit and **k** back part Ac 5:3
would **k** me from being baptized? Ac 8:36
them to **k** the law of Moses! Ac 15:5
If you **k** yourselves from these Ac 15:29
the jailer to **k** them securely Ac 16:23
but **k** on speaking and don't be Ac 18:9
you must **k** calm and not do Ac 19:36
the weak and to **k** in mind the Ac 20:35
that they should **k** themselves Ac 21:25
the centurion **k** Paul under guard Ac 24:23
K it to yourself before God. Rm 14:22
his heart to **k** his own virgin, 1Co 7:37
all things and **k** the traditions 1Co 11:2
does not **k** a record of wrongs; 1Co 13:5
that person should **k** silent in 1Co 14:28
kept myself, and will **k** myself, 2Co 11:9
obligated to **k** the entire law. Gl 5:3
circumcised don't **k** the law Gl 6:13
that your love will **k** on growing Php 1:9
to **k** away from every brother who 2Th 3:6
sins of others. **K** yourself pure. 1Tm 5:22
k the commandment without spot 1Tm 6:14

remind you to **k** ablaze the gift 2Tm 1:6
K in mind Jesus Christ, risen 2Tm 2:8
k a clear head about everything, 2Tm 4:5
I wanted to **k** him with me, Phm 13
for they **k** watch over your souls Heb 13:17
distress and to **k** oneself Jms 1:27
Go in peace, **k** warm, and eat Jms 2:16
see good days must **k** his tongue 1Pt 3:10
k your love for one another at 1Pt 4:8
they will **k** you from being 2Pt 1:8
trials and to **k** the unrighteous 2Pt 2:9
because we **k** His commands and 1Jn 3:22
for God is: to **k** His commands. 1Jn 5:3
who did not **k** their own position Jd 6
k yourselves in the love of God, Jd 21
prophecy and **k** what is written Rv 1:3
and heard; **k** it, and repent. Rv 3:3
I will also **k** you from the hour Rv 3:10
those who **k** the commandments of Rv 12:17
k the commandments of God and Rv 14:12
those who **k** the words of this Rv 22:9

KEEPER *(8)*

of Harhas, **k** of the wardrobe. 2Kg 22:14
the Levite, the **k** of the East 2Ch 31:14
of Hasrah, **k** of the wardrobe. 2Ch 34:22
to Asaph, **k** of the king's Neh 2:8
they made me a **k** of the Sg 1:6
the record **k**, came out to him Is 36:3
the record **k**, came to Hezekiah Is 36:22
and My Father is the vineyard **k**. Jn 15:1

KEEPING *(40)*

father in **k** with your oath." Gn 50:6
he makes in **k** with the ritual Nm 6:21
of this people in **k** with the Nm 14:19
of your life by **k** all His Dt 6:2
k all His commands I am giving Dt 13:18
your God by **k** His commands Dt 30:10
in **k** with all that Moses had Jos 4:10
in **k** with all that the LORD had Jos 11:23
k with the LORD's instruction. Jos 17:4
What is **k** you here?" Jdg 18:3
k the gracious covenant with 1Kg 8:23
k with the LORD's word through 1Ch 11:3
perseveres in **k** My commandments 1Ch 28:7
k His gracious covenant with 2Ch 6:14
compassion in **k** with Your Neh 13:22
there is great reward in **k** them. Ps 19:11
in **k** with Your faithful love, Ps 25:7
in **k** with Your righteousness, Ps 35:24
in **k** with Your great compassion, Ps 69:16
committed to **k** Your statutes! Ps 119:5
his way pure? By **k** Your word. Ps 119:9
In **k** with Your faithful love, Ps 119:149
give me life, in **k** with Your Ps 119:149
not **k** the terms of the covenant Jr 34:18
in **k** with all Your righteous Dn 9:16
you are not **k** My ways but are Mal 2:9
we gained by **k** His requirements Mal 3:14
k with the time he had learned Mt 2:16
k the tradition of the elders. Mk 7:3
the fields and **k** watch at night Lk 2:8
but **k** God's commandments does. 1Co 7:19
in **k** with the authority the Lord 2Co 13:10
diligently **k** the unity of the Eph 4:3
instruction in **k** with the 1Tm 1:18
in **k** with what He has said: Heb 4:3
k our eyes on Jesus, the source Heb 12:2
and respect, **k** your conscience 1Pt 3:16
to know Him: by **k** His commands. 1Jn 2:3
Him," without **k** His commands, is 1Jn 2:4
in **k** with a command we have 2Jn 4

KEEPS *(41)*

community that **k** complaining Nm 14:27
faithful God who **k** His gracious Dt 7:9
see this man who **k** coming out? 1Sm 17:25
God who **k** His gracious covenant Neh 1:5
God who **k** His gracious covenant Neh 9:32
let it go but **k** it in his mouth Jb 20:13
and someone **k** watch over ⌊his⌋ Jb 21:32
He **k** company with evildoers and Jb 34:8
k his word whatever the cost, Ps 15:4
He **k** His eye on the nations. Ps 66:7
He **k** us alive and does not allow Ps 66:9
man with understanding **k** silent. Pr 11:12
the trustworthy **k** a confidence. Pr 11:13
and one who **k** a cool head is a Pr 17:27
wise when he **k** silent, Pr 17:28
The one who **k** commands preserves Pr 19:16

mouth and tongue **k** himself out Pr 21:23
A discerning son **k** the law, Pr 28:7
but one who **k** the law will be Pr 29:18
life because God **k** him occupied Ec 5:20
The one who **k** a command will not Ec 8:5
who **k** the Sabbath without Is 56:2
and **k** his hand from doing any Is 56:2
A leopard **k** watch over their Jr 5:6
for profit but **k** his hand from Ezk 18:8
My statutes and **k** My ordinances, Ezk 18:9
He **k** his hand from ⌊harming⌋ the Ezk 18:17
has committed, **k** all My statutes Ezk 18:21
God who **k** His gracious covenant Dn 9:4
this widow **k** pestering me, Lk 18:5
Yet none of you **k** the law! Jn 7:19
If anyone **k** My word, he will Jn 8:51
say, 'If anyone **k** My word, he Jn 8:52
commands and **k** them is the one Jn 14:21
an uncircumcised man **k** the law's Rm 2:26
For whoever **k** the entire law, Jms 2:10
But whoever **k** His word, truly in 1Jn 2:5
The one who **k** His commands 1Jn 3:24
One who is born of God **k** him, 1Jn 5:18
the one who **k** My works to the Rv 2:26
is the one who **k** the prophetic Rv 22:7

KEHELATHAH *(2)*
from Rissah and camped at **K**. Nm 33:22
departed from **K** and camped at Nm 33:23

KEILAH *(18)*
K, Achzib, and Mareshah—nine Jos 15:44
fighting against **K** and raiding 1Sm 23:1
the Philistines and rescue **K**." 1Sm 23:2
much more if we go to **K** against 1Sm 23:3
Go at once to **K**, for I will hand 1Sm 23:4
David and his men went to **K**, 1Sm 23:5
rescued the inhabitants of **K**. 1Sm 23:5
of Ahimelech fled to David at **K**, 1Sm 23:6
Saul that David had gone to **K**, 1Sm 23:7
to go to war at **K** and besiege 1Sm 23:8
intends to come to **K** and destroy 1Sm 23:10
the citizens of **K** hand me over 1Sm 23:11
the citizens of **K** hand me and my 1Sm 23:12
left **K** at once and moved from 1Sm 23:13
that David had escaped from **K**, 1Sm 23:13
the father of **K** the Garmite and 1Ch 4:19
over half the district of **K**, Neh 3:17
over half the district of **K**. Neh 3:18

KELAIAH *(1)*
(AKA KELITA)
Shimei, **K** (that is Kelita) Ezr 10:23

KELITA *(3)*
(AKA KELAIAH)
Kelaiah (that is **K**), Pethahiah, Ezr 10:23
Maaseiah, **K**, Azariah, Jozabad Neh 8:7
Hodiah, **K**, Pelaiah, Hanan, Neh 10:10

KEMUEL *(3)*
his brother Buz, **K** the father of Gn 22:21
K son of Shiphtan, a leader from Nm 34:24
the Levites, Hashabiah son of **K**; 1Ch 27:17

KENAN *(5)*
90 years old when he fathered **K**. Gn 5:9
815 years after the birth of **K**, Gn 5:10
K was 70 years old when he Gn 5:12
K lived 840 years after the Gn 5:13
K, Mahalalel, Jared, 1Ch 1:2

KENAN'S *(1)*
So **K** life lasted 910 years; Gn 5:14

KENATH *(2)*
and captured **K** with its villages Nm 32:42
along with **K** and its villages— 1Ch 2:23

KENAZ *(10)*
Omar, Zepho, Gatam, and **K**. Gn 36:11
Chiefs Teman, Omar, Zepho, **K**, Gn 36:15
K, Teman, Mibzar, Gn 36:42
Caleb's brother, **K**, captured it, Jos 15:17
Othniel son of **K**, Caleb's Jdg 1:13
LORD raised up Othniel son of **K**, Jdg 3:9
and Othniel son of **K** died. Jdg 3:11
Omar, Zephi, Gatam, and **K**; 1Ch 1:36
K, Teman, Mibzar, 1Ch 1:53
Elah, and Naam. Elah's son: **K**. 1Ch 4:15

KENAZ'S *(1)*
K sons: Othniel and Seraiah. 1Ch 4:13

KENITE *(5)*
The descendants of the **K**, Moses' Jdg 1:16
Now Heber the **K** had moved away Jdg 4:11
of Heber the **K**, because there Jdg 4:17
and the family of Heber the **K**. Jdg 4:17
women, the wife of Heber the **K**; Jdg 5:24

KENITES *(8)*
⌊the land of⌋ the **K**, Kenizzites, Gn 15:19
Next he saw the **K** and proclaimed Nm 24:21
had moved away from the **K**, Jdg 4:11
He warned the **K**, "Since you 1Sm 15:6
So the **K** withdrew from the 1Sm 15:6
the south country of the **K**." 1Sm 27:10
and in the towns of the **K**; 1Sm 30:29
These are the **K** who came from 1Ch 2:55

KENIZZITE *(3)*
Jephunneh the **K** and Joshua son Nm 32:12
of Jephunneh the **K** said to him, Jos 14:6
of Jephunneh the **K** as an Jos 14:14

KENIZZITES *(1)*
of⌋ the Kenites, **K**, Kadmonites, Gn 15:19

KEPT *(181)*
I have also **k** you from sinning Gn 20:6
As I have **k** faith with you, Gn 21:23
to My voice and **k** My mandate, Gn 26:5
became rich and **k** getting richer Gn 26:13
but his father **k** the matter ⌊in Gn 37:11
The man **k** asking about us and Gn 43:7
aside to be **k** until morning.' Ex 16:23
of the altar is **k** burning on it. Lv 6:9
on the altar is to be **k** burning; Lv 6:12
Fire must be **k** burning on the Lv 6:13
testimony to be **k** as a sign for Nm 17:10
offerings ⌊**k**⌋ from the fire Nm 18:9
ashes must be **k** by the Israelite Nm 19:9
You **k** hearing the sound of the Dt 4:12
loved you and **k** the oath He Dt 7:8
for they **k** Your word and Dt 33:9
they **k** the Passover on the Jos 5:10
the LORD has **k** me alive ⌊these⌋ Jos 14:10
travelers **k** to the side roads Jdg 5:6
but **k** the 300 who took the Jdg 7:8
and he **k** the vow he had made Jdg 11:39
them the women they had **k** alive Jdg 21:14
the LORD had **k** her from 1Sm 1:5
because the LORD had **k** Hannah 1Sm 1:6
You have not **k** the command 1Sm 13:13
but David **k** going back and forth 1Sm 17:15
Saul **k** David with him from that 1Sm 18:2
only if they have **k** themselves 1Sm 21:4
that women are being **k** from us, 1Sm 21:5
it is the LORD who **k** you from 1Sm 25:26
you **k** me from participating 1Sm 25:33
Abner **k** acquiring more power in 2Sm 3:6
length ⌊of those⌋ to be **k** alive. 2Sm 8:2
horses, and he **k** 100 chariots. 2Sm 8:4
The mule under him **k** going, 2Sm 18:9
She **k** the birds of the sky from 2Sm 21:10
I have **k** the ways of the LORD 2Sm 22:22
I have **k** all His ordinances in 2Sm 22:23
before Him and **k** myself from 2Sm 22:24
son of Haggith **k** exalting 1Kg 1:5
have you not **k** the LORD's oath 1Kg 2:43
You have **k** what You promised to 1Kg 8:24
and who **k** My commandments 1Kg 11:34
who **k** My commandments and 1Kg 14:8
The ravens **k** bringing him bread 1Kg 17:6
they **k** on raving until the 1Kg 18:29
watched, he **k** crying out, "My 2Kg 2:12
k bringing her ⌊containers⌋, 2Kg 4:5
containers⌋, and she **k** pouring. 2Kg 4:5
Him but **k** the commandments 2Kg 18:6
But the people **k** silent; 2Kg 18:36
had ever been **k** from the time 2Kg 23:22
and they **k** a genealogical record 1Ch 4:33
horses, and he **k** 100 chariots. 1Ch 18:4
You have **k** what You promised to 2Ch 6:15
the king's ships **k** going to 2Ch 9:21
armed forces, they **k** singing: 2Ch 20:21
fathers have not **k** the word of 2Ch 34:21
But they **k** ridiculing God's 2Ch 36:16
You and have not **k** the commands, Neh 1:7
These nobles **k** mentioning Neh 6:19
You have **k** Your promise, for You Neh 9:8
of the sanctuary are **k** and where Neh 10:39
slaves, I would have **k** silent. Est 7:4
I have **k** to His way and not Jb 23:11
I have **k** the ways of the LORD Ps 18:21
I have **k** all His ordinances in Ps 18:22
toward Him and **k** myself from Ps 18:23
When I **k** silent, my bones became Ps 32:3
They are **k** safe forever, but the Ps 37:28
I **k** silent, even from ⌊speaking⌋ Ps 39:2
these things, and I **k** silent; Ps 50:21
You have **k** me from closing my Ps 77:4
they **k** sinning and did not Ps 78:32
they **k** His decrees and the Ps 99:7
Your precepts be diligently **k**. Ps 119:4
for I have **k** Your decrees. Ps 119:22
I have **k** my feet from every evil Ps 119:101
say, "I have **k** my heart pure; Pr 20:9
wealth **k** by its owner to his Ec 5:13
I have not **k** my own vineyard. Sg 1:6
I have **k** silent from ages past; Is 42:14
Have I not **k** silent for such a Is 57:11
and have **k** all his commands Jr 35:18
where he **k** him in custody until Jr 52:11
My statutes or **k** My ordinances; Ezk 5:7
have not even **k** the ordinances Ezk 5:7
You have not **k** charge of My holy Ezk 44:8
k charge of My sanctuary when Ezk 44:15
who **k** My charge and did not go Ezk 48:11
he wanted and **k** alive anyone he Dn 5:19
k trying to find a charge Dn 6:4
As I **k** watching, thrones were Dn 7:9
but I **k** the matter to myself." Dn 7:28
So the LORD **k** the disaster in Dn 9:14
They **k** sacrificing to the Baals Hs 11:2
and have not **k** His statutes. Am 2:4
you have not **k** ⌊them⌋. Return to Mal 3:7
I will declare things **k** secret Mt 13:35
region came and **k** crying out, Mt 15:22
and **k** on giving them to the Mt 15:36
"I have **k** all these," the young Mt 19:20
those who followed **k** shouting: Mt 21:9
And the crowds **k** saying, "This Mt 21:11
Jesus **k** silent. Then the high Mt 26:63
But they **k** shouting, "Crucify Mt 27:23
and **k** hitting Him on the head. Mt 27:30
with Him **k** taunting Him. Mt 27:44
And he **k** begging Him not to send Mk 5:10
demon-possessed **k** begging Him to Mk 5:18
and **k** begging Him, "My little Mk 5:23
k giving them to His disciples Mk 6:41
she **k** asking Him to drive the Mk 7:26
and **k** on giving ⌊them⌋ to His Mk 8:6
They **k** this word to themselves, Mk 9:10
have **k** all these from my youth. Mk 10:20
those who followed **k** shouting: Mk 11:9
But he **k** insisting, "If I have Mk 14:31
But He **k** silent and did not Mk 14:61
They **k** hitting Him on the head Mk 15:19
He **k** making signs to them and Lk 1:22
conceived and **k** herself in Lk 1:24
His mother **k** all these things in Lk 2:51
amazement and **k** saying to one Lk 4:36
had departed **k** begging Him to be Lk 8:38
k giving them to the disciples Lk 9:16
They **k** silent, and in those days Lk 9:36
But they **k** silent. He took the Lk 14:4
in that town **k** coming to him, Lk 18:3
to heaven but **k** striking his Lk 18:13
have **k** all these from my youth, Lk 18:21
he **k** crying out all the more, Lk 18:39
I have **k** it hidden away in a Lk 19:20
later, another **k** insisting, "This Lk 22:59
Him, they **k** asking, "Prophesy! Lk 22:64
But they **k** insisting, "He stirs Lk 23:5
So he **k** asking Him questions, Lk 23:9
but they **k** shouting, "Crucify! Lk 23:21
But they **k** up the pressure, Lk 23:23
and even the leaders **k** scoffing: Lk 23:35
But you have **k** the fine wine Jn 2:10
the disciples **k** urging Him, Jn 4:31
He **k** saying, "I'm the one!" Jn 9:9
eyes also have **k** this man from Jn 11:37
she has **k** it for the day of My Jn 12:7
to meet Him. They **k** shouting: Jn 12:13
Since Judas **k** the money-bag, Jn 13:29
just as I have **k** My Father's Jn 15:10
they **k** My word, they will also Jn 15:20
and they have **k** Your word. Jn 17:6
other disciples **k** telling him, Jn 20:25
he **k** back part of the proceeds Ac 5:2
angels and yet have not **k** it." Ac 7:53
and **k** confounding the Jews who Ac 9:22
So Peter was **k** in prison, but Ac 12:5

But she **k** insisting that it was Ac 12:15
Peter, however, **k** on knocking, Ac 12:16
And there they **k** evangelizing. Ac 14:7
sleep as Paul **k** on speaking. Ac 20:9
ordered that he be **k** under guard Ac 23:35
Paul should be **k** at Caesarea, Ac 25:4
him to be **k** in custody until Ac 25:21
and the severe storm **k** raging; Ac 27:20
But the centurion **k** them from Ac 27:43
what people have **k** secret, Rm 2:16
sacred secret **k** silent for long Rm 16:25
I have **k** myself, and will keep 2Co 11:9
they simply **k** hearing: Gl 1:23
body be **k** sound and blameless 1Th 5:23
the race, I have **k** the faith. 2Tm 4:7
the marriage bed **k** undefiled, Heb 13:4
and unfading, **k** in heaven for 1Pt 1:4
delivered them to be **k** in chains 2Pt 2:4
k until the day of judgment 2Pt 3:7
Father and **k** by Jesus Christ. Jd 1
He has **k**, with eternal chains Jd 6
strength, have **k** My word, and Rv 3:8
Because you have **k** My command Rv 3:10
for they have **k** their virginity. Rv 14:4
her burning and **k** crying out: Rv 18:18
on their heads and **k** crying out, Rv 18:19

KEREN-HAPPUCH *(1)*
second Keziah, and his third **K**. Jb 42:14

KERIOTH *(2)*
K, Bozrah, and all the towns of Jr 48:24
will consume the citadels of **K**. Am 2:2

KERIOTH-HEZRON *(1)*
(AKA HAZOR)
K (that is, Hazor), Jos 15:25

KERNELS *(2)*
of grain, crushed **k**, roasted on Lv 2:14
its crushed **k** and oil with all Lv 2:16

KEROS'S *(2)*
K descendants, Siaha's Ezr 2:44
K descendants, Sia's descendants, Neh 7:47

KETTLE *(1)*
the container or **k** or caldron or 1Sm 2:14

KETTLES *(1)*
in pots, in **k**, and in bowls; 2Ch 35:13

KETURAH *(3)*
another wife, whose name was **K**, Gn 25:1
All these were sons of **K**. Gn 25:4
The sons born to **K**, Abraham's 1Ch 1:32

KETURAH'S *(1)*
All of these were **K** sons. 1Ch 1:33

KEY *(6)*
they took the **k** and opened the Jdg 3:25
I will place the **k** of the House Is 22:22
taken away the **k** of knowledge! Lk 11:52
the One who has the **k** of David, Rv 3:7
The **k** to the shaft of the abyss Rv 9:1
heaven with the **k** to the abyss Rv 20:1

KEYS *(2)*
give you the **k** of the kingdom Mt 16:19
and I hold the **k** of death and Rv 1:18

KEZIAH *(1)*
his second **K**, and his third Jb 42:14

KIBROTH-HATTAAVAH *(5)*
So they named that place **K**, Nm 11:34
From **K** the people moved on to Nm 11:35
of Sinai and camped at **K**. Nm 33:16
departed from **K** and camped at Nm 33:17
LORD at Taberah, Massah, and **K**. Dt 9:22

KIBZAIM *(1)*
K with its pasturelands, and Jos 21:22

KICK *(1)*
hard for you to **k** against the Ac 26:14

KID *(1)*
lambs, and **k** goats, plus 3,000 2Ch 35:7

KIDNAPPED *(4)*
For I was **k** from the land of the Gn 40:15
They also had **k** the women and 1Sm 30:2
sons, and daughters had been **k**. 1Sm 30:3
the Carmelite, had also been **k**. 1Sm 30:5

KIDNAPPER *(1)*
or sells him, the **k** must die. Dt 24:7

KIDNAPPERS *(1)*
homosexuals, for **k**, liars, 1Tm 1:10

KIDNAPPING *(1)*
a man is discovered **k** one of his Dt 24:7

KIDNAPS *(1)*
Whoever **k** a person must be put Ex 21:16

KIDNEYS *(19)*
and the two **k** with the fat on Ex 29:13
the two **k** and the fat on them, Ex 29:22
and the two **k** with the fat on Lv 3:4
lobe of the liver with the **k**. Lv 3:4
the two **k** with the fat on them Lv 3:10
lobe of the liver above the **k**. Lv 3:10
and the two **k** with the fat on Lv 3:15
lobe of the liver with the **k**. Lv 3:15
and the two **k** with the fat on Lv 4:9
lobe of the liver with the **k**, Lv 4:9
and the two **k** with the fat on Lv 7:4
lobe of the liver with the **k**. Lv 7:4
and the two **k** with their fat, Lv 8:16
and the two **k** with their fat— Lv 8:25
the fat, the **k**, and the fatty Lv 9:10
entrails⌋, the **k**, and the fatty Lv 9:19
pierces my **k** without mercy and Jb 16:13
with the fat of the **k** of rams. Is 34:6
He pierced my **k** with His arrows. Lm 3:13

KIDRON *(12)*
king was crossing the **K** Valley, 2Sm 15:23
do leave and cross the **K** Valley, 1Kg 2:37
and burned it in the **K** Valley. 1Kg 15:13
fields of the **K** and carried 2Kg 23:4
temple to the **K** Valley outside 2Kg 23:6
He burned it at the **K** Valley, 2Kg 23:6
their dust into the **K** Valley. 2Kg 23:12
and burned it in the **K** Valley. 2Ch 15:16
them outside to the **K** Valley. 2Ch 29:16
threw them into the **K** Valley. 2Ch 30:14
as far as the **K** Valley to the Jr 31:40
disciples across the **K** Valley, Jn 18:1

KILL *(192)*
whoever finds me will **k** me." Gn 4:14
found him would not **k** him. Gn 4:15
They will **k** me but let you Gn 12:12
to **k** the righteous with the Gn 18:25
will **k** me because of my wife. Gn 20:11
the place will **k** me on account Gn 26:7
then I will **k** my brother Jacob." Gn 27:41
himself by planning to **k** you. Gn 27:42
them, they plotted to **k** him. Gn 37:18
let's **k** him and throw him into Gn 37:20
do we gain if we **k** our brother Gn 37:26
You can **k** my two sons if I don't Gn 42:37
For in their anger they **k** men, Gn 49:6
return from the **k**—he crouches; Gn 49:9
child is a son, **k** him, but if Ex 1:16
you planning to **k** me as you Ex 2:14
about this, he tried to **k** Moses. Ex 2:15
who wanted to **k** you are dead." Ex 4:19
I will **k** your firstborn son!" Ex 4:23
a sword in their hand to **k** us!" Ex 5:21
us out of Egypt to **k** us and our Ex 17:3
and I will **k** you with the sword; Ex 22:24
Do not **k** the innocent and the Ex 23:7
an evil intent to **k** them in the Ex 32:12
and each of you **k** his brother, Ex 32:27
you are also to **k** the animal. Lv 20:15
you are to **k** the woman and the Lv 20:16
this, please **k** me right now. Nm 11:15
If You **k** this people with a Nm 14:15
milk and honey to **k** us in the Nm 16:13
in my hand, I'd **k** you now!" Nm 22:29
K each of the men who aligned Nm 25:5
k all the male children and kill Nm 31:17
children and **k** every woman who Nm 31:17
himself is to **k** the murderer; Nm 35:19
he finds him, he is to **k** him. Nm 35:19
of blood is to **k** the murderer Nm 35:21
that could **k** a person and he Nm 35:23
brought them out to **k** them in Dt 9:28
Instead, you must **k** him. Dt 13:9
a bribe to **k** an innocent person Dt 27:25
and they did not **k** them. Jos 9:26
kind of men did you **k** at Tabor?" Jdg 8:18
them live, I would not **k** you." Jdg 8:19
firstborn, "Get up and **k** them." Jdg 8:20
Get up and **k** us yourself, Jdg 8:21
had helped him **k** his brothers. Jdg 9:24
Draw your sword and **k** me, Jdg 9:54
the LORD had intended to **k** us, Jdg 13:23
that you yourselves won't **k** me." Jdg 15:12
said, "we won't **k** you, but we Jdg 15:13
until dawn; then we will **k** him." Jdg 16:2
They intended to **k** me, but they Jdg 20:5
Go and **k** the inhabitants of Jdg 21:10
the LORD intended to **k** them. 1Sm 2:25
to us to **k** us and our people! 1Sm 5:10
so it won't **k** us and our people 1Sm 5:11
us those men so we can **k** them!" 1Sm 11:12
K men and women, children and 1Sm 15:3
will hear ⌊about it⌋ and **k** me!" 1Sm 16:2
if I win against him and **k** him, 1Sm 17:9
fur, strike it down, and **k** it. 1Sm 17:35
sheath, and used it to **k** him. 1Sm 17:51
and all his servants to **k** David. 1Sm 19:1
My father Saul intends to **k** you. 1Sm 19:2
watch for him and **k** him in the 1Sm 19:11
him on his bed so I can **k** him." 1Sm 19:15
me go! Why should I **k** you?' " 1Sm 19:17
wrong, then **k** me yourself; 1Sm 20:8
his spear at Jonathan to **k** him, 1Sm 20:33
was determined to **k** David. 1Sm 20:33
Turn and **k** the priests of the 1Sm 22:17
⌊Someone⌋ advised ⌊me⌋ to **k** you, 1Sm 24:10
cut it off, but I didn't **k** you. 1Sm 24:11
me over to you, you didn't **k** me. 1Sm 24:18
that you won't **k** me or turn me 1Sm 30:15
Stand over me and **k** me, for I'm 2Sm 1:9
and said, "Come here and **k** him!" 2Sm 1:15
when wicked men **k** a righteous 2Sm 4:11
you to strike Amnon, then **k** him. 2Sm 13:28
If I am guilty, let him **k** me." 2Sm 14:32
had tried to **k** them in his zeal 2Sm 21:2
new armor, intended to **k** David. 2Sm 21:16
he will not **k** his servant with 1Kg 1:51
'I will never **k** you with the 1Kg 2:8
first woman, and don't **k** him. 1Kg 3:27
Solomon tried to **k** Jeroboam, 1Kg 11:40
me of my guilt and to **k** my son?" 1Kg 17:18
doesn't find you, he will **k** me. 1Kg 18:12
is here!" ' He will **k** me!" 1Kg 18:14
leave me, a lion will **k** you." 1Kg 20:36
My father, should I **k** them? 2Kg 6:21
I kill them? I will **k** them." 2Kg 6:21
Elisha replied, "Don't **k** them. 2Kg 6:22
Do you **k** those you have captured 2Kg 6:22
if they **k** us, we will die." 2Kg 7:4
You will **k** their young men with 2Kg 8:12
and officers, "Go in and **k** them. 2Kg 10:25
the first to **k** a Jebusite will 1Ch 11:6
so that she did not **k** him. 2Ch 22:11
them and can **k** them and stop Neh 4:11
they are coming to **k** you. Neh 6:10
are coming to **k** you tonight! Neh 6:10
destroy, **k**, and annihilate all Est 3:13
to destroy, **k**, and annihilate Est 8:11
a viper's fangs will **k** him. Jb 20:16
rises at dawn to **k** the poor and Jb 24:14
who seek to **k** me be disgraced Ps 35:4
righteous and seeks to **k** him; Ps 37:32
Do not **k** them; otherwise, my Ps 59:11
They **k** the widow and the Ps 94:6
if only You would **k** the wicked— Ps 139:19
set an ambush and **k** someone. Pr 1:11
set an ambush to **k** themselves; Pr 1:18
the inexperienced will **k** them, Pr 1:32
craving will **k** him because his Pr 21:25
a time to **k** and a time to heal; Ec 3:3
and He will **k** the wicked with a Is 11:4
but I will **k** your root with Is 14:30
and the Lord GOD will **k** you; Is 65:15
the sword to **k**, the dogs to drag Jr 15:3
he didn't **k** me in the womb so Jr 20:17
and he will **k** them before your Jr 29:21
you, you will **k** me, won't you? Jr 38:15
will not **k** you or hand you over Jr 38:16
from us and we won't **k** you. Jr 38:25
Let me go **k** Ishmael son of Jr 40:15
Ishmael, "Don't **k** us, for we Jr 41:8
and did not **k** them along with Jr 41:8
you **k** those who should not die Ezk 13:19
They will **k** their sons and Ezk 23:47
the presence of those who **k** you? Ezk 28:9
in the hands of those who **k** you. Ezk 28:9
Don't **k** the wise men of Babylon! Dn 2:24
I will **k** the precious offspring Hs 9:16
the land and **k** all its officials Am 2:3
Then I will **k** the rest of them Am 9:1

command the sword to **k** them. Am 9:4
filled up its dens with the **k**, Nah 2:12
fear those who **k** the body but Mt 10:28
but are not able to **k** the soul; Mt 10:28
Though he wanted to **k** him, Mt 14:5
will **k** Him, and on the third Mt 17:23
let's **k** him and take his Mt 21:38
of them you will **k** and crucify, Mt 23:34
and they will **k** you. Mt 24:9
in a treacherous way and **k** Him. Mt 26:4
do evil, to save life or to **k**?" Mk 3:4
against him and wanted to **k** him. Mk 6:19
They will **k** Him, and after He is Mk 9:31
flog Him, and **k** Him, and He will Mk 10:34
Come, let's **k** him, and the Mk 12:7
way to arrest and **k** Him. Mk 14:1
them they will **k** and persecute, Lk 11:49
don't fear those who **k** the body, Lk 12:4
of here! Herod wants to **k** You!" Lk 13:31
Him, they will **k** Him, and He Lk 18:33
Let's **k** him, so the inheritance Lk 20:14
They will **k** some of you. Lk 21:16
trying all the more to **k** Him: Jn 5:18
the Jews were trying to **k** Him. Jn 7:1
Why do you want to **k** Me?" Jn 7:19
responded. "Who wants to **k** You?" Jn 7:20
this the man they want to **k**? Jn 7:25
He won't **k** Himself, will He Jn 8:22
you are trying to **k** Me because Jn 8:37
But now you are trying to **k** Me, Jn 8:40
steal and to **k** and to destroy. Jn 10:10
day on they plotted to **k** Him. Jn 11:53
decided to also **k** Lazarus, Jn 12:10
nail Him to a cross and **k** Him. Ac 2:23
enraged and wanted to **k** them. Ac 5:33
you want to **k** me, the same way Ac 7:28
the Jews conspired to **k** him, Ac 9:23
and night intending to **k** him, Ac 9:24
but they attempted to **k** him. Ac 9:29
him, "Get up, Peter; **k** and eat!" Ac 10:13
me, 'Get up, Peter; **k** and eat!' Ac 11:7
and was going to **k** himself, Ac 16:27
As they were trying to **k** him, Ac 21:31
following and yelling, "**K** him!" Ac 21:36
near, we are ready to **k** him." Ac 23:15
eat or drink until they **k** him. Ac 23:21
ambush along the road to **k** him. Ac 25:3
complex and were trying to **k** me. Ac 26:21
plan was to **k** the prisoners so Ac 27:42
those who **k** their fathers and 1Tm 1:9
I will **k** her children with the Rv 2:23
of the earth, to **k** by the sword, Rv 6:8
were not permitted to **k** them, Rv 9:5
were released to **k** a third of Rv 9:15
them, conquer them, and **k** them. Rv 11:7

KILLED *(214)*

his brother Abel and **k** him. Gn 4:8
For I **k** a man for wounding me, Gn 4:23
of Abel, since Cain **k** him." Gn 4:25
city, and **k** every male. Gn 34:25
k Hamor and his son Shechem Gn 34:26
kill me as you **k** the Egyptian?" Ex 2:14
LORD **k** every firstborn ⌊male⌋ Ex 13:15
"You have **k** the LORD's people!" Nm 16:41
who has been **k** by the sword or Nm 19:16
or a person who had been **k**. Nm 19:18
would have **k** you by now and let Nm 22:33
leader who was **k** the day the Nm 25:18
Moses, and **k** every male. Nm 31:7
they **k** the Midianite kings— Nm 31:8
They also **k** Balaam son of Beor Nm 31:8
prisoners who have **k** a person or Nm 31:19
for the one who **k** a person was Nm 35:28
one who has **k** a person return Nm 35:28
manslaughter and **k** his neighbor Dt 4:42
having **k** his neighbor Dt 19:4
and it is not known who **k** him, Dt 21:1
man and the virgin ⌊will be **k**⌋ Dt 32:25
the Israelites **k** with the sword. Jos 10:11
Moses had **k** him and the chiefs Jos 13:21
death, they also **k** the diviner, Jos 13:22
for he **k** his neighbor Jos 20:5
they **k** Oreb at the rock of Oreb Jdg 7:25
who had been **k** were 120,000 Jdg 8:10
of Penuel and **k** the men of the Jdg 8:17
So Gideon got up, **k** Zebah and Jdg 8:21
in Ophrah and **k** his 70 brothers, Jdg 9:5
k his 70 sons on top of a large Jdg 9:18
Abimelech, who **k** them, and on Jdg 9:24
and **k** the people who were in it. Jdg 9:45
say about me, 'A woman **k** him.' " Jdg 9:54
seized him and **k** him at the Jdg 12:6
Ashkelon and **k** 30 of their men Jdg 14:19
took it, and **k** 1,000 men with it Jdg 15:15
of a donkey I have **k** 1,000 men. Jdg 15:16
And the dead he **k** at his death Jdg 16:30
than those he had **k** in his life. Jdg 16:30
They **k** them with their swords Jdg 18:27
and Israel **k** 5,000 men on the Jdg 20:45
and **k** them with their Jdg 20:48
servant has **k** lions and bears 1Sm 17:36
down the Philistine and **k** him. 1Sm 17:50
Saul has **k** his thousands, but 1Sm 18:7
went out and **k** 200 Philistines 1Sm 18:27
lives, David will not be **k**." 1Sm 19:6
Why is he to be **k**? What has he 1Sm 20:32
you **k** in the valley of Elah, 1Sm 21:9
Saul has **k** his thousands, but 1Sm 21:11
he **k** 85 men who wore linen 1Sm 22:18
that Saul had **k** the priests 1Sm 22:21
how he has **k** the mediums and 1Sm 28:9
a trap for me to get me **k**?" 1Sm 28:9
Saul has **k** his thousands, but 1Sm 29:5
had **k** no one but had carried 1Sm 30:2
Many were **k** on Mount Gilboa. 1Sm 31:1
and his sons and **k** his sons, 1Sm 31:2
over him and **k** him because I 2Sm 1:10
'I **k** the LORD's anointed.' " 2Sm 1:16
but they had **k** 360 of the 2Sm 2:31
brother Abishai **k** Abner because 2Sm 3:30
bedroom and stabbed and **k** him. 2Sm 4:7
and they **k** Rechab and Baanah. 2Sm 4:12
and David **k** 700 of their 2Sm 10:18
think they have **k** all the young 2Sm 13:32
one struck the other and **k** him. 2Sm 14:6
over the one who **k** his brother 2Sm 14:7
Absalom, struck him, and **k** him. 2Sm 18:15
any man be **k** in Israel today? 2Sm 19:22
when he **k** the Gibeonites." 2Sm 21:1
Philistines **k** Saul at Gilboa. 2Sm 21:12
the Philistine, and **k** him. 2Sm 21:17
Sibbecai the Hushathite **k** Saph, 2Sm 21:18
the Bethlehemite **k** Goliath the 2Sm 21:19
David's brother Shimei, **k** him. 2Sm 21:21
Gath and were **k** by David and his 2Sm 21:22
800 ⌊men⌋ he **k** at one time. 2Sm 23:8
against 300 ⌊men⌋ and **k** them, 2Sm 23:18
Benaiah **k** two sons of Ariel of 2Sm 23:20
pit on a snowy day and **k** a lion. 2Sm 23:20
He also **k** an Egyptian, a huge 2Sm 23:21
and then **k** him with his own 2Sm 23:21
"but please don't have him **k**!" 1Kg 3:26
k the Canaanites who lived in 1Kg 9:16
until he had **k** every male in 1Kg 11:16
party when David **k** the Zobaites. 1Kg 11:24
met him along the way and **k** him. 1Kg 13:24
and it has mauled him and **k** him, 1Kg 13:26
Baasha **k** Nadab and reigned in 1Kg 15:28
in, struck Elah down, and **k** him. 1Kg 16:10
how he had **k** all the prophets 1Kg 19:1
and **k** Your prophets with the 1Kg 19:10
and **k** Your prophets with the 1Kg 19:14
a lion found him and **k** him. 1Kg 20:36
clashed swords and **k** each other. 2Kg 3:23
against my master and **k** him. 2Kg 10:9
Jehu **k** all who remained of the 2Kg 10:11
who were being **k** and ⌊put⌋ him 2Kg 11:2
from Athaliah and was not **k**. 2Kg 11:2
pieces, and they **k** Mattan, the 2Kg 11:18
against him and **k** him at 2Kg 12:20
Amaziah **k** his servants who had 2Kg 14:5
Amaziah **k** 10,000 Edomites in the 2Kg 14:7
down publicly, **k** him, and became 2Kg 15:10
He **k** him and became king in his 2Kg 15:14
He **k** Pekahiah and became king 2Kg 15:25
attacked him, **k** him, and became 2Kg 15:30
them, which **k** some of them. 2Kg 17:25
the king and **k** him in his own 2Kg 21:23
when Neco saw him he **k** him. 2Kg 23:29
⌊they **k**⌋ the Jews and the 2Kg 25:25
Hagrites were **k** because it was 1Ch 5:22
in the land **k** Ezer and Elead 1Ch 7:21
them and were **k** on Mount Gilboa. 1Ch 10:1
and his sons and **k** Saul's sons 1Ch 10:2
against 300 and **k** them at one 1Ch 11:11
They **k** the Philistines, and the 1Ch 11:14
against 300 ⌊men⌋ and **k** them, 1Ch 11:20
Benaiah **k** two ⌊sons of⌋ Ariel of 1Ch 11:22
pit on a snowy day and **k** a lion. 1Ch 11:22
He also **k** an Egyptian who was 1Ch 11:23
and then **k** him with his own 1Ch 11:23
and David **k** 7,000 of their 1Ch 19:18
He also **k** Shophach, commander 1Ch 19:18
the Hushathite **k** Sippai, 1Ch 20:4
son of Jair **k** Lahmi the brother 1Ch 20:5
David's brother Shimei, **k** him. 1Ch 20:7
giant in Gath **k** by David and his 1Ch 20:8
choice men of Israel were **k**. 2Ch 13:17
and also have **k** your brothers, 2Ch 21:13
to the camp had **k** all the older 2Ch 22:1
serving Ahaziah, and he **k** them. 2Ch 22:8
him to Jehu, and they **k** him. 2Ch 22:9
who were being **k** and put him 2Ch 22:11
images into pieces and **k** Mattan, 2Ch 23:17
extended to him, but **k** his son. 2Ch 24:22
him, and **k** him on his bed, 2Ch 24:25
son of Remaliah **k** 120,000 in 2Ch 28:6
named Zichri **k** the king's son 2Ch 28:7
k their choice young men with 2Ch 36:17
They **k** the Passover lamb for Ezr 6:20
their backs and **k** Your prophets Neh 9:26
of Susa the Jews **k** and destroyed Est 9:6
They **k** these 10 sons of Haman Est 9:10
of people **k** in the fortress Est 9:11
the Jews have **k** and destroyed Est 9:12
of Adar and **k** 300 men in Susa, Est 9:15
They **k** 75,000 of those who hated Est 9:16
and He **k** some of their best men. Ps 78:31
When He **k** ⌊some of⌋ them, Ps 78:34
He **k** their vines with hail and Ps 78:47
I'll be **k** in the streets!" Pr 22:13
they were not **k** in battle. Is 22:2
Was he **k** like those killed by Is 27:7
he killed like those **k** by Him? Is 27:7
with evil intent will be **k**— Is 29:20
he **k** the one the king of Babylon Jr 41:2
day after he had **k** Gedaliah, Jr 41:4
after Ishmael had **k** Gedaliah son Jr 41:16
He has **k** everyone who was loved, Lm 2:4
and prophets be **k** in the Lord's Lm 2:20
You have **k** ⌊them⌋ in the day of Lm 2:21
You have **k** without compassion. Lm 3:43
daughters, and **k** her with the Ezk 23:10
would not be **k** with the rest Dn 2:18
raging flames **k** those men who Dn 3:22
He **k** anyone he wanted and kept Dn 5:19
the king of the Chaldeans was **k**, Dn 5:30
the beast was **k** and its body Dn 7:11
I have **k** them with the words of Hs 6:5
I **k** your young men with the Am 4:10
and scribes, be **k**, and be raised Mt 16:21
slaves, beat one, **k** another, and Mt 21:35
out of the vineyard, and **k** him. Mt 21:39
them outrageously and **k** them. Mt 22:6
scribes, be **k**, and rise after Mk 8:31
and after He is **k**, He will rise Mk 9:31
another, and they **k** that one. Mk 12:5
they beat some and they **k** some. Mk 12:5
seized him, **k** him, and threw Mk 12:8
and scribes, be **k**, and be raised Lk 9:22
and your fathers **k** them. Lk 11:47
fathers, for they **k** them, and Lk 11:48
tower in Siloam fell on and **k**— Lk 13:4
out of the vineyard and **k** him. Lk 20:15
And you **k** the source of life, Ac 3:15
He was **k**, and all his partisans Ac 5:36
the same way you **k** the Egyptian Ac 7:28
They even **k** those who announced Ac 7:52
yet they **k** Him by hanging Him on Ac 10:39
and he **k** James, John's brother, Ac 12:2
they asked Pilate to have Him **k**. Ac 13:28
clothes of those who **k** him.' Ac 22:20
to drink until they had **k** Paul. Ac 23:12
anything until we have **k** Paul. Ac 23:14
and was about to be **k** by them, Ac 23:27
me, and through it **k** me. Rm 7:11
they have **k** Your prophets, Rm 11:3
and were **k** by the destroyer. 1Co 10:10
as being chastened yet not **k**; 2Co 6:9
They **k** both the Lord Jesus and 1Th 2:15
who was **k** among you, where Rv 2:13
going to be **k** just as they had Rv 6:11
human race was **k** by these three Rv 9:18
who were not **k** by these plagues, Rv 9:20

them, he must be **k** in this way. Rv 11:5
people were **k** in the earthquake Rv 11:13
anyone is to be **k** with a sword, Rv 13:10
with a sword he will be **k**. Rv 13:10
the image of the beast to be **k**. Rv 13:15
The rest were **k** with the sword Rv 19:21

KILLER *(1)*
peace, Zimri, **k** of your master? 2Kg 9:31

KILLING *(19)*
who is guilty of **k** someone; Nm 35:31
had finished **k** everyone living Jos 8:24
father, by **k** his 70 brothers, Jdg 9:56
k about 30 men of Israel on the Jdg 20:31
strike them down, **k** about 30 men Jdg 20:39
returned from **k** the Philistine, 1Sm 17:57
returning from **k** the Philistine, 1Sm 18:6
innocent blood by **k** David for no 1Sm 19:5
no part in the **k** of Abner son 2Sm 3:37
I am staying with by **k** her son?" 1Kg 17:20
k and giving life that this man 2Kg 5:7
which are **k** them because the 2Kg 17:26
his position by **k** with the sword 2Ch 21:4
to the sword, **k** and destroying Est 9:5
don't be intent on **k** him. Pr 19:18
set them apart for the day of **k**. Jr 12:3
the city after him and start **k**; Ezk 9:5
So they went out **k** ⌊people⌋ in Ezk 9:7
While they were **k**, I was left Ezk 9:8

KILLS *(30)*
whoever **k** Cain will suffer Gn 4:15
and it **k** a man or a woman, Ex 21:29
If a man **k** anyone, he must be Lv 24:17
Whoever **k** an animal is to make Lv 24:18
Whoever **k** an animal is to make Lv 24:21
but whoever **k** a person is to be Lv 24:21
the one who **k** someone may flee Nm 35:6
so that a person who **k** someone Nm 35:11
the one who **k** someone will not Nm 35:12
so that anyone who **k** a person Nm 35:15
protect the one who **k** someone Nm 35:25
If the one who **k** someone ever Nm 35:26
of his city of refuge and **k** him, Nm 35:27
If anyone **k** a person, the Nm 35:30
of someone who **k** a person and Dt 19:4
is the one who **k** his neighbor Dt 27:24
so that a person who **k** someone Jos 20:3
so that anyone who **k** a person Jos 20:9
in a fight against me and **k** me, 1Sm 17:9
make the man who **k** him very 1Sm 17:25
the man who **k** that Philistine 1Sm 17:26
be done for the man who **k** him." 1Sm 17:27
For anger **k** a fool, and jealousy Jb 5:2
Even if He **k** me, I will hope in Jb 13:15
he **k** the innocent in secret Ps 10:8
slaughters an ox, one **k** a man; Is 66:3
The city who **k** the prophets and Mt 23:37
The city who **k** the prophets and Lk 13:34
when anyone who **k** you will think Jn 16:2
for the letter **k**, but the Spirit 2Co 3:6

KINAH *(1)*
K, Dimonah, Adadah, Jos 15:22

KIND *(85)*
winged bird according to its **k**. Gn 1:21
the ground according to its **k**— Gn 6:20
with you every **k** of food that is Gn 6:21
on the earth according to its **k**, Gn 7:14
some of every **k** of clean animal Gn 8:20
animal and every **k** of clean bird Gn 8:20
your father—the **k** he loves. Gn 27:9
What **k** of dream is this that you Gn 37:10
and ability in every **k** of craft Ex 35:31
work in every **k** of artistic Ex 35:33
They can do every **k** of craft and Ex 35:35
every **k** of raven, Lv 11:15
and plant any **k** of tree for food Lv 19:23
the same **k** of grain offering Nm 28:8
every **k** of raven, Dt 14:14
Asherah of any **k** of wood next to Dt 16:21
a loan of any **k** to your neighbor Dt 24:10
k of men did you kill at Tabor? Jdg 8:18
Why are you so **k** to notice me, Ru 2:10
you have been so **k** to me, Ru 2:13
to do every **k** of bronze work. 1Kg 7:14
by speaking **k** words to them, 1Kg 12:7
people skilled in every **k** of 1Ch 22:15
articles for every **k** of service; 1Ch 28:14
articles for every **k** of service; 1Ch 28:14
If you will be **k** to these people 2Ch 10:7
by speaking **k** words to them, 2Ch 10:7
or any **k** of grain to sell Neh 10:31
are **k** and ready to forgive, Ps 86:5
A **k** man benefits himself, but a Pr 11:17
but one who is **k** to the needy Pr 14:31
it for one who is **k** to the poor. Pr 28:8
planted every **k** of fruit tree Ec 2:5
from Judah every **k** of security: Is 3:1
from bowls to every **k** of jar. Is 22:24
favorably on this **k** of person: Is 66:2
their abominations of every **k**. Ezk 6:9
Birds of every **k** will nest under Ezk 17:23
your⌋ great wealth of every **k**. Ezk 27:12
your great wealth of every **k**, Ezk 27:18
k of precious stone covered Ezk 28:13
as food to every **k** of predatory Ezk 39:4
Tell every **k** of bird and all the Ezk 39:17
of every **k** and contribution Ezk 44:30
of every **k** from all your gifts Ezk 44:30
Every ⌊**k** of⌋ living creature Ezk 47:9
in every **k** of literature Dn 1:17
visions and dreams of every **k**. Dn 1:17
drum, and every **k** of music, you Dn 3:5
harp, and every **k** of music, Dn 3:7
and every **k** of music must fall Dn 3:10
drum, and every **k** of music, fall Dn 3:15
of it, every **k** of wild animal. Zph 2:14
replied with **k** and comforting Zch 1:13
say every **k** of evil against Mt 5:11
asked, "What **k** of man is this? Mt 8:27
It collected every **k** ⌊of fish⌋, Mt 13:47
this **k** does not come out except Mt 17:21
the **k** that hasn't taken place Mt 24:21
This **k** can come out by nothing Mk 9:29
the **k** that hasn't been from the Mk 13:19
wondering what **k** of greeting Lk 1:29
who and what **k** of woman this is Lk 7:39
rue, and every **k** of herb, and Lk 11:42
signify what **k** of death He was Jn 12:33
signify by what **k** of death he Jn 21:19
He wrote a letter of this **k**: Ac 23:25
By what **k** of law? By one Rm 3:27
in me coveting of every **k**. Rm 7:8
and the **k** of sexual immorality 1Co 5:1
patient; love is **k**. Love does 1Co 13:4
What **k** of body will they have 1Co 15:35
who are in any **k** of affliction, 2Co 1:4
We have this **k** of confidence 2Co 3:4
of every **k** of impurity with Eph 4:19
be **k** and compassionate to one Eph 4:32
and every **k** of discernment, Php 1:9
You know what **k** of men we were 1Th 1:5
about us what **k** of reception we 1Th 1:9
and to be **k**, always showing Ti 3:2
For this is the **k** of high priest Heb 7:26
we have this **k** of high priest, Heb 8:1
forgets what **k** of man he was. Jms 1:24
is disorder and every **k** of evil. Jms 3:16
with every **k** of precious stone Rv 21:19

KINDLE *(8)*
and He will **k** a burning fire Is 10:16
Look, all you who **k** a fire, who Is 50:11
My anger will **k** a fire that will Jr 15:14
I will **k** a fire in its forest Jr 21:14
will **k** a fire in the temples of Jr 43:12
Pile on the logs and **k** the fire! Ezk 24:10
will go out, **k** fires, and burn Ezk 39:9
no longer **k** a useless ⌊fire Mal 1:10

KINDLED *(4)*
For fire has been **k** because of Dt 32:22
wrath that is **k** against us 2Kg 22:13
My wrath will be **k** against this 2Kg 22:17
see that I, Yahweh, have **k** it. Ezk 20:48

KINDLES *(4)*
and briers and **k** the forest Is 9:18
a torrent of brimstone, **k** it. Is 30:33
he **k** a fire and bakes bread; Is 44:15
fire **k** the brushwood, and fire Is 64:2

KINDLING *(2)*
a quarrelsome man for **k** strife. Pr 26:21
will make the pile of **k** large. Ezk 24:9

KINDLY *(7)*
them and spoke **k** to them. Gn 50:21
her to speak **k** to her and bring Jdg 19:3
He spoke **k** to him and set his 2Kg 25:28
do not deal **k** with the widow. Jb 24:21
deal ⌊**k**⌋ with me because of Your Ps 109:21
He spoke **k** to him and set his Jr 52:32
treated Paul **k** and allowed him Ac 27:3

KINDNESS *(42)*
shown me great **k** by saving my Gn 19:19
and show **k** to my master Abraham. Gn 24:12
You have shown **k** to my master." Gn 24:14
withheld His **k** and faithfulness Gn 24:27
going to show **k** and faithfulness Gn 24:49
of all the **k** and faithfulness Gn 32:10
Joseph and extended **k** to him. Gn 39:21
show **k** to me by mentioning Gn 40:14
will also show **k** to my family, Jos 2:12
because I showed **k** to you. Jos 2:12
we will show **k** and faithfulness Jos 2:14
They did not show **k** to the house Jdg 8:35
not forsaken his **k** to the living Ru 2:20
shown more **k** now than before Ru 3:10
Since you showed **k** to all the 1Sm 15:6
this special **k** to Saul your lord 2Sm 2:5
show special **k** and faithfulness 2Sm 2:6
family I can show **k** to because 2Sm 9:1
I can show the **k** of God to?" 2Sm 9:3
to show you **k** because of your 2Sm 9:7
I'll show **k** to Hanun son of 2Sm 10:2
as his father showed **k** to me." 2Sm 10:2
LORD show you **k** and 2Sm 15:20
are kings ⌊who show⌋ special **k**. 1Kg 20:31
I'll show **k** to Hanun son of 1Ch 19:2
his father showed **k** to me." 1Ch 19:2
remember the **k** that Zechariah's 2Ch 24:22
one show him **k**, and let no one Ps 109:12
For he did not think to show **k**, Ps 109:16
whoever shows **k** to the poor will Pr 14:21
K to the poor is a loan to the Pr 19:17
human cords, with ropes of **k**. Hs 11:4
showed us extraordinary **k**, Ac 28:2
you despise the riches of His **k**, Rm 2:4
that God's **k** is intended to lead Rm 2:4
consider God's **k** and severity: Rm 11:22
but God's **k** toward you—if Rm 11:22
you—if you remain in His **k**. Rm 11:22
by patience, by **k**, by the Holy 2Co 6:6
patience, **k**, goodness, faith Gl 5:22
grace in ⌊His⌋ **k** to us in Christ Eph 2:7
compassion, **k**, humility, Col 3:12

KINDRED *(1)*
for the welfare of all his **k**. Est 10:3

KINDS *(60)*
in it, according to their **k**." Gn 1:11
to their **k** and trees bearing Gn 1:12
in it, according to their **k**. Gn 1:12
the water, according to their **k**. Gn 1:21
creatures according to their **k**: Gn 1:24
the earth according to their **k**." Gn 1:24
the earth according to their **k**, Gn 1:25
livestock according to their **k**, Gn 1:25
the ground according to their **k**. Gn 1:25
made all **k** of bronze and iron Gn 4:22
the birds according to their **k**, Gn 6:20
livestock according to their **k**, Gn 6:20
wildlife according to their **k**, Gn 7:14
livestock according to their **k**, Gn 7:14
with wings according to their **k**. Gn 7:14
with all **k** of his master's Gn 24:10
and in all **k** of fieldwork. Ex 1:14
and all **k** of gold jewelry— Ex 35:22
eat all these ⌊**k**⌋ of land Lv 11:2
kite, the various **k** of falcon, Lv 11:14
the gull, the various **k** of hawk, Lv 11:16
stork, the various **k** of heron, Lv 11:19
may eat these **k** of all the Lv 11:21
the various **k** of locust, the Lv 11:22
the various **k** of katydid, Lv 11:22
the various **k** of cricket, Lv 11:22
the various **k** of grasshopper. Lv 11:22
the various **k** of large lizard, Lv 11:29
two different **k** of your Lv 19:19
your fields with two **k** of seed, Lv 19:19
made of two **k** of material. Lv 19:19
kite, the various **k** of falcon, Dt 14:13
the gull, the various **k** of hawk, Dt 14:15
stork, the various **k** of heron, Dt 14:18
Egyptians with all **k** of plagues 1Sm 4:8
LORD with all ⌊**k** of⌋ fir wood 2Sm 6:5
40 camel-loads of all **k** of goods 2Kg 8:9
battle with all **k** of weapons of 1Ch 12:33
brought⌋ all **k** of items of gold, 1Ch 18:10

colors, all **k** of precious stones 1Ch 29:2
how to do all **k** of engraving and 2Ch 2:14
and stalls for all **k** of cattle, 2Ch 32:28
abundance of all **k** of wine was Neh 5:18
k of goods were being brought Neh 13:15
fish and all **k** of merchandise Neh 13:16
who sell all **k** of goods camped Neh 13:20
supplying all **k** of produce; Ps 144:13
We'll find all **k** of valuable Pr 1:13
will ordain four **k** ⌊of judgment⌋ Jr 15:3
and all **k** of precious stones for Ezk 27:22
consist of many different **k**, Ezk 47:10
All ⌊**k** of⌋ trees providing food Ezk 47:12
different **k** of languages, to 1Co 12:10
various **k** of languages. 1Co 12:28
many different **k** of languages 1Co 14:10
with all **k** of false miracles, 2Th 2:9
is a root of all **k** of evil, 1Tm 6:10
astray by various **k** of strange Heb 13:9
all **k** of fragrant wood products; Rv 18:12
of life bearing 12 **k** of fruit, Rv 22:2

KING *(2328)*

those days Amraphel **k** of Shinar, Gn 14:1
of Shinar, Arioch **k** of Ellasar, Gn 14:1
Chedorlaomer **k** of Elam, and Gn 14:1
of Elam, and Tidal **k** of Goiim Gn 14:1
war against Bera **k** of Sodom, Gn 14:2
of Sodom, Birsha **k** of Gomorrah, Gn 14:2
of Gomorrah, Shinab **k** of Admah, Gn 14:2
and Shemeber **k** of Zeboiim, Gn 14:2
as well as the **k** of Bela (that Gn 14:2
Then the **k** of Sodom, the king of Gn 14:8
of Sodom, the **k** of Gomorrah, Gn 14:8
of Gomorrah, the **k** of Admah, the Gn 14:8
king of Admah, the **k** of Zeboiim, Gn 14:8
and the **k** of Bela (that is Gn 14:8
against Chedorlaomer **k** of Elam, Gn 14:9
of Elam, Tidal **k** of Goiim, Gn 14:9
of Goiim, Amraphel **k** of Shinar, Gn 14:9
and Arioch **k** of Ellasar—four Gn 14:9
the **k** of Sodom went out to meet Gn 14:17
Melchizedek, **k** of Salem, brought Gn 14:18
Then the **k** of Sodom said to Gn 14:21
Abram said to the **k** of Sodom, Gn 14:22
So Abimelech **k** of Gerar had Gn 20:2
to Abimelech, **k** of the Gn 26:1
Abimelech **k** of the Philistines Gn 26:8
of Edom before any **k** ruled over Gn 36:31
the **k** of Egypt's cupbearer and Gn 40:1
their master, the **k** of Egypt. Gn 40:1
and the baker of the **k** of Egypt, Gn 40:5
service of Pharaoh **k** of Egypt. Gn 41:46
A new **k**, who had not known Ex 1:8
Then the **k** of Egypt said to the Ex 1:15
not do as the **k** of Egypt had Ex 1:17
So the **k** of Egypt summoned the Ex 1:18
long time, the **k** of Egypt died. Ex 2:23
must go to the **k** of Egypt and Ex 3:18
I know that the **k** of Egypt will Ex 3:19
The **k** of Egypt said to them, Ex 5:4
tell Pharaoh **k** of Egypt to let Ex 6:11
and Pharaoh **k** of Egypt to bring Ex 6:13
spoke to Pharaoh **k** of Egypt in Ex 6:27
tell Pharaoh **k** of Egypt Ex 6:29
the **k** of Egypt was told that Ex 14:5
the heart of Pharaoh **k** of Egypt, Ex 14:8
from Kadesh to the **k** of Edom, Nm 20:14
When the Canaanite **k** of Arad, Nm 21:1
say to Sihon **k** of the Amorites Nm 21:21
city of Sihon **k** of the Amorites Nm 21:26
the former **k** of Moab and had Nm 21:26
to Sihon the Amorite **k**. Nm 21:29
and Og **k** of Bashan came out Nm 21:33
did to Sihon **k** of the Amorites Nm 21:34
was Moab's **k** at that time, Nm 22:4
son of Zippor, **k** of Moab, sent Nm 22:10
the **k** of Moab, from the eastern Nm 23:7
rejoicing over the **K** among them. Nm 23:21
His **k** will be greater than Agag, Nm 24:7
of Sihon **k** of the Amorites Nm 32:33
the kingdom of Og **k** of Bashan, Nm 32:33
time the Canaanite **k** of Arad, Nm 33:40
Sihon **k** of the Amorites, Dt 1:4
Heshbon, and Og **k** of Bashan, who Dt 1:4
Sihon the Amorite, **k** of Heshbon, Dt 2:24
of peace to Sihon **k** of Heshbon Dt 2:26
But Sihon **k** of Heshbon would not Dt 2:30
Bashan, and Og **k** of Bashan, with Dt 3:1
did to Sihon **k** of the Amorites Dt 3:2
handed over Og **k** of Bashan and Dt 3:3
had done to Sihon **k** of Heshbon, Dt 3:6
Only Og **k** of Bashan was left of Dt 3:11
land of Sihon **k** of the Amorites Dt 4:46
and the land of Og **k** of Bashan, Dt 4:47
the power of Pharaoh **k** of Egypt. Dt 7:8
to Pharaoh **k** of Egypt and all Dt 11:3
to appoint a **k** over us like all Dt 17:14
over you the **k** the LORD your God Dt 17:15
Appoint a **k** from your brothers. Dt 17:15
you and your **k** that you have Dt 28:36
Sihon **k** of Heshbon and Og king Dt 29:7
Heshbon and Og **k** of Bashan came Dt 29:7
So He became **K** in Jeshurun when Dt 33:5
The **k** of Jericho was told, Jos 2:2
the **k** of Jericho sent ⌊word⌋ Jos 2:3
Jericho, its **k**, and its fighting Jos 6:2
handed over to you the **k** of Ai, Jos 8:1
Treat Ai and its **k** as you did Jos 8:2
as you did Jericho and its **k**; Jos 8:2
When the **k** of Ai saw ⌊the Jos 8:14
they captured the **k** of Ai alive Jos 8:23
body of⌋ the **k** of Ai on a tree Jos 8:29
Sihon **k** of Heshbon and Og king Jos 9:10
of Heshbon and Og **k** of Bashan, Jos 9:10
Now Adoni-zedek **k** of Jerusalem Jos 10:1
Ai and its **k** as he had done to Jos 10:1
had done to Jericho and its **k**, Jos 10:1
Adoni-zedek **k** of Jerusalem sent Jos 10:3
⌊word⌋ to Hoham **k** of Hebron, Jos 10:3
of Hebron, Piram **k** of Jarmuth, Jos 10:3
of Jarmuth, Japhia **k** of Lachish, Jos 10:3
and Debir **k** of Eglon, saying, Jos 10:3
with the sword, including its **k**. Jos 10:28
he treated the **k** of Makkedah as Jos 10:28
as he had the **k** of Jericho. Jos 10:28
it and its **k** over to Israel. Jos 10:30
treated Libnah's **k** as he had the Jos 10:30
king as he had the **k** of Jericho. Jos 10:30
that time Horam **k** of Gezer went Jos 10:33
it and struck down its **k**, Jos 10:37
its **k** and all its villages. Jos 10:39
and its **k** as he had treated Jos 10:39
he had treated Libnah and its **k**. Jos 10:39
Jabin **k** of Hazor heard ⌊this Jos 11:1
Jobab **k** of Madon, the kings of Jos 11:1
down its **k** with the sword, Jos 11:10
Sihon **k** of the Amorites lived in Jos 12:2
k of Bashan, of the remnant of Jos 12:4
border of Sihon, **k** of Heshbon. Jos 12:5
the **k** of Jericho one the king of Jos 12:9
king of Jericho one the **k** of Ai, Jos 12:9
the **k** of Jerusalem one the king Jos 12:10
Jerusalem one the **k** of Hebron Jos 12:10
the **k** of Jarmuth one the king of Jos 12:11
Jarmuth one the **k** of Lachish one Jos 12:11
the **k** of Eglon one the king of Jos 12:12
of Eglon one the **k** of Gezer one Jos 12:12
the **k** of Debir one the king of Jos 12:13
of Debir one the **k** of Geder one Jos 12:13
the **k** of Hormah one the king of Jos 12:14
of Hormah one the **k** of Arad one Jos 12:14
the **k** of Libnah one the king of Jos 12:15
Libnah one the **k** of Adullam one Jos 12:15
the **k** of Makkedah one the king Jos 12:16
Makkedah one the **k** of Bethel one Jos 12:16
the **k** of Tappuah one the king of Jos 12:17
Tappuah one the **k** of Hepher one Jos 12:17
the **k** of Aphek one the king of Jos 12:18
Aphek one the **k** of Lasharon one Jos 12:18
the **k** of Madon one the king of Jos 12:19
of Madon one the **k** of Hazor one Jos 12:19
the **k** of Shimron-meron one the Jos 12:20
one the **k** of Achshaph one Jos 12:20
the **k** of Taanach one the king of Jos 12:21
Taanach one the **k** of Megiddo one Jos 12:21
the **k** of Kedesh one the king of Jos 12:22
Kedesh one the **k** of Jokneam in Jos 12:22
the **k** of Dor in Naphoth-dor one Jos 12:23
one the **k** of Goiim in Gilgal Jos 12:23
the **k** of Tirzah one ⌊the total Jos 12:24
of Sihon **k** of the Amorites Jos 13:10
of Sihon **k** of the Amorites Jos 13:21
kingdom of Sihon **k** of Heshbon. Jos 13:27
the kingdom of Og **k** of Bashan, Jos 13:30
of Zippor, **k** of Moab, set out Jos 24:9
Cushan-rishathaim **k** of Aram of Jdg 3:8
k of Aram to him, Jdg 3:10
He gave Eglon **k** of Moab power Jdg 3:12
served Eglon **k** of Moab 18 years. Jdg 3:14
sent him to Eglon **k** of Moab with Jdg 3:15
the tribute to Eglon **k** of Moab, Jdg 3:17
and said, "**K** ⌊Eglon⌋, I have Jdg 3:19
The **k** called for silence, Jdg 3:19
and the **k** stood up from his Jdg 3:20
the hand of Jabin **k** of Canaan, Jdg 4:2
peace between Jabin **k** of Hazor Jdg 4:17
subdued Jabin **k** of Canaan before Jdg 4:23
against Jabin **k** of Canaan until Jdg 4:24
"Each resembled the son of a **k**." Jdg 8:18
make Abimelech **k** at the oak of Jdg 9:6
to anoint a **k** over themselves Jdg 9:8
are anointing me as **k** over you, Jdg 9:15
honestly in making Abimelech **k**, Jdg 9:16
k over the lords of Shechem Jdg 9:18
to the **k** of the Ammonites Jdg 11:12
The **k** of the Ammonites said to Jdg 11:13
to the **k** of the Ammonites Jdg 11:14
messengers to the **k** of Edom, Jdg 11:17
but the **k** of Edom would not Jdg 11:17
messengers⌋ to the **k** of Moab, Jdg 11:17
to Sihon **k** of the Amorites, Jdg 11:19
of the Amorites, **k** of Heshbon. Jdg 11:19
Balak son of Zippor, **k** of Moab? Jdg 11:25
But the **k** of the Ammonites would Jdg 11:28
days there was no **k** in Israel; Jdg 17:6
days, there was no **k** in Israel, Jdg 18:1
when there was no **k** in Israel, Jdg 19:1
days there was no **k** in Israel; Jdg 21:25
He will give power to His **k**; 1Sm 2:10
appoint a **k** to judge us the same 1Sm 8:5
"Give us a **k** to judge us," 1Sm 8:6
have rejected Me as their **k**. 1Sm 8:7
rights of the **k** who will rule 1Sm 8:9
who were asking him for a **k**. 1Sm 8:10
rights of the **k** who will rule 1Sm 8:11
because of the **k** you've chosen 1Sm 8:18
We must have a **k** over us. 1Sm 8:19
our **k** will judge us, go out 1Sm 8:20
"Appoint a **k** for them." 1Sm 8:22
'You must set a **k** over us.' 1Sm 10:19
shouted, "Long live the **k**!" 1Sm 10:24
presence they made Saul **k**. 1Sm 11:15
to me and placed a **k** over you. 1Sm 12:1
see that the **k** is leading you. 1Sm 12:2
and to the **k** of Moab. 1Sm 12:9
saw that Nahash **k** of the 1Sm 12:12
we must have a **k** rule over us'— 1Sm 12:12
the LORD your God is your **k**. 1Sm 12:12
Now here is the **k** you've chosen, 1Sm 12:13
is the **k** the LORD has placed 1Sm 12:13
you and the **k** who rules over 1Sm 12:14
requesting a **k** for yourselves. 1Sm 12:17
requesting a **k** for ourselves." 1Sm 12:19
you and your **k** will be swept 1Sm 12:25
30 years old when he became **k**, 1Sm 13:1
anoint you as **k** over His people 1Sm 15:1
captured Agag **k** of Amalek alive 1Sm 15:8
I regret that I made Saul **k**, 1Sm 15:11
LORD anointed you **k** over Israel 1Sm 15:17
back Agag, **k** of Amalek, and I 1Sm 15:20
LORD, He has rejected you as **k**. 1Sm 15:23
you from being **k** over Israel." 1Sm 15:26
"Bring me Agag **k** of Amalek." 1Sm 15:32
He had made Saul **k** over Israel. 1Sm 15:35
rejected him as **k** over Israel? 1Sm 16:1
selected a **k** from his sons." 1Sm 16:1
k will make the man who kills 1Sm 17:25
The **k** will also make the 1Sm 17:25
⌊My⌋ **k**, as surely as you live, 1Sm 17:55
The **k** said, "Find out whose son 1Sm 17:56
cities of Israel to meet **K** Saul, 1Sm 18:6
the **k** is pleased with you, 1Sm 18:22
'The **k** desires no other 1Sm 18:25
payment to the **k** to become his 1Sm 18:27
The **k** should not sin against his 1Sm 19:4
to sit down and eat with the **k**. 1Sm 20:5
the **k** sat down to eat the meal. 1Sm 20:24
the priest, "The **k** gave me a 1Sm 21:2
and went to **K** Achish of Gath. 1Sm 21:10
this David, the **k** of the land? 1Sm 21:11
very afraid of **K** Achish of Gath, 1Sm 21:12
where he said to the **k** of Moab, 1Sm 22:3
in the care of the **k** of Moab, 1Sm 22:4
k sent ⌊messengers⌋ to summon 1Sm 22:11

All of them came to the **k**. 1Sm 22:11
Ahimelech replied to the **k**: 1Sm 22:14
don't let the **k** make an 1Sm 22:15
But the **k** said, "You will die, 1Sm 22:16
Then the **k** ordered the guards 1Sm 22:17
So the **k** said to Doeg, "Go and 1Sm 22:18
yourself will be **k** over Israel, 1Sm 23:17
whenever the **k** wants to come 1Sm 23:20
be to hand him over to the **k**." 1Sm 23:20
called to Saul, "My lord the **k**!" 1Sm 24:8
Who has the **k** of Israel come 1Sm 24:14
know for certain you will be **k**, 1Sm 24:20
in his house, feasting like a **k**. 1Sm 25:36
Who are you who calls to the **k**?" 1Sm 26:14
protect your lord the **k** when one 1Sm 26:15
my lord and **k**," David said. 1Sm 26:17
my lord the **k** please hear the 1Sm 26:19
for the **k** of Israel has come out 1Sm 26:20
son of Maoch, the **k** of Gath. 1Sm 27:2
But the **k** said to her, "Don't be 1Sm 28:13
servant of **K** Saul of Israel. 1Sm 29:3
the enemies of my lord the **k**?" 1Sm 29:8
anointed David **k** over the house 2Sm 2:4
has anointed me **k** over them." 2Sm 2:7
He made him **k** over Gilead, 2Sm 2:9
that David was **k** in Hebron over 2Sm 2:11
the daughter of **K** Talmai of 2Sm 3:3
wanted David to be **k** over you. 2Sm 3:17
all Israel to my lord the **k**. 2Sm 3:21
son of Ner came to see the **k**, 2Sm 3:23
the king, the **k** dismissed him, 2Sm 3:23
Joab went to the **k** and said, 2Sm 3:24
And **K** David walked behind the 2Sm 3:31
k wept aloud at Abner's tomb. 2Sm 3:32
and the **k** sang a lament for 2Sm 3:33
everything the **k** did pleased 2Sm 3:36
convinced that the **k** had no part 2Sm 3:37
Then the **k** said to his soldiers, 2Sm 3:38
even though I am the anointed **k**, 2Sm 3:39
day while the **k** was taking his 2Sm 4:5
at Hebron and said to the **k**, 2Sm 4:8
my lord the **k** against Saul and 2Sm 4:8
Even while Saul was **k** over us, 2Sm 5:2
Israel came to the **k** at Hebron. 2Sm 5:3
K David made a covenant with 2Sm 5:3
anointed David **k** over Israel. 2Sm 5:3
The **k** and his men marched to 2Sm 5:6
K Hiram of Tyre sent envoys to 2Sm 5:11
established him as **k** over Israel 2Sm 5:12
had been anointed **k** over Israel, 2Sm 5:17
It was reported to **K** David: 2Sm 6:12
window and saw **K** David leaping 2Sm 6:16
How the **k** of Israel honored 2Sm 6:20
When the **k** had settled into his 2Sm 7:1
k said to Nathan the prophet, 2Sm 7:2
Nathan told the **k**, "Go and do 2Sm 7:3
Then **K** David went in, sat in the 2Sm 7:18
son of Rehob, **k** of Zobah, who 2Sm 8:3
came to assist **K** Hadadezer of 2Sm 8:5
K David also took huge 2Sm 8:8
When **K** Toi of Hamath heard that 2Sm 8:9
son Joram to **K** David to greet 2Sm 8:10
K David also dedicated these to 2Sm 8:11
son of Rehob, **k** of Zobah. 2Sm 8:12
David, and the **k** said to him, 2Sm 9:2
So the **k** asked, "Is there anyone 2Sm 9:3
said to the **k**, "There is still 2Sm 9:3
The **k** asked him, "Where is he?" 2Sm 9:4
answered the **k**, "You'll find him 2Sm 9:4
So **K** David had him brought from 2Sm 9:5
Then the **k** summoned Saul's 2Sm 9:9
said to the **k**, "Your servant 2Sm 9:11
do all my lord the **k** commands." 2Sm 9:11
later the **k** of the Ammonites 2Sm 10:1
son Hanun became **k** in his place. 2Sm 10:1
The **k** said, "Stay in Jericho 2Sm 10:5
1,000 men from the **k** of Maacah, 2Sm 10:6
a gift from the **k** followed him. 2Sm 11:8
telling the **k** all the details 2Sm 11:19
'I anointed you **k** over Israel, 2Sm 12:7
crown from the head of their **k**, 2Sm 12:30
When the **k** came to see him, 2Sm 13:6
speak to the **k**, for he won't 2Sm 13:13
When **K** David heard about all 2Sm 13:21
Then he went to the **k** and said, 2Sm 13:24
Will the **k** and his servants 2Sm 13:24
The **k** replied to Absalom, 2Sm 13:25
The **k** asked him, "Why should he 2Sm 13:26

In response the **k** stood up, 2Sm 13:31
now, my lord the **k**, don't take 2Sm 13:33
said to the **k**, "Look, the king's 2Sm 13:35
Then the **k** and all his servants 2Sm 13:36
son of Ammihud, **k** of Geshur. 2Sm 13:37
Then **K** David longed to go to 2Sm 13:39
to the **k** and speak these words 2Sm 14:3
woman from Tekoa came to the **k**, 2Sm 14:4
and said, "Help me, my **k**!" 2Sm 14:4
matter?" the **k** asked her. "To 2Sm 14:5
The **k** told the woman, "Go home. 2Sm 14:8
woman of Tekoa said to the **k**, 2Sm 14:9
My lord the **k**, may any blame be 2Sm 14:9
and may the **k** and his throne be 2Sm 14:9
to you," the **k** said, "bring him 2Sm 14:10
may the **k** invoke the LORD your 2Sm 14:11
speak a word to my lord the **k**?" 2Sm 14:12
When the **k** spoke as he did about 2Sm 14:13
The **k** has not brought back his 2Sm 14:13
to my lord the **k** because the 2Sm 14:15
speak to the **k**. Perhaps the king 2Sm 14:15
Perhaps the **k** will grant his 2Sm 14:15
k will surely listen in order 2Sm 14:16
of my lord the **k** bring relief, 2Sm 14:17
for my lord the **k** is able to 2Sm 14:17
Then the **k** answered the woman, 2Sm 14:18
"Let my lord the **k** speak," 2Sm 14:18
The **k** asked, "Did Joab put you 2Sm 14:19
my lord the **k**, no one can turn 2Sm 14:19
from all my lord the **k** says. 2Sm 14:19
Then the **k** said to Joab, "I 2Sm 14:21
in homage and praised the **k**. 2Sm 14:22
you, my lord the **k**, because the 2Sm 14:22
because the **k** has granted the 2Sm 14:22
However, the **k** added, "He may 2Sm 14:24
house, but he did not see the **k**. 2Sm 14:24
two years but never saw the **k**. 2Sm 14:28
in order to send him to the **k**, 2Sm 14:29
to send you to the **k** to ask: 2Sm 14:32
So now, let me see the **k**. 2Sm 14:32
Joab went to the **k** and told him. 2Sm 14:33
came to the **k** and bowed down 2Sm 14:33
face to the ground before the **k**. 2Sm 14:33
Then the **k** kissed Absalom. 2Sm 14:33
before the **k** for settlement, 2Sm 15:2
but the **k** does not have anyone 2Sm 15:3
who came to the **k** for a 2Sm 15:6
said to the **k**, "Please let me go 2Sm 15:7
"Go in peace," the **k** said to him. 2Sm 15:9
has become **k** in Hebron!' " 2Sm 15:10
Whatever my lord the **k** decides, 2Sm 15:15
Then the **k** set out, and his 2Sm 15:16
So the **k** set out, and all the 2Sm 15:17
from Gath—marched past the **k**. 2Sm 15:18
The **k** said to Ittai the Gittite, 2Sm 15:19
stay with the **k** since you're 2Sm 15:19
vowed to the **k**, "As surely as 2Sm 15:21
and as my lord the **k** lives, 2Sm 15:21
wherever my lord the **k** is, 2Sm 15:21
As the **k** was crossing the Kidron 2Sm 15:23
Then the **k** instructed Zadok, 2Sm 15:25
The **k** also said to Zadok the 2Sm 15:27
I will be your servant, my **k**! 2Sm 15:34
The **k** said to Ziba, "Why do you 2Sm 16:2
son?" the **k** asked. "Why, he's 2Sm 16:3
replied to the **k**, "for he said, 2Sm 16:3
The **k** said to Ziba, "All that 2Sm 16:4
favorably on me, my lord the **k**!" 2Sm 16:4
When **K** David got to Bahurim, 2Sm 16:5
son of Zeruiah said to the **k**, 2Sm 16:9
dead dog curse my lord the **k**? 2Sm 16:9
The **k** replied, "Sons of Zeruiah, 2Sm 16:10
k and all the people with him 2Sm 16:14
to Absalom, "Long live the **k**! 2Sm 16:16
live the king! Long live the **k**!" 2Sm 16:16
I will strike down only the **k** 2Sm 17:2
or the **k** and all the people with 2Sm 17:16
would go and inform **K** David, 2Sm 17:17
and went and informed **K** David. 2Sm 17:21
The **k** said to the troops, 2Sm 18:2
is best," the **k** replied to them. 2Sm 18:4
The **k** commanded Joab, Abishai, 2Sm 18:5
we heard the **k** command you, 2Sm 18:12
nothing is hidden from the **k**— 2Sm 18:13
run and tell the **k** the good news 2Sm 18:19
tell the **k** what you have seen. 2Sm 18:21
He called out and told the **k**. 2Sm 18:25
The **k** said, "If he's alone, he 2Sm 18:25

bringing good news," said the **k**. 2Sm 18:26
good news," the **k** commented. 2Sm 18:27
Ahimaaz called out to the **k**, 2Sm 18:28
down to the **k** with his face to 2Sm 18:28
rebelled against my lord the **k**." 2Sm 18:28
The **k** asked, "Is the young man 2Sm 18:29
k said, "Move aside and stand 2Sm 18:30
May my lord the **k** hear the good 2Sm 18:31
The **k** asked the Cushite, "Is the 2Sm 18:32
of my lord the **k** and to all who 2Sm 18:32
k was deeply moved and went 2Sm 18:33
to Joab, "The **k** is weeping. 2Sm 19:1
"The **k** is grieving over his son." 2Sm 19:2
But the **k** hid his face and cried 2Sm 19:4
the house to the **k** and said, 2Sm 19:5
So the **k** got up and sat in the 2Sm 19:8
the **k** is sitting in the gate." 2Sm 19:8
The **k** delivered us from the 2Sm 19:9
nothing about restoring the **k**?" 2Sm 19:10
K David sent word to the priests, 2Sm 19:11
to restore the **k** to his palace? 2Sm 19:11
has reached the **k** at his house. 2Sm 19:11
be the last to restore the **k**?' 2Sm 19:12
and they sent word to the **k**: 2Sm 19:14
Then the **k** returned. When he 2Sm 19:15
to meet the **k** and escort him 2Sm 19:15
men of Judah to meet **K** David. 2Sm 19:16
to the Jordan ahead of the **k**. 2Sm 19:17
and do whatever the **k** desired. 2Sm 19:18
Jordan, he fell down before the **k** 2Sm 19:18
my lord the **k** left Jerusalem. 2Sm 19:19
May the **k** not take it to heart. 2Sm 19:19
down to meet my lord the **k**." 2Sm 19:20
that today I'm **k** over Israel?" 2Sm 19:22
So the **k** said to Shimei, "You 2Sm 19:23
Then the **k** gave him his oath. 2Sm 19:23
also went down to meet the **k**. 2Sm 19:24
from the day the **k** left until 2Sm 19:24
from Jerusalem to meet the **k**, 2Sm 19:25
meet the king, the **k** asked him, 2Sm 19:25
"My lord the **k**," he replied, "my 2Sm 19:26
may ride it and go with the **k**'— 2Sm 19:26
your servant to my lord the **k**. 2Sm 19:27
But my lord the **k** is like the 2Sm 19:27
death from my lord the **k**, 2Sm 19:28
on making appeals to the **k**?" 2Sm 19:28
The **k** said to him, "Why keep on 2Sm 19:29
Mephibosheth said to the **k**, 2Sm 19:30
my lord the **k** has come to his 2Sm 19:30
accompanied the **k** to the Jordan 2Sm 19:31
needs of the **k** while he stayed 2Sm 19:32
The **k** said to Barzillai, "Cross 2Sm 19:33
Barzillai replied to the **k**, 2Sm 19:34
go up to Jerusalem with the **k**? 2Sm 19:34
added burden to my lord the **k**? 2Sm 19:35
going with the **k** a little way 2Sm 19:36
why should the **k** repay me with 2Sm 19:36
cross over with my lord the **k**. 2Sm 19:37
The **k** replied, "Chimham will 2Sm 19:38
Jordan, and then the **k** crossed. 2Sm 19:39
The **k** kissed Barzillai and 2Sm 19:39
The **k** went on to Gilgal, and 2Sm 19:40
half of Israel's escorted the **k**. 2Sm 19:40
the men of Israel came to the **k**. 2Sm 19:41
transport the **k** and his 2Sm 19:41
Because the **k** is our relative. 2Sm 19:42
We have 10 shares in the **k**, 2Sm 19:43
to speak of restoring our **k**?" 2Sm 19:43
remained loyal to their **k**. 2Sm 20:2
The **k** said to Amasa, "Summon 2Sm 20:4
has rebelled against **K** David. 2Sm 20:21
returned to the **k** in Jerusalem. 2Sm 20:22
replied to the **k**, "As for the 2Sm 21:5
The **k** answered, "I will hand 2Sm 21:6
But the **k** took Armoni and 2Sm 21:8
did everything the **k** commanded. 2Sm 21:14
a tower of salvation for His **k**; 2Sm 22:51
So the **k** said to Joab, the 2Sm 24:2
replied to the **k**, "May the LORD 2Sm 24:3
while my lord the **k** looks on! 2Sm 24:3
my lord the **k** want to do this? 2Sm 24:3
Joab gave the **k** the total of the 2Sm 24:9
and saw the **k** and his servants 2Sm 24:20
bowed to the **k** with his face to 2Sm 24:20
has my lord the **k** come to his 2Sm 24:21
My lord the **k** may take whatever 2Sm 24:22
⌊My⌋ **k**, Araunah gives everything 2Sm 24:23
gives everything here to the **k**." 2Sm 24:23

he said to the **k**, "May the LORD 2Sm 24:23
The **k** answered Araunah, "No, I 2Sm 24:24
Now **K** David was old and getting 1Kg 1:1
young virgin for my lord the **k**. 1Kg 1:2
is to attend the **k** and be his 1Kg 1:2
my lord the **k** will get warm." 1Kg 1:2
and brought her to the **k**. 1Kg 1:3
himself, saying, "I will be **k**!" 1Kg 1:5
of Judah, the servants of the **k**, 1Kg 1:9
has become **k** and our lord David 1Kg 1:11
K David and say to him, 1Kg 1:13
to him, 'My lord **k**, did you not 1Kg 1:13
Solomon is to become **k** after me, 1Kg 1:13
So why has Adonijah become **k**?' 1Kg 1:13
still there speaking with the **k**, 1Kg 1:14
went to the **k** in his bedroom. 1Kg 1:15
the **k** was very old, Abishag 1Kg 1:15
down and paid homage to the **k**, 1Kg 1:16
Solomon is to become **k** after me, 1Kg 1:17
Now look, Adonijah has become **k**. 1Kg 1:18
And, my lord **k**, you didn't know 1Kg 1:18
Now, my lord **k**, the eyes of all 1Kg 1:20
of my lord the **k** after him. 1Kg 1:20
when my lord the **k** rests with 1Kg 1:21
was still speaking with the **k**, 1Kg 1:22
and it was announced to the **k**, 1Kg 1:23
"My lord **k**," Nathan said, "did 1Kg 1:24
is to become **k** after me, 1Kg 1:24
invited all the sons of the **k**, 1Kg 1:25
saying, 'Long live **K** Adonijah!' 1Kg 1:25
my lord the **k** would not have let 1Kg 1:27
K David responded by saying, 1Kg 1:28
The **k** swore an oath and said, 1Kg 1:29
Solomon is to become **k** after me, 1Kg 1:30
homage to the **k**, and said, "May 1Kg 1:31
my lord **K** David live forever! 1Kg 1:31
K David then said, "Call in 1Kg 1:32
The **k** said to them, "Take my 1Kg 1:33
to anoint him as **k** over Israel. 1Kg 1:34
and say, 'Long live **K** Solomon!' 1Kg 1:34
who is to become **k** in my place; 1Kg 1:35
of Jehoiada replied to the **k**. 1Kg 1:36
of my lord the **k**, so affirm it. 1Kg 1:36
the LORD was with my lord the **k**, 1Kg 1:37
the throne of my lord **K** David." 1Kg 1:37
Solomon ride on **K** David's mule, 1Kg 1:38
Long live **K** Solomon!" 1Kg 1:39
Our lord **K** David has made 1Kg 1:43
King David has made Solomon **k**. 1Kg 1:43
the **k** has sent Zadok the priest, 1Kg 1:44
have anointed him **k** in Gihon. 1Kg 1:45
congratulate our lord **K** David, 1Kg 1:47
Then the **k** bowed in worship on 1Kg 1:47
And the **k** went on to say this: 1Kg 1:48
Adonijah fears **K** Solomon, and he 1Kg 1:51
'Let **K** Solomon first swear to me 1Kg 1:51
So **K** Solomon sent for him, 1Kg 1:53
and paid homage to **K** Solomon, 1Kg 1:53
All Israel expected me to be **k**, 1Kg 2:15
Please speak to **K** Solomon since 1Kg 2:17
"I will speak to the **k** for you." 1Kg 2:18
went to **K** Solomon to speak 1Kg 2:19
The **k** stood up to greet her, 1Kg 2:19
mother," the **k** replied, "for I 1Kg 2:20
K Solomon answered his mother, 1Kg 2:22
Then **K** Solomon gave the order to 1Kg 2:25
The **k** said to Abiathar the 1Kg 2:26
It was reported to **K** Solomon: 1Kg 2:29
This is what the **k** says: 1Kg 2:30
took a message back to the **k**, 1Kg 2:30
The **k** said to him, "Do just as 1Kg 2:31
Then the **k** appointed Benaiah son 1Kg 2:35
Then the **k** summoned Shimei and 1Kg 2:36
said to the **k**, "The sentence is 1Kg 2:38
do as my lord the **k** has spoken." 1Kg 2:38
Achish son of Maacah, **k** of Gath. 1Kg 2:39
the **k** summoned Shimei and said 1Kg 2:42
The **k** also said, "You yourself 1Kg 2:44
but **K** Solomon will be blessed, 1Kg 2:45
Then the **k** commanded Benaiah 1Kg 2:46
with Pharaoh **k** of Egypt by 1Kg 3:1
k went to Gibeon to sacrifice 1Kg 3:4
made Your servant **k** in my father 1Kg 3:7
came to the **k** and stood before 1Kg 3:16
So they argued before the **k**. 1Kg 3:22
The **k** replied, "This woman says, 1Kg 3:23
The **k** continued, "Bring me a 1Kg 3:24
they brought the sword to the **k**. 1Kg 3:24

spoke to the **k** because she felt 1Kg 3:26
k responded, "Give the living 1Kg 3:27
the judgment the **k** had given, 1Kg 3:28
in awe of the **k** because they saw 1Kg 3:28
K Solomon ruled over Israel, 1Kg 4:1
a priest and adviser to the **k**; 1Kg 4:5
for the **k** and his household; 1Kg 4:7
of Sihon **k** of the Amorites 1Kg 4:19
Amorites and of Og **k** of Bashan. 1Kg 4:19
food for **K** Solomon and for 1Kg 4:27
who came to **K** Solomon's table. 1Kg 4:27
⌊sent⌋ by every **k** on earth who 1Kg 4:34
k of Tyre sent his servants 1Kg 5:1
been anointed **k** in his father's 1Kg 5:1
Then **K** Solomon drafted forced 1Kg 5:13
The **k** commanded them to quarry 1Kg 5:17
The temple that **K** Solomon built 1Kg 6:2
K Solomon had Hiram brought 1Kg 7:13
So he came to **K** Solomon and 1Kg 7:14
was doing for **K** Solomon on the 1Kg 7:40
that Hiram made for **K** Solomon at 1Kg 7:45
k had them cast in clay molds 1Kg 7:46
So all the work **K** Solomon did in 1Kg 7:51
in the presence of **K** Solomon in 1Kg 8:2
K Solomon and the entire 1Kg 8:5
The **k** turned around and blessed 1Kg 8:14
The **k** and all Israel with him 1Kg 8:62
In this manner the **k** and all the 1Kg 8:63
the **k** consecrated the middle of 1Kg 8:64
blessed the **k** and went home to 1Kg 8:66
Hiram **k** of Tyre having supplied 1Kg 9:11
K Solomon gave Hiram 20 towns 1Kg 9:11
had sent the **k** 9,000 pounds 1Kg 9:14
forced labor that **K** Solomon had 1Kg 9:15
Pharaoh **k** of Egypt had attacked 1Kg 9:16
K Solomon put together a fleet 1Kg 9:26
for the **k** to explain to her 1Kg 10:3
She said to the **k**, "The report I 1Kg 10:6
He has made you **k** to carry out 1Kg 10:9
she gave the **k** four and a half 1Kg 10:10
of Sheba gave to **K** Solomon. 1Kg 10:10
The **k** made the almug wood into 1Kg 10:12
K Solomon gave the queen of 1Kg 10:13
K Solomon made 200 large 1Kg 10:16
The **k** put them in the House of 1Kg 10:17
The **k** also made a large ivory 1Kg 10:18
All of **K** Solomon's drinking cups 1Kg 10:21
for the **k** had ships of Tarshish 1Kg 10:22
K Solomon surpassed all the 1Kg 10:23
and with the **k** in Jerusalem. 1Kg 10:26
The **k** made silver as common in 1Kg 10:27
K Solomon loved many foreign 1Kg 11:1
Egypt, to Pharaoh **k** of Egypt, 1Kg 11:18
his master Hadadezer **k** of Zobah 1Kg 11:23
there, and became **k** in Damascus. 1Kg 11:24
he rebelled against the **k**: 1Kg 11:27
will reign as **k** over all you 1Kg 11:37
and you will be **k** over Israel. 1Kg 11:37
to Shishak **k** of Egypt, where 1Kg 11:40
Rehoboam became **k** in his place. 1Kg 11:43
gone to Shechem to make him **k**. 1Kg 12:1
he had fled from **K** Solomon's 1Kg 12:2
Then **K** Rehoboam consulted with 1Kg 12:6
third day, as the **k** had ordered: 1Kg 12:12
Then the **k** answered the people 1Kg 12:13
The **k** did not listen to the 1Kg 12:15
saw that the **k** had not listened 1Kg 12:16
Then **K** Rehoboam sent Adoram, 1Kg 12:18
K Rehoboam managed to get into 1Kg 12:18
and made him **k** over all Israel. 1Kg 12:20
son of Solomon, **k** of Judah, to 1Kg 12:23
their lord, Rehoboam **k** of Judah. 1Kg 12:27
and go back to the **k** of Judah." 1Kg 12:27
So the **k** sought advice. 1Kg 12:28
When the **k** heard the word that 1Kg 13:4
Then the **k** responded to the man 1Kg 13:6
Then the **k** declared to the man 1Kg 13:7
that he had spoken to the **k**. 1Kg 13:11
me becoming **k** over this people 1Kg 14:2
up for Himself a **k** over Israel, 1Kg 14:14
son Nadab became **k** in his place. 1Kg 14:20
41 years old when he became **k**; 1Kg 14:21
In the fifth year of **K** Rehoboam, 1Kg 14:25
Shishak **k** of Egypt went to war 1Kg 14:25
K Rehoboam made bronze shields 1Kg 14:27
Whenever the **k** entered the 1Kg 14:28
Abijam became **k** in his place. 1Kg 14:31
year of ⌊Israel's⌋ **K** Jeroboam 1Kg 15:1

Abijam became **k** over Judah; 1Kg 15:1
son Asa became **k** in his place. 1Kg 15:8
year of Israel's **K** Jeroboam, 1Kg 15:9
Jeroboam, Asa became **k** of Judah; 1Kg 15:9
Asa and Baasha **k** of Israel 1Kg 15:16
Israel's **K** Baasha went to war 1Kg 15:17
anyone access to Judah's **K** Asa. 1Kg 15:17
K Asa sent them to Ben-hadad 1Kg 15:18
of Hezion **k** of Aram who lived 1Kg 15:18
with Baasha **k** of Israel so that 1Kg 15:19
listened to **K** Asa and sent 1Kg 15:20
Then **K** Asa gave a command to 1Kg 15:22
K Asa built Geba of Benjamin 1Kg 15:22
became **k** in his place. 1Kg 15:24
of Jeroboam became **k** over Israel 1Kg 15:25
second year of Judah's **K** Asa; 1Kg 15:25
the third year of Judah's **K** Asa, 1Kg 15:28
Baasha became **k**, he struck down 1Kg 15:29
Asa and Baasha **k** of Israel 1Kg 15:32
the third year of Judah's **K** Asa, 1Kg 15:33
Ahijah became **k** over all Israel 1Kg 15:33
son Elah became **k** in his place. 1Kg 16:6
year of Judah's **K** Asa, 1Kg 16:8
of Baasha became **k** over Israel 1Kg 16:8
year of Judah's **K** Asa, 1Kg 16:10
Zimri became **k** in his place. 1Kg 16:10
When he became **k**, as soon as he 1Kg 16:11
year of Judah's **K** Asa, 1Kg 16:15
Zimri became **k** for seven days in 1Kg 16:15
but had also struck down the **k**, 1Kg 16:16
k over Israel that very day in 1Kg 16:16
to make him **k**, and half followed 1Kg 16:21
So Tibni died and Omri became **k**. 1Kg 16:22
year of Judah's **K** Asa, 1Kg 16:23
Omri became **k** over Israel; 1Kg 16:23
son Ahab became **k** in his place. 1Kg 16:28
son of Omri became **k** over Israel 1Kg 16:29
year of Judah's **K** Asa; 1Kg 16:29
of Ethbaal **k** of the Sidonians, 1Kg 16:31
to anoint Hazael as **k** over Aram. 1Kg 19:15
son of Nimshi as **k** over Israel 1Kg 19:16
Ben-hadad **k** of Aram assembled 1Kg 20:1
the city to Ahab **k** of Israel and 1Kg 20:2
Then the **k** of Israel answered, 1Kg 20:4
Just as you say, my lord **k**: 1Kg 20:4
Then the **k** of Israel called for 1Kg 20:7
my lord the **k**, 'Everything you 1Kg 20:9
The **k** of Israel answered, 1Kg 20:11
came to Ahab **k** of Israel and 1Kg 20:13
but Ben-hadad **k** of Aram escaped 1Kg 20:20
Then the **k** of Israel marched out 1Kg 20:21
approached the **k** of Israel and 1Kg 20:22
in the spring the **k** of Aram will 1Kg 20:22
the **k** of Aram's servants said 1Kg 20:23
remove each **k** from his position 1Kg 20:24
The **k** listened to them and did 1Kg 20:25
and said to the **k** of Israel, 1Kg 20:28
let's go out to the **k** of Israel. 1Kg 20:31
heads, went to the **k** of Israel, 1Kg 20:32
waited for the **k** on the road. 1Kg 20:38
the **k** was passing by, he cried 1Kg 20:39
he cried out to the **k** and said, 1Kg 20:39
The **k** of Israel said to him, 1Kg 20:40
The **k** of Israel recognized that 1Kg 20:41
The **k** of Israel left for home 1Kg 20:43
the palace of Ahab **k** of Samaria. 1Kg 21:1
"You have cursed God and **k**!" 1Kg 21:10
"Naboth has cursed God and **k**!" 1Kg 21:13
and go to meet Ahab **k** of Israel, 1Kg 21:18
Jehoshaphat **k** of Judah went to 1Kg 22:2
went to visit the **k** of Israel. 1Kg 22:2
The **k** of Israel had said to his 1Kg 22:3
from the hand of the **k** of Aram?" 1Kg 22:3
replied to the **k** of Israel, 1Kg 22:4
said to the **k** of Israel, 1Kg 22:5
So the **k** of Israel gathered the 1Kg 22:6
will hand it over to the **k**." 1Kg 22:6
The **k** of Israel said to 1Kg 22:8
"The **k** shouldn't say that!" 1Kg 22:8
So the **k** of Israel called an 1Kg 22:9
Now the **k** of Israel and 1Kg 22:10
and Jehoshaphat **k** of Judah, 1Kg 22:10
will hand it over to the **k**." 1Kg 22:12
unanimously favorable for the **k**. 1Kg 22:13
he went to the **k**, and the king 1Kg 22:15
the king, and the **k** asked him, 1Kg 22:15
will hand it over to the **k**." 1Kg 22:15
But the **k** said to him, "How many 1Kg 22:16

So the **k** of Israel said to 1Kg 22:18
Then the **k** of Israel ordered, 1Kg 22:26
say, 'This is what the **k** says: 1Kg 22:27
Then the **k** of Israel and Judah's 1Kg 22:29
and Judah's **K** Jehoshaphat went 1Kg 22:29
But the **k** of Israel said to 1Kg 22:30
So the **k** of Israel disguised 1Kg 22:30
the **k** of Aram had ordered his 1Kg 22:31
at all except the **k** of Israel." 1Kg 22:31
"He must be the **k** of Israel!" 1Kg 22:32
that he was not the **k** of Israel, 1Kg 22:33
and struck the **k** of Israel 1Kg 22:34
and the **k** was propped up in his 1Kg 22:35
So the **k** died and was brought to 1Kg 22:37
They buried the **k** in Samaria. 1Kg 22:37
Ahaziah became **k** in his place. 1Kg 22:40
son of Asa became **k** over Judah 1Kg 22:41
fourth year of Israel's **K** Ahab. 1Kg 22:41
35 years old when he became **k**; 1Kg 22:42
made peace with the **k** of Israel. 1Kg 22:44
There was no **k** in Edom; 1Kg 22:47
in Edom; a deputy served as **k**. 1Kg 22:47
Jehoram became **k** in his place. 1Kg 22:50
son of Ahab became **k** over Israel 1Kg 22:51
year of Judah's **K** Jehoshaphat; 1Kg 22:51
messengers of the **k** of Samaria 2Kg 1:3
messengers returned to the **k**, 2Kg 1:5
'Go back to the **k** who sent you 2Kg 1:6
The **k** asked them: "What sort of 2Kg 1:7
K Ahaziah sent a captain of 50 2Kg 1:9
of God, the **k** declares, 'Come 2Kg 1:9
So the **k** sent another captain of 2Kg 1:11
God, this is what the **k** says: 2Kg 1:11
Then the **k** sent a third captain 2Kg 1:13
and went down with him to the **k**. 2Kg 1:15
Then Elijah said to **K** Ahaziah, 2Kg 1:16
Joram became **k** in his place. 2Kg 1:17
year of Judah's **K** Jehoram son 2Kg 1:17
son of Ahab became **k** over Israel 2Kg 3:1
year of Judah's **K** Jehoshaphat; 2Kg 3:1
K Mesha of Moab was a sheep 2Kg 3:4
used to pay the **k** of Israel 2Kg 3:4
the **k** of Moab rebelled against 2Kg 3:5
against the **k** of Israel. 2Kg 3:5
So **K** Joram marched out from 2Kg 3:6
⌊a message⌋ to **K** Jehoshaphat 2Kg 3:7
The **k** of Moab has rebelled 2Kg 3:7
So the **k** of Israel, the king of 2Kg 3:9
king of Israel, the **k** of Judah, 2Kg 3:9
and the **k** of Edom set out. 2Kg 3:9
Then the **k** of Israel said, 2Kg 3:10
servants of the **k** of Israel 2Kg 3:11
So the **k** of Israel and 2Kg 3:12
and the **k** of Edom went to him 2Kg 3:12
Elisha said to **K** ⌊Joram⌋ of 2Kg 3:13
But the **k** of Israel replied, 2Kg 3:13
have respect for **K** Jehoshaphat 2Kg 3:14
When the **k** of Moab saw that the 2Kg 3:26
break through to the **k** of Edom, 2Kg 3:26
was to become **k** in his place, 2Kg 3:27
your behalf to the **k** or to the 2Kg 4:13
of the army for the **k** of Aram, 2Kg 5:1
Therefore, the **k** of Aram said, 2Kg 5:5
with you⌋ to the **k** of Israel." 2Kg 5:5
the letter to the **k** of Israel, 2Kg 5:6
When the **k** of Israel read the 2Kg 5:7
heard that the **k** of Israel tore 2Kg 5:8
he sent ⌊a message⌋ to the **k**, 2Kg 5:8
my master, ⌊the **k** of Aram⌋, goes 2Kg 5:18
When the **k** of Aram was waging 2Kg 6:8
sent ⌊word⌋ to the **k** of Israel: 2Kg 6:9
the **k** of Israel sent ⌊word⌋ to 2Kg 6:10
of God repeatedly warned the **k**, 2Kg 6:10
so the **k** would be on his guard. 2Kg 6:10
k of Aram was enraged because 2Kg 6:11
of us is for the **k** of Israel?" 2Kg 6:11
said, "No one, my lord the **k**. 2Kg 6:12
tells the **k** of Israel even the 2Kg 6:12
So the **k** said, "Go and see where 2Kg 6:13
When the **k** of Israel saw them, 2Kg 6:21
K Ben-hadad of Aram brought all 2Kg 6:24
the **k** of Israel was passing by 2Kg 6:26
to him, "My lord the **k**, help!" 2Kg 6:26
Then the **k** asked her, "What's 2Kg 6:28
When the **k** heard the woman's 2Kg 6:30
The **k** sent a man ahead of him, 2Kg 6:32
The **k** of Israel must have hired 2Kg 7:6
So the **k** got up in the night and 2Kg 7:12
and the **k** sent them after the 2Kg 7:14
returned and told the **k**. 2Kg 7:15
The **k** had appointed the captain, 2Kg 7:17
when the **k** came to him. 2Kg 7:17
man of God had said to the **k**, 2Kg 7:18
to appeal to the **k** for her house 2Kg 8:3
The **k** had been speaking to 2Kg 8:4
he was telling the **k** how Elisha 2Kg 8:5
to appeal to the **k** for her house 2Kg 8:5
My lord the **k**, this is the woman 2Kg 8:5
When the **k** asked the woman, 2Kg 8:6
So the **k** appointed a court 2Kg 8:6
while Ben-hadad **k** of Aram was 2Kg 8:7
was sick, and the **k** was told, 2Kg 8:7
So the **k** said to Hazael, "Take a 2Kg 8:8
son, Ben-hadad **k** of Aram, has 2Kg 8:9
that you will be **k** over Aram." 2Kg 8:13
year of Israel's **K** Joram son of 2Kg 8:16
Jehoshaphat became **k** of Judah, 2Kg 8:16
32 years old when he became **k**; 2Kg 8:17
and appointed their own **k**. 2Kg 8:20
Ahaziah became **k** in his place. 2Kg 8:24
year of Israel's **K** Joram son of 2Kg 8:25
of Jehoram became **k** of Judah. 2Kg 8:25
22 years old when he became **k**; 2Kg 8:26
of Israel's **K** Omri. 2Kg 8:26
fight against Hazael **k** of Aram 2Kg 8:28
K Joram returned to Jezreel to 2Kg 8:29
fought against Aram's **K** Hazael. 2Kg 8:29
Then Judah's **K** Ahaziah son of 2Kg 8:29
"I anoint you **k** over Israel." ' 2Kg 9:3
'I anoint you **k** over the LORD's 2Kg 9:6
I anoint you **k** over Israel.' " 2Kg 9:12
and proclaimed, "Jehu is **k**!" 2Kg 9:13
guard against Hazael **k** of Aram. 2Kg 9:14
But **K** Joram had returned to 2Kg 9:15
fought against Aram's **K** Hazael. 2Kg 9:15
commanders⌋ wish ⌊to make me **k**⌋, 2Kg 9:15
and Ahaziah **k** of Judah had gone 2Kg 9:16
This is what the **k** asks: 2Kg 9:18
This is what the **k** asks: 2Kg 9:19
Then Joram **k** of Israel and 2Kg 9:21
and Ahaziah **k** of Judah set out, 2Kg 9:21
K Ahaziah of Judah saw ⌊what 2Kg 9:27
Ahaziah had become **k** over Judah. 2Kg 9:29
We will not make anyone **k**. 2Kg 10:5
sons," the **k** said, "Pile them 2Kg 10:8
of Ahaziah **k** of Judah and asked 2Kg 10:13
Jehoahaz became **k** in his place. 2Kg 10:35
⌊who was⌋ **K** Jehoram's daughter 2Kg 11:2
surround the **k** with weapons in 2Kg 11:8
be with the **k** in all his daily 2Kg 11:8
of hundreds **K** David's spears 2Kg 11:10
in hand surrounding the **k**— 2Kg 11:11
the testimony, and made him **k**. 2Kg 11:12
and cried, "Long live the **k**!" 2Kg 11:12
there was the **k** standing by the 2Kg 11:14
the trumpeters were by the **k**, 2Kg 11:14
the LORD, the **k**, and the people 2Kg 11:17
between the **k** and the people. 2Kg 11:17
brought the **k** from the LORD's 2Kg 11:19
years old when he became **k**. 2Kg 12:21
year of Jehu, Joash became **k**; 2Kg 12:1
year ⌊of the reign⌋ of **K** Joash, 2Kg 12:6
So **K** Joash called Jehoiada the 2Kg 12:7
time Hazael **k** of Aram marched 2Kg 12:17
So **K** Joash of Judah took all the 2Kg 12:18
sent ⌊them⌋ to Hazael **k** of Aram. 2Kg 12:18
Amaziah became **k** in his place. 2Kg 12:21
year of Judah's **K** Joash son of 2Kg 13:1
son of Jehu became **k** over Israel 2Kg 13:1
power of Hazael **k** of Aram and 2Kg 13:3
oppression the **k** of Aram 2Kg 13:4
because the **k** of Aram had 2Kg 13:7
Jehoash became **k** in his place. 2Kg 13:9
year of Judah's **K** Joash, 2Kg 13:10
of Jehoahaz became **k** over Israel 2Kg 13:10
war against Judah's **K** Amaziah, 2Kg 13:12
Jehoash **k** of Israel went down 2Kg 13:14
Elisha said to the **k** of Israel, 2Kg 13:16
So the **k** put his hand on it, 2Kg 13:16
and he said to the **k** of Israel, 2Kg 13:18
k of Aram oppressed Israel 2Kg 13:22
K Hazael of Aram died, and his 2Kg 13:24
Ben-hadad became **k** in his place. 2Kg 13:24
year of Israel's **K** Jehoash son 2Kg 14:1
son of Joash became **k** of Judah. 2Kg 14:1
25 years old when he became **k**; 2Kg 14:2
had murdered his father the **k**. 2Kg 14:5
of Jehu, **k** of Israel, saying, 2Kg 14:8
K Jehoash of Israel sent ⌊word⌋ 2Kg 14:9
word⌋ to Amaziah **k** of Judah, 2Kg 14:9
so **K** Jehoash of Israel advanced. 2Kg 14:11
He and **K** Amaziah of Judah faced 2Kg 14:11
K Jehoash of Israel captured 2Kg 14:13
captured Judah's **K** Amaziah son 2Kg 14:13
war against Amaziah **k** of Judah, 2Kg 14:15
Jeroboam became **k** in his place. 2Kg 14:16
Judah's **K** Amaziah son of Joash 2Kg 14:17
death of Israel's **K** Jehoash son 2Kg 14:17
and made him **k** in place of his 2Kg 14:21
Amaziah⌋ the **k** rested with his 2Kg 14:22
year of Judah's **K** Amaziah son of 2Kg 14:23
of Jehoash became **k** of Israel in 2Kg 14:23
Zechariah became **k** in his place. 2Kg 14:29
year of Israel's **K** Jeroboam, 2Kg 15:1
of Amaziah became **k** of Judah. 2Kg 15:1
16 years old when he became **k**; 2Kg 15:2
LORD afflicted the **k**, and he had 2Kg 15:5
Jotham became **k** in his place. 2Kg 15:7
year of Judah's **K** Azariah, 2Kg 15:8
of Jeroboam became **k** over Israel 2Kg 15:8
and became **k** in his place. 2Kg 15:10
year of Judah's **K** Uzziah, 2Kg 15:13
Shallum son of Jabesh became **k**; 2Kg 15:13
him and became **k** in his place. 2Kg 15:14
year of Judah's **K** Azariah, 2Kg 15:17
of Gadi became **k** over Israel; 2Kg 15:17
Pul **k** of Assyria invaded the 2Kg 15:19
to give to the **k** of Assyria. 2Kg 15:20
So the **k** of Assyria withdrew and 2Kg 15:20
Pekahiah became **k** in his place. 2Kg 15:22
year of Judah's **K** Azariah, 2Kg 15:23
of Menahem became **k** over Israel 2Kg 15:23
and became **k** in his place. 2Kg 15:25
year of Judah's **K** Azariah, 2Kg 15:27
of Remaliah became **k** over Israel 2Kg 15:27
the days of Pekah **k** of Israel, 2Kg 15:29
Tiglath-pileser **k** of Assyria 2Kg 15:29
and became **k** in his place in the 2Kg 15:30
year of Israel's **K** Pekah son of 2Kg 15:32
son of Uzziah became **k** of Judah. 2Kg 15:32
25 years old when he became **k**; 2Kg 15:33
sending Rezin **k** of Aram and 2Kg 15:37
son Ahaz became **k** in his place. 2Kg 15:38
son of Jotham became **k** of Judah. 2Kg 16:1
20 years old when he became **k**; 2Kg 16:2
Then Aram's **K** Rezin and Israel's 2Kg 16:5
Rezin and Israel's **K** Pekah son 2Kg 16:5
that time Rezin **k** of Aram 2Kg 16:6
to Tiglath-pileser **k** of Assyria, 2Kg 16:7
from the power of the **k** of Aram 2Kg 16:7
of Aram and of the **k** of Israel, 2Kg 16:7
them⌋ to the **k** of Assyria as 2Kg 16:8
So the **k** of Assyria listened to 2Kg 16:9
K Ahaz went to Damascus to 2Kg 16:10
Tiglath-pileser **k** of Assyria. 2Kg 16:10
K Ahaz sent a model of the altar 2Kg 16:10
the instructions⌋ **K** Ahaz sent 2Kg 16:11
the time **K** Ahaz came back from 2Kg 16:11
When the **k** came back from 2Kg 16:12
Then **K** Ahaz commanded Uriah 2Kg 16:15
everything **K** Ahaz commanded. 2Kg 16:16
Then **K** Ahaz cut off the frames 2Kg 16:17
To satisfy the **k** of Assyria, 2Kg 16:18
the outer entrance for the **k**. 2Kg 16:18
Hezekiah became **k** in his place. 2Kg 16:20
twelfth year of Judah's **K** Ahaz, 2Kg 17:1
son of Elah became **k** over Israel 2Kg 17:1
Shalmaneser **k** of Assyria 2Kg 17:3
But the **k** of Assyria discovered 2Kg 17:4
envoys to So **k** of Egypt and had 2Kg 17:4
money to the **k** of Assyria as 2Kg 17:4
k of Assyria arrested him and 2Kg 17:4
Then the **k** of Assyria invaded 2Kg 17:5
the **k** of Assyria captured 2Kg 17:6
power of Pharaoh **k** of Egypt and 2Kg 17:7
made Jeroboam son of Nebat **k**. 2Kg 17:21
Then the **k** of Assyria brought 2Kg 17:24
spoke to the **k** of Assyria, 2Kg 17:26
Then the **k** of Assyria issued a 2Kg 17:27
year of Israel's **K** Hoshea son of 2Kg 18:1
son of Ahaz became **k** of Judah. 2Kg 18:1
25 years old when he became **k**; 2Kg 18:2
against the **k** of Assyria and did 2Kg 18:7
the fourth year of **K** Hezekiah, 2Kg 18:9

year of Israel's **K** Hoshea son of 2Kg 18:9
Shalmaneser **k** of Assyria marched 2Kg 18:9
ninth year of Israel's **K** Hoshea, 2Kg 18:10
The **k** of Assyria deported the 2Kg 18:11
fourteenth year of **K** Hezekiah, 2Kg 18:13
Sennacherib **k** of Assyria 2Kg 18:13
So Hezekiah **k** of Judah sent word 2Kg 18:14
sent word to the **k** of Assyria at 2Kg 18:14
The **k** of Assyria demanded from 2Kg 18:14
demanded from **K** Hezekiah of 2Kg 18:14
and gave it to the **k** of Assyria. 2Kg 18:16
Then the **k** of Assyria sent the 2Kg 18:17
from Lachish to **K** Hezekiah at 2Kg 18:17
Then they called for the **k**, 2Kg 18:18
this is what the great **k**, 2Kg 18:19
great king, the **k** of Assyria, 2Kg 18:19
is how Pharaoh **k** of Egypt is to 2Kg 18:21
with my master the **k** of Assyria. 2Kg 18:23
Hear the word of the great **k**, 2Kg 18:28
great king, the **k** of Assyria. 2Kg 18:28
This is what the **k** says: 2Kg 18:29
over to the **k** of Assyria.' 2Kg 18:30
is what the **k** of Assyria says 2Kg 18:31
the power of the **k** of Assyria? 2Kg 18:33
When **K** Hezekiah heard ⌊their 2Kg 19:1
his master the **k** of Assyria sent 2Kg 19:4
the servants of **K** Hezekiah went 2Kg 19:5
that the **k** of Assyria's 2Kg 19:6
heard that the **k** of Assyria had 2Kg 19:8
The **k** had heard this about 2Kg 19:9
this about Tirhakah **k** of Cush: 2Kg 19:9
this to Hezekiah **k** of Judah: 2Kg 19:10
handed over to the **k** of Assyria. 2Kg 19:10
Where is the **k** of Hamath, the 2Kg 19:13
of Hamath, the **k** of Arpad, the 2Kg 19:13
the **k** of the city of Sepharvaim, 2Kg 19:13
Sennacherib **k** of Assyria.' 2Kg 19:20
says about the **k** of Assyria: 2Kg 19:32
Sennacherib **k** of Assyria broke 2Kg 19:36
became **k** in his place. 2Kg 19:37
the hand of the **k** of Assyria. 2Kg 20:6
son of Baladan, **k** of Babylon, 2Kg 20:12
Isaiah came to **K** Hezekiah and 2Kg 20:14
palace of the **k** of Babylon.' " 2Kg 20:18
Manasseh became **k** in his place. 2Kg 20:21
12 years old when he became **k**; 2Kg 21:1
as **K** Ahab of Israel had done; 2Kg 21:3
Since Manasseh **k** of Judah has 2Kg 21:11
son Amon became **k** in his place. 2Kg 21:18
22 years old when he became **k**; 2Kg 21:19
against the **k** and killed him in 2Kg 21:23
against **K** Amon and made his 2Kg 21:24
his son Josiah **k** in his place. 2Kg 21:24
Josiah became **k** in his place. 2Kg 21:26
years old when he became **k**; 2Kg 22:1
the eighteenth year of **K** Josiah, 2Kg 22:3
the **k** sent the court secretary 2Kg 22:3
went to the **k** and reported, 2Kg 22:9
the court secretary told the **k**, 2Kg 22:10
it in the presence of the **k**. 2Kg 22:10
When the **k** heard the words of 2Kg 22:11
book that the **k** of Judah has 2Kg 22:16
Say this to the **k** of Judah who 2Kg 22:18
Then they reported to the **k**. 2Kg 22:20
So the **k** sent ⌊messengers⌋, 2Kg 23:1
Then the **k** went to the LORD's 2Kg 23:2
the **k** stood by the pillar and 2Kg 23:3
Then the **k** commanded Hilkiah the 2Kg 23:4
The **k** tore down the altars that 2Kg 23:12
The **k** also defiled the high 2Kg 23:13
which Solomon **k** of Israel had 2Kg 23:13
The **k** commanded all the people, 2Kg 23:21
the eighteenth year of **K** Josiah, 2Kg 23:23
him there was no **k** like him who 2Kg 23:25
Neco **k** of Egypt marched 2Kg 23:29
marched up to the **k** of Assyria 2Kg 23:29
K Josiah went to confront him, 2Kg 23:29
and made him **k** in place of his 2Kg 23:30
23 years old when he became **k**; 2Kg 23:31
son of Josiah **k** in place of his 2Kg 23:34
25 years old when he became **k**; 2Kg 23:36
Nebuchadnezzar **k** of Babylon 2Kg 24:1
became **k** in his place. 2Kg 24:6
Now the **k** of Egypt did not march 2Kg 24:7
for the **k** of Babylon took 2Kg 24:7
that belonged to the **k** of Egypt, 2Kg 24:7
18 years old when he became **k**; 2Kg 24:8
of Nebuchadnezzar **k** of Babylon 2Kg 24:10

K Nebuchadnezzar of Babylon 2Kg 24:11
Jehoiachin **k** of Judah, along 2Kg 24:12
surrendered to the **k** of Babylon. 2Kg 24:12
So the **k** of Babylon took him 2Kg 24:12
Solomon **k** of Israel had made 2Kg 24:13
The **k** of Babylon also brought 2Kg 24:16
Then the **k** of Babylon made 2Kg 24:17
k in his place and changed his 2Kg 24:17
21 years old when he became **k**; 2Kg 24:18
against the **k** of Babylon. 2Kg 24:20
K Nebuchadnezzar of Babylon 2Kg 25:1
under siege until **K** Zedekiah's 2Kg 25:2
As the **k** made his way along the 2Kg 25:4
seized the **k** and brought him up 2Kg 25:6
him up to the **k** of Babylon at 2Kg 25:6
the **k** of Babylon blinded 2Kg 25:7
year of **K** Nebuchadnezzar, 2Kg 25:8
Nebuchadnezzar, **k** of Babylon, 2Kg 25:8
a servant of the **k** of Babylon, 2Kg 25:8
defected to the **k** of Babylon, 2Kg 25:11
them to the **k** of Babylon at 2Kg 25:20
The **k** of Babylon put them to 2Kg 25:21
Nebuchadnezzar **k** of Babylon 2Kg 25:22
heard that the **k** of Babylon had 2Kg 25:23
land and serve the **k** of Babylon, 2Kg 25:24
exile of Judah's **K** Jehoiachin, 2Kg 25:27
Evil-merodach **k** of Babylon, 2Kg 25:27
year he became **k**, pardoned King 2Kg 25:27
pardoned **K** Jehoiachin of Judah 2Kg 25:27
presence of the **k** of Babylon for 2Kg 25:29
was given to him by the **k**, 2Kg 25:30
of Edom before any **k** ruled over 1Ch 1:43
daughter of **K** Talmai of Geshur, 1Ch 3:2
there in the service of the **k**. 1Ch 4:23
cities until David became **k**. 1Ch 4:31
in the days of **K** Hezekiah of 1Ch 4:41
Tiglath-pileser **k** of Assyria 1Ch 5:6
reigns of Judah's **K** Jotham and 1Ch 5:17
Jotham and Israel's **K** Jeroboam. 1Ch 5:17
k of Assyria to take the 1Ch 5:26
when Saul was **k**, you led us out 1Ch 11:2
Israel came to the **k** at Hebron. 1Ch 11:3
anointed David **k** over Israel, 1Ch 11:3
reign to make him **k** according to 1Ch 11:10
name to come and make David **k**. 1Ch 12:31
to make David **k** over all Israel. 1Ch 12:38
of one mind to make David **k**. 1Ch 12:38
K Hiram of Tyre sent envoys to 1Ch 14:1
established him as **k** over Israel 1Ch 14:2
been anointed **k** over all Israel 1Ch 14:8
window and saw **K** David dancing 1Ch 15:29
the nations, "The LORD is **K**!" 1Ch 16:31
Then **K** David went in, sat in the 1Ch 17:16
also defeated **K** Hadadezer of 1Ch 18:3
came to assist **K** Hadadezer of 1Ch 18:5
When **K** Tou of Hamath heard that 1Ch 18:9
entire army of **K** Hadadezer of 1Ch 18:9
son Hadoram to **K** David to greet 1Ch 18:10
K David also dedicated these to 1Ch 18:11
K Nahash of the Ammonites died, 1Ch 19:1
his son became **k** in his place. 1Ch 19:1
The **k** said, "Stay in Jericho 1Ch 19:5
chariots and the **k** of Maacah 1Ch 19:7
crown from the head of their **k**, 1Ch 20:2
lord the **k**, aren't they all my 1Ch 21:3
My lord the **k** may do whatever he 1Ch 21:23
K David answered Ornan, "No, I 1Ch 21:24
son Solomon as **k** over Israel. 1Ch 23:1
presence of the **k** and the 1Ch 24:6
did in the presence of **K** David, 1Ch 24:31
under the authority of the **k**. 1Ch 25:2
had been dedicated by **K** David, 1Ch 26:26
and for the service of the **k**. 1Ch 26:30
K David appointed them over the 1Ch 26:32
relating to God and the **k**. 1Ch 26:32
who served the **k** in every matter 1Ch 27:1
Historical Record of **K** David. 1Ch 27:24
in charge of **K** David's property. 1Ch 27:31
cattle of the **k** and his sons, 1Ch 28:1
Then **K** David rose to his feet 1Ch 28:2
household to be **k** over Israel 1Ch 28:4
to make me **k** over all Israel. 1Ch 28:4
Then **K** David said to all the 1Ch 29:1
K David also rejoiced greatly. 1Ch 29:9
homage to the LORD and the **k**. 1Ch 29:20
made David's son Solomon **k**; 1Ch 29:22
throne as **k** in place of his 1Ch 29:23
and all of **K** David's sons as 1Ch 29:24

their allegiance to **K** Solomon. 1Ch 29:24
bestowed⌋ on any **k** over Israel 1Ch 29:25
of Jesse was **k** over all Israel 1Ch 29:26
Solomon became **k** in his place. 1Ch 29:28
the events of **K** David's ⌊reign⌋ 1Ch 29:29
You have made me **k** in his place. 2Ch 1:8
have made me **k** over a people as 2Ch 1:9
over whom I have made you **k**, 2Ch 1:11
and with the **k** in Jerusalem. 2Ch 1:14
The **k** made silver and gold as 2Ch 1:15
sent ⌊word⌋ to **K** Hiram of Tyre: 2Ch 2:3
Then **K** Hiram of Tyre wrote a 2Ch 2:11
He set you over them as **k**. 2Ch 2:11
He gave **K** David a wise son with 2Ch 2:12
was doing for **K** Solomon in God's 2Ch 4:11
made them for **K** Solomon for the 2Ch 4:16
k had them cast in clay molds 2Ch 4:17
K Solomon and the entire 2Ch 5:6
Then the **k** turned and blessed 2Ch 6:3
The **k** and all the people were 2Ch 7:4
K Solomon offered a sacrifice of 2Ch 7:5
this manner the **k** and all the 2Ch 7:5
which **K** David had made to praise 2Ch 7:6
These were **K** Solomon's deputies: 2Ch 8:10
house of David **k** of Israel 2Ch 8:11
and delivered it to **K** Solomon. 2Ch 8:18
She said to the **k**, "The report I 2Ch 9:5
on his throne as **k** for the LORD 2Ch 9:8
you over them as **k** to carry out 2Ch 9:8
she gave the **k** four and a half 2Ch 9:9
of Sheba gave to **K** Solomon. 2Ch 9:9
The **k** made the algum wood into 2Ch 9:11
K Solomon gave the queen of 2Ch 9:12
more than she had brought the **k**. 2Ch 9:12
K Solomon made 200 large shields 2Ch 9:15
The **k** put them in the House of 2Ch 9:16
The **k** also made a large ivory 2Ch 9:17
All of **K** Solomon's drinking cups 2Ch 9:20
K Solomon surpassed all the 2Ch 9:22
and with the **k** in Jerusalem. 2Ch 9:25
The **k** made silver as common in 2Ch 9:27
Rehoboam became **k** in his place. 2Ch 9:31
gone to Shechem to make him **k**. 2Ch 10:1
he had fled from **K** Solomon's 2Ch 10:2
Then **K** Rehoboam consulted with 2Ch 10:6
just as the **k** had ordered, 2Ch 10:12
the **k** answered them harshly. 2Ch 10:13
K Rehoboam rejected the elders' 2Ch 10:13
The **k** did not listen to the 2Ch 10:15
saw that the **k** had not listened 2Ch 10:16
the people answered the **k**: 2Ch 10:16
Then **K** Rehoboam sent Hadoram, 2Ch 10:18
K Rehoboam managed to get up 2Ch 10:18
son of Solomon, **k** of Judah, to 2Ch 11:3
intending to make him **k**. 2Ch 11:22
in the fifth year of **K** Rehoboam, 2Ch 12:2
Shishak **k** of Egypt went to war 2Ch 12:2
of Israel and the **k** humbled 2Ch 12:6
K Shishak of Egypt went to war 2Ch 12:9
K Rehoboam made bronze shields 2Ch 12:10
Whenever the **k** entered the 2Ch 12:11
K Rehoboam established his royal 2Ch 12:13
41 years old when he became **k**; 2Ch 12:13
Abijah became **k** in his place. 2Ch 12:16
year of ⌊Israel's⌋ **K** Jeroboam, 2Ch 13:1
Abijah became **k** over Judah; 2Ch 13:1
son Asa became **k** in his place. 2Ch 14:1
K Asa also removed Maacah, 2Ch 15:16
Israel's **K** Baasha went to war 2Ch 16:1
or coming—to Judah's **K** Asa. 2Ch 16:1
sent it to Aram's **K** Ben-hadad, 2Ch 16:2
with Israel's **K** Baasha so that 2Ch 16:3
listened to **K** Asa and sent 2Ch 16:4
Then **K** Asa brought all Judah, 2Ch 16:6
the seer came to **K** Asa of Judah 2Ch 16:7
depended on the **k** of Aram and 2Ch 16:7
the army of the **k** of Aram has 2Ch 16:7
Jehoshaphat became **k** in his 2Ch 17:1
were the ones who served the **k**, 2Ch 17:19
Israel's **K** Ahab asked Judah's 2Ch 18:3
asked Judah's **K** Jehoshaphat, 2Ch 18:3
said to the **k** of Israel, 2Ch 18:4
So the **k** of Israel gathered the 2Ch 18:5
God will hand it over to the **k**." 2Ch 18:5
The **k** of Israel said to 2Ch 18:7
"The **k** shouldn't say that," 2Ch 18:7
So the **k** of Israel called an 2Ch 18:8
Now the **k** of Israel and King 2Ch 18:9

king of Israel and **K** Jehoshaphat 2Ch 18:9
will hand it over to the **k**.” 2Ch 18:11
unanimously favorable for the **k**. 2Ch 18:12
he went to the **k**, and the king 2Ch 18:14
the king, and the **k** asked him, 2Ch 18:14
But the **k** said to him, “How many 2Ch 18:15
So the **k** of Israel said to 2Ch 18:17
will entice Ahab **k** of Israel to 2Ch 18:19
Then the **k** of Israel ordered, 2Ch 18:25
say, ‘This is what the **k** says: 2Ch 18:26
Then the **k** of Israel and Judah’s 2Ch 18:28
and Judah’s **K** Jehoshaphat went 2Ch 18:28
But the **k** of Israel said to 2Ch 18:29
So the **k** of Israel disguised 2Ch 18:29
the **k** of Aram had ordered his 2Ch 18:30
great, except the **k** of Israel.” 2Ch 18:30
“He must be the **k** of Israel!” 2Ch 18:31
that he was not the **k** of Israel, 2Ch 18:32
and struck the **k** of Israel 2Ch 18:33
and the **k** of Israel propped 2Ch 18:34
Jehoshaphat **k** of Judah returned 2Ch 19:1
him and said to **K** Jehoshaphat, 2Ch 19:2
in all matters related to the **k**, 2Ch 19:11
of Jerusalem, and **K** Jehoshaphat. 2Ch 20:15
Jehoshaphat became **k** over Judah. 2Ch 20:31
35 years old when he became **k**; 2Ch 20:31
Judah’s **K** Jehoshaphat made an 2Ch 20:35
with Israel’s **K** Ahaziah, 2Ch 20:35
Jehoram became **k** in his place. 2Ch 21:1
sons of Jehoshaphat, **k** of Judah. 2Ch 21:2
32 years old when he became **k**; 2Ch 21:5
and appointed their own **k**. 2Ch 21:8
or in the ways of Asa **k** of Judah 2Ch 21:12
32 years old when he became **k**; 2Ch 21:20
youngest son, **k** in his place, 2Ch 22:1
of Jehoram became **k** of Judah. 2Ch 22:1
22 years old when he became **k**; 2Ch 22:2
son of Israel’s **K** Ahab to fight 2Ch 22:5
fight against Hazael, **k** of Aram, 2Ch 22:5
fought against Aram’s **K** Hazael. 2Ch 22:6
Then Judah’s **K** Ahaziah son of 2Ch 22:6
the daughter of **K** Jehoram and 2Ch 22:11
with the **k** in God’s temple. 2Ch 23:3
surround the **k** with weapons in 2Ch 23:7
be with the **k** in all his daily 2Ch 23:7
of hundreds **K** David’s spears, 2Ch 23:9
in hand surrounding the **k**— 2Ch 23:10
the testimony, and made him **k**. 2Ch 23:11
and cried, “Long live the **k**!” 2Ch 23:11
those praising the **k**, she went 2Ch 23:12
there was the **k** standing by his 2Ch 23:13
the trumpeters were by the **k**, 2Ch 23:13
himself, the **k**, and the people 2Ch 23:16
and brought the **k** down from the 2Ch 23:20
and seated the **k** on the throne 2Ch 23:20
years old when he became **k**; 2Ch 24:1
the **k** called Jehoiada the high 2Ch 24:6
Then the **k** and Jehoiada gave it 2Ch 24:12
the money to the **k** and Jehoiada, 2Ch 24:14
came and paid homage to the **k**. 2Ch 24:17
Then the **k** listened to them, 2Ch 24:17
K Joash didn’t remember the 2Ch 24:22
plunder to the **k** of Damascus. 2Ch 24:23
Amaziah became **k** in his place. 2Ch 24:27
Amaziah became **k** ⌊when he was⌋ 2Ch 25:1
had murdered his father the **k**. 2Ch 25:3
to him and said, “**K**, do not let 2Ch 25:7
to him, the **k** asked, “Have we 2Ch 25:16
K Amaziah of Judah took counsel 2Ch 25:17
of Jehu, **k** of Israel, saying, 2Ch 25:17
K Jehoash of Israel sent ⌊word⌋ 2Ch 25:18
sent ⌊word⌋ to **K** Amaziah of 2Ch 25:18
So **K** Jehoash of Israel advanced. 2Ch 25:21
He and **K** Amaziah of Judah faced 2Ch 25:21
K Jehoash of Israel captured 2Ch 25:23
captured Judah’s **K** Amaziah son 2Ch 25:23
Judah’s **K** Amaziah son of Joash 2Ch 25:25
death of Israel’s **K** Jehoash son 2Ch 25:25
and made him **k** in place of his 2Ch 26:1
Amaziah⌋ the **k** rested with his 2Ch 26:2
16 years old when he became **k**; 2Ch 26:3
to help the **k** against the enemy 2Ch 26:13
stand against **K** Uzziah and said, 2Ch 26:18
So **K** Uzziah was diseased to the 2Ch 26:21
Jotham became **k** in his place. 2Ch 26:23
25 years old when he became **k**; 2Ch 27:1
war against the **k** of the 2Ch 27:5
25 years old when he became **k**; 2Ch 27:8

son Ahaz became **k** in his place. 2Ch 27:9
20 years old when he became **k**; 2Ch 28:1
Ahaz over to the **k** of Aram. 2Ch 28:5
handed over to the **k** of Israel, 2Ch 28:5
Elkanah who was second to the **k**. 2Ch 28:7
At that time **K** Ahaz asked the 2Ch 28:16
Ahaz asked the **k** of Assyria for 2Ch 28:16
because of **K** Ahaz of Judah, 2Ch 28:19
Tiglath-pileser **k** of Assyria 2Ch 28:20
palace of the **k** and of the 2Ch 28:21
the plunder to the **k** of Assyria, 2Ch 28:21
K Ahaz himself became more 2Ch 28:22
Hezekiah became **k** in his place. 2Ch 28:27
25 years old when he became **k**; 2Ch 29:1
went inside to **K** Hezekiah and 2Ch 29:18
utensils that **K** Ahaz rejected 2Ch 29:19
K Hezekiah got up early, 2Ch 29:20
the presence of the **k** and the 2Ch 29:23
for the **k** said that the burnt 2Ch 29:24
of David **k** of Israel. 2Ch 29:27
the **k** and all those present with 2Ch 29:29
K Hezekiah and the officials 2Ch 29:30
For the **k** and his officials and 2Ch 30:2
pleased the **k** and the 2Ch 30:4
the hand of the **k** and his 2Ch 30:6
command of the **k** and his 2Ch 30:12
for Hezekiah **k** of Judah 2Ch 30:24
son of David, the **k** of Israel. 2Ch 30:26
The **k** contributed from his own 2Ch 31:3
by appointment of **K** Hezekiah 2Ch 31:13
Sennacherib **k** of Assyria came 2Ch 32:1
the **k** of Assyria or before 2Ch 32:7
on the words of **K** Hezekiah of 2Ch 32:8
Sennacherib **k** of Assyria with 2Ch 32:9
against **K** Hezekiah of Judah 2Ch 32:9
This is what **K** Sennacherib of 2Ch 32:10
the power of the **k** of Assyria”? 2Ch 32:11
K Hezekiah and the prophet 2Ch 32:20
in the camp of the **k** of Assyria. 2Ch 32:21
the **k** of Assyria returned with 2Ch 32:21
from the power of **K** Sennacherib 2Ch 32:22
gifts to **K** Hezekiah of Judah 2Ch 32:23
Manasseh became **k** in his place. 2Ch 32:33
12 years old when he became **k**; 2Ch 33:1
commanders of the **k** of Assyria. 2Ch 33:11
son Amon became **k** in his place. 2Ch 33:20
22 years old when he became **k**; 2Ch 33:21
against **K** Amon and made his 2Ch 33:25
his son Josiah **k** in his place. 2Ch 33:25
years old when he became **k**; 2Ch 34:1
Shaphan took the book to the **k**, 2Ch 34:16
the court secretary told the **k**, 2Ch 34:18
it in the presence of the **k**. 2Ch 34:18
When the **k** heard the words of 2Ch 34:19
and those the **k** had designated 2Ch 34:22
the presence of the **k** of Judah, 2Ch 34:24
Say this to the **k** of Judah who 2Ch 34:26
Then they reported to the **k**. 2Ch 34:28
So the **k** sent ⌊messengers⌋ and 2Ch 34:29
Then the **k** went up to the LORD’s 2Ch 34:30
Next the **k** stood at his post and 2Ch 34:31
son of David **k** of Israel. 2Ch 35:3
of David **k** of Israel and that 2Ch 35:4
to the command of **K** Josiah. 2Ch 35:16
Neco **k** of Egypt marched up to 2Ch 35:20
between you and me, **k** of Judah? 2Ch 35:21
The archers shot **K** Josiah, 2Ch 35:23
and made him **k** in Jerusalem 2Ch 36:1
23 years old when he became **k**; 2Ch 36:2
The **k** of Egypt deposed him in 2Ch 36:3
Then ⌊Neco⌋ **k** of Egypt made 2Ch 36:4
brother Eliakim **k** over Judah and 2Ch 36:4
25 years old when he became **k**; 2Ch 36:5
Nebuchadnezzar **k** of Babylon 2Ch 36:6
became **k** in his place. 2Ch 36:8
18 years old when he became **k**; 2Ch 36:9
brother Zedekiah **k** over Judah 2Ch 36:10
21 years old when he became **k**; 2Ch 36:11
against **K** Nebuchadnezzar 2Ch 36:13
them the **k** of the Chaldeans 2Ch 36:17
treasures of the **k** and his 2Ch 36:18
first year of Cyrus **k** of Persia, 2Ch 36:22
the mind of **K** Cyrus of Persia 2Ch 36:22
This is what **K** Cyrus of Persia 2Ch 36:23
first year of Cyrus **k** of Persia, Ezr 1:1
the mind of **K** Cyrus to issue Ezr 1:1
This is what **K** Cyrus of Persia Ezr 1:2
K Cyrus also brought out the Ezr 1:7

K Cyrus of Persia had them Ezr 1:8
captive exiles **K** Nebuchadnezzar Ezr 2:1
them by **K** Cyrus of Persia. Ezr 3:7
as **K** David of Israel had Ezr 3:10
Him since the time **K** Esar-haddon Ezr 4:2
of Israel, as **K** Cyrus, the king Ezr 4:3
k of Persia has commanded us. Ezr 4:3
the reign of **K** Cyrus of Persia Ezr 4:5
the reign of **K** Darius of Persia Ezr 4:5
the time of ⌊**K**⌋ Artaxerxes Ezr 4:7
wrote to **K** Artaxerxes. Ezr 4:7
wrote a letter to **K** Artaxerxes Ezr 4:8
To **K** Artaxerxes from your Ezr 4:11
be known to the **k** that the Jews Ezr 4:12
be known to the **k** that if that Ezr 4:13
an oath of loyalty to the **k**, Ezr 4:14
we have sent to inform the **k** Ezr 4:14
advise the **k** that if this city Ezr 4:16
The **k** sent a reply to his chief Ezr 4:17
as the text of **K** Artaxerxes’ Ezr 4:23
of the reign of **K** Darius of Ezr 4:24
in the region, sent to **K** Darius. Ezr 5:6
as follows: To **K** Darius: All Ezr 5:7
known to the **k** that we went to Ezr 5:8
which a great **k** of Israel built Ezr 5:11
them over to **K** Nebuchadnezzar Ezr 5:12
year of Cyrus **k** of Babylon, Ezr 5:13
by the appointment of **K** Cyrus. Ezr 5:14
it pleases the **k**, let a search Ezr 5:17
was issued by **K** Cyrus to rebuild Ezr 5:17
K Darius gave the order, and Ezr 6:1
In the first year of **K** Cyrus, Ezr 6:3
the life of the **k** and his sons. Ezr 6:10
overthrow any **k** or people who Ezr 6:12
carried out what **K** Darius had Ezr 6:13
and **K** Artaxerxes of Persia. Ezr 6:14
year of the reign of **K** Darius. Ezr 6:15
during the reign of **K** Artaxerxes Ezr 7:1
The **k** had granted him everything Ezr 7:6
seventh year of **K** Artaxerxes. Ezr 7:7
the seventh year of the **k**. Ezr 7:8
of the letter **K** Artaxerxes gave Ezr 7:11
Artaxerxes, **k** of kings, to Ezra Ezr 7:12
are sent by the **k** and his seven Ezr 7:14
and gold the **k** and his Ezr 7:15
I, **K** Artaxerxes, issue a decree Ezr 7:21
the realm of the **k** and his sons. Ezr 7:23
your God and the law of the **k**, Ezr 7:26
shown favor to me before the **k**, Ezr 7:28
the reign of **K** Artaxerxes: Ezr 8:1
to ask the **k** for infantry Ezr 8:22
the house of our God that the **k**, Ezr 8:25
twentieth year of **K** Artaxerxes, Neh 2:1
the wine and gave it to the **k**. Neh 2:1
the **k** said to me, “Why are you Neh 2:2
replied to the **k**, “May the king Neh 2:3
king, “May the **k** live forever! Neh 2:3
Then the **k** asked me, “What is Neh 2:4
answered the **k**, “If it pleases Neh 2:5
If it pleases the **k**, and if your Neh 2:5
The **k**, with the queen seated Neh 2:6
and it pleased the **k** to send me. Neh 2:6
said to the **k**: “If it pleases Neh 2:7
If it pleases the **k**, let me have Neh 2:7
The **k** granted my ⌊requests⌋, Neh 2:8
The **k** had also sent officers of Neh 2:9
and what the **k** had said to me. Neh 2:18
you rebelling against the **k**?” Neh 2:19
from the upper palace of the **k**, Neh 3:25
from the day **K** Artaxerxes Neh 5:14
you are to become their **k** Neh 6:6
“There is a **k** in Judah.” Neh 6:7
rumors will be heard by the **k**. Neh 6:7
deported by **K** Nebuchadnezzar Neh 7:6
the land of Sihon **k** of Heshbon Neh 9:22
of the land of Og **k** of Bashan. Neh 9:22
command of the **k** regarding them Neh 11:23
had returned to **K** Artaxerxes of Neh 13:6
that I asked the **k** for a leave Neh 13:6
Didn’t **K** Solomon of Israel sin Neh 13:26
There was not a **k** like him among Neh 13:26
God made him **k** over all Israel Neh 13:26
those days **K** Ahasuerus reigned Est 1:2
the **k** held a week-long banquet Est 1:5
The **k** had ordered every wine Est 1:8
for the women of **K** Ahasuerus’ Est 1:9
when the **k** was feeling good from Est 1:10
The **k** became furious and his Est 1:12

The **k** consulted the wise men who Est 1:13
access to the **k** and occupied Est 1:14
⌊The **k** asked,⌋ "According to the Est 1:15
refused to obey **K** Ahasuerus' Est 1:15
presence of the **k** and his Est 1:16
has defied not only the **k**, Est 1:16
are in every one of **K** Ahasuerus' Est 1:16
'**K** Ahasuerus ordered Queen Est 1:17
is not to enter **K** Ahasuerus' Est 1:19
The decree the **k** issues will be Est 1:20
k and his counselors approved Est 1:21
K Ahasuerus' rage had cooled Est 2:1
young virgins for the **k**. Est 2:2
Let the **k** appoint commissioners Est 2:3
who pleases the **k** will reign in Est 2:4
This suggestion pleased the **k**, Est 2:4
captives when **K** Nebuchadnezzar Est 2:6
of Babylon took **K** Jeconiah of Est 2:6
turn to go to **K** Ahasuerus, Est 2:12
young woman would go to the **k**, Est 2:13
She never went to the **k** again, Est 2:14
her turn came to go to the **k**, Est 2:15
Esther was taken to **K** Ahasuerus Est 2:16
The **k** loved Esther more than all Est 2:17
The **k** held a great banquet for Est 2:18
to assassinate **K** Ahasuerus. Est 2:21
and she told the **k** on Mordecai's Est 2:22
K Ahasuerus honored Haman, Est 3:1
because the **k** had commanded this Est 3:2
in **K** Ahasuerus' twelfth year, Est 3:7
Then Haman informed **K** Ahasuerus, Est 3:8
If the **k** approves, let an order Est 3:9
The **k** removed his signet ring Est 3:10
the **k** told Haman, "The money Est 3:11
in the name of **K** Ahasuerus and Est 3:12
The **k** and Haman sat down to Est 3:15
instruct her to approach the **k**, Est 4:8
approaches the **k** in the inner Est 4:11
Only if the **k** extends the golden Est 4:11
before the **k** for the last 30 Est 4:11
I will go to the **k** even if it is Est 4:16
The **k** was sitting on his royal Est 5:1
soon as the **k** saw Queen Esther Est 5:2
k extended the golden scepter Est 5:2
Queen Esther?" the **k** asked her. Est 5:3
it pleases the **k**," Esther Est 5:4
may the **k** and Haman come today Est 5:4
The **k** commanded, "Hurry, and get Est 5:5
So the **k** and Haman went to the Est 5:5
the wine, the **k** asked Esther, Est 5:6
the **k** approves of me and if it Est 5:8
if it pleases the **k** to grant my Est 5:8
may the **k** and Haman come to the Est 5:8
I will do what the **k** has asked." Est 5:8
all how the **k** had promoted him Est 5:11
me to join the **k** at the banquet Est 5:12
tomorrow to join her with the **k**. Est 5:12
Ask the **k** in the morning to hang Est 5:14
banquet with the **k** and enjoy Est 5:14
That night sleep escaped the **k**, Est 6:1
to be brought and read to the **k**. Est 6:1
to assassinate **K** Ahasuerus. Est 6:2
The **k** inquired, "What honor and Est 6:3
k asked, "Who's in the court?" Est 6:4
to ask the **k** to hang Mordecai Est 6:4
Have him enter," the **k** ordered. Est 6:5
and the **k** asked him, "What Est 6:6
the man the **k** wants to honor? Est 6:6
Who is it the **k** would want to Est 6:6
Haman told the **k**, "For the man Est 6:7
For the man the **k** wants to honor Est 6:7
that the **k** himself has worn Est 6:8
and a horse the **k** himself has Est 6:8
the man the **k** wants to honor, Est 6:9
the man the **k** wants to honor. Est 6:9
The **k** told Haman, "Hurry, and do Est 6:10
the man the **k** wants to honor. Est 6:11
eunuchs of the **k** arrived and Est 6:14
The **k** and Haman came to feast Est 7:1
wine, the **k** asked Esther, Est 7:2
approval, my **k**, and if the king Est 7:3
king, and if the **k** is pleased, Est 7:3
be worth burdening the **k**." Est 7:4
K Ahasuerus spoke up and asked Est 7:5
before the **k** and queen. Est 7:6
the **k** arose from where they were Est 7:7
he realized the **k** was planning Est 7:7
Just as the **k** returned from the Est 7:8
The **k** exclaimed, "Would he Est 7:8
the report that saved the **k**." Est 7:9
The **k** commanded, "Hang him on Est 7:9
same day **K** Ahasuerus awarded Est 8:1
The **k** removed his signet ring he Est 8:2
Esther addressed the **k** again. Est 8:3
k extended the golden scepter Est 8:4
got up and stood before the **k**. Est 8:4
it pleases the **k**, and I have Est 8:5
right to the **k** and I am pleasing Est 8:5
K Ahasuerus said to Esther the Est 8:7
wrote in **K** Ahasuerus' name Est 8:10
the provinces of **K** Ahasuerus, Est 8:12
each of **K** Ahasuerus' provinces Est 9:2
of Susa was reported to the **k**. Est 9:11
The **k** said to Queen Esther, Est 9:12
it pleases the **k**, may the Jews Est 9:13
The **k** gave the orders for this Est 9:14
the Jews in all of **K** Ahasuerus' Est 9:20
matter was brought before the **k**, Est 9:25
K Ahasuerus imposed a tax Est 10:1
to which the **k** had promoted him Est 10:2
was second only to **K** Ahasuerus, Est 10:3
like a **k** prepared for battle. Jb 15:24
away to the **k** of terrors. Jb 18:14
I lived as a **k** among his troops, Jb 29:25
says to a **k**, "Worthless man!" Jb 34:18
he is **k** over all the proud Jb 41:34
I have consecrated My **K** on Zion, Ps 2:6
of my cry, my **K** and my God, for Ps 5:2
The LORD is **K** forever and ever; Ps 10:16
gives great victories to His **k**; Ps 18:50
LORD, give victory to the **k**! Ps 20:9
k finds joy in Your strength. Ps 21:1
For the **k** relies on the LORD; Ps 21:7
the **K** of glory will come in. Ps 24:7
Who is this **K** of glory? Ps 24:8
the **K** of glory will come in. Ps 24:9
Who is He, this **K** of glory? Ps 24:10
of Hosts, He is the **K** of glory. Ps 24:10
LORD sits enthroned, **K** forever. Ps 29:10
k is not saved by a large army; Ps 33:16
are my **K**, my God, who ordains Ps 44:4
as I recite my verses to the **k**; Ps 45:1
and the **k** will desire your Ps 45:11
garments she is led to the **k**; Ps 45:14
a great **K** over all the earth. Ps 47:2
praise to our **K**, sing praise! Ps 47:6
for God is **K** of all the earth. Ps 47:7
is the city of the great **K**. Ps 48:2
But the **k** will rejoice in God; Ps 63:11
of my God, my **K**, in the Ps 68:24
Your justice to the **k** and Your Ps 72:1
God my **k** is from ancient times, Ps 74:12
LORD of Hosts, my **K** and my God. Ps 84:3
our **k** to the Holy One of Israel. Ps 89:18
God, a great **K** above all gods. Ps 95:3
the presence of the LORD, our **K**. Ps 98:6
The mighty **K** loves justice. Ps 99:4
k sent ⌊for him⌋ and released Ps 105:20
Sihon **k** of the Amorites, Og king Ps 135:11
Amorites, Og **k** of Bashan, and Ps 135:11
Sihon **k** of the Amorites His love Ps 136:19
and Og **k** of Bashan—His love is Ps 136:20
You, my God the **K**, and praise Ps 145:1
of Zion rejoice in their **K**. Ps 149:2
son of David, **k** of Israel: Pr 1:1
A **k** favors a wise servant, Pr 14:35
verdict is on the lips of a **k**; Pr 16:10
A **k** sitting on a throne to judge Pr 20:8
wise **k** separates out the wicked Pr 20:26
and faithfulness deliver a **k**; Pr 20:28
lips—the **k** is his friend. Pr 22:11
as well as the **k**, and don't Pr 24:21
of Hezekiah, **k** of Judah, copied Pr 25:1
about yourself before the **k**, Pr 25:6
By justice a **k** brings stability Pr 29:4
A **k** who judges the poor with Pr 29:14
a servant when he becomes **k**, Pr 30:22
locusts have no **k**, yet all of Pr 30:27
and a **k** at the head of his army. Pr 30:31
The words of **K** Lemuel, an oracle Pr 31:1
son of David, **k** in Jerusalem. Ec 1:1
have been **k** over Israel in Ec 1:12
be like who comes after the **k**? Ec 2:12
old but foolish **k** who no longer Ec 4:13
For he came from prison to be **k**, Ec 4:14
the **k** is served by the field. Ec 5:9
A great **k** came against it, Ec 9:14
when your **k** is a household Ec 10:16
when your **k** is a son of nobles Ec 10:17
Do not curse the **k** even in your Ec 10:20
that the **k** would bring me to his Sg 1:4
While the **k** is on his couch, Sg 1:12
K Solomon made a sedan chair for Sg 3:9
and gaze at **K** Solomon, wearing Sg 3:11
k could be held captive in your Sg 7:5
In the year that **K** Uzziah died, Is 6:1
because my eyes have seen the **K**, Is 6:5
son of Uzziah **k** of Judah: Is 7:1
Rezin **k** of Aram, along with Is 7:1
of Remaliah, **k** of Israel, waged Is 7:1
Tabeel's son as **k** in it." Is 7:6
the **k** of Assyria ⌊is coming⌋. Is 7:17
River—the **k** of Assyria—to Is 7:20
off to the **k** of Assyria." Is 8:4
the **k** of Assyria and all his Is 8:7
curse their **k** and their God. Is 8:21
will punish the **k** of Assyria for Is 10:12
about the **k** of Babylon and say Is 14:4
In the year that **K** Ahaz died, Is 14:28
and a strong **k** will rule it. Is 19:4
sent by Sargon **k** of Assyria, Is 20:1
the **k** of Assyria will lead the Is 20:4
us⌋ from the **k** of Assyria! Is 20:6
years—the life span of one **k**. Is 23:15
will reign as **k** on Mount Zion Is 24:23
ready for the **k** for a long time Is 30:33
a **k** will reign righteously, Is 32:1
will see the **k** in his beauty; Is 33:17
our lawgiver, the LORD is our **K**. Is 33:22
will be left to proclaim a **k**, Is 34:12
fourteenth year of **K** Hezekiah, Is 36:1
Sennacherib **k** of Assyria Is 36:1
Then the **k** of Assyria sent the Is 36:2
from Lachish to **K** Hezekiah at Is 36:2
great **k**, the king of Assyria, Is 36:4
great king, the **k** of Assyria, Is 36:4
is how Pharaoh **k** of Egypt is to Is 36:6
my master, the **k** of Assyria. Is 36:8
to the words of the great **k**, Is 36:13
great king, the **k** of Assyria! Is 36:13
The **k** says: "Don't let Hezekiah Is 36:14
over to the **k** of Assyria.'" Is 36:15
For the **k** of Assyria says: Is 36:16
the hand of the **k** of Assyria? Is 36:18
When **K** Hezekiah heard ⌊their Is 37:1
his master, the **k** of Assyria, Is 37:4
When **K** Hezekiah's servants came Is 37:5
which the **k** of Assyria's Is 37:6
heard that the **k** had left Is 37:8
that the **k** of Assyria was Is 37:8
The **k** had heard this about Is 37:9
this about Tirhakah, **k** of Cush: Is 37:9
this to Hezekiah **k** of Judah: Is 37:10
handed over to the **k** of Assyria. Is 37:10
Where is the **k** of Hamath, the Is 37:13
of Hamath, the **k** of Arpad, the Is 37:13
the **k** of the city of Sepharvaim, Is 37:13
about Sennacherib **k** of Assyria, Is 37:21
says about the **k** of Assyria: Is 37:33
Sennacherib **k** of Assyria broke Is 37:37
became **k** in his place. Is 37:38
the hand of the **k** of Assyria; Is 38:6
by Hezekiah **k** of Judah after Is 38:9
son of Baladan, **k** of Babylon, Is 39:1
prophet came to **K** Hezekiah and Is 39:3
palace of the **k** of Babylon.'" Is 39:7
your arguments," says Jacob's **K**. Is 41:21
the Creator of Israel, your **K**. Is 43:15
K of Israel and its Redeemer, Is 44:6
You went to the **k** with oil and Is 57:9
Josiah son of Amon, **k** of Judah. Jr 1:2
son of Josiah, **k** of Judah, until Jr 1:3
son of Josiah, **k** of Judah, when Jr 1:3
and each ⌊**k**⌋ will set up his Jr 1:15
In the days of **K** Josiah the LORD Jr 3:6
the **k** and the officials will Jr 4:9
in Zion, her **K** not in her midst? Jr 8:19
not fear You, **K** of the nations? Jr 10:7
is the living God and eternal **K**. Jr 10:10
Say to the **k** and the queen Jr 13:18
of Hezekiah, the **k** of Judah, for Jr 15:4
Judah over to the **k** of Babylon, Jr 20:4
the LORD when **K** Zedekiah sent Jr 21:1
Nebuchadnezzar **k** of Babylon is Jr 21:2

using to fight the **k** of Babylon Jr 21:4
declaration—"'**K** Zedekiah of Jr 21:7
hand over to **K** Nebuchadnezzar Jr 21:7
handed over to the **k** of Babylon, Jr 21:10
the house of the **k** of Judah ⌊say Jr 21:11
to the palace of the **k** of Judah Jr 22:1
of the LORD, **k** of Judah, you who Jr 22:2
the house of the **k** of Judah: Jr 22:6
son of Josiah, **k** of Judah, who Jr 22:11
Josiah his father as **k**: Jr 22:11
Are you a **k** because you excel in Jr 22:15
son of Josiah, **k** of Judah: Jr 22:18
Jehoiakim, the **k** of Judah, were Jr 22:24
to Nebuchadnezzar **k** of Babylon Jr 22:25
reign wisely as **k** and administer Jr 23:5
Nebuchadnezzar **k** of Babylon had Jr 24:1
son of Jehoiakim **k** of Judah, Jr 24:1
deal with Zedekiah **k** of Judah, Jr 24:8
son of Josiah, **k** of Judah (which Jr 25:1
of Nebuchadnezzar **k** of Babylon Jr 25:1
son of Amon, **k** of Judah, until Jr 25:3
Nebuchadnezzar **k** of Babylon, Jr 25:9
will serve the **k** of Babylon for Jr 25:11
I will punish the **k** of Babylon Jr 25:12
k of Egypt, his officers, Jr 25:19
the **k** of Sheshach will drink Jr 25:26
son of Josiah, **k** of Judah, this Jr 26:1
days of Hezekiah **k** of Judah and Jr 26:18
Did Hezekiah **k** of Judah and all Jr 26:19
K Jehoiakim, all his warriors, Jr 26:21
and the **k** tried to put him to Jr 26:21
But **K** Jehoiakim sent men to Jr 26:22
and took him to **K** Jehoiakim, Jr 26:23
son of Josiah, **k** of Judah, this Jr 27:1
Send ⌊word⌋ to the **k** of Edom, Jr 27:3
of Edom, the **k** of Moab, the king Jr 27:3
of Moab, the **k** of the Ammonites Jr 27:3
Ammonites, the **k** of Tyre, and Jr 27:3
and the **k** of Sidon through Jr 27:3
coming to Zedekiah **k** of Judah in Jr 27:3
Nebuchadnezzar, **k** of Babylon. Jr 27:6
Nebuchadnezzar **k** of Babylon and Jr 27:8
the yoke of the **k** of Babylon, Jr 27:8
Don't serve the **k** of Babylon! Jr 27:9
the yoke of the **k** of Babylon and Jr 27:11
spoke to Zedekiah **k** of Judah in Jr 27:12
the yoke of the **k** of Babylon, Jr 27:12
does not serve the **k** of Babylon? Jr 27:13
not serve the **k** of Babylon,' Jr 27:14
Serve the **k** of Babylon and live! Jr 27:17
in the palace of the **k** of Judah, Jr 27:18
Nebuchadnezzar **k** of Babylon did Jr 27:20
son of Jehoiakim, **k** of Judah, Jr 27:20
in the palace of the **k** of Judah, Jr 27:21
reign of Zedekiah **k** of Judah, Jr 28:1
the yoke of the **k** of Babylon. Jr 28:2
Nebuchadnezzar **k** of Babylon took Jr 28:3
of Jehoiakim, **k** of Judah, and Jr 28:4
the yoke of the **k** of Babylon.'" Jr 28:4
of Nebuchadnezzar, **k** of Babylon, Jr 28:11
Nebuchadnezzar **k** of Babylon, Jr 28:14
⌊This was⌋ after **K** Jeconiah, Jr 29:2
Zedekiah **k** of Judah had sent Jr 29:3
to Nebuchadnezzar **k** of Babylon. Jr 29:3
concerning the **k** sitting on Jr 29:16
to Nebuchadnezzar **k** of Babylon, Jr 29:21
whom the **k** of Babylon roasted in Jr 29:22
up David their **k** for them." Jr 30:9
year of Zedekiah **k** of Judah, Jr 32:1
the army of the **k** of Babylon was Jr 32:2
in the palace of the **k** of Judah. Jr 32:2
Zedekiah **k** of Judah had Jr 32:3
this city over to Babylon's **k**, Jr 32:3
Zedekiah **k** of Judah will not Jr 32:4
be handed over to Babylon's **k**. Jr 32:4
to Babylon's **k** Nebuchadnezzar, Jr 32:28
to Babylon's **k** through sword, Jr 32:36
Nebuchadnezzar, **k** of Babylon, Jr 34:1
to Zedekiah, **k** of Judah, and Jr 34:2
city over to the **k** of Babylon, Jr 34:2
will meet the **k** of Babylon eye Jr 34:3
word, Zedekiah, **k** of Judah. Jr 34:4
words to Zedekiah **k** of Judah in Jr 34:6
while the **k** of Babylon's army Jr 34:7
the LORD after **K** Zedekiah made Jr 34:8
hand Zedekiah **k** of Judah and his Jr 34:21
to the **k** of Babylon's army that Jr 34:21
son of Josiah, **k** of Judah: Jr 35:1

Nebuchadnezzar **k** of Babylon Jr 35:11
son of Josiah, **k** of Judah, this Jr 36:1
of Josiah, **k** of Judah, in the Jr 36:9
tell the **k** all these things. Jr 36:16
came to the **k** at the courtyard Jr 36:20
in the hearing of the **k**. Jr 36:20
The **k** sent Jehudi to get the Jr 36:21
the hearing of the **k** and all the Jr 36:21
who were standing by the **k**. Jr 36:21
the **k** was sitting in his winter Jr 36:22
k and all of his servants did Jr 36:24
had urged the **k** not to burn the Jr 36:25
Then the **k** commanded Jerahmeel Jr 36:26
the **k** had burned the scroll Jr 36:27
Jehoiakim **k** of Judah burned. Jr 36:28
concerning Jehoiakim **k** of Judah: Jr 36:29
The **k** of Babylon will certainly Jr 36:29
concerning Jehoiakim **k** of Judah: Jr 36:30
Jehoiakim, Judah's **k**, had burned Jr 36:32
Josiah reigned as **k** in the land Jr 37:1
Nebuchadnezzar **k** of Babylon made Jr 37:1
king of Babylon made him **k**. Jr 37:1
K Zedekiah sent Jehucal son of Jr 37:3
what you will say to Judah's **k**, Jr 37:7
K Zedekiah later sent ⌊for him⌋ Jr 37:17
over to the **k** of Babylon." Jr 37:17
Jeremiah said to **K** Zedekiah, Jr 37:18
'The **k** of Babylon will not come Jr 37:19
please listen, my lord the **k**. Jr 37:20
So **K** Zedekiah gave orders, Jr 37:21
over to the **k** of Babylon's army Jr 38:3
officials then said to the **k**, Jr 38:4
K Zedekiah said, "Here he is; Jr 38:5
hands since the **k** can't do Jr 38:5
While the **k** was sitting at the Jr 38:7
palace and spoke to the **k**: Jr 38:8
My lord **k**, these men have been Jr 38:9
So the **k** commanded Ebed-melech, Jr 38:10
K Zedekiah sent for Jeremiah the Jr 38:14
The **k** said to Jeremiah, "I am Jr 38:14
K Zedekiah swore to Jeremiah in Jr 38:16
officials of the **k** of Babylon, Jr 38:17
officials of the **k** of Babylon, Jr 38:18
But **K** Zedekiah said to Jeremiah, Jr 38:19
of Judah's **k** will be brought Jr 38:22
officials of the **k** of Babylon Jr 38:22
seized by the **k** of Babylon and Jr 38:23
'Tell us what you said to the **k**; Jr 38:25
what did the **k** say to you?' Jr 38:25
before the **k** my petition that he Jr 38:26
to them the **k** had commanded, Jr 38:27
year of Zedekiah **k** of Judah, Jr 39:1
K Nebuchadnezzar of Babylon Jr 39:1
officials of the **k** of Babylon Jr 39:3
of the officials of Babylon's **k**. Jr 39:3
Zedekiah **k** of Judah and all the Jr 39:4
Babylon's **k**, at Riblah in the Jr 39:5
The **k** passed sentence on him Jr 39:5
At Riblah the **k** of Babylon Jr 39:6
K Nebuchadnezzar of Babylon gave Jr 39:11
the captains of the **k** of Babylon Jr 39:13
whom the **k** of Babylon has Jr 40:5
heard that the **k** of Babylon had Jr 40:7
land and serve the **k** of Babylon, Jr 40:9
heard that the **k** of Babylon had Jr 40:11
that Baalis, **k** of the Ammonites, Jr 40:14
the one the **k** of Babylon had Jr 41:2
a large one that **K** Asa had made Jr 41:9
with Baasha **k** of Israel. Jr 41:9
the daughters of the **k**— Jr 41:10
whom the **k** of Babylon had Jr 41:18
afraid of the **k** of Babylon whom Jr 42:11
Nebuchadnezzar **k** of Babylon, Jr 43:10
Egypt's **k**, to his enemies Jr 44:30
handed over Judah's **K** Zedekiah Jr 44:30
to Babylon's **K** Nebuchadnezzar, Jr 44:30
son of Josiah, **k** of Judah: Jr 45:1
Neco, Egypt's **k**, which was Jr 46:2
by Nebuchadnezzar **k** of Babylon Jr 46:2
year of Judah's **K** Jehoiakim son Jr 46:2
Nebuchadnezzar **k** of Babylon to Jr 46:13
k of Egypt was all noise; Jr 46:17
to Nebuchadnezzar **k** of Babylon Jr 46:26
Babylon's **k**, defeated, this is Jr 49:28
Nebuchadnezzar **k** of Babylon has Jr 49:30
reign of Zedekiah **k** of Judah. Jr 49:34
will destroy the **k** and officials Jr 49:38
him was the **k** of Assyria; Jr 50:17

was Nebuchadnezzar **k** of Babylon. Jr 50:17
to punish the **k** of Babylon and Jr 50:18
as I punished the **k** of Assyria. Jr 50:18
The **k** of Babylon has heard Jr 50:43
announce to the **k** of Babylon Jr 51:31
Babylon with Zedekiah **k** of Judah Jr 51:59
21 years old when he became **k**; Jr 52:1
against the **k** of Babylon. Jr 52:3
K Nebuchadnezzar of Babylon Jr 52:4
under siege until **K** Zedekiah's Jr 52:5
army pursued the **k** and overtook Jr 52:8
seized the **k** and brought him to Jr 52:9
him to the **k** of Babylon at Jr 52:9
At Riblah the **k** of Babylon Jr 52:10
k of Babylon brought Zedekiah Jr 52:11
year of **K** Nebuchadnezzar, Jr 52:12
Nebuchadnezzar, **k** of Babylon— Jr 52:12
of the **k** of Babylon. Jr 52:12
defected to the **k** of Babylon, Jr 52:15
carts that **K** Solomon had made Jr 52:20
them to the **k** of Babylon at Jr 52:26
The **k** of Babylon put them to Jr 52:27
exile of Judah's **K** Jehoiachin, Jr 52:31
Evil-merodach **k** of Babylon, Jr 52:31
pardoned **K** Jehoiachin of Judah Jr 52:31
presence of the **k** of Babylon for Jr 52:33
to him by the **k** of Babylon, Jr 52:34
He has despised **k** and priest in Lm 2:6
Her **k** and her leaders ⌊live⌋ Lm 2:9
the fifth year of **K** Jehoiachin's Ezk 1:2
k will mourn; the prince will Ezk 7:27
The **k** of Babylon came to Ezk 17:12
took its **k** and officials, Ezk 17:12
this **k** revolted against him by Ezk 17:15
in the land of the **k** who put him Ezk 17:16
him away to the **k** of Babylon. Ezk 19:9
sword of Babylon's **k** can take, Ezk 21:19
For the **k** of Babylon stands at Ezk 21:21
The **k** of Babylon has laid siege Ezk 24:2
about to bring **K** Nebuchadnezzar Ezk 26:7
of Babylon, **k** of kings, against Ezk 26:7
lament for the **k** of Tyre and say Ezk 28:12
face toward Pharaoh **k** of Egypt Ezk 29:2
you, Pharaoh **k** of Egypt, the Ezk 29:3
Nebuchadnezzar **k** of Babylon Ezk 29:18
to Nebuchadnezzar **k** of Babylon, Ezk 29:19
of Nebuchadnezzar **k** of Babylon. Ezk 30:10
the arm of Pharaoh **k** of Egypt. Ezk 30:21
I am against Pharaoh **k** of Egypt. Ezk 30:22
arms of Babylon's **k** and place My Ezk 30:24
the arms of Babylon's **k**, Ezk 30:25
of Babylon's **k** and he wields it Ezk 30:25
say to Pharaoh **k** of Egypt and to Ezk 31:2
for Pharaoh **k** of Egypt and say Ezk 32:2
of Babylon's **k** will come against Ezk 32:11
and one **k** will rule over all of Ezk 37:22
David will be **k** over them, Ezk 37:24
reign of Jehoiakim **k** of Judah, Dn 1:1
Nebuchadnezzar **k** of Babylon came Dn 1:1
Jehoiakim **k** of Judah over to Dn 1:2
k ordered Ashpenaz, the chief Dn 1:3
The **k** assigned them daily Dn 1:5
My lord the **k** assigned your food Dn 1:10
endanger my life with the **k**." Dn 1:10
the time that the **k** had said to Dn 1:18
k interviewed them, and among Dn 1:19
that the **k** consulted them about Dn 1:20
until the first year of **K** Cyrus. Dn 1:21
So the **k** gave orders to summon Dn 2:2
to tell the **k** his dreams. Dn 2:2
came and stood before the **k**, Dn 2:2
The Chaldeans spoke to the **k** Dn 2:4
May the **k** live forever. Dn 2:4
The **k** replied to the Chaldeans, Dn 2:5
May the **k** tell the dream to his Dn 2:7
The **k** replied, "I know for Dn 2:8
The Chaldeans answered the **k**, Dn 2:10
make known what the **k** requests. Dn 2:10
Consequently, no **k**, however Dn 2:10
What the **k** is asking is so Dn 2:11
the **k** became violently angry and Dn 2:12
the decree from the **k** so harsh?" Dn 2:15
and asked the **k** to give him some Dn 2:16
he could give the **k** the Dn 2:16
whom the **k** had assigned to Dn 2:24
me before the **k**, and I will give Dn 2:24
before the **k** and said to him, Dn 2:25
exiles who can let the **k** know Dn 2:25

The **k** said in reply to Daniel, Dn 2:26
Daniel answered the **k**: Dn 2:27
known to the **k** the mystery he Dn 2:27
and He has let **K** Nebuchadnezzar Dn 2:28
might be made known to the **k**, Dn 2:30
My **k**, as you were watching, a Dn 2:31
we will tell the **k** its Dn 2:36
Majesty, you are **k** of kings. Dn 2:37
has told the **k** what will happen Dn 2:45
Then **K** Nebuchadnezzar fell down, Dn 2:46
The **k** said to Daniel, "Your God Dn 2:47
Then the **k** promoted Daniel and Dn 2:48
request, the **k** appointed Dn 2:49
K Nebuchadnezzar made a gold Dn 3:1
K Nebuchadnezzar sent word to Dn 3:2
of the statue **K** Nebuchadnezzar Dn 3:2
of the statue the **k** had set up. Dn 3:3
statue that **K** Nebuchadnezzar Dn 3:5
statue that **K** Nebuchadnezzar Dn 3:7
They said to **K** Nebuchadnezzar, Dn 3:9
May the **k** live forever. Dn 3:9
You as **k** have issued a decree Dn 3:10
men have ignored you, the **k**; Dn 3:12
men were brought before the **k**. Dn 3:13
and Abednego replied to the **k**, Dn 3:16
us from the power of you, the **k**. Dn 3:17
we want you as **k** to know that we Dn 3:18
Then **K** Nebuchadnezzar jumped up Dn 3:24
Majesty," they replied to the **k**. Dn 3:24
Then the **k** rewarded Shadrach, Dn 3:30
K Nebuchadnezzar, To those of Dn 4:1
dream that I, **K** Nebuchadnezzar, Dn 4:18
The **k** said, "Belteshazzar, don't Dn 4:19
that tree is you, the **k**. Dn 4:22
The **k** saw an observer, a holy Dn 4:23
passed against my lord the **k**: Dn 4:24
my advice seem good to you my **k**. Dn 4:27
happened to **K** Nebuchadnezzar. Dn 4:28
the **k** exclaimed, "Is this not Dn 4:30
K Nebuchadnezzar, to you it is Dn 4:31
and glorify the **K** of heaven, Dn 4:37
K Belshazzar held a great feast Dn 5:1
so that the **k** and his nobles, Dn 5:2
and the **k** and his nobles, Dn 5:3
As the **k** watched the hand that Dn 5:5
The **k** called out to bring in the Dn 5:7
Then **K** Belshazzar became even Dn 5:9
outcry of the **k** and his nobles, Dn 5:10
"May the **k** live forever," she Dn 5:10
predecessor, **K** Nebuchadnezzar, Dn 5:11
Your own predecessor, the **k**, Dn 5:11
one the **k** named Belteshazzar, Dn 5:12
Daniel was brought before the **k**. Dn 5:13
The **k** said to him, "Are you Dn 5:13
predecessor the **k** brought from Dn 5:13
Then Daniel answered the **k**, Dn 5:17
inscription for the **k** and make Dn 5:17
Belshazzar the **k** of the Dn 5:30
them so that the **k** would not be Dn 6:2
so the **k** planned to set him over Dn 6:3
to the **k** and said to him Dn 6:6
May **K** Darius live forever. Dn 6:6
agreed that the **k** should Dn 6:7
you, the **k**, will be thrown Dn 6:7
So **K** Darius signed the document. Dn 6:9
approached the **k** and asked about Dn 6:12
you, the **k**, will be thrown Dn 6:12
The **k** answered, "As a law of Dn 6:12
Then they replied to the **k**, Dn 6:13
ignored you, the **k**, and the Dn 6:13
As soon as the **k** heard this, Dn 6:14
went to the **k** and said to him Dn 6:15
You as **k** know it is a law of the Dn 6:15
ordinance the **k** establishes can Dn 6:15
the **k** gave the order, and they Dn 6:16
The **k** said to Daniel, "May your Dn 6:16
The **k** sealed it with his own Dn 6:17
Then the **k** went to his palace Dn 6:18
light of dawn the **k** got up and Dn 6:19
God," the **k** said, "has your Dn 6:20
Then Daniel spoke with the **k**: Dn 6:21
May the **k** live forever. Dn 6:21
a crime against you my **k**." Dn 6:22
The **k** was overjoyed and gave Dn 6:23
The **k** then gave the command, Dn 6:24
Then **K** Darius wrote to those of Dn 6:25
year of Belshazzar **k** of Babylon, Dn 7:1
the third year of **K** Belshazzar's Dn 8:1
goat represents the **k** of Greece, Dn 8:21
his eyes represents the first **k**. Dn 8:21
sin, an insolent **k**, skilled in Dn 8:23
third year of Cyrus **k** of Persia, Dn 10:1
Then a warrior **k** will arise; Dn 11:3
The **k** of the South will grow Dn 11:5
daughter of the **k** of the South Dn 11:6
will go to the **k** of the North to Dn 11:6
the place of the **k** of the South, Dn 11:7
fortress of the **k** of the North. Dn 11:7
away from the **k** of the North, Dn 11:8
kingdom of the **k** of the South Dn 11:9
k of the South will march out Dn 11:11
fight with the **k** of the North, Dn 11:11
The **k** of the North will again Dn 11:13
up against the **k** of the South. Dn 11:14
Then the **k** of the North will Dn 11:15
The **k** of the North who comes Dn 11:16
against the **k** of the South. Dn 11:25
The **k** of the South will prepare Dn 11:25
The **k** of the North will return Dn 11:28
Then the **k** will do whatever he Dn 11:36
the **k** of the South will engage Dn 11:40
the **k** of the North will storm Dn 11:40
son of Joash, **k** of Israel. Hs 1:1
many days without **k** or prince, Hs 3:4
their God and David their **k**. Hs 3:5
a delegation⌋ to the great **k**. Hs 5:13
please the **k** with their evil Hs 7:3
the day of our **k**, the princes Hs 7:5
the burden of the **k** and leaders. Hs 8:10
We have no **k**! For we do not fear Hs 10:3
What can a **k** do for us?" Hs 10:3
as an offering to the great **k**. Hs 10:6
Samaria's **k** will disappear like Hs 10:7
At dawn the **k** of Israel will be Hs 10:15
Egypt and Assyria will be his **k**, Hs 11:5
now is your **k**, that he may save Hs 13:10
Give me a **k** and leaders? Hs 13:10
I give you a **k** in My anger and Hs 13:11
and take away ⌊a **k**⌋ in My wrath. Hs 13:11
the days of Uzziah, **k** of Judah, Am 1:1
son of Joash, **k** of Israel, two Am 1:1
Their **k** and his princes will go Am 1:15
lime the bones of the **k** of Edom. Am 2:1
Sakkuth your **k** and Kaiwan your Am 5:26
word⌋ to Jeroboam **k** of Israel, Am 7:10
word reached the **k** of Nineveh, Jnh 3:6
order of the **k** and his nobles: Jnh 3:7
Their **K** will pass through before Mc 2:13
Is there no **k** with you? Mc 4:9
what Balak **k** of Moab proposed, Mc 6:5
K of Assyria, your shepherds Nah 3:18
Josiah son of Amon, **k** of Judah. Zph 1:1
The **K** of Israel, the LORD, is Zph 3:15
In the second year of **K** Darius, Hg 1:1
in the second year of **K** Darius. Hg 1:15
In the fourth year of **K** Darius, Zch 7:1
will cease to be a **k** in Gaza, Zch 9:5
See, your **K** is coming to you; Zch 9:9
over to his neighbor and his **k**. Zch 11:6
the days of Uzziah **k** of Judah. Zch 14:5
will become **k** over all the earth Zch 14:9
after year to worship the **K**, Zch 14:16
to Jerusalem to worship the **K**, Zch 14:17
I am a great **K**," says the LORD Mal 1:14
and Jesse fathered **K** David. Mt 1:6
of Judea in the days of **K** Herod, Mt 2:1
who has been born **K** of the Jews? Mt 2:2
When **K** Herod heard this, he was Mt 2:3
After hearing the **k**, they went Mt 2:9
it is the city of the great **K**. Mt 5:35
Although the **k** regretted it, Mt 14:9
be compared to a **k** who wanted to Mt 18:23
See, your **K** is coming to you Mt 21:5
be compared to a **k** who gave a Mt 22:2
k was enraged, so he sent out Mt 22:7
But when the **k** came in to view Mt 22:11
Then the **k** told the attendants, Mt 22:13
Then the **K** will say to those on Mt 25:34
And the **K** will answer them, Mt 25:40
"Are You the **K** of the Jews?" Mt 27:11
Him: "Hail, **K** of the Jews!" Mt 27:29
JESUS THE **K** OF THE JEWS Mt 27:37
He is the **K** of Israel! Let Him Mt 27:42
K Herod heard of this, because Mk 6:14
The **k** said to the girl, "Ask me Mk 6:22
she hurried to the **k** and said, Mk 6:25
Though the **k** was deeply Mk 6:26
The **k** immediately sent for an Mk 6:27
"Are You the **K** of the Jews?" Mk 15:2
to release the **K** of the Jews for Mk 15:9
One you call the **K** of the Jews?" Mk 15:12
Him, "Hail, **K** of the Jews!" Mk 15:18
against Him was THE **K** OF THE Mk 15:26
Messiah, the **K** of Israel, come Mk 15:32
In the days of **K** Herod of Judea, Lk 1:5
Or what **k**, going to war against Lk 14:31
going to war against another **k**, Lk 14:31
to be **k** and then return Lk 19:12
received the authority to be **k**, Lk 19:15
Blessed is the **K** who comes in Lk 19:38
He Himself is the Messiah, a **K**." Lk 23:2
"Are You the **K** of the Jews?" Lk 23:3
If You are the **K** of the Jews, Lk 23:37
THIS IS THE **K** OF THE JEWS Lk 23:38
You are the **K** of Israel!" Jn 1:49
take Him by force to make Him **k**, Jn 6:15
of the Lord—the **K** of Israel!" Jn 12:13
your **K** is coming, sitting on a Jn 12:15
"Are You the **K** of the Jews?" Jn 18:33
"You are a **k** then?" Pilate asked. Jn 18:37
that I'm a **k**," Jesus replied. Jn 18:37
to you the **K** of the Jews?" Jn 18:39
and said, "Hail, **K** of the Jews!" Jn 19:3
himself a **k** opposes Caesar! Jn 19:12
told the Jews, "Here is your **k**!" Jn 19:14
"Should I crucify your **k**?" Jn 19:15
"We have no **k** but Caesar!" Jn 19:15
NAZARENE THE **K** OF THE Jn 19:19
write, 'The **K** of the Jews,' Jn 19:21
'I am the **K** of the Jews.' " Jn 19:21
sight of Pharaoh, **k** of Egypt, Ac 7:10
a different **k** ruled over Egypt Ac 7:18
About that time **K** Herod cruelly Ac 12:1
they asked for a **k**, so God gave Ac 13:21
He raised up David as their **k**, Ac 13:22
saying that there is another **k**— Ac 17:7
K Agrippa and Bernice arrived in Ac 25:13
presented Paul's case to the **k**, Ac 25:14
K Agrippa and all men present Ac 25:24
before you, **K** Agrippa, so that Ac 25:26
myself fortunate, **K** Agrippa, Ac 26:2
being accused by the Jews, O **k**! Ac 26:7
on the road, O **k**, I saw a light Ac 26:13
Therefore, **K** Agrippa, I was not Ac 26:19
For the **k** knows about these Ac 26:26
K Agrippa, do you believe the Ac 26:27
So the **k**, the governor, Bernice, Ac 26:30
governor under **K** Aretas guarded 2Co 11:32
Now to the **K** eternal, immortal, 1Tm 1:17
only Sovereign, the **K** of kings, 1Tm 6:15
Melchizedek—**K** of Salem, priest Heb 7:1
name means "**k** of righteousness, Heb 7:2
then also, "**k** of Salem," meaning Heb 7:2
of Salem," meaning "**k** of peace"; Heb 7:2
They had as their **k** the angel of Rv 9:11
are Your ways, **K** of the Nations. Rv 15:3
is Lord of lords and **K** of kings. Rv 17:14
K OF KINGS AND LORD OF Rv 19:16

KING'S *(241)*

Shaveh (that is, the **K** Valley). Gn 14:17
where the **k** prisoners were Gn 39:20
We will travel the **K** Highway; Nm 20:17
will travel the **K** Highway until Nm 21:22
that I should become the **k** 1Sm 18:18
you should become the **k** 1Sm 18:22
in your sight to become the **k** 1Sm 18:23
he was pleased to become the **k** 1Sm 18:26
he didn't come to the **k** table." 1Sm 20:29
weapons since the **k** mission was 1Sm 21:8
He is the **k** son-in-law, captain 1Sm 22:14
But the **k** servants would not 1Sm 22:17
where are the **k** spear and water 1Sm 26:16
answered, "Here is the **k** spear; 1Sm 26:22
just like one of the **k** sons. 2Sm 9:11
he always ate at the **k** table. 2Sm 9:13
if the **k** anger gets stirred up 2Sm 11:20
and some of the **k** soldiers died. 2Sm 11:24
Why are you, the **k** son, so 2Sm 13:4
is what the **k** virgin daughters 2Sm 13:18
Absalom invited all the **k** sons. 2Sm 13:23
sent Amnon and all the **k** sons. 2Sm 13:27
the rest of⌋ the **k** sons got up, 2Sm 13:29
struck down all the **k** sons; 2Sm 13:30
young men, the **k** sons, because 2Sm 13:32

says all the **k** sons are dead. 2Sm 13:33
Look, the **k** sons have come! 2Sm 13:35
the **k** sons entered and wept 2Sm 13:36
observed that the **k** mind was on 2Sm 14:1
The **k** servants said to him, 2Sm 15:15
hear from the **k** palace to Zadok 2Sm 15:35
are for the **k** household to ride 2Sm 16:2
people heard the **k** orders to all 2Sm 18:5
raise my hand against the **k** son. 2Sm 18:12
a pillar in the **K** Valley, 2Sm 18:18
because the **k** son is dead." 2Sm 18:20
Joab sent the **k** servant and your 2Sm 18:29
all came into the **k** presence. 2Sm 19:8
to bring the **k** household across 2Sm 19:18
anything of the **k** or been 2Sm 19:42
Yet the **k** order prevailed over 2Sm 24:4
the army left the **k** presence to 2Sm 24:4
and she became the **k** caregiver. 1Kg 1:4
He invited all the **k** sons, 1Kg 1:19
He came into the **k** presence and 1Kg 1:23
my lord the **k** throne after him. 1Kg 1:27
she came into the **k** presence and 1Kg 1:28
they came into the **k** presence. 1Kg 1:32
have had him ride on the **k** mule. 1Kg 1:44
The **k** servants have also gone to 1Kg 1:47
throne placed for the **k** mother. 1Kg 2:19
temple and the **k** palace and into 1Kg 10:12
The **k** traders bought them from 1Kg 10:28
and the **k** hand was restored to 1Kg 13:6
the entrance to the **k** palace. 1Kg 14:27
city, and to Joash, the **k** son, 1Kg 22:26
captain, the **k** right-hand man, 2Kg 7:2
Let's go tell the **k** household." 2Kg 7:9
was reported to the **k** household. 2Kg 7:11
and spread it over the **k** face. 2Kg 8:15
since she's a **k** daughter." 2Kg 9:34
All 70 of the **k** sons were being 2Kg 10:6
they took the **k** sons and 2Kg 10:7
the heads of the **k** sons," 2Kg 10:8
down to greet the **k** sons and the 2Kg 10:13
Ahaziah from the **k** sons who were 2Kg 11:2
He showed them the **k** son 2Kg 11:4
protection for the **k** palace. 2Kg 11:5
brought out the **k** son, put the 2Kg 11:12
Entrance to the **k** palace, 2Kg 11:16
They entered the **k** palace by way 2Kg 11:19
by the sword in the **k** palace. 2Kg 11:20
the **k** secretary and the high 2Kg 12:10
temple and in the **k** palace, 2Kg 12:18
put his hands on the **k** hands. 2Kg 13:16
the treasuries of the **k** palace, 2Kg 14:14
while Jotham, the **k** son, was 2Kg 15:5
at the citadel of the **k** palace. 2Kg 15:25
of the **k** palace and sent 2Kg 16:8
and the **k** burnt offering and his 2Kg 16:15
the treasuries of the **k** palace. 2Kg 18:15
a word, for the **k** command was, 2Kg 18:36
and the **k** servant Asaiah: 2Kg 22:12
the treasures of the **k** palace, 2Kg 24:13
Also, he took the **k** mother, the 2Kg 24:15
king's mother, the **k** wives, his 2Kg 24:15
the two walls near the **k** garden, 2Kg 25:4
temple, the **k** palace, and all 2Kg 25:9
at the **K** Gate on the east 1Ch 9:18
chief officials at the **k** side. 1Ch 18:17
Yet the **k** order prevailed over 1Ch 21:4
count because the **k** command was 1Ch 21:6
of Heman, the **k** seer, were 1Ch 25:5
were under the **k** authority. 1Ch 25:6
in charge of the **k** storehouses. 1Ch 27:25
of Hachmoni attended the **k** sons. 1Ch 27:32
Ahithophel was the **k** counselor. 1Ch 27:33
the Archite was the **k** friend. 1Ch 27:33
was the commander of the **k** army. 1Ch 27:34
the divisions in the **k** service, 1Ch 28:1
in charge of the **k** work gave 1Ch 29:6
k traders would get them from 2Ch 1:16
assembled in the **k** presence at 2Ch 5:3
aside from the **k** command 2Ch 8:15
temple and for the **k** palace and 2Ch 9:11
for the **k** ships kept going to 2Ch 9:21
the entrance to the **k** palace. 2Ch 12:10
city, and to Joash, the **k** son, 2Ch 18:25
found in the **k** palace and also 2Ch 21:17
the **k** daughter, rescued 2Ch 22:11
Ahaziah from the **k** sons who 2Ch 22:11
to them, "Here is the **k** son! 2Ch 23:3
third are to be at the **k** palace, 2Ch 23:5

They brought out the **k** son, 2Ch 23:11
Horses' Gate to the **k** palace, 2Ch 23:15
entered the **k** palace through 2Ch 23:20
the **k** command a chest was made 2Ch 24:8
the Levites to the **k** overseers, 2Ch 24:11
the **k** secretary and the high 2Ch 24:11
and stoned him at the **k** command 2Ch 24:21
we made you the **k** counselor? 2Ch 25:16
the treasures of the **k** palace, 2Ch 25:24
one of the **k** commanders. 2Ch 26:11
was over the **k** household 2Ch 26:21
killed the **k** son Maaseiah, 2Ch 28:7
according to the **k** command by 2Ch 29:15
David, Gad the **k** seer, and 2Ch 29:25
and according to the **k** command, 2Ch 30:6
and the **k** servant Asaiah, 2Ch 34:20
according to the **k** command. 2Ch 35:10
Heman, and Jeduthun the **k** seer. 2Ch 35:15
Let the **k** decision regarding Ezr 5:17
the Assyrian **k** attitude toward Ezr 6:22
it into the **k** mind to glorify Ezr 7:27
also delivered the **k** edicts to Ezr 8:36
time,⌋ I was the **k** cupbearer. Neh 1:11
keeper of the **k** forest, so that Neh 2:8
and gave them the **k** letters. Neh 2:9
Fountain Gate and the **K** Pool, Neh 2:14
of Shelah near the **k** garden, Neh 3:15
money to pay the **k** tax on our Neh 5:4
was the **k** agent in every matter Neh 11:24
freely, according to the **k** Est 1:7
come at the **k** command that was Est 1:12
thing⌋ to all the **k** officials, Est 1:18
If it meets the **k** approval, Est 1:19
The **k** personal attendants Est 2:2
of Hegai, the **k** eunuch, who is Est 2:3
When the **k** command and edict Est 2:8
the **k** eunuch in charge of the Est 2:14
the **k** trusted official in charge Est 2:15
gifts worthy of the **k** bounty. Est 2:18
was sitting at the **K** Gate. Est 2:19
was sitting at the **K** Gate, Est 2:21
who guarded the ⌊**k**⌋ entrance, Est 2:21
daily events in the **k** presence. Est 2:23
staff at the **K** Gate bowed down Est 3:2
royal staff at the **K** Gate asked Est 3:3
you disobeying the **k** command?" Est 3:3
so that they defy the **k** laws. Est 3:8
is not in the **k** best interest to Est 3:8
only went as far as the **K** Gate, Est 4:2
from entering the **K** Gate. Est 4:2
where the **k** command and edict Est 4:3
one of the **k** eunuchs assigned to Est 4:5
square in front of the **K** Gate. Est 4:6
because you are in the **k** palace. Est 4:13
saw Mordecai at the **K** Gate, Est 5:9
sitting at the **K** Gate all the Est 5:13
who guarded the ⌊**k**⌋ entrance, Est 6:2
The **k** personal attendants Est 6:3
The **k** attendants answered him, Est 6:5
of one of the **k** most noble Est 6:9
who is sitting at the **K** Gate. Est 6:10
Mordecai returned to the **K** Gate, Est 6:12
the statement left the **k** mouth, Est 7:8
Then the **k** anger subsided. Est 7:10
entered the **k** presence because Est 8:1
reside⌋ in all the **k** provinces. Est 8:5
may write in the **k** name whatever Est 8:8
written in the **k** name and sealed Est 8:8
k edict gave the Jews in each Est 8:11
haste, at the **k** urgent command. Est 8:14
out from the **k** presence clothed Est 8:15
wherever the **k** command and his Est 8:17
The **k** command and law went into Est 9:1
the hearts of the **k** enemies; Ps 45:5
they enter the **k** palace. Ps 45:15
Add days to the **k** life; Ps 61:6
Your righteousness to the **k** son. Ps 72:1
population is a **k** splendor, Pr 14:28
Righteous lips are a **k** delight, Pr 16:13
k fury is a messenger of death, Pr 16:14
When a **k** face lights up, there Pr 16:15
A **k** rage is like a lion's roar, Pr 19:12
A **k** terrible wrath is like the Pr 20:2
A **k** heart is a water channel in Pr 21:1
the wicked from the **k** presence, Pr 25:5
Keep the **k** command. Concerning Ec 8:2
For the **k** word is authoritative, Ec 8:4
at all, for the **k** command was, Is 36:21

went up from the **k** palace to the Jr 26:10
chamber in the **k** palace. Jr 36:12
commanded Jerahmeel the **k** son, Jr 36:26
cistern of Malchiah the **k** son, Jr 38:6
employed in the **k** palace, Jr 38:7
went from the **k** palace and spoke Jr 38:8
and went to the **k** palace to a Jr 38:11
by way of the **k** garden through Jr 39:4
next burned down the **k** palace Jr 39:8
and one of the **k** chief officers, Jr 41:1
women, children, **k** daughters, Jr 43:6
⌊this is⌋ the **K** declaration; Jr 46:18
⌊This is⌋ the **K** declaration; Jr 48:15
⌊This is⌋ the **K** declaration; Jr 51:57
the two walls near the **k** garden, Jr 52:7
LORD's temple, the **k** palace, all Jr 52:13
of serving in the **k** palace— Dn 1:4
were to serve in the **k** court. Dn 1:5
himself with the **k** food or with Dn 1:8
men who are eating the **k** food, Dn 1:13
men who were eating the **k** food. Dn 1:15
began to serve in the **k** court. Dn 1:19
the commander of the **k** guard, Dn 2:14
Arioch, the **k** officer, "Why is Dn 2:15
have let us know the **k** mystery. Dn 2:23
Daniel remained at the **k** court. Dn 2:49
the **k** command was so urgent Dn 3:22
and the **k** advisers gathered Dn 3:27
They violated the **k** command and Dn 3:28
words were still in the **k** mouth, Dn 4:31
plaster of the **k** palace wall Dn 5:5
So all the **k** wise men came in, Dn 5:8
and went about the **k** business. Dn 8:27
after the cutting of the **k** hay. Am 7:1
for it is the **k** sanctuary and a Am 7:13
officials, the **k** sons, and all Zph 1:8
was in charge of the **k** bedroom, Ac 12:20
with food from the **k** country. Ac 12:20
they didn't fear the **k** edict. Heb 11:23
not being afraid of the **k** anger, Heb 11:27

KINGDOM *(310)*

His **k** started with Babylon, Gn 10:10
guilt on me and on my **k**? Gn 20:9
you will be My **k** of priests and Ex 19:6
and his **k** will be exalted. Nm 24:7
the **k** of Sihon king of the Nm 32:33
Amorites and the **k** of Og king of Nm 32:33
of Argob, the **k** of Og in Bashan. Dt 3:4
cities of Og's **k** in Bashan. Dt 3:10
and all Bashan, the **k** of Og. Dt 3:13
the whole **k** of Og in Bashan, Jos 13:12
and all the **k** of Sihon king of Jos 13:21
the rest of the **k** of Sihon king Jos 13:27
all the **k** of Og king of Bashan, Jos 13:30
more can he have but the **k**?" 1Sm 18:8
and the **k** of Israel will be 1Sm 24:20
to transfer the **k** from the house 2Sm 3:10
I and my **k** are forever innocent 2Sm 3:28
had exalted his **k** for the sake 2Sm 5:12
and I will establish his **k**. 2Sm 7:12
the throne of his **k** forever. 2Sm 7:13
Your house and **k** will endure 2Sm 7:16
restore my father's **k** to me.' " 2Sm 16:3
handed the **k** over to your son 2Sm 16:8
So the **k** was established in 1Kg 2:46
no man in any **k** will be your 1Kg 3:13
ever been made in any other **k**. 1Kg 10:20
I will tear the **k** away from you 1Kg 11:11
tear the entire **k** away from him. 1Kg 11:13
to tear the **k** out of Solomon's 1Kg 11:31
take the whole **k** from his hand 1Kg 11:34
tribes of the **k** from his son's 1Kg 11:35
to restore the **k** to Rehoboam son 1Kg 12:21
the **k** might return to the house 1Kg 12:26
tore the **k** away from the house 1Kg 14:8
is no nation or **k** where my lord 1Kg 18:10
he made that **k** or nation swear 1Kg 18:10
As soon as the **k** was firmly in 2Kg 14:5
to strengthen his grip on the **k**. 2Kg 15:19
and turned the **k** over to David 1Ch 10:14
to turn Saul's **k** over to him, 1Ch 12:23
and that his **k** had been exalted 1Ch 14:2
and from one **k** to another, 1Ch 16:20
and I will establish his **k**. 1Ch 17:11
over My house and My **k** forever, 1Ch 17:14
the throne of his **k** over Israel 1Ch 22:10
of the LORD's **k** over Israel. 1Ch 28:5
establish his **k** forever if he 1Ch 28:7

LORD, is the **k**, and You are 1Ch 29:11
strengthened his hold on his **k**. 2Ch 1:1
ever been made in any other **k**. 2Ch 9:19
they strengthened the **k** of Judah 2Ch 11:17
against the LORD's **k** in the hand 2Ch 13:8
the **k** experienced peace under 2Ch 14:5
established the **k** in his hand. 2Ch 17:5
Then Jehoshaphat's **k** was quiet, 2Ch 20:30
but he gave the **k** to Jehoram 2Ch 21:3
himself over his father's **k**, 2Ch 21:4
to exercise power over the **k**. 2Ch 22:9
the king on the throne of the **k**. 2Ch 23:20
As soon as the **k** was firmly in 2Ch 25:3
as a sin offering for the **k**, 2Ch 29:21
any nation or **k** has been able to 2Ch 32:15
him back to Jerusalem, to his **k**. 2Ch 33:13
until the rise of the Persian **k**. 2Ch 36:20
his entire **k** and also ⌊to put it 2Ch 36:22
his entire **k** and ⌊to put it⌋ Ezr 1:1
any of the Israelites in my **k**, Ezr 7:13
When they were in their **k**, Neh 9:35
wealth of his **k** and the Est 1:4
the highest positions in the **k**. Est 1:14
be heard throughout his vast **k**, Est 1:20
in each province of his **k**, Est 2:3
Jews, throughout Ahasuerus' **k**. Est 3:6
in every province of your **k**, Est 3:8
come to the **k** for such a time Est 4:14
to half the **k**, will be given Est 5:3
to half the **k**, will be done." Est 5:6
to half the **k**, will be done." Est 7:2
provinces of the **k** of Ahasuerus, Est 9:30
scepter of Your **k** is a scepter Ps 45:6
and His **k** rules over all. Ps 103:19
and from one **k** to another, Ps 105:13
glory of Your **k** and will declare Ps 145:11
the glorious splendor of Your **k**. Ps 145:12
k is an everlasting kingdom; Ps 145:13
kingdom is an everlasting **k**; Ps 145:13
he was born poor in his **k**. Ec 4:14
throne of David and over his **k**, Is 9:7
Ephraim, and a **k** from Damascus. Is 17:3
against city, **k** against kingdom. Is 19:2
against city, kingdom against **k**. Is 19:2
nation and the **k** that will not Is 60:12
a nation or a **k** that I will Jr 18:7
build and plant a nation or a **k**. Jr 18:9
the nation or **k** that does not Jr 27:8
defiled the **k** and its leaders Lm 2:2
so the **k** might be humble and not Ezk 17:14
There they will be a lowly **k**. Ezk 29:14
and mediums in his entire **k**. Dn 1:20
there will arise another **k**, Dn 2:39
another, a third **k**, of bronze, Dn 2:39
A fourth **k** will be as strong as Dn 2:40
will be a divided **k**, though some Dn 2:41
part of the **k** will be strong, Dn 2:42
will set up a **k** that will never Dn 2:44
and this **k** will not be left to Dn 2:44
His **k** is an eternal kingdom, Dn 4:3
His kingdom is an eternal **k**, Dn 4:3
High is ruler over the **k** of men. Dn 4:17
of the wise men of my **k** can make Dn 4:18
High is ruler over the **k** of men, Dn 4:25
your **k** will be restored to you Dn 4:26
declared that the **k** has departed Dn 4:31
High is ruler over the **k** of men, Dn 4:32
and His **k** is from generation to Dn 4:34
to me for the glory of my **k**. Dn 4:36
I was reestablished over my **k**, Dn 4:36
highest position in the **k**." Dn 5:7
is a man in your **k** who has the Dn 5:11
highest position in the **k**." Dn 5:16
ruler over the **k** of men and sets Dn 5:21
days of⌋ your **k** and brought it Dn 5:26
that⌋ your **k** has been divided Dn 5:28
be the third ruler in the **k**. Dn 5:29
received the **k** at the age of 62 Dn 5:31
appoint 120 satraps over the **k**, Dn 6:1
against Daniel regarding the **k**. Dn 6:4
All the administrators of the **k**, Dn 6:7
His **k** will never be destroyed, Dn 6:26
to rule, and glory, and a **k**; Dn 7:14
and His **k** is one that will not Dn 7:14
will receive the **k** and possess Dn 7:18
ones took possession of the **k**. Dn 7:22
will be a fourth **k** on the earth, Dn 7:23
kings who will rise from this **k**. Dn 7:24
The **k**, dominion, and greatness Dn 7:27
His **k** will be an everlasting Dn 7:27
will be an everlasting **k**, Dn 7:27
over the **k** of the Chaldeans Dn 9:1
prince of the **k** of Persia Dn 10:13
against the **k** of Greece. Dn 11:2
his **k** will be broken up and Dn 11:4
not be the same **k** that he ruled, Dn 11:4
because his **k** will be uprooted Dn 11:4
and will rule a **k** greater than Dn 11:5
who will enter the **k** of the king Dn 11:9
of his whole **k** and will reach Dn 11:17
for the glory of the **k**; Dn 11:20
and seize the **k** by intrigue. Dn 11:21
put an end to the **k** of the house Hs 1:4
Lord GOD are on the sinful **k**, Am 9:8
but the **k** will be the LORD's. Ob 21
because the **k** of heaven has come Mt 3:2
because the **k** of heaven has come Mt 4:17
the good news of the **k**, Mt 4:23
because the **k** of heaven is Mt 5:3
because the **k** of heaven is Mt 5:10
called least in the **k** of heaven. Mt 5:19
called great in the **k** of heaven. Mt 5:19
never enter the **k** of heaven. Mt 5:20
Your **k** come. Your will be done Mt 6:10
For Yours is the **k** and the power Mt 6:13
seek first the **k** of God and His Mt 6:33
will enter the **k** of heaven, Mt 7:21
and Jacob in the **k** of heaven. Mt 8:11
the sons of the **k** will be thrown Mt 8:12
the good news of the **k**, Mt 9:35
'The **k** of heaven has come near.' Mt 10:7
the least in the **k** of heaven is Mt 11:11
the **k** of heaven has been Mt 11:12
Every **k** divided against itself Mt 12:25
How then will his **k** stand? Mt 12:26
then the **k** of God has come to Mt 12:28
secrets of the **k** of heaven have Mt 13:11
the word about the **k** and doesn't Mt 13:19
The **k** of heaven may be compared Mt 13:24
The **k** of heaven is like a Mt 13:31
The **k** of heaven is like yeast Mt 13:33
these are the sons of the **k**. Mt 13:38
gather from His **k** everything Mt 13:41
the sun in their Father's **k**. Mt 13:43
The **k** of heaven is like Mt 13:44
the **k** of heaven is like a Mt 13:45
the **k** of heaven is like a large Mt 13:47
in the **k** of heaven is like Mt 13:52
you the keys of the **k** of heaven, Mt 16:19
the Son of Man coming in His **k**." Mt 16:28
is greatest in the **k** of heaven?" Mt 18:1
never enter the **k** of heaven. Mt 18:3
the greatest in the **k** of heaven. Mt 18:4
the **k** of heaven can be compared Mt 18:23
way because of the **k** of heaven. Mt 19:12
because the **k** of heaven is made Mt 19:14
person to enter the **k** of heaven! Mt 19:23
person to enter the **k** of God." Mt 19:24
For the **k** of heaven is like a Mt 20:1
other on Your left, in Your **k**." Mt 20:21
are entering the **k** of God before Mt 21:31
the **k** of God will be taken away Mt 21:43
The **k** of heaven may be compared Mt 22:2
You lock up the **k** of heaven from Mt 23:13
nation, and **k** against kingdom. Mt 24:7
nation, and kingdom against **k**. Mt 24:7
good news of the **k** will be Mt 24:14
Then the **k** of heaven will be Mt 25:1
inherit the **k** prepared for you Mt 25:34
way in My Father's **k** with you." Mt 26:29
and the **k** of God has come near. Mk 1:15
a **k** is divided against itself, Mk 3:24
itself, that **k** cannot stand. Mk 3:24
secret of the **k** of God has been Mk 4:11
"The **k** of God is like this," Mk 4:26
can we illustrate the **k** of God, Mk 4:30
will give you, up to half my **k**." Mk 6:23
until they see the **k** of God come Mk 9:1
to enter the **k** of God with one Mk 9:47
for the **k** of God belongs to such Mk 10:14
not welcome the **k** of God like a Mk 10:15
wealth to enter the **k** of God!" Mk 10:23
it is to enter the **k** of God! Mk 10:24
person to enter the **k** of God." Mk 10:25
is the coming **k** of our father Mk 11:10
are not far from the **k** of God." Mk 12:34
nation, and **k** against kingdom. Mk 13:8
nation, and kingdom against **k**. Mk 13:8
in a new way in the **k** of God." Mk 14:25
looking forward to the **k** of God, Mk 15:43
and His **k** will have no end. Lk 1:33
news about the **k** of God to the Lk 4:43
because the **k** of God is yours. Lk 6:20
the least in the **k** of God is Lk 7:28
the good news of the **k** of God. Lk 8:1
secrets of the **k** of God have Lk 8:10
to proclaim the **k** of God and to Lk 9:2
to them about the **k** of God, Lk 9:11
until they see the **k** of God." Lk 9:27
the news of the **k** of God." Lk 9:60
back is fit for the **k** of God." Lk 9:62
'The **k** of God has come near you.' Lk 10:9
the **k** of God has come near.' Lk 10:11
be honored as holy. Your **k** come. Lk 11:2
Every **k** divided against itself Lk 11:17
himself, how will his **k** stand? Lk 11:18
then the **k** of God has come to Lk 11:20
But seek His **k**, and these things Lk 12:31
delights to give you the **k**. Lk 12:32
What is the **k** of God like, Lk 13:18
can I compare the **k** of God to? Lk 13:20
the prophets in the **k** of God but Lk 13:28
at the table in the **k** of God. Lk 13:29
in the **k** of God is blessed! Lk 14:15
news of the **k** of God has been Lk 16:16
when the **k** of God will come, Lk 17:20
The **k** of God is not coming with Lk 17:20
the **k** of God is among you." Lk 17:21
because the **k** of God belongs to Lk 18:16
not welcome the **k** of God like a Lk 18:17
wealth to enter the **k** of God! Lk 18:24
person to enter the **k** of God." Lk 18:25
because of the **k** of God, Lk 18:29
thought the **k** of God was going Lk 19:11
nation, and **k** against kingdom. Lk 21:10
nation, and kingdom against **k**. Lk 21:10
that the **k** of God is near. Lk 21:31
is fulfilled in the **k** of God." Lk 22:16
vine until the **k** of God comes." Lk 22:18
I bestow on you a **k**, just as My Lk 22:29
and drink at My table in My **k**. Lk 22:30
me when You come into Your **k**!" Lk 23:42
looking forward to the **k** of God. Lk 23:51
he cannot see the **k** of God." Jn 3:3
he cannot enter the **k** of God. Jn 3:5
"My **k** is not of this world," Jn 18:36
If My **k** were of this world, Jn 18:36
k does not have its origin here. Jn 18:36
and speaking about the **k** of God. Ac 1:3
You restoring the **k** to Israel?" Ac 1:6
news about the **k** of God and the Ac 8:12
on our way into the **k** of God." Ac 14:22
things related to the **k** of God. Ac 19:8
I went about preaching the **k**, Ac 20:25
witnessed about the **k** of God. Ac 28:23
proclaiming the **k** of God and Ac 28:31
for the **k** of God is not eating Rm 14:17
For the **k** of God is not in talk 1Co 4:20
unjust will not inherit God's **k**? 1Co 6:9
swindlers will inherit God's **k**. 1Co 6:10
hands over the **k** to God the 1Co 15:24
cannot inherit the **k** of God, 1Co 15:50
will not inherit the **k** of God. Gl 5:21
in the **k** of the Messiah Eph 5:5
us into the **k** of the Son He Col 1:13
my co-workers for the **k** of God, Col 4:11
you into His own **k** and glory. 1Th 2:12
be counted worthy of God's **k**, 2Th 1:5
and by His appearing and His **k**, 2Tm 4:1
me safely into His heavenly **k**. 2Tm 4:18
scepter of Your **k** is a scepter Heb 1:8
are receiving a **k** that cannot be Heb 12:28
and heirs of the **k** that He has Jms 2:5
into the eternal **k** of our Lord 2Pt 1:11
and made us a **k**, priests to His Rv 1:6
the tribulation, **k**, and Rv 1:9
You made them a **k** and priests to Rv 5:10
k of the world has become the Rv 11:15
has become the ⌊**k**⌋ of our Lord Rv 11:15
the power and the **k** of our God Rv 12:10
and his **k** was plunged into Rv 16:10
who have not yet received a **k**, Rv 17:12
and to give their **k** to the beast Rv 17:17

KINGDOMS *(55)*

same to all the **k** you are about	Dt 3:21
to all the **k** of the earth.	Dt 28:25
been the leader of all these **k**.	Jos 11:10
and all the **k** that were	1Sm 10:18
over all the **k** from the	1Kg 4:21
of all the **k** of the earth.	2Kg 19:15
so that all the **k** of the earth	2Kg 19:19
Israel and all the **k** of the	1Ch 29:30
and serving the **k** of the land."	2Ch 12:8
was on all the **k** of the lands	2Ch 17:10
over all the **k** of the nations?	2Ch 20:6
was on all the **k** of the lands	2Ch 20:29
given me all the **k** of the earth	2Ch 36:23
given me all the **k** of the earth	Ezr 1:2
You gave them **k** and peoples and	Neh 9:22
Nations rage, **k** topple;	Ps 46:6
Sing to God, you **k** of the earth;	Ps 68:32
on the **k** that don't call on Your	Ps 79:6
peoples and **k** are assembled to	Ps 102:22
my hand seized the idolatrous **k**,	Is 10:10
uproar among the **k**, like nations	Is 13:4
the jewel of the **k**, the glory of	Is 13:19
to tremble, who shook the **k**,	Is 14:16
the sea; He made **k** tremble. The	Is 23:11
with all the **k** of the world	Is 23:17
of all the **k** of the earth.	Is 37:16
so that all the **k** of the earth	Is 37:20
longer be called mistress of **k**.	Is 47:5
over nations and **k** to uproot and	Jr 1:10
the clans and **k** of the north."	Jr 1:15
nations and among all their **k**,	Jr 10:7
horror to all the **k** of the earth	Jr 15:4
to all the **k** of the earth,	Jr 24:9
all the **k** of the world which are	Jr 25:26
against many lands and great **k**.	Jr 28:8
to all the **k** of the earth—	Jr 29:18
all the earthly **k** under his	Jr 34:1
a horror to all the earth's **k**.	Jr 34:17
About Kedar and the **k** of Hazor,	Jr 49:28
with you I will bring **k** to ruin.	Jr 51:20
Summon **k** against her—Ararat,	Jr 51:27
the lowliest of **k** and will never	Ezk 29:15
no longer be divided into two **k**.	Ezk 37:22
crush all these **k** and bring them	Dn 2:44
different from all the other **k**.	Dn 7:23
greatness of the **k** under all of	Dn 7:27
shattered horn represent four **k**.	Dn 8:22
end of their **k**, when the rebels	Dn 8:23
Are you better than these **k**?	Am 6:2
to nations, your shame to **k**.	Nah 3:5
to assemble **k**, in order to pour	Zph 3:8
the power of the Gentile **k**.	Hg 2:22
showed Him all the **k** of the	Mt 4:8
showed Him all the **k** of the	Lk 4:5
faith conquered **k**, administered	Heb 11:33

KINGS *(319)*

and the **k** who were with him	Gn 14:5
Ellasar—four **k** against five.	Gn 14:9
and ⌊as⌋ the **k** of Sodom and	Gn 14:10
The ⌊four **k**⌋ took all the goods	Gn 14:11
and the **k** who were with him,	Gn 14:17
nations and **k** come from you.	Gn 17:6
k of peoples will come from her."	Gn 17:16
and **k** will descend from you.	Gn 35:11
These are the **k** who ruled in the	Gn 36:31
they killed the Midianite **k**—	Nm 31:8
and Reba, the five **k** of Midian.	Nm 31:8
the two Amorite **k** across the	Dt 3:8
God has done to these two **k**.	Dt 3:21
two Amorite **k** who were across	Dt 4:47
will hand their **k** over to you,	Dt 7:24
and Og, the **k** of the Amorites,	Dt 31:4
the two Amorite **k** you completely	Jos 2:10
all the Amorite **k** across the	Jos 5:1
all the Canaanite **k** near the sea	Jos 5:1
When all the **k** heard ⌊about	Jos 9:1
the two Amorite **k** beyond the	Jos 9:10
the five Amorite **k**—the kings	Jos 10:5
kings—the **k** of Jerusalem,	Jos 10:5
all the Amorite **k** living in the	Jos 10:6
five ⌊defeated⌋ **k** had fled and	Jos 10:16
The five **k** have been found;	Jos 10:17
men by it to guard the **k**.	Jos 10:18
bring those five **k** to me out of	Jos 10:22
brought the five **k** of Jerusalem,	Jos 10:23
they had brought the **k** to him,	Jos 10:24
feet on the necks of these **k**."	Jos 10:24
with all their **k**, leaving no	Jos 10:40
all these **k** and their land	Jos 10:42
the **k** of Shimron and Achshaph,	Jos 11:1
and the **k** of the north in the	Jos 11:2
All these **k** joined forces;	Jos 11:5
all these **k** and their cities	Jos 11:12
all their **k** and struck them	Jos 11:17
all these **k** for a long time.	Jos 11:18
down the following **k** of the land	Jos 12:1
the following **k** of the land	Jos 12:7
one ⌊the total number of⌋ all **k**:	Jos 12:24
the two Amorite **k** before you.	Jos 24:12
Seventy **k** with their thumbs and	Jdg 1:7
Listen, **k**! Pay attention,	Jdg 5:3
K came and fought. Then the	Jdg 5:19
Then the **k** of Canaan fought at	Jdg 5:19
and Zalmunna, the **k** of Midian."	Jdg 8:5
captured these two **k** of Midian	Jdg 8:12
garments on the **k** of Midian,	Jdg 8:26
Edom, the **k** of Zobah,	1Sm 14:47
belongs to the **k** of Judah today.	1Sm 27:6
When all the **k** who were	2Sm 10:19
the spring when **k** march out ⌊to	2Sm 11:1
and over all the **k** west of the	1Kg 4:24
all the Arabian **k** and governors	1Kg 10:15
surpassed all the **k** of the world	1Kg 10:23
to all the **k** of the Hittites	1Kg 10:29
and to the **k** of Aram through	1Kg 10:29
Historical Record of Israel's **K**.	1Kg 14:19
Historical Record of Judah's **K**.	1Kg 14:29
Historical Record of Judah's **K**.	1Kg 15:7
Historical Record of Judah's **K**.	1Kg 15:23
Historical Record of Israel's **K**.	1Kg 15:31
Historical Record of Israel's **K**.	1Kg 16:5
Historical Record of Israel's **K**.	1Kg 16:14
Historical Record of Israel's **K**.	1Kg 16:20
Historical Record of Israel's **K**.	1Kg 16:27
than all the **k** of Israel who	1Kg 16:33
Thirty-two **k**, along with horses	1Kg 20:1
while he and the **k** were drinking	1Kg 20:12
and the 32 **k** who were helping	1Kg 20:16
heard that the **k** of the house	1Kg 20:31
of Israel are **k** ⌊who show⌋	1Kg 20:31
Historical Record of Israel's **K**.	1Kg 22:39
Historical Record of Judah's **K**.	1Kg 22:45
Historical Record of Israel's **K**.	2Kg 1:18
LORD has summoned us three **k**,	2Kg 3:10
us three **k** to hand us over	2Kg 3:13
heard that the **k** had come up to	2Kg 3:21
The **k** have clashed swords and	2Kg 3:23
have hired the **k** of the Hittites	2Kg 7:6
Hittites and the **k** of Egypt to	2Kg 7:6
in the way of the **k** of Israel,	2Kg 8:18
Historical Record of Israel's **K**.	2Kg 8:23
k couldn't stand against him;	2Kg 10:4
Historical Record of Israel's **K**.	2Kg 10:34
sat on the throne of the **k**.	2Kg 11:19
Judah's **k** Jehoshaphat,	2Kg 12:18
Historical Record of Judah's **K**.	2Kg 12:19
Historical Record of Israel's **K**.	2Kg 13:8
Historical Record of Israel's **K**.	2Kg 13:12
in Samaria with the **k** of Israel.	2Kg 13:13
Historical Record of Israel's **K**.	2Kg 14:15
in Samaria with the **k** of Israel.	2Kg 14:16
Historical Record of Judah's **K**.	2Kg 14:18
Historical Record of Israel's **K**.	2Kg 14:28
his fathers, the **k** of Israel.	2Kg 14:29
Historical Record of Judah's **K**.	2Kg 15:6
Historical Record of Israel's **K**.	2Kg 15:11
Historical Record of Israel's **K**.	2Kg 15:15
Historical Record of Israel's **K**.	2Kg 15:21
Historical Record of Israel's **K**.	2Kg 15:26
Historical Record of Israel's **K**.	2Kg 15:31
Historical Record of Judah's **K**.	2Kg 15:36
in the way of the **k** of Israel.	2Kg 16:3
Historical Record of Judah's **K**.	2Kg 16:19
but not like the **k** of Israel who	2Kg 17:2
the customs the **k** of Israel had	2Kg 17:8
not one of the **k** of Judah was	2Kg 18:5
heard what the **k** of Assyria have	2Kg 19:11
true that the **k** of Assyria have	2Kg 19:17
Historical Record of Judah's **K**.	2Kg 20:20
Historical Record of Judah's **K**.	2Kg 21:17
Historical Record of Judah's **K**.	2Kg 21:25
priests the **k** of Judah had	2Kg 23:5
horses that the **k** of Judah had	2Kg 23:11
chamber that the **k** of Judah had	2Kg 23:12
which the **k** of Israel had made	2Kg 23:19
entire time of the **k** of Israel	2Kg 23:22
Historical Record of Judah's **K**.	2Kg 23:28
Historical Record of Judah's **K**.	2Kg 24:5
thrones of the **k** who were with	2Kg 25:28
These were the **k** who ruled in	1Ch 1:43
in the Book of the **K** of Israel.	1Ch 9:1
He rebuked **k** on their behalf:	1Ch 16:21
city while the **k** who had come	1Ch 19:9
the spring when **k** march out ⌊to	1Ch 20:1
this for the **k** who were before	2Ch 1:12
to all the **k** of the Hittites	2Ch 1:17
and to the **k** of Aram through	2Ch 1:17
All the Arabian **k** and governors	2Ch 9:14
surpassed all the **k** of the world	2Ch 9:22
All the **k** of the world wanted an	2Ch 9:23
over all the **k** from the	2Ch 9:26
the Book of the **K** of Judah and	2Ch 16:11
in the Book of Israel's **K**.	2Ch 20:34
in the way of the **k** of Israel,	2Ch 21:6
in the way of the **k** of Israel,	2Ch 21:13
but not in the tombs of the **k**.	2Ch 21:20
David with the **k** because he had	2Ch 24:16
bury him in the tombs of the **k**.	2Ch 24:25
Writing of the Book of the **K**.	2Ch 24:27
the Book of the **K** of Judah and	2Ch 25:26
in the Book of the **K** of Israel	2Ch 27:7
the ways of the **k** of Israel and	2Ch 28:2
the gods of the **k** of Aram are	2Ch 28:23
the Book of the **K** of Judah and	2Ch 28:26
the grasp of the **k** of Assyria.	2Ch 30:6
Why should the **k** of Assyria come	2Ch 32:4
the Book of the **K** of Judah and	2Ch 32:32
in the Events of Israel's **K**.	2Ch 33:18
that Judah's **K** had destroyed.	2Ch 34:11
None of the **k** of Israel ever	2Ch 35:18
in the Book of the **K** of Israel	2Ch 35:27
about in the Book of Israel's **K**.	2Ch 36:8
harmful to **k** and provinces.	Ezr 4:15
uprisings against **k** since	Ezr 4:19
Powerful **k** have also ruled over	Ezr 4:20
king of **k**, to Ezra the priest	Ezr 7:12
along with our **k** and priests,	Ezr 9:7
the surrounding **k**, and to the	Ezr 9:7
the presence of the Persian **k**,	Ezr 9:9
and handed their **k** and the	Neh 9:24
us, our **k** and leaders, our	Neh 9:32
of the Assyrian **k** until today.	Neh 9:32
Our **k**, leaders, priests, and	Neh 9:34
goes to the **k** You have set over	Neh 9:37
events of the **k** of Media and	Est 10:2
with the **k** and counselors of the	Jb 3:14
bonds put on by **k** and ties a	Jb 12:18
them forever with enthroned **k**,	Jb 36:7
The **k** of the earth take their	Ps 2:2
So now, **k**, be wise; receive	Ps 2:10
Look! The **k** assembled; they	Ps 48:4
The **k** of the armies flee—	Ps 68:12
scattered **k** in the land,	Ps 68:14
k will bring tribute to You.	Ps 68:29
May the **k** of Tarshish and the	Ps 72:10
the **k** of Sheba and Seba offer	Ps 72:10
And let all **k** bow down to him,	Ps 72:11
is feared by the **k** of the earth.	Ps 76:12
greatest of the **k** of the earth.	Ps 89:27
and all the **k** of the earth Your	Ps 102:15
He rebuked **k** on their behalf:	Ps 105:14
will crush **k** on the day of His	Ps 110:5
decrees before **k** and not be	Ps 119:46
and slaughtered mighty **k**:	Ps 135:10
Bashan, and all the **k** of Canaan.	Ps 135:11
struck down great **k** His love is	Ps 136:17
and slaughtered famous **k**—	Ps 136:18
All the **k** on earth will give You	Ps 138:4
the One who gives victory to **k**,	Ps 144:10
k of the earth and all peoples,	Ps 148:11
binding their **k** with chains and	Ps 149:8
is by me that **k** reign and rulers	Pr 8:15
behavior is detestable to **k**,	Pr 16:12
will stand in the presence of **k**.	Pr 22:29
the glory of **k** to investigate	Pr 25:2
so the hearts of **k** cannot be	Pr 25:3
efforts on those who destroy **k**.	Pr 31:3
It is not for **k**, Lemuel, it is	Pr 31:4
it is not for **k** to drink wine or	Pr 31:4
the treasure of **k** and provinces.	Ec 2:8
Ahaz, and Hezekiah, **k** of Judah.	Is 1:1
land of the two **k** you dread will	Is 7:16
Aren't all my commanders **k**?	Is 10:8

makes all the **k** of the nations Is 14:9
All the **k** of the nations lie in Is 14:18
wise, a student of eastern **k**." Is 19:11
heaven above and **k** of the earth Is 24:21
heard what the **k** of Assyria have Is 37:11
true that the **k** of Assyria have Is 37:18
over to him, and he subdues **k**. Is 41:2
to unloose the loins of **k**, Is 45:1
K will see and stand up, and Is 49:7
K will be your foster fathers, Is 49:23
K will shut their mouths because Is 52:15
and **k** to the brightness of your Is 60:3
and their **k** will serve you. Is 60:10
with their **k** being led ⌊in Is 60:11
and nurse at the breast of **k**; Is 60:16
and all **k** your glory. Is 62:2
against the **k** of Judah, its Jr 1:18
They, their **k**, their officials, Jr 2:26
the bones of the **k** of Judah, Jr 8:1
the **k** who reign for David on his Jr 13:13
which the **k** of Judah enter Jr 17:19
word of the LORD, **k** of Judah, Jr 17:20
k and princes will enter through Jr 17:25
k of Judah and residents of Jr 19:3
and the **k** of Judah have never Jr 19:4
houses of the **k** of Judah will Jr 19:13
of the **k** of Judah over to Jr 20:5
then **k** sitting on David's throne Jr 22:4
and great **k** will enslave them Jr 25:14
of Judah, its **k** and its Jr 25:18
all the **k** of the land of Uz; Jr 25:20
all the **k** of the land of the Jr 25:20
all the **k** of Tyre, all the kings Jr 25:22
of Tyre, all the **k** of Sidon, Jr 25:22
and the **k** of the coastlands Jr 25:22
all the **k** of Arabia, and all the Jr 25:24
and all the **k** of the mixed Jr 25:24
the **k** of Zimri, all the kings Jr 25:25
Zimri, all the **k** of Elam, and Jr 25:25
of Elam, and all the **k** of Media; Jr 25:25
the **k** of the north, both near Jr 25:26
and great **k** will enslave him Jr 27:7
they, their **k**, their officials, Jr 32:32
and the palaces of Judah's **k**, Jr 33:4
the former **k** who preceded you. Jr 34:5
evils of Judah's **k**, the evils of Jr 44:9
our fathers, our **k**, and our Jr 44:17
fathers, your **k**, your officials, Jr 44:21
gods, and her **k**—Pharaoh and Jr 46:25
and many **k** will be stirred Jr 50:41
the mind of the **k** of the Medes Jr 51:11
against her—the **k** of Media, Jr 51:28
thrones of the **k** who were with Jr 52:32
The **k** of the earth and all the Lm 4:12
Babylon, king of **k**, against Tyre Ezk 26:7
You enriched the **k** of the earth Ezk 27:33
Their **k** shudder with fear; Ezk 27:35
a spectacle of you before **k**. Ezk 28:17
and their **k** will shudder with Ezk 32:10
her **k** and all her princes, Ezk 32:29
and their **k** will no longer Ezk 43:7
corpses of their **k** at their high Ezk 43:7
corpses of their **k** far from Me, Ezk 43:9
He removes **k** and establishes Dn 2:21
removes kings and establishes **k**. Dn 2:21
Your Majesty, you are king of **k**. Dn 2:37
the days of those **k**, the God of Dn 2:44
gods, Lord of **k**, and a revealer Dn 2:47
four **k** who will rise from the Dn 7:17
10 horns are 10 **k** who will rise Dn 7:24
after them and subdue three **k**. Dn 7:24
represents the **k** of Media and Dn 8:20
who spoke in Your name to our **k**, Dn 9:6
to us, our **k**, our leaders, Dn 9:8
left there with the **k** of Persia. Dn 10:13
Three more **k** will arise in Dn 11:2
The two **k**, whose hearts are bent Dn 11:27
Ahaz, and Hezekiah, **k** of Judah, Hs 1:1
rulers. All their **k** fall; not Hs 7:7
installed **k**, but not through Hs 8:4
Ahaz, and Hezekiah, **k** of Judah. Mc 1:1
a deception to the **k** of Israel. Mc 1:14
They mock **k**, and rulers are a Hab 1:10
governors and **k** because of Me, Mt 10:18
Who do earthly **k** collect tariffs Mt 17:25
governors and **k** because of Me, Mk 13:9
many prophets and **k** wanted to Lk 10:24
brought before **k** and governors Lk 21:12
The **k** of the Gentiles dominate Lk 22:25
The **k** of the earth took their Ac 4:26
before Gentiles, **k**, and the sons Ac 9:15
begun to reign as **k** without us— 1Co 4:8
for **k** and all those who are in 1Tm 2:2
the King of **k**, and the Lord of 1Tm 6:15
returned from defeating the **k**, Heb 7:1
the ruler of the **k** of the earth. Rv 1:5
Then the **k** of the earth, the Rv 6:15
nations, languages, and **k**." Rv 10:11
the way for the **k** from the east. Rv 16:12
who travel to the **k** of the whole Rv 16:14
The **k** of the earth committed Rv 17:2
They are also seven **k**: Rv 17:10
saw are 10 **k** who have not yet Rv 17:12
authority as **k** with the beast Rv 17:12
is Lord of lords and King of **k**. Rv 17:14
empire over the **k** of the earth." Rv 17:18
k of the earth have committed Rv 18:3
The **k** of the earth who have Rv 18:9
KING OF **K** AND LORD OF Rv 19:16
that you may eat the flesh of **k**, Rv 19:18
the beast, the **k** of the earth, Rv 19:19
the **k** of the earth will bring Rv 21:24

KINGS' *(5)*
burial ground of the **k** cemetery, 2Ch 26:23
K daughters are among your Ps 45:9
frogs, even in their **k** chambers. Ps 105:30
yet it lives in **k** palaces. Pr 30:28
soft clothes are in **k** palaces. Mt 11:8

KINGSHIP *(13)*
had said about the matter of **k**. 1Sm 10:16
to the people the rights of **k**. 1Sm 10:25
so we can renew the **k** there." 1Sm 11:14
Saul assumed the **k** over Israel, 1Sm 14:47
has torn the **k** of Israel away 1Sm 15:28
you and your **k** are not secure. 1Sm 20:31
has torn the **k** out of your hand 1Sm 28:17
his **k** was firmly established. 1Kg 2:12
"You know the **k** was mine," 1Kg 2:15
but then the **k** was turned over 1Kg 2:15
might as well ask the **k** for him, 1Kg 2:22
Israel gave the **k** over Israel to 2Ch 13:5
for **k** belongs to the LORD; Ps 22:28

KINSMEN *(1)*
whether of his **k** or his friends. 1Kg 16:11

KIR *(5)*
its people to **K** but put Rezin to 2Kg 16:9
K in Moab is devastated, Is 15:1
and **K** uncovered the shield. Is 22:6
of Aram will be exiled to **K**. Am 1:5
and the Arameans from **K**? Am 9:7

KIR-HARESETH *(2)*
(AKA KIR-HERES)
the buildings of **K** were left. 2Kg 3:25
for the raisin cakes of **K**. Is 16:7

KIR-HERES *(3)*
(AKA KIR-HARESETH)
does⌋ my innermost being for **K**. Is 16:11
he will moan for the men of **K**. Jr 48:31
like flutes for the people of **K**. Jr 48:36

KIRIATH *(1)*
(AKA BAALAH, KIRIATHARIM, KIRIATH-BAAL, KIRIATH-JEARIM)
Gibeah, and **K**—14 cities, with Jos 18:28

KIRIATH-ARBA *(9)*
(AKA HEBRON)
Sarah died in **K** (that is, Hebron Gn 23:2
his father Isaac at Mamre in **K** Gn 35:27
Hebron's name used to be **K**; Jos 14:15
K (that is, Hebron; Jos 15:13
Humtah, **K** (that is, Hebron), and Jos 15:54
of Ephraim, and **K** (that is, Jos 20:7
They gave them **K** (that is, Jos 21:11
Hebron was formerly named **K** Jdg 1:10
lived in **K** and its villages, Neh 11:25

KIRIATH-BAAL *(2)*
(AKA BAALAH, KIRIATH, KIRIATHARIM, KIRIATH-JEARIM)
K (that is, Kiriath-jearim), and Jos 15:60
and ended at **K** (that is, Jos 18:14

KIRIATH-HUZOTH *(1)*
with Balak, and they came to **K**. Nm 22:39

KIRIATH-JEARIM *(17)*
(AKA BAALAH, KIRIATH, KIRIATHARIM, KIRIATH-BAAL)
Chephirah, Beeroth, and **K**. Jos 9:17
curved to Baalah (that is, **K**). Jos 15:9
that is, **K**), and Rabbah—two Jos 15:60
Kiriath-baal (that is, **K**), a Jos 18:14
side began at the edge of **K**, Jos 18:15
up and camped at **K** in Judah. Jdg 18:12
it is west of **K**. Jdg 18:12
to the residents of **K**, 1Sm 6:21
So the men of **K** came for the ark 1Sm 7:1
the ark had been taken to **K**. 1Sm 7:2
Shobal fathered **K**; 1Ch 2:50
of Shobal the father of **K**: 1Ch 2:52
families of **K**—the Ithrites, 1Ch 2:53
to bring the ark of God from **K**. 1Ch 13:5
that is, **K**), which belongs 1Ch 13:6
ark of God from **K** to the place 2Ch 1:4
Uriah son of Shemaiah from **K**. Jr 26:20

KIRIATH-JEARIM'S *(1)*
K, Chephirah's, and Beeroth's Neh 7:29

KIRIATH-SANNAH *(1)*
(AKA DEBIR, KIRIATH-SEPHER)
Dannah, **K** (that is, Debir), Jos 15:49

KIRIATH-SEPHER *(4)*
(AKA DEBIR, KIRIATH-SANNAH)
Debir whose name used to be **K**, Jos 15:15
strikes down and captures **K**." Jos 15:16
Debir was formerly named **K** Jdg 1:11
strikes down and captures **K**, Jdg 1:12

KIRIATHAIM *(6)*
(AKA KARTAN)
rebuilt Heshbon, Elealeh, **K**, Nm 32:37
K, Sibmah, Zereth-shahar on the Jos 13:19
and **K** and its pasturelands. 1Ch 6:76
K will be put to shame; Jr 48:1
K, Beth-gamul, Beth-meon, Jr 48:23
Baal-meon, and **K**. Ezk 25:9

KIRIATHARIM'S *(1)*
(AKA BAALAH, KIRIATH, KIRIATH-BAAL, KIRIATH-JEARIM)
K, Chephirah's, and Beeroth's Ezr 2:25

KISH *(21)*
Benjamin named **K** son of Abiel, 1Sm 9:1
of Saul's father **K** wandered off. 1Sm 9:3
K said to his son Saul, "Take 1Sm 9:3
has happened to the son of **K**? 1Sm 10:11
Saul son of **K** was selected. 1Sm 10:21
father was **K**. Abner's father 1Sm 14:51
in the tomb of Saul's father **K**. 2Sm 21:14
son, then Zur, **K**, Baal, Nadab, 1Ch 8:30
Ner fathered **K**, Kish fathered 1Ch 8:33
fathered Kish, **K** fathered Saul, 1Ch 8:33
son, then Zur, **K**, Baal, Ner, 1Ch 9:36
Ner fathered **K**, Kish fathered 1Ch 9:39
fathered Kish, **K** fathered Saul, 1Ch 9:39
the presence of Saul son of **K**. 1Ch 12:1
Mahli's sons: Eleazar and **K**. 1Ch 23:21
the sons of **K**, married them. 1Ch 23:22
From **K**, ⌊from⌋ Kish's sons: 1Ch 24:29
Saul son of **K**, Abner son of Ner 1Ch 26:28
K son of Abdi and Azariah son of 2Ch 29:12
Shimei, son of **K**, a Benjaminite. Est 2:5
God gave them Saul the son of **K**, Ac 13:21

KISH'S *(1)*
From Kish, ⌊from⌋ **K** sons: 1Ch 24:29

KISHI *(1)*
(AKA KUSHAIAH)
Ethan son of **K**, son of Abdi, son 1Ch 6:44

KISHION *(2)*
(AKA KEDESH)
Rabbith, **K**, Ebez, Jos 19:20
K with its pasturelands, Jos 21:28

KISHON *(6)*
army at the Wadi **K** ⌊to fight⌋ Jdg 4:7
of the Nations to the Wadi **K**. Jdg 4:13
The river **K** swept them away, Jdg 5:21
the ancient river, the river **K**. Jdg 5:21
to the Wadi **K** and slaughtered 1Kg 18:40
Sisera and Jabin at the **K** River. Ps 83:9

KISS *(19)*
Please come closer and **k** me, Gn 27:26
even let me **k** my grandchildren Gn 31:28
Amasa by the beard to **k** him. 2Sm 20:9
Please let me **k** my father and 1Kg 19:20
enticed and I threw them a **k**, Jb 31:27

answer gives a **k** on the lips. Pr 24:26
that he would **k** me with the Sg 1:2
find you in public and **k** you, Sg 8:1
men who sacrifice **k** the calves." Hs 13:2
The One I **k**, He's the One; Mt 26:48
"The One I **k**," he said, "He's Mk 14:44
You gave Me no **k**, but she hasn't Lk 7:45
He came near Jesus to **k** Him, Lk 22:47
the Son of Man with a **k**?" Lk 22:48
Greet one another with a holy **k**. Rm 16:16
Greet one another with a holy **k**. 1Co 16:20
Greet one another with a holy **k**. 2Co 13:12
all the brothers with a holy **k**. 1Th 5:26
one another with a **k** of love. 1Pt 5:14

KISSED *(22)*
So he came closer and **k** him. Gn 27:27
Then Jacob **k** Rachel and wept Gn 29:11
meet him, hugged him, and **k** him. Gn 29:13
k his grandsons and daughters, Gn 31:55
his arms around him, and **k** him. Gn 33:4
Joseph **k** each of his brothers as Gn 45:15
and he **k** and embraced them. Gn 48:10
father's face, wept and **k** him. Gn 50:1
the mountain of God and **k** him. Ex 4:27
bowed down, and then **k** him. Ex 18:7
She **k** them, and they wept Ru 1:9
and Orpah **k** her mother-in-law, Ru 1:14
on Saul's head, **k** him, and said, 1Sm 10:1
he and Jonathan **k** each other and 1Sm 20:41
Then the king **k** Absalom. 2Sm 14:33
took hold of him, and **k** him. 2Sm 15:5
The king **k** Barzillai and blessed 2Sm 19:39
every mouth that has not **k** him." 1Kg 19:18
Greetings, Rabbi!"—and **k** Him. Mt 26:49
and said, "Rabbi!"—and **k** Him. Mk 14:45
arms around his neck, and **k** him. Lk 15:20
And embracing Paul, they **k** him, Ac 20:37

KISSES *(3)*
She grabs him and **k** him; Pr 7:13
but the **k** of an enemy are Pr 27:6
kiss me with the **k** of his mouth! Sg 1:2

KISSING *(2)*
k them and anointing them with Lk 7:38
hasn't stopped **k** My feet since I Lk 7:45

KITCHENS *(1)*
These are the **k** where those who Ezk 46:24

KITE *(2)*
the **k**, the various kinds of Lv 11:14
the **k**, the various kinds of Dt 14:13

KITRON *(1)*
residents of **K** or the residents Jdg 1:30

KITTIM *(4)*
(AKA CYPRUS)
Tarshish, **K**, and Dodanim. Gn 10:4
will come from the coast of **K**; Nm 24:24
Tarshish, **K**, and Rodanim. 1Ch 1:7
of **K** will come against him, Dn 11:30

KNEAD *(2)*
K three measures of fine flour Gn 18:6
and the women **k** dough to make Jr 7:18

KNEADED *(2)*
also took flour, **k** it, and baked 1Sm 28:24
She took dough, **k** it, made cakes 2Sm 13:8

KNEADING *(5)*
and into your ovens and **k** bowls. Ex 8:3
with their **k** bowls wrapped up in Ex 12:34
Your basket and **k** bowl will be Dt 28:5
Your basket and **k** bowl will be Dt 28:17
fire⌋ from the **k** of the dough Hs 7:4

KNEE *(6)*
have bowed the **k** to Ashtoreth, 1Kg 11:33
every **k** that has not bowed to 1Kg 19:18
Every **k** will bow to Me, every Is 45:23
and every **k** will turn to water. Ezk 21:7
Lord, every **k** will bow to Me, Rm 14:11
of Jesus every **k** should bow— Php 2:10

KNEEL *(6)*
made the camels **k** beside a well Gn 24:11
to the dust will **k** before Him— Ps 22:29
May desert tribes **k** before him Ps 72:9
let us **k** before the LORD our Ps 95:6
Then they **k** and bow down to it. Is 46:6
and all of you will **k** down to be Is 65:12

KNEELING *(2)*
got up from **k** before the altar 1Kg 8:54
After **k** down on the beach to Ac 21:5

KNEELS *(1)*
with everyone who **k** to drink." Jdg 7:5

KNEES *(21)*
his ⌊father's⌋ **k** and bowed with Gn 48:12
you on your **k** and thighs with Dt 28:35
and put his face between his **k**. 1Kg 18:42
and fell on his **k** in front of 2Kg 1:13
I fell on my **k** and spread out my Ezr 9:5
did the **k** receive me, and why Jb 3:12
and braced the **k** that were Jb 4:4
My **k** are weak from fasting, Ps 109:24
hands, steady the shaking **k**! Is 35:3
and all ⌊their⌋ **k** will turn to Ezk 7:17
came up to ⌊my⌋ **k**. He measured Ezk 47:4
and his **k** knocked together. Dn 5:6
a day he got down on his **k**, Dn 6:10
and raised me to my hands and **k**. Dn 10:10
Hearts melt, **k** tremble, loins Nah 2:10
to their **k**, they worshiped Mt 2:11
Him and, on his **k**, begged Him: Mk 1:40
on their **k**, they were paying Mk 15:19
he fell at Jesus' **k** and said, Lk 5:8
reason I bow my **k** before the Eph 3:14
your tired hands and weakened **k**, Heb 12:12

KNELT *(15)*
Balaam **k** and bowed with his face Nm 22:31
of the people **k** to drink water. Jdg 7:6
k down in front of the entire 2Ch 6:13
came up and **k** before Him, Mt 8:2
came and **k** down before Him Mt 9:18
But she came, **k** before Him, and Mt 15:25
and **k** down before Him. Mt 17:14
She **k** down to ask Him for Mt 20:20
And they **k** down before Him and Mt 27:29
he ran and **k** down before Him. Mk 5:6
a man ran up, **k** down before Him, Mk 10:17
stone's throw, **k** down, and began Lk 22:41
he **k** down and cried out with Ac 7:60
He **k** down, prayed, and turning Ac 9:40
he **k** down and prayed with all of Ac 20:36

KNEW *(83)*
and they **k** they were naked; Gn 3:7
Adam **k** his wife Eve intimately, Gn 4:1
Cain **k** his wife intimately, Gn 4:17
k his wife intimately again, Gn 4:25
So Noah **k** that the water on the Gn 8:11
But Onan **k** that the offspring Gn 38:9
whom the LORD **k** face to face. Dt 34:10
to Beer-sheba **k** that Samuel was 1Sm 3:20
Everyone who **k** him previously 1Sm 10:11
so he **k** that his father was 1Sm 20:33
and David **k** the arrangement. 1Sm 20:39
For they **k** he was fleeing, 1Sm 22:17
I **k** that Doeg the Edomite was 1Sm 22:22
out spies and **k** for certain that 1Sm 26:4
them, no one **k**, and no one woke 1Sm 26:12
Then Saul **k** that it was Samuel, 1Sm 28:14
because I **k** that after he had 2Sm 1:10
Then David **k** that the LORD had 2Sm 5:12
where he **k** the best ⌊enemy⌋ 2Sm 11:16
for they **k** nothing about the 2Sm 15:11
the times and **k** what Israel 1Ch 12:32
Then David **k** that the LORD had 1Ch 14:2
realized that we **k** their scheme Neh 4:15
for You **k** how arrogantly they Neh 9:10
If only I **k** how to find Him, Jb 23:3
Yet I also **k** that one fate comes Ec 2:14
Before I **k** it, my desire put me Sg 6:12
not claim, "I already **k** them!" Is 48:7
For I **k** that you were very Is 48:8
of suffering who **k** what sickness Is 53:3
in the law no longer **k** Me, Jr 2:8
The LORD informed me, so I **k**. Jr 11:18
Then I **k** that this was the Jr 32:8
Gedaliah, when no one **k** ⌊yet⌋, Jr 41:4
all the men who **k** that their Jr 44:15
even though you **k** all this. Dn 5:22
but they never **k** that I healed Hs 11:3
I **k** you in the wilderness, Hs 13:5
For the men **k** he was fleeing Jnh 1:10
I **k** that You are a merciful and Jnh 4:2
were watching me **k** that it was Zch 11:11
to them, 'I never **k** you! Mt 7:23
they **k** He was speaking about Mt 21:45
If you **k** that I reap where I Mt 25:26
he **k** they had handed Him over Mt 27:18
to speak, because they **k** Him. Mk 1:34
Because they **k** He had said this Mk 12:12
For he **k** it was because of envy Mk 15:10
because they **k** He was the Lk 4:41
But He **k** their thoughts and told Lk 6:8
because they **k** she was dead. Lk 8:53
that slave who **k** his master's Lk 12:47
⌊If⌋ you **k** I was a tough man, Lk 19:22
If you **k** this day what ⌊would Lk 19:42
because they **k** He had told this Lk 20:19
But all who **k** Him, including the Lk 23:49
who had drawn the water **k**. Jn 2:9
to them, since He **k** them all Jn 2:24
He Himself **k** what was in man. Jn 2:25
When Jesus **k** that the Pharisees Jn 4:1
If you **k** the gift of God, Jn 4:10
lying there and **k** he had already Jn 5:6
for He Himself **k** what He was Jn 6:6
Jesus **k** that they were about Jn 6:15
side of the sea **k** there had been Jn 6:22
⌊They also **k**⌋ that Jesus had not Jn 6:22
For Jesus **k** from the beginning Jn 6:64
If you **k** Me, you would also know Jn 8:19
that if anyone **k** where He was, Jn 11:57
Jesus **k** that His hour had come Jn 13:1
k that the Father had given Jn 13:3
For He **k** who would betray Him. Jn 13:11
at the table **k** why He told him Jn 13:28
Jesus **k** they wanted to question Jn 16:19
Him, also **k** the place, because Jn 18:2
when Jesus **k** that everything was Jn 19:28
because they **k** it was the Lord. Jn 21:12
he **k** that God had sworn an oath Ac 2:30
were amazed and **k** that they had Ac 4:13
since they all **k** that his father Ac 16:3
although he **k** only John's Ac 18:25
For though they **k** God, they did Rm 1:21
of the rulers of this age **k** it, 1Co 2:8

KNIFE *(6)*
the fire and the sacrificial **k**, Gn 22:6
and took the **k** to slaughter his Gn 22:10
he picked up a **k**, took hold of Jdg 19:29
and stick a **k** in your throat if Pr 23:2
off the shoots with a pruning **k**, Is 18:5
with a scribe's **k** and throw the Jr 36:23

KNIT *(2)*
You **k** me together in my mother's Ps 139:13
fitted and **k** together by every Eph 4:16

KNIVES *(9)*
their **k** are vicious weapons. Gn 49:5
Make flint **k** and circumcise the Jos 5:2
made flint **k** and circumcised Jos 5:3
themselves with **k** and spears, 1Kg 18:28
silver basins, 29 silver **k**, Ezr 1:9
whose fangs are **k**, devouring Pr 30:14
and their spears into pruning **k**. Is 2:4
and your pruning **k** into spears. Jl 3:10
and their spears into pruning **k**. Mc 4:3

KNOCK *(7)*
When you **k** down the fruit from Dt 24:20
k the teeth out of their mouths; Ps 58:6
whitewash and **k** it to the ground Ezk 13:14
Then I will **k** your bow from your Ezk 39:3
k them down on the heads of all Am 9:1
stand outside and **k** on the door, Lk 13:25
I stand at the door and **k**. Rv 3:20

KNOCKED *(3)*
shook and his knees **k** together. Dn 5:6
the demon **k** him down and threw Lk 9:42
He **k** at the door in the gateway, Ac 12:13

KNOCKING *(4)*
My love is **k**! Open to me, my Sg 5:2
Keep **k**, and the door will be Mt 7:7
Keep **k**, and the door will be Lk 11:9
however, kept on **k**, and when Ac 12:16

KNOCKS *(4)*
he **k** out the tooth of his male Ex 21:27
to the one who **k**, the door will Mt 7:8
to the one who **k**, the door will Lk 11:10
so that when he comes and **k**, Lk 12:36

KNOW *(891)*
"I don't **k**," he replied. Gn 4:9
I **k** what a beautiful woman you Gn 12:11
can I **k** that I will possess it? Gn 15:8

said to Abram, "**K** this for	Gn 15:13
did not **k** when she lay down or	Gn 19:33
did not **k** when she lay down or	Gn 19:35
I **k** that you did this with a	Gn 20:6
k that you will certainly die,	Gn 20:7
I don't **k** who did this thing.	Gn 21:26
For now I **k** that you fear God,	Gn 22:12
By this I will **k** that You have	Gn 24:14
old and do not **k** the day of my	Gn 27:2
this place, and I did not **k** it."	Gn 28:16
"Do you **k** Laban son of Nahor?"	Gn 29:5
They answered, "We **k** ⌊him⌋."	Gn 29:5
k how hard I have worked for you.	Gn 30:26
You **k** what I have done for you	Gn 30:29
You **k** that I've worked hard for	Gn 31:6
Jacob did not **k** that Rachel had	Gn 31:32
brothers, you **k**, are pasturing	Gn 37:13
for he did not **k** that she was	Gn 38:16
And he did not **k** her intimately	Gn 38:26
is how I will **k** if you are	Gn 42:33
and I will **k** that you are not	Gn 42:34
could we **k** that he would say,	Gn 43:7
We don't **k** who put our money in	Gn 43:22
Didn't you **k** that a man like me	Gn 44:15
'You **k** that my wife bore me two	Gn 44:27
your face ⌊and **k**⌋ you are still	Gn 46:30
you **k** of any capable men among	Gn 47:6
and said, "I **k**, my son, I know!	Gn 48:19
and said, "I know, my son, I **k**!	Gn 48:19
and I **k** about their sufferings.	Ex 3:7
I **k** that the king of Egypt will	Ex 3:19
I **k** that he can speak well.	Ex 4:14
I do not **k** the LORD, and what's	Ex 5:2
You will **k** that I am Yahweh your	Ex 6:7
Egyptians will **k** that I am the	Ex 7:5
is how you will **k** that I am the	Ex 7:17
you may **k** there is no one like	Ex 8:10
This way you will **k** that I,	Ex 8:22
Then you will **k** there is no one	Ex 9:14
so that you may **k** the earth is	Ex 9:29
I **k** that you still do not fear	Ex 9:30
you will **k** that I am the LORD.	Ex 10:2
will not **k** what we will use to	Ex 10:26
so that you may **k** that the LORD	Ex 11:7
Egyptians will **k** that I am the	Ex 14:4
Egyptians will **k** that I am the	Ex 14:18
evening you will **k** that it was	Ex 16:6
Then you will **k** that I am the	Ex 16:12
they didn't **k** what it was.	Ex 16:15
Now I **k** that the LORD is greater	Ex 18:11
you yourselves **k** how it feels to	Ex 23:9
And they will **k** that I am the	Ex 29:46
so that you will **k** that I am the	Ex 31:13
k what has happened to him!	Ex 32:1
yourself **k** that the people are	Ex 32:22
k what has happened to him!	Ex 32:23
have not let me **k** whom You will	Ex 33:12
You said, 'I **k** you by name, and	Ex 33:12
and I will **k** You and find favor	Ex 33:13
My sight, and I **k** you by name."	Ex 33:17
understanding to **k** how to do all	Ex 36:1
generations may **k** that I made	Lv 23:43
you **k** where we should camp	Nm 10:31
You will **k** My displeasure.	Nm 14:34
is how you will **k** that the LORD	Nm 16:28
then you will **k** that these men	Nm 16:30
'You **k** all the hardships that	Nm 20:14
for I **k** that those you bless are	Nm 22:6
for I did not **k** that You were	Nm 22:34
sons who don't **k** good from evil,	Dt 1:39
I **k** that you have a lot of	Dt 3:19
that you would **k** that the LORD	Dt 4:35
K that Yahweh your God is God,	Dt 7:9
of Egypt that you **k** about,	Dt 7:15
and test you to **k** what was in	Dt 8:2
You **k** about them and you have	Dt 9:2
testing you to **k** whether you	Dt 13:3
trees that you **k** do not produce	Dt 20:20
near you or you don't **k** him,	Dt 22:2
people you don't **k** will eat your	Dt 28:33
that you might **k** that I am the	Dt 29:6
you **k** how we lived in the land	Dt 29:16
who do not **k** ⌊the law⌋ will	Dt 31:13
For I **k** what they are prone to	Dt 31:21
For I **k** how rebellious and	Dt 31:27
For I **k** that after my death you	Dt 31:29
but I didn't **k** where they were	Jos 2:4
and I don't **k** where they were	Jos 2:5
I **k** that the LORD has given you	Jos 2:9
so they will **k** that I will be	Jos 3:7
You will **k** that the living God	Jos 3:10
the earth may **k** that the LORD's	Jos 4:24
But he did not **k** there was an	Jos 8:14
You **k** what the LORD promised	Jos 14:6
He knows, and may Israel also **k**.	Jos 22:22
Today we **k** that the LORD is	Jos 22:31
k for certain that the LORD your	Jos 23:13
you **k** with all your heart and	Jos 23:14
rose up who did not **k** the LORD	Jdg 2:10
I will **k** that You will deliver	Jdg 6:37
Manoah did not **k** He was the	Jdg 13:16
and mother did not **k** this was	Jdg 14:4
you wouldn't **k** my riddle now!	Jdg 14:18
But he did not **k** that the LORD	Jdg 16:20
Now I **k** that the LORD will be	Jdg 17:13
God so we will **k** if we will have	Jdg 18:5
Did you **k** that there are an	Jdg 18:14
did not **k** that disaster was	Jdg 20:34
people you didn't previously **k**.	Ru 2:11
let the man **k** you are there	Ru 3:3
people in my town **k** that you are	Ru 3:11
so that I will **k**, because there	Ru 4:4
we will **k** that it was not His	1Sm 6:9
so that you will **k** and see what	1Sm 12:17
troops did not **k** that Jonathan	1Sm 14:3
I will let you **k** what you are to	1Sm 16:3
I **k** your arrogance and your evil	1Sm 17:28
the world will **k** that Israel has	1Sm 17:46
assembly will **k** that it is not	1Sm 17:47
live, I don't **k**," Abner replied	1Sm 17:55
'Jonathan must not **k** of this,	1Sm 20:3
you will **k** he has evil	1Sm 20:7
Don't I **k** that you are siding	1Sm 20:30
He did not **k** anything; only	1Sm 20:39
let anyone **k** anything about	1Sm 21:2
you until I **k** what God will do	1Sm 22:3
Now I **k** for certain you will be	1Sm 24:20
who are from I don't **k** where?"	1Sm 25:11
David, "You **k**, of course, that	1Sm 28:1
You surely **k** what Saul has done,	1Sm 28:9
How do you **k** Saul and his son	2Sm 1:5
You **k** that Abner son of Ner came	2Sm 3:25
You must **k** that a great leader	2Sm 3:38
You **k** Your servant, Lord GOD.	2Sm 7:20
You **k** your father and his men.	2Sm 17:8
it so nobody would **k** anything.	2Sm 17:19
but I don't **k** what ⌊it was⌋."	2Sm 18:29
today I **k** that if Absalom were	2Sm 19:6
troops so I can **k** their number."	2Sm 24:2
our lord David does not **k** ⌊it⌋?	1Kg 1:11
my lord king, you didn't **k** ⌊it⌋.	1Kg 1:18
your servant **k** who will sit on	1Kg 1:27
You also **k** what Joab son of	1Kg 2:5
You **k** how to deal with him to	1Kg 2:9
"You **k** the kingship was mine,"	1Kg 2:15
k for sure that you will	1Kg 2:37
k for sure that you will	1Kg 2:42
You yourself **k** all the evil that	1Kg 2:44
You **k** my father David was not	1Kg 5:3
for you **k** that not a man among	1Kg 5:6
ways, since You **k** his heart, for	1Kg 8:39
for You alone **k** every human	1Kg 8:39
on earth will **k** Your name,	1Kg 8:43
Israel do and **k** that this temple	1Kg 8:43
the earth may **k** that the LORD is	1Kg 8:60
so they won't **k** that you're	1Kg 14:2
Now I **k** you are a man of God	1Kg 17:24
you off to some place I don't **k**.	1Kg 18:12
this people will **k** that You,	1Kg 18:37
so that you may **k** that I am the	1Kg 20:13
Then you will **k** that I am the	1Kg 20:28
Don't you **k** that Ramoth-gilead	1Kg 22:3
Do you **k** that today the LORD	2Kg 2:3
He said, "Yes, I **k**. Be quiet."	2Kg 2:3
Do you **k** that today the LORD	2Kg 2:5
He said, "Yes, I **k**. Be quiet."	2Kg 2:5
You **k** that your servant feared	2Kg 4:1
I **k** that the one who often	2Kg 4:9
and he will **k** there is a prophet	2Kg 5:8
I **k** there's no God in the whole	2Kg 5:15
They **k** we are starving, so they	2Kg 7:12
Because I **k** the evil you will do	2Kg 8:12
k the sort and their ranting.	2Kg 9:11
K, then, that not a word the	2Kg 10:10
Samaria do not **k** the custom of	2Kg 17:26
the people don't **k** the custom of	2Kg 17:26
of the earth may **k** that You are	2Kg 19:19
But I **k** your sitting down,	2Kg 19:27
servant? You **k** Your servant.	1Ch 17:18
to me so I can **k** their number."	1Ch 21:2
Solomon my son, **k** the God of	1Ch 28:9
I **k**, my God, that You test the	1Ch 29:17
for I **k** that your servants know	2Ch 2:8
that your servants **k** how to cut	2Ch 2:8
ways, since You **k** his heart, for	2Ch 6:30
for You alone **k** the human heart,	2Ch 6:30
of the earth will **k** Your name,	2Ch 6:33
Israel do and **k** that this temple	2Ch 6:33
Don't you **k** that the LORD God of	2Ch 13:5
We do not **k** what to do, but we	2Ch 20:12
I **k** that God intends to destroy	2Ch 25:16
Don't you **k** what I and my	2Ch 32:13
came to **k** that the LORD is	2Ch 33:13
Euphrates who **k** the laws of your	Ezr 7:25
anyone who does not **k** ⌊them⌋.	Ezr 7:25
did not **k** where I had gone	Neh 2:16
They won't **k** or see anything	Neh 4:11
royal provinces **k** that one law	Est 4:11
You will **k** that your tent is	Jb 5:24
You will also **k** that your	Jb 5:25
only⌋ yesterday and **k** nothing.	Jb 8:9
I **k** what you've said is true,	Jb 9:2
I **k** You will not acquit me.	Jb 9:28
Let me **k** why You prosecute me.	Jb 10:2
even though You **k** that I am not	Jb 10:7
I **k** that this was Your hidden	Jb 10:13
K then that God has chosen to	Jb 11:6
than Sheol—what can you **k**?	Jb 11:8
Who doesn't **k** the things you are	Jb 12:3
these does not **k** that the hand	Jb 12:9
Everything you **k**, I also know;	Jb 13:2
Everything you know, I also **k**;	Jb 13:2
my⌋ case; I **k** that I am right.	Jb 13:18
receive honor, he does not **k** it;	Jb 14:21
What do you **k** that we don't?	Jb 15:9
of the one who does not **k** God.	Jb 18:21
But I **k** my living Redeemer,	Jb 19:25
so that you may **k** there is a	Jb 19:29
Don't you **k** that ever since	Jb 20:4
Those who **k** him will ask,	Jb 20:7
We don't want to **k** Your ways.	Jb 21:14
himself, so that he may **k** ⌊it⌋.	Jb 21:19
Look, I **k** your thoughts, the	Jb 21:27
What does God **k**? Can He judge	Jb 22:13
Why do those who **k** Him never see	Jb 24:1
No man can **k** its value, since it	Jb 28:13
I **k** that You will lead me to	Jb 30:23
and afraid to tell you what I **k**.	Jb 32:6
I too will declare what I **k**."	Jb 32:10
yes, I will tell what I **k**.	Jb 32:17
I do not **k** how to give ⌊such⌋	Jb 32:22
what they **k** with sincerity.	Jb 33:3
not I! So declare what you **k**.	Jb 34:33
so that all men may **k** His work.	Jb 37:7
Do you **k** how God directs His	Jb 37:15
Certainly you **k**! Who stretched	Jb 38:5
Tell ⌊Me⌋, if you **k** all this.	Jb 38:18
⌊Do you **k**⌋ where darkness lives,	Jb 38:19
Don't you **k**? You were already	Jb 38:21
Do you **k** the laws of heaven?	Jb 38:33
you **k** when mountain goats give	Jb 39:1
so you can **k** the time they give	Jb 39:2
I **k** that You can do anything and	Jb 42:2
too wonderful for me to **k**.	Jb 42:3
K that the LORD has set apart	Ps 4:3
Those who **k** Your name trust in	Ps 9:10
let the nations **k** they are only	Ps 9:20
Now I **k** that the LORD gives	Ps 20:6
me about things I do not **k**.	Ps 35:11
I did not **k** tore at me and did	Ps 35:15
love over those who **k** You,	Ps 36:10
Let me **k** how transitory I am.	Ps 39:4
mouth closed—as You **k**, LORD.	Ps 40:9
By this I **k** that You delight in	Ps 41:11
fighting⌋—and **k** that I am God,	Ps 46:10
k every bird of the mountains ,	Ps 50:11
I call. This I **k**: God is for me.	Ps 56:9
Then they will **k** to the ends of	Ps 59:13
God, You **k** my foolishness, and	Ps 69:5
You **k** the insults I endure—	Ps 69:19
They say, "How can God **k**?	Ps 73:11
the Most High **k** everything?"	Ps 73:11
yet to be born—might **k**.	Ps 78:6
They do not **k** or understand;	Ps 82:5

May they **k** that You alone— Ps 83:18
I will mention those who **k** Me: Ps 87:4
the people who **k** the joyful Ps 89:15
A stupid person does not **k**, Ps 92:6
they do not **k** My ways.' Ps 95:10
so they may **k** that this is Your Ps 109:27
I **k**, LORD, that Your judgments Ps 119:75
You, those who **k** Your decrees, Ps 119:79
so that I may **k** Your decrees. Ps 119:125
For I **k** that the LORD is great; Ps 135:5
You **k** when I sit down and when I Ps 139:2
my tongue, You **k** all about it, Ps 139:4
and I **k** ⌊this⌋ very well Ps 139:14
Search me, God, and **k** my heart; Ps 139:23
test me and **k** my concerns. Ps 139:23
I **k** that the LORD upholds the Ps 140:12
is weak within me, You **k** my way. Ps 142:3
they do not **k** ⌊His⌋ judgments. Ps 147:20
they don't **k** what makes them Pr 4:19
she doesn't **k** that her ways are Pr 5:6
doesn't **k** it will cost him his Pr 7:23
But he doesn't **k** that the Pr 9:18
of the righteous **k** what is Pr 10:32
They beat me, but I didn't **k** it! Pr 23:35
"But we didn't **k** about this," Pr 24:12
He who protects your life **k**? Pr 24:12
for you don't **k** what a day might Pr 27:1
K well the condition of your Pr 27:23
he doesn't **k** that poverty will Pr 28:22
the name of His Son—if you **k**? Pr 30:4
applied my mind to **k** wisdom and Ec 1:17
I **k** that there is nothing better Ec 3:12
I **k** that all God does will last Ec 3:14
for you **k** that many times you Ec 7:22
I turned my thoughts to **k**, Ec 7:25
and to **k** that wickedness is Ec 7:25
I also **k** that it will go well Ec 8:12
my mind to **k** wisdom and to Ec 8:16
if the wise man claims to **k** it, Ec 8:17
People don't **k** whether ⌊to Ec 9:1
For the living **k** that they will Ec 9:5
but the dead don't **k** anything. Ec 9:5
certainly does not **k** his time: Ec 9:12
they don't **k** how to go to the Ec 10:15
you don't **k** what disaster may Ec 11:2
Just as you don't **k** the path of Ec 11:5
so you don't **k** the work of God Ec 11:5
because you don't **k** which will Ec 11:6
but **k** that for all of these Ec 11:9
If you do not **k**, most beautiful Sg 1:8
but⌋ Israel does not **k**; Is 1:3
take place so that we can **k** it!" Is 5:19
of Samaria—will **k** it. Is 9:9
Egypt will **k** the LORD on that Is 19:21
who are near, **k** My strength." Is 33:13
of the earth may **k** that You are Is 37:20
But I **k** your sitting down, Is 37:28
you not **k**? Have you not heard? Is 40:21
you not **k**? Have you not heard? Is 40:28
so that all may see and **k**, Is 41:20
reflect on it and **k** the outcome. Is 41:22
we will **k** that you are gods. Is 41:23
that we might **k**, and from times Is 41:26
blind by a way they did not **k**; Is 42:16
fire, but he did not **k** ⌊it⌋; Is 42:25
so that you may **k** and believe Me Is 43:10
no ⌊other⌋ Rock; I do not **k** any. Is 44:8
do not see or **k** ⌊anything⌋, Is 44:9
so that you may **k** that I, the Is 45:3
to you, though you do not **k** Me. Is 45:4
you, though you do not **k** Me, Is 45:5
that all may **k** from the rising Is 45:6
never be a widow or **k** the loss Is 47:8
you will not **k** how to avert it. Is 47:11
Because I **k** that you are Is 48:4
Then you will **k** that I am the Is 49:23
Then all flesh will **k** that I, Is 49:26
instructed to **k** how to sustain Is 50:4
and I **k** I will not be put to Is 50:7
to Me, you who **k** righteousness, Is 51:7
My people will **k** My name; Is 52:6
they will **k**⌋ on that day that I Is 52:6
summon a nation you do not **k**, Is 55:5
who do not **k** you will run to Is 55:5
all of them, they **k** nothing; Is 56:10
day and delight to **k** My ways, Is 58:2
who walks on them will **k** peace. Is 59:8
us, and we **k** our iniquities: Is 59:12

you will **k** that I, the LORD, am Is 60:16
Abraham does not **k** us and Israel Is 63:16
don't **k** how to speak since I am Jr 1:6
fools; they do not **k** Me. They Jr 4:22
but they do not **k** how to do what Jr 4:22
Surely they **k** the way of the Jr 5:5
you do not **k** and whose speech Jr 5:15
so you may **k** and assay their way Jr 6:27
people do not **k** the requirements Jr 8:7
deception they refuse to **k** Me. Jr 9:6
I **k**, LORD, that a man's way of Jr 10:23
I didn't **k** that they had devised Jr 11:19
As for You, You **k** me, LORD; Jr 12:3
Don't we **k** that every jar should Jr 13:12
travel to a land they do not **k**. Jr 14:18
enemies in a land you do not **k**, Jr 15:14
k, LORD; remember me and take Jr 15:15
K that I suffer disgrace for Jr 15:15
will make them **k** My power and My Jr 16:21
then they will **k** that My name is Jr 16:21
enemies in a land you do not **k**, Jr 17:4
You **k** my words were spoken in Jr 17:16
k all their deadly plots against Jr 18:23
this not what it means to **k** Me? Jr 22:16
will give them a heart to **k** Me, Jr 24:7
k for certain that if you put Jr 26:15
I **k** the plans I have for you" Jr 29:11
K the LORD, for they will all Jr 31:34
for they will all **k** Me, from the Jr 31:34
wondrous things you do not **k**. Jr 33:3
Don't let anyone **k** about these Jr 38:24
No one will **k** it. Why should he Jr 40:15
K for certain that I have Jr 42:19
k for certain that by the sword, Jr 42:22
and your fathers did not **k**. Jr 44:3
a while, will **k** whose word Jr 44:28
so you may **k** that My words of Jr 44:29
I **k** his outburst. ⌊This is⌋ the Jr 48:30
but you did not even **k** it. Jr 50:24
they will **k** that a prophet has Ezk 2:5
them, they will **k** that I, the Ezk 5:13
and you will **k** that I am the Ezk 6:7
And they will **k** that I am the Ezk 6:10
You will ⌊all⌋ **k** that I am the Ezk 6:13
they will **k** that I am Yahweh. Ezk 6:14
you will **k** that I am the LORD. Ezk 7:4
Then you will **k** that it is I, Ezk 7:9
Then they will **k** that I am the Ezk 7:27
and I **k** the thoughts that arise Ezk 11:5
Then you will **k** that I am the Ezk 11:10
you will **k** that I am the LORD, Ezk 11:12
They will **k** that I am the LORD Ezk 12:15
they will **k** that I am the LORD. Ezk 12:16
you will **k** that I am the LORD. Ezk 12:20
Then you will **k** that I am the Ezk 13:9
Then you will **k** that I am the Ezk 13:14
Then you will **k** that I am the Ezk 13:21
you will **k** that I am the LORD. Ezk 13:23
Then you will **k** that I am the Ezk 14:8
and you will **k** that it was not Ezk 14:23
you will **k** that I am the LORD Ezk 15:7
and you will **k** that I am the Ezk 16:62
Don't you **k** what these things Ezk 17:12
Then you will **k** that I, Yahweh, Ezk 17:21
the field will **k** that I am the Ezk 17:24
they will **k** that I am the LORD Ezk 20:12
so you may **k** that I am the LORD Ezk 20:20
so they would **k** that I am the Ezk 20:26
Then you will **k** that I am the Ezk 20:38
you will **k** that I am the LORD. Ezk 20:42
You will **k** that I am the LORD, Ezk 20:44
So all the people will **k** that I, Ezk 21:5
you will **k** that I am the LORD. Ezk 22:16
you will **k** that I, the LORD, Ezk 22:22
Then you will **k** that I am the Ezk 23:49
you will **k** that I am the Lord Ezk 24:24
k that on the day I take their Ezk 24:25
they will **k** that I am the LORD. Ezk 24:27
you will **k** that I am the LORD. Ezk 25:5
you will **k** that I am the LORD. Ezk 25:7
they will **k** that I am the LORD. Ezk 25:11
So they will **k** My vengeance." Ezk 25:14
They will **k** that I am the LORD Ezk 25:17
they will **k** that I am the LORD. Ezk 26:6
All those who **k** you among the Ezk 28:19
They will **k** that I am the LORD Ezk 28:22
Then they will **k** that I am the Ezk 28:23
Then they will **k** that I am the Ezk 28:24

Then they will **k** that I am the Ezk 28:26
of Egypt will **k** that I am the Ezk 29:6
Then they will **k** that I am the Ezk 29:9
Then they will **k** that I am the Ezk 29:16
they will **k** that I am the LORD. Ezk 29:21
They will **k** that I am the LORD Ezk 30:8
and they will **k** that I am the Ezk 30:19
They will **k** that I am the LORD Ezk 30:25
they will **k** that I am the LORD." Ezk 30:26
in countries you do not **k**. Ezk 32:9
then they will **k** that I am the Ezk 32:15
They will **k** that I am the LORD Ezk 33:29
then they will **k** that a prophet Ezk 33:33
They will **k** that I am the LORD Ezk 34:27
they will **k** that I, the LORD Ezk 34:30
Then you will **k** that I am the Ezk 35:4
Then you will **k** that I am the Ezk 35:9
you will **k** that I, the LORD, Ezk 35:12
Then they will **k** that I am the Ezk 35:15
Then you will **k** that I am the Ezk 36:11
nations will **k** that I am Yahweh Ezk 36:23
remain around you will **k** that I, Ezk 36:36
they will **k** that I am the LORD. Ezk 36:38
Lord GOD, ⌊only⌋ You **k**." Ezk 37:3
you will **k** that I am the LORD. Ezk 37:6
You will **k** that I am the LORD, Ezk 37:13
Then you will **k** that I am the Ezk 37:14
the nations will **k** that I, Ezk 37:28
securely, will you not **k** ⌊this⌋ Ezk 38:14
so that the nations may **k** Me, Ezk 38:16
Then they will **k** that I am the Ezk 38:23
Then they will **k** that I am the Ezk 39:6
the nations will **k** that I am the Ezk 39:7
of Israel will **k** that I am the Ezk 39:22
nations will **k** that the house Ezk 39:23
They will **k** that I am the LORD Ezk 39:28
I **k** for certain you are trying Dn 2:8
and I will **k** you can give me Dn 2:9
You have let me **k** what we asked Dn 2:23
You have let us **k** the king's Dn 2:23
can let the king **k** the Dn 2:25
Nebuchadnezzar **k** what will Dn 2:28
has let you **k** what will happen. Dn 2:29
as king to **k** that we will not Dn 3:18
because I **k** that you have a Dn 4:9
the living will **k** that the Most Dn 4:17
You as king **k** it is a law of the Dn 6:15
he let me **k** the interpretation Dn 7:16
I wanted to **k** the true meaning Dn 7:19
also wanted to **k**⌋ about the 10 Dn 7:20
K and understand this: From the Dn 9:25
Do you **k** why I've come to you? Dn 10:20
the people who **k** their God will Dn 11:32
a god his fathers did not **k**— Dn 11:38
and you will **k** the LORD. Hs 2:20
I **k** Ephraim, and Israel is not Hs 5:3
and they do not **k** the LORD. Hs 5:4
Let us strive to **k** the LORD. Hs 6:3
out to Me: My God, we **k** You! Hs 8:2
you **k** no God but Me, and no Hs 13:4
You will **k** that I am present in Jl 2:27
Then you will **k** that I am the Jl 3:17
For I **k** your crimes are many and Am 5:12
Then we will **k** who is to blame Jnh 1:7
for I **k** that I'm to blame for Jnh 1:12
you supposed to **k** what is just? Mc 3:1
But they do not **k** the LORD's Mc 4:12
Then you will **k** that the LORD of Zch 2:9
and you will **k** that the LORD of Zch 2:11
"Don't you **k** what they are?" Zch 4:5
Then you will **k** that the LORD of Zch 4:9
"Don't you **k** what these are?" Zch 4:13
and you will **k** that the LORD of Zch 6:15
Then you will **k** that I sent you Mal 2:4
but did not **k** her intimately Mt 1:25
your left hand **k** what your right Mt 6:3
k how to give good gifts to your Mt 7:11
But so you may **k** that the Son of Mt 9:6
have been given for you to **k**, Mt 13:11
Do You **k** that the Pharisees took Mt 15:12
You **k** how to read the Mt 16:3
You don't **k** what you're asking. Mt 20:22
You **k** that the rulers of the Mt 20:25
answered Jesus, "We don't **k**." Mt 21:27
we **k** that You are truthful and Mt 22:16
you don't **k** the Scriptures Mt 22:29
you **k** that summer is near. Mt 24:32
They didn't **k** until the flood Mt 24:39

since you don't **k** what day your Mt 24:42
But **k** this: If the homeowner had Mt 24:43
and at an hour he does not **k**. Mt 24:50
I assure you: I do not **k** you!' Mt 25:12
you don't **k** either the day Mt 25:13
and said, 'Master, I **k** you. Mt 25:24
You **k** that the Passover takes Mt 26:2
I don't **k** what you're talking Mt 26:70
an oath, "I don't **k** the man!" Mt 26:72
an oath, "I do not **k** the man!" Mt 26:74
make it as secure as you **k** how." Mt 27:65
because I **k** you are looking for Mt 28:5
k who You are—the Holy One of Mk 1:24
But so you may **k** that the Son of Mk 2:10
and grows—he doesn't **k** how. Mk 4:27
that no one should **k** about this Mk 5:43
and did not want anyone to **k** it, Mk 7:24
he did not **k** what he should say Mk 9:6
He did not want anyone to **k** it. Mk 9:30
You **k** the commandments: Mk 10:19
You don't **k** what you're asking. Mk 10:38
You **k** that those who are Mk 10:42
answered Jesus, "We don't **k**." Mk 11:33
we **k** You are truthful and defer Mk 12:14
you don't **k** the Scriptures Mk 12:24
you **k** that summer is near. Mk 13:28
happening, **k** that He is near Mk 13:29
For you don't **k** when the time is Mk 13:33
you don't **k** when the master Mk 13:35
They did not **k** what to say to Mk 14:40
I don't **k** or understand what Mk 14:68
I don't **k** this man you're Mk 14:71
so that you may **k** the certainty Lk 1:4
"How can I **k** this?" Zechariah Lk 1:18
but His parents did not **k** it. Lk 2:43
Didn't you **k** that I had to be in Lk 2:49
k who You are—the Holy One of Lk 4:34
But so you may **k** that the Son of Lk 5:24
would **k** who and what kind of Lk 7:39
have been given for you to **k**, Lk 8:10
k that power has gone out from Me. Lk 8:46
to our feet. **K** this for certain: Lk 10:11
k how to give good gifts to your Lk 11:13
who walk over them don't **k** it." Lk 11:44
But **k** this: if the homeowner had Lk 12:39
and at an hour he does not **k**. Lk 12:46
one who did not **k** and did things Lk 12:48
You **k** how to interpret the Lk 12:56
why don't you **k** how to interpret Lk 12:56
'I don't **k** you or where you're Lk 13:25
I don't **k** you or where you're Lk 13:27
k what I'll do so that when I'm Lk 16:4
You **k** the commandments: Lk 18:20
that they did not **k** its origin. Lk 20:7
we **k** that You speak and teach Lk 20:21
deny three times that you **k** Me!" Lk 22:34
"Woman, I don't **k** Him!" Lk 22:57
I don't **k** what you're talking Lk 22:60
they do not **k** what they are Lk 23:34
who doesn't **k** the things that Lk 24:18
you, but you don't **k** ⌊Him⌋. Jn 1:26
I didn't **k** Him, but I came Jn 1:31
I didn't **k** Him, but He who sent Jn 1:33
"How do you **k** me?" Nathanael Jn 1:48
did not **k** where it came from— Jn 2:9
we **k** that You have come from God Jn 3:2
but you don't **k** where it comes Jn 3:8
and don't **k** these things?" Jn 3:10
speak what We **k** and We testify Jn 3:11
worship what you do not **k**. Jn 4:22
what we do **k**, because salvation Jn 4:22
"I **k** that Messiah is coming" Jn 4:25
to eat that you don't **k** about." Jn 4:32
ourselves and **k** that this really Jn 4:42
was cured did not **k** who it was, Jn 5:13
and I **k** that the testimony He Jn 5:32
but I **k** you—that you have no Jn 5:42
whose father and mother we **k**? Jn 6:42
to believe and **k** that You are Jn 6:69
How does He **k** the Scriptures, Jn 7:15
the authorities **k** He is the Jn 7:26
But we **k** where this man is from. Jn 7:27
nobody will **k** where He is from." Jn 7:27
You **k** Me and you know where I am Jn 7:28
You know Me and you **k** where I am Jn 7:28
Me is true. You don't **k** Him; Jn 7:28
I **k** Him because I am from Him, Jn 7:29
which doesn't **k** the law, is Jn 7:49

because I **k** where I came from Jn 8:14
you don't **k** where I come from Jn 8:14
You **k** neither Me nor My Father," Jn 8:19
you would also **k** My Father." Jn 8:19
They did not **k** He was speaking Jn 8:27
then you will **k** that I am ⌊He⌋, Jn 8:28
You will **k** the truth, and the Jn 8:32
I **k** you are descendants of Jn 8:37
Now we **k** You have a demon. Jn 8:52
never known Him, but I **k** Him. Jn 8:55
If I were to say I don't **k** Him, Jn 8:55
But I do **k** Him, and I keep His Jn 8:55
asked. "I don't **k**," he said. Jn 9:12
We **k** this is our son and that he Jn 9:20
But we don't **k** how he now sees, Jn 9:21
and we don't **k** who opened his Jn 9:21
We **k** that this man is a sinner!" Jn 9:24
or not He's a sinner, I don't **k**. Jn 9:25
One thing I do **k**: I was blind, Jn 9:25
We **k** that God has spoken to Jn 9:29
we don't **k** where He's from!" Jn 9:29
You don't **k** where He is from, Jn 9:30
We **k** that God doesn't listen to Jn 9:31
I **k** My own sheep, and they know Jn 10:14
My own sheep, and they **k** Me, Jn 10:14
knows Me, and I **k** the Father. Jn 10:15
My voice, I **k** them, and they Jn 10:27
way you will **k** and understand Jn 10:38
Yet even now I **k** that whatever Jn 11:22
I **k** that he will rise again in Jn 11:24
I **k** that You always hear Me, Jn 11:42
to them, "You **k** nothing at all! Jn 11:49
doesn't **k** where he's going Jn 12:35
I **k** that His command is eternal Jn 12:50
but afterwards you will **k**." Jn 13:7
Do you **k** what I have done for Jn 13:12
If you **k** these things, you are Jn 13:17
I **k** those I have chosen. Jn 13:18
all people will **k** that you are Jn 13:35
You **k** the way where I am going." Jn 14:4
we don't **k** where You're going. Jn 14:5
going. How can we **k** the way?" Jn 14:5
If you **k** Me, you will also know Jn 14:7
you will also **k** My Father. Jn 14:7
now on you do **k** Him and have Jn 14:7
it doesn't see Him or **k** Him. Jn 14:17
But you do **k** Him, because He Jn 14:17
day you will **k** that I am in My Jn 14:20
that the world may **k** that I love Jn 14:31
slave doesn't **k** what his master Jn 15:15
they don't **k** the One who sent Jn 15:21
We don't **k** what He's talking Jn 16:18
we **k** that You know everything Jn 16:30
know that You **k** everything and Jn 16:30
that they may **k** You, the only Jn 17:3
Now they **k** that all things You Jn 17:7
the world may **k** You have sent Me Jn 17:23
Look, they **k** what I said." Jn 18:21
you to let you **k** I find no Jn 19:4
Don't You **k** that I have the Jn 19:10
and we don't **k** where they have Jn 20:2
and I don't **k** where they've put Jn 20:13
she did not **k** it was Jesus. Jn 20:14
did not **k** it was Jesus. Jn 21:4
to Him, "You **k** that I love You. Jn 21:15
to Him, "You **k** that I love You. Jn 21:16
said, "Lord, You **k** everything! Jn 21:17
You **k** that I love You." Jn 21:17
We **k** that his testimony is true. Jn 21:24
not for you to **k** times or Ac 1:7
You, Lord, **k** the hearts of all; Ac 1:24
Him, just as you yourselves **k**. Ac 2:22
house of Israel **k** with certainty Ac 2:36
man strong, whom you see and **k**. Ac 3:16
k that you did it in ignorance, Ac 3:17
over Egypt who did not **k** Joseph. Ac 7:18
we don't **k** what's become of him. Ac 7:40
You **k** it's forbidden for a Ac 10:28
You **k** the events that took place Ac 10:37
and he did not **k** that what took Ac 12:9
Now I **k** for certain that the Ac 12:11
we want to **k** what these ideas Ac 17:20
them, "Jesus I **k**, and Paul I Ac 19:15
you **k** that our prosperity is Ac 19:25
of them did not **k** why they had Ac 19:32
there who doesn't **k** that the Ac 19:35
You **k**, from the first day I set Ac 20:18
And now I **k** that none of you, Ac 20:25

I **k** that after my departure Ac 20:29
yourselves **k** that these hands Ac 20:34
everyone will **k** that what they Ac 21:24
He replied, "Do you **k** Greek? Ac 21:37
has appointed you to **k** His will, Ac 22:14
they **k** that in synagogue after Ac 22:19
"I did not **k**, brothers," Paul Ac 23:5
Wanting to **k** the charge for Ac 23:28
Because I **k** you have been a Ac 24:10
All the Jews **k** my way of life Ac 26:4
the prophets? I **k** you believe." Ac 26:27
I want you to **k**, brothers, that Rm 1:13
Although they **k** full well God's Rm 1:32
k that God's judgment on those Rm 2:2
and **k** His will, and approve the Rm 2:18
Now we **k** that whatever the law Rm 3:19
because we **k** that affliction Rm 5:3
For we **k** that our old self was Rm 6:6
because we **k** that Christ, having Rm 6:9
Do you not **k** that if you offer Rm 6:16
For we **k** that the law is Rm 7:14
For I **k** that nothing good lives Rm 7:18
For we **k** that the whole creation Rm 8:22
we do not **k** what to pray for Rm 8:26
We **k** that all things work Rm 8:28
Or do you not **k** what the Rm 11:2
I **k** and am persuaded by the Lord Rm 14:14
But I **k** that when I come to you, Rm 15:29
I don't **k** if I baptized anyone 1Co 1:16
the world did not **k** God through 1Co 1:21
I determined to **k** nothing among 1Co 2:2
in order to **k** what has been 1Co 2:12
is not able to **k** it since it is 1Co 2:14
Don't you **k** that you are God's 1Co 3:16
I will **k** not the talk but the 1Co 4:19
Don't you **k** that a little yeast 1Co 5:6
Or do you not **k** that the saints 1Co 6:2
Do you not **k** that we will judge 1Co 6:3
you not **k** that the unjust will 1Co 6:9
you not **k** that your bodies are 1Co 6:15
Do you not **k** that anyone joined 1Co 6:16
Do you not **k** that your body is a 1Co 6:19
how do you **k** whether you will 1Co 7:16
how do you **k** whether you will 1Co 7:16
k that "we all have knowledge. 1Co 8:1
he does not yet **k** it as he ought 1Co 8:2
yet know it as he ought to **k** it. 1Co 8:2
we **k** that "an idol is nothing in 1Co 8:4
Do you not **k** that those who 1Co 9:13
Do you not **k** that the runners in 1Co 9:24
I want you to **k**, brothers, that 1Co 10:1
I want you to **k** that Christ is 1Co 11:3
You **k** how, when you were pagans, 1Co 12:2
we **k** in part, and we prophesy 1Co 13:9
Now I **k** in part, but then I will 1Co 13:12
but then I will **k** fully, as I am 1Co 13:12
if I do not **k** the meaning of the 1Co 14:11
since he does not **k** what you are 1Co 14:16
k the household of Stephanas: 1Co 16:15
because we **k** that as you share 2Co 1:7
that you should **k** the abundant 2Co 2:4
I may **k** your proven character, 2Co 2:9
For we **k** that if our earthly 2Co 5:1
confident and **k** that while we 2Co 5:6
we do not **k** anyone in a purely 2Co 5:16
we no longer **k** Him like that. 2Co 5:16
One who did not **k** sin to be sin 2Co 5:21
want you to **k**, brothers, about 2Co 8:1
For you **k** the grace of our Lord 2Co 8:9
For I **k** your eagerness, and I 2Co 9:2
I **k** a man in Christ who was 2Co 12:2
or out of the body, I don't **k**; 2Co 12:2
I **k** that this man—whether in 2Co 12:3
or out of the body I do not **k**, 2Co 12:3
I want you to **k**, brothers, that Gl 1:11
to Jerusalem to get to **k** Cephas, Gl 1:18
we **k** that no one is justified Gl 2:16
when you didn't **k** God, you were Gl 4:8
now, since you **k** God, or rather Gl 4:9
you **k** that previously I preached Gl 4:13
because I don't **k** what to do Gl 4:20
so you may **k** what is the hope Eph 1:18
and to **k** the Messiah's love that Eph 3:19
For **k** and recognize this: Eph 5:5
because you **k** that both their Eph 6:9
you also may **k** how I am and what Eph 6:21
to let you **k** how we are and to Eph 6:22
I want you to **k**, brothers, that Php 1:12

because I **k** this will lead to my Php 1:19
and I don't **k** which one I should Php 1:22
I **k** that I will remain and Php 1:25
But you **k** his proven character, Php 2:22
⌊My goal⌋ is to **k** Him and the Php 3:10
I **k** both how to have a little, Php 4:12
and I **k** how to have a lot. Php 4:12
k that in the early days of the Php 4:15
For I want you to **k** how great a Col 2:1
since you **k** that you too have a Col 4:1
so that you may **k** how you should Col 4:6
so that you may **k** how we are, Col 4:8
You **k** what kind of men we were 1Th 1:5
you yourselves **k**, brothers, that 1Th 2:1
Philippi, as you **k**, we were 1Th 2:2
speech, as you **k**, or had greedy 1Th 2:5
As you **k**, like a father with his 1Th 2:11
For you yourselves **k** that we are 1Th 3:3
and as you **k**, it happened. 1Th 3:4
For you **k** what commands we gave 1Th 4:2
the Gentiles who don't **k** God. 1Th 4:5
you yourselves **k** very well that 1Th 5:2
those who don't **k** God and on 2Th 1:8
you **k** what currently restrains 2Th 2:6
you yourselves **k** how you must 2Th 3:7
Now we **k** that the law is good, 1Tm 1:8
We **k** that the law is not meant 1Tm 1:9
anyone does not **k** how to manage 1Tm 3:5
that you will **k** how people ought 1Tm 3:15
who believe and **k** the truth. 1Tm 4:3
because I **k** whom I have believed 2Tm 1:12
This you **k**: all those in Asia 2Tm 1:15
you **k** how much he ministered 2Tm 1:18
them repentance to **k** the truth. 2Tm 2:25
But **k** this: difficult times will 2Tm 3:1
They profess to **k** God, but they Ti 1:16
brother, saying, '**K** the Lord,' Heb 8:11
because they will all **k** Me, Heb 8:11
For we **k** the One who has said, Heb 10:30
For you **k** that later, when he Heb 12:17
you not **k** that friendship with Jms 4:4
You don't even **k** what tomorrow Jms 4:14
he should **k** that whoever turns a Jms 5:20
For you **k** that you were redeemed 1Pt 1:18
even though you **k** them and are 2Pt 1:12
First of all, you should **k** this: 2Pt 1:20
sure that we have come to **k** Him: 1Jn 2:3
I have come to **k** Him," without 1Jn 2:4
This is how we **k** we are in Him: 1Jn 2:5
and doesn't **k** where he's going, 1Jn 2:11
you have come to **k** the One who 1Jn 2:13
you have come to **k** the Father. 1Jn 2:14
you have come to **k** the One who 1Jn 2:14
We **k** from this that it is the 1Jn 2:18
because you don't **k** the truth, 1Jn 2:21
because you do **k** it, and because 1Jn 2:21
If you **k** that He is righteous, 1Jn 2:29
righteous, you **k** this as well: 1Jn 2:29
world does not **k** us is that it 1Jn 3:1
know us is that it didn't **k** Him. 1Jn 3:1
We **k** that when He appears, 1Jn 3:2
You **k** that He was revealed so 1Jn 3:5
We **k** that we have passed from 1Jn 3:14
and you **k** that no murderer has 1Jn 3:15
is how we have come to **k** love: 1Jn 3:16
is how we will **k** we are of the 1Jn 3:19
And the way we **k** that He remains 1Jn 3:24
This is how you **k** the Spirit of 1Jn 4:2
From this we **k** the Spirit of 1Jn 4:6
does not love does not **k** God, 1Jn 4:8
This is how we **k** that we remain 1Jn 4:13
we have come to **k** and to believe 1Jn 4:16
This is how we **k** that we love 1Jn 5:2
so that you may **k** that you have 1Jn 5:13
And if we **k** that He hears 1Jn 5:15
we **k** that we have what we have 1Jn 5:15
We **k** that everyone who has been 1Jn 5:18
We **k** that we are of God, and the 1Jn 5:19
And we **k** that the Son of God has 1Jn 5:20
so that we may **k** the true One. 1Jn 5:20
who have come to **k** the truth— 2Jn 1
and you **k** that our testimony is 3Jn 12
though you **k** all these things: Jd 5
and what they **k** by instinct, Jd 10
I **k** your works, your labor, and Rv 2:2
k your tribulation and poverty, Rv 2:9
⌊I **k**⌋ the slander of those who Rv 2:9
I **k** where you live—where Rv 2:13
I **k** your works—your love, Rv 2:19
churches will **k** that I am the Rv 2:23
stars says: I **k** your works; you Rv 3:1
I **k** your works. Because you have Rv 3:8
they will **k** that I have loved Rv 3:9
I **k** your works, that you are Rv 3:15
and you don't **k** that you are Rv 3:17
I said to him, "Sir, you **k**." Rv 7:14

KNOWING *(44)*

be like God, **k** good and evil." Gn 3:5
like one of Us, **k** good and evil, Gn 3:22
sins and without **k** ⌊it⌋ violates Lv 5:17
the Angel of God, **k** everything 2Sm 14:20
each man **k** his own afflictions 1Kg 8:38
each man **k** his own affliction 2Ch 6:29
it will deny ⌊**k**⌋ him, saying, "I Jb 8:18
without **k** who will get them. Ps 39:6
K their works and their Is 66:18
K their thoughts, He told them: Mt 12:25
k what had happened to her, Mk 5:33
k he was a righteous and holy Mk 6:20
But **k** their hypocrisy, He said Mk 12:15
Elijah"—not **k** what he said. Lk 9:33
k the thoughts of their hearts, Lk 9:47
K their thoughts, He told them: Lk 11:17
k in Himself that His disciples Jn 6:61
all this time without your **k** Me, Jn 14:9
k everything that was about to Jn 18:4
came in, not **k** what had happened Ac 5:7
not **k** what I will encounter Ac 20:22
Besides this, **k** the time, it is Rm 13:11
k that your labor in the Lord is 1Co 15:58
every place the scent of **k** Him. 2Co 2:14
k that the One who raised the 2Co 4:14
K, then, the fear of the Lord, 2Co 5:11
k that whatever good each one Eph 6:8
k that I am appointed for the Php 1:16
value of **k** Christ Jesus my Php 3:8
k that you will receive the Col 3:24
k your election, brothers loved 1Th 1:4
k that they breed quarrels. 2Tm 2:23
k those from whom you learned, 2Tm 3:14
k that such a person is Ti 3:11
through **k** every good thing Phm 6
k that you will do even more Phm 21
k that you yourselves have a Heb 10:34
he went out, not **k** where he was Heb 11:8
angels as guests without **k** it. Heb 13:2
k that the testing of your faith Jms 1:3
k that we will receive a Jms 3:1
k that the same sufferings are 1Pt 5:9
k that I will soon lay aside my 2Pt 1:14
than, after **k** it, to turn back 2Pt 2:21

KNOWLEDGE *(134)*

the tree of the **k** of good and Gn 2:9
the tree of the **k** of good and Gn 2:17
of God and has **k** from the Most Nm 24:16
for the LORD is a God of **k**, 1Sm 2:3
without my father David's **k**. 1Kg 2:32
and **k** to do every kind of bronze 1Kg 7:14
me wisdom and **k** so that I may 2Ch 1:10
wisdom and **k** that you may judge 2Ch 1:11
wisdom and **k** are given to you. 2Ch 1:12
become public **k** to all the women Est 1:17
and edict became public **k**, Est 2:8
mountains without their **k**, Jb 9:5
teach God **k**, since He judges Jb 21:22
Job speaks without **k**; Jb 34:35
and multiplies words without **k**. Jb 35:16
I will get my **k** from afar and Jb 36:3
who has perfect **k** is with you. Jb 36:4
of death⌋ and die without **k**. Jb 36:12
God is exalted beyond our **k**; Jb 36:26
works of Him who has perfect **k**? Jb 37:16
after night they communicate **k**. Ps 19:2
the One who teaches man **k**— Ps 94:10
extraordinary **k** is beyond me. Ps 139:6
k and discretion to a young man— Pr 1:4
the LORD is the beginning of **k**; Pr 1:7
mocking and ⌊you⌋ fools hate **k**? Pr 1:22
they hated **k**, didn't choose to Pr 1:29
LORD and discover the **k** of God. Pr 2:5
His mouth come **k** and Pr 2:6
and **k** will delight your heart. Pr 2:10
By His **k** the watery depths broke Pr 3:20
and your lips safeguard **k**. Pr 5:2
right to those who discover **k**. Pr 8:9
and **k** rather than pure gold. Pr 8:10
and have **k** and discretion. Pr 8:12
and the **k** of the Holy One is Pr 9:10
wise store up **k**, but the mouth Pr 10:14
but through **k** the righteous are Pr 11:9
loves instruction loves **k**, Pr 12:1
A shrewd person conceals **k**, Pr 12:23
but **k** ⌊comes⌋ easily to the Pr 14:6
will gain no **k** from his speech Pr 14:7
the sensible are crowned with **k**. Pr 14:18
of the wise makes **k** attractive, Pr 15:2
lips of the wise broadcast **k**, Pr 15:7
A discerning mind seeks **k**, Pr 15:14
of the discerning acquires **k**, Pr 18:15
Even zeal is not good without **k**, Pr 19:2
the discerning, and he gains **k**. Pr 19:25
will stray from the words of **k**. Pr 19:27
a wise man, he acquires **k**. Pr 21:11
LORD's eyes keep watch over **k**, Pr 22:12
and apply your mind to my **k**. Pr 22:17
sayings about counsel and **k**, Pr 22:20
and listen to words of **k**. Pr 23:12
by **k** the rooms are filled with Pr 24:4
and a man of **k** than one of Pr 24:5
and I have no **k** of the Holy One. Pr 30:3
grasped wisdom and **k**." Ec 1:16
my mind to know wisdom and **k**, Ec 1:17
as **k** increases, grief increases. Ec 1:18
done with wisdom, **k**, and skill, Ec 2:21
gives wisdom, **k**, and joy, but to Ec 2:26
advantage of **k** is that wisdom Ec 7:12
no work, planning, **k**, or wisdom Ec 9:10
constantly taught the people **k**; Ec 12:9
into exile because they lack **k**; Is 5:13
a Spirit of **k** and of the fear of Is 11:2
as full of the **k** of the LORD as Is 11:9
The reckless mind will gain **k**, Is 32:4
of salvation, wisdom, and **k**. Is 33:6
Who taught Him **k** and showed Him Is 40:14
and makes their **k** foolishness; Is 44:25
god who cannot save, have no **k**. Is 45:20
wisdom and **k** led you astray. Is 47:10
He will be satisfied with His **k**. Is 53:11
shepherd you with **k** and skill. Jr 3:15
our husbands' **k** that we made Jr 44:19
four young men **k** and Dn 1:17
to the wise and **k** to those who Dn 2:21
spirit, **k** and perception, Dn 5:12
about, and **k** will increase." Dn 12:4
and no **k** of God in the land! Hs 4:1
are destroyed for lack of **k**. Hs 4:6
Because you have rejected **k**, Hs 4:6
the **k** of God rather than burnt Hs 6:6
filled with the **k** of the LORD's Hab 2:14
lips of a priest should guard **k**, Mal 2:7
give His people **k** of salvation Lk 1:77
have taken away the key of **k**! Lk 11:52
the proceeds with his wife's **k**, Ac 5:2
to have God in their **k**, Rm 1:28
full expression of **k** and truth— Rm 2:20
the law ⌊comes⌋ the **k** of sin. Rm 3:20
for God, but not according to **k**. Rm 10:2
of the wisdom and the **k** of God! Rm 11:33
filled with all **k**, and able to Rm 15:14
in all speaking and all **k**— 1Co 1:5
We know that "we all have **k**." 1Co 8:1
K inflates with pride, but love 1Co 8:1
not everyone has this **k**. 1Co 8:7
one who has this **k**, dining in an 1Co 8:10
died, is ruined by your **k**. 1Co 8:11
a message of **k** by the same 1Co 12:8
all mysteries and all **k**, 1Co 13:2
for **k**, it will come to an end. 1Co 13:8
a revelation or **k** or prophecy 1Co 14:6
light of the **k** of God's glory 2Co 4:6
by purity, by **k**, by patience, by 2Co 6:6
in speech, in **k**, in all 2Co 8:7
raised up against the **k** of God, 2Co 10:5
certainly not ⌊untrained⌋ in **k**. 2Co 11:6
and revelation in the **k** of Him. Eph 1:17
Messiah's love that surpasses **k**, Eph 3:19
faith and in the **k** of God's Son, Eph 4:13
on growing in **k** and every kind Php 1:9
filled with the **k** of His will in Col 1:9
and growing in the **k** of God. Col 1:10
have the **k** of God's mystery— Col 2:2
of wisdom and **k** are hidden. Col 2:3
being renewed in **k** according to Col 3:10
to come to the **k** of the truth. 1Tm 2:4

from the “**k**” that falsely bears 1Tm 6:20
to come to a **k** of the truth. 2Tm 3:7
elect and the **k** of the truth Ti 1:1
receiving the **k** of the truth, Heb 10:26
to you through the **k** of God and 2Pt 1:2
through the **k** of Him who called 2Pt 1:3
with goodness, goodness with **k**, 2Pt 1:5
k with self-control, 2Pt 1:6
in the **k** of our Lord Jesus 2Pt 1:8
through the **k** of our Lord 2Pt 2:20
in the grace and **k** of our Lord 2Pt 3:18
Holy One, and you all have **k**. 1Jn 2:20

KNOWLEDGEABLE *(4)*

and listen to me, you **k** ones. Jb 34:2
but **k** lips are a rare treasure. Pr 20:15
with a discerning and **k** person, Pr 28:2
all wisdom, **k**, perceptive, and Dn 1:4

KNOWLEDGEABLY *(1)*

Every sensible person acts **k**, Pr 13:16

KNOWN *(154)*

who had not **k** a man intimately Gn 24:16
God has made all this **k** to you, Gn 41:39
who had not **k** Joseph, came to Ex 1:8
What I did is certainly **k**. Ex 2:14
make My name Yahweh **k** to them. Ex 6:3
to make My name **k** in all the Ex 9:16
it is **k** that the ox was in the Ex 21:36
How will it be **k** that I and Your Ex 33:16
regard to the command becomes **k**, Lv 4:14
or **k** about something he has Lv 5:1
men from Israel **k** to you as Nm 11:16
I make Myself **k** to him in a Nm 12:6
you and your fathers had not **k**, Dt 8:3
that your fathers had not **k**, Dt 8:16
LORD ever since I have **k** you. Dt 9:24
other gods you have not **k**. Dt 11:28
which you have not **k**, ‘and let Dt 13:2
you nor your fathers have **k**, Dt 13:6
gods,’ which you have not **k**, Dt 13:13
and it is not **k** who killed him, Dt 21:1
you nor your fathers have **k**, Dt 28:36
you nor your fathers have **k**. Dt 28:64
down to gods they had not **k**— Dt 29:26
they had not **k**, new gods that Dt 32:17
Don’t let it be **k** that a woman Ru 3:14
a people I had not **k** serve me. 2Sm 22:44
today let it be **k** that You are 1Kg 18:36
making **k** all these great 1Ch 17:19
Let it be **k** to the king that the Ezr 4:12
Let it now be **k** to the king that Ezr 4:13
Let it be **k** to the king that we Ezr 5:8
a people I had not **k** serve me. Ps 18:43
Make Your ways **k** to me, LORD; Ps 25:4
You have **k** the troubles of my Ps 31:7
my every desire is **k** to You; Ps 38:9
God is **k** as a stronghold in its Ps 48:3
that Your way may be **k** on earth, Ps 67:2
God is **k** in Judah; His name is Ps 76:1
we have heard and **k** and that our Ps 78:3
Your servants be **k** among the Ps 79:10
wonders be **k** in the darkness Ps 88:12
The LORD has made His victory **k**; Ps 98:2
and its place is no longer **k**. Ps 103:16
His name, to make His power **k**. Ps 106:8
You have searched me and **k** me. Ps 139:1
fool’s displeasure is **k** at once, Pr 12:16
she is **k** even among fools. Pr 14:33
young man is **k** by his actions— Pr 20:11
Her husband is **k** at the city Pr 31:23
long ago, and who man is, is **k**. Ec 6:10
When it became **k** to the house of Is 7:2
Let this be **k** throughout the Is 12:5
will make Himself **k** to Egypt, Is 19:21
Your faithfulness **k** to children Is 38:19
them on paths they have not **k**. Is 42:16
things that you have not **k**. Is 48:6
have never **k**; For a long time Is 48:8
were **k** as a rebel from birth. Is 48:8
They have not **k** the path of Is 59:8
will be **k** among the nations, Is 61:9
will make **k** the LORD’s faithful Is 63:7
make Your name **k** to Your enemies Is 64:2
other gods that you have not **k**? Jr 7:9
and their fathers have not **k**. Jr 9:16
the kings of Judah have never **k**. Jr 19:4
into a land they have not **k**? Jr 22:28
and made Myself **k** to them in the Ezk 20:5
I had made Myself **k** to Israel by Ezk 20:9
make Myself **k** among them when Ezk 35:11
GOD—“let this be **k** to you. Ezk 36:32
My holy name **k** among My people Ezk 39:7
and its interpretation **k** to me, Dn 2:6
and its interpretation **k** to me.” Dn 2:6
earth can make **k** what the king Dn 2:10
one can make it **k** to him except Dn 2:11
able to make **k** to the king the Dn 2:27
might be made **k** to the king, Dn 2:30
dream’s interpretation **k** to me. Dn 4:6
make its interpretation **k** to me. Dn 4:7
make the interpretation **k** to me. Dn 4:18
or make **k** its interpretation Dn 5:8
make its interpretation **k** to me, Dn 5:15
the interpretation **k** to him. Dn 5:17
I have **k** only you out of all the Am 3:2
make ⌊it⌋ **k** in these years. Hab 3:2
the nations that had not **k** them, Zch 7:14
will be a day **k** ⌊only⌋ to Yahweh Zch 14:7
hidden that won’t be made **k**. Mt 10:26
If you had **k** what this means: Mt 12:7
warned them not to make Him **k**, Mt 12:16
for a tree is **k** by its fruit. Mt 12:33
homeowner had **k** what time the Mt 24:43
warn them not to make Him **k**. Mk 3:12
Jesus’ name had become well **k**. Mk 6:14
the Lord has made **k** to us.” Lk 2:15
each tree is **k** by its own fruit Lk 6:44
won’t be made **k** and come to Lk 8:17
hidden that won’t be made **k**. Lk 12:2
the homeowner had **k** at what hour Lk 12:39
and how He was made **k** to them in Lk 24:35
You’ve never **k** Him, but I know Jn 8:55
I have made **k** to you everything Jn 15:15
they haven’t **k** the Father or Me. Jn 16:3
them and have **k** for certain that Jn 17:8
The world has not **k** You. Jn 17:25
However, I have **k** You, and these Jn 17:25
and these have **k** that You sent Jn 17:25
made Your name **k** to them and Jn 17:26
to them and will make it **k**, Jn 17:26
the one **k** to the high priest, Jn 18:16
This became **k** to all the Ac 1:19
who was also **k** as Justus, and Ac 1:23
let this be **k** to you and pay Ac 2:14
let it be **k** to all of you and to Ac 4:10
family became **k** to Pharaoh. Ac 7:13
but their plot became **k** to Saul. Ac 9:24
This became **k** throughout all Ac 9:42
let it be **k** to you, brothers, Ac 13:38
which have been **k** from long ago. Ac 15:18
This became **k** to everyone who Ac 19:17
had previously **k** me for quite Ac 26:5
let it be **k** to you that this Ac 28:28
since what can be **k** about God is Rm 1:19
path of peace they have not **k**. Rm 3:17
would not have **k** sin if it were Rm 7:7
I would not have **k** what it is to Rm 7:7
wrath and to make His power **k**, Rm 9:22
did this to make **k** the riches of Rm 9:23
For who has **k** the mind of the Rm 11:34
revealed and made **k** through the Rm 16:26
for if they had **k** it, they would 1Co 2:8
who has **k** the Lord’s mind, 1Co 2:16
loves God, he is **k** by Him. 1Co 8:3
know fully, as I am fully **k**. 1Co 13:12
how will what is spoken be **k**? 1Co 14:9
Even if we have **k** Christ in a 2Co 5:16
or rather have become **k** by God, Gl 4:9
He made **k** to us the mystery of Eph 1:9
mystery was made **k** to me by Eph 3:3
This was not made **k** to people in Eph 3:5
may now be made **k** through the Eph 3:10
my mouth to make **k** with boldness Eph 6:19
that it has become **k** throughout Php 1:13
graciousness be **k** to everyone. Php 4:5
your requests be made **k** to God. Php 4:6
to make God’s message fully **k**, Col 1:25
wanted to make **k** to those among Col 1:27
and is well **k** for good works— 1Tm 5:10
childhood you have **k** the sacred 2Tm 3:15
and they have not **k** My ways.” Heb 3:10
when we made **k** to you the power 2Pt 1:16
for them not to have **k** the way 2Pt 2:21
sins has not seen Him or **k** Him. 1Jn 3:6
who haven’t **k** the deep things of Rv 2:24

KNOWS *(88)*

God **k** that when you eat it your Gn 3:5
My lord **k** that the children are Gn 33:13
to this day **k** where his grave Dt 34:6
He **k**, and may Israel also know. Jos 22:22
of the iniquity he **k** about: 1Sm 3:13
someone who **k** how to play the 1Sm 16:16
of Bethlehem who **k** how to play 1Sm 16:18
father certainly **k** that you have 1Sm 20:3
my father Saul **k** it is true.” 1Sm 23:17
and stupidity is all he **k**. 1Sm 25:25
wept because I thought, ‘Who **k**? 2Sm 12:22
your servant **k** I have found 2Sm 14:22
all Israel **k** that your father 2Sm 17:10
For your servant **k** that I have 2Sm 19:20
a man among us **k** how to cut 1Kg 5:6
He **k** how to work with gold, 2Ch 2:14
He **k** how to do all kinds of 2Ch 2:14
Who **k**, perhaps you have come to Est 4:14
Surely He **k** which people are Jb 11:11
He **k** the day of darkness is at Jb 15:23
Yet He **k** the way I have taken; Jb 23:10
No bird of prey **k** that path; Jb 28:7
wisdom, and He **k** its location. Jb 28:23
since He **k** the secrets of the Ps 44:21
And none of us **k** how long this Ps 74:9
exalt him because he **k** My name. Ps 91:14
The LORD **k** man’s thoughts; Ps 94:11
For He **k** what we are made of, Ps 103:14
the sun **k** when to set. Ps 104:19
but He **k** the haughty from afar. Ps 138:6
she is gullible and **k** nothing. Pr 9:13
The heart **k** its own bitterness, Pr 14:10
k what disaster these two can Pr 24:22
righteous person **k** the rights Pr 29:7
And who **k** whether he will be a Ec 2:19
Who **k** if the spirit of people Ec 3:21
poor person who **k** how to conduct Ec 6:8
For who **k** what is good for man Ec 6:12
and who **k** the interpretation of Ec 8:1
a wise heart **k** the right time Ec 8:5
Yet no one **k** what will happen, Ec 8:7
No one **k** what will happen, Ec 10:14
The ox **k** its owner, and the Is 1:3
before the boy **k** to reject what Is 7:16
before the boy **k** how to call out Is 8:4
say, “Who sees us? Who **k** us?” Is 29:15
stork in the sky **k** her seasons. Jr 8:7
that he understands and **k** Me— Jr 9:24
am He who **k**, and I am a witness. Jr 29:23
everyone who **k** his name. Jr 48:17
He **k** what is in the darkness, Dn 2:22
k? He may turn and relent and Jl 2:14
Who **k**? God may turn and relent; Jnh 3:9
and no one **k** where they are. Nah 3:17
one who does wrong **k** no shame. Zph 3:5
your Father **k** the things you Mt 6:8
heavenly Father **k** that you need Mt 6:32
No one **k** the Son except the Mt 11:27
and no one **k** the Father except Mt 11:27
that day and hour no one **k**— Mt 24:36
that day or hour no one **k**— Mk 13:32
No one **k** who the Son is except Lk 10:22
and your Father **k** that you need Lk 12:30
others, but God **k** your hearts. Lk 16:15
from him and **k** what he’s doing, Jn 7:51
as the Father **k** Me, and I know Jn 10:15
he **k** he is telling the truth. Jn 19:35
And God, who **k** the heart, Ac 15:8
For the king **k** about these Ac 26:26
the hearts **k** the Spirit’s Rm 8:27
For who among men **k** the concerns 1Co 2:11
no one **k** the concerns of God 1Co 2:11
The Lord **k** the reasonings of the 1Co 3:20
If anyone thinks he **k** anything, 1Co 8:2
I don’t love you? God **k** I do! 2Co 11:11
Lord Jesus, **k** I am not lying. 2Co 11:31
the body, I don’t know; God **k**. 2Co 12:2
the body I do not know, God **k**— 2Co 12:3
each of you **k** how to possess 1Th 4:4
The Lord **k** those who are His, 2Tm 2:19
for the person who **k** to do good Jms 4:17
then the Lord **k** how to rescue 2Pt 2:9
our hearts and **k** all things. 1Jn 3:20
Anyone who **k** God listens to us; 1Jn 4:6
has been born of God and **k** God. 1Jn 4:7
that no one **k** except the one who Rv 2:17
he **k** he has a short time. Rv 12:12
that no one **k** except Himself. Rv 19:12

KOA *(1)*
Pekod, Shoa, and **K**; and all the Ezk 23:23

KOHATH *(14)*
Gershon, **K**, and Merari. Gn 46:11
Gershon, **K**, and Merari. Ex 6:16
The sons of **K**: Amram, Izhar, Ex 6:18
and Uzziel. **K** lived 133 years. Ex 6:18
Gershon, **K**, and Merari. Nm 3:17
the Uzzielite clan came from **K**; Nm 3:27
of Izhar, son of **K**, son of Levi, Nm 16:1
the Kohathite clan from **K**; Nm 26:57
K was the ancestor of Amram. Nm 26:58
descendants of **K** received 10 Jos 21:5
Gershom, **K**, and Merari. 1Ch 6:1
Gershom, **K**, and Merari. 1Ch 6:16
of Izhar, son of **K**, son of Levi, 1Ch 6:38
Gershom, **K**, and Merari. 1Ch 23:6

KOHATH'S *(7)*
K sons by their clans were Amram, Nm 3:19
clans of **K** descendants, Jos 21:20
for the clans of **K** other Jos 21:26
K sons: Amram, Izhar, Hebron, 1Ch 6:2
K sons: Amram, Izhar, Hebron and 1Ch 6:18
K sons: his son Amminadab, his 1Ch 6:22
K sons: Amram, Izhar, Hebron, 1Ch 23:12

KOHATHITE *(7)*
the family of the **K** clans was Nm 3:30
not allow the **K** tribal clans to Nm 4:18
registered men of the **K** clans, Nm 4:37
the **K** clan from Kohath; Nm 26:57
lot came out for the **K** clans: Jos 21:4
of Aaron from the **K** clans of the Jos 21:10
sons from the **K** family for their 1Ch 6:54

KOHATHITES *(18)*
these were the **K**. Nm 3:27
The clans of the **K** camped on the Nm 3:29
a census of the **K** by their clans Nm 4:2
The service of the **K** at the tent Nm 4:4
The **K** will come and carry them, Nm 4:15
duties of the **K** regarding the Nm 4:15
The **K** are not to go in and look Nm 4:20
registered the **K** by their clans Nm 4:34
he did not give ⌊any⌋ to the **K**, Nm 7:9
The **K** then set out, transporting Nm 10:21
sons. From the **K**: Heman the 1Ch 6:33
To the rest of the **K**, 10 towns 1Ch 6:61
families of the **K** were given 1Ch 6:66
rest of the families of the **K**. 1Ch 6:70
From the **K**, Uriel the leader and 1Ch 15:5
sons of the **K** and the 2Ch 20:19
Joel son of Azariah from the **K**; 2Ch 29:12
from the **K** as supervisors. 2Ch 34:12

KOHATHITES' *(1)*
Some of the **K** relatives were 1Ch 9:32

KOLAIAH *(2)*
Pedaiah, son of **K**, son of Neh 11:7
to Ahab son of **K** and to Zedekiah Jr 29:21

KORAH *(23)*
bore Jeush, Jalam, and **K**. Gn 36:5
Jeush, Jalam, and **K** to Edom. Gn 36:14
K, Gatam, and Amalek. These are Gn 36:16
Chiefs Jeush, Jalam, and **K**. Gn 36:18
K, Nepheg, and Zichri. Ex 6:21
The sons of **K**: Assir, Elkanah, Ex 6:24
Now **K** son of Izhar, son of Nm 16:1
Then he said to **K** and all his Nm 16:5
K, you and all your followers Nm 16:6
Moses also told **K**, "Now listen, Nm 16:8
So Moses told **K**, "You and all Nm 16:16
After **K** assembled the whole Nm 16:19
away from the dwellings of **K**, Nm 16:24
away from the dwellings of **K**, Nm 16:27
and become like **K** and his Nm 16:40
died because of the **K** incident. Nm 16:49
and swallowed them with **K**, Nm 26:10
The sons of **K**, however, did not Nm 26:11
Reuel, Jeush, Jalam, and **K**. 1Ch 1:35
K, Tappuah, Rekem, and Shema. 1Ch 2:43
his son **K**, his son Assir, 1Ch 6:22
son of Ebiasaph, son of **K**, 1Ch 6:37
son of **K** and his relatives from 1Ch 9:19

KORAH'S *(4)*
households, all **K** people, and Nm 16:32
they and **K** followers fought Nm 26:9
he was not among **K** followers, Nm 27:3
have perished in **K** rebellion. Jd 11

KORAHITE *(2)*
Mushite clan, and the **K** clan. Nm 26:58
the firstborn of Shallum the **K**, 1Ch 9:31

KORAHITES *(6)*
These are the clans of the **K**. Ex 6:24
household, the **K**, were assigned 1Ch 9:19
Joezer, and Jashobeam, the **K**; 1Ch 12:6
From the **K**: Meshelemiah son 1Ch 26:1
the sons of the **K** and Merarites. 1Ch 26:19
and the **K** stood up to praise 2Ch 20:19

KORE *(3)*
Shallum son of **K**, son of 1Ch 9:19
son of **K**, one of the sons 1Ch 26:1
K son of Imnah the Levite, 2Ch 31:14

KOUM *(1)*
and said to her, "Talitha **k**!" Mk 5:41

KOZ *(1)*
K fathered Anub, Zobebah, and 1Ch 4:8

KUE *(4)*
were imported from Egypt and **K**. 1Kg 10:28
bought them from **K** at the going 1Kg 10:28
horses came from Egypt and **K**. 2Ch 1:16
get them from **K** at the going 2Ch 1:16

KUSHAIAH *(1)*
(AKA KISHI)
the Merarites, Ethan son of **K**. 1Ch 15:17

L

LAADAH *(1)*
father of Lecah, **L** the father 1Ch 4:21

LABAN *(55)*
Rebekah had a brother named **L**, Gn 24:29
and **L** ran out to the man at the Gn 24:29
L said, "Come, you who are Gn 24:31
So **L** said, "Speak on." Gn 24:33
L and Bethuel answered, "This is Gn 24:50
and sister of **L** the Aramean. Gn 25:20
once to my brother **L** in Haran, Gn 27:43
Marry one of the daughters of **L**, Gn 28:2
to **L** son of Bethuel the Aramean, Gn 28:5
"Do you know **L** son of Nahor?" Gn 29:5
When **L** heard the news about his Gn 29:13
L said to him, "Yes, you are my Gn 29:14
L said to him, "Just because Gn 29:15
Now **L** had two daughters: Gn 29:16
so he answered **L**, "I'll work for Gn 29:18
L replied, "Better that I give Gn 29:19
Jacob said to **L**, "Give me my Gn 29:21
So **L** invited all the men of the Gn 29:22
L took his daughter Leah and Gn 29:23
And **L** gave his slave Zilpah to Gn 29:24
So he said to **L**, "What is this Gn 29:25
L answered, "It is not the Gn 29:26
and **L** gave him his daughter Gn 29:28
And **L** gave his slave Bilhah to Gn 29:29
he worked for **L** another seven Gn 29:30
Jacob said to **L**, "Send me on my Gn 30:25
But **L** said to him, "If I have Gn 30:27
Then **L** said, "Name your wages, Gn 30:28
L asked, "What should I give you? Gn 30:31
"Good," said **L**. "Let it be as Gn 30:34
That day **L** removed the streaked Gn 30:35
belonged to **L** and the stronger Gn 30:42
seen all that **L** has been doing Gn 31:12
When **L** had gone to shear his Gn 31:19
Jacob deceived **L** the Aramean, Gn 31:20
On the third day **L** was told that Gn 31:22
But God came to **L** the Aramean in Gn 31:24
When **L** overtook Jacob, Jacob had Gn 31:25
L and his brothers also pitched Gn 31:25
Then **L** said to Jacob, "What have Gn 31:26
So **L** went into Jacob's tent, Gn 31:33
L searched the whole tent but Gn 31:34
So **L** searched, but could not Gn 31:35
and brought charges against **L**. Gn 31:36
he said to **L**. "What is my sin, Gn 31:36
Then **L** answered Jacob, "The Gn 31:43
L named the mound Gn 31:47
Then **L** said, "This mound is a Gn 31:48
L also said to Jacob, "Look at Gn 31:51
L got up early in the morning, Gn 31:55
Then **L** left to return home. Gn 31:55
staying with **L** and have been Gn 32:4
whom **L** gave to his daughter Leah Gn 46:18
whom **L** gave to his daughter Gn 46:25
Paran and Tophel, **L**, Hazeroth, Dt 1:1

LABAN'S *(8)*
saw his uncle **L** daughter Rachel Gn 29:10
and watered his uncle **L** sheep. Gn 29:10
shepherding the rest of **L** flock. Gn 30:36
dark sheep in **L** flocks. Gn 30:40
didn't put them with **L** sheep. Gn 30:40
heard what **L** sons were saying Gn 31:1
Jacob saw from **L** face that his Gn 31:2
had taken **L** household idols Gn 31:34

LABOR *(108)*
I will intensify your **l** pains; Gn 3:16
means of painful **l** all the days Gn 3:17
the agonizing **l** of our hands, Gn 5:29
birth, and her **l** was difficult. Gn 35:16
difficult **l**, the midwife said Gn 35:17
to oppress them with forced **l**. Ex 1:11
with difficult **l** in brick and Ex 1:14
and observed their forced **l**. Ex 2:11
because of their difficult **l**, Ex 2:23
God because of the difficult **l**. Ex 2:23
from the forced **l** of the Ex 6:6
from the forced **l** of the Ex 6:7
their broken spirit and hard **l**. Ex 6:9
You are to **l** six days and do all Ex 20:9
You are to **l** six days but you Ex 34:21
not force him to do slave **l**. Lv 25:39
You are to **l** six days and do all Dt 5:13
and forced us to do hard **l**. Dt 26:6
imposed forced **l** on the Jos 17:13
you a land you did not **l** for, Jos 24:13
as forced **l** but never drove Jdg 1:28
them and served as forced **l**. Jdg 1:30
served as their forced **l**. Jdg 1:33
were made to serve as forced **l**. Jdg 1:35
because her **l** pains came on her 1Sm 4:19
axes, and to **l** at brickmaking. 2Sm 12:31
was in charge of forced **l**; 2Sm 20:24
of Abda, in charge of forced **l**. 1Kg 4:6
the **l** force numbered 30,000 men. 1Kg 5:13
was in charge of the forced **l**. 1Kg 5:14
the forced **l** that King Solomon 1Kg 9:15
imposed forced **l** on them; 1Kg 9:21
over the entire **l** force of the 1Kg 11:28
who was in charge of forced **l**, 1Kg 12:18
imposed forced **l** on them; 2Ch 8:8
was in charge of the forced **l**, 2Ch 10:18
in charge of the **l** on the LORD's 2Ch 24:12
consigned to forced **l** on earth? Jb 7:1
guilty, why should I **l** in vain? Jb 9:29
the fruit of his **l** without Jb 20:18
Have you watched the deer in **l**? Jb 39:1
no fear that her **l** may have been Jb 39:16
agony like that of a woman in **l**, Ps 48:6
fruit of their **l** to the locust. Ps 78:46
by the fruit of Your **l**. Ps 104:13
work and to his **l** until evening. Ps 104:23
broke their spirits with hard **l**; Ps 107:12
its builders **l** over it in vain; Ps 127:1
The **l** of the righteous leads to Pr 10:16
laziness will lead to forced **l**. Pr 12:24
it through **l** will multiply it Pr 13:11
Give her the reward of her **l**, Pr 31:31
saw that all **l** and all skillful Ec 4:4
good in all the **l** one does under Ec 5:18
reward, and rejoice in his **l**. Ec 5:19
All man's **l** is for his stomach, Ec 6:7
him in his **l** during the years Ec 8:15
be in anguish like a woman in **l**. Is 13:8
and the hard **l** you were forced Is 14:3
like the pain of a woman in **l**. Is 21:3
not been in **l** or given birth. Is 23:4
men will be put to forced **l**. Is 31:8
I will groan like a woman in **l**, Is 42:14
you who have not been in **l**! Is 54:1
They will not **l** without success Is 65:23
Zion was in **l**, she gave birth; Is 66:7
Yet as soon as Zion was in **l**, Is 66:8
I hear a cry like a woman in **l**, Jr 4:31
us—pain like a woman in **l**. Jr 6:24
l pains seize you, as ⌊they Jr 13:21
as ⌊they do⌋ a woman in **l**? Jr 13:21
will groan when **l** pains come on Jr 22:23
on you, agony like a woman in **l**. Jr 22:23
like a woman in **l** and every face Jr 30:6
Distress and **l** pains have seized Jr 49:24
seized her like a woman in **l**. Jr 49:24
him—pain, like a woman in **l**. Jr 50:43
Young men **l** at millstones; Lm 5:13

made his army l strenuously Ezk 29:18
from Tyre for the l he expended Ezk 29:18
L pains come on him. He is not a Hs 13:13
you did not l over and did not Jnh 4:10
grips you like a woman in l? Mc 4:9
Zion, like a woman in l. Mc 4:10
she who is in l has given birth; Mc 5:3
the peoples l ⌊only⌋ to fuel Hab 2:13
they don't l or spin thread. Mt 6:28
they don't l or spin thread. Lk 12:27
to reap what you didn't l for; Jn 4:38
have benefited from their l." Jn 4:38
a woman is in l she has pain Jn 16:21
together with l pains until now. Rm 8:22
reward according to his own l. 1Co 3:8
l, working with our own hands. 1Co 4:12
that your l in the Lord is 1Co 15:58
l and hardship, many sleepless 2Co 11:27
that perhaps my l for you has Gl 4:11
who are not in l, for the Gl 4:27
run in vain or l for nothing. Php 2:16
I l for this, striving with His Col 1:29
your work of faith, l of love, 1Th 1:3
you remember our l and hardship, 1Th 2:9
you and that our l might be for 1Th 3:5
l pains on a pregnant woman, 1Th 5:3
those who l among you and lead 1Th 5:12
In fact, we l and strive for 1Tm 4:10
your works, your l, and your Rv 2:2
and cried out in l and agony to Rv 12:2

LABORED *(11)*

and everything you have l for. Dt 28:33
and what I had l to achieve, Ec 2:11
work at which I l under the sun Ec 2:18
my work that I l at skillfully Ec 2:19
my work I had l at under the sun Ec 2:20
have l in vain, I have spent my Is 49:4
your new wine you have l for. Is 62:8
peoples will have l for nothing; Jr 51:58
of Egypt as the pay he l for, Ezk 29:20
others have l, and you have Jn 4:38
instead, we l and toiled, 2Th 3:8

LABORER *(3)*

a load and became a forced l. Gn 49:15
The strength of the l fails, Neh 4:10
The l is worthy of his wages. 1Tm 5:18

LABORERS *(4)*

become forced l for you and Dt 20:11
this day, but they are forced l. Jos 16:10
forced l from all Israel; 1Kg 5:13
The l who carried the loads Neh 4:17

LABORING *(1)*

shown you that by l like this, Ac 20:35

LABORS *(10)*

their work? Get to your l!" Ex 5:4
his efforts he l at under the Ec 1:3
efforts that he l with under the Ec 2:22
though a man l hard to explore Ec 8:17
The ironworker l over the coals, Is 44:12
who works and l with them. 1Co 16:16
by riots, by l, by sleepless 2Co 6:5
measure about other people's l. 2Co 10:15
with far more l, many more 2Co 11:23
let them rest from their l, Rv 14:13

LACHISH *(24)*

Japhia king of L, and Debir king Jos 10:3
Hebron, Jarmuth, L, and Eglon— Jos 10:5
Hebron, Jarmuth, L, and Eglon to Jos 10:23
Israel with him crossed to L. Jos 10:31
LORD handed L over to Israel, Jos 10:32
king of Gezer went to help L, Jos 10:33
crossed from L to Eglon and all Jos 10:34
day, just as he had done to L. Jos 10:35
of Jarmuth one the king of L one Jos 12:11
L, Bozkath, Eglon, Jos 15:39
in Jerusalem, and he fled to L. 2Kg 14:19
⌊men⌋ were sent after him to L, 2Kg 14:19
to the king of Assyria at L, 2Kg 18:14
from L to King Hezekiah at 2Kg 18:17
the king of Assyria had left L, 2Kg 19:8
Adoraim, L, Azekah, 2Ch 11:9
in Jerusalem, and he fled to L. 2Ch 25:27
⌊men⌋ were sent after him to L, 2Ch 25:27
all his armed forces besieged L, 2Ch 32:9
in L with its fields and Azekah Neh 11:30
from L to King Hezekiah at Is 36:2
heard that the king had left L, Is 37:8
against L and Azekah, for Jr 34:7
the chariot, you residents of L. Mc 1:13

LACK *(34)*

suppose the 50 righteous l five. Gn 18:28
the whole city for l of five?" Gn 18:28
where you will l nothing; Dt 8:9
and a l of everything. Dt 28:48
them for l of anything ⌊else⌋ Dt 28:57
There is nothing we l." Jdg 19:19
What do you l here with me for 1Kg 11:22
anyone dying for l of clothing Jb 31:19
and wander about for l of food? Jb 38:41
shepherd; there is nothing I l. Ps 23:1
those who fear Him l nothing. Ps 34:9
lions l food and go hungry, Ps 34:10
LORD will not l any good thing. Ps 34:10
but fools die for l of sense. Pr 10:21
and I l man's ability to Pr 30:2
and he will not l anything good. Pr 31:11
exile because they l knowledge; Is 5:13
or l compassion for the child of Is 49:15
because of l of water and die Is 50:2
because the fields l produce. Lm 4:9
So they will l bread and water; Ezk 4:17
scattered for l of a shepherd; Ezk 34:5
since ⌊they⌋ l a shepherd, Ezk 34:8
destroyed for l of knowledge. Hs 4:6
told Him. "What do I still l?" Mt 19:20
said to him, "You l one thing: Mk 10:21
him, "You still l one thing: Lk 18:22
or sandals, did you l anything?" Lk 22:35
not l diligence; be fervent in Rm 12:11
that you do not l any spiritual 1Co 1:7
of your l of self-control 1Co 7:5
they l understanding. 2Co 10:12
their l of understanding will 2Tm 3:9
so that they will l nothing. Ti 3:13

LACKED *(5)*

years, and you have l nothing.' Dt 2:7
40 years and they l nothing. Neh 9:21
offerings, we have l everything, Jr 44:18
withered, since it l moisture. Lk 8:6
l the opportunity ⌊to show it⌋ Php 4:10

LACKING *(16)*

is a nation l sense with no Dt 32:28
There was nothing l in the land Jdg 18:7
where nothing on earth is l." Jdg 18:10
the youths, a young man l sense. Pr 7:7
the vineyard of a man l sense. Pr 24:30
what is l cannot be counted. Ec 1:15
never let oil be l on your head. Ec 9:8
none will be l its mate, because Is 34:16
and his food will not be l. Is 51:14
you still l in understanding? Mt 15:16
Are you also as l in Mk 7:18
food, cold, and l clothing. 2Co 11:27
up what was l in your ministry Php 2:30
my flesh what is l in Christ's Col 1:24
what is l in your faith? 1Th 3:10
mature and complete, l nothing. Jms 1:4

LACKS *(14)*

who commits adultery l sense; Pr 6:32
To the one who l sense, she says Pr 9:4
To the one who l sense, she says Pr 9:16
the back of the one who l sense. Pr 10:13
for his neighbor l sense, Pr 11:12
chases fantasies l sense. Pr 12:11
A leader who l understanding is Pr 28:16
honor so that he l nothing of Ec 6:2
road, his heart l sense, and he Ec 10:3
it never l mixed wine. Sg 7:2
a nation that l understanding. Rm 10:19
Now if any of you l wisdom, Jms 1:5
clothes and l daily food, Jms 2:15
The person who l these things is 2Pt 1:9

LADAN *(6)*

his son L, his son Ammihud, his 1Ch 7:26
The Gershomites: L and Shimei. 1Ch 23:7
the heads of the families of L. 1Ch 23:9
From the sons of L, who were the 1Ch 26:21
through L and were the heads 1Ch 26:21
belonging to L the Gershonite: 1Ch 26:21

LADAN'S *(1)*

L sons: Jehiel was the first, 1Ch 23:8

LADIES-IN-WAITING *(1)*

her l moan like the sound of Nah 2:7

LADLES *(3)*

basins, l, and firepans; 1Kg 7:50
basins, l, and firepans— 2Ch 4:22
and l and articles of gold and 2Ch 24:14

LADY *(3)*

girl when she ousts her l. Pr 30:23
To the elect l and her children, 2Jn 1
now I urge you, l—not as if I 2Jn 5

LAEL *(1)*

family was Eliasaph son of L. Nm 3:24

LAG *(1)*

will l behind all the nations Jr 50:12

LAHAD *(1)*

Jahath fathered Ahumai and L. 1Ch 4:2

LAHMAM *(1)*

Cabbon, L, Chitlish, Jos 15:40

LAHMI *(1)*

son of Jair killed L the brother 1Ch 20:5

LAID *(86)*

and l the pieces opposite each Gn 15:10
offering and l it on his son Gn 22:6
he l its bases, positioned its Ex 40:18
Aaron and his sons l their hands Lv 8:14
Aaron and his sons l their hands Lv 8:18
Aaron and his sons l their hands Lv 8:22
l his hands on him, and Nm 27:23
Moses had l his hands on him Dt 34:9
They l siege to it and attacked Jos 10:31
They l siege to it and attacked Jos 10:34
Ammonite came up and l siege to 1Sm 11:1
She l him at her breast, and she 1Kg 3:20
temple was l in ⌊Solomon's⌋ 1Kg 6:37
of God and l it on the donkey 1Kg 13:29
Then he l the corpse in his own 1Kg 13:30
firstborn, he l its foundation, 1Kg 16:34
staying, and l him on his own 1Kg 17:19
she went up and l him on the bed 2Kg 4:21
since Joram was l up there and 2Kg 9:16
They l siege to the city and 2Kg 25:1
foundation ⌊was l⌋ for the 2Ch 8:16
They l him out in a coffin that 2Ch 16:14
who l their hands on them. 2Ch 29:23
He l siege to the fortified 2Ch 32:1
temple had not ⌊yet⌋ been l. Ezr 3:6
builders had l the foundation Ezr 3:10
of the LORD's house had been l. Ezr 3:11
came and l the foundation Ezr 5:16
what my God had l on my heart to Neh 2:12
I would have l down in peace; Jb 3:13
He l out the horizon on the Jb 26:10
Or who l its cornerstone Jb 38:6
for He l its foundation on the Ps 24:2
when He l out the horizon on the Pr 8:27
when He l out the foundations of Pr 8:29
Since you have been l low, Is 14:8
Look, I have l a stone in Zion, Is 28:16
Its foundation will be l. Is 44:28
heavens and l the foundations Is 51:13
the foundations l long ago; Is 58:12
They have l waste his land. Jr 2:15
entire army and l siege to it. Jr 39:1
Babylon, I l a trap for you, and Jr 50:24
They l siege to the city and Jr 52:4
He has l siege against me, Lm 3:5
instant without a hand l on it. Lm 4:6
of Babylon has l siege to Ezk 24:2
of Israel when it was l waste, Ezk 25:3
down and be l to rest with the Ezk 32:19
hordes will be l to rest among Ezk 32:32
and the hand I have l on them. Ezk 39:21
a paved surface l out all around Ezk 40:17
was to be l on the tables. Ezk 40:43
to Jerusalem and l siege to it. Dn 1:1
I have l waste their streets, Zph 3:6
of the LORD's temple was l; Hg 2:18
hands have l the foundation of Zch 4:9
foundations were l for the Zch 8:9
l the foundation of the earth, Zch 12:1
then they l their robes on them, Mt 21:7
except that He l His hands on a Mk 6:5
they l the sick in the Mk 6:56
He l His hands on them and Mk 10:16
in cloth and l Him in a feeding Lk 2:7
As He l His hands on each one of Lk 4:40
dug deep and l the foundation Lk 6:48
Then He l His hands on her, Lk 13:13

after he has **l** the foundation Lk 14:29
you never **l** a hand on Me. Lk 22:53
and **l** the cross on him to carry Lk 23:26
Yet no one **l** a hand on Him Jn 7:30
but no one **l** hands on Him. Jn 7:44
from supper, **l** aside His robe, Jn 13:4
l them at the apostles' feet. Ac 4:35
and **l** it at the apostles' feet. Ac 4:37
portion of it and **l** it at the Ac 5:2
who prayed and **l** their hands on Ac 6:6
the witnesses **l** their robes at Ac 7:58
Peter and John **l** their hands on Ac 8:17
prayed, and **l** hands on them, Ac 13:3
when Paul had **l** his hands on Ac 19:6
builder I have **l** a foundation, 1Co 3:10
than what has been **l**— 1Co 3:11
He **l** down His life for us. 1Jn 3:16
He **l** His right hand on me, Rv 1:17
The city is **l** out in a square; Rv 21:16

LAIN *(1)*

general of his army, had **l** down. 1Sm 26:5

LAIR *(3)*

He has left his **l** to make your Jr 4:7
growl from its **l** unless it has Am 3:4
is the lions' **l**, or the feeding Nah 2:11

LAIRS *(4)*

⌊their⌋ **l** and stay in their Jb 37:8
and lie in wait within their **l**? Jb 38:40
in their **l**, there will be Is 35:7
and its **l** with mauled prey. Nah 2:12

LAISH *(6)*

(AKA DAN, LESHEM)

The five men left and came to **L**. Jdg 18:7
out the land of **L** told their Jdg 18:14
him, they went to **L**, to a quiet Jdg 18:27
The city was formerly named **L**. Jdg 18:29
to Palti son of **L**, who was from 1Sm 25:44
her husband, Paltiel son of **L**. 2Sm 3:15

LAISHAH *(1)*

Gallim! Listen, L! Anathoth is Is 10:30

LAKE *(12)*

to the other side ⌊of the **l**⌋." Mk 4:35
He was standing by **L** Gennesaret. Lk 5:1
two boats at the edge of the **l**; Lk 5:2
to the other side of the **l**." Lk 8:22
windstorm came down on the **l**; Lk 8:23
bank into the **l** and drowned. Lk 8:33
alive into the **l** of fire that Rv 19:20
thrown into the **l** of fire and Rv 20:10
were thrown into the **l** of fire. Rv 20:14
the second death, the **l** of fire. Rv 20:14
was thrown into the **l** of fire. Rv 20:15
will be in the **l** that burns with Rv 21:8

LAKKUM *(1)*

as far as **L**, and ended at Jos 19:33

LAMB *(93)*

but where is the **l** for the burnt Gn 22:7
will provide the **l** for the burnt Gn 22:8
and slaughter the Passover **l**. Ex 12:21
In the morning offer one **l**, Ex 29:39
at twilight offer the other **l**. Ex 29:39
the first **l** offer two quarts Ex 29:40
offer the second **l** at twilight. Ex 29:41
is presenting a **l** for his Lv 3:7
brings as a sin offering is a **l**, Lv 4:32
as the fat of the **l** is removed Lv 4:35
female **l** or goat from the flock Lv 5:6
a calf and a **l**, male yearlings Lv 9:3
a year-old male **l** for a burnt Lv 12:6
an unblemished year-old ewe **l**, Lv 14:10
take one male **l** and present it Lv 14:12
slaughter the male **l** at the Lv 14:13
to take one male **l** for a Lv 14:21
will take the male **l** for the Lv 14:24
the male **l** for the restitution Lv 14:25
year-old male **l** without blemish Lv 23:12
a year-old male **l** as a Nm 6:12
year-old male **l** as a burnt Nm 6:14
year-old female **l** as a sin Nm 6:14
and one male **l** a year old, Nm 7:15
and one male **l** a year old, Nm 7:21
and one male **l** a year old, Nm 7:27
and one male **l** a year old, Nm 7:33
and one male **l** a year old, Nm 7:39
and one male **l** a year old, Nm 7:45
and one male **l** a year old, Nm 7:51
and one male **l** a year old, Nm 7:57
and one male **l** a year old, Nm 7:63
and one male **l** a year old, Nm 7:69
and one male **l** a year old, Nm 7:75
and one male **l** a year old, Nm 7:81
offering or sacrifice of each **l**. Nm 15:5
for each ox, ram, **l**, or goat. Nm 15:11
Offer one **l** in the morning and Nm 28:4
and the other **l** at twilight, Nm 28:4
is to be a quart with each **l**. Nm 28:7
Offer the second **l** at twilight, Nm 28:8
as a grain offering for each **l**. Nm 28:13
and one quart with each male **l**. Nm 28:14
took a young **l** and offered it as 1Sm 7:9
carried off a **l** from the flock, 1Sm 17:34
rescued ⌊the **l**⌋ from its mouth 1Sm 17:35
one small ewe **l** that he had 2Sm 12:3
the poor man's **l** and prepared it 2Sm 12:4
must pay four lambs for that **l**." 2Sm 12:6
the Passover **l** on the fourteenth 2Ch 30:15
the Passover **l** for themselves, Ezr 6:20
The wolf will live with the **l**, Is 11:6
Like a **l** led to the slaughter Is 53:7
The wolf and the **l** will feed Is 65:25
one sacrifices a **l**, one breaks a Is 66:3
like a docile **l** led to slaughter Jr 11:19
is a stray **l**, chased by lions Jr 50:17
year-old male **l** as a daily burnt Ezk 46:13
will offer the **l**, the grain Ezk 46:15
them like a **l** in an open meadow? Hs 4:16
they sacrifice the Passover **l**, Mk 14:12
when the Passover **l** had to be Lk 22:7
Here is the **L** of God, who takes Jn 1:29
he said, "Look! The **L** of God!" Jn 1:36
and as a **l** is silent before its Ac 8:32
like that of a **l** without defect 1Pt 1:19
a slaughtered **l** standing between Rv 5:6
elders fell down before the **L**. Rv 5:8
The **L** who was slaughtered is Rv 5:12
and to the **L**, forever and ever Rv 5:13
Then I saw the **L** open one of the Rv 6:1
and from the wrath of the **L**, Rv 6:16
the throne and before the **L**. Rv 7:9
on the throne, and to the **L**! Rv 7:10
white in the blood of the **L**. Rv 7:14
Because the **L** who is at the Rv 7:17
blood of the **L** and by the word Rv 12:11
of life of the **L** who was Rv 13:8
he had two horns like a **l**, Rv 13:11
there on Mount Zion stood the **L**, Rv 14:1
who follow the **L** wherever He Rv 14:4
firstfruits for God and the **L**. Rv 14:4
and in the sight of the **L**, Rv 14:10
Moses, and the song of the **L**: Rv 15:3
will make war against the **L**, Rv 17:14
but the **L** will conquer them Rv 17:14
the marriage of the **L** has come, Rv 19:7
to the marriage feast of the **L**!" Rv 19:9
the bride, the wife of the **L**." Rv 21:9
Almighty and the **L** are its Rv 21:22
it, and its lamp is the **L**. Rv 21:23
the throne of God and of the **L** Rv 22:1
of God and of the **L** will be in Rv 22:3

LAMB'S *(2)*

12 names of the **L** 12 apostles. Rv 21:14
written in the **L** book of life. Rv 21:27

LAMBS *(94)*

seven ewe **l** from the flock. Gn 21:28
set apart these seven ewe **l**?" Gn 21:29
the seven ewe **l** from my hand so Gn 21:30
dark-colored sheep among the **l**, Gn 30:32
or any **l** that are not black, Gn 30:33
dark-colored sheep among the **l**, Gn 30:35
separated the **l** and made the Gn 30:40
altar every day: two year-old **l**. Ex 29:38
take two unblemished male **l**, Lv 14:10
unblemished male **l** a year old, Lv 23:18
and two male **l** a year old as a Lv 23:19
will wave the **l** with the bread Lv 23:20
and the two **l** will be holy to Lv 23:20
and five male **l** a year old, Nm 7:17
and five male **l** a year old, Nm 7:23
and five male **l** a year old, Nm 7:29
and five male **l** a year old, Nm 7:35
and five male **l** a year old, Nm 7:41
and five male **l** a year old, Nm 7:47
and five male **l** a year old, Nm 7:53
and five male **l** a year old, Nm 7:59
and five male **l** a year old, Nm 7:65
and five male **l** a year old, Nm 7:71
and five male **l** a year old, Nm 7:77
and five male **l** a year old, Nm 7:83
and 12 male **l** a year old, with Nm 7:87
goats, and 60 male **l** a year old. Nm 7:88
year-old male **l** as a regular Nm 28:3
two unblemished year-old male **l**, Nm 28:9
seven male **l** a year old— Nm 28:11
and seven male **l** a year old. Nm 28:19
quarts with each of the seven **l** Nm 28:21
and seven male **l** a year old, Nm 28:27
quarts with each of the seven **l** Nm 28:29
seven male **l** a year old— Nm 29:2
with each of the seven male **l**. Nm 29:4
and seven male **l** a year old. Nm 29:8
quarts with each of the seven **l**. Nm 29:10
rams, and 14 male **l** a year old. Nm 29:13
quarts with each of the 14 **l**. Nm 29:15
and 14 male **l** a year old— Nm 29:17
bulls, rams, and **l**, in Nm 29:18
rams, 14 male **l** a year old— Nm 29:20
bulls, rams, and **l**, in Nm 29:21
rams, 14 male **l** a year old— Nm 29:23
bulls, rams, and **l**, in Nm 29:24
rams, 14 male **l** a year old— Nm 29:26
bulls, rams, and **l**, in Nm 29:27
rams, 14 male **l** a year old— Nm 29:29
bulls, rams, and **l**, in Nm 29:30
and 14 male **l** a year old— Nm 29:32
bulls, rams, and **l**, in Nm 29:33
seven male **l** a year old— Nm 29:36
bulls, rams, and **l**, in Nm 29:37
with the fat of **l**, rams from Dt 32:14
must pay four **l** for that lamb." 2Sm 12:6
of Israel 100,000 **l** and the wool 2Kg 3:4
rams, and 1,000 **l**, along with 1Ch 29:21
rams, seven **l**, and seven male 2Ch 29:21
slaughtered the **l** and sprinkled 2Ch 29:22
70 bulls, 100 rams, and 200 **l**; 2Ch 29:32
the Passover ⌊**l**⌋ for every 2Ch 30:17
consecrate ⌊the **l**⌋ to the LORD. 2Ch 30:17
the Passover ⌊**l**⌋ on the 2Ch 35:1
Slaughter the Passover ⌊**l**⌋, 2Ch 35:6
30,000 sheep, **l**, and kid goats, 2Ch 35:7
slaughtered the Passover ⌊**l**⌋, 2Ch 35:11
the Passover ⌊**l**⌋ with fire 2Ch 35:13
and **l** for burnt offerings to the Ezr 6:9
rams, and 400 **l**, as well as 12 Ezr 6:17
rams, and **l** as needed, along Ezr 7:17
96 rams, and 77 **l**, along with 12 Ezr 8:35
little ones run around like **l**; Jb 21:11
like rams, the hills, like **l**. Ps 114:4
like rams? Hills, like **l**? Ps 114:6
l will provide your clothing, Pr 27:26
of bulls, **l**, or male goats. Is 1:11
L will graze as ⌊if in⌋ their Is 5:17
Send **l** to the ruler of the land, Is 16:1
with the blood of **l** and goats, Is 34:6
He gathers the **l** in His arms and Is 40:11
flock's little **l** will certainly Jr 49:20
flock's little **l** will be dragged Jr 50:45
them down like **l** to the Jr 51:40
with you in **l**, rams, and goats. Ezk 27:21
rams, **l**, male goats, and bulls, Ezk 39:18
six unblemished **l** and an Ezk 46:4
with the **l** will be whatever Ezk 46:5
as well as six **l** and a ram Ezk 46:6
he can afford with the **l**, Ezk 46:7
he wants to give with the **l**, Ezk 46:11
and dine on **l** from the flock and Am 6:4
you out like **l** among wolves. Lk 10:3
"Feed My **l**," He told him. Jn 21:15

LAME *(34)*

man who is blind, **l**, facially Lv 21:18
if it is **l** or blind or has any Dt 15:21
to flee, he fell and became **l**. 2Sm 4:4
the blind and **l** can repel you," 2Sm 5:6
to reach the **l** and the blind who 2Sm 5:8
blind and the **l** will never enter 2Sm 5:8
son who is **l** in both feet." 2Sm 9:3
table. He was **l** in both feet. 2Sm 9:13
king'—for your servant is **l**. 2Sm 19:26
they did their **l** dance around 1Kg 18:26
to the blind and feet to the **l**. Jb 29:15
a fool is like **l** legs that hang Pr 26:7
divided, the **l** will plunder it Is 33:23
the **l** will leap like a deer, Is 35:6

blind and the l will be with Jr 31:8
I will assemble the l and gather Mc 4:6
will make the l into a remnant, Mc 4:7
I will save the l and gather the Zph 3:19
you present a l or sick ⌊animal⌋ Mal 1:8
bring stolen, l, or sick animals Mal 1:13
blind see, the l walk, those Mt 11:5
with them the l, the blind, Mt 15:30
restored, the l walking, and the Mt 15:31
you to enter life maimed or l, Mt 18:8
The blind and the l came to Him Mt 21:14
to enter life l than to have two Mk 9:45
sight, the l walk, those with Lk 7:22
are poor, maimed, l, or blind. Lk 14:13
poor, maimed, blind, and l!' Lk 14:21
sick—blind, l, and paralyzed Jn 5:3
a man who was l from his Ac 3:2
paralyzed and l were healed. Ac 8:7
in his feet, l from birth, and Ac 14:8
so that what is l may not be Heb 12:13

LAMECH *(11)*
and Methushael fathered L. Gn 4:18
L took two wives for himself, Gn 4:19
L said to his wives: Adah and Gn 4:23
wives of L, pay attention to my Gn 4:23
then for L it will be Gn 4:24
years old when he fathered L. Gn 5:25
782 years after the birth of L, Gn 5:26
L was 182 years old when he Gn 5:28
L lived 595 years after Noah's Gn 5:30
Enoch, Methuselah, L, 1Ch 1:3
Shem, ⌊son⌋ of Noah, ⌊son⌋ of L, Lk 3:36

LAMECH'S *(1)*
So L life lasted 777 years; Gn 5:31

LAMENT *(35)*
the following l for Saul and his 2Sm 1:17
and the king sang a l for Abner: 2Sm 3:33
You turned my l into dancing; Ps 30:11
but the widows could not l. Ps 78:64
and no cry of l in our public Ps 144:14
you will l when your physical Pr 5:11
Then her gates will l and mourn; Is 3:26
cast hooks into the Nile will l, Is 19:8
and you will l out of a broken Is 65:14
son, a bitter l, for suddenly Jr 6:26
weeping and a l over the Jr 9:10
to raise a l over us so that Jr 9:18
daughters a l and one another Jr 9:20
Don't go to l or sympathize with Jr 16:5
No l will be made for them, Jr 16:6
heard in Ramah, a l with bitter Jr 31:15
be the l for you, for I have Jr 34:5
with sackcloth, and l; Jr 49:3
l for the princes of Israel Ezk 19:1
This is a l and should be used Ezk 19:14
and should be used as a l." Ezk 19:14
you must not l or weep or let Ezk 24:16
You will not l or weep but will Ezk 24:23
Then they will l for you and say Ezk 26:17
Now, son of man, l for Tyre. Ezk 27:2
In their wailing they l for you, Ezk 27:32
l for the king of Tyre and say Ezk 28:12
l for Pharaoh king of Egypt and Ezk 32:2
This is a l that will be Ezk 32:16
Dress ⌊in sackcloth⌋ and l, Jl 1:13
for you, a l, house of Israel: Am 5:1
of this I will l and wail; Mc 1:8
against you, and l mournfully, Mc 2:4
we sang a l, but you didn't Mt 11:17
sang a l, but you didn't weep! Lk 7:32

LAMENTATION *(5)*
the practices of fasting and l. Est 9:31
For a sound of l is heard from Jr 9:19
mourning and l within Daughter Lm 2:5
⌊words of⌋ l, mourning, and woe Ezk 2:10
and all your songs into l; Am 8:10

LAMENTED *(3)*
Jordan, they l and wept loudly Gn 50:10
fasted, wept, and l, and many Est 4:3
you fasted and l in the fifth Zch 7:5

LAMENTING *(3)*
Beth-ezel is l; its support is Mc 1:11
players and a crowd l loudly. Mt 9:23
who were mourning and l Him. Lk 23:27

LAMP *(38)*
order to keep the l burning Ex 27:20
are to tend the l from evening Ex 27:21
so that the l will burn Lv 24:2
has oversight of the l oil, Nm 4:16
the l of God had gone out, 1Sm 3:3
not extinguish the l of Israel." 2Sm 21:17
LORD, You are my l; the LORD 2Sm 22:29
will always have a l before Me 1Kg 11:36
God gave him a l in Jerusalem to 1Kg 15:4
a chair, and a l there for him. 2Kg 4:10
to give a l to David and to 2Kg 8:19
to give a l to David and to 2Ch 21:7
and the l beside him is put out. Jb 18:6
How often is the l of the wicked Jb 21:17
when His l shone above my head, Jb 29:3
LORD, You light my l; my God Ps 18:28
Your word is a l for my feet and Ps 119:105
prepared a l for My anointed Ps 132:17
commandment is a l, teaching is Pr 6:23
but the l of the wicked is Pr 13:9
his l will go out in deep Pr 20:20
breath is the l of the LORD, Pr 20:27
The l that guides the wicked— Pr 21:4
the l of the wicked will be put Pr 24:20
and her l never goes out at Pr 31:18
and the light of the l. Jr 25:10
No one lights a l and puts it Mt 5:15
The eye is the l of the body. Mt 6:22
Is a l brought in to be put Mk 4:21
lighting a l, covers it with Lk 8:16
No one lights a l and puts it in Lk 11:33
Your eye is the l of the body. Lk 11:34
a l shines its light on you. Lk 11:36
not light a l, sweep the house Lk 15:8
was a burning and shining l, Jn 5:35
as to a l shining in a dismal 2Pt 1:19
light of a l will never shine Rv 18:23
it, and its l is the Lamb. Rv 21:23

LAMPLIGHT *(1)*
will not need l or sunlight, Rv 22:5

LAMPS *(32)*
Make seven l on it. Its lamps Ex 25:37
Its l are to be set up so they Ex 25:37
morning when he tends the l. Ex 30:7
Aaron sets up the l at twilight, Ex 30:8
utensils and l as well as the Ex 35:14
also made its seven l, snuffers, Ex 37:23
with its l arranged and all its Ex 39:37
the lampstand and set up its l. Ex 40:4
set up the l before the LORD, Ex 40:25
tend the l on the pure ⌊gold Lv 24:4
for light, with its l, snuffers, Nm 4:9
set up the l, the seven lamps Nm 8:2
the seven l are to give light in Nm 8:2
he set up its l ⌊to give light⌋ Nm 8:3
the gold flowers, l, and tongs; 1Kg 7:49
lampstands and their gold l, 1Ch 28:15
of each lampstand and its l; 1Ch 28:15
each silver lampstand and its l, 1Ch 28:15
and their l of pure gold to burn 2Ch 4:20
the flowers, l, and gold tongs— 2Ch 4:21
They light the l of the gold 2Ch 13:11
extinguished the l, did not burn 2Ch 29:7
Jerusalem with l and punish the Zph 1:12
It has seven l on it and seven Zch 4:2
for each of the l on its top. Zch 4:2
who took their l and went out to Mt 25:1
When the foolish took their l, Mt 25:3
in their flasks with their l. Mt 25:4
got up and trimmed their l. Mt 25:7
because our l are going out.' Mt 25:8
for service and have your l lit. Lk 12:35
There were many l in the room Ac 20:8

LAMPSTAND *(39)*
You are to make a l out of pure, Ex 25:31
branches of the l from one side Ex 25:32
branches of the l from the other Ex 25:32
branches that extend from the l. Ex 25:33
blossoms on the l ⌊shaft⌋ along Ex 25:34
branches that extend from the l, Ex 25:35
The l with all these utensils is Ex 25:39
the veil and the l on the south Ex 26:35
utensils, the l with its Ex 30:27
the pure ⌊gold⌋ l with all its Ex 31:8
l for light with its utensils Ex 35:14
Then he made the l out of pure Ex 37:17
branches of the l from one side Ex 37:18
branches of the l from the other Ex 37:18
that extended from the l. Ex 37:19
On the l shaft there were four Ex 37:20
pure ⌊gold⌋ l, with its lamps Ex 39:37
bring in the l and set up its Ex 40:4
He also put the l in the tent of Ex 40:24
the pure ⌊gold⌋ l in the LORD's Lv 24:4
the table, the l, the altars, Nm 3:31
and cover the l used for light, Nm 4:9
give light in front of the l." Nm 8:2
in front of the l just as the Nm 8:3
This is the way the l was made: Nm 8:4
The l was made according to the Nm 8:4
weight of each l and its lamps; 1Ch 28:15
of each silver l and its lamps, 1Ch 28:15
to the service of each l; 1Ch 28:15
of the gold l every evening. 2Ch 13:11
palace wall next to the l. Dn 5:5
see a solid gold l there with a Zch 4:2
on the right and left of the l?" Zch 4:11
but rather on a l, and it gives Mt 5:15
Isn't it to be put on a l? Mk 4:21
but puts it on a l so that those Lk 8:16
basket, but on a l, so that Lk 11:33
place," were the l, the table, Heb 9:2
and remove your l from its place Rv 2:5

LAMPSTANDS *(11)*
the pure gold l in front of the 1Kg 7:49
of the gold l and their gold 1Ch 28:15
made the 10 gold l according to 2Ch 4:7
the l and their lamps of pure 2Ch 4:20
the pots, the l, the pans, Jr 52:19
I turned I saw seven gold l, Rv 1:12
and among the l was One like the Rv 1:13
of the seven gold l, is this: Rv 1:20
and the seven l are the seven Rv 1:20
among the seven gold l says: Rv 2:1
and the two l that stand before Rv 11:4

LANCE *(1)*
with a flashing spear and a l. Jb 39:23

LANCES *(1)*
on! Polish the l; put on armor! Jr 46:4

LAND *(1835)*
and let the dry l appear." Gn 1:9
God called the dry l "earth," Gn 1:10
field had yet ⌊grown⌋ on the l, Gn 2:5
had not made it rain on the l, Gn 2:5
the entire surface of the l. Gn 2:6
the entire l of the Havilah, Gn 2:11
Gold from that l is pure; Gn 2:12
encircles the entire l of Cush. Gn 2:13
but Cain cultivated the l. Gn 4:2
If you work the l, it will never Gn 4:12
and lived in the l of Nod, Gn 4:16
everything on dry l died. Gn 7:22
and Calneh, in the l of Shinar. Gn 10:10
From that l he went to Assyria Gn 10:11
a valley in the l of Shinar and Gn 11:2
Haran died in his native l, Gn 11:28
to go to the l of Canaan. Gn 11:31
out from your l, your relatives Gn 12:1
house to the l that I will show Gn 12:1
set out for the l of Canaan. Gn 12:5
they came to the l of Canaan, Gn 12:5
passed through the l to the site Gn 12:6
the Canaanites were in the l. Gn 12:6
I will give this l to your Gn 12:7
There was a famine in the l, Gn 12:10
the famine in the l was severe. Gn 12:10
But the l was unable to support Gn 13:6
Perizzites were living in the l. Gn 13:7
Isn't the whole l before you? Gn 13:9
garden and the l of Egypt. Gn 13:10
Abram lived in the l of Canaan, Gn 13:12
forever all the l that you see. Gn 13:15
one end of the l to the other, Gn 13:17
to give you this l to possess." Gn 15:7
strangers in a l that does not Gn 15:13
I give this l to your offspring, Gn 15:18
⌊the l of⌋ the Kenites, Gn 15:19
had lived in the l of Canaan 10 Gn 16:3
I will give the l where you are Gn 17:8
all the l of Canaan—as Gn 17:8
over the l when Lot reached Gn 19:23
and all the l of the plain, Gn 19:28
up from the l like the smoke Gn 19:28
no man in the l to sleep with us Gn 19:31
as is⌋ the custom of all the l. Gn 19:31
said, "Look, my l is before you. Gn 20:15

for him from the **l** of Egypt.	Gn 21:21
returned to the **l** of the	Gn 21:32
foreigner in the **l** of the	Gn 21:34
you love, go to the **l** of Moriah,	Gn 22:2
is, Hebron) in the **l** of Canaan,	Gn 23:2
Hittites, the people of the **l**.	Gn 23:7
down to the people of the **l**	Gn 23:12
presence of the people of the **l**,	Gn 23:13
L worth 400 shekels of silver—	Gn 23:15
is, Hebron) in the **l** of Canaan.	Gn 23:19
will go to my **l** and my family to	Gn 24:4
to follow me to this **l**?	Gn 24:5
son go back to the **l** you came	Gn 24:5
house and from my native **l**,	Gn 24:7
I will give this **l** to your	Gn 24:7
the Canaanites in whose **l** I live	Gn 24:37
son Isaac, to the **l** of the East.	Gn 25:6
famine in the **l** in addition to	Gn 26:1
Live in the **l** that I tell you	Gn 26:2
stay in this **l** as a foreigner,	Gn 26:3
Isaac sowed seed in that **l**,	Gn 26:12
we will be fruitful in the **l**."	Gn 26:22
and from the richness of the **l**—	Gn 27:28
away from the richness of the **l**,	Gn 27:39
may possess the **l** where you live	Gn 28:4
the **l** God gave to Abraham."	Gn 28:4
offspring the **l** that you are now	Gn 28:13
I will bring you back to this **l**,	Gn 28:15
Go back to the **l** of your fathers	Gn 31:3
up, leave this **l**, and return to	Gn 31:13
and return to your native **l**.' "	Gn 31:13
to go to the **l** of his father	Gn 31:18
brother Esau in the **l** of Seir,	Gn 32:3
'Go back to your **l** and to your	Gn 32:9
with us. The **l** is before you.	Gn 34:10
live in our **l** and move about	Gn 34:21
to the inhabitants of the **l**,	Gn 34:30
is, Bethel) in the **l** of Canaan.	Gn 35:6
The **l** that I gave to Abraham and	Gn 35:12
I will give the **l** to your	Gn 35:12
born to him in the **l** of Canaan.	Gn 36:5
he went to a **l** away from his	Gn 36:6
l where they stayed could not	Gn 36:7
of Eliphaz in the **l** of Edom.	Gn 36:16
of Reuel in the **l** of Edom.	Gn 36:17
the inhabitants of the **l**:	Gn 36:20
sons of Seir, in the **l** of Edom.	Gn 36:21
divisions, in the **l** of Seir.	Gn 36:30
ruled in the **l** of Edom before	Gn 36:31
Husham from the **l** of the	Gn 36:34
in the **l** they possessed.	Gn 36:43
lived in the **l** where his father	Gn 37:1
had stayed, the **l** of Canaan.	Gn 37:1
from the **l** of the Hebrews,	Gn 40:15
as these in all the **l** of Egypt.	Gn 41:19
throughout the **l** of Egypt.	Gn 41:29
in the **l** of Egypt will be	Gn 41:30
The famine will devastate the **l**.	Gn 41:30
abundance in the **l** will not be	Gn 41:31
and set him over the **l** of Egypt.	Gn 41:33
over the **l** and take one-fifth	Gn 41:34
harvest⌋ of the **l** of Egypt	Gn 41:34
reserve for the **l** during the	Gn 41:36
take place in the **l** of Egypt.	Gn 41:36
you over all the **l** of Egypt."	Gn 41:41
him over all the **l** of Egypt.	Gn 41:43
or foot in all the **l** of Egypt."	Gn 41:44
went throughout the **l** of Egypt.	Gn 41:45
throughout the **l** of Egypt.	Gn 41:46
of abundance the **l** produced	Gn 41:47
food in the **l** of Egypt during	Gn 41:48
in the **l** of my affliction.	Gn 41:52
in the **l** of Egypt came to	Gn 41:53
throughout the **l** of Egypt there	Gn 41:54
came to all the **l** of Egypt,	Gn 41:55
was severe in the **l** of Egypt.	Gn 41:56
famine was in the **l** of Canaan.	Gn 42:5
the **l** of Canaan to buy food,	Gn 42:7
to see the weakness of the **l**."	Gn 42:9
to see the weakness of the **l**."	Gn 42:12
of one man in the **l** of Canaan.	Gn 42:13
father Jacob in the **l** of Canaan,	Gn 42:29
our father in the **l** of Canaan.	Gn 42:32
the famine in the **l** was severe.	Gn 43:1
products of the **l** in your packs	Gn 43:11
to you from the **l** of Canaan the	Gn 44:8
been in the **l** these two years	Gn 45:6
within the **l** and to keep you	Gn 45:7
ruler over all the **l** of Egypt.	Gn 45:8
settle in the **l** of Goshen and be	Gn 45:10
go on back to the **l** of Canaan.	Gn 45:17
you the best of the **l** of Egypt,	Gn 45:18
eat from the richness of the **l**.'	Gn 45:18
wagons from the **l** of Egypt for	Gn 45:19
best of all the **l** of Egypt is	Gn 45:20
father Jacob in the **l** of Canaan.	Gn 45:25
ruler over all the **l** of Egypt!"	Gn 45:26
had acquired in the **l** of Canaan.	Gn 46:6
Onan died in the **l** of Canaan.	Gn 46:12
to Joseph in the **l** of Egypt.	Gn 46:20
they came to the **l** of Goshen,	Gn 46:28
who were in the **l** of Canaan,	Gn 46:31
to settle in the **l** of Goshen,	Gn 46:34
come from the **l** of Canaan and	Gn 47:1
and are now in the **l** of Goshen."	Gn 47:1
to live in the **l** for a while	Gn 47:4
no grazing **l** for your servants'	Gn 47:4
famine in the **l** of Canaan has	Gn 47:4
settle in the **l** of Goshen."	Gn 47:4
the **l** of Egypt is open before	Gn 47:6
in the best part of the **l**.	Gn 47:6
can live in the **l** of Goshen.	Gn 47:6
brothers in the **l** of Egypt and	Gn 47:11
in the best part of the **l**,	Gn 47:11
the land, the **l** of Rameses, as	Gn 47:11
The **l** of Egypt and the land of	Gn 47:13
Egypt and the **l** of Canaan were	Gn 47:13
be found in the **l** of Egypt and	Gn 47:14
of Egypt and the **l** of Canaan in	Gn 47:14
money from the **l** of Egypt and	Gn 47:15
of Egypt and the **l** of Canaan was	Gn 47:15
except our bodies and our **l**.	Gn 47:18
of you—both us and our **l**?	Gn 47:19
Buy us and our **l** in exchange for	Gn 47:19
Then we with our **l** will become	Gn 47:19
and so that the **l** won't become	Gn 47:19
acquired all the **l** in Egypt for	Gn 47:20
The **l** became Pharaoh's,	Gn 47:20
The only **l** he didn't acquire was	Gn 47:22
they did not sell their **l**.	Gn 47:22
you and your **l** for Pharaoh.	Gn 47:23
seed for you. Sow it in the **l**.	Gn 47:23
effect today in the **l** of Egypt,	Gn 47:26
the priests' **l** does not belong	Gn 47:26
settled in the **l** of Egypt,	Gn 47:27
lived in the **l** of Egypt 17 years	Gn 47:28
to me at Luz in the **l** of Canaan	Gn 48:3
I will give this **l** as an eternal	Gn 48:4
to you in the **l** of Egypt before	Gn 48:5
from Ephrath in the **l** of Canaan.	Gn 48:7
to be numerous within the **l**.	Gn 48:16
back to the **l** of your fathers	Gn 48:21
and that the **l** was pleasant,	Gn 49:15
near Mamre, in the **l** of Canaan.	Gn 49:30
for myself in the **l** of Canaan.'	Gn 50:5
elders of the **l** of Egypt went	Gn 50:7
were left in the **l** of Goshen.	Gn 50:8
of the **l** saw the mourning	Gn 50:11
carried him to the **l** of Canaan	Gn 50:13
you up from this **l** to the land	Gn 50:24
this land to the **l** He promised	Gn 50:24
so that the **l** was filled with	Ex 1:7
went to live in the **l** of Midian,	Ex 2:15
a stranger in a foreign **l**."	Ex 2:22
bring them from that **l** to a good	Ex 3:8
land to a good and spacious **l**,	Ex 3:8
l flowing with milk and honey—	Ex 3:8
of Egypt to the **l** of the	Ex 3:17
a **l** flowing with milk and honey.	Ex 3:17
and set out for the **l** of Egypt.	Ex 4:20
people of the **l** are so numerous	Ex 5:5
throughout the **l** of Egypt to	Ex 5:12
them out of his **l** because of My	Ex 6:1
to give them the **l** of Canaan,	Ex 6:4
the **l** they lived in as	Ex 6:4
you to the **l** that I swore to	Ex 6:8
the Israelites go from his **l**."	Ex 6:11
out of the **l** of Egypt.	Ex 6:13
out of the **l** of Egypt according	Ex 6:26
to Moses in the **l** of Egypt,	Ex 6:28
the Israelites go from his **l**.	Ex 7:2
and wonders in the **l** of Egypt.	Ex 7:3
out of the **l** of Egypt by great	Ex 7:4
blood throughout the **l** of Egypt,	Ex 7:19
blood throughout the **l** of Egypt.	Ex 7:21
to come up onto the **l** of Egypt."	Ex 8:5
up and covered the **l** of Egypt.	Ex 8:6
frogs up onto the **l** of Egypt.	Ex 8:7
was a terrible odor in the **l**.	Ex 8:14
throughout the **l** of Egypt."	Ex 8:16
gnats throughout the **l** of Egypt.	Ex 8:17
so will the **l** where they live	Ex 8:21
treatment to the **l** of Goshen,	Ex 8:22
that I, the LORD, am in the **l**.	Ex 8:22
Egypt the **l** was ruined because	Ex 8:24
will do this thing in the **l**."	Ex 9:5
dust over the entire **l** of Egypt.	Ex 9:9
throughout the **l** of Egypt."	Ex 9:9
hail throughout the **l** of Egypt—	Ex 9:22
of the field in the **l** of Egypt."	Ex 9:22
rained hail on the **l** of Egypt.	Ex 9:23
occurred in the **l** of Egypt since	Ex 9:24
Throughout the **l** of Egypt,	Ex 9:25
was in the **l** of Goshen where	Ex 9:26
no longer poured down on the **l**.	Ex 9:33
surface of the **l** so that no one	Ex 10:5
one will be able to see the **l**.	Ex 10:5
occupied the **l** until today."	Ex 10:6
your hand over the **l** of Egypt	Ex 10:12
it and eat every plant in the **l**,	Ex 10:12
his staff over the **l** of Egypt,	Ex 10:13
east wind over the **l** all that	Ex 10:13
over the entire **l** of Egypt and	Ex 10:14
of the whole **l** so that the land	Ex 10:15
land so that the **l** was black,	Ex 10:15
field throughout the **l** of Egypt.	Ex 10:15
be darkness over the **l** of Egypt,	Ex 10:21
throughout the **l** of Egypt for	Ex 10:22
was feared in the **l** of Egypt,	Ex 11:3
in the **l** of Egypt will die,	Ex 11:5
through all the **l** of Egypt such	Ex 11:6
multiplied in the **l** of Egypt."	Ex 11:9
the Israelites go out of his **l**.	Ex 11:10
and Aaron in the **l** of Egypt:	Ex 12:1
through the **l** of Egypt on that	Ex 12:12
male⌋ in the **l** of Egypt,	Ex 12:12
when I strike the **l** of Egypt.	Ex 12:13
ranks out of the **l** of Egypt.	Ex 12:17
resident or native of the **l**,	Ex 12:19
you enter the **l** that the LORD	Ex 12:25
male⌋ in the **l** of Egypt,	Ex 12:29
went out from the **l** of Egypt.	Ex 12:41
them out of the **l** of Egypt.	Ex 12:42
become like a native of the **l**.	Ex 12:48
out of the **l** of Egypt according	Ex 12:51
you into the **l** of the Canaanites	Ex 13:5
a **l** flowing with milk and honey,	Ex 13:5
you into the **l** of the Canaanites	Ex 13:11
male⌋ in the **l** of Egypt,	Ex 13:15
the road to the **l** of the	Ex 13:17
left the **l** of Egypt in battle	Ex 13:18
around the **l** in confusion;	Ex 14:3
and turned the sea into dry **l**.	Ex 14:21
they had left the **l** of Egypt.	Ex 16:1
LORD's hand in the **l** of Egypt,	Ex 16:3
you out of the **l** of Egypt;	Ex 16:6
you out of the **l** of Egypt.' "	Ex 16:32
they came to an inhabited **l**.	Ex 16:35
the border of the **l** of Canaan.	Ex 16:35
been a stranger in a foreign **l**"	Ex 18:3
and he journeyed to his own **l**.	Ex 18:27
had left the **l** of Egypt,	Ex 19:1
you out of the **l** of Egypt,	Ex 20:2
long life in the **l** that the LORD	Ex 20:12
foreigners in the **l** of Egypt.	Ex 22:21
foreigners in the **l** of Egypt.	Ex 23:9
Sow your **l** for six years and	Ex 23:10
of your **l** to the house	Ex 23:19
you to ⌊the **l** of⌋ the Amorites	Ex 23:23
miscarry or be barren in your **l**.	Ex 23:26
the **l** would become desolate,	Ex 23:29
and take possession of the **l**.	Ex 23:30
of the **l** under your control	Ex 23:31
They must not remain in your **l**,	Ex 23:33
them out of the **l** of Egypt,	Ex 29:46
us up from the **l** of Egypt—	Ex 32:1
you up from the **l** of Egypt!"	Ex 32:4
up from the **l** of Egypt have	Ex 32:7
you up from the **l** of Egypt.' "	Ex 32:8
out of the **l** of Egypt with	Ex 32:11
offspring all this **l** that I have	Ex 32:13
us up from the **l** of Egypt—	Ex 32:23
brought up from the **l** of Egypt,	Ex 33:1
to the **l** I promised to Abraham,	Ex 33:1

⌊Go up⌋ to a l flowing with milk Ex 33:3
of the l that you are going Ex 34:12
with the inhabitants of the l, Ex 34:15
will covet your l when you go up Ex 34:24
of your l to the house Ex 34:26
all these ⌊kinds⌋ of l animals. Lv 11:2
you up from the l of Egypt to be Lv 11:45
you enter the l of Canaan that I Lv 14:34
in a house in the l you possess, Lv 14:34
wrongdoings into a desolate l, Lv 16:22
the practices of the l of Egypt, Lv 18:3
practices of the l of Canaan, Lv 18:3
The l has become defiled, so I Lv 18:25
and the l will vomit out its Lv 18:25
who were in the l prior to you Lv 18:27
and the l has become defiled. Lv 18:27
you defile the l, it will vomit Lv 18:28
you reap the harvest of your l, Lv 19:9
come into the l and plant any Lv 19:23
or the l will be prostituted and Lv 19:29
lives with you in your l, Lv 19:33
foreigners in the l of Egypt; Lv 19:34
you out of the l of Egypt. Lv 19:36
that the l where I am bringing Lv 20:22
inherit their l, since I will Lv 20:24
a l flowing with milk and honey. Lv 20:24
detestable by any l animal, Lv 20:25
not sacrifice ⌊them⌋ in your l. Lv 22:24
you out of the l of Egypt to be Lv 22:33
you enter the l I am giving you Lv 23:10
you reap the harvest of your l, Lv 23:22
gathered the produce of the l. Lv 23:39
them out of the l of Egypt; Lv 23:43
you enter the l I am giving you, Lv 25:2
the l will observe a Sabbath to Lv 25:2
rest for the l in the seventh Lv 25:4
year of complete rest for the l. Lv 25:5
⌊Whatever⌋ the l ⌊produces Lv 25:6
and the wild animals in your l. Lv 25:7
it throughout your l on the Day Lv 25:9
freedom in the l for all its Lv 25:10
you may live securely in the l. Lv 25:18
Then the l will yield its fruit, Lv 25:19
and live securely in the l. Lv 25:19
The l is not to be permanently Lv 25:23
and temporary residents on My l. Lv 25:23
redemption of any l you occupy. Lv 25:24
obtains enough to redeem his l, Lv 25:26
out of the l of Egypt to give Lv 25:38
to give you the l of Canaan and Lv 25:38
I brought out of the l of Egypt. Lv 25:42
you—those born in your l. Lv 25:45
I brought out of the l of Egypt; Lv 25:55
stone in your l to bow down to Lv 26:1
the l will yield its produce, Lv 26:4
eat and live securely in your l. Lv 26:5
I will give peace to the l, Lv 26:6
dangerous animals from the l, Lv 26:6
sword will pass through your l. Lv 26:6
you out of the l of Egypt, Lv 26:13
iron and your l like bronze, Lv 26:19
Your l will not yield its Lv 26:20
the trees of the l will not bear Lv 26:20
I also will devastate the l, Lv 26:32
So your l will become desolate, Lv 26:33
Then the l will make up for its Lv 26:34
are in the l of your enemies. Lv 26:34
At that time the l will rest and Lv 26:34
l of your enemies will devour Lv 26:38
them into the l of their enemies Lv 26:41
and I will remember the l. Lv 26:42
For the l abandoned by them will Lv 26:43
they are in the l of their Lv 26:44
I brought out of the l of Egypt Lv 26:45
departure from the l of Egypt: Nm 1:1
firstborn in the l of Egypt, Nm 3:13
firstborn in the l of Egypt. Nm 8:17
departure from the l of Egypt, Nm 9:1
and the native of the l." Nm 9:14
into battle in your l against an Nm 10:9
go to my own l and my relatives. Nm 10:30
to the l that You swore to Nm 11:12
scout out the l of Canaan I am Nm 13:2
Moses sent to scout out the l, Nm 13:16
to scout out the l of Canaan, Nm 13:17
See what the l is like, and Nm 13:18
Is the l they live in good or Nm 13:19
the l fertile or unproductive? Nm 13:20

back some fruit from the l." Nm 13:20
scouted out the l from the Nm 13:21
from scouting out the l. Nm 13:25
showed them the fruit of the l. Nm 13:26
went into the l where you sent Nm 13:27
living in the l are strong, Nm 13:28
living in the l of the Negev; Nm 13:29
of the l because we can Nm 13:30
about the l they had scouted: Nm 13:32
The l we passed through to Nm 13:32
we had died in the l of Egypt, Nm 14:2
us into this l to die by the Nm 14:3
those who scouted out the l, Nm 14:6
The l we passed through and Nm 14:7
explored is an extremely good l. Nm 14:7
He will bring us into this l, Nm 14:8
a l flowing with milk and honey, Nm 14:8
afraid of the people of the l, Nm 14:9
to⌋ the inhabitants of this l. Nm 14:14
people into the l He swore to Nm 14:16
ever see the l I swore to ⌊give Nm 14:23
him into the l where he has gone Nm 14:24
will enter the l I promised to Nm 14:30
plunder into the l you rejected, Nm 14:31
40 days that you scouted the l, Nm 14:34
Moses sent to scout out the l, Nm 14:36
a bad report about the l— Nm 14:36
about the l were struck down Nm 14:37
men who went to scout out the l. Nm 14:38
you enter the l I am giving you Nm 15:2
you enter the l where I am Nm 15:18
you eat from the food of the l. Nm 15:19
you out of the l of Egypt to be Nm 15:41
us up from a l flowing with milk Nm 16:13
bring us to a l flowing with Nm 16:14
of all that is in their l, Nm 18:13
have an inheritance in their l; Nm 18:20
into the l I have given them Nm 20:12
let us travel through your l. Nm 20:17
must not travel through our l, Nm 20:18
on the border of the l of Edom, Nm 20:23
not enter the l I have given Nm 20:24
Red Sea to bypass the l of Edom, Nm 21:4
Let us travel through your l. Nm 21:22
of his l from the Arnon to Nm 21:24
control of all his l as far as Nm 21:26
Israel lived in the Amorites' l. Nm 21:31
with his whole army and his l. Nm 21:34
they took possession of his l. Nm 21:35
in the l of his people. Nm 22:5
surface of the l and are living Nm 22:5
and drive them out of the l, Nm 22:6
they cover the surface of the l. Nm 22:11
Go back to your l, because the Nm 22:13
who came out of the l of Egypt." Nm 26:4
they died in the l of Canaan. Nm 26:19
The l is to be divided among Nm 26:53
The l must be divided by lot; Nm 26:55
and see the l that I have given Nm 27:12
is ⌊good⌋ l for livestock, Nm 32:4
let this l be given to your Nm 32:5
crossing into the l the LORD has Nm 32:7
from Kadesh-barnea to see the l. Nm 32:8
as Eshcol Valley and saw the l, Nm 32:9
from entering the l the LORD had Nm 32:9
will see the l I swore ⌊to give Nm 32:11
of the inhabitants of the l. Nm 32:17
and the l is subdued before the Nm 32:22
And this l will belong to you as Nm 32:22
and the l is subdued before you, Nm 32:29
to give them the l of Gilead as Nm 32:29
must accept l in Canaan with Nm 32:30
the LORD into the l of Canaan, Nm 32:32
the l including its cities with Nm 32:33
went out of the l of Egypt by Nm 33:1
on the edge of the l of Edom. Nm 33:37
went out of the l of Egypt. Nm 33:38
in the Negev in the l of Canaan, Nm 33:40
the Jordan into the l of Canaan, Nm 33:51
inhabitants of the l before you, Nm 33:52
of the l and settle in it Nm 33:53
have given you the l to possess. Nm 33:53
to receive the l as an Nm 33:54
inhabitants of the l before you, Nm 33:55
you in the l where you will Nm 33:55
When you enter the l of Canaan, Nm 34:2
will be your l ⌊defined⌋ by its Nm 34:12
This is the l you are to receive Nm 34:13

distribute the l as an Nm 34:17
each tribe to distribute the l. Nm 34:18
Israelites in the l of Canaan. Nm 34:29
the Jordan into the l of Canaan, Nm 35:10
cities in the l of Canaan to be Nm 35:14
return to the l he possesses. Nm 35:28
and live in the l before the Nm 35:32
not defile the l where you are, Nm 35:33
for bloodshed defiles the l, Nm 35:33
atonement for the l because of Nm 35:33
Do not make the l unclean where Nm 35:34
lord to give the l as an Nm 36:2
the Jordan in the l of Moab, Dt 1:5
the l of the Canaanites and to Dt 1:7
I have set the l before you. Dt 1:8
of the l the LORD swore to Dt 1:8
God has set the l before you. Dt 1:21
may explore the l for us and Dt 1:22
of Eshcol, scouting the l. Dt 1:24
fruit from the l in their hands, Dt 1:25
'The l the LORD our God is Dt 1:25
us out of the l of Egypt to Dt 1:27
see the good l I swore to give Dt 1:35
descendants the l on which he Dt 1:36
give them the l, and they will Dt 1:39
not give you any of their l, Dt 2:5
any of their l as a possession Dt 2:9
did in the l of its possession Dt 2:12
the Ammonites' l as a possession Dt 2:19
as the l of the Rephaim. Dt 2:20
Heshbon, and his l over to you. Dt 2:24
'Let us travel through your l; Dt 2:27
Jordan into the l the LORD our Dt 2:29
not let us travel through his l, Dt 2:30
to give Sihon and his l to you. Dt 2:31
not go near the Ammonites' l, Dt 2:37
with his whole army and his l. Dt 3:2
time we took the l from the two Dt 3:8
we took possession of this l. Dt 3:12
be called the l of the Rephaim. Dt 3:13
has given you this l to possess. Dt 3:18
of the l the LORD your God Dt 3:20
the beautiful l on the other Dt 3:25
to inherit this l that you will Dt 3:28
possession of the l the LORD, Dt 4:1
them in the l you are entering Dt 4:5
follow in the l you are about to Dt 4:14
enter the good l the LORD your Dt 4:21
I am going to die in this l. Dt 4:22
take possession of this good l. Dt 4:22
have been in the l a long time, Dt 4:25
perish from the l you are about Dt 4:26
give you their l as an Dt 4:38
live long in the l the LORD your Dt 4:40
the wilderness on the plateau l, Dt 4:43
Beth-peor in the l of Sihon king Dt 4:46
possession of his l and the land Dt 4:47
of his land and the l of Og king Dt 4:47
you out of the l of Egypt, Dt 5:6
were a slave in the l of Egypt, Dt 5:15
prosper in the l the LORD your Dt 5:16
them⌋ in the l I am giving them Dt 5:31
life in the l you will possess Dt 5:33
them⌋ in the l you are about to Dt 6:1
promised you a l flowing with Dt 6:3
you into the l He swore to your Dt 6:10
a ⌊l with⌋ large and beautiful Dt 6:10
you out of the l of Egypt, Dt 6:12
possess the good l the LORD your Dt 6:18
and give us the l that He swore Dt 6:23
you into the l you are entering Dt 7:1
the l He swore to your fathers Dt 7:13
of the l the LORD swore to Dt 8:1
is bringing you into a good l, Dt 8:7
a l with streams of water, Dt 8:7
a l of wheat, barley, vines, Dt 8:8
a l of olive oil and honey; Dt 8:8
a l where you will eat food Dt 8:9
l whose rocks are iron and from Dt 8:9
for the good l He has given you Dt 8:10
you out of the l of Egypt, Dt 8:14
a thirsty l where there was no Dt 8:15
of this l because of my Dt 9:4
of their l because of your Dt 9:5
you this good l to possess Dt 9:6
you left the l of Egypt until Dt 9:7
possess the l I have given you' Dt 9:23
those in the l you brought us Dt 9:28

them into the l He had promised Dt 9:28
a l with streams of water. Dt 10:7
possess the l I swore to give Dt 10:11
foreigners in the l of Egypt. Dt 10:19
king of Egypt and all his l; Dt 11:3
and possess the l you are to Dt 11:8
long in the l the LORD swore Dt 11:9
a l flowing with milk and honey. Dt 11:9
For the l you are entering to Dt 11:10
is not like the l of Egypt, Dt 11:10
But the l you are entering to Dt 11:11
to possess is a l of mountains Dt 11:11
is a l the LORD your God cares Dt 11:12
rain for your l in season, Dt 11:14
l will not yield its produce, Dt 11:17
from the good l the LORD is Dt 11:17
be many in the l the LORD swore Dt 11:21
you in all the l where you set Dt 11:25
you into the l you are entering Dt 11:29
road in the l of the Canaanites Dt 11:30
of the l the LORD your God Dt 11:31
in the l that the LORD, Dt 12:1
and live in the l the LORD your Dt 12:10
as long as you live in your l. Dt 12:19
them out and live in their l, Dt 12:29
you out of the l of Egypt and Dt 13:5
you out of the l of Egypt, Dt 13:10
bless you in the l the LORD your Dt 15:4
gates in the l the LORD your God Dt 15:7
to be poor people in the l; Dt 15:11
and poor brother in your l.' Dt 15:11
were a slave in the l of Egypt Dt 15:15
you left the l of Egypt in a Dt 16:3
the day you left the l of Egypt. Dt 16:3
and possess the l the LORD your Dt 16:20
you enter the l the LORD your Dt 17:14
you enter the l the LORD your Dt 18:9
nations whose l He is giving you Dt 19:1
within the l the LORD your God Dt 19:2
and divide the l the LORD your Dt 19:3
you all the l He promised to Dt 19:8
bloodshed in the l the LORD your Dt 19:10
receive in the l the LORD your Dt 19:14
you out of the l of Egypt, Dt 20:1
a field in the l the LORD your Dt 21:1
not defile the l the LORD your Dt 21:23
a foreign resident in his l. Dt 23:7
you do in the l you are entering Dt 23:20
guilt on the l the LORD your God Dt 24:4
within a town in your l. Dt 24:14
were a slave in the l of Egypt. Dt 24:22
live long in the l the LORD your Dt 25:15
you in the l the LORD your God Dt 25:19
you enter the l the LORD your Dt 26:1
harvest from the l the LORD your Dt 26:2
entered the l the LORD swore Dt 26:3
this place and gave us this l, Dt 26:9
a l flowing with milk and honey. Dt 26:9
Israel and the l You have given Dt 26:15
a l flowing with milk and honey. Dt 26:15
Jordan into the l the LORD your Dt 27:2
to enter the l the LORD your God Dt 27:3
a l flowing with milk and honey, Dt 27:3
bless you in the l the LORD your Dt 28:8
produce in the l the LORD swore Dt 28:11
give your l rain in its season Dt 28:12
you from the l you are entering Dt 28:21
the rain of your l into falling Dt 28:24
and the wild animals of the l, Dt 28:26
come down throughout your l. Dt 28:52
throughout the l the LORD your Dt 28:52
from the l you are entering Dt 28:63
the Israelites in the l of Moab, Dt 29:1
officials, and to his entire l. Dt 29:2
took their l and gave it as an Dt 29:8
we lived in the l of Egypt and Dt 29:16
the well-watered ⌊l⌋ as well as Dt 29:19
land⌋ as well as the dry ⌊l⌋. Dt 29:19
plagues of the l and the Dt 29:22
the LORD done this to this l? Dt 29:24
them out of the l of Egypt. Dt 29:25
anger burned against this l, Dt 29:27
from their l in ⌊His⌋ anger, Dt 29:28
into another l where they are Dt 29:28
you into the l your fathers Dt 30:5
you in the l you are entering Dt 30:16
long in the l you are entering Dt 30:18
life in the l the LORD swore Dt 30:20

and their l when He destroyed Dt 31:4
people into the l the LORD swore Dt 31:7
you live in the l you are Dt 31:13
gods of the l they are entering Dt 31:16
into the l I swore to ⌊give⌋ Dt 31:20
⌊a l⌋ flowing with milk and Dt 31:20
them into the l I swore ⌊to give Dt 31:21
into the l I swore to them, Dt 31:23
He found him in a desolate l, Dt 32:10
the heights of the l and eat the Dt 32:13
devours the l and its produce, Dt 32:22
purify His l and His people. Dt 32:43
long in the l you are crossing Dt 32:47
Abarim ⌊range⌋ in the l of Moab, Dt 32:49
and view the l of Canaan I am Dt 32:49
will view the l from a distance Dt 32:52
May his l be blessed by the LORD Dt 33:13
gifts of the l and everything Dt 33:16
untroubled in a l of grain and Dt 33:28
the LORD showed him all the l: Dt 34:1
the l of Ephraim and Manasseh, Dt 34:2
all the l of Judah as far as the Dt 34:2
This is the l I promised Dt 34:4
died there in the l of Moab, Dt 34:5
valley in the l of Moab facing Dt 34:6
to do against the l of Egypt— Dt 34:11
his officials, and to all his l, Dt 34:11
the Jordan to the l I am giving Jos 1:2
all the l of the Hittites— Jos 1:4
distribute the l I swore to Jos 1:6
of the l the LORD your God Jos 1:11
and He will give you this l.' Jos 1:13
remain in the l Moses gave you Jos 1:14
too possess the l the LORD your Jos 1:15
then return to the l of your Jos 1:15
Go and scout the l, especially Jos 2:1
tonight to investigate the l." Jos 2:2
to investigate the entire l." Jos 2:3
given you this l and that dread Jos 2:9
who lives in the l is panicking Jos 2:9
when the LORD gives us the l." Jos 2:14
we enter the l, you tie this Jos 2:18
handed over the entire l to us." Jos 2:24
who lives in the l is also Jos 2:24
them see the l He had sworn to Jos 5:6
a l flowing with milk and honey. Jos 5:6
grain from the produce of the l. Jos 5:11
ate from the produce of the l, Jos 5:12
crops of the l of Canaan that Jos 5:12
two men who had scouted the l, Jos 6:22
fame spread throughout the l. Jos 6:27
them, "Go up and scout the l." Jos 7:2
live in the l hear about this Jos 7:9
of Ai, his people, city, and l. Jos 8:1
We have come from a distant l. Jos 9:6
come from a far away l because Jos 9:9
inhabitants of our l told us, Jos 9:11
you all the l and to destroy Jos 9:24
inhabitants of the l before you. Jos 9:24
and all the l of Goshen as far Jos 10:41
and their l in one campaign Jos 10:42
of Hermon in the l of Mizpah. Jos 11:3
So Joshua took all this l— Jos 11:16
the Negev, all the l of Goshen, Jos 11:16
were left in the l of the Jos 11:22
So Joshua took the entire l, Jos 11:23
After this, the l had rest from Jos 11:23
kings of the l and took Jos 12:1
of their l beyond the Jordan Jos 12:1
gave their l as an inheritance Jos 12:6
kings of the l beyond the Jordan Jos 12:7
gave their l as an inheritance Jos 12:7
great deal of the l remains to Jos 13:1
This is the l that remains: Jos 13:2
all the l of the Canaanites: Jos 13:4
the l of the Gebalites; Jos 13:5
distribute the l as an Jos 13:6
divide this l as an inheritance Jos 13:7
of Sihon who lived in the l. Jos 13:21
and half the l of the Ammonites Jos 13:25
⌊Their l also included⌋ the Jos 13:27
gave them in the l of Canaan. Jos 14:1
No portion of the l was given to Jos 14:4
Moses, and they divided the l. Jos 14:5
Kadesh-barnea to scout the l, Jos 14:7
'The l where you have set foot Jos 14:9
After this, the l had rest from Jos 14:15
have given me l in the Negev, Jos 15:19

besides the l of Gilead and Jos 17:5
The l of Gilead belonged to the Jos 17:6
determined to stay in this l. Jos 17:12
there in the l of the Perizzites Jos 17:15
the l had been subdued by them. Jos 18:1
of the l that the LORD, Jos 18:3
They are to go and survey the l, Jos 18:4
portions of l and brought it to Jos 18:6
down a description of the l, Jos 18:8
Go and survey the l, write a Jos 18:8
through the l, and described Jos 18:9
distributed the l to the Jos 18:10
distributing the l into its Jos 19:49
they finished dividing up the l. Jos 19:51
at Shiloh in the l of Canaan: Jos 21:2
Israel all the l He had sworn to Jos 21:43
homes in your own l that Moses Jos 22:4
Shiloh in the l of Canaan to go Jos 22:9
to go to their own l of Gilead, Jos 22:9
the Jordan in the l of Canaan, Jos 22:10
frontier of the l of Canaan at Jos 22:11
of Manasseh, in the l of Gilead. Jos 22:13
Manasseh, in the l of Gilead, Jos 22:15
But if the l you possess is Jos 22:19
cross over to the l the LORD Jos 22:19
and Gadites in the l of Gilead Jos 22:32
Israelites in the l of Canaan Jos 22:32
them to ravage the l where the Jos 22:33
can take possession of their l, Jos 23:5
from this good l the LORD your Jos 23:13
from this good l the LORD your Jos 23:15
this good l He has given you. Jos 23:16
him throughout the l of Canaan, Jos 24:3
you to the l of the Amorites Jos 24:8
possessed their l, and I Jos 24:8
I gave you a l you did not labor Jos 24:13
in whose l you are living. Jos 24:15
fathers out of the l of Egypt, Jos 24:17
the Amorites who lived in the l. Jos 24:18
in the parcel of l Jacob had Jos 24:32
have handed the l over to him." Jdg 1:2
have given me l in the Negev, Jdg 1:15
went to the l of the Hittites Jdg 1:26
refused to leave this l. Jdg 1:27
who were living in the l. Jdg 1:32
who were living in the l, Jdg 1:33
you into the l I had promised Jdg 2:1
people who are living in this l, Jdg 2:2
to take possession of the l, Jdg 2:6
the l was peaceful 40 years, Jdg 3:11
and the l was peaceful 80 years. Jdg 3:30
And the l was peaceful 40 years. Jdg 5:31
destroyed the produce of the l, Jdg 6:4
they entered the l to waste it. Jdg 6:5
before you and gave you their l. Jdg 6:9
of the Amorites whose l you live Jdg 6:10
The l was peaceful 40 years Jdg 8:28
from the central part of the l, Jdg 9:37
Jordan in the l of the Amorites Jdg 10:8
and lived in the l of Tob. Jdg 11:3
get Jephthah from the l of Tob. Jdg 11:5
to fight against me in my l?" Jdg 11:12
they seized my l from the Arnon Jdg 11:13
not take away the l of Moab or Jdg 11:15
of Moab or the l of the Jdg 11:15
let us travel through your l,' Jdg 11:17
east side of the l of Moab and Jdg 11:18
through your l to our country,' Jdg 11:19
of the entire l of the Amorites Jdg 11:21
in Aijalon in the l of Zebulun. Jdg 12:12
in Pirathon in the l of Ephraim, Jdg 12:15
who destroyed our l and who Jdg 16:24
to spy out the l and explore it. Jdg 18:2
them, "Go and explore the l." Jdg 18:2
lacking in the l and no Jdg 18:7
have seen the l, and it is very Jdg 18:9
and take possession of the l! Jdg 18:9
people and a wide-open l, Jdg 18:10
to spy out the l of Laish told Jdg 18:14
spy out the l went in and took Jdg 18:17
time of the exile from the l. Jdg 18:30
came out of the l of Egypt to Jdg 19:30
and from the l of Gilead came Jdg 20:1
at Shiloh in the l of Canaan. Jdg 21:12
and go to the l of Benjamin. Jdg 21:21
there was a famine in the l. Ru 1:1
to live in the l of Moab for a Ru 1:1
They entered the l of Moab and Ru 1:2

prepared to leave the l of Moab, Ru 1:6
leading back to the l of Judah. Ru 1:7
back from the l of Moab with her Ru 1:22
the portion of l belonging to Ru 2:3
with Naomi from the l of Moab. Ru 2:6
mother, and the l of your birth, Ru 2:11
has returned from the l of Moab, Ru 4:3
a piece of l that belonged to Ru 4:3
day you buy the l from Naomi, Ru 4:5
had been in the l of the 1Sm 6:1
mice that are destroying the l. 1Sm 6:5
you, your gods, and your l. 1Sm 6:5
When they came to the l of Zuph, 1Sm 9:5
a man from the l of Benjamin. 1Sm 9:16
at Zelzah in the l of Benjamin. 1Sm 10:2
them throughout the l of Israel 1Sm 11:7
up from the l of Egypt, 1Sm 12:6
horn throughout the l saying, 1Sm 13:3
Jordan to the l of Gad and 1Sm 13:7
road leading to the l of Shual. 1Sm 13:17
be found in all the l of Israel, 1Sm 13:19
has brought trouble to the l. 1Sm 14:29
this David, the king of the l? 1Sm 21:11
and return to the l of Judah." 1Sm 22:5
Philistines have raided the l!" 1Sm 23:27
to the l of the Philistines 1Sm 27:1
Shur as far as the l of Egypt. 1Sm 27:8
Whenever David attacked the l, 1Sm 27:9
and spiritists from the l. 1Sm 28:3
mediums and spiritists in the l. 1Sm 28:9
to return to the l of the 1Sm 29:11
taken from the l of the 1Sm 30:16
Philistines and the l of Judah. 1Sm 30:16
throughout the l of the 1Sm 31:9
to say to David, "Whose l is it? 2Sm 3:12
Jebusites who inhabited the l. 2Sm 5:6
that of the greatest in the l. 2Sm 7:9
arrived in the l of the 2Sm 10:2
would appoint me judge in the l. 2Sm 15:4
camped in the l of Gilead. 2Sm 17:26
has fled from the l because of 2Sm 19:9
and Ziba are to divide the l." 2Sm 19:29
at Zela in the l of Benjamin in 2Sm 21:14
God answered prayer for the l. 2Sm 21:14
and to the l of the Hittites 2Sm 24:6
had gone through the whole l, 2Sm 24:8
of famine to come on your l, 2Sm 24:13
a plague in your l three days? 2Sm 24:13
prayer on behalf of the l, 2Sm 24:25
Socoh and the whole l of Hepher 1Kg 4:10
son of Uri, in the l of Gilead, 1Kg 4:19
one deputy in the l of Judah. 1Kg 4:19
to the l of the Philistines 1Kg 4:21
came out from the l of Egypt, 1Kg 6:1
they came out of the l of Egypt. 1Kg 8:9
them out of the l of Egypt. 1Kg 8:21
them to the l You gave their 1Kg 8:34
rain on Your l that You gave 1Kg 8:36
they live on the l You gave our 1Kg 8:40
from a distant l because of Your 1Kg 8:41
senses in the l where they were 1Kg 8:47
You in their captors' l: 1Kg 8:47
heart in the l of their enemies 1Kg 8:48
of their l that You gave 1Kg 8:48
Israel from the l I gave them, 1Kg 9:7
this to this l and this temple 1Kg 9:8
ancestors out of the l of Egypt. 1Kg 9:9
20 towns in the l of Galilee. 1Kg 9:11
he called them the L of Cabul, 1Kg 9:13
else in the l of his dominion. 1Kg 9:19
remained in the l after them, 1Kg 9:21
of the Red Sea in the l of Edom. 1Kg 9:26
kings and governors of the l. 1Kg 10:15
be given⌋ food, and gave him l. 1Kg 11:18
you out of the l of Egypt." 1Kg 12:28
shrine prostitutes in the l. 1Kg 14:24
from the l and removed all 1Kg 15:12
and the whole l of Naphtali. 1Kg 15:20
there had been no rain in the l. 1Kg 17:7
on the surface of the l.'" 1Kg 17:14
rain on the surface of the l." 1Kg 18:1
throughout the l to every spring 1Kg 18:5
They divided the l between them 1Kg 18:6
the elders of the l and said, 1Kg 20:7
in the plot of l at Jezreel: 1Kg 21:23
and each man to his own l! 1Kg 22:36
removed from the l the rest of 1Kg 22:46
is bad and the l unfruitful." 2Kg 2:19
good piece of l with stones." 2Kg 3:19
of Edom and filled the l. 2Kg 3:20
went into the l and struck down 2Kg 3:24
to cover every good piece of l. 2Kg 3:25
him and returned to their l. 2Kg 3:27
there was a famine in the l. 2Kg 4:38
from the l of Israel a young 2Kg 5:2
girl from the l of Israel had 2Kg 5:4
not come into Israel's l again. 2Kg 6:23
it has already come to the l." 2Kg 8:1
foreigners in the l of the 2Kg 8:2
returned from the l of the 2Kg 8:3
in the plot of l at Jezreel— 2Kg 9:10
Jehu at the plot of l of Naboth 2Kg 9:21
I repay you on this plot of l,' 2Kg 9:26
and throw him on the plot of l." 2Kg 9:26
'In the plot of l at Jezreel, 2Kg 9:36
in the plot of l at Jezreel so 2Kg 9:37
eastward, all the l of Gilead— 2Kg 10:33
while Athaliah ruled over the l. 2Kg 11:3
people of the l were rejoicing 2Kg 11:14
the people of the l went to the 2Kg 11:18
and all the people of the l, 2Kg 11:19
the people of the l rejoiced, 2Kg 11:20
to come into the l in the spring 2Kg 13:20
governing the people of the l. 2Kg 15:5
king of Assyria invaded the l, 2Kg 15:19
and did not stay there in the l. 2Kg 15:20
—all the l of Naphtali— 2Kg 15:29
of all the people of the l, 2Kg 16:15
of Assyria invaded the whole l, 2Kg 17:5
them out of the l of Egypt from 2Kg 17:7
the custom of the God of the l. 2Kg 17:26
the custom of the God of the l." 2Kg 17:26
the custom of the God of the l." 2Kg 17:27
you from the l of Egypt with 2Kg 17:36
'Attack this l and destroy it.'" 2Kg 18:25
you away to a l like your own 2Kg 18:32
away to a land like your own l— 2Kg 18:32
a l of grain and new wine, 2Kg 18:32
a l of bread and vineyards, 2Kg 18:32
a l of olive trees and honey— 2Kg 18:32
delivered his l from the power 2Kg 18:33
delivered his l from my power? 2Kg 18:35
return to his own l where I will 2Kg 19:7
and escaped to the l of Ararat. 2Kg 19:37
wander from the l I gave to 2Kg 21:8
that were seen in the l of Judah 2Kg 23:24
at Riblah in the l of Hamath to 2Kg 23:33
imposed on the l a fine of 7,500 2Kg 23:33
taxed the l to give the money. 2Kg 23:35
gold from the people of the l, 2Kg 23:35
not march out of his l again, 2Kg 24:7
for the poorest people of the l, 2Kg 24:14
leading men of the l into exile 2Kg 24:15
the people of the l had no food. 2Kg 25:3
poorest of the l to be 2Kg 25:12
people of the l for military 2Kg 25:19
at Riblah in the l of Hamath. 2Kg 25:21
went into exile from its l. 2Kg 25:21
he left in the l of Judah. 2Kg 25:22
Live in the l and serve the king 2Kg 25:24
ruled in the l of Edom before 1Ch 1:43
Husham from the l of the 1Ch 1:45
23 towns in the l of Gilead. 1Ch 2:22
pasture, and the l was broad, 1Ch 4:40
increased in the l of Gilead. 1Ch 5:9
them in the l of Bashan as far 1Ch 5:11
settled in the l from Bashan to 1Ch 5:23
Hebron in the l of Judah and its 1Ch 6:55
were born in the l killed Ezer 1Ch 7:21
throughout the l of the 1Ch 10:9
who inhabited the l were there. 1Ch 11:4
I will give the l of Canaan to 1Ch 16:18
that of the greatest in the l. 1Ch 17:8
in the l of the Ammonites 1Ch 19:2
overthrow, and spy on the l?" 1Ch 19:3
and destroyed the Ammonites' l. 1Ch 20:1
a plague on the l, the angel of 1Ch 21:12
that were in the l of Israel, 1Ch 22:2
the l has been subdued before 1Ch 22:18
this good l and leave it as 1Ch 28:8
foreign men in the l of Israel, 2Ch 2:17
Israel out of the l of Egypt, 2Ch 6:5
them to the l You gave them 2Ch 6:25
rain on Your l that You gave 2Ch 6:27
they live on the l You gave our 2Ch 6:31
from a distant l because of Your 2Ch 6:32
senses in the l where they were 2Ch 6:37
You in their captors' l, 2Ch 6:37
and heart in the l of their 2Ch 6:38
of their l that You gave 2Ch 6:38
grasshopper to consume the l, 2Ch 7:13
their sin, and heal their l. 2Ch 7:14
this to this l and this temple 2Ch 7:21
them out of the l of Egypt. 2Ch 7:22
else in the l of his dominion. 2Ch 8:6
remained in the l after them, 2Ch 8:8
the seashore in the l of Edom. 2Ch 8:17
been seen in the l of Judah. 2Ch 9:11
governors of the l also brought 2Ch 9:14
to the l of the Philistines 2Ch 9:26
serving the kingdoms of the l." 2Ch 12:8
reign the l experienced peace 2Ch 14:1
Because the l experienced peace, 2Ch 14:6
The l is still ours because we 2Ch 14:7
idols from the whole l of Judah 2Ch 15:8
set garrisons in the l of Judah 2Ch 17:2
from the l and have decided 2Ch 19:3
cities of the l of Judah, 2Ch 19:5
of this l before Your people 2Ch 20:7
lived in the l and have built 2Ch 20:8
came out of the l of Egypt, 2Ch 20:10
While Athaliah ruled over the l, 2Ch 22:12
people of the l were rejoicing 2Ch 23:13
the people of the l and brought 2Ch 23:20
the people of the l rejoiced, 2Ch 23:21
governing the people of the l. 2Ch 26:21
and will return to this l. 2Ch 30:9
city to city in the l of Ephraim 2Ch 30:10
who came from the l of Israel, 2Ch 30:25
that flowed through the l; 2Ch 32:4
deliver their l from my power? 2Ch 32:13
gods of the peoples of the l, 2Ch 32:19
returned with shame to his l. 2Ch 32:21
sign that happened in the l, 2Ch 32:31
upon the l where I stationed 2Ch 33:8
throughout the l of Israel 2Ch 34:7
to cleanse the l and the temple, 2Ch 34:8
and fined the l 7,500 pounds of 2Ch 36:3
Jeremiah and the l enjoyed its 2Ch 36:21
already in the l discouraged Ezr 4:4
already in the l wrote an Ezr 4:6
tribute, duty, or l tax, and the Ezr 4:13
and l tax were paid to them. Ezr 4:20
Gentiles of the l in order to Ezr 6:21
and l tax must not be imposed on Ezr 7:24
The l you are entering to Ezr 9:11
to possess is an impure l. Ezr 9:11
eat the good things of the l, Ezr 9:12
as plunder to a l of captivity. Neh 4:4
governor in the l of Judah— Neh 5:14
the work. We didn't buy any l. Neh 5:16
him to give the l of the Neh 9:8
and all the people of his l, Neh 9:10
and possess the l You had sworn Neh 9:15
possession of the l of Sihon Neh 9:22
Heshbon and of the l of Og king Neh 9:22
them to the l You told their Neh 9:23
went in and possessed the l: Neh 9:24
who inhabited the l before them Neh 9:24
cities and fertile l and took Neh 9:25
and fertile l You set before Neh 9:35
slaves in the l You gave our Neh 9:36
also leave ⌊the l⌋ uncultivated Neh 10:31
of our l and of every fruit Neh 10:35
groups of the l professed Est 8:17
tax throughout the l even to the Est 10:1
are spread out in the l. Jb 1:10
before I go to a l of darkness Jb 10:21
is⌋ a l of blackness like the Jb 10:22
them, they destroy the l. Jb 12:15
wash away the soil from the l, Jb 14:19
the l was given to them alone Jb 15:19
will not spread over the l. Jb 15:29
while the l belonged to a Jb 22:8
poor of the l are forced into Jb 24:4
section of the l is cursed, Jb 24:18
be found in the l of the living. Jb 28:13
gnawed the dry l, the desolate Jb 30:3
They were forced to leave the l. Jb 30:8
If my l cries out against me and Jb 31:38
punishment, for His l, or for Jb 37:13
south wind brings calm to the l, Jb 37:17
bring rain on an uninhabited l, Jb 38:26
could be found in all the l, Jb 42:15

nations will perish from His **l**. Ps 10:16
holy people who are in the **l**, Ps 16:3
descendants will inherit the **l**. Ps 25:13
goodness in the **l** of the living. Ps 27:13
who live peacefully in the **l**. Ps 35:20
in the **l** and live securely. Ps 37:3
in the LORD will inherit the **l**. Ps 37:9
inherit the **l** and will enjoy Ps 37:11
by Him will inherit the **l**, Ps 37:22
inherit the **l** and dwell in it Ps 37:29
will exalt you to inherit the **l**. Ps 37:34
he will be blessed in the **l**. Ps 41:2
remember You from the **l** of Ps 42:6
not take the **l** by their sword Ps 44:3
them princes throughout the **l**. Ps 45:16
you from the **l** of the living. Ps 52:5
you weigh out violence in the **l**. Ps 58:2
have shaken the **l** and split it Ps 60:2
for You in a **l** that is dry, Ps 63:1
He turned the sea into dry **l**, Ps 66:6
rebellious live in a scorched **l**. Ps 68:6
scattered kings in the **l**, Ps 68:14
be plenty of grain in the **l**; Ps 72:16
throughout the **l** where God met Ps 74:8
dark places of the **l** are full of Ps 74:20
fathers, in the **l** of Egypt, the Ps 78:12
He brought them to His holy **l**, Ps 78:54
it took root and filled the **l**. Ps 80:9
went throughout the **l** of Egypt. Ps 81:5
you up from the **l** of Egypt. Ps 81:10
You showed favor to Your **l**; Ps 85:1
that glory may dwell in our **l**. Ps 85:9
and our **l** will yield its crops. Ps 85:12
in the **l** of oblivion? Ps 88:12
His hands formed the dry **l**. Ps 95:5
faithful of the **l** so that they Ps 101:6
destroy all the wicked of the **l**, Ps 101:8
I will give the **l** of Canaan to Ps 105:11
against the **l** and destroyed Ps 105:16
as a foreigner in the **l** of Ham. Ps 105:23
and wonders in the **l** of Ham. Ps 105:27
Their **l** was overrun with frogs, Ps 105:30
lightning throughout their **l**. Ps 105:32
in their **l** and consumed Ps 105:35
all the firstborn in their **l**, Ps 105:36
wonderful works in the **l** of Ham, Ps 106:22
the pleasant **l** and did not Ps 106:24
so the **l** became polluted with Ps 106:38
and fruitful **l** into salty Ps 107:34
dry **l** into springs of water. Ps 107:35
will be powerful in the **l**; Ps 112:2
the LORD in the **l** of the living. Ps 116:9
not remain over the **l** allotted Ps 125:3
He gave their **l** as an Ps 135:12
He spread the **l** on the waters. Ps 136:6
and gave their **l** as an Ps 136:21
let a slanderer stay in the **l**. Ps 140:11
portion in the **l** of the living." Ps 142:5
I am like parched **l** before You. Ps 143:6
ways to the **l** of the departed Pr 2:18
the upright will inhabit the **l**, Pr 2:21
will be cut off from the **l**, Pr 2:22
He made the **l**, the fields, Pr 8:26
who works his **l** will have plenty Pr 12:11
from a distant **l** is like cold Pr 25:25
When a **l** is in rebellion, it has Pr 28:2
who works his **l** will have plenty Pr 28:19
a king brings stability to a **l**, Pr 29:4
from the **l** and the needy Pr 30:14
sits among the elders of the **l**. Pr 31:23
from the **l** is taken by all Ec 5:9
Woe to you, **l**, when your king is Ec 10:16
are you, **l**, when your king Ec 10:17
cooing is heard in our **l**. Sg 2:12
Your **l** is desolate, your cities Is 1:7
eat the good things of the **l**. Is 1:19
Their **l** is full of silver and Is 2:7
their **l** is full of horses, Is 2:7
Their **l** is full of idols; Is 2:8
the fruit of the **l** will be the Is 4:2
and you alone are left in the **l**. Is 5:8
one looks at the **l**, there will Is 5:30
the **l** is ruined and desolate, Is 6:11
great emptiness in the **l**. Is 6:12
a tenth will remain in the **l**, Is 6:13
the **l** of the two kings you dread Is 7:16
bee that is in the **l** of Assyria. Is 7:18
survivor in the **l** will eat Is 7:22
the whole **l** will be thorns Is 7:24
streams will fill your entire **l**, Is 8:8
They will wander through the **l**, Is 8:21
the distressed **l** will not be Is 9:1
when He humbled the **l** of Zebulun Is 9:1
Zebulun and the **l** of Naphtali. Is 9:1
to the **l** east of the Jordan, Is 9:1
living in the **l** of darkness, Is 9:2
The **l** is scorched by the wrath Is 9:19
throughout the **l** the Lord GOD Is 10:23
for the oppressed of the **l**. Is 11:4
strike the **l** with discipline Is 11:4
for the **l** will be as full of the Is 11:9
came up from the **l** of Egypt. Is 11:16
They are coming from a far **l**, Is 13:5
each one will flee to his own **l**. Is 13:14
will settle them on their own **l**. Is 14:1
female slaves in the LORD's **l**. Is 14:2
destroyed your **l** and slaughtered Is 14:20
up to possess a **l** or fill the Is 14:21
I will break Assyria in My **l**; Is 14:25
and for the survivors in the **l**. Is 15:9
lambs to the ruler of the **l**, Is 16:1
have vanished from the **l**. Is 16:4
The **l** of buzzing insect wings Is 18:1
whose **l** is divided by rivers. Is 18:2
for the wild animals of the **l**. Is 18:6
whose **l** is divided by rivers— Is 18:7
The **l** of Judah will terrify Is 19:17
cities in the **l** of Egypt will Is 19:18
in the center of the **l** of Egypt Is 19:19
LORD of Hosts in the **l** of Egypt. Is 19:20
a blessing within the **l**. Is 19:24
desert, from the **l** of terror. Is 21:1
inhabitants of the **l** of Tema Is 21:14
and sling you into a wide **l**. Is 22:18
them from the **l** of Cyprus. Is 23:1
Overflow your **l** like the Nile, Is 23:10
Look at the **l** of Chaldeans— Is 23:13
like heat in a dry **l**, You subdue Is 25:5
will be sung in the **l** of Judah: Is 26:1
Your judgments are ⌊in⌋ the **l**, Is 26:9
a righteous **l** he acts unjustly Is 26:10
all the borders of the **l**. Is 26:15
lost in the **l** of Assyria will Is 27:13
dispersed in the **l** of Egypt; Is 27:13
it across the **l** with ⌊His⌋ hand. Is 28:2
of destruction for the whole **l**. Is 28:22
Through a **l** of trouble and Is 30:6
water in a dry **l** and the shade Is 32:2
of a massive rock in an arid **l**. Is 32:2
The **l** mourns and withers; Is 33:9
beauty; you will see a vast **l**. Is 33:17
slaughter in the **l** of Edom. Is 34:6
Their **l** will be soaked with Is 34:7
her **l** will become burning pitch. Is 34:9
and the dry **l** will be glad; Is 35:1
and the thirsty **l** springs of Is 35:7
I attacked this **l** to destroy it Is 36:10
'Attack this **l** and destroy it.' " Is 36:10
you away to a **l** like your land, Is 36:17
you away to a land like your **l**, Is 36:17
a **l** of grain and new wine, Is 36:17
a **l** of bread and vineyards. Is 36:17
delivered his **l** from the hand Is 36:18
delivered his **l** from my hand, Is 36:20
a rumor and return to his own **l**, Is 37:7
and escaped to the **l** of Ararat. Is 37:38
the LORD in the **l** of the living; Is 38:11
of water and dry **l** into springs Is 41:18
pour water on the thirsty **l**, Is 44:3
somewhere in a **l** of darkness. Is 45:19
to restore the **l**, to make them Is 49:8
west, and from the **l** of Sinim. Is 49:12
places and your **l** marked by Is 49:19
off from the **l** of the living; Is 53:8
will inherit the **l** and possess Is 57:13
satisfy you in a parched **l**, Is 58:11
ride over the heights of the **l**, Is 58:14
of camels will cover your **l**— Is 60:6
again be heard of in your **l**; Is 60:18
they will possess the **l** forever; Is 60:21
will possess double in their **l**, Is 61:7
and your **l** will not be called Is 62:4
is in Her, and your **l** Married; Is 62:4
and your **l** will be married. Is 62:4
blessed in the **l** will be blessed Is 65:16
swears in the **l** will swear by Is 65:16
Can a **l** be born in one day, Is 66:8
north on all who live in the **l**. Jr 1:14
walls against the whole **l**— Jr 1:18
the wilderness, in a **l** not sown. Jr 2:2
brought us from the **l** of Egypt, Jr 2:6
through a **l** of deserts and Jr 2:6
through a **l** of drought and Jr 2:6
a **l** no one traveled through and Jr 2:6
to a fertile **l** to eat its fruit Jr 2:7
you entered, you defiled My **l**; Jr 2:7
They have laid waste his **l**. Jr 2:15
to Israel or a **l** of dense Jr 2:31
Wouldn't such a **l** become totally Jr 3:1
You have defiled the **l** with your Jr 3:2
she defiled the **l** and committed Jr 3:9
multiply and increase in the **l**, Jr 3:16
from the **l** of the north to Jr 3:18
the north to the **l** I have given Jr 3:18
sons and give you a desirable **l**, Jr 3:19
the ram's horn throughout the **l**. Jr 4:5
his lair to make your **l** a waste. Jr 4:7
are coming from a distant **l**; Jr 4:16
for the whole **l** is destroyed. Jr 4:20
whole **l** will be a desolation, Jr 4:27
served foreign gods in your **l**, Jr 5:19
strangers in a **l** that is not Jr 5:19
thing has taken place in the **l**. Jr 5:30
you a desolation, a **l** devoid of Jr 6:8
against the residents of the **l**. Jr 6:12
or sweet cane from a distant **l**? Jr 6:20
is coming from a northern **l**; Jr 6:22
the **l** I gave to your ancestors Jr 7:7
ancestors out of the **l** of Egypt, Jr 7:22
came out of the **l** of Egypt until Jr 7:25
for the wild animals of the **l**, Jr 7:33
for the **l** will become a desolate Jr 7:34
steeds, the whole **l** quakes. Jr 8:16
to devour the **l** and everything Jr 8:16
dear people from a far away **l**: Jr 8:19
faithfulness prevail in the **l**, Jr 9:3
over the wilderness grazing **l**, Jr 9:10
Why is the **l** destroyed and Jr 9:12
for we have abandoned the **l**; Jr 9:19
from the **l** to the north. Jr 10:22
them out of the **l** of Egypt, Jr 11:4
to give ⌊them⌋ a **l** flowing with Jr 11:5
them out of the **l** of Egypt until Jr 11:7
off from the **l** of the living so Jr 11:19
long will the **l** mourn and the Jr 12:4
If you stumble in a peaceful **l**, Jr 12:5
they have trampled My plot of **l**. Jr 12:10
the **l** is desolate, but no one Jr 12:11
to uproot them from their **l**, Jr 12:14
to his inheritance and to his **l**. Jr 12:15
to fill all who live in this **l**— Jr 13:13
no rain ⌊has fallen⌋ on the **l**. Jr 14:4
are You like an alien in the **l**, Jr 14:8
be sword or famine in this **l**: Jr 14:15
travel to a **l** they do not know. Jr 14:18
wild animals of the **l** to devour Jr 15:3
fork at the gates of the **l**. Jr 15:7
and conflict in all the **l**. Jr 15:10
enemies in a **l** you do not know, Jr 15:14
who father them in this **l**: Jr 16:3
for the wild animals of the **l**. Jr 16:4
die in this **l** without burial. Jr 16:6
you from this **l** into a land that Jr 16:13
this land into a **l** that you and Jr 16:13
Israelites from the **l** of Egypt, Jr 16:14
from the **l** of the north Jr 16:15
them to their **l** that I gave to Jr 16:15
because they have polluted My **l**. Jr 16:18
enemies in a **l** you do not know, Jr 17:4
in a salt **l** where no one lives. Jr 17:6
from the **l** of Benjamin and from Jr 17:26
They have made their **l** a horror, Jr 18:16
for the wild animals of the **l**. Jr 19:7
again and see his native **l**. Jr 22:10
never seeing this **l** again." Jr 22:12
birth to you into another **l**, Jr 22:26
return to the **l** they long to Jr 22:27
and cast into a **l** they have not Jr 22:28
return them to their grazing **l**. Jr 23:3
and righteousness in the **l**. Jr 23:5
Israelites from the **l** of Egypt, Jr 23:7
Israel from the **l** of the north Jr 23:8
dwell once more in their own **l**." Jr 23:8
For the **l** is full of adulterers; Jr 23:10

the l mourns because of the Jr 23:10
has spread throughout the l. Jr 23:15
place to the l of the Chaldeans Jr 24:5
and will return them to this l. Jr 24:6
in this l and those living Jr 24:8
those living in the l of Egypt. Jr 24:8
from the l I gave to them Jr 24:10
Live in the l the LORD gave to Jr 25:5
will bring them against this l, Jr 25:9
This whole l will become a Jr 25:11
the l of the Chaldeans, Jr 25:12
bring on that l all My words I Jr 25:13
all the kings of the l of Uz; Jr 25:20
the kings of the l of the Jr 25:20
roars loudly over His grazing l; Jr 25:30
Peaceful grazing l will become Jr 25:37
for their l has become a Jr 25:38
elders of the l stood up and Jr 26:17
and against this l in words like Jr 26:20
the time for his own l comes, Jr 27:7
you will be removed from your l. Jr 27:10
I will leave it in its own l, Jr 27:11
them to the l I gave to their Jr 30:3
from the l of their captivity! Jr 30:10
bring them from the northern l. Jr 31:8
will return from the enemy's l. Jr 31:16
creates something new in the l— Jr 31:22
this word in the l of Judah and Jr 31:23
them out of the l of Egypt— Jr 31:32
Anathoth in the l of Benjamin, Jr 32:8
again be bought in this l.' Jr 32:15
wonders in the l of Egypt and do Jr 32:20
gave them this l You swore ⌊to Jr 32:22
a l flowing with milk and honey. Jr 32:22
in this l with all My mind Jr 32:41
bought in this l about which you Jr 32:43
called on in the l of Benjamin, Jr 32:44
fortunes of the l as in former Jr 33:11
be a grazing l where shepherds Jr 33:12
the Negev, the l of Benjamin— Jr 33:13
and righteousness in the l. Jr 33:15
them out of the l of Egypt, Jr 34:13
the people of the l who passed Jr 34:19
for the wild animals of the l. Jr 34:20
of Babylon marched into the l, Jr 35:11
Live in the l that I gave you Jr 35:15
destroy this l and cause it to Jr 36:29
as king in the l of Judah in Jr 37:1
the people of the l did not obey Jr 37:2
to return to its own l of Egypt. Jr 37:7
to go to the l of Benjamin to Jr 37:12
come against you and this l'? Jr 37:19
at Riblah in the l of Hamath. Jr 39:5
left in the l of Judah some of Jr 39:10
the whole l is in front of you. Jr 40:4
people who remained in the l. Jr 40:6
Ahikam over the l and that he Jr 40:7
poorest of the l who had not Jr 40:7
Live in the l and serve the king Jr 40:9
and came to the l of Judah, Jr 40:12
Babylon had appointed in the l. Jr 41:2
Babylon had appointed in the l. Jr 41:18
you will indeed stay in this l, Jr 42:10
We will not stay in this l, Jr 42:13
we'll go to the l of Egypt where Jr 42:14
you there in the l of Egypt, Jr 42:16
LORD to stay in the l of Judah. Jr 43:4
to live in the l of Judah for a Jr 43:5
went to the l of Egypt because Jr 43:7
and strike down the l of Egypt— Jr 43:11
He will clean the l of Egypt as Jr 43:12
temple in the l of Egypt and Jr 43:13
Jews living in the l of Egypt— Jr 44:1
and in the l of Pathros: Jr 44:1
gods in the l of Egypt where Jr 44:8
were committed in the l of Judah Jr 44:9
to go to the l of Egypt to live Jr 44:12
of them in the l of Egypt will Jr 44:12
living in the l of Egypt just as Jr 44:13
while there in the l of Egypt— Jr 44:14
return to the l of Judah where Jr 44:14
were living in the l of Egypt at Jr 44:15
people of the l—did the LORD Jr 44:21
so your l has become a waste, Jr 44:22
Judah who are in the l of Egypt. Jr 44:24
who live in the l of Egypt: Jr 44:26
of Judah in all the l of Egypt, Jr 44:26
who is in the l of Egypt will Jr 44:27
return from the l of Egypt to Jr 44:28
of Egypt to the l of Judah only Jr 44:28
going to the l of Egypt to live Jr 44:28
about to uproot—the whole l! Jr 45:4
in the northern l by the Jr 46:10
to defeat the l of Egypt: Jr 46:13
and to the l of our birth, Jr 46:16
from the l of their captivity! Jr 46:27
overflow the l and everything Jr 47:2
inhabitant of the l will wail. Jr 47:2
has come to the l of the plateau Jr 48:21
all the towns of the l of Moab, Jr 48:24
field and from the l of Moab. Jr 48:33
perennially watered grazing l. Jr 49:19
away from her ⌊l⌋ in a flash. Jr 49:19
and their grazing l will be made Jr 49:20
Babylon, the l of the Chaldeans Jr 50:1
it will make her l desolate. Jr 50:3
their righteous grazing l, Jr 50:7
depart from the Chaldeans' l. Jr 50:8
nations—a dry l, a wilderness, Jr 50:12
each will flee to his own l. Jr 50:16
Babylon and his l just as I Jr 50:18
return Israel to his grazing l, Jr 50:19
Go against the l of Merathaim, Jr 50:21
The sound of war is in the l— Jr 50:22
of Hosts in the l of the Jr 50:25
escapees from the l of Babylon Jr 50:28
For it is a l of carved images, Jr 50:38
perennially watered grazing l. Jr 50:44
away from her ⌊l⌋ in a flash. Jr 50:44
against the l of the Chaldeans: Jr 50:45
the grazing l will be made Jr 50:45
her and strip her l bare, Jr 51:2
fall in the l of the Chaldeans Jr 51:4
though their l is full of guilt Jr 51:5
Let each of us go to his own l, Jr 51:9
Raise a signal flag in the l; Jr 51:27
to make the l of Babylon an Jr 51:29
dry and arid l, a land where no Jr 51:43
and arid land, a l where no one Jr 51:43
report is proclaimed in the l, Jr 51:46
violence in the l with ruler Jr 51:46
Her entire l will suffer shame, Jr 51:47
will groan throughout her l. Jr 51:52
from the l of the Chaldeans! Jr 51:54
the people of the l had no food. Jr 52:6
at Riblah in the l of Hamath, Jr 52:9
people of the l Nebuzaradan, Jr 52:16
people of the l for military Jr 52:25
at Riblah in the l of Hamath. Jr 52:27
went into exile from its l. Jr 52:27
prisoners of the l beneath one's Lm 3:34
you resident of the l of Uz! Lm 4:21
in the l of the Chaldeans by the Ezk 1:3
I will make the l a desolate Ezk 6:14
GOD says to the l of Israel: Ezk 7:2
on the four corners of the l. Ezk 7:2
on you, inhabitants of the l. Ezk 7:7
for the l is filled with crimes Ezk 7:23
people of the l will tremble. Ezk 7:27
The LORD has abandoned the l." Ezk 8:12
also fill the l with violence Ezk 8:17
the l is full of bloodshed, Ezk 9:9
The LORD has abandoned the l; Ezk 9:9
this l has been given to us as a Ezk 11:15
I will give you the l of Israel. Ezk 11:17
so that you cannot see the l. Ezk 12:6
cannot see the l with his eyes. Ezk 12:12
to Babylon, the l of the Ezk 12:13
Then say to the people of the l: Ezk 12:19
of Jerusalem in the l of Israel: Ezk 12:19
for their l will be stripped of Ezk 12:19
and the l will become a Ezk 12:20
have about the l of Israel, Ezk 12:22
will not enter the l of Israel. Ezk 13:9
if a l sins against Me by acting Ezk 14:13
through the l and depopulate Ezk 14:15
but the l would be desolate. Ezk 14:16
a sword against that l and say: Ezk 14:17
into that l and pour out My Ezk 14:19
I will make the l desolate Ezk 15:8
were in the l of the Canaanites Ezk 16:3
to Chaldea, the l of merchants, Ezk 16:29
it to the l of merchants, Ezk 17:4
away the leading men of the l, Ezk 17:13
in the l of the king who put him Ezk 17:16
concerning the l of Israel: Ezk 18:2
with hooks to the l of Egypt. Ezk 19:4
The l and everything in it Ezk 19:7
in a dry and thirsty l. Ezk 19:13
known to them in the l of Egypt. Ezk 20:5
them out of the l of Egypt into Ezk 20:6
of Egypt into a l I had searched Ezk 20:6
⌊a l⌋ flowing with milk and Ezk 20:6
them within the l of Egypt. Ezk 20:8
them out of the l of Egypt and Ezk 20:10
them into the l I had given Ezk 20:15
them into the l that I swore to Ezk 20:28
wilderness of the l of Egypt, Ezk 20:36
out of the l where they live Ezk 20:38
will not enter the l of Israel. Ezk 20:38
of them, will serve Me in the l. Ezk 20:40
I lead you into the l of Israel, Ezk 20:42
the l I swore to give your Ezk 20:42
the forest l in the Negev, Ezk 20:46
against the l of Israel, Ezk 21:2
originate from the same l. Ezk 21:19
in the l of your origin. Ezk 21:30
will be ⌊spilled⌋ in the l. Ezk 21:32
You are a l that has not been Ezk 22:24
people of the l have practiced Ezk 22:29
behalf of the l so that I might Ezk 22:30
Chaldea, the l of their birth. Ezk 23:15
a prostitute in the l of Egypt Ezk 23:19
which began in the l of Egypt, Ezk 23:27
an end to indecency in the l, Ezk 23:48
about the l of Israel when it Ezk 25:3
over the l of Israel with Ezk 25:6
cities, the pride of the l: Ezk 25:9
splendor in the l of the living. Ezk 26:20
Judah and the l of Israel were Ezk 27:17
they will live in their own l, Ezk 28:25
l of Egypt will be a desolate Ezk 29:9
I will turn the l of Egypt into Ezk 29:10
I will make the l of Egypt a Ezk 29:12
them back to the l of Pathros, Ezk 29:14
Pathros, the l of their origin Ezk 29:14
going to give the l of Egypt to Ezk 29:19
have given him the l of Egypt as Ezk 29:20
men of the covenant l will fall Ezk 30:5
be brought in to destroy the l. Ezk 30:11
and fill the l with the slain. Ezk 30:11
and sell the l into the hands Ezk 30:12
on the l and everything Ezk 30:12
be a prince from the l of Egypt. Ezk 30:13
I will instill fear in that l. Ezk 30:13
it against the l of Egypt. Ezk 30:25
abandon you on the l and hurl Ezk 32:4
will drench the l with the flow Ezk 32:6
will bring darkness on your l. Ezk 32:8
When I make the l of Egypt a Ezk 32:15
terror in the l of the living. Ezk 32:23
terror in the l of the living. Ezk 32:24
spread in the l of the living. Ezk 32:25
spread in the l of the living. Ezk 32:26
once⌋ in the l of the living. Ezk 32:27
terror in the l of the living, Ezk 32:32
I bring the sword against a l, Ezk 33:2
people of that l select a man Ezk 33:2
against the l and blows his Ezk 33:3
the ruins in the l of Israel are Ezk 33:24
he received possession of the l. Ezk 33:24
the l has been given to us as a Ezk 33:24
receive possession of the l? Ezk 33:25
receive possession of the l? Ezk 33:26
I will make the l a desolate Ezk 33:28
when I make the l a desolate Ezk 33:29
and bring them into their own l. Ezk 34:13
the inhabited places of the l. Ezk 34:13
dangerous animals in the l, Ezk 34:25
the l will yield its produce; Ezk 34:27
flock will be secure in their l. Ezk 34:27
of the l will not consume Ezk 34:28
be victims of famine in the l. Ezk 34:29
who took My l as their own Ezk 36:5
concerning the l of Israel and Ezk 36:6
of Israel lived in their l, Ezk 36:17
blood they had shed on the l, Ezk 36:18
had to leave His l ⌊in exile⌋. Ezk 36:20
will bring you into your own l. Ezk 36:24
live in the l that I gave your Ezk 36:28
desolate l will be cultivated Ezk 36:34
This l that was desolate has Ezk 36:35
lead you into the l of Israel. Ezk 37:12
I will settle you in your own l. Ezk 37:14

and bring them into their own l. Ezk 37:21
make them one nation in the l, Ezk 37:22
will live in the l that I gave Ezk 37:25
toward Gog, of the l of Magog, Ezk 38:2
you will enter a l that has been Ezk 38:8
be like a cloud covering the l. Ezk 38:9
go up against a l of open Ezk 38:11
like a cloud covering the l. Ezk 38:16
you against My l so that the Ezk 38:16
comes against the l of Israel"— Ezk 38:18
earthquake in the l of Israel. Ezk 38:19
them in order to cleanse the l. Ezk 39:12
people of the l will bury ⌊them Ezk 39:13
to pass through the l and bury Ezk 39:14
through the l and one of them Ezk 39:15
So they will cleanse the l. Ezk 39:16
in their l with no one to Ezk 39:26
them to their own l after having Ezk 39:28
took me to the l of Israel and Ezk 40:2
When you divide the l by lot as Ezk 45:1
holy portion of the l, eight and Ezk 45:1
entire tract of l will be holy. Ezk 45:1
a holy area of the l to be used Ezk 45:4
to the holy donation ⌊of l⌋. Ezk 45:6
donation ⌊of l⌋ and the city's Ezk 45:7
will be his l as a possession Ezk 45:8
the ⌊rest of the⌋ l to the house Ezk 45:8
people of the l must take part Ezk 45:16
and all the people of the l. Ezk 45:22
people of the l will also bow Ezk 46:3
the people of the l come before Ezk 46:9
to⌋ divide the l as an Ezk 47:13
So this l will fall to you as an Ezk 47:14
is to be the border of the l: Ezk 47:15
Gilead and the l of Israel; Ezk 47:18
divide this l among yourselves Ezk 47:21
of the ⌊holy⌋ donation of the l, Ezk 48:12
this choice ⌊part⌋ of the l, Ezk 48:14
He will own ⌊the l⌋ adjacent to Ezk 48:21
This is the l you are to allot Ezk 48:29
them to the l of Babylon, Dn 1:2
east and toward the beautiful l. Dn 8:9
and all the people of the l. Dn 9:6
people out of the l of Egypt Dn 9:15
and then return to his own l. Dn 11:9
in the beautiful l with total Dn 11:16
to the fortresses of his own l, Dn 11:19
return to his l with great Dn 11:28
then return to his own l. Dn 11:28
and distributing l as a reward. Dn 11:39
also invade the beautiful l, Dn 11:41
and not even the l of Egypt will Dn 11:42
for the whole l has been Hs 1:2
ruler, and go up from the l. Hs 1:11
a desert and like a parched l, Hs 2:3
she came out of the l of Egypt. Hs 2:15
of war in the l and will enable Hs 2:18
sow her in the l for Myself, Hs 2:23
the inhabitants of the l: Hs 4:1
no knowledge of God in the l! Hs 4:1
For this reason the l mourns, Hs 4:3
spring showers that water the l. Hs 6:3
for this in the l of Egypt. Hs 7:16
not stay in the l of the LORD. Hs 9:3
The better his l produced, Hs 10:1
not return to the l of Egypt and Hs 11:5
doves from the l of Assyria. Hs 11:11
God ever since the l of Egypt. Hs 12:9
Jacob fled to the l of Aram. Hs 12:12
God ever since the l of Egypt; Hs 13:4
wilderness, in the l of drought. Hs 13:5
all you inhabitants of the l. Jl 1:2
For a nation has invaded My l, Jl 1:6
the l grieves; indeed, Jl 1:10
residents of the l at the house Jl 1:14
the residents of the l tremble, Jl 2:1
The l in front of them is like Jl 2:3
jealous for His l and spared His Jl 2:18
him to a dry and desolate l, Jl 2:20
be afraid, l; rejoice and be Jl 2:21
countries and divided up My l. Jl 3:2
of Judah in whose l they shed Jl 3:19
judge from the l and kill all Am 2:3
you from the l of Egypt and led Am 2:10
to possess the l of the Amorite. Am 2:10
I brought from the l of Egypt: Am 3:1
Does a bird l in a trap on the Am 3:5
the citadels in the l of Egypt: Am 3:9
An enemy will surround the l; Am 3:11
She lies abandoned on her l, Am 5:2
eating the vegetation of the l, Am 7:2
great deep and devoured the l. Am 7:4
The l cannot endure all his Am 7:10
Flee to the l of Judah. Am 7:12
and your l will be divided up Am 7:17
do away with the poor of the l, Am 8:4
won't the l quake and all who Am 8:8
darken the l in the daytime. Am 8:9
send a famine through the l: Am 8:11
Israel from the l of Egypt, Am 9:7
I will plant them on their l, Am 9:15
from the l I have given them Am 9:15
will possess ⌊the l of⌋ the Ob 19
who made the sea and the dry l." Jnh 1:9
rowed hard to get back to dry l, Jnh 1:13
and it vomited Jonah onto dry l. Jnh 2:10
out the allotted l of my people. Mc 2:4
to divide the l by casting lots. Mc 2:5
When Assyria invades our l, Mc 5:5
shepherd the l of Assyria with Mc 5:6
the l of Nimrod with a drawn Mc 5:6
Assyria when it invades our l, Mc 5:6
cities of your l and tear down Mc 5:11
you up from the l of Egypt and Mc 6:4
people have vanished from the l; Mc 7:2
your exodus from the l of Egypt. Mc 7:15
gates of your l are wide open to Nah 3:13
strips ⌊the l⌋ and flies away. Nah 3:16
curtains of the l of Midian Hab 3:7
you, Canaan, l of the Zph 2:5
the dew and the l its crops. Hg 1:10
all you people of the l"— Hg 2:4
earth, the sea and the dry l. Hg 2:6
horns against the l of Judah to Zch 1:21
Leave the l of the north"— Zch 2:6
as His portion in the Holy L, Zch 2:12
guilt of this l in a single day Zch 3:9
is going out over the whole l, Zch 5:3
is their iniquity in all the l." Zch 5:6
for it in the l of Shinar," Zch 5:11
is going to the l of the north, Zch 6:6
going to the l of the south." Zch 6:6
going to the l of the north have Zch 6:8
My Spirit in the northern l." Zch 6:8
people of the l and the priests Zch 7:5
and the l was left desolate Zch 7:14
a pleasant l into a desolation Zch 7:14
My people from the l of the east Zch 8:7
the east and the l of the west. Zch 8:7
the l will yield its produce, Zch 8:12
is against the l of Hadrach, Zch 9:1
a crown, sparkling over His l. Zch 9:16
them back from the l of Egypt Zch 10:10
them to the l of Gilead and to Zch 10:10
on the inhabitants of the l"— Zch 11:6
They will devastate the l, Zch 11:6
shepherd in the l who will not Zch 11:16
The l will mourn, every family Zch 12:12
names of the idols from the l, Zch 13:2
the unclean spirit from the l. Zch 13:2
In the whole l—the LORD's Zch 13:8
All the l from Geba to Rimmon Zch 14:10
for you will be a delightful l," Mal 3:12
and strike the l with a curse." Mal 4:6
Bethlehem, in the l of Judah, Mt 2:6
and go to the l of Israel, Mt 2:20
and entered the l of Israel. Mt 2:21
L of Zebulun and land of Mt 4:15
of Zebulun and l of Naphtali, Mt 4:15
of judgment for the l of Sodom Mt 10:15
tolerable for the l of Sodom on Mt 11:24
was already over a mile from l, Mt 14:24
they came to l at Gennesaret. Mt 14:34
travel over l and sea to make Mt 23:15
darkness came over the whole l. Mt 27:45
ran there by l from all the Mk 6:33
and He was alone on the l. Mk 6:47
they came to l at Gennesaret and Mk 6:53
over the whole l until three Mk 15:33
famine came over all the l. Lk 4:25
to put out a little from the l. Lk 5:3
they brought the boats to l, Lk 5:11
He got out on l, a Lk 8:27
A rich man's l was very Lk 12:16
distress in the l and wrath Lk 21:23
over the whole l until three, Lk 23:44
since they were not far from l Jn 21:8
they got out on l, they saw a Jn 21:9
and come to the l that I will Ac 7:3
came out of the l of the Ac 7:4
move to this l in which you now Ac 7:4
an exile in the l of Midian, Ac 7:29
and signs in the l of Egypt, Ac 7:36
us out of the l of Egypt, Ac 7:40
throughout the l of Judea and Ac 8:1
their stay in the l of Egypt, Ac 13:17
nations in the l of Canaan, Ac 13:19
He gave their l to them as an Ac 13:19
since he himself was going by l. Ac 20:13
thought they were approaching l. Ac 27:27
they did not recognize the l, Ac 27:39
overboard first and get to l. Ac 27:43
this way, all got safely to l. Ac 27:44
may have a long life in the l. Eph 6:3
lead them out of the l of Egypt. Heb 8:9
a foreigner in the l of promise, Heb 11:9
remembering that l they came Heb 11:15
they now aspire to a better l— Heb 11:16
as though they were on dry l. Heb 11:29
on the l and have indulged Jms 5:5
months it did not rain on the l. Jms 5:17
gave rain and the l produced its Jms 5:18
on the sea, his left on the l, Rv 10:2
and on the l raised his right Rv 10:5
on the sea and on the l." Rv 10:8

LAND'S *(8)*

some of the l produce as Gn 4:3
Every tenth of the l produce, Lv 27:30
first of the l produce that You Dt 26:10
your trees and your l produce. Dt 28:42
has handed the l inhabitants 1Ch 22:18
A tenth of our l ⌊produce⌋ from Neh 10:37
slinging out the l residents at Jr 10:18
some of the l seed and put it Ezk 17:5

LANDHOLDING *(2)*

is not part of his inherited l, Lv 27:22
or his inherited l, can be sold Lv 27:28

LANDING *(1)*

On l at Caesarea, he went up and Ac 18:22

LANDOWNER *(4)*

heaven is like a l who brings Mt 13:52
heaven is like a l who went out Mt 20:1
they began to complain to the l: Mt 20:11
was a man, a l, who planted Mt 21:33

LANDOWNER'S *(1)*

The l slaves came to him and Mt 13:27

LANDS *(50)*

peoples spread out into their l. Gn 10:5
their own l and their nations. Gn 10:20
in their l and their nations. Gn 10:31
give all these l to you and your Gn 26:3
give your offspring all these l, Gn 26:4
survive in the l of their Lv 26:36
survive in the l of your enemies Lv 26:39
they surveyed the l of Jazer and Nm 32:1
the peoples whose l we traveled Jos 24:17
and around the l of Edom and Jdg 11:18
the gods of the l has delivered 2Kg 18:35
the nations and their l. 2Kg 19:17
fame spread throughout the l, 1Ch 14:17
and glorious in all the l. 1Ch 22:5
kingdoms of the ⌊surrounding⌋ l. 1Ch 29:30
the peoples of ⌊other⌋ l do? 2Ch 13:9
residents of the l had many 2Ch 15:5
of the l that surrounded 2Ch 17:10
kingdoms of the l when they 2Ch 20:29
the hills and in the fertile l. 2Ch 26:10
to all the peoples of the l? 2Ch 32:13
gods of the l been able to 2Ch 32:13
gods of the l that did not 2Ch 32:17
from all the l belonging to 2Ch 34:33
produce⌋ from our l belongs to Neh 10:37
gave them the l of the nations, Ps 105:44
them throughout the l. Ps 106:27
has gathered them from the l— Ps 107:3
attention, all you distant l; Is 8:9
gods of these l ⌊ever⌋ delivered Is 36:20
all these countries and their l Is 37:18
from all the other l where He Jr 16:15
flock from all the l where I Jr 23:3
and the grazing l in the Jr 23:10
placed all these l under the Jr 27:6
against many l and great Jr 28:8

them from all the l where I have Jr 32:37
all the other l also heard that Jr 40:11
and all the l they rule. Jr 51:28
the most beautiful of all l. Ezk 20:6
the most beautiful of all l, Ezk 20:15
and a mockery to all the l. Ezk 22:4
a desolation among desolate l, Ezk 29:12
be desolate among desolate l, Ezk 30:7
nations and two l will be mine, Ezk 35:10
horsemen come from distant ⌊l⌋. Hab 1:8
and violence against l, Hab 2:8
and violence against l, Hab 2:17
remember Me in the distant l; Zch 10:9
those who owned l or houses sold Ac 4:34

LANDSCAPE (1)

while the Arameans filled the l. 1Kg 20:27

LANES (1)

the highways and l and make them Lk 14:23

LANGUAGE (52)

Each ⌊group⌋ had its own l. Gn 10:5
had the same l and vocabulary. Gn 11:1
people all having the same l, Gn 11:6
confuse their l so that they Gn 11:7
LORD confused the l of the whole Gn 11:9
a nation whose l you don't Dt 28:49
children spoke the l of Ashdod Neh 13:24
each ethnic group in its own l, Est 1:22
and speak in the l of his own Est 1:22
each ethnic group in its own l. Est 3:12
each ethnic group in its own l, Est 8:9
Jews in their own script and l. Est 8:9
you choose the l of the crafty. Jb 15:5
I heard an unfamiliar l: Ps 81:5
a people who spoke a foreign l— Ps 114:1
nation with a strange l, Is 18:2
nation with a strange l, Is 18:7
will speak the l of Canaan and Is 19:18
speech and in a foreign l. Is 28:11
who stammer in a l that is not Is 33:19
a nation whose l you do not know Jr 5:15
or difficult l but to the house Ezk 3:5
speech or difficult l, Ezk 3:6
the Chaldean l and literature. Dn 1:4
People of every nation and l, Dn 3:4
of every nation and l fell down Dn 3:7
or l who says anything offensive Dn 3:29
nation, and l, who live in all Dn 4:1
and l who live in all the earth: Dn 6:25
nation, and l should serve Him. Dn 7:14
nations of every l will grab the Zch 8:23
and not using any figurative l. Jn 16:29
that in their own l that field Ac 1:19
them speaking in his own l. Ac 2:6
each of us, in our own native l? Ac 2:8
saying in the Lycaonian l, Ac 14:11
addressed them in the Hebrew l: Ac 21:40
addressing them in the Hebrew l, Ac 22:2
to me in the Hebrew l, Ac 26:14
in ⌊another⌋ l is not speaking 1Co 14:2
in ⌊another⌋ l builds himself up 1Co 14:4
not know the meaning of the l, 1Co 14:11
in ⌊another⌋ l should pray that 1Co 14:13
For if I pray in ⌊another⌋ l, 1Co 14:14
10,000 words in ⌊another⌋ l. 1Co 14:19
another⌋ l, or an interpretation 1Co 14:26
person speaks in ⌊another⌋ l, 1Co 14:27
and filthy l from your mouth. Col 3:8
every tribe and l and people Rv 5:9
people, and l, which no one Rv 7:9
tribe, people, l, and nation. Rv 13:7
nation, tribe, l, and people. Rv 14:6

LANGUAGES (27)

to their l, in their own Gn 10:20
to their l, in their lands Gn 10:31
to gather all nations and l; Is 66:18
and l were terrified and fearful Dn 5:19
they will speak in new l; Mk 16:17
began to speak in different l, Ac 2:4
in our own l the magnificent Ac 2:11
in ⌊other⌋ l and declaring Ac 10:46
with ⌊other⌋ l and to prophesy. Ac 19:6
kinds of l, to another, 1Co 12:10
to another, interpretation of l. 1Co 12:10
managing, various kinds of l. 1Co 12:28
Do all speak in l? 1Co 12:30
If I speak the l of men and of 1Co 13:1
as for l, they will cease; 1Co 13:8
all of you spoke in other l, 1Co 14:5
than the person who speaks in l, 1Co 14:5
to you speaking in ⌊other⌋ l, 1Co 14:6
kinds of l in the world, 1Co 14:10
speak in ⌊other⌋ l more than all 1Co 14:18
people of other l and by the 1Co 14:21
in other l is intended as 1Co 14:22
all are speaking in ⌊other⌋ l, 1Co 14:23
forbid speaking in ⌊other⌋ l. 1Co 14:39
peoples, nations, l, and kings." Rv 10:11
peoples, tribes, l, and nations Rv 11:9
multitudes, nations, and l. Rv 17:15

LANGUISH (1)

her gates l. ⌊Her people⌋ are Jr 14:2

LANGUISHED (1)

Your inheritance when it l. Ps 68:9

LANGUISHES (1)

and everyone who lives in it l, Hs 4:3

LANTERNS (1)

Pharisees and came there with l, Jn 18:3

LAODICEA (6)

for those in L, and for all who Col 2:1
for those in L, and for those Col 4:13
greetings to the brothers in L, Col 4:15
you also read the letter from L. Col 4:16
Sardis, Philadelphia, and L." Rv 1:11
angel of the church in L write: Rv 3:14

LAODICEANS (1)

also in the church of the L; Col 4:16

LAP (6)

asleep on her l and called a man Jdg 16:19
him on her l, and took care Ru 4:16
child sat on her l until noon 2Kg 4:20
The lot is cast into the l, Pr 16:33
hip, and bounced on ⌊her⌋ l. Is 66:12
will be poured into your l. Lk 6:38

LAPPED (2)

of those who l with their hands Jdg 7:6
with the 300 men who l and hand Jdg 7:7

LAPPIDOTH (1)

was a prophet and the wife of L, Jdg 4:4

LAPS (2)

everyone who l water with his Jdg 7:5
on their sons' l after them, Jr 32:18

LARGE (160)

God created the l sea-creatures Gn 1:21
A l stone covered the opening of Gn 29:2
the region is l enough for them. Gn 34:21
been such a l number of locusts Ex 10:14
the various kinds of l lizard, Lv 11:29
the cities are l and fortified. Nm 13:28
confront them with a l force of Nm 20:20
the inheritance for a l ⌊tribe⌋, Nm 26:54
Gadites had a very l number of Nm 32:1
for a l clan and decrease Nm 33:54
the cities are l, fortified to Dt 1:28
besides a l number of rural Dt 3:5
a ⌊land with⌋ l and beautiful Dt 6:10
your herds and flocks grow l, Dt 8:13
than you ⌊with⌋ l cities Dt 9:1
not acquire very l amounts of Dt 17:17
you must set up l stones and Dt 27:2
raised over him a l pile of Jos 7:26
gate and put a l pile of rocks Jos 8:29
Gibeon was a l city like one Jos 10:2
the LORD threw l hailstones on Jos 10:11
Roll l stones against the mouth Jos 10:18
l stones were placed against Jos 10:27
as well as l fortified cities. Jos 14:12
descendants was too l for them. Jos 19:9
and a l quantity of clothing. Jos 22:8
the tribe of Manasseh built a l, Jos 22:10
also took a l stone and set it Jos 24:26
Jerubbaal, on top of a l stone. Jdg 9:5
his 70 sons on top of a l stone, Jdg 9:18
and stopped there near a l rock. 1Sm 6:14
and placed them on the l rock. 1Sm 6:15
The l rock on which the ark of 1Sm 6:18
a l stone over here at once. 1Sm 14:33
came to the l cistern at Secu, 1Sm 19:22
raid and brought a l amount of 2Sm 3:22
rich man had a l number of sheep 2Sm 12:2
David took away a l quantity of 2Sm 12:30
branches of a l oak tree, 2Sm 18:9
threw him into a l pit in the 2Sm 18:17
king commanded them to quarry l, 1Kg 5:17
The foundation was made of l, 1Kg 7:10
Jerusalem with a very l retinue, 1Kg 10:2
from Ophir a l quantity of almug 1Kg 10:11
Solomon made 200 l shields of 1Kg 10:16
king also made a l ivory throne 1Kg 10:18
around the altar l enough to 1Kg 18:32
Put on the l pot and make stew 2Kg 4:38
there was a l amount of money 2Kg 12:10
David took away a l quantity of 1Ch 20:2
brought a l quantity of cedar 1Ch 22:4
of the priests and the l court, 2Ch 4:9
Jerusalem with a very l retinue, 2Ch 9:1
Solomon made 200 l shields of 2Ch 9:15
king also made a l ivory throne 2Ch 9:17
He also put l shields and spears 2Ch 11:12
Judah bearing l shields and 2Ch 14:8
there was a l amount of money 2Ch 24:11
and ⌊catapult⌋ l stones for use 2Ch 26:15
A very l assembly of people was 2Ch 30:13
For a l number of the people— 2Ch 30:18
gathered ⌊them⌋ into l piles. 2Ch 31:6
divisions, whether l or small. 2Ch 31:15
God's temple, l and small, the 2Ch 36:18
an extremely l assembly of Ezr 10:1
So I called a l assembly Neh 5:7
The city was l and spacious, Neh 7:4
I appointed two l processions Neh 12:31
had prepared a l room for him Neh 13:5
and a very l number of servants. Jb 1:3
do not let a l ransom lead you Jb 36:18
A king is not saved by a l army; Ps 33:16
Your shields—l and small— Ps 35:2
living things both l and small. Ps 104:25
A l population is a king's Pr 14:28
and built l siege works against Ec 9:14
Take a l piece of parchment and Is 8:1
in spite of a very l population. Is 16:14
fragment l enough to take fire Is 30:14
down was a l one that King Asa Jr 41:9
Pick up some l stones and set Jr 43:9
Deploy small shields and l; Jr 46:3
rims were l and frightening Ezk 1:18
give him horses and a l army. Ezk 17:15
make the pile of kindling l. Ezk 24:9
the small ledge to the l ledge, Ezk 43:14
I saw a very l number of trees Ezk 47:7
The tree grew l and strong; Dn 4:11
saw, which grew l and strong, Dn 4:20
strong, with l iron teeth. Dn 7:7
powerful, the l horn was Dn 8:8
and the l horn between his eyes Dn 8:21
and assemble a l number of armed Dn 11:10
With a l army he will stir up Dn 11:25
an extremely l and powerful army Dn 11:25
way and in your l number of Hs 10:13
camp is very l; Those who carry Jl 2:11
The l house will be smashed to Am 6:11
Nineveh was an extremely l city, Jnh 3:3
L crowds followed Him from Mt 4:25
the mountain, l crowds followed Mt 8:1
When Jesus saw l crowds around Mt 8:18
a l herd of pigs was feeding. Mt 8:30
Such l crowds gathered around Mt 13:2
of heaven is like a l net thrown Mt 13:47
and l crowds came to Him, having Mt 15:30
pieces—seven l baskets full. Mt 15:37
4,000 and how many l baskets you Mt 16:10
L crowds followed Him, and He Mt 19:2
Jericho, a l crowd followed Him Mt 20:29
very l crowd spread their robes Mt 21:8
A l mob, with swords and clubs, Mt 26:47
the soldiers a l sum of money Mt 28:12
and a very l crowd gathered Mk 4:1
and produces l branches, so that Mk 4:32
Now a l herd of pigs was there, Mk 5:11
a l crowd gathered around Him Mk 5:21
and a l crowd was following and Mk 5:24
days there was again a l crowd, Mk 8:1
collected seven l baskets of Mk 8:8
many l baskets full of pieces Mk 8:20
they saw a l crowd around them Mk 9:14
His disciples and a l crowd, Mk 10:46
And the l crowd was listening Mk 12:37
people were putting in l sums. Mk 12:41
will show you a l room upstairs, Mk 14:15
which was very l—had been Mk 16:4
and l crowds would come together Lk 5:15

Now there was a **l** crowd of tax Lk 5:29
level place with a **l** crowd of Lk 6:17
His disciples and a **l** crowd were Lk 7:11
A **l** crowd from the city was also Lk 7:12
As a **l** crowd was gathering, Lk 8:4
A **l** herd of pigs was there, Lk 8:32
the mountain, a **l** crowd met Him. Lk 9:37
A man was giving a **l** banquet and Lk 14:16
Then he will show you a **l**, Lk 22:12
Then a **l** crowd of the Jews Jn 12:9
when the **l** crowd that had come Jn 12:12
it dies, it produces a **l** crop. Jn 12:24
because of the **l** number of fish. Jn 21:6
ashore, full of **l** fish—153 of Jn 21:11
and a **l** group of priests became Ac 6:7
him in a **l** basket through Ac 9:25
that resembled a **l** sheet being Ac 10:11
that resembled a **l** sheet being Ac 11:5
and a **l** number who believed Ac 11:21
and **l** numbers of people were Ac 11:24
the church and taught **l** numbers, Ac 11:26
and made a **l** profit for her Ac 16:16
for a **l** amount of money. Ac 22:28
concerning this **l** sum 2Co 8:20
Look at what **l** letters I have Gl 6:11
Now in a **l** house there are not 2Tm 2:20
also have such a **l** cloud of Heb 12:1
though very **l** and driven by Jms 3:4
Consider how **l** a forest a small Jms 3:5
And a **l** sword was given to him. Rv 6:4
He was given a **l** amount of Rv 8:3
a stone like a **l** millstone and Rv 18:21

LARGER *(14)*
was five times **l** than any of Gn 43:34
by lot among the **l** and smaller Nm 26:56
more from a **l** ⌊tribe⌋ and less Nm 35:8
The people are **l** and taller than Dt 1:28
and an army **l** than yours, do not Dt 20:1
your house, a **l** and a smaller. Dt 25:14
was **l** than Ai, and all its men Jos 10:2
The **l** room he paneled with 2Ch 3:5
their feet and faced the **l** room. 2Ch 3:13
of the standard **l** capacity Ezk 45:11
one standard **l** capacity measure Ezk 45:14
one standard **l** capacity measure Ezk 45:14
a multitude **l** than the first. Dn 11:13
Is their territory **l** than yours? Am 6:2

LASEA *(1)*
Fair Havens near the city of **L**. Ac 27:8

LASH *(1)*
stretched him out for the **l**, Ac 22:25

LASHA *(1)*
Admah, and Zeboiim, as far as **L**. Gn 10:19

LASHARON *(1)*
of Aphek one the king of **L** one Jos 12:18

LASHES *(6)*
number ⌊of **l**⌋ appropriate for Dt 25:2
He may be flogged with 40 **l**, Dt 25:3
flogged with more **l** than these, Dt 25:3
than a hundred **l** into a fool. Pr 17:10
L and wounds purge away evil, Pr 20:30
from the Jews 40 **l** minus one. 2Co 11:24

LAST *(116)*
This one, at **l**, is bone of my Gn 2:23
I slept with my father **l** night. Gn 19:34
He took his **l** breath and died at Gn 25:8
He took his **l** breath and died, Gn 25:17
and said, "At **l**, my husband will Gn 29:34
but **l** night the God of your Gn 31:29
He issued His verdict **l** night." Gn 31:42
next, and Rachel and Joseph **l**. Gn 33:2
With her **l** breath—for she was Gn 35:18
He took his **l** breath and died, Gn 35:29
to Joseph, "At **l** I can die, now Gn 46:30
on the edge of the **l** curtain in Ex 26:4
on the edge of the **l** curtain in Ex 36:11
of years since the **l** Jubilee. Lv 25:15
redemption will **l** until a year Lv 25:29
of redemption will **l** a year. Lv 25:29
are to move out **l**, with their Nm 2:31
your strength **l** as long as you Dt 33:25
and when every **l** one of them had Jos 8:24
feast, and at **l**, on the seventh Jdg 14:17
and the **l** division headed down 1Sm 13:18
the LORD said to me **l** night." 1Sm 15:16
They stopped at the **l** house 2Sm 15:17
should you be the **l** to restore 2Sm 19:11
should you be the **l** to restore 2Sm 19:12
These are the **l** words of David: 2Sm 23:1
to the **l** words of David, 1Ch 23:27
and Manasseh, to the **l** one. 2Ch 31:1
these are the **l** ones, from Ezr 8:13
from the first day to the **l**. Neh 8:18
the king for the **l** 30 days." Est 4:11
like a shadow and does not **l**. Jb 14:2
he breathes his **l**—where is he? Jb 14:10
He will stand on the dust at **l**. Jb 19:25
his prosperity will not **l**. Jb 20:21
inheritance will **l** forever. Ps 37:18
his⌋ assets, man will not **l**; Ps 49:12
us knows how long this will **l**. Ps 74:9
their doom would **l** forever. Ps 81:15
Our lives **l** seventy years or, Ps 90:10
all God does will **l** forever; Ec 3:14
the **l** days the mountain of the Is 2:2
has turned my **l** glimmer of hope Is 21:4
agreement with Sheol will not **l**. Is 28:18
and with the **l**—I am He." Is 41:4
I am the first and I am the **l**. Is 44:6
I am the first, I am also the **l**. Is 48:12
But My salvation will **l** forever, Is 51:6
My righteousness will **l** forever, Is 51:8
every **l** one for his own gain. Is 56:11
she breathed her ⌊**l**⌋ breath. Jr 15:9
jar so they will **l** a long time. Jr 32:14
fortunes of Moab in the **l** days. Jr 48:47
the **l** days, I will restore the Jr 49:39
l who has crunched his bones Jr 50:17
In the **l** years you will enter a Ezk 38:8
It will happen in the **l** days, Ezk 38:16
what will happen in the **l** days. Dn 2:28
and the longer one came up **l**. Dn 8:3
the events of⌋ this vision **l**— Dn 8:13
to your people in the **l** days, Dn 10:14
to His goodness in the **l** days. Hs 3:5
every **l** ⌊one⌋ of you with Am 4:2
the **l** days the mountain of the Mc 4:1
until you have paid the **l** penny! Mt 5:26
that man's **l** condition is worse Mt 12:45
many who are first will be **l**, Mt 19:30
will be last, and the **l** first. Mt 19:30
with the **l** and ending with Mt 20:8
'These **l** men put in one hour, Mt 20:12
to give this **l** man the same as I Mt 20:14
So the **l** will be first, and the Mt 20:16
will be first, and the first **l**." Mt 20:16
Then **l** of all the woman died. Mt 22:27
Then the **l** deception will be Mt 27:64
he must be **l** of all and servant Mk 9:35
many who are first will be **l**, Mk 10:31
will be last, and the **l** first." Mk 10:31
L of all, the woman died too. Mk 12:22
a loud cry and breathed His **l**. Mk 15:37
saw the way He breathed His **l**, Mk 15:39
that man's **l** condition is worse Lk 11:26
until you have paid the **l** cent." Lk 12:59
some are **l** who will be first, Lk 13:30
some are first who will be **l**." Lk 13:30
Saying this, He breathed His **l**. Lk 23:46
raise them up on the **l** day. Jn 6:39
will raise him up on the **l** day." Jn 6:40
will raise him up on the **l** day. Jn 6:44
will raise him up on the **l** day, Jn 6:54
On the **l** and most important day Jn 7:37
the resurrection at the **l** day." Jn 11:24
will judge him on the **l** day. Jn 12:48
And it will be in the **l** days, Ac 2:17
I may now at **l** succeed in coming Rm 1:10
apostles, in **l** place, like men 1Co 4:9
L of all, as to one abnormally 1Co 15:8
The **l** enemy to be abolished is 1Co 15:26
the **l** Adam became a life-giving 1Co 15:45
of an eye, at the **l** trumpet. 1Co 15:52
has been prepared since **l** year," 2Co 9:2
that now at **l** you have renewed Php 4:10
times will come in the **l** days. 2Tm 3:1
these **l** days, He has spoken to Heb 1:2
up treasure in the **l** days! Jms 5:3
to be revealed in the **l** time. 1Pt 1:5
the **l** state is worse for them 2Pt 2:20
come in the **l** days to scoff, 2Pt 3:3
Children, it is the **l** hour. 1Jn 2:18
from this that it is the **l** hour. 1Jn 2:18
I am the First and the **L**, Rv 1:17
First and the **L**, the One who was Rv 2:8
Your **l** works are greater than Rv 2:19
angels with the seven **l** plagues, Rv 15:1
filled with the seven **l** plagues, Rv 21:9
First and the **L**, the Beginning Rv 22:13

LASTED *(13)*
So Adam's life **l** 930 years; Gn 5:5
So Seth's life **l** 912 years; Gn 5:8
So Enosh's life **l** 905 years; Gn 5:11
So Kenan's life **l** 910 years; Gn 5:14
So Mahalalel's life **l** 895 years; Gn 5:17
So Jared's life **l** 962 years; Gn 5:20
So Enoch's life **l** 365 years. Gn 5:23
Methuselah's life **l** 969 years; Gn 5:27
So Lamech's life **l** 777 years; Gn 5:31
So Noah's life **l** 950 years; Gn 9:29
My pilgrimage has **l** 130 years. Gn 47:9
of the altar **l** seven days 2Ch 7:9
the godless has **l** only a moment? Jb 20:5

LASTING *(7)*
severe and **l** plagues, and Dt 28:59
establish a **l** dynasty for him 1Sm 2:35
to make a **l** dynasty for my 1Sm 25:28
build you a **l** dynasty just as 1Kg 11:38
He gave them **l** shame. Ps 78:66
l wealth and righteousness. Pr 8:18
there is no **l** remembrance of the Ec 2:16

LASTS *(4)*
For His anger **l** only a moment, Ps 30:5
his throne as long as heaven **l**. Ps 89:29
not even a crown **l** for all time. Pr 27:24
the food that **l** for eternal life Jn 6:27

LATCHED *(1)*
so they quickly **l** onto the hint 1Kg 20:33

LATE *(12)*
the early and **l** rains, and you Dt 11:14
So they waited until **l** afternoon Jdg 19:8
you get up early and stay up **l**, Ps 127:2
both early and **l**, in its season, Jr 5:24
certainly come and not be **l**. Hab 2:3
wilderness, and it is already **l**. Mt 14:15
it was already **l**, His disciples Mk 6:35
wilderness, and it is already **l**! Mk 6:35
it was already **l**, He went out to Mk 11:11
L in the day, the Twelve Lk 9:12
the early and the **l** rains. Jms 5:7
trees in **l** autumn—fruitless, Jd 12

LATELY *(1)*
Have you not **l** called Me: Jr 3:4

LATER *(51)*
Seven days **l** the waters of the Gn 7:10
L, you can continue on." Gn 18:5
L, Leah bore a daughter and Gn 30:21
three months **l** Judah was told, Gn 38:24
Two years **l** Pharaoh had a dream: Gn 41:1
Years **l**, after Moses had grown Ex 2:11
L, Moses and Aaron went in and Ex 5:1
since they are **l** crops. Ex 9:32
if he can ⌊**l**⌋ get up and walk Ex 21:19
of it, but ⌊**l**⌋ recognizes ⌊it⌋ Lv 5:3
of it, but ⌊**l**⌋ recognizes it, Lv 5:4
L, Moses inquired about the male Lv 10:16
LORD your God in **l** days and obey Dt 4:30
L, I brought you to the land Jos 24:8
L, the trees said to the Jdg 9:12
time **l**, the Ammonites fought Jdg 11:4
L on, during the wheat harvest, Jdg 15:1
time **l**, he fell in love with Jdg 16:4
L, when Boaz arrived from Ru 2:4
About 10 days **l**, the LORD struck 1Sm 25:38
Some time **l**, David inquired of 2Sm 2:1
heard ⌊about it⌋ **l** and said: 2Sm 3:28
Some time **l** the king of the 2Sm 10:1
Two years **l**, Absalom's 2Sm 13:23
Some time **l**, King Ben-hadad of 2Kg 6:24
Some time **l**, King Nahash of the 1Ch 19:1
It was only **l** that I asked the Neh 13:6
time **l**, when King Ahasuerus' Est 2:1
be written for a **l** generation, Ps 102:18
away! Come back **l**. I'll give it Pr 3:28
that you may be wise in **l** life. Pr 19:20
rashly and **l** to reconsider his Pr 20:25
a person will **l** find more favor Pr 28:23
his youth will become arrogant **l** Pr 29:21
who come **l** will not rejoice Ec 4:16
A long time **l** the LORD said to Jr 13:6

King Zedekiah **l** sent ⌊for him⌋ Jr 37:17
Yet **I** he changed his mind and Mt 21:29
L the rest of the virgins also Mt 25:11
He will rise three days **l**." Mk 9:31
L, He appeared to the Eleven Mk 16:14
Not many days **l**, the younger son Lk 15:13
l you can eat and drink'? Lk 17:8
but **l** he said to himself, Lk 18:4
About an hour **l**, another kept Lk 22:59
Me now, but you will follow **l**." Jn 13:36
430 years **l**, does not revoke Gl 3:17
not have spoken **l** about another Heb 4:8
L on, however, it yields the Heb 12:11
you know that **l**, when he wanted Heb 12:17
l destroyed those who did not Jd 5

LATIN *(1)*
written in Hebrew, **L**, and Greek. Jn 19:20

LATRINE *(1)*
temple of Baal and made it a **l**— 2Kg 10:27

LATTER *(2)*
LORD blessed the **l** part of Job's Jb 42:12
that in the **l** times some will 1Tm 4:1

LATTICE *(3)*
she ⌊peered⌋ through the **l**, Jdg 5:28
my house I looked through my **l**. Pr 7:6
windows, peering through the **l**. Sg 2:9

LATTICED *(1)*
through the **l** window of his 2Kg 1:2

LATTICEWORK *(3)*
the pillars had gratings of **l**, 1Kg 7:17
by bronze **l** and pomegranates, Jr 52:22
around the **l** numbered 100. Jr 52:23

LAUGH *(12)*
Why did Sarah **l**, saying, 'Can I Gn 18:13
"I did not **l**," she said, because Gn 18:15
But He replied, "No, you did **l**." Gn 18:15
God has made me **l**, and everyone Gn 21:6
who hears will **l** with me." Gn 21:6
You will **l** at destruction and Jb 5:22
But You **l** at them, LORD; Ps 59:8
in turn, will **l** at your calamity Pr 1:26
and she can **l** at the time to Pr 31:25
a time to weep and a time to **l**; Ec 3:4
They **l** at every fortress and Hab 1:10
weep now, because you will **l**. Lk 6:21

LAUGHED *(3)*
to the ground, **l**, and thought in Gn 17:17
So she **l** to herself: Gn 18:12
the inhabitants **l** at them and 2Ch 30:10

LAUGHING *(5)*
looked at her, **l** over her Lm 1:7
And they started **l** at Him. Mt 9:24
They started **l** at Him, but He Mk 5:40
you who are **l** now, because you Lk 6:25
They started **l** at Him, because Lk 8:53

LAUGHINGSTOCK *(9)*
otherwise we will become a **l**. Gn 38:23
I am a **l** to my friends, by Jb 12:4
and upright man is a **l**. Jb 12:4
the nations, a **l** among the Ps 44:14
I am a **l** all the time; Jr 20:7
and he will also become a **l**. Jr 48:26
Wasn't Israel a **l** to you? Jr 48:27
will become a **l** and a shock to Jr 48:39
I am a **l** to all my people, Lm 3:14

LAUGHS *(5)*
l at the horse and its rider. Jb 39:18
He **l** at fear, since he is afraid Jb 39:22
and he **l** at the whirring of a Jb 41:29
The One enthroned in heaven **l**; Ps 2:4
Lord **l** at him because He sees Ps 37:13

LAUGHTER *(8)*
your mouth with **l** and your lips Jb 8:21
mouths were filled with **l** then, Ps 126:2
Even in **l** a heart may be sad, Pr 14:13
I said about **l**, "It is madness," Ec 2:2
better than **l**, for when a face Ec 7:3
pot, so is the **l** of the fool. Ec 7:6
A feast is prepared for **l**, Ec 10:19
Your **l** must change to mourning Jms 4:9

LAUNCH *(2)*
Should I **l** an attack against 1Sm 23:2
L an attack against the 1Sm 23:2

LAUNDERER *(1)*
white as no **l** on earth could Mk 9:3

LAUREL *(1)*
plants a **l**, and the rain makes Is 44:14

LAVISH *(3)*
So David made **l** preparations 1Ch 22:5
or be persuaded by **l** gifts. Pr 6:35
He will **l** plunder, loot, and Dn 11:24

LAVISHED *(3)*
You **l** your sexual favors on Ezk 16:15
I **l** silver and gold on her, Hs 2:8
that He **l** on us with all wisdom Eph 1:8

LAVISHLY *(3)*
He has **l** sacrificed oxen, 1Kg 1:19
went down and **l** sacrificed oxen 1Kg 1:25
linen, feasting **l** every day. Lk 16:19

LAW *(385)*
made it a **l**, still in effect Gn 47:26
same **l** will apply to both the Ex 12:49
so that the **l** of the LORD may be Ex 13:9
with according to this same **l**. Ex 21:31
tablets with the **l** and commands Ex 24:12
This is the **l** of the burnt Lv 6:9
Now this is the **l** of the grain Lv 6:14
This is the **l** of the sin Lv 6:25
Now this is the **l** of the Lv 7:1
the **l** is the same for both. Lv 7:7
Now this is the **l** of the Lv 7:11
This is the **l** for the burnt Lv 7:37
This is the **l** concerning Lv 11:46
This is the **l** for a woman giving Lv 12:7
This is the **l** concerning a Lv 13:59
This is the **l** concerning the Lv 14:2
This is the **l** for someone who Lv 14:32
This is the **l** for any skin Lv 14:54
This is the **l** regarding skin Lv 14:57
This is the **l** for someone with a Lv 15:32
have the same **l** for the foreign Lv 24:22
This is the **l** regarding jealousy Nm 5:29
This is the **l** of the Nazirite: Nm 6:13
same **l** and the same ordinance Nm 15:16
have the same **l** for the person Nm 15:29
This is the **l** when a person dies Nm 19:14
Moses began to explain this **l**, Dt 1:5
this entire **l** I set before you Dt 4:8
This is the **l** Moses gave the Dt 4:44
Here is the **l** concerning a case Dt 19:4
words of this **l** on the stones Dt 27:3
words of this **l** on the Dt 27:8
words of this **l** into practice.' Dt 27:26
to obey all the words of this **l**, Dt 28:58
recorded in the book of this **l**, Dt 28:61
written in this book of the **l**. Dt 29:21
follow all the words of this **l**. Dt 29:29
this book of the **l** and return to Dt 30:10
wrote down this **l** and gave it to Dt 31:9
to read this **l** aloud before all Dt 31:11
follow all the words of this **l**. Dt 31:12
do not know ⌊the **l**⌋ will listen Dt 31:13
every single word of this **l**, Dt 31:24
this book of the **l** and place it Dt 31:26
follow all the words of this **l**. Dt 32:46
in the book of the **l** of Moses: Jos 8:31
Joshua copied the **l** of Moses, Jos 8:32
aloud all the words of the **l**— Jos 8:34
is written in the book of the **l**. Jos 8:34
in the book of the **l** of Moses, Jos 23:6
in the book of the **l** of God; Jos 24:26
policy⌋ as a **l** and an ordinance 1Sm 30:25
is written in the **l** of Moses, 1Kg 2:3
his heart the **l** of the LORD God 2Kg 10:31
the book of the **l** of Moses where 2Kg 14:6
to all the **l** I commanded your 2Kg 17:13
l and commandments the LORD 2Kg 17:34
whole **l** that My servant Moses 2Kg 21:8
the book of the **l** in the LORD's 2Kg 22:8
the words of the book of the **l**, 2Kg 22:11
the words of the **l** that were 2Kg 23:24
according to all the **l** of Moses, 2Kg 23:25
written in the **l** of the LORD, 1Ch 16:40
may keep the **l** of the LORD your 1Ch 22:12
way to walk in My **L** as you have 2Ch 6:16
he abandoned the **l** of the LORD— 2Ch 12:1
teaching priest, and without **l**, 2Ch 15:3
of bloodguilt, **l**, commandment, 2Ch 19:10
it is written in the **l** of Moses, 2Ch 23:18
as it is written in the **L**, 2Ch 25:4
to the **l** of Moses the man 2Ch 30:16
as written in the **l** of the LORD. 2Ch 31:3
energy to the **l** of the LORD. 2Ch 31:4
in the **l** and in the commandment, 2Ch 31:21
Moses—all the **l**, statutes, 2Ch 33:8
the book of the **l** of the LORD 2Ch 34:14
the book of the **l** in the LORD's 2Ch 34:15
king heard the words of the **l**, 2Ch 34:19
is written in the **l** of the LORD, 2Ch 35:26
written in the **l** of Moses the Ezr 3:2
skilled in the **l** of Moses, Ezr 7:6
to study the **l** of the LORD, Ezr 7:10
an expert in the **l** of the God of Ezr 7:12
according to the **l** of your God, Ezr 7:14
and expert in the **l** of the God Ezr 7:21
does not keep the **l** of your God Ezr 7:26
your God and the **l** of the king, Ezr 7:26
it be done according to the **l**. Ezr 10:3
the book of the **l** of Moses that Neh 8:1
priest brought the **l** before the Neh 8:2
to the book of the **l**. Neh 8:3
explained the **l** to the people as Neh 8:7
read the book of the **l** of God, Neh 8:8
they heard the words of the **l**. Neh 8:9
to study the words of the **l**. Neh 8:13
written in the **l** how the LORD Neh 8:14
the book of the **l** of God every Neh 8:18
the book of the **l** of the LORD Neh 9:3
and a **l** through Your servant Neh 9:14
They flung Your **l** behind their Neh 9:26
them to turn back to Your **l**, Neh 9:29
not obey Your **l** or listen to Neh 9:34
peoples to ⌊obey⌋ the **l** of God— Neh 10:28
to follow the **l** of God given Neh 10:29
as it is written in the **l**. Neh 10:34
by the **l**, and will bring Neh 10:36
they heard the **l**, they separated Neh 13:3
with experts in **l** and justice. Est 1:13
to the **l**, what should be Est 1:15
issued as **l** throughout every Est 3:14
and the **l** was issued in the Est 3:15
since ⌊the **l**⌋ prohibited anyone Est 4:2
know that one **l** applies to every Est 4:11
even if it is against the **l**. Est 4:16
to be issued as **l** in every Est 8:13
The **l** was also issued in the Est 8:14
command and his **l** reached, Est 8:17
command and **l** went into effect Est 9:1
tomorrow to carry out today's **l**, Est 9:13
so a **l** was announced in Susa, Est 9:14
Jacob and set up a **l** in Israel, Ps 78:5
and refused to live by His **l**. Ps 78:10
discipline and teach from Your **l** Ps 94:12
one that creates trouble by **l**— Ps 94:20
according to the **l** of the LORD! Ps 119:1
see wonderful things in Your **l**. Ps 119:18
I will always keep Your **l**, Ps 119:44
night, LORD, and I keep Your **l**. Ps 119:55
me, I did not forget Your **l**. Ps 119:61
⌊for⌋ they have broken Your **l**. Ps 119:126
reign and rulers enact just **l**; Pr 8:15
who reject the **l** praise the Pr 28:4
who keep the **l** battle against Pr 28:4
A discerning son keeps the **l**, Pr 28:7
ear away from hearing the **l**— Pr 28:9
who keeps the **l** will be happy. Pr 29:18
To the **l** and to the testimony! Is 8:20
L after law, law after law, line Is 28:10
Law after **l**, law after law, line Is 28:10
Law after law, **l** after law, line Is 28:10
law, law after **l**, line after Is 28:10
L after law, law after law, line Is 28:13
Law after **l**, law after law, line Is 28:13
Law after law, **l** after law, line Is 28:13
law, law after **l**, line after Is 28:13
experts in the **l** no longer knew Jr 2:8
They have rejected My **l**. Jr 6:19
the **l** of the LORD is with us? Jr 8:8
abandoned My **l** I set in front Jr 9:13
Me and did not keep My **l**. Jr 16:11
the **l** will never be lost from Jr 18:18
according to My **l** that I set Jr 26:4
I will place My **l** within them Jr 31:33
or live according to Your **l**. Jr 32:23
or walked by My **l** or My statutes Jr 44:10
voice and didn't walk in His **l**, Jr 44:23
violence to My **l** and profane My Ezk 22:26
This is the **l** of the temple: Ezk 43:12
this is the **l** of the temple. Ezk 43:12
concerning the **l** of his God." Dn 6:5

a **l** of the Medes and Persians, Dn 6:8
As a **l** of the Medes and Dn 6:12
king know it is a **l** of the Medes Dn 6:15
broken Your **l** and turned away Dn 9:11
curse written in the **l** of Moses, Dn 9:11
it is written in the **l** of Moses, Dn 9:13
forgotten the **l** of your God, Hs 4:6
covenant and rebel against My **l**. Hs 8:1
him ten thousand points of My **l**, Hs 8:12
have rejected the **l** of the LORD Am 2:4
This is why the **l** is ineffective Hab 1:4
not to obey the **l** or the words Zch 7:12
destroy the **L** or the Prophets. Mt 5:17
pass from the **l** until all things Mt 5:18
this is the **L** and the Prophets. Mt 7:12
and the **l** prophesied until Mt 11:13
read in the **L** that on Sabbath Mt 12:5
an expert in the **l**, asked a Mt 22:35
in the **l** is the greatest?" Mt 22:36
the **L** and the Prophets depend Mt 22:40
important matters of the **l**— Mt 23:23
according to the **l** of Moses were Lk 2:22
is written in the **l** of the Lord: Lk 2:23
is stated in the **l** of the Lord: Lk 2:24
what was customary under the **l**, Lk 2:27
according to the **l** of the Lord, Lk 2:39
teachers of the **l** were sitting Lk 5:17
experts in the **l** had not been Lk 7:30
expert in the **l** stood up to test Lk 10:25
"What is written in the **l**?" Lk 10:26
experts in the **l** answered Him, Lk 11:45
also to you experts in the **l**! Lk 11:46
Woe to you experts in the **l**! Lk 11:52
Jesus asked the **l** experts and Lk 14:3
The **L** and the Prophets were Lk 16:16
a letter in the **l** to drop out. Lk 16:17
about Me in the **L** of Moses, Lk 24:44
for although the **l** was given Jn 1:17
One Moses wrote about in the **l** Jn 1:45
Didn't Moses give you the **l**? Jn 7:19
Yet none of you keeps the **l**! Jn 7:19
so that the **l** of Moses won't be Jn 7:23
know the **l**, is accursed!" Jn 7:49
Our **l** doesn't judge a man before Jn 7:51
In the **l** Moses commanded us to Jn 8:5
in your **l** it is written that Jn 8:17
Isn't it written in your **l**, Jn 10:34
from the **l** that the Messiah Jn 12:34
written in their **l** might be Jn 15:25
judge Him according to your **l**." Jn 18:31
"We have a **l**," the Jews replied Jn 19:7
according to that **l** He must die, Jn 19:7
a teacher of the **l** who was Ac 5:34
this holy place and the **l**. Ac 6:13
You received the **l** under the Ac 7:53
reading of the **L** and the Ac 13:15
from through the **l** of Moses. Ac 13:39
them to keep the **l** of Moses!" Ac 15:5
worship God contrary to the **l**!" Ac 18:13
names, and your own **l**, see to it Ac 18:15
they are all zealous for the **l**. Ac 21:20
careful about observing the **l**. Ac 21:24
people, our **l**, and this place Ac 21:28
view of our patriarchal **l**. Ac 22:3
a devout man according to the **l**, Ac 22:12
judging me according to the **l**, Ac 23:3
of the **l** are you ordering Ac 23:3
disputed matters in their **l**, Ac 23:29
to judge him according to our **l**. Ac 24:6
are written in the **L** and in the Ac 24:14
Neither against the Jewish **l**, Ac 25:8
Jesus from both the **L** of Moses Ac 28:23
without the **l** will also perish Rm 2:12
will also perish without the **l**, Rm 2:12
under the **l** will be judged Rm 2:12
the law will be judged by the **l**. Rm 2:12
hearers of the **l** are not Rm 2:13
doers of the **l** will be declared Rm 2:13
do not have the **l**, instinctively Rm 2:14
do what the **l** demands, Rm 2:14
they are a **l** to themselves even Rm 2:14
though they do not have the **l**. Rm 2:14
the work of the **l** is written on Rm 2:15
and rest in the **l**, and boast in Rm 2:17
being instructed from the **l**, Rm 2:18
having in the **l** the full Rm 2:20
boast in the **l**, do you dishonor Rm 2:23
dishonor God by breaking the **l**? Rm 2:23
you if you observe the **l**, Rm 2:25
fulfills the **l**, will judge you Rm 2:27
letter ⌊of the **l**⌋ and Rm 2:27
whatever the **l** says speaks to Rm 3:19
those who are subject to the **l**, Rm 3:19
His sight by the works of the **l**, Rm 3:20
for through the **l** ⌊comes⌋ the Rm 3:20
now, apart from the **l**, God's Rm 3:21
attested by the **L** and the Rm 3:21
By what kind of **l**? By one of Rm 3:27
the contrary, by a **l** of faith. Rm 3:27
by faith apart from works of **l**. Rm 3:28
then cancel the **l** through faith? Rm 3:31
the contrary, we uphold the **l**. Rm 3:31
the world was not through the **l**, Rm 4:13
who are of the **l** are heirs, Rm 4:14
For the **l** produces wrath; Rm 4:15
where there is no **l**, there is no Rm 4:15
only to those who are of the **l**, Rm 4:16
was in the world before the **l**, Rm 5:13
account when there is no **l**. Rm 5:13
The **l** came along to multiply the Rm 5:20
are not under **l** but under grace Rm 6:14
are not under **l** but under grace Rm 6:15
to those who understand **l**, Rm 7:1
unaware that the **l** has authority Rm 7:1
is released from the **l** regarding Rm 7:2
dies, she is free from that **l**. Rm 7:3
in relation to the **l** through the Rm 7:4
through the **l** in every part of Rm 7:5
have been released from the **l**, Rm 7:6
not in the old letter of the **l**. Rm 7:6
then? Is the **l** sin? Absolutely Rm 7:7
sin if it were not for the **l**. Rm 7:7
to covet if the **l** had not said, Rm 7:7
apart from the **l** sin is dead. Rm 7:8
I was alive apart from the **l**, Rm 7:9
So then, the **l** is holy, and the Rm 7:12
we know that the **l** is spiritual; Rm 7:14
agree with the **l** that it is good Rm 7:16
I joyfully agree with God's **l**. Rm 7:22
I see a different **l** in the parts Rm 7:23
war against the **l** of my mind and Rm 7:23
me prisoner to the **l** of sin in Rm 7:23
am a slave to the **l** of God, Rm 7:25
with my flesh, to the **l** of sin. Rm 7:25
the Spirit's **l** of life in Christ Rm 8:2
you free from the **l** of sin and Rm 8:2
What the **l** could not do since it Rm 8:3
not submit itself to God's **l**, Rm 8:7
the giving of the **l**, the temple Rm 9:4
the **l** for righteousness, Rm 9:31
has not achieved the **l**. Rm 9:31
the end of the **l** for Rm 10:4
that is from the **l**: Rm 10:5
another has fulfilled the **l**. Rm 13:8
is the fulfillment of the **l**. Rm 13:10
someone dare go to **l** before the 1Co 6:1
goes to **l** against brother 1Co 6:6
Doesn't the **l** also say the same 1Co 9:8
it is written in the **l** of Moses, 1Co 9:9
under the **l**, like one under 1Co 9:20
one under the **l**—though I 1Co 9:20
I myself am not under the **l**— 1Co 9:20
law—to win those under the **l**. 1Co 9:20
To those who are outside the **l**, 1Co 9:21
one outside the **l**—not being 1Co 9:21
not being outside God's **l**, 1Co 9:21
but under the **l** of Christ— 1Co 9:21
to win those outside the **l**. 1Co 9:21
written in the **l**: By people of 1Co 14:21
submissive, as the **l** also says. 1Co 14:34
and the power of sin is the **l**. 1Co 15:56
the works of the **l** but by faith Gl 2:16
and not by the works of the **l**, Gl 2:16
works of the **l** no human being Gl 2:16
For through the **l** I have died to Gl 2:19
the law I have died to the **l**, Gl 2:19
comes through the **l**, Gl 2:21
the works of the **l** or by hearing Gl 3:2
the works of the **l** or by hearing Gl 3:5
the works of the **l** are under a Gl 3:10
written in the book of the **l**. Gl 3:10
justified before God by the **l**, Gl 3:11
But the **l** is not based on faith; Gl 3:12
the curse of the **l** by becoming a Gl 3:13
the **l**, which came 430 years Gl 3:17
the inheritance is from the **l**, Gl 3:18
Why the **l** then? It was added Gl 3:19
⌊The **l**⌋ was ordered through Gl 3:19
Is the **l** therefore contrary to Gl 3:21
For if a **l** had been given that Gl 3:21
would certainly be by the **l**. Gl 3:21
we were confined under the **l**, Gl 3:23
The **l**, then, was our guardian Gl 3:24
of a woman, born under the **l**, Gl 4:4
to redeem those under the **l**, Gl 4:5
you who want to be under the **l**, Gl 4:21
the law, don't you hear the **l**? Gl 4:21
obligated to keep the entire **l**. Gl 5:3
justified by the **l** are alienated Gl 5:4
For the entire **l** is fulfilled in Gl 5:14
Spirit, you are not under the **l**. Gl 5:18
such things there is no **l**. Gl 5:23
will fulfill the **l** of Christ. Gl 6:2
don't keep the **l** themselves; Gl 6:13
did away with the **l** of the Eph 2:15
as to the **l**, a Pharisee; Php 3:5
righteousness that is in the **l**, Php 3:6
of my own from the **l**, Php 3:9
want to be teachers of the **l**, 1Tm 1:7
Now we know that the **l** is good, 1Tm 1:8
know that the **l** is not meant for 1Tm 1:9
about the **l**, for they are Ti 3:9
according to the **l** to collect a Heb 7:5
it the people received the **l** Heb 7:11
must be a change of **l** as well. Heb 7:12
for the **l** perfected nothing Heb 7:19
For the **l** appoints as high Heb 7:28
came after the **l**, ⌊appoints⌋ a Heb 7:28
the gifts prescribed by the **l**. Heb 8:4
the people according to the **l**, Heb 9:19
According to the **l** almost Heb 9:22
Since the **l** has ⌊only⌋ a shadow Heb 10:1
are offered according to the **l** Heb 10:8
If anyone disregards Moses' **l**, Heb 10:28
into the perfect **l** of freedom Jms 1:25
carry out the royal **l** prescribed Jms 2:8
by the **l** as transgressors Jms 2:9
For whoever keeps the entire **l**, Jms 2:10
be judged by the **l** of freedom. Jms 2:12
criticizes the **l** and judges the Jms 4:11
the law and judges the **l**. Jms 4:11
if you judge the **l**, you are not Jms 4:11
not a doer of the **l** but a judge. Jms 4:11
commits sin also breaks the **l**; 1Jn 3:4
sin is the breaking of **l**. 1Jn 3:4

LAW'S *(2)*
man keeps the **l** requirements, Rm 2:26
order that the **l** requirement Rm 8:4

LAWBREAKER *(4)*
but if you are a **l**, your Rm 2:25
you who are a **l** in spite of Rm 2:27
down, I show myself to be a **l**. Gl 2:18
but you do murder, you are a **l**. Jms 2:11

LAWBREAKERS *(1)*
Depart from Me, you **l**!' Mt 7:23

LAWFUL *(19)*
doing what is not **l** to do on the Mt 12:2
which is not **l** for him or for Mt 12:4
"Is it **l** to heal on the Sabbath?" Mt 12:10
is **l** to do good on the Sabbath. Mt 12:12
"It's not **l** for you to have her!" Mt 14:4
Is it **l** for a man to divorce his Mt 19:3
it **l** to pay taxes to Caesar or Mt 22:17
It's not **l** to put it into the Mt 27:6
what is not **l** on the Sabbath?" Mk 2:24
which is not **l** for anyone to eat Mk 2:26
Is it **l** on the Sabbath to do Mk 3:4
It is not **l** for you to have your Mk 6:18
Is it **l** for a man to divorce Mk 10:2
it **l** to pay taxes to Caesar or Mk 12:14
what is not **l** on the Sabbath?" Lk 6:2
which is not **l** for any but the Lk 6:4
it **l** on the Sabbath to do good Lk 6:9
Is it **l** to heal on the Sabbath Lk 14:3
Is it **l** for us to pay taxes to Lk 20:22

LAWGIVER *(2)*
the LORD is our **l**, the LORD is Is 33:22
There is one **l** and judge who is Jms 4:12

LAWLESS *(9)*
Then some **l** men joined Jephthah Jdg 11:3
you used **l** people to nail Him to Ac 2:23
those whose **l** acts are forgiven Rm 4:7
and then the **l** one will be 2Th 2:8

coming ⌊of the **l** one⌋ is based 2Th 2:9
but for the **l** and rebellious, 1Tm 1:9
their sins and their **l** acts. Heb 10:17
carousing, and **l** idolatry. 1Pt 4:3
by day with the **l** deeds he saw 2Pt 2:8

LAWLESSNESS *(9)*

sin and those guilty of **l**. Mt 13:41
you are full of hypocrisy and **l**. Mt 23:28
Because **l** will multiply, the Mt 24:12
and to greater and greater **l**, Rm 6:19
between righteousness and **l**? 2Co 6:14
and the man of **l** is revealed, 2Th 2:3
the mystery of **l** is already at 2Th 2:7
us from all **l** and to cleanse for Ti 2:14
loved righteousness and hated **l**; Heb 1:9

LAWS *(17)*

them⌋ God's statutes and **l**." Ex 18:16
them about the statutes and **l**, Ex 18:20
and **l** the LORD established Lv 26:46
the ordinances, the **l**, and the 2Kg 17:37
who know the **l** of your God and Ezr 7:25
be recorded in the **l** of Persia Est 1:19
Their **l** are different from Est 3:8
so that they defy the king's **l**. Est 3:8
Do you know the **l** of heaven? Jb 38:33
His statutes and obey His **l**. Ps 105:45
and writing oppressive **l** Is 10:1
design specifications, and **l**. Ezk 43:11
the statutes and **l** of the LORD's Ezk 44:5
must observe My **l** and statutes Ezk 44:24
religious festivals and **l**, Dn 7:25
I will put My **l** into their Heb 8:10
I will put My **l** on their hearts, Heb 10:16

LAWSUIT *(5)*

not testify in a **l** and go along Ex 23:2
to a poor person in his **l**. Ex 23:3
to the poor among you in his **l**. Ex 23:6
or suppressing a person's **l**— Lm 3:36
to the LORD's **l**, you mountains Mc 6:2

LAWSUITS *(4)*

bloodshed, **l**, or assaults— Dt 17:8
then **l** and dishonor will cease. Pr 22:10
So **l** break out like poisonous Hs 10:4
you that you have **l** against one 1Co 6:7

LAWYER *(2)*

elders and a **l** named Tertullus. Ac 24:1
help Zenas the **l** and Apollos on Ti 3:13

LAY *(97)*

know when she **l** down or when she Gn 19:33
know when she **l** down or when she Gn 19:35
Do not **l** a hand on the boy or do Gn 22:12
at his head, and **l** down in that Gn 28:11
but don't **l** a hand on him"— Gn 37:22
and not **l** a hand on him, Gn 37:27
and his sons must **l** their hands Ex 29:10
his sons are to **l** their hands Ex 29:15
and his sons must **l** their hands Ex 29:19
in the table and **l** out its Ex 40:4
He is to **l** his hand on the head Lv 1:4
He is to **l** his hand on the head Lv 3:2
must **l** his hand on the head of Lv 3:8
He must **l** his hand on its head Lv 3:13
l his hand on the bull's head, Lv 4:4
assembly are to **l** their hands Lv 4:15
He is to **l** his hand on the head Lv 4:24
He is to **l** his hand on the head Lv 4:29
He is to **l** his hand on the head Lv 4:33
Aaron will **l** both his hands on Lv 16:21
who heard ⌊him⌋ **l** their hands on Lv 24:14
the Israelites **l** their hands on Nm 8:10
the Levites are to **l** their hands Nm 8:12
in him, and **l** your hands on him Nm 27:18
war against you, **l** siege to it. Dt 20:12
When you **l** siege to a city for a Dt 20:19
He will **l** its foundation ⌊at the Jos 6:26
territory **l** between Judah's Jos 18:11
he fell, he **l** down at her feet; Jdg 5:27
uncovered his feet, and **l** down. Ru 3:7
So she **l** down at his feet until Ru 3:14
So he went and **l** down. 1Sm 3:5
Samuel went and **l** down in his 1Sm 3:9
Samuel **l** down until the morning; 1Sm 3:15
collapsed ⌊and **l**⌋ naked all that 1Sm 19:24
Saul will never **l** a hand on you. 1Sm 23:17
of the troops, **l** siege to the 2Sm 12:28
So Amnon **l** down and pretended 2Sm 13:6
his clothes, and **l** down on the 2Sm 13:31
son died because she **l** on him. 1Kg 3:19
stones to **l** the foundation 1Kg 5:17
l my bones beside his bones, 1Kg 13:31
Then he **l** down and slept under 1Kg 19:5
ate and drank and **l** down again. 1Kg 19:6
they will **l** their hands on and 1Kg 20:6
He **l** down on his bed, turned 1Kg 21:4
l down in sackcloth and walked 1Kg 21:27
he went up and **l** on the boy: 2Kg 4:34
for your brothers, the **l** people, 2Ch 35:5
for all the **l** people who were 2Ch 35:7
houses of the **l** people to offer 2Ch 35:12
brought ⌊them⌋ to the **l** people. 2Ch 35:13
and many **l** on sackcloth and Est 4:3
you must not **l** a hand on Job Jb 1:12
to **l** his hand on both of us. Jb 9:33
L a hand on him. You will Jb 41:8
rebuke you and **l** out the case Ps 50:21
both chariot and horse **l** still. Ps 76:6
Advance, Elam! **L** siege, you Is 21:2
will **l** and hatch her eggs and Is 34:15
I will **l** waste mountains and Is 42:15
and **l** your foundations in Is 54:11
that hatches eggs it didn't **l**. Jr 17:11
to thousands but **l** the fathers' Jr 32:18
Then **l** siege against it: Ezk 4:2
I will **l** the corpses of the Ezk 6:5
to you ⌊as you **l**⌋ in your blood: Ezk 16:6
to you ⌊as you **l**⌋ in your blood: Ezk 16:6
She **l** down among the lions; Ezk 19:2
its boughs **l** broken in all the Ezk 31:12
your mind ⌊as you **l**⌋ in bed were Dn 2:28
overcome and **l** sick for days. Dn 8:27
Man has no place to **l** His head." Mt 8:20
but come and **l** Your hand on her, Mt 9:18
and see the place where He **l**. Mt 28:6
Come and **l** Your hands on her so Mk 5:23
Jesus to **l** His hand on him Mk 7:32
they will **l** hands on the sick, Mk 16:18
Man has no place to **l** His head." Lk 9:58
they will **l** their hands on you Lk 21:12
Within these **l** a multitude of Jn 5:3
I **l** down My life for the sheep. Jn 10:15
but I **l** it down on My own. Jn 10:18
I have the right to **l** it down, Jn 10:18
I will **l** down my life for You!" Jn 13:37
Will you **l** down your life for Jn 13:38
someone would **l** down his life Jn 15:13
the streets and **l** them on beds Ac 5:15
so that anyone I **l** hands on may Ac 8:19
and no one will **l** a hand on you Ac 18:10
because no one can **l** any other 1Co 3:11
too quick to **l** hands on anyone 1Tm 5:22
let us **l** aside every weight and Heb 12:1
for the joy that **l** before Him Heb 12:2
l a stone in Zion, a chosen and 1Pt 2:6
I will soon **l** aside my tent, 2Pt 1:14
We should also **l** down our lives 1Jn 3:16

LAYER *(3)*

there was a **l** of dew all around Ex 16:13
When the **l** of dew evaporated, Ex 16:14
penetrate his double **l** of armor? Jb 41:13

LAYERS *(2)*

with three **l** of cut stones and Ezr 6:4
of David, constructed in **l**. Sg 4:4

LAYING *(9)*

l the beams of His palace on the Ps 104:3
on his eyes and **l** His hands on Mk 8:23
because I am **l** down My life so I Jn 10:17
given through the **l** on of the Ac 8:18
and praying and **l** his hands on Ac 28:8
with the **l** on of hands by the 1Tm 4:14
through the **l** on of my hands. 2Tm 1:6
not **l** again the foundation of Heb 6:1
ritual washings, **l** on of hands, Heb 6:2

LAYOUT *(1)*

its **l** with its exits and Ezk 43:11

LAYS *(2)*

the heavens and **l** the foundation Am 9:6
good shepherd **l** down his life Jn 10:11

LAZARUS *(16)*

a poor man named **L**, covered with Lk 16:20
way off, with **L** at his side. Lk 16:23
on me and send **L** to dip the tip Lk 16:24
just as **L** received bad things, Lk 16:25
a man was sick, **L**, from Bethany, Jn 11:1
was her brother **L** who was sick. Jn 11:2
loved Martha, her sister, and **L**. Jn 11:5
Our friend **L** has fallen asleep, Jn 11:11
told them plainly, "**L** has died. Jn 11:14
He found that **L** had already been Jn 11:17
a loud voice, "**L**, come out!" Jn 11:43
came to Bethany where **L** was, Jn 12:1
and **L** was one of those reclining Jn 12:2
but also to see **L** the one He had Jn 12:9
priests decided to also kill **L**, Jn 12:10
when He called **L** out of the tomb Jn 12:17

LAZINESS *(3)*

but **l** will lead to forced labor. Pr 12:24
L induces deep sleep, and a lazy Pr 19:15
Because of **l** the roof caves in, Ec 10:18

LAZY *(7)*

A **l** man doesn't roast his game, Pr 12:27
one who is truly **l** in his work Pr 18:9
and a **l** person will go hungry. Pr 19:15
to him, 'You evil, **l** slave! Mt 25:26
warn those who are **l**, comfort 1Th 5:14
liars, evil beasts, **l** gluttons. Ti 1:12
so that you won't become **l**, Heb 6:12

LEAD *(80)*

so that you may **l** My people, Ex 3:10
did not **l** them along the road Ex 13:17
of cloud to **l** them on their way Ex 13:21
They sank like **l** in the mighty Ex 15:10
You will **l** the people You have Ex 15:13
l the people to the place I told Ex 32:34
told me, '**L** this people up,' Ex 33:12
bronze, iron, tin, and **l**— Nm 31:22
in order to **l** us in and give us Dt 6:23
military commanders to **l** it. Dt 20:9
This will **l** to the destruction Dt 29:19
When the leaders **l** in Israel, Jdg 5:2
Which man will **l** the fight Jdg 10:18
L me where I can feel the Jdg 16:26
began to **l**⌋ the Israelites 1Sm 7:6
"Will you **l** me to these raiders?" 1Sm 30:15
and I will **l** you to them." 1Sm 30:15
Azaziah were to **l** the music with 1Ch 15:21
so that I may **l** these people, 2Ch 1:10
have taken the **l** in this Ezr 9:2
his own feet **l** him into a net, Jb 18:8
forever by an iron stylus and **l**! Jb 19:24
that You will **l** me to death— Jb 30:23
let a large ransom **l** you astray. Jb 36:18
so you can **l** it back to its Jb 38:20
season and **l** the Bear and her Jb 38:32
l me in Your righteousness, Ps 5:8
way, LORD, and **l** me on a level Ps 27:11
You **l** and guide me because of Ps 31:3
truth; let them **l** me. Let them Ps 43:3
ever—He will **l** us eternally." Ps 48:14
city? Who will **l** me to Edom? Ps 60:9
L me to a rock that is high Ps 61:2
with fairness and **l** the nations Ps 67:4
l the way, with musicians Ps 68:25
city? Who will **l** me to Edom? Ps 108:10
even there Your hand will **l** me; Ps 139:10
l me in the everlasting way. Ps 139:24
gracious Spirit **l** me on level Ps 143:10
by me, princes **l**, as do nobles Pr 8:16
laziness will **l** to forced labor Pr 12:24
of wicked men **l** them astray. Pr 12:26
A fool's lips **l** to strife, Pr 18:6
diligent certainly **l** to profit, Pr 21:5
rich—both **l** only to poverty Pr 22:16
I would **l** you, I would take you, Sg 8:2
and a child will **l** them. Is 11:6
of Assyria will **l** the captives Is 20:4
the peoples to **l** ⌊them⌋ astray. Is 30:28
I will **l** the blind by a way they Is 42:16
and **l** them to springs of water. Is 49:10
I will **l** him and comfort him and Is 57:18
The LORD will always **l** you, Is 58:11
the ships of Tarshish in the **l**, Is 60:9
blow, blasting the **l** with fire. Jr 6:29
I will **l** them to wadis ⌊filled⌋ Jr 31:9
like the rams that **l** the flock. Jr 50:8
I will **l** you into the wilderness Ezk 20:35
When I **l** you into the land of Ezk 20:42
tin, iron, and **l** inside the Ezk 22:18
silver, copper, iron, **l**, and tin Ezk 22:20
and **l** for your merchandise. Ezk 27:12
and **l** you into the land of Ezk 37:12
and **l** you up from the remotest Ezk 39:2
and those who **l** many to Dn 12:3

to persuade her, l her to the Hs 2:14
prophets who l my people astray Mc 3:5
Then a l cover was lifted, Zch 5:7
and pushed the l weight over its Zch 5:8
signs and wonders to l astray, Mt 24:24
signs and wonders to l astray, Mk 13:22
the Sabbath, and l it to water? Lk 13:15
It will l to an opportunity for Lk 21:13
someone to l him by the hand. Ac 13:11
is intended to l you to Rm 2:4
I know this will l to my Php 1:19
to seek to l a quiet life, 1Th 4:11
among you and l you in the Lord 1Th 5:12
so that we may l a tranquil and 1Tm 2:2
by their hand to l them out of Heb 8:9

LEADER *(96)*

made you a l and judge over us? Ex 2:14
God or curse a l among your Ex 22:28
When a l sins and Lv 4:22
l of the descendants of Judah Nm 2:3
The l of the Issacharites is Nm 2:5
l of the Zebulunites is Eliab Nm 2:7
l of the Reubenites is Elizur Nm 2:10
The l of the Simeonites is Nm 2:12
The l of the Gadites is Eliasaph Nm 2:14
The l of the Ephraimites is Nm 2:18
The l of the Manassites is Nm 2:20
The l of the Benjaminites is Nm 2:22
The l of the Danites is Ahiezer Nm 2:25
The l of the Asherites is Pagiel Nm 2:27
l of the Naphtalites is Ahira Nm 2:29
and the l of the Gershonite Nm 3:24
and the l of the family of the Nm 3:30
The l of the family of the Nm 3:35
Each day have one l present his Nm 7:11
son of Zuar, l of Issachar, Nm 7:18
son of Helon, l of the Nm 7:24
son of Shedeur, l of the Nm 7:30
of Zurishaddai, l of the Nm 7:36
son of Deuel, l of the Gadites, Nm 7:42
son of Ammihud, l of the Nm 7:48
son of Pedahzur, l of the Nm 7:54
son of Gideoni, l of the Nm 7:60
Ammishaddai, l of the Danites, Nm 7:66
son of Ochran, l of the Nm 7:72
son of Enan, l of the Nm 7:78
one man who is a l among them Nm 13:2
Let's appoint a l and go back to Nm 14:4
the l of a Simeonite ancestral Nm 25:14
the Midianite l who was killed Nm 25:18
Take one l from each tribe to Nm 34:18
a l from the tribe of Dan; Nm 34:22
a l from the tribe of Manasseh, Nm 34:23
a l from the tribe of Ephraim; Nm 34:24
a l from the tribe of Zebulun; Nm 34:25
a l from the tribe of Issachar; Nm 34:26
a l from the tribe of Asher; Nm 34:27
a l from the tribe of Naphtali." Nm 34:28
I can no longer act as your l. Dt 31:2
formerly been the l of all these Jos 11:10
one family l for each tribe of Jos 22:14
country, and he became their l. Jdg 3:27
He will be the l of all the Jdg 10:18
and you will become l of all the Jdg 11:8
them to me, I will be your l." Jdg 11:9
themselves as l and commander, Jdg 11:11
not become the l of the tribes 1Sm 15:17
him, and he became their l. 1Sm 22:2
know that a great l has fallen 2Sm 3:38
of Zeruiah, was l of the Three. 2Sm 23:18
Hezekiah, the l of My people, 2Kg 20:5
a l of Judah's descendants. 1Ch 2:10
was a l of the Reubenites, 1Ch 5:6
son of Eleazar had been their l, 1Ch 9:20
brother, was the l of the Three. 1Ch 11:20
Thirty and ⌊a l⌋ over the Thirty 1Ch 12:4
to Jehoiada, l of the house of 1Ch 12:27
Uriel the l and 120 of his 1Ch 15:5
Asaiah the l and 220 of his 1Ch 15:6
Joel the l and 130 of his 1Ch 15:7
Shemaiah the l and 200 of his 1Ch 15:8
Eliel the l and 80 of his 1Ch 15:9
Amminadab the l and 112 of his 1Ch 15:10
the l of the Levites in music, 1Ch 15:22
the music l of the singers. 1Ch 15:27
month, and Mikloth was the l; 1Ch 27:4
chose Judah as l, and from the 1Ch 28:4
and to every l in all Israel— 2Ch 1:2
Maacah as chief, l among his 2Ch 11:22
brave warrior, l, and commander 2Ch 32:21
to Iddo, the l at Casiphia, with Ezr 8:17
and appointed a l to return to Neh 9:17
the l who began the thanksgiving Neh 11:17
l of the Levites in Jerusalem Neh 11:22
sang, with Jezrahiah as the l. Neh 12:42
Without l, administrator, or Pr 6:7
A destitute l who oppresses the Pr 28:3
A l who lacks understanding is Pr 28:16
You have a cloak—you be our l! Is 3:6
make me the l of the people!" Is 3:7
will send them a savior and l, Is 19:20
a l and commander for the Is 55:4
the groves following their l, Is 66:17
Jacob's l will be one of them; Jr 30:21
them, the LORD as their l. Mc 2:13
You crush the l of the house of Hab 3:13
you will come a l who will Mt 2:6
the synagogue l, "Don't be Mk 5:36
He was a l of the synagogue. Lk 8:41
But the l of the synagogue, Lk 13:14
Crispus, the l of the synagogue, Ac 18:8
Sosthenes, the l of the Ac 18:17

LEADER'S *(4)*

When Jesus came to the l house, Mt 9:23
the synagogue l house and said, Mk 5:35
They came to the l house, and He Mk 5:38
from the synagogue l ⌊house⌋, Lk 8:49

LEADERS *(189)*

He will father 12 tribal l, Gn 17:20
12 l of their clans. Gn 25:16
will seize the l of Moab; Ex 15:15
and all the l of the community Ex 16:22
and made them l over the people Ex 18:25
and all the l of the community Ex 34:31
The l brought onyx and gemstones Ex 35:27
they are l of their ancestral Nm 1:16
of⌋ the 12 l of Israel; Nm 1:44
of the Levite l was Eleazar son Nm 3:32
and the l of the community Nm 4:34
and the l of Israel registered Nm 4:46
the l of Israel, the heads of Nm 7:2
were the tribal l who supervised Nm 7:2
from every two l and an ox from Nm 7:3
The l also presented the Nm 7:10
The l presented their offerings Nm 7:10
gift from the l of Israel for Nm 7:84
sounded, only the l, the heads Nm 10:4
All the men were l in Israel. Nm 13:3
men who were l of the community Nm 16:2
from all the l of their Nm 17:2
each of their l gave him a staff Nm 17:6
for each of the l of their Nm 17:6
Take all the l of the people and Nm 25:4
priest, the l, and the entire Nm 27:2
told the l of the Israelite Nm 30:1
and all the l of the community Nm 31:13
the family l of the community Nm 31:26
and the l of the community and Nm 32:2
the family l of the Israelite Nm 32:28
family l from the clan of the Nm 36:1
Moses and the l who were over Nm 36:1
and I will make them your l. Dt 1:13
So I took the l of your tribes, Dt 1:15
and set them over you as l: Dt 1:15
your tribal l and elders when Dt 5:23
God—your l, tribes, elders Dt 29:10
the heads of the enemy l." Dt 32:42
Jeshurun when the l of the Dt 33:5
came ⌊with⌋ the l of the people; Dt 33:21
and the l of the community swore Jos 9:15
because the l of the community Jos 9:18
grumbled against the l. Jos 9:18
the l answered them, "We have Jos 9:19
as the l had promised them. Jos 9:21
of Nun, and the l, saying, "The Jos 17:4
⌊They sent⌋ 10 l with him— Jos 22:14
answered the l of the Israelite Jos 22:21
the priest and the community l, Jos 22:30
the priest and the l returned Jos 22:32
its elders, l, judges, and Jos 23:2
Israel's elders, l, judges, and Jos 24:1
When the l lead in Israel, Jdg 5:2
heart is with the l of Israel, Jdg 5:9
The l came down from Machir, Jdg 5:14
The Philistine l went to her and Jdg 16:5
The Philistine l brought her Jdg 16:8
message to the Philistine l: Jdg 16:18
The Philistine l came to her Jdg 16:18
the Philistine l gathered Jdg 16:23
the l of the Philistines were Jdg 16:27
fell on the l and all the people Jdg 16:30
The l of all the people and of Jdg 20:2
said, "All you l of the troops, 1Sm 14:38
As the Philistine l were passing 1Sm 29:2
But the l don't think you are 1Sm 29:6
Philistine l think is wrong." 1Sm 29:7
two men who were l of raiding 2Sm 4:2
the Ammonite l said to Hanun 2Sm 10:3
from the l of Jabesh-gilead 2Sm 21:12
the ancestral l of the 1Kg 8:1
men of the provincial l.' " 1Kg 20:14
young men of the provincial l, 1Kg 20:15
the provincial l marched out 1Kg 20:17
of the provincial l and the army 1Kg 20:19
name were l in their families. 1Ch 4:38
Ishi, as their l to Mount Seir. 1Ch 4:42
and chiefs among the l. 1Ch 7:40
and made them l of his troops. 1Ch 12:18
David consulted with all his l, 1Ch 13:1
David told the l of the Levites 1Ch 15:16
the Ammonite l said to Hanun, 1Ch 19:3
ordered all the l of Israel to 1Ch 22:17
he gathered all the l of Israel, 1Ch 23:2
Since more l were found among 1Ch 24:4
Those were the l of the tribes 1Ch 27:22
Jerusalem all the l of Israel: 1Ch 28:1
the l of the tribes, the leaders 1Ch 28:1
the l of the divisions in the 1Ch 28:1
and the l and all the people are 1Ch 28:21
Then the l of the households, 1Ch 29:6
the l of the tribes of Israel, 1Ch 29:6
All the l and the mighty men, 1Ch 29:24
and put l in them with supplies 2Ch 11:11
Rehoboam and the l of Judah who 2Ch 12:5
So the l of Israel and the king 2Ch 12:6
All the l and all the people 2Ch 24:10
destroyed all the l of the 2Ch 24:23
some men who were l of the 2Ch 28:12
and Jehiel, l of God's temple, 2Ch 35:8
All the l of the priests and the 2Ch 36:14
So the family l of Judah and Ezr 1:5
of the family l gave freewill Ezr 2:68
and family l, who had seen Ezr 3:12
and the l of the families Ezr 4:2
and the other l of Israel's Ezr 4:3
the names of their l for your Ezr 5:10
Israelite l to return with me Ezr 7:28
are the family l and the Ezr 8:1
Then I summoned the l: Ezr 8:16
by David and the l for the work Ezr 8:20
his counselors, his l, and all Ezr 8:25
the l approached me and said: Ezr 9:1
The l and officials have taken Ezr 9:2
decision of the l and elders, Ezr 10:8
Let our l represent the entire Ezr 10:14
selected men who were family l, Ezr 10:16
Some of the family l gave to the Neh 7:70
of the family l gave 20,000 gold Neh 7:71
the family l of all the people, Neh 8:13
us, our kings and l, our priests Neh 9:32
Our kings, l, priests, and Neh 9:34
containing the names of⌋ our l, Neh 9:38
The l of the people were: Neh 10:14
Now the l of the people stayed Neh 11:1
relatives, the l of families: Neh 11:13
from the l of the Levites, Neh 11:16
These were the l of the priests Neh 12:7
the l of the priestly families Neh 12:12
the l of the families of the Neh 12:22
descendants, the l of families, Neh 12:23
l of the Levites—Hashabiah, Neh 12:24
I brought the l of Judah up on Neh 12:31
half the l of Judah followed: Neh 12:32
there were l of the singers and Neh 12:46
and overthrows established l. Jb 12:19
the world's l of reason, Jb 12:24
For the l of the earth belong to Ps 47:9
He humbles the spirit of l; Ps 76:12
all their tribal l like Zebah Ps 83:11
He will crush l over the entire Ps 110:6
I will make youths their l, Is 3:4
My people, your l mislead you; Is 3:12
the elders and l of His people: Is 3:14
l of the people mislead ⌊them⌋ Is 9:16

⌊The l⌋ have made Egypt stagger Is 19:14
close friends as l over you, Jr 13:21
officers, his l, all his people Jr 25:19
the dust⌋, you l of the flock. Jr 25:34
escape, for the l of the flock. Jr 25:35
the wail of the l of the flock, Jr 25:36
Her l are like stags that find Lm 1:6
defiled the kingdom and its l. Lm 2:2
Her king and her l ⌊live⌋ among Lm 2:9
son of Benaiah, l of the people. Ezk 11:1
Warrior I will speak from the Ezk 32:21
All the l of the north and all Ezk 32:30
to our kings, l, fathers, and Dn 9:6
our kings, our l, and our Dn 9:8
Israel's l fervently love Hs 4:18
Their l will fall by the sword Hs 7:16
have appointed l, but without My Hs 8:4
the burden of the king and l. Hs 8:10
all their l are rebellious. Hs 9:15
Give me a king and l? Hs 13:10
Now listen, l of Jacob, you Mc 3:1
Listen to this, l of the house Mc 3:9
Her l issue rulings for a bribe, Mc 3:11
shepherds, even eight l of men. Mc 5:5
so I will punish the l. Zch 10:3
each of⌋ the l of Judah will Zch 12:5
I will make the l of Judah like Zch 12:6
least among the l of Judah: Mt 2:6
one of the l came and knelt down Mt 9:18
the synagogue l, named Jairus, Mk 5:22
and the l of the people were Lk 19:47
priests, the l, and the people, Lk 23:13
and even the l kept scoffing: Lk 23:35
priests and l handed Him over Lk 24:20
just as your l also did. Ac 3:17
the l of the synagogue sent Ac 13:15
priests and the l of the Jews Ac 25:2
together the l of the Jews. Ac 28:17
to those recognized ⌊as l⌋— Gl 2:2
elders who are good l should be 1Tm 5:17
Remember your l who have spoken Heb 13:7
Obey your l and submit to them, Heb 13:17
Greet all your l and all the Heb 13:24

LEADERS' *(1)*
because of their l willingness 1Ch 29:9

LEADERSHIP *(2)*
under the l of Moses and Aaron Nm 33:1
a youth with no experience in l. 1Kg 3:7

LEADING *(40)*
fords of the Jordan l to Moab, Jdg 3:28
So Gaal went out l the lords of Jdg 9:39
of the Jordan l to Ephraim. Jdg 12:5
man who was l him by the hand, Jdg 16:26
along the road l back to the Ru 1:7
can see that the king is l you. 1Sm 12:2
the Ophrah road l to the land of 1Sm 13:17
because he was l their troops. 1Sm 18:16
prophesying with Samuel l them, 1Sm 19:20
of Hadadezer's army, l them. 2Sm 10:16
beside the road l to the city 2Sm 15:2
Three of the 30 l ⌊warriors⌋ 2Sm 23:13
and the l men of the land into 2Kg 24:15
of Hadadezer's army, l them. 1Ch 19:16
under their l men, had duties 1Ch 26:12
instruments were l the praise. 2Ch 23:13
I selected 12 of the l priests, Ezr 8:24
house before the l priests, Ezr 8:29
got up and made the l priests, Ezr 10:5
l the festive procession to the Ps 42:4
the youngest, l them, the rulers Ps 68:27
l him in a way that is not good. Pr 16:29
God while He was l you along the Jr 2:17
them and l My people astray Jr 23:32
took away the l men of the land Ezk 17:13
the road l to other nations, Mt 10:5
and the l men of Galilee. Mk 6:21
house of one of the l Pharisees, Lk 14:1
Twelve named Judas was l them. Lk 22:47
and the l men of the city Ac 13:50
both l men among the brothers. Ac 15:22
which is a l city of that Ac 16:12
well as a number of the l women. Ac 17:4
belonging to the l man of the Ac 28:7
either of sin l to death or of Rm 6:16
or of obedience l to Rm 6:16
generosity; l, with diligence Rm 12:8
are a scent of death l to death, 2Co 2:16
a scent of life l to life. 2Co 2:16
be regretted and l to salvation, 2Co 7:10

LEADS *(35)*
is the one who l a blind person Dt 27:18
the road that l to the desert. 2Sm 15:23
l counselors away barefoot and Jb 12:17
He l priests away barefoot and Jb 12:19
nations, then l them away. Jb 12:23
What road l to ⌊the place⌋ where Jb 38:24
the way of the wicked l to ruin. Ps 1:6
He l me beside quiet waters. Ps 23:2
l me along the right paths for Ps 23:3
He l the humble in what is right Ps 25:9
He l out the prisoners to Ps 68:6
of the righteous l to life; Pr 10:16
activity of the wicked l to sin. Pr 10:16
righteousness ⌊l⌋ to life, Pr 11:19
but pursuing evil ⌊l⌋ to death. Pr 11:19
hope of the wicked ⌊l to⌋ wrath. Pr 11:23
from the wicked ⌊l to⌋ deceit. Pr 12:5
but another path l to death. Pr 12:28
Arrogance l to nothing but Pr 13:10
endless talk l only to poverty Pr 14:23
the path of life l upward, Pr 15:24
own foolishness l him astray, Pr 19:3
The fear of the LORD l to life; Pr 19:23
The one who l the upright into Pr 28:10
He gently l those that are Is 40:11
who l you in the way you should Is 48:17
of promiscuity l them astray; Hs 4:12
is broad that l to destruction, Mt 7:13
the road that l to life, Mt 7:14
and whoever l, like the one Lk 22:26
sheep by name and l them out. Jn 10:3
iron gate that l into the city, Ac 12:10
which ⌊l to⌋ reckless actions, Eph 5:18
way profitable and l to the ruin 2Tm 2:14
the truth that l to godliness, Ti 1:1

LEAF *(6)*
a plucked olive l in her beak. Gn 8:11
a wind-driven l will put them to Lv 26:36
You frighten a wind-driven l? Jb 13:25
and whose l does not wither Ps 1:3
all of us wither like a l, Is 64:6
and even the l will wither. Jr 8:13

LEAFY *(6)*
fronds, boughs of l trees, and Lv 23:40
and ⌊other⌋ l trees to make Neh 8:15
under every l tree you lie down Jr 2:20
green tree and every l oak— Ezk 6:13
saw any high hill or l tree, Ezk 20:28
and others spread l branches cut Mk 11:8

LEAGUE *(1)*
They are in l with foreigners. Is 2:6

LEAH *(28)*
older was named L, and the Gn 29:16
L had delicate eyes, but Rachel Gn 29:17
his daughter L and gave her to Gn 29:23
to his daughter L as her slave. Gn 29:24
When morning came, there was L! Gn 29:25
he loved Rachel more than L. Gn 29:30
the LORD saw that L was unloved, Gn 29:31
L conceived, gave birth to a son, Gn 29:32
Then L stopped having children. Gn 29:35
When L saw that she had stopped Gn 30:9
L said, "What good fortune!" Gn 30:11
L said, "I am happy that the Gn 30:13
he brought them to his mother L, Gn 30:14
But L replied to her, "Isn't it Gn 30:15
L went out to meet him and said, Gn 30:16
God listened to L, and she Gn 30:17
L said, "God has rewarded me for Gn 30:18
Then L conceived again and bore Gn 30:19
given me a good gift," L said. Gn 30:20
L bore a daughter and named her Gn 30:21
had Rachel and L called to the Gn 31:4
Then Rachel and L answered him, Gn 31:14
he divided the children among L, Gn 33:1
slaves first, L and her sons Gn 33:2
L and her children also Gn 33:7
Laban gave to his daughter L— Gn 46:18
there, and I buried L there. Gn 49:31
your house like Rachel and L, Ru 4:11

LEAH'S *(8)*
L slave Zilpah bore Jacob a son. Gn 30:10
When L slave Zilpah bore Jacob a Gn 30:12
tent, then L tent, and then Gn 31:33
Then he left L tent and entered Gn 31:33
L daughter whom she bore to Gn 34:1
L sons were Reuben (Jacob's Gn 35:23
The sons of L slave Zilpah were Gn 35:26
These were L sons born to Jacob Gn 46:15

LEAKS *(3)*
of negligent hands the house l. Ec 10:18
within you, repairing your l. Ezk 27:9
who repair your l, those who Ezk 27:27

LEAN *(5)*
so I can l against them." Jdg 16:26
and l on the God of Israel; Is 48:2
the LORD; let him l on his God. Is 50:10
the fat sheep and the l sheep. Ezk 34:20
Yet they l on the LORD, saying, Mc 3:11

LEANED *(6)*
so he l his shoulder to bear a Gn 49:15
the temple and l against them, Jdg 16:29
I have l on You from birth; Ps 71:6
they l on you, you shattered Ezk 29:7
So he l back against Jesus and Jn 13:25
the one who had l back against Jn 21:20

LEANING *(6)*
Then Joseph, l over his father's Gn 50:1
around outside ⌊l⌋ on his staff, Ex 21:19
there was Saul, l on his spear. 2Sm 1:6
as if he were a l wall or a Ps 62:3
the wilderness, l on the one she Sg 8:5
l on the top of his staff. Heb 11:21

LEANS *(3)*
which if a man l on it will go 2Kg 18:21
He l on his web, but it doesn't Jb 8:15
the hand of anyone who l on it. Is 36:6

LEAP *(7)*
with my God I can l over a wall. 2Sm 22:30
and I would l for joy in Jb 6:10
Do you make him l like a locust? Jb 39:20
with my God I can l over a wall. Ps 18:29
and wild goats will l about. Is 13:21
the lame will l like a deer, Is 35:6
in that day and l for joy! Lk 6:23

LEAPED *(4)*
Then flames l from the LORD's Lv 10:2
greeting, the baby l inside her, Lk 1:41
the baby l for joy inside me! Lk 1:44
had the evil spirit l on them, Ac 19:16

LEAPING *(4)*
a young lion, l out of Bashan. Dt 33:22
saw King David l and dancing 2Sm 6:16
Here he comes, l over the Sg 2:8
them—walking, l, and praising Ac 3:8

LEAPS *(1)*
at this and l from my chest. Jb 37:1

LEARN *(39)*
that they may l to fear Me all Dt 4:10
L and follow them carefully. Dt 5:1
that you might l that man does Dt 8:3
you will always l to fear the Dt 14:23
that he may l to fear the LORD Dt 17:19
listen and l to fear the LORD Dt 31:12
will listen and l to fear the Dt 31:13
courtyard to l how Esther was Est 2:11
to Mordecai to l what he was Est 4:5
would l how He would answer me; Jb 23:5
heart when I l Your righteous Ps 119:7
so that I could l Your statutes. Ps 119:71
so that I can l Your commands. Ps 119:73
L to be shrewd, you who are Pr 8:5
man, and he will l more. Pr 9:9
the inexperienced l a lesson; Pr 19:25
or you will l his ways and Pr 22:25
L to do what is good. Seek Is 1:17
the world will l righteousness. Is 26:9
he does not l righteousness. Is 26:10
l what ⌊the charge⌋ is against Jr 6:18
Do not l the way of the nations Jr 10:2
will diligently l the ways of My Jr 12:16
L how the wildflowers of the Mt 6:28
Go and l what this means: Mt 9:13
take up My yoke and l from Me, Mt 11:29
Now l this parable from the fig Mt 24:32
L this parable from the fig Mk 13:28
May we l about this new teaching Ac 17:19
so that you may l from us the 1Co 4:6
everyone may l and everyone may 1Co 14:31
And if they want to l something, 1Co 14:35

I only want to **l** this from you: Gl 3:2
A woman should **l** in silence with 1Tm 2:11
they should **l** to practice their 1Tm 5:4
time, they also **l** to be idle, 1Tm 5:13
people must also **l** to devote Ti 3:14
you willing to **l** that faith Jms 2:20
no one could **l** the song except Rv 14:3

LEARNED *(30)*
his drinking and **l** what his Gn 9:24
I have **l** by divination that the Gn 30:27
Jacob **l** that there was grain Gn 42:1
When David **l** that Saul was 1Sm 23:9
When Mordecai **l** of the plot, Est 2:22
And when he **l** of Mordecai's Est 3:6
When Mordecai **l** all that had Est 4:1
Long ago I **l** from Your decrees Ps 119:152
l that this too is a pursuit of Ec 1:17
of⌋ man-made rules **l** ⌊by rote⌋— Is 29:13
After he **l** to tear prey, he Ezk 19:3
After he **l** to tear prey, he Ezk 19:6
When Daniel **l** that the document Dn 6:10
the time he had **l** from the wise Mt 2:16
the wise and **l** and revealed them Mt 11:25
the wise and the **l** and have Lk 10:21
listened to and **l** from the Jn 6:45
of the Jews **l** He was there. Jn 12:9
him because I **l** that he is a Ac 23:27
when he **l** he was from Cilicia, Ac 23:34
we then **l** that the island was Ac 28:1
to the doctrine you have **l**. Rm 16:17
is not how you **l** about the Eph 4:20
Do what you have **l** and received Php 4:9
for I have **l** to be content in Php 4:11
I have **l** the secret ⌊of being Php 4:12
You **l** this from Epaphras, our Col 1:7
in what you have **l** and firmly 2Tm 3:14
knowing those from whom you **l**, 2Tm 3:14
He **l** obedience through what He Heb 5:8

LEARNING *(4)*
will listen and increase his **l**, Pr 1:5
and pleasant speech increases **l**. Pr 16:21
and increases **l** with its speech. Pr 16:23
always **l** and never able to come 2Tm 3:7

LEARNS *(1)*
By the time he **l** to reject what Is 7:15

LEASE *(1)*
and **l** his vineyard to other Mt 21:41

LEASED *(4)*
He **l** the vineyard to tenants. Sg 8:11
He **l** it to tenant farmers and Mt 21:33
Then he **l** it to tenant farmers Mk 12:1
a vineyard, **l** it to tenant Lk 20:9

LEASH *(1)*
put him on a **l** for your girls? Jb 41:5

LEAST *(31)*
one who took the **l** gathered 33 Nm 11:32
my clan the **l** important of all 1Sm 9:21
among the **l** of my master's 2Kg 18:24
the **l** of them was a match for a 1Ch 12:14
from the greatest to the **l**, Est 1:5
from the **l** to the greatest." Est 1:20
I am the **l** intelligent of men, Pr 30:2
The **l** will become a thousand, Is 60:22
For from the **l** to the greatest Jr 6:13
for from the **l** to the greatest, Jr 8:10
from the **l** to the greatest of Jr 31:34
from the **l** to the greatest Jr 42:1
from the **l** to the greatest Jr 42:8
From the **l** to the greatest, Jr 44:12
the greatest of them to the **l**. Jnh 3:5
are by no means **l** among the Mt 2:6
breaks one of the **l** of these Mt 5:19
will be called **l** in the kingdom Mt 5:19
but the **l** in the kingdom of Mt 11:11
for one of the **l** of these Mt 25:40
do for one of the **l** of these, Mt 25:45
but the **l** in the kingdom of God Lk 7:28
For whoever is **l** among you— Lk 9:48
at **l** his shadow might fall on Ac 5:15
from the **l** of them to the Ac 8:10
to others, at **l** I am to you, for 1Co 9:2
For I am the **l** of the apostles, 1Co 15:9
if ⌊you do⌋, at **l** accept me as a 2Co 11:16
to me—the **l** of all the saints Eph 3:8
unless she is at **l** 60 years old, 1Tm 5:9
from the **l** to the greatest of Heb 8:11

LEATHER *(19)*
wood, clothing, **l**, sackcloth, or Lv 11:32
or in **l** or anything made of Lv 13:48
leather or anything made of **l**— Lv 13:48
in the fabric, the **l**, the warp, Lv 13:49
the woof, or any **l** article, it Lv 13:49
the woof, or the **l**, regardless Lv 13:51
linen, or any **l** article, which Lv 13:52
warp or woof, or any **l** article, Lv 13:53
the fabric, the **l**, or the warp Lv 13:56
woof, or any **l** article, it has Lv 13:57
or woof, or any **l** article, which Lv 13:58
or woof, or any **l** article, in Lv 13:59
Any clothing or **l** on which there Lv 15:17
garments, **l** goods, things made Nm 31:20
man with a **l** belt around his 2Kg 1:8
and provided you with **l** sandals. Ezk 16:10
garment with a **l** belt around his Mt 3:4
garment with a **l** belt around his Mk 1:6
in Joppa with Simon, a **l** tanner. Ac 9:43

LEAVE *(233)*
said to Isaac, "**L** us, for you Gn 26:16
I will not **l** you until I have Gn 28:15
Get up, **l** this land, and return Gn 31:13
and **l** some distance between the Gn 32:16
me **l** some of my people with you. Gn 33:15
Only if you **l** something ⌊with Gn 38:17
you will not **l** this place unless Gn 42:15
L one brother with me, take Gn 42:33
'The boy cannot **l** his father. Gn 44:22
he were to **l**, his father would Gn 44:22
against us, and **l** the country." Ex 1:10
then did you **l** the man behind? Ex 2:20
"As soon as I **l** you," Moses said, Ex 8:29
Pharaoh said to him, "**L** me! Ex 10:28
L, you and all the people who Ex 11:8
After that, I will **l**.' " Ex 11:8
said, "Get up, **l** my people, both Ex 12:31
you asked, and **l**, and this will Ex 12:32
L us alone so that we may serve Ex 14:12
no one is to **l** his place on the Ex 16:29
seventh he is to **l** as a free man Ex 21:2
arrives alone, he is to **l** alone; Ex 21:3
his wife is to **l** with him. Ex 21:3
and the man must **l** alone. Ex 21:4
do not want to **l** as a free man, Ex 21:5
she is not to **l** as the male Ex 21:7
her, she may **l** free of charge, Ex 21:11
it rest and **l** it uncultivated Ex 23:11
animals may consume what they **l**. Ex 23:11
Now **l** Me alone, so that My anger Ex 32:10
Go, **l** here, you and the people Ex 33:1
would not **l** the inside of the Ex 33:11
But He will not **l** ⌊the guilty⌋ Ex 34:7
he may not **l** any of it until Lv 7:15
holy place, and **l** them there. Lv 16:23
L them for the poor and the Lv 19:10
must not **l** the sanctuary or he Lv 21:12
L them for the poor and the Lv 23:22
may **l** them to your sons after Lv 25:46
they may not **l** any of it until Nm 9:12
"Please don't **l** us," Moses said, Nm 10:31
'Why did we ever **l** Egypt?' " Nm 11:20
But He will not **l** ⌊the guilty⌋ Nm 14:18
and Moses did not **l** the camp. Nm 14:44
He will once again **l** this people Nm 32:15
He will not **l** you, destroy you, Dt 4:31
L Me alone, and I will destroy Dt 9:14
I don't want to **l** you,' because Dt 15:16
Let him **l** and return home. Dt 20:5
Let him **l** and return home. Dt 20:6
Let him **l** and return home. Dt 20:7
Let him **l** and return home, Dt 20:8
you are not to **l** his corpse on Dt 21:23
They will **l** you no grain, new Dt 28:51
will not **l** you or forsake you. Dt 31:6
will not **l** you or forsake you. Dt 31:8
I will not **l** you or forsake you. Jos 1:5
refused to **l** this land. Jdg 1:27
Amorites refused to **l** Har-heres, Jdg 1:35
Please do not **l** this place until Jdg 6:18
turn back and **l** Mount Gilead.' Jdg 7:3
strength will **l** me, and I will Jdg 16:17
prepared to **l**, putting their Jdg 18:21
morning of the fifth day to **l**, Jdg 19:8
went out to **l** on his journey, Jdg 19:27
each of you **l** the vineyards and Jdg 21:21
prepared to **l** the land of Moab, Ru 1:6
persuade me to **l** you or go back Ru 1:16
field, and don't **l** this one, but Ru 2:8
for her and **l** ⌊them⌋ for her to Ru 2:16
Today when you **l** me, you'll find 1Sm 10:2
Saul turned around to **l** Samuel, 1Sm 10:9
came out of Egypt, go on and **l**! 1Sm 15:6
and the evil spirit would **l** him. 1Sm 16:23
Who did you **l** those few sheep 1Sm 17:28
L and return to the land of Judah. 1Sm 22:5
he did not **l** a single person 1Sm 27:9
love will never **l** him as I 2Sm 7:15
sword will never **l** your house 2Sm 12:10
Amnon said, "Everyone **l** me!" 2Sm 13:9
L quickly, or he will overtake 2Sm 15:14
L him alone and let him curse 2Sm 16:11
but don't **l** there ⌊and go⌋ 1Kg 2:36
the day you do **l** and cross the 1Kg 2:37
'On the day you **l** and go 1Kg 2:42
May He not abandon us or **l** us. 1Kg 8:57
Let me **l**, so I can go to 1Kg 11:21
replied, "but please let me **l**." 1Kg 11:22
He did not **l** Jeroboam anyone 1Kg 15:29
He did not **l** him a single male, 1Kg 16:11
L here, turn eastward, and hide 1Kg 17:3
But when I **l** you, the Spirit of 1Kg 18:12
But I will **l** 7,000 in Israel— 1Kg 19:18
When you **l** me, a lion will kill 1Kg 20:36
of the LORD **l** me to speak to you 1Kg 22:24
live, I will not **l** you." 2Kg 2:2
live, I will not **l** you." 2Kg 2:4
live, I will not **l** you." 2Kg 2:6
of God said, "**L** her alone—she 2Kg 4:27
live, I will not **l** you." 2Kg 4:30
this good land and **l** it as an 1Ch 28:8
He won't **l** you or forsake you 1Ch 28:20
of the LORD **l** me to speak to you 2Ch 18:23
L the sanctuary, for you have 2Ch 26:18
L the construction of this house Ezr 6:7
and **l** ⌊it⌋ as an inheritance to Ezr 9:12
cease while I **l** it and go down Neh 6:3
We will also **l** ⌊the land⌋ Neh 10:31
the king for a **l** of absence Neh 13:6
Do not **l** out anything you have Est 6:10
and naked I will **l** this life. Jb 1:21
L me alone, for my days are a Jb 7:16
or **l** me alone until I swallow my Jb 7:19
L me alone, so that I can smile Jb 10:20
such words to **l** your mouth? Jb 15:13
they say to God: "**L** us alone! We Jb 21:14
who said to God, "**L** us alone!" Jb 22:17
They were forced to **l** the land. Jb 30:8
They **l** and do not return. Jb 39:4
Would you **l** it to do your hard Jb 39:11
to the ground and **l** my honor in Ps 7:5
they **l** their surplus to their Ps 17:14
do not **l** me or abandon me, Ps 27:9
LORD will not **l** him in his hand Ps 37:33
Then they **l** their wealth to Ps 49:10
deceit never **l** its marketplace Ps 55:11
do not **l** me to my oppressors. Ps 119:121
loyalty and faithfulness **l** you. Pr 3:3
L inexperience behind, and you Pr 9:6
because I must **l** it to the man Ec 2:18
L his presence, and don't Ec 8:3
you, don't **l** your place, for Ec 10:4
Where will you **l** your wealth? Is 10:3
out of the way! **L** the pathway. Is 30:11
L Babylon, flee from the Is 48:20
and devastate you will **l** you. Is 49:17
L, leave, go out from there! Is 52:11
Leave, **l**, go out from there! Is 52:11
For you will not **l** in a hurry, Is 52:12
You will **l** your name behind as a Is 65:15
As they **l**, they will see the Is 66:24
called by Your name. Don't **l** us! Jr 14:9
the kings of Judah enter and **l**, Jr 17:19
of Lebanon ever **l** the highland Jr 18:14
I will **l** it in its own land, Jr 27:11
by no means **l** you unpunished. Jr 30:11
Chaldeans will **l** us for good, Jr 37:9
for good, for they will not **l**. Jr 37:9
started to⌋ **l** Jerusalem to go to Jr 37:12
and he will **l** there unscathed. Jr 43:12
by no means **l** you unpunished. Jr 46:28
wouldn't they **l** some gleanings? Jr 49:9
forgive those I **l** as a remnant. Jr 50:20
destroy her. **L** her no survivors. Jr 50:26
L Babylon; save your lives, each Jr 51:6

They will l you childless, Ezk 5:17
Yet I will l a remnant when you Ezk 6:8
jewelry, and l you stark naked. Ezk 16:39
for, and l you stark naked Ezk 23:29
I will l you in the desert, Ezk 29:5
yet they had to l His land ⌊in Ezk 36:20
I will l none of them behind. Ezk 39:28
l them in the holy chambers, Ezk 44:19
and when they l, he will leave. Ezk 46:10
and when they leave, he will l. Ezk 46:10
But l the stump with its roots Dn 4:15
but l the stump with its roots Dn 4:23
command to l the tree's stump Dn 4:26
Persia, and when I l, the prince Dn 10:20
attached to idols; l him alone! Hs 4:17
his Lord will l his bloodguilt Hs 12:14
and relent and l a blessing Jl 2:14
the bridegroom l his bedroom, Jl 2:16
wouldn't they l some grapes? Ob 5
Get up and l, for this is not Mc 2:10
through the gate, and l by it. Mc 2:13
For now you will l the city and Mc 4:10
LORD will never l ⌊the guilty⌋ Nah 1:3
which l nothing for the morning. Zph 3:3
will l a meek and humble people Zph 3:12
L the land of the north"— Zch 2:6
l your gift there in front of Mt 5:24
begged Him to l their region. Mt 8:34
"L," He said, "because the girl Mt 9:24
and stay there until you l. Mt 10:11
feet when you l that house or Mt 10:14
L them alone! They are blind Mt 15:14
he l the 99 on the hillside Mt 18:12
reason a man will l his father Mt 19:5
Then Jesus said, "L the children Mt 19:14
My brothers to l for Galilee, Mt 28:10
to beg Him to l their region. Mk 5:17
there until you l that place. Mk 6:10
to you, when you l there, shake Mk 6:11
reason a man will l his father Mk 10:7
Then Jesus said, "L her alone. Mk 14:6
did not l the temple complex, Lk 2:37
L us alone! What do You have to Lk 4:34
region asked Him to l them, Lk 8:37
stay there and l from there. Lk 9:4
you, when you l that town, shake Lk 9:5
to him, 'Sir, l it this year Lk 13:8
does not l the 99 in the open Lk 15:4
and they will not l one stone on Lk 19:44
Those inside the city must l it, Lk 21:21
day He decided to l for Galilee. Jn 1:43
L here and go to Judea so Your Jn 7:3
Jesus answered, "L her alone; Jn 12:7
I will not l you as orphans; Jn 14:18
Peace I l with you. My peace I Jn 14:27
do. "Get up; let's l this place. Jn 14:31
home, and you will l Me alone. Jn 16:32
them not to l Jerusalem, Ac 1:4
You will not l my soul in Hades, Ac 2:27
ordered them to l the Sanhedrin, Ac 4:15
from these men and l them alone. Ac 5:38
by making them l their infants Ac 7:19
He did not l Himself without Ac 14:17
they urged them to l town. Ac 16:39
ordered all the Jews to l Rome. Ac 18:2
replied, "L for now, but when Ac 24:25
they began to l after Paul made Ac 28:25
instead, l room for His wrath. Rm 12:19
you would have to l the world. 1Co 5:10
a wife is not to l her husband. 1Co 7:10
But if she does l, she must 1Co 7:11
a husband is not to l his wife. 1Co 7:11
with him, he must not l her. 1Co 7:12
she must not l her husband. 1Co 7:13
unbeliever leaves, let him l. 1Co 7:15
reason a man will l his father Eph 5:31
were forced to l you for a short 1Th 2:17
I will never l you or forsake Heb 13:5

LEAVENED *(12)*
eats what is l from the first Ex 12:15
If anyone eats something l, Ex 12:19
Do not eat anything l; Ex 12:20
their dough before it was l, Ex 12:34
Nothing l may be eaten. Ex 13:3
l may be found among you, Ex 13:7
My sacrifices with anything l. Ex 23:18
My sacrifice with anything l. Ex 34:25
his offering cakes of l bread, Lv 7:13
must not eat l bread with it. Dt 16:3
of the dough until it is l. Hs 7:4
Offer l bread as a thank Am 4:5

LEAVENS *(1)*
A little yeast l the whole lump Gl 5:9

LEAVES *(37)*
This is why a man l his father Gn 2:24
they sewed fig l together and Gn 3:7
place until he l after he has Lv 16:17
a Levite l one of your towns Dt 18:6
He l a shining wake behind him; Jb 41:32
races, my strength l me, and Ps 38:10
of my head, and my courage l me. Ps 40:12
his breath l him, he returns Ps 146:4
A good man l an inheritance to Pr 13:22
for the one who l the path; Pr 15:10
a driving rain that l no food. Pr 28:3
an oak whose l are withered, Is 1:30
which l a stump when felled, Is 6:13
He l the hungry empty and Is 32:6
and Carmel shake off ⌊their⌋ l. Is 33:9
all wither as l wither on the Is 34:4
his wife and she l him to marry Jr 3:1
Anyone who l them will be torn Jr 5:6
All its fresh l will wither! Ezk 17:9
gate must be closed after he l. Ezk 46:12
Their l will not wither, and Ezk 47:12
food and their l for medicine." Ezk 47:12
Its l were beautiful, its fruit Dn 4:12
strip off its l and scatter its Dn 4:14
whose l were beautiful and its Dn 4:21
found nothing on it except l. Mt 21:19
becomes tender and sprouts l, Mt 24:32
the distance a fig tree with l, Mk 11:13
nothing but l, because it was Mk 11:13
brother dies, l his wife behind, Mk 12:19
wife behind, and l no child, his Mk 12:19
becomes tender and sprouts l, Mk 13:28
him, it hardly ever l him. Lk 9:39
they put out ⌊l⌋ you can see for Lk 21:30
l them and runs away when he Jn 10:12
the unbeliever l, let him leave. 1Co 7:15
l of the tree are for healing Rv 22:2

LEAVING *(36)*
But l his garment in her hand, Gn 39:12
as they were l, he said to them Gn 45:24
in the month of Abib, you are l. Ex 13:4
after l his house she goes and Dt 24:2
no one l or entering. Jos 6:1
l the city exposed while they Jos 8:17
everyone in it, l no survivors. Jos 10:28
with his people, l no survivors Jos 10:33
everyone in it, l no survivors. Jos 10:39
all their kings, l no survivors. Jos 10:40
them down, l no survivors. Jos 11:8
them, l no one alive. Jos 11:14
l nothing undone of all that the Jos 11:15
priests—l him no survivors. 2Kg 10:11
destroy us, l no survivors? Ezr 9:14
their clothes and l them naked. Jb 22:6
l great emptiness in the land. Is 6:12
l yourselves without a remnant. Jr 44:7
acted promiscuously, l your God. Hs 9:1
the LORD is l His place and Mc 1:3
not l them root or branches. Mal 4:1
As they were l Jericho, a large Mt 20:29
After l them, He went away again Mt 26:44
many saw them l and recognized Mk 6:33
Again, l the region of Tyre, He Mk 7:31
And as He was l Jericho with His Mk 10:46
and he died, l no offspring. Mk 12:21
tried to keep Him from l them. Lk 4:42
So, l everything behind, he got Lk 5:28
up, and fled, l him half dead. Lk 10:30
am l the world and going to the Jn 16:28
As they were l, they begged that Ac 13:42
After l the jail, they came to Ac 16:40
Cyprus, l it on the left, Ac 21:3
l the elementary message about Heb 6:1
for you, l you an example, 1Pt 2:21

LEB-QAMAI *(1)*
(AKA CHALDEA)
and against the population of L. Jr 51:1

LEBANA'S *(1)*
L descendants, Hagaba's Neh 7:48

LEBANAH'S *(1)*
L descendants, Hagabah's Ezr 2:45

LEBANESE *(1)*
lived in the L mountains from Jdg 3:3

LEBANON *(70)*
the Canaanites and to L as far Dt 1:7
that good hill country and L. Dt 3:25
the wilderness to L and from the Dt 11:24
wilderness and L to the great Jos 1:4
the Mediterranean Sea toward L— Jos 9:1
the Valley of L at the foot of Jos 11:17
the valley of L to Mount Halak, Jos 12:7
and all L east from Baal-gad Jos 13:5
hill country from L to Jos 13:6
and consume the cedars of L." Jdg 9:15
the cedar in L to the hyssop 1Kg 4:33
cedars from L be cut down for 1Kg 5:6
logs⌋ down from L to the sea, 1Kg 5:9
sent 10,000 to L each month in 1Kg 5:14
they were in L, two months they 1Kg 5:14
the House of the Forest of L. 1Kg 7:2
Jerusalem, L, or anywhere else 1Kg 9:19
in the House of the Forest of L. 1Kg 10:17
the Forest of L were pure gold. 1Kg 10:21
thistle that was in L once sent 2Kg 14:9
to the cedar that was in L, 2Kg 14:9
animal that was in L passed by 2Kg 14:9
to the far recesses of L. 2Kg 19:23
algum logs from L, for I know 2Ch 2:8
know how to cut the trees of L. 2Ch 2:8
cut logs from L, as many as you 2Ch 2:16
Jerusalem, L, or anywhere else 2Ch 8:6
in the House of the Forest of L. 2Ch 9:16
the Forest of L were pure gold. 2Ch 9:20
that was in L sent ⌊a message⌋ 2Ch 25:18
to the cedar that was in L, 2Ch 25:18
animal that was in L passed by 2Ch 25:18
wood from L to Joppa by sea Ezr 3:7
LORD shatters the cedars of L. Ps 29:5
He makes L skip like a calf, Ps 29:6
May its crops be like L. Ps 72:16
and grow like a cedar tree in L. Ps 92:12
the cedars of L that He planted. Ps 104:16
for himself with wood from L. Sg 3:9
with me from L, my bride—with Sg 4:8
my bride—with me from L! Sg 4:8
is like the fragrance of L. Sg 4:11
flowing water streaming from L. Sg 4:15
is like L, as majestic as Sg 5:15
the tower of L looking toward Sg 7:4
against all the cedars of L, Is 2:13
L with its majesty will fall. Is 10:34
the cedars of L rejoice over you Is 14:8
a little while L will become Is 29:17
L is ashamed and decayed. Is 33:9
The glory of L will be given to Is 35:2
to the far recesses of L. Is 37:24
L is not enough for fuel, or its Is 40:16
glory of L will come to you— Is 60:13
Does the snow of L ever leave Jr 18:14
or⌋ the summit of L, but I will Jr 22:6
Go up to L and cry out; Jr 22:20
residents of L, nestled among Jr 22:23
colors came to L and took the Ezk 17:3
a cedar from L to make a mast Ezk 27:5
a cedar in L, with beautiful Ezk 31:3
I made L mourn on account of it, Ezk 31:15
and best of L, were comforted Ezk 31:16
root like ⌊the cedars of⌋ L. Hs 14:5
like ⌊the forest of⌋ L. Hs 14:6
will be like the wine of L. Hs 14:7
even the flower of L withers. Nah 1:4
against L will overwhelm Hab 2:17
to the land of Gilead and to L, Zch 10:10
your gates, L, and fire will Zch 11:1

LEBAOTH *(1)*
(AKA BETH-BIRI, BETH-LEBAOTH)
L, Shilhim, Ain, and Rimmon—29 Jos 15:32

LEBO-HAMATH *(4)*
border from L as far as the Sea 2Kg 14:25
way of Hethlon and L to Zedad, Ezk 47:15
border up to a point opposite L. Ezk 47:20
to L as far as Hazar-enon, Ezk 48:1

LEBONAH *(1)*
to Shechem, and south of L." Jdg 21:19

LECAH *(1)*
Er the father of L, Laadah the 1Ch 4:21

LECTURE *(1)*
day in the l hall of Tyrannus Ac 19:9

LED (114)

the LORD has l me on the journey Gn 24:27
l the flock to the far side of Ex 3:1
So He l the people around toward Ex 13:18
Then Moses l Israel on from the Ex 15:22
that you have l them into ⌊such Ex 32:21
Why have you l us up from Egypt Nm 20:5
Why have you l us up from Egypt Nm 21:5
do not be l astray to bow down Dt 4:19
LORD your God l you on the Dt 8:2
He l you through the great and Dt 8:15
l the inhabitants of their city Dt 13:13
l us to this place and gave us Dt 26:9
I l you 40 years in the Dt 29:5
and you are l astray to bow down Dt 30:17
The LORD alone l him, with no Dt 32:12
of Israel l the troops up to Jos 8:10
l him throughout the land of Jos 24:3
out of Egypt and l you into the Jdg 2:1
new ropes and l him away from Jdg 15:13
I have l you from my youth until 1Sm 12:2
l your ancestors out of Egypt 1Sm 12:8
1,000 men. David l the troops 1Sm 18:13
So he l him, and there were the 1Sm 30:16
were the one who l us out ⌊to 2Sm 5:2
This l to sin; the people walked 1Kg 12:30
And he l them to Samaria. 2Kg 6:19
Then Jeroboam l Israel away from 2Kg 17:21
you l us out ⌊to battle⌋ and 1Ch 11:2
Joab l the army and destroyed 1Ch 20:1
and he l Judah astray. 2Ch 21:11
his position and l his people to 2Ch 25:11
grew arrogant and it l to his 2Ch 26:16
l them with a pillar of cloud Neh 9:12
things, being l astray, for what Jb 15:31
garments she is l to the king; Ps 45:14
They are l in with gladness and Ps 45:15
You l Your people like a flock Ps 77:20
l them with a cloud by day and Ps 78:14
He l His people out like sheep Ps 78:52
He l them safely, and they were Ps 78:53
He l them through the depths as Ps 106:9
l them by the right path to go Ps 107:7
and l Israel through, His love Ps 136:14
He l His people in the Ps 136:16
chieftains have l Egypt astray. Is 19:13
deceived mind has l him astray, Is 44:20
and knowledge l you astray. Is 47:10
thirst when He l them through Is 48:21
Like a lamb l to the slaughter Is 53:7
kings being l ⌊in procession⌋. Is 60:11
and l them through the depths Is 63:13
You l Your people this way to Is 63:14
who l us through the wilderness, Jr 2:6
you will be l out from here with Jr 2:37
a docile lamb l to slaughter. Jr 11:19
brought and l the descendants Jr 23:8
by Baal and l My people Israel Jr 23:13
but you have l these people to Jr 28:15
have l your own selves astray Jr 42:20
shepherds have l them astray, Jr 50:6
Since they have l My people Ezk 13:10
Then they l him away with hooks Ezk 19:4
him with hooks and l him away to Ezk 19:9
land of Egypt and l them into Ezk 20:10
He l me all around them. Ezk 37:2
Seven steps l up to the gate, Ezk 40:22
deep, and 10 steps l up to it. Ezk 40:49
Then the man l me out by way of Ezk 42:1
he l me out by way of the gate Ezk 42:15
l me to the gate, the one that Ezk 43:1
outer court and l me past its Ezk 46:21
the north gate and l me around Ezk 47:2
third of a mile and l me through Ezk 47:3
of a mile⌋ and l me through the Ezk 47:4
of a mile⌋ and l me through ⌊the Ezk 47:4
Then he l me back to the bank Ezk 47:6
I l them with human cords, Hs 11:4
followed have l them astray. Am 2:4
land of Egypt and l you 40 years Am 2:10
It l them until it came and Mt 2:9
Jesus was l up by the Spirit Mt 4:1
until He has l justice to Mt 12:20
and l them up on a high mountain Mt 17:1
had arrested Jesus l Him away to Mt 26:57
they l Him away and handed Him Mt 27:2
and l Him away to crucify Him. Mt 27:31
and John and l them up on a high Mk 9:2
They l Jesus away to the high Mk 14:53
they l Him away and handed Him Mk 15:1
the soldiers l Him away into Mk 15:16
and l Him out to crucify Him. Mk 15:20
and was l by the Spirit in the Lk 4:1
sword and be l captive into all Lk 21:24
They seized Him, l Him away, and Lk 22:54
As they l Him away, they seized Lk 23:26
were also l away to be executed Lk 23:32
Then He l them out as far as Lk 24:50
First they l Him to Annas, Jn 18:13
man l them out and performed Ac 7:36
He was l like a sheep to the Ac 8:32
by the hand and l him into Ac 9:8
they l him to the room upstairs. Ac 9:39
and l them out of it with a Ac 13:17
time ago and l 4,000 Assassins Ac 21:38
I was l by the hand by those who Ac 22:11
him by the hand, l him aside, Ac 23:19
All those l by God's Spirit are Rm 8:14
you were l to dumb idols— 1Co 12:2
to dumb idols—being l astray. 1Co 12:2
your grief l to repentance. 2Co 7:9
But if you are l by the Spirit, Gl 5:18
l along by a variety of passions, 2Tm 3:6
Don't be l astray by various Heb 13:9
that you are not l away by the 2Pt 3:17

LEDGE (9)

the altar's l, so that the mesh Ex 27:5
of bronze mesh under its l, Ex 38:4
to the lower l is three and a Ezk 43:14
width ⌊of the l⌋ is 21 inches. Ezk 43:14
from the small l to the large Ezk 43:14
the small ledge to the large l. Ezk 43:14
The l is 24 and a half feet long Ezk 43:17
the four corners of the l, Ezk 43:20
four corners of the altar's l, Ezk 45:19

LEDGES (2)

provided offset l for the temple 1Kg 6:6
There were l on the wall of the Ezk 41:6

LEECH (1)

The l has two daughters: Pr 30:15

LEEKS (1)

cucumbers, melons, l, onions, Nm 11:5

LEFT (466)

Only Noah was l, and those that Gn 7:23
75 years old when he l Haran. Gn 12:4
you go⌋ to the l, I will go to Gn 13:9
the right, I will go to the l." Gn 13:9
him out and l him outside Gn 19:16
She l and wandered in the Gn 21:14
she l the boy under one of the Gn 21:15
l and returned to the land of Gn 21:32
the servant took Rebekah and l. Gn 24:61
So Isaac l there, camped in the Gn 26:17
way, and they l him in peace. Gn 26:31
and Jacob had l the presence of Gn 27:30
Jacob l Beer-sheba and went Gn 28:10
he l Leah's tent and entered Gn 31:33
Then Laban l to return home. Gn 31:55
Jacob was l alone, and a man Gn 32:24
that time Judah l his brothers Gn 38:1
She got up and l, then removed Gn 38:19
items he had l with the woman, Gn 38:20
He l all that he owned under Gn 39:6
that he had l his garment with Gn 39:13
he l his garment with me and ran Gn 39:15
he l his garment with me and ran Gn 39:18
Joseph l Pharaoh's presence and Gn 41:46
on their donkeys and l there. Gn 42:26
is dead and he alone is l. Gn 42:38
only one of his mother's sons l, Gn 44:20
One l—I said that he must have Gn 44:28
Jacob l Beer-sheba. The sons of Gn 46:5
There is nothing l for our lord Gn 47:18
hand Ephraim toward Israel's l, Gn 48:13
and with his l hand Manasseh Gn 48:13
put his l on Manasseh's head, Gn 48:14
their cattle were l in the land Gn 50:8
When they l Pharaoh, they Ex 5:20
Then Moses l Pharaoh's presence Ex 8:30
and his people; not one was l. Ex 8:31
word seriously l their servants Ex 9:21
When I have l the city, I will Ex 9:29
eat the remainder l to you that Ex 10:5
he turned and l Pharaoh's Ex 10:6
everything that the hail l." Ex 10:12
the trees that the hail had l. Ex 10:15
Nothing green was l on the trees Ex 10:15
Moses l Pharaoh's presence and Ex 10:18
a single locust was l in all the Ex 10:19
a hoof will be l behind because Ex 10:26
And he l Pharaoh's presence Ex 11:8
the Israelites l the land of Ex 13:18
by night never l its place in Ex 13:22
them on their right and their l. Ex 14:22
them on their right and their l. Ex 14:29
after they had l the land of Ex 16:1
some people l part of it until Ex 16:20
and everything l over set aside Ex 16:23
community l the Wilderness Ex 17:1
Israelites had l the land of Ex 19:1
the flap that is l over from the Ex 26:12
other of what is l over along Ex 26:13
of the bread is l until morning, Ex 29:34
morning, burn up what is l over. Ex 29:34
community l Moses' presence. Ex 35:20
and what is l over may be eaten Lv 7:16
offering that is l over from the Lv 10:12
oil and pour it into his l palm. Lv 14:15
the oil in his l palm and Lv 14:16
What is l of the oil in the Lv 14:18
some of the oil into his l palm. Lv 14:26
the oil in his l palm seven Lv 14:27
What is l of the oil in the Lv 14:29
If many years are still l, Lv 25:51
to the years l until the ⌊next⌋ Lv 27:18
burned against them, and He l. Nm 12:9
the right or the l until we have Nm 20:17
whole army until no one was l, Nm 21:35
to turn to the right or the l. Nm 22:26
of them was l except Caleb son Nm 26:65
They l and went up into the hill Dt 1:24
not turn to the right or the l. Dt 2:27
and children. We l no survivors. Dt 2:34
until there was no survivor l. Dt 3:3
of Bashan was l of the remnant Dt 3:11
aside to the right or the l. Dt 5:32
from the day you l the land of Dt 9:7
because you l the land of Egypt Dt 16:3
life the day you l the land of Dt 16:3
the right or the l from the Dt 17:11
command to the right or the l, Dt 17:20
the journey after you l Egypt. Dt 24:9
It is to be l for the foreign Dt 24:19
you must not glean what is l. Dt 24:21
the journey after you l Egypt. Dt 25:17
the right or the l from all the Dt 28:14
has nothing l during the siege Dt 28:55
you will be l with only a few Dt 28:62
is gone and no one is l— Dt 32:36
his vitality had not l ⌊him⌋. Dt 34:7
from it to the right or the l, Jos 1:7
So they l, and they came to the Jos 2:1
soon as they l to pursue them, Jos 2:7
next morning and l Acacia Grove Jos 3:1
Not a man was l in Ai or Bethel Jos 8:17
burned Ai and l it a permanent Jos 8:28
on the day we l to come to you. Jos 9:12
to the sword, and l no survivors Jos 10:30
at Eglon, he l no survivors. Jos 10:37
them; he l no one alive. Then Jos 11:11
No Anakim were l in the land of Jos 11:22
Israelites were l who had not Jos 18:2
So the men l, went through the Jos 18:9
of Manasseh l the Israelites at Jos 22:9
turn from it to the right or l Jos 23:6
nations Joshua l when he died. Jdg 2:21
The LORD l these nations and did Jdg 2:23
the LORD l in order to test Jdg 3:1
The LORD l them to test Israel, Jdg 3:4
and all his attendants l him. Jdg 3:19
Ehud reached with his l hand, Jdg 3:21
Sisera l his chariot and fled on Jdg 4:15
not a single man was l. Jdg 4:16
l nothing for Israel to eat, Jdg 6:4
their torches in their l hands, Jdg 7:20
were all those l of the entire Jdg 8:10
So she l with her friends and Jdg 11:38
l ⌊the road⌋ to see the lion's Jdg 14:8
and his strength l him. Jdg 16:19
know that the LORD had l him. Jdg 16:20
hand and the other on his l. Jdg 16:29
The man l the town of Bethlehem Jdg 17:8
five men l and came to Laish. Jdg 18:7

What do I have l? How can you	Jdg 18:24
to him and l him for her	Jdg 19:2
about wives for those who are l,	Jdg 21:16
A man l Bethlehem in Judah with	Ru 1:1
and she was l with her two sons.	Ru 1:3
and Naomi was l without her two	Ru 1:5
She l the place where she had	Ru 1:7
I l full, but the LORD has	Ru 1:21
So Ruth l and entered the field	Ru 2:3
⌊how⌋ you l your father and	Ru 2:11
satisfied and had ⌊some⌋ l over.	Ru 2:14
out what she had l over from her	Ru 2:18
who has not l you without a	Ru 4:14
Anyone who is l in your family	1Sm 2:36
send Israel away, and Israel l?	1Sm 6:6
to the right or to the l.	1Sm 6:12
no two of them were l together.	1Sm 11:11
not know that Jonathan had l.	1Sm 14:3
and determine who has l us."	1Sm 14:17
Spirit of the LORD had l Saul,	1Sm 16:14
l the flock with someone to keep	1Sm 17:20
David l his supplies in the care	1Sm 17:22
with David but had l from Saul.	1Sm 18:12
he and Samuel l and stayed at	1Sm 19:18
Then David l, and Jonathan went	1Sm 20:42
So David l Gath and took refuge	1Sm 22:1
So he l them in the care of the	1Sm 22:4
So David l and went to the	1Sm 22:5
l Keilah at once and moved from	1Sm 23:13
Then Saul l the cave and went on	1Sm 24:7
had any men l by morning light.	1Sm 25:34
they got up and l that night.	1Sm 28:25
they had no strength l to weep.	1Sm 30:4
him and had been l at the Wadi	1Sm 30:21
right or the l in his pursuit	2Sm 2:19
to your right or l, seize one	2Sm 2:21
Then Joab l David and sent	2Sm 3:26
the people l, each to his own	2Sm 6:19
Is there anyone l of Saul's	2Sm 9:3
So Uriah l the palace, and a	2Sm 11:8
the messenger l. When he arrived	2Sm 11:22
leave me!" And everyone l him.	2Sm 13:9
to the right or l from all my	2Sm 14:19
But he l behind 10 concubines to	2Sm 15:16
warriors on David's right and l.	2Sm 16:6
concubines he l to take care	2Sm 16:21
even one will be l of all the	2Sm 17:12
So the two l quickly and came to	2Sm 17:18
my lord the king l Jerusalem.	2Sm 19:19
day the king l until the day he	2Sm 19:24
my life are l that I should go	2Sm 19:34
concubines he had l to take care	2Sm 20:3
they l Jerusalem to pursue Sheba	2Sm 20:7
the army l the king's presence	2Sm 24:4
he set up the l pillar and named	1Kg 7:21
temple and five on the l side.	1Kg 7:39
Solomon l all the utensils	1Kg 7:47
on the right and five on the l;	1Kg 7:49
return to me." So the people l.	1Kg 12:5
When he l, a lion met him along	1Kg 13:24
wife got up and l and went to	1Kg 14:17
Elijah l and lived by the Wadi	1Kg 17:5
Judah, he l his servant there,	1Kg 19:3
I alone am l, and they are	1Kg 19:10
alone am l, and they're looking	1Kg 19:14
Elijah l there and found Elisha	1Kg 19:19
Elisha l the oxen, ran to follow	1Kg 19:20
Then he l, followed Elijah, and	1Kg 19:21
the messengers l and took word	1Kg 20:9
When he l him, a lion found him	1Kg 20:36
king of Israel l for home	1Kg 20:43
right hand and at His l hand.	1Kg 22:19
who were l from the days of his	1Kg 22:46
certainly die.' " Then Elijah l.	2Kg 1:4
which parted to the right and l.	2Kg 2:8
parted to the right and the l,	2Kg 2:14
of Kir-hareseth were l.	2Kg 3:25
So she l. After she had shut the	2Kg 4:5
man of God, shut him in, and l.	2Kg 4:21
she picked up her son and l.	2Kg 4:37
they will have some l over.' "	2Kg 4:43
they ate and had some l over.	2Kg 4:44
But Naaman got angry and l,	2Kg 5:11
So he turned and l in a rage.	2Kg 5:12
dismissed the men, and they l.	2Kg 5:24
so they have l the camp to hide	2Kg 7:12
horses that are l in the city.	2Kg 7:13
from the day she l the country	2Kg 8:6
Hazael l Elisha and went to his	2Kg 8:14
When he l there, he found	2Kg 10:15
not a man l who did not come.	2Kg 10:21
of the temple to the l side,	2Kg 11:11
Jehoahaz did not have an army l,	2Kg 13:7
king of Assyria had l Lachish,	2Kg 19:8
of Assyria broke camp and l.	2Kg 19:36
nothing will be l,' says the	2Kg 20:17
not turn to the right or the l.	2Kg 22:2
city (on the l at the city gate)	2Kg 23:8
So they l his bones undisturbed	2Kg 23:18
people who were l in the city,	2Kg 25:11
of the guards l some of the	2Kg 25:12
the people he l in the land of	2Kg 25:22
the army, l and went to Egypt,	2Kg 25:26
On the l, their relatives were	1Ch 6:44
either their right or l hand,	1Ch 12:2
So David l Asaph and his	1Ch 16:37
⌊He also l⌋ Obed-edom and his 68	1Ch 16:38
⌊David l⌋ Zadok the priest and	1Ch 16:39
the people l for their homes,	1Ch 16:43
Joab l and traveled throughout	1Ch 21:4
he l the threshing floor and	1Ch 21:21
on the right and one on the l.	2Ch 3:17
and the one on the l Boaz.	2Ch 3:17
on the right and five on the l.	2Ch 4:6
on the right and five on the l.	2Ch 4:7
on the right and five on the l.	2Ch 4:8
in three days." So the people l.	2Ch 10:5
for the Levites l their	2Ch 11:14
right hand and at His l hand.	2Ch 18:18
not a son was l to him except	2Ch 21:17
of the temple to the l side,	2Ch 23:10
had many wounds, they l him.	2Ch 24:25
The army l the captives and the	2Ch 28:14
there is plenty l over because	2Ch 31:10
abundance is what is l over."	2Ch 31:10
God l him to test him and	2Ch 32:31
aside to the right or the l.	2Ch 34:2
none of them l their tasks.	2Ch 35:15
and that no gap was l in it—	Neh 6:1
to his l were Pedaiah, Mishael,	Neh 8:4
procession went to the l,	Neh 12:38
The couriers l, spurred on by	Est 3:15
That day Haman l full of joy and	Est 5:9
the statement l the king's mouth	Est 7:8
So Satan l the LORD's presence	Jb 2:7
Nothing is l for him to consume;	Jb 20:21
feed on what is l in his tent.	Jb 20:26
consumed what they l behind."	Jb 22:20
Their vigor had l them.	Jb 30:2
answer; words have l them.	Jb 32:15
Egypt was glad when they l,	Ps 105:38
in her l, riches and honor.	Pr 3:16
turn to the right or to the l;	Pr 4:27
but a youth l to himself is a	Pr 29:15
but a fool's heart to the l.	Ec 10:2
His l hand is under my head,	Sg 2:6
I was crushed that he had l.	Sg 5:6
His l hand is under my head,	Sg 8:3
of Hosts had not l us a few	Is 1:9
and whoever is l in Jerusalem	Is 4:3
and you alone are l in the land.	Is 5:8
eaten on the l, but they are	Is 9:20
And those who are l will be few	Is 16:14
gleanings will be l in Israel,	Is 17:6
They will all be l for the birds	Is 18:6
what is ⌊l⌋ of the night?	Is 21:11
what is ⌊l⌋ of the night?"	Is 21:11
turn to the right or to the l,	Is 30:21
No nobles will be l to proclaim	Is 34:12
that the king had l Lachish,	Is 37:8
of Assyria broke camp and l.	Is 37:37
will be l,' says the LORD	Is 39:6
See, I was l by myself—but	Is 49:21
out to the right and to the l,	Is 54:3
He has l his lair to make your	Jr 4:7
I looked, and no man was l;	Jr 4:25
abandoned; no inhabitant is l.	Jr 4:29
You have l Me. ⌊This is⌋ the	Jr 15:6
there is no place l to bury.	Jr 19:11
He has l this place—he will	Jr 22:11
He has l His den like a lion,	Jr 25:38
the metalsmiths had l Jerusalem.	Jr 29:2
only they were l among Judah's	Jr 34:7
Pharaoh's army had l Egypt,	Jr 37:5
They l the city at night by way	Jr 39:4
They l along the route to the	Jr 39:4
l in the land of Judah some of	Jr 39:10
of Babylon had l a remnant in	Jr 40:11
They l, stopping in Geruth	Jr 41:17
Moab has been l quiet since his	Jr 48:11
Judah are not l widowed by their	Jr 51:5
They l the city by night by way	Jr 52:7
people who were l in the city,	Jr 52:15
l to be vinedressers and farmers.	Jr 52:16
me to pieces; He l me desolate.	Lm 3:11
The elders have l the city gate,	Lm 5:14
has l our hearts; our dancing	Lm 5:15
the face of an ox on the l,	Ezk 1:10
l in bitterness and in an angry	Ezk 3:14
down on your l side and place	Ezk 4:4
were killing, I was l alone.	Ezk 9:8
the vision I had seen l me,	Ezk 11:24
there will be survivors l in it,	Ezk 14:22
turn to the l—wherever your	Ezk 21:16
daughters you l behind will fall	Ezk 24:21
cut it down and l it lying.	Ezk 31:12
peoples of the earth l its shade	Ezk 31:12
bow from your l hand and make	Ezk 39:3
they will be l for salt.	Ezk 47:11
will not be l to another people	Dn 2:44
with its feet whatever was l.	Dn 7:7
with its feet whatever was l.	Dn 7:19
I was l alone, looking at this	Dn 10:8
No strength was l in me;	Dn 10:8
me after I had been l there with	Dn 10:13
What the devouring locust has l,	Jl 1:4
what the swarming locust has l,	Jl 1:4
and what the young locust has l,	Jl 1:4
will have ⌊only⌋ a hundred l,	Am 5:3
have ⌊only⌋ ten l in the house	Am 5:3
there are 10 men l in one house,	Am 6:9
Jonah l the city and sat down	Jnh 4:5
between their right and their l,	Jnh 4:11
you until there is no one l.	Zph 2:5
Who is l among you who saw this	Hg 2:3
still seed l in the granary?	Hg 2:19
bowl and the other on its l."	Zch 4:3
right and l of the lampstand?	Zch 4:11
the land was l desolate behind	Zch 7:14
them on the right and the l,	Zch 12:6
but a third will be l in it.	Zch 13:8
Then the Devil l Him, and	Mt 4:11
He l Nazareth behind and went to	Mt 4:13
Immediately they l their nets	Mt 4:20
Immediately they l the boat and	Mt 4:22
don't let your l hand know what	Mt 6:3
her hand, and the fever l her.	Mt 8:15
weeds among the wheat, and l.	Mt 13:25
these parables, He l there.	Mt 13:53
When Jesus l there, He withdrew	Mt 15:21
Then He l them and went away.	Mt 16:4
have l everything and followed	Mt 19:27
And everyone who has l houses,	Mt 19:29
right and the other on Your l,	Mt 20:21
at My right and l is not Mine to	Mt 20:23
Then He l them, went out of the	Mt 21:17
So they l Him and went away.	Mt 22:22
he l his wife to his brother.	Mt 22:25
your house is l to you desolate.	Mt 23:38
As Jesus l and was going out of	Mt 24:1
stone will be l here on another	Mt 24:2
one will be taken and one l.	Mt 24:40
one will be taken and one l.	Mt 24:41
right, and the goats on the l.	Mt 25:33
also say to those on the l,	Mt 25:41
on the right and one on the l.	Mt 27:38
He l after rolling a great stone	Mt 27:60
Immediately they l their nets	Mk 1:18
and they l their father Zebedee	Mk 1:20
As soon as they l the synagogue,	Mk 1:29
The fever l her, and she began	Mk 1:31
Immediately the disease l him,	Mk 1:42
So they l the crowd and took Him	Mk 4:36
He l them, got on board ⌊the	Mk 8:13
Then they l that place and made	Mk 9:30
have l everything and followed	Mk 10:28
there is no one who has l house,	Mk 10:29
and at Your l in Your glory."	Mk 10:37
at My right or l is not Mine to	Mk 10:40
So they l Him and went away.	Mk 12:12
wife, and dying, l no offspring.	Mk 12:20
The seven also l no offspring.	Mk 12:22
stone will be l here on another	Mk 13:2
a journey, who l his house, gave	Mk 13:34

but he **l** the linen cloth behind Mk 14:52
on His right and one on His **l**. Mk 15:27
Then the angel **l** her. Lk 1:38
the angels had **l** them and Lk 2:15
After He **l** the synagogue, He Lk 4:38
rebuked the fever, and it **l** her. Lk 4:39
fishermen had **l** them and were Lk 5:2
the boats to land, **l** everything, Lk 5:11
immediately the disease **l** him. Lk 5:13
After John's messengers **l**, Lk 7:24
my sister has **l** me to serve Lk 10:40
When He **l** there, the scribes and Lk 11:53
with sores, was **l** at his gate. Lk 16:20
But on the day Lot **l** Sodom, Lk 17:29
taken and the other will be **l**. Lk 17:34
will be taken and the other **l**. Lk 17:35
taken, and the other will be **l**." Lk 17:36
we have **l** what we had and Lk 18:28
is no one who has **l** a house, Lk 18:29
were sent **l** and found it just Lk 19:32
seven died and **l** no children. Lk 20:31
stone will be **l** on another that Lk 21:6
on the right and one on the **l**. Lk 23:33
l them and was carried up into Lk 24:51
He **l** Judea and went again to Jn 4:3
Then the woman **l** her water jar, Jn 4:28
They **l** the town and made their Jn 4:30
two days He **l** there for Galilee Jn 4:43
in the morning the fever **l** him," Jn 4:52
loaves that were **l** over by those Jn 6:13
heard this, they **l** one by one, Jn 8:9
Only He was **l**, with the woman in Jn 8:9
He has not **l** Me alone, because I Jn 8:29
So he **l**, washed, and came back Jn 9:7
that Judas **l** to go to his own Ac 1:25
He was not **l** in Hades, and His Ac 2:31
and when he was **l** outside, Ac 7:21
So Ananias **l** and entered the Ac 9:17
and immediately the angel **l** him. Ac 12:10
l them and went back to Ac 13:13
The next day he **l** with Barnabas Ac 14:20
those who are **l** of mankind may Ac 15:17
he **l** from Athens and went to Ac 18:1
So he **l** there and went to the Ac 18:7
reached Ephesus he **l** them there, Ac 18:19
and the diseases **l** them, and the Ac 19:12
time until dawn. Then he **l**. Ac 20:11
it on the **l**, we sailed on to Ac 21:3
we **l** to continue our journey, Ac 21:5
The next day we **l** and came to Ac 21:8
Jews, Felix **l** Paul in prison. Ac 24:27
a man who was **l** as a prisoner Ac 25:14
when they had **l** they talked with Ac 26:31
anchors, they **l** them in the sea Ac 27:40
same way also **l** natural sexual Rm 1:27
of Hosts had not **l** us a seed, Rm 9:29
am the only one **l**, and they are Rm 11:3
have **l** 7,000 men for Myself who Rm 11:4
to them and **l** for Macedonia. 2Co 2:13
on the right hand and the **l**, 2Co 6:7
gospel, when I **l** Macedonia, no Php 4:15
better to be **l** alone in Athens 1Th 3:1
The real widow, **l** all alone, has 1Tm 5:5
bring the cloak I **l** in Troas 2Tm 4:13
Trophimus I **l** sick at Miletus. 2Tm 4:20
The reason I **l** you in Crete was Ti 1:5
to set right what was **l** undone Ti 1:5
He **l** nothing not subject to him. Heb 2:8
By faith he **l** Egypt behind, Heb 11:27
on the sea, his **l** on the land, Rv 10:2
with the woman and **l** to wage war Rv 12:17
The fruit you craved has **l** you. Rv 18:14

LEFT-HANDED *(2)*
son of Gera, a **l** Benjaminite, as Jdg 3:15
men who were **l** among all these Jdg 20:16

LEFTOVER *(5)*
the **l** half curtain is to hang Ex 26:12
up 12 baskets full of **l** pieces! Mt 14:20
they collected the **l** pieces— Mt 15:37
seven large baskets of **l** pieces. Mk 8:8
up 12 baskets of **l** pieces. Lk 9:17

LEFTOVERS *(1)*
Collect the **l** so that nothing is Jn 6:12

LEGAL *(8)*
This is the **l** statute that the Nm 19:2
This is the **l** statute the LORD Nm 31:21
was the **l** guardian of his Est 2:7
It's not **l** for us to put Jn 18:31
that are not **l** for us as Romans Ac 16:21
must be decided in a **l** assembly. Ac 19:39
Is it **l** for you to scourge a man Ac 22:25
based on a **l** command concerning Heb 7:16

LEGALLY *(6)*
make any matter ⌊**l**⌋ binding Ru 4:7
was ⌊the method of⌋ **l** binding a Ru 4:7
The **l** required portions for the Neh 12:44
married woman is **l** bound to her Rm 7:2
through angels was **l** binding, Heb 2:2
which has been **l** enacted on Heb 8:6

LEGION *(3)*
"My name is **L**," he answered Him, Mk 5:9
been demon-possessed by the **l**, Mk 5:15
"**L**," he said—because many Lk 8:30

LEGIONS *(1)*
with more than 12 **l** of angels? Mt 26:53

LEGITIMATELY *(1)*
is good, provided one uses it **l**. 1Tm 1:8

LEGS *(16)*
as well as its **l** and inner Ex 12:9
the four corners at its four **l**. Ex 25:26
the four corners at its four **l**. Ex 37:13
have jointed **l** above their feet Lv 11:21
between her **l** and the children Dt 28:57
is like lame **l** that hang limp. Pr 26:7
His **l** are alabaster pillars set Sg 5:15
the hair on the **l**, and to remove Is 7:20
Their **l** were straight, and the Ezk 1:7
spread your **l** to everyone who Ezk 16:25
its **l** were iron, and its feet Dn 2:33
snatches two **l** or a piece of an Am 3:12
have the men's **l** broken and that Jn 19:31
and broke the **l** of the first man Jn 19:32
not break His **l** since they saw Jn 19:33
his **l** were like fiery pillars, Rv 10:1

LEHABIM *(2)*
Ludim, Anamim, **L**, Naphtuhim, Gn 10:13
Ludim, Anamim, **L**, Naphtuhim, 1Ch 1:11

LEHEM *(1)*
Moabites and returned to **L**. 1Ch 4:22

LEHI *(4)*
camped in Judah, and raided **L**. Jdg 15:9
When he came to **L**, the Jdg 15:14
place ⌊in the ground⌋ at **L**, Jdg 15:19
which is in **L** to this day. Jdg 15:19

LEMUEL *(2)*
words of King **L**, an oracle that Pr 31:1
not for kings, **L**, it is not for Pr 31:4

LEMÁ *(2)*
Elí, Elí, **l** sabachtháni?" Mt 27:46
Eloi, Eloi, **l** sabachtháni?" Mk 15:34

LEND *(14)*
If you **l** money to My people— Ex 22:25
You are not to **l** him your silver Lv 25:37
you will **l** to many nations but Dt 15:6
You will **l** to many nations, Dt 28:12
He will **l** to you, but you won't Dt 28:44
to you, but you won't **l** to him. Dt 28:44
who does not **l** his money at Ps 15:5
they **l** support to the sons of Ps 83:8
I did not **l** or borrow, yet Jr 15:10
He doesn't **l** at interest or for Ezk 18:8
And if you **l** to those from whom Lk 6:34
Even sinners **l** to sinners to be Lk 6:34
is⌋ good, and **l**, expecting Lk 6:35
l me three loaves of bread, Lk 11:5

LENDER *(3)*
He will give a reward to the **l**. Pr 19:17
borrower is a slave to the **l**. Pr 22:7
and seller, **l** and borrower, Is 24:2

LENDING *(2)*
been **l** them money and grain. Neh 5:10
generous, always **l**, and his Ps 37:26

LENDS *(2)*
come to a man who **l** generously Ps 112:5
and **l** at interest or for profit, Ezk 18:13

LENGTH *(49)*
This is the **l** of Abraham's life: Gn 25:7
This is the **l** of Ishmael's life: Gn 25:17
The **l** of each curtain should be Ex 26:2
The **l** of each curtain should be Ex 26:8
over along the **l** of the tent Ex 26:13
The **l** of each plank is to be 15 Ex 26:16
The **l** of the courtyard is to be Ex 27:18
The **l** of each curtain was 42 Ex 36:9
The **l** of each curtain was 45 Ex 36:15
The **l** of each plank was 15 feet, Ex 36:21
spun linen, 150 feet in **l**, Ex 38:9
side were also 150 feet in **l**, Ex 38:11
the west side were 75 feet in **l**, Ex 38:12
sunrise were also 75 feet in **l**. Ex 38:13
unfairly in measurements of **l**, Lv 19:35
l of time that David was king 2Sm 2:11
death and one **l** ⌊of those⌋ to be 2Sm 8:2
The ⌊**l** of⌋ time David reigned 1Kg 2:11
The **l** of Solomon's reign in 1Kg 11:42
The **l** of Jeroboam's reign was 22 1Kg 14:20
l of Jehu's reign over Israel 2Kg 10:36
measurements of volume and **l**. 1Ch 23:29
The **l** of his reign over Israel 1Ch 29:27
the **l** was 90 feet, and the width 2Ch 3:3
its **l** corresponded to the width 2Ch 3:8
overall **l** of the wings of the 2Ch 3:11
l of days forever and ever. Ps 21:4
have made my days short in **l**, Ps 39:5
in the **l** of its limbs, for Ezk 31:7
was the standard **l** plus three Ezk 40:5
to the **l** of the gates; Ezk 40:18
north, ⌊both⌋ its **l** and width. Ezk 40:20
measured the **l** of the great hall Ezk 41:2
then measured the **l** of the room Ezk 41:4
the building's **l** was 157 and a Ezk 41:12
measured the **l** of the building Ezk 41:15
its **l** and sides were of wood. Ezk 41:22
Along the **l** ⌊of the chambers⌋, Ezk 42:2
Their **l** and width, as well as Ezk 42:11
of the altar in units of **l** Ezk 43:13
the standard **l** plus three inches Ezk 43:13
⌊Its⌋ **l** will correspond to one Ezk 45:7
The total **l** will be eight and Ezk 48:13
remainder of the **l** alongside the Ezk 48:18
to determine its width and **l**." Zch 2:2
areas and exhorted them at **l**, Ac 20:2
saints what is the **l** and width, Eph 3:18
its **l** and width are the same. Rv 21:16
Its **l**, width, and height are Rv 21:16

LENGTHEN *(5)*
for the shadow to **l** 10 steps. 2Kg 20:10
they will not **l** their days like Ec 8:13
l your ropes, and drive your Is 54:2
He will not **l** your exile. Lm 4:22
and **l** their tassels. Mt 23:5

LENGTHENING *(2)*
My days are like a **l** shadow, Ps 102:11
I fade away like a **l** shadow; Ps 109:23

LENGTHS *(2)*
every two cord **l** ⌊of those⌋ to 2Sm 8:2
who go to great **l** to hide their Is 29:15

LENIENT *(1)*
I come again, I will not be **l**, 2Co 13:2

LENT *(1)*
what he has **l** his neighbor. Dt 15:2

LENTIL *(1)*
gave bread and **l** stew to Esau; Gn 25:34

LENTILS *(3)*
flour, roasted grain, beans, **l**, 2Sm 17:28
there was a field full of **l**. 2Sm 23:11
barley, beans, **l**, millet, and Ezk 4:9

LEOPARD *(6)*
and the **l** will lie down with the Is 11:6
A **l** keeps watch over their Jr 5:6
his skin, or a **l** his spots? Jr 13:23
It was like a **l** with four wings Dn 7:6
will lurk like a **l** on the path. Hs 13:7
The beast I saw was like a **l**, Rv 13:2

LEOPARDS *(2)*
from the mountains of the **l**. Sg 4:8
swifter than **l** and more fierce Hab 1:8

LEPROSY *(1)*
an infection or **l** or a man who 2Sm 3:29

LESHEM *(2)*
(AKA DAN, LAISH)
went up and fought against **L**, Jos 19:47
and renamed **L** after their Jos 19:47

LESS *(19)*
and the poor may not give **l**, Ex 30:15
tribe⌋ and **l** from a smaller one Nm 35:8

Because their **L** brothers had 2Ch 35:15
the **L** supporting them. Ezr 10:15
the same way, a **L**, when he Lk 10:32
a **L** and a Cypriot by birth, Ac 4:36

LEVITES *(242)*

the clans of the **L** according to Ex 6:19
And all the **L** gathered around Ex 32:26
The **L** did as Moses commanded, Ex 32:28
the work of the **L** under the Ex 38:21
the **L** always have the right to Lv 25:32
one of the **L** can redeem— Lv 25:33
But the **L** were not registered Nm 1:47
the **L** over the tabernacle Nm 1:50
the **L** are to take it down, Nm 1:51
a campsite, the **L** are to set it Nm 1:51
The **L** are to camp around the Nm 1:53
But the **L** were not registered Nm 2:33
Assign the **L** to Aaron and his Nm 3:9
I have taken the **L** from the Nm 3:12
the womb. The **L** belong to Me, Nm 3:12
Register the **L** by their Nm 3:15
You are to take the **L** for Me— Nm 3:41
Take the **L** in place of every Nm 3:45
cattle. The **L** belong to Me; I Nm 3:45
Israelites who outnumber the **L**, Nm 3:46
of the ones redeemed by the **L**. Nm 3:49
Among the **L**, take a census of Nm 4:2
to be wiped out from the **L**. Nm 4:18
all the **L** by their clans Nm 4:46
and give this offering to the **L**, Nm 7:5
and oxen and gave them to the **L**. Nm 7:6
Take the **L** from among the Nm 8:6
Bring the **L** before the tent of Nm 8:9
present the **L** before the LORD Nm 8:10
to present the **L** before the LORD Nm 8:11
the **L** are to lay their hands Nm 8:12
to make atonement for the **L**. Nm 8:12
are to have the **L** stand before Nm 8:13
to separate the **L** from the rest Nm 8:14
so that the **L** will belong to Me. Nm 8:14
that the **L** may come to serve Nm 8:15
I have taken the **L** in place of Nm 8:18
have given the **L** exclusively to Nm 8:19
community did ⌊this⌋ to the **L**. Nm 8:20
commanded Moses regarding the **L**. Nm 8:20
The **L** purified themselves and Nm 8:21
the **L** came to do their work at Nm 8:22
Moses concerning the **L**. Nm 8:22
In regard to the **L**: Nm 8:24
deal with the **L** regarding their Nm 8:26
is you **L** who have gone too far! Nm 16:7
also told Korah, "Now listen, **L**! Nm 16:8
all your fellow **L** who are with Nm 16:10
your fellow **L** from the Nm 18:6
have given the **L** every tenth in Nm 18:21
The **L** will do the work of the Nm 18:23
The **L** will not receive an Nm 18:23
Speak to the **L** and tell them: Nm 18:26
credited to you **L** as the produce Nm 18:30
These were the **L** registered by Nm 26:57
give them to the **L** who perform Nm 31:30
gave them to the **L** who perform Nm 31:47
property for the **L** to live in Nm 35:2
are to give the **L** ⌊will extend⌋ Nm 35:4
you give the **L** will include six Nm 35:6
you give the **L** will be 48, Nm 35:7
cities to the **L** in proportion to Nm 35:8
all his fellow **L** who minister Dt 18:7
The **L** will proclaim in a loud Dt 27:14
he commanded the **L** who carried Dt 31:25
inheritance among them to the **L**. Jos 14:3
given to the **L** except cities to Jos 14:4
But the **L** among you do not get a Jos 18:7
gave the **L** these cities with Jos 21:3
The **L** who were the descendants Jos 21:4
around them to the **L** by lot, Jos 21:8
the Kohathite clans of the **L**, Jos 21:10
who were **L**, came from the tribe Jos 21:20
who were the remaining **L**: Jos 21:34
their pasturelands for the **L**. Jos 21:41
The **L** removed the ark of the 1Sm 6:15
and all the **L** with him were 2Sm 15:24
priests and the **L** brought the 1Kg 8:4
class of people who were not **L**. 1Kg 12:31
relatives the **L** were assigned to 1Ch 6:48
and their pasturelands to the **L**. 1Ch 6:64
priests, **L**, and temple servants 1Ch 9:2
The **L**: Shemaiah son of Hasshub, 1Ch 9:14
from the camp of the **L**. 1Ch 9:18
who were **L**, were entrusted with 1Ch 9:26
From the **L**: 4,600 1Ch 12:26
priests and **L** in their cities 1Ch 13:2
No one but the **L** may carry the 1Ch 15:2
descendants of Aaron and the **L**: 1Ch 15:4
and Abiathar and the **L** Uriel, 1Ch 15:11
us because you **L** were not ⌊with⌋ 1Ch 15:13
priests and the **L** consecrated 1Ch 15:14
Then the **L** carried the ark of 1Ch 15:15
leaders of the **L** to appoint 1Ch 15:16
So the **L** appointed Heman son of 1Ch 15:17
the leader of the **L** in music, 1Ch 15:22
God helped the **L** who were 1Ch 15:26
as were all the **L** who were 1Ch 15:27
some of the **L** to be ministers 1Ch 16:4
Israel, the priests, and the **L**. 1Ch 23:2
L 30 years old and above were 1Ch 23:3
L no longer need to carry the 1Ch 23:26
the **L** 20 years old or more were 1Ch 23:27
of the priests and the **L**. 1Ch 24:6
the sons of the **L** according to 1Ch 24:30
families of the priests and **L**— 1Ch 24:31
There were six **L** each day on the 1Ch 26:17
From the **L**, Ahijah was in charge 1Ch 26:20
for the **L**, Hashabiah son of 1Ch 27:17
of the priests and the **L**; 1Ch 28:13
priests and the **L** for all the 1Ch 28:21
and the **L** picked up the ark. 2Ch 5:4
and the **L** brought them up 2Ch 5:5
as were the **L** with the musical 2Ch 7:6
of the **L** over their 2Ch 8:14
priests and the **L** concerning any 2Ch 8:15
The priests and **L** from all their 2Ch 11:13
the **L** left their pasturelands 2Ch 11:14
followed the **L** to Jerusalem to 2Ch 11:16
descendants of Aaron and the **L**, 2Ch 13:9
the **L** ⌊serve⌋ at their tasks. 2Ch 13:10
The **L** with them were Shemaiah, 2Ch 17:8
and Jehoram, were with these **L**. 2Ch 17:8
some of the **L** and priests and 2Ch 19:8
and the **L** are officers in your 2Ch 19:11
Then the **L** from the sons of the 2Ch 20:19
They gathered the **L** from all the 2Ch 23:2
priests and **L** who are coming on 2Ch 23:4
priests and those **L** who serve; 2Ch 23:6
the priests and **L** and said, 2Ch 24:5
However, the **L** did not hurry. 2Ch 24:5
you required the **L** to bring from 2Ch 24:6
brought by the **L** to the king's 2Ch 24:11
the priests and **L** and gathered 2Ch 29:4
He said to them, "Hear me, **L**. 2Ch 29:5
Then the **L** stood up: 2Ch 29:12
the **L** received them and took 2Ch 29:16
stationed the **L** in the LORD's 2Ch 29:25
The **L** stood with the instruments 2Ch 29:26
told the **L** to sing praise to 2Ch 29:30
the **L** were more conscientious 2Ch 29:34
The priests and **L** were ashamed, 2Ch 30:15
from the hand of the **L**, 2Ch 30:16
and so the **L** were in charge of 2Ch 30:17
the **L** and the priests praised 2Ch 30:21
all the **L** who performed 2Ch 30:22
of Judah with the priests and **L**, 2Ch 30:25
priests and the **L** stood to bless 2Ch 30:27
the priests and **L** for the burnt 2Ch 31:2
service among the priests and **L**. 2Ch 31:2
the priests and **L** so that they 2Ch 31:4
priests and **L** about the piles 2Ch 31:9
families and the **L** 20 years old 2Ch 31:17
The **L** and the doorkeepers had 2Ch 34:9
and Obadiah the **L** from the 2Ch 34:12
L were all skilled on musical 2Ch 34:12
Some of the **L** were secretaries, 2Ch 34:13
well as the priests and the **L**— 2Ch 34:30
He said to the **L** who taught all 2Ch 35:3
the tribal household of the **L**. 2Ch 35:5
people, the priests, and the **L**. 2Ch 35:8
officers of the **L**, donated 5,000 2Ch 35:9
Passover sacrifices for the **L**, 2Ch 35:9
posts and the **L** in their 2Ch 35:10
while the **L** were skinning the 2Ch 35:11
So the **L** made preparations for 2Ch 35:14
the priests, the **L**, all Judah, 2Ch 35:18
along with the priests and **L**— Ezr 1:5
The **L** ⌊included⌋: Jeshua's and Ezr 2:40
The priests, **L**, singers, Ezr 2:70
priests, the **L**, and all who had Ezr 3:8
appointed the **L** who were 20 Ezr 3:8
brothers, the **L**, joined together Ezr 3:9
and the **L** descended from Asaph, Ezr 3:10
the older priests, **L**, and family Ezr 3:12
the priests, the **L**, and the rest Ezr 6:16
and the **L** by their groups Ezr 6:18
the priests and **L** were Ezr 6:20
Israelites, priests, **L**, singers, Ezr 7:7
including their priests and **L**, Ezr 7:13
on any priests, **L**, singers, Ezr 7:24
priests, but found no **L** there. Ezr 8:15
leaders for the work of the **L**. Ezr 8:20
leading priests, **L**, and heads Ezr 8:29
So the priests and **L** took charge Ezr 8:30
The **L** Jozabad son of Jeshua and Ezr 8:33
and the **L** have not separated Ezr 9:1
priests, **L**, and all Israel Ezr 10:5
The **L**: Jozabad, Shimei, Kelaiah Ezr 10:23
Next to him the **L** made repairs Neh 3:17
their fellow ⌊**L**⌋ made repairs Neh 3:18
singers, and **L** were appointed. Neh 7:1
The **L** ⌊included⌋: Jeshua's Neh 7:43
So the priests, **L**, gatekeepers, Neh 7:73
Pelaiah, who were **L**, explained Neh 8:7
and the **L** who were instructing Neh 8:9
the **L** quieted all the people, Neh 8:11
along with the priests and **L**, Neh 8:13
built⌋ for the **L** and cried out Neh 9:4
Then the **L**—Jeshua, Kadmiel, Neh 9:5
of⌋ our leaders, **L**, and priests. Neh 9:38
The **L** were: Jeshua son of Neh 10:9
the priests, **L**, singers, Neh 10:28
the priests, **L**, and people for Neh 10:34
from our lands belongs to the **L**, Neh 10:37
for the **L** are to collect the Neh 10:37
accompany the **L** when they Neh 10:38
and the **L** must take a tenth of Neh 10:38
Israelites and the **L** are to Neh 10:39
priests, **L**, temple servants, Neh 11:3
The **L**: Shemaiah son of Hasshub, Neh 11:15
from the leaders of the **L**, Neh 11:16
All the **L** in the holy city: Neh 11:18
and the **L** were in all the Neh 11:20
leader of the **L** in Jerusalem was Neh 11:22
divisions of **L** were in Benjamin. Neh 11:36
the priests and **L** who went up Neh 12:1
The **L**: Jeshua, Binnui, Kadmiel, Neh 12:8
families of the **L** and priests Neh 12:22
leaders of the **L**—Hashabiah, Neh 12:24
sent for the **L** wherever they Neh 12:27
the priests and **L** had purified Neh 12:30
the priests and **L** were gathered Neh 12:44
the priests and **L** who were Neh 12:44
aside daily portions for the **L**, Neh 12:47
and the **L** set aside daily Neh 12:47
and oil prescribed for the **L**, Neh 13:5
portions for the **L** had not been Neh 13:10
each of the **L** and the singers Neh 13:10
I gathered the **L** and singers Neh 13:11
Pedaiah of the **L**, with Hanan son Neh 13:13
I instructed the **L** to purify Neh 13:22
of the priesthood and the **L**. Neh 13:29
to each of the priests and **L**. Neh 13:30
some of them as priests and **L**," Is 66:21
David and the **L** who minister to Jr 33:22
Surely the **L** who wandered away Ezk 44:10
wide for the **L** who minister Ezk 45:5
not go astray as the **L** did when Ezk 48:11
to the territory of the **L**. Ezk 48:12
the **L** ⌊will have an area⌋ eight Ezk 48:13
sent priests and **L** to ask him, Jn 1:19

LEVITES' *(4)*

is to move out with the **L** camp, Nm 2:17
and the **L** cattle in place of Nm 3:41
and the **L** cattle in place of Nm 3:45
These are the **L** families 1Ch 6:19

LEVITICAL *(18)*

Concerning the **L** cities, the Lv 25:32
houses in the **L** cities are their Lv 25:33
are to go to the **L** priests and Dt 17:9
the presence of the **L** priests. Dt 17:18
The **L** priests, the whole tribe Dt 18:1
everything the **L** priests Dt 24:8
Moses and the **L** priests spoke to Dt 27:9
God carried by the **L** priests, Jos 3:3
facing the **L** priests who carried Jos 8:33
L singers of Asaph, of Heman, 2Ch 5:12
into the hands of the **L** priests, 2Ch 23:18

The **L** priests will never fail to Jr 33:18
and the **L** priests will not be My Jr 33:21
offering to the **L** priests who Ezk 43:19
But the **L** priests descended from Ezk 44:15
Except for the **L** property and Ezk 48:22
came through the **L** priesthood Heb 7:11
many have become ⌊**L**⌋ priests, Heb 7:23

LEWDNESS *(1)*
actions, deceit, **l**, stinginess, Mk 7:22

LIABLE *(1)*
the army or be **l** for any duty. Dt 24:5

LIAR *(13)*
out to be a **l** who has falsely Dt 19:18
can prove me a **l** and show that Jb 24:25
alarm I said, "Everyone is a **l**." Ps 116:11
a **l** pays attention to a Pr 17:4
and you will be proved a **l**. Pr 30:6
because he is a **l** and the father Jn 8:44
Him, I would be a **l** like you. Jn 8:55
everyone is a **l**, as it is Rm 3:4
we make Him a **l**, and His word is 1Jn 1:10
commands, is a **l**, and the truth 1Jn 2:4
Who is the **l**, if not the one who 1Jn 2:22
hates his brother, he is a **l**. 1Jn 4:20
believe God has made Him a **l**, 1Jn 5:10

LIARS *(9)*
from the womb; **l** err from birth. Ps 58:3
the mouths of **l** will be shut. Ps 63:11
children, you race of **l**, Is 57:4
is a liar and the father of **l**. Jn 8:44
kidnappers, **l**, perjurers, and 1Tm 1:10
the hypocrisy of **l** whose 1Tm 4:2
are always **l**, evil beasts, lazy Ti 1:12
and you have found them to be **l**. Rv 2:2
and all **l**—their share will Rv 21:8

LIBERALLY *(1)*
Israelites gave **l** of the best 2Ch 31:5

LIBERATED *(3)*
and having been **l** from sin, Rm 6:18
you have been **l** from sin and Rm 6:22
Christ has **l** us into freedom. Gl 5:1

LIBERATION *(1)*
l and deliverance will come to Est 4:14

LIBERATOR *(1)*
The **L** will come from Zion; Rm 11:26

LIBERTY *(1)*
to proclaim **l** to the captives, Is 61:1

LIBNAH *(18)*
Rimmon-perez and camped at **L**. Nm 33:20
departed from **L** and camped at Nm 33:21
from Makkedah to **L** and fought Jos 10:29
to Libnah and fought against **L**. Jos 10:29
From **L**, Joshua and all Israel Jos 10:31
sword, just as he had done to **L**. Jos 10:32
he had treated **L** and its king. Jos 10:39
the king of **L** one the king of Jos 12:15
L, Ether, Ashan, Jos 15:42
its pasturelands, **L** with its Jos 21:13
L also rebelled at that time. 2Kg 8:22
found him fighting against **L**. 2Kg 19:8
of Jeremiah; ⌊she was⌋ from **L**. 2Kg 23:31
of Jeremiah; ⌊she was⌋ from **L**. 2Kg 24:18
a city of refuge), **L** and its 1Ch 6:57
L also rebelled at that time 2Ch 21:10
Assyria was fighting against **L**. Is 37:8
of Jeremiah; ⌊she was⌋ from **L**. Jr 52:1

LIBNAH'S *(1)*
He treated **L** king as he had the Jos 10:30

LIBNI *(5)*
L and Shimei, by their clans. Ex 6:17
by their clans: **L** and Shimei. Nm 3:18
of Gershom's sons: **L** and Shimei. 1Ch 6:17
his son **L**, his son Jahath, his 1Ch 6:20
his son **L**, his son Shimei, 1Ch 6:29

LIBNITE *(2)*
The **L** clan and the Shimeite clan Nm 3:21
the **L** clan, the Hebronite clan, Nm 26:58

LIBRARY *(1)*
searched in the **l** of Babylon Ezr 6:1

LIBYA *(3)*
plus **L** and the men of the Ezk 30:5
Put and **L** were among her allies. Nah 3:9
and the parts of **L** near Cyrene; Ac 2:10

LIBYANS *(3)*
him from Egypt—**L**, Sukkiim, 2Ch 12:3
Cushites and **L** a vast army with 2Ch 16:8
The **L** and Cushites will also be Dn 11:43

LICE *(1)*
shepherd picks **l** off his garment Jr 43:12

LICK *(5)*
dogs will also **l** your blood!' " 1Kg 21:19
him and his enemies **l** the dust. Ps 72:9
and **l** the dust at your feet. Is 49:23
They will **l** the dust like a Mc 7:17
dogs would come and **l** his sores. Lk 16:21

LICKED *(3)*
and it **l** up the water that was 1Kg 18:38
where the dogs **l** Naboth's blood, 1Kg 21:19
The dogs **l** up his blood, and the 1Kg 22:38

LID *(2)*
without a **l** tied on it is Nm 19:15
a hole in its **l**, and set it 2Kg 12:9

LIE *(123)*
When I **l** down with my fathers, Gn 47:30
deceptively or **l** to one another. Lv 19:11
and you will **l** down with nothing Lv 26:6
all your corpses **l** ⌊scattered⌋ Nm 14:33
of Ar and **l** along the border Nm 21:15
They will not **l** down until they Nm 23:24
when you **l** down and when you get Dt 6:7
when you **l** down and when you get Dt 11:19
will make him **l** down and be Dt 25:2
watery depths that **l** beneath; Dt 33:13
L in ambush behind the city, Jos 8:4
uncover his feet, and **l** down. Ru 3:4
he went to **l** down at the end of Ru 3:7
Now, **l** down until morning." Ru 3:13
replied. "Go and **l** down." So he 1Sm 3:5
he replied. "Go and **l** down." 1Sm 3:6
He told Samuel, "Go and **l** down. 1Sm 3:9
Israel does not **l** or change His 1Sm 15:29
after making them **l** down on the 2Sm 8:2
the evening to **l** down on his cot 2Sm 11:13
L down on your bed and pretend 2Sm 13:5
She is to **l** by your side so that 1Kg 1:2
to the room upstairs to **l** down. 2Kg 4:11
But they replied, "⌊That's⌋ a **l**! 2Kg 9:12
at me; would I **l** to your face? Jb 6:28
When I **l** down I think: When will Jb 7:4
For soon I will **l** down in the Jb 7:21
about and **l** down in safety. Jb 11:18
You will **l** down without fear, Jb 11:19
but it will **l** down with him in Jb 20:11
But they both **l** in the dust, Jb 21:26
Would I **l** about my case? Jb 34:6
their dens and **l** in wait within Jb 38:40
wherever corpses **l**, it is there. Jb 39:30
I **l** down and sleep; I wake again Ps 3:5
is worthless and pursue a **l**? Ps 4:2
I will both **l** down and sleep in Ps 4:8
l to one another; they speak Ps 12:2
He lets me **l** down in green Ps 23:2
I **l** down with those who devour Ps 57:4
you **l** among the sheepfolds, Ps 68:13
holiness; I will not **l** to David. Ps 89:35
they go back and **l** down in their Ps 104:22
for their deceit is a **l**. Ps 119:118
When you **l** down, you will not be Pr 3:24
you will **l** down, and your sleep Pr 3:24
when you **l** down, they will watch Pr 6:22
Sheol and Abaddon **l** open before Pr 15:11
Also, if two **l** down together, Ec 4:11
the tree falls, there it will **l**. Ec 11:3
Until cities **l** in ruins without Is 6:11
the leopard will **l** down with the Is 11:6
young ones will **l** down together, Is 11:7
wild animals will **l** down there, Is 13:21
of the nations **l** in splendor, Is 14:18
will **l** down in safety, Is 14:30
They will **l** down without fear. Is 17:2
all those who **l** in wait with Is 29:20
your strength will **l** in quiet Is 30:15
together (they **l** down, they do Is 43:17
there a **l** in my right hand? Is 44:20
you will **l** down in a place of Is 50:11
they **l** at the head of every Is 51:20
L down, so we can walk over you. Is 51:23
they dream, **l** down, and love to Is 56:10
a place for cattle to **l** down, Is 65:10
leafy tree you **l** down ⌊like⌋ Jr 2:20
Let us **l** down in our shame; Jr 3:25
for his cast images are a **l**; Jr 10:14
are prophesying a **l** in My name. Jr 14:14
who prophesy a **l** in My name have Jr 23:25
they prophesy a **l** to you so that Jr 27:10
they are prophesying a **l** to you. Jr 27:14
They are prophesying a **l** to you. Jr 27:16
these people to trust in a **l**. Jr 28:15
prophesying a **l** to you in My Jr 29:21
and have spoken a **l** in My name, Jr 29:23
him, and made you trust a **l**, Jr 29:31
"⌊That's⌋ a **l**," Jeremiah replied. Jr 37:14
saying about Ishmael is a **l**." Jr 40:16
Jeremiah, "You are speaking a **l**! Jr 43:2
L low, residents of Dedan, for I Jr 49:8
L low, residents of Hazor— Jr 49:30
for his cast images are a **l**; Jr 51:17
her slain will **l** fallen within Jr 51:47
of the temple **l** scattered at Lm 4:1
Then **l** down on your left side Ezk 4:4
of days you **l** on your side. Ezk 4:4
the number of days ⌊you **l** down⌋, Ezk 4:5
these days, **l** down again, Ezk 4:6
of days you **l** on your side, Ezk 4:9
altars will **l** in ruins and be Ezk 6:6
when their slain **l** among their Ezk 6:13
live, when you **l** to My people, Ezk 13:19
their cities will **l** among ruined Ezk 30:7
You will **l** among the Ezk 31:18
the uncircumcised **l** slain by the Ezk 32:21
They do not **l** down with the Ezk 32:27
shattered and will **l** down among Ezk 32:28
They **l** down with the Ezk 32:29
They **l** down uncircumcised with Ezk 32:30
There they will **l** down in a good Ezk 34:14
My flock and let them **l** down." Ezk 34:15
The seeds **l** shriveled in their Jl 1:17
They **l** on beds ⌊inlaid with⌋ Am 6:4
about the end and will not **l**. Hab 2:3
They will **l** down in the evening Zph 2:7
Herds will **l** down in the middle Zph 2:14
for wild animals to **l** down! Zph 2:15
Their cities **l** devastated, Zph 3:6
they will pasture and **l** down, Zph 3:13
he tells a **l**, he speaks from Jn 8:44
your heart to **l** to the Holy Ac 5:3
the truth of God for a **l**, Rm 1:25
But if by my **l** God's truth is Rm 3:7
Do not **l** to one another, since Col 3:9
God, who cannot **l**, promised Ti 1:2
it is impossible for God to **l**, Heb 6:18
don't brag and **l** in defiance of Jms 3:14
and because no **l** comes from the 1Jn 2:21
and is true and is not a **l**; 1Jn 2:27
dead bodies will **l** in the public Rv 11:8
No **l** was found in their mouths; Rv 14:5

LIED *(3)*
l to Him with their tongues, Ps 78:36
that you **l** and didn't remember Is 57:11
have not **l** to men but to God! Ac 5:4

LIES *(78)*
he **l** down like a lion and like a Gn 49:9
of the deep that **l** below, Gn 49:25
something lost and **l** about it; Lv 6:3
Whoever **l** down in the house is Lv 14:47
the discharge **l** on will be Lv 15:4
Anything she **l** on during her Lv 15:20
every bed he **l** on will become Lv 15:24
Any bed she **l** on during the days Lv 15:26
during the time it **l** desolate, Lv 26:34
long as it **l** desolate, it will Lv 26:35
not a man who **l**, or a son of man Nm 23:19
he **l** down like a lion or a Nm 24:9
his neighbor, **l** in ambush for Dt 19:11
He **l** down like a lion and tears Dt 33:20
have mocked me and told me **l**! Jdg 16:10
me all along and told me **l**! Jdg 16:13
When he **l** down, notice the place Ru 3:4
of Israel **l** slain on your 2Sm 1:19
Jonathan ⌊**l**⌋ slain on your 2Sm 1:25
are buried **l** in ruins and its Neh 2:3
Jerusalem **l** in ruins and its Neh 2:17
lying, or can I not recognize **l**? Jb 6:30
But you coat ⌊the truth⌋ with **l**; Jb 13:4
so man **l** down never to rise Jb 14:12
A rope **l** hidden for him on the Jb 18:10
disaster **l** ready for him to Jb 18:12
root of the problem **l** with him?" Jb 19:28

l down wealthy, but will do so Jb 27:19
He l under the lotus plants, Jb 40:21
You destroy those who tell l; Ps 5:6
The wicked l in wait for the Ps 37:32
or to those who run after l! Ps 40:4
heal him on the bed where he l. Ps 41:3
rise again from where he l!" Ps 41:8
They utter curses and l. Ps 59:12
one who tells l will remain in Ps 101:7
arrogant have smeared me with l, Ps 119:69
shame for slandering me with l; Ps 119:78
people persecute me with l— Ps 119:86
mouths speak l, whose right Ps 144:8
foreigners whose mouths speak l, Ps 144:11
a dishonest witness utters l. Pr 14:5
one who utters l is deceitful. Pr 14:25
much worse are l for a ruler. Pr 17:7
who utters l will not escape. Pr 19:5
and one who utters l perishes. Pr 19:9
ruler listens to l, all his Pr 29:12
Everything l ahead of them. Ec 9:1
to destroy the needy with l, Is 32:7
have spoken l, and you mutter Is 59:3
that was dear to us l in ruins. Is 64:11
l and not faithfulness prevail Jr 9:3
taught their tongues to speak l; Jr 9:5
Our fathers inherited only l, Jr 16:19
commit adultery and walk in l. Jr 23:14
of the prophets prophesying l, Jr 23:26
which l desolate ⌊and has⌋ Lm 5:18
to My people, who listen to l. Ezk 13:19
the righteous person with l, Ezk 13:22
⌊now that⌋ she l in ruins, Ezk 26:2
will speak l at the same table Dn 11:27
evil, the princes with their l. Hs 7:3
them⌋, they speak l against Me. Hs 7:13
you have eaten the fruit of l. Hs 10:13
Ephraim surrounds me with l, Hs 11:12
multiplies l and violence. Hs 12:1
The l that their ancestors Am 2:4
She l abandoned on her land, Am 5:2
of spirit comes and invents l: Mc 2:11
and its residents speak l; Mc 6:12
the woman who l in your arms. Mc 7:5
a cast image, a teacher of l. Hab 2:18
no longer do wrong or tell l; Zph 3:13
while this house l in ruins?" Hg 1:4
My house still l in ruins, Hg 1:9
a veil l over their hearts, 2Co 3:15
the race that l before us, Heb 12:1
the scroll that l open in the Rv 10:8

LIFE *(612)*

having the breath of l in it. Gn 1:30
the breath of l into his Gn 2:7
the tree of l in the midst Gn 2:9
eat dust all the days of your l. Gn 3:14
labor all the days of your l. Gn 3:17
also take from the tree of l, Gn 3:22
guard the way to the tree of l. Gn 3:24
So Adam's l lasted 930 years; Gn 5:5
So Seth's l lasted 912 years; Gn 5:8
So Enosh's l lasted 905 years; Gn 5:11
So Kenan's l lasted 910 years; Gn 5:14
So Mahalalel's l lasted 895 Gn 5:17
So Jared's l lasted 962 years; Gn 5:20
So Enoch's l lasted 365 years. Gn 5:23
So Methuselah's l lasted 969 Gn 5:27
So Lamech's l lasted 777 years; Gn 5:31
with the breath of l in it. Gn 6:17
six hundredth year of Noah's l, Gn 7:11
the breath of l in it entered Gn 7:15
the spirit of l in its nostrils Gn 7:22
require the l of every animal Gn 9:5
man for your l and your blood. Gn 9:5
will require the l of each man's Gn 9:5
man's brother for a man's l. Gn 9:5
So Noah's l lasted 950 years; Gn 9:29
and my l will be spared on your Gn 12:13
great kindness by saving my l. Gn 19:19
were all⌋ the years of her l. Gn 23:1
is the length of Abraham's l: Gn 25:7
is the length of Ishmael's l: Gn 25:17
They made l bitter for Isaac and Gn 26:35
I'm sick of my l because of Gn 27:46
one of them, what good is my l?" Gn 27:46
He said, "Let's not take his l." Gn 37:21
his l is wrapped up with the Gn 44:30
is wrapped up with the boy's l— Gn 44:30
me ahead of you to preserve l. Gn 45:5
and his l span was 147 years. Gn 47:28
shepherd all my l to this day, Gn 48:15
may have a long l in the land Ex 20:12
he will serve his master for l. Ex 21:6
then you must give l for life, Ex 21:23
then you must give life for l, Ex 21:23
price for his l in the full Ex 21:30
the l of a creature is in the Lv 17:11
Since the l of every creature is Lv 17:14
because the l of every creature Lv 17:14
jeopardize your neighbor's l; Lv 19:16
restitution for it, l for life. Lv 24:18
restitution for it, life for l. Lv 24:18
you can make them slaves for l. Lv 25:46
to fail and your l to ebb away. Lv 26:16
ridden all your l until today? Nm 22:30
end of my ⌊l⌋ be like theirs. Nm 23:10
a ransom for the l of a murderer Nm 35:31
have a long l in the land you Dt 5:33
days of your l by keeping all Dt 6:2
so that you may have a long l. Dt 6:2
the blood is the l, and you must Dt 12:23
not eat the l with the meat. Dt 12:23
he will become your slave for l. Dt 15:17
rest of your l the day you left Dt 16:3
from it all the days of his l, Dt 17:19
and flees there to save his l, Dt 19:4
l for life, eye for eye, tooth Dt 19:21
life for l, eye for eye, tooth Dt 19:21
is like taking a l as security. Dt 24:6
Your l will hang in doubt before Dt 28:66
set before you l and prosperity, Dt 30:15
have set before you l and death, Dt 30:19
Choose l so that you and your Dt 30:19
For He is your l, and He will Dt 30:20
will prolong your l in the land Dt 30:20
I bring death and I give l; Dt 32:39
to you but they are your l, Dt 32:47
revered him throughout his l, Jos 4:14
you, risked his l, and delivered Jdg 9:17
I took my l in my own hands and Jdg 12:3
those he had killed in his l. Jdg 16:30
L⌋ is much too bitter for you Ru 1:13
will renew your l and sustain Ru 4:15
the LORD all the days of his l, 1Sm 1:11
LORD brings death and gives l; 1Sm 2:6
Philistines all of Samuel's l. 1Sm 7:13
judged Israel throughout his l. 1Sm 7:15
He took his l in his hands when 1Sm 19:5
so that he wants to take my l?" 1Sm 20:1
wants to take my l wants to take 1Sm 22:23
my life wants to take your l. 1Sm 22:23
Saul had come out to take his l. 1Sm 23:15
hunting me down to take my l. 1Sm 24:11
'Long l to you, and peace to you, 1Sm 25:6
Throughout your l, may evil not 1Sm 25:28
you and attempts to take your l, 1Sm 25:29
lord's l will be tucked safely 1Sm 25:29
you considered my l precious. 1Sm 26:21
your l valuable today, 1Sm 26:24
LORD consider my l valuable and 1Sm 26:24
I took my l in my hands and did 1Sm 28:21
wounded, but my l still lingers. 2Sm 1:9
not parted in l or in death. 2Sm 1:23
who intended to take your l. 2Sm 4:8
has redeemed my l from every 2Sm 4:9
as you live and by your l, 2Sm 11:11
death for the l of the brother 2Sm 14:7
But God would not take away a l; 2Sm 14:14
whether it means l or death, 2Sm 15:21
to take my l—how much more 2Sm 16:11
If I had jeopardized my own l— 2Sm 18:13
who rescued your l and the lives 2Sm 19:5
years of my l are left that I 2Sm 19:34
Save your l and the life of your 1Kg 1:12
your life and the l of your son 1Kg 1:12
who has redeemed my l from every 1Kg 1:29
request at the cost of his l. 1Kg 2:23
not ask for long l or riches for 1Kg 3:11
your equal during your entire l. 1Kg 3:13
I will give you a long l." 1Kg 3:14
Solomon all the days of his l. 1Kg 4:21
the days of his l because of My 1Kg 11:34
him all the days of his l, 1Kg 15:5
all the days of Rehoboam's l. 1Kg 15:6
with the LORD his entire l. 1Kg 15:14
let this boy's l return to him!" 1Kg 17:21
and the boy's l returned to him, 1Kg 17:22
don't make your l like the life 1Kg 19:2
life like the l of one of them 1Kg 19:2
and immediately ran for his l. 1Kg 19:3
LORD, take my l, for I'm no 1Kg 19:4
looking for me to take my l." 1Kg 19:10
looking for me to take my l." 1Kg 19:14
Perhaps he will spare your l." 1Kg 20:31
says, 'Please spare my l.' " 1Kg 20:32
will be your l in place of his 1Kg 20:39
be your life in place of his l, 1Kg 20:39
will be your l in place of his 1Kg 20:42
place of his l and your people 1Kg 20:42
please let my l and the lives of 2Kg 1:13
this time let my l be precious 2Kg 1:14
there was no sound or sign of l, 2Kg 4:31
and giving l that this man 2Kg 5:7
whose son he had restored to l, 2Kg 8:1
restored the dead ⌊son⌋ to l, 2Kg 8:5
had restored to l came to appeal 2Kg 8:5
the son Elisha restored to l." 2Kg 8:5
will forfeit⌋ his l for theirs." 2Kg 10:24
I will add 15 years to your l. 2Kg 20:6
Babylon for the rest of his l. 2Kg 25:29
each day, for the rest of his l. 2Kg 25:30
or for the l of those who hate 2Ch 1:11
have not even requested long l, 2Ch 1:11
was wholehearted his entire l. 2Ch 15:17
temple throughout Jehoiada's l. 2Ch 24:14
why should you lose your l?" 2Ch 25:16
and pray for the l of the king Ezr 6:10
given us new l and light to our Ezr 9:8
giving us new l, so that we can Ezr 9:9
stones back to l from the mounds Neh 4:2
You give l to all of them, Neh 9:6
spare my l—[this is] my Est 7:3
Esther for his l because he Est 7:7
in Jewish l and their memory Est 9:28
and naked I will leave this l. Jb 1:21
he owns in exchange for his l. Jb 2:4
your power; only spare his l." Jb 2:6
and l to those whose existence Jb 3:20
⌊Why is l given⌋ to a man whose Jb 3:23
integrity of your l your hope? Jb 4:6
Remember that my l is ⌊but⌋ a Jb 7:7
rather than l in this body. Jb 7:15
this is the joy of his way of l; Jb 8:19
about myself; I renounce my l. Jb 9:21
I am disgusted with my l. Jb 10:1
You gave me l and faithful love, Jb 10:12
and Your care has guarded my l. Jb 10:12
⌊Your⌋ l will be brighter than Jb 11:17
The l of every living thing is Jb 12:10
understanding comes with long l. Jb 12:12
and take my l in my own hands Jb 13:14
dies, will he come back to l? Jb 14:14
they have no assurance of l. Jb 24:22
when God takes away his l? Jb 27:8
Now my l is poured out before my Jb 30:16
asking for his l with a curse. Jb 31:30
of the Almighty gives me l. Jb 33:4
l from crossing the river ⌊of Jb 33:18
and his l to the executioners. Jb 33:22
may shine with the light of l. Jb 33:30
their l ⌊ends⌋ among male cult Jb 36:14
you ever in your l commanded the Jb 38:12
⌊on⌋ a desert with no human l, Jb 38:26
latter part of Job's l more than Jb 42:12
You reveal the path of l to me; Ps 16:11
whose portion is in this l: Ps 17:14
asked You for l, and You gave it Ps 21:4
Deliver my l from the sword, Ps 22:20
my very l from the power of the Ps 22:20
one who cannot preserve his l. Ps 22:29
renews my l; He leads me along Ps 23:3
pursue me all the days of my l, Ps 23:6
He will live a good l, and his Ps 25:13
or my l along with men of Ps 26:9
LORD is the stronghold of my l— Ps 27:1
the LORD all the days of my l, Ps 27:4
have known the troubles of my l Ps 31:7
my l is consumed with grief, Ps 31:10
they plotted to take my l. Ps 31:13
course of my l is in Your power Ps 31:15
is the man who delights in l, Ps 34:12
loving a long l to enjoy what is Ps 34:12
redeems the l of His servants Ps 34:22
Rescue my l from their ravages, Ps 35:17

my very l from the young lions. Ps 35:17
Those who seek my l set traps, Ps 38:12
the end of my l and the number Ps 39:4
and my l span as nothing in Your Ps 39:5
seek to take my l be disgraced Ps 40:14
a prayer to the God of my l. Ps 42:8
will redeem my l from the power Ps 49:15
and violent men seek my l. Ps 54:3
Lord is the sustainer of my l. Ps 54:4
while they wait to take my l. Ps 56:6
before God in the light of l. Ps 56:13
Add days to the king's l; Ps 61:6
faithful love is better than l. Ps 63:3
who seek to destroy my l will go Ps 63:9
Protect my l from the terror of Ps 64:1
from the book of l and not be Ps 69:28
those who seek my l be disgraced Ps 70:2
not give the l of Your dove to Ps 74:19
Protect my l, for I am faithful. Ps 86:2
Bring joy to Your servant's l, Ps 86:4
You deliver my l from the depths Ps 86:13
gang of ruthless men seeks my l. Ps 86:14
and my l is near Sheol. Ps 88:3
Remember how short my l is. Ps 89:47
end their l; they sleep. They Ps 90:5
him with a long l and show him Ps 91:16
against the l of the righteous Ps 94:21
take me in the middle of my l! Ps 102:24
He redeems your l from the Pit; Ps 103:4
will sing to the LORD all my l; Ps 104:33
My l is down in the dust; Ps 119:25
give me l through Your word. Ps 119:25
You about my l, and You listened Ps 119:26
give me l in Your ways. Ps 119:37
Give me l through Your Ps 119:40
Your promise has given me l. Ps 119:50
of⌊ my song during my earthly l. Ps 119:54
They almost ended my l on earth, Ps 119:87
me l in accordance with Your Ps 119:88
have given me l through them. Ps 119:93
give me l through Your word. Ps 119:107
My l is constantly in danger, Ps 119:109
LORD, give me l, in keeping with Ps 119:149
give me l, as You promised. Ps 119:154
give me l, according to Your Ps 119:156
LORD, give me l, according to Ps 119:159
He will protect your l. Ps 121:7
all the days of your l, Ps 128:5
the blessing—l forevermore. Ps 133:3
preserve my l from the anger Ps 138:7
I will praise the LORD all my l; Ps 146:2
none reach the paths of l. Pr 2:19
days, a full l, and well-being. Pr 3:2
Long l is in her right hand; Pr 3:16
She is a tree of l to those who Pr 3:18
They will be l for you and Pr 3:22
Guard it, for it is your l. Pr 4:13
For they are l to those who find Pr 4:22
for it is the source of l. Pr 4:23
doesn't consider the path of l; Pr 5:6
the end of your l, you will Pr 5:11
instructions are the way to l. Pr 6:23
goes after ⌊your⌋ very l. Pr 6:26
know it will cost him his l. Pr 7:23
finds me finds l and obtains Pr 8:35
years will be added to your l. Pr 9:11
righteous is a fountain of l, Pr 10:11
of the righteous leads to l; Pr 10:16
instruction is on the path to l, Pr 10:17
The fear of the LORD prolongs l, Pr 10:27
righteousness ⌊leads⌋ to l, Pr 11:19
of the righteous is a tree of l, Pr 11:30
There is l in the path of Pr 12:28
guards his mouth protects his l; Pr 13:3
are a ransom for a man's l, Pr 13:8
fulfilled desire is a tree of l. Pr 13:12
instruction is a fountain of l, Pr 13:14
of the LORD is a fountain of l, Pr 14:27
tranquil heart is l to the body, Pr 14:30
that heals is a tree of l, Pr 15:4
the path of l leads upward, Pr 15:24
face lights up, there is l; Pr 16:15
guards his way protects his l. Pr 16:17
is a fountain of l for its Pr 16:22
his lips are a trap for his l. Pr 18:7
L and death are in the power of Pr 18:21
that you may be wise in later l. Pr 19:20
The fear of the LORD leads to l; Pr 19:23

and faithful love will find l, Pr 21:21
along with wealth, honor, and l. Pr 22:4
will rescue his l from Sheol. Pr 23:14
to your father who gave you l, Pr 23:22
He who protects your l know? Pr 24:12
refreshes the l of his masters. Pr 25:13
unjust gain prolongs his l. Pr 28:16
wine to one whose l is bitter. Pr 31:6
not evil, all the days of her l. Pr 31:12
my body enjoy l with wine and Ec 2:3
I hated l because the work that Ec 2:17
who can enjoy l apart from Him? Ec 2:25
to rejoice and enjoy the good l. Ec 3:12
few days of his l God has given Ec 5:18
the days of his l because God Ec 5:20
knows what is good for man in l, Ec 6:12
of his futile l that he spends Ec 6:12
preserves the l of its owner. Ec 7:12
In my futile l I have seen Ec 7:15
times and prolongs his l, Ec 8:12
Enjoy l with the wife you love Ec 9:9
all the days of your fleeting l, Ec 9:9
is your portion in l and in your Ec 9:9
wine makes l happy, and money Ec 10:19
and the prime of l are fleeting. Ec 11:10
70 years—the l span of one Is 23:15
and human l disregarded. Is 33:8
going to add 15 years to your l. Is 38:5
the prime of my l I must go to Is 38:10
rolled up my l like a weaver; Is 38:12
of them is the l of my spirit as Is 38:16
people on it and l to those who Is 42:5
and peoples in place of your l. Is 43:4
Your way of l and your actions Jr 4:18
they want to take your l. Jr 4:30
for my l is weary because of the Jr 4:31
know and assay their way of l. Jr 6:27
will be chosen over l by all the Jr 8:3
a man's way of l is not his own; Jr 10:23
who want to take your l. Jr 11:21
the love of My l into the hand Jr 12:7
those who want to take their l. Jr 19:7
those who want to take their l, Jr 19:9
He rescues the l of the needy Jr 20:13
sorrow, to end my l in shame? Jr 20:18
to you the way of l and the way Jr 21:8
retain his l like the spoils Jr 21:9
want to take your l, to Jr 22:25
Their way of l has become evil, Jr 23:10
your evil way of l and from your Jr 25:5
each from his evil way of l— Jr 26:3
risk his l to approach Me? Jr 30:21
l will be like an irrigated Jr 31:12
those who want to take their l. Jr 34:20
those who want to take their l, Jr 34:21
must live in tents your whole l, Jr 35:7
haven't drunk wine our whole l— Jr 35:8
each one from his evil way of l, Jr 35:15
will keep his l like the spoils Jr 38:2
given us this l, I will not kill Jr 38:16
men who want to take your l." Jr 38:16
will keep your l like the spoils Jr 39:18
to those who want to take his l, Jr 44:30
one who wanted to take his l.' " Jr 44:30
grant you your l like the spoils Jr 45:5
has come, your l thread is cut. Jr 51:13
Babylon for the rest of his l. Jr 52:33
death, for the rest of his l. Jr 52:34
my cause, Lord; You redeem my l. Lm 3:58
breath of our l, was captured Lm 4:20
way in order to save his l— Ezk 3:18
but you will have saved your l. Ezk 3:19
and you will have saved your l." Ezk 3:21
preserve his l because of his Ezk 7:13
from his evil way to save his l, Ezk 13:22
Look, every l belongs to Me. Ezk 18:4
The l of the father is like the Ezk 18:4
is like the l of the son— Ezk 18:4
right, he will preserve his l. Ezk 18:27
that did not bring them l. Ezk 20:25
tremble every moment for his l. Ezk 32:10
he would have saved his l. Ezk 33:5
but you will have saved your l. Ezk 33:9
the statutes of l without Ezk 33:15
in you so that you come to l. Ezk 37:6
and they came to l and stood on Ezk 37:10
there will be l everywhere the Ezk 47:9
endanger my l with the king." Dn 1:10

the whole course of your l. Dn 5:23
an extension of l was granted to Dn 7:12
some to eternal l, and some to Dn 12:2
the brave will not save his l. Am 2:14
a horse will not save his l. Am 2:15
perish because of this man's l, Jnh 1:14
You raised my l from the Pit, Jnh 2:6
As my l was fading away, I Jnh 2:7
please take my l from me, for it Jnh 4:3
with him was one of l and peace, Mal 2:5
sought the child's l are dead." Mt 2:20
worry about your l, what you Mt 6:25
Isn't l more than food and the Mt 6:25
the road that leads to l, Mt 7:14
finding his l will lose it, Mt 10:39
anyone losing his l because of Mt 10:39
to save his l will lose it, Mt 16:25
whoever loses his l because of Mt 16:25
the whole world yet loses his l? Mt 16:26
man give in exchange for his l? Mt 16:26
you to enter l maimed or lame, Mt 18:8
for you to enter l with one eye, Mt 18:9
must I do to have eternal l?" Mt 19:16
If you want to enter into l, Mt 19:17
more and will inherit eternal l. Mt 19:29
and to give His l—a ransom for Mt 20:28
the righteous into eternal l." Mt 25:46
do evil, to save l or to kill?" Mk 3:4
to save his l will lose it, Mk 8:35
whoever loses his l because of Mk 8:35
the whole world yet lose his l? Mk 8:36
man give in exchange for his l? Mk 8:37
for you to enter l maimed than Mk 9:43
for you to enter l lame than to Mk 9:45
must I do to inherit eternal l?" Mk 10:17
eternal l in the age to come. Mk 10:30
and to give His l—a ransom for Mk 10:45
to save l or to destroy it?" Lk 6:9
and save the l of his slave. Lk 7:3
pleasures of l, and produce no Lk 8:14
to save his l will lose it, Lk 9:24
whoever loses his l because of Lk 9:24
must I do to inherit eternal l?" Lk 10:25
greed because one's l is not in Lk 12:15
very night your l is demanded of Lk 12:20
worry about your l, what you Lk 12:22
For l is more than food and the Lk 12:23
and even his own l—he cannot Lk 14:26
that during your l you received Lk 16:25
to make his l secure will lose Lk 17:33
loses his l will preserve it Lk 17:33
must I do to inherit eternal l?" Lk 18:18
eternal l in the age to come. Lk 18:30
and worries of l, or that day Lk 21:34
L was in Him, and that life was Jn 1:4
and that l was the light of men. Jn 1:4
in Him will have eternal l. Jn 3:15
not perish but have eternal l. Jn 3:16
in the Son has eternal l, Jn 3:36
in the Son will not see l; Jn 3:36
up within him for eternal l." Jn 4:14
gathering fruit for eternal l, Jn 4:36
the dead and gives them l, Jn 5:21
Son also gives l to anyone He Jn 5:21
Me has eternal l and will not Jn 5:24
but has passed from death to l. Jn 5:24
as the Father has l in Himself, Jn 5:26
to the Son to have l in Himself. Jn 5:26
resurrection of l, but those who Jn 5:29
you have eternal l in them, Jn 5:39
come to Me that you may have l. Jn 5:40
food that lasts for eternal l, Jn 6:27
and gives l to the world." Jn 6:33
am the bread of l," Jesus told Jn 6:35
in Him may have eternal l, Jn 6:40
who believes has eternal l. Jn 6:47
I am the bread of l. Jn 6:48
give for the l of the world is Jn 6:51
you do not have l in yourselves. Jn 6:53
drinks My blood has eternal l, Jn 6:54
Spirit is the One who gives l. Jn 6:63
to you are spirit and are l. Jn 6:63
You have the words of eternal l. Jn 6:68
but will have the light of l." Jn 8:12
that they may have l and have it Jn 10:10
lays down his l for the sheep. Jn 10:11
I lay down My l for the sheep. Jn 10:15
laying down My l so I may take Jn 10:17

them eternal **l**, and they will Jn 10:28
I am the resurrection and the **l**. Jn 11:25
who loves his **l** will lose it, Jn 12:25
who hates his **l** in this world Jn 12:25
will keep it for eternal **l**. Jn 12:25
that His command is eternal **l**. Jn 12:50
I will lay down my **l** for You!" Jn 13:37
Will you lay down your **l** for Me? Jn 13:38
the way, the truth, and the **l**. Jn 14:6
lay down his **l** for his friends. Jn 15:13
give eternal **l** to all You have Jn 17:2
This is eternal **l**: that they may Jn 17:3
you may have **l** in His name. Jn 20:31
revealed the paths of **l** to me; Ac 2:28
And you killed the source of **l**, Ac 3:15
the people all about this **l**." Ac 5:20
For His **l** is taken from the Ac 8:33
in **l** to even the Gentiles! Ac 11:18
John was completing his **l** work, Ac 13:25
unworthy of eternal **l**, Ac 13:46
appointed to eternal **l** believed. Ac 13:48
gives everyone **l** and breath and Ac 17:25
alarmed, for his **l** is in him!" Ac 20:10
But I count my **l** of no value to Ac 20:24
I have lived my **l** before God in Ac 23:1
know my way of **l** from my youth, Ac 26:4
eternal **l** to those who by Rm 2:7
gives **l** to the dead and calls Rm 4:17
will we be saved by His **l**! Rm 5:10
reign in **l** through the one man, Rm 5:17
in eternal **l** through Jesus Rm 5:21
too may walk in a new way of **l**. Rm 6:4
and the end is eternal **l**! Rm 6:22
God is eternal **l** in Christ Jesus Rm 6:23
came, sin sprang to **l** Rm 7:9
was meant for **l** resulted in Rm 7:10
Spirit's law of **l** in Christ Rm 8:2
of the Spirit is **l** and peace. Rm 8:6
but the Spirit is **l** because of Rm 8:10
mortal bodies to **l** through His Rm 8:11
that neither death nor **l**, Rm 8:38
they are trying to take my **l**! Rm 11:3
mean but **l** from the dead? Rm 11:15
died and came to **l** for this: Rm 14:9
risked their own necks for my **l**. Rm 16:4
or the world or **l** or death or 1Co 3:22
of things pertaining to this **l**? 1Co 6:3
have cases pertaining to this **l**, 1Co 6:4
must live his **l** in the situation 1Co 7:17
remain in the **l** situation in 1Co 7:20
will have trouble in this **l**, 1Co 7:28
hope in Christ for this **l** only, 1Co 15:19
not come to **l** unless it dies. 1Co 15:36
so that we even despaired of **l**. 2Co 1:8
a scent of **l** leading to life. 2Co 2:16
a scent of life leading to **l**. 2Co 2:16
but the Spirit produces **l**. 2Co 3:6
so that the **l** of Jesus may also 2Co 4:10
so that Jesus' **l** may also be 2Co 4:11
death works in us, but **l** in you. 2Co 4:12
may be swallowed up by **l**. 2Co 5:4
my former way of **l** in Judaism: Gl 1:13
The **l** I now live in the flesh, Gl 2:20
given that was able to give **l**, Gl 3:21
reap eternal **l** from the Spirit. Gl 6:8
excluded from the **l** of God, Eph 4:18
took off your former way of **l**, Eph 4:22
may have a long **l** in the land. Eph 6:3
body, whether by **l** or by death. Php 1:20
live your **l** in a manner worthy Php 1:27
Hold firmly the message of **l**. Php 2:16
risking his **l** to make up what Php 2:30
names are in the book of **l**. Php 4:3
and your **l** is hidden with the Col 3:3
who is your **l**, is revealed, then Col 3:4
to seek to lead a quiet **l**, 1Th 4:11
believe in Him for eternal **l**. 1Tm 1:16
and quiet **l** in all godliness 1Tm 2:2
for the present **l** and also for 1Tm 4:8
life and also for the **l** to come. 1Tm 4:8
hold of eternal **l**, to which you 1Tm 6:12
of God, who gives **l** to all, and 1Tm 6:13
may take hold of **l** that is real. 1Tm 6:19
promise of **l** in Christ Jesus: 2Tm 1:1
has brought **l** and immortality 2Tm 1:10
in the concerns of everyday **l**. 2Tm 2:4
live a godly **l** in Christ Jesus 2Tm 3:12
the hope of eternal **l** that God, Ti 1:2
with the hope of eternal **l**. Ti 3:7
During His earthly **l**, He offered Heb 5:7
beginning of days nor end of **l**, Heb 7:3
power of an indestructible **l**. Heb 7:16
who have faith and obtain **l**. Heb 10:39
he was nearing the end of his **l**, Heb 11:22
their dead raised to **l** again. Heb 11:35
Your **l** should be free from the Heb 13:5
the crown of **l** that He has Jms 1:12
sets the course of **l** on fire, Jms 3:6
bring—what your **l** will be! Jms 4:14
way will save his **l** from death Jms 5:20
your empty way of **l** inherited 1Pt 1:18
as co-heirs of the grace of **l**, 1Pt 3:7
wants to love **l** and to see good 1Pt 3:10
your Christian **l** will be put to 1Pt 3:16
required for **l** and godliness, 2Pt 1:3
concerning the Word of **l**— 1Jn 1:1
that **l** was revealed, and we have 1Jn 1:2
you the eternal **l** that was with 1Jn 1:2
Himself made to us: eternal **l**. 1Jn 2:25
from death to **l** because we love 1Jn 3:14
has eternal **l** residing in him. 1Jn 3:15
He laid down His **l** for us. 1Jn 3:16
God has given us eternal **l**, 1Jn 5:11
life, and this **l** is in His Son. 1Jn 5:11
The one who has the Son has **l**. 1Jn 5:12
the Son of God does not have **l**. 1Jn 5:12
know that you have eternal **l**. 1Jn 5:13
and God will give **l** to him— 1Jn 5:16
is the true God and eternal **l**. 1Jn 5:20
Lord Jesus Christ for eternal **l**. Jd 21
right to eat from the tree of **l**, Rv 2:7
One who was dead and came to **l**, Rv 2:8
I will give you the crown of **l**. Rv 2:10
his name from the book of **l**, Rv 3:5
the breath of **l** from God entered Rv 11:11
in the book of **l** of the Lamb who Rv 13:8
and all **l** in the sea died. Rv 16:3
in the book of **l** from the Rv 17:8
They came to **l** and reigned with Rv 20:4
not come to **l** until the 1,000 Rv 20:5
is the book of **l**, and the dead Rv 20:12
in the book of **l** was thrown Rv 20:15
written in the Lamb's book of **l**. Rv 21:27
was the tree of **l** bearing 12 Rv 22:2
to the tree of **l** and may enter Rv 22:14
of the tree of **l** and the holy Rv 22:19

LIFE'S *(1)*
for with You is **l** fountain. Ps 36:9

LIFE-BREATH *(2)*
God who holds your **l** in His hand Dn 5:23
us⌋ with a remnant of His **l**? Mal 2:15

LIFE-GIVING *(3)*
that listens to **l** rebukes will Pr 15:31
act there is **l** justification for Rm 5:18
the last Adam became a **l** Spirit. 1Co 15:45

LIFEBLOOD *(2)*
not eat meat with its **l** in it. Gn 9:4
since it is the **l** that makes Lv 17:11

LIFELESS *(3)*
bodies on the **l** bodies of your Lv 26:30
sacrifices offered to **l** gods. Ps 106:28
land will become **l** because of Jr 25:37

LIFELESSNESS *(1)*
with the **l** of their detestable Jr 16:18

LIFESTYLE *(1)*
and the pride in one's **l**— 1Jn 2:16

LIFETIME *(16)*
during his father Terah's **l**. Gn 11:28
her during her ⌊sister's⌋ **l**. Lv 18:18
throughout Joshua's **l** and during Jos 24:31
throughout Joshua's **l** and during Jdg 2:7
it during your **l** because of your 1Kg 11:12
bring the disaster during his **l**, 1Kg 21:29
his house during his son's **l**." 1Kg 21:29
peace and security during my **l**? 2Kg 20:19
earth was divided during his **l**, 1Ch 1:19
throughout the **l** of Zechariah, 2Ch 26:5
on them during Hezekiah's **l**. 2Ch 32:26
a moment, but His favor, a **l**. Ps 30:5
praises himself during his **l**— Ps 49:18
peace and security during my **l**. Is 39:8
will be like the **l** of a tree. Is 65:22
will not be successful in his **l**. Jr 22:30

LIFETIMES *(2)*
and during the **l** of the elders Jos 24:31
and during the **l** of the elders Jdg 2:7

LIFT *(60)*
days Pharaoh will **l** up your head Gn 40:13
Pharaoh will **l** up your head— Gn 40:19
As for you, **l** up your staff, Ex 14:16
you must help him **l** it up. Dt 22:4
Each of you **l** a stone onto his Jos 4:5
He will **l** up the horn of His 1Sm 2:10
would not **l** a hand to execute 1Sm 22:17
⌊I will never⌋ **l** my hand against 1Sm 24:6
I won't **l** my hand against my 1Sm 24:10
for who can **l** a hand against the 1Sm 26:9
I will never **l** my hand against 1Sm 26:11
willing to **l** my hand against 1Sm 26:23
were not afraid to **l** your hand 2Sm 1:14
embarrassed to **l** my face toward Ezr 9:6
nobles did not **l** a finger to Neh 3:5
I cannot **l** up my head. Jb 10:15
your heart and **l** up your hands Jb 11:13
Almighty and **l** up your face to Jb 22:26
and you say, "**L** ⌊them⌋ up," God Jb 22:29
You **l** me up on the wind and make Jb 30:22
l Yourself up against the fury Ps 7:6
L me up from the gates of death, Ps 9:13
up, LORD God! **L** up Your hand. Do Ps 10:12
at your victory and **l** the banner Ps 20:5
L up your heads, you gates! Ps 24:7
L up your heads, you gates! Ps 24:9
when I **l** up my hands toward Your Ps 28:2
Your name, I will **l** up my hands. Ps 63:4
wicked, 'Do not **l** up your horn. Ps 75:4
Do not **l** up your horn against Ps 75:5
warriors was able to **l** a hand. Ps 76:5
L up a song—play the Ps 81:2
the floods **l** up their pounding Ps 93:3
He will **l** up His head. Ps 110:7
I will **l** up my hands to Your Ps 119:48
I **l** my eyes to You, the One Ps 123:1
L up your hands in the holy Ps 134:2
to insight and **l** your voice to Pr 2:3
his companion can **l** him up; Ec 4:10
without another to **l** him up. Ec 4:10
When you **l** up your hands ⌊in Is 1:15
staff could wave those who **l** it! Is 10:15
if a rod could **l** what isn't wood Is 10:15
He will **l** up a banner for the Is 11:12
L up a banner on a barren Is 13:2
Now I will **l** Myself up. Is 33:10
They **l** it to their shoulder and Is 46:7
I will **l** up My hand to the Is 49:22
they **l** up their voices Is 52:8
L up a signal flag toward Zion. Jr 4:6
L up your hands to Him for the Lm 2:19
Let us **l** up our hearts and ⌊our⌋ Lm 3:41
l ⌊the bags⌋ to ⌊your⌋ shoulder Ezk 12:6
among them will **l** ⌊his bags⌋ to Ezk 12:12
I will **l** your skirts over your Nah 3:5
all who try to **l** it will injure Zch 12:3
take hold of it and **l** it out? Mt 12:11
willing to **l** a finger to move Mt 23:4
stand up and **l** up your heads, Lk 21:28
When you **l** up the Son of Man, Jn 8:28

LIFTED *(51)*
increased and **l** up the ark so Gn 7:17
He **l** up the heads of the chief Gn 40:20
⌊my⌋ hand is ⌊**l** up⌋ toward the Ex 17:16
that is **l** up from the ram Ex 29:27
Aaron **l** up his hands toward the Lv 9:22
the cloud was **l** up above the Nm 9:17
when the cloud **l** in the morning, Nm 9:21
they moved out when the cloud **l**. Nm 9:21
But when it was **l**, they set out. Nm 9:22
the cloud was **l** up above the Nm 10:11
my horn is **l** up by the LORD. 1Sm 2:1
So the prophet **l** the corpse of 1Kg 13:29
your⌋ voice and **l** your eyes in 2Kg 19:22
and mourners are **l** to safety. Jb 5:11
because You have **l** me up and Ps 30:1
has **l** up his heel against me. Ps 41:9
of the righteous will be **l** up." Ps 75:10
My hands were **l** up all night Ps 77:2
Your right hand is **l** high. Ps 89:13
You have **l** high the right hand Ps 89:42
You have **l** up my horn like that Ps 92:10
The floods have **l** up, LORD, the Ps 93:3
floods have **l** up their voice; Ps 93:3

against all that is l up— Is 2:12
lofty and l up, against all Is 2:13
hand is l up ⌊to take action⌋ Is 26:11
voice against and l your eyes in Is 37:23
Every valley will be l up, Is 40:4
be raised and l up and greatly Is 52:13
l them up and carried them all Is 63:9
up with the ropes and l him out Jr 38:13
The Spirit then l me up, and I Ezk 3:12
the Spirit l me up and took me Ezk 3:14
Then the Spirit l me up between Ezk 8:3
and when they l their wings to Ezk 10:16
The cherubim l their wings and Ezk 10:19
The Spirit then l me up and Ezk 11:1
beside them, l their wings, Ezk 11:22
The Spirit l me up and brought Ezk 11:24
Then the Spirit l me up and Ezk 43:5
It was l up from the ground, Dn 7:4
hand will be l up against your Mc 5:9
lead cover was l, and there was Zch 5:7
and they l up the basket between Zch 5:9
'Be l up and thrown into the sea, Mt 21:21
'Be l up and thrown into the sea, Mk 11:23
Just as Moses l up the snake in Jn 3:14
so the Son of Man must be l up, Jn 3:14
if I am l up from the earth I Jn 12:32
'The Son of Man must be l up'? Jn 12:34
it is not l, because it is set 2Co 3:14

LIFTING *(2)*

and l up His hands He blessed Lk 24:50
l up holy hands without anger or 1Tm 2:8

LIFTS *(8)*

and l him up on His pinions. Dt 32:11
from the dust and l the needy 1Sm 2:8
and the One who l up my head. Ps 3:3
earth melts when He l His voice. Ps 46:6
But He l the needy out of their Ps 107:41
from the dust and l the needy Ps 113:7
He l up the islands like fine Is 40:15
its voice and l its waves high. Hab 3:10

LIGAMENT *(1)*

together by every supporting l, Eph 4:16

LIGAMENTS *(1)*

together by its l and tendons, Col 2:19

LIGHT *(227)*

Let there be l," and there was Gn 1:3
be light," and there was l. Gn 1:3
God saw that the l was good, Gn 1:4
separated the l from the Gn 1:4
God called the l "day," and He Gn 1:5
sky to provide l on the earth." Gn 1:15
the greater l to have dominion Gn 1:16
the lesser l to have dominion Gn 1:16
sky to provide l on the earth, Gn 1:17
and to separate l from darkness. Gn 1:18
with a blinding l so that they Gn 19:11
At morning l, the men were sent Gn 44:3
Israelites had l where they Ex 10:23
of fire to give them l at night, Ex 13:21
oil for the l; spices for the Ex 25:6
from crushed olives for the l, Ex 27:20
Do not l a fire in any of your Ex 35:3
oil for the l; spices for the Ex 35:8
lampstand for l with its Ex 35:14
as well as the oil for the l; Ex 35:14
as the spice and oil for the l, Ex 35:28
as well as the oil for the l; Ex 39:37
oil of beaten olives for the l, Lv 24:2
cover the lampstand used for l, Nm 4:9
lamps are to give l in front Nm 8:2
its lamps ⌊to give l⌋ in front Nm 8:3
your bag, one heavy and one l. Dt 25:13
it was getting l, she collapsed Jdg 19:26
had any men left by morning l." 1Sm 25:34
anything to him until morning l. 1Sm 25:36
up early, go as soon as it's l." 1Sm 29:10
like the morning l when the sun 2Sm 23:4
on the wood but not l the fire. 1Kg 18:23
on the wood but not l the fire. 1Kg 18:23
your god but don't l the fire." 1Kg 18:25
silent and wait until morning l, 2Kg 7:9
They l the lamps of the gold 2Ch 13:11
us new life and l to our eyes. Ezr 9:8
what can we say in l of this? Ezr 9:10
care about it, or l shine on it. Jb 3:4
Why is l given to one burdened Jb 3:20
where even the l is like the Jb 10:22
the deepest darkness into the l. Jb 12:22
around in darkness without l; Jb 12:25
day and ⌊made⌋ l ⌊seem⌋ near Jb 17:12
the l of the wicked is Jb 18:5
The l in his tent grows dark, Jb 18:6
He is driven from l to darkness Jb 18:18
and l will shine on your ways. Jb 22:28
those who rebel against the l. Jb 24:13
in, never experiencing the l. Jb 24:16
His l not shine on everyone? Jb 25:3
boundary between l and darkness. Jb 26:10
may bring to l what is hidden. Jb 28:11
through darkness by His l! Jb 29:3
thrilled at the l of my Jb 29:24
I looked for l, darkness came. Jb 30:26
I exert against you will be l. Jb 33:7
I will continue to see the l." Jb 33:28
he may shine with the l of life. Jb 33:30
L is withheld from the wicked, Jb 38:15
is the road to the home of l? Jb 38:19
the place⌋ where l is dispersed? Jb 38:24
His snorting flashes with l, Jb 41:18
LORD, You l my lamp; my God Ps 18:28
radiant, making the eyes l up. Ps 19:8
LORD is my l and my salvation Ps 27:1
In Your l we will see light. Ps 36:9
In Your light we will see l. Ps 36:9
and even the l of my eyes has Ps 38:10
Send Your l and Your truth; Ps 43:3
arm, and the l of Your face, for Ps 44:3
they will never see the l. Ps 49:19
before God in the l of life. Ps 56:13
with a fiery l throughout the Ps 78:14
walk in the l of Your presence Ps 89:15
sins in the l of Your presence. Ps 90:8
L dawns for the righteous, Ps 97:11
wraps Himself in l as if it were Ps 104:2
gave⌋ a fire to l up the night. Ps 105:39
L shines in the darkness for the Ps 112:4
LORD is God and has given us l. Ps 118:27
for my feet and a l on my path. Ps 119:105
of Your words brings l and gives Ps 119:130
and the l around me will become Ps 139:11
darkness and l are alike to You. Ps 139:12
righteous is like the l of dawn, Pr 4:18
teaching is a l, and corrective Pr 6:23
The l of the righteous shines Pr 13:9
the LORD gives l to the eyes of Pr 29:13
advantage of l over darkness. Ec 2:13
L is sweet, and it is pleasing Ec 11:7
the sun and the l are darkened, Ec 12:2
and let us walk in the LORD's l. Is 2:5
darkness for l and light for Is 5:20
for light and l for darkness, Is 5:20
l will be obscured by clouds. Is 5:30
in darkness have seen a great l; Is 9:2
of darkness, a l has dawned. Is 9:2
Israel's L will become a fire, Is 10:17
will not give their l. Is 13:10
like the l of seven days— Is 30:26
people ⌊and⌋ a l to the nations, Is 42:6
darkness to l in front of them Is 42:16
I form l and create darkness, Is 45:7
make you a l for the nations Is 49:6
walks in darkness, and has no l? Is 50:10
walk in the l of your fire and Is 50:11
justice for a l to the nations. Is 51:4
Then your l will appear like the Is 58:8
then your l will shine in the Is 58:10
We hope for l, but there is Is 59:9
shine, for your l has come, Is 60:1
Nations will come to your l, Is 60:3
will no longer be your l by day, Is 60:19
LORD will be your everlasting l, Is 60:19
LORD will be your everlasting l, Is 60:20
shines like a bright l, Is 62:1
heavens, and their l was gone. Jr 4:23
wood, the fathers l the fire, Jr 7:18
You wait for l, but He brings Jr 13:16
and the l of the lamp. Jr 25:10
who gives the sun for l by day, Jr 31:35
moon and stars for l by night, Jr 31:35
walk in darkness instead of l. Lm 3:2
and brilliant l all around it. Ezk 1:4
a brilliant l all around Him. Ezk 1:27
the brilliant l all around was Ezk 1:28
the moon will not give its l. Ezk 32:7
darkness, and l dwells with Him Dn 2:22
At the first l of dawn the king Dn 6:19
It will be darkness and not l. Am 5:18
LORD be darkness rather than l, Am 5:20
At morning l they accomplish it Mc 2:1
darkness, the LORD will be my l. Mc 7:8
He will bring me into the l; Mc 7:9
⌊His⌋ brilliance is like l; Hab 3:4
On that day there will be no l; Zch 14:6
but there will be l at evening. Zch 14:7
in darkness have seen a great l, Mt 4:16
of death, l has dawned. Mt 4:16
You are the l of the world. Mt 5:14
and it gives l for all who are Mt 5:15
let your l shine before men, Mt 5:16
whole body will be full of l. Mt 6:22
So if the l within you is Mt 6:23
you in the dark, speak in the l. Mt 10:27
is easy and My burden is l." Mt 11:30
became as white as the l. Mt 17:2
the moon will not shed its l; Mt 24:29
hidden except to come to l. Mk 4:22
the moon will not shed its l; Mk 13:24
a l for revelation to the Lk 2:32
those who come in may see the l. Lk 8:16
be made known and come to l. Lk 8:17
those who come in may see its l. Lk 11:33
whole body is also full of l. Lk 11:34
that the l in you is not Lk 11:35
your whole body is full of l, Lk 11:36
whole body will be full of l, Lk 11:36
a lamp shines its l on you." Lk 11:36
the dark will be heard in the l, Lk 12:3
coin, does not l a lamp, sweep Lk 15:8
than the sons of l ⌊in dealing⌋ Lk 16:8
because the sun's l failed. Lk 23:45
and that life was the l of men. Jn 1:4
That l shines in the darkness, Jn 1:5
witness to testify about the l, Jn 1:7
He was not the l, but he came to Jn 1:8
he came to testify about the l. Jn 1:8
The true l, who gives light to Jn 1:9
who gives l to everyone, was Jn 1:9
the l has come into the world, Jn 3:19
rather than the l because their Jn 3:19
hates the l and avoids it, Jn 3:20
by the truth comes to the l, Jn 3:21
you were willing to enjoy his l. Jn 5:35
I am the l of the world. Jn 8:12
but will have the l of life." Jn 8:12
world, I am the l of the world." Jn 9:5
he sees the l of this world. Jn 11:9
because the l is not in him." Jn 11:10
The l will be with you only a Jn 12:35
you have the l so that darkness Jn 12:35
While you have the l, believe in Jn 12:36
believe in the l so that you may Jn 12:36
that you may become sons of l." Jn 12:36
have come as a l into the world Jn 12:46
a l from heaven suddenly flashed Ac 9:3
and a l shone in the cell. Ac 12:7
you as a l for the Gentiles, Ac 13:47
noon an intense l from heaven Ac 22:6
who were with me saw the l, Ac 22:9
of the brightness of that l, Ac 22:11
I saw a l from heaven brighter Ac 26:13
from darkness to l and from the Ac 26:18
would proclaim l to our people Ac 26:23
for the blind, a l to those in Rm 2:19
and put on the armor of l. Rm 13:12
both bring to l what is hidden 1Co 4:5
cannot see the l of the gospel 2Co 4:4
"L shall shine out of darkness"— 2Co 4:6
to give the l of the knowledge 2Co 4:6
For our momentary l affliction 2Co 4:17
fellowship does l have with 2Co 6:14
is disguised as an angel of l. 2Co 11:14
and to shed l for all about the Eph 3:9
but now ⌊you are⌋ l in the Lord. Eph 5:8
Walk as children of l— Eph 5:8
fruit of the l ⌊results⌋ in all Eph 5:9
exposed by the l is made clear, Eph 5:13
makes everything clear is l. Eph 5:14
saints' inheritance in the l. Col 1:12
all sons of l and sons of the 1Th 5:5
dwelling in unapproachable l, 1Tm 6:16
immortality to l through the 2Tm 1:10
darkness into His marvelous l. 1Pt 2:9
is l, and there is absolutely 1Jn 1:5

we walk in the l as He Himself 1Jn 1:7
light as He Himself is in the l, 1Jn 1:7
away and the true l is already 1Jn 2:8
says he is in the l but hates 1Jn 2:9
his brother remains in the l, 1Jn 2:10
third of the day was without l, Rv 8:12
the l of a lamp will never shine Rv 18:23
The nations will walk in its l, Rv 21:24
the Lord God will give them l. Rv 22:5

LIGHTEN *(7)*
this way you will l your load, Ex 18:22
l your father's harsh service 1Kg 12:4
L the yoke your father put on us'? 1Kg 12:9
l your father's harsh service 2Ch 10:4
L the yoke your father put on us'? 2Ch 10:9
into the sea to l the load. Jnh 1:5
they began to l the ship by Ac 27:38

LIGHTER *(2)*
but you, make it l on us!' 1Kg 12:10
but you, make it l on us!' 2Ch 10:10

LIGHTING *(1)*
No one, after l a lamp, covers Lk 8:16

LIGHTLY *(4)*
Naaman off l by not accepting 2Kg 5:20
do not view l all the hardships Neh 9:32
of blows will be beaten l. Lk 12:48
take the Lord's discipline l, Heb 12:5

LIGHTNING *(40)*
L struck the earth, and the LORD Ex 9:23
with l flashing through it, Ex 9:24
was thunder and l, a thick cloud Ex 19:16
witnessed the thunder and l, Ex 20:18
with l from His right hand for Dt 33:2
⌊He hurled⌋ l bolts and routed 2Sm 22:15
A l storm struck from heaven. Jb 1:16
the rain and a path for the l, Jb 28:26
He spreads His l around Him and Jb 36:30
His⌋ hands with l and commands Jb 36:32
His l to the ends of the earth. Jb 37:3
not restrain the l when His Jb 37:4
He scatters His l through them. Jb 37:11
clouds or makes their l flash? Jb 37:15
rain or clears the way for l, Jb 38:25
you send out l bolts, and they Jb 38:35
He hurled l bolts and routed Ps 18:14
l lit up the world. Ps 77:18
and their cattle to l bolts. Ps 78:48
His l lights up the world; Ps 97:4
and l throughout their land. Ps 105:32
He makes l for the rain and Ps 135:7
Flash ⌊Your⌋ l and scatter the Ps 144:6
l and hail, snow and cloud, Ps 148:8
He makes l for the rain and Jr 10:13
He makes l for the rain and Jr 51:16
bright, with l coming out of it Ezk 1:13
and forth like flashes of l. Ezk 1:14
polished to flash like l! Ezk 21:10
It is ready to flash like l; Ezk 21:15
to consume, to flash like l. Ezk 21:28
face like the brilliance of l, Dn 10:6
My judgment strikes like l. Hs 6:5
they dart back and forth like l. Nah 2:4
and His arrow will fly like l. Zch 9:14
For as the l comes from the east Mt 24:27
His appearance was like l, Mt 28:3
fall from heaven like a l flash. Lk 10:18
as the l flashes from horizon Lk 17:24
the throne came flashes of l, Rv 4:5

LIGHTNINGS *(3)*
rumblings, l, and an earthquake Rv 8:5
There were l, rumblings, Rv 11:19
There were l, rumblings, and Rv 16:18

LIGHTS *(12)*
Let there be l in the expanse of Gn 1:14
They will be l in the expanse of Gn 1:15
God made the two great l— Gn 1:16
His lightning l up the world; Ps 97:4
He made the great l: His love is Ps 136:7
a king's face l up, there is Pr 16:15
all the shining l in the heavens Ezk 32:8
one l a lamp and puts it under Mt 5:15
No one l a lamp and puts it in Lk 11:33
to horizon and l up the sky, Lk 17:24
Then the jailer called for l, Ac 16:29
down from the Father of l; Jms 1:17

LIKE *(1591)*
(See pp. xi-xii.)

LIKE-MINDED *(2)*
have no one else l who will Php 2:20
you should be l and sympathetic 1Pt 3:8

LIKED *(2)*
son Jonathan l David very much, 1Sm 19:1
Pharaoh l Hadad so much that he 1Kg 11:19

LIKEN *(1)*
What can I l you to, so that I Lm 2:13

LIKENESS *(15)*
Our image, according to Our l. Gn 1:26
He made him in the l of God; Gn 5:1
he fathered ⌊a child⌋ in his l, Gn 5:3
The l of oxen was below it, 2Ch 4:3
What l will you compare Him to? Is 40:18
makes it according to a human l, Is 44:13
with human l touched my lips. Dn 10:16
with human l touched me again Dn 10:18
did not sin in the l of Adam's Rm 5:14
with Him in the l of His death, Rm 6:5
also be in the l of His Rm 6:5
to God's ⌊l⌋ in righteousness Eph 4:24
a slave, taking on the l of men. Php 2:7
into the l of His glorious Php 3:21
men who are made in God's l. Jms 3:9

LIKEWISE *(15)*
(See pp. xi-xii.)

LIKHI *(1)*
Ahian, Shechem, L, and Aniam. 1Ch 7:19

LILIES *(8)*
the portico were shaped like l, 1Kg 7:19
the pillars were shaped like l. 1Kg 7:22
he feeds among the l. Sg 2:16
gazelle, that feed among the l. Sg 4:5
His lips are l, dripping with Sg 5:13
in the gardens and gather l. Sg 6:2
he feeds among the l. Sg 6:3
mound of wheat surrounded by l. Sg 7:2

LILY *(5)*
brim of a cup or of a l blossom. 1Kg 7:26
brim of a cup or a l blossom. 2Ch 4:5
of Sharon, a l of the valleys. Sg 2:1
Like a l among thorns, so is my Sg 2:2
blossom like the l and take root Hs 14:5

LIMB *(9)*
has an elongated or stunted l, Lv 22:23
He tore them l from limb with a Jdg 15:8
them limb from l with a great Jdg 15:8
into 12 pieces, l by limb, and Jdg 19:29
pieces, limb by l, and sent her Jdg 19:29
you will be torn l from limb, Dn 2:5
you will be torn limb from l, Dn 2:5
will be torn l from limb and his Dn 3:29
torn limb from l and his house Dn 3:29

LIMBS *(6)*
firstborn consumes his l. Jb 18:13
his l are like iron rods. Jb 40:18
I cannot be silent about his l, Jb 41:12
length of its l, for its roots Ezk 31:7
it beautiful with its many l, Ezk 31:9
Its l fell on the mountains and Ezk 31:12

LIME *(1)*
because he burned to l the bones Am 2:1

LIMIT *(11)*
of oil, and salt without l. Ezr 7:22
setting a l for the soles of my Jb 13:27
He established a l for the rain Jb 28:26
only Job were tested to the l, Jb 34:36
I have seen a l to all Ps 119:96
but Your command is without l. Ps 119:96
when He set a l for the sea so Pr 8:29
There is no l to all the people Ec 4:16
and there is no l to their Is 2:7
and there is no l to their Is 2:7
there is no l to His Is 40:28

LIMITED *(13)*
Moses, "Is the LORD's power l? Nm 11:23
of the wind and l the water by Jb 28:25
time, your strength is l. Pr 24:10
those days were l, no one would Mt 24:22
those days will be l because of Mt 24:22
Unless the Lord l those days, Mk 13:20
But He l those days because of Mk 13:20
do since it was l by the flesh, Rm 8:3
the time is l, so from now on 1Co 7:29
You are not l by us, but you are 2Co 6:12
but you are l by your own 2Co 6:12
of the body has a l benefit, 1Tm 4:8
Because you have l strength, Rv 3:8

LIMITS *(4)*
on the eastern l of Jericho. Jos 4:19
discover the l of the Almighty Jb 11:7
You have set l he cannot pass, Jb 14:5
or⌋ settle at the western l, Ps 139:9

LIMP *(1)*
is like lame legs that hang l. Pr 26:7

LIMPING *(1)*
passed by Penuel—l on his hip. Gn 32:31

LINE *(44)*
and preserve our father's l." Gn 19:32
we can preserve our father's l." Gn 19:34
so that the loops l up together. Ex 26:5
Sea draw a l to Mount Hor; Nm 34:7
Hor draw a l to the entrance Nm 34:8
draw a l from Hazar-enan to Nm 34:10
you come out to l up in battle 1Sm 17:8
and ran to the battle l. 1Sm 17:22
battle l and shouted his 1Sm 17:23
quickly to the battle l to meet 1Sm 17:48
was a battle l in front of him 2Sm 10:9
measuring l ⌊used on⌋ Samaria 2Kg 21:13
was a battle l in front of him 1Ch 19:10
a measuring l across it? Jb 38:5
I will establish his l forever, Ps 89:29
Let the l of his descendants be Ps 109:13
ancient property l that your Pr 22:28
move an ancient property l, Pr 23:10
after law, l after line, line Is 28:10
law, line after l, line after Is 28:10
line after line, l after line, a Is 28:10
line after l, a little here, Is 28:10
after law, l after line, line Is 28:13
law, line after l, line after Is 28:13
line after line, l after line, a Is 28:13
line after l, a little here, Is 28:13
measuring l and righteousness Is 28:17
out a measuring l and a plumb Is 34:11
line and a plumb l over her for Is 34:11
portion with a measuring l. Is 34:17
stretches out a measuring l, Is 44:13
A measuring l will once again Jr 31:39
They will l up in battle Jr 50:9
L up in battle formation around Jr 50:14
out a measuring l and did not Lm 2:8
with a measuring l in his hand, Ezk 47:3
wall with a plumb l in His hand. Am 7:7
I replied, "A plumb l." Am 7:8
setting a plumb l among My Am 7:8
divided up with a measuring l. Am 7:17
and a measuring l will be Zch 1:16
with a measuring l in his hand. Zch 2:1
see the plumb l in Zerubbabel's Zch 4:10
the house and family l of David, Lk 2:4

LINEAGE *(2)*
outside the l of Aaron should Nm 16:40
without this l collected tithes Heb 7:6

LINED *(19)*
went out and l up for battle in Gn 14:8
so that the loops l up with each Ex 36:12
The Philistines l up in battle 1Sm 4:2
then they l up in battle 1Sm 17:2
the Philistines l up in battle 1Sm 17:21
marched out and l up in battle 2Sm 10:8
of Israel and l up in battle 2Sm 10:9
Abishai who l up in battle 2Sm 10:10
the Arameans l up in formation 2Sm 10:17
Then he l 30 feet of the rear of 1Kg 6:16
these warriors, l up in battle 1Ch 12:38
marched out and l up in battle 1Ch 19:9
of Israel and l up in battle 1Ch 19:10
they l up in battle formation 1Ch 19:11
up to them and l up in battle 1Ch 19:17
When David l up to engage the 1Ch 19:17
against him and l up in battle 2Ch 14:10
l up like men in battle Jr 6:23
l up like men in battle Jr 50:42

LINEN *(102)*
him with fine l garments, Gn 41:42
yarn; fine l and goat hair; Ex 25:4
must make them of finely spun l, Ex 26:1

and finely spun l with a design	Ex 26:31
scarlet yarn, and finely spun l.	Ex 26:36
courtyard out of finely spun l.	Ex 27:9
scarlet yarn, and finely spun l.	Ex 27:16
of it made⌋ of finely spun l.	Ex 27:18
and scarlet yarn; and fine l.	Ex 28:5
finely spun l embroidered with	Ex 28:6
yarn, and of finely spun l.	Ex 28:8
yarn, and of finely spun l.	Ex 28:15
to weave the tunic from fine l,	Ex 28:39
a turban of fine l, and make	Ex 28:39
them l undergarments to cover	Ex 28:42
yarn; fine l and goat hair;	Ex 35:6
yarn, fine l or goat hair, ram	Ex 35:23
and scarlet yarn, and fine l.	Ex 35:25
and scarlet yarn and fine l;	Ex 35:35
made them of finely spun l,	Ex 36:8
scarlet yarn, and finely spun l.	Ex 36:35
and finely spun l for the	Ex 36:37
courtyard were of finely spun l,	Ex 38:9
courtyard were of finely spun l.	Ex 38:16
scarlet yarn, and finely spun l.	Ex 38:18
and scarlet yarn, and fine l.	Ex 38:23
yarn, and of finely spun l.	Ex 39:2
and the fine l in a skillful	Ex 39:3
of finely spun l, just as the	Ex 39:5
yarn, and of finely spun l.	Ex 39:8
fine woven l for Aaron and his	Ex 39:27
the ornate headbands of fine l,	Ex 39:28
of finely spun l of embroidered	Ex 39:29
to put on his l robe and linen	Lv 6:10
linen robe and l undergarments.	Lv 6:10
mildew—in wool or l fabric,	Lv 13:47
the warp or woof of l or wool,	Lv 13:48
the warp or woof in wool or l,	Lv 13:52
in wool or l fabric,	Lv 13:59
He is to wear a holy l tunic,	Lv 16:4
and l undergarments are to be on	Lv 16:4
must tie a l sash ⌊around him⌋	Lv 16:4
wrap his head with a l turban.	Lv 16:4
take off the l garments he wore	Lv 16:23
He will put on the l garments,	Lv 16:32
clothes made of both wool and l.	Dt 22:11
give you 30 l garments and 30	Jdg 14:12
must give me 30 l garments and	Jdg 14:13
presence and wore a l ephod.	1Sm 2:18
killed 85 men who wore l ephods.	1Sm 22:18
the LORD wearing a l ephod .	2Sm 6:14
of the guild of l workers at	1Ch 4:21
was dressed in a robe of fine l,	1Ch 15:27
David also wore a l ephod.	1Ch 15:27
blue, crimson yarn, and fine l.	2Ch 2:14
and crimson yarn and fine l,	2Ch 3:14
dressed in fine l, with cymbals,	2Ch 5:12
White and violet l hangings were	Est 1:6
and purple l cords to silver	Est 1:6
and a purple robe of fine l.	Est 8:15
richly colored l from Egypt.	Pr 7:16
clothing is fine l and purple.	Pr 31:22
She makes and sells l garments;	Pr 31:24
garments, l clothes, turbans,	Is 3:23
and buy yourself l underwear and	Jr 13:1
them, clothed in l, with writing	Ezk 9:2
clothed in l with the writing	Ezk 9:3
clothed in l with the writing	Ezk 9:11
the man clothed in l and said,	Ezk 10:2
commanded the man clothed in l,	Ezk 10:6
hands of the man clothed in l,	Ezk 10:7
you in fine l and covered you	Ezk 16:10
clothing was ⌊made⌋ of fine l,	Ezk 16:13
fine embroidered l from Egypt,	Ezk 27:7
cloth, fine l, coral, and rubies	Ezk 27:16
with a l cord and a measuring	Ezk 40:3
court they must wear l garments;	Ezk 44:17
must wear l turbans on their	Ezk 44:18
their heads and l undergarments	Ezk 44:18
there was a man dressed in l,	Dn 10:5
said to the man dressed in l,	Dn 12:6
I heard the man dressed in l,	Dn 12:7
I will take away My wool and l,	Hs 2:9
wrapped it in clean, fine l,	Mt 27:59
having a l cloth wrapped around	Mk 14:51
but he left the l cloth behind	Mk 14:52
After he bought some fine l,	Mk 15:46
down and wrapped Him in the l.	Mk 15:46
dress in purple and fine l,	Lk 16:19
it in fine l and placed it	Lk 23:53
in, he saw only the l cloths.	Lk 24:12
and foot with l strips and with	Jn 11:44
and wrapped it in l cloths with	Jn 19:40
he saw the l cloths lying there,	Jn 20:5
tomb and saw the l cloths lying	Jn 20:6
lying with the l cloths but was	Jn 20:7
in clean, bright l, with gold	Rv 15:6
fine fabrics of l, purple, silk,	Rv 18:12
clothed in fine l, purple, and	Rv 18:16
was permitted to wear fine l,	Rv 19:8
For the fine l represents the	Rv 19:8
horses, wearing pure white l.	Rv 19:14

LINES *(1)*

The boundary l have fallen for	Ps 16:6

LINGER *(4)*

why did you l at the ships?	Jdg 5:17
Those who l over wine, those who	Pr 23:30
of beer, who l into the evening,	Is 5:11
for anyone or l for mankind.	Mc 5:7

LINGERS *(1)*

wounded, but my life still l.'	2Sm 1:9

LINTEL *(3)*

doorposts and the l of the	Ex 12:7
and brush the l and the two	Ex 12:22
the blood on the l and the two	Ex 12:23

LINUS *(1)*

as do Pudens, L, Claudia, and	2Tm 4:21

LION *(85)*

Judah is a young l—my son, you	Gn 49:9
lies down like a l and like a	Gn 49:9
They rouse themselves like a l.	Nm 23:24
down like a l or a lioness—	Nm 24:9
lies down like a l and tears off	Dt 33:20
Dan is a young l, leaping out of	Dt 33:22
a young l came roaring at	Jdg 14:5
and he tore the l apart with his	Jdg 14:6
What is stronger than a l?	Jdg 14:18
Whenever a l or a bear came and	1Sm 17:34
from the paw of the l and the	1Sm 17:37
the heart of a l will melt	2Sm 17:10
on a snowy day and killed a l.	2Sm 23:20
a l met him along the way and	1Kg 13:24
the l was standing beside the	1Kg 13:24
road and the l standing beside	1Kg 13:25
The LORD has given him to the l,	1Kg 13:26
donkey and the l standing beside	1Kg 13:28
The l had not eaten the corpse	1Kg 13:28
leave me, a l will kill you."	1Kg 20:36
a l found him and killed him.	1Kg 20:36
on a snowy day and killed a l.	1Ch 11:22
The l may roar and the fierce	Jb 4:10
may roar and the fierce l growl,	Jb 4:10
strong l dies if ⌊it catches⌋	Jb 4:11
hunt me like a l and again	Jb 10:16
no l has ever prowled over it.	Jb 28:8
or they will tear me like a l,	Ps 7:2
in secret like a l in a thicket.	Ps 10:9
They are like a l eager to tear,	Ps 17:12
a young l lurking in ambush.	Ps 17:12
Save me from the mouth of the l!	Ps 22:21
tread on the l and the cobra;	Ps 91:13
the young l and the serpent.	Ps 91:13
is like the roaring of a l;	Pr 20:2
says, "There's a l outside!	Pr 22:13
There's a l in the road—	Pr 26:13
a l in the public square!"	Pr 26:13
righteous are as bold as a l.	Pr 28:1
like a roaring l or a charging	Pr 28:15
a l, which is mightiest among	Pr 30:30
dog is better than a dead l.	Ec 9:4
calf, the young l, and the	Is 11:6
and the l will eat straw like an	Is 11:7
a l for those who escape from	Is 15:9
of lioness and l, of viper and	Is 30:6
As a l or young lion growls over	Is 31:4
lion or young l growls over its	Is 31:4
There will be no l there, and no	Is 35:9
break all my bones like a l;	Is 38:13
the l will eat straw like the	Is 65:25
your prophets like a ravaging l.	Jr 2:30
l has gone up from his thicket;	Jr 4:7
a l from the forest will strike	Jr 5:6
Me like a l in the forest.	Jr 12:8
He has left His den like a l,	Jr 25:38
it will be like a l coming up	Jr 49:19
it will be like a l coming up	Jr 50:44
they will growl like l cubs.	Jr 51:38
in ambush, a l in hiding;	Lm 3:10
the face of a l on the right,	Ezk 1:10
that of a l, and the fourth	Ezk 10:14
cubs, and he became a young l.	Ezk 19:3
her cubs and made him a young l.	Ezk 19:5
lions, and he became a young l.	Ezk 19:6
like a roaring l tearing ⌊its⌋	Ezk 22:25
yourself to a l of the nations,	Ezk 32:2
was like a l but had eagle's	Dn 7:4
For I am like a l to Ephraim and	Hs 5:14
and like a young l to the house	Hs 5:14
roar like a l. When He roars,	Hs 11:10
So I will be like a l to them;	Hs 13:7
its teeth are the teeth of a l,	Jl 1:6
Does a l roar in the forest when	Am 3:4
Does a young l growl from its	Am 3:4
A l has roared; who will not	Am 3:8
who flees from a l only to have	Am 5:19
like a l among animals of the	Mc 5:8
like a young l among flocks of	Mc 5:8
where the l and lioness prowled,	Nah 2:11
The l mauled whatever its cubs	Nah 2:12
around like a roaring l,	1Pt 5:8
living creature was like a l;	Rv 4:7
The L from the tribe of Judah,	Rv 5:5
a loud voice like a roaring l.	Rv 10:3

LION'S *(9)*

the road⌋ to see the l carcass,	Jdg 14:8
the honey from the l carcass.	Jdg 14:9
A king's rage is like a l roar,	Pr 19:12
Their roaring is like a l;	Is 5:29
and a l face turned toward it on	Ezk 41:19
of an ear from the l mouth,	Am 3:12
prowled, and the l cub, with	Nah 2:11
I was rescued from the l mouth.	2Tm 4:17
his mouth was like a l mouth.	Rv 13:2

LIONESS *(10)*

down like a lion and like a l—	Gn 49:9
A people rise up like a l;	Nm 23:24
lies down like a lion or a l—	Nm 24:9
the cubs of the l are scattered.	Jb 4:11
you hunt prey for a l or satisfy	Jb 38:39
and distress, of l and lion, of	Is 30:6
your mother? A l! She lay down	Ezk 19:2
will devour them there like a l,	Hs 13:8
and it has the fangs of a l.	Jl 1:6
where the lion and l prowled,	Nah 2:11

LIONESSES *(1)*

and strangled ⌊prey⌋ for its l.	Nah 2:12

LIONS *(35)*

servant has killed l and bears;	1Sm 17:36
than eagles, stronger than l.	2Sm 1:23
between the cross-pieces were l,	1Kg 7:29
and below the l and oxen were	1Kg 7:29
cherubim, l, and palm trees	1Kg 7:36
and two l standing beside the	1Kg 10:19
Twelve l were standing there on	1Kg 10:20
So the LORD sent l among them,	2Kg 17:25
He has sent l among them, which	2Kg 17:26
faces were like the faces of l,	1Ch 12:8
and two l standing beside the	2Ch 9:18
Twelve l were standing there on	2Ch 9:19
the fangs of young l are broken.	Jb 4:10
satisfy the appetite of young l	Jb 38:39
mouths against me—l, mauling	Ps 22:13
Young l lack food and go hungry,	Ps 34:10
my very life from the young l.	Ps 35:17
I am in the midst of l;	Ps 57:4
The young l roar for their prey	Ps 104:21
the dens of the l, from the	Sg 4:8
they roar like young l;	Is 5:29
The young l have roared at him;	Jr 2:15
is a stray lamb, chased by l.	Jr 50:17
will roar together like young l;	Jr 51:38
She lay down among the l;	Ezk 19:2
her cubs among the young l.	Ezk 19:2
among the l, and he became	Ezk 19:6
able to rescue you from the l?"	Dn 6:20
before the l overpowered them	Dn 6:24
Daniel from the power of the l."	Dn 6:27
feeding ground of the young l,	Nah 2:11
sword will devour your young l.	Nah 2:13
within her are roaring l;	Zph 3:3
Listen to the roar of young l,	Zch 11:3
promises, shut the mouths of l,	Heb 11:33

LIONS' *(10)*

tear out the young l fangs.	Ps 58:6
will be thrown into the l den.	Dn 6:7

will be thrown into the l den?” Dn 6:12
and threw him into the l den. Dn 6:16
got up and hurried to the l den. Dn 6:19
His angel and shut the l mouths. Dn 6:22
and thrown into the l den— Dn 6:24
Where is the l lair, or the Nah 2:11
their teeth were like l teeth; Rv 9:8
of the horses were like l heads, Rv 9:17

LIP-SERVICE *(1)*

mouths to honor Me with l— Is 29:13

LIPS *(98)*

must not be heard on your l. Ex 23:13
nothing that came from her l, Nm 30:12
do whatever comes from your l, Dt 23:23
presence, Eli watched her l. 1Sm 1:12
and although her l were moving, 1Sm 1:13
laughter and your l with a shout Jb 8:21
your own l testify against you. Jb 15:6
from my l would bring relief Jb 16:5
from the commands of His l; Jb 23:12
my l will not speak unjustly, Jb 27:4
I must open my l and respond. Jb 32:20
and my l speak what they know Jb 33:3
with flattering l and deceptive Ps 12:2
all flattering l and the tongue Ps 12:3
our l are our own—who can be Ps 12:4
not speak their names with my l. Ps 16:4
prayer—from l free of deceit. Ps 17:1
word of Your l I have avoided Ps 17:4
not denied the request of his l. Ps 21:2
Let lying l be quieted; Ps 31:18
praise will always be on my l. Ps 34:1
evil and your l from deceitful Ps 34:13
grace flows from your l. Ps 45:2
to take My covenant on your l? Ps 50:16
Lord, open my l, and my mouth Ps 51:15
sharp words from their l. Ps 59:7
mouths is the word of their l, Ps 59:12
My l will glorify You because Ps 63:3
will praise You with joyful l. Ps 63:5
that my l promised and my mouth Ps 66:14
My l will shout for joy when I Ps 71:23
or change what My l have said. Ps 89:34
and he spoke rashly with his l. Ps 106:33
With my l I proclaim all the Ps 119:13
from Your l is better for me Ps 119:72
My l pour out praise, for You Ps 119:171
me from lying l and a deceitful Ps 120:2
viper's venom is under their l. Ps 140:3
trouble their l cause overwhelm Ps 140:9
keep watch at the door of my l. Ps 141:3
don't let your l talk deviously. Pr 4:24
and your l safeguard knowledge Pr 5:2
Though the l of the forbidden Pr 5:3
trapped by the words of your l— Pr 6:2
and what my l say is right. Pr 8:6
is detestable to my l. Pr 8:7
but foolish l will be destroyed. Pr 10:8
and foolish l will be destroyed. Pr 10:10
is found on the l of the Pr 10:13
who conceals hatred has lying l, Pr 10:18
one who controls his l is wise. Pr 10:19
l of the righteous feed many, Pr 10:21
The l of the righteous know what Pr 10:32
Truthful l endure forever, Pr 12:19
Lying l are detestable to the Pr 12:22
who opens his l invites his own Pr 13:3
but the l of the wise protect Pr 14:3
The l of the wise broadcast Pr 15:7
verdict is on the l of a king; Pr 16:10
l are a king's delight, Pr 16:13
compresses his l brings about Pr 16:30
not appropriate on a fool's l; Pr 17:7
discerning, when he seals his l. Pr 17:28
A fool's l lead to strife, Pr 18:6
and his l are a trap for his Pr 18:7
with the product of his l. Pr 18:20
has deceitful l and is a fool. Pr 19:1
but knowledgeable l are a rare Pr 20:15
a pure heart and gracious l— Pr 22:11
they are constantly on your l. Pr 22:18
cheer when your l say what is Pr 23:16
answer gives a kiss on the l. Pr 24:26
Don't deceive with your l. Pr 24:28
Smooth l with an evil heart are Pr 26:23
a stranger, and not your own l. Pr 27:2
but the l of a fool consume him. Ec 10:12
Your l are like a scarlet cord, Sg 4:3
Your l drip ⌊sweetness like⌋ the Sg 4:11
His l are lilies, dripping with Sg 5:13
gliding past my l and teeth! Sg 7:9
man of unclean l and live among Is 6:5
among a people of unclean l, Is 6:5
that this has touched your l, Is 6:7
with a command from His l. Is 11:4
His l are full of fury, and His Is 30:27
your l have spoken lies, and you Is 59:3
ever on their l, but far from Jr 12:2
human likeness touched my l. Dn 10:16
You with praise from our l. Hs 14:2
my l quivered at the sound. Hab 3:16
wrong was found on his l. Mal 2:6
For the l of a priest should Mal 2:7
people honor Me with their l, Mt 15:8
people honor Me with their l, Mk 7:6
Vipers' venom is under their l. Rm 3:13
and by the l of foreigners, 1Co 14:21
fruit of our l that confess His Heb 13:15
evil and his l from speaking 1Pt 3:10

LIQUID *(9)*

12 and a half pounds of l myrrh, Ex 30:23
any drinkable l in any container Lv 11:34
and an honest l measure; Lv 19:36
and an honest l measure. Ezk 45:10
measure and the l measure will Ezk 45:11
with the l measure containing Ezk 45:11
quota of oil in l measures will Ezk 45:14
cor equals⌋ 10 l measures ⌊or⌋ Ezk 45:14
since 10 l measures equal one Ezk 45:14

LIST *(5)*

old or more, and l their names. Nm 3:40
This is the l of David's 1Ch 11:11
This is the l of the men who 1Ch 25:1
This is the l of the Israelites, 1Ch 27:1
support l unless she is at 1Tm 5:9

LISTED *(8)*

month old or more l by name was Nm 3:43
were among those l, but had not Nm 11:26
are the stages ⌊l⌋ by their Nm 33:2
He is not l in the genealogy 1Ch 5:1
22,034 were l in their 1Ch 7:7
sons of Jediael l by heads of 1Ch 7:11
The number of men l in their 1Ch 7:40
the year or be l in the calendar Jb 3:6

LISTEN *(399)*

says to you, l to her, because Gn 21:12
L to us, lord. You are God's Gn 23:6
l to me and ask Ephron son of Gn 23:8
No, my lord. L to me. I give you Gn 23:11
of the land, “Please l to me. Gn 23:13
My lord, l to me. Land worth 400 Gn 23:15
said to her son Jacob, “L! Gn 27:6
said to him, “L, your brother Gn 27:42
So now, my son, l to me. Gn 27:43
if you will not l to us and be Gn 34:17
said to them, “L to this dream I Gn 37:6
L,” he went on, “I have heard Gn 42:2
with us, but we would not l. Gn 42:21
But you wouldn't l. Now we must Gn 42:22
together and l, sons of Jacob; Gn 49:2
l to your father Israel: Gn 49:2
They will l to what you say. Ex 3:18
two signs or l to what you say, Ex 4:9
they did not l to him because Ex 6:9
the Israelites will not l to me, Ex 6:12
then how will Pharaoh l to me, Ex 6:12
how will Pharaoh l to me?” Ex 6:30
Pharaoh will not l to you, Ex 7:4
and he did not l to them, as the Ex 7:13
and he would not l to them, Ex 7:22
heart and would not l to them, Ex 8:15
and he would not l to them, Ex 8:19
heart and he did not l to them, Ex 9:12
Pharaoh will not l to you, Ex 11:9
But they didn't l to Moses; Ex 16:20
l to me; I will give you some Ex 18:19
Now if you will l to Me and Ex 19:5
us, and we will l,” they said to Ex 20:19
I will l because I am Ex 22:27
to Him and l to His voice. Ex 23:21
He said: “L to what I say: If Nm 12:6
told Korah, “Now l, Levites! Nm 16:8
said to them, “L, you rebels! Nm 20:10
get up and l; son of Zippor, Nm 23:18
l to small and great alike. Dt 1:17
spoke to you, but you didn't l. Dt 1:43
but He didn't l to your requests Dt 1:45
of you and would not l to me. Dt 3:26
l to the statutes and ordinances Dt 4:1
l to the statutes and ordinances Dt 5:1
Go near and l to everything the Dt 5:27
we will l and obey.' Dt 5:27
L, Israel, and be careful to Dt 6:3
L, Israel: The LORD our God, the Dt 6:4
If you l to and are careful to Dt 7:12
L, Israel: Today you are about Dt 9:1
do not l to that prophet's words Dt 13:3
His commands and l to His voice; Dt 13:4
not yield to him or l to him. Dt 13:8
refusing to l either to the Dt 17:12
to drive out l to Dt 18:14
own brothers. You must l to him. Dt 18:15
does not l to My words that Dt 18:19
say to them: 'L, Israel: Today Dt 20:3
and doesn't l to them even after Dt 21:18
your God would not l to Balaam, Dt 23:5
Be silent, Israel, and l! Dt 27:9
downward if you l to the LORD Dt 28:13
and you do not l and you are led Dt 30:17
so that they may l and learn to Dt 31:12
law⌋ will l and learn to fear Dt 31:13
l, earth, to the words of my Dt 32:1
Come closer and l to the words Jos 3:9
but I would not l to Balaam. Jos 24:10
they did not l to their judges Jdg 2:17
L, kings! Pay attention, princes! Jdg 5:3
L to what they say, and then you Jdg 7:11
He said, “L, I had a dream: Jdg 7:13
L to me, lords of Shechem, and Jdg 9:7
Shechem, and may God l to you: Jdg 9:7
the king of Edom would not l. Jdg 11:17
would not l to Jephthah's Jdg 11:28
But the men would not l to him, Jdg 19:25
said to Ruth, “L, my daughter. Ru 2:8
would not l to their father, 1Sm 2:25
L to the people and everything 1Sm 8:7
L to them, but you must solemnly 1Sm 8:9
people refused to l to Samuel. 1Sm 8:19
“L to them,” the LORD told 1Sm 8:22
l to the words of the LORD. 1Sm 15:1
L, my father doesn't do anything, 1Sm 20:2
his servants, “L, men of 1Sm 22:7
Saul said, “L, son of Ahitub! 1Sm 22:12
Why do you l to the words of 1Sm 24:9
L to the words of your servant. 1Sm 25:24
Now please l to your servant. 1Sm 28:22
to him, and he wouldn't l to us. 2Sm 12:18
But he refused to l to her, 2Sm 13:14
But he refused to l to her. 2Sm 13:16
king will surely l in order to 2Sm 14:16
not have anyone to l to you.” 2Sm 15:3
called out from the city, “L! 2Sm 20:16
city, “Listen! L! Please tell 2Sm 20:16
“L to the words of your servant,” 2Sm 20:17
of his wisdom, to l to Solomon's 1Kg 4:34
L to Your servant's prayer and 1Kg 8:28
king did not l to the people, 1Kg 12:15
said to him, “Don't l or agree.” 1Kg 20:8
you did not l to the voice 1Kg 20:36
Then he said, “L, all you people 1Kg 22:28
would not l, so King Jehoash 2Kg 14:11
But they would not l. 2Kg 17:14
they would not l but continued 2Kg 17:40
they did not l to the voice 2Kg 18:12
They did not l, and they did not 2Kg 18:12
Don't l to Hezekiah, for this is 2Kg 18:31
But don't l to Hezekiah when he 2Kg 18:32
L closely, LORD, and hear; 2Kg 19:16
they did not l; Manasseh caused 2Kg 21:9
feet and said, “L to me, my 1Ch 28:2
L to Your servant's prayer and 2Ch 6:19
The king did not l to the people 2Ch 10:15
Then he said, “L, all you people 2Ch 18:27
and he said, “L carefully, all 2Ch 20:15
them, but they would not l. 2Ch 24:19
would not l, for this ⌊turn 2Ch 25:20
L to me and return the captives 2Ch 28:11
his people, but they didn't l. 2Ch 33:10
did not l to Neco's words from 2Ch 35:22
L, our God, for we are despised. Neh 4:4
and all who could l with Neh 8:2
and did not l to Your commands. Neh 9:16
They refused to l and did not Neh 9:17

prophets, but they would not **l**. Neh 9:30
obey Your law or **l** to Your Neh 9:34
he still would not **l** to them, Est 3:4
argument, and **l** to my defense. Jb 13:6
Do you **l** in on the council of Jb 15:8
L to me and I will inform you. Jb 15:17
Therefore I say, "**L** to me. Jb 32:10
my speech, and **l** to all my words Jb 33:1
Pay attention, Job, and **l** to me. Jb 33:31
If not, then **l** to me; Jb 33:33
you wise men, and **l** to me, you Jb 34:2
Therefore **l** to me, you men of Jb 34:10
l to what I have to say. Jb 34:16
God does not **l** to empty ⌊cries⌋, Jb 35:13
Just **l** to His thunderous voice Jb 37:2
L to this, Job. Stop and Jb 37:14
⌊You said,⌋ "**L** now, and I will Jb 42:4
L to my words, LORD; consider my Ps 5:1
You will **l** carefully, Ps 10:17
l to my prayer—from lips free Ps 17:1
will answer me; **l** closely to me; Ps 17:6
L to the sound of my pleading Ps 28:2
LORD, **l** and be gracious to me; Ps 30:10
L closely to me; rescue me Ps 31:2
Come, children, **l** to me; Ps 34:11
prayer, LORD, and **l** to my cry Ps 39:12
You open my ears to **l**. Ps 40:6
L, daughter, pay attention and Ps 45:10
l, all who inhabit the world, Ps 49:1
L, My people, and I will speak; Ps 50:7
l to the words of my mouth. Ps 54:2
l to my prayer and do not ignore Ps 55:1
that does not **l** to the sound of Ps 58:5
Come and **l**, all who fear God, Ps 66:16
l closely to me and save me. Ps 71:2
my instruction; **l** to what I say. Ps 78:1
L, Shepherd of Israel, who Ps 80:1
L, My people, and I will Ps 81:8
if you would only **l** to Me! Ps 81:8
But My people did not **l** to Me; Ps 81:11
My people would **l** to Me and Ps 81:13
hear my prayer; **l**, God of Jacob. Ps 84:8
I will **l** to what God will say; Ps 85:8
L, LORD, and answer me, for I am Ps 86:1
l to my plea for mercy. Ps 86:6
Your presence; **l** to my cry. Ps 88:2
day of trouble. **L** closely to me; Ps 102:2
and did not **l** to the LORD's Ps 106:25
Lord, **l** to my voice; let Your Ps 130:2
L, LORD, to my cry for help. Ps 140:6
L to my voice when I call on You. Ps 141:1
the people will **l** to my words, Ps 141:6
L to my cry, for I am very weak. Ps 142:6
Your faithfulness **l** to my plea, Ps 143:1
a wise man will **l** and increase Pr 1:5
L, my son, to your father's Pr 1:8
L, ⌊my⌋ sons, to a father's Pr 4:1
L, my son. Accept my words, and Pr 4:10
l closely to my sayings. Pr 4:20
l closely to my understanding Pr 5:1
now, ⌊my⌋ sons, **l** to me, and Pr 5:7
my teachers or **l** closely to my Pr 5:13
Now, ⌊my⌋ sons, **l** to me, and pay Pr 7:24
L, for I speak of noble things, Pr 8:6
And now, ⌊my⌋ sons, **l** to me; Pr 8:32
L to instruction and be wise; Pr 8:33
a mocker doesn't **l** to rebuke. Pr 13:1
L to counsel and receive Pr 19:20
L closely, pay attention to the Pr 22:17
to instruction and **l** to words of Pr 23:12
L, my son, and be wise; Pr 23:19
L to your father who gave you Pr 23:22
It is better to **l** to rebuke from Ec 7:5
person than to **l** to the song Ec 7:5
L! My love ⌊is approaching⌋. Sg 2:8
L, heavens, and pay attention, Is 1:2
L to the instruction of our God, Is 1:10
countless prayers, I will not **l**. Is 1:15
Isaiah said, "**L**, house of David! Is 7:13
of Gallim! **L**, Laishah! Anathoth Is 10:30
L, a tumult on the mountains, Is 13:4
L, an uproar among the kingdoms, Is 13:4
When a trumpet sounds, **l**! Is 18:3
But they would not **l**. Is 28:12
L and hear my voice. Pay Is 28:23
ears of those who hear will **l**. Is 32:3
complacent women; **l** to me. Pay Is 32:9
L! Their warriors cry loudly in Is 33:7

You nations, come here and **l**; Is 34:1
L to the words of the great king, Is 36:13
Don't **l** to Hezekiah. For the Is 36:16
L closely, LORD, and hear; Is 37:17
L, you deaf! Look, you blind, so Is 42:18
ears are open, he does not **l**." Is 42:20
him **l** and obey in the future. Is 42:23
they would not **l** to His Is 42:24
And now **l**, Jacob My servant, Is 44:1
L to Me, house of Jacob, all the Is 46:3
L to me, you hardhearted, far Is 46:12
L to this, house of Jacob— Is 48:1
L to Me, Jacob, and Israel, the Is 48:12
All of you, assemble and **l**! Is 48:14
Approach Me and **l** to this. Is 48:16
Coastlands, **l** to me; distant Is 49:1
My ear to **l** like those being Is 50:4
L to Me, you who pursue Is 51:1
My people, and **l** to Me, My Is 51:4
L to Me, you who know Is 51:7
So **l** to this, afflicted and Is 51:21
L carefully to Me, and eat what Is 55:2
l, so that you will live. Is 55:3
from you so that He does not **l**. Is 59:2
such a warning that they will **l**? Jr 6:10
L for the sound of the ram's Jr 6:17
But they protested: We won't **l**! Jr 6:17
Therefore **l**, you nations and you Jr 6:18
L, earth! I am about to bring Jr 6:19
time again but you wouldn't **l**, Jr 7:13
beg Me, for I will not **l** to you. Jr 7:16
Yet they didn't **l** or pay Jr 7:24
they wouldn't **l** to Me or pay Jr 7:26
to them, they will not **l** to you. Jr 7:27
that would not **l** to the voice Jr 7:28
L—the cry of my dear people Jr 8:19
L! A noise—it is coming—a Jr 10:22
L to the words of this covenant, Jr 11:2
who refuse to **l** to Me, who walk Jr 13:10
L and pay attention. Do not be Jr 13:15
if you will not **l**, my innermost Jr 13:17
They wouldn't **l** or pay attention Jr 17:23
However, if you **l** to Me, says Jr 17:24
If you do not **l** to Me to Jr 17:27
said: I will not **l**. This has Jr 22:21
Do not **l** to the words of the Jr 23:16
Perhaps they will **l** and return— Jr 26:3
If you do not **l** to Me by living Jr 26:4
again, though you did not **l**, Jr 26:5
do not **l** to your prophets, Jr 27:9
Do not **l** to the words of the Jr 27:14
'Do not **l** to the words of your Jr 27:16
Do not **l** to them. Serve the king Jr 27:17
Only **l** to this message I am Jr 28:7
prophet Hananiah, "**L**, Hananiah! Jr 28:15
and don't **l** to the dreams you Jr 29:8
pray to Me, and I will **l** to you. Jr 29:12
they do not **l** and receive Jr 32:33
scroll, he would not **l** to them. Jr 36:25
them about but they did not **l**." Jr 36:31
Irijah would not **l** to him but Jr 37:14
So now please **l**, my lord the Jr 37:20
you won't **l** to me anyway." Jr 38:15
they did not **l** or pay attention Jr 44:5
we are not going to **l** to you! Jr 44:16
His command. **L**, all you people; Lm 1:18
Whether they **l** or refuse ⌊to Ezk 2:5
they listen or refuse ⌊to **l**⌋— Ezk 2:5
them whether they **l** or refuse Ezk 2:7
they listen or refuse ⌊to **l**⌋, Ezk 2:7
you, son of man, **l** to what I Ezk 2:8
to them, they would **l** to you. Ezk 3:6
not want to **l** to you because Ezk 3:7
they do not want to **l** to Me. Ezk 3:7
l carefully to all My words that Ezk 3:10
whether they **l** or refuse ⌊to Ezk 3:11
they listen or refuse ⌊to **l**⌋." Ezk 3:11
who listens, **l**, and let the one Ezk 3:27
voice, I will not **l** to them." Ezk 8:18
lie to My people, who **l** to lies. Ezk 13:19
Now **l**, house of Israel: Ezk 18:25
and were unwilling to **l** to Me. Ezk 20:8
you will surely **l** to Me, Ezk 20:39
your eyes, **l** with your ears, Ezk 40:4
your eyes and **l** with your ears Ezk 44:5
L, my God, and hear. Open Your Dn 9:18
Lord, **l** and act! My God, Dn 9:19
house of Israel! **L**, royal house! Hs 5:1

l, all you inhabitants of the Jl 1:2
L to this message that the LORD Am 3:1
L and testify against the house Am 3:13
L to this message, you cows of Am 4:1
L to this message that I am Am 5:1
will not **l** to the music of your Am 5:23
L, all you peoples; pay Mc 1:2
Now **l**, leaders of Jacob, you Mc 3:1
L to this, leaders of the house Mc 3:9
l to what the LORD is saying: Mc 6:1
L to the LORD's lawsuit, you Mc 6:2
call for help and You do not **l**, Hab 1:2
L, the Day of the LORD—there Zph 1:14
they did not **l** or pay attention Zch 1:4
L, Joshua the high priest, you Zch 3:8
they would not **l**, so when they Zch 7:13
I would not **l**," says the LORD Zch 7:13
L! The Lord will impoverish her Zch 9:4
L to the wail of the shepherds, Zch 11:3
L to the roar of young lions, Zch 11:3
If you don't **l**, and if you don't Mal 2:2
welcome you or **l** to your words, Mt 10:14
Anyone who has ears should **l**! Mt 11:15
Anyone who has ears should **l**!" Mt 13:9
they do not **l** or understand. Mt 13:13
You will **l** and listen, yet never Mt 13:14
You will listen and **l**, yet never Mt 13:14
l to the parable of the sower: Mt 13:18
Anyone who has ears should **l**! Mt 13:43
He told them, "**L** and understand: Mt 15:10
I take delight in Him. **L** to Him! Mt 17:5
But if he won't **l**, take one or Mt 18:16
L! We are going up to Jerusalem. Mt 20:18
L to another parable: Mt 21:33
L, I have told you." Mt 28:7
L! Consider the sower who went Mk 4:3
who has ears to hear should **l**!" Mk 4:9
they may **l** and listen, yet not Mk 4:12
may listen and **l**, yet not Mk 4:12
has ears to hear, he should **l**!" Mk 4:23
and people refuse to **l** to you, Mk 6:11
He told them, "**L** to Me, all of Mk 7:14
has ears to hear, he should **l**!" Mk 7:16
is My beloved Son; **l** to Him! Mk 9:7
L! We are going up to Jerusalem. Mk 10:33
Jesus answered: **L**, Israel! The Mk 12:29
l! You will become silent and Lk 1:20
l: You will conceive and give Lk 1:31
Today as you **l**, this Scripture Lk 4:21
But I say to you who **l**: Lk 6:27
who has ears to hear should **l**!" Lk 8:8
Therefore, take care how you **l**. Lk 8:18
Son, the Chosen One; **l** to Him! Lk 9:35
worker, '**L**, for three years Lk 13:7
who has ears to hear should **l**!" Lk 14:35
were approaching to **l** to Him. Lk 15:1
they should **l** to them.' Lk 16:29
'If they don't **l** to Moses and Lk 16:31
L to what the unjust judge says. Lk 18:6
Twelve aside and told them, "**L**! Lk 18:31
"**L**," He said to them, "when Lk 22:10
L ⌊to what⌋ I'm telling you: Jn 4:35
Because you cannot **l** to My word. Jn 8:43
why you don't **l**, because you are Jn 8:47
he said, "and you didn't **l**. Jn 9:27
that God doesn't **l** to sinners, Jn 9:31
but the sheep didn't **l** to them. Jn 10:8
and they will **l** to My voice. Jn 10:16
Why do you **l** to Him?" Jn 10:20
Men of Israel, **l** to these words: Ac 2:22
You must **l** to Him in everything Ac 3:22
who will not **l** to that Prophet Ac 3:23
God ⌊for us⌋ to **l** to you rather Ac 4:19
and fathers," he said, "**l**: Ac 7:2
Israel, and you who fear God, **l**! Ac 13:16
responded: "Brothers, **l** to me! Ac 15:13
l now to my defense before you." Ac 22:1
I beg you to **l** to me patiently. Ac 26:3
you but all who **l** to me today Ac 26:29
'You will **l** and listen, yet Ac 28:26
'You will listen and **l**, yet Ac 28:26
to the Gentiles; they will **l**!" Ac 28:28
then, they will not **l** to Me, 1Co 14:21
L! I am telling you a mystery: 1Co 15:51
L, my dear brothers: Didn't God Jms 2:5
not from God does not **l** to us. 1Jn 4:6
has an ear should **l** to what the Rv 2:7
has an ear should **l** to what the Rv 2:11

has an ear should l to what the Rv 2:17
has an ear should l to what the Rv 2:29
has an ear should l to what the Rv 3:6
has an ear should l to what the Rv 3:13
L! I stand at the door and knock. Rv 3:20
has an ear should l to what the Rv 3:22
anyone has an ear, he should l: Rv 13:9

LISTENED *(51)*

Because you l to your wife's Gn 3:17
because Abraham l to My voice Gn 26:5
And Jacob l to his father and Gn 28:7
God l to Leah, and she conceived Gn 30:17
He l to her and opened her womb. Gn 30:22
able-bodied men l to Hamor and Gn 34:24
but so far you have not l. Ex 7:16
Moses l to his father-in-law and Ex 18:24
The LORD l to Israel's request, Nm 21:3
the LORD l to me on that Dt 9:19
The LORD also l to me on this Dt 10:10
when the LORD l to the voice of Jos 10:14
God l to Manoah, and the Angel Jdg 13:9
Samuel l to all the people's 1Sm 8:21
I have carefully l to everything 1Sm 12:1
brother Eliab l as he spoke to 1Sm 17:28
Saul l to Jonathan's advice and 1Sm 19:6
woman urged him, he l to them. 1Sm 28:23
that the king had not l to them, 1Kg 12:16
So they l to what the LORD 1Kg 12:24
Ben-hadad l to King Asa and sent 1Kg 15:20
So the LORD l to Elijah's voice, 1Kg 17:22
The king l to them and did so. 1Kg 20:25
king of Assyria l to him and 2Kg 16:9
As they l, he read all the words 2Kg 23:2
that the king had not l to them, 2Ch 10:16
So they l to what the LORD 2Ch 11:4
Ben-hadad l to King Asa and sent 2Ch 16:4
Then the king l to them, 2Ch 24:17
and have not l to my advice." 2Ch 25:16
All the people l attentively to Neh 8:3
Men l to me with expectation, Jb 29:21
I l to your insights as you Jb 32:11
but l when he cried to Him for Ps 22:24
the Lord would not have l. Ps 66:18
However, God has l; Ps 66:19
about my life, and You l to me; Ps 119:26
no one has l, no eye has seen Is 64:4
indeed, you have never l to Me. Jr 22:21
they have not l to My words"— Jr 29:19
And you too have not l." Jr 29:19
and I l to the One who was Ezk 2:2
live because he l to ⌊your⌋ Ezk 3:21
As I l the wheels were called Ezk 10:13
We have not l to Your servants Dn 9:6
because they have not l to Him; Hs 9:17
The LORD took notice and l. Mal 3:16
Everyone who has l to and Jn 6:45
fell silent and l to Barnabas Ac 15:12
They l to him up to this word. Ac 22:22
he sent for Paul and l to him on Ac 24:24

LISTENING *(26)*

Now Sarah was l at the entrance Gn 18:10
Now Rebekah was l to what Isaac Gn 27:5
the sheepfolds l to the playing Jdg 5:16
LORD, for Your servant is l.'" 1Sm 3:9
Speak, for Your servant is l." 1Sm 3:10
He answered, "I'm l." 2Sm 20:17
l to them whenever they call to 1Kg 8:52
l closely to wisdom and Pr 2:2
If you stop l to instruction, Pr 19:27
are l for your voice— Sg 8:13
Keep l, but do not understand; Is 6:9
his ears from l to murderous Is 33:15
l to the voice of His servant? Is 50:10
I will not be l when they call Jr 11:14
not l or accepting discipline. Jr 17:23
My sight by not l to My voice, Jr 18:10
and by l to the words of My Jr 26:5
discipline by l to My words?" Jr 35:13
large crowd was l to Him with Mk 12:37
l to them and asking them Lk 2:46
feet and was l to what He said. Lk 10:39
were l to all these things and Lk 16:14
As they were l to this, He went Lk 19:11
While all the people were l, Lk 20:45
who worshiped God, was l. Ac 16:14
the prisoners were l to them. Ac 16:25

LISTENS *(20)*

For the LORD l to the needy and Ps 69:33
But whoever l to me will live Pr 1:33
Anyone who l to me is happy, Pr 8:34
whoever l to counsel is wise. Pr 12:15
An ear that l to life-giving Pr 15:31
but whoever l to correction Pr 15:32
A wicked person l to malicious Pr 17:4
gives an answer before he l— Pr 18:13
but the one who l will speak Pr 21:28
If a ruler l to lies, all his Pr 29:12
Let the one who l, listen, and Ezk 3:27
he l to you, you have won your Mt 18:15
Whoever l to you listens to Me. Lk 10:16
Whoever listens to you l to Me. Lk 10:16
who stands by and l for him, Jn 3:29
is from God l to God's words. Jn 8:47
and does His will, He l to him. Jn 9:31
is of the truth l to My voice." Jn 18:37
world, and the world l to them. 1Jn 4:5
Anyone who knows God l to us; 1Jn 4:6

LIT *(6)*

darkness, yet it l up the night. Ex 14:20
lightning l up the world. Ps 77:18
in the firebrands you have l! Is 50:11
service and have your lamps l. Lk 12:35
They l a fire in the middle of Lk 22:55
they l a fire and took us all Ac 28:2

LITERATURE *(2)*

the Chaldean language and l. Dn 1:4
in every kind of l and wisdom. Dn 1:17

LITTER *(1)*

Solomon's royal l surrounded by Sg 3:7

LITTERED *(1)*

the whole way was l with clothes 2Kg 7:15

LITTERS *(1)*

and chariots, in l, and on mules Is 66:20

LITTLE *(163)*

Let a l water be brought, that Gn 18:4
let me have a l water from your Gn 24:17
let me drink a l water from your Gn 24:43
you had very l before I came, Gn 30:30
care of you and your l ones." Gn 50:21
saw the child—a l boy, crying. Ex 2:6
Some gathered a lot, some a l. Ex 16:17
gathered a l had no shortage. Ex 16:18
a l while they will stone me!" Ex 17:4
drive them out l by little ahead Ex 23:30
out little by l ahead of you Ex 23:30
the l owl, the cormorant, the Lv 11:17
Our wives and l children will Nm 14:3
l children, wives, livestock, Nm 32:26
Your l children who you said Dt 1:39
nations before you l by little. Dt 7:22
nations before you little by l. Dt 7:22
the l owl, the long-eared owl, Dt 14:16
seed in the field but harvest l, Dt 28:38
including the women, l children, Jos 8:35
Please give me a l water to Jdg 4:19
she rested a l in the shelter." Ru 2:7
made him a l robe and took it 1Sm 2:19
because I tasted a l honey. 1Sm 14:29
I tasted a l honey with the end 1Sm 14:43
king, I have l power today. 2Sm 3:39
so far was a l thing to You, 2Sm 7:19
David had gone a l beyond the 2Sm 16:1
with the king a l way across the 2Sm 19:36
'My l finger is thicker than my 1Kg 12:10
bring me a l water in a cup 1Kg 17:10
In a l while, the sky grew dark 1Kg 18:45
them like two l flocks of goats 1Kg 20:27
dash their l ones to pieces. 2Kg 8:12
served Baal a l, but Jehu will 2Kg 10:18
This was a l thing to You, 1Ch 17:17
'My l finger is thicker than my 2Ch 10:10
will grant them a l deliverance. 2Ch 12:7
alone, so that I can smile a l Jb 10:20
They let their l ones run around Jb 21:11
Be patient with me a l longer, Jb 36:2
You made him l less than God and Ps 8:5
l while, and the wicked will be Ps 37:10
Better the l that the righteous Ps 37:16
myself like a l weaned child Ps 131:2
its mother; I am like a l child. Ps 131:2
who takes your l ones and dashes Ps 137:9
A l sleep, a little slumber, a Pr 6:10
little sleep, a l slumber, a Pr 6:10
a l folding of the arms to rest, Pr 6:10
of the wicked is of l value. Pr 10:20
Better a l with the fear of the Pr 15:16
Better a l with righteousness Pr 16:8
will vomit the l you've eaten Pr 23:8
a l sleep, a little slumber, a Pr 24:33
little sleep, a l slumber, a Pr 24:33
a l folding of the arms to rest, Pr 24:33
whether he eats l or much; Ec 5:12
a l folly outweighs wisdom and Ec 10:1
the l foxes that ruin the Sg 2:15
In just a l while My wrath will Is 10:25
have no compassion on l ones; Is 13:18
Hide for a l while until the Is 26:20
after line, a l here, a little Is 28:10
line, a little here, a l there." Is 28:10
after line, a l here, a little Is 28:13
little here, a l there," so they Is 28:13
that⌋ in just a l while Lebanon Is 29:17
In a l more than a year you Is 32:10
had a possession for a l while, Is 63:18
her l ones will cry out. Jr 48:4
The flock's l lambs will Jr 49:20
the flock's l lambs will be Jr 50:45
In just a l while her harvest Jr 51:33
L children beg for bread, but no Lm 4:4
⌊older⌋ women and l children, Ezk 9:6
yet for a l while I have been a Ezk 11:16
another horn, a l one, came up Dn 7:8
one of them a l horn emerged Dn 8:9
for in a l while I will avenge Hs 1:4
their l ones will be dashed to Hs 13:16
planted much but harvested l. Hg 1:6
but then it amounted to l. Hg 1:9
Once more, in a l while, I am Hg 2:6
for I was a l angry, but they Zch 1:15
turn My hand against the l ones. Zch 13:7
more for you—you of l faith? Mt 6:30
you fearful, you of l faith?" Mt 8:26
one of these l ones because he Mt 10:42
to him, "You of l faith, why did Mt 14:31
Jesus said, "You of l faith! Mt 16:8
"Because of your l faith," Mt 17:20
of one of these l ones who Mt 18:6
down on one of these l ones, Mt 18:10
that one of these l ones perish. Mt 18:14
Going a l farther, He fell Mt 26:39
After a l while those standing Mt 26:73
Going on a l farther, He saw Mk 1:19
My l daughter is at death's Mk 5:23
is translated, "L girl, I say to Mk 5:41
a woman whose l daughter had an Mk 7:25
welcomes one l child such as Mk 9:37
of one of these l ones who Mk 9:42
were bringing l children to Him Mk 10:13
Let the l children come to Me. Mk 10:14
of God like a l child will never Mk 10:15
in two tiny coins worth very l. Mk 12:42
Then He went a l farther, fell Mk 14:35
After a l while those standing Mk 14:70
to put out a l from the land. Lk 5:3
But the one who is forgiven l, Lk 7:47
is forgiven little, loves l." Lk 7:47
took a l child and had him stand Lk 9:47
welcomes this l child in My name Lk 9:48
not able to do even a l thing, Lk 12:26
He do for you—you of l faith? Lk 12:28
be afraid, l flock, because Lk 12:32
in very l is also faithful Lk 16:10
in very l is also unrighteous Lk 16:10
one of these l ones to stumble. Lk 17:2
Let the l children come to Me, Lk 18:16
of God like a l child will never Lk 18:17
After a l while, someone else Lk 22:58
for each of them to have a l." Jn 6:7
be with you only a l longer. Jn 12:35
I am with you a l while longer. Jn 13:33
In a l while the world will see Jn 14:19
A l while and you will no longer Jn 16:16
a l while and you will see Me. Jn 16:16
'A l while and you will not see Jn 16:17
a l while and you will see Me' Jn 16:17
this He is saying, 'A l while'? Jn 16:18
'A l while and you will not see Jn 16:19
a l while and you will see Me' Jn 16:19
be taken outside for a l while. Ac 5:34
the shelter of a l island called Ac 27:16
they had sailed a l farther and Ac 27:28
It is of l importance that I 1Co 4:3
know that a l yeast permeates 1Co 5:6

though only for a l while. 2Co 7:8
who gathered l did not have too 2Co 8:15
little did not have too l. 2Co 8:15
put up with a l foolishness from 2Co 11:1
a fool, so I too may boast a l. 2Co 11:16
A l yeast leavens the whole lump Gl 5:9
we will no longer be l children, Eph 4:14
I know both how to have a l, Php 4:12
but use a l wine because of your 1Tm 5:23
For in yet a very l while, Heb 10:37
that appears for a l while, Jms 4:14
you after you have suffered a l. 1Pt 5:10
My l children, I am writing you 1Jn 2:1
writing to you, l children, 1Jn 2:12
So now, l children, remain in 1Jn 2:28
L children, let no one deceive 1Jn 3:7
L children, we must not love in 1Jn 3:18
are from God, l children, and 1Jn 4:4
L children, guard yourselves 1Jn 5:21
told to rest a l while longer Rv 6:11
and he had a l scroll opened in Rv 10:2
him to give me the l scroll. Rv 10:9
Then I took the l scroll from Rv 10:10
he must remain for a l while. Rv 17:10

LIVE *(575)*

life, and eat, and l forever." Gn 3:22
down to Egypt to l there for a Gn 12:10
They will kill me but let you l. Gn 12:12
and went to l beside the oaks Gn 13:18
he will l at odds with all his Gn 16:12
L in My presence and be devout. Gn 17:1
could l in Your presence! Gn 17:18
he was afraid to l in Zoar. Gn 19:30
pray for you and you will l. Gn 20:7
the Canaanites among whom I l, Gn 24:3
the Canaanites in whose land I l Gn 24:37
L in the land that I tell you Gn 26:2
will l by your sword, and you Gn 27:40
land where you l as an alien, Gn 28:4
anyone ⌊here⌋, he will not l! Gn 31:32
L with us. The land is before Gn 34:10
for ourselves, l with you, and Gn 34:16
Let them l in our land and move Gn 34:21
will agree to l with us and be Gn 34:22
them, and they will l with us." Gn 34:23
many ⌊for them⌋ to l together, Gn 36:7
Tamar went to l in her father's Gn 38:11
so that we will l and not die." Gn 42:2
God—do this and you will l. Gn 42:18
be on our way so that we may l, Gn 43:8
have come to l in the land for Gn 47:4
can l in the land of Goshen. Gn 47:6
so that we can l and not die, Gn 47:19
Zebulun will l by the seashore Gn 49:13
if it's a daughter, she may l." Ex 1:16
told them; they let the boys l. Ex 1:17
done this and let the boys l?" Ex 1:18
but let every daughter l." Ex 1:22
Pharaoh and went to l in the Ex 2:15
so will the land where they l. Ex 8:21
I have let you l for this Ex 9:16
them the way to l and what they Ex 18:20
neither animal or man will l. Ex 19:13
must sell the l ox and divide Ex 21:35
must not allow a sorceress to l. Ex 22:18
for no one can see Me and l." Ex 33:20
the people you l among will see Ex 34:10
generations, wherever you l: Lv 3:17
Wherever you l, you must not eat Lv 7:26
He must l alone in a place Lv 13:46
order that two l clean birds, Lv 14:4
is to take the l bird together Lv 14:6
and release the l bird over the Lv 14:7
yarn, and the l bird, dip them Lv 14:51
water, the l bird, the cedar Lv 14:52
to release the l bird into the Lv 14:53
is to present the l male goat. Lv 16:20
the head of the l goat and Lv 16:21
foreigners who l among them who Lv 17:8
foreigners who l among them who Lv 17:10
where you used to l, or follow Lv 18:3
a person will l if he does them. Lv 18:5
bringing you to l will not vomit Lv 20:22
to the LORD wherever you l. Lv 23:3
your generations wherever you l. Lv 23:14
wherever you l throughout your Lv 23:21
your generations wherever you l. Lv 23:31
You are to l in booths for seven Lv 23:42
of Israel must l in booths, Lv 23:42
the Israelites l in booths when Lv 23:43
that you may l securely in the Lv 25:18
and l securely in the land. Lv 25:19
he can continue to l among you. Lv 25:35
let your brother l among you. Lv 25:36
food to eat and l securely in Lv 26:5
and enabled you to l in freedom. Lv 26:13
who come to l there will be Lv 26:32
that they may l and not die when Nm 4:19
people who l there are strong Nm 13:18
the land they l in good or bad? Nm 13:19
the cities they l in encampments Nm 13:19
and Amorites l in the hill Nm 13:29
and the Canaanites l by the sea Nm 13:29
surely as I l and as the whole Nm 14:21
As surely as I l, declares the Nm 14:28
you by now and let her l." Nm 22:33
who can l when God does this? Nm 24:23
"Have you let every female l?" Nm 31:15
in the land where you will l. Nm 33:55
the Levites to l in and Nm 35:2
The cities will be for them to l Nm 35:3
and he must l there until the Nm 35:25
was supposed to l in his city of Nm 35:28
your generations wherever you l. Nm 35:29
him to return and l in the land Nm 35:32
unclean where you l and where I Nm 35:34
of Esau, who l in Seir. Dt 2:4
of Esau, who l in Seir. Dt 2:8
Esau who l in Seir did for us, Dt 2:29
and the Moabites who l in Ar, Dt 2:29
so that you may l, enter, and Dt 4:1
from your mind as long as you l. Dt 4:9
all the days they l on the earth Dt 4:10
You will not l long there, Dt 4:26
so that you may l long in the Dt 4:40
so that you may l long and so Dt 5:16
so that you may l, prosper, and Dt 5:33
so that you may l and increase, Dt 8:1
man does not l on bread alone Dt 8:3
and build beautiful houses to l Dt 8:12
so that you may l long in the Dt 11:9
Canaanites, who l in the Arabah, Dt 11:30
all the days you l on the earth. Dt 12:1
the Jordan and l in the land the Dt 12:10
you and you l in security, Dt 12:10
as long as you l in your land. Dt 12:19
them out and l in their land, Dt 12:29
LORD your God is giving you to l Dt 13:12
so that you will l and possess Dt 16:20
of it, l in it, and say, Dt 17:14
them out and l in their cities Dt 19:1
to one of these cities and l. Dt 19:5
taken prisoner, l in your house, Dt 21:13
does not l near you or you Dt 22:2
that you may prosper and l long. Dt 22:7
with them as long as you l. Dt 23:6
Let him l among you wherever he Dt 23:16
When brothers l on the same Dt 25:5
so that you may l long in the Dt 25:15
possession of it and l in it, Dt 26:1
build a house but not l in it. Dt 28:30
your soul, so that you will l. Dt 30:6
so that you may l and multiply, Dt 30:16
and will not l long in the land Dt 30:18
you and your descendants may l, Dt 30:19
as long as you l in the land you Dt 31:13
As surely as I l forever, Dt 32:40
them you will l long in the land Dt 32:47
Let Reuben l and not die though Dt 33:6
strength last as long as you l. Dt 33:25
against you as long as you l. Jos 1:5
with her in the house will l, Jos 6:17
and all who l in the land hear Jos 7:9
"Perhaps you l among us. Jos 9:7
and made a treaty to let them l, Jos 9:15
we will let them l, so that no Jos 9:20
They also said, "Let them l." Jos 9:21
telling us you l far away from Jos 9:22
when in fact you l among us? Jos 9:22
and Maacath l in Israel to this Jos 13:13
the Levites except cities to l Jos 14:4
So the Jebusites l in Jerusalem Jos 15:63
the Canaanites l in Ephraim to Jos 16:10
him a place to l among them. Jos 20:4
that we be given cities to l Jos 21:2
not build, though you l in them; Jos 24:13
They went to l among the people. Jdg 1:16
of the Amorites whose land you l Jdg 6:10
you had let them l, I would not Jdg 8:19
went back to l at his house. Jdg 8:29
and two sons to l in the land of Ru 1:1
and wherever you l, I will live; Ru 1:16
and wherever you live, I will l; Ru 1:16
as sure as you l, my lord, I am 1Sm 1:26
shouted, "Long l the king!" 1Sm 10:24
surely as you l, I don't know," 1Sm 17:55
lives and as you yourself l, 1Sm 20:3
I continue to l, treat me with 1Sm 20:14
lives and as you yourself l, 1Sm 25:26
towns, so I can l there. 1Sm 27:5
your servant l in the royal city 1Sm 27:5
man or woman l to be brought to 1Sm 27:11
and still l there as aliens 2Sm 4:3
you to build a house for Me to l 2Sm 7:5
that they may l there and not be 2Sm 7:10
surely as you l and by your life 2Sm 11:11
gracious to me and let him l.' 2Sm 12:22
As surely as you l, my lord the 2Sm 14:19
to Absalom, "Long l the king! 2Sm 16:16
live the king! Long l the king!" 2Sm 16:16
saying, 'Long l King Adonijah!' 1Kg 1:25
my lord King David l forever!" 1Kg 1:31
and say, 'Long l King Solomon!' 1Kg 1:34
Long l King Solomon!" 1Kg 1:39
in Jerusalem and l there, 1Kg 2:36
this woman and I l in the same 1Kg 3:17
will l among the Israelites and 1Kg 6:13
own palace where he would l, 1Kg 7:8
But will God indeed l on earth? 1Kg 8:27
the days they l on the land You 1Kg 8:40
lives and as you yourself l, 2Kg 2:2
lives and as you yourself l, 2Kg 2:4
lives and as you yourself l, 2Kg 2:6
your sons can l on the rest." 2Kg 4:7
lives and as you yourself l, 2Kg 4:30
the place where we l under your 2Kg 6:1
ourselves a place to l there." 2Kg 6:2
If they let us l, we will live; 2Kg 7:4
If they let us live, we will l; 2Kg 7:4
and go and l as a foreigner 2Kg 8:1
Whoever is missing will not l." 2Kg 10:19
and cried, "Long l the king!" 2Kg 11:12
and they l there until today. 2Kg 16:6
Have him go and l there so he 2Kg 17:27
so that you may l and not die. 2Kg 18:32
L in the land and serve the king 2Kg 25:24
escaped and still l there today. 1Ch 4:43
The first to l in their towns on 1Ch 9:2
that they may l there and not be 1Ch 17:9
cedars to build him a house to l 2Ch 2:3
will God indeed l on earth with 2Ch 6:18
the days they l on the land You 2Ch 6:31
My wife must not l in the house 2Ch 8:11
the Arabs who l near the 2Ch 21:16
and cried, "Long l the king!" 2Ch 23:11
the Arabs that l in Gur-baal, 2Ch 26:7
king, "May the king l forever! Neh 2:3
and the home where I will l." Neh 2:8
grain so that we can eat and l." Neh 5:2
can I enter the temple and l? Neh 6:11
a person will l if he does them. Neh 9:29
ten to come and l in Jerusalem, Neh 11:1
volunteered to l in Jerusalem. Neh 11:2
scepter will that person l. Est 4:11
the rural Jews who l in villages Est 9:19
up! I will not l forever. Leave Jb 7:16
I would still l in terror of all Jb 9:28
no survivor where he used to l. Jb 18:19
Why do the wicked continue to l, Jb 21:7
not accuse ⌊me⌋ as long as I l! Jb 27:6
place appointed for all who l. Jb 30:23
LORD, make me l in safety. Ps 4:8
Who can l on Your holy mountain? Ps 15:1
May your hearts l forever! Ps 22:26
of the LORD as long as I l. Ps 23:6
He will l a good life, and his Ps 25:13
my eyes, and I l by Your truth. Ps 26:3
But I l with integrity; Ps 26:11
against those who l peacefully Ps 35:20
in the land and l securely. Ps 37:3
so that he may l forever and not Ps 49:9
will not l out half their Ps 55:23
will l in Your tent forever and Ps 61:4
will praise You as long as I l; Ps 63:4

bring near to l in Your courts! Ps 65:4
Those who l far away are awed by Ps 65:8
the rebellious l in a scorched Ps 68:6
The LORD will l ⌊there⌋ forever! Ps 68:16
the LORD God might l ⌊there⌋. Ps 68:18
may no one l in their tents. Ps 69:25
will l there and possess it. Ps 69:35
who love His name will l in it. Ps 69:36
May he l long! May gold from Ps 72:15
and refused to l by His law. Ps 78:10
of my God than to l in the tents Ps 84:10
from those who l with integrity. Ps 84:11
and I will l by Your truth. Ps 86:11
and do not l by My ordinances, Ps 89:30
What man can l and never see Ps 89:48
the world and those who l in it, Ps 98:7
I will l with integrity of heart Ps 101:2
deceitfully will l in my palace; Ps 101:7
birds of the sky l beside ⌊the Ps 104:12
sing praise to my God while I l. Ps 104:33
to a city where they could l. Ps 107:4
go to a city where they could l. Ps 107:7
a city where they can l. Ps 107:36
⌊out to Him⌋ as long as I l. Ps 116:2
but I will l and proclaim what Ps 118:17
l according to the law of the Ps 119:1
Your servant so that I might l; Ps 119:17
come to me so that I may l, Ps 119:77
as You promised, and I will l; Ps 119:116
me understanding, and I will l. Ps 119:144
Let me l, and I will praise You; Ps 119:175
is when brothers can l together! Ps 133:1
If I l at the eastern horizon Ps 139:9
upright will l in Your presence Ps 140:13
making me l in darkness like Ps 143:3
of Your name, Yahweh, let me l. Ps 143:11
sing to the LORD as long as I l. Ps 146:2
to me will l securely and be Pr 1:33
for those who l with integrity Pr 2:7
Keep my commands and l. Pr 4:4
and you will l many years. Pr 4:10
Keep my commands and l; Pr 7:2
behind, and you will l; Pr 9:6
the one who hates bribes will l. Pr 15:27
Better to l on the corner of a Pr 21:9
Better to l in a wilderness than Pr 21:19
and you'll never l it down. Pr 25:10
Better to l on the corner of a Pr 25:24
children and l many years. Ec 6:3
in their hearts while they l— Ec 9:3
since a l dog is better than a Ec 9:4
if a man should l many years, Ec 11:8
who are destined to l— Is 4:3
unclean lips and l among a Is 6:5
The wolf will l with the lamb, Is 11:6
and you who l on the earth, Is 18:3
go to those who l in the LORD's Is 23:18
those who l in lofty places Is 26:5
The dead do not l; departed Is 26:14
Your dead will l; their bodies Is 26:19
For you people will l on Zion in Is 30:19
of these ⌊promises⌋ people l, Is 38:16
me to health and let me l. Is 38:16
them out like a tent to l Is 40:22
As I l"—the LORD's declaration Is 49:18
went down to Egypt to l there, Is 52:4
listen, so that you will l. Is 55:3
I l in a high and holy place, Is 57:15
of streets where people l. Is 58:12
but we l in the night. Is 59:9
no longer l only a few days, Is 65:20
an old man not l out his days. Is 65:20
build houses and l ⌊in them⌋; Is 65:21
build and others l ⌊in them⌋; Is 65:22
north on all who l in the land. Jr 1:14
wicked men l among My people. Jr 5:26
allow you to l in this place. Jr 7:3
allow you to l in this place, Jr 7:7
You l in ⌊a world⌋ of deception. Jr 9:6
ground, you who l under siege. Jr 10:17
do the treacherous l at ease? Jr 12:1
to fill all who l in this land— Jr 13:13
and all who l in your house, Jr 20:6
you will l and will retain Jr 21:9
"As I l," says the LORD, "though Jr 22:24
L in the land the LORD gave to Jr 25:5
serve him and his people, and l! Jr 27:12
Serve the king of Babylon and l! Jr 27:17
Build houses and l ⌊in them⌋. Jr 29:5
its cities will l in it together Jr 31:24
Your voice or l according to Jr 32:23
place and make them l in safety. Jr 32:37
you must l in tents your whole Jr 35:7
so you may l a long time on the Jr 35:7
built houses to l in and do not Jr 35:9
L in the land that I gave you Jr 35:15
to the Chaldeans will l. Jr 38:2
spoils ⌊of war⌋ and will l.' Jr 38:2
then you will l, this city will Jr 38:17
go well for you and you can l. Jr 38:20
L in the land and serve the king Jr 40:9
I am going to l in Mizpah to Jr 40:10
and l in the cities you have Jr 40:10
for food, and we'll l there, Jr 42:14
go to Egypt and l there for a Jr 42:15
go to Egypt to l there for a Jr 42:17
desired to go to l for a while." Jr 42:22
go to Egypt to l there for a Jr 43:2
been banished to l in the land Jr 43:5
you have gone to l for a while. Jr 44:8
land of Egypt to l there for a Jr 44:12
those going to l for a while Jr 44:14
they are longing to return to l, Jr 44:14
you Judeans who l in the land Jr 44:26
land of Egypt to l there for a Jr 44:28
As I l—⌊this is⌋ the King's Jr 46:18
L in the cliffs, residents of Jr 48:28
You who l in the clefts of the Jr 49:16
the LORD, "no one will l there; Jr 49:18
even a gate bar; they l alone. Jr 49:31
No one will l there; no human Jr 49:33
to those who l in Babylon. Jr 50:34
against those who l in Babylon, Jr 50:35
creatures will l with jackals, Jr 50:39
ostriches will also l in her. Jr 50:39
so no one will l there; Jr 50:40
against those who l in Babylon. Jr 51:12
so that no one will l in it— Jr 51:62
and her leaders ⌊l⌋ among the Lm 2:9
We will l under his protection Lm 4:20
you and you l among scorpions. Ezk 2:6
he will indeed l because he Ezk 3:21
"Therefore, as I l"—⌊this is⌋ Ezk 5:11
Wherever you l the cities will Ezk 6:6
and wherever they l I will make Ezk 6:14
will escape and l on the Ezk 7:16
the violence of all who l there. Ezk 12:19
spare those who should not l, Ezk 13:19
were in it, as I l"—the Ezk 14:16
were in it, as I l"—the Ezk 14:18
were in it, as I l"—the Ezk 14:20
in your blood: L! Yes, I said to Ezk 16:6
as you lay⌋ in your blood: L! Ezk 16:6
"As I l"—the declaration of Ezk 16:48
"As I l"—⌊this is⌋ the Ezk 17:16
As I l, I will bring down on his Ezk 17:19
As I l"—⌊this is⌋ the Ezk 18:3
he will certainly l." ⌊This is⌋ Ezk 18:9
or for profit, will he l? Ezk 18:13
live? He will not l! Since he Ezk 18:13
iniquity. He will certainly l. Ezk 18:17
statutes, he will certainly l. Ezk 18:19
and right, he will certainly l; Ezk 18:21
He will l because of the Ezk 18:22
that the wicked do, will he l? Ezk 18:24
He will certainly l because he Ezk 18:28
the Lord GOD. "So repent and l! Ezk 18:32
As I l, I will not be consulted Ezk 20:3
who does them will l by them. Ezk 20:11
who does them will l by them. Ezk 20:13
who does them will l by them. Ezk 20:21
As I l"—⌊this is⌋ the Ezk 20:31
As I l"—the declaration of the Ezk 20:33
the land where they l as foreign Ezk 20:38
People who ⌊l⌋ in you eat at the Ezk 22:9
People who ⌊l⌋ in you accept Ezk 22:12
then they will l in their own Ezk 28:25
They will l there securely, Ezk 28:26
They will l securely when I Ezk 28:26
I strike down all who l there, Ezk 32:15
As I l"—the declaration of the Ezk 33:11
should turn from his way and l. Ezk 33:11
person that he will surely l, Ezk 33:13
iniquity—he will certainly l; Ezk 33:15
and right; he will certainly l. Ezk 33:16
he will l because of this. Ezk 33:19
those who l in the ruins in the Ezk 33:24
As surely as I l, those who are Ezk 33:27
As I l"—the declaration of the Ezk 34:8
so that they may l securely in Ezk 34:25
They will l securely, and no one Ezk 34:28
therefore, as I l"—⌊this is⌋ Ezk 35:6
therefore, as I l"—the Ezk 35:11
Then you will l in the land that Ezk 36:28
Son of man, can these bones l?" Ezk 37:3
to enter you, and you will l. Ezk 37:5
these slain so that they may l!" Ezk 37:9
you, and you will l, and I will Ezk 37:14
They will l in the land that I Ezk 37:25
They will l in it forever with Ezk 37:25
all of them ⌊now⌋ l securely. Ezk 38:8
and who l at the center Ezk 38:12
Magog and those who l securely Ezk 39:6
when they l securely in their Ezk 39:26
their possession for towns to l Ezk 45:5
that swarms will l wherever the Ezk 47:9
May the king l forever. Dn 2:4
Wherever people l—or wild Dn 2:38
May the king l forever. Dn 3:9
language, who l in all the earth Dn 4:1
from people to l with the wild Dn 4:25
from people to l with the wild Dn 4:32
"May the king l forever," she Dn 5:10
May King Darius l forever. Dn 6:6
May the king l forever. Dn 6:21
language who l in all the earth Dn 6:25
You must l with me many days. Hs 3:3
Israelites must l many days Hs 3:4
up so we can l in His presence Hs 6:2
will make you l in tents again, Hs 12:9
will return and l beneath his Hs 14:7
Israelites who l in Samaria will Am 3:12
house of Israel: Seek Me and l! Am 5:4
Seek Yahweh and l, or He will Am 5:6
you will never l in the houses Am 5:11
and not evil so that you may l, Am 5:14
you who l in clefts of the rock Ob 3
better for me to die than to l." Jnh 4:3
better for me to die than to l." Jnh 4:8
against you who l in Mareshah. Mc 1:15
They will l securely, for then Mc 5:4
They l alone in a scrubland, Mc 7:14
the world and all who l in it. Nah 1:5
one will l by his faith. Hab 2:4
cities, and all who l in them. Hab 2:8
cities, and all who l in them. Hab 2:17
houses but never l ⌊in them⌋, Zph 1:13
Therefore, as I l—the Zph 2:9
yourselves to l in your paneled Hg 1:4
And do the prophets l forever? Zch 1:5
to Zion and l in Jerusalem. Zch 8:3
them ⌊back⌋ to l in Jerusalem. Zch 8:8
mongrel people will l in Ashdod, Zch 9:6
children will l and return. Zch 10:9
People will l there, and never Zch 14:11
must not l on bread alone but Mt 4:4
and went to l in Capernaum Mt 4:13
people who l in darkness have Mt 4:16
hand on her, and she will l." Mt 9:18
her so she can get well and l." Mk 5:23
Your disciples l according to Mk 7:5
she possessed—all she had to l Mk 12:44
shine on those who l in darkness Lk 1:79
Man must not l on bread alone." Lk 4:4
dressed and l in luxury are in Lk 7:25
"Do this and you will l." Lk 10:28
the people who l in Jerusalem? Lk 13:4
has put in all she had to l Lk 21:4
come on all who l on the face Lk 21:35
told him, "your son will l." Jn 4:50
had told him, "Your son will l." Jn 4:53
and those who hear will l. Jn 5:25
of this bread he will l forever. Jn 6:51
Father sent Me and I l because Jn 6:57
on Me will l because of Me. Jn 6:57
eats this bread will l forever." Jn 6:58
in Me, even if he dies, will l. Jn 11:25
Because I l, you will live too. Jn 14:19
Because I live, you will l too. Jn 14:19
let no one l in it; and Let Ac 1:20
those who l in Mesopotamia, Ac 2:9
to all who l in Jerusalem, Ac 4:16
to this land in which you now l. Ac 7:4
and does not l in shrines made Ac 17:24

nation of men to l all over the Ac 17:26
the boundaries of where they l, Ac 17:26
For in Him we l and move and Ac 17:28
it's a disgrace for him to l!" Ac 22:22
that he should not l any longer. Ac 25:24
does not allow him to l!" Ac 28:4
The righteous will l by faith. Rm 1:17
who died to sin still l in it? Rm 6:2
that we will also l with Him, Rm 6:8
to the flesh to l according to Rm 8:12
for if you l according to the Rm 8:13
deeds of the body, you will l. Rm 8:13
these things will l by them. Rm 10:5
on your part, l at peace with Rm 12:18
If we l, we live to the Lord; Rm 14:8
If we live, we l to the Lord; Rm 14:8
whether we l or die, we belong Rm 14:8
I l, says the Lord, every knee Rm 14:11
she is willing to l with him, 1Co 7:12
and he is willing to l with her, 1Co 7:13
each one must l his life in the 1Co 7:17
For we who l are always given 2Co 4:11
that those who l should no 2Co 5:15
no longer l for themselves, 2Co 5:15
as dying and look—we l; 2Co 6:9
die together and to l together. 2Co 7:3
you we will l with Him by God's 2Co 13:4
l like a Gentile and not like a Gl 2:14
compel Gentiles to l like Jews?" Gl 2:14
the law, that I might l to God. Gl 2:19
and I no longer l, but Christ Gl 2:20
The life I now l in the flesh, Gl 2:20
I l by faith in the Son of God, Gl 2:20
the righteous will l by faith. Gl 3:11
these things will l by them. Gl 3:12
If we l by the Spirit, we must Gl 5:25
Now if I l on in the flesh, Php 1:22
l your life in a manner worthy Php 1:27
we should l up to whatever Php 3:16
observe those who l according to Php 3:17
that many l as enemies of the Php 3:18
why do you l as if you still Col 2:20
For now we l, if you stand firm 1Th 3:8
we will l together with Him. 1Th 5:10
Him, we will also l with Him; 2Tm 2:11
those who want to l a godly life 2Tm 3:12
lusts and to l in a sensible, Ti 2:12
righteous one will l by faith; Heb 10:38
to the Father of spirits and l? Heb 12:9
He has caused to l in us yearns Jms 4:5
we will l and do this or that." Jms 4:15
God's slaves, ⌊l⌋ as free people 1Pt 2:16
we might l for righteousness; 1Pt 2:24
by the way their wives l, 1Pt 3:1
l with your wives with 1Pt 3:7
in order to l the remaining time 1Pt 4:2
they might l by God in the 1Pt 4:6
from those who l in error. 2Pt 2:18
so that we might l through Him. 1Jn 4:9
know where you l—where Satan's Rv 2:13
test those who l on the earth. Rv 3:10
from those who l on the earth?" Rv 6:10
Woe to those who l on the earth, Rv 8:13
Those who l on the earth will Rv 11:10
those who l on the earth. Rv 11:10
those who l on the earth will Rv 13:8
and those who l on it to worship Rv 13:12
deceives those who l on the Rv 13:14
those who l on the earth to Rv 13:14
and those who l on the earth Rv 17:2
Those who l on the earth whose Rv 17:8
men, and He will l with them. Rv 21:3

LIVED *(216)*

presence and l in the land of Gn 4:16
Adam l 800 years after the birth Gn 5:4
Seth l 807 years after the birth Gn 5:7
l 815 years after the birth Gn 5:10
l 840 years after the birth Gn 5:13
Mahalalel l 830 years after the Gn 5:16
l 800 years after the birth Gn 5:19
Methuselah l 782 years after the Gn 5:26
Lamech l 595 years after Noah's Gn 5:30
Now Noah l 350 years after the Gn 9:28
Shem l 100 years and fathered Gn 11:10
Shem l 500 years and fathered Gn 11:11
Arpachshad l 35 years and Gn 11:12
l 403 years and fathered Gn 11:13
Shelah l 30 years and fathered Gn 11:14
Shelah l 403 years and fathered Gn 11:15
Eber l 34 years and fathered Gn 11:16
Eber l 430 years and fathered Gn 11:17
Peleg l 30 years and fathered Gn 11:18
Peleg l 209 years and fathered Gn 11:19
Reu l 32 years and fathered Gn 11:20
Reu l 207 years and fathered Gn 11:21
Serug l 30 years and fathered Gn 11:22
Serug l 200 years and fathered Gn 11:23
Nahor l 29 years and fathered Gn 11:24
Nahor l 119 years and fathered Gn 11:25
Terah l 70 years and fathered Gn 11:26
Terah l 205 years and died in Gn 11:32
Abram l in the land of Canaan, Gn 13:12
but Lot l in the cities of the Gn 13:12
Amorites who l in Hazazon-tamar Gn 14:7
after Abram had l in the land of Gn 16:3
the cities where Lot had l. Gn 19:29
from Zoar and l in the mountains Gn 19:30
his two daughters l in a cave. Gn 19:30
and Shur. While he l in Gerar, Gn 20:1
And Abraham l as a foreigner in Gn 21:34
Now Sarah l 127 years; Gn 23:1
who l near Beer-lahai-roi. Gn 25:11
He l in opposition to all his Gn 25:18
valley of Gerar, and l there. Gn 26:17
Isaac l 180 years. Gn 35:28
l in the mountains of Seir. Gn 36:8
Jacob l in the land where his Gn 37:1
"How many years have you l?" Gn 47:8
They l off the allotment Pharaoh Gn 47:22
Now Jacob l in the land of Egypt Gn 47:28
in Egypt. Joseph l 110 years. Gn 50:22
land they l in as foreigners. Ex 6:4
and Merari. Levi l 137 years. Ex 6:16
and Uzziel. Kohath l 133 years. Ex 6:18
and Moses. Amram l 137 years. Ex 6:20
had light where they l. Ex 10:23
Israelites l in Egypt was 430 Ex 12:40
your Sabbaths when you l there. Lv 26:35
Canaanites who l in that ⌊part Nm 14:45
and we l in Egypt many years, Nm 20:15
of Arad, who l in the Negev, Nm 21:1
the cities and l in all these Nm 21:25
So Israel l in the Amorites' Nm 21:31
the Amorites, who l in Heshbon." Nm 21:34
cities where the Midianites l, Nm 31:10
who l in the Negev in the land Nm 33:40
the Amorites, who l in Heshbon, Dt 1:4
Bashan, who l in Ashtaroth, at Dt 1:4
Amorites who l there came out Dt 1:44
Anakim, had previously l there. Dt 2:10
had previously l in Seir, Dt 2:12
The Rephaim l there previously, Dt 2:20
of Esau who l in Seir, Dt 2:22
out and have l in their place Dt 2:22
l in villages as far as Gaza, Dt 2:23
the Amorites, who l in Heshbon.' Dt 3:2
the fire as you have, and l? Dt 4:33
He l in Heshbon, and Moses and Dt 4:46
the fire, as we have, and l? Dt 5:26
with a few people and l there. Dt 26:5
you know how we l in the land of Dt 29:16
since she l in a house that was Jos 2:15
of the Amorites l in Heshbon. Jos 12:2
of the Rephaim, l in Ashtaroth Jos 12:4
of Sihon who l in the land. Jos 13:21
Jebusites who l in Jerusalem. Jos 15:63
the Canaanites who l in Gezer. Jos 16:10
possession of it, l there, and Jos 19:47
He rebuilt the city and l in it. Jos 19:50
the Reubenites and Gadites l. Jos 22:33
l beyond the Euphrates River and Jos 24:2
you l in the wilderness a long Jos 24:7
the Amorites who l beyond the Jos 24:8
the Amorites who l in the land. Jos 24:18
three sons of Anak who l there. Jdg 1:20
The Jebusites have l among the Jdg 1:21
Canaanites have l among them in Jdg 1:29
so the Canaanites l among them Jdg 1:30
The Asherites l among the Jdg 1:32
They l among the Canaanites who Jdg 1:33
Hivites who l in the Lebanese Jdg 3:3
was Sisera who l in Harosheth Jdg 4:2
and l there because of his Jdg 9:21
from Issachar and l in Shamir in Jdg 10:1
his brothers and l in the land Jdg 11:3
Amorites who l in that country Jdg 11:21
While Israel l 300 years in Jdg 11:26
who l in the Sorek Valley. Jdg 16:4
his priest and l in Micah's Jdg 17:12
rebuilt the city and l in it. Jdg 18:28
their cities, and l in them. Jdg 21:23
After they l in Moab about 10 Ru 1:4
she l with her mother-in-law. Ru 2:23
around you, and you l securely. 1Sm 12:11
today I have not l in a house; 2Sm 7:6
Mephibosheth l in Jerusalem 2Sm 9:13
l and grew up with him and his 2Sm 12:3
So Tamar l as a desolate woman 2Sm 13:20
a vow when I l in Geshur of Aram 2Sm 15:8
And Shimei l in Jerusalem for a 1Kg 2:38
Judah and Israel l in safety 1Kg 4:25
Canaanites who l in the city, 1Kg 9:16
Genubath ⌊l⌋ there along with 1Kg 11:20
to Damascus, l there, and became 1Kg 11:24
country of Ephraim and l there. 1Kg 12:25
city where the old prophet l. 1Kg 13:25
king of Aram who l in Damascus, 1Kg 15:18
Elijah left and l by the Wadi 1Kg 17:5
life returned to him, and he l. 1Kg 17:22
and nobles who l with Naboth in 1Kg 21:8
and nobles who l in his city, 1Kg 21:11
woman who ⌊l⌋ there persuaded 2Kg 4:8
her household l as foreigners 2Kg 8:2
son of Joash l 15 years after 2Kg 14:17
He l in a separate house, while 2Kg 15:5
They had l according to the 2Kg 17:8
LORD their God but l according 2Kg 17:19
of Samaria and l in its cities. 2Kg 17:24
When they first l there, they 2Kg 17:25
deported came and l in Bethel, 2Kg 17:28
in the cities where they l, 2Kg 17:29
⌊home⌋ and l in Nineveh. 2Kg 19:36
She l in Jerusalem in the Second 2Kg 22:14
of scribes who l in Jabez— 1Ch 2:55
They l there in the service of 1Ch 4:23
They l in Beer-sheba, Moladah, 1Ch 4:28
Hamites had l there previously 1Ch 4:40
And they l in their tents 1Ch 5:10
The sons of Gad l next to them 1Ch 5:11
They l in Gilead, in Bashan and 1Ch 5:16
they l there in the Hagrites' 1Ch 5:22
son of Israel l in these towns. 1Ch 7:29
genealogies, and l in Jerusalem. 1Ch 8:28
fathered Gibeon and l in Gibeon. 1Ch 8:29
These also l opposite their 1Ch 8:32
of Elkanah who l in the villages 1Ch 9:16
genealogies, and l in Jerusalem. 1Ch 9:34
fathered Gibeon and l in Gibeon. 1Ch 9:35
These also l opposite their 1Ch 9:38
today I have not l in a house; 1Ch 17:5
Ben-hadad, who l in Damascus, 2Ch 16:2
Jehoshaphat l in Jerusalem, 2Ch 19:4
They have l in the land and have 2Ch 20:8
son of Joash l 15 years after 2Ch 25:25
l in quarantine with a serious 2Ch 26:21
its villages, and they l there. 2Ch 28:18
the people who l in Jerusalem to 2Ch 31:4
Judahites who l in the cities 2Ch 31:6
She l in Jerusalem in the Second 2Ch 34:22
the Jews who l nearby arrived, Neh 4:12
exile made booths and l in them. Neh 8:17
of Judah each l on his own Neh 11:3
The temple servants l on Ophel; Neh 11:21
descendants l in Kiriath-arba Neh 11:25
wherever they l and brought them Neh 12:27
Where are the tents the wicked l Jb 21:28
and an influential man l on it. Jb 22:8
I l as a king among his troops, Jb 29:25
born; you have l so long! Jb 38:21
Job l 140 years after this and Jb 42:16
because I have l with integrity Ps 26:1
Jacob l as a foreigner in the Ps 105:23
that I have l among the tents of Ps 120:5
I have l too long with those who Ps 120:6
be inhabited or l in from Is 13:20
⌊home⌋ and l in Nineveh. Is 37:37
through and where no one l? Jr 2:6
But we have l in tents and have Jr 35:10
be inhabited or l in through all Jr 50:39
We have l to see ⌊it⌋." Lm 2:16
who l with her daughters to the Ezk 16:46
who l with her daughters to the Ezk 16:46
great nations l in its shade. Ezk 31:6
allies they had l in its shade Ezk 31:17

house of Israel l in their land, Ezk 36:17
Jacob, where your fathers l. Ezk 37:25
of the air l in its branches Dn 4:12
under it the wild animals l, Dn 4:21
the birds of the air l— Dn 4:21
he l with the wild donkeys, Dn 5:21
'If we had l in the days of our Mt 23:30
He l in the tombs. No one was Mk 5:3
on all those who l around them, Lk 1:65
having l with her husband seven Lk 2:36
Bethlehem, where David once l?" Jn 7:42
the Jews who l in Damascus by Ac 9:22
to the saints who l in Lydda. Ac 9:32
So all who l in Lydda and Sharon Ac 9:35
to the brothers who l in Judea. Ac 11:29
to everyone who l in Ephesus, Ac 19:17
I have l my life before God in Ac 23:1
our religion I l as a Pharisee. Ac 26:5
all previously l among them in Eph 2:3
faith that first l in your 2Tm 1:5
You have l luxuriously on the Jms 5:5
for as he l among them, that 2Pt 2:8
who had the sword wound yet l. Rv 13:14
herself and l luxuriously, Rv 18:7
immorality and l luxuriously Rv 18:9

LIVER *(14)*

fatty lobe of the l, and the two Ex 29:13
lobe of the l, the two kidneys Ex 29:22
lobe of the l with the kidneys Lv 3:4
lobe of the l above the kidneys Lv 3:10
lobe of the l with the kidneys Lv 3:15
lobe of the l with the kidneys Lv 4:9
lobe of the l with the kidneys Lv 7:4
fatty lobe of the l, and the two Lv 8:16
fatty lobe of the l, and the two Lv 8:25
fatty lobe of the l from the sin Lv 9:10
and the fatty lobe of the l— Lv 9:19
the flashing tip out of his l. Jb 20:25
until an arrow pierces its l, Pr 7:23
the idols, and observes the l. Ezk 21:21

LIVES *(186)*

of them said, "Run for your l! Gn 19:17
surely as Pharaoh l, you will Gn 42:15
then as surely as Pharaoh l, Gn 42:16
said, "You have saved our l. Gn 47:25
and made their l bitter with Ex 1:14
to the LORD to atone for your l. Ex 30:15
the LORD to atone for your l." Ex 30:16
on the altar for your l, Lv 17:11
no foreigner who l among you may Lv 17:12
the foreigner who l among you. Lv 18:26
a foreigner l with you in your Lv 19:33
the foreigner who l with you as Lv 19:34
or a foreigner who l among you. Nm 15:29
at the cost of their own l, Nm 16:38
foreigner who l within your Dt 5:14
with a person, yet he still l. Dt 5:24
towns where he l in Israel and Dt 18:6
divorce her as long as he l. Dt 22:19
divorce her as long as he l. Dt 22:29
Jacob l untroubled in a land of Dt 33:28
and everyone who l in the land Jos 2:9
will spare the l of my father, Jos 2:13
⌊We will give⌋ our l for yours. Jos 2:14
Everyone who l in the land is Jos 2:24
and she l in Israel to this day. Jos 6:25
feared for our l because of you, Jos 9:24
was a people risking their l, Jdg 5:18
As the LORD l, if you had let Jdg 8:19
your family will lose your l." Jdg 18:25
you, as the LORD l, I will. Ru 3:13
as long as he l, he is given to 1Sm 1:28
as the LORD l who saves Israel, 1Sm 14:39
No, as the LORD l, not a hair of 1Sm 14:45
as the LORD l, David will not be 1Sm 19:6
surely as the LORD l and as you 1Sm 20:3
as the LORD l, it is safe for 1Sm 20:21
day Jesse's son l on earth you 1Sm 20:31
for the l of everyone in your 1Sm 22:22
Nabal, for he l up to his name: 1Sm 25:25
surely as the LORD l and as you 1Sm 25:26
your enemies' l like ⌊stones⌋ 1Sm 25:29
as the LORD God of Israel l, 1Sm 25:34
As the LORD l, the LORD will 1Sm 26:10
the LORD l, all of you deserve 1Sm 26:16
as the LORD l, nothing bad will 1Sm 28:10
him, "As the LORD l, you are an 1Sm 29:6
"As God l," Joab replied, "if 2Sm 2:27
As surely as the LORD l, 2Sm 4:9
as the LORD l, the man who did 2Sm 12:5
"As the LORD l," he vowed, "not 2Sm 14:11
as the LORD l and as my lord 2Sm 15:21
lives and as my lord the king l, 2Sm 15:21
your life and the l of your sons 2Sm 19:5
The LORD l—may my rock be 2Sm 22:47
of men who risked their l?" 2Sm 23:17
As the LORD l, who has redeemed 1Kg 1:29
now, as the LORD l, the One who 1Kg 2:24
As the LORD God of Israel l, 1Kg 17:1
LORD your God l, I don't have 1Kg 17:12
the LORD your God l, there is no 1Kg 18:10
LORD of Hosts l, before whom I 1Kg 18:15
said, "As the LORD l, I will say 1Kg 22:14
let my life and the l of these 2Kg 1:13
As the LORD l and as you 2Kg 2:2
As the LORD l and as you 2Kg 2:4
As the LORD l and as you 2Kg 2:6
LORD of Hosts l, I stand before 2Kg 3:14
As the LORD l and as you 2Kg 4:30
As the LORD l, I stand before 2Kg 5:16
As the LORD l, I will run after 2Kg 5:20
and they had fled for their l. 2Kg 7:7
these men who risked their l?" 1Ch 11:19
it at the risk of their l. 1Ch 11:19
said, "As the LORD l, I will say 2Ch 18:13
wherever he l, be assisted Ezr 1:4
As God l, who has deprived me of Jb 27:2
⌊Do you know⌋ where darkness l, Jb 38:19
It l on a cliff where it spends Jb 39:28
one who l honestly, practices Ps 15:2
The LORD l—may my rock be Ps 18:46
and save the l of the poor. Ps 72:13
for their l are precious in his Ps 72:14
do not forget the l of Your poor Ps 74:19
delivered their l to the plague. Ps 78:50
Our l last seventy years or, Ps 90:10
The one who l under the Ps 91:1
He protects the l of His godly Ps 97:10
they attack their own l. Pr 1:18
it takes the l of those who Pr 1:19
he trusts you and l near you. Pr 3:29
The one who l with integrity Pr 10:9
lives with integrity l securely, Pr 10:9
of life, but violence takes l. Pr 11:30
Whoever l with integrity fears Pr 14:2
A truthful witness rescues l, Pr 14:25
The one who l with integrity is Pr 20:7
a poor man who l with integrity Pr 28:6
one who l with integrity will Pr 28:18
yet it l in kings' palaces. Pr 30:28
during the few days of their l. Ec 2:3
how long he l, if he is not Ec 6:3
And if he l a thousand years Ec 6:6
a wicked man who l long in spite Ec 7:15
He l in a godless way and speaks Is 32:6
The one who l righteously and Is 33:15
the days of our l at the house Is 38:20
beds—everyone who l uprightly. Is 57:2
and Exalted One who l forever, Is 57:15
For My people's l will be like Is 65:22
swear, As the LORD l, in truth, Jr 4:2
say, "As the LORD l," they are Jr 5:2
As the LORD l,' just as they Jr 12:16
As the LORD l who brought the Jr 16:14
As the LORD l who brought the Jr 16:15
in a salt land where no one l. Jr 17:6
those who want to take their l. Jr 21:7
As the LORD l who brought the Jr 23:7
As the LORD l, who brought and Jr 23:8
As the LORD l, who has given us Jr 38:16
saying, As the Lord GOD l. Jr 44:26
those who want to take their l— Jr 46:26
Flee! Save your l! Be like a Jr 48:6
those who want to take their l. Jr 49:37
save your l, each of you! Jr 51:6
where no one l, where no human Jr 51:43
Save your l, each of you, from Jr 51:45
l among the nations but finds Lm 1:3
as their l fade away in the arms Lm 2:12
Him for the l of your children Lm 2:19
at the risk of our l because of Lm 5:9
abandoned us for ⌊our⌋ entire l? Lm 5:20
height in order to ensnare l. Ezk 13:18
you ensnare the l of My people Ezk 13:18
constructed to destroy many l. Ezk 17:17
he turns from his ways and l? Ezk 18:23
and destroying l in order to get Ezk 22:27
comes and takes away their l, Ezk 33:6
whatever tribe the foreigner l, Ezk 47:23
and risked their l rather than Dn 3:28
and glorified Him who l forever: Dn 4:34
swore by Him who l eternally Dn 12:7
everyone who l in it languishes Hs 4:3
swear an oath: As the LORD l! Hs 4:15
say, "As your god l, Dan," or "As Am 8:14
"As the way of Beer-sheba l"— Am 8:14
city that l in security, Zph 2:15
By your endurance gain your l. Lk 21:19
But anyone who l by the truth Jn 3:21
and drinks My blood l in Me, Jn 6:56
Everyone who l and believes in Jn 11:26
The Father who l in Me does His Jn 14:10
have risked their l for the name Ac 15:26
the ship, but also of our l." Ac 27:10
be no loss of any of your l, Ac 27:22
but in that He l, He lives to Rm 6:10
in that He lives, He l to God. Rm 6:10
over someone as long as he l? Rm 7:1
bound to her husband while he l. Rm 7:2
know that nothing good l in me, Rm 7:18
but it is the sin that l in me. Rm 7:20
For those whose l are according Rm 8:5
but those whose l are according Rm 8:5
Those whose l are in the flesh Rm 8:8
the Spirit of God l in you. Rm 8:9
Jesus from the dead l in you, Rm 8:11
through His Spirit who l in you. Rm 8:11
For none of us l to himself, Rm 14:7
that the Spirit of God l in you? 1Co 3:16
but He l by God's power. 2Co 13:4
longer live, but Christ l in me. Gl 2:20
of God but also our own l, 1Th 2:8
is dead even while she l. 1Tm 5:6
the Holy Spirit who l in us, 2Tm 1:14
slavery all their l by the fear Heb 2:15
Now everyone who l on milk is Heb 5:13
⌊Scripture⌋ testifies that he l. Heb 7:8
since He always l to intercede Heb 7:25
observe the outcome of their l, Heb 13:7
observe your pure, reverent l. 1Pt 3:2
lay down our l for our brothers 1Jn 3:16
killed among you, where Satan l. Rv 2:13
the One who l forever and ever, Rv 4:9
the One who l forever and ever, Rv 4:10
by the One who l forever and Rv 10:6
did not love their l in the face Rv 12:11
of God who l forever and ever Rv 15:7

LIVESTOCK *(94)*

l, creatures that crawl, and the Gn 1:24
the l according to their kinds, Gn 1:25
The man gave names to all the l, Gn 2:20
more than any l and more than Gn 3:14
from the l according to their Gn 6:20
all l according to their kinds, Gn 7:14
the earth, birds, l, wildlife, Gn 7:21
from mankind to l, to creatures Gn 7:23
and all the l that were with him Gn 8:1
you—birds, l, creatures that Gn 8:17
All wildlife, all l, every bird, Gn 8:19
you—birds, l, and all wildlife Gn 9:10
was very rich in l, silver, and Gn 13:2
of Abram's l and the herdsmen Gn 13:7
and the herdsmen of Lot's l. Gn 13:7
took all the l and possessions Gn 31:18
suited to the l and the children Gn 33:14
and all their l become ours? Gn 34:23
herds, all his l, and all the Gn 36:6
indeed they raise l. Gn 46:32
have raised l from our youth Gn 46:34
put them in charge of my l." Gn 47:6
Joseph said, "Give me your l. Gn 47:16
food in exchange for your l." Gn 47:16
they brought their l to Joseph, Gn 47:17
in exchange for all their l. Gn 47:17
that all our l belongs to our Gn 47:18
against your l in the field— Ex 9:3
between the l of Israel Ex 9:4
of Israel and the l of Egypt, Ex 9:4
the Egyptian l died, but none Ex 9:6
none among the Israelite l died. Ex 9:6
one of the Israelite l was dead. Ex 9:7
to bring your l and all that you Ex 9:19
servants and l flee to shelters Ex 9:20
servants and l in the field. Ex 9:21

Even our l must go with us; Ex 10:26
as every firstborn of the l. Ex 11:5
and every firstborn of the l. Ex 12:29
along with a huge number of l, Ex 12:38
of the l you own that are Ex 13:12
of man to the firstborn of l. Ex 13:15
children, and our l with thirst?" Ex 17:3
slave, your l, or the foreigner Ex 20:10
including all your male l, Ex 34:19
offering to the LORD from the l, Lv 1:2
or unclean l, or an unclean Lv 5:2
two different kinds of your l, Lv 19:19
as food for your l and the wild Lv 25:7
ravage your l, and reduce your Lv 26:22
consecrate a firstborn of the l, Lv 27:26
If it is one of the unclean l, Lv 27:27
All the l for the burnt offering Nm 7:87
All the l for the fellowship Nm 7:88
for us and our l to die here? Nm 20:4
for the community and their l." Nm 20:8
the community and their l drank. Nm 20:11
goats, all the l, and give them Nm 31:30
the people and the l from the Nm 31:47
had a very large number of l. Nm 32:1
region was a ⌊good⌋ one for l. Nm 32:1
good⌋ land for l, and your Nm 32:4
and your servants own l." Nm 32:4
here for our l and cities for Nm 32:16
children, wives, l, and all our Nm 32:26
We took only the l and the spoil Dt 2:35
we took all the l and the spoil Dt 3:7
children, and l—I know that Dt 3:19
know that you have a lot of l— Dt 3:19
any of your l, or the foreigner Dt 5:14
or female among you or your l. Dt 7:14
grass in your fields for your l. Dt 11:15
as well as its l with the sword. Dt 13:15
and the offspring of your l, Dt 28:4
of your l, and your soil's Dt 28:11
of your l and your soil's Dt 28:51
of your l, and your soil's Dt 30:9
and l may remain in the land Jos 1:14
its spoil and l for yourselves. Jos 8:2
for their cattle and l. Jos 14:4
their pasturelands for our l." Jos 21:2
small children, l, and Jdg 18:21
their l away, and inflicted 1Sm 23:5
driven ahead of the other l, 1Sm 30:20
They captured the Hagrites' l— 1Ch 5:21
gold, goods, and l, along with a Ezr 1:4
gold, goods, l, and valuables, Ezr 1:6
bodies and our l as they please. Neh 9:37
firstborn of our sons and our l, Neh 10:36
over their l to hail and their Ps 78:48
to grow for the l and ⌊provides⌋ Ps 104:14
does not let their l decrease. Ps 107:38
number of people and l in it." Zch 2:4
himself, as did his sons and l." Jn 4:12

LIVING *(254)*

water swarm with l creatures, Gn 1:20
and every l creature that moves Gn 1:21
the earth produce l creatures Gn 1:24
and the man became a l being. Gn 2:7
the man called a l creature, Gn 2:19
she was the mother of all the l. Gn 3:20
ark two of every l thing of all Gn 6:19
the earth every l thing I have Gn 7:4
wiped out every l thing that was Gn 7:23
Bring out every l thing of all Gn 8:17
down every l thing as I have Gn 8:21
you will be in every l creature Gn 9:2
Every l creature will be food Gn 9:3
and with every l creature that Gn 9:10
you and every l creature with Gn 9:12
you and every l creature of all Gn 9:15
God and every l creature of all Gn 9:16
Perizzites were l in the land. Gn 13:7
for he was l in Sodom, and they Gn 14:12
A Well of the L One Who Sees Me. Gn 16:14
he was l in the Negev region. Gn 24:62
Israel was l in that region, Gn 35:22
father, and one is no longer l." Gn 42:13
One is no longer l, and the Gn 42:32
Is my father still l?" Gn 45:3
and see if they are still l." Ex 4:18
Goshen, where My people are l; Ex 8:22
things and ⌊other⌋ l creatures Lv 11:10
all l creatures that move in the Lv 11:46
or foreigner l among them, Lv 17:13
or foreigner l in Israel who Lv 20:2
their families l among you— Lv 25:45
resident ⌊l⌋ among you prospers Lv 25:47
your brother ⌊l⌋ near him Lv 25:47
to the foreigner l among you, Lv 25:47
the descendants of Anak, were l. Nm 13:22
the people l in the land are Nm 13:28
The Amalekites are l in the land Nm 13:29
are l in the lowlands, Nm 14:25
between the dead and the l, Nm 16:48
The firstborn of every l thing, Nm 18:15
the land and are l right across Nm 22:5
There is a people l alone; Nm 23:9
the voice of the l God speaking Dt 5:26
and every l thing with them. Dt 11:6
must not let any l thing survive Dt 20:16
and foreigners l within your Dt 31:12
know that the l God is among you Jos 3:10
killing everyone l in Ai who had Jos 8:24
their neighbors, l among them. Jos 9:16
Israel and were ⌊l⌋ among them. Jos 10:1
the Amorite kings l in the hill Jos 10:6
destroyed every l being, Jos 10:40
in whose land you are l. Jos 24:15
who were l in the hill country Jdg 1:9
Canaanites who were l in Hebron Jdg 1:10
who were l in Zephath, Jdg 1:17
people who were l in the valley Jdg 1:19
who were l in Jerusalem. Jdg 1:21
Canaanites who were l in Gezer, Jdg 1:29
who were l in the land, Jdg 1:32
who were l in the land, Jdg 1:33
people who are l in this land, Jdg 2:2
who were there were l securely, Jdg 18:7
a Levite l in a remote part of Jdg 19:1
the place where she had been l, Ru 1:7
kindness to the l or the dead." Ru 2:20
defy the armies of the l God?" 1Sm 17:26
defied the armies of the l God." 1Sm 17:36
time we were l among them. 1Sm 25:15
LORD your God protects the l. 1Sm 25:29
David was l in the wilderness 1Sm 26:3
am l in a cedar house while the 2Sm 7:2
All those l in Ziba's house were 2Sm 9:12
day of their death, l as widows. 2Sm 20:3
My son is the l one; 1Kg 3:22
my son is the l one." 1Kg 3:22
Cut the l boy in two and give 1Kg 3:25
give her the l baby," she said, 1Kg 3:26
Give the l baby to the first 1Kg 3:27
the Israelites l in the cities 1Kg 12:17
old prophet was l in Bethel. 1Kg 13:11
"I am l among my own people." 2Kg 4:13
Assyria sent to mock the l God, 2Kg 19:4
has sent to mock the l God. 2Kg 19:16
the families l in Geba and who 1Ch 8:6
am l in a cedar house while the 1Ch 17:1
the Israelites l in the cities 2Ch 10:17
and those who were l in Judah, 2Ch 30:25
of their colleagues l in Samaria Ezr 4:17
temple servants l on Ophel ⌊made Neh 3:26
The Tyrians l there were Neh 13:16
kingdom, yet l in isolation. Est 3:8
life of every l thing is in His Jb 12:10
But I know my l Redeemer, and He Jb 19:25
be found in the land of the l. Jb 28:13
the eyes of every l thing and Jb 28:21
They are l on the slopes of the Jb 30:6
every l thing would perish Jb 34:15
goodness in the land of the l. Ps 27:13
I thirst for God, the l God. Ps 42:2
you from the land of the l. Ps 52:5
and flesh cry out for the l God. Ps 84:2
l things both large and small. Ps 104:25
the LORD in the land of the l. Ps 116:9
portion in the land of the l." Ps 142:5
the desire of every l thing. Ps 145:16
every l thing praise His holy Ps 145:21
more than the l, who are still Ec 4:2
I saw all the l who move about Ec 4:15
and the l should take it to Ec 7:2
is joined with all the l, Ec 9:4
For the l know that they will Ec 9:5
the dead on behalf of the l? Is 8:19
on those l in the land of Is 9:2
sent to mock the l God, and will Is 37:4
has sent to mock the l God. Is 37:17
the LORD in the land of the l; Is 38:11
The l, only the living can thank Is 38:19
only the l can thank You, Is 38:19
cut off from the land of the l; Is 53:8
one of the priests l in Anathoth Jr 1:1
the fountain of l water, and dug Jr 2:13
is the l God and eternal King. Jr 10:10
the land of the l so that his Jr 11:19
the fountain of l water, Jr 17:13
pervert the words of the l God, Jr 23:36
land and those l in the land Jr 24:8
listen to Me by l according to Jr 26:4
all the people l in this city— Jr 29:16
his ⌊descendants⌋ l among these Jr 29:32
So we have been l in Jerusalem." Jr 35:11
for all the Jews l in the land Jr 44:1
will punish those l in the land Jr 44:13
people who were l in the land Jr 44:15
disaster on every l creature'— Jr 45:5
at ease, one l in security. Jr 49:31
one will be l in it—both man Jr 50:3
and against those l in Pekod. Jr 50:21
should ⌊any⌋ l person complain Lm 3:39
form of four l creatures came Ezk 1:5
The form of the l creatures was Ezk 1:13
forth between the l creatures; Ezk 1:13
I looked at the l creatures, Ezk 1:15
So when the l creatures moved, Ezk 1:19
spirit of the l creatures was Ezk 1:20
spirit of the l creatures was Ezk 1:21
the heads of the l creatures. Ezk 1:22
sound of the l creatures' wings Ezk 3:13
who were l by the Chebar Canal, Ezk 3:15
these were the l creatures I had Ezk 10:15
spirit of the l creatures was Ezk 10:17
These were the l creatures I had Ezk 10:20
you are l among a rebellious Ezk 12:2
house of Israel who are l there. Ezk 12:10
the nations they were l among, Ezk 20:9
splendor in the land of the l. Ezk 26:20
terror in the land of the l. Ezk 32:23
terror in the land of the l. Ezk 32:24
spread in the land of the l. Ezk 32:25
spread in the land of the l. Ezk 32:26
was ⌊once⌋ in the land of the l. Ezk 32:27
My terror in the land of the l, Ezk 32:32
people who are l securely, Ezk 38:11
all of them l without walls and Ezk 38:11
Every ⌊kind of⌋ l creature that Ezk 47:9
for the foreigners l among you, Ezk 47:22
have more wisdom than anyone l, Dn 2:30
This is so the l will know that Dn 4:17
servant of the l God," the king Dn 6:20
For He is the l God, and He Dn 6:26
be called: Sons of the l God. Hs 1:10
Earn your l and give ⌊your⌋ Am 7:12
who are l with Daughter Babylon. Zch 2:7
that day l water will flow out Zch 14:8
for those l in the shadowland Mt 4:16
Messiah, the Son of the l God!" Mt 16:16
God of the dead, but of the l." Mt 22:32
By the l God I place You under Mt 26:63
God of the dead but of the l. Mk 12:27
l without blame according to all Lk 1:6
his estate in foolish l. Lk 15:13
God of the dead but of the l, Lk 20:38
because all are l to Him." Lk 20:38
for the l among the dead? Lk 24:5
and He would give you l water." Jn 4:10
where do you get this 'l water'? Jn 4:11
don't have His word l in you, Jn 5:38
I am the l bread that came down Jn 6:51
Just as the l Father sent Me and Jn 6:57
streams of l water flow from Jn 7:38
There were Jews l in Jerusalem, Ac 2:5
He received l oracles to give to Ac 7:38
the Judge of the l and the dead. Ac 10:42
worthless things to the l God, Ac 14:15
man while her husband is l, Rm 7:3
doing it, but it is sin l in me. Rm 7:17
be called sons of the l God. Rm 9:26
your bodies as a l sacrifice, Rm 12:1
over both the dead and the l. Rm 14:9
not fleshly and l like ordinary 1Co 3:3
a man is l with his father's 1Co 5:1
as long as her husband is l. 1Co 7:39
earn their l by the gospel. 1Co 9:14
first man Adam became a l being; 1Co 15:45

with the Spirit of the l God; 2Co 3:3
are the sanctuary of the l God, 2Co 6:16
l is Christ and dying is gain. Php 1:21
things when you were l in them. Col 3:7
to serve the l and true God, 1Th 1:9
is the church of the l God, 1Tm 3:15
have put our hope in the l God, 1Tm 4:10
to judge the l and the dead, 2Tm 4:1
and pleasures, l in malice and Ti 3:3
that departs from the l God. Heb 3:12
word of God is l and effective Heb 4:12
dead works to serve the l God? Heb 9:14
force while the testator is l. Heb 9:17
by the new and l way that He has Heb 10:20
into the hands of the l God! Heb 10:31
l in tents with Isaac and Jacob, Heb 11:9
the city of the l God (the Heb 12:22
new birth into a l hope through 1Pt 1:3
through the l and enduring word 1Pt 1:23
to Him, a l stone—rejected 1Pt 2:4
yourselves, as l stones, are 1Pt 2:5
to judge the l and the dead. 1Pt 4:5
and the L One. I was dead, but Rv 1:18
throne were four l creatures Rv 4:6
The first l creature was like a Rv 4:7
the second l creature was like a Rv 4:7
the third l creature had a face Rv 4:7
and the fourth l creature was Rv 4:7
Each of the four l creatures had Rv 4:8
Whenever the four l creatures give Rv 4:9
and the four l creatures and Rv 5:6
the four l creatures and the 24 Rv 5:8
and also of the l creatures, Rv 5:11
The four l creatures said, Rv 5:14
one of the four l creatures say Rv 6:1
heard the second l creature say, Rv 6:3
heard the third l creature say, Rv 6:5
among the four l creatures say, Rv 6:6
of the fourth l creature say, Rv 6:7
who had the seal of the l God. Rv 7:2
and the four l creatures, and Rv 7:11
them to springs of l waters, Rv 7:17
third of the l creatures in the Rv 8:9
and before the four l creatures Rv 14:3
One of the four l creatures gave Rv 15:7
and the four l creatures fell Rv 19:4
the spring of l water as a gift. Rv 21:6
showed me the river of l water, Rv 22:1
take the l water as a gift Rv 22:17

LIZARD *(4)*
the various kinds of large l, Lv 11:29
the monitor l, the common lizard Lv 11:30
lizard, the common l, the skink, Lv 11:30
a l can be caught in your hands, Pr 30:28

LO-DEBAR *(4)*
(AKA DEBIR)
You'll find him in L at the 2Sm 9:4
of Machir son of Ammiel in L. 2Sm 9:5
Machir son of Ammiel from L, 2Sm 17:27
you who rejoice over L and say, Am 6:13

LOAD *(11)*
L your animals and go on back to Gn 45:17
shoulder to bear a l and became Gn 49:15
way you will lighten your l, Ex 18:22
lying ⌊helpless⌋ under its l, Ex 23:5
the l on it will be destroyed. Is 22:25
do not pick up a l and bring it Jr 17:21
must not carry a l out of your Jr 17:22
not carrying a l while entering Jr 17:27
into the sea to lighten the l. Jnh 1:5
You l people with burdens that Lk 11:46
will have to carry his own l. Gl 6:5

LOADED *(9)*
l the grain on their donkeys Gn 42:26
and each one l his donkey and Gn 44:13
took a donkey l with bread, 1Sm 16:20
to keep it, l up, and set out as 1Sm 17:20
figs, and l them on donkeys. 1Sm 25:18
saddled donkeys l with 200 2Sm 16:1
The ⌊images⌋ you carry are l, Is 46:1
full and heavily l in the heart Ezk 27:25
all those l with silver will be Zph 1:11

LOADING *(1)*
of grain and l ⌊them⌋ on donkeys Neh 13:15

LOADS *(5)*
carried the l worked with one Neh 4:17
and do not bring l through the Jr 17:24
boys stumble under ⌊l of⌋ wood. Lm 5:13
and l himself with goods taken Hab 2:6
tie up heavy l that are hard to Mt 23:4

LOAF *(14)*
take one l of bread, one cake of Ex 29:23
each l is to be made with four Lv 24:5
are to offer a l from your first Nm 15:20
l of barley bread came tumbling Jdg 7:13
l turned the tent upside down Jdg 7:13
piece of silver or a l of bread. 1Sm 2:36
he distributed a l of bread, 2Sm 6:19
make me a small l from it and 1Kg 17:13
his head was a l of bread baked 1Kg 19:6
and women, a l of bread, a date 1Ch 16:3
will bring ⌊a l⌋ from our first Neh 10:37
fee is only a l of bread, Pr 6:26
He was given a l of bread each Jr 37:21
and had only one l with them in Mk 8:14

LOAN *(7)*
him and freely l him enough for Dt 15:8
When you make a l of any kind to Dt 24:10
you are making the l to brings Dt 24:11
to the poor is a l to the LORD, Pr 19:17
interest or profit ⌊on a l⌋. Ezk 18:17
and profit ⌊on a l⌋ and brutally Ezk 22:12
him, and forgave him the l. Mt 18:27

LOANS *(1)*
who put up security for l. Pr 22:26

LOATHE *(5)*
and do not l His discipline; Pr 3:11
They will l themselves because Ezk 6:9
you will l yourselves for all Ezk 20:43
and you will l yourselves for Ezk 36:31
I l Jacob's pride and hate his Am 6:8

LOATHED *(2)*
over Aram, but he l Israel. 1Kg 11:25
They l all food and came near Ps 107:18

LOAVES *(39)*
out of Egypt into unleavened l, Ex 12:39
Bring two l of bread from your Lv 23:17
flour and bake it into 12 l; Lv 24:5
Please give some l of bread to Jdg 8:5
one bringing three l of bread, 1Sm 10:3
and give you two ⌊l of⌋ bread, 1Sm 10:4
along with these l of bread for 1Sm 17:17
Give me five l of bread or 1Sm 21:3
taking 200 l of bread, two skins 1Sm 25:18
loaded with 200 l of bread, 2Sm 16:1
Take with you 10 l of bread, 1Kg 14:3
full of 20 l of barley bread 2Kg 4:42
I to set 20 l before 100 men?" 2Kg 4:43
only have five l and two fish Mt 14:17
took the five l and the two fish Mt 14:19
He broke the l and gave them to Mt 14:19
"How many l do you have?" Mt 15:34
took the seven l and the fish, Mt 15:36
remember the five l for the Mt 16:9
Or the seven l for the 4,000 and Mt 16:10
them, "How many l do you have? Mk 6:38
took the five l and the two fish Mk 6:41
He blessed and broke the l. Mk 6:41
who ate the l were 5,000 men. Mk 6:44
had not understood about the l. Mk 6:52
"How many l do you have?" Mk 8:5
the seven l, He gave thanks Mk 8:6
thanks, broke the ⌊l⌋, and kept Mk 8:6
served the ⌊l⌋ to the crowd. Mk 8:6
broke the five l for the 5,000, Mk 8:19
broke the seven l for the 4,000, Mk 8:20
more than five l and two fish," Lk 9:13
took the five l and the two fish Lk 9:16
lend me three l of bread, Lk 11:5
has five barley l and two fish— Jn 6:9
Jesus took the l, and after Jn 6:11
the five barley l that were left Jn 6:13
you ate the l and were filled. Jn 6:26
table, and the presentation l. Heb 9:2

LOBE *(13)*
the fatty l of the liver, Ex 29:13
the fatty l of the liver, Ex 29:22
remove the fatty l of the liver Lv 3:4
and the fatty l of the liver Lv 3:10
remove the fatty l of the liver Lv 3:15
remove the fatty l of the liver Lv 4:9
remove the fatty l of the liver Lv 7:4
the fatty l of the liver, Lv 8:16
the fatty l of the liver, Lv 8:25
the fatty l of the liver from Lv 9:10
and the fatty l of the liver— Lv 9:19
put ⌊it⌋ on the l of the right Lv 14:14
put some on the l of the right Lv 14:17

LOCAL *(5)*
and ⌊the l women⌋ exclaimed Ru 1:19
In the l church at Antioch there Ac 13:1
both we and the l people begged Ac 21:12
The l people showed us Ac 28:2
When the l people saw the Ac 28:4

LOCALITIES *(1)*
to their families and their l, Gn 36:40

LOCATED *(6)*
It is l between Kadesh and Gn 16:14
LORD where the ark of God was l. 1Sm 3:3
and where is understanding l? Jb 28:12
and where is understanding l? Jb 28:20
that provokes jealousy was l. Ezk 8:3
who is l at the entrance of the Ezk 27:3

LOCATION *(3)*
He came to the l of the arrow 1Sm 20:37
see that the city's l is good, 2Kg 2:19
to wisdom, and He knows its l. Jb 28:23

LOCATIONS *(1)*
judge Israel at all these l. 1Sm 7:16

LOCK *(2)*
by day they l themselves in, Jb 24:16
You l up the kingdom of heaven Mt 23:13

LOCKED *(10)*
upstairs room l and thought he Jdg 3:24
They l themselves in and went up Jdg 9:51
you are⌋ a l garden—a locked Sg 4:12
a l garden and a sealed spring. Sg 4:12
else—he l John up in prison. Lk 3:20
door is already l, and my Lk 11:7
the doors l because of their Jn 20:19
Even though the doors were l, Jn 20:26
We found the jail securely l, Ac 5:23
and I l up many of the saints in Ac 26:10

LOCKING *(1)*
closing and l the doors of the Jdg 3:23

LOCUST *(23)*
Not a single l was left in all Ex 10:19
various kinds of l, the various Lv 11:22
mildew, l, or grasshopper 1Kg 8:37
mildew, l, or grasshopper 2Ch 6:28
Do you make him leap like a l? Jb 39:20
fruit of their labor to the l. Ps 78:46
I am shaken off like a l. Ps 109:23
What the devouring l has left, Jl 1:4
left, the swarming l has eaten; Jl 1:4
what the swarming l has left, Jl 1:4
has left, the young l has eaten; Jl 1:4
and what the young l has left, Jl 1:4
the destroying l has eaten. Jl 1:4
years that the swarming l ate, Jl 2:25
ate, the young l, the destroying Jl 2:25
the destroying l, and the Jl 2:25
the devouring l—My great army Jl 2:25
the l devoured your many gardens Am 4:9
devour you like the young l. Nah 3:15
yourselves like the young l, Nah 3:15
multiply like the swarming l! Nah 3:15
young l strips ⌊the land⌋ and Nah 3:16
are like the swarming l, Nah 3:17

LOCUSTS *(24)*
I will bring l into your Ex 10:4
of Egypt and the l will come up Ex 10:12
east wind had brought in the l. Ex 10:13
The l went up over the entire Ex 10:14
been such a large number of l, Ex 10:14
carried off the l and blew them Ex 10:19
because l will devour it. Dt 28:38
tents like a great swarm of l. Jdg 6:5
in the valley like a swarm of l, Jdg 7:12
He spoke and l came—young Ps 105:34
came—young l without number. Ps 105:34
l have no king, yet all of them Pr 30:27
be gathered as l are gathered; Is 33:4
it like an infestation of l. Is 33:4
they are more numerous than l; Jr 46:23
fill you up with men as with l, Jr 51:14
up horses like a swarm of l. Jr 51:27
forming a swarm of l at the time Am 7:1
When the l finished eating the Am 7:2

your scribes like clouds of l, Nah 3:17
his food was l and wild honey. Mt 3:4
waist and ate l and wild honey. Mk 1:6
out of the smoke l came to the Rv 9:3
of the l was like horses Rv 9:7

LOD (2)
(AKA LYDDA)
built Ono and L and its villages 1Ch 8:12
L, and Ono, the valley of the Neh 11:35

LOD'S (2)
L, Hadid's, and Ono's people 725 Ezr 2:33
L, Hadid's, and Ono's people 721 Neh 7:37

LODGE (2)
evil cannot l with You. Ps 5:4
gone to l with a sinful man! Lk 19:7

LODGED (2)
where they l for the night, Gn 42:27
place where we l for the night Gn 43:21

LODGING (7)
had a traveler's l place in the Jr 9:2
countryside to find food and l, Lk 9:12
He is l with Simon, a tanner, Ac 10:6
also named Peter, was l there. Ac 10:18
invited them in and gave them l. Ac 10:23
He is l in Simon the tanner's Ac 10:32
many came to him at his l. Ac 28:23

LOFTINESS (2)
and the l of men will be brought Is 2:11
the l of men will be humbled; Is 2:17

LOFTY (15)
highest stars—how l they are! Jb 22:12
Your l judgments are beyond his Ps 10:5
Sheol, far from their l abode. Ps 49:14
me. It is l; I am unable to Ps 139:6
against all that is proud and l, Is 2:12
of Lebanon, l and lifted up, Is 2:13
against all the l hills, Is 2:14
seated on a high and l throne, Is 6:1
those who live in l places— Is 26:5
bed on a high and l mountain; Is 57:7
and see from Your l home— Is 63:15
sprig⌋ from the l top of the Ezk 17:22
shady foliage, and of l height. Ezk 31:3
will be on Israel's l mountains. Ezk 34:14
still in ⌊their⌋ l residence, Hab 3:11

LOG (7)
can each get a l and can build 2Kg 6:2
notice the l in your own eye Mt 7:3
look, there's a l in your eye? Mt 7:4
take the l out of your eye, Mt 7:5
notice the l in your own eye Lk 6:41
don't see the l in your eye? Lk 6:42
take the l out of your eye, Lk 6:42

LOGS (10)
also sent⌋ cedar l, carpenters, 2Sm 5:11
will bring ⌊the l⌋ down from 1Kg 5:9
and cypress l and gold for his 1Kg 9:11
along with cedar l, stonemasons, 1Ch 14:1
and innumerable cedar l, because 1Ch 22:4
quantity of cedar l to David. 1Ch 22:4
and algum l from Lebanon, for 2Ch 2:8
to prepare l for me in abundance 2Ch 2:9
We will cut l from Lebanon, 2Ch 2:16
Pile on the l and kindle the Ezk 24:10

LOINCLOTHS (1)
and made l for themselves. Gn 3:7

LOINS (13)
with the fat on them at the l; Lv 3:4
with the fat on them at the l, Lv 3:10
with the fat on them at the l, Lv 3:15
with the fat on them at the l. Lv 4:9
with the fat on them at the l; Lv 7:4
Smash the l of his adversaries Dt 33:11
is thicker than my father's l! 1Kg 12:10
is thicker than my father's l. 2Ch 10:10
strength of his l and the power Jb 40:16
For my l are full of burning Ps 38:7
and let their l continually Ps 69:23
to unloose the l of kings, Is 45:1
knees tremble, l shake, every Nah 2:10

LOIS (1)
lived in your grandmother L, 2Tm 1:5

LONE (1)
Seeing a l fig tree by the road, Mt 21:19

LONG (346)
The ark will be 450 feet l, Gn 6:15
As l as the earth endures, Gn 8:22
support them as l as they stayed Gn 13:6
because you l for your father Gn 31:30
After a l time Judah's wife, Gn 38:12
him, and wept for a l time. Gn 46:29
for embalming takes that l, Gn 50:3
a l time, the king of Egypt Ex 2:23
How l will you refuse to humble Ex 10:3
How l must this man be a snare Ex 10:7
came near the other all night l. Ex 14:20
How l will you refuse to keep My Ex 16:28
the ram's horn sounds a l blast, Ex 19:13
may have a l life in the land Ex 20:12
45 inches l, 27 inches wide Ex 25:10
45 inches l and 27 inches wide. Ex 25:17
36 inches l, 18 inches wide Ex 25:23
and a half feet l, and seven and Ex 27:1
linen, 150 feet l on that side. Ex 27:9
on the north side 150 ⌊feet⌋ l. Ex 27:11
on the west side 75 feet l, Ex 27:12
nine inches l and nine inches Ex 28:16
18 inches l and 18 inches wide; Ex 30:2
45 inches l, 27 inches wide Ex 37:1
45 inches l and 27 inches wide. Ex 37:6
36 inches l, 18 inches wide Ex 37:10
18 inches l and 18 inches wide; Ex 37:25
and a half feet l and seven and Ex 38:1
It was 30 feet l, and like the Ex 38:18
nine inches l and nine inches Ex 39:9
remain unclean as l as he has Lv 13:46
l as it lies desolate, it will Lv 26:35
let the hair of his head grow l. Nm 6:5
l as the cloud stayed over the Nm 9:18
not set out as l as the cloud Nm 9:22
both are sounded in l blasts, Nm 10:3
you are to sound l blasts, Nm 10:7
How l will these people despise Nm 14:11
How l will they not trust in Me Nm 14:11
How l ⌊must I endure⌋ this evil Nm 14:27
at this mountain l enough. Dt 1:6
in Kadesh as l as you did. Dt 1:46
this hill country l enough; Dt 2:3
feet six inches l and six feet Dt 3:11
from your mind as l as you live. Dt 4:9
have been in the land a l time, Dt 4:25
You will not live l there, Dt 4:26
that you may live l in the land Dt 4:40
you may live l and so that you Dt 5:16
have a l life in the land you Dt 5:33
so that you may have a l life. Dt 6:2
that you may live l in the land Dt 11:9
so that as l as the heavens are Dt 11:21
as l as you live in your land. Dt 12:19
siege to a city for a l time, Dt 20:19
that you may prosper and live l. Dt 22:7
divorce her as l as he lives. Dt 22:19
divorce her as l as he lives. Dt 22:29
with them as l as you live. Dt 23:6
that you may live l in the land Dt 25:15
will not live l in the land you Dt 30:18
LORD your God as l as you live Dt 31:13
consider the years l past. Dt 32:7
you will live l in the land you Dt 32:47
him all day l, and he rests Dt 33:12
strength last as l as you live. Dt 33:25
against you as l as you live. Jos 1:5
from the extremely l journey." Jos 9:13
all these kings for a l time. Jos 11:18
How l will you delay going out Jos 18:3
l time after the LORD had given Jos 23:1
'L ago your ancestors, including Jos 24:2
in the wilderness a l time. Jos 24:7
double-edged sword 18 inches l. Jdg 3:16
is his chariot so l in coming? Jdg 5:28
it was there⌋ as l as the house Jdg 18:31
How l are you going to be drunk? 1Sm 1:14
as l as he lives, he is given 1Sm 1:28
shouted, "L live the king!" 1Sm 10:24
How l are you going to mourn for 1Sm 16:1
'L life to you, and peace to you, 1Sm 25:6
How l before you tell the troops 2Sm 2:26
of David was l and drawn out, 2Sm 3:1
for the dead for a l time. 2Sm 14:2
to Absalom, "L live the king! 2Sm 16:16
live the king! L live the king!" 2Sm 16:16
they're saying, 'L live King 1Kg 1:25
horn and say, 'L live King 1Kg 1:34
"L live King Solomon! 1Kg 1:39
lived in Jerusalem for a l time. 1Kg 2:38
did not ask for l life or riches 1Kg 3:11
I will give you a l life." 1Kg 3:14
for the LORD was 90 feet l, 1Kg 6:2
was 30 feet l extending across 1Kg 6:3
most holy place, was 60 feet l. 1Kg 6:17
of the sanctuary was 30 feet l, 1Kg 6:20
was seven and a half feet l, 1Kg 6:24
was seven and a half feet l. 1Kg 6:24
It was 150 feet l, 75 feet wide, 1Kg 7:2
pillars 75 feet l and 45 feet 1Kg 7:6
costly stones 12 and 15 feet l. 1Kg 7:10
Each water cart was six feet l, 1Kg 7:27
poles were so l that their ends 1Kg 8:8
After a l time, the word of the 1Kg 18:1
How l will you hesitate between 1Kg 18:21
can there be as l as there is so 2Kg 9:22
and cried, "L live the king!" 2Kg 11:12
designed it l ago; I planned it 2Kg 19:25
father Ephraim mourned a l time, 1Ch 7:22
have not even requested l life, 2Ch 1:11
made a bronze altar 30 feet l, 2Ch 4:1
poles were so l that their ends 2Ch 5:9
seven and a half feet l, 2Ch 6:13
and cried, "L live the king!" 2Ch 23:11
How l will your journey take, Neh 2:6
For l ago, in the days of David Neh 12:46
l will you go on saying these Jb 8:2
understanding comes with l life. Jb 12:12
You would l for the work of Your Jb 14:15
How l until you stop talking? Jb 18:2
How l will you torment me and Jb 19:2
as l as my breath is still in me Jb 27:3
not accuse ⌊me⌋ as l as I live! Jb 27:6
Do not l for the night when Jb 36:20
born; you have lived so l! Jb 38:21
l, exalted men, will my honor Ps 4:2
⌊How l⌋ will you love what is Ps 4:2
terror. And You, LORD—how l? Ps 6:3
l will You continually forget Ps 13:1
How l will You hide Your face Ps 13:1
How l will I store up anxious Ps 13:2
How l will my enemy dominate me? Ps 13:2
of the LORD as l as I live. Ps 23:6
I wait for You all day l. Ps 25:5
from my groaning all day l. Ps 32:3
loving a l life to enjoy what is Ps 34:12
Lord, how l will You look on? Ps 35:17
Your praise all day l. Ps 35:28
all day l I go around in Ps 38:6
they plot treachery all day l. Ps 38:12
with a muzzle as l as the wicked Ps 39:1
of water, so I l for You, God. Ps 42:1
all day l people say to me, Ps 42:3
while all day l they say to me, Ps 42:10
in their days, in days l ago: Ps 44:1
We boast in God all day l; Ps 44:8
disgrace is before me all day l, Ps 44:15
of You we are slain all day l; Ps 44:22
the One enthroned from l ago, Ps 55:19
and oppresses me all day l. Ps 56:1
They twist my words all day l; Ps 56:5
How l will you threaten a man? Ps 62:3
will praise You as l as I live; Ps 63:4
and honor to You all day l. Ps 71:8
and Your salvation all day l, Ps 71:15
Your righteousness all day l, Ps 71:24
endures, and as l as the moon, Ps 72:5
May he live l! May gold from Ps 72:15
and may he be blessed all day l. Ps 72:15
as l as the sun shines, may his Ps 72:17
For I am afflicted all day l, Ps 73:14
You purchased l ago and redeemed Ps 74:2
us knows how l this will last. Ps 74:9
God, how l will the foe mock? Ps 74:10
bring against You all day l. Ps 74:22
were lifted up all night l; Ps 77:2
days of old, years l past. Ps 77:5
How l, LORD? Will You be angry Ps 79:5
l will You be angry with Your Ps 80:4
How l will you judge unjustly Ps 82:2
I l and yearn for the courts of Ps 84:2
for I call to You all day l. Ps 86:3
I cry out to You all day l; Ps 88:9
me like water all day l; Ps 88:17
rejoice in Your name all day l, Ps 89:16

his throne as l as heaven lasts. Ps 89:29
How l, LORD? Will You hide Ps 89:46
LORD—how l? Turn and have Ps 90:13
him with a l life and show him Ps 91:16
LORD, how l will the wicked— Ps 94:3
how l will the wicked gloat? Ps 94:3
My enemies taunt me all day l; Ps 102:8
L ago You established the earth, Ps 102:25
⌊out to Him⌋ as l as I live. Ps 116:2
How I l for Your precepts! Ps 119:40
judgments from l ago and find Ps 119:52
I l for Your salvation; Ps 119:81
It is my meditation all day l. Ps 119:97
mouth because I l for Your Ps 119:131
L ago I learned from Your Ps 119:152
I for Your salvation, LORD, and Ps 119:174
have lived too l with those who Ps 120:6
they made their furrows l. Ps 129:3
They stir up wars all day l. Ps 140:2
in darkness like those l dead. Ps 143:3
should go, because I l for You. Ps 143:8
sing to the LORD as l as I live. Ps 146:2
How l, foolish ones, will you Pr 1:22
⌊How l⌋ will ⌊you⌋ mockers enjoy Pr 1:22
L life is in her right hand; Pr 3:16
How l will you stay in bed, Pr 6:9
he went on a l journey. Pr 7:19
before His works of l ago. Pr 8:22
filled with craving all day l, Pr 21:26
No matter how l he lives, if he Ec 6:3
exists was given its name l ago, Ec 6:10
man who lives l in spite of his Ec 7:15
the One who created it l ago. Is 22:11
plans ⌊formed⌋ l ago, with Is 25:1
I l for You in the night; Is 26:9
for the king for a l time now. Is 30:33
designed it l ago; I planned it Is 37:26
told you and declared it l ago? Is 44:8
Who predicted this l ago? Is 45:21
Remember what happened l ago, Is 46:9
and from l ago what is not yet Is 46:10
declared the past events l ago; Is 48:3
I declared to you l ago; Is 48:5
been created now, and not l ago; Is 48:7
For a l time your ears have not Is 48:8
as in generations of l ago. Is 51:9
dread all day l because of the Is 51:13
blasphemed all day l. Is 52:5
for such a l time and you do Is 57:11
the foundations laid l ago; Is 58:12
hands all day l to a rebellious Is 65:2
a fire that burns all day l. Is 65:5
For l ago I broke your yoke; Jr 2:20
I l to make you ⌊My⌋ sons and Jr 3:19
How l will you harbor malicious Jr 4:14
How l must I see the signal flag Jr 4:21
the evening shadows grow l. Jr 6:4
l will the land mourn and the Jr 12:4
A l time later the LORD said to Jr 13:6
You are unclean—for how l yet? Jr 13:27
the land they l to return to." Jr 22:27
How l will this continue in the Jr 23:26
exile will be l. Build houses Jr 29:28
How l will you turn here and Jr 31:22
jar so they will last a l time. Jr 32:14
you may live a l time on the Jr 35:7
How l will you gash yourself? Jr 47:5
How l will you be restless? Jr 47:6
me desolate, sick all day l. Lm 1:13
His hand against me all day l. Lm 3:3
mocked by their songs all day l. Lm 3:14
opponents attack me all day l. Lm 3:62
what was sold as l as he and the Ezk 7:13
great wings, l pinions, and full Ezk 17:3
its boughs grew l as it spread Ezk 31:5
After a l time you will be Ezk 38:8
Israel, which had l been a ruin. Ezk 38:8
about 10 feet l and 10 feet deep Ezk 40:7
87 and a half feet l and 43 and Ezk 40:21
was 87 and a half feet l and 43 Ezk 40:25
was 87 and a half feet l and 43 Ezk 40:29
three-quarter feet l and eight Ezk 40:30
was 87 and a half feet l and 43 Ezk 40:33
was 87 and a half feet l and 43 Ezk 40:36
⌊each⌋ 31 and a half inches l, Ezk 40:42
175 feet l and 175 feet wide. Ezk 40:47
it was 175 feet l. In addition, Ezk 41:13
its walls, were 175 feet l. Ezk 41:13
and three and a half feet l. Ezk 41:22
a half feet wide and 175 feet l, Ezk 42:4
it was 87 and a half feet l. Ezk 42:7
court were 87 and a half feet l, Ezk 42:8
great hall were 175 feet ⌊l⌋. Ezk 42:8
⌊feet⌋ l and 875 ⌊feet⌋ wide, Ezk 42:20
21 feet l by 21 feet wide. Ezk 43:16
and a half feet l by 24 and a Ezk 43:17
heads or let their hair grow l, Ezk 44:20
and one-third ⌊miles⌋ l and six Ezk 45:1
one-third ⌊miles⌋ l and three Ezk 45:3
one-third ⌊miles⌋ l and three Ezk 45:5
eight and one-third ⌊miles⌋ l, Ezk 45:6
70 ⌊feet⌋ l by 52 and a half Ezk 46:22
and as l as one of the ⌊tribal⌋ Ezk 48:8
one-third ⌊miles⌋ l and three Ezk 48:9
miles l⌋ on the northern Ezk 48:10
miles⌋ l on the southern Ezk 48:10
one-third ⌊miles⌋ l and three Ezk 48:13
eight and one-third ⌊miles l⌋, Ezk 48:15
two horns were l, but one was Dn 8:3
How l will ⌊the events of⌋ this Dn 8:13
How l until the end of these Dn 12:6
How l will they be incapable of Hs 8:5
Woe to you who l for the Day of Am 5:18
to our fathers from days l ago. Mc 7:20
l, LORD, must I call for help Hab 1:2
"How l, LORD of Hosts, Zch 1:12
"30 feet l and 15 feet wide." Zch 5:2
Now a l way off from them, Mt 8:30
in sackcloth and ashes l ago! Mt 11:21
How l will I be with you? Mt 17:17
How l must I put up with you? Mt 17:17
houses and make l prayers just Mt 23:14
After a l time the master of Mt 25:19
As l as they have the groom with Mk 2:19
of them have come a l distance." Mk 8:3
How l will I be with you? Mk 9:19
How l must I put up with you? Mk 9:19
How l has this been happening to Mk 9:21
want to go around in l robes, Mk 12:38
houses and say l prayers just Mk 12:40
man dressed in a l white robe Mk 16:5
he stayed so l in the sanctuary Lk 1:21
hard all night l and caught Lk 5:5
For a l time he had worn no Lk 8:27
How l will I be with you and put Lk 9:41
they would have repented l ago, Lk 10:13
the son was still a l way off, Lk 15:20
up and saw Abraham a l way off, Lk 16:23
coming when you will l to see Lk 17:22
and went away for a l time. Lk 20:9
to go around in l robes and who Lk 20:46
houses and say l prayers just Lk 20:47
a l time he had wanted to see Lk 23:8
had already been there a l time, Jn 5:6
As l as I am in the world, Jn 9:5
How l are You going to keep us Jn 10:24
Not l ago Theudas rose up, Ac 5:36
with his sorceries for a l time. Ac 8:11
have been known from l ago. Ac 15:18
them with a l message. Ac 15:32
But not l afterwards, a fierce Ac 27:14
they waited a l time and saw Ac 28:6
He promised l ago through His Rm 1:2
over someone as l as he lives? Rm 7:1
All day l I have spread out My Rm 10:21
secret kept silent for l ages, Rm 16:25
is bound as l as her husband 1Co 7:39
that if a man has l hair it is a 1Co 11:14
but that if a woman has l hair, 1Co 11:15
I say that as l as the heir is Gl 4:1
you may have a l life in the Eph 6:3
I l to see you so that I may be 2Tm 1:4
L ago God spoke to the fathers Heb 1:1
David after such a l time, Heb 4:7
as l as I am in this tent, 2Pt 1:13
pronounced⌋ l ago, is not idle, 2Pt 2:3
l ago the heavens and the earth 2Pt 3:5
for this judgment l ago, Jd 4
dressed in a l robe, and with Rv 1:13
how l until You judge and avenge Rv 6:10
they will l to die, but death Rv 9:6

LONG-EARED *(2)*

owl, the cormorant, the l owl, Lv 11:17
little owl, the l owl, the white Dt 14:16

LONG-SLEEVED *(2)*

Tamar was wearing a l garment, 2Sm 13:18
and tore the l garment she was 2Sm 13:19

LONGED *(7)*

Then King David l to go to 2Sm 13:39
them to the harbor they l for. Ps 107:30
and I have not l for the fatal Jr 17:16
fathers, the god l for by women, Dn 11:37
righteous people l to see the Mt 13:17
He l to eat his fill from the Lk 15:16
He l to be filled with what fell Lk 16:21

LONGER *(230)*

Your name will no l be Abram, Gn 17:5
"Your name will no l be Jacob," Gn 32:28
you will no l be named Jacob, Gn 35:10
father, and one is no l living." Gn 42:13
One is no l living, and the Gn 42:32
Joseph could no l keep his Gn 45:1
you will no l excel, because you Gn 49:4
when she could no l hide him, Ex 2:3
you don't need to stay any l." Ex 9:28
and rain no l poured down on the Ex 9:33
They must no l offer their Lv 17:7
you would no l be their slaves. Lv 26:13
man, it is no l redeemable. Lv 27:20
in the work and no l serve. Nm 8:25
a month, or l, the Israelites Nm 9:22
voice of the LORD our God any l. Dt 5:25
and don't be stiff-necked any l. Dt 10:16
they will no l do anything evil Dt 13:11
and no l behave arrogantly. Dt 17:13
or see this great fire any l, Dt 18:16
I can no l act as your leader. Dt 31:2
our God is no l with us?' Dt 31:17
I will no l be with you unless Jos 7:12
they could no l resist their Jdg 2:14
will no l drive out before them Jdg 2:21
and they were no l a threat. Jdg 8:28
she ate and no l appeared 1Sm 1:18
the LORD now says, "No l!" 1Sm 2:30
to Gath, he no l searched for 1Sm 27:4
of Saul, no l anointed with oil 2Sm 1:21
they no l pursued Israel or 2Sm 2:28
but he took l than the time 2Sm 20:5
l will death or unfruitfulness 2Kg 2:21
servant will no l offer a burnt 2Kg 5:17
should I trust the LORD any l?" 2Kg 6:33
the Levites no l need to carry 1Ch 23:26
Jeroboam no l retained his power 2Ch 13:20
we will no l be a disgrace." Neh 2:17
looks on me will no l see me. Jb 7:8
hometown will no l remember him. Jb 7:10
of the wicked will exist no l. Jb 8:22
blameless, I no l care about Jb 9:21
terror will no l frighten me. Jb 9:34
measure is l than the earth Jb 11:9
He will no l be rich; Jb 15:29
his household will no l see him. Jb 20:9
dismayed and can no l answer; Jb 32:15
stand ⌊there⌋ and no l answer? Jb 32:16
I will no ⌊l⌋ act wickedly. Jb 34:31
Be patient with me a little l, Jb 36:2
There is no l a prophet. Ps 74:9
name will no l be remembered." Ps 83:4
whom You no l remember, and who Ps 88:5
and its place is no l known. Ps 103:16
king who no l pays attention to Ec 4:13
There is no l a reward for them Ec 9:5
and there is no l a portion for Ec 9:6
of Jacob will no l depend on the Is 10:20
Ephraim will no l be envious of Is 11:13
Look, Damascus is no l a city. Is 17:1
is no l anything to restrain Is 23:10
a people who no l exist. Is 23:13
They no l sing and drink wine; Is 24:9
of barbarians is no l a city; Is 25:2
it and will no l conceal her Is 26:21
Jacob will no l be ashamed and Is 29:22
and his face will no l be pale. Is 29:22
will not hide Himself any l. Is 30:20
A fool will no l be called a Is 32:5
will no l see the barbarians, Is 33:19
on humanity any l with the Is 38:11
For you will no l be called Is 47:1
For you will no l be called Is 47:5
the unclean will no l enter you. Is 52:1
and you will no l remember the Is 54:4
The sun will no l be your light Is 60:19

Your sun will no **l** set, and your Is 60:20
will no **l** be called Deserted, Is 62:4
I will no **l** give your grain to Is 62:8
will no **l** be heard in her. Is 65:19
infant will no **l** live only a few Is 65:20
experts in the law no **l** knew Me, Jr 2:8
we will no **l** come to You? Jr 2:31
no one will say any **l**: Jr 3:16
They can no **l** feel humiliation. Jr 6:15
if you no **l** oppress the alien, Jr 7:6
the widow and no **l** shed innocent Jr 7:6
place⌋ will no **l** be called Jr 7:32
They can no **l** feel humiliation. Jr 8:12
Is the LORD no **l** in Zion, her Jr 8:19
sound of cattle is no **l** heard. Jr 9:10
name will no **l** be remembered." Jr 11:19
when it will no **l** be said: Jr 16:14
place will no **l** be called Jr 19:6
Him or speak any **l** in His name, Jr 20:9
They will no **l** be afraid or Jr 23:4
when it will no **l** be said: Jr 23:7
But no **l** refer to the burden of Jr 23:36
they no **l** look for you, for I Jr 30:14
and they will no **l** grow weak Jr 31:12
No **l** will one teach his neighbor Jr 31:34
contempt and no **l** regarded as a Jr 33:24
not to enslave them any **l**— Jr 34:10
The LORD can no **l** bear your evil Jr 44:22
There is no **l** praise for Moab; Jr 48:2
Is there no **l** wisdom in Teman? Jr 49:7
neighbors. He will exist no **l**. Jr 49:10
nations will no **l** stream to him; Jr 51:44
"They can stay here no **l**." Lm 4:15
they no **l** exist, but we bear Lm 5:7
For there will no **l** be any false Ezk 12:24
It will no **l** be delayed. Ezk 12:25
My words will be delayed any **l**. Ezk 12:28
they will no **l** be prey in your Ezk 13:21
you will no **l** see false visions Ezk 13:23
of Israel may no **l** stray from Ezk 14:11
Me and no **l** defile themselves Ezk 14:11
I will be silent and no **l** angry. Ezk 16:42
you will no **l** use this proverb Ezk 18:3
so his roar could no **l** be heard Ezk 19:9
so that it no **l** has a strong Ezk 19:14
and you will no **l** defile My holy Ezk 20:39
you will speak and no **l** be mute. Ezk 24:27
your lyres will no **l** be heard. Ezk 26:13
that you will no **l** be inhabited Ezk 26:20
horror, and you will no **l** exist. Ezk 26:21
of Israel will no **l** be hurt by Ezk 28:24
There will no **l** be a prince from Ezk 30:13
was opened and I was no **l** mute. Ezk 33:22
will no **l** feed themselves, Ezk 34:10
they will no **l** be prey for you Ezk 34:22
They will no **l** be prey for the Ezk 34:28
and they will no **l** be victims of Ezk 34:29
will no **l** endure the insults Ezk 34:29
You will no **l** deprive them of Ezk 36:12
you will no **l** devour men and Ezk 36:14
I will no **l** allow the insults of Ezk 36:15
you will no **l** cause your nation Ezk 36:15
that you will no **l** experience Ezk 36:30
They will no **l** be two nations Ezk 37:22
and will no **l** be divided into Ezk 37:22
and will no **l** allow it to be Ezk 39:7
I will no **l** hide My face from Ezk 39:29
kings will no **l** defile My holy Ezk 43:7
princes will no **l** oppress My Ezk 45:8
but one was **l** than the other, Dn 8:3
and the **l** one came up last. Dn 8:3
for I will no **l** have compassion Hs 1:6
My husband, and no **l** call Me: Hs 2:16
they will no **l** be remembered by Hs 2:17
I will no **l** love them; Hs 9:15
and we will no **l** proclaim: Hs 14:3
and I will no **l** make you a Jl 2:19
I will no **l** spare them: Am 7:8
I will no **l** spare them. Am 8:2
you, I will afflict you no **l**. Nah 1:12
what is not his—how much **l**? Hab 2:6
Israel will no **l** do wrong or Zph 3:13
you need no **l** fear harm. Zph 3:15
I will no **l** have compassion on Zch 11:6
I will no **l** shepherd you. Zch 11:9
they will no **l** be remembered. Zch 13:2
there will no **l** be a Canaanite Zch 14:21
you would no **l** kindle a useless Mal 1:10
because He no **l** respects your Mal 2:13
It's no **l** good for anything but Mt 5:13
So they are no **l** two, but one Mt 19:6
Jesus could no **l** enter a town Mk 1:45
you no **l** let him do anything for Mk 7:12
they no **l** saw anyone with them Mk 9:8
So they are no **l** two, but one Mk 10:8
one dared to question Him any **l**. Mk 12:34
will no **l** drink of the fruit of Mk 14:25
no **l** worthy to be called your Lk 15:19
no **l** worthy to be called your Lk 15:21
you can no **l** be ⌊my⌋ manager.' Lk 16:2
And they no **l** dared to ask Him Lk 20:40
We no **l** believe because of what Jn 4:42
back and no **l** accompanied Him. Jn 6:66
Jesus no **l** walked openly Jn 11:54
be with you only a little **l**. Jn 12:35
I am with you a little while **l**. Jn 13:33
the world will see Me no **l**, Jn 14:19
I will not talk with you much **l**, Jn 14:30
Father and you will no **l** see Me; Jn 16:10
while and you will no **l** see Me; Jn 16:16
she no **l** remembers the suffering Jn 16:21
when I will no **l** speak to you Jn 16:25
I am no **l** in the world, but they Jn 17:11
eunuch did not see him any **l**. Ac 8:39
asked him to stay for a **l** time, Ac 18:20
that he should not live any **l**. Ac 25:24
that we may no **l** be enslaved to Rm 6:6
raised from the dead, no **l** dies. Rm 6:9
Death no **l** rules over Him. Rm 6:9
So now I am no **l** the one doing Rm 7:17
I am no **l** the one doing it, Rm 7:20
let us no **l** criticize one Rm 14:13
you are no **l** walking according Rm 14:15
But now I no **l** have any work to Rm 15:23
who live should no **l** live for 2Co 5:15
yet now we no **l** know Him like 2Co 5:16
I no **l** live, but Christ lives Gl 2:20
it is no **l** from the promise; Gl 3:18
we are no **l** under a guardian, Gl 3:25
So you are no **l** a slave, but a Gl 4:7
So then you are no **l** foreigners Eph 2:19
Then we will no **l** be little Eph 4:14
You should no **l** walk as the Eph 4:17
The thief must no **l** steal. Eph 4:28
when we could no **l** stand it, 1Th 3:1
when I could no **l** stand it, 1Th 3:5
no **l** as a slave, but more than a Phm 16
no **l** have any consciousness Heb 10:2
there is no **l** an offering for Heb 10:18
there no **l** remains a sacrifice Heb 10:26
in the flesh, no **l** for human 1Pt 4:2
a little while **l** until ⌊the Rv 6:11
no **l** will they hunger; Rv 7:16
no **l** will they thirst; Rv 7:16
no **l** will the sun strike them, Rv 7:16
There will no **l** be an interval Rv 10:6
place for them in heaven any **l**. Rv 12:8
buys their merchandise any **l**— Rv 18:11
that he would no **l** deceive the Rv 20:3
away, and the sea existed no **l**. Rv 21:1
Death will exist no **l**; Rv 21:4
pain will exist no **l**, because Rv 21:4
there will no **l** be any curse. Rv 22:3
will no **l** exist, and people Rv 22:5

LONGING *(8)*

by **l** for Your judgments. Ps 119:20
is still thirsty, **l** for water. Is 29:8
where they are **l** to return to Jr 44:14
eyes and the **l** of their hearts, Ezk 24:25
l to put on our house from 2Co 5:2
He announced to us your deep **l**, 2Co 7:7
fear, what deep **l**, what zeal, 2Co 7:11
he has been **l** for all of you Php 2:26

LONGINGLY *(2)*

wife looked **l** at Joseph and said Gn 39:7
you will not look **l** at them or Ezk 23:27

LONGS *(4)*

Like a slave he **l** for shade; Jb 7:2
stranger. My heart **l** within me. Jb 19:27
place the one who **l** for it." Ps 12:5
a deer **l** for streams of water, Ps 42:1

LOOK *(576)*

God also said, "**L**, I have given Gn 1:29
for food and delightful to **l** at, Gn 3:6
and I will **l** at it and remember Gn 9:16
came down to **l** over the city Gn 11:5
his wife Sarai, "**L**, I know what Gn 12:11
L from the place where you are. Gn 13:14
L north and south, east and west, Gn 13:14
continued, "**L**, You have given Gn 15:3
L at the sky and count the Gn 15:5
L, I've got two daughters who Gn 19:8
Don't **l** back and don't stop Gn 19:17
L, this town is close enough for Gn 19:20
the younger, "**L**, I slept with my Gn 19:34
Abimelech said, "**L**, my land is Gn 20:15
Sarah he said, "**L**, I am giving Gn 20:16
"**L**," said Esau, "I'm about to Gn 25:32
He said, "**L**, I am old and do not Gn 27:2
his mother, "**L**, my brother Esau Gn 27:11
birthright, and **l**, now he has Gn 27:36
L, I have made him a master over Gn 27:37
L, your dwelling place will be Gn 27:39
L, I am with you and will watch Gn 28:15
Then Jacob said, "**L**, it is still Gn 29:7
And He said, '**L** up and see: Gn 31:12
L at this mound and the marker I Gn 31:51
And **l**, he is behind us.' " Gn 32:18
to also say, '**L**, your servant Gn 32:20
"**L**," he said, "I had another Gn 37:9
master's wife, "**L**, my master Gn 39:8
"**L**," she said to them, "my Gn 39:14
let Pharaoh **l** for a discerning Gn 41:33
L! Your eyes and my brother Gn 45:12
Then Israel said to Joseph, "**L**! Gn 48:21
to his people, "**L**, the Israelite Ex 1:9
must go over and **l** at this Ex 3:3
saw that he had gone over to **l**, Ex 3:4
he was afraid to **l** at God. Ex 3:6
Pharaoh also said, "**L**, the Ex 5:5
L, your servants are being Ex 5:16
L out—you are planning evil. Ex 10:10
L, I have appointed by name Ex 31:2
to the LORD, "**L**, You have told Ex 33:12
L, I am making a covenant. Ex 34:10
L, the LORD has appointed by Ex 35:30
the priest will **l**, and if the Lv 13:13
not need to **l** for yellow hair Lv 13:36
of the country **l** the other way Lv 20:4
not to go in and **l** at the holy Nm 4:20
the LORD **l** with favor on you and Nm 6:26
nothing to **l** at but this manna! Nm 11:6
as tassels for you to **l** at, Nm 15:39
to Moses, "**L**, we're perishing! Nm 17:12
L, I have selected your fellow Nm 18:6
to Aaron, "**L**, I have put you Nm 18:8
L, I have given the Levites Nm 18:21
Now **l**, we are in Kadesh, a city Nm 20:16
L, a people has come out of Nm 22:5
'**L**, a people has come out of Nm 22:11
You made me **l** like a fool. Nm 22:29
L, I came out to oppose you, Nm 22:32
said to him, "**L**, I have come to Nm 22:38
my enemies, but **l**, you have only Nm 23:11
you richly, but **l**, the LORD has Nm 24:11
top of Pisgah and **l** to the west, Dt 3:27
L, I have taught you statutes Dt 4:5
When you **l** to the heavens and Dt 4:19
You said, '**L**, the LORD our God Dt 5:24
to you and not **l** on them with Dt 7:16
L, today I set before you a Dt 11:26
You must not **l** on him with pity Dt 19:13
L down from Your holy dwelling, Dt 26:15
among you will **l** grudgingly at Dt 28:54
of Jericho was told, "**L**, some of Jos 2:2
to Joshua, "**L**, I have handed Jos 6:2
L, I have handed over to you the Jos 8:1
But take a **l**, it is now dry and Jos 9:12
filled them, but **l**, they are Jos 9:13
it⌋ said, "**L**, the Reubenites, Jos 22:11
L at the replica of the LORD's Jos 22:28
L, my family is the weakest in Jdg 6:15
saying, "**L**, Gaal son of Ebed, Jdg 9:31
said to Zebul, "**L**, people are Jdg 9:36
the mountains **l** like men to you. Jdg 9:36
L, people are coming down from Jdg 9:37
"**L**," he said, "I haven't even Jdg 14:16
to him, "**L**, night is coming. Jdg 19:9
L, all of you are Israelites. Jdg 20:7
They also said, "**L**, there's an Jdg 21:19
Naomi said, "**L**, your Ru 1:15
L, the days are coming when I 1Sm 2:31
said to him, "**L**, you are old, 1Sm 8:5

you and go l for the donkeys. 1Sm 9:3
"L," the attendant said, "there's 1Sm 9:6
"To l for the donkeys," Saul 1Sm 10:14
L, this is the king the LORD has 1Sm 12:13
said, "L, the Hebrews are 1Sm 14:11
Just l at how I have renewed 1Sm 14:29
L, the troops are sinning 1Sm 14:33
obeying the LORD? L: to obey is 1Sm 15:22
Do not l at his appearance or 1Sm 16:7
presence to l for someone who 1Sm 16:16
and tell him, 'L, the king is 1Sm 18:22
have come to l favorably on me 1Sm 20:3
David told him, "L, tomorrow is 1Sm 20:5
young man, 'L, the arrows are 1Sm 20:21
'L, the arrows are beyond you!' 1Sm 20:22
L! You can see the man is crazy, 1Sm 21:14
L, the Philistines are fighting 1Sm 23:1
said to him, "L, we're afraid 1Sm 23:3
L and find out all the places 1Sm 23:23
and his men went to l for ⌊him⌋. 1Sm 23:25
men and went to l for David and 1Sm 24:2
said to him, "L, this is the day 1Sm 24:4
who say, 'L, David intends 1Sm 24:9
L at the corner of your robe in 1Sm 24:11
L and recognize that there is no 1Sm 24:11
L, David sent messengers from 1Sm 25:14
anointed. Now l around; where 1Sm 26:16
her, "What does he l like?" 1Sm 28:14
said to him, "L, your servant 1Sm 28:21
How could I ever l your brother 2Sm 2:22
L here, Abner came to you. 2Sm 3:24
told me, 'L, Saul is dead,' 2Sm 4:10
the prophet, "L, I am living 2Sm 7:2
They said, "L, while the baby 2Sm 12:18
to the king, "L, the king's sons 2Sm 13:35
"L," Absalom explained to Joab, 2Sm 14:32
said to him, "L, your claims are 2Sm 15:3
Zadok the priest, "L, return to 2Sm 15:27
May you l favorably on me, 2Sm 16:4
L, you are in trouble because 2Sm 16:8
his servants, "L, my own son, my 2Sm 16:11
out to the gatekeeper, "L! 2Sm 18:26
L, the king is sitting in the 2Sm 19:8
I have sinned. But l! Today I am 2Sm 19:20
They l, but there is no one to 2Sm 22:42
them⌊—they l⌋ to the LORD, 2Sm 22:42
to the LORD, "L, I am the one 2Sm 24:17
Now l, Adonijah has become king. 1Kg 1:18
priest. And l! They're eating 1Kg 1:25
L, Adonijah fears King Solomon, 1Kg 1:51
informed, "L, your slaves are 1Kg 2:39
from Tyre to l over the towns 1Kg 9:12
now l after your own house! 1Kg 12:16
L, I have sent you a gift of 1Kg 15:19
L, I have commanded a woman 1Kg 17:9
Elijah said, "L, your son is 1Kg 17:23
"Go up and l toward the sea." 1Kg 18:43
instructed him, "L, the words 1Kg 22:13
of Judah, I would not l at you; 2Kg 3:14
Say to her, 'L, you've gone to 2Kg 4:13
attendant Gehazi, "L, there's 2Kg 4:25
L, when the messenger comes, 2Kg 6:32
man of God, "L, ⌊even if⌋ the 2Kg 7:2
man of God, "L, ⌊even if⌋ the 2Kg 7:19
l for Jehu son of Jehoshaphat, 2Kg 9:2
and reasoned, "L, two kings 2Kg 10:4
L carefully to see that there 2Kg 10:23
L, you now trust in Egypt, the 2Kg 18:21
L, he has set out to fight 2Kg 19:9
L, you have heard what the kings 2Kg 19:11
your tears. L, I will heal you 2Kg 20:5
our ancestors l on it and judge. 1Ch 12:17
said to Nathan the prophet, "L! 1Ch 17:1
l after your own house now! 2Ch 10:16
L, God and His priests are with 2Ch 13:12
L, I have sent you silver and 2Ch 16:3
instructed him, "L, the words 2Ch 18:12
L how they repay us by coming to 2Ch 20:11
what to do, but we l to You. 2Ch 20:12
You have said, 'L, I have 2Ch 25:19
said to them, "L, the LORD God 2Ch 28:9
and l on me with compassion in Neh 13:22
the Jew, "L, I have given Est 8:7
L! You have instructed many and Jb 4:3
caravans of Tema l ⌊for these Jb 6:19
But now, please l at me; Jb 6:28
Your eyes will l for me, but I Jb 7:8
Will You ever l away from me, Jb 7:19

L, God does not reject a person Jb 8:20
of strength, l, He is the Mighty Jb 9:19
that You l for my wrongdoing and Jb 10:6
You will l carefully about and Jb 11:18
L, my eyes have seen all this; Jb 13:1
l away from him and let him rest Jb 14:6
my eyes will l at ⌊Him⌋, and not Jb 19:27
L at me and shudder; put ⌊your⌋ Jb 21:5
L, I know your thoughts, the Jb 21:27
And l at the highest stars— Jb 22:12
He said to mankind, "L! Jb 28:28
stand up, You ⌊merely⌋ l at me. Jb 30:20
then could I l at a young woman Jb 31:1
L, I waited for your conclusions; Jb 32:11
He will l at men and say, Jb 33:27
L at the heavens and see; Jb 35:5
L, God shows Himself exalted by Jb 36:22
L, God is exalted beyond our Jb 36:26
L, He spreads His lightning Jb 36:30
cannot ⌊even⌋ l at the sun when Jb 37:21
He does not l favorably on any Jb 37:24
l on every proud person and Jb 40:11
L on every proud person and Jb 40:12
L at Behemoth, which I made Jb 40:15
L at the strength of his loins Jb 40:16
L on us with favor, LORD. Ps 4:6
son of man that You l after him? Ps 8:4
l, the wicked string the bow; Ps 11:2
people l and stare at me. Ps 22:17
Those who l to Him are radiant Ps 34:5
Lord, how long will You l on? Ps 35:17
me without cause l at me Ps 35:19
though you l for him, he will Ps 37:10
L! The kings assembled; they Ps 48:4
The righteous will l on with awe Ps 52:6
LORD, l! They set an ambush for Ps 59:3
L, they spew from their mouths— Ps 59:7
God will let me l down on my Ps 59:10
l on us with favor Selah Ps 67:1
L, He thunders with His powerful Ps 68:33
L at them—the wicked! Ps 73:12
L! He struck the rock and water Ps 78:20
l ⌊on us⌋ with favor, and we Ps 80:3
l ⌊on us⌋ with favor, and we Ps 80:7
L down from heaven and see; Ps 80:14
l ⌊on us⌋ with favor, and we Ps 80:19
l on the face of Your anointed Ps 84:9
will l down from heaven. Ps 85:11
My eyes l down on my enemies; Ps 92:11
the end he will l in triumph on Ps 112:8
stoops down to l on the heavens Ps 113:6
I will l in triumph on those who Ps 118:7
my eyes ⌊l⌋ to You, Lord GOD. Ps 141:8
L to the right and see: Ps 142:4
All eyes l to You, and You give Ps 145:15
Let your eyes l forward; Pr 4:25
I'll l for another ⌊drink⌋." Pr 23:35
anything, "L, this is new"? Ec 1:10
to myself, "L, I have amassed Ec 1:16
L at the tears of those who are Ec 4:1
"L," says the Teacher, "this I Ec 7:27
approaching⌋. L! Here he comes, Sg 2:8
L, he is standing behind our Sg 2:9
come back, that we may l at you! Sg 6:13
as you ⌊l⌋ at the dance of the Sg 6:13
I will refuse to l at you; Is 1:15
The l on their faces testifies Is 3:9
L—how quickly and swiftly they Is 5:26
They will l toward the earth and Is 8:22
and the proud l in his eyes." Is 10:12
L, the Lord GOD of Hosts will Is 10:33
They will l at each other, Is 13:8
L, the day of the LORD is coming Is 13:9
L! I am stirring up the Medes Is 13:17
they will not l with pity on Is 13:18
they will l closely at you: Is 14:16
L, Damascus is no longer a city. Is 17:1
day people will l to their Maker Is 17:7
They will not l to the altars Is 17:8
is raised on the mountains, l! Is 18:3
I will quietly l out from My Is 18:4
L, the LORD rides on a swift Is 19:1
L, this is what has happened to Is 20:6
L, riders come—horsemen in Is 21:9
I said, "L away from me! Is 22:4
but you did not l to the One who Is 22:11
But l: joy and gladness, Is 22:13
L, young man! The LORD is about Is 22:17

L at the land of Chaldeans— Is 23:13
L, the LORD is stripping the Is 24:1
will be said, "L, this is our Is 25:9
For l, the LORD is coming from Is 26:21
L, the Lord has a strong and Is 28:2
L, I have laid a stone in Zion, Is 28:16
L, Yahweh comes from far away, Is 30:27
They do not l to the Holy One of Is 31:1
L at Zion, the city of our Is 33:20
L, you are trusting in Egypt, Is 36:6
L! I am putting a spirit in him Is 37:7
L, you have heard what the kings Is 37:11
L, I am going to add 15 years to Is 38:5
I will not l on humanity any Is 38:11
L, the nations are like a drop Is 40:15
L up and see: who created these? Is 40:26
You will l for those who contend Is 41:12
L, you are nothing and your work Is 41:24
say to Zion: L! Here they are! Is 41:27
When I l, there is no one; Is 41:28
L, all of them are a delusion; Is 41:29
L, you blind, so that you may Is 42:18
L, I am about to do something Is 43:19
L, all its worshipers will be Is 44:11
L, they are like stubble; Is 47:14
L, I have refined you, but not Is 48:10
L, I have inscribed you on the Is 49:16
L up, and look around. They all Is 49:18
Look up, and l around. They all Is 49:18
L, I will lift up My hand to the Is 49:22
L, you were sold for your Is 50:1
L, I dry up the sea by My rebuke; Is 50:2
L, all you who kindle a fire, Is 50:11
L to the rock from which you Is 51:1
L to Abraham your father, and to Is 51:2
and they will l to My strength. Is 51:5
L up to the heavens, and look at Is 51:6
and l at the earth beneath; Is 51:6
His people—"L, I have removed Is 51:22
that He did not l like a man, Is 52:14
that we should l at Him, Is 53:2
L, I have created the craftsman Is 54:16
not say, "L, I am a dried-up Is 56:3
L, you do as you please on the Is 58:3
l, darkness covers the earth, Is 60:2
Raise your eyes and l around: Is 60:4
L, the LORD has proclaimed to Is 62:11
L, your salvation is coming, His Is 62:11
L down from heaven and see from Is 63:15
Please l—all of us are Your Is 64:9
I will l favorably on this kind Is 66:2
L, the LORD will come with fire— Is 66:15
L, I don't know how to speak Jr 1:6
L, I have filled your mouth with Jr 1:9
over to Cyprus and take a l. Jr 2:10
L at your behavior in the valley; Jr 2:23
who l for her will not become Jr 2:24
L to the barren heights and see. Jr 3:2
the brazen l of a prostitute Jr 3:3
I will not l on you with anger, Jr 3:12
L, he advances like clouds; Jr 4:13
Warn the nations: L! Proclaim to Jr 4:16
of Jerusalem. L and take note; Jr 5:1
don't Your eyes ⌊l for⌋ Jr 5:3
L, their ear is uncircumcised, Jr 6:10
Stand by the roadways and l. Jr 6:16
L, an army is coming from a Jr 6:22
⌊But⌋ l, you keep trusting in Jr 7:8
L, My anger—My burning wrath— Jr 7:20
L, I am slinging out the land's Jr 10:18
L up and see those coming from Jr 13:20
to the field, l—those slain Jr 14:18
I enter the city, l—those ill Jr 14:18
L, each one of you was following Jr 16:12
L, I am presenting to you the Jr 21:8
L, a storm from the LORD! Jr 23:19
L, very soon now the articles of Jr 27:16
they no longer l for you, for I Jr 30:14
L, a storm from the LORD! Jr 30:23
"L, the days are coming"—⌊this Jr 31:31
"L, the days are coming"—the Jr 31:38
L, I am about to hand this city Jr 32:3
L! Siege ramps have come against Jr 32:24
has happened. L, You can see it! Jr 32:24
L, I am the LORD, the God of all Jr 32:27
"L, the days are coming"—⌊this Jr 33:14
Take him, l after him, and don't Jr 39:12
L—the whole land is in front Jr 40:4

l, they are a ruin today without Jr 44:2
they never l back, terror is Jr 46:5
L, waters are rising from the Jr 47:2
Therefore l, the days are coming Jr 48:12
Stand by the highway and l, Jr 48:19
Therefore l, the days are coming Jr 49:2
L, I am about to bring terror on Jr 49:5
L, I will certainly make you Jr 49:15
L, it will be like a lion coming Jr 49:19
L! It will be like an eagle Jr 49:22
be put to shame. L! She will lag Jr 50:12
L, I am against you, you Jr 50:31
L! A people comes from the north. Jr 50:41
L, it will be like a lion coming Jr 50:44
L, I am against you, devastating Jr 51:25
Therefore, l, the days are Jr 51:47
Therefore, l, the days are Jr 51:52
LORD, l on my affliction, for Lm 1:9
l and see how I have become Lm 1:11
you who pass by? L and see! Is Lm 1:12
all you people; l at my pain. My Lm 1:18
l and consider who You have done Lm 2:20
when they rise, l, I am mocked Lm 3:63
L, and see our disgrace! Lm 5:1
by ⌊the l on⌋ their faces, Ezk 2:6
L, I have made your face as hard Ezk 3:8
by ⌊the l on⌋ their faces, Ezk 3:9
replied to me, "L, I will let Ezk 4:15
I will not l on you with pity or Ezk 7:4
L, one disaster after another is Ezk 7:5
against you. L, it is coming! Ezk 7:6
I will not l on ⌊you⌋ with pity Ezk 7:9
L, the day is coming! Doom has Ezk 7:10
Son of man, l toward the north. Ezk 8:5
an exile's bags while they l Ezk 12:4
And while they l on, lift ⌊the Ezk 12:6
L, everyone who uses proverbs Ezk 16:44
L, every life belongs to Me. Ezk 18:4
L, every prince of Israel within Ezk 22:6
Now l, I clap My hands together Ezk 22:13
and you will not l longingly at Ezk 23:27
them. And l how they came! You Ezk 23:40
L, the house of Judah is like Ezk 25:8
Lord GOD says: L! I am against Ezk 28:22
L, I am against you, Pharaoh Ezk 29:3
L, it has not been bandaged— Ezk 30:21
Lord GOD says: L! I am against Ezk 30:22
L, I am against the shepherds. Ezk 34:10
for My flock and l for them. Ezk 34:11
flock, so I will l for My flock. Ezk 34:12
Lord GOD says: L! I am against Ezk 35:3
L, I speak in My burning zeal Ezk 36:6
L! I am on your side; I will Ezk 36:9
house of Israel. L how they say: Ezk 37:11
L, I am against you, Gog, chief Ezk 38:3
L, I am against you, Gog, chief Ezk 39:1
Son of man, l with your eyes, Ezk 40:4
l with your eyes and listen with Ezk 44:5
exclaimed, "L! I see four men, Dn 3:25
the promiscuous l from her face Hs 2:2
L, I am about to send you grain, Jl 2:19
L, I am about to rouse them up Jl 3:7
L, I am about to crush ⌊you⌋ in Am 2:13
L, the days are coming when you Am 4:2
But l, I am raising up a nation Am 6:14
L, the eyes of the Lord GOD are Am 9:8
L, I will make you insignificant Ob 2
yet I will l once more toward Jnh 2:4
L, the LORD is leaving His place Mc 1:3
as for me, I will l to the LORD; Mc 7:7
My eyes will l at her in Mc 7:10
L to the mountains—the feet of Nah 1:15
the plazas. They l like torches; Nah 2:4
L, your troops are women among Nah 3:13
You force me to l at injustice? Hab 1:3
L at the nations and observe— Hab 1:5
L! I am raising up the Chaldeans, Hab 1:6
eyes are too pure to l on evil, Hab 1:13
L, his ego is inflated; Hab 2:4
order to l at their nakedness! Hab 2:15
it teach? L! It may be plated Hab 2:19
How does it l to you now? Hg 2:3
L up and see what this is that Zch 5:5
L, I will make Jerusalem a cup Zch 12:2
and they will l at Me whom they Zch 12:10
also say: "L, what a nuisance! Mal 1:13
L, I am going to rebuke your Mal 2:3
L, I am going to send you Elijah Mal 4:5

L at the birds of the sky: Mt 6:26
do you l at the speck in your Mt 7:3
your eye,' and l, there's a log Mt 7:4
L, I'm sending you out like Mt 10:16
L, those who wear soft clothes Mt 11:8
L, I am sending My messenger Mt 11:10
and they say, 'L, a glutton Mt 11:19
said to Him, "L, Your disciples Mt 12:2
and l—something greater than Mt 12:41
and l—something greater than Mt 12:42
Someone told Him, "L, Your Mt 12:47
and you will l and look, yet Mt 13:14
you will look and l, yet never Mt 13:14
See that you don't l down on one Mt 18:10
to Him, "L, we have left Mt 19:27
L, I've prepared my dinner; Mt 22:4
tells you then, 'L, here is the Mt 24:23
So if they tell you, 'L, he's in Mt 24:26
'L, he's in the inner rooms!' Mt 24:26
L, I've earned five more talents. Mt 25:20
L, I've earned two more talents.' Mt 25:22
L, you have what is yours.' Mt 25:25
resting? L, the time is near. Mt 26:45
L, now you've heard the Mt 26:65
L, I am sending My messenger Mk 1:2
said to Him, "L, why are they Mk 2:24
and told Him, "L, Your mother, Mk 3:32
so that they may l and look, Mk 4:12
so that they may look and l, Mk 4:12
do you have? Go l." When they Mk 6:38
l to me like trees walking." Mk 8:24
to tell Him, "L, we have left Mk 10:28
and said to Him, "Rabbi, l! Mk 11:21
Bring Me a denarius to l at." Mk 12:15
said to Him, "Teacher, l! Mk 13:1
anyone tells you, 'L, here is Mk 13:21
is the Messiah! L—there!' do Mk 13:21
L, the Son of Man is being Mk 14:41
L how many things they are Mk 15:4
they said, "L, He's calling for Mk 15:35
be afraid, for l, I proclaim to Lk 2:10
Why do you l at the speck in Lk 6:41
should we l for someone else?" Lk 7:19
should we l for someone else?' Lk 7:20
L, those who are splendidly Lk 7:25
L, I am sending My messenger Lk 7:27
and you say, 'L, a glutton Lk 7:34
beg You to l at my son, because Lk 9:38
L, I have given you the Lk 10:19
of Solomon, and l—something Lk 11:31
proclamation, and l—something Lk 11:32
to them, "Go tell that fox, 'L! Lk 13:32
to his father, 'L, I have been Lk 15:29
no one will say, 'L here!' Lk 17:21
They will say to you, 'L there!' Lk 17:23
Look there!' or 'L here!' Don't Lk 17:23
Peter said, "L, we have left Lk 18:28
to the Lord, "L, I'll give half Lk 19:8
L at the fig tree, and all the Lk 21:29
But l, the hand of the one Lk 22:21
Simon, Simon, l out! Satan has Lk 22:31
they said, "l, here are two Lk 22:38
L, the days are coming when they Lk 23:29
he stooped to l in, he saw only Lk 24:12
L at My hands and My feet, Lk 24:39
And l, I am sending you what My Lk 24:49
Jesus passing by, he said, "L! Jn 1:36
your eyes and l at the fields, Jn 4:35
Yet, l! He's speaking publicly Jn 7:26
You will l for Me, but you will Jn 7:34
'You will l for Me, and you will Jn 7:36
you will l for Me, and you will Jn 8:21
Daughter Zion; l! your King is Jn 12:15
L—the world has gone after Him! Jn 12:19
You will l for Me, and just as I Jn 13:33
L: An hour is coming, and has Jn 16:32
L, they know what I said." Jn 18:21
said to them, "L, I'm bringing Jn 19:4
They will l at the One they Jn 19:37
she stooped to l into the tomb. Jn 20:11
amazed, saying, "L, aren't all Ac 2:7
intently and said, "L at us." Ac 3:4
of the Lord? L! The feet of Ac 5:9
came and reported to them, "L! Ac 5:25
And l, you have filled Jerusalem Ac 5:28
he was approaching to l at it, Ac 7:31
tremble and did not dare to l. Ac 7:32
L! I see the heavens opened and Ac 7:56

eunuch said, "L, there's water! Ac 8:36
Now, l! The Lord's hand is Ac 13:11
not the One. But l! Someone is Ac 13:25
L, you scoffers, marvel and Ac 13:41
Caesar. And, l! God has Ac 27:24
and you will l and look, yet Ac 28:26
you will look and l, yet never Ac 28:26
it is written: L! I am putting Rm 9:33
eats must not l down on one who Rm 14:3
why do you l down on your Rm 14:10
L at the people of Israel. 1Co 10:18
do you l down on the church of 1Co 11:22
no one should l down on him; 1Co 16:11
not able to l directly at Moses' 2Co 3:7
Israel could not l at the end of 2Co 3:13
away, and l, new things have 2Co 5:17
L, now is the acceptable time; 2Co 6:2
l, now is the day of salvation. 2Co 6:2
as dying and l—we live; 2Co 6:9
L at what is obvious. If anyone 2Co 10:7
L! I am ready to come to you 2Co 12:14
L at what large letters I have Gl 6:11
Everyone should l out not ⌊only⌋ Php 2:4
"L, the days are coming," says Heb 8:8
to l after orphans and widows in Jms 1:27
If you l with favor on the man Jms 2:3
L! The pay that you withheld Jms 5:4
L, the judge stands at the door! Jms 5:9
Angels desire to l into these 1Pt 1:12
in Scripture: L! I lay a stone 1Pt 2:6
L at how great a love the Father 1Jn 3:1
about them: L! The Lord comes Jd 14
L! He is coming with the clouds, Rv 1:7
I was dead, but l—I am alive Rv 1:18
L, the Devil is about to throw Rv 2:10
L! I will throw her into a Rv 2:22
denied My name, l, I have placed Rv 3:8
the scroll or even to l in it. Rv 5:3
the scroll or even to l in it. Rv 5:4
to me, "Stop crying. L! The Lion Rv 5:5
L, I am coming like a thief. Rv 16:15
the throne: L! God's dwelling Rv 21:3
seated on the throne said, "L! Rv 21:5
L, I am coming quickly! Rv 22:7
L! I am coming quickly, and My Rv 22:12

LOOKED *(144)*

l out and saw that the entire Gn 13:10
she l down on her mistress. Gn 16:4
pregnant, she has l down on me. Gn 16:5
He l up, and he saw three men Gn 18:2
from there and l out over Sodom, Gn 18:16
But his wife l back and became a Gn 19:26
He l down toward Sodom and Gn 19:28
third day Abraham l up and saw Gn 22:4
Abraham l up and saw a ram Gn 22:13
Rebekah l up, and when she saw Gn 24:64
of the Philistines l down from Gn 26:8
He l and saw a well in a field. Gn 29:2
Now Jacob l up and saw Esau Gn 33:1
When Esau l up and saw the women Gn 33:5
They l up, and there was a Gn 37:25
his master's wife l longingly at Gn 39:7
he saw that they l distraught. Gn 40:6
When he l up and saw his brother Gn 43:29
The men l at each other in Gn 43:33
As Moses l, he saw that the bush Ex 3:2
the Israelites l up and saw the Ex 14:10
the LORD l down on the Egyptian Ex 14:24
and he l at the bronze snake, Nm 21:9
When Balaam l up and saw Israel Nm 24:2
l up and saw a man standing in Jos 5:13
The men of Ai turned and l back, Jos 8:20
They l and found the doors of Jdg 3:24
Sisera's mother l through the Jdg 5:28
He l, and the people were coming Jdg 9:43
l like the awe-inspiring Angel Jdg 13:6
he l up and saw the traveler Jdg 19:17
city, Benjamin l behind them, Jdg 20:40
and when they l up and saw the 1Sm 6:13
because they l inside the ark 1Sm 6:19
in Gibeah of Benjamin l, 1Sm 14:16
the Philistine l and saw David, 1Sm 17:42
cistern at Secu, l around, and 1Sm 19:22
When Saul l behind him, David 1Sm 24:8
daughter Michal l down from the 2Sm 6:16
who was standing watch l up, 2Sm 13:34
watchman l out and saw a man 2Sm 18:24
Araunah l down and saw the king 2Sm 24:20

when I l closely at him I 1Kg 3:21
So he went up, l, and said, 1Kg 18:43
Then he l, and there at his head 1Kg 19:6
who l for three days but did not 2Kg 2:17
He turned around, l at them, and 2Kg 2:24
He l and saw that the mountain 2Kg 6:17
l and discovered ⌊they were⌋ 2Kg 6:20
and l down from the window. 2Kg 9:30
He l up toward the window and 2Kg 9:32
or three eunuchs l down at him, 2Kg 9:32
As she l, there was the king 2Kg 11:14
daughter Michal l down from the 1Ch 15:29
the city, the LORD l, relented 1Ch 21:15
David l up and saw the angel 1Ch 21:16
and when Ornan l and saw David, 1Ch 21:21
they l toward the multitude, 2Ch 20:24
Then Jehu l for Ahaziah, and 2Ch 22:9
As she l, there was the king 2Ch 23:13
When they l from a distance, Jb 2:12
when I l for light, darkness Jb 30:26
people have l at it from a Jb 36:25
They l, and froze with fear; Ps 48:5
and my eye has l down on my Ps 54:7
l down from His holy heights— Ps 102:19
The sea l and fled; the Jordan Ps 114:3
of my house I l through my Pr 7:6
I l, and received instruction: Pr 24:32
hall, and he l on me with love. Sg 2:4
He l for justice but saw Is 5:7
On that day you l to the weapons Is 22:8
I l, but there was no one to Is 63:5
I l at the earth, and it was Jr 4:23
⌊I l⌋ to the heavens, and their Jr 4:23
I l at the mountains, and they Jr 4:24
I l, and no man was left; Jr 4:25
I l, and the fertile field was a Jr 4:26
At this I awoke and l around. Jr 31:26
The adversaries l at her, Lm 1:7
failing ⌊as we l⌋ in vain for Lm 4:17
I l and there was a whirlwind Ezk 1:4
I l at the living creatures, Ezk 1:15
with what l like fire enclosing Ezk 1:27
I also saw what l like fire. Ezk 1:27
So I l and saw a hand reaching Ezk 2:9
I l, and there was a form that Ezk 8:2
up was something that l bright, Ezk 8:2
I l to the north, and there was Ezk 8:5
and when I l there was a hole in Ezk 8:7
I went in and l, and there Ezk 8:10
Then I l, and there above the Ezk 10:1
I l, and there were four wheels Ezk 10:9
faces l like the same faces Ezk 10:22
all of them l like officers, Ezk 23:15
I l, tendons appeared on them, Ezk 37:8
I l, and the glory of the LORD Ezk 44:4
end of 10 days they l better and Dn 1:15
Nebuchadnezzar, l up to heaven, Dn 4:34
second one, that l like a bear. Dn 7:5
I l up, and there was a ram Dn 8:3
I l up, and there was a man Dn 10:5
I, Daniel, l, and two others Dn 12:5
I l out in the night and saw a Zch 1:8
Then I l up and saw four horns. Zch 1:18
I l up and saw a man with a Zch 2:1
I l up again and saw a flying Zch 5:1
Then I l up and saw two women Zch 5:9
Then I l up again and saw four Zch 6:1
When they l up they saw no one Mt 17:8
But Jesus l at them and said, Mt 19:26
l up and said, "I see people— Mk 8:24
Jesus l around and said to His Mk 10:23
himself, she l at him and said, Mk 14:67
has l with favor in these days Lk 1:25
because He has l with favor on Lk 1:48
he l up and saw Abraham a long Lk 16:23
righteous and l down on everyone Lk 18:9
the place, He l up and said to Lk 19:5
But He l at them and said, Lk 20:17
chief priests l for a way to get Lk 20:19
l up and saw the rich dropping Lk 21:1
firelight, and l closely at him, Lk 22:56
the Lord turned and l at Peter. Lk 22:61
walking and l⌋ discouraged. Lk 24:17
when Jesus l up and noticed a Jn 6:5
these things, l up to heaven, Jn 17:1
l at him intently and said, Ac 3:4
the Sanhedrin l intently at him Ac 6:15
When I l closely and considered Ac 11:6
very hour I l up and saw him. Ac 22:13
Paul l intently at the Sanhedrin Ac 23:1
After this I l, and there in Rv 4:1
and the One seated l like jasper Rv 4:3
A rainbow that l like an emerald Rv 4:3
Then I l, and heard the voice of Rv 5:11
l, and there was a white horse. Rv 6:2
And I l, and there was a black Rv 6:5
And I l, and there was a pale Rv 6:8
After this I l, and there was a Rv 7:9
l, and I heard an eagle, flying Rv 8:13
I l, and there on Mount Zion Rv 14:1
Then I l, and there was a white Rv 14:14
After this I l, and the heavenly Rv 15:5

LOOKING *(92)*

the field, and l up, he saw Gn 24:63
asked him, "What are you l for?" Gn 37:15
"I'm l for my brothers," Joseph Gn 37:16
Why do you keep l at each other? Gn 42:1
L all around and seeing no one, Ex 2:12
cherubim were l toward the mercy Ex 37:9
stone without l that could kill Nm 35:23
your brother comes l for it; Dt 22:2
eyes grow weary l for them every Dt 28:32
show you the man you are l for." Jdg 4:22
tribe was l for territory to Jdg 18:1
donkeys you went l for have been 1Sm 10:2
and they are l for me to take my 1Kg 19:10
l for me to take my life. 1Kg 19:14
this one is only l for trouble, 1Kg 20:7
Now the men were l for a sign of 1Kg 20:33
you to the man you're l for." 2Kg 6:19
My eyes fail, l for my God. Ps 69:3
Turn my eyes from l at what is Ps 119:37
eyes grow weary ⌊l⌋ for what You Ps 119:82
eyes grow weary ⌊l for⌋ Your Ps 119:123
those who go l for mixed wine. Pr 23:30
Why are you l at the Shulammite, Sg 6:13
of Lebanon l toward Damascus Sg 7:4
keep l, but do not perceive. Is 6:9
enraged, and, l upward, will Is 8:21
My eyes grow weak l upward. Is 38:14
he saw your faces l thinner than Dn 1:10
was left alone, l at this great Dn 10:8
waterless places l for rest but Mt 12:43
because l they do not see, Mt 13:13
two fish, and l up to heaven, He Mt 14:19
Although they were l for a way Mt 21:46
time he started l for a good Mt 26:16
Sanhedrin were l for false Mt 26:59
Him were there, l on from a Mt 27:55
I know you are l for Jesus who Mt 28:5
said, "Everyone's l for You!" Mk 1:37
l around at them with anger Mk 3:5
And l about at those who were Mk 3:34
He was l around to see who had Mk 5:32
two fish, and l up to heaven, He Mk 6:41
Then, l up to heaven, He sighed Mk 7:34
around and l at His disciples, Mk 8:33
Then suddenly, l around, they no Mk 9:8
Then, l at him, Jesus loved him Mk 10:21
L at them, Jesus said, "With men Mk 10:27
After l around at everything, Mk 11:11
it and started l for a way to Mk 11:18
they were l for a way to arrest Mk 12:12
the scribes were l for a Mk 14:1
So he started l for a good Mk 14:11
Sanhedrin were l for testimony Mk 14:55
were also women l on from a Mk 15:40
who was himself l forward to the Mk 15:43
L up, they observed that the Mk 16:4
You are l for Jesus the Mk 16:6
l forward to Israel's Lk 2:25
Him to all who were l forward to Lk 2:38
Then they began l for Him among Lk 2:44
After l around at them all, Lk 6:10
Then l up at His disciples, Lk 6:20
so that L they may not see, Lk 8:10
two fish, and l up to heaven, He Lk 9:16
waterless places l for rest, Lk 11:24
He came l for fruit on it and Lk 13:6
I have come l for fruit on this Lk 13:7
the people were l for a way to Lk 19:47
scribes were l for a way to put Lk 22:2
offer⌋ and started l for a good Lk 22:6
and was l forward to the kingdom Lk 23:51
Why are you l for the living Lk 24:5
them, "What are you l for?" Jn 1:38
went to Capernaum l for Jesus. Jn 6:24
are l for Me, not because you Jn 6:26
The Jews were l for Him at the Jn 7:11
They were l for Jesus and asking Jn 11:56
started l at one another— Jn 13:22
them, "Who is it you're l for?" Jn 18:4
"Who is it you're l for?" Jn 18:7
So if you're l for Me, let these Jn 18:8
Who is it you are l for?" Jn 20:15
do you stand l up into heaven? Ac 1:11
L intently at him, he became Ac 10:4
Three men are here l for you. Ac 10:19
Here I am, the one you're l for. Ac 10:21
by those who were not l for Me; Rm 10:20
did not find what it was l for, Rm 11:7
For he was l forward to the city Heb 11:10
is like a man l at his own face Jms 1:23
l for anyone he can devour. 1Pt 5:8
adultery and always l for sin, 2Pt 2:14

LOOKOUT *(5)*

Balak took him to L Field on top Nm 23:14
eyes are on the l for the Ps 10:8
has said to me, "Go, post a l; Is 21:6
Then the l reported, "Lord, I Is 21:8
station myself on the l tower. Hab 2:1

LOOKS *(29)*

anyone who is bitten l at it, Nm 21:8
border road that l out over the 1Sm 13:18
first man runs l to me like the 2Sm 18:27
while my lord the king l on! 2Sm 24:3
eye of anyone who l on me will Jb 7:8
l for a home among the stones. Jb 8:17
He l to the ends of the earth Jb 28:24
anyone capture him while he l Jb 40:24
The LORD l down from heaven on Ps 14:2
The LORD l down from heaven; Ps 33:13
God l down from heaven on the Ps 53:2
He l at the earth, and it Ps 104:32
but if someone l for trouble, Pr 11:27
harvest time he l, and there is Pr 20:4
a backbiting tongue, angry l. Pr 25:23
and whoever l after his master Pr 27:18
its eyes and pretentious its l. Pr 30:13
and the one who l at the clouds Ec 11:4
When one l at the land, there Is 5:30
He l for a skilled craftsman to Is 40:20
the LORD l down from heaven Lm 3:50
As a shepherd l for his sheep on Ezk 34:12
and the fourth l like a son of Dn 3:25
He l and startles the nations. Hab 3:6
everyone who l at a woman to Mt 5:28
the plow and l back is fit for Lk 9:62
saying, "but he l like him." Jn 9:9
for he l at himself, goes away, Jms 1:24
But the one who l intently into Jms 1:25

LOOM *(3)*

my head with the web of a l—" Jdg 16:13
the pin, with the l and the web. Jdg 16:14
He cuts me off from the l. Is 38:12

LOOMED *(1)*

a form l before my eyes. Jb 4:16

LOOPS *(13)*

Make l of blue yarn on the edge Ex 26:4
Make 50 l on the one curtain and Ex 26:5
curtain and make 50 l on the Ex 26:5
so that the l line up together. Ex 26:5
Make 50 l on the edge of the one Ex 26:10
and make 50 l on the edge of the Ex 26:10
through the l and join the tent Ex 26:11
He made l of blue yarn on the Ex 36:11
He made 50 l on the one curtain Ex 36:12
one curtain and 50 l on the edge Ex 36:12
so that the l lined up with each Ex 36:12
He made 50 l on the edge of the Ex 36:17
first⌋ set and 50 l on the edge Ex 36:17

LOOSE *(11)*

does not come l from the ephod. Ex 28:28
did not come l from the ephod. Ex 39:21
your hair hang l and do not tear Lv 10:6
torn and his hair hanging l, Lv 13:45
Terrors are turned l against me; Jb 30:15
He lets it l beneath the entire Jb 37:3
belt is l, and no sandal strap Is 5:27
and whatever you l on earth is Mt 16:19
and whatever you l on earth is Mt 18:18
to them, "L him and let him go. Jn 11:44
and everyone's chains came l. Ac 16:26

LOOSED *(4)*
earth is already l in heaven." Mt 16:19
on earth is already l in heaven. Mt 18:18
not seek to be l. Are you loosed 1Co 7:27
Are you l from a wife? 1Co 7:27

LOOSEN *(1)*
the Pleiades or l the belt of Jb 38:31

LOOSENED *(3)*
Because God has l my bowstring Jb 30:11
You have l my bonds. Ps 116:16
nor will any of its cords be l. Is 33:20

LOOSENING *(1)*
the same time l the ropes that Ac 27:40

LOOT *(4)*
carried off a great supply of l. 2Ch 14:13
rescue them, and l, with no one Is 42:22
will take the l from those who Ezk 39:10
lavish plunder, l, and wealth on Dn 11:24

LOOTED *(4)*
houses will be l, and their Is 13:16
is a people plundered and l, Is 42:22
those who l them and plunder Ezk 39:10
the houses l, and the women Zch 14:2

LORD *(1228)*
(See also LORD Yahweh.)
But Abram said, "L GOD, what can Gn 15:2
But he said, "L GOD, how can I Gn 15:8
he said, "My l, if I have found Gn 18:3
shriveled up and my l is old, Gn 18:12
ventured to speak to the L— Gn 18:27
said, "Let the L not be angry, Gn 18:30
have ventured to speak to the L, Gn 18:31
said, "Let the L not be angry, Gn 18:32
said to them, "No, L—please. Gn 19:18
her, so he said, "L, would you Gn 20:4
Listen to us, l. You are God's Gn 23:6
No, my l. Listen to me. I give Gn 23:11
My l, listen to me. Land worth Gn 23:15
She replied, "Drink, my l." Gn 24:18
You are to say to my l Esau, Gn 32:4
this message⌋ to inform my l, Gn 32:5
are a gift sent to my l Esau. Gn 32:18
with you, my l," he answered. Gn 33:8
My l knows that the children are Gn 33:13
my l go ahead of his servant. Gn 33:14
until I come to my l at Seir." Gn 33:14
Please indulge me, my l." Gn 33:15
No, my l. Your servants have Gn 42:10
man who is the l of the country Gn 42:30
man who is the l of the country Gn 42:33
Why does my l say these things? Gn 44:7
"What can we say to my l?" Gn 44:16
speak personally to my l. Gn 44:18
My l asked his servants, 'Do you Gn 44:19
and we answered my l, 'We have Gn 44:20
we said to my l, 'The boy cannot Gn 44:22
l of his entire household, Gn 45:8
God has made me l of all Egypt. Gn 45:9
hide from our l that the money Gn 47:18
our livestock belongs to our l. Gn 47:18
left for our l except our bodies Gn 47:18
LORD, "Please, L, I have never Ex 4:10
said, "Please, L, send someone Ex 4:13
LORD and asked, "L, why have You Ex 5:22
L, Your hands have established Ex 15:17
are to appear before the L GOD. Ex 23:17
enraged, my l," Aaron replied. Ex 32:22
he said, "My L, if I have indeed Ex 34:9
Your sight, my L, please go with Ex 34:9
are to appear before the L GOD, Ex 34:23
Moses, my l, stop them!" Nm 11:28
to Moses, "My l, please don't Nm 12:11
will do just as my l commands. Nm 32:25
to the battle as my l orders." Nm 32:27
commanded my l to give the land Nm 36:2
l was further commanded by the Nm 36:2
L GOD, You have begun to show Dt 3:24
L GOD, do not annihilate Your Dt 9:26
the God of gods and L of lords, Dt 10:17
covenant of the L of all the Jos 3:11
the LORD, the L of all the earth Jos 3:13
What does my L want to say to Jos 5:14
"Oh, L GOD," Joshua said, "why Jos 7:7
What can I say, L, now that Jos 7:8
and there was their l lying dead Jdg 3:25
and said to him, "Come in, my l. Jdg 4:18
to Him, "Please, L, how can I Jdg 6:15
LORD, he said, "Oh no, L GOD! Jdg 6:22
and said, "Please L, let the man Jdg 13:8
L GOD, please remember me. Jdg 16:28
"My l," she said, "you have been Ru 2:13
"No, my l," Hannah replied. 1Sm 1:15
"Please, my l," she said, "as 1Sm 1:26
you live, my l, I am the woman 1Sm 1:26
Let our l command your servants 1Sm 16:16
at your service, my l," he said. 1Sm 22:12
never do such a thing to my l, 1Sm 24:6
called to Saul, "My l the king!" 1Sm 24:8
won't lift my hand against my l, 1Sm 24:10
is mine, my l, but please let 1Sm 25:24
My l should pay no attention to 1Sm 25:25
Now my l, as surely as the LORD 1Sm 25:26
trouble for my l be like Nabal. 1Sm 25:26
servant has brought to my l, 1Sm 25:27
the young men who follow my l. 1Sm 25:27
dynasty for my l because he 1Sm 25:28
does for my l all the good He 1Sm 25:30
conscience for my l because of 1Sm 25:31
LORD does good things for my l, 1Sm 25:31
you protect your l the king when 1Sm 26:15
since you didn't protect your l, 1Sm 26:16
is my voice, my l and king," 1Sm 26:17
Why is my l pursuing his 1Sm 26:18
my l the king please hear the 1Sm 26:19
the enemies of my l the king?" 1Sm 29:8
I've brought them here to my l." 2Sm 1:10
to Saul your l when you buried 2Sm 2:5
for though Saul your l is dead, 2Sm 2:7
all Israel to my l the king. 2Sm 3:21
vengeance to my l the king 2Sm 4:8
that place the L Bursts Out. 2Sm 5:20
Who am I, L GOD, and what is 2Sm 7:18
thing to You, L GOD, for You 2Sm 7:19
a revelation for mankind, L GOD. 2Sm 7:19
You know Your servant, L GOD. 2Sm 7:20
is why You are great, L GOD. 2Sm 7:22
L GOD, You are God; Your words 2Sm 7:28
For You, L GOD, have spoken, and 2Sm 7:29
do all my l the king commands. 2Sm 9:11
leaders said to Hanun their l, 2Sm 10:3
My l must not think they have 2Sm 13:32
now, my l the king, don't take 2Sm 13:33
to the king, "My l the king, may 2Sm 14:9
speak a word to my l the king?" 2Sm 14:12
matter to my l the king because 2Sm 14:15
the word of my l the king bring 2Sm 14:17
for my l the king is able to 2Sm 14:17
"Let my l the king speak," 2Sm 14:18
as you live, my l the king, no 2Sm 14:19
from all my l the king says. 2Sm 14:19
but my l has wisdom like the 2Sm 14:20
with you, my l the king, because 2Sm 14:22
fulfill a vow I made to the L. 2Sm 15:7
Whatever my l the king decides, 2Sm 15:15
and as my l the king lives, 2Sm 15:21
wherever my l the king is, 2Sm 15:21
favorably on me, my l the king!" 2Sm 16:4
dead dog curse my l the king? 2Sm 16:9
rebelled against my l the king." 2Sm 18:28
May my l the king hear the good 2Sm 18:31
enemies of my l the king and to 2Sm 18:32
said to him, "My l, don't hold 2Sm 19:19
on the day my l the king left 2Sm 19:19
down to meet my l the king." 2Sm 19:20
"My l the king," he replied, "my 2Sm 19:26
your servant to my l the king. 2Sm 19:27
But my l the king is like the 2Sm 19:27
death from my l the king, 2Sm 19:28
since my l the king has come to 2Sm 19:30
added burden to my l the king? 2Sm 19:35
cross over with my l the king. 2Sm 19:37
while my l the king looks on! 2Sm 24:3
But why does my l the king want 2Sm 24:3
Why has my l the king come to 2Sm 24:21
My l the king may take whatever 2Sm 24:22
young virgin for my l the king. 1Kg 1:2
side so that my l the king will 1Kg 1:2
king and our l David does not 1Kg 1:11
say to him, 'My l king, did you 1Kg 1:13
She replied, "My l, you swore to 1Kg 1:17
And, my l king, you didn't know 1Kg 1:18
Now, my l king, the eyes of all 1Kg 1:20
throne of my l the king after 1Kg 1:20
when my l the king rests with 1Kg 1:21
"My l king," Nathan said, "did 1Kg 1:24
I'm certain my l the king would 1Kg 1:27
will sit on my l the king's 1Kg 1:27
my l King David live forever! 1Kg 1:31
the God of my l the king, so 1Kg 1:36
the LORD was with my l the king, 1Kg 1:37
the throne of my l King David." 1Kg 1:37
Our l King David has made 1Kg 1:43
congratulate our l King David, 1Kg 1:47
the ark of the L GOD in the 1Kg 2:26
do as my l the king has spoken. 1Kg 2:38
pleased the L that Solomon had 1Kg 3:10
said, "Please my l, this woman 1Kg 3:17
"My l, give her the living baby," 1Kg 3:26
For You, L GOD, have set them 1Kg 8:53
people will return to their l, 1Kg 12:27
said, "Is it you, my l Elijah?" 1Kg 18:7
Go tell your l, 'Elijah is here!' 1Kg 18:8
kingdom where my l has not sent 1Kg 18:10
Go tell your l, "Elijah is here! 1Kg 18:11
reported to my l what I did when 1Kg 18:13
Go tell your l, "Elijah is here! 1Kg 18:14
Just as you say, my l king: 1Kg 20:4
Say to my l the king, 1Kg 20:9
and the L will hand it over to 1Kg 22:6
Even though our l can see that 2Kg 2:19
Then she said, "No, my l. 2Kg 4:16
Did I ask my l for a son? 2Kg 4:28
said, "No one, my l the king. 2Kg 6:12
to him, "My l the king, help! 2Kg 6:26
for the L had caused the Aramean 2Kg 7:6
Gehazi said, "My l the king, 2Kg 8:5
asked, "Why is my l weeping?" 2Kg 8:12
have mocked the L through your 2Kg 19:23
that place the L Bursts Out. 1Ch 14:11
l the king, aren't they all my 1Ch 21:3
Why does my l want to do this? 1Ch 21:3
My l the king may do whatever he 1Ch 21:23
and the craftsmen of my l, 2Ch 2:14
Now, let my l send the wheat, 2Ch 2:15
up and rebelled against his l. 2Ch 13:6
counsel of my l and of those who Ezr 10:3
Please, L, let Your ear be Neh 1:11
the great and awe-inspiring L, Neh 4:14
since today is holy to our L. Neh 8:10
and statutes of the LORD our L. Neh 10:29
The fear of the L—that is Jb 28:28
laughs; the L ridicules them. Ps 2:4
LORD, our L, how magnificent is Ps 8:1
You made him l over the works of Ps 8:6
LORD, our L, how magnificent is Ps 8:9
said to the LORD, "You are my L; Ps 16:2
will be told about the L. Ps 22:30
I sought favor from my L: Ps 30:8
L, how long will You look on? Ps 35:17
L, do not be far from me. Ps 35:22
The L laughs at him because He Ps 37:13
L, my every desire is known to Ps 38:9
You will answer, L my God. Ps 38:15
Hurry to help me, L, my Savior. Ps 38:22
Now, L, what do I wait for? Ps 39:7
and needy; the L thinks of me. Ps 40:17
down to him, for he is your l. Ps 45:11
L, open my lips, and my mouth Ps 51:15
the L is the sustainer of my Ps 54:4
L, confuse and confound their Ps 55:9
will praise You, L, among the Ps 57:9
bring them down, L, our shield. Ps 59:11
the L would not have listened. Ps 66:18
The L gave the command; Ps 68:11
the L is among them in the Ps 68:17
May the L be praised! Day after Ps 68:19
from death belongs to the L GOD. Ps 68:20
The L said, "I will bring ⌊them⌋ Ps 68:22
sing praise to the L, Selah Ps 68:32
because of me, L GOD of Hosts; Ps 69:6
You are my hope, L GOD, my Ps 71:5
of the mighty acts of the L GOD; Ps 71:16
from a dream, L, when arising, Ps 73:20
I have made the L GOD my refuge, Ps 73:28
day of trouble I sought the L. Ps 77:2
Will the L reject forever and Ps 77:7
Then the L awoke as if from Ps 78:65
they have hurled at You, L. Ps 79:12
gracious to me, L, for I call to Ps 86:3
since I set my hope on You, L. Ps 86:4
For You, L, are kind and ready Ps 86:5
L, there is no one like You Ps 86:8
before You, L, and will honor Ps 86:9

all my heart, **L** my God, and will	Ps 86:12
But You, **L**, are a compassionate	Ps 86:15
L, where are the former acts of	Ps 89:49
Remember, **L**, the ridicule	Ps 89:50
L, You have been our refuge in	Ps 90:1
favor of the **L** our God be on us	Ps 90:17
presence of the **L** of all the	Ps 97:5
But You, GOD my **L**, deal ⌊kindly⌋	Ps 109:21
The LORD declared to my **L**:	Ps 110:1
The **L** is at Your right hand;	Ps 110:5
presence of the **L**, at the	Ps 114:7
L, listen to my voice; let Your	Ps 130:2
sins, **L**, who could stand	Ps 130:3
I ⌊wait⌋ for the **L** more than	Ps 130:6
our **L** is greater than all gods.	Ps 135:5
Give thanks to the **L** of lords.	Ps 136:3
L GOD, my strong Savior, You	Ps 140:7
my eyes ⌊look⌋ to You, **L** GOD.	Ps 141:8
Our **L** is great, vast in power;	Ps 147:5
Therefore the **L** GOD of Hosts,	Is 1:24
The **L** GOD of Hosts is about to	Is 3:1
says the **L** GOD of Hosts.	Is 3:15
L will put scabs on the heads	Is 3:17
On that day the **L** will strip	Is 3:18
when the **L** has washed away the	Is 4:4
I saw the **L** seated on a high and	Is 6:1
heard the voice of the **L** saying:	Is 6:8
Then I said, "Until when, **L**?"	Is 6:11
This is what the **L** GOD says:	Is 7:7
the **L** Himself will give you a	Is 7:14
On that day the **L** will use a	Is 7:20
the **L** will certainly bring	Is 8:7
The **L** sent a message against	Is 9:8
Therefore the **L** does not rejoice	Is 9:17
But when the **L** finishes all His	Is 10:12
Therefore the **L** GOD of Hosts	Is 10:16
the land the **L** GOD of Hosts is	Is 10:23
the **L** GOD of Hosts says this:	Is 10:24
the **L** GOD of Hosts will chop off	Is 10:33
On that day the **L** will ⌊extend⌋	Is 11:11
of the **L** GOD of Hosts.	Is 19:4
For the **L** has said to me,	Is 21:6
lookout reported, "**L**, I stand	Is 21:8
For the **L** said this to me:	Is 21:16
For the **L** GOD of Hosts had a day	Is 22:5
On that day the **L** GOD of Hosts	Is 22:12
The **L** GOD of Hosts has spoken.	Is 22:14
The **L** GOD of Hosts said:	Is 22:15
disgrace to the house of your **l**.	Is 22:18
The **L** GOD will wipe away the	Is 25:8
L has a strong and mighty one	Is 28:2
Therefore the **L** GOD said:	Is 28:16
heard from the **L** GOD of Hosts	Is 28:22
The **L** said: Because these people	Is 29:13
For the **L** GOD, the Holy One of	Is 30:15
The **L** will give you meager bread	Is 30:20
upward. **L**, I am oppressed	Is 38:14
L, because of these ⌊promises⌋	Is 38:16
the **L** GOD comes with strength,	Is 40:10
And now the **L** GOD has sent me	Is 48:16
The **L** has forgotten me!"	Is 49:14
This is what the **L** GOD says:	Is 49:22
L GOD has given Me the tongue	Is 50:4
The **L** GOD has opened My ear,	Is 50:5
The **L** GOD will help Me;	Is 50:7
truth, the **L** GOD will help Me;	Is 50:9
This is what your **L** says—	Is 51:22
For this is what the **L** GOD says:	Is 52:4
the declaration of the **L** GOD,	Is 56:8
Spirit of the **L** GOD is on Me,	Is 61:1
so the **L** GOD will cause	Is 61:11
this is what the **L** GOD says:	Is 65:13
and the **L** GOD will kill you;	Is 65:15
But I protested, "Oh no, **L** GOD!	Jr 1:6
of the **L** GOD of Hosts.	Jr 2:19
⌊This is⌋ the **L** GOD's	Jr 2:22
I said, "Oh no, **L** GOD, You have	Jr 4:10
this is what the **L** GOD of Hosts	Jr 5:14
this is what the **L** GOD says:	Jr 7:20
And I replied, "Oh no, **L** GOD!	Jr 14:13
mourn for him, saying, Woe, **l**!	Jr 22:18
Ah, **L** GOD! You Yourself made the	Jr 32:17
Yet You, **L** GOD, have said to me:	Jr 32:25
you. Alas, **l**! will be the lament	Jr 34:5
please listen, my **l** the king.	Jr 37:20
My **l** king, these men have been	Jr 38:9
saying, As the **L** GOD lives.	Jr 44:26
That day belongs to the **L**,	Jr 46:10
it will be a sacrifice to the **L**,	Jr 46:10
is⌋ the declaration of the **L**,	Jr 49:5
is a task of the **L** GOD of Hosts	Jr 50:25
of the **L** GOD of Hosts—	Jr 50:31
the **L** has broken my strength.	Lm 1:14
L has rejected all the mighty	Lm 1:15
The **L** has trampled Virgin	Lm 1:15
How the **L** has overshadowed	Lm 2:1
compassion the **L** has swallowed	Lm 2:2
The **L** is like an enemy;	Lm 2:5
The **L** has rejected His altar,	Lm 2:7
of the people cry out to the **L**.	Lm 2:18
For the **L** will not reject ⌊us⌋	Lm 3:31
the **L** does not approve ⌊of these	Lm 3:36
unless the **L** has ordained ⌊it⌋?	Lm 3:37
You defend my cause, **L**;	Lm 3:58
This is what the **L** GOD says.	Ezk 2:4
This is what the **L** GOD says,	Ezk 3:11
This is what the **L** GOD says.	Ezk 3:27
But I said, "Ah, **L** GOD, I have	Ezk 4:14
This is what the **L** GOD says:	Ezk 5:5
this is what the **L** GOD says:	Ezk 5:7
this is what the **L** GOD says:	Ezk 5:8
the declaration of the **L** GOD—	Ezk 5:11
hear the word of the **L** GOD!	Ezk 6:3
This is what the **L** GOD says to	Ezk 6:3
This is what the **L** GOD says:	Ezk 6:11
this is what the **L** GOD says to	Ezk 7:2
This is what the **L** GOD says:	Ezk 7:5
the hand of the **L** GOD came down	Ezk 8:1
and cried out, "Ah, **L** GOD!	Ezk 9:8
this is what the **L** GOD says:	Ezk 11:7
the declaration of the **L** GOD.	Ezk 11:8
loud voice: "Ah, **L** GOD! Will You	Ezk 11:13
This is what the **L** GOD says:	Ezk 11:16
This is what the **L** GOD says:	Ezk 11:17
the declaration of the **L** GOD.	Ezk 11:21
This is what the **L** GOD says:	Ezk 12:10
is what the **L** GOD says about	Ezk 12:19
This is what the **L** GOD says:	Ezk 12:23
the declaration of the **L** GOD.	Ezk 12:25
This is what the **L** GOD says:	Ezk 12:28
the declaration of the **L** GOD.	Ezk 12:28
This is what the **L** GOD says:	Ezk 13:3
this is what the **L** GOD says:	Ezk 13:8
the declaration of the **L** GOD.	Ezk 13:8
will know that I am the **L** GOD.	Ezk 13:9
So this is what the **L** GOD says:	Ezk 13:13
the declaration of the **L** GOD.	Ezk 13:16
This is what the **L** GOD says:	Ezk 13:18
this is what the **L** GOD says:	Ezk 13:20
This is what the **L** GOD says:	Ezk 14:4
This is what the **L** GOD says:	Ezk 14:6
the declaration of the **L** GOD.	Ezk 14:11
the declaration of the **L** GOD.	Ezk 14:14
the declaration of the **L** GOD—	Ezk 14:16
the declaration of the **L** GOD—	Ezk 14:18
the declaration of the **L** GOD—	Ezk 14:20
For this is what the **L** GOD says:	Ezk 14:21
the declaration of the **L** GOD.	Ezk 14:23
this is what the **L** GOD says:	Ezk 15:6
the declaration of the **L** GOD.	Ezk 15:8
This is what the **L** GOD says to	Ezk 16:3
the declaration of the **L** GOD.	Ezk 16:8
the declaration of the **L** GOD.	Ezk 16:14
the declaration of the **L** GOD.	Ezk 16:19
the declaration of the **L** GOD—	Ezk 16:23
the declaration of the **L** GOD—	Ezk 16:30
This is what the **L** GOD says:	Ezk 16:36
the declaration of the **L** GOD.	Ezk 16:43
the declaration of the **L** GOD—	Ezk 16:48
For this is what the **L** GOD says:	Ezk 16:59
the declaration of the **L** GOD.	Ezk 16:63
This is what the **L** GOD says:	Ezk 17:3
This is what the **L** GOD says:	Ezk 17:9
the declaration of the **L** GOD—	Ezk 17:16
this is what the **L** GOD says:	Ezk 17:19
This is what the **L** GOD says:	Ezk 17:22
the declaration of the **L** GOD—	Ezk 18:3
the declaration of the **L** GOD.	Ezk 18:9
the declaration of the **L** GOD.	Ezk 18:23
the declaration of the **L** GOD.	Ezk 18:30
the declaration of the **L** GOD.	Ezk 18:32
This is what the **L** GOD says:	Ezk 20:3
the declaration of the **L** GOD.	Ezk 20:3
This is what the **L** GOD says:	Ezk 20:5
This is what the **L** GOD says:	Ezk 20:27
This is what the **L** GOD says:	Ezk 20:30
the declaration of the **L** GOD—	Ezk 20:31
the declaration of the **L** GOD—	Ezk 20:33
the declaration of the **L** GOD.	Ezk 20:36
this is what the **L** GOD says:	Ezk 20:39
the declaration of the **L** GOD—	Ezk 20:40
the declaration of the **L** GOD.	Ezk 20:44
This is what the **L** GOD says:	Ezk 20:47
Then I said, "Ah, **L** GOD, they	Ezk 20:49
the declaration of the **L** GOD.	Ezk 21:7
This is what the **L** says!	Ezk 21:9
the declaration of the **L** GOD.	Ezk 21:13
this is what the **L** GOD says:	Ezk 21:24
This is what the **L** GOD says:	Ezk 21:26
This is what the **L** GOD says	Ezk 21:28
This is what the **L** GOD says:	Ezk 22:3
the declaration of the **L** GOD.	Ezk 22:12
this is what the **L** GOD says:	Ezk 22:19
This is what the **L** GOD says,	Ezk 22:28
the declaration of the **L** GOD.	Ezk 22:31
this is what the **L** GOD says:	Ezk 23:22
For this is what the **L** GOD says:	Ezk 23:28
This is what the **L** GOD says:	Ezk 23:32
the declaration of the **L** GOD.	Ezk 23:34
this is what the **L** GOD says:	Ezk 23:35
This is what the **L** GOD says:	Ezk 23:46
will know that I am the **L** GOD."	Ezk 23:49
This is what the **L** GOD says:	Ezk 24:3
this is what the **L** GOD says:	Ezk 24:6
this is what the **L** GOD says:	Ezk 24:9
the declaration of the **L** GOD.	Ezk 24:14
This is what the **L** GOD says:	Ezk 24:21
will know that I am the **L** GOD.	Ezk 24:24
Hear the word of the **L** GOD:	Ezk 25:3
This is what the **L** GOD says:	Ezk 25:3
For this is what the **L** GOD says:	Ezk 25:6
This is what the **L** GOD says:	Ezk 25:8
This is what the **L** GOD says:	Ezk 25:12
this is what the **L** GOD says:	Ezk 25:13
the declaration of the **L** GOD.	Ezk 25:14
This is what the **L** GOD says:	Ezk 25:15
this is what the **L** GOD says:	Ezk 25:16
this is what the **L** GOD says:	Ezk 26:3
the declaration of the **L** GOD.	Ezk 26:5
For this is what the **L** GOD says:	Ezk 26:7
the declaration of the **L** GOD.	Ezk 26:14
is what the **L** GOD says to Tyre	Ezk 26:15
For this is what the **L** GOD says:	Ezk 26:19
the declaration of the **L** GOD.	Ezk 26:21
This is what the **L** GOD says:	Ezk 27:3
This is what the **L** GOD says:	Ezk 28:2
this is what the **L** GOD says:	Ezk 28:6
the declaration of the **L** GOD.	Ezk 28:10
This is what the **L** GOD says:	Ezk 28:12
This is what the **L** GOD says:	Ezk 28:22
will know that I am the **L** GOD.	Ezk 28:24
This is what the **L** GOD says:	Ezk 28:25
This is what the **L** GOD says:	Ezk 29:3
this is what the **L** GOD says:	Ezk 29:8
For this is what the **L** GOD says:	Ezk 29:13
will know that I am the **L** GOD."	Ezk 29:16
this is what the **L** GOD says:	Ezk 29:19
the declaration of the **L** GOD.	Ezk 29:20
This is what the **L** GOD says:	Ezk 30:2
the declaration of the **L** GOD.	Ezk 30:6
This is what the **L** GOD says:	Ezk 30:10
This is what the **L** GOD says:	Ezk 30:13
this is what the **L** GOD says:	Ezk 30:22
this is what the **L** GOD says:	Ezk 31:10
This is what the **L** GOD says:	Ezk 31:15
the declaration of the **L** GOD.	Ezk 31:18
This is what the **L** GOD says:	Ezk 32:3
the declaration of the **L** GOD.	Ezk 32:8
For this is what the **L** GOD says:	Ezk 32:11
the declaration of the **L** GOD.	Ezk 32:14
the declaration of the **L** GOD.	Ezk 32:16
the declaration of the **L** GOD.	Ezk 32:31
the declaration of the **L** GOD.	Ezk 32:32
the declaration of the **L** GOD—	Ezk 33:11
This is what the **L** GOD says:	Ezk 33:25
This is what the **L** GOD says:	Ezk 33:27
This is what the **L** GOD says to	Ezk 34:2
the declaration of the **L** GOD—	Ezk 34:8
This is what the **L** GOD says:	Ezk 34:10
For this is what the **L** GOD says:	Ezk 34:11
the declaration of the **L** GOD.	Ezk 34:15
The **L** GOD says to you, My flock:	Ezk 34:17
is what the **L** GOD says to them	Ezk 34:20
the declaration of the **L** GOD.	Ezk 34:30

the declaration of the **L** GOD. Ezk 34:31
This is what the **L** GOD says: Ezk 35:3
the declaration of the **L** GOD— Ezk 35:6
the declaration of the **L** GOD— Ezk 35:11
This is what the **L** GOD says: Ezk 35:14
This is what the **L** GOD says: Ezk 36:2
This is what the **L** GOD says: Ezk 36:3
hear the word of the **L** GOD. Ezk 36:4
This is what the **L** GOD says to Ezk 36:4
This is what the **L** GOD says: Ezk 36:5
This is what the **L** GOD says: Ezk 36:6
this is what the **L** GOD says: Ezk 36:7
This is what the **L** GOD says: Ezk 36:13
the declaration of the **L** GOD. Ezk 36:14
the declaration of the **L** GOD. Ezk 36:15
This is what the **L** GOD says: Ezk 36:22
the declaration of the **L** GOD— Ezk 36:23
the declaration of the **L** GOD— Ezk 36:32
This is what the **L** GOD says: Ezk 36:33
This is what the **L** GOD says: Ezk 36:37
I replied, "**L** GOD, ⌊only⌋ You Ezk 37:3
This is what the **L** GOD says to Ezk 37:5
This is what the **L** GOD says: Ezk 37:9
This is what the **L** GOD says: Ezk 37:12
This is what the **L** GOD says: Ezk 37:19
This is what the **L** GOD says: Ezk 37:21
This is what the **L** GOD says: Ezk 38:3
This is what the **L** GOD says: Ezk 38:10
This is what the **L** GOD says: Ezk 38:14
This is what the **L** GOD says: Ezk 38:17
the declaration of the **L** GOD— Ezk 38:18
the declaration of the **L** GOD— Ezk 38:21
This is what the **L** GOD says: Ezk 39:1
the declaration of the **L** GOD. Ezk 39:5
the declaration of the **L** GOD. Ezk 39:8
the declaration of the **L** GOD. Ezk 39:10
the declaration of the **L** GOD. Ezk 39:13
this is what the **L** GOD says: Ezk 39:17
the declaration of the **L** GOD. Ezk 39:20
So this is what the **L** GOD says: Ezk 39:25
the declaration of the **L** GOD. Ezk 39:29
this is what the **L** GOD says: Ezk 43:18
the declaration of the **L** GOD. Ezk 43:19
the declaration of the **L** GOD. Ezk 43:27
This is what the **L** GOD says: Ezk 44:6
This is what the **L** GOD says: Ezk 44:9
the declaration of the **L** GOD— Ezk 44:12
the declaration of the **L** GOD— Ezk 44:15
the declaration of the **L** GOD. Ezk 44:27
This is what the **L** GOD says: Ezk 45:9
the declaration of the **L** GOD. Ezk 45:9
the declaration of the **L** GOD. Ezk 45:15
This is what the **L** GOD says: Ezk 45:18
This is what the **L** GOD says: Ezk 46:1
This is what the **L** GOD says: Ezk 46:16
This is what the **L** GOD says: Ezk 47:13
the declaration of the **L** GOD. Ezk 47:23
the declaration of the **L** GOD. Ezk 48:29
The **L** handed Jehoiakim king of Dn 1:2
My **l** the king assigned your food Dn 1:10
indeed God of gods, **L** of kings, Dn 2:47
answered, "My **l**, may the dream Dn 4:19
passed against my **l** the king: Dn 4:24
against the **L** of heaven. Dn 5:23
to the **L** God to seek Him Dn 9:3
Ah, **L**—the great and Dn 9:4
L, righteousness belongs to You, Dn 9:7
belong to the **L** our God, Dn 9:9
Now, **L** our God, who brought Your Dn 9:15
L, in keeping with all Your Dn 9:16
L, hear! Lord, forgive! Lord, Dn 9:19
Lord, hear! **L**, forgive! Lord, Dn 9:19
forgive! **L**, listen and act! Dn 9:19
front of me, "My **l**, because of Dn 10:16
with someone like you, my **l**? Dn 10:17
said, "Let my **l** speak, for you Dn 10:19
So I asked, "My **l**, what will be Dn 12:8
so his **L** will leave his Hs 12:14
perish. The **L** GOD has spoken. Am 1:8
the **L** GOD does nothing without Am 3:7
not fear? The **L** GOD has spoken; Am 3:8
Therefore, the **L** GOD says: Am 3:11
the declaration of the **L** GOD, Am 3:13
The **L** GOD has sworn by His Am 4:2
the **L** GOD says: The city that Am 5:3
the God of Hosts, the **L**, says: Am 5:16
The **L** GOD has sworn by Himself— Am 6:8
is⌋ the declaration of the **L**, Am 6:14
The **L** GOD showed me this: Am 7:1
the land, I said, "**L** GOD, please Am 7:2
The **L** GOD showed me this: Am 7:4
The **L** GOD was calling for a Am 7:4
I said, "**L** GOD, please stop! Am 7:5
happen either," said the **L** GOD. Am 7:6
The **L** was standing there by a Am 7:7
Then the **L** said, "I am setting Am 7:8
The **L** GOD showed me this: Am 8:1
wailing"—the **L** GOD's Am 8:3
the declaration of the **L** GOD— Am 8:9
the declaration of the **L** GOD— Am 8:11
The **L**, the GOD of Hosts—He Am 9:5
the eyes of the **L** GOD are on the Am 9:8
This is what the **L** GOD has said Ob 1
The **L** GOD will be a witness Mc 1:2
against you, the **L**, from His Mc 1:2
to the **L** of all the earth. Mc 4:13
declaration of the **L** of Hosts. Nah 2:13
declaration of the **L** of Hosts. Nah 3:5
Yahweh my **L** is my strength; Hab 3:19
in the presence of the **L** GOD, Zph 1:7
I asked, "What are these, my **l**?" Zch 1:9
with me, "What are these, my **l**?" Zch 4:4
with me. I said, "No, my **l**." Zch 4:5
"No, my **l**," I replied. Zch 4:13
who stand by the **L** of the whole Zch 4:14
with me, "What are these, my **l**?" Zch 6:4
themselves to the **L** of the whole Zch 6:5
The **L** will impoverish her and Zch 9:4
The **L** GOD will sound the trumpet Zch 9:14
a defective ⌊animal⌋ to the **L**. Mal 1:14
the **L** you seek will suddenly Mal 3:1
an angel of the **L** suddenly Mt 1:20
was spoken by the **L** through the Mt 1:22
an angel of the **L** suddenly Mt 2:13
was spoken by the **L** through the Mt 2:15
an angel of the **L** suddenly Mt 2:19
Prepare the way for the **L**; Mt 3:3
Do not test the **L** your God." Mt 4:7
Worship the **L** your God, and Mt 4:10
must keep your oaths to the **L**. Mt 5:33
who says to Me, '**L**, Lord!' Mt 7:21
who says to Me, 'Lord, **L**!' Mt 7:21
say to Me, '**L**, Lord, didn't we Mt 7:22
say to Me, 'Lord, **L**, didn't we Mt 7:22
Him, saying, "**L**, if You are Mt 8:2
L, my servant is lying at home Mt 8:6
"**L**," the centurion replied, "I Mt 8:8
"**L**," another of His disciples Mt 8:21
Him up, saying, "**L**, save ⌊us⌋! Mt 8:25
"Yes, **L**," they answered Him. Mt 9:28
pray to the **L** of the harvest to Mt 9:38
You, Father, **L** of heaven and Mt 11:25
Son of Man is **L** of the Sabbath. Mt 12:8
"**L**, if it's You," Peter answered Mt 14:28
sink he cried out, "**L**, save me!" Mt 14:30
mercy on me, **L**, Son of David! Mt 15:22
Him, and said, "**L**, help me!" Mt 15:25
"Yes, **L**," she said, "yet even Mt 15:27
began to rebuke Him, "Oh no, **L**! Mt 16:22
said to Jesus, "**L**, it's good for Mt 17:4
"**L**," he said, "have mercy on my Mt 17:15
Him and said, "**L**, how many times Mt 18:21
they cried out, "**L**, have mercy Mt 20:30
all the more, "**L**, have mercy on Mt 20:31
"**L**," they said to Him, "open our Mt 20:33
say that the **L** needs them, Mt 21:3
who comes in the name of the **L**! Mt 21:9
came from the **L** and is wonderful Mt 21:42
Love the **L** your God with all Mt 22:37
by the Spirit, calls Him '**L**': Mt 22:43
The **L** declared to my Lord, Mt 22:44
The Lord declared to my **L**, Mt 22:44
David calls Him '**L**,' how then Mt 22:45
who comes in the name of the **L**!" Mt 23:39
know what day your **L** is coming. Mt 24:42
answer Him, '**L**, when did we see Mt 25:37
will answer, '**L**, when did we see Mt 25:44
say to Him, "Surely not I, **L**?" Mt 26:22
field, as the **L** directed me. Mt 27:10
an angel of the **L** descended from Mt 28:2
Prepare the way for the **L**; Mk 1:3
the Son of Man is **L** even of the Mk 2:28
how much the **L** has done for you Mk 5:19
replied to Him, "**L**, even the Mk 7:28
'The **L** needs it and will send it Mk 11:3
who comes in the name of the **L**! Mk 11:9
came from the **L** and is wonderful Mk 12:11
The **L** our God, The Lord is One. Mk 12:29
The Lord our God, The **L** is One. Mk 12:29
the **L** your God with all your Mk 12:30
The **L** declared to my Lord, Mk 12:36
The Lord declared to my **L**, Mk 12:36
David himself calls Him '**L**'; Mk 12:37
Unless the **L** limited those days, Mk 13:20
the **L** Jesus was taken up into Mk 16:19
the **L** working with them and Mk 16:20
and requirements of the **L**. Lk 1:6
of the **L** and burn incense Lk 1:9
angel of the **L** appeared to him Lk 1:11
sight of the **L** and will never Lk 1:15
of Israel to the **L** their God. Lk 1:16
ready for the **L** a prepared Lk 1:17
The **L** has done this for me. Lk 1:25
woman! The **L** is with you." Lk 1:28
and the **L** God will give Him the Lk 1:32
the mother of my **L** should come Lk 1:43
her by the **L** will be fulfilled! Lk 1:45
the greatness of the **L**, Lk 1:46
heard that the **L** had shown her Lk 1:58
Praise the **L**, the God of Israel, Lk 1:68
go before the **L** to prepare His Lk 1:76
an angel of the **L** stood before Lk 2:9
the glory of the **L** shone around Lk 2:9
is Messiah the **L**, was born for Lk 2:11
the **L** has made known to us. Lk 2:15
to present Him to the **L** Lk 2:22
is written in the law of the **L**: Lk 2:23
male will be dedicated to the **L** Lk 2:23
is stated in the law of the **L**: Lk 2:24
according to the law of the **L**, Lk 2:39
Prepare the way for the **L**; Lk 3:4
Worship the **L** your God, and Lk 4:8
Do not test the **L** your God." Lk 4:12
The Spirit of the **L** is on Me, Lk 4:18
because I'm a sinful man, **L**!" Lk 5:8
L, if You are willing, You can Lk 5:12
Son of Man is **L** of the Sabbath. Lk 6:5
do you call Me '**L**, Lord,' and Lk 6:46
call Me 'Lord, **L**,' and don't do Lk 6:46
to tell Him, "**L**, don't trouble Lk 7:6
When the **L** saw her, He had Lk 7:13
sent them to the **L**, asking, "Are Lk 7:19
they said, "**L**, do You want us Lk 9:54
"**L**," he said, "first let me go Lk 9:59
will follow You, **L**, but first Lk 9:61
the **L** appointed 70 others, Lk 10:1
pray to the **L** of the harvest to Lk 10:2
joy, saying, "**L**, even the demons Lk 10:17
You, Father, **L** of heaven and Lk 10:21
the **L** your God with all your Lk 10:27
up and asked, "**L**, don't You care Lk 10:40
The **L** answered her, "Martha, Lk 10:41
said to Him, "**L**, teach us to Lk 11:1
But the **L** said to him: Lk 11:39
"**L**," Peter asked, "are You Lk 12:41
The **L** said: "Who then is the Lk 12:42
But the **L** answered him and said, Lk 13:15
"**L**," someone asked Him, "are Lk 13:23
saying, '**L**, open up for us! Lk 13:25
who comes in the name of the **L**!" Lk 13:35
The apostles said to the **L**, Lk 17:5
seed," the **L** said, "you can say Lk 17:6
"Where, **L**?" they asked Him. He Lk 17:37
Then the **L** said, "Listen to what Lk 18:6
"**L**," he said, "I want to see!" Lk 18:41
stood there and said to the **L**, Lk 19:8
my possessions to the poor, **L**! Lk 19:8
say this: 'The **L** needs it.' " Lk 19:31
"The **L** needs it," they said. Lk 19:34
who comes in the name of the **L**. Lk 19:38
he calls the **L** the God of Lk 20:37
The **L** declared to my Lord, Lk 20:42
The Lord declared to my **L**, Lk 20:42
David calls Him '**L**'; how then Lk 20:44
"**L**," he told Him, "I'm ready to Lk 22:33
"**L**," they said, "look, here are Lk 22:38
they asked, "**L**, should we strike Lk 22:49
Then the **L** turned and looked at Lk 22:61
remembered the word of the **L**, Lk 22:61
find the body of the **L** Jesus. Lk 24:3
The **L** has certainly been raised, Lk 24:34
Make straight the way of the **L**— Jn 1:23
bread after the **L** gave thanks. Jn 6:23
answered, "**L**, who will we go Jn 6:68

"No one, L," she answered. Jn 8:11
"I believe, L!" he said, and he Jn 9:38
who anointed the L with fragrant Jn 11:2
"L, the one You love is sick." Jn 11:3
to Him, "L, if he has fallen Jn 11:12
said to Jesus, "L, if You had Jn 11:21
"Yes, L," she told Him, "I Jn 11:27
told Him, "L, if You had been Jn 11:32
"L," they told Him, "come and see. Jn 11:34
told Him, "L, he already stinks Jn 11:39
who comes in the name of the L— Jn 12:13
L, who has believed our message? Jn 12:38
the arm of the L been revealed Jn 12:38
who asked Him, "L, are You going Jn 13:6
said to Him, "L, not only my Jn 13:9
You call Me Teacher and L. Jn 13:13
if I, your L and Teacher, have Jn 13:14
and asked Him, "L, who is it?" Jn 13:25
"L," Simon Peter said to Him, Jn 13:36
"L," Peter asked, "why can't I Jn 13:37
"L," Thomas said, "we don't know Jn 14:5
"L," said Philip, "show us the Jn 14:8
to Him, "L, how is it You're Jn 14:22
taken the L out of the tomb, Jn 20:2
they've taken away my L," Jn 20:13
disciples, "I have seen the L!" Jn 20:18
rejoiced when they saw the L. Jn 20:20
him, "We have seen the L!" Jn 20:25
to Him, "My L and my God!" Jn 20:28
said to Peter, "It is the L!" Jn 21:7
Peter heard that it was the L, Jn 21:7
because they knew it was the L. Jn 21:12
"Yes, L," he said to Him, "You Jn 21:15
"Yes, L," he said to Him, "You Jn 21:16
He said, "L, You know Jn 21:17
and asked, "L, who is the one Jn 21:20
said to Jesus, "L—what about Jn 21:21
they asked Him, "L, at this time Ac 1:6
the whole time the L Jesus went Ac 1:21
prayed, "You, L, know the hearts Ac 1:24
remarkable day of the L comes; Ac 2:20
the name of the L will be saved. Ac 2:21
I saw the L ever before me; Ac 2:25
The L said to my Lord, 'Sit at Ac 2:34
Lord said to my L, 'Sit at My Ac 2:34
crucified, both L and Messiah!" Ac 2:36
many as the L our God will call. Ac 2:39
every day the L added to them Ac 2:47
come from the presence of the L, Ac 3:19
The L your God will raise up for Ac 3:22
against the L and against His Ac 4:26
And now, L, consider their Ac 4:29
the resurrection of the L Jesus, Ac 4:33
to test the Spirit of the L? Ac 5:9
added to the L in increasing Ac 5:14
an angel of the L opened the Ac 5:19
at it, the voice of the L came: Ac 7:31
Then the L said to him: Ac 7:33
the L, or what is My resting Ac 7:49
"L Jesus, receive my spirit!" Ac 7:59
a loud voice, "L, do not charge Ac 7:60
in the name of the L Jesus. Ac 8:16
pray to the L that the intent Ac 8:22
"Please pray to the L for me," Ac 8:24
and spoken the message of the L, Ac 8:25
angel of the L spoke to Philip Ac 8:26
Spirit of the L carried Philip Ac 8:39
against the disciples of the L, Ac 9:1
"Who are You, L?" he said. "I am Ac 9:5
And the L said to him in a Ac 9:10
Here I am, L!" he said. Ac 9:10
Straight," the L said to him, "to Ac 9:11
"L," Ananias answered, "I have Ac 9:13
But the L said to him, "Go! Ac 9:15
Brother Saul, the L Jesus, who Ac 9:17
had seen the L, and that He had Ac 9:27
boldly in the name of the L. Ac 9:28
in the fear of the L and in the Ac 9:31
saw him and turned to the L. Ac 9:35
and many believed in the L. Ac 9:42
and said, "What is it, L?" Ac 10:4
"No, L!" Peter said. "For I have Ac 10:14
have been commanded by the L." Ac 10:33
Jesus Christ—He is L of all. Ac 10:36
'No, L!' I said. 'For nothing Ac 11:8
I remembered the word of the L, Ac 11:16
believed on the L Jesus Christ, Ac 11:17
the good news about the L Jesus. Ac 11:20
who believed turned to the L. Ac 11:21
remain true to the L with a firm Ac 11:23
of people were added to the L. Ac 11:24
an angel of the L appeared, Ac 12:7
certain that the L has sent His Ac 12:11
them how the L had brought him Ac 12:17
an angel of the L struck him Ac 12:23
to the L and fasting, Ac 13:2
the straight paths of the L? Ac 13:10
at the teaching about the L. Ac 13:12
to hear the message of the L. Ac 13:44
is what the L has commanded us Ac 13:47
glorified the message of the L, Ac 13:48
message of the L spread through Ac 13:49
reliance on the L, who testified Ac 14:3
them to the L in whom they had Ac 14:23
the grace of the L Jesus, Ac 15:11
left of mankind may seek the L— Ac 15:17
the L who does these things, Ac 15:17
the name of our L Jesus Christ. Ac 15:26
the message of the L. Ac 15:35
preached the message of the L, Ac 15:36
grace of the L by the brothers Ac 15:40
The L opened her heart to pay Ac 16:14
consider me a believer in the L, Ac 16:15
Believe on the L Jesus, and you Ac 16:31
message of the L to him along Ac 16:32
He is L of heaven and earth and Ac 17:24
believed the L, along with his Ac 18:8
Then the L said to Paul in a Ac 18:9
instructed in the way of the L; Ac 18:25
in the name of the L Jesus. Ac 19:5
Greeks, heard the word of the L. Ac 19:10
the name of the L Jesus over Ac 19:13
the name of the L Jesus was Ac 19:17
serving the L with all humility, Ac 20:19
God and faith in our L Jesus. Ac 20:21
I received from the L Jesus, Ac 20:24
mind the words of the L Jesus, Ac 20:35
for the name of the L Jesus." Ac 21:13
I answered, 'Who are You, L?' Ac 22:8
I said, 'What should I do, L?' Ac 22:10
And the L told me, 'Get up and Ac 22:10
But I said, 'L, they know that Ac 22:19
the L stood by him and said, Ac 23:11
But I said, 'Who are You, L?' Ac 26:15
Lord?' "And the L replied: 'I am Ac 26:15
concerning the L Jesus Christ Ac 28:31
Jesus Christ our L, who was a Rm 1:3
Father and the L Jesus Christ. Rm 1:7
the man whom the L will never Rm 4:8
Jesus our L from the dead. Rm 4:24
God through our L Jesus Christ. Rm 5:1
God through our L Jesus Christ, Rm 5:11
life through Jesus Christ our L. Rm 5:21
life in Christ Jesus our L. Rm 6:23
God through Jesus Christ our L! Rm 7:25
that is in Christ Jesus our L! Rm 8:39
for the L will execute His Rm 9:28
the L of Hosts had not left us Rm 9:29
mouth, "Jesus is L," and believe Rm 10:9
since the same L of all is rich Rm 10:12
the name of the L will be saved. Rm 10:13
For Isaiah says, L, who has Rm 10:16
L, they have killed Your Rm 11:3
who has known the mind of the L? Rm 11:34
fervent in spirit; serve the L. Rm 12:11
I will repay, says the L. Rm 12:19
But put on the L Jesus Christ, Rm 13:14
Before his own L he stands or Rm 14:4
For the L is able to make him Rm 14:4
the day, observes it to the L. Rm 14:6
eats to the L, since he gives Rm 14:6
it is to the L that he does not Rm 14:6
If we live, we live to the L; Rm 14:8
and if we die, we die to the L. Rm 14:8
live or die, we belong to the L. Rm 14:8
live, says the L, every knee Rm 14:11
persuaded by the L Jesus that Rm 14:14
Father of our L Jesus Christ Rm 15:6
Praise the L, all you Gentiles; Rm 15:11
through the L Jesus Christ and Rm 15:30
her in the L in a manner worthy Rm 16:2
my dear friend in the L. Rm 16:8
of Narcissus who are in the L. Rm 16:11
who have worked hard in the L. Rm 16:12
has worked very hard in the L. Rm 16:12
Greet Rufus, chosen in the L; Rm 16:13
not serve our L Christ but their Rm 16:18
The grace of our L Jesus be with Rm 16:20
penned this epistle in the L, Rm 16:22
grace of our L Jesus Christ be Rm 16:24
the name of Jesus Christ our L— 1Co 1:2
Father and the L Jesus Christ. 1Co 1:3
of our L Jesus Christ. 1Co 1:7
the day of our L Jesus Christ. 1Co 1:8
His Son, Jesus Christ our L. 1Co 1:9
the name of our L Jesus Christ, 1Co 1:10
who boasts must boast in the L. 1Co 1:31
have crucified the L of glory. 1Co 2:8
has the role the L has given. 1Co 3:5
L knows the reasonings of the 1Co 3:20
One who evaluates me is the L. 1Co 4:4
before the L comes, who will 1Co 4:5
and faithful child in the L. 1Co 4:17
you soon, if the L wills, and I 1Co 4:19
In the name of our L Jesus, 1Co 5:4
with the power of our L Jesus, 1Co 5:4
be saved in the Day of the L. 1Co 5:5
the name of the L Jesus Christ 1Co 6:11
sexual immorality but for the L, 1Co 6:13
Lord, and the L for the body. 1Co 6:13
raised up the L and will also 1Co 6:14
joined to the L is one spirit 1Co 6:17
not I, but the L—a wife is not 1Co 7:10
to the rest I, not the L, say: 1Co 7:12
situation the L assigned when 1Co 7:17
is called by the L as a slave is 1Co 7:22
I have no command from the L, 1Co 7:25
about the things of the L— 1Co 7:32
Lord—how he may please the L. 1Co 7:32
about the things of the L, 1Co 7:34
be devoted to the L without 1Co 7:35
she wants—only in the L. 1Co 7:39
and one L, Jesus Christ, through 1Co 8:6
Have I not seen Jesus our L? 1Co 9:1
Are you not my work in the L? 1Co 9:1
seal of my apostleship in the L. 1Co 9:2
the L has commanded that those 1Co 9:14
the cup of the L and the cup 1Co 10:21
we provoking the L to jealousy? 1Co 10:22
However, in the L, woman is not 1Co 11:11
received from the L what I also 1Co 11:23
betrayed, the L Jesus took bread 1Co 11:23
the cup of the L in an unworthy 1Co 11:27
the body and blood of the L. 1Co 11:27
we are disciplined by the L, 1Co 11:32
can say, "Jesus is L," except by 1Co 12:3
ministries, but the same L. 1Co 12:5
not listen to Me, says the L. 1Co 14:21
I have in Christ Jesus our L: 1Co 15:31
through our L Jesus Christ! 1Co 15:57
labor in the L is not in vain. 1Co 15:58
time with you, if the L allows. 1Co 16:7
greet you heartily in the L, 1Co 16:19
If anyone does not love the L, 1Co 16:22
The grace of our L Jesus be with 1Co 16:23
Father and the L Jesus Christ. 2Co 1:2
Father of our L Jesus Christ, 2Co 1:3
in the day of our L Jesus. 2Co 1:14
door was opened to me by the L. 2Co 2:12
a person turns to the L, 2Co 3:16
Now the L is the Spirit; 2Co 3:17
where the Spirit of the L is, 2Co 3:17
the glory of the L and are being 2Co 3:18
this is from the L who is the 2Co 3:18
ourselves but Jesus Christ as L, 2Co 4:5
raised the L Jesus will raise 2Co 4:14
body we are away from the L— 2Co 5:6
the body and at home with the L. 2Co 5:8
the fear of the L, we persuade 2Co 5:11
and be separate, says the L; 2Co 6:17
to Me, says the L Almighty. 2Co 6:18
themselves especially to the L, 2Co 8:5
the grace of our L Jesus Christ: 2Co 8:9
the glory of the L Himself and 2Co 8:19
before the L but also before 2Co 8:21
which the L gave for building 2Co 10:8
who boasts must boast in the L. 2Co 10:17
but the one the L commends. 2Co 10:18
I don't speak as the L would, 2Co 11:17
God and Father of the L Jesus, 2Co 11:31
and revelations of the L. 2Co 12:1
pleaded with the L three times 2Co 12:8
the authority the L gave me for 2Co 13:10
The grace of the L Jesus Christ, 2Co 13:13

Father and our **L** Jesus Christ, Gl 1:3
the **L** I have confidence in you Gl 5:10
the cross of our **L** Jesus Christ, Gl 6:14
grace of our **L** Jesus Christ be Gl 6:18
Father and the **L** Jesus Christ. Eph 1:2
Father of our **L** Jesus Christ, Eph 1:3
faith in the **L** Jesus and your Eph 1:15
the God of our **L** Jesus Christ, Eph 1:17
into a holy sanctuary in the **L**, Eph 2:21
in the Messiah, Jesus our **L**, Eph 3:11
prisoner in the **L**, urge you to Eph 4:1
one **L**, one faith, one baptism, Eph 4:5
I say this and testify in the **L**: Eph 4:17
now ⌊you are⌋ light in the **L**. Eph 5:8
what is pleasing to the **L**. Eph 5:10
music to the **L** in your heart, Eph 5:19
the name of our **L** Jesus Christ, Eph 5:20
your own husbands as to the **L**, Eph 5:22
obey your parents in the **L**, Eph 6:1
and instruction of the **L**. Eph 6:4
as to the **L** and not to men, Eph 6:7
receive this back from the **L**. Eph 6:8
by the **L** and by His vast Eph 6:10
and faithful servant in the **L**, Eph 6:21
Father and the **L** Jesus Christ. Eph 6:23
love for our **L** Jesus Christ. Eph 6:24
Father and the **L** Jesus Christ. Php 1:2
brothers in the **L** have gained Php 1:14
confess that Jesus Christ is **L**, Php 2:11
I hope in the **L** Jesus to send Php 2:19
convinced in the **L** that I myself Php 2:24
welcome him in the **L** with all Php 2:29
my brothers, rejoice in the **L**. Php 3:1
of knowing Christ Jesus my **L**. Php 3:8
a Savior, the **L** Jesus Christ. Php 3:20
firm in the **L**, dear friends. Php 4:1
urge Syntyche to agree in the **L**. Php 4:2
Rejoice in the **L** always. Php 4:4
to everyone. The **L** is near. Php 4:5
rejoiced in the **L** greatly that Php 4:10
grace of the **L** Jesus Christ be Php 4:23
Father of our **L** Jesus Christ, Col 1:3
you may walk worthy of the **L**, Col 1:10
received Christ Jesus the **L**, Col 2:6
Just as the **L** has forgiven you, Col 3:13
in the name of the **L** Jesus, Col 3:17
as is fitting in the **L**. Col 3:18
for this is pleasing in the **L**. Col 3:20
wholeheartedly, fearing the **L**. Col 3:22
done for the **L** and not for men, Col 3:23
of an inheritance from the **L**— Col 3:24
Lord—you serve the **L** Christ. Col 3:24
and a fellow slave in the **L**, Col 4:7
you have received in the **L**, Col 4:17
Father and the **L** Jesus Christ. 1Th 1:1
of hope in our **L** Jesus Christ, 1Th 1:3
of us and of the **L** when, 1Th 1:6
They killed both the **L** Jesus and 1Th 2:15
presence of our **L** Jesus at His 1Th 2:19
if you stand firm in the **L**. 1Th 3:8
Himself, and our **L** Jesus, direct 1Th 3:11
And may the **L** cause you to 1Th 3:12
coming of our **L** Jesus with all 1Th 3:13
encourage you in the **L** Jesus, 1Th 4:1
we gave you through the **L** Jesus. 1Th 4:2
because the **L** is an avenger of 1Th 4:6
you by a revelation from the **L**: 1Th 4:15
For the **L** Himself will descend 1Th 4:16
clouds to meet the **L** in the air; 1Th 4:17
so we will always be with the **L**. 1Th 4:17
the Day of the **L** will come just 1Th 5:2
through our **L** Jesus Christ, 1Th 5:9
lead you in the **L** and admonish 1Th 5:12
coming of our **L** Jesus Christ. 1Th 5:23
you by the **L** that this letter 1Th 5:27
grace of our **L** Jesus Christ be 1Th 5:28
Father and the **L** Jesus Christ. 2Th 1:1
Father and the **L** Jesus Christ. 2Th 1:2
of the **L** Jesus from heaven 2Th 1:7
obey the gospel of our **L** Jesus. 2Th 1:8
the name of our **L** Jesus will be 2Th 1:12
our God and the **L** Jesus Christ. 2Th 1:12
the coming of our **L** Jesus Christ 2Th 2:1
that the Day of the **L** has come. 2Th 2:2
L Jesus will destroy him with 2Th 2:8
brothers loved by the **L**, because 2Th 2:13
the glory of our **L** Jesus Christ. 2Th 2:14
May our **L** Jesus Christ Himself 2Th 2:16

But the **L** is faithful; He will 2Th 3:3
confidence in the **L** about you, 2Th 3:4
May the **L** direct your hearts to 2Th 3:5
the name of our **L** Jesus Christ, 2Th 3:6
people, by the **L** Jesus Christ, 2Th 3:12
May the **L** of peace Himself give 2Th 3:16
The **L** be with all of you. 2Th 3:16
grace of our **L** Jesus Christ be 2Th 3:18
Father and Christ Jesus our **L**. 1Tm 1:2
thanks to Christ Jesus our **L**, 1Tm 1:12
the grace of our **L** overflowed, 1Tm 1:14
teaching of our **L** Jesus Christ 1Tm 6:3
appearing of our **L** Jesus Christ, 1Tm 6:14
of kings, and the **L** of lords, 1Tm 6:15
Father and Christ Jesus our **L**. 2Tm 1:2
of the testimony about our **L**, 2Tm 1:8
May the **L** grant mercy to the 2Tm 1:16
May the **L** grant that he obtain 2Tm 1:18
mercy from the **L** on that day. 2Tm 1:18
for the **L** will give you 2Tm 2:7
The **L** knows those who are His, 2Tm 2:19
the name of the **L** must turn away 2Tm 2:19
who call on the **L** from a pure 2Tm 2:22
Yet the **L** rescued me from them 2Tm 3:11
the **L**, the righteous Judge, 2Tm 4:8
The **L** will repay him according 2Tm 4:14
But the **L** stood with me and 2Tm 4:17
The **L** will rescue me from every 2Tm 4:18
The **L** be with your spirit. 2Tm 4:22
Father and the **L** Jesus Christ. Phm 3
faith toward the **L** Jesus and for Phm 5
both in the flesh and in the **L**. Phm 16
I have joy from you in the **L**; Phm 20
grace of the **L** Jesus Christ be Phm 25
the beginning, **L**, You Heb 1:10
by the **L** and was confirmed Heb 2:3
that our **L** came from Judah Heb 7:14
The **L** has sworn, and He will not Heb 7:21
which the **L** set up, and not man Heb 8:2
coming," says the **L**, "when I Heb 8:8
I disregarded them," says the **L**. Heb 8:9
after those days," says the **L**: Heb 8:10
Know the **L**,' because they Heb 8:11
after those days, says the **L**: Heb 10:16
The **L** will judge His people. Heb 10:30
for the **L** disciplines the one He Heb 12:6
it no one will see the **L**. Heb 12:14
boldly say: The **L** is my helper; Heb 13:6
up from the dead our **L** Jesus— Heb 13:20
God and of the **L** Jesus Christ: Jms 1:1
to receive anything from the **L**. Jms 1:7
in our glorious **L** Jesus Christ Jms 2:1
it we bless our **L** and Father, Jms 3:9
Humble yourselves before the **L**, Jms 4:10
say, "If the **L** wills, we will Jms 4:15
the ears of the **L** of Hosts. Jms 5:4
seen the outcome from the **L**: Jms 5:11
the **L** is very compassionate and Jms 5:11
olive oil in the name of the **L**. Jms 5:14
and the **L** will raise him up; Jms 5:15
Father of our **L** Jesus Christ. 1Pt 1:3
word of the **L** endures forever 1Pt 1:25
have tasted that the **L** is good. 1Pt 2:3
institution because of the **L**, 1Pt 2:13
obeyed Abraham, calling him **l**. 1Pt 3:6
the eyes of the **L** are on the 1Pt 3:12
the face of the **L** is against 1Pt 3:12
the Messiah as **L** in your hearts, 1Pt 3:15
of God and of Jesus our **L**. 2Pt 1:2
knowledge of our **L** Jesus Christ. 2Pt 1:8
kingdom of our **L** and Savior 2Pt 1:11
as our **L** Jesus Christ has also 2Pt 1:14
coming of our **L** Jesus Christ; 2Pt 1:16
then the **L** knows how to rescue 2Pt 2:9
against them before the **L**. 2Pt 2:11
of our **L** and Savior Jesus 2Pt 2:20
of our **L** and Savior ⌊given 2Pt 3:2
with the **L** one day is like 1,000 2Pt 3:8
L does not delay His promise, 2Pt 3:9
the Day of the **L** will come like 2Pt 3:10
patience of our **L** as ⌊an 2Pt 3:15
of our **L** and Savior Jesus 2Pt 3:18
denying our only Master and **L**, Jd 4
the **L**, having first of all saved Jd 5
but said, "The **L** rebuke you!" Jd 9
L comes with thousands of His Jd 14
apostles of our **L** Jesus Christ; Jd 17
mercy of our **L** Jesus Christ for Jd 21

through Jesus Christ our **L**, Jd 25
Omega," says the **L** God, "the One Rv 1:8
holy, holy, **L** God, the Almighty Rv 4:8
Our **L** and God, You are worthy to Rv 4:11
O **L**, holy and true, how long Rv 6:10
stand before the **L** of the earth. Rv 11:4
also their **L** was crucified. Rv 11:8
kingdom⌋ of our **L** and of His Rv 11:15
We thank You, **L** God, the Rv 11:17
dead who die in the **L** from now Rv 14:13
are Your works, **L** God, the Rv 15:3
L, who will not fear and glorify Rv 15:4
Yes, **L** God, the Almighty, true Rv 16:7
because He is **L** of lords and Rv 17:14
because the **L** God who judges her Rv 18:8
because our **L** God, the Almighty, Rv 19:6
OF KINGS AND **L** OF LORDS Rv 19:16
because the **L** God the Almighty Rv 21:22
because the **L** God will give them Rv 22:5
the **L**, the God of the spirits Rv 22:6
quickly." Amen! Come, **L** Jesus! Rv 22:20
The grace of the **L** Jesus be with Rv 22:21

LORD (Yahweh) *(5452)*
(See also LORD.)

the time that the **L** God made the Gn 2:4
for the **L** God had not made it Gn 2:5
Then the **L** God formed the man Gn 2:7
The **L** God planted a garden in Gn 2:8
The **L** God caused to grow out of Gn 2:9
L God took the man and placed Gn 2:15
the **L** God commanded the man, Gn 2:16
Then the **L** God said, "It is not Gn 2:18
So the **L** God formed out of the Gn 2:19
So the **L** God caused a deep sleep Gn 2:21
Then the **L** God made the rib He Gn 2:22
animals that the **L** God had made. Gn 3:1
the sound of the **L** God walking Gn 3:8
from the **L** God among the trees Gn 3:8
So the **L** God called out to the Gn 3:9
So the **L** God asked the woman, Gn 3:13
Then the **L** God said to the Gn 3:14
The **L** God made clothing out of Gn 3:21
The **L** God said, "Since man has Gn 3:22
So the **L** God sent him away from Gn 3:23
produce as an offering to the **L**. Gn 4:3
L had regard for Abel and his Gn 4:4
Then the **L** said to Cain, "Why Gn 4:6
Then the **L** said to Cain, "Where Gn 4:9
answered the **L**, "My punishment Gn 4:13
Then the **L** replied to him, Gn 4:15
to call on the name of the **L**. Gn 4:26
by the ground the **L** has cursed." Gn 5:29
And the **L** said, "My Spirit will Gn 6:3
When the **L** saw that man's Gn 6:5
the **L** regretted that He had made Gn 6:6
Then the **L** said, "I will wipe Gn 6:7
favor in the eyes of the **L**. Gn 6:8
Then the **L** said to Noah, "Enter Gn 7:1
that the **L** commanded him. Gn 7:5
Then the **L** shut him in. Gn 7:16
Noah built an altar to the **L**. Gn 8:20
When the **L** smelled the pleasing Gn 8:21
Praise the **L**, the God of Shem; Gn 9:26
hunter in the sight of the **L**. Gn 10:9
hunter in the sight of the **L**." Gn 10:9
the **L** came down to look over Gn 11:5
The **L** said, "If, as one people Gn 11:6
So the **L** scattered them from Gn 11:8
for there the **L** confused the Gn 11:9
from there the **L** scattered them Gn 11:9
The **L** said to Abram: Go out from Gn 12:1
went, as the **L** had told him, Gn 12:4
But the **L** appeared to Abram and Gn 12:7
there to the **L** who had appeared Gn 12:7
an altar to the **L** and worshiped Gn 12:8
But the **L** struck Pharaoh and his Gn 12:17
And Abram worshiped the **L** there. Gn 13:4
sinning greatly against the **L**. Gn 13:13
from him, the **L** said to Abram, Gn 13:14
he built an altar to the **L**. Gn 13:18
my hand in an oath to the **L**, Gn 14:22
the word of the **L** came to Abram Gn 15:1
the word of the **L** came to him: Gn 15:4
believed the **L**, and He credited Gn 15:6
I am the **L** who brought you from Gn 15:7
Then the **L** said to Abram, Gn 15:13
that day the **L** made a covenant Gn 15:18
Since the **L** has prevented me Gn 16:2

the **L** judge between me and you.	Gn 16:5
The Angel of the **L** found her by	Gn 16:7
the Angel of the **L** said to her,	Gn 16:9
Angel of the **L** also said to her	Gn 16:10
the Angel of the **L** said to her:	Gn 16:11
the **L** has heard your ⌊cry of⌋	Gn 16:11
she named the **L** who spoke to her	Gn 16:13
years old, the **L** appeared to him	Gn 17:1
Then the **L** appeared to Abraham	Gn 18:1
The **L** said, "I will certainly	Gn 18:10
the **L** asked Abraham, "Why did	Gn 18:13
anything impossible for the **L**?	Gn 18:14
Then the **L** said, "Should I hide	Gn 18:17
the way of the **L** by doing what	Gn 18:19
This is how the **L** will fulfill	Gn 18:19
Then the **L** said, "The outcry	Gn 18:20
remained standing before the **L**.	Gn 18:22
The **L** said, "If at Sodom I find	Gn 18:26
When the **L** had finished speaking	Gn 18:33
people is great before the **L**,	Gn 19:13
the **L** has sent us to destroy it.	Gn 19:13
the **L** is about to destroy the	Gn 19:14
Then the **L** rained burning sulfur	Gn 19:24
from the **L** out of the sky.	Gn 19:24
where he had stood before the **L**.	Gn 19:27
for the **L** had completely closed	Gn 20:18
The **L** came to Sarah as He had	Gn 21:1
and the **L** did for Sarah what He	Gn 21:1
and there he worshiped the **L**,	Gn 21:33
the Angel of the **L** called to him	Gn 22:11
that place The **L** Will Provide,	Gn 22:14
the Angel of the **L** called to	Gn 22:15
Myself I have sworn, says the **L**:	Gn 22:16
and the **L** had blessed him in	Gn 24:1
I will have you swear by the **L**,	Gn 24:3
The **L**, the God of heaven, who	Gn 24:7
"**L**, God of my master Abraham,"	Gn 24:12
whether or not the **L** had made	Gn 24:21
bowed down, worshiped the **L**,	Gn 24:26
Praise the **L**, the God of my	Gn 24:27
the **L** has led me on the journey	Gn 24:27
you who are blessed by the **L**.	Gn 24:31
The **L** has greatly blessed my	Gn 24:35
'The **L** before whom I have walked	Gn 24:40
L, God of my master Abraham, if	Gn 24:42
be the woman the **L** has appointed	Gn 24:44
worshiped the **L**, and praised	Gn 24:48
and praised the **L**, the God of my	Gn 24:48
answered, "This is from the **L**;	Gn 24:50
just as the **L** has spoken."	Gn 24:51
to the ground before the **L**.	Gn 24:52
since the **L** has made my journey	Gn 24:56
prayed to the **L** on behalf of his	Gn 25:21
The **L** heard his prayer, and his	Gn 25:21
So she went to inquire of the **L**.	Gn 25:22
And the **L** said to her: Two	Gn 25:23
The **L** appeared to him and said,	Gn 26:2
was sown⌋. The **L** blessed him,	Gn 26:12
For now the **L** has made room for	Gn 26:22
and the **L** appeared to him that	Gn 26:24
worshiped the **L**, and pitched his	Gn 26:25
how the **L** has been with you.	Gn 26:28
You are now blessed by the **L**."	Gn 26:29
Because the **L** your God worked it	Gn 27:20
a field that the **L** has blessed.	Gn 27:27
The **L** was standing there beside	Gn 28:13
I am the **L**, the God of your	Gn 28:13
Surely the **L** is in this place,	Gn 28:16
then the **L** will be my God.	Gn 28:21
When the **L** saw that Leah was	Gn 29:31
The **L** has seen my affliction;	Gn 29:32
The **L** heard that I am unloved	Gn 29:33
"This time I will praise the **L**."	Gn 29:35
May the **L** add another son to me.	Gn 30:24
that the **L** has blessed me	Gn 30:27
The **L** has blessed you because of	Gn 30:30
Then the **L** said to him, "Go back	Gn 31:3
May the **L** watch between you and	Gn 31:49
Isaac, the **L** who said to me,	Gn 32:9
and the **L** put him to death.	Gn 38:7
The **L** was with Joseph, and he	Gn 39:2
saw that the **L** was with him	Gn 39:3
and that the **L** made everything	Gn 39:3
the **L** blessed the Egyptian's	Gn 39:5
But the **L** was with Joseph and	Gn 39:21
because the **L** was with him,	Gn 39:23
and the **L** made everything that	Gn 39:23
I wait for Your salvation, **L**.	Gn 49:18

Angel of the **L** appeared to him	Ex 3:2
When the **L** saw that he had gone	Ex 3:4
the **L** said, "I have observed	Ex 3:7
The **L**, the God of the Hebrews,	Ex 3:18
may sacrifice to the **L** our God.	Ex 3:18
The **L** did not appear to you'?"	Ex 4:1
The **L** asked him, "What is that	Ex 4:2
but the **L** told him, "Stretch out	Ex 4:4
so they will believe that the **L**,	Ex 4:5
In addition the **L** said to him,	Ex 4:6
But Moses replied to the **L**,	Ex 4:10
The **L** said to him, "Who made the	Ex 4:11
or blind? Is it not I, the **L**?	Ex 4:11
Now in Midian the **L** told Moses,	Ex 4:19
L instructed Moses, "When you	Ex 4:21
This is what the **L** says:	Ex 4:22
that the **L** confronted him	Ex 4:24
Now the **L** had said to Aaron,	Ex 4:27
everything the **L** had sent him to	Ex 4:28
everything the **L** had said to	Ex 4:30
heard that the **L** had paid	Ex 4:31
This is what the **L**, the God of	Ex 5:1
Who is the **L** that I should obey	Ex 5:2
do not know the **L**, and what's	Ex 5:2
may sacrifice to the **L** our God,	Ex 5:3
'Let us go sacrifice to the **L**.'	Ex 5:17
May the **L** take note of you and	Ex 5:21
went back to the **L** and asked,	Ex 5:22
But the **L** replied to Moses,	Ex 6:1
as a possession. I am the **L**."	Ex 6:8
Then the **L** spoke to Moses,	Ex 6:10
Then the **L** spoke to Moses and	Ex 6:13
Aaron and Moses whom the **L** told,	Ex 6:26
On the day the **L** spoke to Moses	Ex 6:28
He said to him, "I am the **L**;	Ex 6:29
The **L** answered Moses, "See, I	Ex 7:1
that I am the **L** when I stretch	Ex 7:5
just as the **L** commanded them.	Ex 7:6
The **L** said to Moses and Aaron,	Ex 7:8
did just as the **L** had commanded.	Ex 7:10
to them, as the **L** had said.	Ex 7:13
Then the **L** said to Moses,	Ex 7:14
The **L**, the God of the Hebrews,	Ex 7:16
This is what the **L** says:	Ex 7:17
you will know that I am the **L**.	Ex 7:17
So the **L** said to Moses, "Tell	Ex 7:19
did just as the **L** had commanded;	Ex 7:20
to them, as the **L** had said.	Ex 7:22
after the **L** struck the Nile	Ex 7:25
Then the **L** said to Moses,	Ex 8:1
This is what the **L** says:	Ex 8:1
The **L** then said to Moses,	Ex 8:5
Ask the **L** that He remove the	Ex 8:8
they can sacrifice to the **L**."	Ex 8:8
is no one like the **L** our God,	Ex 8:10
cried out to the **L** for help	Ex 8:12
The **L** did as Moses had said:	Ex 8:13
to them, as the **L** had said.	Ex 8:15
Then the **L** said to Moses,	Ex 8:16
to them, as the **L** had said.	Ex 8:19
The **L** said to Moses, "Get up	Ex 8:20
This is what the **L** says:	Ex 8:20
that I, the **L**, am in the land	Ex 8:22
And the **L** did this. Thick swarms	Ex 8:24
sacrifice to the **L** our God is	Ex 8:26
sacrifice to the **L** our God as He	Ex 8:27
and sacrifice to the **L** your God	Ex 8:28
appeal to the **L**, and tomorrow	Ex 8:29
go and sacrifice to the **L**."	Ex 8:29
presence and appealed to the **L**.	Ex 8:30
The **L** did as Moses had said:	Ex 8:31
Then the **L** said to Moses,	Ex 9:1
This is what the **L**, the God of	Ex 9:1
the **L** will make a distinction	Ex 9:4
And the **L** set a time, saying,	Ex 9:5
Tomorrow the **L** will do this	Ex 9:5
The **L** did this the next day.	Ex 9:6
Then the **L** said to Moses and	Ex 9:8
But the **L** hardened Pharaoh's	Ex 9:12
them, as the **L** had told Moses.	Ex 9:12
Then the **L** said to Moses,	Ex 9:13
This is what the **L**, the God of	Ex 9:13
the word of the **L** made their	Ex 9:20
Then the **L** said to Moses,	Ex 9:22
and the **L** sent thunder and hail.	Ex 9:23
the **L** rained hail on the land	Ex 9:23
The **L** is the Righteous One,	Ex 9:27
Make an appeal to the **L**.	Ex 9:28

I will extend my hands to the **L**.	Ex 9:29
still do not fear the **L** God."	Ex 9:30
and extended his hands to the **L**.	Ex 9:33
as the **L** had said through Moses.	Ex 9:35
Then the **L** said to Moses,	Ex 10:1
you will know that I am the **L**."	Ex 10:2
him, "This is what the **L**, the	Ex 10:3
may worship the **L** their God.	Ex 10:7
"Go, worship the **L** your God,"	Ex 10:8
May the **L** be with you if I	Ex 10:10
men may go and worship the **L**,	Ex 10:11
The **L** then said to Moses,	Ex 10:12
and the **L** sent an east wind over	Ex 10:13
sinned against the **L** your God	Ex 10:16
an appeal to the **L** your God,	Ex 10:17
presence and appealed to the **L**.	Ex 10:18
Then the **L** changed the wind to a	Ex 10:19
But the **L** hardened Pharaoh's	Ex 10:20
Then the **L** said to Moses,	Ex 10:21
and said, "Go, worship the **L**.	Ex 10:24
to prepare for the **L** our God.	Ex 10:25
them to worship the **L** our God.	Ex 10:26
to worship the **L** until we get	Ex 10:26
But the **L** hardened Pharaoh's	Ex 10:27
The **L** said to Moses, "I will	Ex 11:1
The **L** gave the people favor in	Ex 11:3
This is what the **L** says:	Ex 11:4
may know that the **L** makes a	Ex 11:7
The **L** said to Moses, "Pharaoh	Ex 11:9
but the **L** hardened Pharaoh's	Ex 11:10
The **L** said to Moses and Aaron in	Ex 12:1
beast. I am the **L**; I will	Ex 12:12
it as a festival to the **L**.	Ex 12:14
When the **L** passes through to	Ex 12:23
land that the **L** will give you as	Ex 12:25
the Passover sacrifice to the **L**,	Ex 12:27
did just as the **L** had commanded	Ex 12:28
at midnight the **L** struck every	Ex 12:29
worship the **L** as you have asked.	Ex 12:31
And the **L** gave the people such	Ex 12:36
the divisions of the **L** went out	Ex 12:41
of vigil in honor of the **L**,	Ex 12:42
same night is in honor of the **L**,	Ex 12:42
The **L** said to Moses and Aaron,	Ex 12:43
did just as the **L** had commanded	Ex 12:50
On that same day the **L** brought	Ex 12:51
The **L** spoke to Moses:	Ex 13:1
the **L** brought you out of here	Ex 13:3
When the **L** brings you into the	Ex 13:5
is to be a festival to the **L**.	Ex 13:6
of what the **L** did for me when I	Ex 13:8
the law of the **L** may be in your	Ex 13:9
for the **L** brought you out of	Ex 13:9
When the **L** brings you into the	Ex 13:11
present to the **L** every firstborn	Ex 13:12
His⌋ hand the **L** brought us out	Ex 13:14
the **L** killed every firstborn	Ex 13:15
sacrifice to the **L** all the	Ex 13:15
the **L** brought us out of Egypt	Ex 13:16
The **L** went ahead of them in a	Ex 13:21
Then the **L** spoke to Moses:	Ex 14:1
will know that I am the **L**."	Ex 14:4
The **L** hardened the heart of	Ex 14:8
and cried out to the **L** for help.	Ex 14:10
The **L** will fight for you;	Ex 14:14
L said to Moses, "Why are you	Ex 14:15
that I am the **L** when I receive	Ex 14:18
The **L** drove the sea ⌊back⌋ with	Ex 14:21
L looked down on the Egyptian	Ex 14:24
because the **L** is fighting for	Ex 14:25
Then the **L** said to Moses,	Ex 14:26
the **L** overthrew them in the sea.	Ex 14:27
That day the **L** saved Israel from	Ex 14:30
power that the **L** used against	Ex 14:31
people feared the **L** and believed	Ex 14:31
sang this song to the **L**.	Ex 15:1
will sing to the **L**, for He is	Ex 15:1
L is my strength and my song;	Ex 15:2
L is a warrior; Yahweh is His	Ex 15:3
L, Your right hand is glorious	Ex 15:6
L, Your right hand shattered the	Ex 15:6
L, who is like You among the	Ex 15:11
people pass by, **L**, until the	Ex 15:16
L, You have prepared the place	Ex 15:17
The **L** will reign forever and	Ex 15:18
the **L** brought the waters of the	Ex 15:19
Sing to the **L**, for He is highly	Ex 15:21
cried out to the **L**, and the LORD	Ex 15:25

and the **L** showed him a tree.	Ex 15:25
carefully obey the **L** your God,	Ex 15:26
For I am the **L** who heals you."	Ex 15:26
Then the **L** said to Moses,	Ex 16:4
that it was the **L** who brought	Ex 16:6
The **L** will give you meat to eat	Ex 16:8
against us but against the **L**."	Ex 16:8
Come before the **L**, for He has	Ex 16:9
The **L** spoke to Moses,	Ex 16:11
know that I am the **L** your God."	Ex 16:12
the bread the **L** has given you to	Ex 16:15
is what the **L** has commanded:	Ex 16:16
This is what the **L** has said:	Ex 16:23
rest, a holy Sabbath to the **L**.	Ex 16:23
today is a Sabbath to the **L**.	Ex 16:25
Then the **L** said to Moses,	Ex 16:28
that the **L** has given you	Ex 16:29
is what the **L** has commanded:	Ex 16:32
it before the **L** to be preserved	Ex 16:33
As the **L** commanded Moses,	Ex 16:34
"Why are you testing the **L**?"	Ex 17:2
Then Moses cried out to the **L**,	Ex 17:4
The **L** answered Moses, "Go on	Ex 17:5
and because they tested the **L**,	Ex 17:7
"Is the **L** among us or not?"	Ex 17:7
The **L** then said to Moses,	Ex 17:14
named it, "The **L** Is My Banner."	Ex 17:15
The **L** will be at war with Amalek	Ex 17:16
and how the **L** had brought Israel	Ex 18:1
all that the **L** had done to	Ex 18:8
and how the **L** delivered them.	Ex 18:8
good things the **L** had done for	Ex 18:9
"Blessed is the **L**," Jethro	Ex 18:10
know that the **L** is greater than	Ex 18:11
and the **L** called to him from the	Ex 19:3
words that the **L** had commanded	Ex 19:7
do all that the **L** has spoken."	Ex 19:8
people's words back to the **L**.	Ex 19:8
The **L** said to Moses, "I am going	Ex 19:9
the people's words to the **L**.	Ex 19:9
And the **L** told Moses, "Go to the	Ex 19:10
third day the **L** will come down	Ex 19:11
because the **L** came down on it	Ex 19:18
The **L** came down on Mount Sinai,	Ex 19:20
Then the **L** summoned Moses to	Ex 19:20
The **L** directed Moses, "Go down	Ex 19:21
to break through to see the **L**;	Ex 19:21
who come near the **L** must purify	Ex 19:22
or the **L** will break out	Ex 19:22
But Moses responded to the **L**,	Ex 19:23
And the **L** replied to him,	Ex 19:24
through to come up to the **L**,	Ex 19:24
I am the **L** your God, who brought	Ex 20:2
for I, the **L** your God, am a	Ex 20:5
the name of the **L** your God,	Ex 20:7
because the **L** will punish anyone	Ex 20:7
is a Sabbath to the **L** your God.	Ex 20:10
For the **L** made the heavens and	Ex 20:11
Therefore the **L** blessed the	Ex 20:11
the land that the **L** your God is	Ex 20:12
Then the **L** told Moses, "This is	Ex 20:22
oath before the **L** between the	Ex 22:11
except the **L** alone, is to be	Ex 22:20
to the house of the **L** your God.	Ex 23:19
Worship the **L** your God, and He	Ex 23:25
Go up to the **L**, you and Aaron,	Ex 24:1
alone is to approach the **L**,	Ex 24:2
commands of the **L** and all the	Ex 24:3
that the **L** has commanded."	Ex 24:3
down all the words of the **L**.	Ex 24:4
fellowship offerings to the **L**.	Ex 24:5
that the **L** has commanded."	Ex 24:7
that the **L** has made with you	Ex 24:8
The **L** said to Moses, "Come up to	Ex 24:12
glory of the **L** settled on Mount	Ex 24:16
The **L** spoke to Moses:	Ex 25:1
until morning before the **L**.	Ex 27:21
before the **L** as a reminder.	Ex 28:12
continual reminder before the **L**.	Ex 28:29
whenever he comes before the **L**.	Ex 28:30
over his heart before the **L**.	Ex 28:30
before the **L** and when he exits,	Ex 28:35
of a seal: HOLY TO THE **L**	Ex 28:36
may find acceptance with the **L**.	Ex 28:38
before the **L** at the entrance	Ex 29:11
it is a burnt offering to the **L**.	Ex 29:18
aroma, a fire offering to the **L**.	Ex 29:18
bread that is before the **L**;	Ex 29:23
offering before the **L**.	Ex 29:24
a pleasing aroma before the **L**;	Ex 29:25
it is a fire offering to the **L**.	Ex 29:25
offering before the **L**;	Ex 29:26
their contribution to the **L**.	Ex 29:28
aroma, a fire offering to the **L**.	Ex 29:41
tent of meeting before the **L**,	Ex 29:42
know that I am the **L** their God,	Ex 29:46
them. I am the **L** their God.	Ex 29:46
before the **L** throughout your	Ex 30:8
is especially holy to the **L**."	Ex 30:10
The **L** spoke to Moses:	Ex 30:11
for himself to the **L** as they are	Ex 30:12
is a contribution to the **L**.	Ex 30:13
give this contribution to the **L**.	Ex 30:14
to the **L** to atone for your	Ex 30:15
before the **L** to atone for your	Ex 30:16
The **L** spoke to Moses:	Ex 30:17
burning up an offering to the **L**,	Ex 30:20
The **L** spoke to Moses:	Ex 30:22
The **L** said to Moses: "Take	Ex 30:34
by you as sacred to the **L**.	Ex 30:37
The **L** also spoke to Moses:	Ex 31:1
The **L** said to Moses:	Ex 31:12
that I am the **L** who sets you	Ex 31:13
rest, dedicated to the **L**.	Ex 31:15
in six days the **L** made the	Ex 31:17
a festival to the **L** tomorrow."	Ex 32:5
The **L** spoke to Moses: "Go down	Ex 32:7
The **L** also said to Moses:	Ex 32:9
interceded with the **L** his God:	Ex 32:11
L, why does Your anger burn	Ex 32:11
So the **L** changed His mind about	Ex 32:14
is for the **L**, ⌊come⌋ to me."	Ex 32:26
This is what the **L**, the God of	Ex 32:27
have been dedicated to the **L**,	Ex 32:29
Now I will go up to the **L**;	Ex 32:30
returned to the **L** and said,	Ex 32:31
The **L** replied to Moses:	Ex 32:33
And the **L** inflicted a plague on	Ex 32:35
The **L** spoke to Moses: "Go, leave	Ex 33:1
For the **L** said to Moses:	Ex 33:5
to consult the **L** would go to the	Ex 33:7
and ⌊the **L**⌋ would speak with	Ex 33:9
The **L** spoke with Moses face to	Ex 33:11
said to the **L**, "Look, You have	Ex 33:12
The **L** answered Moses, "I will do	Ex 33:17
L said, "Here is a place near	Ex 33:21
The **L** said to Moses, "Cut two	Ex 34:1
just as the **L** had commanded him.	Ex 34:4
The **L** came down in a cloud,	Ex 34:5
Then the **L** passed in front of	Ex 34:6
And the **L** responded: "Look, I am	Ex 34:10
to another god because the **L**,	Ex 34:14
to appear before the **L** your God.	Ex 34:24
to the house of the **L** your God.	Ex 34:26
The **L** also said to Moses,	Ex 34:27
there with the **L** 40 days and 40	Ex 34:28
of his speaking with the **L**.	Ex 34:29
everything the **L** had told him	Ex 34:32
went before the **L** to speak with	Ex 34:34
he went to speak with the **L**.	Ex 34:35
things that the **L** has commanded	Ex 35:1
of complete rest to the **L**.	Ex 35:2
is what the **L** has commanded:	Ex 35:4
an offering for the **L** among you.	Ex 35:5
that the **L** has commanded:	Ex 35:10
offering to the **L** to construct	Ex 35:21
offering of gold to the **L**.	Ex 35:22
or bronze brought it to the **L**.	Ex 35:24
a freewill offering to the **L**,	Ex 35:29
for all the work that the **L**,	Ex 35:29
the **L** has appointed by name	Ex 35:30
everything the **L** has commanded.	Ex 36:1
The **L** has given them wisdom and	Ex 36:1
whose heart the **L** had placed	Ex 36:2
the work the **L** commanded to be	Ex 36:5
that the **L** commanded Moses.	Ex 38:22
just as the **L** had commanded	Ex 39:1
just as the **L** had commanded	Ex 39:5
just as the **L** had commanded	Ex 39:7
did⌋ just as the **L** had commanded	Ex 39:21
just as the **L** had commanded	Ex 39:26
did⌋ just as the **L** had commanded	Ex 39:29
on a seal: HOLY TO THE **L**	Ex 39:30
just as the **L** had commanded	Ex 39:31
just as the **L** had commanded	Ex 39:32
everything the **L** had commanded	Ex 39:42
done just as the **L** commanded.	Ex 39:43
The **L** spoke to Moses:	Ex 40:1
just as the **L** had commanded him.	Ex 40:16
just as the **L** had commanded	Ex 40:19
just as the **L** had commanded him.	Ex 40:21
the bread on it before the **L**,	Ex 40:23
just as the **L** had commanded him.	Ex 40:23
set up the lamps before the **L**,	Ex 40:25
just as the **L** had commanded him.	Ex 40:25
just as the **L** had commanded him.	Ex 40:27
just as the **L** had commanded him.	Ex 40:29
just as the **L** had commanded	Ex 40:32
the glory of the **L** filled the	Ex 40:34
the glory of the **L** filled the	Ex 40:35
For the cloud of the **L** was over	Ex 40:38
Then the **L** summoned Moses and	Lv 1:1
offering to the **L** from the	Lv 1:2
he may be accepted by the **L**.	Lv 1:3
slaughter the bull before the **L**;	Lv 1:5
of a pleasing aroma to the **L**.	Lv 1:9
side of the altar before the **L**.	Lv 1:11
of a pleasing aroma to the **L**.	Lv 1:13
If his gift to the **L** is a burnt	Lv 1:14
of a pleasing aroma to the **L**.	Lv 1:17
offering as a gift to the **L**,	Lv 2:1
of a pleasing aroma to the **L**.	Lv 2:2
of the fire offerings to the **L**.	Lv 2:3
you bring to the **L** the grain	Lv 2:8
of a pleasing aroma to the **L**.	Lv 2:9
of the fire offerings to the **L**.	Lv 2:10
present to the **L** is to be made	Lv 2:11
as a fire offering to the **L**.	Lv 2:11
them to the **L** as an offering	Lv 2:12
of firstfruits to the **L**,	Lv 2:14
as a fire offering to the **L**.	Lv 2:16
without blemish before the **L**.	Lv 3:1
as a fire offering to the **L**:	Lv 3:3
of a pleasing aroma to the **L**.	Lv 3:5
sacrifice to the **L** is from the	Lv 3:6
is to present it before the **L**.	Lv 3:7
offering to the **L** ⌊consisting	Lv 3:9
food, a fire offering to the **L**.	Lv 3:11
is to present it before the **L**.	Lv 3:12
as a fire offering to the **L**:	Lv 3:14
All fat belongs to the **L**.	Lv 3:16
Then the **L** spoke to Moses:	Lv 4:1
is to present to the **L** a young,	Lv 4:3
tent of meeting before the **L**,	Lv 4:4
and slaughter it before the **L**.	Lv 4:4
times before the **L** in front of	Lv 4:6
that is before the **L** in the tent	Lv 4:7
head before the **L** and it is to	Lv 4:15
to be slaughtered before the **L**.	Lv 4:15
times before the **L** in front of	Lv 4:17
that is before the **L** in the tent	Lv 4:18
commands of the **L** his God by	Lv 4:22
is slaughtered before the **L**.	Lv 4:24
as a pleasing aroma to the **L**.	Lv 4:31
the fire offerings to the **L**.	Lv 4:35
sin he has committed to the **L**:	Lv 5:6
bring to the **L** two turtledoves	Lv 5:7
the fire offerings to the **L**;	Lv 5:12
Then the **L** spoke to Moses:	Lv 5:14
restitution offering to the **L**:	Lv 5:15
is indeed guilty before the **L**."	Lv 5:19
The **L** spoke to Moses:	Lv 6:1
and offends the **L** by deceiving	Lv 6:2
restitution offering to the **L**:	Lv 6:6
on his behalf before the **L**,	Lv 6:7
The **L** spoke to Moses:	Lv 6:8
it before the **L** in front of the	Lv 6:14
as a pleasing aroma to the **L**.	Lv 6:15
the fire offerings to the **L**.	Lv 6:18
The **L** spoke to Moses:	Lv 6:19
present to the **L** on the day that	Lv 6:20
a pleasing aroma to the **L**.	Lv 6:21
a permanent portion for the **L**.	Lv 6:22
The **L** spoke to Moses:	Lv 6:24
before the **L** at the place where	Lv 6:25
as a fire offering to the **L**;	Lv 7:5
someone may present to the **L**:	Lv 7:11
as a contribution to the **L**.	Lv 7:14
The **L** spoke to Moses:	Lv 7:22
offering presented to the **L**,	Lv 7:25
The **L** spoke to Moses:	Lv 7:28
sacrifice to the **L** must bring an	Lv 7:29
offering to the **L** from his	Lv 7:29
the fire offerings to the **L**.	Lv 7:30

offering before the **L**.	Lv 7:30
offerings to the **L** for Aaron and	Lv 7:35
to serve the **L** as priests.	Lv 7:35
The **L** commanded this to be given	Lv 7:36
which the **L** commanded Moses on	Lv 7:38
offerings to the **L** in the	Lv 7:38
The **L** spoke to Moses:	Lv 8:1
did as the **L** commanded him,	Lv 8:4
is what the **L** has commanded to	Lv 8:5
as the **L** had commanded Moses.	Lv 8:9
as the **L** had commanded Moses.	Lv 8:13
as the **L** had commanded Moses.	Lv 8:17
offering to the **L** as He had	Lv 8:21
before the **L** he took one cake	Lv 8:26
them before the **L** as a	Lv 8:27
aroma, a fire offering to the **L**.	Lv 8:28
before the **L** as a presentation	Lv 8:29
ram as the **L** had commanded him.	Lv 8:29
The **L** commanded what has been	Lv 8:34
everything the **L** had commanded	Lv 8:36
and present ⌊them⌋ before the **L**.	Lv 9:2
to sacrifice before the **L**;	Lv 9:4
For today the **L** is going to	Lv 9:4
forward and stood before the **L**.	Lv 9:5
is what the **L** commanded you to	Lv 9:6
of the **L** may appear to you.	Lv 9:6
for them, as the **L** commanded."	Lv 9:7
as the **L** had commanded Moses.	Lv 9:10
offering before the **L**,	Lv 9:21
glory of the **L** appeared to all	Lv 9:23
came out from the **L** and consumed	Lv 9:24
unauthorized fire before the **L**,	Lv 10:1
them to death before the **L**.	Lv 10:2
This is what the **L** meant when He	Lv 10:3
and the **L** will become angry with	Lv 10:6
when the **L** sent the fire.	Lv 10:6
The **L** spoke to Aaron:	Lv 10:8
that the **L** has given to them	Lv 10:11
the fire offerings to the **L**,	Lv 10:12
the fire offerings to the **L**,	Lv 10:13
offering before the **L**.	Lv 10:15
children, as the **L** commanded."	Lv 10:15
atonement for them before the **L**.	Lv 10:17
burnt offering before the **L**.	Lv 10:19
The **L** spoke to Moses and Aaron:	Lv 11:1
For I am the **L** your God, so you	Lv 11:44
For I am the **L**, who brought you	Lv 11:45
The **L** spoke to Moses:	Lv 12:1
them before the **L** and make	Lv 12:7
The **L** spoke to Moses and Aaron:	Lv 13:1
The **L** spoke to Moses:	Lv 14:1
before the **L** at the entrance to	Lv 14:11
offering before the **L**.	Lv 14:12
finger seven times before the **L**.	Lv 14:16
atonement for him before the **L**.	Lv 14:18
tent of meeting before the **L**.	Lv 14:23
offering before the **L**.	Lv 14:24
palm seven times before the **L**.	Lv 14:27
atonement for him before the **L**.	Lv 14:29
before the **L** for the one to be	Lv 14:31
The **L** spoke to Moses and Aaron:	Lv 14:33
The **L** spoke to Moses and Aaron:	Lv 15:1
before the **L** at the entrance	Lv 15:14
him before the **L** because of his	Lv 15:15
her before the **L** because of her	Lv 15:30
The **L** spoke to Moses after the	Lv 16:1
the presence of the **L** and died.	Lv 16:1
The **L** said to Moses: "Tell your	Lv 16:2
before the **L** at the entrance	Lv 16:7
one lot for the **L** and the other	Lv 16:8
lot for the **L** and sacrifice it	Lv 16:9
alive before the **L** to make	Lv 16:10
before the **L** and two handfuls	Lv 16:12
on the fire before the **L**,	Lv 16:13
is before the **L** and make	Lv 16:18
from all your sins before the **L**.	Lv 16:30
done as the **L** commanded Moses	Lv 16:34
The **L** spoke to Moses:	Lv 17:1
is what the **L** has commanded:	Lv 17:2
an offering to the **L** before His	Lv 17:4
bring to the **L** the sacrifices	Lv 17:5
fellowship sacrifices to the **L**.	Lv 17:5
as a pleasing aroma to the **L**.	Lv 17:6
to sacrifice it to the **L**,	Lv 17:9
The **L** spoke to Moses:	Lv 18:1
tell them: I am the **L** your God.	Lv 18:2
them; I am the **L** your God.	Lv 18:4
if he does them. I am the **L**.	Lv 18:5
sexual intercourse; I am the **L**.	Lv 18:6
name of your God; I am the **L**.	Lv 18:21
by them; I am the **L** your God."	Lv 18:30
The **L** spoke to Moses:	Lv 19:1
because I, the **L** your God, am	Lv 19:2
Sabbaths; I am the **L** your God.	Lv 19:3
yourselves; I am the **L** your God.	Lv 19:4
a fellowship sacrifice to the **L**,	Lv 19:5
profaned what is holy to the **L**.	Lv 19:8
resident; I am the **L** your God.	Lv 19:10
name of your God; I am the **L**.	Lv 19:12
to fear your God; I am the **L**.	Lv 19:14
neighbor's life; I am the **L**.	Lv 19:16
as yourself; I am the **L**.	Lv 19:18
to the **L** at the entrance	Lv 19:21
behalf before the **L** with the ram	Lv 19:22
as a praise offering to the **L**.	Lv 19:24
for you; I am the **L** your God.	Lv 19:25
marks on yourselves; I am the **L**.	Lv 19:28
revere My sanctuary; I am the **L**.	Lv 19:30
by them; I am the **L** your God.	Lv 19:31
old. Fear your God; I am the **L**.	Lv 19:32
of Egypt; I am the **L** your God.	Lv 19:34
I am the **L** your God, who brought	Lv 19:36
and do them; I am the **L**."	Lv 19:37
The **L** spoke to Moses:	Lv 20:1
holy, for I am the **L** your God.	Lv 20:7
I am the **L** who sets you apart.	Lv 20:8
I am the **L** your God who set you	Lv 20:24
because I, the **L**, am holy, and I	Lv 20:26
The **L** said to Moses: "Speak to	Lv 21:1
the fire offerings to the **L**,	Lv 21:6
because I, the **L** who sets you	Lv 21:8
his God is on him; I am the **L**.	Lv 21:12
I am the **L** who sets him apart.	Lv 21:15
The **L** spoke to Moses:	Lv 21:16
the fire offerings to the **L**.	Lv 21:21
I am the **L** who sets them apart.	Lv 21:23
The **L** spoke to Moses:	Lv 22:1
My holy name; I am the **L**.	Lv 22:2
Israelites consecrate to the **L**,	Lv 22:3
from My presence; I am the **L**.	Lv 22:3
unclean by it; I am the **L**.	Lv 22:8
I am the **L** who sets them apart.	Lv 22:9
the Israelites give to the **L**	Lv 22:15
I am the **L** who sets them apart.	Lv 22:16
The **L** spoke to Moses:	Lv 22:17
of vows to the **L** as burnt	Lv 22:18
to the **L** to fulfill a vow	Lv 22:21
animal⌋ to the **L** that is blind,	Lv 22:22
as a fire offering to the **L**.	Lv 22:22
present to the **L** anything that	Lv 22:24
The **L** spoke to Moses:	Lv 22:26
gift, a fire offering to the **L**.	Lv 22:27
a thank offering to the **L**,	Lv 22:29
until morning; I am the **L**.	Lv 22:30
and do them; I am the **L**.	Lv 22:31
I am the **L** who sets you apart,	Lv 22:32
to be your God; I am the **L**."	Lv 22:33
The **L** spoke to Moses:	Lv 23:1
the times of the **L** that you will	Lv 23:2
a Sabbath to the **L** wherever you	Lv 23:3
Passover to the **L** comes in the	Lv 23:5
Bread to the **L** is on the	Lv 23:6
to the **L** for seven days.	Lv 23:8
The **L** spoke to Moses:	Lv 23:9
before the **L** so that you may	Lv 23:11
as a burnt offering to the **L**.	Lv 23:12
oil as a fire offering to the **L**,	Lv 23:13
offering of new grain to the **L**.	Lv 23:16
yeast, as firstfruits to the **L**.	Lv 23:17
be a burnt offering to the **L**,	Lv 23:18
of a pleasing aroma to the **L**.	Lv 23:18
offering before the **L**;	Lv 23:20
be holy to the **L** for the priest.	Lv 23:20
resident; I am the **L** your God."	Lv 23:22
The **L** spoke to Moses:	Lv 23:23
a fire offering to the **L**."	Lv 23:25
The **L** again spoke to Moses:	Lv 23:26
a fire offering to the **L**.	Lv 23:27
before the **L** your God.	Lv 23:28
The **L** spoke to Moses:	Lv 23:33
of Booths to the **L** begins on the	Lv 23:34
to the **L** for seven days.	Lv 23:36
a fire offering to the **L**.	Lv 23:36
fire offerings to the **L**,	Lv 23:37
that you give to the **L**.	Lv 23:38
before the **L** your God for seven	Lv 23:40
festival to the **L** seven days	Lv 23:41
of Egypt; I am the **L** your God."	Lv 23:43
The **L** spoke to Moses:	Lv 24:1
before the **L** outside the veil	Lv 24:3
pure ⌊gold⌋ table before the **L**.	Lv 24:6
and a fire offering to the **L**.	Lv 24:7
out before the **L** every Sabbath	Lv 24:8
the fire offerings to the **L**;	Lv 24:9
Then the **L** spoke to Moses:	Lv 24:13
the name of the **L** is to be put	Lv 24:16
because I am the **L** your God."	Lv 24:22
as the **L** had commanded Moses	Lv 24:23
The **L** spoke to Moses on Mount	Lv 25:1
will observe a Sabbath to the **L**.	Lv 25:2
year, a Sabbath to the **L**:	Lv 25:4
God, for I am the **L** your God.	Lv 25:17
I am the **L** your God, who brought	Lv 25:38
of Egypt; I am the **L** your God.	Lv 25:55
to it, for I am the **L** your God.	Lv 26:1
honor My sanctuary; I am the **L**.	Lv 26:2
I am the **L** your God, who brought	Lv 26:13
since I am the **L** their God.	Lv 26:44
to be their God; I am the **L**."	Lv 26:45
and laws the **L** established	Lv 26:46
The **L** spoke to Moses:	Lv 27:1
vow to the **L** that involves	Lv 27:2
brought as an offering to the **L**,	Lv 27:9
he gives to the **L** will be holy.	Lv 27:9
brought as an offering to the **L**,	Lv 27:11
his house as holy to the **L**,	Lv 27:14
consecrates to the **L** any part of	Lv 27:16
be holy to the **L** like a field	Lv 27:21
to the **L** a field he has	Lv 27:22
day as a holy offering to the **L**.	Lv 27:23
or flock, to the **L**, because a	Lv 27:26
already⌋ belongs to the **L**.	Lv 27:26
apart to the **L** from all he owns	Lv 27:28
is especially holy to the **L**.	Lv 27:28
the trees, belongs to the **L**;	Lv 27:30
the LORD; it is holy to the **L**.	Lv 27:30
rod, will be holy to the **L**.	Lv 27:32
commands the **L** gave Moses for	Lv 27:34
The **L** spoke to Moses in the tent	Nm 1:1
just as the **L** commanded Moses.	Nm 1:19
For the **L** had told Moses:	Nm 1:48
just as the **L** had commanded	Nm 1:54
The **L** spoke to Moses and Aaron:	Nm 2:1
just as the **L** had commanded	Nm 2:33
the **L** commanded Moses;	Nm 2:34
at the time the **L** spoke with	Nm 3:1
fire before the **L** in the	Nm 3:4
The **L** spoke to Moses:	Nm 3:5
The **L** spoke to Moses:	Nm 3:11
they are Mine; I am the **L**."	Nm 3:13
The **L** spoke to Moses in the	Nm 3:14
obedience to the **L** as he had	Nm 3:16
L told Moses: "Register every	Nm 3:40
for Me—I am the **L**—in place	Nm 3:41
as the **L** commanded him.	Nm 3:42
The **L** spoke to Moses again:	Nm 3:44
belong to Me; I am the **L**.	Nm 3:45
his sons in obedience to the **L**,	Nm 3:51
just as the **L** commanded Moses.	Nm 3:51
The **L** spoke to Moses and Aaron:	Nm 4:1
Then the **L** spoke to Moses and	Nm 4:17
The **L** spoke to Moses:	Nm 4:21
was as the **L** commanded Moses.	Nm 4:49
The **L** instructed Moses:	Nm 5:1
did as the **L** instructed Moses.	Nm 5:4
The **L** spoke to Moses:	Nm 5:5
toward the **L** and is guilty.	Nm 5:6
goes to the **L** for the priest,	Nm 5:8
The **L** spoke to Moses:	Nm 5:11
and have her stand before the **L**.	Nm 5:16
the woman stand before the **L**,	Nm 5:18
'May the **L** make you into an	Nm 5:21
wave the offering before the **L**,	Nm 5:25
the woman stand before the **L**,	Nm 5:30
The **L** instructed Moses:	Nm 6:1
to consecrate himself to the **L**,	Nm 6:2
he consecrates himself to the **L**;	Nm 6:5
he consecrates himself to the **L**.	Nm 6:6
is holy to the **L** during the time	Nm 6:8
to the **L** and to bring	Nm 6:12
offering to the **L** of one	Nm 6:14
before the **L** and sacrifice	Nm 6:16
a fellowship sacrifice to the **L**,	Nm 6:17
offering before the **L**.	Nm 6:20

his offering to the **L** for his Nm 6:21
The **L** spoke to Moses: Nm 6:22
The **L** bless you and protect you; Nm 6:24
L make His face shine on you, Nm 6:25
the **L** look with favor on you and Nm 6:26
before the **L** six covered carts Nm 7:3
The **L** said to Moses, Nm 7:4
The **L** told Moses, "Each day have Nm 7:11
of meeting to speak with the **L**, Nm 7:89
The **L** spoke to Moses: Nm 8:1
just as the **L** had commanded Nm 8:3
pattern the **L** had shown Moses Nm 8:4
The **L** spoke to Moses: Nm 8:5
the Levites before the **L**, Nm 8:10
before the **L** as a presentation Nm 8:11
as a burnt offering to the **L**, Nm 8:12
them before the **L** as a Nm 8:13
to them the **L** commanded Moses Nm 8:20
them before the **L** as a Nm 8:21
to them as the **L** had commanded Nm 8:22
The **L** spoke to Moses: Nm 8:23
the **L** told Moses in the Nm 9:1
everything as the **L** had Nm 9:5
what the **L** commands for you. Nm 9:8
Then the **L** spoke to Moses: Nm 9:9
observe the Passover to the **L**. Nm 9:10
observe the Passover to the **L**, Nm 9:14
The **L** spoke to Moses: Nm 10:1
before the **L** your God and be Nm 10:9
your God: I am the **L** your God." Nm 10:10
for the place the **L** promised: Nm 10:29
for the **L** has promised good Nm 10:29
good the **L** does for us we Nm 10:32
mountain of the **L** on a three-day Nm 10:33
the cloud of the **L** was over them Nm 10:34
say: Arise, **L**! Let Your enemies Nm 10:35
Return, **L**, to the countless Nm 10:36
before the **L** about hardship. Nm 11:1
When the **L** heard, His anger Nm 11:1
fire from the **L** blazed among Nm 11:1
he prayed to the **L**, and the fire Nm 11:2
tents. The **L** was very angry; Nm 11:10
Moses asked the **L**, "Why have Nm 11:11
L answered Moses, "Bring Me Nm 11:16
you cried before the **L**: Nm 11:18
The **L** will give you meat and Nm 11:18
rejected the **L** who is among you Nm 11:20
The **L** answered Moses, "Is the Nm 11:23
the people the words of the **L**. Nm 11:24
the **L** descended in the cloud Nm 11:25
and the **L** would place His Spirit Nm 11:29
sent by the **L** came up and blew Nm 11:31
the **L** struck them with a very Nm 11:33
Does the **L** speak only through Nm 12:2
And the **L** heard ⌊it⌋. Nm 12:2
Suddenly the **L** said to Moses, Nm 12:4
Then the **L** descended in a pillar Nm 12:5
a prophet among you from the **L**, Nm 12:6
he sees the form of the **L**. Nm 12:8
Then Moses cried out to the **L**, Nm 12:13
The **L** answered Moses, "If her Nm 12:14
The **L** spoke to Moses: Nm 13:1
Why is the **L** bringing us into Nm 14:3
If the **L** is pleased with us, Nm 14:8
Only don't rebel against the **L**, Nm 14:9
from them, and the **L** is with us. Nm 14:9
glory of the **L** appeared to all Nm 14:10
The **L** said to Moses, "How long Nm 14:11
But Moses replied to the **L**, Nm 14:13
heard that You, **L**, are among Nm 14:14
people, how You, **L**, are seen Nm 14:14
'Since the **L** wasn't able to Nm 14:16
The **L** is slow to anger and rich Nm 14:18
L responded, "I have pardoned Nm 14:20
Then the **L** spoke to Moses and Nm 14:26
declares the **L**, I will do to you Nm 14:28
I, the **L**, have spoken. I swear Nm 14:35
land were struck down by the **L**. Nm 14:37
go to the place the **L** promised, Nm 14:40
because the **L** is not among you Nm 14:42
The **L** won't be with you, since Nm 14:43
The **L** instructed Moses: Nm 15:1
offering to the **L** from the herd Nm 15:3
a pleasing aroma for the **L**, Nm 15:3
offering to the **L** must also Nm 15:4
as a pleasing aroma to the **L**. Nm 15:7
a fellowship offering to the **L**, Nm 15:8
of pleasing aroma to the **L**. Nm 15:10

as a pleasing aroma to the **L**. Nm 15:13
as a pleasing aroma to the **L**. Nm 15:14
will be alike before the **L**. Nm 15:15
The **L** instructed Moses: Nm 15:17
to the **L** when you eat Nm 15:19
are to give the **L** a contribution Nm 15:21
that the **L** spoke to Moses— Nm 15:22
all that the **L** has commanded you Nm 15:23
from the day the **L** issued the Nm 15:23
as a pleasing aroma to the **L**, Nm 15:24
one made by fire to the **L**, Nm 15:25
offering before the **L** for their Nm 15:25
atonement before the **L** on behalf Nm 15:28
resident, blasphemes the **L**. Nm 15:30
Then the **L** told Moses, "The man Nm 15:35
as the **L** had commanded Moses. Nm 15:36
The **L** said to Moses, Nm 15:37
I am the **L** your God who brought Nm 15:41
your God; I am the **L** your God." Nm 15:41
holy, and the **L** is among them. Nm 16:3
morning the **L** will reveal who Nm 16:5
incense on them before the **L**. Nm 16:7
the man the **L** chooses will be Nm 16:7
have conspired against the **L**! Nm 16:11
became angry and said to the **L**, Nm 16:15
appear before the **L** tomorrow— Nm 16:16
his firepan before the **L**— Nm 16:17
the glory of the **L** appeared to Nm 16:19
The **L** spoke to Moses and Aaron, Nm 16:20
The **L** replied to Moses, Nm 16:23
know that the **L** sent me to do Nm 16:28
then the **L** has not sent me. Nm 16:29
But if the **L** brings about Nm 16:30
these men have despised the **L**." Nm 16:30
out from the **L** and consumed Nm 16:35
Then the **L** spoke to Moses: Nm 16:36
presented them before the **L**, Nm 16:38
just as the **L** commanded him Nm 16:40
before the **L** and become like Nm 16:40
and the **L** said to Moses, Nm 16:44
wrath has come from the **L**; Nm 16:46
The **L** instructed Moses: Nm 17:1
staffs before the **L** in the tent Nm 17:7
The **L** told Moses, "Put Aaron's Nm 17:10
did as the **L** commanded him. Nm 17:11
The **L** said to Aaron, "You, your Nm 18:1
assigned by the **L** to work at the Nm 18:6
Then the **L** spoke to Aaron, Nm 18:8
give to the **L** as their Nm 18:12
which they bring to the **L**, Nm 18:13
to the **L**⌋ belongs to you. Nm 18:14
to the **L** belongs to you. Nm 18:15
for a pleasing aroma to the **L**. Nm 18:17
present to the **L** as a perpetual Nm 18:19
before the **L** for you as well Nm 18:19
The **L** told Aaron, "You will not Nm 18:20
present to the **L** as a Nm 18:24
The **L** instructed Moses, Nm 18:25
of it as an offering to the **L**— Nm 18:26
offering to the **L** from every Nm 18:28
priest as an offering to the **L**. Nm 18:28
offering due the **L** from all your Nm 18:29
The **L** spoke to Moses and Aaron, Nm 19:1
that the **L** has commanded: Nm 19:2
defiles the tabernacle of the **L**. Nm 19:13
defiled the sanctuary of the **L**. Nm 19:20
brothers perished before the **L**. Nm 20:3
glory of the **L** appeared to them Nm 20:6
The **L** spoke to Moses, Nm 20:7
But the **L** said to Moses and Nm 20:12
Israelites quarreled with the **L**, Nm 20:13
When we cried out to the **L**, Nm 20:16
The **L** said to Moses and Aaron at Nm 20:23
Moses did as the **L** commanded, Nm 20:27
Then Israel made a vow to the **L**, Nm 21:2
The **L** listened to Israel's Nm 21:3
Then the **L** sent poisonous snakes Nm 21:6
against the **L** and against you. Nm 21:7
with the **L** so that He will Nm 21:7
Then the **L** said to Moses, Nm 21:8
the well the **L** told Moses about, Nm 21:16
But the **L** said to Moses, "Do not Nm 21:34
you the answer the **L** tells me." Nm 22:8
because the **L** has refused to let Nm 22:13
command of the **L** my God to do Nm 22:18
what else the **L** has to tell me. Nm 22:19
Angel of the **L** took His stand Nm 22:22
the Angel of the **L** standing on Nm 22:23

the Angel of the **L** stood in a Nm 22:24
the Angel of the **L** and pressed Nm 22:25
Angel of the **L** went ahead and Nm 22:26
donkey saw the Angel of the **L**, Nm 22:27
Then the **L** opened the donkey's Nm 22:28
Then the **L** opened Balaam's eyes, Nm 22:31
the Angel of the **L** standing in Nm 22:31
The Angel of the **L** asked him, Nm 22:32
said to the Angel of the **L**, Nm 22:34
Angel of the **L** said to Balaam, Nm 22:35
Maybe the **L** will meet with me. Nm 23:3
Then the **L** put a message in Nm 23:5
someone the **L** has not denounced? Nm 23:8
what the **L** puts in my mouth? Nm 23:12
I seek ⌊the **L**⌋ over there." Nm 23:15
The **L** met with Balaam and put a Nm 23:16
asked him, "What did the **L** say?" Nm 23:17
The **L** their God is with them, Nm 23:21
Whatever the **L** says, I must do?" Nm 23:26
pleased the **L** to bless Israel, Nm 24:1
like aloes the **L** has planted, Nm 24:6
the **L** has denied you a reward." Nm 24:11
I will say whatever the **L** says. Nm 24:13
The **L** said to Moses, "Take all Nm 25:4
before the **L** so that His burning Nm 25:4
The **L** spoke to Moses, Nm 25:10
The **L** told Moses: Nm 25:16
the **L** said to Moses and Eleazar Nm 26:1
as the **L** had commanded Moses Nm 26:4
followers fought against the **L**. Nm 26:9
The **L** spoke to Moses, Nm 26:52
unauthorized fire before the **L**. Nm 26:61
For the **L** had said to them that Nm 26:65
gathered together against the **L**. Nm 27:3
brought their case before the **L**, Nm 27:5
and the **L** answered him, Nm 27:6
as the **L** commanded Moses. Nm 27:11
Then the **L** said to Moses, Nm 27:12
So Moses appealed to the **L**, Nm 27:15
May the **L**, the God of the Nm 27:16
The **L** replied to Moses, "Take Nm 27:18
will consult the **L** for him with Nm 27:21
did as the **L** commanded him. Nm 27:22
as the **L** had spoken through Nm 27:23
The **L** spoke to Moses, Nm 28:1
you are to present to the **L**: Nm 28:3
aroma, a fire offering to the **L**. Nm 28:6
beer to the **L** in the sanctuary Nm 28:7
a pleasing aroma to the **L**. Nm 28:8
a burnt offering to the **L**: Nm 28:11
aroma, a fire offering to the **L**. Nm 28:13
as a sin offering to the **L**, Nm 28:15
Passover to the **L** comes in the Nm 28:16
a burnt offering to the **L**: Nm 28:19
a pleasing aroma to the **L**. Nm 28:24
new grain to the **L** at your Nm 28:26
for a pleasing aroma to the **L**: Nm 28:27
as a pleasing aroma to the **L**: Nm 29:2
aroma, a fire offering to the **L**. Nm 29:6
a burnt offering to the **L**, Nm 29:8
a seven-day festival for the **L**. Nm 29:12
as a pleasing aroma to the **L**: Nm 29:13
as a pleasing aroma to the **L**: Nm 29:36
these to the **L** at your appointed Nm 29:39
everything the **L** had commanded Nm 29:40
is what the **L** has commanded: Nm 30:1
a vow to the **L** or swears an oath Nm 30:2
a vow to the **L** or puts ⌊herself Nm 30:3
The **L** will absolve her because Nm 30:5
and the **L** will forgive her. Nm 30:8
and the **L** will absolve her. Nm 30:12
that the **L** commanded Moses Nm 30:16
The **L** spoke to Moses, Nm 31:1
as the **L** had commanded Moses, Nm 31:7
against the **L** in the Peor Nm 31:16
statute the **L** commanded Moses: Nm 31:21
The **L** told Moses, Nm 31:25
tribute for the **L** from what Nm 31:28
as a contribution to the **L**. Nm 31:29
did as the **L** commanded Moses. Nm 31:31
tribute to the **L** was 675 from Nm 31:37
the tribute to the **L** was 72; Nm 31:38
the tribute to the **L** was 61; Nm 31:39
tribute to the **L** was 32 people. Nm 31:40
as a contribution for the **L**, Nm 31:41
as the **L** had commanded Moses. Nm 31:41
as the **L** had commanded him. Nm 31:47
presented to the **L** an offering Nm 31:50

for ourselves before the **L**.” Nm 31:50
they offered to the **L**, Nm 31:52
for the Israelites before the **L**. Nm 31:54
which the **L** struck down before Nm 32:4
the land the **L** has given them? Nm 32:7
the land the **L** had given them. Nm 32:9
did follow the **L** completely.’ Nm 32:12
for battle before the **L**, Nm 32:20
Jordan before the **L** until He has Nm 32:21
land is subdued before the **L**— Nm 32:22
to the **L** and to Israel. Nm 32:22
as a possession before the **L**. Nm 32:22
certainly sin against the **L**; Nm 32:23
war before the **L** and will go Nm 32:27
battle formation before the **L**, Nm 32:29
What the **L** has spoken to your Nm 32:31
before the **L** into the land Nm 32:32
male the **L** had struck down Nm 33:4
for the **L** had executed judgment Nm 33:4
The **L** spoke to Moses in the Nm 33:50
The **L** spoke to Moses, Nm 34:1
the **L** commanded to be given Nm 34:13
The **L** spoke to Moses, Nm 34:16
are the ones the **L** commanded to Nm 34:29
L again spoke to Moses in the Nm 35:1
The **L** said to Moses, Nm 35:9
for I, the **L**, reside among the Nm 35:34
The **L** commanded my lord to give Nm 36:2
commanded by the **L** to give our Nm 36:2
Israelites at the word of the **L**, Nm 36:5
This is what the **L** has commanded Nm 36:6
did as the **L** commanded Moses. Nm 36:10
and ordinances the **L** commanded Nm 36:13
the **L** had commanded him Dt 1:3
The **L** our God spoke to us at Dt 1:6
of the land the **L** swore to give Dt 1:8
The **L** your God has so multiplied Dt 1:10
May the **L**, the God of your Dt 1:11
just as the **L** our God had Dt 1:19
the **L** our God is giving us. Dt 1:20
the **L** your God has set the land Dt 1:21
take possession of it as the **L**, Dt 1:21
‘The land the **L** our God is Dt 1:25
the command of the **L** your God. Dt 1:26
‘The **L** brought us out of the Dt 1:27
The **L** your God who goes before Dt 1:30
how the **L** your God carried Dt 1:31
did not trust the **L** your God, Dt 1:32
When the **L** heard your words, Dt 1:34
he followed the **L** completely.’ Dt 1:36
The **L** was angry with me also Dt 1:37
‘We have sinned against the **L**. Dt 1:41
just as the **L** our God commanded Dt 1:41
But the **L** said to me, ‘Tell Dt 1:42
wept before the **L**, but He didn’t Dt 1:45
Red Sea, as the **L** had told me, Dt 2:1
The **L** then said to me, Dt 2:2
For the **L** your God has blessed Dt 2:7
The **L** your God has been with you Dt 2:7
The **L** said to me, ‘Show no Dt 2:9
its possession the **L** gave them. Dt 2:12
⌊The **L** said,⌋ ‘Now get up and Dt 2:13
as the **L** had sworn to them. Dt 2:14
the **L** spoke to me, Dt 2:17
The **L** destroyed the Rephaim at Dt 2:21
⌊The **L** also said,⌋ ‘Get up, move Dt 2:24
the land the **L** our God is giving Dt 2:29
for the **L** your God made his Dt 2:30
Then the **L** said to me, ‘See, I Dt 2:31
The **L** our God handed him over to Dt 2:33
The **L** our God gave everything to Dt 2:36
everything that the **L** our God Dt 2:37
But the **L** said to me, ‘Do not Dt 3:2
the **L** our God also handed over Dt 3:3
L your God has given you this Dt 3:18
until the **L** gives rest to your Dt 3:20
of the land the **L** your God is Dt 3:20
everything the **L** your God has Dt 3:21
L will do the same to all the Dt 3:21
for the **L** your God fights for Dt 3:22
At that time I begged the **L**: Dt 3:23
But the **L** was angry with me on Dt 3:26
L said to me, ‘That’s enough! Dt 3:26
possession of the land the **L**, Dt 4:1
commands of the **L** your God I am Dt 4:2
seen what the **L** did at Baal-peor Dt 4:3
for the **L** your God destroyed Dt 4:3
faithful to the **L** your God are Dt 4:4
ordinances as the **L** my God has Dt 4:5
to it as the **L** our God is ⌊to us Dt 4:7
stood before the **L** your God at Dt 4:10
at Horeb, the **L** said to me, Dt 4:10
Then the **L** spoke to you from the Dt 4:12
that time the **L** commanded me to Dt 4:14
on the day the **L** spoke to you at Dt 4:15
The **L** your God has provided them Dt 4:19
But the **L** selected you and Dt 4:20
The **L** was angry with me on your Dt 4:21
the good land the **L** your God is Dt 4:21
covenant of the **L** your God that Dt 4:23
the **L** your God is a consuming Dt 4:24
in the sight of the **L** your God, Dt 4:25
The **L** will scatter you among the Dt 4:27
nations where the **L** your God Dt 4:27
will search for the **L** your God, Dt 4:29
return to the **L** your God in Dt 4:30
because the **L** your God is a Dt 4:31
as the **L** your God did for you in Dt 4:34
would know that the **L** is God; Dt 4:35
mind that the **L** is God in heaven Dt 4:39
in the land the **L** your God is Dt 4:40
The **L** our God made a covenant Dt 5:2
The **L** spoke to you face to face Dt 5:4
between the **L** and you to report Dt 5:5
report the word of the **L** to you, Dt 5:5
I am the **L** your God, who brought Dt 5:6
because I, the **L** your God, am Dt 5:9
the name of the **L** your God, Dt 5:11
because the **L** will punish anyone Dt 5:11
as the **L** your God has commanded Dt 5:12
is a Sabbath to the **L** your God. Dt 5:14
and the **L** your God brought you Dt 5:15
That is why the **L** your God has Dt 5:15
as the **L** your God has commanded Dt 5:16
in the land the **L** your God is Dt 5:16
The **L** spoke these commands in a Dt 5:22
the **L** our God has shown us His Dt 5:24
the voice of the **L** our God any Dt 5:25
everything the **L** our God says. Dt 5:27
everything the **L** our God tells Dt 5:27
The **L** heard your words when you Dt 5:28
to do as the **L** your God has Dt 5:32
instruction the **L** your God has Dt 5:33
the **L** your God has instructed Dt 6:1
you may fear the **L** your God all Dt 6:2
because the **L**, the God of your Dt 6:3
The **L** our God, the LORD is One. Dt 6:4
The LORD our God, the **L** is One. Dt 6:4
the **L** your God with all your Dt 6:5
When the **L** your God brings you Dt 6:10
to forget the **L** who brought you Dt 6:12
the **L** your God, worship Him, Dt 6:13
for the **L** your God, who is among Dt 6:15
the **L** your God will become angry Dt 6:15
not test the **L** your God as you Dt 6:16
the commands of the **L** your God, Dt 6:17
good land the **L** your God swore Dt 6:18
before you, as the **L** has said. Dt 6:19
the **L** our God has commanded Dt 6:20
the **L** brought us out of Egypt Dt 6:21
our eyes the **L** inflicted great Dt 6:22
The **L** commanded us to follow all Dt 6:24
to fear the **L** our God for our Dt 6:24
commands before the **L** our God, Dt 6:25
When the **L** your God brings you Dt 7:1
and when the **L** your God delivers Dt 7:2
belonging to the **L** your God. Dt 7:6
The **L** your God has chosen you to Dt 7:6
The **L** was devoted to you and Dt 7:7
But because the **L** loved you and Dt 7:8
the **L** your God will keep His Dt 7:12
The **L** will remove all sickness Dt 7:15
all the peoples the **L** your God Dt 7:16
what the **L** your God did to Dt 7:18
by which the **L** your God brought Dt 7:19
The **L** your God will do the same Dt 7:19
L your God will also send the Dt 7:20
of them, for the **L** your God, a Dt 7:21
The **L** your God will drive out Dt 7:22
The **L** your God will give them Dt 7:23
is abhorrent to the **L** your God. Dt 7:25
of the land the **L** swore to your Dt 8:1
that the **L** your God led you Dt 8:2
comes from the mouth of the **L**. Dt 8:3
in mind that the **L** your God has Dt 8:5
commands of the **L** your God by Dt 8:6
For the **L** your God is bringing Dt 8:7
will praise the **L** your God for Dt 8:10
don’t forget the **L** your God by Dt 8:11
you forget the **L** your God who Dt 8:14
that the **L** your God gives Dt 8:18
ever forget the **L** your God and Dt 8:19
the nations the **L** is about to Dt 8:20
you do not obey the **L** your God. Dt 8:20
that today the **L** your God will Dt 9:3
swiftly, as the **L** has told you. Dt 9:3
When the **L** your God drives them Dt 9:4
‘The **L** brought me in to take Dt 9:4
the **L** will drive out these Dt 9:4
the **L** your God will drive out Dt 9:5
that the **L** your God is not Dt 9:6
how you provoked the **L** your God Dt 9:7
against the **L** from the day you Dt 9:7
You provoked the **L** at Horeb, Dt 9:8
covenant the **L** made with you, Dt 9:9
assembly the **L** gave me the two Dt 9:10
which the **L** spoke to you from Dt 9:10
The **L** gave me the two stone Dt 9:11
The **L** said to me, ‘Get up and go Dt 9:12
The **L** also said to me, ‘I have Dt 9:13
sinned against the **L** your God; Dt 9:16
from the way the **L** had commanded Dt 9:16
presence of the **L** for 40 days Dt 9:18
fierce anger the **L** had directed Dt 9:19
the **L** listened to me on that Dt 9:19
L was angry enough with Aaron Dt 9:20
to provoke the **L** at Taberah, Dt 9:22
When the **L** sent you from Dt 9:23
the command of the **L** your God. Dt 9:23
against the **L** ever since I have Dt 9:24
presence of the **L** 40 days and 40 Dt 9:25
because the **L** had threatened to Dt 9:25
I prayed to the **L**: Lord GOD, do Dt 9:26
‘Because the **L** wasn’t able to Dt 9:28
The **L** said to me at that time, Dt 10:1
the **L** wrote on the tablets what Dt 10:4
the fire. The **L** gave them to me, Dt 10:4
there, as the **L** commanded me.” Dt 10:5
At that time the **L** set apart the Dt 10:8
stand before the **L** to serve Him, Dt 10:8
the **L** is his inheritance, as the Dt 10:9
as the **L** your God told him. Dt 10:9
L also listened to me on this Dt 10:10
Then the **L** said to me, ‘Get up. Dt 10:11
what does the **L** your God ask of Dt 10:12
except to fear the **L** your God by Dt 10:12
to worship the **L** your God with Dt 10:12
belong to the **L** your God, as Dt 10:14
Yet the **L** was devoted to your Dt 10:15
For the **L** your God is the God of Dt 10:17
You are to fear the **L** your God Dt 10:20
and now the **L** your God has made Dt 10:22
love the **L** your God and always Dt 11:1
discipline of the **L** your God: Dt 11:2
every great work the **L** has done. Dt 11:7
in the land the **L** swore to your Dt 11:9
is a land the **L** your God cares Dt 11:12
to love the **L** your God and Dt 11:13
good land the **L** is giving you. Dt 11:17
in the land the **L** swore to give Dt 11:21
to love the **L** your God, walk Dt 11:22
the **L** will drive out all these Dt 11:23
the **L** your God will put fear and Dt 11:25
commands of the **L** your God I am Dt 11:27
the commands of the **L** your God, Dt 11:28
When the **L** your God brings you Dt 11:29
of the land the **L** your God is Dt 11:31
in the land that the **L**, Dt 12:1
worship the **L** your God this way Dt 12:4
the place the **L** your God chooses Dt 12:5
the presence of the **L** your God Dt 12:7
because the **L** your God has Dt 12:7
inheritance the **L** your God is Dt 12:9
in the land the **L** your God is Dt 12:10
then the **L** your God will choose Dt 12:11
offerings you vow to the **L**. Dt 12:11
rejoice before the **L** your God— Dt 12:12
the place the **L** chooses in one Dt 12:14
the blessing the **L** your God has Dt 12:15
the presence of the **L** your God Dt 12:18
the place the **L** your God chooses Dt 12:18
Rejoice before the **L** your God in Dt 12:18
When the **L** your God enlarges Dt 12:20
place where the **L** your God Dt 12:21

go to the place the **L** chooses.	Dt 12:26
on the altar of the **L** your God.	Dt 12:27
the altar of the **L** your God,	Dt 12:27
in the sight of the **L** your God.	Dt 12:28
When the **L** your God annihilates	Dt 12:29
do the same to the **L** your God,	Dt 12:31
detestable thing the **L** hates.	Dt 12:31
the **L** your God is testing you	Dt 13:3
you love the **L** your God with all	Dt 13:3
must follow the **L** your God and	Dt 13:4
against the **L** your God who	Dt 13:5
from the way the **L** your God has	Dt 13:5
you away from the **L** your God who	Dt 13:10
your cities the **L** your God is	Dt 13:12
its spoil for the **L** your God.	Dt 13:16
so that the **L** will turn from His	Dt 13:17
if you obey the **L** your God,	Dt 13:18
in the sight of the **L** your God.	Dt 13:18
You are sons of the **L** your God;	Dt 14:1
belonging to the **L** your God.	Dt 14:2
The **L** has chosen you to be His	Dt 14:2
belonging to the **L** your God.	Dt 14:21
the presence of the **L** your God	Dt 14:23
learn to fear the **L** your God.	Dt 14:23
place where the **L** your God	Dt 14:24
you and since the **L** your God has	Dt 14:24
the place the **L** your God chooses	Dt 14:25
the presence of the **L** your God	Dt 14:26
the **L** your God will bless you	Dt 14:29
because the **L** is certain to	Dt 15:4
in the land the **L** your God is	Dt 15:4
you obey the **L** your God and are	Dt 15:5
When the **L** your God blesses you	Dt 15:6
in the land the **L** your God is	Dt 15:7
cry out to the **L** against you,	Dt 15:9
of this the **L** your God will	Dt 15:10
him whatever the **L** your God has	Dt 15:14
of Egypt and the **L** your God	Dt 15:15
Then the **L** your God will bless	Dt 15:18
to the **L** your God every	Dt 15:19
to eat it before the **L** your God	Dt 15:20
God in the place the **L** chooses.	Dt 15:20
sacrifice it to the **L** your God.	Dt 15:21
the Passover to the **L** your God,	Dt 16:1
because the **L** your God brought	Dt 16:1
Sacrifice to the **L** your God a	Dt 16:2
place where the **L** chooses to	Dt 16:2
of the towns the **L** your God is	Dt 16:5
place where the **L** your God	Dt 16:6
the place the **L** your God chooses	Dt 16:7
assembly to the **L** your God,	Dt 16:8
of Weeks to the **L** your God with	Dt 16:10
to how the **L** your God has	Dt 16:10
Rejoice before the **L** your God in	Dt 16:11
festival for the **L** your God in	Dt 16:15
because the **L** your God will	Dt 16:15
a year before the **L** your God in	Dt 16:16
before the **L** empty-handed.	Dt 16:16
the blessing the **L** your God has	Dt 16:17
your towns the **L** your God is	Dt 16:18
land the **L** your God is giving	Dt 16:20
will build for the **L** your God,	Dt 16:21
the **L** your God hates them.	Dt 16:22
sacrifice to the **L** your God an	Dt 17:1
is detestable to the **L** your God.	Dt 17:1
towns that the **L** your God will	Dt 17:2
in the sight of the **L** your God	Dt 17:2
the place the **L** your God chooses	Dt 17:8
you at the place the **L** chooses.	Dt 17:10
serving the **L** your God or to	Dt 17:12
the land the **L** your God is	Dt 17:14
the king the **L** your God chooses	Dt 17:15
for the **L** has told you,	Dt 17:16
may learn to fear the **L** his God,	Dt 17:19
his brothers, the **L** is his	Dt 18:2
the **L** your God has chosen him	Dt 18:5
go to the place the **L** chooses,	Dt 18:6
the name of the **L** his God like	Dt 18:7
there in the presence of the **L**.	Dt 18:7
the land the **L** your God is	Dt 18:9
things is detestable to the **L**,	Dt 18:12
the **L** your God is driving out	Dt 18:12
blameless before the **L** your God.	Dt 18:13
the **L** your God has not permitted	Dt 18:14
The **L** your God will raise up for	Dt 18:15
from the **L** your God at Horeb	Dt 18:16
voice of the **L** our God or see	Dt 18:16
the **L** said to me, 'They have	Dt 18:17

a message the **L** has not spoken?'	Dt 18:21
a message the **L** has not spoken.	Dt 18:22
When the **L** your God annihilates	Dt 19:1
the land the **L** your God is	Dt 19:2
divide the land the **L** your God	Dt 19:3
If the **L** your God enlarges your	Dt 19:8
the **L** your God and walking	Dt 19:9
in the land the **L** your God is	Dt 19:10
in the land the **L** your God is	Dt 19:14
presence of the **L** before the	Dt 19:17
of them, for the **L** your God, who	Dt 20:1
the **L** your God is the One who	Dt 20:4
the **L** your God hands it over	Dt 20:13
enemies that the **L** your God has	Dt 20:14
these people the **L** your God is	Dt 20:16
as the **L** your God has commanded	Dt 20:17
you sin against the **L** your God.	Dt 20:18
in the land the **L** your God is	Dt 21:1
for the **L** your God has chosen	Dt 21:5
L, forgive Your people Israel	Dt 21:8
enemies and the **L** your God hands	Dt 21:10
the land the **L** your God is	Dt 21:23
is detestable to the **L** your God.	Dt 22:5
Yet the **L** your God would not	Dt 23:5
you because the **L** your God loves	Dt 23:5
For the **L** your God walks	Dt 23:14
the house of the **L** your God to	Dt 23:18
detestable to the **L** your God.	Dt 23:18
so that the **L** your God may bless	Dt 23:20
make a vow to the **L** your God,	Dt 23:21
you promised to the **L** your God.	Dt 23:23
would be detestable to the **L**.	Dt 24:4
on the land the **L** your God is	Dt 24:4
what the **L** your God did to	Dt 24:9
to you before the **L** your God.	Dt 24:13
cry out to the **L** against you,	Dt 24:15
and the **L** your God redeemed you	Dt 24:18
so that the **L** your God may bless	Dt 24:19
in the land the **L** your God is	Dt 25:15
is detestable to the **L** your God.	Dt 25:16
When the **L** your God gives you	Dt 25:19
in the land the **L** your God is	Dt 25:19
the land the **L** your God is	Dt 26:1
from the land the **L** your God is	Dt 26:2
place where the **L** your God	Dt 26:2
to the **L** your God that I	Dt 26:3
the land the **L** swore to our	Dt 26:3
the altar of the **L** your God.	Dt 26:4
the presence of the **L** your God:	Dt 26:5
So we called out to the **L**,	Dt 26:7
and the **L** heard our cry and saw	Dt 26:7
Then the **L** brought us out of	Dt 26:8
that You, **L**, have given me.	Dt 26:10
before the **L** your God and bow	Dt 26:10
good things the **L** your God has	Dt 26:11
the presence of the **L** your God:	Dt 26:13
I have obeyed the **L** my God;	Dt 26:14
L your God is commanding you	Dt 26:16
affirmed that the **L** is your God	Dt 26:17
today the **L** has affirmed that	Dt 26:18
people to the **L** your God as He	Dt 26:19
into the land the **L** your God is	Dt 27:2
the land the **L** your God is	Dt 27:3
honey, as the **L**, the God of your	Dt 27:3
stones there to the **L** your God—	Dt 27:5
the altar of the **L** your God and	Dt 27:6
to the **L** your God on it.	Dt 27:6
the presence of the **L** your God.	Dt 27:7
the people of the **L** your God.	Dt 27:9
Obey the **L** your God and follow	Dt 27:10
which is detestable to the **L**,	Dt 27:15
obey the **L** your God and are	Dt 28:1
the **L** your God will put you far	Dt 28:1
because you obey the **L** your God:	Dt 28:2
The **L** will cause the enemies who	Dt 28:7
The **L** will grant you a blessing	Dt 28:8
in the land the **L** your God is	Dt 28:8
The **L** will establish you as His	Dt 28:9
commands of the **L** your God and	Dt 28:9
The **L** will make you prosper	Dt 28:11
in the land the **L** swore to your	Dt 28:11
The **L** will open for you His	Dt 28:12
The **L** will make you the head and	Dt 28:13
you listen to the **L** your God's	Dt 28:13
you do not obey the **L** your God	Dt 28:15
The **L** will send against you	Dt 28:20
The **L** will make pestilence cling	Dt 28:21
The **L** will afflict you with	Dt 28:22

The **L** will turn the rain of your	Dt 28:24
The **L** will cause you to be	Dt 28:25
The **L** will afflict you with the	Dt 28:27
The **L** will afflict you with	Dt 28:28
The **L** will afflict you on your	Dt 28:35
The **L** will bring you and your	Dt 28:36
where the **L** will drive you.	Dt 28:37
did not obey the **L** your God and	Dt 28:45
didn't serve the **L** your God with	Dt 28:47
your enemies the **L** will send	Dt 28:48
The **L** will bring a nation from	Dt 28:49
land the **L** your God has given	Dt 28:52
and daughters the **L** your God has	Dt 28:53
The **L** will also inflict you with	Dt 28:61
you did not obey the **L** your God.	Dt 28:62
Just as the **L** was glad to cause	Dt 28:63
the **L** will scatter you among	Dt 28:64
There the **L** will give you a	Dt 28:65
L will take you back in ships	Dt 28:68
covenant the **L** commanded Moses	Dt 29:1
everything the **L** did in Egypt to	Dt 29:2
to this day the **L** has not given	Dt 29:4
know that I am the **L** your God.	Dt 29:6
today before the **L** your God—	Dt 29:10
the covenant of the **L** your God,	Dt 29:12
presence of the **L** our God and	Dt 29:15
away from the **L** our God to go	Dt 29:18
The **L** will not be willing to	Dt 29:20
The **L** will blot out his name	Dt 29:20
sicknesses the **L** has inflicted	Dt 29:22
which the **L** demolished in His	Dt 29:23
'Why has the **L** done this to this	Dt 29:24
abandoned the covenant of the **L**,	Dt 29:25
that the **L** had not permitted	Dt 29:26
The **L** uprooted them from their	Dt 29:28
things belong to the **L** our God,	Dt 29:29
nations where the **L** your God has	Dt 30:1
return to the **L** your God and	Dt 30:2
peoples where the **L** your God has	Dt 30:3
The **L** your God will bring you	Dt 30:5
The **L** your God will circumcise	Dt 30:6
L your God will put all these	Dt 30:7
The **L** your God will make you	Dt 30:9
the **L** will again delight in your	Dt 30:9
when you obey the **L** your God by	Dt 30:10
today to love the **L** your God,	Dt 30:16
and the **L** your God may bless you	Dt 30:16
love the **L** your God, obey Him,	Dt 30:20
in the land the **L** swore to give	Dt 30:20
The **L** has told me, 'You will not	Dt 31:2
The **L** your God is the One who	Dt 31:3
ahead of you, as the **L** has said.	Dt 31:3
The **L** will deal with them as He	Dt 31:4
The **L** will deliver them over to	Dt 31:5
it is the **L** your God who goes	Dt 31:6
the land the **L** swore to give to	Dt 31:7
The **L** is the One who will go	Dt 31:8
the presence of the **L** your God	Dt 31:11
to fear the **L** your God and be	Dt 31:12
to fear the **L** your God as long	Dt 31:13
The **L** said to Moses, "The time	Dt 31:14
the **L** appeared at the tent in a	Dt 31:15
The **L** said to Moses, "You are	Dt 31:16
The **L** commissioned Joshua son of	Dt 31:23
the covenant of the **L** your God,	Dt 31:26
are rebelling against the **L** now,	Dt 31:27
Is this how you repay the **L**,	Dt 32:6
L alone led him, with no help	Dt 32:12
When the **L** saw ⌊this⌋, He	Dt 32:19
wasn't the **L** who did all this.	Dt 32:27
unless the **L** had given them up?	Dt 32:30
The **L** will indeed vindicate His	Dt 32:36
same day the **L** spoke to Moses,	Dt 32:48
The **L** came from Sinai and	Dt 33:2
L, hear Judah's cry and bring	Dt 33:7
L, bless his possessions, and	Dt 33:11
be blessed by the **L** with the dew	Dt 33:13
you, a people saved by the **L**?	Dt 33:29
and the **L** showed him all the	Dt 34:1
The **L** then said to him, "This is	Dt 34:4
the servant of the **L** died there	Dt 34:5
land of Moab, as the **L** had said.	Dt 34:5
and did as the **L** had commanded	Dt 34:9
whom the **L** knew face to face.	Dt 34:10
and wonders the **L** sent him to do	Dt 34:11
L spoke to Joshua son of Nun,	Jos 1:1
for the **L** your God is with you	Jos 1:9
of the land the **L** your God is	Jos 1:11

'The L your God will give you Jos 1:13
until the L gives our brothers Jos 1:15
land the L your God is giving Jos 1:15
And may the L your God be with Jos 1:17
I know that the L has given you Jos 2:9
have heard how the L dried up Jos 2:10
for the L your God is God in Jos 2:11
to me by the L that you will Jos 2:12
when the L gives us the land. Jos 2:14
The L has handed over the entire Jos 2:24
covenant of the L your God Jos 3:3
because the L will do wonders Jos 3:5
The L spoke to Joshua: Jos 3:7
to the words of the L your God." Jos 3:9
who carry the ark of the L, Jos 3:13
Jordan, the L spoke to Joshua Jos 4:1
to the ark of the L your God in Jos 4:5
just as the L had told Joshua. Jos 4:8
that the L had commanded Jos 4:10
with the ark of the L crossed in Jos 4:11
On that day the L exalted Joshua Jos 4:14
The L told Joshua, Jos 4:15
For the L your God dried up the Jos 4:23
just as the L your God did to Jos 4:23
may always fear the L your God." Jos 4:24
sea heard how the L had dried up Jos 5:1
that time the L said to Joshua, Jos 5:2
because they did not obey the L. Jos 5:6
So the L vowed never to let them Jos 5:6
The L then said to Joshua, Jos 5:9
The L said to Joshua, "Look, I Jos 6:2
in front of the ark of the L." Jos 6:6
go ahead of the ark of the L." Jos 6:7
before the L moved forward Jos 6:8
So the ark of the L was carried Jos 6:11
priests took the ark of the L, Jos 6:12
in front of the ark of the L. Jos 6:13
went behind the ark of the L. Jos 6:13
the L has given you the city. Jos 6:16
apart to the L for destruction Jos 6:17
dedicated to the L and must go Jos 6:19
before the L is the man who Jos 6:26
And the L was with Joshua, Jos 6:27
the ark of the L with his face Jos 7:6
The L then said to Joshua, Jos 7:10
this is what the L, the God of Jos 7:13
The tribe the L selects is to Jos 7:14
clan the L selects is to come Jos 7:14
The family the L selects is to Jos 7:14
give glory to the L, the God of Jos 7:19
I have sinned against the L, Jos 7:20
Today the L will trouble you!" Jos 7:25
Then the L turned from His Jos 7:26
The L said to Joshua, "Do not be Jos 8:1
for the L your God has handed it Jos 8:7
Then the L said to Joshua, Jos 8:18
an altar on Mount Ebal to the L, Jos 8:30
to the L and sacrificed Jos 8:31
reputation of the L your God. Jos 9:9
sworn an oath to them by the L, Jos 9:18
sworn an oath to them by the L, Jos 9:19
servants that the L your God had Jos 9:24
The L said to Joshua, "Do not be Jos 10:8
The L threw them into confusion Jos 10:10
the L threw large hailstones on Jos 10:11
On the day the L gave the Jos 10:12
spoke to the L in the presence Jos 10:12
when the L listened to the voice Jos 10:14
because the L fought for Israel. Jos 10:14
for the L your God has handed Jos 10:19
the L will do this to all the Jos 10:25
L also handed it and its king Jos 10:30
The L handed Lachish over to Jos 10:32
being, as the L, the God of Jos 10:40
the L, the God of Israel, Jos 10:42
The L said to Joshua, "Do not be Jos 11:6
L handed them over to Israel, Jos 11:8
them as the L had told him; Jos 11:9
Just as the L had commanded His Jos 11:15
of all that the L had commanded Jos 11:15
just as the L had commanded Jos 11:20
all that the L had told Moses. Jos 11:23
years, and the L said to him, Jos 13:1
offerings made by fire to the L, Jos 13:14
The L, the God of Israel, was Jos 13:33
by lot as the L commanded Jos 14:2
did as the L commanded Moses, Jos 14:5
know what the L promised Moses Jos 14:6
remained loyal to the L my God. Jos 14:8
loyal to the L my God.' Jos 14:9
the L has kept me alive ⌊these⌋ Jos 14:10
since the L spoke this word to Jos 14:10
hill country the L promised ⌊me⌋ Jos 14:12
Perhaps the L will be with me Jos 14:12
them out as the L promised." Jos 14:12
he remained loyal to the L, Jos 14:14
The L commanded Moses to give us Jos 17:4
the L has greatly blessed us. Jos 17:14
of the land that the L, Jos 18:3
the presence of the L our God. Jos 18:6
is the priesthood of the L. Jos 18:7
in the presence of the L." Jos 18:8
the presence of the L where he Jos 18:10
Then the L spoke to Joshua, Jos 20:1
The L commanded through Moses Jos 21:2
as the L had commanded through Jos 21:8
the L gave Israel all the land Jos 21:43
The L gave them rest on every Jos 21:44
for the L handed over all their Jos 21:44
good promises the L had made to Jos 21:45
the command of the L your God. Jos 22:3
to love the L your God, walk in Jos 22:5
away from the L and building an Jos 22:16
rebellion against the L today? Jos 22:16
you would turn away from the L? Jos 22:18
you rebel against the L today, Jos 22:18
the land the L possesses where Jos 22:19
rebel against the L or against Jos 22:19
than the altar of the L our God. Jos 22:19
The L is the God of gods! Jos 22:22
The L is the God of gods! Jos 22:22
or treachery against the L Jos 22:22
May the L Himself hold us Jos 22:23
do you have with the L, Jos 22:24
For the L has made the Jordan a Jos 22:25
You have no share in the L!' Jos 22:25
to stop fearing the L. Jos 22:25
worship of the L in His presence Jos 22:27
'You have no share in the L!' Jos 22:27
rebel against the L or turn away Jos 22:29
than the altar of the L our God, Jos 22:29
we know that the L is among us, Jos 22:31
between us that the L is God. Jos 22:34
after the L had given Israel Jos 23:1
everything the L your God did to Jos 23:3
it was the L your God who was Jos 23:3
The L your God will force them Jos 23:5
as the L your God promised you. Jos 23:5
faithful to the L your God, Jos 23:8
The L has driven out great and Jos 23:9
because the L your God was Jos 23:10
to love the L your God for your Jos 23:11
certain that the L your God will Jos 23:13
good land the L your God has Jos 23:13
promises the L your God made to Jos 23:14
good thing the L your God Jos 23:15
good land the L your God has Jos 23:15
the covenant of the L your God, Jos 23:16
This is what the L, the God of Jos 24:2
Your fathers cried out to the L, Jos 24:7
fear the L and worship Him in Jos 24:14
and in Egypt, and worship the L. Jos 24:14
please you to worship the L, Jos 24:15
family, we will worship the L." Jos 24:15
not abandon the L to worship Jos 24:16
For the L our God brought us and Jos 24:17
L drove out before us all the Jos 24:18
We too will worship the L, Jos 24:18
not be able to worship the L, Jos 24:19
If you abandon the L and worship Jos 24:20
"We will worship the L." Jos 24:21
have chosen to worship the L." Jos 24:22
and offer your hearts to the L, Jos 24:23
worship the L our God and obey Jos 24:24
next to the sanctuary of the L. Jos 24:26
all the words the L said to us, Jos 24:27
worshiped the L throughout Jos 24:31
all the works the L had done for Jos 24:31
Israelites inquired of the L, Jdg 1:1
The L answered, "Judah is to go. Jdg 1:2
the L handed the Canaanites and Jdg 1:4
The L was with Judah and enabled Jdg 1:19
Bethel, and the L was with them. Jdg 1:22
The Angel of the L went up from Jdg 2:1
Angel of the L had spoken these Jdg 2:4
sacrifices there to the L. Jdg 2:5
worshiped the L throughout Jdg 2:7
servant of the L, died at the Jdg 2:8
not know the L or the works He Jdg 2:10
abandoned the L, the God of Jdg 2:12
to them. They infuriated the L, Jdg 2:12
the L was against them and Jdg 2:15
L raised up judges, who saved Jdg 2:16
Whenever the L raised up a judge Jdg 2:18
the L was with him and saved the Jdg 2:18
The L was moved to pity whenever Jdg 2:18
The L left these nations and did Jdg 2:23
the nations the L left in order Jdg 3:1
The L left them to test Israel, Jdg 3:4
they forgot the L their God and Jdg 3:7
Israelites cried out to the L. Jdg 3:9
the L raised up Othniel son of Jdg 3:9
The Spirit of the L was on him, Jdg 3:10
and the L handed over Jdg 3:10
Israelites cried out to the L, Jdg 3:15
because the L has handed over Jdg 3:28
sight of the L after Ehud had Jdg 4:1
So the L sold them into the hand Jdg 4:2
Israelites cried out to the L, Jdg 4:3
him, "Hasn't the L, the God of Jdg 4:6
because the L will sell Sisera Jdg 4:9
is the day the L has handed Jdg 4:14
Hasn't the L gone before you?" Jdg 4:14
The L threw Sisera, all his Jdg 4:15
people volunteer, praise the L. Jdg 5:2
will sing to the L; I will sing Jdg 5:3
praise to the L God of Israel. Jdg 5:3
L, when You came from Seir, when Jdg 5:4
mountains melted before the L, Jdg 5:5
Sinai before the L, the God of Jdg 5:5
of the people. Praise the L! Jdg 5:9
the righteous acts of the L, Jdg 5:11
says the Angel of the L, Jdg 5:23
they did not come to help the L, Jdg 5:23
to help the L against the mighty Jdg 5:23
L, may all your enemies perish Jdg 5:31
was evil in the sight of the L. Jdg 6:1
So the L handed them over to Jdg 6:1
Israelites cried out to the L. Jdg 6:6
the L sent a prophet to them. Jdg 6:8
This is what the L God of Israel Jdg 6:8
you: I am the L your God. Do not Jdg 6:10
Angel of the L came, and He sat Jdg 6:11
Angel of the L appeared to him Jdg 6:12
The L is with you, mighty Jdg 6:12
Sir, if the L is with us, why Jdg 6:13
'Hasn't the L brought us out of Jdg 6:13
But now the L has abandoned us Jdg 6:13
The L turned to him and said, Jdg 6:14
be with you," the L said to him. Jdg 6:16
Angel of the L extended the tip Jdg 6:21
the Angel of the L vanished from Jdg 6:21
that He was the Angel of the L, Jdg 6:22
Angel of the L face to face!" Jdg 6:22
But the L said to him, "Peace to Jdg 6:23
an altar to the L there and Jdg 6:24
very night the L said to him, Jdg 6:25
altar to the L your God on the Jdg 6:26
and did as the L had told him. Jdg 6:27
Spirit of the L enveloped Gideon Jdg 6:34
The L said to Gideon, "You have Jdg 7:2
Then the L said to Gideon, Jdg 7:4
and the L said to Gideon, Jdg 7:5
The L said to Gideon, "I will Jdg 7:7
That night the L said to him, Jdg 7:9
for the L has handed the Jdg 7:15
sword of the L and of Gideon!' Jdg 7:18
sword of the L and of Gideon!" Jdg 7:20
the L set the swords of each man Jdg 7:22
when the L has handed Zebah and Jdg 8:7
As the L lives, if you had let Jdg 8:19
the L will rule over you." Jdg 8:23
not remember the L their God who Jdg 8:34
was evil in the sight of the L. Jdg 10:6
They abandoned the L and did not Jdg 10:6
so they cried out to the L, Jdg 10:10
The L said to the Israelites, Jdg 10:11
among them and worshiped the L, Jdg 10:16
and the L gives them to me Jdg 11:9
The L is our witness if we don't Jdg 11:10
the presence of the L at Mizpah. Jdg 11:11
Then the L God of Israel handed Jdg 11:21
The L God of Israel has now Jdg 11:23
everything the L our God drives Jdg 11:24

Let the **L** ⌊who is⌋ the Judge Jdg 11:27
Spirit of the **L** came on Jephthah Jdg 11:29
Jephthah made this vow to the **L**: Jdg 11:30
Ammonites will belong to the **L**, Jdg 11:31
and the **L** handed them over to Jdg 11:32
my word to the **L** and cannot take Jdg 11:35
have given your word to the **L**. Jdg 11:36
for the **L** brought vengeance on Jdg 11:36
the **L** handed them over to me. Jdg 12:3
so the **L** handed them over to the Jdg 13:1
The Angel of the **L** appeared to Jdg 13:3
Manoah prayed to the **L** and said, Jdg 13:8
Angel of the **L** answered Manoah Jdg 13:13
The Angel of the **L** said to him, Jdg 13:16
offering, offer it to the **L**." Jdg 13:16
know He was the Angel of the **L**. Jdg 13:16
the Angel of the **L** asked him, Jdg 13:18
offered them on a rock to the **L**, Jdg 13:19
Angel of the **L** went up in its Jdg 13:20
Angel of the **L** did not appear Jdg 13:21
that it was the Angel of the **L**. Jdg 13:21
If the **L** had intended to kill Jdg 13:23
boy grew, and the **L** blessed him. Jdg 13:24
Spirit of the **L** began to direct Jdg 13:25
not know this was from the **L**, Jdg 14:4
the Spirit of the **L** took control Jdg 14:6
The Spirit of the **L** took control Jdg 14:19
The Spirit of the **L** took control Jdg 15:14
thirsty and called out to the **L**: Jdg 15:18
know that the **L** had left him. Jdg 16:20
He called out to the **L**: Jdg 16:28
you are blessed by the **L**!" Jdg 17:2
the silver to the **L** for my son's Jdg 17:3
know that the **L** will be good to Jdg 17:13
The **L** is watching over the Jdg 18:6
I'm going to the house of the **L**. Jdg 19:18
one body before the **L** at Mizpah. Jdg 20:1
And the **L** answered, "Judah will Jdg 20:18
wept before the **L** until evening, Jdg 20:23
And the **L** answered: "Fight Jdg 20:23
they wept and sat before the **L**. Jdg 20:26
fellowship offerings to the **L**. Jdg 20:26
Israelites inquired of the **L**. Jdg 20:27
stop?" The **L** answered: "Fight, Jdg 20:28
The **L** defeated Benjamin in the Jdg 20:35
out, "Why, **L** God of Israel, Jdg 21:3
come to the **L** with the assembly? Jdg 21:5
come to the **L** at Mizpah would Jdg 21:5
sworn to the **L** not to give them Jdg 21:7
didn't come to the **L** at Mizpah?" Jdg 21:8
because the **L** had made this gap Jdg 21:15
festival to the **L** in Shiloh, Jdg 21:19
in Moab that the **L** had paid Ru 1:6
May the **L** show faithful love to Ru 1:8
May the **L** enable each of you to Ru 1:9
the **L** do this to me, and even Ru 1:17
but the **L** has brought me back Ru 1:21
since the **L** has pronounced Ru 1:21
harvesters, "The **L** be with you." Ru 2:4
"The **L** bless you," they Ru 2:4
the **L** reward you for what you Ru 2:12
reward from the **L** God of Israel, Ru 2:12
May ⌊the **L**⌋ bless the man who Ru 2:19
May he be blessed by the **L**, Ru 2:20
said, "May the **L** bless you, my Ru 3:10
you, as the **L** lives, I will. Ru 3:13
May the **L** make the woman who is Ru 4:11
offspring the **L** will give you Ru 4:12
the **L** enabled her to conceive, Ru 4:13
Praise the **L**, who has not left Ru 4:14
sacrifice to the **L** of Hosts at 1Sm 1:3
even though the **L** had kept her 1Sm 1:5
because the **L** had kept Hannah 1Sm 1:6
prayed to the **L** and wept with 1Sm 1:10
she pleaded, "**L** of Hosts, if You 1Sm 1:11
give him to the **L** all the days 1Sm 1:11
out my heart before the **L**. 1Sm 1:15
to bow and to worship the **L**. 1Sm 1:19
and the **L** remembered her. 1Sm 1:19
"I requested him from the **L**." 1Sm 1:20
and his vow offering to the **L**, 1Sm 1:21
May the **L** confirm your word." 1Sm 1:23
beside you praying to the **L**. 1Sm 1:26
and since the **L** gave me what I 1Sm 1:27
I now give the boy to the **L**. 1Sm 1:28
he lives, he is given to the **L**." 1Sm 1:28
bowed and worshiped the **L** there. 1Sm 1:28
My heart rejoices in the **L**; 1Sm 2:1

my horn is lifted up by the **L**. 1Sm 2:1
There is no one holy like the **L**. 1Sm 2:2
for the **L** is a God of knowledge, 1Sm 2:3
The **L** brings death and gives 1Sm 2:6
The **L** brings poverty and gives 1Sm 2:7
who oppose the **L** will be 1Sm 2:10
The **L** will judge the ends of the 1Sm 2:10
boy served the **L** in the presence 1Sm 2:11
they had no regard for the **L** 1Sm 2:12
severe in the presence of the **L**, 1Sm 2:17
May the **L** give you children by 1Sm 2:20
the one she has given to the **L**." 1Sm 2:20
The **L** paid attention to Hannah's 1Sm 2:21
up in the presence of the **L**. 1Sm 2:21
but if a man sins against the **L**, 1Sm 2:25
since the **L** intended to kill 1Sm 2:25
favor with the **L** and with men. 1Sm 2:26
This is what the **L** says: 1Sm 2:27
Therefore, the **L**, the God of 1Sm 2:30
Me forever, the **L** now says, "No 1Sm 2:30
served the **L** in Eli's presence 1Sm 3:1
days the word of the **L** was rare 1Sm 3:1
tabernacle of the **L** where the 1Sm 3:3
Then the **L** called Samuel, and he 1Sm 3:4
again the **L** called, "Samuel! 1Sm 3:6
had not yet experienced the **L**, 1Sm 3:7
the word of the **L** had not yet 1Sm 3:7
third time, the **L** called Samuel. 1Sm 3:8
that the **L** was calling the boy 1Sm 3:8
say, 'Speak, **L**, for Your servant 1Sm 3:9
The **L** came, stood there, and 1Sm 3:10
L said to Samuel, "I am about 1Sm 3:11
Eli responded, "He is the **L**. 1Sm 3:18
and the **L** was with him and let 1Sm 3:19
a confirmed prophet of the **L**. 1Sm 3:20
The **L** continued to appear in 1Sm 3:21
Why did the **L** let us be defeated 1Sm 4:3
the covenant of the **L** of Hosts, 1Sm 4:4
covenant of the **L** entered the 1Sm 4:5
the ark of the **L** had entered 1Sm 4:6
ground before the ark of the **L**. 1Sm 5:3
ground before the ark of the **L**. 1Sm 5:4
The **L** severely oppressed the 1Sm 5:6
When the ark of the **L** had been 1Sm 6:1
we do with the ark of the **L**? 1Sm 6:2
Take the ark of the **L**, place it 1Sm 6:8
it is the **L** who has made this 1Sm 6:9
the ark of the **L** on the cart, 1Sm 6:11
as a burnt offering to the **L**. 1Sm 6:14
removed the ark of the **L**, 1Sm 6:15
and made sacrifices to the **L**. 1Sm 6:15
As a guilt offering to the **L**, 1Sm 6:17
the ark of the **L** was placed is 1Sm 6:18
looked inside the ark of the **L**. 1Sm 6:19
because the **L** struck them with 1Sm 6:19
the presence of this holy **L** God? 1Sm 6:20
have returned the ark of the **L**. 1Sm 6:21
the ark of the **L** and took it to 1Sm 7:1
of Israel began to seek the **L**. 1Sm 7:2
returning to the **L** with all your 1Sm 7:3
dedicate yourselves to the **L**, 1Sm 7:3
and only worshiped the **L**. 1Sm 7:4
pray to the **L** on your behalf. 1Sm 7:5
"We have sinned against the **L**." 1Sm 7:6
out to the **L** our God for us, 1Sm 7:8
a whole burnt offering to the **L**. 1Sm 7:9
cried out to the **L** on behalf of 1Sm 7:9
Israel, and the **L** answered him. 1Sm 7:9
The **L** thundered loudly against 1Sm 7:10
L has helped us to this point. 1Sm 7:12
built an altar to the **L** there. 1Sm 7:17
sinful, so he prayed to the **L**. 1Sm 8:6
But the **L** told him, "Listen to 1Sm 8:7
but the **L** won't answer you on 1Sm 8:18
and then repeated them to the **L**. 1Sm 8:21
to them," the **L** told Samuel. 1Sm 8:22
the **L** had informed Samuel, 1Sm 9:15
saw Saul, the **L** told him, "Here 1Sm 9:17
Hasn't the **L** anointed you ruler 1Sm 10:1
Spirit of the **L** will control you 1Sm 10:6
the people to the **L** at Mizpah 1Sm 10:17
This is what the **L**, the God of 1Sm 10:18
before the **L** by your tribes 1Sm 10:19
They again inquired of the **L**, 1Sm 10:22
The **L** replied, "There he is, 1Sm 10:22
see the one the **L** has chosen? 1Sm 10:24
placed in the presence of the **L**. 1Sm 10:25
the terror of the **L** fell on the 1Sm 11:7

for today the **L** has provided 1Sm 11:13
before the **L** and His anointed: 1Sm 12:3
The **L** is a witness against you, 1Sm 12:5
people, "The **L**, who appointed 1Sm 12:6
judge you before the **L** about all 1Sm 12:7
ancestors cried out to the **L**, 1Sm 12:8
But they forgot the **L** their God, 1Sm 12:9
cried out to the **L** and said, 1Sm 12:10
abandoned the **L** and worshiped 1Sm 12:10
So the **L** sent Jerubbaal, Barak, 1Sm 12:11
even though the **L** your God is 1Sm 12:12
the king the **L** has placed over 1Sm 12:13
If you fear the **L**, worship and 1Sm 12:14
you will follow the **L** your God. 1Sm 12:14
you disobey the **L** and rebel 1Sm 12:15
thing that the **L** will do before 1Sm 12:16
call on the **L** and He will send 1Sm 12:17
called on the **L**, and on that day 1Sm 12:18
on that day the **L** sent thunder 1Sm 12:18
greatly feared the **L** and Samuel. 1Sm 12:18
Pray to the **L** your God for your 1Sm 12:19
turn away from following the **L**. 1Sm 12:20
worship the **L** with all your 1Sm 12:20
The **L** will not abandon His 1Sm 12:22
sin against the **L** by ceasing to 1Sm 12:23
fear the **L** and worship Him 1Sm 12:24
which the **L** your God gave you 1Sm 13:13
this time that the **L** would have 1Sm 13:13
The **L** has found a man loyal to 1Sm 13:14
and the **L** has appointed him as 1Sm 13:14
not done what the **L** commanded. 1Sm 13:14
Perhaps the **L** will help us. 1Sm 14:6
can keep the **L** from saving, 1Sm 14:6
because the **L** has handed them 1Sm 14:10
for the **L** has handed them over 1Sm 14:12
So the **L** saved Israel that day. 1Sm 14:23
against the **L** by eating ⌊meat⌋ 1Sm 14:33
against the **L** by eating ⌊meat 1Sm 14:34
Saul built an altar to the **L**; 1Sm 14:35
he had built an altar to the **L**. 1Sm 14:35
surely as the **L** lives who saves 1Sm 14:39
said to the **L**, "God of Israel 1Sm 14:41
No, as the **L** lives, not a hair 1Sm 14:45
The **L** sent me to anoint you as 1Sm 15:1
listen to the words of the **L**. 1Sm 15:1
is what the **L** of Hosts says: 1Sm 15:2
word of the **L** came to Samuel: 1Sm 15:10
cried out to the **L** ⌊all⌋ night. 1Sm 15:11
Saul said, "May the **L** bless you. 1Sm 15:13
a sacrifice to the **L** your God, 1Sm 15:15
you what the **L** said to me last 1Sm 15:16
The **L** anointed you king over 1Sm 15:17
So why didn't you obey the **L**? 1Sm 15:19
"But I did obey the **L**!" 1Sm 15:20
on the mission the **L** gave me: 1Sm 15:20
sacrifice to the **L** your God at 1Sm 15:21
the **L** take pleasure in burnt 1Sm 15:22
as much as in obeying the **L**? 1Sm 15:22
have rejected the word of the **L**, 1Sm 15:23
with me so I can worship the **L**." 1Sm 15:25
you rejected the word of the **L**, 1Sm 15:26
L has rejected you from being 1Sm 15:26
The **L** has torn the kingship of 1Sm 15:28
bow and worship the **L** your God. 1Sm 15:30
and Saul bowed down to the **L**. 1Sm 15:31
pieces before the **L** at Gilgal. 1Sm 15:33
and the **L** regretted He had made 1Sm 15:35
The **L** said to Samuel, "How long 1Sm 16:1
The **L** answered, "Take a young 1Sm 16:2
come to sacrifice to the **L**.' 1Sm 16:2
did what the **L** directed and went 1Sm 16:4
I've come to sacrifice to the **L**. 1Sm 16:5
But the **L** said to Samuel, 1Sm 16:7
does not see what the **L** sees, 1Sm 16:7
but the **L** sees the heart." 1Sm 16:7
The **L** hasn't chosen this one 1Sm 16:8
The **L** hasn't chosen this one 1Sm 16:9
L hasn't chosen any of these. 1Sm 16:10
Then the **L** said, "Anoint him, 1Sm 16:12
the Spirit of the **L** took control 1Sm 16:13
Spirit of the **L** had left Saul, 1Sm 16:14
spirit from the **L** began to 1Sm 16:14
and the **L** is with him." 1Sm 16:18
The **L** who rescued me from the 1Sm 17:37
and may the **L** be with you." 1Sm 17:37
in the name of the **L** of Hosts, 1Sm 17:45
the **L** will hand you over to me. 1Sm 17:46
or by spear that the **L** saves, 1Sm 17:47

because the **L** was with David but 1Sm 18:12
because the **L** was with him. 1Sm 18:14
that the **L** was with David 1Sm 18:28
and the **L** brought about a great 1Sm 19:5
As surely as the **L** lives, 1Sm 19:6
spirit from the **L** came on Saul 1Sm 19:9
surely as the **L** lives and as you 1Sm 20:3
covenant before the **L** with you. 1Sm 20:8
By the **L**, the God of Israel, if 1Sm 20:12
May the **L** be with you, just as 1Sm 20:13
even when the **L** cuts off every 1Sm 20:15
May the **L** hold David's enemies 1Sm 20:16
because as the **L** lives, it is 1Sm 20:21
for the **L** is sending you away. 1Sm 20:22
the **L** will be a witness between 1Sm 20:23
the name of the **L** when we said: 1Sm 20:42
L will be ⌊a witness⌋ between 1Sm 20:42
been removed from before the **L**. 1Sm 21:6
before the **L**, was there that day 1Sm 21:7
inquired of the **L** for him and 1Sm 22:10
priests of the **L** because they 1Sm 22:17
to execute the priests of the **L**. 1Sm 22:17
had killed the priests of the **L**. 1Sm 22:21
So David inquired of the **L**: 1Sm 23:2
The **L** answered David, "Launch 1Sm 23:2
inquired of the **L**, and the LORD 1Sm 23:4
LORD, and the **L** answered him: 1Sm 23:4
David said, "**L** God of Israel, 1Sm 23:10
L God of Israel, please tell 1Sm 23:11
The **L** answered, "He will come 1Sm 23:11
"They will," the **L** responded. 1Sm 23:12
"May you be blessed by the **L**," 1Sm 23:21
the day the **L** told you about: 1Sm 24:4
his men, "I swear before the **L**: 1Sm 24:6
eyes that the **L** handed you over 1Sm 24:10
May the **L** judge between you 1Sm 24:12
and may the **L** take vengeance on 1Sm 24:12
May the **L** be judge and decide 1Sm 24:15
the **L** handed me over to you, 1Sm 24:18
the **L** repay you with good for 1Sm 24:19
to me by the **L** that you will not 1Sm 24:21
surely as the **L** lives and as you 1Sm 25:26
it is the **L** who kept you from 1Sm 25:26
for the **L** is certain to make a 1Sm 25:28
place where the **L** your God 1Sm 25:29
When the **L** does for my lord all 1Sm 25:30
And when the **L** does good things 1Sm 25:31
Praise to the **L** God of Israel, 1Sm 25:32
as surely as the **L** God of Israel 1Sm 25:34
days later, the **L** struck Nabal 1Sm 25:38
Praise the **L** who championed my 1Sm 25:39
The **L** brought Nabal's evil deeds 1Sm 25:39
added, "As the **L** lives, the LORD 1Sm 26:10
the **L** will certainly strike him 1Sm 26:10
because of the **L**, I will never 1Sm 26:11
sleep from the **L** came over them. 1Sm 26:12
As the **L** lives, all of you 1Sm 26:16
If it is the **L** who has incited 1Sm 26:19
cursed in the presence of the **L**, 1Sm 26:19
inheritance of the **L** saying, 1Sm 26:19
the **L** repay every man for his 1Sm 26:23
though the **L** handed you over 1Sm 26:23
so may the **L** consider my life 1Sm 26:24
inquired of the **L**, but the LORD 1Sm 28:6
but the **L** did not answer him in 1Sm 28:6
Then Saul swore to her by the **L**: 1Sm 28:10
As surely as the **L** lives, 1Sm 28:10
Since the **L** has turned away from 1Sm 28:16
The **L** has done exactly what He 1Sm 28:17
The **L** has torn the kingship out 1Sm 28:17
did not obey the **L** and did not 1Sm 28:18
therefore the **L** has done this to 1Sm 28:18
The **L** will also hand Israel over 1Sm 28:19
the **L** will hand Israel's army 1Sm 28:19
him, "As the **L** lives, you are 1Sm 29:6
found strength in the **L** his God. 1Sm 30:6
and David asked the **L**: 1Sm 30:8
The **L** replied to him, "Pursue 1Sm 30:8
with what the **L** has given us. 1Sm 30:23
later, David inquired of the **L**: 2Sm 2:1
The **L** answered him, "Go." 2Sm 2:1
"To Hebron," the **L** replied. 2Sm 2:1
to them, "The **L** bless you, 2Sm 2:5
may the **L** show special kindness 2Sm 2:6
David what the **L** swore to him: 2Sm 3:9
because the **L** has spoken 2Sm 3:18
innocent before the **L** concerning 2Sm 3:28
May the **L** repay the evildoer 2Sm 3:39
the **L** has granted vengeance 2Sm 4:8
As surely as the **L** lives, 2Sm 4:9
L also said to you, 'You will 2Sm 5:2
and the **L** God of Hosts was with 2Sm 5:10
knew that the **L** had established 2Sm 5:12
Then David inquired of the **L**: 2Sm 5:19
The **L** replied to David, 2Sm 5:19
the **L** has burst out against my 2Sm 5:20
So David inquired of the **L**, 2Sm 5:23
for then the **L** will have marched 2Sm 5:24
exactly as the **L** commanded him, 2Sm 5:25
the name of the **L** of Hosts who 2Sm 6:2
before the **L** with all ⌊kinds 2Sm 6:5
David feared the **L** that day and 2Sm 6:9
ark of the **L** ever come to me? 2Sm 6:9
the ark of the **L** to the city 2Sm 6:10
The ark of the **L** remained in his 2Sm 6:11
and the **L** blessed Obed-edom and 2Sm 6:11
The **L** has blessed Obed-edom's 2Sm 6:12
the ark of the **L** advanced six 2Sm 6:13
before the **L** wearing a linen 2Sm 6:14
up the ark of the **L** with shouts 2Sm 6:15
As the ark of the **L** was entering 2Sm 6:16
and dancing before the **L**, 2Sm 6:16
the ark of the **L** and set it in 2Sm 6:17
in the name of the **L** of Hosts. 2Sm 6:18
before the **L** who chose me over 2Sm 6:21
I will celebrate before the **L**, 2Sm 6:21
palace and the **L** had given him 2Sm 7:1
heart, for the **L** is with you." 2Sm 7:3
word of the **L** came to Nathan: 2Sm 7:4
say, 'This is what the **L** says: 2Sm 7:5
is what the **L** of Hosts says: 2Sm 7:8
The **L** declares to you: 2Sm 7:11
The **L** Himself will make a house 2Sm 7:11
forever, and You, **L**, have become 2Sm 7:24
Now, **L** God, fulfill the promise 2Sm 7:25
L of Hosts is God over Israel. 2Sm 7:26
since You, **L** of Hosts, God of 2Sm 7:27
The **L** made David victorious 2Sm 8:6
also dedicated these to the **L**, 2Sm 8:11
The **L** made David victorious 2Sm 8:14
the **L** considered what David had 2Sm 11:27
So the **L** sent Nathan to David. 2Sm 12:1
As surely as the **L** lives, 2Sm 12:5
This is what the **L** God of Israel 2Sm 12:7
command of the **L** by doing what I 2Sm 12:9
This is what the **L** says, 2Sm 12:11
"I have sinned against the **L**." 2Sm 12:13
The **L** has taken away your sin; 2Sm 12:13
you treated the **L** with such 2Sm 12:14
The **L** struck the baby that 2Sm 12:15
The **L** may be gracious to me and 2Sm 12:22
him Solomon. The **L** loved him, 2Sm 12:24
him Jedidiah, because of the **L**. 2Sm 12:25
the king invoke the **L** your God, 2Sm 14:11
"As the **L** lives," he vowed, 2Sm 14:11
May the **L** your God be with you. 2Sm 14:17
the **L** really brings me back to 2Sm 15:8
I will worship the **L** in Hebron." 2Sm 15:8
May the **L** show you kindness 2Sm 15:20
surely as the **L** lives and as my 2Sm 15:21
"**L**," David pleaded, "please 2Sm 15:31
The **L** has paid you back for all 2Sm 16:8
and the **L** has handed the kingdom 2Sm 16:8
way because the **L** told him, 2Sm 16:10
me⌋; the **L** has told him to 2Sm 16:11
Perhaps the **L** will see my 2Sm 16:12
the side of the one that the **L**, 2Sm 16:18
Since the **L** had decreed that 2Sm 17:14
news that the **L** has delivered 2Sm 18:19
May the **L** your God be praised! 2Sm 18:28
today the **L** has delivered you 2Sm 18:31
I swear by the **L** that if you 2Sm 19:7
so David inquired of the **L**. 2Sm 21:1
The **L** answered, "It is because 2Sm 21:1
presence of the **L** at Gibeah of 2Sm 21:6
the oath of the **L** that was 2Sm 21:7
hill in the presence of the **L**; 2Sm 21:9
this song to the **L** on the day 2Sm 22:1
LORD on the day the **L** rescued 2Sm 22:1
The **L** is my rock, my fortress, 2Sm 22:2
I called to the **L**, who is worthy 2Sm 22:4
called to the **L** in my distress; 2Sm 22:7
The **L** thundered from heaven; 2Sm 22:14
exposed at the rebuke of the **L**, 2Sm 22:16
but the **L** was my support. 2Sm 22:19
The **L** rewarded me according to 2Sm 22:21
the ways of the **L** and have not 2Sm 22:22
So the **L** repaid me according to 2Sm 22:25
L, You are my lamp; the LORD 2Sm 22:29
the **L** illuminates my darkness. 2Sm 22:29
the word of the **L** is pure. 2Sm 22:31
For who is God besides the **L**? 2Sm 22:32
look⌋ to the **L**, but He does not 2Sm 22:42
The **L** lives—may my rock be 2Sm 22:47
will praise You, **L**, among the 2Sm 22:50
Spirit of the **L** spoke through me 2Sm 23:2
The **L** brought about a great 2Sm 23:10
So the **L** brought about a great 2Sm 23:12
he poured it out to the **L**. 2Sm 23:16
David said, "**L**, I would never do 2Sm 23:17
May the **L** your God multiply the 2Sm 24:3
He said to the **L**, "I have sinned 2Sm 24:10
Now, **L**, because I've been very 2Sm 24:10
revelation from the **L** had come 2Sm 24:11
David, 'This is what the **L** says: 2Sm 24:12
So the **L** sent a plague on Israel 2Sm 24:15
the **L** relented concerning the 2Sm 24:16
The angel of the **L** was then at 2Sm 24:16
said to the **L**, "Look, I am the 2Sm 24:17
an altar to the **L** on the 2Sm 24:18
just as the **L** had commanded. 2Sm 24:19
to build an altar to the **L**, 2Sm 24:21
May the **L** your God accept you. 2Sm 24:23
not offer to the **L** my God burnt 2Sm 24:24
an altar to the **L** there and 2Sm 24:25
Then the **L** answered prayer on 2Sm 24:25
servant by the **L** your God, 1Kg 1:17
said, "As the **L** lives, who has 1Kg 1:29
to you by the **L** God of Israel: 1Kg 1:30
May the **L**, the God of my lord 1Kg 1:36
Just as the **L** was with my lord 1Kg 1:37
'May the **L** God of Israel be 1Kg 1:48
to the **L** your God to walk 1Kg 2:3
and so that the **L** will carry out 1Kg 2:4
and I swore to him by the **L**: 1Kg 2:8
for the **L** gave it to him. 1Kg 2:15
Solomon took an oath by the **L**: 1Kg 2:23
And now, as the **L** lives, the One 1Kg 2:24
The **L** will bring back his own 1Kg 2:32
be peace from the **L** forever." 1Kg 2:33
you swear by the **L** and warn you, 1Kg 2:42
the **L** has brought back your evil 1Kg 2:44
before the **L** forever." 1Kg 2:45
Solomon loved the **L** by walking 1Kg 3:3
At Gibeon the **L** appeared to 1Kg 3:5
L my God, You have now made 1Kg 3:7
for the name of the **L** his God. 1Kg 5:3
him until the **L** put his enemies 1Kg 5:3
The **L** my God has now given me 1Kg 5:4
for the name of the **L** my God, 1Kg 5:5
to what the **L** promised my father 1Kg 5:5
May the **L** be praised today! 1Kg 5:7
The **L** gave Solomon wisdom, 1Kg 5:12
the temple for the **L** in the four 1Kg 6:1
for the **L** was 90 feet long, 1Kg 6:2
word of the **L** came to Solomon 1Kg 6:11
brought the ark of the **L**, 1Kg 8:4
where the **L** made a covenant with 1Kg 8:9
the glory of the **L** filled the 1Kg 8:11
The **L** said that He would dwell 1Kg 8:12
May the **L** God of Israel be 1Kg 8:15
the name of the **L** God of Israel. 1Kg 8:17
But the **L** said to my father 1Kg 8:18
The **L** has fulfilled what He 1Kg 8:20
of Israel, as the **L** promised. 1Kg 8:20
the name of the **L** God of Israel. 1Kg 8:20
the altar of the **L** in front of 1Kg 8:22
L God of Israel, there is no God 1Kg 8:23
Therefore, **L** God of Israel, keep 1Kg 8:25
Now **L** God of Israel, please 1Kg 8:26
his petition, **L** my God, so that 1Kg 8:28
pray to the **L** in the direction 1Kg 8:44
prayer and petition to the **L**, 1Kg 8:54
before the altar of the **L**, 1Kg 8:54
May the **L** be praised! He has 1Kg 8:56
May the **L** our God be with us as 1Kg 8:57
with before the **L** be near the 1Kg 8:59
LORD be near the **L** our God day 1Kg 8:59
may know that the **L** is God. 1Kg 8:60
devoted to the **L** our God to walk 1Kg 8:61
fellowship offerings to the **L**: 1Kg 8:63
before the **L** was too small to 1Kg 8:64
the presence of the **L** our God, 1Kg 8:65
that the **L** had done for His 1Kg 8:66

building the temple of the **L**,	1Kg 9:1
the **L** appeared to Solomon a	1Kg 9:2
The **L** said to him: I have heard	1Kg 9:3
Why did the **L** do this to this	1Kg 9:8
abandoned the **L** their God who	1Kg 9:9
the **L** brought all this ruin on	1Kg 9:9
altar he had built for the **L**,	1Kg 9:25
the name of the **L** and came to	1Kg 10:1
May the **L** your God be praised!	1Kg 10:9
the nations that the **L** had told	1Kg 11:2
his heart away ⌊from the **L**⌋.	1Kg 11:3
completely with the **L** his God,	1Kg 11:4
did not completely follow the **L**.	1Kg 11:6
The **L** was angry with Solomon,	1Kg 11:9
away from the **L** God of Israel,	1Kg 11:9
do what the **L** had commanded.	1Kg 11:10
Then the **L** said to Solomon,	1Kg 11:11
So the **L** raised up Hadad the	1Kg 11:14
this is what the **L** God of Israel	1Kg 11:31
came from the **L** to carry out His	1Kg 12:15
which the **L** had spoken through	1Kg 12:15
'This is what the **L** says:	1Kg 12:24
to what the **L** said and went back	1Kg 12:24
from the **L** while Jeroboam was	1Kg 13:1
by a revelation from the **L**:	1Kg 13:2
this is what the **L** says, 'A son	1Kg 13:2
sign that the **L** has spoken:	1Kg 13:3
had given by the word of the **L**.	1Kg 13:5
the favor of the **L** your God and	1Kg 13:6
pleaded for the favor of the **L**,	1Kg 13:6
by the word of the **L**:	1Kg 13:9
to me by the word of the **L**:	1Kg 13:17
to me by the word of the **L**:	1Kg 13:18
the word of the **L** came to the	1Kg 13:20
This is what the **L** says:	1Kg 13:21
command of the **L** and did not	1Kg 13:21
that the **L** your God commanded	1Kg 13:21
disobeyed the command of the **L**.	1Kg 13:26
The **L** has given him to the lion,	1Kg 13:26
the word of the **L** that He spoke	1Kg 13:26
from the **L** against the altar	1Kg 13:32
But the **L** had said to Ahijah,	1Kg 14:5
'This is what the **L** God of	1Kg 14:7
eat, for the **L** has said it!'	1Kg 14:11
pleasing to the **L** God of Israel.	1Kg 14:13
The **L** will raise up for Himself	1Kg 14:14
the **L** will strike Israel ⌊and	1Kg 14:15
Asherah poles, provoking the **L**.	1Kg 14:15
the word of the **L** He had spoken	1Kg 14:18
the city the **L** had chosen from	1Kg 14:21
the nations the **L** had	1Kg 14:24
devoted to the **L** his God as his	1Kg 15:3
the **L** his God gave him a lamp in	1Kg 15:4
with the **L** his entire life.	1Kg 15:14
the word of the **L** He had spoken	1Kg 15:29
had provoked the **L** God of Israel	1Kg 15:30
the word of the **L** came to Jehu	1Kg 16:1
the word of the **L** also came	1Kg 16:7
the word of the **L** He had spoken	1Kg 16:12
provoking the **L** God of Israel	1Kg 16:13
provoking the **L** God of Israel	1Kg 16:26
to provoke the **L** God of Israel	1Kg 16:33
the word of the **L** He had spoken	1Kg 16:34
As the **L** God of Israel lives,	1Kg 17:1
from the **L** came to him:	1Kg 17:2
So he did what the **L** commanded.	1Kg 17:5
the word of the **L** came to him:	1Kg 17:8
said, "As the **L** your God lives,	1Kg 17:12
this is what the **L** God of Israel	1Kg 17:14
until the day the **L** sends rain	1Kg 17:14
the word of the **L** He had spoken	1Kg 17:16
he cried out to the **L** and said,	1Kg 17:20
and said, "My **L** God, have You	1Kg 17:20
He cried out to the **L** and said,	1Kg 17:21
and said, "My **L** God, please let	1Kg 17:21
So the **L** listened to Elijah's	1Kg 17:22
the word of the **L** came to Elijah	1Kg 18:1
a man who greatly feared the **L**	1Kg 18:3
the **L** your God lives, there is	1Kg 18:10
Spirit of the **L** may carry you	1Kg 18:12
have feared the **L** from my youth.	1Kg 18:12
100 of the prophets of the **L**,	1Kg 18:13
said, "As the **L** of Hosts lives,	1Kg 18:15
only remaining prophet of the **L**,	1Kg 18:22
the word of the **L** had come,	1Kg 18:31
and said, "**L** God of Abraham,	1Kg 18:36
Answer me, **L**! Answer me so that	1Kg 18:37
power of the **L** was on Elijah,	1Kg 18:46

L, take my life, for I'm no	1Kg 19:4
the angel of the **L** returned a	1Kg 19:7
the word of the **L** came to him,	1Kg 19:9
zealous for the **L** God of Hosts,	1Kg 19:10
At that moment, the **L** passed	1Kg 19:11
shattering cliffs before the **L**,	1Kg 19:11
but the **L** was not in the wind.	1Kg 19:11
but the **L** was not in the	1Kg 19:11
but the **L** was not in the fire.	1Kg 19:12
zealous for the **L** God of Hosts,"	1Kg 19:14
Then the **L** said to him, "Go and	1Kg 19:15
This is what the **L** says:	1Kg 20:13
may know that I am the **L**.' "	1Kg 20:13
This is what the **L** says:	1Kg 20:14
This is what the **L** says:	1Kg 20:28
The **L** is a god of the mountains	1Kg 20:28
will know that I am the **L**.' "	1Kg 20:28
prophet by the word of the **L**,	1Kg 20:35
listen to the voice of the **L**,	1Kg 20:36
This is what the **L** says:	1Kg 20:42
the word of the **L** came to Elijah	1Kg 21:17
him, 'This is what the **L** says:	1Kg 21:19
him, 'This is what the **L** says:	1Kg 21:19
This is what the **L** says:	1Kg 21:21
The **L** also speaks of Jezebel:	1Kg 21:23
whom the **L** had dispossessed	1Kg 21:26
the word of the **L** came to Elijah	1Kg 21:28
still one man who can ask the **L**,	1Kg 22:8
This is what the **L** says:	1Kg 22:11
for the **L** will hand it over to	1Kg 22:12
said, "As the **L** lives, I will	1Kg 22:14
say whatever the **L** says to me."	1Kg 22:14
L will hand it over to the king.	1Kg 22:15
the truth in the name of the **L**?"	1Kg 22:16
And the **L** said, 'They have no	1Kg 22:17
hear the word of the **L**:	1Kg 22:19
I saw the **L** sitting on His	1Kg 22:19
And the **L** said, 'Who will entice	1Kg 22:20
stood before the **L**, and said, 'I	1Kg 22:21
The **L** asked him, 'How?'	1Kg 22:22
L has put a lying spirit into	1Kg 22:23
the **L** has pronounced disaster	1Kg 22:23
Spirit of the **L** leave me to	1Kg 22:24
L has not spoken through me."	1Kg 22:28
the word of the **L** that He had	1Kg 22:38
He provoked the **L** God of Israel	1Kg 22:53
angel of the **L** said to Elijah	2Kg 1:3
this is what the **L** says:	2Kg 1:4
This is what the **L** says:	2Kg 1:6
angel of the **L** said to Elijah,	2Kg 1:15
This is what the **L** says:	2Kg 1:16
word of the **L** that Elijah had	2Kg 1:17
come for the **L** to take Elijah	2Kg 2:1
L is sending me on to Bethel.	2Kg 2:2
As the **L** lives and as you	2Kg 2:2
that today the **L** will take your	2Kg 2:3
the **L** is sending me to Jericho."	2Kg 2:4
As the **L** lives and as you	2Kg 2:4
that today the **L** will take your	2Kg 2:5
L is sending me to the Jordan.	2Kg 2:6
As the **L** lives and as you	2Kg 2:6
"Where is the **L** God of Elijah?"	2Kg 2:14
Spirit of the **L** has carried him	2Kg 2:16
This is what the **L** says:	2Kg 2:21
them in the name of the **L**.	2Kg 2:24
the **L** has summoned us three	2Kg 3:10
there a prophet of the **L** here?	2Kg 3:11
inquire of the **L** through him."	2Kg 3:11
it is the **L** who has summoned	2Kg 3:13
As the **L** of Hosts lives, I	2Kg 3:14
This is what the **L** says:	2Kg 3:16
the **L** says, 'You will not see	2Kg 3:17
that your servant feared the **L**.	2Kg 4:1
and the **L** has hidden it from me.	2Kg 4:27
As the **L** lives and as you	2Kg 4:30
of them, and prayed to the **L**.	2Kg 4:33
for this is what the **L** says:	2Kg 4:43
and as the **L** had promised,	2Kg 4:44
the **L** had given victory to Aram.	2Kg 5:1
said, "As the **L** lives, I stand	2Kg 5:16
matter may the **L** pardon your	2Kg 5:18
may the **L** pardon your servant in	2Kg 5:18
As the **L** lives, I will run after	2Kg 5:20
Elisha prayed, "**L**, please open	2Kg 6:17
So the **L** opened the servant's	2Kg 6:17
prayed to the **L**, "Please strike	2Kg 6:18
Elisha said, "**L**, open these	2Kg 6:20
So the **L** opened their eyes.	2Kg 6:20

If the **L** doesn't help you,	2Kg 6:27
This disaster is from the **L**.	2Kg 6:33
I trust the **L** any longer?"	2Kg 6:33
said, "Hear the word of the **L**!	2Kg 7:1
This is what the **L** says:	2Kg 7:1
⌊even if⌋ the **L** were to make	2Kg 7:2
according to the word of the **L**.	2Kg 7:16
⌊even if⌋ the **L** were to make	2Kg 7:19
For the **L** has announced a	2Kg 8:1
Inquire of the **L** through him,	2Kg 8:8
But the **L** has shown me that he	2Kg 8:10
The **L** has shown me that you will	2Kg 8:13
The **L** was unwilling to destroy	2Kg 8:19
This is what the **L** says:	2Kg 9:3
This is what the **L** God of Israel	2Kg 9:6
of all the servants of the **L**.	2Kg 9:7
said, 'This is what the **L** says:	2Kg 9:12
and the **L** uttered this oracle	2Kg 9:25
according to the word of the **L**,	2Kg 9:26
not a word the **L** spoke against	2Kg 10:10
for the **L** has done what He	2Kg 10:10
me and see my zeal for the **L**!"	2Kg 10:16
the word of the **L** spoken to	2Kg 10:17
servants of the **L** here among you	2Kg 10:23
the **L** said to Jehu,	2Kg 10:30
the law of the **L** God of Israel.	2Kg 10:31
those days the **L** began to reduce	2Kg 10:32
made a covenant between the **L**,	2Kg 11:17
favor, and the **L** heard him, for	2Kg 13:4
the **L** gave Israel a deliverer,	2Kg 13:5
but the **L** was gracious to them	2Kg 13:23
of Moses where the **L** commanded,	2Kg 14:6
according to the word the **L**,	2Kg 14:25
the **L** saw that the affliction	2Kg 14:26
the **L** had not said He would blot	2Kg 14:27
The **L** afflicted the king, and he	2Kg 15:5
The word of the **L** that He spoke	2Kg 15:12
those days the **L** began sending	2Kg 15:37
sight of the **L** his God like his	2Kg 16:2
the nations the **L** had	2Kg 16:3
that was before the **L** in front	2Kg 16:14
against the **L** their God who had	2Kg 17:7
that the **L** had dispossessed	2Kg 17:8
right against the **L** their God.	2Kg 17:9
nations that the **L** had driven	2Kg 17:11
evil things, provoking the **L**.	2Kg 17:11
although the **L** had told them,	2Kg 17:12
the **L** warned Israel and Judah	2Kg 17:13
did not believe the **L** their God.	2Kg 17:14
nations the **L** had commanded	2Kg 17:15
commandments of the **L** their	2Kg 17:16
L was very angry with Israel,	2Kg 17:18
of the **L** their God but lived	2Kg 17:19
So the **L** rejected all the	2Kg 17:20
When the **L** tore Israel from the	2Kg 17:21
following the **L** and caused them	2Kg 17:21
the **L** removed Israel from His	2Kg 17:23
there, they did not fear the **L**.	2Kg 17:25
So the **L** sent lions among them,	2Kg 17:25
them how they should fear the **L**.	2Kg 17:28
they feared the **L**, but they also	2Kg 17:32
They feared the **L**, but they also	2Kg 17:33
them fear the **L** or observe their	2Kg 17:34
and commandments the **L**	2Kg 17:34
The **L** made a covenant with them	2Kg 17:35
fear the **L**, who brought you	2Kg 17:36
but fear the **L** your God, and He	2Kg 17:39
feared the **L** but also served	2Kg 17:41
trusted in the **L** God of Israel;	2Kg 18:5
fast to the **L** and did not turn	2Kg 18:6
commandments the **L** had	2Kg 18:6
The **L** was with him, and wherever	2Kg 18:7
to the voice of the **L** their God	2Kg 18:12
Moses the servant of the **L**.	2Kg 18:12
We trust in the **L** our God.	2Kg 18:22
The **L** said to me, 'Attack this	2Kg 18:25
you to trust in the **L** by saying:	2Kg 18:30
Certainly the **L** will deliver us!	2Kg 18:30
saying: The **L** will deliver us	2Kg 18:32
So how is the **L** to deliver	2Kg 18:35
Perhaps the **L** your God will hear	2Kg 19:4
words that the **L** your God has	2Kg 19:4
your master this, 'The **L** says:	2Kg 19:6
and spread it out before the **L**.	2Kg 19:14
Hezekiah prayed before the **L**:	2Kg 19:15
L God of Israel who is enthroned	2Kg 19:15
Listen closely, **L**, and hear;	2Kg 19:16
open Your eyes, **L**, and see;	2Kg 19:16

L, it is true that the kings of 2Kg 19:17
Now, **L** our God, please save us 2Kg 19:19
know that You are the **L** God— 2Kg 19:19
The **L**, the God of Israel says: 2Kg 19:20
is the word the **L** has spoken 2Kg 19:21
The zeal of the **L** of Hosts will 2Kg 19:31
this is what the **L** says about 2Kg 19:32
enter this city, declares the **L**. 2Kg 19:33
the angel of the **L** went out and 2Kg 19:35
This is what the **L** says: 2Kg 20:1
to the wall and prayed to the **L**, 2Kg 20:2
Please **L**, remember how I have 2Kg 20:3
the word of the **L** came to him: 2Kg 20:4
'This is what the **L** God of your 2Kg 20:5
the sign that the **L** will heal me 2Kg 20:8
you from the **L** that He will do 2Kg 20:9
the prophet called out to the **L**, 2Kg 20:11
Hear the word of the **L**: 2Kg 20:16
will be left,' says the **L**. 2Kg 20:17
The word of the **L** that you have 2Kg 20:19
that the **L** had dispossessed 2Kg 21:2
temple, where the **L** had said, 2Kg 21:4
temple that the **L** had spoken 2Kg 21:7
the nations the **L** had destroyed 2Kg 21:9
The **L** spoke through His servants 2Kg 21:10
this is what the **L** God of Israel 2Kg 21:12
He abandoned the **L** God of his 2Kg 21:22
not walk in the way of the **L**. 2Kg 21:22
Go and inquire of the **L** for me, 2Kg 22:13
This is what the **L** God of Israel 2Kg 22:15
This is what the **L** says: 2Kg 22:16
sent you to inquire of the **L**: 2Kg 22:18
This is what the **L** God of Israel 2Kg 22:18
before the **L** when you heard what 2Kg 22:19
have heard you—declares the **L**. 2Kg 22:19
presence of the **L** to follow the 2Kg 23:3
to follow the **L** and to keep His 2Kg 23:3
the altar of the **L** in Jerusalem; 2Kg 23:9
to the word of the **L** proclaimed 2Kg 23:16
had made to provoke ⌊the **L**⌋. 2Kg 23:19
Passover of the **L** your God as 2Kg 23:21
observed to the **L** in Jerusalem. 2Kg 23:23
turned to the **L** with all his 2Kg 23:25
the **L** did not turn from the 2Kg 23:26
For the **L** had said, "I will also 2Kg 23:27
The **L** sent Chaldean, Aramean, 2Kg 24:2
the word of the **L** He had spoken 2Kg 24:2
and the **L** would not forgive. 2Kg 24:4
into exile when the **L** sent Judah 1Ch 6:15
leader, and the **L** was with him. 1Ch 9:20
to the **L** because he did not 1Ch 10:13
but he did not inquire of the **L**. 1Ch 10:14
So the **L** put him to death and 1Ch 10:14
L your God also said to you, 1Ch 11:2
and the **L** of Hosts was with him. 1Ch 11:9
and the **L** gave them a great 1Ch 11:14
he poured it out to the **L**. 1Ch 11:18
if this is from the **L** our God, 1Ch 13:2
by the name of the **L** who dwells 1Ch 13:6
and the **L** blessed his family and 1Ch 13:14
knew that the **L** had established 1Ch 14:2
The **L** replied, "Go, and I will 1Ch 14:10
and the **L** caused all the nations 1Ch 14:17
because the **L** has chosen them to 1Ch 15:2
the ark of the **L** and to minister 1Ch 15:2
the ark of the **L** to the place he 1Ch 15:3
ark of the **L** God of Israel to 1Ch 15:12
For the **L** our God burst out ⌊in 1Ch 15:13
the ark of the **L** God of Israel. 1Ch 15:14
according to the word of the **L**: 1Ch 15:15
covenant of the **L** from the house 1Ch 15:25
ark of the covenant of the **L**, 1Ch 15:26
of the **L** up with shouts, 1Ch 15:28
covenant of the **L** was entering 1Ch 15:29
the people in the name of the **L**. 1Ch 16:2
before the ark of the **L**, 1Ch 16:4
celebrate the **L** God of Israel, 1Ch 16:4
be given to the **L** by Asaph and 1Ch 16:7
thanks to the **L**; call on His 1Ch 16:8
of those who seek the **L** rejoice. 1Ch 16:10
Search for the **L** and for His 1Ch 16:11
He is the **L** our God; His 1Ch 16:14
Sing to the **L**, all the earth. 1Ch 16:23
For the **L** is great and is highly 1Ch 16:25
but the **L** made the heavens. 1Ch 16:26
Ascribe to the **L**, families of 1Ch 16:28
ascribe to the **L** glory and 1Ch 16:28
Ascribe to the **L** the glory of 1Ch 16:29

Worship the **L** in the splendor of 1Ch 16:29
the nations, "The **L** is King!" 1Ch 16:31
will shout for joy before the **L**, 1Ch 16:33
thanks to the **L**, for He is good; 1Ch 16:34
May the **L**, the God of Israel, be 1Ch 16:36
"Amen" and "Praise the **L**." 1Ch 16:36
of the **L** at the high place 1Ch 16:39
to the **L** on the altar of burnt 1Ch 16:40
was written in the law of the **L**, 1Ch 16:40
name to give thanks to the **L**— 1Ch 16:41
say, 'This is what the **L** says: 1Ch 17:4
is what the **L** of Hosts says: 1Ch 17:7
to you that the **L** Himself will 1Ch 17:10
Who am I, **L** God, and what is 1Ch 17:16
as a man of distinction, **L** God. 1Ch 17:17
L, You have done all this 1Ch 17:19
L, there is no one like You, and 1Ch 17:20
forever, and You, **L**, have become 1Ch 17:22
Now, **L**, let the word that You 1Ch 17:23
the saying, 'The **L** of Hosts, the 1Ch 17:24
L, You indeed are God, and You 1Ch 17:26
For You, **L**, have blessed it, and 1Ch 17:27
The **L** made David victorious 1Ch 18:6
also dedicated these to the **L**, 1Ch 18:11
The **L** made David victorious 1Ch 18:13
May the **L** multiply the number of 1Ch 21:3
Then the **L** instructed Gad, 1Ch 21:9
David, 'This is what the **L** says: 1Ch 21:10
This is what the **L** says: 1Ch 21:11
days of the sword of the **L**— 1Ch 21:12
the angel of the **L** bringing 1Ch 21:12
the **L** sent a plague on Israel, 1Ch 21:14
the city, the **L** looked, relented 1Ch 21:15
The angel of the **L** was then 1Ch 21:15
angel of the **L** standing between 1Ch 21:16
L God, please let Your hand be 1Ch 21:17
the angel of the **L** ordered Gad 1Ch 21:18
an altar to the **L** on the 1Ch 21:18
spoken in the name of the **L**. 1Ch 21:19
build an altar to the **L** on it. 1Ch 21:22
take for the **L** what belongs to 1Ch 21:24
an altar to the **L** there and 1Ch 21:26
called on the **L**, and He answered 1Ch 21:26
Then the **L** spoke to the angel, 1Ch 21:27
saw that the **L** answered him at 1Ch 21:28
time the tabernacle of the **L**, 1Ch 21:29
This is the house of the **L** God, 1Ch 22:1
be built for the **L** must be 1Ch 22:5
a house for the **L** God of Israel. 1Ch 22:6
for the name of the **L** my God, 1Ch 22:7
the word of the **L** came to me: 1Ch 22:8
my son, may the **L** be with you, 1Ch 22:11
the house of the **L** your God, 1Ch 22:11
may the **L** give you insight and 1Ch 22:12
keep the law of the **L** your God. 1Ch 22:12
ordinances the **L** commanded 1Ch 22:13
provide for the house of the **L**— 1Ch 22:14
and may the **L** be with you." 1Ch 22:16
The **L** your God is with you, 1Ch 22:18
before the **L** and His people. 1Ch 22:18
heart to seek the **L** your God. 1Ch 22:19
building the **L** God's sanctuary 1Ch 22:19
be built for the name of the **L**." 1Ch 22:19
are to praise the **L** with the 1Ch 23:5
in the presence of the **L**, 1Ch 23:13
The **L** God of Israel has given 1Ch 23:25
give thanks and praise to the **L**, 1Ch 23:30
to the **L** on the Sabbaths, 1Ch 23:31
as the **L** God of Israel had 1Ch 24:19
thanks and praise to the **L**. 1Ch 25:3
and skillful in music for the **L**, 1Ch 25:7
the work of the **L** and for the 1Ch 26:30
for the **L** had said He would make 1Ch 27:23
Yet the **L** God of Israel chose me 1Ch 28:4
for the **L** has given me many sons 1Ch 28:5
assembly of the **L**, and in the 1Ch 28:8
of the **L** your God so that 1Ch 28:8
for the **L** searches every heart 1Ch 28:9
now that the **L** has chosen you to 1Ch 28:10
for the **L** God, my God, is with 1Ch 28:20
be for man, but for the **L** God. 1Ch 29:1
himself to the **L** today?" 1Ch 29:5
had given to the **L** with a whole 1Ch 29:9
David praised the **L** in the sight 1Ch 29:10
L God of our father Israel, 1Ch 29:10
Yours, **L**, is the greatness and 1Ch 29:11
Yours, **L**, is the kingdom, and 1Ch 29:11
L our God, all this wealth that 1Ch 29:16

L God of Abraham, Isaac, and 1Ch 29:18
Praise the **L** your God." 1Ch 29:20
praised the **L** God of their 1Ch 29:20
homage to the **L** and the king. 1Ch 29:20
sacrifices to the **L** and burnt 1Ch 29:21
and burnt offerings to the **L**: 1Ch 29:21
The **L** highly exalted Solomon in 1Ch 29:25
The **L** his God was with him and 2Ch 1:1
L God, let Your promise to my 2Ch 1:9
the name of the **L** and a royal 2Ch 2:1
name of the **L** my God in order 2Ch 2:4
festivals of the **L** our God. 2Ch 2:4
Because the **L** loves His people, 2Ch 2:11
the **L** God of Israel, who made 2Ch 2:12
a temple for the **L** and a royal 2Ch 2:12
where the **L** had appeared to 2Ch 3:1
covenant of the **L** up from the 2Ch 5:2
where the **L** had made a covenant 2Ch 5:10
and thank the **L** with one voice. 2Ch 5:13
instruments, in praise to the **L**: 2Ch 5:13
the glory of the **L** filled God's 2Ch 5:14
The **L** said He would dwell in 2Ch 6:1
May the **L** God of Israel be 2Ch 6:4
the name of the **L** God of Israel. 2Ch 6:7
the **L** said to my father David, 2Ch 6:8
So the **L** has fulfilled what He 2Ch 6:10
of Israel, as the **L** promised. 2Ch 6:10
the name of the **L** God of Israel. 2Ch 6:10
the altar of the **L** in front of 2Ch 6:12
L God of Israel, there is no God 2Ch 6:14
Therefore, **L** God of Israel, keep 2Ch 6:16
Now, **L** God of Israel, please 2Ch 6:17
his petition, **L** my God, so that 2Ch 6:19
Arise, **L** God, ⌊come⌋ to Your 2Ch 6:41
Your priests, **L** God, be clothed 2Ch 6:41
L God, do not reject Your 2Ch 6:42
the glory of the **L** filled the 2Ch 7:1
the glory of the **L** filled the 2Ch 7:2
LORD filled the temple of the **L**. 2Ch 7:2
the glory of the **L** came on the 2Ch 7:3
worshiped and praised the **L**: 2Ch 7:3
musical instruments of the **L**, 2Ch 7:6
David had made to praise the **L**— 2Ch 7:6
the goodness the **L** had done for 2Ch 7:10
Then the **L** appeared to Solomon 2Ch 7:12
Why did the **L** do this to this 2Ch 7:21
abandoned the **L** God of their 2Ch 7:22
ark of the **L** has come are holy. 2Ch 8:11
offerings to the **L** on the LORD's 2Ch 8:12
May the **L** your God be praised! 2Ch 9:8
as king for the **L** your God. 2Ch 9:8
order that the **L** might carry out 2Ch 10:15
the word of the **L** came to 2Ch 11:2
'This is what the **L** says: 2Ch 11:4
to what the **L** said and turned 2Ch 11:4
them serve as priests of the **L**. 2Ch 11:14
to seek the **L** their God followed 2Ch 11:16
sacrifice to the **L** God of their 2Ch 11:16
he abandoned the law of the **L**— 2Ch 12:1
they were unfaithful to the **L**, 2Ch 12:2
This is what the **L** says: 2Ch 12:5
and said, "The **L** is righteous." 2Ch 12:6
When the **L** saw that they had 2Ch 12:7
the city the **L** had chosen from 2Ch 12:13
in his heart to seek the **L**. 2Ch 12:14
know that the **L** God of Israel 2Ch 13:5
you banish the priests of the **L**, 2Ch 13:9
But as for us, the **L** is our God. 2Ch 13:10
to the **L** are descendants 2Ch 13:10
incense to the **L** every morning 2Ch 13:11
requirements of the **L** our God, 2Ch 13:11
fight against the **L** God of your 2Ch 13:12
so they cried out to the **L**. 2Ch 13:14
because they depended on the **L**, 2Ch 13:18
the **L** struck him and he died. 2Ch 13:20
in the sight of the **L** his God. 2Ch 14:2
Judah to seek the **L** God of their 2Ch 14:4
because the **L** gave him rest. 2Ch 14:6
because we sought the **L** our God. 2Ch 14:7
Asa cried out to the **L** his God: 2Ch 14:11
L, there is no one besides You 2Ch 14:11
us, **L** our God, for we depend 2Ch 14:11
this multitude. **L**, You are our 2Ch 14:11
So the **L** routed the Cushites 2Ch 14:12
before the **L** and before His 2Ch 14:13
the terror of the **L** was on them. 2Ch 14:14
The **L** is with you when you are 2Ch 15:2
turned to the **L** God of Israel 2Ch 15:4

the altar of the **L** that was in 2Ch 15:8
saw that the **L** his God was with 2Ch 15:9
sacrificed to the **L** 700 cattle 2Ch 15:11
to seek the **L** God of their 2Ch 15:12
not seek the **L** God of Israel 2Ch 15:13
oath to the **L** in a loud voice, 2Ch 15:14
So the **L** gave them rest on every 2Ch 15:15
not depended on the **L** your God, 2Ch 16:7
When you depended on the **L**, 2Ch 16:8
the eyes of the **L** range 2Ch 16:9
didn't seek the **L** but the 2Ch 16:12
Now the **L** was with Jehoshaphat 2Ch 17:3
So the **L** established the kingdom 2Ch 17:5
The terror of the **L** was on all 2Ch 17:10
volunteer of the **L**, and 200,000 2Ch 17:16
still one man who can ask the **L**, 2Ch 18:7
This is what the **L** says: 2Ch 18:10
for the **L** will hand it over to 2Ch 18:11
said, "As the **L** lives, I will 2Ch 18:13
the truth in the name of the **L**?" 2Ch 18:15
And the **L** said, 'They have no 2Ch 18:16
hear the word of the **L**. 2Ch 18:18
I saw the **L** sitting on His 2Ch 18:18
And the **L** said, 'Who will entice 2Ch 18:19
stood before the **L**, and said, 'I 2Ch 18:20
The **L** asked him, 'How?' 2Ch 18:20
L has put a lying spirit into 2Ch 18:22
the **L** has pronounced disaster 2Ch 18:22
Spirit of the **L** leave me to 2Ch 18:23
L has not spoken through me." 2Ch 18:27
cried out and the **L** helped him. 2Ch 18:31
and love those who hate the **L**? 2Ch 19:2
them back to the **L** God of their 2Ch 19:4
but for the **L**, who is with you 2Ch 19:6
the terror of the **L** be on you. 2Ch 19:7
bribes with the **L** our God." 2Ch 19:7
fear of the **L**, with integrity 2Ch 19:9
guilt before the **L** and wrath 2Ch 19:10
in all matters related to the **L**, 2Ch 19:11
may the **L** be with those who do 2Ch 19:11
so he resolved to seek the **L**. 2Ch 20:3
who gathered to seek the **L**. 2Ch 20:4
L God of our ancestors, are You 2Ch 20:6
before the **L** with their infants 2Ch 20:13
Spirit of the **L** came on Jahaziel 2Ch 20:14
This is what the **L** says: 2Ch 20:15
and see the salvation of the **L**. 2Ch 20:17
for the **L** is with you.'" 2Ch 20:17
before the **L** to worship Him. 2Ch 20:18
up to praise the **L** God of Israel 2Ch 20:19
Believe in the **L** your God, 2Ch 20:20
to sing for the **L** and some to 2Ch 20:21
thanks to the **L**, for His 2Ch 20:21
the **L** set an ambush against the 2Ch 20:22
for there they praised the **L**. 2Ch 20:26
the **L** enabled them to rejoice 2Ch 20:27
heard that the **L** had fought 2Ch 20:29
L has broken up what you have 2Ch 20:37
the covenant the **L** had made with 2Ch 21:7
David since the **L** had promised 2Ch 21:7
had abandoned the **L** God of his 2Ch 21:10
This is what the **L** God of your 2Ch 21:12
L is now about to strike your 2Ch 21:14
L put it into the mind of the 2Ch 21:16
the **L** afflicted him in his 2Ch 21:18
whom the **L** had anointed to 2Ch 22:7
sought the **L** with all his heart. 2Ch 22:9
as the **L** promised concerning 2Ch 23:3
obey the requirement of the **L**. 2Ch 23:6
to the **L** as it is written 2Ch 23:18
wilderness be brought to the **L**. 2Ch 24:9
the temple of the **L** God of their 2Ch 24:18
to bring them back to the **L**; 2Ch 24:19
you have abandoned the **L**, 2Ch 24:20
the **L** see and demand an account. 2Ch 24:22
the **L** handed over a vast army to 2Ch 24:24
had abandoned the **L** God of their 2Ch 24:24
Moses, where the **L** commanded— 2Ch 25:4
for the **L** is not with Israel— 2Ch 25:7
The **L** is able to give you much 2Ch 25:9
turned from following the **L**, 2Ch 25:27
the time that he sought the **L**, 2Ch 26:5
against the **L** his God by going 2Ch 26:16
with 80 brave priests of the **L**, 2Ch 26:17
to offer incense to the **L**— 2Ch 26:18
receive honor from the **L** God." 2Ch 26:18
out because the **L** had afflicted 2Ch 26:20
waver in obeying the **L** his God. 2Ch 27:6

the nations the **L** had 2Ch 28:3
the **L** his God handed Ahaz over 2Ch 28:5
had abandoned the **L** God of their 2Ch 28:6
prophet of the **L** named Oded was 2Ch 28:9
the **L** God of your ancestors 2Ch 28:9
guilty before the **L** your God? 2Ch 28:10
on us from the **L** to add to our 2Ch 28:13
For the **L** humbled Judah because 2Ch 28:19
and was unfaithful to the **L**. 2Ch 28:19
became more unfaithful to the **L**. 2Ch 28:22
the temple of the **L** God of your 2Ch 29:5
in the sight of the **L** our God. 2Ch 29:6
the wrath of the **L** was on Judah 2Ch 29:8
with the **L** God of Israel so 2Ch 29:10
the **L** has chosen you to stand 2Ch 29:11
by the words of the **L** to cleanse 2Ch 29:15
the whole temple of the **L**, 2Ch 29:18
in front of the altar of the **L**." 2Ch 29:19
them on the altar of the **L**. 2Ch 29:21
was from the **L** through His 2Ch 29:25
the song of the **L** and the 2Ch 29:27
praise to the **L** in the words 2Ch 29:30
you are consecrated to the **L**. 2Ch 29:31
for a burnt offering to the **L**. 2Ch 29:32
Passover of the **L** God of Israel. 2Ch 30:1
Passover of the **L** in the second 2Ch 30:2
Passover of the **L** God of Israel 2Ch 30:5
return to the **L** God of Abraham, 2Ch 30:6
unfaithful to the **L** God of their 2Ch 30:7
Give your allegiance to the **L**, 2Ch 30:8
Serve the **L** your God so that He 2Ch 30:8
for when you return to the **L**, 2Ch 30:9
For the **L** your God is gracious 2Ch 30:9
officials by the word of the **L**. 2Ch 30:12
consecrate ⌊the lambs⌋ to the **L**. 2Ch 30:17
the good **L** provide atonement 2Ch 30:18
the **L** God of his ancestors, 2Ch 30:19
So the **L** heard Hezekiah and 2Ch 30:20
praised the **L** day after day with 2Ch 30:21
skillfully before the **L**. 2Ch 30:22
thanks to the **L** God of their 2Ch 30:22
the gates of the camp of the **L**, 2Ch 31:2
as written in the law of the **L**. 2Ch 31:3
energy to the law of the **L**. 2Ch 31:4
consecrated to the **L** their God. 2Ch 31:6
praised the **L** and His people 2Ch 31:8
because the **L** has blessed His 2Ch 31:10
to the **L** and the consecrated 2Ch 31:14
and true before the **L** his God. 2Ch 31:20
we have the **L** our God to help 2Ch 32:8
The **L** our God will deliver us 2Ch 32:11
against the **L** God and against 2Ch 32:16
to mock the **L** God of Israel, 2Ch 32:17
and the **L** sent an angel who 2Ch 32:21
So the **L** saved Hezekiah and the 2Ch 32:22
offering to the **L** to Jerusalem 2Ch 32:23
prayed to the **L**, and He spoke to 2Ch 32:24
that the **L** had dispossessed 2Ch 33:2
temple, where the **L** had said: 2Ch 33:4
the nations the **L** had destroyed 2Ch 33:9
The **L** spoke to Manasseh and his 2Ch 33:10
the favor of the **L** his God and 2Ch 33:12
came to know that the **L** is God. 2Ch 33:13
the altar of the **L** and offered 2Ch 33:16
to serve the **L** God of Israel. 2Ch 33:16
but only to the **L** their God. 2Ch 33:17
the name of the **L** God of Israel, 2Ch 33:18
before the **L** like his father 2Ch 33:23
the temple of the **L** his God. 2Ch 34:8
of the law of the **L** ⌊written⌋ by 2Ch 34:14
Inquire of the **L** for me and for 2Ch 34:21
the word of the **L** in order to do 2Ch 34:21
This is what the **L** God of Israel 2Ch 34:23
'This is what the **L** says: 2Ch 34:24
sent you to inquire of the **L**: 2Ch 34:26
'This is what the **L** God of 2Ch 34:26
heard'—this is the **L** speaking. 2Ch 34:27
to follow the **L** and to keep His 2Ch 34:31
Israel to serve the **L** their God. 2Ch 34:33
following the **L** God of their 2Ch 34:33
Israel the holy things of the **L**, 2Ch 35:3
now serve the **L** your God and His 2Ch 35:3
word of the **L** through Moses." 2Ch 35:6
lay people to offer to the **L**, 2Ch 35:12
service of the **L** was established 2Ch 35:16
offerings on the altar of the **L**, 2Ch 35:16
is written in the law of the **L**, 2Ch 35:26
in the sight of the **L** his God. 2Ch 36:5

sight of the **L** his God and did 2Ch 36:12
to the **L** God of Israel. 2Ch 36:13
But the **L** God of their ancestors 2Ch 36:15
the word of the **L** through 2Ch 36:21
the word of the **L** spoken through 2Ch 36:22
The **L** put it into the mind of 2Ch 36:22
The **L**, the God of heaven, has 2Ch 36:23
may the **L** his God be with him. 2Ch 36:23
the word of the **L** spoken through Ezr 1:1
The **L** put it into the mind of Ezr 1:1
The **L**, the God of heaven, has Ezr 1:2
and build the house of the **L**, Ezr 1:3
on it to the **L** even though they Ezr 3:3
offerings brought to the **L**. Ezr 3:5
offer burnt offerings to the **L**, Ezr 3:6
their positions to praise the **L**, Ezr 3:10
and thanksgiving to the **L**: Ezr 3:11
of praise to the **L** because the Ezr 3:11
building a temple for the **L**, Ezr 4:1
alone must build ⌊it⌋ for the **L**, Ezr 4:3
land in order to worship the **L**, Ezr 6:21
because the **L** had made them Ezr 6:22
Moses, which the **L**, the God of Ezr 7:6
the hand of the **L** his God was on Ezr 7:6
heart to study the law of the **L**, Ezr 7:10
Praise the **L** God of our fathers, Ezr 7:27
the house of the **L** in Jerusalem, Ezr 7:27
strengthened by the **L** my God, Ezr 7:28
are holy to the **L**, and the Ezr 8:28
offering to the **L** God of your Ezr 8:28
was a burnt offering for the **L**. Ezr 8:35
out my hands to the **L** my God. Ezr 9:5
has come from the **L** our God to Ezr 9:8
L God of Israel, You are Ezr 9:15
confession to the **L** God of your Ezr 10:11
I said, **L** God of heaven, the Neh 1:5
Amen," and they praised the **L**. Neh 5:13
Moses that the **L** had given Neh 8:1
blessed the **L**, the great God, Neh 8:6
worshiped the **L** with their faces Neh 8:6
day is holy to the **L** your God. Neh 8:9
comes from⌋ rejoicing in the **L**." Neh 8:10
the law how the **L** had commanded Neh 8:14
the law of the **L** their God for Neh 9:3
and worship of the **L** their God. Neh 9:3
out loudly to the **L** their God. Neh 9:4
Bless the **L** your God from Neh 9:5
You alone are the **L**. You created Neh 9:6
are the **L** God who chose Abram Neh 9:7
and statutes of the **L** our Lord. Neh 10:29
bread displayed before the **L**, Neh 10:33
on the altar of the **L** our God, Neh 10:34
present themselves before the **L**, Jb 1:6
The **L** asked Satan, "Where have Jb 1:7
Then the **L** said to Satan, Jb 1:8
answered the **L**, "Does Job fear Jb 1:9
"Very well," the **L** told Satan, Jb 1:12
The **L** gives, and the LORD takes Jb 1:21
gives, and the **L** takes away. Jb 1:21
Praise the name of the **L**. Jb 1:21
present themselves before the **L**, Jb 2:1
to present himself before the **L**. Jb 2:1
The **L** asked Satan, "Where have Jb 2:2
Then the **L** said to Satan, Jb 2:3
Satan answered the **L**. Jb 2:4
well," the **L** told Satan, "he Jb 2:6
the hand of the **L** has done this? Jb 12:9
Then the **L** answered Job from the Jb 38:1
The **L** answered Job: Jb 40:1
Then Job answered the **L**: Jb 40:3
Then the **L** answered Job from the Jb 40:6
Then Job replied to the **L**: Jb 42:1
the **L** had finished speaking Jb 42:7
and did as the **L** had told them, Jb 42:9
the **L** accepted Job's ⌊prayer⌋ Jb 42:9
L restored his prosperity and Jb 42:10
the adversity the **L** had brought Jb 42:11
So the **L** blessed the latter part Jb 42:12
For the **L** watches over the way Ps 1:6
against the **L** and His Anointed Ps 2:2
the **L** with reverential awe, Ps 2:11
L, how my foes increase! Ps 3:1
But You, **L**, are a shield around Ps 3:3
aloud to the **L**, and He answers Ps 3:4
again because the **L** sustains me. Ps 3:5
Rise up, **L**! Save me, my God! You Ps 3:7
Salvation belongs to the **L**; Ps 3:8
Know that the **L** has set apart Ps 4:3

the L will hear when I call to Ps 4:3
and trust in the L. Ps 4:5
Look on us with favor, L. Ps 4:6
for You alone, L, make me live Ps 4:8
to my words, L; consider my Ps 5:1
At daybreak, L, You hear my Ps 5:3
the L abhors a man of bloodshed Ps 5:6
L, lead me in Your righteousness, Ps 5:8
For You, L, bless the righteous Ps 5:12
L, do not rebuke me in Your Ps 6:1
to me, L, for I am weak; Ps 6:2
heal me, L, for my bones are Ps 6:2
terror. And You, L—how long? Ps 6:3
Turn, L! Rescue me; save me Ps 6:4
for the L has heard the sound of Ps 6:8
L has heard my plea for help; Ps 6:9
the L accepts my prayer. Ps 6:9
L my God, I seek refuge in You; Ps 7:1
L my God, if I have done this, Ps 7:3
Rise up, L, in Your anger; Ps 7:6
The L judges the peoples; Ps 7:8
vindicate me, L, according to my Ps 7:8
I will thank the L for His Ps 7:17
sing about the name of the L, Ps 7:17
L, our Lord, how magnificent is Ps 8:1
L, our Lord, how magnificent is Ps 8:9
I will thank the L with all my Ps 9:1
the L sits enthroned forever; Ps 9:7
The L is a refuge for the Ps 9:9
abandoned those who seek You, L. Ps 9:10
Sing to the L, who dwells in Ps 9:11
gracious to me, L; consider my Ps 9:13
The L has revealed Himself; Ps 9:16
Rise up, L! Do not let man Ps 9:19
terror in them, L; let the Ps 9:20
L, why do You stand so far away? Ps 10:1
curses and despises the L. Ps 10:3
Rise up, L God! Lift up Your Ps 10:12
The L is King forever and ever; Ps 10:16
L, You have heard the desire of Ps 10:17
I have taken refuge in the L. Ps 11:1
The L is in His holy temple; Ps 11:4
The L examines the righteous and Ps 11:5
For the L is righteous; Ps 11:7
Help, L, for no faithful one Ps 12:1
May the L cut off all flattering Ps 12:3
I will now rise up," says the L. Ps 12:5
words of the L are pure words, Ps 12:6
You, L, will guard us; You will Ps 12:7
L, how long will You continually Ps 13:1
me and answer, L, my God. Ps 13:3
will sing to the L because He Ps 13:6
The L looks down from heaven on Ps 14:2
they do not call on the L. Ps 14:4
but the L is his refuge. Ps 14:6
When the L restores His captive Ps 14:7
L, who can dwell in Your tent? Ps 15:1
the one rejected by the L, Ps 15:4
but honors those who fear the L, Ps 15:4
I said to the L, "You are my Ps 16:2
L, You are my portion and my cup Ps 16:5
will praise the L who counsels Ps 16:7
I keep the L in mind always. Ps 16:8
L, hear a just cause; pay Ps 17:1
Rise up, L! Confront him; bring Ps 17:13
Your hand, L, ⌊save me⌋ from Ps 17:14
I love You, L, my strength. Ps 18:1
The L is my rock, my fortress, Ps 18:2
I called to the L, who is worthy Ps 18:3
called to the L in my distress, Ps 18:6
The L thundered from heaven; Ps 18:13
at Your rebuke, L, at the blast Ps 18:15
but the L was my support. Ps 18:18
The L rewarded me according to Ps 18:20
the ways of the L and have not Ps 18:21
So the L repaid me according to Ps 18:24
L, You light my lamp; my God Ps 18:28
the word of the L is pure. Ps 18:30
For who is God besides the L? Ps 18:31
they cry ⌊to the L⌋, but He does Ps 18:41
The L lives—may my rock be Ps 18:46
will praise You, L, among the Ps 18:49
instruction of the L is perfect, Ps 19:7
of the L is trustworthy, Ps 19:7
The precepts of the L are right, Ps 19:8
commandment of the L is radiant, Ps 19:8
The fear of the L is pure, Ps 19:9
ordinances of the L are reliable Ps 19:9
to You, L, my rock and my Ps 19:14
May the L answer you in a day of Ps 20:1
May the L fulfill all your Ps 20:5
I know that the L gives victory Ps 20:6
in the name of the L our God. Ps 20:7
L, give victory to the king! Ps 20:9
L, the king finds joy in Your Ps 21:1
For the king relies on the L; Ps 21:7
the L will engulf them in His Ps 21:9
Be exalted, L, in Your strength; Ps 21:13
relies on the L; let Him rescue Ps 22:8
let the L deliver him, since He Ps 22:8
But You, L, don't be far away. Ps 22:19
You who fear the L, praise Him! Ps 22:23
who seek the L will praise Him. Ps 22:26
will remember and turn to the L. Ps 22:27
for kingship belongs to the L; Ps 22:28
The L is my shepherd; there is Ps 23:1
the house of the L as long as I Ps 23:6
inhabitants, belong to the L; Ps 24:1
ascend the mountain of the L? Ps 24:3
receive blessing from the L, Ps 24:5
The L, strong and mighty, the Ps 24:8
and mighty, the L, mighty in Ps 24:8
The L of Hosts, He is the King Ps 24:10
L, I turn my hope to You. Ps 25:1
Make Your ways known to me, L; Ps 25:4
Remember, L, Your compassion and Ps 25:6
me because of Your goodness, L. Ps 25:7
The L is good and upright; Ps 25:8
of Your name, L, forgive my sin, Ps 25:11
is the person who fears the L? Ps 25:12
counsel of the L is for those Ps 25:14
My eyes are always on the L, Ps 25:15
Vindicate me, L, because I have Ps 26:1
trusted in the L without Ps 26:1
Test me, L, and try me; Ps 26:2
and go around Your altar, L, Ps 26:6
L, I love the house where You Ps 26:8
will praise the L in the Ps 26:12
The L is my light and my Ps 27:1
The L is the stronghold of my Ps 27:1
have asked one thing from the L; Ps 27:4
the house of the L all the days Ps 27:4
beauty of the L and seeking ⌊Him Ps 27:4
sing and make music to the L. Ps 27:6
L, hear my voice when I call; Ps 27:7
L, I will seek Your face. Ps 27:8
abandon me, the L cares for me. Ps 27:10
show me Your way, L, and lead me Ps 27:11
Wait for the L; be courageous Ps 27:14
heart be strong. Wait for the L. Ps 27:14
L, I call to You; my rock, do Ps 28:1
consider what the L has done or Ps 28:5
May the L be praised, for He has Ps 28:6
The L is my strength and my Ps 28:7
The L is the strength of His Ps 28:8
Give the L—you heavenly beings Ps 29:1
give the L glory and strength. Ps 29:1
Give the L the glory due His Ps 29:2
worship the L in the splendor of Ps 29:2
The voice of the L is above the Ps 29:3
thunders—the L, above vast Ps 29:3
the voice of the L in power, Ps 29:4
the voice of the L in splendor. Ps 29:4
The voice of the L breaks the Ps 29:5
the L shatters the cedars of Ps 29:5
voice of the L flashes flames Ps 29:7
The voice of the L shakes the Ps 29:8
the L shakes the wilderness of Ps 29:8
voice of the L makes the deer Ps 29:9
L sat enthroned at the flood; Ps 29:10
the L sits enthroned, King Ps 29:10
The L gives His people strength; Ps 29:11
the L blesses His people with Ps 29:11
will exalt You, L, because You Ps 30:1
L my God, I cried to You for Ps 30:2
L, You brought me up from Sheol; Ps 30:3
Sing to the L, you His faithful Ps 30:4
L, when You showed Your favor, Ps 30:7
L, I called to You; I sought Ps 30:8
L, listen and be gracious to me; Ps 30:10
to me; L, be my helper." Ps 30:10
L my God, I will praise You Ps 30:12
L, I seek refuge in You; Ps 31:1
You redeem me, L, God of truth. Ps 31:5
idols, but I trust in the L. Ps 31:6
gracious to me, L, because I am Ps 31:9
I trust in You, L; I say, "You Ps 31:14
L, do not let me be disgraced Ps 31:17
May the L be praised, for He has Ps 31:21
Love the L, all His faithful Ps 31:23
The L protects the loyal, but Ps 31:23
you who put your hope in the L. Ps 31:24
is the man the L does not charge Ps 32:2
my transgressions to the L," Ps 32:5
who trusts in the L will have Ps 32:10
Be glad in the L and rejoice, Ps 32:11
Rejoice in the L, you righteous Ps 33:1
Praise the L with the lyre; Ps 33:2
For the word of the L is right, Ps 33:4
were made by the word of the L, Ps 33:6
earth tremble before the L; Ps 33:8
The L frustrates the counsel of Ps 33:10
counsel of the L stands forever, Ps 33:11
the nation whose God is the L— Ps 33:12
The L looks down from heaven; Ps 33:13
the eye of the L is on those who Ps 33:18
wait for the L; He is our help Ps 33:20
rest on us, L, for we put our Ps 33:22
will praise the L at all times; Ps 34:1
boast in the L; the humble will Ps 34:2
I sought the L, and He answered Ps 34:4
and the L heard ⌊him⌋ and saved Ps 34:6
angel of the L encamps around Ps 34:7
and see that the L is good. Ps 34:8
Fear the L, you His saints, for Ps 34:9
who seek the L will not lack any Ps 34:10
teach you the fear of the L. Ps 34:11
The eyes of the L are on the Ps 34:15
The face of the L is set against Ps 34:16
cry out, and the L hears, and Ps 34:17
The L is near the brokenhearted; Ps 34:18
but the L delivers him from them Ps 34:19
The L redeems the life of His Ps 34:22
Oppose my opponents, L; Ps 35:1
the angel of the L driving them Ps 35:5
angel of the L pursuing them. Ps 35:6
Then I will rejoice in the L; Ps 35:9
will say, "L, who is like You Ps 35:10
You saw it, L; do not be silent. Ps 35:22
to my cause, my God and my L! Ps 35:23
Vindicate me, L, my God, in Ps 35:24
say, "The L be exalted, who Ps 35:27
L, Your faithful love ⌊reaches⌋ Ps 36:5
L, You preserve man and beast. Ps 36:6
Trust in the L and do what is Ps 37:3
delight in the L, and He will Ps 37:4
Commit your way to the L; Ps 37:5
silent before the L and wait Ps 37:7
their hope in the L will inherit Ps 37:9
the L supports the righteous. Ps 37:17
The L watches over the blameless Ps 37:18
steps are established by the L, Ps 37:23
because the L holds his hand. Ps 37:24
For the L loves justice and will Ps 37:28
the L will not leave him in his Ps 37:33
Wait for the L and keep His way, Ps 37:34
of the righteous is from the L, Ps 37:39
The L helps and delivers them; Ps 37:40
L, do not punish me in Your Ps 38:1
I put my hope in You, L; Ps 38:15
L, do not abandon me; my God, do Ps 38:21
L, reveal to me the end of my Ps 39:4
Hear my prayer, L, and listen to Ps 39:12
I waited patiently for the L, Ps 40:1
and put their trust in the L. Ps 40:3
his trust in the L and has not Ps 40:4
L my God, You have done many Ps 40:5
mouth closed—as You know, L. Ps 40:9
L, do not withhold Your Ps 40:11
L, be pleased to deliver me; Ps 40:13
deliver me; hurry to help me, L. Ps 40:13
say, The L is great!" Ps 40:16
the L will save him in a day of Ps 41:1
The L will keep him and preserve Ps 41:2
The L will sustain him on his Ps 41:3
I said, "L, be gracious to me; Ps 41:4
You, L, be gracious to me and Ps 41:10
May the L, the God of Israel, be Ps 41:13
L will send His faithful love Ps 42:8
up, L! Why are You sleeping? Ps 44:23
The L of Hosts is with us; Ps 46:7
the works of the L, who brings Ps 46:8
The L of Hosts is with us; Ps 46:11
For the L Most High is Ps 47:2

of joy, the **L**, amid the sound	Ps 47:5
The **L** is great and is highly	Ps 48:1
in the city of the **L** of Hosts,	Ps 48:8
God, the **L** God speaks; He	Ps 50:1
Your name, **L**, because it is	Ps 54:6
to God, and the **L** will save me.	Ps 55:16
Cast your burden on the **L**,	Ps 55:22
I praise, in the **L**, whose word I	Ps 56:10
L, tear out the young lions'	Ps 58:6
L, look! They set an ambush for	Ps 59:3
You, **L** God of Hosts, God of	Ps 59:5
But You laugh at them, **L**;	Ps 59:8
faithful love belongs to You, **L**.	Ps 62:12
rejoice in the **L** and take refuge	Ps 64:10
The **L** will live ⌊there⌋ forever!	Ps 68:16
so that the **L** God might live	Ps 68:18
⌊praise⌋ the **L** from the fountain	Ps 68:26
But as for me, **L**, my prayer to	Ps 69:13
Answer me, **L**, for Your faithful	Ps 69:16
please the **L** more than an ox	Ps 69:31
For the **L** listens to the needy	Ps 69:33
deliver me. Hurry to help me, **L**!	Ps 70:1
my deliverer; **L**, do not delay.	Ps 70:5
L, I seek refuge in You;	Ps 71:1
the **L** God, the God of Israel,	Ps 72:18
the enemy has mocked the **L**,	Ps 74:18
your vows to the **L** your God;	Ps 76:11
generation the praises of the **L**,	Ps 78:4
the **L** heard and became furious;	Ps 78:21
How long, **L**? Will You be angry	Ps 79:5
L God of Hosts, how long will	Ps 80:4
Restore us, **L** God of Hosts;	Ps 80:19
who hate the **L** would pretend	Ps 81:15
they will seek Your name, **L**.	Ps 83:16
Your dwelling place, **L** of Hosts.	Ps 84:1
yearn for the courts of the **L**;	Ps 84:2
Your altars, **L** of Hosts, my King	Ps 84:3
L God of Hosts, hear my prayer;	Ps 84:8
For the **L** God is a sun and	Ps 84:11
The **L** gives grace and glory;	Ps 84:11
L of Hosts, happy is the person	Ps 84:12
L, You showed favor to Your land;	Ps 85:1
faithful love, **L**, and give us	Ps 85:7
surely the **L** will declare peace	Ps 85:8
the **L** will provide what is good,	Ps 85:12
Listen, **L**, and answer me, for I	Ps 86:1
L, hear my prayer; listen to my	Ps 86:6
me Your way, **L**, and I will live	Ps 86:11
because You, **L**, have helped	Ps 86:17
The **L** loves the gates of Zion	Ps 87:2
the peoples, the **L** will record,	Ps 87:6
L, God of my salvation, I cry	Ps 88:1
L, I cry out to You all day long;	Ps 88:9
But I call to You for help, **L**;	Ps 88:13
L, why do You reject me?	Ps 88:14
⌊The **L** said,⌋ "I have made a	Ps 89:3
L, the heavens praise Your	Ps 89:5
skies can compare with the **L**?	Ps 89:6
heavenly beings is like the **L**?	Ps 89:6
L God of Hosts, who is strong	Ps 89:8
who is strong like You, **L**?	Ps 89:8
L, they walk in the light of	Ps 89:15
our shield belongs to the **L**,	Ps 89:18
How long, **L**? Will You hide	Ps 89:46
have ridiculed, **L**, how they have	Ps 89:51
May the **L** be praised forever.	Ps 89:52
L—how long? Turn and have	Ps 90:13
I will say to the **L**, "My refuge	Ps 91:2
Because you have made the **L**—	Ps 91:9
It is good to praise the **L**,	Ps 92:1
made me rejoice, **L**, by what You	Ps 92:4
are Your works, **L**, how profound	Ps 92:5
But You, **L**, are exalted forever.	Ps 92:8
For indeed, **L**, Your enemies—	Ps 92:9
Planted in the house of the **L**,	Ps 92:13
declare: "The **L** is just; He is	Ps 92:15
The **L** reigns! He is robed in	Ps 93:1
The **L** is robed, enveloped in	Ps 93:1
have lifted up, **L**, the floods	Ps 93:3
the **L** on high is majestic.	Ps 93:4
L, Your testimonies are	Ps 93:5
L, God of vengeance—God of	Ps 94:1
L, how long will the wicked—	Ps 94:3
L, they crush Your people;	Ps 94:5
They say, "The **L** doesn't see it.	Ps 94:7
The **L** knows man's thoughts;	Ps 94:11
L, happy is the man You	Ps 94:12
L will not forsake His people	Ps 94:14
If the **L** had not been my help,	Ps 94:17
love will support me, **L**.	Ps 94:18
But the **L** is my refuge;	Ps 94:22
The **L** our God will destroy them.	Ps 94:23
let us shout joyfully to the **L**,	Ps 95:1
the **L** is a great God, a great	Ps 95:3
us kneel before the **L** our Maker.	Ps 95:6
Sing a new song to the **L**;	Ps 96:1
sing to the **L**, all the earth.	Ps 96:1
Sing to the **L**, praise His name;	Ps 96:2
For the **L** is great and is highly	Ps 96:4
but the **L** made the heavens.	Ps 96:5
Ascribe to the **L**, you families	Ps 96:7
ascribe to the **L** glory and	Ps 96:7
Ascribe to the **L** the glory of	Ps 96:8
Worship the **L** in the splendor of	Ps 96:9
nations: "The **L** reigns. The	Ps 96:10
before the **L**, for He is coming—	Ps 96:13
The **L** reigns! Let the earth	Ps 97:1
wax at the presence of the **L**—	Ps 97:5
because of Your judgments, **L**.	Ps 97:8
For You, **L**, are the Most High	Ps 97:9
You who love the **L**, hate evil!	Ps 97:10
Be glad in the **L**, you righteous	Ps 97:12
a new song to the **L**, for He has	Ps 98:1
L has made His victory known;	Ps 98:2
Shout to the **L**, all the earth;	Ps 98:4
Sing to the **L** with the lyre,	Ps 98:5
in the presence of the **L**,	Ps 98:6
before the **L**, for He is coming	Ps 98:9
The **L** reigns! Let the peoples	Ps 99:1
The **L** is great in Zion;	Ps 99:2
Exalt the **L** our God; bow in	Ps 99:5
called to the **L**, and He answered	Ps 99:6
L our God, You answered them.	Ps 99:8
Exalt the **L** our God; bow in	Ps 99:9
for the **L** our God is holy.	Ps 99:9
Shout triumphantly to the **L**,	Ps 100:1
Serve the **L** with gladness;	Ps 100:2
Acknowledge that the **L** is God.	Ps 100:3
For the **L** is good, and His love	Ps 100:5
I will sing praise to You, **L**.	Ps 101:1
L, hear my prayer; let my cry	Ps 102:1
But You, **L**, are enthroned	Ps 102:12
will fear the name of the **L**,	Ps 102:15
for the **L** will rebuild Zion;	Ps 102:16
people will praise the **L**:	Ps 102:18
the **L** gazed out from heaven to	Ps 102:19
name of the **L** in Zion and His	Ps 102:21
are assembled to serve the **L**.	Ps 102:22
praise the **L**, and all that is	Ps 103:1
soul, praise the **L**, and do not	Ps 103:2
The **L** executes acts of	Ps 103:6
The **L** is compassionate and	Ps 103:8
so the **L** has compassion on those	Ps 103:13
The **L** has established His throne	Ps 103:19
Praise the **L**, ⌊all⌋ His angels	Ps 103:20
Praise the **L**, all His armies,	Ps 103:21
Praise the **L**, all His works in	Ps 103:22
He rules. My soul, praise the **L**!	Ps 103:22
soul, praise the **L**! LORD my God,	Ps 104:1
L my God, You are very great;	Ps 104:1
The trees of the **L** flourish,	Ps 104:16
How countless are Your works, **L**!	Ps 104:24
glory of the **L** endure forever;	Ps 104:31
may the **L** rejoice in His works.	Ps 104:31
will sing to the **L** all my life;	Ps 104:33
I will rejoice in the **L**.	Ps 104:34
soul, praise the **L**! Hallelujah!	Ps 104:35
thanks to the **L**, call on His	Ps 105:1
of those who seek the **L** rejoice.	Ps 105:3
Search for the **L** and for His	Ps 105:4
He is the **L** our God; His	Ps 105:7
the word of the **L** tested him.	Ps 105:19
The **L** made His people very	Ps 105:24
thanks to the **L**, for He is good;	Ps 106:1
Remember me, **L**, when You show	Ps 106:4
provoked the **L** with their deeds	Ps 106:29
angered ⌊the **L**⌋ at the waters	Ps 106:32
peoples as the **L** had commanded	Ps 106:34
Save us, **L** our God, and gather	Ps 106:47
May the **L**, the God of Israel, be	Ps 106:48
thanks to the **L**, for He is good;	Ps 107:1
redeemed of the **L** proclaim that	Ps 107:2
out to the **L** in their trouble	Ps 107:6
thanks to the **L** for His faithful	Ps 107:8
out to the **L** in their trouble	Ps 107:13
thanks to the **L** for His faithful	Ps 107:15
out to the **L** in their trouble	Ps 107:19
thanks to the **L** for His faithful	Ps 107:21
out to the **L** in their trouble	Ps 107:28
thanks to the **L** for His faithful	Ps 107:31
will praise You, **L**, among the	Ps 108:3
be remembered before the **L**,	Ps 109:14
sins always remain before the **L**,	Ps 109:15
Help me, **L** my God; save me	Ps 109:26
and that You, **L**, have done it.	Ps 109:27
thank the **L** with my mouth;	Ps 109:30
The **L** declared to my Lord:	Ps 110:1
The **L** will extend Your mighty	Ps 110:2
The **L** has sworn an oath and will	Ps 110:4
will praise the **L** with all my	Ps 111:1
The **L** is gracious and	Ps 111:4
The fear of the **L** is the	Ps 111:10
is the man who fears the **L**,	Ps 112:1
is confident, trusting in the **L**.	Ps 112:7
Give praise, servants of the **L**;	Ps 113:1
praise the name of the **L**.	Ps 113:1
name of the **L** be praised both	Ps 113:2
the name of the **L** be praised.	Ps 113:3
The **L** is exalted above all the	Ps 113:4
Who is like the **L** our God—	Ps 113:5
Not to us, **L**, not to us, but to	Ps 115:1
Israel, trust in the **L**!	Ps 115:9
House of Aaron, trust in the **L**!	Ps 115:10
You who fear the **L**, trust in the	Ps 115:11
fear the LORD, trust in the **L**!	Ps 115:11
L remembers us and will bless	Ps 115:12
bless those who fear the **L**—	Ps 115:13
May the **L** add to ⌊your numbers⌋,	Ps 115:14
May you be blessed by the **L**,	Ps 115:15
not the dead who praise the **L**,	Ps 115:17
we will praise the **L**, both now	Ps 115:18
love the **L** because He has heard	Ps 116:1
I called on the name of the **L**:	Ps 116:4
name of the LORD: "**L**, save me!"	Ps 116:4
The **L** is gracious and righteous;	Ps 116:5
The **L** guards the inexperienced;	Ps 116:6
for the **L** has been good to you.	Ps 116:7
For You, ⌊**L**,⌋ rescued me from	Ps 116:8
walk before the **L** in the land	Ps 116:9
can I repay the **L** all the good	Ps 116:12
of salvation and worship the **L**.	Ps 116:13
my vows to the **L** in the presence	Ps 116:14
L, I am indeed Your servant;	Ps 116:16
and will worship the **L**.	Ps 116:17
I will fulfill my vows to the **L**,	Ps 116:18
Praise the **L**, all nations!	Ps 117:1
thanks to the **L**, for He is good;	Ps 118:1
Let those who fear the **L** say,	Ps 118:4
I called to the **L** in distress;	Ps 118:5
the **L** answered me ⌊and put me⌋	Ps 118:5
The **L** is for me; I will not be	Ps 118:6
With the **L** for me as my helper,	Ps 118:7
refuge in the **L** than to trust	Ps 118:8
refuge in the **L** than to trust	Ps 118:9
the name of the **L** I destroyed	Ps 118:10
the name of the **L** I destroyed	Ps 118:11
the name of the **L** I destroyed	Ps 118:12
me fall, but the **L** helped me.	Ps 118:13
L is my strength and my song;	Ps 118:14
proclaim what the **L** has done.	Ps 118:17
L disciplined me severely but	Ps 118:18
them and give thanks to the **L**.	Ps 118:19
This is the gate of the **L**;	Ps 118:20
came from the **L**; it is wonderful	Ps 118:23
This is the day the **L** has made;	Ps 118:24
L, save us! LORD, please grant	Ps 118:25
L, please grant us success!	Ps 118:25
who comes in the name of the **L**.	Ps 118:26
the house of the **L** we bless you.	Ps 118:26
The **L** is God and has given us	Ps 118:27
thanks to the **L**, for He is good;	Ps 118:29
according to the law of the **L**!	Ps 119:1
L, may You be praised; teach me	Ps 119:12
L, do not put me to shame.	Ps 119:31
Teach me, **L**, the meaning of Your	Ps 119:33
come to me, **L**, Your salvation	Ps 119:41
L, I remember Your judgments	Ps 119:52
in the night, **L**, and I keep Your	Ps 119:55
The **L** is my portion; I have	Ps 119:57
L, the earth is filled with Your	Ps 119:64
L, You have treated Your servant	Ps 119:65
I know, **L**, that Your judgments	Ps 119:75
L, Your word is forever;	Ps 119:89
L, give me life through Your	Ps 119:107

L, please accept my willing	Ps 119:108
It is time for the **L** to act,	Ps 119:126
You are righteous, **L**, and Your	Ps 119:137
answer me, **L**. I will obey Your	Ps 119:145
L, give me life, in keeping with	Ps 119:149
You are near, **L**, and all Your	Ps 119:151
Your compassions are many, **L**;	Ps 119:156
L, give me life, according to	Ps 119:159
L, I hope for Your salvation and	Ps 119:166
Let my cry reach You, **L**;	Ps 119:169
for Your salvation, **L**, and Your	Ps 119:174
my distress I called to the **L**,	Ps 120:1
L, deliver me from lying lips	Ps 120:2
help comes from the **L**, the Maker	Ps 121:2
The **L** protects you; the LORD is	Ps 121:5
the **L** is a shelter right by your	Ps 121:5
The **L** will protect you from all	Ps 121:7
The **L** will protect your coming	Ps 121:8
us go to the house of the **L**."	Ps 122:1
tribes of the **L**, go up to give	Ps 122:4
thanks to the name of the **L**.	Ps 122:4
of the house of the **L** our God,	Ps 122:9
eyes are on the **L** our God until	Ps 123:2
Show us favor, **L**, show us favor,	Ps 123:3
the **L** had not been on our side	Ps 124:1
the **L** had not been on our side	Ps 124:2
Praise the **L**, who has not let us	Ps 124:6
help is in the name of the **L**,	Ps 124:8
trust in the **L** are like Mount	Ps 125:1
And the **L** surrounds His people,	Ps 125:2
what is good, **L**, to the good, to	Ps 125:4
the **L** will banish them with the	Ps 125:5
When the **L** restored the fortunes	Ps 126:1
The **L** has done great things for	Ps 126:2
The **L** had done great things for	Ps 126:3
our fortunes, **L**, like	Ps 126:4
Unless the **L** builds a house,	Ps 127:1
the **L** watches over a city,	Ps 127:1
indeed a heritage from the **L**,	Ps 127:3
is everyone who fears the **L**,	Ps 128:1
who fears the **L** will be blessed	Ps 128:4
May the **L** bless you from Zion,	Ps 128:5
The **L** is righteous; He has cut	Ps 129:4
bless you in the name of the **L**.	Ps 129:8
of the depths I call to You, **L**!	Ps 130:1
L, if You considered sins, Lord,	Ps 130:3
wait for the **L**; I wait, and put	Ps 130:5
Israel, put your hope in the **L**.	Ps 130:7
is faithful love with the **L**,	Ps 130:7
L, my heart is not proud;	Ps 131:1
put your hope in the **L**, both now	Ps 131:3
L, remember David and all the	Ps 132:1
how he swore an oath to the **L**,	Ps 132:2
until I find a place for the **L**,	Ps 132:5
Arise, **L**, come to Your resting	Ps 132:8
The **L** swore an oath to David,	Ps 132:11
For the **L** has chosen Zion;	Ps 132:13
there the **L** has appointed the	Ps 133:3
Now praise the **L**, all you	Ps 134:1
you servants of the **L** who stand	Ps 134:1
holy place, and praise the **L**!	Ps 134:2
May the **L**, Maker of heaven and	Ps 134:3
Praise the name of the **L**.	Ps 135:1
praise, you servants of the **L**	Ps 135:1
who stand in the house of the **L**,	Ps 135:2
Praise the **L**, for the LORD is	Ps 135:3
the LORD, for the **L** is good;	Ps 135:3
For the **L** has chosen Jacob for	Ps 135:4
For I know that the **L** is great;	Ps 135:5
The **L** does whatever He pleases	Ps 135:6
L, Your name ⌊endures⌋ forever,	Ps 135:13
Your reputation, **L**, through all	Ps 135:13
For the **L** will judge His people	Ps 135:14
House of Israel, praise the **L**!	Ps 135:19
House of Aaron, praise the **L**!	Ps 135:19
House of Levi, praise the **L**!	Ps 135:20
who revere the **L**, praise the	Ps 135:20
revere the LORD, praise the **L**!	Ps 135:20
May the **L** be praised from Zion;	Ps 135:21
thanks to the **L**, for He is good.	Ps 136:1
Remember, **L**, ⌊what⌋ the Edomites	Ps 137:7
You thanks, **L**, when they hear	Ps 138:4
Though the **L** is exalted, He	Ps 138:6
The **L** will fulfill ⌊His purpose⌋	Ps 138:8
L, Your love is eternal;	Ps 138:8
L, You have searched me and	Ps 139:1
You know all about it, **L**.	Ps 139:4
L, don't I hate those who hate	Ps 139:21
Rescue me, **L**, from evil men.	Ps 140:1
Protect me, **L**, from the clutches	Ps 140:4
say to the **L**, "You are my God."	Ps 140:6
Listen, **L**, to my cry for help.	Ps 140:6
L, do not grant the desires of	Ps 140:8
I know that the **L** upholds the	Ps 140:12
L, I call on You; hurry to	Ps 141:1
L, set up a guard for my mouth;	Ps 141:3
aloud to the **L**; I plead aloud	Ps 142:1
plead aloud to the **L** for mercy.	Ps 142:1
I cry to You, **L**; I say, "You are	Ps 142:5
L, hear my prayer. In Your	Ps 143:1
me quickly, **L**; my spirit fails.	Ps 143:7
Rescue me from my enemies, **L**;	Ps 143:9
May the **L** my rock be praised,	Ps 144:1
L, what is man, that You care	Ps 144:3
L, part Your heavens and come	Ps 144:5
the people whose God is the **L**.	Ps 144:15
The **L** is gracious and	Ps 145:8
The **L** is good to everyone;	Ps 145:9
have made will praise You, **L**;	Ps 145:10
The **L** is faithful in all His	Ps 145:13
The **L** helps all who fall;	Ps 145:14
The **L** is righteous in all His	Ps 145:17
The **L** is near all who call out	Ps 145:18
The **L** guards all those who love	Ps 145:20
My soul, praise the **L**.	Ps 146:1
I will praise the **L** all my life;	Ps 146:2
will sing to the **L** as long as I	Ps 146:2
whose hope is in the **L** his God,	Ps 146:5
hungry. The **L** frees prisoners	Ps 146:7
The **L** opens ⌊the eyes of⌋ the	Ps 146:8
The **L** raises up those who are	Ps 146:8
The **L** loves the righteous.	Ps 146:8
The **L** protects foreigners and	Ps 146:9
The **L** reigns forever; Zion, your	Ps 146:10
The **L** rebuilds Jerusalem;	Ps 147:2
The **L** helps the afflicted but	Ps 147:6
Sing to the **L** with thanksgiving;	Ps 147:7
The **L** values those who fear Him,	Ps 147:11
Exalt the **L**, Jerusalem;	Ps 147:12
Praise the **L** from the heavens;	Ps 148:1
them praise the name of the **L**,	Ps 148:5
Praise the **L** from the earth,	Ps 148:7
them praise the name of the **L**,	Ps 148:13
Sing to the **L** a new song, His	Ps 149:1
For the **L** takes pleasure in His	Ps 149:4
that breathes praise the **L**.	Ps 150:6
The fear of the **L** is the	Pr 1:7
didn't choose to fear the **L**,	Pr 1:29
the fear of the **L** and discover	Pr 2:5
For the **L** gives wisdom;	Pr 2:6
Trust in the **L** with all your	Pr 3:5
fear the **L** and turn away from	Pr 3:7
the **L** with your possessions	Pr 3:9
for the **L** disciplines the one He	Pr 3:12
L founded the earth by wisdom	Pr 3:19
the **L** will be your confidence	Pr 3:26
devious are detestable to the **L**,	Pr 3:32
Six things the **L** hates;	Pr 6:16
To fear the **L** is to hate evil.	Pr 8:13
The **L** made me at the beginning	Pr 8:22
and obtains favor from the **L**,	Pr 8:35
The fear of the **L** is the	Pr 9:10
The **L** will not let the righteous	Pr 10:3
The fear of the **L** prolongs life,	Pr 10:27
The way of the **L** is a stronghold	Pr 10:29
scales are detestable to the **L**,	Pr 11:1
minds are detestable to the **L**,	Pr 11:20
good obtain favor from the **L**,	Pr 12:2
lips are detestable to the **L**,	Pr 12:22
with integrity fears the **L**,	Pr 14:2
the fear of the **L** one has strong	Pr 14:26
The fear of the **L** is a fountain	Pr 14:27
eyes of the **L** are everywhere,	Pr 15:3
wicked is detestable to the **L**,	Pr 15:8
The **L** detests the way of the	Pr 15:9
Abaddon lie open before the **L**—	Pr 15:11
the fear of the **L** than great	Pr 15:16
The **L** destroys the house of the	Pr 15:25
The **L** detests the plans of an	Pr 15:26
The **L** is far from the wicked,	Pr 15:29
The fear of the **L** is wisdom's	Pr 15:33
of the tongue is from the **L**.	Pr 16:1
but the **L** weighs the motives.	Pr 16:2
to the **L** and your plans	Pr 16:3
L has prepared everything for	Pr 16:4
heart is detestable to the **L**;	Pr 16:5
from evil by the fear of the **L**.	Pr 16:6
When a man's ways please the **L**,	Pr 16:7
but the **L** determines his steps.	Pr 16:9
trusts in the **L** will be happy.	Pr 16:20
every decision is from the **L**.	Pr 16:33
but the **L** is a tester of hearts.	Pr 17:3
both are detestable to the **L**.	Pr 17:15
The name of the **L** is a strong	Pr 18:10
and obtains favor from the **L**.	Pr 18:22
his heart rages against the **L**.	Pr 19:3
a sensible wife is from the **L**.	Pr 19:14
to the poor is a loan to the **L**,	Pr 19:17
The fear of the **L** leads to life;	Pr 19:23
both are detestable to the **L**.	Pr 20:10
eye—the **L** made them both.	Pr 20:12
Wait on the **L**, and He will	Pr 20:22
weights are detestable to the **L**,	Pr 20:23
steps are determined by the **L**,	Pr 20:24
breath is the lamp of the **L**,	Pr 20:27
but the **L** evaluates the motives.	Pr 21:2
to the **L** than sacrifice.	Pr 21:3
will prevail⌋ against the **L**.	Pr 21:30
but victory comes from the **L**.	Pr 21:31
in common: the **L** made them both.	Pr 22:2
of humility is fear of the **L**,	Pr 22:4
cursed by the **L** will fall into	Pr 22:14
your confidence may be in the **L**.	Pr 22:19
the **L** will take up their case	Pr 22:23
instead, always fear the **L**.	Pr 23:17
the **L** will see, be displeased,	Pr 24:18
My son, fear the **L**, as well as	Pr 24:21
and the **L** will reward you.	Pr 25:22
those who seek the **L** understand	Pr 28:5
trusts in the **L** will prosper.	Pr 28:25
the **L** gives light to the eyes of	Pr 29:13
trusts in the **L** is protected.	Pr 29:25
man receives justice from the **L**.	Pr 29:26
You, saying, "Who is the **L**?"	Pr 30:9
who fears the **L** will be praised.	Pr 31:30
earth, for the **L** has spoken:	Is 1:2
They have abandoned the **L**;	Is 1:4
the **L** of Hosts had not left us	Is 1:9
the word of the **L**, you rulers of	Is 1:10
to Me?" asks the **L**. "I have had	Is 1:11
us discuss this," says the **L**.	Is 1:18
the mouth of the **L** has spoken.	Is 1:20
who abandon the **L** will perish.	Is 1:28
go up to the mountain of the **L**,	Is 2:3
word of the **L** from Jerusalem.	Is 2:3
the terror of the **L** and from His	Is 2:10
the **L** alone will be exalted on	Is 2:11
belonging to the **L** of Hosts is	Is 2:12
the **L** alone will be exalted on	Is 2:17
the terror of the **L** and from His	Is 2:19
the terror of the **L** and from His	Is 2:21
spoken and acted against the **L**,	Is 3:8
L rises to argue the case and	Is 3:13
The **L** brings ⌊this⌋ charge	Is 3:14
The **L** also says: Because the	Is 3:16
and the **L** will shave their	Is 3:17
branch of the **L** will be	Is 4:2
Then the **L** will create a cloud	Is 4:5
the vineyard of the **L** of Hosts	Is 5:7
my hearing the **L** of Hosts ⌊has	Is 5:9
But the **L** of Hosts is exalted by	Is 5:16
instruction of the **L** of Hosts,	Is 5:24
holy, holy is the **L** of Hosts;	Is 6:3
seen the King, the **L** of Hosts.	Is 6:5
and the **L** drives the people far	Is 6:12
Then the **L** said to Isaiah,	Is 7:3
Then the **L** spoke again to Ahaz:	Is 7:10
for a sign from the **L** your God—	Is 7:11
I will not test the **L**."	Is 7:12
The **L** will bring on you, your	Is 7:17
that day the **L** will whistle to	Is 7:18
Then the **L** said to me, "Take a	Is 8:1
The **L** said to me, "Name him	Is 8:3
The **L** spoke to me again:	Is 8:5
is what the **L** said to me with	Is 8:11
regard only the **L** of Hosts as	Is 8:13
wait for the **L**, who is hiding	Is 8:17
children the **L** has given me to	Is 8:18
Israel from the **L** of Hosts who	Is 8:18
The zeal of the **L** of Hosts will	Is 9:7
The **L** has raised up Rezin's	Is 9:11
did not seek the **L** of Hosts.	Is 9:13
So the **L** cut off Israel's head	Is 9:14
by the wrath of the **L** of Hosts,	Is 9:19

will faithfully depend on the **L**, Is 10:20
And the **L** of Hosts will brandish Is 10:26
Spirit of the **L** will rest on Him Is 11:2
and of the fear of the **L**. Is 11:2
will be in the fear of the **L**. Is 11:3
knowledge of the **L** as the sea is Is 11:9
The **L** will divide the Gulf of Is 11:15
will praise You, **L**, although You Is 12:1
Yah, the **L**, is my strength Is 12:2
thanks to the **L**; proclaim His Is 12:4
Sing to the **L**, for He has done Is 12:5
The **L** of Hosts is mobilizing an Is 13:4
the **L** and the weapons of His Is 13:5
For the day of the **L** is near. Is 13:6
the day of the **L** is coming— Is 13:9
at the wrath of the **L** of Hosts, Is 13:13
For the **L** will have compassion Is 14:1
When the **L** gives you rest from Is 14:3
L has broken the staff of the Is 14:5
declaration of the **L** of Hosts— Is 14:22
declaration of the **L** of Hosts. Is 14:23
The **L** of Hosts has sworn: Is 14:24
The **L** of Hosts Himself has Is 14:27
The **L** has founded Zion, and His Is 14:32
message that the **L** previously Is 16:13
And now the **L** says, "In three Is 16:14
declaration of the **L** of Hosts. Is 17:3
is⌋ the declaration of the **L**, Is 17:6
For, the **L** said to me: I will Is 18:4
brought to the **L** of Hosts from Is 18:7
of the name of the **L** of Hosts. Is 18:7
the **L** rides on a swift cloud and Is 19:1
reveal what the **L** of Hosts has Is 19:12
The **L** has mixed within her a Is 19:14
hand of the **L** of Hosts when He Is 19:16
of what the **L** of Hosts has Is 19:17
swear loyalty to the **L** of Hosts. Is 19:18
an altar to the **L** in the center Is 19:19
pillar to the **L** near her border Is 19:19
and witness to the **L** of Hosts in Is 19:20
out to the **L** because of their Is 19:20
The **L** will make Himself known to Is 19:21
will know the **L** on that day. Is 19:21
vows to the **L** and fulfill them Is 19:21
L will strike Egypt, striking Is 19:22
return to the **L** and He will hear Is 19:22
The **L** of Hosts will bless them, Is 19:25
that time the **L** had spoken Is 20:2
L said, "As My servant Isaiah Is 20:3
have heard from the **L** of Hosts, Is 21:10
For the **L**, the God of Israel, Is 21:17
The **L** of Hosts has revealed Is 22:14
The **L** is about to shake you Is 22:17
declaration of the **L** of Hosts— Is 22:25
Indeed, the **L** has spoken. Is 22:25
The **L** of Hosts planned it, Is 23:9
The **L** has commanded that the Is 23:11
the **L** will restore Tyre and she Is 23:17
will be dedicated to the **L**. Is 23:18
L is stripping the earth bare Is 24:1
for the **L** has spoken this Is 24:3
the west the majesty of the **L**. Is 24:14
in the east honor the **L**! Is 24:15
west ⌊honor⌋ the name of the **L**, Is 24:15
that day the **L** will punish the Is 24:21
because the **L** of Hosts will Is 24:23
L, You are my God; I will exalt Is 25:1
The **L** of Hosts will prepare a Is 25:6
earth, for the **L** has spoken. Is 25:8
us. This is the **L**; we have Is 25:9
Trust in the **L** forever, because Is 26:4
in Yah, the **L**, is an everlasting Is 26:4
Yes, **L**, we wait for You in the Is 26:8
not see the majesty of the **L**. Is 26:10
L, Your hand is lifted up ⌊to Is 26:11
L, You will establish peace for Is 26:12
L, our God, other lords than You Is 26:13
You have added to the nation, **L**. Is 26:15
L, they went to You in their Is 26:16
pains, so we were before You, **L**. Is 26:17
the **L** is coming from His place Is 26:21
that day the **L** with His harsh, Is 27:1
I, the **L**, watch over it; Is 27:3
Did the **L** strike Israel as He Is 27:7
On that day the **L** will thresh Is 27:12
will worship the **L** at Jerusalem Is 27:13
On that day the **L** of Hosts will Is 28:5
the word of the **L** came to them: Is 28:13

hear the word of the **L**, Is 28:14
For the **L** will rise up as ⌊He Is 28:21
also comes from the **L** of Hosts. Is 28:29
visited by the **L** of Hosts with Is 29:6
For the **L** has poured out on you Is 29:10
to hide their plans from the **L**. Is 29:15
have joy after joy in the **L**, Is 29:19
the **L** who redeemed Abraham says Is 29:22
Therefore the **L** is waiting to Is 30:18
for the **L** is a just God. Is 30:18
the day that the **L** bandages His Is 30:26
up to the mountain of the **L**, Is 30:29
And the **L** will make the splendor Is 30:30
shattered by the voice of the **L**. Is 30:31
staff that the **L** brings down on Is 30:32
breath of the **L**, like a torrent Is 30:33
When the **L** raises His hand ⌊to Is 31:3
this is what the **L** said to me: Is 31:4
so the **L** of Hosts will come down Is 31:4
so the **L** of Hosts will protect Is 31:5
and speaks falsely about the **L**. Is 32:6
L, be gracious to us! We wait Is 33:2
The **L** is exalted, for He dwells Is 33:5
The fear of the **L** is Zion's Is 33:6
Now I will rise up," says the **L**. Is 33:10
One, the **L**, will be for us, Is 33:21
For the **L** is our Judge, the LORD Is 33:22
our Judge, the **L** is our lawgiver Is 33:22
our lawgiver, the **L** is our King. Is 33:22
The **L** is angry with all the Is 34:2
For the **L** has a sacrifice in Is 34:6
the **L** has a day of vengeance, Is 34:8
⌊The **L**⌋ will stretch out a Is 34:11
and read the scroll of the **L**: Is 34:16
will see the glory of the **L**, Is 35:2
ransomed of the **L** will return Is 35:10
We trust in the **L** our God. Is 36:7
The **L** said to me, 'Attack this Is 36:10
persuade you to trust the **L**, Is 36:15
'The **L** will surely deliver us. Is 36:15
saying, 'The **L** will deliver us Is 36:18
the **L** should deliver Jerusalem? Is 36:20
and went to the house of the **L**. Is 37:1
Perhaps the **L** your God will hear Is 37:4
words that the **L** your God has Is 37:4
to your master, 'The **L** says: Is 37:6
and spread it out before the **L**. Is 37:14
Hezekiah prayed to the **L**: Is 37:15
L of Hosts, God of Israel, who Is 37:16
Listen closely, **L**, and hear; Is 37:17
open Your eyes, **L**, and see; Is 37:17
L, it is true that the kings of Is 37:18
Now, **L** our God, save us from his Is 37:20
may know that You are the **L**— Is 37:20
The **L**, the God of Israel, says: Is 37:21
is the word the **L** has spoken Is 37:22
have mocked the **L** through your Is 37:24
The zeal of the **L** of Hosts will Is 37:32
this is what the **L** says about Is 37:33
the angel of the **L** went out and Is 37:36
This is what the **L** says: Is 38:1
to the wall and prayed to the **L**. Is 38:2
said, "Please, **L**, remember how I Is 38:3
word of the **L** came to Isaiah: Is 38:4
this is what the **L** God of your Is 38:5
to you from the **L** that the LORD Is 38:7
LORD that the **L** will do what He Is 38:7
I will never see the **L**, the LORD Is 38:11
the **L** in the land of the living; Is 38:11
The **L** will save me; we will play Is 38:20
our lives at the house of the **L**. Is 38:20
Hear the word of the **L** of Hosts: Is 39:5
will be left,' says the **L**. Is 39:6
The word of the **L** that you have Is 39:8
the way of the **L** in the Is 40:3
the glory of the **L** will appear, Is 40:5
the mouth of the **L** has spoken. Is 40:5
breath of the **L** blows on them; Is 40:7
directed the Spirit of the **L**, Is 40:13
My way is hidden from the **L**, Is 40:27
trust in the **L** will renew their Is 40:31
The **L** hands nations over to him, Is 41:2
I, the **L**, am the first, and with Is 41:4
For I, the **L** your God, hold your Is 41:13
But you will rejoice in the **L**; Is 41:16
I, the **L**, will answer them; Is 41:17
the hand of the **L** has done this, Is 41:20
"Submit your case," says the **L**. Is 41:21

This is what God the **L** says— Is 42:5
I, the **L**, have called you for a Is 42:6
Sing a new song to the **L**; Is 42:10
Let them give glory to the **L**, Is 42:12
The **L** advances like a warrior; Is 42:13
blind like the servant of the **L**? Is 42:19
L was pleased, because of His Is 42:21
Was it not the **L**? Have we not Is 42:24
Now this is what the **L** says— Is 43:1
For I the **L** your God, the Holy Is 43:3
I, I am the **L**, and there is no Is 43:11
is what the **L**, your Redeemer, Is 43:14
I am the **L**, your Holy One, the Is 43:15
is what the **L** says—who makes Is 43:16
the word of the **L** your Maker who Is 44:2
This is what the **L**, the King of Is 44:6
Redeemer, the **L** of Hosts, says: Is 44:6
heavens, for the **L** has acted; Is 44:23
For the **L** has redeemed Jacob, Is 44:23
is what the **L**, your Redeemer Is 44:24
I am the **L**, who made everything; Is 44:24
The **L** says this to Cyrus, His Is 45:1
know that I, the **L**, the God of Is 45:3
I am the **L**, and there is no Is 45:5
I am the **L**, and there is no Is 45:6
I, the **L**, do all these things. Is 45:7
I, the **L**, have created it. Is 45:8
This is what the **L**, the Holy One Is 45:11
a bribe," says the **L** of Hosts. Is 45:13
This is what the **L** says: Is 45:14
be saved by the **L** with an Is 45:17
For this is what the **L** says— Is 45:18
I am the **L**, and there is no Is 45:18
I, the **L**, speak truthfully; Is 45:19
Was it not I, the **L**? There is no Is 45:21
Only in the **L** is righteousness Is 45:24
and find glory through the **L**. Is 45:25
the **L** of Hosts is His name. Is 47:4
by the name of the **L** and declare Is 48:1
these things? The **L** loves him; Is 48:14
is what the **L**, your Redeemer, Is 48:17
I am the **L** your God, who teaches Is 48:17
The **L** has redeemed His servant Is 48:20
says the **L**, "for the wicked Is 48:22
The **L** called me before I was Is 49:1
my vindication is with the **L**, Is 49:4
now, says the **L**, who formed me Is 49:5
honored in the sight of the **L**, Is 49:5
This is what the **L**, the Redeemer Is 49:7
because of the **L**, who is Is 49:7
This is what the **L** says: Is 49:8
For the **L** has comforted His Is 49:13
Zion says, "The **L** has abandoned Is 49:14
you will know that I am the **L**; Is 49:23
For this is what the **L** says: Is 49:25
that I, the **L**, am your Savior Is 49:26
This is what the **L** says: Is 50:1
Who among you fears the **L**, Is 50:10
him trust in the name of the **L**; Is 50:10
you who seek the **L**: Is 51:1
For the **L** will comfort Zion; Is 51:3
desert like the garden of the **L**. Is 51:3
ransomed of the **L** will return Is 51:11
But you have forgotten the **L**, Is 51:13
I am the **L** your God who stirs Is 51:15
His fury from the hand of the **L**; Is 51:17
For this is what the **L** says: Is 52:3
see when the **L** returns to Zion. Is 52:8
For the **L** has comforted His Is 52:9
The **L** has displayed His holy arm Is 52:10
who carry the vessels of the **L**. Is 52:11
because the **L** is going before Is 52:12
the arm of the **L** been revealed Is 53:1
and the **L** has punished Him for Is 53:6
Yet the **L** was pleased to crush Is 53:10
the will of the **L** will succeed Is 53:10
the married woman," says the **L**. Is 54:1
For the **L** has called you, like a Is 54:6
says the **L** your Redeemer. Is 54:8
says your compassionate **L**. Is 54:10
will be taught by the **L**, Is 54:13
the **L** your God, even the Holy Is 55:5
the **L** while He may be found; Is 55:6
return to the **L**, so He may have Is 55:7
a name for the **L** as an Is 55:13
This is what the **L** says: Is 56:1
converted to the **L** should say, Is 56:3
The **L** will exclude me from His Is 56:3

For the **L** says this: "For the	Is 56:4
foreigners who convert to the **L**,	Is 56:6
The **L** says, "Peace, peace to	Is 57:19
and a day acceptable to the **L**?	Is 58:5
you call, the **L** will answer;	Is 58:9
The **L** will always lead you,	Is 58:11
holy ⌊day⌋ of the **L** honorable;	Is 58:13
will delight yourself in the **L**,	Is 58:14
the mouth of the **L** has spoken.	Is 58:14
and deception against the **L**,	Is 59:13
The **L** saw that there was no	Is 59:15
the name of the **L** in the west,	Is 59:19
driven by the wind of the **L**.	Is 59:19
covenant with them," says the **L**:	Is 59:21
now on and forever," says the **L**.	Is 59:21
glory of the **L** shines over you	Is 60:1
but the **L** will shine over you,	Is 60:2
proclaim the praises of the **L**.	Is 60:6
for the honor of the **L** your God,	Is 60:9
will call you the City of the **L**,	Is 60:14
that I, the **L**, am your Savior	Is 60:16
but the **L** will be your	Is 60:19
for the **L** will be your	Is 60:20
nation. I am the **L**; I will	Is 60:22
because the **L** has anointed Me to	Is 61:1
by the **L**, to glorify Him.	Is 61:3
For I the **L** love justice;	Is 61:8
are a people the **L** has blessed.	Is 61:9
I greatly rejoice in the **L**,	Is 61:10
for the **L** delights in you,	Is 62:4
who remind the **L**, no rest for	Is 62:6
The **L** has sworn with His right	Is 62:8
will eat it and praise the **L**,	Is 62:9
the **L** has proclaimed to the end	Is 62:11
of all the **L** has done for us—	Is 63:7
Spirit of the **L** gave them rest.	Is 63:14
You, **L**, are our Father;	Is 63:16
Why, **L**, do You make us stray	Is 63:17
Yet **L**, You are our Father;	Is 64:8
L, do not be terribly angry or	Is 64:9
L, after all this, will You	Is 64:12
fathers together," says the **L**.	Is 65:7
The **L** says this: As the new wine	Is 65:8
But you who abandon the **L**,	Is 65:11
blessed by the **L** along with	Is 65:23
holy mountain," says the **L**.	Is 65:25
This is what the **L** says:	Is 66:1
word, hear the word of the **L**:	Is 66:5
Let the **L** be glorified, so that	Is 66:5
voice of the **L**, paying back His	Is 66:6
it⌋?" says the **L**; "or will I who	Is 66:9
For this is what the **L** says:	Is 66:12
the **L** will come with fire—	Is 66:15
For the **L** will execute judgment	Is 66:16
and many will be slain by the **L**.	Is 66:16
as a gift to the **L** on horses and	Is 66:20
Jerusalem, says the **L**, just as	Is 66:20
vessel to the house of the **L**.	Is 66:20
and Levites," says the **L**.	Is 66:21
Sabbath to another," says the **L**.	Is 66:23
The word of the **L** came to him in	Jr 1:2
The word of the **L** came to me:	Jr 1:4
Then the **L** said to me: Do not	Jr 1:7
Then the **L** reached out His hand,	Jr 1:9
the word of the **L** came to me,	Jr 1:11
The **L** said to me, "You have seen	Jr 1:12
the word of the **L** came to me	Jr 1:13
Then the **L** said to me, "Disaster	Jr 1:14
The word of the **L** came to me:	Jr 2:1
that this is what the **L** says:	Jr 2:2
was holy to the **L**, the	Jr 2:3
word of the **L**, house of Jacob	Jr 2:4
Here is what the **L** says:	Jr 2:5
Where is the **L** who brought us	Jr 2:6
Where is the **L**? The experts	Jr 2:8
abandoning the **L** your God while	Jr 2:17
to abandon the **L** your God and to	Jr 2:19
attention to the word of the **L**!	Jr 2:31
head since the **L** has rejected	Jr 2:37
of King Josiah the **L** asked me,	Jr 3:6
The **L** announced to me,	Jr 3:11
rebelled against the **L** your God.	Jr 3:13
the name of the **L** in Jerusalem.	Jr 3:17
have forgotten the **L** their God.	Jr 3:21
for You are the **L** our God.	Jr 3:22
Israel is only in the **L** our God.	Jr 3:23
sinned against the **L** our God,	Jr 3:25
the voice of the **L** our God."	Jr 3:25

swear, As the **L** lives, in truth	Jr 4:2
is what the **L** says to the men	Jr 4:3
Circumcise yourselves to the **L**;	Jr 4:4
because of the **L** and His burning	Jr 4:26
For this is what the **L** says:	Jr 4:27
say, "As the **L** lives," they are	Jr 5:2
L, don't Your eyes ⌊look for⌋	Jr 5:3
understand the way of the **L**,	Jr 5:4
they know the way of the **L**,	Jr 5:5
for they do not belong to the **L**.	Jr 5:10
contradicted the **L** and insisted,	Jr 5:12
offense has the **L** our God done	Jr 5:19
Let's fear the **L** our God, who	Jr 5:24
is what the **L** of Hosts says:	Jr 6:6
is what the **L** of Hosts says:	Jr 6:9
the word of the **L** has become	Jr 6:10
they will collapse, says the **L**.	Jr 6:15
This is what the **L** says:	Jr 6:16
this is what the **L** says:	Jr 6:21
This is what the **L** says:	Jr 6:22
for the **L** has rejected them.	Jr 6:30
came to Jeremiah from the **L**:	Jr 7:1
house of the **L** and there call	Jr 7:2
the word of the **L**, all ⌊you	Jr 7:2
these gates to worship the **L**.	Jr 7:2
This is what the **L** of Hosts,	Jr 7:3
This is the temple of the **L**,	Jr 7:4
the temple of the **L**, the temple	Jr 7:4
the LORD, the temple of the **L**.	Jr 7:4
This is what the **L** of Hosts,	Jr 7:21
the voice of the **L** their God and	Jr 7:28
for the **L** has rejected and	Jr 7:29
declaration of the **L** of Hosts.	Jr 8:3
This is what the **L** says:	Jr 8:4
know the requirements of the **L**.	Jr 8:7
the law of the **L** is with us?	Jr 8:8
have rejected the word of the **L**,	Jr 8:9
they will collapse, says the **L**.	Jr 8:12
for the **L** our God has condemned	Jr 8:14
we have sinned against the **L**.	Jr 8:14
Is the **L** no longer in Zion,	Jr 8:19
is what the **L** of Hosts says:	Jr 9:7
Who has the **L** spoken to, that he	Jr 9:12
The **L** said, "It is because they	Jr 9:13
this is what the **L** of Hosts,	Jr 9:15
is what the **L** of Hosts says:	Jr 9:17
Now hear the word of the **L**,	Jr 9:20
This is what the **L** says:	Jr 9:22
This is what the **L** says:	Jr 9:23
that I am the **L**, showing	Jr 9:24
word that the **L** has spoken to	Jr 10:1
This is what the **L** says:	Jr 10:2
L, there is no one like You.	Jr 10:6
But the **L** is the true God;	Jr 10:10
the **L** of Hosts is His name.	Jr 10:16
For this is what the **L** says:	Jr 10:18
don't seek the **L**. Therefore they	Jr 10:21
I know, **L**, that a man's way of	Jr 10:23
Discipline me, **L**, but with	Jr 10:24
came to Jeremiah from the **L**:	Jr 11:1
This is what the **L**, the God of	Jr 11:3
I answered, "Amen, **L**."	Jr 11:5
The **L** said to me, "Proclaim all	Jr 11:6
The **L** said to me, "A conspiracy	Jr 11:9
this is what the **L** says:	Jr 11:11
The **L** named you a flourishing	Jr 11:16
The **L** of Hosts who planted you	Jr 11:17
The **L** informed me, so I knew.	Jr 11:18
But, **L** of Hosts, who judges	Jr 11:20
is what the **L** says concerning	Jr 11:21
prophesy in the name of the **L**,	Jr 11:21
is what the **L** of Hosts says:	Jr 11:22
be righteous, **L**, even if I bring	Jr 12:1
As for You, You know me, **L**;	Jr 12:3
for the **L** has a sword that	Jr 12:12
This is what the **L** says:	Jr 12:14
name, 'As the **L** lives,' just as	Jr 12:16
This is what the **L** said to me:	Jr 13:1
underwear as the **L** instructed me	Jr 13:2
the word of the **L** came to me a	Jr 13:3
as the **L** commanded me.	Jr 13:5
time later the **L** said to me,	Jr 13:6
the word of the **L** came to me:	Jr 13:8
This is what the **L** says:	Jr 13:9
This is what the **L**, the God of	Jr 13:12
them, This is what the **L** says:	Jr 13:13
be proud, for the **L** has spoken.	Jr 13:15
glory to the **L** your God before	Jr 13:16

The word of the **L** that came to	Jr 14:1
against us, **L**, act for Your	Jr 14:7
You are among us, **L**, and we are	Jr 14:9
is what the **L** says concerning	Jr 14:10
So the **L** does not accept them.	Jr 14:10
Then the **L** said to me, "Do not	Jr 14:11
But the **L** said to me, "These	Jr 14:14
is what the **L** says concerning	Jr 14:15
our wickedness, **L**, the guilt of	Jr 14:20
Are You not the **L** our God?	Jr 14:22
Then the **L** said to me:	Jr 15:1
This is what the **L** says:	Jr 15:2
L said: Assuredly, I will set	Jr 15:11
know, **L**; remember me and take	Jr 15:15
by Your name, **L** God of Hosts.	Jr 15:16
this is what the **L** says:	Jr 15:19
The word of the **L** came to me:	Jr 16:1
is what the **L** says concerning	Jr 16:3
For this is what the **L** says:	Jr 16:5
For this is what the **L** of Hosts,	Jr 16:9
Why has the **L** declared all this	Jr 16:10
committed against the **L** our God?	Jr 16:10
As the **L** lives who brought the	Jr 16:14
As the **L** lives who brought the	Jr 16:15
L, my strength and my stronghold,	Jr 16:19
This is what the **L** says:	Jr 17:5
and turns his heart from the **L**.	Jr 17:5
is the man who trusts in the **L**,	Jr 17:7
confidence indeed is the **L**.	Jr 17:7
I, the **L**, examine the mind, I	Jr 17:10
L, the hope of Israel, all who	Jr 17:13
fountain of living water, the **L**.	Jr 17:13
me, **L**, and I will be healed;	Jr 17:14
Where is the word of the **L**?	Jr 17:15
This is what the **L** said to me,	Jr 17:19
word of the **L**, kings of Judah	Jr 17:20
This is what the **L** says:	Jr 17:21
to Me, says the **L**, and do not	Jr 17:24
offerings to the house of the **L**.	Jr 17:26
came to Jeremiah from the **L**:	Jr 18:1
The word of the **L** came to me:	Jr 18:5
This is what the **L** says:	Jr 18:11
this is what the **L** says:	Jr 18:13
Pay attention to me, **L**.	Jr 18:19
You, **L**, know all their deadly	Jr 18:23
This is what the **L** says:	Jr 19:1
word of the **L**, kings of Judah	Jr 19:3
This is what the **L** of Hosts,	Jr 19:3
is what the **L** of Hosts says:	Jr 19:11
is⌋ the declaration of the **L**—	Jr 19:12
where the **L** had sent him to	Jr 19:14
This is what the **L** of Hosts,	Jr 19:15
officer in the house of the **L**,	Jr 20:1
The **L** does not call you Pashhur,	Jr 20:3
for this is what the **L** says,	Jr 20:4
You deceived me, **L**, and I was	Jr 20:7
the word of the **L** has become for	Jr 20:8
But the **L** is with me like a	Jr 20:11
L of Hosts, testing the	Jr 20:12
Sing to the **L**! Praise the LORD,	Jr 20:13
Praise the **L**, for He rescues the	Jr 20:13
the cities the **L** overthrew	Jr 20:16
Jeremiah from the **L** when King	Jr 21:1
Ask the **L** on our behalf, since	Jr 21:2
Perhaps the **L** will perform for	Jr 21:2
'This is what the **L**, the God of	Jr 21:4
'This is what the **L** says:	Jr 21:8
'Hear the word of the **L**!	Jr 21:11
David, this is what the **L** says:	Jr 21:12
This is what the **L** says:	Jr 22:1
word of the **L**, king of Judah,	Jr 22:2
This is what the **L** says:	Jr 22:3
is what the **L** says concerning	Jr 22:6
Why did the **L** do such a thing to	Jr 22:8
the covenant of the **L** their God	Jr 22:9
is what the **L** says concerning	Jr 22:11
is what the **L** says concerning	Jr 22:18
live," says the **L**, "though you,	Jr 22:24
earth, hear the word of the **L**!	Jr 22:29
This is what the **L** says:	Jr 22:30
this is what the **L**, the God of	Jr 23:2
The **L** Is Our Righteousness.	Jr 23:6
As the **L** lives who brought the	Jr 23:7
As the **L** lives, who brought and	Jr 23:8
because of the **L**, because of His	Jr 23:9
this is what the **L** of Hosts says	Jr 23:15
is what the **L** of Hosts says:	Jr 23:16
despise Me: The **L** has said: You	Jr 23:17

council of the **L** to see and hear Jr 23:18
Look, a storm from the **L**! Jr 23:19
What is the burden of the **L**? Jr 23:33
burden of the **L**, I will punish Jr 23:34
What has the **L** answered? Jr 23:35
or What has the **L** spoken? Jr 23:35
refer to the burden of the **L**, Jr 23:36
living God, the **L** of Hosts, our Jr 23:36
What has the **L** answered you? Jr 23:37
and What has the **L** spoken? Jr 23:37
The burden of the **L**, then this Jr 23:38
then this is what the **L** says: Jr 23:38
The burden of the **L**, and I Jr 23:38
not to say, The burden of the **L**, Jr 23:38
the **L** showed me two baskets of Jr 24:1
before the temple of the **L**. Jr 24:1
The **L** said to me, "What do you Jr 24:3
The word of the **L** came to me: Jr 24:4
This is what the **L**, the God of Jr 24:5
to know Me, that I am the **L**. Jr 24:7
this is what the **L** says: Jr 24:8
word of the **L** has come to me, Jr 25:3
The **L** sent all His servants the Jr 25:4
the land the **L** gave to you and Jr 25:5
is what the **L** of Hosts says: Jr 25:8
This is what the **L**, the God of Jr 25:15
everyone the **L** sent me to. Jr 25:17
This is what the **L** of Hosts, Jr 25:27
is what the **L** of Hosts says: Jr 25:28
declaration of the **L** of Hosts. Jr 25:29
The **L** roars from on high; Jr 25:30
earth because the **L** brings a Jr 25:31
is what the **L** of Hosts says: Jr 25:32
slain by the **L** on that day will Jr 25:33
for the **L** is destroying their Jr 25:36
this word came from the **L**: Jr 26:1
This is what the **L** says: Jr 26:2
This is what the **L** says: Jr 26:4
words in the temple of the **L**. Jr 26:7
the address the **L** had commanded Jr 26:8
prophesy in the name of the **L**, Jr 26:9
The **L** sent me to prophesy all Jr 26:12
voice of the **L** your God so that Jr 26:13
is certain the **L** has sent me to Jr 26:15
in the name of the **L** our God!" Jr 26:16
is what the **L** of Hosts says: Jr 26:18
he not fear the **L** and plead for Jr 26:19
and did not the **L** relent Jr 26:19
in the name of the **L**— Jr 26:20
came to Jeremiah from the **L**: Jr 27:1
This is what the **L** said to me: Jr 27:2
This is what the **L** of Hosts, Jr 27:4
plague as the **L** has threatened Jr 27:13
This is what the **L** says, Jr 27:16
the word of the **L** is with them, Jr 27:18
with the **L** of Hosts not to Jr 27:18
this is what the **L** of Hosts says Jr 27:19
this is what the **L** of Hosts, Jr 27:21
remain in the temple of the **L**, Jr 27:21
temple of the **L** in the presence Jr 28:1
This is what the **L** of Hosts, Jr 28:2
standing in the temple of the **L**. Jr 28:5
Amen! May the **L** do so. May the Jr 28:6
the **L** make the words you have Jr 28:6
one whom the **L** has truly sent. Jr 28:9
This is what the **L** says: Jr 28:11
The word of the **L** came to Jr 28:12
This is what the **L** says: Jr 28:13
For this is what the **L** of Hosts, Jr 28:14
The **L** did not send you, but you Jr 28:15
this is what the **L** says: Jr 28:16
rebellion against the **L**.'" Jr 28:16
This is what the **L** of Hosts, Jr 29:4
Pray to the **L** on its behalf, Jr 29:7
For this is what the **L** of Hosts, Jr 29:8
For this is what the **L** says: Jr 29:10
The **L** has raised up prophets for Jr 29:15
is what the **L** says concerning Jr 29:16
is what the **L** of Hosts says: Jr 29:17
word of the **L**, all you exiles Jr 29:20
This is what the **L** of Hosts, Jr 29:21
May the **L** make you like Zedekiah Jr 29:22
This is what the **L** of Hosts, Jr 29:25
The **L** has appointed you priest Jr 29:26
officer in the temple of the **L**, Jr 29:26
the word of the **L** came to Jr 29:30
is what the **L** says concerning Jr 29:31
this is what the **L** says: Jr 29:32

rebellion against the **L**." Jr 29:32
came to Jeremiah from the **L**. Jr 30:1
This is what the **L**, the God of Jr 30:2
the words the **L** spoke to Israel Jr 30:4
Yes, this is what the **L** says: Jr 30:5
declaration of the **L** of Hosts— Jr 30:8
will serve the **L** their God and I Jr 30:9
For this is what the **L** says: Jr 30:12
This is what the **L** says: Jr 30:18
Look, a storm from the **L**! Jr 30:23
This is what the **L** says: Jr 31:2
the **L** appeared to him from far Jr 31:3
go up to Zion, to the **L** our God! Jr 31:6
For this is what the **L** says: Jr 31:7
L, save Your people, the remnant Jr 31:7
the word of the **L**, and tell it Jr 31:10
for the **L** has ransomed Jacob and Jr 31:11
This is what the **L** says: Jr 31:15
This is what the **L** says: Jr 31:16
return, for you, **L**, are my God. Jr 31:18
For the **L** creates something new Jr 31:22
This is what the **L** of Hosts, Jr 31:23
May the **L** bless you, righteous Jr 31:23
and to plant them," says the **L**. Jr 31:28
Know the **L**, for they will all Jr 31:34
This is what the **L** says: Jr 31:35
the **L** of Hosts is His name: Jr 31:35
This is what the **L** says: Jr 31:37
Gate will be rebuilt for the **L**. Jr 31:38
east—will be holy to the **L**. Jr 31:40
from the **L** in the tenth year Jr 32:1
This is what the **L** says: Jr 32:3
The word of the **L** came to me: Jr 32:6
courtyard as the **L** had said and Jr 32:8
that this was the word of the **L**. Jr 32:8
'This is what the **L** of Hosts, Jr 32:14
For this is what the **L** of Hosts, Jr 32:15
of Neriah, I prayed to the **L**: Jr 32:16
whose name is the **L** of Hosts, Jr 32:18
the word of the **L** came to Jr 32:26
Look, I am the **L**, the God of all Jr 32:27
this is what the **L** says: Jr 32:28
this is what the **L**, the God of Jr 32:36
For this is what the **L** says: Jr 32:42
the word of the **L** came to Jr 33:1
The **L** who made the earth, Jr 33:2
the **L** who forms it to establish Jr 33:2
it, the **L** is His name, says Jr 33:2
this is what the **L**, the God of Jr 33:4
This is what the **L** says: Jr 33:10
Praise the **L** of Hosts, for Jr 33:11
of Hosts, for the **L** is good; Jr 33:11
to the temple of the **L**. Jr 33:11
as in former times, says the **L**. Jr 33:11
is what the **L** of Hosts says: Jr 33:12
and Judah's cities, says the **L**. Jr 33:13
The **L** Is Our Righteousness. Jr 33:16
For this is what the **L** says: Jr 33:17
The word of the **L** came to Jr 33:19
This is what the **L** says: Jr 33:20
The word of the **L** came to Jr 33:23
The **L** has rejected the two Jr 33:24
This is what the **L** says: Jr 33:25
Jeremiah from the **L** when Jr 34:1
This is what the **L**, the God of Jr 34:2
This is what the **L** says: Jr 34:2
is what the **L** says concerning Jr 34:4
Jeremiah from the **L** after King Jr 34:8
the word of the **L** came to Jr 34:12
came to Jeremiah from the **L**: Jr 34:12
This is what the **L**, the God of Jr 34:13
this is what the **L** says: Jr 34:17
Jeremiah from the **L** in the days Jr 35:1
temple of the **L** to offer them Jr 35:2
the temple of the **L** to a chamber Jr 35:4
the word of the **L** came to Jr 35:12
This is what the **L** of Hosts, Jr 35:13
this is what the **L**, the God of Jr 35:17
This is what the **L** of Hosts, Jr 35:18
this is what the **L** of Hosts, Jr 35:19
came to Jeremiah from the **L**: Jr 36:1
all the words the **L** had spoken Jr 36:4
enter the temple of the **L**, Jr 36:5
words of the **L** in the hearing Jr 36:6
the temple of the **L** on a day of Jr 36:6
petition will come before the **L**, Jr 36:7
fury that the **L** has pronounced Jr 36:7
proclaimed a fast before the **L**. Jr 36:9

words of the **L** from the scroll Jr 36:11
but the **L** had hidden them. Jr 36:26
the word of the **L** came to Jr 36:27
This is what the **L** says: Jr 36:29
is what the **L** says concerning Jr 36:30
the words of the **L** that He spoke Jr 37:2
pray to the **L** our God for us!" Jr 37:3
The word of the **L** came to Jr 37:6
This is what the **L**, the God of Jr 37:7
This is what the **L** says: Jr 37:9
"Is there a word from the **L**?" Jr 37:17
This is what the **L** says: Jr 38:2
This is what the **L** says: Jr 38:3
private, "As the **L** lives, who Jr 38:16
This is what the **L**, the God of Jr 38:17
the voice of the **L** in what I am Jr 38:20
verdict that the **L** has shown me: Jr 38:21
Now the word of the **L** had come Jr 39:15
This is what the **L** of Hosts, Jr 39:16
from the **L** after Nebuzaradan Jr 40:1
The **L** your God decreed this Jr 40:2
and the **L** has fulfilled ⌊it⌋. Jr 40:3
sinned against the **L** and have Jr 40:3
to bring to the temple of the **L**. Jr 41:5
pray to the **L** your God on our Jr 42:2
that the **L** your God may tell us Jr 42:3
now pray to the **L** your God Jr 42:4
word that the **L** answers you I Jr 42:4
every word the **L** your God sends Jr 42:5
may the **L** be a true and faithful Jr 42:5
voice of the **L** our God to whom Jr 42:6
the voice of the **L** our God!" Jr 42:6
the word of the **L** came to Jr 42:7
This is what the **L** says, the God Jr 42:9
the voice of the **L** your God, Jr 42:13
then hear the word of the **L**, Jr 42:15
This is what the **L** of Hosts, Jr 42:15
For this is what the **L** of Hosts, Jr 42:18
The **L** has spoken concerning you, Jr 42:19
who sent me to the **L** your God, Jr 42:20
'Pray to the **L** our God on our Jr 42:20
for all that the **L** our God says, Jr 42:20
the voice of the **L** your God in Jr 42:21
the words of the **L** their God— Jr 43:1
these words the **L** their God had Jr 43:1
The **L** our God has not sent you Jr 43:2
voice of the **L** to stay in the Jr 43:4
did not obey the voice of the **L**. Jr 43:7
the word of the **L** came to Jr 43:8
This is what the **L** of Hosts, Jr 43:10
This is what the **L** of Hosts, Jr 44:2
this is what the **L**, the God of Jr 44:7
this is what the **L** of Hosts, Jr 44:11
to us in the name of the **L**, Jr 44:16
did the **L** not remember them? Jr 44:21
The **L** can no longer bear your Jr 44:22
against the **L** and didn't obey Jr 44:23
the word of the **L**, all Judah who Jr 44:24
This is what the **L** of Hosts, Jr 44:25
the word of the **L**, all you Jr 44:26
name, says the **L**, that My name Jr 44:26
This is what the **L** says: Jr 44:30
This is what the **L**, the God of Jr 45:2
because the **L** has added misery Jr 45:3
This is what the **L** says: Jr 45:4
The word of the **L** that came to Jr 46:1
is⌋ the word the **L** spoke to Jr 46:13
for the **L** has thrust him down. Jr 46:15
the **L** of Hosts is His name. Jr 46:18
The **L** of Hosts, the God of Jr 46:25
the word of the **L** that came to Jr 47:1
This is what the **L** says: Jr 47:2
the **L** is about to destroy the Jr 47:4
Ah, sword of the **L**! How long Jr 47:6
it rest when the **L** has given it Jr 47:7
this is what the **L** of Hosts, Jr 48:1
annihilated, as the **L** has said. Jr 48:8
the **L** of Hosts is His name. Jr 48:15
exalted himself against the **L**. Jr 48:26
For this is what the **L** says: Jr 48:40
exalted himself against the **L**. Jr 48:42
this is what the **L** says: Jr 49:1
their dispossessors, says the **L**. Jr 49:2
is what the **L** of Hosts says: Jr 49:7
For this is what the **L** says: Jr 49:12
have heard a message from the **L**; Jr 49:14
says the **L**, "no one will live Jr 49:18
the plans that the **L** has drawn Jr 49:20

declaration of the **L** of Hosts. Jr 49:26
this is what the **L** says: Jr 49:28
the word of the **L** that came to Jr 49:34
is what the **L** of Hosts says: Jr 49:35
The word the **L** spoke about Jr 50:1
and will seek the **L** their God. Jr 50:4
to the **L** in an everlasting Jr 50:5
they have sinned against the **L**, Jr 50:7
hope of their ancestors, the **L**. Jr 50:7
she has sinned against the **L**. Jr 50:14
this is what the **L** of Hosts, Jr 50:18
you fought against the **L**. Jr 50:24
The **L** opened His armory and Jr 50:25
the vengeance of the **L** our God, Jr 50:28
acted arrogantly against the **L**, Jr 50:29
is what the **L** of Hosts says: Jr 50:33
the **L** of Hosts is His name. Jr 50:34
the plans that the **L** has drawn Jr 50:45
This is what the **L** says: Jr 51:1
their God, the **L** of Hosts, Jr 51:5
The **L** has brought about our Jr 51:10
in Zion what the **L** our God has Jr 51:10
The **L** has put it into the mind Jr 51:11
For the **L** has both planned and Jr 51:12
The **L** of Hosts has sworn by Jr 51:14
the **L** of Hosts is His name. Jr 51:19
For this is what the **L** of Hosts, Jr 51:33
this is what the **L** says: Jr 51:36
Remember the **L** from far away, Jr 51:50
For the **L** is going to devastate Jr 51:55
for the **L** is a God of Jr 51:56
the **L** of Hosts is His name. Jr 51:57
is what the **L** of Hosts says: Jr 51:58
You must say, '**L**, You have Jr 51:62
for the **L** has made her suffer Lm 1:5
L, look on my affliction, for Lm 1:9
L, look and see how I have Lm 1:11
which the **L** made ⌊me⌋ suffer on Lm 1:12
L has issued a decree against Lm 1:17
L is in the right, for I have Lm 1:18
L, see how I am in distress. Lm 1:20
The **L** has abolished appointed Lm 2:6
the house of the **L** as on the day Lm 2:7
The **L** determined to destroy the Lm 2:8
receive no vision from the **L**. Lm 2:9
The **L** has done what He planned; Lm 2:17
L, look and consider who You Lm 2:20
as well as my hope from the **L**. Lm 3:18
The **L** is my portion, therefore I Lm 3:24
The **L** is good to those who wait Lm 3:25
for deliverance from the **L**. Lm 3:26
ways, and turn back to the **L**. Lm 3:40
until the **L** looks down from Lm 3:50
L, You see the wrong done to me; Lm 3:59
L, You hear their insults, all Lm 3:61
they deserve, **L**, according to Lm 3:64
The **L** has exhausted His wrath, Lm 4:11
L Himself has scattered them; Lm 4:16
You, **L**, are enthroned forever; Lm 5:19
L, restore us to Yourself, so we Lm 5:21
the word of the **L** came directly Ezk 1:3
the glory of the **L** in His place! Ezk 3:12
the word of the **L** came to me: Ezk 3:16
hand of the **L** was on me there Ezk 3:22
The **L** said, "This is how the Ezk 4:13
know that I, the **L**, have spoken Ezk 5:13
rebukes. I, the **L**, have spoken. Ezk 5:15
I, the **L**, have spoken." Ezk 5:17
The word of the **L** came to me: Ezk 6:1
you will know that I am the **L**. Ezk 6:7
they will know that I am the **L**; Ezk 6:10
that I am the **L** when their slain Ezk 6:13
the word of the **L** came to me: Ezk 7:1
you will know that I am the **L**." Ezk 7:4
it is I, the **L**, who strikes. Ezk 7:9
they will know that I am the **L**. Ezk 7:27
The **L** said to me, "Son of man, Ezk 8:5
saying: The **L** does not see us Ezk 8:12
The **L** has abandoned the land." Ezk 8:12
Jerusalem," the **L** said to him, Ezk 9:4
The **L** has abandoned the land; Ezk 9:9
The **L** spoke to the man clothed Ezk 10:2
glory of the **L** rose from above Ezk 10:4
After the **L** commanded the man Ezk 10:6
the glory of the **L** moved away Ezk 10:18
The **L** said to me, "Son of man, Ezk 11:2
the Spirit of the **L** came on me, Ezk 11:5
This is what the **L** says: Ezk 11:5
you will know that I am the **L**. Ezk 11:10
you will know that I am the **L**, Ezk 11:12
The word of the **L** came to me Ezk 11:14
away from the **L**; this land has Ezk 11:15
The glory of the **L** rose up from Ezk 11:23
the things the **L** had shown me. Ezk 11:25
The word of the **L** came to me: Ezk 12:1
Then the word of the **L** came to Ezk 12:8
that I am the **L** when I disperse Ezk 12:15
they will know that I am the **L**." Ezk 12:16
The word of the **L** came to me: Ezk 12:17
you will know that I am the **L**." Ezk 12:20
the word of the **L** came to me: Ezk 12:21
I, the **L**, will speak whatever Ezk 12:25
The word of the **L** came to me: Ezk 12:26
The word of the **L** came to me: Ezk 13:1
Hear the word of the **L**! Ezk 13:2
in battle on the day of the **L**. Ezk 13:5
when the **L** did not send them, Ezk 13:6
you will know that I am the **L**. Ezk 13:14
you will know that I am the **L**. Ezk 13:21
you will know that I am the **L**." Ezk 13:23
the word of the **L** came to me: Ezk 14:2
prophet, I, the **L**, will answer Ezk 14:4
of Me, I, the **L**, will answer him Ezk 14:7
you will know that I am the **L**. Ezk 14:8
it was I, the **L**, who deceived Ezk 14:9
The word of the **L** came to me: Ezk 14:12
the word of the **L** came to me: Ezk 15:1
know that I am the **L** when I turn Ezk 15:7
The word of the **L** came to me Ezk 16:1
hear the word of the **L**! Ezk 16:35
you will know that I am the **L**, Ezk 16:62
The word of the **L** came to me: Ezk 17:1
The word of the **L** came to me: Ezk 17:11
field will know that I am the **L**. Ezk 17:24
The word of the **L** came to me: Ezk 18:1
elders came to consult the **L**, Ezk 20:1
the word of the **L** came to me: Ezk 20:2
saying: I am the **L** your God. Ezk 20:5
of Egypt. I am the **L** your God. Ezk 20:7
that I am the **L** who sets them Ezk 20:12
I am the **L** your God. Follow My Ezk 20:19
know that I am the **L** your God. Ezk 20:20
they would know that I am the **L**. Ezk 20:26
you will know that I am the **L**. Ezk 20:38
you will know that I am the **L**. Ezk 20:42
You will know that I am the **L**, Ezk 20:44
The word of the **L** came to me: Ezk 20:45
Hear the word of the **L**! Ezk 20:47
The word of the **L** came to me Ezk 21:1
This is what the **L** says: Ezk 21:3
know that I, the **L**, have taken Ezk 21:5
The word of the **L** came to me: Ezk 21:8
I, the **L**, have spoken." Ezk 21:17
the word of the **L** came to me: Ezk 21:18
for I, the **L**, have spoken." Ezk 21:32
The word of the **L** came to me: Ezk 22:1
I, the **L**, have spoken, and I Ezk 22:14
you will know that I am the **L**." Ezk 22:16
The word of the **L** came to me: Ezk 22:17
that I, the **L**, have poured out Ezk 22:22
The word of the **L** came to me: Ezk 22:23
when the **L** has not spoken. Ezk 22:28
The word of the **L** came to me Ezk 23:1
Then the **L** said to me: Ezk 23:36
The word of the **L** came to me in Ezk 24:1
I, the **L**, have spoken. It is Ezk 24:14
the word of the **L** came to me: Ezk 24:15
The word of the **L** came to me: Ezk 24:20
will know that I am the **L**.' " Ezk 24:27
the word of the **L** came to me: Ezk 25:1
you will know that I am the **L**." Ezk 25:5
you will know that I am the **L**." Ezk 25:7
they will know that I am the **L**." Ezk 25:11
that I am the **L** when I take My Ezk 25:17
the word of the **L** came to me: Ezk 26:1
they will know that I am the **L**." Ezk 26:6
for I, the **L**, have spoken." Ezk 26:14
The word of the **L** came to me: Ezk 27:1
The word of the **L** came to me: Ezk 28:1
The word of the **L** came to me: Ezk 28:11
The word of the **L** came to me: Ezk 28:20
that I am the **L** when I execute Ezk 28:22
they will know that I am the **L**. Ezk 28:23
know that I am the **L** their God." Ezk 28:26
the word of the **L** came to me: Ezk 29:1
Egypt will know that I am the **L**, Ezk 29:6
they will know that I am the **L**. Ezk 29:9
the word of the **L** came to me: Ezk 29:17
they will know that I am the **L**." Ezk 29:21
The word of the **L** came to me: Ezk 30:1
day belonging to the **L** is near. Ezk 30:3
This is what the **L** says: Ezk 30:6
that I am the **L** when I set fire Ezk 30:8
I, the **L**, have spoken. Ezk 30:12
they will know that I am the **L**. Ezk 30:19
the word of the **L** came to me: Ezk 30:20
that I am the **L** when I place My Ezk 30:25
they will know that I am the **L**." Ezk 30:26
the word of the **L** came to me: Ezk 31:1
the word of the **L** came to me: Ezk 32:1
they will know that I am the **L**. Ezk 32:15
the word of the **L** came to me: Ezk 32:17
The word of the **L** came to me: Ezk 33:1
the hand of the **L** had been on me Ezk 33:22
the word of the **L** came to me: Ezk 33:23
know that I am the **L** when I make Ezk 33:29
is that comes from the **L**! Ezk 33:30
The word of the **L** came to me: Ezk 34:1
hear the word of the **L**. Ezk 34:7
hear the word of the **L**! Ezk 34:9
I, the **L**, will be their God, and Ezk 34:24
them. I, the **L**, have spoken. Ezk 34:24
that I am the **L** when I break Ezk 34:27
know that I, the **L** their God, am Ezk 34:30
The word of the **L** came to me: Ezk 35:1
you will know that I am the **L**. Ezk 35:4
you will know that I am the **L**. Ezk 35:9
them—though the **L** was there— Ezk 35:10
that I, the **L**, have heard all Ezk 35:12
they will know that I am the **L**. Ezk 35:15
Israel, hear the word of the **L**. Ezk 36:1
you will know that I am the **L**. Ezk 36:11
The word of the **L** came to me: Ezk 36:16
These are the people of the **L**, Ezk 36:20
know that I, the **L**, have rebuilt Ezk 36:36
I, the **L**, have spoken and I will Ezk 36:36
they will know that I am the **L**." Ezk 36:38
The hand of the **L** was on me, Ezk 37:1
bones, hear the word of the **L**! Ezk 37:4
you will know that I am the **L**." Ezk 37:6
You will know that I am the **L**, Ezk 37:13
you will know that I am the **L**. Ezk 37:14
is⌋ the declaration of the **L**. Ezk 37:14
The word of the **L** came to me: Ezk 37:15
that I, the **L**, sanctify Israel Ezk 37:28
The word of the **L** came to me: Ezk 38:1
they will know that I am the **L**. Ezk 38:23
they will know that I am the **L**. Ezk 39:6
will know that I am the **L**, Ezk 39:7
know that I am the **L** their God. Ezk 39:22
that I am the **L** their God when I Ezk 39:28
approach the **L** to serve Him." Ezk 40:46
table that stands before the **L**." Ezk 41:22
who approach the **L** will eat the Ezk 42:13
The glory of the **L** entered the Ezk 43:4
the glory of the **L** filled the Ezk 43:5
must present them before the **L**; Ezk 43:24
as a burnt offering to the **L**. Ezk 43:24
L said to me: "This gate will Ezk 44:2
it, because the **L**, the God of Ezk 44:2
to eat a meal before the **L**. Ezk 44:3
the glory of the **L** filled His Ezk 44:4
The **L** said to me: "Son of man, Ezk 44:5
to the **L**⌋ will belong to Ezk 44:29
set aside a donation to the **L**, Ezk 45:1
who draw near to serve the **L**. Ezk 45:4
offering to the **L** on each of the Ezk 45:23
before the **L** at the entrance Ezk 46:3
presents to the **L** on the Sabbath Ezk 46:4
come before the **L** at the Ezk 46:9
as a freewill offering to the **L**, Ezk 46:12
a daily burnt offering to the **L**; Ezk 46:13
a grain offering to the **L**. Ezk 46:14
portion you donate ⌊to the **L**⌋, Ezk 48:8
donate to the **L** will be eight Ezk 48:9
land, for it is holy to the **L**. Ezk 48:14
to the word of the **L** to Jeremiah Dn 9:2
I prayed to the **L** my God and Dn 9:4
L, public shame belongs to us, Dn 9:8
the voice of the **L** our God by Dn 9:10
not appeased the **L** our God by Dn 9:13
So the **L** kept the disaster in Dn 9:14
for the **L** our God is righteous Dn 9:14
The word of the **L** that came to Hs 1:1

When the **L** first spoke to Hosea,	Hs 1:2
promiscuous by abandoning the **L**.	Hs 1:2
Then the **L** said to him:	Hs 1:4
daughter, and the **L** said to him:	Hs 1:6
deliver them by the **L** their God.	Hs 1:7
Then the **L** said: Name him Not My	Hs 1:9
and you will know the **L**.	Hs 2:20
the **L** said to me, "Go again;	Hs 3:1
just as the **L** loves the	Hs 3:1
and seek the **L** their God and	Hs 3:5
with awe to the **L** and to His	Hs 3:5
the word of the **L**, people of	Hs 4:1
for the **L** has a case against the	Hs 4:1
their devotion to the **L**.	Hs 4:10
swear an oath: As the **L** lives!	Hs 4:15
Can the **L** now shepherd them like	Hs 4:16
and they do not know the **L**.	Hs 5:4
to seek the **L** but do not find	Hs 5:6
betrayed the **L**; indeed, they	Hs 5:7
Come, let us return to the **L**.	Hs 6:1
Let us strive to know the **L**.	Hs 6:3
not return to the **L** their God,	Hs 7:10
against the house of the **L**,	Hs 8:1
the **L** does not accept them.	Hs 8:13
not stay in the land of the **L**.	Hs 9:3
their wine offerings to the **L**,	Hs 9:4
not enter the house of the **L**.	Hs 9:4
Give them, **L**—What should You	Hs 9:14
The **L** will break down their	Hs 10:2
For we do not fear the **L**.	Hs 10:3
to seek the **L** until He comes	Hs 10:12
They will follow the **L**;	Hs 11:10
The **L** also has a dispute with	Hs 12:2
I have been the **L** your God ever	Hs 12:9
The **L** brought Israel from Egypt	Hs 12:13
I have been the **L** your God ever	Hs 13:4
a wind from the **L** rising up from	Hs 13:15
return to the **L** your God, for	Hs 14:1
with you and return to the **L**.	Hs 14:2
For the ways of the **L** are right,	Hs 14:9
The word of the **L** that came to	Jl 1:1
cut off from the house of the **L**;	Jl 1:9
who are ministers of the **L**,	Jl 1:9
at the house of the **L** your God,	Jl 1:14
your God, and cry out to the **L**.	Jl 1:14
Day of the **L** is near and will	Jl 1:15
I call to You, **L**, for fire has	Jl 1:19
for the Day of the **L** is coming;	Jl 2:1
The **L** raises His voice in the	Jl 2:11
the Day of the **L** is terrible and	Jl 2:11
and return to the **L** your God.	Jl 2:13
and wine to the **L** your God.	Jl 2:14
on Your people, **L**, and do not	Jl 2:17
Then the **L** became jealous for	Jl 2:18
The **L** answered His people:	Jl 2:19
for the **L** has done great things.	Jl 2:21
and be glad in the **L** your God,	Jl 2:23
and that I am the **L** your God,	Jl 2:27
awe-inspiring Day of the **L** comes.	Jl 2:31
as the **L** promised, among	Jl 2:32
among the survivors the **L** calls.	Jl 2:32
nation, for the **L** has spoken.	Jl 3:8
down Your warriors there, **L**.	Jl 3:11
For the Day of the **L** is near in	Jl 3:14
The **L** will roar from Zion and	Jl 3:16
But the **L** will be a refuge for	Jl 3:16
know that I am the **L** your God,	Jl 3:17
for the **L** dwells in Zion.	Jl 3:21
The **L** roars from Zion and raises	Am 1:2
The **L** says: I will not relent	Am 1:3
exiled to Kir. The **L** has spoken.	Am 1:5
The **L** says: I will not relent	Am 1:6
The **L** says: I will not relent	Am 1:9
The **L** says: I will not relent	Am 1:11
The **L** says: I will not relent	Am 1:13
together. The **L** has spoken.	Am 1:15
The **L** says: I will not relent	Am 2:1
with him. The **L** has spoken.	Am 2:3
The **L** says: I will not relent	Am 2:4
the law of the **L** and have not	Am 2:4
The **L** says: I will not relent	Am 2:6
message that the **L** has spoken	Am 3:1
in a city, hasn't the **L** done it?	Am 3:6
The **L** says: As the shepherd	Am 3:12
For the **L** says to the house of	Am 5:4
live, and the **L**, the God of	Am 5:14
Perhaps the **L**, the God of Hosts,	Am 5:15
among you. The **L** has spoken.	Am 5:17
who long for the Day of the **L**!	Am 5:18
the Day of the **L** be for you?	Am 5:18
the Day of the **L** be darkness	Am 5:20
For the **L** commands: The large	Am 6:11
The **L** relented concerning this.	Am 7:3
The **L** relented concerning this.	Am 7:6
L asked me, "What do you see,	Am 7:8
But the **L** took me from following	Am 7:15
Now hear the word of the **L**.	Am 7:16
this is what the **L** says:	Am 7:17
The **L** said to me, "The end has	Am 8:2
The **L** has sworn by the Pride of	Am 8:7
of hearing the words of the **L**.	Am 8:11
seeking the word of the **L**,	Am 8:12
I saw the **L** standing beside the	Am 9:1
have heard a message from the **L**;	Ob 1
For the Day of the **L** is near,	Ob 15
of Esau, for the **L** has spoken.	Ob 18
The word of the **L** came to Jonah	Jnh 1:1
Then the **L** hurled a violent wind	Jnh 1:4
So they called out to the **L**:	Jnh 1:14
The men feared the **L** even more,	Jnh 1:16
to the **L** and made vows.	Jnh 1:16
the **L** appointed a great fish	Jnh 1:17
prayed to the **L** his God from	Jnh 2:1
called to the **L** in my distress,	Jnh 2:2
my life from the Pit, **L** my God!	Jnh 2:6
fading away, I remembered the **L**.	Jnh 2:7
Salvation is from the **L**!	Jnh 2:9
Then the **L** commanded the fish,	Jnh 2:10
the word of the **L** came to Jonah	Jnh 3:1
prayed to the **L**: "Please, LORD,	Jnh 4:2
Please, **L**, isn't this what I	Jnh 4:2
And now, **L**, please take my life	Jnh 4:3
L asked, "Is it right for you	Jnh 4:4
the **L** God appointed a plant,	Jnh 4:6
So the **L** said, "You cared about	Jnh 4:10
The word of the **L** that came to	Mc 1:1
the **L** is leaving His place and	Mc 1:3
has come from the **L** to the gate	Mc 1:12
Therefore, the **L** says: I am now	Mc 2:3
assembly of the **L** to divide the	Mc 2:5
the Spirit of the **L** impatient?	Mc 2:7
them, the **L** as their leader	Mc 2:13
Then they will cry out to the **L**,	Mc 3:4
is what the **L** says concerning	Mc 3:5
power by the Spirit of the **L**,	Mc 3:8
lean on the **L**, saying, "Isn't	Mc 3:11
saying, "Isn't the **L** among us?	Mc 3:11
go up to the mountain of the **L**,	Mc 4:2
word of the **L** from Jerusalem.	Mc 4:2
the mouth of the **L** of Hosts has	Mc 4:4
Then the **L** will rule over them	Mc 4:7
there the **L** will redeem you from	Mc 4:10
what they plundered to the **L**,	Mc 4:13
peoples like dew from the **L**,	Mc 5:7
listen to what the **L** is saying:	Mc 6:1
because the **L** has a case against	Mc 6:2
bring before the **L** when I come	Mc 6:6
Would the **L** be pleased with	Mc 6:7
it is the **L** requires of you:	Mc 6:8
The voice of the **L** calls out to	Mc 6:9
as for me, I will look to the **L**;	Mc 7:7
darkness, the **L** will be my light	Mc 7:8
"Where is the **L** your God?"	Mc 7:10
tremble before the **L** our God;	Mc 7:17
The **L** is a jealous and avenging	Nah 1:2
the **L** takes vengeance and is	Nah 1:2
L takes vengeance against His	Nah 1:2
The **L** is slow to anger but great	Nah 1:3
the **L** will never leave the	Nah 1:3
The **L** is good, a stronghold in a	Nah 1:7
Whatever you plot against the **L**,	Nah 1:9
who plots evil against the **L**,	Nah 1:11
This is what the **L** says:	Nah 1:12
The **L** has issued an order	Nah 1:14
For the **L** will restore the	Nah 2:2
long, **L**, must I call for help	Hab 1:2
L, You appointed them to execute	Hab 1:12
The **L** answered me: Write down	Hab 2:2
Is it not from the **L** of Hosts,	Hab 2:13
But the **L** is in His holy temple;	Hab 2:20
L, I have heard the report about	Hab 3:2
L, I stand in awe of Your deeds.	Hab 3:2
Are You angry at the rivers, **L**?	Hab 3:8
yet I will triumph in the **L**;	Hab 3:18
The word of the **L** that came to	Zph 1:1
loyalty to the **L** but also pledge	Zph 1:5
turn back from following the **L**,	Zph 1:6
do not seek the **L** or inquire of	Zph 1:6
for the Day of the **L** is near.	Zph 1:7
the **L** has prepared a sacrifice;	Zph 1:7
The **L** will not do good or evil.	Zph 1:12
The great Day of the **L** is near,	Zph 1:14
the Day of the **L**—there the	Zph 1:14
they have sinned against the **L**.	Zph 1:17
Seek the **L**, all you humble of	Zph 2:3
word of the **L** is against you,	Zph 2:5
for the **L** their God will return	Zph 2:7
declaration of the **L** of Hosts,	Zph 2:9
the people of the **L** of Hosts.	Zph 2:10
The **L** will be terrifying to them	Zph 2:11
She has not trusted in the **L**;	Zph 3:2
The righteous **L** is in her;	Zph 3:5
The **L** has removed your	Zph 3:15
of Israel, the **L**, is among you;	Zph 3:15
The **L** your God is among you,	Zph 3:17
the word of the **L** came through	Hg 1:1
The **L** of Hosts says this:	Hg 1:2
house of the **L** to be rebuilt."	Hg 1:2
The word of the **L** came through	Hg 1:3
the **L** of Hosts says this:	Hg 1:5
The **L** of Hosts says this:	Hg 1:7
and be glorified," says the **L**.	Hg 1:8
declaration of the **L** of Hosts.	Hg 1:9
the voice of the **L** their God and	Hg 1:12
because the **L** their God had sent	Hg 1:12
So the people feared the **L**.	Hg 1:12
The **L** stirred up the spirit of	Hg 1:14
the word of the **L** came through	Hg 2:1
declaration of the **L** of Hosts.	Hg 2:4
For the **L** of Hosts says this:	Hg 2:6
glory," says the **L** of Hosts.	Hg 2:7
declaration of the **L** of Hosts.	Hg 2:8
the first," says the **L** of Hosts.	Hg 2:9
declaration of the **L** of Hosts.	Hg 2:9
the word of the **L** came to Haggai	Hg 2:10
is what the **L** of Hosts says:	Hg 2:11
The word of the **L** came to Haggai	Hg 2:20
declaration of the **L** of Hosts—	Hg 2:23
declaration of the **L** of Hosts.	Hg 2:23
the word of the **L** came to the	Zch 1:1
The **L** was extremely angry with	Zch 1:2
is what the **L** of Hosts says:	Zch 1:3
declaration of the **L** of Hosts—	Zch 1:3
to you, says the **L** of Hosts.	Zch 1:3
is what the **L** of Hosts says:	Zch 1:4
As the **L** of Hosts purposed to	Zch 1:6
the word of the **L** came to the	Zch 1:7
are the ones the **L** has sent to	Zch 1:10
Angel of the **L** standing among	Zch 1:11
the Angel of the **L** responded,	Zch 1:12
How long, **L** of Hosts, will You	Zch 1:12
The **L** replied with kind and	Zch 1:13
Proclaim: The **L** of Hosts says: I	Zch 1:14
this is what the **L** says:	Zch 1:16
declaration of the **L** of Hosts—	Zch 1:16
is what the **L** of Hosts says:	Zch 1:17
L will once more comfort Zion	Zch 1:17
Then the **L** showed me four	Zch 1:20
The declaration of the **L**:	Zch 2:5
For the **L** of Hosts says this:	Zch 2:8
know that the **L** of Hosts has	Zch 2:9
themselves to the **L** on that day	Zch 2:11
know that the **L** of Hosts has	Zch 2:11
The **L** will take possession of	Zch 2:12
people be silent before the **L**,	Zch 2:13
before the Angel of the **L**,	Zch 3:1
The **L** said to Satan: "The LORD	Zch 3:2
The **L** rebuke you, Satan!	Zch 3:2
May the **L** who has chosen	Zch 3:2
the Angel of the **L** was standing	Zch 3:5
Angel of the **L** charged Joshua:	Zch 3:6
is what the **L** of Hosts says:	Zch 3:7
declaration of the **L** of Hosts—	Zch 3:9
declaration of the **L** of Hosts.	Zch 3:10
word of the **L** to Zerubbabel:	Zch 4:6
Spirit,' says the **L** of Hosts.	Zch 4:6
the word of the **L** came to me:	Zch 4:8
know that the **L** of Hosts has	Zch 4:9
These seven eyes of the **L**,	Zch 4:10
declaration of the **L** of Hosts—	Zch 5:4
earth, and the **L** said, "Go,	Zch 6:7
The word of the **L** came to me:	Zch 6:9
is what the **L** of Hosts says:	Zch 6:12
know that the **L** of Hosts has	Zch 6:15

you fully obey the **L** your God." Zch 6:15
the word of the **L** came to Zch 7:1
house of the **L** of Hosts as well Zch 7:3
the word of the **L** of Hosts came Zch 7:4
words that the **L** proclaimed Zch 7:7
The word of the **L** came to Zch 7:8
The **L** of Hosts says this: Zch 7:9
words that the **L** of Hosts had Zch 7:12
anger came from the **L** of Hosts. Zch 7:12
listen," says the **L** of Hosts. Zch 7:13
The word of the **L** of Hosts came: Zch 8:1
The **L** of Hosts says this: Zch 8:2
The **L** says this: "I will return Zch 8:3
the mountain of the **L** of Hosts, Zch 8:3
The **L** of Hosts says this: Zch 8:4
The **L** of Hosts says this: Zch 8:6
declaration of the **L** of Hosts. Zch 8:6
The **L** of Hosts says this: Zch 8:7
The **L** of Hosts says this: Zch 8:9
the house of the **L** of Hosts. Zch 8:9
declaration of the **L** of Hosts. Zch 8:11
For the **L** of Hosts says this: Zch 8:14
relent," says the **L** of Hosts, Zch 8:14
the word of the **L** of Hosts came Zch 8:18
The **L** of Hosts says this: Zch 8:19
The **L** of Hosts says this: Zch 8:20
and to seek the **L** of Hosts. Zch 8:21
come to seek the **L** of Hosts in Zch 8:22
The **L** of Hosts says this: Zch 8:23
The word of the **L** is against the Zch 9:1
the eyes of men are on the **L**— Zch 9:1
the **L** will appear over them, Zch 9:14
The **L** of Hosts will defend them. Zch 9:15
The **L** their God will save them Zch 9:16
Ask the **L** for rain in the season Zch 10:1
The **L** makes the rain clouds, Zch 10:1
the **L** of Hosts has tended His Zch 10:3
because the **L** is with them, Zch 10:5
For I am the **L** their God, and I Zch 10:6
hearts will rejoice in the **L**. Zch 10:7
I will strengthen them in the **L**, Zch 10:12
The **L** my God says this: Zch 11:4
Praise the **L** because I have Zch 11:5
that it was the word of the **L**. Zch 11:11
the potter," the **L** said to me— Zch 11:13
it into the house of the **L**, Zch 11:13
The **L** also said to me: Zch 11:15
The word of the **L** concerning Zch 12:1
of the **L**, who stretched out Zch 12:1
strength through the **L** of Hosts, Zch 12:5
The **L** will save the tents of Zch 12:7
that day the **L** will defend the Zch 12:8
the Angel of the **L**, before them. Zch 12:8
declaration of the **L** of Hosts— Zch 13:2
falsely in the name of the **L**. Zch 13:3
declaration of the **L** of Hosts. Zch 13:7
will say: The **L** is our God." Zch 13:9
A day of the **L** is coming when Zch 14:1
Then the **L** will go out to fight Zch 14:3
Then the **L** my God will come and Zch 14:5
be the plague the **L** strikes all Zch 14:12
panic from the **L** will be among Zch 14:13
the King, the **L** of Hosts, and to Zch 14:16
the King, the **L** of Hosts, rain Zch 14:17
be the plague the **L** inflicts Zch 14:18
HOLY TO THE **L** will be on Zch 14:20
the house of the **L** will be like Zch 14:20
will be holy to the **L** of Hosts. Zch 14:21
in the house of the **L** of Hosts. Zch 14:21
The word of the **L** to Israel Mal 1:1
"I have loved you," says the **L**. Mal 1:2
the **L** of Hosts says this: Mal 1:4
the people the **L** has cursed Mal 1:4
L is great, ⌊even⌋ beyond the Mal 1:5
says the **L** of Hosts to you Mal 1:6
you favor?" asks the **L** of Hosts. Mal 1:8
you favor?" asks the **L** of Hosts. Mal 1:9
you," says the **L** of Hosts, "and Mal 1:10
nations," says the **L** of Hosts. Mal 1:11
scorn it," says the **L** of Hosts. Mal 1:13
from your hands?" asks the **L**. Mal 1:13
King," says the **L** of Hosts, "and Mal 1:14
name," says the **L** of Hosts, "I Mal 2:2
continue," says the **L** of Hosts. Mal 2:4
the messenger of the **L** of Hosts. Mal 2:7
of Levi," says the **L** of Hosts. Mal 2:8
the **L** cut off any descendants Mal 2:12
an offering to the **L** of Hosts. Mal 2:12
Because the **L** has been a Mal 2:14
says the **L** God of Israel, Mal 2:16
injustice," says the **L** of Hosts. Mal 2:16
wearied the **L** with your words Mal 2:17
is coming," says the **L** of Hosts. Mal 3:1
to the **L** in righteousness Mal 3:3
will please the **L** as in days of Mal 3:4
fear Me," says the **L** of Hosts. Mal 3:5
to you," says the **L** of Hosts. Mal 3:7
this way," says the **L** of Hosts. Mal 3:10
be barren," says the **L** of Hosts. Mal 3:11
land," says the **L** of Hosts. Mal 3:12
Me are harsh," says the **L**. Mal 3:13
before the **L** of Hosts? Mal 3:14
who feared the **L** spoke to one Mal 3:16
The **L** took notice and listened. Mal 3:16
Mine," says the **L** of Hosts, "a Mal 3:17
them," says the **L** of Hosts, "not Mal 4:1
preparing," says the **L** of Hosts. Mal 4:3
and awesome Day of the **L** comes. Mal 4:5

LORD'S *(55)*
(See also LORD'S Yahweh's.)

also will become my **l** slaves." Gn 44:9
We are now my **l** slaves—both we Gn 44:16
remain here as my **l** slave, Gn 44:33
favor in our **l** eyes and will be Gn 47:25
may My **L** power be magnified Nm 14:17
commander of the **L** army said to Jos 5:15
didn't see my **l** young men whom 1Sm 25:25
my **l** life will be tucked safely 1Sm 25:29
bloodshed or my **l** revenge. 1Sm 25:31
wash the feet of my **l** servants." 1Sm 25:41
Take your **l** soldiers and pursue 2Sm 20:6
the ark of the **L** covenant, 1Kg 3:15
aren't they all my **l** servants? 1Ch 21:3
water before the **L** presence. Lm 2:19
be killed in the **L** sanctuary? Lm 2:20
The **L** way isn't fair. Ezk 18:25
The **L** way isn't fair. Ezk 18:29
L way isn't fair, even though Ezk 33:17
The **L** way isn't fair. Ezk 33:20
sanctuary for the **L** sake. Dn 9:17
The **L** table is defiled, and its Mal 1:12
he did as the **L** angel had Mt 1:24
"I am the **L** slave," said Mary. Lk 1:38
For, indeed, the **L** hand was with Lk 1:66
before he saw the **L** Messiah. Lk 2:26
the year of the **L** favor. Lk 4:19
And the **L** power to heal was in Lk 5:17
also sat at the **L** feet and was Lk 10:39
The **L** hand was with them, and a Ac 11:21
The **L** hand is against you: Ac 13:11
In this way the **L** message Ac 19:20
said, "The **L** will be done!" Ac 21:14
has known the **L** mind, that he 1Co 2:16
as a slave is the **L** freedman. 1Co 7:22
as one who by the **L** mercy is 1Co 7:25
other apostles, the **L** brothers, 1Co 9:5
share in the **L** table and the 1Co 10:21
earth is the **L**, and all that is 1Co 10:26
not really to eat the **L** Supper. 1Co 11:20
you proclaim the **L** death until 1Co 11:26
I write to you is the **L** command. 1Co 14:37
always excelling in the **L** work, 1Co 15:58
because he is doing the **L** work, 1Co 16:10
except James, the **L** brother. Gl 1:19
understand what the **L** will is. Eph 5:17
For the **L** message rang out from 1Th 1:8
still alive at the **L** coming will 1Th 4:15
from the **L** presence and from 2Th 1:9
that the **L** message may spread 2Th 3:1
The **L** slave must not quarrel, 2Tm 2:24
do not take the **L** discipline Heb 12:5
be patient until the **L** coming. Jms 5:7
because the **L** coming is near. Jms 5:8
who spoke in the **L** name as an Jms 5:10
was in the Spirit on the **L** day, Rv 1:10

LORD'S (Yahweh's) *(962)*
(See also LORD'S.)

a male child with the **L** help." Gn 4:1
went out from the **L** presence and Gn 4:16
like the **L** garden and the land Gn 13:10
because of the **L** compassion for Gn 19:16
be provided on the **L** mountain." Gn 22:14
you in the **L** presence before Gn 27:7
was evil in the **L** sight, and the Gn 38:7
he did was evil in the **L** sight, Gn 38:10
The **L** blessing was on all that Gn 39:5
Then the **L** anger burned against Ex 4:14
Moses said in the **L** presence: Ex 6:12
Moses replied in the **L** presence, Ex 6:30
then the **L** hand will bring a Ex 9:3
didn't take the **L** word seriously Ex 9:21
you may know the earth is the **L**. Ex 9:29
we must hold the **L** festival." Ex 10:9
it is the **L** Passover. Ex 12:11
to celebrate the **L** Passover, Ex 12:48
that are males will be the **L**. Ex 13:12
firm and see the **L** salvation He Ex 14:13
had died by the **L** hand in the Ex 16:3
will see the **L** glory because He Ex 16:7
a cloud, the **L** glory appeared. Ex 16:10
next according to the **L** command. Ex 17:1
lifted up⌋ toward the **L** throne. Ex 17:16
The appearance of the **L** glory to Ex 24:17
live among will see the **L** work, Ex 34:10
bring this as the **L** offering: Ex 35:5
any of the **L** commands and does Lv 4:2
any of the **L** commands and incur Lv 4:13
violating one of the **L** commands, Lv 4:27
to any of the **L** holy things, Lv 5:15
any of the **L** commands concerning Lv 5:17
eats meat from the **L** fellowship Lv 7:20
eats meat from the **L** fellowship Lv 7:21
and keep the **L** charge so that Lv 8:35
leaped from the **L** presence and Lv 10:2
the **L** anointing oil is on you. Lv 10:7
been acceptable in the **L** sight?" Lv 10:19
the blood on the **L** altar at the Lv 17:6
These are the **L** appointed times, Lv 23:4
These are the **L** appointed times Lv 23:37
offerings for the **L** Sabbaths, Lv 23:38
are to celebrate the **L** festival Lv 23:39
declared the **L** appointed times Lv 23:44
lampstand in the **L** presence. Lv 24:4
until the **L** decision could be Lv 24:12
Abihu died in the **L** presence Nm 3:4
clans at the **L** command was Nm 3:39
them at the **L** command through Nm 4:37
At the **L** command Moses and Nm 4:41
them at the **L** command through Nm 4:45
At the **L** command they were Nm 4:49
they may perform the **L** work. Nm 8:11
presenting the **L** offering at its Nm 9:7
present the **L** offering at its Nm 9:13
At the **L** command the Israelites Nm 9:18
at the **L** command they camped. Nm 9:18
carried out the **L** requirement Nm 9:19
camp at the **L** command and set Nm 9:20
and set out at the **L** command. Nm 9:20
They camped at the **L** command, Nm 9:23
they set out at the **L** command. Nm 9:23
carried out the **L** requirement Nm 9:23
to the **L** command through Nm 10:13
the ark of the **L** covenant Nm 10:33
because the **L** fire had blazed Nm 11:3
Moses, "Is the **L** power limited? Nm 11:23
If only all the **L** people were Nm 11:29
the **L** anger burned against the Nm 11:33
The **L** anger burned against them, Nm 12:9
of Paran at the **L** command. Nm 13:3
is filled with the **L** glory, Nm 14:21
going against the **L** command? Nm 14:41
the ark of the **L** covenant and Nm 14:44
despised the **L** word and broken Nm 15:31
remember all the **L** commands and Nm 15:39
above the **L** assembly?" Nm 16:3
the work at the **L** tabernacle, Nm 16:9
"You have killed the **L** people!" Nm 16:41
it, and the **L** glory appeared. Nm 16:42
staffs from the **L** presence to Nm 17:9
comes near the **L** tabernacle will Nm 17:13
you brought the **L** assembly into Nm 20:4
staff from the **L** presence just Nm 20:9
in the Book of the **L** Wars: Nm 21:14
not go against the **L** command, Nm 24:13
and the **L** anger burned against Nm 25:3
so that the **L** community won't be Nm 27:17
to inflict the **L** vengeance on Nm 31:3
came against the **L** community. Nm 31:16
the duties of the **L** tabernacle." Nm 31:30
the duties of the **L** tabernacle, Nm 31:47
So the **L** anger burned that day, Nm 32:10
The **L** anger burned against Nm 32:13
evil in the **L** sight was gone. Nm 32:13
even more to the **L** burning anger Nm 32:14

At the **L** command, Moses wrote Nm 33:2
At the **L** command, Aaron the Nm 33:38
rebelled against the **L** command Dt 1:43
the **L** hand was against them, Dt 2:15
right and good in the **L** sight, Dt 6:18
Then the **L** anger will burn Dt 7:4
was evil in the **L** sight and Dt 9:18
carry the ark of the **L** covenant, Dt 10:8
Keep the **L** commands and statutes Dt 10:13
Then the **L** anger will burn Dt 11:17
what is right in the **L** sight. Dt 12:25
because the **L** release of debts Dt 15:2
will eat the **L** fire offerings; Dt 18:1
minister in the **L** name from now Dt 18:5
a prophet speaks in the **L** name, Dt 18:22
blessings in the **L** name, Dt 21:5
what is right in the **L** sight. Dt 21:9
off may enter the **L** assembly. Dt 23:1
birth may enter the **L** assembly; Dt 23:2
may enter the **L** assembly. Dt 23:2
may enter the **L** assembly; Dt 23:3
may ever enter the **L** assembly. Dt 23:3
may enter the **L** assembly. Dt 23:8
you are called by the **L** name, Dt 28:10
Therefore the **L** anger burned Dt 29:27
the ark of the **L** covenant, Dt 31:9
the ark of the **L** covenant, Dt 31:25
do what is evil in the **L** sight, Dt 31:29
For I will proclaim the **L** name. Dt 32:3
But the **L** portion is His people, Dt 32:9
The **L** beloved rests securely on Dt 33:12
carried out the **L** justice and Dt 33:21
full of the **L** blessing, take Dt 33:23
death of Moses the **L** servant, Jos 1:1
what Moses the **L** servant Jos 1:13
what Moses the **L** servant gave Jos 1:15
the ark of the **L** covenant stood Jos 3:17
of the ark of the **L** covenant. Jos 4:7
of Jericho in the **L** presence. Jos 4:13
the ark of the **L** covenant came Jos 4:18
know that the **L** hand is mighty, Jos 4:24
as commander of the **L** army." Jos 5:14
the ark of the **L** covenant Jos 6:8
must go into the **L** treasury." Jos 6:19
the treasury of the **L** house. Jos 6:24
and the **L** anger burned against Jos 7:1
he has violated the **L** covenant Jos 7:15
them out in the **L** presence. Jos 7:23
Follow the **L** command—see ⌊that Jos 8:8
to the **L** command that He Jos 8:27
just as Moses the **L** servant had Jos 8:31
the ark of the **L** covenant facing Jos 8:33
As Moses the **L** servant had Jos 8:33
but did not seek the **L** counsel. Jos 9:14
and for the **L** altar at the place Jos 9:27
as Moses the **L** servant had Jos 11:12
For it was the **L** intention to Jos 11:20
Moses the **L** servant and the Jos 12:6
And Moses the **L** servant gave Jos 12:6
as Moses the **L** servant had given Jos 13:8
when Moses the **L** servant sent me Jos 14:7
based on the **L** instruction to Jos 15:13
keeping with the **L** instruction. Jos 17:4
Moses the **L** servant gave them. Jos 18:7
By the **L** command, they gave him Jos 19:50
at Shiloh in the **L** presence at Jos 19:51
by the **L** command, gave Jos 21:3
Moses the **L** servant commanded Jos 22:2
that Moses the **L** servant gave Jos 22:4
that Moses the **L** servant gave Jos 22:5
to the **L** command through Jos 22:9
is what the **L** entire community Jos 22:16
a plague on the **L** community, Jos 22:17
where the **L** tabernacle stands, Jos 22:19
replica of the **L** altar that our Jos 22:28
Israelites from the **L** power." Jos 22:31
the **L** anger will burn against Jos 23:16
things, the **L** servant, Joshua Jos 24:29
had seen all the **L** great works Jdg 2:7
what was evil in the **L** sight. Jdg 2:11
The **L** anger burned against Jdg 2:14
in obedience to the **L** commands. Jdg 2:17
The **L** anger burned against Jdg 2:20
would keep the **L** way by walking Jdg 2:22
would keep the **L** commands He had Jdg 3:4
what was evil in the **L** sight; Jdg 3:7
The **L** anger burned against Jdg 3:8
what was evil in the **L** sight. Jdg 3:12
what was evil in the **L** sight. Jdg 3:12
Then the **L** people went down to Jdg 5:11
L people came down to me with Jdg 5:13
So the **L** anger burned against Jdg 10:7
what was evil in the **L** sight, Jdg 13:1
because the **L** hand has turned Ru 1:13
Phinehas, were the **L** priests. 1Sm 1:3
she went up to the **L** house, 1Sm 1:7
doorpost of the **L** tabernacle. 1Sm 1:9
was praying in the **L** presence, 1Sm 1:12
appear in the **L** presence and to 1Sm 1:22
him to the **L** house at Shiloh 1Sm 1:24
of the earth are the **L**; 1Sm 2:8
they treated the **L** offering with 1Sm 2:17
served in the **L** presence and 1Sm 2:18
I hear from the **L** people is not 1Sm 2:24
opened the doors of the **L** house. 1Sm 3:15
the ark of the **L** covenant from 1Sm 4:3
the **L** hand was against the city 1Sm 5:9
poured it out in the **L** presence. 1Sm 7:6
The **L** hand was against the 1Sm 7:13
told all the **L** words to the 1Sm 8:10
and there in the **L** presence they 1Sm 11:15
offerings in the **L** presence, 1Sm 11:15
rebel against the **L** command, 1Sm 12:14
the **L** hand will be against you 1Sm 12:15
committed in the **L** sight by 1Sm 12:17
I haven't sought the **L** favor. 1Sm 13:12
son of Eli the **L** priest at 1Sm 14:3
carried out the **L** instructions." 1Sm 15:13
what was evil in the **L** sight?" 1Sm 15:19
the **L** command and your 1Sm 15:24
Certainly the **L** anointed one is 1Sm 16:6
saves, for the battle is the **L**. 1Sm 17:47
for me and fight the **L** battles." 1Sm 18:17
me with the **L** faithful love, 1Sm 20:14
a covenant in the **L** presence. 1Sm 23:18
to my lord, the **L** anointed. 1Sm 24:6
since he is the **L** anointed." 1Sm 24:6
since he is the **L** anointed. 1Sm 24:10
because he fights the **L** battles. 1Sm 25:28
against the **L** anointed and be 1Sm 26:9
my hand against the **L** anointed. 1Sm 26:11
your lord, the **L** anointed. 1Sm 26:16
ground far from the **L** presence, 1Sm 26:20
my hand against the **L** anointed, 1Sm 26:23
the plunder of the **L** enemies." 1Sm 30:26
son Jonathan, the **L** people, and 2Sm 1:12
hand to destroy the **L** anointed?" 2Sm 1:14
'I killed the **L** anointed.' " 2Sm 1:16
at Hebron in the **L** presence, 2Sm 5:3
Then the **L** anger burned against 2Sm 6:7
of the **L** outburst against 2Sm 6:8
offerings in the **L** presence. 2Sm 6:17
ruler over the **L** people Israel. 2Sm 6:21
in, sat in the **L** presence, and 2Sm 7:18
May the **L** will be done." 2Sm 10:12
went to the **L** house, and 2Sm 12:20
If I find favor in the **L** eyes, 2Sm 15:25
he ridiculed the **L** anointed?" 2Sm 19:21
you devour the **L** inheritance?" 2Sm 20:19
blessing on the **L** inheritance?" 2Sm 21:3
Gibeah of Saul, the **L** chosen." 2Sm 21:6
L anger burned against Israel 2Sm 24:1
us fall into the **L** hands because 2Sm 24:14
from being the **L** priest, 1Kg 2:27
fulfilled the **L** prophecy He had 1Kg 2:27
Joab fled to the **L** tabernacle 1Kg 2:28
has fled to the **L** tabernacle and 1Kg 2:29
you not kept the **L** oath and the 1Kg 2:43
palace, the **L** temple, and the 1Kg 3:1
a temple for the **L** name had not 1Kg 3:2
the ark of the **L** covenant there. 1Kg 6:19
of the **L** temple was laid 1Kg 6:37
courtyard of the **L** temple and 1Kg 7:12
King Solomon on the **L** temple: 1Kg 7:40
Solomon at the **L** temple ⌊were 1Kg 7:45
the equipment in the **L** temple: 1Kg 7:48
Solomon did in the **L** temple was 1Kg 7:51
the treasuries of the **L** temple. 1Kg 7:51
the ark of the **L** covenant from 1Kg 8:1
the ark of the **L** covenant to its 1Kg 8:6
the cloud filled the **L** temple, 1Kg 8:10
where the **L** covenant is that He 1Kg 8:21
sacrifices in the **L** presence. 1Kg 8:62
dedicated the **L** temple. 1Kg 8:63
in front of the **L** temple because 1Kg 8:64
L temple and the royal palace 1Kg 9:10
imposed to build the **L** temple, 1Kg 9:15
with them in the **L** presence. 1Kg 9:25
he offered at the **L** temple, 1Kg 10:5
because of the **L** eternal love 1Kg 10:9
into steps for the **L** temple and 1Kg 10:12
what was evil in the **L** sight, 1Kg 11:6
sacrifices in the **L** temple in 1Kg 12:27
did what was evil in the **L** eyes. 1Kg 14:22
the treasuries of the **L** temple 1Kg 14:26
the king entered the **L** temple, 1Kg 14:28
what was right in the **L** eyes, 1Kg 15:5
what was right in the **L** eyes, 1Kg 15:11
gifts into the **L** temple: 1Kg 15:15
the treasuries of the **L** temple 1Kg 15:18
was evil in the **L** sight and 1Kg 15:26
was evil in the **L** sight and 1Kg 15:34
evil he had done in the **L** sight, 1Kg 16:7
what was evil in the **L** sight and 1Kg 16:19
what was evil in the **L** sight; 1Kg 16:25
evil in the **L** sight more than 1Kg 16:30
of God and the **L** word in your 1Kg 17:24
slaughtered the **L** prophets. 1Kg 18:4
slaughtered the **L** prophets? 1Kg 18:13
abandoned the **L** commandments 1Kg 18:18
he repaired the **L** altar that had 1Kg 18:30
the mountain in the **L** presence." 1Kg 19:11
do what is evil in the **L** sight. 1Kg 21:20
do what was evil in the **L** sight, 1Kg 21:25
please ask what the **L** will is." 1Kg 22:5
what was right in the **L** sight. 1Kg 22:43
what was evil in the **L** sight. 1Kg 22:52
what was evil in the **L** sight, 2Kg 3:2
"The **L** words are with him." 2Kg 3:12
the **L** hand came on Elisha. 2Kg 3:15
This is easy in the **L** sight. 2Kg 3:18
what was evil in the **L** sight. 2Kg 8:18
was evil in the **L** sight like the 2Kg 8:27
you king over the **L** people, 2Kg 9:6
this is the **L** message, 'so will 2Kg 9:26
of land,' this is the **L** message. 2Kg 9:26
fulfills⌋ the **L** word that He 2Kg 9:36
in the **L** temple six years 2Kg 11:3
come to him in the **L** temple, 2Kg 11:4
protection for the **L** temple. 2Kg 11:7
that were in the **L** temple. 2Kg 11:10
to the people at the **L** temple. 2Kg 11:13
put to death in the **L** temple." 2Kg 11:15
they would be the **L** people and 2Kg 11:17
guards for the **L** temple. 2Kg 11:18
the king from the **L** temple. 2Kg 11:19
what was right in the **L** sight. 2Kg 12:2
money brought to the **L** temple, 2Kg 12:4
given for the **L** temple, 2Kg 12:4
side as one enters the **L** temple; 2Kg 12:9
money brought into the **L** temple. 2Kg 12:9
would go to the **L** temple and 2Kg 12:10
those who oversaw the **L** temple. 2Kg 12:11
those working on the **L** temple— 2Kg 12:11
damage to the **L** temple and for 2Kg 12:12
were made for the **L** temple from 2Kg 12:13
repaired the **L** temple with it. 2Kg 12:14
brought to the **L** temple since it 2Kg 12:16
the treasuries of the **L** temple 2Kg 12:18
was evil in the **L** sight and 2Kg 13:2
So the **L** anger burned against 2Kg 13:3
Jehoahaz sought the **L** favor, 2Kg 13:4
what was evil in the **L** sight. 2Kg 13:11
said, "The **L** arrow of victory 2Kg 13:17
what was right in the **L** sight, 2Kg 14:3
utensils found in the **L** temple 2Kg 14:14
what was evil in the **L** sight. 2Kg 14:24
was right in the **L** sight just as 2Kg 15:3
was evil in the **L** sight as his 2Kg 15:9
what was evil in the **L** sight. 2Kg 15:18
was evil in the **L** sight and did 2Kg 15:24
what was evil in the **L** sight. 2Kg 15:28
was right in the **L** sight just as 2Kg 15:34
the Upper Gate of the **L** temple. 2Kg 15:35
and gold found in the **L** temple 2Kg 16:8
his⌋ altar and the **L** temple, 2Kg 16:14
removed from the **L** temple the 2Kg 16:18
what was evil in the **L** sight, 2Kg 17:2
was evil in the **L** sight and 2Kg 17:17
was right in the **L** sight just as 2Kg 18:3
the silver found in the **L** temple 2Kg 18:15
the doors of the **L** sanctuary 2Kg 18:16
it without the **L** ⌊approval⌋? 2Kg 18:25
and went into the **L** temple. 2Kg 19:1

then went up to the **L** temple, 2Kg 19:14
you will go up to the **L** temple. 2Kg 20:5
will go up to the **L** temple on 2Kg 20:8
what was evil in the **L** sight, 2Kg 21:2
build altars in the **L** temple, 2Kg 21:4
both courtyards of the **L** temple. 2Kg 21:5
amount of evil in the **L** sight, 2Kg 21:6
what was evil in the **L** sight. 2Kg 21:16
was evil in the **L** sight as his 2Kg 21:20
right in the **L** sight and walked 2Kg 22:2
to the **L** temple, saying, 2Kg 22:3
brought into the **L** temple— 2Kg 22:4
those who oversee the **L** temple. 2Kg 22:5
workmen in the **L** temple to 2Kg 22:5
of the law in the **L** temple," 2Kg 22:8
those who oversee the **L** temple." 2Kg 22:9
For great is the **L** wrath that is 2Kg 22:13
went to the **L** temple with all 2Kg 23:2
had been found in the **L** temple. 2Kg 23:2
to bring out of the **L** temple all 2Kg 23:4
pole from the **L** temple to the 2Kg 23:6
that were in the **L** temple, 2Kg 23:7
at the entrance of the **L** temple 2Kg 23:11
two courtyards of the **L** temple. 2Kg 23:12
priest found in the **L** temple. 2Kg 23:24
was evil in the **L** sight just as 2Kg 23:32
was evil in the **L** sight just as 2Kg 23:37
only at the **L** command to remove 2Kg 24:3
was evil in the **L** sight as his 2Kg 24:9
treasures of the **L** temple and 2Kg 24:13
had made for the **L** sanctuary, 2Kg 24:13
was evil in the **L** sight just as 2Kg 24:19
Because of the **L** anger, it came 2Kg 24:20
He burned the **L** temple, the 2Kg 25:9
bronze pillars of the **L** temple, 2Kg 25:13
which were in the **L** temple, 2Kg 25:13
had made for the **L** temple, 2Kg 25:16
was evil in the **L** sight, so He 1Ch 2:3
the music in the **L** temple after 1Ch 6:31
Solomon built the **L** temple in 1Ch 6:32
assigned to the **L** camp as 1Ch 9:19
to the gates of the **L** house, 1Ch 9:23
he did not keep the **L** word. 1Ch 10:13
at Hebron in the **L** presence, 1Ch 11:3
keeping with the **L** word through 1Ch 11:3
according to the **L** word about 1Ch 11:10
according to the **L** word, were as 1Ch 12:23
Then the **L** anger burned against 1Ch 13:10
of the **L** outburst against 1Ch 13:11
the ark of the **L** covenant to 1Ch 16:37
the ark of the **L** covenant is 1Ch 17:1
in, sat in the **L** presence, and 1Ch 17:16
May the **L** will be done." 1Ch 19:13
me fall into the **L** hands because 1Ch 21:13
of the sword of the **L** angel. 1Ch 21:30
bring the ark of the **L** covenant 1Ch 22:19
of the work on the **L** temple, 1Ch 23:4
in the service of the **L** temple. 1Ch 23:24
the service of the **L** temple, 1Ch 23:28
regularly in the **L** presence 1Ch 23:31
in the service of the **L** temple." 1Ch 23:32
when they entered the **L** temple, 1Ch 24:19
for the music in the **L** temple, 1Ch 25:6
for ministering in the **L** temple, 1Ch 26:12
the treasuries of the **L** temple. 1Ch 26:22
for the repair of the **L** temple. 1Ch 26:27
the ark of the **L** covenant and as 1Ch 28:2
the throne of the **L** kingdom over 1Ch 28:5
for the courts of the **L** house, 1Ch 28:12
work of service in the **L** house; 1Ch 28:13
of service of the **L** house; 1Ch 28:13
cover the ark of the **L** covenant. 1Ch 28:18
By the **L** hand on me, He 1Ch 28:19
service of the **L** house is 1Ch 28:20
treasury of the **L** house under 1Ch 29:8
great joy in the **L** presence that 1Ch 29:22
anointed him as the **L** ruler, 1Ch 29:22
sat on the **L** throne as king 1Ch 29:23
which the **L** servant Moses had 2Ch 1:3
in front of the **L** tabernacle. 2Ch 1:5
there in the **L** presence on the 2Ch 1:6
began to build the **L** temple in 2Ch 3:1
King Solomon for the **L** temple. 2Ch 4:16
Solomon did for the **L** temple was 2Ch 5:1
the ark of the **L** covenant to its 2Ch 5:7
the temple, the **L** temple, was 2Ch 5:13
where the **L** covenant is that He 2Ch 6:11
to enter the **L** temple because 2Ch 7:2

sacrifices in the **L** presence. 2Ch 7:4
in front of the **L** temple because 2Ch 7:7
finished the **L** temple and the 2Ch 7:11
to do for the **L** temple and for 2Ch 7:11
had built the **L** temple and his 2Ch 8:1
the LORD on the **L** altar he had 2Ch 8:12
laid⌋ for the **L** temple until it 2Ch 8:16
So the **L** temple was completed. 2Ch 8:16
he offered at the **L** temple, 2Ch 9:4
walkways for the **L** temple and 2Ch 9:11
the **L** message came to Shemaiah: 2Ch 12:7
the treasuries of the **L** temple 2Ch 12:9
the king entered the **L** temple, 2Ch 12:11
L anger turned away from him, 2Ch 12:12
against the **L** kingdom in the 2Ch 13:8
the vestibule of the **L** ⌊temple⌋. 2Ch 15:8
treasuries of the **L** temple and 2Ch 16:2
His mind rejoiced in the **L** ways, 2Ch 17:6
the book of the **L** instruction 2Ch 17:9
please ask what the **L** will is." 2Ch 18:4
of this, the **L** wrath is on you. 2Ch 19:2
rendering⌋ the **L** judgments and 2Ch 19:8
Jerusalem in the **L** temple before 2Ch 20:5
Jerusalem to the **L** temple with 2Ch 20:28
what was right in the **L** sight. 2Ch 20:32
what was evil in the **L** sight, 2Ch 21:6
was evil in the **L** sight like the 2Ch 22:4
the courtyards of the **L** temple. 2Ch 23:5
one is to enter the **L** temple but 2Ch 23:6
to the troops in the **L** temple. 2Ch 23:12
her to death in the **L** temple." 2Ch 23:14
that they would be the **L** people. 2Ch 23:16
the oversight of the **L** temple 2Ch 23:18
had appointed over the **L** temple, 2Ch 23:18
gates of the **L** temple so that 2Ch 23:19
the king down from the **L** temple. 2Ch 23:20
what was right in the **L** sight. 2Ch 24:2
heart to renovate the **L** temple. 2Ch 24:4
imposed by⌋ the **L** servant Moses 2Ch 24:6
broke into the **L** temple and even 2Ch 24:7
things of the **L** temple for the 2Ch 24:7
the gate of the **L** temple. 2Ch 24:8
of the labor on the **L** temple, 2Ch 24:12
to renovate the **L** temple, 2Ch 24:12
to repair the **L** temple. 2Ch 24:12
articles for the **L** temple with 2Ch 24:14
offerings in the **L** temple 2Ch 24:14
the **L** commands and you 2Ch 24:20
the courtyard of the **L** temple. 2Ch 24:21
the restoration of the **L** temple, 2Ch 24:27
was right in the **L** sight but not 2Ch 25:2
So the **L** anger was against 2Ch 25:15
was right in the **L** sight as his 2Ch 26:4
going into the **L** sanctuary to 2Ch 26:16
priests in the **L** temple beside 2Ch 26:19
from access to the **L** temple, 2Ch 26:21
was right in the **L** sight as his 2Ch 27:2
he didn't enter the **L** sanctuary. 2Ch 27:2
the Upper Gate of the **L** temple, 2Ch 27:3
right in the **L** sight like his 2Ch 28:1
the **L** fierce wrath is on you. 2Ch 28:11
Ahaz plundered the **L** temple and 2Ch 28:21
shut the doors of the **L** temple, 2Ch 28:24
was right in the **L** sight just as 2Ch 29:2
the doors of the **L** temple and 2Ch 29:3
away from the **L** tabernacle, 2Ch 29:6
LORD to cleanse the **L** temple. 2Ch 29:15
entrance of the **L** temple to 2Ch 29:16
they found in the **L** sanctuary to 2Ch 29:16
the courtyard of the **L** temple. 2Ch 29:16
the vestibule of the **L** ⌊temple⌋. 2Ch 29:17
consecrated the **L** temple for 2Ch 29:17
and went up to the **L** temple. 2Ch 29:20
the Levites in the **L** temple with 2Ch 29:25
offerings to the **L** temple." 2Ch 29:31
the service of the **L** temple was 2Ch 29:35
to come to the **L** temple in 2Ch 30:1
burnt offerings to the **L** temple. 2Ch 30:15
the offering to the **L** temple, 2Ch 31:10
chambers in the **L** temple, 2Ch 31:11
would enter the **L** temple for 2Ch 31:16
so the **L** wrath didn't come on 2Ch 32:26
what was evil in the **L** sight, 2Ch 33:2
He built altars in the **L** temple, 2Ch 33:4
both courtyards of the **L** temple. 2Ch 33:5
deal of evil in the **L** sight, 2Ch 33:6
and the idol from the **L** temple, 2Ch 33:15
on the mountain of the **L** temple 2Ch 33:15

was evil in the **L** sight just as 2Ch 33:22
right in the **L** sight and walked 2Ch 34:2
those who oversaw the **L** temple. 2Ch 34:10
were working in the **L** temple, 2Ch 34:10
been deposited in the **L** temple, 2Ch 34:14
of the law in the **L** temple," 2Ch 34:15
found in the **L** temple and have 2Ch 34:17
For great is the **L** wrath that is 2Ch 34:21
went up to the **L** temple with all 2Ch 34:30
had been found in the **L** temple. 2Ch 34:30
a covenant in the **L** presence to 2Ch 34:31
Josiah observed the **L** Passover 2Ch 35:1
them to serve in the **L** temple. 2Ch 35:2
utensils of the **L** temple to 2Ch 36:7
what was evil in the **L** sight. 2Ch 36:9
utensils of the **L** temple. 2Ch 36:10
the prophet at the **L** command. 2Ch 36:12
they defiled the **L** temple that 2Ch 36:14
until the **L** wrath was so stirred 2Ch 36:16
the treasures of the **L** temple, 2Ch 36:18
and rebuild the **L** house in Ezr 1:5
the articles of the **L** house that Ezr 1:7
arrived at the **L** house in Ezr 2:68
and for all the **L** appointed holy Ezr 3:5
of the **L** temple had not Ezr 3:6
the work on the **L** house. Ezr 3:8
the foundation of the **L** temple, Ezr 3:10
of the **L** house had been Ezr 3:11
in matters of the **L** commandments Ezr 7:11
chambers of the **L** house before Ezr 8:29
fruit tree to the **L** house year Neh 10:35
went out from the **L** presence. Jb 1:12
So Satan left the **L** presence and Jb 2:7
delight is in the **L** instruction, Ps 1:2
I will declare the **L** decree: Ps 2:7
the **L** throne is in heaven. Ps 11:4
All the **L** ways ⌊show⌋ faithful Ps 25:10
that I will see the **L** goodness Ps 27:13
is full of the **L** unfailing love. Ps 33:5
with me the **L** greatness; Ps 34:3
the **L** enemies, like the glory of Ps 37:20
there is a cup in the **L** hand, Ps 75:8
I will remember the **L** works; Ps 77:11
sing about the **L** faithful love Ps 89:1
all evildoers from the **L** city. Ps 101:8
to eternity the **L** faithful love Ps 103:17
can declare the **L** mighty acts Ps 106:2
and of Aaron, the **L** holy one. Ps 106:16
did not listen to the **L** voice. Ps 106:25
Therefore the **L** anger burned Ps 106:40
They saw the **L** works, His Ps 107:24
consider the **L** acts of faithful Ps 107:43
Let this be the **L** payment to my Ps 109:20
The **L** works are great, studied Ps 111:2
heavens are the **L**, but the earth Ps 115:16
ones is valuable in the **L** sight. Ps 116:15
in the courts of the **L** house— Ps 116:19
the **L** faithfulness endures Ps 117:2
The **L** right hand strikes with Ps 118:15
The **L** right hand is raised! Ps 118:16
L right hand strikes with power! Ps 118:16
"May the **L** blessing be on you." Ps 129:8
stand in the **L** house at night! Ps 134:1
we sing the **L** song on foreign Ps 137:4
They will sing of the **L** ways, Ps 138:5
ways, for the **L** glory is great. Ps 138:5
mouth will declare the **L** praise; Ps 145:21
not despise the **L** instruction, Pr 3:11
The **L** curse is on the household Pr 3:33
ways are before the **L** eyes, Pr 5:21
The **L** blessing enriches, and Pr 10:22
balances and scales are the **L**; Pr 16:11
but the **L** decree will prevail. Pr 19:21
a water channel in the **L** hand: Pr 21:1
The **L** eyes keep watch over Pr 22:12
mountain of the **L** house will be Is 2:2
and let us walk in the **L** light. Is 2:5
do not perceive the **L** actions, Is 5:12
Therefore the **L** anger burns Is 5:25
and female slaves in the **L** land. Is 14:2
posterity"—the **L** declaration. Is 14:22
who live in the **L** presence, Is 23:18
the **L** power will rest on this Is 25:10
⌊This is⌋ the **L** declaration. Is 30:1
do not obey the **L** instruction. Is 30:9
and they do not seek the **L** help. Is 31:1
⌊This is⌋ the **L** declaration— Is 31:9
The **L** sword is covered with Is 34:6

it without the L ⌊approval⌋? Is 36:10
up to the L house and spread Is 37:14
⌊This is⌋ the L declaration. Is 37:34
I will go up to the L temple?" Is 38:22
from the L hand double for Is 40:2
help you—the L declaration. Is 41:14
witnesses"—the L declaration— Is 43:10
witnesses"—the L declaration— Is 43:12
say: I am the L; another will Is 44:5
The L, and name ⌊himself⌋ by the Is 44:5
As I live"—the L declaration— Is 49:18
on the strength of the L power. Is 51:9
They are full of the L fury, Is 51:20
I here"—the L declaration— Is 52:5
wail"—the L declaration— Is 52:5
the heritage of the L servants, Is 54:17
⌊This is⌋ the L declaration. Is 54:17
⌊This is⌋ the L declaration. Is 55:8
to Him, love the L name, and are Is 56:6
the L glory will be your rear Is 58:8
the L hand is not too short to Is 59:1
⌊This is⌋ the L declaration. Is 59:20
the year of the L favor, Is 61:2
will be called the L priests; Is 61:6
new name that the L mouth will Is 62:2
a glorious crown in the L hand, Is 62:3
the Holy People, the L Redeemed; Is 62:12
make known the L faithful love Is 63:7
love ⌊and⌋ the L praiseworthy Is 63:7
⌊This is⌋ the L declaration. Is 66:2
the L power will be revealed Is 66:14
⌊This is⌋ the L declaration. Is 66:17
before Me"—the L declaration— Is 66:22
⌊This is⌋ the L declaration. Jr 1:8
⌊This is⌋ the L declaration. Jr 1:15
⌊This is⌋ the L declaration. Jr 1:19
⌊This is⌋ the L declaration. Jr 2:3
⌊This is⌋ the L declaration. Jr 2:9
⌊This is⌋ the L declaration. Jr 2:12
⌊This is⌋ the L declaration. Jr 2:29
⌊This is⌋ the L declaration. Jr 3:1
⌊This is⌋ the L declaration. Jr 3:10
⌊This is⌋ the L declaration. Jr 3:12
⌊This is⌋ the L declaration. Jr 3:12
⌊This is⌋ the L declaration. Jr 3:13
⌊this is⌋ the L declaration— Jr 3:14
days"—the L declaration—"no Jr 3:16
The ark of the L covenant. Jr 3:16
be called, The L Throne, and all Jr 3:17
⌊This is⌋ the L declaration. Jr 3:20
⌊this is⌋ the L declaration— Jr 4:1
for the L burning anger has not Jr 4:8
⌊this is⌋ the L declaration— Jr 4:9
⌊This is⌋ the L declaration. Jr 4:17
⌊This is⌋ the L declaration. Jr 5:9
⌊This is⌋ the L declaration. Jr 5:11
for the ⌊L⌋ word is not in them. Jr 5:13
⌊This is⌋ the L declaration. Jr 5:15
⌊this is⌋ the L declaration— Jr 5:18
⌊This is⌋ the L declaration. Jr 5:22
⌊This is⌋ the L declaration. Jr 5:29
But I am full of the L wrath; Jr 6:11
⌊This is⌋ the L declaration. Jr 6:12
⌊This is⌋ the L declaration. Jr 7:11
⌊this is⌋ the L declaration— Jr 7:13
⌊This is⌋ the L declaration. Jr 7:19
⌊This is⌋ the L declaration. Jr 7:30
coming"—the L declaration— Jr 7:32
⌊this is⌋ the L declaration— Jr 8:1
⌊This is⌋ the L declaration. Jr 8:13
⌊This is⌋ the L declaration. Jr 8:17
⌊This is⌋ the L declaration. Jr 9:3
⌊This is⌋ the L declaration. Jr 9:6
⌊This is⌋ the L declaration. Jr 9:9
⌊This is⌋ the L declaration. Jr 9:24
coming"—the L declaration— Jr 9:25
because of the L burning anger. Jr 12:13
⌊This is⌋ the L declaration. Jr 12:17
⌊this is the L declaration⌋— Jr 13:11
sons alike"—the L declaration. Jr 13:14
for the L flock has been taken Jr 13:17
⌊this is⌋ the L declaration— Jr 13:25
⌊this is⌋ the L declaration— Jr 15:3
⌊This is⌋ the L declaration. Jr 15:6
⌊This is⌋ the L declaration. Jr 15:9
⌊This is⌋ the L declaration. Jr 15:20
⌊this is⌋ the L declaration— Jr 16:5
Me"—the L declaration— Jr 16:11

coming"—the L declaration— Jr 16:14
fishermen"—the L declaration— Jr 16:16
⌊this is⌋ the L declaration. Jr 18:6
⌊this is⌋ the L declaration— Jr 19:6
the courtyard of the L temple, Jr 19:14
Benjamin Gate in the L temple. Jr 20:2
⌊this is⌋ the L declaration— Jr 21:7
⌊this is⌋ the L declaration— Jr 21:10
⌊this is⌋ the L declaration— Jr 21:13
⌊this is⌋ the L declaration. Jr 21:14
⌊this is⌋ the L declaration— Jr 22:5
⌊This is⌋ the L declaration. Jr 22:16
⌊This is⌋ the L declaration. Jr 23:1
evil acts"—the L declaration. Jr 23:2
⌊This is⌋ the L declaration. Jr 23:4
⌊this is⌋ the L declaration— Jr 23:5
coming"—the L declaration— Jr 23:7
⌊This is⌋ the L declaration. Jr 23:11
⌊This is⌋ the L declaration. Jr 23:12
own minds, not from the L mouth. Jr 23:16
The L anger will not turn back Jr 23:20
⌊this is⌋ the L declaration— Jr 23:23
—the L declaration. Jr 23:24
—the L declaration. Jr 23:24
—the L declaration. Jr 23:28
like fire"—the L declaration— Jr 23:29
prophets"—the L declaration— Jr 23:30
prophets"—the L declaration— Jr 23:31
dreams"—the L declaration— Jr 23:32
⌊this is⌋ the L declaration. Jr 23:32
⌊this is⌋ the L declaration. Jr 23:33
⌊this is⌋ the L declaration— Jr 25:7
⌊this is⌋ the L declaration— Jr 25:9
⌊this is⌋ the L declaration— Jr 25:12
the cup from the L hand and made Jr 25:17
⌊This is⌋ the L declaration. Jr 25:31
because of the L burning anger. Jr 25:37
of the L temple and speak Jr 26:2
Jeremiah at the L temple. Jr 26:9
palace to the L temple and sat Jr 26:10
LORD and plead for the L favor, Jr 26:19
⌊this is⌋ the L declaration— Jr 27:8
⌊This is⌋ the L declaration. Jr 27:11
⌊this is⌋ the L declaration— Jr 27:15
articles of the L temple will be Jr 27:16
that remain in the L temple, Jr 27:18
⌊This is⌋ the L declaration. Jr 27:22
articles of the L temple that Jr 28:3
⌊this is⌋ the L declaration— Jr 28:4
articles of the L temple and all Jr 28:6
⌊This is⌋ the L declaration. Jr 29:9
⌊this is⌋ the L declaration— Jr 29:11
by you"—the L declaration— Jr 29:14
you"—the L declaration. Jr 29:14
⌊this is⌋ the L declaration— Jr 29:19
⌊This is⌋ the L declaration. Jr 29:19
⌊This is⌋ the L declaration. Jr 29:23
⌊This is⌋ the L declaration— Jr 29:32
⌊this is⌋ the L declaration— Jr 30:3
and Judah"—the L declaration. Jr 30:3
⌊this is⌋ the L declaration— Jr 30:10
⌊this is⌋ the L declaration— Jr 30:11
⌊this is⌋ the L declaration— Jr 30:17
⌊This is⌋ the L declaration. Jr 30:21
L burning anger will not turn Jr 30:24
⌊this is⌋ the L declaration— Jr 31:1
joy because of the L goodness, Jr 31:12
⌊This is⌋ the L declaration. Jr 31:14
⌊this is⌋ the L declaration— Jr 31:16
⌊this is⌋ the L declaration— Jr 31:17
⌊This is⌋ the L declaration. Jr 31:20
⌊this is⌋ the L declaration— Jr 31:27
⌊this is⌋ the L declaration— Jr 31:31
them"—the L declaration. Jr 31:32
those days"—the L declaration. Jr 31:33
of them"—the L declaration. Jr 31:34
⌊this is⌋ the L declaration— Jr 31:36
⌊this is⌋ the L declaration. Jr 31:37
coming"—the L declaration— Jr 31:38
⌊this is⌋ the L declaration. Jr 32:5
⌊this is⌋ the L declaration— Jr 32:30
⌊This is⌋ the L declaration. Jr 32:44
⌊this is⌋ the L declaration— Jr 33:14
Yet hear the L word, Zedekiah, Jr 34:4
⌊This is⌋ the L declaration. Jr 34:5
⌊this is⌋ the L declaration— Jr 34:17
⌊this is⌋ the L declaration— Jr 34:22
⌊this is⌋ the L declaration. Jr 35:13

At the L temple he read the Jr 36:8
temple he read the L words from Jr 36:8
Then at the L temple, in the Jr 36:10
of the New Gate of the L temple, Jr 36:10
third entrance of the L temple. Jr 38:14
⌊this is⌋ the L declaration— Jr 39:17
⌊This is⌋ the L declaration. Jr 39:18
⌊this is⌋ the L declaration— Jr 42:11
didn't obey the L voice and Jr 44:23
⌊this is⌋ the L declaration— Jr 44:29
⌊this is⌋ the L declaration— Jr 45:5
⌊This is⌋ the L declaration. Jr 46:5
⌊this is⌋ the L declaration— Jr 46:23
⌊This is⌋ the L declaration. Jr 46:26
⌊this is⌋ the L declaration— Jr 46:28
one who does the L business Jr 48:10
⌊this is⌋ the L declaration— Jr 48:12
⌊This is⌋ the L declaration. Jr 48:25
⌊This is⌋ the L declaration. Jr 48:30
⌊this is⌋ the L declaration— Jr 48:35
⌊This is⌋ the L declaration. Jr 48:38
⌊This is⌋ the L declaration. Jr 48:43
⌊This is⌋ the L declaration. Jr 48:44
⌊This is⌋ the L declaration. Jr 48:47
⌊this is⌋ the L declaration— Jr 49:2
⌊This is⌋ the L declaration. Jr 49:6
sworn"—the L declaration— Jr 49:13
⌊This is⌋ the L declaration. Jr 49:16
⌊this is⌋ the L declaration— Jr 49:30
⌊This is⌋ the L declaration. Jr 49:31
⌊This is⌋ the L declaration. Jr 49:32
⌊This is⌋ the L declaration. Jr 49:37
⌊This is⌋ the L declaration. Jr 49:38
⌊This is⌋ the L declaration. Jr 49:39
⌊this is⌋ the L declaration— Jr 50:4
⌊This is⌋ the L declaration. Jr 50:10
Because of the L wrath, she will Jr 50:13
Since this is the L vengeance, Jr 50:15
⌊this is⌋ the L declaration— Jr 50:20
⌊this is⌋ the L declaration— Jr 50:21
⌊This is⌋ the L declaration. Jr 50:30
⌊this is⌋ the L declaration— Jr 50:35
⌊this is⌋ the L declaration— Jr 50:40
is the time of the L vengeance— Jr 51:6
golden cup in the L hand making Jr 51:7
for it is the L vengeance, Jr 51:11
⌊This is⌋ the L declaration. Jr 51:24
⌊this is⌋ the L declaration— Jr 51:25
⌊This is⌋ the L declaration. Jr 51:26
because the L purposes against Jr 51:29
⌊This is⌋ the L declaration. Jr 51:39
you, from the L burning anger. Jr 51:45
⌊This is⌋ the L declaration. Jr 51:48
the holy places of the L temple. Jr 51:51
⌊this is⌋ the L declaration— Jr 51:52
⌊This is⌋ the L declaration. Jr 51:53
was evil in the L sight just as Jr 52:2
Because of the L anger, it came Jr 52:3
He burned the L temple, the Jr 52:13
pillars for the L temple and the Jr 52:17
that were in the L temple, Jr 52:17
had made for the L temple, Jr 52:20
on the day of the L anger no one Lm 2:22
Because of⌋ the L faithful love Lm 3:22
L anointed, the breath of our Lm 4:20
And the L hand was on him there. Ezk 1:3
of the form of the L glory. Ezk 1:28
and the L hand was on me Ezk 3:14
The L glory was present there, Ezk 3:23
them in the day of the L wrath. Ezk 7:19
the north gate of the L house, Ezk 8:14
the inner court of the L house, Ezk 8:16
at the entrance of the L temple, Ezk 8:16
backs to the L temple and their Ezk 8:16
the brightness of the L glory. Ezk 10:4
the eastern gate of the L house. Ezk 10:19
the eastern gate of the L house, Ezk 11:1
⌊This is⌋ the L declaration, Ezk 13:6
⌊This is⌋ the L declaration, Ezk 13:7
the L declaration. Ezk 16:58
very day the L hand was on me, Ezk 40:1
and laws of the L temple. Ezk 44:5
The L sanctuary will be in the Ezk 48:10
⌊This is⌋ the L declaration. Hs 2:13
that day—the L declaration— Hs 2:16
respond—the L declaration. Hs 2:21
on the day of the L feast? Hs 9:5
⌊This is⌋ the L declaration. Hs 11:11

⌊this is⌋ the L declaration— Jl 2:12
priests, the L ministers, weep Jl 2:17
will issue from the L house, Jl 3:18
⌊This is⌋ the L declaration. Am 2:11
on that day—the L declaration. Am 2:16
right—the L declaration— Am 3:10
to an end—the L declaration. Am 3:15
⌊This is⌋ the L declaration. Am 4:3
⌊This is⌋ the L declaration. Am 4:5
to Me—the L declaration. Am 4:6
to Me—the L declaration. Am 4:8
to Me—the L declaration. Am 4:9
to Me—the L declaration. Am 4:10
to Me—the L declaration. Am 4:11
⌊This is⌋ the L declaration. Am 9:7
of Jacob—the L declaration— Am 9:8
⌊this is⌋ the L declaration— Am 9:12
are coming—the L declaration— Am 9:13
⌊This is⌋ the L declaration. Ob 4
that day—the L declaration— Ob 8
but the kingdom will be the L. Ob 21
to Tarshish from the L presence. Jnh 1:3
Tarshish, from the L presence. Jnh 1:3
was fleeing from the L presence, Jnh 1:10
according to the L command. Jnh 3:3
mountain of the L house will be Mc 4:1
⌊this is⌋ the L declaration— Mc 4:6
do not know the L intentions Mc 4:12
that day—the L declaration—I Mc 5:10
Listen to the L lawsuit, you Mc 6:2
the L righteous acts. Mc 6:5
must endure the L rage until He Mc 7:9
the knowledge of the L glory, Hab 2:14
The cup in the L right hand will Hab 2:16
⌊this is⌋ the L declaration. Zph 1:2
the earth—the L declaration. Zph 1:3
the day of the L sacrifice I Zph 1:8
that day—the L declaration— Zph 1:10
them on the day of the L wrath. Zph 1:18
burning of the L anger overtakes Zph 2:2
the day of the L anger overtakes Zph 2:2
on the day of the L anger. Zph 2:3
for Me—the L declaration— Zph 3:8
Haggai, the L messenger, Hg 1:13
delivered the L message to the Hg 1:13
with you"—the L declaration. Hg 1:13
Zerubbabel"—the L declaration. Hg 2:4
the land"—the L declaration. Hg 2:4
before Me"—the L declaration. Hg 2:14
on another in the L temple, Hg 2:15
turn to Me"—the L declaration. Hg 2:17
of the L temple was laid; Hg 2:18
servant"—the L declaration— Hg 2:23
to Me"—the L declaration. Zch 1:4
the north"—the L declaration— Zch 2:6
of heaven"—the L declaration. Zch 2:6
among you"—the L declaration. Zch 2:10
place and build the L temple. Zch 6:12
He will build the L temple; Zch 6:13
will reside in the L temple as a Zch 6:14
come and build the L temple, Zch 6:15
men to plead for the L favor Zch 7:2
all this"—the L declaration. Zch 8:17
to plead for the L favor and to Zch 8:21
and to plead for the L favor." Zch 8:22
the land"—the L declaration. Zch 11:6
that day"—the L declaration— Zch 12:4
whole land—the L declaration— Zch 13:8
⌊This is⌋ the L declaration. Mal 1:2
"The L table is contemptible." Mal 1:7
has profaned the L sanctuary, Mal 2:11
cover the L altar with tears, Mal 2:13
evil is good in the L sight, Mal 2:17

LORDING *(1)*
not l it over those entrusted to 1Pt 5:3

LORDS *(24)*
and said, "My l, turn aside to Gn 19:2
Ar of Moab, the l of Arnon's Nm 21:28
the God of gods and Lord of l, Dt 10:17
of all the l of Shechem, Jdg 9:2
of all the l of Shechem, Jdg 9:3
Then all the l of Shechem and of Jdg 9:6
Listen to me, l of Shechem, and Jdg 9:7
king over the l of Shechem Jdg 9:18
and consume the l of Shechem and Jdg 9:20
fire come from the l of Shechem Jdg 9:20
Abimelech and the l of Shechem. Jdg 9:23
and on the l of Shechem, who Jdg 9:24
l of Shechem rebelled against Jdg 9:25
the l of Shechem trusted him. Jdg 9:26
out leading the l of Shechem Jdg 9:39
When all the l of the Tower of Jdg 9:46
that all the l of the Tower Jdg 9:47
and l of the city fled there. Jdg 9:51
Give thanks to the Lord of l. Ps 136:3
other l than You have ruled over Is 26:13
are many "gods" and many "l"— 1Co 8:5
of kings, and the Lord of l, 1Tm 6:15
He is Lord of l and King of Rv 17:14
OF KINGS AND LORD OF L Rv 19:16

LOSE *(26)*
should I l you both in one day? Gn 27:45
your family will l your lives." Jdg 18:25
Foreigners l heart and come 2Sm 22:46
why should you l your life?" 2Ch 25:16
of Purim will not l their Est 9:28
Foreigners l heart and come Ps 18:45
My son, don't l sight of them. Pr 3:21
Don't l sight of them; keep them Pr 4:21
officials will l their courage. Jr 4:9
if the salt should l its taste, Mt 5:13
better that you l one of the Mt 5:29
better that you l one of the Mt 5:30
finding his life will l it, Mt 10:39
He will never l his reward!" Mt 10:42
to save his life will l it, Mt 16:25
to save his life will l it, Mk 8:35
the whole world yet l his life? Mk 8:36
He will never l his reward. Mk 9:41
if the salt should l its flavor, Mk 9:50
to save his life will l it, Lk 9:24
but if salt should l its taste, Lk 14:34
make his life secure will l it, Lk 17:33
that I should l none of those He Jn 6:39
who loves his life will l it, Jn 12:25
won't grow weary and l heart. Heb 12:3
so that you don't l what we have 2Jn 8

LOSES *(11)*
If a man l the hair of his head, Lv 13:40
Or if he l the hair at his Lv 13:41
the grasshopper l its spring, Ec 12:5
but whoever l his life because Mt 16:25
the whole world yet l his life? Mt 16:26
but whoever l his life because Mk 8:35
but whoever l his life because Lk 9:24
yet l or forfeits himself? Lk 9:25
has 100 sheep and l one of them, Lk 15:4
coins, if she l one coin, does Lk 15:8
and whoever l his life will Lk 17:33

LOSING *(1)*
and anyone l his life because of Mt 10:39

LOSS *(15)*
myself bore the l. You demanded Gn 31:39
the l is covered by its rental Ex 22:15
bitter over ⌊the l of⌋ their 1Sm 30:6
blood will not increase the l, 2Sm 14:11
widow or know the l of children. Is 47:8
l of children and widowhood. Is 47:9
because of ⌊the l of⌋ his father Jr 16:7
Since I was at a l in a dispute Ac 25:20
toward damage and heavy l, Ac 27:10
and sustain this damage and l. Ac 27:21
there will be no l of any of Ac 27:22
didn't experience any l from us. 2Co 7:9
to be a l because of Christ Php 3:7
everything to be a l in view of Php 3:8
suffered the l of all things Php 3:8

LOSSES *(1)*
and inflicted heavy l on them. 1Sm 23:5

LOST *(42)*
he must pay for his l work time Ex 21:19
anything ⌊else⌋ l, and someone Ex 22:9
finds something l and lies about Lv 6:3
to him, or the l item he found, Lv 6:4
We're l; we're all lost Nm 17:12
We're lost; we're all l! Nm 17:12
your brother has l and you have Dt 22:3
we heard this, we l heart, and Jos 2:11
they l heart and their courage Jos 5:1
they l their courage and were 1Sm 17:11
yourself like the army you l— 1Kg 20:25
intimidated and l their Neh 6:16
if I hold back, what have I l? Jb 16:6
I wander like a l sheep; Ps 119:176
be l in her love forever. Pr 5:19
and be l because of his great Pr 5:23
search and a time to count as l; Ec 3:6
That wealth was l in a bad Ec 5:14
and those l in the land of Is 27:13
given them will be l to them. Jr 8:13
will never be l from the priest Jr 18:18
My people are l sheep; their Jr 50:6
My future is l, as well as my Lm 3:18
her hope was l, she took another Ezk 19:5
the strays, or sought the l. Ezk 34:4
I will seek the l, bring back Ezk 34:16
will not seek the l or heal the Zch 11:16
to the l sheep of the house of Mt 10:6
sent only to the l sheep of the Mt 15:24
of Man has come to save the l. Mt 18:11
and the wine is l as well as the Mk 2:22
and go after the l one until he Lk 15:4
I have found my l sheep!' Lk 15:6
have found the silver coin I l!' Lk 15:9
he was l and is found!' Lk 15:24
he was l and is found.' " Lk 15:32
come to seek and to save the l." Lk 19:10
a hair of your head will be l. Lk 21:18
them and not one of them is l, Jn 17:12
I have not l one of those You Jn 18:9
a hair will be l from the head Ac 27:34
up, it will be l, but he will be 1Co 3:15

LOT *(60)*
(See also LOT proper noun.)
gathered a l, some a little. Ex 16:17
who gathered a l had no surplus, Ex 16:18
one l for the LORD and the other Lv 16:8
goat chosen by l for the LORD Lv 16:9
goat chosen by l for Azazel is Lv 16:10
The land must be divided by l; Nm 26:55
be divided by l among the larger Nm 26:56
inheritance by l according to Nm 33:54
place the l indicates for Nm 33:54
to receive by l as an Nm 34:13
inheritance by l to the Nm 36:2
that you have a l of livestock— Dt 3:19
inheritance was by l as the LORD Jos 14:2
You will not have just one l, Jos 17:17
The l came up for the tribe of Jos 18:11
second l came out for Simeon, Jos 19:1
third l came up for Zebulun's Jos 19:10
The fourth l came out for the Jos 19:17
The fifth l came out for the Jos 19:24
The sixth l came out for Jos 19:32
The seventh l came out for the Jos 19:40
Israelite tribes by l at Shiloh Jos 19:51
The l came out for the Kohathite Jos 21:4
13 cities by l from the tribes Jos 21:4
10 cities by l from the clans Jos 21:5
13 cities by l from the clans Jos 21:6
around them to the Levites by l, Jos 21:8
they received the first l. Jos 21:10
we will go against it by l. Jdg 20:9
Cast ⌊the l⌋ between me and my 1Sm 14:42
but Jehu will serve him a l. 2Kg 10:18
the ⌊first⌋ l was for them. 1Ch 6:54
Manasseh ⌊were assigned⌋ by l. 1Ch 6:61
assigned⌋ by l 12 towns from 1Ch 6:63
assigned by l the towns named 1Ch 6:65
were divided impartially by l, 1Ch 24:5
The first l fell to Jehoiarib, 1Ch 24:7
The first l for Asaph fell to 1Ch 25:9
The l for the east ⌊gate⌋ fell 1Ch 26:14
and his l came out for the north 1Ch 26:14
and his sons' ⌊l⌋ was the 1Ch 26:15
that is, the l) was cast before Est 3:7
(that is, the l) to crush and Est 9:24
is the wicked man's l from God, Jb 20:29
is a wicked man's l from God, Jb 27:13
inheritance by l and settled Ps 78:55
Throw in your l with us, and Pr 1:14
The l is cast into the lap, Pr 16:33
⌊Casting⌋ the l ends quarrels Pr 18:18
plunder us and the l of those Is 17:14
He has ordained a l for them; Is 34:17
indeed, they are your l. Is 57:6
This is your l, what I have Jr 13:25
the land by l as an inheritance Ezk 45:1
and the l singled out Jonah. Jnh 1:7
that he was chosen by l, Lk 1:9
And there was a l of discussion Jn 7:12
and the l fell to Matthias. Ac 1:26
and I know how to have a l. Php 4:12
not drinking a l of wine, not 1Tm 3:8

LOT (proper noun) *(34)*
and Haran, and Haran fathered **L**. Gn 11:27
his grandson **L** (Haran's son), Gn 11:31
told him, and **L** went with him. Gn 12:4
Sarai, his nephew **L**, all the Gn 12:5
and all he had, and **L** with him. Gn 13:1
Now **L**, who was traveling with Gn 13:5
Abram said to **L**, "Please, let's Gn 13:8
L looked out and saw that the Gn 13:10
So **L** chose the entire Jordan Gn 13:11
Then **L** journeyed eastward, Gn 13:11
but **L** lived in the cities of the Gn 13:12
After **L** had separated from him, Gn 13:14
Abram's nephew **L** and his Gn 14:12
his relative **L** and his goods, Gn 14:16
the evening as **L** was sitting at Gn 19:1
When **L** saw ⌊them⌋, he got up to Gn 19:1
They called out to **L** and said, Gn 19:5
L went out to them at the Gn 19:6
put pressure on **L** and came up to Gn 19:9
brought **L** into the house with Gn 19:10
Then the angels said to **L**, Gn 19:12
So **L** went out and spoke to his Gn 19:14
crack of dawn the angels urged **L** Gn 19:15
But **L** said to them, "No, Lord— Gn 19:18
the land when **L** reached Zoar. Gn 19:23
and brought **L** out of the middle Gn 19:29
the cities where **L** had lived. Gn 19:29
L departed from Zoar and lived Gn 19:30
to the descendants of **L**.' " Dt 2:9
to the descendants of **L**.' " Dt 2:19
lend support to the sons of **L**. Ps 83:8
same as it was in the days of **L**: Lk 17:28
But on the day **L** left Sodom, Lk 17:29
and if He rescued righteous **L**, 2Pt 2:7

LOT'S *(3)*
and the herdsmen of **L** livestock. Gn 13:7
So both of **L** daughters became Gn 19:36
Remember **L** wife! Lk 17:32

LOTAN *(4)*
L, Shobal, Zibeon, Anah, Gn 36:20
The sons of **L** were Hori and Gn 36:22
Chiefs **L**, Shobal, Zibeon, Anah, Gn 36:29
L, Shobal, Zibeon, Anah, Dishon, 1Ch 1:38

LOTAN'S *(3)*
and Heman. Timna was **L** sister. Gn 36:22
L sons: Hori and Homam. Timna 1Ch 1:39
and Homam. Timna was **L** sister. 1Ch 1:39

LOTS *(24)*
Aaron casts **l** for the two goats Lv 16:8
will cast **l** for you here in the Jos 18:6
I will then cast **l** for you here Jos 18:8
Joshua cast **l** for them at Shiloh Jos 18:10
They also cast **l** the same way as 1Ch 24:31
cast **l** impartially for their 1Ch 25:8
They cast **l** according to their 1Ch 26:13
They also cast **l** for his son 1Ch 26:14
have cast **l** among the priests, Neh 10:34
the people cast **l** for one out of Neh 11:1
you would cast ⌊**l**⌋ for a Jb 6:27
and they cast **l** for my clothing. Ps 22:18
l should not be cast for its Ezk 24:6
They cast **l** for My people; Jl 3:3
gate and cast **l** for Jerusalem, Ob 11
Let's cast **l**. Then we will know Jnh 1:7
So they cast **l**, and the lot Jnh 1:7
to divide the land by casting **l**. Mc 2:5
They cast **l** for her dignitaries, Nah 3:10
His clothes by casting **l**. Mt 27:35
casting **l** for them to decide Mk 15:24
divided His clothes and cast **l**. Lk 23:34
and they cast **l** for My clothing. Jn 19:24
Then they cast **l** for them, Ac 1:26

LOTUS *(2)*
He lies under the **l** plants, Jb 40:21
L plants cover him with their Jb 40:22

LOUD *(66)*
cried out with a **l** and bitter Gn 27:34
and I screamed as **l** as I could. Gn 39:14
and there was a **l** wailing Ex 12:30
mountain, and a **l** trumpet sound, Ex 19:16
community broke into **l** cries, Nm 14:1
commands in a **l** voice to your Dt 5:22
proclaim in a **l** voice to every Dt 27:14
raised such a **l** shout that the 1Sm 4:5
this **l** shout in the Hebrews' 1Sm 4:6
of Israel with a **l** voice: 1Kg 8:55
oath to the LORD in a **l** voice, 2Ch 15:14
of Israel shouting in a **l** voice. 2Ch 20:19
after day with **l** instruments. 2Ch 30:21
responded with a **l** voice: Ezr 10:12
She is **l** and defiant; her feet Pr 7:11
neighbor with a **l** voice early Pr 27:14
earthquake, and **l** noise, storm, Is 29:6
out in My ears with a **l** voice, Ezk 8:18
to me directly with a **l** voice, Ezk 9:1
and cried out with a **l** voice: Ezk 11:13
and a **l** crashing from the hills. Zph 1:10
out His angels with a **l** trumpet, Mt 24:31
Jesus cried out with a **l** voice, Mt 27:46
again with a **l** voice and gave up Mt 27:50
shouted with a **l** voice, and came Mk 1:26
And he cried out with a **l** voice, Mk 5:7
Jesus cried out with a **l** voice, Mk 15:34
Jesus let out a **l** cry and Mk 15:37
Then she exclaimed with a **l** cry: Lk 1:42
who cried out with a **l** voice, Lk 4:33
and said in a **l** voice, "What do Lk 8:28
and, with a **l** voice, gave glory Lk 17:15
joyfully with a **l** voice for all Lk 19:37
demanding with **l** voices that He Lk 23:23
Jesus called out with a **l** voice, Lk 23:46
He shouted with a **l** voice, Jn 11:43
and cried out with a **l** voice, Ac 7:60
crying out with a **l** voice, Ac 8:7
⌊Paul⌋ said in a **l** voice, Ac 14:10
Paul called out in a **l** voice, Ac 16:28
The shouting grew **l**, and some of Ac 23:9
Festus exclaimed in a **l** voice, Ac 26:24
appeals, with **l** cries and tears Heb 5:7
will pass away with a **l** noise, 2Pt 3:10
I heard behind me a **l** voice like Rv 1:10
angel proclaiming in a **l** voice, Rv 5:2
They said with a **l** voice: Rv 5:12
They cried out with a **l** voice: Rv 6:10
cried out in a **l** voice to the Rv 7:2
And they cried out in a **l** voice: Rv 7:10
saying in a **l** voice, "Woe! Rv 8:13
he cried out with a **l** voice like Rv 10:3
they heard a **l** voice from heaven Rv 11:12
there were **l** voices in heaven Rv 11:15
Then I heard a **l** voice in heaven Rv 12:10
like the rumbling of **l** thunder. Rv 14:2
He spoke with a **l** voice: Rv 14:7
them and spoke with a **l** voice: Rv 14:9
crying out in a **l** voice to the Rv 14:15
called with a **l** voice to the one Rv 14:18
Then I heard a **l** voice from the Rv 16:1
and a **l** voice came out of the Rv 16:17
like the **l** voice of a vast Rv 19:1
like the rumbling of **l** thunder, Rv 19:6
and he cried out in a **l** voice, Rv 19:17
Then I heard a **l** voice from the Rv 21:3

LOUDER *(2)*
the trumpet grew **l** and louder, Ex 19:19
the trumpet grew louder and **l**, Ex 19:19

LOUDLY *(37)*
as she sat nearby, she wept **l**. Gn 21:16
my father!" And Esau wept **l**. Gn 27:38
Jacob kissed Rachel and wept **l**. Gn 29:11
But he wept so **l** that the Gn 45:2
lamented and wept **l**, and Joseph Gn 50:10
sound a trumpet **l** in the seventh Lv 25:9
Israelites, the people wept **l**. Jdg 2:4
They wept **l** and bitterly, Jdg 21:2
kissed them, and they wept **l**. Ru 1:9
Again they wept **l**, and Orpah Ru 1:14
The LORD thundered **l** against the 1Sm 7:10
with him wept **l** until they had 1Sm 30:4
king's sons entered and wept **l**. 2Sm 13:36
was weeping **l** while all the 2Sm 15:23
said, "Shout **l**, for he's a god 1Kg 18:27
They shouted **l**, and cut 1Kg 18:28
and called out **l** in Hebrew. 2Kg 18:28
they called out **l** in Hebrew to 2Ch 32:18
wept **l** when they saw the Ezr 3:12
the people were shouting so **l**. Ezr 3:13
cried out **l** to the LORD their Neh 9:4
city, and cried **l** and bitterly. Est 4:1
warriors cry **l** in the streets; Is 33:7
and called out **l** in Hebrew: Is 36:13
good news, raise your voice **l**. Is 40:9
Cry out **l**, don't hold back! Is 58:1
have roared **l**. They have laid Jr 2:15
land. Cry out **l** and say: Jr 4:5
they have cried out **l** after you. Jr 12:6
roars **l** over His grazing land; Jr 25:30
herald **l** proclaimed, "People of Dn 3:4
He called out **l**: Cut down the Dn 4:14
and **l** proclaim your freewill Am 4:5
Now, why are you shouting **l**? Mc 4:9
Zion; shout **l**, Israel! Be glad Zph 3:14
players and a crowd lamenting **l**. Mt 9:23
people weeping and wailing **l**. Mk 5:38

LOVE *(565)*
Isaac, whom you **l**, go to the Gn 22:2
food that I **l** and bring it to me Gn 27:4
to him because of his **l** for her. Gn 29:20
my husband will **l** me now." Gn 29:32
will deal with me in faithful **l**. Gn 47:29
redeemed with Your faithful **l**; Ex 15:13
showing faithful **l** to a thousand Ex 20:6
of those who **l** Me and keep My Ex 20:6
'I **l** my master, my wife, and my Ex 21:5
rich in faithful **l** and truth, Ex 34:6
faithful **l** to a thousand Ex 34:7
but **l** your neighbor as yourself; Lv 19:18
You are to **l** him as yourself, Lv 19:34
to anger and rich in faithful **l**, Nm 14:18
greatness of Your faithful **l**, Nm 14:19
showing faithful **l** to a thousand Dt 5:10
of those who **l** Me and keep My Dt 5:10
L the LORD your God with all Dt 6:5
with those who **l** Him and keep Dt 7:9
He will **l** you, bless you, and Dt 7:13
all His ways, to **l** Him, and to Dt 10:12
You also must **l** the foreigner, Dt 10:19
l the LORD your God and always Dt 11:1
to **l** the LORD your God and Dt 11:13
to follow—to **l** the LORD your Dt 11:22
know whether you **l** the LORD your Dt 13:3
and you will **l** Him with all your Dt 30:6
today to **l** the LORD your God, Dt 30:16
l the LORD your God, obey Him, Dt 30:20
to **l** the LORD your God, walk in Jos 22:5
very diligent to **l** the LORD your Jos 23:11
But may those who **l** Him be like Jdg 5:31
You hate me and don't **l** me! Jdg 14:16
he fell in **l** with a woman named Jdg 16:4
can you say, 'I **l** you,' " she Jdg 16:15
show faithful **l** to you as you Ru 1:8
and all his servants **l** you. 1Sm 18:22
me with the LORD's faithful **l**, 1Sm 20:14
faithful **l** from my household 1Sm 20:15
swore to David in his **l** for him, 1Sm 20:17
Your **l** for me was more wonderful 2Sm 1:26
than the **l** of a woman ⌊for me 2Sm 1:26
But My faithful **l** will never 2Sm 7:15
replied, "I'm in **l** with Tamar, 2Sm 13:4
than the **l** he had loved her 2Sm 13:15
l your enemies and hate those 2Sm 19:6
and hate those who **l** you! 2Sm 19:6
and faithful **l** to Your servant, 1Kg 3:6
and faithful **l** for him by giving 1Kg 3:6
the LORD's eternal **l** for Israel. 1Kg 10:9
His faithful **l** endures forever. 1Ch 16:34
His faithful **l** endures forever 1Ch 16:41
away My faithful **l** from him as I 1Ch 17:13
great faithful **l** to my father 2Ch 1:8
His faithful **l** endures forever; 2Ch 5:13
His faithful **l** endures forever 2Ch 7:3
His faithful **l** endures forever 2Ch 7:6
the wicked and **l** those who hate 2Ch 19:2
His faithful **l** endures forever 2Ch 20:21
and his deeds of faithful **l**, 2Ch 32:32
of faithful **l** according to what 2Ch 35:26
His faithful **l** to Israel endures Ezr 3:11
with those who **l** Him and keep Neh 1:5
to anger and rich in faithful **l**, Neh 9:17
with Your abundant, faithful **l**. Neh 13:22
You gave me life and faithful **l**, Jb 10:12
those I **l** have turned against Jb 19:19
His land, or for His faithful **l**. Jb 37:13
long⌋ will you **l** what is Ps 4:2
abundance of Your faithful **l**; Ps 5:7
may those who **l** Your name boast Ps 5:11
me because of Your faithful **l**. Ps 6:4
have trusted in Your faithful **l**; Ps 13:5
the wonders of Your faithful **l**, Ps 17:7
I **l** You, LORD, my strength. Ps 18:1
the faithful **l** of the Most High Ps 21:7
faithful **l** will pursue me all Ps 23:6
compassion and Your faithful **l**, Ps 25:6
in keeping with Your faithful **l**, Ps 25:7

show⌋ faithful l and truth to Ps 25:10
Your faithful l is before my Ps 26:3
I l the house where You dwell, Ps 26:8
Your faithful l because You have Ps 31:7
save me by Your faithful l. Ps 31:16
His faithful l to me in a city Ps 31:21
L the LORD, all His faithful Ps 31:23
have faithful l surrounding him. Ps 32:10
full of the LORD's unfailing l. Ps 33:5
who depend on His faithful l Ps 33:18
May Your faithful l rest on us, Ps 33:22
Your faithful l ⌊reaches⌋ to Ps 36:5
Your faithful l is so valuable Ps 36:7
Your faithful l over those who Ps 36:10
conceal Your constant l and Ps 40:10
Your constant l and truth will Ps 40:11
let those who l Your salvation Ps 40:16
will send His faithful l by day; Ps 42:8
us because of Your faithful l. Ps 44:26
You l righteousness and hate Ps 45:7
we contemplate Your faithful l. Ps 48:9
according to Your faithful l; Ps 51:1
God's faithful l is constant. Ps 52:1
You l evil instead of good, Ps 52:3
You l any words that destroy, Ps 52:4
God's faithful l forever and Ps 52:8
sends His faithful l and truth. Ps 57:3
For Your faithful l is as high Ps 57:10
Your faithful l in the morning. Ps 59:16
that those You l may be rescued. Ps 60:5
appoint faithful l and truth to Ps 61:7
and faithful l belongs to You, Ps 62:12
Your faithful l is better than Ps 63:3
turned His faithful l from me. Ps 66:20
faithful l, God, answer me Ps 69:13
for Your faithful l is good; Ps 69:16
and those who l His name will Ps 69:36
let those who l Your salvation Ps 70:4
His faithful l ceased forever? Ps 77:8
Your faithful l, LORD, and give Ps 85:7
Faithful l and truth will join Ps 85:10
in faithful l to all who call Ps 86:5
Your faithful l for me is great Ps 86:13
in faithful l and truth. Ps 86:15
Will Your faithful l be declared Ps 88:11
the LORD's faithful l forever; Ps 89:1
Faithful l is built up forever; Ps 89:2
faithful l and truth go before Ps 89:14
and l will be with him Ps 89:24
preserve My faithful l for him, Ps 89:28
My faithful l from him or betray Ps 89:33
Your faithful l that You swore Ps 89:49
Your faithful l so that we may Ps 90:14
Your faithful l in the morning Ps 92:2
Your faithful l will support me Ps 94:18
You who l the LORD, hate evil! Ps 97:10
His l and faithfulness Ps 98:3
is good, and His l is eternal; Ps 100:5
sing of faithful l and justice; Ps 101:1
with faithful l and compassion. Ps 103:4
to anger and full of faithful l. Ps 103:8
is His faithful l toward those Ps 103:11
LORD's faithful l is toward Ps 103:17
His faithful l endures forever. Ps 106:1
Your many acts of faithful l; Ps 106:7
the abundance of His faithful l. Ps 106:45
His faithful l endures forever. Ps 107:1
for His faithful l and His Ps 107:8
for His faithful l and His Ps 107:15
for His faithful l and His Ps 107:21
for His faithful l and His Ps 107:31
the LORD's acts of faithful l. Ps 107:43
Your faithful l is higher than Ps 108:4
that those You l may be rescued. Ps 108:6
return for my l they accuse me, Ps 109:4
for good, and hatred for my l. Ps 109:5
the goodness of Your faithful l. Ps 109:21
me according to Your faithful l Ps 109:26
because of Your faithful l, Ps 115:1
l the LORD because He has heard Ps 116:1
great is His faithful l to us; Ps 117:2
His faithful l endures forever. Ps 118:1
"His faithful l endures forever." Ps 118:2
"His faithful l endures forever." Ps 118:3
"His faithful l endures forever." Ps 118:4
His faithful l endures forever. Ps 118:29
Let Your faithful l come to me, Ps 119:41
in Your commands, which I l. Ps 119:47

commands, which I l, and will Ps 119:48
is filled with Your faithful l; Ps 119:64
May Your faithful l comfort me, Ps 119:76
accordance with Your faithful l, Ps 119:88
How I l Your teaching! It is my Ps 119:97
but I l Your instruction. Ps 119:113
therefore, I l Your decrees. Ps 119:119
based on Your faithful l; Ps 119:124
I l Your commandments more Ps 119:127
toward those who l Your name. Ps 119:132
In keeping with Your faithful l, Ps 119:149
Consider how I l Your precepts; Ps 119:159
according to Your faithful l. Ps 119:159
⌊but⌋ I l Your instruction. Ps 119:163
to those who l Your instruction; Ps 119:165
Your decrees and l them greatly. Ps 119:167
May those who l you prosper; Ps 122:6
is faithful l with the LORD, Ps 130:7
He is good. His l is eternal. Ps 136:1
God of gods. His l is eternal. Ps 136:2
Lord of lords. His l is eternal. Ps 136:3
great wonders. His l is eternal. Ps 136:4
skillfully. His l is eternal. Ps 136:5
on the waters. His l is eternal. Ps 136:6
great lights: His l is eternal. Ps 136:7
rule by day, His l is eternal. Ps 136:8
rule by night. His l is eternal. Ps 136:9
the Egyptians His l is eternal. Ps 136:10
among them His l is eternal. Ps 136:11
arm. His l is eternal. Ps 136:12
the Red Sea His l is eternal. Ps 136:13
through, His l is eternal. Ps 136:14
the Red Sea. His l is eternal. Ps 136:15
wilderness. His l is eternal. Ps 136:16
great kings His l is eternal. Ps 136:17
famous kings—His l is eternal. Ps 136:18
the Amorites His l is eternal. Ps 136:19
of Bashan—His l is eternal. Ps 136:20
inheritance, His l is eternal. Ps 136:21
His servant. His l is eternal. Ps 136:22
humiliation His l is eternal. Ps 136:23
from our foes. His l is eternal. Ps 136:24
creature. His l is eternal. Ps 136:25
God of heaven! His l is eternal. Ps 136:26
Your constant l and faithfulness Ps 138:2
LORD, Your l is eternal; Ps 138:8
it is ⌊an act of⌋ faithful l; Ps 141:5
Your faithful l in the morning, Ps 143:8
in Your faithful l destroy my Ps 143:12
is my faithful l and my fortress Ps 144:2
anger and great in faithful l. Ps 145:8
LORD guards all those who l Him, Ps 145:20
their hope in His faithful l. Ps 147:11
ones, will you l ignorance? Pr 1:22
l her, and she will guard you. Pr 4:6
be lost in her l forever. Pr 5:19
Let's feast on each other's l! Pr 7:18
I l those who love me, and those Pr 8:17
I love those who l me, and those Pr 8:17
inheritance to those who l me, Pr 8:21
all who hate me l death." Pr 8:36
a wise man, and he will l you. Pr 9:8
but l covers all offenses. Pr 10:12
there are many who l the rich. Pr 14:20
mocker doesn't l one who Pr 15:12
where there is l than a fattened Pr 15:17
conceals an offense promotes l, Pr 17:9
and those who l it will eat its Pr 18:21
l sleep, or you will become Pr 20:13
and faithful l will find life, Pr 21:21
open reprimand than concealed l. Pr 27:5
a time to l and a time to hate; Ec 3:8
whether ⌊to expect⌋ l or hate. Ec 9:1
Their l, their hate, and their Ec 9:6
with the wife you l all the days Ec 9:9
For your l is more delightful Sg 1:2
praise your l more than wine. Sg 1:4
Tell me, you, the one I l: Sg 1:7
My l is a sachet of myrrh to me, Sg 1:13
My l is a cluster of henna Sg 1:14
How handsome you are, my l. Sg 1:16
so is my l among the young men. Sg 2:3
and he looked on me with l. Sg 2:4
stir up or awaken l until the Sg 2:7
Listen! My l ⌊is approaching⌋. Sg 2:8
l is like a gazelle or a young Sg 2:9
My l calls to me: Arise, my Sg 2:10
My l is mine and I am his; Sg 2:16

turn ⌊to me⌋, my l, and be like Sg 2:17
at night I sought the one I l; Sg 3:1
I will seek the one I l. Sg 3:2
"Have you seen the one I l?" Sg 3:3
them when I found the one I l. Sg 3:4
stir up or awaken l until the Sg 3:5
is inlaid with l by the young Sg 3:10
delightful your l is, my sister, Sg 4:10
Your l is much better than wine, Sg 4:10
Let my l come to his garden and Sg 4:16
Drink, be intoxicated with l! Sg 5:1
A sound! My l is knocking! Open Sg 5:2
My l thrust his hand through the Sg 5:4
I rose to open for my l. Sg 5:5
opened to my l, but my love had Sg 5:6
but my l had turned and gone Sg 5:6
if you find my l, tell him that Sg 5:8
makes the one you l better than Sg 5:9
My l is fit and strong, notable Sg 5:10
This is my l, and this is my Sg 5:16
Where has your l gone, most Sg 6:1
l has gone down to his garden, Sg 6:2
I am my love's and my l is mine; Sg 6:3
how pleasant, ⌊my⌋ l, with such Sg 7:6
smoothly for my l gliding past Sg 7:9
I belong to my l, and his desire Sg 7:10
Come, my l, let's go to the Sg 7:11
There I will give you my l. Sg 7:12
treasured them up for you, my l. Sg 7:13
stir up or awaken l until the Sg 8:4
For l is as strong as death; Sg 8:6
ardent l is as unrelenting as Sg 8:6
waters cannot extinguish l; Sg 8:7
to give all his wealth for l, Sg 8:7
Hurry ⌊to me⌋, my l, and be like Sg 8:14
They all l graft and chase after Is 1:23
I will sing about the one I l, Is 5:1
The one I l had a vineyard on a Is 5:1
be established by faithful l. Is 16:5
but Your l ⌊has delivered⌋ me Is 38:17
honored, and I l you, I will Is 43:4
on you with everlasting l," Is 54:8
l will not be removed from you Is 54:10
to Him, l the LORD's name Is 56:6
dream, lie down, and l to sleep. Is 56:10
For I the LORD l justice; Is 61:8
LORD's faithful l ⌊and⌋ the Is 63:7
the abundance of His faithful l. Is 63:7
because of His l and compassion; Is 63:9
rejoice over her, all who l her. Is 66:10
youth, your l as a bride—how Jr 2:2
I l strangers, and I will Jr 2:25
How skillfully you pursue l; Jr 2:33
for I am unfailing in My l. Jr 3:12
My people l it like this. Jr 5:31
showing faithful l, justice, Jr 9:24
I have given the l of My life Jr 12:7
Truly they l to wander; Jr 14:10
My⌋ faithful l and compassion. Jr 16:5
both yourself and those you l. Jr 20:4
loved you with an everlasting l; Jr 31:3
to extend faithful l to you. Jr 31:3
You show faithful l to thousands Jr 32:18
His faithful l endures forever Jr 33:11
LORD's faithful l we do not Lm 3:22
to His abundant, faithful l. Lm 3:32
were indeed at the age for l. Ezk 16:8
to the bed of l, and defiled her Ezk 23:17
express l with their mouths, Ezk 33:31
like a singer of l songs who has Ezk 33:32
with those who l Him and keep Dn 9:4
justice, l, and compassion. Hs 2:19
show l to a woman who is loved Hs 3:1
other gods and l raisin cakes." Hs 3:1
no faithful l, and no knowledge Hs 4:1
leaders fervently l disgrace. Hs 4:18
Ephraim has paid for l. Hs 8:9
I will no longer l them; Hs 9:15
yourselves and reap faithful l; Hs 10:12
Maintain l and justice, and Hs 12:6
I will freely l them, for My Hs 14:4
in faithful l, and He relents Jl 2:13
what you Israelites l ⌊to do⌋! Am 4:5
Hate evil and l good; establish Am 5:15
idols forsake faithful l, Jnh 2:8
rich in faithful l, and One who Jnh 4:2
You hate good and l evil. Mc 3:2
act justly, to l faithfulness, Mc 6:8

He delights in faithful **l**. Mc 7:18
Jacob and faithful **l** to Abraham, Mc 7:20
⌊you⌋ quietness with His **l**. Zph 3:17
Show faithful **l** and compassion Zch 7:9
and do not **l** perjury, for I hate Zch 8:17
Therefore, **l** truth and peace." Zch 8:19
L your neighbor and hate your Mt 5:43
l your enemies and pray for Mt 5:44
For if you **l** those who love you, Mt 5:46
For if you love those who **l** you, Mt 5:46
because they **l** to pray standing Mt 6:5
will hate one and **l** the other, Mt 6:24
and **l** your neighbor as yourself. Mt 19:19
L the Lord your God with all Mt 22:37
L your neighbor as yourself. Mt 22:39
They **l** the place of honor at Mt 23:6
the **l** of many will grow cold. Mt 24:12
L the Lord your God with all Mk 12:30
L your neighbor as yourself. Mk 12:31
to **l** Him with all your heart, Mk 12:33
and to **l** your neighbor as Mk 12:33
L your enemies, do good to those Lk 6:27
If you **l** those who love you, Lk 6:32
If you love those who **l** you, Lk 6:32
Even sinners **l** those who love Lk 6:32
sinners love those who **l** them. Lk 6:32
But **l** your enemies, do ⌊what is⌋ Lk 6:35
which of them will **l** him more?" Lk 7:42
L the Lord your God with all Lk 10:27
bypass justice and **l** for God. Lk 11:42
You **l** the front seat in the Lk 11:43
will hate one and **l** the other, Lk 16:13
long robes and who **l** greetings Lk 20:46
you have no **l** for God within Jn 5:42
Father, you would **l** Me, because Jn 8:42
"Lord, the one You **l** is sick." Jn 11:3
new commandment: **l** one another. Jn 13:34
you must also **l** one another. Jn 13:34
if you have **l** for one another." Jn 13:35
If you **l** Me, you will keep My Jn 14:15
also will **l** him and will reveal Jn 14:21
Father will **l** him, and We will Jn 14:23
one who doesn't **l** Me will not Jn 14:24
may know that I **l** the Father. Jn 14:31
also loved you. Remain in My **l**. Jn 15:9
you will remain in My **l**, Jn 15:10
commands and remain in His **l**. Jn 15:10
l one another as I have loved Jn 15:12
No one has greater **l** than this, Jn 15:13
I command you: **l** one another. Jn 15:17
the world would **l** ⌊you as⌋ its Jn 15:19
so the **l** You have loved Me with Jn 17:26
do you **l** Me more than these?" Jn 21:15
to Him, "You know that I **l** You." Jn 21:15
son of John, do you **l** Me?" Jn 21:16
to Him, "You know that I **l** You." Jn 21:16
son of John, do you **l** Me?" Jn 21:17
the third time, "Do you **l** Me?" Jn 21:17
You know that I **l** You." Jn 21:17
because God's **l** has been poured Rm 5:5
proves His own **l** for us in that Rm 5:8
for the good of those who **l** God: Rm 8:28
us from the **l** of Christ? Rm 8:35
us from the **l** of God that is Rm 8:39
L must be without hypocrisy. Rm 12:9
to one another with brotherly **l**. Rm 12:10
except to **l** one another, for Rm 13:8
You shall **l** your neighbor as Rm 13:9
L does no wrong to a neighbor. Rm 13:10
L, therefore, is the fulfillment Rm 13:10
longer walking according to **l**. Rm 14:15
and through the **l** of the Spirit, Rm 15:30
prepared for those who **l** Him. 1Co 2:9
or in **l** and a spirit of 1Co 4:21
with pride, but **l** builds up. 1Co 8:1
but do not have **l**, I am a 1Co 13:1
but do not have **l**, I am nothing. 1Co 13:2
do not have **l**, I gain nothing 1Co 13:3
L is patient; love is kind. Love 1Co 13:4
Love is patient; **l** is kind. Love 1Co 13:4
love is kind. **L** does not envy; 1Co 13:4
L never ends. But as for 1Co 13:8
faith, hope, and **l**. But the 1Co 13:13
But the greatest of these is **l**. 1Co 13:13
Pursue **l** and desire spiritual 1Co 14:1
action⌋ must be done with **l**. 1Co 16:14
If anyone does not **l** the Lord, 1Co 16:22
l be with all of you in Christ 1Co 16:24

the abundant **l** I have for you. 2Co 2:4
you to confirm your **l** to him. 2Co 2:8
For Christ's **l** compels us, 2Co 5:14
the Holy Spirit, by sincere **l**, 2Co 6:6
in your **l** for us—excel also 2Co 8:7
the genuineness of your **l**. 2Co 8:8
the proof of your **l** and of our 2Co 8:24
Because I don't **l** you? God knows 2Co 11:11
I **l** you more, am I to be loved 2Co 12:15
and the God of **l** and peace will 2Co 13:11
Jesus Christ, and the **l** of God, 2Co 13:13
is faith working through **l**. Gl 5:6
but serve one another through **l**. Gl 5:13
You shall **l** your neighbor as Gl 5:14
the fruit of the Spirit is **l**, Gl 5:22
and blameless in His sight. In **l** Eph 1:4
Jesus and your **l** for all the Eph 1:15
of His great **l** that He had for Eph 2:4
and firmly established in **l**, Eph 3:17
height and depth ⌊of God's **l**⌋, Eph 3:18
the Messiah's **l** that surpasses Eph 3:19
accepting one another in **l**, Eph 4:2
But speaking the truth in **l**, Eph 4:15
up itself in **l** by the proper Eph 4:16
And walk in **l**, as the Messiah Eph 5:2
Husbands, **l** your wives, just as Eph 5:25
husbands should **l** their wives as Eph 5:28
one of you is to **l** his wife as Eph 5:33
the brothers, and **l** with faith, Eph 6:23
who have undying **l** for our Lord Eph 6:24
that your **l** will keep on growing Php 1:9
do so out of **l**, knowing that I Php 1:16
consolation of **l**, if any Php 2:1
having the same **l**, sharing the Php 2:2
and of the **l** you have for all Col 1:4
us about your **l** in the Spirit. Col 1:8
and joined together in **l**, Col 2:2
all, ⌊put on⌋ **l**—the perfect Col 3:14
l your wives and don't become Col 3:19
faith, labor of **l**, and endurance 1Th 1:3
news about your faith and **l**, 1Th 3:6
overflow with **l** for one another 1Th 3:12
About brotherly **l**: you don't 1Th 4:9
taught by God to **l** one another. 1Th 4:9
of faith and **l** on our chests, 1Th 5:8
highly in **l** because of their 1Th 5:13
the **l** of every one of you for 2Th 1:3
not accept the **l** of the truth 2Th 2:10
hearts to God's **l** and Christ's 2Th 3:5
instruction is **l** from a pure 1Tm 1:5
the faith and **l** that are in 1Tm 1:14
in faith, **l**, and holiness, with 1Tm 2:15
in conduct, in **l**, in faith, in 1Tm 4:12
For the **l** of money is a root of 1Tm 6:10
godliness, faith, **l**, endurance, 1Tm 6:11
but one of power, **l**, and sound 2Tm 1:7
in the faith and **l** that are in 2Tm 1:13
faith, **l**, and peace, along 2Tm 2:22
without **l** for what is good, 2Tm 3:3
patience, **l**, and endurance, 2Tm 3:10
in faith, **l**, and endurance. Ti 2:2
young women to **l** their husbands Ti 2:4
goodness and **l** for man appeared Ti 3:4
those who **l** us in the faith Ti 3:15
hear of your **l** and faith toward Phm 5
and encouragement from your **l**, Phm 7
instead, on the basis of **l**. Phm 9
work and the **l** you showed for Heb 6:10
to promote **l** and good works, Heb 10:24
Let brotherly **l** continue. Heb 13:1
be free from the **l** of money. Heb 13:5
has promised to those who **l** Him. Jms 1:12
has promised to those who **l** Him? Jms 2:5
You shall **l** your neighbor as Jms 2:8
You **l** Him, though you have not 1Pt 1:8
for sincere **l** of the brothers, 1Pt 1:22
l one another earnestly from a 1Pt 1:22
everyone. **L** the brotherhood 1Pt 2:17
should **l** believers, and be 1Pt 3:8
who wants to **l** life and to see 1Pt 3:10
keep your **l** for one another at 1Pt 4:8
since **l** covers a multitude of 1Pt 4:8
one another with a kiss of **l**. 1Pt 5:14
and brotherly affection with **l**. 2Pt 1:7
truly in him the **l** of God is 1Jn 2:5
Do not **l** the world or the things 1Jn 2:15
l for the Father is not in him. 1Jn 2:15
at how great a **l** the Father has 1Jn 3:1

one who does not **l** his brother. 1Jn 3:10
we should **l** one another, 1Jn 3:11
life because we **l** our brothers. 1Jn 3:14
who does not **l** remains in death 1Jn 3:14
is how we have come to know **l**: 1Jn 3:16
how can God's **l** reside in him? 1Jn 3:17
we must not **l** in word or speech, 1Jn 3:18
l one another as He commanded 1Jn 3:23
friends, let us **l** one another, 1Jn 4:7
another, because **l** is from God, 1Jn 4:7
one who does not **l** does not know 1Jn 4:8
not know God, because God is **l**. 1Jn 4:8
God's **l** was revealed among us in 1Jn 4:9
L consists in this: not that we 1Jn 4:10
we also must **l** one another. 1Jn 4:11
If we **l** one another, God remains 1Jn 4:12
in us and His **l** is perfected in 1Jn 4:12
believe the **l** that God has for 1Jn 4:16
is **l**, and the one who remains 1Jn 4:16
who remains in **l** remains in God, 1Jn 4:16
l is perfected with us so that 1Jn 4:17
no fear in **l**; instead, perfect 1Jn 4:18
perfect **l** drives out fear, 1Jn 4:18
has not reached perfection in **l**. 1Jn 4:18
We **l** because He first loved us. 1Jn 4:19
anyone says, "I **l** God," yet 1Jn 4:20
who does not **l** his brother whom 1Jn 4:20
seen cannot **l** God whom he has 1Jn 4:20
God must also **l** his brother. 1Jn 4:21
we know that we **l** God's children 1Jn 5:2
when we **l** God and obey His 1Jn 5:2
For this is what **l** for God is: 1Jn 5:3
children, whom I **l** in truth— 2Jn 1
of the Father, in truth and **l**. 2Jn 3
that we **l** one another. 2Jn 5
And this is **l**: that we walk 2Jn 6
beginning: you must walk in **l**. 2Jn 6
friend Gaius, whom I **l** in truth. 3Jn 1
to your **l** before the church 3Jn 6
and **l** be multiplied to you. Jd 2
reefs at your **l** feasts. Jd 12
keep yourselves in the **l** of God, Jd 21
abandoned the **l** ⌊you had⌋ at Rv 2:4
works—your **l**, faithfulness, Rv 2:19
As many as I **l**, I rebuke and Rv 3:19
for they did not **l** their lives Rv 12:11

LOVE'S *(2)*

I am my **l** and my love is mine; Sg 6:3
L flames are fiery flames— Sg 8:6

LOVED *(110)*

l her, and he was comforted Gn 24:67
Isaac **l** Esau because he had a Gn 25:28
wild game, but Rebekah **l** Jacob. Gn 25:28
the delicious food his father **l**. Gn 27:14
Jacob **l** Rachel, so he answered Gn 29:18
he **l** Rachel more than Leah. Gn 29:30
He **l** the young girl and spoke Gn 34:3
Israel **l** Joseph more than his Gn 37:3
their father **l** him more than all Gn 37:4
Because He **l** your fathers, Dt 4:37
because the LORD **l** you and kept Dt 7:8
to your fathers and **l** them. Dt 10:15
one **l** and the other unloved, Dt 21:15
and both the **l** and the unloved Dt 21:15
the son of the **l** ⌊wife⌋ as his Dt 21:16
he **l** her even though the LORD 1Sm 1:5
and **l** him as much as he loved 1Sm 18:1
him as much as he **l** himself. 1Sm 18:1
David because he **l** him as much 1Sm 18:3
and Judah **l** David because he 1Sm 18:16
Saul's daughter Michal **l** David, 1Sm 18:20
that his daughter Michal **l** him, 1Sm 18:28
because he **l** him as he loved 1Sm 20:17
he loved him as he **l** himself. 1Sm 20:17
and Jonathan, **l** and delightful, 2Sm 1:23
him Solomon. The LORD **l** him, 2Sm 12:24
than the love he had **l** her with. 2Sm 13:15
Solomon **l** the LORD by walking in 1Kg 3:3
Solomon **l** many foreign women 1Kg 11:1
to these women and **l** ⌊them⌋. 1Kg 11:2
Your God **l** Israel enough to 2Ch 9:8
Rehoboam **l** Maacah daughter of 2Ch 11:21
was **l** by his God and God made Neh 13:26
The king **l** Esther more than all Est 2:17
My **l** ones and friends stand back Ps 38:11
Judah, Mount Zion, which He **l**. Ps 78:68
distanced **l** one and neighbor Ps 88:18
He **l** cursing—let it fall on Ps 109:17

song about my l one's vineyard: Is 5:1
them. You have l their bed; you Is 57:8
which they have l, served, Jr 8:2
I have l you with an everlasting Jr 31:3
has killed everyone who was l, Lm 2:4
all those you l as well as all Ezk 16:37
a woman who is l by another man Hs 3:1
You have l the wages of a Hs 9:1
like the thing they l. Hs 9:10
was a child, I l him, and out of Hs 11:1
"I have l you," says the LORD. Mal 1:2
How have You l us?" "Wasn't Esau Mal 1:2
"Even so, I l Jacob, Mal 1:2
Jesus l him and said to him, Mk 10:21
that's why she l much. Lk 7:47
For God l the world in this way: Jn 3:16
people l darkness rather than Jn 3:19
Jesus l Martha, her sister, and Jn 11:5
Jews said, "See how He l him!" Jn 11:36
For they l praise from men more Jn 12:43
Having l His own who were in the Jn 13:1
the world, He l them to the end Jn 13:1
the one Jesus l, was reclining Jn 13:23
Just as I have l you, you must Jn 13:34
loves Me will be l by My Father. Jn 14:21
If you l Me, you would have Jn 14:28
the Father has l me, I have also Jn 15:9
has loved me, I have also l you. Jn 15:9
one another as I have l you. Jn 15:12
because you have l Me and have Jn 16:27
Me and have l them as You have Jn 17:23
loved them as You have l Me. Jn 17:23
given Me because You l Me before Jn 17:24
love You have l Me with may be Jn 17:26
disciple He l standing there, Jn 19:26
the one Jesus l, and said to Jn 20:2
the one Jesus l, said to Peter, Jn 21:7
disciple Jesus l following them. Jn 21:20
are in Rome, l by God, called Rm 1:7
victorious through Him who l us. Rm 8:37
Jacob I have l, but Esau I have Rm 9:13
they are l because of their Rm 11:28
you more, am I to be l less? 2Co 12:15
l me and gave Himself for me. Gl 2:20
of God, as dearly l children. Eph 5:1
the Messiah also l us and gave Eph 5:2
as also Christ l the church and Eph 5:25
dearly l brother and faithful Eph 6:21
way, my dearly l brothers, my Php 4:1
our much l fellow slave. Col 1:7
ones, holy and l, put on Col 3:12
Tychicus, a l brother, a Col 4:7
a faithful and l brother, who is Col 4:9
Luke, the l physician, and Demas Col 4:14
election, brothers l by God. 1Th 1:4
for you, brothers l by the Lord, 2Th 2:13
has l us and given us eternal 2Th 2:16
are believers and dearly l. 1Tm 6:2
To Timothy, my dearly l child. 2Tm 1:2
those who have l His appearing. 2Tm 4:8
because he l this present world, 2Tm 4:10
a slave—as a dearly l brother. Phm 16
You have l righteousness and Heb 1:9
deceived, my dearly l brothers. Jms 1:16
My dearly l brothers, understand Jms 1:19
who l the wages of 2Pt 2:15
not that we l God, but that He 1Jn 4:10
that He l us and sent His Son 1Jn 4:10
if God l us in this way, 1Jn 4:11
We love because He first l us. 1Jn 4:19
l by God the Father and kept by Jd 1
will know that I have l you. Rv 3:9

LOVELINESS *(1)*
Whom do you surpass in l? Ezk 32:19

LOVELY *(9)*
How l is Your dwelling place, Ps 84:1
for praise is pleasant and l. Ps 147:1
yet l like the curtains of Sg 1:5
is sweet, and your face is l. Sg 2:14
cord, and your mouth is l. Sg 4:3
my darling, l as Jerusalem, Sg 6:4
grand and l ones without Is 5:9
l and beautiful they will be! Zch 9:17
pure, whatever is l, whatever is Php 4:8

LOVEMAKING *(1)*
drink deeply of l until morning. Pr 7:18

LOVER *(4)*
since he was a l of the soil, 2Ch 26:10
He hates the l of violence. Ps 11:5
now hear this, l of luxury, who Is 47:8
as a woman may betray her l, Jr 3:20

LOVERS *(25)*
nothing. Your l reject you; they Jr 4:30
all your l have been crushed. Jr 22:20
and your l will go into Jr 22:22
All your l have forgotten you; Jr 30:14
not one⌋ from all her l. Lm 1:2
I called to my l, but they Lm 1:19
you gave gifts to all your l. Ezk 16:33
of prostitution with your l, Ezk 16:36
gather all the l you pleased— Ezk 16:37
will never again pay fees for l. Ezk 16:41
after her l, the Assyrians: Ezk 23:5
I handed her over to her l, Ezk 23:9
after their l, whose sexual Ezk 23:20
to incite your l against you, Ezk 23:22
will go after my l, the men who Hs 2:5
will pursue her l but not catch Hs 2:7
her shame in the sight of her l, Hs 2:10
wages that her l have given her. Hs 2:12
went after her l, but forgot Me. Hs 2:13
though they hire ⌊l⌋ among the Hs 8:10
who were l of money, were Lk 16:14
For people will be l of self, 2Tm 3:2
lovers of self, l of money, 2Tm 3:2
l of pleasure rather than lovers 2Tm 3:4
pleasure rather than l of God, 2Tm 3:4

LOVES *(67)*
for your father—the kind he l. Gn 27:9
left, and his father l him.' Gn 44:20
and l the foreign resident, Dt 10:18
because he l you and your Dt 15:16
because the LORD your God l you. Dt 23:5
Indeed He l the people. Dt 33:3
who l you and is better to you Ru 4:15
Because the LORD l His people, 2Ch 2:11
righteous; He l righteous deeds Ps 11:7
He l righteousness and justice; Ps 33:5
For the LORD l justice and will Ps 37:28
the pride of Jacob, whom He l. Ps 47:4
LORD l the gates of Zion more Ps 87:2
The mighty King l justice. Ps 99:4
pure, and Your servant l it. Ps 119:140
He gives sleep to the one He l. Ps 127:2
The LORD l the righteous. Ps 146:8
LORD disciplines the one He l, Pr 3:12
Whoever l instruction loves Pr 12:1
loves instruction l knowledge, Pr 12:1
the one who l him disciplines Pr 13:24
but He l the one who pursues Pr 15:9
he l one who speaks honestly. Pr 16:13
A friend l at all times, and a Pr 17:17
who l to offend loves strife; Pr 17:19
who loves to offend l strife; Pr 17:19
acquires good sense l himself; Pr 19:8
The one who l pleasure will Pr 21:17
whoever l wine and oil will not Pr 21:17
The one who l a pure heart and Pr 22:11
A man who l wisdom brings joy to Pr 29:3
The one who l money is never Ec 5:10
and whoever l wealth ⌊is⌋ never Ec 5:10
leaning on the one she l? Sg 8:5
things? The LORD l him; he will Is 48:14
as the LORD l the Israelites Hs 3:1
young cow that l to thresh, Hs 10:11
A merchant l to extort with Hs 12:7
which He l, and has married Mal 2:11
person who l father or mother Mt 10:37
the person who l son or daughter Mt 10:37
because he l our nation and has Lk 7:5
is forgiven little, l little." Lk 7:47
The Father l the Son and has Jn 3:35
For the Father l the Son and Jn 5:20
This is why the Father l Me, Jn 10:17
The one who l his life will lose Jn 12:25
keeps them is the one who l Me. Jn 14:21
And the one who l Me will be Jn 14:21
If anyone l Me, he will keep My Jn 14:23
For the Father Himself l you, Jn 16:27
for the one who l another has Rm 13:8
But if anyone l God, he is known 1Co 8:3
for God l a cheerful giver. 2Co 9:7
He who l his wife loves himself. Eph 5:28
He who loves his wife l himself. Eph 5:28
the kingdom of the Son He l, Col 1:13
Lord disciplines the one He l, Heb 12:6
one who l his brother remains 1Jn 2:10
If anyone l the world, love for 1Jn 2:15
and everyone who l has been born 1Jn 4:7
the one who l God must also love 1Jn 4:21
everyone who l the parent also 1Jn 5:1
the parent also l his child. 1Jn 5:1
who l to have first place among 3Jn 9
To Him who l us and has set us Rv 1:5
and everyone who l and practices Rv 22:15

LOVESICK *(2)*
me with apricots, for I am l. Sg 2:5
my love, tell him that I am l. Sg 5:8

LOVING *(5)*
l the LORD your God and walking Dt 19:9
l a long life to enjoy what is Ps 34:12
A l doe, a graceful fawn—let Pr 5:19
and l instruction is on her Pr 31:26
but hospitable, l what is good, Ti 1:8

LOVINGLY *(1)*
Because he is l devoted to Me, Ps 91:14

LOW *(18)*
its value, whether high or l; Lv 27:12
its value, whether high or l. Lv 27:14
or an ox l over its fodder? Jb 6:5
they are brought l and shrivel Jb 24:24
I am bent over and brought l; Ps 38:6
both l and high, rich and poor Ps 49:2
is brought l, and man is humbled Is 2:9
of men will be brought l; Is 2:11
human pride will be brought l, Is 2:17
is brought l, man is humbled, Is 5:15
Since you have been laid l, Is 14:8
His pride will be brought l, Is 25:11
will come from l in the dust. Is 29:4
Lie l, residents of Dedan, for I Jr 49:8
l, residents of Hazor—⌊this Jr 49:30
l in height with its branches Ezk 17:6
tree, and make the l tree tall. Ezk 17:24
and hill will be made l; Lk 3:5

LOWER *(25)*
it with l, middle, and upper Gn 6:16
'Please l your water jug so that Gn 24:14
yarn on its l hem and all around Ex 28:33
around the l hem of the robe. Ex 28:34
yarn on the l hem of the robe. Ex 39:24
around the l hem of the robe. Ex 39:26
while you sink l and lower. Dt 28:43
while you sink lower and l. Dt 28:43
her the upper and l springs. Jos 15:19
as the border of l Beth-horon, Jos 16:3
the hill south of L Beth-horon. Jos 18:13
both the upper and l springs. Jdg 1:15
rebuilt Gezer, L Beth-horon, 1Kg 9:17
who built L and Upper Beth-horon 1Ch 7:24
Beth-horon and L Beth-horon— 2Ch 8:5
rock, as hard as a l millstone! Jb 41:24
collected water from the l pool. Is 22:9
⌊this⌋ was the l pavement. Ezk 40:18
the front of the l gate to the Ezk 40:19
than from the l and middle Ezk 42:5
more than the l and middle Ezk 42:6
ground to the l ledge is three Ezk 43:14
descended to the l parts of the Eph 4:9
You made him l than the angels Heb 2:7
made l than the angels for a Heb 2:9

LOWERED *(13)*
She quickly l her jug to her Gn 24:18
She quickly l her jug from her Gn 24:46
each one quickly l his sack to Gn 44:11
So she l David from the window, 1Sm 19:12
clothes and l them by ropes to Jr 38:11
stood still, they l their wings. Ezk 1:24
stood still, they l their wings. Ezk 1:25
they l the stretcher on which Mk 2:4
up on the roof and l him on the Lk 5:19
by night and l him in a large Ac 9:25
large sheet being l to the earth Ac 10:11
large sheet being l from heaven Ac 11:5
Syrtis, they l the drift-anchor Ac 27:17

LOWERING *(1)*
courtyard, l Jeremiah with Jr 38:6

LOWEST *(9)*
will be the l of slaves to his Gn 9:25
The l chamber was seven and a 1Kg 6:6

door for the **l** side chamber was 1Kg 6:8
people⌋ behind the **l** sections of Neh 4:13
put me in the **l** part of the Pit, Ps 88:6
go up from the **l** story to the Ezk 41:7
gone down to the **l** part of the Jnh 1:5
proceed to take the **l** place. Lk 14:9
go and recline in the **l** place, Lk 14:10

LOWING *(1)*
one highway, **l** as they went; 1Sm 6:12

LOWLANDS *(3)*
Canaanites are living in the **l**, Nm 14:25
hill country, the **l**, the Negev Dt 1:7
both in the **l** and the plain, 2Ch 26:10

LOWLIEST *(2)*
Egypt will be the **l** of kingdoms Ezk 29:15
and sets over it the **l** of men. Dn 4:17

LOWLY *(9)*
He sets the **l** on high, and Jb 5:11
to save all the **l** of the earth. Ps 76:9
Better to be **l** of spirit with Pr 16:19
the rich remain in **l** positions. Ec 10:6
the oppressed and **l** of spirit, Is 57:15
the spirit of the **l** and revive Is 57:15
exalt the **l** and bring down the Ezk 21:26
There they will be a **l** kingdom. Ezk 29:14
their thrones and exalted the **l**. Lk 1:52

LOYAL *(12)*
but I remained **l** to the LORD my Jos 14:8
have remained **l** to the LORD my Jos 14:9
he remained **l** to the LORD, Jos 14:14
LORD has found a man **l** to Him, 1Sm 13:14
time I've been **l** to the house 2Sm 3:8
remained **l** to their king. 2Sm 20:2
the **l** have disappeared from the Ps 12:1
protects the **l**, but fully repays Ps 31:23
heart was not **l** and whose spirit Ps 78:8
vision to Your **l** ones and said: Ps 89:19
the way of His **l** followers. Pr 2:8
you shepherds who are **l** to Me, Jr 3:15

LOYALTY *(25)*
your **l** to me wherever we go, Gn 20:13
covenant **l** for a thousand Dt 7:9
keep His covenant **l** with you, Dt 7:12
for his righteousness and his **l**. 1Sm 26:23
"Is this your **l** to your friend?" 2Sm 16:17
He shows **l** to His anointed, 2Sm 22:51
Show **l** to the sons of Barzillai 1Kg 2:7
remember the **l** of Your servant 2Ch 6:42
taken an oath of **l** to the king, Ezr 4:14
should receive **l** from his Jb 6:14
He shows **l** to His anointed, Ps 18:50
Never let **l** and faithfulness Pr 3:3
plan good find **l** and Pr 14:22
atoned for by **l** and faithfulness Pr 16:6
should be **l** to the covenant Pr 19:22
Many a man proclaims his own **l**, Pr 20:6
L and faithfulness deliver a Pr 20:28
through **l** he maintains his Pr 20:28
Canaan and swear **l** to the LORD Is 19:18
I remember the **l** of your youth, Jr 2:2
Your **l** is like the morning mist Hs 6:4
I desire **l** and not sacrifice, Hs 6:6
You will show **l** to Jacob and Mc 7:20
who bow and pledge **l** to the LORD Zph 1:5
but also pledge **l** to Milcom; Zph 1:5

LUCIUS *(2)*
called Niger, **L** the Cyrenian, Ac 13:1
my co-worker, and **L**, Jason, and Rm 16:21

LUD *(5)*
Asshur, Arpachshad, **L**, and Aram. Gn 10:22
Arpachshad, **L**, Aram, Uz, Hul, 1Ch 1:17
Tarshish, Put, **L** (who are Is 66:19
⌊Men of⌋ Persia, **L**, and Put were Ezk 27:10
Cush, Put, and **L**, and all the Ezk 30:5

LUDIM *(3)*
Egypt fathered **L**, Anamim, Gn 10:13
fathered **L**, Anamim, Lehabim 1Ch 1:11
and the **L**, who are able to Jr 46:9

LUHITH *(2)*
go up the slope of **L** weeping; Is 15:5
on the ascent to **L** they will be Jr 48:5

LUKE *(3)*
L, the loved physician, and Col 4:14
Only **L** is with me. Bring Mark 2Tm 4:11
Demas, and **L**, my co-workers. Phm 24

LUKEWARM *(1)*
because you are **l**, and neither Rv 3:16

LULL *(1)*
There was a **l** of three years 1Kg 22:1

LUMBER *(1)*
hills, bring down **l**, and build Hg 1:8

LUMP *(4)*
"Bring a **l** of pressed figs." 2Kg 20:7
Let them take a **l** of figs and Is 38:21
make from the same **l** one piece Rm 9:21
leavens the whole **l** of dough. Gl 5:9

LUNCH *(1)*
When you give a **l** or a dinner, Lk 14:12

LURE *(2)*
Then I will **l** Sisera commander Jdg 4:7
doctrines to **l** the disciples Ac 20:30

LURED *(2)*
He **l** you from the jaws of Jb 36:16
You **l** us into a trap; You placed Ps 66:11

LURES *(3)*
that no one **l** you with riches; Jb 36:18
she **l** with her flattering talk. Pr 7:21
A violent man **l** his neighbor, Pr 16:29

LURK *(2)*
They stir up strife, they **l**; Ps 56:6
I will **l** like a leopard on the Hs 13:7

LURKED *(1)*
wife or I have **l** at his door, Jb 31:9

LURKING *(1)*
like a young lion **l** in ambush. Ps 17:12

LURKS *(3)*
He **l** in secret like a lion in a Ps 10:9
He **l** in order to seize the Ps 10:9
squares, she **l** at every corner Pr 7:12

LUSH *(3)*
Our bed is **l** with foliage; Sg 1:16
Israel is a **l** vine; it yields Hs 10:1
wine from the **l** vineyards you Am 5:11

LUST *(13)*
Don't **l** in your heart for her Pr 6:25
who burn with **l** among the oaks, Is 57:5
heart was inflamed ⌊with **l**⌋"— Ezk 16:30
Because your **l** was poured out Ezk 16:36
and poured out their **l** on her. Ezk 23:8
depraved in her **l** than Oholah, Ezk 23:11
and defiled her with their **l**. Ezk 23:17
at a woman to **l** for her has Mt 5:28
in their **l** for one another. Rm 1:27
impurity, **l**, evil desire, Col 3:5
the **l** of the flesh, the lust of 1Jn 2:16
of the flesh, the **l** of the eyes, 1Jn 2:16
with its **l** is passing away, 1Jn 2:17

LUSTED *(7)*
their eyes that **l** after their Ezk 6:9
She **l** after her lovers, the Ezk 23:5
all those she **l** after and with Ezk 23:7
lovers, the Assyrians she **l** for. Ezk 23:9
She **l** after the Assyrians: Ezk 23:12
sight of them she **l** after them Ezk 23:16
and **l** after their lovers, whose Ezk 23:20

LUSTER *(1)*
The **l** of the wheels was like the Ezk 10:9

LUSTFUL *(2)*
and your ⌊**l**⌋ neighings, Jr 13:27
not with **l** desires, like the 1Th 4:5

LUSTS *(2)*
and worldly **l** and to live Ti 2:12
to scoff, following their own **l**, 2Pt 3:3

LUTE *(1)*
with a **l** I will praise You for Ps 71:22

LUXURIOUS *(3)*
in scarlet, with **l** things, who 2Sm 1:24
and jackals, in the **l** palaces. Is 13:22
sat on a **l** couch with a table Ezk 23:41

LUXURIOUSLY *(3)*
You have lived **l** on the land and Jms 5:5
glorified herself and lived **l**, Rv 18:7
and lived **l** with her will weep Rv 18:9

LUXURY *(4)*
L is not appropriate for a fool— Pr 19:10
this, lover of **l**, who sits Is 47:8
and live in **l** are in royal Lk 7:25
wealthy from her excessive **l**. Rv 18:3

LUZ *(8)*
(AKA BETHEL)
previously the city was named **L**. Gn 28:19
all who were with him came to **L** Gn 35:6
appeared to me at **L** in the land Gn 48:3
it went to **L** and proceeded to Jos 16:2
there the border went toward **L**, Jos 18:13
to the southern slope of **L** Jos 18:13
the town was formerly named **L** Jdg 1:23
built a town, and named it **L**. Jdg 1:26

LYCAONIAN *(2)*
and fled to the **L** towns called Ac 14:6
saying in the **L** language, Ac 14:11

LYCIA *(1)*
Pamphylia, we reached Myra in **L**. Ac 27:5

LYDDA *(3)*
(AKA LOD)
to the saints who lived in **L**. Ac 9:32
who lived in **L** and Sharon saw Ac 9:35
Since **L** was near Joppa, the Ac 9:38

LYDIA *(1)*
A woman named **L**, a dealer in Ac 16:14

LYDIA'S *(1)*
they came to **L** house where they Ac 16:40

LYE *(3)*
and cleanse my hands with **l**, Jb 9:30
you wash with **l** and use a great Jr 2:22
fire and like cleansing **l**. Mal 3:2

LYING *(86)*
of sheep were **l** there beside it Gn 29:2
a strong donkey **l** down between Gn 49:14
who hates you **l** ⌊helpless⌋ under Ex 23:5
its Sabbaths by **l** desolate Lv 26:43
victim is found **l** in a field in Dt 21:1
was their lord **l** dead on the Jdg 3:25
was Sisera **l** dead with a tent Jdg 4:22
notice the place where he's **l**, Ru 3:4
and there **l** at his feet was a Ru 3:8
was failing, was **l** in his room. 1Sm 3:2
Samuel was **l** down in the 1Sm 3:3
broken off and **l** on the 1Sm 5:4
Saul was **l** inside the inner 1Sm 26:5
and Saul was **l** there asleep in 1Sm 26:7
the troops were **l** around him. 1Sm 26:7
Ish-bosheth was **l** on his bed in 2Sm 4:7
spent the night **l** on the ground. 2Sm 12:16
house while Amnon was **l** down. 2Sm 13:8
go and become a **l** spirit in the 1Kg 22:22
the LORD has put a **l** spirit into 1Kg 22:23
the boy **l** dead on his bed. 2Kg 4:32
go and become a **l** spirit in the 2Ch 18:21
the LORD has put a **l** spirit into 2Ch 18:22
were corpses **l** on the ground; 2Ch 20:24
Am I **l**, or can I not recognize Jb 6:30
Let **l** lips be quieted; Ps 31:18
l instead of speaking truthfully. Ps 52:3
They take pleasure in **l**; Ps 62:4
like the slain **l** in the grave, Ps 88:5
speak against me with **l** tongues. Ps 109:2
deliver me from **l** lips and a Ps 120:2
arrogant eyes, a **l** tongue, hands Pr 6:17
a **l** witness who gives false Pr 6:19
who conceals hatred has **l** lips, Pr 10:18
forever, but a **l** tongue, only a Pr 12:19
L lips are detestable to the Pr 12:22
righteous hate **l**, but the wicked Pr 13:5
fortune through a **l** tongue is a Pr 21:6
A **l** witness will perish, but the Pr 21:28
out at sea or **l** down on the top Pr 23:34
A **l** tongue hates those it Pr 26:28
is the prophet, the **l** teacher. Is 9:15
and uttering **l** words from the Is 59:13
watch like fowlers **l** in wait. Jr 5:26
l pen of scribes has produced Jr 8:8
and old are **l** on the ground Lm 2:21
visions and speak **l** divinations. Ezk 13:6
and speak a **l** divination when Ezk 13:7
falsely and had **l** visions." Ezk 13:8
visions and speak **l** divinations. Ezk 13:9
you and saw you **l** in your blood, Ezk 16:6
stark naked and **l** in your blood. Ezk 16:22
visions and **l** divinations about Ezk 21:29
false visions and **l** divinations, Ezk 22:28
great monster **l** in the middle Ezk 29:3
cut it down and left it **l**. Ezk 31:12
instead of **l** desolate in the Ezk 36:34

of my mind as I was **l** in bed, Dn 4:10
As I was **l** in my bed, I also saw Dn 4:13
his mind as he was **l** in his bed. Dn 7:1
Cursing, **l**, murder, stealing, Hs 4:2
my servant is **l** at home Mt 8:6
his mother-in-law **l** in bed with Mt 8:14
a paralytic **l** on a stretcher. Mt 9:2
mother-in-law was **l** in bed with Mk 1:30
on which the paralytic was **l**. Mk 2:4
found her child **l** on the bed, Mk 7:30
in cloth and **l** in a feeding Lk 2:12
baby who was **l** in the feeding Lk 2:16
picked up what he had been **l** on, Lk 5:25
they were **l** in wait for Him to Lk 11:54
Jesus saw him **l** there and knew Jn 5:6
and a stone was **l** against it. Jn 11:38
he saw the linen cloths **l** there, Jn 20:5
saw the linen cloths **l** there. Jn 20:6
head was not **l** with the linen Jn 20:7
where Jesus' body had been **l**. Jn 20:12
with fish **l** on it, and bread Jn 21:9
truth in Christ—I am not **l**; Rm 9:1
Lord Jesus, knows I am not **l**. 2Co 11:31
what I write to you, I'm not **l**. Gl 1:20
you put away **l**, Speak the truth Eph 4:25
am not **l**), and a teacher of the 1Tm 2:7
we are **l** and are not practicing 1Jn 1:6
not, but are **l**—note this—I Rv 3:9
who loves and practices **l**. Rv 22:15

LYRE *(22)*
who play the **l** and the flute. Gn 4:21
tambourine and **l** and rejoicing Jb 21:12
My **l** is ⌊used⌋ for mourning and Jb 30:31
Praise the LORD with the **l**; Ps 33:2
I will praise You with the **l**, Ps 43:4
I explain my riddle with a **l**. Ps 49:4
up, harp and **l**! I will wake up Ps 57:8
the melodious **l**, and the harp. Ps 81:2
harp and the music of a **l**. Ps 92:3
Sing to the LORD with the **l**, Ps 98:5
with the **l** and melodious song. Ps 98:5
up, harp and **l**! I will wake up Ps 108:2
play the **l** to our God, Ps 147:7
to Him with tambourine and **l**. Ps 149:3
praise Him with harp and **l**. Ps 150:3
At their feasts they have **l**, Is 5:12
⌊the sound of⌋ a **l** for Moab, Is 16:11
The joyful **l** has ceased. Is 24:8
flute, zither, **l**, harp, drum, Dn 3:5
flute, zither, **l**, harp, and Dn 3:7
flute, zither, **l**, harp, drum, Dn 3:10
flute, zither, **l**, harp, drum, Dn 3:15

LYRES *(20)*
singing, with tambourines and **l**, Gn 31:27
tambourines, flutes, and **l**. 1Sm 10:5
⌊instruments⌋, **l**, harps, 2Sm 6:5
harps and **l** for the singers. 1Kg 10:12
God with songs and with **l**, 1Ch 13:8
harps, **l**, and cymbals. 1Ch 15:16
the music with **l** according to 1Ch 15:21
and the playing of harps and **l**. 1Ch 15:28
Jeiel played the harps and **l**, 1Ch 16:5
to prophesy accompanied by **l**, 1Ch 25:1
to the accompaniment of **l**, 1Ch 25:3
and **l** for the service of God's 1Ch 25:6
harps and **l**, were standing 2Ch 5:12
harps and **l** for the singers. 2Ch 9:11
with harps, **l**, and trumpets. 2Ch 20:28
and **l** according to the command 2Ch 29:25
by cymbals, harps, and **l**. Neh 12:27
we hung up our **l** on the poplar Ps 137:2
the sound⌋ of tambourines and **l**; Is 30:32
sound of your **l** will no longer Ezk 26:13

LYSANIAS *(1)*
and **L** tetrarch of Abilene, Lk 3:1

LYSIAS *(3)*
L, To the most excellent Ac 23:26
L the commander came and took Ac 24:7
When **L** the commander comes Ac 24:22

LYSTRA *(6)*
towns called **L** and Derbe, Ac 14:6
In **L** a man without strength in Ac 14:8
they returned to **L**, to Iconium, Ac 14:21
Then he went on to Derbe and **L**, Ac 16:1
The brothers at **L** and Iconium Ac 16:2
me in Antioch, Iconium, and **L**. 2Tm 3:11

M

MAACAH *(21)*
(AKA MICAIAH)
Tebah, Gaham, Tahash, and **M**. Gn 22:24
son of **M** the daughter of King 2Sm 3:3
1,000 men from the king of **M**, 2Sm 10:6
men of Tob and **M** were in the 2Sm 10:8
ran away to Achish son of **M**, 1Kg 2:39
mother's name was **M** daughter of 1Kg 15:2
was **M** daughter of Abishalom 1Kg 15:10
his grandmother **M** from being 1Kg 15:13
concubine **M** was the mother 1Ch 2:48
Absalom son of **M**, daughter of 1Ch 3:2
The name of his sister was **M**. 1Ch 7:15
Machir's wife **M** gave birth to a 1Ch 7:16
His wife's name was **M**. 1Ch 8:29
His wife's name was **M**. 1Ch 9:35
Hanan son of **M**, Joshaphat the 1Ch 11:43
and the king of **M** with his army, 1Ch 19:7
Simeonites, Shephatiah son of **M**; 1Ch 27:16
married **M** daughter of Absalom. 2Ch 11:20
Rehoboam loved **M** daughter of 2Ch 11:21
Abijah son of **M** as chief, 2Ch 11:22
also removed **M**, his grandmother 2Ch 15:16

MAACATH *(1)*
Geshur and **M** live in Israel to Jos 13:13

MAACATHITE *(5)*
to the Geshurite and **M** border, Jos 12:5
son of Ahasbai son of the **M**, 2Sm 23:34
and Jaazaniah son of the **M**— 2Kg 25:23
the father of⌋ Eshtemoa the **M**. 1Ch 4:19
and Jezaniah son of the **M**— Jr 40:8

MAACATHITES *(3)*
border of the Geshurites and **M**. Dt 3:14
of the Geshurites and **M**, Jos 13:11
drive out the Geshurites and **M**. Jos 13:13

MAADAI *(1)*
descendants: **M**, Amram, Uel, Ezr 10:34

MAADIAH *(1)*
Mijamin, **M**, Bilgah, Neh 12:5

MAAI *(1)*
Gilalai, **M**, Nethanel, Judah Neh 12:36

MAARATH *(1)*
M, Beth-anoth, and Eltekon—six Jos 15:59

MAASAI *(1)*
M son of Adiel, son of Jahzerah, 1Ch 9:12

MAASEIAH *(23)*
Eliab, Benaiah, **M**, Mattithiah, 1Ch 15:18
Unni, Eliab, **M**, and Benaiah were 1Ch 15:20
son of Obed, **M** son of Adaiah, 2Ch 23:1
secretary and **M** the officer 2Ch 26:11
Zichri killed the king's son **M**, 2Ch 28:7
along with **M** the governor of the 2Ch 34:8
M, Eliezer, Jarib, and Gedaliah. Ezr 10:18
M, Elijah, Shemaiah, Jehiel, and Ezr 10:21
Elioenai, **M**, Ishmael, Nethanel, Ezr 10:22
Chelal, Benaiah, **M**, Mattaniah, Ezr 10:30
Beside them Azariah son of **M**, Neh 3:23
and **M** stood beside him on his Neh 8:4
Hodiah, **M**, Kelita, Azariah, Neh 8:7
Rehum, Hashabnah, **M**, Neh 10:25
and **M** son of Baruch, son of Neh 11:5
son of **M**, son of Ithiel, Neh 11:7
Eliakim, **M**, Miniamin, Micaiah, Neh 12:41
and **M**, Shemaiah, Eleazar, Uzzi, Neh 12:42
Zephaniah son of **M** to Jeremiah, Jr 21:1
and to Zedekiah son of **M**, Jr 29:21
the priest Zephaniah son of **M**, Jr 29:25
the chamber of **M** son of Shallum Jr 35:4
and Zephaniah son of **M**, Jr 37:3

MAATH *(1)*
⌊son⌋ of **M**, ⌊son⌋ of Mattathias, Lk 3:26

MAAZ *(1)*
firstborn: **M**, Jamin, and Eker. 1Ch 2:27

MAAZIAH *(2)*
and the twenty-fourth to **M**. 1Ch 24:18
M, Bilgai, and Shemaiah. Neh 10:8

MACEDONIA *(22)*
"Cross over to **M** and help us!" Ac 16:9
made efforts to set out for **M**, Ac 16:10
city of that district of **M**. Ac 16:12
and Timothy came down from **M**, Ac 18:5
to pass through **M** and Achaia and Ac 19:21
and Erastus, to **M**, he himself Ac 19:22
good-bye, departed to go to **M**. Ac 20:1
was made to go back through **M**. Ac 20:3
for **M** and Achaia were pleased to Rm 15:26
to you after I pass through **M**— 1Co 16:5
I will be traveling through **M**— 1Co 16:5
to go on to **M** with your help, 2Co 1:16
to you again from **M** and be given 2Co 1:16
good-bye to them and left for **M**. 2Co 2:13
we came into **M**, we had no rest. 2Co 7:5
granted to the churches of **M**: 2Co 8:1
who came from **M** supplied my 2Co 11:9
when I left **M**, no church shared Php 4:15
the believers in **M** and Achaia. 1Th 1:7
you, not only in **M** and Achaia, 1Th 1:8
in the entire region of **M**. 1Th 4:10
As I urged you when I went to **M**, 1Tm 1:3

MACEDONIAN *(2)*
M man was standing and pleading Ac 16:9
a **M** of Thessalonica, Ac 27:2

MACEDONIANS *(3)*
M who were Paul's traveling Ac 19:29
and I brag about you to the **M**: 2Co 9:2
For if any **M** should come with me 2Co 9:4

MACHBANNAI *(1)*
Jeremiah tenth, and **M** eleventh. 1Ch 12:13

MACHBENAH *(1)*
the father of **M** and Gibea. 1Ch 2:49

MACHI *(1)*
Geuel son of **M** from the tribe of Nm 13:15

MACHIR *(21)*
Manasseh's son **M** were Gn 50:23
the Machirite clan from **M**. Nm 26:29
from Machir. **M** fathered Gilead; Nm 26:29
Gilead, son of **M**, son of Nm 27:1
descendants of **M** son of Nm 32:39
the clan of⌋ **M** son of Manasseh Nm 32:40
the son of **M**, son of Manasseh— Nm 36:1
I gave Gilead to **M**, Dt 3:15
of **M** son of Manasseh, Jos 13:31
descendants of **M** by their clans. Jos 13:31
Gilead and Bashan came to **M**, Jos 17:1
Gilead, son of **M**, son of Jos 17:3
The leaders came down from **M**, Jdg 5:14
the house of **M** son of Ammiel." 2Sm 9:4
the house of **M** son of Ammiel 2Sm 9:5
M son of Ammiel from Lo-debar, 2Sm 17:27
the daughter of **M** the father of 1Ch 2:21
the sons of **M** father of Gilead 1Ch 2:23
Asriel and **M** the father of 1Ch 7:14
M took wives from Huppim and 1Ch 7:15
the sons of Gilead son of **M**, 1Ch 7:17

MACHIR'S *(1)*
M wife Maacah gave birth to a 1Ch 7:16

MACHIRITE *(1)*
the **M** clan from Machir. Nm 26:29

MACHNADEBAI *(1)*
M, Shashai, Sharai, Ezr 10:40

MACHPELAH *(6)*
me the cave of **M** that belongs to Gn 23:9
Ephron's field at **M** near Mamre— Gn 23:17
of the field at **M** near Mamre Gn 23:19
him in the cave of **M** near Mamre, Gn 25:9
The cave is in the field of **M**, Gn 49:30
in the cave at **M** in the field Gn 50:13

MAD *(5)*
be driven **m** by what you see. Dt 28:34
barefoot and makes judges go **m**. Jb 12:17
and they go **m** because of Jr 50:38
therefore, the nations go **m**. Jr 51:7
much study is driving you **m**!" Ac 26:24

MADAI *(2)*
Gomer, Magog, **M**, Javan, Tubal, Gn 10:2
Gomer, Magog, **M**, Javan, Tubal, 1Ch 1:5

MADE *(966)*
So God **m** the expanse and Gn 1:7
God **m** the two great lights— Gn 1:16
So God **m** the wildlife of the Gn 1:25
God saw all that He had **m**, Gn 1:31
that the LORD God **m** the earth Gn 2:4
LORD God had not **m** it rain on Gn 2:5
the LORD God **m** the rib He had Gn 2:22
animals that the LORD God had **m**. Gn 3:1
together and **m** loincloths for Gn 3:7
The LORD God **m** clothing out of Gn 3:21
who **m** all kinds of bronze and Gn 4:22

He **m** him in the likeness of God;	Gn 5:1
that He had **m** man on the earth,	Gn 6:6
for I regret that I **m** them."	Gn 6:7
every living thing I have **m**."	Gn 7:4
window of the ark that he had **m**,	Gn 8:6
for God **m** man in His image.	Gn 9:6
can never say, 'I **m** Abram rich.'	Gn 14:23
day the LORD **m** a covenant with	Gn 15:18
Sarah said, "God has **m** me laugh,	Gn 21:6
the two of them **m** a covenant.	Gn 21:27
After they had **m** a covenant at	Gn 21:32
He **m** the camels kneel beside a	Gn 24:11
not the LORD had **m** his journey	Gn 24:21
since the LORD has **m** my journey	Gn 24:56
now the LORD has **m** room for us,	Gn 26:22
They **m** life bitter for Isaac and	Gn 26:35
and his mother **m** the delicious	Gn 27:14
bread she had **m** to her son Jacob	Gn 27:17
had also **m** some delicious food	Gn 27:31
I have **m** him a master over you,	Gn 27:37
Then Jacob **m** a vow: "If God will	Gn 28:20
the lambs and **m** the flocks face	Gn 30:40
marker and **m** a solemn vow to	Gn 31:13
they took stones and **m** a mound,	Gn 31:46
and he **m** a robe of many colors	Gn 37:3
that the LORD **m** everything he	Gn 39:3
and the LORD **m** everything that	Gn 39:23
Since God has **m** all this known	Gn 41:39
God has **m** me forget all my	Gn 41:51
God has **m** me fruitful in the	Gn 41:52
They **m** their way down to Egypt	Gn 43:15
He has **m** me a father to Pharaoh,	Gn 45:8
God has **m** me lord of all Egypt.	Gn 45:9
So Joseph **m** it a law, still in	Gn 47:26
strong arms were **m** agile by the	Gn 49:24
my father **m** me take an oath,	Gn 50:5
So Joseph **m** the Israelites take	Gn 50:25
and **m** their lives bitter with	Ex 1:14
Who **m** you a leader and judge	Ex 2:14
to him, "Who **m** the human mouth?	Ex 4:11
you have **m** us reek in front	Ex 5:21
have **m** you like God to Pharaoh,	Ex 7:1
of the LORD **m** their servants	Ex 9:20
Joseph had **m** the Israelites	Ex 13:19
to swerve and **m** them drive with	Ex 14:25
He **m** a statute and ordinance for	Ex 15:25
like wafers ⌊**m**⌋ with honey.	Ex 16:31
all Israel and **m** them leaders	Ex 18:25
For the LORD **m** the heavens and	Ex 20:11
that the LORD has **m** with you	Ex 24:8
like a pavement **m** of sapphire	Ex 24:10
It is to be **m** of one piece:	Ex 25:31
is to be **m** from 75 pounds	Ex 25:39
⌊all of it **m**⌋ of finely spun	Ex 27:18
courtyard are to be **m** of bronze.	Ex 27:19
one cake of bread ⌊**m**⌋ with oil,	Ex 29:23
atonement was **m** at the ⌊time	Ex 29:33
six days the LORD **m** the heavens	Ex 31:17
m it into an image of a calf.	Ex 32:4
then he **m** an announcement:	Ex 32:5
they have **m** for themselves an	Ex 32:8
he took the calf they had **m**,	Ex 32:20
they have **m** for themselves a god	Ex 32:31
did with the calf Aaron had **m**.	Ex 32:35
for I have **m** a covenant with you	Ex 34:27
doing the work **m** the tabernacle	Ex 36:8
Bezalel **m** them of finely spun	Ex 36:8
He **m** loops of blue yarn on the	Ex 36:11
He **m** 50 loops on the one curtain	Ex 36:12
He also **m** 50 gold clasps and	Ex 36:13
He **m** curtains of goat hair for a	Ex 36:14
he also **m** 11 of them.	Ex 36:14
He **m** 50 loops on the edge of the	Ex 36:17
m 50 bronze clasps to join the	Ex 36:18
also **m** a covering for the tent	Ex 36:19
He **m** upright planks of acacia	Ex 36:20
m planks for the tabernacle as	Ex 36:23
and he **m** 40 silver bases to put	Ex 36:24
the north side, he **m** 20 planks,	Ex 36:25
the tabernacle he **m** six planks.	Ex 36:27
He also **m** two additional planks	Ex 36:28
He **m** five crossbars of acacia	Ex 36:31
He **m** the central crossbar run	Ex 36:33
them with gold and **m** their rings	Ex 36:34
Then he **m** the veil with blue,	Ex 36:35
m it with a design of cherubim	Ex 36:35
For it he **m** four posts of acacia	Ex 36:36
He **m** a screen embroidered with	Ex 36:37
m the ark of acacia wood,	Ex 37:1
and out and **m** a gold molding all	Ex 37:2
He **m** poles of acacia wood and	Ex 37:4
He **m** a mercy seat of pure gold,	Ex 37:6
He **m** two cherubim of gold;	Ex 37:7
m them of hammered work at the	Ex 37:7
He **m** the cherubim ⌊of one piece⌋	Ex 37:8
pure gold and **m** a gold molding	Ex 37:11
He **m** a three-inch frame all	Ex 37:12
around it and **m** a gold molding	Ex 37:12
He **m** the poles for carrying the	Ex 37:15
also **m** the utensils that would	Ex 37:16
Then he **m** the lampstand out of	Ex 37:17
He **m** it ⌊all⌋ of one piece:	Ex 37:17
He also **m** its seven lamps,	Ex 37:23
He **m** it and all its utensils of	Ex 37:24
He **m** the altar of incense out of	Ex 37:25
Then he **m** a gold molding all	Ex 37:26
He **m** two gold rings for it under	Ex 37:27
m the poles of acacia wood and	Ex 37:28
He also **m** the holy anointing oil	Ex 37:29
He **m** horns for it on its four	Ex 38:2
He **m** all the altar's utensils:	Ex 38:3
he **m** all its utensils of bronze.	Ex 38:3
He also **m** the poles of acacia	Ex 38:6
He **m** the bronze basin and its	Ex 38:8
Then he **m** the courtyard.	Ex 38:9
m everything that the LORD	Ex 38:22
44 pounds he **m** the hooks for the	Ex 38:28
He **m** with it the bases for the	Ex 38:30
They **m** specially woven garments	Ex 39:1
Bezalel **m** the ephod of gold,	Ex 39:2
They **m** shoulder pieces for	Ex 39:4
He also **m** the embroidered	Ex 39:8
They **m** the breastpiece square	Ex 39:9
They **m** braided chains of pure	Ex 39:15
They **m** two ⌊other⌋ gold rings	Ex 39:19
They **m** two ⌊more⌋ gold rings and	Ex 39:20
They **m** the woven robe of the	Ex 39:22
They **m** pomegranates of finely	Ex 39:24
They **m** bells of pure gold and	Ex 39:25
They **m** the tunics of fine woven	Ex 39:27
⌊They also **m**⌋ the turban and the	Ex 39:28
They also **m** a plate, the holy	Ex 39:30
it must be ⌊**m**⌋ of fine flour,	Lv 2:4
bread ⌊**m**⌋ of fine flour	Lv 2:5
it must be **m** of fine flour with	Lv 2:7
grain offering **m** in any of these	Lv 2:8
the LORD is to be **m** with yeast,	Lv 2:11
one cake of bread ⌊**m**⌋ with oil,	Lv 8:26
and **m** a sin offering with it as	Lv 9:15
of fat portions **m** by fire,	Lv 10:15
and the patch **m** raw by the burn	Lv 13:24
or anything **m** of leather—	Lv 13:48
after he has **m** atonement for	Lv 16:17
will be **m** for you on this	Lv 16:30
put on a garment **m** of two kinds	Lv 19:19
touches anything **m** unclean by a	Lv 22:4
each of them **m** from four quarts	Lv 23:17
may know that I **m** the Israelites	Lv 23:43
loaf is to be **m** with four quarts	Lv 24:5
could be **m** clear to them.	Lv 24:12
a covering **m** of manatee skin	Nm 4:6
a covering **m** of manatee skin	Nm 4:8
a covering **m** of manatee skin	Nm 4:10
a covering **m** of manatee skin	Nm 4:11
a covering **m** of manatee skin	Nm 4:12
a covering **m** of manatee skin	Nm 4:14
the covering **m** of manatee skin	Nm 4:25
not drink vinegar **m** from wine or	Nm 6:3
cakes **m** from fine flour	Nm 6:15
is the way the lampstand was **m**:	Nm 8:4
The lampstand was **m** according to	Nm 8:4
Aaron also **m** atonement for them	Nm 8:21
one **m** by fire to the LORD,	Nm 15:25
he **m** atonement for the people.	Nm 16:47
Then Israel **m** a vow to the LORD,	Nm 21:2
So Moses **m** a bronze snake and	Nm 21:9
You **m** me look like a fool.	Nm 22:29
for his God and **m** atonement for	Nm 25:13
she herself **m** are binding,	Nm 30:6
rash commitment she herself **m**,	Nm 30:8
house has **m** a vow or put	Nm 30:10
goods, things **m** of goat hair,	Nm 31:20
all the articles **m** out of gold.	Nm 31:51
and He **m** them wander in the	Nm 32:13
the LORD your God **m** his spirit	Dt 2:30
His bed was **m** of iron. Isn't it	Dt 3:11
your God that He **m** with you,	Dt 4:23
LORD our God **m** a covenant with	Dt 5:2
covenant the LORD **m** with you,	Dt 9:9
they have **m** a cast image for	Dt 9:12
you had **m** a calf image for	Dt 9:16
took the sinful calf you had **m**,	Dt 9:21
So I **m** an ark of acacia wood,	Dt 10:3
the tablets in the ark I had **m**.	Dt 10:5
your God has **m** you as numerous	Dt 10:22
when He **m** the waters of the Red	Dt 11:4
not wear clothes **m** of both wool	Dt 22:11
the nations He has **m** in praise,	Dt 26:19
covenant He had **m** with them at	Dt 29:1
images and idols ⌊**m**⌋ of wood,	Dt 29:17
which He had **m** with them when	Dt 29:25
the covenant I have **m** with them.	Dt 31:16
with what your hands have **m**."	Dt 31:29
He **m** him ride on the heights of	Dt 32:13
the God who **m** him and scorned	Dt 32:15
from this oath you **m** us swear,	Jos 2:17
from the oath you **m** us swear."	Jos 2:20
So Joshua **m** flint knives and	Jos 5:3
with them and **m** a treaty to let	Jos 9:15
that day he **m** them woodcutters	Jos 9:27
Gibeon had **m** peace with Israel	Jos 10:1
they have **m** peace with Joshua	Jos 10:4
No city **m** peace with the	Jos 11:19
the offerings **m** by fire to the	Jos 13:14
the LORD had **m** to the house	Jos 21:45
For the LORD has **m** the Jordan a	Jos 22:25
LORD's altar that our fathers **m**,	Jos 22:28
LORD your God **m** to you has	Jos 23:14
that day Joshua **m** a covenant for	Jos 24:25
they **m** the Canaanites serve as	Jdg 1:28
the Amorites were **m** to serve as	Jdg 1:35
covenant that I **m** with their	Jdg 2:20
Ehud **m** himself a double-edged	Jdg 3:16
the Israelites **m** hiding places	Jdg 6:2
After they **m** a thorough	Jdg 6:29
Gideon **m** an ephod from all this	Jdg 8:27
the Baals and **m** Baal-berith	Jdg 8:33
large stone, and **m** Abimelech,	Jdg 9:18
the Ammonites **m** war with Israel,	Jdg 11:5
Jephthah **m** this vow to the LORD:	Jdg 11:30
kept the vow he had **m** about her.	Jdg 11:39
He **m** it into a carved image	Jdg 17:4
and he **m** an ephod and household	Jdg 17:5
the gods I had **m** and the priest,	Jdg 18:24
gods Micah had **m** and the priest	Jdg 18:27
carved image that he had **m**,	Jdg 18:31
the woman **m** her way back,	Jdg 19:26
from all Israel **m** a frontal	Jdg 20:34
because the LORD had **m** this gap	Jdg 21:15
Almighty has **m** me very bitter.	Ru 1:20
year his mother **m** him a little	1Sm 2:19
the LORD who has **m** this terrible	1Sm 6:9
offerings and **m** sacrifices to	1Sm 6:15
presence they **m** Saul king.	1Sm 11:15
Your father **m** the troops	1Sm 14:28
I regret that I **m** Saul king,	1Sm 15:11
sword has **m** women childless	1Sm 15:33
regretted He had **m** Saul king	1Sm 15:35
Jonathan **m** a covenant with David	1Sm 18:3
David and **m** him commander	1Sm 18:13
Then Jonathan **m** a covenant with	1Sm 20:16
the two of them **m** a covenant	1Sm 23:18
Since he has **m** himself	1Sm 27:12
He **m** him king over Gilead,	2Sm 2:9
David **m** a covenant with them	2Sm 5:3
that You have **m** to Your servant	2Sm 7:25
The LORD **m** David victorious	2Sm 8:6
David **m** a reputation for himself	2Sm 8:13
The LORD **m** David victorious	2Sm 8:14
they **m** peace with Israel and	2Sm 10:19
dough, kneaded it, **m** cakes in	2Sm 13:8
cakes she had **m** and went to her	2Sm 13:10
the people have **m** me afraid.	2Sm 14:15
fulfill a vow I **m** to the Lord.	2Sm 15:7
For your servant **m** a vow when I	2Sm 15:8
Today you have **m** it clear that	2Sm 19:6
He **m** darkness a canopy around	2Sm 22:12
You have **m** my enemies retreat	2Sm 22:41
King David has **m** Solomon king.	1Kg 1:43
His promise that He **m** to me:	1Kg 2:4
has not **m** this request at	1Kg 2:23
m me a dynasty as He promised	1Kg 2:24
Solomon **m** an alliance with	1Kg 3:1
You have now **m** Your servant king	1Kg 3:7

each one **m** provision for one 1Kg 4:7
and the two of them **m** a treaty. 1Kg 5:12
He also **m** windows with beveled 1Kg 6:4
And he **m** side chambers all 1Kg 6:5
which I **m** to your father David. 1Kg 6:12
sanctuary he **m** two cherubim 15 1Kg 6:23
he **m** olive wood doors. 1Kg 6:31
two doors were **m** of olive wood. 1Kg 6:32
he **m** four-sided olive wood 1Kg 6:33
doors were **m** of cypress wood; 1Kg 6:34
He **m** the hall of pillars 75 feet 1Kg 7:6
m the Hall of the Throne where 1Kg 7:7
And he **m** a house like this hall 1Kg 7:8
The foundation was **m** of large, 1Kg 7:10
He also **m** two capitals of cast 1Kg 7:16
wreaths **m** of chainwork—seven 1Kg 7:17
He **m** the pillars with two 1Kg 7:18
He **m** the cast ⌊metal⌋ reservoir, 1Kg 7:23
Then he **m** 10 bronze water carts. 1Kg 7:27
m as a pedestal 27 inches wide. 1Kg 7:31
In this way he **m** the 10 water 1Kg 7:37
Then he **m** 10 bronze basins— 1Kg 7:38
Then Hiram **m** the basins, the 1Kg 7:40
that Hiram **m** for King Solomon at 1Kg 7:45
temple ⌊were **m**⌋ of burnished 1Kg 7:45
Solomon also **m** all the equipment 1Kg 7:48
where the LORD **m** a covenant with 1Kg 8:9
is that He **m** with our ancestors 1Kg 8:21
good promises He **m** through His 1Kg 8:56
my words I have **m** my petition 1Kg 8:59
petition you have **m** before Me. 1Kg 9:3
He has **m** you king to carry out 1Kg 10:9
The king **m** the almug wood into 1Kg 10:12
Solomon **m** 200 large shields 1Kg 10:16
He **m** 300 small shields of 1Kg 10:17
The king also **m** a large ivory 1Kg 10:18
it had ever been **m** in any other 1Kg 10:20
The king **m** silver as common in 1Kg 10:27
and he **m** cedar as abundant as 1Kg 10:27
Your father **m** our yoke harsh. 1Kg 12:4
'Your father **m** our yoke heavy, 1Kg 12:10
My father **m** your yoke heavy, 1Kg 12:14
assembly and **m** him king over 1Kg 12:20
Then he **m** two gold calves, 1Kg 12:28
Jeroboam **m** a festival in the 1Kg 12:32
he **m** this offering in Bethel to 1Kg 12:32
He **m** a festival for the 1Kg 12:33
because they **m** their Asherah 1Kg 14:15
gold shields that Solomon had **m**. 1Kg 14:26
King Rehoboam **m** bronze shields 1Kg 14:27
idols that his fathers had **m**. 1Kg 15:12
because she had **m** an obscene 1Kg 15:13
the dust and **m** you ruler over My 1Kg 16:2
then all Israel **m** Omri, the army 1Kg 16:16
Ahab also **m** an Asherah pole. 1Kg 16:33
he **m** that kingdom or nation 1Kg 18:10
around the altar they had **m**. 1Kg 18:26
Then he **m** a trench around the 1Kg 18:32
So he **m** a treaty with him and 1Kg 20:34
of Chenaanah **m** iron horns and 1Kg 22:11
Jehoshaphat also **m** peace with 1Kg 22:44
Jehoshaphat **m** ships of Tarshish 1Kg 22:48
pillar of Baal his father had **m**. 2Kg 3:2
it there, and **m** the iron float. 2Kg 6:6
of Baal and **m** it a latrine— 2Kg 10:27
where he **m** a covenant with them 2Kg 11:4
the testimony, and **m** him king. 2Kg 11:12
Then Jehoiada **m** a covenant 2Kg 11:17
or silver were **m** for the LORD's 2Kg 12:13
and **m** him king in place of his 2Kg 14:21
He even **m** his son pass through 2Kg 16:3
Uriah the priest had **m** it. 2Kg 16:11
His covenant He had **m** with their 2Kg 17:15
They **m** for themselves molded 2Kg 17:16
They **m** their sons and daughters 2Kg 17:17
Israel **m** Jeroboam son of Nebat 2Kg 17:21
that the Samaritans had **m**. 2Kg 17:29
of Babylon **m** Succoth-benoth, 2Kg 17:30
men of Cuth **m** Nergal, the men 2Kg 17:30
the men of Hamath **m** Ashima, 2Kg 17:30
the Avvites **m** Nibhaz and Tartak, 2Kg 17:31
LORD **m** a covenant with them 2Kg 17:35
covenant that I have **m** with you. 2Kg 17:38
the bronze snake that Moses **m**, 2Kg 18:4
You **m** the heavens and the earth. 2Kg 19:15
not gods but **m** by human hands 2Kg 19:18
his might and how he **m** the pool 2Kg 20:20
He **m** an Asherah, as King Ahab of 2Kg 21:3

He **m** his son pass through the 2Kg 21:6
of Asherah he **m** in the temple 2Kg 21:7
King Amon and **m** his son Josiah 2Kg 21:24
by the pillar and **m** a covenant 2Kg 23:3
all the articles **m** for Baal, 2Kg 23:4
that the kings of Judah had **m**— 2Kg 23:12
that Manasseh had **m** in the two 2Kg 23:12
who caused Israel to sin, had **m**. 2Kg 23:15
kings of Israel had **m** to provoke 2Kg 23:19
and **m** him king in place of his 2Kg 23:30
Pharaoh Neco **m** Eliakim son 2Kg 23:34
of Israel had **m** for the LORD's 2Kg 24:13
the king of Babylon **m** Mattaniah, 2Kg 24:17
As the king **m** his way along the 2Kg 25:4
Solomon had **m** for the LORD's 2Kg 25:16
David **m** a covenant with them at 1Ch 11:3
received them and **m** them leaders 1Ch 12:18
had come and **m** a raid in the 1Ch 14:9
the Philistines **m** a raid in the 1Ch 14:13
covenant⌋ He **m** with Abraham, 1Ch 16:16
but the LORD **m** the heavens. 1Ch 16:26
m Your people Israel Your own 1Ch 17:22
The LORD **m** David victorious 1Ch 18:6
from which Solomon **m** the bronze 1Ch 18:8
The LORD **m** David victorious 1Ch 18:13
realized they had **m** themselves 1Ch 19:6
they **m** peace with David and 1Ch 19:19
which Moses **m** in the desert, 1Ch 21:29
So David **m** lavish preparations 1Ch 22:5
that I have **m** for worship." 1Ch 23:5
of David's reign a search was **m**, 1Ch 26:31
I had **m** preparations to build, 1Ch 28:2
my ability I've **m** provision for 1Ch 29:2
for which I have **m** provision." 1Ch 29:19
m David's son Solomon king; 1Ch 29:22
Moses had **m** in the wilderness 2Ch 1:3
Uri, son of Hur, had **m**, in front 2Ch 1:5
and You have **m** me king in his 2Ch 1:8
For You have **m** me king over a 2Ch 1:9
over whom I have **m** you king, 2Ch 1:11
The king **m** silver and gold as 2Ch 1:15
and he **m** cedar as abundant as 2Ch 1:15
who **m** the heavens and the earth, 2Ch 2:12
m 70,000 of them porters, 2Ch 2:18
Then he **m** the most holy place; 2Ch 3:8
He **m** two cherubim of sculptured 2Ch 3:10
He **m** the veil of blue, purple, 2Ch 3:14
of the temple he **m** two pillars, 2Ch 3:15
He had **m** chainwork in the inner 2Ch 3:16
He **m** 100 pomegranates and 2Ch 3:16
m a bronze altar 30 feet long, 2Ch 4:1
Then he **m** the cast ⌊metal⌋ 2Ch 4:2
m 10 basins for washing and he 2Ch 4:6
He **m** the 10 gold lampstands 2Ch 4:7
m 10 tables and placed them in 2Ch 4:8
He also **m** 100 gold bowls. 2Ch 4:8
m the courtyard of the priests 2Ch 4:9
Then Huram **m** the pots, the 2Ch 4:11
also **m** the water carts and the 2Ch 4:14
Huram-abi **m** them for King 2Ch 4:16
⌊All these were **m**⌋ of polished 2Ch 4:16
Solomon **m** all these utensils in 2Ch 4:18
Solomon also **m** all the equipment 2Ch 4:19
the LORD had **m** a covenant with 2Ch 5:10
is that He **m** with the Israelites 2Ch 6:11
For Solomon had **m** a bronze 2Ch 6:13
King David had **m** to praise the 2Ch 7:6
that Solomon had **m** could not 2Ch 7:7
LORD's altar he had **m** in front 2Ch 8:12
The king **m** the algum wood into 2Ch 9:11
King Solomon **m** 200 large shields 2Ch 9:15
He **m** 300 small shields of 2Ch 9:16
The king also **m** a large ivory 2Ch 9:17
it had ever been **m** in any other 2Ch 9:19
The king **m** silver as common in 2Ch 9:27
and he **m** cedar as abundant as 2Ch 9:27
Your father **m** our yoke harsh. 2Ch 10:4
'Your father **m** our yoke heavy, 2Ch 10:10
My father **m** your yoke heavy, 2Ch 10:14
and the ⌊gold⌋ calves he had **m**. 2Ch 11:15
gold shields that Solomon had **m**. 2Ch 12:9
King Rehoboam **m** bronze shields 2Ch 12:10
that Jeroboam **m** for you as gods. 2Ch 13:8
No one **m** war with him in those 2Ch 14:6
because she had **m** an obscene 2Ch 15:16
then they **m** a great fire in his 2Ch 16:14
and he **m** an alliance with Ahab 2Ch 18:1
of Chenaanah **m** iron horns and 2Ch 18:10

Jehoshaphat **m** an alliance with 2Ch 20:35
and they **m** the ships in 2Ch 20:36
has broken up what you have **m**." 2Ch 20:37
the LORD had **m** with David, 2Ch 21:7
of Jerusalem **m** Ahaziah, 2Ch 22:1
They **m** a circuit throughout 2Ch 23:2
whole assembly **m** a covenant with 2Ch 23:3
the testimony, and **m** him king. 2Ch 23:11
Then Jehoiada **m** a covenant 2Ch 23:16
a chest was **m** and placed outside 2Ch 24:8
who **m** articles for the LORD's 2Ch 24:14
Have we **m** you the king's 2Ch 25:16
and **m** him king in place of his 2Ch 26:1
for ⌊God⌋ **m** ⌊him⌋ very powerful. 2Ch 26:8
He **m** skillfully designed devices 2Ch 26:15
of Israel and **m** cast images 2Ch 28:2
and **m** himself altars on every 2Ch 28:24
m high places in every city of 2Ch 28:25
and He **m** them an object of 2Ch 29:8
so that He **m** them an object 2Ch 30:7
m an abundance of weapons and 2Ch 32:5
which were **m** by human hands. 2Ch 32:19
and he **m** himself treasuries for 2Ch 32:27
He **m** warehouses for the harvest 2Ch 32:28
He **m** cities for himself, and he 2Ch 32:29
He **m** Asherah poles, and he 2Ch 33:3
image of the idol he had **m**, 2Ch 33:7
that his father Manasseh had **m**, 2Ch 33:22
King Amon and **m** his son Josiah 2Ch 33:25
at his post and **m** a covenant 2Ch 34:31
they **m** preparations for 2Ch 35:14
the Levites **m** preparations for 2Ch 35:14
brothers had **m** preparations for 2Ch 35:15
son of Josiah and **m** him king in 2Ch 36:1
king of Egypt **m** Jehoahaz's 2Ch 36:4
Then he **m** Jehoiachin's brother 2Ch 36:10
who had **m** him swear allegiance 2Ch 36:13
of Judah and **m** them afraid to Ezr 4:4
should be **m** in your fathers' Ezr 4:15
house will be **m** into a garbage Ezr 6:11
the LORD had **m** them joyful, Ezr 6:22
Ezra got up and **m** the leading Ezr 10:5
Uriah, son of Hakkoz, **m** repairs. Neh 3:4
son of Meshezabel, **m** repairs. Neh 3:4
Zadok son of Baana **m** repairs. Neh 3:4
them the Tekoites **m** repairs, Neh 3:5
the goldsmith, **m** repairs, and Neh 3:8
son of the perfumer **m** repairs. Neh 3:8
of Jerusalem, **m** repairs. Neh 3:9
son of Harumaph **m** repairs across Neh 3:10
son of Hashabneiah **m** repairs. Neh 3:10
of Pahath-moab **m** repairs to Neh 3:11
of Jerusalem, **m** repairs—he and Neh 3:12
He also **m** repairs to the wall of Neh 3:15
m repairs up to ⌊a point⌋ Neh 3:16
the Levites **m** repairs ⌊under⌋ Neh 3:17
m repairs for his district. Neh 3:17
Levites⌋ **m** repairs ⌊under⌋ Neh 3:18
m repairs to another section Neh 3:19
m repairs to another section, Neh 3:21
the surrounding area **m** repairs. Neh 3:22
and Hasshub **m** repairs opposite Neh 3:23
m repairs beside his house. Neh 3:23
son of Henadad **m** repairs to Neh 3:24
son of Uzai ⌊**m** repairs⌋ opposite Neh 3:25
living on Ophel ⌊**m** repairs⌋ Neh 3:26
him the Tekoites **m** repairs to Neh 3:27
of the priests **m** repairs above Neh 3:28
son of Immer **m** repairs opposite Neh 3:29
of the East Gate, **m** repairs. Neh 3:29
son of Zalaph **m** repairs to Neh 3:30
of Berechiah **m** repairs opposite Neh 3:30
m repairs to the house of the Neh 3:31
and merchants **m** repairs between Neh 3:32
After I **m** an inspection, I stood Neh 4:14
the priests and **m** everyone take Neh 5:12
wooden platform **m** for this Neh 8:4
and **m** booths for themselves on Neh 8:16
from exile **m** booths and lived Neh 8:17
m a covenant with him to give Neh 9:8
You **m** a name for Yourself that Neh 9:10
his God and God **m** him king over Neh 13:26
Let a search be **m** for beautiful Est 2:2
on her head and **m** her queen in Est 2:17
house that he **m** for Mordecai, Est 7:9
formed three bands, **m** a raid on Jb 1:17
came over me and **m** all my bones Jb 4:14
stone, or my flesh **m** of bronze? Jb 6:12

So I have been **m** to inherit Jb 7:3
Why have You **m** me Your target, Jb 7:20
by like boats **m** of papyrus, Jb 9:26
your defenses are **m** of clay. Jb 13:12
has **m** me an object of scorn to Jb 17:6
into day and ⌊**m**⌋ light ⌊seem⌋ Jb 17:12
God has **m** my heart faint; Jb 23:16
Almighty who has **m** me bitter, Jb 27:2
and I **m** the widow's heart Jb 29:13
have **m** a covenant with my eyes. Jb 31:1
servants when they **m** a complaint Jb 31:13
not the One who **m** me in the womb Jb 31:15
The Spirit of God has **m** me, Jb 33:4
when I **m** the clouds its garment Jb 38:9
I **m** the wilderness its home, Jb 39:6
which I **m** along with you. Jb 40:15
strung His bow and **m** it ready. Ps 7:12
but fell into the hole he had **m**. Ps 7:15
You **m** him little less than God Ps 8:5
You **m** him lord over the works of Ps 8:6
have fallen into the pit they **m**; Ps 9:15
He **m** darkness His hiding place, Ps 18:11
You have **m** my enemies retreat Ps 18:40
You **m** me stand like a strong Ps 30:7
The heavens were **m** by the word Ps 33:6
have **m** my days short in length, Ps 39:5
those who **m** a covenant with Me Ps 50:5
You have **m** Your people suffer Ps 60:3
wine to drink that **m** us stagger. Ps 60:3
They will be **m** to stumble; Ps 64:8
I have **m** the Lord GOD my refuge, Ps 73:28
You **m** summer and winter. Ps 74:17
the stone and **m** water flow down Ps 78:16
He **m** the east wind blow in the Ps 78:26
He **m** ⌊them⌋ fall in His camp, Ps 78:28
He **m** their days end in futility, Ps 78:33
the shoot that You **m** strong for Ps 80:15
of man You have **m** strong for Ps 80:17
nations You have **m** will come and Ps 86:9
You have **m** me repulsive to them. Ps 88:8
I have **m** a covenant with My Ps 89:3
You have **m** all his enemies Ps 89:42
have **m** his splendor cease and Ps 89:44
Because you have **m** the LORD— Ps 91:9
For You have **m** me rejoice, Ps 92:4
sea is His; He **m** it. His hands Ps 95:5
but the LORD **m** the heavens. Ps 96:5
LORD has **m** His victory known; Ps 98:2
He **m** us, and we are His—His Ps 100:3
For He knows what we are **m** of, Ps 103:14
He **m** the moon to mark the Ps 104:19
In wisdom You have **m** them all; Ps 104:24
⌊the covenant⌋ He **m** with Abraham, Ps 105:9
m him master of his household, Ps 105:21
The LORD **m** His people very Ps 105:24
He **m** them more numerous than Ps 105:24
At Horeb they **m** a calf and Ps 106:19
and gold, **m** by human hands. Ps 115:4
This is the day the LORD has **m**; Ps 118:24
Your hands **m** me and formed me; Ps 119:73
they **m** their furrows long. Ps 129:3
and gold, **m** by human hands. Ps 135:15
He **m** the heavens skillfully. Ps 136:5
He **m** the great lights: His love Ps 136:7
remarkably and wonderfully **m**. Ps 139:14
from You when I was **m** in secret, Ps 139:15
rests⌋ on all He has **m**. Ps 145:9
All You have **m** will praise You, Ps 145:10
I've **m** fellowship offerings; Pr 7:14
The LORD **m** me at the beginning Pr 8:22
He **m** the land, the fields, Pr 8:26
Man cannot be **m** secure by Pr 12:3
eye—the LORD **m** them both. Pr 20:12
in common: the LORD **m** them both. Pr 22:2
I **m** gardens and parks for myself Ec 2:5
He has **m** everything appropriate Ec 3:11
out what He has **m** crooked? Ec 7:13
God has **m** the one as well as the Ec 7:14
that God **m** people upright, Ec 7:29
they **m** me a keeper of the Sg 1:6
King Solomon **m** a sedan chair for Sg 3:9
He **m** its posts of silver, its Sg 3:10
to what their fingers have **m**. Is 2:8
which they **m** to worship, to Is 2:20
the altars they **m** with their Is 17:8
altars they **m** with their fingers Is 17:8
leaders⌋ have **m** Egypt stagger Is 19:14
Those who **m** Cush their hope and Is 20:5

You **m** a reservoir between the Is 22:11
not look to the One who **m** it, Is 22:11
the sea; He **m** kingdoms tremble Is 23:11
its palaces. They **m** it a ruin. Is 23:13
and we have **m** an agreement with Is 28:15
because we have **m** falsehood our Is 28:15
How can what is **m** say about its Is 29:16
your own hands have sinfully **m**. Is 31:7
him, but not one **m** by man. Is 31:8
You **m** the heavens and the earth. Is 37:16
not gods but **m** by human hands— Is 37:19
him; indeed, I have **m** him." Is 43:7
I am the LORD, who **m** everything; Is 44:24
m the earth, and created man on Is 45:12
He formed the earth and **m** it; Is 45:18
I have **m** ⌊you⌋, and I will carry Is 46:4
m your yoke very heavy on the Is 47:6
m water flow for them from the Is 48:21
m my words like a sharp sword; Is 49:2
He **m** me like a sharpened arrow; Is 49:2
I blessed him and **m** him many. Is 51:2
m the sea-bed into a road for Is 51:10
You **m** your back like the ground, Is 51:23
m His grave with the wicked, Is 53:9
to crush Him, and He **m** Him sick. Is 53:10
Since I have **m** him a witness to Is 55:4
went up, and **m** your bed wide, Is 57:8
and you have **m** a bargain for Is 57:8
breath ⌊of man⌋, which I have **m**. Is 57:16
your sins have **m** Him hide ⌊His⌋ Is 59:2
They have **m** their roads crooked; Is 59:8
I **m** them drunk with My wrath and Is 63:6
from us and **m** us melt because Is 64:7
My hand **m** all these things, Is 66:2
One who has **m** you a fortified Jr 1:18
you **m** My inheritance detestable. Jr 2:7
your gods you **m** for yourself? Jr 2:28
It will never again be **m**. Jr 3:16
They **m** their faces harder than Jr 5:3
I **m** My name dwell at first. Jr 7:12
by worthless idols ⌊**m** of⌋ wood! Jr 10:8
He **m** the earth by His power, Jr 10:12
of Judah will be **m** desolate, Jr 10:22
him off and **m** his homeland Jr 10:25
broke My covenant I **m** with their Jr 11:10
They have **m** it a desolation. Jr 12:11
of the land. I **m** ⌊them⌋ Jr 15:7
I **m** their widows more numerous Jr 15:8
No lament will be **m** for them, Jr 16:6
so he **m** it into another jar, Jr 18:4
nation I have **m** an announcement Jr 18:8
They have **m** their land a horror, Jr 18:16
abandoned Me and **m** this a Jr 19:4
hand and **m** all the nations Jr 25:17
outstretched arm, I **m** the earth, Jr 27:5
send him, and **m** you trust a lie Jr 29:31
like the covenant I **m** with their Jr 31:32
You Yourself **m** the heavens and Jr 32:17
You **m** a name for Yourself, Jr 32:20
The LORD who **m** the earth, Jr 33:2
King Zedekiah **m** a covenant with Jr 34:8
I **m** a covenant with your Jr 34:13
m a covenant before Me at the Jr 34:15
the covenant they **m** before Me, Jr 34:18
king of Babylon **m** him king. Jr 37:1
for it had been **m** into a prison. Jr 37:15
King Asa had **m** in the encounter Jr 41:9
that we **m** sacrificial cakes Jr 44:19
vows we have **m** to burn incense Jr 44:25
land will be **m** desolate because Jr 49:20
land will be **m** desolate because Jr 50:45
He **m** the earth by His power, Jr 51:15
They **m** their way along the route Jr 52:7
Solomon had **m** for the LORD's Jr 52:20
for the LORD has **m** her suffer Lm 1:5
which the LORD **m** ⌊me⌋ suffer on Lm 1:12
my bones; He **m** it descend. He Lm 1:13
He **m** me desolate, sick all day Lm 1:13
He **m** the ramparts and walls Lm 2:8
He has **m** me dwell in darkness Lm 3:6
He has **m** my paths crooked. Lm 3:9
teeth on gravel and **m** me cower Lm 3:16
You have **m** us disgusting filth Lm 3:45
m a treaty with Egypt and with Lm 5:6
I have **m** your face as hard as Ezk 3:8
I have **m** your forehead like a Ezk 3:9
I have **m** you a watchman over the Ezk 3:17
they **m** their abhorrent images Ezk 7:20

I have **m** these into something Ezk 7:20
For I have **m** you a sign to the Ezk 12:6
it could not be **m** into a useful Ezk 15:5
can it ever be **m** into anything Ezk 15:5
m you thrive like plants of the Ezk 16:7
clothing was ⌊**m**⌋ of fine linen, Ezk 16:13
garments and **m** colorful high Ezk 16:16
beautiful jewelry **m** from the Ezk 16:17
you **m** male images so that you Ezk 16:17
a mound and **m** yourself an Ezk 16:24
beyond theirs and **m** your sisters Ezk 16:51
since you have **m** your sisters Ezk 16:52
the covenant I **m** with you in the Ezk 16:60
family and **m** a covenant with Ezk 17:13
of her cubs and **m** him a young Ezk 19:5
house and **m** Myself known to Ezk 20:5
sight I had **m** Myself known to Ezk 20:9
When they **m** every firstborn pass Ezk 20:26
from the idols you have **m**. Ezk 22:4
I have **m** you a disgrace to the Ezk 22:4
gain you have **m** and against Ezk 22:13
and **m** her promiscuous acts worse Ezk 23:11
They have even **m** the children Ezk 23:37
They **m** your oars of oaks from Ezk 27:6
They **m** your deck of cypress wood Ezk 27:6
Your sail was ⌊**m** of⌋ fine Ezk 27:7
I **m** a spectacle of you before Ezk 28:17
is my own; I **m** ⌊it⌋ for myself. Ezk 29:3
have been a staff ⌊**m**⌋ of reed to Ezk 29:6
shattered and **m** all their hips Ezk 29:7
The Nile is my own; I **m** ⌊it⌋, Ezk 29:9
king of Babylon **m** his army labor Ezk 29:18
Every head was **m** bald and every Ezk 29:18
underground springs **m** it tall, Ezk 31:4
I **m** it beautiful with its many Ezk 31:9
I **m** Lebanon mourn on account of Ezk 31:15
I **m** the nations quake at the Ezk 31:16
I have **m** you a watchman for the Ezk 33:7
Because they have **m** you desolate Ezk 36:3
altar was **m** of wood, five and Ezk 41:22
on them anything **m** of wool when Ezk 44:17
houses will be **m** a garbage dump. Dn 2:5
might be **m** known to the king, Dn 2:30
over to you and **m** you ruler over Dn 2:38
He **m** him ruler over the entire Dn 2:48
Nebuchadnezzar **m** a gold statue, Dn 3:1
down and worship the statue I **m**. Dn 3:15
and his house **m** a garbage dump. Dn 3:29
their gods **m** of gold and silver Dn 5:4
praised the gods **m** of silver and Dn 5:23
Daniel and **m** every effort until Dn 6:14
this horn **m** war with the holy Dn 7:21
m some of the stars and some of Dn 8:10
m itself great, even up to the Dn 8:11
he touched me, **m** me stand up, Dn 8:18
a mighty hand and **m** Your name Dn 9:15
After an alliance is **m** with him, Dn 11:23
plots will be **m** against him. Dn 11:25
a craftsman **m** it, and it is not Hs 8:6
the better they **m** the sacred Hs 10:1
have become; I **m** it all myself. Hs 12:8
idols skillfully **m** from their Hs 13:2
But you **m** the Nazirites drink Am 2:12
The One who **m** the Pleiades and Am 5:8
you have **m** for yourselves. Am 5:26
who **m** the sea and the dry land." Jnh 1:9
to the LORD and **m** vows. Jnh 1:16
He **m** himself a shelter there and Jnh 4:5
You have **m** your merchants more Nah 3:16
You have **m** mankind like the fish Hab 1:14
the promise I **m** to you when you Hg 2:5
angry, but they **m** it worse. Zch 1:15
the mountains were **m** of bronze. Zch 6:1
They **m** their hearts like a rock Zch 7:12
covenant I had **m** with all the Zch 11:10
So I in turn have **m** you despised Mal 2:9
taste, how can it be **m** salty? Mt 5:13
I am willing; be **m** clean." Mt 8:3
touch His robe, I'll be **m** well!" Mt 9:21
"Your faith has **m** you well." Mt 9:22
the woman was **m** well from that Mt 9:22
hidden that won't be **m** known. Mt 10:26
Immediately He **m** the disciples Mt 14:22
it were **m** perfectly well. Mt 14:36
in the beginning **m** them male and Mt 19:4
are eunuchs who were **m** by men, Mt 19:12
who have **m** themselves that Mt 19:12
of heaven is **m** up of people like Mt 19:14

and you **m** them equal to us who Mt 20:12
that the tomb be **m** secure until Mt 27:64
they went and **m** the tomb secure Mt 27:66
and **m** His way to a deserted Mk 1:35
He told him. "Be **m** clean." Mk 1:41
cloth, and a worse tear is **m**. Mk 2:21
Sabbath was **m** for man and not Mk 2:27
His robes, I'll be **m** well!" Mk 5:28
your faith has **m** you well. Mk 5:34
Immediately He **m** His disciples Mk 6:45
who touched it was **m** well. Mk 6:56
a result, He **m** all foods clean Mk 7:19
that place and **m** their way Mk 9:30
of creation God **m** them male and Mk 10:6
you have **m** it a den of thieves! Mk 11:17
this sanctuary **m** by ⌊human⌋ Mk 14:58
build another not **m** by hands.' " Mk 14:58
the Lord has **m** known to us." Lk 2:15
mountain and hill will be **m** low; Lk 3:5
He went out and **m** His way to a Lk 4:42
be **m** clean," and immediately the Lk 5:13
by unclean spirits were **m** well. Lk 6:18
that won't be **m** known and come Lk 8:17
your faith has **m** you well. Lk 8:48
and she will be **m** well." Lk 8:50
Mary has **m** the right choice, Lk 10:42
Didn't He who **m** the outside make Lk 11:40
hidden that won't be **m** known. Lk 12:2
taste, how will it be **m** salty? Lk 14:34
Your faith has **m** you well." Lk 17:19
how much they had **m** in business. Lk 19:15
your mina has **m** five minas.' Lk 19:18
you have **m** it a den of thieves! Lk 19:46
He went out and **m** His way as Lk 22:39
and how He was **m** known to them Lk 24:35
and the statement Jesus had **m**. Jn 2:22
the town and **m** their way to Him Jn 4:30
The man who **m** me well told me, Jn 5:11
it was Jesus who had **m** him well. Jn 5:15
at Me because I **m** a man entirely Jn 7:23
What is this remark He **m**: Jn 7:36
m some mud from the saliva, Jn 9:6
The man called Jesus **m** mud, Jn 9:11
day that Jesus **m** the mud and Jn 9:14
because I have **m** known to you Jn 15:15
May they be **m** completely one, Jn 17:23
I **m** Your name known to them and Jn 17:26
police had **m** a charcoal fire, Jn 18:18
He **m** Himself the Son of God. Jn 19:7
moment Pilate **m** every effort to Jn 19:12
that God has **m** this Jesus, Ac 2:36
or godliness we had **m** him walk? Ac 3:12
His name has **m** this man strong, Ac 3:16
covenant that God **m** with your Ac 3:25
are the One who **m** the heaven, Ac 4:24
that God had **m** to Abraham, Ac 7:17
even **m** a calf in those days, Ac 7:41
what their hands had **m**. Ac 7:41
images that you **m** to worship. Ac 7:43
in sanctuaries **m** with hands, Ac 7:48
that Dorcas had **m** while she was Ac 9:39
What God has **m** clean, you must Ac 10:15
What God has **m** clean, you must Ac 11:9
of Stephen **m** their way as far Ac 11:19
was being **m** earnestly to God Ac 12:5
promise that was **m** to our Ac 13:32
covenant blessings **m** to David. Ac 13:34
When an attempt was **m** by both Ac 14:5
living God, who **m** the heaven, Ac 14:15
that town and **m** many disciples, Ac 14:21
early days God **m** a choice among Ac 15:7
He **m** no distinction between us Ac 15:9
we immediately **m** efforts to set Ac 16:10
prediction and **m** a large profit Ac 16:16
The God who **m** the world and Ac 17:24
not live in shrines **m** by hands. Ac 17:24
one man He has **m** every nation of Ac 17:26
the Jews **m** a united attack Ac 18:12
silversmith who **m** silver shrines Ac 19:24
that gods **m** by hand are not Ac 19:26
so a decision was **m** to go back Ac 20:3
for each of them would be **m**. Ac 21:26
while Paul **m** the defense that, Ac 25:8
of the promise **m** by God to our Ac 26:6
after Paul **m** one statement: Ac 28:25
through what He has **m**. Rm 1:20
faith is **m** empty and the promise Rm 4:14
I have **m** you the father of many Rm 4:17
the many were **m** sinners, Rm 5:19
the many will be **m** righteous. Rm 5:19
but I am **m** out of flesh, sold Rm 7:14
would have been **m** like Gomorrah. Rm 9:29
now revealed and **m** known Rm 16:26
by Him you were **m** rich in 1Co 1:5
Hasn't God **m** the world's wisdom 1Co 1:20
I have **m** myself a slave to all, 1Co 9:19
we were all **m** to drink of one 1Co 12:13
in Christ all will be **m** alive. 1Co 15:22
from the earth and **m** of dust; 1Co 15:47
Like the man **m** of dust, so are 1Co 15:48
so are those who are **m** of dust; 1Co 15:48
the image of the man **m** of dust, 1Co 15:49
will need to be **m** when I come. 1Co 16:2
these men have **m** up for your 1Co 16:17
I **m** up my mind about this: 2Co 2:1
He has **m** us competent to be 2Co 3:6
God, a house not **m** with hands, 2Co 5:1
m the One who did not know sin 2Co 5:21
for us might be **m** plain to you 2Co 7:12
we were **m** to rejoice even more 2Co 7:13
For if I have **m** any boast to him 2Co 7:14
we have always **m** that clear to 2Co 11:6
is **m** to stumble, and I do not 2Co 11:29
which I **m** every effort to do. Gl 2:10
you now going to be **m** complete Gl 3:3
the promise was **m** would come. Gl 3:19
He **m** known to us the mystery of Eph 1:9
we were also **m** His inheritance Eph 1:11
m us alive with the Messiah even Eph 2:5
who **m** both groups one and tore Eph 2:14
The mystery was **m** known to me by Eph 3:3
This was not **m** known to people Eph 3:5
I was **m** a servant of this Eph 3:7
may now be **m** known through Eph 3:10
which He **m** in the Messiah, Eph 3:11
exposed by the light is **m** clear, Eph 5:13
your requests be **m** known to God. Php 4:6
He **m** you alive with Him and Col 2:13
desired and **m** every effort to 1Th 2:17
previously **m** about you, 1Tm 1:18
thanksgivings be **m** for everyone, 1Tm 2:1
called and have **m** a good 1Tm 6:12
has now been **m** evident through 2Tm 1:10
might be fully **m** through me, 2Tm 4:17
through whom He **m** the universe. Heb 1:2
You **m** him lower than the angels Heb 2:7
m lower than the angels for a Heb 2:9
For when God **m** a promise to Heb 6:13
He with an oath **m** by the One who Heb 7:21
covenant that I **m** with their Heb 8:9
tabernacle not **m** with hands Heb 9:11
enter a sanctuary **m** with hands Heb 9:24
His enemies are **m** His footstool. Heb 10:13
seen has been **m** from things that Heb 11:3
would not be **m** perfect without Heb 11:40
of righteous people **m** perfect, Heb 12:23
men who are **m** in God's likeness Jms 3:9
the fleshly realm but **m** alive in 1Pt 3:18
also went and **m** a proclamation 1Pt 3:19
myths when we **m** known to you the 2Pt 1:16
it might be **m** clear that none 1Jn 2:19
promise that He Himself **m** to us: 1Jn 2:25
children—are **m** evident. 1Jn 3:10
believe God has **m** Him a liar, 1Jn 5:10
and **m** us a kingdom, priests to Rv 1:6
You **m** them a kingdom and priests Rv 5:10
like sackcloth **m** of goat hair; Rv 6:12
their robes and **m** them white Rv 7:14
because they had been **m** bitter. Rv 8:11
who **m** all nations drink the wine Rv 14:8
gate was **m** of a single pearl. Rv 21:21
the filthy go on being **m** filthy; Rv 22:11
the holy go on being **m** holy." Rv 22:11

MADLY *(1)*
The chariots dash **m** through the Nah 2:4

MADMAN *(5)*
He acted like a **m** around them, 1Sm 21:13
of Nimshi—he drives like a **m**." 2Kg 9:20
a **m** who throws flaming darts Pr 26:18
for every **m** who acts like Jr 29:26
talking like a **m**—I'm a better 2Co 11:23

MADMANNAH *(1)*
Ziklag, **M**, Sansannah, Jos 15:31

MADMANNAH'S *(1)*
mother of Shaaph, **M** father, and 1Ch 2:49

MADMEN *(1)*
You **m** will also be silenced; Jr 48:2

MADMENAH *(1)*
M has fled. The inhabitants of Is 10:31

MADNESS *(9)*
LORD will afflict you with **m**, Dt 28:28
and knowledge, **m** and folly; Ec 1:17
laughter, "It is **m**," and about Ec 2:2
wisdom, **m**, and folly, for Ec 2:12
is stupidity and folly is **m**. Ec 7:25
and **m** is in their hearts while Ec 9:3
end of his speaking is evil **m**. Ec 10:13
with panic and its rider with **m**. Zch 12:4
and restrained the prophet's **m**. 2Pt 2:16

MADON *(2)*
Jobab king of **M**, the kings of Jos 11:1
the king of **M** one the king of Jos 12:19

MAGADAN *(1)*
and went to the region of **M**. Mt 15:39

MAGBISH'S *(1)*
M people 156 Ezr 2:30

MAGDALENE *(12)*
were Mary **M**, Mary the mother Mt 27:56
Mary **M** and the other Mary were Mt 27:61
Mary **M** and the other Mary went Mt 28:1
were Mary **M**, Mary the mother Mk 15:40
Mary **M** and Mary the mother Mk 15:47
over, Mary **M**, Mary the mother Mk 16:1
He appeared first to Mary **M**, Mk 16:9
Mary, called **M** (seven demons had Lk 8:2
Mary **M**, Joanna, Mary the mother Lk 24:10
the wife of Clopas, and Mary **M**. Jn 19:25
the week Mary **M** came to the tomb Jn 20:1
Mary **M** went and announced to the Jn 20:18

MAGDIEL *(2)*
M, and Iram. These are Edom's Gn 36:43
M, and Iram. These were Edom's 1Ch 1:54

MAGGOT *(1)*
less man, who is a **m**, and the Jb 25:6

MAGGOTS *(4)*
smell or have any **m** in it. Ex 16:24
is clothed with **m** and encrusted Jb 7:5
M are spread out under you, Is 14:11
for their **m** will never die, Is 66:24

MAGIC *(5)*
is no **m** curse against Jacob Nm 23:23
seems like a **m** stone to its Pr 17:8
the women who sew ⌊**m**⌋ bands on Ezk 13:18
against your ⌊**m**⌋ bands that you Ezk 13:20
had practiced **m** collected their Ac 19:19

MAGICIAN *(1)*
cunning **m**, and necromancer. Is 3:3

MAGICIANS *(9)*
all the **m** of Egypt and all Gn 41:8
this to the **m**, but no one can Gn 41:24
sorcerers—the **m** of Egypt, and Ex 7:11
But the **m** of Egypt did the same Ex 7:22
But the **m** did the same thing by Ex 8:7
The **m** tried to produce gnats Ex 8:18
of God," the **m** said to Pharaoh. Ex 8:19
The **m** could not stand before Ex 9:11
were on the **m** as well as on all Ex 9:11

MAGISTRATES *(9)*
the judges and **m** from Tripolis, Ezr 4:9
appoint **m** and judges to judge Ezr 7:25
judges, **m**, and all the rulers Dn 3:2
judges, **m**, and all the rulers Dn 3:3
them before the chief **m**, Ac 16:20
and the chief **m** stripped off Ac 16:22
the chief **m** sent the police to Ac 16:35
The **m** have sent orders for you Ac 16:36
reported these words to the **m**. Ac 16:38

MAGNIFICENCE *(1)*
despised and her **m** come to the Ac 19:27

MAGNIFICENT *(10)*
from the hand of these **m** gods? 1Sm 4:8
kingdom and the **m** splendor of Est 1:4
powerful and **m** accomplishments Est 10:2
m is Your name throughout the Ps 8:1
m is Your name throughout the Ps 8:9
For You are their **m** strength; Ps 89:17
How **m** are Your works, LORD, how Ps 92:5
against your **m** wisdom and will Ezk 28:7

this **m** price I was valued by Zch 11:13
languages the **m** acts of God." Ac 2:11

MAGNIFIED *(3)*
Lord's power be **m** just as You Nm 14:17
confirmed and **m** forever in the 1Ch 17:24
name of the Lord Jesus was **m**. Ac 19:17

MAGNIFY *(5)*
Does a saw **m** itself above the Is 10:15
to **m** ⌊His⌋ instruction and make Is 42:21
will exalt and **m** himself above Dn 11:36
because he will **m** himself above Dn 11:37
the Gentiles, I **m** my ministry, Rm 11:13

MAGNITUDE *(2)*
by the **m** of your iniquities Ezk 28:18
because of the **m** of your guilt Hs 9:7

MAGOG *(5)*
Gomer, **M**, Madai, Javan, Tubal, Gn 10:2
Gomer, **M**, Madai, Javan, Tubal, 1Ch 1:5
of the land of **M**, the chief Ezk 38:2
send fire against **M** and those Ezk 39:6
earth, Gog and **M**, to gather them Rv 20:8

MAGOR-MISSABIB *(1)*
not call you Pashhur, but **M**, Jr 20:3

MAGPIASH *(1)*
M, Meshullam, Hezir, Neh 10:20

MAHALAB *(1)*
at the sea, including **M**, Achzib, Jos 19:29

MAHALALEEL *(1)*
(AKA MAHALALEL)
Jared, ⌊son⌋ of **M**, ⌊son⌋ of Lk 3:37

MAHALALEL *(6)*
(AKA MAHALALEEL)
70 years old when he fathered **M**. Gn 5:12
840 years after the birth of **M**, Gn 5:13
M was 65 years old when he Gn 5:15
M lived 830 years after the Gn 5:16
Kenan, **M**, Jared, 1Ch 1:2
Shephatiah, son of **M**, of Perez's Neh 11:4

MAHALALEL'S *(1)*
So **M** life lasted 895 years; Gn 5:17

MAHALATH *(2)*
his other wives, **M** daughter of Gn 28:9
Rehoboam married **M**, daughter 2Ch 11:18

MAHANAIM *(13)*
So he called that place **M**. Gn 32:2
and from **M** to the border of Jos 13:26
From **M** through all Bashan— Jos 13:30
its pasturelands, **M** with its Jos 21:38
Ish-bosheth and moved him to **M**. 2Sm 2:8
marched out from **M** to Gibeon. 2Sm 2:12
all morning, and arrived at **M**. 2Sm 2:29
had arrived at **M** by the time 2Sm 17:24
When David came to **M**, Shobi 2Sm 17:27
the king while he stayed in **M**. 2Sm 19:32
against me the day I went to **M**. 1Kg 2:8
Ahinadab son of Iddo, ⌊in⌋ **M**; 1Kg 4:14
its pasturelands, **M** and its 1Ch 6:80

MAHARAI *(3)*
the Ahohite, **M** the Netophathite, 2Sm 23:28
M the Netophathite, Heled son of 1Ch 11:30
month, was **M** the Netophathite 1Ch 27:13

MAHATH *(3)*
son of **M**, son of Amasai, 1Ch 6:35
M son of Amasai and Joel son of 2Ch 29:12
Ismachiah, **M**, and Benaiah were 2Ch 31:13

MAHAVITE *(1)*
Eliel the **M**, Jeribai and 1Ch 11:46

MAHAZIOTH *(2)*
Mallothi, Hothir, and **M**. 1Ch 25:4
twenty-third to **M**, his sons, and 1Ch 25:30

MAHER-SHALAL-HASH-BAZ *(2)*
on it with an ordinary pen: **M**. Is 8:1
LORD said to me, "Name him **M**, Is 8:3

MAHLAH *(5)*
Zelophehad's daughters were **M**, Nm 26:33
M, Noah, Hoglah, Milcah, and Nm 27:1
M, Tirzah, Hoglah, Milcah, and Nm 36:11
M, Noah, Hoglah, Milcah, and Jos 17:3
birth to Ishhod, Abiezer, and **M**. 1Ch 7:18

MAHLI *(11)*
sons of Merari: **M** and Mushi. Ex 6:19
by their clans were **M** and Mushi. Nm 3:20
Merari's sons: **M** and Mushi. 1Ch 6:19
M, his son Libni, his son Shimei, 1Ch 6:29
son of **M**, son of Mushi, son of 1Ch 6:47
Merari's sons: **M** and Mushi. 1Ch 23:21
M, Eder, and Jeremoth—three. 1Ch 23:23
M and Mushi, ⌊and from⌋ his sons, 1Ch 24:26
M: Eleazar, who had no sons. 1Ch 24:28
M, Eder, and Jerimoth. 1Ch 24:30
from the descendants of **M**, Ezr 8:18

MAHLI'S *(1)*
and Mushi. **M** sons: Eleazar 1Ch 23:21

MAHLITE *(2)*
The **M** clan and the Mushite clan Nm 3:33
clan, the **M** clan, the Mushite Nm 26:58

MAHLON *(3)*
his two sons were **M** and Chilion. Ru 1:2
both **M** and Chilion also died, Ru 1:5
to Elimelech, Chilion, and **M**. Ru 4:9

MAHLON'S *(1)*
the Moabitess, **M** widow, as my Ru 4:10

MAHOL *(1)*
Calcol, and Darda, sons of **M**. 1Kg 4:31

MAHSEIAH *(2)*
Baruch son of Neriah, son of **M**. Jr 32:12
Seraiah son of Neriah son of **M**, Jr 51:59

MAIMED *(5)*
blind, injured, **m**, or has a Lv 22:22
for you to enter life **m** or lame, Mt 18:8
to enter life **m** than to have two Mk 9:43
who are poor, **m**, lame, or blind. Lk 14:13
here the poor, **m**, blind, and Lk 14:21

MAIN *(7)*
"We will go on the **m** road," Nm 20:19
the **m** camp to the north of the Jos 8:13
days of Jael, the **m** ways were Jdg 5:6
the city, at the **m** entrance, she Pr 8:3
out from its **m** branch and has Ezk 19:14
because he was the **m** speaker. Ac 14:12
Now the **m** point of what is being Heb 8:1

MAINLAND *(2)*
villages on the **m** will be Ezk 26:6
on the **m** with the sword. Ezk 26:8

MAINTAIN *(5)*
I will **m** my integrity until I Jb 27:5
M ⌊your⌋ competence and Pr 3:21
so that ⌊you⌋ may **m** discretion Pr 5:2
M love and justice, and always Hs 12:6
in order to **m** your tradition! Mk 7:9

MAINTAINED *(3)*
Your word and **m** Your covenant. Dt 33:9
Benjaminites **m** their allegiance 1Ch 12:29
Because you **m** an ancient hatred Ezk 35:5

MAINTAINING *(1)*
m faithful love to a thousand Ex 34:7

MAINTAINS *(2)*
through loyalty he **m** his throne. Pr 20:28
anyone who **m** this, who keeps Is 56:2

MAJESTIC *(19)*
to take the product of **m** trees— Lv 23:40
him curdled milk in a **m** bowl. Jdg 5:25
God thunders with His **m** voice. Jb 37:4
resplendent and **m** ⌊coming down⌋ Ps 76:4
the sea—the LORD on high is **m**. Ps 93:4
that He does is splendid and **m**; Ps 111:3
Lebanon, as **m** as the cedars. Sg 5:15
LORD and from His **m** splendor. Is 2:10
LORD and from His **m** splendor, Is 2:19
LORD and from His **m** splendor, Is 2:21
Woe to the **m** crown of Ephraim's Is 28:1
The **m** crown of Ephraim's Is 28:3
For there the **m** One, the LORD, Is 33:21
and **m** vessels will not pass. Is 33:21
fruit, and become a **m** cedar. Ezk 17:23
and to display my **m** glory?" Dn 4:30
in the **m** name of Yahweh His God. Mc 5:4
them like His **m** steed in battle. Zch 10:3
came to Him from the **M** Glory: 2Pt 1:17

MAJESTY *(37)*
adversaries by Your great **m**. Ex 15:7
your aid on the clouds in His **m**. Dt 33:26
Splendor and **m** are before Him; 1Ch 16:27
and the splendor and the **m**, 1Ch 29:11
him such royal **m** as had not been 1Ch 29:25
Would God's **m** not terrify you? Jb 13:11
because of His **m** I could not do Jb 31:23
awesome **m** surrounds Him. Jb 37:22
yourself with **m** and splendor, Jb 40:10
covered the heavens with Your **m**. Ps 8:1
confer **m** and splendor on him. Ps 21:5
In your **m** and splendor— Ps 45:3
His **m** is over Israel, His power Ps 68:34
He is robed in **m**; The LORD is Ps 93:1
Splendor and **m** are before Him; Ps 96:6
are clothed with **m** and splendor. Ps 104:1
His **m** covers heaven and earth. Ps 148:13
Lebanon with its **m** will fall. Is 10:34
in the west the **m** of the LORD. Is 24:14
does not see the **m** of the LORD. Is 26:10
scatter when You rise in Your **m**. Is 33:3
saying, Woe, lord! Woe, his **m**! Jr 22:18
His beautiful ornaments for **m**, Ezk 7:20
Your **M**, while you were in your Dn 2:29
Your **M**, you are king of kings. Dn 2:37
of course, Your **M**," they replied Dn 3:24
Your **M**, and this is Dn 4:24
and my **m** and splendor returned Dn 4:36
Your **M**, the Most High God gave Dn 5:18
and **m** to your predecessor Dn 5:18
Therefore, Your **M**, establish the Dn 6:8
will restore the **m** of Jacob, Nah 2:2
Jacob, yes, the **m** of Israel, Nah 2:2
the right hand of the **M** on high. Heb 1:3
throne of the **M** in the heavens, Heb 8:1
we were eyewitnesses of His **m**. 2Pt 1:16
Lord, be glory, **m**, power, and Jd 25

MAJOR *(1)*
time there was a **m** disturbance Ac 19:23

MAJORITY *(3)*
to that time the **m** of the 1Ch 12:29
the **m** decided to set sail from Ac 27:12
by the **m** is sufficient for 2Co 2:6

MAKAZ *(1)*
Ben-deker, in **M**, Shaalbim, 1Kg 4:9

MAKE *(804)*
Let Us **m** man in Our image, Gn 1:26
will **m** a helper who is like him. Gn 2:18
M yourself an ark of gofer wood. Gn 6:14
M rooms in the ark, and cover it Gn 6:14
This is how you are to **m** it: Gn 6:15
You are to **m** a roof, finishing Gn 6:16
M it with lower, middle, and Gn 6:16
from now I will **m** it rain on the Gn 7:4
let us **m** oven-fired bricks." Gn 11:3
Let us **m** a name for ourselves; Gn 11:4
will **m** you into a great nation, Gn 12:2
you, I will **m** your name great, Gn 12:2
I will **m** your offspring like the Gn 13:16
for I will **m** you the father of Gn 17:5
I will **m** you extremely fruitful Gn 17:6
and will **m** nations and kings Gn 17:6
I will **m** him fruitful and will Gn 17:20
and I will **m** him into a great Gn 17:20
of fine flour and **m** bread." Gn 18:6
I will also **m** a nation of the Gn 21:13
I will **m** him a great nation." Gn 21:18
bless you and **m** your offspring Gn 22:17
M sure that you don't take my Gn 24:6
with you and **m** your journey Gn 24:40
if only You will **m** my journey Gn 24:42
I will **m** your offspring as Gn 26:4
Let us **m** a covenant with you: Gn 26:28
m me the delicious food that Gn 27:4
some game and **m** some delicious Gn 27:7
and I will **m** them into a Gn 27:9
bless you and **m** you fruitful Gn 28:3
Come now, let's **m** a covenant, Gn 31:44
and I will **m** your offspring like Gn 32:12
Hebrew man to us to **m** fun of us. Gn 39:14
to us came to me to **m** fun of me, Gn 39:17
us, seize us, **m** us slaves, and Gn 43:18
for I will **m** you a great nation Gn 46:3
'I will **m** you fruitful and Gn 48:4
will **m** many nations ⌊come from⌋ Gn 48:4
May God **m** you like Ephraim and Gn 48:20
m sure you do in front of Ex 4:21
yet they say to us, '**M** bricks!' Ex 5:16
but I did not **m** My name Yahweh Ex 6:3
M the choice rather than me ⌊by Ex 8:9
will **m** a distinction between My Ex 8:23
go very far. **M** an appeal for me. Ex 8:28
the LORD will **m** a distinction Ex 9:4
power and to **m** My name known Ex 9:16

M an appeal to the LORD.	Ex 9:28
sin once more and **m** an appeal to	Ex 10:17
M sure you never see my face	Ex 10:28
this wilderness to **m** this whole	Ex 16:3
and I **m** a decision between one	Ex 18:16
Do not **m** an idol for yourself,	Ex 20:4
You must not **m** gods of silver to	Ex 20:23
must not **m** ⌊gods of gold⌋ for	Ex 20:23
You must **m** an earthen altar for	Ex 20:24
If you **m** a stone altar for Me,	Ex 20:25
A thief must **m** full restitution.	Ex 22:3
the fire must **m** full restitution	Ex 22:6
does not have to **m** restitution.	Ex 22:11
he must **m** restitution to its	Ex 22:12
not have to **m** restitution for	Ex 22:13
the man must **m** full restitution.	Ex 22:14
does not have to **m** restitution.	Ex 22:15
I will **m** all your enemies turn	Ex 23:27
You must not **m** a covenant with	Ex 23:32
else they will **m** you sin against	Ex 23:33
They are to **m** a sanctuary for Me	Ex 25:8
You must **m** ⌊it⌋ according to all	Ex 25:9
They are to **m** an ark of acacia	Ex 25:10
Also **m** a gold molding all around	Ex 25:11
M poles of acacia wood and	Ex 25:13
M a mercy seat of pure gold,	Ex 25:17
M two cherubim of gold;	Ex 25:18
m them of hammered work at the	Ex 25:18
M one cherub at one end and one	Ex 25:19
M the cherubim of one piece with	Ex 25:19
pure gold and **m** a gold molding	Ex 25:24
M a three-inch frame all around	Ex 25:25
around it and **m** a gold molding	Ex 25:25
M four gold rings for it, and	Ex 25:26
M the poles of acacia wood and	Ex 25:28
You are also to **m** its plates and	Ex 25:29
M them out of pure gold.	Ex 25:29
You are to **m** a lampstand out of	Ex 25:31
M seven lamps on it. Its lamps	Ex 25:37
Be careful to **m** ⌊everything⌋	Ex 25:40
You must **m** them of finely spun	Ex 26:1
M loops of blue yarn on the edge	Ex 26:4
M 50 loops on the one curtain	Ex 26:5
the one curtain and **m** 50 loops	Ex 26:5
Also **m** 50 gold clasps and join	Ex 26:6
You are to **m** curtains of goat	Ex 26:7
m 11 of these curtains.	Ex 26:7
M 50 loops on the edge of the	Ex 26:10
m 50 loops on the edge of the	Ex 26:10
M 50 bronze clasps; put the	Ex 26:11
M a covering for the tent from	Ex 26:14
You are to **m** upright planks of	Ex 26:15
M the planks for the tabernacle	Ex 26:18
and **m** 40 silver bases under the	Ex 26:19
and **m** six planks for the west	Ex 26:22
M two additional planks for the	Ex 26:23
You are to **m** five crossbars of	Ex 26:26
and **m** their rings of gold as the	Ex 26:29
You are to **m** a veil of blue,	Ex 26:31
the veil will **m** a separation for	Ex 26:33
the tent you are to **m** a screen	Ex 26:36
M five posts of acacia wood for	Ex 26:37
M horns for it on its four	Ex 27:2
M its pots for removing ashes,	Ex 27:3
m all its utensils of bronze.	Ex 27:3
and **m** four bronze rings on the	Ex 27:4
Then **m** poles for the altar,	Ex 27:6
They are to **m** it just as it was	Ex 27:8
You are to **m** the courtyard for	Ex 27:9
⌊**M** the hangings⌋ on the south of	Ex 27:9
Then ⌊**m** the hangings⌋ on the	Ex 27:11
⌊**M**⌋ the hangings of the	Ex 27:12
M the hangings of the courtyard	Ex 27:13
⌊**M**⌋ the hangings on one side ⌊of	Ex 27:14
And **m** the hangings on the other	Ex 27:15
M holy garments for your brother	Ex 28:2
to **m** Aaron's garments for	Ex 28:3
the garments that they must **m**:	Ex 28:4
They are to **m** holy garments for	Ex 28:4
They are to **m** the ephod of	Ex 28:6
you will **m** them of braided cord	Ex 28:14
You are to **m** an embroidered	Ex 28:15
M it with the same workmanship	Ex 28:15
m it of gold, of blue, purple,	Ex 28:15
You are to **m** braided chains of	Ex 28:22
M two ⌊other⌋ gold rings and put	Ex 28:26
M two ⌊more⌋ gold rings and	Ex 28:27
You are to **m** the robe of the	Ex 28:31
M pomegranates of blue, purple,	Ex 28:33
You are to **m** a plate of pure	Ex 28:36
fine linen, **m** a turban of fine	Ex 28:39
and **m** an embroidered sash.	Ex 28:39
M tunics, sashes, and headbands	Ex 28:40
M them linen undergarments to	Ex 28:42
M them out of fine wheat flour,	Ex 29:2
altar when you **m** atonement for	Ex 29:36
days you must **m** atonement for	Ex 29:37
You are to **m** an altar for the	Ex 30:1
of incense; **m** it of acacia wood	Ex 30:1
m a gold molding all around it.	Ex 30:3
M two gold rings for it under	Ex 30:4
M the poles of acacia wood and	Ex 30:5
M a bronze basin for washing and	Ex 30:18
you must not **m** anything like it	Ex 30:32
you must not **m** ⌊any⌋ for	Ex 30:37
in order to **m** all that I have	Ex 31:6
They must **m** ⌊them⌋ according to	Ex 31:11
m us a god who will go before us	Ex 32:1
Then I will **m** you into a great	Ex 32:10
'I will **m** your offspring as	Ex 32:13
'**M** us a god who will go before	Ex 32:23
don't **m** us go up from here.	Ex 33:15
careful not to **m** a treaty with	Ex 34:12
Do not **m** a treaty with the	Ex 34:15
Do not **m** cast images of gods for	Ex 34:17
you come and **m** everything that	Ex 35:10
and ⌊to **m**⌋ the holy garments.	Ex 35:21
no man or woman **m** anything else	Ex 36:6
on his behalf to **m** atonement for	Lv 1:4
the priest will **m** atonement on	Lv 4:20
the priest will **m** atonement on	Lv 4:26
the priest will **m** atonement on	Lv 4:31
the priest will **m** atonement on	Lv 4:35
the priest will **m** atonement on	Lv 5:6
the priest will **m** atonement on	Lv 5:10
the priest will **m** atonement on	Lv 5:13
must **m** restitution for his sin	Lv 5:16
the priest will **m** atonement on	Lv 5:16
the priest will **m** atonement on	Lv 5:18
must **m** full restitution for it	Lv 6:5
the priest will **m** atonement on	Lv 6:7
tent of meeting to **m** atonement	Lv 6:30
in order to **m** atonement for you	Lv 8:34
m atonement for yourself and the	Lv 9:7
offering and **m** atonement for	Lv 9:7
community and **m** atonement for	Lv 10:17
These will **m** you unclean.	Lv 11:24
the LORD and **m** atonement on her	Lv 12:7
the priest will **m** atonement on	Lv 12:8
priest will **m** an examination,	Lv 13:20
priest is to **m** an examination.	Lv 13:39
the priest will **m** atonement for	Lv 14:18
sin offering and **m** atonement for	Lv 14:19
The priest will **m** atonement for	Lv 14:20
in order to **m** atonement for him	Lv 14:21
be cleansed to **m** atonement for	Lv 14:29
the priest will **m** atonement	Lv 14:31
this way he will **m** atonement for	Lv 14:53
the priest will **m** atonement for	Lv 15:15
the priest will **m** atonement for	Lv 15:30
sin offering and **m** atonement for	Lv 16:6
the LORD to **m** purification with	Lv 16:10
time he enters to **m** atonement	Lv 16:17
the LORD and **m** atonement for it.	Lv 16:18
he will **m** atonement for himself	Lv 16:24
most⌋ holy place to **m** atonement,	Lv 16:27
of his father will **m** atonement.	Lv 16:32
altar and will **m** atonement for	Lv 16:33
m atonement for the Israelites	Lv 16:34
it to you to **m** atonement on the	Lv 17:11
You are not to **m** any of your	Lv 18:21
turn to idols or **m** cast images	Lv 19:4
The priest will **m** atonement on	Lv 19:22
You are not to **m** gashes on your	Lv 19:28
You are not to **m** yourselves	Lv 20:25
A priest is not to **m** himself	Lv 21:1
He may **m** himself unclean for his	Lv 21:3
He is not to **m** himself unclean	Lv 21:4
Priests may not **m** bald spots on	Lv 21:5
or **m** gashes on their bodies.	Lv 21:5
dead person or **m** himself unclean	Lv 21:11
day you are to **m** a proclamation	Lv 23:21
of Atonement to **m** atonement for	Lv 23:28
animal is to **m** restitution for	Lv 24:18
animal is to **m** restitution for	Lv 24:21
If you **m** a sale to your neighbor	Lv 25:14
You are to **m** the purchase from	Lv 25:15
you can **m** them slaves for life.	Lv 25:46
Do not **m** idols for yourselves,	Lv 26:1
m you fruitful and multiply you,	Lv 26:9
out the old to **m** room for the	Lv 26:10
I will **m** your sky like iron and	Lv 26:19
the land will **m** up for its	Lv 26:34
land will rest and **m** up for its	Lv 26:34
by them will **m** up for its	Lv 26:43
replace it or **m** a substitution	Lv 27:10
he is not to **m** a substitution	Lv 27:33
But if he does **m** a substitution,	Lv 27:33
the priest will **m** atonement for	Nm 5:8
the priest must **m** the woman take	Nm 5:21
'May the LORD **m** you into an	Nm 5:21
burnt offering to **m** atonement on	Nm 6:11
LORD **m** His face shine on you,	Nm 6:25
to **m** atonement for the Levites.	Nm 8:12
of meeting and to **m** atonement on	Nm 8:19
M two trumpets of hammered	Nm 10:2
I **m** Myself known to him in a	Nm 12:6
Then I will **m** you into a greater	Nm 14:12
that they **m** against Me.	Nm 14:27
and you **m** a fire offering to the	Nm 15:3
priest must then **m** atonement for	Nm 15:25
must then **m** atonement before	Nm 15:28
they are to **m** tassels for the	Nm 15:38
m them into hammered sheets as	Nm 16:38
community and **m** atonement for	Nm 16:46
M a snake ⌊image⌋ and mount it	Nm 21:8
sin offering to **m** atonement for	Nm 28:22
one male goat to **m** atonement for	Nm 28:30
sin offering to **m** atonement for	Nm 29:5
to **m** atonement for ourselves	Nm 31:50
Don't **m** us cross the Jordan."	Nm 32:5
Do not **m** the land unclean where	Nm 35:34
and I will **m** them your leaders.	Dt 1:13
act corruptly and **m** an idol for	Dt 4:16
and **m** an idol for yourselves in	Dt 4:23
m an idol in the form of	Dt 4:25
He did not **m** this covenant with	Dt 5:3
Do not **m** an idol for yourself in	Dt 5:8
M no treaty with them and show	Dt 7:2
Then I will **m** you into a nation	Dt 9:14
the mountain and **m** a wooden ark.	Dt 10:1
cut yourselves or **m** a bald spot	Dt 14:1
among you is to **m** his son or	Dt 18:10
The judges are to **m** a careful	Dt 19:18
you must **m** an offer of peace.	Dt 20:10
if it does not **m** peace with you	Dt 20:12
m sure you return it to your	Dt 22:1
m a railing around your roof,	Dt 22:8
M tassels on the four corners of	Dt 22:12
If you **m** a vow to the LORD your	Dt 23:21
When you **m** a loan of any kind to	Dt 24:10
judge will **m** him lie down and	Dt 25:2
The LORD will **m** you prosper	Dt 28:11
The LORD will **m** you the head and	Dt 28:13
The LORD will **m** pestilence cling	Dt 28:21
commanded Moses to **m** with the	Dt 29:1
LORD your God will **m** you prosper	Dt 30:9
Didn't He **m** you and sustain you?	Dt 32:6
I will **m** My arrows drunk with	Dt 32:42
M flint knives and circumcise	Jos 5:2
and **m** a confession to Him.	Jos 7:19
Please **m** a treaty with us."	Jos 9:6
How can we **m** a treaty with you?"	Jos 9:7
Please **m** a treaty with us." '	Jos 9:11
their gods or **m** an oath to them	Jos 23:7
You are not to **m** a covenant with	Jdg 2:2
allow me to **m** one more test with	Jdg 6:39
Let me **m** a request of you:	Jdg 8:24
proceeded to **m** Abimelech king	Jdg 9:6
tie him up, and **m** him helpless.	Jdg 16:5
tie you up and **m** you helpless?"	Jdg 16:6
benefit to **m** a carved image	Jdg 17:3
party in order to **m** any matter	Ru 4:7
May the LORD **m** the woman who is	Ru 4:11
went up to **m** the annual	1Sm 1:21
M images of your tumors and of	1Sm 6:5
to **m** his weapons of war or the	1Sm 8:12
to him, "**M** a treaty with us,	1Sm 11:1
I'll **m** one with you on this	1Sm 11:2
has determined to **m** you His own	1Sm 12:22
Hebrews will **m** swords or spears.	1Sm 13:19
his father **m** the troops swear	1Sm 14:27
king will **m** the man who kills	1Sm 17:25
king will also **m** the household	1Sm 17:25

you think⌋ he'll **m** all of you 1Sm 22:7
let the king **m** an accusation 1Sm 22:15
is certain to **m** a lasting 1Sm 25:28
M your covenant with me, and you 2Sm 3:12
I will **m** a covenant with you. 2Sm 3:13
They will **m** a covenant with you, 2Sm 3:21
Do not **m** a frontal assault. 2Sm 5:23
will **m** a name for you like that 2Sm 7:9
Himself will **m** a house for you. 2Sm 7:11
for Himself, to **m** a name for 2Sm 7:23
Tamar come and **m** a couple of 2Sm 13:6
and I would **m** sure he received 2Sm 15:4
should I **m** you wander around 2Sm 15:20
Why does this **m** you angry? 2Sm 19:42
the wall to **m** it collapse, 2Sm 20:15
with Solomon and **m** his throne 1Kg 1:37
'May your God **m** the name of 1Kg 1:47
and may He **m** his throne greater 1Kg 1:47
Didn't I **m** you swear by the LORD 1Kg 2:42
and I will **m** them into rafts to 1Kg 5:9
gone to Shechem to **m** him king. 1Kg 12:1
but you, **m** it lighter on us! 1Kg 12:10
have proceeded to **m** for yourself 1Kg 14:9
and I will **m** your house like the 1Kg 16:3
of Ginath, to **m** him king, and 1Kg 16:21
Only **m** me a small loaf from it 1Kg 17:13
you may **m** some for yourself and 1Kg 17:13
if I don't **m** your life like 1Kg 19:2
I will **m** your house like the 1Kg 21:22
times must I **m** you swear not to 1Kg 22:16
so let's **m** a small room upstairs 2Kg 4:10
large pot and **m** stew for the 2Kg 4:38
the LORD were to **m** windows in 2Kg 7:2
the LORD were to **m** windows in 2Kg 7:19
I will **m** the house of Ahab like 2Kg 9:9
commanders⌋ wish ⌊to **m** me king⌋, 2Kg 9:15
We will not **m** anyone king. 2Kg 10:5
So now **m** a bargain with my 2Kg 18:23
'**M** peace with me and surrender 2Kg 18:31
I will **m** you go back the way you 2Kg 19:28
no one could **m** his son or his 2Kg 23:10
of incense to **m** atonement for 1Ch 6:49
in his reign to **m** him king 1Ch 11:10
name to come and **m** David king. 1Ch 12:31
to **m** David king over 1Ch 12:38
of one mind to **m** David king. 1Ch 12:38
will **m** a name for you like that 1Ch 17:8
to **m** a name for Yourself through 1Ch 17:21
deal of iron to **m** the nails for 1Ch 22:3
I must **m** provision for it." 1Ch 22:5
had said He would **m** Israel as 1Ch 27:23
was pleased to **m** me king over 1Ch 28:4
in Your hand to **m** great and to 1Ch 29:12
to **m** the people work. 2Ch 2:18
I will **m** it an object of scorn 2Ch 7:20
gone to Shechem to **m** him king. 2Ch 10:1
but you, **m** it lighter on us! 2Ch 10:10
every city to **m** them very strong 2Ch 11:12
intending to **m** him king. 2Ch 11:22
and **m** your own priests like the 2Ch 13:9
times must I **m** you swear not to 2Ch 18:15
with him to **m** ships to go to 2Ch 20:36
⌊But⌋ God will **m** you stumble 2Ch 25:8
to help or to **m** one stumble. 2Ch 25:8
heart now to **m** a covenant with 2Ch 29:10
to **m** atonement for all Israel, 2Ch 29:24
for joining and to **m** beams— 2Ch 34:11
and **m** preparations for your 2Ch 35:6
don't **m** Him destroy you!" 2Ch 35:21
Let us therefore **m** a covenant Ezr 10:3
m a confession to the LORD God Ezr 10:11
M their insults return on their Neh 4:4
other⌋ leafy trees to **m** booths, Neh 8:15
the wicked cease to **m** trouble, Jb 3:17
against me and **m** me inherit the Jb 13:26
M arrangements! Put up security Jb 17:3
When you **m** a decision, it will Jb 22:28
on the wind and **m** me ride ⌊it⌋; Jb 30:22
made me in the womb also **m** them? Jb 31:15
Do you **m** him leap like a locust? Jb 39:20
command and **m** its nest on high Jb 39:27
Will he **m** a covenant with you so Jb 41:4
No arrow can **m** him flee; Jb 41:28
and I will **m** the nations Your Ps 2:8
You alone, LORD, **m** me live in Ps 4:8
m Your way straight before me. Ps 5:8
You will **m** them ⌊burn⌋ like a Ps 21:9
M Your ways known to me, LORD; Ps 25:4

I will sing and **m** music to the Ps 27:6
m music to Him with a Ps 33:2
do not **m** me the taunt of fools. Ps 39:8
You **m** us retreat from the foe, Ps 44:10
You **m** no profit from selling Ps 44:12
You **m** us an object of reproach Ps 44:13
You **m** us a joke among the Ps 44:14
you will **m** them princes Ps 45:16
a thief, you **m** friends with him Ps 50:18
who would not **m** God his refuge, Ps 52:7
and night they **m** the rounds on Ps 55:10
I will **m** my thank offerings to Ps 56:12
m them homeless wanderers and Ps 59:11
You **m** east and west shout for Ps 65:8
glory of His name; **m** His praise Ps 66:2
and drunkards **m** up songs about Ps 69:12
M their fortification desolate; Ps 69:25
You **m** them fall into ruin. Ps 73:18
M Your way to the everlasting Ps 74:3
M and keep your vows to the LORD Ps 76:11
our enemies **m** fun of us. Ps 80:6
how Your enemies **m** an uproar; Ps 83:2
M their nobles like Oreb and Ps 83:11
M them like tumbleweed, my God, Ps 83:13
they **m** it a source of Ps 84:6
I will also **m** him My firstborn, Ps 89:27
M us rejoice for as many days as Ps 90:15
There the birds **m** their nests; Ps 104:17
His name, to **m** His power known Ps 106:8
oath⌋ that He would **m** them fall Ps 106:26
hand until I **m** Your enemies Your Ps 110:1
They cannot **m** a sound with their Ps 115:7
Those who **m** them are just like Ps 115:8
You pushed me hard to **m** me fall, Ps 118:13
M my steps steady through Your Ps 119:133
I will **m** My home here because I Ps 132:14
There I will **m** a horn grow for Ps 132:17
Those who **m** them are just like Ps 135:18
if I **m** my bed in Sheol, You are Ps 139:8
They **m** their tongues as sharp as Ps 140:3
men who plan to **m** me stumble. Ps 140:4
with dancing and **m** music to Him Ps 149:3
unless they **m** someone stumble. Pr 4:16
Understanding **m** her voice heard? Pr 8:1
Idle hands **m** one poor, but Pr 10:4
Don't **m** friends with an angry Pr 22:24
M your case with your opponent Pr 25:9
yet they **m** their homes in the Pr 30:26
impulsive to **m** a speech before Ec 5:2
When you **m** a vow to God, don't Ec 5:4
Dead flies **m** a perfumer's oil Ec 10:1
We will **m** gold jewelry for you, Sg 1:11
I will **m** my way to the mountain Sg 4:6
I will **m** youths their leaders, Is 3:4
m me the leader of the people! Is 3:7
I will **m** it a wasteland. Is 5:6
it will fail. **M** a prediction; it Is 8:10
to **m** the earth a desolation and Is 13:9
I will **m** man scarcer than gold, Is 13:12
Therefore I will **m** the heavens Is 13:13
They will **m** captives of their Is 14:2
m myself like the Most High. Is 14:14
I will **m** her a swampland and a Is 14:23
us counsel and **m** a decision. Is 16:3
The LORD will **m** Himself known to Is 19:21
they will **m** vows to the LORD and Is 19:21
let it **m** peace with Me—make Is 27:5
peace with Me—**m** peace with Me. Is 27:5
will come and **m** fires with them, Is 27:11
And I will **m** justice the Is 28:17
its maker, "He didn't **m** me"? Is 29:16
not Mine, They **m** an alliance, Is 30:1
And the LORD will **m** the splendor Is 30:30
partridge will **m** her nest there; Is 34:15
Now **m** a deal with my master, Is 36:8
M peace with me and surrender to Is 36:16
I will **m** you go back the way you Is 37:29
I am going to **m** the sun's shadow Is 38:8
m an end of me from day until Is 38:12
m an end of me day and night. Is 38:13
father will **m** Your faithfulness Is 38:19
m a straight highway for our God Is 40:3
I will **m** you into a sharp Is 41:15
them⌋, and **m** hills like chaff. Is 41:15
or shout or **m** His voice heard Is 42:2
and I **m** you a covenant for the Is 42:6
instruction and **m** it glorious. Is 42:21
will **m** a way in the wilderness, Is 43:19

him say so and **m** a case before Is 44:7
All who **m** idols are nothing, Is 44:9
I will **m** something detestable Is 44:19
I **m** success and create disaster; Is 45:7
you compare Me or **m** Me equal to? Is 46:5
will also **m** you a light for the Is 49:6
to **m** them possess the desolate Is 49:8
I will **m** all My mountains into a Is 49:11
m room for me so that I may Is 49:20
I will **m** your oppressors eat Is 49:26
in black and **m** sackcloth their Is 50:3
He will **m** her wilderness like Is 51:3
When You **m** Him a restitution Is 53:10
I will **m** your battlements of Is 54:12
I will **m** an everlasting covenant Is 55:3
it will **m** a name for the LORD as Is 55:13
⌊hoping⌋ to **m** your voice heard Is 58:4
and I will **m** you ride over the Is 58:14
will **m** you an object of eternal Is 60:15
reward them and **m** an everlasting Is 61:8
I will **m** known the LORD's Is 63:7
this way to **m** a glorious name Is 63:14
You **m** us stray from Your ways? Is 63:17
to **m** Your name known to Your Is 64:2
will **m** peace flow to her like a Is 66:12
which I will **m**, will endure Is 66:22
I long to **m** you ⌊My⌋ sons and Jr 3:19
left his lair to **m** your land a Jr 4:7
I am going to **m** My words become Jr 5:14
I will **m** you a desolation, Jr 6:8
knead dough to **m** cakes for the Jr 7:18
I will **m** Jerusalem a heap of Jr 9:11
I will **m** the cities of Judah a Jr 9:11
gods that did not **m** the heavens Jr 10:11
will **m** them a horror to all the Jr 15:4
Then I will **m** you serve your Jr 15:14
Then I will **m** you a fortified Jr 15:20
Can one **m** gods for himself? Jr 16:20
this time I will **m** them know My Jr 16:21
I will **m** you serve your enemies Jr 17:4
harm to you and **m** plans against Jr 18:11
⌊idols⌋ that **m** them stumble Jr 18:15
let's **m** plans against Jeremiah, Jr 18:18
I will **m** them fall by the sword Jr 19:7
I will **m** this city desolate, Jr 19:8
I will **m** them eat the flesh of Jr 19:9
'I am about to **m** you a terror to Jr 20:4
they **m** plans to cause My people Jr 23:27
will **m** them an object of horror Jr 24:9
destroy them and **m** them a Jr 25:9
and I will **m** it a ruin forever. Jr 25:12
My hand and **m** all the nations Jr 25:15
to **m** them a desolate ruin, Jr 25:18
will **m** this temple like Shiloh. Jr 26:6
I will **m** this city an object of Jr 26:6
M fetters and yoke bars for Jr 27:2
the LORD **m** the words you have Jr 28:6
place you will **m** an iron yoke Jr 28:13
plague and will **m** them like Jr 29:17
will **m** them a horror to all the Jr 29:18
May the LORD **m** you like Zedekiah Jr 29:22
when I will **m** a new covenant Jr 31:31
covenant I will **m** with the house Jr 31:33
Valley of Hinnom to **m** their sons Jr 32:35
to this place and **m** them live in Jr 32:37
I will **m** with them an Jr 32:40
offerings, and to **m** sacrifices." Jr 33:18
I will **m** the descendants of My Jr 33:22
I will **m** you a horror to all the Jr 34:17
I will **m** Judah's cities a Jr 34:22
in order to **m** their way into Jr 41:17
M Moab a salt marsh, for she Jr 48:9
M him drunk, because he has Jr 48:26
I will **m** the shout of battle Jr 49:2
I will certainly **m** you Jr 49:15
it will **m** her land desolate. Jr 50:3
to **m** the land of Babylon an Jr 51:29
her sea and **m** her fountain run Jr 51:36
and I will **m** them drunk so that Jr 51:39
I will **m** him vomit what he Jr 51:44
I will **m** her princes and sages Jr 51:57
will **m** your tongue stick to the Ezk 3:26
container and **m** them into bread Ezk 4:9
you can **m** your bread over that. Ezk 4:15
I will **m** you a ruin and a Ezk 5:14
they live I will **m** the land a Ezk 6:14
every hand and who **m** veils for Ezk 13:18
against that one and **m** him a Ezk 14:8

MAKER *(24)*

MAKERS *(1)*

MAKES *(108)*

When someone **m** a special vow to Lv 27:2
as the priest **m** the valuation Lv 27:12
swearing when He **m** your thigh Nm 5:21
When he **m** her drink the water, Nm 5:27
a man or woman **m** a special vow, Nm 6:2
whatever vow he **m** in keeping Nm 6:21
and when he **m** atonement for him, Nm 15:28
When a man **m** a vow to the LORD Nm 30:2
during her youth **m** a vow to the Nm 30:3
the person who **m** a carved idol Dt 27:15
told me what **m** your strength so Jdg 16:15
my own son **m** a covenant with 1Sm 22:8
refuge; He **m** my way perfect. 2Sm 22:33
He **m** my feet like ⌊the feet of⌋ 2Sm 22:34
He **m** ⌊the stars⌋: the Bear, Jb 9:9
barefoot and **m** judges go mad. Jb 12:17
m nations great, then destroys Jb 12:23
and **m** them wander in a trackless Jb 12:24
He **m** them stagger like drunken Jb 12:25
the smell of water **m** it thrive Jb 14:9
and my understanding **m** me reply. Jb 20:3
of the earth and **m** us wiser than Jb 35:11
For He **m** waterdrops evaporate; Jb 36:27
His clouds or **m** their lightning Jb 37:15
He **m** the depths seethe like a Jb 41:31
he **m** the sea like an ointment Jb 41:31
strength and **m** my way perfect. Ps 18:32
He **m** my feet like the feet of a Ps 18:33
He **m** Lebanon skip like a calf, Ps 29:6
voice of the LORD **m** the deer Ps 29:9
on his bed he **m** malicious plans. Ps 36:4
He **m** wars cease throughout the Ps 46:9
wine that **m** man's heart glad— Ps 104:15
the stork **m** its home in the pine Ps 104:17
on nobles and **m** them wander Ps 107:40
suffering and **m** their families Ps 107:41
Your command **m** me wiser than Ps 119:98
nothing **m** them stumble. Ps 119:165
He **m** lightning for the rain and Ps 135:7
don't know what **m** them stumble. Pr 4:19
Delayed hope **m** the heart sick, Pr 13:12
tongue of the wise **m** knowledge Pr 15:2
joyful heart **m** a face cheerful, Pr 15:13
He **m** even his enemies to be at Pr 16:7
for it **m** wings for itself and Pr 23:5
She **m** her own bed coverings; Pr 31:22
She **m** and sells linen garments; Pr 31:24
Wisdom **m** the wise man stronger Ec 7:19
laughter, and wine **m** life happy, Ec 10:19
work of God who **m** everything. Ec 11:5
What **m** the one you love better Sg 5:9
What **m** him better than another, Sg 5:9
m all the kings of the nations Is 14:9
when he **m** all the altar stones Is 27:9
gold and **m** silver welds ⌊for Is 40:19
to nothing and **m** the judges Is 40:23
He **m** ⌊them⌋ like dust ⌊with⌋ his Is 41:2
LORD says—who **m** a way in the Is 43:16
Who **m** a god or casts a metal Is 44:10
He **m** it according to a human Is 44:13
laurel, and the rain **m** it grow. Is 44:14
he even **m** it into a god and Is 44:15
he **m** it an idol and bows down to Is 44:15
He **m** a god or his idol with the Is 44:17
prophets and **m** fools of diviners Is 44:25
the wise and **m** their knowledge Is 44:25
and he **m** it into a god. Is 46:6
No one **m** claims justly; Is 59:4
establishes and **m** her Jerusalem Is 62:7
He **m** lightning for the rain and Jr 10:13
gloom and **m** thick darkness. Jr 13:16
who **m** ⌊human⌋ flesh his strength Jr 17:5
He who **m** a fortune unjustly is Jr 17:11
who **m** his fellow man serve Jr 22:13
the sea and **m** its waves roar— Jr 31:35
He **m** lightning for the rain and Jr 51:16
has come and who **m** idols for Ezk 22:3
m restitution for what he has Ezk 33:15
on ⌊anything that **m** them⌋ sweat. Ezk 44:18
When the prince **m** a freewill Ezk 46:12
the rebellion that **m** desolate, Dn 8:13
He **m** a covenant with Assyria, Hs 12:1
the One who **m** the dawn out of Am 4:13
and He **m** all the rivers run dry. Nah 1:4
trusts in it and **m** idols that Hab 2:18
m my feet like those of a deer Hab 3:19
The LORD **m** the rain clouds, Zch 10:1
in his flock and **m** a vow but Mal 1:14
garment and **m** the tear worse. Mt 9:16
He even **m** deaf people hear, Mk 7:37
has a spirit that **m** him unable Mk 9:17
Anyone who **m** himself a king Jn 19:12
do anything that **m** your brother Rm 14:21
For who **m** you so superior? 1Co 4:7
if the trumpet **m** an unclear 1Co 14:8
really were **m** no difference to Gl 2:6
ratified, or **m** additions to it. Gl 3:15
for what **m** everything clear is Eph 5:14
He **m** His angels winds, and His Heb 1:7
He judges and **m** war. Rv 19:11

MAKHELOTH *(2)*

from Haradah and camped at **M**. Nm 33:25
departed from **M** and camped at Nm 33:26

MAKING *(80)*

the covenant I am **m** between Me Gn 9:12
m me odious to the inhabitants Gn 34:30
people with straw for **m** bricks, Ex 5:7
from them as they were **m** before; Ex 5:8
you finished **m** your prescribed Ex 5:14
As for the incense you are **m**, Ex 30:37
Look, I am **m** a covenant. Ex 34:10
for the task of **m** the sanctuary. Ex 36:3
it by **m** atonement for it Lv 8:15
daughter by **m** her a prostitute Lv 19:29
wild beasts, **m** himself unclean Lv 22:8
to what the one **m** the vow can Lv 27:8
they have been **m** about you." Nm 17:5
But if you refrain from **m** a vow, Dt 23:22
the man you are **m** the loan to Dt 24:11
which He is **m** with you today, Dt 29:12
I am **m** this covenant and this Dt 29:14
days after **m** the treaty with Jos 9:16
honestly in **m** Abimelech king, Jdg 9:16
M a vow, she pleaded, "LORD of 1Sm 1:11
m yourselves fat with the best 1Sm 2:29
and after **m** them lie down on the 2Sm 8:2
to the point of **m** himself sick 2Sm 13:2
I have to keep on **m** appeals to 2Sm 19:28
m them like dust at threshing. 2Kg 13:7
were still **m** their own gods and 2Kg 17:29
m known all these great 1Ch 17:19
and for **m** burnt offerings 2Ch 24:14
we are **m** a binding agreement in Neh 9:38
is trustworthy, **m** the Ps 19:7
are right, **m** the heart glad; Ps 19:8
is radiant, **m** the eyes light Ps 19:8
m me secure while at my mother's Ps 22:9
me evil for good, **m** me desolate. Ps 35:12
m your righteousness shine like Ps 37:6
on a rock, **m** my steps secure Ps 40:2
waters ⌊above⌋, **m** the clouds His Ps 104:3
and **m** the winds His messengers, Ps 104:4
m his face shine with oil— Ps 104:15
⌊**m** her⌋ the joyful mother of Ps 113:9
m a vow to the Mighty One of Ps 132:2
m me live in darkness like those Ps 143:3
Fools mock at **m** restitution, Pr 14:9
M a fortune through a lying Pr 21:6
no end to the **m** of many books, Ec 12:12
earth bare and **m** it desolate. Is 24:1
it: What are you **m**? Or does your Is 45:9
and **m** it germinate and sprout, Is 55:10
jar that he was **m** from the clay Jr 18:4
its residents, **m** this city like Jr 19:12
of Babylon is **m** war against us. Jr 21:2
They are **m** you worthless. Jr 23:16
LORD's hand **m** the whole earth Jr 51:7
every street and **m** your elevated Ezk 16:31
m your children pass through the Ezk 20:31
m them rulers over many and Dn 11:39
false oaths while **m** covenants. Hs 10:4
wrath and even **m** them drunk, Hab 2:15
⌊By not **m** the payments⌋ of 10 Mal 3:8
you are **m** it a den of thieves! Mt 21:13
Why are you **m** a commotion and Mk 5:39
He kept **m** signs to them and Lk 1:22
teaching and **m** His way to Lk 13:22
After **m** a whip out of cords, Jn 2:15
heard He was **m** and baptizing Jn 4:1
His own Father, **m** Himself equal Jn 5:18
m her stand in the center. Jn 8:3
forefathers by **m** them leave Ac 7:19
he was **m** his defense this way, Ac 26:24
after **m** a circuit along the Ac 28:13
m our sanctification complete in 2Co 7:1
For we are **m** provision for what 2Co 8:21
m the most of the time, because Eph 5:16
singing and **m** music to the Lord Eph 5:19
Himself by **m** peace through the Col 1:20
toward outsiders, **m** the most of Col 4:5
After **m** purification for sins, Heb 1:3
Holy Spirit was **m** it clear that Heb 9:8
m them an example to those who 2Pt 2:6
I am **m** everything new." Rv 21:5

MAKKEDAH *(9)*

down as far as Azekah and **M**. Jos 10:10
themselves in the cave at **M**. Jos 10:16
are hiding in the cave at **M**." Jos 10:17
to Joshua in the camp at **M**. Jos 10:21
Joshua captured **M** and struck it Jos 10:28
the king of **M** as he had the king Jos 10:28
him crossed from **M** to Libnah and Jos 10:29
the king of **M** one the king of Jos 12:16
Naamah, and **M**—16 cities, with Jos 15:41

MALACHI *(1)*

of the LORD to Israel through **M**. Mal 1:1

MALCAM *(1)*

Jobab, Zibia, Mesha, **M**, 1Ch 8:9

MALCHIAH *(1)*

(AKA MALCHIJAH)

the cistern of **M** the king's son, Jr 38:6

MALCHIEL *(3)*

Beriah's sons were Heber and **M**. Gn 46:17
the Malchielite clan from **M**. Nm 26:45
Heber, and **M**, who fathered 1Ch 7:31

MALCHIELITE *(1)*

the **M** clan from Malchiel. Nm 26:45

MALCHIJAH *(15)*

(AKA MALCHIAH)

son of Baaseiah, son of **M**, 1Ch 6:40
son of Pashhur, son of **M**; 1Ch 9:12
the fifth to **M**, the sixth to 1Ch 24:9
Ramiah, Izziah, **M**, Mijamin, Ezr 10:25
Eleazar, **M**, and Benaiah; Ezr 10:25
Isshijah, **M**, Shemaiah, Shimeon Ezr 10:31
M son of Harim and Hasshub son Neh 3:11
M son of Rechab, ruler over the Neh 3:14
Next to him **M**, one of the Neh 3:31
Pedaiah, Mishael, **M**, Hashum, Neh 8:4
Pashhur, Amariah, **M**, Neh 10:3
son of Pashhur, son of **M** Neh 11:12
Jehohanan, **M**, Elam, and Ezer Neh 12:42
Pashhur son of **M** and the priest Jr 21:1
Pashhur son of **M** heard the words Jr 38:1

MALCHIRAM *(1)*

M, Pedaiah, Shenazzar, Jekamiah, 1Ch 3:18

MALCHISHUA *(5)*

were Jonathan, Ishvi, and **M**. 1Sm 14:49
sons, Jonathan, Abinadab, and **M**. 1Sm 31:2
fathered Jonathan, **M**, Abinadab, 1Ch 8:33
fathered Jonathan, **M**, Abinadab, 1Ch 9:39
sons Jonathan, Abinadab, and **M**. 1Ch 10:2

MALCHUS *(1)*

The slave's name was **M**. Jn 18:10

MALE *(251)*

He created them **m** and female. Gn 1:27
I have had a **m** child with the Gn 4:1
He created them **m** and female. Gn 5:2
of all flesh, **m** and female, to Gn 6:19
seven pairs, a **m** and its female, Gn 7:2
not clean, a **m** and its female, Gn 7:2
and seven pairs, **m** and female, Gn 7:3
two of each, **m** and female, Gn 7:9
m and female of all flesh, Gn 7:16
flocks and herds, **m** and female Gn 12:16
female donkeys, **m** and female Gn 12:16
every **m** among you at eight days Gn 17:12
If any **m** is not circumcised in Gn 17:14
every **m** among the members of Gn 17:23
and cattle and **m** and female Gn 20:14
silver and gold, **m** and female Gn 24:35
and spotted **m** goats and all Gn 30:35
had many flocks, **m** and female Gn 30:43
donkeys, flocks, **m** and female Gn 32:5
goats, 20 **m** goats, 200 ewes Gn 32:14
donkeys, and 10 **m** donkeys. Gn 32:15
city, and killed every **m**. Gn 34:25
every firstborn ⌊**m**⌋ in the land Ex 11:5
animal, a year-old **m**; Ex 12:5
every firstborn ⌊**m**⌋ in the land Ex 12:12
every firstborn ⌊**m**⌋ in the land Ex 12:29

MALES *(20)*

MALICE *(10)*

MALICIOUS *(13)*

his mouth are **m** and deceptive; Ps 36:3
on his bed he makes **m** plans. Ps 36:4
but destruction awaits the **m**. Pr 10:29
wicked person listens to **m** talk; Pr 17:4
finger-pointing and **m** speaking, Is 58:9
you harbor **m** thoughts within Jr 4:14
slandering us with **m** words. 3Jn 10

MALICIOUSLY *(5)*
me without cause look at me **m**. Ps 35:19
My enemies speak **m** about me: Ps 41:5
They mock, and they speak **m**; Ps 73:8
forward and **m** accuse the Jews Dn 3:8
men who had **m** accused Daniel Dn 6:24

MALIGNING *(1)*
You sit, **m** your brother, Ps 50:20

MALLET *(1)*
right hand, for a workman's **m**. Jdg 5:26

MALLOTHI *(2)*
Joshbekashah, **M**, Hothir, and 1Ch 25:4
the nineteenth to **M**, his sons, 1Ch 25:26

MALLOW *(1)*
They plucked **m** among the shrubs, Jb 30:4

MALLUCH *(6)*
(AKA MALLUCHI)
of Kishi, son of Abdi, son of **M**, 1Ch 6:44
Meshullam, **M**, Adaiah, Jashub, Ezr 10:29
Benjamin, **M**, and Shemariah; Ezr 10:32
Hattush, Shebaniah, **M**, Neh 10:4
M, Harim, Baanah. Neh 10:27
Amariah, **M**, Hattush, Neh 12:2

MALLUCHI *(1)*
(AKA MALLUCH)
Jonathan of **M**, Joseph of Neh 12:14

MALTA *(1)*
that the island was called **M**. Ac 28:1

MAMRE *(10)*
(AKA HEBRON)
beside the oaks of **M** at Hebron, Gn 13:18
oaks belonging to **M** the Amorite, Gn 14:13
Eshcol, and **M**—they can take Gn 14:24
at the oaks of **M** while he was Gn 18:1
field at Machpelah near **M**— Gn 23:17
of the field at Machpelah near **M** Gn 23:19
in the cave of Machpelah near **M**, Gn 25:9
Isaac at **M** in Kiriath-arba Gn 35:27
Machpelah, near **M**, in the land Gn 49:30
Machpelah in the field near **M**, Gn 50:13

MAN *(1745)*
Let Us make **m** in Our image, Gn 1:26
So God created **m** in His own Gn 1:27
and there was no **m** to work the Gn 2:5
God formed the **m** out of the dust Gn 2:7
and the **m** became a living being. Gn 2:7
He placed the **m** He had formed. Gn 2:8
God took the **m** and placed him Gn 2:15
the LORD God commanded the **m**, Gn 2:16
not good for the **m** to be alone. Gn 2:18
each to the **m** to see what he Gn 2:19
whatever the **m** called a living Gn 2:19
The **m** gave names to all the Gn 2:20
for the **m** no helper was found Gn 2:20
a deep sleep to come over the **m**, Gn 2:21
taken from the **m** into a woman Gn 2:22
woman and brought her to the **m**. Gn 2:22
And the **m** said: This one, at Gn 2:23
woman, for she was taken from **m**. Gn 2:23
is why a **m** leaves his father Gn 2:24
Both the **m** and his wife were Gn 2:25
Then the **m** and his wife heard Gn 3:8
out to the **m** and said to him, Gn 3:9
Then the **m** replied, "The woman Gn 3:12
Since **m** has become like one of Gn 3:22
He drove **m** out, and east of the Gn 3:24
I killed a **m** for wounding me, Gn 4:23
On the day that God created **m**, Gn 5:1
blessed them and called them **m**. Gn 5:2
daughters of **m** were beautiful, Gn 6:2
God came to the daughters of **m**, Gn 6:4
that He had made **m** on the earth, Gn 6:6
m, whom I created, together with Gn 6:7
was a righteous **m**, blameless Gn 6:9
curse the ground because of **m**, Gn 8:21
animal and every **m** for your life Gn 9:5
his blood will be shed by **m**, Gn 9:6
for God made **m** in His image. Gn 9:6
Noah, a **m** of the soil, was the Gn 9:20
the first powerful **m** on earth. Gn 10:8
m will be ⌊like⌋ a wild ass. Gn 16:12
that **m** will be cut off from his Gn 17:14
be born to a hundred-year-old **m**? Gn 17:17
it to a young **m**, who hurried to Gn 18:7
had sexual relations with a **m**. Gn 19:8
and there is no **m** in the land to Gn 19:31
had not known a **m** intimately. Gn 24:16
while the **m** silently watched her Gn 24:21
the **m** took a gold ring weighing Gn 24:22
Then the **m** bowed down, Gn 24:26
ran out to the **m** at the spring. Gn 24:29
words—"The **m** said this to me!" Gn 24:30
went to the **m**. He was standing Gn 24:30
So the **m** came to the house, Gn 24:32
"Will you go with this **m**?" Gn 24:58
the camels, and followed the **m**. Gn 24:61
Who is that **m** in the field Gn 24:65
Jacob was a quiet **m** who stayed Gn 25:27
harms this **m** or his wife will Gn 26:11
and the **m** became rich and kept Gn 26:13
my brother Esau is a hairy **m**, Gn 27:11
but I am a **m** with smooth skin. Gn 27:11
her to you than to some other **m**. Gn 29:19
And the **m** became very rich. Gn 30:43
and a **m** wrestled with him until Gn 32:24
When the **m** saw that He could not Gn 32:25
name?" the **m** asked. "Jacob!" Gn 32:27
uncircumcised **m** is a disgrace to Gn 34:14
The young **m** did not delay doing Gn 34:19
The young **m** ⌊was working⌋ with Gn 37:2
m found him there, wandering in Gn 37:15
moved on from here," the **m** said. Gn 37:17
pregnant by the **m** to whom these Gn 38:25
and he became a successful **m**, Gn 39:2
brought a Hebrew **m** to us to make Gn 39:14
and the other **m** was hanged." Gn 41:13
and wise **m** and set him over Gn 41:33
m who has the spirit of God in Gn 41:38
We are all sons of one **m**. Gn 42:11
the sons of one **m** in the land of Gn 42:13
The **m** who is the lord of the Gn 42:30
The **m** who is the lord of the Gn 42:33
The **m** specifically warned us: Gn 43:3
not go, for the **m** said to us, Gn 43:5
did you tell the **m** that you had Gn 43:6
The **m** kept asking about us and Gn 43:7
them down to the **m** as a gift— Gn 43:11
and go back at once to the **m**. Gn 43:13
cause the **m** to be merciful to Gn 43:14
The **m** did as Joseph had said and Gn 43:17
The **m** brought the men into Gn 43:24
you know that a **m** like me could Gn 44:15
m in whose possession the cup Gn 44:17
with us, we cannot see the **m**.' Gn 44:26
Now a **m** from the family of Levi Ex 2:1
over us?" the **m** replied. "Are Ex 2:14
then did you leave the **m** behind? Ex 2:20
Moses agreed to stay with the **m**, Ex 2:21
festering boils on **m** and beast. Ex 9:10
m and beast and every plant of Ex 9:22
in the field, both **m** and beast. Ex 9:25
long must this **m** be a snare to Ex 10:7
the **m** Moses was feared in the Ex 11:3
whether **m** or beast, not ⌊even Ex 11:7
land of Egypt, both **m** and beast. Ex 12:12
But any slave a **m** has purchased Ex 12:44
Israelites, both **m** and animal; Ex 13:2
firstborn of **m** to the firstborn Ex 13:15
between one **m** and another. Ex 18:16
neither animal or **m** will live. Ex 19:13
leave as a free **m** without paying Ex 21:2
and the **m** must leave alone. Ex 21:4
not want to leave as a free **m**,' Ex 21:5
When a **m** sells his daughter as a Ex 21:7
and the injured **m** does not die Ex 21:18
When a **m** strikes his male or Ex 21:20
When a **m** strikes the eye of his Ex 21:26
an ox gores a **m** or a woman to Ex 21:28
and it kills a **m** or a woman, Ex 21:29
When a **m** uncovers a pit or digs Ex 21:33
When a **m** steals an ox or a sheep Ex 22:1
When a **m** lets a field or Ex 22:5
When a **m** gives his neighbor Ex 22:7
When a **m** gives his neighbor a Ex 22:10
and the other **m** does not have to Ex 22:11
When a **m** borrows ⌊an animal⌋ Ex 22:14
m must make full restitution. Ex 22:14
the **m** does not have to make Ex 22:15
When a **m** seduces a virgin who Ex 22:16
Each **m** who is registered, 20 Ex 30:14
the **m** who brought us up from the Ex 32:1
the **m** who brought us up from the Ex 32:23
'Every **m** fasten his sword to his Ex 32:27
since each **m** went against his Ex 32:29
just as a **m** speaks with his Ex 33:11
the young **m** Joshua son of Nun, Ex 33:11
Let no **m** or woman make anything Ex 36:6
two-fifths of an ounce per **m**, Ex 38:26
When a **m** or woman has an Lv 13:29
When a **m** or a woman has white Lv 13:38
If a **m** loses the hair of his Lv 13:40
the **m** is afflicted with a skin Lv 13:44
When any **m** has a discharge from Lv 15:2
Any bed the **m** with the discharge Lv 15:4
that the **m** with the discharge Lv 15:6
the body of the **m** with a Lv 15:7
the **m** with the discharge spits Lv 15:8
Any saddle the **m** with the Lv 15:9
If the **m** with the discharge Lv 15:11
clay pot that the **m** with the Lv 15:12
When the **m** with the discharge Lv 15:13
When a **m** has an emission of Lv 15:16
If a **m** sleeps with a woman and Lv 15:18
If a **m** sleeps with her, and Lv 15:24
m who has an emission of semen, Lv 15:32
and a **m** who sleeps with an Lv 15:33
wilderness by the **m** appointed Lv 16:21
The **m** who released the goat for Lv 16:26
sleep with a **m** as with a woman Lv 18:22
If a **m** has sexual intercourse Lv 19:20
designated for ⌊another⌋ **m**, Lv 19:20
against that **m** and cut him off Lv 20:3
way when that **m** gives any of his Lv 20:4
against that **m** and his family, Lv 20:5
If a **m** commits adultery with a Lv 20:10
If a **m** sleeps with his father's Lv 20:11
If a **m** sleeps with his Lv 20:12
If a **m** sleeps with a man as with Lv 20:13
sleeps with a **m** as with a woman Lv 20:13
If a **m** marries a woman and her Lv 20:14
If a **m** has sexual intercourse Lv 20:15
If a **m** marries his sister, Lv 20:17
a **m** sleeps with a menstruating Lv 20:18
If a **m** sleeps with his aunt, Lv 20:20
If a **m** marries his brother's Lv 20:21
m or a woman who is a medium or Lv 20:27
No **m** who has any defect is to Lv 21:18
m who is blind, lame, facially Lv 21:18
no **m** who has a broken foot or Lv 21:19
If any **m** from any of your Lv 22:3
No **m** of Aaron's descendants who Lv 22:4
person or by a **m** who has an Lv 22:4
the **m** who touches any of these Lv 22:6
is married to a **m** outside a Lv 22:12
Any **m** of the house of Israel or Lv 22:18
When a **m** presents a fellowship Lv 22:21
woman's son and an Israelite **m**. Lv 24:10
If a **m** kills anyone, he must be Lv 24:17
If any **m** inflicts a permanent Lv 24:19
If a **m** has no family redeemer, Lv 25:26
balance to the **m** he sold it to, Lv 25:27
If a **m** sells a residence in a Lv 25:29
with him like a **m** hired year by Lv 25:53
When a **m** consecrates his house Lv 27:14
If a **m** consecrates to the LORD Lv 27:16
if he has sold it to another **m**, Lv 27:20
Nothing that a **m** permanently Lv 27:28
a **m** decides to redeem any part Lv 27:31
m from each tribe is to be with Nm 1:4
each **m** with his encampment and Nm 1:52
each **m** by his clan and by his Nm 2:34
to Myself, both **m** and animal; Nm 3:13
go in and assign each **m** his task Nm 4:19
When a **m** or woman commits any Nm 5:6
then the **m** is to bring his wife Nm 5:15
'If no **m** has slept with you, Nm 5:19
yourself and a **m** other than your Nm 5:20
a **m** or woman makes a special Nm 6:2
is Mine, both **m** and animal. Nm 8:17
a **m** enters the service in the Nm 8:24
But the **m** who is ceremonially Nm 9:13
m will bear the consequences Nm 9:13
A young **m** ran and reported to Nm 11:27
Moses was a very humble **m**, Nm 12:3
more so than any **m** on the face Nm 12:3

Send one **m** who is a leader among Nm 13:2
they found a **m** gathering wood on Nm 15:32
The **m** is to be put to death. Nm 15:35
Then the **m** the LORD chooses will Nm 16:7
Each **m** took his firepan, placed Nm 16:18
flesh, when one **m** sins, will you Nm 16:22
The staff of the **m** I choose will Nm 17:5
and each **m** took his own staff. Nm 17:9
every living thing, **m** or animal, Nm 18:15
redeem the firstborn of **m**, Nm 18:15
A **m** who is clean is to gather up Nm 19:9
is not a **m** who lies, or a son Nm 23:19
or a son of **m** who changes His Nm 23:19
oracle of the **m** whose eyes are Nm 24:3
oracle of the **m** whose eyes are Nm 24:15
An Israelite **m** came bringing a Nm 25:6
the Israelite **m** into the tent, Nm 25:8
the Israelite **m** and the woman— Nm 25:8
name of the slain Israelite **m**, Nm 25:14
When a **m** dies without having a Nm 27:8
appoint a **m** over the community Nm 27:16
a **m** who has the Spirit in him, Nm 27:18
When a **m** makes a vow to the Nm 30:2
between a **m** and his wife, Nm 30:16
had sexual relations with a **m**, Nm 31:17
had sexual relations with a **m**. Nm 31:35
the gold articles each **m** found— Nm 31:50
every **m** in battle formation Nm 32:29
If a **m** has in his hand a stone Nm 35:17
strikes another **m** and he dies, Nm 35:17
If a **m** has in his hand a wooden Nm 35:18
between a **m** and his brother Dt 1:16
among you, one **m** for each tribe. Dt 1:23
you as a **m** carries his son Dt 1:31
day God created **m** on the earth Dt 4:32
might learn that **m** does not live Dt 8:3
you just as a **m** disciplines his Dt 8:5
fellow Hebrew, a **m** or woman, is Dt 15:12
If a **m** or woman among you in one Dt 17:2
your gates that **m** or woman who Dt 17:5
'Has any **m** built a new house and Dt 20:5
and another **m** dedicate it. Dt 20:5
Has any **m** planted a vineyard and Dt 20:6
and another **m** enjoy its fruit. Dt 20:6
Has any **m** become engaged to a Dt 20:7
battle and another **m** marry her.' Dt 20:7
'Is there any **m** who is afraid or Dt 20:8
If a **m** has two wives, one loved Dt 21:15
when that **m** gives what he has to Dt 21:16
If a **m** has a stubborn and Dt 21:18
and a **m** is not to put on a Dt 22:5
If a **m** marries a woman, has Dt 22:13
my daughter to this **m** as a wife, Dt 22:16
will take the **m** and punish him. Dt 22:18
because that **m** gave an Israelite Dt 22:19
If a **m** is discovered having Dt 22:22
both the **m** who had sex with the Dt 22:22
who is a virgin engaged to a **m**, Dt 22:23
and ⌊another⌋ **m** encounters her Dt 22:23
city and the **m** because he has Dt 22:24
But if the **m** encounters the Dt 22:25
only the **m** who raped her must Dt 22:25
like one in which a **m** attacks Dt 22:26
If a **m** encounters a young woman, Dt 22:28
m who raped her must give the Dt 22:29
A **m** is not to marry his father's Dt 22:30
No **m** whose ⌊testicles⌋ have been Dt 23:1
If there is a **m** among you who is Dt 23:10
no Israelite **m** is to be a cult Dt 23:17
If a **m** marries a woman, but she Dt 24:1
and the second **m** hates her, Dt 24:3
When a **m** takes a bride, he must Dt 24:5
If a **m** is discovered kidnapping Dt 24:7
while the **m** you are making Dt 24:11
If he is a poor **m**, you must not Dt 24:12
wife of the dead **m** may not marry Dt 25:5
But if the **m** doesn't want to Dt 25:7
what is done to a **m** who will not Dt 25:9
house of the **m** whose sandal was Dt 25:10
grope as a blind **m** gropes in the Dt 28:29
but another **m** will rape her. Dt 28:30
refined **m** among you will look Dt 28:54
sure there is no **m**, woman, clan, Dt 29:18
the young **m** and the virgin ⌊will Dt 32:25
infant and the gray-haired **m**. Dt 32:25
How could one **m** pursue a Dt 32:30
that Moses, the **m** of God, gave Dt 33:1
of Israel, one **m** for each tribe. Jos 3:12
people, one **m** for each tribe, Jos 4:2
one **m** for each tribe, Jos 4:4
up and saw a **m** standing in front Jos 5:13
advance, each **m** straight ahead." Jos 6:5
the city, each **m** straight ahead, Jos 6:20
sword—every **m** and woman, both Jos 6:21
the LORD is the **m** who undertakes Jos 6:26
is to come forward **m** by man. Jos 7:14
is to come forward man by **m**. Jos 7:14
family come forward **m** by man, Jos 7:18
family come forward man by **m**, Jos 7:18
Not a **m** was left in Ai or Bethel Jos 8:17
listened to the voice of a **m**, Jos 10:14
promised Moses the **m** of God at Jos 14:6
the greatest **m** among the Anakim Jos 14:15
of Gilead, who was a **m** of war. Jos 17:1
The spies saw a **m** coming out of Jdg 1:24
released the **m** and his entire Jdg 1:25
Then the **m** went to the land of Jdg 1:26
who was an extremely fat **m**. Jdg 3:17
not a single **m** was left. Jdg 4:16
If a **m** comes and asks you, Jdg 4:20
asks you, 'Is there a **m** here?' Jdg 4:20
show you the **m** you are looking Jdg 4:22
down ⌊as if it were⌋ one **m**." Jdg 6:16
there was a **m** telling his friend Jdg 7:13
the swords of each **m** in the army Jdg 7:22
a **m** is judged by his strength. Jdg 8:21
or that one **m** rule over you?' Jdg 9:2
oil that honors both God and **m**, Jdg 9:9
wine that cheers both God and **m**, Jdg 9:13
Which **m** will lead the fight Jdg 10:18
never been intimate with a **m**. Jdg 11:39
was a certain **m** from Zorah, Jdg 13:2
her husband, "A **m** of God came to Jdg 13:6
let the **m** of God you sent come Jdg 13:8
The **m** who came to me today has Jdg 13:10
he came to the **m**, he asked, "Are Jdg 13:11
You the **m** who spoke to my wife? Jdg 13:11
and given her to another **m**." Jdg 15:6
weak and be like any other **m**." Jdg 16:7
weak and be like any other **m**." Jdg 16:11
weak and be like any other **m**." Jdg 16:17
lap and called a **m** to shave off Jdg 16:19
to the young **m** who was leading Jdg 16:26
There was a **m** from the hill Jdg 17:1
This **m** Micah had a shrine, Jdg 17:5
There was a young **m**, a Levite, Jdg 17:7
The **m** left the town of Bethlehem Jdg 17:8
and agreed to stay with the **m**, Jdg 17:11
and the young **m** became like one Jdg 17:11
the young **m** became his priest Jdg 17:12
the girl's father said to the **m**, Jdg 19:6
The **m** got up to go, but his Jdg 19:7
The **m** got up to go with his Jdg 19:9
But the **m** was unwilling to spend Jdg 19:10
m had his two saddled donkeys Jdg 19:10
old **m** came in from his work in Jdg 19:16
square, the old **m** asked, "Where Jdg 19:17
and the young **m** with your Jdg 19:19
"Peace to you," said the old **m**. Jdg 19:20
said to the old **m** who was the Jdg 19:22
Bring out the **m** who came to your Jdg 19:22
this **m** has come into my house. Jdg 19:23
this horrible thing to this **m**." Jdg 19:24
the **m** seized his concubine and Jdg 19:25
So the **m** put her on his donkey Jdg 19:28
female who has slept with a **m**." Jdg 21:11
had sexual relations with a **m**, Jdg 21:12
A **m** left Bethlehem in Judah with Ru 1:1
was a prominent **m** of noble Ru 2:1
bless the **m** who noticed you. Ru 2:19
The name of the **m** I worked with Ru 2:19
The **m** is a close relative. Ru 2:20
but don't let the **m** know you are Ru 3:3
everything the **m** had done for Ru 3:16
the wife of the deceased **m**, Ru 4:5
a **m** removed his sandal and gave Ru 4:7
There was a **m** from 1Sm 1:1
This **m** would go up from his town 1Sm 1:3
for a **m** does not prevail by ⌊his 1Sm 2:9
When any **m** offered a sacrifice, 1Sm 2:13
and say to the **m** who was 1Sm 2:15
If that **m** said to him, "The fat 1Sm 2:16
If a **m** sins against another man, 1Sm 2:25
If a man sins against another **m**, 1Sm 2:25
if a **m** sins against the LORD, 1Sm 2:25
A **m** of God came to Eli and said 1Sm 2:27
m from your ⌊family⌋ I do not 1Sm 2:33
and each **m** fled to his tent. 1Sm 4:10
a Benjaminite **m** ran from the 1Sm 4:12
When the **m** entered the city to 1Sm 4:13
The **m** quickly came and reported 1Sm 4:14
The **m** said to Eli, "I'm the one 1Sm 4:16
an influential **m** of Benjamin 1Sm 9:1
Saul, an impressive young **m**. 1Sm 9:2
there's a **m** of God in this city 1Sm 9:6
what do we take the **m**? 1Sm 9:7
no gift to take to the **m** of God. 1Sm 9:7
I'll give it to the **m** of God, 1Sm 9:8
a **m** who was going to inquire of 1Sm 9:9
the city where the **m** of God was. 1Sm 9:10
will send you a **m** from the land 1Sm 9:16
Here is the **m** I told you about; 1Sm 9:17
Then a **m** who was from there 1Sm 10:12
"Has the **m** come here yet?" 1Sm 10:22
has found a **m** loyal to Him, 1Sm 13:14
Cursed is the **m** who eats food 1Sm 14:24
is the **m** who eats food today, 1Sm 14:28
'Each **m** must bring me his ox or 1Sm 14:34
noticed any strong or brave **m**, 1Sm 14:52
is not **m** who changes his mind. 1Sm 15:29
M does not see what the LORD 1Sm 16:7
for **m** sees what is visible, 1Sm 16:7
is also a valiant **m**, a warrior, 1Sm 16:18
Send me a **m** so we can fight each 1Sm 17:10
reign was ⌊already⌋ an old **m**. 1Sm 17:12
an Israelite **m** had declared, 1Sm 17:25
Do you see this **m** who keeps 1Sm 17:25
will make the **m** who kills him 1Sm 17:25
be done for the **m** who kills that 1Sm 17:26
done for the **m** who kills him." 1Sm 17:27
out whose son this young **m** is!" 1Sm 17:56
Whose son are you, young **m**?" 1Sm 17:58
I am a poor **m** who is common." 1Sm 18:23
will send the young **m** ⌊and say⌋, 1Sm 20:21
expressly say to the young **m**, 1Sm 20:21
A small young **m** was with him. 1Sm 20:35
to the young **m**, "Run and find 1Sm 20:36
As the young **m** ran, Jonathan 1Sm 20:36
Jonathan's young **m** picked up 1Sm 20:38
to the young **m** who was with him 1Sm 20:40
When the young **m** had gone, 1Sm 20:41
You can see the **m** is crazy," 1Sm 21:14
every **m** who was desperate, 1Sm 22:2
When a **m** finds his enemy, does 1Sm 24:19
A **m** in Maon had a business in 1Sm 25:2
was a very rich **m** with 3,000 1Sm 25:2
but the **m**, a Calebite, was 1Sm 25:3
belonged to this **m** in the 1Sm 25:21
to this worthless **m** Nabal, 1Sm 25:25
Abner, "You're a **m**, aren't you? 1Sm 26:15
the LORD repay every **m** for his 1Sm 26:23
Each **m** had his family with him, 1Sm 27:3
alive, either **m** or woman, but he 1Sm 27:9
did not let a **m** or woman live to 1Sm 27:11
"An old **m** is coming up," 1Sm 28:14
Send that **m** back and let him 1Sm 29:4
lives, you are an honorable **m**. 1Sm 29:6
the slave of an Amalekite **m**," 1Sm 30:13
the third day a **m** with torn 2Sm 1:2
the young **m** who had brought 2Sm 1:5
of the young **m** who had brought 2Sm 1:13
Then each **m** grabbed his opponent 2Sm 2:16
or leprosy or a **m** who can only 2Sm 3:29
a righteous **m** in his own house 2Sm 4:11
The rich **m** had a large number of 2Sm 12:2
the poor **m** had nothing except 2Sm 12:3
a traveler came to the rich **m**, 2Sm 12:4
but the rich **m** could not bring 2Sm 12:4
with the **m** and said to Nathan 2Sm 12:5
the **m** who did this deserves to 2Sm 12:5
to David, "You are the **m**! 2Sm 12:7
Jonadab was a very shrewd **m**, 2Sm 13:3
the young **m** who was standing 2Sm 13:34
the hand of this **m** who would 2Sm 14:16
bring back the young **m** Absalom. 2Sm 14:21
No **m** in all Israel was as 2Sm 14:25
a **m** belonging to the family of 2Sm 16:5
except⌋ the **m** you're seeking, 2Sm 17:3
even a brave **m** with the heart of 2Sm 17:10
a young **m** did see them and 2Sm 17:18
to the house of a **m** in Bahurim. 2Sm 17:18
was the son of a **m** named Ithra 2Sm 17:25
Treat the young **m** Absalom gently 2Sm 18:5
The **m** replied to Joab, "Even if 2Sm 18:12

the young **m** Absalom for me. 2Sm 18:12
You are not the **m** to take good 2Sm 18:20
out and saw a **m** running alone. 2Sm 18:24
watchman saw another **m** running 2Sm 18:26
Another **m** is running alone!" 2Sm 18:26
way the first **m** runs looks to me 2Sm 18:27
This is a good **m**; he comes with 2Sm 18:27
the young **m** Absalom all right? 2Sm 18:29
the young **m** Absalom all right? 2Sm 18:32
become of the young **m** happen to 2Sm 18:32
not a **m** will remain with you 2Sm 19:7
the **m** we anointed over us, 2Sm 19:10
Should any **m** be killed in Israel 2Sm 19:22
Barzillai was a very old **m**— 2Sm 19:32
since he was a very wealthy **m**, 2Sm 19:32
Now a wicked **m**, a Benjaminite 2Sm 20:1
Each **m** to his tent, Israel! 2Sm 20:1
and the **m** had seen that all the 2Sm 20:12
There is a **m** named Sheba son of 2Sm 20:21
Deliver this one **m**, and I will 2Sm 20:21
As for the **m** who annihilated us 2Sm 21:5
A huge **m** was there with six 2Sm 21:20
the blameless **m** You prove 2Sm 22:26
of the **m** raised on high, 2Sm 23:1
The **m** who touches them must be 2Sm 23:7
son of a brave **m** from Kabzeel, 2Sm 23:20
from Kabzeel, a **m** of many 2Sm 23:20
killed an Egyptian, a huge **m**. 2Sm 23:21
for you are an excellent **m**, 1Kg 1:42
If he is a **m** of character, 1Kg 1:52
fail to have a **m** on the throne 1Kg 2:4
for you are a wise **m**. 1Kg 2:9
so that no **m** in any kingdom will 1Kg 3:13
each **m** under his own vine and 1Kg 4:25
Each **m** brought the barley and 1Kg 4:28
know that not a **m** among us knows 1Kg 5:6
and his father was a **m** of Tyre, 1Kg 7:14
fail to have a **m** to sit before 1Kg 8:25
When a **m** sins against his 1Kg 8:31
each **m** knowing his own 1Kg 8:38
and repay the **m**, according to 1Kg 8:39
fail to have a **m** on the throne 1Kg 9:5
Every **m** would bring his annual 1Kg 10:25
the **m** Jeroboam was capable, 1Kg 11:28
the young **m** because he was 1Kg 11:28
came to Shemaiah, the **m** of God: 1Kg 12:22
A **m** of God came from Judah to 1Kg 13:1
The **m** of God cried out against 1Kg 13:2
word that the **m** of God had cried 1Kg 13:4
sign that the **m** of God had given 1Kg 13:5
king responded to the **m** of God, 1Kg 13:6
So the **m** of God pleaded for the 1Kg 13:6
king declared to the **m** of God, 1Kg 13:7
But the **m** of God replied, 1Kg 13:8
deeds that the **m** of God had done 1Kg 13:11
taken by the **m** of God who had 1Kg 13:12
He followed the **m** of God and 1Kg 13:14
Are you the **m** of God who came 1Kg 13:14
and the **m** of God went back with 1Kg 13:19
cried out to the **m** of God who 1Kg 13:21
is the **m** of God who disobeyed 1Kg 13:26
corpse of the **m** of God thrown 1Kg 13:28
corpse of the **m** of God and laid 1Kg 13:29
grave where the **m** of God is 1Kg 13:31
to Elijah, "**M** of God, what do 1Kg 17:18
I know you are a **m** of God and 1Kg 17:24
Obadiah was a **m** who greatly 1Kg 18:3
Then the **m** of God approached 1Kg 20:28
But the **m** refused to strike 1Kg 20:35
found another **m** and said to him, 1Kg 20:37
So the **m** struck him, inflicting 1Kg 20:37
a **m** turned aside and brought 1Kg 20:39
to me and said, 'Guard this **m**! 1Kg 20:39
your hand the **m** I had devoted to 1Kg 20:42
There is still one **m** who can ask 1Kg 22:8
But a **m** drew his bow without 1Kg 22:34
Each **m** to his own city, and each 1Kg 22:36
and each **m** to his own land! 1Kg 22:36
A **m** came to meet us and said, 2Kg 1:6
What sort of **m** came up to meet 2Kg 1:7
A hairy **m** with a leather belt 2Kg 1:8
announced, "**M** of God, the king 2Kg 1:9
50, "If I am a **m** of God, may 2Kg 1:10
and announced, "**M** of God, this 2Kg 1:11
If I am a **m** of God, may fire 2Kg 1:12
begged him, "**M** of God, please 2Kg 1:13
She went and told the **m** of God, 2Kg 4:7
by here is a holy **m** of God, 2Kg 4:9
M of God, do not deceive your 2Kg 4:16
him on the bed of the **m** of God, 2Kg 4:21
hurry to the **m** of God and then 2Kg 4:22
went to the **m** of God at Mount 2Kg 4:25
When the **m** of God saw her at a 2Kg 4:25
she came up to the **m** of God at 2Kg 4:27
her away, but the **m** of God said, 2Kg 4:27
him, and if a **m** greets you, 2Kg 4:29
death in the pot, **m** of God!" 2Kg 4:40
A **m** from Baal-shalishah came to 2Kg 4:42
came to the **m** of God with his 2Kg 4:42
was a great **m** in his master's 2Kg 5:1
The **m** was a brave warrior, 2Kg 5:1
life that this **m** expects me to 2Kg 5:7
me to cure a **m** of his skin 2Kg 5:7
When Elisha the **m** of God heard 2Kg 5:8
to the command of the **m** of God. 2Kg 5:14
went back to the **m** of God, 2Kg 5:15
as his right-hand **m**, bow in the 2Kg 5:18
of Elisha the **m** of God, 2Kg 5:20
there when the **m** got down from 2Kg 5:26
Then the **m** of God asked, "Where 2Kg 6:6
the place, the **m** of God cut a 2Kg 6:6
But the **m** of God sent ⌊word⌋ to 2Kg 6:9
the place the **m** of God had told 2Kg 6:10
The **m** of God repeatedly warned 2Kg 6:10
servant of the **m** of God got up 2Kg 6:15
take you to the **m** you're looking 2Kg 6:19
The king sent a **m** ahead of him, 2Kg 6:32
king's right-hand **m**, responded 2Kg 7:2
responded to the **m** of God, 2Kg 7:2
was not a ⌊single⌋ **m** there, 2Kg 7:5
right-hand **m**, to be in charge 2Kg 7:17
just as the **m** of God had 2Kg 7:17
When the **m** of God had said to 2Kg 7:18
had answered the **m** of God, 2Kg 7:19
and did what the **m** of God said. 2Kg 8:2
the servant of the **m** of God, 2Kg 8:4
"The **m** of God has come here." 2Kg 8:7
you and go meet the **m** of God. 2Kg 8:8
was ashamed. The **m** of God wept, 2Kg 8:11
Each **m** quickly took his garment 2Kg 9:13
there was not a **m** left who did 2Kg 10:21
m of God was angry with him 2Kg 13:19
the Israelites were burying a **m**, 2Kg 13:21
they threw the **m** into Elisha's 2Kg 13:21
the **m** revived and stood up! 2Kg 13:21
which if a **m** leans on it will go 2Kg 18:21
Say to the **m** who sent you to Me: 2Kg 22:15
proclaimed by the **m** of God who 2Kg 23:16
tomb of the **m** of God who came 2Kg 23:17
each **m** according to his 2Kg 23:35
son of a brave **m** from Kabzeel, 1Ch 11:22
from Kabzeel, a **m** of many 1Ch 11:22
regard me as a **m** of distinction, 1Ch 17:17
there was a **m** of extraordinary 1Ch 20:6
he will be a **m** of rest. I will 1Ch 22:9
As for Moses the **m** of God, 1Ch 23:14
was a mighty **m** among the Thirty 1Ch 27:6
he was a **m** of understanding and 1Ch 27:32
you are a **m** of war and have 1Ch 28:3
Every willing **m** of any skill 1Ch 28:21
the temple will not be for **m**, 1Ch 29:1
a skillful **m** who has 2Ch 2:13
His father is a **m** of Tyre. 2Ch 2:14
not chosen a **m** to be ruler over 2Ch 6:5
fail to have a **m** to sit before 2Ch 6:16
God indeed live on earth with **m**? 2Ch 6:18
If a **m** sins against his neighbor 2Ch 6:22
m knowing his own affliction 2Ch 6:29
and repay the **m** according to all 2Ch 6:30
fail to have a **m** on the throne 2Ch 7:18
command of David, the **m** of God. 2Ch 8:14
Israel, each **m** to your tent; 2Ch 10:16
came to Shemaiah, the **m** of God: 2Ch 11:2
death, young or old, **m** or woman. 2Ch 15:13
There is still one **m** who can ask 2Ch 18:7
But a **m** drew his bow without 2Ch 18:33
for you do not judge for **m**, 2Ch 19:6
a **m** of God came to him and said, 2Ch 25:7
Amaziah said to the **m** of God, 2Ch 25:9
The **m** of God replied, "The LORD 2Ch 25:9
the law of Moses the **m** of God. 2Ch 30:16
Say to the **m** who sent you to Me, 2Ch 34:23
no pity on young **m** and virgin 2Ch 36:17
the law of Moses the **m** of God. Ezr 3:2
in Babylon to a **m** named Ezr 5:14
concerning any **m** who interferes Ezr 6:11
a **m** of insight from the Ezr 8:18
him in the presence of this **m**. Neh 1:11
Should a **m** like me run away? Neh 6:11
was a faithful **m** who feared God Neh 7:2
as David the **m** of God had Neh 12:24
of David, the **m** of God. Neh 12:36
that every **m** should be master of Est 1:22
Jewish **m** was in the fortress of Est 2:5
applies to every **m** or woman who Est 4:11
be done for the **m** the king wants Est 6:6
For the **m** the king wants to Est 6:7
them clothe the **m** the king wants Est 6:9
is done for the **m** the king wants Est 6:9
is done for the **m** the king wants Est 6:11
There was a **m** in the country of Jb 1:1
He was a **m** of perfect integrity, Jb 1:1
was the greatest **m** among all the Jb 1:3
is like him, a **m** of perfect Jb 1:8
is like him, a **m** of perfect Jb 2:3
A **m** will give up everything he Jb 2:4
and each **m** tore his robe and Jb 2:12
life given⌋ to a **m** whose path is Jb 3:23
a **m** more pure than his Maker?" Jb 4:17
how happy the **m** is God corrects Jb 5:17
A despairing **m** should receive Jb 6:14
like a hired **m** he waits for his Jb 7:2
What is **m**, that You think so Jb 7:17
For He is not a **m** like me, Jb 9:32
or Your years like those of a **m**, Jb 10:5
But a stupid **m** will gain Jb 11:12
as a wild donkey is born a **m**! Jb 11:12
upright **m** is a laughingstock. Jb 12:4
Him as you would deceive a **m**? Jb 13:9
M wears out like something Jb 13:28
M born of woman is short of days Jb 14:1
But a **m** dies and fades away; Jb 14:10
so **m** lies down never to rise Jb 14:12
When a **m** dies, will he come back Jb 14:14
Does a wise **m** answer with empty Jb 15:2
What is **m**, that he should be Jb 15:14
A wicked **m** writhes in pain all Jb 15:20
between a **m** and God just as Jb 16:21
God just as a **m** ⌊pleads⌋ for his Jb 16:21
a **m** informs on his friends for Jb 17:5
have become a **m** people spit at. Jb 17:6
not find a wise **m** among you. Jb 17:10
from ⌊the time⌋ **m** was placed on Jb 20:4
is my complaint against a **m**? Jb 21:4
evil **m** is spared from the day Jb 21:30
Can a **m** be of ⌊any⌋ use to God? Jb 22:2
Can even a wise **m** be of use to Jb 22:2
to a powerful **m** and an Jb 22:8
an influential **m** lived on it. Jb 22:8
There an upright **m** could reason Jb 23:7
much less **m**, who is a maggot, Jb 25:6
and the son of **m**, who is a worm! Jb 25:6
the godless **m** have when he is Jb 27:8
m can know its value, since it Jb 28:13
rescued the poor **m** who cried out Jb 29:12
The dying **m** blessed me, and I Jb 29:13
against a ruined **m** when he cries Jb 30:24
grind ⌊grain⌋ for another **m**, Jb 31:10
is a spirit in **m** and the breath Jb 32:8
let God deal with him, not **m**." Jb 32:13
since God is greater than **m**. Jb 33:12
That **m** will behold His face with Jb 33:26
things two or three times to a **m** Jb 33:29
What **m** is like Job? He drinks Jb 34:7
A **m** gains nothing when he Jb 34:9
says to a king, "Worthless **m**!" Jb 34:18
Can a **m** speak when he is Jb 37:20
Get ready to answer Me like a **m**; Jb 38:3
Get ready to answer Me like a **m**; Jb 40:7
How happy is the **m** who does not Ps 1:1
the LORD abhors a **m** of bloodshed Ps 5:6
what is **m** that You remember him, Ps 8:4
the son of **m** that You look after Ps 8:4
LORD! Do not let **m** prevail; let Ps 9:19
the blameless **m** You prove Ps 18:25
But I am a worm and not a **m**, Ps 22:6
How happy is the **m** the LORD does Ps 32:2
This poor **m** cried, and the LORD Ps 34:6
happy is the **m** who takes refuge Ps 34:8
Who is the **m** who delights in Ps 34:12
LORD, You preserve **m** and beast. Ps 36:6
by the **m** who carries out evil Ps 37:7
that the righteous **m** has than Ps 37:16
violent **m** well-rooted like a Ps 37:35

for the **m** of peace will have a Ps 37:37
I am like a **m** who does not hear Ps 38:14
every mortal **m** is only a vapor. Ps 39:5
m walks about like a mere shadow. Ps 39:6
discipline a **m** with punishment Ps 39:11
every **m** is a mere vapor. Ps 39:11
happy is the **m** who has put his Ps 40:4
from the deceitful and unjust **m**. Ps 43:1
his⌋ assets, **m** will not last; Ps 49:12
be afraid when a **m** gets rich, Ps 49:16
m with valuable possessions but Ps 49:20
Here is the **m** who would not make Ps 52:7
it is you, a **m** who is my peer, Ps 55:13
to me, God, for **m** tramples me; Ps 56:1
not fear. What can **m** do to me? Ps 56:4
not fear. What can **m** do to me? Ps 56:11
How long will you threaten a **m**? Ps 62:3
The inner **m** and the heart are Ps 64:6
hand be with the **m** at Your right Ps 80:17
with the son of **m** You have made Ps 80:17
I am like a **m** without strength, Ps 88:4
no wicked **m** will oppress him. Ps 89:22
What **m** can live and never see Ps 89:48
One who teaches **m** knowledge— Ps 94:10
happy is the **m** You discipline Ps 94:12
for **m**, his days are like grass Ps 103:15
crops for **m** to cultivate, Ps 104:14
M goes out to his work and to Ps 104:23
He had sent a **m** ahead of them— Ps 105:17
Happy is the **m** who fears the Ps 112:1
Good will come to a **m** who lends Ps 112:5
The wicked **m** will see ⌊it⌋ and Ps 112:10
be afraid. What can **m** do to me? Ps 118:6
in the LORD than to trust in **m**. Ps 118:8
How can a young **m** keep his way Ps 119:9
Happy is the **m** who has filled Ps 127:5
this very way the **m** who fears Ps 128:4
hunt down a violent **m**. Ps 140:11
LORD, what is **m**, that You care Ps 144:3
him, the son of **m**, that You Ps 144:3
M is like a breath; his days are Ps 144:4
nobles, in **m**, who cannot save. Ps 146:3
does not value the power of a **m**. Ps 147:10
and discretion to a young **m**— Pr 1:4
wise **m** will listen and increase Pr 1:5
and a discerning **m** will obtain Pr 1:5
in the sight of God and **m**. Pr 3:4
Happy is a **m** who finds wisdom Pr 3:13
envy a violent **m** or choose any Pr 3:31
a wicked **m**, who goes around Pr 6:12
Can a **m** embrace fire and his Pr 6:27
Can a **m** walk on coals without Pr 6:28
youths, a young **m** lacking sense. Pr 7:7
a wicked **m** will get hurt. Pr 9:7
rebuke a wise **m**, and he will Pr 9:8
Instruct a wise **m**, and he will Pr 9:9
teach a righteous **m**, and he will Pr 9:9
wisdom is for a **m** of Pr 10:23
but a **m** with understanding keeps Pr 11:12
A kind **m** benefits himself, Pr 11:17
but a cruel **m** brings disaster on Pr 11:17
wicked **m** earns an empty wage, Pr 11:18
but He condemns a **m** who schemes. Pr 12:2
M cannot be made secure by Pr 12:3
A **m** is praised for his insight, Pr 12:8
A righteous **m** cares about his Pr 12:10
An evil **m** is trapped by ⌊his⌋ Pr 12:13
A **m** will be satisfied with good Pr 12:14
A righteous **m** is careful in Pr 12:26
A lazy **m** doesn't roast his game, Pr 12:27
to a diligent **m**, his wealth is Pr 12:27
a **m** will enjoy good things, Pr 13:2
m pretends to be rich but has Pr 13:7
but a poor **m** hears no threat. Pr 13:8
good **m** leaves an inheritance to Pr 13:22
A righteous **m** eats until he is Pr 13:25
Stay away from a foolish **m**; Pr 14:7
a way that seems right to a **m**, Pr 14:12
and a good **m**, what his ⌊deeds Pr 14:14
A wise **m** is cautious and turns Pr 14:16
quick-tempered **m** acts foolishly Pr 14:17
and a **m** who schemes is hated. Pr 14:17
A poor **m** is hated even by his Pr 14:20
A hot-tempered **m** stirs up Pr 15:18
but a **m** slow to anger calms Pr 15:18
but a **m** with understanding walks Pr 15:21
A **m** takes joy in giving an Pr 15:23
detests the plans of an evil **m**, Pr 15:26

of the heart belong to **m**, Pr 16:1
death, but a wise **m** appeases it. Pr 16:14
a way that seems right to a **m**, Pr 16:25
A worthless **m** digs up evil, Pr 16:27
A contrary **m** spreads conflict, Pr 16:28
A violent **m** lures his neighbor, Pr 16:29
An evil **m** seeks only rebellion; Pr 17:11
Better for a **m** to meet a bear Pr 17:12
A **m** fathers a fool to his own Pr 17:21
wicked **m** secretly takes a bribe Pr 17:23
cool head is a **m** of Pr 17:27
a wicked **m** comes, shame does Pr 18:3
doors for a **m** and brings him Pr 18:16
m who finds a wife finds a good Pr 18:22
The poor **m** pleads, but the rich Pr 18:23
A **m** with many friends may be Pr 18:24
Better a poor **m** who walks in Pr 19:1
but a poor **m** is separated from Pr 19:4
brothers of a poor **m** hate him; Pr 19:7
to be a poor **m** than a perjurer. Pr 19:22
is honorable for a **m** to resolve Pr 20:3
but a **m** of understanding draws Pr 20:5
Many a **m** proclaims his own Pr 20:6
who can find a trustworthy **m**? Pr 20:6
Even a young **m** is known by his Pr 20:11
gained by fraud is sweet to a **m**, Pr 20:17
the ways of a **m** seem right to Pr 21:2
when one teaches a wise **m**, Pr 21:11
The **m** who strays from the way of Pr 21:16
pleasure will become a poor **m**; Pr 21:17
but a foolish **m** consumes them. Pr 21:20
A wicked **m** puts on a bold face, Pr 21:29
but the upright **m** considers his Pr 21:29
a **m** cursed by the LORD will fall Pr 22:14
Don't rob a poor **m** because he is Pr 22:22
make friends with an angry **m**, Pr 22:24
a companion of a hot-tempered **m**, Pr 22:24
Do you see a **m** skilled in his Pr 22:29
and a **m** of knowledge than one of Pr 24:5
an ambush, wicked **m**, at the camp Pr 24:15
at the camp of the righteous **m**; Pr 24:15
a righteous **m** falls seven times Pr 24:16
I'll repay the **m** for what he has Pr 24:29
vineyard of a **m** lacking sense. Pr 24:30
The **m** who boasts about a gift Pr 25:14
A **m** giving false testimony Pr 25:18
A **m** who does not control his Pr 25:28
you see a **m** who is wise in his Pr 26:12
so is the **m** who deceives his Pr 26:19
is a quarrelsome **m** for kindling Pr 26:21
A **m** wandering from his home is Pr 27:8
and one **m** sharpens another. Pr 27:17
smelter, and a **m**, by the praise Pr 27:21
Better a poor **m** who lives with Pr 28:6
than a rich **m** who distorts right Pr 28:6
rich **m** is wise in his own eyes, Pr 28:11
but a poor **m** who has discernment Pr 28:11
A **m** burdened by bloodguilt will Pr 28:17
A faithful **m** will have many Pr 28:20
yet a **m** may sin for a piece of Pr 28:21
A greedy **m** is in a hurry for Pr 28:22
a companion to a **m** who destroys. Pr 28:24
A **m** who loves wisdom brings joy Pr 29:3
but a **m** ⌊who demands⌋ Pr 29:4
A **m** who flatters his neighbor Pr 29:5
An evil **m** is caught by sin, Pr 29:6
If a wise **m** goes to court with a Pr 29:9
but a wise **m** holds it in check. Pr 29:11
Do you see a **m** who speaks too Pr 29:20
An angry **m** stirs up conflict, Pr 29:22
and a hot-tempered **m** increases Pr 29:22
fear of **m** is a snare, but the Pr 29:25
a **m** receives justice from the Pr 29:26
An unjust **m** is detestable to the Pr 29:27
and the way of a **m** with a young Pr 30:19
What does a **m** gain for all his Ec 1:3
are wearisome; **m** is unable to Ec 1:8
what will the **m** be like who Ec 2:12
The wise **m** has eyes in his head, Ec 2:14
remembrance of the wise **m**, Ec 2:16
that the wise **m** dies just like Ec 2:16
it to the **m** who comes after Ec 2:18
he will be a wise **m** or a fool? Ec 2:19
For there is a **m** whose work was Ec 2:21
his portion to a **m** who has not Ec 2:21
For what does a **m** get with all Ec 2:22
better for **m** than to eat, Ec 2:24
For to the **m** who is pleasing in Ec 2:26

but **m** cannot discover the work Ec 3:11
riches and wealth to every **m**, Ec 5:19
gives a **m** riches, wealth, and Ec 6:2
m may father a hundred children Ec 6:3
does the wise **m** have over the Ec 6:8
ago, and who **m** is, is known. Ec 6:10
What is the advantage for **m**? Ec 6:11
what is good for **m** in life, Ec 6:12
Who can tell **m** what will happen Ec 6:12
so that **m** cannot discover Ec 7:14
is a righteous **m** who perishes Ec 7:15
is a wicked **m** who lives long Ec 7:15
makes the wise **m** stronger than Ec 7:19
no righteous **m** on the earth who Ec 7:20
I have found one ⌊true⌋ **m**, Ec 7:28
a time when one **m** has authority Ec 8:9
better for **m** under the sun Ec 8:15
concluded⌋ that **m** is unable to Ec 8:17
Even though a **m** labors hard to Ec 8:17
if the wise **m** claims to know Ec 8:17
m certainly does not know his Ec 9:12
Now a poor wise **m** was found in Ec 9:15
no one remembered that poor **m**. Ec 9:15
of the poor **m** is despised, Ec 9:16
mouth of a wise **m** are gracious, Ec 10:12
For if a **m** should live many Ec 11:8
Rejoice, young **m**, while you are Ec 11:9
for **m** is headed to his eternal Ec 12:5
to the Teacher being a wise **m**, Ec 12:9
If a **m** were to give all his Sg 8:7
brought low, and **m** is humbled. Is 2:9
no more trust in **m**, who has only Is 2:22
one another, **m** against man, Is 3:5
man against **m**, neighbor against Is 3:5
A **m** will even seize his brother Is 3:6
seven women will seize one **m**, Is 4:1
brought low, **m** is humbled, and Is 5:15
because I am a **m** of unclean lips Is 6:5
On that day a **m** will raise a Is 7:21
A **m** will go there with bow and Is 7:24
I will make **m** scarcer than gold, Is 13:12
Is this the **m** who caused the Is 14:16
Look, young **m**! The LORD is about Is 22:17
him, but not one made by **m**. Is 31:8
It serves as fuel for **m**. Is 44:15
the earth, and created **m** on it. Is 45:12
a **m** for My purpose from a far Is 46:11
of a mighty **m** will be taken, Is 49:25
that you should fear **m** who dies, Is 51:12
or a son of **m** who is given up Is 51:12
that He did not look like a **m**, Is 52:14
a **m** of suffering who knew what Is 53:3
and with a rich **m** at His death, Is 53:9
Happy is the **m** who does this, Is 56:2
the breath ⌊of **m**⌋, which I have Is 57:16
He saw that there was no **m**— Is 59:16
For as a young **m** marries a Is 62:5
or an old **m** not live out his Is 65:20
slaughters an ox, one kills a **m**; Is 66:3
If a **m** divorces his wife and she Jr 3:1
I looked, and no **m** was left; Jr 4:25
on this place, on **m** and beast, Jr 7:20
his mouth a **m** speaks peaceably Jr 9:8
Who is the **m** wise enough to Jr 9:12
curse be on the **m** who does not Jr 11:3
Why are You like a helpless **m**, Jr 14:9
a **m** who incites dispute and Jr 15:10
Cursed is the **m** who trusts in Jr 17:5
Blessed is the **m** who trusts in Jr 17:7
Cursed be the **m** who brought the Jr 20:15
that **m** be like the cities the Jr 20:16
of this city, both **m** and beast. Jr 21:6
makes his fellow **m** serve without Jr 22:13
Is this **m** Coniah a despised, Jr 22:28
Record this **m** as childless, Jr 22:30
m who will not be successful in Jr 22:30
like a **m** overcome by wine, Jr 23:9
Can a **m** hide himself in secret Jr 23:24
will punish that **m** and his Jr 23:34
is what each **m** is to say to his Jr 23:35
This **m** deserves the death Jr 26:11
This **m** doesn't deserve the death Jr 26:16
Another **m** was also prophesying Jr 26:20
do I see every **m** with his hands Jr 30:6
a female will shelter a **m**. Jr 31:22
with the seed of **m** and the seed Jr 31:27
a desolation without **m** or beast; Jr 32:43
ruin, without **m** or beast—that Jr 33:10

that are a desolation without **m**, Jr 33:10
place—without **m** or beast—and Jr 33:12
never fail to have a **m** sitting Jr 33:17
fail to have a **m** always before Jr 33:18
each **m** would free his male and Jr 34:9
each **m** for his brother and for Jr 34:17
of Igdaliah, a **m** of God, who had Jr 35:4
fail to have a **m** to always stand Jr 35:19
it to be without **m** or beast? Jr 36:29
the king, "This **m** ought to die, Jr 38:4
This **m** is not seeking the Jr 38:4
You are cutting off **m** and woman, Jr 44:7
and every **m** of Judah who is in Jr 44:27
banished, each **m** headlong, with Jr 49:5
both **m** and beast will escape. Jr 50:3
you I will smash **m** and woman; Jr 51:22
smash the old **m** and the youth; Jr 51:22
the young **m** and the virgin. Jr 51:22
will live in it—**m** or beast. Jr 51:62
I am the **m** who has seen Lm 3:1
is good for a **m** to bear the yoke Lm 3:27
justice to a **m** in the presence Lm 3:35
complain, ⌊any⌋ **m**, because Lm 3:39
of⌋ their faces was that of a **m**, Ezk 1:10
to me, "Son of **m**, stand up on Ezk 2:1
Son of **m**, I am sending you to Ezk 2:3
But you, son of **m**, do not be Ezk 2:6
you, son of **m**, listen to what Ezk 2:8
Son of **m**, eat what you find Ezk 3:1
"Son of **m**," he said to me, "eat Ezk 3:3
Son of **m**, go to the house of Ezk 3:4
Son of **m**, listen carefully to Ezk 3:10
Son of **m**, I have made you a Ezk 3:17
And you, son of **m**, they will put Ezk 3:25
Now you, son of **m**, take a brick, Ezk 4:1
to me, "Son of **m**, I am going to Ezk 4:16
Now you, son of **m**, take a sharp Ezk 5:1
Son of **m**, turn your face toward Ezk 6:2
Son of **m**, this is what the Lord Ezk 7:2
that had the appearance of a **m**. Ezk 8:2
to me, "Son of **m**, look toward Ezk 8:5
me, "Son of **m**, do you see what Ezk 8:6
to me, "Son of **m**, dig through Ezk 8:8
me, "Son of **m**, do you see what Ezk 8:12
"Do you see ⌊this⌋, son of **m**? Ezk 8:15
"Do you see ⌊this⌋, son of **m**? Ezk 8:17
There was another **m** among them, Ezk 9:2
called to the **m** clothed in linen Ezk 9:3
Then the **m** clothed in linen with Ezk 9:11
spoke to the **m** clothed in linen Ezk 10:2
of the temple when the **m** went Ezk 10:3
commanded the **m** clothed in linen Ezk 10:6
the **m** went in and stood beside Ezk 10:6
hands of the **m** clothed in linen Ezk 10:7
that of a **m**, the third that Ezk 10:14
to me, "Son of **m**, these are the Ezk 11:2
them. Prophesy, son of **m**!" Ezk 11:4
Son of **m**, your own relatives, Ezk 11:15
Son of **m**, you are living among a Ezk 12:2
Son of **m**, pack your bags for Ezk 12:3
Son of **m**, hasn't the house of Ezk 12:9
Son of **m**, eat your bread with Ezk 12:18
Son of **m**, what is this proverb Ezk 12:22
Son of **m**, notice that the house Ezk 12:27
Son of **m**, prophesy against the Ezk 13:2
Now, son of **m**, turn toward the Ezk 13:17
Son of **m**, these men have set up Ezk 14:3
Son of **m**, if a land sins against Ezk 14:13
out ⌊both⌋ **m** and animal from Ezk 14:13
I wipe out ⌊both⌋ **m** and animal Ezk 14:17
out ⌊both⌋ **m** and animal from Ezk 14:19
out ⌊both⌋ **m** and animal from Ezk 14:21
Son of **m**, how does the wood of Ezk 15:2
Son of **m**, explain Jerusalem's Ezk 16:2
Son of **m**, pose a riddle and Ezk 17:2
Now suppose a **m** is righteous and Ezk 18:5
Now suppose the **m** has a violent Ezk 18:10
Son of **m**, speak with the elders Ezk 20:3
you pass judgment, son of **m**? Ezk 20:4
Therefore, son of **m**, speak to Ezk 20:27
Son of **m**, face the south and Ezk 20:46
Son of **m**, turn your face toward Ezk 21:2
But you, son of **m**, groan! Ezk 21:6
Son of **m**, prophesy: This is what Ezk 21:9
and wail, son of **m**, for it is Ezk 21:12
Therefore, son of **m**, prophesy Ezk 21:14
Now you, son of **m**, mark out two Ezk 21:19
Now prophesy, son of **m**, and say: Ezk 21:28

Now, son of **m**, will you pass Ezk 22:2
One **m** within you commits an Ezk 22:11
Son of **m**, the house of Israel Ezk 22:18
Son of **m**, say to her: You are a Ezk 22:24
searched for a **m** among them who Ezk 22:30
Son of **m**, there were two women, Ezk 23:2
Son of **m**, will you pass judgment Ezk 23:36
Son of **m**, write down today's Ezk 24:2
Son of **m**, I am about to take the Ezk 24:16
Son of **m**, know that on the day Ezk 24:25
Son of **m**, turn your face toward Ezk 25:2
and cut off both **m** and animal Ezk 25:13
Son of **m**, because Tyre said Ezk 26:2
Now, son of **m**, lament for Tyre. Ezk 27:2
Son of **m**, say to the ruler of Ezk 28:2
Yet you are a **m** and not a god, Ezk 28:2
you will be ⌊shown to be⌋ a **m**, Ezk 28:9
Son of **m**, lament for the king of Ezk 28:12
Son of **m**, turn your face toward Ezk 28:21
Son of **m**, turn your face toward Ezk 29:2
you and wipe out **m** and animal Ezk 29:8
Son of **m**, Nebuchadnezzar king Ezk 29:18
Son of **m**, prophesy and say: Ezk 30:2
Son of **m**, I have broken the arm Ezk 30:21
him as a mortally wounded **m**. Ezk 30:24
Son of **m**, say to Pharaoh king of Ezk 31:2
Son of **m**, lament for Pharaoh Ezk 32:2
Son of **m**, wail over the hordes Ezk 32:18
Son of **m**, speak to your people Ezk 33:2
land select a **m** from among them, Ezk 33:2
for you, son of **m**, I have made Ezk 33:7
for you, son of **m**, say to the Ezk 33:10
Now, son of **m**, say to your Ezk 33:12
my mouth before the **m** came to Ezk 33:22
Son of **m**, those who live in the Ezk 33:24
Now, son of **m**, your people are Ezk 33:30
Son of **m**, prophesy against the Ezk 34:2
Son of **m**, turn your face toward Ezk 35:2
Son of **m**, prophesy to the Ezk 36:1
Son of **m**, while the house of Ezk 36:17
me, "Son of **m**, can these bones Ezk 37:3
the breath, prophesy, son of **m**. Ezk 37:9
me, "Son of **m**, these bones are Ezk 37:11
Son of **m**, take a single stick Ezk 37:16
Son of **m**, turn your face toward Ezk 38:2
son of **m**, and say to Gog Ezk 38:14
for you, son of **m**, prophesy Ezk 39:1
Son of **m**, this is what the Lord Ezk 39:17
and I saw a **m** whose appearance Ezk 40:3
Son of **m**, look with your eyes, Ezk 40:4
Then the **m** said to me: "This Ezk 40:45
Then the **m** measured the temple; Ezk 41:13
m told me, "This is the table Ezk 41:22
Then the **m** led me out by way of Ezk 42:1
Then the **m** said to me, "The Ezk 42:13
While the **m** was standing beside Ezk 43:6
Son of **m**, this is the place of Ezk 43:7
As for you, son of **m**, describe Ezk 43:10
Son of **m**, this is what the Lord Ezk 43:18
m then brought me back toward Ezk 44:1
Then the **m** brought me by way of Ezk 44:4
Son of **m**, pay attention; Ezk 44:5
As the **m** went out east with a Ezk 47:3
Do you see ⌊this⌋, son of **m**?" Ezk 47:6
I have found a **m** among the Dn 2:25
No wise **m**, medium, Dn 2:27
be changed from that of a **m**, Dn 4:16
There is a **m** in your kingdom who Dn 5:11
any god or **m** except you, Dn 6:7
for 30 days any **m** who petitions Dn 6:12
any god or **m** except you, Dn 6:12
its feet like a **m**, and given a Dn 7:4
One like a son of **m** coming with Dn 7:13
someone who appeared to be a **m**. Dn 8:15
explain the vision to this **m**." Dn 8:16
"Son of **m**," he said to me, Dn 8:17
the **m** I had seen in the first Dn 9:21
and there was a **m** dressed in Dn 10:5
you are a **m** treasured ⌊by God⌋. Dn 10:11
One said to the **m** dressed in Dn 12:6
I heard the **m** dressed in linen Dn 12:7
is loved by another **m** and is an Hs 3:1
promiscuous or belong to any **m**, Hs 3:3
and the inspired **m** is insane, Hs 9:7
I am God and not **m**, the Holy One Hs 11:9
each **m** proceeds on his own path. Jl 2:8
A **m** and his father have sexual Am 2:7
and reveals His thoughts to **m**, Am 4:13

It will be like a **m** who flees Am 5:19
No **m** or beast, herd or flock, is Jnh 3:7
both **m** and beast must be covered Jnh 3:8
They deprive a **m** of his home, Mc 2:2
If a **m** of spirit comes and Mc 2:11
But each **m** will sit under his Mc 4:4
the powerful **m** communicates his Mc 7:3
up against you. **M** the Nah 2:1
an arrogant **m** is never at rest. Hab 2:5
I will sweep away **m** and animal; Zph 1:3
If a **m** is carrying consecrated Hg 2:12
night and saw a **m** riding on a Zch 1:8
Then the **m** standing among the Zch 1:10
up and saw a **m** with a measuring Zch 2:1
Run and tell this young **m**: Zch 2:4
Isn't this **m** a burning stick Zch 3:2
is a **m** whose name is Branch; Zch 6:12
days neither **m** nor beast had Zch 8:10
the robe of a Jewish **m** tightly, Zch 8:23
the spirit of **m** within him. Zch 12:1
If a **m** still prophesies, his Zch 13:3
a **m** purchased me as a servant Zch 13:5
the **m** who is My associate Zch 13:7
To the **m** who does this, may the Mal 2:12
Will a **m** rob God? Yet you are Mal 3:8
on them as a **m** has compassion on Mal 3:17
a righteous **m**, and not wanting Mt 1:19
M must not live on bread alone Mt 4:4
m among you, if his son asks Mt 7:9
like a sensible **m** who built his Mt 7:24
like a foolish **m** who built his Mt 7:26
Right away a **m** with a serious Mt 8:2
I too am a **m** under authority, Mt 8:9
but the Son of **M** has no place to Mt 8:20
asked, "What kind of **m** is this? Mt 8:27
that the Son of **M** has authority Mt 9:6
He saw a **m** named Matthew sitting Mt 9:9
demon-possessed **m** who was unable Mt 9:32
been driven out, the **m** spoke. Mt 9:33
before the Son of **M** comes. Mt 10:23
I came to turn a **m** against his Mt 10:35
A **m** dressed in soft clothes? Mt 11:8
The Son of **M** came eating and Mt 11:19
For the Son of **M** is Lord of the Mt 12:8
There He saw a **m** who had a Mt 12:10
them, "What **m** among you, if he Mt 12:11
A **m** is worth far more than a Mt 12:12
Then He told the **m**, "Stretch out Mt 12:13
demon-possessed **m** who was blind Mt 12:22
so that the **m** could both speak Mt 12:22
The **m** drives out demons only by Mt 12:24
he first ties up the strong **m**? Mt 12:29
a word against the Son of **M**, Mt 12:32
A good **m** produces good things Mt 12:35
and an evil **m** produces evil Mt 12:35
so the Son of **M** will be in the Mt 12:40
unclean spirit comes out of a **m**, Mt 12:43
compared to a **m** who sowed good Mt 13:24
seed that a **m** took and sowed Mt 13:31
the good seed is the Son of **M**; Mt 13:37
The Son of **M** will send out His Mt 13:41
that a **m** found and reburied. Mt 13:44
into the mouth that defiles a **m**, Mt 15:11
of the mouth, this defiles a **m**." Mt 15:11
the heart, and this defiles a **m**. Mt 15:18
are the things that defile a **m**, Mt 15:20
hands does not defile a **m**." Mt 15:20
say that the Son of **M** is?" Mt 16:13
will it benefit a **m** if he gains Mt 16:26
what will a **m** give in exchange Mt 16:26
the Son of **M** is going to come Mt 16:27
see the Son of **M** coming in His Mt 16:28
until the Son of **M** is raised Mt 17:9
way the Son of **M** is going to Mt 17:12
a **m** approached and knelt down Mt 17:14
The Son of **M** is about to be Mt 17:22
but woe to that **m** by whom the Mt 18:7
the Son of **M** has come to save Mt 18:11
If a **m** has 100 sheep, and one of Mt 18:12
it lawful for a **m** to divorce his Mt 19:3
this reason a **m** will leave his Mt 19:5
together, **m** must not separate. Mt 19:6
of a **m** with his wife is Mt 19:10
these," the young **m** told Him. Mt 19:20
When the young **m** heard that Mt 19:22
when the Son of **M** sits on His Mt 19:28
to give this last **m** the same as Mt 20:14
The Son of **M** will be handed over Mt 20:18

as the Son of **M** did not come to	Mt 20:28
do you think? A **m** had two sons.	Mt 21:28
Then the **m** went to the other and	Mt 21:30
There was a **m**, a landowner, who	Mt 21:33
he saw a **m** there who was not	Mt 22:11
clothes?' The **m** was speechless.	Mt 22:12
said, if a **m** dies, having no	Mt 22:24
m on the housetop must not come	Mt 24:17
And a **m** in the field must not go	Mt 24:18
be the coming of the Son of **M**.	Mt 24:27
sign of the Son of **M** will appear	Mt 24:30
will see the Son of **M** coming on	Mt 24:30
coming of the Son of **M** will be.	Mt 24:37
coming of the Son of **M** will be:	Mt 24:39
because the Son of **M** is coming	Mt 24:44
it is just like a **m** going on a	Mt 25:14
the **m** who had received five	Mt 25:16
same way the **m** with two earned	Mt 25:17
But the **m** who had received one	Mt 25:18
The **m** who had received five	Mt 25:20
Then the **m** with two talents also	Mt 25:22
Then the **m** who had received one	Mt 25:24
a difficult **m**, reaping where you	Mt 25:24
When the Son of **M** comes in His	Mt 25:31
and the Son of **M** will be handed	Mt 26:2
a **m** who had a serious skin	Mt 26:6
the **m** called Judas Iscariot—	Mt 26:14
into the city to a certain **m**,"	Mt 26:18
The Son of **M** will go just as it	Mt 26:24
woe to that **m** by whom the Son	Mt 26:24
whom the Son of **M** is betrayed!	Mt 26:24
better for that **m** if he had not	Mt 26:24
The Son of **M** is being betrayed	Mt 26:45
stated, "This **m** said, 'I can	Mt 26:61
see the Son of **M** seated at the	Mt 26:64
m was with Jesus the Nazarene!	Mt 26:71
an oath, "I don't know the **m**!"	Mt 26:72
an oath, "I do not know the **m**!"	Mt 26:74
to do with that righteous **m**,	Mt 27:19
found a Cyrenian **m** named Simon.	Mt 27:32
They forced this **m** to carry His	Mt 27:32
"This **m** really was God's Son!"	Mt 27:54
a rich **m** from Arimathea named	Mt 27:57
Just then a **m** with an unclean	Mk 1:23
Then a **m** with a serious skin	Mk 1:40
that the Son of **M** has authority	Mk 2:10
was made for **m** and not man for	Mk 2:27
man and not **m** for the Sabbath	Mk 2:27
the Son of **M** is Lord even	Mk 2:28
and a **m** was there who had a	Mk 3:1
He told the **m** with the paralyzed	Mk 3:3
He told the **m**, "Stretch out your	Mk 3:5
he first ties up the strong **m**.	Mk 3:27
A **m** scatters seed on the ground;	Mk 4:26
a **m** with an unclean spirit came	Mk 5:2
Come out of the **m**, you unclean	Mk 5:8
Jesus and saw the **m** who had been	Mk 5:15
demon-possessed **m** and ⌊told⌋	Mk 5:16
the **m** who had been	Mk 5:18
did this **m** get these things?	Mk 6:2
he was a righteous and holy **m**.	Mk 6:20
'If a **m** tells his father or	Mk 7:11
going into a **m** from the outside	Mk 7:18
to Him a deaf **m** who also had a	Mk 7:32
brought a blind **m** to Him and	Mk 8:22
He took the blind **m** by the hand	Mk 8:23
that the Son of **M** must suffer	Mk 8:31
it benefit a **m** to gain the whole	Mk 8:36
What can a **m** give in exchange	Mk 8:37
Son of **M** will also be ashamed	Mk 8:38
until the Son of **M** had risen	Mk 9:9
about the Son of **M** that He must	Mk 9:12
the crowd, one **m** answered Him,	Mk 9:17
The Son of **M** is being betrayed	Mk 9:31
lawful for a **m** to divorce ⌊his	Mk 10:2
this reason a **m** will leave his	Mk 10:7
together, **m** must not separate.	Mk 10:9
on a journey, a **m** ran up, knelt	Mk 10:17
The Son of **M** will be handed over	Mk 10:33
even the Son of **M** did not come	Mk 10:45
the blind **m** and said to him	Mk 10:49
the blind **m** told Him, "I want to	Mk 10:51
A **m** planted a vineyard, put a	Mk 12:1
m on the housetop must not come	Mk 13:15
And a **m** in the field must not go	Mk 13:16
the Son of **M** coming in clouds	Mk 13:26
It is like a **m** on a journey,	Mk 13:34
a **m** carrying a water jug will	Mk 14:13
For the Son of **M** will go just as	Mk 14:21
woe to that **m** by whom the Son	Mk 14:21
whom the Son of **M** is betrayed!	Mk 14:21
better for that **m** if he had not	Mk 14:21
the Son of **M** is being betrayed	Mk 14:41
certain young **m**, having a linen	Mk 14:51
see the Son of **M** seated at the	Mk 14:62
nearby, "This **m** is one of them!"	Mk 14:69
don't know this **m** you're talking	Mk 14:71
They forced a **m** coming in from	Mk 15:21
"This **m** really was God's Son!"	Mk 15:39
they saw a young **m** dressed in a	Mk 16:5
I am an old **m**, and my wife is	Lk 1:18
engaged to a **m** named Joseph,	Lk 1:27
not been intimate with a **m**?"	Lk 1:34
There was a **m** in Jerusalem whose	Lk 2:25
This **m** was righteous and devout,	Lk 2:25
M must not live on bread alone."	Lk 4:4
there was a **m** with an unclean	Lk 4:33
because I'm a sinful **m**, Lord!"	Lk 5:8
a **m** was there who had a serious	Lk 5:12
on a stretcher a **m** who was	Lk 5:18
Who is this **m** who speaks	Lk 5:21
that the Son of **M** has authority	Lk 5:24
the paralyzed **m**, "I tell you:	Lk 5:24
Son of **M** is Lord of the Sabbath.	Lk 6:5
A **m** was there whose right hand	Lk 6:6
told the **m** with the paralyzed	Lk 6:8
evil, because of the Son of **M**.	Lk 6:22
good **m** produces good out of the	Lk 6:45
An evil **m** produces evil out of	Lk 6:45
He is like a **m** building a house,	Lk 6:48
act is like a **m** who built a	Lk 6:49
For I too am a **m** placed under	Lk 7:8
a dead **m** was being carried out.	Lk 7:12
He said, "Young **m**, I tell you,	Lk 7:14
The dead **m** sat up and began to	Lk 7:15
A **m** dressed in soft robes?	Lk 7:25
The Son of **M** has come eating and	Lk 7:34
to himself, "This **m**, if He were	Lk 7:39
Who is this **m** who even forgives	Lk 7:49
demon-possessed **m** from the town	Lk 8:27
spirit to come out of the **m**.	Lk 8:29
came out of the **m** and entered	Lk 8:33
and found the **m** the demons had	Lk 8:35
demon-possessed **m** was delivered.	Lk 8:36
The **m** from whom the demons had	Lk 8:38
then, a **m** named Jairus came.	Lk 8:41
The Son of **M** must suffer many	Lk 9:22
is a **m** benefited if he gains	Lk 9:25
the Son of **M** will be ashamed of	Lk 9:26
Just then a **m** from the crowd	Lk 9:38
the Son of **M** is about to be	Lk 9:44
but the Son of **M** has no place to	Lk 9:58
A **m** was going down from	Lk 10:30
when he saw ⌊the **m**⌋, he had	Lk 10:33
be a neighbor to the **m** who fell	Lk 10:36
came out, the **m** who had been	Lk 11:14
When a strong **m**, fully armed,	Lk 11:21
unclean spirit comes out of a **m**,	Lk 11:24
the Son of **M** will be to this	Lk 11:30
the Son of **M** will also	Lk 12:8
the Son of **M** will be forgiven,	Lk 12:10
because the Son of **M** is coming	Lk 12:40
A **m** had a fig tree that was	Lk 13:6
seed that a **m** took and sowed	Lk 13:19
of Him was a **m** whose body was	Lk 14:2
He took the **m**, healed him, and	Lk 14:4
'Give your place to this **m**,'	Lk 14:9
A **m** was giving a large banquet	Lk 14:16
'This **m** started to build and	Lk 14:30
This **m** welcomes sinners and eats	Lk 15:2
What **m** among you, who has 100	Lk 15:4
He also said: "A **m** had two sons.	Lk 15:11
There was a rich **m** who received	Lk 16:1
was a rich **m** who would dress	Lk 16:19
But a poor **m** named Lazarus,	Lk 16:20
One day the poor **m** died and was	Lk 16:22
The rich **m** also died and was	Lk 16:22
one of the days of the Son of **M**,	Lk 17:22
so the Son of **M** will be in His	Lk 17:24
be in the days of the Son of **M**:	Lk 17:26
day the Son of **M** is revealed.	Lk 17:30
that day, a **m** on the housetop,	Lk 17:31
Likewise the **m** who is in the	Lk 17:31
didn't fear God or respect **m**.	Lk 18:2
I don't fear God or respect **m**,	Lk 18:4
when the Son of **M** comes, will He	Lk 18:8
about the Son of **M** will be	Lk 18:31
blind **m** was sitting by the road	Lk 18:35
There was a **m** named Zacchaeus	Lk 19:2
crowd, since he was a short **m**.	Lk 19:3
gone to lodge with a sinful **m**!"	Lk 19:7
the Son of **M** has come to seek	Lk 19:10
want this **m** to rule over us!	Lk 19:14
of you, for you're a tough **m**:	Lk 19:21
⌊If⌋ you knew I was a tough **m**,	Lk 19:22
A **m** planted a vineyard, leased	Lk 20:9
see the Son of **M** coming in a	Lk 21:27
to stand before the Son of **M**."	Lk 21:36
a **m** carrying a water jug will	Lk 22:10
For the Son of **M** will go away as	Lk 22:22
but woe to that **m** by whom He is	Lk 22:22
the Son of **M** with a kiss?"	Lk 22:48
"This **m** was with Him too."	Lk 22:56
of them too!" "**M**, I am not!"	Lk 22:58
This **m** was certainly with Him,	Lk 22:59
But Peter said, "**M**, I don't know	Lk 22:60
the Son of **M** will be seated at	Lk 22:69
We found this **m** subverting our	Lk 23:2
no grounds for charging this **m**."	Lk 23:4
asked if the **m** was a Galilean.	Lk 23:6
brought me this **m** as one who	Lk 23:14
to charge this **m** with those	Lk 23:14
out together, "Take this **m** away!	Lk 23:18
What has this **m** done wrong?	Lk 23:22
this **m** has done nothing wrong.	Lk 23:41
"This **m** really was righteous!"	Lk 23:47
and righteous **m** named Joseph,	Lk 23:50
'The Son of **M** must be betrayed	Lk 24:7
There was a **m** named John who was	Jn 1:6
or of the will of **m**, but of God.	Jn 1:13
After me comes a **m** who has	Jn 1:30
and descending on the Son of **M**."	Jn 1:51
need anyone to testify about **m**;	Jn 2:25
He Himself knew what was in **m**.	Jn 2:25
There was a **m** from the Pharisees	Jn 3:1
This **m** came to Him at night and	Jn 3:2
from heaven—the Son of **M**.	Jn 3:13
so the Son of **M** must be lifted	Jn 3:14
and the **m** you now have is not	Jn 4:18
see a **m** who told me everything I	Jn 4:29
When this **m** heard that Jesus had	Jn 4:47
The **m** believed what Jesus said	Jn 4:50
m was there who had been sick	Jn 5:5
"Sir," the sick **m** answered, "I	Jn 5:7
I don't have a **m** to put me into	Jn 5:7
Instantly the **m** got well, picked	Jn 5:9
Jews said to the **m** who had been	Jn 5:10
The **m** who made me well told me,	Jn 5:11
Who is this **m** who told you,	Jn 5:12
But the **m** who was cured did not	Jn 5:13
The **m** went and reported to the	Jn 5:15
because He is the Son of **M**.	Jn 5:27
the Son of **M** will give you,	Jn 6:27
How can this **m** give us His flesh	Jn 6:52
of the Son of **M** and drink His	Jn 6:53
the Son of **M** ascending to where	Jn 6:62
were saying, "He's a good **m**."	Jn 7:12
circumcise a **m** on the Sabbath.	Jn 7:22
If a **m** receives circumcision on	Jn 7:23
because I made a **m** entirely well	Jn 7:23
Isn't this the **m** they want to	Jn 7:25
we know where this **m** is from.	Jn 7:27
more signs than this **m** has done,	Jn 7:31
"No **m** ever spoke like this!"	Jn 7:46
doesn't judge a **m** before it	Jn 7:51
When you lift up the Son of **M**,	Jn 8:28
a **m** who has told you the truth	Jn 8:40
He saw a **m** blind from birth.	Jn 9:1
sinned, this **m** or his parents,	Jn 9:2
Neither this **m** nor his parents	Jn 9:3
this the **m** who sat begging?	Jn 9:8
The **m** called Jesus made mud,	Jn 9:11
They brought the **m** who used to	Jn 9:13
said, "This **m** is not from God,	Jn 9:16
How can a sinful **m** perform such	Jn 9:16
Again they asked the blind **m**,	Jn 9:17
they summoned the **m** who had been	Jn 9:24
know that this **m** is a sinner!"	Jn 9:24
But this **m**—we don't know where	Jn 9:29
amazing thing," the **m** told them.	Jn 9:30
If this **m** were not from God,	Jn 9:33
that they had thrown the **m** out,	Jn 9:35
"Do you believe in the Son of **M**?"	Jn 9:35
The hired **m**, since he is not the	Jn 10:12

he is a hired **m** and doesn't care Jn 10:13
You—being a **m**—make Yourself Jn 10:33
said about this **m** was true." Jn 10:41
Now a **m** was sick, Lazarus, from Jn 11:1
have kept this **m** from dying?" Jn 11:37
The dead **m** came out bound hand Jn 11:44
do since this **m** does many signs Jn 11:47
that one **m** should die for Jn 11:50
the Son of **M** to be glorified. Jn 12:23
'The Son of **M** must be lifted up'? Jn 12:34
up'? Who is this Son of **M**?" Jn 12:34
Now the Son of **M** is glorified, Jn 13:31
that one **m** should die for Jn 18:14
relative of the **m** whose ear Jn 18:26
do you bring against this **m**?" Jn 18:29
If this **m** weren't a criminal, Jn 18:30
"Not this **m**, but Barabbas!" Jn 18:40
said to them, "Here is the **m**!" Jn 19:5
you release this **m**, you are not Jn 19:12
of the first **m** and of the other Jn 19:32
Now this **m** acquired a field with Ac 1:18
Nazarene was a **m** pointed out to Ac 2:22
And a **m** who was lame from his Ac 3:2
His name has made this **m** strong, Ac 3:16
good deed done to a disabled **m**— Ac 4:9
by Him this **m** is standing here Ac 4:10
since they saw the **m** who had Ac 4:14
for the **m** was over 40 years old Ac 4:22
But a **m** named Ananias, with Ac 5:1
God exalted this **m** to His right Ac 5:31
After this **m**, Judas the Galilean Ac 5:37
That **m** also perished, and all Ac 5:37
a **m** full of faith and the Holy Ac 6:5
This **m** does not stop speaking Ac 6:13
the oppressed **m** by striking down Ac 7:24
m led them out and performed Ac 7:36
and the Son of **M** standing at the Ac 7:56
feet of a young **m** named Saul. Ac 7:58
A **m** named Simon had previously Ac 8:9
This **m** is called the Great Power Ac 8:10
was an Ethiopian **m**, a eunuch and Ac 8:27
ask for a **m** from Tarsus named Ac 9:11
he has seen a **m** named Ananias Ac 9:12
from many people about this **m**, Ac 9:13
For this **m** is My chosen Ac 9:15
Isn't this the **m** who, in Ac 9:21
There he found a **m** named Aeneas, Ac 9:33
There was a **m** in Caesarea named Ac 10:1
He was a devout **m** and feared God Ac 10:2
an upright and God-fearing **m**, Ac 10:22
Stand up! I myself am also a **m**." Ac 10:26
for a Jewish **m** to associate with Ac 10:28
Just then a **m** in a dazzling robe Ac 10:30
raised up this **m** on the third Ac 10:40
he was a good **m**, full of the Ac 11:24
voice of a god and not of a **m**!" Ac 12:22
Paulus, an intelligent **m**. Ac 13:7
m summoned Barnabas and Saul Ac 13:7
a **m** of the tribe of Benjamin, Ac 13:21
of Jesse, a **m** after My heart, Ac 13:22
that through this **m** forgiveness Ac 13:38
Lystra a **m** without strength in Ac 14:8
take along this **m** who had Ac 15:38
a Macedonian **m** was standing and Ac 16:9
From one **m** He has made every Ac 17:26
by the **M** He has appointed. Ac 17:31
found a Jewish **m** named Aquila, Ac 18:2
to the house of a **m** named Titius Ac 18:7
"This **m**," they said, "persuades Ac 18:13
eloquent **m** who was powerful in Ac 18:24
This **m** had been instructed in Ac 18:25
Then the **m** who had the evil Ac 19:16
this **m** Paul has persuaded and Ac 19:26
What **m** is there who doesn't know Ac 19:35
and a young **m** named Eutychus was Ac 20:9
This **m** had four virgin daughters Ac 21:9
will bind the **m** who owns this Ac 21:11
This is the **m** who teaches Ac 21:28
I am a Jewish **m** from Tarsus of Ac 21:39
I am a Jewish **m**, born in Tarsus Ac 22:3
a devout **m** according to the law, Ac 22:12
to scourge a **m** who is a Roman Ac 22:25
For this **m** is a Roman citizen." Ac 22:26
We find nothing evil in this **m**. Ac 23:9
Take this young **m** to the Ac 23:17
me to bring this young **m** to you, Ac 23:18
the young **m** and instructed him Ac 23:22
When this **m** had been seized by Ac 23:27
there was a plot against the **m**, Ac 23:30
found this **m** to be a plague, Ac 24:5
there is any wrong in this **m**." Ac 25:5
There's a **m** who was left as a Ac 25:14
custom to give any **m** up before Ac 25:16
and ordered the **m** to be brought Ac 25:17
a dead **m** whom Paul claimed to be Ac 25:19
like to hear the **m** myself." Ac 25:22
you see this **m** about whom the Ac 25:24
This **m** is doing nothing that Ac 26:31
This **m** could have been released Ac 26:32
This **m** is probably a murderer, Ac 28:4
to the leading **m** of the island, Ac 28:7
for images resembling mortal **m**, Rm 1:23
uncircumcised **m** keeps the law's Rm 2:26
A **m** who is physically Rm 2:27
conclude that a **m** is justified Rm 3:28
blessing of the **m** to whom God Rm 4:6
How happy the **m** whom the Lord Rm 4:8
entered the world through one **m**, Rm 5:12
many by the grace of the one **m**, Rm 5:15
reigned through that one **m**, Rm 5:17
reign in life through the one **m**, Rm 5:17
to another **m** while her husband Rm 7:3
she gives herself to another **m**, Rm 7:3
What a wretched **m** I am! Who will Rm 7:24
it is wrong for a **m** to cause Rm 14:20
Blessed is the **m** who does not Rm 14:22
concerns of a **m** except the 1Co 2:11
spirit of the **m** that is in him? 1Co 2:11
But the natural **m** does not 1Co 2:14
a **m** is living with his father's 1Co 5:1
It is good for a **m** not to have 1Co 7:1
each **m** should have his own wife, 1Co 7:2
called as a free **m** is Christ's 1Co 7:22
is fine for a **m** to stay as he is 1Co 7:26
unmarried **m** is concerned about 1Co 7:32
But a married **m** is concerned 1Co 7:33
But if any **m** thinks he is acting 1Co 7:36
Christ is the head of every **m**, 1Co 11:3
and the **m** is the head of the 1Co 11:3
Every **m** who prays or prophesies 1Co 11:4
A **m**, in fact, should not cover 1Co 11:7
For **m** did not come from woman, 1Co 11:8
woman, but woman came from **m**; 1Co 11:8
and **m** was not created for woman, 1Co 11:9
for woman, but woman for **m**. 1Co 11:9
woman is not independent of **m**, 1Co 11:11
and **m** is not independent of 1Co 11:11
For just as woman came from **m**, 1Co 11:12
from man, so **m** comes through 1Co 11:12
you that if a **m** has long hair it 1Co 11:14
So a **m** should examine himself; 1Co 11:28
When I became a **m**, I put aside 1Co 13:11
since death came through a **m**, 1Co 15:21
the dead also comes through a **m**. 1Co 15:21
The first **m** Adam became a living 1Co 15:45
The first **m** was from the earth 1Co 15:47
the second **m** is from heaven. 1Co 15:47
Like the **m** made of dust, so are 1Co 15:48
the heavenly **m**, so are those who 1Co 15:48
the image of the **m** made of dust, 1Co 15:49
the image of the heavenly **m**. 1Co 15:49
I know a **m** in Christ who was 2Co 12:2
I know that this **m**—whether in 2Co 12:3
which a **m** is not allowed to 2Co 12:4
from men or by **m**, but by Jesus Gl 1:1
I testify to every **m** who gets Gl 5:3
For whatever a **m** sows he will Gl 6:7
Himself one new **m** from the two, Eph 2:15
His Spirit in the inner **m**, Eph 3:16
into a mature **m** with a stature Eph 4:13
the old **m** that is corrupted by Eph 4:22
on the new **m**, the one created Eph 4:24
this reason a **m** will leave his Eph 5:31
had come as a **m** in His external Php 2:7
put off the old **m** with his Col 3:9
and have put on the new **m**, Col 3:10
rejects this does not reject **m**, 1Th 4:8
first and the **m** of lawlessness 2Th 2:3
a persecutor, and an arrogant **m**. 1Tm 1:13
one mediator between God and **m**, 1Tm 2:5
God and man, a **m**, Christ Jesus, 1Tm 2:5
or to have authority over a **m**; 1Tm 2:12
rebuke an older **m**, but exhort 1Tm 5:1
you, **m** of God, run from these 1Tm 6:11
so that the **m** of God may be 2Tm 3:17
and love for **m** appeared from God Ti 3:4
as an elderly **m** and now also as Phm 9
is **m**, that You remember him, Heb 2:6
or the son of **m**, that You care Heb 2:6
consider how great this **m** was, Heb 7:4
the Lord set up, and not **m**. Heb 8:2
But this **m**, after offering one Heb 10:12
was approved as a righteous **m**, Heb 11:4
And therefore from one **m**— Heb 11:12
be afraid. What can **m** do to me? Heb 13:6
An indecisive **m** is unstable in Jms 1:8
rich **m** will wither away while Jms 1:11
Blessed is a **m** who endures Jms 1:12
is like a **m** looking at his own Jms 1:23
forgets what kind of **m** he was. Jms 1:24
For suppose a **m** comes into your Jms 2:2
and a poor **m** dressed in dirty Jms 2:2
favor on the **m** wearing the fine Jms 2:3
and yet you say to the poor **m**, Jms 2:3
Yet you dishonored that poor **m**. Jms 2:6
Foolish **m**! Are you willing to Jms 2:20
You see that a **m** is justified by Jms 2:24
is a mature **m** who is also able Jms 3:2
tamed and has been tamed by **m**, Jms 3:7
but no **m** can tame the tongue. Jms 3:8
have murdered—the righteous **m**; Jms 5:6
Elijah was a **m** with a nature Jms 5:17
ever came by the will of **m**; 2Pt 1:21
that righteous **m** tormented 2Pt 2:8
was One like the Son of **M**, Rv 1:13
fell at His feet like a dead **m**. Rv 1:17
creature had a face like a **m**; Rv 4:7
a scorpion when it strikes a **m**. Rv 9:5
because it is the number of a **m**. Rv 13:18
One like the Son of **M** was seated Rv 14:14
like no other since **m** has been Rv 16:18

MAN'S *(102)*

LORD saw that **m** wickedness was Gn 6:5
though **m** inclination is evil Gn 8:21
the life of each **m** brother for a Gn 9:5
each man's brother for a **m** life. Gn 9:5
Whoever sheds **m** blood, his blood Gn 9:6
Now return the **m** wife, for he is Gn 20:7
return each **m** money to his sack, Gn 42:25
there in each **m** sack was his bag Gn 42:35
When a **m** ox injures his Ex 21:35
If any **m** wife goes astray, Nm 5:12
Write each **m** name on his staff. Nm 17:2
relations with ⌊another⌋ **m** wife, Dt 22:22
goes and becomes another **m** wife, Dt 24:2
and the **m** concubine now. Jdg 19:24
doorway of the **m** house where her Jdg 19:26
m name was Elimelech, and his Ru 1:2
to perpetuate the **m** name on his Ru 4:5
the deceased **m** name on his Ru 4:10
household of that **m** father 1Sm 17:25
The **m** name was Nabal, and his 1Sm 25:3
except for each **m** wife and 1Sm 30:22
he took the poor **m** lamb and 2Sm 12:4
as small as a **m** hand coming 1Kg 18:44
a despairing **m** words are ⌊mere⌋ Jb 6:26
Since **m** days are determined and Jb 14:5
land, so You destroy a **m** hope. Jb 14:19
is the wicked **m** lot from God, Jb 20:29
This is a wicked **m** lot from God, Jb 27:13
His eyes ⌊watch⌋ over a **m** ways, Jb 34:21
A **m** steps are established by the Ps 37:23
The LORD knows **m** thoughts; Ps 94:11
wine that makes **m** heart glad— Ps 104:15
and bread that sustains **m** heart. Ps 104:15
For a **m** ways are before the Pr 5:21
wicked **m** iniquities entrap him; Pr 5:22
who sleeps with another **m** wife; Pr 6:29
A rich **m** wealth is his fortified Pr 10:15
the work of a **m** hands will Pr 12:14
Anxiety in a **m** heart weighs it Pr 12:25
are a ransom for a **m** life, Pr 13:8
A wise **m** instruction is a Pr 13:14
The sensible **m** wisdom is to Pr 14:8
All a **m** ways seem right in his Pr 16:2
When a **m** ways please the LORD, Pr 16:7
A **m** heart plans his way, but the Pr 16:9
The words of a **m** mouth are deep Pr 18:4
A rich **m** wealth is his fortified Pr 18:11
his downfall a **m** heart is proud, Pr 18:12
A **m** spirit can endure sickness, Pr 18:14
of his mouth a **m** stomach is Pr 18:20
A **m** own foolishness leads him Pr 19:3
Many plans are in a **m** heart, Pr 19:21

A **m** desire should be loyalty to Pr 19:22
Counsel in a **m** heart is deep Pr 20:5
A **m** steps are determined by the Pr 20:24
A guilty **m** conduct is crooked, Pr 21:8
The **m** oration to Ithiel, to Pr 30:1
and I lack **m** ability to Pr 30:2
is due to a **m** jealousy of his Ec 4:4
All **m** labor is for his stomach, Ec 6:7
A **m** wisdom brightens his face, Ec 8:1
even though **m** troubles are heavy Ec 8:6
A wise **m** heart ⌊goes⌋ to the Ec 10:2
and every **m** heart will melt. Is 13:7
that a **m** way of life is not his Jr 10:23
for each **m** word becomes his Jr 23:36
and every **m** sword will be Ezk 38:21
rod in the **m** hand was six units Ezk 40:5
the fingers of a **m** hand appeared Dn 5:5
were eyes in this horn like a **m**, Dn 7:8
perish because of this **m** life, Jnh 1:14
and a **m** enemies will be the Mt 10:36
enter a strong **m** house and steal Mt 12:29
that **m** last condition is worse Mt 12:45
about God's concerns, but **m**." Mt 16:23
I am innocent of this **m** blood. Mt 27:24
enter a strong **m** house and rob Mk 3:27
fingers in the **m** ears and Mk 7:33
placed His hands on the **m** eyes, Mk 8:25
about God's concerns, but **m**!" Mk 8:33
for us that if a **m** brother dies, Mk 12:19
that **m** last condition is worse Lk 11:26
A rich **m** land was very Lk 12:16
what fell from the rich **m** table, Lk 16:21
for us that if a **m** brother has a Lk 20:28
I don't receive **m** testimony, Jn 5:34
You're that **m** disciple, but Jn 9:28
opened the blind **m** eyes also Jn 11:37
the dead **m** sister, told Him Jn 11:39
one of this **m** disciples too, Jn 18:17
to bring this **m** blood on us!" Ac 5:28
and we went into the **m** house. Ac 11:12
From this **m** descendants, Ac 13:23
if by the one **m** trespass the Rm 5:15
gift is not like the one **m** sin, Rm 5:16
Since by the one **m** trespass, Rm 5:17
as through one **m** disobedience Rm 5:19
through the one **m** obedience the Rm 5:19
has never come into a **m** heart, 1Co 2:9
and glory, but woman is **m** glory. 1Co 11:7
for **m** anger does not accomplish Jms 1:20
turned to blood like a dead **m**, Rv 16:3

MAN-MADE (2)
you will worship **m** gods of wood Dt 4:28
consists of⌋ **m** rules learned Is 29:13

MANAEN (1)
the Cyrenian, **M**, a close friend Ac 13:1

MANAGE (4)
and Abednego to **m** the province Dn 2:49
have appointed to **m** the province Dn 3:12
not know how to **m** his own 1Tm 3:5
have children, **m** their 1Tm 5:14

MANAGED (3)
household who **m** all he owned, Gn 24:2
King Rehoboam **m** to get into the 1Kg 12:18
King Rehoboam **m** to get up into 2Ch 10:18

MANAGEMENT (3)
Give an account of your **m**, Lk 16:2
is taking the **m** away from me? Lk 16:3
so that when I'm removed from **m**, Lk 16:4

MANAGER (7)
and sensible **m** his master will Lk 12:42
that his **m** was squandering his Lk 16:1
he called the **m** in and asked, Lk 16:2
you can no longer be ⌊my⌋ **m**.' Lk 16:2
Then the **m** said to himself, Lk 16:3
the unrighteous **m** because he had Lk 16:8
as God's **m**, must be blameless Ti 1:7

MANAGERS (3)
of Christ and **m** of God's 1Co 4:1
is expected of **m** that each one 1Co 4:2
as good **m** of the varied grace of 1Pt 4:10

MANAGES (1)
one who **m** his own household 1Tm 3:4

MANAGING (2)
helping, **m**, various kinds 1Co 12:28
m their children and their own 1Tm 3:12

MANAHATH (3)
M, Ebal, Shepho, and Onam. Gn 36:23
M, Ebal, Shephi, and Onam. 1Ch 1:40
Geba and who were deported to **M**: 1Ch 8:6

MANAHATHITES (2)
Haroeh, half of the **M**, 1Ch 2:52
and half of the **M**, the Zorites, 1Ch 2:54

MANASSEH (132)
Joseph named the firstborn **M**, Gn 41:51
M and Ephraim were born to Gn 46:20
his two sons, **M** and Ephraim. Gn 48:1
Ephraim and **M** belong to me just Gn 48:5
his left hand **M** toward Israel's Gn 48:13
although **M** was the firstborn. Gn 48:14
make you like Ephraim and **M**," Gn 48:20
putting Ephraim before **M**. Gn 48:20
Gamaliel son of Pedahzur from **M**; Nm 1:10
The descendants of **M**: Nm 1:34
the tribe of **M** numbered 32,200 Nm 1:35
The tribe of **M** will be next to Nm 2:20
the division of the tribe of **M**, Nm 10:23
son of Susi from the tribe of **M** Nm 13:11
clans ⌊from⌋ **M** and Ephraim: Nm 26:28
son of **M** from the clans of Nm 27:1
of Manasseh from the clans of **M**, Nm 27:1
the tribe of **M** son of Joseph— Nm 32:33
Machir son of **M** went to Gilead, Nm 32:39
⌊the clan of⌋ Machir son of **M**, Nm 32:40
a descendant of **M**, went and Nm 32:41
the tribe of **M** has received its Nm 34:14
a leader from the tribe of **M**, Nm 34:23
of Machir, son of **M**—one of the Nm 36:1
descendants of **M** son of Joseph, Nm 36:12
half the tribe of **M** the rest of Dt 3:13
a descendant of **M**, took over the Dt 3:14
and half the tribe of **M**. Dt 29:8
and such are the thousands of **M**. Dt 33:17
the land of Ephraim and **M**, Dt 34:2
and half the tribe of **M**: Jos 1:12
the tribe of **M** went in battle Jos 4:12
and half the tribe of **M**. Jos 12:6
tribes and half the tribe of **M**." Jos 13:7
And to half the tribe of **M**, Jos 13:29
descendants of Machir son of **M**, Jos 13:31
two tribes, **M** and Ephraim. Jos 14:4
So Ephraim and **M**, the sons of Jos 16:4
of the descendants of **M**— Jos 16:9
for the tribe of **M** as Joseph's Jos 17:1
firstborn of **M** and the father Jos 17:1
descendants of **M** son of Joseph, Jos 17:2
Machir, son of **M**, had no sons, Jos 17:3
tracts fell to **M**, besides the Jos 17:5
The border of **M** went from Asher Jos 17:7
region of Tappuah belonged to **M**, Jos 17:8
M had Beth-shean with its towns, Jos 17:11
descendants of **M** could not Jos 17:12
is, Ephraim and **M**), "You have Jos 17:17
the tribe of **M** have taken their Jos 18:7
Dan, and half the tribe of **M**. Jos 21:5
half the tribe of **M** in Bashan. Jos 21:6
half the tribe of **M** ⌊they gave⌋: Jos 21:25
From half the tribe of **M**, Jos 21:27
and half the tribe of **M**, Jos 22:1
half the tribe of **M** in Bashan, Jos 22:7
half the tribe of **M** left the Jos 22:9
the tribe of **M** built a large, Jos 22:10
half the tribe of **M** have built Jos 22:11
half the tribe of **M**, in the land Jos 22:13
half the tribe of **M**, in the land Jos 22:15
half the tribe of **M** answered the Jos 22:21
Gad, and **M** had to say, they Jos 22:30
Gad, and **M**, "Today we know Jos 22:31
At that time **M** failed to take Jdg 1:27
my family is the weakest in **M**, Jdg 6:15
messengers throughout all of **M**, Jdg 6:35
Asher, and **M**, and they pursued Jdg 7:23
traveled through Gilead and **M**, Jdg 11:29
territories of⌋ Ephraim and **M**." Jdg 12:4
the villages of Jair son of **M**, 1Kg 4:13
and his son **M** became king in his 2Kg 20:21
M was 12 years old when he 2Kg 21:1
M set up the carved image of 2Kg 21:7
M caused them to stray so that 2Kg 21:9
Since **M** king of Judah has 2Kg 21:11
M also shed so much innocent 2Kg 21:16
M rested with his fathers and 2Kg 21:18
sight as his father **M** had done. 2Kg 21:20
altars that **M** had made in the 2Kg 23:12
provocations **M** had provoked 2Kg 23:26
It was because of the sins of **M**, 2Kg 24:3
his son Hezekiah, his son **M**, 1Ch 3:13
half the tribe of **M** had 44,760 1Ch 5:18
half the tribe of **M** settled in 1Ch 5:23
half the tribe of **M** into exile. 1Ch 5:26
half tribe of **M** ⌊were assigned⌋ 1Ch 6:61
and **M** in Bashan according to 1Ch 6:62
half the tribe of **M**, Aner and 1Ch 6:70
families of half the tribe of **M**. 1Ch 6:71
Gilead son of Machir, son of **M**. 1Ch 7:17
the borders of the sons of **M**, 1Ch 7:29
and **M** settled in Jerusalem: 1Ch 9:3
men from **M** defected to him: 1Ch 12:20
chiefs of thousands in **M**. 1Ch 12:20
From half the tribe of **M**: 1Ch 12:31
and half the tribe of **M**: 1Ch 12:37
half the tribe of **M** as overseers 1Ch 26:32
half the tribe of **M**, Joel son of 1Ch 27:20
half the tribe of **M** in Gilead, 1Ch 27:21
of⌋ Ephraim, **M**, and Simeon who 2Ch 15:9
to Ephraim and **M** to come to the 2Ch 30:1
of Ephraim and **M** as far as 2Ch 30:10
some from Asher, **M**, and Zebulun 2Ch 30:11
many from Ephraim, **M**, Issachar, 2Ch 30:18
as well as in Ephraim and **M**, 2Ch 31:1
His son **M** became king in his 2Ch 32:33
M was 12 years old when he 2Ch 33:1
M set up a carved image of the 2Ch 33:7
So **M** caused Judah and the 2Ch 33:9
LORD spoke to **M** and his people, 2Ch 33:10
They captured **M** with hooks, 2Ch 33:11
M came to know that the LORD 2Ch 33:13
M rested with his fathers, 2Ch 33:20
just as his father **M** had done. 2Ch 33:22
that his father **M** had made, 2Ch 33:22
his father **M** humbled himself 2Ch 33:23
the same⌋ in the cities of **M**, 2Ch 34:6
had collected ⌊money⌋ from **M**, 2Ch 34:9
Bezalel, Binnui, and **M**; Ezr 10:30
Jeremai, **M**, and Shimei; Ezr 10:33
Gilead is Mine, **M** is Mine, and Ps 60:7
of Ephraim, Benjamin, and **M**. Ps 80:2
Gilead is Mine, **M** is Mine, and Ps 108:8
M is with Ephraim, and Ephraim Is 9:21
Ephraim, and Ephraim with **M**; Is 9:21
because of **M** son of Hezekiah Jr 15:4
west, will be **M**—one ⌊portion⌋ Ezk 48:4
Next to the territory of **M**, Ezk 48:5
Hezekiah fathered **M**, Manasseh Mt 1:10
Manasseh, **M** fathered Amon, Mt 1:10
12,000 from the tribe of **M**, Rv 7:6

MANASSEH'S (17)
put his left on **M** head, although Gn 48:14
it from Ephraim's head to **M**. Gn 48:17
the sons of **M** son Machir were Gn 50:23
M descendants: the Machirite Nm 26:29
These were **M** clans, numbered by Nm 26:34
half the tribe of **M** descendants Jos 13:29
for the rest of **M** descendants Jos 17:2
because **M** daughters received an Jos 17:6
belonged to the rest of **M** sons. Jos 17:6
itself⌋ on **M** border belonged to Jos 17:8
to Ephraim among **M** cities. Jos 17:9
M border was on the north side Jos 17:9
to the south and **M** to the north, Jos 17:10
Golan in Bashan from **M** tribe. Jos 20:8
rest of the events of **M** ⌊reign⌋, 2Kg 21:17
M sons through his Aramean 1Ch 7:14
rest of the events of **M** ⌊reign⌋, 2Ch 33:18

MANASSITES (5)
leader of the **M** is Gamaliel son Nm 2:20
leader of the **M**, ⌊presented an Nm 7:54
in Bashan, belonging to the **M**. Dt 4:43
and the **M**—from Aroer which 2Kg 10:33
Some **M** defected to David when 1Ch 12:19

MANATEE (13)
ram skins dyed red and **m** skins; Ex 25:5
and a covering of **m** skins on top Ex 26:14
ram skins dyed red and **m** skins; Ex 35:7
ram skins dyed red or **m** skins, Ex 35:23
and a covering of **m** skins on top Ex 36:19
red and the covering of **m** skins; Ex 39:34
this a covering made of **m** skin, Nm 4:6
with a covering made of **m** skin, Nm 4:8
covering made of **m** skin and put Nm 4:10
with a covering made of **m** skin, Nm 4:11
with a covering made of **m** skin, Nm 4:12

covering made of **m** skin over it Nm 4:14
covering made of **m** skin on top Nm 4:25

MANDATE *(3)*
to My voice and kept My **m**, Gn 26:5
always keep His **m** and His Dt 11:1
They will keep My **m**. Ezk 44:16

MANDRAKES *(6)*
and found some **m** in the field. Gn 30:14
give me some of your son's **m**." Gn 30:14
also want to take my son's **m**?" Gn 30:15
in exchange for your son's **m**." Gn 30:15
have hired you with my son's **m**." Gn 30:16
The **m** give off a fragrance, Sg 7:13

MANE *(1)*
Do you adorn his neck with a **m**? Jb 39:19

MANIFESTATION *(1)*
A **m** of the Spirit is given to 1Co 12:7

MANIFESTED *(1)*
He was **m** in the flesh, justified 1Tm 3:16

MANKIND *(33)*
When **m** began to multiply on the Gn 6:1
will not remain with **m** forever, Gn 6:3
on the earth, as well as all **m**. Gn 7:21
ground, from **m** to livestock, to Gn 7:23
For who out of all **m** has heard Dt 5:26
out the memory of them from **m**, Dt 32:26
And this is a revelation for **m**, 2Sm 7:19
But **m** is born for trouble as Jb 5:7
m consigned to forced labor Jb 7:1
I done to You, Watcher of **m**? Jb 7:20
as well as the breath of all **m**. Jb 12:10
He said to **m**, "Look! Jb 28:28
together and **m** would return to Jb 34:15
All **m** has seen it; people have Jb 36:25
out and shower abundantly on **m**. Jb 36:28
serve as His signature to all **m**, Jb 37:7
His acts toward **m** are Ps 66:5
return **m** to the dust, saying, Ps 90:3
call out to you; my cry is to **m**. Pr 8:4
land and the needy from among **m**. Pr 30:14
since that is the end of all **m**, Ec 7:2
and **m** more rare than the gold of Is 13:12
All **m** will come to worship Me, Is 66:23
they will be a horror to all **m**." Is 66:24
is the man who trusts in **m**, Jr 17:5
day both in Israel and among **m**. Jr 32:20
affliction or suffering on **m**. Lm 3:33
wait for anyone or linger for **m**. Mc 5:7
You have made **m** like the fish of Hab 1:14
will cut off **m** from the face of Zph 1:3
I will bring distress on **m**, Zph 1:17
who are left of **m** may seek the Ac 15:17
whom none of **m** has seen or can 1Tm 6:16

MANNA *(18)*
of Israel named the substance **m**. Ex 16:31
and put two quarts of **m** in it. Ex 16:33
Israelites ate **m** for 40 years, Ex 16:35
They ate **m** until they reached Ex 16:35
nothing to look at but this **m**!" Nm 11:6
The **m** resembled coriander seed, Nm 11:7
at night, the **m** would fall with Nm 11:9
then He gave you **m** to eat, Dt 8:3
wilderness with **m** that your Dt 8:16
of the land, the **m** ceased. Jos 5:12
there was no more **m** for the Jos 5:12
withhold Your **m** from their Neh 9:20
He rained **m** for them to eat; Ps 78:24
fathers ate the **m** in the Jn 6:31
fathers ate the **m** in the Jn 6:49
is not like the **m** your fathers Jn 6:58
was a gold jar containing the **m**, Heb 9:4
the victor some of the hidden **m**. Rv 2:17

MANNER *(6)*
In this **m** the king and all the 1Kg 8:63
In this **m** the king and all the 2Ch 7:5
inhabitants will die in like **m**. Is 51:6
in the Lord in a **m** worthy of the Rm 16:2
live your life in a **m** worthy of Php 1:27
journey in a **m** worthy of God, 3Jn 6

MANOAH *(16)*
family of Dan, whose name was **M**; Jdg 13:2
M prayed to the LORD and said, Jdg 13:8
God listened to **M**, and the Angel Jdg 13:9
and her husband **M** was not with Jdg 13:9
So **M** got up and followed his Jdg 13:11
Then **M** asked, "When Your words Jdg 13:12
Angel of the LORD answered **M**, Jdg 13:13
stay here," **M** told Him, "and we Jdg 13:15
For **M** did not know He was the Jdg 13:16
M said to Him, "What is Your Jdg 13:17
M took a young goat and a grain Jdg 13:19
thing while **M** and his wife were Jdg 13:19
When **M** and his wife saw ⌊this⌋, Jdg 13:20
appear again to **M** and his wife. Jdg 13:21
Then **M** realized that it was the Jdg 13:21
in the tomb of his father **M**. Jdg 16:31

MANSLAUGHTER *(10)*
who committed **m** and killed his Dt 4:42
who commits **m** can flee to these Dt 19:3
pursue the one who committed **m**, Dt 19:6
one who committed **m** over to him, Jos 20:5
who committed **m** may return home Jos 20:6
for the one who commits **m**, Jos 21:13
for the one who commits **m**, Jos 21:21
for the one who commits **m**, Jos 21:27
for the one who commits **m**, Jos 21:32
for the one who commits **m**, Jos 21:38

MANTLE *(9)*
spread out a **m**, and everyone Jdg 8:25
he tucked his **m** under his belt 1Kg 18:46
his face in his **m** and went out 1Kg 19:13
by him and threw his **m** over him. 1Kg 19:19
Elijah took his **m**, rolled it up, 2Kg 2:8
picked up the **m** that had fallen 2Kg 2:13
Then he took the **m** Elijah had 2Kg 2:14
Tuck your **m** under your belt, 2Kg 4:29
Tuck your **m** under your belt, 2Kg 9:1

MANURE *(7)*
will be like **m** on the surface 2Kg 9:37
they became **m** for the ground. Ps 83:10
become like **m** on the surface Jr 8:2
will fall like **m** on the surface Jr 9:22
but will be like **m** on the face Jr 16:4
will be like **m** on the surface Jr 25:33
for the soil or for the **m** pile; Lk 14:35

MANY *(548)*
for they had so **m** possessions Gn 13:6
Siddim contained **m** asphalt pits, Gn 14:10
will go out with **m** possessions. Gn 15:14
they will be too **m** to count." Gn 16:10
become the father of **m** nations. Gn 17:4
you the father of **m** nations. Gn 17:5
of the Philistines for **m** days. Gn 21:34
herds of cattle, and **m** slaves, Gn 26:14
He had **m** flocks, male and female Gn 30:43
were too **m** ⌊for them⌋ to live Gn 36:7
made a robe of **m** colors for him. Gn 37:3
the robe of **m** colors that he had Gn 37:23
the robe of **m** colors to their Gn 37:32
and mourned for his son **m** days. Gn 37:34
"How **m** years have you lived?" Gn 47:8
will make **m** nations ⌊come from⌋ Gn 48:4
the survival of **m** people. Gn 50:20
otherwise **m** of them will die. Ex 19:21
walks on all fours or on **m** feet, Lv 11:42
of her blood for **m** days, Lv 15:25
If **m** years are still left, Lv 25:51
over the tabernacle **m** days, Nm 9:19
are strong or weak, few or **m**. Nm 13:18
each of them, no matter how **m**. Nm 15:12
and we lived in Egypt **m** years, Nm 20:15
them so that **m** Israelites died Nm 21:6
hill country of Seir for **m** days. Dt 2:1
He drives out **m** nations before Dt 7:1
children may be **m** in the land Dt 11:21
will lend to **m** nations but not Dt 15:6
you will rule over **m** nations, Dt 15:6
must not acquire **m** horses for Dt 17:16
to Egypt to acquire **m** horses, Dt 17:16
must not acquire **m** wives for Dt 17:17
continue ruling **m** years over Dt 17:20
you may eat as **m** grapes as you Dt 23:24
You will lend to **m** nations, Dt 28:12
M troubles and afflictions will Dt 31:17
And when **m** troubles and Dt 31:21
We have **m** people, because the Jos 17:14
"If you have so **m** people," Jos 17:15
You have **m** people and great Jos 17:17
You have too **m** people for Me to Jdg 7:2
There are still too **m** people. Jdg 7:4
offspring, since he had **m** wives. Jdg 8:30
M wounded died as far as the Jdg 9:40
the LORD and wept with **m** tears. 1Sm 1:10
woman with **m** sons pines away. 1Sm 2:5
saving, whether by **m** or by few." 1Sm 14:6
M slaves these days are running 1Sm 25:10
M were killed on Mount Gilboa. 1Sm 31:1
M of the troops have fallen and 2Sm 1:4
and Hadadezer had fought **m** wars. 2Sm 8:10
there were **m** people coming from 2Sm 13:34
How **m** years of my life are left 2Sm 19:34
Kabzeel, a man of **m** exploits. 2Sm 23:20
because there were so **m**; 1Kg 7:47
because there were so **m**. 1Kg 8:5
Solomon loved **m** foreign women 1Kg 11:1
her household ate for **m** days. 1Kg 17:15
How **m** times must I make you 1Kg 22:16
he gathered as **m** wild gourds as 2Kg 4:39
With my **m** chariots I have gone 2Kg 19:23
did not have **m** children, 1Ch 4:27
M of the Hagrites were killed 1Ch 5:22
for they had **m** wives and 1Ch 7:4
They had **m** sons and grandsons— 1Ch 8:40
Kabzeel, a man of **m** exploits. 1Ch 11:22
Hadadezer had fought **m** wars. 1Ch 18:10
You also have **m** workers: 1Ch 22:15
and Beriah did not have **m** sons, 1Ch 23:11
the LORD has given me **m** sons— 1Ch 28:5
from Lebanon, as **m** as you need, 2Ch 2:16
because there were so **m**. 2Ch 5:6
and sought **m** wives for them. 2Ch 11:23
and captured **m** sheep and camels. 2Ch 14:15
For **m** years Israel has been 2Ch 15:3
of the lands had **m** conflicts. 2Ch 15:5
vast army with very **m** chariots 2Ch 16:8
Ahab sacrificed **m** sheep and 2Ch 18:2
How **m** times must I make you 2Ch 18:15
given them **m** gifts of silver, 2Ch 21:3
be struck⌋ with **m** illnesses, 2Ch 21:15
saw that Joash had **m** wounds, 2Ch 24:25
his sons, the **m** oracles about 2Ch 24:27
Since he had **m** cattle both in 2Ch 26:10
in the desert and dug **m** wells. 2Ch 26:10
him and took **m** captives to 2Ch 28:5
for there were **m** in the assembly 2Ch 30:17
of the people—**m** from Ephraim, 2Ch 30:18
and **m** priests consecrated 2Ch 30:24
M people gathered and stopped up 2Ch 32:4
M were bringing an offering to 2Ch 32:23
But **m** of the older priests, Ezr 3:12
but **m** ⌊others⌋ shouted joyfully. Ezr 3:12
that was built **m** years ago, Ezr 5:11
buy with this money as **m** bulls, Ezr 7:17
But there are **m** people, and it Ezr 10:13
of Judah sent **m** letters to Neh 6:17
m in Judah were bound by oath Neh 6:18
and rescued them **m** times in Your Neh 9:28
patient with them for **m** years, Neh 9:30
a king like him among **m** nations. Neh 13:26
m young women gathered at the Est 2:8
m lay on sackcloth and ashes. Est 4:3
glorious wealth and his **m** sons. Est 5:11
m of the ethnic groups of the Est 8:17
popular with **m** of his relatives. Est 10:3
You have instructed **m** and have Jb 4:3
offspring will be **m** and your Jb 5:25
and **m** will seek your favor. Jb 11:19
How **m** iniquities and sins have I Jb 13:23
have heard **m** things like these. Jb 16:2
and He has **m** more things like Jb 23:14
There are **m** who attack me. Ps 3:1
M say about me, "There is no Ps 3:2
M are saying, "Who can show us Ps 4:6
out because of their **m** crimes, Ps 5:10
M bulls surround me; strong ones Ps 22:12
I have heard the gossip of **m**; Ps 31:13
M pains come to the wicked, Ps 32:10
M adversities come to the one Ps 34:19
I will exalt You among **m** people. Ps 35:18
abundance of **m** wicked people. Ps 37:16
m hate me for no reason. Ps 38:19
M will see and fear, and put Ps 40:3
You have done **m** things—Your Ps 40:5
how I walked with **m**, leading the Ps 42:4
Though **m** are against me, He will Ps 55:18
for **m** arrogantly fight against Ps 56:2
his years span **m** generations. Ps 61:6
Bashan is a mountain of **m** peaks. Ps 68:15
become an ominous sign to **m**, Ps 71:7
me to experience **m** troubles Ps 71:20
rejoice for as **m** days as You Ps 90:15

for as **m** years as we have seen Ps 90:15
than the roar of **m** waters— Ps 93:4
let the **m** coasts and islands be Ps 97:1
remember Your **m** acts of faithful Ps 106:7
rescued them **m** times, but they Ps 106:43
praise Him in the presence of **m**. Ps 109:30
How **m** days ⌊must⌋ Your servant Ps 119:84
Your compassions are **m**, LORD; Ps 119:156
My persecutors and foes are **m**. Ps 119:157
He struck down **m** nations and Ps 135:10
for they will bring you **m** days, Pr 3:2
and you will live **m** years. Pr 4:10
she has brought **m** down to death; Pr 7:26
by Wisdom your days will be **m**, Pr 9:11
When there are **m** words, sin is Pr 10:19
lips of the righteous feed **m**, Pr 10:21
but with **m** counselors there is Pr 11:14
but there are **m** who love the Pr 14:20
with **m** advisers they succeed. Pr 15:22
A man with **m** friends may be Pr 18:24
Wealth attracts **m** friends, Pr 19:4
M seek the favor of a ruler, Pr 19:6
M plans are in a man's heart, Pr 19:21
M a man proclaims his own Pr 20:6
victory comes with **m** counselors. Pr 24:6
it has **m** rulers, but with Pr 28:2
man will have **m** blessings, Pr 28:20
eyes away will receive **m** curses. Pr 28:27
m reprimands will be broken Pr 29:1
M seek a ruler's favor, but a Pr 29:26
M women are capable, but you Pr 31:29
I also owned **m** herds of cattle Ec 2:7
for myself, and **m** concubines, Ec 2:8
and a fool's voice from **m** words. Ec 5:3
For **m** dreams bring futility, Ec 5:7
bring futility, also **m** words. Ec 5:7
children and live **m** years. Ec 6:3
For when there are **m** words, Ec 6:11
for you know that **m** times you Ec 7:22
but they pursued **m** schemes." Ec 7:29
after **m** days you may find it. Ec 11:1
if a man should live **m** years, Ec 11:8
darkness, since they will be **m**. Ec 11:8
and arranged **m** proverbs. Ec 12:9
no end to the making of **m** books, Ec 12:12
and **m** peoples will come and say, Is 2:3
arbitration for **m** peoples. Is 2:4
m houses will become desolate, Is 5:9
M will stumble over these; Is 8:15
and to cut off **m** nations. Is 10:7
roar of **m** peoples—they roar Is 17:12
like the raging of **m** waters. Is 17:13
saw that there were **m** breaches Is 22:9
on **m** waters. Tyre's revenue was Is 23:3
sing **m** a song, and you Is 23:16
after **m** days they will be Is 24:22
With my **m** chariots I have gone Is 37:24
board, new, with **m** teeth. Is 41:15
Though seeing **m** things, you do Is 42:20
Maker—one clay pot among **m**. Is 45:9
in spite of your **m** sorceries and Is 47:9
spells and your **m** sorceries, Is 47:12
out with your **m** consultations. Is 47:13
I blessed him and made him **m**. Is 51:2
Just as **m** were appalled at You— Is 52:14
so He will sprinkle **m** nations. Is 52:15
servant will justify **m**, Is 53:11
give Him the **m** as a portion, Is 53:12
bore the sin of **m** and interceded Is 53:12
became weary on your **m** journeys, Is 57:10
devastations of **m** generations. Is 61:4
even the **m** good things ⌊He has Is 63:7
and **m** will be slain by the LORD. Is 66:16
the prostitute with **m** partners— Jr 3:1
their rebellious acts are **m**, Jr 5:6
carried out so **m** evil schemes? Jr 11:15
M shepherds have destroyed My Jr 12:10
Indeed, our rebellions are **m**; Jr 14:7
about to send for **m** fishermen"— Jr 16:16
Then I will send for **m** hunters, Jr 16:16
M nations will pass by this city Jr 22:8
For **m** nations and great kings Jr 25:14
and then **m** nations and great Jr 27:7
plague against **m** lands and great Jr 28:8
And **m** other words like them were Jr 36:32
dungeon and stayed there **m** days. Jr 37:16
few of us remain out of the **m**, Jr 42:2
great nation and **m** kings will be Jr 50:41
You who reside by **m** waters, Jr 51:13
because of her **m** transgressions. Lm 1:5
my groans are **m**, and I am sick Lm 1:22
not ⌊being sent⌋ to **m** peoples Ezk 3:6
sees concerns **m** years ⌊from now⌋ Ezk 12:27
him⌋ according to his **m** idols, Ezk 14:4
you in the sight of **m** women. Ezk 16:41
full plumage of **m** colors came to Ezk 17:3
strength and **m** people will not Ezk 17:9
constructed to destroy **m** lives. Ezk 17:17
as well as its **m** branches. Ezk 19:11
may melt and **m** may stumble. Ezk 21:15
will raise up **m** nations against Ezk 26:3
of the peoples to **m** coasts and Ezk 27:3
m coasts and islands were your Ezk 27:15
seas, you satisfied **m** peoples. Ezk 27:33
it beautiful with its **m** limbs, Ezk 31:9
with an assembly of **m** peoples, Ezk 32:3
trouble the hearts of **m** peoples, Ezk 32:9
I will cause **m** nations to be Ezk 32:10
cattle that are beside **m** waters. Ezk 32:13
land. But we are **m**; the land has Ezk 33:24
and spoke **m** words against Me. Ezk 35:13
There were a great **m** of them on Ezk 37:2
its troops—**m** peoples are with Ezk 38:6
and regathered from **m** peoples to Ezk 38:8
and **m** peoples with you will Ezk 38:9
you and **m** peoples with you, Ezk 38:15
troops and the **m** peoples who are Ezk 38:22
in the sight of **m** nations. Ezk 38:23
them in the sight of **m** nations. Ezk 39:27
consist of **m** different kinds Ezk 47:10
and gave him **m** generous gifts. Dn 2:48
of⌋ peace, he will destroy **m**; Dn 8:25
it refers to **m** days ⌊in the Dn 8:26
covenant with **m** for one week, Dn 9:27
a great army and **m** supplies. Dn 11:13
In those times **m** will rise up Dn 11:14
and islands and capture **m**. Dn 11:18
away, and **m** will fall slain Dn 11:26
will give understanding to **m**, Dn 11:33
but **m** others will join them Dn 11:34
rulers over **m** and distributing Dn 11:39
chariots, horsemen, and **m** ships. Dn 11:40
beautiful land, and **m** will fall. Dn 11:41
to destroy and annihilate **m**. Dn 11:44
M of those who sleep in the dust Dn 12:2
those who lead **m** to Dn 12:3
M will roam about, and knowledge Dn 12:4
M will be purified, cleansed, Dn 12:10
You must live with me **m** days. Hs 3:3
must live **m** days without king Hs 3:4
prophets and granted **m** visions; Hs 12:10
locust devoured your **m** gardens Am 4:9
your crimes are **m** and your sins Am 5:12
M dead bodies, thrown Am 8:3
left, as well as **m** animals?" Jnh 4:11
and **m** nations will come and say, Mc 4:2
disputes among **m** peoples and Mc 4:3
M nations have now assembled Mc 4:11
so you can crush **m** peoples. Mc 4:13
will be among **m** peoples like dew Mc 5:7
nations, among **m** peoples, like Mc 5:8
you have plundered **m** nations, Hab 2:8
by wiping out **m** peoples and Hab 2:10
M nations will join themselves Zch 2:11
as we have done these **m** years?" Zch 7:3
the residents of **m** cities; Zch 8:20
M peoples and strong nations Zch 8:22
fairness and turned **m** from sin. Mal 2:6
You have caused **m** to stumble by Mal 2:8
When he saw **m** of the Pharisees Mt 3:7
be heard for their **m** words. Mt 6:7
and there are **m** who go through Mt 7:13
On that day **m** will say to Me, Mt 7:22
do **m** miracles in Your name?' Mt 7:22
I tell you that **m** will come from Mt 8:11
they brought to Him **m** who were Mt 8:16
m tax collectors and sinners Mt 9:10
are worth more than **m** sparrows. Mt 10:31
Then He told them **m** things in Mt 13:3
M prophets and righteous people Mt 13:17
He did not do **m** miracles there Mt 13:58
And as **m** as touched it were made Mt 14:36
unable to speak, and **m** others. Mt 15:30
"How **m** loaves do you have?" Mt 15:34
the 5,000 and how **m** baskets you Mt 16:9
4,000 and how **m** large baskets Mt 16:10
Jerusalem and suffer **m** things Mt 16:21
how **m** times could my brother sin Mt 18:21
him? As **m** as seven times? Mt 18:21
you, not as **m** as seven," Jesus Mt 18:22
because he had **m** possessions. Mt 19:22
m who are first will be last, Mt 19:30
give His life—a ransom for **m**." Mt 20:28
For **m** are invited, but few are Mt 22:14
For **m** will come in My name, Mt 24:5
and they will deceive **m**. Mt 24:5
Then **m** will take offense, betray Mt 24:10
M false prophets will rise up Mt 24:11
will rise up and deceive **m**. Mt 24:11
the love of **m** will grow cold. Mt 24:12
put you in charge of **m** things. Mt 25:21
put you in charge of **m** things. Mt 25:23
it is shed for **m** for the Mt 26:28
even though **m** false witnesses Mt 26:60
were opened and **m** bodies of the Mt 27:52
holy city, and appeared to **m**. Mt 27:53
M women who had followed Jesus Mt 27:55
and He healed **m** who were sick Mk 1:34
diseases and drove out **m** demons. Mk 1:34
So **m** people gathered together Mk 2:2
m tax collectors and sinners Mk 2:15
there were **m** who were following Mk 2:15
He had healed **m**, all who had Mk 3:10
He taught them **m** things in Mk 4:2
to them with **m** parables like Mk 4:33
Him, "because we are **m**." Mk 5:9
endured much under **m** doctors. Mk 5:26
and **m** who heard Him were Mk 6:2
they were driving out **m** demons, Mk 6:13
m sick people with oil, Mk 6:13
For **m** people were coming and Mk 6:31
but **m** saw them leaving and Mk 6:33
He began to teach them **m** things. Mk 6:34
How **m** loaves do you have? Mk 6:38
And there are **m** other customs Mk 7:4
you do **m** other similar things. Mk 7:13
"How **m** loaves do you have?" Mk 8:5
how **m** baskets full of pieces of Mk 8:19
how **m** large baskets full of Mk 8:20
Son of Man must suffer **m** things, Mk 8:31
He must suffer **m** things and be Mk 9:12
And **m** times it has thrown him Mk 9:22
corpse, so that **m** said, "He's Mk 9:26
because he had **m** possessions. Mk 10:22
m who are first will be last, Mk 10:31
give His life—a ransom for **m**." Mk 10:45
M people told him to keep quiet, Mk 10:48
M people spread their robes on Mk 11:8
⌊He⌋ also ⌊sent⌋ **m** others; Mk 12:5
M rich people were putting in Mk 12:41
M will come in My name, saying, Mk 13:6
and they will deceive **m**. Mk 13:6
the covenant; it is shed for **m**. Mk 14:24
m were giving false testimony Mk 14:56
began to accuse Him of **m** things. Mk 15:3
Look how **m** things they are Mk 15:4
M other women had come up with Mk 15:41
M have undertaken to compile a Lk 1:1
and **m** will rejoice at his birth. Lk 1:14
He will turn **m** of the sons of Lk 1:16
and rise of **m** in Israel and to Lk 2:34
the thoughts of **m** hearts may be Lk 2:35
along with **m** other exhortations, Lk 3:18
certainly **m** widows in Israel Lk 4:25
there were **m** in Israel who had Lk 4:27
demons were coming out of **m**, Lk 4:41
time Jesus healed **m** people of Lk 7:21
granted sight to **m** blind people. Lk 7:21
her **m** sins have been forgiven; Lk 7:47
and **m** others who were supporting Lk 8:3
M times it had seized him, Lk 8:29
m demons had entered him. Lk 8:30
Man must suffer **m** things and be Lk 9:22
I tell you that **m** prophets and Lk 10:24
was distracted by her **m** tasks, Lk 10:40
and upset about **m** things, Lk 10:41
cross-examine Him about **m** Lk 11:53
a crowd of **m** thousands came Lk 12:1
are worth more than **m** sparrows! Lk 12:7
You have **m** goods stored up for Lk 12:19
goods stored up for **m** years. Lk 12:19
m will try to enter and won't be Lk 13:24
a large banquet and invited **m**. Lk 14:16
m days later, the younger son Lk 15:13

'How **m** of my father's hired Lk 15:17
been slaving **m** years for you, Lk 15:29
He must suffer **m** things and be Lk 17:25
will not receive **m** times more at Lk 18:30
For **m** will come in My name, Lk 21:8
they were saying **m** other Lk 22:65
m trusted in His name when they Jn 2:23
Now **m** Samaritans from that town Jn 4:39
M more believed because of what Jn 4:41
but what are they for so **m**?" Jn 6:9
when **m** of His disciples heard Jn 6:60
that moment **m** of His disciples Jn 6:66
m from the crowd believed in Him Jn 7:31
I have **m** things to say and to Jn 8:26
these things, **m** believed in Him. Jn 8:30
M of them were saying, "He has a Jn 10:20
I have shown you **m** good works Jn 10:32
M came to Him and said, "John Jn 10:41
And **m** believed in Him there. Jn 10:42
M of the Jews had come to Martha Jn 11:19
Therefore **m** of the Jews who came Jn 11:45
do since this man does **m** signs? Jn 11:47
and **m** went up to Jerusalem from Jn 11:55
was the reason **m** of the Jews Jn 12:11
performed so **m** signs in their Jn 12:37
m did believe in Him even among Jn 12:42
house are **m** dwelling places; Jn 14:2
I still have **m** things to tell Jn 16:12
M of the Jews read this sign, Jn 19:20
Jesus performed **m** other signs in Jn 20:30
Even though there were so **m**, Jn 21:11
there are also **m** other things Jn 21:25
alive to them by **m** convincing Ac 1:3
Spirit not **m** days from now." Ac 1:5
m as the Lord our God will call. Ac 2:39
And with **m** other words he Ac 2:40
and **m** wonders and signs were Ac 2:43
But **m** of those who heard the Ac 4:4
M signs and wonders were being Ac 5:12
out of **m** who were possessed, Ac 8:7
m who were paralyzed and lame Ac 8:7
evangelizing **m** villages of the Ac 8:25
have heard from **m** people about Ac 9:13
After **m** days had passed, the Ac 9:23
and **m** believed in the Lord. Ac 9:42
Peter stayed on **m** days in Joppa Ac 9:43
did **m** charitable deeds for the Ac 10:2
and found that **m** had come Ac 10:27
where **m** had assembled and were Ac 12:12
He appeared for **m** days to those Ac 13:31
m of the Jews and devout Ac 13:43
that town and made **m** disciples, Ac 14:21
pass through **m** troubles on our Ac 14:22
along with **m** others, remained Ac 15:35
And she did this for **m** days. Ac 16:18
had inflicted **m** blows on them, Ac 16:23
m of them believed, Ac 17:12
and **m** of the Corinthians, when Ac 18:8
I have **m** people in this city. Ac 18:10
having stayed on for **m** days, Ac 18:18
And **m** who had become believers Ac 19:18
while **m** of those who had Ac 19:19
There were **m** lamps in the room Ac 20:8
we were staying there **m** days, Ac 21:10
m thousands of Jews there are Ac 21:20
of this nation for **m** years, Ac 24:10
After **m** years, I came to bring Ac 24:17
and brought **m** serious charges Ac 25:7
Since they stayed there **m** days, Ac 25:14
was necessary to do **m** things in Ac 26:9
and I locked up **m** of the saints Ac 26:10
Sailing slowly for **m** days, Ac 27:7
For **m** days neither sun nor stars Ac 27:20
Since **m** were going without food, Ac 27:21
So they heaped **m** honors on us, Ac 28:10
m came to him at his lodging. Ac 28:23
you the father of **m** nations. Rm 4:17
became the father of **m** nations, Rm 4:18
one man's trespass the **m** died, Rm 5:15
overflowed to the **m** by the grace Rm 5:15
but from **m** trespasses came the Rm 5:16
disobedience the **m** were made Rm 5:19
obedience the **m** will be made Rm 5:19
the firstborn among **m** brothers. Rm 8:29
Now as we have **m** parts in one Rm 12:4
way we who are **m** are one body Rm 12:5
been prevented **m** times from Rm 15:22
desired for **m** years to come to Rm 15:23
she has been a benefactor of **m**— Rm 16:2
not **m** are wise from a human 1Co 1:26
perspective, not **m** powerful, not 1Co 1:26
powerful, not **m** of noble birth. 1Co 1:26
but you can't have **m** fathers. 1Co 4:15
as there are **m** "gods" and many 1Co 8:5
are many "gods" and **m** "lords"— 1Co 8:5
we who are **m** are one body, 1Co 10:17
the profit of **m**, that they may 1Co 10:33
This is why **m** are sick and ill 1Co 11:30
among you, and **m** have fallen 1Co 11:30
the body is one and has **m** parts, 1Co 12:12
body, though **m**, are one body— 1Co 12:12
the body is not one part but **m**. 1Co 12:14
Now there are **m** parts, yet one 1Co 12:20
are doubtless **m** different kinds 1Co 14:10
opened for me—yet **m** oppose me. 1Co 16:9
may be given by **m** on our behalf 2Co 1:11
us through ⌊the prayers of⌋ **m**. 2Co 1:11
I wrote to you with **m** tears— 2Co 2:4
not like the **m** who make a trade 2Co 2:17
as poor yet enriching **m**; 2Co 6:10
tested, in **m** circumstances, 2Co 8:22
also overflowing in **m** acts of 2Co 9:12
Since **m** boast from a human 2Co 11:18
far more labors, **m** more 2Co 11:23
beatings, near death **m** times. 2Co 11:23
hardship, **m** sleepless nights, 2Co 11:27
will grieve for **m** who sinned 2Co 12:21
Judaism beyond **m** contemporaries Gl 1:14
as though referring to **m**, Gl 3:16
For as **m** of you as have been Gl 3:27
children of the desolate are **m**, Gl 4:27
that **m** live as enemies of the Php 3:18
and **m** foolish and harmful 1Tm 6:9
pierced themselves with **m** pains. 1Tm 6:10
confession before **m** witnesses. 1Tm 6:12
in the presence of **m** witnesses, 2Tm 2:2
there are also **m** rebellious Ti 1:10
in bringing **m** sons to glory, Heb 2:10
Now **m** have become ⌊Levitical⌋ Heb 7:23
this to offer Himself **m** times, Heb 9:25
have had to suffer **m** times since Heb 9:26
once to bear the sins of **m**, Heb 9:28
trouble and by it, defiling **m**. Heb 12:15
Not **m** should become teachers, Jms 3:1
for we all stumble in **m** ways. Jms 3:2
M will follow their unrestrained 2Pt 2:2
even now **m** antichrists have 1Jn 2:18
because **m** false prophets have 1Jn 4:1
M deceivers have gone out into 2Jn 7
Though I have **m** things to write 2Jn 12
I have **m** things to write you, 3Jn 13
tolerated ⌊**m** things⌋ because Rv 2:3
As **m** as I love, I rebuke and Rv 3:19
the voice of **m** angels around Rv 5:11
m of the people died from the Rv 8:11
chariots with **m** horses rushing Rv 9:9
prophesy again about **m** peoples, Rv 10:11
prostitute who sits on **m** waters. Rv 17:1
and on His head were **m** crowns. Rv 19:12

MAOCH *(1)*
men and went to Achish son of **M**, 1Sm 27:2

MAON *(6)*
M, Carmel, Ziph, Juttah, Jos 15:55
wilderness near **M** in the Arabah 1Sm 23:24
stayed in the Wilderness of **M**. 1Sm 23:25
A man in **M** had a business in 1Sm 25:2
Shammai's son was **M**, and Maon 1Ch 2:45
was Maon, and **M** fathered 1Ch 2:45

MAONITES *(1)*
Amalekites, and **M** oppressed you, Jdg 10:12

MAR *(1)*
of your head or **m** the edge of Lv 19:27

MARA *(1)*
Call me **M**," she answered, "for Ru 1:20

MARAH *(6)*
They came to **M**, but they could Ex 15:23
the water at **M** because it was Ex 15:23
that is why it was named **M**. Ex 15:23
for them at **M** and He tested them Ex 15:25
of Etham and camped at **M**. Nm 33:8
departed from **M** and came to Elim Nm 33:9

MARALAH *(1)*
border went up westward to **M**, Jos 19:11

MARANATHA *(1)*
the Lord, a curse be on him. **M**! 1Co 16:22

MARAUDERS *(5)*
them over to **m** who raided them. Jdg 2:14
them from the power of their **m**, Jdg 2:16
They helped David against the **m**, 1Ch 12:21
and **m** have vanished from the Is 16:4
came to you, if **m** by night—how Ob 5

MARAUDING *(3)*
will be attacked by ⌊**m**⌋ bands, Gn 49:19
Now **m** bands of Moabites used to 2Kg 13:20
suddenly they saw a **m** band, 2Kg 13:21

MARBLE *(4)*
and a great quantity of **m**. 1Ch 29:2
to silver rods on **m** columns. Est 1:6
pavement of red feldspar, **m**, Est 1:6
wood, brass, iron, and **m**; Rv 18:12

MARCH *(39)*
was the order of **m** for the Nm 10:28
They will **m** out against you from Dt 28:7
You will **m** out against them from Dt 28:25
M around the city with all the Jos 6:3
m around the city seven times, Jos 6:4
Move forward, **m** around the city, Jos 6:7
M on, my soul, in strength! Jdg 5:21
anyone who doesn't **m** behind Saul 1Sm 11:7
your men must **m** out in the army 1Sm 28:1
when kings **m** out ⌊to war⌋, 2Sm 11:1
"**M** on," David replied to Ittai. 2Sm 15:22
"I will also **m** out with you." 2Sm 18:2
You are not to **m** up and fight 1Kg 12:24
of Aram will **m** up against you." 1Kg 20:22
They replied, "**M** up, and the 1Kg 22:6
M up to Ramoth-gilead and 1Kg 22:12
told him, "**M** up and succeed. 1Kg 22:15
entice Ahab to **m** up and fall at 1Kg 22:20
M up and save me from the power 2Kg 16:7
Egypt did not **m** out of his land 2Kg 24:7
trees, then **m** out to battle, for 1Ch 14:15
when kings **m** out ⌊to war⌋, 1Ch 20:1
You are not to **m** up and fight 2Ch 11:4
persuaded him to **m** up to 2Ch 18:2
They replied, "**M** up, and God 2Ch 18:5
M up to Ramoth-gilead and 2Ch 18:11
Micaiah said, "**M** up and succeed 2Ch 18:14
of Israel to **m** up and fall at 2Ch 18:19
do not **m** out with our armies. Ps 44:9
do not **m** out with our armies. Ps 60:10
do not **m** out with our armies. Ps 108:11
yet all of them **m** in ranks; Pr 30:27
He will **m** over rulers as if they Is 41:25
the South will **m** out to fight Dn 11:11
will never again **m** through you; Nah 1:15
You **m** across the earth with Hab 3:12
those who **m** back and forth, Zch 9:8
no oppressor will **m** against them Zch 9:8
and they will **m** in His name— Zch 10:12

MARCHED *(51)*
seven trumpets **m** in front of the Jos 6:13
second day they **m** around the Jos 6:14
at dawn and **m** around the city Jos 6:15
only day they **m** around the city Jos 6:15
From there he **m** against the Jos 15:15
the men of Judah **m** down to fight Jdg 1:9
Judah also **m** against the Jdg 1:10
From there they **m** against the Jdg 1:11
when You **m** from the fields of Jdg 5:4
their rulers **m** up toward Israel. 1Sm 7:7
assembled and **m** to the battle, 1Sm 14:20
David **m** out ⌊with the army⌋, 1Sm 18:5
son of Saul **m** out from Mahanaim 2Sm 2:12
soldiers **m** out and met them 2Sm 2:13
Abner and his men **m** through the 2Sm 2:29
the Jordan, **m** all morning, 2Sm 2:29
Joab and his men **m** all night and 2Sm 2:32
king and his men **m** to Jerusalem 2Sm 5:6
LORD will have **m** out ahead of 2Sm 5:24
Ammonites **m** out and lined up 2Sm 10:8
all his servants **m** past him. 2Sm 15:18
him from Gath—**m** past the king. 2Sm 15:18
the Gittite **m** past with all his 2Sm 15:22
all the troops **m** out by hundreds 2Sm 18:4
David's forces **m** into the field 2Sm 18:6
all the warriors **m** out under 2Sm 20:7
with all Israel **m** up from 1Kg 16:17
He **m** up, besieged Samaria, and 1Kg 20:1
They **m** out at noon while 1Kg 20:16

provincial leaders **m** out first. 1Kg 20:17
If they have **m** out in peace, 1Kg 20:18
if they have **m** out for battle, 1Kg 20:18
army behind them **m** out from the 1Kg 20:19
of Israel **m** out and attacked 1Kg 20:21
Your servant **m** out into the 1Kg 20:39
So King Joram **m** out from Samaria 2Kg 3:6
together and **m** up to besiege 2Kg 6:24
king of Aram **m** up and fought 2Kg 12:17
to him and **m** up to Damascus 2Kg 16:9
the whole land, **m** up to Samaria, 2Kg 17:5
of Assyria **m** against Samaria 2Kg 18:9
king of Egypt **m** up to the king 2Kg 23:29
of Babylon **m** up to Jerusalem 2Kg 24:10
and all Israel **m** to Jerusalem 1Ch 11:4
God will have **m** out ahead of you 1Ch 14:15
The Ammonites **m** out and lined up 1Ch 19:9
So Asa **m** out against him and 2Ch 14:10
king of Egypt **m** up to fight at 2Ch 35:20
of his tent and **m** away to the Jb 18:14
when You **m** through the desert, Ps 68:7
king of Babylon **m** into the land, Jr 35:11

MARCHES *(5)*
The city that **m** out a thousand Am 5:3
and the one that **m** out a hundred Am 5:3
it **m** against our fortresses, Mc 5:5
when it **m** against our territory. Mc 5:6
nation that **m** across the earth's Hab 1:6

MARCHING *(8)*
after **m** all night from Gilgal. Jos 10:9
as the army was **m** out to its 1Sm 17:20
hear the sound of **m** in the tops 2Sm 5:24
all the people were **m** past. 2Sm 15:23
the people were **m** past on the 2Sm 15:23
the people had finished **m** past. 2Sm 15:24
"Men are **m** out of Samaria." 1Kg 20:17
hear the sound of **m** in the tops 1Ch 14:15

MARDUK *(1)*
(AKA BEL, MERODACH)
put to shame; **M** is devastated; Jr 50:2

MARE *(1)*
to a **m** among Pharaoh's chariots. Sg 1:9

MARES *(1)*
bred from the royal racing **m**. Est 8:10

MARESHAH *(8)*
Achzib, and **M**—nine cities, Jos 15:44
Ziph, and **M**, his second son, 1Ch 2:42
the father of **M**, the families 1Ch 4:21
Gath, **M**, Ziph, 2Ch 11:8
They came as far as **M**. 2Ch 14:9
in the Valley of Zephathah at **M**. 2Ch 14:10
of Dodavahu of **M** prophesied 2Ch 20:37
against you who live in **M**. Mc 1:15

MARINE *(1)*
like **m** creatures that have no Hab 1:14

MARITAL *(2)*
or **m** rights of the first wife. Ex 21:10
fulfill his **m** duty to his wife, 1Co 7:3

MARK *(18)*
(See also MARK proper noun.)
He placed a **m** on Cain so that Gn 4:15
be a distinguishing **m** for you; Ex 12:13
voice of the LORD, **m** my words: 1Kg 20:36
and commands it to hit its **m**. Jb 36:32
made the moon to **m** the seasons; Ps 104:19
and put a **m** on the foreheads of Ezk 9:4
come near anyone who has the **m**. Ezk 9:6
m out two roads that the sword Ezk 21:19
M out a road that the sword can Ezk 21:20
I don't see the **m** of the nails Jn 20:25
finger into the **m** of the nails, Jn 20:25
be given a **m** on his right hand Rv 13:16
buy or sell unless he has the **m**: Rv 13:17
and receives a **m** on his forehead Rv 14:9
who receives the **m** of his name. Rv 14:11
people who had the **m** of the Rv 16:2
who accepted the **m** of the beast Rv 19:20
not accepted the **m** on their Rv 20:4

MARK (proper noun) *(8)*
mother of John **M**, where many had Ac 12:12
on which they took John **M**. Ac 12:25
wanted to take along John **M**. Ac 15:37
and Barnabas took **M** with him and Ac 15:39
you, as does **M**, Barnabas' Col 4:10
Bring **M** with you, for he is 2Tm 4:11
M, Aristarchus, Demas, and Luke, Phm 24
greetings, as does **M**, my son. 1Pt 5:13

MARKED *(3)*
of his hand or **m** off the heavens Is 40:12
and your land **m** by ruins— Is 49:19
The answer **m** Jerusalem appears Ezk 21:22

MARKER *(14)*
his head and set it up as a **m**. Gn 28:18
have set up as a **m** will be God's Gn 28:22
oil on the stone **m** and made a Gn 31:13
a stone and set it up as a **m**. Gn 31:45
mound and the **m** I have set up Gn 31:51
witness and the **m** is a witness Gn 31:52
mound and this **m** to do me harm. Gn 31:52
Jacob set up a **m** at the place Gn 35:14
had spoken to him—a stone **m**. Gn 35:14
Jacob set up a **m** on her grave; Gn 35:20
it is the **m** at Rachel's grave to Gn 35:20
move your neighbor's boundary **m**, Dt 19:14
his neighbor's boundary **m**.' Dt 27:17
he will erect a **m** next to it Ezk 39:15

MARKERS *(3)*
The wicked displace boundary **m**. Jb 24:2
Set up road **m** for yourself; Jr 31:21
like those who move boundary **m**; Hs 5:10

MARKET *(2)*
the Sabbath, so we may **m** wheat? Am 8:5
that is sold in the meat **m**, 1Co 10:25

MARKETPLACE *(9)*
and deceit never leave its **m**. Ps 55:11
secured with cords in your **m**. Ezk 27:24
standing in the **m** doing nothing. Mt 20:3
When they come from the **m**, Mk 7:4
sitting in the **m** and calling to Lk 7:32
My Father's house into a **m**!" Jn 2:16
them into the **m** to the Ac 16:19
from the **m** and formed a mob, Ac 17:5
in the **m** every day with those Ac 17:17

MARKETPLACES *(7)*
you may set up **m** for yourself 1Kg 20:34
sitting in the **m** who call out to Mt 11:16
greetings in the **m**, and to be Mt 23:7
the sick in the **m** and begged Him Mk 6:56
and who want greetings in the **m**, Mk 12:38
and greetings in the **m**. Lk 11:43
and who love greetings in the **m**, Lk 20:46

MARKETS *(1)*
and islands were your regular **m**. Ezk 27:15

MARKS *(2)*
or put tattoo **m** on yourselves; Lv 19:28
I carry the **m** of Jesus on my Gl 6:17

MAROTH *(1)*
residents of **M** anxiously wait Mc 1:12

MARRIAGE *(29)*
younger ⌊daughter in **m**⌋ before Gn 29:26
Zipporah to Moses ⌊in **m**⌋. Ex 2:21
who was not promised in **m**, Ex 22:16
related to him by **m** and so Lv 21:4
not violate his father's **m** bed. Dt 22:30
violated his father's **m** bed.' Dt 27:20
30 daughters in **m** ⌊to men⌋ Jdg 12:9
daughter to a Benjaminite in **m**." Jdg 21:1
his daughter in **m** to his servant 1Ch 2:35
an alliance with Ahab through **m**. 2Ch 18:1
to their sons in **m** or take their Ezr 9:12
our daughters in **m** to the Neh 10:30
daughters in **m** to their sons Neh 13:25
to men ⌊in **m**⌋ so that they may Jr 29:6
a daughter in **m** to destroy it, Dn 11:17
she was your **m** partner and your Mal 2:14
nor are given in **m** but are like Mt 22:30
and giving in **m**, until the day Mt 24:38
nor are given in **m** but are like Mk 12:25
husband seven years after her **m**, Lk 2:36
and giving in **m** until the day Lk 17:27
age marry and are given in **m**. Lk 20:34
marry nor are given in **m**. Lk 20:35
promised you in **m** to one husband 2Co 11:2
They forbid **m** and demand 1Tm 4:3
M must be respected by all, Heb 13:4
and the **m** bed kept undefiled, Heb 13:4
because the **m** of the Lamb has Rv 19:7
to the **m** feast of the Lamb! Rv 19:9

MARRIAGEABLE *(1)*
if she is past **m** age, and so it 1Co 7:36

MARRIED *(52)*
taken, for she is a **m** woman." Gn 20:3
so Esau went to Ishmael and **m**, Gn 28:9
family of Levi **m** a Levite woman. Ex 2:1
Amram **m** his father's sister Ex 6:20
Aaron **m** Elisheba, daughter of Ex 6:23
Aaron's son Eleazar **m** one of the Ex 6:25
adultery with a **m** woman— Lv 20:10
daughter is **m** to a man outside Lv 22:12
of the Cushite woman he **m** Nm 12:1
for he had **m** a Cushite woman Nm 12:1
m cousins on their father's side. Nm 36:11
They **m** ⌊men⌋ from the clans of Nm 36:12
to a woman and not **m** her? Dt 20:7
'I **m** this woman and was intimate Dt 22:14
bring joy to the wife he has **m**. Dt 24:5
David also **m** Ahinoam of Jezreel, 1Sm 25:43
Ithra had **m** Abigail daughter of 2Sm 17:25
he also had **m** a daughter of 1Kg 4:15
a trivial matter, he **m** Jezebel, 1Kg 16:31
died, Caleb **m** Ephrath, and she 1Ch 2:19
Hezron had **m** her when he was 60 1Ch 2:21
Mered had **m** her. His Judean 1Ch 4:18
who **m** Moabites and returned to 1Ch 4:22
the sons of Kish, **m** them. 1Ch 23:22
Rehoboam **m** Mahalath, daughter 2Ch 11:18
m Maacah daughter of Absalom. 2Ch 11:20
towns who have **m** foreign women Ezr 10:14
men who had **m** foreign women. Ezr 10:17
found to have **m** foreign women Ezr 10:18
of these had **m** foreign women, Ezr 10:44
son Jehohanan had **m** the daughter Neh 6:18
Jews who had **m** women from Neh 13:23
the children of the **m** woman," Is 54:1
is in Her, and your land **M**; Is 62:4
in you, and your land will be **m**. Is 62:4
even though I had **m** them"— Jr 31:32
So he went and **m** Gomer daughter Hs 1:3
and has **m** the daughter of a Mal 2:11
angel had commanded him. He **m** Mt 1:24
The first got **m** and died. Mt 22:25
For they all had **m** her." Mt 22:28
Philip's wife, whom he had **m**. Mk 6:17
since the seven had **m** her?" Mk 12:23
I just got **m**, and therefore Lk 14:20
For all seven had **m** her." Lk 20:33
m woman is legally bound to her Rm 7:2
I command the **m**—not I, but the 1Co 7:10
if you do get **m**, you have not 1Co 7:28
But a **m** man is concerned about 1Co 7:33
But a **m** woman is concerned about 1Co 7:34
is not sinning; they can get **m**. 1Co 7:36
is free to be **m** to anyone she 1Co 7:39

MARRIES *(17)*
If Jacob **m** a Hittite woman like Gn 27:46
If a man **m** a woman and her Lv 20:14
If a man **m** his sister, whether Lv 20:17
If a man **m** his brother's wife, Lv 20:21
If a woman **m** while her vows or Nm 30:6
If a man **m** a woman, has sexual Dt 22:13
If a man **m** a woman, but she Dt 24:1
an unloved woman when she **m**, Pr 30:23
For as a young man **m** a virgin, Is 62:5
And whoever **m** a divorced woman Mt 5:32
immorality, and **m** another, Mt 19:9
his wife and **m** another commits Mk 10:11
her husband and **m** another, Mk 10:12
his wife and **m** another woman Lk 16:18
everyone who **m** a woman divorced Lk 16:18
and if a virgin **m**, she has not 1Co 7:28
So then he who **m** his virgin does 1Co 7:38

MARROW *(2)*
and his bones are full of **m**. Jb 21:24
soul, spirit, joints, and **m**; Heb 4:12

MARRY *(38)*
were going to **m** his daughters. Gn 19:14
M one of the daughters of Laban, Gn 28:2
not to **m** a Canaanite woman. Gn 28:6
You are not to **m** her son's Lv 18:17
You are not to **m** a woman as a Lv 18:18
are not to **m** a woman defiled Lv 21:7
He is to **m** a woman who is a Lv 21:13
He is not to **m** a widow, a Lv 21:14
He is to **m** a virgin from his own Lv 21:14
they **m** any of the men from the Nm 36:3
of the tribe into which they **m**. Nm 36:3
of the tribe into which they **m**, Nm 36:4
They may **m** anyone they like Nm 36:6

provided they **m** within a clan Nm 36:6
Israelite tribe must **m** someone Nm 36:8
battle and another man **m** her.' Dt 20:7
A man is not to **m** his father's Dt 22:30
away may not **m** her again after Dt 24:4
dead man may not **m** a stranger Dt 25:5
if the man doesn't want to **m** his Dt 25:7
says, 'I don't want to **m** her,' Dt 25:8
virgin, so your sons will **m** you; Is 62:5
and she leaves him to **m** another, Jr 3:1
You must not **m** or have sons or Jr 16:2
He is not to **m** a widow or a Ezk 44:22
but must **m** a virgin from the Ezk 44:22
Go and **m** a promiscuous wife and Hs 1:2
this, it's better not to **m**!" Mt 19:10
his brother is to **m** his wife and Mt 22:24
they neither **m** nor are given in Mt 22:30
they neither **m** nor are given in Mk 12:25
sons of this age **m** and are given Lk 20:34
the dead neither **m** nor are given Lk 20:35
they should **m**, for it is better 1Co 7:9
it is better to **m** than to burn 1Co 7:9
who does not **m** will do better. 1Co 7:38
by desire, they want to **m**, 1Tm 5:11
I want younger women to **m**, 1Tm 5:14

MARRYING *(7)*
to speak to Abigail about **m** him. 1Sm 25:39
king of Egypt by **m** Pharaoh's 1Kg 3:1
to our God by **m** foreign women Ezr 10:2
unfaithful by **m** foreign women, Ezr 10:10
our God by **m** foreign women?" Neh 13:27
and drinking, **m** and giving Mt 24:38
m and giving in marriage until Lk 17:27

MARSENA *(1)*
Tarshish, Meres, **M**, and Memucan. Est 1:14

MARSH *(2)*
grow where there is no **m**? Jb 8:11
Make Moab a salt **m**, for she will Jr 48:9

MARSHAL *(1)*
Appoint a **m** against her; Jr 51:27

MARSHAL'S *(1)*
those who carry a **m** staff ⌊came⌋ Jdg 5:14

MARSHES *(3)*
into islands, and dry up **m**. Is 42:15
been seized, the **m** set on fire, Jr 51:32
its swamps and **m** will not be Ezk 47:11

MARSHY *(1)*
in the protection of **m** reeds. Jb 40:21

MARTHA *(13)*
a woman named **M** welcomed Him Lk 10:38
But **M** was distracted by her many Lk 10:40
answered her, "**M**, Martha, you Lk 10:41
her, "Martha, **M**, you are worried Lk 10:41
of Mary and her sister **M**. Jn 11:1
Jesus loved **M**, her sister, and Jn 11:5
Jews had come to **M** and Mary to Jn 11:19
soon as **M** heard that Jesus was Jn 11:20
Then **M** said to Jesus, "Lord, if Jn 11:21
M said, "I know that he will Jn 11:24
the place where **M** had met Him. Jn 11:30
M, the dead man's sister, told Jn 11:39
M was serving them, and Lazarus Jn 12:2

MARVEL *(1)*
you scoffers, **m** and vanish away, Ac 13:41

MARVELOUS *(1)*
of darkness into His **m** light. 1Pt 2:9

MARVELOUSLY *(2)*
for he was **m** helped until he 2Ch 26:15
God thunders **m** with His voice; Jb 37:5

MARVELS *(1)*
in Egypt and His **m** in the region Ps 78:43

MARY *(53)*
Joseph the husband of **M**, Mt 1:16
His mother **M** had been engaged Mt 1:18
afraid to take **M** as your wife, Mt 1:20
saw the child with **M** His mother, Mt 2:11
Isn't His mother called **M**, Mt 13:55
Among them were **M** Magdalene, Mt 27:56
M the mother of James and Joseph, Mt 27:56
M Magdalene and the other Mary Mt 27:61
and the other **M** were seated Mt 27:61
M Magdalene and the other Mary Mt 28:1
and the other **M** went to view the Mt 28:1
the son of **M**, and the brother Mk 6:3
Among them were **M** Magdalene, Mk 15:40
M the mother of James the Mk 15:40
Now **M** Magdalene and Mary the Mk 15:47
Magdalene and **M** the mother Mk 15:47
was over, **M** Magdalene, Mary Mk 16:1
Mary Magdalene, **M** the mother of Mk 16:1
appeared first to **M** Magdalene, Mk 16:9
The virgin's name was **M**. Lk 1:27
not be afraid, **M**, for you have Lk 1:30
M asked the angel, "How can this Lk 1:34
"I am the Lord's slave," said **M**. Lk 1:38
In those days **M** set out and Lk 1:39
M said: My soul proclaims the Lk 1:46
M stayed with her about three Lk 1:56
to be registered along with **M**, Lk 2:5
off and found both **M** and Joseph, Lk 2:16
M was treasuring up all these Lk 2:19
them and told His mother **M**: Lk 2:34
M, called Magdalene (seven Lk 8:2
sister named **M**, who also sat at Lk 10:39
M has made the right choice, Lk 10:42
M Magdalene, Joanna, Mary the Lk 24:10
Magdalene, Joanna, **M** the mother Lk 24:10
the village of **M** and her sister Jn 11:1
M was the one who anointed the Jn 11:2
to Martha and **M** to comfort them Jn 11:19
But **M** remained seated in the Jn 11:20
back and called her sister **M**, Jn 11:28
her saw that **M** got up quickly Jn 11:31
When **M** came to where Jesus was Jn 11:32
who came to **M** and saw what He Jn 11:45
Then **M** took a pound of fragrant Jn 12:3
mother's sister, **M** the wife of Jn 19:25
wife of Clopas, and **M** Magdalene. Jn 19:25
day of the week **M** Magdalene came Jn 20:1
But **M** stood outside facing the Jn 20:11
Jesus said, "**M**." Turning around, Jn 20:16
M Magdalene went and announced Jn 20:18
including **M** the mother of Jesus, Ac 1:14
he went to the house of **M**, Ac 12:12
Greet **M**, who has worked very Rm 16:6

MARY'S *(1)*
When Elizabeth heard **M** greeting, Lk 1:41

MASH *(1)*
(AKA MESHECH)
Uz, Hul, Gether, and **M**. Gn 10:23

MASHAL *(1)*
they received⌋ **M** and its 1Ch 6:74

MASON'S *(2)*
Samaria and the **m** level ⌊used 2Kg 21:13
and righteousness the **m** level." Is 28:17

MASONS *(4)*
m, and the stonecutters—and 2Kg 12:12
and **m** to buy timber and quarried 2Kg 22:6
stonecutters, **m**, carpenters, and 1Ch 22:15
who were hiring **m** and carpenters 2Ch 24:12

MASREKAH *(2)*
from **M** ruled in his place. Gn 36:36
from **M** ruled in his place. 1Ch 1:47

MASS *(3)*
will stand up ⌊in⌋ a **m**." Jos 3:13
up ⌊in⌋ a **m** that extended as Jos 3:16
for the **m** of people were Ac 21:36

MASSA *(2)*
Mishma, Dumah, **M**, Gn 25:14
Mishma, Dumah, **M**, Hadad, Tema, 1Ch 1:30

MASSACRE *(3)*
It is a sword for **m**, a sword for Ezk 21:14
sword for great **m**—it surrounds Ezk 21:14
He gave orders to **m** all the male Mt 2:16

MASSAH *(5)*
He named the place **M** and Meribah Ex 17:7
God as you tested ⌊Him⌋ at **M**. Dt 6:16
the LORD at Taberah, **M**, and Dt 9:22
tested him at **M** and contended Dt 33:8
on that day at **M** in the Ps 95:8

MASSES *(2)*
and the **m** are parched with Is 5:13
dignitaries, her **m**, her crowds, Is 5:14

MASSIVE *(8)*
chariots, and a **m** army there. 2Kg 6:14
with a **m** army, from Lachish 2Kg 18:17
the shade of a **m** rock in an arid Is 32:2
with a **m** army, from Lachish Is 36:2
I will build myself a **m** palace, Jr 22:14
and their **m** herds of cattle will Jr 49:32
look! What **m** stones! What Mk 13:1
⌊The city⌋ had a **m** high wall, Rv 21:12

MAST *(3)*
down on the top of a ship's **m**. Pr 23:34
the base of the **m** or spread out Is 33:23
Lebanon to make a **m** for you. Ezk 27:5

MASTER *(146)*
is for you, but you must **m** it." Gn 4:7
hand under his **m** Abraham's thigh Gn 24:9
"LORD, God of my **m** Abraham," Gn 24:12
show kindness to my **m** Abraham. Gn 24:12
have shown kindness to my **m**." Gn 24:14
God of my **m** Abraham, who has Gn 24:27
and faithfulness from my **m**. Gn 24:27
LORD has greatly blessed my **m**, Gn 24:35
a son to my **m** in her old age, Gn 24:36
My **m** put me under this oath: Gn 24:37
But I said to my **m**, 'Suppose the Gn 24:39
LORD, God of my **m** Abraham, if Gn 24:42
the God of my **m** Abraham, who Gn 24:48
and faithfulness to my **m**, Gn 24:49
he said, "Send me to my **m**." Gn 24:54
away so that I may go to my **m**." Gn 24:56
servant answered, "It is my **m**." Gn 24:65
Be **m** over your brothers; Gn 27:29
I have made him a **m** over you, Gn 27:37
the household of his Egyptian **m**. Gn 39:2
When his **m** saw that the LORD was Gn 39:3
my **m** does not concern himself Gn 39:8
her until his **m** came home. Gn 39:16
When his **m** heard the story his Gn 39:19
and his baker offended their **m**, Gn 40:1
cup that my **m** drinks from and Gn 44:5
his **m** gives him a wife and she Ex 21:4
her children belong to her **m**, Ex 21:4
'I love my **m**, my wife, and my Ex 21:5
his **m** is to bring him to the Ex 21:6
His **m** must pierce his ear with Ex 21:6
he will serve his **m** for life. Ex 21:6
If she is displeasing to her **m**, Ex 21:8
of silver to the slave's **m**, Ex 21:32
a slave to his **m** when he has Dt 23:15
has escaped from his **m** to you. Dt 23:15
the servant said to his **m**, Jdg 19:11
But his **m** replied to him, Jdg 19:12
the man's house where her **m** was. Jdg 19:26
her **m** got up in the morning, Jdg 19:27
the arrow and returned to his **m**. 1Sm 20:38
the wilderness to greet our **m**, 1Sm 25:14
trouble for our **m** and his entire 1Sm 25:17
My **m** abandoned me when I got 1Sm 30:13
kill me or turn me over to my **m**, 1Sm 30:15
and my **m** Joab and his soldiers 2Sm 11:11
fled from his **m** Hadadezer king 1Kg 11:23
the LORD said, 'They have no **m**; 1Kg 22:17
will take your **m** away from you?" 2Kg 2:3
will take your **m** away from you?" 2Kg 2:5
them go and search for your **m**. 2Kg 2:16
If only my **m** would go to the 2Kg 5:3
and told his **m** what the girl 2Kg 5:4
When my **m**, ⌊the king of Aram⌋, 2Kg 5:18
My **m** has let this Aramean 2Kg 5:20
My **m** has sent me to say, 'I have 2Kg 5:22
Gehazi came and stood by his **m**. 2Kg 5:25
"Oh, my **m**, it was borrowed!" 2Kg 6:5
Elisha, "Oh, my **m**, what are we 2Kg 6:15
and drink and go to their **m**." 2Kg 6:22
away, and they went to their **m**. 2Kg 6:23
left Elisha and went to his **m**, 2Kg 8:14
house of your **m** Ahab so that I 2Kg 9:7
peace, Zimri, killer of your **m**?" 2Kg 9:31
against my **m** and killed him. 2Kg 10:9
a bargain with my **m** the king of 2Kg 18:23
Has my **m** sent me only to your 2Kg 18:27
me only to your **m** and to you to 2Kg 18:27
whom his **m** the king of Assyria 2Kg 19:4
Tell your **m** this, 'The LORD 2Kg 19:6
if he defects to his **m** Saul." 1Ch 12:19
the LORD said, 'They have no **m**; 2Ch 18:16
man should be **m** of his own house Est 1:22
slave is set free from his **m**. Jb 3:19
are our own—who can be our **m**?" Ps 12:4
He made him **m** of his household, Ps 105:21
after his **m** will be honored Pr 27:18
slander a servant to his **m**, Pr 30:10
jewelry, the handiwork of a **m**. Sg 7:1
servant and **m**, female servant Is 24:2
Now make a deal with my **m**, Is 36:8

Has my **m** sent me to speak these Is 36:12
words to your **m** and to you, Is 36:12
Rabshakeh, whom his **m**, the king Is 37:4
this to your **m**, 'The LORD says Is 37:6
for I am your **m**, and I will take Jr 3:14
father, and a servant his **m**. Mal 1:6
And if I am a **m**, where is ⌊your⌋ Mal 1:6
teacher, or a slave above his **m**. Mt 10:24
teacher and a slave like his **m**. Mt 10:25
him and said, '**M**, didn't you sow Mt 13:27
it back, his **m** commanded that Mt 18:25
Then the **m** of that slave had Mt 18:27
to their **m** everything that Mt 18:31
him, his **m** said to him, 'You Mt 18:32
And his **m** got angry and handed Mt 18:34
you have one **M**, the Messiah. Mt 23:10
whom his **m** has put in charge of Mt 24:45
That slave whose **m** finds him Mt 24:46
in his heart, 'My **m** is delayed,' Mt 24:48
that slave's **m** will come on a Mt 24:50
came and said, '**M**, master, open Mt 25:11
'Master, **m**, open up for us! Mt 25:11
long time the **m** of those slaves Mt 25:19
and said, '**M**, you gave me five Mt 25:20
His **m** said to him, 'Well done, Mt 25:21
He said, '**M**, you gave me two Mt 25:22
His **m** said to him, 'Well done, Mt 25:23
and said, '**M**, I know you. Mt 25:24
But his **m** replied to him, Mt 25:26
know when the **m** of the house is Mk 13:35
Now, **M**, You can dismiss Your Lk 2:29
"**M**," Simon replied, "we've Lk 5:5
up, saying, "**M**, Master, we're Lk 8:24
Master, **M**, we're going to Lk 8:24
Peter said, "**M**, the crowds are Lk 8:45
said to Jesus, "**M**, it's good for Lk 9:33
responded, "**M**, we saw someone Lk 9:49
waiting for their **m** to return Lk 12:36
slaves the **m** will find alert Lk 12:37
manager his **m** will put in charge Lk 12:42
That slave whose **m** finds him Lk 12:43
'My **m** is delaying his coming,' Lk 12:45
that slave's **m** will come on a Lk 12:46
reported these things to his **m**. Lk 14:21
the **m** of the house told his Lk 14:21
'**M**,' the slave said, 'what you Lk 14:22
Then the **m** told the slave, Lk 14:23
since my **m** is taking the Lk 16:3
'How much do you owe my **m**?' Lk 16:5
The **m** praised the unrighteous Lk 16:8
saying, "Jesus, **M**, have mercy on Lk 17:13
and said, '**M**, your mina has Lk 19:16
came and said, '**M**, your mina has Lk 19:18
came and said, '**M**, here is your Lk 19:20
to him, '**M**, he has 10 minas. Lk 19:25
slave is not greater than his **m**, Jn 13:16
know what his **m** is doing. Jn 15:15
is not greater than his **m**.' Jn 15:20
said, "**M**, You are the One who Ac 4:24
as a skilled **m** builder I have 1Co 3:10
their and your **M** is in heaven, Eph 6:9
that you too have a **M** in heaven. Col 4:1
useful to the **M**, prepared for 2Tm 2:21
denying the **M** who bought them 2Pt 2:1
and denying our only **M** and Lord, Jd 4

MASTER'S *(38)*

took 10 of his **m** camels and Gn 24:10
kinds of his **m** goods in hand. Gn 24:10
to the house of my **m** relatives." Gn 24:27
Sarah, my **m** wife, bore a son to Gn 24:36
LORD has appointed for my **m** son. Gn 24:44
daughter of my **m** brother for his Gn 24:48
her be a wife for your **m** son, Gn 24:51
favor in his **m** sight and became Gn 39:4
some time his **m** wife looked Gn 39:7
refused and said to his **m** wife, Gn 39:8
custody with him in his **m** house, Gn 40:7
and silver from your **m** house? Gn 44:8
he regain his **m** favor than with 1Sm 29:4
given to your **m** grandson all 2Sm 9:9
crops⌋ so your **m** grandson will 2Sm 9:10
Mephibosheth, your **m** grandson, 2Sm 9:10
palace with all his **m** servants; 2Sm 11:9
on his cot with his **m** servants, 2Sm 11:13
I gave your **m** house to you and 2Sm 12:8
you and your **m** wives into your 2Sm 12:8
"Where is your **m** son?" 2Sm 16:3
man in his **m** sight and highly 2Kg 5:1
sound of his **m** feet behind him? 2Kg 6:32
Jehu came out to his **m** servants, 2Kg 9:11
since your **m** sons are with you 2Kg 10:2
most qualified of your **m** sons, 2Kg 10:3
and fight for your **m** house. 2Kg 10:3
heads of your **m** sons at this 2Kg 10:6
the least of my **m** servants and 2Kg 18:24
a servant's eyes on His **m** hand, Ps 123:2
the donkey its **m** feeding-trough, Is 1:3
the weakest of my **m** officers, Is 36:9
who fill their **m** house with Zph 1:9
the ground, and hid his **m** money. Mt 25:18
Share your **m** joy!' Mt 25:21
many things. Share your **m** joy!' Mt 25:23
who knew his **m** will and didn't Lk 12:47
each one of his **m** debtors. Lk 16:5

MASTERS *(18)*

are running away from their **m**. 1Sm 25:10
he refreshes the life of his **m**. Pr 25:13
and those from **m** of collections Ec 12:11
Egypt into the hands of harsh **m**, Is 19:4
Command them ⌊to go⌋ to their **m**, Jr 27:4
is what you must say to your **m**: Jr 27:4
adversaries have become ⌊her⌋ **m**; Lm 1:5
No one can be a slave of two **m**, Mt 6:24
And do not be called **m** either, Mt 23:10
slave can be the slave of two **m**, Lk 16:13
obey your human **m** with fear and Eph 6:5
And **m**, treat them the same way, Eph 6:9
obey your human **m** in everything; Col 3:22
M, supply your slaves with what Col 4:1
regard their own **m** to be worthy 1Tm 6:1
have believing **m** should not be 1Tm 6:2
to their **m** in everything, Ti 2:9
to your **m** with all respect, 1Pt 2:18

MASTERS' *(2)*

you and your **m** servants who 1Sm 29:10
that fall from their **m** table!" Mt 15:27

MATCH *(3)*

of them was a **m** for a hundred, 1Ch 12:14
the plane trees **m** its boughs. Ezk 31:8
new garment will not **m** the old. Lk 5:36

MATCHES *(1)*

Your wrath **m** the fear that is Ps 90:11

MATE *(3)*

to an animal to **m** with it; Lv 18:23
gather there, each with its **m**. Is 34:15
none will be lacking its **m**, Is 34:16

MATERIAL *(6)*

garment made of two kinds of **m**. Lv 19:19
Your decrees and not to **m** gain. Ps 119:36
to minister to Jews in **m** needs. Rm 15:27
if we reap **m** things from you 1Co 9:11
godliness is a way to **m** gain. 1Tm 6:5
The building **m** of its wall was Rv 21:18

MATERIALS *(2)*

The **m** were sufficient for them Ex 36:7
of blue and embroidered **m**, Ezk 27:24

MATERNAL *(1)*

and to all his **m** grandfather's Jdg 9:1

MATES *(1)*

near any animal and **m** with it, Lv 20:16

MATING *(3)*

males were **m** with the females. Gn 31:10
males that are **m** with the flocks Gn 31:12
will find her in her **m** season. Jr 2:24

MATRED *(2)*

daughter of **M** daughter of Gn 36:39
was Mehetabel daughter of **M**, 1Ch 1:50

MATRITE *(1)*

and the **M** clan was selected. 1Sm 10:21

MATTAN *(3)*

and they killed **M**, the priest of 2Kg 11:18
images into pieces and killed **M**, 2Ch 23:17
Shephatiah son of **M**, Gedaliah Jr 38:1

MATTANAH *(2)*

went⌋ from the wilderness to **M**, Nm 21:18
M to Nahaliel, from Nahaliel Nm 21:19

MATTANIAH *(16)*
(AKA ZEDEKIAH)

the king of Babylon made **M**, 2Kg 24:17
Galal, and **M**, son of Mica, son 1Ch 9:15
Bukkiah, **M**, Uzziel, Shebuel, 1Ch 25:4
the ninth ⌊to⌋ **M**, his sons, and 1Ch 25:16
son of Jeiel, son of **M**, a Levite 2Ch 20:14
Zechariah and **M** from the 2Ch 29:13
M, Zechariah, Jehiel, Abdi, Ezr 10:26
Eliashib, **M**, Jeremoth, Zabad, Ezr 10:27
Maaseiah, **M**, Bezalel, Binnui, Ezr 10:30
M, Mattenai, Jaasu, Ezr 10:37
M son of Mica, son of Zabdi, son Neh 11:17
son of **M**, son of Mica, Neh 11:22
Judah, and **M**—he and his Neh 12:8
⌊This included⌋ **M**, Bakbukiah, Neh 12:25
son of **M**, son of Micaiah Neh 12:35
Zaccur, son of **M** to assist them, Neh 13:13

MATTATHA *(1)*

Menna, ⌊son⌋ of **M**, ⌊son⌋ of Lk 3:31

MATTATHIAS *(2)*

⌊son⌋ of **M**, ⌊son⌋ of Amos, ⌊son⌋ Lk 3:25
Maath, ⌊son⌋ of **M**, ⌊son⌋ of Lk 3:26

MATTATTAH *(1)*

Mattenai, **M**, Zabad, Eliphelet, Ezr 10:33

MATTENAI *(3)*

M, Mattattah, Zabad, Eliphelet, Ezr 10:33
Mattaniah, **M**, Jaasu, Ezr 10:37
M of Joiarib, Uzzi of Jedaiah, Neh 12:19

MATTER *(81)*

your request about this **m** too, Gn 19:21
oath to him concerning this **m**. Gn 24:9
we have no choice in the **m**. Gn 24:50
his father kept the **m** ⌊in mind⌋. Gn 37:11
it means that the **m** has been Gn 41:32
and the **m** escapes the notice of Lv 4:13
each of them, no **m** how many. Nm 15:12
speak to Me again about this **m**. Dt 3:26
What's the **m** with you that you Jdg 18:23
'What's the **m** with you?'" Jdg 18:24
to make any **m** ⌊legally⌋ binding Ru 4:7
said about the **m** of kingship. 1Sm 10:16
What's the **m** with the people? 1Sm 11:5
would he hide this **m** from me? 1Sm 20:2
As for the **m** you and I have 1Sm 20:23
'Don't let this **m** upset you 2Sm 11:25
with such contempt in this **m**, 2Sm 12:14
"What's the **m**?" the king asked 2Sm 14:5
spoke as he did about this **m**, 2Sm 14:13
to present this **m** to my lord the 2Sm 14:15
knew nothing about the whole **m**. 2Sm 15:11
to Joab, "No **m** what, please let 2Sm 18:22
"No **m** what I want to run!" 2Sm 18:23
except in the **m** of Uriah the 1Kg 15:5
son of Nebat were a trivial **m**, 1Kg 16:31
in a particular **m** may the LORD 2Kg 5:18
pardon your servant in this **m**." 2Kg 5:18
was enraged because of this **m**, 2Kg 6:11
king asked her, "What's the **m**?" 2Kg 6:28
in every **m** relating to God 1Ch 26:32
the king in every **m** to do with 1Ch 27:1
concerning any **m** or concerning 2Ch 8:15
You have been foolish in this **m**, 2Ch 16:9
with you in the **m** of judgment. 2Ch 19:6
See that you not neglect this **m**. Ezr 4:22
instructions about this ⌊**m**⌋. Ezr 5:5
⌊this **m**⌋ be sent to us. Ezr 5:17
for this **m** is your Ezr 10:4
because of this **m** and because of Ezr 10:9
rebelled terribly in this **m**. Ezr 10:13
of our God concerning this **m**." Ezr 10:14
month to investigate the **m**, Ezr 10:16
seriously considering the **m**, Neh 5:7
agent in every **m** concerning the Neh 11:24
if the **m** seems right to the king Est 8:5
when the **m** was brought before Est 9:25
If it is a **m** of strength, look, Jb 9:19
If it is a **m** of justice, who can Jb 9:19
that you are wrong in this ⌊**m**⌋, Jb 33:12
to take the **m** into Your hands. Ps 10:14
understands a **m** finds success, Pr 16:20
God to conceal a **m** and the glory Pr 25:2
of kings to investigate a **m**. Pr 25:2
Don't take a **m** to court hastily. Pr 25:8
No **m** how long he lives, if he is Ec 6:3
end of a **m** is better than its Ec 7:8
knows the interpretation of a **m**? Ec 8:1
creature may report the **m**. Ec 10:20
the conclusion of the **m** is: Ec 12:13
What's the **m** with you? Is 22:1
them in this **m** and tested them Dn 1:14
In every **m** of wisdom and Dn 1:20
and Azariah about the **m**, Dn 2:17

you **m** purchase male and female Lv 25:44
m also purchase them from the Lv 25:45
These **m** become your property. Lv 25:45
You **m** leave them to your sons Lv 25:46
of his brothers **m** redeem him. Lv 25:48
uncle or cousin **m** redeem him, Lv 25:49
from his clan **m** redeem him. Lv 25:49
prospers, he **m** redeem himself. Lv 25:49
the animals that **m** be brought as Lv 27:9
He **m** not replace it or make a Lv 27:10
animals that **m** not be brought as Lv 27:11
so that they **m** live and not die Nm 4:19
'**M** the LORD make you into an Nm 5:21
M this water that brings a curse Nm 5:22
the Nazirite **m** drink wine. Nm 6:20
that they **m** perform the LORD's Nm 8:11
that the Levites **m** come to serve Nm 8:15
He **m** assist his brothers to Nm 8:26
he **m** still observe the Passover Nm 9:10
they **m** not leave any of it until Nm 9:12
after that she **m** be brought back Nm 12:14
m My Lord's power be magnified Nm 14:17
so that they **m** be forgiven, Nm 15:25
so that you **m** remember all the Nm 15:39
community so I **m** consume them Nm 16:21
"The earth **m** swallow us too!" Nm 16:34
so that I **m** consume them Nm 16:45
that you **m** put an end to their Nm 17:10
they **m** join you and serve with Nm 18:2
person **m** come near you. Nm 18:4
altar so that wrath **m** not fall Nm 18:5
Every male **m** eat it; it is to be Nm 18:10
person in your house **m** eat it. Nm 18:11
person in your house **m** eat them. Nm 18:13
household **m** eat it anywhere. Nm 18:31
after that he **m** enter the camp, Nm 19:7
people so I **m** give them water. Nm 21:16
I **m** be able to defeat them and Nm 22:6
m be able to fight against them Nm 22:11
so that I **m** find out what else Nm 22:19
His burning anger **m** turn away Nm 25:4
M the LORD, the God of the Nm 27:16
Her husband **m** confirm or cancel Nm 30:13
that you **m** enter the camp." Nm 31:24
afterwards you **m** return and be Nm 32:22
who kills someone **m** flee there; Nm 35:6
unintentionally **m** flee there. Nm 35:11
unintentionally **m** flee there. Nm 35:15
high priest **m** the one who has Nm 35:28
They **m** marry anyone they like Nm 36:6
M the LORD, the God of your Dt 1:11
so that they **m** explore the land Dt 1:22
You **m** purchase food from them Dt 2:6
so that you **m** eat, and buy water Dt 2:6
exchange for silver so we **m** eat, Dt 2:28
water for silver so we **m** drink. Dt 2:28
Then each of you **m** return to his Dt 3:20
so that you **m** live, enter, Dt 4:1
so that you **m** keep the commands Dt 4:2
so that you **m** follow them in the Dt 4:5
so that they **m** learn to fear Me Dt 4:10
the earth and **m** instruct their Dt 4:10
after you **m** prosper and so Dt 4:40
and so that you **m** live long in Dt 4:40
female slaves **m** rest as you do. Dt 5:14
so that you **m** live long and so Dt 5:16
and so that you **m** prosper in the Dt 5:16
so that they **m** follow ⌊them⌋ in Dt 5:31
so that you **m** live, prosper, Dt 5:33
so that you **m** follow ⌊them⌋ in Dt 6:1
this⌋ so that you **m** fear the Dt 6:2
and so that you **m** have a long Dt 6:2
so that you **m** prosper and Dt 6:3
that you **m** prosper and so that Dt 6:18
and so that you **m** enter and Dt 6:18
so that you **m** live and increase, Dt 8:1
and **m** enter and take possession Dt 8:1
You **m** say to yourself, 'My power Dt 8:17
so that they **m** enter and possess Dt 10:11
so that you **m** have the strength Dt 11:8
and so that you **m** live long in Dt 11:9
your children **m** be many in the Dt 11:21
you **m** slaughter and eat meat Dt 12:15
are clean or unclean **m** eat it, Dt 12:15
Within your gates you **m** not eat: Dt 12:17
you **m** eat it whenever you want. Dt 12:20
you **m** slaughter any of your herd Dt 12:21
and you **m** eat it within your Dt 12:21

you **m** eat it as the gazelle and Dt 12:22
clean and the unclean **m** eat it. Dt 12:22
God, but you **m** eat the meat. Dt 12:27
after you **m** prosper forever, Dt 12:28
These are the animals you **m** eat: Dt 14:4
You **m** eat any animal that has Dt 14:6
You **m** eat everything from the Dt 14:9
but you **m** not eat anything that Dt 14:10
You **m** eat every clean bird, Dt 14:11
are the ones you **m** not eat: Dt 14:12
for you; they **m** not be eaten. Dt 14:19
But you **m** eat every clean flying Dt 14:20
m give it to a resident alien Dt 14:21
gates, and he **m** eat it, or you Dt 14:21
or you **m** sell it to a foreigner. Dt 14:21
m spend the money on anything Dt 14:26
widow within your gates **m** come, Dt 14:29
You **m** collect ⌊something⌋ from a Dt 15:3
person and the clean ⌊**m** eat it⌋, Dt 15:22
so that you **m** remember for the Dt 16:3
so that he **m** learn to fear the Dt 17:19
he **m** serve in the name of the Dt 18:7
You **m** say to yourself, 'How can Dt 18:21
that person **m** flee to one of Dt 19:5
he **m** die in battle and another Dt 20:5
Otherwise he **m** die in battle and Dt 20:6
Otherwise he **m** die in battle and Dt 20:7
But you **m** take the women, Dt 20:14
You **m** enjoy the spoil of your Dt 20:14
But you **m** destroy the trees that Dt 20:20
You **m** cut them down to build Dt 20:20
you **m** have sexual relations with Dt 21:13
You **m** take the young for Dt 22:7
so that you **m** prosper and live Dt 22:7
been cut off **m** enter the LORD's Dt 23:1
birth **m** enter the LORD's Dt 23:2
m enter the LORD's assembly. Dt 23:2
or Moabite **m** enter the LORD's Dt 23:3
m ever enter the LORD's assembly. Dt 23:3
generation **m** enter the LORD's Dt 23:8
m not come anywhere inside the Dt 23:10
sun sets he **m** come inside the Dt 23:11
You **m** charge a foreigner Dt 23:20
the LORD your God **m** bless you Dt 23:20
you **m** eat as many grapes as you Dt 23:24
you **m** pluck heads of grain with Dt 23:25
he **m** write her a divorce Dt 24:1
sent her away **m** not marry her Dt 24:4
LORD your God **m** bless you in all Dt 24:19
He **m** be flogged with 40 lashes, Dt 25:3
of the dead man **m** not marry a Dt 25:5
so that you **m** live long in the Dt 25:15
so that they **m** eat in your towns Dt 26:12
so that you **m** enter into the Dt 29:12
that you **m** enter into His oath Dt 29:12
and so that He **m** establish you Dt 29:13
people and He **m** be your God as Dt 29:13
he **m** bless himself in his mind, Dt 29:19
that we **m** follow all the words Dt 29:29
to us so that we **m** follow it?' Dt 30:12
to us so that we **m** follow it?' Dt 30:13
heart, so that you **m** follow it. Dt 30:14
so that you **m** live and multiply, Dt 30:16
the LORD your God **m** bless you in Dt 30:16
you and your descendants **m** live, Dt 30:19
so that they **m** listen and learn Dt 31:12
so that I **m** commission him." Dt 31:14
that this song **m** be a witness Dt 31:19
so that it **m** remain there as a Dt 31:26
so that I **m** speak these words Dt 31:28
so that you **m** command your Dt 32:46
but **m** You be a help against his Dt 33:7
M his land be blessed by the Dt 33:13
M these rest on the head of Dt 33:16
M Asher be the most blessed of Dt 33:24
m he be the most favored among Dt 33:24
M the bolts of your gate be iron Dt 33:25
so that you **m** carefully observe Jos 1:8
and livestock **m** remain in the Jos 1:14
You **m** then return to the land of Jos 1:15
And **m** the LORD your God be with Jos 1:17
people of the earth **m** know that Jos 4:24
so that you **m** always fear the Jos 4:24
you **m** plunder its spoil and Jos 8:2
or accidentally **m** flee there. Jos 20:3
manslaughter **m** return home to Jos 20:6
unintentionally **m** flee there and Jos 20:9
knows, and **m** Israel also know. Jos 22:22

M the LORD Himself hold us Jos 22:23
So your descendants **m** cause our Jos 22:25
so that we **m** carry out the Jos 22:27
m all your enemies perish as Jdg 5:31
But **m** those who love Him be like Jdg 5:31
and trembling **m** turn back and Jdg 7:3
of Shechem, and **m** God listen to Jdg 9:7
m fire come out from the bramble Jdg 9:15
Abimelech and **m** he also rejoice Jdg 9:19
m fire come from Abimelech and Jdg 9:20
and **m** fire come from the lords Jdg 9:20
true that you **m** possess whatever Jdg 11:24
and we **m** possess everything the Jdg 11:24
so that we **m** honor You when Your Jdg 13:17
M the LORD show faithful love to Ru 1:8
M the LORD enable each of you to Ru 1:9
M the LORD do this to me, and Ru 1:17
M the LORD reward you for what Ru 2:12
and **m** you receive a full reward Ru 2:12
M ⌊the LORD⌋ bless the man who Ru 2:19
M he be blessed by the LORD, Ru 2:20
Then he said, "**M** the LORD bless Ru 3:10
M the LORD make the woman who Ru 4:11
M you be powerful in Ephrathah Ru 4:11
M your house become like the Ru 4:12
M his name be famous in Israel. Ru 4:14
m the God of Israel grant the 1Sm 1:17
M your servant find favor with 1Sm 1:18
M the LORD confirm your word." 1Sm 1:23
M the LORD give you children by 1Sm 2:20
M God punish you and do so 1Sm 3:17
so I **m** judge you before the LORD 1Sm 12:7
M God punish me severely if you 1Sm 14:44
him, Saul said, "**M** the LORD 1Sm 15:13
and **m** the LORD be with you." 1Sm 17:37
then **m** God punish Jonathan and 1Sm 20:13
M the LORD be with you, just as 1Sm 20:13
M the LORD hold David's 1Sm 20:16
the young men **m** eat it only if 1Sm 21:4
"**M** you be blessed by the LORD," 1Sm 23:21
M the LORD judge between you 1Sm 24:12
m the LORD take vengeance on 1Sm 24:12
M the LORD be judge and decide 1Sm 24:15
M He take notice and plead my 1Sm 24:15
M the LORD repay you with good 1Sm 24:19
M God punish me, and even more 1Sm 25:22
M your enemies and those who 1Sm 25:26
m evil not be found in you. 1Sm 25:28
m you remember ⌊me⌋ your 1Sm 25:31
m my lord the king please hear 1Sm 26:19
then **m** He accept an offering. 1Sm 26:19
m they be cursed in the presence 1Sm 26:19
M the LORD repay every man for 1Sm 26:23
so **m** the LORD consider my life 1Sm 26:24
They **m** take them and go." 1Sm 30:22
m the LORD show special kindness 2Sm 2:6
M God punish Abner and do so 2Sm 3:9
M it hang over Joab's head and 2Sm 3:29
and **m** the house of Joab never be 2Sm 3:29
M God punish me and do so 2Sm 3:35
M the LORD repay the evildoer 2Sm 3:39
that they **m** live there and not 2Sm 7:10
M the LORD's will be done." 2Sm 10:12
He **m** do something desperate." 2Sm 12:18
The LORD **m** be gracious to me 2Sm 12:22
brother so we **m** put him to death 2Sm 14:7
m any blame be on me and my 2Sm 14:9
and **m** the king and his throne be 2Sm 14:9
m the king invoke the LORD your 2Sm 14:11
m your servant speak a word to 2Sm 14:12
M the word of my lord the king 2Sm 14:17
M the LORD your God be with 2Sm 14:17
He **m** return to his house, 2Sm 14:24
but he **m** not see my face." 2Sm 14:24
M the LORD show you kindness 2Sm 15:20
M you look favorably on me, 2Sm 16:4
You **m** do it another day, but 2Sm 18:20
M the LORD your God be praised! 2Sm 18:28
M my lord the king hear the good 2Sm 18:31
M what has become of the young 2Sm 18:32
M God punish me and do so 2Sm 19:13
M the king not take it to heart. 2Sm 19:19
myself so that I **m** ride it and 2Sm 19:26
return so that I **m** die in my own 2Sm 19:37
over to us so we **m** hang them 2Sm 21:6
The LORD lives—**m** my rock be 2Sm 22:47
M the LORD your God multiply the 2Sm 24:3
on the people **m** be halted." 2Sm 24:21

lord the king **m** take whatever he 2Sm 24:22
M the LORD your God accept you 2Sm 24:23
M my lord King David live 1Kg 1:31
M the LORD, the God of my lord 1Kg 1:36
so **m** He be with Solomon and 1Kg 1:37
'**M** your God make the name of 1Kg 1:47
and **m** He make his throne greater 1Kg 1:47
'**M** the LORD God of Israel be 1Kg 1:48
then asked, "**M** I talk with you? 1Kg 2:14
M God punish me and do so 1Kg 2:23
M the LORD be praised today! 1Kg 5:7
M the LORD God of Israel be 1Kg 8:15
so that You **m** hear the cry and 1Kg 8:28
that Your eyes **m** watch over this 1Kg 8:29
so that You **m** hear the prayer 1Kg 8:29
M You hear in Your dwelling 1Kg 8:30
place in heaven. **M** You hear and 1Kg 8:30
m You hear in heaven and act. 1Kg 8:32
M You judge Your servants, 1Kg 8:32
m You hear in heaven and forgive 1Kg 8:34
M You restore them to the land 1Kg 8:34
m You hear in heaven and forgive 1Kg 8:36
that You **m** teach them the good 1Kg 8:36
M You send rain on Your land 1Kg 8:36
m You hear in heaven, Your 1Kg 8:39
place, and **m** You forgive, act, 1Kg 8:39
so that they **m** fear You all the 1Kg 8:40
m You hear in heaven, Your 1Kg 8:43
m You hear their prayer and 1Kg 8:45
m You hear in heaven, Your 1Kg 8:49
M You forgive Your people who 1Kg 8:50
and **m** You give them compassion 1Kg 8:50
so that they **m** be compassionate 1Kg 8:50
M Your eyes be open to Your 1Kg 8:52
M the LORD be praised! He has 1Kg 8:56
M the LORD our God be with us as 1Kg 8:57
M He not abandon us or leave us. 1Kg 8:57
M He incline our hearts toward 1Kg 8:58
M my words I have made my 1Kg 8:59
that He **m** uphold His servant's 1Kg 8:59
the earth **m** know that the LORD 1Kg 8:60
M the LORD your God be praised! 1Kg 10:9
so that my hand **m** be restored to 1Kg 13:6
house so that he **m** eat bread and 1Kg 13:18
you **m** make some for yourself 1Kg 17:13
of the LORD **m** carry you off to 1Kg 18:12
M the gods punish me and do so 1Kg 19:2
M the gods punish me and do so 1Kg 20:10
so that you **m** know that I am 1Kg 20:13
you **m** set up marketplaces for 1Kg 20:34
m fire come down from heaven 2Kg 1:10
m fire come down from heaven 2Kg 1:12
matter **m** the LORD pardon 2Kg 5:18
m the LORD pardon your servant 2Kg 5:18
M God punish me and do so 2Kg 6:31
so that I **m** avenge the blood 2Kg 9:7
one of you **m** eat from his own 2Kg 18:31
and every one **m** drink water from 2Kg 18:31
so that you **m** live and not die. 2Kg 18:32
of the earth **m** know that You are 2Kg 19:19
priest so that he **m** total up the 2Kg 22:4
m the God of our ancestors look 1Ch 12:17
but the Levites **m** carry the ark 1Ch 15:2
so that you **m** bring the ark 1Ch 15:12
so that we **m** give thanks to 1Ch 16:35
M the LORD, the God of Israel, 1Ch 16:36
that they **m** live there and not 1Ch 17:9
M the house of Your servant 1Ch 17:24
house that it **m** continue before 1Ch 17:27
M the LORD's will be done." 1Ch 19:13
M the LORD multiply the number 1Ch 21:3
plot so that I **m** build an altar 1Ch 21:22
on the people **m** be halted." 1Ch 21:22
lord the king **m** do whatever he 1Ch 21:23
Now, my son, **m** the LORD be with 1Ch 22:11
m you succeed in building the 1Ch 22:11
m the LORD give you insight and 1Ch 22:12
Israel so that you **m** keep the 1Ch 22:12
and **m** the LORD be with you." 1Ch 22:16
so that you **m** bring the ark 1Ch 22:19
God so that you **m** possess this 1Ch 28:8
David said, "**M** You be praised, 1Ch 29:10
so that I **m** lead these people, 2Ch 1:10
that you **m** judge My people 2Ch 1:11
M the LORD God of Israel, who 2Ch 2:12
any design that **m** be given him. 2Ch 2:14
M the LORD God of Israel be 2Ch 6:4
so that You **m** hear the cry and 2Ch 6:19

so that You **m** hear the prayer 2Ch 6:20
M You hear in Your dwelling 2Ch 6:21
place in heaven. **M** You hear and 2Ch 6:21
m You hear in heaven and act. 2Ch 6:23
M You judge Your servants, 2Ch 6:23
m You hear in heaven and forgive 2Ch 6:25
M You restore them to the land 2Ch 6:25
m You hear in heaven and forgive 2Ch 6:27
that You **m** teach them the good 2Ch 6:27
M You send rain on Your land 2Ch 6:27
m You hear in heaven, Your 2Ch 6:30
and **m** You forgive and repay the 2Ch 6:30
so that they **m** fear You and walk 2Ch 6:31
m You hear in heaven in Your 2Ch 6:33
m You hear their prayer and 2Ch 6:35
m You hear in heaven, in Your 2Ch 6:39
M You forgive Your people who 2Ch 6:39
M Your priests, LORD God, be 2Ch 6:41
and **m** Your godly people rejoice 2Ch 6:41
so that My name **m** be there 2Ch 7:16
M the LORD your God be praised! 2Ch 9:8
so that they **m** recognize 2Ch 12:8
and seven rams **m** become a priest 2Ch 13:9
m the terror of the LORD be on 2Ch 19:7
m the LORD be with those who do 2Ch 19:11
they **m** enter because they are 2Ch 23:6
M the LORD see and demand an 2Ch 24:22
fierce wrath **m** turn away from 2Ch 29:10
so that He **m** return to those 2Ch 30:6
God so that He **m** turn His fierce 2Ch 30:8
M the good LORD provide 2Ch 30:18
among you of His people **m** go 2Ch 36:23
m the LORD his God be with him. 2Ch 36:23
His people, **m** his God be with Ezr 1:3
m he go to Jerusalem in Judah Ezr 1:3
You **m** have no part with us in Ezr 4:3
M the God who caused His name to Ezr 6:12
go to Jerusalem, **m** go with you. Ezr 7:13
You **m** do whatever seems best to Ezr 7:18
You **m** use the royal treasury to Ezr 7:20
to the king, "**M** the king live Neh 2:3
buried, so that I **m** rebuild it." Neh 2:5
M God likewise shake from his Neh 5:13
M he be shaken out and have Neh 5:13
and **m** it be exalted above all Neh 9:5
so that they **m** assemble all the Est 2:3
m the king and Haman come today Est 5:4
m the king and Haman come to the Est 5:8
You **m** write in the king's name Est 8:8
m the Jews who are in Susa also Est 9:13
and **m** ⌊the bodies of⌋ Haman's 10 Est 9:13
M the day I was born perish, Jb 3:3
M God above not care about it, Jb 3:4
M darkness and gloom reclaim it, Jb 3:5
M an eclipse of the sun terrify Jb 3:5
M it not appear among the days Jb 3:6
Yes, **m** that night be barren; Jb 3:7
m no joyful shout be heard in it. Jb 3:7
M its morning stars grow dark. Jb 3:9
M it wait for daylight but have Jb 3:9
m it not see the breaking of Jb 3:9
The lion **m** roar and the fierce Jb 4:10
m my cry for help find no Jb 16:18
so that you **m** know there is a Jb 19:29
His bones **m** be full of youthful Jb 20:11
spoken, you **m** continue mocking Jb 21:3
himself, so that he **m** know ⌊it⌋. Jb 21:19
M my enemy be like the wicked Jb 27:7
he **m** heap ⌊it⌋ up, but the Jb 27:17
Food **m** come from the earth, Jb 28:5
so that he **m** bring to light Jb 28:11
but a person **m** not notice it. Jb 33:14
A person **m** be disciplined on his Jb 33:19
so he **m** shine with the light of Jb 33:30
so that all men **m** know His work. Jb 37:7
You **m** come this far, but no Jb 38:11
so it **m** seize the edges of the Jb 38:13
that a foot **m** crush them or that Jb 39:15
some wild animal **m** trample them. Jb 39:15
that her labor **m** have been in Jb 39:16
for His anger **m** ignite at any Ps 2:12
m Your blessing be on Your Ps 3:8
M You shelter them, and may Ps 5:11
and **m** those who love Your name Ps 5:11
m an enemy pursue and overtake Ps 7:5
m he trample me to the ground Ps 7:5
so that I **m** declare all Your Ps 9:14
of the earth **m** terrify ⌊them⌋ Ps 10:18

M the LORD cut off all Ps 12:3
The LORD lives—**m** my rock be Ps 18:46
M the words of my mouth and the Ps 19:14
M the LORD answer you in a day Ps 20:1
m the name of Jacob's God Ps 20:1
M He send you help from the Ps 20:2
M He remember all your offerings Ps 20:3
M He give you what your heart Ps 20:4
M the LORD fulfill all your Ps 20:5
M He answer us on the day that Ps 20:9
M your hearts live forever! Ps 22:26
Who **m** ascend the mountain of the Ps 24:3
Who **m** stand in His holy place? Ps 24:3
M integrity and uprightness keep Ps 25:21
M the LORD be praised, for He Ps 28:6
Weeping **m** spend the night, Ps 30:5
M the LORD be praised, for He Ps 31:21
at a time that You **m** be found. Ps 32:6
M Your faithful love rest on us, Ps 33:22
ways so that I **m** not sin with my Ps 39:1
from me so that I **m** be cheered Ps 39:13
M the LORD, the God of Israel, Ps 41:13
M your right hand show your Ps 45:4
that he **m** live forever and not Ps 49:9
those You love **m** be rescued. Ps 60:5
m his years span many Ps 61:6
M he sit enthroned before God Ps 61:7
M God be praised! He has not Ps 66:20
M God be gracious to us and Ps 67:1
so that Your way **m** be known on Ps 67:2
M the Lord be praised! Day after Ps 68:19
that your foot **m** wade in blood Ps 68:23
dogs' tongues **m** have their share Ps 68:23
to His people. **M** God be praised! Ps 68:35
m no one live in their tents. Ps 69:25
M my adversaries be disgraced Ps 71:13
m those who seek my harm be Ps 71:13
M the mountains bring prosperity Ps 72:3
M he vindicate the afflicted Ps 72:4
M he continue while the sun Ps 72:5
M he be like rain that falls on Ps 72:6
M the righteous flourish in his Ps 72:7
m he rule from sea to sea and Ps 72:8
M desert tribes kneel before him Ps 72:9
M the kings of Tarshish and the Ps 72:10
M he live long! May gold from Ps 72:15
M gold from Sheba be given to Ps 72:15
M prayer be offered for him Ps 72:15
m he be blessed all day long. Ps 72:15
M there be plenty of grain in Ps 72:16
m it wave on the tops of the Ps 72:16
M its crops be like Lebanon. Ps 72:16
M people flourish in the cities Ps 72:16
M his name endure forever; Ps 72:17
the sun shines, **m** his fame Ps 72:17
M all nations be blessed by him Ps 72:17
M the LORD God, the God of Ps 72:18
M His glorious name be praised Ps 72:19
My flesh and my heart **m** fail, Ps 73:26
M they know that You alone— Ps 83:18
Your people **m** rejoice in You? Ps 85:6
so that glory **m** dwell in our Ps 85:9
M my prayer reach Your presence; Ps 88:2
M the LORD be praised forever. Ps 89:52
so that we **m** develop wisdom Ps 90:12
love so that we **m** shout with joy Ps 90:14
so that they **m** sit down with me Ps 101:6
the way of integrity **m** serve me. Ps 101:6
M the glory of the LORD endure Ps 104:31
m the LORD rejoice in His works. Ps 104:31
M my meditation be pleasing to Ps 104:34
M sinners vanish from the earth Ps 104:35
so that I **m** enjoy the prosperity Ps 106:5
so that we **m** give thanks to Your Ps 106:47
M the LORD, the God of Israel, Ps 106:48
those You love **m** be rescued. Ps 108:6
so they **m** know that this is Your Ps 109:27
M the LORD add to ⌊your numbers⌋ Ps 115:14
M you be blessed by the LORD, Ps 115:15
so that I **m** not sin against Ps 119:11
LORD, **m** You be praised; teach me Ps 119:12
eyes so that I **m** see wonderful Ps 119:18
M Your faithful love comfort me, Ps 119:76
M Your compassion come to me Ps 119:77
come to me so that I **m** live, Ps 119:77
M my heart be blameless Ps 119:80
so that I **m** obey my God's Ps 119:115
so that I **m** know Your decrees. Ps 119:125

M Your hand be ready to help me Ps 119:173
m Your judgments help me. Ps 119:175
M those who love you prosper; Ps 122:6
m there be peace within your Ps 122:7
M the LORD bless you from Zion, Ps 128:5
M the LORD's blessing be on you. Ps 129:8
so that You **m** be revered. Ps 130:4
M Your priests be clothed with Ps 132:9
m Your godly people shout for Ps 132:9
M the LORD, Maker of heaven and Ps 134:3
M the LORD be praised from Zion; Ps 135:21
m my right hand forget ⌊its Ps 137:5
M my tongue stick to the roof of Ps 137:6
M my prayer be set before You as Ps 141:2
M Your gracious Spirit lead me Ps 143:10
M the LORD my rock be praised, Ps 144:1
so that He **m** guard the paths of Pr 2:8
that you **m** gain understanding, Pr 4:1
so that ⌊you⌋ **m** maintain Pr 5:2
in laughter a heart **m** be sad, Pr 14:13
be sad, and joy **m** end in grief. Pr 14:13
so that he **m** avoid going down to Pr 15:24
with many friends **m** be harmed, Pr 18:24
He **m** pursue ⌊them with⌋ words, Pr 19:7
so that you **m** be wise in later Pr 19:20
confidence **m** be in the LORD. Pr 22:19
so that you **m** give a dependable Pr 22:21
yet a man **m** sin for a piece of Pr 28:21
m ravens of the valley pluck it Pr 30:17
so that God **m** test them and they Ec 3:18
them and they **m** see for Ec 3:18
man **m** father a hundred children Ec 6:3
face is sad, a heart **m** be glad. Ec 7:3
or you **m** hear your servant Ec 7:21
who digs a pit **m** fall into it, Ec 10:8
through a wall **m** be bitten by a Ec 10:8
stones **m** be hurt by them Ec 10:9
who splits trees **m** be endangered Ec 10:9
bird of the sky **m** carry the Ec 10:20
winged creature **m** report the Ec 10:20
after many days you **m** find it. Ec 11:1
what disaster **m** happen on earth. Ec 11:2
back, that we **m** look at you! Sg 6:13
M your breasts be like clusters Sg 7:8
so that we **m** walk in His paths. Is 2:3
of the earth **m** know that You are Is 37:20
skin, so that he **m** recover." Is 38:21
Youths **m** faint and grow weary, Is 40:30
so that all **m** see and know, Is 41:20
so that we **m** reflect on it and Is 41:22
you blind, so that you **m** see. Is 42:18
so that people **m** hear and say, Is 43:9
that you **m** know and believe Me Is 43:10
so that you **m** be vindicated. Is 43:26
so that you **m** know that I, Is 45:3
so that all **m** know from the Is 45:6
room for me so that I **m** settle. Is 49:20
the LORD while He **m** be found; Is 55:6
so He **m** have compassion on him, Is 55:7
of the nations **m** be brought into Is 60:11
hands, so that I **m** be glorified. Is 60:21
so that you **m** nurse and be Is 66:11
as a woman **m** betray her lover, Jr 3:20
you **m** know and assay their way Jr 6:27
so that it **m** go well with you. Jr 7:23
spoken to, that he **m** explain it? Jr 9:12
so that our eyes **m** overflow with Jr 9:18
day and night **m** ⌊they⌋ not stop, Jr 14:17
said, "Amen! **M** the LORD do so. Jr 28:6
M the LORD make the words you Jr 28:6
come true and **m** He restore the Jr 28:6
so that they **m** bear sons Jr 29:6
M the LORD make you like Jr 29:22
M the LORD bless you, righteous Jr 31:23
where shepherds **m** rest flocks. Jr 33:12
My servant David **m** be broken so Jr 33:21
He **m** serve you six years, but Jr 34:14
so you **m** live a long time on the Jr 35:7
M my petition come before you. Jr 37:20
They **m** hand me over to them to Jr 38:19
so it **m** go well for you and you Jr 38:20
M our petition come before you; Jr 42:2
LORD your God **m** tell us the way Jr 42:3
m the LORD be a true and Jr 42:5
so that it **m** go well with us. Jr 42:6
so you **m** know that My words of Jr 44:29
M you not become faint-hearted Jr 51:46
so that they **m** become like me. Lm 1:21

you to, so that I **m** console you, Lm 2:13
M Your curse be on them! Lm 3:65
us to Yourself, so we **m** return; Lm 5:21
so they **m** follow My statutes, Ezk 11:20
so that I **m** take hold of the Ezk 14:5
of Israel **m** no longer stray Ezk 14:11
They **m** have escaped from the Ezk 15:7
so that it **m** bear branches, Ezk 17:23
But you **m** ask: Why doesn't the Ezk 18:19
you **m** know that I am the LORD Ezk 20:20
their hearts **m** melt and many may Ezk 21:15
may melt and many **m** stumble. Ezk 21:15
so that they **m** live securely in Ezk 34:25
slain so that they **m** live!" Ezk 37:9
so that the nations **m** know Me, Ezk 38:16
sons of Levi who **m** approach the Ezk 40:46
so that they **m** be ashamed of Ezk 43:10
sight so that they **m** observe its Ezk 43:11
statutes and **m** carry them out. Ezk 43:11
burnt offerings **m** be sacrificed Ezk 43:18
it and blood **m** be sprinkled on Ezk 43:18
heart and flesh, **m** enter My Ezk 44:9
are the ones who **m** enter My Ezk 44:16
They **m** not shave their heads or Ezk 44:20
No priest **m** drink wine before he Ezk 44:21
priest **m** not come ⌊near⌋ a dead Ezk 44:25
m defile himself for a father, Ezk 44:25
that a blessing **m** rest on your Ezk 44:30
The priests **m** not eat any bird Ezk 44:31
M the king live forever. Dn 2:4
M the king tell the dream to his Dn 2:7
M the name of God be praised Dn 2:20
and that you **m** understand the Dn 2:30
Nebuchadnezzar, "**M** the king live Dn 3:9
M your prosperity increase. Dn 4:1
m the dream apply to those who Dn 4:19
m my advice seem good to you my Dn 4:27
"**M** the king live forever," Dn 5:10
king, "You **m** keep your gifts, Dn 5:17
M King Darius live forever. Dn 6:6
to Daniel, "**M** your God, whom Dn 6:16
M the king live forever. Dn 6:21
M your prosperity abound. Dn 6:25
m Your anger and wrath turn away Dn 9:16
fall so that they **m** be refined, Dn 11:35
that he **m** save you in all your Hs 13:10
so that we **m** repay You with Hs 14:2
He **m** turn and relent and leave a Jl 2:14
and not evil so that you **m** live, Am 5:14
Moon be over so we **m** sell grain, Am 8:5
Sabbath, so we **m** market wheat? Am 8:5
so that they **m** possess the Am 9:12
the sea so it **m** quiet down for Jnh 1:12
knows? God **m** turn and relent; Jnh 3:9
He **m** turn from His burning anger Jnh 3:9
ways so we **m** walk in His paths. Mc 4:2
so that you **m** acknowledge the Mc 6:5
tablets so one **m** easily read it. Hab 2:2
It **m** be plated with gold and Hab 2:19
all of them **m** call on the name Zph 3:9
M the LORD who has chosen Zch 3:2
Though it **m** seem incredible to Zch 8:6
M a sword strike his arm and his Zch 11:17
M his arm wither away and his Zch 11:17
residents **m** not be greater than Zch 12:7
They **m** build, but I will Mal 1:4
covenant with Levi **m** continue," Mal 2:4
m the LORD cut off any Mal 2:12
so that there **m** be food in My Mal 3:10
so that they **m** see your good Mt 5:16
so that you **m** be sons of your Mt 5:45
that your giving **m** be in secret. Mt 6:4
But so you **m** know that the Son Mt 9:6
of heaven **m** be compared to Mt 13:24
every fact **m** be established. Mt 18:16
these two sons of mine **m** sit, Mt 20:21
M no fruit ever come from you Mt 21:19
of heaven **m** be compared to Mt 22:2
outside of it **m** also become Mt 23:26
your escape **m** not be in winter Mt 24:20
the Passover so You **m** eat it?" Mt 26:17
His disciples **m** come, steal Him, Mt 27:64
so that I **m** preach there too. Mk 1:38
But so you **m** know that the Son Mk 2:10
blasphemies they **m** blaspheme. Mk 3:28
so that they **m** look and look, Mk 4:12
they **m** listen and listen, yet Mk 4:12
the pigs, so we **m** enter them." Mk 5:12

Because of this reply, you **m** go. Mk 7:29
M no one ever eat fruit from you Mk 11:14
or there **m** be rioting among the Mk 14:2
the Passover so You **m** eat it?" Mk 14:12
so that we **m** see and believe." Mk 15:32
so that you **m** know the certainty Lk 1:4
M it be done to me according to Lk 1:38
of many hearts **m** be revealed." Lk 2:35
But so you **m** know that the Son Lk 5:24
so that Looking they **m** not see, Lk 8:10
hearing they **m** not understand. Lk 8:10
that they **m** not believe and be Lk 8:12
who come in **m** see the light. Lk 8:16
who come in **m** see its light. Lk 11:33
this generation **m** be held Lk 11:50
person than you **m** have been Lk 14:8
both of you **m** come and say to Lk 14:9
so that my house **m** be filled. Lk 14:23
they **m** welcome you into eternal Lk 16:9
that you **m** have strength to Lk 21:36
that you **m** eat and drink at My Lk 22:30
you that your faith **m** not fail. Lk 22:32
Pray that you **m** not enter into Lk 22:40
that his deeds **m** not be exposed. Jn 3:20
that his works **m** be shown to be Jn 3:21
things so that you **m** be saved. Jn 5:34
come to Me that you **m** have life. Jn 5:40
to do so we **m** see and believe Jn 6:30
believes in Him **m** have eternal Jn 6:40
so that anyone **m** eat of it and Jn 6:50
Sir, that I **m** believe in Him? Jn 9:36
come that they **m** have life and Jn 10:10
My life so I **m** take it up again Jn 10:17
the Son of God **m** be glorified Jn 11:4
there so that you **m** believe. Jn 11:15
go so that we **m** die with Him." Jn 11:16
so they **m** believe You sent Me." Jn 11:42
light so that you **m** become sons Jn 12:36
that where I am you **m** be also. Jn 14:3
that the Father **m** be glorified Jn 14:13
it does happen you **m** believe. Jn 14:29
that the world **m** know that I Jn 14:31
so that My joy **m** be in you and Jn 15:11
you and your joy **m** be complete. Jn 15:11
time comes you **m** remember I told Jn 16:4
that your joy **m** be complete. Jn 16:24
so that in Me you **m** have peace. Jn 16:33
so that the Son **m** glorify You, Jn 17:1
so He **m** give eternal life to all Jn 17:2
that they **m** know You, the only Jn 17:3
so that they **m** be one as We are Jn 17:11
the Scripture **m** be fulfilled. Jn 17:12
world so that they **m** have My joy Jn 17:13
so they also **m** be sanctified by Jn 17:19
M they all be one, as You, Jn 17:21
M they also be one in Us, so the Jn 17:21
so the world **m** believe You sent Jn 17:21
M they be one as We are one. Jn 17:22
M they be made completely one, Jn 17:23
the world **m** know You have sent Jn 17:23
loved Me with **m** be in them and I Jn 17:26
be in them and I **m** be in them. Jn 17:26
so that you also **m** believe. Jn 19:35
so that you **m** believe Jesus is Jn 20:31
believing you **m** have life in His Jn 20:31
that your sins **m** be wiped out so Ac 3:19
seasons of refreshing **m** come Ac 3:19
He **m** send Jesus, who has been Ac 3:20
that Your slaves **m** speak Your Ac 4:29
You **m** even be found fighting Ac 5:39
lay hands on **m** receive the Holy Ac 8:19
M your silver be destroyed with Ac 8:20
of your heart **m** be forgiven you. Ac 8:22
you have said **m** happen to me." Ac 8:24
with all your heart you **m**." Ac 8:37
on him so he **m** regain his sight. Ac 9:12
sent me so you **m** regain your Ac 9:17
of mankind **m** seek the Lord— Ac 15:17
M we learn about this new Ac 17:19
our business **m** be discredited, Ac 19:27
goddess Artemis **m** be despised Ac 19:27
so that I **m** finish my course and Ac 20:24
I **m** have something to write. Ac 25:26
eyes that they **m** turn from Ac 26:18
that they **m** receive forgiveness Ac 26:18
m now at last succeed in coming Rm 1:10
that I **m** impart to you some Rm 1:11
That You **m** be justified in Your Rm 3:4

us do evil so that good **m** come"? Rm 3:8
that every mouth **m** be shut and Rm 3:19
the whole world **m** become subject Rm 3:19
righteousness **m** be credited to Rm 4:11
so that it **m** be according to Rm 4:16
in order that grace **m** multiply? Rm 6:1
so we too **m** walk in a new way of Rm 6:4
over the body **m** be abolished, Rm 6:6
so that we **m** no longer be Rm 6:6
that you **m** belong to another— Rm 7:4
that we **m** bear fruit for God. Rm 7:4
that we **m** serve in the new way Rm 7:6
Him so that we **m** also be Rm 8:17
so that I **m** display My power in Rm 9:17
and that My name **m** be proclaimed Rm 9:17
they also now **m** receive mercy. Rm 11:31
so that He **m** have mercy on all. Rm 11:32
that you **m** discern what is the Rm 12:2
believes he **m** eat anything, Rm 14:2
the Scriptures we **m** have hope. Rm 15:4
Now **m** the God of endurance and Rm 15:5
that you **m** glorify the God and Rm 15:6
that Gentiles **m** glorify God for Rm 15:9
Now **m** the God of hope fill you Rm 15:13
so that you **m** overflow with hope Rm 15:13
of the Gentiles **m** be acceptable, Rm 15:16
that I **m** be rescued from the Rm 15:31
for Jerusalem **m** be acceptable to Rm 15:31
I **m** come to you with joy and be Rm 15:32
matter she **m** require your help. Rm 16:2
mind, that he **m** instruct Him? 1Co 2:16
so that you **m** learn from us the 1Co 4:6
so that his spirit **m** be saved in 1Co 5:5
so that you **m** be a new batch, 1Co 5:7
Satan **m** tempt you because of 1Co 7:5
Lord—how he **m** please the Lord 1Co 7:32
how he **m** please his wife— 1Co 7:33
so that she **m** be holy both in 1Co 7:34
how she **m** please her husband. 1Co 7:34
and so that you **m** be devoted to 1Co 7:35
so that I **m** by all means save 1Co 9:22
that I **m** become a partner in its 1Co 9:23
in such a way that you **m** win. 1Co 9:24
of many, that they **m** be saved. 1Co 10:33
among you **m** be recognized. 1Co 11:19
so that we **m** not be condemned 1Co 11:32
above all that you **m** prophesy. 1Co 14:1
that the church **m** be built up. 1Co 14:5
For you **m** very well be giving 1Co 14:17
so that everyone **m** learn and 1Co 14:31
and everyone **m** be encouraged. 1Co 14:31
so that God **m** be all in all. 1Co 15:28
that you **m** send me on my way 1Co 16:6
so that we **m** be able to comfort 2Co 1:4
that thanks **m** be given by many 2Co 1:11
this one **m** be overwhelmed by 2Co 2:7
so I **m** know your proven 2Co 2:9
so that we **m** not be taken 2Co 2:11
power **m** be from God and not 2Co 4:7
life of Jesus **m** also be revealed 2Co 4:10
Jesus' life **m** also be revealed 2Co 4:11
m cause thanksgiving to overflow 2Co 4:15
that mortality **m** be swallowed up 2Co 5:4
that each **m** be repaid for what 2Co 5:10
so that you **m** have a reply for 2Co 5:12
so there **m** also be a completion 2Co 8:11
not that there **m** be relief for 2Co 8:13
their abundance **m** also become 2Co 8:14
need, that there **m** be equality. 2Co 8:14
you **m** excel in every good work. 2Co 9:8
that we **m** preach the gospel to 2Co 10:16
your minds **m** be corrupted from a 2Co 11:3
so I too **m** boast a little. 2Co 11:16
Christ's power **m** reside in me. 2Co 12:9
and I **m** not be found by you to 2Co 12:20
there **m** be quarreling, jealousy, 2Co 12:20
not that we **m** appear to pass the 2Co 13:7
but that you **m** do what is right, 2Co 13:7
though we ⌊**m** appear⌋ to fail 2Co 13:7
M peace be on all those who Gl 6:16
of your heart **m** be enlightened Eph 1:18
enlightened so you **m** know what Eph 1:18
wisdom **m** now be made known Eph 3:10
⌊I pray⌋ that He **m** grant you, Eph 3:16
that the Messiah **m** dwell in your Eph 3:17
m be able to comprehend with all Eph 3:18
so you **m** be filled with all the Eph 3:19
that it **m** go well with you and Eph 6:3

and that you **m** have a long life Eph 6:3
so that you **m** be able to resist Eph 6:13
that the message **m** be given to Eph 6:19
so that you also **m** know how I am Eph 6:21
your confidence **m** grow in Christ Php 1:26
so that you **m** be blameless and Php 2:15
so that I also **m** be encouraged Php 2:19
him so that you **m** rejoice when Php 2:28
again and I **m** be less anxious Php 2:28
filth, so that I **m** gain Christ Php 3:8
asking that you **m** be filled with Col 1:9
so that you **m** walk worthy of the Col 1:10
M you be strengthened with all Col 1:11
so that we **m** present everyone Col 1:28
so that they **m** have all the Col 2:2
For I **m** be absent in body, Col 2:5
for us that God **m** open a door to Col 4:3
so that I **m** reveal it as I am Col 4:4
that you **m** know how you should Col 4:6
so that you **m** know how we are, Col 4:8
and so that he **m** encourage your Col 4:8
so that they **m** be saved. 1Th 2:16
m our God and Father Himself, 1Th 3:11
And **m** the Lord cause you to 1Th 3:12
M He make your hearts blameless 1Th 3:13
so that you **m** walk properly in 1Th 4:12
Now **m** the God of peace Himself 1Th 5:23
m your spirit, soul, and body 1Th 5:23
M the grace of our Lord Jesus 1Th 5:28
M our Lord Jesus Christ Himself 2Th 2:16
Lord's message **m** spread rapidly 2Th 3:1
and that we **m** be delivered from 2Th 3:2
M the Lord direct your hearts to 2Th 3:5
they **m** eat their own bread. 2Th 3:12
him, so that he **m** be ashamed. 2Th 3:14
M the Lord of peace Himself give 2Th 3:16
so that you **m** command certain 1Tm 1:3
by them you **m** strongly engage 1Tm 1:18
so that they **m** be taught not to 1Tm 1:20
so that we **m** lead a tranquil and 1Tm 2:2
your progress **m** be evident to 1Tm 4:15
so that they **m** take hold of life 1Tm 6:19
you so that I **m** be filled with 2Tm 1:4
M the Lord grant mercy to the 2Tm 1:16
M the Lord grant that he obtain 2Tm 1:18
that they also **m** obtain 2Tm 2:10
Then they **m** come to their senses 2Tm 2:26
the man of God **m** be complete, 2Tm 3:17
M it not be counted against them. 2Tm 4:16
they **m** be sound in the faith Ti 1:13
m not pay attention to Jewish Ti 1:14
so that they **m** encourage the Ti 2:4
that they **m** adorn the teaching Ti 2:10
we **m** become heirs with the hope Ti 3:7
in the faith **m** become effective Phm 6
m I have joy from you in the Phm 20
so that we **m** receive mercy and Heb 4:16
m receive what was promised. Heb 10:36
what is lame **m** not be dislocated Heb 12:13
we **m** serve God acceptably, Heb 12:28
Therefore, we **m** boldly say: Heb 13:6
to pray that I **m** be restored to Heb 13:19
Now **m** the God of peace, who Heb 13:20
so that you **m** be mature and Jms 1:4
so that you **m** spend it on your Jms 4:3
so that you **m** be healed. Jms 5:16
M grace and peace be multiplied 1Pt 1:2
by fire—**m** result in praise 1Pt 1:7
so that you **m** grow by it in 1Pt 2:2
so that you **m** proclaim the 1Pt 2:9
do evil, they **m**, by observing 1Pt 2:12
they **m** be won over without a 1Pt 3:1
in everything God **m** be glorified 1Pt 4:11
so that you **m** also rejoice with 1Pt 4:13
so that He **m** exalt you in due 1Pt 5:6
M grace and peace be multiplied 2Pt 1:2
through them you **m** share in the 2Pt 1:4
my departure you **m** be able to 2Pt 1:15
so that you **m** have fellowship 1Jn 1:3
so that our joy **m** be complete. 1Jn 1:4
things so that you **m** not sin. 1Jn 2:1
He appears we **m** have boldness 1Jn 2:28
us so that we **m** have confidence 1Jn 4:17
so that you **m** know that you have 1Jn 5:13
so that we **m** know the true One. 1Jn 5:20
but you **m** receive a full reward. 2Jn 8
so that our joy **m** be complete. 2Jn 12
I pray that you **m** prosper in 3Jn 2

M mercy, peace, and love be Jd 2
the fire so that you **m** be rich, Rv 3:18
so that you **m** be dressed and Rv 3:18
on your eyes so that you **m** see. Rv 3:18
so that He **m** open the scroll Rv 5:5
so that he **m** not go naked, Rv 16:15
so that you **m** eat the flesh of Rv 19:18
so that they **m** have the right to Rv 22:14
of life and **m** enter the city Rv 22:14

MAYBE *(8)*
M the LORD will meet with me. Nm 23:3
M it will be agreeable to God Nm 23:27
M he'll tell us which way we 1Sm 9:6
M he's thinking it over; 1Kg 18:27
m he has wandered away; 1Kg 18:27
or **m** he's on the road. 1Kg 18:27
M the Spirit of the LORD has 2Kg 2:16
M this god will consider us, Jnh 1:6

ME *(4023)*
(See pp. xi-xii.)

ME-JARKON *(1)*
M, and Rakkon, with the Jos 19:46

ME-ZAHAB *(2)*
of Matred daughter of **M**. Gn 36:39
of Matred, daughter of **M**. 1Ch 1:50

MEADOW *(2)*
them like a lamb in an open **m**? Hs 4:16
planted in a **m**, so Ephraim will Hs 9:13

MEADOWS *(1)*
to Acacia **M** on the plains of Nm 33:49

MEAGER *(2)*
It shared his **m** food and drank 2Sm 12:3
will give you **m** bread and water Is 30:20

MEAL *(26)*
A **m** was set before him, but he Gn 24:33
a delicious **m** for your father Gn 27:9
his relatives to eat a **m**. Gn 31:54
So they ate a **m** and spent the Gn 31:54
Then they sat down to eat a **m**. Gn 37:25
were going to eat a **m** there, Gn 43:25
he said, "Serve the **m**." Gn 43:31
of Israel to eat a **m** with Moses' Ex 18:12
over from her **m** and gave ⌊it⌋ to Ru 2:18
the king sat down to eat the **m**. 1Sm 20:24
son come to the **m** either 1Sm 20:27
house and prepare a **m** for him." 2Sm 13:7
"Bring the **m** to the bedroom," 2Sm 13:10
fine flour and 300 bushels of **m**, 1Kg 4:22
Then Elisha said, "Get some **m**." 2Kg 4:41
quarts of fine **m** ⌊will sell⌋ for 2Kg 7:1
six quarts of fine **m** ⌊sold⌋ for 2Kg 7:16
quarts of fine **m** ⌊will sell⌋ for 2Kg 7:18
Better a **m** of vegetables where Pr 15:17
Take millstones and grind **m**; Is 47:2
They ate a **m** together there in Jr 41:1
from Minnith, **m**, honey, oil, Ezk 27:17
to eat a **m** before the LORD Ezk 44:3
prepare the Passover **m** for us, Lk 22:8
his house, set a **m** before them, Ac 16:34
in exchange for one **m**. Heb 12:16

MEALS *(1)*
will always eat **m** at my table." 2Sm 9:7

MEALTIME *(1)*
At **m** Boaz told her, "Come over Ru 2:14

MEAN *(18)*
What do you **m** by this whole Gn 33:8
dreams **m** the same thing. Gn 41:25
The dreams **m** the same thing. Gn 41:26
'What does this ritual **m** to you?' Ex 12:26
asks you, 'What does this **m**?' Ex 13:14
'What do these stones **m** to you?' Jos 4:6
and soldiers **m** nothing to you. 2Sm 19:6
you know what these things **m**? Ezk 17:12
What do you **m** by using this Ezk 18:2
things you are doing **m** for us?" Ezk 24:19
us what you **m** by these things? Ezk 37:18
"What does this parable **m**?" Lk 8:9
the vision he had seen might **m**, Ac 10:17
to know what these ideas **m**." Ac 17:20
will their acceptance **m** but life Rm 11:15
I do not **m** your own conscience, 1Co 10:29
and uncircumcision **m** nothing; Gl 6:15
He ascended" **m** except that He Eph 4:9

MEANING *(17)*
and each dream had its own **m**. Gn 40:5

each dream had its own **m**. Gn 41:11
Manasseh, **m**, "God has made me Gn 41:51
Ephraim, **m**, "God has made Gn 41:52
'What is the **m** of the decrees, Dt 6:20
'What is the **m** of these stones?' Jos 4:21
and giving the **m** so that the Neh 8:8
understand the **m** of Your Ps 119:27
LORD, the **m** of Your statutes, Ps 119:33
him the true **m** of all this. Dn 7:16
to know the true **m** of the fourth Dn 7:19
This is the **m** of the parable: Lk 8:11
Then what is the **m** of this Lk 20:17
in the world, and all have **m**. 1Co 14:10
not know the **m** of the language 1Co 14:11
of Salem," **m** "king of peace" Heb 7:2
you the secret **m** of the woman Rv 17:7

MEANINGLESS *(2)*
For they are not **m** words to you Dt 32:47
man's thoughts; they are **m**. Ps 94:11

MEANS *(42)*
from it by **m** of painful labor Gn 3:17
no one can tell me what it **m**." Gn 41:24
it **m** that the matter has been Gn 41:32
receive glory by **m** of Pharaoh Ex 14:4
receive glory by **m** of Pharaoh, Ex 14:17
carry the ⌊**m** of⌋ decisions for Ex 28:30
have sufficient **m** for a sheep, Lv 12:8
with a gift suited to his **m**, Dt 16:17
whether it **m** life or death, 2Sm 15:21
and by **m** of his idols has also 2Kg 21:11
them by **m** of their torment Jb 36:15
this not what it **m** to know Me? Jr 22:16
but I will by no **m** leave you Jr 30:11
but I will by no **m** leave you Jr 46:28
the highest by **m** of the middle Ezk 41:7
MENE ⌊**m** that⌋ God has numbered Dn 5:26
TEKEL ⌊**m** that⌋ you have been Dn 5:27
PERES ⌊**m** that⌋ your kingdom has Dn 5:28
are by no **m** least among the Mt 2:6
Go and learn what this **m**: Mt 9:13
If you had known what this **m**: Mt 12:7
by the sanctuary, it **m** nothing. Mt 23:16
oath by the altar, it **m** nothing. Mt 23:18
Golgotha (which **m** Skull Place), Mt 27:33
Golgotha (which **m** Skull Place). Mk 15:22
for yourselves by **m** of the Lk 16:9
Rabbi" (which **m** "Teacher"), Jn 1:38
(which **m** "Anointed One"), Jn 1:41
called Cephas" (which **m** "Rock"). Jn 1:42
of Siloam" (which **m** "Sent"). Jn 9:7
—which **m** "Teacher." Jn 20:16
man—by what **m** he was healed— Ac 4:9
a redeemer by **m** of the angel who Ac 7:35
to the elders by **m** of Barnabas Ac 11:30
no **m** referring to this world's 1Co 5:10
by all **m** take the opportunity. 1Co 7:21
that I may by all **m** save some. 1Co 9:22
by **m** of the diligence of others, 2Co 8:8
angels by **m** of a mediator. Gl 3:19
this **m** fruitful work for me; Php 1:22
This **m** one must not transgress 1Th 4:6
name **m** "king of righteousness, Heb 7:2

MEANT *(6)*
is what the LORD **m** when He said: Lv 10:3
what "rising from the dead" **m**. Mk 9:10
and asked what these things **m**. Lk 15:26
by, he inquired what this **m**. Lk 18:36
that was **m** for life resulted Rm 7:10
the law is not **m** for a righteous 1Tm 1:9

MEANTIME *(1)*
In the **m** the disciples kept Jn 4:31

MEANWHILE *(25)*
(See pp. xi-xii.)

MEASURE *(51)*
has not yet reached its full **m**." Gn 15:16
it because it was beyond **m**. Gn 41:49
an honest dry **m**, and an honest Lv 19:36
measure, and an honest liquid **m**; Lv 19:36
M 1,000 yards outside the city Nm 35:5
six feet wide by a standard **m**. Dt 3:11
come out and **m** ⌊the distance⌋ Dt 21:2
honest dry **m**, so that you may Dt 25:15
all these articles was beyond **m**. 2Kg 25:16
Their **m** is longer than the earth Jb 11:9
wind and limited the water by **m**, Jb 28:25
gave them a full **m** of tears to Ps 80:5
of the earth in a **m** or weighed Is 40:12
Who will you **m** Me with, so that Is 46:5
all these articles was beyond **m**. Jr 52:20
are also to drink water by **m**, Ezk 4:11
and in dread drink water by **m**. Ezk 4:16
Let them **m** ⌊its⌋ pattern, Ezk 43:10
you will **m** off an area eight and Ezk 45:3
an honest dry **m**, and an honest Ezk 45:10
measure, and an honest liquid **m**. Ezk 45:10
The dry **m** and the liquid measure Ezk 45:11
the liquid **m** will be uniform, Ezk 45:11
the liquid **m** containing five Ezk 45:11
and the dry **m** ⌊holding⌋ half Ezk 45:11
the standard larger capacity **m**. Ezk 45:11
one standard larger capacity **m**, Ezk 45:14
one standard larger capacity **m**. Ezk 45:14
you will **m** from the ⌊northern⌋ Ezk 47:18
reached the full **m** of their sin, Dn 8:23
can reduce the **m** while Am 8:5
accursed short **m** in the house Mc 6:10
To **m** Jerusalem to determine its Zch 2:2
a blessing for you without **m**. Mal 3:10
they were overjoyed beyond **m**. Mt 2:10
and with the **m** you use, it will Mt 7:2
the **m** of your fathers' sins! Mt 23:32
By the **m** you use, it will be Mk 4:24
a good **m**—pressed down, shaken Lk 6:38
For with the **m** you use, it will Lk 6:38
He gives the Spirit without **m**. Jn 3:34
might become sinful beyond **m**. Rm 7:13
distributed a **m** of faith to each Rm 12:3
boast beyond **m**, but according 2Co 10:13
according to the **m** of the area 2Co 10:13
bragging beyond **m** about other 2Co 10:15
to the **m** of the Messiah's Eph 4:7
even greater **m** of godlessness. 2Tm 2:16
Go and **m** God's sanctuary and the Rv 11:1
Don't **m** it, because it is given Rv 11:2
measuring rod to **m** the city, Rv 21:15

MEASURED *(63)*
When they **m** it by quarts, the Ex 16:18
silver shekels ⌊**m**⌋ by the Lv 27:3
will be ⌊**m**⌋ by the standard Lv 27:25
⌊shekels **m**⌋ by the standard Nm 3:50
⌊**m**⌋ by the standard sanctuary Nm 7:13
⌊**m**⌋ by the standard sanctuary Nm 7:19
⌊**m**⌋ by the standard sanctuary Nm 7:25
⌊**m**⌋ by the standard sanctuary Nm 7:31
⌊**m**⌋ by the standard sanctuary Nm 7:37
⌊**m**⌋ by the standard sanctuary Nm 7:43
⌊**m**⌋ by the standard sanctuary Nm 7:49
⌊**m**⌋ by the standard sanctuary Nm 7:55
⌊**m**⌋ by the standard sanctuary Nm 7:61
⌊**m**⌋ by the standard sanctuary Nm 7:67
⌊**m**⌋ by the standard sanctuary Nm 7:73
⌊**m**⌋ by the standard sanctuary Nm 7:79
60 pounds ⌊**m**⌋ by the standard Nm 7:85
four ounces ⌊**m**⌋ by the standard Nm 7:86
he **m** them off with a cord. 2Sm 8:2
He **m** every two cord lengths ⌊of 2Sm 8:2
Who has **m** the waters in the Is 40:12
above can be **m** and the Jr 31:37
the sand of the sea cannot be **m**. Jr 33:22
He **m** the thickness of the ⌊wall⌋ Ezk 40:5
He **m** the threshold of the gate; Ezk 40:6
Next he **m** the portico of the Ezk 40:8
he **m** the width of the gate's Ezk 40:11
Then he **m** the gateway from the Ezk 40:13
Next, he **m** the pilasters—105 Ezk 40:14
Then he **m** the distance from the Ezk 40:19
He **m** the gate of the outer court Ezk 40:20
He **m** the distance from gate to Ezk 40:23
He **m** its pilasters and portico; Ezk 40:24
He **m** from gate to gate on the Ezk 40:27
When he **m** the south gate, it had Ezk 40:28
When he **m** the gate, it had the Ezk 40:32
When he **m** ⌊it⌋, it had the same Ezk 40:35
Next he **m** the court. Ezk 40:47
the temple and **m** the pilasters Ezk 40:48
great hall and **m** the pilasters; Ezk 41:1
also **m** the length of the great Ezk 41:2
next room⌋ and **m** the pilasters Ezk 41:3
He then **m** the length of the room Ezk 41:4
he **m** the wall of the temple; Ezk 41:5
Then the man **m** the temple; Ezk 41:13
Next he **m** the length of the Ezk 41:15
that faced east and **m** all around Ezk 42:15
He **m** the east side with a Ezk 42:16
He **m** the north side; Ezk 42:17
He **m** the south side; Ezk 42:18
to the west side and **m** 875 feet Ezk 42:19
He **m** the temple complex on all Ezk 42:20
he **m** off a third of a mile and Ezk 47:3
he **m** off a third ⌊of a mile⌋ Ezk 47:4
He **m** off another third ⌊of a Ezk 47:4
he **m** off a third of a ⌊mile⌋ Ezk 47:5
which cannot be **m** or counted. Hs 1:10
you use, it will be **m** to you. Mt 7:2
it will be **m** and added to you. Mk 4:24
it will be **m** back to you." Lk 6:38
man with a stature **m** by Christ's Eph 4:13
He **m** the city with the rod at Rv 21:16
Then he **m** its wall, 144 cubits Rv 21:17

MEASUREMENT *(2)*
Their **m** will be one-tenth of the Ezk 45:11
144 cubits according to human **m**, Rv 21:17

MEASUREMENTS *(19)*
curtains are to have the same **m**. Ex 26:2
curtains are to have the same **m**. Ex 26:8
all the curtains had the same **m**. Ex 36:9
All 11 curtains had the same **m**. Ex 36:15
not act unfairly in **m** of length, Lv 19:35
and all **m** of volume and length. 1Ch 23:29
with the same **m**, and the Ezk 40:10
either side also had the same **m**. Ezk 40:10
the same **m** as the first gate: Ezk 40:21
trees had the same **m** as those of Ezk 40:22
had the same **m** as the others. Ezk 40:24
it had the same **m** as the others. Ezk 40:28
had the same **m** as the others. Ezk 40:29
it had the same **m** as the others. Ezk 40:32
had the same **m** as the others. Ezk 40:33
it had the same **m** as the others, Ezk 40:35
their exits, **m**, and entrances, Ezk 42:11
These are the **m** of the altar in Ezk 43:13
These are the city's **m**: Ezk 48:16

MEASURES *(16)*
Knead three **m** of fine flour and Gn 18:6
are to be in equal **m**. Ex 30:34
differing dry **m** in your house, Dt 25:14
he shoveled six ⌊**m**⌋ of barley Ru 3:15
gave me these six ⌊**m**⌋ of barley, Ru 3:17
weights and varying **m**— Pr 20:10
of oil in liquid **m** will be one Ezk 45:14
10 liquid **m** ⌊or⌋ one standard Ezk 45:14
since 10 liquid **m** equal one Ezk 45:14
which **m** one and a half ⌊miles⌋, Ezk 48:30
which **m** one and a half ⌊miles⌋, Ezk 48:33
He **m** out the allotted land of my Mc 2:4
came to a ⌊grain⌋ heap of 20 **m**, Hg 2:16
to dip 50 **m** from the vat, Hg 2:16
'A hundred **m** of oil,' he said. Lk 16:6
'A hundred **m** of wheat,' Lk 16:7

MEASURING *(25)*
that he stopped **m** it because it Gn 41:49
over Jerusalem the **m** line ⌊used 2Kg 21:13
stretched a **m** line across it? Jb 38:5
will make justice the **m** line and Is 28:17
stretch out a **m** line and a plumb Is 34:11
their portion with a **m** line. Is 34:17
stretches out a **m** line, Is 44:13
A **m** line will once again stretch Jr 31:39
stretched out a **m** line and did Lm 2:8
cord and a **m** rod in his hand Ezk 40:3
The **m** rod in the man's hand was Ezk 40:5
When he finished **m** inside the Ezk 42:15
the east side with a **m** rod; Ezk 42:16
it was 875 feet by the **m** rod. Ezk 42:16
it was 875 feet by the **m** rod. Ezk 42:17
it was 875 feet by the **m** rod. Ezk 42:18
measured 875 feet by the **m** rod. Ezk 42:19
out east with a **m** line in his Ezk 47:3
be divided up with a **m** line. Am 7:17
and a **m** line will be stretched Zch 1:16
a man with a **m** line in his hand Zch 2:1
a **m** basket that is approaching. Zch 5:6
in **m** themselves by themselves 2Co 10:12
I was given a **m** reed like a rod, Rv 11:1
me had a gold **m** rod to measure Rv 21:15

MEAT *(85)*
you must not eat **m** with its Gn 9:4
are to eat the **m** that night; Ex 12:8
take any of the **m** outside the Ex 12:46
we sat by pots of **m** and ate all Ex 16:3
LORD will give you **m** to eat this Ex 16:8
At twilight you will eat **m**, Ex 16:12

and its **m** may not be eaten, Ex 21:28
must not eat the **m** of a mauled Ex 22:31
shovels, basins, **m** forks, and Ex 27:3
sons are to eat the **m** of the ram Ex 29:32
If any of the **m** of ordination or Ex 29:34
shovels, basins, **m** forks, and Ex 38:3
The **m** of his thanksgiving Lv 7:15
the sacrificial **m** by the third Lv 7:17
any of the **m** of his fellowship Lv 7:18
M that touches anything unclean Lv 7:19
is clean may eat any ⌊other⌋ **m**. Lv 7:19
one who eats **m** from the LORD's Lv 7:20
and eats **m** from the LORD's Lv 7:21
Boil the **m** at the entrance to Lv 8:31
what remains of the **m** and bread. Lv 8:32
any of their **m** or touch their Lv 11:8
you must not eat any of their **m**, Lv 11:11
and said, "Who will feed us **m**? Nm 11:4
Where can I get **m** to give all Nm 11:13
to me: 'Give us **m** to eat!' Nm 11:13
and you will eat **m** because you Nm 11:18
will feed us **m**? We really had Nm 11:18
will give you **m** and you will eat Nm 11:18
will give them **m**, and they will Nm 11:21
While the **m** was still between Nm 11:33
people who had craved ⌊the **m**⌋. Nm 11:34
But their **m** belongs to you. Nm 18:18
slaughter and eat **m** within any Dt 12:15
'I want to eat **m**' because you Dt 12:20
have a strong desire to eat **m**, Dt 12:20
not eat the life with the **m**. Dt 12:23
Present the **m** and blood of your Dt 12:27
your God, but you may eat the **m**. Dt 12:27
not eat their **m** or touch their Dt 14:8
and none of the **m** you sacrifice Dt 16:4
He placed the **m** in a basket and Jdg 6:19
Take the **m** with the unleavened Jdg 6:20
and touched the **m** and the Jdg 6:21
and consumed the **m** and the Jdg 6:21
portions of the **m** to his wife 1Sm 1:4
a three-pronged **m** fork while the 1Sm 2:13
fork while the **m** was boiling 1Sm 2:13
whatever the **m** fork brought up. 1Sm 2:14
the priest ⌊some⌋ **m** to roast, 1Sm 2:15
won't accept boiled **m** from you— 1Sm 2:15
the portion of **m** that I gave you 1Sm 9:23
ate ⌊**m**⌋ with the blood ⌊still 1Sm 14:32
by eating ⌊**m**⌋ with the blood 1Sm 14:33
by eating ⌊**m**⌋ with the blood 1Sm 14:34
and my **m** that I butchered for my 1Sm 25:11
him bread and **m** in the morning 1Kg 17:6
he cooked the **m** and gave it to 1Kg 19:21
or furnish **m** for His people? Ps 78:20
He rained **m** on them like dust, Ps 78:27
She has prepared her **m**; Pr 9:2
those who gorge themselves on **m**. Pr 23:20
They carve ⌊**m**⌋ on the right, Is 9:20
sheep, eating of **m**, and drinking Is 22:13
wine, choice **m**, finely aged wine Is 25:6
and he roasts **m** on that half. Is 44:16
its coals, I roasted **m** and ate. Is 44:19
leader, eating **m** from pigs, Is 66:17
and eat the **m** yourselves, Jr 7:21
Can holy **m** prevent your disaster Jr 11:15
And impure **m** has never entered Ezk 4:14
is the pot, and we are the **m**. Ezk 11:3
have put within it are the **m**, Ezk 11:7
you will not be the **m** within it. Ezk 11:11
Place the pieces of **m** in it, Ezk 24:4
Cook the **m** well and mix in the Ezk 24:10
You eat ⌊**m**⌋ with blood ⌊in it⌋, Ezk 33:25
no **m** or wine entered my mouth, Dn 10:3
pot, like **m** in a caldron." Mc 3:3
consecrated **m** in the fold of his Hg 2:12
is a noble thing not to eat **m**, Rm 14:21
never again eat **m**, so that I 1Co 8:13
that is sold in the **m** market, 1Co 10:25
to eat **m** sacrificed to idols and Rv 2:14
and to eat **m** sacrificed to idols Rv 2:20

MEATFORKS *(1)*
the firepans, **m**, shovels, and Nm 4:14

MEBUNNAI *(1)*
(AKA SIBBECAI)
Anathothite, **M** the Hushathite, 2Sm 23:27

MECHERATHITE *(1)*
Hepher the **M**, Ahijah the 1Ch 11:36

MECONAH *(1)*
Ziklag and **M** and its villages, Neh 11:28

MEDAD *(2)*
one named Eldad and the other **M**; Nm 11:26
Eldad and **M** are prophesying in Nm 11:27

MEDAN *(2)*
Jokshan, **M**, Midian, Ishbak Gn 25:2
Jokshan, **M**, Midian, Ishbak 1Ch 1:32

MEDDLER *(1)*
a thief, an evildoer, or as a **m**. 1Pt 4:15

MEDDLES *(1)*
A passerby who **m** in a quarrel Pr 26:17

MEDE *(3)*
and Darius the **M** received the Dn 5:31
Ahasuerus, was a **M** by birth, and Dn 9:1
the first year of Darius the **M**, Dn 11:1

MEDEBA *(5)*
which reaches as far as **M**. Nm 21:30
all the **M** plateau as far as Jos 13:9
the whole plateau as far as **M**, Jos 13:16
who came and camped near **M**. 1Ch 19:7
Moab wails on Nebo and at **M**. Is 15:2

MEDES *(10)*
and in the cities of the **M**. 2Kg 17:6
and in the cities of the **M**, 2Kg 18:11
stirring up the **M** against them, Is 13:17
Lay siege, you **M**! I will put an Is 21:2
kings of the **M** because His plan Jr 51:11
given to the **M** and Persians." Dn 5:28
as a law of the **M** and Persians, Dn 6:8
As a law of the **M** and Persians, Dn 6:12
is a law of the **M** and Persians Dn 6:15
Parthians, **M**, Elamites; Ac 2:9

MEDIA *(9)*
the province of **M** that a scroll Ezr 6:2
of Persia and **M**, the nobles, Est 1:3
of Persia and **M** who had personal Est 1:14
of Persia and **M** who hear about Est 1:18
in the laws of Persia and **M**, Est 1:19
of the kings of **M** and Persia? Est 10:2
of Elam, and all the kings of **M**; Jr 25:25
the kings of **M**, her governors Jr 51:28
the kings of **M** and Persia. Dn 8:20

MEDIATOR *(8)*
on his side, one **m** out of a Jb 33:23
a trap at the gate for the **m**, Is 29:21
through angels by means of a **m**. Gl 3:19
Now a **m** is not for just one Gl 3:20
is one God and one **m** between God 1Tm 2:5
degree He is the **m** of a better Heb 8:6
He is the **m** of a new covenant, Heb 9:15
to Jesus (**m** of a new covenant), Heb 12:24

MEDIATORS *(1)*
and your **m** have rebelled against Is 43:27

MEDICINE *(3)*
heart is good **m**, but a broken Pr 17:22
⌊no⌋ **m** has been applied and no Ezk 30:21
food and their leaves for **m**." Ezk 47:12

MEDITATE *(11)*
I **m** on You during the night Ps 63:6
God; I groan; I **m**; my spirit Ps 77:3
I **m** in my heart, and my spirit Ps 77:6
have done and **m** on Your actions Ps 77:12
I will **m** on Your precepts and Ps 119:15
so that I can **m** on Your wonders. Ps 119:27
and will **m** on Your statutes. Ps 119:48
I will **m** on Your precepts. Ps 119:78
the night to **m** on Your promise Ps 119:148
I **m** on all You have done; Ps 143:5
Your mind will **m** on the ⌊past⌋ Is 33:18

MEDITATES *(1)*
and he **m** on it day and night. Ps 1:2

MEDITATING *(1)*
in her heart and **m** on them. Lk 2:19

MEDITATION *(6)*
of God⌋ and hinder **m** before Him. Jb 15:4
mouth and the **m** of my heart be Ps 19:14
my heart's **m** ⌊brings⌋ Ps 49:3
May my **m** be pleasing to Him; Ps 104:34
It is my **m** all day long. Ps 119:97
because Your decrees are my **m**. Ps 119:99

MEDITERRANEAN *(22)*
from the Red Sea to the **M** Sea, Ex 23:31
where it will end at the **M** Sea. Nm 34:5
be the coastline of the **M** Sea; Nm 34:6
From the **M** Sea draw a line to Nm 34:7
Euphrates River to the **M** Sea. Dt 11:24
of Judah as far as the **M** Sea, Dt 34:2
—and west to the **M** Sea. Jos 1:4
the coast of the **M** Sea toward Jos 9:1
the border ended at the **M** Sea. Jos 15:4
Jabneel, and ended at the **M** Sea. Jos 15:11
was the coastline of the **M** Sea. Jos 15:12
and the coastline of the **M** Sea. Jos 15:47
Gezer, and ended at the **M** Sea. Jos 16:3
of Kanah and ended at the **M** Sea. Jos 16:8
brook and ended at the **M** Sea. Jos 17:9
Jordan westward to the **M** Sea. Jos 23:4
like the fish of the **M** Sea. Ezk 47:10
will extend from the **M** Sea by Ezk 47:15
of Egypt⌋ as far as the **M** Sea. Ezk 47:19
the west side the **M** Sea will be Ezk 47:20
of Egypt⌋, and out to the **M** Sea. Ezk 48:28
his rear guard into the **M** Sea. Jl 2:20

MEDIUM *(7)*
woman who is a **m** or a spiritist Lv 20:27
a **m** or a familiar spirit, Dt 18:11
Find me a woman who is a **m**, 1Sm 28:7
is a woman at Endor who is a **m**." 1Sm 28:7
even consulted a **m** for guidance, 1Ch 10:13
diviner-priest, **m**, or Chaldean. Dn 2:10
No wise man, **m**, diviner-priest, Dn 2:27

MEDIUMS *(13)*
Do not turn to **m** or consult Lv 19:31
Whoever turns to **m** or spiritists Lv 20:6
had removed the **m** and spiritists 1Sm 28:3
has killed the **m** and spiritists 1Sm 28:9
and consulted **m** and spiritists. 2Kg 21:6
removed the **m**, the spiritists, 2Kg 23:24
and consulted **m** and spiritists. 2Ch 33:6
and **m** in his entire Dn 1:20
diviner-priests, **m**, sorcerers, Dn 2:2
diviner-priests, **m**, Chaldeans, Dn 4:7
called out to bring in the **m**, Dn 5:7
of the diviners, **m**, Chaldeans, Dn 5:11
the wise men and **m** were brought Dn 5:15

MEEK *(1)*
I will leave a **m** and humble Zph 3:12

MEET *(115)*
went out to **m** him in the Valley Gn 14:17
of the tent to **m** them and bowed Gn 18:2
saw ⌊them⌋, he got up to **m** them. Gn 19:1
servant ran to **m** her and said, Gn 24:17
in the field coming to **m** us?" Gn 24:65
he ran to **m** him, hugged him Gn 29:13
Leah went out to **m** him and said, Gn 30:16
he is coming to **m** you—and he Gn 32:6
Esau ran to **m** him, hugged him Gn 33:4
up to Goshen to **m** his father Gn 46:29
he is on his way now to **m** you. Ex 4:14
and **m** Moses in the wilderness. Ex 4:27
who stood ⌊waiting⌋ to **m** them. Ex 5:20
stand ready to **m** him by the bank Ex 7:15
So Moses went out to **m** his Ex 18:7
people out of the camp to **m** God, Ex 19:17
will **m** with you there above the Ex 25:22
where I will **m** you to speak with Ex 29:42
will also **m** with the Israelites Ex 29:43
where I will **m** with you. Ex 30:6
where I will **m** with you. Ex 30:36
testimony where I **m** with you. Nm 17:4
he went out to **m** him at the Nm 22:36
Maybe the LORD will **m** with me. Nm 23:3
community went to **m** them Nm 31:13
they did not **m** you with food Dt 23:4
go and **m** them and say, "We are Jos 9:11
who ⌊also⌋ came to **m** him. Jdg 6:35
coming out to **m** him with Jdg 11:34
came to **m** him shouting. Jdg 15:14
out from Gibeah to **m** them and Jdg 20:25
went out to **m** the Philistines 1Sm 4:1
God at Bethel will **m** you there, 1Sm 10:3
you will **m** a group of prophets 1Sm 10:5
battle line to **m** the Philistine. 1Sm 17:48
cities of Israel to **m** King Saul, 1Sm 18:6
Ahimelech was afraid to **m** David, 1Sm 21:1
who sent you to **m** me today! 1Sm 25:32
had not come quickly to **m** me, 1Sm 25:34
came out to **m** him and to meet 1Sm 30:21
him and to **m** the troops with 1Sm 30:21
Michal came out to **m** him. 2Sm 6:20

he sent ⌊someone⌋ to **m** them, 2Sm 10:5
there to **m** him was Hushai the 2Sm 15:32
was right there to **m** him. 2Sm 16:1
he happened to **m** David's 2Sm 18:9
came to Gilgal to **m** the king and 2Sm 19:15
men of Judah to **m** King David. 2Sm 19:16
down to **m** my lord the king. 2Sm 19:20
also went down to **m** the king. 2Sm 19:24
from Jerusalem to **m** the king, 2Sm 19:25
he came down to **m** me at the 1Kg 2:8
You then can **m** my needs by 1Kg 5:9
Obadiah went to **m** Ahab and 1Kg 18:16
Then Ahab went to **m** Elijah. 1Kg 18:16
all Israel to **m** me at Mount 1Kg 18:19
Get up and go to **m** Ahab king of 1Kg 21:18
Go and **m** the messengers of the 2Kg 1:3
A man came to **m** us and said, 2Kg 1:6
man came up to **m** you and spoke 2Kg 1:7
They came to **m** him and bowed 2Kg 2:15
Run out to **m** her and ask, 2Kg 4:26
If you **m** anyone, don't ⌊stop to⌋ 2Kg 4:29
went back to **m** Elisha and told 2Kg 4:31
the chariot to **m** him and asked, 2Kg 5:21
down from his chariot to **m** you? 2Kg 5:26
you and go **m** the man of God. 2Kg 8:8
Hazael went to **m** Elisha, taking 2Kg 8:9
and send him to **m** them and have 2Kg 9:17
went to **m** Jehu and said, 2Kg 9:18
son of Rechab ⌊coming⌋ to **m** him. 2Kg 10:15
Come, let us **m** face to face." 2Kg 14:8
to Damascus to **m** Tiglath-pileser 2Kg 16:10
went out to **m** them and said to 1Ch 12:17
so he sent ⌊someone⌋ to **m** them, 1Ch 19:5
he went out to **m** Asa and said to 2Ch 15:2
out with Joram to **m** Jehu son of 2Ch 22:7
Come, let us **m** face to face." 2Ch 25:17
He went out to **m** the army that 2Ch 28:9
have to supply ⌊to **m**⌋ the needs Ezr 7:20
let's **m** together in the villages Neh 6:2
Let us **m** at the house of God Neh 6:10
they did not **m** the Israelites Neh 13:2
For You **m** him with rich Ps 21:3
faithful God will come to **m** me; Ps 59:10
A woman came to **m** him, dressed Pr 7:10
I came out to **m** you, to search Pr 7:15
for a man to **m** a bear robbed Pr 17:12
Shear-jashub to **m** Ahaz at the Is 7:3
the land of Tema **m** the refugees Is 21:14
The wild beasts will **m** hyenas, Is 34:14
these prophets will **m** their end. Jr 14:15
face to face and **m** eye to eye. Jr 32:4
You will **m** the king of Babylon Jr 34:3
came out of Mizpah to **m** them, Jr 41:6
while; they will **m** their end. Jr 44:12
they will **m** their end by famine. Jr 44:12
of Egypt will **m** his end by sword Jr 44:27
Messenger races to **m** messenger, Jr 51:31
and herald to **m** herald, to Jr 51:31
he will **m** his end with no one Dn 11:45
together without agreeing to **m**? Am 3:3
Israel, prepare to **m** your God! Am 4:12
another angel went out to **m** him. Zch 2:3
whole town went out to **m** Jesus. Mt 8:34
and went out to **m** the groom. Mt 25:1
the groom! Come out to **m** him.' Mt 25:6
carrying a water jug will **m** you. Mk 14:13
could not **m** with Him because Lk 8:19
carrying a water jug will **m** you. Lk 22:10
was coming, she went to **m** Him. Jn 11:20
branches and went out to **m** Him. Jn 12:13
they would all **m** in Solomon's Ac 5:12
and had come to **m** us as far as Ac 28:15
in the clouds to **m** the Lord in 1Th 4:17

MEETING *(154)*

the tent of **m** outside the veil Ex 27:21
enter the tent of **m** or approach Ex 28:43
to the tent of **m** and wash them Ex 29:4
to the front of the tent of **m**, Ex 29:10
the entrance to the tent of **m**. Ex 29:11
enters the tent of **m** to minister Ex 29:30
the entrance to the tent of **m**. Ex 29:32
the tent of **m** before the LORD, Ex 29:42
the tent of **m** and the altar; Ex 29:44
the service of the tent of **m**. Ex 30:16
the tent of **m** and the altar, Ex 30:18
enter the tent of **m** or approach Ex 30:20
you are to anoint the tent of **m**, Ex 30:26
the testimony in the tent of **m**, Ex 30:36
the tent of **m**, the ark of the Ex 31:7
he called it the tent of **m**. Ex 33:7
to the tent of **m** that was Ex 33:7
the tent of **m** for every use, Ex 35:21
the entrance to the tent of **m**. Ex 38:8
the entrance to the tent of **m**, Ex 38:30
the tent of **m**, was finished. Ex 39:32
the tabernacle, the tent of **m**; Ex 39:40
the tent of **m**, on the first day Ex 40:2
the tabernacle, the tent of **m**, Ex 40:6
the tent of **m** and the altar, Ex 40:7
to the tent of **m** and wash them Ex 40:12
in the tent of **m** on the north Ex 40:22
in the tent of **m** opposite the Ex 40:24
the gold altar in the tent of **m**, Ex 40:26
the tent of **m**, and offered the Ex 40:29
the tent of **m** and the altar Ex 40:30
to the tent of **m** and approached Ex 40:32
The cloud covered the tent of **m**, Ex 40:34
the tent of **m** because the cloud Ex 40:35
spoke to him from the tent of **m**: Lv 1:1
to the tent of **m** so that he may Lv 1:3
the entrance to the tent of **m**. Lv 1:5
the entrance to the tent of **m**. Lv 3:2
it before the tent of **m**. Lv 3:8
it before the tent of **m**. Lv 3:13
the tent of **m** before the LORD, Lv 4:4
and bring it into the tent of **m**. Lv 4:5
the LORD in the tent of **m**. Lv 4:7
the entrance to the tent of **m**. Lv 4:7
bring it before the tent of **m**. Lv 4:14
bull's blood into the tent of **m**. Lv 4:16
the LORD in the tent of **m**. Lv 4:18
the entrance to the tent of **m**. Lv 4:18
the courtyard of the tent of **m**. Lv 6:16
the courtyard of the tent of **m**. Lv 6:26
into the tent of **m** to make Lv 6:30
the entrance to the tent of **m**." Lv 8:3
the entrance to the tent of **m**. Lv 8:4
the tent of **m** and eat it there Lv 8:31
to the tent of **m** for seven days, Lv 8:33
to the tent of **m** day and night Lv 8:35
to the front of the tent of **m**, Lv 9:5
then entered the tent of **m**. Lv 9:23
the tent of **m** or you will die, Lv 10:7
when you enter the tent of **m**, Lv 10:9
to the tent of **m** a year-old male Lv 12:6
the entrance to the tent of **m**. Lv 14:11
the tent of **m** before the LORD. Lv 14:23
the entrance to the tent of **m**, Lv 15:14
the entrance to the tent of **m**. Lv 15:29
the entrance to the tent of **m**. Lv 16:7
for the tent of **m** that remains Lv 16:16
in the tent of **m** from the time Lv 16:17
the tent of **m**, and the altar, he Lv 16:20
Aaron is to enter the tent of **m**, Lv 16:23
the tent of **m** and the altar Lv 16:33
to the tent of **m** to present ⌊it⌋ Lv 17:4
to the tent of **m** and offer them Lv 17:5
the tent of **m** and burn the fat Lv 17:6
to the tent of **m** to sacrifice it Lv 17:9
the entrance to the tent of **m**. Lv 19:21
the testimony in the tent of **m**. Lv 24:3
in the tent of **m** in the Nm 1:1
the tent of **m** at a distance Nm 2:2
tent of **m** is to move out with Nm 2:17
the tent of **m** by attending to Nm 3:7
of the tent of **m** and perform Nm 3:8
duties at the tent of **m** involved Nm 3:25
the entrance to the tent of **m**, Nm 3:25
of the tent of **m** toward the Nm 3:38
to do work at the tent of **m**. Nm 4:3
at the tent of **m** concerns the Nm 4:4
regarding the tent of **m**. Nm 4:15
to do work at the tent of **m**. Nm 4:23
the tent of **m** with its covering Nm 4:25
the entrance to the tent of **m**, Nm 4:25
clans at the tent of **m**, Nm 4:28
to do the work of the tent of **m**. Nm 4:30
their service at the tent of **m**: Nm 4:31
all their work at the tent of **m**, Nm 4:33
for work at the tent of **m**. Nm 4:35
could serve at the tent of **m**. Nm 4:37
for work at the tent of **m**. Nm 4:39
could serve at the tent of **m**. Nm 4:41
for work at the tent of **m**. Nm 4:43
the tent of **m** and transporting Nm 4:47
the entrance to the tent of **m**. Nm 6:10
the entrance to the tent of **m**. Nm 6:13
the entrance to the tent of **m**, Nm 6:18
in the work of the tent of **m**, Nm 7:5
the tent of **m** to speak with Nm 7:89
the tent of **m** and assemble Nm 8:9
to serve ⌊at⌋ the tent of **m**, Nm 8:15
at the tent of **m** and to make Nm 8:19
at the tent of **m** in the presence Nm 8:22
in the work at the tent of **m**. Nm 8:24
at the tent of **m**, Nm 8:26
the entrance to the tent of **m**. Nm 10:3
to the tent of **m** and have them Nm 11:16
come out to the tent of **m**." Nm 12:4
the Israelites at the tent of **m**. Nm 14:10
the tent of **m** along with Moses Nm 16:18
the entrance to the tent of **m**, Nm 16:19
turned toward the tent of **m**, Nm 16:42
to the front of the tent of **m**, Nm 16:43
the entrance to the tent of **m**, Nm 16:50
them in the tent of **m** in front Nm 17:4
you and guard the tent of **m**, Nm 18:4
LORD to work at the tent of **m**. Nm 18:6
the work of the tent of **m**. Nm 18:21
again come near the tent of **m**, Nm 18:22
do the work of the tent of **m**, Nm 18:23
for your work at the tent of **m**. Nm 18:31
the front of the tent of **m**. Nm 19:4
to the doorway of the tent of **m**. Nm 20:6
the entrance to the tent of **m**. Nm 25:6
to the tent of **m** and said, Nm 27:2
into the tent of **m** as a memorial Nm 31:54
yourselves at the tent of **m**, Dt 31:14
themselves at the tent of **m**, Dt 31:14
it set up the tent of **m** there; Jos 18:1
the entrance to the tent of **m**. Jos 19:51
the entrance to the tent of **m**. 1Sm 2:22
for the appointed **m** with David. 1Sm 20:35
LORD, the tent of **m**, and the 1Kg 8:4
the tent of **m**, until Solomon 1Ch 6:32
the entrance to the tent of **m**. 1Ch 9:21
to the tent of **m**, 1Ch 23:32
Gibeon because God's tent of **m**, 2Ch 1:3
bronze altar at the tent of **m**; 2Ch 1:6
in front of the tent of **m**, 2Ch 1:13
ark, the tent of **m**, and the holy 2Ch 5:5
roared in the **m** place where You Ps 74:4
destroying His place of **m**. Lm 2:6
As they were **m** in Galilee, Mt 17:22
priests had a **m** with the elders, Mk 15:1
themselves ⌊to **m**⌋ together Ac 2:46
woman to speak in the church **m**. 1Co 14:35
comes into your **m** wearing a gold Jms 2:2

MEETINGS *(1)*

not staying away from our **m**, Heb 10:25

MEETS *(6)*

brother Esau **m** you and asks, Gn 32:17
If it **m** the king's approval, Est 1:19
in the morning my prayer **m** You. Ps 88:13
the church that **m** in their home. Rm 16:5
the church that **m** in their home. 1Co 16:19
the church that **m** in your house. Phm 2

MEGIDDO *(12)*

of Taanach one the king of **M** one Jos 12:21
of **M** with its towns— Jos 17:11
residents of **M** and its villages Jdg 1:27
at Taanach by the waters of **M**, Jdg 5:19
in Taanach, **M**, and all 1Kg 4:12
and Hazor, **M**, and Gezer. 1Kg 9:15
but he fled to **M** and died there. 2Kg 9:27
and at **M** when Neco saw him he 2Kg 23:29
From **M** his servants carried his 2Kg 23:30
its villages, **M** and its villages 1Ch 7:29
to the Valley of **M** to fight. 2Ch 35:22
Hadad-rimmon in the plain of **M**. Zch 12:11

MEHETABEL *(3)*

wife's name was **M** daughter of Gn 36:39
wife's name was **M** daughter of 1Ch 1:50
of Delaiah, son of **M**, who was Neh 6:10

MEHIDA'S *(2)*

descendants, **M** descendants, Ezr 2:52
descendants, **M** descendants, Neh 7:54

MEHIR *(1)*

brother of Shuhah fathered **M**, 1Ch 4:11

MEHOLATHITE *(2)*

given to Adriel the **M** as a wife. 1Sm 18:19
to Adriel son of Barzillai the **M** 2Sm 21:8

MEHUJAEL *(2)*
Irad fathered **M**, Mehujael Gn 4:18
fathered Mehujael, **M** fathered Gn 4:18

MEHUMAN *(1)*
commanded **M**, Biztha, Harbona, Est 1:10

MELATIAH *(1)*
Next to them **M** the Gibeonite, Neh 3:7

MELCHI *(2)*
Levi, ⌊son⌋ of **M**, ⌊son⌋ of Lk 3:24
⌊son⌋ of **M**, ⌊son⌋ of Addi, ⌊son⌋ Lk 3:28

MELCHIZEDEK *(10)*
Then **M**, king of Salem, brought Gn 14:18
You are a priest like **M**." Ps 110:4
forever in the order of **M**. Heb 5:6
high priest "in the order of **M**." Heb 5:10
forever in the order of **M**." Heb 6:20
For this **M**—King of Salem, Heb 7:1
his forefather when **M** met him. Heb 7:10
to arise in the order of **M**, Heb 7:11
if another priest like **M** arises, Heb 7:15
forever in the order of **M**. Heb 7:17

MELEA *(1)*
of **M**, ⌊son⌋ of Menna, ⌊son⌋ Lk 3:31

MELECH *(2)*
Pithon, **M**, Tarea, and Ahaz. 1Ch 8:35
Pithon, **M**, Tahrea, and Ahaz. 1Ch 9:41

MELODIOUS *(3)*
tambourine, the **m** lyre, and the Ps 81:2
lyre, with the lyre and **m** song. Ps 98:5
in her, thanksgiving and **m** song. Is 51:3

MELONS *(1)*
the cucumbers, **m**, leeks, onions, Nm 11:5

MELT *(16)*
hearts won't **m** like his own.' Dt 20:8
people's hearts to **m** with fear, Jos 14:8
of a lion will **m** because all 2Sm 17:10
The mountains **m** like wax at the Ps 97:5
and every man's heart will **m**. Is 13:7
Egypt's heart will **m** within it. Is 19:1
us and made us **m** because of our Is 64:7
heart will **m**, and every hand Ezk 21:7
their hearts may **m** and many may Ezk 21:15
to blow fire on them and **m** them, Ezk 22:20
put you ⌊inside⌋, and **m** you. Ezk 22:20
its impurity will **m** inside it; Ezk 24:11
mountains will **m** beneath Him, Mc 1:4
before Him, and the hills **m**; Nah 1:5
Hearts **m**, knees tremble, loins Nah 2:10
elements will **m** with the heat. 2Pt 3:12

MELTED *(7)*
but when the sun grew hot, it **m**. Ex 16:21
people's hearts **m** and became Jos 7:5
The mountains **m** before the LORD, Jdg 5:5
and heat snatch away the **m** snow, Jb 24:19
you will be **m** within the city Ezk 22:21
As silver is **m** inside a furnace, Ezk 22:22
you will be **m** inside the city. Ezk 22:22

MELTING *(2)*
heart is like wax, **m** within me. Ps 22:14
their courage **m** away in anguish, Ps 107:26

MELTS *(5)*
ice, and the snow **m** into them. Jb 6:16
the earth **m** when He lifts His Ps 46:6
As wax **m** before the fire, so the Ps 68:2
He sends His word and **m** them; Ps 147:18
it **m**, and all who dwell on it Am 9:5

MEMBER *(5)*
or to a **m** of the foreigner's Lv 25:47
a prominent **m** of the Sanhedrin Mk 15:43
named Joseph, a **m** of the Lk 23:50
So if one **m** suffers, all the 1Co 12:26
if one **m** is honored, all the 1Co 12:26

MEMBERS *(21)*
male among the **m** of Abraham's Gn 17:23
a grudge against **m** of your Lv 19:18
The **m** of the royal staff at the Est 3:3
Haven't the **m** of my household Jb 31:31
whose sexual **m** were like those Ezk 23:20
much more the **m** of his household Mt 10:25
will be the **m** of his household. Mt 10:36
and all the **m** of the Ac 4:6
individually **m** of one another. Rm 12:5
by **m** of Chloe's household, 1Co 1:11
your bodies are the **m** of Christ? 1Co 6:15
should I take the **m** of Christ 1Co 6:15
and make them **m** of a prostitute? 1Co 6:15
but that the **m** would have the 1Co 12:25
all the **m** suffer with it; 1Co 12:26
all the **m** rejoice with it. 1Co 12:26
Christ, and individual **m** of it. 1Co 12:27
the saints, and **m** of God's Eph 2:19
co-heirs, **m** of the same body, Eph 3:6
because we are **m** of one another. Eph 4:25
since we are **m** of His body. Eph 5:30

MEMORABLE *(1)*
Your **m** sayings are proverbs of Jb 13:12

MEMORIAL *(15)*
This day is to be a **m** for you, Ex 12:14
of the ephod as **m** stones for Ex 28:12
of the ephod as **m** stones for Ex 39:7
will burn this **m** portion of it Lv 2:2
will remove the **m** portion from Lv 2:9
it as its **m** portion and burn Lv 5:12
and burn its **m** portion on the Lv 6:15
it may serve as a **m** portion for Lv 24:7
offering as a **m** portion and burn Nm 5:26
of meeting as a **m** for the Nm 31:54
will always be a **m** for the Jos 4:7
a **m** and a name better than sons Is 56:5
set up your **m** behind the door Is 57:8
LORD's temple as a **m** to Heldai, Zch 6:14
come up as a **m** offering before Ac 10:4

MEMORIES *(1)*
you always have good **m** of us, 1Th 3:6

MEMORY *(16)*
blot out the **m** of Amalek under Ex 17:14
blot out the **m** of Amalek from Dt 25:19
and blot out the **m** of them from Dt 32:26
to preserve the **m** of my name." 2Sm 18:18
life and their **m** will not fade Est 9:28
⌊All⌋ **m** of him perishes from the Jb 18:17
and the very **m** of them has Ps 9:6
gone from **m** like a dead person— Ps 31:12
to erase all **m** of them from the Ps 34:16
let Him cut off ⌊all⌋ **m** of them Ps 109:15
There is no **m** of those who came Ec 1:11
will also be no **m** among those Ec 1:11
them because the **m** of them is Ec 9:5
have wiped out all **m** of them. Is 26:14
will also be told in **m** of her." Mt 26:13
will also be told in **m** of her." Mk 14:9

MEMPHIS *(8)*
the princes of **M** are deceived. Is 19:13
The men of **M** and Tahpanhes have Jr 2:16
Tahpanhes, **M**, and in the land Jr 44:1
Proclaim it in **M** and in Jr 46:14
For **M** will become a desolation, Jr 46:19
an end to the false gods in **M**. Ezk 30:13
and **M** will face foes in broad Ezk 30:16
them, and **M** will bury them. Hs 9:6

MEMUCAN *(2)*
Tarshish, Meres, Marsena, and **M**. Est 1:14
M said in the presence of the Est 1:16

MEMUCAN'S *(1)*
and he followed **M** advice. Est 1:21

MEN *(1228)*
They were the powerful **m** of old, Gn 6:4
men of old, the famous **m**. Gn 6:4
tower that the **m** were building. Gn 11:5
gave ⌊his⌋ **m** orders about him, Gn 12:20
Now the **m** of Sodom were evil, Gn 13:13
he assembled his 318 trained **m**, Gn 14:14
share of the **m** who came with me Gn 14:24
And all the **m** of his household— Gn 17:27
and he saw three **m** standing near Gn 18:2
and set ⌊them⌋ before the **m**. Gn 18:8
The **m** got up from there and Gn 18:16
The **m** turned from there and went Gn 18:22
the **m** of the city of Sodom, Gn 19:4
Where are the **m** who came to you Gn 19:5
don't do anything to these **m**, Gn 19:8
They struck the **m** who were at Gn 19:11
for him, the **m** grabbed his hand, Gn 19:16
and the **m** were terrified. Gn 20:8
two of his young **m** and his son Gn 22:3
Abraham said to his young **m**, Gn 22:5
went back to his young **m**, Gn 22:19
of the **m** of the town are Gn 24:13
and the feet of the **m** with him. Gn 24:32
Then he and the **m** with him ate Gn 24:54
and Abraham's servant and his **m**. Gn 24:59
When the **m** of the place asked Gn 26:7
The **m** of the place will kill me Gn 26:7
Jacob asked the **m** at the well, Gn 29:4
invited all the **m** of the place Gn 29:22
and he has 400 **m** with him." Gn 32:6
with God and with **m** and have Gn 32:28
coming toward him with 400 **m**. Gn 33:1
city and spoke to the **m** there. Gn 34:20
"These **m** are peaceful toward us," Gn 34:21
the **m** will agree to live with Gn 34:22
if all our **m** are circumcised as Gn 34:22
the able-bodied **m** listened to Gn 34:24
the able-bodied **m** were Gn 34:24
He asked the **m** of the place, Gn 38:21
furthermore, the **m** of the place Gn 38:22
of Egypt and all its wise **m**. Gn 41:8
you are honest **m**, let one of you Gn 42:19
We are honest **m** and not spies. Gn 42:31
I will know if you are honest **m**: Gn 42:33
you are not spies but honest **m**. Gn 42:34
The **m** took this gift, double the Gn 43:15
Take the **m** to ⌊my⌋ house. Gn 43:16
But the **m** were afraid because Gn 43:18
man brought the **m** into Joseph's Gn 43:24
Since the **m** had heard that they Gn 43:25
The **m** looked at each other in Gn 43:33
the **m** were sent off with their Gn 44:3
Pursue the **m**, and when you Gn 44:4
The **m** are shepherds; indeed they Gn 46:32
of any capable **m** among them, Gn 47:6
For in their anger they kill **m**, Gn 49:6
for all the **m** who wanted to kill Ex 4:19
Impose heavier work on the **m**. Ex 5:9
the wise **m** and sorcerers— Ex 7:11
Let the **m** go, so that they may Ex 10:7
only the **m** may go and worship Ex 10:11
that both **m** and women should Ex 11:2
Select some **m** for us, and go Ex 17:9
from all the people able **m**, Ex 18:21
chose able **m** from all Israel Ex 18:25
When **m** quarrel and one strikes Ex 21:18
When **m** get in a fight, and hit a Ex 21:22
he sent out young Israelite **m**, Ex 24:5
each of the **m** must pay a ransom Ex 30:12
and about 3,000 **m** fell dead that Ex 32:28
Both **m** and women came; all who Ex 35:22
all the **m** and women whose hearts Ex 35:29
the registered group, 603,550 **m**. Ex 38:26
For the **m** who were in the land Lv 18:27
the names of the **m** who are to Nm 1:5
These are the **m** called from the Nm 1:16
Aaron took these **m** who had been Nm 1:17
These are the **m** Moses and Aaron Nm 1:44
m from 30 years old to 50 years Nm 4:3
Register **m** from 30 years old to Nm 4:23
Register **m** from 30 years old to Nm 4:30
m from 30 years old to 50 years Nm 4:35
The **m** registered by their clans Nm 4:36
registered **m** of the Kohathite Nm 4:37
m from 30 years old to 50 years Nm 4:39
The **m** registered by their clans Nm 4:40
the registered **m** of the Nm 4:41
The **m** of the Merarite clans were Nm 4:42
The **m** registered by their clans Nm 4:44
the registered **m** of the Merarite Nm 4:45
registered **m** numbered 8,580. Nm 4:48
were ⌊some⌋ **m** who were unclean Nm 9:6
These **m** came before Moses and Nm 9:6
Bring Me 70 **m** from Israel known Nm 11:16
He brought 70 **m** from the elders Nm 11:24
Two **m** had remained in the camp, Nm 11:26
Send **m** to scout out the land of Nm 13:2
the **m** were leaders in Israel. Nm 13:3
the names of the **m** Moses sent to Nm 13:16
was carried on a pole by two **m**. Nm 13:23
m went back to Moses, Aaron, Nm 13:26
But the **m** who had gone up with Nm 13:31
saw in it are **m** of great size. Nm 13:32
none of the **m** who have seen My Nm 14:22
So the **m** Moses sent to scout out Nm 14:36
those **m** who spread the report Nm 14:37
alive of those **m** who went to Nm 14:38
Israelite **m** who were leaders Nm 16:2
gouge out the eyes of these **m**? Nm 16:14
the tents of these wicked **m**. Nm 16:26
these **m** die ⌊naturally⌋ as all Nm 16:29
know that these **m** have despised Nm 16:30
consumed the 250 **m** who were Nm 16:35

"Who are these **m** with you?" Nm 22:9
Since these **m** have come to Nm 22:20
Go with the **m**, but you are to Nm 22:35
Kill each of the **m** who aligned Nm 25:5
registered **m** numbered 43,730 Nm 26:7
and the fire consumed 250 **m**. Nm 26:10
clans, numbering 22,200 **m**. Nm 26:14
numbered⌋ by their registered **m**: Nm 26:18
numbered⌋ by their registered **m**: Nm 26:22
numbered⌋ by their registered **m**: Nm 26:25
numbered⌋ by their registered **m**: Nm 26:27
numbered by their registered **m**: Nm 26:34
numbered⌋ by their registered **m**: Nm 26:37
numbered by their registered **m**: Nm 26:41
their registered **m** were 64,400. Nm 26:43
numbered⌋ by their registered **m**: Nm 26:47
numbered by their registered **m**: Nm 26:50
Israelite **m** numbered 601,730. Nm 26:51
Equip some of your **m** for war. Nm 31:3
Send 1,000 **m** to war from each Nm 31:4
the fighting **m** who went out to Nm 31:28
separated from the **m** who fought, Nm 31:42
of the fighting **m** under our Nm 31:49
none of the **m** 20 years old or Nm 32:11
one of your armed **m** crosses the Nm 32:21
are the names of the **m** who are Nm 34:17
These are the names of the **m**: Nm 34:19
any of the **m** from the ⌊other Nm 36:3
They married ⌊**m**⌋ from the clans Nm 36:12
respected **m** from each of your Dt 1:13
and respected **m**, and set them Dt 1:15
'Let's send **m** ahead of us, Dt 1:22
I selected 12 **m** from among you, Dt 1:23
'None of these **m** in this evil Dt 1:35
of fighting **m** had perished Dt 2:14
the fighting **m** had died among Dt 2:16
destroying the **m**, women, and Dt 3:6
your fighting **m** will cross over Dt 3:18
that wicked **m** have sprung up Dt 13:13
Then all the **m** of his city will Dt 21:21
and the **m** of her city will stone Dt 22:21
If there is a dispute between **m**, Dt 25:1
If two **m** are fighting with each Dt 25:11
officials, all the **m** of Israel, Dt 29:10
the people—**m**, women, children, Dt 31:12
your fighting **m** must cross over Jos 1:14
secretly sent two **m** as spies Jos 2:1
the Israelite **m** have come here Jos 2:2
Bring out the **m** who came to you Jos 2:3
taken the two **m** and hidden them Jos 2:4
"Yes, the **m** did come to me, Jos 2:4
to close, the **m** went out, and I Jos 2:5
m pursued them along the road Jos 2:7
Before the **m** fell asleep, she Jos 2:8
The **m** answered her, "⌊We will Jos 2:14
so that the **m** pursuing you won't Jos 2:16
The **m** said to her, "We will be Jos 2:17
So the two **m** went into the hill Jos 2:22
Then the **m** returned, came down Jos 2:23
Now choose 12 **m** from the tribes Jos 3:12
Choose 12 **m** from the people, Jos 4:2
summoned the 12 **m** selected Jos 4:4
The 12 **m** took stones from the Jos 4:8
the Israelite **m** again." Jos 5:2
the Israelite **m** at Jos 5:3
males—all the **m** of war—had Jos 5:4
the nation's **m** of war who came Jos 5:6
and its fighting **m** over to you. Jos 6:2
the city with all the **m** of war, Jos 6:3
because she hid the **m** we sent. Jos 6:17
to the two **m** who had scouted Jos 6:22
So the young **m** who had scouted Jos 6:23
she hid the **m** Joshua had sent to Jos 6:25
sent **m** from Jericho to Ai, Jos 7:2
So the **m** went up and scouted Jos 7:2
2,000 or 3,000 **m** to attack Ai. Jos 7:3
So about 3,000 **m** went up there, Jos 7:4
but they fled from the **m** of Ai. Jos 7:4
The **m** of Ai struck down about 36 Jos 7:5
30,000 fighting **m** and sent them Jos 8:3
taken about 5,000 **m** and set them Jos 8:12
the **m** of the city hurried and Jos 8:14
m in ambush rose quickly from Jos 8:19
The **m** of Ai turned and looked Jos 8:20
saw that the ⌊**m** in⌋ ambush had Jos 8:21
and struck down the **m** of Ai. Jos 8:21
The **m** in the ambush came out of Jos 8:22
and the **m** of Ai were ⌊trapped⌋ Jos 8:22

that day, both **m** and women, was Jos 8:25
said to him and the **m** of Israel, Jos 9:6
The **m** of Israel replied to the Jos 9:7
Then the **m** ⌊of Israel⌋ took some Jos 9:14
and all its **m** were warriors. Jos 10:2
Then the **m** of Gibeon sent ⌊word⌋ Jos 10:6
including all the fighting **m**, Jos 10:7
and station **m** by it to guard the Jos 10:18
summoned all the **m** of Israel and Jos 10:24
three **m** from each tribe Jos 18:4
As the **m** prepared to go, Joshua Jos 18:8
So the **m** left, went through the Jos 18:9
struck down 10,000 **m** in Bezek. Jdg 1:4
The **m** of Judah fought against Jdg 1:8
the **m** of Judah marched down to Jdg 1:9
had gone up with the **m** of Judah Jdg 1:16
all strong and able-bodied **m**. Jdg 3:29
with you 10,000 **m** from the Jdg 4:6
10,000 **m** followed him, and Jdg 4:10
with 10,000 **m** following him. Jdg 4:14
and the **m** of the city to do Jdg 6:27
When the **m** of the city got up in Jdg 6:28
Then the **m** of the city said to Jdg 6:30
hands to their mouths was 300 **m**, Jdg 7:6
with the 300 **m** who lapped and Jdg 7:7
he divided the 300 **m** into three Jdg 7:16
each of the **m** a trumpet in one Jdg 7:16
and the 100 **m** who were with him Jdg 7:19
When Gideon's **m** blew their 300 Jdg 7:22
Then the **m** of Israel were called Jdg 7:23
So all the **m** of Ephraim were Jdg 7:24
The **m** of Ephraim said to him, Jdg 8:1
and the 300 **m** came to the Jordan Jdg 8:4
He said to the **m** of Succoth, Jdg 8:5
The **m** of Penuel answered just as Jdg 8:8
just as the **m** of Succoth had Jdg 8:8
He also told the **m** of Penuel, Jdg 8:9
their army of about 15,000 **m**, Jdg 8:10
a youth from the **m** of Succoth Jdg 8:14
he went to the **m** of Succoth and Jdg 8:15
bread to your exhausted **m**?'" Jdg 8:15
disciplined the **m** of Succoth Jdg 8:16
and killed the **m** of the city. Jdg 8:17
What kind of **m** did you kill at Jdg 8:18
'Is it better for you that 70 **m**, Jdg 9:2
and reckless **m** with this money, Jdg 9:4
You are to serve the **m** of Hamor, Jdg 9:28
mountains look like **m** to you." Jdg 9:36
died—about 1,000 **m** and women. Jdg 9:49
and all the **m**, women, and lords Jdg 9:51
the evil of the **m** of Shechem on Jdg 9:57
some lawless **m** joined Jephthah Jdg 11:3
The **m** of Ephraim were called Jdg 12:1
gathered all of the **m** of Gilead. Jdg 12:4
in marriage ⌊to **m**⌋ outside the Jdg 12:9
young **m** were accustomed to do. Jdg 14:10
they brought 30 **m** to accompany Jdg 14:11
the **m** of the city said to him: Jdg 14:18
and killed 30 of their **m**. Jdg 14:19
to one of the **m** who had Jdg 14:20
to one of the **m** who accompanied Jdg 15:2
the **m** of Judah said, "Why have Jdg 15:10
Then 3,000 **m** of Judah went to Jdg 15:11
and killed 1,000 **m** with it. Jdg 15:15
a donkey I have killed 1,000 **m**. Jdg 15:16
While the **m** in ambush were Jdg 16:9
But while the **m** in ambush were Jdg 16:12
temple was full of **m** and women; Jdg 16:27
about 3,000 **m** and women were Jdg 16:27
out five brave **m** from all their Jdg 18:2
The five **m** left and came to Jdg 18:7
When the **m** went back to their Jdg 18:8
The five **m** who had gone to spy Jdg 18:14
The 600 Danite **m** were standing Jdg 18:16
Then the five **m** who had gone to Jdg 18:17
gate with the 600 **m** armed with Jdg 18:17
m who were in the houses near Jdg 18:22
you that you mobilized ⌊the **m**⌋?" Jdg 18:23
or angry **m** will attack you, Jdg 18:25
and the **m** of that place were Jdg 19:16
perverted **m** of the city Jdg 19:22
But the **m** would not listen to Jdg 19:25
We will take 10 **m** out of every Jdg 20:10
So all the **m** of Israel gathered Jdg 20:11
of Israel sent **m** throughout the Jdg 20:12
the perverted **m** in Gibeah so we Jdg 20:13
armed **m** from their cities, Jdg 20:15
besides 700 choice **m** rallied by Jdg 20:15

were 700 choice **m** who were Jdg 20:16
400,000 armed **m**, every one Jdg 20:17
m of Israel went out to fight Jdg 20:20
slaughtered 22,000 **m** of Israel Jdg 20:21
on the field; all were armed **m**. Jdg 20:25
killing about 30 **m** of Israel on Jdg 20:31
So all the **m** of Israel got up Jdg 20:33
10,000 choice **m** from all Israel Jdg 20:34
25,100 **m** of Benjamin; Jdg 20:35
of Benjamin; all were armed **m**. Jdg 20:35
The **m** of Israel had retreated Jdg 20:36
The **m** in ambush had rushed Jdg 20:37
m of Israel had a prearranged Jdg 20:38
signal with the **m** in ambush: Jdg 20:38
the **m** of Israel would return to Jdg 20:39
killing about 30 **m** of Israel, Jdg 20:39
Then the **m** of Israel returned, Jdg 20:41
and the **m** of Benjamin were Jdg 20:41
before the **m** of Israel toward Jdg 20:42
There were 18,000 **m** who died Jdg 20:44
killed 5,000 **m** on the highways. Jdg 20:45
that day were 25,000 armed **m**; Jdg 20:46
But 600 **m** escaped into the Jdg 20:47
The **m** of Israel turned back Jdg 20:48
m of Israel had sworn an oath Jdg 21:1
the young **m** not to touch you Ru 2:9
jars the young **m** have filled." Ru 2:9
Boaz ordered his young **m**, Ru 2:15
the **m** she had worked ⌊with⌋ Ru 2:19
with my young **m** until they have Ru 2:21
you have not pursued younger **m**, Ru 3:10
Boaz took 10 **m** of the city's Ru 4:2
Eli's sons were wicked **m**; 1Sm 2:12
favor with the LORD and with **m**. 1Sm 2:26
down about 4,000 **m** on the 1Sm 4:2
the people sent ⌊**m**⌋ to Shiloh to 1Sm 4:4
Show some courage and be **m**, 1Sm 4:9
served you. Now be **m** and fight!" 1Sm 4:9
When the **m** of Ashdod saw what 1Sm 5:7
the **m** of Ashdod moved the ark. 1Sm 5:8
He afflicted the **m** of the city, 1Sm 5:9
The **m** who did not die were 1Sm 5:12
The **m** did this: They took two 1Sm 6:10
That day the **m** of Beth-shemesh 1Sm 6:15
down the **m** of Beth-shemesh 1Sm 6:19
struck down 70 **m** ⌊out of⌋ 50,000 1Sm 6:19
down 70 men ⌊out of⌋ 50,000 **m**. 1Sm 6:19
The **m** of Beth-shemesh asked, 1Sm 6:20
So the **m** of Kiriath-jearim came 1Sm 7:1
Then the **m** of Israel charged out 1Sm 7:11
your best young **m**, and your 1Sm 8:16
Samuel told the **m** of Israel, 1Sm 8:22
of the 30 or so **m** who had been 1Sm 9:22
you'll find two **m** at Rachel's 1Sm 10:2
m going up to God at Bethel 1Sm 10:3
brave **m** whose hearts God had 1Sm 10:26
some wicked **m** said, "How can 1Sm 10:27
All the **m** of Jabesh said to him, 1Sm 11:1
the words of the **m** from Jabesh. 1Sm 11:5
and 30,000 **m** from Judah. 1Sm 11:8
this to the **m** of Jabesh-gilead 1Sm 11:9
messengers told the **m** of Jabesh, 1Sm 11:9
Then the **m** of Jabesh said to 1Sm 11:10
us those **m** so we can kill them! 1Sm 11:12
Saul and all the **m** of Israel 1Sm 11:15
He chose 3,000 **m** from Israel for 1Sm 13:2
The **m** of Israel saw that they 1Sm 13:6
who were with him, about 600 **m**. 1Sm 13:15
of these uncircumcised **m**. 1Sm 14:6
over to the **m** and then let them 1Sm 14:8
The **m** of the garrison called to 1Sm 14:12
down about 20 **m** in a half-acre 1Sm 14:14
all the Israelite **m** who had been 1Sm 14:22
the **m** of Israel were worn out 1Sm 14:24
Kill **m** and women, children and 1Sm 15:3
and 10,000 **m** from Judah. 1Sm 15:4
One of the young **m** answered, 1Sm 16:18
and the **m** of Israel gathered 1Sm 17:2
one of your **m** and have him come 1Sm 17:8
Saul and all the **m** of Israel are 1Sm 17:19
all the Israelite **m** saw Goliath, 1Sm 17:24
spoke to the **m** who were 1Sm 17:26
listened as he spoke to the **m**, 1Sm 17:28
The **m** of Israel and Judah 1Sm 17:52
him commander over 1,000 **m**. 1Sm 18:13
David and his **m** went out and 1Sm 18:27
my⌋ young **m** at a certain place. 1Sm 21:2
but the young **m** may eat it only 1Sm 21:4

their leading **m**, had duties for 1Ch 26:12
1,700 capable **m**, had assigned 1Ch 26:30
capable **m** were found among 1Ch 26:31
2,700 capable **m** who were heads 1Ch 26:32
count the **m** aged 20 or under 1Ch 27:23
fighting **m**, and all the brave 1Ch 28:1
the leaders and the mighty **m**, 1Ch 29:24
he assigned 70,000 **m** as porters, 2Ch 2:2
80,000 **m** as stonecutters in the 2Ch 2:2
of all the foreign **m** in the land 2Ch 2:17
So all the **m** of Israel were 2Ch 5:3
happy are your **m**. How happy are 2Ch 9:7
with the young **m** who had grown 2Ch 10:8
Then the young **m** who had grown 2Ch 10:10
in order with 400,000 choice **m**. 2Ch 13:3
of 800,000 choice **m** in battle 2Ch 13:3
and wicked **m** gathered around him 2Ch 13:7
and the **m** of Judah raised the 2Ch 13:15
When the **m** of Judah raised the 2Ch 13:15
500,000 choice **m** of Israel were 2Ch 13:17
of one million **m** and 300 2Ch 14:9
had fighting **m**, brave warriors 2Ch 17:13
prophets, 400 **m**, and asked them 2Ch 18:5
Then all the **m** of Judah and 2Ch 20:27
They each brought their **m**— 2Ch 23:8
army came with only a few **m**, 2Ch 24:24
300,000 choice **m** who could serve 2Ch 25:5
for the **m** of the division that 2Ch 25:13
⌊**m**⌋ were sent after him to 2Ch 25:27
day—all brave **m**—because they 2Ch 28:6
some **m** who were leaders of the 2Ch 28:12
Then the **m** who were designated 2Ch 28:15
⌊There were⌋ **m** who were 2Ch 31:19
The **m** were doing the work with 2Ch 34:12
temple with all the **m** of Judah 2Ch 34:30
all the singing **m** and singing 2Ch 35:25
choice young **m** with the sword 2Ch 36:17
assisted by the **m** of that region Ezr 1:4
of the Israelite **m** ⌊included⌋: Ezr 2:2
Netophah's **m** 56 Ezr 2:22
Anathoth's **m** 128 Ezr 2:23
Michmas's **m** 122 Ezr 2:27
Bethel's and Ai's **m** 223 Ezr 2:28
m from the region west of the Ezr 4:11
an order for these **m** to stop, Ezr 4:21
These **m** wouldn't stop them until Ezr 5:5
full to these **m** out of the royal Ezr 6:8
and 150 **m** with him who were Ezr 8:3
descendants, and 200 **m** with him; Ezr 8:4
descendants, and 300 **m** with him; Ezr 8:5
descendants, and 50 **m** with him; Ezr 8:6
descendants, and 70 **m** with him; Ezr 8:7
descendants, and 80 **m** with him; Ezr 8:8
descendants, and 218 **m** with him; Ezr 8:9
descendants, and 160 **m** with him; Ezr 8:10
descendants, and 28 **m** with him; Ezr 8:11
descendants, and 110 **m** with him; Ezr 8:12
Shemaiah, and 60 **m** with them; Ezr 8:13
descendants, and 70 **m** with them. Ezr 8:14
his sons and brothers, 18 **m**, Ezr 8:18
brothers and their sons, 20 **m**. Ezr 8:19
large assembly of Israelite **m**, Ezr 10:1
So all the **m** of Judah and Ezr 10:9
selected **m** who were family Ezr 10:16
with all the **m** who had married Ezr 10:17
arrived with **m** from Judah, Neh 1:2
and ⌊took⌋ a few **m** with me. Neh 2:12
The **m** of Jericho built next to Neh 3:2
and the **m** of Gibeon and Mizpah, Neh 3:7
and the powerful **m** of Samaria, Neh 4:2
half of my **m** did the work while Neh 4:16
while half of the **m** were holding Neh 4:21
brothers, my **m**, and the guards Neh 4:23
of the Israelite **m** ⌊included⌋: Neh 7:7
Bethlehem's and Netophah's **m** 188 Neh 7:26
Anathoth's **m** 128 Neh 7:27
Beth-azmaveth's **m** 42 Neh 7:28
Chephirah's, and Beeroth's **m** 743 Neh 7:29
Ramah's and Geba's **m** 621 Neh 7:30
Michmas's **m** 122 Neh 7:31
Bethel's and Ai's **m** 123 Neh 7:32
the other Nebo's **m** 52 Neh 7:33
law before the assembly of **m**, Neh 8:2
until noon before the **m**, Neh 8:3
all the **m** who volunteered Neh 11:2
in Jerusalem, was 468 capable **m**. Neh 11:6
and their relatives, capable **m**: Neh 11:14
that same day **m** were placed in Neh 12:44

some of my **m** at the gates, Neh 13:19
some of their **m**, and pulled out Neh 13:25
the wise **m** who understood Est 1:13
both **m** were hanged on the Est 2:23
Jews killed and destroyed 500 **m**, Est 9:6
have killed and destroyed 500 **m**, Est 9:12
Adar and killed 300 **m** in Susa, Est 9:15
when deep sleep descends on **m**, Jb 4:13
them stagger like drunken **m**. Jb 12:25
are with us, **m** older than your Jb 15:10
declared by wise **m** and was not Jb 15:18
God hands me over to unjust **m**; Jb 16:11
path that wicked **m** have walked? Jb 22:15
From the city, **m** groan; the Jb 24:12
the young **m** saw me and withdrew, Jb 29:8
while older **m** stood to their Jb 29:8
M listened to me with Jb 29:21
they mock me, **m** younger than I Jb 30:1
Foolish **m**, without even a name! Jb 30:8
and let other **m** sleep with her. Jb 31:10
So these three **m** quit answering Jb 32:1
the three **m** could not answer Jb 32:5
He will look at **m** and say, Jb 33:27
words, you wise **m**, and listen to Jb 34:2
and walks with wicked **m**. Jb 34:8
to me, you **m** of understanding Jb 34:10
and to nobles, "Wicked **m**!" Jb 34:18
that godless **m** should not rule Jb 34:30
Reasonable **m** will say to me, Jb 34:34
with the wise **m** who hear me, Jb 34:34
are ⌊like⌋ those of wicked **m**. Jb 34:36
because of the pride of evil **m**. Jb 35:12
so that all **m** may know His work. Jb 37:7
Now **m** cannot ⌊even⌋ look at the Jb 37:21
Therefore, **m** fear Him. He does Jb 37:24
long, exalted **m**, will my honor Ps 4:2
nations know they are only **m**. Ps 9:20
that **m** of the earth may terrify Ps 10:18
LORD, ⌊save me⌋ from **m**, from men Ps 17:14
from men, from **m** of the world, Ps 17:14
You rescue me from violent **m**. Ps 18:48
scorned by **m** and despised by Ps 22:6
life along with **m** of bloodshed Ps 26:9
a shelter from the schemes of **m**, Ps 31:20
You are the most handsome of **m**; Ps 45:2
For one can see that wise **m** die; Ps 49:10
and violent **m** seek my life. Ps 54:3
m of bloodshed and treachery Ps 55:23
down with those who devour **m**. Ps 57:4
and save me from **m** of bloodshed. Ps 59:2
Powerful **m** attack me, but not Ps 59:3
M are only a vapor; exalted men, Ps 62:9
a vapor; exalted **m**, an illusion. Ps 62:9
You let **m** ride over our heads; Ps 66:12
It was like **m** in a thicket of Ps 74:5
He killed some of their best **m**. Ps 78:31
down Israel's choice young **m**. Ps 78:31
tent where He resided among **m**. Ps 78:60
consumed His chosen young **m**, Ps 78:63
will die like **m** and fall like Ps 82:7
of ruthless **m** seeks my life. Ps 86:14
and staggered like drunken **m**, Ps 107:27
on our side when **m** attacked us, Ps 124:2
m will never be put to shame Ps 127:5
you bloodthirsty **m**, stay away Ps 139:19
Rescue me, LORD, from evil **m**. Ps 140:1
Keep me safe from violent **m** Ps 140:1
from violent **m** who plan to make Ps 140:4
acts with **m** who commit sin. Ps 141:4
young **m** as well as young women, Ps 148:12
violent **m** gain ⌊only⌋ riches. Pr 11:16
wicked desire what evil **m** have, Pr 12:12
ways of wicked **m** lead them Pr 12:26
glory of young **m** is their Pr 20:29
splendor of old **m** is gray hair. Pr 20:29
in the presence of unknown **m**. Pr 22:29
among **m** who are unfaithful. Pr 23:28
Don't envy evil **m** or desire to Pr 24:1
which the **m** of Hezekiah, king Pr 25:1
than seven **m** who can answer Pr 26:16
m do not understand justice, Pr 28:5
Bloodthirsty **m** hate an honest Pr 29:10
I am the least intelligent of **m**, Pr 30:2
concubines, the delights of **m**. Ec 2:8
a small city with few **m** in it. Ec 9:14
the strong **m** stoop, the women Ec 12:3
so is my love among the young **m**. Sg 2:3
loftiness of **m** will be brought Is 2:11

loftiness of **m** will be humbled Is 2:17
Your **m** will fall by the sword, Is 3:25
of Jerusalem and **m** of Judah, Is 5:3
of Israel, and the **m** of Judah, Is 5:7
you to try the patience of **m**? Is 7:13
over Israel's young **m** and has no Is 9:17
bows will cut young **m** to pieces. Is 13:18
Where then are your wise **m**? Is 19:12
raised young **m** ⌊or⌋ brought up Is 23:4
prostitute forgotten ⌊by **m**⌋. Is 23:16
of their wise **m** will vanish, Is 29:14
house of wicked **m** and against Is 31:2
Egyptians are **m**, not God; Is 31:3
young **m** will be put to forced Is 31:8
and not to the **m** who sit on the Is 36:12
him, "What did these **m** say? Is 39:3
The **m** who came to you—where Is 39:3
and young **m** stumble and fall, Is 40:30
you worm Jacob, you **m** of Israel: Is 41:14
the Sabeans, **m** of stature, will Is 45:14
do not fear disgrace by **m**, Is 51:7
was despised and rejected by **m**, Is 53:3
faithful **m** are swept away, Is 57:1
bodies of the **m** who have Is 66:24
The **m** of Memphis and Tahpanhes Jr 2:16
the LORD says to the **m** of Judah Jr 4:3
m of Judah and residents of Jr 4:4
for wicked **m** live among My Jr 5:26
They set a trap; they catch **m**. Jr 5:26
on the gang of young **m** as well. Jr 6:11
lined up like **m** in battle Jr 6:23
give their wives to other **m**, Jr 8:10
streets, young **m** from the Jr 9:21
and tell them to the **m** of Judah Jr 11:2
discovered among the **m** of Judah Jr 11:9
The young **m** will die by the Jr 11:22
mother of young **m** a destroyer at Jr 15:8
their officials, the **m** of Judah, Jr 17:25
say to the **m** of Judah and to the Jr 18:11
their young **m** struck down by the Jr 18:21
King Jehoiakim sent **m** to Egypt: Jr 26:22
certain other⌋ **m** with him ⌊went⌋ Jr 26:22
daughters to **m** ⌊in marriage⌋ so Jr 29:6
young and old **m** ⌊rejoice⌋ Jr 31:13
the sons of **m** in order to give Jr 32:19
their prophets, the **m** of Judah, Jr 32:32
⌊their own⌋ **m** I strike down in Jr 33:5
say to the **m** of Judah and the Jr 35:13
and on the **m** of Judah all the Jr 36:31
them only the badly wounded **m**, Jr 37:10
these **m** have been evil in all Jr 38:9
Take from here 30 **m** under your Jr 38:10
took the **m** under his authority Jr 38:11
over to these **m** who want to take Jr 38:16
handed over to the **m** you fear. Jr 39:17
they and their **m**—heard that Jr 40:7
had put him in charge of the **m**, Jr 40:7
Maacathite—they and their **m**. Jr 40:8
an oath to them and their **m**, Jr 40:9
came with 10 **m** to Gedaliah son Jr 41:1
and the 10 **m** who were with him Jr 41:2
80 **m** came from Shechem, Shiloh, Jr 41:5
Nethaniah and the **m** with him Jr 41:7
there were 10 **m** among them who Jr 41:8
corpses of the **m** he had struck Jr 41:9
took all their **m** and went to Jr 41:12
Johanan with eight **m** and went to Jr 41:15
son of Ahikam—**m**, soldiers, Jr 41:16
the other arrogant **m** responded Jr 43:2
the **m**, women, children, king's Jr 43:6
in the sight of the Judean **m** Jr 43:9
all the **m** who knew that their Jr 44:15
people—the **m**, women, and all Jr 44:20
and you **m** fulfilled it by your Jr 44:25
mighty **m** ⌊ready⌋ for battle? Jr 48:14
of its young **m** have gone down to Jr 48:15
moan for the **m** of Kir-heres. Jr 48:31
her young **m** will fall in her Jr 49:26
her young **m** will fall in her Jr 50:30
lined up like **m** in battle Jr 50:42
Don't spare her young **m**; Jr 51:3
you up with **m** as with locusts Jr 51:14
and 60 **m** from the common people Jr 52:25
all the mighty **m** within me. Lm 1:15
My young **m** and women have gone Lm 1:18
young **m** and women have fallen Lm 2:21
Young **m** labor at millstones; Lm 5:13
gate, the young **m**, their music. Lm 5:14

Violent **m** will enter it and Ezk 7:22
were about 25 **m** at the entrance Ezk 8:16
And I saw six **m** coming from the Ezk 9:2
foreheads of the **m** who sigh and Ezk 9:4
the old **m**, the young men Ezk 9:6
men, the young **m** and women, as Ezk 9:6
the gate's entrance were 25 **m**. Ezk 11:1
these are the **m** who plan evil Ezk 11:2
these **m** have set up idols in Ezk 14:3
these three **m**—Noah, Daniel, Ezk 14:14
if⌋ these three **m** were in it, Ezk 14:16
if⌋ these three **m** were in it, Ezk 14:18
acts with Egyptian **m**, Ezk 16:26
the Assyrian **m** because you were Ezk 16:28
M give gifts to all prostitutes, Ezk 16:33
away the leading **m** of the land, Ezk 17:13
out true justice between **m**. Ezk 18:8
will hand you over to brutal **m**, Ezk 21:31
There are **m** within you who Ezk 22:9
M within you have sexual Ezk 22:10
all of them desirable young **m**, Ezk 23:6
when **m** slept with her in her Ezk 23:8
all of them desirable young **m**. Ezk 23:12
desirable young **m**, all of them Ezk 23:23
they sent for **m** who came from Ezk 23:40
brought in, along with common **m**. Ezk 23:42
But righteous **m** will judge them Ezk 23:45
Your wise **m** were within you, Ezk 27:8
and its wise **m** were within you, Ezk 27:9
⌊**M** of⌋ Persia, Lud, and Put were Ezk 27:10
M of Arvad and Helech were Ezk 27:11
M of Dedan were also your Ezk 27:15
ruthless **m** from the nations. Ezk 28:7
Libya and the **m** of the covenant Ezk 30:5
ruthless **m** from the nations, Ezk 30:11
land into the hands of evil **m**. Ezk 30:12
The young **m** of On and Pi-beseth Ezk 30:17
ruthless **m** from the nations, Ezk 31:12
them ruthless **m** from the nations Ezk 32:12
You devour **m** and deprive your Ezk 36:13
longer devour **m** and deprive your Ezk 36:14
will appoint **m** on a full-time Ezk 39:14
flesh of mighty **m** and drink the Ezk 39:18
mighty **m** and all the warriors. Ezk 39:20
young **m** without any physical Dn 1:4
of the other young **m** your age. Dn 1:10
of the young **m** who are eating Dn 1:13
all the young **m** who were eating Dn 1:15
these four young **m** knowledge Dn 1:17
all the wise **m** of Babylon. Dn 2:12
that the wise **m** were to be Dn 2:13
execute the wise **m** of Babylon. Dn 2:14
the rest of Babylon's wise **m**. Dn 2:18
destroy the wise **m** of Babylon. Dn 2:24
kill the wise **m** of Babylon! Dn 2:24
over all the wise **m** of Babylon. Dn 2:48
These **m** have ignored you, the Dn 3:12
So these **m** were brought before Dn 3:13
So these **m**, in their trousers, Dn 3:21
killed those **m** who carried Dn 3:22
And these three **m**, Shadrach, Dn 3:23
throw three **m**, bound, into the Dn 3:24
I see four **m**, not tied, walking Dn 3:25
effect on the bodies of these **m**: Dn 3:27
all the wise **m** of Babylon to me Dn 4:6
is ruler over the kingdom of **m**. Dn 4:17
sets over it the lowliest of **m**. Dn 4:17
none of the wise **m** of my kingdom Dn 4:18
is ruler over the kingdom of **m**, Dn 4:25
is ruler over the kingdom of **m**, Dn 4:32
said to these wise **m** of Babylon, Dn 5:7
all the king's wise **m** came in, Dn 5:8
Now the wise **m** and mediums were Dn 5:15
the kingdom of **m** and sets anyone Dn 5:21
these **m** said, "We will never Dn 6:5
Then these **m** went as a group and Dn 6:11
Then these **m** went to the king Dn 6:15
and those **m** who had maliciously Dn 6:24
the **m** of Judah, the residents of Dn 9:7
The **m** who were with me did not Dn 10:7
the **m** who give me my food and Hs 2:5
for the **m** themselves go off with Hs 4:14
Let the **m** who sacrifice kiss the Hs 13:2
scale walls as **m** of war⌊do⌋. Jl 2:7
your old **m** will have dreams, Jl 2:28
and your young **m** will see Jl 2:28
let all the **m** of war advance and Jl 3:9
of your young **m** as Nazirites. Am 2:11

your young **m** with the sword, Am 4:10
if there are 10 **m** left in one Am 6:9
the young **m** also, will faint Am 8:13
Then the **m** were even more afraid Jnh 1:10
For the **m** knew he was fleeing Jnh 1:10
the **m** rowed hard to get back to Jnh 1:13
The **m** feared the LORD even more, Jnh 1:16
m of Nineveh believed in God. Jnh 3:5
even eight leaders of **m**. Mc 5:5
He has told you **m** what is good Mc 6:8
the valiant **m** are dressed in Nah 2:3
and punish the **m** who settle down Zph 1:12
are reckless—treacherous **m**. Zph 3:4
these **m** are a sign that I am Zch 3:8
and their **m** to plead for the Zch 7:2
Old **m** and women will again sit Zch 8:4
10 **m** from nations of every Zch 8:23
the eyes of **m** are on the LORD Zch 9:1
will make the young **m** flourish, Zch 9:17
wise **m** from the east arrived Mt 2:1
the wise **m** and asked them Mt 2:7
been outwitted by the wise **m**, Mt 2:16
he had learned from the wise **m**. Mt 2:16
thrown out and trampled on by **m**. Mt 5:13
let your light shine before **m**, Mt 5:16
The **m** were amazed and asked, Mt 8:27
demon-possessed **m** met Him as Mt 8:28
Then the **m** who tended them fled. Mt 8:33
Just then some **m** brought to Him Mt 9:2
had given such authority to **m**. Mt 9:8
there, two blind **m** followed Him, Mt 9:27
the blind **m** approached Him, Mt 9:28
will acknowledge Me before **m**, Mt 10:32
But whoever denies Me before **m**, Mt 10:33
these **m** went away, Jesus began Mt 11:7
The **m** of Nineveh will stand up Mt 12:41
who ate were about 5,000 **m**, Mt 14:21
When the **m** of that place Mt 14:35
as doctrines the commands of **m**." Mt 15:9
Now those who ate were 4,000 **m**, Mt 15:38
be betrayed into the hands of **m**. Mt 17:22
are eunuchs who were made by **m**, Mt 19:12
With **m** this is impossible, Mt 19:26
To those **m** he said, 'You also go Mt 20:4
'These last **m** put in one hour, Mt 20:12
and the **m** of high position Mt 20:25
were two blind **m** sitting by the Mt 20:30
heaven or from **m**?" They began to Mt 21:25
we say, 'From **m**,' we're afraid Mt 21:26
destroy those terrible **m**," Mt 21:41
Then two **m** will be in the field: Mt 24:40
to what these **m** are testifying Mt 26:62
that they became like dead **m**. Mt 28:4
with the hired **m** and followed Mk 1:20
a paralytic, carried by four **m**. Mk 2:3
m who tended them ran off and Mk 5:14
and the leading **m** of Galilee. Mk 6:21
who ate the loaves were 5,000 **m**. Mk 6:44
as doctrines the commands of **m**. Mk 7:7
you keep the tradition of **m**." Mk 7:8
About 4,000 ⌊**m**⌋ were there. Mk 8:9
betrayed into the hands of **m**. Mk 9:31
said, "With **m** it is impossible Mk 10:27
and their **m** of high positions Mk 10:42
baptism from heaven or from **m**? Mk 11:30
we say, 'From **m**' "—they were Mk 11:32
to what these **m** are testifying Mk 14:60
Just then some **m** came, carrying Lk 5:18
When the **m** reached Him, they Lk 7:20
When the **m** who tended them saw Lk 8:34
For about 5,000 **m** were there. Lk 9:14
two **m** were talking with Him— Lk 9:30
and the two **m** who were standing Lk 9:32
As the two **m** were departing from Lk 9:33
betrayed into the hands of **m**." Lk 9:44
judgment with the **m** of this Lk 11:31
The **m** of Nineveh will rise up at Lk 11:32
who acknowledges Me before **m**, Lk 12:8
Me before **m** will be denied Lk 12:9
one of those **m** who were invited Lk 14:24
10 **m** with serious skin diseases Lk 17:12
Two **m** went up to the temple Lk 18:10
impossible with **m** is possible Lk 18:27
of John from heaven or from **m**?" Lk 20:4
we say, 'From **m**,' all the people Lk 20:6
The **m** who were holding Jesus Lk 22:63
suddenly two **m** stood by them in Lk 24:4
among the dead?" asked the **m**. Lk 24:5

into the hands of sinful **m**, Lk 24:7
that life was the light of **m**. Jn 1:4
went into town, and told the **m**, Jn 4:28
I do not accept glory from **m**, Jn 5:41
The **m** numbered about 5,000. Jn 6:10
starting with the older **m**. Jn 8:9
the witness of two **m** is valid. Jn 8:17
praise from **m** more than praise Jn 12:43
Your name to the **m** You gave Me Jn 17:6
looking for Me, let these **m** go." Jn 18:8
"**M**," Jesus called to them, "you Jn 21:5
suddenly two **m** in white clothes Ac 1:10
They said, "**M** of Galilee, why do Ac 1:11
from among the **m** who have Ac 1:21
devout **m** from every nation under Ac 2:5
Jewish **m** and all you residents Ac 2:14
your young **m** will see visions, Ac 2:17
your old **m** will dream dreams. Ac 2:17
M of Israel, listen to these Ac 2:22
M of Israel, why are you amazed Ac 3:12
number of the **m** came to about Ac 4:4
were uneducated and untrained **m**, Ac 4:13
What should we do with these **m**? Ac 4:16
have not lied to **m** but to God!" Ac 5:4
The young **m** got up, wrapped ⌊his Ac 5:6
When the young **m** came in, they Ac 5:10
crowds of both **m** and women. Ac 5:14
The **m** you put in jail are Ac 5:25
We must obey God rather than **m**. Ac 5:29
and ordered the **m** to be taken Ac 5:34
said to them, "**M** of Israel, be Ac 5:35
you're going to do to these **m**. Ac 5:35
of about 400 **m** rallied to him. Ac 5:36
away from these **m** and leave them Ac 5:38
this plan or this work is of **m**, Ac 5:38
among you seven **m** of good Ac 6:3
Then they induced **m** to say, Ac 6:11
saying, '**M**, you are brothers. Ac 7:26
But devout **m** buried Stephen and Ac 8:2
house, drag off **m** and women, and Ac 8:3
both **m** and women were baptized. Ac 8:12
the Way, either **m** or women, he Ac 9:2
m who were traveling with him Ac 9:7
and sent two **m** to him who begged Ac 9:38
Now send **m** to Joppa and call for Ac 10:5
the **m** who had been sent by Ac 10:17
Three **m** are here looking for Ac 10:19
went down to the **m** and said, Ac 10:21
m and ate with them! Ac 11:3
three **m** who had been sent to me Ac 11:11
and Cyrenian **m**, who came to Ac 11:20
M of Israel, and you who fear Ac 13:16
and the leading **m** of the city. Ac 13:50
down to us in the form of **m**!" Ac 14:11
M! Why are you doing these Ac 14:15
We are **m** also, with the same Ac 14:15
Some **m** came down from Judea and Ac 15:1
to select **m** from among them Ac 15:22
both leading **m** among the Ac 15:22
to select **m** and send them to Ac 15:25
These **m** are the slaves of the Ac 16:17
These **m** are seriously disturbing Ac 16:20
to say, "Release those **m**!" Ac 16:35
These **m** who have turned the Ac 17:6
Greek women as well as **m**. Ac 17:12
and said: "**M** of Athens! I see Ac 17:22
every nation of **m** to live all Ac 17:26
some **m** joined him and believed, Ac 17:34
there were about 12 **m** in all. Ac 19:7
M, you know that our prosperity Ac 19:25
down, he said, "**M** of Ephesus! Ac 19:35
brought these **m** here who are not Ac 19:37
These **m** went on ahead and waited Ac 20:5
And **m** from among yourselves will Ac 20:30
have four **m** who have obligated Ac 21:23
Take these **m**, purify yourself Ac 21:24
Paul took the **m**, having purified Ac 21:26
shouting, "**M** of Israel, help! Ac 21:28
and putting both **m** and women in Ac 22:4
m went to the chief priests Ac 23:14
m who have bound themselves Ac 23:21
When these **m** entered Caesarea Ac 23:33
These **m** presented their case Ac 24:1
which these **m** themselves also Ac 24:15
conscience toward God and **m**. Ac 24:16
let these **m** here state what Ac 24:20
let the **m** of authority among you Ac 25:5
nothing to what these **m** accuse Ac 25:11

and prominent **m** of the city. Ac 25:23
and all **m** present with us Ac 25:24
told them, "**M**, I can see that Ac 27:10
You **m** should have followed my Ac 27:21
take courage, **m**, because I Ac 27:25
Unless these **m** stay in the ship, Ac 27:31
is not from **m** but from God. Rm 2:29
this way death spread to all **m**, Rm 5:12
have left 7,000 **m** for Myself who Rm 11:4
to God and approved by **m**. Rm 14:18
For who among **m** knows the 1Co 2:11
are you not ⌊typical⌋ **m**? 1Co 3:4
So no one should boast in **m**, 1Co 3:21
place, like **m** condemned to die 1Co 4:9
world and to angels and to **m**. 1Co 4:9
do not become slaves of **m**. 1Co 7:23
languages of **m** and of angels, 1Co 13:1
is not speaking to **m** but to God, 1Co 14:2
because these **m** have made up for 1Co 16:17
the Lord but also before **m**. 2Co 8:21
apostle—not from **m** or by man, Gl 1:1
certain **m** came from James. Gl 2:12
order to please **m**, but as slaves Eph 6:6
as to the Lord and not to **m**, Eph 6:7
taking on the likeness of **m**. Php 2:7
all joy and hold **m** like him in Php 2:29
in order to please **m**, but ⌊work⌋ Col 3:22
done for the Lord and not for **m**, Col 3:23
what kind of **m** we were among you 1Th 1:5
not to please **m**, but rather God, 1Th 2:4
from wicked and evil **m**. 2Th 3:2
I want the **m** in every place to 1Tm 2:8
a father, younger **m** as brothers, 1Tm 5:1
among **m** whose minds are 1Tm 6:5
to faithful **m** who will be able 2Tm 2:2
m who are corrupt in mind, 2Tm 3:8
the commandments of **m** who reject Ti 1:14
Older **m** are to be Ti 2:2
the young **m** to be sensible Ti 2:6
priest taken from **m** is appointed Heb 5:1
For **m** swear by something greater Heb 6:16
m who will die receive tithes; Heb 7:8
as high priests **m** who are weak, Heb 7:28
Some **m** were tortured, not Heb 11:35
with it we curse **m** who are made Jms 3:9
rejected by **m** but chosen and 1Pt 2:4
stone that causes **m** to stumble, 1Pt 2:8
be judged by **m** in the fleshly 1Pt 4:6
you younger **m**, be subject to 1Pt 5:5
Holy Spirit, **m** spoke from God. 2Pt 1:21
and destruction of ungodly **m**. 2Pt 3:7
you, young **m**, because you have 1Jn 2:13
to you, young **m**, because you are 1Jn 2:14
If we accept the testimony of **m**, 1Jn 5:9
we ought to support such **m**, 3Jn 8
For certain **m**, who were Jd 4
These **m** have the power to close Rv 11:6
the flesh of mighty **m**, the flesh Rv 19:18
dwelling is with **m**, and He will Rv 21:3

MEN'S *(9)*
Fill the **m** bags with as much Gn 44:1
The young **m** bodies are 1Sm 21:5
according to the young **m** advice: 1Kg 12:14
these **m** eyes and let them see. 2Kg 6:20
according to the young **m** advice, 2Ch 10:14
full of dead **m** bones and every Mt 23:27
Pilate have the **m** legs broken Jn 19:31
not be based on **m** wisdom but on 1Co 2:5
their faces were like **m** faces; Rv 9:7

MENAHEM *(7)*
Then **M** son of Gadi came up 2Kg 15:14
from Tirzah, **M** attacked Tiphsah, 2Kg 15:16
M son of Gadi became king over 2Kg 15:17
so **M** gave Pul 75,000 pounds of 2Kg 15:19
Then **M** exacted 20 ounces of 2Kg 15:20
M rested with his fathers, 2Kg 15:22
Pekahiah son of **M** became king 2Kg 15:23

MENAHEM'S *(1)*
rest of the events of **M** ⌊reign⌋, 2Kg 15:21

MENDED *(2)*
old wineskins, cracked and **m**. Jos 9:4
jar that can never again be **m**. Jr 19:11

MENDING *(2)*
their father, **m** their nets, and Mt 4:21
were in their boat **m** their nets. Mk 1:19

MENE *(3)*
was inscribed: **M**, MENE, TEKEL, Dn 5:25
inscribed: MENE, **M**, TEKEL, Dn 5:25
M ⌊means that⌋ God has numbered Dn 5:26

MENNA *(1)*
Melea, ⌊son⌋ of **M**, ⌊son⌋ of Lk 3:31

MENSTRUAL *(10)*
the days of her **m** impurity. Lv 12:2
she is⌋ during her ⌊**m**⌋ impurity. Lv 12:5
like her bed during **m** impurity; Lv 15:26
be unclean as in her **m** period. Lv 15:26
a woman who is in her **m** period; Lv 15:33
during her **m** impurity to have Lv 18:19
throw them away like **m** cloths, Is 30:22
a woman during her **m** impurity. Ezk 18:6
women during their **m** impurity. Ezk 22:10
before Me was like **m** impurity. Ezk 36:17

MENSTRUATING *(1)*
sleeps with a **m** woman and has Lv 20:18

MENSTRUATION *(5)*
because of her **m** for seven days. Lv 15:19
lies on during her **m** will become Lv 15:20
blood from⌋ her **m** gets on him, Lv 15:24
it is not the time of her **m**, Lv 15:25
is⌋ during the days of her **m**. Lv 15:25

MENTAL *(1)*
blindness, and **m** confusion, Dt 28:28

MENTION *(8)*
I will **m** those who know Me: Ps 87:4
won't **m** Him or speak any longer Jr 20:9
witness that I constantly **m** you, Rm 1:9
we, not to **m** you, would be 2Co 9:4
Not to **m** other things, there is 2Co 11:28
shameful even to **m** what is done Eph 5:12
my God when I **m** you in my Phm 4
not to **m** to you that you owe me Phm 19

MENTIONED *(6)*
not overthrow the town you **m**. Gn 19:21
When he **m** the ark of God, Eli 1Sm 4:18
these **m** by name were leaders in 1Ch 4:38
whenever Judah is **m**, Egypt will Is 19:17
I have never commanded or **m**; Jr 19:5
m the exodus of the sons of Heb 11:22

MENTIONING *(3)*
to me by **m** me to Pharaoh, Gn 40:14
These nobles kept **m** Tobiah's Neh 6:19
and quartz are not worth **m**. Jb 28:18

MENTORS *(1)*
or listen closely to my **m**. Pr 5:13

MEONOTHAI *(2)*
Othniel's sons: Hathath and **M**. 1Ch 4:13
M fathered Ophrah, and Seraiah 1Ch 4:14

MEPHAATH *(4)*
Jahaz, Kedemoth, **M**, Jos 13:18
and **M** with its pasturelands— Jos 21:37
and **M** and its pasturelands. 1Ch 6:79
plateau—to Holon, Jahzah, **M**, Jr 48:21

MEPHIBOSHETH *(14)*
(AKA MERIB-BAAL)
His name was **M**. 2Sm 4:4
M son of Jonathan son of Saul 2Sm 9:6
David said, "**M**!" 2Sm 9:6
M bowed down and said, "What is 2Sm 9:8
But **M**, your master's grandson, 2Sm 9:10
So **M** ate at David's table just 2Sm 9:11
M had a young son whose name 2Sm 9:12
M lived in Jerusalem because he 2Sm 9:13
that belongs to **M** is now yours!" 2Sm 16:4
M, Saul's grandson, also went 2Sm 19:24
asked him, "**M**, why didn't you 2Sm 19:25
M said to the king, "Instead, 2Sm 19:30
spared **M**, the son of Saul's 2Sm 21:7
But the king took Armoni and **M**, 2Sm 21:8

MEPHIBOSHETH'S *(2)*
in Ziba's house were **M** servants. 2Sm 9:12
the summit, Ziba, **M** servant, was 2Sm 16:1

MERAB *(4)*
M, his firstborn, and Michal, 1Sm 14:49
Here is my oldest daughter **M**. 1Sm 18:17
give Saul's daughter **M** to David, 1Sm 18:19
sons whom **M** daughter of Saul 2Sm 21:8

MERAIAH *(1)*
M of Seraiah, Hananiah of Neh 12:12

MERAIOTH *(6)*
Zerahiah fathered **M**; 1Ch 6:6
M fathered Amariah; 1Ch 6:7
his son **M**, his son Amariah, his 1Ch 6:52
Zadok, son of **M**, son of Ahitub, 1Ch 9:11
Zadok, son of **M**, son of Ahitub, Neh 11:11
Adna of Harim, Helkai of **M**, Neh 12:15

MERAIOTH'S *(1)*
son, Azariah's son, **M** son, Ezr 7:3

MERARI *(12)*
Gershon, Kohath, and **M**. Gn 46:11
Gershon, Kohath, and **M**. Ex 6:16
The sons of **M**: Mahli and Mushi. Ex 6:19
Gershon, Kohath, and **M**. Nm 3:17
the Mushite clan came from **M**; Nm 3:33
the Merarite clan from **M**. Nm 26:57
clans of the descendants of **M**, Jos 21:34
Gershom, Kohath, and **M**. 1Ch 6:1
Gershom, Kohath, and **M**. 1Ch 6:16
of Mushi, son of **M**, son of Levi. 1Ch 6:47
Gershom, Kohath, and **M**. 1Ch 23:6
from the descendants of **M**, Ezr 8:19

MERARI'S *(10)*
M sons by their clans were Mahli Nm 3:20
assigned duties of **M** descendants Nm 3:36
M descendants received 12 cities Jos 21:7
to the clans of **M** descendants, Jos 21:40
M sons: Mahli and Mushi. These 1Ch 6:19
M sons: Mahli, his son Libni, 1Ch 6:29
their relatives were **M** sons: 1Ch 6:44
M sons: Mahli and Mushi. 1Ch 23:21
M sons: Mahli and Mushi, ⌊and 1Ch 24:26
M sons, by his son Jaaziah: 1Ch 24:27

MERARITE *(6)*
these were the **M** clans. Nm 3:33
family of the **M** clans was Zuriel Nm 3:35
service of the **M** clans regarding Nm 4:33
The men of the **M** clans were Nm 4:42
registered men of the **M** clans; Nm 4:45
the **M** clan from Merari. Nm 26:57

MERARITES *(12)*
As for the **M**, you are to Nm 4:29
and gave the **M** four carts and Nm 7:8
Gershonites and the **M** set out, Nm 10:17
The **M** ⌊were assigned⌋ by lot 12 1Ch 6:63
The rest of the **M** ⌊received⌋: 1Ch 6:77
son of Hashabiah of the **M**; 1Ch 9:14
from the **M**, Asaiah the leader 1Ch 15:6
and from their relatives the **M**, 1Ch 15:17
from the **M**, also had sons: 1Ch 26:10
the sons of the Korahites and **M**. 1Ch 26:19
son of Jehallelel from the **M**; 2Ch 29:12
Obadiah the Levites from the **M**, 2Ch 34:12

MERATHAIM *(1)*
the land of **M**, and against those Jr 50:21

MERCENARIES *(1)*
Even her **m** among her are like Jr 46:21

MERCHANDISE *(15)*
her for money or treat her as **m**, Dt 21:14
merchants, traders' **m**, and all 1Kg 10:15
peoples bring **m** or any kind of Neh 10:31
all kinds of **m** and selling them Neh 13:16
of Egypt and the **m** of Cush and Is 45:14
as spoil and plunder your **m**. Ezk 26:12
iron, tin, and lead for your **m**. Ezk 27:12
horses, and mules for your **m**. Ezk 27:14
coral, and rubies for your **m**. Ezk 27:16
Javan from Uzal dealt in your **m**; Ezk 27:19
of precious stones for your **m**. Ezk 27:22
Your wealth, **m**, and goods, your Ezk 27:27
When your **m** was unloaded from Ezk 27:33
no one buys their **m** any longer— Rv 18:11
m of gold, silver, precious Rv 18:12

MERCHANT *(7)*
is like the **m** ships, bringing Pr 31:14
every fragrant powder of the **m**? Sg 3:6
She was the **m** among the nations. Is 23:3
m of the peoples to many coasts Ezk 27:3
Dedan was your **m** in saddlecloths Ezk 27:20
A **m** loves to extort with Hs 12:7
heaven is like a **m** in search of Mt 13:45

MERCHANTS *(25)*
what came from **m**, traders' 1Kg 10:15
brought by the **m** and traders. 2Ch 9:14
the temple servants and the **m**, Neh 3:31
goldsmiths and **m** made repairs Neh 3:32
Once or twice the **m** and those Neh 13:20
traveling **m** of Sheba hope for Jb 6:19
him or divide him among the **m**? Jb 41:6

she delivers belts to the **m**. Pr 31:24
the coastland, you **m** of Sidon; Is 23:2
whose **m** are the honored ones of Is 23:8
the land of **m**, but you were not Ezk 16:29
brought it to the land of **m**, Ezk 17:4
Tubal, and Meshech were your **m**. Ezk 27:13
Men of Dedan were also your **m**; Ezk 27:15
the land of Israel were your **m**. Ezk 27:17
m of Sheba and Raamah traded Ezk 27:22
Eden, the **m** of Sheba, Asshur Ezk 27:23
They were your **m** in choice Ezk 27:24
Dedan and the **m** of Tarshish with Ezk 38:13
have made your **m** more numerous Nah 3:16
for all the **m** will be silenced; Zph 1:11
the **m** of the earth have grown Rv 18:3
m of the earth will also weep Rv 18:11
m of these things, who became Rv 18:15
because your **m** were the nobility Rv 18:23

MERCIES *(5)*
hands because His **m** are great, 2Sm 24:14
because His **m** are very great, 1Ch 21:13
not perish, for His **m** never end. Lm 3:22
brothers, by the **m** of God, I Rm 12:1
the Father of **m** and the God of 2Co 1:3

MERCIFUL *(11)*
the man to be **m** to you so that Gn 43:14
LORD your God is gracious and **m**; 2Ch 30:9
but ⌊even⌋ the **m** acts of the Pr 12:10
that You are a **m** and Jnh 4:2
Blessed are the **m**, because they Mt 5:7
of our God's **m** compassion, Lk 1:78
m, just as your Father also is Lk 6:36
just as your Father also is **m**. Lk 6:36
could become a **m** and faithful Heb 2:17
For I will be **m** to their Heb 8:12
is very compassionate and **m**. Jms 5:11

MERCIFULLY *(1)*
He has dealt **m** with our fathers Lk 1:72

MERCY *(116)*
Make a **m** seat of pure gold, Ex 25:17
at the two ends of the **m** seat. Ex 25:18
piece with the **m** seat at its two Ex 25:19
covering the **m** seat with their Ex 25:20
should be toward the **m** seat. Ex 25:20
Set the **m** seat on top of the ark Ex 25:21
with you there above the **m** seat, Ex 25:22
Put the **m** seat on the ark of the Ex 26:34
in front of the **m** seat that is Ex 30:6
the **m** seat that is on top of it, Ex 31:7
its poles, the **m** seat, and the Ex 35:12
He made a **m** seat of pure gold, Ex 37:6
at the two ends of the **m** seat, Ex 37:7
of one piece⌋ with the **m** seat, Ex 37:8
covering the **m** seat with their Ex 37:9
were looking toward the **m** seat. Ex 37:9
with its poles and the **m** seat; Ex 39:35
He set the **m** seat on top of the Ex 40:20
front of the **m** seat on the ark Lv 16:2
in the cloud above the **m** seat. Lv 16:2
covers the **m** seat that is over Lv 16:13
the east side of the **m** seat; Lv 16:14
before the **m** seat seven times Lv 16:14
it against the **m** seat and in Lv 16:15
from above the **m** seat that was Nm 7:89
with them and show them no **m**. Dt 7:2
burning anger and grant you **m**, Dt 13:17
completely destroyed without **m**, Jos 11:20
with You for **m** in this temple, 1Kg 8:33
and plead for **m** before You in 2Ch 6:24
will receive⌋ **m** in the presence 2Ch 30:9
God and ask the Almighty for **m**, Jb 8:5
I could only beg my judge for **m**. Jb 9:15
kidneys without **m** and pours my Jb 16:13
Have **m** on me, my friends, have Jb 19:21
friends, have **m**, for God's hand Jb 19:21
It blasts at him without **m**, Jb 27:22
he beg you for **m** or speak softly Jb 41:3
listen to my plea for **m**. Ps 86:6
He has heard my appeal for **m**. Ps 116:1
I plead aloud to the LORD for **m**. Ps 142:1
he will show no **m** when he takes Pr 6:34
and renounces them will find **m**. Pr 28:13
LORD is waiting to show you **m**, Is 30:18
showed them no **m**; you made your Is 47:6
yet I will show **m** to you with My Is 60:10
weeping and begging for **m**, Jr 3:21
They are cruel and show no **m**. Jr 6:23
I will allow no **m**, pity, or Jr 13:14
They are cruel and show no **m**. Jr 50:42
of heaven for **m** concerning this Dn 2:18
by showing **m** to the needy. Dn 4:27
slaughter nations without **m**? Hab 1:17
In ⌊Your⌋ wrath remember **m**! Hab 3:2
You withhold **m** from Jerusalem Zch 1:12
because they will be shown **m**. Mt 5:7
I desire **m** and not sacrifice. Mt 9:13
shouting, "Have **m** on us, Son of Mt 9:27
I desire **m** and not sacrifice, Mt 12:7
out, "Have **m** on me, Lord, Son Mt 15:22
he said, "have **m** on my son, Mt 17:15
also have had **m** on your fellow Mt 18:33
slave, as I had **m** on you?' Mt 18:33
out, "Lord, have **m** on us, Son of Mt 20:30
more, "Lord, have **m** on us, Son Mt 20:31
the law—justice, **m**, and faith. Mt 23:23
and how He has had **m** on you." Mk 5:19
of David, Jesus, have **m** on me!" Mk 10:47
the more, "Have **m** on me, Son of Mk 10:48
His **m** is from generation to Lk 1:50
Israel, mindful of His **m**, Lk 1:54
Lord had shown her His great **m**, Lk 1:58
"The one who showed **m** to him," Lk 10:37
'Have **m** on me and send Lazarus Lk 16:24
Jesus, Master, have **m** on us!" Lk 17:13
Son of David, have **m** on me!" Lk 18:38
Son of David, have **m** on me!" Lk 18:39
I will show **m** to whom I show Rm 9:15
show mercy to whom I show **m**, Rm 9:15
effort, but on God who shows **m**. Rm 9:16
He shows **m** to whom He wills, Rm 9:18
on objects of **m** that He prepared Rm 9:23
have received **m** through their Rm 11:30
resulting⌋ in **m** to you, so that Rm 11:31
they also now may receive **m**. Rm 11:31
so that He may have **m** on all. Rm 11:32
showing **m**, with cheerfulness. Rm 12:8
may glorify God for His **m**. Rm 15:9
by the Lord's **m** is trustworthy. 1Co 7:25
have received **m**, we do not give 2Co 4:1
and **m** also be on the Israel of Gl 6:16
is abundant in **m**, because of His Eph 2:4
Spirit, if any affection and **m**, Php 2:1
God had **m** on him, and not Php 2:27
Grace, **m**, and peace from God the 1Tm 1:2
acted in unbelief, I received **m**, 1Tm 1:13
I received **m** because of this, 1Tm 1:16
Grace, **m**, and peace from God the 2Tm 1:2
Lord grant **m** to the household 2Tm 1:16
that he obtain **m** from the Lord 2Tm 1:18
according to His **m**, through the Ti 3:5
we may receive **m** and find grace Heb 4:16
it overshadowing the **m** seat. Heb 9:5
law, he dies without **m**, based on Heb 10:28
is without **m** to the one who Jms 2:13
to the one who hasn't shown **m**. Jms 2:13
M triumphs over judgment. Jms 2:13
full of **m** and good fruits, Jms 3:17
to His great **m**, He has given us 1Pt 1:3
had not received **m**, but now you 1Pt 2:10
but now you have received **m**. 1Pt 2:10
Grace, **m**, and peace will be with 2Jn 3
May **m**, peace, and love be Jd 2
expecting the **m** of our Lord Jd 21
Have **m** on some who doubt; Jd 22
on others have **m** in fear, hating Jd 23

MERE *(8)*
your servant, a **m** dog, do this 2Kg 8:13
You think **m** words are strategy 2Kg 18:20
not let a **m** mortal hinder You. 2Ch 14:11
man's words are ⌊**m**⌋ wind? Jb 6:26
man walks about like a **m** shadow. Ps 39:6
every man is a **m** vapor. Ps 39:11
preparedness are **m** words. Is 36:5
They speak ⌊**m**⌋ words, taking Hs 10:4

MERED *(2)*
Jether, **M**, Epher, and Jalon. 1Ch 4:17
Bithiah; **M** had married her. 1Ch 4:18

MERED'S *(1)*
M wife Bithiah gave birth to 1Ch 4:17

MERELY *(4)*
her father had **m** spit in her Nm 12:14
we had **m** been sold as male and Est 7:4
I stand up, You ⌊**m**⌋ look at me. Jb 30:20
divisions and are **m** natural, Jd 19

MEREMOTH *(6)*
into the care of **M** the priest, Ezr 8:33
Vaniah, **M**, Eliashib, Ezr 10:36
Next to them **M** son of Uriah, Neh 3:4
Beside him **M** son of Uriah, Neh 3:21
Harim, **M**, Obadiah, Neh 10:5
Shecaniah, Rehum, **M**, Neh 12:3

MERES *(1)*
Admatha, Tarshish, **M**, Marsena, Est 1:14

MERIB-BAAL *(4)*
(AKA MEPHIBOSHETH)
son was **M**, and Merib-baal 1Ch 8:34
and **M** fathered Micah. 1Ch 8:34
son was **M**, and Merib-baal 1Ch 9:40
and **M** fathered Micah. 1Ch 9:40

MERIBAH *(8)*
(AKA MERIBATH-KADESH)
the place Massah and **M** because Ex 17:7
These are the waters of **M**, Nm 20:13
My command at the waters of **M**. Nm 20:24
were the waters of **M** of Kadesh Nm 27:14
with him at the waters of **M**. Dt 33:8
I tested you at the waters of **M**. Ps 81:7
not harden your hearts as at **M**, Ps 95:8
the LORD⌋ at the waters of **M**, Ps 106:32

MERIBATH-KADESH *(3)*
(AKA MERIBAH)
at the waters of **M** in the Dt 32:51
from Tamar to the waters of **M**, Ezk 47:19
from Tamar to the waters of **M**, Ezk 48:28

MERITED *(1)*
charge that **m** death or chains. Ac 23:29

MERODACH-BALADAN *(2)*
At that time **M** son of Baladan, 2Kg 20:12
At that time **M** son of Baladan, Is 39:1

MEROM *(2)*
the waters of **M** to attack Israel Jos 11:5
at the waters of **M** and attacked Jos 11:7

MERONOTHITE *(2)*
Jehdeiah the **M** was in charge of 1Ch 27:30
Jadon the **M**, and the men Neh 3:7

MEROZ *(1)*
"Curse **M**," says the Angel of the Jdg 5:23

MESH *(5)*
a grate for it of bronze **m**, Ex 27:4
rings on the **m** at its four Ex 27:4
so that the **m** comes halfway up Ex 27:5
of bronze **m** under its ledge Ex 38:4
a net, and he strays into its **m**. Jb 18:8

MESHA *(4)*
extended from **M** to Sephar, Gn 10:30
King **M** of Moab was a sheep 2Kg 3:4
M, his firstborn, fathered Ziph, 1Ch 2:42
Jobab, Zibia, **M**, Malcam, 1Ch 8:9

MESHACH *(15)*
(AKA MISHAEL)
to Mishael, **M**; and to Azariah, Dn 1:7
Shadrach, **M**, and Abednego to Dn 2:49
Shadrach, **M**, and Abednego. Dn 3:12
in Shadrach, **M**, and Abednego. Dn 3:13
"Shadrach, **M**, and Abednego, Dn 3:14
Shadrach, **M**, and Abednego Dn 3:16
Shadrach, **M**, and Abednego. Dn 3:19
tie up Shadrach, **M**, and Abednego Dn 3:20
Shadrach, **M**, and Abednego up Dn 3:22
men, Shadrach, **M**, and Abednego Dn 3:23
Shadrach, **M**, and Abednego, you Dn 3:26
So Shadrach, **M**, and Abednego Dn 3:26
of Shadrach, **M**, and Abednego! Dn 3:28
God of Shadrach, **M**, and Abednego Dn 3:29
Shadrach, **M**, and Abednego Dn 3:30

MESHECH *(9)*
(AKA MASH)
Javan, Tubal, **M**, and Tiras. Gn 10:2
Javan, Tubal, **M**, and Tiras. 1Ch 1:5
Aram, Uz, Hul, Gether, and **M**. 1Ch 1:17
misery that I have stayed in **M**, Ps 120:5
and **M** were your merchants. Ezk 27:13
M and Tubal are there, with all Ezk 32:26
the chief prince of **M** and Tubal. Ezk 38:2
chief prince of **M** and Tubal. Ezk 38:3
chief prince of **M** and Tubal. Ezk 39:1

MESHELEMIAH *(4)*
(AKA SHELEMIAH)
Zechariah son of **M** was the 1Ch 9:21

M son of Kore, one of the sons 1Ch 26:1
M had sons: Zechariah the 1Ch 26:2
M also had sons and brothers who 1Ch 26:9

MESHEZABEL *(3)*
son of **M**, made repairs. Neh 3:4
M, Zadok, Jaddua, Neh 10:21
Pethahiah son of **M**, of the Neh 11:24

MESHILLEMITH *(1)*
son of **M**, son of Immer; 1Ch 9:12

MESHILLEMOTH *(2)*
Berechiah son of **M**, Jehizkiah 2Ch 28:12
Ahzai, son of **M**, son of Immer, Neh 11:13

MESHOBAB *(1)*
M, Jamlech, Joshah son of 1Ch 4:34

MESHULLAM *(25)*
(AKA SHALLUM)
Azaliah, son of **M**, to the LORD's 2Kg 22:3
M and Hananiah, with their 1Ch 3:19
Michael, **M**, Sheba, Jorai, Jacan, 1Ch 5:13
Zebadiah, **M**, Hizki, Heber, 1Ch 8:17
Sallu son of **M**, son of Hodaviah, 1Ch 9:7
M son of Shephatiah, son of 1Ch 9:8
Hilkiah, son of **M**, son of Zadok, 1Ch 9:11
of Jahzerah, son of **M**, son of 1Ch 9:12
and Zechariah and **M** from the 2Ch 34:12
Zechariah, and **M**, as well as Ezr 8:16
with **M** and Shabbethai the Levite Ezr 10:15
M, Malluch, Adaiah, Jashub, Ezr 10:29
Beside them **M** son of Berechiah, Neh 3:4
of Paseah and **M** son of Besodeiah Neh 3:6
After them **M** son of Berechiah Neh 3:30
the daughter of **M** son of Neh 6:18
Hash-baddanah, Zechariah, and **M**. Neh 8:4
M, Abijah, Mijamin, Neh 10:7
Magpiash, **M**, Hezir, Neh 10:20
Sallu son of **M**, son of Joed, son Neh 11:7
Hilkiah, son of **M**, son of Zadok, Neh 11:11
M of Ezra, Jehohanan of Neh 12:13
of Iddo, **M** of Ginnethon, Neh 12:16
M, Talmon, and Akkub were Neh 12:25
Azariah, Ezra, **M**, Neh 12:33

MESHULLEMETH *(1)*
name was **M** daughter of Haruz 2Kg 21:19

MESOPOTAMIA *(2)*
those who live in **M**, in Judea Ac 2:9
father Abraham when he was in **M**, Ac 7:2

MESSAGE *(165)*
have sent ⌊this **m**⌋ to inform my Gn 32:5
sent her father-in-law ⌊this **m**⌋: Gn 38:25
So they sent this **m** to Joseph, Gn 50:16
wept when their **m** came to him. Gn 50:17
of Moab, sent ⌊this **m**⌋ to me: Nm 22:10
speak only the **m** God puts in my Nm 22:38
the LORD put a **m** in Balaam's Nm 23:5
Balaam and put a **m** in his mouth. Nm 23:16
speak in My name a **m** I have not Dt 18:20
recognize a **m** the LORD has not Dt 18:21
and the **m** does not come true or Dt 18:22
that is a **m** the LORD has not Dt 18:22
But the **m** is very near you, Dt 30:14
this news⌋, he sent ⌊a **m**⌋ to: Jos 11:1
I have a secret **m** for you." Jdg 3:19
country of Ephraim with this **m**: Jdg 7:24
Jephthah's **m** that he sent him. Jdg 11:28
sent this **m** to the Philistine Jdg 16:18
congregation sent a **m** of peace Jdg 21:13
"What was the **m** He gave you?" 1Sm 3:17
and He sent ⌊a **m**⌋ through Nathan 2Sm 12:25
tribes of Israel with this **m**: 2Sm 15:10
Benaiah took a **m** back to the 1Kg 2:30
Solomon sent ⌊this **m**⌋ to Hiram: 1Kg 5:2
saying, "I have heard your **m**; 1Kg 5:8
What **m** do you advise that we 1Kg 12:9
for a **m** came to me by the word 1Kg 13:17
Then he sent ⌊a **m**⌋ to King 2Kg 3:7
he sent ⌊a **m**⌋ to the king, 2Kg 5:8
said, "I have a **m** for you, 2Kg 9:5
is the LORD's **m**, 'so will I 2Kg 9:26
of land,' this is the LORD's **m**. 2Kg 9:26
guardians sent ⌊a **m**⌋ to Jehu: 2Kg 10:5
sent ⌊a **m**⌋ to the cedar that 2Kg 14:9
of Amoz sent ⌊a **m**⌋ to Hezekiah: 2Kg 19:20
out and send the **m** to the rest 1Ch 13:2
What **m** do you advise we send 2Ch 10:9
the LORD's **m** came to Shemaiah: 2Ch 12:7
Lebanon sent ⌊a **m**⌋ to the cedar 2Ch 25:18
and spread the **m** throughout all 2Ch 30:5
with a **m** for him and his Ezr 8:17
and Geshem sent me a **m**: Neh 6:2
sent me this same **m** a fifth time Neh 6:5
Their **m** has gone out to all the Ps 19:4
one who sends a **m** by a fool's Pr 26:6
bird of the sky may carry the **m**, Ec 10:20
The Lord sent a **m** against Jacob; Is 9:8
This is the **m** that the LORD Is 16:13
for the LORD has spoken this **m**. Is 24:3
cause you to understand the **m**. Is 28:19
rejected this **m** and have trusted Is 30:12
of Amoz sent ⌊a **m**⌋ to Hezekiah: Is 37:21
confirms the **m** of His servant Is 44:26
His **m** becomes a fire burning in Jr 20:9
yet they ran ⌊with a **m**⌋. Jr 23:21
listen to this **m** I am speaking Jr 28:7
Send ⌊a **m**⌋ to all the exiles, Jr 29:31
I have heard a **m** from the LORD; Jr 49:14
speak whatever **m** I will speak, Ezk 12:25
I will speak a **m** and bring it to Ezk 12:25
m I speak will be fulfilled." Ezk 12:28
the fulfillment of ⌊their⌋ **m**. Ezk 13:6
is deceived and speaks a **m**, Ezk 14:9
hear what the **m** is that comes Ezk 33:30
is the interpretation of the **m**: Dn 5:26
So consider the **m** and understand Dn 9:23
a **m** was revealed to Daniel, Dn 10:1
The **m** was true and was about a Dn 10:1
He understood the **m** and had Dn 10:1
Listen to this **m** that the LORD Am 3:1
Listen to this **m**, you cows of Am 4:1
Listen to this **m** that I am Am 5:1
We have heard a **m** from the LORD; Ob 1
preach the **m** that I tell you. Jnh 3:2
the LORD's **m** to the people, Hg 1:13
he sent ⌊a **m**⌋ by his disciples Mt 11:2
He was speaking the **m** to them. Mk 2:2
reported the **m** they were told Lk 2:17
because His **m** had authority. Lk 4:32
to one another, "What is this **m**? Lk 4:36
So the sisters sent a **m** to Him: Jn 11:3
Lord, who has believed our **m**? Jn 12:38
believe in Me through their **m**. Jn 17:20
accepted his **m** were baptized, Ac 2:41
those who heard the **m** believed, Ac 4:4
may speak Your **m** with complete Ac 4:29
to speak God's **m** with boldness. Ac 4:31
proclaiming the **m** of good news. Ac 8:4
Samaria had welcomed God's **m**, Ac 8:14
and spoken the **m** of the Lord, Ac 8:25
house and to hear a **m** from you." Ac 10:22
He sent the **m** to the sons of Ac 10:36
on all those who heard the **m**. Ac 10:44
had welcomed God's **m** also. Ac 11:1
speaking the **m** to no one except Ac 11:19
Then God's **m** flourished and Ac 12:24
proclaimed God's **m** in the Jewish Ac 13:5
and desired to hear God's **m**. Ac 13:7
if you have any **m** of Ac 13:15
the **m** of this salvation has been Ac 13:26
to hear the **m** of the Lord. Ac 13:44
that God's **m** be spoken to you Ac 13:46
and glorified the **m** of the Lord, Ac 13:48
So the **m** of the Lord spread Ac 13:49
testified to the **m** of His grace Ac 14:3
After they spoke the **m** in Perga, Ac 14:25
hear the gospel **m** and believe. Ac 15:7
strengthened them with a long **m**. Ac 15:32
proclaiming the **m** of the Lord. Ac 15:35
have preached the **m** of the Lord, Ac 15:36
speaking the **m** in the province Ac 16:6
they spoke the **m** of the Lord to Ac 16:32
welcomed the **m** with eagerness Ac 17:11
out that God's **m** had been Ac 17:13
preaching the **m** and solemnly Ac 18:5
this way the Lord's **m** flourished Ac 19:20
extended his **m** until midnight. Ac 20:7
God and to the **m** of His grace, Ac 20:32
The **m** is near you, in your mouth Rm 10:8
This is the **m** of faith that we Rm 10:8
Lord, who has believed our **m**? Rm 10:16
through the **m** about Christ. Rm 10:17
perishing the **m** of the cross is 1Co 1:18
foolishness of the **m** preached. 1Co 1:21
one is given a **m** of wisdom 1Co 12:8
a **m** of knowledge by the same 1Co 12:8
you hold to the **m** I proclaimed 1Co 15:2
m to you is not "Yes and no." 2Co 1:18
a trade in God's **m** ⌊for profit⌋, 2Co 2:17
in deceit or distorting God's **m**, 2Co 4:2
committed the **m** of 2Co 5:19
by the **m** of truth, by the power 2Co 6:7
is taught the **m** must share his Gl 6:6
that the **m** may be given to me Eph 6:19
more to speak the **m** fearlessly. Php 1:14
Hold firmly the **m** of life. Php 2:16
this hope⌋ in the **m** of truth, Col 1:5
to make God's **m** fully known, Col 1:25
the **m** about the Messiah dwell Col 3:16
may open a door to us for the **m**, Col 4:3
you welcomed the **m** with the joy 1Th 1:6
For the Lord's **m** rang out from 1Th 1:8
received the **m** about God that 1Th 2:13
welcomed it not as a human **m**, 1Th 2:13
it truly is, the **m** of God, which 1Th 2:13
spirit or by a **m** or by a letter 2Th 2:2
by our **m** or by our letter. 2Th 2:15
that the Lord's **m** may spread 2Th 3:1
but God's **m** is not bound. 2Tm 2:9
proclaim the **m**; persist in it 2Tm 4:2
time revealed His **m** in the Ti 1:3
to the faithful **m** as taught, Ti 1:9
so that God's **m** will not be Ti 2:5
Your **m** is to be sound beyond Ti 2:8
For if the **m** spoken through Heb 2:2
but the **m** they heard did not Heb 4:2
with the **m** about righteousness, Heb 5:13
the elementary **m** about the Heb 6:1
birth by the **m** of truth so that Jms 1:18
stumble by disobeying the **m**; 1Pt 2:8
some disobey the ⌊Christian⌋ **m**, 1Pt 3:1
without a **m** by the way their 1Pt 3:1
Now this is the **m** we have heard 1Jn 1:5
command is the **m** you have heard. 1Jn 2:7
For this is the **m** you have heard 1Jn 3:11

MESSAGES *(1)*
He sent letters with **m** of peace Est 9:30

MESSENGER *(39)*
The **m** answered, "Israel has fled 1Sm 4:17
Then a **m** came to Saul saying, 1Sm 23:27
He commanded the **m**, "When 2Sm 11:19
the **m** left. When he arrived, 2Sm 11:22
m reported to David, "The men 2Sm 11:23
David told the **m**, "Say this to 2Sm 11:25
So Jezebel sent a **m** to Elijah, 1Kg 19:2
The **m** who went to call Micaiah 1Kg 22:13
sent him a **m**, who said, "Go 2Kg 5:10
but before the **m** got to him, 2Kg 6:32
Look, when the **m** comes, shut the 2Kg 6:32
with them, the **m** came down to 2Kg 6:33
The **m** reached them but hasn't 2Kg 9:18
When the **m** came and told him, 2Kg 10:8
The **m** who went to call Micaiah 2Ch 18:12
Mordecai told ⌊the **m**⌋ to reply Est 4:13
a **m** came to Job and reported: Jb 1:14
when another ⌊**m**⌋ came and Jb 1:16
That **m** was still speaking when Jb 1:17
when another ⌊**m**⌋ came and Jb 1:18
A wicked **m** falls into trouble, Pr 13:17
A king's fury is a **m** of death, Pr 16:14
a cruel **m** will be sent against Pr 17:11
a trustworthy **m** is like the Pr 25:13
presence of the **m** that it was Ec 5:6
or deaf like My **m** I am sending? Is 42:19
M races to meet messenger, Jr 51:31
Messenger races to meet **m**, Jr 51:31
away when a **m** was dispatched Ezk 23:40
Haggai, the LORD's **m**, delivered Hg 1:13
because he is the **m** of the LORD Mal 2:7
going to send My **m**, and he will Mal 3:1
the **M** of the covenant you desire Mal 3:1
I am sending My **m** ahead of You; Mt 11:10
I am sending My **m** ahead of You, Mk 1:2
I am sending My **m** ahead of You; Lk 7:27
and a **m** is not greater than the Jn 13:16
a **m** of Satan to torment me so I 2Co 12:7
well as your **m** and minister to Php 2:25

MESSENGERS *(88)*
Jacob sent **m** ahead of him to his Gn 32:3
When the **m** returned to Jacob, Gn 32:6
Pharaoh sent ⌊**m**⌋ who saw that Ex 9:7
Moses sent **m** from Kadesh to the Nm 20:14
Israel sent **m** to say to Sihon Nm 21:21
he sent **m** to Balaam son of Beor Nm 22:5

tell the **m** you sent me: Nm 24:12
So I sent **m** with an offer of Dt 2:26
So Joshua sent **m** who ran to the Jos 7:22
He sent **m** throughout all of Jdg 6:35
He also sent **m** throughout Asher, Jdg 6:35
Gideon sent **m** throughout the Jdg 7:24
So he sent **m** secretly to Jdg 9:31
Jephthah sent **m** to the king of Jdg 11:12
Ammonites said to Jephthah's **m**, Jdg 11:13
Jephthah again sent **m** to the Jdg 11:14
Israel sent **m** to the king of Jdg 11:17
They also sent ⌊**m**⌋ to the king Jdg 11:17
Then Israel sent **m** to Sihon king Jdg 11:19
They sent **m** to the residents of 1Sm 6:21
and let us send **m** throughout the 1Sm 11:3
When the **m** came to Gibeah, 1Sm 11:4
land of Israel by **m** who said, 1Sm 11:7
He told the **m** who had come, 1Sm 11:9
So the **m** told the men of 1Sm 11:9
Saul dispatched **m** to Jesse and 1Sm 16:19
When the **m** arrived, to their 1Sm 19:16
The king sent ⌊**m**⌋ to summon 1Sm 22:11
David sent **m** from the wilderness 1Sm 25:14
Then David sent **m** to speak to 1Sm 25:39
the donkey following David's **m**. 1Sm 25:42
and sent **m** throughout the land 1Sm 31:9
David sent **m** to the men of 2Sm 2:5
Abner sent **m** as his 2Sm 3:12
Then David sent **m** to say to 2Sm 3:14
David and sent **m** after Abner. 2Sm 3:26
Hadadezer sent ⌊**m**⌋ to bring the 2Sm 10:16
David sent **m** to get her, and 2Sm 11:4
Joab sent **m** to David to say, 2Sm 12:27
Then Absalom sent **m** throughout 2Sm 15:10
He sent **m** into the city to Ahab 1Kg 20:2
The **m** then returned and said, 1Kg 20:5
I have sent ⌊**m**⌋ to you, saying: 1Kg 20:5
So he said to Ben-hadad's **m**, 1Kg 20:9
So the **m** left and took word 1Kg 20:9
Ben-hadad sent ⌊**m**⌋ to him and 1Kg 20:10
So he sent **m** instructing them: 2Kg 1:2
Go and meet the **m** of the king of 2Kg 1:3
The **m** returned to the king, 2Kg 1:5
you have sent **m** to inquire 2Kg 1:16
let ⌊**m**⌋ take five of the horses 2Kg 7:13
⌊The **m**⌋ are like the whole 2Kg 7:13
⌊The **m**⌋ took two chariots with 2Kg 7:14
m returned and told the king. 2Kg 7:15
Then Jehu sent ⌊**m**⌋ throughout 2Kg 10:21
Jehoiada sent ⌊**m**⌋ and brought in 2Kg 11:4
then sent **m** to Jehoash son 2Kg 14:8
Ahaz sent **m** to Tiglath-pileser 2Kg 16:7
So he again sent **m** to Hezekiah, 2Kg 19:9
letter from the hand of the **m**, 2Kg 19:14
mocked the Lord through your **m**. 2Kg 19:23
So the king sent ⌊**m**⌋, and they 2Kg 23:1
and sent **m** throughout the land 1Ch 10:9
So David sent **m** to console him 1Ch 19:2
they sent **m** to bring out the 1Ch 19:16
the king sent ⌊**m**⌋ and gathered 2Ch 34:29
But Neco sent **m** to him, saying, 2Ch 35:21
them by the hand of his **m**, 2Ch 36:15
they kept ridiculing God's **m**, 2Ch 36:16
So I sent **m** to them, saying, "I Neh 6:3
calamity—a band of deadly **m**. Ps 78:49
and making the winds His **m**, Ps 104:4
be given to the **m** from that Is 14:32
Go, swift **m**, to a nation tall Is 18:2
Zoan and his **m** reach as far as Is 30:4
the **m** of peace weep bitterly. Is 33:7
this, he sent **m** to Hezekiah, Is 37:9
took the letter from the **m**, Is 37:14
fulfills the counsel of His **m**; Is 44:26
Sidon through **m** who are coming Jr 27:3
them and sent **m** to them in Ezk 23:16
m will go out from Me in ships Ezk 30:9
the sound of your **m** will never Nah 2:13
After John's **m** left, He began to Lk 7:24
He sent **m** ahead of Him, and on Lk 9:52
You have sent ⌊**m**⌋ to John, Jn 5:33
they are the **m** of the churches, 2Co 8:23
she received the **m** and sent them Jms 2:25

MESSIAH *(116)*
(AKA CHRIST)

Jerusalem until **M** the Prince Dn 9:25
62 weeks the **M** will be cut off Dn 9:26
to Jesus who is called the **M**. Mt 1:16
exile to Babylon until the **M**, Mt 1:17
them where the **M** would be born. Mt 2:4
in prison what the **M** was doing, Mt 11:2
You are the **M**, the Son of the Mt 16:16
tell no one that He was the **M**. Mt 16:20
What do you think about the **M**? Mt 22:42
how then can the **M** be his Son" Mt 22:45
you have one Master, the **M**. Mt 23:10
I am the **M**,' and they will Mt 24:5
then, 'Look, here is the **M**!' Mt 24:23
You are the **M**, the Son of God! Mt 26:63
and said, "Prophesy to us, **M**! Mt 26:68
or Jesus who is called **M**?" Mt 27:17
with Jesus, who is called **M**?" Mt 27:22
answered Him, "You are the **M**!" Mk 8:29
since you belong to the **M**— Mk 9:41
say that the **M** is the Son of Mk 12:35
how then can the **M** be his Son?" Mk 12:37
tells you, 'Look, here is the **M**! Mk 13:21
Him, "Are You the **M**, the Son of Mk 14:61
Let the **M**, the King of Israel, Mk 15:32
a Savior, who is **M** the Lord, was Lk 2:11
before he saw the Lord's **M**. Lk 2:26
whether John might be the **M**. Lk 3:15
because they knew He was the **M**. Lk 4:41
Peter answered, "God's **M**!" Lk 9:20
they say that the **M** is the Son Lk 20:41
how then can the **M** be his Son?" Lk 20:44
If You are the **M**, tell us." Lk 22:67
saying that He Himself is the **M**, Lk 23:2
save Himself if this is God's **M**, Lk 23:35
Aren't You the **M**? Save Yourself Lk 23:39
Didn't the **M** have to suffer Lk 24:26
the **M** would suffer and rise from Lk 24:46
he declared: "I am not the **M**." Jn 1:20
you baptize if you aren't the **M**, Jn 1:25
told him, "We have found the **M**!" Jn 1:41
I am not the **M**, but I've been Jn 3:28
"I know that **M** is coming" Jn 4:25
Could this be the **M**?" Jn 4:29
authorities know He is the **M**? Jn 7:26
When the **M** comes, nobody will Jn 7:27
said, "When the **M** comes, He Jn 7:31
Others said, "This is the **M**!" Jn 7:41
Surely the **M** doesn't come from Jn 7:41
that the **M** comes from David's Jn 7:42
if anyone confessed Him as **M**, Jn 9:22
You are the **M**, tell us plainly. Jn 10:24
You are the **M**, the Son of God, Jn 11:27
the law that the **M** will remain Jn 12:34
you may believe Jesus is the **M**, Jn 20:31
the resurrection of the **M**: Ac 2:31
you crucified, both Lord and **M**!" Ac 2:36
name of Jesus the **M** for the Ac 2:38
that His **M** would suffer—He Ac 3:18
has been appointed **M** for you. Ac 3:20
the Lord and against His **M**. Ac 4:26
good news that the **M** is Jesus. Ac 5:42
and preached the **M** to them. Ac 8:5
proving that this One is the **M**. Ac 9:22
showing that the **M** had to suffer Ac 17:3
This is the **M**, Jesus, whom I am Ac 17:3
to the Jews that the **M** is Jesus. Ac 18:5
Scriptures that Jesus is the **M**. Ac 18:28
that the **M** must suffer, and that Ac 26:23
the ⌊crucified⌋ body of the **M**, Rm 7:4
off from the **M** for the benefit Rm 9:3
came the **M**, who is God over Rm 9:5
serves the **M** in this way is Rm 14:18
For even the **M** did not please Rm 15:3
just as the **M** also accepted you, Rm 15:7
news about the **M** from Jerusalem Rm 15:19
everything together in the **M**, Eph 1:10
our hope in the **M** might bring Eph 1:12
power⌋ in the **M** by raising Him Eph 1:20
alive with the **M** even though we Eph 2:5
time you were without the **M**, Eph 2:12
near by the blood of the **M**. Eph 2:13
about the mystery of the **M**. Eph 3:4
incalculable riches of the **M**, Eph 3:8
made in the **M**, Jesus our Lord, Eph 3:11
and that the **M** may dwell in your Eph 3:17
not how you learned about the **M**, Eph 4:20
as the **M** also loved us and gave Eph 5:2
the kingdom of the **M** and of God. Eph 5:5
and the **M** will shine on you. Eph 5:14
of the **M** on your behalf, Col 1:7
in the circumcision of the **M**. Col 2:11
the substance is the **M**. Col 2:17
you have been raised with the **M**, Col 3:1
above, where the **M** is, seated at Col 3:1
is hidden with the **M** in God. Col 3:3
When the **M**, who is your life, is Col 3:4
And let the peace of the **M**, Col 3:15
message about the **M** dwell richly Col 3:16
to speak the mystery of the **M**— Col 4:3
of the **M** if we hold firmly Heb 3:14
the **M** did not exalt Himself to Heb 5:5
elementary message about the **M**, Heb 6:1
Now the **M** has appeared, high Heb 9:11
more will the blood of the **M**, Heb 9:14
For the **M** did not enter a Heb 9:24
so also the **M**, having been Heb 9:28
the sake of the **M** to be greater Heb 11:26
set apart the **M** as Lord in your 1Pt 3:15
the sufferings of the **M** rejoice, 1Pt 4:13
to the sufferings of the **M**, 1Pt 5:1
who denies that Jesus is the **M**? 1Jn 2:22
Jesus is the **M** has been born 1Jn 5:1
of our Lord and of His **M**, Rv 11:15
of His **M** have now come, Rv 12:10
with the **M** for 1,000 years Rv 20:4
be priests of God and the **M**, Rv 20:6

MESSIAH'S *(2)*

and to know the **M** love that Eph 3:19
to the measure of the **M** gift. Eph 4:7

MESSIAHS *(2)*

False **m** and false prophets will Mt 24:24
For false **m** and false prophets Mk 13:22

MESSIANIC *(2)*

the **M** Age, when the Son of Man Mt 19:28
in advance to the **m** sufferings 1Pt 1:11

MET *(39)*

his way, and God's angels **m** him. Gn 32:1
by this whole procession I **m**?" Gn 33:8
of the Hebrews, has **m** with us. Ex 3:18
So he went and **m** him at the Ex 4:27
of the Hebrews has **m** with us. Ex 5:3
God **m** with him and Balaam said Nm 23:4
The LORD **m** with Balaam and put Nm 23:16
They **m** you along the way and Dt 25:18
and **m** the brook east of Jokneam. Jos 19:11
a group of prophets **m** him. 1Sm 10:10
the elders of the town **m** him, 1Sm 16:4
coming toward her and **m** them. 1Sm 25:20
marched out and **m** them by the 2Sm 2:13
the Shilonite **m** Jeroboam on the 1Kg 11:29
a lion **m** him along the way and 1Kg 13:24
the road, Elijah suddenly **m** him. 1Kg 18:7
and **m** Jehu at the plot of land 2Kg 9:21
Jehu **m** the relatives of Ahaziah 2Kg 10:13
They **m** together to go and offer Jb 2:11
place where You **m** with us. Ps 74:4
the land where God **m** with us. Ps 74:8
and famine we have **m** our end." Jr 44:18
men **m** Him as they came Mt 8:28
Just then Jesus **m** them and said, Mt 28:9
came out of the tombs and **m** Him. Mk 5:2
man from the town **m** Him. Lk 8:27
mountain, a large crowd **m** Him. Lk 9:37
serious skin diseases **m** Him. Lk 17:12
his slaves **m** him saying that his Jn 4:51
place where Martha had **m** Him. Jn 11:30
is also why the crowd **m** Him, Jn 12:18
Jesus often **m** there with His Jn 18:2
Cornelius **m** him, fell at his Ac 10:25
year they **m** with the church Ac 11:26
a slave girl **m** us who had a Ac 16:16
from them and **m** separately with Ac 19:9
When he **m** us at Assos, we took Ac 20:14
who **m** Abraham and blessed him as Heb 7:1
when Melchizedek **m** him. Heb 7:10

METAL *(9)*

He made the cast ⌊**m**⌋ reservoir, 1Kg 7:23
and hubs were all of cast **m**. 1Kg 7:33
he made the cast ⌊**m**⌋ reservoir, 2Ch 4:2
as hard as a cast **m** mirror? Jb 37:18
like cast **m** and the clods Jb 38:38
solid as **m** and immovable. Jb 41:23
and worshiped the cast **m** image. Ps 106:19
a god or casts a **m** image for no Is 44:10
with their **m** images and their Dn 11:8

METAL-PLATED *(1)*

in idols and say to **m** images: Is 42:17

METALSMITHS *(4)*
and all the craftsmen and **m**. 2Kg 24:14
and 1,000 craftsmen and **m**— 2Kg 24:16
craftsmen and **m** from Jerusalem Jr 24:1
and the **m** had left Jerusalem. Jr 29:2

METALWORKER *(2)*
and a **m** plates with gold and Is 40:19
The craftsman encourages the **m**; Is 41:7

METHEG-AMMAH *(1)*
and took **M** from Philistine 2Sm 8:1

METHOD *(1)*
This was ⌊the **m** of⌋ legally Ru 4:7

METHUSELAH *(6)*
65 years old when he fathered **M**. Gn 5:21
the birth of **M**, Enoch walked Gn 5:22
M was 187 years old when he Gn 5:25
M lived 782 years after the Gn 5:26
Enoch, **M**, Lamech, 1Ch 1:3
of **M**, ⌊son⌋ of Enoch, ⌊son⌋ Lk 3:37

METHUSELAH'S *(1)*
So **M** life lasted 969 years; Gn 5:27

METHUSHAEL *(2)*
fathered **M**, and Methushael Gn 4:18
and **M** fathered Lamech Gn 4:18

MEUNIM *(1)*
tents and the **M** who were found 1Ch 4:41

MEUNIM'S *(2)*
descendants, **M** descendants, Ezr 2:50
descendants, **M** descendants, Neh 7:52

MEUNITES *(2)*
together with some of the **M**, 2Ch 20:1
live in Gur-baal, and the **M**. 2Ch 26:7

MEZOBAITE *(1)*
Eliel, Obed, and Jaasiel the **M**. 1Ch 11:47

MIBHAR *(1)*
of Nathan, **M** son of Hagri, 1Ch 11:38

MIBSAM *(3)*
then Kedar, Adbeel, **M**, Gn 25:13
firstborn, Kedar, Adbeel, **M**, 1Ch 1:29
Shallum, his son **M**, and his son 1Ch 4:25

MIBZAR *(2)*
Kenaz, Teman, **M**, Gn 36:42
Kenaz, Teman, **M**, 1Ch 1:53

MICA *(5)*
(AKA MICAH)
a young son whose name was **M**. 2Sm 9:12
son of **M**, son of Zichri, 1Ch 9:15
M, Rehob, Hashabiah, Neh 10:11
son of **M**, son of Zabdi, Neh 11:17
Mattaniah, son of **M**, of the Neh 11:22

MICAH *(20)*
(AKA MICA, MICAIAH)
hill country of Ephraim named **M**. Jdg 17:1
This man **M** had a shrine, and he Jdg 17:5
you come from?" **M** asked him. He Jdg 17:9
M replied, "Stay with me and be Jdg 17:10
M consecrated the Levite, and Jdg 17:12
Then **M** said, "Now I know that Jdg 17:13
far as the home of **M** and spent Jdg 18:2
He told them what **M** had for him Jdg 18:4
the home of **M** and greeted him. Jdg 18:15
them, and said to **M**, "What's the Jdg 18:23
and **M** turned to go back home, Jdg 18:26
taken the gods **M** had made and Jdg 18:27
his son **M**, his son Reaiah, his 1Ch 5:5
and Merib-baal fathered **M**. 1Ch 8:34
and Merib-baal fathered **M**. 1Ch 9:40
M was first, and Isshiah second. 1Ch 23:20
Uzziel's sons: **M**; from Micah's 1Ch 24:24
son of **M**, Shaphan the court 2Ch 34:20
M the Moreshite prophesied in Jr 26:18
that came to **M** the Moreshite— Mc 1:1

MICAH'S *(12)*
silver, and it was in **M** house. Jdg 17:4
he came to **M** home in the hill Jdg 17:8
his priest and lived in **M** house. Jdg 17:12
While they were near **M** home, Jdg 18:3
Ephraim and arrived at **M** house. Jdg 18:13
they entered **M** house and took Jdg 18:18
were some distance from **M** house, Jdg 18:22
for themselves **M** carved image Jdg 18:31
M sons: Pithon, Melech, Tarea, 1Ch 8:35
M sons: Pithon, Melech, Tahrea, 1Ch 9:41
Micah; from **M** sons: Shamir. 1Ch 24:24
M brother: Isshiah; from 1Ch 24:25

MICAIAH *(31)*
(AKA MAACAH, MICAH)
He is **M** son of Imlah." 1Kg 22:8
"Hurry ⌊and get⌋ **M** son of Imlah!" 1Kg 22:9
went to call **M** instructed him, 1Kg 22:13
But **M** said, "As the LORD lives, 1Kg 22:14
asked him, "**M**, should we go to 1Kg 22:15
M told him, "March up and 1Kg 22:15
So **M** said: I saw all Israel 1Kg 22:17
Then **M** said, "Therefore, hear 1Kg 22:19
came up, hit **M** in the face, 1Kg 22:24
M replied, "You will soon see 1Kg 22:25
Take **M** and return him to Amon, 1Kg 22:26
But **M** said, "If you ever return 1Kg 22:28
Achbor son of **M**, Shaphan the 2Kg 22:12
name was **M** daughter of Uriel 2Ch 13:2
Nethanel, and **M**—to teach in 2Ch 17:7
He is **M** son of Imlah." 2Ch 18:7
"Hurry ⌊and get⌋ **M** son of Imlah!" 2Ch 18:8
went to call **M** instructed him, 2Ch 18:12
But **M** said, "As the LORD lives, 2Ch 18:13
asked him, "**M**, should we go to 2Ch 18:14
M said, "March up and succeed, 2Ch 18:14
So **M** said: I saw all Israel 2Ch 18:16
Then **M** said, "Therefore, hear 2Ch 18:18
came up, hit **M** in the face, 2Ch 18:23
M replied, "You will soon see 2Ch 18:24
Take **M** and return him to Amon, 2Ch 18:25
But **M** said, "If you ever return 2Ch 18:27
son of **M**, son of Zaccur, Neh 12:35
Maaseiah, Miniamin, **M**, Elioenai, Neh 12:41
When **M** son of Gemariah, son of Jr 36:11
M reported to them all the words Jr 36:13

MICE *(4)*
and five gold **m** ⌊corresponding 1Sm 6:4
tumors and of your **m** that are 1Sm 6:5
the gold **m** and the images 1Sm 6:11
number of gold **m** also 1Sm 6:18

MICHAEL *(15)*
Sethur son of **M** from the tribe Nm 13:13
M, Meshullam, Sheba, Jorai, 1Ch 5:13
Gilead, son of **M**, son of 1Ch 5:14
son of **M**, son of Baaseiah, son 1Ch 6:40
M, Obadiah, Joel, Isshiah. 1Ch 7:3
M, Ishpah, and Joha were 1Ch 8:16
Jediael, **M**, Jozabad, Elihu, 1Ch 12:20
for Issachar, Omri son of **M**; 1Ch 27:18
Azariah, **M**, and Shephatiah; 2Ch 21:2
Zebadiah son of **M** from Ezr 8:8
M, one of the chief princes, Dn 10:13
me against them except **M**, Dn 10:21
At that time **M** the great prince Dn 12:1
Yet **M** the archangel, when he was Jd 9
M and his angels fought against Rv 12:7

MICHAL *(16)*
firstborn, and **M**, the younger. 1Sm 14:49
Saul's daughter **M** loved David, 1Sm 18:20
his daughter **M** to David as his 1Sm 18:27
that his daughter **M** loved him, 1Sm 18:28
But his wife **M** warned David: 1Sm 19:11
Then **M** took the household idol 1Sm 19:13
to seize David, **M** said, "He's 1Sm 19:14
Saul asked **M**, "Why did you 1Sm 19:17
But Saul gave his daughter **M**, 1Sm 25:44
Saul's daughter **M** here when you 2Sm 3:13
Saul, "Give me back my wife, **M**. 2Sm 3:14
Saul's daughter **M** looked down 2Sm 6:16
Saul's daughter **M** came out to 2Sm 6:20
replied to **M**, "I was dancing 2Sm 6:21
Saul's daughter **M** had no child 2Sm 6:23
Saul's daughter **M** looked down 1Ch 15:29

MICHMAS'S *(2)*
M men 122 Ezr 2:27
M men 122 Neh 7:31

MICHMASH *(9)*
with Saul at **M** and in Bethel's 1Sm 13:2
They went up and camped at **M**, 1Sm 13:5
Philistines were gathering at **M**, 1Sm 13:11
Philistines were camped at **M**. 1Sm 13:16
took control of the pass at **M**. 1Sm 13:23
in front of **M** and the other to 1Sm 14:5
that day from **M** all the way to 1Sm 14:31
from Geba, **M**, Aija, and Bethel— Neh 11:31
storing his equipment at **M**. Is 10:28

MICHMETHATH *(2)*
the border went westward from **M**; Jos 16:6
from Asher to **M** near Shechem. Jos 17:7

MICHRI *(1)*
Elah son of Uzzi, son of **M**; 1Ch 9:8

MID-HEAVEN *(3)*
eagle, flying in **m**, saying in a Rv 8:13
I saw another angel flying in **m**, Rv 14:6
to all the birds flying in **m**, Rv 19:17

MIDAIR *(1)*
going, so he was suspended in **m**. 2Sm 18:9

MIDCOURSE *(1)*
He has broken my strength in **m**; Ps 102:23

MIDDAY *(4)*
the king was taking his **m** nap. 2Sm 4:5
brighter and brighter until **m**. Pr 4:18
At **m**, while on the road, O king, Ac 26:13
was shining like the sun at **m**. Rv 1:16

MIDDIN *(1)*
Beth-arabah, **M**, Secacah, Jos 15:61

MIDDLE *(79)*
the tree in the **m** of the garden, Gn 3:3
it with lower, **m**, and upper Gn 6:16
split them down the **m**, and laid Gn 15:10
Lot out of the **m** of the upheaval Gn 19:29
run through the **m** of the planks Ex 26:28
run through the **m** of the planks Ex 36:33
which is in the **m** of the camps. Nm 2:17
I'm in the **m** of a people with Nm 11:21
ran into the **m** of the assembly, Nm 16:47
crossed through the **m** of the sea Nm 33:8
the **m** of the valley was the Dt 3:16
when in the **m** of the whole Dt 11:6
its spoil in the **m** of the city Dt 13:16
ground in the **m** of the Jordan, Jos 3:17
place in the **m** of the Jordan Jos 4:3
your God in the **m** of the Jordan. Jos 4:5
stones from the **m** of the Jordan, Jos 4:8
12 stones in the **m** of the Jordan Jos 4:9
standing in the **m** of the Jordan Jos 4:10
up from the **m** of the Jordan, Jos 4:18
sun stopped in the **m** of the sky Jos 10:13
along the **m** of the valley, Jos 12:2
the city in the **m** of the valley, Jos 13:9
the city in the **m** of the valley, Jos 13:16
beginning of the **m** watch after Jdg 7:19
hold of the two **m** pillars Jdg 16:29
aside to the **m** of the gateway, 2Sm 3:27
blood in the **m** of the highway, 2Sm 20:12
his stand in the **m** of the field, 2Sm 23:12
the town in the **m** of the valley, 2Sm 24:5
She got up in the **m** of the night 1Kg 3:20
feet wide, the **m** was nine feet 1Kg 6:6
a stairway to the **m** ⌊chamber⌋, 1Kg 6:8
and from the **m** to the third. 1Kg 6:8
and in the **m** of the temple their 1Kg 6:27
out of the **m** of an iron furnace. 1Kg 8:51
consecrated the **m** of the 1Kg 8:64
their stand in the **m** of the plot 1Ch 11:14
consecrated the **m** of the 2Ch 7:7
went into the **m** of the city, Est 4:1
suddenly in the **m** of the night; Jb 34:20
not take me in the **m** of my life! Ps 102:24
a tower in the **m** of it and even Is 5:2
out his arms in the **m** of it, Is 25:11
springs in the **m** of the plains. Is 41:18
the **m** of his days ⌊his riches⌋ Jr 17:11
entered and sat at the **M** Gate: Jr 39:3
it into the **m** of the Euphrates Jr 51:63
its ends, and the **m** is charred. Ezk 15:4
silenced in the **m** of the sea? Ezk 27:32
lying in the **m** of his Nile, Ezk 29:3
you up from the **m** of your Nile, Ezk 29:4
speak from the **m** of Sheol about Ezk 32:21
me down in the **m** of the valley; Ezk 37:1
highest by means of the **m** one. Ezk 41:7
from the lower and **m** stories of Ezk 42:5
than the lower and **m** stories. Ezk 42:6
will be in the **m** of it. Ezk 48:8
will be in the **m** of it. Ezk 48:10
The city will be in the **m** of it. Ezk 48:15
temple will be in the **m** of it. Ezk 48:21
property in the **m** of the area Ezk 48:22
a tree in the **m** of the earth, Dn 4:10
calling from the **m** of the Ulai: Dn 8:16
but in the **m** of the week he will Dn 9:27

a flock in the **m** of its fold. Mc 2:12
will lie down in the **m** of it, Zph 2:14
In the **m** of the night there was Mt 25:6
boat was in the **m** of the sea, Mk 6:47
tiles into the **m** of the crowd Lk 5:19
he comes in the **m** of the night, Lk 12:38
a fire in the **m** of the courtyard Lk 22:55
sanctuary was split down the **m**. Lk 23:45
side, with Jesus in the **m**. Jn 19:18
burst open in the **m**, and all his Ac 1:18
stood in the **m** of the Areopagus Ac 17:22
and in the **m** of the night the Ac 27:27
In the **m** and around the throne Rv 4:6
down the **m** of the broad street Rv 22:2

MIDIAN *(40)*
Jokshan, Medan, **M**, Ishbak, and Gn 25:2
He defeated **M** in the field of Gn 36:35
went to live in the land of **M**, Ex 2:15
Now the priest of **M** had seven Ex 2:16
Jethro, the priest of **M**. Ex 3:1
Now in **M** the LORD told Moses, Ex 4:19
the priest of **M**, heard about Ex 18:1
said to the elders of **M**, Nm 22:4
of Moab and **M** departed with fees Nm 22:7
head of an ancestral house in **M**. Nm 25:15
will go against **M** to inflict Nm 31:3
war against **M**, as the LORD had Nm 31:7
and Reba, the five kings of **M**. Nm 31:8
killed him and the chiefs of **M**— Jos 13:21
them over to **M** seven years, Jdg 6:1
Because of **M**, the Israelites Jdg 6:2
poverty stricken because of **M**, Jdg 6:6
cried out to Him because of **M**, Jdg 6:7
us and handed us over to **M**." Jdg 6:13
Israel from the power of **M**. Jdg 6:14
You will strike **M** down ⌊as if it Jdg 6:16
The camp of **M** was north of them, Jdg 7:1
The camp of **M** was below him in Jdg 7:8
and Zeeb, the two princes of **M**; Jdg 7:25
and Zeeb, the two princes of **M**. Jdg 8:3
and Zalmunna, the kings of **M**." Jdg 8:5
these two kings of **M** and routed Jdg 8:12
us from the power of **M**." Jdg 8:22
garments on the kings of **M**, Jdg 8:26
So **M** was subdued before the Jdg 8:28
you from the hand of **M**, Jdg 9:17
men set out from **M** and went to 1Kg 11:18
Jokshan, Medan, **M**, Ishbak, and 1Ch 1:32
who defeated **M** in the country of 1Ch 1:46
with them as ⌊You did⌋ with **M**, Ps 83:9
as ⌊You did⌋ on the day of **M**. Is 9:4
when He⌋ struck **M** at the rock of Is 10:26
young camels of **M** and Ephah— Is 60:6
of the land of **M** tremble. Hab 3:7
an exile in the land of **M**, Ac 7:29

MIDIAN'S *(2)*
And **M** sons were Ephah, Epher, Gn 25:4
M sons: Ephah, Epher, Hanoch, 1Ch 1:33

MIDIANITE *(12)*
When **M** traders passed by, they Gn 37:28
father-in-law Reuel the **M**: Nm 10:29
came bringing a **M** woman to his Nm 25:6
struck dead with the **M** woman, Nm 25:14
of the slain **M** woman was Cozbi, Nm 25:15
daughter of the **M** leader who was Nm 25:18
they killed the **M** kings—Evi, Nm 31:8
took the **M** women and their Nm 31:9
came tumbling into the **M** camp, Jdg 7:13
the entire **M** camp over to him. Jdg 7:14
handed the **M** camp over to you. Jdg 7:15
and the entire ⌊**M**⌋ army fled, Jdg 7:21

MIDIANITES *(15)*
the **M** sold Joseph in Egypt to Gn 37:36
Attack the **M** and strike them Nm 25:17
the Israelites against the **M**. Nm 31:2
the cities where the **M** lived, Nm 31:10
crops, the **M**, Amalekites, Jdg 6:3
For the **M** came with their cattle Jdg 6:5
in order to hide it from the **M**. Jdg 6:11
All the **M**, Amalekites, and Jdg 6:33
Me to hand the **M** over to you, Jdg 7:2
and hand the **M** over to you. Jdg 7:7
Now the **M**, Amalekites, and all Jdg 7:12
and they pursued the **M**. Jdg 7:23
intercept the **M** and take control Jdg 7:24
while they were pursuing the **M**. Jdg 7:25
went to fight against the **M**?" Jdg 8:1

MIDNIGHT *(9)*
'About **m** I will go throughout Ex 11:4
Now at **m** the LORD struck every Ex 12:29
in bed until **m** when he got up, Jdg 16:3
At **m**, Boaz was startled, turned Ru 3:8
rise at **m** to thank You for Your Ps 119:62
evening or at **m** or at the Mk 13:35
to him at **m** and says to him, Lk 11:5
About **m** Paul and Silas were Ac 16:25
he extended his message until **m**. Ac 20:7

MIDST *(6)*
of life in the **m** of the garden, Gn 2:9
out into the **m** of the battle. 1Kg 20:39
In the **m** of the congregation, 2Ch 20:14
I am in the **m** of lions; Ps 57:4
in Zion, her King not in her **m**? Jr 8:19
the blood she shed is in her **m**. Ezk 24:7

MIDWIFE *(3)*
labor, the **m** said to her, "Don't Gn 35:17
and the **m** took it and tied a Gn 38:28
before a **m** can get to them. Ex 1:19

MIDWIVES *(6)*
of Egypt said to the Hebrew **m**, Ex 1:15
Hebrew **m**, however, feared God Ex 1:17
summoned the **m** and asked them, Ex 1:18
The **m** said to Pharaoh, "The Ex 1:19
good to the **m**, and the people Ex 1:20
Since the **m** feared God, He gave Ex 1:21

MIGDAL-EL *(1)*
Iron, **M**, Horem, Beth-anath, and Jos 19:38

MIGDAL-GAD *(1)*
Zenan, Hadashah, **M**, Jos 15:37

MIGDOL *(6)*
between **M** and the sea; Ex 14:2
and they camped before **M**. Nm 33:7
land of Egypt—at **M**, Tahpanhes, Jr 44:1
in Egypt, and proclaim it in **M**! Jr 46:14
desolate waste from **M** to Syene, Ezk 29:10
From **M** to Syene they will fall Ezk 30:6

MIGHT *(196)*
I thought I **m** die on account Gn 26:9
he thought, "He **m** die too, like Gn 38:11
"Something **m** happen to him." Gn 42:4
so that I **m** dwell among them. Ex 29:46
I **m** destroy you on the way." Ex 33:3
so that He **m** humble you and test Dt 8:2
that you **m** learn that man does Dt 8:3
that in the end He **m** cause you Dt 8:16
of his anger **m** pursue the one Dt 19:6
so that you **m** know that I am the Dt 29:6
that these foes **m** misunderstand Dt 32:27
your descendants **m** say to our Jos 22:24
to you, or else Israel **m** brag: Jdg 7:2
of Jerubbaal **m** come to justice Jdg 9:24
bare hands as he **m** have torn a Jdg 14:6
He pushed with all his **m**, Jdg 16:30
with all his **m** before the LORD 2Sm 6:14
you **m** as well ask the kingship 1Kg 2:22
from Your people Israel **m** have— 1Kg 8:38
kingdom **m** return to the house 1Kg 12:26
along with all his **m**, all his 1Kg 15:23
all his accomplishments and **m**, 1Kg 16:5
and the **m** he exercised, 1Kg 16:27
tree and prayed that he **m** die. 1Kg 19:4
along with the **m** he exercised 1Kg 22:45
accomplishments and all his **m**, 2Kg 10:34
his accomplishments and his **m**, 2Kg 13:8
his **m**, and how he waged 2Kg 14:15
with all his **m** and how he made 2Kg 20:20
with all their **m** before God with 1Ch 13:8
In Your hand are power and **m**, 1Ch 29:12
his reign, his **m**, and the 1Ch 29:30
from your people Israel **m** have— 2Ch 6:29
that the LORD **m** carry out His 2Ch 10:15
Power and **m** are in Your hand, 2Ch 20:6
order that he **m** capture the city 2Ch 32:18
so that they **m** be given to 2Ch 35:12
so that we **m** humble ourselves Ezr 8:21
that they **m** get ready for that Est 3:14
so that Hathach **m** show it to Est 4:8
that someone **m** arbitrate between Jb 16:21
we will sing and praise Your **m**. Ps 21:13
and vindicate me by Your **m**! Ps 54:1
He rules forever by His **m**; Ps 66:7
the LORD God **m** live ⌊there⌋. Ps 68:18
of the LORD, His **m**, and the Ps 78:4
yet to be born—**m** know. Ps 78:6
so that they **m** put their Ps 78:7
drove the south wind by His **m**. Ps 78:26
so that they **m** declare the name Ps 102:21
so that they **m** keep His statutes Ps 105:45
Your servant so that I **m** live; Ps 119:17
kingdom and will declare Your **m**, Ps 145:11
don't know what a day **m** bring. Pr 27:1
I **m** have too much and deny You, Pr 30:9
or I **m** have nothing and steal, Pr 30:9
otherwise they **m** see with their Is 6:10
so that we **m** know, and from Is 41:26
times past, so that we **m** say: Is 41:26
so that Israel **m** be gathered to Is 49:5
up proudly in His great **m**? Is 63:1
Where is Your zeal and Your **m**? Is 63:15
orphans, so they **m** prosper, and Jr 5:28
mighty must not boast in his **m**; Jr 9:23
so that they **m** be My people for Jr 13:11
m be able to do what is good, Jr 13:23
so that your shame **m** be seen. Jr 13:26
them know My power and My **m**; Jr 16:21
At one moment I **m** announce Jr 18:7
so that we **m** prevail against him Jr 20:10
so that my mother **m** have been my Jr 20:17
order that you **m** provoke Me to Jr 25:7
that I **m** relent concerning the Jr 26:3
God so that He **m** relent Jr 26:13
nations that they **m** serve Jr 28:14
then I **m** also reject the seed of Jr 33:26
bow, the source of their **m**. Jr 49:35
case so that He **m** bring rest to Jr 50:34
Their **m** is exhausted; they Jr 51:30
so that it **m** stand in battle Ezk 13:5
bed, so that he **m** water it. Ezk 17:7
so the kingdom **m** be humble and Ezk 17:14
exalt itself but **m** keep his Ezk 17:14
Egypt so they **m** give him horses Ezk 17:15
land so that I **m** not destroy it, Ezk 22:30
here so that I **m** show ⌊it⌋ to Ezk 40:4
interpretation **m** be made known Dn 2:30
order that they **m** make the Dn 4:6
strength or by **m**, but by My Zch 4:6
the prophet **m** be fulfilled: Mt 2:15
prophet Isaiah **m** be fulfilled: Mt 8:17
Him, how they **m** destroy Him. Mt 12:14
prophet Isaiah **m** be fulfilled: Mt 12:17
otherwise they **m** see with their Mt 13:15
you **m** also uproot the wheat with Mt 13:29
the prophet **m** be fulfilled: Mt 13:35
to give her whatever she **m** ask. Mt 14:7
Him that they **m** only touch the Mt 14:36
benefit you **m** have received Mt 15:5
they **m** collapse on the way. Mt 15:32
to Him so He **m** put His hands Mt 19:13
the prophet **m** be fulfilled: Mt 21:4
This **m** have been sold for a Mt 26:9
Him, how they **m** destroy Him. Mk 3:6
otherwise, they **m** turn back— Mk 4:12
begged Him that they **m** touch Mk 6:56
benefit you **m** have received Mk 7:11
to Him so He **m** touch them, Mk 10:13
he **m** come suddenly and find you Mk 13:36
this oil **m** have been sold for Mk 14:5
the hour **m** pass from Him. Mk 14:35
whether John **m** be the Messiah. Lk 3:15
another what they **m** do to Jesus. Lk 6:11
because they **m** invite you back, Lk 14:12
to Him so He **m** touch them, Lk 18:15
so that they **m** give him some Lk 20:10
so that all **m** believe through Jn 1:7
with water so He **m** be revealed Jn 1:31
world that He **m** judge the world Jn 3:17
the world **m** be saved through Jn 3:17
order that they **m** have evidence Jn 8:6
that God's works **m** be displayed Jn 9:3
in their law **m** be fulfilled: Jn 15:25
that Jesus' words **m** be fulfilled Jn 18:32
the Scripture **m** be fulfilled, Jn 19:28
Pilate that he **m** remove Jesus' Jn 19:38
least his shadow **m** fall on some Ac 5:15
afraid the people **m** stone them. Ac 5:26
and asked that he **m** provide a Ac 7:46
that they **m** receive the Holy Ac 8:15
he **m** bring them as prisoners to Ac 9:2
the vision he had seen **m** mean, Ac 10:17
so that they **m** seek God, and Ac 17:27
and perhaps they **m** reach out and Ac 17:27

feared that Paul **m** be torn apart — Ac 23:10
that he **m** summon him to — Ac 25:3
to me today **m** become as I am— — Ac 26:29
fearing we **m** run aground in some — Ac 27:29
otherwise they **m** see with their — Ac 28:27
order that I **m** have a fruitful — Rm 1:13
perhaps someone **m** even dare to — Rm 5:7
commandment sin **m** become sinful — Rm 7:13
according to election **m** stand, — Rm 9:11
off so that I **m** be grafted — Rm 11:19
He **m** rule over both the dead — Rm 14:9
so He **m** bring to nothing the — 1Co 1:28
that your faith **m** not be based — 1Co 2:5
committed this act **m** be removed — 1Co 5:2
so that we **m** become the — 2Co 5:21
for us **m** be made plain to — 2Co 7:12
His poverty you **m** become rich. — 2Co 8:9
myself so that you **m** be exalted, — 2Co 11:7
so that I **m** not be running, — Gl 2:2
so that we **m** be justified by — Gl 2:16
the law, that I **m** live to God. — Gl 2:19
in Jesus Christ **m** be given to — Gl 3:22
so that we **m** receive adoption as — Gl 4:5
are disturbing you **m** also get — Gl 5:12
in the Messiah **m** bring praise to — Eph 1:12
in the coming ages He **m** display — Eph 2:7
so that He **m** create in Himself — Eph 2:15
so⌋ that He **m** reconcile both — Eph 2:16
that He **m** fill all things. — Eph 4:10
Pray that I **m** be bold enough in — Eph 6:20
according to His glorious **m**, — Col 1:11
so that He **m** come to have first — Col 1:18
that our labor **m** be for nothing. — 1Th 3:5
that you **m** obtain the glory of — 2Th 2:14
Christ Jesus **m** demonstrate the — 1Tm 1:16
he **m** become conceited and fall — 1Tm 3:6
to whom be honor and eternal **m**. — 1Tm 6:16
the proclamation **m** be fully made — 2Tm 4:17
and all the Gentiles **m** hear. — 2Tm 4:17
have believed God **m** be careful — Ti 3:8
the gospel he **m** serve me in your — Phm 13
that your good deed **m** not be out — Phm 14
so that you **m** get him back — Phm 15
God's grace He **m** taste death for — Heb 2:9
His death He **m** destroy the one — Heb 2:14
fled for refuge **m** have strong — Heb 6:18
who are called **m** receive the — Heb 9:15
that He **m** now appear in the — Heb 9:24
the firstborn **m** not touch them. — Heb 11:28
so that they **m** gain a better — Heb 11:35
what is not shaken **m** remain. — Heb 12:27
so that He **m** sanctify the people — Heb 13:12
we **m** live for righteousness; — 1Pt 2:24
that He **m** bring you to God, — 1Pt 3:18
although they **m** be judged by men — 1Pt 4:6
they **m** live by God in the — 1Pt 4:6
who are greater in **m** and power, — 2Pt 2:11
out so that it **m** be made clear — 1Jn 2:19
so that He **m** take away sins, — 1Jn 3:5
so that we **m** live through Him — 1Jn 4:9
give birth he **m** devour her child — Rv 12:4
that with it He **m** strike the — Rv 19:15

MIGHTIER *(1)*
a greater and **m** nation than they — Nm 14:12

MIGHTIEST *(1)*
which is **m** among beasts and — Pr 30:30

MIGHTY *(106)*
the hands of the **M** One of Jacob, — Gn 49:24
sank like lead in the **m** waters. — Ex 15:10
deeds and **m** acts like Yours? — Dt 3:24
the great, **m**, and awesome God — Dt 10:17
for all the **m** ⌊acts of⌋ power — Dt 34:12
know that the LORD's hand is **m**, — Jos 4:24
all the people give a **m** shout. — Jos 6:5
LORD against the **m** warriors." — Jdg 5:23
LORD is with you, **m** warrior." — Jdg 6:12
How the **m** have fallen! — 2Sm 1:19
shield of the **m** was defiled— — 2Sm 1:21
slain, from the bodies of the **m**. — 2Sm 1:22
How the **m** have fallen in the — 2Sm 1:25
How the **m** have fallen and the — 2Sm 1:27
of Your great name, **m** hand, and — 1Kg 8:42
great and **m** wind was tearing at — 1Kg 19:11
This Benaiah was a **m** man among — 1Ch 27:6
All the leaders and the **m** men, — 1Ch 29:24
great name and Your **m** hand and — 2Ch 6:32
arranged his **m** army of 800,000 — 2Ch 13:3
struck them with a **m** blow, — 2Ch 13:17
You to help the **m** and those — 2Ch 14:11
God—the great, **m**, and — Neh 9:32
strength, look, He is the **M** One! — Jb 9:19
drags away the **m** by His power; — Jb 24:22
can understand His **m** thunder? — Jb 26:14
you condemn the **m** Righteous One, — Jb 34:17
Even the **m** are removed without — Jb 34:20
He shatters the **m** without an — Jb 34:24
for help from the arm of the **m**. — Jb 35:9
Yes, God is **m**, but He despises — Jb 36:5
rains, His **m** torrential rains, — Jb 37:6
rises, the **m** are terrified; — Jb 41:25
heaven with **m** victories from — Ps 20:6
LORD, strong and **m**, the LORD, — Ps 24:8
mighty, the LORD, **m** in battle. — Ps 24:8
M warrior, strap your sword at — Ps 45:3
speak righteously, you **m** ones? — Ps 58:1
because of the **m** acts of the — Ps 71:16
and the **m** cedars with its — Ps 80:10
You have a **m** arm; Your hand is — Ps 89:13
the **m** breakers of the sea— — Ps 93:4
The **m** King loves justice. — Ps 99:4
the LORD's **m** acts or proclaim — Ps 106:2
will extend Your **m** scepter from — Ps 110:2
a vow to the **M** One of Jacob: — Ps 132:2
for the **M** One of Jacob." — Ps 132:5
nations and slaughtered **m** kings: — Ps 135:10
and will proclaim Your **m** acts. — Ps 145:4
all⌋ people of Your **m** acts and — Ps 145:12
Praise Him in His **m** heavens. — Ps 150:1
and bring down its **m** fortress. — Pr 21:22
hyraxes are not a **m** people, — Pr 30:26
warriors from the **m** of Israel. — Sg 3:7
M waters cannot extinguish love; — Sg 8:7
of Hosts, the **M** One of Israel, — Is 1:24
against them the **m** rushing — Is 8:7
Counselor, **M** God, Eternal Father — Is 9:6
like a **m** warrior, I subjugated — Is 10:13
remnant of Jacob, to the **M** God. — Is 10:21
with His **m** wind and will — Is 11:15
like that of a **m** people! — Is 13:4
like the raging of **m** waters. — Is 17:12
Lord has a strong and **m** one— — Is 28:2
young bulls with the **m** bulls. — Is 34:7
the army and the **m** one together — Is 43:17
the prey be taken from the **m**, — Is 49:24
captives of a **m** man will be — Is 49:25
Redeemer, the **M** One of Jacob." — Is 49:26
He will receive the **m** as spoil, — Is 53:12
Redeemer, the **M** One of Jacob. — Is 60:16
the smallest a **m** nation. — Is 60:22
they are all **m** warriors. — Jr 5:16
of the neighing of **m** steeds, — Jr 8:16
the **m** must not boast in his — Jr 9:23
outstretched hand and a **m** arm, — Jr 21:5
great and **m** God whose name is — Jr 32:18
great in counsel and **m** in deed, — Jr 32:19
are warriors—**m** men ⌊ready⌋ for — Jr 48:14
How the **m** scepter is shattered, — Jr 48:17
He will silence her **m** voice. — Jr 51:55
all the **m** men within me. — Lm 1:15
wings like the roar of **m** waters, — Ezk 1:24
and your **m** pillars will fall to — Ezk 26:11
you so that the **m** waters cover — Ezk 26:19
daughters of **m** nations down to — Ezk 32:18
riding horses—a **m** horde, a — Ezk 38:15
eat the flesh of **m** men and drink — Ezk 39:18
of **m** men and all the warriors." — Ezk 39:20
like the roar of **m** waters, — Ezk 43:2
miracles, and how **m** His wonders! — Dn 4:3
of Egypt with a **m** hand and made — Dn 9:15
like a **m** army deployed for war. — Jl 2:5
because the **M** One has done great — Lk 1:49
He has done a **m** deed with His — Lk 1:51
has toppled the **m** from their — Lk 1:52
led them out of it with a **m** arm. — Ac 13:17
weak, became **m** in battle, and — Heb 11:34
under the **m** hand of God, — 1Pt 5:6
I also saw a **m** angel proclaiming — Rv 5:2
I saw another **m** angel coming — Rv 10:1
He cried in a **m** voice: — Rv 18:2
Lord God who judges her is **m**. — Rv 18:8
great city, Babylon, the **m** city! — Rv 18:10
Then a **m** angel picked up a stone — Rv 18:21
the flesh of **m** men, the flesh of — Rv 19:18

MIGRATED *(1)*
As people **m** from the east, — Gn 11:2

MIGRATION *(1)*
and crane are aware of their **m**, — Jr 8:7

MIGRON *(2)*
tree in **M** on the outskirts — 1Sm 14:2
to Aiath and has gone through **M**, — Is 10:28

MIJAMIN *(4)*
to Malchijah, the sixth to **M**, — 1Ch 24:9
Izziah, Malchijah, **M**, Eleazar, — Ezr 10:25
Meshullam, Abijah, **M**, — Neh 10:7
M, Maadiah, Bilgah, — Neh 12:5

MIKLOTH *(4)*
and **M** who fathered Shimeah. — 1Ch 8:32
Gedor, Ahio, Zechariah, and **M**. — 1Ch 9:37
M fathered Shimeam. These also — 1Ch 9:38
month, and **M** was the leader; — 1Ch 27:4

MIKNEIAH *(2)*
Eliphelehu, **M**, and the — 1Ch 15:18
Eliphelehu, **M**, Obed-edom, Jeiel, — 1Ch 15:21

MILALAI *(1)*
Azarel, **M**, Gilalai, Maai, — Neh 12:36

MILCAH *(11)*
and Nahor's wife was named **M**. — Gn 11:29
the father of both **M** and Iscah. — Gn 11:29
M also has borne sons to your — Gn 22:20
M bore these eight to Nahor, — Gn 22:23
daughter of Bethuel son of **M**, — Gn 24:15
daughter of Bethuel son of **M**, — Gn 24:24
of Nahor, whom **M** bore to him.' — Gn 24:47
Noah, Hoglah, **M**, and Tirzah. — Nm 26:33
Noah, Hoglah, **M**, and Tirzah. — Nm 27:1
Tirzah, Hoglah, **M**, and Noah, — Nm 36:11
Noah, Hoglah, **M**, and Tirzah. — Jos 17:3

MILCOM *(7)*
(AKA MOLECH)
Sidonians, and **M**, the detestable — 1Kg 11:5
Moab, and for **M**, the detestable — 1Kg 11:7
god of Moab, and to **M**, the god — 1Kg 11:33
for **M**, the abomination of the — 2Kg 23:13
Why then has **M** dispossessed Gad — Jr 49:1
because **M** will go into exile — Jr 49:3
but also pledge loyalty to **M**; — Zph 1:5

MILDEW *(16)*
fabric is contaminated with **m**— — Lv 13:47
is a **m** contamination and is to — Lv 13:49
the contamination is harmful **m**; — Lv 13:51
is harmful **m** it must be burned — Lv 13:52
law concerning a **m** contamination — Lv 13:59
and I place a **m** contamination in — Lv 14:34
Something like **m** contamination — Lv 14:35
in the house, it is harmful **m**; — Lv 14:44
law for any skin disease or **m**, — Lv 14:54
for **m** in clothing or on a house, — Lv 14:55
regarding skin disease and **m**." — Lv 14:57
heat, drought, blight, and **m**; — Dt 28:22
when there is blight, **m**, locust, — 1Kg 8:37
when there is blight, **m**, locust, — 2Ch 6:28
I struck you with blight and **m**; — Am 4:9
with blight, **m**, and hail, but — Hg 2:17

MILE *(8)*
of a **m**⌋ wide and eight — Ezk 45:6
off a third of a **m** and led me — Ezk 47:3
off a third ⌊of a **m**⌋ and led me — Ezk 47:4
third ⌊of a **m**⌋ and led me — Ezk 47:4
measured off a third of a ⌊**m**⌋, — Ezk 47:5
of a **m**⌋ wide and eight — Ezk 48:15
anyone forces you to go one **m**, — Mt 5:41
was already over a **m** from land, — Mt 14:24

MILES *(38)*
and one-third ⌊**m**⌋ long and six — Ezk 45:1
and six and two-thirds ⌊**m**⌋ wide. — Ezk 45:1
and one-third ⌊**m**⌋ long and three — Ezk 45:3
three and one-third ⌊**m**⌋ wide, — Ezk 45:3
and one-third ⌊**m**⌋ long and three — Ezk 45:5
three and one-third ⌊**m**⌋ wide for — Ezk 45:5
eight and one-third ⌊**m**⌋ long, — Ezk 45:6
eight and one-third ⌊**m**⌋ wide, — Ezk 48:8
and one-third ⌊**m**⌋ long and three — Ezk 48:9
three and one-third ⌊**m**⌋ wide. — Ezk 48:9
eight and one-third ⌊**m** long⌋ on — Ezk 48:10
and one-third ⌊**m**⌋ wide on the — Ezk 48:10
and one-third ⌊**m**⌋ wide on the — Ezk 48:10
eight and one-third ⌊**m**⌋ long on — Ezk 48:10
and one-third ⌊**m**⌋ long and three — Ezk 48:13
three and one-third ⌊**m**⌋ wide. — Ezk 48:13
and one-third ⌊**m**⌋ and the width — Ezk 48:13
width three and one-third ⌊**m**⌋. — Ezk 48:13

eight and one-third ⌊**m** long⌋, Ezk 48:15
one and a half ⌊**m**⌋ on the north Ezk 48:16
one and a half ⌊**m**⌋ on the south Ezk 48:16
one and a half ⌊**m**⌋ on the east Ezk 48:16
one and a half ⌊**m**⌋ on the west Ezk 48:16
and one-third ⌊**m**⌋ to the east Ezk 48:18
and one-third ⌊**m**⌋ to the west. Ezk 48:18
eight and one-third ⌊**m**⌋ by eight Ezk 48:20
by eight and one-third ⌊**m**⌋; Ezk 48:20
one-third ⌊**m**⌋ of the donation Ezk 48:21
one-third ⌊**m** of the donation⌋ Ezk 48:21
measures one and a half ⌊**m**⌋, Ezk 48:30
which is one and a half ⌊**m**⌋, Ezk 48:32
measures one and a half ⌊**m**⌋, Ezk 48:33
which is one and a half ⌊**m**⌋, Ezk 48:34
of the city⌋ will be six ⌊**m**⌋, Ezk 48:35
about seven **m** from Jerusalem. Lk 24:13
had rowed about three or four **m**, Jn 6:19
Jerusalem (about two **m** away). Jn 11:18
horses' bridles for about 180 **m**. Rv 14:20

MILETUS *(3)*
and the day after, we came to **M**. Ac 20:15
Now from **M**, he sent to Ephesus Ac 20:17
Trophimus I left sick at **M**. 2Tm 4:20

MILITARY *(55)*
according to their **m** divisions. Ex 12:51
or more by their **m** divisions— Nm 1:3
to camp by their **m** divisions, Nm 1:52
Judah's **m** divisions will camp on Nm 2:3
His **m** division numbers 74,600. Nm 2:4
His **m** division numbers 54,400. Nm 2:6
His **m** division numbers 57,400. Nm 2:8
number in their **m** divisions who Nm 2:9
Reuben's **m** divisions will camp Nm 2:10
His **m** division numbers 46,500. Nm 2:11
His **m** division numbers 59,300. Nm 2:13
His **m** division numbers 45,650. Nm 2:15
number in their **m** divisions who Nm 2:16
Ephraim's **m** divisions will camp Nm 2:18
His **m** division numbers 40,500. Nm 2:19
His **m** division numbers 32,200. Nm 2:21
His **m** division numbers 35,400. Nm 2:23
total in their **m** divisions who Nm 2:24
Dan's **m** divisions will camp on Nm 2:25
His **m** division numbers 62,700. Nm 2:26
His **m** division numbers 41,500. Nm 2:28
His **m** division numbers 53,400. Nm 2:30
the camps by their **m** divisions Nm 2:32
The **m** divisions of the camp of Nm 10:14
The **m** divisions of the camp of Nm 10:18
Next the **m** divisions of the camp Nm 10:22
The **m** divisions of the camp of Nm 10:25
by their **m** divisions as they Nm 10:28
returning from the **m** campaign. Nm 31:14
Egypt by their **m** divisions under Nm 33:1
they will appoint **m** commanders Dt 20:9
Take the whole **m** force with you Jos 8:1
and the whole **m** force set out to Jos 8:3
m force was stationed in this Jos 8:13
So Joshua and his whole **m** force, Jos 10:7
and said to the **m** commanders who Jos 10:24
and his whole **m** force surprised Jos 11:7
Saul had his own **m** clothes put 1Sm 17:38
on over the **m** clothes and tried 1Sm 17:39
along with his **m** tunic, his 1Sm 18:4
brought their **m** units together 1Sm 28:1
all their **m** units together at 1Sm 29:1
brought all his **m** units together 2Kg 6:24
people of the land for **m** duty; 2Kg 25:19
genealogies for **m** service was 1Ch 7:40
with all the **m** weapons of war. 1Ch 12:37
on rotated **m** duty each month 1Ch 27:1
He set **m** commanders over the 2Ch 32:6
against them the **m** commanders 2Ch 33:11
He also placed **m** commanders in 2Ch 33:14
your plans and **m** preparedness Is 36:5
people of the land for **m** duty; Jr 52:25
a ramp, pitch **m** camps, and place Ezk 4:2
for his nobles, **m** commanders, Mk 6:21
nobles, the **m** commanders, the Rv 6:15

MILK *(50)*
Then Abraham took curds and **m**, Gn 18:8
30 **m** camels with their young, Gn 32:15
and his teeth are whiter than **m**. Gn 49:12
land flowing with **m** and honey— Ex 3:8
a land flowing with **m** and honey. Ex 3:17
a land flowing with **m** and honey, Ex 13:5
a young goat in its mother's **m**. Ex 23:19
a land flowing with **m** and honey. Ex 33:3
a young goat in its mother's **m**." Ex 34:26
a land flowing with **m** and honey. Lv 20:24
it is flowing with **m** and honey, Nm 13:27
a land flowing with **m** and honey, Nm 14:8
flowing with **m** and honey to kill Nm 16:13
flowing with **m** and honey or give Nm 16:14
a land flowing with **m** and honey. Dt 6:3
a land flowing with **m** and honey. Dt 11:9
a young goat in its mother's **m**. Dt 14:21
a land flowing with **m** and honey. Dt 26:9
a land flowing with **m** and honey. Dt 26:15
a land flowing with **m** and honey, Dt 27:3
land⌋ flowing with **m** and honey, Dt 31:20
the herd and **m** from the flock, Dt 32:14
a land flowing with **m** and honey. Jos 5:6
She opened a container of **m**, Jdg 4:19
she gave him **m**. She brought him Jdg 5:25
him curdled **m** in a majestic bowl Jdg 5:25
cart and two **m** cows that have 1Sm 6:7
They took two **m** cows, hitched 1Sm 6:10
pour me out like **m** and curdle me Jb 10:10
enough goat's **m** for your food— Pr 27:27
churning of **m** produces butter Pr 30:33
Honey and **m** are under your Sg 4:11
I drink my wine with my **m**. Sg 5:1
washed in **m** and set like jewels. Sg 5:12
the abundant **m** they give he will Is 7:22
Infants ⌊just⌋ weaned from **m**? Is 28:9
buy wine and **m** without money and Is 55:1
will nurse on the **m** of nations, Is 60:16
a land flowing with **m** and honey, Jr 11:5
a land flowing with **m** and honey. Jr 32:22
than snow, whiter than **m**; Lm 4:7
land⌋ flowing with **m** and honey, Ezk 20:6
flowing with **m** and honey— Ezk 20:15
eat your fruit and drink your **m**. Ezk 25:4
and the hills will flow with **m**. Jl 3:18
I fed you **m**, not solid food, 1Co 3:2
not drink the **m** from the flock? 1Co 9:7
You need **m**, not solid food. Heb 5:12
who lives on **m** is inexperienced Heb 5:13
the unadulterated spiritual **m**, 1Pt 2:2

MILL *(3)*
while the sound of the **m** fades; Ec 12:4
women will be grinding at the **m**: Mt 24:41
the sound of a **m** will never be Rv 18:22

MILLET *(1)*
beans, lentils, **m**, and spelt. Ezk 4:9

MILLION *(2)*
with an army of one **m** men and 2Ch 14:9
of mounted troops was 200 **m**; Rv 9:16

MILLSTONE *(8)*
or an upper **m** as security for a Dt 24:6
portion of a **m** on Abimelech's Jdg 9:53
drop an upper **m** on him from the 2Sm 11:21
as a rock, as hard as a lower **m**! Jb 41:24
if a heavy **m** were hung around Mt 18:6
if a heavy **m** were hung around Mk 9:42
for him if a **m** were hung around Lk 17:2
stone like a large **m** and threw Rv 18:21

MILLSTONES *(5)*
girl who is behind the **m**, Ex 11:5
not take a pair of **m** or an upper Dt 24:6
Take **m** and grind meal; Is 47:2
the sound of the **m** and the light Jr 25:10
Young men labor at **m**; Lm 5:13

MINA *(5)*
Your **m** will equal 60 shekels. Ezk 45:12
m has earned 10 more minas.' Lk 19:16
your **m** has made five minas.' Lk 19:18
said, 'Master, here is your **m**. Lk 19:20
'Take the **m** away from him and Lk 19:24

MINAS *(7)*
2,200 silver **m** to the treasury Neh 7:71
2,000 silver **m**, and 67 priestly Neh 7:72
gave them 10 **m**, and told them, Lk 19:13
your mina has earned 10 more **m**.' Lk 19:16
your mina has made five **m**.' Lk 19:18
it to the one who has 10 **m**.' Lk 19:24
to him, 'Master, he has 10 **m**.' Lk 19:25

MIND *(133)*
every scheme his **m** thought of Gn 6:5
father kept the matter ⌊in **m**⌋. Gn 37:11
and change Your **m** about this Ex 32:12
LORD changed His **m** about the Ex 32:14
that brings sin to **m**. Nm 5:15
a son of man who changes His **m**. Nm 23:19
slip from your **m** as long as you Dt 4:9
and keep in **m** that the LORD is Dt 4:39
Keep in **m** that the LORD your God Dt 8:5
not given you a **m** to understand, Dt 29:4
he may bless himself in his **m**, Dt 29:19
whatever is in My heart and **m**. 1Sm 2:35
does not lie or change His **m**, 1Sm 15:29
is not man who changes his **m**." 1Sm 15:29
the king's **m** was on Absalom. 2Sm 14:1
His ordinances in **m** and have not 2Sm 22:23
Me with their whole **m** and heart, 1Kg 2:4
You with their whole **m** and heart 1Kg 8:48
everything that was on her **m**. 1Kg 10:2
with all his **m** and with all his 2Kg 23:3
with all his **m** and with all his 2Kg 23:25
Israel put it into the **m** of Pul 1Ch 5:26
was also of one **m** to make David 1Ch 12:38
in your **m** and heart to seek 1Ch 22:19
a whole heart and a willing **m**, 1Ch 28:9
he had in **m** for the courts 1Ch 28:12
You with their whole **m** and heart 2Ch 6:38
everything that was on her **m**. 2Ch 9:1
with all their **m** and all their 2Ch 15:12
had sworn it with all their **m**. 2Ch 15:15
His **m** rejoiced in the LORD's 2Ch 17:6
put it into the **m** of the 2Ch 21:16
put it into the **m** of King Cyrus 2Ch 36:22
put it into the **m** of King Cyrus Ezr 1:1
it into the king's **m** to glorify Ezr 7:27
inventing them in your own **m**." Neh 6:8
God put it into my **m** to assemble Neh 7:5
But I also have a **m**; I am not Jb 12:3
more things like these in **m**. Jb 23:14
If He put His **m** to it and Jb 34:14
or gave the **m** understanding? Jb 38:36
me, agony in my **m** every day? Ps 13:2
I keep the LORD in **m** always. Ps 16:8
His ordinances in **m** and have not Ps 18:22
has not set his **m** on what is Ps 24:4
examine my heart and **m**. Ps 26:2
they have conspired with one **m**; Ps 83:5
me an undivided **m** to fear Your Ps 86:11
For wisdom will enter your **m**, Pr 2:10
but a twisted **m** is despised. Pr 12:8
A discerning **m** seeks knowledge, Pr 15:14
The **m** of the righteous person Pr 15:28
with a twisted **m** will not Pr 17:20
The **m** of the discerning acquires Pr 18:15
apply your **m** to my knowledge. Pr 22:17
keep your **m** on the right course. Pr 23:19
I applied my **m** to seek and Ec 1:13
and my **m** has thoroughly grasped Ec 1:16
applied my **m** to know wisdom and Ec 1:17
explored with my **m** how to let my Ec 2:3
m still guiding me with wisdom Ec 2:3
at night, his **m** does not rest. Ec 2:23
and a bribe destroys the **m**. Ec 7:7
applying my **m** to all the work Ec 8:9
I applied my **m** to know wisdom Ec 8:16
perfect peace the **m** ⌊that is⌋ Is 26:3
The reckless **m** will gain Is 32:4
and his **m** plots iniquity. Is 32:6
Your **m** will meditate on the Is 33:18
⌊His⌋ deceived **m** has led him Is 44:20
not be remembered or come to **m**. Is 65:17
never come to **m**, and no one will Jr 3:16
tests heart and **m**, let me see Jr 11:20
examine the **m**, I test the heart Jr 17:10
and seeing the heart and **m**, Jr 20:12
the highway in **m**, the way you Jr 31:21
land with all My **m** and heart. Jr 32:41
them? He brought this to **m**. Jr 44:21
put it into the **m** of the kings Jr 51:11
let Jerusalem come to your **m**. Jr 51:50
call this to **m**, and therefore I Lm 3:21
thoughts that arise in your **m**. Ezk 11:5
what you have in **m** will never Ezk 20:32
thoughts will arise in your **m**, Ezk 38:10
came into⌋ your **m** ⌊as you lay⌋ Dn 2:28
came ⌊to your **m**⌋ about what will Dn 2:29
the thoughts of your **m**. Dn 2:30
and visions in my **m** alarmed me. Dn 4:5
visions of my **m** as I was lying Dn 4:10
the visions of my **m** an observer, Dn 4:13
Let his **m** be changed from that Dn 4:16
be given the **m** of an animal for Dn 4:16

his **m** was like an animal's, Dn 5:21
he set his **m** on rescuing Daniel Dn 6:14
visions in his **m** as he was lying Dn 7:1
like a man, and given a human **m**. Dn 7:4
visions in my **m** terrified me. Dn 7:15
and in his own **m** he will make Dn 8:25
the disaster in **m** and brought it Dn 9:14
later he changed his **m** and went. Mt 21:29
your soul, and with all your **m**. Mt 22:37
they said, "He's out of His **m**." Mk 3:21
dressed and in his right **m**; Mk 5:15
with all your **m**, and with all Mk 12:30
dressed and in his right **m**. Lk 8:35
strength, and with all your **m**; Lk 10:27
with one **m** to what Philip Ac 8:6
weak and to keep in **m** the words Ac 20:35
You're out of your **m**, Paul! Ac 26:24
not out of my **m**, most excellent Ac 26:25
to a worthless **m** to do what is Rm 1:28
the law of my **m** and taking me Rm 7:23
with my **m** I myself am a slave to Rm 7:25
who has known the **m** of the Lord? Rm 11:34
by the renewing of your **m**, Rm 12:2
be fully convinced in his own **m**. Rm 14:5
with a united **m** and voice. Rm 15:6
who has known the Lord's **m**, 1Co 2:16
But we have the **m** of Christ. 1Co 2:16
I made up my **m** about this: 2Co 2:1
For if we are out of our **m**, 2Co 5:13
have a sound **m**, it is for you. 2Co 5:13
be of the same **m**, be at peace, 2Co 13:11
spirit, with one **m**, working side Php 1:27
and hostile in **m** because of your Col 1:21
without cause by his fleshly **m**. Col 2:18
a quiet life, to **m** your own 1Th 4:11
easily upset in **m** or troubled, 2Th 2:2
Keep in **m** Jesus Christ, risen 2Tm 2:8
who are corrupt in **m**, worthless 2Tm 3:8
both their **m** and conscience are Ti 1:15
and He will not change His **m**, Heb 7:21
Here is the **m** with wisdom: Rv 17:9

MIND-SET *(4)*
For the **m** of the flesh is death, Rm 8:6
but the **m** of the Spirit is life Rm 8:6
the **m** of the flesh is hostile Rm 8:7
the hearts knows the Spirit's **m**, Rm 8:27

MINDFUL *(1)*
servant Israel, **m** of His mercy, Lk 1:54

MINDS *(34)*
will change their **m** and return Ex 13:17
changed their **m** about the people Ex 14:5
closed their **m** to understanding Jb 17:4
with twisted **m** are detestable to Pr 11:20
Dull the **m** of these people; Is 6:10
with their **m**, turn back, and be Is 6:10
and their **m** so they cannot Is 44:18
the deceit of their own **m**. Jr 14:14
speak visions from their own **m**, Jr 23:16
in the **m** of the prophets Jr 23:26
of the deceit of their own **m**? Jr 23:26
and go out of their **m** because of Jr 25:16
changed their **m** and took back Jr 34:11
changed your **m** and profaned My Jr 34:16
change your **m** then and believe Mt 21:32
debating in their **m** whether John Lk 3:15
make up your **m** not to prepare Lk 21:14
so that your **m** are not dulled Lk 21:34
He opened their **m** to understand Lk 24:45
poisoned the **m** of the Gentiles Ac 14:2
changed their **m** and said he was Ac 28:6
their senseless **m** were darkened. Rm 1:21
say that you are out of your **m**? 1Co 14:23
But their **m** were closed. 2Co 3:14
has blinded the **m** of the 2Co 4:4
your **m** may be corrupted from a 2Co 11:3
renewed in the spirit of your **m**; Eph 4:23
and your **m** in Christ Jesus Php 4:7
Set your **m** on what is above, Col 3:2
among men whose **m** are depraved 1Tm 6:5
I will put My laws into their **m**, Heb 8:10
I will write them on their **m**, Heb 10:16
get your **m** ready for action, 1Pt 1:13
One who examines **m** and hearts, Rv 2:23

MINE *(60)*
Everything you see is **m**! Gn 31:43
these daughters of **m** or for the Gn 31:43
came to you in Egypt are now **m**. Gn 48:5
signs of **M** among them, Ex 10:1
both man and animal; it is **M**." Ex 13:2
although all the earth is **M**, Ex 19:5
That's **m**, the case between the Ex 22:9
apart from the nations to be **M**. Lv 20:26
sold because it is **M**, Lv 25:23
they are **M**; I am the LORD. Nm 3:13
among the Israelites is **M**, Nm 8:17
whose hills you will **m** copper. Dt 8:9
these words of **M** on your hearts Dt 11:18
said, "The guilt is **m**, my lord, 1Sm 25:24
has a field right next to **m**, 2Sm 14:30
"You know the kingship was **m**," 1Kg 2:15
He will not be **m** or yours. 1Kg 3:26
'Your silver and your gold are **m**! 1Kg 20:3
and children are **m** as well!' " 1Kg 20:3
"Is your heart one with **m**?" 2Kg 10:15
Surely there is a **m** for silver Jb 28:1
every animal of the forest is **M**, Ps 50:10
creatures of the field are **M**. Ps 50:11
world and everything in it is **M**. Ps 50:12
of any sin or rebellion of **m**. Ps 59:3
For no fault of **m**, they run and Ps 59:4
Gilead is **M**, Manasseh is Mine, Ps 60:7
Manasseh is **M**, and Ephraim is Ps 60:7
Gilead is **M**, Manasseh is Mine, Ps 108:8
Manasseh is **M**, and Ephraim is Ps 108:8
My love is **m** and I am his; Sg 2:16
I am my love's and my love is **m**; Sg 6:3
out a plan, but not **M**, They make Is 30:1
you by your name; you are **M**. Is 43:1
whose word stands, **M** or theirs! Jr 44:28
any pain like **m**, which was dealt Lm 1:12
with you, and you became **M**." Ezk 16:8
They became **M** and gave birth to Ezk 23:4
even though she was **M**. Ezk 23:5
nations and two lands will be **m**, Ezk 35:10
"They will be **M**," says the LORD Mal 3:17
these words of **M** and acts on Mt 7:24
these words of **M** and doesn't act Mt 7:26
these two sons of **m** may sit, Mt 20:21
right and left is not **M** to give; Mt 20:23
least of these brothers of **M**, Mt 25:40
right or left is not **M** to give; Mk 10:40
a friend of **m** on a journey has Lk 11:6
this son of **m** was dead and is Lk 15:24
bring here these enemies of **m**, Lk 19:27
So this joy of **m** is complete. Jn 3:29
My teaching isn't **M** but is from Jn 7:16
that you hear is not **M** but is Jn 14:24
from what is **M** and declare it to Jn 16:14
Everything the Father has is **M**. Jn 16:15
from what is **M** and will declare Jn 16:15
and Yours are **M**, and I have been Jn 17:10
other's faith, both yours and **m**. Rm 1:12
also his mother—and **m**. Rm 16:13
this boasting of **m** will not be 2Co 11:10

MINER *(2)*
A **m** puts an end to the darkness; Jb 28:3
The **m** strikes the flint and Jb 28:9

MINERS *(1)*
the **m** swing back and forth. Jb 28:4

MINGLE *(1)*
like bread and **m** my drinks with Ps 102:9

MINGLED *(1)*
but **m** with the nations and Ps 106:35

MINIAMIN *(3)*
Eden, **M**, Jeshua, Shemaiah, 2Ch 31:15
Abijah, Piltai of Moadiah, of **M**, Neh 12:17
Maaseiah, **M**, Micaiah, Elioenai Neh 12:41

MINISTER *(26)*
the altar to **m** in the sanctuary Ex 28:43
of meeting to **m** in the sanctuary Ex 29:30
the altar to **m** by burning up Ex 30:20
the community to **m** to them? Nm 16:9
to stand and **m** in the LORD's Dt 18:5
fellow Levites who **m** there in Dt 18:7
the LORD and to **m** before Him 1Ch 15:2
covenant to **m** regularly before 1Ch 16:37
of the LORD, to **m** to Him, and to 1Ch 23:13
praise and to **m** before the 2Ch 8:14
to the LORD, **m** to Him, love Is 56:6
Levites who **m** to Me innumerable. Jr 33:22
have removed the clothes they **m** Ezk 42:14
of wool when they **m** at the gates Ezk 44:17
inner court to **m** in the Ezk 44:27
the priests who **m** in the Ezk 45:4
the Levites who **m** in the temple; Ezk 45:5
where those who **m** at the temple Ezk 46:24
to be a **m** of Christ Jesus to the Rm 15:16
are obligated to **m** to Jews in Rm 15:27
pay ⌊from them⌋ to **m** to you. 2Co 11:8
messenger and **m** to my need— Php 2:25
is a faithful **m** of the Messiah Col 1:7
I, Paul, have become a **m** of it. Col 1:23
have become its **m**, according to Col 1:25
m of the sanctuary and the true Heb 8:2

MINISTERED *(4)*
They **m** with song in front of the 1Ch 6:32
Because they **m** to the house of Ezk 44:12
from Galilee and **m** to Him were Mt 27:55
know how much he **m** at Ephesus. 2Tm 1:18

MINISTERING *(11)*
garments for **m** in the sanctuary Ex 35:19
garments for **m** in the sanctuary Ex 39:41
were not able to continue **m**, 1Kg 8:11
had duties for **m** in the LORD's 1Ch 26:12
were not able to continue **m**, 2Ch 5:14
the priests **m** to the LORD are 2Ch 13:10
gates and **m** at the temple. Ezk 44:11
off the clothes they have been **m** Ezk 44:19
As they were **m** to the Lord and Ac 13:2
they not all **m** spirits sent out Heb 1:14
after day **m** and offering time Heb 10:11

MINISTERS *(12)*
⌊worn by⌋ Aaron whenever he **m**, Ex 28:35
Levites to be **m** before the ark 1Ch 16:4
and to be His **m** and burners of 2Ch 29:11
should bring us **m** for the house Ezr 8:17
speak of you as **m** of our God; Is 61:6
priests will not be My **m**. Jr 33:21
priests, who are **m** of the LORD, Jl 1:9
wail, you **m** of the altar. Jl 1:13
in sackcloth, you **m** of my God, Jl 1:13
the LORD's **m**, weep between Jl 2:17
competent to be **m** of a new 2Co 3:6
as God's **m**, we commend 2Co 6:4

MINISTRIES *(1)*
are different **m**, but the same 1Co 12:5

MINISTRY *(38)*
garments for **m** in the sanctuary Ex 39:1
to be used for **m**, just as the Ex 39:26
in the **m** of God's temple 1Ch 9:13
articles for **m** and for making 2Ch 24:14
offerings, for **m**, for giving 2Ch 31:2
days of his **m** were completed, Lk 1:23
As He began ⌊His **m**⌋, Jesus was Lk 3:23
was allotted a share in this **m**." Ac 1:17
prayer and to the preaching **m**." Ac 6:4
my course and the **m** I received Ac 20:24
the Gentiles through his **m**. Ac 21:19
have a fruitful **m** among you, Rm 1:13
to the Gentiles, I magnify my **m**, Rm 11:13
for effective **m** has opened for 1Co 16:9
Now if the **m** of death, chiseled 2Co 3:7
how will the **m** of the Spirit not 2Co 3:8
For if the **m** of condemnation had 2Co 3:9
the **m** of righteousness overflows 2Co 3:9
since we have this **m**, as we have 2Co 4:1
and gave us the **m** of 2Co 5:18
that the **m** will not be blamed. 2Co 6:3
sharing in the **m** to the saints, 2Co 8:4
the churches for his gospel **m**. 2Co 8:18
concerning the **m** to the saints, 2Co 9:1
For the **m** of this service is not 2Co 9:12
of the area ⌊of **m**⌋ that God has 2Co 10:13
our area ⌊of **m**⌋ will be greatly 2Co 10:15
in someone else's area ⌊of **m**⌋. 2Co 10:16
of the saints in the work of **m**, Eph 4:12
in the gospel **m** like a son with Php 2:22
was lacking in your **m** to me. Php 2:30
attention to the **m** you have Col 4:17
appointing me to the **m**— 1Tm 1:12
an evangelist, fulfill your **m**. 2Tm 4:5
for he is useful to me in the **m**. 2Tm 4:11
has now obtained a superior **m**, Heb 8:6
regulations for **m** and an earthly Heb 9:1
repeatedly, performing their **m**. Heb 9:6

MINNI *(1)*
her—Ararat, **M**, and Ashkenaz. Jr 51:27

MINNITH *(2)*
to the entrance of **M** and to Jdg 11:33
They exchanged wheat from **M**, Ezk 27:17

MINOR *(2)*
judge every **m** case themselves Ex 18:22
every **m** case they would judge Ex 18:26

MINT *(2)*
pay a tenth of **m**, dill, and Mt 23:23
a tenth of **m**, rue, and every Lk 11:42

MINUS *(1)*
from the Jews 40 lashes **m** one. 2Co 11:24

MIRACLE *(3)*
Perform a **m**, tell Aaron: Ex 7:9
will perform a **m** in My name who Mk 9:39
to see some **m** performed by Him. Lk 23:8

MIRACLES *(23)*
Egypt with all My **m** that I will Ex 3:20
tell you about the **m** and wonders Dn 4:2
great are His **m**, and how mighty Dn 4:3
and do many **m** in Your name?' Mt 7:22
where most of His **m** were done, Mt 11:20
For if the **m** that were done in Mt 11:21
For if the **m** that were done in Mt 11:23
wisdom and these **m** come to Him? Mt 13:54
did not do many **m** there because Mt 13:58
how are these **m** performed by His Mk 6:2
was not able to do any **m** there, Mk 6:5
For if the **m** that were done in Lk 10:13
for all the **m** they had seen: Lk 19:37
out to you by God with **m**, Ac 2:22
and great **m** that were being Ac 8:13
extraordinary **m** by Paul's hands, Ac 19:11
the performing of **m**, to another, 1Co 12:10
teachers, next, **m**, then gifts 1Co 12:28
Are all teachers? Do all do **m**? 1Co 12:29
signs but also wonders and **m**. 2Co 12:12
the Spirit and work **m** among you Gl 3:5
with all kinds of false **m**, 2Th 2:9
wonders, various **m**, and Heb 2:4

MIRACULOUS *(8)*
I may do these **m** signs of Mine Ex 10:1
performed **m** signs among them, Ex 10:2
to him and gave him a **m** sign. 2Ch 32:24
inquire about the **m** sign that 2Ch 32:31
display Your **m** power against me Jb 10:16
performed His **m** signs in Egypt Ps 78:43
performed His **m** signs among Ps 105:27
by the power of **m** signs and Rm 15:19

MIRAGE *(1)*
have become like a **m** to me— Jr 15:18

MIRE *(2)*
its waters churn up **m** and muck. Is 57:20
Your feet sank into the **m**, Jr 38:22

MIRIAM *(13)*
Then **M** the prophetess, Aaron's Ex 15:20
M sang to them: Sing to the LORD, Ex 15:21
M and Aaron criticized Moses Nm 12:1
Aaron, and **M**, "You three come Nm 12:4
tent, and summoned Aaron and **M**. Nm 12:5
So **M** was confined outside the Nm 12:15
move on until **M** was brought Nm 12:15
M died and was buried there. Nm 20:1
Moses, and their sister **M**. Nm 26:59
your God did to **M** on the journey Dt 24:9
wife Bithiah gave birth to **M**, 1Ch 4:17
Moses, and **M**. Aaron's sons: 1Ch 6:3
Aaron, and **M** ahead of you. Mc 6:4

MIRIAM'S *(1)*
M ⌊skin⌋ suddenly became Nm 12:10

MIRMAH *(1)*
Sachia, and **M**. These were his 1Ch 8:10

MIRROR *(3)*
skies as hard as a cast metal **m**? Jb 37:18
as in a **m**, but then face to 1Co 13:12
looking at his own face in a **m**; Jms 1:23

MIRRORS *(1)*
the ⌊bronze⌋ **m** of the women who Ex 38:8

MIRY *(1)*
Rescue me from the **m** mud; Ps 69:14

MISCARRIED *(3)*
and female goats have not **m**, Gn 31:38
was I not hidden like a **m** child, Jb 3:16
like a woman's **m** ⌊child⌋, they Ps 58:8

MISCARRIES *(1)*
a womb that **m** and breasts that Hs 9:14

MISCARRY *(2)*
No woman will **m** or be barren in Ex 23:26
their cows calve and do not **m**. Jb 21:10

MISDEEDS *(1)*
them, but punished their **m**. Ps 99:8

MISERABLE *(7)*
king's son, so **m** every morning? 2Sm 13:4
You are all **m** comforters. Jb 16:2
the days of the oppressed are **m**, Pr 15:15
people this **m** task to keep them Ec 1:13
This too is futile and a **m** task. Ec 4:8
Listen, Laishah! Anathoth is **m**. Is 10:30
Be **m** and mourn and weep. Jms 4:9

MISERIES *(1)*
wail over the **m** that are coming Jms 5:1

MISERY *(12)*
have observed the **m** of My people Ex 3:7
up from the **m** of Egypt to the Ex 3:17
and that He had seen their **m**, Ex 4:31
let me see my **m** ⌊any more⌋." Nm 11:15
heard our cry and saw our **m**, Dt 26:7
He became weary of Israel's **m**. Jdg 10:16
You have brought great **m** on me. Jdg 11:35
full weight of **m** will crush him. Jb 20:22
What **m** that I have stayed in Ps 120:5
but the wicked are full of **m**. Pr 12:21
the LORD has added **m** to my pain! Jr 45:3
gloat over their **m** in the day of Ob 13

MISFORTUNE *(4)*
there had been **m** in his home. 1Ch 7:23
the wicked and **m** to evildoers? Jb 31:3
who rejoice at my **m** be disgraced Ps 35:26
my enemies have heard of my **m**; Lm 1:21

MISFORTUNES *(1)*
experience many troubles and **m**, Ps 71:20

MISHAEL *(8)*
(AKA MESHACH)
M, Elzaphan, and Sithri. Ex 6:22
Moses summoned **M** and Elzaphan, Lv 10:4
were Pedaiah, **M**, Malchijah, Neh 8:4
Hananiah, **M**, and Azariah. Dn 1:6
Shadrach; to **M**, Meshach; and to Dn 1:7
Hananiah, **M**, and Azariah, Dn 1:11
Hananiah, **M**, and Azariah. Dn 1:19
friends Hananiah, **M**, and Azariah Dn 2:17

MISHAL *(2)*
and **M** and reached westward to Jos 19:26
M with its pasturelands, Abdon Jos 21:30

MISHAM *(1)*
Eber, **M**, and Shemed who built 1Ch 8:12

MISHMA *(3)*
M, Dumah, Massa, Gn 25:14
M, Dumah, Massa, Hadad, Tema, 1Ch 1:30
his son Mibsam, and his son **M**. 1Ch 4:25

MISHMA'S *(1)*
M sons: his son Hammuel, his son 1Ch 4:26

MISHMANNAH *(1)*
M fourth, Jeremiah fifth, 1Ch 12:10

MISHRAITES *(1)*
Puthites, Shumathites, and **M**. 1Ch 2:53

MISLEAD *(5)*
don't let him **m** you like this. 2Ch 32:15
My people, your leaders **m** you; Is 3:12
leaders of the people **m** ⌊them⌋, Is 9:16
and those they **m** are swallowed Is 9:16
does not **m** you by saying, Is 36:18

MISLEADING *(2)*
Isn't Hezekiah **m** you to give you 2Ch 32:11
for you that were empty and **m**. Lm 2:14

MISLEADS *(1)*
to Hezekiah when he **m** you, 2Kg 18:32

MISLED *(3)*
has your heart **m** you, and why do Jb 15:12
trusted friends **m** you and Jr 38:22
persuaded and **m** a considerable Ac 19:26

MISMATCHED *(1)*
Do not be **m** with unbelievers. 2Co 6:14

MISPAR *(1)*
Bilshan, **M**, Bigvai, Rehum, Ezr 2:2

MISPERETH *(1)*
Bilshan, **M**, Bigvai, Nehum, Neh 7:7

MISREPHOTH-MAIM *(2)*
as far as Great Sidon and **M**, Jos 11:8
hill country from Lebanon to **M**, Jos 13:6

MISS *(4)*
a stone at a hair and not **m**. Jdg 20:16
no one will remember or **m** it. Jr 3:16
how I deeply **m** all of you with Php 1:8
so that none of you should **m** it. Heb 4:1

MISSED *(1)*
you'll be **m** because your seat 1Sm 20:18

MISSES *(2)*
If your father **m** me at all, 1Sm 20:6
the one who **m** a hundred years Is 65:20

MISSILES *(1)*
dodge the **m**, never stopping. Jl 2:8

MISSING *(18)*
command, and not one of us is **m**. Nm 31:49
tribe is ⌊**m**⌋ in Israel today? Jdg 21:3
of theirs was **m** the whole time 1Sm 25:7
of ours was **m** the whole time we 1Sm 25:15
He was not **m** anything, yet he 1Sm 25:21
of theirs⌋ was **m** from the 1Sm 30:19
19 of David's soldiers were **m**, 2Sm 2:30
If he is ever **m**, it will be your 1Kg 20:39
None must be **m**, for I have a 2Kg 10:19
Whoever is **m** will not live." 2Kg 10:19
nothing will be **m** when you Jb 5:24
having a twin, and not one **m**. Sg 4:2
having a twin, and not one **m**. Sg 6:6
there is no one **m** from ⌊the Is 14:31
Not one of them will be **m**, Is 34:16
strength, not one of them is **m**. Is 40:26
Truth is **m**, and whoever turns Is 59:15
or dismayed, nor will any be **m**." Jr 23:4

MISSION *(11)*
If you don't report our **m**, Jos 2:14
if you report our **m**, we are free Jos 2:20
responsibilities and **m** be?" Jdg 13:12
then sent you on a **m** and said: 1Sm 15:18
I went on the **m** the LORD gave 1Sm 15:20
gave me a **m**, but he told me, 1Sm 21:2
about the **m** I'm sending you 1Sm 21:2
even on an ordinary **m**, 1Sm 21:5
since the king's **m** was urgent." 1Sm 21:8
and he will succeed in his **m**. Is 48:15
had completed their relief **m**, Ac 12:25

MIST *(6)*
distill the rain into its **m**, Jb 36:27
a lying tongue is a vanishing **m**, Pr 21:6
a cloud, and your sins like a **m**. Is 44:22
like the morning **m** and like the Hs 6:4
they will be like the morning **m**, Hs 13:3
Suddenly a **m** and darkness fell Ac 13:11

MISTAKE *(4)*
your bags. Perhaps it was a **m**. Gn 43:12
thought it was a **m** and took his Gn 48:17
have sinned, my **m** concerns only Jb 19:4
the messenger that it was a **m**. Ec 5:6

MISTREAT *(6)*
If you **m** my daughters or take Gn 31:50
You must not **m** any widow or Ex 22:22
If you do **m** them, they will no Ex 22:23
within your gates. Do not **m** him. Dt 23:16
and you **m** me without shame. Jb 19:3
you, pray for those who **m** you. Lk 6:28

MISTREATED *(9)*
Then Sarai **m** her so much that Gn 16:6
from them or **m** a single one Nm 16:15
the Egyptians **m** and afflicted us Dt 26:6
Whom have I wronged or **m**? 1Sm 12:3
us, you haven't **m** us, and you 1Sm 12:4
And Asa **m** some of the people at 2Ch 16:10
When he saw one of them being **m**, Ac 7:24
destitute, afflicted, and **m**. Heb 11:37
them, and the **m**, as though you Heb 13:3

MISTREATING *(2)*
Why are you **m** each other?' Ac 7:26
the one who was **m** his neighbor Ac 7:27

MISTREATMENT *(1)*
mistress and submit to her **m**." Gn 16:9

MISTRESS *(8)*
she looked down on her **m**. Gn 16:4
running away from my **m** Sarai." Gn 16:8
go back to your **m** and submit to Gn 16:9
She said to her **m**, "If only my 2Kg 5:3

servant and **m**, buyer and seller Is 24:2
longer be called **m** of kingdoms. Is 47:5
I will be the **m** forever. Is 47:7
the attractive **m** of sorcery, Nah 3:4

MISTRESS'S *(1)*
girl's eyes on her **m** hand, Ps 123:2

MISTS *(1)*
without water, **m** driven by a 2Pt 2:17

MISUNDERSTAND *(1)*
that these foes might **m** and say: Dt 32:27

MISUSE *(2)*
Do not **m** the name of the LORD Ex 20:7
Do not **m** the name of the LORD Dt 5:11

MISUSES *(2)*
punish anyone who **m** His name. Ex 20:7
punish anyone who **m** His name. Dt 5:11

MITHKAH *(2)*
from Terah and camped at **M**. Nm 33:28
departed from **M** and camped at Nm 33:29

MITHNITE *(1)*
son of Maacah, Joshaphat the **M**, 1Ch 11:43

MITHREDATH *(2)*
supervision of **M** the treasurer, Ezr 1:8
Persia, Bishlam, **M**, Tabeel and Ezr 4:7

MITYLENE *(1)*
took him on board and came to **M**. Ac 20:14

MIX *(4)*
meat well and **m** in the spices! Ezk 24:10
peoples will **m** with one another Dn 2:43
iron does not **m** with fired clay Dn 2:43
m a double portion for her. Rv 18:6

MIXED *(61)*
unleavened cakes **m** with oil, Ex 29:2
of fine flour **m** with one quart Ex 29:40
unleavened cakes **m** with oil or Lv 2:4
made⌋ of fine flour **m** with oil. Lv 2:5
whether dry or **m** with oil, Lv 7:10
cakes **m** with olive oil, Lv 7:12
cakes of fine flour **m** with oil. Lv 7:12
and a grain offering **m** with oil. Lv 9:4
of fine flour **m** with olive oil, Lv 14:10
of fine flour **m** with olive oil Lv 14:21
of fine flour **m** with oil as a Lv 23:13
made from fine flour **m** with oil, Nm 6:15
full of fine flour **m** with oil Nm 7:13
full of fine flour **m** with oil Nm 7:19
full of fine flour **m** with oil Nm 7:25
full of fine flour **m** with oil Nm 7:31
full of fine flour **m** with oil Nm 7:37
full of fine flour **m** with oil Nm 7:43
full of fine flour **m** with oil Nm 7:49
full of fine flour **m** with oil Nm 7:55
full of fine flour **m** with oil Nm 7:61
full of fine flour **m** with oil Nm 7:67
full of fine flour **m** with oil Nm 7:73
full of fine flour **m** with oil Nm 7:79
of fine flour **m** with oil, Nm 8:8
of fine flour **m** with a quart of Nm 15:4
of fine flour **m** with a third Nm 15:6
of fine flour **m** with two quarts Nm 15:9
a grain offering **m** with a quart Nm 28:5
of fine flour **m** with oil as a Nm 28:9
of fine flour **m** with oil as a Nm 28:12
of fine flour **m** with oil as a Nm 28:12
of fine flour **m** with oil as a Nm 28:13
to be of fine flour **m** with oil; Nm 28:20
of fine flour **m** with oil, Nm 28:28
of fine flour **m** with oil, Nm 29:3
to be of fine flour **m** with oil, Nm 29:9
to be of fine flour **m** with oil, Nm 29:14
the priests' sons **m** the spices. 1Ch 9:30
people has become **m** with the Ezr 9:2
all those of **m** descent from Neh 13:3
meat; she has **m** her wine; she Pr 9:2
and drink the wine I have **m**. Pr 9:5
those who go looking for **m** wine. Pr 23:30
it never lacks **m** wine. Sg 7:2
The LORD has **m** within her a Is 19:14
fill bowls of **m** wine for Destiny Is 65:11
and all the **m** peoples; Jr 25:20
kings of the **m** peoples who have Jr 25:24
You saw the iron **m** with clay, Dn 2:41
You saw the iron **m** with clay— Dn 2:43
himself to get **m** up with the Hs 7:8
woman took and **m** into 50 pounds Mt 13:33
gave Him wine **m** with gall to Mt 27:34
to give Him wine **m** with myrrh, Mk 15:23
blood Pilate had **m** with their Lk 13:1
woman took and **m** into 50 pounds Lk 13:21
and fire, **m** with blood, were Rv 8:7
which is **m** full strength in the Rv 14:10
like a sea of glass **m** with fire, Rv 15:2
In the cup in which she **m**, Rv 18:6

MIXING *(2)*
the baking, the **m**, and all 1Ch 23:29
who are fearless at **m** beer, Is 5:22

MIXTURE *(2)*
it spread through the entire **m**." Lk 13:21
bringing a **m** of about 75 pounds Jn 19:39

MIXTURES *(1)*
spices and various **m** of prepared 2Ch 16:14

MIZAR *(1)*
peaks of Hermon, from Mount **M**. Ps 42:6

MIZPAH *(42)*
(AKA JEGAR-SAHADUTHA, GALEED)
and ⌊also⌋ **M**, for he said, "May Gn 31:49
foot of Hermon in the land of **M**. Jos 11:3
assembled and camped at **M**. Jdg 10:17
the presence of the LORD at **M**. Jdg 11:11
and then through **M** of Gilead. Jdg 11:29
the Ammonites from **M** of Gilead. Jdg 11:29
Jephthah went to his home in **M**, Jdg 11:34
one body before the LORD at **M**. Jdg 20:1
the Israelites had gone up to **M**. Jdg 20:3
Israel had sworn an oath at **M**: Jdg 21:1
to the LORD at **M** would certainly Jdg 21:5
didn't come to the LORD at **M**?" Jdg 21:8
all Israel at **M**, and I will pray 1Sm 7:5
gathered at **M**, they drew water 1Sm 7:6
Israelites at **M** as ⌊their⌋ judge 1Sm 7:6
Israelites had gathered at **M**, 1Sm 7:7
charged out of **M** and pursued 1Sm 7:11
it upright between **M** and Shen. 1Sm 7:12
and **M** and would judge Israel at 1Sm 7:16
the people to the LORD at **M** 1Sm 10:17
of Benjamin and **M** with them. 1Kg 15:22
they came to Gedaliah at **M**. 2Kg 25:23
who were with him at **M**. 2Kg 25:25
he built Geba and **M** with them. 2Ch 16:6
and the men of Gibeon and **M**, Neh 3:7
ruler over the district of **M**, Neh 3:15
ruler over **M**, made repairs to Neh 3:19
to Gedaliah son of Ahikam at **M**, Jr 40:6
they came to Gedaliah at **M**. Jr 40:8
going to live in **M** to represent Jr 40:10
to Gedaliah at **M**, and harvested Jr 40:12
the field came to Gedaliah at **M** Jr 40:13
to Gedaliah in private at **M**, Jr 40:15
to Gedaliah son of Ahikam at **M**. Jr 41:1
ate a meal together there in **M**, Jr 41:1
who were with Gedaliah at **M**, Jr 41:3
came out of **M** to meet them, Jr 41:6
of the people of **M** including the Jr 41:10
who remained in **M** over whom Jr 41:10
captive from **M** turned around Jr 41:14
then took from **M** all the remnant Jr 41:16
been a snare at **M** and a net Hs 5:1

MIZPEH *(4)*
east as far as the valley of **M**. Jos 11:8
Dilan, **M**, Jokthe-el, Jos 15:38
M, Chephirah, Mozah, Jos 18:26
David went to **M** of Moab where 1Sm 22:3

MIZRAIM *(2)*
Cush, **M**, Put, and Canaan. 1Ch 1:8
M fathered Ludim, Anamim, 1Ch 1:11

MIZZAH *(3)*
Nahath, Zerah, Shammah, and **M**. Gn 36:13
Nahath, Zerah, Shammah, and **M**. Gn 36:17
Nahath, Zerah, Shammah, and **M**. 1Ch 1:37

MNASON *(1)*
with us and brought us to **M**, Ac 21:16

MOAB *(153)*
birth to a son and named him **M**. Gn 19:37
Midian in the field of **M**; Gn 36:35
will seize the leaders of **M**; Ex 15:15
that borders **M** on the east. Nm 21:11
border between **M** and the Nm 21:13
and lie along the border of **M**. Nm 21:15
territory of **M** near the Pisgah Nm 21:20
former king of **M** and had taken Nm 21:26
consumed Ar of **M**, the lords of Nm 21:28
Woe to you, **M**! You have been Nm 21:29
the plains of **M** near the Jordan Nm 22:1
M was terrified of the people Nm 22:3
The elders of **M** and Midian Nm 22:7
the officials of **M** stayed with Nm 22:8
of Zippor, king of **M**, sent ⌊this Nm 22:10
officials of **M** arose, returned Nm 22:14
went with the officials of **M**. Nm 22:21
with all the officials of **M**. Nm 23:6
the king of **M**, from the eastern Nm 23:7
with the officials of **M**. Nm 23:17
forehead of **M** and strike down Nm 24:17
relations with the women of **M**. Nm 25:1
in the plains of **M** by the Jordan Nm 26:3
on the plains of **M** by the Jordan Nm 26:63
on the plains of **M** by the Jordan Nm 31:12
Iye-abarim on the border of **M**. Nm 33:44
on the plains of **M** by the Jordan Nm 33:48
Meadows on the plains of **M**. Nm 33:49
in the plains of **M** by the Jordan Nm 33:50
in the plains of **M** by the Jordan Nm 35:1
in the plains of **M** by the Jordan Nm 36:13
the Jordan in the land of **M**, Dt 1:5
the road to the Wilderness of **M**. Dt 2:8
'Show no hostility toward **M**, Dt 2:9
to cross the border of **M** at Ar. Dt 2:18
the Israelites in the land of **M**, Dt 29:1
Abarim ⌊range⌋ in the land of **M**, Dt 32:49
the plains of **M** to Mount Nebo, Dt 34:1
died there in the land of **M**, Dt 34:5
in the land of **M** facing Dt 34:6
in the plains of **M** 30 days. Dt 34:8
on the plains of **M** beyond the Jos 13:32
Zippor, king of **M**, set out to Jos 24:9
Eglon king of **M** power over Jdg 3:12
served Eglon king of **M** 18 years. Jdg 3:14
to Eglon king of **M** with tribute Jdg 3:15
the tribute to Eglon king of **M**, Jdg 3:17
of the Jordan leading to **M**, Jdg 3:28
M became subject to Israel that Jdg 3:30
Aram, Sidon, and **M**, and the gods Jdg 10:6
away the land of **M** or the land Jdg 11:15
messengers⌋ to the king of **M**, Jdg 11:17
around the lands of Edom and **M**. Jdg 11:18
side of the land of **M** and camped Jdg 11:18
enter into the territory of **M**, Jdg 11:18
the Arnon was the boundary of **M**. Jdg 11:18
Balak son of Zippor, king of **M**? Jdg 11:25
in the land of **M** for a while. Ru 1:1
the land of **M** and ⌊settled⌋ Ru 1:2
they lived in **M** about 10 years, Ru 1:4
prepared to leave the land of **M**, Ru 1:6
she had heard in **M** that the LORD Ru 1:6
back from the land of **M** with her Ru 1:22
with Naomi from the land of **M**. Ru 2:6
has returned from the land of **M**, Ru 4:3
and to the king of **M**. 1Sm 12:9
against **M**, the Ammonites, 1Sm 14:47
to Mizpeh of **M** where he said to 1Sm 22:3
where he said to the king of **M**, 1Sm 22:3
in the care of the king of **M**, 1Sm 22:4
from Edom, **M**, the Ammonites, 2Sm 8:12
killed two sons of Ariel of **M**, 2Sm 23:20
idol of **M**, and for Milcom, 1Kg 11:7
the god of **M**, and to Milcom, 1Kg 11:33
M rebelled against Israel. 2Kg 1:1
King Mesha of **M** was a sheep 2Kg 3:4
the king of **M** rebelled against 2Kg 3:5
The king of **M** has rebelled 2Kg 3:7
go with me to fight against **M**?" 2Kg 3:7
only to hand us over to **M**." 2Kg 3:10
kings to hand us over to **M**." 2Kg 3:13
He will also hand **M** over to you. 2Kg 3:18
All **M** had heard that the kings 2Kg 3:21
other. So, to the spoil, **M**!" 2Kg 3:23
When the king of **M** saw that the 2Kg 3:26
the detestable idol of **M**; 2Kg 23:13
Midian in the country of **M**, 1Ch 1:46
in the country of **M** after he had 1Ch 8:8
killed two ⌊sons of⌋ Ariel of **M**, 1Ch 11:22
from Edom, **M**, the Ammonites, 1Ch 18:11
from Ashdod, Ammon, and **M**. Neh 13:23
M is My washbasin; on Edom I Ps 60:8
Ishmaelites, **M** and the Hagrites Ps 83:6
M is My washbasin; on Edom I Ps 108:9
their power over Edom and **M**, Is 11:14
oracle against **M**: Ar in Moab is Is 15:1
Ar in **M** is devastated, destroyed Is 15:1

in **M** is devastated, destroyed Is 15:1
M wails on Nebo and at Medeba. Is 15:2
the soldiers of **M** cry out, Is 15:4
My heart cries out over **M**, Is 15:5
throughout the territory of **M**. Is 15:8
for those who escape from **M**, Is 15:9
daughters of **M** will be at the Is 16:2
be a refuge for **M** from the Is 16:4
Therefore let **M** wail; let every Is 16:7
every one of them wail for **M**. Is 16:7
the sound of⌋ a lyre for **M**, Is 16:11
M appears on the high place, Is 16:12
previously announced about **M**. Is 16:13
But **M** will be trampled in his Is 25:10
the Ammonites, **M**, all those who Jr 9:26
Edom, **M**, and the Ammonites; Jr 25:21
of Edom, the king of **M**, the king Jr 27:3
all the Judeans in **M** and among Jr 40:11
About **M**, this is what the LORD Jr 48:1
There is no longer praise for **M**; Jr 48:2
M will be shattered; her little Jr 48:4
M a salt marsh, for she will Jr 48:9
M has been left quiet since his Jr 48:11
M will be put to shame because Jr 48:13
The destroyer of **M** and its towns Jr 48:15
destroyer of **M** has come against Jr 48:18
M is put to shame, indeed Jr 48:20
the Arnon that **M** is destroyed. Jr 48:20
all the towns of the land of **M**, Jr 48:24
M will wallow in his own vomit, Jr 48:26
in the cliffs, residents of **M**! Jr 48:28
Therefore, I will wail over **M**. Jr 48:31
I will cry out for **M**, all of it; Jr 48:31
field and from the land of **M**. Jr 48:33
In **M**, I will stop"—⌊this is⌋ Jr 48:35
heart moans like flutes for **M**, Jr 48:36
the rooftops of **M** and in her Jr 48:38
I have shattered **M** like a jar no Jr 48:38
How **M** has turned his back! Jr 48:39
M will become a laughingstock Jr 48:39
and spread his wings against **M**. Jr 48:40
M will be destroyed as a people Jr 48:42
trap await you, resident of **M**. Jr 48:43
bring against **M** the year of Jr 48:44
Woe to you, **M**! The people of Jr 48:46
the fortunes of **M** in the last Jr 48:47
The judgment on **M** ends here. Jr 48:47
Because **M** and Seir said: Ezk 25:8
execute judgments against **M**, Ezk 25:11
Edom, **M**, and the prominent Dn 11:41
from punishing **M** for three Am 2:1
I will send fire against **M**, Am 2:2
M will die with a tumult, with Am 2:2
what Balak king of **M** proposed, Mc 6:5
taunting of **M** and the insults Zph 2:8
M will be like Sodom and the Zph 2:9

MOAB'S *(9)*
of Zippor was **M** king at that Nm 22:4
We have heard of **M** pride— Is 16:6
M splendor will become an object Is 16:14
M calamity is near at hand; Jr 48:16
M horn is chopped off; Jr 48:25
We have heard of **M** pride, great Jr 48:29
the heart of **M** warriors will be Jr 48:41
will devour **M** forehead and the Jr 48:45
to expose **M** flank beginning Ezk 25:9

MOABITE *(10)*
Arnon was the **M** border between Nm 21:13
meet him at the **M** city on the Nm 22:36
No Ammonite or **M** may enter the Dt 23:3
Her sons took **M** women as their Ru 1:4
She is the young **M** woman who Ru 2:6
M, Ammonite, Edomite, Sidonian, 1Kg 11:1
Aramean, **M**, and Ammonite 2Kg 24:2
sons of Elnaam, Ithmah the **M**, 1Ch 11:46
son of the **M** woman Shimrith. 2Ch 24:26
no Ammonite or **M** should ever Neh 13:1

MOABITES *(19)*
is the father of the **M** of today. Gn 19:37
So the **M** said to the elders of Nm 22:4
though the **M** called them Emim. Dt 2:11
us, and the **M** who live in Ar, Dt 2:29
your enemies, the **M**, to you." Jdg 3:28
they struck down about 10,000 **M**, Jdg 3:29
defeated the **M**, and after making 2Sm 8:2
So the **M** became David's subjects 2Sm 8:2
and the **M** saw that the water 2Kg 3:22
the **M** came to Israel's camp, 2Kg 3:24
the land and struck down the **M**. 2Kg 3:24
marauding bands of **M** used to 2Kg 13:20
who married **M** and returned to 1Ch 4:22
defeated the **M**, and they became 1Ch 18:2
After this, the **M** and Ammonites, 2Ch 20:1
are the Ammonites, **M**, and ⌊the 2Ch 20:10
the Ammonites, **M**, and ⌊the 2Ch 20:22
Ammonites and **M** turned against 2Ch 20:23
Ammonites, **M**, Egyptians, Ezr 9:1

MOABITESS *(5)*
her daughter-in-law Ruth the **M**. Ru 1:22
Ruth the **M** asked Naomi, "Will Ru 2:2
Ruth the **M** said, "He also told Ru 2:21
will also acquire Ruth the **M**, Ru 4:5
I will also acquire Ruth the **M**, Ru 4:10

MOADIAH *(1)*
Piltai of **M**, of Miniamin, Neh 12:17

MOAN *(5)*
Therefore I **m** like ⌊the sound Is 16:11
or⌋ a crane; I **m** like a dove. My Is 38:14
like bears and **m** like doves. Is 59:11
he will **m** for the men of Jr 48:31
m like the sound Nah 2:7

MOANING *(2)*
I have heard Ephraim **m**: Jr 31:18
all of them **m**, each over his own Ezk 7:16

MOANS *(2)*
My heart **m** like flutes for Moab, Jr 48:36
and My heart **m** like flutes for Jr 48:36

MOAT *(1)*
be rebuilt with a plaza and a **m**, Dn 9:25

MOB *(8)*
wicked, from the **m** of evildoers, Ps 64:2
will bring a **m** against you to Ezk 16:40
large **m**, with swords and clubs, Mt 26:47
With him was a **m**, with swords Mk 14:43
suddenly a **m** was there, and one Lk 22:47
Then the **m** joined in the attack Ac 16:22
the marketplace and formed a **m**, Ac 17:5
Some in the **m** were shouting one Ac 21:34

MOB'S *(1)*
because of the **m** violence, Ac 21:35

MOBILIZE *(1)*
His sons will **m** for war and Dn 11:10

MOBILIZED *(9)*
the next morning and **m** them. Jos 8:10
houses near it **m** and caught up Jdg 18:22
with you that you **m** ⌊the men⌋?" Jdg 18:23
m 180,000 choice warriors from 1Kg 12:21
Ben-hadad **m** the Arameans and 1Kg 20:26
The Israelites **m**, gathered 1Kg 20:27
at that time and **m** all Israel. 2Kg 3:6
he **m** the house of Judah and 2Ch 11:1
who have been **m** around you; Ezk 38:7

MOBILIZING *(1)*
of Hosts is **m** an army for war Is 13:4

MOCK *(19)*
sent to **m** the living God, 2Kg 19:4
has sent to **m** the living God. 2Kg 19:16
wrote letters to **m** the LORD God 2Ch 32:17
When I stand up, they **m** me. Jb 19:18
the innocent **m** them, ⌊saying⌋, Jb 22:19
But now they **m** me, men younger Jb 30:1
They **m**, and they speak Ps 73:8
God, how long will the foe **m**? Ps 74:10
will **m** when terror strikes you, Pr 1:26
mocks those who **m**, but gives Pr 3:34
if you **m**, you alone will bear Pr 9:12
Fools **m** at making restitution, Pr 14:9
So now, do not **m**, or your Is 28:22
sent to **m** the living God, Is 37:4
has sent to **m** the living God. Is 37:17
far away from you will **m** you, Ezk 22:5
not boastfully **m** in the day of Ob 12
They **m** kings, and rulers are a Hab 1:10
they will **m** Him, spit on Him, Mk 10:34

MOCKED *(26)*
You have **m** me and told me lies! Jdg 16:10
You have **m** me all along and told Jdg 16:13
time you have **m** me and not told Jdg 16:15
At noon Elijah **m** them. 1Kg 18:27
Who is it you **m** and blasphemed? 2Kg 19:22
You have **m** the Lord through 2Kg 19:23
laughed at them and **m** them. 2Ch 30:10
this⌋, they **m** and despised us, Neh 2:19
he became furious. He **m** the Jews Neh 4:1
Now I am **m** by their songs; Jb 30:9
the enemy has **m** the LORD, and a Ps 74:18
is it you have **m** and blasphemed? Is 37:23
You have **m** the LORD through your Is 37:24
are worthless, a work to be **m**. Jr 10:15
are worthless, a work to be **m**. Jr 51:18
m by their songs all day long. Lm 3:14
look, I am **m** by their songs. Lm 3:63
over to the Gentiles to be **m**, Mt 20:19
down before Him and **m** Him: Mt 27:29
When they had **m** Him, they Mt 27:31
and elders, **m** Him and said, Mt 27:41
When they had **m** Him, they Mk 15:20
and He will be **m**, insulted, spit Lk 18:32
with contempt, **m** Him, dressed Lk 23:11
The soldiers also **m** Him. Lk 23:36
God is not **m**. For whatever a man Gl 6:7

MOCKER *(11)*
one who corrects a **m** will bring Pr 9:7
Don't rebuke a **m**, or he will Pr 9:8
a **m** doesn't listen to rebuke. Pr 13:1
m seeks wisdom and doesn't find Pr 14:6
m doesn't love one who corrects Pr 15:12
a **m**, and the inexperienced Pr 19:25
Wine is a **m**, beer is a brawler, Pr 20:1
When a **m** is punished, the Pr 21:11
person, named "**M**," acts with Pr 21:24
Drive out a **m**, and conflict goes Pr 22:10
and a **m** is detestable to people. Pr 24:9

MOCKERS *(6)*
Surely **m** surround me and my eyes Jb 17:2
sinners, or join a group of **m**! Ps 1:1
long⌋ will ⌊you⌋ **m** enjoy mocking Pr 1:22
Judgments are prepared for **m**, Pr 19:29
M inflame a city, but the wise Pr 29:8
you **m** who rule this people in Is 28:14

MOCKERY *(6)*
godless **m** they gnashed their Ps 35:16
a source of **m** and ridicule to Ps 44:13
a source of **m** and ridicule to Ps 79:4
nations and a **m** to all the lands Ezk 22:4
plunder and a **m** to the rest Ezk 36:4
with **m** and riddles about him? Hab 2:6

MOCKING *(6)*
saw the son **m**—the one Hagar Gn 21:9
have spoken, you may continue **m**. Jb 21:3
mockers enjoy **m** and ⌊you⌋ fools Pr 1:22
Who is it you are **m**? Is 57:4
the scribes were **m** Him to one Mk 15:31
Jesus started **m** and beating Him. Lk 22:63

MOCKINGS *(1)*
experienced **m** and scourgings, Heb 11:36

MOCKS *(5)*
m the despair of the innocent. Jb 9:23
Everyone who sees me **m** me; Ps 22:7
He **m** those who mock, but gives Pr 3:34
The one who **m** the poor insults Pr 17:5
A worthless witness **m** justice, Pr 19:28

MODEL *(3)*
to the **m** of them you have Ex 25:40
King Ahaz sent a **m** of the altar 2Kg 16:10
hands (only a **m** of the true one) Heb 9:24

MODEST *(2)*
even if your beginnings were **m**, Jb 8:7
dress themselves in **m** clothing, 1Tm 2:9

MOISTEN *(1)*
gallon of oil to **m** the fine Ezk 46:14

MOISTURE *(2)*
He saturates clouds with **m**; Jb 37:11
it withered, since it lacked **m**. Lk 8:6

MOLADAH *(4)*
Amam, Shema, **M**, Jos 15:26
Beer-sheba (or Sheba), **M**, Jos 19:2
in Beer-sheba, **M**, Hazar-shual, 1Ch 4:28
in Jeshua, **M**, Beth-pelet, Neh 11:26

MOLDED *(1)*
made for themselves **m** images— 2Kg 17:16

MOLDING *(10)*
make a gold **m** all around it. Ex 25:11
and make a gold **m** all around it. Ex 25:24
and make a gold **m** for it all Ex 25:25
make a gold **m** all around it. Ex 30:3
for it under the **m** on two of its Ex 30:4
and made a gold **m** all around it. Ex 37:2

and made a gold **m** all around it. Ex 37:11
and made a gold **m** all around its Ex 37:12
he made a gold **m** all around it. Ex 37:26
for it under the **m** on two of its Ex 37:27

MOLDS *(2)*
cast in clay **m** in the Jordan 1Kg 7:46
cast in clay **m** in the Jordan 2Ch 4:17

MOLECH *(7)*
(AKA MILCOM)
pass through ⌊the fire⌋ to **M**. Lv 18:21
his children to **M** must be put to Lv 20:2
he gave his offspring to **M**, Lv 20:3
gives any of his children to **M**, Lv 20:4
prostituting themselves with **M**. Lv 20:5
pass through the fire to **M**. 2Kg 23:10
pass through ⌊the fire⌋ to **M**— Jr 32:35

MOLES *(1)*
worship, to the **m** and the bats. Is 2:20

MOLID *(1)*
who bore him Ahban and **M**. 1Ch 2:29

MOLOCH *(1)*
up the tent of **M** and the star Ac 7:43

MOMENT *(37)*
I went with you for a single **m**, Ex 33:5
even for a **m**, or they will die. Nm 4:20
At that very **m** the chariots and 2Sm 1:6
At that **m**, while you are still 1Kg 1:14
At that **m**, while she was still 1Kg 1:22
At that **m**, the LORD passed by. 1Kg 19:11
The **m** they began ⌊their⌋ shouts 2Ch 20:22
for a brief **m**, grace has come Ezr 9:8
and put him to the test every **m**. Jb 7:18
the godless has lasted only a **m**? Jb 20:5
exalted for a **m**, then they are Jb 24:24
His anger may ignite at any **m**. Ps 2:12
For His anger lasts only a **m**, Ps 30:5
but a lying tongue, only a **m**. Pr 12:19
I deserted you for a brief **m**, Is 54:7
I hid My face from you for a **m**, Is 54:8
my tent curtains, in a **m**. Jr 4:20
At one **m** I might announce Jr 18:7
he let the opportune **m** pass. Jr 46:17
tremble every **m** for his life. Ezk 32:10
stunned for a **m**, and his Dn 4:19
At that **m** the sentence against Dn 4:33
At that **m** the fingers of a man's Dn 5:5
servant was cured that very **m**. Mt 8:13
woman was made well from that **m**. Mt 9:22
And from that **m** her daughter Mt 15:28
and from that **m** the boy was Mt 17:18
from this **m** I will not drink of Mt 26:29
that **m** one of those with Jesus Mt 26:51
At that very **m**, she came up and Lk 2:38
of the world in a **m** of time. Lk 4:5
that **m** many of His disciples Jn 6:66
From that **m** Pilate made every Jn 19:12
that very **m**, three men who had Ac 11:11
the appointed **m**, Christ died for Rm 5:6
in a **m**, in the twinkling of an 1Co 15:52
At that **m** a violent earthquake Rv 11:13

MOMENTARY *(1)*
For our **m** light affliction is 2Co 4:17

MONEY *(132)*
purchased with **m** from any Gn 17:12
as well as one purchased with **m**, Gn 17:13
house or purchased with his **m**— Gn 17:23
with **m** from a foreigner Gn 17:27
and has certainly spent our **m**. Gn 31:15
return each man's **m** to his sack, Gn 42:25
he saw his **m** there at the top Gn 42:27
brothers, "My **m** has been Gn 42:28
man's sack was his bag of **m**! Gn 42:35
father saw their bags of **m**, Gn 42:35
Take twice as much **m** with you. Gn 43:12
Return the **m** that was returned Gn 43:12
the amount of **m**, and Benjamin. Gn 43:15
because of the **m** that was Gn 43:18
each one's **m** was at the top of Gn 43:21
It was the full amount of our **m**, Gn 43:21
additional **m** with us to buy Gn 43:22
know who put our **m** in the bags." Gn 43:22
I received your **m**." Then he Gn 43:23
put each one's **m** at the top of Gn 44:1
bag, along with his grain **m**." Gn 44:2
land of Canaan the **m** we found at Gn 44:8
collected all the **m** to be found Gn 47:14
he brought the **m** to Pharaoh's Gn 47:14
the **m** from the land of Egypt Gn 47:15
in front of you? The **m** is gone!" Gn 47:15
Since the **m** is gone, I will give Gn 47:16
lord that the **m** is gone and that Gn 47:18
without any exchange of **m**. Ex 21:11
he must pay **m** to its owner, Ex 21:34
his neighbor **m** or goods to keep Ex 22:7
If you lend **m** to My people— Ex 22:25
Take the atonement **m** from the Ex 30:16
purchases someone with his **m**, Lv 22:11
Give the **m** to Aaron and his sons Nm 3:48
the redemption **m** from those in Nm 3:49
He collected the **m** from the Nm 3:50
redemption **m** to Aaron and his Nm 3:51
exchange it for **m**, take the Dt 14:25
money, take the **m** in your hand, Dt 14:25
may spend the **m** on anything you Dt 14:26
sell her for **m** or treat her as Dt 21:14
your brother interest on **m**, Dt 23:19
with the **m** under the cloak." Jos 7:21
his tent, with the **m** underneath. Jos 7:22
king of Moab with tribute ⌊**m**⌋. Jdg 3:15
and reckless men with this **m**, Jdg 9:4
her and brought the **m** with them. Jdg 16:18
asking for **m** from Saul or his 2Sm 21:4
a time to accept **m** and clothes, 2Kg 5:26
All the dedicated **m** brought to 2Kg 12:4
temple, census **m**, money from 2Kg 12:4
census money, **m** from vows, and 2Kg 12:4
and all **m** voluntarily given for 2Kg 12:4
don't take any **m** from your 2Kg 12:7
would not take **m** from the people 2Kg 12:8
threshold put all the **m** brought 2Kg 12:9
large amount of **m** in the chest, 2Kg 12:10
and count the **m** found there and 2Kg 12:10
put the counted **m** into the hands 2Kg 12:11
temple from the **m** brought 2Kg 12:13
who received the **m** to pay those 2Kg 12:15
The **m** from the restitution 2Kg 12:16
vassal and paid him tribute **m**. 2Kg 17:3
not paid tribute **m** to the king 2Kg 17:4
he may total up the **m** brought 2Kg 22:4
⌊the **m**⌋ the doorkeepers have 2Kg 22:4
them for the **m** put into their 2Kg 22:7
emptied out the **m** that was found 2Kg 22:9
he taxed the land to give the **m**. 2Kg 23:35
and collect **m** from all Israel 2Ch 24:5
there was a large amount of **m**, 2Ch 24:11
and gathered the **m** in abundance. 2Ch 24:11
rest of the **m** to the king and 2Ch 24:14
Ammonites gave Uzziah tribute **m**, 2Ch 26:8
and gave him the **m** brought into 2Ch 34:9
had collected ⌊**m**⌋ from Manasseh, 2Ch 34:9
brought out the **m** that had been 2Ch 34:14
emptied out the **m** that was found 2Ch 34:17
They gave **m** to the stonecutters Ezr 3:7
buy with this **m** as many bulls, Ezr 7:17
We have borrowed **m** to pay the Neh 5:4
been lending them **m** and grain. Neh 5:10
with the percentage of the **m**, Neh 5:11
The **m** and people are given to Est 3:11
exact amount of **m** Haman had Est 4:7
does not lend his **m** at interest Ps 15:5
and we'll all share our **m**"— Pr 1:14
He took a bag of **m** with him and Pr 7:20
a fool have **m** in his hand with Pr 17:16
If you have no **m** to pay, even Pr 22:27
The one who loves **m** is never Ec 5:10
money is never satisfied with **m**, Ec 5:10
protection as **m** is protection, Ec 7:12
and **m** is the answer for Ec 10:19
you without **m**, come, buy, and Is 55:1
milk without **m** and without cost Is 55:1
do you spend **m** on what is not Is 55:2
and I weighed out to him the **m**— Jr 32:9
practice divination for **m**. Mc 3:11
be slaves of God and of **m**. Mt 6:24
overturned the **m** changers' Mt 21:12
ground, and hid his master's **m**. Mt 25:18
deposited my **m** with the bankers Mt 25:27
have received my **m** back with Mt 25:27
treasury, since it is blood **m**." Mt 27:6
the soldiers a large sum of **m** Mt 28:12
they took the **m** and did as they Mt 28:15
bag, no **m** in their belts. Mk 6:8
overturned the **m** changers' Mk 11:15
crowd dropped **m** into the Mk 12:41
Don't take **m** from anyone by Lk 3:14
traveling bag, no bread, no **m**; Lk 9:3
the unrighteous **m** so that when Lk 16:9
faithful with the unrighteous **m**, Lk 16:11
be slaves to both God and **m**." Lk 16:13
were lovers of **m**, were listening Lk 16:14
had given the **m** to so he could Lk 19:15
didn't you put my **m** in the bank? Lk 19:23
also found⌋ the **m** changers Jn 2:14
poured out the **m** changers' coins Jn 2:15
brought the **m**, and laid it at Ac 4:37
hands, he offered them **m**, Ac 8:18
of God could be obtained with **m**! Ac 8:20
for a large amount of **m**." Ac 22:28
hoping that **m** would be given Ac 24:26
a lot of wine, not greedy for **m**, 1Tm 3:8
For the love of **m** is a root of 1Tm 6:10
self, lovers of **m**, boastful, 2Tm 3:2
not a bully, not greedy for **m**, Ti 1:7
be free from the love of **m**. Heb 13:5
not for the **m** but eagerly; 1Pt 5:2

MONEY-BAG *(5)*
Don't carry a **m**, traveling bag, Lk 10:4
When I sent you out without **m**, Lk 22:35
whoever has a **m** should take it, Lk 22:36
charge of the **m** and would steal Jn 12:6
Judas kept the **m**, some thought Jn 13:29

MONEY-BAGS *(1)*
Make **m** for yourselves that won't Lk 12:33

MONEY-BELTS *(1)*
silver, or copper for your **m**. Mt 10:9

MONEYLENDER *(1)*
you must not be like a **m** to him; Ex 22:25

MONGREL *(1)*
A **m** people will live in Ashdod, Zch 9:6

MONITOR *(1)*
the gecko, the **m** lizard, the Lv 11:30

MONOPOLY *(1)*
of God, or have a **m** on wisdom? Jb 15:8

MONSTER *(6)*
sea or a sea **m**, that You keep Jb 7:12
will slay the **m** that is in the Is 27:1
pieces, who pierced the sea **m**? Is 51:9
has swallowed me like a sea **m**; Jr 51:34
the great **m** lying in the middle Ezk 29:3
you are like a **m** in the seas. Ezk 32:2

MONSTERS *(2)*
of the sea **m** in the waters; Ps 74:13
all sea **m** and ocean depths, Ps 148:7

MONSTROUS *(1)*
a mere dog, do this **m** thing?" 2Kg 8:13

MONTH *(235)*
in the second **m**, on the Gn 7:11
on the seventeenth day of the **m**, Gn 7:11
came to rest in the seventh **m**, Gn 8:4
on the seventeenth day of the **m**, Gn 8:4
to recede until the tenth **m**; Gn 8:5
in the tenth **m**, on the first day Gn 8:5
on the first day of the **m**, Gn 8:5
in the first **m**, on the first day Gn 8:13
on the first day of the **m**, Gn 8:13
day of the second **m**, Gn 8:14
Jacob had stayed with him a **m**, Gn 29:14
This **m** is to be the beginning of Ex 12:2
it is the first **m** of your year. Ex 12:2
day of this **m** they must each Ex 12:3
the fourteenth day of this **m**; Ex 12:6
bread in the first ⌊**m**⌋, Ex 12:18
day of the **m** until the evening Ex 12:18
Today, in the **m** of Abib, you are Ex 13:4
carry out this ritual in this **m**. Ex 13:5
of the second **m** after they had Ex 16:1
In the third **m**, on the same day Ex 19:1
same day ⌊of the **m**⌋ that the Ex 19:1
appointed time in the **m** of Abib, Ex 23:15
you came out of Egypt in that **m**. Ex 23:15
time in the **m** of Abib as I Ex 34:18
out of Egypt in the **m** of Abib. Ex 34:18
on the first day of the first **m**. Ex 40:2
up in the first **m** of the second Ex 40:17
on the first ⌊day⌋ of the **m**. Ex 40:17
In the seventh **m**, on the tenth Lv 16:29
tenth ⌊day⌋ of the **m** you are to Lv 16:29
the LORD comes in the first **m**, Lv 23:5
on the fourteenth day of the **m**. Lv 23:5

the fifteenth day of the same **m**. Lv 23:6
In the seventh **m**, on the first Lv 23:24
on the first ⌊day⌋ of the **m**, Lv 23:24
day⌋ of this seventh **m** is the Lv 23:27
ninth ⌊day⌋ of the **m** until the Lv 23:32
of this seventh **m** and continues Lv 23:34
of the seventh **m** for seven days Lv 23:39
celebrate it in the seventh **m**. Lv 23:41
trumpet loudly in the seventh **m**, Lv 25:9
on the tenth ⌊day⌋ of the **m**; Lv 25:9
is from one **m** to five years old Lv 27:6
of the second **m** of the second Nm 1:1
the first day of the second **m**. Nm 1:18
every male one **m** old or more." Nm 3:15
every male one **m** old or more, Nm 3:22
every male one **m** old or more, Nm 3:28
every male one **m** old or more, Nm 3:34
males one **m** old or more that Nm 3:39
Israelites one **m** old or more, Nm 3:40
males one **m** old or more listed Nm 3:43
the first **m** of the second year Nm 9:1
day of this **m** at twilight; Nm 9:3
it in the first **m** on the Nm 9:5
to observe it in the second **m**, Nm 9:11
it was two days, a **m**, or longer, Nm 9:22
in the second **m** on the twentieth Nm 10:11
on the twentieth ⌊day⌋ of the **m**, Nm 10:11
but for a whole **m**—until it Nm 11:20
and they will eat for a **m**.' Nm 11:21
of Zin in the first **m**, Nm 20:1
every male one **m** old or more; Nm 26:62
the LORD comes in the first **m**, Nm 28:16
on the fourteenth day of the **m**. Nm 28:16
day of this **m** there will be Nm 28:17
assembly in the seventh **m**, Nm 29:1
on the first ⌊day⌋ of the **m**, Nm 29:1
of this seventh **m** and practice Nm 29:7
fifteenth day of the seventh **m**; Nm 29:12
from Rameses in the first **m**, Nm 33:3
on the fifteenth day of the **m**. Nm 33:3
of the fifth **m** in the fortieth Nm 33:38
in the eleventh **m**, on the first Dt 1:3
the first of the **m**, Moses told Dt 1:3
Observe the **m** of Abib and Dt 16:1
Egypt by night in the **m** of Abib. Dt 16:1
her father and mother a full **m**. Dt 21:13
on the tenth day of the first **m**, Jos 4:19
of the fourteenth day of the **m**, Jos 5:10
for one **m** out of the year. 1Kg 4:7
for a **m** in turn provided 1Kg 4:27
to Lebanon each **m** in shifts; 1Kg 5:14
one **m** they were in Lebanon, 1Kg 5:14
in the second **m**, in the month of 1Kg 6:1
second month, in the **m** of Ziv. 1Kg 6:1
fourth year in the **m** of Ziv. 1Kg 6:37
eleventh year in the eighth **m**, 1Kg 6:38
month, in the **m** of Bul, the 1Kg 6:38
King Solomon in the seventh **m**, 1Kg 8:2
m of Ethanim at the festival. 1Kg 8:2
in the eighth **m** on the fifteenth 1Kg 12:32
on the fifteenth day of the **m**, 1Kg 12:32
fifteenth day of the eighth **m**, 1Kg 12:33
the **m** he had decided on his own. 1Kg 12:33
he reigned in Samaria a full **m**. 2Kg 15:13
on the tenth day of the tenth **m**, 2Kg 25:1
of the ⌊fourth⌋ **m** the famine was 2Kg 25:3
the seventh day of the fifth **m**, 2Kg 25:8
In the seventh **m**, however, 2Kg 25:25
day of the twelfth **m** of the 2Kg 25:27
Jordan in the first **m** when it 1Ch 12:15
military duty each **m** throughout 1Ch 27:1
first division, for the first **m**; 1Ch 27:2
army commanders for the first **m**. 1Ch 27:3
the division for the second **m**, 1Ch 27:4
for the third **m**, was Benaiah son 1Ch 27:5
for the fourth **m**, was Joab's 1Ch 27:7
for the fifth **m**, was the 1Ch 27:8
for the sixth **m**, was Ira son 1Ch 27:9
for the seventh **m**, was Helez the 1Ch 27:10
for the eighth **m**, was Sibbecai 1Ch 27:11
for the ninth **m**, was Abiezer 1Ch 27:12
for the tenth **m**, was Maharai 1Ch 27:13
for the eleventh **m**, was Benaiah 1Ch 27:14
for the twelfth **m**, was Heldai 1Ch 27:15
of the second **m** in the fourth 2Ch 3:2
this was in the seventh **m**. 2Ch 5:3
of the seventh **m** he sent the 2Ch 7:10
in the third **m** of the fifteenth 2Ch 15:10
reign, in the first **m**, he opened 2Ch 29:3
on the first day of the first **m**, 2Ch 29:17
eighth day of the **m** they came to 2Ch 29:17
of the first **m** they finished. 2Ch 29:17
of the LORD in the second **m** 2Ch 30:2
Bread in the second **m**. 2Ch 30:13
fourteenth day of the second **m**. 2Ch 30:15
In the third **m** they began 2Ch 31:7
they finished in the seventh **m**. 2Ch 31:7
fourteenth day of the first **m**. 2Ch 35:1
By the seventh **m**, the Israelites Ezr 3:1
beginning of each **m** and for all Ezr 3:5
of the seventh **m** they began to Ezr 3:6
In the second **m** of the second Ezr 3:8
third day of the **m** of Adar in Ezr 6:15
fourteenth day of the first **m**. Ezr 6:19
to Jerusalem in the fifth **m**, Ezr 7:8
day of the first **m** and arrived Ezr 7:9
on the first day of the fifth **m**. Ezr 7:9
day⌋ of the first **m** to go to Ezr 8:31
twentieth ⌊day⌋ of the ninth **m**, Ezr 10:9
of the tenth **m** to investigate Ezr 10:16
of the first **m** they had dealt Ezr 10:17
During the **m** of Chislev in the Neh 1:1
During the **m** of Nisan in the Neh 2:1
twenty-fifth day of the **m** Elul. Neh 6:15
When the seventh **m** came and the Neh 8:1
the first day of the seventh **m**, Neh 8:2
the festival of the seventh **m**. Neh 8:14
day of this **m** the Israelites Neh 9:1
the royal palace in the tenth **m**, Est 2:16
the tenth month, the **m** Tebeth, Est 2:16
In the first **m**, the month of Est 3:7
first month, the **m** of Nisan, in Est 3:7
Haman for each day in each **m**, Est 3:7
and it fell on the twelfth **m**, Est 3:7
the twelfth month, the **m** Adar. Est 3:7
thirteenth day of the first **m**, Est 3:12
day of Adar, the twelfth **m**. Est 3:13
twenty-third day of the third **m** Est 8:9
that is, the **m** Sivan), the royal Est 8:9
thirteenth day of the twelfth **m**, Est 8:12
the twelfth month, the **m** Adar. Est 8:12
thirteenth day of the twelfth **m**, Est 9:1
the twelfth month, the **m** Adar. Est 9:1
day of the **m** of Adar and killed Est 9:15
day of the **m** of Adar and rested Est 9:17
the fourteenth days of the **m**. Est 9:18
on the fifteenth day of the **m**, Est 9:18
day of the **m** of Adar as ⌊a time⌋ Est 9:19
days of the **m** Adar every year Est 9:21
That was the **m** when their sorrow Est 9:22
the fifth **m** of the eleventh Jr 1:3
in the fifth **m** of the fourth Jr 28:1
died that year in the seventh **m**. Jr 28:17
in the ninth **m**, all the people Jr 36:9
it was the ninth **m**, the king was Jr 36:22
Judah, in the tenth **m**, King Jr 39:1
In the fourth **m** of Zedekiah's Jr 39:2
on the ninth day of the **m**, Jr 39:2
In the seventh **m**, Ishmael son of Jr 41:1
on the tenth day of the tenth **m**, Jr 52:4
of the fourth **m** the famine was Jr 52:6
the tenth day of the fifth **m**— Jr 52:12
day of the twelfth **m** of the Jr 52:31
in the fourth ⌊**m**⌋, on the fifth Ezk 1:1
on the fifth ⌊day⌋ of the **m**, Ezk 1:1
On the fifth ⌊day⌋ of the **m**— Ezk 1:2
in the sixth ⌊**m**⌋, on the fifth Ezk 8:1
on the fifth ⌊day⌋ of the **m**, Ezk 8:1
in the fifth ⌊**m**⌋, on the tenth Ezk 20:1
on the tenth ⌊day⌋ of the **m**, Ezk 20:1
in the tenth **m**, on the tenth Ezk 24:1
on the tenth ⌊day⌋ of the **m**: Ezk 24:1
on the first ⌊day⌋ of the **m**, Ezk 26:1
in the tenth ⌊**m**⌋ on the twelfth Ezk 29:1
on the twelfth ⌊day⌋ of the **m**, Ezk 29:1
year in the first ⌊**m**⌋, Ezk 29:17
on the first ⌊day⌋ of the **m**, Ezk 29:17
in the first ⌊**m**⌋, on the seventh Ezk 30:20
on the seventh ⌊day⌋ of the **m**, Ezk 30:20
in the third ⌊**m**⌋, on the first Ezk 31:1
on the first ⌊day⌋ of the **m**, Ezk 31:1
in the twelfth **m**, on the first Ezk 32:1
on the first ⌊day⌋ of the **m**, Ezk 32:1
on the fifteenth ⌊day⌋ of the **m**, Ezk 32:17
in the tenth ⌊**m**⌋, on the fifth Ezk 33:21
on the fifth ⌊day⌋ of the **m**, Ezk 33:21
tenth day of the **m** in the Ezk 40:1
In the first ⌊**m**⌋, on the first Ezk 45:18
on the first ⌊day⌋ of the **m**, Ezk 45:18
day⌋ of the **m** for everyone who Ezk 45:20
In the first ⌊**m**⌋, on the Ezk 45:21
on the fourteenth day of the **m**, Ezk 45:21
fifteenth day of the seventh **m**, Ezk 45:25
m they will bear fresh fruit Ezk 47:12
twenty-fourth day of the first **m**, Dn 10:4
on the first day of the sixth **m**, Hg 1:1
twenty-fourth day of the sixth **m**, Hg 1:15
day of the seventh **m**, Hg 2:1
day of the ninth ⌊**m**⌋, Hg 2:10
twenty-fourth day of the ninth **m**, Hg 2:18
the twenty-fourth day of the **m**: Hg 2:20
In the eighth **m**, in the second Zch 1:1
day of the eleventh **m**, Zch 1:7
month, which is the **m** of Shebat, Zch 1:7
the fourth day of the ninth **m**, Zch 7:1
in the fifth **m** as we have done Zch 7:3
The fast of the fourth ⌊**m**⌋, Zch 8:19
In one **m** I got rid of three Zch 11:8
the sixth **m**, the angel Gabriel Lk 1:26
is the sixth **m** for her who was Lk 1:36
the hour, day, **m**, and year were Rv 9:15
producing its fruit every **m**. Rv 22:2

MONTH-OLD *(1)*

price for a **m** male according to Nm 18:16

MONTHLY *(4)*

I am having my **m** period." Gn 31:35
This is the **m** burnt offering for Nm 28:14
addition to the **m** and regular Nm 29:6
who predict **m** what will happen Is 47:13

MONTHS *(56)*

About three **m** later Judah was Gn 38:24
she hid him for three **m**. Ex 2:2
be the beginning of **m** for you; Ex 12:2
the beginning of each of your **m**. Nm 10:10
each of your **m** present a burnt Nm 28:11
for all the **m** of the year. Nm 28:14
Let me wander two **m** through the Jdg 11:37
And he sent her away two **m**. Jdg 11:38
the end of two **m**, she returned Jdg 11:39
there for a period of four **m**. Jdg 19:2
Rimmon and stayed there four **m**. Jdg 20:47
of the Philistines for seven **m**, 1Sm 6:1
amounted to a year and four **m**. 1Sm 27:7
Judah was seven years and six **m**. 2Sm 2:11
Judah seven years and six **m**, 2Sm 5:5
remained in his house three **m**, 2Sm 6:11
the end of nine **m** and 20 days. 2Sm 24:8
your foes three **m** while they 2Sm 24:13
in Lebanon, two **m** they were at 1Kg 5:14
Israel had remained there six **m**, 1Kg 11:16
Israel in Samaria for six **m**. 2Kg 15:8
he reigned three **m** in Jerusalem. 2Kg 23:31
he reigned three **m** in Jerusalem. 2Kg 24:8
he ruled seven years and six **m**, 1Ch 3:4
family in his house for three **m**, 1Ch 13:14
three **m** of devastation by your 1Ch 21:12
he reigned three **m** in Jerusalem. 2Ch 36:2
reigned three **m** and 10 days in 2Ch 36:9
of myrrh for six **m** and then with Est 2:12
cosmetics for ⌊another⌋ six **m**. Est 2:12
made to inherit **m** of futility, Jb 7:3
number of his **m** depends on You, Jb 14:5
the number of his **m** has run out? Jb 21:21
If only I could be as in **m** gone Jb 29:2
you count the **m** they are Jb 39:2
will spend seven **m** burying them Ezk 39:12
at the end of the seven **m**. Ezk 39:14
At the end of 12 **m**, as he was Dn 4:29
still three **m** until harvest. Am 4:7
in the seventh ⌊**m**⌋ for these 70 Zch 7:5
herself in seclusion for five **m**. Lk 1:24
stayed with her about three **m**; Lk 1:56
years and six **m** while a great Lk 4:25
'There are still four more **m**, Jn 4:35
in his father's home three **m**, Ac 7:20
stayed there a year and six **m**, Ac 18:11
boldly over a period of three **m**, Ac 19:8
and stayed three **m**. When he was Ac 20:3
After three **m** we set sail in an Ac 28:11
special⌋ days, **m**, seasons, and Gl 4:10
by his parents for three **m**, Heb 11:23
years and six **m** it did not rain Jms 5:17
to torment ⌊them⌋ for five **m**; Rv 9:5
power to harm people for five **m**. Rv 9:10

trample the holy city for 42 **m**. Rv 11:2
given authority to act for 42 **m**. Rv 13:5

MONUMENT *(3)*
where he set up a **m** for himself. 1Sm 15:12
still called Absalom's **M** today. 2Sm 18:18
he said, "What is this **m** I see?" 2Kg 23:17

MONUMENTS *(3)*
decorate the **m** of the righteous Mt 23:29
You build **m** to the prophets, Lk 11:47
them, and you build their **m**. Lk 11:48

MOOD *(2)*
was in a good **m** and very drunk, 1Sm 25:36
he is in a good **m** from the wine. 2Sm 13:28

MOON *(55)*
time the sun, **m**, and 11 stars Gn 37:9
see the sun, **m**, and stars—all Dt 4:19
down to the sun, **m**, or all the Dt 17:3
Gibeon, and **m**, over the valley Jos 10:12
stood still and the **m** stopped, Jos 10:13
is the New **M**, and I'm supposed 1Sm 20:5
him, "Tomorrow is the New **M**; 1Sm 20:18
At the New **M**, the king sat down 1Sm 20:24
after the New **M**, the second day 1Sm 20:27
that second day of the New **M**, 1Sm 20:34
It's neither New **M** or Sabbath." 2Kg 4:23
to the sun, **m**, constellations 2Kg 23:5
the Sabbath and New **M** offerings, Neh 10:33
If even the **m** does not shine and Jb 25:5
shining or at the **m** moving in Jb 31:26
fingers, the **m** and the stars, Ps 8:3
as long as the **m**, throughout all Ps 72:5
abound until the **m** is no more. Ps 72:7
established the **m** and the sun. Ps 74:16
during the new **m** and during the Ps 81:3
new moon and during the full **m**, Ps 81:3
like the **m**, established forever, Ps 89:37
He made the **m** to mark the Ps 104:19
you by day, or the **m** by night. Ps 121:6
m and stars to rule by night. Ps 136:9
Him, sun and **m**; praise Him, all Ps 148:3
home at the time of the full **m**." Pr 7:20
and the **m** and the stars, Ec 12:2
beautiful as the **m**, bright as Sg 6:10
rises, and the **m** will not shine. Is 13:10
The **m** will be put to shame and Is 24:23
of the **m** will not shine Is 60:19
set, and your **m** will not fade; Is 60:20
from one New **M** to another, Is 66:23
to the sun, the **m**, and the whole Jr 8:2
fixed order of **m** and stars for Jr 31:35
and the **m** will not give its Ezk 32:7
opened on the day of the New **M**. Ezk 46:1
the day of the New **M**, ⌊the burnt Ezk 46:6
Now the New **M** will devour them Hs 5:7
The sun and **m** grow dark, and the Jl 2:10
and the **m** to blood before Jl 2:31
The sun and **m** will grow dark, Jl 3:15
will the New **M** be over so we may Am 8:5
Sun and **m** stand still in ⌊their⌋ Hab 3:11
and the **m** will not shed its Mt 24:29
and the **m** will not shed its Mk 13:24
signs in the sun, **m**, and stars; Lk 21:25
and the **m** to blood, before Ac 2:20
another of the **m**, and another 1Co 15:41
or a new **m** or a sabbath day Col 2:16
the entire **m** became like blood; Rv 6:12
a third of the **m**, and a third Rv 8:12
with the **m** under her feet, Rv 12:1
the sun or the **m** to shine on it, Rv 21:23

MOONLIGHT *(2)*
The **m** will be as bright as the Is 30:26
sunlight and **m** will diminish. Zch 14:6

MOONS *(9)*
Sabbaths, New **M**, and appointed 1Ch 23:31
the Sabbaths and the New **M**, 2Ch 2:4
Sabbaths, New **M**, and the three 2Ch 8:13
Sabbaths, of the New **M**, and of 2Ch 31:3
New **M** and Sabbaths, and the Is 1:13
I hate your New **M** and prescribed Is 1:14
festivals, New **M**, and Sabbaths— Ezk 45:17
gate on the Sabbaths and New **M**. Ezk 46:3
feasts, New **M**, and Sabbaths— Hs 2:11

MORAL *(5)*
matter of a crime or of **m** evil, Ac 18:14
as slaves to **m** impurity, Rm 6:19
sexual immorality, **m** impurity, Gl 5:19
if there is any **m** excellence and Php 4:8
of all **m** filth and evil Jms 1:21

MORALE *(1)*
weakening the **m** of the warriors Jr 38:4

MORALLY *(1)*
mind to do what is **m** wrong. Rm 1:28

MORALS *(1)*
"Bad company corrupts good **m**." 1Co 15:33

MORDECAI *(55)*
Reelaiah, **M**, Bilshan, Mispar, Ezr 2:2
Raamiah, Nahamani, **M**, Bilshan, Neh 7:7
of Susa named **M** son of Jair, Est 2:5
M was the legal guardian of his Est 2:7
M had adopted her as his own Est 2:7
M had ordered her not to. Est 2:10
Every day **M** took a walk in front Est 2:11
the uncle of **M** who had adopted Est 2:15
M was sitting at the King's Gate. Est 2:19
background, as **M** had directed. Est 2:20
those days while **M** was sitting Est 2:21
When **M** learned of the plot, Est 2:22
But **M** would not bow down or pay Est 3:2
at the King's Gate asked **M**, Est 3:3
Haman saw that **M** was not bowing Est 3:5
not to do away with **M** alone. Est 3:6
When **M** learned all that had Est 4:1
sent clothes for **M** to wear so he Est 4:4
him to **M** to learn what he Est 4:5
went out to **M** in the city square Est 4:6
M told him everything that had Est 4:7
M also gave him a copy of the Est 4:8
and commanded him to tell **M**, Est 4:10
response was reported to **M**. Est 4:12
M told ⌊the messenger⌋ to reply Est 4:13
Esther sent this reply to **M**: Est 4:15
So **M** went and did everything Est 4:17
when Haman saw **M** at the King's Est 5:9
and **M** didn't rise or tremble in Est 5:9
was filled with rage toward **M**. Est 5:9
me since I see **M** the Jew sitting Est 5:13
in the morning to hang **M** on it. Est 5:14
report of how **M** had informed Est 6:2
been given to **M** for this ⌊act⌋?" Est 6:3
king to hang **M** on the gallows Est 6:4
and a horse for **M** the Jew, Est 6:10
He clothed **M** and paraded him Est 6:11
Then **M** returned to the King's Est 6:12
to him, "If **M**, before whom you Est 6:13
house that he made for **M**, Est 7:9
gallows he had prepared for **M**. Est 7:10
M entered the king's presence Est 8:1
revealed her relationship to **M**. Est 8:1
from Haman and gave it to **M**, Est 8:2
the Queen and to **M** the Jew, Est 8:7
written exactly as **M** ordered for Est 8:9
M wrote in King Ahasuerus' name Est 8:10
M went out from the king's Est 8:15
because they were afraid of **M**. Est 9:3
For **M** ⌊exercised⌋ great power in Est 9:4
M recorded these events and sent Est 9:20
as **M** had written them to do. Est 9:23
along with **M** the Jew, wrote this Est 9:29
time just as **M** the Jew and Queen Est 9:31
M the Jew was second only to Est 10:3

MORDECAI'S *(7)*
She obeyed **M** orders, as she Est 2:20
she told the king on **M** behalf. Est 2:22
Haman to see if **M** actions would Est 3:4
he learned of **M** ethnic identity, Est 3:6
out to destroy all of **M** people, Est 3:6
came and repeated **M** response to Est 4:9
account of **M** great rank to which Est 10:2

MORE *(461)*
you are cursed **m** than any Gn 3:14
livestock and **m** than any wild Gn 3:14
above them⌋ **m** than 20 feet. Gn 7:20
waited seven **m** days and sent out Gn 8:10
and I will speak one **m** time. Gn 18:32
Now we'll do **m** harm to you than Gn 19:9
he loved Rachel **m** than Leah. Gn 29:30
loved Joseph **m** than his other Gn 37:3
father loved him **m** than all his Gn 37:4
brothers, they hated him even **m**. Gn 37:5
hated him even **m** because of his Gn 37:8
She is **m** in the right than I, Gn 38:26
will be five **m** years without Gn 45:6
will be five **m** years of famine. Gn 45:11
Israelite people are **m** numerous Ex 1:9
But the **m** they oppressed them, Ex 1:12
the **m** they multiplied and spread Ex 1:12
and what's **m**, I will not let Ex 5:2
and there will be no **m** hail, Ex 9:29
my sin once **m** and make an appeal Ex 10:17
I will bring one **m** plague on Ex 11:1
Make two ⌊**m**⌋ gold rings and Ex 28:27
years old or **m**, must give this Ex 30:14
The wealthy may not give **m**, Ex 30:15
are bringing **m** than is needed Ex 36:5
There was **m** than enough. Ex 36:7
years old or **m** who had crossed Ex 38:26
They made two ⌊**m**⌋ gold rings and Ex 39:20
If the person is 60 years or **m**, Lv 27:7
20 years old or **m** by their Nm 1:3
of those 20 years old or **m**, Nm 1:18
of every male 20 years old or **m**, Nm 1:20
of every male 20 years old or **m**, Nm 1:22
of those 20 years old or **m**, Nm 1:24
of those 20 years old or **m**, Nm 1:26
of those 20 years old or **m**, Nm 1:28
of those 20 years old or **m**, Nm 1:30
of those 20 years old or **m**, Nm 1:32
of those 20 years old or **m**, Nm 1:34
of those 20 years old or **m**, Nm 1:36
of those 20 years old or **m**, Nm 1:38
of those 20 years old or **m**, Nm 1:40
of those 20 years old or **m**, Nm 1:42
Israelites 20 years old or **m**, Nm 1:45
every male one month old or **m**." Nm 3:15
every male one month old or **m**, Nm 3:22
every male one month old or **m**, Nm 3:28
every male one month old or **m**, Nm 3:34
month old or **m** that Moses and Nm 3:39
Israelites one month old or **m**, Nm 3:40
month old or **m** listed by name Nm 3:43
25 years old or **m**, a man enters Nm 8:24
let me see my misery ⌊any **m**⌋." Nm 11:15
m so than any man on the face of Nm 12:3
of you 20 years old or **m**— Nm 14:29
they are **m** powerful than I Nm 22:6
again who were **m** numerous and Nm 22:15
Once **m** he proclaimed his poem: Nm 24:23
20 years old or **m** who can serve Nm 26:2
of⌋ those 20 years old or **m**, Nm 26:4
every male one month old or **m**; Nm 26:62
men 20 years old or **m** who came Nm 32:11
adding even **m** to the LORD's Nm 32:14
you should take **m** from a larger Nm 35:8
increase you a thousand times **m**, Dt 1:11
added nothing **m**. He wrote them Dt 5:22
seven nations **m** numerous and Dt 7:1
because you were **m** numerous than Dt 7:7
stronger and **m** numerous than Dt 9:14
to add three **m** cities to these Dt 19:9
with 40 lashes, but no **m**. Dt 25:3
is flogged with **m** lashes than Dt 25:3
and multiply you **m** than ⌊He did⌋ Dt 30:5
much **m** ⌊will you rebel⌋ after Dt 31:27
Since there was no **m** manna for Jos 5:12
M of them died from the hail Jos 10:11
They spoke no **m** about going to Jos 22:33
would act even **m** corruptly than Jdg 2:19
let me speak one **m** time. Jdg 6:39
me to make one **m** test with the Jdg 6:39
younger sister **m** beautiful than Jdg 15:2
Come one **m** time, for he has told Jdg 16:18
Strengthen me, God, just once **m**. Jdg 16:28
his death were **m** than those he Jdg 16:30
Gidom and struck 2,000 **m** dead. Jdg 20:45
to have any **m** sons who could Ru 1:11
to me, and even **m**, if anything Ru 1:17
You have shown **m** kindness now Ru 3:10
who are starving ⌊hunger⌋ no **m**. 1Sm 2:5
honored your sons **m** than Me, 1Sm 2:29
was no one **m** impressive among 1Sm 9:2
m can he have but the kingdom? 1Sm 18:8
became even **m** afraid of David. 1Sm 18:29
David was **m** successful than all 1Sm 18:30
each other, though David wept **m**. 1Sm 20:41
how much **m** if we go to Keilah 1Sm 23:3
You are **m** righteous than I, 1Sm 24:17
even **m** if I let any of his men 1Sm 25:22
He doesn't answer me any **m**, 1Sm 28:15
love for me was **m** wonderful than 2Sm 1:26
kept acquiring **m** power in the 2Sm 3:6
the people wept over him even **m**. 2Sm 3:34

much **m** when wicked men kill 2Sm 4:11
became **m** and more powerful, 2Sm 5:10
became more and **m** powerful, 2Sm 5:10
took **m** concubines and wives 2Sm 5:13
and **m** sons and daughters were 2Sm 5:13
myself even **m** and humiliate 2Sm 6:22
What **m** can David say to You? 2Sm 7:20
I would have given you even **m**. 2Sm 12:8
much **m** now this Benjaminite! 2Sm 16:11
the forest claimed **m** people than 2Sm 18:8
Bichri will do **m** harm to us than 2Sm 20:6
100 times **m** than they are— 2Sm 24:3
name of Solomon **m** famous than 1Kg 1:47
struck down two men **m** righteous 1Kg 2:32
and seven ⌊**m**⌋ days—14 days 1Kg 8:65
You behaved **m** wickedly than all 1Kg 14:9
to jealous anger **m** than all that 1Kg 14:22
he did **m** evil than all who were 1Kg 16:25
the LORD's sight **m** than all who 1Kg 16:30
Ahab did **m** to provoke the LORD 1Kg 16:33
a prophet of Yahweh here any **m**? 1Kg 22:7
replied, "There aren't any **m**." 2Kg 4:6
How much **m** ⌊should you do it⌋ 2Kg 5:13
Jabez was **m** honorable than his 1Ch 4:9
David steadily grew **m** powerful, 1Ch 11:9
David took **m** wives in Jerusalem, 1Ch 14:3
the father of **m** sons and 1Ch 14:3
What **m** can David say to You for 1Ch 17:18
you will need to add **m** to them. 1Ch 22:14
20 years old or **m**, who worked in 1Ch 23:24
20 years old or **m** were to be 1Ch 23:27
Since **m** leaders were found among 1Ch 24:4
far **m** than she had brought the 2Ch 9:12
of Absalom **m** than all his wives 2Ch 11:21
a prophet of Yahweh here any **m**? 2Ch 18:6
until nobody could carry any **m**. 2Ch 20:25
20 years old or **m** for all Judah 2Ch 25:5
to give you much **m** than this." 2Ch 25:9
himself became **m** unfaithful to 2Ch 28:22
Levites were **m** conscientious to 2Ch 29:34
decided to observe seven **m** days, 2Ch 30:23
there are **m** with us than with 2Ch 32:7
servants said **m** against the LORD 2Ch 32:16
20 years old or **m** to supervise Ezr 3:8
and require nothing **m** from them. Neh 5:12
man who feared God **m** than most. Neh 7:2
in **m** contempt and fury. Est 1:18
woman who is **m** worthy than she. Est 1:19
king loved Esther **m** than all the Est 2:17
won **m** favor and approval from Est 2:17
"What's **m**," Haman added, "Queen Est 5:12
would want to honor **m** than me?" Est 6:6
he became **m** and more powerful. Est 9:4
he became more and **m** powerful. Est 9:4
search for it **m** than for hidden Jb 3:21
Can a person be **m** righteous than Jb 4:17
or a man **m** pure than his Maker?" Jb 4:17
how much **m** those who dwell in Jb 4:19
My days pass **m** swiftly than a Jb 7:6
up until the heavens are no **m**; Jb 14:12
saw him will see ⌊him⌋ no **m**, Jb 20:9
of His mouth **m** than my daily Jb 23:12
and He has many **m** things like Jb 23:14
they are remembered no **m**. Jb 24:20
wealthy, but will do so no **m**; Jb 27:19
gives us **m** understanding than Jb 35:11
for there is still **m** to be said Jb 36:2
of Job's life **m** than the earlier Jb 42:12
You have put **m** joy in my heart Ps 4:7
earth may terrify ⌊them⌋ no **m**. Ps 10:18
They are **m** desirable than gold— Ps 19:10
and the wicked will be no **m**; Ps 37:10
they are **m** than can be told. Ps 40:5
They are **m** than the hairs of my Ps 40:12
has anointed you, **m** than your Ps 45:7
without cause are **m** numerous Ps 69:4
please the LORD **m** than an ox, Ps 69:31
m than a bull with horns and Ps 69:31
and will praise You **m** and more. Ps 71:14
and will praise You more and **m**. Ps 71:14
abound until the moon is no **m**. Ps 72:7
the gates of Zion **m** than all the Ps 87:2
m awe-inspiring than all who Ps 89:7
earth and the wicked be no **m**. Ps 104:35
He made them **m** numerous than Ps 105:24
I have **m** insight than all my Ps 119:99
I understand **m** than the elders Ps 119:100
commandments **m** than gold, Ps 119:127

for we've had **m** than enough Ps 123:3
We've had **m** than enough scorn Ps 123:4
for the Lord **m** than watchmen for Ps 130:6
m than watchmen for the morning. Ps 130:6
for she is **m** profitable than Pr 3:14
She is **m** precious than jewels; Pr 3:15
man, and he will learn **m**. Pr 9:9
the wicked are no **m**, but the Pr 10:25
gives freely, yet gains **m**; Pr 11:24
much **m** the wicked and sinful. Pr 11:31
—how much **m**, human hearts. Pr 15:11
person **m** than a hundred Pr 17:10
how much **m** do his friends keep Pr 19:7
and just is **m** acceptable to Pr 21:3
how much **m** so when he brings it Pr 21:27
There is **m** hope for a fool than Pr 26:12
will later find **m** favor than one Pr 28:23
There is **m** hope for a fool than Pr 29:20
and remember his trouble no **m**. Pr 31:7
She is far **m** precious than Pr 31:10
m than all who were before me in Ec 2:7
already died, **m** than the living, Ec 4:2
What is **m**, he eats in darkness Ec 5:17
it has **m** rest than he. Ec 6:5
And I find **m** bitter than death Ec 7:26
are heeded **m** than the shouts Ec 9:17
then one must exert **m** strength; Ec 10:10
your love is **m** delightful than Sg 1:2
praise your love **m** than wine. Sg 1:4
Why do you want **m** beatings? Is 1:5
Put no **m** trust in man, who has Is 2:22
What **m** could I have done for My Is 5:4
until there is no **m** room and you Is 5:8
and mankind **m** rare than the gold Is 13:12
on Dibon even **m** ⌊than this⌋— Is 15:9
You will not rejoice any **m**, Is 23:12
In a little **m** than a year you Is 32:10
and remember your sins no **m**. Is 43:25
one will be **m** than the children Is 54:1
shown herself **m** righteous than Jr 3:11
your hand once **m** like a grape Jr 6:9
they did **m** evil than their Jr 7:26
departed from me and are no **m**. Jr 10:20
their widows **m** numerous than Jr 15:8
did **m** evil than your fathers. Jr 16:12
The heart is **m** deceitful than Jr 17:9
dwell once **m** in their own land. Jr 23:8
children because they are no **m**. Jr 31:15
there will once **m** be a grazing Jr 33:12
there is no **m** bread in the city. Jr 38:9
for they are **m** numerous than Jr 46:23
with **m** than the weeping for Jr 48:32
instruction is no **m**, and even Lm 2:9
bodies were **m** ruddy than coral, Lm 4:7
regards them no **m**. The priests Lm 4:16
Take some **m** of them, throw them Ezk 5:4
ordinances with **m** wickedness Ezk 5:6
My statutes **m** than the countries Ezk 5:6
you have been **m** insubordinate Ezk 5:7
The wall is no **m** and neither are Ezk 13:15
you behaved **m** corruptly than Ezk 16:47
For they appear **m** righteous than Ezk 16:52
you committed **m** abhorrently than Ezk 16:52
she was ⌊even⌋ **m** depraved in her Ezk 23:11
them or remember Egypt any **m**. Ezk 23:27
reproach of the peoples any **m**; Ezk 36:15
themselves any **m** with their Ezk 37:23
one side and two ⌊**m**⌋ tables on Ezk 40:40
took away **m** space from them Ezk 42:5
from the ground **m** than the lower Ezk 42:6
because I have **m** wisdom than Dn 2:30
seven times **m** than was customary Dn 3:19
and even **m** greatness came to me. Dn 4:36
became even **m** terrified, Dn 5:9
and that was **m** visible than the Dn 7:20
Three **m** kings will arise in Dn 11:2
will grow **m** powerful and will Dn 11:5
will stumble, fall, and be no **m**. Dn 11:19
The **m** they multiplied, the more Hs 4:7
the **m** they sinned against Me. Hs 4:7
The **m** his fruit increased, Hs 10:1
the **m** he increased the altars. Hs 10:1
⌊The **m**⌋ they called them, Hs 11:2
⌊the **m**⌋ they departed from Me. Hs 11:2
I have anything **m** to do with Hs 14:8
rebel even **m** at Gilgal! Am 4:4
of the house, "Any **m** with you?" Am 6:10
men were even **m** afraid and said Jnh 1:10

raging against them **m** and more. Jnh 1:13
raging against them more and **m**. Jnh 1:13
The men feared the LORD even **m**, Jnh 1:16
will look once **m** toward Your Jnh 2:4
which has **m** than 120,000 people Jnh 4:11
not have any **m** fortune-tellers. Mc 5:12
your merchants **m** numerous than Nah 3:16
than leopards and **m** fierce than Hab 1:8
up one who is **m** righteous than Hab 1:13
they became **m** corrupt in all Zph 3:7
Once **m**, in a little while, I am Hg 2:6
LORD will once **m** comfort Zion Zch 1:17
because they were no **m**. Mt 2:18
after me is **m** powerful than I. Mt 3:11
Anything **m** than this is from Mt 5:37
Isn't life **m** than food and the Mt 6:25
and the body **m** than clothing? Mt 6:25
Aren't you worth **m** than they? Mt 6:26
won't He do much **m** for you— Mt 6:30
how much **m** will your Father in Mt 7:11
will be **m** tolerable on the day Mt 10:15
how much **m** the members of his Mt 10:25
you are worth **m** than many Mt 10:31
father or mother **m** than Me is Mt 10:37
son or daughter **m** than Me is not Mt 10:37
you, and far **m** than a prophet. Mt 11:9
it will be **m** tolerable for Tyre Mt 11:22
it will be **m** tolerable for the Mt 11:24
man is worth far **m** than a sheep, Mt 12:12
spirits **m** evil than itself, Mt 12:45
whoever has, ⌊**m**⌋ will be given Mt 13:12
and he will have **m** than enough. Mt 13:12
over that sheep **m** than over the Mt 18:13
take one or two **m** with you, Mt 18:16
100 times **m** and will inherit Mt 19:29
they assumed they would get **m**, Mt 20:10
but they cried out all the **m**, Mt 20:31
other slaves, **m** than the first Mt 21:36
Once **m** Jesus spoke to them in Mt 22:1
one dared to question Him any **m**. Mt 22:46
neglected the **m** important Mt 23:23
them to work, and earned five **m**. Mt 25:16
the man with two earned two **m**. Mt 25:17
presented five **m** talents, and Mt 25:20
I've earned five **m** talents.' Mt 25:20
I've earned two **m** talents.' Mt 25:22
who has, **m** will be given, Mt 25:29
and he will have **m** than enough. Mt 25:29
saying the same thing once **m**. Mt 26:44
at once with **m** than 12 legions Mt 26:53
Crucify Him!" all the **m**. Mt 27:23
Someone **m** powerful than I will Mk 1:7
that there was no **m** room, Mk 2:2
was able to restrain him any **m**— Mk 5:3
Why bother the Teacher any **m**?" Mk 5:35
but the **m** He would order them, Mk 7:36
the **m** they would proclaim it. Mk 7:36
He began teaching them once **m**. Mk 10:1
So they were even **m** astonished, Mk 10:26
will not receive 100 times **m**, Mk 10:30
but he was crying out all the **m**, Mk 10:48
far **m** ⌊important⌋ than all the Mk 12:33
has put in **m** than all those Mk 12:43
been sold for **m** than 300 denarii Mk 14:5
Crucify Him!" all the **m**. Mk 15:14
Don't collect any **m** than what Lk 3:13
coming who is **m** powerful than I Lk 3:16
news about Him spread even **m**, Lk 5:15
you, and far **m** than a prophet. Lk 7:26
which of them will love him **m**?" Lk 7:42
I suppose the one he forgave **m**." Lk 7:43
whoever has, **m** will be given to Lk 8:18
We have no **m** than five loaves Lk 9:13
day it will be **m** tolerable for Lk 10:12
But it will be **m** tolerable for Lk 10:14
how much **m** will the heavenly Lk 11:13
spirits **m** evil than itself, Lk 11:26
He said, "Even **m**, those who hear Lk 11:28
and after that can do nothing **m**. Lk 12:4
you are worth **m** than many Lk 12:7
For life is **m** than food and the Lk 12:23
and the body **m** than clothing. Lk 12:23
you worth much **m** than the birds? Lk 12:24
how much **m** will He do for you— Lk 12:28
And even **m** will be expected of Lk 12:48
who has been entrusted with **m**. Lk 12:48
Galileans were **m** sinful than all Lk 13:2
think they were **m** sinful than Lk 13:4

because a **m** distinguished person Lk 14:8
there will be **m** joy in heaven Lk 15:7
hands have **m** than enough food Lk 15:17
this age are **m** astute than the Lk 16:8
many times **m** at this time, Lk 18:30
he kept crying out all the **m**, Lk 18:39
mina has earned 10 **m** minas.' Lk 19:16
who has, **m** will be given; Lk 19:26
has put in **m** than all of them Lk 21:3
He prayed **m** fervently, and His Lk 22:44
Jesus responded, "No **m** of this!" Lk 22:51
Why do we need any **m** testimony, Lk 22:71
and baptizing **m** disciples than Jn 4:1
'There are still four **m** months, Jn 4:35
Many **m** believed because of what Jn 4:41
Do not sin any **m**, so that Jn 5:14
trying all the **m** to kill Him: Jn 5:18
won't perform **m** signs than this Jn 7:31
from now on do not sin any **m**." Jn 8:11
stayed two **m** days in the place Jn 11:6
Fear no **m**, Daughter Zion; Jn 12:15
praise from men **m** than praise Jn 12:43
so that it will produce **m** fruit. Jn 15:2
he was **m** afraid than ever. Jn 19:8
do you love Me **m** than these?" Jn 21:15
Saul grew **m** capable, and kept Ac 9:22
here were **m** open-minded than Ac 17:11
way of God to him **m** accurately. Ac 18:26
'It is **m** blessed to give than to Ac 20:35
What's **m**, he also brought Greeks Ac 21:28
There were **m** than 40 who had Ac 23:13
his case **m** thoroughly. Ac 23:15
a somewhat **m** careful inquiry Ac 23:20
there are **m** than 40 of them Ac 23:21
that it is no **m** than 12 days Ac 24:11
had spent not **m** than eight or 10 Ac 25:6
With yet **m** difficulty we sailed Ac 27:8
Much **m** then, since we have now Rm 5:9
then how⌊ much **m**, having been Rm 5:10
how much **m** have the grace of God Rm 5:15
much **m** will those who receive Rm 5:17
grace multiplied even **m**, Rm 5:20
died, but even **m**, has been Rm 8:34
things we are **m** than victorious Rm 8:37
much **m** will their full number Rm 11:12
tree, how much **m** will these— Rm 11:24
think of himself **m** highly than Rm 12:3
written to you **m** boldly on some Rm 15:15
over you, don't we even **m**? 1Co 9:12
all, in order to win **m** people. 1Co 9:19
contrary, all the **m**, those parts 1Co 12:22
but even **m** that you prophesied. 1Co 14:5
languages **m** than all of you 1Co 14:18
I worked **m** than any of them, 1Co 15:10
should be pitied **m** than anyone. 1Co 15:19
of the Spirit not be **m** glorious? 2Co 3:8
overflows with even **m** glory. 2Co 3:9
endures will be even **m** glorious. 2Co 3:11
through **m** and more people 2Co 4:15
through more and **m** people, 2Co 4:15
so that I rejoiced even **m**. 2Co 7:7
to rejoice even **m** over the joy 2Co 7:13
and now even **m** diligent because 2Co 8:22
if I boast some **m** about our 2Co 10:8
with far **m** labors, many more 2Co 11:23
labors, many **m** imprisonments, 2Co 11:23
boast all the **m** about my 2Co 12:9
I love you **m**, am I to be loved 2Co 12:15
m numerous than those of the Gl 4:27
with a desire for **m** and more. Eph 4:19
with a desire for more and **m**. Eph 4:19
and dare even **m** to speak the Php 1:14
in the flesh is **m** necessary for Php 1:24
others as **m** important than Php 2:3
but now even **m** in my absence, Php 2:12
in the flesh, I have **m**: Php 3:4
M than that, I also consider Php 3:8
as you are doing—do so even **m**. 1Th 4:1
you, brothers, to do so even **m**, 1Th 4:10
as a slave, but **m** than a slave— Phm 16
to me, but even **m** to you, both Phm 16
you will do even **m** than I say. Phm 21
pay even **m** attention to what Heb 2:1
worthy of **m** glory than Moses, Heb 3:3
as the builder has **m** honor than Heb 3:3
purpose even **m** clearly to the Heb 6:17
the greater and **m** perfect Heb 9:11
how much **m** will the blood of the Heb 9:14
and all the **m** as you see the day Heb 10:25
what **m** can I say? Time is too Heb 11:32
submit even **m** to the Father of Heb 12:9
Yet once **m** I will shake not only Heb 12:26
Yet once **m**," indicates Heb 12:27
of your faith—**m** valuable than 1Pt 1:7
are still two **m** woes to come Rv 9:12

MOREH *(3)*

of Shechem, at the oak of **M**. Gn 12:6
Gilgal, near the oaks of **M**? Dt 11:30
the hill of **M**, in the valley. Jdg 7:1

MOREOVER *(8)*

M, Isaac's slaves dug in the Gn 26:19
M, because of my delight in the 1Ch 29:3
M, keep Your servant from Ps 19:13
M, your skirts are stained with Jr 2:34
M, you will be led out from here Jr 2:37
M, wine betrays; an arrogant man Hab 2:5
M, some women from our group Lk 24:22
M my flesh will rest in hope, Ac 2:26

MORESHETH-GATH *(1)*

send farewell gifts to **M**; Mc 1:14

MORESHITE *(2)*

Micah the **M** prophesied in the Jr 26:18
LORD that came to Micah the **M**— Mc 1:1

MORIAH *(2)*

to the land of **M**, and offer him Gn 22:2
on Mount **M** where the LORD had 2Ch 3:1

MORNING *(222)*

Evening came, and then **m**: Gn 1:5
Evening came, and then **m**: Gn 1:8
Evening came, and then **m**: Gn 1:13
Evening came, and then **m**: Gn 1:19
Evening came, and then **m**: Gn 1:23
Evening came, and then **m**: Gn 1:31
Early in the **m** Abraham went to Gn 19:27
Early in the **m** Abimelech got up, Gn 20:8
Early in the **m** Abraham got up, Gn 21:14
early in the **m** Abraham got up, Gn 22:3
When they got up in the **m**, Gn 24:54
up early in the **m** and swore an Gn 26:31
Early in the **m** Jacob took the Gn 28:18
When **m** came, there was Leah! Gn 29:25
Laban got up early in the **m**, Gn 31:55
Joseph came to them in the **m**, Gn 40:6
When **m** came, he was troubled, so Gn 41:8
m light, the men were sent off Gn 44:3
In the **m** he devours the prey, Gn 49:27
Go to Pharaoh in the **m**. Ex 7:15
up early in the **m** and present Ex 8:20
up early in the **m** and present Ex 9:13
m the east wind had brought in Ex 10:13
let any of it remain until **m**; Ex 12:10
of it that does remain until **m**. Ex 12:10
the door of his house until **m**. Ex 12:22
during the **m** watch, the LORD Ex 14:24
in the **m** you will see the LORD's Ex 16:7
and abundant bread in the **m**, Ex 16:8
and in the **m** you will eat bread Ex 16:12
the **m** there was a layer of dew Ex 16:13
let any of it remain until **m**." Ex 16:19
people left part of it until **m**, Ex 16:20
They gathered it every **m**. Ex 16:21
set aside to be kept until **m**.' " Ex 16:23
it aside until **m** as Moses Ex 16:24
Moses from **m** until evening. Ex 18:13
you from **m** until evening?" Ex 18:14
third day, when **m** came, there Ex 19:16
must not remain until **m**. Ex 23:18
early the next **m** and set up an Ex 24:4
evening until **m** before the LORD. Ex 27:21
of the bread is left until **m**, Ex 29:34
In the **m** offer one lamb, and at Ex 29:39
the one in the **m**, as a pleasing Ex 29:41
burn it every **m** when he tends Ex 30:7
Early the next **m** they arose, Ex 32:6
Be prepared by **m**. Come up Mount Ex 34:2
Sinai in the **m** and stand before Ex 34:2
early in the **m**, and taking the Ex 34:4
must not remain until **m**. Ex 34:25
offerings **m** after morning. Ex 36:3
offerings morning after **m**. Ex 36:3
hearth all night until **m**, Lv 6:9
Every **m** the priest will burn Lv 6:12
half of it in the **m** and half in Lv 6:20
may not leave any of it until **m**. Lv 7:15
to the **m** burnt offering. Lv 9:17
not remain with you until **m**. Lv 19:13
let any of it remain until **m**; Lv 22:30
evening until **m** before the LORD Lv 24:3
any of it until **m** or break any Nm 9:12
tabernacle from evening until **m**. Nm 9:15
only⌋ from evening until **m**; Nm 9:21
when the cloud lifted in the **m**, Nm 9:21
up early the next **m** and went up Nm 14:40
Tomorrow **m** the LORD will reveal Nm 16:5
got up the next **m** and said to Nm 22:13
got up in the **m**, Balaam saddled Nm 22:21
In the **m**, Balak took Balaam and Nm 22:41
one lamb in the **m** and the other Nm 28:4
and drink offering as in the **m**. Nm 28:8
these with the **m** burnt offering Nm 28:23
first day is to remain until **m**. Dt 16:4
return to your tents in the **m**. Dt 16:7
In the **m** you will say, 'If only Dt 28:67
will say, 'If only it were **m**!' Dt 28:67
early the next **m** and left Acacia Jos 3:1
Joshua got up early the next **m**. Jos 6:12
In the **m** you must present Jos 7:14
Joshua got up early the next **m**. Jos 7:16
early the next **m** and mobilized Jos 8:10
and went out early in the **m**, Jos 8:14
men of the city got up in the **m**, Jdg 6:28
case will be put to death by **m**! Jdg 6:31
When he got up early in the **m**, Jdg 6:38
early in the **m** and prepared to Jdg 19:5
up early in the **m** of the fifth Jdg 19:8
abused her all night until **m**. Jdg 19:25
Early that **m**, the woman made her Jdg 19:26
When her master got up in the **m**, Jdg 19:27
In the **m**, the Israelites set out Jdg 20:19
remained from early **m** until now, Ru 2:7
and in the **m**, if he wants to Ru 3:13
Now, lie down until **m**." Ru 3:13
his feet until **m** but got up Ru 3:14
next **m** Elkanah and Hannah got 1Sm 1:19
Samuel lay down until the **m**; 1Sm 3:15
Ashdod got up early the next **m**, 1Sm 5:3
they got up early the next **m**, 1Sm 5:4
When I send you off in the **m**, 1Sm 9:19
During the **m** watch, they invaded 1Sm 11:11
and plunder them until **m**. 1Sm 14:36
Early in the **m** Samuel got up to 1Sm 15:12
Every **m** and evening for 40 days 1Sm 17:16
So David got up early in the **m**, 1Sm 17:20
your guard in the **m** and hide in 1Sm 19:2
for him and kill him in the **m**. 1Sm 19:11
the **m** Jonathan went out to the 1Sm 20:35
of his men ⌊survive⌋ until **m**." 1Sm 25:22
had any men left by **m** light." 1Sm 25:34
anything to him until **m** light. 1Sm 25:36
In the **m** when Nabal sobered up, 1Sm 25:37
up early in the **m**, you and your 1Sm 29:10
up early in the **m** to return to 1Sm 29:11
their brothers until **m**." 2Sm 2:27
marched all **m**, and arrived at 2Sm 2:29
The next **m** David wrote a letter 2Sm 11:14
son, so miserable every **m**? 2Sm 13:4
is like the **m** light when the sun 2Sm 23:4
the sun rises on a cloudless **m**, 2Sm 23:4
When David got up in the **m**, 2Sm 24:11
Israel from that **m** until the 2Sm 24:15
got up in the **m** to nurse my son 1Kg 3:21
That **m**, when I looked closely at 1Kg 3:21
and meat in the **m** and in the 1Kg 17:6
name of Baal from **m** until noon, 1Kg 18:26
the grain offering the ⌊next⌋ **m**, 2Kg 3:20
When they got up early in the **m**, 2Kg 3:22
silent and wait until **m** light, 2Kg 7:9
entrance of the gate until **m**." 2Kg 10:8
The next **m** when he went out and 2Kg 10:9
altar the **m** burnt offering, 2Kg 16:15
the people got up the ⌊next⌋ **m**— 2Kg 19:35
in charge of opening it every **m**. 1Ch 9:27
regularly, **m** and evening, to 1Ch 16:40
to stand every **m** to give thanks 1Ch 23:30
for the evening and the **m**, 2Ch 2:4
the LORD every **m** and every 2Ch 13:11
In the **m** they got up early and 2Ch 20:20
for the regular **m** and evening 2Ch 31:3
for the **m** and evening on it Ezr 3:3
and in the **m** she would return to Est 2:14
the king in the **m** to hang Est 5:14
early in the **m** to offer burnt Jb 1:5
May its **m** stars grow dark. Jb 3:9

him every **m**, and put him to Jb 7:18
darkness will be like the **m**. Jb 11:17
For the **m** is like death's shadow Jb 24:17
while the **m** stars sang together Jb 38:7
life commanded the **m** or assigned Jb 38:12
but there is joy in the **m**. Ps 30:5
will help her when the **m** dawns. Ps 46:5
will rule over them in the **m**, Ps 49:14
and groan, **m**, noon, and night, Ps 55:17
Your faithful love in the **m**. Ps 59:16
day long, and punished every **m**. Ps 73:14
in the **m** my prayer meets You. Ps 88:13
like grass that grows in the **m**— Ps 90:5
in the **m** it sprouts and grows; Ps 90:6
Satisfy us in the **m** with Your Ps 90:14
faithful love in the **m** and Your Ps 92:2
Every **m** I will destroy all the Ps 101:8
more than watchmen for the **m**— Ps 130:6
more than watchmen for the **m**. Ps 130:6
Your faithful love in the **m**, Ps 143:8
deeply of lovemaking until **m**. Pr 7:18
a loud voice early in the **m**, Pr 27:14
and your princes feast in the **m**. Ec 10:16
In the **m** sow your seed, and at Ec 11:6
rise early in the **m** in pursuit Is 5:11
Shining **m** star, how you have Is 14:12
and in the **m** you will help your Is 17:11
Before **m**—it is gone! Is 17:14
watchman said, "**M** has come, and Is 21:12
will be covered with the **m** dew, Is 26:19
it will pass through every **m**— Is 28:19
strength every **m**, and our Is 33:2
the people got up the ⌊next⌋ **m**— Is 37:36
I thought until the **m**: Is 38:13
He awakens ⌊Me⌋ each **m**; Is 50:4
outcry in the **m** and a war cry at Jr 20:16
Administer justice every **m**, Jr 21:12
They are new every **m**; Lm 3:23
of the LORD came to me in the **m**: Ezk 12:8
I spoke to the people in the **m**, Ezk 24:18
The next **m** I did just as I was Ezk 24:18
the man came to me in the **m**. Ezk 33:22
you will offer it every **m**. Ezk 46:13
offering every **m** along with it: Ezk 46:14
and the oil every **m** as a regular Ezk 46:15
is like the **m** mist and like Hs 6:4
the **m** it blazes like a flaming Hs 7:6
they will be like the **m** mist, Hs 13:3
Bring your sacrifices every **m**, Am 4:4
At **m** light they accomplish it Mc 2:1
which leave nothing for the **m**. Zph 3:3
His justice **m** by morning; Zph 3:5
His justice morning by **m**; Zph 3:5
three in the **m**, He came toward Mt 14:25
And in the **m**, 'Today will be Mt 16:3
early in the **m** to hire workers Mt 20:1
he went out about nine in the **m**, Mt 20:3
Early in the **m**, as He was Mt 21:18
met them and said, "Good **m**!" Mt 28:9
Very early in the **m**, while it Mk 1:35
three in the **m** He came toward Mk 6:48
Early in the **m**, as they were Mk 11:20
the rooster or early in the **m**. Mk 13:35
As soon as it was **m**, the chief Mk 15:1
it was nine in the **m** when they Mk 15:25
early in the **m**, on the first day Mk 16:2
come early in the **m** to hear Him Lk 21:38
very early in the **m**, they came Lk 24:1
It was about 10 in the **m**. Jn 1:39
in the **m** the fever left him, Jn 4:52
It was early **m**. They did not Jn 18:28
and it was about six in the **m**. Jn 19:14
since it's only nine in the **m**. Ac 2:15
day dawns and the **m** star arises 2Pt 1:19
I will also give him the **m** star. Rv 2:28
of David, the Bright **M** Star." Rv 22:16

MORNINGS *(2)*
For 2,300 evenings and **m**; Dn 8:14
evenings and the **m** that has been Dn 8:26

MORON *(1)*
But whoever says, 'You **m**!' Mt 5:22

MORTAL *(8)*
Do not let a mere **m** hinder You." 2Ch 14:11
every **m** man is only a vapor. Ps 39:5
God for images resembling **m** man, Rm 1:23
let sin reign in your **m** body, Rm 6:12
also bring your **m** bodies to life Rm 8:11
and this **m** must be clothed with 1Co 15:53
and this **m** is clothed with 1Co 15:54
also be revealed in our **m** flesh. 2Co 4:11

MORTALITY *(1)*
so that **m** may be swallowed up by 2Co 5:4

MORTALLY *(3)*
me, for I'm **m** wounded, but my 2Sm 1:9
the **m** wounded cry for help, Jb 24:12
before him as a **m** wounded man. Ezk 30:24

MORTALS *(1)*
whose dwelling is not with **m**." Dn 2:11

MORTAR *(7)*
for stone and asphalt for **m**. Gn 11:3
difficult labor in brick and **m**, Ex 1:14
stones or crushed ⌊it⌋ in a **m**, Nm 11:8
a fool in a **m** with a pestle Pr 27:22
will set your stones in black **m**, Is 54:11
set them in the **m** of the brick Jr 43:9
into the clay and tread the **m**; Nah 3:14

MORTGAGING *(1)*
saying, "We are **m** our fields, Neh 5:3

MOSAIC *(1)*
arranged⌋ on a **m** pavement of red Est 1:6

MOSERAH *(1)*
from Beeroth Bene-jaakan to **M**. Dt 10:6

MOSEROTH *(2)*
Hashmonah and camped at **M**. Nm 33:30
departed from **M** and camped at Nm 33:31

MOSES *(817)*
She named him **M**, "Because," she Ex 2:10
later, after **M** had grown up, he Ex 2:11
Then **M** became afraid and Ex 2:14
about this, he tried to kill **M**. Ex 2:15
But **M** fled from Pharaoh and went Ex 2:15
but **M** came to their rescue and Ex 2:17
M agreed to stay with the man, Ex 2:21
Zipporah to **M** ⌊in marriage⌋. Ex 2:21
Meanwhile **M** was shepherding the Ex 3:1
M looked, he saw that the bush Ex 3:2
So **M** thought: I must go over and Ex 3:3
him from the bush, "**M**, Moses!" Ex 3:4
him from the bush, "Moses, **M**!" Ex 3:4
M hid his face because he was Ex 3:6
But **M** asked God, "Who am I that Ex 3:11
Then **M** asked God, "If I go to Ex 3:13
replied to **M**, "I AM WHO I AM. Ex 3:14
God also said to **M**, "Say this to Ex 3:15
Then **M** answered, "What if they Ex 4:1
became a snake. **M** ran from it, Ex 4:3
But **M** replied to the LORD, Ex 4:10
M said, "Please, Lord, send Ex 4:13
LORD's anger burned against **M**, Ex 4:14
Then **M** went back to his Ex 4:18
Jethro said to **M**, "Go in peace. Ex 4:18
Now in Midian the LORD told **M**, Ex 4:19
So **M** took his wife and sons, Ex 4:20
And **M** took God's staff in his Ex 4:20
LORD instructed **M**, "When you go Ex 4:21
Go and meet **M** in the wilderness. Ex 4:27
M told Aaron everything the LORD Ex 4:28
Then **M** and Aaron went and Ex 4:29
LORD had said to **M** and performed Ex 4:30
M and Aaron went in and said to Ex 5:1
said to them, "**M** and Aaron, why Ex 5:4
they confronted **M** and Aaron, Ex 5:20
So **M** went back to the LORD and Ex 5:22
But the LORD replied to **M**, Ex 6:1
God spoke to **M**, telling him, "I Ex 6:2
M told this to the Israelites, Ex 6:9
Then the LORD spoke to **M**, Ex 6:10
But **M** said in the LORD's Ex 6:12
LORD spoke to **M** and Aaron and Ex 6:13
and she bore him Aaron and **M**. Ex 6:20
this Aaron and **M** whom the LORD Ex 6:26
M and Aaron were the ones who Ex 6:27
the LORD spoke to **M** in the land Ex 6:28
But **M** replied in the LORD's Ex 6:30
LORD answered **M**, "See, I have Ex 7:1
So **M** and Aaron did ⌊this⌋; Ex 7:6
M was 80 years old and Aaron 83 Ex 7:7
The LORD said to **M** and Aaron, Ex 7:8
M and Aaron went in to Pharaoh Ex 7:10
the LORD said to **M**, "Pharaoh is Ex 7:14
the LORD said to **M**, "Tell Aaron: Ex 7:19
M and Aaron did just as the LORD Ex 7:20
the LORD said to **M**, "Go in to Ex 8:1
then said to **M**, "Tell Aaron: Ex 8:5
Pharaoh summoned **M** and Aaron and Ex 8:8
M said to Pharaoh, "Make the Ex 8:9
M replied, "As you have said, so Ex 8:10
After **M** and Aaron went out from Ex 8:12
M cried out to the LORD for help Ex 8:12
The LORD did as **M** had said: Ex 8:13
the LORD said to **M**, "Tell Aaron: Ex 8:16
LORD said to **M**, "Get up early Ex 8:20
Pharaoh summoned **M** and Aaron Ex 8:25
But **M** said, "It would not be Ex 8:26
as I leave you," **M** said, "I will Ex 8:29
Then **M** left Pharaoh's presence Ex 8:30
The LORD did as **M** had said: Ex 8:31
the LORD said to **M**, "Go in to Ex 9:1
the LORD said to **M** and Aaron, Ex 9:8
and **M** is to throw it toward Ex 9:8
M threw it toward heaven, and it Ex 9:10
stand before **M** because of the Ex 9:11
to them, as the LORD had told **M**. Ex 9:12
LORD said to **M**, "Get up early Ex 9:13
the LORD said to **M**, "Stretch out Ex 9:22
So **M** stretched out his staff Ex 9:23
Pharaoh sent for **M** and Aaron. Ex 9:27
M said to him, "When I have left Ex 9:29
M went out from Pharaoh and the Ex 9:33
as the LORD had said through **M**. Ex 9:35
LORD said to **M**, "Go to Pharaoh Ex 10:1
M and Aaron went in to Pharaoh Ex 10:3
So **M** and Aaron were brought back Ex 10:8
M replied, "We will go with our Ex 10:9
LORD then said to **M**, "Stretch Ex 10:12
M stretched out his staff over Ex 10:13
urgently sent for **M** and Aaron Ex 10:16
M left Pharaoh's presence and Ex 10:18
the LORD said to **M**, "Stretch out Ex 10:21
So **M** stretched out his hand Ex 10:22
Pharaoh summoned **M** and said, Ex 10:24
M responded, "You must also let Ex 10:25
you've said," **M** replied, "I will Ex 10:29
LORD said to **M**, "I will bring Ex 11:1
And the man **M** was feared in the Ex 11:3
M said, "This is what the LORD Ex 11:4
LORD said to **M**, "Pharaoh will Ex 11:9
M and Aaron did all these Ex 11:10
The LORD said to **M** and Aaron in Ex 12:1
Then **M** summoned all the elders Ex 12:21
had commanded **M** and Aaron. Ex 12:28
He summoned **M** and Aaron during Ex 12:31
The LORD said to **M** and Aaron, Ex 12:43
had commanded **M** and Aaron. Ex 12:50
The LORD spoke to **M**: Ex 13:1
Then **M** said to the people, Ex 13:3
M took the bones of Joseph with Ex 13:19
Then the LORD spoke to **M**: Ex 14:1
They said to **M**: "Is it because Ex 14:11
But **M** said to the people, Ex 14:13
The LORD said to **M**, "Why are you Ex 14:15
Then **M** stretched out his hand Ex 14:21
the LORD said to **M**, "Stretch out Ex 14:26
So **M** stretched out his hand over Ex 14:27
in Him and in His servant **M**. Ex 14:31
Then **M** and the Israelites sang Ex 15:1
Then **M** led Israel on from the Ex 15:22
The people grumbled to **M**, Ex 15:24
grumbled against **M** and Aaron Ex 16:2
LORD said to **M**, "I am going to Ex 16:4
So **M** and Aaron said to all the Ex 16:6
M continued, "The LORD will give Ex 16:8
Then **M** told Aaron, "Say to the Ex 16:9
The LORD spoke to **M**, Ex 16:11
M told them, "It is the bread Ex 16:15
M said to them, "No one is to Ex 16:19
But they didn't listen to **M**; Ex 16:20
Therefore **M** was angry with them. Ex 16:20
came and reported ⌊this⌋ to **M**. Ex 16:22
until morning as **M** commanded, Ex 16:24
"Eat it today," **M** said, "because Ex 16:25
LORD said to **M**, "How long will Ex 16:28
M said, "This is what the LORD Ex 16:32
M told Aaron, "Take a container Ex 16:33
commanded **M**, Aaron placed Ex 16:34
So the people complained to **M**: Ex 17:2
to me?" **M** replied to them. Ex 17:2
water, and grumbled against **M**. Ex 17:3
Then **M** cried out to the LORD, Ex 17:4
LORD answered **M**, "Go on ahead Ex 17:5
M did this in the sight of the Ex 17:6
M said to Joshua, "Select some Ex 17:9

Joshua did as **M** had told him,	Ex 17:10
Amalek, while **M**, Aaron, and Hur	Ex 17:10
While **M** held up his hand, Israel	Ex 17:11
then said to **M**, "Write this down	Ex 17:14
And **M** built an altar and named	Ex 17:15
had done for **M** and His people	Ex 18:1
Gershom (because **M** had said, "I	Ex 18:3
He sent word to **M**, "I, your	Ex 18:6
So **M** went out to meet his	Ex 18:7
M recounted to his father-in-law	Ex 18:8
The next day **M** sat down to judge	Ex 18:13
they stood around **M** from morning	Ex 18:13
M replied to his father-in-law,	Ex 18:15
M listened to his father-in-law	Ex 18:24
So **M** chose able men from all	Ex 18:25
cases they would bring to **M**,	Ex 18:26
Then **M** said goodbye to his	Ex 18:27
M went up ⌊the mountain⌋ to God,	Ex 19:3
After **M** came back, He summoned	Ex 19:7
So **M** brought the people's words	Ex 19:8
LORD said to **M**, "I am going to	Ex 19:9
Then **M** reported the people's	Ex 19:9
And the LORD told **M**, "Go to the	Ex 19:10
Then **M** came down from the	Ex 19:14
Then **M** brought the people out of	Ex 19:17
M spoke and God answered him in	Ex 19:19
the LORD summoned **M** to the top	Ex 19:20
LORD directed **M**, "Go down and	Ex 19:21
But **M** responded to the LORD,	Ex 19:23
So **M** went down to the people and	Ex 19:25
they said to **M**, "but don't let	Ex 20:19
M responded to the people,	Ex 20:20
a distance as **M** approached the	Ex 20:21
the LORD told **M**, "This is what	Ex 20:22
Then He said to **M**, "Go up to the	Ex 24:1
M alone is to approach the LORD,	Ex 24:2
M came and told the people all	Ex 24:3
And **M** wrote down all the words	Ex 24:4
M took half the blood and set it	Ex 24:6
M took the blood, sprinkled it	Ex 24:8
Then **M** went up with Aaron,	Ex 24:9
LORD said to **M**, "Come up to Me	Ex 24:12
So **M** arose with his assistant	Ex 24:13
When **M** went up the mountain,	Ex 24:15
He called to **M** from the cloud.	Ex 24:16
M entered the cloud as he went	Ex 24:18
The LORD spoke to **M**:	Ex 25:1
The LORD spoke to **M**:	Ex 30:11
The LORD spoke to **M**:	Ex 30:17
The LORD spoke to **M**:	Ex 30:22
LORD said to **M**: "Take fragrant	Ex 30:34
The LORD also spoke to **M**:	Ex 31:1
The LORD said to **M**:	Ex 31:12
speaking with **M** on Mount Sinai,	Ex 31:18
people saw that **M** delayed in	Ex 32:1
go before us because this **M**,	Ex 32:1
LORD spoke to **M**: "Go down at	Ex 32:7
The LORD also said to **M**:	Ex 32:9
But **M** interceded with the LORD	Ex 32:11
Then **M** turned and went down the	Ex 32:15
he said to **M**, "There is a sound	Ex 32:17
M replied: It's not the sound	Ex 32:18
M became enraged and threw the	Ex 32:19
Then **M** asked Aaron, "What did	Ex 32:21
go before us because this **M**,	Ex 32:23
M saw that the people were out	Ex 32:25
And **M** stood at the camp's	Ex 32:26
The Levites did as **M** commanded,	Ex 32:28
Afterwards **M** said, "Today you	Ex 32:29
The following day **M** said to the	Ex 32:30
So **M** returned to the LORD and	Ex 32:31
The LORD replied to **M**:	Ex 32:33
LORD spoke to **M**: "Go, leave here	Ex 33:1
For the LORD said to **M**:	Ex 33:5
Now **M** took a tent and set it up	Ex 33:7
Whenever **M** went out to the tent,	Ex 33:8
would watch **M** until he entered	Ex 33:8
When **M** entered the tent, the	Ex 33:9
the LORD⌋ would speak with **M**.	Ex 33:9
LORD spoke with **M** face to face,	Ex 33:11
Then **M** would return to the camp,	Ex 33:11
M said to the LORD, "Look, You	Ex 33:12
not go," **M** responded to Him,	Ex 33:15
LORD answered **M**, "I will do this	Ex 33:17
Then **M** said, "Please, let me see	Ex 33:18
LORD said to **M**, "Cut two stone	Ex 34:1
M cut two stone tablets like the	Ex 34:4
M immediately bowed down to the	Ex 34:8

LORD also said to **M**, "Write down	Ex 34:27
M was there with the LORD 40	Ex 34:28
M descended from Mount Sinai—	Ex 34:29
and all the Israelites saw **M**,	Ex 34:30
But **M** called out to them, so	Ex 34:31
to him, and **M** spoke to them.	Ex 34:31
M had finished speaking with	Ex 34:33
But whenever **M** went before the	Ex 34:34
Then **M** would put the veil over	Ex 34:35
M assembled the entire Israelite	Ex 35:1
Then **M** said to the entire	Ex 35:4
LORD, through **M**, had commanded	Ex 35:29
M then said to the Israelites:	Ex 35:30
So **M** summoned Bezalel, Oholiab,	Ex 36:2
and said to **M**, "The people are	Ex 36:5
After **M** gave an order, they sent	Ex 36:6
that the LORD commanded **M**.	Ex 38:22
as the LORD had commanded **M**.	Ex 39:1
as the LORD had commanded **M**.	Ex 39:5
as the LORD had commanded **M**.	Ex 39:7
as the LORD had commanded **M**.	Ex 39:21
as the LORD had commanded **M**.	Ex 39:26
as the LORD had commanded **M**.	Ex 39:29
as the LORD had commanded **M**.	Ex 39:31
as the LORD had commanded **M**.	Ex 39:32
brought the tabernacle to **M**:	Ex 39:33
the LORD had commanded **M**.	Ex 39:42
M inspected all the work they	Ex 39:43
commanded. Then **M** blessed them.	Ex 39:43
The LORD spoke to **M**:	Ex 40:1
M did everything just as the	Ex 40:16
M set up the tabernacle:	Ex 40:18
as the LORD had commanded **M**.	Ex 40:19
M took the testimony and placed	Ex 40:20
M placed the table in the tent	Ex 40:22
M also installed the gold altar	Ex 40:26
M, Aaron, and his sons washed	Ex 40:31
as the LORD had commanded **M**.	Ex 40:32
Next **M** set up the surrounding	Ex 40:33
So **M** finished the work.	Ex 40:33
M was unable to enter the tent	Ex 40:35
LORD summoned **M** and spoke to him	Lv 1:1
Then the LORD spoke to **M**:	Lv 4:1
Then the LORD spoke to **M**:	Lv 5:14
The LORD spoke to **M**:	Lv 6:1
The LORD spoke to **M**:	Lv 6:8
The LORD spoke to **M**:	Lv 6:19
The LORD spoke to **M**:	Lv 6:24
The LORD spoke to **M**:	Lv 7:22
The LORD spoke to **M**:	Lv 7:28
commanded **M** on Mount Sinai	Lv 7:38
The LORD spoke to **M**:	Lv 8:1
So **M** did as the LORD commanded	Lv 8:4
M said to them, "This is what	Lv 8:5
Then **M** presented Aaron and his	Lv 8:6
as the LORD had commanded **M**.	Lv 8:9
Then **M** took the anointing oil	Lv 8:10
Then **M** presented Aaron's sons,	Lv 8:13
as the LORD had commanded **M**.	Lv 8:13
Then **M** slaughtered ⌊it⌋, took	Lv 8:15
M took all the fat that was on	Lv 8:16
as the LORD had commanded **M**.	Lv 8:17
M slaughtered it and sprinkled	Lv 8:19
M cut the ram into pieces and	Lv 8:20
the LORD as He had commanded **M**.	Lv 8:21
M slaughtered ⌊it⌋, took some of	Lv 8:23
M also presented Aaron's sons	Lv 8:24
Then **M** sprinkled the blood on	Lv 8:24
M took them from their hands	Lv 8:28
M took some of the anointing	Lv 8:30
M said to Aaron and his sons,	Lv 8:31
LORD had commanded through **M**.	Lv 8:36
the eighth day **M** summoned Aaron,	Lv 9:1
brought what **M** had commanded to	Lv 9:5
M said, "This is what the LORD	Lv 9:6
Then **M** said to Aaron, "Approach	Lv 9:7
as the LORD had commanded **M**.	Lv 9:10
the LORD, as **M** had commanded.	Lv 9:21
M and Aaron then entered the	Lv 9:23
M said to Aaron, "This is what	Lv 10:3
M summoned Mishael and Elzaphan	Lv 10:4
outside the camp, as **M** had said.	Lv 10:5
M said to Aaron and his sons	Lv 10:6
So they did as **M** said.	Lv 10:7
has given to them through **M**."	Lv 10:11
M spoke to Aaron and his	Lv 10:12
M inquired about the male goat	Lv 10:16
Aaron replied to **M**, "See, today	Lv 10:19

When **M** heard this, it was	Lv 10:20
The LORD spoke to **M** and Aaron:	Lv 11:1
The LORD spoke to **M**:	Lv 12:1
The LORD spoke to **M** and Aaron:	Lv 13:1
The LORD spoke to **M**:	Lv 14:1
The LORD spoke to **M** and Aaron:	Lv 14:33
The LORD spoke to **M** and Aaron:	Lv 15:1
LORD spoke to **M** after the death	Lv 16:1
The LORD said to **M**: "Tell your	Lv 16:2
done as the LORD commanded **M**.	Lv 16:34
The LORD spoke to **M**:	Lv 17:1
The LORD spoke to **M**:	Lv 18:1
The LORD spoke to **M**:	Lv 19:1
The LORD spoke to **M**:	Lv 20:1
The LORD said to **M**: "Speak to	Lv 21:1
The LORD spoke to **M**:	Lv 21:16
M said ⌊this⌋ to Aaron and his	Lv 21:24
The LORD spoke to **M**:	Lv 22:1
The LORD spoke to **M**:	Lv 22:17
The LORD spoke to **M**:	Lv 22:26
The LORD spoke to **M**:	Lv 23:1
The LORD spoke to **M**:	Lv 23:9
The LORD spoke to **M**:	Lv 23:23
The LORD again spoke to **M**:	Lv 23:26
The LORD spoke to **M**:	Lv 23:33
So **M** declared the LORD's	Lv 23:44
The LORD spoke to **M**:	Lv 24:1
and they brought him to **M**.	Lv 24:11
Then the LORD spoke to **M**:	Lv 24:13
After **M** spoke to the Israelites,	Lv 24:23
as the LORD had commanded **M**.	Lv 24:23
LORD spoke to **M** on Mount Sinai:	Lv 25:1
through **M** on Mount Sinai.	Lv 26:46
The LORD spoke to **M**:	Lv 27:1
the LORD gave **M** for the	Lv 27:34
The LORD spoke to **M** in the tent	Nm 1:1
M and Aaron took these men who	Nm 1:17
just as the LORD commanded **M**.	Nm 1:19
These are the men **M** and Aaron	Nm 1:44
For the LORD had told **M**:	Nm 1:48
as the LORD had commanded **M**.	Nm 1:54
The LORD spoke to **M** and Aaron:	Nm 2:1
as the LORD had commanded **M**.	Nm 2:33
the LORD commanded **M**;	Nm 2:34
of Aaron and **M** at the time the	Nm 3:1
spoke with **M** on Mount Sinai.	Nm 3:1
The LORD spoke to **M**:	Nm 3:5
The LORD spoke to **M**:	Nm 3:11
LORD spoke to **M** in the	Nm 3:14
M registered them in obedience	Nm 3:16
M, Aaron, and his sons, who	Nm 3:38
old or more that **M** and Aaron	Nm 3:39
The LORD told **M**: "Register every	Nm 3:40
So **M** registered every firstborn	Nm 3:42
The LORD spoke to **M** again:	Nm 3:44
So **M** collected the redemption	Nm 3:49
just as the LORD commanded **M**.	Nm 3:51
The LORD spoke to **M** and Aaron:	Nm 4:1
the LORD spoke to **M** and Aaron:	Nm 4:17
The LORD spoke to **M**:	Nm 4:21
So **M**, Aaron, and the leaders of	Nm 4:34
M and Aaron registered them at	Nm 4:37
at the LORD's command through **M**.	Nm 4:37
the LORD's command **M** and Aaron	Nm 4:41
M and Aaron registered them at	Nm 4:45
at the LORD's command through **M**.	Nm 4:45
M, Aaron, and the leaders of	Nm 4:46
under the direction of **M**,	Nm 4:49
was as the LORD commanded **M**.	Nm 4:49
The LORD instructed **M**:	Nm 5:1
did as the LORD instructed **M**.	Nm 5:4
The LORD spoke to **M**:	Nm 5:5
The LORD spoke to **M**:	Nm 5:11
The LORD instructed **M**:	Nm 6:1
The LORD spoke to **M**:	Nm 6:22
On the day **M** finished setting up	Nm 7:1
The LORD said to **M**,	Nm 7:4
So **M** took the carts and oxen and	Nm 7:6
The LORD told **M**, "Each day have	Nm 7:11
When **M** entered the tent of	Nm 7:89
The LORD spoke to **M**:	Nm 8:1
as the LORD had commanded **M**.	Nm 8:3
pattern the LORD had shown **M**.	Nm 8:4
The LORD spoke to **M**:	Nm 8:5
M, Aaron, and the entire	Nm 8:20
the LORD commanded **M** regarding	Nm 8:20
had commanded **M** concerning	Nm 8:22
The LORD spoke to **M**:	Nm 8:23

LORD told **M** in the Wilderness Nm 9:1
So **M** told the Israelites to Nm 9:4
as the LORD had commanded **M**. Nm 9:5
men came before **M** and Aaron the Nm 9:6
M replied to them, "Wait here Nm 9:8
Then the LORD spoke to **M**: Nm 9:9
to His command through **M**. Nm 9:23
The LORD spoke to **M**: Nm 10:1
the LORD's command through **M**. Nm 10:13
M said to Hobab, son of Moses' Nm 10:29
leave us," **M** said, "since you Nm 10:31
the ark set out, **M** would say: Nm 10:35
Then the people cried out to **M**, Nm 11:2
M heard the people, family after Nm 11:10
was very angry; **M** was also Nm 11:10
So **M** asked the LORD, "Why have Nm 11:11
LORD answered **M**, "Bring Me 70 Nm 11:16
M replied, "I'm in the middle Nm 11:21
LORD answered **M**, "Is the LORD's Nm 11:23
M went out and told the people Nm 11:24
Spirit that was on **M** and placed Nm 11:25
young man ran and reported to **M**, Nm 11:27
assistant to **M** since his youth, Nm 11:28
responded, "**M**, my lord, stop Nm 11:28
M asked him, "Are you jealous Nm 11:29
M returned to the camp along Nm 11:30
and Aaron criticized **M** because Nm 12:1
the LORD speak only through **M**? Nm 12:2
M was a very humble man, more so Nm 12:3
Suddenly the LORD said to **M**, Nm 12:4
Not so with My servant **M**; Nm 12:7
to speak against My servant **M**?" Nm 12:8
and said to **M**, "My lord, please Nm 12:11
Then **M** cried out to the LORD, Nm 12:13
LORD answered **M**, "If her father Nm 12:14
The LORD spoke to **M**: Nm 13:1
M sent them from the Wilderness Nm 13:3
names of the men **M** sent to scout Nm 13:16
M renamed Hoshea son of Nun, Nm 13:16
When **M** sent them to scout out Nm 13:17
The men went back to **M**, Aaron, Nm 13:26
reported to **M**: "We went into Nm 13:27
in the presence of **M** and said, Nm 13:30
complained about **M** and Aaron, Nm 14:2
Then **M** and Aaron fell down with Nm 14:5
LORD said to **M**, "How long will Nm 14:11
But **M** replied to the LORD, Nm 14:13
the LORD spoke to **M** and Aaron: Nm 14:26
So the men **M** sent to scout out Nm 14:36
When **M** reported these words to Nm 14:39
But **M** responded, "Why are you Nm 14:41
covenant and **M** did not leave Nm 14:44
The LORD instructed **M**: Nm 15:1
The LORD instructed **M**: Nm 15:17
that the LORD spoke to **M**— Nm 15:22
has commanded you through **M**, Nm 15:23
gathering wood brought him to **M**, Nm 15:33
the LORD told **M**, "The man is to Nm 15:35
as the LORD had commanded **M**. Nm 15:36
The LORD said to **M**, Nm 15:37
and they rebelled against **M**. Nm 16:2
together against **M** and Aaron and Nm 16:3
When **M** heard ⌊this⌋, he fell Nm 16:4
M also told Korah, "Now listen, Nm 16:8
M sent for Dathan and Abiram, Nm 16:12
Then **M** became angry and said to Nm 16:15
So **M** told Korah, "You and all Nm 16:16
meeting along with **M** and Aaron. Nm 16:18
The LORD spoke to **M** and Aaron, Nm 16:20
M and Aaron fell facedown and Nm 16:22
The LORD replied to **M**, Nm 16:23
M got up and went to Dathan and Nm 16:25
Then **M** said, "This is how you Nm 16:28
Then the LORD spoke to **M**: Nm 16:36
commanded him through **M**. Nm 16:40
complained about **M** and Aaron, Nm 16:41
M and Aaron turned toward the Nm 16:42
M and Aaron went to the front of Nm 16:43
and the LORD said to **M**, Nm 16:44
Then **M** told Aaron, "Take your Nm 16:46
his firepan as **M** had ordered, Nm 16:47
returned to **M** at the entrance Nm 16:50
The LORD instructed **M**: Nm 17:1
So **M** spoke to the Israelites, Nm 17:6
M placed the staffs before the Nm 17:7
The next day **M** entered the tent Nm 17:8
M then brought out all the Nm 17:9
LORD told **M**, "Put Aaron's rod Nm 17:10
So **M** did as the LORD commanded Nm 17:11
the Israelites declared to **M**, Nm 17:12
The LORD instructed **M**, Nm 18:25
The LORD spoke to **M** and Aaron, Nm 19:1
assembled against **M** and Aaron. Nm 20:2
quarreled with **M** and said, Nm 20:3
Then **M** and Aaron went from the Nm 20:6
The LORD spoke to **M**, Nm 20:7
So **M** took the staff from the Nm 20:9
M and Aaron summoned the Nm 20:10
of the rock, and **M** said to them, Nm 20:10
M raised his hand and struck Nm 20:11
the LORD said to **M** and Aaron, Nm 20:12
M sent messengers from Kadesh Nm 20:14
The LORD said to **M** and Aaron at Nm 20:23
M did as the LORD commanded, Nm 20:27
After **M** removed Aaron's Nm 20:28
M and Eleazar came down from Nm 20:28
people spoke against God and **M**: Nm 21:5
people then came to **M** and said, Nm 21:7
And **M** interceded for the Nm 21:7
LORD said to **M**, "Make a snake Nm 21:8
So **M** made a bronze snake and Nm 21:9
the well the LORD told **M** about, Nm 21:16
After **M** sent spies to Jazer, Nm 21:32
the LORD said to **M**, "Do not fear Nm 21:34
LORD said to **M**, "Take all the Nm 25:4
So **M** told Israel's judges, Nm 25:5
in the sight of **M** and the whole Nm 25:6
The LORD spoke to **M**, Nm 25:10
The LORD told **M**: Nm 25:16
LORD said to **M** and Eleazar son Nm 26:1
So **M** and Eleazar the priest said Nm 26:3
had commanded **M** and the Nm 26:4
who fought against **M** and Aaron; Nm 26:9
The LORD spoke to **M**, Nm 26:52
Aaron, **M**, and their sister Nm 26:59
ones registered by **M** and Eleazar Nm 26:63
been registered by **M** and Aaron Nm 26:64
They stood before **M**, Eleazar the Nm 27:2
M brought their case before the Nm 27:5
as the LORD commanded **M**." Nm 27:11
the LORD said to **M**, "Go up this Nm 27:12
So **M** appealed to the LORD, Nm 27:15
LORD replied to **M**, "Take Joshua Nm 27:18
M did as the LORD commanded Nm 27:22
the LORD had spoken through **M**. Nm 27:23
The LORD spoke to **M**, Nm 28:1
So **M** told the Israelites Nm 29:40
M told the leaders of the Nm 30:1
LORD commanded **M** concerning Nm 30:16
The LORD spoke to **M**, Nm 31:1
So **M** spoke to the people, Nm 31:3
M sent 1,000 from each tribe to Nm 31:6
as the LORD had commanded **M**, Nm 31:7
spoils of war to **M**, Eleazar the Nm 31:12
M, Eleazar the priest, and all Nm 31:13
But **M** became furious with the Nm 31:14
statute the LORD commanded **M**: Nm 31:21
The LORD told **M**, Nm 31:25
So **M** and Eleazar the priest did Nm 31:31
did as the LORD commanded **M**. Nm 31:31
M gave the tribute to Eleazar Nm 31:41
as the LORD had commanded **M**. Nm 31:41
which **M** separated from the men Nm 31:42
M took one out of ⌊every⌋ 50, Nm 31:47
and of hundreds, approached **M** Nm 31:48
M and Eleazar the priest Nm 31:51
M and Eleazar the priest Nm 31:54
and Reubenites came to **M**, Nm 32:2
But **M** asked the Gadites and Nm 32:6
M replied to them, "If you do Nm 32:20
and Reubenites answered **M**, Nm 32:25
So **M** gave orders about them to Nm 32:28
M told them, "If the Gadites and Nm 32:29
So **M** gave them—the Gadites, Nm 32:33
M gave Gilead to ⌊the clan of⌋ Nm 32:40
the leadership of **M** and Aaron. Nm 33:1
M wrote down the starting points Nm 33:2
LORD spoke to **M** in the plains Nm 33:50
The LORD spoke to **M**, Nm 34:1
So **M** commanded the Israelites, Nm 34:13
The LORD spoke to **M**, Nm 34:16
again spoke to **M** in the plains Nm 35:1
The LORD said to **M**, Nm 35:9
and addressed **M** and the leaders Nm 36:1
So **M** commanded the Israelites at Nm 36:5
did as the LORD commanded **M**. Nm 36:10
through **M** in the plains Nm 36:13
are the words **M** spoke to all Dt 1:1
M told the Israelites everything Dt 1:3
M began to explain this law, Dt 1:5
Then **M** set apart three cities Dt 4:41
This is the law **M** gave the Dt 4:44
and ordinances **M** proclaimed to Dt 4:45
M and the Israelites defeated Dt 4:46
M summoned all Israel and said Dt 5:1
M and the elders of Israel Dt 27:1
M and the Levitical priests Dt 27:9
On that day **M** commanded the Dt 27:11
LORD commanded **M** to make with Dt 29:1
M summoned all Israel and said Dt 29:2
Then **M** continued to speak these Dt 31:1
M then summoned Joshua and said Dt 31:7
M wrote down this law and gave Dt 31:9
M commanded them, "At the end of Dt 31:10
The LORD said to **M**, "The time of Dt 31:14
When **M** and Joshua went and Dt 31:14
LORD said to **M**, "You are about Dt 31:16
M wrote down this song on that Dt 31:22
When **M** had finished writing down Dt 31:24
M recited aloud every single Dt 31:30
M came with Joshua son of Nun Dt 32:44
After **M** finished reciting all Dt 32:45
same day the LORD spoke to **M**, Dt 32:48
This is the blessing that **M**, Dt 33:1
M gave us instruction, a Dt 33:4
Then **M** went up from the plains Dt 34:1
M the servant of the LORD died Dt 34:5
M was 120 years old when he died; Dt 34:7
wept for **M** in the plains Dt 34:8
mourning for **M** came to an end. Dt 34:8
because **M** had laid his hands on Dt 34:9
did as the LORD had commanded **M**. Dt 34:9
arisen again in Israel like **M**, Dt 34:10
terrifying deeds that **M** Dt 34:12
the death of **M** the LORD's Jos 1:1
son of Nun, who had served **M**: Jos 1:1
M My servant is dead. Jos 1:2
treads, just as I promised **M**. Jos 1:3
with you, just as I was with **M**. Jos 1:5
My servant **M** commanded you. Jos 1:7
Remember what **M** the LORD's Jos 1:13
in the land **M** gave you on this Jos 1:14
of what **M** the LORD's servant Jos 1:15
as we obeyed **M** in everything. Jos 1:17
be with you, as He was with **M**. Jos 1:17
with you just as I was with **M**. Jos 3:7
with all that **M** had commanded Jos 4:10
Israelites, as **M** had instructed Jos 4:12
his life, as they had revered **M**. Jos 4:14
just as **M** the LORD's servant had Jos 8:31
in the book of the law of **M**: Jos 8:31
Joshua copied the law of **M**, Jos 8:32
As **M** the LORD's servant had Jos 8:33
word of all that **M** had commanded Jos 8:35
His servant **M** to give you all Jos 9:24
as **M** the LORD's servant had Jos 11:12
had commanded His servant **M**, Jos 11:15
servant Moses, **M** commanded Jos 11:15
that the LORD had commanded **M**. Jos 11:15
as the LORD had commanded **M**. Jos 11:20
all that the LORD had told **M**. Jos 11:23
M the LORD's servant and the Jos 12:6
And **M** the LORD's servant gave Jos 12:6
the inheritance **M** gave them Jos 13:8
just as **M** the LORD's servant had Jos 13:8
M struck them down and drove Jos 13:12
Reubenites by their clans, **M** Jos 13:15
M had killed him and the chiefs Jos 13:21
Gadites by their clans, **M** gave Jos 13:24
by their clans, **M** gave Jos 13:29
were the portions **M** gave ⌊them⌋ Jos 13:32
But **M** did not give a portion to Jos 13:33
commanded through **M** for the nine Jos 14:2
because **M** had given the Jos 14:3
did as the LORD commanded **M**, Jos 14:5
LORD promised **M** the man of God Jos 14:6
40 years old when **M** the LORD's Jos 14:7
On that day **M** promised me, Jos 14:9
this word to **M** while Israel was Jos 14:10
as I was the day **M** sent me out. Jos 14:11
The LORD commanded **M** to give us Jos 17:4
which **M** the LORD's servant gave Jos 18:7
as I instructed you through **M**, Jos 20:2
through **M** that we be given Jos 21:2

LORD had commanded through **M**. Jos 21:8
done everything **M** the LORD's Jos 22:2
own land that **M** the LORD's Jos 22:4
instruction that **M** the LORD's Jos 22:5
M had given ⌊territory⌋ to half Jos 22:7
to the LORD's command through **M**. Jos 22:9
in the book of the law of **M**, Jos 23:6
Then I sent **M** and Aaron, Jos 24:5
Caleb, just as **M** had promised. Jdg 1:20
given their fathers through **M**. Jdg 3:4
Gershom, son of **M**, and his sons Jdg 18:30
appointed **M** and Aaron and who 1Sm 12:6
and He sent them **M** and Aaron, 1Sm 12:8
This is written in the law of **M**, 1Kg 2:3
tablets that **M** had put there at 1Kg 8:9
Your servant **M** when You brought 1Kg 8:53
His servant **M** has failed. 1Kg 8:56
of the law of **M** where the LORD 2Kg 14:6
the bronze snake that **M** made, 2Kg 18:4
the LORD had commanded **M**. 2Kg 18:6
He had commanded **M** the servant 2Kg 18:12
My servant **M** commanded them. 2Kg 21:8
according to all the law of **M**, 2Kg 23:25
children: Aaron, **M**, and Miriam. 1Ch 6:3
to all that **M** the servant of God 1Ch 6:49
God the way **M** had commanded 1Ch 15:15
which **M** made in the desert, 1Ch 21:29
LORD commanded **M** for Israel. 1Ch 22:13
sons: Aaron and **M**. Aaron, along 1Ch 23:13
for **M** the man of God, his sons 1Ch 23:14
the LORD's servant **M** had made 2Ch 1:3
tablets that **M** had put ⌊in it⌋ 2Ch 5:10
commandment of **M** for Sabbaths, 2Ch 8:13
it is written in the law of **M**, 2Ch 23:18
servant **M** and the assembly 2Ch 24:6
tax God's servant **M** ⌊imposed⌋ on 2Ch 24:9
in the book of **M**, where the LORD 2Ch 25:4
to the law of **M** the man of God. 2Ch 30:16
commanded them through **M**— 2Ch 33:8
LORD ⌊written⌋ by the hand of **M**. 2Ch 34:14
the word of the LORD through **M**." 2Ch 35:6
is written in the book of **M**; 2Ch 35:12
in the law of **M** the man of God. Ezr 3:2
is written in the book of **M**. Ezr 6:18
scribe skilled in the law of **M**, Ezr 7:6
You gave Your servant **M**. Neh 1:7
You commanded Your servant **M**: Neh 1:8
of the law of **M** that the LORD Neh 8:1
commanded through **M** that the Neh 8:14
a law through Your servant **M**. Neh 9:14
God's servant **M** and to carefully Neh 10:29
time the book of **M** was read Neh 13:1
by the hand of **M** and Aaron. Ps 77:20
M and Aaron were among His Ps 99:6
He revealed His ways to **M**, Ps 103:7
sent **M** His servant, and Aaron, Ps 105:26
were envious of **M** and of Aaron, Ps 106:16
M His chosen one had not stood Ps 106:23
and **M** suffered because of them; Ps 106:32
⌊the days⌋ of **M** ⌊and⌋ his people. Is 63:11
Even if **M** and Samuel should Jr 15:1
curse written in the law of **M**, Dn 9:11
it is written in the law of **M**, Dn 9:13
sent **M**, Aaron, and Miriam ahead Mc 6:4
the instruction of **M** My servant, Mal 4:4
the gift that **M** prescribed, Mt 8:4
M and Elijah appeared to them, Mt 17:3
for You, one for **M**, and one for Mt 17:4
did **M** command ⌊us⌋ to give Mt 19:7
M permitted you to divorce your Mt 19:8
Teacher, **M** said, if a man dies, Mt 22:24
are seated in the chair of **M**. Mt 23:2
and offer what **M** prescribed for Mk 1:44
M said: Honor your father and Mk 7:10
Elijah appeared to them with **M**, Mk 9:4
for You, one for **M**, and one for Mk 9:5
"What did **M** command you?" Mk 10:3
M permitted us to write divorce Mk 10:4
M wrote for us that if a man's Mk 12:19
you read in the book of **M**, Mk 12:26
to the law of **M** were finished, Lk 2:22
and offer what **M** prescribed for Lk 5:14
talking with Him—**M** and Elijah. Lk 9:30
for You, one for **M**, and one for Lk 9:33
'They have **M** and the prophets; Lk 16:29
don't listen to **M** and the Lk 16:31
M wrote for us that if a man's Lk 20:28
M even indicated ⌊in the Lk 20:37
Then beginning with **M** and all Lk 24:27
about Me in the Law of **M**, Lk 24:44
the law was given through **M**; Jn 1:17
have found the One **M** wrote about Jn 1:45
Just as **M** lifted up the snake in Jn 3:14
Your accuser is **M**, on whom you Jn 5:45
if you believed **M**, you would Jn 5:46
M didn't give you the bread from Jn 6:32
Didn't **M** give you the law? Jn 7:19
M has given you circumcision— Jn 7:22
that it comes from **M** but from Jn 7:22
the law of **M** won't be broken Jn 7:23
In the law **M** commanded us to Jn 8:5
but we're **M'** disciples. Jn 9:28
know that God has spoken to **M**. Jn 9:29
M said: The Lord your God will Ac 3:22
words against **M** and God!" Ac 6:11
that **M** handed down to us. Ac 6:14
At this time **M** was born, and he Ac 7:20
So **M** was educated in all the Ac 7:22
M fled and became an exile in Ac 7:29
When **M** saw it, he was amazed at Ac 7:31
M began to tremble and did not Ac 7:32
This **M**, whom they rejected when Ac 7:35
This is the **M** who said to the Ac 7:37
As for this **M** who brought us out Ac 7:40
He who spoke to **M** commanded Ac 7:44
from through the law of **M**. Ac 13:39
to the custom prescribed by **M**, Ac 15:1
them to keep the law of **M**!" Ac 15:5
M has had in every city those Ac 15:21
among the Gentiles to abandon **M**, Ac 21:21
prophets and **M** said would take Ac 26:22
both the Law of **M** and the Ac 28:23
death reigned from Adam to **M**, Rm 5:14
He tells **M**: I will show mercy Rm 9:15
For **M** writes about the Rm 10:5
First, **M** said: I will make Rm 10:19
it is written in the law of **M**, 1Co 9:9
baptized into **M** in the cloud 1Co 10:2
not like **M**, who used to put a 2Co 3:13
day, whenever **M** is read, a veil 2Co 3:15
Jannes and Jambres resisted **M**, 2Tm 3:8
just as **M** was in all God's Heb 3:2
worthy of more glory than **M**, Heb 3:3
M was faithful as a servant in Heb 3:5
who came out of Egypt under **M**? Heb 3:16
about that tribe **M** said nothing Heb 7:14
M was warned when he was about Heb 8:5
proclaimed by **M** to all the Heb 9:19
By faith **M**, after he was born, Heb 11:23
faith **M**, when he had grown up, Heb 11:24
was so terrifying that **M** said, Heb 12:21
in a debate about **M'** body, Jd 9
the song of God's servant **M**, Rv 15:3

MOSES' *(25)*

and threw it at **M** feet. Ex 4:25
acted on **M** word and asked Ex 12:35
When **M** hands grew heavy, they Ex 17:12
M father-in-law Jethro, the Ex 18:1
Now Jethro, **M** father-in-law, had Ex 18:2
in Zipporah, **M** wife, after he Ex 18:2
M father-in-law Jethro, along Ex 18:5
along with **M** wife and sons, Ex 18:5
Then Jethro, **M** father-in-law, Ex 18:12
to eat a meal with **M** Ex 18:12
When **M** father-in-law saw Ex 18:14
M father-in-law said to him, Ex 18:17
would see that **M** face was Ex 34:35
community left **M** presence. Ex 35:20
They took from **M** presence all Ex 36:3
that was recorded at **M** command. Ex 38:21
it was **M** portion of the Lv 8:29
son of **M** father-in-law Reuel the Nm 10:29
of the Kenite, **M** father-in-law, Jdg 1:16
the sons of Hobab, **M** Jdg 4:11
M sons: Gershom and Eliezer. 1Ch 23:15
a descendant of **M** son Gershom, 1Ch 26:24
glorious arm at **M** right hand, Is 63:12
look directly at **M** face because 2Co 3:7
If anyone disregards **M** law, Heb 10:28

MOST *(146)*

serpent was the **m** cunning of all Gn 3:1
he was a priest to God **M** High. Gn 14:18
Abram is blessed by God **M** High, Gn 14:19
give praise to God **M** High who Gn 14:20
to the LORD, God **M** High, Creator Gn 14:22
he was the **m** important in all Gn 34:19
holy place and the **m** holy place. Ex 26:33
testimony in the **m** holy place. Ex 26:34
sin offering is **m** holy and must Lv 6:25
to enter the ⌊**m**⌋ holy place in Lv 16:3
will purify the ⌊**m**⌋ holy place Lv 16:16
in the ⌊**m**⌋ holy place until Lv 16:17
purifying the ⌊**m**⌋ holy place, Lv 16:20
he entered the ⌊**m**⌋ holy place, Lv 16:23
into the ⌊**m**⌋ holy place to Lv 16:27
and purify the **m** holy place. Lv 16:33
concerns the **m** holy objects. Nm 4:4
come near the **m** holy objects: Nm 4:19
offering will be **m** holy for you Nm 18:9
to eat it as a **m** holy offering. Nm 18:10
has knowledge from the **M** High, Nm 24:16
The **m** sensitive and refined man Dt 28:54
m sensitive and refined woman Dt 28:56
When the **M** High gave the nations Dt 32:8
Asher be the **m** blessed of the Dt 33:24
he be the **m** favored among his Dt 33:24
Jael is **m** blessed of women, Jdg 5:24
she is **m** blessed among Jdg 5:24
the **M** High projected His voice. 2Sm 22:14
Was he not the **m** honored of the 2Sm 23:19
He was the **m** honored of the 2Sm 23:23
it was the **m** famous high place 1Kg 3:4
sanctuary, the **m** holy place. 1Kg 6:16
in front of the **m** holy place, 1Kg 6:17
that is, the **m** holy place) and 1Kg 7:50
to the **m** holy place beneath the 1Kg 8:6
committed the **m** detestable acts 1Kg 21:26
select the **m** qualified of your 2Kg 10:3
the work of the **m** holy place. 1Ch 6:49
was the **m** honored of the Three 1Ch 11:21
He was the **m** honored of the 1Ch 11:25
to consecrate the **m** holy things, 1Ch 23:13
Then he made the **m** holy place; 2Ch 3:8
work, for the **m** holy place, and 2Ch 3:10
inner doors to the **m** holy place, 2Ch 4:22
the temple, to the **m** holy place, 2Ch 5:7
not to eat the **m** holy things Ezr 2:63
man who feared God more than **m**. Neh 7:2
not to eat the **m** holy things Neh 7:65
m trusted ones were Carshena, Est 1:14
of the king's **m** noble officials Est 6:9
name of the LORD, the **M** High. Ps 7:17
sing about Your name, **M** High. Ps 9:2
the **M** High projected His voice. Ps 18:13
love of the **M** High he is not Ps 21:7
You are the **m** handsome of men; Ps 45:2
dwelling place of the **M** High. Ps 46:4
For the LORD **M** High is Ps 47:2
and pay your vows to the **M** High. Ps 50:14
I call to God **M** High, to God who Ps 57:2
are not afflicted like **m** people. Ps 73:5
the **M** High know everything?" Ps 73:11
hand of the **M** High has changed. Ps 77:10
the desert against the **M** High. Ps 78:17
rock, the **M** High God, their Ps 78:35
tested the **M** High God, Ps 78:56
you are all sons of the **M** High. Ps 82:6
are the **M** High over all the Ps 83:18
The **M** High Himself will Ps 87:5
protection of the **M** High dwells Ps 91:1
my refuge, the **M** High—your Ps 91:9
praise to Your name, **M** High, Ps 92:1
are the **M** High over all the Ps 97:9
the counsel of the **M** High. Ps 107:11
you do not know, **m** beautiful of Sg 1:8
than another, **m** beautiful of Sg 5:9
your love gone, **m** beautiful of Sg 6:1
make myself like the **M** High." Is 14:14
the **m** beautiful inheritance of Jr 3:19
has done a **m** terrible thing. Jr 18:13
incurable; your wound **m** severe. Jr 30:12
sleep had been **m** pleasant to me. Jr 31:26
'This city will **m** certainly be Jr 38:3
her from the **m** distant places. Jr 50:26
in the presence of the **M** High, Lm 3:35
from the mouth of the **M** High? Lm 3:38
will bring the **m** evil of nations Ezk 7:24
the **m** beautiful of all lands. Ezk 20:6
the **m** beautiful of all lands, Ezk 20:15
"This is the **m** holy place." Ezk 41:4
will eat the **m** holy offerings. Ezk 42:13
deposit the **m** holy offerings Ezk 42:13
things or the **m** holy things. Ezk 44:13

sanctuary, the **m** holy place, Ezk 45:3
a **m** holy place adjacent to the Ezk 48:12
you servants of the **M** High God— Dn 3:26
and wonders the **M** High God has Dn 4:2
know that the **M** High is ruler Dn 4:17
sentence of the **M** High that has Dn 4:24
that the **M** High is ruler over Dn 4:25
that the **M** High is ruler over Dn 4:32
I praised the **M** High and honored Dn 4:34
the **M** High God gave sovereignty, Dn 5:18
that the **M** High God is ruler Dn 5:21
holy ones of the **M** High will Dn 7:18
of the holy ones of the **M** High, Dn 7:22
against the **M** High and oppress Dn 7:25
the holy ones of the **M** High. Dn 7:25
the holy ones of the **M** High. Dn 7:27
and to anoint the **m** holy place. Dn 9:24
Even the **m** courageous of the Am 2:16
the **m** upright is worse than a Mc 7:4
towns where **m** of His miracles Mt 11:20
is the greatest and **m** important Mt 22:38
Jesus, Son of the **M** High God? Mk 5:7
is the **m** important of all? Mk 12:28
"This is the **m** important," Mk 12:29
orderly sequence, **m** honorable Lk 1:3
be called the Son of the **M** High, Lk 1:32
the power of the **M** High will Lk 1:35
You are the **m** blessed of women, Lk 1:42
called a prophet of the **M** High, Lk 1:76
you will be sons of the **M** High. Lk 6:35
You Son of the **M** High God? Lk 8:28
On the last and **m** important day Jn 7:37
the **M** High does not dwell in Ac 7:48
the slaves of the **M** High God, Ac 16:17
and **m** of them did not know why Ac 19:32
grieving **m** of all over his Ac 20:38
To the **m** excellent governor Ac 23:26
all places, **m** excellent Felix, Ac 24:3
out of my mind, **m** excellent Ac 26:25
was not pleased with **m** of them, 1Co 10:5
two, or at the **m** three, each in 1Co 14:27
on to you as **m** important what I 1Co 15:3
m of whom remain to the present, 1Co 15:6
zeal has stirred up **m** of them. 2Co 9:2
I will **m** gladly boast all the 2Co 12:9
I will **m** gladly spend and be 2Co 12:15
the **m** of the time, because Eph 5:16
M of the brothers in the Lord Php 1:14
making the **m** of the time. Col 4:5
And **m** certainly, the mystery of 1Tm 3:16
I will **m** certainly bless you, Heb 6:14
priest of the **M** High God, who Heb 7:1
up in your **m** holy faith Jd 20

MOTH *(7)*
dust, who are crushed like a **m**! Jb 4:19
like a **m** what is precious Ps 39:11
a garment; a **m** will devour them Is 50:9
For the **m** will devour them like Is 51:8
where **m** and rust destroy and Mt 6:19
where neither **m** nor rust Mt 6:20
comes near and no **m** destroys. Lk 12:33

MOTH'S *(1)*
he built is like a **m** ⌊cocoon⌋ or Jb 27:18

MOTH-EATEN *(2)*
rotten, like a **m** garment. Jb 13:28
your clothes are **m**; Jms 5:2

MOTHER *(226)*
his father and **m** and bonds with Gn 2:24
she was the **m** of all the living Gn 3:20
though not the daughter of my **m**, Gn 20:12
his **m** got a wife for him from Gn 21:21
gifts to her brother and her **m**. Gn 24:53
But her brother and **m** said, Gn 24:55
the tent of his **m** Sarah and took Gn 24:67
Jacob answered Rebekah his **m**, Gn 27:11
His **m** said to him, "Your curse Gn 27:13
them and brought them to his **m**, Gn 27:14
his **m** made the delicious food Gn 27:14
of Rebekah, the **m** of Jacob and Gn 28:5
to his father and **m** and went to Gn 28:7
he brought them to his **m** Leah, Gn 30:14
Are your **m** and brothers and I Gn 37:10
went and called the boy's **m**. Ex 2:8
father and your **m** so that you Ex 20:12
father or his **m** must be put to Ex 21:15
father or his **m** must be put to Ex 21:17
by having sex with your **m**. Lv 18:7
She is your **m**; you must not have Lv 18:7
is to respect his **m** and father. Lv 19:3
anyone curses his father or **m**, Lv 20:9
He has cursed his father or **m**; Lv 20:9
a man marries a woman and her **m**, Lv 20:14
his **m**, father, son, daughter, or Lv 21:2
even⌋ for his father or **m**. Lv 21:11
with its **m** for seven days; Lv 22:27
an Israelite **m** and an Egyptian Lv 24:10
himself for his father or **m**, Nm 6:7
Honor your father and your **m**, Dt 5:16
the son of your **m**, or your son Dt 13:6
her father and **m** a full month. Dt 21:13
his father or **m** and doesn't Dt 21:18
his father and **m** must take hold Dt 21:19
and the **m** is sitting on the Dt 22:6
must not take the **m** along with Dt 22:6
be sure to let the **m** go free, Dt 22:7
woman's father and **m** will take Dt 22:15
who dishonors his father or **m**.' Dt 27:16
He said about his father and **m**, Dt 33:9
of my father, **m**, brothers, Jos 2:13
your father, **m**, brothers, and Jos 2:18
and her father, **m**, brothers, and Jos 6:23
Deborah, I arose, a **m** in Israel. Jdg 5:7
Sisera's **m** looked through the Jdg 5:28
my brothers, the sons of my **m**! Jdg 8:19
and told his father and his **m**: Jdg 14:2
his father and **m** said to him, Jdg 14:3
his father and **m** did not know Jdg 14:4
with his father and **m** and came Jdg 14:5
his father or **m** what he had done Jdg 14:6
he returned to his father and **m**, Jdg 14:9
explained it to my father or **m**, Jdg 14:16
He said to his **m**, "The 1,100 Jdg 17:2
Then his **m** said, "My son, you Jdg 17:2
1,100 pieces of silver to his **m**, Jdg 17:3
mother, and his **m** said, "I Jdg 17:3
he returned the silver to his **m**, Jdg 17:4
⌊how⌋ you left your father and **m**, Ru 2:11
year his **m** made him a little 1Sm 2:19
your **m** will be childless among 1Sm 15:33
and to the disgrace of your **m**? 1Sm 20:30
my father and **m** stay with you 1Sm 22:3
a sister to Zeruiah, Joab's **m**. 2Sm 17:25
the tomb of my father and **m**. 2Sm 19:37
city that is like a **m** in Israel. 2Sm 20:19
Solomon's **m**, "Have you not heard 1Kg 1:11
came to Bathsheba, Solomon's **m**. 1Kg 2:13
throne placed for the king's **m**. 1Kg 2:19
ahead and⌋ ask, **m**," the king 1Kg 2:20
King Solomon answered his **m**, 1Kg 2:22
don't kill him. She is his **m**." 1Kg 3:27
being queen **m** because she had 1Kg 15:13
house, and gave him to his **m**. 1Kg 17:23
let me kiss my father and **m**, 1Kg 19:20
the way of his **m**, and in the way 1Kg 22:52
but not like his father and **m**, 2Kg 3:2
of your father and your **m**!" 2Kg 3:13
servant, "Carry him to his **m**." 2Kg 4:19
him up and took him to his **m**. 2Kg 4:20
The boy's **m** said ⌊to Elisha⌋, 2Kg 4:30
witchcraft from your **m** Jezebel?" 2Kg 9:22
Ahaziah's **m**, saw that her son 2Kg 11:1
along with his **m**, his servants, 2Kg 24:12
took the king's **m**, the king's 2Kg 24:15
Amasa's **m** was Abigail, and his 1Ch 2:17
Atarah, who was the **m** of Onam. 1Ch 2:26
Ephah was the **m** of Haran, 1Ch 2:46
Maacah was the **m** of Sheber and 1Ch 2:48
She was also the **m** of Shaaph, 1Ch 2:49
His **m** named him Jabez and said, 1Ch 4:9
being queen **m** because she had 2Ch 15:16
for his **m** gave him evil advice. 2Ch 22:3
Ahaziah's **m**, saw that her son 2Ch 22:10
she didn't have a father or **m**. Est 2:7
When her father and **m** died, Est 2:7
to the worm: My **m** or my sister, Jb 17:14
if my father and **m** abandon me, Ps 27:10
grief, like one mourning a **m**. Ps 35:14
sinful when my **m** conceived me. Ps 51:5
her⌋ the joyful **m** of children. Ps 113:9
little weaned child with its **m**; Ps 131:2
tender and precious to my **m**, Pr 4:3
foolish son, heartache to his **m**. Pr 10:1
a foolish one despises his **m**. Pr 15:20
evicts his **m** is a disgraceful Pr 19:26
Whoever curses his father or **m**— Pr 20:20
despise your **m** when she is old. Pr 23:22
Let your father and **m** have joy, Pr 23:25
robs his father or **m** and says, Pr 28:24
himself is a disgrace to his **m**. Pr 29:15
father and does not bless its **m**. Pr 30:11
and despises obedience to a **m**, Pr 30:17
an oracle that his **m** taught him: Pr 31:1
crown his **m** placed on him the Sg 3:11
she is the favorite of her **m**, Sg 6:9
the house of my **m** who taught me. Sg 8:2
There your **m** conceived you; Sg 8:5
how to call out father or **m**, Is 8:4
or to ⌊his⌋ **m**: What are you Is 45:10
and your **m** was put away because Is 50:1
As a **m** comforts her son, so I Is 66:13
Say to the king and the queen **m**: Jr 13:18
against the **m** of young men Jr 15:8
The **m** of seven grew faint; Jr 15:9
Woe is me, my **m**, that you gave Jr 15:10
⌊the loss of⌋ his father or **m**. Jr 16:7
The day my **m** bore me—let it Jr 20:14
so that my **m** might have been Jr 20:17
you and the **m** who gave birth Jr 22:26
Jeconiah, the queen **m**, the court Jr 29:2
your **m** will be utterly Jr 50:12
an Amorite and your **m** a Hittite. Ezk 16:3
Like **m**, like daughter. Ezk 16:44
You are the daughter of your **m**, Ezk 16:45
Your **m** was a Hittite and your Ezk 16:45
What was your **m**? A lioness! She Ezk 19:2
Your **m** was like a vine in your Ezk 19:10
Father and **m** are treated with Ezk 22:7
women, daughters of the same **m**, Ezk 23:2
for a father, a **m**, a son, a Ezk 44:25
Rebuke your **m**; rebuke ⌊her⌋. For Hs 2:2
For their **m** is promiscuous; Hs 2:5
And I will destroy your **m**. Hs 4:5
a daughter opposes her **m**, and a Mc 7:6
father and his **m** who bore him Zch 13:3
father and his **m** who bore him Zch 13:3
His **m** Mary had been engaged Mt 1:18
saw the child with Mary His **m**, Mt 2:11
child and His **m**, flee to Egypt, Mt 2:13
child and His **m** during the night Mt 2:14
child and His **m** and go to the Mt 2:20
the child and His **m**, and entered Mt 2:21
a daughter against her **m**, a Mt 10:35
loves father or **m** more than Me Mt 10:37
suddenly His **m** and brothers were Mt 12:46
Your **m** and Your brothers are Mt 12:47
is My **m** and who are My brothers? Mt 12:48
Here are My **m** and My brothers! Mt 12:49
is My brother and sister and **m**." Mt 12:50
Isn't His **m** called Mary, and His Mt 13:55
prompted by her **m**, she answered, Mt 14:8
girl, who carried it to her **m**. Mt 14:11
Honor your father and your **m**; Mt 15:4
of father or **m** must be put to Mt 15:4
Whoever tells his father or **m**, Mt 15:5
his father and **m** and be joined Mt 19:5
honor your father and your **m**; Mt 19:19
sisters, father or **m**, children, Mt 19:29
Then the **m** of Zebedee's sons Mt 20:20
Mary the **m** of James and Joseph, Mt 27:56
and the **m** of Zebedee's sons. Mt 27:56
His **m** and His brothers came, Mk 3:31
Look, Your **m**, Your brothers, Mk 3:32
"Who are My **m** and My brothers?" Mk 3:33
Here are My **m** and My brothers! Mk 3:34
is My brother and sister and **m**." Mk 3:35
child's father, **m**, and those who Mk 5:40
she went out and said to her **m**, Mk 6:24
Then the girl gave it to her **m**. Mk 6:28
Honor your father and your **m**; Mk 7:10
of father or **m** must be put to Mk 7:10
'If a man tells his father or **m**: Mk 7:11
do anything for his father or **m**. Mk 7:12
his father and **m** and be joined Mk 10:7
honor your father and **m**." Mk 10:19
or sisters, **m** or father, Mk 10:29
Mary the **m** of James the younger Mk 15:40
and Mary the **m** of Joses were Mk 15:47
Magdalene, Mary the **m** of James, Mk 16:1
the **m** of my Lord should come Lk 1:43
But his **m** responded, "No! Lk 1:60
His father and **m** were amazed at Lk 2:33
them and told His **m** Mary: Lk 2:34
and His **m** said to Him, "Son, Lk 2:48

His **m** kept all these things in Lk 2:51
and Jesus gave him to his **m**. Lk 7:15
Then His **m** and brothers came to Lk 8:19
Your **m** and Your brothers are Lk 8:20
My **m** and My brothers are those Lk 8:21
and the child's father and **m**. Lk 8:51
against father, **m** against Lk 12:53
against **m**, mother-in-law Lk 12:53
not hate his own father and **m**, Lk 14:26
honor your father and **m**." Lk 18:20
Joanna, Mary the **m** of James, and Lk 24:10
Jesus' **m** was there, and Jn 2:1
out, Jesus' **m** told Him, "They Jn 2:3
His **m** told the servants. Jn 2:5
with His **m**, His brothers, Jn 2:12
whose father and **m** we know? Jn 6:42
the cross of Jesus were His **m**, Jn 19:25
Jesus saw His **m** and the disciple Jn 19:26
said to His **m**, "Woman, here is Jn 19:26
the disciple, "Here is your **m**." Jn 19:27
including Mary the **m** of Jesus, Ac 1:14
of Mary, the **m** of John Mark, Ac 12:12
also his **m**—and mine. Rm 16:13
above is free, and she is our **m**. Gl 4:26
his father and **m** and be joined Eph 5:31
your father and **m**—which is the Eph 6:2
as a nursing **m** nurtures her own 1Th 2:7
then in your **m** Eunice, and that 2Tm 1:5
without father, **m**, or genealogy, Heb 7:3
THE **M** OF PROSTITUTES Rv 17:5

MOTHER'S *(74)*

and told her **m** household about Gn 24:28
comforted after his **m** ⌊death⌋. Gn 24:67
may your **m** sons bow down to you Gn 27:29
house of Bethuel, your **m** father. Gn 28:2
of Laban, your **m** brother. Gn 28:2
Benjamin, his **m** son, he asked, Gn 43:29
the only one of his **m** sons left, Gn 44:20
boil a young goat in its **m** milk. Ex 23:19
a young goat in its **m** milk." Ex 34:26
father's daughter or your **m**, Lv 18:9
intercourse with your **m** sister, Lv 18:13
she is your **m** close relative. Lv 18:13
daughter or his **m** daughter, Lv 20:17
with your **m** sister or your Lv 20:19
His **m** name was Shelomith, a Lv 24:11
he comes out of his **m** womb." Nm 12:12
boil a young goat in its **m** milk. Dt 14:21
daughter or his **m** daughter.' Dt 27:22
to his **m** brothers at Shechem Jdg 9:1
His **m** relatives spoke all these Jdg 9:3
of you go back to your **m** home. Ru 1:8
widowed **m** name was Zeruah. 1Kg 11:26
Rehoboam's **m** name was 1Kg 14:21
His **m** name was Naamah the 1Kg 14:31
His **m** name was Maacah daughter 1Kg 15:2
His **m** name was Azubah daughter 1Kg 22:42
His **m** name was Athaliah, 2Kg 8:26
sons and the queen **m** sons." 2Kg 10:13
His **m** name was Zibiah, who was 2Kg 12:1
His **m** name was Jehoaddan and 2Kg 14:2
His **m** name was Jecoliah; 2Kg 15:2
His **m** name was Jerusha daughter 2Kg 15:33
His **m** name was Abi daughter of 2Kg 18:2
His **m** name was Hephzibah. 2Kg 21:1
His **m** name was Meshullemeth 2Kg 21:19
His **m** name was Jedidah the 2Kg 22:1
m name was Hamutal daughter 2Kg 23:31
m name was Zebidah daughter 2Kg 23:36
m name was Nehushta daughter 2Kg 24:8
m name was Hamutal daughter 2Kg 24:18
Rehoboam's **m** name was 2Ch 12:13
His **m** name was Micaiah daughter 2Ch 13:2
His **m** name was Azubah daughter 2Ch 20:31
His **m** name was Athaliah, 2Ch 22:2
His **m** name was Zibiah; 2Ch 24:1
His **m** name was Jehoaddan; 2Ch 25:1
His **m** name was Jecoliah; 2Ch 26:3
His **m** name was Jerushah daughter 2Ch 27:1
His **m** name was Abijah daughter 2Ch 29:1
Naked I came from my **m** womb, Jb 1:21
shut the doors of my ⌊**m**⌋ womb, Jb 3:10
me secure while at my **m** breast. Ps 22:9
been my God from my **m** womb. Ps 22:10
brother, slandering your **m** son. Ps 50:20
and a foreigner to my **m** sons Ps 69:8
You took me from my **m** womb. Ps 71:6
do not let his **m** sin be blotted Ps 109:14
knit me together in my **m** womb. Ps 139:13
don't reject your **m** teaching, Pr 1:8
don't reject your **m** teaching. Pr 6:20
As he came from his **m** womb, Ec 5:15
My **m** sons were angry with me; Sg 1:6
I brought him to my **m** house— Sg 3:4
one who nursed at my **m** breasts, Sg 8:1
me while I was in my **m** womb. Is 49:1
Where is your **m** divorce Is 50:1
His **m** name was Hamutal daughter Jr 52:1
born that way from their **m** womb, Mt 19:12
while still in his **m** womb. Lk 1:15
He was his **m** only son, and she Lk 7:12
Can he enter his **m** womb a second Jn 3:4
His mother, His **m** sister, Mary Jn 19:25
lame from his **m** womb was carried Ac 3:2
who from my **m** womb set me apart Gl 1:15

MOTHER-IN-LAW *(18)*

the one who sleeps with his **m**.' Dt 27:23
kissed her **m**, but Ruth clung Ru 1:14
have done for your **m** since your Ru 2:11
where her **m** saw what she had Ru 2:18
Then her **m** said to her, "Where Ru 2:19
Ruth told her **m** about the men Ru 2:19
And she lived with her **m**. Ru 2:23
Ruth's **m** Naomi said to her, Ru 3:1
everything her **m** had instructed Ru 3:6
She went to her **m**, Naomi, who Ru 3:16
go back to your **m** empty-handed.' Ru 3:17
daughter-in-law is against her **m**; Mc 7:6
He saw his **m** lying in bed with a Mt 8:14
a daughter-in-law against her **m**; Mt 10:35
Simon's **m** was lying in bed with Mk 1:30
Simon's **m** was suffering from a Lk 4:38
m against her daughter-in-law, Lk 12:53
and daughter-in-law against **m**." Lk 12:53

MOTHER-OF-PEARL *(1)*

feldspar, marble, **m**, and Est 1:6

MOTHERS *(14)*

and attack me, the **m**, and their Gn 32:11
with their **m** for seven days, Ex 22:30
and their queens your nursing **m**. Is 49:23
concerning the **m** who bear them Jr 16:3
They cry out to their **m**: Lm 2:12
away in the arms of their **m**. Lm 2:12
fatherless; our **m** are widows. Lm 5:3
M will be dashed to pieces along Hs 10:14
and nursing **m** in those days! Mt 24:19
and sisters, **m** and children, Mk 10:30
and nursing **m** in those days! Mk 13:17
and nursing **m** in those days, Lk 21:23
who kill their fathers and **m**, 1Tm 1:9
older women as **m**, and with all 1Tm 5:2

MOTIONED *(5)*

So they **m** to his father to find Lk 1:62
Simon Peter **m** to him to find out Jn 13:24
Paul **m** with his hand and spoke: Ac 13:16
the steps and **m** with his hand to Ac 21:40
the governor **m** to him to speak, Ac 24:10

MOTIONING *(2)*

M to them with his hand to be Ac 12:17
So **m** with his hand, Alexander Ac 19:33

MOTIVATED *(1)*

God had **m**—prepared to go Ezr 1:5

MOTIVES *(5)*

but the LORD weighs the **m**. Pr 16:2
but the LORD evaluates the **m**. Pr 21:2
he brings it with ulterior **m**! Pr 21:27
whether out of false **m** or true, Php 1:18
or had greedy **m**—God is our 1Th 2:5

MOUND *(15)*

they took stones and made a **m**, Gn 31:46
mound, then ate there by the **m**. Gn 31:46
named the **m** Jegar-sahadutha Gn 31:47
This **m** is a witness between me Gn 31:48
Look at this **m** and the marker I Gn 31:51
This **m** is a witness and the Gn 31:52
not pass beyond this **m** to you, Gn 31:52
beyond this **m** and this marker Gn 31:52
must remain a **m** of ruins forever Dt 13:16
piled a huge **m** of stones over 2Sm 18:17
Your waist is a **m** of wheat Sg 7:2
city will be rebuilt on its **m**; Jr 30:18
It will become a desolate **m**, Jr 49:2
built yourself a **m** and made Ezk 16:24
building your **m** at the head of Ezk 16:31

MOUNDS *(5)*

stood on their **m** except Hazor, Jos 11:13
to life from the **m** of rubble?" Neh 4:2
pile her up like **m** of grain and Jr 50:26
will level your **m** and tear down Ezk 16:39
heaps of slain, **m** of corpses, Nah 3:3

MOUNT *(146)*

and overtook him at **M** Gilead. Gn 31:23
will come down on **M** Sinai in the Ex 19:11
M Sinai was completely enveloped Ex 19:18
The LORD came down on **M** Sinai, Ex 19:20
people cannot come up **M** Sinai, Ex 19:23
of the LORD settled on **M** Sinai, Ex 24:16
M them, surrounded with gold Ex 28:11
speaking with Moses on **M** Sinai, Ex 31:18
jewelry from **M** Horeb ⌊onward⌋. Ex 33:6
Come up **M** Sinai in the morning Ex 34:2
hand, he climbed **M** Sinai, just Ex 34:4
Moses descended from **M** Sinai— Ex 34:29
LORD had told him on **M** Sinai. Ex 34:32
with gemstones to **m** on the ephod Ex 35:9
and gemstones to **m** on the ephod Ex 35:27
to it in order to **m** ⌊it⌋ on the Ex 39:31
Moses on **M** Sinai on the day Lv 7:38
LORD spoke to Moses on **M** Sinai: Lv 25:1
through Moses on **M** Sinai. Lv 26:46
for the Israelites on **M** Sinai. Lv 27:34
spoke with Moses on **M** Sinai. Nm 3:1
community came to **M** Hor. Nm 20:22
and Aaron at **M** Hor on the border Nm 20:23
Eleazar and bring them up **M** Hor. Nm 20:25
they climbed **M** Hor in the sight Nm 20:27
they set out from **M** Hor by way Nm 21:4
⌊image⌋ and **m** it on a pole. Nm 21:8
established at **M** Sinai for a Nm 28:6
and camped at **M** Shepher. Nm 33:23
departed from **M** Shepher and Nm 33:24
and camped at **M** Hor on the edge Nm 33:37
priest climbed **M** Hor and died Nm 33:38
years old when he died on **M** Hor. Nm 33:39
departed from **M** Hor and camped Nm 33:41
Sea draw a line to **M** Hor; Nm 34:7
from **M** Hor draw a line to the Nm 34:8
Kadesh-barnea by way of **M** Seir. Dt 1:2
Arnon Valley as far as **M** Hermon, Dt 3:8
Arnon Valley as far as **M** Sion Dt 4:48
blessing at **M** Gerizim and the Dt 11:29
Gerizim and the curse at **M** Ebal. Dt 11:29
set up these stones on **M** Ebal, Dt 27:4
will stand on **M** Gerizim to bless Dt 27:12
will stand on **M** Ebal to deliver Dt 27:13
Go up **M** Nebo in the Abarim Dt 32:49
Aaron died on **M** Hor and was Dt 32:50
on them⌋ from **M** Paran and came Dt 33:2
the plains of Moab to **M** Nebo, Dt 34:1
an altar on **M** Ebal to the LORD Jos 8:30
in front of **M** Gerizim and half Jos 8:33
and half in front of **M** Ebal, Jos 8:33
from **M** Halak, which ascends to Jos 11:17
Lebanon at the foot of **M** Hermon. Jos 11:17
the Arnon Valley to **M** Hermon, Jos 12:1
He ruled over **M** Hermon, Salecah, Jos 12:5
valley of Lebanon to **M** Halak, Jos 12:7
from Baal-gad below **M** Hermon to Jos 13:5
all **M** Hermon, and all Jos 13:11
went to the cities of **M** Ephron, Jos 15:9
westward from Baalah to **M** Seir, Jos 15:10
the northern slope of **M** Jearim Jos 15:10
proceeded to **M** Baalah, went to Jos 15:11
of Ephraim north of **M** Gaash. Jos 24:30
of Ephraim, north of **M** Gaash. Jdg 2:9
mountains from **M** Baal-hermon as Jdg 3:3
deploy ⌊the troops⌋ on **M** Tabor, Jdg 4:6
of Abinoam had gone up **M** Tabor. Jdg 4:12
came down from **M** Tabor with Jdg 4:14
back and leave **M** Gilead.'" Jdg 7:3
climbed to the top of **M** Gerizim, Jdg 9:7
with him went up to **M** Zalmon. Jdg 9:48
Many were killed on **M** Gilboa. 1Sm 31:1
his three sons dead on **M** Gilboa. 1Sm 31:8
"I happened to be on **M** Gilboa," 2Sm 1:6
the slope of the **M** of Olives, 2Sm 15:30
Israel to meet me at **M** Carmel, 1Kg 18:19
the prophets at **M** Carmel. 1Kg 18:20
there Elisha went to **M** Carmel, 2Kg 2:25
to the man of God at **M** Carmel. 2Kg 4:25
and survivors from **M** Zion. 2Kg 19:31
south of the **M** of Destruction, 2Kg 23:13

as their leaders to **M** Seir. 1Ch 4:42
that is, Senir or **M** Hermon). 1Ch 5:23
and were killed on **M** Gilboa. 1Ch 10:1
and his sons dead on **M** Gilboa. 1Ch 10:8
in Jerusalem on **M** Moriah where 2Ch 3:1
Then Abijah stood on **M** Zemaraim 2Ch 13:4
and ⌊the inhabitants of⌋ **M** Seir. 2Ch 20:10
inhabitants of⌋ **M** Seir who came 2Ch 20:22
the inhabitants of **M** Seir and 2Ch 20:23
came down on **M** Sinai, and spoke Neh 9:13
peaks of Hermon, from **M** Mizar. Ps 42:6
M Zion on the slopes of the Ps 48:2
M Zion is glad. The towns of Ps 48:11
M Bashan is God's towering Ps 68:15
M Bashan is a mountain of many Ps 68:15
⌊Remember⌋ **M** Zion where You Ps 74:2
tribe of Judah, **M** Zion, which He Ps 78:68
in the LORD are like **M** Zion. Ps 125:1
goats streaming down **M** Gilead. Sg 4:1
head crowns you like **M** Carmel, Sg 7:5
entire site of **M** Zion and over Is 4:5
of Hosts who dwells on **M** Zion. Is 8:18
His work against **M** Zion and Is 10:12
will sit on the **m** of the ⌊gods'⌋ Is 14:13
by rivers—to **M** Zion, the place Is 18:7
reign as king on **M** Zion in Is 24:23
up as ⌊He did⌋ at **M** Perazim. Is 28:21
who go to battle against **M** Zion. Is 29:8
to fight on **M** Zion and on its Is 31:4
and survivors from **M** Zion. Is 37:32
malice from **M** Ephraim. Jr 4:15
the temple **m** a forested hill. Jr 26:18
the horses; **m** the steeds; take Jr 46:4
because of **M** Zion, which lies Lm 5:18
your face toward **M** Seir and Ezk 35:2
I am against you, **M** Seir. Ezk 35:3
I will make **M** Seir a desolate Ezk 35:7
a desolation, **M** Seir, and ⌊so Ezk 35:15
escape for those on **M** Zion and Jl 2:32
will be a deliverance on **M** Zion, Ob 17
will ascend **M** Zion to rule over Ob 21
of the temple **m** will be a Mc 3:12
over them in **M** Zion from this Mc 4:7
the Holy One from **M** Paran. Hab 3:3
will stand on the **M** of Olives, Zch 14:4
The **M** of Olives will be split in Zch 14:4
the Jordan. The Sermon on the **M** Mt 4:25
to Bethphage at the **M** of Olives, Mt 21:1
was sitting on the **M** of Olives, Mt 24:3
went out to the **M** of Olives. Mt 26:30
Bethany near the **M** of Olives, Mk 11:1
sitting on the **M** of Olives Mk 13:3
went out to the **M** of Olives. Mk 14:26
place called the **M** of Olives, Lk 19:29
the path down the **M** of Olives, Lk 19:37
what is called the **M** of Olives. Lk 21:37
way as usual to the **M** of Olives, Lk 22:39
Jesus went to the **M** of Olives. Jn 8:1
from the **m** called Olive Grove Ac 1:12
to him in the desert of **M** Sinai, Ac 7:30
who spoke to him on **M** Sinai, Ac 7:38
One is from **M** Sinai and bears Gl 4:24
Now Hagar is **M** Sinai in Arabia Gl 4:25
you have come to **M** Zion, to the Heb 12:22
and there on **M** Zion stood the Rv 14:1

MOUNTAIN *(186)*

be provided on the LORD's **m**." Gn 22:14
on the **m** and invited his Gn 31:54
and spent the night on the **m**. Gn 31:54
you the one **m** slope that I took Gn 48:22
and came to Horeb, the **m** of God. Ex 3:1
will all worship God at this **m**." Ex 3:12
met him at the **m** of God and Ex 4:27
plant them on the **m** of Your Ex 15:17
he was camped at the **m** of God. Ex 18:5
camped there in front of the **m**. Ex 19:2
Moses went up ⌊the **m**⌋ to God, Ex 19:3
LORD called to him from the **m**: Ex 19:3
all around the ⌊**m**⌋ and say: Ex 19:12
go up on the **m** or touch its base Ex 19:12
who touches the **m** will be put to Ex 19:12
blast, they may go up the **m**." Ex 19:13
down from the **m** to the people Ex 19:14
thick cloud on the **m**, and a loud Ex 19:16
they stood at the foot of the **m**. Ex 19:17
and the whole **m** shook violently. Ex 19:18
Sinai, at the top of the **m**. Ex 19:20
Moses to the top of the **m**, Ex 19:20
around the **m** and consider it Ex 19:23
and the **m** ⌊surrounded by⌋ smoke. Ex 20:18
of Israel at the base of the **m**. Ex 24:4
up to Me on the **m** and stay there Ex 24:12
and went up the **m** of God. Ex 24:13
Moses went up the **m**, the cloud Ex 24:15
the cloud as he went up the **m**, Ex 24:18
remained on the **m** 40 days and 40 Ex 24:18
you have been shown on the **m**. Ex 25:40
you have been shown on the **m**. Ex 26:30
as it was shown to you on the **m**. Ex 27:8
in coming down from the **m**, Ex 32:1
and went down the **m** with the two Ex 32:15
them at the base of the **m**. Ex 32:19
must be seen anywhere on the **m**. Ex 34:3
to graze in front of that **m**." Ex 34:3
hands as he descended the **m**— Ex 34:29
set out from the **m** of the LORD Nm 10:33
died there on top of the **m**. Nm 20:28
Eleazar came down from the **m**. Nm 20:28
Go up this **m** of the Abarim Nm 27:12
stayed at this **m** long enough. Dt 1:6
and stood at the base of the **m**, Dt 4:11
a **m** blazing with fire into the Dt 4:11
to face from the fire on the **m**. Dt 5:4
fire and did not go up the **m**. Dt 5:5
and thick darkness on the **m**; Dt 5:22
and while the **m** was blazing with Dt 5:23
When I went up the **m** to receive Dt 9:9
I stayed on the **m** 40 days and 40 Dt 9:9
to you from the fire on the **m**. Dt 9:10
So I went back down the **m**, Dt 9:15
that came down from the **m**. Dt 9:21
to Me on the **m** and make a wooden Dt 10:1
and climbed the **m** with the two Dt 10:3
to you on the **m** from the fire. Dt 10:4
went back down the **m** and placed Dt 10:5
I stayed on the **m** 40 days and 40 Dt 10:10
the antelope, and the **m** sheep. Dt 14:5
die on the **m** that you go up, Dt 32:50
They summon the peoples to a **m**; Dt 33:19
to the top of the **m** overlooking Jdg 16:3
one side of the **m** and David and 1Sm 23:26
the donkey down a **m** pass hidden 1Sm 25:20
on top of the **m** at a distance; 1Sm 26:13
of him from the side of the **m**. 2Sm 13:34
God, my **m** where I seek refuge. 2Sm 22:3
nights to Horeb, the **m** of God. 1Kg 19:8
and stand on the **m** in the LORD's 1Kg 19:11
up to the man of God at the **m**, 2Kg 4:27
saw that the **m** was covered with 2Kg 6:17
he saw the tombs there on the **m**. 2Kg 23:16
had built on the **m** of the LORD's 2Ch 33:15
on their surrounding **m** shrines. 2Ch 34:6
as a **m** collapses and crumbles Jb 14:18
Drenched by **m** rains, they huddle Jb 24:8
you know when **m** goats give birth Jb 39:1
My King on Zion, My holy **m**." Ps 2:6
He answers me from His holy **m**. Ps 3:4
Escape to the **m** like a bird! Ps 11:1
Who can live on Your holy **m**? Ps 15:1
my God, my **m** where I seek refuge Ps 18:2
may ascend the **m** of the LORD? Ps 24:3
made me stand like a strong **m**; Ps 30:7
for me, a **m** fortress to save Ps 31:2
is like the highest **m**; Ps 36:6
them bring me to Your holy **m**, Ps 43:3
the city of our God. His holy **m**, Ps 48:1
Bashan is God's towering **m**; Ps 68:15
Bashan is a **m** of many peaks. Ps 68:15
gaze with envy, you **m** peaks, at Ps 68:16
at the **m** God desired for His Ps 68:16
the **m** His right hand acquired. Ps 78:54
hand, and the **m** peaks are His. Ps 95:4
bow in worship at His holy **m**, Ps 99:9
make my way to the **m** of myrrh Sg 4:6
last days the **m** of the LORD's Is 2:2
us go up to the **m** of the LORD, Is 2:3
his fist at the **m** of Daughter Is 10:32
or destroy on My entire holy **m**, Is 11:9
Lift up a banner on a barren **m**. Is 13:2
I will tread him down on My **m**. Is 14:25
desert to the **m** of Daughter Zion Is 16:1
for all the peoples on this **m**— Is 25:6
On this **m** ⌊He⌋ will destroy the Is 25:7
power will rest on this **m**. Is 25:10
LORD at Jerusalem on the holy **m**. Is 27:13
on every high **m** and every raised Is 30:25
going up to the **m** of the LORD, Is 30:29
and every **m** and hill will be Is 40:4
of good news, go up on a high **m**. Is 40:9
them to My holy **m** and let them Is 56:7
your bed on a high and lofty **m**; Is 57:7
the land and possess My holy **m**. Is 57:13
forget My holy **m**, who prepare Is 65:11
or destroy on My entire holy **m**," Is 65:25
to My holy **m** Jerusalem, says Is 66:20
down on every **m** and hill and out Jr 16:16
righteous settlement, holy **m**. Jr 31:23
you who occupy the **m** summit, Jr 49:16
have wandered from **m** to hill; Jr 50:6
you, devastating **m**—⌊this is⌋ Jr 51:25
turn you into a burned-out **m**. Jr 51:25
stood on the **m** east of the city Ezk 11:23
plant ⌊it⌋ on a high towering **m**. Ezk 17:22
Israel's high **m** so that it may Ezk 17:23
not eat at the **m** ⌊shrines⌋ or Ezk 18:6
the son eats at the **m** ⌊shrines⌋, Ezk 18:11
not eat at the **m** ⌊shrines⌋ or Ezk 18:15
For on My holy **m**, Israel's high Ezk 20:40
Israel's high **m**"—the Ezk 20:40
in you eat at the **m** ⌊shrines⌋; Ezk 22:9
You were on the holy **m** of God; Ezk 28:14
in disgrace from the **m** of God, Ezk 28:16
set me down on a very high **m**. Ezk 40:2
on top of the **m** will be Ezk 43:12
became a great **m** and filled the Dn 2:35
off from the **m** without a hand Dn 2:45
city Jerusalem, Your holy **m**; Dn 9:16
the holy **m** of my God— Dn 9:20
sea and the beautiful holy **m**, Dn 11:45
sound the alarm on My holy **m**! Jl 2:1
who dwells in Zion, My holy **m**. Jl 3:17
as you have drunk on My holy **m**, Ob 16
last days the **m** of the LORD's Mc 4:1
us go up to the **m** of the LORD, Mc 4:2
sea to sea and **m** to mountain. Mc 7:12
sea to sea and mountain to **m**. Mc 7:12
enables me to walk on **m** heights! Hab 3:19
again be haughty on My holy **m**. Zph 3:11
'What are you, great **m**? Zch 4:7
the **m** of the LORD of Hosts, Zch 8:3
LORD of Hosts, and the Holy **M**." Zch 8:3
so that half the **m** will move to Zch 14:4
You will flee by My **m** valley, Zch 14:5
to a very high **m** and showed Him Mt 4:8
went up on the **m**, and after He Mt 5:1
When He came down from the **m**, Mt 8:1
went up on the **m** by Himself to Mt 14:23
He went up on a **m** and sat there, Mt 15:29
up on a high **m** by themselves. Mt 17:1
were coming down from the **m**, Mt 17:9
tell this **m**, 'Move from here Mt 17:20
but even if you tell this **m**, Mt 21:21
the **m** where Jesus had directed Mt 28:16
He went up the **m** and summoned Mk 3:13
He went away to the **m** to pray. Mk 6:46
up on a high **m** by themselves to Mk 9:2
were coming down from the **m**, Mk 9:9
If anyone says to this **m**, Mk 11:23
every **m** and hill will be made Lk 3:5
went out to the **m** to pray and Lk 6:12
and went up on the **m** to pray. Lk 9:28
when they came down from the **m**, Lk 9:37
Our fathers worshiped on this **m**, Jn 4:20
neither on this **m** nor in Jn 4:21
Jesus went up a **m** and sat down Jn 6:3
again to the **m** by Himself. Jn 6:15
that was shown to you on the **m**. Heb 8:5
if even an animal touches the **m**, Heb 12:20
we were with Him on the holy **m**. 2Pt 1:18
and every **m** and island was moved Rv 6:14
like a great **m** ablaze with fire Rv 8:8
a great and high **m** and showed me Rv 21:10

MOUNTAINS *(162)*

all the high **m** under the whole Gn 7:19
The **m** were covered as the waters Gn 7:20
the month, on the **m** of Ararat. Gn 8:4
the tops of the **m** were visible. Gn 8:5
the Horites in the **m** of Seir, Gn 14:6
but the rest fled to the **m**. Gn 14:10
Run to the **m**, or you will be Gn 19:17
But I can't run to the **m**; Gn 19:19
lived in the **m** along with his Gn 19:30
on one of the **m** I will tell you Gn 22:2
Edom) lived in the **m** of Seir. Gn 36:8

the Edomites in the **m** of Seir. Gn 36:9
kill them in the **m** and wipe them Ex 32:12
of Moab, from the eastern **m**: Nm 23:7
is a land of **m** and valleys, Dt 11:11
these **m** across the Jordan, Dt 11:30
on the high **m**, on the hills, Dt 12:2
the foundations of the **m**. Dt 32:22
of the ancient **m** and the bounty Dt 33:15
in the Lebanese **m** from Mount Jdg 3:3
The **m** melted before the LORD, Jdg 5:5
places for themselves in the **m**, Jdg 6:2
the tops of the **m** to ambush and Jdg 9:25
shadows of the **m** look like men Jdg 9:36
through the **m** with my friends Jdg 11:37
as she wandered through the **m**. Jdg 11:38
pursues a partridge in the **m**." 1Sm 26:20
M of Gilboa, let no dew or rain 2Sm 1:21
80,000 stonecutters in the **m**, 1Kg 5:15
tearing at the **m** and was 1Kg 19:11
is a god of the **m** and not a god 1Kg 20:28
him on one of the **m** or into one 2Kg 2:16
gone up to the heights of the **m**, 2Kg 19:23
as swift as gazelles on the **m**. 1Ch 12:8
men as stonecutters in the **m**, 2Ch 2:2
80,000 stonecutters in the **m**, 2Ch 2:18
He removes **m** without their Jb 9:5
and transforms the **m** at ⌊their⌋ Jb 28:9
It roams the **m** for its Jb 39:8
foundations of the **m** trembled; Ps 18:7
trembles and the **m** topple into Ps 46:2
foam and the **m** quake with its Ps 46:3
I know every bird of the **m**, Ps 50:11
establish the **m** by Your power, Ps 65:6
the **m** bring prosperity to the Ps 72:3
it wave on the tops of the **m**. Ps 72:16
coming down⌋ from the **m** of prey. Ps 76:4
The **m** were covered by its shade, Ps 80:10
as a flame blazes through **m**, Ps 83:14
His foundation is on the holy **m**. Ps 87:1
Before the **m** were born, before Ps 90:2
The **m** melt like wax at the Ps 97:5
let the **m** shout together for joy Ps 98:8
the waters stood above the **m**. Ps 104:6
m rose and valleys sank—to the Ps 104:8
they flow between the **m**. Ps 104:10
He waters the **m** from His palace; Ps 104:13
The high **m** are for the wild Ps 104:18
He touches the **m**, and they pour Ps 104:32
The **m** skipped like rams, the Ps 114:4
M, that you skipped like rams? Ps 114:6
I raise my eyes toward the **m**. Ps 121:1
Jerusalem—the **m** surround her. Ps 125:2
Hermon falling on the **m** of Zion. Ps 133:3
the **m**, and they will smoke. Ps 144:5
m and all hills, fruit trees and Ps 148:9
forth before the **m** and hills Pr 8:25
leaping over the **m**, bounding Sg 2:8
a young stag on the divided **m**. Sg 2:17
from the **m** of the leopards. Sg 4:8
a young stag on the **m** of spices. Sg 8:14
at the top of the **m** and will be Is 2:2
all the high **m**, against all Is 2:14
the **m** quaked, and their corpses Is 5:25
tumult on the **m**, like that of a Is 13:4
a banner is raised on the **m**, Is 18:3
shouting and crying to the **m**; Is 22:5
the **m** flow with their blood. Is 34:3
gone up to the heights of the **m**, Is 37:24
or weighed the **m** in a balance Is 40:12
You will thresh **m** and pulverize Is 41:15
I will lay waste **m** and hills, Is 42:15
out into singing, **m**, forest, and Is 44:23
will make all My **m** into a road, Is 49:11
M break into joyful shouts! Is 49:13
beautiful on the **m** are the feet Is 52:7
Though the **m** move and the hills Is 54:10
the **m** and the hills will break Is 55:12
so that **m** would quake at Your Is 64:1
and the **m** quaked at Your Is 64:3
incense on the **m** and reproached Is 65:7
and heirs to My **m** from Judah; Is 65:9
from the **m**, but the salvation Jr 3:23
I looked at the **m**, and they were Jr 4:24
weeping and a lament over the **m**, Jr 9:10
feet stumble on the **m** at dusk. Jr 13:16
My **m** in the countryside. Jr 17:3
again on the **m** of Samaria; Jr 31:5
among the **m** and like Carmel Jr 46:18
them the wrong way in the **m**. Jr 50:6
us over the **m** and ambushed us Lm 4:19
your face toward the **m** of Israel Ezk 6:2
M of Israel, hear the word of Ezk 6:3
GOD says to the **m** and the hills, Ezk 6:3
be panic on the **m** and not Ezk 7:7
and live on the **m** like doves Ezk 7:16
be heard on the **m** of Israel. Ezk 19:9
limbs fell on the **m** and in every Ezk 31:12
your flesh on the **m** and fill the Ezk 32:5
of your blood, ⌊even⌋ to the **m**; Ezk 32:6
The **m** of Israel will become Ezk 33:28
on all the **m** and every high Ezk 34:6
them on the **m** of Israel, Ezk 34:13
will be on Israel's lofty **m**. Ezk 34:14
rich pasture on the **m** of Israel. Ezk 34:14
will fill its **m** with the slain; Ezk 35:8
uttered against the **m** of Israel, Ezk 35:12
prophesy to the **m** of Israel and Ezk 36:1
M of Israel, hear the word of Ezk 36:1
therefore, **m** of Israel, hear the Ezk 36:4
GOD says to the **m** and hills, Ezk 36:4
and say to the **m** and hills, Ezk 36:6
You, **m** of Israel, will put forth Ezk 36:8
land, on the **m** of Israel, and Ezk 37:22
many peoples to the **m** of Israel, Ezk 38:8
The **m** will be thrown down, Ezk 38:20
sword against him on all My **m** Ezk 38:21
you against the **m** of Israel. Ezk 39:2
will fall on the **m** of Israel. Ezk 39:4
great feast on the **m** of Israel; Ezk 39:17
will say to the **m**, "Cover us!" Hs 10:8
the dawn spreading over the **m**; Jl 2:2
They bound on the tops of the **m**. Jl 2:5
In that day the **m** will drip with Jl 3:18
Assemble on the **m** of Samaria and Am 3:9
who forms the **m**, creates the Am 4:13
The **m** will drip with sweet wine, Am 9:13
to the foundations of the **m**; Jnh 2:6
The **m** will melt beneath Him, Mc 1:4
at the top of the **m** and will be Mc 4:1
plead ⌊your⌋ case before the **m**, Mc 6:1
you **m** and enduring foundations Mc 6:2
The **m** quake before Him, and the Nah 1:5
Look to the **m**—the feet of one Nah 1:15
across the **m** with no one to Nah 3:18
The age-old **m** break apart; Hab 3:6
The **m** see You and shudder; Hab 3:10
coming from between two **m**. Zch 6:1
And the **m** were made of bronze. Zch 6:1
valley of the **m** will extend to Zch 14:5
I turned his **m** into a wasteland, Mal 1:3
in Judea must flee to the **m**! Mt 24:16
tombs and in the **m** and cutting Mk 5:5
in Judea must flee to the **m**! Mk 13:14
in Judea must flee to the **m**! Lk 21:21
will begin to say to the **m**, Lk 23:30
that I can move **m**, but do not 1Co 13:2
in deserts, **m**, caves, and holes Heb 11:38
and among the rocks of the **m**. Rv 6:15
said to the **m** and to the rocks Rv 6:16
fled, and the **m** disappeared. Rv 16:20
heads are seven **m** on which the Rv 17:9

MOUNTAINSIDE *(1)*

like water cascading down a **m**. Mc 1:4

MOUNTAINTOP *(3)*

like a consuming fire on the **m**. Ex 24:17
and stand before Me on the **m**. Ex 34:2
solitary⌋ pole on a **m** or a Is 30:17

MOUNTAINTOPS *(5)*

are coming down from the **m**!" Jdg 9:36
woods and **m** that were abandoned Is 17:9
let them cry out from the **m**. Is 42:11
on all the **m**, and under every Ezk 6:13
sacrifice on the **m**, and they Hs 4:13

MOUNTED *(7)*

women got up, **m** the camels, Gn 24:61
Then they **m** the onyx stones Ex 39:6
They **m** four rows of gemstones on Ex 39:10
bronze snake and **m** it on a pole. Nm 21:9
the documents by **m** couriers, Est 8:10
you, gentle, and **m** on a donkey, Mt 21:5
The number of **m** troops was 200 Rv 9:16

MOUNTING *(4)*

gemstones for **m** on the ephod Ex 25:7
gemstones for **m**, and to carve Ex 31:5
gemstones for **m**, and to carve Ex 35:33
stones for⌋ **m**, antimony, stones 1Ch 29:2

MOUNTINGS *(1)*

Your **m** and settings were crafted Ezk 28:13

MOUNTS *(1)*

Also provide **m** so they can put Ac 23:24

MOURN *(51)*

went in to **m** for Sarah and to Gn 23:2
may **m** over that tragedy when the Lv 10:6
and **m** for her father and mother Dt 21:13
my friends and **m** my virginity." Jdg 11:37
are you going to **m** for Saul, 1Sm 16:1
Israel assembled to **m** for him, 1Sm 25:1
on sackcloth, and **m** over Abner." 2Sm 3:31
the city to **m** and to bury him. 1Kg 13:29
All Israel will **m** for him and 1Kg 14:13
your God. Do not **m** or weep." For Neh 8:9
one who comforts those who **m**. Jb 29:25
a time to **m** and a time to dance; Ec 3:4
her gates will lament and **m**; Is 3:26
M, you who are completely Is 16:7
Then the fishermen will **m**. Is 19:8
M, inhabitants of the coastland, Is 23:2
vengeance; to comfort all who **m**, Is 61:2
provide for those who **m** in Zion; Is 61:3
with her, all who **m** over her— Is 66:10
m and wail, for the LORD's Jr 4:8
of this, the earth will **m**; Jr 4:28
M ⌊as you would for⌋ an only son, Jr 6:26
dear people. I **m**; horror has Jr 8:21
and summon the women who **m**; Jr 9:17
will the land **m** and the grass Jr 12:4
the dead; do not **m** for him. Weep Jr 22:10
will not **m** for him, ⌊saying, Jr 22:18
They will not **m** for him, saying, Jr 22:18
M for him, all you surrounding Jr 48:17
roads to Zion **m**, for no one Lm 1:4
rejoice and the seller not **m**, Ezk 7:12
The king will **m**; the prince will Ezk 7:27
I made Lebanon **m** on account of Ezk 31:15
the people will **m** over it, Hs 10:5
are ministers of the LORD, **m**. Jl 1:9
the pastures of the shepherds **m**, Am 1:2
farmer will be called on to **m**, Am 5:16
quake and all who dwell in it **m**? Am 8:8
and all who dwell on it **m**; Am 9:5
jackals and **m** like ostriches. Mc 1:8
Should we **m** and fast in the Zch 7:3
will **m** for Him as one mourns Zch 12:10
The land will **m**, every family by Zch 12:12
are those who **m**, because they Mt 5:4
sang a lament, but you didn't **m**! Mt 11:17
the peoples of the earth will **m**; Mt 24:30
because you will **m** and weep. Lk 6:25
Be miserable and **m** and weep. Jms 4:9
of the earth will **m** over Him. Rv 1:7
will weep and **m** over her when Rv 18:9
will also weep and **m** over her, Rv 18:11

MOURNED *(20)*

and **m** for his son many days. Gn 37:34
the Egyptians **m** for him 70 days Gn 50:3
and Joseph **m** seven days for his Gn 50:10
they **m** and didn't put on their Ex 33:4
of Israel **m** for him 30 days Nm 20:29
her friends and **m** her virginity Jdg 11:38
Samuel **m** for Saul, and the LORD 1Sm 15:35
all Israel had **m** for him and 1Sm 28:3
They **m**, wept, and fasted until 2Sm 1:12
Uriah had died, she **m** for him. 2Sm 11:26
And David **m** for his son every 2Sm 13:37
own grave, and they **m** over him: 1Kg 13:30
and all Israel **m** for him, 1Kg 14:18
father Ephraim **m** a long time, 1Ch 7:22
and Jerusalem **m** for Josiah. 2Ch 35:24
m for a number of days, fasting Neh 1:4
m and fasted, but it brought me Ps 69:10
They will not be **m** or buried but Jr 16:4
They will not be **m**, gathered, or Jr 25:33
Stephen and **m** deeply over him. Ac 8:2

MOURNER *(1)*

provided for the **m** to comfort Jr 16:7

MOURNERS *(7)*

and **m** are lifted to safety. Jb 5:11
and **m** will walk around in the Ec 12:5
him and comfort him and his **m**, Is 57:18
mustache or eat the bread of **m**." Ezk 24:17
mustache or eat the bread of **m**. Ezk 24:22

will be like the bread of **m**; Hs 9:4
and professional **m** to wail. Am 5:16

MOURNFULLY *(2)*
you, and lament **m**, saying: Mc 2:4
and walking **m** before the LORD of Mal 3:14

MOURNING *(49)*
The days of **m** for my father are Gn 27:41
go down to Sheol to my son, **m**." Gn 37:35
When Judah had finished **m**, Gn 38:12
When the days of **m** were over, Gn 50:4
land saw the **m** at the threshing Gn 50:11
This is a solemn **m** on the part Gn 50:11
not eaten any of it while in **m**, Dt 26:14
of weeping and **m** for Moses came Dt 34:8
the time of **m** ended, David had 2Sm 11:27
told her, "Pretend to be in **m**: 2Sm 14:2
dress in **m** clothes and don't put 2Sm 14:2
who has been **m** for the dead for 2Sm 14:2
He's **m** over Absalom." 2Sm 19:1
was turned into **m** for all the 2Sm 19:2
because he was **m** over the Ezr 10:6
There was great **m** among the Est 4:3
and their **m** into a holiday. Est 9:22
is ⌊used⌋ for **m** and my flute for Jb 30:31
with grief, like one **m** a mother. Ps 35:14
all day long I go around in **m**. Ps 38:6
go to a house of **m** than to go to Ec 7:2
of the wise is in a house of **m**, Ec 7:4
and there will be **m** and crying, Is 29:2
your breasts ⌊in **m**⌋ for the Is 32:12
oil instead of **m**, and splendid Is 61:3
people⌋ are on the ground in **m**; Jr 14:2
house where a **m** feast is taking Jr 16:5
I will turn their **m** into joy, Jr 31:13
everyone is **m** because I have Jr 48:38
has multiplied **m** and lamentation Lm 2:5
our dancing has turned to **m**. Lm 5:15
of⌋ lamentation, **m**, and woe were Ezk 2:10
do not observe **m** rites for the Ezk 24:17
with deep anguish and bitter **m**. Ezk 27:31
they lament for you, **m** over you: Ezk 27:32
was **m** for three full weeks. Dn 10:2
⌊**m**⌋ for the husband of her youth. Jl 1:8
with fasting, weeping, and **m**. Jl 2:12
your feasts into **m** and all your Am 8:10
that grief like **m** for an only Am 8:10
On that day the **m** in Jerusalem Zch 12:11
great as the **m** of Hadad-rimmon Zch 12:11
and great **m**, Rachel weeping Mt 2:18
as they were **m** and weeping. Mk 16:10
was crying and **m** for her. Lk 8:52
women who were **m** and lamenting Lk 23:27
must change to **m** and your joy to Jms 4:9
of her torment, weeping and **m**, Rv 18:15
kept crying out, weeping, and **m**: Rv 18:19

MOURNS *(9)*
own body and **m** only for himself Jb 14:22
The earth **m** and withers; Is 24:4
new wine **m**; the vine withers. Is 24:7
The land **m** and withers; Is 33:9
It **m**, desolate, before Me. Jr 12:11
Judah **m**; her gates languish. Jr 14:2
the land **m** because of the curse, Jr 23:10
For this reason the land **m**, Hs 4:3
for Him as one **m** for an only Zch 12:10

MOUSE *(1)*
the weasel, the **m**, the various Lv 11:29

MOUSTACHE *(1)*
trimmed his **m**, or washed his 2Sm 19:24

MOUTH *(271)*
opened its **m** to receive your Gn 4:11
to him, "Who made the human **m**? Ex 4:11
of the LORD may be in your **m**; Ex 13:9
must cover his **m** and cry out, Lv 13:45
ground opens its **m** and swallows Nm 16:30
earth opened its **m** and swallowed Nm 16:32
the LORD opened the donkey's **m**, Nm 22:28
the message God puts in my **m**." Nm 22:38
message in Balaam's **m** and said, Nm 23:5
what the LORD puts in my **m**?" Nm 23:12
and put a message in his **m**. Nm 23:16
earth opened its **m** and swallowed Nm 26:10
comes from the **m** of the LORD. Dt 8:3
earth opened its **m** and swallowed Dt 11:6
I will put My words in his **m**, Dt 18:18
in your **m** and in your heart, Dt 30:14
earth, to the words of my **m**. Dt 32:1
must not depart from your **m**; Jos 1:8
out of your **m** until the time I Jos 6:10
against the **m** of the cave, Jos 10:18
said, "Open the **m** of the cave, Jos 10:22
against the **m** of the cave, Jos 10:27
Dead Sea to the **m** of the Jordan. Jos 15:5
the sea at the **m** of the Jordan. Jos 15:5
Keep your **m** shut. Come with Jdg 18:19
My **m** boasts over my enemies, 1Sm 2:1
words⌋ come out of your **m**, 1Sm 2:3
rescued ⌊the lamb⌋ from its **m**. 1Sm 17:35
because your own **m** testified 2Sm 1:16
it over the **m** of the well, 2Sm 17:19
fire ⌊came⌋ from His **m**; 2Sm 22:9
word in your **m** is the truth." 1Kg 17:24
to Baal and every **m** that has not 1Kg 19:18
spirit in the **m** of all his 1Kg 22:22
spirit into the **m** of all these 1Kg 22:23
he put **m** to mouth, eye to eye, 2Kg 4:34
he put mouth to **m**, eye to eye, 2Kg 4:34
your nose and My bit in your **m**; 2Kg 19:28
spirit in the **m** of all his 2Ch 18:21
spirit into the **m** of these 2Ch 18:22
Neco's words from the **m** of God, 2Ch 35:22
the statement left the king's **m**, Est 7:8
and injustice shuts its **m**. Jb 5:16
I will not restrain my **m**. Jb 7:11
yet fill your **m** with laughter Jb 8:21
my own **m** would condemn me; Jb 9:20
my **m** would declare me guilty. Jb 9:20
Your own **m** condemns you, not I; Jb 15:6
such words to leave your **m**? Jb 15:13
depart by the breath of God's **m**. Jb 15:30
I would encourage you with my **m**, Jb 16:5
even if I beg him with my own **m**. Jb 19:16
sweet in his **m** and he conceals Jb 20:12
let it go but keeps it in his **m**, Jb 20:13
put ⌊your⌋ hand over ⌊your⌋ **m**. Jb 21:5
Receive instruction from His **m**, Jb 22:22
and fill my **m** with arguments. Jb 23:4
the words of His **m** more than my Jb 23:12
breath came out of your ⌊**m**⌋? Jb 26:4
allowed my **m** to sin by asking Jb 31:30
I am going to open my **m**; Jb 33:2
Job opens his **m** in vain and Jb 35:16
rumbling that comes from His **m**. Jb 37:2
I place my hand over my **m**. Jb 40:4
the Jordan surges up to his **m**. Jb 40:23
torches shoot from his **m**; Jb 41:19
and flames pour out of his **m**. Jb 41:21
deceit, and violence fill his **m**; Ps 10:7
that my **m** will not sin. Ps 17:3
fire ⌊came⌋ from His **m**; Ps 18:8
the words of my **m** and the Ps 19:14
sticks to the roof of my **m**. Ps 22:15
Save me from the **m** of the lion! Ps 22:21
stars, by the breath of His **m**. Ps 33:6
The words of his **m** are malicious Ps 36:3
The **m** of the righteous utters Ps 37:30
person who does not open his **m**. Ps 38:13
and has no arguments in his **m**. Ps 38:14
I will guard my **m** with a muzzle Ps 39:1
do not open my **m** because of what Ps 39:9
He put a new song in my **m**, Ps 40:3
I do not keep my **m** closed— Ps 40:9
My **m** speaks wisdom; my heart's Ps 49:3
You unleash your **m** for evil and Ps 50:19
and my **m** will declare Your Ps 51:15
listen to the words of my **m**. Ps 54:2
my **m** will praise You with joyful Ps 63:5
promised and my **m** spoke during Ps 66:14
I cried out to Him with my **m**, Ps 66:17
let the Pit close its **m** over me. Ps 69:15
My **m** is full of praise and honor Ps 71:8
My **m** will tell about Your Ps 71:15
your **m** wide, and I will fill Ps 81:10
with my **m** I will proclaim Your Ps 89:1
and all injustice shuts its **m**. Ps 107:42
thank the LORD with my **m**; Ps 109:30
all the judgments from Your **m**. Ps 119:13
the word of truth from my **m**, Ps 119:43
⌊sweeter⌋ than honey to my **m**. Ps 119:103
pant with open **m** because I long Ps 119:131
to the roof of my **m** if I do not Ps 137:6
LORD, set up a guard for my **m**; Ps 141:3
scattered at the **m** of Sheol. Ps 141:7
My **m** will declare the LORD's Ps 145:21
from His **m** come knowledge and Pr 2:6
away from the words of my **m**. Pr 4:5
Don't let your **m** speak Pr 4:24
away from the words of my **m**. Pr 5:7
ensnared by the words of your **m**. Pr 6:2
attention to the words of my **m**. Pr 7:24
For my **m** tells the truth, and Pr 8:7
the words of my **m** are righteous; Pr 8:8
but the **m** of the wicked conceals Pr 10:6
The **m** of the righteous is a Pr 10:11
but the **m** of the wicked conceals Pr 10:11
but the **m** of the fool hastens Pr 10:14
The **m** of the righteous produces Pr 10:31
but the **m** of the wicked, ⌊only Pr 10:32
With his **m** the ungodly destroys Pr 11:9
down by the **m** of the wicked. Pr 11:11
with good by the words of his **m**, Pr 12:14
the words of his **m**, a man will Pr 13:2
who guards his **m** protects his Pr 13:3
but the **m** of fools blurts out Pr 15:2
but the **m** of fools feeds on Pr 15:14
but the **m** of the wicked blurts Pr 15:28
m should not err in judgment. Pr 16:10
instructs its **m** and increases Pr 16:23
of a man's **m** are deep waters Pr 18:4
and his **m** provokes a beating. Pr 18:6
A fool's **m** is his devastation, Pr 18:7
fruit of his **m** a man's stomach Pr 18:20
even bring it back to his **m**. Pr 19:24
a wicked **m** swallows iniquity. Pr 19:28
afterwards his **m** is full of Pr 20:17
avoid someone with a big **m**. Pr 20:19
guards his **m** and tongue keeps Pr 21:23
The **m** of the forbidden woman is Pr 22:14
does not open his **m** at the gate. Pr 24:7
A proverb in the **m** of a fool is Pr 26:7
A proverb in the **m** of a fool is Pr 26:9
too weary to bring it to his **m**. Pr 26:15
and a flattering **m** causes ruin. Pr 26:28
and not your own **m**—a stranger, Pr 27:2
eats and wipes her **m** and says, Pr 30:20
put your hand over your **m**. Pr 30:32
She opens her **m** with wisdom, Pr 31:26
Do not let your **m** bring guilt on Ec 5:6
words from the **m** of a wise man Ec 10:12
of the words of his **m** is folly, Ec 10:13
me with the kisses of his **m**! Sg 1:2
cord, and your **m** is lovely. Sg 4:3
His **m** is sweetness. He is Sg 5:16
Your **m** is like fine wine— Sg 7:9
For the **m** of the LORD has Is 1:20
He touched my **m** ⌊with it⌋ and Is 6:7
and every **m** speaks folly. Is 9:17
land with discipline from His **m**, Is 11:4
the Nile, by the **m** of the river, Is 19:7
He has ordered it by my **m**, Is 34:16
your nose and My bit in your **m**; Is 37:29
the **m** of the LORD has spoken. Is 40:5
has gone from My **m**, a word that Is 45:23
they came out of My **m**; Is 48:3
I have put My words in your **m**, Is 51:16
yet He did not open His **m**. Is 53:7
shearers, He did not open His **m**. Is 53:7
comes from My **m** will not return Is 55:11
opening your **m** and sticking out Is 57:4
For the **m** of the LORD has Is 58:14
words that I have put in your **m**, Is 59:21
will not depart from your **m**, Is 59:21
or from the **m** of your children, Is 59:21
or from the **m** of your children's Is 59:21
that the LORD's **m** will announce. Is 62:2
hand, touched my **m**, and told me: Jr 1:9
filled your **m** with My words. Jr 1:9
its **m** tilted from the north ⌊to Jr 1:13
My words become fire in your **m**. Jr 5:14
his **m** a man speaks peaceably Jr 9:8
attention to the word of His **m**. Jr 9:20
minds, not from the LORD's **m**. Jr 23:16
nests inside the **m** of a cave. Jr 48:28
Let him put his **m** in the dust— Lm 3:29
come from the **m** of the Most High Lm 3:38
the roof of his **m** from thirst. Lm 4:4
Open your **m** and eat what I am Ezk 2:8
So I opened my **m**, and He fed me Ezk 3:2
was as sweet as honey in my **m**. Ezk 3:3
When you hear a word from My **m**, Ezk 3:17
stick to the roof of your **m**, Ezk 3:26
I will open your **m**, and you will Ezk 3:27
meat has never entered my **m**." Ezk 4:14

never open your **m** again because Ezk 16:63
that day your **m** will be opened Ezk 24:27
When you hear a word from My **m**, Ezk 33:7
He opened my **m** before the man Ezk 33:22
So my **m** was opened and I was no Ezk 33:22
boasted against Me with your **m**, Ezk 35:13
were still in the king's **m**, Dn 4:31
placed over the **m** of the den. Dn 6:17
ribs in its **m** between its teeth Dn 7:5
and it had a **m** that spoke Dn 7:8
and a **m** that spoke arrogantly, Dn 7:20
no meat or wine entered my **m**, Dn 10:3
opened my **m** and said to the one Dn 10:16
names of the Baals from her **m**; Hs 2:17
them with the words of My **m**. Hs 6:5
⌊Put⌋ the horn to your **m**! Hs 8:1
it has been taken from your **m**. Jl 1:5
of an ear from the lion's **m**, Am 3:12
For the **m** of the LORD of Hosts Mc 4:4
Seal your **m** from the woman who Mc 7:5
right into the **m** of the eater! Nah 3:12
True instruction was in his **m**, Mal 2:6
seek instruction from his **m**, Mal 2:7
that comes from the **m** of God." Mt 4:4
For the **m** speaks from the Mt 12:34
I will open My **m** in parables; Mt 13:35
goes into the **m** that defiles a Mt 15:11
but what comes out of the **m**, Mt 15:11
whatever goes into the **m** passes Mt 15:17
comes out of the **m** comes from Mt 15:18
When you open its **m** you'll find Mt 17:27
he foams at the **m**, grinds his Mk 9:18
rolled around, foaming at the **m**. Mk 9:20
Immediately his **m** was opened and Lk 1:64
as He spoke by the **m** of His holy Lk 1:70
words that came from His **m**, Lk 4:22
for his **m** speaks from the Lk 6:45
until he foams at the **m**; Lk 9:39
heard it ourselves from His **m**?" Lk 22:71
hyssop and held it up to His **m**. Jn 19:29
through the **m** of David spoke Ac 1:16
the **m** of all the prophets Ac 3:18
spoke about by the **m** of His holy Ac 3:21
the **m** of our father David Your Ac 4:25
so He does not open His **m**. Ac 8:32
unclean has ever entered my **m**!' Ac 11:8
that by my **m** the Gentiles would Ac 15:7
the same things by word of **m**. Ac 15:27
as Paul was about to open his **m**, Ac 18:14
to him to strike him on the **m**. Ac 23:2
Their **m** is full of cursing and Rm 3:14
so that every **m** may be shut and Rm 3:19
in your **m** and in your heart. Rm 10:8
if you confess with your **m**, Rm 10:9
and with the **m** one confesses, Rm 10:10
talk should come from your **m**, Eph 4:29
when I open my **m** to make known Eph 6:19
and filthy language from your **m**. Col 3:8
breath of His **m** and will bring 2Th 2:8
I was rescued from the lion's **m**. 2Tm 4:17
Out of the same **m** come blessing Jms 3:10
no deceit was found in His **m**; 1Pt 2:22
His **m** came a sharp two-edged Rv 1:16
them with the sword of My **m**. Rv 2:16
going to vomit you out of My **m**. Rv 3:16
be as sweet as honey in your **m**." Rv 10:9
was as sweet as honey in my **m**, Rv 10:10
From his **m** the serpent spewed Rv 12:15
opened its **m** and swallowed up Rv 12:16
dragon had spewed from his **m**. Rv 12:16
and his **m** was like a lion's Rv 13:2
his mouth was like a lion's **m**. Rv 13:2
A **m** was given to him to speak Rv 13:5
coming⌋ from the dragon's **m**, Rv 16:13
from the beast's **m**, and from the Rv 16:13
and from the **m** of the false Rv 16:13
From His **m** came a sharp sword, Rv 19:15
came from the **m** of the rider Rv 19:21

MOUTHING *(1)*

Where is your **m** off now? Jdg 9:38

MOUTHS *(52)*

hands to their **m** was 300 men, Jdg 7:6
Your manna from their **m**, Neh 9:20
They open their **m** against me and Jb 16:10
and covered their **m** with ⌊their⌋ Jb 29:9
stuck to the roof of their **m**. Jb 29:10
and opened their **m** as for spring Jb 29:23
stronghold from the **m** of Ps 8:2
their **m** speak arrogantly. Ps 17:10
They open their **m** against me— Ps 22:13
They open their **m** wide against Ps 35:21
knock the teeth out of their **m**; Ps 58:6
spew from their **m**—sharp words Ps 59:7
The sin of their **m** is the word Ps 59:12
with their **m**, but they curse Ps 62:4
for the **m** of liars will be shut. Ps 63:11
They set their **m** against heaven, Ps 73:9
the food was still in their **m**, Ps 78:30
they deceived Him with their **m**, Ps 78:36
and deceitful **m** open against me; Ps 109:2
They have **m**, but cannot speak, Ps 115:5
Our **m** were filled with laughter Ps 126:2
They have **m**, but cannot speak, Ps 135:16
there is no breath in their **m**. Ps 135:17
whose **m** speak lies, whose right Ps 144:8
foreigners whose **m** speak lies, Ps 144:11
be in their **m** and a two-edged Ps 149:6
consumed Israel with open **m**. Is 9:12
Me with their **m** to honor Me with Is 29:13
shut their **m** because of Him, Is 52:15
it has disappeared from their **m**. Jr 7:28
women have spoken with your **m**, Jr 44:25
open their **m** against you. Lm 2:16
enemies open their **m** against us. Lm 3:46
they express love with their **m**, Ezk 33:31
flock from their **m** so that they Ezk 34:10
His angel and shut the lions' **m**. Dn 6:22
one who puts nothing in their **m**. Mc 3:5
all cover their **m** because there Mc 3:7
in their **m** are deceitful. Mc 6:12
⌊their⌋ hands over ⌊their⌋ **m**, Mc 7:16
will not be found in their **m**. Zph 3:13
blood from their **m** and the Zch 9:7
tongues will rot in their **m**. Zch 14:12
praise from the **m** of children Mt 21:16
promises, shut the **m** of lions, Heb 11:33
bits into the **m** of horses to Jms 3:3
their **m** utter arrogant words, Jd 16
and from their **m** came fire, Rv 9:17
sulfur that came from their **m**. Rv 9:18
is in their **m** and in their tails Rv 9:19
comes from their **m** and consumes Rv 11:5
No lie was found in their **m**; Rv 14:5

MOVE *(45)*

You will **m** on your belly and eat Gn 3:14
said, "Let's **m** on, and I'll go Gn 33:12
here, **m** about, and acquire Gn 34:10
in our land and **m** about in it, Gn 34:21
father's hand to **m** it from Gn 48:17
they did not **m** from where they Ex 10:23
creatures that **m** in the water, Lv 11:46
Whenever the tabernacle is to **m**, Nm 1:51
186,400; they will **m** out first. Nm 2:9
they will **m** out second. Nm 2:16
of meeting is to **m** out with the Nm 2:17
They are to **m** out just as they Nm 2:17
108,100; they will **m** out third. Nm 2:24
they are to **m** out last, with Nm 2:31
Whenever the camp is about to **m** Nm 4:5
whenever the camp is to **m** Nm 4:15
people did not **m** on until Miriam Nm 12:15
said,⌋ 'Get up, **m** out, and cross Dt 2:24
You must not **m** your neighbor's Dt 19:14
you will only **m** upward and never Dt 28:13
to the people, "**M** forward, march Jos 6:7
said to Barak, "**M** on, for this Jdg 4:14
Let's **m** on to Gibeah." Jdg 19:12
was not willing to **m** the ark of 2Sm 6:10
king said, "**M** aside and stand 2Sm 18:30
David did not **m** the ark of God 1Ch 13:13
then He will **m** even now on your Jb 8:6
There the ships **m** about, and Ps 104:26
Don't **m** an ancient property line Pr 22:28
m an ancient property line, Pr 23:10
all the living who **m** about under Ec 4:15
the mountains **m** and the hills Is 54:10
those who **m** with the flocks— Jr 31:24
destroyer will **m** against every Jr 48:8
like those who **m** boundary Hs 5:10
I will **m** against them with My Zch 2:9
the mountain will **m** to the north Zch 14:4
mountain, '**M** from here to there, Mt 17:20
here to there,' and it will **m**. Mt 17:20
to lift a finger to **m** them. Mt 23:4
to you, 'Friend, **m** up higher.' Lk 14:10
God had him **m** to this land in Ac 7:4
in Him we live and **m** and exist, Ac 17:28
so that I can **m** mountains, 1Co 13:2
but I will **m** on to visions and 2Co 12:1

MOVED *(50)*

From there he **m** on to the hill Gn 12:8
So Abram **m** his tent and went to Gn 13:18
He **m** from there and dug another, Gn 26:22
"They've **m** on from here," the Gn 37:17
and Joseph **m** the people to the Gn 47:21
forces, **m** and went behind Ex 14:19
pillar of cloud **m** from in front Ex 14:19
whose heart was **m** and whose Ex 35:21
whose hearts were **m** spun the Ex 35:26
everyone whose heart **m** him, Ex 36:2
in this way and **m** out the same Nm 2:34
m out when the cloud lifted. Nm 9:21
the people **m** on to Hazeroth and Nm 11:35
As the cloud **m** away from the Nm 12:10
before the LORD **m** forward and Jos 6:8
The LORD was **m** to pity whenever Jdg 2:18
Heber the Kenite had **m** away from Jdg 4:11
God should be **m** to Gath," 1Sm 5:8
So the men of Ashdod **m** the ark. 1Sm 5:8
After they had **m** it, the LORD's 1Sm 5:9
They've **m** the ark of Israel's 1Sm 5:10
at once and **m** from place to 1Sm 23:13
and **m** him to Mahanaim 2Sm 2:8
king was deeply **m** and went up 2Sm 18:33
he **m** Amasa from the highway to 2Sm 20:12
daughter **m** from the city 1Kg 9:24
I have **m** from tent to tent and 1Ch 17:5
I will never be **m**—from Ps 10:6
these things will never be **m**. Ps 15:5
heart is **m** by a noble theme as Ps 45:1
did not turn as they **m**; Ezk 1:9
went without turning as they **m**. Ezk 1:12
When they **m**, they went in any of Ezk 1:17
without pivoting as they **m**. Ezk 1:17
So when the living creatures **m**, Ezk 1:19
moved, the wheels **m** beside them, Ezk 1:19
the creatures **m**, the wheels Ezk 1:21
creatures moved, the wheels **m**; Ezk 1:21
When they **m**, I heard the sound Ezk 1:24
When they **m**, they would go in Ezk 10:11
without pivoting as they **m**. Ezk 10:11
cherubim **m**, the wheels moved Ezk 10:16
moved, the wheels **m** beside them, Ezk 10:16
glory of the LORD **m** away from Ezk 10:18
He **m** on from there to teach and Mt 11:1
M with compassion, Jesus touched Mt 20:34
M with compassion, Jesus reached Mk 1:41
in His spirit and deeply **m**. Jn 11:33
instead, **m** by the Holy Spirit, 2Pt 1:21
and island was **m** from its place. Rv 6:14

MOVES *(5)*

creature that **m** and swarms Gn 1:21
anything that **m** on its belly or Lv 11:42
is the one who **m** his neighbor's Dt 27:17
a slug that **m** along in slime, Ps 58:8
and everything that **m** in them, Ps 69:34

MOVING *(12)*

m from one place to the next Ex 17:1
m from one place to the next Nm 10:12
and although her lips were **m**, 1Sm 1:13
I have been **m** around with the 2Sm 7:6
or at the moon **m** in splendor, Jb 31:26
was **m** back and forth between Ezk 1:13
the direction the Spirit was **m**. Ezk 1:20
M on from there, He entered Mt 12:9
M on from there, Jesus passed Mt 15:29
Then, **m** on, He saw Levi the son Mk 2:14
Don't be **m** from house to house. Lk 10:7
waiting for the **m** of the water, Jn 5:3

MOWED *(1)*

they will still be **m** down, Nah 1:12

MOZA *(5)*

mother of Haran, **M**, and Gazez. 1Ch 2:46
and Zimri, and Zimri fathered **M**. 1Ch 8:36
M fathered Binea. His son was 1Ch 8:37
and Zimri; Zimri fathered **M**. 1Ch 9:42
M fathered Binea. His son was 1Ch 9:43

MOZAH *(1)*

Mizpeh, Chephirah, **M**, Jos 18:26

MUCH *(131)*

her so **m** that she ran away Gn 16:6
you are **m** too powerful for us. Gn 26:16

did you cause me so **m** trouble?" Gn 43:6
Take twice as **m** money with you. Gn 43:12
bags with as **m** food as they can Gn 44:1
be twice as **m** as they gather Ex 16:5
'Gather as **m** of it as each Ex 16:16
gathered as **m** as he needed to Ex 16:18
gathered as **m** as he needed to Ex 16:21
they gathered twice as **m** food, Ex 16:22
myrrh, half as **m** (six and a Ex 30:23
myself. They are too **m** for me. Nm 11:14
You will sow **m** seed in the field Dt 28:38
m more ⌊will you rebel⌋ after Dt 31:27
because she had nagged him so **m**. Jdg 14:17
my life⌋ is **m** too bitter for you Ru 1:13
How **m** better if the troops had 1Sm 14:30
would have been **m** greater." 1Sm 14:30
sacrifices as **m** as in obeying 1Sm 15:22
and loved him as **m** as he loved 1Sm 18:1
he loved him as **m** as himself. 1Sm 18:3
son Jonathan liked David very **m**, 1Sm 19:1
how **m** more if we go to Keilah 1Sm 23:3
m more when wicked men kill 2Sm 4:11
sending me away is **m** worse than 2Sm 13:16
m more now this Benjaminite! 2Sm 16:11
m less this temple I have built. 1Kg 8:27
liked Hadad so **m** that he gave 1Kg 11:19
journey will be too **m** for you." 1Kg 19:7
How **m** more ⌊should you do it⌋ 2Kg 5:13
as there is so **m** prostitution 2Kg 9:22
also shed so **m** innocent blood 2Kg 21:16
'You have shed **m** blood and waged 1Ch 22:8
you have shed so **m** blood on the 1Ch 22:8
because there is so **m** of it. 1Ch 22:14
m less this temple I have built. 2Ch 6:18
days because there was so **m**. 2Ch 20:25
to give you **m** more than this. 2Ch 25:9
For we have **m** guilt, and fierce 2Ch 28:13
m less will your gods deliver 2Ch 32:15
since there is so **m** rubble. Neh 4:10
to serve as **m** as each person Est 1:8
are filled with **m** joy and are Jb 3:22
how **m** more those who dwell in Jb 4:19
him and pay so **m** attention to Jb 7:17
how **m** less one who is revolting Jb 15:16
how **m** less man, who is a maggot, Jb 25:6
my own hand has acquired ⌊so⌋ **m**, Jb 31:25
m less when you complain that Jb 35:14
himself ⌊too **m**⌋ to discover and Ps 36:2
Your decrees as **m** as in all Ps 119:14
he must pay seven times as **m**; Pr 6:31
m more the wicked and sinful. Pr 11:31
the LORD—how **m** more, human Pr 15:11
how **m** better it is than gold! Pr 16:16
m worse are lies for a ruler. Pr 17:7
how **m** more do his friends keep Pr 19:7
how **m** less for a slave to rule Pr 19:10
how **m** more so when he brings it Pr 21:27
with those who drink too **m** wine, Pr 23:20
is not good to eat too **m** honey, Pr 25:27
I might have too **m** and deny You, Pr 30:9
with **m** wisdom is much sorrow; Ec 1:18
with much wisdom is **m** sorrow; Ec 1:18
result from **m** work and a fool's Ec 5:3
whether he eats little or **m**; Ec 5:12
his days, with **m** sorrow, Ec 5:17
one sinner can destroy **m** good. Ec 9:18
and **m** study wearies the body. Ec 12:12
Your love is **m** better than wine, Sg 4:10
own pleasure, or talking too **m**; Is 58:13
How **m** worse will it be when I Ezk 14:21
How **m** less can it ever be made Ezk 15:5
and scorn, for it holds ⌊so⌋ **m**. Ezk 23:32
what is not his—how **m** longer? Hab 2:6
You have planted **m** but harvested Hg 1:6
You expected **m**, but then it Hg 1:9
won't He do **m** more for you— Mt 6:30
how **m** more will your Father in Mt 7:11
how **m** more the members of his Mt 10:25
where there wasn't **m** soil, Mt 13:5
Don't You hear how **m** they are Mt 27:13
where it didn't have **m** soil, Mk 4:5
to them how **m** the Lord has done Mk 5:19
Decapolis how **m** Jesus had done Mk 5:20
endured **m** under many doctors. Mk 5:26
that's why she loved **m**. Lk 7:47
and give him as **m** as he needs. Lk 11:8
how **m** more will the heavenly Lk 11:13
Aren't you worth **m** more than the Lk 12:24
how **m** more will He do for you— Lk 12:28
M will be required of everyone Lk 12:48
everyone who has been given **m**. Lk 12:48
'How **m** do you owe my master?' Lk 16:5
another, 'How **m** do you owe?' Lk 16:7
little is also faithful in **m**, Lk 16:10
little is also unrighteous in **m**. Lk 16:10
I'll pay back four times as **m**!" Lk 19:8
find out how **m** they had made Lk 19:15
the fish, as **m** as they wanted. Jn 6:11
will not talk with you **m** longer, Jn 14:30
and I in him produces **m** fruit, Jn 15:5
you produce **m** fruit and prove Jn 15:8
how **m** harm he has done to Your Ac 9:13
show him how **m** he must suffer Ac 9:16
After there had been **m** debate, Ac 15:7
Too **m** study is driving you mad!" Ac 26:24
now **m** time had passed, and the Ac 27:9
For I want very **m** to see you, Rm 1:11
M more then, since we have now Rm 5:9
Son, ⌊then how⌋ **m** more, having Rm 5:10
how **m** more have the grace of God Rm 5:15
m more will those who receive Rm 5:17
endured with **m** patience objects Rm 9:22
m more will their full number Rm 11:12
tree, how **m** more will these Rm 11:24
in fear, and in **m** trembling. 1Co 2:3
is it too **m** if we reap material 1Co 9:11
consider how **m** diligence this 2Co 7:11
who gathered **m** did not have too 2Co 8:15
much did not have too **m**, 2Co 8:15
you suffer so **m** for nothing— Gl 3:4
Epaphras, our **m** loved fellow Col 1:7
Spirit, and with **m** assurance. 1Th 1:5
We cared so **m** for you that we 1Th 2:8
you know how **m** he ministered at 2Tm 1:18
not addicted to **m** wine. Ti 2:3
how **m** more will the blood of the Heb 9:14
How **m** worse punishment, do you Heb 10:29
m as she glorified herself and Rv 18:7
give her that **m** torment and Rv 18:7

MUCK *(1)*
its waters churn up mire and **m**. Is 57:20

MUD *(18)*
them like **m** in the streets. 2Sm 22:43
then You dip me in a pit ⌊of **m**⌋, Jb 9:31
me into the **m**, and I have become Jb 30:19
spreading the **m** like a threshing Jb 41:30
them like **m** in the streets. Ps 18:42
sunk in deep **m**, and there is no Ps 69:2
Rescue me from the miry **m**; Ps 69:14
over rulers as if they were **m**, Is 41:25
cistern, only **m**, and Jeremiah Jr 38:6
and Jeremiah sank in the **m**. Jr 38:6
trampled like **m** in the streets. Mc 7:10
down the **m** of the streets. Zch 10:5
made some **m** from the saliva, Jn 9:6
and spread the **m** on his eyes. Jn 9:6
The man called Jesus made **m**, Jn 9:11
Jesus made the **m** and opened his Jn 9:14
"He put **m** on my eyes," he told Jn 9:15
itself, wallows in the **m**." 2Pt 2:22

MUDDIED *(2)*
wicked is like a **m** spring or a Pr 25:26
and drink what your feet have **m**. Ezk 34:19

MUDDLED *(1)*
they are **m** in ⌊their⌋ visions, Is 28:7

MUDDY *(3)*
pit, out of the **m** clay, and set Ps 40:2
your feet, and **m** the rivers." Ezk 32:2
Must you also **m** the rest with Ezk 34:18

MULBERRY *(1)*
you can say to this **m** tree, Lk 17:6

MULE *(8)*
got up, and each fled on his **m**. 2Sm 13:29
riding on his **m** when he happened 2Sm 18:9
the **m** went under the tangled 2Sm 18:9
The **m** under him kept going, 2Sm 18:9
son Solomon ride on my own **m**, 1Kg 1:33
Solomon ride on King David's **m**, 1Kg 1:38
had him ride on the king's **m**. 1Kg 1:44
Do not be like a horse or **m**, Ps 32:9

MULE-LOADS *(1)*
please let two **m** of dirt be 2Kg 5:17

MULES *(9)*
spices, and horses and **m**. 1Kg 10:25
the horses and **m** alive and not 1Kg 18:5
donkeys, camels, **m**, and oxen— 1Ch 12:40
and horses and **m**—as an annual 2Ch 9:24
They had 736 horses, 245 **m**, Ezr 2:66
They had 736 horses, 245 **m**, Neh 7:68
litters, and on **m** and camels, to Is 66:20
and **m** for your merchandise. Ezk 27:14
the horses, **m**, camels, donkeys, Zch 14:15

MULTI-FACETED *(1)*
so that God's **m** wisdom may now Eph 3:10

MULTICOLORED *(1)*
materials, and **m** carpets, which Ezk 27:24

MULTIPLIED *(28)*
increased rapidly, **m**, and became Ex 1:7
the more they **m** and spread so Ex 1:12
and the people **m** and became very Ex 1:20
My wonders may be **m** in the land Ex 11:9
your God has so **m** you that today Dt 1:10
Canaan, and **m** his descendants. Jos 24:3
our land and who **m** our dead. Jdg 16:24
the people **m** their unfaithful 2Ch 36:14
You **m** their descendants like the Neh 9:23
with oil and **m** your perfumes; Is 57:9
have **m** before You, Is 59:12
You have **m** remedies in vain; Jr 46:11
has **m** mourning and lamentation Lm 2:5
You have **m** your slain in this Ezk 11:6
You have **m** your abominations Ezk 16:51
Yet she **m** her acts of Ezk 23:19
Its branches **m**, and its boughs Ezk 31:5
The more they **m**, the more they Hs 4:7
When Ephraim **m** his altars for Hs 8:11
Judah has also **m** fortified Hs 8:14
in Jerusalem **m** greatly, Ac 6:7
people flourished and **m** in Egypt Ac 7:17
God's message flourished and **m**. Ac 12:24
where sin **m**, grace multiplied Rm 5:20
multiplied, grace **m** even more, Rm 5:20
May grace and peace be **m** to you. 1Pt 1:2
and peace be **m** to you through 2Pt 1:2
peace, and love be **m** to you. Jd 2

MULTIPLIES *(4)*
a whirlwind and **m** my wounds Jb 9:17
in vain and **m** words without Jb 35:16
Yet the fool **m** words. Ec 10:14
He continually **m** lies and Hs 12:1

MULTIPLY *(50)*
them, "Be fruitful, **m**, and fill Gn 1:22
let the birds **m** on the earth." Gn 1:22
Be fruitful, **m**, fill the earth, Gn 1:28
mankind began to **m** on the earth Gn 6:1
be fruitful and **m** on the earth." Gn 8:17
Be fruitful and **m** and fill the Gn 9:1
But you, be fruitful and **m**; Gn 9:7
out over the earth and **m** on it." Gn 9:7
I will greatly **m** your offspring, Gn 16:10
and I will **m** you greatly." Gn 17:2
fruitful and will **m** him greatly. Gn 17:20
bless you and **m** your offspring Gn 26:24
fruitful and **m** you so that you Gn 28:3
Be fruitful and **m**. A nation, Gn 35:11
otherwise they will **m** ⌊further⌋, Ex 1:10
Pharaoh's heart and **m** My signs Ex 7:3
animals would **m** against you. Ex 23:29
make you fruitful and **m** you, Lv 26:9
will **m** your plagues seven times Lv 26:21
you may prosper and **m** greatly, Dt 6:3
love you, bless you, and **m** you. Dt 7:13
and your silver and gold **m**, Dt 8:13
and **m** you as He swore to your Dt 13:17
you to prosper and to **m** you, Dt 28:63
to prosper and **m** you more than Dt 30:5
so that you may live and **m**, Dt 30:16
LORD your God **m** the troops 100 2Sm 24:3
May the LORD **m** the number of 1Ch 21:3
against me and **m** Your anger Jb 10:17
my own nest and **m** ⌊my⌋ days as Jb 29:18
If you **m** your transgressions, Jb 35:6
another ⌊god⌋ for themselves **m**; Ps 16:4
them, and they **m** greatly; Ps 107:38
their families ⌊**m**⌋ like flocks. Ps 107:41
it through labor will **m** it. Pr 13:11
the ones who consume them **m**; Ec 5:11
When you **m** and increase in the Jr 3:16
and daughters. **M** there; do not Jr 29:6
I will **m** them, and they will not Jr 30:19
and **m** the widows within her. Ezk 22:25

I will **m** them in number like a Ezk 36:37
I will establish and **m** them, Ezk 37:26
will be promiscuous but not **m**; Hs 4:10
M yourselves like the young Nah 3:15
m like the swarming locust! Nah 3:15
Because lawlessness will **m**, Mt 24:12
came along to **m** the trespass. Rm 5:20
sin in order that grace may **m**? Rm 6:1
will provide and **m** your seed 2Co 9:10
you, and I will greatly **m** you. Heb 6:14

MULTIPLYING *(2)*
while **m** his words against God. Jb 34:37
number of the disciples was **m**, Ac 6:1

MULTITUDE *(37)*
a **m** as numerous as the sand on Jos 11:4
one of the whole **m** of the people 2Sm 6:19
like the whole **m** of Israelites 2Kg 7:13
You are a vast **m** and have with 2Ch 13:8
we have come against this **m**. 2Ch 14:11
A vast **m** from beyond the Dead 2Ch 20:2
before this vast **m** that comes 2Ch 20:12
because of this vast **m**, 2Ch 20:15
toward the **m**, and there were 2Ch 20:24
or before all the **m** with him, 2Ch 32:7
There is gold and a **m** of jewels, Pr 20:15
The **m** of your foes will be like Is 29:5
and the **m** of the ruthless, Is 29:5
The **m** of all the nations going Is 29:7
So will be the **m** of all the Is 29:8
none of their **m**, none of their Ezk 7:11
for wrath is on all her **m**. Ezk 7:12
for My wrath is on all her **m**. Ezk 7:14
his words like the sound of a **m**. Dn 10:6
raise a great **m**, but the Dn 11:11
but the **m** will be handed over to Dn 11:11
When the **m** is carried off, Dn 11:12
will again raise a **m** larger than Dn 11:13
and a great **m** followed from Mk 3:7
The great **m** came to Him because Mk 3:8
there was a **m** of the heavenly Lk 2:13
and a great **m** of people from all Lk 6:17
A great **m** of the people followed Lk 23:27
these lay a **m** of the sick— Jn 5:3
the **m** came together and was Ac 2:6
Now the **m** of those who believed Ac 4:32
a **m** came together from the towns Ac 5:16
death and cover a **m** of sins. Jms 5:20
since love covers a **m** of sins. 1Pt 4:8
there was a vast **m** from every Rv 7:9
voice of a vast **m** in heaven, Rv 19:1
like the voice of a vast **m**, Rv 19:6

MULTITUDES *(4)*
have heard the gossip of the **m**, Jr 20:10
M, multitudes in the valley of Jl 3:14
m in the valley of decision! Jl 3:14
seated, are peoples, **m**, nations, Rv 17:15

MUPPIM *(1)*
(AKA SHUPHAM)
Ehi, Rosh, **M**, Huppim, and Ard. Gn 46:21

MURDER *(24)*
Do not **m**. Ex 20:13
neighbor to **m** him by scheming Ex 21:14
person will be charged with **m**. Lv 17:4
Do not **m**. Dt 5:17
If a **m** victim is found lying in Dt 21:1
They will **m** me and go back to 1Kg 12:27
foreigner and **m** the fatherless. Ps 94:6
and they hurry to commit **m**. Pr 1:16
Do you steal, **m**, commit Jr 7:9
Cursing, lying, **m**, stealing, and Hs 4:2
ancestors, Do not **m**, and whoever Mt 5:21
Jesus answered, Do not **m**; Mt 19:18
Do not **m**; do not commit Mk 10:19
who had committed **m** during the Mk 15:7
do not **m**; do not steal; Lk 18:20
place in the city, and for **m**. Lk 23:19
into prison for rebellion and **m**. Lk 23:25
threats and **m** against the Ac 9:1
full of envy, **m**, disputes, Rm 1:29
you shall not **m**, you shall not Rm 13:9
adultery, also said, Do not **m**. Jms 2:11
adultery, but you do **m**, you are Jms 2:11
You **m** and covet and cannot Jms 4:2
And why did he **m** him? 1Jn 3:12

MURDERED *(13)*
the husband of the **m** woman, Jdg 20:4
you **m** him with the Ammonite's 2Sm 12:9
the life of the brother he **m**. 2Sm 14:7
m them ⌊in a time⌋ of peace to 1Kg 2:5
his sword, Joab **m** Abner son of 1Kg 2:32
Have you **m** and also taken 1Kg 21:19
servants who had **m** his father 2Kg 14:5
servants who had **m** his father 2Ch 25:3
of those who **m** the prophets. Mt 23:31
you **m** between the sanctuary Mt 23:35
whom you had **m** by hanging Him Ac 5:30
you have **m**—the righteous man Jms 5:6
the evil one and **m** his brother. 1Jn 3:12

MURDERER *(19)*
and death results, he is a **m**; Nm 35:16
the **m** must be put to death. Nm 35:16
the **m** must be put to death. Nm 35:17
the **m** must be put to death. Nm 35:18
blood himself is to kill the **m**; Nm 35:19
to death; he is a **m**. The avenger Nm 35:21
is to kill the **m** when he finds Nm 35:21
m is to be put to death based Nm 35:30
the life of a **m** who is guilty Nm 35:31
out, get out, you worthless **m**! 2Sm 16:7
in trouble because you're a **m**!" 2Sm 16:8
you see how this **m** has sent 2Kg 6:32
The **m** rises at dawn to kill the Jb 24:14
was a **m** from the beginning and Jn 8:44
asked to have a **m** given to you. Ac 3:14
This man is probably a **m**, Ac 28:4
should suffer as a **m**, a thief, 1Pt 4:15
who hates his brother is a **m**, 1Jn 3:15
know that no **m** has eternal life 1Jn 3:15

MURDERERS *(8)*
the children of the **m** to death, 2Kg 14:6
once dwelt in her—but now, **m**! Is 1:21
life is weary because of the **m**! Jr 4:31
destroyed those **m**, and burned Mt 22:7
betrayers and **m** you have now Ac 7:52
fathers and mothers, for **m**, 1Tm 1:9
vile, **m**, sexually immoral Rv 21:8
immoral, the **m**, the idolaters, Rv 22:15

MURDEROUS *(1)*
listening to **m** plots and shuts Is 33:15

MURDERS *(6)*
attacks his neighbor and **m** him. Dt 22:26
band of priests **m** on the road to Hs 6:9
and whoever **m** will be subject to Mt 5:21
evil thoughts, **m**, adulteries, Mt 15:19
sexual immoralities, thefts, **m**, Mk 7:21
they did not repent of their **m**, Rv 9:21

MURMUR *(1)*
He stilled the storm to a **m**, Ps 107:29

MURMURING *(1)*
slander and **m** of my opponents Lm 3:62

MUSCLE *(2)*
eat the thigh **m** that is at the Gn 32:32
hip socket at the thigh **m**. Gn 32:32

MUSCLES *(1)*
the power in the **m** of his belly. Jb 40:16

MUSED *(1)*
as I **m**, a fire burned. Ps 39:3

MUSHI *(6)*
Merari: Mahli and **M**. These are Ex 6:19
by their clans were Mahli and **M**. Nm 3:20
sons: Mahli and **M**. These are the 1Ch 6:19
Mahli, son of **M**, son of Merari, 1Ch 6:47
sons: Mahli and **M**. Mahli's sons: 1Ch 23:21
and **M**, ⌊and from⌋ his sons, 1Ch 24:26

MUSHI'S *(2)*
M sons: Mahli, Eder, and 1Ch 23:23
M sons: Mahli, Eder, and 1Ch 24:30

MUSHITE *(2)*
Mahlite clan and the **M** clan came Nm 3:33
Mahlite clan, the **M** clan, and Nm 26:58

MUSIC *(22)*
in charge of the **m** in the LORD's 1Ch 6:31
were to lead the **m** with lyres 1Ch 15:21
the leader of the Levites in **m**, 1Ch 15:22
to direct the **m** because he was 1Ch 15:22
the **m** leader of the singers. 1Ch 15:27
authority for the **m** in the 1Ch 25:6
and skillful in **m** for the LORD, 1Ch 25:7
sing and make **m** to the LORD. Ps 27:6
m to Him with a ten-stringed Ps 33:2
At night I remember my **m**; Ps 77:6
harp and the **m** of a lyre. Ps 92:3
dancing and make **m** to Him with Ps 149:3
⌊along with⌋ the **m** of your harps. Is 14:11
who walks ⌊to the **m**⌋ of a flute, Is 30:29
gate, the young men, their **m**. Lm 5:14
every kind of **m**, you are to fall Dn 3:5
every kind of **m**, people of every Dn 3:7
every kind of **m** must fall down Dn 3:10
and every kind of **m**, fall down Dn 3:15
listen to the **m** of your harps. Am 5:23
house, he heard **m** and dancing. Lk 15:25
singing and making **m** to the Lord Eph 5:19

MUSICAL *(8)*
accompanied by **m** instruments— 1Ch 15:16
to play and **m** instruments of God 1Ch 16:42
cymbals, and **m** instruments, in 2Ch 5:13
Levites with the **m** instruments 2Ch 7:6
singers with **m** instruments were 2Ch 23:13
all skilled on **m** instruments. 2Ch 34:12
with the **m** instruments of David, Neh 12:36
their own **m** instruments like Am 6:5

MUSICIAN *(2)*
Now, bring me a **m**." 2Kg 3:15
While the **m** played, the LORD's 2Kg 3:15

MUSICIANS *(2)*
lead the way, with **m** following; Ps 68:25
sound of harpists, **m**, flutists, Rv 18:22

MUST *(1038)*
but you **m** not eat from the tree Gn 2:17
'You **m** not eat it or touch it, Gn 3:3
and evil, he **m** not reach out, Gn 3:22
for you, but you **m** master it." Gn 4:7
and I **m** hide myself from Your Gn 4:14
you **m** not eat meat with its Gn 9:4
You **m** go back to your mistress Gn 16:9
of your males **m** be circumcised. Gn 17:10
You **m** circumcise the flesh of Gn 17:11
with money, **m** be circumcised. Gn 17:13
and said, "You **m** come with me, Gn 30:16
We **m** get up and go to Bethel. Gn 35:3
Now we **m** account for his blood!" Gn 42:22
to them, "If it **m** be so, then do Gn 43:11
of your father **m** have put Gn 43:23
have it, he **m** die, and we also Gn 44:9
I said that he **m** have been torn Gn 44:28
You **m** bury me there in the tomb Gn 50:5
You **m** throw every son born to Ex 1:22
I **m** go over and look at this Ex 3:3
m go to the king of Egypt and Ex 3:18
They **m** go and gather straw for Ex 5:7
but you **m** produce the same Ex 5:18
m say whatever I command you; Ex 7:2
your brother **m** declare it to Ex 7:2
We **m** go a distance of three days Ex 8:27
Pharaoh **m** not act deceptively Ex 8:29
How long **m** this man be a snare Ex 10:7
because we **m** hold the LORD's Ex 10:9
and your herds **m** stay behind." Ex 10:24
You **m** also let us have Ex 10:25
Even our livestock **m** go with us; Ex 10:26
of this month they **m** each select Ex 12:3
m have an unblemished animal, Ex 12:5
They **m** take some of the blood Ex 12:7
m burn up any part of it that Ex 12:10
Here is how you **m** eat it: Ex 12:11
and you **m** celebrate it as a Ex 12:14
You **m** eat unleavened bread for Ex 12:15
the first day you **m** remove yeast Ex 12:15
seventh day **m** be cut off from Ex 12:15
m observe this day throughout Ex 12:17
Yeast **m** not be found in your Ex 12:19
m be cut off from the community Ex 12:19
of Israel **m** celebrate it. Ex 12:47
his household **m** be circumcised, Ex 12:48
you **m** carry out this ritual in Ex 13:5
seven days you **m** eat unleavened Ex 13:6
You **m** redeem every firstborn of Ex 13:13
you **m** redeem every firstborn Ex 13:13
then you **m** take my bones with Ex 13:19
you **m** camp in front of Ex 14:2
fight for you; you **m** be quiet." Ex 14:14
way to live and what they **m** do. Ex 18:20
is what you **m** say to the house Ex 19:3
They **m** wash their clothes Ex 19:10
near the LORD **m** purify Ex 19:22
and the people **m** not break Ex 19:24
You **m** not bow down to them or Ex 20:5
m not do any work—you, your Ex 20:10

You **m** not make gods of silver to Ex 20:23
m not make ⌊gods of gold⌋ for Ex 20:23
You **m** make an earthen altar for Ex 20:24
you **m** not build it out of cut Ex 20:25
You **m** not go up to My altar on Ex 20:26
that you **m** set before them: Ex 21:1
and the man **m** leave alone. Ex 21:4
His master **m** pierce his ear with Ex 21:6
then he **m** let her be redeemed. Ex 21:8
he **m** deal with her according to Ex 21:9
wife, he **m** not reduce the food Ex 21:10
that he dies **m** be put to death Ex 21:12
you **m** take him from My altar to Ex 21:14
or his mother **m** be put to death. Ex 21:15
a person **m** be put to death Ex 21:16
or his mother **m** be put to death. Ex 21:17
he **m** pay for his lost work time Ex 21:19
abuse, the owner **m** be punished. Ex 21:20
the one who hit her **m** be fined Ex 21:22
and he **m** pay according to Ex 21:22
then you **m** give life for life, Ex 21:23
he **m** let the slave go free in Ex 21:26
he **m** let the slave go free in Ex 21:27
death, the ox **m** be stoned, and Ex 21:28
a woman, the ox **m** be stoned, and Ex 21:29
and its owner **m** also be put to Ex 21:29
m give 30 shekels of silver to Ex 21:32
master, and the ox **m** be stoned. Ex 21:32
owner of the pit **m** give Ex 21:34
he **m** pay money to its owner, Ex 21:34
they **m** sell the live ox and Ex 21:35
they **m** also divide the dead Ex 21:35
it, he **m** compensate fully Ex 21:36
m repay five cattle for the ox Ex 22:1
A thief **m** make full restitution. Ex 22:3
possession, he **m** repay double. Ex 22:4
he **m** repay with the best of his Ex 22:5
who started the fire **m** make full Ex 22:6
if caught, **m** repay double. Ex 22:7
of the house **m** present himself Ex 22:8
judges condemn **m** repay double to Ex 22:9
there **m** be an oath before the Ex 22:11
Its owner **m** accept ⌊the oath⌋, Ex 22:11
he **m** make restitution to its Ex 22:12
the man **m** make full restitution. Ex 22:14
he **m** certainly pay the bridal Ex 22:16
he **m** pay an amount in silver Ex 22:17
You **m** not allow a sorceress to Ex 22:18
an animal **m** be put to death. Ex 22:19
You **m** not exploit a foreign Ex 22:21
You **m** not mistreat any widow or Ex 22:22
you **m** not be like a moneylender Ex 22:25
you **m** not charge him interest. Ex 22:25
You **m** not blaspheme God or curse Ex 22:28
You **m** not hold back ⌊offerings Ex 22:29
You **m** not eat the meat of a Ex 22:31
You **m** not spread a false report. Ex 23:1
You **m** not follow a crowd in Ex 23:2
or donkey, you **m** return it to Ex 23:4
helping it, you **m** help with it. Ex 23:5
You **m** not deny justice to the Ex 23:6
You **m** not take a bribe, for a Ex 23:8
You **m** not oppress a foreign Ex 23:9
You **m** not invoke the names of Ex 23:13
m not be heard on your lips. Ex 23:13
You **m** not offer the blood of My Ex 23:18
offering **m** not remain until Ex 23:18
You **m** not boil a young goat in Ex 23:19
You **m** not bow down to their gods Ex 23:24
You **m** not make a covenant with Ex 23:32
They **m** not remain in your land, Ex 23:33
You **m** make ⌊it⌋ according to all Ex 25:9
they **m** not be removed from it. Ex 25:15
a calyx **m** be under the ⌊first⌋ Ex 25:35
and firepans **m** be of pure gold. Ex 25:38
You **m** make them of finely spun Ex 26:1
Each plank **m** be connected Ex 26:17
The altar **m** be square, seven and Ex 27:1
it **m** be four and a half feet Ex 27:1
bands of the posts **m** be silver. Ex 27:10
bands of the posts **m** be silver. Ex 27:11
bases of the posts **m** be bronze. Ex 27:18
the garments that they **m** make: Ex 28:4
It **m** have two shoulder pieces Ex 28:7
on the ephod **m** be of one piece Ex 28:8
m be square and folded double, Ex 28:16
Each stone **m** be engraved like a Ex 28:21
The robe **m** be ⌊worn by⌋ Aaron Ex 28:35
they **m** extend from the waist to Ex 28:42
These **m** be ⌊worn by⌋ Aaron and Ex 28:43
You **m** also bring his sons, Ex 29:8
and his sons **m** lay their hands Ex 29:10
and his sons **m** lay their hands Ex 29:19
in the sanctuary **m** wear them for Ex 29:30
They **m** eat those things by which Ex 29:33
person **m** not eat ⌊them⌋, Ex 29:33
It **m** not be eaten because it is Ex 29:34
seven days you **m** make atonement Ex 29:37
It **m** be square, 18 inches long Ex 30:2
it **m** be 36 inches high. Ex 30:2
Its horns **m** be of one piece. Ex 30:2
Aaron **m** burn fragrant incense on Ex 30:7
he **m** burn it every morning when Ex 30:7
at twilight, he **m** burn incense. Ex 30:8
You **m** not offer unauthorized Ex 30:9
each of the men **m** pay a ransom Ex 30:12
is registered **m** pay half a Ex 30:13
m give this contribution to the Ex 30:14
and his sons **m** wash their hands Ex 30:19
they **m** wash with water so that Ex 30:20
They **m** wash their hands and feet Ex 30:21
It **m** not be used for ⌊ordinary⌋ Ex 30:32
and you **m** not make anything like Ex 30:32
holy, and it **m** be holy to you. Ex 30:32
person **m** be cut off from his Ex 30:33
It **m** be especially holy to you. Ex 30:36
you **m** not make ⌊any⌋ for Ex 30:37
its fragrance **m** be cut off from Ex 30:38
They **m** make ⌊them⌋ according to Ex 31:11
You **m** observe My Sabbaths, Ex 31:13
profanes it **m** be put to death. Ex 31:14
that person **m** be cut off from Ex 31:14
seventh day there **m** be a Sabbath Ex 31:15
Sabbath day **m** be put to death Ex 31:15
The Israelites **m** observe the Ex 31:16
no one **m** be seen anywhere on the Ex 34:3
you **m** tear down their altars, Ex 34:13
You **m** redeem the firstborn of a Ex 34:20
You **m** redeem all the firstborn Ex 34:20
six days but you **m** rest on the Ex 34:21
you **m** even rest during plowing Ex 34:21
Festival **m** not remain until Ex 34:25
You **m** not boil a young goat in Ex 34:26
does work on it **m** be executed. Ex 35:2
He **m** bring it to the entrance to Lv 1:3
he **m** skin the burnt offering Lv 1:6
The offerer **m** wash its entrails Lv 1:9
Then the priest **m** bring it to Lv 1:15
m twist off its head and burn Lv 1:15
gift **m** consist of fine flour. Lv 2:1
it **m** be ⌊made⌋ of fine flour, Lv 2:4
it **m** be unleavened bread ⌊made⌋ Lv 2:5
it **m** be made of fine flour with Lv 2:7
you **m** not omit from your grain Lv 2:13
you **m** present fresh heads of Lv 2:14
he **m** present one without blemish Lv 3:1
he **m** present a male or female Lv 3:6
He **m** lay his hand on the head of Lv 3:8
m lay his hand on its head and Lv 3:13
m not eat any fat or any blood. Lv 3:17
He **m** bring the bull to the Lv 4:4
anointed priest **m** then take some Lv 4:5
The priest **m** apply some of the Lv 4:7
He **m** pour out the rest of the Lv 4:7
he **m** bring to a ceremonially Lv 4:12
and **m** burn it on a wood fire. Lv 4:12
the assembly **m** present a young Lv 4:14
He **m** pour out the rest of the Lv 4:18
Then the priest **m** take some of Lv 4:25
its blood he **m** pour out at the Lv 4:25
He **m** burn all its fat on the Lv 4:26
Then the priest **m** take some of Lv 4:30
He **m** pour out the rest of its Lv 4:30
Then the priest **m** take some of Lv 4:34
He **m** pour out the rest of its Lv 4:34
He **m** bring his restitution for Lv 5:6
He **m** twist its head at the back Lv 5:8
m prepare the second ⌊bird⌋ as Lv 5:10
He **m** not put olive oil or Lv 5:11
he **m** bring his restitution Lv 5:15
m make restitution for his sin Lv 5:16
He **m** bring an unblemished ram Lv 5:18
he **m** return what he stole or Lv 6:4
m make full restitution for it Lv 6:5
Then he **m** bring his restitution Lv 6:6
offering itself **m** remain on the Lv 6:9
Then he **m** take off his garments, Lv 6:11
kept burning; it **m** not go out. Lv 6:12
Fire **m** be kept burning on the Lv 6:13
continually; it **m** not go out. Lv 6:13
It **m** not be baked with yeast; Lv 6:17
Aaron and his sons **m** present to Lv 6:20
You **m** present it as a grain Lv 6:21
It **m** be completely burned as a Lv 6:22
most holy and **m** be slaughtered Lv 6:25
It **m** be eaten in a holy place, Lv 6:26
then you **m** wash that garment in Lv 6:27
offering is boiled **m** be broken; Lv 6:28
it **m** be scoured and rinsed with Lv 6:28
holy place; it **m** be burned up. Lv 6:30
offering **m** be slaughtered at Lv 7:2
offerer **m** present all the fat Lv 7:3
From the cakes he **m** present one Lv 7:14
of fellowship **m** be eaten on the Lv 7:15
by the third day **m** be burned up. Lv 7:17
anything unclean **m** not be eaten; Lv 7:19
that person **m** be cut off from Lv 7:20
that person **m** be cut off from Lv 7:21
purpose, but you **m** not eat it. Lv 7:24
who eats ⌊it⌋ **m** be cut off from Lv 7:25
you **m** not eat the blood of any Lv 7:26
that person **m** be cut off from Lv 7:27
to the LORD **m** bring an offering Lv 7:29
m burn up what remains of the Lv 8:32
m not go outside the entrance Lv 8:33
You **m** remain at the entrance to Lv 8:35
m not go outside the entrance Lv 10:7
You **m** distinguish between the Lv 10:10
You **m** eat it in a holy place Lv 10:13
you **m** not eat any of their meat, Lv 11:11
you **m** detest their carcasses. Lv 11:11
They **m** not be eaten because they Lv 11:13
their carcasses **m** wash his Lv 11:25
their carcasses **m** wash his Lv 11:28
become unclean; you **m** break it. Lv 11:33
oven or stove, it **m** be smashed; Lv 11:35
its carcass **m** wash his clothes Lv 11:40
its carcass **m** wash his clothes Lv 11:40
detestable; they **m** not be eaten. Lv 11:41
so you **m** consecrate yourselves Lv 11:44
You **m** not defile yourselves by Lv 11:44
so you **m** be holy because I am Lv 11:45
of his foreskin **m** be circumcised Lv 12:3
She **m** not touch any holy thing Lv 12:4
he **m** pronounce him unclean. Lv 13:3
the priest **m** quarantine the Lv 13:4
the priest **m** quarantine him for Lv 13:5
m present himself again to the Lv 13:7
then the priest **m** pronounce him Lv 13:8
and the priest **m** pronounce him Lv 13:11
he **m** pronounce him unclean. Lv 13:15
turns white, he **m** go to the Lv 13:16
the priest **m** pronounce the Lv 13:17
the person **m** present himself to Lv 13:19
the priest **m** pronounce him Lv 13:20
priest **m** quarantine him seven Lv 13:21
the priest **m** pronounce him Lv 13:22
The priest **m** pronounce him Lv 13:25
priest **m** quarantine him seven Lv 13:26
the priest **m** pronounce him Lv 13:27
the priest **m** examine the Lv 13:30
priest **m** pronounce the person Lv 13:30
the priest **m** quarantine the Lv 13:31
the person **m** shave himself but Lv 13:33
Then the priest **m** quarantine the Lv 13:33
The priest **m** pronounce him Lv 13:44
and he **m** cover his mouth and cry Lv 13:45
He **m** live alone in a place Lv 13:46
mildew it **m** be burned up. Lv 13:52
not spread, you **m** burn up the Lv 13:55
m cut the contaminated section Lv 13:56
You **m** burn up whatever is Lv 13:57
to be cleansed **m** wash his Lv 14:8
but he **m** remain outside his tent Lv 14:8
the eighth day he **m** take two Lv 14:10
and he **m** wave them as a Lv 14:12
The priest **m** sacrifice the sin Lv 14:19
He **m** then sacrifice one type of Lv 14:30
The priest **m** order them to clear Lv 14:36
the priest **m** order that the Lv 14:40
that is scraped off **m** be dumped Lv 14:41
they **m** take different stones Lv 14:42
priest **m** come and examine it. Lv 14:44
It **m** be torn down with its Lv 14:45

discharge touches **m** be broken, Lv 15:12
wooden utensil **m** be rinsed with Lv 15:12
He **m** take two turtledoves or two Lv 15:14
of semen **m** be washed with Lv 15:17
he **m** wash his clothes and bathe Lv 15:27
the eighth day she **m** take two Lv 15:29
You **m** keep the Israelites from Lv 15:31
He **m** tie a linen sash ⌊around Lv 16:4
he **m** bathe his body with water Lv 16:4
Then he **m** take a firepan full of Lv 16:12
he **m** do the same with its blood Lv 16:15
Then he **m** go out and sacrifice Lv 16:24
m be brought outside the camp Lv 16:27
and you **m** practice self-denial; Lv 16:31
has shed blood and **m** be cut off Lv 17:4
They **m** no longer offer their Lv 17:7
that person **m** be cut off from Lv 17:9
may be eaten **m** drain its blood Lv 17:13
You **m** not eat the blood of any Lv 17:14
whoever eats it **m** be cut off. Lv 17:14
You **m** not follow their customs. Lv 18:3
m not have sexual intercourse Lv 18:7
You **m** not commit any of these Lv 18:26
these abominations **m** be cut off Lv 18:29
You **m** keep My instruction to not Lv 18:30
on the third day **m** be burned up. Lv 19:6
That person **m** be cut off from Lv 19:8
You **m** not strip your vineyard Lv 19:10
You **m** not steal. You must not Lv 19:11
You **m** not act deceptively or lie Lv 19:11
You **m** not swear falsely by My Lv 19:12
You **m** not oppress your neighbor Lv 19:13
a hired hand **m** not remain with Lv 19:13
You **m** not curse the deaf or put Lv 19:14
You **m** not act unjustly when Lv 19:15
You **m** not go about spreading Lv 19:16
you **m** not jeopardize your Lv 19:16
You **m** not hate your brother in Lv 19:17
You **m** not crossbreed two Lv 19:19
freedom, there **m** be punishment. Lv 19:20
he **m** bring his ram as a Lv 19:21
all its fruit **m** be consecrated Lv 19:24
m keep My Sabbaths and revere Lv 19:30
your land, you **m** not oppress him Lv 19:33
You **m** regard the foreigner who Lv 19:34
You **m** not act unfairly in Lv 19:35
You **m** keep all My statutes and Lv 19:37
to Molech **m** be put to death; Lv 20:2
or mother, he **m** be put to death. Lv 20:9
adulteress **m** be put to death. Lv 20:10
Both of them **m** be put to death; Lv 20:11
both of them **m** be put to death. Lv 20:12
They **m** be put to death; Lv 20:13
he and they **m** be burned with Lv 20:14
an animal, he **m** be put to death; Lv 20:15
They **m** be put to death; Lv 20:16
They **m** be cut off publicly from Lv 20:17
Both of them **m** be cut off from Lv 20:18
m not have sexual intercourse Lv 20:19
You **m** not follow the statutes of Lv 20:23
Therefore you **m** distinguish the Lv 20:25
a spiritist **m** be put to death. Lv 20:27
of their God. They **m** be holy. Lv 21:6
her father; she **m** be burned up. Lv 21:9
m not dishevel his hair or tear Lv 21:10
He **m** not go near any dead person Lv 21:11
He **m** not leave the sanctuary or Lv 21:12
he **m** not go near the curtain or Lv 21:23
He **m** not eat an animal that died Lv 22:8
They **m** keep My instruction, Lv 22:9
m add a fifth to its value and Lv 22:14
The priests **m** not profane the Lv 22:15
m offer an unblemished male from Lv 22:19
there **m** be no defect in it. Lv 22:21
you **m** not sacrifice ⌊them⌋ in Lv 22:24
it **m** remain with its mother for Lv 22:27
You **m** not profane My holy name; Lv 22:32
I **m** be treated as holy among the Lv 22:32
seventh day there **m** be a Sabbath Lv 23:3
seven days you **m** eat unleavened Lv 23:6
you **m** not do any daily work." Lv 23:8
You **m** not eat bread, roasted Lv 23:14
You **m** not do any daily work, Lv 23:25
you **m** present a fire offering Lv 23:25
he **m** be cut off from his people. Lv 23:29
and you **m** practice self-denial. Lv 23:32
m celebrate it in the seventh Lv 23:41
of Israel **m** live in booths, Lv 23:42

He **m** regularly tend the lamps on Lv 24:4
the whole community **m** stone him. Lv 24:16
anyone, he **m** be put to death Lv 24:17
It **m** be a year of complete rest Lv 25:5
m be released at the Jubilee, Lv 25:33
you **m** not force him to do slave Lv 25:39
you **m** not rule over one another Lv 25:46
he **m** pay his redemption price in Lv 25:51
You **m** keep My Sabbaths and honor Lv 26:2
he **m** present the person before Lv 27:8
the animal **m** be presented before Lv 27:11
he **m** add a fifth to the Lv 27:13
m add a fifth to the valuation Lv 27:15
m add a fifth to the valuation Lv 27:19
it **m** be ransomed according to Lv 27:27
ransomed; he **m** be put to death Lv 27:29
he **m** add one-fifth to its value. Lv 27:31
near ⌊it⌋ **m** be put to death Nm 1:51
sanctuary⌋ **m** be put to death. Nm 3:10
Then they **m** place it with all Nm 4:10
You **m** send away both male or Nm 5:3
the priest **m** make the woman Nm 5:21
And the woman **m** reply, Nm 5:22
He **m** not drink vinegar made from Nm 6:3
m not drink any grape juice or Nm 6:3
You **m** not cut his hair Nm 6:5
He **m** be holy until the time is Nm 6:5
He **m** not go near a dead body Nm 6:6
m shave his head on the day of Nm 6:9
On that day he **m** consecrate his Nm 6:11
he **m** be brought to the entrance Nm 6:13
he **m** fulfill whatever vow he Nm 6:21
This is what you **m** do to them Nm 8:7
but he **m** not do the work Nm 8:26
m observe it at its appointed Nm 9:3
They **m** observe the Passover Nm 9:12
We **m** go up and take possession Nm 13:30
we **m** have seemed the same to Nm 13:33
How long ⌊**m** I endure⌋ this evil Nm 14:27
to the LORD **m** also present a Nm 15:4
m be four quarts of fine flour Nm 15:6
quarts of oil **m** be presented Nm 15:9
This is how you **m** prepare each Nm 15:12
The priest **m** then make atonement Nm 15:25
The priest **m** then make atonement Nm 15:28
because there **m** be one staff for Nm 17:3
They **m** not come near the Nm 18:3
But you **m** certainly redeem the Nm 18:15
you **m** not redeem the firstborn Nm 18:17
Israelites **m** never again come Nm 18:22
you **m** present part of it as an Nm 18:26
m present the entire offering Nm 18:29
you **m** not defile the Israelites' Nm 18:32
cow **m** be burned in his sight. Nm 19:5
Then the priest **m** wash his Nm 19:7
burned the cow **m** also wash his Nm 19:8
The ashes **m** be kept by the Nm 19:9
the cow's ashes **m** wash his Nm 19:10
purified **m** wash his clothes Nm 19:19
M we bring water out of this Nm 20:10
You **m** not travel through our Nm 20:18
"You **m** not travel through." Nm 20:20
you **m** only do what I tell you. Nm 22:20
I **m** speak only the message God Nm 22:38
Whatever the LORD says, I **m** do?" Nm 23:26
The land **m** be divided by lot; Nm 26:55
you **m** not do any work Nm 29:7
you **m** not do any daily work. Nm 29:12
You **m** offer these to the LORD at Nm 29:39
obligation, he **m** not break his Nm 30:2
m do whatever he has promised. Nm 30:2
It **m** still be purified with the Nm 31:23
m accept land in Canaan with Nm 32:30
you **m** drive out all the Nm 33:52
which you **m** provide so that the Nm 35:6
the murderer **m** be put to death. Nm 35:16
the murderer **m** be put to death. Nm 35:17
the murderer **m** be put to death. Nm 35:18
struck him **m** be put to death; Nm 35:21
and he **m** live there until the Nm 35:25
someone; he **m** be put to death. Nm 35:31
to the Israelites **m** not transfer Nm 36:7
Israelite tribe **m** marry someone Nm 36:8
you, so you **m** be very careful. Dt 2:4
You **m** not add anything to what I Dt 4:2
You **m** not bow down to them or Dt 5:9
m not do any work—you, your Dt 5:14
you **m** completely destroy them. Dt 7:2

m destroy all the peoples the Dt 7:16
You **m** burn up the carved images Dt 7:25
You **m** not bring any abhorrent Dt 7:26
You **m** carefully follow every Dt 8:1
You also **m** love the foreigner, Dt 10:19
You **m** understand today that it Dt 11:2
you **m** go to the place the LORD Dt 12:5
You **m** offer your burnt offerings Dt 12:14
and there you **m** do everything I Dt 12:14
but you **m** not eat the blood; Dt 12:16
You **m** eat them in the presence Dt 12:18
and you **m** not eat the life with Dt 12:23
m not do the same to the LORD Dt 12:31
m be careful to do everything Dt 12:32
You **m** follow the LORD your God Dt 13:4
You **m** keep His commands and Dt 13:4
you **m** worship Him and remain Dt 13:4
or dreamer **m** be put to death, Dt 13:5
You **m** purge the evil from you. Dt 13:5
you **m** not yield to him or listen Dt 13:8
Instead, you **m** kill him. Dt 13:9
m strike down the inhabitants Dt 13:15
The city **m** remain a mound of Dt 13:16
You **m** not eat any detestable Dt 14:3
m not eat their meat or touch Dt 14:8
You **m** not boil a young goat in Dt 14:21
seven years you **m** cancel debts. Dt 15:1
but you **m** forgive whatever your Dt 15:3
you **m** not be hardhearted or Dt 15:7
'You **m** willingly open your hand Dt 15:11
m set him free in the seventh Dt 15:12
You **m** consecrate to the LORD Dt 15:19
you **m** not sacrifice it to the Dt 15:21
But you **m** not eat its blood; Dt 15:23
m not eat leavened bread with Dt 16:3
m only sacrifice the Passover Dt 16:6
You **m** eat unleavened bread for Dt 16:8
and you **m** not do any work. Dt 16:8
Everyone ⌊**m** appear⌋ with a gift Dt 16:17
You **m** not sacrifice to the LORD Dt 17:1
you **m** investigate it thoroughly. Dt 17:4
you **m** bring out to your gates Dt 17:5
You **m** purge the evil from you. Dt 17:7
m go up to the place the LORD Dt 17:8
You **m** abide by the verdict they Dt 17:10
You **m** abide by the instruction Dt 17:11
your God or to the judge, **m** die. Dt 17:12
m purge the evil from Israel. Dt 17:12
he **m** not acquire many horses for Dt 17:16
He **m** not acquire many wives for Dt 17:17
He **m** not acquire very large Dt 17:17
You **m** be blameless before the Dt 18:13
brothers. You **m** listen to him. Dt 18:15
gods—that prophet **m** die.' Dt 18:20
of his city **m** send ⌊for him⌋, Dt 19:12
You **m** not look on him with pity Dt 19:13
You **m** not move your neighbor's Dt 19:14
A fact **m** be established by the Dt 19:15
in the dispute **m** stand in the Dt 19:17
you **m** do to him as he intended Dt 19:19
You **m** purge the evil from you. Dt 19:19
You **m** not show pity: life for Dt 19:21
you **m** make an offer of peace. Dt 20:10
you **m** strike down all its males Dt 20:13
you **m** not let any living thing Dt 20:16
You **m** completely destroy them— Dt 20:17
you **m** not destroy its trees by Dt 20:19
You **m** not cut them down. Dt 20:19
elders and judges **m** come out and Dt 21:2
You **m** purge from yourselves the Dt 21:9
She **m** shave her head, trim her Dt 21:12
but you **m** not sell her for money Dt 21:14
He **m** acknowledge the firstborn, Dt 21:17
and mother **m** take hold of him Dt 21:19
You **m** purge the evil from you, Dt 21:21
You **m** not defile the land the Dt 21:23
straying, you **m** not ignore it; Dt 22:1
found. You **m** not ignore ⌊it⌋ Dt 22:3
the road, you **m** not ignore it; Dt 22:4
you **m** help him lift it up. Dt 22:4
you **m** not take the mother along Dt 22:6
You **m** purge the evil from you. Dt 22:21
the woman and the woman **m** die. Dt 22:22
m purge the evil from Israel. Dt 22:22
you **m** take the two of them out Dt 22:24
You **m** purge the evil from you. Dt 22:24
the man who raped her **m** die. Dt 22:25
who raped her **m** give the young Dt 22:29

she **m** become his wife because	Dt 22:29
he **m** not violate his father's	Dt 22:30
the night, he **m** go outside the	Dt 23:10
he **m** wash with water,	Dt 23:11
You **m** have a place outside the	Dt 23:12
m have a digging tool in your	Dt 23:13
so your encampments **m** be holy.	Dt 23:14
He **m** not see anything improper	Dt 23:14
you **m** not charge your brother	Dt 23:20
but you **m** not put ⌊any⌋ in your	Dt 23:24
but you **m** not put a sickle to	Dt 23:25
m not bring guilt on the land	Dt 24:4
he **m** not go out with the army or	Dt 24:5
sells him, the kidnapper **m** die.	Dt 24:7
You **m** purge the evil from you.	Dt 24:7
m stand outside while the man	Dt 24:11
you **m** not sleep in ⌊the garment⌋	Dt 24:12
you **m** not go over the branches	Dt 24:20
you **m** not glean what is left.	Dt 24:21
she **m** go to the elders at the	Dt 25:7
her hand. You **m** not show pity.	Dt 25:12
You **m** not have two different	Dt 25:13
You **m** not have two differing dry	Dt 25:14
You **m** have a full and honest	Dt 25:15
you **m** take some of the first of	Dt 26:2
that time, you **m** say to him,	Dt 26:3
You **m** be careful to follow them	Dt 26:16
you **m** set up large stones and	Dt 27:2
you **m** not use any iron tool on	Dt 27:5
and you **m** do to them exactly as	Dt 31:5
book of instruction **m** not depart	Jos 1:8
your fighting men **m** cross over	Jos 1:14
you **m** break camp and follow it.	Jos 3:3
to the LORD and **m** go into the	Jos 6:19
the morning you **m** present	Jos 7:14
things set apart **m** be burned,	Jos 7:15
they **m** not hand the one who	Jos 20:5
He **m** die, because he tore down	Jdg 6:30
m never cut his hair, because	Jdg 13:5
m not eat anything that comes	Jdg 13:14
And she **m** not eat anything	Jdg 13:14
Your wife **m** do everything I have	Jdg 13:14
M you go to the uncircumcised	Jdg 14:3
you **m** give me 30 linen garments	Jdg 14:13
M I now die of thirst and fall	Jdg 15:18
There **m** be heirs for the	Jdg 21:17
The fat **m** be burned first;	1Sm 2:16
of Israel's God **m** not stay here	1Sm 5:7
It **m** return to its place so it	1Sm 5:11
you **m** not send it without ⌊an	1Sm 6:3
You **m** return it with a guilt	1Sm 6:3
but you **m** solemnly warn them and	1Sm 8:9
We **m** have a king over us.	1Sm 8:19
comes because he **m** bless the	1Sm 9:13
'You **m** set a king over us.'	1Sm 10:19
we **m** have a king rule over us'—	1Sm 12:12
'Each man **m** bring me his ox or	1Sm 14:34
said, "We **m** consult God here.	1Sm 14:36
of my son Jonathan, he **m** die!"	1Sm 14:39
said to Saul, "**M** Jonathan die,	1Sm 14:45
'Jonathan **m** not know of this,	1Sm 20:3
he **m** be ceremonially unclean—	1Sm 20:26
carefully what you **m** do,	1Sm 25:17
you and your men **m** march out in	1Sm 28:1
He **m** not go down with us into	1Sm 29:4
'He **m** not go into battle with us.	1Sm 29:9
you **m** not do this with what the	1Sm 30:23
M the sword devour forever?	2Sm 2:26
You **m** know that a great leader	2Sm 3:38
the Jebusites **m** go through the	2Sm 5:8
We **m** prove ourselves strong for	2Sm 10:12
m pay four lambs for that lamb.	2Sm 12:6
My lord **m** not think they have	2Sm 13:32
thought: I **m** speak to the king	2Sm 14:15
The people **m** be hungry,	2Sm 17:29
"You **m** not go!" the people	2Sm 18:3
You **m** never again go out with us	2Sm 21:17
You **m** not extinguish the lamp of	2Sm 21:17
who touches them **m** be armed	2Sm 23:7
you **m** be bringing good news."	1Kg 1:42
and they **m** not intermarry with	1Kg 11:2
Each of you **m** return home,	1Kg 12:24
'You **m** not eat bread or drink	1Kg 13:9
'You **m** not eat bread or drink	1Kg 13:17
you **m** bury me in the grave where	1Kg 13:31
How many times **m** I make you	1Kg 22:16
"He **m** be the king of Israel!"	1Kg 22:32
you **m** attack every fortified	2Kg 3:19
You **m** cut down every good tree	2Kg 3:19
You **m** ruin every good piece of	2Kg 3:19
The king of Israel **m** have hired	2Kg 7:6
None **m** be missing, for I have a	2Kg 10:19
You **m** completely surround the	2Kg 11:8
m be with the king in all his	2Kg 11:8
Fathers **m** not be put to death	2Kg 14:6
and children **m** not be put to	2Kg 14:6
told them, "You **m** not do this."	2Kg 17:12
You **m** worship at this altar in	2Kg 18:22
and your relatives **m** consecrate	1Ch 15:12
We **m** prove ourselves strong for	1Ch 19:13
for the LORD **m** be exceedingly	1Ch 22:5
I **m** make provision for it."	1Ch 22:5
My wife **m** not live in the house	2Ch 8:11
Each of you **m** return home,	2Ch 11:4
How many times **m** I make you	2Ch 18:15
"He **m** be the king of Israel!"	2Ch 18:31
He **m** reign, just as the LORD	2Ch 23:3
You **m** completely surround the	2Ch 23:7
m be with the king in all his	2Ch 23:7
Fathers **m** not die because of	2Ch 25:4
and children **m** not die because	2Ch 25:4
You **m** not bring the captives	2Ch 28:13
You **m** worship before one altar,	2Ch 32:12
and you **m** burn incense on it"?	2Ch 32:12
since we alone **m** build ⌊it⌋ for	Ezr 4:3
to Babylon **m** also be returned.	Ezr 6:5
you **m** stay away from that place,	Ezr 6:6
decree concerning what you **m** do,	Ezr 6:8
You **m** deliver to the God of	Ezr 7:19
heaven asks of you **m** be provided	Ezr 7:21
the God of heaven **m** be done	Ezr 7:23
and land tax **m** not be imposed on	Ezr 7:24
of Aaronic descent **m** accompany	Neh 10:38
and the Levites **m** take a tenth	Neh 10:38
You **m** not give your daughters in	Neh 13:25
you **m** not lay a hand on Job	Jb 1:12
me and my eyes **m** gaze at their	Jb 17:2
his own hands **m** give back his	Jb 20:10
wealth but **m** vomit it up;	Jb 20:15
He **m** return the fruit of his	Jb 20:18
I **m** speak so that I can find	Jb 32:20
I **m** open my lips and respond.	Jb 32:20
His⌋? You **m** choose, not I! So	Jb 34:33
that **m** be controlled with bit	Ps 32:9
Why **m** I go about in sorrow	Ps 42:9
Why **m** I go about in sorrow	Ps 43:2
I did not steal, I **m** repay.	Ps 69:4
We **m** not hide them from their	Ps 78:4
but **m** tell a future generation	Ps 78:4
There **m** not be a strange god	Ps 81:9
you **m** not bow down to a foreign	Ps 81:9
All the gods **m** worship Him.	Ps 97:7
How many days ⌊**m**⌋ Your servant	Ps 119:84
Your heart **m** hold on to my	Pr 4:4
he **m** pay seven times as much;	Pr 6:31
he **m** give up all the wealth in	Pr 6:31
the sun because I **m** leave it to	Ec 2:18
but he **m** give his portion to a	Ec 2:21
then one **m** exert more strength;	Ec 10:10
of my life I **m** go to the gates	Is 38:10
How long **m** I see the signal flag	Jr 4:21
This city **m** be punished.	Jr 6:6
m walk in every way I command	Jr 7:23
You **m** therefore declare to them:	Jr 7:28
The wise **m** not boast in his	Jr 9:23
the mighty **m** not boast in his	Jr 9:23
the rich **m** not boast in his	Jr 9:23
They **m** be carried because they	Jr 10:5
suffering, but I **m** bear it."	Jr 10:19
m tell them: This is what the	Jr 11:3
You **m** not prophesy in the name	Jr 11:21
we go? you **m** tell them: This	Jr 15:2
It is they who **m** return to you;	Jr 15:19
you **m** not return to them.	Jr 15:19
You **m** not marry or have sons or	Jr 16:2
You **m** not enter the house where	Jr 16:8
You **m** not carry a load out of	Jr 17:22
but you **m** consecrate the Sabbath	Jr 17:22
But you **m** say to this people,	Jr 21:8
You **m** say to the prophet:	Jr 23:37
LORD of Hosts says: You **m** drink!	Jr 25:28
him, yelling, "You **m** surely die!	Jr 26:8
This is what you **m** say to your	Jr 27:4
m not serve the king of Babylon,	Jr 27:14
You **m** confine him in stocks and	Jr 29:26
each of you **m** free his Hebrew	Jr 34:14
but then you **m** send him out free	Jr 34:14
and your sons **m** never drink wine	Jr 35:6
You **m** not build a house or sow	Jr 35:7
you **m** live in tents your whole	Jr 35:7
so you **m** go and read from the	Jr 36:6
You **m** also read them in the	Jr 36:6
We **m** surely tell the king all	Jr 36:16
and Jeremiah **m** hide yourselves	Jr 36:19
'You **m** not go to Egypt to live	Jr 43:2
to drink the cup **m** drink it,	Jr 49:12
for you **m** drink ⌊it⌋ too.	Jr 49:12
Babylon **m** fall ⌊because of⌋ the	Jr 51:49
You **m** say, 'LORD, You have	Jr 51:62
We **m** pay for the water we drink;	Lm 5:4
to them, and you **m** say to them:	Ezk 2:4
You **m** turn your face toward the	Ezk 4:7
so that I **m** depart from My	Ezk 8:6
that they **m** also fill the land	Ezk 8:17
You **m** also bear your disgrace,	Ezk 16:52
You yourself **m** bear the	Ezk 16:58
Each of you **m** throw away the	Ezk 20:7
you **m** bear the consequences of	Ezk 23:35
But you **m** not lament or weep or	Ezk 24:16
M you also trample the rest of	Ezk 34:18
M you also muddy the rest with	Ezk 34:18
they **m** not go out from the holy	Ezk 42:14
You **m** take some of its blood and	Ezk 43:20
Then you **m** take away the bull	Ezk 43:21
and it **m** be burned outside the	Ezk 43:21
You **m** present them before the	Ezk 43:24
unblemished, **m** also be offered.	Ezk 43:25
He **m** enter by way of the portico	Ezk 44:3
They **m** not approach Me to serve	Ezk 44:13
inner court they **m** wear linen	Ezk 44:17
they **m** not have on them anything	Ezk 44:17
They **m** wear linen turbans on	Ezk 44:18
they **m** take off the clothes they	Ezk 44:19
but **m** carefully trim their hair.	Ezk 44:20
but **m** marry a virgin from the	Ezk 44:22
They **m** teach My people the	Ezk 44:23
They **m** observe My laws and	Ezk 44:24
he **m** present his sin offering."	Ezk 44:27
m set aside a donation to the	Ezk 45:1
you **m** set aside an area one and	Ezk 45:6
You **m** have honest balances,	Ezk 45:10
of the land **m** take part in this	Ezk 45:16
The priest **m** take some of the	Ezk 45:19
You **m** do the same thing on the	Ezk 45:20
that faces east **m** be closed	Ezk 46:1
but the gate **m** not be closed	Ezk 46:2
he **m** go in by way of the gate's	Ezk 46:8
gate to worship **m** go out by way	Ezk 46:9
the south gate **m** go out by way	Ezk 46:9
No one **m** return through the gate	Ezk 46:9
but **m** go out by the opposite	Ezk 46:9
that faces east **m** be opened for	Ezk 46:12
and the gate **m** be closed after	Ezk 46:12
You **m** offer an unblemished	Ezk 46:13
You **m** also prepare a grain	Ezk 46:14
The prince **m** not take any of the	Ezk 46:18
They **m** not sell or exchange any	Ezk 48:14
they **m** not transfer this choice	Ezk 48:14
every kind of music **m** fall down	Dn 3:10
people **m** tremble in fear before	Dn 6:26
Now you **m** seal up the vision	Dn 8:26
I **m** return at once to fight	Dn 10:20
You **m** live with me many days.	Hs 3:3
the Israelites **m** live many days	Hs 3:4
now they **m** bear their guilt.	Hs 10:2
But you **m** return to your God.	Hs 12:6
Yahweh's name **m** not be invoked."	Am 6:10
They **m** not eat or drink water.	Jnh 3:7
man and beast **m** be covered with	Jnh 3:8
everyone **m** call out earnestly	Jnh 3:8
Each **m** turn from his evil ways	Jnh 3:8
I **m** endure the LORD's rage until	Mc 7:9
m I call for help and You do not	Hab 1:2
Now I **m** quietly wait for the day	Hab 3:16
These are the things you **m** do:	Zch 8:16
m not live on bread alone but	Mt 4:4
divorces his wife **m** give her a	Mt 5:31
You **m** not break your oath,	Mt 5:33
but you **m** keep your oaths to the	Mt 5:33
m not be like the hypocrites,	Mt 6:5
or mother **m** be put to death	Mt 15:4
that He **m** go to Jerusalem	Mt 16:21
come with Me, he **m** deny himself,	Mt 16:24
say that Elijah **m** come first?"	Mt 17:10

How long **m** I put up with you? Mt 17:17
For offenses **m** come, but woe to Mt 18:7
together, man **m** not separate." Mt 19:6
what good **m** I do to have eternal Mt 19:16
It **m** not be like that among you. Mt 20:26
among you **m** be your servant Mt 20:26
first among you **m** be your slave; Mt 20:27
these things **m** take place, Mt 24:6
then those in Judea **m** flee to Mt 24:16
on the housetop **m** not come down Mt 24:17
man in the field **m** not go back Mt 24:18
This is why you also **m** be ready, Mt 24:44
that say it **m** happen this way?" Mt 26:54
or mother **m** be put to death Mk 7:10
the Son of Man **m** suffer many Mk 8:31
My follower, he **m** deny himself, Mk 8:34
say that Elijah **m** come first?" Mk 9:11
of Man that He **m** suffer many Mk 9:12
How long **m** I put up with you? Mk 9:19
he **m** be last of all and servant Mk 9:35
together, man **m** not separate." Mk 10:9
m I do to inherit eternal life? Mk 10:17
But it **m** not be like that among Mk 10:43
among you **m** be your servant Mk 10:43
first among you **m** be a slave to Mk 10:44
these things **m** take place, Mk 13:7
And the good news **m** first be Mk 13:10
then those in Judea **m** flee to Mk 13:14
on the housetop **m** not come down Mk 13:15
man in the field **m** not go back Mk 13:16
And you **m** watch! I have told you Mk 13:23
the Scriptures **m** be fulfilled." Mk 14:49
has two shirts **m** share with Lk 3:11
one who has food **m** do the same." Lk 3:11
Man **m** not live on bread alone." Lk 4:4
I **m** proclaim the good news about Lk 4:43
The Son of Man **m** suffer many Lk 9:22
come with Me, he **m** deny himself, Lk 9:23
m I do to inherit eternal life? Lk 10:25
that very hour what **m** be said." Lk 12:12
You **m** be like people waiting for Lk 12:36
Yet I **m** travel today, tomorrow, Lk 13:33
and I **m** go out and see it. Lk 14:18
I repent,' you **m** forgive him." Lk 17:4
first He **m** suffer many things Lk 17:25
m not come down to get them. Lk 17:31
is in the field **m** not turn back. Lk 17:31
m I do to inherit eternal life? Lk 18:18
today I **m** stay at your house. Lk 19:5
these things **m** take place first, Lk 21:9
Then those in Judea **m** flee to Lk 21:21
inside the city **m** leave it, Lk 21:21
in the country **m** not enter it, Lk 21:21
But it **m** not be like that among Lk 22:26
greatest among you **m** become like Lk 22:26
what is written **m** be fulfilled Lk 22:37
'The Son of Man **m** be betrayed Lk 24:7
and the Psalms **m** be fulfilled." Lk 24:44
you that you **m** be born again. Jn 3:7
the Son of Man **m** be lifted up, Jn 3:14
He **m** increase, but I must Jn 3:30
increase, but I **m** decrease." Jn 3:30
who worship Him **m** worship in Jn 4:24
m do the works of Him who sent Jn 9:4
I **m** bring them also, and they Jn 10:16
serves Me, he **m** follow Me. Jn 12:26
'The Son of Man **m** be lifted up'? Jn 12:34
the Scripture **m** be fulfilled: Jn 13:18
you **m** also love one another. Jn 13:34
Your heart **m** not be troubled. Jn 14:1
Your heart **m** not be troubled or Jn 14:27
according to that law He **m** die, Jn 19:7
Scripture that He **m** rise from Jn 20:9
"Brothers, what **m** we do?" Ac 2:37
Heaven **m** welcome Him until the Ac 3:21
m listen to Him in everything Ac 3:22
people by which we **m** be saved." Ac 4:12
We **m** obey God rather than men. Ac 5:29
you will be told what you **m** do." Ac 9:6
much he **m** suffer for My name! Ac 9:16
clean, you **m** not call common. Ac 10:15
shown me that I **m** not call any Ac 10:28
clean, you **m** not call common. Ac 11:9
Sirs, what **m** I do to be saved? Ac 16:30
he said, "I **m** see Rome as well! Ac 19:21
you **m** keep calm and not do Ac 19:36
it **m** be decided in a legal Ac 19:39
You **m** not speak evil of a ruler Ac 23:5
so you **m** also testify in Rome." Ac 23:11
that the Messiah **m** suffer, Ac 26:23
You **m** stand before Caesar. Ac 27:24
m run aground on a certain island. Ac 27:26
preach, "You **m** not steal"—do Rm 2:21
"You **m** not commit adultery"— Rm 2:22
God **m** be true, but everyone is a Rm 3:4
Love **m** be without hypocrisy. Rm 12:9
Everyone **m** submit to the Rm 13:1
Therefore, you **m** submit, not Rm 13:5
One who eats **m** not look down on Rm 14:3
who does not eat **m** not criticize Rm 14:3
Each one **m** be fully convinced in Rm 14:5
we **m** pursue what promotes peace Rm 14:19
Each one of us **m** please his Rm 15:2
one who boasts **m** boast in the 1Co 1:31
But each one **m** be careful how he 1Co 3:10
he **m** become foolish so that he 1Co 3:18
she **m** remain unmarried or be 1Co 7:11
with him, he **m** not leave her. 1Co 7:12
she **m** not leave her husband. 1Co 7:13
each one **m** live his life in the 1Co 7:17
age, and so it **m** be, he can do 1Co 7:36
thinks he stands **m** be careful 1Co 10:12
There **m**, indeed, be factions 1Co 11:19
All things **m** be done for 1Co 14:26
turn, and someone **m** interpret. 1Co 14:27
everything **m** be done decently 1Co 14:40
For He **m** reign until He puts all 1Co 15:25
corruptible **m** be clothed with 1Co 15:53
this mortal **m** be clothed with 1Co 15:53
every ⌊action⌋ **m** be done with 1Co 16:14
For we **m** all appear before the 2Co 5:10
one who boasts **m** boast in the 2Co 10:17
we **m** also follow the Spirit. Gl 5:25
We **m** not become conceited, Gl 5:26
the message **m** share his goods Gl 6:6
So we **m** not get tired of doing Gl 6:9
we **m** work for the good of all, Gl 6:10
The thief **m** no longer steal. Eph 4:28
he **m** do honest work with his own Eph 4:28
insult and slander **m** be removed Eph 4:31
This is why you **m** take up the Eph 6:13
But now you **m** also put away all Col 3:8
you, so also you **m** ⌊forgive⌋. Col 3:13
us how you **m** walk and please 1Th 4:1
This means one **m** not transgress 1Th 4:6
then, we **m** not sleep, like the 1Th 5:6
we **m** stay awake and be sober. 1Th 5:6
we **m** be sober and put the armor 1Th 5:8
We **m** always thank God for you, 2Th 1:3
But we **m** always thank God for 2Th 2:13
know how you **m** imitate us: 2Th 3:7
therefore, **m** be above reproach, 1Tm 3:2
He **m** not be a new convert, 1Tm 3:6
m have a good reputation among 1Tm 3:7
And they **m** also be tested first; 1Tm 3:10
Wives, too, **m** be worthy of 1Tm 3:11
Deacons **m** be husbands of one 1Tm 3:12
You **m** not muzzle an ox that is 1Tm 5:18
yoke as slaves **m** regard their 1Tm 6:1
the name of the Lord **m** turn away 2Tm 2:19
The Lord's slave **m** not quarrel, 2Tm 2:24
but **m** be gentle to everyone, 2Tm 2:24
God's manager, **m** be blameless, Ti 1:7
But you **m** speak what is Ti 2:1
And our people **m** also learn to Ti 3:14
all God's angels **m** worship Him. Heb 1:6
We **m** therefore pay even more Heb 2:1
to whom we **m** give an account Heb 4:13
he **m** make a sin offering for Heb 5:3
there **m** be a change of law as Heb 7:12
the testator **m** be established. Heb 9:16
near to Him **m** believe that He Heb 11:6
the mountain, it **m** be stoned! Heb 12:20
Marriage **m** be respected by all, Heb 13:4
But endurance **m** do its complete Jms 1:4
everyone **m** be quick to hear, Jms 1:19
Your laughter **m** change to Jms 4:9
also **m** be patient. Strengthen Jms 5:8
Your "yes" **m** be "yes," and your Jms 5:12
and your "no" **m** be "no," Jms 5:12
see good days **m** keep his tongue 1Pt 3:10
and he **m** turn away from evil and 1Pt 3:11
He **m** seek peace and pursue it, 1Pt 3:11
the beginning **m** remain in you. 1Jn 2:24
we **m** not love in word or speech, 1Jn 3:18
we also **m** love one another. 1Jn 4:11
who loves God **m** also love his 1Jn 4:21
beginning: you **m** walk in love. 2Jn 6
His slaves what **m** quickly take Rv 1:1
show you what **m** take place after Rv 4:1
You **m** prophesy again about many Rv 10:11
he **m** be killed in this way. Rv 11:5
understanding **m** calculate the Rv 13:18
he **m** remain for a little while. Rv 17:10
he **m** be released for a short Rv 20:3
His servants what **m** quickly take Rv 22:6

MUSTACHE *(2)*
cover ⌊your⌋ **m** or eat the bread Ezk 24:17
cover ⌊your⌋ **m** or eat the bread Ezk 24:22

MUSTARD *(5)*
is like a **m** seed that a man Mt 13:31
have faith the size of a **m** seed, Mt 17:20
It's like a **m** seed that, when Mk 4:31
It's like a **m** seed that a man Lk 13:19
faith the size of a **m** seed," Lk 17:6

MUTE *(10)*
Who makes him **m** or deaf, seeing Ex 4:11
tongue of the **m** will sing for Is 35:6
all of them are **m** dogs, they Is 56:10
and you will be **m** and unable to Ezk 3:26
will speak and no longer be **m**. Ezk 24:27
opened and I was no longer **m**. Ezk 33:22
Wake up! or to **m** stone: Come Hab 2:19
to it, "You **m** and deaf spirit, I Mk 9:25
driving out a demon that was **m**. Lk 11:14
the man who had been **m**, spoke, Lk 11:14

MUTILATE *(1)*
out for those who **m** the flesh. Php 3:2

MUTTER *(2)*
the spiritists who chirp and **m**," Is 8:19
lies, and you **m** injustice. Is 59:3

MUTTERING *(1)*
heard the crowd **m** these things Jn 7:32

MUTUALLY *(1)*
to be **m** encouraged by each Rm 1:12

MUZZLE *(4)*
Do not **m** an ox while it treads Dt 25:4
my mouth with a **m** as long as the Ps 39:1
Do not **m** an ox while it treads 1Co 9:9
You must not **m** an ox that is 1Tm 5:18

MY *(4512)*
(See pp. xi-xii.)

MY-PEOPLE *(1)*
M," and she who is Rm 9:25

MYRA *(1)*
we reached **M** in Lycia. Ac 27:5

MYRIADS *(1)*
to **m** of angels in festive Heb 12:22

MYRRH *(16)*
and a half pounds of liquid **m**, Ex 30:23
with oil of **m** for six months Est 2:12
M, aloes, and cassia ⌊perfume⌋ Ps 45:8
I've perfumed my bed with **m**, Pr 7:17
My love is a sachet of **m** to me, Sg 1:13
scented with **m** and frankincense Sg 3:6
the mountain of **m** and the hill Sg 4:6
frankincense, **m** and aloes, with Sg 4:14
I gather my **m** with my spices. Sg 5:1
dripped with **m**, my fingers with Sg 5:5
with flowing **m** on the handles Sg 5:5
lilies, dripping with flowing **m**. Sg 5:13
gold, frankincense, and **m**. Mt 2:11
to give Him wine mixed with **m**, Mk 15:23
about 75 pounds of **m** and aloes. Jn 19:39
spice, incense, **m**, and Rv 18:13

MYRTLE *(5)*
wild olive, **m**, palm, and ⌊other Neh 8:15
of the brier, a **m** will come up; Is 55:13
standing among the **m** trees in Zch 1:8
among the **m** trees explained, Zch 1:10
LORD standing among the **m** trees, Zch 1:11

MYRTLES *(1)*
acacias, **m**, and olive trees Is 41:19

MYSELF *(128)*
(See pp. xi-xii.)

MYSIA *(2)*
they came to **M**, they tried to go Ac 16:7
So, bypassing **M**, they came down Ac 16:8

MYSTERIES *(8)*
He reveals **m** from the darkness Jb 12:22

I will speak **m** from the past— Ps 78:2
a God in heaven who reveals **m**, Dn 2:28
The revealer of **m** has let you Dn 2:29
a revealer of **m**, since you were Dn 2:47
Christ and managers of God's **m**. 1Co 4:1
understand all **m** and all 1Co 13:2
he speaks **m** in the Spirit. 1Co 14:2

MYSTERIOUS *(1)*
inner man and the heart are **m**. Ps 64:6

MYSTERY *(23)*
for mercy concerning this **m**, Dn 2:18
m was then revealed to Daniel Dn 2:19
have let us know the king's **m**. Dn 2:23
the king the **m** he asked about. Dn 2:27
this **m** has been revealed to me, Dn 2:30
you were able to reveal this **m**." Dn 2:47
gods and that no **m** puzzles you, Dn 4:9
you to be unaware of this **m**: Rm 11:25
God's hidden wisdom in a **m**, 1Co 2:7
I am telling you a **m**: 1Co 15:51
known to us the **m** of His will, Eph 1:9
The **m** was made known to me by Eph 3:3
about the **m** of the Messiah. Eph 3:4
of the **m** hidden for ages Eph 3:9
This **m** is profound, but I am Eph 5:32
boldness the **m** of the gospel. Eph 6:19
the **m** hidden for ages and Col 1:26
the glorious wealth of this **m**, Col 1:27
have the knowledge of God's **m**— Col 2:2
to speak the **m** of the Messiah— Col 4:3
For the **m** of lawlessness is 2Th 2:7
holding the **m** of the faith with 1Tm 3:9
the **m** of godliness is great: 1Tm 3:16

MYTHS *(5)*
pay attention to **m** and endless 1Tm 1:4
do with irreverent and silly **m**. 1Tm 4:7
truth and will turn aside to **m**. 2Tm 4:4
attention to Jewish **m** and the Ti 1:14
contrived **m** when we made known 2Pt 1:16

N

NAAM *(1)*
Iru, Elah, and **N**. Elah's son: 1Ch 4:15

NAAMAH *(5)*
Tubal-cain's sister was **N**. Gn 4:22
Beth-dagon, **N**, and Makkedah— Jos 15:41
name was **N** the Ammonite. 1Kg 14:21
name was **N** the Ammonite. 1Kg 14:31
name was **N** the Ammonite. 2Ch 12:13

NAAMAN *(21)*
(AKA RAPHA)
Ashbel, Gera, **N**, Ehi, Rosh, Gn 46:21
descendants ⌊from⌋ Ard and **N**: Nm 26:40
the Naamite clan from **N**. Nm 26:40
N, commander of the army for the 2Kg 5:1
So **N** went and told his master 2Kg 5:4
you my servant **N** for you to cure 2Kg 5:6
So **N** came with his horses and 2Kg 5:9
N got angry and left, saying, 2Kg 5:11
N went down and dipped himself 2Kg 5:14
N and his whole company went 2Kg 5:15
N urged him to accept it, 2Kg 5:16
N responded, "If not, please let 2Kg 5:17
After **N** had traveled a short 2Kg 5:19
let this Aramean **N** off lightly 2Kg 5:20
Gehazi pursued **N**. When Naaman 2Kg 5:21
When **N** saw someone running 2Kg 5:21
But **N** insisted, "Please, accept 2Kg 5:23
N gave them to two of his young 2Kg 5:23
Abishua, **N**, Ahoah, 1Ch 8:4
N, Ahijah, and Gera. Gera 1Ch 8:7
was healed—only **N** the Syrian." Lk 4:27

NAAMAN'S *(2)*
a young girl who served **N** wife. 2Kg 5:2
N skin disease will cling to you 2Kg 5:27

NAAMATHITE *(4)*
and Zophar the **N**—heard about Jb 2:11
Then Zophar the **N** replied: Jb 11:1
Then Zophar the **N** replied: Jb 20:1
and Zophar the **N** went and did as Jb 42:9

NAAMITE *(1)*
the **N** clan from Naaman. Nm 26:40

NAARAH *(3)*
it descended to Ataroth and **N**, Jos 16:7
and had two wives, Helah and **N**. 1Ch 4:5
N bore him Ahuzzam, Hepher, 1Ch 4:6

NAARAH'S *(1)*
Haahashtari. These were **N** sons. 1Ch 4:6

NAARAI *(1)*
(AKA PAARAI)
the Carmelite, **N** son of Ezbai, 1Ch 11:37

NAARAN *(1)*
N to the east, Gezer and its 1Ch 7:28

NABAL *(18)*
man's name was **N**, and his wife's 1Sm 25:3
he heard that **N** was shearing 1Sm 25:4
you come to **N**, greet him in my 1Sm 25:5
these things to **N** on David's 1Sm 25:9
N asked them, "Who is David? 1Sm 25:10
she did not tell her husband **N**. 1Sm 25:19
to this worthless man **N**, 1Sm 25:25
His name is **N**, and stupidity is 1Sm 25:25
trouble for my lord be like **N**. 1Sm 25:26
N wouldn't have had any men left 1Sm 25:34
Abigail went to **N**, and there he 1Sm 25:36
N was in a good mood and very 1Sm 25:36
the morning when **N** sobered up, 1Sm 25:37
later, the LORD struck **N** dead. 1Sm 25:38
David heard that **N** was dead, 1Sm 25:39
the widow of **N** the Carmelite, 1Sm 30:5
the widow of **N** the Carmelite. 2Sm 2:2
the widow of **N** the Carmelite; 2Sm 3:3

NABAL'S *(5)*
One of **N** young men informed 1Sm 25:14
men informed Abigail, **N** wife: 1Sm 25:14
my cause against **N** insults and 1Sm 25:39
LORD brought **N** evil deeds back 1Sm 25:39
and Abigail of Carmel, **N** widow. 1Sm 27:3

NABOTH *(20)*
N the Jezreelite had a vineyard; 1Kg 21:1
Ahab spoke to **N**, saying, "Give 1Kg 21:2
N said to Ahab, "I will never 1Kg 21:3
because of what **N** the Jezreelite 1Kg 21:4
I spoke to **N** the Jezreelite," 1Kg 21:6
vineyard of **N** the Jezreelite. 1Kg 21:7
who lived with **N** in his city. 1Kg 21:8
a fast and seat **N** at the head 1Kg 21:9
a fast and seated **N** at the head 1Kg 21:12
against **N** in the presence 1Kg 21:13
"**N** has cursed God and king!" 1Kg 21:13
"**N** has been stoned to death." 1Kg 21:14
heard that **N** had been stoned to 1Kg 21:15
the vineyard of **N** the Jezreelite 1Kg 21:15
for silver, since **N** isn't alive, 1Kg 21:15
Ahab heard that **N** was dead, 1Kg 21:16
the vineyard of **N** the Jezreelite 1Kg 21:16
of land of **N** the Jezreelite. 2Kg 9:21
belonging to **N** the Jezreelite. 2Kg 9:25
saw the blood of **N** and the blood 2Kg 9:26

NABOTH'S *(2)*
You'll find him in **N** vineyard, 1Kg 21:18
where the dogs licked **N** blood, 1Kg 21:19

NACON'S *(1)*
(AKA CHIDON)
they came to **N** threshing floor, 2Sm 6:6

NADAB *(21)*
bore him **N** and Abihu, Eleazar Ex 6:23
you and Aaron, **N**, and Abihu, and Ex 24:1
up with Aaron, **N**, and Abihu, and Ex 24:9
Aaron, his sons **N** and Abihu, Ex 28:1
Aaron's sons **N** and Abihu each Lv 10:1
N, the firstborn, and Abihu, Nm 3:2
But **N** and Abihu died in the Nm 3:4
N, Abihu, Eleazar, and Ithamar Nm 26:60
but **N** and Abihu died when they Nm 26:61
and his son **N** became king in his 1Kg 14:20
N son of Jeroboam became king 1Kg 15:25
N did what was evil in the 1Kg 15:26
of Issachar conspired against **N**, 1Kg 15:27
while **N** and all Israel 1Kg 15:27
Baasha killed **N** and reigned in 1Kg 15:28
Shammai's sons: **N** and Abishur. 1Ch 2:28
N, Abihu, Eleazar, and Ithamar. 1Ch 6:3
son, then Zur, Kish, Baal, **N**, 1Ch 8:30
then Zur, Kish, Baal, Ner, **N**, 1Ch 9:36
sons were **N**, Abihu, Eleazar, 1Ch 24:1
N and Abihu died before their 1Ch 24:2

NADAB'S *(2)*
rest of the events of **N** ⌊reign⌋, 1Kg 15:31
N sons: Seled and Appaim. Seled 1Ch 2:30

NAGGAI *(1)*
⌊son⌋ of Esli, ⌊son⌋ of **N**, Lk 3:25

NAGGED *(2)*
because she had **n** him so much. Jdg 14:17
Because she **n** him day after day Jdg 16:16

NAGGING *(5)*
and a wife's **n** is an endless Pr 19:13
to share a house with a **n** wife. Pr 21:9
than with a **n** and hot-tempered Pr 21:19
in a house shared with a **n** wife. Pr 25:24
day and a **n** wife are alike. Pr 27:15

NAHALAL *(2)*
Kattath, **N**, Shimron, Idalah, Jos 19:15
and **N** with its pasturelands— Jos 21:35

NAHALIEL *(2)*
Mattanah to **N**, from Nahaliel Nm 21:19
to Nahaliel, from **N** to Bamoth, Nm 21:19

NAHALOL *(1)*
of Kitron or the residents of **N**, Jdg 1:30

NAHAM *(1)*
Hodiah's wife, the sister of **N**: 1Ch 4:19

NAHAMANI *(1)*
Azariah, Raamiah, **N**, Mordecai, Neh 7:7

NAHARAI *(2)*
the Ammonite, **N** the Beerothite, 2Sm 23:37
the Ammonite, **N** the Beerothite, 1Ch 11:39

NAHASH *(9)*
N the Ammonite came up and laid 1Sm 11:1
N the Ammonite replied, "I'll 1Sm 11:2
the men of Jabesh said to ⌊**N**⌋, 1Sm 11:10
when you saw that **N** king of the 1Sm 12:12
show kindness to Hanun son of **N**, 2Sm 10:2
married Abigail daughter of **N**. 2Sm 17:25
Shobi son of **N** from Rabbah of 2Sm 17:27
King **N** of the Ammonites died, 1Ch 19:1
show kindness to Hanun son of **N**, 1Ch 19:2

NAHATH *(5)*
N, Zerah, Shammah, and Mizzah. Gn 36:13
Chiefs **N**, Zerah, Shammah, and Gn 36:17
N, Zerah, Shammah, and Mizzah. 1Ch 1:37
his son Zophai, his son **N**, 1Ch 6:26
Jehiel, Azaziah, **N**, Asahel, 2Ch 31:13

NAHBI *(1)*
N son of Vophsi from the tribe Nm 13:14

NAHOR *(18)*
lived 30 years and fathered **N**. Gn 11:22
he fathered **N**, Serug lived 200 Gn 11:23
N lived 29 years and fathered Gn 11:24
N lived 119 years and fathered Gn 11:25
fathered Abram, **N**, and Haran. Gn 11:26
fathered Abram, **N**, and Haran, Gn 11:27
Abram and **N** took wives: Gn 11:29
borne sons to your brother **N**: Gn 22:20
Milcah bore these eight to **N**, Gn 22:23
he set out for the town of **N**, Gn 24:10
wife of Abraham's brother **N**— Gn 24:15
of Milcah, whom she bore to **N**." Gn 24:24
daughter of Bethuel son of **N**, Gn 24:47
"Do you know Laban son of **N**?" Gn 29:5
and the gods of **N**—the gods of Gn 31:53
the father of Abraham and **N**, Jos 24:2
Serug, **N**, Terah, 1Ch 1:26
son⌋ of Terah, ⌊son⌋ of **N**, Lk 3:34

NAHOR'S *(1)*
and **N** wife was named Milcah. Gn 11:29

NAHSHON *(12)*
of Amminadab and sister of **N**. Ex 6:23
N son of Amminadab from Judah; Nm 1:7
of Judah is **N** son of Amminadab. Nm 2:3
first day was **N** son of Amminadab Nm 7:12
the offering of **N** son of Nm 7:17
N son of Amminadab was over Nm 10:14
fathered **N**, who fathered Ru 4:20
Amminadab fathered **N**, a leader 1Ch 2:10
N fathered Salma, and Salma 1Ch 2:11
fathered **N**, Nahshon fathered Mt 1:4
Nahshon, **N** fathered Salmon, Mt 1:4
⌊son⌋ of Salmon, ⌊son⌋ of **N**, Lk 3:32

NAHUM *(2)*
the vision of **N** the Elkoshite. Nah 1:1
Amos, ⌊son⌋ of **N**, ⌊son⌋ of Esli, Lk 3:25

NAIL *(1)*
people to **n** Him to a cross Ac 2:23

NAILING *(1)*
of the way by **n** it to the cross Col 2:14

NAILS *(9)*
must shave her head, trim her **n**, Dt 21:12
iron to make the **n** for the doors 1Ch 22:3
weight of the **n** was 20 ounces 2Ch 3:9
are like firmly embedded **n**. Ec 12:11
fastens it with **n** so that it Is 41:7
is fastened with hammer and **n**, Jr 10:4
feathers⌋ and his **n** like birds' Dn 4:33
the mark of the **n** in His hands, Jn 20:25
finger into the mark of the **n**, Jn 20:25

NAIN *(1)*
on His way to a town called **N**. Lk 7:11

NAIOTH *(6)*
and Samuel left and stayed at **N**. 1Sm 19:18
that David was at **N** in Ramah, 1Sm 19:19
"At **N** in Ramah," someone said. 1Sm 19:22
So he went to **N** in Ramah. 1Sm 19:23
until he entered **N** in Ramah. 1Sm 19:23
David fled from **N** in Ramah and 1Sm 20:1

NAKED *(40)*
the man and his wife were **n**, Gn 2:25
and they knew they were **n**; Gn 3:7
I was afraid because I was **n**, Gn 3:10
Who told you that you were **n**? Gn 3:11
his father **n** and told his two Gn 9:22
they did not see their father **n**. Gn 9:23
to cover ⌊their⌋ **n** bodies; Ex 28:42
and lay⌋ **n** all that day 1Sm 19:24
clothes for their **n** ones from 2Ch 28:15
N I came from my mother's womb, Jb 1:21
and **n** I will leave this life. Jb 1:21
clothes and leaving them **n**. Jb 22:6
spend the night **n**, having no Jb 24:7
clothing, they wander about **n**. Jb 24:10
Sheol is **n** before God, and Jb 26:6
he will go again, **n** as he came; Ec 5:15
did so, going **n** and barefoot— Is 20:2
Isaiah has gone **n** and barefoot Is 20:3
and old alike, **n** and barefoot, Is 20:4
clothe the **n** when you see him, Is 58:7
hair grew, but you were stark **n**. Ezk 16:7
you were stark **n** and lying in Ezk 16:22
so they see you completely **n**. Ezk 16:37
jewelry, and leave you stark **n**. Ezk 16:39
and covers the **n** with clothing. Ezk 18:7
and covers the **n** with clothing. Ezk 18:16
leave you stark **n**, so that the Ezk 23:29
will strip her **n** and expose her Hs 2:3
will flee **n** on that day— Am 2:16
I will walk barefoot and **n**. Mc 1:8
I was **n** and you clothed Me; Mt 25:36
was **n** and you didn't clothe Me, Mt 25:43
cloth wrapped around his **n** body, Mk 14:51
cloth behind and ran away **n**. Mk 14:52
out of that house **n** and wounded. Ac 19:16
clothed, we will not be found **n**. 2Co 5:3
all things are **n** and exposed to Heb 4:13
pitiful, poor, blind, and **n**, Rv 3:17
clothed so that he may not go **n**, Rv 16:15
will make her desolate and **n**, Rv 17:16

NAKEDNESS *(16)*
they covered their father's **n**. Gn 9:23
so that your **n** is not exposed on Ex 20:26
in famine, thirst, **n**, and a lack Dt 28:48
Your **n** will be uncovered, and Is 47:3
her, for they have seen her **n**. Lm 1:8
over you and covered your **n**. Ezk 16:8
out and your **n** exposed by your Ezk 16:36
expose your **n** to them so they Ezk 16:37
exposed her **n**, seized her sons Ezk 23:10
promiscuity and exposed her **n**, Ezk 23:18
which were to cover her **n**. Hs 2:9
in shameful **n**, you residents Mc 1:11
and display your **n** to nations, Nah 3:5
in order to look at their **n**! Hab 2:15
or famine or **n** or danger or Rm 8:35
your shameful **n** not be exposed, Rv 3:18

NAME *(753)*
The **n** of the first is Pishon, Gn 2:11
The **n** of the second river is Gn 2:13
The **n** of the third river is the Gn 2:14
living creature, that was its **n**. Gn 2:19
to call on the **n** of the LORD. Gn 4:26
Let us make a **n** for ourselves; Gn 11:4
Therefore its **n** is called Gn 11:9
will make your **n** great, and you Gn 12:2
You will **n** him Ishmael, for the Gn 16:11
Abram gave the **n** Ishmael to the Gn 16:15
Your **n** will no longer be Abram, Gn 17:5
but your **n** will be Abraham, Gn 17:5
Sarai, for Sarah will be her **n**. Gn 17:15
a son, and you will **n** him Isaac. Gn 17:19
Therefore the **n** of the city is Gn 19:22
whose **n** was Reumah, also Gn 22:24
wife, whose **n** was Keturah, Gn 25:1
Therefore the **n** of the city is Gn 26:33
Laban said, "**N** your wages, and I Gn 30:28
"What is your **n**?" the man asked. Gn 32:27
"Your **n** will no longer be Jacob," Gn 32:28
Him, "Please tell me Your **n**." Gn 32:29
Why do you ask My **n**? Gn 32:29
said to him: Your **n** is Jacob; Gn 35:10
but Israel will be your **n**. Gn 35:10
the **n** of his city was Dinhabah. Gn 36:32
the **n** of his city was Avith. Gn 36:35
and his wife's **n** was Mehetabel Gn 36:39
firstborn, and her **n** was Tamar. Gn 38:6
gave Joseph the **n** Gn 41:45
be called by my **n** and the names Gn 48:16
Jacob, by the **n** of the Shepherd Gn 49:24
they ask me, 'What is His **n**?' Ex 3:13
you. This is My **n** forever; this Ex 3:15
to speak in Your **n** he has caused Ex 5:23
did not make My **n** Yahweh known Ex 6:3
and to make My **n** known in all Ex 9:16
is a warrior; Yahweh is His **n**. Ex 15:3
not misuse the **n** of the LORD Ex 20:7
punish anyone who misuses His **n**. Ex 20:7
I cause My **n** to be remembered Ex 20:24
rebellion, for My **n** is in Him. Ex 23:21
have appointed by **n** Bezalel son Ex 31:2
I know you by **n**, and you have Ex 33:12
My sight, and I know you by **n**." Ex 33:17
proclaim the **n** Yahweh before you Ex 33:19
and proclaimed ⌊His⌋ **n** Yahweh. Ex 34:5
has appointed by **n** Bezalel son Ex 35:30
not profane the **n** of your God; Lv 18:21
must not swear falsely by My **n**, Lv 19:12
profaning the **n** of your God; Lv 19:12
and profaning My holy **n**. Lv 20:3
not profane the **n** of their God, Lv 21:6
they do not profane My holy **n**; Lv 22:2
You must not profane My holy **n**; Lv 22:32
son cursed and blasphemed the **N**, Lv 24:11
His mother's **n** was Shelomith, Lv 24:11
blasphemes the **n** of the LORD is Lv 24:16
blasphemes the **N**, he is to be Lv 24:16
who had been designated by **n**, Nm 1:17
These were Levi's sons by **n**: Nm 3:17
or more listed by **n** was 22,273. Nm 3:43
to assign by **n** the items that Nm 4:32
they will put My **n** on the Nm 6:27
Write each man's **n** on his staff. Nm 17:2
Write Aaron's **n** on Levi's staff, Nm 17:3
n of the slain Israelite man, Nm 25:14
The **n** of the slain Midianite Nm 25:15
the **n** of Asher's daughter was Nm 26:46
The **n** of Amram's wife was Nm 26:59
Why should the **n** of our father Nm 27:4
called it Nobah after his own **n**. Nm 32:42
He called Bashan by his own **n**, Dt 3:14
not misuse the **n** of the LORD Dt 5:11
punish anyone who misuses His **n**. Dt 5:11
and take ⌊your⌋ oaths in His **n**. Dt 6:13
blot out their **n** under heaven. Dt 9:14
bless in His **n**, as it is today Dt 10:8
to Him and take oaths in His **n**. Dt 10:20
to put His **n** for His dwelling Dt 12:5
the place to have His **n** dwell. Dt 12:11
chooses to put His **n** is too far Dt 12:21
He chooses to have His **n** dwell, Dt 14:23
to put His **n** is too far away Dt 14:24
chooses to have His **n** dwell. Dt 16:2
God chooses to have His **n** dwell. Dt 16:6
He chooses to have His **n** dwell— Dt 16:11
minister in the LORD's **n** from Dt 18:5
serve in the **n** of the LORD his Dt 18:7
My words that he speaks in My **n**. Dt 18:19
speak in My **n** a message I have Dt 18:20
speaks in the **n** of other gods— Dt 18:20
prophet speaks in the LORD's **n**, Dt 18:22
blessings in the LORD's **n**, Dt 21:5
gives her a bad **n**, saying, 'I Dt 22:14
an Israelite virgin a bad **n**. Dt 22:19
will carry on the **n** of the dead Dt 25:6
so his **n** will not be blotted out Dt 25:6
his brother's **n** in Israel. Dt 25:7
his ⌊family⌋ **n** in Israel will Dt 25:10
God chooses to have His **n** dwell. Dt 26:2
you are called by the LORD's **n**, Dt 28:10
this glorious and awesome **n**— Dt 28:58
blot out his **n** under heaven, Dt 29:20
I will proclaim the LORD's **n**. Dt 32:3
wipe out our **n** from the earth. Jos 7:9
will You do about Your great **n**?" Jos 7:9
Hebron's **n** used to be Jos 14:15
of Debir whose **n** used to be Jos 15:15
cities by **n** from the tribes Jos 21:9
That is its **n** to this day. Jdg 1:26
of Dan, whose **n** was Manoah; Jdg 13:2
and He didn't tell me His **n**. Jdg 13:6
What is Your **n**, so that we may Jdg 13:17
"Why do you ask My **n**," the Jdg 13:18
after the **n** of their ancestor Jdg 18:29
The man's **n** was Elimelech, Ru 1:2
and his wife's **n** was Naomi. Ru 1:2
The **n** of the man I worked with Ru 2:19
Boaz called him by **n** and said, Ru 4:1
the man's **n** on his property." Ru 4:5
man's **n** on his property, Ru 4:10
so that his **n** will not disappear Ru 4:10
May his **n** be famous in Israel. Ru 4:14
n was Elkanah son of Jeroham, 1Sm 1:1
firstborn son's **n** was Joel and 1Sm 8:2
His great **n** and because He has 1Sm 12:22
n of Saul's wife was Ahinoam 1Sm 14:50
The **n** of the commander of his 1Sm 14:50
against you in the **n** of the LORD 1Sm 17:45
So his **n** became very famous. 1Sm 18:30
pledged in the **n** of the LORD 1Sm 20:42
His **n** was Doeg the Edomite, 1Sm 21:7
His **n** was Abiathar, and he fled 1Sm 22:20
wipe out my **n** from my father's 1Sm 24:21
The man's **n** was Nabal, and his 1Sm 25:3
and his wife's **n**, Abigail. 1Sm 25:3
to Nabal, greet him in my **n**. 1Sm 25:5
Nabal, for he lives up to his **n**: 1Sm 25:25
His **n** is Nabal, and stupidity is 1Sm 25:25
a concubine whose **n** was Rizpah 2Sm 3:7
His **n** was Mephibosheth. 2Sm 4:4
The ark is called by the **N**, 2Sm 6:2
the **n** of the LORD of Hosts who 2Sm 6:2
the people in the **n** of the LORD 2Sm 6:18
will make a **n** for you like that 2Sm 7:9
He will build a house for My **n**, 2Sm 7:13
to make a **n** for Himself, 2Sm 7:23
so that Your **n** will be exalted 2Sm 7:26
a young son whose **n** was Mica. 2Sm 9:12
n or posterity on earth. 2Sm 14:7
His **n** was Shimei son of Gera, 2Sm 16:5
to preserve the memory of my **n**." 2Sm 18:18
So he gave the pillar his **n**. 2Sm 18:18
I will sing about Your **n**. 2Sm 22:50
God make the **n** of Solomon more 1Kg 1:47
Solomon more famous than your **n**, 1Kg 1:47
for the LORD's **n** had not been 1Kg 3:2
temple for the **n** of the LORD his 1Kg 5:3
temple for the **n** of the LORD my 1Kg 5:5
build the temple for My **n**.' 1Kg 5:5
so that My **n** would be there. 1Kg 8:16
temple for the **n** of the LORD God 1Kg 8:17
to build a temple for My **n**, 1Kg 8:18
will build it for My **n**." 1Kg 8:19
temple for the **n** of the LORD God 1Kg 8:20
My **n** will be there, and so that 1Kg 8:29
return to You and praise Your **n**, 1Kg 8:33
this place and praise Your **n**, 1Kg 8:35
distant land because of Your **n**— 1Kg 8:41
they will hear of Your great **n**, 1Kg 8:42
on earth will know Your **n**, 1Kg 8:43
have built is called by Your **n**. 1Kg 8:43
temple I have built for Your **n**, 1Kg 8:44
temple I have built for Your **n**, 1Kg 8:48
to put My **n** there forever; 1Kg 9:3
I have sanctified for My **n**. 1Kg 9:7
connected with the **n** of the LORD 1Kg 10:1
widowed mother's **n** was Zeruah. 1Kg 11:26
for Myself to put My **n** there. 1Kg 11:36
tribes of Israel to put His **n**. 1Kg 14:21
Rehoboam's mother's **n** was 1Kg 14:21
His mother's **n** was Naamah the 1Kg 14:31

His mother's **n** was Maacah	1Kg 15:2
His grandmother's **n** was Maacah	1Kg 15:10
Samaria based on the **n** Shemer,	1Kg 16:24
you call on the **n** of your god,	1Kg 18:24
I will call on the **n** of Yahweh.	1Kg 18:24
Then call on the **n** of your god	1Kg 18:25
and called on the **n** of Baal from	1Kg 18:26
"Israel will be your **n**"—	1Kg 18:31
the stones in the **n** of Yahweh.	1Kg 18:32
in Ahab's **n** and sealed them	1Kg 21:8
the truth in the **n** of the LORD?"	1Kg 22:16
His mother's **n** was Azubah	1Kg 22:42
them in the **n** of the LORD.	2Kg 2:24
and call on the **n** of Yahweh his	2Kg 5:11
His mother's **n** was Athaliah,	2Kg 8:26
His mother's **n** was Zibiah,	2Kg 12:1
His mother's **n** was Jehoaddan and	2Kg 14:2
⌊which is its **n**⌋ to this very	2Kg 14:7
would blot out the **n** of Israel	2Kg 14:27
His mother's **n** was Jecoliah;	2Kg 15:2
His mother's **n** was Jerusha	2Kg 15:33
His mother's **n** was Abi daughter	2Kg 18:2
His mother's **n** was Hephzibah.	2Kg 21:1
is where I will put My **n**."	2Kg 21:4
establish My **n** forever in this	2Kg 21:7
His mother's **n** was Meshullemeth	2Kg 21:19
His mother's **n** was Jedidah the	2Kg 22:1
I said, 'My **n** will be there.'	2Kg 23:27
His mother's **n** was Hamutal	2Kg 23:31
Eliakim's **n** to Jehoiakim.	2Kg 23:34
His mother's **n** was Zebidah	2Kg 23:36
His mother's **n** was Nehushta	2Kg 24:8
and changed his **n** to Zedekiah.	2Kg 24:17
His mother's **n** was Hamutal	2Kg 24:18
and the **n** of his brother was	1Ch 1:19
and his wife's **n** was Mehetabel	1Ch 1:50
servant whose **n** was Jarha.	1Ch 2:34
mentioned by **n** were leaders	1Ch 4:38
recorded by **n** came in the days	1Ch 4:41
The **n** of his sister was Maacah.	1Ch 7:15
His wife's **n** was Maacah.	1Ch 8:29
His wife's **n** was Maacah.	1Ch 9:35
designated by **n** to come and	1Ch 12:31
called by the **n** of the LORD who	1Ch 13:6
the people in the **n** of the LORD.	1Ch 16:2
LORD; call on His **n**; proclaim	1Ch 16:8
Honor His holy **n**; let the hearts	1Ch 16:10
to the LORD the glory of His **n**;	1Ch 16:29
to Your holy **n** and rejoice in	1Ch 16:35
designated by **n** to give thanks	1Ch 16:41
will make a **n** for you like that	1Ch 17:8
to make a **n** for Yourself through	1Ch 17:21
Let your **n** be confirmed and	1Ch 17:24
spoken in the **n** of the LORD.	1Ch 21:19
a house for the **n** of the LORD my	1Ch 22:7
house for My **n** because you have	1Ch 22:8
for his **n** will be Solomon,	1Ch 22:9
who will build a house for My **n**.	1Ch 22:10
be built for the **n** of the LORD."	1Ch 22:19
blessings in His **n** forever.	1Ch 23:13
registration by **n** in the	1Ch 23:24
a house for My **n** because you are	1Ch 28:3
and praise Your glorious **n**.	1Ch 29:13
for Your holy **n** comes from Your	1Ch 29:16
a temple for the **n** of the LORD	2Ch 2:1
temple for the **n** of the LORD my	2Ch 2:4
so that My **n** would be there,	2Ch 6:5
so that My **n** will be there,	2Ch 6:6
temple for the **n** of the LORD God	2Ch 6:7
to build a temple for My **n**,	2Ch 6:8
will build the temple for My **n**."	2Ch 6:9
temple for the **n** of the LORD God	2Ch 6:10
You said You would put Your **n**;	2Ch 6:20
to You⌋ and praise Your **n**,	2Ch 6:24
this place and praise Your **n**,	2Ch 6:26
of Your great **n** and Your mighty	2Ch 6:32
of the earth will know Your **n**,	2Ch 6:33
have built is called by Your **n**.	2Ch 6:33
that I have built for Your **n**,	2Ch 6:34
temple I have built for Your **n**,	2Ch 6:38
are called by My **n** humble	2Ch 7:14
temple so that My **n** may be there	2Ch 7:16
sanctified for My **n** I will	2Ch 7:20
tribes of Israel to put His **n**.	2Ch 12:13
Rehoboam's mother's **n** was	2Ch 12:13
His mother's **n** was Micaiah	2Ch 13:2
and in Your **n** we have come	2Ch 14:11
the truth in the **n** of the LORD?"	2Ch 18:15
in it for Your **n** and have said,	2Ch 20:8
for Your **n** is in this temple.	2Ch 20:9
His mother's **n** was Azubah	2Ch 20:31
His mother's **n** was Athaliah,	2Ch 22:2
His mother's **n** was Zibiah;	2Ch 24:1
His mother's **n** was Jehoaddan;	2Ch 25:1
His mother's **n** was Jecoliah;	2Ch 26:3
His mother's **n** was Jerushah	2Ch 27:1
were designated by **n** took charge	2Ch 28:15
His mother's **n** was Abijah	2Ch 29:1
registered by **n** to distribute	2Ch 31:19
where My **n** will remain forever.	2Ch 33:4
establish My **n** forever in this	2Ch 33:7
to him in the **n** of the LORD God	2Ch 33:18
Eliakim's **n** to Jehoiakim.	2Ch 36:4
and was called by their **n**.	Ezr 2:61
the **n** of the God of Israel who	Ezr 5:1
who caused His **n** to dwell there	Ezr 6:12
All were identified by **n**.	Ezr 8:20
identified⌋ by **n**, to represent	Ezr 10:16
I chose to have My **n** dwell."	Neh 1:9
who delight to revere Your **n**.	Neh 1:11
and was called by their **n**.	Neh 7:63
Your glorious **n**, and may it be	Neh 9:5
and changed his **n** to Abraham.	Neh 9:7
You made a **n** for Yourself that	Neh 9:10
her and summoned her by **n**.	Est 2:14
written in the **n** of King	Est 3:12
in the king's **n** whatever pleases	Est 8:8
in the king's **n** and sealed with	Est 8:8
in King Ahasuerus' **n** and sealed	Est 8:10
Praise the **n** of the LORD.	Jb 1:21
the earth; he has no **n** abroad.	Jb 18:17
Foolish men, without even a **n**!	Jb 30:8
who love Your **n** boast about You.	Ps 5:11
sing about the **n** of the LORD,	Ps 7:17
magnificent is Your **n** throughout	Ps 8:1
magnificent is Your **n** throughout	Ps 8:9
sing about Your **n**, Most High.	Ps 9:2
erased their **n** forever and ever	Ps 9:5
who know Your **n** trust in You	Ps 9:10
I will sing about Your **n**.	Ps 18:49
may the **n** of Jacob's God protect	Ps 20:1
the banner in the **n** of our God.	Ps 20:5
pride in the **n** of the LORD our	Ps 20:7
proclaim Your **n** to my brothers;	Ps 22:22
Because of Your **n**, LORD, forgive	Ps 25:11
the LORD the glory due His **n**;	Ps 29:2
ones, and praise His holy **n**.	Ps 30:4
and guide me because of Your **n**.	Ps 31:3
because we trust in His holy **n**.	Ps 33:21
let us exalt His **n** together.	Ps 34:3
through Your **n** we trample our	Ps 44:5
we will praise Your **n** forever.	Ps 44:8
had forgotten the **n** of our God	Ps 44:20
will cause your **n** to be	Ps 45:17
Your **n**, God, like Your praise,	Ps 48:10
I will put my hope in Your **n**,	Ps 52:9
save me by Your **n**, and vindicate	Ps 54:1
praise Your **n**, LORD, because	Ps 54:6
to those who fear Your **n**.	Ps 61:5
will continually sing of Your **n**,	Ps 61:8
at Your **n**, I will lift up my	Ps 63:4
Sing the glory of His **n**;	Ps 66:2
will sing praise to Your **n**."	Ps 66:4
praises to His **n**. Exalt Him who	Ps 68:4
the clouds—His **n** is Yahweh—	Ps 68:4
will praise God's **n** with song	Ps 69:30
who love His **n** will live in it.	Ps 69:36
May his **n** endure forever;	Ps 72:17
May His glorious **n** be praised	Ps 72:19
the dwelling place of Your **n**.	Ps 74:7
the enemy insult Your **n** forever?	Ps 74:10
people has insulted Your **n**.	Ps 74:18
poor and needy praise Your **n**.	Ps 74:21
to You, for Your **n** is near.	Ps 75:1
His **n** is great in Israel.	Ps 76:1
that don't call on Your **n**,	Ps 79:6
us—for the glory of Your **n**.	Ps 79:9
for our sins, because of Your **n**.	Ps 79:9
and we will call on Your **n**.	Ps 80:18
that Israel's **n** will no longer	Ps 83:4
so that they will seek Your **n**,	Ps 83:16
alone—whose **n** is Yahweh—are	Ps 83:18
Lord, and will honor Your **n**.	Ps 86:9
undivided mind to fear Your **n**.	Ps 86:11
and will honor Your **n** forever.	Ps 86:12
Hermon shout for joy at Your **n**.	Ps 89:12
rejoice in Your **n** all day long,	Ps 89:16
and through My **n** his horn will	Ps 89:24
exalt him because he knows My **n**.	Ps 91:14
praise to Your **n**, Most High,	Ps 92:1
Sing to the LORD, praise His **n**;	Ps 96:2
to the LORD the glory of His **n**;	Ps 96:8
ones, and praise His holy **n**.	Ps 97:12
Your great and awe-inspiring **n**.	Ps 99:3
among those calling on His **n**.	Ps 99:6
thanks to Him and praise His **n**.	Ps 100:4
will fear the **n** of the LORD,	Ps 102:15
might declare the **n** of the LORD	Ps 102:21
is within me, praise His holy **n**.	Ps 103:1
to the LORD, call on His **n**;	Ps 105:1
Honor His holy **n**; let the hearts	Ps 105:3
He saved them because of His **n**,	Ps 106:8
to Your holy **n** and rejoice in	Ps 106:47
their **n** be blotted out in the	Ps 109:13
with me because of Your **n**;	Ps 109:21
His **n** is holy and awe-inspiring.	Ps 111:9
praise the **n** of the LORD.	Ps 113:1
Let the **n** of the LORD be praised	Ps 113:2
the **n** of the LORD be praised.	Ps 113:3
but to Your **n** give glory because	Ps 115:1
I called on the **n** of the LORD:	Ps 116:4
in the **n** of the LORD I destroyed	Ps 118:10
in the **n** of the LORD I destroyed	Ps 118:11
in the **n** of the LORD I destroyed	Ps 118:12
who comes in the **n** of the LORD.	Ps 118:26
I remember Your **n** in the night,	Ps 119:55
toward those who love Your **n**.	Ps 119:132
thanks to the **n** of the LORD.	Ps 122:4
help is in the **n** of the LORD,	Ps 124:8
bless you in the **n** of the LORD.	Ps 129:8
Praise the **n** of the LORD.	Ps 135:1
sing praise to His **n**, for it is	Ps 135:3
LORD, Your **n** ⌊endures⌋ forever,	Ps 135:13
thanks to Your **n** for Your	Ps 138:2
exalted Your **n** and Your promise	Ps 138:2
righteous will praise Your **n**;	Ps 140:13
so that I can praise Your **n**.	Ps 142:7
Because of Your **n**, Yahweh, let	Ps 143:11
and praise Your **n** forever and	Ps 145:1
will honor Your **n** forever and	Ps 145:2
praise His holy **n** forever and	Ps 145:21
them praise the **n** of the LORD,	Ps 148:5
them praise the **n** of the LORD,	Ps 148:13
for His **n** alone is exalted.	Ps 148:13
them praise His **n** with dancing	Ps 149:3
the **n** of the wicked will rot.	Pr 10:7
The **n** of the LORD is a strong	Pr 18:10
A good **n** is to be chosen over	Pr 22:1
What is His **n**, and what is the	Pr 30:4
and what is the **n** of His Son—	Pr 30:4
profaning the **n** of my God.	Pr 30:9
and his **n** is shrouded in	Ec 6:4
exists was given its **n** long ago,	Ec 6:10
A good **n** is better than fine	Ec 7:1
your **n** is perfume poured out.	Sg 1:3
Just let us be called by your **n**.	Is 4:1
have a son, and **n** him Immanuel.	Is 7:14
N him Maher-shalal-hash-baz,	Is 8:3
proclaim His **n**! Celebrate His	Is 12:4
Declare that His **n** is exalted.	Is 12:4
the place of the **n** of the LORD	Is 18:7
west ⌊honor⌋ the **n** of the LORD,	Is 24:15
will praise Your **n**, for You have	Is 25:1
desire is for Your **n** and renown.	Is 26:8
but we remember Your **n** alone.	Is 26:13
will honor My **n**, they will honor	Is 29:23
He calls all of them by **n**.	Is 40:26
from the east who invokes My **n**.	Is 41:25
I am Yahweh, that is My **n**;	Is 42:8
I have called you by your **n**;	Is 43:1
called by My **n** and created for	Is 43:7
⌊himself⌋ by the **n** of Jacob;	Is 44:5
and **n** ⌊himself⌋ by the name of	Is 44:5
himself⌋ by the **n** of Israel."	Is 44:5
of Israel call you by your **n**.	Is 45:3
call you by your **n**, because of	Is 45:4
I give a **n** to you, though you do	Is 45:4
the LORD of Hosts is His **n**.	Is 47:4
called by the **n** Israel and have	Is 48:1
who swear by the **n** of the LORD	Is 48:1
His **n** is Yahweh of Hosts.	Is 48:2
My anger for the honor of My **n**,	Is 48:9
their **n** would not be cut off or	Is 48:19
him trust in the **n** of the LORD;	Is 50:10

waves roar—His **n** is Yahweh of Is 51:15
and My **n** is continually Is 52:5
My people will know My **n**; Is 52:6
His **n** is Yahweh of Hosts— Is 54:5
it will make a **n** for the LORD as Is 55:13
memorial and a **n** better than Is 56:5
an everlasting **n** that will never Is 56:5
love the LORD's **n**, and are His Is 56:6
whose **n** is Holy says this: Is 57:15
They will fear the **n** of the LORD Is 59:19
But you will **n** your walls Is 60:18
by a new **n** that the LORD's Is 62:2
make a glorious **n** for Yourself. Is 63:14
times, Your **n** is our Redeemer. Is 63:16
like those not called by Your **n**. Is 63:19
to make Your **n** known to Your Is 64:2
calls on Your **n**, striving to Is 64:7
that was not called by My **n**. Is 65:1
will leave your **n** behind as a Is 65:15
give His servants another **n**. Is 65:15
offspring and your **n** endure. Is 66:22
to the **n** of the LORD in Jr 3:17
house called by My **n** and insist: Jr 7:10
is called by My **n**, become a den Jr 7:11
I made My **n** dwell at first. Jr 7:12
house that is called by My **n**— Jr 7:14
called by My **n** and defiled it. Jr 7:30
Your **n** is great in power. Jr 10:6
the LORD of Hosts is His **n**. Jr 10:16
that don't call on Your **n**, Jr 10:25
so that his **n** will no longer be Jr 11:19
prophesy in the **n** of the LORD, Jr 11:21
to swear by My **n**, 'As the LORD Jr 12:16
and we are called by Your **n**. Jr 14:9
are prophesying a lie in My **n**. Jr 14:14
prophets who prophesy in My **n**, Jr 14:15
Because of Your **n**, don't despise Jr 14:21
for I am called by Your **n**, Jr 15:16
will know that My **n** is Yahweh." Jr 16:21
or speak any longer in His **n**, Jr 20:9
a lie in My **n** have said: Jr 23:25
to forget My **n** as their fathers Jr 23:27
fathers forgot My **n** through Baal Jr 23:27
on the city that bears My **n**, Jr 25:29
prophesy in the **n** of the LORD, Jr 26:9
to us in the **n** of the LORD our Jr 26:16
in the **n** of the LORD— Jr 26:20
are prophesying falsely in My **n**; Jr 27:15
falsely to you in My **n**. Jr 29:9
a lie to you in My **n**: Jr 29:21
and have spoken a lie in My **n**, Jr 29:23
You in your own **n** have sent out Jr 29:25
the LORD of Hosts is His **n**: Jr 31:35
mighty God whose **n** is the LORD Jr 32:18
You made a **n** for Yourself, Jr 32:20
is called by My **n** and have Jr 32:34
the LORD is His **n**, says this: Jr 33:2
bear on My behalf a **n** of joy, Jr 33:9
Me at the temple called by My **n**. Jr 34:15
your minds and profaned My **n**. Jr 34:16
whose **n** was Irijah son of Jr 37:13
to us in the **n** of the LORD, Jr 44:16
'I have sworn by My great **n**, Jr 44:26
that My **n** will never again be Jr 44:26
the LORD of Hosts is His **n**. Jr 46:18
the LORD of Hosts is His **n**. Jr 48:15
everyone who knows his **n**. Jr 48:17
the LORD of Hosts is His **n**. Jr 50:34
the LORD of Hosts is His **n**. Jr 51:19
the LORD of Hosts is His **n**. Jr 51:57
His mother's **n** was Hamutal Jr 52:1
I called on Your **n**, Yahweh, from Lm 3:55
I acted for the sake of My **n**, Ezk 20:9
But I acted because of My **n**, Ezk 20:14
hand and acted because of My **n**, Ezk 20:22
defile My holy **n** with your gifts Ezk 20:39
you because of My **n** rather than Ezk 20:44
My holy **n**, because it was Ezk 36:20
I had concern for My holy **n**, Ezk 36:21
but for My holy **n**, which you Ezk 36:22
the holiness of My great **n**, Ezk 36:23
the **n** you have profaned among Ezk 36:23
make My holy **n** known among My Ezk 39:7
I will be jealous for My holy **n**. Ezk 39:25
defile My holy **n** by their Ezk 43:7
defiling My holy **n** by the Ezk 43:8
and the **n** of the city from that Ezk 48:35
he gave the **n** Belteshazzar; Dn 1:7
May the **n** of God be praised Dn 2:20
whose **n** was Belteshazzar, Dn 2:26
after the **n** of my god— Dn 4:8
Daniel, whose **n** is Belteshazzar, Dn 4:19
spoke in Your **n** to our kings, Dn 9:6
and made Your **n** ⌊renowned⌋ as it Dn 9:15
and the city called by Your **n**. Dn 9:18
people are called by Your **n**. Dn 9:19
N him Jezreel, for in a little Hs 1:4
N her No Compassion, for I will Hs 1:6
N him Not My People, for you are Hs 1:9
God of Hosts; Yahweh is His **n**. Hs 12:5
will praise the **n** of Yahweh your Jl 2:26
calls on the **n** of Yahweh will Jl 2:32
same girl, profaning My holy **n**. Am 2:7
the God of Hosts, is His **n**. Am 4:13
of the earth—Yahweh is His **n**. Am 5:8
the God of Hosts, is His **n**. Am 5:27
because Yahweh's **n** must not be Am 6:10
of the earth. Yahweh is His **n**. Am 9:6
that are called by My **n**— Am 9:12
walk in the **n** of their gods, Mc 4:5
will walk in the **n** of Yahweh our Mc 4:5
in the majestic **n** of Yahweh His Mc 5:4
and it is wise to fear Your **n** Mc 6:9
no offspring to carry on your **n**. Nah 1:14
may call on the **n** of Yahweh and Zph 3:9
will trust in the **n** of Yahweh. Zph 3:12
one who swears falsely by My **n**. Zch 5:4
Here is a man whose **n** is Branch; Zch 6:12
and they will march in His **n**— Zch 10:12
falsely in the **n** of the LORD. Zch 13:3
will call on My **n**, and I will Zch 13:9
Yahweh alone, and His **n** alone. Zch 14:9
you priests, who despise My **n**." Mal 1:6
"How have we despised Your **n**?" Mal 1:6
For My **n** will be great among the Mal 1:11
presented in My **n** in every place Mal 1:11
place because My **n** will be great Mal 1:11
and My **n** will be feared among Mal 1:14
take it to heart to honor My **n**," Mal 2:2
Me and stood in awe of My **n**. Mal 2:5
and had high regard for His **n**. Mal 3:16
But for you who fear My **n**, Mal 4:2
and you are to **n** Him Jesus, Mt 1:21
and they will **n** Him Immanuel, Mt 1:23
Your **n** be honored as holy. Mt 6:9
didn't we prophesy in Your **n**, Mt 7:22
drive out demons in Your **n**, Mt 7:22
do many miracles in Your **n**?' Mt 7:22
by everyone because of My **n**. Mt 10:22
will put their hope in His **n**. Mt 12:21
like this in My **n** welcomes Me. Mt 18:5
are gathered together in My **n**, Mt 18:20
because of My **n** will receive 100 Mt 19:29
who comes in the **n** of the Lord! Mt 21:9
who comes in the **n** of the Lord!" Mt 23:39
For many will come in My **n**, Mt 24:5
by all nations because of My **n**. Mt 24:9
them in the **n** of the Father Mt 28:19
To Simon, He gave the **n** Peter; Mk 3:16
He gave the **n** "Boanerges" Mk 3:17
"What is your **n**?" He asked him. Mk 5:9
"My **n** is Legion," he answered Mk 5:9
because Jesus' **n** had become well Mk 6:14
as this in My **n** welcomes Me. Mk 9:37
driving out demons in Your **n**, Mk 9:38
a miracle in My **n** who can soon Mk 9:39
water to drink because of My **n**, Mk 9:41
who comes in the **n** of the Lord! Mk 11:9
will come in My **n**, saying, 'I am Mk 13:6
by everyone because of My **n**. Mk 13:13
In My **n** they will drive out Mk 16:17
Aaron, and her **n** was Elizabeth. Lk 1:5
a son, and you will **n** him John. Lk 1:13
The virgin's **n** was Mary. Lk 1:27
and you will call His **n** JESUS. Lk 1:31
for me, and His **n** is holy. Lk 1:49
were going to **n** him Zechariah, Lk 1:59
of your relatives has that **n**." Lk 1:61
HIS **N** IS JOHN And they were all Lk 1:63
the **n** given by the angel before Lk 2:21
in Jerusalem whose **n** was Simeon. Lk 2:25
and slander your **n** as evil, Lk 6:22
"What is your **n**?" Jesus asked Lk 8:30
child in My **n** welcomes Me. Lk 9:48
driving out demons in Your **n**, Lk 9:49
demons submit to us in Your **n**." Lk 10:17
Your **n** be honored as holy. Lk 11:2
who comes in the **n** of the Lord!" Lk 13:35
who comes in the **n** of the Lord. Lk 19:38
For many will come in My **n**, Lk 21:8
and governors because of My **n**. Lk 21:12
by everyone because of My **n**, Lk 21:17
proclaimed in His **n** to all the Lk 24:47
to those who believe in His **n**, Jn 1:12
trusted in His **n** when they saw Jn 2:23
believed in the **n** of the One and Jn 3:18
I have come in My Father's **n**, Jn 5:43
someone else comes in his own **n**, Jn 5:43
own sheep by **n** and leads them Jn 10:3
in My Father's **n** testify about Jn 10:25
who comes in the **n** of the Lord— Jn 12:13
Father, glorify Your **n**!" Jn 12:28
you ask in My **n**, I will do it so Jn 14:13
If you ask Me anything in My **n**, Jn 14:14
Father will send Him in My **n**— Jn 14:26
you ask the Father in My **n**, Jn 15:16
to you on account of My **n**, Jn 15:21
you ask the Father in My **n**, Jn 16:23
have asked for nothing in My **n**. Jn 16:24
that day you will ask in My **n**. Jn 16:26
revealed Your **n** to the men You Jn 17:6
them by Your **n** that You have Jn 17:11
them by Your **n** that You have Jn 17:12
I made Your **n** known to them and Jn 17:26
The slave's **n** was Malchus. Jn 18:10
you may have life in His **n**. Jn 20:31
calls on the **n** of the Lord will Ac 2:21
the **n** of Jesus the Messiah for Ac 2:38
In the **n** of Jesus Christ the Ac 3:6
By faith in His **n**, His name has Ac 3:16
His **n** has made this man strong, Ac 3:16
power or in what **n** have you done Ac 4:7
that by the **n** of Jesus Christ Ac 4:10
there is no other **n** under heaven Ac 4:12
to anyone in this **n** again." Ac 4:17
teach at all in the **n** of Jesus. Ac 4:18
through the **n** of Your holy Ac 4:30
you not to teach in this **n**? Ac 5:28
not to speak in the **n** of Jesus Ac 5:40
dishonored on behalf of the **n**. Ac 5:41
God and the **n** of Jesus Christ, Ac 8:12
baptized in the **n** of the Lord Ac 8:16
arrest all who call on Your **n**." Ac 9:14
to carry My **n** before Gentiles, Ac 9:15
much he must suffer for My **n**!" Ac 9:16
those who called on this **n**, Ac 9:21
spoken boldly in the **n** of Jesus. Ac 9:27
boldly in the **n** of the Lord. Ac 9:28
that through His **n** everyone who Ac 10:43
in the **n** of Jesus Christ Ac 10:48
is how his **n** is translated, Ac 13:8
the Gentiles a people for His **n**. Ac 15:14
Gentiles who are called by My **n**, Ac 15:17
for the **n** of our Lord Jesus Ac 15:26
you in the **n** of Jesus Christ to Ac 16:18
baptized in the **n** of the Lord Ac 19:5
to pronounce the **n** of the Lord Ac 19:13
and the **n** of the Lord Jesus was Ac 19:17
for the **n** of the Lord Jesus Ac 21:13
your sins by calling on His **n**.' Ac 22:16
in opposition to the **n** of Jesus Ac 26:9
the nations, on behalf of His **n**, Rm 1:5
The **n** of God is blasphemed among Rm 2:24
and that My **n** may be proclaimed Rm 9:17
calls on the **n** of the Lord will Rm 10:13
I will sing psalms to Your **n**. Rm 15:9
call on the **n** of Jesus Christ 1Co 1:2
in the **n** of our Lord Jesus 1Co 1:10
were you baptized in Paul's **n**? 1Co 1:13
you had been baptized in my **n**. 1Co 1:15
In the **n** of our Lord Jesus, 1Co 5:4
who bears the **n** of brother who 1Co 5:11
justified in the **n** of the Lord 1Co 6:11
Father in the **n** of our Lord Eph 5:20
and gave Him the **n** that is above Php 2:9
the name that is above every **n**, Php 2:9
so that at the **n** of Jesus every Php 2:10
in the **n** of the Lord Jesus Col 3:17
so that the **n** of our Lord Jesus 2Th 1:12
in the **n** of our Lord Jesus 2Th 3:6
so that God's **n** and His teaching 1Tm 6:1
that falsely bears that **n**. 1Tm 6:20
who names the **n** of the Lord must 2Tm 2:19
just as the **n** He inherited is Heb 1:4

proclaim Your **n** to My brothers; Heb 2:12
showed for His **n** when you served Heb 6:10
his **n** means "king of Heb 7:2
of our lips that confess His **n**. Heb 13:15
the noble **n** that you bear? Jms 2:7
in the Lord's **n** as an example Jms 5:10
olive oil in the **n** of the Lord. Jms 5:14
ridiculed for the **n** of Christ, 1Pt 4:14
should glorify God with that **n**. 1Pt 4:16
forgiven on account of His **n**. 1Jn 2:12
believe in the **n** of His Son 1Jn 3:23
believe in the **n** of the Son of 1Jn 5:13
set out for the sake of the **n**, 3Jn 7
Greet the friends by **n**. 3Jn 14
many things⌋ because of My **n**, Rv 2:3
on to My **n** and did not deny Rv 2:13
the stone a new **n** is inscribed Rv 2:17
never erase his **n** from the book Rv 3:5
acknowledge his **n** before My Rv 3:5
not denied My **n**, look, I have Rv 3:8
write on him the **n** of My God, Rv 3:12
the **n** of the city of My God— Rv 3:12
from My God—and My new **n**. Rv 3:12
The **n** of the star is Wormwood, Rv 8:11
his **n** in Hebrew is Abaddon, Rv 9:11
in Greek he has the **n** Apollyon. Rv 9:11
and to those who fear Your **n**, Rv 11:18
blaspheme His **n** and His dwelling Rv 13:6
everyone whose **n** was not written Rv 13:8
the beast's **n** or the number of Rv 13:17
name or the number of his **n**. Rv 13:17
who had His **n** and His Father's Rv 14:1
His Father's **n** written on their Rv 14:1
who receives the mark of his **n**. Rv 14:11
number of his **n**, were standing Rv 15:2
not fear and glorify Your **n**? Rv 15:4
blasphemed the **n** of God who had Rv 16:9
a cryptic **n** was written: Rv 17:5
He had a **n** written that no one Rv 19:12
and His **n** is called the Word of Rv 19:13
on His thigh He has a **n** written: Rv 19:16
and His **n** will be on their Rv 22:4

NAME'S *(2)*

the right paths for His **n** sake. Ps 23:3
us, LORD, act for Your **n** sake. Jr 14:7

NAMED *(221)*

Adam **n** his wife Eve because she Gn 3:20
he **n** the city Enoch after his Gn 4:17
one **n** Adah and the other named Gn 4:19
Adah and the other **n** Zillah. Gn 4:19
His brother was **n** Jubal; Gn 4:21
birth to a son and **n** him Seth, Gn 4:25
Seth also, and he **n** him Enosh. Gn 4:26
to his image, and **n** him Seth. Gn 5:3
And he **n** him Noah, saying, "This Gn 5:29
One was **n** Peleg, for during his Gn 10:25
his brother was **n** Joktan. Gn 10:25
Abram's wife was **n** Sarai, and Gn 11:29
and Nahor's wife was **n** Milcah. Gn 11:29
owned an Egyptian slave **n** Hagar. Gn 16:1
So she **n** the LORD who spoke to Gn 16:13
That is why she **n** the spring, Gn 16:14
birth to a son and **n** him Moab. Gn 19:37
a son, and she **n** him Ben-ammi. Gn 19:38
Abraham **n** his son who was born Gn 21:3
Abraham **n** that place The LORD Gn 22:14
Rebekah had a brother **n** Laban, Gn 24:29
a fur coat, and they **n** him Esau. Gn 25:25
hand. So he was **n** Jacob. Isaac Gn 25:26
is why he was ⌊also⌋ **n** Edom. Gn 25:30
So he **n** the well Quarrel Gn 26:20
one also, so he **n** it Hostility. Gn 26:21
He **n** it Open Spaces and said, Gn 26:22
Isn't he rightly **n** Jacob? Gn 27:36
and **n** the place Bethel, though Gn 28:19
previously the city was **n** Luz. Gn 28:19
the older was **n** Leah, and the Gn 29:16
and the younger was **n** Rachel. Gn 29:16
to a son, and **n** him Reuben, for Gn 29:32
So she **n** him Simeon. Gn 29:33
Therefore he was **n** Levi. Gn 29:34
Therefore she **n** him Judah. Gn 29:35
me a son," and she **n** him Dan. Gn 30:6
won," and she **n** him Naphtali. Gn 30:8
fortune!" and she **n** him Gad. Gn 30:11
me happy," so she **n** him Asher. Gn 30:13
and she **n** him Issachar. Gn 30:18
sons," and she **n** him Zebulun. Gn 30:20
bore a daughter and **n** her Dinah. Gn 30:21
She **n** him Joseph: "May the LORD Gn 30:24
Laban **n** the mound Gn 31:47
but Jacob **n** it Galeed. Gn 31:47
Jacob then **n** the place Peniel, Gn 32:30
So Jacob **n** it Oak of Weeping. Gn 35:8
you will no longer be **n** Jacob, Gn 35:10
your name. So He **n** him Israel. Gn 35:10
Jacob **n** the place where God had Gn 35:15
was dying—she **n** him Ben-oni, Gn 35:18
near an Adullamite **n** Hirah. Gn 38:1
daughter of a Canaanite **n** Shua; Gn 38:2
birth to a son, and he **n** him Er. Gn 38:3
birth to a son, and **n** him Onan. Gn 38:4
to another son and **n** him Shelah. Gn 38:5
out ⌊first⌋!" So he was **n** Perez. Gn 38:29
hand, came out, and was **n** Zerah. Gn 38:30
An Egyptian ⌊**n**⌋ Potiphar, an Gn 39:1
Joseph **n** the firstborn Manasseh, Gn 41:51
And the second son he **n** Ephraim, Gn 41:52
the place is **n** Abel-mizraim. Gn 50:11
one of whom was **n** Shiphrah and Ex 1:15
She **n** him Moses, "Because," she Ex 2:10
to a son whom he **n** Gershom, Ex 2:22
that is why it was **n** Marah. Ex 15:23
house of Israel **n** the substance Ex 16:31
n the place Massah and Meribah Ex 17:7
Moses built an altar and **n** it, Ex 17:15
one of whom was **n** Gershom Ex 18:3
So that place was **n** Taberah, Nm 11:3
one **n** Eldad and the other Medad; Nm 11:26
So they **n** that place Nm 11:34
So they **n** the place Hormah. Nm 21:3
a prostitute **n** Rahab, and stayed Jos 2:1
and Gadites **n** the altar: Jos 22:34
was formerly **n** Kiriath-arba Jdg 1:10
was formerly **n** Kiriath-sepher Jdg 1:11
So they **n** the town Hormah. Jdg 1:17
the town was formerly **n** Luz Jdg 1:23
built a town, and **n** it Luz. Jdg 1:26
So they **n** that place Bochim and Jdg 2:5
a son, and he **n** him Abimelech. Jdg 8:31
birth to a son and **n** him Samson. Jdg 13:24
the jawbone and **n** that place Jdg 15:17
That is why he **n** it En-hakkore, Jdg 15:19
in love with a woman **n** Delilah, Jdg 16:4
hill country of Ephraim **n** Micah. Jdg 17:1
They **n** the city Dan, after the Jdg 18:29
The city was formerly **n** Laish. Jdg 18:29
one was **n** Orpah and the second Ru 1:4
Orpah and the second was **n** Ruth. Ru 1:4
on her husband's side **n** Boaz. Ru 2:1
to Naomi," and they **n** him Obed. Ru 4:17
first **n** Hannah and the second 1Sm 1:2
She **n** him Samuel, because ⌊she 1Sm 1:20
She **n** the boy Ichabod, saying, 1Sm 4:21
He **n** it Ebenezer, explaining, 1Sm 7:12
man of Benjamin **n** Kish son of 1Sm 9:1
He had a son **n** Saul, an 1Sm 9:2
One was **n** Bozez and the other 1Sm 14:4
Then a champion **n** Goliath, 1Sm 17:4
from Bethlehem of Judah **n** Jesse. 1Sm 17:12
suddenly the champion **n** Goliath, 1Sm 17:23
that place was **n** the Rock of 1Sm 23:28
in Gibeon, is **n** Field of Blades 2Sm 2:16
one **n** Baanah and the other 2Sm 4:2
which he **n** the city of David. 2Sm 5:9
he **n** that place the Lord Bursts 2Sm 5:20
so he **n** that place an Outburst 2Sm 6:8
servant of Saul's family **n** Ziba. 2Sm 9:2
to a son and **n** him Solomon. 2Sm 12:24
the prophet, who **n** him Jedidiah, 2Sm 12:25
and it will be **n** after me. 2Sm 12:28
had a beautiful sister **n** Tamar, 2Sm 13:1
Amnon had a friend **n** Jonadab, 2Sm 13:3
and a daughter **n** Tamar, who was 2Sm 14:27
the son of a man **n** Ithra the 2Sm 17:25
a Benjaminite **n** Sheba son of 2Sm 20:1
There is a man **n** Sheba son of 2Sm 20:21
right pillar and **n** it Jachin; 1Kg 7:21
the left pillar and **n** it Boaz. 1Kg 7:21
house of David, **n** Josiah, and he 1Kg 13:2
He **n** the city he built Samaria 1Kg 16:24
One of them was **n** Peleg, because 1Ch 1:19
Bela's town was **n** Dinhabah. 1Ch 1:43
Hadad's town was **n** Avith. 1Ch 1:46
Hadad's city was **n** Pai, and his 1Ch 1:50
had another wife **n** Atarah, 1Ch 2:26
Abishur's wife was **n** Abihail, 1Ch 2:29
their sister was **n** Hazzelelponi. 1Ch 4:3
His mother **n** him Jabez and said, 1Ch 4:9
lot the towns **n** above from the 1Ch 6:65
descendant was **n** Zelophehad, 1Ch 7:15
a son, and she **n** ⌊him⌋ Peresh. 1Ch 7:16
His brother was **n** Sheresh, 1Ch 7:16
he **n** him Beriah, because there 1Ch 7:23
so he **n** that place Outburst 1Ch 13:11
Uzzah, as it is ⌊still **n**⌋ today. 1Ch 13:11
n that place the Lord Bursts 1Ch 14:11
his sons were **n** among the tribe 1Ch 23:14
He **n** the one on the right Jachin 2Ch 3:17
warrior **n** Zichri killed 2Ch 28:7
of the LORD **n** Oded was there. 2Ch 28:9
Babylon to a man **n** Sheshbazzar, Ezr 5:14
fortress of Susa **n** Mordecai son Est 2:5
man in the country of Uz **n** Job. Jb 1:1
He **n** his first ⌊daughter⌋ Jb 42:14
though they have **n** estates after Ps 49:11
arrogant person, **n** "Mocker," Pr 21:24
will be **n** Wonderful Counselor, Is 9:6
For they are **n** after the Holy Is 48:2
He **n** me while I was in my Is 49:1
The LORD **n** you a flourishing Jr 11:16
This is what He will be **n**: Jr 23:6
and this is what she will be **n**: Jr 33:16
The older one was **n** Oholah, Ezk 23:4
be a city **n** Hamonah ⌊there⌋. Ezk 39:16
the city being **n** for the tribes Ezk 48:31
n Belteshazzar after the name of Dn 4:8
the one the king **n** Belteshazzar, Dn 5:12
Daniel, who was **n** Belteshazzar. Dn 10:1
to a son. And he **n** Him Jesus. Mt 1:25
saw a man **n** Matthew sitting at Mt 9:9
found a Cyrenian man **n** Simon. Mt 27:32
from Arimathea **n** Joseph came, Mt 27:57
—He also **n** them apostles—to Mk 3:14
leaders, **n** Jairus, came, Mk 5:22
came to a place **n** Gethsemane, Mk 14:32
There was one **n** Barabbas, who Mk 15:7
Abijah's division **n** Zechariah. Lk 1:5
engaged to a man **n** Joseph, Lk 1:27
He was **n** JESUS—the name Lk 2:21
tax collector **n** Levi sitting at Lk 5:27
them—He also **n** them apostles: Lk 6:13
whom He also **n** Peter, and Andrew Lk 6:14
Just then, a man **n** Jairus came. Lk 8:41
a woman **n** Martha welcomed Him Lk 10:38
had a sister **n** Mary, who also Lk 10:39
a poor man **n** Lazarus, covered Lk 16:20
There was a man **n** Zacchaeus who Lk 19:2
of the Twelve **n** Judas was Lk 22:47
good and righteous man **n** Joseph, Lk 23:50
The one **n** Cleopas answered Him, Lk 24:18
There was a man **n** John who was Jn 1:6
from the Pharisees **n** Nicodemus, Jn 3:1
whom the apostles **n** Barnabas, Ac 4:36
But a man **n** Ananias, with Ac 5:1
A Pharisee **n** Gamaliel, a teacher Ac 5:34
the feet of a young man **n** Saul. Ac 7:58
A man **n** Simon had previously Ac 8:9
there was a disciple **n** Ananias. Ac 9:10
for a man from Tarsus **n** Saul, Ac 9:11
has seen a man **n** Ananias coming Ac 9:12
There he found a man **n** Aeneas, Ac 9:33
there was a disciple **n** Tabitha, Ac 9:36
a man in Caesarea **n** Cornelius, Ac 10:1
for Simon, who is also **n** Peter. Ac 10:5
who was also **n** Peter, was Ac 10:18
Simon here, who is also **n** Peter. Ac 10:32
for Simon, who is also **n** Peter. Ac 11:13
one of them, **n** Agabus, stood up Ac 11:28
and a servant **n** Rhoda came to Ac 12:13
false prophet **n** Bar-Jesus. Ac 13:6
there was a disciple **n** Timothy, Ac 16:1
A woman **n** Lydia, a dealer in Ac 16:14
a woman **n** Damaris, and others Ac 17:34
he found a Jewish man **n** Aquila, Ac 18:2
house of a man **n** Titius Justus, Ac 18:7
A Jew **n** Apollos, a native Ac 18:24
For a person **n** Demetrius, a Ac 19:24
and a young man **n** Eutychus was Ac 20:9
prophet **n** Agabus came down from Ac 21:10
Someone **n** Ananias, a devout man Ac 22:12
elders and a lawyer **n** Tertullus. Ac 24:1
to a centurion **n** Julius, Ac 27:1
of the island, **n** Publius, who Ac 28:7

where Christ has not been **n**, Rm 15:20
in heaven and on earth is **n**. Eph 3:15
The horseman on it was **n** Death, Rv 6:8

NAMELY *(1)*
n the righteousness that comes Rm 9:30

NAMES *(96)*
The man gave **n** to all the Gn 2:20
These are the **n** of Ishmael's Gn 25:13
their **n** according to the family Gn 25:13
these are their **n** by their Gn 25:16
them the same **n** his father had Gn 26:18
These are the **n** of Esau's sons: Gn 36:10
are the **n** of Esau's chiefs, Gn 36:40
their localities, by their **n**: Gn 36:40
These are the **n** of the Gn 46:8
under the **n** of their brothers Gn 48:6
my name and the **n** of my fathers Gn 48:16
These are the **n** of the sons of Ex 1:1
These are the **n** of the sons of Ex 6:16
not invoke the **n** of other gods; Ex 23:13
on them the **n** of Israel's sons: Ex 28:9
of their **n** on the first stone Ex 28:10
remaining six **n** on the second Ex 28:10
stones with the **n** of Israel's Ex 28:11
will carry their **n** on his two Ex 28:12
to the **n** of Israel's sons Ex 28:21
with one of the **n** of the 12 Ex 28:21
is to carry the **n** of Israel's Ex 28:29
with the **n** of Israel's sons Ex 39:6
to the **n** of Israel's sons. Ex 39:14
with one of the **n** of the 12 Ex 39:14
counting the **n** of every male one Nm 1:2
These are the **n** of the men who Nm 1:5
one by one the **n** of those 20 Nm 1:18
one by one the **n** of every male Nm 1:20
one by one the **n** of every male Nm 1:22
counting the **n** of those 20 years Nm 1:24
counting the **n** of those 20 years Nm 1:26
counting the **n** of those 20 years Nm 1:28
counting the **n** of those 20 years Nm 1:30
counting the **n** of those 20 years Nm 1:32
counting the **n** of those 20 years Nm 1:34
counting the **n** of those 20 years Nm 1:36
counting the **n** of those 20 years Nm 1:38
counting the **n** of those 20 years Nm 1:40
counting the **n** of those 20 years Nm 1:42
These are the **n** of Aaron's sons: Nm 3:2
These are the **n** of Aaron's sons, Nm 3:3
These were the **n** of Gershon's Nm 3:18
old or more, and list their **n**. Nm 3:40
These were their **n**: Shammua son Nm 13:4
were the **n** of the men Moses Nm 13:16
The **n** of Zelophehad's daughters Nm 26:33
based on the number of **n**. Nm 26:53
according to the **n** of their Nm 26:55
These were the **n** of his Nm 27:1
(whose **n** were changed), Nm 32:38
They gave **n** to the cities they Nm 32:38
These are the **n** of the men who Nm 34:17
These are the **n** of the men: Nm 34:19
wipe out their **n** under heaven. Dt 7:24
wipe out their **n** from every Dt 12:3
are the **n** of his daughters: Jos 17:3
not call on the **n** of their gods Jos 23:7
down for him the ⌊**n** of the⌋ 77 Jdg 8:14
n of his two sons were Mahlon Ru 1:2
The **n** of his two daughters were: 1Sm 14:49
the war, and their **n** were Eliab, 1Sm 17:13
These are the **n** of those born to 2Sm 5:14
These are the **n** of David's 2Sm 23:8
These were their **n**: Ben-hur, in 1Kg 4:8
These ⌊**n**⌋ are from ancient 1Ch 4:22
These are the **n** of Gershom's 1Ch 6:17
sons, and these were their **n**: 1Ch 8:38
sons, and these were their **n**: 1Ch 9:44
These are the **n** of the children 1Ch 14:4
What are the **n** of the workers Ezr 5:4
We also asked them for their **n**, Ezr 5:10
down the **n** of their leaders Ezr 5:10
descendants, and their **n** are: Ezr 8:13
the **n** of⌊ our leaders, Neh 9:38
not speak their **n** with my lips. Ps 16:4
He gives **n** to all of them. Ps 147:4
for their **n**, Oholah represents Ezk 23:4
these are the **n** of the tribes: Ezk 48:1
gave them ⌊different⌋ **n**: Dn 1:7
I will remove the **n** of the Baals Hs 2:17
longer be remembered by their **n**. Hs 2:17
the **n** of the pagan priests along Zph 1:4
I will erase the **n** of the idols Zch 13:2
These are the **n** of the 12 Mt 10:2
rejoice that your **n** are written Lk 10:20
words, **n**, and your own law, Ac 18:15
whose **n** are in the book Php 4:3
and Everyone who **n** the name of 2Tm 2:19
firstborn whose **n** have been Heb 12:23
on his heads were blasphemous **n**. Rv 13:1
was covered with blasphemous **n**, Rv 17:3
the earth whose **n** were not Rv 17:8
⌊on the gates⌋, **n** were inscribed, Rv 21:12
the **n** of the 12 tribes of the Rv 21:12
were the 12 **n** of the Lamb's 12 Rv 21:14

NAOMI *(24)*
and his wife's name was **N**. Ru 1:2
and **N** was left without her two Ru 1:5
But **N** replied, "Return home, my Ru 1:11
N said, "Look, your Ru 1:15
When **N** saw that Ruth was Ru 1:18
exclaimed, "Can this be **N**?" Ru 1:19
"Don't call me **N**. Call me Mara," Ru 1:20
do you call me **N**, since the LORD Ru 1:21
So **N** came back from the land of Ru 1:22
Now **N** had a relative on her Ru 2:1
Ruth the Moabitess asked **N**, Ru 2:2
N answered her, "Go ahead, my Ru 2:2
returned with **N** from the land Ru 2:6
Then **N** said to her Ru 2:20
N continued, "The man is a Ru 2:20
So **N** said to her daughter-in-law Ru 2:22
mother-in-law **N** said to her, Ru 3:1
mother-in-law, **N**, who asked Ru 3:16
the redeemer, "**N**, who has Ru 4:3
the day you buy the land from **N**, Ru 4:5
am buying from **N** everything that Ru 4:9
Then the women said to **N**, Ru 4:14
N took the child, placed him on Ru 4:16
"A son has been born to **N**," Ru 4:17

NAOMI'S *(1)*
N husband Elimelech died, and Ru 1:3

NAP *(1)*
king was taking his midday **n**. 2Sm 4:5

NAPHATH *(1)*
towns—the three ⌊cities⌋ of **N**. Jos 17:11

NAPHATH-DOR *(1)*
in all **N** (Taphath daughter 1Kg 4:11

NAPHISH *(3)*
Tema, Jetur, **N**, and Kedemah. Gn 25:15
Jetur, **N**, and Kedemah. 1Ch 1:31
Hagrites, Jetur, **N**, and Nodab. 1Ch 5:19

NAPHOTH-DOR *(1)*
king of Dor in **N** one the king Jos 12:23

NAPHTALI *(45)*
and won," and she named him **N**. Gn 30:8
slave Bilhah were Dan and **N**. Gn 35:25
N is a doe set free that bears Gn 49:21
Dan and **N**; Gad and Asher. Ex 1:4
Ahira son of Enan from **N**. Nm 1:15
The descendants of **N**: Nm 1:42
the tribe of **N** numbered 53,400 Nm 1:43
The tribe of **N** ⌊will be next⌋. Nm 2:29
the division of the tribe of **N**. Nm 10:27
of Vophsi from the tribe of **N**; Nm 13:14
These were the **N** clans numbered Nm 26:50
a leader from the tribe of **N**." Nm 34:28
Gad, Asher, Zebulun, Dan, and **N**. Dt 27:13
He said about **N**: Naphtali, Dt 33:23
N, enjoying approval, full of Dt 33:23
of **N**, the land of Ephraim and Dt 34:2
hill country of **N** in Galilee, Jos 20:7
Issachar, Asher, **N**, and half the Jos 21:6
From the tribe of **N** ⌊they gave⌋: Jos 21:32
N did not drive out the Jdg 1:33
Kedesh in **N** and said to him, Jdg 4:6
Zebulun and **N** to Kedesh; Jdg 4:10
their lives, **N** also, on the Jdg 5:18
Zebulun, and **N**, who ⌊also⌋ came Jdg 6:35
of Israel were called from **N**, Jdg 7:23
Ahimaaz, in **N** (he also had 1Kg 4:15
widow's son from the tribe of **N**, 1Kg 7:14
and the whole land of **N**. 1Kg 15:20
all the land of **N**—and deported 2Kg 15:29
Benjamin, **N**, Gad, and Asher. 1Ch 2:2
Issachar, Asher, **N**, and Manasseh 1Ch 6:62
the tribe of **N** ⌊they received⌋ 1Ch 6:76
From **N**: 1,000 commanders 1Ch 12:34
and **N** came bringing food on 1Ch 12:40
for **N**, Jerimoth son of Azriel; 1Ch 27:19
and all the storage cities of **N**. 2Ch 16:4
and as far as **N** ⌊and⌋ on their 2Ch 34:6
of Zebulun, the rulers of **N**. Ps 68:27
of Zebulun and the land of **N**. Is 9:1
west, will be **N**—one ⌊portion⌋ Ezk 48:3
Next to the territory of **N**, Ezk 48:4
and one, the gate of **N**. Ezk 48:34
in the region of Zebulun and **N**. Mt 4:13
Land of Zebulun and land of **N**, Mt 4:15
12,000 from the tribe of **N**, Rv 7:6

NAPHTALI'S *(5)*
N sons: Jahzeel, Guni, Jezer, Gn 46:24
N descendants by their clans: Nm 26:48
lot came out for **N** descendants Jos 19:32
of the tribe of **N** descendants by Jos 19:39
N sons: Jahziel, Guni, Jezer, 1Ch 7:13

NAPHTALITES *(3)*
The leader of the **N** is Ahira son Nm 2:29
Enan, leader of the **N**, Nm 7:78
men from the **N** and Zebulunites? Jdg 4:6

NAPHTUHIM *(2)*
Ludim, Anamim, Lehabim, **N**, Gn 10:13
Ludim, Anamim, Lehabim, **N**, 1Ch 1:11

NARCISSUS *(1)*
household of **N** who are in the Rm 16:11

NARD *(4)*
choicest fruits, henna with **n**— Sg 4:13
n and saffron, calamus and Sg 4:14
and expensive fragrant oil of **n**. Mk 14:3
expensive **n**—anointed Jesus' Jn 12:3

NARRATIVE *(2)*
to compile a **n** about the events Lk 1:1
I wrote the first **n**, Theophilus, Ac 1:1

NARROW *(8)*
stood in a **n** passage between Nm 22:24
and stood in a **n** place where Nm 22:26
it became too **n** for my animal to Neh 2:14
a forbidden woman is a **n** well; Pr 23:27
have overtaken her in **n** places. Lm 1:3
Enter through the **n** gate. Mt 7:13
How **n** is the gate and difficult Mt 7:14
to enter through the **n** door, Lk 13:24

NARROWER *(1)*
upper chambers were **n** because Ezk 42:5

NARROWS *(1)*
The one who **n** his eyes is Pr 16:30

NATHAN *(41)*
Shammua, Shobab, **N**, Solomon, 2Sm 5:14
the king said to **N** the prophet, 2Sm 7:2
So **N** told the king, "Go and do 2Sm 7:3
the word of the LORD came to **N**: 2Sm 7:4
N spoke all these words and this 2Sm 7:17
So the LORD sent **N** to David. 2Sm 12:1
with the man and said to **N**: 2Sm 12:5
N replied to David, "You are the 2Sm 12:7
responded to **N**, "I have sinned 2Sm 12:13
Then **N** replied to David, 2Sm 12:13
N went home. The LORD struck 2Sm 12:15
message⌋ through **N** the prophet, 2Sm 12:25
Igal son of **N** from Zobah, Bani 2Sm 23:36
son of Jehoiada, **N** the prophet, 1Kg 1:8
he did not invite **N** the prophet, 1Kg 1:10
Then **N** said to Bathsheba, 1Kg 1:11
with the king, **N** the prophet 1Kg 1:22
king, "**N** the prophet is here. 1Kg 1:23
"My lord king," **N** said, "did you 1Kg 1:24
Zadok the priest, **N** the prophet, 1Kg 1:32
the priest and **N** the prophet are 1Kg 1:34
Zadok the priest, **N** the prophet, 1Kg 1:38
Zadok the priest, **N** the prophet, 1Kg 1:44
priest and **N** the prophet have 1Kg 1:45
Azariah son of **N**, in charge of 1Kg 4:5
Zabud son of **N**, a priest and 1Kg 4:5
Attai fathered **N**, and Nathan 1Ch 2:36
Nathan, and **N** fathered Zabad. 1Ch 2:36
Shimea, Shobab, **N**, and Solomon. 1Ch 3:5
Joel the brother of **N**, Mibhar 1Ch 11:38
Shammua, Shobab, **N**, Solomon, 1Ch 14:4
he said to **N** the prophet, 1Ch 17:1
So **N** told David, "Do all that is 1Ch 17:2
night the word of God came to **N**: 1Ch 17:3
N recounted all these words and 1Ch 17:15
the Events of **N** the Prophet, 1Ch 29:29

in the Events of **N** the Prophet, 2Ch 9:29
king's seer, and **N** the prophet. 2Ch 29:25
Jarib, Elnathan, **N**, Zechariah, Ezr 8:16
Shelemiah, **N**, Adaiah, Ezr 10:39
son⌋ of **N**, ⌊son⌋ of David, Lk 3:31

NATHAN'S *(1)*
the family of **N** house by itself Zch 12:12

NATHAN-MELECH *(1)*
by the chamber of **N** the court 2Kg 23:11

NATHANAEL *(6)*
(AKA BARTHOLOMEW)
Philip found **N** and told him, Jn 1:45
of Nazareth?" **N** asked him. "Come Jn 1:46
Then Jesus saw **N** coming toward Jn 1:47
you know me?" **N** asked. "Before Jn 1:48
"Rabbi," **N** replied, "You are the Jn 1:49
called "Twin"), **N** from Cana of Jn 21:2

NATION *(157)*
I will make you into a great **n**, Gn 12:2
I will judge the **n** they serve, Gn 15:14
I will make him into a great **n**. Gn 17:20
become a great and powerful **n**, Gn 18:18
you destroy a **n** even though it Gn 20:4
also make a **n** of the slave's Gn 21:13
for I will make him a great **n**." Gn 21:18
A **n**, indeed an assembly of Gn 35:11
I will make you a great **n** there. Gn 46:3
will become a populous **n**." Gn 48:19
Egypt since it had become a **n**. Ex 9:24
of priests and My holy **n**. Ex 19:6
I will make you into a great **n**." Ex 32:10
that this **n** is Your people." Ex 33:13
in all the earth or in any **n**. Ex 34:10
and mightier **n** than they are." Nm 14:12
'This great **n** is indeed a wise Dt 4:6
For what great **n** is there that Dt 4:7
And what great **n** has righteous Dt 4:8
go and take a **n** as his own out Dt 4:34
as his own out of ⌊another⌋ **n**, Dt 4:34
make you into a **n** stronger and Dt 9:14
great, powerful, and populous **n**. Dt 26:5
appointed to a **n** neither you nor Dt 28:36
will bring a **n** from far away, Dt 28:49
a **n** whose language you don't Dt 28:49
a ruthless **n**, showing no respect Dt 28:50
enrage them with a foolish **n**. Dt 32:21
Israel is a **n** lacking sense with Dt 32:28
until the entire **n** had finished Jos 3:17
After the entire **n** had finished Jos 4:1
After the entire **n** had been Jos 5:8
until the **n** took vengeance on Jos 10:13
Because this **n** has violated My Jdg 2:20
God came to one **n** on earth in 2Sm 7:23
there is no **n** or kingdom where 1Kg 18:10
that kingdom or **n** swear they had 1Kg 18:10
strike this **n** with blindness." 2Kg 6:18
But ⌊the people of⌋ each **n**, 2Kg 17:29
wandering from **n** to nation and 1Ch 16:20
from nation to **n** and from one 1Ch 16:20
You came to one **n** on earth to 1Ch 17:21
N was crushed by nation and city 2Ch 15:6
was crushed by **n** and city by 2Ch 15:6
no god of any **n** or kingdom has 2Ch 32:15
Happy is the **n** whose God is the Ps 33:12
my cause against an ungodly **n**; Ps 43:1
them out as a **n** so that Israel's Ps 83:4
wandering from **n** to nation and Ps 105:13
from nation to **n** and from one Ps 105:13
rejoice in the joy of Your **n**, Ps 106:5
He has not done this for any **n**; Ps 147:20
exalts a **n**, but sin is a Pr 14:34
Oh—sinful **n**, people weighed Is 1:4
enlarged the **n** and increased its Is 9:3
send him against a godless **n**; Is 10:6
to the messengers from that **n**? Is 14:32
to a **n** tall and smooth-skinned, Is 18:2
a powerful **n** with a strange Is 18:2
a powerful **n** with a strange Is 18:7
gates so a righteous **n** can come Is 26:2
You have added to the **n**, LORD. Is 26:15
You have added to the **n**; Is 26:15
work of My hands within his ⌊**n**⌋, Is 29:23
people, and listen to Me, My **n**; Is 51:4
will summon a **n** you do not know Is 55:5
like a **n** that does what is right Is 58:2
For the **n** and the kingdom that Is 60:12
the smallest a mighty **n**. Is 60:22
to a **n** that was not called by My Is 65:1
or a **n** be delivered in an Is 66:8
Has a **n** ⌊ever⌋ exchanged its Jr 2:11
Myself on such a **n** as this? Jr 5:9
about to bring a **n** from far away Jr 5:15
is an established **n**, an ancient Jr 5:15
an ancient **n**, a nation whose Jr 5:15
a **n** whose language you do not Jr 5:15
Myself on such a **n** as this? Jr 5:29
a great **n** will be awakened from Jr 6:22
This is the **n** that would not Jr 7:28
against a **n** such as this? Jr 9:9
will uproot and destroy that **n**." Jr 12:17
concerning a **n** or a kingdom that Jr 18:7
if that **n** I have made an Jr 18:8
and plant a **n** or a kingdom. Jr 18:9
king of Babylon and that **n'**— Jr 25:12
goes forth from **n** to nation. Jr 25:32
goes forth from nation to **n**. Jr 25:32
As for the **n** or kingdom that Jr 27:8
that **n** I will punish by sword, Jr 27:8
But as for the **n** that will put Jr 27:11
and that **n** will till it and Jr 27:11
against any **n** that does not Jr 27:13
cease to be a **n** before Me Jr 31:36
regarded as a **n** among them. Jr 33:24
go up against a **n** at ease, Jr 49:31
will not be a **n** to which Elam's Jr 49:36
For a **n** from the north will come Jr 50:3
A great **n** and many kings will be Jr 50:41
towers for a **n** that refused to Lm 4:17
and deprive your **n** of children, Ezk 36:13
and deprive your **n** of children." Ezk 36:14
longer cause your **n** to stumble." Ezk 36:15
make them one **n** in the land, Ezk 37:22
People of every **n** and language, Dn 3:4
people of every **n** and language Dn 3:7
any people, **n**, or language who Dn 3:29
every people, **n**, and language, Dn 4:1
of every people, **n**, and language Dn 6:25
of every people, **n**, and language Dn 7:14
They will rise from that **n**, Dn 8:22
rise to power with a small **n**. Dn 11:23
For a **n** has invaded My land, Jl 1:6
to a distant **n**, for the LORD has Jl 3:8
I am raising up a **n** against you, Am 6:14
a disaster against this **n**; Mc 2:3
N will not take up the sword Mc 4:3
not take up the sword against **n**, Mc 4:3
far removed into a strong **n**. Mc 4:7
impetuous **n** that marches across Hab 1:6
gather together, undesirable **n**, Zph 2:1
of the seacoast, **n** of the Zph 2:5
of My **n** will dispossess Zph 2:9
and so is this **n** before Me"— Hg 2:14
you—the whole **n**—are ⌊still⌋ Mal 3:9
and given to a **n** producing its Mt 21:43
For **n** will rise up against Mt 24:7
nation will rise up against **n**, Mt 24:7
For **n** will rise up against Mk 13:8
nation will rise up against **n**, Mk 13:8
he loves our **n** and has built us Lk 7:5
N will be raised up against Lk 21:10
will be raised up against **n**, Lk 21:10
found this man subverting our **n**, Lk 23:2
both our place and our **n**." Jn 11:48
rather than the whole **n** perish." Jn 11:50
was going to die for the **n**, Jn 11:51
and not for the **n** only, but also Jn 11:52
Your own **n** and the chief priests Jn 18:35
men from every **n** under heaven. Ac 2:5
will judge the **n** that they will Ac 7:7
with the whole Jewish **n**, Ac 10:22
but in every **n** the person who Ac 10:35
has made every **n** of men to live Ac 17:26
benefit of this **n** by your Ac 24:2
judge of this **n** for many years, Ac 24:10
gifts and offerings to my **n**, Ac 24:17
among my own **n** and in Jerusalem. Ac 26:4
had any accusation against my **n**. Ac 28:19
of those who are not a **n**; Rm 10:19
make you angry by a **n** that lacks Rm 10:19
of the **n** of Israel, of the tribe Php 3:5
a holy **n**, a people for His 1Pt 2:9
and language and people and **n**. Rv 5:9
a vast multitude from every **n**, Rv 7:9
tribe, people, language, and **n**. Rv 13:7
to every **n**, tribe, language Rv 14:6

NATION'S *(1)*
until all the **n** men of war who Jos 5:6

NATIONAL *(2)*
Have any of the **n** gods of the 2Ch 32:13
like the **n** gods of the lands 2Ch 32:17

NATIONALITY *(1)*
terror of them fell on every **n**. Est 9:2

NATIONHOOD *(1)*
Come, let's cut her off from **n**. Jr 48:2

NATIONS *(513)*
by their clans, in their **n**. Gn 10:5
in their own lands and their **n**. Gn 10:20
in their lands and their **n**. Gn 10:31
family records, in their **n**. Gn 10:32
The **n** on earth spread out from Gn 10:32
become the father of many **n**. Gn 17:4
make you the father of many **n**. Gn 17:5
and will make **n** and kings come Gn 17:6
her, and she will produce **n**; Gn 17:16
and all the **n** of the earth will Gn 18:18
And all the **n** of the earth will Gn 22:18
Two **n** are in your womb; Gn 25:23
and all the **n** of the earth will Gn 26:4
serve you and **n** bow down to you. Gn 27:29
an assembly of **n**, will come from Gn 35:11
will make many **n** ⌊come from⌋ you Gn 48:4
confusion all the **n** you come to. Ex 23:27
I will drive out **n** before you Ex 34:24
the **n** I am driving out before Lv 18:24
vomited out the **n** that were Lv 18:28
statutes of the **n** I am driving Lv 20:23
you apart from the **n** to be Mine. Lv 20:26
are to be from the **n** around you; Lv 25:44
I will scatter you among the **n**, Lv 26:33
You will perish among the **n**; Lv 26:38
sight of the **n** to be their God Lv 26:45
the **n** that have heard of Your Nm 14:15
not consider itself among the **n**. Nm 23:9
feed on enemy **n** and gnaw their Nm 24:8
Amalek was first among the **n**, Nm 24:20
among the **n** where the LORD your Dt 4:27
out before you **n** greater and Dt 4:38
drives out many **n** before you— Dt 7:1
seven **n** more numerous and Dt 7:1
'These **n** are greater than I; Dt 7:17
drive out these **n** before you Dt 7:22
Like the **n** the LORD is about to Dt 8:20
go and drive out **n** greater and Dt 9:1
drive out these **n** before you Dt 9:4
drive out these **n** before you Dt 9:5
out all these **n** before you, Dt 11:23
you will drive out **n** greater and Dt 11:23
where the **n** you are driving Dt 12:2
annihilates the **n** before you, Dt 12:29
'How did these **n** worship their Dt 12:30
lend to many **n** but not borrow; Dt 15:6
you will rule over many **n**, Dt 15:6
us like all the **n** around us,' Dt 17:14
detestable customs of those **n**. Dt 18:9
driving out the **n** before you Dt 18:12
Though these **n** you are about to Dt 18:14
annihilates the **n** whose land He Dt 19:1
not among the cities of these **n**. Dt 20:15
far above all the **n** He has made Dt 26:19
above all the **n** of the earth. Dt 28:1
lend to many **n**, but you will not Dt 28:12
find no peace among those **n**, Dt 28:65
through the **n** where you traveled Dt 29:16
and worship the gods of those **n**. Dt 29:18
All the **n** will ask, 'Why has the Dt 29:24
are⌋ in all the **n** where the LORD Dt 30:1
will destroy these **n** before you, Dt 31:3
High gave the **n** their Dt 32:8
Rejoice, you **n**, over His people, Dt 32:43
to all these **n** on your account Jos 23:3
these remaining **n** to you as an Jos 23:4
all the **n** I have destroyed Jos 23:4
with these **n** remaining among you Jos 23:7
great and powerful **n** before you, Jos 23:9
rest of these **n** remaining among Jos 23:12
to drive these **n** out before you. Jos 23:13
them any of the **n** Joshua left Jdg 2:21
LORD left these **n** and did not Jdg 2:23
These are the **n** the LORD left in Jdg 3:1
⌊These **n** included:⌋ the five Jdg 3:3
who lived in Harosheth of the **N**. Jdg 4:2
Harosheth of the **N** to the Wadi Jdg 4:13

as far as Harosheth of the **N**, Jdg 4:16
same as all the other **n** have." 1Sm 8:5
we'll be like all the other **n**: 1Sm 8:20
driving out **n** and their gods 2Sm 7:23
from all the **n** he had subdued— 2Sm 8:11
have appointed me the head of **n**; 2Sm 22:44
praise You, LORD, among the **n**; 2Sm 22:50
to all the surrounding **n**. 1Kg 4:31
the **n** that the LORD had told 1Kg 11:2
of the **n** the LORD had 1Kg 14:24
of the **n** the LORD had 2Kg 16:3
customs of the **n** that the LORD 2Kg 17:8
just like those **n** that the LORD 2Kg 17:11
the surrounding **n** the LORD had 2Kg 17:15
The **n** that you have deported and 2Kg 17:26
custom of the **n** where they had 2Kg 17:33
These **n** feared the LORD but also 2Kg 17:41
the gods of the **n** ever delivered 2Kg 18:33
Did the gods of the **n** that my 2Kg 19:12
rescue them—⌊**n** such as⌋ Gozan, 2Kg 19:12
the **n** and their lands. 2Kg 19:17
of the **n** that the LORD had 2Kg 21:2
evil than the **n** the LORD had 2Kg 21:9
the gods of the **n** God had 1Ch 5:25
caused all the **n** to be terrified 1Ch 14:17
Declare His glory among the **n**, 1Ch 16:24
and let them say among the **n**, 1Ch 16:31
us from the **n** so that we may 1Ch 16:35
by driving out **n** before Your 1Ch 17:21
had carried off from all the **n**— 1Ch 18:11
over all the kingdoms of the **n**? 2Ch 20:6
practices of the **n** the LORD had 2Ch 28:3
gods of these **n** that my fathers 2Ch 32:14
eyes of all the **n** after that. 2Ch 32:23
practices of the **n** that the LORD 2Ch 33:2
evil than the **n** the LORD had 2Ch 33:9
detestable practices of the **n**, 2Ch 36:14
the surrounding **n** at my table. Neh 5:17
It is reported among the **n**— Neh 6:6
the surrounding **n** were Neh 6:16
a king like him among many **n**. Neh 13:26
He makes **n** great, then destroys Jb 12:23
He enlarges **n**, then leads them Jb 12:23
over both individuals and **n**, Jb 34:29
the night when **n** will disappear Jb 36:20
For He judges the **n** with these; Jb 36:31
Why do the **n** rebel and the Ps 2:1
I will make the **n** Your Ps 2:8
You have rebuked the **n**: Ps 9:5
The **n** have fallen into the pit Ps 9:15
all the **n** that forget God. Ps 9:17
let the **n** be judged in Your Ps 9:19
the **n** know they are only men. Ps 9:20
the **n** will perish from His land. Ps 10:16
have appointed me the head of **n**; Ps 18:43
praise You, LORD, among the **n**; Ps 18:49
families of the **n** will bow down Ps 22:27
He rules over the **n**. Ps 22:28
frustrates the counsel of the **n**; Ps 33:10
drove out the **n** with Your hand; Ps 44:2
and scatter us among the **n**. Ps 44:11
You make us a joke among the **n**, Ps 44:14
N rage, kingdoms topple; Ps 46:6
exalted among the **n**, exalted on Ps 46:10
under us and **n** under our feet. Ps 47:3
God reigns over the **n**; Ps 47:8
bring down the **n** in wrath. Ps 56:7
sing praises to You among the **n**. Ps 57:9
rise up to punish all the **n**; Ps 59:5
You ridicule all the **n**. Ps 59:8
waves, and the tumult of the **n**. Ps 65:7
He keeps His eye on the **n**. Ps 66:7
Your salvation among all **n**. Ps 67:2
Let the **n** rejoice and shout for Ps 67:4
and lead the **n** on earth. Ps 67:4
down to him, all **n** serve him. Ps 72:11
May all **n** be blessed by him and Ps 72:17
He drove out **n** before them. Ps 78:55
the **n** have invaded Your Ps 79:1
Your wrath on the **n** that don't Ps 79:6
Why should the **n** ask, "Where is Ps 79:10
servants be known among the **n**. Ps 79:10
drove out the **n** and planted it. Ps 80:8
for all the **n** belong to You. Ps 82:8
the **n** You have made will come Ps 86:9
One who instructs **n**, the One who Ps 94:10
Declare His glory among the **n**, Ps 96:3
Say among the **n**: "The LORD Ps 96:10
in the sight of the **n**. Ps 98:2
Then the **n** will fear the name of Ps 102:15
He gave them the lands of the **n**, Ps 105:44
their descendants among the **n**, Ps 106:27
mingled with the **n** and adopted Ps 106:35
He handed them over to the **n**; Ps 106:41
us from the **n**, so that we may Ps 106:47
sing praises to You among the **n**. Ps 108:3
He will judge the **n**, heaping up Ps 110:6
them the inheritance of the **n**. Ps 111:6
LORD is exalted above all the **n**, Ps 113:4
Why should the **n** say, "Where is Ps 115:2
Praise the LORD, all **n**! Ps 117:1
All the **n** surrounded me; Ps 118:10
Then they said among the **n**, Ps 126:2
down many **n** and slaughtered Ps 135:10
The idols of the **n** are of silver Ps 135:15
on the **n** and punishment Ps 149:7
All **n** will stream to it, Is 2:2
disputes among the **n** and provide Is 2:4
N will not take up the sword Is 2:4
up the sword against ⌊other⌋ **n**, Is 2:4
for the distant **n** and whistles Is 5:26
Jordan, and to Galilee of the **n**. Is 9:1
destroy and to cut off many **n**. Is 10:7
the borders of **n** and plundered Is 10:13
to seize the wealth of the **n**. Is 10:14
The **n** will seek Him, and His Is 11:10
up a banner for the **n** and gather Is 11:12
like **n** being gathered together! Is 13:4
The **n** will escort Israel and Is 14:2
It subdued the **n** in rage with Is 14:6
kings of the **n** rise from their Is 14:9
destroyer of **n**, you have been Is 14:12
kings of the **n** lie in splendor Is 14:18
stretched out against all the **n**. Is 14:26
rulers of the **n** have trampled Is 16:8
raging of the **n**—they rage like Is 17:12
The **n** rage like the raging of Is 17:13
was the merchant among the **n**. Is 23:3
it will be on earth among the **n**: Is 24:13
the sheet covering all the **n**; Is 25:7
of all the **n** going out to battle Is 29:7
of all the **n** who go to battle Is 29:8
comes⌋ to sift the **n** in a sieve Is 30:28
the **n** scatter when You rise in Is 33:3
You **n**, come here and listen; Is 34:1
LORD is angry with all the **n**— Is 34:2
the gods of the **n** delivered his Is 36:18
Did the gods of the **n** that my Is 37:12
the **n** are like a drop in a Is 40:15
All the **n** are as nothing before Is 40:17
The LORD hands **n** over to him, Is 41:2
He will bring justice to the **n**. Is 42:1
people ⌊and⌋ a light to the **n**, Is 42:6
All the **n** are gathered together, Is 43:9
grasped to subdue **n** before him, Is 45:1
near, you fugitives of the **n**. Is 45:20
also make you a light for the **n**, Is 49:6
I will lift up My hand to the **n**, Is 49:22
My justice for a light to the **n**. Is 51:4
will bring justice to the **n**. Is 51:5
arm in the sight of all the **n**; Is 52:10
so He will sprinkle many **n**. Is 52:15
will dispossess **n** and inhabit Is 54:3
and **n** who do not know you will Is 55:5
a house of prayer for all **n**." Is 56:7
N will come to your light, Is 60:3
wealth of the **n** will come to you Is 60:5
wealth of the **n** may be brought Is 60:11
those **n** will be annihilated. Is 60:12
You will nurse on the milk of **n**, Is 60:16
will eat the wealth of the **n**, Is 61:6
will be known among the **n**, Is 61:9
to spring up before all the **n**. Is 61:11
N will see your righteousness, Is 62:2
no one from the **n** was with Me. Is 63:3
I crushed **n** in My anger; Is 63:6
so that **n** will tremble at Your Is 64:2
the wealth of **n** like a flood; Is 66:12
to gather all **n** and languages; Is 66:18
survivors from them to the **n**— Is 66:19
proclaim My glory among the **n**. Is 66:19
from all the **n** as a gift to the Is 66:20
you a prophet to the **n**. Jr 1:5
set you over **n** and kingdoms to Jr 1:10
and all the **n** will be gathered Jr 3:17
inheritance of all the **n**. Jr 3:19
then the **n** will be blessed by Jr 4:2
a destroyer of **n** has set out. Jr 4:7
Warn the **n**: Look! Proclaim to Jr 4:16
listen, you **n** and you witnesses, Jr 6:18
scatter them among **n** that they Jr 9:16
All these **n** are uncircumcised, Jr 9:26
the way of the **n** or be terrified Jr 10:2
although the **n** are terrified by Jr 10:2
not fear You, King of the **n**? Jr 10:7
people of the **n** and among all Jr 10:7
the **n** cannot endure His rage. Jr 10:10
Your wrath on the **n** that don't Jr 10:25
idols of the **n** bring rain? Jr 14:22
the **n** will come to You from the Jr 16:19
Ask among the **n**, Who has heard Jr 18:13
Many **n** will pass by this city Jr 22:8
against all these surrounding **n**, Jr 25:9
and these **n** will serve the king Jr 25:11
prophesied against all the **n**. Jr 25:13
For many **n** and great kings will Jr 25:14
make all the **n** I am sending you Jr 25:15
made all the **n** drink ⌊from it⌋ Jr 25:17
brings a case against the **n**. Jr 25:31
for all the **n** of the earth." Jr 26:6
All **n** will serve him, his son, Jr 27:7
and then many **n** and great kings Jr 27:7
from the neck of all the **n**.' " Jr 28:11
of all these **n** that they might Jr 28:14
from all the **n** and places where Jr 29:14
among all the **n** where I will Jr 29:18
on all the **n** where I have Jr 30:11
shout for the chief of the **n**! Jr 31:7
N, hear the word of the LORD, Jr 31:10
before all the **n** of the earth, Jr 33:9
and all other **n** were fighting Jr 34:1
and all the **n** from the time I Jr 36:2
from all the **n** where they had Jr 43:5
insult among all the **n** of earth. Jr 44:8
Prophecies Against the **N** Jr 45:5
the prophet about the **n**: Jr 46:1
The **n** have heard of your Jr 46:12
on all the **n** where I have Jr 46:28
surrounding ⌊**n**⌋, everyone who Jr 48:17
envoy has been sent among the **n**: Jr 49:14
you insignificant among the **n**, Jr 49:15
Announce to the **n**; proclaim and Jr 50:2
of great **n** from the north Jr 50:9
She will lag behind all the **n**— Jr 50:12
Babylon has become among the **n**! Jr 50:23
a cry will be heard among the **n**. Jr 50:46
The **n** drank her wine; Jr 51:7
therefore, the **n** go mad. Jr 51:7
With you I will smash **n**; Jr 51:20
blow a ram's horn among the **n**; Jr 51:27
set apart the **n** against her. Jr 51:27
Set apart the **n** for battle Jr 51:28
Babylon has become among the **n**! Jr 51:41
The **n** will no longer stream to Jr 51:44
the **n** will exhaust themselves Jr 51:58
great among the **n** has become Lm 1:1
lives among the **n** but finds no Lm 1:3
has even seen the **n** enter her Lm 1:10
her leaders ⌊live⌋ among the **n**, Lm 2:9
said among the **n**, "They can stay Lm 4:15
his protection among the **n**. Lm 4:20
the rebellious **n** who have Ezk 2:3
the **n** where I will banish them. Ezk 4:13
in the center of the **n**, Ezk 5:5
with more wickedness than the **n**, Ezk 5:6
than the **n** around you— Ezk 5:7
ordinances of the **n** around you— Ezk 5:7
you in the sight of the **n**. Ezk 5:8
disgrace among the **n** around you, Ezk 5:14
to the **n** around you when I Ezk 5:15
you are scattered among the **n**, Ezk 6:8
Me among the **n** where they are Ezk 6:9
the most evil of **n** to take Ezk 7:24
ordinances of the **n** around you." Ezk 11:12
away among the **n** and scattered Ezk 11:16
among the **n** and scatter them Ezk 12:15
among the **n** where they go. Ezk 12:16
among the **n** because of your Ezk 16:14
When the **n** heard about him, Ezk 19:4
Then the **n** from the surrounding Ezk 19:8
the eyes of the **n** they were Ezk 20:9
the eyes of the **n** in whose sight Ezk 20:14
the eyes of the **n** in whose sight Ezk 20:22
among the **n** and scatter them Ezk 20:23

us be like the **n**, like the	Ezk 20:32
you in the sight of the **n**.	Ezk 20:41
disgrace to the **n** and a mockery	Ezk 22:4
you among the **n** and scatter you	Ezk 22:15
profaned in the sight of the **n**.	Ezk 22:16
an alliance of **n** and with	Ezk 23:24
like a prostitute with the **n**,	Ezk 23:30
Prophecies Against the **N**	Ezk 24:27
give you as plunder to the **n**.	Ezk 25:7
Judah is like all the ⌊other⌋ **n**,	Ezk 25:8
not be remembered among the **n**.	Ezk 25:10
raise up many **n** against you,	Ezk 26:3
will become plunder for the **n**,	Ezk 26:5
you, ruthless men from the **n**.	Ezk 28:7
you among the **n** are appalled at	Ezk 28:19
them in the sight of the **n**,	Ezk 28:25
among the **n** and scatter them	Ezk 29:12
from the **n** where they were	Ezk 29:13
again exalt itself over the **n**.	Ezk 29:15
they cannot rule over the **n**.	Ezk 29:15
a time ⌊of doom⌋ for the **n**.	Ezk 30:3
men from the **n**, will be brought	Ezk 30:11
among the **n** and scatter them	Ezk 30:23
among the **n** and scatter them	Ezk 30:26
all the great **n** lived in its	Ezk 31:6
to hand it over to a ruler of **n**;	Ezk 31:11
men from the **n**, cut it down and	Ezk 31:12
I made the **n** quake at the sound	Ezk 31:16
lived in its shade among the **n**.	Ezk 31:17
yourself to a lion of the **n**,	Ezk 32:2
your destruction among the **n**,	Ezk 32:9
will cause many **n** to be appalled	Ezk 32:10
of them ruthless men from the **n**.	Ezk 32:12
women of the **n** will chant it.	Ezk 32:16
daughters of mighty **n** down to	Ezk 32:18
no longer be prey for the **n**,	Ezk 34:28
endure the insults of the **n**.	Ezk 34:29
These two **n** and two lands will	Ezk 35:10
the rest of the **n** and an object	Ezk 36:3
to the rest of the **n** all around.	Ezk 36:4
rest of the **n** and all of Edom	Ezk 36:5
endured the insults of the **n**.	Ezk 36:6
swear that the **n** all around you	Ezk 36:7
the insults of the **n** to be heard	Ezk 36:15
I dispersed them among the **n**,	Ezk 36:19
came to the **n** where they went	Ezk 36:20
among the **n** where they went.	Ezk 36:21
among the **n** where you went.	Ezk 36:22
has been profaned among the **n**—	Ezk 36:23
n will know that I am Yahweh"	Ezk 36:23
you from the **n** and gather you	Ezk 36:24
reproach among the **n** on account	Ezk 36:30
Then the **n** that remain around	Ezk 36:36
out of the **n** where they have	Ezk 37:21
no longer be two **n** and will no	Ezk 37:22
forever, the **n** will know that I	Ezk 37:28
a people gathered from the **n**,	Ezk 38:12
land so that the **n** may know Me,	Ezk 38:16
Myself in the sight of many **n**.	Ezk 38:23
Then the **n** will know that I am	Ezk 39:7
display My glory among the **n**,	Ezk 39:21
and all the **n** will see the	Ezk 39:21
And the **n** will know that the	Ezk 39:23
them in the sight of many **n**.	Ezk 39:27
having exiled them among the **n**.	Ezk 39:28
all peoples, **n**, and languages	Dn 5:19
occurred since **n** came into being	Dn 12:1
to get mixed up with the **n**.	Hs 7:8
are among the **n** like discarded	Hs 8:8
they hire ⌊lovers⌋ among the **n**,	Hs 8:10
rejoice jubilantly as the **n** do,	Hs 9:1
become wanderers among the **n**.	Hs 9:17
n will be gathered against them	Hs 10:10
N writhe in horror before them;	Jl 2:6
an object of scorn among the **n**.	Jl 2:17
make you a disgrace among the **n**.	Jl 2:19
gather all the **n** and take them	Jl 3:2
The **n** have scattered the	Jl 3:2
Proclaim this among the **n**:	Jl 3:9
quickly, all you surrounding **n**;	Jl 3:11
Let the **n** be roused and come to	Jl 3:12
to judge all the surrounding **n**.	Jl 3:12
wickedness of the **n** is great.	Jl 3:13
people in this first of the **n**,	Am 6:1
house of Israel among all the **n**,	Am 9:9
and all the **n** that are called	Am 9:12
envoy has been sent among the **n**:	Ob 1
you insignificant among the **n**;	Ob 2
LORD is near, against all the **n**.	Ob 15
so all the **n** will drink	Ob 16
and many **n** will come and say,	Mc 4:2
for strong **n** that are far away.	Mc 4:3
n have now assembled against	Mc 4:11
of Jacob will be among the **n**,	Mc 5:8
wrath against the **n** that have	Mc 5:15
N will see and be ashamed of all	Mc 7:16
betrays **n** by her prostitution	Nah 3:4
and display your nakedness to **n**,	Nah 3:5
Look at the **n** and observe—	Hab 1:5
slaughter **n** without mercy?	Hab 1:17
He gathers all the **n** to himself;	Hab 2:5
Since you have plundered many **n**,	Hab 2:8
He looks and startles the **n**.	Hab 3:6
You trample down the **n** in wrath.	Hab 3:12
coastlands of the **n** will bow in	Zph 2:11
I have cut off **n**; their corner	Zph 3:6
For My decision is to gather **n**,	Zph 3:8
I will shake all the **n** so that	Hg 2:7
of all the **n** will come,	Hg 2:7
angry with the **n** that are at	Zch 1:15
the horns of the **n** that raised	Zch 1:21
glory against the **n** who are	Zch 2:8
Many **n** will join themselves to	Zch 2:11
all the **n** that had not known	Zch 7:14
have been a curse among the **n**,	Zch 8:13
and strong **n** will come to seek	Zch 8:22
10 men from **n** of every language	Zch 8:23
He will proclaim peace to the **n**.	Zch 9:10
Though I sow them among the **n**,	Zch 10:9
when all the **n** of the earth	Zch 12:3
horses of the **n** with blindness.	Zch 12:4
destroy all the **n** that come	Zch 12:9
gather all the **n** against	Zch 14:2
against those **n** as He fights	Zch 14:3
the surrounding **n** will be	Zch 14:14
from the **n** that came against	Zch 14:16
inflicts on the **n** who do not go	Zch 14:18
and all the **n** that do not go up	Zch 14:19
name will be great among the **n**,	Mal 1:11
name will be great among the **n**,"	Mal 1:11
name will be feared among the **n**.	Mal 1:14
Then all the **n** will consider you	Mal 3:12
the road leading to other **n**,	Mt 10:5
witness to them and to the **n**.	Mt 10:18
will proclaim justice to the **n**.	Mt 12:18
The **n** will put their hope in His	Mt 12:21
be hated by all **n** because of My	Mt 24:9
world as a testimony to all **n**.	Mt 24:14
the **n** will be gathered before	Mt 25:32
and make disciples of all **n**,	Mt 28:19
a house of prayer for all **n**?	Mk 11:17
first be proclaimed to all **n**.	Mk 13:10
be led captive into all the **n**,	Lk 21:24
on the earth among **n** bewildered	Lk 21:25
in His name to all the **n**,	Lk 24:47
dispossessed the **n** that God	Ac 7:45
destroying seven **n** in the land	Ac 13:19
allowed all the **n** to go their	Ac 14:16
of faith among all the **n**,	Rm 1:5
made you the father of many **n**.	Rm 4:17
he became the father of many **n**,	Rm 4:18
obedience of faith among all **n**—	Rm 16:26
the **n** will be blessed in you.	Gl 3:8
give him authority over the **n**—	Rv 2:26
many peoples, **n**, languages,	Rv 10:11
because it is given to the **n**,	Rv 11:2
and **n** will view their bodies for	Rv 11:9
The **n** were angry, but Your wrath	Rv 11:18
to shepherd all **n** with an iron	Rv 12:5
who made all **n** drink the wine of	Rv 14:8
are Your ways, King of the **N**.	Rv 15:3
because all the **n** will come and	Rv 15:4
and the cities of the **n** fell.	Rv 16:19
multitudes, **n**, and languages.	Rv 17:15
all the **n** have drunk the wine	Rv 18:3
because all the **n** were deceived	Rv 18:23
with it He might strike the **n**.	Rv 19:15
deceive the **n** until the 1,000	Rv 20:3
out to deceive the **n** at the four	Rv 20:8
The **n** will walk in its light,	Rv 21:24
and honor of the **n** into it.	Rv 21:26
the tree are for healing the **n**,	Rv 22:2

NATIVE *(19)*

Haran died in his **n** land, in Ur	Gn 11:28
house and from my **n** land,	Gn 24:7
and return to your **n** land.'"	Gn 31:13
resident or **n** of the land,	Ex 12:19
become like a **n** of the land.	Ex 12:48
to both the **n** and the foreigner	Ex 12:49
both the **n** and the foreigner who	Lv 16:29
whether the **n** or the foreigner,	Lv 17:15
not the **n** or the foreigner who	Lv 18:26
the foreign resident or the **n**.	Lv 24:16
the foreign resident and the **n**,	Lv 24:22
resident and the **n** of the land."	Nm 9:14
whether **n** or foreign resident,	Nm 15:30
like a flourishing **n** tree.	Ps 37:35
return again and see his **n** land.	Jr 22:10
of us, in our own **n** language?	Ac 2:8
named Aquila, a **n** of Pontus, who	Ac 18:2
named Apollos, a **n** Alexandrian,	Ac 18:24
cut off from your **n** wild olive,	Rm 11:24

NATIVE-BORN *(3)*

with you as the **n** among you.	Lv 19:34
All the **n** of Israel must live in	Lv 23:42
treat them like **n** Israelites;	Ezk 47:22

NATURAL *(12)*

animal that died a **n** death or	Lv 17:15
He was speaking about **n** sleep.	Jn 11:13
females exchanged **n** sexual	Rm 1:26
way also left **n** sexual	Rm 1:27
did not spare the **n** branches,	Rm 11:21
will these—the **n** branches—be	Rm 11:24
But the **n** man does not welcome	1Co 2:14
a **n** body, raised a spiritual	1Co 15:44
If there is a **n** body, there is	1Co 15:44
is not first, but the **n**;	1Co 15:46
we had **n** fathers discipline us,	Heb 12:9
divisions and are merely **n**,	Jd 19

NATURALLY *(5)*

animal that dies **n** or is mauled	Lv 7:24
animal that died **n** or was mauled	Lv 22:8
these men die ⌊**n**⌋ as all people	Nm 16:29
that died **n** or was mauled	Ezk 4:14
animal that died **n** or was mauled	Ezk 44:31

NATURE *(14)*

being jealous by **n**, is a jealous	Ex 34:14
from his own **n**, because he is	Jn 8:44
with the same **n** as you, and we	Ac 14:15
that the divine **n** is like gold	Ac 17:29
His eternal power and divine **n**,	Rm 1:20
and against **n** were grafted into	Rm 11:24
Does not even **n** itself teach you	1Co 11:14
things that by **n** are not gods.	Gl 4:8
and by **n** we were children under	Eph 2:3
of God's **n** dwells bodily,	Col 2:9
the exact expression of His **n**,	Heb 1:3
was a man with a **n** like ours;	Jms 5:17
of their weaker **n** yet showing	1Pt 3:7
you may share in the divine **n**,	2Pt 1:4

NAUSEATING *(1)*

nostrils and becomes **n** to you—	Nm 11:20

NAVEL *(1)*

Your **n** is a rounded bowl;	Sg 7:2

NAZARENE *(18)*

that He will be called a **N**.	Mt 2:23
"This man was with Jesus the **N**!"	Mt 26:71
have to do with us, Jesus—**N**?	Mk 1:24
heard that it was Jesus the **N**,	Mk 10:47
You also were with that **N**,	Mk 14:67
You are looking for Jesus the **N**,	Mk 16:6
have to do with us, Jesus—**N**?	Lk 4:34
"Jesus the **N** is passing by,"	Lk 18:37
things concerning Jesus the **N**,	Lk 24:19
"Jesus the **N**," they answered.	Jn 18:5
"Jesus the **N**," they said.	Jn 18:7
JESUS THE **N** THE KING OF	Jn 19:19
This Jesus the **N** was a man	Ac 2:22
the name of Jesus Christ the **N**,	Ac 3:6
the name of Jesus Christ the **N**—	Ac 4:10
that Jesus, this **N**, will destroy	Ac 6:14
I am Jesus the **N**, whom you are	Ac 22:8
to the name of Jesus the **N**.	Ac 26:9

NAZARENES *(1)*

ringleader of the sect of the **N**!	Ac 24:5

NAZARETH *(12)*

a town called **N** to fulfill what	Mt 2:23
left **N** behind and went to live	Mt 4:13
Jesus from **N** in Galilee!"	Mt 21:11
Jesus came from **N** in Galilee and	Mk 1:9
to a town in Galilee called **N**,	Lk 1:26
from the town of **N** in Galilee,	Lk 2:4

Galilee, to their own town of **N**. Lk 2:39
and came to **N** and was obedient Lk 2:51
He came to **N**, where He had been Lk 4:16
the son of Joseph, from **N**!" Jn 1:45
anything good come out of **N**?" Jn 1:46
anointed Jesus of **N** with the Ac 10:38

NAZIRITE *(10)*
a special vow, a **N** vow, to Nm 6:2
atonement on behalf of the **N**, Nm 6:11
This is the law of the **N**: Nm 6:13
The **N** is to shave his Nm 6:18
the hands of the **N** after he has Nm 6:19
that, the **N** may drink wine. Nm 6:20
the ritual of the **N** who vows his Nm 6:21
boy will be a **N** to God from Jdg 13:5
boy will be a **N** to God from Jdg 13:7
because I am a **N** to God from Jdg 16:17

NAZIRITE'S *(1)*
and sacrifice the **N** sin offering Nm 6:16

NAZIRITES *(2)*
and some of your young men as **N**. Am 2:11
you made the **N** drink wine and Am 2:12

NEAH *(2)*
to Rimmon, curving around to **N**. Jos 19:13
circled around **N** on the north to Jos 19:14

NEAPOLIS *(1)*
Samothrace, the next day to **N**, Ac 16:11

NEAR *(248)*
(See pp. xi-xii.)

NEARBY *(14)*
Then she went and sat down **n**, Gn 21:16
So as she sat **n**, she wept Gn 21:16
even though it was **n**; Ex 13:17
from the victim to the **n** cities. Dt 21:2
country—whether distant or **n**— 1Kg 8:46
them to a distant or **n** country, 2Ch 6:36
the Jews who lived **n** arrived, Neh 4:12
and the donkeys grazing **n**, Jb 1:14
a neighbor **n** than a brother Pr 27:10
there is no one **n** to comfort Lm 1:16
of the LORD was standing **n**. Zch 3:5
began to tell those standing **n**, Mk 14:69
and since the tomb was **n**. Jn 19:42
And those standing **n** said, Ac 23:4

NEARED *(2)*
sun set as they **n** Gibeah in Jdg 19:14
Just as He **n** the gate of the Lk 7:12

NEARER *(1)*
our salvation is **n** than when we Rm 13:11

NEAREST *(5)*
the neighbor **n** his house are to Ex 12:4
his **n** relative may come and Lv 25:25
to the **n** relative of his Nm 27:11
of the city **n** to the victim are Dt 21:3
of the city **n** to the victim will Dt 21:6

NEARIAH *(2)*
Igal, Bariah, **N**, and Shaphat— 1Ch 3:22
went with Pelatiah, **N**, Rephaiah, 1Ch 4:42

NEARIAH'S *(1)*
N sons: Elioenai, Hizkiah, and 1Ch 3:23

NEARING *(3)*
he traveled and was **n** Damascus, Ac 9:3
were traveling and **n** the city, Ac 10:9
as he was **n** the end of his life, Heb 11:22

NEARLY *(4)*
my steps **n** went astray. Ps 73:2
the crowds were **n** crushing Him. Lk 8:42
The night is **n** over, and the Rm 13:12
he was so sick that he **n** died. Php 2:27

NEARNESS *(1)*
they delight in the **n** of God." Is 58:2

NEBAI *(1)*
Hariph, Anathoth, **N**, Neh 10:19

NEBAIOTH *(5)*
N, Ishmael's firstborn, then Gn 25:13
She was the sister of **N**. Gn 28:9
of Ishmael and sister of **N**. Gn 36:3
N, Ishmael's firstborn, Kedar, 1Ch 1:29
the rams of **N** will serve you and Is 60:7

NEBALLAT *(1)*
Hadid, Zeboim, **N**, Neh 11:34

NEBAT *(25)*
Jeroboam son of **N**, was an 1Kg 11:26
Jeroboam son of **N** heard ⌊about 1Kg 12:2
Shilonite to Jeroboam son of **N**. 1Kg 12:15
King Jeroboam son of **N**, 1Kg 15:1
the house of Jeroboam son of **N**: 1Kg 16:3
Jeroboam son of **N** and the sins 1Kg 16:26
Jeroboam son of **N** were a trivial 1Kg 16:31
Jeroboam son of **N** and like the 1Kg 21:22
in the way of Jeroboam son of **N**, 1Kg 22:52
Jeroboam son of **N** had caused 2Kg 3:3
Jeroboam son of **N** and like the 2Kg 9:9
Jeroboam son of **N** had caused 2Kg 10:29
Jeroboam son of **N** had caused 2Kg 13:2
Jeroboam son of **N** had caused 2Kg 13:11
Jeroboam son of **N** had caused 2Kg 14:24
Jeroboam son of **N** had caused 2Kg 15:9
Jeroboam son of **N** had caused 2Kg 15:18
Jeroboam son of **N** had caused 2Kg 15:24
Jeroboam son of **N** had caused 2Kg 15:28
made Jeroboam son of **N** king. 2Kg 17:21
place that Jeroboam son of **N**, 2Kg 23:15
concerning Jeroboam son of **N**. 2Ch 9:29
son of **N** heard ⌊about it 2Ch 10:2
Shilonite to Jeroboam son of **N**. 2Ch 10:15
But Jeroboam son of **N**, a servant 2Ch 13:6

NEBO *(10)*
Elealeh, Sebam, **N**, and Beon, Nm 32:3
as well as **N** and Baal-meon Nm 32:38
in the Abarim ⌊range⌋ facing **N**. Nm 33:47
Go up Mount **N** in the Abarim Dt 32:49
the plains of Moab to Mount **N**, Dt 34:1
Aroer as far as **N** and Baal-meon. 1Ch 5:8
Moab wails on **N** and at Medeba. Is 15:2
Bel crouches; **N** cowers. Their Is 46:1
Woe to **N**, because it is about to Jr 48:1
Dibon, **N**, Beth-diblathaim, Jr 48:22

NEBO'S *(3)*
N people 52 Ezr 2:29
N descendants: Jeiel, Mattithiah, Ezr 10:43
the other **N** men 52 Neh 7:33

NEBUCHADNEZZAR *(90)*
N king of Babylon attacked, 2Kg 24:1
servants of **N** king of Babylon 2Kg 24:10
Then King **N** of Babylon came to 2Kg 24:11
N deported Jehoiachin to 2Kg 24:15
King **N** of Babylon advanced 2Kg 25:1
the nineteenth year of King **N**, 2Kg 25:8
N king of Babylon appointed 2Kg 25:22
into exile at the hands of **N**. 1Ch 6:15
Now **N** king of Babylon attacked 2Ch 36:6
Also **N** took some of the utensils 2Ch 36:7
In the spring **N** sent ⌊for him⌋ 2Ch 36:10
against King **N** who had made 2Ch 36:13
LORD's house that **N** had taken Ezr 1:7
exiles King **N** of Babylon had Ezr 2:1
them over to King **N** of Babylon, Ezr 5:12
of God's house that **N** had taken Ezr 5:14
of God's house that **N** took from Ezr 6:5
deported by King **N** of Babylon. Neh 7:6
when King **N** of Babylon took Est 2:6
N king of Babylon is making Jr 21:2
works so that ⌊**N**⌋ will withdraw Jr 21:2
hand over to King **N** of Babylon, Jr 21:7
to **N** king of Babylon and the Jr 22:25
After **N** king of Babylon had Jr 24:1
first year of **N** king of Babylon Jr 25:1
My servant **N** king of Babylon Jr 25:9
the authority of My servant **N**, Jr 27:6
does not serve **N** king of Babylon Jr 27:8
those **N** king of Babylon did not Jr 27:20
temple that **N** king of Babylon Jr 28:3
I will break the yoke of **N**, Jr 28:11
might serve **N** king of Babylon Jr 28:14
all the people **N** had deported Jr 29:1
to Babylon to **N** king of Babylon. Jr 29:3
them over to **N** king of Babylon, Jr 29:21
was the eighteenth year of **N**. Jr 32:1
to Babylon's king **N**, and he will Jr 32:28
Jeremiah from the LORD when **N**, Jr 34:1
when **N** king of Babylon marched Jr 35:11
for **N** king of Babylon made him Jr 37:1
King **N** of Babylon advanced Jr 39:1
him to **N**, Babylon's king, Jr 39:5
King **N** of Babylon gave orders Jr 39:11
My servant **N** king of Babylon, Jr 43:10
Zedekiah to Babylon's King **N**, Jr 44:30
River by **N** king of Babylon Jr 46:2
the coming of **N** king of Babylon Jr 46:13
to **N** king of Babylon and his Jr 46:26
Hazor, which **N**, Babylon's king Jr 49:28
for **N** king of Babylon has drawn Jr 49:30
his bones was **N** king of Babylon. Jr 50:17
N of Babylon has devoured me; Jr 51:34
King **N** of Babylon advanced Jr 52:4
the nineteenth year of King **N**, Jr 52:12
These are the people **N** deported: Jr 52:28
to bring King **N** of Babylon, Ezk 26:7
N king of Babylon made his army Ezk 29:18
of Egypt to **N** king of Babylon Ezk 29:19
the hand of **N** king of Babylon. Ezk 30:10
N king of Babylon came to Dn 1:1
N carried them to the land of Dn 1:2
official presented them to **N**. Dn 1:18
N had dreams that troubled him, Dn 2:1
He has let King **N** know what will Dn 2:28
Then King **N** fell down, paid Dn 2:46
King **N** made a gold statue, Dn 3:1
King **N** sent word to assemble the Dn 3:2
of the statue King **N** had set up. Dn 3:2
before the statue **N** had set up. Dn 3:3
statue that King **N** has set up. Dn 3:5
statue that King **N** had set up. Dn 3:7
said to King **N**, "May the king Dn 3:9
a furious rage **N** gave orders to Dn 3:13
N asked them, "Shadrach, Meshach, Dn 3:14
the king, "**N**, we don't need to Dn 3:16
Then **N** was filled with rage, Dn 3:19
Then King **N** jumped up in alarm. Dn 3:24
N then approached the door of Dn 3:26
N exclaimed, "Praise to the God Dn 3:28
N, To those of every people, Dn 4:1
I, **N**, was at ease in my house Dn 4:4
the dream that I, King **N**, had. Dn 4:18
All this happened to King **N**. Dn 4:28
King **N**, to you it is declared Dn 4:31
sentence against **N** was executed. Dn 4:33
those days, I, **N**, looked up to Dn 4:34
Now I, **N**, praise, exalt, and Dn 4:37
that his predecessor **N** had taken Dn 5:2
King **N**, appointed him Dn 5:11
majesty to your predecessor **N**. Dn 5:18

NEBUCHADNEZZAR'S *(1)*
in **N** twenty-third year, Jr 52:30

NEBUSHAZBAN *(1)*
of the guard, **N** the Rab-saris, Jr 39:13

NEBUZARADAN *(16)*
of Babylon, **N**, the commander 2Kg 25:8
N, the commander of the guards, 2Kg 25:11
N, the commander of the guards, 2Kg 25:20
N, the commander of the guards, Jr 39:9
⌊However,⌋ **N**, the commander of Jr 39:10
⌊Speaking⌋ through **N**, captain of Jr 39:11
N, captain of the guard, Jr 39:13
Jeremiah from the LORD after **N**, Jr 40:1
turned ⌊to go, **N** said to him:⌋ Jr 40:5
remained in Mizpah over whom **N**, Jr 41:10
and everyone whom **N**, captain of Jr 43:6
of Babylon—**N**, the commander Jr 52:12
N, the commander of the guards, Jr 52:15
the poor people of the land **N**, Jr 52:16
N, the commander of the guards, Jr 52:26
year, **N**, the commander Jr 52:30

NECESSARY *(18)*
but one thing is **n**. Lk 10:42
is **n** that one become a witness Ac 1:22
It was **n** that God's message be Ac 13:46
It is **n** to pass through many Ac 14:22
It is **n** to circumcise them and Ac 15:5
on you than these **n** things: Ac 15:28
it is **n** to help the weak and to Ac 20:35
supposed it was **n** to do many Ac 26:9
that seem to be weaker are **n**. 1Co 12:22
I considered it **n** to urge the 2Co 9:5
If boasting is **n**, I will boast 2Co 11:30
It is **n** to boast; it is not 2Co 12:1
in the flesh is more **n** for you. Php 1:24
I considered it **n** to send you Php 2:25
It is **n** to silence them; Ti 1:11
it was **n** for this ⌊priest Heb 8:3
Therefore it was **n** for the Heb 9:23
I found it **n** to write and exhort Jd 3

NECESSITY *(1)*
not out of regret or out of **n**, 2Co 9:7

NECK *(50)*
and the smooth part of his **n**. Gn 27:16
will break his yoke from your **n**. Gn 27:40

a gold chain around his **n**. Gn 41:42
do not redeem it, break its **n**. Ex 13:13
do not redeem ⌊it⌋, break its **n**. Ex 34:20
the back of the **n** without Lv 5:8
break the cow's **n** there by the Dt 21:4
heifer whose **n** has been broken Dt 21:6
iron yoke on your **n** until He has Dt 28:48
garment or two for my **n**?" Jdg 5:30
and heavy, his **n** broke and he 1Sm 4:18
scruff of the **n** and smashed me Jb 16:12
me by the **n** of my garment. Jb 30:18
Do you adorn his **n** with a mane? Jb 39:19
Strength resides in his **n**, Jb 41:22
for the water has risen to my **n**. Ps 69:1
his **n** was put in an iron collar. Ps 105:18
a ⌊gold⌋ chain around your **n**. Pr 1:9
Tie them around your **n**; Pr 3:3
you and adornment for your **n**. Pr 3:22
tie them around your **n**. Pr 6:21
jewelry, your **n** with its Sg 1:10
Your **n** is like the tower of Sg 4:4
Your **n** is like a tower of ivory, Sg 7:4
through, reaching up to the **n**; Is 8:8
and his yoke from your **n**. Is 10:27
torrent that rises to the **n**. Is 30:28
and your **n** is iron and your Is 48:4
Remove the bonds from your **n**, Is 52:2
a lamb, one breaks a dog's **n**; Is 66:3
yourself and put them on your **n**. Jr 27:2
not place its **n** under the yoke Jr 27:8
will put its **n** under the yoke Jr 27:11
yoke bar from the **n** of Jeremiah Jr 28:10
the **n** of all the nations.'" Jr 28:11
yoke bar from the **n** of Jeremiah Jr 28:12
iron yoke on the **n** of all these Jr 28:14
yoke from your **n** and snap your Jr 30:8
they have been placed on my **n**, Lm 1:14
and a chain around your **n**. Ezk 16:11
have a gold chain around his **n**, Dn 5:7
have a gold chain around your **n**, Dn 5:16
a gold chain around his **n**, Dn 5:29
will place a yoke on her fine **n**. Hs 10:11
waters engulfed me up to the **n**; Jnh 2:5
and strip ⌊him⌋ from foot to **n**. Hab 3:13
hung around his **n** and he were Mt 18:6
hung around his **n** and he were Mk 9:42
threw his arms around his **n**, Lk 15:20
hung around his **n** and he were Lk 17:2

NECKLACE *(3)*
pride is their **n**, and violence Ps 73:6
jewelry, your neck with its **n**. Sg 1:10
eyes, with one jewel of your **n**. Sg 4:9

NECKLACES *(2)*
earrings, rings, **n**, and all Ex 35:22
earrings, and **n**—to make Nm 31:50

NECKS *(11)*
be on the **n** of your enemies; Gn 49:8
feet on the **n** of these kings. Jos 10:24
and put their feet on their **n**. Jos 10:24
were on the **n** of their camels Jdg 8:21
chains on the **n** of their camels Jdg 8:26
stiffened their **n**, and would not Neh 9:29
Put your **n** under the yoke of the Jr 27:12
put you to the **n** of the profane Ezk 21:29
you cannot free your **n** from it. Mc 2:3
on the disciples' **n** a yoke that Ac 15:10
risked their own **n** for my life. Rm 16:4

NECO *(11)*
Pharaoh **N** king of Egypt marched 2Kg 23:29
at Megiddo when **N** saw him he 2Kg 23:29
Pharaoh **N** imprisoned him at 2Kg 23:33
Then Pharaoh **N** made Eliakim 2Kg 23:34
But **N** took Jehoahaz and went to 2Kg 23:34
to give it to Pharaoh **N**. 2Kg 23:35
N king of Egypt marched up to 2Ch 35:20
But **N** sent messengers to him, 2Ch 35:21
Then ⌊**N**⌋ king of Egypt made 2Ch 36:4
But **N** took his brother Jehoahaz 2Ch 36:4
Egypt and the army of Pharaoh **N**, Jr 46:2

NECO'S *(1)*
did not listen to **N** words from 2Ch 35:22

NECROMANCER *(1)*
cunning magician, and **n**. Is 3:3

NEDABIAH *(1)*
Jekamiah, Hoshama, and **N**. 1Ch 3:18

NEED *(76)*
You don't **n** to give me anything. Gn 30:31
me and I have everything I **n**." Gn 33:11
you don't **n** to stay any longer." Ex 9:28
preparing what people **n** to eat— Ex 12:16
He **n** not quarantine him, for he Lv 13:11
priest does not **n** to look for Lv 13:36
enough for whatever **n** he has. Dt 15:8
take care of everything you **n**. Jdg 19:20
to His people's ⌊**n**⌋ by providing Ru 1:6
paid attention to Hannah's ⌊**n**⌋, 1Sm 2:21
My hand doesn't **n** to be against 1Sm 18:17
but you will **n** to add more to 1Ch 22:14
the Levites no longer **n** to carry 1Ch 23:26
as many as you ⌊**n**⌋, and bring them 2Ch 2:16
God does not ⌊**n** to⌋ examine a Jb 34:23
a robber, your **n**, like a bandit. Pr 6:11
a robber, your **n**, like a bandit. Pr 24:34
find honey, eat only what you **n**; Pr 25:16
to the poor will not be in **n**, Pr 28:27
feed me with the food I **n**. Pr 30:8
we don't **n** to give you an answer Dn 3:16
you **n** no longer fear harm. Zph 3:15
I **n** to be baptized by You, Mt 3:14
the things you **n** before you ask Mt 6:8
Father knows that you **n** them. Mt 6:32
who are well don't **n** a doctor, Mt 9:12
"They don't **n** to go away," Mt 14:16
Why do we still **n** witnesses? Mt 26:65
who are well don't **n** a doctor, Mk 2:17
doctor, but the sick ⌊do **n** one⌋. Mk 2:17
when he was in **n** and hungry— Mk 2:25
Why do we still **n** witnesses? Mk 14:63
The healthy don't **n** a doctor, Lk 5:31
Father knows that you **n** them. Lk 12:30
people who don't **n** repentance. Lk 15:7
parable on the **n** for them to Lk 18:1
Why do we **n** any more testimony, Lk 22:71
We **n** to give an answer to those Jn 1:22
He did not **n** anyone to testify Jn 2:25
doesn't **n** to wash anything Jn 13:10
"Buy what we **n** for the festival," Jn 13:29
and don't **n** anyone to question Jn 16:30
to all, as anyone had a **n**. Ac 2:45
each person as anyone had a **n**. Ac 4:35
to the hand, "I don't **n** you!" 1Co 12:21
to the feet, "I don't **n** you!" 1Co 12:21
parts have no **n** ⌊of clothing⌋. 1Co 12:24
will **n** to be made when 1Co 16:2
we **n** letters of recommendation 2Co 3:1
is ⌊available⌋ for their **n**, 2Co 8:14
become ⌊available⌋ for your **n**, 2Co 8:14
always having everything you **n**, 2Co 9:8
I will not **n** to be bold with 2Co 10:2
I was present with you and in **n**, 2Co 11:9
to share with anyone in **n**. Eph 4:28
the building up of someone in **n**, Eph 4:29
messenger and minister to my **n**— Php 2:25
I don't say this out of **n**, Php 4:11
whether in abundance or in **n**. Php 4:12
gifts⌋ for my **n** several times. Php 4:16
so we don't **n** to say anything. 1Th 1:8
you don't **n** me to write you 1Th 4:9
you do not **n** anything to be 1Th 5:1
who doesn't **n** to be ashamed, 2Tm 2:15
works for cases of urgent **n**, Ti 3:14
you **n** someone to teach you again Heb 5:12
You **n** milk, not solid food. Heb 5:12
what further **n** was there for Heb 7:11
is the kind of high priest we **n**: Heb 7:26
He doesn't **n** to offer sacrifices Heb 7:27
For you **n** endurance, so that Heb 10:36
and you don't **n** anyone to teach 1Jn 2:27
his brother in **n** but shuts off 1Jn 3:17
wealthy, and **n** nothing,' and you Rv 3:17
The city does not **n** the sun or Rv 21:23
and people will not **n** lamplight Rv 22:5

NEEDED *(13)*
gathered as much as he **n** to eat. Ex 16:18
gathered as much as he **n** to eat, Ex 16:21
more than is **n** for the Ex 36:5
to the seed **n** to sow it, Lv 27:16
of women they **n** from the dancers Jdg 21:23
of your God as **n** year by year, 2Ch 24:5
Whatever is **n**—young bulls, Ezr 6:9
and lambs as **n**, along with their Ezr 7:17
people will not be **n** to pull it Ezk 17:9
its cubs **n** and strangled Nah 2:12
and cured those who **n** healing. Lk 9:11
as though He **n** anything, since Ac 17:25
sailed, they gave us what we **n**. Ac 28:10

NEEDLE *(3)*
the eye of a **n** than for a rich Mt 19:24
the eye of a **n** than for a rich Mk 10:25
the eye of a **n** than for a rich Lk 18:25

NEEDLESS *(1)*
lord because of **n** bloodshed or 1Sm 25:31

NEEDS *(19)*
of it as each person **n** to eat. Ex 16:16
everything that **n** to be done Nm 4:26
Your wife **n** to do everything I Jdg 13:13
provided for the **n** of the king 2Sm 19:32
can meet my **n** by providing my 1Kg 5:9
to meet⌋ the **n** of the house of Ezr 7:20
I satisfied their **n**, yet they Jr 5:7
should say that the Lord **n** them, Mt 21:3
'The Lord **n** it and will send it Mk 11:3
up and give him as much as he **n**. Lk 11:8
say this: 'The Lord **n** it.'" Lk 19:31
"The Lord **n** it," they said. Lk 19:34
hands have provided for my **n**, Ac 20:34
with the saints in their **n**; Rm 12:13
minister to Jews in material **n**. Rm 15:27
supplying the **n** of the saints, 2Co 9:12
from Macedonia supplied my **n**. 2Co 11:9
supply all your **n** according to Php 4:19
don't give them what the body **n**, Jms 2:16

NEEDY *(42)*
a hired hand who is poor and **n**, Dt 24:14
and lifts the **n** from the garbage 1Sm 2:8
He saves the **n** from their sharp Jb 5:15
They push the **n** off the road; Jb 24:4
at dawn to kill the poor and **n**, Jb 24:14
father to the **n**, and I examined Jb 29:16
my soul not grieved for the **n**? Jb 30:25
clothing or a **n** person without Jb 31:19
the poor or the **n** from one who Ps 35:10
afflicted and **n** and to slaughter Ps 37:14
afflicted and **n**; the Lord thinks Ps 40:17
listens to the **n** and does not Ps 69:33
am afflicted and **n**; hurry to me, Ps 70:5
the poor and **n** praise Your name Ps 74:21
justice for the **n** and the Ps 82:3
Rescue the poor and **n**; Ps 82:4
answer me, for I am poor and **n**. Ps 86:1
But He lifts the **n** out of their Ps 107:41
For I am poor and **n**; my heart is Ps 109:22
at the right hand of the **n**, Ps 109:31
and lifts the **n** from the garbage Ps 113:7
I will satisfy its **n** with bread. Ps 132:15
of the poor, justice for the **n**. Ps 140:12
who is kind to the **n** honors Him. Pr 14:31
the land and the **n** from among Pr 30:14
cause of the oppressed and **n**. Pr 31:9
she extends her hands to the **n**. Pr 31:20
to destroy the **n** with lies, Is 32:7
The poor and the **n** seek water, Is 41:17
defended the rights of the **n**. Jr 5:28
the life of the **n** from the hand Jr 20:13
up the case of the poor and **n**, Jr 22:16
didn't support the poor and **n**. Ezk 16:49
he oppresses the poor and **n**, Ezk 18:12
the poor and **n** and unlawfully Ezk 22:29
by showing mercy to the **n**. Dn 4:27
for silver and a **n** person for a Am 2:6
and block the path of the **n**. Am 2:7
the poor and crush the **n**, Am 4:1
trample on the **n** and do away Am 8:4
with silver and the **n** for a pair Am 8:6
there was not a **n** person among Ac 4:34

NEGATIVE *(1)*
So they gave a **n** report to the Nm 13:32

NEGEV *(34)*
journeyed by stages to the **N**. Gn 12:9
went up from Egypt to the **N**— Gn 13:1
by stages from the **N** to Bethel, Gn 13:3
the region of the **N** and settled Gn 20:1
he was living in the **N** region. Gn 24:62
up this way to the **N**, then go up Nm 13:17
up through the **N** and came to Nm 13:22
are living in the land of the **N**; Nm 13:29
who lived in the **N**, heard that Nm 21:1
who lived in the **N** in the land Nm 33:40
lowlands, the **N** and the sea Dt 1:7
the **N**, and the region from the Dt 34:3

hill country, the **N**, the Judean Jos 10:40
country, all the **N**, all the land Jos 11:16
and the **N** of the Hittites, Jos 12:8
you have given me land in the **N**, Jos 15:19
the border of Edom in the **N**: Jos 15:21
country, the **N**, and the Judean Jdg 1:9
you have given me land in the **N**, Jdg 1:15
which was in the **N** of Arad. Jdg 1:16
raided the **N** and attacked and 1Sm 30:1
Ramoth of the **N**, and in Jattir; 1Sm 30:27
they went to the **N** of Judah at 2Sm 24:7
foothills and the **N** of Judah and 2Ch 28:18
like watercourses in the **N**. Ps 126:4
storms that pass over the **N**, Is 21:1
about the animals of the **N**: Is 30:6
cities of the **N** are under siege Jr 13:19
and from the **N** bringing burnt Jr 17:26
cities of the **N**—because I will Jr 32:44
the cities of the **N**, the land of Jr 33:13
the forest land in the **N**, Ezk 20:46
⌊People from⌋ the **N** will possess Ob 19
possess the cities of the **N**. Ob 20

NEGLECT *(8)*
the people to **n** their work? Ex 5:4
be careful not to **n** the Levite, Dt 12:19
See that you not **n** this matter. Ezr 4:22
We will not **n** the house of our Neh 10:39
not **n** the gift that is in you; 1Tm 4:14
we escape if we **n** such a great Heb 2:3
Don't **n** to show hospitality, Heb 13:2
Don't **n** to do good and to share, Heb 13:16

NEGLECTED *(4)*
Solomon's table. They **n** nothing. 1Kg 4:27
has the house of God been **n**?" Neh 13:11
since you **n** all my counsel and Pr 1:25
you have **n** the more important Mt 23:23

NEGLECTING *(2)*
been done without **n** the others. Mt 23:23
have done without **n** the others. Lk 11:42

NEGLIGENCE *(1)*
and no **n** or corruption was found Dn 6:4

NEGLIGENT *(2)*
sons, don't be **n** now, for the 2Ch 29:11
and because of **n** hands the house Ec 10:18

NEGOTIATE *(1)*
child and **n** a price to ⌊sell⌋ Jb 6:27

NEHELAMITE *(3)*
Shemaiah the **N** you are to say, Jr 29:24
says concerning Shemaiah the **N**. Jr 29:31
Shemaiah the **N** and his Jr 29:32

NEHEMIAH *(8)*
Jeshua, **N**, Seraiah, Reelaiah Ezr 2:2
The words of **N** son of Hacaliah: Neh 1:1
After him **N** son of Azbuk, ruler Neh 3:16
Jeshua, **N**, Azariah, Raamiah, Neh 7:7
N the governor, Ezra the priest Neh 8:9
N the governor, son of Hacaliah, Neh 10:1
in the days of **N** the governor Neh 12:26
in the days of Zerubbabel and **N**, Neh 12:47

NEHUM *(1)*
(AKA REHUM)
Bigvai, **N**, and Baanah. Neh 7:7

NEHUSHTA *(1)*
mother's name was **N** daughter of 2Kg 24:8

NEHUSHTAN *(1)*
up to that time. He called it **N**. 2Kg 18:4

NEIEL *(1)*
north toward Beth-emek and **N**, Jos 19:27

NEIGH *(1)*
grain and **n** like stallions, Jr 50:11

NEIGHBOR *(84)*
"Why are you attacking your **n**?" Ex 2:13
will ask her **n** and any woman Ex 3:22
person and the **n** nearest his Ex 12:4
false testimony against your **n**. Ex 20:16
anything that belongs to your **n**. Ex 20:17
acts against his **n** to murder him Ex 21:14
a man gives his **n** money or goods Ex 22:7
must repay double to his **n**. Ex 22:9
When a man gives his **n** a donkey, Ex 22:10
borrows ⌊an animal⌋ from his **n**, Ex 22:14
his friend, and his **n**.'" Ex 32:27
by deceiving his **n** in regard to Lv 6:2
or a robbery; or defrauds his **n**; Lv 6:2
not oppress your **n** or rob ⌊him⌋. Lv 19:13
judge your **n** fairly. Lv 19:15
Rebuke your **n** directly, and you Lv 19:17
but love your **n** as yourself; Lv 19:18
a permanent injury on his **n**, Lv 24:19
a sale to your **n** or a purchase Lv 25:14
purchase from your **n** based on Lv 25:15
and killed his **n** accidentally Dt 4:42
testimony against your **n**. Dt 5:20
anything that belongs to your **n**. Dt 5:21
cancel what he has lent his **n**. Dt 15:2
anything⌋ from his **n** or brother, Dt 15:2
having killed his **n** accidentally Dt 19:4
forest with his **n** to cut timber, Dt 19:5
strikes his **n** so that he dies Dt 19:5
did not previously hate his **n**. Dt 19:6
But if someone hates his **n**, Dt 19:11
attacks his **n** and murders him Dt 22:26
a loan of any kind to your **n**, Dt 24:10
one who kills his **n** in secret.' Dt 27:24
for he killed his **n** accidentally Jos 20:5
n women said, "A son has been Ru 4:17
given it to your **n** who is better 1Sm 15:28
and given it to your **n** David. 1Sm 28:17
against his **n** and is forced to 1Kg 8:31
against his **n** and is forced to 2Ch 6:22
his friend or discredit his **n**, Ps 15:3
loved one and **n** from me; Ps 88:18
who secretly slanders his **n**; Ps 101:5
Don't say to your **n**, "Go away! Pr 3:28
plan any harm against your **n**, Pr 3:29
security for your **n** or entered Pr 6:1
yourself, and plead with your **n**. Pr 6:3
the ungodly destroys his **n**, Pr 11:9
contempt for his **n** lacks sense, Pr 11:12
careful in dealing with his **n**, Pr 12:26
poor man is hated even by his **n**, Pr 14:20
The one who despises his **n** sins, Pr 14:21
A violent man lures his **n**, Pr 16:29
has no consideration for his **n**. Pr 21:10
against your **n** without cause. Pr 24:28
against his **n** is like a club, Pr 25:18
man who deceives his **n** and says, Pr 26:19
better a **n** nearby than a brother Pr 27:10
one blesses his **n** with a loud Pr 27:14
who flatters his **n** spreads a net Pr 29:5
against man, **n** against neighbor Is 3:5
against man, neighbor against **n**; Is 3:5
one teach his **n** or his brother, Jr 31:34
proclaiming freedom for his **n**. Jr 34:15
for his brother and for his **n**. Jr 34:17
will invite his **n** to ⌊sit⌋ under Zch 3:10
I turned everyone against his **n**. Zch 8:10
in your hearts against your **n**, Zch 8:17
over to his **n** and his king. Zch 11:6
Love your **n** and hate your enemy. Mt 5:43
and love your **n** as yourself. Mt 19:19
Love your **n** as yourself. Mt 22:39
Love your **n** as yourself. Mk 12:31
and to love your **n** as yourself, Mk 12:33
and your **n** as yourself. Lk 10:27
asked Jesus, "And who is my **n**?" Lk 10:29
proved to be a **n** to the man who Lk 10:36
his **n** pushed him away Ac 7:27
shall love your **n** as yourself. Rm 13:9
Love does no wrong to a **n**. Rm 13:10
must please his **n** for his good, Rm 15:2
shall love your **n** as yourself. Gl 5:14
each one to his **n**, because we Eph 4:25
shall love your **n** as yourself, Jms 2:8
But who are you to judge your **n**? Jms 4:12

NEIGHBOR'S *(25)*
Do not covet your **n** house. Ex 20:17
not covet your **n** wife, his male Ex 20:17
ox injures his **n** ox and it dies, Ex 21:35
not he has taken his **n** property. Ex 22:8
not he has taken his **n** property. Ex 22:11
you ever take your **n** cloak as Ex 22:26
intercourse with your **n** wife, Lv 18:20
must not jeopardize your **n** life; Lv 19:16
adultery with his **n** wife— Lv 20:10
not desire your **n** wife or covet Dt 5:21
wife or covet your **n** house, Dt 5:21
not move your **n** boundary marker, Dt 19:14
he has violated his **n** fiancée. Dt 22:24
When you enter your **n** vineyard, Dt 23:24
you enter your **n** standing grain, Dt 23:25
put a sickle to your **n** grain. Dt 23:25
who moves his **n** boundary marker. Dt 27:17
seduced by ⌊my **n**⌋ wife or I have Jb 31:9
put yourself in your **n** power: Pr 6:3
Seldom set foot in your **n** house; Pr 25:17
not defile his **n** wife or come Ezk 18:6
shrines⌋ and defiles his **n** wife, Ezk 18:11
He does not defile his **n** wife. Ezk 18:15
an abomination with his **n** wife; Ezk 22:11
of you has defiled his **n** wife. Ezk 33:26

NEIGHBORING *(2)*
and Gomorrah and their **n** towns— Jr 50:40
go on to the **n** villages so that Mk 1:38

NEIGHBORS *(28)*
should ask their **n** for gold and Ex 11:2
and their **n** in the Arabah, Dt 1:7
the Gibeonites were their **n**, Jos 9:16
from everyone—from all your **n**. 2Kg 4:3
their **n** from as far away as 1Ch 12:40
All their **n** supported them with Ezr 1:6
in friendly ways with their **n**, Ps 28:3
my adversaries and even by my **n**. Ps 31:11
an object of reproach to our **n**, Ps 44:13
an object of reproach to our **n**, Ps 79:4
sevenfold to our **n** the reproach Ps 79:12
You set us at strife with our **n**; Ps 80:6
he has become a joke to his **n**. Ps 89:41
and **n** will ⌊also⌋ perish. Jr 6:21
all My evil **n** who attack Jr 12:14
along with his relatives and **n**. Jr 49:10
overthrown along with their **n**," Jr 49:18
Jacob that his **n** should be his Lm 1:17
well-endowed **n**, and increased Ezk 16:26
and brutally extort your **n**. Ezk 22:12
from all their **n** who treat them Ezk 28:24
all their **n** who treat them Ezk 28:26
to him who gives his **n** drink, Hab 2:15
Then her **n** and relatives heard Lk 1:58
or your rich **n**, because they Lk 14:12
his friends and **n** together, Lk 15:6
women friends and **n** together, Lk 15:9
His **n** and those who formerly had Jn 9:8

NEIGHBORS' *(1)*
with their **n** wives and have Jr 29:23

NEIGHING *(2)*
n after someone else's wife. Jr 5:8
sound of the **n** of mighty steeds Jr 8:16

NEIGHINGS *(1)*
adulteries and your ⌊lustful⌋ **n**, Jr 13:27

NEITHER *(51)*
and not die—**n** we, nor you, nor Gn 43:8
So **n** group came near the other Ex 14:20
n animal or man will live. Ex 19:13
N you nor a foreigner are to Lv 22:25
N should you accept a ransom for Nm 35:32
which **n** you nor your fathers Dt 13:6
to a nation **n** you nor your Dt 28:36
which **n** you nor your fathers Dt 28:64
"**N**," He replied. "I have now Jos 5:14
It's **n** New Moon or Sabbath." 2Kg 4:23
to help Israel, **n** bond nor free. 2Kg 14:26
Give me **n** poverty nor wealth; Pr 30:8
land, where **n** of you were born, Jr 22:26
is no more and **n** are those who Ezk 13:15
n will the wickedness of the Ezk 33:12
those days **n** man nor beast had Zch 8:10
N should you swear by your head, Mt 5:36
where **n** moth nor rust destroys, Mt 6:20
n can a bad tree produce good Mt 7:18
N will I tell you by what Mt 21:27
resurrection they **n** marry nor Mt 22:30
hour no one knows—**n** the angels Mt 24:36
n will your Father in heaven Mk 11:26
N will I tell you by what Mk 11:33
they **n** marry nor are given in Mk 12:25
n the angels in heaven nor the Mk 13:32
n can those from there cross Lk 16:26
N will I tell you by what Lk 20:8
from the dead **n** marry nor are Lk 20:35
N has Herod, because he sent Him Lk 23:15
the Father **n** on this mountain Jn 4:21
crowd saw that **n** Jesus nor His Jn 6:24
"**N** do I condemn you," said Jesus. Jn 8:11
"You know **n** Me nor My Father," Jn 8:19
N this man nor his parents sinned, Jn 9:3
n can you unless you remain in Jn 15:4
I have **n** silver nor gold, Ac 3:6
a yoke that **n** our forefathers Ac 15:10
N is He served by human hands, Ac 17:25

n to eat nor to drink until they Ac 23:12
N can they provide evidence to Ac 24:13
N against the Jewish law, Ac 25:8
For many days **n** sun nor stars Ac 27:20
persuaded that **n** death nor life, Rm 8:38
N are they all children because Rm 9:7
So then **n** the one who plants nor 1Co 3:7
in Christ Jesus **n** circumcision Gl 5:6
having **n** beginning of days nor Heb 7:3
N can a saltwater spring yield Jms 3:12
that you are **n** cold nor hot. Rv 3:15
lukewarm, and **n** hot nor cold, I Rv 3:16

NEKODA'S *(4)*
descendants, **N** descendants, Ezr 2:48
descendants, **N** descendants 652 Ezr 2:60
descendants, **N** descendants, Neh 7:50
and **N** descendants 642 Neh 7:62

NEMUEL *(3)*
(AKA JEMUEL)
sons of Eliab were **N**, Dathan, Nm 26:9
the Nemuelite clan from **N**; Nm 26:12
N, Jamin, Jarib, Zerah, and 1Ch 4:24

NEMUELITE *(1)*
the **N** clan from Nemuel; Nm 26:12

NEPHEG *(4)*
Korah, **N**, and Zichri. Ex 6:21
Ibhar, Elishua, **N**, Japhia, 2Sm 5:15
Nogah, **N**, Japhia, 1Ch 3:7
Nogah, **N**, Japhia, 1Ch 14:6

NEPHEW *(2)*
his wife Sarai, his **n** Lot, all Gn 12:5
also took Abram's **n** Lot and his Gn 14:12

NEPHILIM *(3)*
The **N** were on the earth both in Gn 6:4
We even saw the **N** there." Nm 13:33
Anak were descended from the **N**. Nm 13:33

NEPHISHESIM'S *(1)*
descendants, **N** descendants, Neh 7:52

NEPHTOAH *(2)*
the spring of the Waters of **N**, Jos 15:9
the spring at the Waters of **N**. Jos 18:15

NEPHUSIM'S *(1)*
descendants, **N** descendants, Ezr 2:50

NER *(16)*
was Abner son of Saul's uncle **N**. 1Sm 14:50
father was **N** son of Abiel. 1Sm 14:51
where Saul and Abner son of **N**, 1Sm 26:5
troops and to Abner son of **N**: 1Sm 26:14
Abner son of **N**, commander of 2Sm 2:8
Abner son of **N** and soldiers of 2Sm 2:12
Abner son of **N** came to see the 2Sm 3:23
Abner son of **N** came to deceive 2Sm 3:25
the blood of Abner son of **N**. 2Sm 3:28
the killing of Abner son of **N**. 2Sm 3:37
Abner son of **N** and Amasa son of 1Kg 2:5
Joab murdered Abner son of **N**, 1Kg 2:32
N fathered Kish, Kish fathered 1Ch 8:33
then Zur, Kish, Baal, **N**, Nadab, 1Ch 9:36
N fathered Kish, Kish fathered 1Ch 9:39
Abner son of **N**, and Joab son 1Ch 26:28

NEREUS *(1)*
and Julia, **N** and his sister, Rm 16:15

NERGAL *(1)*
men of Cuth made **N**, the men of 2Kg 17:30

NERGAL-SHAREZER *(3)*
N, Samgar-nebo, Sarsechim the Jr 39:3
Rab-saris, **N** the Rab-mag, and Jr 39:3
Rab-saris, **N** the Rab-mag, and Jr 39:13

NERI *(1)*
son⌋ of Shealtiel, ⌊son⌋ of **N**, Lk 3:27

NERIAH *(10)*
agreement to Baruch son of **N**, Jr 32:12
to Baruch, son of **N**, I prayed to Jr 32:16
summoned Baruch son of **N**. Jr 36:4
Baruch son of **N** did everything Jr 36:8
Baruch son of **N** took the scroll Jr 36:14
and gave it to Baruch son of **N**, Jr 36:32
Baruch son of **N** is inciting you Jr 43:3
prophet and Baruch son of **N**— Jr 43:6
to Baruch son of **N** when he wrote Jr 45:1
son of **N** son of Mahseiah, Jr 51:59

NEST *(16)*
your **n** is set in the cliffs. Nm 24:21
across a bird's **n** with chicks or Dt 22:6
watches over His **n** like an eagle Dt 32:11
die in my own **n** and multiply ⌊my Jb 29:18
command and make its **n** on high? Jb 39:27
a **n** for herself where she places Ps 84:3
a bird wandering from its **n**. Pr 27:8
out, as if into a **n**, to seize Is 10:14
forced from the **n**, the daughters Is 16:2
partridge will make her **n** there; Is 34:15
elevate your **n** like the eagle, Jr 49:16
of every kind will **n** under it, Ezk 17:23
and make your **n** among the stars, Ob 4
house to place his **n** on high, Hab 2:9
sky come and **n** in its branches. Mt 13:32
of the sky can **n** in its shade." Mk 4:32

NESTED *(3)*
of the sky **n** in its branches Ezk 31:6
birds of the sky **n** on its fallen Ezk 31:13
of the sky **n** in its branches. Lk 13:19

NESTLED *(1)*
of Lebanon, **n** among the cedars, Jr 22:23

NESTS *(4)*
There the birds make their **n**; Ps 104:17
a dove that **n** inside the mouth Jr 48:28
and birds of the sky have **n**, Mt 8:20
and birds of the sky have **n**, Lk 9:58

NET *(37)*
his own feet lead him into a **n**, Jb 18:8
me and caught me in His **n**. Jb 19:6
is caught in the **n** they have Ps 9:15
and drags him in his **n**. Ps 10:9
will pull my feet out of the **n**. Ps 25:15
me from the **n** that is secretly Ps 31:4
They hid their **n** for me without Ps 35:7
let the **n** that he hid ensnare Ps 35:8
They prepared a **n** for my steps; Ps 57:6
deliver you from the hunter's **n**, Ps 91:3
like a bird from the hunter's **n**; Ps 124:7
the **n** is torn, and we have Ps 124:7
they spread a **n** along the path Ps 140:5
to spread a **n** where any bird can Pr 1:17
spreads a **n** for his feet. Pr 29:5
her heart a **n**, and her hands Ec 7:26
like fish caught in a cruel **n**, Ec 9:12
street like an antelope in a **n**. Is 51:20
He spread a **n** for my feet and Lm 1:13
But I will spread My **n** over him, Ezk 12:13
I will spread My **n** over him, Ezk 17:20
They spread their **n** over him; Ezk 19:8
I will spread My **n** over you with Ezk 32:3
they will haul you up in My **n**. Ezk 32:3
at Mizpah and a **n** spread out on Hs 5:1
I will spread My **n** over them; Hs 7:12
they hunt each other with a **n**. Mc 7:2
gather them in their fishing **n**; Hab 1:15
burn incense to their fishing **n**, Hab 1:16
empty their **n** and continually Hab 1:17
were casting a **n** into the sea, Mt 4:18
like a large **n** thrown into the Mt 13:47
were casting a **n** into the sea, Mk 1:16
Cast the **n** on the right side of Jn 21:6
dragging the **n** full of fish. Jn 21:8
got up and hauled the **n** ashore, Jn 21:11
so many, the **n** was not torn. Jn 21:11

NETAIM *(1)*
and residents of **N** and Gederah. 1Ch 4:23

NETHANEL *(14)*
N son of Zuar from Issachar; Nm 1:8
Issacharites is **N** son of Zuar. Nm 2:5
On the second day **N** son of Zuar, Nm 7:18
the offering of **N** son of Zuar. Nm 7:23
N son of Zuar was over the Nm 10:15
N fourth, Raddai fifth, 1Ch 2:14
Joshaphat, **N**, Amasai, Zechariah, 1Ch 15:24
Shemaiah son of **N**, a Levite, 1Ch 24:6
Sachar the fourth, **N** the fifth, 1Ch 26:4
Zechariah, **N**, and Micaiah—to 2Ch 17:7
and his brothers Shemaiah and **N**, 2Ch 35:9
Maaseiah, Ishmael, **N**, Jozabad, Ezr 10:22
of Hilkiah, and **N** of Jedaiah. Neh 12:21
Gilalai, Maai, **N**, Judah, and Neh 12:36

NETHANIAH *(20)*
included⌋ Ishmael son of **N**, 2Kg 25:23
Ishmael son of **N**, son of 2Kg 25:25
Zaccur, Joseph, **N**, and Asarelah, 1Ch 25:2
the fifth ⌊to⌋ **N**, his sons, and 1Ch 25:12
were Shemaiah, **N**, Zebadiah, 2Ch 17:8
Baruch through Jehudi son of **N**, Jr 36:14
included⌋ Ishmael son of **N**, Jr 40:8
Ishmael son of **N** to strike you Jr 40:14
Let me go kill Ishmael son of **N**. Jr 40:15
Ishmael son of **N**, son of Jr 41:1
Ishmael son of **N** and the 10 men Jr 41:2
Ishmael son of **N** came out of Jr 41:6
Ishmael son of **N** and the men Jr 41:7
Ishmael son of **N** filled ⌊it⌋ Jr 41:9
Ishmael son of **N** took them Jr 41:10
that Ishmael son of **N** had done, Jr 41:11
Ishmael son of **N** and found him Jr 41:12
Ishmael son of **N** escaped from Jr 41:15
Ishmael son of **N** after Ishmael Jr 41:16
Ishmael son of **N** had struck down Jr 41:18

NETOPHAH'S *(2)*
N men 56 Ezr 2:22
Bethlehem's and **N** men 188 Neh 7:26

NETOPHAHITE *(1)*
Heleb son of Baanah the **N**, 2Sm 23:29

NETOPHATHITE *(7)*
the Ahohite, Maharai the **N**, 2Sm 23:28
Seraiah son of Tanhumeth the **N**, 2Kg 25:23
Maharai the **N**, Heled son of 1Ch 11:30
Heled son of Baanah the **N**, 1Ch 11:30
was Maharai the **N**, a Zerahite; 1Ch 27:13
was Heldai the **N**, of Othniel's 1Ch 27:15
of Ephai the **N**, and Jezaniah son Jr 40:8

NETOPHATHITES *(3)*
Bethlehem, the **N**, 1Ch 2:54
lived in the villages of the **N**. 1Ch 9:16
from the villages of the **N**, Neh 12:28

NETS *(13)*
wicked fall into their own **n**, Ps 141:10
those who spread **n** on the water Is 19:8
a place in the sea to spread **n**, Ezk 26:5
you will be a place to spread **n**. Ezk 26:14
places where **n** are spread out to Ezk 47:10
they left their **n** and followed Mt 4:20
mending their **n**, and He called Mt 4:21
they left their **n** and followed Mk 1:18
in their boat mending their **n**. Mk 1:19
them and were washing their **n**. Lk 5:2
let down your **n** for a catch." Lk 5:4
Your word, I'll let down the **n**." Lk 5:5
and their **n** began to tear. Lk 5:6

NEVER *(390)*
(See pp. xi-xii.)

NEVERTHELESS *(21)*
(See pp. xi-xii.)

NEW *(174)*
abundance of grain and **n** wine. Gn 27:28
him with grain and **n** wine. Gn 27:37
A **n** king, who had not known Ex 1:8
or ⌊any⌋ **n** grain until this very Lv 23:14
an offering of **n** grain to the Lv 23:16
the old to make room for the **n**. Lv 26:10
olive oil, **n** wine, and grain Nm 18:12
an offering of **n** grain to the Nm 28:26
your grain, **n** wine, and oil— Dt 7:13
your grain, **n** wine, and oil. Dt 11:14
of your grain, **n** wine, or oil; Dt 12:17
of your grain, **n** wine, and oil, Dt 14:23
of your grain, **n** wine, and oil, Dt 18:4
any man built a **n** house and not Dt 20:5
If you build a **n** house, make a Dt 22:8
you no grain, **n** wine, oil, young Dt 28:51
gentle rain on **n** grass and Dt 32:2
n gods that had just arrived, Dt 32:17
in a land of grain and **n** wine; Dt 33:28
wineskins were **n** when we filled Jos 9:13
Israel chose **n** gods, then war Jdg 5:8
him up with two **n** ropes and led Jdg 15:13
tie me up with **n** ropes that have Jdg 16:11
Delilah took **n** ropes, tied him Jdg 16:12
the house of your ⌊**n**⌋ husband." Ru 1:9
prepare one **n** cart and two milk 1Sm 6:7
tomorrow is the **N** Moon, and I'm 1Sm 20:5
him, "Tomorrow is the **N** Moon; 1Sm 20:18
At the **N** Moon, the king sat down 1Sm 20:24
day after the **N** Moon, the second 1Sm 20:27
that second day of the **N** Moon, 1Sm 20:34
the ark of God on a **n** cart and 2Sm 6:3
pounds and who wore **n** armor, 2Sm 21:16
wrapped himself with a **n** cloak, 1Kg 11:29
took hold of the **n** cloak he had 1Kg 11:30

Bring me a **n** bowl and put salt 2Kg 2:20
It's neither **N** Moon or Sabbath." 2Kg 4:23
a land of grain and **n** wine, 2Kg 18:32
set the ark of God on a **n** cart. 1Ch 13:7
on the Sabbaths, **N** Moons, and 1Ch 23:31
the Sabbaths and the **N** Moons, 2Ch 2:4
Moses for Sabbaths, **N** Moons, and 2Ch 8:13
temple before the **n** courtyard. 2Ch 20:5
of the Sabbaths, of the **N** Moons, 2Ch 31:3
has given us **n** life and light Ezr 9:8
giving us **n** life, so that we Ezr 9:9
money, grain, **n** wine, and olive Neh 5:11
Sabbath and **N** Moon offerings, Neh 10:33
and of the **n** wine and oil. Neh 10:37
of grain, **n** wine, and oil to Neh 10:39
tenths of grain, **n** wine, and oil Neh 13:5
of the grain, **n** wine, and oil Neh 13:12
You produce **n** witnesses against Jb 10:17
about to burst like **n** wineskins. Jb 32:19
their grain and **n** wine abound. Ps 4:7
Sing a **n** song to Him; play Ps 33:3
He put a **n** song in my mouth, Ps 40:3
during the **n** moon and during Ps 81:3
Sing a **n** song to the LORD; Ps 96:1
Sing a **n** song to the LORD, Ps 98:1
I will sing a **n** song to You; Ps 144:9
Sing to the LORD a **n** song, Ps 149:1
vats will overflow with **n** wine. Pr 3:10
is removed and **n** growth appears Pr 27:25
is nothing **n** under the sun. Ec 1:9
anything, "Look, this is **n**"? Ec 1:10
delicacy—**n** as well as old. Sg 7:13
N Moons and Sabbaths, and the Is 1:13
I hate your **N** Moons and Is 1:14
The **n** wine mourns; the vine Is 24:7
a land of grain and **n** wine, Is 36:17
board, **n**, with many teeth Is 41:15
Now I declare **n** events; I Is 42:9
Sing a **n** song to the LORD; Is 42:10
I am about to do something **n**; Is 43:19
I will announce **n** things to you, Is 48:6
will be called by a **n** name that Is 62:2
not drink your **n** wine you have Is 62:8
the **n** wine is found in a bunch Is 65:8
I will create a **n** heaven and a Is 65:17
a new heaven and a **n** earth; Is 65:17
For just as the **n** heavens and Is 66:22
the new heavens and the **n** earth, Is 66:22
from one **N** Moon to another, Is 66:23
their fields to **n** occupants, Jr 8:10
roads—to walk on ⌊**n**⌋ paths, Jr 18:15
at the entrance of the **N** Gate. Jr 26:10
the grain, the **n** wine, the fresh Jr 31:12
something **n** in the land— Jr 31:22
I will make a **n** covenant with Jr 31:31
opening of the **N** Gate of the Jr 36:10
They are **n** every morning; Lm 3:23
heart and put a **n** spirit within Ezk 11:19
yourselves a **n** heart and a new Ezk 18:31
a new heart and a **n** spirit. Ezk 18:31
will give you a **n** heart and put Ezk 36:26
heart and put a **n** spirit within Ezk 36:26
for the festivals, **N** Moons, and Ezk 45:17
opened on the day of the **N** Moon. Ezk 46:1
on the Sabbaths and **N** Moons. Ezk 46:3
On the day of the **N** Moon, Ezk 46:6
the grain, the **n** wine, and the Hs 2:8
its time and My **n** wine in its Hs 2:9
feasts, **N** Moons, and Sabbaths Hs 2:11
the grain, the **n** wine, and the Hs 2:22
and **n** wine take away ⌊one's⌋ Hs 4:11
Now the **N** Moon will devour them Hs 5:7
and the **n** wine will fail them. Hs 9:2
His **n** branches will spread, Hs 14:6
destroyed; the **n** wine is dried Jl 1:10
you grain, **n** wine, and olive Jl 2:19
overflow with **n** wine and olive Jl 2:24
When will the **N** Moon be over so Am 8:5
on the grain, **n** wine, olive oil, Hg 1:11
flourish, and **n** wine, the young Zch 9:17
And no one puts **n** wine into old Mt 9:17
But they put **n** wine into fresh Mt 9:17
what is **n** and what is old. Mt 13:52
I drink it in a **n** way in My Mt 26:29
and placed it in his **n** tomb, Mt 27:60
A **n** teaching with authority! Mk 1:27
the **n** patch pulls away from the Mk 2:21
And no one puts **n** wine into old Mk 2:22
n wine is for fresh wineskins. Mk 2:22
I drink it in a **n** way in the Mk 14:25
they will speak in **n** languages; Mk 16:17
patch from a **n** garment and puts Lk 5:36
not only will he tear the **n**, Lk 5:36
piece from the **n** garment will Lk 5:36
And no one puts **n** wine into old Lk 5:37
the **n** wine will burst the skins, Lk 5:37
But **n** wine should be put into Lk 5:38
old wine, wants **n**, because he Lk 5:39
This cup is the **n** covenant Lk 22:20
I give you a **n** commandment: Jn 13:34
A **n** tomb was in the garden; Jn 19:41
said, "They're full of **n** wine!" Ac 2:13
about this **n** teaching you're Ac 17:19
telling or hearing something **n**. Ac 17:21
too may walk in a **n** way of life. Rm 6:4
may serve in the **n** way of the Rm 7:6
so that you may be a **n** batch, 1Co 5:7
This cup is the **n** covenant in My 1Co 11:25
to be ministers of a **n** covenant, 2Co 3:6
Christ, there is a **n** creation; 2Co 5:17
away, and look, **n** things have 2Co 5:17
instead is a **n** creation. Gl 6:15
in Himself one **n** man from the Eph 2:15
you put on the **n** man, the one Eph 4:24
a festival or a **n** moon or a Col 2:16
and have put on the **n** man, Col 3:10
He must not be a **n** convert, 1Tm 3:6
an itch to hear something **n**. 2Tm 4:3
I will make a **n** covenant with Heb 8:8
saying, a **n** ⌊covenant⌋, He has Heb 8:13
is the mediator of a **n** covenant, Heb 9:15
by the **n** and living way that He Heb 10:20
mediator of a **n** covenant), and Heb 12:24
He gave us a **n** birth by the Jms 1:18
He has given us a **n** birth into a 1Pt 1:3
we wait for **n** heavens and a new 2Pt 3:13
for new heavens and a **n** earth, 2Pt 3:13
am not writing you a **n** command, 1Jn 2:7
I am writing you a **n** command, 1Jn 2:8
I were writing you a **n** command, 2Jn 5
on the stone a **n** name is Rv 2:17
of My God—the **n** Jerusalem, Rv 3:12
from My God—and My **n** name. Rv 3:12
And they sang a **n** song: You are Rv 5:9
They sang a **n** song before the Rv 14:3
Then I saw a **n** heaven and a new Rv 21:1
saw a new heaven and a **n** earth, Rv 21:1
the Holy City, **n** Jerusalem, Rv 21:2
I am making everything **n**." Rv 21:5

NEWBORN *(6)*

herds, and the **n** of your flocks, Dt 7:13
herds and the **n** of your flocks. Dt 28:4
herds, and the **n** of your flocks. Dt 28:18
or **n** of your flocks until they Dt 28:51
they deliver their **n**. Jb 39:3
Like **n** infants, desire the 1Pt 2:2

NEWLY *(3)*

and a **n** created people will Ps 102:18
like a flock of **n** shorn ⌊sheep⌋ Sg 4:2
n cut grain after the reaper Jr 9:22

NEWS *(91)*

Laban heard the **n** about his Gn 29:13
When the **n** reached Pharaoh's Gn 45:16
the people heard this bad **n**, Ex 33:4
king of Hazor heard ⌊this **n**⌋, Jos 11:1
she heard the **n** about the 1Sm 4:19
And all Israel heard the **n**, 1Sm 13:4
spread the good **n** in the temples 1Sm 31:9
he was a bearer of good **n**, 2Sm 4:10
was my reward to him for his **n**! 2Sm 4:10
king the good **n** that the LORD 2Sm 18:19
the man to take good **n** today. 2Sm 18:20
today you aren't taking good **n**, 2Sm 18:20
If he's alone, he bears good **n**." 2Sm 18:25
one is also bringing good **n**," 2Sm 18:26
he comes with good **n**," the king 2Sm 18:27
lord the king hear the good **n**: 2Sm 18:31
you must be bringing good **n**." 1Kg 1:42
The **n** reached Joab. Since he had 1Kg 2:28
disguised? I have bad **n** for you. 1Kg 14:6
Today is a day of good **n**. 2Kg 7:9
and ⌊the **n**⌋ was reported to the 2Kg 7:11
spread the good **n** to their idols 1Ch 10:9
and spread this **n** throughout all Neh 8:15
came and reported the **n** to her, Est 4:4
heard **n** of it with our ears. Jb 28:22
of women brought the good **n**: Ps 68:11
He will not fear bad **n**; Ps 112:7
good **n** strengthens the bones. Pr 15:30
Good **n** from a distant land is Pr 25:25
When the **n** reaches Egypt, they Is 23:5
anguish over the **n** about Tyre. Is 23:5
herald of good **n**, go up on a Is 40:9
herald of good **n**, raise your Is 40:9
a herald of good **n** to Jerusalem. Is 41:27
who brings **n** of good things, Is 52:7
Me to bring good **n** to the poor. Is 61:1
who brought the **n** to my father, Jr 20:15
Because of the **n** that is coming. Ezk 21:7
come to you and report the **n**. Ezk 24:26
with the **n** that reaches their Hs 7:12
bringing good **n** and proclaiming Nah 1:15
who hear the **n** about you will Nah 3:19
the good **n** of the kingdom, Mt 4:23
Then the **n** about Him spread Mt 4:24
this **n** spread throughout that Mt 9:26
out and spread the **n** about Him Mt 9:31
the good **n** of the kingdom, Mt 9:35
the poor are told the good **n**. Mt 11:5
This good **n** of the kingdom will Mt 24:14
ran to tell His disciples the **n**. Mt 28:8
preaching the good **n** of God: Mk 1:14
and believe in the good **n**!" Mk 1:15
it widely and to spread the **n**, Mk 1:45
And the good **n** must first be Mk 13:10
to you and tell you this good **n**. Lk 1:19
to you good **n** of great joy that Lk 2:10
proclaimed good **n** to the people. Lk 3:18
n about Him spread throughout Lk 4:14
Me to preach good **n** to the poor. Lk 4:18
And **n** about Him began to go out Lk 4:37
the good **n** about the kingdom Lk 4:43
But the **n** about Him spread even Lk 5:15
have the good **n** preached to them Lk 7:22
the good **n** of the kingdom Lk 8:1
the good **n** and healing Lk 9:6
and spread the **n** of the kingdom Lk 9:60
the good **n** of the kingdom of God Lk 16:16
and proclaiming the good **n**, Lk 20:1
the good **n** that the Messiah is Ac 5:42
the message of good **n**. Ac 8:4
the good **n** about the kingdom Ac 8:12
tell him the good **n** about Jesus, Ac 8:35
the good **n** of peace through Ac 10:36
the good **n** about the Lord Jesus Ac 11:20
to you the good **n** of the promise Ac 13:32
are proclaiming good **n** to you, Ac 14:15
telling the good **n** about Jesus Ac 17:18
had heard the **n** about us and had Ac 28:15
singled out for God's good **n**— Rm 1:1
you because the **n** of your faith Rm 1:8
the good **n** about His Son, Rm 1:9
preach the good **n** to you also Rm 1:15
as a priest of God's good **n**. Rm 15:16
the good **n** about the Messiah Rm 15:19
foretold the good **n** to Abraham, Gl 3:8
the good **n** of peace to you who Eph 2:17
when I hear **n** about you. Php 2:19
tell you all the **n** about me. Col 4:7
brought us good **n** about your 1Th 3:6
the good **n** just as they did Heb 4:2
received the good **n** did not Heb 4:6

NEXT *(181)*

to you at this time **n** year." Gn 17:21
The **n** day the firstborn said to Gn 19:34
Leah and her sons **n**, and Rachel Gn 33:2
they came the **n** year and said to Gn 47:18
territory will be **n** to Sidon. Gn 49:13
n day he went out and saw two Ex 2:13
The LORD did this the **n** day. Ex 9:6
one place to the **n** according to Ex 17:1
n day Moses sat down to judge Ex 18:13
rose early the **n** morning and set Ex 24:4
rings should be **n** to the frame Ex 25:27
and petals, on the **n** branch. Ex 25:33
bases under the **n** plank for its Ex 26:19
the edge that is **n** to the inner Ex 28:26
Early the **n** morning they arose, Ex 32:6
The rings were **n** to the frame as Ex 37:14
and petals, on the **n** branch. Ex 37:19
the edge that is **n** to the inner Ex 39:19
N Moses set up the surrounding Ex 40:33
over may be eaten on the **n** day. Lv 7:16
N he presented the second ram, Lv 8:22

N he presented the grain Lv 9:17
N he will take the two goats and Lv 16:7
sacrifice ⌊it⌋ or on the **n** day, Lv 19:6
left until the ⌊**n**⌋ Year of Lv 27:18
of Issachar will camp **n** to it. Nm 2:5
tribe of Zebulun ⌊will be **n**⌋. Nm 2:7
of Simeon will camp **n** to it. Nm 2:12
The tribe of Gad ⌊will be **n**⌋. Nm 2:14
of Manasseh will be **n** to it. Nm 2:20
tribe of Benjamin ⌊will be **n**⌋. Nm 2:22
of Asher will camp **n** to it. Nm 2:27
tribe of Naphtali ⌊will be **n**⌋. Nm 2:29
N the Levites are to lay their Nm 8:12
place to the **n** until the cloud Nm 10:12
N the military divisions of the Nm 10:22
and all the **n** day gathering Nm 11:32
up early the **n** morning and went Nm 14:40
The **n** day the entire Israelite Nm 16:41
The **n** day Moses entered the tent Nm 17:8
got up the **n** morning and said Nm 22:13
N he saw the Kenites and Nm 24:21
kind of wood **n** to the altar you Dt 16:21
early the **n** morning and left Jos 3:1
as Adam, a city **n** to Zarethan. Jos 3:16
got up early the **n** morning. Jos 6:12
got up early the **n** morning. Jos 7:16
started early the **n** morning and Jos 8:10
N, Joshua and all Israel with Jos 10:36
of Ai, which is **n** to Bethel one Jos 12:9
under the oak **n** to the sanctuary Jos 24:26
The **n** day when the people went Jdg 9:42
The **n** day the people got up Jdg 21:4
it⌋, and I am **n** after you." Ru 4:4
n morning Elkanah and Hannah 1Sm 1:19
and placed it **n** to his statue. 1Sm 5:2
got up early the **n** morning, 1Sm 5:3
they got up early the **n** morning, 1Sm 5:4
The **n** day Saul organized the 1Sm 11:11
The **n** division headed toward the 1Sm 13:18
to Shur, which is **n** to Egypt. 1Sm 15:7
Abinadab, the **n**, and Shammah, 1Sm 17:13
n day an evil spirit from God 1Sm 18:10
tomorrow or the **n** day and I find 1Sm 20:12
until the evening of the **n** day. 1Sm 30:17
The **n** day when the Philistines 1Sm 31:8
he died there **n** to the ark of 2Sm 6:7
in Jerusalem that day and the **n**. 2Sm 11:12
The **n** morning David wrote a 2Sm 11:14
has a field right **n** to mine, 2Sm 14:30
which is **n** to En-rogel. 1Kg 1:9
N, Solomon overlaid the interior 1Kg 6:21
surface **n** to the grating, 1Kg 7:20
supports, each **n** to a wreath. 1Kg 7:30
N, he arranged the wood, cut up 1Kg 18:33
was in Jezreel **n** to the palace 1Kg 21:1
it is right **n** to my palace. 1Kg 21:2
grain offering the ⌊**n**⌋ morning, 2Kg 3:20
At this time **n** year you will 2Kg 4:16
and I said to her the **n** day, 2Kg 6:29
under his clothes **n** to his skin. 2Kg 6:30
The **n** day Hazael took a heavy 2Kg 8:15
The **n** morning when he went out 2Kg 10:9
people got up the ⌊**n**⌋ morning— 2Kg 19:35
N, the king stood by the pillar 2Kg 23:3
sons of Gad lived **n** to them in 1Ch 5:11
The **n** day when the Philistines 1Ch 10:8
n to him, Jehohanan the 2Ch 17:15
n to him, Amasiah son of Zichri, 2Ch 17:16
n to him, Jehozabad and 180,000 2Ch 17:18
N the king stood at his post and 2Ch 34:31
of Jericho built **n** to Eliashib, Neh 3:2
and **n** to them Zaccur son of Imri Neh 3:2
N to them Meremoth son of Uriah, Neh 3:4
N to them Zadok son of Baana Neh 3:4
N to them Melatiah the Gibeonite, Neh 3:7
and **n** to him Hananiah son of the Neh 3:8
N to them Rephaiah son of Hur, Neh 3:9
N to him Hattush the son of Neh 3:10
N to him the Levites made Neh 3:17
N to him Ezer son of Jeshua, Neh 3:19
n to him the priests from the Neh 3:22
N to him the Tekoites made Neh 3:27
N to him Hananiah son of Neh 3:30
N to him Malchijah, one of the Neh 3:31
the **n** generation will be told Ps 22:30
blotted out in the **n** generation. Ps 109:13
works to the **n** and will proclaim Ps 145:4
people got up the ⌊**n**⌋ morning— Is 37:36
The **n** day, when Pashhur released Jr 20:3
The Chaldeans **n** burned down the Jr 39:8
and then another the **n** year. Jr 51:46
N He said to me: "Son of man, Ezk 3:10
n morning I did just as I was Ezk 24:18
erect a marker **n** to it until Ezk 39:15
the temple side **n** to the gate's Ezk 40:7
N he measured the portico of the Ezk 40:8
N, he measured the pilasters— Ezk 40:14
n the north ⌊is described⌋. Ezk 40:19
N he measured the court. Ezk 40:47
N he brought me into the great Ezk 41:1
went inside ⌊the **n** room⌋ and Ezk 41:3
N he measured the length of the Ezk 41:15
threshold **n** to My threshold Ezk 43:8
N he brought me into the outer Ezk 46:21
N he brought me out by way of Ezk 47:2
N to the territory of Dan, Ezk 48:2
N to the territory of Asher, Ezk 48:3
N to the territory of Naphtali, Ezk 48:4
N to the territory of Manasseh, Ezk 48:5
N to the territory of Ephraim, Ezk 48:6
N to the territory of Reuben, Ezk 48:7
N to the territory of Judah, Ezk 48:8
N to the territory of the Ezk 48:13
n to the eight and one-third Ezk 48:21
eastern border and **n** to the Ezk 48:21
N to the territory of Benjamin, Ezk 48:24
N to the territory of Simeon, Ezk 48:25
N to the territory of Issachar, Ezk 48:26
N to the territory of Zebulun, Ezk 48:27
N to the territory of Gad toward Ezk 48:28
palace wall **n** to the lampstand. Dn 5:5
their children the **n** generation. Jl 1:3
dawn came the **n** day, God Jnh 4:7
N I took my staff called Favor Zch 11:10
The **n** day, which followed the Mt 27:62
n day when they came out from Mk 11:12
The **n** day, when they came down Lk 9:37
and had him stand **n** to Him. Lk 9:47
The **n** day he took out two Lk 10:35
it will bear fruit **n** year, Lk 13:9
and the **n** day, because it Lk 13:33
N he asked another, 'How much do Lk 16:7
The **n** day John saw Jesus coming Jn 1:29
Again the **n** day, John was Jn 1:35
n day He decided to leave for Jn 1:43
The **n** day, the crowd that had Jn 6:22
The **n** day, when the large crowd Jn 12:12
N, He poured water into a basin Jn 13:5
them in custody until the **n** day, Ac 4:3
The **n** day, their rulers, elders, Ac 4:5
n day he showed up while they Ac 7:26
n day, as they were traveling Ac 10:9
The **n** day he got up and set out Ac 10:23
The **n** day he left with Barnabas Ac 14:20
the **n** day to Neapolis Ac 16:11
whose house was **n** door to the Ac 18:7
was about to depart the **n** day, Ac 20:7
the **n** day we arrived off Chios. Ac 20:15
to Cos, the **n** day to Rhodes, Ac 21:1
The **n** day we left and came to Ac 21:8
Then the **n** day, Paul took the Ac 21:26
The **n** day, since he wanted to Ac 22:30
were standing **n** to him to strike Ac 23:2
The **n** day, they returned to the Ac 23:32
The **n** day, seated at the judge's Ac 25:6
The **n** day I sat at the judge's Ac 25:17
the **n** day, Agrippa and Bernice Ac 25:23
The **n** day we put in at Sidon, Ac 27:3
to jettison the cargo the **n** day. Ac 27:18
third teachers, **n**, miracles, 1Co 12:28

NEZIAH'S *(2)*
N descendants, and Hatipha's Ezr 2:54
N descendants, Hatipha's Neh 7:56

NEZIB *(1)*
Iphtah, Ashnah, **N**, Jos 15:43

NIBHAZ *(1)*
the Avvites made **N** and Tartak, 2Kg 17:31

NIBSHAN *(1)*
N, the City of Salt, and En-gedi Jos 15:62

NICANOR *(1)*
Prochorus, **N**, Timon, Parmenas, Ac 6:5

NICODEMUS *(5)*
man from the Pharisees named **N**, Jn 3:1
he is old?" **N** asked Him. "Can Jn 3:4
can these things be?" asked **N**. Jn 3:9
N—the one who came to Him Jn 7:50
N (who had previously come to Jn 19:39

NICOLAITANS *(2)*
you hate the practices of the **N**, Rv 2:6
hold to the teaching of the **N**. Rv 2:15

NICOLAUS *(1)*
Parmenas, and **N**, a proselyte Ac 6:5

NICOPOLIS *(1)*
every effort to come to me in **N**, Ti 3:12

NIGER *(1)*
(AKA SIMEON)
who was called **N**, Lucius the Ac 13:1

NIGHT *(318)*
and He called the darkness "**n**." Gn 1:5
to separate the day from the **n**. Gn 1:14
to have dominion over the **n**— Gn 1:16
to dominate the day and the **n**, Gn 1:18
and day and **n** will not cease." Gn 8:22
deployed against them by **n**, Gn 14:15
wash your feet, and spend the **n**. Gn 19:2
spend the **n** in the square." Gn 19:2
father to drink wine that **n**, Gn 19:33
I slept with my father last **n**. Gn 19:34
That **n** they again got their Gn 19:35
in a dream by **n** and said to him, Gn 20:3
house for us to spend the **n**?" Gn 24:23
and a place to spend the **n**." Gn 24:25
ate and drank and spent the **n**. Gn 24:54
appeared to him that **n** and said, Gn 26:24
and spent the **n** there because Gn 28:11
So Jacob slept with her that **n**. Gn 30:16
the Aramean in a dream at **n**. Gn 31:24
last **n** the God of your father Gn 31:29
what was stolen by day or by **n**. Gn 31:39
me by day and the frost by **n**, Gn 31:40
He issued His verdict last **n**." Gn 31:42
and spent the **n** on the mountain. Gn 31:54
He spent the **n** there and took Gn 32:13
he remained in the camp that **n**. Gn 32:21
During the **n** Jacob got up and Gn 32:22
Both had a dream on the same **n**, Gn 40:5
and I had dreams on the same **n**; Gn 41:11
where they lodged for the **n**, Gn 42:27
lodged for the **n** and opened our Gn 43:21
That **n** God spoke to Israel in a Gn 46:2
all that day and through the **n**. Ex 10:13
They are to eat the meat that **n**; Ex 12:8
Egypt on that **n** and strike every Ex 12:12
During the **n** Pharaoh got up, Ex 12:30
and Aaron during the **n** and said, Ex 12:31
It was a **n** of vigil in honor of Ex 12:42
This same **n** is in honor of the Ex 12:42
a **n** vigil for all the Israelites Ex 12:42
of fire to give them light at **n**, Ex 13:21
that they could travel day or **n**. Ex 13:21
of fire by **n** never left its Ex 13:22
darkness, yet it lit up the **n**. Ex 14:20
came near the other all **n** long. Ex 14:20
wind all that **n** and turned the Ex 14:21
a fire inside the cloud by **n**, Ex 40:38
hearth all **n** until morning, Lv 6:9
meeting day and **n** for seven days Lv 8:35
it, appearing like fire at **n**. Nm 9:16
Or if it remained a day and a **n**, Nm 9:21
the dew fell on the camp at **n**, Nm 11:9
that day and **n** and all the next Nm 11:32
and the people wept that **n**. Nm 14:1
and in a pillar of fire by **n**. Nm 14:14
Spend the **n** here, and I will Nm 22:8
to Balaam at **n** and said to him, Nm 22:20
the fire by **n** and in the cloud Dt 1:33
out of Egypt by **n** in the month Dt 16:1
a bodily emission during the **n**, Dt 23:10
You will be in dread **n** and day, Dt 28:66
you are to recite it day and **n**, Jos 1:8
place where you spend the **n**.'" Jos 4:3
the camp and spent the **n** there. Jos 6:11
men and sent them out at **n**. Jos 8:3
he spent that **n** with the troops Jos 8:9
And that **n** Joshua went into the Jos 8:13
marching all **n** from Gilgal. Jos 10:9
On that very **n** the LORD said to Jdg 6:25
in the daytime, he did it at **n**. Jdg 6:27
That **n** God did ⌊as Gideon Jdg 6:40
That **n** the LORD said to him, Jdg 7:9
with him got up at **n** and waited Jdg 9:34
him all that **n** at the city gate Jdg 16:2

of Micah and spent the **n** there. Jdg 18:2
and spent the **n** there again. Jdg 19:7
said to him, "Look, **n** is coming. Jdg 19:9
spend the **n**. See, the day is Jdg 19:9
the **n** here, enjoy yourself, Jdg 19:9
was unwilling to spend the **n**. Jdg 19:10
city and spend the **n** here?" Jdg 19:11
spend the **n** in Gibeah or Ramah. Jdg 19:13
go in and spend the **n** in Gibeah. Jdg 19:15
into their home to spend the **n**. Jdg 19:15
spend the **n** in the square." Jdg 19:20
abused her all **n** until morning. Jdg 19:25
my concubine to spend the **n**. Jdg 20:4
and surrounded the house at **n**. Jdg 20:5
his ox that **n** and slaughtered it 1Sm 14:34
cried out to the LORD ⌊all⌋ **n**. 1Sm 15:11
the LORD said to me last **n**." 1Sm 15:16
and escaped. That **n** he ran away. 1Sm 19:10
all that day and all that **n**. 1Sm 19:24
in the field until the third **n**. 1Sm 20:5
both day and **n**, the entire time 1Sm 25:16
That **n**, David and Abishai came 1Sm 26:7
They came to the woman at **n**, 1Sm 28:8
had any food all day and all **n**. 1Sm 28:20
they got up and left that **n**. 1Sm 28:25
journeyed all **n**, and retrieved 1Sm 31:12
through the Arabah all that **n**. 2Sm 2:29
men marched all **n** and reached 2Sm 2:32
by way of the Arabah all **n**. 2Sm 4:7
But that **n** the word of the LORD 2Sm 7:4
and spent the **n** lying on the 2Sm 12:16
spend the **n** with the people 2Sm 17:8
'Don't spend the **n** at the 2Sm 17:16
day and the wild animals by **n**. 2Sm 21:10
to Solomon in a dream at **n**. 1Kg 3:5
During the **n** this woman's son 1Kg 3:19
middle of the **n** and took my son 1Kg 3:20
over this temple **n** and day, 1Kg 8:29
near the LORD our God day and **n**, 1Kg 8:59
a cave there and spent the **n**. 1Kg 19:9
They went by **n** and surrounded 2Kg 6:14
got up in the **n** and said to his 2Kg 7:12
Then at **n** he set out to attack 2Kg 8:21
n the angel of the LORD went 2Kg 19:35
fled⌋ by **n** by way of the gate 2Kg 25:4
They spent the **n** in the vicinity 1Ch 9:27
they were on duty day and **n**. 1Ch 9:33
But that **n** the word of God came 1Ch 17:3
That **n** God appeared to Solomon 2Ch 1:7
over this temple day and **n**, 2Ch 6:20
to Solomon at **n** and said to him: 2Ch 7:12
Then at **n** he set out to attack 2Ch 21:9
burnt offerings and fat until **n**. 2Ch 35:14
Eliashib, where he spent the **n**. Ezr 10:6
to You day and **n** for Your Neh 1:6
I got up at **n** and ⌊took⌋ a few Neh 2:12
I went out at **n** through the Neh 2:13
So I went up at **n** by way of the Neh 2:15
guard because of them day and **n**. Neh 4:9
spend the **n** inside Jerusalem Neh 4:22
guard by **n** and work by day. Neh 4:22
and with a pillar of fire by **n**, Neh 9:12
And during the **n** the pillar of Neh 9:19
drink for three days, **n** and day. Est 4:16
That **n** sleep escaped the king, Est 6:1
and the **n** when they said, Jb 3:3
darkness had taken that **n** away! Jb 3:6
Yes, may that **n** be barren; Jb 3:7
that **n** did not shut the doors Jb 3:10
thoughts from visions in the **n**, Jb 4:13
grope at noon as if it were **n**. Jb 5:14
turned **n** into day and ⌊made⌋ Jb 17:12
away like a vision in the **n**. Jb 20:8
they spend the **n** naked, having Jb 24:7
and by **n** he becomes a thief. Jb 24:14
storm wind sweeps him away at **n**. Jb 27:20
will rest on my branches all **n**. Jb 29:19
the desolate wasteland by **n**. Jb 30:3
N pierces my bones, and my Jb 30:17
to spend the **n** on the street, Jb 31:32
a vision in the **n**, when deep Jb 33:15
suddenly in the middle of the **n**; Jb 34:20
and overthrows ⌊them⌋ by **n**, Jb 34:25
us⌋ with songs in the **n**, Jb 35:10
not long for the **n** when nations Jb 36:20
it spend the **n** by your feeding Jb 39:9
a cliff where it spends the **n**; Jb 39:28
he meditates on it day and **n**. Ps 1:2
and drench my bed every **n**. Ps 6:6
at **n** my conscience instructs Ps 16:7
You have visited by **n**; Ps 17:3
n after night they communicate Ps 19:2
night after **n** they communicate Ps 19:2
not answer, by **n**, yet I have no Ps 22:2
spend the **n**, but there is joy Ps 30:5
day and **n** Your hand was heavy Ps 32:4
have been my food day and **n**, Ps 42:3
song will be with me in the **n**— Ps 42:8
day and **n** they make the rounds Ps 55:10
noon, and **n**, and He hears my Ps 55:17
on You during the **n** watches Ps 63:6
The day is Yours, also the **n**; Ps 74:16
hands were lifted up all **n** long; Ps 77:2
At **n** I remember my music; Ps 77:6
a fiery light throughout the **n**. Ps 78:14
I cry out before You day and **n**. Ps 88:1
like a few hours of the **n**. Ps 90:4
not fear the terror of the **n**, Ps 91:5
and Your faithfulness at **n**, Ps 92:2
and it becomes **n**, when all the Ps 104:20
gave⌋ a fire to light up the **n**. Ps 105:39
I remember Your name in the **n**, Ps 119:55
each watch of the **n** to meditate Ps 119:148
you by day, or the moon by **n**. Ps 121:6
stand in the LORD's house at **n**! Ps 134:1
the moon and stars to rule by **n**. Ps 136:9
light around me will become **n**"— Ps 139:11
The **n** shines like the day; Ps 139:12
evening, in the dark of the **n**. Pr 7:9
will sleep at **n** without danger. Pr 19:23
it is still **n** and provides food Pr 31:15
her lamp never goes out at **n**. Pr 31:18
even at **n**, his mind does not Ec 2:23
do not close in sleep day or **n** Ec 8:16
spending the **n** between my Sg 1:13
In my bed at **n** I sought the one Sg 3:1
against the terror of the **n**. Sg 3:8
my hair with droplets of the **n**. Sg 5:2
spend the **n** among the henna Sg 7:11
of fire by **n** over the entire Is 4:5
"We will spend the **n** at Geba." Is 10:29
is devastated, destroyed in a **n**. Is 15:1
is devastated, destroyed in a **n**. Is 15:1
with shade that is as dark as **n**. Is 16:3
and I stay at my post all **n**. Is 21:8
what is ⌊left⌋ of the **n**? Is 21:11
what is ⌊left⌋ of the **n**?" Is 21:11
Morning has come, and also **n**. Is 21:12
camp for the **n** in the scrublands Is 21:13
I long for You in the **n**; Is 26:9
I guard it **n** and day so that no Is 27:3
morning—every day and every **n**. Is 28:19
like a dream, a vision in the **n**. Is 29:7
like that on the **n** of a holy Is 30:29
It will never go out—day or **n**. Is 34:10
an end of me from day until **n**. Is 38:12
You make an end of me day and **n**. Is 38:13
and your **n** will be like noonday. Is 58:10
but we live in the **n**. Is 59:9
be shut day or **n** so that the Is 60:11
will never be silent, day or **n**. Is 62:6
Rise up, let's attack by **n**. Jr 6:5
weep day and **n** over the slain Jr 9:1
stopping only for the **n**? Jr 14:8
day and **n** may ⌊they⌋ not stop, Jr 14:17
other gods both day and **n**, Jr 16:13
moon and stars for light by **n**, Jr 31:35
covenant with the **n** so that day Jr 33:20
so that day and **n** cease to come Jr 33:20
day and with the **n** and fail to Jr 33:25
heat of day and the frost of **n**. Jr 36:30
left the city at **n** by way of the Jr 39:4
Were thieves to come in the **n**, Jr 49:9
left the city by **n** by way of the Jr 52:7
She weeps aloud during the **n**, Lm 1:2
run down like a river day and **n**. Lm 2:18
cry out in the **n**, from the first Lm 2:19
from the first watch of the **n**. Lm 2:19
to Daniel in a vision at **n**, Dn 2:19
That very **n** Belshazzar the king Dn 5:30
palace and spent the **n** fasting. Dn 6:18
In my vision at **n** I was watching Dn 7:2
I was watching in the **n** visions, Dn 7:7
watching in the **n** visions, Dn 7:13
will also stumble with you by **n**. Hs 4:5
Their anger smolders all **n**; Hs 7:6
and spend the **n** in sackcloth, Jl 1:13
dawn and darkens day into **n**, Am 5:8
if marauders by **n**—how ravaged Ob 5
It appeared in a **n** and perished Jnh 4:10
in a night and perished in a **n**. Jnh 4:10
it will be **n** for you—without Mc 3:6
fierce than wolves of the **n**. Hab 1:8
her judges are wolves of the **n**, Zph 3:3
dealt with us." The **N** Visions Zch 1:6
looked out in the **n** and saw a Zch 1:8
without day or **n**, but there will Zch 14:7
and His mother during the **n**, Mt 2:14
Bethany, and spent the **n** there. Mt 21:17
middle of the **n** there was a Mt 25:6
came during the **n** and stole Him Mt 28:13
sleeps and rises—**n** and day, Mk 4:27
And always, **n** and day, he was Mk 5:5
today, this very **n**, before the Mk 14:30
watch at **n** over their flock Lk 2:8
serving God **n** and day with Lk 2:37
hard all **n** long and caught Lk 5:5
and spent all **n** in prayer to God Lk 6:12
very **n** your life is demanded Lk 12:20
he comes in the middle of the **n**, Lk 12:38
that **n** two will be in one bed: Lk 17:34
who cry out to Him day and **n**? Lk 18:7
and spend the **n** on what is Lk 21:37
man came to Him at **n** and said, Jn 3:2
N is coming when no one can work. Jn 9:4
If anyone walks during the **n**, Jn 11:10
out immediately. And it was **n**. Jn 13:30
had previously come to Him at **n** Jn 19:39
but that **n** they caught nothing. Jn 21:3
doors of the jail during the **n**, Ac 5:19
gates day and **n** intending to Ac 9:24
took him by **n** and lowered him Ac 9:25
On the **n** before Herod was to Ac 12:6
During the **n** a vision appeared Ac 16:9
hour of the **n** and washed their Ac 16:33
soon as it was **n**, the brothers Ac 17:10
Lord said to Paul in a **n** vision, Ac 18:9
remembering that **n** and day for Ac 20:31
The following **n**, the Lord stood Ac 23:11
during the **n**, the soldiers took Ac 23:31
earnestly serve Him **n** and day. Ac 26:7
For this **n** an angel of the God I Ac 27:23
When the fourteenth **n** came, Ac 27:27
the middle of the **n** the sailors Ac 27:27
The **n** is nearly over, and the Rm 13:12
on the **n** when He was betrayed, 1Co 11:23
have spent a **n** and a day in the 2Co 11:25
Working **n** and day so that we 1Th 2:9
pray earnestly **n** and day to see 1Th 3:10
come just like a thief in the **n**. 1Th 5:2
not of the **n** or of darkness. 1Th 5:5
sleep, sleep at **n**, and those who 1Th 5:7
who get drunk are drunk at **n**. 1Th 5:7
toiled, working **n** and day, so 2Th 3:8
and continues **n** and day in her 1Tm 5:5
you in my prayers **n** and day. 2Tm 1:3
Day and **n** they never stop, Rv 4:8
Him day and **n** in His sanctuary Rv 7:15
light, and the **n** as well. Rv 8:12
them before our God day and **n**. Rv 12:10
no rest day or **n** for those who Rv 14:11
day and **n** forever and ever Rv 20:10
it will never be **n** there. Rv 21:25
N will no longer exist, and Rv 22:5

NIGHTFALL *(1)*

At **n**, when the gate was about to Jos 2:5

NIGHTS *(21)*

on the earth 40 days and 40 **n**, Gn 7:4
on the earth 40 days and 40 **n**. Gn 7:12
the mountain 40 days and 40 **n**. Ex 24:18
with the LORD 40 days and 40 **n**; Ex 34:28
the mountain 40 days and 40 **n**. Dt 9:9
the end of the 40 days and 40 **n**. Dt 9:11
the LORD for 40 days and 40 **n**; Dt 9:18
days and 40 **n** because the LORD Dt 9:25
40 days and 40 **n** like the first Dt 10:10
drank, and spent the **n** there. Jdg 19:4
for three days and three **n**. 1Sm 30:12
40 days and 40 **n** to Horeb, 1Kg 19:8
with him seven days and **n**, Jb 2:13
troubled **n** have been assigned Jb 7:3
spending **n** in secret places, Is 65:4
the fish three days and three **n**. Jnh 1:17
He had fasted 40 days and 40 **n**, Mt 4:2

fish three days and three **n**. Mt 12:40
earth three days and three **n**. Mt 12:40
by sleepless **n**, by times of 2Co 6:5
many sleepless **n**, hunger and 2Co 11:27

NILE *(43)*
He was standing beside the **N**, Gn 41:1
came up from the **N** and began to Gn 41:2
up from the **N** and stood beside Gn 41:3
cows along the bank of the **N**. Gn 41:3
standing on the bank of the **N**, Gn 41:17
came up from the **N** and began to Gn 41:18
born to the Hebrews into the **N**, Ex 1:22
the reeds by the bank of the **N**. Ex 2:3
to bathe at the **N** while her Ex 2:5
some water from the **N** and pour Ex 4:9
take from the **N** will become Ex 4:9
meet him by the bank of the **N**. Ex 7:15
water in the **N** with the staff Ex 7:17
The fish in the **N** will die, Ex 7:18
and struck the water in the **N**, Ex 7:20
the water in the **N** was turned to Ex 7:20
The fish in the **N** died, and the Ex 7:21
dug around the **N** for water to Ex 7:24
after the LORD struck the **N**. Ex 7:25
The **N** will swarm with frogs; Ex 8:3
and remain only in the **N**." Ex 8:9
will remain only in the **N**." Ex 8:11
you struck the **N** with in your Ex 17:5
streams of the **N** and to the bee Is 7:18
The reeds by the **N**, by the mouth Is 19:7
areas of the **N** will wither, Is 19:7
hooks into the **N** will lament, Is 19:8
Shihor—the harvest of the **N**. Is 23:3
Overflow your land like the **N**, Is 23:10
to drink the waters of the **N**? Jr 2:18
rising like the **N**, like rivers Jr 46:7
rises like the **N**, and its waters Jr 46:8
lying in the middle of his **N**, Ezk 29:3
who says: My **N** is my own; I made Ezk 29:3
up from the middle of your **N**, Ezk 29:4
said: The **N** is my own; I made Ezk 29:9
I am against you and your **N**. Ezk 29:10
All of it will rise like the **N**; Am 8:8
subside like the **N** in Egypt. Am 8:8
rises like the **N** and subsides Am 9:5
subsides like the **N** of Egypt. Am 9:5
that sat along the **N** with water Nah 3:8
the depths of the **N** will dry up. Zch 10:11

NIMRAH *(1)*
(AKA BETH-NIMRAH)
Dibon, Jazer, **N**, Heshbon, Nm 32:3

NIMRIM *(2)*
The waters of **N** are desolate; Is 15:6
even the waters of **N** have become Jr 48:34

NIMROD *(4)*
Cush fathered **N**, who was the Gn 10:8
it is said, "Like **N**, a powerful Gn 10:9
Cush fathered **N**, who was the 1Ch 1:10
land of **N** with a drawn blade. Mc 5:6

NIMSHI *(5)*
anoint Jehu son of **N** as king 1Kg 19:16
son of Jehoshaphat, son of **N**. 2Kg 9:2
son of **N**, conspired against 2Kg 9:14
is like that of Jehu son of **N**— 2Kg 9:20
Joram to meet Jehu son of **N**, 2Ch 22:7

NINE *(25)*
n inches long and nine inches Ex 28:16
inches long and **n** inches wide. Ex 28:16
n inches long and nine inches Ex 39:9
inches long and **n** inches wide. Ex 39:9
the fifth day ⌊present⌋ **n** bulls, Nm 29:26
be given to the **n** and a half Nm 34:13
to the **n** tribes and half Jos 13:7
Moses for the **n** and a half Jos 14:2
and Mareshah—**n** cities, with Jos 15:44
and Zior—**n** cities, with their Jos 15:54
n cities from these two tribes. Jos 21:16
He was **n** feet, nine inches tall 1Sm 17:4
He was nine feet, **n** inches tall 1Sm 17:4
at the end of **n** months and 20 2Sm 24:8
the middle was **n** feet wide, 1Kg 6:6
cart was a band **n** inches high 1Kg 7:35
Samaria; ⌊he reigned⌋ **n** years. 2Kg 17:1
Eliada, and Eliphelet—**n** sons. 1Ch 3:8
with a rim of **n** inches around Ezk 43:13
90 feet high and **n** feet wide. Dn 3:1
went out about **n** in the morning, Mt 20:3
Now it was **n** in the morning when Mk 15:25
10 cleansed? Where are the **n**? Lk 17:17
it's only **n** in the morning. Ac 2:15
to go to Caesarea at **n** tonight. Ac 23:23

NINE-TENTHS *(1)*
while the other **n** remained in Neh 11:1

NINETEENTH *(4)*
which was the **n** year of King 2Kg 25:8
n to Pethahiah, the twentieth 1Ch 24:16
the **n** to Mallothi, his sons, and 1Ch 25:26
which was the **n** year of King Jr 52:12

NINETY-YEAR-OLD *(1)*
Sarah, a **n** woman, give birth? Gn 17:17

NINEVEH *(22)*
he went to Assyria and built **N**, Gn 10:11
between **N** and the great city Gn 10:12
returned ⌊home⌋ and lived in **N**. 2Kg 19:36
returned ⌊home⌋ and lived in **N**. Is 37:37
the great city of **N** and preach Jnh 1:2
the great city of **N** and preach Jnh 3:2
got up and went to **N** according Jnh 3:3
Now **N** was an extremely large Jnh 3:3
In 40 days **N** will be overthrown! Jnh 3:4
The men of **N** believed in God. Jnh 3:5
When word reached the king of **N**, Jnh 3:6
Then he issued a decree in **N**: Jnh 3:7
care about the great city of **N**, Jnh 4:11
The oracle concerning **N**. Nah 1:1
completely destroy **N** with an Nah 1:8
gone out from **N**, who plots evil Nah 1:11
N has been like a pool of water Nah 2:8
you, saying: **N** is devastated; Nah 3:7
He will make **N** a desolate ruin, Zph 2:13
men of **N** will stand up at the Mt 12:41
a sign to the people of **N**, Lk 11:30
The men of **N** will rise up at the Lk 11:32

NINTH *(24)*
evening of the **n** ⌊day⌋ of the Lv 23:32
this until the **n** year when its Lv 25:22
On the **n** day Abidan son of Nm 7:60
the **n** year of Hoshea, the king 2Kg 17:6
which was the **n** year of Israel's 2Kg 18:10
In the **n** year of Zedekiah's 2Kg 25:1
By the **n** day of the ⌊fourth⌋ 2Kg 25:3
Johanan eighth, Elzabad **n**, 1Ch 12:12
the **n** to Jeshua, the tenth to 1Ch 24:11
the **n** ⌊to⌋ Mattaniah, his sons, 1Ch 25:16
The **n**, for the ninth month, was 1Ch 27:12
ninth, for the **n** month, was 1Ch 27:12
twentieth ⌊day⌋ of the **n** month, Ezr 10:9
Judah, in the **n** month, all the Jr 36:9
it was the **n** month, the king Jr 36:22
the **n** year of Zedekiah king of Jr 39:1
on the **n** day of the month, Jr 39:2
In the **n** year of Zedekiah's Jr 52:4
By the **n** day of the fourth month Jr 52:6
LORD came to me in the **n** year, Ezk 24:1
day of the **n** ⌊month⌋, Hg 2:10
twenty-fourth day of the **n** month, Hg 2:18
the fourth day of the **n** month, Zch 7:1
beryl, the **n** topaz, the tenth Rv 21:20

NIPPLES *(3)*
and their virgin **n** caressed. Ezk 23:3
her virgin **n**, and poured out Ezk 23:8
caressed your **n** to enjoy your Ezk 23:21

NISAN *(2)*
(AKA ABIB)
the month of **N** in the twentieth Neh 2:1
the month of **N**, in King Est 3:7

NISROCH *(2)*
in the temple of his god **N**, 2Kg 19:37
in the temple of his god **N**, Is 37:38

NO *(1546)*
(See pp. xi-xii.)

NOADIAH *(2)*
of Jeshua and **N** son of Binnui Ezr 8:33
also **N** the prophetess and the Neh 6:14

NOAH *(48)*
he named him **N**, saying, "This Gn 5:29
N was 500 years old, and he Gn 5:32
N, however, found favor in the Gn 6:8
are the family records of **N**. Gn 6:9
N was a righteous man, blameless Gn 6:9
N walked with God Gn 6:9
And **N** fathered three sons: Gn 6:10
God said to **N**, "I have decided Gn 6:13
N did this. He did everything Gn 6:22
LORD said to **N**, "Enter the ark Gn 7:1
And **N** did everything that the Gn 7:5
N was 600 years old when the Gn 7:6
N, his sons, his wife, and his Gn 7:7
the ark with **N**, just as God had Gn 7:9
that same day **N** along with his Gn 7:13
in it entered the ark with **N**. Gn 7:15
Only **N** was left, and those that Gn 7:23
God remembered **N**, as well as all Gn 8:1
40 days **N** opened the window Gn 8:6
So **N** waited seven more days and Gn 8:10
So **N** knew that the water on the Gn 8:11
Then **N** removed the ark's cover Gn 8:13
Then God spoke to **N**, Gn 8:15
So **N**, along with his sons, his Gn 8:18
Then **N** built an altar to the Gn 8:20
God blessed **N** and his sons and Gn 9:1
Then God said to **N** and his sons Gn 9:8
God said to **N**, "This is the sign Gn 9:17
N, a man of the soil, was the Gn 9:20
When **N** awoke from his drinking Gn 9:24
Now **N** lived 350 years after the Gn 9:28
were Mahlah, **N**, Hoglah, Milcah, Nm 26:33
Mahlah, **N**, Hoglah, Milcah, and Nm 27:1
Milcah, and **N**, the daughters Nm 36:11
Mahlah, **N**, Hoglah, Milcah, and Jos 17:3
N, Noah's sons: Shem, Ham, and 1Ch 1:4
is like the days of **N** to Me: Is 54:9
the waters of **N** would never Is 54:9
three men—**N**, Daniel, and Job Ezk 14:14
⌊if⌋ **N**, Daniel, and Job were Ezk 14:20
As the days of **N** were, so the Mt 24:37
until the day **N** boarded the ark. Mt 24:38
Shem, ⌊son⌋ of **N**, ⌊son⌋ of Lk 3:36
Just as it was in the days of **N**, Lk 17:26
until the day **N** boarded the ark, Lk 17:27
By faith **N**, after being warned Heb 11:7
the days of **N** while an ark was 1Pt 3:20
but protected **N**, a preacher 2Pt 2:5

NOAH'S *(9)*
lived 595 years after **N** birth, Gn 5:30
six hundredth year of **N** life, Gn 7:11
Ham, and Japheth, **N** wife, and Gn 7:13
N sons who came out of the ark Gn 9:18
These three were **N** sons, and Gn 9:19
So **N** life lasted 950 years; Gn 9:29
the family records of **N** sons, Gn 10:1
These are the clans of **N** sons, Gn 10:32
Noah, **N** sons: Shem, Ham, and 1Ch 1:4

NOB *(6)*
to Ahimelech the priest at **N**. 1Sm 21:1
to Ahimelech son of Ahitub at **N**. 1Sm 22:9
family, who were priests in **N**. 1Sm 22:11
He also struck down **N**, the city 1Sm 22:19
Anathoth, **N**, Ananiah, Neh 11:32
he will stand at **N**, shaking his Is 10:32

NOBAH *(3)*
N went and captured Kenath with Nm 32:42
and called it **N** after his own Nm 32:42
route, east of **N** and Jogbehah, Jdg 8:11

NOBILITY *(3)*
royal family and from the **n**— Dn 1:3
The **n** of Israel will come to Mc 1:15
were the **n** of the earth, Rv 18:23

NOBLE *(22)*
a prominent man of **n** character Ru 2:1
you are a woman of **n** character. Ru 3:11
join with their **n** brothers and Neh 10:29
the **n** women of Persia and Media Est 1:18
of the king's most **n** officials. Est 6:9
they are the **n** ones in whom is Ps 16:3
moved by a **n** theme as I recite Ps 45:1
I speak of **n** things, and what Pr 8:6
or to beat a **n** for his honesty. Pr 17:26
demote you in plain view of a **n**. Pr 25:7
the chariots of my **n** people. Sg 6:12
will no longer be called a **n**, Is 32:5
But a **n** person plans noble Is 32:8
a noble person plans **n** things; Is 32:8
he stands up for **n** causes. Is 32:8
And if you speak **n** ⌊words⌋, Jr 15:19
She has done a **n** thing for Me. Mt 26:10
She has done a **n** thing for Me. Mk 14:6
It is a **n** thing not to eat meat, Rm 14:21
powerful, not many of **n** birth. 1Co 1:26

overseer, he desires a **n** work." 1Tm 3:1
blaspheme the **n** name that you Jms 2:7

NOBLEMAN *(1)*
A **n** traveled to a far country to Lk 19:12

NOBLEMAN'S *(1)*
"Where now is the **n** house?" Jb 21:28

NOBLEMEN *(1)*
seats them with **n** and gives them 1Sm 2:8

NOBLEMEN'S *(1)*
The **n** voices were hushed, and Jb 29:10

NOBLES *(45)*
did not harm the Israelite **n**; Ex 24:11
The **n** of the people hollowed it Nm 21:18
survivors came down to the **n**; Jdg 5:13
the elders and **n** who lived with 1Kg 21:8
elders and **n** who lived in his 1Kg 21:11
hundreds, the **n**, the governors 2Ch 23:20
the Jews, priests, **n**, officials, Neh 2:16
their **n** did not lift a finger Neh 3:5
I stood up and said to the **n**, Neh 4:14
I said to the **n**, the officials, Neh 4:19
I accused the **n** and officials, Neh 5:7
the **n** of Judah sent many letters Neh 6:17
These **n** kept mentioning Tobiah's Neh 6:19
into my mind to assemble the **n**, Neh 7:5
rebuked the **n** of Judah and said Neh 13:17
and Media, the **n**, and the Est 1:3
out contempt on **n** and disarms Jb 12:21
and to **n**, "Wicked men!" Jb 34:18
n of the peoples have assembled Ps 47:9
Make their **n** like Oreb and Zeeb, Ps 83:11
contempt on **n** and makes them Ps 107:40
in order to seat them with **n**— Ps 113:8
with the **n** of His people. Ps 113:8
in the LORD than to trust in **n**. Ps 118:9
Do not trust in **n**, in man, who Ps 146:3
as do **n** ⌊and⌋ all righteous Pr 8:16
is a son of **n** and your princes Ec 10:17
go through the gates of the **n**. Is 13:2
No **n** will be left to proclaim a Is 34:12
Their **n** send their servants for Jr 14:3
along with all the **n** of Judah Jr 27:20
also⌋ slaughtered all Judah's **n**. Jr 39:6
and all the houses of the **n**. Jr 52:13
advisers and my **n** sought me out, Dn 4:36
1,000 of his **n** and drank wine Dn 5:1
so that the king and his **n**, Dn 5:2
and the king and his **n**, wives, Dn 5:3
and his **n** were bewildered. Dn 5:9
outcry of the king and his **n**, Dn 5:10
as you and your **n**, wives, and Dn 5:23
with the signet rings of his **n**, Dn 6:17
By order of the king and his **n**: Jnh 3:7
and all her **n** were bound in Nah 3:10
Herod gave a banquet for his **n**, Mk 6:21
the earth, the **n**, the military Rv 6:15

NOBODY *(8)*
(See pp. xi-xii.)

NOD *(1)*
and lived in the land of **N**, Gn 4:16

NODAB *(1)*
Hagrites, Jetur, Naphish, and **N**. 1Ch 5:19

NOGAH *(2)*
N, Nepheg, Japhia, 1Ch 3:7
N, Nepheg, Japhia, 1Ch 14:6

NOHAH *(1)*
N fourth, and Rapha fifth. 1Ch 8:2

NOISE *(17)*
him heard ⌊the **n**⌋ as they 1Kg 1:41
that's the **n** you heard. 1Kg 1:45
heard the **n** from the guard 2Kg 11:13
heard the **n** from the troops, 2Ch 23:12
scoffs at the **n** of the village Jb 39:7
The **n** of the jubilant has Is 24:8
and loud **n**, storm, tempest, Is 29:6
shouting or subdued by their **n**, Is 31:4
flee at the thunderous **n**; Is 33:3
A **n**—it is coming—a great Jr 10:22
Pharaoh king of Egypt was all **n**; Jr 46:17
commotion like the **n** of an army. Ezk 1:24
shake from the **n** of cavalry, Ezk 26:10
an end to the **n** of your songs, Ezk 26:13
there was a **n**, a rattling sound, Ezk 37:7
from Me the **n** of your songs! Am 5:23
will pass away with a loud **n**, 2Pt 3:10

NOISEMAKERS *(1)*
forehead and the skull of the **n**. Jr 48:45

NOISY *(2)*
The **n** city, the jubilant town, Is 22:2
It will be **n** with people. Mc 2:12

NOMAD *(2)*
a **n** will not pitch his tent Is 13:20
highways like a **n** in the desert. Jr 3:2

NOMADIC *(1)*
the father of the **n** herdsmen. Gn 4:20

NONE *(107)*
(See pp. xi-xii.)

NONEXISTENT *(1)*
their works are **n**; Is 41:29

NONSENSE *(2)*
words seemed like **n** to them, Lk 24:11
thinking became **n**, and their Rm 1:21

NOON *(23)*
for they will eat with me at **n**." Gn 43:16
gift for Joseph's arrival at **n**. Gn 43:25
so that at **n** you will grope as a Dt 28:29
of Baal from morning until **n**, 1Kg 18:26
At **n** Elijah mocked them. 1Kg 18:27
marched out at **n** while Ben-hadad 1Kg 20:16
her lap until **n** and then died. 2Kg 4:20
daybreak until **n** before the men, Neh 8:3
they grope at **n** as if it were Jb 5:14
groan morning, **n**, and night, and Ps 55:17
pestilence that ravages at **n**. Ps 91:6
Where do you let them rest at **n**? Sg 1:7
stumble at **n** as though it were Is 59:10
rise up, let's attack at **n**. Jr 6:4
of young men a destroyer at **n**. Jr 15:8
will make the sun go down at **n**; Am 8:9
Ashdod will be driven out at **n**, Zph 2:4
About **n** and at three, he went Mt 20:5
From **n** until three in the Mt 27:45
it was **n**, darkness came over Mk 15:33
It was now about **n**, and darkness Lk 23:44
pray on the housetop at about **n**. Ac 10:9
about **n** an intense light from Ac 22:6

NOONDAY *(4)*
life will be brighter than **n**; Jb 11:17
dawn, your justice like the **n**. Ps 37:6
⌊Shelter us⌋ at **n** with shade Is 16:3
and your night will be like **n**. Is 58:10

NOONTIME *(1)*
the morning and a war cry at **n** Jr 20:16

NOOSE *(1)*
by the heel; a **n** seizes him. Jb 18:9

NOPHAH *(1)*
caused desolation as far as **N**, Nm 21:30

NOR *(52)*
(See pp. xi-xii.)

NORMAL *(2)*
the sea returned to its **n** depth. Ex 14:27
for it was his **n** procedure to Est 1:13

NORTH *(142)*
Look **n** and south, east and west, Gn 13:14
as Hobah to the **n** of Damascus. Gn 14:15
the east, the **n**, and the south. Gn 28:14
of the tabernacle, the **n** side, Ex 26:20
put the table on the **n** side. Ex 26:35
on the **n** side 150 ⌊feet⌋ Ex 27:11
tabernacle, the **n** side, he made Ex 36:25
hangings⌋ on the **n** side were Ex 38:11
of meeting on the **n** side of the Ex 40:22
it on the **n** side of the altar Lv 1:11
camp on the **n** side under their Nm 2:25
they camped on the **n** side of the Nm 3:35
and 1,000 yards for the **n** side, Nm 35:5
country long enough; turn **n**. Dt 2:3
to the west, **n**, south, and east Dt 3:27
and camped to the **n** of it, Jos 8:11
main camp to the **n** of the city Jos 8:13
the kings of the **n** in the hill Jos 11:2
to the border of Ekron on the **n** Jos 13:3
border on the **n** side was from Jos 15:5
proceeded **n** of Beth-arabah, Jos 15:6
turning **n** to the Gilgal that is Jos 15:7
reached to the slope **n** of Ekron, Jos 15:11
the **n** the border went westward Jos 16:6
was on the **n** side of the brook Jos 17:9
south and Manasseh's to the **n**, Jos 17:10
Asher on the **n** and Issachar Jos 17:10
in their territory in the **n**. Jos 18:5
border on the **n** side began at Jos 18:12
the slope of Jericho on the **n**, Jos 18:12
Then it went **n** to the slope Jos 18:18
continued to the **n** slope of Jos 18:19
Neah on the **n** to Hannathon Jos 19:14
n toward Beth-emek and Neiel, Jos 19:27
and Neiel, and went **n** to Cabul, Jos 19:27
of Ephraim **n** of Mount Gaash. Jos 24:30
of Ephraim, **n** of Mount Gaash. Jdg 2:9
camp of Midian was **n** of them, Jdg 7:1
which is **n** of Bethel, east Jdg 21:19
one stood to the **n** in front of 1Sm 14:5
three facing **n**, three facing 1Kg 7:25
put it on the **n** side of ⌊his⌋ 2Kg 16:14
east, west, **n**, and south. 1Ch 9:24
lot came out for the **n** ⌊gate⌋. 1Ch 26:14
each day on the **n**, four each day 1Ch 26:17
three facing **n**, three facing 2Ch 4:4
When He is at work to the **n**, Jb 23:9
cold from the driving **n** winds. Jb 37:9
Yet out of the **n** He comes, Jb 37:22
the slopes of the **n** is the city Ps 48:2
N and south—You created them. Ps 89:12
west, from the **n** and the south. Ps 107:3
The **n** wind produces rain, and a Pr 25:23
turning to the **n**, turning, Ec 1:6
falls to the south or the **n**, Ec 11:3
Awaken, **n** wind—come, south Sg 4:16
in the remotest parts of the **N**. Is 14:13
of dust is coming from the **n**, Is 14:31
I have raised up one from the **n**, Is 41:25
say to the **n**: Give ⌊them⌋ up Is 43:6
from the **n** and from the west, Is 49:12
from the **n** ⌊to the south⌋. Jr 1:13
out from the **n** on all who live Jr 1:14
clans and kingdoms of the **n**." Jr 1:15
proclaim these words to the **n**, Jr 3:12
the land of the **n** to the land I Jr 3:18
bringing disaster from the **n**— Jr 4:6
disaster threatens from the **n**, Jr 6:1
from the land to the **n**. Jr 10:22
and see those coming from the **n**. Jr 13:20
iron from the **n**, or bronze? Jr 15:12
the land of the **n** and from all Jr 16:15
the land of the **n** and from all Jr 23:8
all the families of the **n**'— Jr 25:9
kings of the **n**, both near and Jr 25:26
In the **n** by the bank of the Jr 46:6
from the **n** is coming against Jr 46:20
rising from the **n** and becoming Jr 47:2
nation from the **n** will come Jr 50:3
nations from the **n** country. Jr 50:9
A people comes from the **n**. Jr 50:41
from the **n** will come against Jr 51:48
a whirlwind coming from the **n**, Ezk 1:4
of the inner gate that faces **n**, Ezk 8:3
Son of man, look toward the **n**." Ezk 8:5
I looked to the **n**, and there was Ezk 8:5
offensive statue **n** of the altar Ezk 8:5
entrance of the **n** gate of the Ezk 8:14
which faces **n**, each with a war Ezk 9:2
her daughters to the **n** of you, Ezk 16:46
south to the **n** will be scorched Ezk 20:47
from the south to the **n**. Ezk 21:4
Tyre from the **n** with horses, Ezk 26:7
the leaders of the **n** and all the Ezk 32:30
parts of the **n** along with all Ezk 38:6
in the remotest parts of the **n**— Ezk 38:15
the remotest parts of the **n**. Ezk 39:2
next the **n** ⌊is described⌋. Ezk 40:19
of the outer court facing **n**, Ezk 40:20
had a gate facing the **n** gate, Ezk 40:23
he brought me to the **n** gate. Ezk 40:35
the entrance of the **n** gate, Ezk 40:40
one beside the **n** gate, facing Ezk 40:44
beside the south gate, facing **n**. Ezk 40:44
that faces **n** is for the priests Ezk 40:46
toward the **n** and another to Ezk 41:11
by way of the **n** gate into the Ezk 42:1
opposite the building to the **n**. Ezk 42:1
there was an entrance on the **n**; Ezk 42:2
their entrances were on the **n**. Ezk 42:4
like the chambers that faced **n**. Ezk 42:11
He measured the **n** side; Ezk 42:17
me by way of the **n** gate to the Ezk 44:4
by way of the **n** gate to worship Ezk 46:9
go out by way of the **n** gate. Ezk 46:9

holy chambers, which faced **n**. Ezk 46:19
by way of the **n** gate and led me Ezk 47:2
the **n** side it will extend from Ezk 47:15
territory of Hamath to the **n**. Ezk 47:17
a half ⌊miles⌋ on the **n** side; Ezk 48:16
feet⌋ to the **n**, 425 ⌊feet⌋ to Ezk 48:17
the **n** side, which measures one Ezk 48:30
will be three gates facing **n**, Ezk 48:31
the west, the **n**, and the south. Dn 8:4
to the king of the **N** to seal the Dn 11:6
fortress of the king of the **N**. Dn 11:7
away from the king of the **N**, Dn 11:8
to fight with the king of the **N**, Dn 11:11
The king of the **N** will again Dn 11:13
the king of the **N** will come, Dn 11:15
The king of the **N** who comes Dn 11:16
The king of the **N** will return to Dn 11:28
the king of the **N** will storm Dn 11:40
east and the **n** will terrify him Dn 11:44
to sea and roam from **n** to east, Am 8:12
hand against the **n** and destroy Zph 2:13
Leave the land of the **n**"— Zch 2:6
is going to the land of the **n**, Zch 6:6
the land of the **n** have pacified Zch 6:8
will move to the **n** and half to Zch 14:4
east and west, from **n** and south, Lk 13:29
gates on the **n**, three gates Rv 21:13

NORTHEASTER *(1)*
wind called the "**n**" rushed down Ac 27:14

NORTHERN *(19)*
This will be your **n** border: Nm 34:7
This will be your **n** border. Nm 34:9
at the **n** end of the Valley of Jos 15:8
to the **n** slope of Mount Jearim Jos 15:10
of Hinnom at the **n** end of the Jos 18:16
ended at the **n** bay of the Dead Jos 18:19
He stretches the **n** ⌊skies⌋ over Jb 26:7
an army is coming from a **n** land; Jr 6:22
to bring them from the **n** land. Jr 31:8
in the **n** land by the Euphrates Jr 46:10
handed over to a **n** people. Jr 46:24
The **n** and southern chambers that Ezk 42:13
This will be the **n** side. Ezk 47:17
measure from the ⌊**n**⌋ border to Ezk 47:18
From the **n** end, along the road Ezk 48:1
at the **n** border of Damascus, Ezk 48:1
miles long⌋ on the **n** side, Ezk 48:10
My Spirit in the **n** land." Zch 6:8
along the **n** coast of Cyprus Ac 27:4

NORTHERNER *(1)*
I will drive the **n** far from you Jl 2:20

NORTHWARD *(1)*
It curved **n** and went to Jos 18:17

NORTHWEST *(1)*
open to the southwest and **n**, Ac 27:12

NOSE *(11)*
the ring on her **n** and the Gn 24:47
My hook in your **n** and My bit in 2Kg 19:28
or pierce his **n** with snares? Jb 40:24
cord through his **n** or pierce his Jb 41:2
and twisting a **n** draws blood, Pr 30:33
Your **n** is like the tower of Sg 7:4
signet rings, **n** rings, Is 3:21
My hook in your **n** and My bit in Is 37:29
putting the branch to their **n**? Ezk 8:17
a ring in your **n**, earrings on Ezk 16:12
will cut off your **n** and ears, Ezk 23:25

NOSES *(1)*
but cannot hear, **n**, but cannot Ps 115:6

NOSTRILS *(14)*
the breath of life into his **n**, Gn 2:7
of the spirit of life in its **n**— Gn 7:22
up at the blast of Your **n**; Ex 15:8
comes out of your **n** and becomes Nm 11:20
rose from His **n**, and consuming 2Sm 22:9
blast of the breath of His **n**. 2Sm 22:16
an end by the breath of His **n**. Jb 4:9
breath from God remains in my **n**, Jb 27:3
billows from his **n** as from a Jb 41:20
rose from His **n**, and consuming Ps 18:8
blast of the breath of Your **n**. Ps 18:15
has only the breath in his **n**. Is 2:22
practices are smoke in My **n**, Is 65:5
of your camp to fill your **n**, Am 4:10

NOT *(5086)*
(See pp. xi-xii.)

NOT-MY-PEOPLE *(1)*
will call "N," "My-People," and Rm 9:25

NOTABLE *(2)*
fit and strong, **n** among ten Sg 5:10
n people in this first of the Am 6:1

NOTE *(33)*
the LORD take **n** of you and judge Ex 5:21
All the people took **n** of this, 2Sm 3:36
Take **n**: their two sons, Zadok's 2Sm 15:36
n that they are written about in 1Kg 14:19
take **n**: I will sweep away Baasha 1Kg 16:3
n that I have sent you my 2Kg 5:6
n that they are written about in 1Ch 29:29
N that my servants will be with 2Ch 2:8
N that the events of Asa's 2Ch 16:11
N that Amariah, the chief 2Ch 19:11
n that they are written about in 2Ch 27:7
n that they are written about in 2Ch 32:32
will He not take **n** ⌊of it⌋? Jb 11:11
but would not take **n** of my sin. Jb 14:16
Almighty does not take **n** of it— Jb 35:13
n its ramparts; tour its Ps 48:13
He took **n** of their distress, Ps 106:44
He takes **n** of the humble; Ps 138:6
Look and take **n**; search in her Jr 5:1
Therefore, take **n**! Days are Jr 7:32
remember me and take **n** of me. Jr 15:15
However, take **n**! The days are Jr 16:14
Therefore, take **n**! The days are Jr 19:6
Therefore, take **n**! I am against Jr 23:30
Take careful **n** of the entrance Ezk 44:5
Take **n**: I have told you in Mt 24:25
Take **n**—your reward is great in Lk 6:23
N this: some are last who will Lk 13:30
Take **n**! I, Paul, tell you that Gl 5:2
letter, take **n** of that person; 2Th 3:14
Take **n**! I will make those from Rv 3:9
but are lying—**n** this—I will Rv 3:9
passed. Take **n**: the third woe Rv 11:14

NOTES *(1)*
make a distinction in the **n**, 1Co 14:7

NOTHING *(285)*
thought of was **n** but evil all Gn 6:5
then **n** they plan to do will be Gn 11:6
I will take **n** except what the Gn 14:24
should you work for me for **n**? Gn 29:15
female slaves, but he found **n**. Gn 31:33
the whole tent but found **n**. Gn 31:34
He has withheld **n** from me except Gn 39:9
I have done **n** that they should Gn 40:15
There is **n** left for our lord Gn 47:18
so that **n** of all that the Ex 9:4
was so severe that **n** like it had Ex 9:24
N green was left on the trees or Ex 10:15
N leavened may be eaten. Ex 13:3
N leavened may be found among Ex 13:7
so that **n** in the house becomes Lv 14:36
down with **n** to frighten ⌊you⌋ Lv 26:6
strength will be used up for **n**. Lv 26:20
N that a man permanently sets Lv 27:28
n to look at but this manna! Nm 11:6
'Let **n** keep you from coming to Nm 22:16
and he says **n** to her, all her Nm 30:4
it⌋ and says **n** to her when he Nm 30:7
about it⌋, says **n** to her, and Nm 30:11
n that came from her lips, Nm 30:12
her husband says **n** at all to her Nm 30:14
because he said **n** to her when he Nm 30:14
years, and you have lacked **n**.' Dt 2:7
He added **n** more. He wrote Dt 5:22
shortage, where you will lack **n**; Dt 8:9
N set apart for destruction is Dt 13:17
poor brother and give him ⌊**n**⌋. Dt 15:9
Do **n** to the young woman, because Dt 22:26
eat because he has **n** left during Dt 28:55
producing **n**, with no plant Dt 29:23
leaving **n** undone of all that the Jos 11:15
They left **n** for Israel to eat, Jdg 6:4
This is **n** less than the sword of Jdg 7:14
There was **n** lacking in the land Jdg 18:7
is a place where **n** on earth is Jdg 18:10
There is **n** we lack." Jdg 19:19
N like this has ever happened or Jdg 19:30
so that **n** will happen to you in Ru 2:22
with him and let **n** he said prove 1Sm 3:19
n like this has happened before. 1Sm 4:7
the region of Shaalim—**n**. 1Sm 9:4
him a gift, but Saul said **n**. 1Sm 10:27
N can keep the LORD from saving, 1Sm 14:6
and **n** of theirs was missing the 1Sm 25:7
harassed and **n** of ours was 1Sm 25:15
man in the wilderness for **n**. 1Sm 25:21
There is **n** better for me than to 1Sm 27:1
n bad will happen to you because 1Sm 28:10
N ⌊of theirs⌋ was missing from 1Sm 30:19
poor man had **n** except one small 2Sm 12:3
for they knew **n** about the whole 2Sm 15:11
and **n** is hidden from the king— 2Sm 18:13
and soldiers mean **n** to you. 2Sm 19:6
why do you say **n** about restoring 2Sm 19:10
offerings that cost ⌊me⌋ **n**." 2Sm 24:24
table. They neglected **n**. 1Kg 4:27
outside so that **n** would be 1Kg 6:6
N was in the ark except the two 1Kg 8:9
n was too difficult for the king 1Kg 10:3
N like it had ever been made in 1Kg 10:20
considered as **n** in Solomon's 1Kg 10:21
"**N**," he replied, "but please 1Kg 11:22
looked, and said, "There's **n**." 1Kg 18:43
of Israel, "We have **n** in common. 2Kg 3:13
Your servant has **n** in the house 2Kg 4:2
And there was **n** bad in the pot. 2Kg 4:41
There was **n** but tethered horses 2Kg 7:10
There was **n** in his palace and in 2Kg 20:13
n will be left,' says the LORD. 2Kg 20:17
offerings that cost ⌊me⌋ **n**." 1Ch 21:24
N was in the ark except the two 2Ch 5:10
n was too difficult for Solomon 2Ch 9:2
N like it had ever been made in 2Ch 9:19
considered as **n** in Solomon's 2Ch 9:20
temple so that **n** unclean could 2Ch 23:19
This is **n** but sadness of heart." Neh 2:2
and require **n** more from them. Neh 5:12
he be shaken out and have **n**!" Neh 5:13
There is **n** to these rumors you Neh 6:8
to those who have **n** prepared, Neh 8:10
40 years and they lacked **n**. Neh 9:21
"**N** has been done for him." Est 6:3
LORD, "Does Job fear God for **n**? Jb 1:9
and **n** will be missing when you Jb 5:24
born only⌋ yesterday and know **n**. Jb 8:9
N he owned remains in his tent. Jb 18:15
N is left for him to consume; Jb 20:21
He hangs the earth on **n**. Jb 26:7
His flesh wastes away to **n**, Jb 33:21
A man gains **n** when he becomes Jb 34:9
fear, since he is afraid of **n**; Jb 39:22
twice, but ⌊now⌋ I can add **n**. Jb 40:5
For there is **n** reliable in what Ps 5:9
account until **n** remains of it. Ps 10:15
tried me and found **n** ⌊evil⌋; Ps 17:3
n is hidden from its heat. Ps 19:6
my shepherd; there is **n** I lack. Ps 23:1
for those who fear Him lack **n**. Ps 34:9
my life span as **n** in Your sight. Ps 39:5
You sell Your people for **n**; Ps 44:12
he dies, he will take **n** at all; Ps 49:17
my hands in innocence for **n**? Ps 73:13
And I desire **n** on earth but You. Ps 73:25
Have You created everyone for **n**? Ps 89:47
of the wicked will come to **n**. Ps 112:10
They do **n** wrong; they follow His Ps 119:3
n makes them stumble. Ps 119:165
n you desire compares with her. Pr 3:15
and **n** desirable can compare with Pr 8:11
she is gullible and knows **n**. Pr 9:13
and struggle adds **n** to it. Pr 10:22
of the wicked comes to **n**. Pr 10:28
his expectation comes to **n**, Pr 11:7
craves, yet has **n**, but the Pr 13:4
pretends to be rich but has **n**; Pr 13:7
Arrogance leads to **n** but strife, Pr 13:10
time he looks, and there is **n**. Pr 20:4
If you do **n** in a difficult time, Pr 24:10
or I might have **n** and steal, Pr 30:9
and says, "I've done **n** wrong." Pr 30:20
there is **n** new under the sun. Ec 1:9
There was **n** to be gained under Ec 2:11
There is **n** better for man than Ec 2:24
that there is **n** better for them Ec 3:12
that there is **n** better than for Ec 3:22
he will take **n** for his efforts Ec 5:15
so that he lacks **n** of all he Ec 6:2
because there is **n** better for Ec 8:15
⌊There will be **n** to do⌋ except Is 10:4

they are good for **n** but shame Is 30:5
all her princes will come to **n**. Is 34:12
There was **n** in his palace and in Is 39:2
n will be left,' says the LORD. Is 39:6
the nations are as **n** before Him; Is 40:17
reduces princes to **n** and makes Is 40:23
become as **n** and will perish. Is 41:11
you will become absolutely **n**. Is 41:12
you are **n** and your work is Is 41:24
I ask them, they have **n** to say. Is 41:28
make idols are **n**, and what they Is 44:9
my strength for **n** and futility; Is 49:4
were sold for **n**, and you will be Is 52:3
My people are taken away for **n**? Is 52:5
blind, all of them, they know **n**; Is 56:10
You beautify yourself for **n**. Jr 4:30
There is **n** but oppression within Jr 6:6
for peace, but there was **n** good; Jr 8:15
or You will reduce me to **n**. Jr 10:24
for peace, but there was **n** good; Jr 14:19
and heart for **n** except your own Jr 22:17
You have **n** that can heal you. Jr 30:13
N is too difficult for You! Jr 32:17
have done **n** but what is evil Jr 32:30
They have done **n** but provoke Me Jr 32:30
him because **n** had been heard. Jr 38:27
of the poor people who owned **n**, Jr 39:10
proclaim, and hide **n**. Jr 50:2
peoples will have labored for **n**; Jr 51:58
Is this **n** to you, all you who Lm 1:12
own spirit and have seen **n**. Ezk 13:3
of the earth are counted as **n**, Dn 4:35
so that **n** in regard to Daniel Dn 6:17
a disaster that **n** like what has Dn 9:12
will be cut off and will have **n**. Dn 9:26
they will certainly come to **n**. Hs 12:11
the ground when it has caught **n**? Am 3:5
Lord GOD does **n** without Am 3:7
you absolutely **n** to eat in all Am 4:6
and Bethel will come to **n**. Am 5:5
one who puts **n** in their mouths Mc 3:5
with **n** to frighten them away? Nah 2:11
exhaust themselves for **n**? Hab 2:13
which leave **n** for the morning. Zph 3:3
with **n** to make ⌊them⌋ afraid. Zph 3:13
Doesn't it seem like **n** to you? Hg 2:3
and **n** wrong was found on his Mal 2:6
N like this has ever been seen Mt 9:33
since there is **n** covered that Mt 10:26
and **n** hidden that won't be made Mt 10:26
Me three days and have **n** to eat. Mt 15:32
N will be impossible for you. Mt 17:20
in the marketplace doing **n**. Mt 20:3
standing here all day doing **n**?' Mt 20:6
to it and found **n** on it except Mt 21:19
by the sanctuary, it means **n**. Mt 23:16
oath by the altar, it means **n**. Mt 23:18
hungry and you gave Me **n** to eat; Mt 25:42
and you gave Me **n** to drink; Mt 25:42
Have **n** to do with that righteous Mt 27:19
See that you say **n** to anyone; Mk 1:44
For **n** is concealed except to be Mk 4:22
and **n** hidden except to come to Mk 4:22
them to take **n** for the road Mk 6:8
N that goes into a person from Mk 7:15
realize that **n** going into a man Mk 7:18
crowd, and they had **n** to eat. Mk 8:1
Me three days and have **n** to eat. Mk 8:2
can come out by **n** but prayer Mk 9:29
to it, He found **n** but leaves, Mk 11:13
And they said **n** to anyone, Mk 16:8
n will be impossible with God. Lk 1:37
He ate **n** during those days, Lk 4:2
all night long and caught **n**! Lk 5:5
and lend, expecting **n** in return. Lk 6:35
For **n** is concealed that won't be Lk 8:17
and **n** hidden that won't be made Lk 8:17
"Take **n** for the road," He told Lk 9:3
n will ever harm you. Lk 10:19
There is **n** covered that won't be Lk 12:2
n hidden that won't be made Lk 12:2
and after that can do **n** more. Lk 12:4
that country, and he had **n**. Lk 15:14
He has done **n** to deserve death. Lk 23:15
but this man has done **n** wrong." Lk 23:41
I can do **n** on My own. Jn 5:30
leftovers so that **n** is wasted." Jn 6:12
and they're saying **n** to Him. Jn 7:26
and that I do **n** on My own. Jn 8:28
Jesus answered, "My glory is **n**. Jn 8:54
to them, "You know **n** at all! Jn 11:49
You've accomplished **n**. Jn 12:19
because you can do **n** without Me. Jn 15:5
you have asked for **n** in My name. Jn 16:24
but that night they caught **n**. Jn 21:3
they had **n** to say in response. Ac 4:14
were dispersed and came to **n**. Ac 5:36
so that **n** you have said may Ac 8:24
eyes were open, he could see **n**. Ac 9:8
'For **n** common or unclean has Ac 11:8
their time on **n** else but telling Ac 17:21
told about you amounts to **n**, Ac 21:24
We find **n** evil in this man. Ac 23:9
but if there is **n** to what these Ac 25:11
have **n** definite to write to the Ac 25:26
saying **n** else than what the Ac 26:22
man is doing **n** that deserves Ac 26:31
without food, having eaten **n**. Ac 27:33
time and saw **n** unusual happen to Ac 28:6
I have done **n** against our people Ac 28:17
For I know that **n** good lives in Rm 7:18
the Lord Jesus that **n** is unclean Rm 14:14
things viewed as **n**—so He might 1Co 1:28
might bring to **n** the things that 1Co 1:28
to know **n** among you except 1Co 2:2
this age, who are coming to **n**. 1Co 2:6
"**N** beyond what is written." 1Co 4:6
"an idol is **n** in the world," 1Co 8:4
and embarrass those who have **n**? 1Co 11:22
but do not have love, I am **n**. 1Co 13:2
but do not have love, I gain **n**. 1Co 13:3
see that he has **n** to fear from 1Co 16:10
writing you **n** other than what 2Co 1:13
as having **n** yet possessing 2Co 6:10
even though I am **n**. 2Co 12:11
pray to God that you do **n** wrong, 2Co 13:7
as important added **n** to me. Gl 2:6
the law, then Christ died for **n**. Gl 2:21
Did you suffer so much for **n**— Gl 3:4
if in fact it was for **n**? Gl 3:4
to be something when he is **n**, Gl 6:3
and uncircumcision mean **n**; Gl 6:15
Do **n** out of rivalry or conceit, Php 2:3
run in vain or labor for **n**. Php 2:16
that our labor might be for **n**. 1Th 3:5
will bring him to **n** with the 2Th 2:8
and **n** should be rejected if it 1Tm 4:4
But have **n** to do with irreverent 1Tm 4:7
doing **n** out of favoritism. 1Tm 5:21
understanding **n**, but having a 1Tm 6:4
For we brought **n** into the world, 1Tm 6:7
world, and we can take **n** out. 1Tm 6:7
and unbelieving **n** is pure; Ti 1:15
having **n** bad to say about us. Ti 2:8
so that they will lack **n**. Ti 3:13
He left **n** not subject to him. Heb 2:8
tribe Moses said **n** concerning Heb 7:14
law perfected **n**), but a better Heb 7:19
mature and complete, lacking **n**. Jms 1:4
name, accepting **n** from pagans. 3Jn 7
and need **n**,' and you don't Rv 3:17
N profane will ever enter it: Rv 21:27

NOTHINGNESS *(1)*

by Him as **n** and emptiness. Is 40:17

NOTICE *(24)*

the Israelites, and He took **n**. Ex 2:25
escapes the **n** of the assembly, Lv 4:13
Why are you so kind to **n** me, Ru 2:10
n the place where he's lying, Ru 3:4
if You will take **n** of Your 1Sm 1:11
N that the reserved piece is set 1Sm 9:24
May He take **n** and plead my case 1Sm 24:15
I wouldn't take **n** of you. 2Kg 3:14
Please **n** that the place where we 2Kg 6:1
N I have taken great pains to 1Ch 22:14
sin, You would **n**, and would not Jb 10:14
You really take **n** of one like Jb 14:3
but a person may not **n** it. Jb 33:14
Awake to help me, and take **n**. Ps 59:4
n that the house of Israel is Ezk 12:27
his strength, but he does not **n**. Hs 7:9
with gray, but he does not **n**. Hs 7:9
N the stone I have set before Zch 3:9
The LORD took **n** and listened. Mal 3:16
give her a written **n** of divorce. Mt 5:31
eye but don't **n** the log in your Mt 7:3
but He could not escape **n**. Mk 7:24
but don't **n** the log in your own Lk 6:41
of these things escapes his **n**, Ac 26:26

NOTICED *(11)*

Esau **n** that Isaac blessed Jacob Gn 28:6
LORD⌋ bless the man who **n** you." Ru 2:19
so whenever Saul **n** any strong or 1Sm 14:52
and Solomon **n** the young man 1Kg 11:28
I passed by and **n** he was gone; Ps 37:36
I **n** among the youths Pr 7:7
ourselves, but You haven't **n**!" Is 58:3
Have you not **n** what these people Jr 33:24
when He **n** how they would choose Lk 14:7
turned and **n** them following Jn 1:38
looked up and **n** a huge crowd Jn 6:5

NOTICES *(1)*

perish forever while no one **n**. Jb 4:20

NOTORIOUS *(4)*

her, she became **n** among women. Ezk 23:10
they had a **n** prisoner called Mt 27:16
judgment of the **n** prostitute who Rv 17:1
has judged the **n** prostitute who Rv 19:2

NOURISHED *(3)*

n him with honey from the rock Dt 32:13
n and held together by its Col 2:19
n by the words of the faith and 1Tm 4:6

NOURISHMENT *(2)*

provides **n** for their children Jb 24:5
household and **n** for your Pr 27:27

NOW *(1032)*

(See pp. xi-xii.)

NOWHERE *(2)*

an undeserved curse goes **n**. Pr 26:2
saw that he was getting **n**, Mt 27:24

NUISANCE *(1)*

Look, what a **n**!" "And you scorn Mal 1:13

NUMBER *(136)*

We are few in **n**; if they unite Gn 34:30
Send one of your **n** to get your Gn 42:16
The total **n** of persons: Gn 46:15
The total **n** of persons belonging Gn 46:26
The total **n** of Jacob's Ex 1:5
your prescribed **n** of bricks Ex 5:14
been such a large **n** of locusts, Ex 10:14
on the combined **n** of people; Ex 12:4
with a huge **n** of livestock, Ex 12:38
according to the **n** of people Ex 16:16
you⌋ the full **n** of your days. Ex 23:26
based on the **n** of years since Lv 25:15
based on the **n** of ⌊remaining⌋ Lv 25:15
to you is a **n** of harvests. Lv 25:16
determined⌋ by the **n** of years. Lv 25:50
The total **n** in their military Nm 2:9
The total **n** in their military Nm 2:16
Ephraim's encampment **n** 108,100; Nm 2:24
The total **n** who belong to Dan's Nm 2:31
total **n** in the camps by their Nm 2:32
The total **n** of all the Levite Nm 3:39
The total **n** of the firstborn Nm 3:43
the entire **n** of you 20 years old Nm 14:29
based on the **n** of the 40 days Nm 14:34
based on the **n** of names. Nm 26:53
lambs, in proportion to their **n**. Nm 29:18
lambs, in proportion to their **n**. Nm 29:21
lambs, in proportion to their **n**. Nm 29:24
lambs, in proportion to their **n**. Nm 29:27
lambs, in proportion to their **n**. Nm 29:30
lambs, in proportion to their **n**. Nm 29:33
lambs, in proportion to their **n**. Nm 29:37
had a very large **n** of livestock. Nm 32:1
The total **n** of cities you give Nm 35:7
besides a large **n** of rural Dt 3:5
presence with the **n** ⌊of lashes⌋ Dt 25:2
according to the **n** of the people Dt 32:8
along with a vast **n** of horses Jos 11:4
one ⌊the total **n** of⌋ all kings: Jos 12:24
a huge **n** of cattle, and silver, Jos 22:8
and their camels were without **n**, Jdg 6:5
The **n** of those who lapped with Jdg 7:6
and took the **n** of women they Jdg 21:23
to⌋ the **n** of Philistine rulers 1Sm 6:4
The **n** of gold mice also 1Sm 6:18
to the **n** of Philistine cities 1Sm 6:18
man had a large **n** of sheep and 2Sm 12:2
troops so I can know their **n**." 2Sm 24:2
according to the **n** of the tribes 1Kg 18:31

also appointed from their **n**, 2Kg 17:32
The **n** of men listed in their 1Ch 7:40
The total **n** of those chosen to 1Ch 9:22
were few in **n**, very few indeed 1Ch 16:19
to me so I can know their **n**." 1Ch 21:2
multiply the **n** of His people 1Ch 21:3
bronze, and iron—beyond **n**. 1Ch 22:16
the total **n** of men was 38,000 by 1Ch 23:3
according to the **n** prescribed 1Ch 23:31
and the **n** was not entered in the 1Ch 27:24
The total **n** of heads of families 2Ch 26:12
The **n** of burnt offerings the 2Ch 29:32
For a large **n** of the people— 2Ch 30:18
The **n** of the Israelite men Ezr 2:2
based on the **n** specified by Ezr 3:4
was ⌊verified⌋ by **n** and weight, Ezr 8:34
I mourned for a **n** of days, Neh 1:4
The **n** of the Israelite men Neh 7:7
The total **n** of Perez's Neh 11:6
On that day the **n** of people Est 9:11
and a very large **n** of servants. Jb 1:3
things, wonders without **n**. Jb 5:9
things, wonders without **n**. Jb 9:10
and the **n** of his months Jb 14:5
when the **n** of his months has run Jb 21:21
who go before him are without **n**. Jb 21:33
see my ways and **n** all my steps? Jb 31:4
the **n** of His years cannot be Jb 36:26
has the wisdom to **n** the clouds? Jb 38:37
of my life and the **n** of my days. Ps 39:4
without **n** have surrounded Ps 40:12
Teach us to **n** our days carefully Ps 90:12
with creatures beyond **n**— Ps 104:25
were few in **n**, very few indeed Ps 105:12
came—young locusts without **n**. Ps 105:34
He counts the **n** of the stars; Ps 147:4
and young women without **n**. Sg 6:8
will be so few in **n** that a child Is 10:19
archers will be few in **n**." Is 21:17
They trust in the **n** of chariots Is 31:1
brings out the starry host by **n**; Is 40:26
the land of Judah only few in **n**, Jr 44:28
for the **n** of days you lie Ezk 4:4
to the **n** of days ⌊you lie Ezk 4:5
it during the **n** of days you lie Ezk 4:9
multiply them in **n** like a flock. Ezk 36:37
a very large **n** of trees along Ezk 47:7
will be a huge **n** of fish because Ezk 47:9
beasts, four in **n**, are four Dn 7:17
prophet that the **n** of years for Dn 9:2
a large **n** of armed forces Dn 11:10
Yet the **n** of the Israelites will Hs 1:10
decrease in **n** under the burden Hs 8:10
and in your large **n** of soldiers, Hs 10:13
My land, powerful and without **n**; Jl 1:6
walls because of the **n** of people Zch 2:4
they caught a great **n** of fish, Lk 5:6
because of the large **n** of fish. Jn 21:6
n of people who were together Ac 1:15
was one of our **n** and was Ac 1:17
and the **n** of the men came to Ac 4:4
as the **n** of the disciples was Ac 6:1
the **n** of the disciples in Ac 6:7
a large **n** who believed turned Ac 11:21
way that a great **n** of both Jews Ac 14:1
and were increased in **n** daily. Ac 16:5
in that city for a **n** of days. Ac 16:12
a great **n** of God-fearing Ac 17:4
as well as a **n** of the leading Ac 17:4
including a **n** of the prominent Ac 17:12
a considerable **n** of people by Ac 19:26
Though the **n** of Israel's sons is Rm 9:27
more will their full **n** bring! Rm 11:12
until the full **n** of the Gentiles Rm 11:25
adding to the **n** of their sins, 1Th 2:16
Their **n** was countless thousands, Rv 5:11
until ⌊the **n** of⌋ their fellow Rv 6:11
And I heard the **n** of those who Rv 7:4
no one could **n**, standing before Rv 7:9
The **n** of mounted troops was 200 Rv 9:16
200 million; I heard their **n**. Rv 9:16
name or the **n** of his name. Rv 13:17
calculate the **n** of the beast, Rv 13:18
because it is the **n** of a man. Rv 13:18
number of a man. His **n** is 666. Rv 13:18
image, and the **n** of his name, Rv 15:2
Their **n** is like the sand of the Rv 20:8

NUMBERED *(51)*

the tribe of Reuben **n** 46,500. Nm 1:21
the tribe of Simeon **n** 59,300. Nm 1:23
for the tribe of Gad **n** 45,650. Nm 1:25
for the tribe of Judah **n** 74,600. Nm 1:27
the tribe of Issachar **n** 54,400. Nm 1:29
the tribe of Zebulun **n** 57,400. Nm 1:31
the tribe of Ephraim **n** 40,500. Nm 1:33
the tribe of Manasseh **n** 32,200. Nm 1:35
the tribe of Benjamin **n** 35,400. Nm 1:37
for the tribe of Dan **n** 62,700. Nm 1:39
for the tribe of Asher **n** 41,500. Nm 1:41
the tribe of Naphtali **n** 53,400. Nm 1:43
All those registered **n** 603,550. Nm 1:46
one month old or more, **n** 7,500. Nm 3:22
one month old or more, **n** 6,200. Nm 3:34
by their clans **n** 2,750. Nm 4:36
their ancestral houses **n** 2,630. Nm 4:40
by their clans **n** 3,200. Nm 4:44
Their registered men **n** 8,580. Nm 4:48
died from the plague **n** 14,700, Nm 16:49
of Jacob or **n** the dust clouds Nm 23:10
who died in the plague **n** 24,000. Nm 25:9
their registered men **n** 43,730. Nm 26:7
the Gadite clans ⌊**n**⌋ by their Nm 26:18
were Judah's clans ⌊**n**⌋ by their Nm 26:22
Issachar's clans ⌊**n**⌋ by their Nm 26:25
Zebulunite clans ⌊**n**⌋ by their Nm 26:27
n by their registered men: Nm 26:34
Ephraimite clans ⌊**n**⌋ by their Nm 26:37
Benjaminite clans **n** by their Nm 26:41
Shuhamite clans ⌊**n**⌋ by their Nm 26:43
the Asherite clans ⌊**n**⌋ by their Nm 26:47
the Naphtali clans **n** by their Nm 26:50
Israelite men **n** 601,730. Nm 26:51
for those who went out to war **n**: Nm 31:36
The troops with him **n** about 600. 1Sm 14:2
too numerous to be **n** or counted. 1Kg 3:8
proverbs, and his songs **n** 1,005. 1Kg 4:32
the labor force **n** 30,000 men. 1Kg 5:13
that could not be counted or **n**, 1Kg 8:5
music for the LORD, they **n** 288. 1Ch 25:7
be counted or **n** because there 2Ch 5:6
He **n** those 20 years old or more 2Ch 25:5
combined assembly **n** 42,360 Ezr 2:64
combined assembly **n** 42,360 Neh 7:66
Can His troops be **n**? Jb 25:3
around the latticework **n** 100. Jr 52:23
that⌋ God has **n** ⌊the days of⌋ Dn 5:26
who was **n** among the Twelve. Lk 22:3
The men **n** about 5,000. Jn 6:10
he was **n** with the 11 apostles. Ac 1:26

NUMBERING *(2)*

Simeonite clans, **n** 22,200 men. Nm 26:14
and his men, **n** about 600, left 1Sm 23:13

NUMBERS *(21)*

and reduce your **n** until your Lv 26:22
His military division **n** 74,600. Nm 2:4
His military division **n** 54,400. Nm 2:6
His military division **n** 57,400. Nm 2:8
His military division **n** 46,500. Nm 2:11
His military division **n** 59,300. Nm 2:13
His military division **n** 45,650. Nm 2:15
His military division **n** 40,500. Nm 2:19
His military division **n** 32,200. Nm 2:21
His military division **n** 35,400. Nm 2:23
His military division **n** 62,700. Nm 2:26
His military division **n** 41,500. Nm 2:28
His military division **n** 53,400. Nm 2:30
The **n** of the armed troops who 1Ch 12:23
Israel in great **n** when they saw 2Ch 15:9
These are their **n** according to 2Ch 17:14
May the LORD add to ⌊your **n**⌋, Ps 115:14
to the Lord in increasing **n**— Ac 5:14
Spirit, and it increased in **n**. Ac 9:31
and large **n** of people were added Ac 11:24
the church and taught large **n**, Ac 11:26

NUMEROUS *(54)*

offspring will be that ⌊**n**⌋." Gn 15:5
your offspring as **n** as the stars Gn 22:17
your offspring as **n** as the stars Gn 26:4
and became fruitful and very **n**. Gn 47:27
'I will make you fruitful and **n**; Gn 48:4
grow to be **n** within the land Gn 48:16
extremely **n** so that the land Ex 1:7
people are more **n** and powerful Ex 1:9
multiplied and became very **n**. Ex 1:20
the people of the land are so **n**, Ex 5:5
you have become **n** and take Ex 23:30
your offspring as **n** as the stars Ex 32:13
the people because they were **n**, Nm 22:3
who were more **n** and higher in Nm 22:15
today you are as **n** as the stars Dt 1:10
a great and **n** people as tall as Dt 2:10
great and **n** people, tall as the Dt 2:21
nations more **n** and powerful than Dt 7:1
were more **n** than all peoples, Dt 7:7
will become too **n** for you. Dt 7:22
stronger and more **n** than they.' Dt 9:14
has made you as **n** as the stars Dt 10:22
Though you were as **n** as the Dt 28:62
a multitude as **n** as the sand on Jos 11:4
and troops as **n** as the sand on 1Sm 13:5
as **n** as the sand by the sea— 2Sm 17:11
a people too **n** to be numbered or 1Kg 3:8
and Israel were as **n** as the sand 1Kg 4:20
Since you are so **n**, choose for 1Kg 18:25
not become as **n** as the Judeans. 1Ch 4:27
or Mount Hermon). They were **n**. 1Ch 5:23
but Rehabiah's sons were very **n**. 1Ch 23:17
make Israel as **n** as the stars 1Ch 27:23
over a people as **n** as the dust 2Ch 1:9
sons, and our daughters are **n**. Neh 5:2
they are **n**, and they hate me Ps 25:19
cause are more **n** than the hairs Ps 69:4
made them more **n** than their foes Ps 105:24
people were as **n** as the sand Is 10:22
gods are as **n** as your cities, Jr 2:28
many, their unfaithful deeds **n**. Jr 5:6
are indeed as **n** as your cities, Jr 11:13
n as the streets of Jerusalem. Jr 11:13
their widows more **n** than the Jr 15:8
They will become fruitful and **n**. Jr 23:3
they are more **n** than locusts; Jr 46:23
will be so **n** that their dust Ezk 26:10
because of your **n** products. Ezk 27:16
because of your **n** products and Ezk 27:18
Though they are strong and **n**, Nah 1:12
merchants more **n** than the stars Nah 3:16
they will be as **n** as they once Zch 10:8
more **n** than those of the woman Gl 4:27
came offspring as **n** as the stars Heb 11:12

NUN *(30)*

the young man Joshua son of **N**, Ex 33:11
Joshua son of **N**, assistant to Nm 11:28
Hoshea son of **N** from the tribe Nm 13:8
Moses renamed Hoshea son of **N**, Nm 13:16
Joshua son of **N** and Caleb son of Nm 14:6
Jephunneh and Joshua son of **N**. Nm 14:30
Joshua son of **N** and Caleb son Nm 14:38
Jephunneh and Joshua son of **N**. Nm 26:65
Joshua son of **N**, a man who has Nm 27:18
Kenizzite and Joshua son of **N**, Nm 32:12
Joshua son of **N**, and the family Nm 32:28
the priest and Joshua son of **N**. Nm 34:17
son of **N**, who attends you, Dt 1:38
commissioned Joshua son of **N**, Dt 31:23
Joshua son of **N** and recited all Dt 32:44
Joshua son of **N** was filled with Dt 34:9
LORD spoke to Joshua son of **N**, Jos 1:1
Joshua son of **N** secretly sent Jos 2:1
to Joshua son of **N** and reported Jos 2:23
So Joshua son of **N** summoned the Jos 6:6
Joshua son of **N**, and the heads Jos 14:1
son of **N**, and the leaders, Jos 17:4
Joshua son of **N** an inheritance Jos 19:49
Joshua son of **N**, and the heads Jos 19:51
Joshua son of **N**, and the heads Jos 21:1
Joshua son of **N**, died at the age Jos 24:29
Joshua son of **N**, the servant of Jdg 2:8
spoken through Joshua son of **N**. 1Kg 16:34
his son **N**, and his son Joshua. 1Ch 7:27
Joshua son of **N** until that day. Neh 8:17

NURSE *(15)*

that Sarah would **n** children? Gn 21:7
their sister Rebekah and her **n**, Gn 24:59
Rebekah's **n**, died and was Gn 35:8
Hebrews to **n** the boy for you? Ex 2:7
this child and **n** him for me, Ex 2:9
His **n** picked him up and fled, 2Sm 4:4
up in the morning to **n** my son, 1Kg 3:21
put⌋ him and his **n** in a bedroom. 2Kg 11:2
put him and his **n** in a bedroom. 2Ch 22:11
were there breasts for me to **n**? Jb 3:12
You will **n** on the milk of Is 60:16
and **n** at the breast of kings; Is 60:16

so that you may **n** and be Is 66:11
you will **n** and be carried on Is 66:12
their⌊ breasts to **n** their young, Lm 4:3

NURSED *(6)*
woman took the boy and **n** him. Ex 2:9
stayed there and **n** her son until 1Sm 1:23
who **n** at my mother's breasts, Sg 8:1
the one who **n** You are blessed! Lk 11:27
and the breasts that never **n**!' Lk 23:29
He was **n** in his father's home Ac 7:20

NURSING *(15)*
and I have **n** sheep and cattle. Gn 33:13
as a **n** woman carries a baby,' Nm 11:12
n child of the poor is seized Jb 24:9
of children and **n** infants, Ps 8:2
gently leads those that are **n**. Is 40:11
Can a woman forget her **n** child, Is 49:15
and their queens your **n** mothers. Is 49:23
a **n** infant will no longer live Is 65:20
The **n** infant's tongue clings to Lm 4:4
even those **n** at the breast. Jl 2:16
of children and **n** infants?" Mt 21:16
women and **n** mothers in those Mt 24:19
women and **n** mothers in those Mk 13:17
women and **n** mothers in those Lk 21:23
as a **n** mother nurtures her own 1Th 2:7

NURTURED *(3)*
be like plants **n** in their youth, Ps 144:12
the infants they have **n**? Lm 2:20
destroyed those I **n** and reared. Lm 2:22

NURTURES *(1)*
nursing mother **n** her own 1Th 2:7

NURTURING *(1)*
n only themselves without fear. Jd 12

NYMPHA *(1)*
and to **N** and the church in her Col 4:15

O

O *(10)*
the desert, **O** house of Israel? Ac 7:42
accused by the Jews, **O** king! Ac 26:7
while on the road, **O** king, I saw Ac 26:13
O Death, where is your victory? 1Co 15:55
O Death, where is your sting? 1Co 15:55
O barren woman who does not give Gl 4:27
Your throne, **O** God, is forever Heb 1:8
—to do Your will, **O** God!" Heb 10:7
O Lord, holy and true, how long Rv 6:10
rejoice, **O** heavens, and you Rv 12:12

OAK *(21)*
of Shechem, at the **o** of Moreh. Gn 12:6
them under the **o** near Shechem. Gn 35:4
under the **o** south of Bethel Gn 35:8
So Jacob named it **O** of Weeping. Gn 35:8
and from the **o** in Zaanannim, Jos 19:33
up there under the **o** next to the Jos 24:26
tent beside the **o** tree of Jdg 4:11
He sat under the **o** that was in Jdg 6:11
offered them to Him under the **o**. Jdg 6:19
king at the **o** of the pillar Jdg 9:6
direction of the Diviners' **O**." Jdg 9:37
you come to the **o** of Tabor. 1Sm 10:3
branches of a large **o** tree, 2Sm 18:9
Absalom hanging in an **o** tree!" 2Sm 18:10
was still alive in the **o** tree, 2Sm 18:14
him sitting under an **o** tree. 1Kg 13:14
bones under the **o** in Jabesh and 1Ch 10:12
become like an **o** whose leaves Is 1:30
Like the terebinth or the **o**, Is 6:13
or he takes a cypress or an **o**. Is 44:14
green tree and every leafy **o**— Ezk 6:13

OAKS *(10)*
live beside the **o** of Mamre at Gn 13:18
who was at the **o** belonging to Gn 14:13
Abraham at the **o** of Mamre while Gn 18:1
Gilgal, near the **o** of Moreh? Dt 11:30
against all the **o** of Bashan, Is 2:13
who burn with lust among the **o**, Is 57:5
made your oars of **o** from Bashan. Ezk 27:6
the hills, and under **o**, poplars, Hs 4:13
and he was as sturdy as the **o**; Am 2:9
Wail, **o** of Bashan, for the Zch 11:2

OAR *(1)*
those who handle an **o** disembark Ezk 27:29

OARS *(1)*
They made your **o** of oaks from Ezk 27:6

OATH *(116)*
my hand in an **o** to the LORD, Gn 14:22
that the two of them swore an **o**. Gn 21:31
you are free from this **o** to me, Gn 24:8
and swore an **o** to him concerning Gn 24:9
My master put me under this **o**: Gn 24:37
free from my **o** if you go to my Gn 24:41
you will be free from my **o**.' Gn 24:41
confirm the **o** that I swore to Gn 26:3
there should be an **o** between two Gn 26:28
and swore an **o** to each other. Gn 26:31
He called it **O**. Therefore the Gn 26:33
my father made me take an **o**, Gn 50:5
father in keeping with your **o**." Gn 50:6
made the Israelites take an **o**: Gn 50:25
the Israelites swear a solemn **o**, Ex 13:19
must be an **o** before the LORD Ex 22:11
Its owner must accept ⌊the **o**⌋, Ex 22:11
may speak rashly in an **o**— Lv 5:4
to take an **o** and will say to Nm 5:19
woman take the **o** with the sworn Nm 5:21
or swears an **o** to put himself Nm 30:2
under an obligation with an **o**, Nm 30:10
that day, and He swore an **o**: Nm 32:10
He grew angry and swore an **o**: Dt 1:34
that He swore to them by **o**, Dt 4:31
and kept the **o** He swore to your Dt 7:8
so that you may enter into His **o** Dt 29:12
and this **o** not only with you Dt 29:14
hears the words of this **o**, Dt 29:19
free from this **o** you made us Jos 2:17
free from the **o** you made us Jos 2:20
community swore an **o** to them. Jos 9:15
had sworn an **o** to them by the Jos 9:18
We have sworn an **o** to them by Jos 9:19
because of the **o** we swore to Jos 9:20
their gods or make an **o** to them; Jos 23:7
Israel had sworn an **o** at Mizpah: Jdg 21:1
For a great **o** had been taken Jdg 21:5
guilty ⌊of breaking your **o**⌋.'" Jdg 21:22
placed the troops under an **o**: 1Sm 14:24
of it because they feared the **o**. 1Sm 14:26
make the troops swear the **o**. 1Sm 14:27
advice and swore an **o**: 1Sm 19:6
still day, but David took an **o**: 2Sm 3:35
Then the king gave him his **o**. 2Sm 19:23
had taken an **o** concerning them, 2Sm 21:2
because of the **o** of the LORD 2Sm 21:7
The king swore an **o** and said, 1Kg 1:29
Solomon took an **o** by the LORD: 1Kg 2:23
the LORD's **o** and the command 1Kg 2:43
and is forced to take an **o**, 1Kg 8:31
comes to take an **o** before Your 1Kg 8:31
with them and put them under **o**. 2Kg 11:4
swore an **o** to them and their 2Kg 25:24
to take an **o** and he comes to 2Ch 6:22
comes to take an **o** before Your 2Ch 6:22
They took an **o** to the LORD in a 2Ch 15:14
All Judah rejoiced over the **o**, 2Ch 15:15
we have taken an **o** of loyalty to Ezr 4:14
Israel take an **o** to do what had Ezr 10:5
been said; so they took the **o**. Ezr 10:5
everyone take an **o** to do this. Neh 5:12
in Judah were bound by **o** to him, Neh 6:18
with a sworn **o** to follow the law Neh 10:29
them to take an **o** before God and Neh 13:25
I have sworn an **o** to David My Ps 89:3
have sworn an **o** by My holiness; Ps 89:35
them ⌊with an **o**⌋ that He would Ps 106:26
has sworn an **o** and will not take Ps 110:4
how he swore an **o** to the LORD, Ps 132:2
The LORD swore an **o** to David, Ps 132:11
Concerning an **o** by God, Ec 8:2
as for the one who takes an **o**, Ec 9:2
so for the one who fears an **o**. Ec 9:2
LORD of Hosts ⌊has taken an **o**⌋: Is 5:9
establish the **o** I swore to your Jr 11:5
an **o** to them and their men, Jr 40:9
have despised the **o** by breaking Ezk 16:59
with him, putting him under **o**. Ezk 17:13
whose **o** he despised and whose Ezk 17:16
despised the **o** by breaking the Ezk 17:18
his head My **o** that he despised Ezk 17:19
I swore an **o** to the descendants Ezk 20:5
who have sworn an **o** to the Ezk 21:23
I swore an **o** against them"— Ezk 44:12
Beth-aven, and do not swear an **o**: Hs 4:15
are ready to be used with an **o**. Hab 3:9
You must not break your **o**, Mt 5:33
you, don't take an **o** at all: Mt 5:34
promised with an **o** to give her Mt 14:7
takes an **o** by the sanctuary Mt 23:16
whoever takes an **o** by the gold Mt 23:16
sanctuary is bound by his **o**.' Mt 23:16
'Whoever takes an **o** by the altar, Mt 23:18
takes an **o** by the gift that Mt 23:18
is on it is bound by his **o**.' Mt 23:18
one who takes an **o** by the altar Mt 23:20
the altar takes an **o** by it and Mt 23:20
who takes an **o** by the sanctuary Mt 23:21
takes an **o** by it and by Him Mt 23:21
who takes an **o** by heaven takes Mt 23:22
takes an **o** by God's throne Mt 23:22
living God I place You under **o**: Mt 26:63
again he denied it with an **o**, Mt 26:72
to curse and to swear with an **o**, Mt 26:74
to curse and to swear with an **o**, Mk 14:71
o that He swore to our father Lk 1:73
had sworn an **o** to him to seat Ac 2:30
them a confirming **o** ends every Heb 6:16
He guaranteed it with an **o**, Heb 6:17
of this ⌊happened⌋ without an **o**. Heb 7:20
became priests without an **o**, Heb 7:20
but He with an **o** made by the One Heb 7:21
promise of the **o**, which came Heb 7:28
or by earth or with any other **o**. Jms 5:12
He swore an **o** by the One who Rv 10:6

OATHS *(7)*
and take ⌊your⌋ **o** in His name. Dt 6:13
to Him and take **o** in His name. Dt 10:20
taking false **o** while making Hs 10:4
must keep your **o** to the Lord. Mt 5:33
because of his **o** and his guests. Mt 14:9
So he swore **o** to her: Mk 6:23
because of his **o** and the guests Mk 6:26

OBADIAH *(21)*
Ahab called for **O**, who was in 1Kg 18:3
O was a man who greatly feared 1Kg 18:3
Ahab said to **O**, "Go throughout 1Kg 18:5
and **O** went the other way by 1Kg 18:6
While **O** was ⌊walking⌋ along the 1Kg 18:7
When **O** recognized him, he fell 1Kg 18:7
But **O** said, "What sin have I 1Kg 18:9
O went to meet Ahab and report 1Kg 18:16
Arnan, **O**, and Shecaniah. 1Ch 3:21
Michael, **O**, Joel, Isshiah. 1Ch 7:3
Ishmael, Sheariah, **O**, and Hanan. 1Ch 8:38
O son of Shemaiah, son of Galal, 1Ch 9:16
Ishmael, Sheariah, **O**, and Hanan. 1Ch 9:44
was the chief, **O** second, Eliab 1Ch 12:9
for Zebulun, Ishmaiah son of **O**; 1Ch 27:19
Ben-hail, **O**, Zechariah, Nethanel 2Ch 17:7
were Jahath and **O** the Levites 2Ch 34:12
O son of Jehiel from Joab's Ezr 8:9
Harim, Meremoth, **O**, Neh 10:5
Mattaniah, Bakbukiah, and **O**. Neh 12:25
The vision of **O**. This is what Ob 1

OBAL *(1)*
(AKA EBAL)
O, Abimael, Sheba, Gn 10:28

OBED *(13)*
to Naomi," and they named him **O**. Ru 4:17
fathered Boaz, who fathered **O**. Ru 4:21
And **O** fathered Jesse, who Ru 4:22
Boaz fathered **O**, and Obed 1Ch 2:12
Obed, and **O** fathered Jesse. 1Ch 2:12
Ephlal, and Ephlal fathered **O**. 1Ch 2:37
O fathered Jehu, and Jehu 1Ch 2:38
Eliel, **O**, and Jaasiel the 1Ch 11:47
Othni, Rephael, **O**, and Elzabad; 1Ch 26:7
Azariah son of **O**, Maaseiah son 2Ch 23:1
Boaz fathered **O** by Ruth, Obed Mt 1:5
Obed by Ruth, **O** fathered Jesse, Mt 1:5
⌊son⌋ of **O**, ⌊son⌋ of Boaz, Lk 3:32

OBED-EDOM *(14)*
to the house of **O** the Gittite. 2Sm 6:10
the LORD blessed **O** and his whole 2Sm 6:11
to the house of **O** the Gittite. 1Ch 13:13
and the gatekeepers **O** and Jeiel. 1Ch 15:18
Mikneiah, **O**, Jeiel, and Azaziah 1Ch 15:21
O and Jehiah were also to be 1Ch 15:24
of the LORD from the house of **O**. 1Ch 15:25
Eliab, Benaiah, **O**, and Jeiel 1Ch 16:5

⌊He also left⌋ **O** and his 68 1Ch 16:38
O son of Jeduthun and Hosah 1Ch 16:38
O also had sons: Shemaiah the 1Ch 26:4
the sons of **O** with their sons 1Ch 26:8
for the work—62 from **O**. 1Ch 26:8
found with **O** in God's temple 2Ch 25:24

OBED-EDOM'S *(4)*
LORD has blessed **O** family and 2Sm 6:12
brought up from **O** house to the 2Sm 6:12
remained with **O** family in his 1Ch 13:14
O was the south ⌊gate⌋, and his 1Ch 26:15

OBEDIENCE *(21)*
comes and the **o** of the peoples Gn 49:10
them in **o** to the LORD as he Nm 3:16
and his sons in **o** to the LORD, Nm 3:51
had walked in **o** to the LORD's Jdg 2:17
went up in **o** to Gad's command 2Sm 24:19
and despises **o** to a mother, Pr 30:17
to draw near in **o** than to offer Ec 5:1
In **o** to this, they entered the Ac 5:21
bring about the **o** of faith among Rm 1:5
the one man's **o** the many will be Rm 5:19
to death or of **o** leading to Rm 6:16
The report of your **o** has reached Rm 16:19
to advance the **o** of faith among Rm 16:26
remembers the **o** of all of you, 2Co 7:15
God for your **o** to the confession 2Co 9:13
captive to the **o** of Christ. 2Co 10:5
once your **o** is complete. 2Co 10:6
Since I am confident of your **o**, Phm 21
He learned **o** through what He Heb 5:8
by the Spirit for **o** and ⌊for 1Pt 1:2
By **o** to the truth, having 1Pt 1:22

OBEDIENT *(10)*
Your servant an **o** heart to judge 1Kg 3:9
do His word, **o** to His command. Ps 103:20
are willing and **o**, you will eat Is 1:19
to Nazareth and was **o** to them. Lk 2:51
priests became **o** to the faith. Ac 6:7
to someone as **o** slaves, Rm 6:16
the Gentiles **o** by word and deed Rm 15:18
if you are **o** in everything. 2Co 2:9
by becoming **o** to the point Php 2:8
As **o** children, do not be 1Pt 1:14

OBEDIENTLY *(1)*
they serve Him **o**, they will end Jb 36:11

OBEY *(140)*
Now **o** every order I give you, Gn 27:8
o me and go get them for me. Gn 27:13
my people will **o** your commands. Gn 41:40
me and will not **o** me but say, Ex 4:1
that I should **o** Him by letting Ex 5:2
will carefully **o** the LORD your Ex 15:26
you will carefully **o** Him and do Ex 23:22
We will do and **o** everything that Ex 24:7
if you do not **o** Me and observe Lv 26:14
these things you will not **o** Me, Lv 26:18
Me and are unwilling to **o** Me, Lv 26:21
you do not **o** Me but act with Lv 26:27
these 10 times and did not **o** Me, Nm 14:22
and do not **o** all these commands Nm 15:22
commands and **o** them and not Nm 15:39
remember and **o** all My commands Nm 15:40
community will **o** ⌊him⌋. Nm 27:20
God in later days and **o** Him. Dt 4:30
we will listen and **o**.' Dt 5:27
if you do not **o** the LORD your Dt 8:20
You did not believe or **o** Him. Dt 9:23
you carefully **o** My commands I am Dt 11:13
you **o** the commands of the LORD Dt 11:27
if you do not **o** the commands of Dt 11:28
Be careful to **o** all these things Dt 12:28
occur⌋ if you **o** the LORD your Dt 13:18
if only you **o** the LORD your God Dt 15:5
son who does not **o** his father or Dt 21:18
he doesn't **o** us. He's a glutton Dt 21:20
and ordinances, and **o** Him. Dt 26:17
O the LORD your God and follow Dt 27:10
you faithfully **o** the LORD your Dt 28:1
because you **o** the LORD your God: Dt 28:2
you **o** the commands of the LORD Dt 28:9
if you do not **o** the LORD your Dt 28:15
you did not **o** the LORD your God Dt 28:45
not careful to **o** all the words Dt 28:58
you did not **o** the LORD your God Dt 28:62
your God and **o** Him with all your Dt 30:2
you will again **o** Him and follow Dt 30:8
when you **o** the LORD your God by Dt 30:10
LORD your God, **o** Him, and remain Dt 30:20
We will **o** you, just as we obeyed Jos 1:17
and does not **o** your words in all Jos 1:18
because they did not **o** the LORD. Jos 5:6
Only carefully **o** the command and Jos 22:5
the LORD our God and **o** Him." Jos 24:24
But you did not **o** Me.' " Jdg 6:10
would not **o** their fellow Jdg 20:13
worship and **o** Him, and if you 1Sm 12:14
So why didn't you **o** the LORD? 1Sm 15:19
"But I did **o** the LORD!" 1Sm 15:20
to **o** is better than sacrifice, 1Sm 15:22
You did not **o** the LORD and did 1Sm 28:18
as soon as they hear, they **o** me. 2Sm 22:45
The sentence is fair; I will **o**.' 1Kg 2:42
if you **o** all I command you, 1Kg 11:38
and if you will **o** me, bring me 2Kg 10:6
not listen, and they did not **o**. 2Kg 18:12
people are to **o** the requirement 2Ch 23:6
of the LORD, **o** ⌊it⌋, and teach Ezr 7:10
and would not **o** Your Neh 9:29
their necks, and would not **o**. Neh 9:29
ancestors did not **o** Your law or Neh 9:34
peoples to ⌊**o**⌋ the law of God— Neh 10:28
to carefully **o** all the commands Neh 10:29
she refused to **o** King Ahasuerus' Est 1:15
they do not **o**, they will cross Jb 36:12
as soon as they hear, they **o** me. Ps 18:44
to Me; Israel did not **o** Me. Ps 81:11
His statutes and **o** His laws. Ps 105:45
and I will **o** it and follow it Ps 119:34
⌊practice⌋: I **o** Your precepts. Ps 119:56
but I **o** Your precepts with all Ps 119:69
and I will **o** the decree You have Ps 119:88
because I **o** Your precepts. Ps 119:100
am resolved to **o** Your statutes Ps 119:112
so that I may **o** my God's Ps 119:115
wonderful; therefore I **o** them. Ps 119:129
I will **o** Your statutes. Ps 119:145
I **o** Your decrees and love them Ps 119:167
I **o** Your precepts and decrees, Ps 119:168
I didn't **o** my teachers or listen Pr 5:13
My son, **o** my words, and treasure Pr 7:1
children who do not **o** the LORD's Is 30:9
many things, you do not **o**. Is 42:20
him listen and **o** in the future. Is 42:23
O Me, and then I will be your Jr 7:23
and did not **o** My voice or walk Jr 9:13
man who does not **o** the words of Jr 11:3
'**O** Me, and do everything that I Jr 11:4
O the words of this covenant and Jr 11:6
time and time again: **O** My voice. Jr 11:7
they would not **o** or pay Jr 11:8
who refused to **o** My words and Jr 11:10
if they will not **o**, then I will Jr 12:17
and glory, but they would not **o**. Jr 13:11
But if you do not **o** these words, Jr 22:5
But you would not **o** Me'— Jr 25:7
ways and deeds and **o** the voice Jr 26:13
but they did not **o** Your voice or Jr 32:23
ancestors did not **o** Me or pay Jr 34:14
would not pay attention or **o** Me. Jr 35:15
of the land did not **o** the words Jr 37:2
O the voice of the LORD in what Jr 38:20
we will **o** the voice of the LORD Jr 42:6
We will certainly **o** the voice of Jr 42:6
so as not to **o** the voice of the Jr 42:13
the armies did not **o** the voice Jr 43:4
because they did not **o** the voice Jr 43:7
LORD and didn't **o** the LORD's Jr 44:23
words, but they don't **o** them. Ezk 33:31
words, but they don't **o** them. Ezk 33:32
and keep My statutes and **o** them. Ezk 37:24
rulers will serve and **o** Him.' Dn 7:27
turned away, refusing to **o** You. Dn 9:11
you fully **o** the LORD your God. Zch 6:15
a rock so as not to **o** the law or Zch 7:12
the winds and the sea **o** Him!" Mt 8:27
spirits, and they **o** Him." Mk 1:27
the wind and the sea **o** Him!" Mk 4:41
and the waves, and they **o** Him!" Lk 8:25
in the sea,' and it will **o** you. Lk 17:6
We must **o** God rather than men. Ac 5:29
has given to those who **o** Him." Ac 5:32
were unwilling to **o** him, Ac 7:39
so that you **o** its desires. Rm 6:12
are slaves of that one you **o**— Rm 6:16
But all did not **o** the gospel. Rm 10:16
o your parents in the Lord, Eph 6:1
o your human masters with fear Eph 6:5
o your parents in everything, Col 3:20
o your human masters in Col 3:22
those who don't **o** the gospel of 2Th 1:8
does not **o** our instruction 2Th 3:14
authorities, to **o**, to be ready Ti 3:1
salvation to all who **o** Him, Heb 5:9
O your leaders and submit to Heb 13:17
of horses to make them **o** us, Jms 3:3
we love God and **o** His commands. 1Jn 5:2

OBEYED *(37)*
because you have **o** My command. Gn 22:18
I have **o** the LORD my God; Dt 26:14
the Israelites **o** him and did as Dt 34:9
as we **o** Moses in everything. Jos 1:17
you and have **o** me in everything Jos 22:2
But you have not **o** Me. Jdg 2:2
afraid of the people, I **o** them. 1Sm 15:24
Look, your servant has **o** you. 1Sm 28:21
have not **o** the words of this 2Kg 22:13
prospered, and all Israel **o** him. 1Ch 29:23
She **o** Mordecai's orders, as she Est 2:20
tree and have not **o** My voice. Jr 3:13
We have not **o** the voice of the Jr 3:25
attention to His word and **o**? Jr 23:18
time again, but you have not **o**. Jr 25:3
but you have not **o** or even paid Jr 25:4
'Because you have not **o** My words, Jr 25:8
any longer—**o** and freed them. Jr 34:10
You have not **o** Me by proclaiming Jr 34:17
We have **o** the voice of Jonadab, Jr 35:8
tents and have **o** and done as our Jr 35:10
they have **o** their ancestor's Jr 35:14
again, and you have not **o** Me! Jr 35:14
but these people have not **o** Me. Jr 35:16
but they have not **o**, and I have Jr 35:17
'Because you have **o** the command Jr 35:18
the LORD and have not **o** Him, Jr 40:3
but you have not **o** the voice of Jr 42:21
and have not **o** the voice of the Dn 9:10
But we have not **o** Him. Dn 9:14
nations that have not **o** ⌊Me⌋. Mc 5:15
She has not **o**; she has not Zph 3:2
of the people **o** the voice of the Hg 1:12
o from the heart that pattern Rm 6:17
just as you have always **o**, Php 2:12
o and went out to a place he was Heb 11:8
just as Sarah **o** Abraham, calling 1Pt 3:6

OBEYING *(7)*
and continue **o** all that is Jos 23:6
as much as in **o** the LORD? 1Sm 15:22
not waver in **o** the LORD his God 2Ch 27:6
of his evil heart, not **o** Me. Jr 16:12
obstinate, not **o** My words.' " Jr 19:15
but are **o** unrighteousness; Rm 2:8
prevented you from **o** the truth? Gl 5:7

OBIL *(1)*
O the Ishmaelite was in charge 1Ch 27:30

OBJECT *(47)*
you into an **o** of your people's Nm 5:21
with an iron **o** and death results Nm 35:16
his hand a wooden **o** capable of Nm 35:18
or throws ⌊an **o**⌋ at him with Nm 35:20
or throws any **o** at him without Nm 35:22
will be an **o** of horror to all Dt 28:25
You will become an **o** of horror, Dt 28:37
will become an **o** of scorn and 1Kg 9:7
I will make it an **o** of scorn and 2Ch 7:20
and He made them an **o** of terror, 2Ch 29:8
He made them an **o** of horror as 2Ch 30:7
He has made me an **o** of scorn to Jb 17:6
have become an **o** of scorn to Jb 30:9
I am an **o** of dread to my Ps 31:11
You make us an **o** of reproach to Ps 44:13
have become an **o** of reproach to Ps 79:4
have become an **o** of ridicule to Ps 109:25
will become an **o** of contempt, Is 16:14
make you an **o** of eternal pride Is 60:15
horror, a perpetual **o** of scorn; Jr 18:16
city desolate, an **o** of scorn. Jr 19:8
I will make them an **o** of horror Jr 24:9
a disgrace, an **o** of scorn, Jr 24:9
an **o** of scorn and cursing— Jr 25:18
this city an **o** of cursing for Jr 26:6
an **o** of scorn and a disgrace Jr 29:18

OBTAINED *(12)*
If I have **o** your approval, Est 7:3
Wealth **o** by fraud will dwindle, Pr 13:11
their God wine **o** through fines. Am 2:8
of God could be **o** with money! Ac 8:20
Since I have **o** help that comes Ac 26:22
we have **o** access by faith into Rm 5:2
have **o** righteousness— Rm 9:30
Abraham **o** the promise. Heb 6:15
But Jesus has now **o** a superior Heb 8:6
having **o** eternal redemption. Heb 9:12
justice, **o** promises, shut Heb 11:33
those who have **o** a faith of 2Pt 1:1

OBTAINING *(1)*
it was desirable for **o** wisdom. Gn 3:6

OBTAINS *(3)*
he prospers and **o** enough to Lv 25:26
me finds life and **o** favor from Pr 8:35
good thing and **o** favor from the Pr 18:22

OBVIOUS *(8)*
so their fasting is **o** to people. Mt 6:16
an **o** sign, evident to all who Ac 4:16
each one's work will become **o**, 1Co 3:13
it is **o** that He who puts 1Co 15:27
Look at what is **o**. If anyone is 2Co 10:7
the works of the flesh are **o**: Gl 5:19
good works are **o**, and those that 1Tm 5:25
that are not ⌊**o**⌋ cannot remain 1Tm 5:25

OCCASION *(5)*
LORD listened to me on that **o**. Dt 9:19
also listened to me on this **o**; Dt 10:10
who was seeking an **o** against the Jdg 14:4
There is an **o** for everything, Ec 3:1
took this **o** to come forward Dn 3:8

OCCASIONS *(3)*
sacrifices and on your joyous **o**, Nm 10:10
to seek omens as on previous **o**, Nm 24:1
all the LORD's appointed holy **o**, Ezr 3:5

OCCULT *(4)*
same thing by their **o** practices. Ex 7:11
same thing by their **o** practices. Ex 7:22
same thing by their **o** practices Ex 8:7
gnats using their **o** practices, Ex 8:18

OCCUPANTS *(1)*
fields to new **o**, for from the Jr 8:10

OCCUPATION *(4)*
you and asks, 'What is your **o**?' Gn 46:33
his brothers, "What is your **o**?" Gn 47:3
grief, and his **o** is sorrowful; Ec 2:23
of the same **o**, stayed with them Ac 18:3

OCCUPIED *(9)*
they will be **o** with it and not Ex 5:9
the time they **o** the land until Ex 10:6
to the king and **o** the highest Est 1:14
miserable task to keep them **o**. Ec 1:13
has given people to keep them **o**. Ec 3:10
God keeps him **o** with the joy of Ec 5:20
David that Aram had **o** Ephraim, Is 7:2
to a chamber ⌊**o** by⌋ the sons Jr 35:4
Paul was **o** with preaching the Ac 18:5

OCCUPY *(6)*
redemption of any land you **o**. Lv 25:24
was looking for territory to **o**. Jdg 18:1
you who **o** the mountain summit, Jr 49:16
flesh, to **o** My sanctuary, you Ezk 44:7
Yet they will **o** My sanctuary, Ezk 44:11
rebuild and **o** ruined cities, Am 9:14

OCCUR *(4)*
This ⌊will **o**⌋ if you obey the Dt 13:18
us, how did this outrage **o**?" Jdg 20:3
will not happen; it will not **o**. Is 7:7
them to you before they **o**." Is 42:9

OCCURRED *(15)*
the one that had **o** in Abraham's Gn 26:1
hail that has ever **o** in Egypt Ex 9:18
nothing like it had **o** in the Ex 9:24
outrage that has **o** among you? Jdg 20:12
has it **o** that one tribe is Jdg 21:3
how this sin has **o** today. 1Sm 14:38
Mordecai learned all that had **o**, Est 4:1
Suddenly I acted, and they **o**. Is 48:3
announced it to you before it **o**, Is 48:5
as never has **o** since nations Dn 12:1
As he sowed, this **o**: Mk 4:4
So a division **o** among the crowd Jn 7:43
When this sound **o**, the multitude Ac 2:6
A violent earthquake **o**; Rv 6:12
severe earthquake **o** like no Rv 16:18

OCCURS *(2)*
and slaughter **o** within you? Ezk 26:15
If a disaster **o** in a city, Am 3:6

OCEAN *(4)*
o depths say, "It's not in me, Jb 28:14
all sea monsters and **o** depths, Ps 148:7
horizon on the surface of the **o**, Pr 8:27
fountains of the **o** gushed forth, Pr 8:28

OCEANS *(1)*
walked in the depths of the **o**? Jb 38:16

OCHRAN *(5)*
Pagiel son of **O** from Asher; Nm 1:13
Asherites is Pagiel son of **O**. Nm 2:27
eleventh day Pagiel son of **O**, Nm 7:72
the offering of Pagiel son of **O**. Nm 7:77
Pagiel son of **O** was over the Nm 10:26

ODDS *(1)*
he will live at **o** with all his Gn 16:12

ODED *(3)*
of God came on Azariah son of **O**. 2Ch 15:1
Azariah son of⌋ **O** the prophet, 2Ch 15:8
of the LORD named **O** was there. 2Ch 28:9

ODIOUS *(1)*
making me **o** to the inhabitants Gn 34:30

ODOR *(1)*
was a terrible **o** in the land. Ex 8:14

OF *(23,487)*
(See pp. xi-xii.)

OFF *(383)*
(See pp. xi-xii.)

OFFEND *(3)*
One who loves to **o** loves strife; Pr 17:19
But, so we won't **o** them, go to Mt 17:27
asked them, "Does this **o** you? Jn 6:61

OFFENDED *(7)*
and his baker **o** their master, Gn 40:1
o brother is ⌊harder to reach⌋ Pr 18:19
was no justice, and He was **o**. Is 59:15
anyone is not **o** because of Me, Mt 11:6
And they were **o** by Him. Mt 13:57
So they were **o** by Him. Mk 6:3
who is not **o** because of Me is Lk 7:23

OFFENDS *(2)*
If someone **o** by sinning Lv 5:15
someone sins and **o** the LORD by Lv 6:2

OFFENSE *(14)*
found guilty of an **o** deserving Dt 21:22
guilty of an **o** deserving death Dt 22:26
Please forgive your servant's **o**, 1Sm 25:28
dump because of this ⌊**o**⌋. Ezr 6:11
conceals an **o** promotes love, Pr 17:9
his virtue is to overlook an **o**. Pr 19:11
For what **o** has the LORD our God Jr 5:19
Pharisees took **o** when they heard Mt 15:12
are an **o** to Me because you're Mt 16:23
to that man by whom the **o** comes. Mt 18:7
many will take **o**, betray one Mt 24:10
I had not committed a capital **o**. Ac 28:18
Give no **o** to the Jews or the 1Co 10:32
that case the **o** of the cross has Gl 5:11

OFFENSES *(7)*
or repaid us according to our **o**. Ps 103:10
but love covers all **o**. Pr 10:12
calmness puts great **o** to rest. Ec 10:4
Woe to the world because of **o**. Mt 18:7
For **o** must come, but woe to that Mt 18:7
His disciples, "**O** will certainly Lk 17:1
is an avenger of all these **o**, 1Th 4:6

OFFENSIVE *(7)*
be careful to avoid anything **o**. Dt 23:9
My breath is **o** to my wife, Jb 19:17
See if there is any **o** way in me; Ps 139:24
where the **o** statue that provokes Ezk 8:3
there was this **o** statue north Ezk 8:5
their **o** offerings there Ezk 20:28
says anything **o** against the God Dn 3:29

OFFER *(159)*
and **o** him there as a burnt Gn 22:2
You must not **o** the blood of My Ex 23:18
what you are to **o** regularly on Ex 29:38
In the morning **o** one lamb, Ex 29:39
at twilight **o** the other lamb. Ex 29:39
the first lamb **o** two quarts of Ex 29:40
You are to **o** the second lamb at Ex 29:41
O a grain offering and a drink Ex 29:41
You must not **o** unauthorized Ex 30:9
He is to **o** this bull just as he Lv 4:20
he will **o** it the same way. Lv 4:20
The priest is to **o** the burnt Lv 14:20
of meeting and **o** them as Lv 17:5
no longer **o** their sacrifices Lv 17:7
When you **o** a fellowship Lv 19:5
must **o** an unblemished male from Lv 22:19
are to **o** a year-old male lamb Lv 23:12
The priest is to **o** one as a sin Nm 6:11
He will also **o** the ram as a Nm 6:17
the priest will **o** the Nm 6:17
you are to **o** a contribution to Nm 15:19
You are to **o** a loaf from your Nm 15:20
o it just like a contribution Nm 15:20
approach to **o** incense before Nm 16:40
O one lamb in the morning and Nm 28:4
O the second lamb at twilight, Nm 28:8
o six quarts with each bull and Nm 28:20
O two quarts with each of the Nm 28:21
O these with the morning burnt Nm 28:23
You are to **o** the same food each Nm 28:24
O ⌊them⌋ with their drink Nm 28:31
O a burnt offering as a pleasing Nm 29:2
Also ⌊**o**⌋ one male goat as a sin Nm 29:5
⌊**O**⌋ one male goat for a sin Nm 29:11
Also ⌊**o**⌋ one male goat as a sin Nm 29:16
Also ⌊**o**⌋ one male goat as a sin Nm 29:19
Also ⌊**o**⌋ one male goat as a sin Nm 29:22
Also ⌊**o**⌋ one male goat as a sin Nm 29:25
Also ⌊**o**⌋ one male goat as a sin Nm 29:28
Also ⌊**o**⌋ one male goat as a sin Nm 29:31
Also ⌊**o**⌋ one male goat as a sin Nm 29:34
Also ⌊**o**⌋ one male goat as a sin Nm 29:38
You must **o** these to the LORD at Nm 29:39
with an **o** of peace to Sihon Dt 2:26
Be careful not to **o** your burnt Dt 12:13
You must **o** your burnt offerings Dt 12:14
the people who **o** a sacrifice, Dt 18:3
you must make an **o** of peace. Dt 20:10
it accepts your **o** of peace and Dt 20:11
your God and **o** burnt offerings Dt 27:6
there they **o** acceptable Dt 33:19
intended⌋ to **o** burnt offerings Jos 22:23
among you and **o** your hearts to Jos 24:23
second bull and **o** it as a burnt Jdg 6:26
I will **o** it as a burnt offering. Jdg 11:31
offering, **o** it to the LORD. Jdg 13:16
together to **o** a great sacrifice Jdg 16:23
with her husband to **o** the annual 1Sm 2:19
to **o** sacrifices on My altar, 1Sm 2:28
come to you to **o** burnt offerings 1Sm 10:8
forced myself to **o** the burnt 1Sm 13:12
in order to **o** a sacrifice to 1Sm 15:15
The people told him about the **o**, 1Sm 17:27
of him and asked about the **o**. 1Sm 17:30
take whatever he wants and **o** it. 2Sm 24:22
for I will not **o** to the LORD my 2Sm 24:24
regularly go to **o** sacrifices 1Kg 12:27
no longer **o** a burnt offering 2Kg 5:17
they went in to **o** sacrifices and 2Kg 10:24
O on the great altar the morning 2Kg 16:15
⌊Also **o**⌋ the burnt offering of 2Kg 16:15
o a prayer for the surviving 2Kg 19:4
to **o** burnt offerings regularly, 1Ch 16:40
to you or **o** burnt offerings 1Ch 21:24
to **o** praise and to 2Ch 8:14
They **o** a burnt offering and 2Ch 13:11
to **o** burnt offerings to the LORD 2Ch 23:18
have no right to **o** incense to 2Ch 26:18
have the right to **o** incense. 2Ch 26:18
censer in his hand to **o** incense, 2Ch 26:19
of Judah to **o** incense to other 2Ch 28:25
and did not **o** burnt offerings in 2Ch 29:7
to **o** them on the altar of the 2Ch 29:21
the lay people to **o** to the LORD, 2Ch 35:12
in order to **o** burnt offerings Ezr 3:2
they began to **o** burnt offerings Ezr 3:6
so that they can **o** sacrifices of Ezr 6:10
and **o** them on the altar at the Ezr 7:17
Will they **o** sacrifices? Neh 4:2
the morning to **o** burnt offerings Jb 1:5
together to go and **o** sympathy Jb 2:11
the tents of those who **o** bribes. Jb 15:34

this be the consolation you **o**. Jb 21:2
So how can you **o** me such futile Jb 21:34
and **o** a burnt offering for Jb 42:8
O sacrifices in righteousness Ps 4:5
I will **o** sacrifices in His tent Ps 27:6
the upright in heart **o** praise. Ps 64:10
I will **o** You fattened sheep as Ps 66:15
kings of Sheba and Seba **o** gifts. Ps 72:10
Let them **o** sacrifices of Ps 107:22
I will **o** You a sacrifice of Ps 116:17
than to **o** the sacrifice as Ec 5:1
even if you **o** countless prayers, Is 1:15
They will **o** sacrifices and Is 19:21
Therefore **o** a prayer for the Is 37:4
went up there to **o** sacrifice. Is 57:7
and if you **o** yourself to the Is 58:10
Do not **o** a cry or a prayer on Jr 7:16
If they **o** burnt offering and Jr 14:12
before Me to **o** burnt offerings, Jr 33:18
of the LORD to **o** them a drink of Jr 35:2
of heaven and **o** drink offerings Jr 44:17
of heaven and to **o** her drink Jr 44:18
is no one to **o** her comfort, Lm 1:2
Let him **o** ⌊his⌋ cheek to the one Lm 3:30
Even jackals **o** ⌊their⌋ breasts Lm 4:3
When you **o** your gifts, making Ezk 20:31
While they **o** false visions and Ezk 21:29
You will **o** a goat for a sin Ezk 43:25
the priests will **o** your burnt Ezk 43:27
before Me to **o** Me fat and blood. Ezk 44:15
the contribution you are to **o**: Ezk 45:13
He is to **o** his burnt offering or Ezk 46:12
You must **o** an unblemished Ezk 46:13
you will **o** it every morning. Ezk 46:13
They will **o** the lamb, the grain Ezk 46:15
I **o** thanks and praise to You, Dn 2:23
Though they **o** sacrificial gifts Hs 8:13
⌊so you can⌋ **o** grain and wine to Jl 2:14
O leavened bread as a thank Am 4:5
Even if you **o** Me your burnt Am 5:22
even what they **o** there is Hg 2:14
dreams and **o** empty comfort. Zch 10:2
and then come and **o** your gift. Mt 5:24
and **o** the gift that Moses Mt 8:4
and **o** what Moses prescribed for Mk 1:44
and to **o** a sacrifice (according Lk 2:24
and **o** what Moses prescribed for Lk 5:14
on the cheek, **o** the other also. Lk 6:29
eating and drinking what they **o**, Lk 10:7
I don't have anything to **o** him.' Lk 11:6
he accepted ⌊the **o**⌋ and started Lk 22:6
crowds, intended to **o** sacrifice. Ac 14:13
am glad to **o** my defense in what Ac 24:10
And do not **o** any parts of it to Rm 6:13
from the dead, **o** yourselves to Rm 6:13
know that if you **o** yourselves to Rm 6:16
so now **o** them as slaves to Rm 6:19
the gospel and **o** it free of 1Co 9:18
to **o** both gifts and sacrifices Heb 5:1
doesn't need to **o** sacrifices Heb 7:27
is appointed to **o** gifts and Heb 8:3
also to have something to **o**. Heb 8:3
not do this to **o** Himself many Heb 9:25
continually **o** year after year Heb 10:1
let us continually **o** up to God a Heb 13:15
holy priesthood to **o** spiritual 1Pt 2:5
of incense to **o** with the prayers Rv 8:3

OFFERED *(105)*

clean bird and **o** burnt offerings Gn 8:20
took the ram and **o** it as a burnt Gn 22:13
Then Jacob **o** a sacrifice on the Gn 31:54
and he **o** sacrifices to the God Gn 46:1
and they **o** burnt offerings and Ex 24:5
they arose, **o** burnt offerings, Ex 32:6
Everyone who **o** a contribution of Ex 35:24
and **o** the burnt offering and the Ex 40:29
are not to be **o** on the altar as Lv 2:12
and they **o** a bull and a ram on Nm 23:2
altars and **o** a bull and a ram Nm 23:4
and **o** a bull and a ram on each Nm 23:14
Balaam said and **o** a bull and a Nm 23:30
goat is to be **o** as a sin Nm 28:15
It is to be **o** with its drink Nm 28:24
contribution they **o** to the LORD, Nm 31:52
or **o** any of it for the dead. Dt 26:14
Then they **o** burnt offerings to Jos 8:31
Bochim and **o** sacrifices there Jdg 2:5
them out and **o** them to Him under Jdg 6:19
second bull **o** up on the altar Jdg 6:28
offering and **o** them on a rock to Jdg 13:19
evening and **o** burnt offerings Jdg 20:26
and **o** burnt offerings and Jdg 21:4
and he **o** her roasted grain. Ru 2:14
Whenever Elkanah **o** a sacrifice, 1Sm 1:4
When any man **o** a sacrifice, 1Sm 2:13
up the cart and **o** the cows as a 1Sm 6:14
Beth-shemesh **o** burnt offerings 1Sm 6:15
a young lamb and **o** it as a whole 1Sm 7:9
Then he **o** the burnt offering. 1Sm 13:9
Then David **o** burnt offerings and 2Sm 6:17
Abiathar **o** ⌊sacrifices⌋ until 2Sm 15:24
Ahithophel **o** this proposal. 2Sm 17:6
LORD there and **o** burnt offerings 2Sm 24:25
He **o** 1,000 burnt offerings on 1Kg 3:4
and **o** burnt offerings and 1Kg 3:15
o tribute and served Solomon 1Kg 4:21
Solomon **o** a sacrifice of 1Kg 8:63
that was where he **o** the burnt 1Kg 8:64
a year Solomon **o** burnt offerings 1Kg 9:25
offerings he **o** at the LORD's 1Kg 10:5
He **o** sacrifices on the altar; 1Kg 12:32
He **o** sacrifices on the altar he 1Kg 12:33
o sacrifices on the altar, 1Kg 12:33
and **o** him as a burnt offering on 2Kg 3:27
He **o** his burnt offering and his 2Kg 16:13
Then they **o** burnt offerings and 1Ch 16:1
LORD there and **o** burnt offerings 1Ch 21:26
Jebusite, he **o** sacrifices there 1Ch 21:28
burnt offerings are **o** to the 1Ch 23:31
day they **o** sacrifices to 1Ch 29:21
Solomon **o** sacrifices there in 2Ch 1:6
o 1,000 burnt offerings on it. 2Ch 1:6
King Solomon **o** a sacrifice of 2Ch 7:5
when David **o** praise with them. 2Ch 7:6
that was where he **o** the burnt 2Ch 7:7
time Solomon **o** burnt offerings 2Ch 8:12
offerings he **o** at the LORD's 2Ch 9:4
They regularly **o** burnt offerings 2Ch 24:14
offering be **o** on the altar. 2Ch 29:27
of the LORD and **o** fellowship and 2Ch 33:16
foundation and **o** burnt offerings Ezr 3:3
⌊**o**⌋ burnt offerings each day, Ezr 3:4
⌊they **o**⌋ the regular burnt Ezr 3:5
of God's house they **o** 100 bulls, Ezr 6:17
who were present had **o**. Ezr 8:25
the captivity **o** burnt offerings Ezr 8:35
⌊they **o**⌋ a ram from the flock Ezr 10:19
that day they **o** great sacrifices Neh 12:43
They **o** him sympathy and comfort Jb 42:11
bulls will be **o** on Your altar. Ps 51:19
May prayer be **o** for him Ps 72:15
ate sacrifices **o** to lifeless Ps 106:28
you have **o** a grain offering; Is 57:6
where they **o** pleasing aromas Ezk 6:13
they **o** their sacrifices and Ezk 20:28
She **o** her sexual favors to them; Ezk 23:7
unblemished, must also be **o**. Ezk 43:25
My temple while you **o** My food— Ezk 44:7
and they **o** a sacrifice to the Jnh 1:16
it on a reed, and **o** Him a drink. Mt 27:48
it on a reed, **o** Him a drink, Mk 15:36
in those days, **o** sacrifice to Ac 7:41
hands, he **o** them money, Ac 8:18
abstain from food **o** to idols, Ac 15:29
For just as you **o** the parts of Rm 6:19
His own Son, but **o** Him up for us Rm 8:32
the firstfruits **o** up are holy, Rm 11:16
About food **o** to idols: 1Co 8:1
About eating food **o** to idols, 1Co 8:4
when they eat food **o** to an idol, 1Co 8:7
to eat food **o** to idols? 1Co 8:10
food **o** to idols is anything, 1Co 10:19
"This is food **o** to an idol," 1Co 10:28
earthly life, He **o** prayers and Heb 5:7
once for all when He **o** Himself. Heb 7:27
and sacrifices are **o** that cannot Heb 9:9
eternal Spirit **o** Himself without Heb 9:14
having been **o** once to bear the Heb 9:28
they have stopped being **o**, Heb 10:2
which are **o** according to the law Heb 10:8
By faith Abel **o** to God a better Heb 11:4
when he was tested, **o** up Isaac; Heb 11:17
by works when he **o** Isaac his son Jms 2:21

OFFERER *(2)*

The **o** must wash its entrails and Lv 1:9
The **o** must present all the fat Lv 7:3

OFFERING *(741)*

produce as an **o** to the LORD. Gn 4:3
And Abel also presented ⌊an **o**⌋— Gn 4:4
had regard for Abel and his **o**, Gn 4:4
have regard for Cain and his **o**. Gn 4:5
him there as a burnt **o** on one of Gn 22:2
wood for a burnt **o** and set out Gn 22:3
for the burnt **o** and laid it on Gn 22:6
is the lamb for the burnt **o**?" Gn 22:7
the lamb for the burnt **o**, Gn 22:8
it as a burnt **o** in place of his Gn 22:13
He poured a drink **o** on it and Gn 35:14
brought a burnt **o** and sacrifices Ex 18:12
of My festival **o** must not remain Ex 23:18
Israelites to take an **o** for Me. Ex 25:2
are to take My **o** from everyone Ex 25:2
This is the **o** you are to receive Ex 25:3
outside the camp; it is a sin **o**. Ex 29:14
it is a burnt **o** to the LORD. Ex 29:18
aroma, a fire **o** to the LORD. Ex 29:18
a presentation **o** before the LORD Ex 29:24
the altar on top of the burnt **o**, Ex 29:25
it is a fire **o** to the LORD. Ex 29:25
a presentation **o** before the LORD Ex 29:26
the presentation **o** that is waved Ex 29:27
a bull as a sin **o** each day for Ex 29:36
and a drink **o** of one quart of Ex 29:40
Offer a grain **o** and a drink Ex 29:41
offering and a drink **o** with it, Ex 29:41
aroma, a fire **o** to the LORD. Ex 29:41
regular burnt **o** throughout your Ex 29:42
be an incense ⌊**o**⌋ before the Ex 30:8
on it, or a burnt or grain **o**; Ex 30:9
are not to pour a drink **o** on it. Ex 30:9
of the sin **o** for atonement. Ex 30:10
by burning up an **o** to the LORD, Ex 30:20
altar of burnt **o** with all its Ex 30:28
altar of burnt **o** with all its Ex 31:9
Take up an **o** for the LORD among Ex 35:5
bring this as the LORD's **o**: Ex 35:5
altar of burnt **o** with its bronze Ex 35:16
and brought an **o** to the LORD to Ex 35:21
a presentation **o** of gold to the Ex 35:22
a freewill **o** to the LORD, Ex 35:29
else as an **o** for the sanctuary. Ex 36:6
altar of burnt **o** from acacia Ex 38:1
the presentation **o** that was used Ex 38:24
the presentation **o** totaled 5,310 Ex 38:29
the altar of burnt **o** in front of Ex 40:6
the altar of burnt **o** and all its Ex 40:10
altar of burnt **o** at the entrance Ex 40:29
offered the burnt **o** and the Ex 40:29
offering and the grain **o** on it, Ex 40:29
of you brings an **o** to the LORD Lv 1:2
may bring your **o** from the herd Lv 1:2
gift is a burnt **o** from the herd, Lv 1:3
head of the burnt **o** so it can be Lv 1:4
must skin the burnt **o** and cut it Lv 1:6
of it on the altar as a burnt **o**, Lv 1:9
a fire **o** of a pleasing aroma to Lv 1:9
gift for a burnt **o** is from the Lv 1:10
it is a burnt **o**, a fire offering Lv 1:13
a fire **o** of a pleasing aroma to Lv 1:13
the LORD is a burnt **o** of birds, Lv 1:14
is to present his **o** from the Lv 1:14
It is a burnt **o**, a fire offering Lv 1:17
a fire **o** of a pleasing aroma to Lv 1:17
presents a grain **o** as a gift to Lv 2:1
a fire **o** of a pleasing aroma to Lv 2:2
of the grain **o** will belong to Lv 2:3
present a grain **o** baked in an Lv 2:4
your gift is a grain **o** prepared Lv 2:5
pour oil on it; it is a grain **o**. Lv 2:6
gift is a grain **o** ⌊prepared⌋ in Lv 2:7
the LORD the grain **o** made in any Lv 2:8
from the grain **o** and burn it Lv 2:9
a fire **o** of a pleasing aroma to Lv 2:9
of the grain **o** will belong to Lv 2:10
No grain **o** that you present to Lv 2:11
honey as a fire **o** to the LORD. Lv 2:11
the LORD as an **o** of firstfruits, Lv 2:12
omit from your grain **o** the salt Lv 2:13
present a grain **o** of firstfruits Lv 2:14
for your grain **o** of firstfruits. Lv 2:14
on it; it is a grain **o**. Lv 2:15
as a fire **o** to the LORD. Lv 2:16
If his **o** is a fellowship Lv 3:1
the head of his **o** and slaughter Lv 3:2

as a fire **o** to the LORD: Lv 3:3
along with the burnt **o** that is Lv 3:5
a fire **o** of a pleasing aroma to Lv 3:5
If his **o** as a fellowship Lv 3:6
is presenting a lamb for his **o**, Lv 3:7
his hand on the head of his **o**, Lv 3:8
as a fire **o** to the LORD Lv 3:9
as food, a fire **o** to the LORD. Lv 3:11
If his **o** is a goat, he is to Lv 3:12
part of his **o** as a fire offering Lv 3:14
as a fire **o** to the LORD: Lv 3:14
a fire **o** for a pleasing aroma. Lv 3:16
bull as a sin **o** for the sin he Lv 4:3
the altar of burnt **o** that is at Lv 4:7
fat from the bull of the sin **o**: Lv 4:8
them on the altar of burnt **o**. Lv 4:10
present a young bull as a sin **o**. Lv 4:14
the altar of burnt **o** that is at Lv 4:18
did with the bull in the sin **o**; Lv 4:20
is the sin **o** for the assembly. Lv 4:21
unblemished male goat as his **o**. Lv 4:23
where the burnt **o** is slaughtered Lv 4:24
before the LORD. It is a sin **o**. Lv 4:24
from the sin **o** with his finger Lv 4:25
horns of the altar of burnt **o**. Lv 4:25
base of the altar of burnt **o**. Lv 4:25
goat as his **o** for the sin that Lv 4:28
head of the sin **o** and slaughter Lv 4:29
it at the place of the burnt **o**. Lv 4:29
horns of the altar of burnt **o**. Lv 4:30
Or if the **o** that he brings as a Lv 4:32
he brings as a sin **o** is a lamb, Lv 4:32
head of the sin **o** and slaughter Lv 4:33
it as a sin **o** at the place where Lv 4:33
the burnt **o** is slaughtered. Lv 4:33
of the sin **o** with his finger Lv 4:34
horns of the altar of burnt **o**. Lv 4:34
goat from the flock as a sin **o**. Lv 5:6
one as a sin **o** and the other as Lv 5:7
and the other as a burnt **o**. Lv 5:7
present the one for the sin **o**. Lv 5:8
blood of the sin **o** on the side Lv 5:9
of the altar; it is a sin **o**. Lv 5:9
bird⌋ as a burnt **o** according to Lv 5:10
fine flour as an **o** for his sin. Lv 5:11
on it, for it is a sin **o**. Lv 5:11
to the LORD; it is a sin **o**. Lv 5:12
the priest, like the grain **o**." Lv 5:13
his restitution **o** to the LORD: Lv 5:15
shekel, as a restitution **o**. Lv 5:15
the ram of the restitution **o**, Lv 5:16
a restitution **o** to the priest. Lv 5:18
It is a restitution **o**; Lv 5:19
his restitution **o** to the LORD: Lv 6:6
a restitution **o** to the priest. Lv 6:6
This is the law of the burnt **o**; Lv 6:9
the burnt **o** itself must remain Lv 6:9
ashes of the burnt **o** the fire Lv 6:10
arrange the burnt **o** on the fire Lv 6:12
this is the law of the grain **o**: Lv 6:14
and olive oil from the grain **o**, Lv 6:15
frankincense that is on the **o**, Lv 6:15
like the sin **o** and the Lv 6:17
offering and the restitution **o**. Lv 6:17
This is the **o** that Aaron and his Lv 6:20
fine flour as a regular grain **o**, Lv 6:20
it as a grain **o** of baked pieces, Lv 6:21
Every grain **o** for a priest will Lv 6:23
priest will be a whole burnt **o**; Lv 6:23
This is the law of the sin **o**. Lv 6:25
The sin **o** is most holy and must Lv 6:25
the burnt **o** is slaughtered. Lv 6:25
it as a sin **o** is to eat it. Lv 6:26
which the sin **o** is boiled must Lv 6:28
But no sin **o** may be eaten if its Lv 6:30
is the law of the restitution **o**; Lv 7:1
The restitution **o** must be Lv 7:2
the burnt **o** is slaughtered, Lv 7:2
altar as a fire **o** to the LORD; Lv 7:5
it is a restitution **o**. Lv 7:5
restitution **o** is like the sin Lv 7:7
offering is like the sin **o**; Lv 7:7
who presents someone's burnt **o**, Lv 7:8
of the burnt **o** he has presented Lv 7:8
Any grain **o** that is baked in an Lv 7:9
But any grain **o**, whether dry or Lv 7:10
present as his **o** cakes of Lv 7:13
portion⌋ of each **o** as a Lv 7:14

the blood of the fellowship **o**; Lv 7:14
offers is a vow or a freewill **o**, Lv 7:16
fat from a fire **o** presented to Lv 7:25
LORD must bring an **o** to the LORD Lv 7:29
a presentation **o** before the LORD Lv 7:30
the fellowship **o** and the fat Lv 7:33
the presentation **o** and the thigh Lv 7:34
This is the law for the burnt **o**, Lv 7:37
the grain **o**, the sin offering, Lv 7:37
the sin **o**, the restitution Lv 7:37
restitution **o**, the ordination Lv 7:37
the ordination **o**, and the Lv 7:37
bull of the sin **o**, the two rams, Lv 8:2
the bull near for the sin **o**, Lv 8:14
head of the bull for the sin **o**. Lv 8:14
the ram for the burnt **o**, Lv 8:18
It was a burnt **o** for a pleasing Lv 8:21
a fire **o** to the LORD as He had Lv 8:21
the LORD as a presentation **o**. Lv 8:27
on the altar with the burnt **o**. Lv 8:28
an ordination **o** for a pleasing Lv 8:28
aroma, a fire **o** to the LORD. Lv 8:28
the LORD as a presentation **o**; Lv 8:29
the ordination **o** as I commanded: Lv 8:31
bull for a sin **o** and a ram for Lv 9:2
and a ram for a burnt **o**, Lv 9:2
'Take a male goat for a sin **o**; Lv 9:3
without blemish, for a burnt **o**; Lv 9:3
for a fellowship **o** to sacrifice Lv 9:4
and a grain **o** mixed with oil. Lv 9:4
your sin **o** and your burnt Lv 9:7
sin offering and your burnt **o**; Lv 9:7
people's **o** and make atonement Lv 9:7
the calf as a sin **o** for himself. Lv 9:8
from the sin **o** on the altar, Lv 9:10
Then he slaughtered the burnt **o**. Lv 9:12
him the burnt **o** piece by piece, Lv 9:13
with the burnt **o** on the altar. Lv 9:14
Aaron presented the people's **o**. Lv 9:15
goat for the people's sin **o**, Lv 9:15
and made a sin **o** with it as he Lv 9:15
the burnt **o** and sacrificed it Lv 9:16
Next he presented the grain **o**, Lv 9:17
addition to the morning burnt **o**. Lv 9:17
a presentation **o** before the LORD Lv 9:21
after sacrificing the sin **o**, Lv 9:22
the burnt **o**, and the fellowship Lv 9:22
offering, and the fellowship **o**. Lv 9:22
consumed the burnt **o** and the fat Lv 9:24
Take the grain **o** that is left Lv 10:12
the presentation **o** and the thigh Lv 10:14
breast of the presentation **o**, Lv 10:15
a presentation **o** before the LORD Lv 10:15
the male goat of the sin **o**, Lv 10:16
you eat the sin **o** in the Lv 10:17
their sin **o** and their burnt Lv 10:19
their burnt **o** before the LORD Lv 10:19
if I had eaten the sin **o** today, Lv 10:19
male lamb for a burnt **o**, Lv 12:6
or a turtledove for a sin **o**, Lv 12:6
one for a burnt **o** and the other Lv 12:8
and the other for a sin **o**. Lv 12:8
grain **o** of three quarts of fine Lv 14:10
present it as a restitution **o**, Lv 14:12
a presentation **o** before the LORD Lv 14:12
where the sin **o** and burnt Lv 14:13
and burnt **o** are slaughtered, Lv 14:13
like the sin **o**, the restitution Lv 14:13
the restitution **o** belongs to the Lv 14:13
the restitution **o** and put ⌊it⌋ Lv 14:14
the blood of the restitution **o**. Lv 14:17
sacrifice the sin **o** and make Lv 14:19
he will slaughter the burnt **o**. Lv 14:19
offer the burnt **o** and the grain Lv 14:20
and the grain **o** on the altar. Lv 14:20
for a restitution **o** to be waved Lv 14:21
with olive oil for a grain **o**, Lv 14:21
one to be a sin **o** and the other Lv 14:22
and the other a burnt **o**. Lv 14:22
the restitution **o** and the Lv 14:24
a presentation **o** before the LORD Lv 14:24
male lamb for the restitution **o**, Lv 14:25
the restitution **o** and put ⌊it⌋ Lv 14:25
the blood of the restitution **o**. Lv 14:28
one as a sin **o** and the other as Lv 14:31
and the other as a burnt **o**, Lv 14:31
together with the grain **o**. Lv 14:31
one as a sin **o** and the other as Lv 15:15

and the other as a burnt **o**. Lv 15:15
one as a sin **o** and the other as Lv 15:30
and the other as a burnt **o**. Lv 15:30
bull for a sin **o** and a ram for Lv 16:3
and a ram for a burnt **o**. Lv 16:3
goats for a sin **o** and one ram Lv 16:5
and one ram for a burnt **o**. Lv 16:5
bull for his sin **o** and make Lv 16:6
and sacrifice it as a sin **o**. Lv 16:9
bull for his sin **o** and makes Lv 16:11
the bull for his sin **o**. Lv 16:11
people's sin **o** and brings its Lv 16:15
his burnt **o** and the people's Lv 16:24
and the people's burnt **o**; Lv 16:24
fat of the sin **o** on the altar. Lv 16:25
for the sin **o** and the goat for Lv 16:27
and the goat for the sin **o**, Lv 16:27
it⌋ as an **o** to the LORD before Lv 17:4
they have been **o** in the open Lv 17:5
offers a burnt **o** or a sacrifice Lv 17:8
a restitution **o** to the LORD at Lv 19:21
the restitution **o** for the sin he Lv 19:22
as a praise **o** to the LORD. Lv 19:24
family is to eat the holy **o**. Lv 22:10
hand is not to eat the holy **o**. Lv 22:10
anyone eats a holy **o** in error, Lv 22:14
give the holy **o** to the priest. Lv 22:14
in Israel who presents his **o**— Lv 22:18
or as a freewill **o** from the herd Lv 22:21
altar as a fire **o** to the LORD. Lv 22:22
as a freewill **o** any animal Lv 22:23
it is not acceptable as a vow **o**. Lv 22:23
as a gift, a fire **o** to the LORD. Lv 22:27
sacrifice a thank **o** to the LORD, Lv 22:29
present a fire **o** to the LORD for Lv 23:8
as a burnt **o** to the LORD. Lv 23:12
Its grain **o** is to be four quarts Lv 23:13
oil as a fire **o** to the LORD, Lv 23:13
its drink **o** will be one quart Lv 23:13
have brought the **o** of your God. Lv 23:14
the sheaf of the presentation **o**. Lv 23:15
then present an **o** of new grain Lv 23:16
settlements as a presentation **o**, Lv 23:17
will be a burnt **o** to the LORD, Lv 23:18
a fire **o** of a pleasing aroma to Lv 23:18
one male goat as a sin **o**, Lv 23:19
a presentation **o** before the LORD Lv 23:20
present a fire **o** to the LORD." Lv 23:25
to present a fire **o** to the LORD. Lv 23:27
present a fire **o** to the LORD for Lv 23:36
present a fire **o** to the LORD. Lv 23:36
bread and a fire **o** to the LORD. Lv 24:7
be brought as an **o** to the LORD, Lv 27:9
be brought as an **o** to the LORD, Lv 27:11
day as a holy **o** to the LORD. Lv 27:23
and pitchers for the drink **o**. Nm 4:7
bread ⌊**o**⌋ is to be on it. Nm 4:7
the daily grain **o**, and the Nm 4:16
also to bring an **o** for her of Nm 5:15
it is a grain **o** of jealousy, Nm 5:15
a grain **o** for remembrance that Nm 5:15
the grain **o** for remembrance Nm 5:18
is the grain **o** of jealousy. Nm 5:18
to take the grain **o** of jealousy Nm 5:25
wave the **o** before the LORD, Nm 5:25
of the grain **o** as a memorial Nm 5:26
one as a sin **o** and the other as Nm 6:11
other as a burnt **o** to make Nm 6:11
male lamb as a restitution **o**. Nm 6:12
to present an **o** to the LORD of Nm 6:14
year-old male lamb as a burnt **o**, Nm 6:14
year-old female lamb as a sin **o**, Nm 6:14
ram as a fellowship **o**, Nm 6:14
Nazirite's sin **o** and burnt Nm 6:16
sin offering and burnt **o**. Nm 6:16
grain **o** and drink offering Nm 6:17
grain offering and drink **o**. Nm 6:17
a presentation **o** before the LORD Nm 6:20
the presentation **o** and the thigh Nm 6:20
who vows his **o** to the LORD for Nm 6:21
houses, presented ⌊an **o**⌋. Nm 7:2
as their **o** before the LORD Nm 7:3
and give this **o** to the Levites, Nm 7:5
present his **o** for the dedication Nm 7:11
presented his **o** on the first day Nm 7:12
His **o** was one silver dish Nm 7:13
mixed with oil for a grain **o**; Nm 7:13
lamb a year old, for a burnt **o**; Nm 7:15

one male goat for a sin **o**; Nm 7:16
This was the **o** of Nahshon son of Nm 7:17
of Issachar, presented ⌊an **o**⌋. Nm 7:18
his **o**, he presented one silver Nm 7:19
mixed with oil for a grain **o**; Nm 7:19
lamb a year old, for a burnt **o**; Nm 7:21
one male goat for a sin **o**; Nm 7:22
This was the **o** of Nethanel son Nm 7:23
Zebulunites, ⌊presented an **o**⌋. Nm 7:24
His **o** was one silver dish Nm 7:25
mixed with oil for a grain **o**; Nm 7:25
lamb a year old, for a burnt **o**; Nm 7:27
one male goat for a sin **o**; Nm 7:28
This was the **o** of Eliab son of Nm 7:29
Reubenites, ⌊presented an **o**⌋. Nm 7:30
His **o** was one silver dish Nm 7:31
mixed with oil for a grain **o**; Nm 7:31
lamb a year old, for a burnt **o**; Nm 7:33
one male goat for a sin **o**; Nm 7:34
This was the **o** of Elizur son of Nm 7:35
Simeonites, ⌊presented an **o**⌋. Nm 7:36
His **o** was one silver dish Nm 7:37
mixed with oil for a grain **o**; Nm 7:37
lamb a year old, for a burnt **o**; Nm 7:39
one male goat for a sin **o**; Nm 7:40
This was the **o** of Shelumiel son Nm 7:41
the Gadites, ⌊presented an **o**⌋. Nm 7:42
His **o** was one silver dish Nm 7:43
mixed with oil for a grain **o**; Nm 7:43
lamb a year old, for a burnt **o**; Nm 7:45
one male goat for a sin **o**; Nm 7:46
This was the **o** of Eliasaph son Nm 7:47
Ephraimites, ⌊presented an **o**⌋. Nm 7:48
His **o** was one silver dish Nm 7:49
mixed with oil for a grain **o**; Nm 7:49
lamb a year old, for a burnt **o**; Nm 7:51
one male goat for a sin **o**; Nm 7:52
This was the **o** of Elishama son Nm 7:53
Manassites, ⌊presented an **o**⌋. Nm 7:54
His **o** was one silver dish Nm 7:55
mixed with oil for a grain **o**; Nm 7:55
lamb a year old, for a burnt **o**; Nm 7:57
one male goat for a sin **o**; Nm 7:58
This was the **o** of Gamaliel son Nm 7:59
Benjaminites, ⌊presented an **o**⌋. Nm 7:60
His **o** was one silver dish Nm 7:61
mixed with oil for a grain **o**; Nm 7:61
lamb a year old, for a burnt **o**; Nm 7:63
one male goat for a sin **o**; Nm 7:64
This was the **o** of Abidan son of Nm 7:65
the Danites, ⌊presented an **o**⌋. Nm 7:66
His **o** was one silver dish Nm 7:67
mixed with oil for a grain **o**; Nm 7:67
lamb a year old, for a burnt **o**; Nm 7:69
one male goat for a sin **o**; Nm 7:70
This was the **o** of Ahiezer son of Nm 7:71
the Asherites, ⌊presented an **o**⌋. Nm 7:72
His **o** was one silver dish Nm 7:73
mixed with oil for a grain **o**; Nm 7:73
lamb a year old, for a burnt **o**; Nm 7:75
one male goat for a sin **o**; Nm 7:76
This was the **o** of Pagiel son of Nm 7:77
Naphtalites, ⌊presented an **o**⌋. Nm 7:78
His **o** was one silver dish Nm 7:79
mixed with oil for a grain **o**; Nm 7:79
lamb a year old, for a burnt **o**; Nm 7:81
one male goat for a sin **o**; Nm 7:82
This was the **o** of Ahira son of Nm 7:83
the burnt **o** totaled 12 bulls, Nm 7:87
and 12 male goats for the sin **o**. Nm 7:87
and its grain **o** of fine flour Nm 8:8
a second young bull for a sin **o**. Nm 8:8
as a presentation **o** from the Nm 8:11
one as a sin **o** and the other as Nm 8:12
other as a burnt **o** to the LORD, Nm 8:12
the LORD as a presentation **o**. Nm 8:13
them as a presentation **o**. Nm 8:15
the LORD as a presentation **o**. Nm 8:21
the LORD's **o** at its appointed Nm 9:7
the LORD's **o** at its appointed Nm 9:13
you make a fire **o** to the LORD Nm 15:3
either a burnt **o** or a sacrifice, Nm 15:3
or as a freewill **o**, or at your Nm 15:3
presenting his **o** to the LORD Nm 15:4
present a grain **o** of two quarts Nm 15:4
wine as a drink **o** with the burnt Nm 15:5
with the burnt **o** or sacrifice of Nm 15:5
prepare a grain **o** with a ram, Nm 15:6
wine for a drink **o** as a pleasing Nm 15:7
bull as a burnt **o** or as a Nm 15:8
as a fellowship **o** to the LORD, Nm 15:8
a grain **o** of six quarts of fine Nm 15:9
two quarts of wine as a drink **o**. Nm 15:10
It is a fire **o** of pleasing aroma Nm 15:10
presents a fire **o** as a pleasing Nm 15:13
prepare a fire **o** as a pleasing Nm 15:14
bull for a burnt **o** as a pleasing Nm 15:24
with its grain **o** and drink Nm 15:24
offering and drink **o** according Nm 15:24
and one male goat as a sin **o**. Nm 15:24
They are to bring their **o**, Nm 15:25
and their sin **o** before the LORD Nm 15:25
year-old female goat as a sin **o**. Nm 15:27
LORD, "Don't respect their **o**. Nm 16:15
the grain **o**, sin offering, Nm 18:9
offering, sin **o**, or restitution Nm 18:9
or restitution **o** will be most Nm 18:9
are to eat it as a most holy **o**. Nm 18:10
fat as a fire **o** for a pleasing Nm 18:17
the presentation **o** and the right Nm 18:18
part of it as an **o** to the LORD— Nm 18:26
Your **o** will be credited to you Nm 18:27
are to present an **o** to the LORD Nm 18:28
the priest as an **o** to the LORD. Nm 18:28
present the entire **o** due the Nm 18:29
remove⌋ impurity; it is a sin **o**. Nm 19:9
of the ashes of the burnt sin **o**, Nm 19:17
by your burnt **o** while I am gone. Nm 23:3
there by his burnt **o** with all Nm 23:6
by your burnt **o** while I seek Nm 23:15
by his burnt **o** with the Nm 23:17
time My **o** and My food as My Nm 28:2
and My food as My fire **o**, Nm 28:2
This is the fire **o** you are to Nm 28:3
male lambs as a regular burnt **o**. Nm 28:3
flour for a grain **o** mixed with a Nm 28:5
a regular burnt **o** established at Nm 28:6
aroma, a fire **o** to the LORD. Nm 28:6
drink **o** is to be a quart with Nm 28:7
Pour out the **o** of beer to the Nm 28:7
kind of grain **o** and drink Nm 28:8
and drink **o** as in the morning Nm 28:8
It is a fire **o**, a pleasing aroma Nm 28:8
mixed with oil as a grain **o**, Nm 28:9
grain offering, and its drink **o**. Nm 28:9
It is the burnt **o** for every Nm 28:10
regular burnt **o** and its drink Nm 28:10
burnt offering and its drink **o**. Nm 28:10
present a burnt **o** to the LORD: Nm 28:11
oil as a grain **o** for each bull, Nm 28:12
oil as a grain **o** for the ram, Nm 28:12
oil as a grain **o** for each lamb. Nm 28:13
It is a burnt **o**, a pleasing Nm 28:13
aroma, a fire **o** to the LORD. Nm 28:13
the monthly burnt **o** for all the Nm 28:14
offered as a sin **o** to the LORD, Nm 28:15
regular burnt **o** with its drink Nm 28:15
burnt offering with its drink **o**. Nm 28:15
Present a fire **o**, a burnt Nm 28:19
offering, a burnt **o** to the LORD: Nm 28:19
The grain **o** with them is to be Nm 28:20
goat for a sin **o** to make Nm 28:22
the morning burnt **o** that is part Nm 28:23
is part of the regular burnt **o**. Nm 28:23
day for seven days as a fire **o**, Nm 28:24
with its drink **o** and the regular Nm 28:24
and the regular burnt **o**. Nm 28:24
you present an **o** of new grain to Nm 28:26
Present a burnt **o** for a pleasing Nm 28:27
with their grain **o** of fine flour Nm 28:28
regular burnt **o** and its grain Nm 28:31
burnt offering and its grain **o**. Nm 28:31
Offer a burnt **o** as a pleasing Nm 29:2
with their grain **o** of fine flour Nm 29:3
goat as a sin **o** to make Nm 29:5
aroma, a fire **o** to the LORD. Nm 29:6
Present a burnt **o** to the LORD, Nm 29:8
Their grain **o** is to be of fine Nm 29:9
one male goat for a sin **o**. Nm 29:11
regular burnt **o** with its grain Nm 29:11
with its grain **o** and drink Nm 29:11
to the sin **o** of atonement. Nm 29:11
Present a burnt **o**, a fire Nm 29:13
a fire **o** as a pleasing aroma to Nm 29:13
Their grain **o** is to be of fine Nm 29:14
offer⌋ one male goat as a sin **o**. Nm 29:16
regular burnt **o** with its grain Nm 29:16
offer⌋ one male goat as a sin **o**. Nm 29:19
regular burnt **o** with its grain Nm 29:19
offer⌋ one male goat as a sin **o**. Nm 29:22
regular burnt **o** with its grain Nm 29:22
offer⌋ one male goat as a sin **o**. Nm 29:25
regular burnt **o** with its grain Nm 29:25
offer⌋ one male goat as a sin **o**. Nm 29:28
regular burnt **o** with its grain Nm 29:28
offer⌋ one male goat as a sin **o**. Nm 29:31
regular burnt **o** with its grain Nm 29:31
offer⌋ one male goat as a sin **o**. Nm 29:34
regular burnt **o** with its grain Nm 29:34
Present a burnt **o**, a fire Nm 29:36
a fire **o** as a pleasing aroma to Nm 29:36
offer⌋ one male goat as a sin **o**. Nm 29:38
regular burnt **o** with its grain Nm 29:38
to the LORD an **o** of the gold Nm 31:50
with a freewill **o** that you give Dt 16:10
not for burnt **o** or sacrifice. Jos 22:26
not for burnt **o** or sacrifice, Jos 22:28
building an altar for burnt **o**, Jos 22:29
offering, grain **o**, or sacrifice, Jos 22:29
it as a burnt **o** with the wood Jdg 6:26
I will offer it as a burnt **o**." Jdg 11:31
you want to prepare a burnt **o**, Jdg 13:16
and a grain **o** and offered them Jdg 13:19
the burnt **o** and the grain Jdg 13:23
and the grain **o** from us, Jdg 13:23
and his vow **o** to the LORD, 1Sm 1:21
the LORD's **o** with contempt. 1Sm 2:17
out by either sacrifice or **o**." 1Sm 3:14
must not send it without ⌊an **o**⌋. 1Sm 6:3
must return it with a guilt **o**, 1Sm 6:3
What guilt **o** should we send back 1Sm 6:4
you're sending Him as a guilt **o**. 1Sm 6:8
cows as a burnt **o** to the LORD. 1Sm 6:14
As a guilt **o** to the LORD, the 1Sm 6:17
as a whole burnt **o** to the LORD. 1Sm 7:9
Samuel was **o** the burnt offering 1Sm 7:10
the burnt **o** as the Philistines 1Sm 7:10
me the burnt **o** and the 1Sm 13:9
Then he offered the burnt **o**. 1Sm 13:9
as he finished **o** the burnt 1Sm 13:10
finished offering the burnt **o**, 1Sm 13:10
myself to offer the burnt **o**." 1Sm 13:12
me, then may He accept an **o**. 1Sm 26:19
had finished **o** the burnt 2Sm 6:18
the burnt **o** and the fellowship 2Sm 6:18
While he was **o** the sacrifices, 2Sm 15:12
I am **o** you three ⌊choices⌋. 2Sm 24:12
oxen for a burnt **o** and the 2Sm 24:22
with him were **o** sacrifices 1Kg 8:62
where he offered the burnt **o**, 1Kg 8:64
the grain **o**, and the fat 1Kg 8:64
incense and **o** sacrifices to 1Kg 11:8
he made this **o** in Bethel to 1Kg 12:32
until the **o** of the evening 1Kg 18:29
pour it on the **o** to be burned 1Kg 18:33
At the time for **o** the ⌊evening⌋ 1Kg 18:36
fell and consumed the burnt **o**, 1Kg 18:38
for the grain **o** the ⌊next⌋ 2Kg 3:20
him as a burnt **o** on the city 2Kg 3:27
offer a burnt **o** or a sacrifice 2Kg 5:17
When he finished **o** the burnt 2Kg 10:25
finished offering the burnt **o**, 2Kg 10:25
the restitution **o** and the sin 2Kg 12:16
and the sin **o** was not brought to 2Kg 12:16
offered his burnt **o** and his 2Kg 16:13
burnt offering and his grain **o**, 2Kg 16:13
out his drink **o**, and sprinkled 2Kg 16:13
great altar the morning burnt **o**, 2Kg 16:15
evening grain **o**, and the king's 2Kg 16:15
the king's burnt **o** and his grain 2Kg 16:15
burnt offering and his grain **o**. 2Kg 16:15
offer⌋ the burnt **o** of all the 2Kg 16:15
their grain **o**, and their drink 2Kg 16:15
of the burnt **o** and all the blood 2Kg 16:15
David had finished **o** the burnt 1Ch 16:2
bring an **o** and come before Him. 1Ch 16:29
I am **o** you three ⌊choices⌋. 1Ch 21:10
and the wheat for the grain **o**— 1Ch 21:23
heaven on the altar of burnt **o**. 1Ch 21:26
altar of burnt **o** were at the 1Ch 21:29
altar of burnt **o** for Israel." 1Ch 22:1
the fine flour for the grain **o**, 1Ch 23:29
parts of the burnt **o** were rinsed 2Ch 4:6
the burnt **o** and the sacrifices 2Ch 7:1

all the people were **o** sacrifices	2Ch 7:4
not accommodate the burnt **o**,	2Ch 7:7
the grain **o**, and the fat	2Ch 7:7
offer a burnt **o** and fragrant	2Ch 13:11
the altar of burnt **o** and all its	2Ch 29:18
as a sin **o** for the kingdom,	2Ch 29:21
brought the sin **o** goats right	2Ch 29:23
blood on the altar for a sin **o**,	2Ch 29:24
the burnt **o** and sin offering	2Ch 29:24
offering and sin **o** were for all	2Ch 29:24
that the burnt **o** be offered	2Ch 29:27
until the burnt **o** was completed.	2Ch 29:28
were for a burnt **o** to the LORD.	2Ch 29:32
drink offerings for the burnt **o**.	2Ch 29:35
bringing the **o** to the LORD's	2Ch 31:10
The **o**, the tenth, and the	2Ch 31:12
were bringing an **o** to the LORD	2Ch 32:23
were busy **o** up burnt offerings	2Ch 35:14
and for **o** burnt offerings	2Ch 35:16
with a freewill **o** for the house	Ezr 1:4
that was given as a freewill **o**.	Ezr 1:6
regular burnt **o** and the	Ezr 3:5
as a place for **o** sacrifices,	Ezr 6:3
as a sin **o** for all Israel—	Ezr 6:17
are a freewill **o** to the LORD God	Ezr 8:28
with 12 male goats as a sin **o**.	Ezr 8:35
this was a burnt **o** for the LORD.	Ezr 8:35
devastated until the evening **o**.	Ezr 9:4
At the evening **o**, I got up from	Ezr 9:5
the daily grain **o**, the regular	Neh 10:33
the regular burnt **o**, the Sabbath	Neh 10:33
the one-tenth **o** in all our	Neh 10:37
a tenth of this **o** to the	Neh 10:38
with the grain **o** and	Neh 13:9
offer a burnt **o** for yourselves.	Jb 42:8
and accept your burnt **o**.	Ps 20:3
not delight in sacrifice and **o**;	Ps 40:6
a whole burnt **o** or a sin	Ps 40:6
whole burnt offering or a sin **o**.	Ps 40:6
Sacrifice a thank **o** to God,	Ps 50:14
sacrifices a thank **o** honors Me,	Ps 50:23
are not pleased with a burnt **o**.	Ps 51:16
sacrifice a freewill **o** to You.	Ps 54:6
bring an **o** and enter His courts.	Ps 96:8
of my hands as the evening **o**.	Ps 141:2
animals enough for a burnt **o**.	Is 40:16
You make Him a restitution **o**,	Is 53:10
poured out a drink **o** to them;	Is 57:6
you have offered a grain **o**;	Is 57:6
one offers a grain **o**, one offers	Is 66:3
bring an **o** in a clean vessel	Is 66:20
burnt **o** and sacrifice.	Jr 7:22
they offer burnt **o** and grain	Jr 14:12
burnt offering and grain **o**,	Jr 14:12
and the drink **o** bowls—whatever	Jr 52:19
The burnt **o** was to be washed	Ezk 40:38
which to slaughter the burnt **o**,	Ezk 40:39
offering, sin **o**, and restitution	Ezk 40:39
sin offering, and restitution **o**.	Ezk 40:39
of cut stone for the burnt **o**,	Ezk 40:42
flesh of the **o** was to be laid	Ezk 40:43
herd as a sin **o** to the Levitical	Ezk 43:19
away the bull for the sin **o**,	Ezk 43:21
male goat as a sin **o**.	Ezk 43:22
them as a burnt **o** to the LORD.	Ezk 43:24
a goat for a sin **o** each day for	Ezk 43:25
he must present his sin **o**."	Ezk 44:27
They will eat the grain **o**,	Ezk 44:29
offering, the sin **o**, and the	Ezk 44:29
offering, and the restitution **o**.	Ezk 44:29
from the sin **o** and apply ⌊it⌋ to	Ezk 45:19
a bull as a sin **o** on behalf of	Ezk 45:22
blemish as a burnt **o** to the LORD	Ezk 45:23
male goat each day for a sin **o**.	Ezk 45:23
provide a grain **o** of half a	Ezk 45:24
The burnt **o** that the prince	Ezk 46:4
grain **o** will be half a bushel	Ezk 46:5
and the grain **o** with the lambs	Ezk 46:5
⌊the burnt **o**⌋ is to be a young,	Ezk 46:6
provide a grain **o** of half a	Ezk 46:7
grain **o** will be half a bushel	Ezk 46:11
the prince makes a freewill **o**,	Ezk 46:12
a burnt **o** or a fellowship	Ezk 46:12
or a fellowship **o** as a freewill	Ezk 46:12
as a freewill **o** to the LORD,	Ezk 46:12
offer his burnt **o** or fellowship	Ezk 46:12
or fellowship **o** just as he does	Ezk 46:12
as a daily burnt **o** to the LORD;	Ezk 46:13
prepare a grain **o** every morning	Ezk 46:14
flour—a grain **o** to the LORD.	Ezk 46:14
lamb, the grain **o**, and the oil	Ezk 46:15
morning as a regular burnt **o**.	Ezk 46:15
the restitution **o** and the sin	Ezk 46:20
offering and the sin **o**,	Ezk 46:20
they will bake the grain **o**,	Ezk 46:20
to present an **o** and incense to	Dn 2:46
about the time of the evening **o**.	Dn 9:21
put a stop to sacrifice and **o**.	Dn 9:27
to Assyria as an **o** to the great	Hs 10:6
leavened bread as a thank **o**,	Am 4:5
people, will bring an **o** to Me.	Zph 3:10
Take ⌊an **o**⌋ from the exiles,	Zch 6:10
will accept no **o** from your hands	Mal 1:10
You bring this as an **o**!	Mal 1:13
if they present an **o** to the LORD	Mal 2:12
So if you are **o** your gift on the	Mt 5:23
They came **o** Him sour wine	Lk 23:36
think he is **o** service to God.	Jn 16:2
up as a memorial **o** before God.	Ac 10:4
days when the **o** for each of them	Ac 21:26
sin's domain, and as a sin **o**,	Rm 8:3
is that the **o** of the Gentiles	Rm 15:16
and fragrant **o** to God.	Eph 5:2
as a drink **o** on the sacrifice	Php 2:17
a fragrant **o**, a welcome	Php 4:18
being poured out as a drink **o**,	2Tm 4:6
must make a sin **o** for himself as	Heb 5:3
there are those **o** the gifts	Heb 8:4
did not want sacrifice and **o**,	Heb 10:5
through the **o** of the body of	Heb 10:10
ministering and **o** time after	Heb 10:11
after **o** one sacrifice for sins	Heb 10:12
For by one **o** He has perfected	Heb 10:14
there is no longer an **o** for sin.	Heb 10:18
the promises was **o** up his unique	Heb 11:17
priest as a sin **o** are burned	Heb 13:11

OFFERINGS *(294)*

offered burnt **o** on the altar.	Gn 8:20
and burnt **o** to prepare for	Ex 10:25
it your burnt **o** and fellowship	Ex 20:24
offerings and fellowship **o**,	Ex 20:24
not hold back ⌊**o** from⌋ your	Ex 22:29
offered burnt **o** and sacrificed	Ex 24:5
as fellowship **o** to the LORD.	Ex 24:5
and bowls for pouring drink **o**.	Ex 25:29
with the holy **o** that the	Ex 28:38
offered burnt **o**, and presented	Ex 32:6
and presented fellowship **o**.	Ex 32:6
bring freewill **o** morning after	Ex 36:3
pitchers for pouring drink **o**.	Ex 37:16
part of the fire **o** to the LORD.	Lv 2:3
part of the fire **o** to the LORD.	Lv 2:10
each of your grain **o** with salt;	Lv 2:13
salt with each of your **o**.	Lv 2:13
with the fire **o** to the LORD.	Lv 4:35
with the fire **o** to the LORD;	Lv 5:12
from the fellowship **o** on it.	Lv 6:12
as their portion from My fire **o**.	Lv 6:17
from the fire **o** to the LORD.	Lv 6:18
touches the **o** will become holy.	Lv 6:18
bring the fire **o** to the LORD.	Lv 7:30
from the fire **o** to the LORD for	Lv 7:35
to present their **o** to the LORD	Lv 7:38
from the fire **o** to the LORD,	Lv 10:12
from the fire **o** to the LORD,	Lv 10:13
with the **o** of fat portions	Lv 10:15
with these **o**, before the LORD at	Lv 14:11
present the fire **o** to the LORD,	Lv 21:6
present the fire **o** to the LORD.	Lv 21:21
the holy **o** of the Israelites	Lv 22:2
the holy **o** that the Israelites	Lv 22:3
from the holy **o** until he is	Lv 22:4
from the holy **o** unless he has	Lv 22:6
then he may eat from the holy **o**,	Lv 22:7
the holy **o** the Israelites	Lv 22:15
if the people eat their holy **o**.	Lv 22:16
of vows to the LORD as burnt **o**—	Lv 22:18
with their grain **o** and drink	Lv 23:18
grain offerings and drink **o**,	Lv 23:18
presenting fire **o** to the LORD,	Lv 23:37
burnt **o** and grain offerings,	Lv 23:37
burnt offerings and grain **o**,	Lv 23:37
and drink **o**, each on its	Lv 23:37
addition to the **o** for the LORD's	Lv 23:38
all your vow **o**, and all your	Lv 23:38
your freewill **o** that you give to	Lv 23:38
him from the fire **o** to the LORD;	Lv 24:9
with their grain **o** and drink	Nm 6:15
grain offerings and drink **o**.	Nm 6:15
presented their **o** in front of	Nm 7:10
with their grain **o**, and 12 male	Nm 7:87
over your burnt **o** and your	Nm 10:10
for all the holy **o** of the	Nm 18:8
of the holiest **o** ⌊kept⌋ from the	Nm 18:9
one of their **o** that they give Me	Nm 18:9
presentation **o** to you and to	Nm 18:11
defile the Israelites' holy **o**,	Nm 18:32
Their drink **o** are to be two	Nm 28:14
with their drink **o** in addition	Nm 28:31
regular burnt **o** with their grain	Nm 29:6
with their grain **o** and drink	Nm 29:6
grain offerings and drink **o**.	Nm 29:6
and drink **o** are in addition to	Nm 29:11
with its grain and drink **o**.	Nm 29:16
grain and drink **o** for the bulls,	Nm 29:18
with its grain and drink **o**.	Nm 29:19
grain and drink **o** for the bulls,	Nm 29:21
with its grain and drink **o**.	Nm 29:22
grain and drink **o** for the bulls,	Nm 29:24
with its grain and drink **o**.	Nm 29:25
grain and drink **o** for the bulls,	Nm 29:27
with its grain and drink **o**.	Nm 29:28
grain and drink **o** for the bulls,	Nm 29:30
with its grain and drink **o**.	Nm 29:31
grain and drink **o** for the bulls,	Nm 29:33
with its grain and drink **o**.	Nm 29:34
grain and drink **o** for the bulls,	Nm 29:37
with its grain and drink **o**.	Nm 29:38
to your vow and freewill **o**,	Nm 29:39
grain, drink, or fellowship **o**."	Nm 29:39
your burnt **o** and sacrifices,	Dt 12:6
your vow **o** and freewill	Dt 12:6
vow offerings and freewill **o**,	Dt 12:6
your burnt **o**, sacrifices,	Dt 12:11
sacrifices, **o** of the tenth,	Dt 12:11
all your choice **o** you vow to the	Dt 12:11
offer your burnt **o** in all the	Dt 12:13
offer your burnt **o** only in the	Dt 12:14
of your vow **o** that you pledge	Dt 12:17
freewill **o**; or your personal	Dt 12:17
to take the holy **o** you have and	Dt 12:26
have and your vow **o** and go to	Dt 12:26
of your burnt **o** on the altar	Dt 12:27
They will eat the LORD's fire **o**;	Dt 18:1
and offer burnt **o** to the LORD	Dt 27:6
are to sacrifice fellowship **o**,	Dt 27:7
drank the wine of their drink **o**?	Dt 32:38
and whole burnt **o** on Your altar.	Dt 33:10
they offered burnt **o** to the LORD	Jos 8:31
sacrificed fellowship **o** on it.	Jos 8:31
the **o** made by fire to the LORD,	Jos 13:14
to offer burnt **o** and grain	Jos 22:23
offerings and grain **o** on it,	Jos 22:23
to sacrifice fellowship **o** on it.	Jos 22:23
His presence with our burnt **o**,	Jos 22:27
sacrifices, and fellowship **o**.	Jos 22:27
offered burnt **o** and fellowship	Jdg 20:26
and fellowship **o** to the LORD.	Jdg 20:26
offered burnt **o** and fellowship	Jdg 21:4
offerings and fellowship **o**.	Jdg 21:4
house all the Israelite fire **o**.	1Sm 2:28
sacrifices and **o** that I require	1Sm 2:29
of all of the **o** of My people	1Sm 2:29
offered burnt **o** and made	1Sm 6:15
offer burnt **o** and to sacrifice	1Sm 10:8
and to sacrifice fellowship **o**.	1Sm 10:8
fellowship **o** in the LORD's	1Sm 11:15
offering and the fellowship **o**."	1Sm 13:9
in burnt **o** and sacrifices as	1Sm 15:22
you, or fields of **o**, for there	2Sm 1:21
offered burnt **o** and fellowship	2Sm 6:17
and fellowship **o** in the LORD's	2Sm 6:17
offering and the fellowship **o**,	2Sm 6:18
my God burnt **o** that cost ⌊me⌋	2Sm 24:24
offered burnt **o** and fellowship	2Sm 24:25
offerings and fellowship **o**.	2Sm 24:25
1,000 burnt **o** on that altar.	1Kg 3:4
offered burnt **o** and fellowship	1Kg 3:15
offerings and fellowship **o**.	1Kg 3:15
of fellowship **o** to the LORD:	1Kg 8:63
the fellowship **o** since the	1Kg 8:64
to accommodate the burnt **o**,	1Kg 8:64
the grain **o**, and the fat	1Kg 8:64
and the fat of the fellowship **o**.	1Kg 8:64

offered burnt **o** and fellowship 1Kg 9:25
and fellowship **o** on the altar he 1Kg 9:25
the burnt **o** he offered at the 1Kg 10:5
to offer sacrifices and burnt **o**. 2Kg 10:24
his fellowship **o** on the altar. 2Kg 16:13
offering, and their drink **o**. 2Kg 16:15
presented the **o** on the altar 1Ch 6:49
of burnt **o** and on the altar 1Ch 6:49
offered burnt **o** and fellowship 1Ch 16:1
and fellowship **o** in God's 1Ch 16:1
the burnt **o** and the fellowship 1Ch 16:2
offerings and the fellowship **o**, 1Ch 16:2
to offer burnt **o** regularly, 1Ch 16:40
the altar of burnt **o** and to do 1Ch 16:40
I give the oxen for the burnt **o**, 1Ch 21:23
or offer burnt **o** that cost ⌊me⌋ 1Ch 21:24
offered burnt **o** and fellowship 1Ch 21:26
offerings and fellowship **o**. 1Ch 21:26
Whenever burnt **o** are offered to 1Ch 23:31
LORD and burnt **o** to the LORD: 1Ch 29:21
their drink **o**, and sacrifices 1Ch 29:21
he offered 1,000 burnt **o** on it. 2Ch 1:6
burnt **o** for the evening 2Ch 2:4
offered the burnt **o** and the fat 2Ch 7:7
the fellowship **o** since the 2Ch 7:7
the fat ⌊of the fellowship **o**⌋. 2Ch 7:7
offered burnt **o** to the LORD 2Ch 8:12
requirement for **o** according to 2Ch 8:13
the burnt **o** he offered at the 2Ch 9:4
to offer burnt **o** to the LORD as 2Ch 23:18
ministry and for making burnt **o**, 2Ch 24:14
offered burnt **o** in the LORD's 2Ch 24:14
not offer burnt **o** in the holy 2Ch 29:7
When the burnt **o** began, the song 2Ch 29:27
When the burnt **o** were completed, 2Ch 29:29
and thank **o** to the LORD's temple 2Ch 29:31
brought sacrifices and thank **o**, 2Ch 29:31
willing hearts brought burnt **o**. 2Ch 29:31
number of burnt **o** the 2Ch 29:32
able to skin all the burnt **o**, 2Ch 29:34
the burnt **o** were abundant, 2Ch 29:35
of the fellowship **o** and with the 2Ch 29:35
with the drink **o** for the burnt 2Ch 29:35
brought burnt **o** to the LORD's 2Ch 30:15
fellowship **o** and giving thanks 2Ch 30:22
for the burnt **o** and fellowship 2Ch 31:2
offerings and fellowship **o**, 2Ch 31:2
morning and evening burnt **o**, 2Ch 31:3
the burnt **o** of the Sabbaths, 2Ch 31:3
over the freewill **o** to God to 2Ch 31:14
fellowship and thank **o** on it. 2Ch 33:16
removed the burnt **o** so that they 2Ch 35:12
offering up burnt **o** and fat 2Ch 35:14
offering burnt **o** on the altar 2Ch 35:16
gave freewill **o** for the house of Ezr 2:68
in order to offer burnt **o** on it, Ezr 3:2
offered burnt **o** for the morning Ezr 3:3
and ⌊offered⌋ burnt **o** each day, Ezr 3:4
offering and the **o** for the Ezr 3:5
as the freewill **o** brought to the Ezr 3:5
to offer burnt **o** to the LORD, Ezr 3:6
and lambs for burnt **o** to the God Ezr 6:9
with the freewill **o** given by the Ezr 7:16
with their grain and drink **o**, Ezr 7:17
offered burnt **o** to the God of Ezr 8:35
the Sabbath and New Moon **o**, Neh 10:33
the sin **o** to atone for Israel, Neh 10:33
firstfruits of our ⌊grain⌋ **o**, Neh 10:37
previously stored the grain **o**, Neh 13:5
offer burnt **o** for all of them. Jb 1:5
pour out their drink **o** of blood, Ps 16:4
all your **o** and accept your Ps 20:3
sacrifices or for your burnt **o**, Ps 50:8
sacrifices, whole burnt **o**; Ps 51:19
I will make my thank **o** to You. Ps 56:12
enter Your house with burnt **o**; Ps 66:13
You fattened sheep as burnt **o**, Ps 66:15
accept my willing **o** of praise, Ps 119:108
I've made fellowship **o**; Pr 7:14
had enough of burnt **o** and rams Is 1:11
Stop bringing useless **o**. Is 1:13
will offer sacrifices and **o**; Is 19:21
sheep for burnt **o** or honored Me Is 43:23
you with **o** or wearied you Is 43:23
Their burnt **o** and sacrifices Is 56:7
Your burnt **o** are not acceptable; Jr 6:20
pour out drink **o** to other gods Jr 7:18
Add your burnt **o** to your other Jr 7:21
bringing burnt **o** and sacrifice, Jr 17:26
grain **o** and frankincense Jr 17:26
and thank **o** to the house of the Jr 17:26
in the fire as burnt **o** to Baal, Jr 19:5
out drink **o** to other gods." Jr 19:13
and where drink **o** have been Jr 32:29
they bring thank **o** to the temple Jr 33:11
before Me to offer burnt **o**, Jr 33:18
to burn grain **o**, and to make Jr 33:18
grain and incense **o** to bring to Jr 41:5
and offer drink **o** to her just as Jr 44:17
heaven and to offer her drink **o**, Jr 44:18
and poured out drink **o** to her, Jr 44:19
and poured out drink **o** to her?" Jr 44:19
and to pour out drink **o** for her. Jr 44:25
their offensive **o** there. Ezk 20:28
poured out their drink **o** there. Ezk 20:28
choicest gifts, all your holy **o**. Ezk 20:40
slaughter the burnt **o** and Ezk 40:42
LORD will eat the most holy **o**. Ezk 42:13
will deposit the most holy **o**— Ezk 42:13
the grain **o**, sin offerings, Ezk 42:13
offerings, sin **o**, and Ezk 42:13
restitution **o**—for the place Ezk 42:13
that burnt **o** may be sacrificed Ezk 43:18
your burnt **o** and fellowship Ezk 43:27
and fellowship **o** on the altar, Ezk 43:27
slaughter the burnt **o** and Ezk 44:11
⌊These are⌋ for the grain **o**, Ezk 45:15
burnt **o**, and fellowship Ezk 45:15
and fellowship **o**, to make Ezk 45:15
Then the burnt **o**, grain Ezk 45:17
offerings, grain **o**, and drink Ezk 45:17
and drink **o** for the festivals, Ezk 45:17
He will provide the sin **o**, Ezk 45:17
grain **o**, burnt offerings Ezk 45:17
burnt **o**, and fellowship Ezk 45:17
and fellowship **o** to make Ezk 45:17
the same sin **o**, burnt offerings, Ezk 45:25
burnt **o**, grain offerings Ezk 45:25
offerings, grain **o**, and oil. Ezk 45:25
his burnt **o** and fellowship Ezk 46:2
offerings and fellowship **o**. Ezk 46:2
and they burn **o** on the hills, Hs 4:13
of God rather than burnt **o**. Hs 6:6
out their wine **o** to the LORD, Hs 9:4
Baals and burning **o** to idols. Hs 11:2
Grain and drink **o** have been cut Jl 1:9
grain and drink **o** are withheld Jl 1:13
loudly proclaim your freewill **o**, Am 4:5
Me your burnt **o** and grain Am 5:22
burnt offerings and grain **o**, Am 5:22
your fellowship **o** of fattened Am 5:22
and grain **o** that you presented Am 5:25
I come before Him with burnt **o**, Mc 6:6
Incense and pure **o** will be Mal 1:11
respects your **o** or receives Mal 2:13
they will present **o** to the LORD Mal 3:3
And the **o** of Judah and Jerusalem Mal 3:4
all the burnt **o** and sacrifices." Mk 12:33
dropping their **o** into the temple Lk 21:1
you bring Me **o** and sacrifices Ac 7:42
gifts and **o** to my nation, Ac 24:17
share in the **o** of the altar? 1Co 9:13
in whole burnt **o** and sin Heb 10:6
whole burnt offerings and sin **o**. Heb 10:6
or delight in sacrifices and **o**, Heb 10:8
whole burnt **o** and sin offerings, Heb 10:8
whole burnt offerings and sin **o**, Heb 10:8

OFFERS (11)

The priest who **o** it as a sin Lv 6:26
be eaten on the day he **o** it; Lv 7:15
If the sacrifice he **o** is a vow Lv 7:16
them who **o** a burnt offering Lv 17:8
collect what he **o** as security. Dt 24:10
one **o** a grain offering, one Is 66:3
offering, one **o** swine's blood; Is 66:3
one **o** incense, one praises an Is 66:3
the one who **o** sacrifices on the Jr 48:35
are tired, and no one **o** us rest. Lm 5:5
which he **o** for himself and for Heb 9:7

OFFICE (7)

to some priestly **o** so I can have 1Sm 2:36
I will remove you from your **o**; Is 22:19
Matthew sitting at the tax **o**, Mt 9:9
Alphaeus sitting at the tax **o**, Mk 2:14
named Levi sitting at the tax **o**, Lk 5:27
priestly **o** have a commandment Heb 7:5
by death from remaining in **o**. Heb 7:23

OFFICER (16)

an **o** of Pharaoh and the captain Gn 37:36
an **o** of Pharaoh and the captain Gn 39:1
and isn't Zebul his **o**? Jdg 9:28
of Israel called an **o** and said, 1Kg 22:9
Then his **o**, Pekah son of 2Kg 15:25
back a single **o** among the least 2Kg 18:24
was the **o** in charge of the 1Ch 26:24
of Israel called an **o** and said, 2Ch 18:8
and Maaseiah the **o** under the 2Ch 26:11
Levite was the **o** in charge of 2Ch 31:12
of Zichri was the **o** over them, Neh 11:9
Immer and chief **o** in the house Jr 20:1
to be the chief **o** in the temple Jr 29:26
an **o** of the guard was there, Jr 37:13
Arioch, the king's **o**, "Why is Dn 2:15
judge to the **o**, and you will be Mt 5:25

OFFICERS (53)

was angry with his two **o**, Gn 40:2
he asked Pharaoh's **o** who were in Gn 40:7
of Egypt, with **o** in each one. Ex 14:7
the elite of his **o** were drowned Ex 15:4
as elders and **o** of the people. Nm 11:16
Moses became furious with the **o**, Nm 31:14
o who were over the thousands Nm 31:48
and tens, and **o** for your tribes. Dt 1:15
The **o** are to address the army, Dt 20:5
The **o** will continue to address Dt 20:8
When the **o** have finished Dt 20:9
tribal elders and **o** before me, Dt 31:28
commanded the **o** of the people: Jos 1:10
three days the **o** went through Jos 3:2
their elders, **o**, and judges, Jos 8:33
judges, and **o**, and said to them, Jos 23:2
judges, and **o**, and they Jos 24:1
successful than all of Saul's **o**. 1Sm 18:30
Hadadezer's **o** and brought them 2Sm 8:7
Joab with his **o** and all Israel. 2Sm 11:1
Tahchemonite was chief of the **o**. 2Sm 23:8
Jehu said to the guards and **o**, 2Kg 10:25
the guards and **o** threw ⌊the 2Kg 10:25
Hadadezer's **o** and brought them 1Ch 18:7
6,000 are to be **o** and judges, 1Ch 23:4
there were **o** of the sanctuary 1Ch 24:5
sanctuary and **o** of God among 1Ch 24:5
presence of the king and the **o**, 1Ch 24:6
David and the **o** of the army also 1Ch 25:1
duties as **o** and judges over 1Ch 26:29
and their **o** who served the king 1Ch 27:1
the Levites are **o** in your 2Ch 19:11
the presence of the **o** and the 2Ch 28:14
secretaries, **o**, and gatekeepers 2Ch 34:13
and Jozabad, **o** of the Levites, 2Ch 35:9
and all his powerful **o**. Ezr 7:28
had also sent **o** of the infantry Neh 2:9
The **o** supported all the people Neh 4:16
and his **o** will be afraid because Is 31:9
the weakest of my master's **o**, Is 36:9
I defiled the **o** of the sanctuary Is 43:28
Judah, his **o**, and the people— Jr 21:7
you, your **o**, and your people Jr 22:2
they, their **o**, and their people. Jr 22:4
of Egypt, his **o**, his leaders, Jr 25:19
and his **o** for their wrongdoing. Jr 36:31
He and his **o** and the people of Jr 37:2
and one of the king's chief **o**, Jr 41:1
king of Babylon and his **o**. Jr 46:26
all of them looked like **o**, Ezk 23:15
and prefects, **o** and Ezk 23:23
He gives orders to his **o**; Nah 2:5
slumber; your **o** sleep. Your Nah 3:18

OFFICERS' (1)

he hears the **o** shouts and the Jb 39:25

OFFICIAL (23)

appointed a court **o** for her, 2Kg 8:6
of Nathan-melech the court **o**, 2Kg 23:11
he took a court **o** who had been 2Kg 25:19
the chief **o** of God's temple; 1Ch 9:11
son of Zichri was the chief **o**; 1Ch 27:16
the Ammonite **o** heard that Neh 2:10
the Ammonite **o**, and Geshem Neh 2:19
the chief **o** of God's house, Neh 11:11
the king's trusted **o** in charge Est 2:15
because one **o** protects another Ec 5:8
one official protects another **o**, Ec 5:8

Cushite court **o** employed in the Jr 38:7
he took a court **o** who had been Jr 52:25
chief **o** gave them ⌊different⌋ Dn 1:7
from the chief **o** not to defile Dn 1:8
and compassion from the chief **o**, Dn 1:9
whom the chief **o** had assigned to Dn 1:11
the chief **o** presented them to Dn 1:18
the **o** and the judge demand a Mc 7:3
a certain royal **o** whose son was Jn 4:46
"Sir," the **o** said to Him, "come Jn 4:49
a eunuch and high **o** of Candace, Ac 8:27
be placed on the **o** support list 1Tm 5:9

OFFICIALS (146)

Pharaoh's **o** saw her and praised Gn 12:15
in front of Pharaoh and his **o**— Ex 5:21
staff before Pharaoh and his **o**, Ex 7:10
the sight of Pharaoh and his **o**, Ex 7:20
of your **o** and your people, Ex 8:3
your people, and all your **o**." Ex 8:4
for you, your **o**, and your people Ex 8:9
houses, your **o**, and your people Ex 8:11
you, your **o**, your people, Ex 8:21
Pharaoh, his **o**, and his people. Ex 8:29
Pharaoh, his **o**, and his people; Ex 8:31
you, your **o**, and your people Ex 9:14
among Pharaoh's **o** who feared the Ex 9:20
But as for you and your **o**, Ex 9:30
his heart, he and his **o**. Ex 9:34
hearts of his **o** so that I may do Ex 10:1
Pharaoh's **o** asked him, "How long Ex 10:7
by Pharaoh's **o** and the people. Ex 11:3
All these **o** of yours will come Ex 11:8
along with all his **o** and all the Ex 12:30
Pharaoh and his **o** changed their Ex 14:5
the people as **o** of thousands, Ex 18:21
the people ⌊as⌋ **o** of thousands, Ex 18:25
So the **o** of Moab stayed with Nm 22:8
morning and said to Balak's **o**, Nm 22:13
The **o** of Moab arose, returned to Nm 22:14
Balak sent **o** again who were more Nm 22:15
and went with the **o** of Moab. Nm 22:21
So Balaam went with Balak's **o**. Nm 22:35
Balaam and the **o** who were with Nm 22:40
offering with all the **o** of Moab. Nm 23:6
offering with the **o** of Moab. Nm 23:17
o for thousands, hundreds, Dt 1:15
judges and **o** for your tribes Dt 16:18
to all his **o**, and to his entire Dt 29:2
tribes, elders, **o**, all the men Dt 29:10
to all his **o**, and to all his Dt 34:11
give them to his **o** and servants. 1Sm 8:15
and David's sons were chief **o**. 2Sm 8:18
and these were his **o**: 1Kg 4:2
and his **o**, surrendered to 2Kg 24:12
wives, his **o**, and the leading 2Kg 24:15
were the chief **o** at the king's 1Ch 18:17
All these were **o** in charge of 1Ch 27:31
and the **o** in charge of all the 1Ch 28:1
with the court **o**, the fighting 1Ch 28:1
the **o** in charge of the king's 1Ch 29:6
sent his **o**—Ben-hail, Obadiah 2Ch 17:7
the city **o**, and went up to 2Ch 29:20
and the **o** told the Levites 2Ch 29:30
king and his **o** and the entire 2Ch 30:2
the hand of the king and his **o**, 2Ch 30:6
the king and his **o** by the word 2Ch 30:12
o contributed 1,000 bulls and 2Ch 30:24
and his **o** came and viewed 2Ch 31:8
with his **o** and his warriors 2Ch 32:3
His **o** also donated willingly for 2Ch 35:8
treasures of the king and his **o**. 2Ch 36:18
also bribed **o** ⌊to act⌋ against Ezr 4:5
colleagues, the **o** in the region, Ezr 5:6
colleagues, the **o** in the region. Ezr 6:6
The leaders and **o** have taken the Ezr 9:2
The **o** did not know where I had Neh 2:16
priests, nobles, **o**, or the rest Neh 2:16
the nobles, the **o**, and the rest Neh 4:14
the nobles, the **o**, and the rest Neh 4:19
I accused the nobles and **o**, Neh 5:7
There were 150 Jews and **o**, Neh 5:17
nobles, the **o**, and the people Neh 7:5
Pharaoh, all his **o**, and all the Neh 9:10
half of the **o** accompanying me Neh 12:40
rebuked the **o**, saying, "Why has Neh 13:11
reign for all his **o** and staff, Est 1:3
and the **o** from the provinces. Est 1:3
beauty to the people and the **o**, Est 1:11
were the seven **o** of Persia and Est 1:14
presence of the king and his **o**, Est 1:16
all the **o** and the peoples who Est 1:16
same thing⌋ to all the king's **o**, Est 1:18
banquet for all his **o** and staff. Est 2:18
position than all the other **o**. Est 3:1
and the **o** of each ethnic group Est 3:12
telling the **o**⌋ to destroy, Est 3:13
All the royal **o** and the people Est 4:11
over the other **o** and the royal Est 5:11
one of the king's most noble **o**. Est 6:9
and the **o** of the 127 provinces Est 8:9
All the **o** of the provinces, Est 9:3
City **o** stopped talking and Jb 29:9
binding his **o** at will and Ps 105:22
against Pharaoh and all his **o**. Ps 135:9
and higher **o** ⌊protect⌋ them. Ec 5:8
of Judah, its **o**, its priests, Jr 1:18
kings, their **o**, their priests, Jr 2:26
king and the **o** will lose their Jr 4:9
the bones of her **o**, the bones Jr 8:1
and on horses with their **o**, Jr 17:25
king of Judah, the **o** of Judah, Jr 24:1
of Judah, his **o**, and the remnant Jr 24:8
kings and its **o**, to make them Jr 25:18
When the **o** of Judah heard these Jr 26:10
said to the **o** and all the people Jr 26:11
to all the **o** and the people, Jr 26:12
Then the **o** and all the people Jr 26:16
and all the **o** heard his words, Jr 26:21
the court **o**, the officials Jr 29:2
the **o** of Judah and Jerusalem, Jr 29:2
kings, their **o**, their priests, Jr 32:32
All the **o** and people who entered Jr 34:10
The **o** of Judah and Jerusalem, Jr 34:19
the court **o**, the priests, Jr 34:19
of Judah and his **o** over to their Jr 34:21
All the **o** were sitting there— Jr 36:12
Hananiah, and all the other **o**. Jr 36:12
Then all the **o** sent ⌊word⌋ to Jr 36:14
The **o** said to Baruch, "You and Jr 36:19
king and all the **o** who were Jr 36:21
Jeremiah and took him to the **o**. Jr 37:14
The **o** were angry at Jeremiah and Jr 37:15
The **o** then said to the king, Jr 38:4
surrender to the **o** of the king Jr 38:17
surrender to the **o** of the king Jr 38:18
brought out to the **o** of the king Jr 38:22
If the **o** hear that I have spoken Jr 38:25
When all the **o** came to Jeremiah Jr 38:27
All the **o** of the king of Babylon Jr 39:3
the rest of the **o** of Babylon's Jr 39:3
and court **o** whom he brought back Jr 41:16
and our **o** did in Judah's cities Jr 44:17
kings, your **o**, and the people Jr 44:21
exile with his priests and **o**. Jr 48:7
together with his priests and **o**. Jr 49:3
the king and **o** from there. Jr 49:38
against her **o**, and against her Jr 50:35
I will smash governors and **o**. Jr 51:23
her governors and all her **o**, Jr 51:28
her governors, **o**, and warriors. Jr 51:57
its king and **o**, and brought them Ezk 17:12
Her **o** within her are like wolves Ezk 22:27
of his court **o**, to bring some Dn 1:3
and kill all its **o** with him. Am 2:3
Your court **o** are like the Nah 3:17
sacrifice I will punish the **o**, Zph 1:8
the brothers before the city **o**, Ac 17:6
and the city **o** who heard these Ac 17:8
of the provincial **o** of Asia, Ac 19:31

OFFICIALS' (3)

palace and his **o** houses. Ex 8:24
your houses, all your **o** houses, Ex 10:6
a chamber near the **o** chamber, Jr 35:4

OFFICIATE (1)

they will **o** as judges and decide Ezk 44:24

OFFSET (1)

also provided **o** ledges for the 1Kg 6:6

OFFSHOOTS (1)

the descendants and the **o**— Is 22:24

OFFSPRING (94)

in order to keep **o** alive on the Gn 7:3
will give this land to your **o**." Gn 12:7
give you and your **o** forever all Gn 13:15
I will make your **o** like the dust Gn 13:16
then your **o** could be counted. Gn 13:16
given me no **o**, so a slave born Gn 15:3
"Your **o** will be that ⌊numerous⌋." Gn 15:5
Your **o** will be strangers in a Gn 15:13
I give this land to your **o**, Gn 15:18
I will greatly multiply your **o**, Gn 16:10
and your **o** after you throughout Gn 17:7
the ⌊God⌋ of your **o** after you. Gn 17:7
to you and your **o** after you I Gn 17:8
you and your **o** after you Gn 17:9
Me and you and your **o** after you: Gn 17:10
The one who is not your **o**, Gn 17:12
covenant for his **o** after him. Gn 17:19
because your **o** will be traced Gn 21:12
son because he is your **o**." Gn 21:13
and make your **o** as numerous as Gn 22:17
Your **o** will possess the gates of Gn 22:17
blessed by your **o** because you Gn 22:18
give this land to your **o**'— Gn 24:7
May your **o** possess the gates of Gn 24:60
these lands to you and your **o**, Gn 26:3
will make your **o** as numerous as Gn 26:4
will give your **o** all these lands Gn 26:4
earth will be blessed by your **o**, Gn 26:4
and multiply your **o** because of Gn 26:24
give you and your **o** the blessing Gn 28:4
you and your **o** the land that you Gn 28:13
Your **o** will be like the dust of Gn 28:14
blessed through you and your **o**. Gn 28:14
I will make your **o** like the sand Gn 32:12
and produce **o** for your brother." Gn 38:8
knew that the **o** would not be his Gn 38:9
not produce **o** for his brother. Gn 38:9
indeed all his **o**, he brought Gn 46:7
God has even let me see your **o**." Gn 48:11
and his **o** will become a populous Gn 48:19
All firstborn **o** of the livestock Ex 13:12
will make your **o** as numerous as Ex 32:13
will give your **o** all this land Ex 32:13
I will give it to your **o**. Ex 33:1
because he gave his **o** to Molech, Lv 20:3
o of Anak were descended from Nm 13:33
LORD for you as well as your **o**." Nm 18:19
and the **o** of your livestock, Dt 28:4
children, the **o** of your Dt 28:11
will eat the **o** of your livestock Dt 28:51
children, the **o** of your Dt 30:9
70 sons, his own **o**, since he had Jdg 8:30
because of the **o** the LORD will Ru 4:12
me and between my **o** and your 1Sm 20:42
offspring and your **o** forever." 1Sm 20:42
king against Saul and his **o**." 2Sm 4:8
son, your own **o**, will build it 1Kg 8:19
you **o** of Israel His servant, 1Ch 16:13
your son, your own **o**, will build 2Ch 6:9
know that your **o** will be many Jb 5:25
Their **o** are healthy and grow up Jb 39:4
earth and their **o** from the human Ps 21:10
establish your **o** forever and Ps 89:4
His **o** will continue forever, Ps 89:36
and their **o** will be established Ps 102:28
You **o** of Abraham His servant, Ps 105:6
but the **o** of the righteous will Pr 11:21
The **o** of evildoers will never be Is 14:20
remnant, **o**, and posterity"— Is 14:22
and My blessing on your **o**. Is 44:3
and the **o** of your body like its Is 48:19
among all the **o** she has brought Is 51:18
o of an adulterer and a Is 57:3
so will your **o** and your name Is 66:22
who are from the **o** of Zadok, Ezk 43:19
a virgin from the **o** of the house Ezk 44:22
the precious **o** of their wombs. Hs 9:16
will be no **o** to carry on your Nah 1:14
One seek? A godly **o**. So watch Mal 2:15
and raise up **o** for his brother. Mt 22:24
Having no **o**, he left his wife to Mt 22:25
and produce **o** for his brother Mk 12:19
a wife, and dying, left no **o**. Mk 12:20
her, and he died, leaving no **o**. Mk 12:21
The seven also left no **o**. Mk 12:22
and produce **o** for his brother Lk 20:28
from David's **o** and from the town Jn 7:42
said, 'For we are also His **o**.' Ac 17:28
God's **o**, then, we shouldn't Ac 17:29
angels, but to help Abraham's **o**. Heb 2:16
received power to conceive **o**, Heb 11:11
came **o** as numerous as the stars Heb 11:12

and set My **o** and incense before Ezk 16:18
fine flour, **o**, and honey that Ezk 16:19
you had set My incense and **o**. Ezk 23:41
meal, honey, **o**, and balm for Ezk 27:17
make their rivers flow like **o**. Ezk 32:14
quota of **o** in liquid measures Ezk 45:14
a gallon of **o** for every half Ezk 45:24
grain offerings, and **o**. Ezk 45:25
as a gallon of **o** for every half Ezk 46:5
a gallon of **o** for every half Ezk 46:7
a gallon of **o** for every half Ezk 46:11
of a gallon of **o** to moisten the Ezk 46:14
and the **o** every morning as a Ezk 46:15
I didn't put any **o** ⌊on my body⌋ Dn 10:3
wool and flax, my **o** and drink. Hs 2:5
grain, the new wine, and the **o**. Hs 2:8
wine, and the **o**, and they will Hs 2:22
and olive **o** is carried to Egypt. Hs 12:1
dried up; and the olive **o** fails. Jl 1:10
grain, new wine, and olive **o**. Jl 2:19
with new wine and olive **o**. Jl 2:24
with ten thousand streams of **o**? Mc 6:7
but not anoint yourself with **o**; Mc 6:15
new wine, olive **o**, and whatever Hg 1:11
stew, wine, **o**, or any other food Hg 2:12
which golden ⌊**o**⌋ pours out?" Zch 4:12
you fast, put **o** on your head, Mt 6:17
they didn't take **o** with them. Mt 25:3
ones took **o** in their flasks Mt 25:4
us some of your **o**, because our Mt 25:8
and buy **o** for yourselves.' Mt 25:9
of very expensive fragrant **o**. Mt 26:7
this fragrant **o** on My body, Mt 26:12
many sick people with **o**, Mk 6:13
expensive fragrant **o** of nard. Mk 14:3
has this fragrant **o** been wasted? Mk 14:4
For this **o** might have been sold Mk 14:5
an alabaster flask of fragrant **o** Lk 7:37
them with the fragrant **o**. Lk 7:38
didn't anoint My head with **o**, Lk 7:46
My feet with fragrant **o**. Lk 7:46
wounds, pouring on **o** and wine. Lk 10:34
'A hundred measures of **o**,' Lk 16:6
with fragrant **o** and wiped His Jn 11:2
took a pound of fragrant **o**— Jn 12:3
with the fragrance of the **o**. Jn 12:3
this fragrant **o** sold for 300 Jn 12:5
companions, with the **o** of joy. Heb 1:9
him with olive **o** in the name of Jms 5:14
harm the olive **o** and the wine." Rv 6:6
wine, olive **o**, fine wheat flour, Rv 18:13

OILS *(1)*

with the finest **o** but do not Am 6:6

OINTMENT *(2)*

he makes the sea like an **o** jar. Jb 41:31
and **o** to spread on your eyes so Rv 3:18

OINTMENTS *(1)*

various mixtures of prepared **o**; 2Ch 16:14

OLD *(320)*

was 130 years **o** when he fathered Gn 5:3
was 105 years **o** when he fathered Gn 5:6
was 90 years **o** when he fathered Gn 5:9
was 70 years **o** when he fathered Gn 5:12
was 65 years **o** when he fathered Gn 5:15
was 162 years **o** when he fathered Gn 5:18
was 65 years **o** when he fathered Gn 5:21
was 187 years **o** when he fathered Gn 5:25
was 182 years **o** when he fathered Gn 5:28
was 500 years **o**, and he fathered Gn 5:32
They were the powerful men of **o**, Gn 6:4
was 600 years **o** when the deluge Gn 7:6
was 75 years **o** when he left Gn 12:4
and be buried at a ripe **o** age. Gn 15:15
was 86 years **o** when Hagar bore Gn 16:16
When Abram was 99 years **o**, Gn 17:1
you at eight days **o** is to be Gn 17:12
was 99 years **o** when the flesh Gn 17:24
was 13 years **o** when the flesh Gn 17:25
and Sarah were **o** and getting Gn 18:11
shriveled up and my lord is **o**, Gn 18:12
really have a baby when I'm **o**?' Gn 18:13
both young and **o**, the whole Gn 19:4
young and **o**, with a blinding Gn 19:11
Our father is **o**, and there is no Gn 19:31
a son to Abraham in his **o** age, Gn 21:2
his son Isaac was eight days **o**, Gn 21:4
was 100 years **o** when his son Gn 21:5
borne him a son in his **o** age." Gn 21:7
Abraham was now **o**, getting on in Gn 24:1
a son to my master in her **o** age, Gn 24:36
breath and died at a ripe **o** age, Gn 25:8
a ripe old age, **o** and contented, Gn 25:8
was 40 years **o** when he took as Gn 25:20
was 60 years **o** when they were Gn 25:26
was 40 years **o**, he took as his Gn 26:34
When Isaac was **o** and his eyes Gn 27:1
am **o** and do not know the day of Gn 27:2
to his people, **o** and full of Gn 35:29
son ⌊born to him⌋ in his **o** age, Gn 37:3
was 30 years **o** when he entered Gn 41:46
brother, the child of his **o** age. Gn 44:20
was poor because of **o** age; Gn 48:10
was 80 years **o** and Aaron 83 when Ex 7:7
go with our young and our **o**; Ex 10:9
20 years **o** or more, must give Ex 30:14
20 years **o** or more who had Ex 38:26
of the elderly and honor the **o**. Lv 19:32
unblemished male lambs a year **o**, Lv 23:18
lambs a year **o** as a fellowship Lv 23:19
You will eat the **o** grain of the Lv 26:10
clear out the **o** to make room for Lv 26:10
a male from 20 to 60 years **o**, Lv 27:3
is from five to 20 years **o**, Lv 27:5
from one month to five years **o**, Lv 27:6
are 20 years **o** or more by their Nm 1:3
of those 20 years **o** or more, Nm 1:18
every male 20 years **o** or more, Nm 1:20
every male 20 years **o** or more, Nm 1:22
of those 20 years **o** or more, Nm 1:24
of those 20 years **o** or more, Nm 1:26
of those 20 years **o** or more, Nm 1:28
of those 20 years **o** or more, Nm 1:30
of those 20 years **o** or more, Nm 1:32
of those 20 years **o** or more, Nm 1:34
of those 20 years **o** or more, Nm 1:36
of those 20 years **o** or more, Nm 1:38
of those 20 years **o** or more, Nm 1:40
of those 20 years **o** or more, Nm 1:42
Israelites 20 years **o** or more, Nm 1:45
every male one month **o** or more." Nm 3:15
every male one month **o** or more, Nm 3:22
every male one month **o** or more, Nm 3:28
every male one month **o** or more, Nm 3:34
males one month **o** or more that Nm 3:39
Israelites one month **o** or more, Nm 3:40
males one month **o** or more listed Nm 3:43
from 30 years **o** to 50 years old Nm 4:3
30 years old to 50 years **o**— Nm 4:3
from 30 years **o** to 50 years old Nm 4:23
from 30 years old to 50 years **o**, Nm 4:23
from 30 years **o** to 50 years old Nm 4:30
from 30 years old to 50 years **o**, Nm 4:30
from 30 years **o** to 50 years old Nm 4:35
from 30 years old to 50 years **o**, Nm 4:35
from 30 years **o** to 50 years old Nm 4:39
from 30 years old to 50 years **o**, Nm 4:39
from 30 years **o** to 50 years old, Nm 4:43
from 30 years old to 50 years **o**, Nm 4:43
from 30 years **o** to 50 years old, Nm 4:47
from 30 years old to 50 years **o**, Nm 4:47
and one male lamb a year **o**, Nm 7:15
and five male lambs a year **o**, Nm 7:17
and one male lamb a year **o**, Nm 7:21
and five male lambs a year **o**, Nm 7:23
and one male lamb a year **o**, Nm 7:27
and five male lambs a year **o**, Nm 7:29
and one male lamb a year **o**, Nm 7:33
and five male lambs a year **o**, Nm 7:35
and one male lamb a year **o**, Nm 7:39
and five male lambs a year **o**, Nm 7:41
and one male lamb a year **o**, Nm 7:45
and five male lambs a year **o**, Nm 7:47
and one male lamb a year **o**, Nm 7:51
and five male lambs a year **o**, Nm 7:53
and one male lamb a year **o**, Nm 7:57
and five male lambs a year **o**, Nm 7:59
and one male lamb a year **o**, Nm 7:63
and five male lambs a year **o**, Nm 7:65
and one male lamb a year **o**, Nm 7:69
and five male lambs a year **o**, Nm 7:71
and one male lamb a year **o**, Nm 7:75
and five male lambs a year **o**, Nm 7:77
and one male lamb a year **o**, Nm 7:81
and five male lambs a year **o**, Nm 7:83
and 12 male lambs a year **o**, Nm 7:87
and 60 male lambs a year **o**. Nm 7:88
From 25 years **o** or more, a man Nm 8:24
at 50 years **o** he is to retire Nm 8:25
of you 20 years **o** or more— Nm 14:29
those 20 years **o** or more who can Nm 26:2
of⌋ those 20 years **o** or more, Nm 26:4
every male one month **o** or more; Nm 26:62
seven male lambs a year **o**— Nm 28:11
and seven male lambs a year **o**. Nm 28:19
and seven male lambs a year **o**, Nm 28:27
seven male lambs a year **o**— Nm 29:2
and seven male lambs a year **o**. Nm 29:8
and 14 male lambs a year **o**. Nm 29:13
and 14 male lambs a year **o**— Nm 29:17
male lambs a year **o**—⌊all⌋ Nm 29:20
male lambs a year **o**—⌊all⌋ Nm 29:23
male lambs a year **o**—⌊all⌋ Nm 29:26
male lambs a year **o**—⌊all⌋ Nm 29:29
and 14 male lambs a year **o**— Nm 29:32
seven male lambs a year **o**— Nm 29:36
men 20 years **o** or more who came Nm 32:11
was 123 years **o** when he died Nm 33:39
for the **o** and not sparing Dt 28:50
saying, "I am now 120 years **o**; Dt 31:2
the days of **o**; consider the Dt 32:7
The God of **o** is ⌊your⌋ dwelling Dt 33:27
was 120 years **o** when he died; Dt 34:7
both young and **o**, and every ox, Jos 6:21
their donkeys and **o** wineskins, Jos 9:4
⌊They wore⌋ **o**, patched sandals Jos 9:5
Joshua was now **o**, advanced in Jos 13:1
You have become **o**, advanced in Jos 13:1
I was 40 years **o** when Moses the Jos 14:7
Here I am today, 85 years **o**. Jos 14:10
them, Joshua was **o**, getting on Jos 23:1
said to them, "I am **o**, getting Jos 23:2
and a second bull seven years **o**. Jdg 6:25
died at a ripe **o** age and was Jdg 8:32
o man came in from his work in Jdg 19:16
city square, the **o** man asked, Jdg 19:17
"Peace to you," said the **o** man. Jdg 19:20
They said to the **o** man who was Jdg 19:22
for I am too **o** to have another Ru 1:12
and sustain you in your **o** age. Ru 4:15
Eli was very **o**. He heard about 1Sm 2:22
in your family will reach **o** age. 1Sm 2:31
will ever again reach **o** age. 1Sm 2:32
At that time Eli was 98 years **o**, 1Sm 4:15
and since he was **o** and heavy, 1Sm 4:18
When Samuel grew **o**, he appointed 1Sm 8:1
Look, you are **o**, and your sons 1Sm 8:5
for me, I'm **o** and gray, and my 1Sm 12:2
was 30 years **o** when he became 1Sm 13:1
reign was ⌊already⌋ an **o** man. 1Sm 17:12
As the **o** proverb says, 1Sm 24:13
"An **o** man is coming up," 1Sm 28:14
was 40 years **o** when he began his 2Sm 2:10
was five years **o** when the report 2Sm 4:4
was 30 years **o** when he began his 2Sm 5:4
Barzillai was a very **o** man— 2Sm 19:32
man—80 years **o**—and since he 2Sm 19:32
now 80 years **o**. Can I discern 2Sm 19:35
Now King David was **o** and getting 1Kg 1:1
Since the king was very **o**, 1Kg 1:15
When Solomon was **o**, his wives 1Kg 11:4
Now a certain **o** prophet was 1Kg 13:11
The **o** prophet deceived him, 1Kg 13:18
the **o** prophet saddled the donkey 1Kg 13:23
city where the **o** prophet lived. 1Kg 13:25
Then the **o** prophet instructed 1Kg 13:27
The **o** prophet came into to the 1Kg 13:29
was 41 years **o** when he became 1Kg 14:21
But in his **o** age he developed a 1Kg 15:23
was 35 years **o** when he became 1Kg 22:42
no son, and her husband is **o**." 2Kg 4:14
He was 32 years **o** when he became 2Kg 8:17
was 22 years **o** when he became 2Kg 8:26
seven years **o** when he became 2Kg 12:21
He was 25 years **o** when he became 2Kg 14:2
was 16 years **o**, and made him 2Kg 14:21
He was 16 years **o** when he became 2Kg 15:2
was 25 years **o** when he became 2Kg 15:33
was 20 years **o** when he became 2Kg 16:2
He was 25 years **o** when he became 2Kg 18:2
was 12 years **o** when he became 2Kg 21:1
was 22 years **o** when he became 2Kg 21:19
was eight years **o** when he became 2Kg 22:1
was 23 years **o** when he became 2Kg 23:31

was 25 years **o** when he became 2Kg 23:36
was 18 years **o** when he became 2Kg 24:8
was 21 years **o** when he became 2Kg 24:18
her when he was 60 years **o**, 1Ch 2:21
When David was **o** and full of 1Ch 23:1
Levites 30 years **o** and above 1Ch 23:3
20 years **o** or more, who worked 1Ch 23:24
20 years **o** or more were to 1Ch 23:27
the young and **o** alike, the 1Ch 25:8
young and **o** alike, for each 1Ch 26:13
died at a good **o** age, full of 1Ch 29:28
was 41 years **o** when he became 2Ch 12:13
death, young or **o**, man or woman. 2Ch 15:13
was 35 years **o** when he became 2Ch 20:31
was 32 years **o** when he became 2Ch 21:5
was 32 years **o** when he became 2Ch 21:20
was 22 years **o** when he became 2Ch 22:2
was seven years **o** when he became 2Ch 24:1
when he was **o** and full of days 2Ch 24:15
he was 130 years **o** at his death. 2Ch 24:15
king ⌊when he was⌋ 25 years **o**; 2Ch 25:1
those 20 years **o** or more for all 2Ch 25:5
who was 16 years **o**, and made him 2Ch 26:1
was 16 years **o** when he became 2Ch 26:3
was 25 years **o** when he became 2Ch 27:1
He was 25 years **o** when he became 2Ch 27:8
was 20 years **o** when he became 2Ch 28:1
was 25 years **o** when he became 2Ch 29:1
three years **o** and above; 2Ch 31:16
Levites 20 years **o** and above, 2Ch 31:17
was 12 years **o** when he became 2Ch 33:1
was 22 years **o** when he became 2Ch 33:21
was eight years **o** when he became 2Ch 34:1
was 23 years **o** when he became 2Ch 36:2
was 25 years **o** when he became 2Ch 36:5
was 18 years **o** when he became 2Ch 36:9
was 21 years **o** when he became 2Ch 36:11
who were 20 years **o** or more to Ezr 3:8
Besodeiah repaired the **O** Gate. Neh 3:6
and by the **O** Gate, the Fish Gate Neh 12:39
people—young and **o**, women and Est 3:13
its roots grow **o** in the ground Jb 14:8
growing **o** and becoming powerful? Jb 21:7
young in years, while you are **o**; Jb 32:6
is not ⌊only⌋ the **o** who are wise Jb 32:9
Job died, **o** and full of days. Jb 42:17
they grow **o** because of all my Ps 6:7
have been young and now I am **o**, Ps 37:25
Don't discard me in my **o** age: Ps 71:9
Even when I am **o** and gray, Ps 71:18
days of **o**, years long past Ps 77:5
will still bear fruit in **o** age, Ps 92:14
I remember the days of **o**; Ps 143:5
as young women, **o** and young Ps 148:12
the splendor of **o** men is gray Pr 20:29
even when he is **o** he will not Pr 22:6
your mother when she is **o**. Pr 23:22
youth than an **o** but foolish king Ec 4:13
delicacy—new as well as **o**. Sg 7:13
Cush, young and **o** alike, naked Is 20:4
pay no attention to things of **o**. Is 43:18
be the same until ⌊your⌋ **o** age, Is 46:4
or an **o** man not live out his Is 65:20
be captured, the **o** with the very Jr 6:11
the old with the very **o**. Jr 6:11
while young and **o** men ⌊rejoice⌋ Jr 31:13
there he took **o** rags and Jr 38:11
Place these **o** rags and clothes Jr 38:12
I will smash the **o** man and the Jr 51:22
was 21 years **o** when he became Jr 52:1
that were ⌊hers⌋ in days of **o**. Lm 1:7
which He ordained in days of **o**. Lm 2:17
⌊Both⌋ young and **o** are lying on Lm 2:21
Slaughter the **o** men, the young Ezk 9:6
your **o** men will have dreams, Jl 2:28
rebuild it as in the days of **o**, Am 9:11
O men and women will again sit Zch 8:4
as in days of **o** and years gone Mal 3:4
who were two years **o** and under, Mt 2:16
No one patches an **o** garment with Mt 9:16
puts new wine into **o** wineskins. Mt 9:17
what is new and what is **o**." Mt 13:52
unshrunk cloth on an **o** garment. Mk 2:21
pulls away from the **o** cloth, Mk 2:21
puts new wine into **o** wineskins. Mk 2:22
was 12 years **o**.) At this they Mk 5:42
For I am an **o** man, and my wife Lk 1:18
conceived a son in her **o** age, Lk 1:36
He was 12 years **o**, they went up Lk 2:42
about 30 years **o** and was thought Lk 3:23
and puts it on an **o** garment. Lk 5:36
garment will not match the **o**. Lk 5:36
puts new wine into **o** wineskins. Lk 5:37
drinking **o** wine, wants new, Lk 5:39
he says, 'The **o** is better.' " Lk 5:39
only daughter about 12 years **o**, Lk 8:42
yourselves that won't grow **o**, Lk 12:33
anyone be born when he is **o**?" Jn 3:4
You aren't 50 years **o** yet, Jn 8:57
when you grow **o**, you will Jn 21:18
your **o** men will dream dreams. Ac 2:17
over 40 years **o** on whom this Ac 4:22
he was about a hundred years **o** Rm 4:19
we know that our **o** self was Rm 6:6
and not in the **o** letter of the Rm 7:6
Clean out the **o** yeast so that 1Co 5:7
feast, not with **o** yeast, or with 1Co 5:8
the reading of the **o** covenant, 2Co 3:14
o things have passed away, 2Co 5:17
the **o** man that is corrupted by Eph 4:22
have put off the **o** man with his Col 3:9
she is at least 60 years **o**, 1Tm 5:9
declared that the first is **o**. Heb 8:13
And what is **o** and aging is about Heb 8:13
but an **o** command that you have 1Jn 2:7
The **o** command is the message you 1Jn 2:7

OLDER *(24)*

Shem, Japheth's **o** brother, also Gn 10:21
the **o** will serve the younger. Gn 25:23
called his **o** son Esau and said Gn 27:1
best clothes of her **o** son Esau, Gn 27:15
the words of her **o** son Esau were Gn 27:42
the **o** was named Leah, and the Gn 29:16
child grew **o**, she brought him Ex 2:10
camp had killed all the **o** sons. 2Ch 22:1
But many of the **o** priests, Ezr 3:12
with us, men **o** than your father Jb 15:10
while **o** men stood to their feet. Jb 29:8
they were ⌊all⌋ **o** than he. Jb 32:4
scribe, and the **o** priests, Is 37:2
as well as the ⌊**o**⌋ women and Ezk 9:6
Your **o** sister was Samaria, Ezk 16:46
you receive your **o** and younger Ezk 16:61
The **o** one was named Oholah, Ezk 23:4
Now his **o** son was in the field; Lk 15:25
by one, starting with the **o** men. Jn 8:9
The **o** will serve the younger. Rm 9:12
not rebuke an **o** man, but exhort 1Tm 5:1
o women as mothers, and with all 1Tm 5:2
O men are to be self-controlled, Ti 2:2
o women are to be reverent in Ti 2:3

OLDEST *(13)*

with the **o** and ending with Gn 44:12
from the youngest to the **o**, 1Sm 5:9
three **o** sons had followed 1Sm 17:13
The three **o** had followed Saul, 1Sm 17:14
David's **o** brother Eliab listened 1Sm 17:28
Here is my **o** daughter Merab. 1Sm 18:17
it from the youngest to the **o**. 1Sm 30:2
from the youngest to the **o**, 1Sm 30:19
from the youngest to the **o**, 2Kg 3:21
from the youngest to the **o**. 2Kg 23:2
from the youngest to the **o**, 2Kg 25:26
wine in their **o** brother's house, Jb 1:13
wine in their **o** brother's house. Jb 1:18

OLIVE *(68)*

a plucked **o** leaf in her beak. Gn 8:11
your vineyard and your **o** grove. Ex 23:11
with one quart of crushed **o** oil, Ex 29:40
), and one gallon of **o** oil. Ex 30:24
He is to pour **o** oil on it, Lv 2:1
He must not put **o** oil or Lv 5:11
of fine flour and **o** oil from the Lv 6:15
cakes mixed with **o** oil, Lv 7:12
of fine flour mixed with **o** oil, Lv 14:10
one-third of a quart of **o** oil. Lv 14:10
the one-third quart of **o** oil, Lv 14:12
of a quart of **o** oil and pour it Lv 14:15
mixed with **o** oil for a grain Lv 14:21
one-third of a quart of **o** oil, Lv 14:21
one-third of a quart of **o** oil, Lv 14:24
all the best of the fresh **o** oil, Nm 18:12
with a quart of beaten **o** oil. Nm 28:5
vineyards and **o** groves that you Dt 6:11
a land of **o** oil and honey; Dt 8:8
down the fruit from your **o** tree, Dt 24:20
and dip his foot in ⌊**o**⌋ oil. Dt 33:24
vineyards and **o** groves you did Jos 24:13
They said to the **o** tree, "Reign Jdg 9:8
But the **o** tree said to them, Jdg 9:9
as the vineyards and **o** groves. Jdg 15:5
and **o** orchards and give them to 1Sm 8:14
15 feet high out of **o** wood. 1Kg 6:23
sanctuary, he made **o** wood doors. 1Kg 6:31
two doors were made of **o** wood. 1Kg 6:32
made four-sided **o** wood doorposts 1Kg 6:33
money and clothes, **o** orchards 2Kg 5:26
a land of **o** trees and honey— 2Kg 18:32
in charge of the **o** and sycamore 1Ch 27:28
charge of the stores of **o** oil. 1Ch 27:28
vineyards, **o** groves, and houses Neh 5:11
and **o** oil that you have been Neh 5:11
and bring back branches of **o**, Neh 8:15
of olive, wild **o**, myrtle, palm, Neh 8:15
vineyards, **o** groves, and fruit Neh 9:25
and like an **o** tree that sheds Jb 15:33
a flourishing **o** tree in the Ps 52:8
like young **o** trees around your Ps 128:3
if an **o** tree had been beaten— Is 17:6
like a harvested **o** tree, like a Is 24:13
acacias, myrtles, and **o** trees. Is 41:19
named you a flourishing **o** tree, Jr 11:16
and **o** oil is carried to Egypt. Hs 12:1
will be like the **o** tree, Hs 14:6
dried up; and the **o** oil fails. Jl 1:10
you grain, new wine, and **o** oil. Jl 2:19
with new wine and **o** oil. Jl 2:24
your fig trees and **o** trees, Am 4:9
though the **o** crop fails and the Hab 3:17
grain, new wine, **o** oil, and Hg 1:11
and the **o** tree have not yet Hg 2:19
are also two **o** trees beside it, Zch 4:3
What are the two **o** trees on the Zch 4:11
are the two **o** branches beside Zch 4:12
from the mount called **O** Grove, Ac 1:12
you, though a wild **o** branch, Rm 11:17
root of the cultivated **o** tree, Rm 11:17
cut off from your native wild **o**, Rm 11:24
into a cultivated **o** tree, Rm 11:24
grafted into their own **o** tree? Rm 11:24
him with **o** oil in the name Jms 5:14
not harm the **o** oil and the wine. Rv 6:6
are the two **o** trees and the two Rv 11:4
wine, **o** oil, fine wheat flour, Rv 18:13

OLIVES *(21)*

from crushed **o** for the light, Ex 27:20
oil of beaten **o** for the light, Lv 24:2
You will have **o** trees throughout Dt 28:40
because your **o** will drop off. Dt 28:40
the slope of the Mount of **O**, 2Sm 15:30
They crush **o** in their presses; Jb 24:11
you will press **o** but not anoint Mc 6:15
will stand on the Mount of **O**, Zch 14:4
The Mount of **O** will be split in Zch 14:4
to Bethphage at the Mount of **O**, Mt 21:1
was sitting on the Mount of **O**, Mt 24:3
they went out to the Mount of **O**. Mt 26:30
and Bethany near the Mount of **O**, Mk 11:1
the Mount of **O** across from the Mk 13:3
they went out to the Mount of **O**. Mk 14:26
the place called the Mount of **O**, Lk 19:29
the path down the Mount of **O**, Lk 19:37
what is called the Mount of **O**. Lk 21:37
way as usual to the Mount of **O**, Lk 22:39
Jesus went to the Mount of **O**. Jn 8:1
fig tree produce **o**, my brothers, Jms 3:12

OLYMPAS *(1)*

his sister, and **O**, and all the Rm 16:15

OMAR *(3)*

were Teman, **O**, Zepho, Gatam, Gn 36:11
Chiefs Teman, **O**, Zepho, Kenaz, Gn 36:15
Teman, **O**, Zephi, Gatam, and 1Ch 1:36

OMEGA *(3)*

"I am the Alpha and the **O**," Rv 1:8
Alpha and the **O**, the Beginning Rv 21:6
the Alpha and the **O**, the First Rv 22:13

OMEN *(1)*

as a sign and **o** against Egypt Is 20:3

OMENS *(4)*

not go to seek **o** as on previous Nm 24:1
interpret **o**, practice sorcery, Dt 18:10
divination and interpreted **o**. 2Kg 17:17
who destroys the **o** of the false Is 44:25

He is the only **o** of his mother's Gn 44:20
O left—I said that he must Gn 44:28
you also take this **o** from me and Gn 44:29
No **o** was with him when he Gn 45:1
the **o** you sold into Egypt. Gn 45:4
the cities from **o** end of Egypt Gn 47:21
This **o** is the firstborn. Gn 48:18
giving you the **o** mountain slope Gn 48:22
his people as **o** of the tribes Gn 49:16
hands of the Mighty **O** of Jacob, Gn 49:24
blessed each **o** with a suitable Gn 49:28
dead, they said to **o** another, "If Gn 50:15
o of whom was named Shiphrah and Ex 1:15
"This is **o** of the Hebrew boys." Ex 2:6
a Hebrew, **o** of his people. Ex 2:11
all around and seeing no **o**, Ex 2:12
He asked the **o** in the wrong, Ex 2:13
Eleazar married **o** of the Ex 6:25
Each **o** threw down his staff, Ex 7:12
know there is no **o** like the LORD Ex 8:10
and his people; not **o** was left. Ex 8:31
not a single **o** of the Israelite Ex 9:7
know there is no **o** like Me in Ex 9:14
The LORD is the Righteous **O**, Ex 9:27
land so that no **o** will be able Ex 10:5
O person could not see another, Ex 10:23
I will bring **o** more plague on Ex 11:1
households, **o** animal per Ex 12:3
house are to select **o** based on Ex 12:4
It is to be eaten in **o** house. Ex 12:46
Egypt, with officers in each **o**. Ex 14:7
it, they asked **o** another, "What Ex 16:15
No **o** is to let any of it remain Ex 16:19
o is to leave his place on the Ex 16:29
moving from **o** place to the next Ex 17:1
o on one side and one on the Ex 17:12
one on **o** side and one on the Ex 17:12
one side and **o** on the other so Ex 17:12
o of whom was named Gershom Ex 18:3
between **o** man and another Ex 18:16
You be the **o** to represent the Ex 18:19
men quarrel and **o** strikes the Ex 21:18
then the **o** who struck ⌊him⌋ will Ex 21:19
the **o** who hit her must be fined Ex 21:22
no **o** is guilty of bloodshed. Ex 22:2
the **o** who started the fire must Ex 22:6
The **o** the judges condemn must Ex 22:9
stolen, while no **o** is watching, Ex 22:10
No **o** is to appear before Me Ex 23:15
rings on **o** side and two rings Ex 25:12
Make **o** cherub at one end and one Ex 25:19
one cherub at **o** end and one Ex 25:19
at one end and **o** cherub at the Ex 25:19
the cherubim of **o** piece with the Ex 25:19
and are to face **o** another. Ex 25:20
It is to be made of **o** piece: Ex 25:31
lampstand from **o** side and three Ex 25:32
branches are to be of **o** piece. Ex 25:36
50 loops on the **o** curtain and Ex 26:5
on the edge of the **o** curtain, Ex 26:10
The half yard on **o** side and the Ex 26:13
for the planks on **o** side of the Ex 26:26
the planks from **o** end to the Ex 26:28
the horns are to be of **o** piece. Ex 27:2
the hangings on **o** side ⌊of the Ex 27:14
on the ephod must be of **o** piece, Ex 28:8
with **o** of the names of the 12 Ex 28:21
Take **o** ram, and Aaron and his Ex 29:15
take **o** loaf of bread, one cake Ex 29:23
o cake of bread ⌊made⌋ with oil, Ex 29:23
and **o** wafer from the basket of Ex 29:23
Any priest who is **o** of his sons Ex 29:30
In the morning offer **o** lamb, Ex 29:39
mixed with **o** quart of crushed Ex 29:40
offering of **o** quart of wine. Ex 29:40
like the **o** in the morning, Ex 29:41
Its horns must be of **o** piece. Ex 30:2
and **o** gallon of olive oil. Ex 30:24
each **o** at the door of his tent, Ex 33:8
each **o** at the door of his tent. Ex 33:10
for no **o** can see Me and live." Ex 33:20
No **o** may go up with you; Ex 34:3
o must be seen anywhere on the Ex 34:3
No **o** is to appear before Me Ex 34:20
No **o** will covet your land when Ex 34:24
the sanctuary came **o** by one from Ex 36:4
came one by **o** from the work they Ex 36:4
50 loops on the **o** curtain and 50 Ex 36:12

bases, two bases under each **o**. Ex 36:30
for the planks on **o** side of the Ex 36:31
the planks from **o** end to the Ex 36:33
rings on **o** side and two rings Ex 37:3
o cherub at one end and one Ex 37:8
one cherub at **o** end and one Ex 37:8
at one end and **o** cherub at the Ex 37:8
the cherubim ⌊of **o** piece⌋ with Ex 37:8
He made it ⌊all⌋ of **o** piece: Ex 37:17
lampstand from **o** side and three Ex 37:18
and branches were of **o** piece. Ex 37:22
Its horns were of **o** piece. Ex 37:25
the horns were of **o** piece. Ex 38:2
The hangings on **o** side ⌊of the Ex 38:14
on the ephod was of **o** piece with Ex 39:5
like a seal with **o** of the names Ex 39:14
must present **o** without blemish Lv 3:1
by violating **o** of the LORD's Lv 4:27
by which **o** can become defiled Lv 5:3
guilt in **o** of these cases, Lv 5:5
o as a sin offering and the Lv 5:7
first present the **o** for the sin Lv 5:8
he must present **o** ⌊portion⌋ of Lv 7:14
to the **o** who presents it Lv 7:18
But the **o** who eats meat from the Lv 7:20
The **o** who presents a fellowship Lv 7:29
the LORD he took **o** cake of Lv 8:26
o cake of bread ⌊made⌋ with oil, Lv 8:26
oil, and **o** wafer, and placed Lv 8:26
any **o** of them dies and falls Lv 11:32
Anything **o** of their carcasses Lv 11:35
If **o** of their carcasses falls on Lv 11:37
on the seed and **o** of their Lv 11:38
If **o** of the animals that you use Lv 11:39
o for a burnt offering and the Lv 12:8
the priest or to **o** of his sons, Lv 13:2
brought for the **o** who is to be Lv 14:4
will order that **o** of the birds Lv 14:5
seven times on the **o** who is to Lv 14:7
The **o** who is to be cleansed must Lv 14:8
priest is to take **o** male lamb Lv 14:12
ear of the **o** to be cleansed, Lv 14:14
ear of the **o** to be cleansed, Lv 14:17
head of the **o** to be cleansed. Lv 14:18
for the **o** to be purified Lv 14:19
he is to take **o** male lamb for a Lv 14:21
o to be a sin offering and the Lv 14:22
earlobe of the **o** to be cleansed, Lv 14:25
earlobe of the **o** to be cleansed, Lv 14:28
the head of the **o** to be cleansed Lv 14:29
then sacrifice **o** type of what he Lv 14:30
o as a sin offering and the Lv 14:31
LORD for the **o** to be cleansed. Lv 14:31
is to slaughter **o** of the birds Lv 14:50
o as a sin offering and the Lv 15:15
is to sacrifice **o** as a sin Lv 15:30
offering and **o** ram for a burnt Lv 16:5
o lot for the LORD and the other Lv 16:8
No **o** may be in the tent of Lv 16:17
The **o** who burns them is to wash Lv 16:28
deceptively or lie to **o** another. Lv 19:11
clean animal from the unclean **o**, Lv 20:25
unclean bird from the clean **o**. Lv 20:25
or **o** defiled by prostitution. Lv 21:14
No **o** outside a priest's family Lv 22:10
the **O** who brought you out of the Lv 22:33
will be **o** quart of wine. Lv 23:13
lambs a year old, **o** young bull, Lv 23:18
also to prepare **o** male goat as a Lv 23:19
Bring the **o** who has cursed to Lv 24:14
brought the **o** who had cursed Lv 24:23
him, do not cheat **o** another. Lv 25:14
You are not to cheat **o** another, Lv 25:17
property⌋ **o** of the Levites can Lv 25:33
not rule over **o** another harshly. Lv 25:46
O of his brothers may redeem him. Lv 25:48
The **o** who purchased him is to Lv 25:50
though no **o** is pursuing you. Lv 26:17
they will flee as **o** flees from a Lv 26:36
fall though no **o** is pursuing Lv 26:36
stumble over **o** another as if Lv 26:37
sword though no **o** is pursuing Lv 26:37
person is from **o** month to five Lv 27:6
But if **o** is too poor to pay the Lv 27:8
to what the **o** making the vow can Lv 27:8
vow involves **o** of the animals Lv 27:9
does substitute **o** animal for Lv 27:10
If the **o** who brought it decides Lv 27:13

But if the **o** who consecrated his Lv 27:15
If the **o** who consecrated the Lv 27:19
will return to the **o** he bought Lv 27:24
But no **o** can consecrate a Lv 27:26
If it is **o** of the unclean Lv 27:27
names of every male **o** by one. Nm 1:2
names of every male one by **o**. Nm 1:2
each **o** the head of his ancestral Nm 1:4
counting **o** by one the names of Nm 1:18
counting one by **o** the names of Nm 1:18
counting **o** by one the names of Nm 1:20
counting one by **o** the names of Nm 1:20
counting **o** by one the names Nm 1:22
counting one by **o** the names of Nm 1:22
every male **o** month old or more. Nm 3:15
every male **o** month old or more, Nm 3:22
every male **o** month old or more, Nm 3:28
every male **o** month old or more, Nm 3:34
the Levite males **o** month old or Nm 3:39
the Israelites **o** month old or Nm 3:40
firstborn males **o** month old or Nm 3:43
each **o** according to his work and Nm 4:49
what each **o** gives to the priest Nm 5:10
is to offer **o** as a sin offering Nm 6:11
to the LORD of **o** unblemished Nm 6:14
o unblemished year-old female Nm 6:14
o unblemished ram as a Nm 6:14
o unleavened cake from the Nm 6:19
the basket, and **o** unleavened Nm 6:19
leaders and an ox from each **o**, Nm 7:3
Each day have **o** leader present Nm 7:11
The **o** who presented his offering Nm 7:12
His offering was **o** silver dish Nm 7:13
quarter pounds and **o** silver Nm 7:13
basin weighing **o** and Nm 7:13
o gold bowl weighing four ounces, Nm 7:14
o young bull, one ram, and one Nm 7:15
one young bull, **o** ram, and one Nm 7:15
and **o** male lamb a year old, Nm 7:15
o male goat for a sin offering; Nm 7:16
he presented **o** silver dish Nm 7:19
quarter pounds and **o** silver Nm 7:19
basin weighing **o** and Nm 7:19
o gold bowl weighing four ounces, Nm 7:20
o young bull, one ram, and one Nm 7:21
one young bull, **o** ram, and one Nm 7:21
and **o** male lamb a year old, Nm 7:21
o male goat for a sin offering; Nm 7:22
His offering was **o** silver dish Nm 7:25
quarter pounds and **o** silver Nm 7:25
basin weighing **o** and Nm 7:25
o gold bowl weighing four ounces, Nm 7:26
o young bull, one ram, and one Nm 7:27
one young bull, **o** ram, and one Nm 7:27
and **o** male lamb a year old, Nm 7:27
o male goat for a sin offering; Nm 7:28
His offering was **o** silver dish Nm 7:31
quarter pounds and **o** silver Nm 7:31
basin weighing **o** and Nm 7:31
o gold bowl weighing four ounces, Nm 7:32
o young bull, one ram, and one Nm 7:33
one young bull, **o** ram, and one Nm 7:33
and **o** male lamb a year old, Nm 7:33
o male goat for a sin offering; Nm 7:34
His offering was **o** silver dish Nm 7:37
quarter pounds and **o** silver Nm 7:37
basin weighing **o** and Nm 7:37
o gold bowl weighing four ounces, Nm 7:38
o young bull, one ram, and one Nm 7:39
one young bull, **o** ram, and one Nm 7:39
and **o** male lamb a year old, Nm 7:39
o male goat for a sin offering; Nm 7:40
His offering was **o** silver dish Nm 7:43
quarter pounds and **o** silver Nm 7:43
basin weighing **o** and Nm 7:43
o gold bowl weighing four ounces, Nm 7:44
o young bull, one ram, and one Nm 7:45
one young bull, **o** ram, and one Nm 7:45
and **o** male lamb a year old, Nm 7:45
o male goat for a sin offering; Nm 7:46
His offering was **o** silver dish Nm 7:49
quarter pounds and **o** silver Nm 7:49
basin weighing **o** and Nm 7:49
o gold bowl weighing four ounces, Nm 7:50
o young bull, one ram, and one Nm 7:51
one young bull, **o** ram, and one Nm 7:51
and **o** male lamb a year old, Nm 7:51
o male goat for a sin offering; Nm 7:52

His offering was **o** silver dish Nm 7:55
quarter pounds and **o** silver Nm 7:55
basin weighing **o** and Nm 7:55
o gold bowl weighing four ounces, Nm 7:56
o young bull, one ram, and one Nm 7:57
one young bull, **o** ram, and one Nm 7:57
and **o** male lamb a year old, Nm 7:57
o male goat for a sin offering; Nm 7:58
His offering was **o** silver dish Nm 7:61
quarter pounds and **o** silver Nm 7:61
basin weighing **o** and Nm 7:61
o gold bowl weighing four ounces, Nm 7:62
o young bull, one ram, and one Nm 7:63
one young bull, **o** ram, and one Nm 7:63
and **o** male lamb a year old, Nm 7:63
o male goat for a sin offering; Nm 7:64
His offering was **o** silver dish Nm 7:67
quarter pounds and **o** silver Nm 7:67
basin weighing **o** and Nm 7:67
o gold bowl weighing four ounces, Nm 7:68
o young bull, one ram, and one Nm 7:69
one young bull, **o** ram, and one Nm 7:69
and **o** male lamb a year old, Nm 7:69
o male goat for a sin offering; Nm 7:70
His offering was **o** silver dish Nm 7:73
quarter pounds and **o** silver Nm 7:73
basin weighing **o** and Nm 7:73
o gold bowl weighing four ounces, Nm 7:74
o young bull, one ram, and one Nm 7:75
one young bull, **o** ram, and one Nm 7:75
and **o** male lamb a year old, Nm 7:75
o male goat for a sin offering; Nm 7:76
His offering was **o** silver dish Nm 7:79
quarter pounds and **o** silver Nm 7:79
basin weighing **o** and Nm 7:79
o gold bowl weighing four ounces, Nm 7:80
o young bull, one ram, and one Nm 7:81
one young bull, **o** ram, and one Nm 7:81
and **o** male lamb a year old, Nm 7:81
o male goat for a sin offering; Nm 7:82
and each basin **o** and Nm 7:85
Sacrifice **o** as a sin offering Nm 8:12
When any **o** of you or your Nm 9:10
However, if **o** is sounded, only Nm 10:4
moving from **o** place to the next Nm 10:12
eat, not for **o** day, or two days Nm 11:19
o named Eldad and the other Nm 11:26
o who took the least gathered Nm 11:32
Send **o** man who is a leader among Nm 13:2
to explore is **o** that devours its Nm 13:32
So they said to **o** another, Nm 14:4
the **o** presenting his offering to Nm 15:4
is to prepare **o** young bull for a Nm 15:24
and **o** male goat as a sin Nm 15:24
o made by fire to the LORD, Nm 15:25
If **o** person sins Nm 15:27
⌊the **o**⌋ He will let come near Nm 16:5
will let the **o** He chooses come Nm 16:5
will be the **o** who is set apart. Nm 16:7
have not taken **o** donkey from Nm 16:15
mistreated a single **o** of them." Nm 16:15
all flesh, when **o** man sins, will Nm 16:22
and take **o** staff from them for Nm 17:2
there must be **o** staff for the Nm 17:3
o for each of the leaders of Nm 17:6
every **o** of their offerings that Nm 18:9
The **o** who burned the cow must Nm 19:8
Then the **o** who gathers up the Nm 19:10
to sprinkle the **o** who touched a Nm 19:18
The **o** who is clean is to Nm 19:19
the **o** being purified must wash Nm 19:19
whole army until no **o** was left, Nm 21:35
the oracle of **o** who hears the Nm 24:4
the oracle of **o** who hears the Nm 24:16
O who comes from Jacob will Nm 24:19
and decrease it for a small **o**. Nm 26:54
every male **o** month old or more; Nm 26:62
there was not **o** of those who had Nm 26:64
Offer **o** lamb in the morning and Nm 28:4
young bulls, **o** ram, seven male Nm 28:11
o and a third quarts with the Nm 28:14
and **o** quart with each male lamb. Nm 28:14
And **o** male goat is to be offered Nm 28:15
young bulls, **o** ram, and seven Nm 28:19
and **o** male goat for a sin Nm 28:22
young bulls, **o** ram, and seven Nm 28:27
o male goat to make atonement Nm 28:30
o young bull, one ram, seven Nm 29:2
young bull, **o** ram, seven male Nm 29:2
Also ⌊offer⌋ **o** male goat as a Nm 29:5
o young bull, one ram, and seven Nm 29:8
one young bull, **o** ram, and seven Nm 29:8
⌊Offer⌋ **o** male goat for a sin Nm 29:11
Also ⌊offer⌋ **o** male goat as a Nm 29:16
Also ⌊offer⌋ **o** male goat as a Nm 29:19
Also ⌊offer⌋ **o** male goat as a Nm 29:22
Also ⌊offer⌋ **o** male goat as a Nm 29:25
Also ⌊offer⌋ **o** male goat as a Nm 29:28
Also ⌊offer⌋ **o** male goat as a Nm 29:31
Also ⌊offer⌋ **o** male goat as a Nm 29:34
o bull, one ram, seven male Nm 29:36
bull, **o** ram, seven male lambs Nm 29:36
Also ⌊offer⌋ **o** male goat as a Nm 29:38
o out of ⌊every⌋ 500 humans, Nm 31:28
take **o** out of every 50 from the Nm 31:30
Moses took **o** out of ⌊every⌋ 50, Nm 31:47
and not **o** of us is missing. Nm 31:49
was a ⌊good⌋ **o** for livestock. Nm 32:1
and every **o** of your armed men Nm 32:21
and decrease it for a small **o**. Nm 33:54
Take **o** leader from each tribe to Nm 34:18
so that the **o** who kills someone Nm 35:6
and less from a smaller **o**. Nm 35:8
so that the **o** who kills someone Nm 35:12
the **o** who struck him must be put Nm 35:21
to protect the **o** who kills Nm 35:25
If the **o** who kills someone ever Nm 35:26
the **o** who killed a person was Nm 35:28
priest may the **o** who has killed Nm 35:28
But no **o** is to be put to death Nm 35:30
on the testimony of **o** witness. Nm 35:30
o of the clans of the sons of Nm 36:1
transfer from **o** tribe to another Nm 36:9
from among you, **o** man for each Dt 1:23
destroyed every **o** of you who Dt 4:3
earth and from **o** end of the Dt 4:32
where **o** could flee who committed Dt 4:42
could flee to **o** of these cities Dt 4:42
The LORD our God, the LORD is **O**. Dt 6:4
to follow every **o** of these Dt 6:25
pay back the **o** who hates Him. Dt 7:10
No **o** will be able to stand Dt 7:24
every **o** of these commands Dt 11:22
No **o** will be able to stand Dt 11:25
chooses in **o** of your tribes, Dt 12:14
from **o** end of the earth to the Dt 13:7
it said about **o** of your cities Dt 13:12
to follow every **o** of these Dt 15:5
o of your brothers within any of Dt 15:7
o is to appear before the LORD Dt 16:16
among you in **o** of your towns Dt 17:2
The **o** condemned to die is to be Dt 17:6
No **o** is to be executed on the Dt 17:6
or **o** who is not of your people. Dt 17:15
a Levite leaves **o** of your towns Dt 18:6
o among you is to make his son Dt 18:10
may flee to **o** of these cities Dt 19:5
might pursue the **o** who committed Dt 19:6
you keep every **o** of these Dt 19:9
and flees to **o** of these cities, Dt 19:11
O witness cannot establish any Dt 19:15
your God is the **O** who goes with Dt 20:4
o loved and the other unloved, Dt 21:15
is just like **o** in which a man Dt 22:26
there was no **o** to rescue her. Dt 22:27
No **o** of illegitimate birth may Dt 23:2
to stay⌋ at home for **o** year, Dt 24:5
kidnapping **o** of his Israelite Dt 24:7
whether **o** of your brothers or Dt 24:14
your brothers or **o** of the Dt 24:14
same property and **o** of them dies Dt 25:5
and the wife of **o** steps in to Dt 25:11
husband from the **o** striking him, Dt 25:11
in your bag, **o** heavy and one Dt 25:13
your bag, one heavy and **o** light. Dt 25:13
'Cursed is the **o** who dishonors Dt 27:16
'Cursed is the **o** who moves his Dt 27:17
'Cursed is the **o** who leads a Dt 27:18
'Cursed is the **o** who denies Dt 27:19
'Cursed is the **o** who sleeps with Dt 27:20
'Cursed is the **o** who has sexual Dt 27:21
'Cursed is the **o** who sleeps with Dt 27:22
'Cursed is the **o** who sleeps with Dt 27:23
'Cursed is the **o** who kills his Dt 27:24
'Cursed is the **o** who accepts a Dt 27:25
against you from **o** direction but Dt 28:7
against them from **o** direction Dt 28:25
and no **o** will scare them away. Dt 28:26
and no **o** will help ⌊you⌋. Dt 28:29
enemies, and no **o** will help you. Dt 28:31
peoples from **o** end of the earth Dt 28:64
but no **o** will buy ⌊you⌋." Dt 28:68
your God is the **O** who will cross Dt 31:3
Joshua is the **o** who will cross Dt 31:3
The LORD is the **O** who will go Dt 31:8
How could **o** man pursue a Dt 32:30
is gone and no **o** is left— Dt 32:36
No **o** can rescue ⌊anyone⌋ from My Dt 32:39
Urim belong to Your faithful **o**; Dt 33:8
The **o** who enlarges Gad's Dt 33:20
and no **o** to this day knows where Dt 34:6
No **o** will be able to stand Jos 1:5
tribes of Israel, **o** man for each Jos 3:12
from the people, **o** man for each Jos 4:2
the Israelites, **o** man for each Jos 4:4
o for each of the Israelite Jos 4:5
o for each of the Israelite Jos 4:8
Israelites—no **o** leaving or Jos 6:1
war, circling the city **o** time. Jos 6:3
Don't let **o** word come out of Jos 6:10
The **o** who is caught with the Jos 7:15
some on **o** side and some on the Jos 8:22
when every last **o** of them had Jos 8:24
a large city like **o** of the royal Jos 10:2
Not **o** of them will be able to Jos 10:8
No **o** could say a thing against Jos 10:21
and their land in **o** campaign, Jos 10:42
them; he left no **o** alive. Then Jos 11:11
them, leaving no **o** alive. Jos 11:14
of Jericho **o** the king of Ai, Jos 12:9
of Ai, which is next to Bethel **o** Jos 12:9
king of Jerusalem **o** the king of Jos 12:10
one the king of Hebron **o** Jos 12:10
king of Jarmuth **o** the king of Jos 12:11
one the king of Lachish **o** Jos 12:11
king of Eglon **o** the king of Jos 12:12
of Eglon one the king of Gezer **o** Jos 12:12
king of Debir **o** the king of Jos 12:13
of Debir one the king of Geder **o** Jos 12:13
of Hormah **o** the king of Arad Jos 12:14
of Hormah one the king of Arad **o** Jos 12:14
the king of Libnah **o** the king of Jos 12:15
Libnah one the king of Adullam **o** Jos 12:15
king of Makkedah **o** the king of Jos 12:16
one the king of Bethel **o** Jos 12:16
king of Tappuah **o** the king of Jos 12:17
Tappuah one the king of Hepher **o** Jos 12:17
the king of Aphek **o** the king of Jos 12:18
Aphek one the king of Lasharon **o** Jos 12:18
king of Madon **o** the king of Jos 12:19
of Madon one the king of Hazor **o** Jos 12:19
of Shimron-meron **o** the king of Jos 12:20
one the king of Achshaph **o** Jos 12:20
king of Taanach **o** the king of Jos 12:21
one the king of Megiddo **o** Jos 12:21
the king of Kedesh **o** the king of Jos 12:22
the king of Jokneam in Carmel **o** Jos 12:22
in Naphoth-dor **o** the king of Jos 12:23
the king of Goiim in Gilgal **o** Jos 12:23
king of Tirzah **o** ⌊the total Jos 12:24
he was **o** of the remaining Jos 13:12
a wife to the **o** who strikes down Jos 15:16
give us only **o** tribal allotment Jos 17:14
You will not have just **o** lot, Jos 17:17
flees to **o** of these cities Jos 20:4
not hand the **o** who committed Jos 20:5
Then the **o** who committed Jos 20:6
of refuge for the **o** who commits Jos 21:13
of refuge for the **o** who commits Jos 21:21
who were **o** of the Levite clans: Jos 21:27
of refuge for the **o** who commits Jos 21:27
of refuge for the **o** who commits Jos 21:32
of refuge for the **o** who commits Jos 21:38
o family leader for each tribe Jos 22:14
was not the only **o** who perished Jos 22:20
and no **o** has been able to stand Jos 23:9
O of you routed a thousand, Jos 23:10
not **o** promise has failed. Jos 23:14
today the **o** you will worship: Jos 24:15
men. Not **o** of them escaped. Jdg 3:29
down ⌊as if it were⌋ **o** man." Jdg 6:16
let me speak **o** more time. Jdg 6:39
allow me to make **o** more test Jdg 6:39
to you, 'This **o** can go with you, Jdg 7:4

'This **o** cannot go with you,' Jdg 7:4
men a trumpet in **o** hand and an Jdg 7:16
you or that **o** man rule over you? Jdg 9:2
and **o** unit is coming from the Jdg 9:37
of Gilead said to **o** another, Jdg 10:18
father, "Let me do this **o** thing: Jdg 11:37
he was buried in **o** of the cities Jdg 12:7
was given to **o** of the men who Jdg 14:20
I gave her to **o** of the men who Jdg 15:2
Come **o** more time, for he has Jdg 16:18
With **o** act of vengeance, let me Jdg 16:28
o on his right hand and the Jdg 16:29
and installed **o** of his sons to Jdg 17:5
man became like **o** of his sons. Jdg 17:11
for the house of **o** person or for Jdg 18:19
There was no **o** to save them, Jdg 18:28
try to reach **o** of these places Jdg 19:13
but no **o** took them into their Jdg 19:15
No **o** has taken me into his home, Jdg 19:18
assembled as **o** body before the Jdg 20:1
every **o** an experienced warrior. Jdg 20:17
o of which goes up to Bethel and Jdg 20:31
it occurred that **o** tribe is Jdg 21:3
out that no **o** from Jabesh-gilead Jdg 21:8
no **o** was there from the Jdg 21:9
o was named Orpah and the second Ru 1:4
don't leave this **o**, but stay Ru 2:8
I am not like **o** of your female Ru 2:13
is **o** of our family redeemers." Ru 2:20
is no **o** holy like the LORD. 1Sm 2:2
There is no **o** besides You! 1Sm 2:2
in place of the **o** she has given 1Sm 2:20
no **o** in your family will ever 1Sm 2:32
My anointed **o** for all time. 1Sm 2:35
O day Eli, whose eyesight was 1Sm 3:2
I'm the **o** who came from the 1Sm 4:16
since there was **o** plague for 1Sm 6:4
prepare **o** new cart and two milk 1Sm 6:7
They stayed on that **o** highway, 1Sm 6:12
had sent back **o** gold tumor for 1Sm 6:17
There was no **o** more impressive 1Sm 9:2
O day the donkeys of Saul's 1Sm 9:3
Take **o** of the attendants with 1Sm 9:3
meet you there, **o** bringing three 1Sm 10:3
o bringing three loaves of bread, 1Sm 10:3
and **o** bringing a skin of wine. 1Sm 10:3
Do you see the **o** the LORD has 1Sm 10:24
There is no **o** like him among the 1Sm 10:24
I'll make **o** with you on this 1Sm 11:2
If no **o** saves us, we will 1Sm 11:3
No **o** will be executed this day, 1Sm 11:13
chosen, the **o** you requested. 1Sm 12:13
O division headed toward the 1Sm 13:17
O was named Bozez and the other 1Sm 14:4
o stood to the north in front of 1Sm 14:5
Then, **o** of the troops said, "Your 1Sm 14:28
So every **o** of the troops 1Sm 14:34
Don't let even **o** remain!" 1Sm 14:36
Not **o** of the troops answered 1Sm 14:39
You will be on **o** side, and I and 1Sm 14:40
the Eternal **O** of Israel does not 1Sm 15:29
for Me the **o** I indicate to you 1Sm 16:3
LORD's anointed **o** is here before 1Sm 16:6
hasn't chosen this **o** either," 1Sm 16:8
hasn't chosen this **o** either." 1Sm 16:9
Anoint him, for he is the **o**." 1Sm 16:12
O of the young men answered, 1Sm 16:18
and **o** young goat and sent them 1Sm 16:20
were standing on **o** hill, 1Sm 17:3
Choose **o** of your men and have 1Sm 17:8
⌊**O** day⌋, Jesse had told his son 1Sm 17:17
will be like **o** of them, 1Sm 17:36
cuts off every **o** of David's 1Sm 20:15
you alone and no **o** is with you?" 1Sm 21:1
O of Saul's servants, detained 1Sm 21:7
for there isn't another **o** here." 1Sm 21:9
you brought this **o** to act crazy 1Sm 21:15
Is this **o** going to come into my 1Sm 21:15
o of the sons of Ahimelech son 1Sm 22:20
for the **o** who wants to take my 1Sm 22:23
Saul went along **o** side of the 1Sm 23:26
O of Nabal's young men 1Sm 25:14
No **o** saw them, no one knew, and 1Sm 26:12
saw them, no **o** knew, and no one 1Sm 26:12
no one knew, and no **o** woke up; 1Sm 26:12
the king when **o** of the people 1Sm 26:15
like **o** who pursues a partridge 1Sm 26:20
o of the young men come over 1Sm 26:22

O of these days I'll be swept 1Sm 27:1
a place in **o** of the outlying 1Sm 27:5
together into **o** army to fight 1Sm 28:1
up for me the **o** I tell you." 1Sm 28:8
had killed no **o** but had carried 1Sm 30:2
The share of the **o** who goes into 1Sm 30:24
share of the **o** who remains with 1Sm 30:24
David summoned **o** of his servants 2Sm 1:15
Should I go to **o** of the towns of 2Sm 2:1
each **o** with his household, 2Sm 2:3
like **o** of the wild gazelles. 2Sm 2:18
seize **o** of the young soldiers, 2Sm 2:21
o thing I require of you: 2Sm 3:13
You fell like **o** who falls victim 2Sm 3:34
o named Baanah and the other 2Sm 4:2
⌊the **O**⌋ who has redeemed my life 2Sm 4:9
were the **o** who led us out ⌊to 2Sm 5:2
cake to each **o** of the whole 2Sm 6:19
is no **o** like You, and there 2Sm 7:22
God came to **o** nation on earth in 2Sm 7:23
to death and **o** length ⌊of those 2Sm 8:2
table just like **o** of the king's 2Sm 9:11
O evening David got up from his 2Sm 11:2
o rich and the other poor. 2Sm 12:1
nothing except **o** small ewe lamb 2Sm 12:3
himself to take **o** of his own 2Sm 12:4
I will be the **o** to capture the 2Sm 12:28
would be like **o** of the immoral 2Sm 13:13
I not the **o** who has commanded 2Sm 13:28
not even **o** of them survived!" 2Sm 13:30
field with no **o** to separate them 2Sm 14:6
o struck the other and killed 2Sm 14:6
'Hand over the **o** who killed his 2Sm 14:7
extinguish my **o** remaining ember 2Sm 14:7
brought back his own banished **o**. 2Sm 14:13
so that the **o** banished from Him 2Sm 14:14
no **o** can turn to the right or 2Sm 14:19
Joab is the **o** who gave orders to 2Sm 14:19
servant is from **o** of the tribes 2Sm 15:2
the side of the **o** that the LORD, 2Sm 16:18
already hiding in **o** of the caves 2Sm 17:9
Not even **o** will be left of all 2Sm 17:12
there was no **o** who had not 2Sm 17:22
out the troops, **o** third under 2Sm 18:2
o third under Joab's brother 2Sm 18:2
and **o** third under Ittai the 2Sm 18:2
O of the men saw ⌊him⌋ and 2Sm 18:10
o is also bringing good news, 2Sm 18:26
So he stood to **o** side. 2Sm 18:30
I am the first **o** of the entire 2Sm 19:20
O of Joab's young men had stood 2Sm 20:11
o of the faithful in Israel, 2Sm 20:19
Deliver this **o** man, and I will 2Sm 20:21
o of the descendants of the 2Sm 21:16
who was **o** of the descendants of 2Sm 21:18
but there is no **o** to save ⌊them⌋ 2Sm 22:42
the **o** anointed by the God of 2Sm 23:1
The **o** who rules the people with 2Sm 23:3
800 ⌊men⌋ he killed at **o** time. 2Sm 23:8
did not become **o** of the Three. 2Sm 23:19
did not become **o** of the Three. 2Sm 23:23
Choose **o** of them, and I will do 2Sm 24:12
take back to the **O** who sent me." 2Sm 24:13
I am the **o** who has sinned; 2Sm 24:17
I am the **o** who has done wrong. 2Sm 24:17
and he is the **o** who is to sit on 1Kg 1:13
and he is the **o** who is to sit on 1Kg 1:17
and he is the **o** who is to sit on 1Kg 1:24
and he is the **o** who is to sit on 1Kg 1:30
is the **o** who is to become king 1Kg 1:35
he is the **o** I have commanded to 1Kg 1:35
He has provided **o** to sit on my 1Kg 1:48
I have just **o** request of you; 1Kg 2:16
I have just **o** small request of 1Kg 2:20
lives, the **O** who established 1Kg 2:24
O woman said, "Please my lord, 1Kg 3:17
No **o** else was with us in the 1Kg 3:18
My son is the living **o**; 1Kg 3:22
your son is the dead **o**." 1Kg 3:22
No, your son is the dead **o**; 1Kg 3:22
my son is the living **o**." 1Kg 3:22
and give half to **o** and half to 1Kg 3:25
But the other **o** said, "He will 1Kg 3:26
each **o** made provision for one 1Kg 4:7
made provision for **o** month out 1Kg 4:7
There was **o** deputy in the land 1Kg 4:19
provisions for **o** day were 150 1Kg 4:22
o month they were in Lebanon, 1Kg 5:14

O wing of the ⌊first⌋ cherub was 1Kg 6:24
wing touched ⌊**o**⌋ wall while 1Kg 6:27
on the **o** grating to cover 1Kg 7:18
each support was **o** piece with 1Kg 7:34
its frames were **o** piece with it. 1Kg 7:35
o basin for each of the 10 water 1Kg 7:38
you are not the **o** to build it; 1Kg 8:19
for there is no **o** who does not 1Kg 8:46
Not **o** of all the good promises 1Kg 8:56
on the six steps, **o** at each end. 1Kg 10:20
I will give **o** tribe to your son 1Kg 11:13
but **o** tribe will remain his 1Kg 11:32
I will give **o** tribe to his son, 1Kg 11:36
No **o** followed the house of David 1Kg 12:20
He set up **o** in Bethel, and put 1Kg 12:29
before **o** of the calves all 1Kg 12:30
Jeroboam as **o** sweeps away dung 1Kg 14:10
for this **o** alone out of 1Kg 14:13
Ahab went **o** way by himself, 1Kg 18:6
They are to choose **o** bull for 1Kg 18:23
yourselves **o** bull and prepare 1Kg 18:25
no sound; no **o** answered. Then 1Kg 18:26
no sound, no **o** answered, no one 1Kg 18:29
answered, no **o** paid attention. 1Kg 18:29
not let even **o** of them escape. 1Kg 18:40
the life of **o** of them by this 1Kg 19:2
see that this **o** is only looking 1Kg 20:7
like the **o** who takes it off. 1Kg 20:11
and each **o** struck down his 1Kg 20:20
100,000 foot soldiers in **o** day. 1Kg 20:29
O of the sons of the prophets 1Kg 20:35
that he was **o** of the prophets. 1Kg 20:41
there was no **o** like Ahab, who 1Kg 21:25
There is still **o** man who can ask 1Kg 22:8
So **o** was saying this and 1Kg 22:20
put him on **o** of the mountains 2Kg 2:16
or into **o** of the valleys." 2Kg 2:16
After they had brought him **o**, 2Kg 2:20
O of the servants of the king 2Kg 3:11
O of the wives of the sons of 2Kg 4:1
Set the full ones to **o** side." 2Kg 4:4
O day Elisha went to Shunem. 2Kg 4:8
I know that the **o** who often 2Kg 4:9
O day he came there and stopped 2Kg 4:11
child grew and **o** day went out to 2Kg 4:18
Please send me **o** of the servants 2Kg 4:22
servants and **o** of the donkeys, 2Kg 4:22
O went out to the field to 2Kg 4:39
Then **o** said, "Please come with 2Kg 6:3
As **o** of them was cutting down a 2Kg 6:5
which **o** of us is for the king of 2Kg 6:11
O of his servants said, "No one, 2Kg 6:12
said, "No **o**, my lord the king 2Kg 6:12
camp and no **o** was there— 2Kg 7:10
But **o** of his servants responded, 2Kg 7:13
he reigned **o** year in Jerusalem. 2Kg 8:26
Elisha called **o** of the sons 2Kg 9:1
Jehu asked, "For which **o** of us?" 2Kg 9:5
at Jezreel—no **o** will bury her. 2Kg 9:10
so that no **o** will ⌊be able⌋ to 2Kg 9:37
"Is your heart **o** with mine?" 2Kg 10:15
for Baal." So they called **o**. 2Kg 10:20
was filled from **o** end to the 2Kg 10:21
o third of you who come on duty 2Kg 11:5
and ⌊another **o**⌋ between the king 2Kg 11:17
right side as **o** enters the 2Kg 12:9
each **o** will be put to death for 2Kg 14:6
There was no **o** to help Israel, 2Kg 14:26
Send back **o** of the priests you 2Kg 17:27
So **o** of the priests they had 2Kg 17:28
not **o** of the kings of Judah was 2Kg 18:5
of silver and **o** ton of gold. 2Kg 18:14
Isn't He the **O** whose high places 2Kg 18:22
Then every **o** of you may eat from 2Kg 18:31
and every **o** may drink water from 2Kg 18:31
Against the Holy **O** of Israel! 2Kg 19:22
O day, while he was worshiping 2Kg 19:37
clean as **o** wipes a bowl— 2Kg 21:13
with it from **o** end to another. 2Kg 21:16
so that no **o** could make his son 2Kg 23:10
and no **o** like him arose after 2Kg 23:25
two pillars, the **o** reservoir, 2Kg 25:16
O pillar was 27 feet tall and 2Kg 25:17
O of them was named Peleg, 1Ch 1:19
300 and killed them at **o** time. 1Ch 11:11
the Ahohite was **o** of the three 1Ch 11:12
did not become **o** of the Three. 1Ch 11:21
did not become **o** of the Three. 1Ch 11:25

was also of **o** mind to make David 1Ch 12:38
No **o** but the Levites may carry 1Ch 15:2
nation and from **o** kingdom to 1Ch 16:20
He allowed no **o** to oppress them; 1Ch 16:21
You are not the **o** to build Me a 1Ch 17:4
a word to even **o** of the judges 1Ch 17:6
who is **o** of your own sons, 1Ch 17:11
it from the **o** who was before 1Ch 17:13
LORD, there is no **o** like You, 1Ch 17:20
You came to **o** nation on earth to 1Ch 17:21
Choose **o** of them for yourself, 1Ch 21:10
take back to the **O** who sent me." 1Ch 21:12
Wasn't I the **o** who gave the 1Ch 21:17
I am the **o** who has sinned and 1Ch 21:17
He is the **o** who will build a 1Ch 22:10
O ancestral house was taken for 1Ch 24:6
Eleazar, and then **o** for Ithamar. 1Ch 24:6
son of Kore, **o** of the sons of 1Ch 26:1
for Judah, Elihu, **o** of David's 1Ch 27:18
Solomon is the **o** who is to build 1Ch 28:6
the wing of **o** was seven and a 2Ch 3:11
o on the right and one on the 2Ch 3:17
on the right and **o** on the left. 2Ch 3:17
He named the **o** on the right 2Ch 3:17
Jachin and the **o** on the left 2Ch 3:17
The **o** reservoir and the 12 oxen 2Ch 4:15
and thank the LORD with **o** voice. 2Ch 5:13
you are not the **o** to build the 2Ch 6:9
for there is no **o** who does not 2Ch 6:36
do not reject Your anointed **o**; 2Ch 6:42
on the six steps, **o** at each end. 2Ch 9:19
in the hand of ⌊**o** of⌋ David's 2Ch 13:8
No **o** made war with him in those 2Ch 14:6
with an army of **o** million men 2Ch 14:9
there is no **o** besides You to 2Ch 14:11
There is still **o** man who can ask 2Ch 18:7
So **o** was saying this and 2Ch 18:19
and no **o** can stand against You. 2Ch 20:6
he reigned **o** year in Jerusalem. 2Ch 22:2
Ahaziah had no **o** to exercise 2Ch 22:9
o third of you, priests and 2Ch 23:4
No **o** is to enter the LORD's 2Ch 23:6
each **o** will die for his own sin. 2Ch 25:4
to help or to make **o** stumble. 2Ch 25:8
o of the king's commanders. 2Ch 26:11
120,000 in Judah in **o** day— 2Ch 28:6
to give them **o** heart to carry 2Ch 30:12
and Manasseh, to the last **o**. 2Ch 31:1
You must worship before **o** altar, 2Ch 32:12
Passover like the **o** that Josiah 2Ch 35:18
of cut stones and **o** of timber. Ezr 6:4
o for each Israelite tribe. Ezr 6:17
though no **o** can stand in Your Ezr 9:15
Hanani, **o** of my brothers, Neh 1:2
I took was the **o** I was riding. Neh 2:12
heaven is the **O** who will grant Neh 2:20
him Malchijah, **o** of the Neh 3:31
every **o** of us returned to his Neh 4:15
loads worked with **o** hand and Neh 4:17
far from **o** another along Neh 4:19
day, **o** ox, six choice sheep, Neh 5:18
cast lots for **o** out of ten to Neh 11:1
O went to the right on the wall, Neh 12:31
of Ashdod or of **o** of the other Neh 13:24
Even **o** of the sons of Jehoiada, Neh 13:28
in every **o** of King Ahasuerus' Est 1:16
There is **o** ethnic group, Est 3:8
o of the king's eunuchs assigned Est 4:5
know that **o** law applies to Est 4:11
invited no **o** but me to join Est 5:12
the charge of **o** of the king's Est 6:9
where is the **o** who would devise Est 7:5
Harbona, **o** of the royal eunuchs, Est 7:9
they send gifts to **o** another. Est 9:19
sending gifts to **o** another and Est 9:22
O day the sons of God came to Jb 1:6
No **o** else on earth is like him, Jb 1:8
O day when Job's sons and Jb 1:13
O day the sons of God came again Jb 2:1
No **o** else on earth is like him, Jb 2:3
but no **o** spoke a word to him Jb 2:13
light given to **o** burdened with Jb 3:20
steadied the **o** who was stumbling Jb 4:4
forever while no **o** notices. Jb 4:20
with no **o** to defend ⌊them⌋. Jb 5:4
denied the words of the Holy **O**. Jb 6:10
so the **o** who goes down to Sheol Jb 7:9
o wanted to take Him to court, Jb 9:3

look, He is the Mighty **O**! Jb 9:19
There is no **o** to judge between Jb 9:33
there is no **o** who can deliver Jb 10:7
with no **o** to humiliate you? Jb 11:3
The **o** who is at ease holds Jb 12:5
take notice of **o** like this? Jb 14:3
pure from what is impure? No **o**! Jb 14:4
be pure, or **o** born of woman, Jb 15:14
how much less **o** who is revolting Jb 15:16
and the **o** whose hands are clean Jb 17:9
the place of the **o** who does not Jb 18:21
regards me as ⌊**o** of⌋ His enemies Jb 19:11
O person dies in excellent Jb 21:23
will ⌊even⌋ rescue the guilty **o**, Jb 22:30
the **O** who establishes harmony in Jb 25:2
How can **o** born of woman be pure? Jb 25:4
who had no **o** to support him. Jb 29:12
like **o** who comforts those who Jb 29:25
Yet no **o** would stretch out ⌊his⌋ Jb 30:24
Did not the **O** who made me in the Jb 31:15
Yet no **o** proved Job wrong; Jb 32:12
not **o** of you refuted his Jb 32:12
I will be partial to no **o**, Jb 32:21
o mediator out of a thousand, Jb 33:23
Could **o** who hates justice govern Jb 34:17
condemn the mighty Righteous **O**, Jb 34:17
that **o** should approach Him in Jb 34:23
But no **o** asks, "Where is God my Jb 35:10
o who has perfect knowledge is Jb 36:4
mighty, but He despises ⌊no **o**⌋; Jb 36:5
careful that no **o** lures you with Jb 36:18
snorting ⌊fills **o** with⌋ terror. Jb 39:20
Will the **o** who contends with the Jb 40:2
No **o** is ferocious ⌊enough⌋ to Jb 41:10
O scale is so close to another Jb 41:16
They are joined to **o** another, Jb 41:17
o would think the deep had white Jb 41:32
Each **o** gave him a qesitah , Jb 42:11
the LORD and His Anointed **O**: Ps 2:2
O enthroned in heaven laughs; Ps 2:4
and the **O** who lifts up my head. Ps 3:3
LORD, bless the righteous **o**; Ps 5:12
apart, with no **o** to rescue me. Ps 7:2
done harm to **o** at peace with me Ps 7:4
The **O** who examines the thoughts Ps 7:9
the **O** who seeks an accounting Ps 9:12
the wicked **o** boasts about his Ps 10:3
the **o** who is greedy curses and Ps 10:3
for no faithful **o** remains; Ps 12:1
lie to **o** another; they speak Ps 12:2
place the **o** who longs for it. Ps 12:5
There is no **o** who does good. Ps 14:1
see if there is **o** who is wise, Ps 14:2
who is wise, **o** who seeks God. Ps 14:2
There is no **o** who does good, Ps 14:3
one who does good, not even **o**. Ps 14:3
The **o** who lives honestly, Ps 15:2
who despises the **o** rejected by Ps 15:4
the **o** who does these things will Ps 15:5
Your Faithful **O** to see the Pit. Ps 16:10
but there is no **o** to save ⌊them⌋ Ps 18:41
It rises from **o** end of the Ps 19:6
near and there is no **o** to help. Ps 22:11
even the **o** who cannot preserve Ps 22:29
The **o** who has clean hands and a Ps 24:4
Not **o** person who waits for You Ps 25:3
I have asked **o** thing from the Ps 27:4
How happy is the **o** whose Ps 32:1
but the **o** who trusts in the LORD Ps 32:10
come to the **o** who is righteous, Ps 34:19
not **o** of them is broken. Ps 34:20
the poor from **o** too strong for Ps 35:10
the needy from **o** who robs him?" Ps 35:10
with grief, like **o** mourning a Ps 35:14
be agitated by **o** who prospers Ps 37:7
Happy is **o** who cares for the Ps 41:1
When **o** ⌊of them⌋ comes to visit, Ps 41:6
whom I trusted, **o** who ate my Ps 41:9
o should forever stop trying— Ps 49:8
For **o** can see that wise men die; Ps 49:10
There is no **o** who does good. Ps 53:1
to see if there is **o** who is wise Ps 53:2
There is no **o** who does good, Ps 53:3
one who does good, not even **o**. Ps 53:3
the **O** enthroned from long ago, Ps 55:19
the **o** who tramples me Ps 57:3
to You, the **O** who hears prayer Ps 65:2
happy is the **o** You choose and Ps 65:4

the hairy head of **o** who goes on Ps 68:21
for comforters, but found no **o**. Ps 69:20
may no **o** live in their tents. Ps 69:25
they persecute the **o** You struck Ps 69:26
there is no **o** to rescue ⌊him⌋. Ps 71:11
with a harp, Holy **O** of Israel. Ps 71:22
Like **o** waking from a dream, Ps 73:20
I am the **O** who steadies its Ps 75:3
He brings down **o** and exalts Ps 75:7
tribute to the awe-inspiring **O**. Ps 76:11
provoked the Holy **O** of Israel. Ps 78:41
there was no **o** to bury ⌊them⌋. Ps 79:3
they have conspired with **o** mind; Ps 83:5
on the face of Your anointed **o**. Ps 84:9
there is no **o** like You among the Ps 86:8
Cush—each **o** was born there. Ps 87:4
This **o** and that one were born in Ps 87:5
one and that **o** were born in her. Ps 87:5
record, "This **o** was born there." Ps 87:6
distanced loved **o** and neighbor Ps 88:18
a covenant with My chosen **o**; Ps 89:3
Rahab like **o** who is slain; Ps 89:10
king to the Holy **O** of Israel. Ps 89:18
I have exalted **o** chosen from the Ps 89:19
The **o** who lives under the Ps 91:1
Can the **O** who shaped the ear not Ps 94:9
O who formed the eye not see? Ps 94:9
The **O** who instructs nations, Ps 94:10
O who teaches man knowledge— Ps 94:10
o that creates trouble by law— Ps 94:20
The **o** who follows the way of Ps 101:6
No **o** who acts deceitfully will Ps 101:7
no **o** who tells lies will remain Ps 101:7
nation and from **o** kingdom to Ps 105:13
He allowed no **o** to oppress them; Ps 105:14
and no **o** among His tribes Ps 105:37
their foes; not **o** of them Ps 106:11
and of Aaron, the LORD's holy **o**. Ps 106:16
Moses His chosen **o** had not stood Ps 106:23
and there was no **o** to help. Ps 107:12
Let no **o** show him kindness, Ps 109:12
and let no **o** be gracious to his Ps 109:12
our God—the **O** enthroned on Ps 113:5
can answer the **o** who taunts me, Ps 119:42
promise like **o** who finds vast Ps 119:162
the **O** enthroned in heaven. Ps 123:1
Though **o** goes along weeping, Ps 126:6
gives sleep to the **o** He loves. Ps 127:2
the arms of the **o** who binds Ps 129:7
a vow to the Mighty **O** of Jacob: Ps 132:2
for the Mighty **O** of Jacob." Ps 132:5
do not reject Your anointed **o**. Ps 132:10
I will set **o** of your descendants Ps 132:11
a lamp for My anointed **o**. Ps 132:17
"Sing us **o** of the songs of Zion." Ps 137:3
happy is the **o** who pays you back Ps 137:8
before a single **o** of them began. Ps 139:16
Let the righteous **o** strike me— Ps 141:5
when **o** plows and breaks up the Ps 141:7
and see: no **o** stands up for me Ps 142:4
for me; no **o** cares about me. Ps 142:4
for no **o** alive is righteous in Ps 143:2
O who gives victory to kings, Ps 144:10
O generation will declare Your Ps 145:4
Happy is the **o** whose help is the Ps 146:5
my hand and no **o** paid attention, Pr 1:24
from the **o** who says perverse Pr 2:12
LORD disciplines the **o** He loves, Pr 3:12
good from the **o** to whom it is Pr 3:27
and **o** who stirs up trouble among Pr 6:19
it is with the **o** who sleeps with Pr 6:29
no **o** who touches her will go Pr 6:29
The **o** who commits adultery lacks Pr 6:32
the **o** who finds me finds life Pr 8:35
but the **o** who sins against me Pr 8:36
To the **o** who lacks sense, Pr 9:4
The **o** who corrects a mocker will Pr 9:7
the **o** who rebukes a wicked man Pr 9:7
of the Holy **O** is understanding. Pr 9:10
To the **o** who lacks sense, Pr 9:16
Idle hands make **o** poor, but Pr 10:4
The **o** who lives with integrity Pr 10:9
back of the **o** who lacks sense Pr 10:13
The **o** who follows instruction is Pr 10:17
but the **o** who rejects correction Pr 10:17
The **o** who conceals hatred has Pr 10:18
but the **o** who controls his lips Pr 10:19
is to the **o** who sends him Pr 10:26

but the **o** who hates such Pr 11:15
the **o** who sows righteousness, Pr 11:18
O person gives freely, yet gains Pr 11:24
and the **o** who gives a drink of Pr 11:25
will come to the **o** who sells it. Pr 11:26
The **o** who searches for what is Pr 11:27
The **o** who brings ruin on his Pr 11:29
but **o** who hates correction is Pr 12:1
The **o** who works his land will Pr 12:11
There is **o** who speaks rashly, Pr 12:18
The **o** who guards his mouth Pr 13:3
the **o** who opens his lips invites Pr 13:3
O man pretends to be rich but Pr 13:7
The **o** who has contempt for Pr 13:13
but the **o** who respects a command Pr 13:13
the **o** who accepts rebuke will Pr 13:18
The **o** who walks with the wise Pr 13:20
The **o** who will not use the rod Pr 13:24
but the **o** who loves him Pr 13:24
but a foolish **o** tears it down Pr 14:1
but the **o** who is devious in his Pr 14:2
The **o** who despises his neighbor Pr 14:21
but **o** who utters lies is Pr 14:25
fear of the LORD **o** has strong Pr 14:26
a quick-tempered **o** promotes Pr 14:29
The **o** who oppresses the poor Pr 14:31
but **o** who is kind to the needy Pr 14:31
anger falls on a disgraceful **o**. Pr 14:35
but He loves the **o** who pursues Pr 15:9
harsh for the **o** who leaves the Pr 15:10
the **o** who hates correction will Pr 15:10
doesn't love **o** who corrects him; Pr 15:12
but a foolish **o** despises his Pr 15:20
brings joy to **o** without sense, Pr 15:21
The **o** who profits dishonestly Pr 15:27
but the **o** who hates bribes will Pr 15:27
o turns from evil by the fear Pr 16:6
and he loves **o** who speaks Pr 16:13
o who guards his way protects Pr 16:17
The **o** who understands a matter Pr 16:20
and the **o** who trusts in the LORD Pr 16:20
The **o** who narrows his eyes is Pr 16:30
the **o** who compresses his lips Pr 16:30
The **o** who mocks the poor insults Pr 17:5
and **o** who rejoices over disaster Pr 17:5
O without sense enters an Pr 17:18
O who loves to offend loves Pr 17:19
o who builds a high threshold Pr 17:19
O with a twisted mind will not Pr 17:20
and **o** with deceitful speech will Pr 17:20
to the **o** who bore him. Pr 17:25
and **o** who keeps a cool head is a Pr 17:27
O who isolates himself pursues Pr 18:1
The **o** who is truly lazy in his Pr 18:9
The **o** who gives an answer before Pr 18:13
but the rich **o** answers roughly. Pr 18:23
and the **o** who acts hastily sins. Pr 19:2
and **o** who utters lies will not Pr 19:5
a friend of **o** who gives gifts. Pr 19:6
The **o** who acquires good sense Pr 19:8
o who safeguards understanding Pr 19:8
and **o** who utters lies perishes. Pr 19:9
The **o** who keeps commands Pr 19:16
o who disregards his ways will Pr 19:16
o will sleep at night without Pr 19:23
o who assaults his father and Pr 19:26
The **o** who lives with integrity Pr 20:7
The **o** who reveals secrets is a Pr 20:19
when **o** teaches a wise man, Pr 21:11
The Righteous **O** considers the Pr 21:12
The **o** who shuts his ears to the Pr 21:13
The **o** who loves pleasure will Pr 21:17
The **o** who pursues righteousness Pr 21:21
The **o** who guards his mouth and Pr 21:23
but the **o** who listens will speak Pr 21:28
the **o** who guards himself stays Pr 22:5
The **o** who sows injustice will Pr 22:8
The **o** who loves a pure heart and Pr 22:11
Don't be **o** of those who enter Pr 22:26
o who fathers a wise son will Pr 23:24
is better than a strong **o**, Pr 24:5
of knowledge than **o** of strength; Pr 24:5
The **o** who plots evil will be Pr 24:8
the **o** who hears will disgrace Pr 25:10
The **o** who sends a message by a Pr 26:6
The **o** who hires a fool, or who Pr 26:10
his is like **o** who grabs a dog Pr 26:17
The **o** who digs a pit will fall Pr 26:27

If **o** blesses his neighbor with a Pr 27:14
The **o** who controls her controls Pr 27:16
and **o** man sharpens another. Pr 27:17
when no **o** is pursuing ⌊them⌋ Pr 28:1
collects it for **o** who is kind to Pr 28:8
The **o** who leads the upright into Pr 28:10
The **o** who conceals his sins will Pr 28:13
Happy is the **o** who is always Pr 28:14
o who hardens his heart falls Pr 28:14
but **o** who hates unjust gain Pr 28:16
until death. Let no **o** help him. Pr 28:17
The **o** who lives with integrity Pr 28:18
but **o** who distorts right and Pr 28:18
The **o** who works his land will Pr 28:19
o in a hurry to get rich will Pr 28:20
O who rebukes a person will Pr 28:23
more favor than **o** who flatters Pr 28:23
The **o** who robs his father or Pr 28:24
The **o** who trusts in himself is a Pr 28:26
but **o** who walks in wisdom will Pr 28:26
The **o** who gives to the poor will Pr 28:27
but **o** who turns his eyes away Pr 28:27
O who becomes stiff-necked, Pr 29:1
but **o** who consorts with Pr 29:3
but the righteous **o** sings and Pr 29:6
but the wicked **o** does not Pr 29:7
but **o** who keeps the law will be Pr 29:18
but the **o** who trusts in the LORD Pr 29:25
and **o** whose way is upright is Pr 29:27
have no knowledge of the Holy **O**. Pr 30:3
Give beer to **o** who is dying, Pr 31:6
and wine to **o** whose life is Pr 31:6
Can **o** say about anything, Ec 1:10
I also knew that **o** fate comes to Ec 2:14
to give to the **o** who is pleasing Ec 2:26
As **o** dies, so dies the other; Ec 3:19
they have no **o** to comfort them. Ec 4:1
they have no **o** to comfort them. Ec 4:1
of them is the **o** who has not yet Ec 4:3
Better **o** handful with rest, Ec 4:6
are better than **o** because they Ec 4:9
but pity the **o** who falls without Ec 4:10
but how can **o** person alone keep Ec 4:11
if somebody overpowers **o** person, Ec 4:12
because **o** official protects Ec 5:8
The **o** who loves money is never Ec 5:10
all the labor **o** does under the Ec 5:18
with the **O** stronger than he Ec 6:10
has made the **o** as well as the Ec 7:14
you grasp the **o** and do not let Ec 7:18
For the **o** who fears God will end Ec 7:18
o who pleases God will escape Ec 7:26
by adding **o** thing to another to Ec 7:27
I have found **o** ⌊true⌋ man, Ec 7:28
The **o** who keeps a command will Ec 8:5
Yet no **o** knows what will happen, Ec 8:7
No **o** has authority over the wind Ec 8:8
at a time when **o** man has Ec 8:9
is **o** fate for the righteous Ec 9:2
for the **o** who sacrifices and the Ec 9:2
sacrifices and the **o** who does Ec 9:2
as for the **o** who takes an oath, Ec 9:2
so for the **o** who fears an oath. Ec 9:2
there is **o** fate for everyone. Ec 9:3
Yet no **o** remembered that poor Ec 9:15
but **o** sinner can destroy much Ec 9:18
The **o** who digs a pit may fall Ec 10:8
and the **o** who breaks through a Ec 10:8
The **o** who quarries stones may be Ec 10:9
the **o** who splits trees may be Ec 10:9
and **o** does not sharpen its edge, Ec 10:10
then **o** must exert more strength; Ec 10:10
No **o** knows what will happen, Ec 10:14
O who watches the wind will not Ec 11:4
the **o** who looks at the clouds Ec 11:4
succeed, whether **o** or the other, Ec 11:6
when **o** rises at the sound of a Ec 12:4
sayings are given by **o** Shepherd. Ec 12:11
Tell me, you, the **o** I love: Sg 1:7
should I be like **o** who veils Sg 1:7
Come away, my beautiful **o**. Sg 2:10
Come away, my beautiful **o**. Sg 2:13
at night I sought the **o** I love; Sg 3:1
I will seek the **o** I love. Sg 3:2
"Have you seen the **o** I love?" Sg 3:3
them when I found the **o** I love. Sg 3:4
chamber of the **o** who conceived Sg 3:4
washing, each **o** having a twin, Sg 4:2

a twin, and not **o** missing. Sg 4:2
my heart with **o** glance of your Sg 4:9
with **o** jewel of your necklace. Sg 4:9
darling, my dove, my perfect **o**. Sg 5:2
What makes the **o** you love better Sg 5:9
washing, each **o** having a twin, Sg 6:6
a twin, and not **o** missing. Sg 6:6
dove, my virtuous **o**, is unique; Sg 6:9
perfect to the **o** who gave her Sg 6:9
o who nursed at my mother's Sg 8:1
you, and no **o** would scorn me. Sg 8:1
leaning on the **o** she loves? Sg 8:5
become like **o** who finds peace Sg 8:10
despised the Holy **O** of Israel; Is 1:4
Hosts, the Mighty **O** of Israel, Is 1:24
The strong **o** will become tinder, Is 1:31
no **o** to quench ⌊the flames⌋. Is 1:31
people will oppress **o** another, Is 3:5
seven women will seize **o** man, Is 4:1
I will sing about the **o** I love, Is 5:1
The **o** I love had a vineyard on a Is 5:1
seed will yield only ⌊**o**⌋ bushel. Is 5:10
of the Holy **O** of Israel take Is 5:19
word of the Holy **O** of Israel. Is 5:24
no **o** slumbers or sleeps. Is 5:27
off, and no **o** can rescue ⌊it⌋ Is 5:29
When **o** looks at the land, there Is 5:30
above Him; each **o** had six wings: Is 6:2
And **o** called to another: Is 6:3
Then **o** of the seraphim flew to Is 6:6
is the elder, the honored **o**; Is 9:15
No **o** has compassion on his Is 9:19
Each **o** eats the flesh of his own Is 9:20
Like **o** gathering abandoned eggs, Is 10:14
itself above the **o** who chops Is 10:15
above the **o** who saws with it Is 10:15
a fire, and its Holy **O**, a flame. Is 10:17
In **o** day it will burn up Is 10:17
depend on the **o** who struck them, Is 10:20
the LORD, the Holy **O** of Israel. Is 10:20
No **o** will harm or destroy on My Is 11:9
the Holy **O** of Israel is among Is 12:6
each **o** will turn to his own Is 13:14
o will flee to his own land. Is 13:14
the rod of the **o** who struck you Is 14:29
and there is no **o** missing from Is 14:31
do not betray the **o** who flees. Is 16:3
let every **o** of them wail for Is 16:7
no **o** is singing or shouting for Is 16:10
No **o** tramples grapes in the Is 16:10
and as if **o** had gleaned heads of Is 17:5
eyes to the Holy **O** of Israel. Is 17:7
to Pharaoh, "I am **o** of the wise, Is 19:11
O of the cities will be called Is 19:18
The treacherous **o** acts Is 21:2
O calls to me from Seir, Is 21:11
Within **o** year, as a hired worker Is 21:16
not look to the **O** who made it, Is 22:11
or consider the **O** who created it Is 22:11
what he opens, no **o** can close; Is 22:22
what he closes, no **o** can open. Is 22:22
years—the life span of **o** king. Is 23:15
The Splendor of the Righteous **O**. Is 24:16
can come in—**o** that remains Is 26:2
day so that no **o** disturbs it. Is 27:3
as He struck the **o** who struck Is 27:7
will be gathered **o** by one. Is 27:12
will be gathered one by **o**. Is 27:12
Lord has a strong and mighty **o**— Is 28:2
of justice to the **o** who sits in Is 28:6
the **o** who believes will be Is 28:16
like a hungry **o** who dreams he is Is 29:8
like a thirsty **o** who dreams he Is 29:8
If it is given to **o** who can read Is 29:11
is given to **o** who cannot read Is 29:12
say about the **o** who formed it, Is 29:16
rejoice in the Holy **O** of Israel. Is 29:19
For the ruthless **o** will vanish, Is 29:20
honor the Holy **O** of Jacob and Is 29:23
Rid us of the Holy **O** of Israel." Is 30:11
the Holy **O** of Israel says: Is 30:12
GOD, the Holy **O** of Israel, has Is 30:15
O thousand ⌊will flee⌋ at the Is 30:17
will flee⌋ at the threat of **o**, Is 30:17
will rejoice like **o** who walks Is 30:29
look to the Holy **O** of Israel and Is 31:1
Return to the **O** the Israelites Is 31:6
each **o** will reject the silver Is 31:7

him, but not **o** made by man. Is 31:8
The **o** who lives righteously and Is 33:15
Where is the **o** who spied out our Is 33:18
the majestic **O**, the LORD, will Is 33:21
o will pass through it forever Is 34:10
and **o** wild goat will call to Is 34:14
Not **o** of them will be missing, Is 34:16
Isn't He the **O** whose high places Is 36:7
every **o** of you will eat from Is 36:16
Has any **o** of the gods of the Is 36:18
Against the Holy **O** of Israel! Is 37:23
O day, while he was worshiping Is 37:38
A voice of **o** crying out: Is 40:3
To **o** who shapes a pedestal, Is 40:20
is My equal?" asks the Holy **O**. Is 40:25
and strength, not **o** of them is Is 40:26
Each **o** helps the other, and says Is 41:6
o who flattens with the hammer Is 41:7
supports⌋ the **o** who strikes the Is 41:7
is the Holy **O** of Israel. Is 41:14
boast in the Holy **O** of Israel. Is 41:16
the Holy **O** of Israel has created Is 41:20
have raised up **o** from the north Is 41:25
o from the east who invokes My Is 41:25
No **o** announced it, no one told Is 41:26
it, no **o** told it, no one Is 41:26
one told it, no **o** heard your Is 41:26
When I look, there is no **o**; Is 41:28
Him, ⌊this is⌋ My Chosen **O**; Is 42:1
is blind like ⌊My⌋ dedicated **o**, Is 42:19
with no **o** to rescue them, Is 42:22
no **o** saying "Give ⌊it⌋ back! Is 42:22
says—the **O** who created you Is 43:1
Jacob, and the **O** who formed you, Is 43:1
your God, the Holy **O** of Israel, Is 43:3
no **o** can take ⌊anything⌋ from Is 43:13
the Holy **O** of Israel says: Is 43:14
LORD, your Holy **O**, the Creator Is 43:15
army and the mighty **o** together Is 43:17
o will say: I am the LORD's; Is 44:5
No **o** reflects, no one has the Is 44:19
no **o** has the perception or Is 44:19
servant and Israel My chosen **o**. Is 45:4
that there is no **o** but Me. Is 45:6
Woe to the **o** who argues with his Is 45:9
his Maker—**o** clay pot among Is 45:9
clay say to the **o** forming it: Is 45:9
absurd is the **o** who says to ⌊his Is 45:10
the Holy **O** of Israel and its Is 45:11
there is no **o** except Me. Is 45:21
it saves no **o** from his trouble. Is 46:7
[I am]God, and no **o** is like Me. Is 46:9
vengeance; I will spare no **o**. Is 47:3
The Holy **O** of Israel is our Is 47:4
I, and no **o** else, will never be Is 47:8
to you suddenly, in **o** day: Is 47:9
you said: No **o** sees me. Your Is 47:10
to yourself: I, and no **o** else. Is 47:10
his own way; no **o** can save you. Is 47:15
and Israel, the **o** called by Me: Is 48:12
the Holy **O** of Israel says: Is 48:17
his Holy **O** says to one who is Is 49:7
One says to **o** who is despised Is 49:7
is despised, to **o** abhorred by Is 49:7
the Holy **O** of Israel—and He Is 49:7
compassionate **O** will guide them, Is 49:10
contend with the **o** who contends Is 49:25
the Mighty **O** of Jacob." Is 49:26
Why was no **o** there when I came? Is 50:2
was there no **o** to answer when I Is 50:2
The **O** who justifies Me is near; Is 50:8
I called him, he was only **o**; Is 51:2
I am the **O** who comforts you. Is 51:12
There is no **o** to guide her among Is 51:18
there is no **o** to take hold of Is 51:18
and drunken **o**—but not with Is 51:21
He was like **o** people turned away Is 53:3
Rejoice, barren **o**, who did not Is 54:1
of the forsaken **o** will be more Is 54:1
and the Holy **O** of Israel is your Is 54:5
even the Holy **O** of Israel, Is 55:5
the wicked **o** abandon his way, Is 55:7
and the sinful **o** his thoughts; Is 55:7
every last **o** for his own gain. Is 56:11
The righteous **o** perishes, and no Is 57:1
and no **o** takes it to heart; Is 57:1
with no **o** realizing that the Is 57:1
the righteous **o** is swept away Is 57:1
High and Exalted **O** who lives Is 57:15
peace to the **o** who is far or Is 57:19
and satisfy the afflicted **o**, Is 58:10
No **o** makes claims justly; Is 59:4
justly; no **o** pleads honestly. Is 59:4
crack **o** open, and a viper is Is 59:5
no **o** who walks on them will know Is 59:8
that there was no **o** interceding; Is 59:16
God, the Holy **O** of Israel, who Is 60:9
Zion of the Holy **O** of Israel. Is 60:14
with no **o** passing through, Is 60:15
Redeemer, the Mighty **O** of Jacob. Is 60:16
this **O** who is splendid in His Is 63:1
Your garments like **o** who treads Is 63:2
and no **o** from the nations was Is 63:3
but there was no **o** to help, Is 63:5
I was amazed that no **o** assisted; Is 63:5
ancient times no **o** has heard, Is 64:4
has heard, no **o** has listened, no Is 64:4
on behalf of the **o** who waits for Is 64:4
You welcome the **o** who joyfully Is 64:5
o calls on Your name, striving Is 64:7
a bunch of grapes, and **o** says: Is 65:8
and the **o** who misses a hundred Is 65:20
o who is humble, submissive in Is 66:2
O slaughters an ox, one kills a Is 66:3
slaughters an ox, **o** kills a man; Is 66:3
o sacrifices a lamb, one breaks Is 66:3
a lamb, **o** breaks a dog's Is 66:3
o offers a grain offering, Is 66:3
grain offering, **o** offers swine's Is 66:3
o offers incense, one praises an Is 66:3
offers incense, **o** praises an Is 66:3
I called and no **o** answered; Is 66:4
Can a land be born in **o** day, Is 66:8
from **o** New Moon to another, Is 66:23
and from **o** Sabbath to another," Is 66:23
o of the priests living in Jr 1:1
I am the **O** who has made you a Jr 1:18
a land no **o** traveled through and Jr 2:6
through and where no **o** lived? Jr 2:6
o from a city and two from a Jr 3:14
no **o** will say any longer: Jr 3:16
and no **o** will remember or miss Jr 3:16
the shameful **o** has consumed what Jr 3:24
and burn with no **o** to extinguish Jr 4:4
you devastated **o**, what are you Jr 4:30
of⌋ anguish like **o** bearing her Jr 4:31
the **O** who set the sand as the Jr 5:22
you act justly toward **o** another, Jr 7:5
with no **o** to scare them off. Jr 7:33
No **o** regrets his evil, asking: Jr 8:6
proceed from **o** evil to another, Jr 9:3
Each **o** betrays his friend; Jr 9:5
friend; no **o** tells the truth. Jr 9:5
that no **o** passes through. Jr 9:10
so no **o** can pass through Jr 9:12
a lament and **o** another a dirge, Jr 9:20
reaper with no **o** to gather ⌊it⌋. Jr 9:22
the **o** who boasts should boast Jr 9:24
LORD, there is no **o** like You. Jr 10:6
there is no **o** like You. Jr 10:7
He is the **O** who formed all Jr 10:16
⌊I have⌋ no **o** to pitch my tent Jr 10:20
o who walks determines his own Jr 10:23
each **o** followed the stubbornness Jr 11:8
but no **o** takes it to heart. Jr 12:11
devours from **o** end of the earth Jr 12:12
to the other. No **o** has peace. Jr 12:12
and return each **o** to his Jr 12:15
siege; no **o** can help ⌊them⌋ Jr 13:19
will be no **o** to bury them— Jr 14:16
each **o** of you was following the Jr 16:12
Can **o** make gods for himself? Jr 16:20
in a salt land where no **o** lives. Jr 17:6
At **o** moment I might announce Jr 18:7
like **o** shatters a potter's jar Jr 19:11
by this city and ask **o** another: Jr 22:8
bitterly for the **o** who has gone Jr 22:10
Woe for the **o** who builds his Jr 22:13
shattered pot, a jar no **o** wants? Jr 22:28
dreams that they tell **o** another, Jr 23:27
but the **o** who has My word should Jr 23:28
O basket ⌊contained⌋ very good Jr 24:2
near and far from **o** another; Jr 25:26
spread⌋ from **o** end of the earth Jr 25:33
be recognized as **o** whom the LORD Jr 28:9
will not be even **o** of his Jr 29:32
quiet with no **o** to frighten him Jr 30:10
No **o** takes up the case for your Jr 30:13
that Zion no **o** cares about. Jr 30:17
leader will be **o** of them; Jr 30:21
The **O** who scattered Israel will Jr 31:10
the power of **o** stronger than he Jr 31:11
⌊This **o** will⌋ not be like the Jr 31:32
No longer will **o** teach his Jr 31:34
O who gives the sun for light Jr 31:35
O great in counsel and mighty Jr 32:19
I will give them **o** heart and one Jr 32:39
one heart and **o** way so that for Jr 32:39
hands of the **o** who counts them Jr 33:13
slaves and no **o** enslave his Jr 34:9
bring them to **o** of the chambers Jr 35:2
o from his evil way of life, Jr 35:15
each **o** of them will turn from Jr 36:3
and each **o** will turn from his Jr 36:7
and tell no **o** where you are." Jr 36:19
He will have no **o** to sit on Jr 36:30
of Nethaniah. No **o** will know it. Jr 40:15
royal family and **o** of the king's Jr 41:1
he killed the **o** the king of Jr 41:2
Gedaliah, when no **o** knew ⌊yet⌋, Jr 41:4
down was a large **o** that King Asa Jr 41:9
o who wanted to take his life. Jr 44:30
quiet with no **o** to frighten him Jr 46:27
every town; not **o** town will Jr 48:8
Cursed is the **o** who does the Jr 48:10
cursed is the **o** who withholds Jr 48:10
been poured from **o** container to Jr 48:11
no **o** will tread with shouts of Jr 48:33
the **o** who offers sacrifices on Jr 48:35
Moab like a jar no **o** wants." Jr 48:38
with no **o** to gather up the Jr 49:5
the LORD, "no **o** will live there; Jr 49:18
a nation at ease, **o** living in Jr 49:31
forever. No **o** will live there; Jr 49:33
No **o** will be living in it— Jr 50:3
o will search for Israel's guilt, Jr 50:20
against the Holy **O** of Israel. Jr 50:29
you, you arrogant **o**—⌊this is⌋ Jr 50:31
fall with no **o** to pick him up. Jr 50:32
so no **o** will live there; Jr 50:40
against the Holy **O** of Israel. Jr 51:5
He is the **O** who formed all Jr 51:19
No **o** will be able to retrieve a Jr 51:26
land where no **o** lives, where no Jr 51:43
for the report will come **o** year, Jr 51:46
wrote on **o** scroll about all Jr 51:60
so that no **o** will live in it Jr 51:62
two pillars, the **o** reservoir, Jr 52:20
O pillar was 27 feet tall, Jr 52:21
O capital, encircled by bronze Jr 52:22
There is no **o** to offer her Lm 1:2
⌊not **o**⌋ from all her lovers. Lm 1:2
for no **o** comes to the appointed Lm 1:4
hand, she had no **o** to help. Lm 1:7
there was no **o** to comfort her. Lm 1:9
there is no **o** nearby to comfort Lm 1:16
me⌋, no **o** to keep me alive Lm 1:16
there is no **o** to comfort her. Lm 1:17
but there is no **o** to comfort me. Lm 1:21
LORD's anger no **o** escaped or Lm 2:22
cheek to the **o** who would strike Lm 3:30
but no **o** gives them ⌊any⌋. Lm 4:4
that no **o** dared to touch their Lm 4:14
tired, and no **o** offers us rest. Lm 5:5
no **o** rescues ⌊us⌋ from their Lm 5:8
each **o** went straight ahead. Ezk 1:9
there was **o** wheel on the ground Ezk 1:15
wings extended **o** toward another. Ezk 1:23
listened to the **O** who was Ezk 2:2
Let the **o** who listens, listen, Ezk 3:27
and let the **o** who refuses, Ezk 3:27
are to burn up **o** third ⌊of it⌋ Ezk 5:2
are to take **o** third and slash Ezk 5:2
are to scatter **o** third to the Ezk 5:2
O third of your people will die Ezk 5:12
o third will fall by the sword Ezk 5:12
I will scatter **o** third to every Ezk 5:12
The **o** who is far off will die by Ezk 6:12
the **o** who is near will fall by Ezk 6:12
and the **o** who remains and is Ezk 6:12
o disaster after another is Ezk 7:5
but no **o** goes to war, for Ezk 7:14
Then **o** of the cherubim reached Ezk 10:7
o wheel beside each cherub. Ezk 10:9

Each **o** had four faces: the first Ezk 10:14
I will give them **o** heart and put Ezk 11:19
turn against that **o** and make him Ezk 14:8
of the **o** who inquires will Ezk 14:10
with no **o** passing through ⌊it⌋ Ezk 14:15
No **o** cared ⌊enough⌋ about you to Ezk 16:5
you to do even **o** of these things Ezk 16:5
no **o** solicited you. Ezk 16:34
a fee instead of **o** being paid to Ezk 16:34
took **o** of the royal family and Ezk 17:13
Will the **o** who does such things Ezk 17:15
who sins is the **o** who will die. Ezk 18:4
who sins is the **o** who will die. Ezk 18:20
will judge each **o** of you Ezk 18:30
She brought up **o** of her cubs, Ezk 19:3
you infamous **o** full of turmoil. Ezk 22:5
O man within you commits an Ezk 22:11
as **o** gathers silver, copper, Ezk 22:20
destroy it, but I found no **o**. Ezk 22:30
The older **o** was named Oholah, Ezk 23:4
had sex with her as **o** does with Ezk 23:44
and will groan to **o** another. Ezk 24:23
both the strong **o** and the one Ezk 30:22
one and the **o** ⌊already⌋ broken, Ezk 30:22
Wicked **o**, you will surely die, Ezk 33:8
Abraham was only **o** person, Ezk 33:24
with no **o** passing through. Ezk 33:28
O person speaks to another, Ezk 33:30
and there was no **o** searching or Ezk 34:6
to judge between **o** sheep and Ezk 34:17
judge between **o** sheep and Ezk 34:22
and no **o** will frighten ⌊them⌋. Ezk 34:28
that they become **o** in your hand. Ezk 37:17
that they become **o** in My hand. Ezk 37:19
I will make them **o** nation in the Ezk 37:22
and **o** king will rule over all of Ezk 37:22
there will be **o** shepherd for all Ezk 37:24
Are you the **o** I spoke about in Ezk 38:17
the LORD, the Holy **O** in Israel. Ezk 39:7
the land and **o** of them sees a Ezk 39:15
land with no **o** to frighten ⌊them Ezk 39:26
from the roof of **o** recess to the Ezk 40:13
to the roof of the ⌊opposite⌋ **o**; Ezk 40:13
gate, like the **o** on the east. Ezk 40:23
its pilasters, **o** on each side. Ezk 40:26
as **o** approaches the entrance of Ezk 40:40
two tables on **o** side and two Ezk 40:40
o beside the north gate, facing Ezk 40:44
the pilasters, **o** on each side. Ezk 40:49
were arranged **o** above another Ezk 41:6
o would go up from the lowest Ezk 41:7
by means of the middle **o**. Ezk 41:7
o entrance toward the north and Ezk 41:11
toward the palm tree on **o** side, Ezk 41:19
panels for **o** door and two for Ezk 41:24
the east side as **o** enters them Ezk 42:9
wall as **o** enters on the east Ezk 42:12
the gate, the **o** that faces east Ezk 43:1
was like the **o** I had seen when Ezk 43:3
and no **o** will enter through it, Ezk 44:2
aside an area **o** and two-thirds Ezk 45:6
correspond to **o** of the ⌊tribal⌋ Ezk 45:7
will be **o** percent of every Ezk 45:14
measures ⌊or⌋ **o** standard larger Ezk 45:14
measures equal **o** standard larger Ezk 45:14
from the flock is **o** animal out Ezk 45:15
o must return through the gate Ezk 46:9
to **o** of his servants, Ezk 46:17
sea, will be Dan—**o** portion. Ezk 48:1
will be Asher—**o** ⌊portion⌋. Ezk 48:2
will be Naphtali—**o** ⌊portion⌋. Ezk 48:3
will be Manasseh—**o** ⌊portion⌋. Ezk 48:4
will be Ephraim—**o** ⌊portion⌋. Ezk 48:5
will be Reuben—**o** ⌊portion⌋. Ezk 48:6
will be Judah—**o** ⌊portion⌋. Ezk 48:7
and as long as **o** of the ⌊tribal⌋ Ezk 48:8
o and two-thirds ⌊of a mile⌋ Ezk 48:15
o and a half ⌊miles⌋ on the Ezk 48:16
o and a half ⌊miles⌋ on the Ezk 48:16
o and a half ⌊miles⌋ on the east Ezk 48:16
and **o** and a half ⌊miles⌋ on the Ezk 48:16
will be Benjamin—**o** ⌊portion⌋. Ezk 48:23
will be Simeon—**o** ⌊portion⌋. Ezk 48:24
will be Issachar—**o** ⌊portion⌋. Ezk 48:25
will be Zebulun—**o** ⌊portion⌋. Ezk 48:26
west, will be Gad—**o** ⌊portion⌋. Ezk 48:27
which measures **o** and a half Ezk 48:30
tribes of Israel: **o**, the gate of Ezk 48:31
gate of Reuben; **o**, the gate of Ezk 48:31
and **o**, the gate of Levi. Ezk 48:31
which is **o** and a half ⌊miles⌋, Ezk 48:32
be three gates: **o**, the gate of Ezk 48:32
o, the gate of Benjamin; Ezk 48:32
Benjamin; and **o**, the gate of Dan Ezk 48:32
which measures **o** and a half Ezk 48:33
be three gates: **o**, the gate of Ezk 48:33
o, the gate of Issachar; Ezk 48:33
and **o**, the gate of Zebulun. Ezk 48:33
which is **o** and a half ⌊miles⌋, Ezk 48:34
be three gates: **o**, the gate of Ezk 48:34
the gate of Gad; **o**, the gate of Ezk 48:34
and **o**, the gate of Naphtali. Ezk 48:34
no **o** was found equal to Daniel, Dn 1:19
there is **o** decree for you. Dn 2:9
No **o** on earth can make known Dn 2:10
that no **o** can make it known Dn 2:11
will mix with **o** another but will Dn 2:43
observer, a holy **o**, coming down Dn 4:13
observer, a holy **o**, coming down Dn 4:23
There is no **o** who can hold back Dn 4:35
the **o** the king named Dn 5:12
o of the Judean exiles that my Dn 5:13
king, "Daniel, **o** of the Judean Dn 6:13
a second **o**, that looked like Dn 7:5
It was raised up on **o** side, Dn 7:5
horn, a little **o**, came up among Dn 7:8
and I saw **O** like a son of man Dn 7:13
His kingdom is **o** that will not Dn 7:14
I approached **o** of those who were Dn 7:16
the **o** different from all the Dn 7:19
after the **o** that had appeared to Dn 8:1
but **o** was longer than the other, Dn 8:3
and the longer **o** came up last. Dn 8:3
and there was no **o** to rescue the Dn 8:7
From **o** of them a little horn Dn 8:9
Then I heard a holy **o** speaking, Dn 8:13
and another holy **o** said to the Dn 8:13
covenant with many for **o** week, Dn 9:27
Then Michael, **o** of the chief Dn 10:13
Suddenly **o** with human likeness Dn 10:16
and said to the **o** standing in Dn 10:16
Then the **o** with human likeness Dn 10:18
No **o** has the courage to support Dn 10:21
o of his commanders will grow Dn 11:5
and the **o** who supported her Dn 11:6
o from her family will rise up, Dn 11:7
wants, and no **o** can oppose him. Dn 11:16
In his place **o** will arise who Dn 11:20
his end with no **o** to help him. Dn 11:45
o on this bank of the river and Dn 12:5
of the river and **o** on the other. Dn 12:5
O said to the man dressed in Dn 12:6
Blessed is the **o** who waits for Dn 12:12
and no **o** will rescue her from My Hs 2:10
o act of bloodshed follows Hs 4:2
But let no **o** dispute; let no one Hs 4:4
let no **o** argue, for My case is Hs 4:4
and no **o** can rescue ⌊them⌋. Hs 5:14
not **o** of them calls on Me. Hs 7:7
O like an eagle comes against Hs 8:1
I will bereave them of each **o**. Hs 9:12
them I was like **o** who eases the Hs 11:4
not man, the Holy **O** among you; Hs 11:9
no **o** can find any crime in me Hs 12:8
who was **o** of the sheep breeders Am 1:1
and the **o** who wields the scepter Am 1:5
and the **o** who wields the scepter Am 1:8
the strong **o** will not prevail by Am 2:14
⌊**o** who is⌋ swift of foot will Am 2:15
the **o** riding a horse will not Am 2:15
every last ⌊**o**⌋ of you with Am 4:2
sent rain on **o** city but no rain Am 4:7
O field received rain while a Am 4:7
the **O** who forms the mountains, Am 4:13
the **O** who makes the dawn out of Am 4:13
with no **o** to raise her up. Am 5:2
and the **o** that marches out a Am 5:3
with no **o** at Bethel to Am 5:6
The **O** who made the Pleiades and Am 5:8
hate the **o** who convicts ⌊the Am 5:10
despise the **o** who speaks with Am 5:10
are 10 men left in **o** house, Am 6:9
nations, as **o** shakes a sieve, Am 9:9
reaper and the **o** who treads Am 9:13
you were just like **o** of them. Ob 11
and **O** who relents from ⌊sending⌋ Jnh 4:2
In that day **o** will take up a Mc 2:4
will be no **o** in the assembly Mc 2:5
bring good to the **o** who walks Mc 2:7
O who breaks open ⌊the way⌋ will Mc 2:13
war against the **o** who puts Mc 3:5
tree with no **o** to frighten ⌊him Mc 4:4
O will come from you to be ruler Mc 5:2
there is no **o** to rescue ⌊them⌋ Mc 5:8
rod and the **O** who ordained it Mc 6:9
For I am like **o** who—when the Mc 7:1
there is no **o** upright among the Mc 7:2
shame, the **o** who said to me, Mc 7:10
O has gone out from Nineveh, Nah 1:11
the feet of **o** bringing good news Nah 1:15
the wicked **o** will never again Nah 1:15
O who scatters is coming up Nah 2:1
they cry,⌋ but no **o** turns back. Nah 2:8
and no **o** knows where they are. Nah 3:17
with no **o** to gather ⌊them⌋ Nah 3:18
My Holy **O**, You will not die. Hab 1:12
You silent while **o** who is wicked Hab 1:13
wicked swallows up **o** who is more Hab 1:13
on tablets so **o** may easily read Hab 2:2
the righteous **o** will live by his Hab 2:4
For the **o** who crafts its shape Hab 2:18
the Holy **O** from Mount Paran. Hab 3:3
you until there is no **o** left. Zph 2:5
and there is no **o** besides me. Zph 2:15
yet the **o** who does wrong knows Zph 3:5
with no **o** to pass through. Zph 3:6
Before **o** stone was placed on Hg 2:15
when **o** came to the winepress to Hg 2:16
Judah so no **o** could raise his Zch 1:21
⌊that⌋ **o** stone are seven eyes. Zch 3:9
and roused me as **o** awakened out Zch 4:1
o on the right of the bowl and Zch 4:3
to what is written on **o** side, Zch 5:3
the house of the **o** who swears Zch 5:4
The **o** with the black horses is Zch 6:6
and compassion to **o** another. Zch 7:9
your hearts against **o** another. Zch 7:10
with no **o** coming or going. Zch 7:14
Speak truth to **o** another; Zch 8:16
residents of **o** city will go to Zch 8:21
calling **o** Favor and the other Zch 11:7
In **o** month I got rid of three Zch 11:8
so that the **o** who is weakest Zch 12:8
mourn for Him as **o** mourns for an Zch 12:10
bitterly for Him as **o** weeps for Zch 12:10
and the hand of **o** will rise Zch 14:13
the previous **o** will strike the Zch 14:15
I wish **o** of you would shut the Mal 1:10
him was **o** of life and peace, Mal 2:5
Don't all of us have **o** Father? Mal 2:10
Father? Didn't **o** God create us? Mal 2:10
treacherously against **o** another, Mal 2:10
Didn't the **o** ⌊God⌋ make ⌊us⌋ Mal 2:15
And what does the **O** seek? Mal 2:15
the LORD spoke to **o** another. Mal 3:16
between **o** who serves God and one Mal 3:18
serves God and **o** who does not Mal 3:18
he is the **o** spoken of through Mt 3:3
A voice of **o** crying out in the Mt 3:3
but the **O** who is coming after me Mt 3:11
No **o** lights a lamp and puts it Mt 5:15
letter or **o** stroke of a letter Mt 5:18
whoever breaks **o** of the least of Mt 5:19
that you lose **o** of the parts of Mt 5:29
that you lose **o** of the parts of Mt 5:30
than this is from the evil **o**. Mt 5:37
for the **o** who wants to sue you Mt 5:40
anyone forces you to go **o** mile, Mt 5:41
Give to the **o** who asks you, Mt 5:42
turn away from the **o** who wants Mt 5:42
but deliver us from the evil **o**. Mt 6:13
No **o** can be a slave of two Mt 6:24
he will hate **o** and love the Mt 6:24
or be devoted to **o** and despise Mt 6:24
was adorned like **o** of these! Mt 6:29
and the **o** who searches finds, Mt 7:8
finds, and to the **o** who knocks, Mt 7:8
but ⌊only⌋ the **o** who does the Mt 7:21
them like **o** who had authority Mt 7:29
I say to this **o**, 'Go!' and he Mt 8:9
violent that no **o** could pass Mt 8:28
No **o** patches an old garment with Mt 9:16
And no **o** puts new wine into old Mt 9:17
suddenly **o** of the leaders came Mt 9:18

"Be sure that no **o** finds out!"	Mt 9:30
But the **o** who endures to the end	Mt 10:22
they persecute you in **o** town,	Mt 10:23
Yet not **o** of them falls to the	Mt 10:29
o who welcomes you welcomes	Mt 10:40
and the **o** who welcomes Me	Mt 10:40
cold water to **o** of these little	Mt 10:42
Are You the **O** who is to come,	Mt 11:3
This is the **o** it is written	Mt 11:10
born of women no **o** greater than	Mt 11:11
No **o** knows the Son except the	Mt 11:27
and no **o** knows the Father except	Mt 11:27
and no **o** will hear His voice in	Mt 12:19
in this age or in the **o** to come.	Mt 12:32
replied to the **o** who told Him,	Mt 12:48
the evil **o** comes and snatches	Mt 13:19
This is the **o** sown along the	Mt 13:19
And the **o** sown on rocky ground—	Mt 13:20
this is **o** who hears the word and	Mt 13:20
the **o** sown among the thorns—	Mt 13:22
this is **o** who hears the word,	Mt 13:22
the **o** sown on the good ground	Mt 13:23
this is **o** who hears and	Mt 13:23
The **O** who sows the good seed is	Mt 13:37
are the sons of the evil **o**,	Mt 13:38
When he found **o** priceless pearl,	Mt 13:46
The **o** who speaks evil of father	Mt 15:4
Jeremiah or **o** of the prophets."	Mt 16:14
orders to tell no **o** that He was	Mt 16:20
o for You, one for Moses, and	Mt 17:4
for You, **o** for Moses, and one	Mt 17:4
for Moses, and **o** for Elijah."	Mt 17:4
up they saw no **o** except Him—	Mt 17:8
this **o** is the greatest in the	Mt 18:4
welcomes **o** child like this	Mt 18:5
downfall of **o** of these little	Mt 18:6
you to enter life with **o** eye,	Mt 18:9
look down on **o** of these little	Mt 18:10
and **o** of them goes astray,	Mt 18:12
in heaven that **o** of these little	Mt 18:14
take **o** or two more with you,	Mt 18:16
o who owed 10,000 talents was	Mt 18:24
out and found **o** of his fellow	Mt 18:28
and the two will become **o** flesh?	Mt 19:5
are no longer two, but **o** flesh.	Mt 19:6
There is only **O** who is good.	Mt 19:17
the workers on **o** denarius for	Mt 20:2
'Because no **o** hired us,'	Mt 20:7
they each received **o** denarius.	Mt 20:9
'These last men put in **o** hour,	Mt 20:12
He replied to **o** of them,	Mt 20:13
o on Your right and the other on	Mt 20:21
I will also ask you **o** question,	Mt 21:24
slaves, beat **o**, killed another	Mt 21:35
went away, **o** to his own farm,	Mt 22:5
You defer to no **o**, for You don't	Mt 22:16
And **o** of them, an expert in the	Mt 22:35
No **o** was able to answer Him at	Mt 22:46
from that day no **o** dared to	Mt 22:46
because you have **o** Teacher,	Mt 23:8
because you have **o** Father,	Mt 23:9
because you have **o** Master,	Mt 23:10
and sea to make **o** proselyte,	Mt 23:15
when he becomes **o**, you make him	Mt 23:15
Therefore the **o** who takes an	Mt 23:20
The **o** who takes an oath by the	Mt 23:21
And the **o** who takes an oath by	Mt 23:22
Not **o** stone will be left here on	Mt 24:2
out that no **o** deceives you.	Mt 24:4
betray **o** another and hate one	Mt 24:10
one another and hate **o** another.	Mt 24:10
But the **o** who endures to the end	Mt 24:13
limited, no **o** would survive.	Mt 24:22
from **o** end of the sky to the	Mt 24:31
that day and hour no **o** knows—	Mt 24:36
o will be taken and one left.	Mt 24:40
one will be taken and **o** left.	Mt 24:40
o will be taken and one left.	Mt 24:41
one will be taken and **o** left.	Mt 24:41
To **o** he gave five talents;	Mt 25:15
and to another, **o**—to each	Mt 25:15
had received **o** talent went off	Mt 25:18
who had received **o** talent also	Mt 25:24
give it to the **o** who has 10	Mt 25:28
from the **o** who does not have,	Mt 25:29
separate them **o** from another,	Mt 25:32
you did for **o** of the least	Mt 25:40
did not do for **o** of the least	Mt 25:45
Then **o** of the Twelve—the man	Mt 26:14
O of you will betray Me."	Mt 26:21
each **o** began to say to Him,	Mt 26:22
The **o** who dipped his hand with	Mt 26:23
you stay awake with Me **o** hour?	Mt 26:40
Judas, **o** of the Twelve,	Mt 26:47
The **O** I kiss, He's the One;	Mt 26:48
The One I kiss, He's the **O**;	Mt 26:48
At that moment **o** of those with	Mt 26:51
You certainly are **o** of them,	Mt 26:73
answer him on even **o** charge,	Mt 27:14
o on the right and one on the	Mt 27:38
on the right and **o** on the left.	Mt 27:38
The **O** who would demolish the	Mt 27:40
Immediately **o** of them ran and	Mt 27:48
A voice of **o** crying out in the	Mk 1:3
them as **o** having authority	Mk 1:22
You are—the Holy **O** of God!"	Mk 1:24
began to argue with **o** another,	Mk 1:27
but the sick ⌊do need **o**⌋.	Mk 2:17
No **o** sews a patch of unshrunk	Mk 2:21
And no **o** puts new wine into old	Mk 2:22
no **o** can enter a strong man's	Mk 3:27
For to the **o** who has, it will be	Mk 4:25
from the **o** who does not have,	Mk 4:25
terrified and asked **o** another,	Mk 4:41
o was able to restrain him any	Mk 5:3
No **o** was strong enough to subdue	Mk 5:4
O of the synagogue leaders,	Mk 5:22
orders that no **o** should know	Mk 5:43
prophet—like **o** of the prophets	Mk 6:15
John, the **o** I beheaded, has	Mk 6:16
He ordered them to tell no **o**,	Mk 7:36
and had only **o** loaf with them	Mk 8:14
others, **o** of the prophets."	Mk 8:28
them to tell no **o** about Him.	Mk 8:30
o for You, one for Moses, and	Mk 9:5
for You, **o** for Moses, and one	Mk 9:5
for Moses, and **o** for Elijah"—	Mk 9:5
them to tell no **o** what they had	Mk 9:9
of the crowd, **o** man answered Him	Mk 9:17
possible to the **o** who believes."	Mk 9:23
arguing with **o** another about who	Mk 9:34
Whoever welcomes **o** little child	Mk 9:37
there is no **o** who will perform	Mk 9:39
downfall of **o** of these little	Mk 9:42
of God with **o** eye than to have	Mk 9:47
and be at peace with **o** another."	Mk 9:50
and the two will become **o** flesh.	Mk 10:8
are no longer two, but **o** flesh.	Mk 10:8
No **o** is good but One—God.	Mk 10:18
No one is good but **O**—God.	Mk 10:18
said to him, "You lack **o** thing:	Mk 10:21
saying to **o** another, "Then who	Mk 10:26
there is no **o** who has left	Mk 10:29
on which no **o** has ever sat.	Mk 11:2
May no **o** ever eat fruit from you	Mk 11:14
I will ask you **o** question;	Mk 11:29
another, and they killed that **o**.	Mk 12:5
He still had **o** to send, a	Mk 12:6
are truthful and defer to no **o**,	Mk 12:14
So they brought **o**. "Whose image	Mk 12:16
O of the scribes approached.	Mk 12:28
The Lord our God, The Lord is **O**.	Mk 12:29
correctly said that He is **O**,	Mk 12:32
there is no **o** else except Him	Mk 12:32
And no **o** dared to question Him	Mk 12:34
o of His disciples said to Him,	Mk 13:1
Not **o** stone will be left here on	Mk 13:2
out that no **o** deceives you.	Mk 13:5
But the **o** who endures to the end	Mk 13:13
those days, no **o** would survive.	Mk 13:20
that day or hour no **o** knows—	Mk 13:32
slaves, gave each **o** his work,	Mk 13:34
indignation to **o** another:	Mk 14:4
Judas Iscariot, **o** of the Twelve,	Mk 14:10
O of you will betray Me—one	Mk 14:18
will betray Me—**o** who is eating	Mk 14:18
and to say to Him **o** by one,	Mk 14:19
and to say to Him one by **o**,	Mk 14:19
⌊It is⌋ **o** of the Twelve—	Mk 14:20
o who is dipping ⌊bread⌋ with	Mk 14:20
Couldn't you stay awake **o** hour?	Mk 14:37
Judas, **o** of the Twelve,	Mk 14:43
"The **O** I kiss," he said, "He's	Mk 14:44
I kiss," he said, "He's the **O**;	Mk 14:44
And **o** of those who stood by drew	Mk 14:47
the Son of the Blessed **O**?"	Mk 14:61
o of the high priest's servants	Mk 14:66
nearby, "This man is **o** of them!"	Mk 14:69
You certainly are **o** of them,	Mk 14:70
There was **o** named Barabbas,	Mk 15:7
to do with the **O** you call the	Mk 15:12
o on His right and one on His	Mk 15:27
on His right and **o** on His left.	Mk 15:27
The **O** who would demolish the	Mk 15:29
mocking Him to **o** another and	Mk 15:31
They were saying to **o** another,	Mk 16:3
the holy **O** to be born will be	Lk 1:35
the Mighty **O** has done great	Lk 1:49
the shepherds said to **o** another,	Lk 2:15
A voice of **o** crying out in the	Lk 3:4
The **o** who has two shirts must	Lk 3:11
and the **o** who has food must do	Lk 3:11
but **O** is coming who is more	Lk 3:16
yet not **o** of them was healed—	Lk 4:27
You are—the Holy **O** of God!"	Lk 4:34
and kept saying to **o** another,	Lk 4:36
His hands on each **o** of them,	Lk 4:40
He got into **o** of the boats,	Lk 5:3
While He was in **o** of the towns,	Lk 5:12
He ordered him to tell no **o**:	Lk 5:14
On **o** of those days while He was	Lk 5:17
No **o** tears a patch from a new	Lk 5:36
And no **o** puts new wine into old	Lk 5:37
And no **o**, after drinking old	Lk 5:39
discussing with **o** another what	Lk 6:11
and from **o** who takes away your	Lk 6:30
But the **o** who hears and does not	Lk 6:49
I say to this **o**, 'Go!' and he	Lk 7:8
Are You the **O** who is to come,	Lk 7:19
'Are You the **O** who is to come,	Lk 7:20
This is the **o** it is written	Lk 7:27
of women no **o** is greater than	Lk 7:28
Then **o** of the Pharisees invited	Lk 7:36
O owed 500 denarii, and the	Lk 7:41
I suppose the **o** he forgave more.	Lk 7:43
the **o** who is forgiven little,	Lk 7:47
traveling from **o** town and	Lk 8:1
No **o**, after lighting a lamp,	Lk 8:16
O day He and His disciples got	Lk 8:22
amazed, asking **o** another, "Who	Lk 8:25
let no **o** enter with Him except	Lk 8:51
them to tell no **o** what had	Lk 8:56
and others that **o** of the ancient	Lk 9:8
that **o** of the ancient prophets	Lk 9:19
them to tell this to no **o**,	Lk 9:21
o for You, one for Moses, and	Lk 9:33
for You, **o** for Moses, and one	Lk 9:33
for Moses, and **o** for Elijah"—	Lk 9:33
This is My Son, the Chosen **O**;	Lk 9:35
days told no **o** what they had	Lk 9:36
among you—this **o** is great."	Lk 9:48
No **o** who puts his hand to the	Lk 9:62
Me rejects the **O** who sent Me."	Lk 10:16
No **o** knows who the Son is except	Lk 10:22
"The **o** who showed mercy to him,"	Lk 10:37
but **o** thing is necessary.	Lk 10:42
o of His disciples said to Him,	Lk 11:1
Suppose **o** of you has a friend	Lk 11:5
and the **o** who searches finds,	Lk 11:10
finds, and to the **o** who knocks,	Lk 11:10
But when **o** stronger than he	Lk 11:22
bore You and the **o** who nursed	Lk 11:27
No **o** lights a lamp and puts it	Lk 11:33
O of the experts in the law	Lk 11:45
burdens with **o** of your fingers.	Lk 11:46
were trampling on **o** another.	Lk 12:1
I will show you the **O** to fear:	Lk 12:5
to you, this is the **O** to fear!	Lk 12:5
Yet not **o** of them is forgotten	Lk 12:6
but the **o** who blasphemes against	Lk 12:10
it is with the **o** who stores up	Lk 12:21
was adorned like **o** of these!	Lk 12:27
But the **o** who did not know and	Lk 12:48
expected of the **o** who has been	Lk 12:48
five in **o** household will be	Lk 12:52
was teaching in **o** of the	Lk 13:10
Doesn't each **o** of you untie his	Lk 13:15
He went through **o** town and	Lk 13:22
O Sabbath, when He went to eat	Lk 14:1
at the house of **o** of the leading	Lk 14:1
o who invited both of you may	Lk 14:9
that when the **o** who invited you	Lk 14:10
and the **o** who humbles himself	Lk 14:11
said to the **o** who had invited	Lk 14:12

When **o** of those who reclined at Lk 14:15
The **o** who will eat bread in the Lk 14:15
The first **o** said to him, 'I have Lk 14:18
not **o** of those men who were Lk 14:24
oppose the **o** who comes against Lk 14:31
every **o** of you who does not say Lk 14:33
100 sheep and loses **o** of them, Lk 15:4
after the lost **o** until he finds Lk 15:4
in heaven over **o** sinner who Lk 15:7
if she loses **o** coin, does not Lk 15:8
God's angels over **o** sinner who Lk 15:10
to work for **o** of the citizens Lk 15:15
but no **o** would give him any. Lk 15:16
me like **o** of your hired hands. Lk 15:19
So he summoned **o** of the servants Lk 15:26
summoned each **o** of his master's Lk 16:5
master?' he asked the first **o**. Lk 16:5
he will hate **o** and love the Lk 16:13
will be devoted to **o** and despise Lk 16:13
away than for **o** stroke of a Lk 16:17
O day the poor man died and was Lk 16:22
but woe to the **o** they come Lk 17:1
him to cause **o** of these little Lk 17:2
Which **o** of you having a slave Lk 17:7
o of them, seeing that he was Lk 17:15
no **o** will say, 'Look here!' Lk 17:21
will long to see **o** of the days Lk 17:22
that night two will be in **o** bed: Lk 17:34
o will be taken and the other Lk 17:34
o will be taken and the other Lk 17:35
o will be taken, and the other Lk 17:36
was a judge in **o** town who didn't Lk 18:2
o a Pharisee and the other a tax Lk 18:10
this **o** went down to his house Lk 18:14
but the **o** who humbles himself Lk 18:14
No **o** is good but One—God. Lk 18:19
No one is good but **O**—God. Lk 18:19
him, "You still lack **o** thing: Lk 18:22
There is no **o** who has left a Lk 18:29
it to the **o** who has 10 minas. Lk 19:24
from the **o** who does not have, Lk 19:26
on which no **o** has ever sat. Lk 19:30
not leave **o** stone on another Lk 19:44
O day as He was teaching the Lk 20:1
they beat that **o** too, treated Lk 20:11
wounded this **o** too and threw him Lk 20:12
come when not **o** stone will be Lk 21:6
the hand of the **o** betraying Me Lk 22:21
leads, like the **o** serving. Lk 22:26
the **o** at the table or the one Lk 22:27
at the table or the **o** serving? Lk 22:27
Isn't it the **o** at the table? Lk 22:27
among you as the **O** who serves. Lk 22:27
as My Father bestowed **o** on Me, Lk 22:29
should sell his robe and buy **o**. Lk 22:36
and **o** of the Twelve named Judas Lk 22:47
Then **o** of them struck the high Lk 22:50
said, "You're **o** of them too!" Lk 22:58
me this man as **o** who subverts Lk 23:14
released the **o** they were asking Lk 23:25
o on the right and one on the Lk 23:33
on the right and **o** on the left. Lk 23:33
is God's Messiah, the Chosen **O**!" Lk 23:35
Then **o** of the criminals hanging Lk 23:39
where no **o** had ever been placed. Lk 23:53
o named Cleopas answered Him, Lk 24:18
that He was the **O** who was about Lk 24:21
from Him not **o** thing was created Jn 1:3
the glory as the **O** and Only Son Jn 1:14
This was the **O** of whom I said, Jn 1:15
'The **O** coming after me has Jn 1:15
No **o** has ever seen God. The One Jn 1:18
The **O** and Only Son—the One who Jn 1:18
O who is at the Father's side Jn 1:18
I am a voice of **o** crying out in Jn 1:23
He is the **O** coming after me, Jn 1:27
is the **O** I told you about: Jn 1:30
'The **O** you see the Spirit Jn 1:33
is the **O** who baptizes with the Jn 1:33
was **o** of the two who heard John Jn 1:40
(which means "Anointed **O**"), Jn 1:41
have found the **O** Moses wrote Jn 1:45
for no **o** could perform these Jn 3:2
No **o** has ascended into heaven Jn 3:13
except the **O** who descended Jn 3:13
He gave His **O** and Only Son, Jn 3:16
the name of the **O** and Only Son Jn 3:18
the **O** you testified about, Jn 3:26

No **o** can receive a single thing Jn 3:27
The **O** who comes from above is Jn 3:31
The **o** who is from the earth is Jn 3:31
The **O** who comes from heaven is Jn 3:31
yet no **o** accepts His testimony. Jn 3:32
The **o** who has accepted His Jn 3:33
o who believes in the Son has Jn 3:36
but the **o** who refuses to believe Jn 3:36
her, "the **O** speaking to you. Jn 4:26
no **o** said, "What do You want? Jn 4:27
The disciples said to **o** another, Jn 4:33
'**O** sows and another reaps.' Jn 4:37
the first **o** who got in after Jn 5:4
O man was there who had been Jn 5:5
judges no **o** but has given all Jn 5:22
you don't believe the **O** He sent. Jn 5:38
accepting glory from **o** another, Jn 5:44
O of His disciples, Andrew, Jn 6:8
knew there had been only **o** boat. Jn 6:22
believe in the **O** He has sent." Jn 6:29
of God is the **O** who comes down Jn 6:33
No **o** who comes to Me will ever Jn 6:35
and no **o** who believes in Me will Jn 6:35
and the **o** who comes to Me I will Jn 6:37
No **o** can come to Me unless the Jn 6:44
except the **O** who is from God. Jn 6:46
The **o** who eats My flesh and Jn 6:56
so the **o** who feeds on Me will Jn 6:57
The **o** who eats this bread will Jn 6:58
Spirit is the **O** who gives life. Jn 6:63
believe and the **o** who would Jn 6:64
told you that no **o** can come to Jn 6:65
that You are the Holy **O** of God!" Jn 6:69
Yet **o** of you is the Devil!" Jn 6:70
Iscariot's son, **o** of the Twelve, Jn 6:71
For no **o** does anything in secret Jn 7:4
but is from the **O** who sent Me. Jn 7:16
The **o** who speaks for himself Jn 7:18
glory of the **O** who sent Him is Jn 7:18
I did **o** work, and you are all Jn 7:21
but the **O** who sent Me is true. Jn 7:28
Yet no **o** laid a hand on Him Jn 7:30
I'm going to the **O** who sent Me. Jn 7:33
Then the Jews said to **o** another, Jn 7:35
The **o** who believes in Me, as the Jn 7:38
but no **o** laid hands on Him. Jn 7:44
o who came to Him previously, Jn 7:50
being **o** of them—said to Jn 7:50
So each **o** went to his house. Jn 7:53
The **o** without sin among you Jn 8:7
this, they left **o** by one, Jn 8:9
left one by **o**, starting with Jn 8:9
Has no **o** condemned you?" Jn 8:10
"No **o**, Lord," she answered. Jn 8:11
human standards. I judge no **o**. Jn 8:15
I am the **O** who testifies about Jn 8:18
But no **o** seized Him, because His Jn 8:20
but the **O** who sent Me is true, Jn 8:26
The **O** who sent Me is with Me. Jn 8:29
"We have **o** Father—God." Jn 8:41
The **o** who is from God listens to Jn 8:47
the **O** who seeks it also judges. Jn 8:50
He is the **O** who glorifies Me. Jn 8:54
is coming when no **o** can work. Jn 9:4
Some said, "He's the **o**." Jn 9:9
He kept saying, "I'm the **o**!" Jn 9:9
of the **o** who had received Jn 9:18
⌊the **o**⌋ you say was born blind? Jn 9:19
I don't know. **O** thing I do know: Jn 9:25
history no **o** has ever heard Jn 9:32
He is the **O** speaking with you." Jn 9:37
The **o** who enters by the door is Jn 10:2
Then there will be **o** flock, Jn 10:16
will be one flock, **o** shepherd. Jn 10:16
No **o** takes it from Me, but I lay Jn 10:18
No **o** will snatch them out of My Jn 10:28
No **o** is able to snatch them out Jn 10:29
The Father and I are **o**." Jn 10:30
to the **O** the Father set Jn 10:36
Mary was the **o** who anointed the Jn 11:2
"Lord, the **o** You love is sick." Jn 11:3
The **o** who believes in Me, even Jn 11:25
O of them, Caiaphas, who was Jn 11:49
advantage that **o** man should die Jn 11:50
and asking **o** another as they Jn 11:56
the **o** Jesus had raised from the Jn 12:1
and Lazarus was **o** of those Jn 12:2
Then **o** of His disciples, Judas Jn 12:4

see Lazarus the **o** He had raised Jn 12:9
the Pharisees said to **o** another, Jn 12:19
The **o** who loves his life will Jn 12:25
and the **o** who hates his life in Jn 12:25
The **o** who walks in darkness Jn 12:35
The **o** who believes in Me Jn 12:44
And the **o** who sees Me sees Him Jn 12:45
The **o** who rejects Me and doesn't Jn 12:48
"**O** who has bathed," Jesus told Jn 13:10
ought to wash **o** another's feet. Jn 13:14
greater than the **o** who sent him. Jn 13:16
The **o** who eats My bread has Jn 13:18
The **o** who receives whomever I Jn 13:20
and the **o** who receives Me Jn 13:20
O of you will betray Me!" Jn 13:21
started looking at **o** another— Jn 13:22
uncertain which **o** He was Jn 13:22
O of His disciples, the one Jn 13:23
disciples, the **o** Jesus loved, Jn 13:23
He's the **o** I give the piece of Jn 13:26
love **o** another. Just as Jn 13:34
you must also love **o** another. Jn 13:34
if you have love for **o** another." Jn 13:35
No **o** comes to the Father except Jn 14:6
The **o** who has seen Me has seen Jn 14:9
The **o** who believes in Me will Jn 14:12
The **o** who has My commands and Jn 14:21
them is the **o** who loves Me. Jn 14:21
And the **o** who loves Me will be Jn 14:21
The **o** who doesn't love Me will Jn 14:24
The **o** who remains in Me and I in Jn 15:5
love **o** another as I have loved Jn 15:12
No **o** has greater love than this, Jn 15:13
I command you: love **o** another. Jn 15:17
don't know the **O** who sent Me. Jn 15:21
The **o** who hates Me also hates My Jn 15:23
them that no **o** else has done, Jn 15:24
O I will send to you from the Jn 15:26
and not **o** of you asks Me, Jn 16:5
His disciples said to **o** another, Jn 16:17
Are you asking **o** another about Jn 16:19
and no **o** will rob you of your Jn 16:22
God, and the **O** You have sent— Jn 17:3
they may be **o** as We are one. Jn 17:11
they may be one as We are **o**. Jn 17:11
them and not **o** of them is lost, Jn 17:12
protect them from the evil **o**. Jn 17:15
they all be **o**, as You, Father Jn 17:21
May they also be **o** in Us, so the Jn 17:21
May they be **o** as We are one. Jn 17:22
May they be one as We are **o**. Jn 17:22
May they be made completely **o**, Jn 17:23
I have not lost **o** of those You Jn 18:9
was the **o** who had advised Jn 18:14
that **o** man should die Jn 18:14
the **o** known to the high priest, Jn 18:16
You aren't **o** of this man's Jn 18:17
o of the temple police standing Jn 18:22
You aren't **o** of His disciples Jn 18:25
O of the high priest's slaves, Jn 18:26
that I release **o** ⌊prisoner⌋ to Jn 18:39
This is why the **o** who handed Me Jn 19:11
with Him, **o** on either side, Jn 19:18
woven in **o** piece from the top. Jn 19:23
So they said to **o** another, Jn 19:24
and of the other **o** who had been Jn 19:32
o of the soldiers pierced His Jn 19:34
Not **o** of His bones will be Jn 19:36
will look at the **O** they pierced. Jn 19:37
no **o** had yet been placed in it. Jn 19:41
disciple, the **o** Jesus loved, Jn 20:2
o at the head and one at the Jn 20:12
at the head and **o** at the feet, Jn 20:12
But **o** of the Twelve, Thomas Jn 20:24
disciple, the **o** Jesus loved, Jn 21:7
was the **o** who had leaned Jn 21:20
who is the **o** that's going to Jn 21:20
if they were written **o** by one, Jn 21:25
if they were written one by **o**, Jn 21:25
For he was **o** of our number and Ac 1:17
desolate; let no **o** live in it; Ac 1:20
necessary that **o** become a Ac 1:22
were all together in **o** place. Ac 2:1
and rested on each **o** of them. Ac 2:3
because each **o** heard them Ac 2:6
saying to **o** another, "What could Ac 2:12
allow Your Holy **O** to see decay. Ac 2:27
to him to seat **o** of his Ac 2:30

that he was the **o** who used to Ac 3:10
denied the Holy and Righteous **O**, Ac 3:14
There is salvation in no **o** else, Ac 4:12
You are the **O** who made the Ac 4:24
were of **o** heart and soul, Ac 4:32
and no **o** said that any of his Ac 4:32
them, we found no **o** inside!" Ac 5:23
When he saw **o** of them being Ac 7:24
But the **o** who was mistreating Ac 7:27
this **o** God sent as a ruler and a Ac 7:35
He is the **o** who was in the Ac 7:38
the coming of the Righteous **O**, Ac 7:52
attention with **o** mind to what Ac 8:6
the sound but seeing no **o**. Ac 9:7
that this **O** is the Messiah. Ac 9:22
who was **o** of those who attended Ac 10:7
Here I am, the **o** you're looking Ac 10:21
that He is the **O** appointed by Ac 10:42
the message to no **o** except Jews. Ac 11:19
Then **o** of them, named Agabus, Ac 11:28
outside and passed **o** street, Ac 12:10
am? I am not the **O**. But look! Ac 13:25
allow Your Holy **O** to see decay. Ac 13:35
But the **O** whom God raised up did Ac 13:37
From **o** man He has made every Ac 17:26
He is not far from each **o** of us. Ac 17:27
and no **o** will lay a hand on you Ac 18:10
traveling through **o** place after Ac 18:23
believe in the **O** who would come Ac 19:4
the very **o** whom the whole Ac 19:27
were shouting **o** thing and some Ac 19:32
bring charges against **o** another. Ac 19:38
warning each **o** of you with tears Ac 20:31
we said good-bye to **o** another. Ac 21:6
and stayed with them **o** day. Ac 21:7
who was **o** of the Seven, Ac 21:8
he related **o** by one what God did Ac 21:19
he related one by **o** what God did Ac 21:19
were shouting **o** thing and some Ac 21:34
voice of the **O** who was speaking Ac 22:9
see the Righteous **O**, and to hear Ac 22:14
realized that **o** part of them Ac 23:6
Then Paul called **o** of the Ac 23:17
about this **o** statement I cried Ac 24:21
no **o** can give me up to them. Ac 25:11
so that no **o** could swim off Ac 27:42
they said to **o** another, "This Ac 28:4
After **o** day a south wind sprang Ac 28:13
after Paul made **o** statement: Ac 28:25
in their lust for **o** another. Rm 1:27
will repay each **o** according to Rm 2:6
is not a Jew who is **o** outwardly, Rm 2:28
is a Jew who is **o** inwardly, Rm 2:29
There is no **o** righteous, not Rm 3:10
is no one righteous, not even **o**; Rm 3:10
there is no **o** who understands, Rm 3:11
there is no **o** who seeks God. Rm 3:11
there is no **o** who does good, Rm 3:12
does good, there is not even **o**. Rm 3:12
righteous the **o** who has faith Rm 3:26
kind of law? By **o** of works? No, Rm 3:27
since there is **o** God who will Rm 3:30
Now to the **o** who works, pay is Rm 4:4
But to the **o** who does not work, Rm 4:5
entered the world through **o** man, Rm 5:12
is a prototype of the Coming **O**. Rm 5:14
For if by the **o** man's trespass Rm 5:15
many by the grace of the **o** man, Rm 5:15
is not like the **o** man's sin, Rm 5:16
because from **o** sin came the Rm 5:16
Since by the **o** man's trespass, Rm 5:17
reigned through that **o** man, Rm 5:17
reign in life through the **o** man, Rm 5:17
as through **o** trespass there is Rm 5:18
so also through **o** righteous act Rm 5:18
just as through **o** man's Rm 5:19
through the **o** man's obedience Rm 5:19
are slaves of that **o** you obey— Rm 6:16
I am no longer the **o** doing it, Rm 7:17
I am no longer the **o** doing it, Rm 7:20
God is the **O** who justifies. Rm 8:33
Who is the **o** who condemns? Rm 8:34
Christ Jesus is the **O** who died, Rm 8:34
works but from the **O** who calls Rm 9:12
say to the **o** who formed it, Rm 9:20
the same lump **o** piece of pottery Rm 9:21
yet the **o** who believes on Him Rm 9:33
The **o** who does these things will Rm 10:5
With the heart **o** believes, Rm 10:10
and with the mouth **o** confesses, Rm 10:10
No **o** who believes on Him will be Rm 10:11
I am the only **o** left, and they Rm 11:3
a measure of faith to each **o**. Rm 12:3
as we have many parts in **o** body, Rm 12:4
are many are **o** body in Christ Rm 12:5
members of **o** another. Rm 12:5
affection to **o** another with Rm 12:10
o another in showing honor. Rm 12:10
Be in agreement with **o** another. Rm 12:16
the **o** who resists the authority Rm 13:2
wrath on the **o** who does wrong. Rm 13:4
except to love **o** another, for Rm 13:8
for the **o** who loves another has Rm 13:8
O person believes he may eat Rm 14:2
but **o** who is weak eats only Rm 14:2
O who eats must not look down on Rm 14:3
look down on **o** who does not eat Rm 14:3
and **o** who does not eat must not Rm 14:3
must not criticize **o** who does, Rm 14:3
O person considers one day to be Rm 14:5
considers **o** day to be above Rm 14:5
Each **o** must be fully convinced Rm 14:5
and no **o** dies to himself Rm 14:7
no longer criticize **o** another, Rm 14:13
to that **o** it is unclean. Rm 14:14
destroy that **o** for whom Christ Rm 14:15
and what builds up **o** another. Rm 14:19
Each **o** of us must please his Rm 15:2
you agreement with **o** another, Rm 15:5
Therefore accept **o** another, Rm 15:7
the **O** who rises to rule the Rm 15:12
and able to instruct **o** another. Rm 15:14
o another with a holy kiss. Rm 16:16
that no **o** can say you had been 1Co 1:15
so that no **o** can boast in His 1Co 1:29
The **o** who boasts must boast in 1Co 1:31
no **o** knows the concerns of God 1Co 2:11
then neither the **o** who plants 1Co 3:7
plants nor the **o** who waters is 1Co 3:7
Now the **o** who plants and the one 1Co 3:8
plants and the **o** who waters are 1Co 3:8
But each **o** must be careful how 1Co 3:10
because no **o** can lay any other 1Co 3:11
No **o** should deceive himself. 1Co 3:18
So no **o** should boast in men, 1Co 3:21
that each **o** be found faithful 1Co 4:2
The **O** who evaluates me is the 1Co 4:4
will come to each **o** from God. 1Co 4:5
pride in favor of **o** person over 1Co 4:6
turn that **o** over to Satan for 1Co 5:5
there is not **o** wise person among 1Co 6:5
have lawsuits against **o** another. 1Co 6:7
a prostitute is **o** body with her? 1Co 6:16
The two will become **o** flesh. 1Co 6:16
the Lord is **o** spirit with Him. 1Co 6:17
Do not deprive **o** another— 1Co 7:5
from God, **o** this and another 1Co 7:7
each **o** must live his life in the 1Co 7:17
an opinion as **o** who by the 1Co 7:25
that "there is no God but **o**." 1Co 8:4
yet for us there is **o** God, 1Co 8:6
o Lord, Jesus Christ, through 1Co 8:6
the **o** who has this knowledge, 1Co 8:10
the law, like **o** under the law— 1Co 9:20
law, like **o** outside the law— 1Co 9:21
but only **o** receives the prize? 1Co 9:24
crown, but we an imperishable **o**. 1Co 9:25
I do not run like **o** who runs 1Co 9:26
or box like **o** who beats the air. 1Co 9:26
Because there is **o** bread, we who 1Co 10:17
we who are many are **o** body, 1Co 10:17
all of us share that **o** bread. 1Co 10:17
No **o** should seek his own ⌊good⌋, 1Co 10:24
If **o** of the unbelievers invites 1Co 10:27
for the **o** who told you, 1Co 10:28
since that is **o** and the same as 1Co 11:5
you come together in **o** place, 1Co 11:20
o takes his own supper ahead 1Co 11:21
and **o** person is hungry while 1Co 11:21
to eat, wait for **o** another. 1Co 11:33
informing you that no **o** speaking 1Co 12:3
cursed," and no **o** can say, "Jesus 1Co 12:3
o is given a message of wisdom 1Co 12:8
of healing by the **o** Spirit, 1Co 12:9
But **o** and the same Spirit is 1Co 12:11
to each **o** as He wills. 1Co 12:11
as the body is **o** and has many 1Co 12:12
though many, are **o** body—so 1Co 12:12
baptized by **o** Spirit into one 1Co 12:13
by one Spirit into **o** body— 1Co 12:13
all made to drink of **o** Spirit. 1Co 12:13
the body is not **o** part but many. 1Co 12:14
parts, each **o** of them, in the 1Co 12:18
are many parts, yet **o** body. 1Co 12:20
So if **o** member suffers, all the 1Co 12:26
if **o** member is honored, all the 1Co 12:26
since no **o** understands him; 1Co 14:2
together, each **o** has a psalm, 1Co 14:26
you can all prophesy **o** by one, 1Co 14:31
you can all prophesy one by **o**, 1Co 14:31
to over 500 brothers at **o** time, 1Co 15:6
of all, as to **o** abnormally born, 1Co 15:8
Foolish **o**! What you sow does not 1Co 15:36
there is **o** flesh for humans, 1Co 15:39
Therefore no **o** should look down 1Co 16:11
o another with a holy kiss. 1Co 16:20
For every **o** of God's promises is 2Co 1:20
Now the **O** who confirms us with 2Co 1:21
cheer me other than the **o** hurt? 2Co 2:2
this **o** may be overwhelmed by 2Co 2:7
knowing that the **O** who raised 2Co 4:14
groan in this **o**, longing to put 2Co 5:2
And the **O** who prepared us for 2Co 5:5
O died for all, then all died. 2Co 5:14
but for the **O** who died for them 2Co 5:15
He made the **O** who did not know 2Co 5:21
have wronged no **o**, corrupted no 2Co 7:2
corrupted no **o**, defrauded no one 2Co 7:2
no one, defrauded no **o**. 2Co 7:2
because of the **o** who did wrong, 2Co 7:12
because of the **o** who was wronged 2Co 7:12
according to what **o** has, 2Co 8:12
precaution so no **o** can find 2Co 8:20
Now the **O** who provides seed for 2Co 9:10
the **o** who boasts must boast in 2Co 10:17
For it is not the **o** commending 2Co 10:18
but the **o** the Lord commends. 2Co 10:18
you in marriage to **o** husband— 2Co 11:2
no **o** should consider me a fool. 2Co 11:16
like a madman—I'm a better **o**: 2Co 11:23
from the Jews 40 lashes minus **o**. 2Co 11:24
eternally blessed **O**, the God and 2Co 11:31
so that no **o** can credit me with 2Co 12:6
o another with a holy kiss. 2Co 13:12
we know that no **o** is justified Gl 2:16
is clear that no **o** is justified Gl 3:11
the **o** who does these things will Gl 3:12
No **o** sets aside even a human Gl 3:15
referring to **o**, who is Christ. Gl 3:16
is not for just **o** person, Gl 3:20
just one person, but God is **o**. Gl 3:20
you are all **o** in Christ Jesus Gl 3:28
o by a slave and the other by a Gl 4:22
But the **o** by the slave was born Gl 4:23
while the **o** by the free woman Gl 4:23
O is from Mount Sinai and bears Gl 4:24
persecuted the **o** born according Gl 4:29
serve **o** another through love. Gl 5:13
law is fulfilled in **o** statement: Gl 5:14
you bite and devour **o** another, Gl 5:15
will be consumed by **o** another. Gl 5:15
provoking **o** another, envying one Gl 5:26
one another, envying **o** another. Gl 5:26
Carry **o** another's burdens; Gl 6:2
The **o** who is taught the message Gl 6:6
because the **o** who sows to his Gl 6:8
but the **o** who sows to the Spirit Gl 6:8
let no **o** cause me trouble, Gl 6:17
purpose of the **O** who works out Eph 1:11
age but also in the **o** to come. Eph 1:21
fullness of the **O** who fills all Eph 1:23
works, so that no **o** can boast. Eph 2:9
remember that at **o** time you were Eph 2:11
made both groups **o** and tore down Eph 2:14
create in Himself **o** new man from Eph 2:15
both to God in **o** body through Eph 2:16
both have access by **o** Spirit to Eph 2:18
accepting **o** another in love, Eph 4:2
There is **o** body and one Spirit, Eph 4:4
There is one body and **o** Spirit, Eph 4:4
were called to **o** hope at your Eph 4:4
o Lord, one faith, one baptism, Eph 4:5
one Lord, **o** faith, one baptism, Eph 4:5
one Lord, one faith, **o** baptism, Eph 4:5

o God and Father of all, who is Eph 4:6
given to each **o** of us according Eph 4:7
The **O** who descended is the same Eph 4:10
the same as the **O** who ascended Eph 4:10
the **o** created according to God's Eph 4:24
truth, each **o** to his neighbor Eph 4:25
we are members of **o** another. Eph 4:25
and compassionate to **o** another, Eph 4:32
forgiving **o** another, just as Eph 4:32
Let no **o** deceive you with empty Eph 5:6
speaking to **o** another in psalms, Eph 5:19
submitting to **o** another in the Eph 5:21
For no **o** ever hates his own Eph 5:29
and the two will become **o** flesh. Eph 5:31
o of you is to love his wife Eph 5:33
that whatever good each **o** does, Eph 6:8
flaming arrows of the evil **o**. Eph 6:16
know which **o** I should choose Php 1:22
Just **o** thing: live your life in Php 1:27
are standing firm in **o** spirit, Php 1:27
one spirit, with **o** mind, working Php 1:27
feelings, focusing on **o** goal. Php 2:2
For I have no **o** else like-minded Php 2:20
I would not have **o** grief on top Php 2:27
but **o** that is through faith in Php 3:9
hold of it. But **o** thing I do: Php 3:13
this so that no **o** will deceive Col 2:4
careful that no **o** takes you Col 2:8
Let no **o** disqualify you, Col 2:18
Do not lie to **o** another, since Col 3:9
o another and forgiving Col 3:13
forgiving **o** another if anyone Col 3:13
you were also called in **o** body, Col 3:15
and admonishing **o** another in all Col 3:16
loved brother, who is **o** of you. Col 4:9
who is **o** of you, a slave Col 4:12
implored each **o** of you to walk 1Th 2:12
so that no **o** will be shaken by 1Th 3:3
with love for **o** another and for 1Th 3:12
This means **o** must not transgress 1Th 4:6
taught by God to love **o** another. 1Th 4:9
encourage **o** another with these 1Th 4:18
encourage **o** another and build 1Th 5:11
to it that no **o** repays evil for 1Th 5:15
is good for **o** another and for 1Th 5:15
love of every **o** of you for one 2Th 1:3
every one of you for **o** another 2Th 1:3
but the **o** now restraining will 2Th 2:7
the lawless **o** will be revealed 2Th 2:8
of the lawless **o**⌋ is based on 2Th 2:9
and guard you from the evil **o**. 2Th 3:3
provided **o** uses it legitimately. 1Tm 1:8
o who was formerly a blasphemer, 1Tm 1:13
For there is **o** God and one 1Tm 2:5
one God and **o** mediator between 1Tm 2:5
the husband of **o** wife, 1Tm 3:2
o who manages his own household 1Tm 3:4
must be husbands of **o** wife, 1Tm 3:12
No **o** should despise your youth; 1Tm 4:12
has been the wife of **o** husband, 1Tm 5:9
the only **O** who has immortality, 1Tm 6:16
but **o** of power, love, 2Tm 1:7
no **o** serving as a soldier gets 2Tm 2:4
no **o** came to my assistance, 2Tm 4:16
the husband of **o** wife, having Ti 1:6
O of their very own prophets Ti 1:12
Let no **o** disregard you. Ti 2:15
to slander no **o**, to avoid Ti 3:2
hateful, detesting **o** another. Ti 3:3
But **o** has somewhere testified: Heb 2:6
For the **O** who sanctifies and Heb 2:11
sanctified all have **o** Father. Heb 2:11
destroy the **o** holding the power Heb 2:14
faithful to the **O** who appointed Heb 3:2
but the **O** who built everything Heb 3:4
so that no **o** will fall into the Heb 4:11
but **O** who has been tested in Heb 4:15
o takes this honor on himself; Heb 5:4
but the **O** who said to Him, Heb 5:5
the **O** who was able to save Him Heb 5:7
since He had no **o** greater to Heb 6:13
But **o** without this lineage Heb 7:6
and blessed the **o** who had the Heb 7:6
In the **o** case, men who will die Heb 7:8
the **O** about whom these things Heb 7:13
from which no **o** has served at Heb 7:13
made by the **O** who said to Him Heb 7:21
have been sought for a second **o**. Heb 8:7

only a model of the true **o** Heb 9:24
But now He has appeared **o** time, Heb 9:26
after offering **o** sacrifice for Heb 10:12
For by **o** offering He has Heb 10:14
concerned about **o** another in Heb 10:24
do you think **o** will deserve who Heb 10:29
For we know the **O** who has said, Heb 10:30
the Coming **O** will come and not Heb 10:37
But My righteous **o** will live by Heb 10:38
for the **o** who draws near to Him Heb 11:6
that the **O** who had promised Heb 11:11
And therefore from **o** man— Heb 11:12
fact, from **o** as good as dead— Heb 11:12
to a better land—a heavenly **o**. Heb 11:16
as **o** who sees Him who is Heb 11:27
Lord disciplines the **o** He loves, Heb 12:6
without it no **o** will see the Heb 12:14
See to it that no **o** falls short Heb 12:15
in exchange for **o** meal. Heb 12:16
do not reject the **O** who speaks; Heb 12:25
instead, we seek the **o** to come. Heb 13:14
but the **o** who is rich ⌊should Jms 1:10
No **o** undergoing a trial should Jms 1:13
the **o** who looks intently into Jms 1:25
yet fails in **o** point, is guilty Jms 2:10
mercy to the **o** who hasn't shown Jms 2:13
and **o** of you says to them, Jms 2:16
You believe that God is **o**; Jms 2:19
Don't criticize **o** another, Jms 4:11
There is **o** lawgiver and judge Jms 4:12
do not complain about **o** another, Jms 5:9
your sins to **o** another and pray Jms 5:16
another and pray for **o** another, Jms 5:16
as the **O** who called you is holy, 1Pt 1:15
as Father the **O** who judges 1Pt 1:17
love **o** another earnestly from a 1Pt 1:22
and the **o** who believes in Him 1Pt 2:6
this **O** has become the 1Pt 2:7
praises of the **O** who called you 1Pt 2:9
Himself to the **O** who judges 1Pt 2:23
For the **o** who wants to love life 1Pt 3:10
because the **O** who suffered in 1Pt 4:1
account to the **O** who stands 1Pt 4:5
your love for **o** another at full 1Pt 4:8
hospitable to **o** another without 1Pt 4:9
with humility toward **o** another, 1Pt 5:5
Greet **o** another with a kiss of 1Pt 5:14
don't let this **o** thing escape 2Pt 3:8
the Lord **o** day is like 1,000 2Pt 3:8
and 1,000 years like **o** day. 2Pt 3:8
have fellowship with **o** another, 1Jn 1:7
Jesus Christ the righteous **O**. 1Jn 2:1
The **o** who says, "I have come to 1Jn 2:4
the **o** who says he remains in Him 1Jn 2:6
o who says he is in the light 1Jn 2:9
The **o** who loves his brother 1Jn 2:10
But the **o** who hates his brother 1Jn 2:11
have come to know the **O** who is 1Jn 2:13
had victory over the evil **o**. 1Jn 2:13
have come to know the **O** who is 1Jn 2:14
had victory over the evil **o**. 1Jn 2:14
but the **o** who does God's will 1Jn 2:17
an anointing from the Holy **O**, 1Jn 2:20
if not the **o** who denies that 1Jn 2:22
the **o** who denies the Father and 1Jn 2:22
No **o** who denies the Son can have 1Jn 2:23
children, let no **o** deceive you! 1Jn 3:7
The **o** who does what is right is 1Jn 3:7
The **o** who commits sin is of the 1Jn 3:8
especially the **o** who does not 1Jn 3:10
we should love **o** another, 1Jn 3:11
was of the evil **o** and murdered 1Jn 3:12
The **o** who does not love remains 1Jn 3:14
and love **o** another as He 1Jn 3:23
The **o** who keeps His commands 1Jn 3:24
because the **O** who is in you is 1Jn 4:4
greater than the **o** who is in the 1Jn 4:4
let us love **o** another, because 1Jn 4:7
The **o** who does not love does not 1Jn 4:8
God sent His **O** and Only Son into 1Jn 4:9
we also must love **o** another. 1Jn 4:11
No **o** has ever seen God. If we 1Jn 4:12
we love **o** another, God remains 1Jn 4:12
and the **o** who remains in love 1Jn 4:16
So the **o** who fears has not 1Jn 4:18
the **o** who loves God must also 1Jn 4:21
who is the **o** who conquers the 1Jn 5:5
world but the **o** who believes 1Jn 5:5

is the **O** who came by water and 1Jn 5:6
Spirit is the **O** who testifies, 1Jn 5:6
The **o** who believes in the Son of 1Jn 5:10
The **o** who does not believe God 1Jn 5:10
The **o** who has the Son has life. 1Jn 5:12
The **o** who doesn't have the Son 1Jn 5:12
but the **O** who is born of God 1Jn 5:18
and the evil **o** does not touch 1Jn 5:18
is under the sway of the evil **o**. 1Jn 5:19
so that we may know the true **O**. 1Jn 5:20
are in the true **O**—that is, in 1Jn 5:20
but **o** we have had from the 2Jn 5
that we love **o** another. 2Jn 5
The **o** who remains in that 2Jn 9
this **o** has both the Father and 2Jn 9
for the **o** who says, "Welcome," 2Jn 11
The **o** who does good is of God; 3Jn 11
the **o** who does evil has not seen 3Jn 11
Blessed is the **o** who reads and Rv 1:3
peace to you from the **O** who is, Rv 1:4
God, "the **O** who is, who was, Rv 1:8
lampstands was **O** like the Son Rv 1:13
the Living **O**. I was dead, but Rv 1:18
The **O** who holds the seven stars Rv 2:1
the **O** who was dead and came to Rv 2:8
The **O** who has the sharp, Rv 2:12
inscribed that no **o** knows except Rv 2:17
except the **o** who receives it Rv 2:17
O whose eyes are like a fiery Rv 2:18
that I am the **O** who examines Rv 2:23
victor and the **o** who keeps My Rv 2:26
The **O** who has the seven spirits Rv 3:1
The Holy **O**, the True One, the Rv 3:7
One, the True **O**, the One who has Rv 3:7
the **O** who has the key of David, Rv 3:7
who opens and no **o** will close, Rv 3:7
and closes and no **o** opens says: Rv 3:7
door that no **o** is able to close Rv 3:8
so that no **o** takes your crown. Rv 3:11
O was seated on the throne, Rv 4:2
and the **O** seated looked like Rv 4:3
thanks to the **O** seated on the Rv 4:9
O who lives forever and ever, Rv 4:9
down before the **O** seated on the Rv 4:10
worship the **O** who lives forever Rv 4:10
right hand of the **O** seated on Rv 5:1
But no **o** in heaven or on earth Rv 5:3
because no **o** was found worthy Rv 5:4
Then **o** of the elders said to me, Rv 5:5
Then I saw **o** like a slaughtered Rv 5:6
right hand of the **O** seated on Rv 5:7
Each **o** had a harp and gold bowls Rv 5:8
and dominion to the **O** seated on Rv 5:13
saw the Lamb open **o** of the seven Rv 6:1
and I heard **o** of the four living Rv 6:1
out, a fiery red **o**, and its Rv 6:4
would slaughter **o** another. Rv 6:4
the face of the **O** seated on the Rv 6:16
which no **o** could number, Rv 7:9
Then **o** of the elders asked me, Rv 7:13
The **O** seated on the throne will Rv 7:15
an oath by the **O** who lives Rv 10:6
and send gifts to **o** another, Rv 11:10
the **o** who deceives the whole Rv 12:9
o who accuses them before our Rv 12:10
O of his heads appeared to be Rv 13:3
so that no **o** can buy or sell Rv 13:17
The **o** who has understanding must Rv 13:18
but no **o** could learn the song Rv 14:3
and **O** like the Son of Man was Rv 14:14
voice to the **O** who was seated Rv 14:15
So the **O** seated on the cloud Rv 14:16
voice to the **o** who had the sharp Rv 14:18
O of the four living creatures Rv 15:7
and no **o** could enter the Rv 15:8
was, the Holy **O**, for You have Rv 16:5
Blessed is the **o** who is alert Rv 16:15
Then **o** of the seven angels who Rv 17:1
have fallen, **o** is, the other has Rv 17:10
kings with the beast for **o** hour. Rv 17:12
These have **o** purpose, and they Rv 17:13
His plan by having **o** purpose, Rv 17:17
her plagues will come in **o** day— Rv 18:8
because no **o** buys their Rv 18:11
written that no **o** knows except Rv 19:12
and holy is the **o** who shares in Rv 20:6
white throne and **O** seated on it. Rv 20:11
Then the **O** seated on the throne Rv 21:5

Then **o** of the seven angels, Rv 21:9
The **o** who spoke with me had a Rv 21:15
no **o** who does what is vile or Rv 21:27
Blessed is the **o** who keeps the Rv 22:7
am the **o** who heard and saw these Rv 22:8
And the **o** who is thirsty should Rv 22:17

ONE'S *(29)*
(See pp. xi-xii.)

ONE-FIFTH *(2)*
land and take **o** ⌊of the harvest Gn 41:34
he must add **o** to its value. Lv 27:31

ONE-HALF *(1)*
two and **o** gallons of flour, 1Sm 1:24

ONE-SIXTH *(1)*
water by measure, **o** of a gallon, Ezk 4:11

ONE-TENTH *(2)*
to collect the **o** offering in all Neh 10:37
will be **o** of the standard Ezk 45:11

ONE-THIRD *(31)*
and **o** of a quart of olive oil. Lv 14:10
along with the **o** quart of olive Lv 14:12
take some of the **o** of a quart of Lv 14:15
o of a quart of olive oil, Lv 14:21
offering and the **o** of a quart of Lv 14:24
and **o** ⌊of a shekel⌋ for 1Sm 13:21
eight and **o** ⌊miles⌋ long and six Ezk 45:1
an area eight and **o** ⌊miles⌋ long Ezk 45:3
and three and **o** ⌊miles⌋ wide, Ezk 45:3
area⌋ eight and **o** ⌊miles⌋ long Ezk 45:5
and three and **o** ⌊miles⌋ wide for Ezk 45:5
and eight and **o** ⌊miles⌋ long, Ezk 45:6
with **o** of a gallon of oil to Ezk 46:14
LORD⌋, eight and **o** ⌊miles⌋ wide, Ezk 48:8
will be eight and **o** ⌊miles⌋ long Ezk 48:9
and three and **o** ⌊miles⌋ wide. Ezk 48:9
will be eight and **o** ⌊miles long⌋ Ezk 48:10
three and **o** ⌊miles⌋ wide on the Ezk 48:10
three and **o** ⌊miles⌋ wide on the Ezk 48:10
and eight and **o** ⌊miles⌋ long on Ezk 48:10
area⌋ eight and **o** ⌊miles⌋ long Ezk 48:13
and three and **o** ⌊miles⌋ wide. Ezk 48:13
will be eight and **o** ⌊miles⌋ and Ezk 48:13
the width three and **o** ⌊miles⌋. Ezk 48:13
and eight and **o** ⌊miles long⌋, Ezk 48:15
will be three and **o** ⌊miles⌋ to Ezk 48:18
east and three and **o** ⌊miles⌋ to Ezk 48:18
be eight and **o** ⌊miles⌋ by eight Ezk 48:20
miles⌋ by eight and **o** ⌊miles⌋; Ezk 48:20
next to the eight and **o** ⌊miles⌋ Ezk 48:21
next to the eight and **o** ⌊miles Ezk 48:21

ONES *(151)*
(See pp. xi-xii.)

ONESELF *(3)*
(See pp. xi-xii.)

ONESIMUS *(2)*
He is with **O**, a faithful and Col 4:9
I fathered while in chains—**O**. Phm 10

ONESIPHORUS *(2)*
mercy to the household of **O**, 2Tm 1:16
Aquila, and the household of **O**. 2Tm 4:19

ONGOING *(1)*
Strife is **o**, and conflict Hab 1:3

ONIONS *(1)*
melons, leeks, **o**, and garlic. Nm 11:5

ONLOOKERS *(1)*
all the **o** will begin to make fun Lk 14:29

ONLY *(409)*
O Noah was left, and those that Gn 7:23
If **o** Ishmael could live in Your Gn 17:18
go there—it's **o** a small place, Gn 19:20
He said, "your **o** ⌊son⌋ Isaac, Gn 22:2
withheld your **o** son from Me." Gn 22:12
have not withheld your **o** son, Gn 22:16
if **o** You will make my journey Gn 24:42
you but have **o** done what was Gn 26:29
Do you **o** have one blessing, Gn 27:38
they seemed like **o** a few days to Gn 29:20
agree with you **o** on this Gn 34:15
be one people **o** on this Gn 34:22
O let us agree with them, and Gn 34:23
O if you leave something ⌊with Gn 38:17
woke up, and it was **o** a dream. Gn 41:7
O with regard to the throne will Gn 41:40
the first time **o** to buy food. Gn 43:20
but **o** the one who is found to Gn 44:10
He is the **o** one of his mother's Gn 44:20
The **o** land he didn't acquire was Gn 47:22
O the priests' land does not Gn 47:26
O their children, their sheep, Gn 50:8
and remain **o** in the Nile." Ex 8:9
will remain **o** in the Nile." Ex 8:11
The **o** place it didn't hail was Ex 9:26
o the men may go and worship the Ex 10:11
o your flocks and your herds Ex 10:24
water, but **o** roasted over fire Ex 12:9
need to eat—you may do **o** that. Ex 12:16
If **o** we had died by the LORD's Ex 16:3
For it is his **o** covering; Ex 22:27
Now if You would **o** forgive their Ex 32:32
is ⌊**o**⌋ the scar from the boil. Lv 13:23
for it is ⌊**o**⌋ the scar from the Lv 13:28
it is ⌊**o**⌋ a rash that has broken Lv 13:39
you may ⌊**o**⌋ eat its produce Lv 25:12
and you are **o** foreigners and Lv 25:23
o a few years remain until the Lv 25:52
tabernacle for ⌊**o**⌋ a few days. Nm 9:20
cloud remained ⌊**o**⌋ from evening Nm 9:21
one is sounded, **o** the leaders, Nm 10:4
If **o** all the LORD's people were Nm 11:29
the LORD speak **o** through Moses? Nm 12:2
If **o** we had died in the land of Nm 14:2
or if **o** we had died in this Nm 14:2
O don't rebel against the LORD, Nm 14:9
O Joshua son of Nun and Caleb Nm 14:38
If **o** we had perished when our Nm 20:3
o let us travel through on foot." Nm 20:19
⌊but **o** up⌋ to the Ammonite Nm 21:24
you must **o** do what I tell you. Nm 22:20
are to say **o** what I tell you. Nm 22:35
I must speak **o** the message God Nm 22:38
you have **o** blessed ⌊them⌋!" Nm 23:11
You will **o** see the outskirts of Nm 23:13
had no sons—**o** daughters. Nm 26:33
O the gold, silver, bronze, iron, Nm 31:22
O after the death of the high Nm 35:28
O let us travel through on foot, Dt 2:28
We took **o** the livestock and the Dt 2:35
O Og king of Bashan was left of Dt 3:11
O be on your guard and Dt 4:9
see a form; there was **o** a voice. Dt 4:12
If **o** they had such a heart to Dt 5:29
burnt offerings **o** in the place Dt 12:14
if **o** you obey the LORD your God Dt 15:5
must **o** sacrifice the Passover Dt 16:6
o the man who raped her must die. Dt 22:25
you will **o** move upward and never Dt 28:13
You will **o** be oppressed and Dt 28:29
You will **o** be oppressed and Dt 28:33
be left with **o** a few people, Dt 28:62
will say, 'If **o** it were evening! Dt 28:67
will say, 'If **o** it were morning! Dt 28:67
and this oath not **o** with you, Dt 29:14
If **o** they were wise, they would Dt 32:29
That was the **o** day they marched Jos 6:15
O Rahab the prostitute and Jos 6:17
If **o** we had been content to Jos 7:7
Israel plundered **o** the cattle Jos 8:27
o distribute the land as an Jos 13:6
had no sons, **o** daughters. Jos 17:3
Why did you give us **o** one tribal Jos 17:14
O carefully obey the command and Jos 22:5
was not the **o** one who perished Jos 22:20
If dew is **o** on the fleece, Jdg 6:37
o the fleece was dry, and dew Jdg 6:40
If **o** these people were in my Jdg 9:29
You see fit; **o** deliver us today! Jdg 10:15
She was his **o** child; he had no Jdg 11:34
O don't spend the night in the Jdg 19:20
boiled meat from you—**o** raw." 1Sm 2:15
O Dagon's torso remained. 1Sm 5:4
to the LORD, and worship **o** Him. 1Sm 7:3
Ashtoreths and **o** worshiped the 1Sm 7:4
o Saul and his son Jonathan had 1Sm 13:22
but they **o** credited me with 1Sm 18:8
o Jonathan and David knew the 1Sm 20:39
men may eat it **o** if they have 1Sm 21:4
us into battle **o** to become our 1Sm 29:4
this will **o** end in bitterness 2Sm 2:26
a man who can **o** work a spindle 2Sm 3:29
sons, because **o** Amnon is dead. 2Sm 13:32
sons are dead. **O** Amnon is dead." 2Sm 13:33
If **o** someone would appoint me 2Sm 15:4
you **o** arrived yesterday; 2Sm 15:20
I will strike down **o** the king 2Sm 17:2
If **o** I had died instead of you, 2Sm 18:33
your servant is **o** going with the 2Sm 19:36
And who is a rock? **O** our God. 2Sm 22:32
but **o** to plunder the dead. 2Sm 23:10
If **o** someone would bring me 2Sm 23:15
if **o** your sons guard their walk 1Kg 8:25
o what is right in My eyes. 1Kg 14:8
Zimri had not **o** conspired but 1Kg 16:16
o a handful of flour in the jar 1Kg 17:12
O make me a small loaf from it 1Kg 17:13
I am the **o** remaining prophet of 1Kg 18:22
that this one is **o** looking for 1Kg 20:7
good about me, but **o** disaster. 1Kg 22:8
good about me, but **o** disaster?" 1Kg 22:18
and feed him **o** bread and water 1Kg 22:27
o to hand us over to Moab." 2Kg 3:10
o the buildings of Kir-hareseth 2Kg 3:25
If **o** my master would go to the 2Kg 5:3
see that he is **o** picking a fight 2Kg 5:7
among you—**o** servants of Baal. 2Kg 10:23
now you will **o** strike down Aram 2Kg 13:19
O the tribe of Judah remained. 2Kg 17:18
master sent me **o** to your master 2Kg 18:27
their ancestors if **o** they will 2Kg 21:8
to Israel **o** at the LORD's 2Kg 24:3
had no sons, **o** daughters, but he 1Ch 2:34
If **o** You would bless me, extend 1Ch 4:10
but he had **o** daughters. 1Ch 7:15
If **o** someone would bring me 1Ch 11:17
having no sons, **o** daughters. 1Ch 23:22
we have given You **o** what comes 1Ch 29:14
o your sons guard their way to 2Ch 6:16
good about me, but **o** disaster. 2Ch 18:7
good about me, but **o** disaster?" 2Ch 18:17
and feed him **o** bread and water 2Ch 18:26
army came with **o** a few men, 2Ch 24:24
o the consecrated priests, 2Ch 26:18
He has **o** human strength, but we 2Ch 32:8
if **o** they will be careful to do 2Ch 33:8
but **o** to the LORD their God. 2Ch 33:17
O Jonathan son of Asahel and Ezr 10:15
The **o** animal I took was the one Neh 2:12
It was **o** later that I asked the Neh 13:6
has defied not **o** the king, Est 1:16
He **o** went as far as the King's Est 4:2
O if the king extends the golden Est 4:11
Jew was second **o** to King Est 10:3
in your power; **o** spare his life. Jb 2:6
Should we accept **o** good from God Jb 2:10
If **o** that day had turned to Jb 3:4
If **o** darkness had taken that Jb 3:6
If **o** my grief could be weighed Jb 6:2
If **o** my request would be granted Jb 6:8
we were ⌊born **o**⌋ yesterday and Jb 8:9
could **o** beg my judge for mercy. Jb 9:15
But if **o** God would speak and Jb 11:5
recalling ⌊it **o**⌋ as waters that Jb 11:16
and their ⌊**o**⌋ hope will be to Jb 11:20
If **o** you would shut up and let Jb 13:5
O grant ⌊these⌋ two things to me, Jb 13:20
If **o** You would hide me in Sheol Jb 14:13
He feels **o** the pain of his own Jb 14:22
body and mourns **o** for himself. Jb 14:22
For ⌊**o**⌋ a few years will pass Jb 16:22
my mistake concerns **o** me. Jb 19:4
godless has lasted **o** a moment? Jb 20:5
If **o** I knew how to find Him, Jb 23:3
o I could be as in months gone Jb 29:2
If **o** I had someone to hear my Jb 31:35
It is not ⌊**o**⌋ the old who are Jb 32:9
If **o** Job were tested to the Jb 34:36
⌊**o**⌋ his Maker can draw the sword Jb 40:19
the nations know they are **o** men. Ps 9:20
And who is a rock? **O** our God. Ps 18:31
O goodness and faithful love Ps 23:6
For His anger lasts **o** a moment, Ps 30:5
agitated—it can **o** bring harm. Ps 37:8
every mortal man is **o** a vapor. Ps 39:5
If **o** I had wings like a dove! Ps 55:6
They **o** plan to bring him down Ps 62:4
Men are **o** a vapor; exalted men, Ps 62:9
o You can atone for our Ps 65:3
that they were ⌊**o**⌋ flesh, Ps 78:39
if you would **o** listen to Me! Ps 81:8
o My people would listen to Me Ps 81:13
darkness is my ⌊**o**⌋ friend. Ps 88:18
You will **o** see it with your eyes Ps 91:8

If **o** my ways were committed to Ps 119:5
my heart fears ⌊**o**⌋ Your word. Ps 119:161
if **o** You would kill the wicked— Ps 139:19
fee is **o** a loaf of bread, Pr 6:26
of the wicked, ⌊**o**⌋ what is Pr 10:32
but violent men gain ⌊**o**⌋ riches. Pr 11:16
what is right, **o** to become poor. Pr 11:24
but a lying tongue, **o** a moment. Pr 12:19
endless talk leads **o** to poverty. Pr 14:23
An evil man seeks **o** rebellion; Pr 17:11
but **o** wants to show off his Pr 18:2
who is reckless **o** becomes poor. Pr 21:5
rich—both lead **o** to poverty. Pr 22:16
find honey, eat **o** what you need; Pr 25:16
and says, "I was **o** joking!" Pr 26:19
O see this: I have discovered Ec 7:29
It is **o** right that they adore Sg 1:4
If **o** I could treat you like my Sg 8:1
who has **o** the breath in his Is 2:22
will yield **o** six gallons, Is 5:10
seed will yield **o** ⌊one⌋ bushel. Is 5:10
are to regard **o** the LORD of Is 8:13
of Hosts as holy. **O** He should be Is 8:13
o He should be held in awe. Is 8:13
the earth and see **o** distress, Is 8:22
⌊**o**⌋ a remnant of them will Is 10:22
O gleanings will be left in Is 17:6
burned, and **o** a few survive. Is 24:6
O desolation remains in the city; Is 24:12
O terror will cause you to Is 28:19
o the living can thank You, Is 38:19
O in the LORD is righteousness Is 45:24
o you had paid attention to My Is 48:18
When I called him, he was **o** one; Is 51:2
be like today, **o** far better!" Is 56:12
If **o** You would tear the heavens Is 64:1
no longer live **o** a few days, Is 65:20
speak since I am ⌊**o**⌋ a youth." Jr 1:6
am ⌊**o**⌋ a youth, for you will go Jr 1:7
all her heart—**o** in pretense." Jr 3:10
O acknowledge your guilt— Jr 3:13
of Israel is **o** in the LORD our Jr 3:23
The prophets become ⌊**o**⌋ wind, Jr 5:13
as you would for⌋ an **o** son, Jr 6:26
healing, but there was **o** terror. Jr 8:15
If **o** I had a traveler's lodging Jr 9:2
stopping **o** for the night? Jr 14:8
healing, but there was **o** terror. Jr 14:19
Our fathers inherited **o** lies, Jr 16:19
of the womb to see ⌊**o**⌋ struggle Jr 20:18
"Am I a God who is **o** near"— Jr 23:23
who has ⌊**o**⌋ a dream should Jr 23:28
O listen to this message I am Jr 28:7
o when the word of the prophet Jr 28:9
for **o** they were left among Jr 34:7
among them **o** the badly wounded Jr 37:10
in the cistern, **o** mud, and Jr 38:6
land of Judah **o** few in number, Jr 44:28
would destroy **o** what they wanted Jr 49:9
themselves ⌊**o** to feed⌋ the fire Jr 51:58
would deliver ⌊**o**⌋ themselves Ezk 14:14
would deliver ⌊**o**⌋ themselves Ezk 14:20
It was **o** a short time before you Ezk 16:47
Abraham was **o** one person, yet he Ezk 33:24
Lord GOD, ⌊**o**⌋ You know." Ezk 37:3
with ⌊**o**⌋ a wall between Me and Ezk 43:8
belongs **o** to his sons; Ezk 46:17
O I, Daniel, saw the vision. Dn 10:7
cities, but **o** for a time. Dn 11:24
have known **o** you out of all the Am 3:2
rescued with ⌊**o**⌋ the corner of Am 3:12
will have ⌊**o**⌋ a hundred left, Am 5:3
strong⌋ will have ⌊**o**⌋ ten left Am 5:3
from a lion **o** to have a bear Am 5:19
the wall **o** to have a snake Am 5:19
mourning for an **o** son and its Am 8:10
they steal **o** what they wanted? Ob 5
O to act justly, to love Mc 6:8
peoples labor ⌊**o**⌋ to fuel the Hab 2:13
is ⌊**o**⌋ a cast image, a teacher Hab 2:18
measures, it ⌊**o**⌋ amounted to 10 Hg 2:16
the vat, it ⌊**o**⌋ amounted to 20. Hg 2:16
mourns for an **o** child and weep Zch 12:10
be a day known ⌊**o**⌋ to Yahweh, Zch 14:7
Not **o** do those who commit Mal 3:15
Lord your God, and serve **o** Him." Mt 4:10
if you greet **o** your brothers, Mt 5:47
⌊**o**⌋ the one who does the will Mt 7:21
But **o** say the word, and my Mt 8:8
to eat, but **o** for the priests Mt 12:4
out demons **o** by Beelzebul, Mt 12:24
But we **o** have five loaves and Mt 14:17
that they might **o** touch the Mt 14:36
I was sent **o** to the lost sheep Mt 15:24
o those it has been given to. Mt 19:11
There is **o** One who is good. Mt 19:17
you will not **o** do what was done Mt 21:21
the Son—except the Father **o**. Mt 24:36
Don't be afraid. **O** believe." Mk 5:36
bread and had **o** one loaf with Mk 8:14
Lord your God, and serve Him **o**." Lk 4:8
was healed—**o** Naaman the Syrian Lk 4:27
not **o** will he tear the new, Lk 5:36
He was his mother's **o** son, Lk 7:12
he had an **o** daughter about 12 Lk 8:42
O believe, and she will be made Lk 8:50
had spoken, **o** Jesus was found. Lk 9:36
because he's my **o** ⌊child⌋. Lk 9:38
we've **o** done our duty.'" Lk 17:10
he saw **o** the linen cloths. Lk 24:12
Are You the **o** visitor in Lk 24:18
as the One and **O** Son from the Jn 1:14
The One and **O** Son—the One who Jn 1:18
you believe ⌊**o**⌋ because I told Jn 1:50
they stayed there **o** a few days. Jn 2:12
He gave His One and **O** Son, Jn 3:16
of the One and **O** Son of God. Jn 3:18
not **o** was He breaking the Jn 5:18
but **o** what He sees the Father Jn 5:19
I judge **o** as I hear, and My Jn 5:30
glory that comes from the **o** God. Jn 5:44
knew there had been **o** one boat. Jn 6:22
I am **o** with you for a short Jn 7:33
O He was left, with the woman in Jn 8:9
A thief comes **o** to steal and to Jn 10:10
for the nation **o**, but also to Jn 11:52
came not **o** because of Jesus, Jn 12:9
be with you **o** a little longer Jn 12:35
Him, "Lord, not **o** my feet, but Jn 13:9
know You, the **o** true God, and Jn 17:3
I pray not **o** for these, but also Jn 17:20
it's **o** nine in the morning. Ac 2:15
they had **o** been baptized in the Ac 8:16
he knew **o** John's baptism. Ac 18:25
and hear that not **o** in Ephesus, Ac 19:26
So not **o** do we run a risk that Ac 19:27
I am ready not **o** to be bound, Ac 21:13
not **o** you but all who listen to Ac 26:29
not **o** of the cargo and the ship, Ac 27:10
your lives, but **o** of the ship. Ac 27:22
die—they not **o** do them, but Rm 1:32
God for Jews **o**? Is He not also Rm 3:29
Is this blessing **o** for the Rm 4:9
not **o** to those who are Rm 4:12
not **o** to those who are of the Rm 4:16
And not **o** that, but we also Rm 5:3
And not **o** that, but we also Rm 5:11
And not **o** that, but we ourselves Rm 8:23
And not **o** that, but also when Rm 9:10
o from the Jews but also from Rm 9:24
o the remnant will be saved; Rm 9:27
I am the **o** one left, and they Rm 11:3
submit, not **o** because of wrath Rm 13:5
who is weak eats **o** vegetables. Rm 14:2
Not **o** do I thank them, but so do Rm 16:4
to the **o** wise God, through Jesus Rm 16:27
but **o** God who gives the growth. 1Co 3:7
she wants—**o** in the Lord. 1Co 7:39
Or is it **o** Barnabas and I who 1Co 9:6
but **o** one receives the prize? 1Co 9:24
there should be **o** two, or at the 1Co 14:27
you, or did it come to you **o**? 1Co 14:36
hope in Christ for this life **o**, 1Co 15:19
in Ephesus with **o** human hope, 1Co 15:32
body, but **o** a seed, perhaps 1Co 15:37
it is set aside ⌊**o**⌋ in Christ. 2Co 3:14
not **o** by his coming, but also 2Co 7:7
though **o** for a little while. 2Co 7:8
ago began not **o** to do something 2Co 8:10
And not **o** that, but he was also 2Co 8:19
not **o** before the Lord but also 2Co 8:21
service is not **o** supplying the 2Co 9:12
not **o** signs but also wonders and 2Co 12:12
the truth, but **o** for the truth. 2Co 13:8
⌊They asked⌋ **o** that we would Gl 2:10
I **o** want to learn this from you: Gl 3:2
o don't use this freedom as an Gl 5:13
but **o** to avoid being persecuted Gl 6:12
o in this age but also in the Eph 1:21
but **o** what is good for the Eph 4:29
Don't ⌊work **o**⌋ while being Eph 6:6
behalf not **o** to believe in Him, Php 1:29
look out not ⌊**o**⌋ for his own Php 2:4
obeyed, not **o** in my presence, Php 2:12
and not **o** on him but also on me, Php 2:27
work **o** while being watched, Col 3:22
did not come to you in word **o**, 1Th 1:5
not **o** in Macedonia and Achaia, 1Th 1:8
with you not **o** the gospel of God 1Th 2:8
invisible, the **o** God, be honor 1Tm 1:17
are not **o** idle, but are also 1Tm 5:13
Don't continue drinking **o** water, 1Tm 5:23
is⌋ the blessed and **o** Sovereign, 1Tm 6:15
the **o** One who has immortality, 1Tm 6:16
there are not **o** gold and silver 2Tm 2:20
day, and not **o** to me, but to all 2Tm 4:8
O Luke is with me. Bring Mark 2Tm 4:11
room, and that **o** once a year, Heb 9:7
and **o** deal with food, Heb 9:10
will is valid **o** when people die Heb 9:17
o a model of the true one Heb 9:24
Since the law has ⌊**o**⌋ a shadow Heb 10:1
I will shake not **o** the earth but Heb 12:26
of the word and not hearers **o**, Jms 1:22
not **o** to the good and gentle but 1Pt 2:18
sins, and not **o** for ours, but 1Jn 2:2
sent His One and **O** Son into the 1Jn 4:9
not by water **o**, but by water and 1Jn 5:6
truth—and not **o** I, but also 2Jn 1
He not **o** refuses to welcome the 3Jn 10
denying our **o** Master and Lord Jd 4
nurturing **o** themselves without Jd 12
to the **o** God our Savior, through Jd 25
but **o** people who do not have Rv 9:4
o those written in the Lamb's Rv 21:27

ONO *(3)*
who built **O** and Lod and its 1Ch 8:12
the villages of the **O** Valley." Neh 6:2
Lod, and **O**, the valley of the Neh 11:35

ONO'S *(2)*
Lod's, Hadid's, and **O** people 725 Ezr 2:33
Lod's, Hadid's, and **O** people 721 Neh 7:37

ONTO *(8)*
to come up **o** the land of Egypt. Ex 8:5
brought frogs up **o** the land of Ex 8:7
throw ⌊them⌋ **o** the fire where Nm 19:6
you lift a stone **o** his shoulder, Jos 4:5
quickly latched **o** the hint and 1Kg 20:33
don't stray **o** her paths. Pr 7:25
brought you **o** the high seas, Ezk 27:26
and it vomited Jonah **o** dry land. Jnh 2:10

ONWARD *(3)*
jewelry from Mount Horeb ⌊**o**⌋. Ex 33:6
commands and **o** throughout your Nm 15:23
His clouds swept **o** with hail and Ps 18:12

ONYCHA *(1)*
stacte, **o**, and galbanum; Ex 30:34

ONYX *(11)*
bdellium and **o** are also there. Gn 2:12
and **o** along with ⌊other⌋ Ex 25:7
Take two **o** stones and engrave on Ex 28:9
a beryl, an **o**, and a jasper. Ex 28:20
and **o** with gemstones to mount on Ex 35:9
leaders brought **o** and gemstones Ex 35:27
they mounted the **o** stones Ex 39:6
a beryl, an **o**, and a jasper. Ex 39:13
wood, as well as **o**, ⌊stones for⌋ 1Ch 29:2
in precious **o** or sapphire. Jb 28:16
diamond, beryl, **o**, and jasper, Ezk 28:13

OOZES *(1)*
My skin forms scabs and then **o**. Jb 7:5

OPEN *(161)*
of the watery depths burst **o**, Gn 7:11
He named it **O** Spaces and said, Gn 26:22
land of Egypt is **o** before you; Gn 47:6
He will tear it **o** by its wings Lv 1:17
bird over the **o** countryside. Lv 14:7
live bird into the **o** countryside Lv 14:53
been offering in the **o** country. Lv 17:5
to be classified as **o** fields. Lv 25:31
The **o** pastureland around their Lv 25:34
the ground beneath them split **o**. Nm 16:31

any **o** container without a lid Nm 19:15
in the **o** field who touches Nm 19:16
are to **o** your hand to him and Dt 15:8
must willingly **o** your hand to Dt 15:11
engaged woman in the **o** country, Dt 22:25
The LORD will **o** for you His Dt 28:12
pursued them into the **o** country, Jos 8:24
Then Joshua said, "**O** the mouth Jos 10:22
to Gibeah through the **o** country. Jdg 20:31
camp and the **o** fields to all the 1Sm 14:15
an Egyptian in the **o** country and 1Sm 30:11
are camping in the **o** field. 2Sm 11:11
earth split **o** from the sound. 1Kg 1:40
May Your eyes be **o** to Your 1Kg 8:52
them were alone in the **o** field. 1Kg 11:29
o his eyes and let him see. 2Kg 6:17
o these men's eyes and let them 2Kg 6:20
camp to hide in the **o** country, 2Kg 7:12
will rip **o** their pregnant women. 2Kg 8:12
O the door and escape. 2Kg 9:3
said, "**O** the east window." 2Kg 13:17
and⌋ ripped **o** all the pregnant 2Kg 15:16
o Your eyes, LORD, and see; 2Kg 19:16
let Your eyes be **o** and Your ears 2Ch 6:40
eyes will now be **o** and My ears 2Ch 7:15
plundering, and **o** shame, as it Ezr 9:7
stamina to stay out in the **o**. Ezr 10:13
Your eyes be **o** and Your ears be Neh 1:6
who had an **o** letter in his hand. Neh 6:5
Do not **o** the gates of Jerusalem Neh 7:3
They **o** their mouths against me Jb 16:10
I must **o** my lips and respond. Jb 32:20
I am going to **o** my mouth; Jb 33:2
and grow up in the **o** field. Jb 39:4
Who can **o** his jaws, surrounded Jb 41:14
their throat is an **o** grave; Ps 5:9
They **o** their mouths against me— Ps 22:13
His ears are **o** to their cry for Ps 34:15
They **o** their mouths wide against Ps 35:21
person who does not **o** his mouth. Ps 38:13
I do not **o** my mouth because of Ps 39:9
You **o** my ears to listen. Ps 40:6
Lord, **o** my lips, and my mouth Ps 51:15
shaken the land and split it **o**. Ps 60:2
O your mouth wide, and I will Ps 81:10
when You **o** Your hand, they are Ps 104:28
deceitful mouths **o** against me; Ps 109:2
O the gates of righteousness for Ps 118:19
O my eyes so that I may see Ps 119:18
freely in an **o** place because I Ps 119:45
I pant with **o** mouth because I Ps 119:131
of thousands in our **o** fields. Ps 144:13
You **o** Your hand and satisfy the Ps 145:16
the watery depths broke **o**, Pr 3:20
Abaddon lie **o** before the LORD Pr 15:11
o your eyes, and you'll have Pr 20:13
he does not **o** his mouth at the Pr 24:7
Better an **o** reprimand than Pr 27:5
O to me, my sister, my darling, Sg 5:2
I rose to **o** for my love. Sg 5:5
consumed Israel with **o** mouths. Is 9:12
what he closes, no one can **o**. Is 22:22
earth is split **o**; the earth is Is 24:19
O the gates so a righteous Is 26:2
cattle will graze in **o** pastures. Is 30:23
o Your eyes, LORD, and see; Is 37:17
I will **o** rivers on the barren Is 41:18
in order to **o** blind eyes, to Is 42:7
his⌋ ears are **o**, he does not Is 42:20
o the doors before him and the Is 45:1
the earth **o** up that salvation Is 45:8
time your ears have not been **o**. Is 48:8
yet He did not **o** His mouth. Is 53:7
He did not **o** His mouth. Is 53:7
crack one **o**, and a viper is Is 59:5
Your gates will always be **o**; Is 60:11
the heavens **o** ⌊and⌋ come down Is 64:1
Their quiver is like an **o** grave; Jr 5:16
and conditions and the **o** copy— Jr 32:11
sealed copy and this **o** copy— Jr 32:14
distant places. **O** her granaries; Jr 50:26
All your enemies **o** their mouths Lm 2:16
All our enemies **o** their mouths Lm 3:46
O your mouth and eat what I am Ezk 2:8
with you, I will **o** your mouth, Ezk 3:27
out into the **o** field because you Ezk 16:5
and never **o** your mouth again Ezk 16:63
fall on the **o** ground and will Ezk 29:5
and hurl you on the **o** field. Ezk 32:4
in the **o** field I have given Ezk 33:27
I am going to **o** your graves and Ezk 37:12
when I **o** your graves and bring Ezk 37:13
up against a land of **o** villages; Ezk 38:11
You will fall on the **o** field, Ezk 39:5
half feet of **o** space all around Ezk 45:2
both⌋ residential and **o** space. Ezk 48:15
The city's **o** space will extend: Ezk 48:17
O Your eyes and see our Dn 9:18
them like a lamb in an **o** meadow? Hs 4:16
cubs and tear **o** the rib cage Hs 13:8
beast that would rip them **o**. Hs 13:8
their pregnant women ripped **o**. Hs 13:16
they ripped **o** the pregnant women Am 1:13
One who breaks **o** ⌊the way⌋ will Mc 2:13
city and camp in the **o** fields. Mc 4:10
land are wide **o** to your enemies. Nah 3:13
the earth's **o** spaces to seize Hab 1:6
O your gates, Lebanon, and fire Zch 11:1
if I will not **o** the floodgates Mal 3:10
I will **o** My mouth in parables; Mt 13:35
When you **o** its mouth you'll find Mt 17:27
they said to Him, "**o** our eyes!" Mt 20:33
Master, master, **o** up for us!' Mt 25:11
could not keep their eyes **o**. Mt 26:43
being torn **o** and the Spirit Mk 1:10
could not keep their eyes **o**. Mk 14:40
up and touched the **o** coffin, Lk 7:14
they can **o** ⌊the door⌋ for him at Lk 12:36
saying, 'Lord, **o** up for us!' Lk 13:25
the 99 in the **o** field and go Lk 15:4
O your eyes and look at the Jn 4:35
How did He **o** your eyes?" Jn 9:26
a demon **o** the eyes of the blind? Jn 10:21
he burst **o** in the middle, Ac 1:18
so He does not **o** His mouth. Ac 8:32
and though his eyes were **o**, Ac 9:8
her joy she did not **o** the gate, Ac 12:14
saw the doors of the prison **o**, Ac 16:27
Paul was about to **o** his mouth, Ac 18:14
to **o** their eyes that they may Ac 26:18
through the **o** sea off Cilicia Ac 27:5
harbor on Crete **o** to the Ac 27:12
Their throat is an **o** grave; Rm 3:13
conscience by an **o** display of 2Co 4:2
We are completely **o** before God, 2Co 5:11
we are completely **o** to your 2Co 5:11
you also should be **o** to us. 2Co 6:13
in the **o** country, dangers 2Co 11:26
to me when I **o** my mouth to make Eph 6:19
us that God may **o** a door to us Col 4:3
His ears are **o** to their request 1Pt 3:12
before you an **o** door that no one Rv 3:8
there in heaven was an **o** door. Rv 4:1
Who is worthy to **o** the scroll Rv 5:2
earth was able to **o** the scroll Rv 5:3
found worthy to **o** the scroll or Rv 5:4
so that He may **o** the scroll and Rv 5:5
the scroll and to **o** its seals; Rv 5:9
saw the Lamb **o** one of the seven Rv 6:1
Then I saw Him **o** the sixth seal. Rv 6:12
scroll that lies **o** in the hand Rv 10:8

OPEN-MINDED *(1)*

here were more **o** than those Ac 17:11

OPENED *(110)*

eyes will be **o** and you will be Gn 3:5
the eyes of both of them were **o**, Gn 3:7
the ground that **o** its mouth to Gn 4:11
floodgates of the sky were **o**, Gn 7:11
After 40 days Noah **o** the window Gn 8:6
Then God **o** her eyes, and she saw Gn 21:19
Leah was unloved, He **o** her womb; Gn 29:31
listened to her and **o** her womb. Gn 30:22
o up ⌊all the storehouses⌋ Gn 41:56
one of them **o** his sack to get Gn 42:27
the night and **o** our bags of Gn 43:21
his sack to the ground and **o** it. Gn 44:11
When she **o** it, she saw the child Ex 2:6
The earth **o** its mouth and Nm 16:32
Then the LORD **o** the donkey's Nm 22:28
Then the LORD **o** Balaam's eyes, Nm 22:31
of the man whose eyes are **o**, Nm 24:3
of the man whose eyes are **o**; Nm 24:15
The earth **o** its mouth and Nm 26:10
camp⌋ the earth **o** its mouth and Dt 11:6
he had still not **o** the doors Jdg 3:25
took the key and **o** the doors— Jdg 3:25
She **o** a container of milk, Jdg 4:19
in the morning, **o** the doors of Jdg 19:27
he **o** the doors of the LORD's 1Sm 3:15
seven times and **o** his eyes. 2Kg 4:35
So the LORD **o** the servant's 2Kg 6:17
So the LORD **o** their eyes. 2Kg 6:20
the young prophet **o** the door and 2Kg 9:10
So he **o** it. Elisha said, 2Kg 13:17
he **o** the doors of the LORD's 2Ch 29:3
Ezra **o** the book in full view of Neh 8:5
As he **o** it, all the people stood Neh 8:5
be closed and not **o** until after Neh 13:19
the rain and **o** their mouths as Jb 29:23
for I **o** my door to the traveler. Jb 31:32
You **o** up springs and streams; Ps 74:15
clouds above and **o** the doors of Ps 78:23
He **o** a rock, and water gushed Ps 105:41
The earth **o** up and swallowed Ps 106:17
I **o** to my love, but my love had Sg 5:6
if the blossom has **o**, if the Sg 7:12
no beak **o** or chirped. Is 10:14
the windows are **o** from above, Is 24:18
the eyes of the blind will be **o**, Is 35:5
The Lord GOD has **o** My ear, Is 50:5
LORD **o** His armory and brought Jr 50:25
the heavens **o** and I saw visions Ezk 1:1
So I **o** my mouth, and He fed me Ezk 3:2
mouth will be **o** ⌊to talk⌋ with Ezk 24:27
He **o** my mouth before the man Ezk 33:22
So my mouth was **o** and I was no Ezk 33:22
whose door ⌊**o**⌋ into the portico Ezk 40:38
The side rooms **o** into the free Ezk 41:11
will not be **o**, and no one will Ezk 44:2
but it will be **o** on the Sabbath Ezk 46:1
the Sabbath day and **o** on the day Ezk 46:1
faces east must be **o** for him. Ezk 46:12
its upper room **o** toward Dn 6:10
convened, and the books were **o**. Dn 7:10
I **o** my mouth and said to the one Dn 10:16
gates are **o**, and the palace Nah 2:6
fountain will be **o** for the house Zch 13:1
Then they **o** their treasures and Mt 2:11
The heavens suddenly **o** for Him, Mt 3:16
and the door will be **o** to you. Mt 7:7
who knocks, the door will be **o**. Mt 7:8
And their eyes were **o**. Mt 9:30
also were **o** and many bodies Mt 27:52
Ephphatha!" (that is, "Be **o**!"). Mk 7:34
Immediately his ears were **o**, Mk 7:35
his mouth was **o** and his tongue Lk 1:64
As He was praying, heaven **o**, Lk 3:21
and the door will be **o** to you. Lk 11:9
who knocks, the door will be **o**. Lk 11:10
their eyes were **o**, and they Lk 24:31
Then He **o** their minds to Lk 24:45
will see heaven **o** and the angels Jn 1:51
"Then how were your eyes **o**?" Jn 9:10
made the mud and **o** his eyes was Jn 9:14
Him, since He **o** your eyes?" Jn 9:17
we don't know who **o** his eyes. Jn 9:21
He is from, yet He **o** my eyes! Jn 9:30
He who **o** the blind man's Jn 11:37
an angel of the Lord **o** the doors Ac 5:19
but when we **o** them, we found no Ac 5:23
I see the heavens **o** and the Son Ac 7:56
She **o** her eyes, saw Peter, and Ac 9:40
He saw heaven **o** and an object Ac 10:11
which **o** to them by itself. Ac 12:10
and when they **o** the door and saw Ac 12:16
and that He had **o** the door of Ac 14:27
The Lord **o** her heart to pay Ac 16:14
all the doors were **o**, Ac 16:26
ministry has **o** for me— 1Co 16:9
a door was **o** to me by the Lord. 2Co 2:12
our heart has been **o** wide. 2Co 6:11
When He **o** the second seal, Rv 6:3
He **o** the third seal, I heard Rv 6:5
When He **o** the fourth seal, Rv 6:7
When He **o** the fifth seal, I saw Rv 6:9
When He **o** the seventh seal, Rv 8:1
He **o** the shaft of the abyss, Rv 9:2
a little scroll **o** in his hand. Rv 10:2
God's sanctuary in heaven was **o**, Rv 11:19
the earth **o** its mouth and Rv 12:16
tabernacle of testimony—was **o**. Rv 15:5
I saw heaven **o**, and there was Rv 19:11
the throne, and books were **o**. Rv 20:12
Another book was **o**, which is the Rv 20:12

OPENING *(22)*
stone covered the **o** of the well. Gn 29:2
the stone from the **o** of the well Gn 29:3
placed back on the well's **o**. Gn 29:3
is rolled from the well's **o**. Gn 29:8
stone from the **o** and watered his Gn 29:10
There should be an **o** at its top Ex 28:32
Around the **o**, there should be a Ex 28:32
collar with an **o** like that for Ex 28:32
There was an **o** in the center of Ex 39:23
around the **o** so that it would Ex 39:23
water cart's **o** inside the crown 1Kg 7:31
The **o** was round, made as a 1Kg 7:31
and⌋ repaired the **o** in the wall 1Kg 11:27
in charge of **o** it every morning 1Ch 9:27
thrust his hand through the **o**, Sg 5:4
Who is it you are **o** your mouth Is 57:4
at the **o** of the New Gate Jr 36:10
that is at the **o** of Pharaoh's Jr 43:9
the lead weight over its **o**. Zch 5:8
heard of someone **o** the eyes of a Jn 9:32
through ⌊an **o** in⌋ the wall. Ac 9:25
bitter water from the same **o**? Jms 3:11

OPENINGS *(2)*
the **o** facing each other in three 1Kg 7:5
The **o** of the recesses faced each Ezk 40:13

OPENLY *(8)*
complaining **o** before the LORD Nm 11:1
with him directly, **o**, and not in Nm 12:8
could no longer enter a town **o**. Mk 1:45
He was **o** talking about this. Mk 8:32
went up, not **o** but secretly. Jn 7:10
longer walked **o** among the Jews Jn 11:54
"I have spoken **o** to the world," Jn 18:20
We have spoken **o** to you, 2Co 6:11

OPENS *(15)*
and the ground **o** its mouth and Nm 16:30
of peace and **o** ⌊its gates⌋ to Dt 20:11
when he **o** his eyes, it is gone. Jb 27:19
Job **o** his mouth in vain and Jb 35:16
o their ears to correction and Jb 36:10
The LORD **o** ⌊the eyes of⌋ the Ps 146:8
the one who **o** his lips invites Pr 13:3
A gift **o** doors for a man and Pr 18:16
She **o** her mouth with wisdom, Pr 31:26
its throat and **o** wide its Is 5:14
what he **o**, no one can close; Is 22:22
The doorkeeper **o** it for him, Jn 10:3
who **o** and no one will close, Rv 3:7
and closes and no one **o** says: Rv 3:7
hears My voice and **o** the door, Rv 3:20

OPERATED *(1)*
sinful passions **o** through the Rm 7:5

OPERATES *(1)*
God's plan, which **o** by faith. 1Tm 1:4

OPHEL *(5)*
extensively on the wall of **O**. 2Ch 27:3
he brought it around the **O**, 2Ch 33:14
living on **O** ⌊made repairs⌋ Neh 3:26
out, as far as the wall of **O**. Neh 3:27
The temple servants lived on **O**; Neh 11:21

OPHIR *(13)*
O, Havilah, and Jobab. Gn 10:29
They went to **O** and acquired gold 1Kg 9:28
carried gold from **O** brought from 1Kg 10:11
brought from **O** a large quantity 1Kg 10:11
of Tarshish to go to **O** for gold, 1Kg 22:48
O, Havilah, and Jobab. 1Ch 1:23
gold (gold of **O**) and 250 tons 1Ch 29:4
with Solomon's servants to **O**, 2Ch 8:18
brought gold from **O** also brought 2Ch 9:10
⌊the gold of⌋ **O** to the stones in Jb 22:24
be valued in the gold of **O**, Jb 28:16
with gold from **O**, stands at your Ps 45:9
more rare than the gold of **O**. Is 13:12

OPHNI *(1)*
Chephar-ammoni, **O**, and Geba— Jos 18:24

OPHRAH *(8)*
Avvim, Parah, **O**, Jos 18:23
sat under the oak that was in **O**, Jdg 6:11
It is in **O** of the Abiezrites Jdg 6:24
from all this and put it in **O**, Jdg 8:27
father Joash in **O** of the Jdg 8:32
house in **O** and killed his 70 Jdg 9:5
toward the **O** road leading to 1Sm 13:17
Meonothai fathered **O**, and 1Ch 4:14

OPINION *(5)*
call the girl and ask her **o**." Gn 24:57
wise in their own **o** and clever Is 5:21
but I do give an **o** as one who by 1Co 7:25
she remains as she is, in my **o**. 1Co 7:40
I am giving an **o** on this because 2Co 8:10

OPINIONS *(2)*
will you hesitate between two **o**? 1Kg 18:21
only wants to show off his **o**. Pr 18:2

OPPONENT *(7)*
man grabbed his **o** by the head 2Sm 2:16
and each one struck down his **o**. 1Kg 20:20
wicked and my **o** like the unjust Jb 27:7
Let my **O** compose ⌊His⌋ Jb 31:35
if your **o** humiliates you? Pr 25:8
case with your **o** without Pr 25:9
so that the **o** will be ashamed, Ti 2:8

OPPONENT'S *(1)*
sword into his **o** side so that 2Sm 2:16

OPPONENTS *(8)*
Surely our **o** are destroyed, Jb 22:20
Oppose my **o**, LORD; Ps 35:1
the tumult of Your **o** that goes Ps 74:23
and separates powerful **o**. Pr 18:18
Hear what my **o** are saying! Jr 18:19
murmuring of my **o** attack me all Lm 3:62
frightened in any way by your **o**. Php 1:28
his **o** with gentleness 2Tm 2:25

OPPORTUNE *(2)*
he let the **o** moment pass. Jr 46:17
Now an **o** time came on his Mk 6:21

OPPORTUNITY *(21)*
for a good **o** to betray Him. Mt 26:16
for a good **o** to betray Him. Mk 14:11
will lead to an **o** for you to Lk 21:13
for a good **o** to betray Him to Lk 22:6
face and has an **o** to give a Ac 25:16
seizing an **o** through the Rm 7:8
seizing an **o** through the Rm 7:11
free, by all means take the **o**. 1Co 7:21
giving you an **o** to be proud of 2Co 5:12
We give no **o** for stumbling to 2Co 6:3
to cut off the **o** of those who 2Co 11:12
who want an **o** to be regarded 2Co 11:12
freedom as an **o** for the flesh, Gl 5:13
as we have **o**, we must work for Gl 6:10
and don't give the Devil an **o**. Eph 4:27
but lacked the **o** ⌊to show it⌋. Php 4:10
the adversary no **o** to accuse us. 1Tm 5:14
no **o** would have been sought for Heb 8:7
they would have had **o** to return. Heb 11:15
find any **o** for repentance, Heb 12:17
Lord as ⌊an **o** for⌋ salvation, 2Pt 3:15

OPPOSE *(12)*
His stand on the path to **o** him. Nm 22:22
came out to **o** you, because what Nm 22:32
Those who **o** the LORD will be 1Sm 2:10
who can **o** Him? He does what He Jb 23:13
But He finds reasons to **o** me; Jb 33:10
O my opponents, LORD; Ps 35:1
he wants, and no one can **o** him. Dn 11:16
Pharisees began to **o** Him Lk 11:53
with 10,000 to **o** the one who Lk 14:31
and began to **o** what Paul was Ac 13:45
and those who **o** it will bring Rm 13:2
opened for me—yet many **o** me. 1Co 16:9

OPPOSED *(11)*
when they **o** them along the way 1Sm 15:2
Jahzeiah son of Tikvah **o** this, Ezr 10:15
Who has **o** Him and come out Jb 9:4
has arrogantly **o** the Almighty. Jb 15:25
of Persia **o** me for 21 days. Dn 10:13
to be a sign that will be **o**— Lk 2:34
o them and tried to turn the Ac 13:8
I **o** him to his face because he Gl 2:11
these are **o** to each other, Gl 5:17
that was against us and **o** to us, Col 2:14
because he strongly **o** our words. 2Tm 4:15

OPPOSES *(3)*
a fool, a daughter **o** her mother, Mc 7:6
makes himself a king **o** Caesar!" Jn 19:12
He **o** and exalts himself above 2Th 2:4

OPPOSING *(3)*
Stop **o** God who is with me; 2Ch 35:21
o payment of taxes to Caesar, Lk 23:2
authority is **o** God's command, Rm 13:2

OPPOSITE *(48)*
(See pp. xi-xii.)

OPPOSITE (noun, *contrary*) *(3)*
them, just the **o** happened. Est 9:1
So you were the **o** of other women Ezk 16:34
paid to you, you were the **o**. Ezk 16:34

OPPOSITION *(4)*
He lived in **o** to all his Gn 25:18
stood in **o** to those coming from 2Ch 28:12
do many things in **o** to the name Ac 26:9
God to you in spite of great **o**. 1Th 2:2

OPPRESS *(32)*
Israelites to **o** them with forced Ex 1:11
a foreign resident or **o** him, Ex 22:21
You must not **o** a foreign Ex 23:9
You must not **o** your neighbor or Lv 19:13
your land, you must not **o** him. Lv 19:33
Do not **o** a hired hand who is Dt 24:14
He allowed no one to **o** them; 1Ch 16:21
not continue to **o** them as they 1Ch 17:9
it good for You to **o**, to reject Jb 10:3
righteousness, He will not **o**. Jb 37:23
"Let us **o** them relentlessly." Ps 74:8
no wicked man will **o** him. Ps 89:22
He allowed no one to **o** them; Ps 105:14
do not let the arrogant **o** me. Ps 119:122
Power is with those who **o** them; Ec 4:1
The people will **o** one another, Is 3:5
Youths **o** My people, and women Is 3:12
will **o** Ariel, and there will be Is 29:2
and those who **o** her—will then Is 29:7
your fast, and **o** all your Is 58:3
if you no longer **o** the alien, Jr 7:6
He doesn't **o** anyone but returns Ezk 18:7
He doesn't **o** anyone, hold Ezk 18:16
will no longer **o** My people but Ezk 45:8
Most High and **o** the holy ones Dn 7:25
women who **o** the poor and crush Am 4:1
They **o** the righteous, take a Am 5:12
and they will **o** you from the Am 6:14
Do not **o** the widow or the Zch 7:10
against those who **o** the widow Mal 3:5
would enslave and **o** them for 400 Ac 7:6
Don't the rich **o** you and drag Jms 2:6

OPPRESSED *(45)*
be enslaved and **o** 400 years. Gn 15:13
the more they **o** them, the more Ex 1:12
You will only be **o** and robbed Dt 28:29
You will only be **o** and crushed Dt 28:33
and he harshly **o** them 20 years. Jdg 4:3
and they **o** Israel. Jdg 6:2
and the power of all who **o** you. Jdg 6:9
Israel was greatly **o**, Jdg 10:9
Maonites **o** you, and you cried Jdg 10:12
The LORD severely **o** the people 1Sm 5:6
king of Aram **o** Israel throughout 2Kg 13:22
he **o** him and did not give him 2Ch 28:20
subordinates also **o** the people, Neh 5:15
to their enemies, who **o** them. Neh 9:27
For he **o** and abandoned the poor; Jb 20:19
loosened my bowstring and **o** me, Jb 30:11
The LORD is a refuge for the **o**, Ps 9:9
For the **o** will not always be Ps 9:18
for the fatherless and the **o**, Ps 10:18
Do not let the **o** turn away in Ps 74:21
rights of the **o** and the Ps 82:3
and justice for all the **o**. Ps 103:6
Their enemies **o** them, and they Ps 106:42
He raises up all who are **o**. Ps 145:14
LORD raises up those who are **o**. Ps 146:8
the days of the **o** are miserable, Pr 15:15
don't crush the **o** at the gate, Pr 22:22
devouring the **o** from the land Pr 30:14
pervert justice for all the **o**. Pr 31:5
the cause of the **o** and needy. Pr 31:9
at the tears of those who are **o**; Ec 4:1
justice for the **o** of the land. Is 11:4
Lord, I am **o**; support me. Is 38:14
then Assyria **o** them without Is 52:4
He was **o** and afflicted, yet He Is 53:7
and with the **o** and lowly of Is 57:15
and revive the heart of the **o**. Is 57:15
yoke, to set the **o** free, and to Is 58:6
and Judeans alike have been **o**. Jr 50:33
and widow are **o** in you. Ezk 22:7
They have **o** the poor and needy Ezk 22:29
Ephraim is **o**, crushed in Hs 5:11

to the blind, to set free the **o**, Lk 4:18
our race and **o** our forefathers Ac 7:19
avenged the **o** man by striking Ac 7:24

OPPRESSES *(5)*
he fights and **o** me all day long. Ps 56:1
The one who **o** the poor insults Pr 14:31
leader who **o** the poor is like Pr 28:3
away from the sword that **o**. Jr 46:16
and ⌊when⌋ he **o** the poor and Ezk 18:12

OPPRESSING *(5)*
way the Egyptians are **o** them. Ex 3:9
those who were **o** and afflicting Jdg 2:18
and perhaps He will stop **o** you, 1Sm 6:5
the kingdoms that were **o** you.' 1Sm 10:18
O the poor to enrich oneself, Pr 22:16

OPPRESSION *(29)*
saw our misery, hardship, and **o**. Dt 26:7
you in the time of your **o**." Jdg 10:14
He saw the **o** the king of Aram 2Kg 13:4
You saw the **o** of our ancestors Neh 9:9
cry out because of severe **o**; Jb 35:9
Because of the **o** of the Ps 12:5
because of the enemy's **o**?" Ps 42:9
sorrow because of the enemy's **o**? Ps 43:2
and forget our affliction and **o**? Ps 44:24
o and deceit never leave its Ps 55:11
no trust in **o**, or false hope Ps 62:10
redeem them from **o** and violence, Ps 72:14
they arrogantly threaten **o**. Ps 73:8
humbled by cruel **o** and sorrow, Ps 107:39
me from human **o**, and I will keep Ps 119:134
all the acts of **o** being done Ec 4:1
If you see **o** of the poor and Ec 5:8
have trusted in **o** and deceit, Is 30:12
meager bread and water during **o**, Is 30:20
away because of **o** and judgment; Is 53:8
will be far from **o**, you will Is 54:14
our God, speaking **o** and revolt, Is 59:13
is nothing but **o** within her. Jr 6:6
and committing extortion and **o**. Jr 22:17
violence and **o** and do what is Ezk 45:9
and the acts of **o** within it. Am 3:9
o will not rise up a second time. Nah 1:9
O and violence are right in Hab 1:3
certainly seen the **o** of My Ac 7:34

OPPRESSIVE *(5)*
in the land and no **o** ruler. Jdg 18:7
the grasp of the unjust and **o**. Ps 71:4
lacks understanding is very **o**, Pr 28:16
statutes and writing **o** laws Is 10:1
and defiled, the **o** city! Zph 3:1

OPPRESSOR *(13)*
not hear the voice of ⌊their⌋ **o**. Jb 3:18
help the poor, and crush the **o**. Ps 72:4
The poor and the **o** have this in Pr 29:13
Correct the **o**. Defend the rights Is 1:17
staff of their **o**, just as ⌊You Is 9:4
How the **o** has quieted down, Is 14:4
When the **o** has gone, destruction Is 16:4
because of the fury of the **o**, Is 51:13
But where is the fury of the **o**? Is 51:13
robbery from the hand of his **o**, Jr 21:12
robbery from the hand of his **o**. Jr 22:3
because of the sword of the **o**, Jr 25:38
and no **o** will march against them Zch 9:8

OPPRESSOR'S *(1)*
Because of the **o** sword, each Jr 50:16

OPPRESSORS *(7)*
crying out because of their **o**, Ex 3:7
do not leave me to my **o**. Ps 119:121
and will rule over their **o**. Is 14:2
to the LORD because of their **o**, Is 19:20
I will make your **o** eat their own Is 49:26
The sons of your **o** will come and Is 60:14
I will punish all his **o**. Jr 30:20

OR *(1942)*
(See pp. xi-xii.)

ORACLE *(29)*
The **o** of Balaam son of Beor, Nm 24:3
the **o** of the man whose eyes are Nm 24:3
the **o** of one who hears the Nm 24:4
The **o** of Balaam son of Beor, Nm 24:15
the **o** of the man whose eyes are Nm 24:15
the **o** of one who hears the Nm 24:16
LORD uttered this **o** against him: 2Kg 9:25
An **o** within my heart concerning Ps 36:1
of Agur son of Jakeh. The **o**. Pr 30:1
an **o** that his mother taught him: Pr 31:1
An **o** against Babylon that Isaiah Is 13:1
King Ahaz died, this **o** came: Is 14:28
An **o** against Moab: Ar in Moab is Is 15:1
An **o** against Damascus: Is 17:1
An **o** against Egypt: Look, the Is 19:1
An **o** against the desert by the Is 21:1
An **o** against Dumah: One calls to Is 21:11
An **o** against Arabia: You will Is 21:13
An **o** against the Valley of Is 22:1
o against Tyre: Wail, ships of Is 23:1
An **o** about the animals of the Is 30:6
the wise, or an **o** from the Jr 18:18
own tongues to deliver an **o**. Jr 23:31
This **o** is about the prince in Ezk 12:10
The **o** concerning Nineveh. Nah 1:1
The **o** that Habakkuk the prophet Hab 1:1
An **O** The word of the LORD is Zch 9:1
An **O** The word of the LORD Zch 12:1
An **o**: The word of the LORD to Mal 1:1

ORACLES *(4)*
his sons, the many **o** about him, 2Ch 24:27
They saw **o** for you that were Lm 2:14
received living **o** to give to us. Ac 7:38
should be⌋ like the **o** of God; 1Pt 4:11

ORATION *(1)*
The man's **o** to Ithiel, to Ithiel Pr 30:1

ORCHARD *(7)*
have been removed from the **o**; Is 16:10
while Lebanon will become an **o**, Is 29:17
and the **o** will seem like a Is 29:17
the desert will become an **o**, Is 32:15
and the **o** will seem like a Is 32:15
will dwell in the **o**. Is 32:16
trees of the **o**—have withered Jl 1:12

ORCHARDS *(3)*
and olive **o** and give them to his 1Sm 8:14
clothes, olive **o** and vineyards, 2Kg 5:26
its forests and **o** as a sickness Is 10:18

ORDAIN *(6)*
then anoint, **o**, and consecrate Ex 28:41
the way you will **o** Aaron and his Ex 29:9
O them for seven days. Ex 29:35
will take seven days to **o** you. Lv 8:33
Whoever comes to **o** himself with 2Ch 13:9
I will **o** four kinds ⌊of Jr 15:3

ORDAINED *(16)*
can be anointed and **o** in them. Ex 29:29
is anointed and **o** to serve as Lv 16:32
head and has been **o** to wear the Lv 21:10
who were **o** to serve as priests. Nm 3:3
desired it, he **o**, and they 1Kg 13:33
the promise He **o** for a thousand 1Ch 16:15
This is ⌊**o**⌋ for Israel forever. 2Ch 2:4
rejoicing and song **o** by David. 2Ch 23:18
the inheritance God **o** for him. Jb 20:29
You have **o** a judgment. Ps 7:6
the promise He **o** for a thousand Ps 105:8
He has **o** His covenant forever. Ps 111:9
He has **o** a lot for them; Is 34:17
which He **o** in days of old. Lm 2:17
unless the Lord has **o** ⌊it⌋? Lm 3:37
to the rod and the One who **o** it. Mc 6:9

ORDAINS *(1)*
who **o** victories for Jacob. Ps 44:4

ORDEAL *(1)*
when the fiery **o** arises among 1Pt 4:12

ORDER *(188)*
in **o** to keep offspring alive on Gn 7:3
Now obey every **o** I give you, Gn 27:8
in **o** to seek your favor.' " Gn 32:5
the Adullamite in **o** to get back Gn 38:20
This **o** was carried out. Gn 42:25
seated before him in **o** by age, Gn 43:33
at a distance in **o** to see what Ex 2:4
king of Egypt in **o** to bring the Ex 6:27
the people in **o** to send them Ex 12:33
of the ark in **o** to carry the ark Ex 25:14
in **o** to keep the lamp burning Ex 27:20
stone, in the **o** of their birth. Ex 28:10
anoint it in **o** to consecrate it Ex 29:36
craftsman in **o** to make all that Ex 31:6
After Moses gave an **o**, they sent Ex 36:6
of the altar in **o** to carry it Ex 38:7
yarn to it in **o** to mount ⌊it⌋ Ex 39:31
done today in **o** to make Lv 8:34
in **o** to distinguish between the Lv 11:47
the priest is to **o** whatever is Lv 13:54
in **o** to pronounce it clean or Lv 13:59
the priest will **o** that two live Lv 14:4
Then the priest will **o** that one Lv 14:5
to be waved in **o** to make Lv 14:21
The priest must **o** them to clear Lv 14:36
priest must **o** that the stones Lv 14:40
or goats in **o** for you to be Lv 22:19
This was the **o** of march for the Nm 10:28
obstinate in **o** to hand him over Dt 2:30
us from there in **o** to lead us in Dt 6:23
in **o** to humble and test you, Dt 8:16
in **o** to confirm His covenant He Dt 8:18
o to keep the promise He swore Dt 9:5
against it in **o** to capture it, Dt 20:19
against your **o** and does not obey Jos 1:18
LORD left in **o** to test Israel, Jdg 3:1
in the wine vat in **o** to hide it Jdg 6:11
other party in **o** to make any Ru 4:7
sheep and cattle in **o** to offer a 1Sm 15:15
on earth in **o** to redeem a people 2Sm 7:23
his emissaries in **o** to scout out 2Sm 10:3
When I **o** you to strike Amnon, 2Sm 13:28
surely listen in **o** to rescue his 2Sm 14:16
sent for Joab in **o** to send him 2Sm 14:29
undermined in **o** to bring about 2Sm 17:14
his affairs in **o** and hanged 2Sm 17:23
Yet the king's **o** prevailed over 2Sm 24:4
from you in **o** to build an altar 2Sm 24:21
Solomon gave the **o** to Benaiah 1Kg 2:25
and bury him in **o** to remove from 1Kg 2:31
at Jerusalem in **o** to bring the 1Kg 8:1
in My sight in **o** to keep My 1Kg 11:38
In **o** to provoke Me, you have 1Kg 14:9
built Ramah in **o** to deny anyone 1Kg 15:17
of sticks in **o** to go prepare it 1Kg 17:12
between them in **o** to cover it. 1Kg 18:6
deceptively in **o** to destroy 2Kg 10:19
your affairs in **o**, for you are 2Kg 20:1
of this book in **o** to do 2Kg 22:13
to other gods in **o** to provoke Me 2Kg 22:17
did this in **o** to carry out the 2Kg 23:24
emissaries in **o** to scout out, 1Ch 19:3
Yet the king's **o** prevailed over 1Ch 21:4
one who gave the **o** to count the 1Ch 21:17
LORD my God in **o** to dedicate it 2Ch 2:4
in **o** to bring the ark of the 2Ch 5:2
in **o** that the LORD might carry 2Ch 10:15
of warriors in **o** with 400,000 2Ch 13:3
built Ramah in **o** to deny 2Ch 16:1
was from God in **o** to hand them 2Ch 25:20
in **o** to seek his God 2Ch 31:21
them in **o** that he might 2Ch 32:18
in **o** to cleanse the land and the 2Ch 34:8
the LORD in **o** to do everything 2Ch 34:21
to other gods in **o** to provoke Me 2Ch 34:25
all his soul in **o** to carry out 2Ch 34:31
in **o** to fight with him he 2Ch 35:22
house of God in **o** to have it Ezr 2:68
Israel's God in **o** to offer burnt Ezr 3:2
an **o** for these men to stop, Ezr 4:21
gave you the **o** to rebuild this Ezr 5:3
gave you the **o** to rebuild this Ezr 5:9
Darius gave the **o**, and they Ezr 6:1
of the land in **o** to worship the Ezr 6:21
o to avert the fierce anger of Ezr 10:14
in **o** that they could discredit Neh 6:13
guard the gates in **o** to keep the Neh 13:22
let an **o** be drawn up authorizing Est 3:9
and the **o** was written exactly as Est 3:12
in **o** to confirm these days of Est 9:31
in **o** to turn a person ⌊from his⌋ Jb 33:17
in **o** to turn him back from the Jb 33:30
He lurks in **o** to seize the Ps 10:9
observing it in **o** to take the Ps 10:14
and earth in **o** to judge His Ps 50:4
brokenhearted in **o** to put them Ps 109:16
in **o** to seat them with nobles— Ps 113:8
gave an **o** that will never pass Ps 148:6
in **o** to teach you true and Pr 22:21
accumulating in **o** to give to the Ec 2:26
His God teaches him **o**; Is 28:26
in **o** to seek shelter under Is 30:2
your affairs in **o**, for you are Is 38:1
o to open blind eyes, to bring Is 42:7
in **o** to plant the heavens, Is 51:16

of Hinnom in **o** to burn their Jr 7:31
in **o** to establish the oath I Jr 11:5
'in **o** that you might provoke Me Jr 25:7
fixed **o** of moon and stars for Jr 31:35
If this fixed **o** departs from My Jr 31:36
sons of men in **o** to give to each Jr 32:19
the fixed **o** of heaven and earth Jr 33:25
in **o** not to enslave them any Jr 34:10
cut in two in **o** to pass between Jr 34:18
o to make their way into Egypt Jr 41:17
for food in **o** to stay alive. Lm 1:11
wicked way in **o** to save his life Ezk 3:18
every height in **o** to ensnare Ezk 13:18
o that the house of Israel may Ezk 14:11
in **o** to wipe out ⌊both⌋ man and Ezk 14:21
abundant waters in **o** to produce Ezk 17:8
his covenant in **o** to endure. Ezk 17:14
their gifts in **o** to devastate Ezk 20:26
rams, give the **o** to slaughter, Ezk 21:22
who slander in **o** to shed blood. Ezk 22:9
bribes in **o** to shed blood. Ezk 22:12
lives in **o** to get unjust gain Ezk 22:27
In **o** to stir up wrath and take Ezk 24:8
o to seize spoil and carry off Ezk 38:12
burying them in **o** to cleanse the Ezk 39:12
the ground, in **o** to cleanse it. Ezk 39:14
approach Me in **o** to serve Me." Ezk 43:19
but in **o** that the interpretation Dn 2:30
to me in **o** that they might Dn 4:6
Then Belshazzar gave an **o**, Dn 5:29
o stands and is irrevocable." Dn 6:12
king gave the **o**, and they Dn 6:16
of Gilead in **o** to enlarge their Am 1:13
the wilderness in **o** to possess Am 2:10
By **o** of the king and his nobles: Jnh 3:7
has issued an **o** concerning you: Nah 1:14
in **o** to look at their nakedness! Hab 2:15
in **o** to pour out My indignation Zph 3:8
a hairy cloak in **o** to deceive. Zch 13:4
He gave the **o** to go to the other Mt 8:18
in **o** to accuse Him they asked Mt 12:10
vacant, swept, and put in **o**. Mt 12:44
In **o** to accuse Him, they were Mk 3:2
command in **o** to maintain your Mk 7:9
but the more He would **o** them, Mk 7:36
the house⌋ swept and put in **o**. Lk 11:25
in **o** that they might have Jn 8:6
in **o** that those who do not see Jn 9:39
we strictly **o** you not to teach Ac 5:28
Receiving such an **o**, he put them Ac 16:24
o that I might have a fruitful Rm 1:13
in sin in **o** that grace may Rm 6:1
into death, in **o** that, just as Rm 6:4
Him in **o** that sin's dominion Rm 6:6
in **o** to be recognized as sin, Rm 7:13
in **o** that the law's requirement Rm 8:4
his good, in **o** to build him up Rm 15:2
in **o** that I will not be building Rm 15:20
in **o** that, as it is written: 1Co 1:31
o to know what has been freely 1Co 2:12
slave to all, in **o** to win more 1Co 9:19
weak, in **o** to win the weak 1Co 9:22
in **o** to teach others also, 1Co 14:19
must be done decently and in **o**. 1Co 14:40
But each in his own **o**: 1Co 15:23
but in **o** that your diligence for 2Co 7:12
in **o** to cut off the opportunity 2Co 11:12
Damascenes in **o** to arrest me, 2Co 11:32
Jesus, in **o** to enslave us. Gl 2:4
circumcised in **o** to boast about Gl 6:13
in **o** to give grace to those who Eph 4:29
watched, in **o** to please men, Eph 6:6
see your good **o** and the strength Col 2:5
watched, in **o** to please men, Col 3:22
of the truth in **o** to be saved. 2Th 2:10
forever in the **o** of Melchizedek. Heb 5:6
"in the **o** of Melchizedek." Heb 5:10
in the **o** of Melchizedek." Heb 6:20
arise in the **o** of Melchizedek, Heb 7:11
as being in the **o** of Aaron? Heb 7:11
forever in the **o** of Melchizedek. Heb 7:17
one another in **o** to promote love Heb 10:24
in **o** to live the remaining time 1Pt 4:2

ORDERED *(68)*

took his firepan as Moses had **o**, Nm 16:47
that you do⌋ as I have **o** you." Jos 8:8
Haven't I **o** the young men not to Ru 2:9
grain⌋, Boaz **o** his young men, "Be Ru 2:15
But Saul **o**, "No one will be 1Sm 11:13
Saul then **o** his servants, 1Sm 18:22
Saul **o** his son Jonathan and all 1Sm 19:1
or what I have **o** you ⌊to do⌋.' 1Sm 21:2
Then the king **o** the guards 1Sm 22:17
and he **o** that the Judahites be 2Sm 1:18
David then **o** Joab and all the 2Sm 3:31
since the day I **o** judges to be 2Sm 7:11
o and secured in every ⌊detail⌋. 2Sm 23:5
o that he ⌊be given⌋ food, 1Kg 11:18
third day, as the king had **o**: 1Kg 12:12
Then Elijah **o** them, "Seize the 1Kg 18:40
Then the king of Israel **o**, 1Kg 22:26
of Aram had **o** his 32 chariot 1Kg 22:31
He **o** his attendant Gehazi, 2Kg 4:12
Then Jehu **o**, "Take them alive." 2Kg 10:14
the priest **o** the commanders 2Kg 11:15
and David **o** that they be burned 1Ch 14:12
since the day I **o** judges to be 1Ch 17:10
of the LORD **o** Gad to tell David 1Ch 21:18
Then David **o** all the leaders of 1Ch 22:17
as the king had **o**, saying, 2Ch 10:12
Then the king of Israel **o**, 2Ch 18:25
king of Aram had **o** his chariot 2Ch 18:30
Then Hezekiah **o** that the burnt 2Ch 29:27
The governor **o** them not to eat Ezr 2:63
The governor **o** them not to eat Neh 7:65
I **o** that the rooms be purified, Neh 13:9
king had **o** every wine steward Est 1:8
'King Ahasuerus **o** Queen Vashti Est 1:17
Mordecai had **o** her not to. Est 2:10
did everything Esther had **o** him. Est 4:17
so he **o** the book recording daily Est 6:1
"Have him enter," the king **o**. Est 6:5
as Mordecai **o** for the Jews, Est 8:9
⌊He **o**⌋ them to celebrate the Est 9:21
because He has **o** it by my mouth, Is 34:16
The king **o** Ashpenaz, the chief Dn 1:3
Then Pilate **o** that it be Mt 27:58
Then He **o** them to tell no one, Mk 7:36
He **o** them to tell no one what Mk 9:9
Then He **o** him to tell no one: Lk 5:14
'what you **o** has been done, Lk 14:22
After they had **o** them to leave Ac 4:15
for them and **o** them not to Ac 4:18
the Sanhedrin and **o** the men to Ac 5:34
they **o** them not to speak in the Ac 5:40
Then he **o** the chariot to stop, Ac 8:38
guards and **o** their execution. Ac 12:19
clothes and **o** them to be beaten Ac 16:22
Claudius had **o** all the Jews to Ac 18:2
and **o** him to be bound with two Ac 21:33
he **o** him to be taken into the Ac 21:34
commander **o** him to be brought Ac 22:24
priest Ananias **o** those who were Ac 23:2
by them and **o** the troops to go Ac 23:10
I also **o** his accusers to state Ac 23:30
to Antipatris as they were **o**. Ac 23:31
And he **o** that he be kept under Ac 23:35
o that the centurion keep Paul Ac 24:23
judge's bench and **o** the man to Ac 25:17
I **o** him to be kept in custody Ac 25:21
so he **o** those who could swim to Ac 27:43
⌊The law⌋ was **o** through angels Gl 3:19

ORDERING *(3)*

issued in Susa **o** their Est 4:8
o the jailer to keep them Ac 16:23
law are you **o** me to be struck? Ac 23:3

ORDERLY *(2)*

to write to you in **o** sequence, Lk 1:3
to them in an **o** sequence, Ac 11:4

ORDERS *(41)*

gave ⌊his⌋ men **o** about him, Gn 12:20
Joseph then gave **o** to fill their Gn 42:25
Therefore give **o** to bring your Ex 9:19
to the battle as my lord **o**." Nm 32:27
So Moses gave **o** about them to Nm 32:28
David gave **o** to the young men, 2Sm 4:12
David sent **o** to Joab: 2Sm 11:6
is the one who gave **o** to me; 2Sm 14:19
heard the king's **o** to all the 2Sm 18:5
So David gave **o** to gather the 1Ch 22:2
gave **o** that the gates be closed Neh 13:19
Mordecai's **o**, as she always Est 2:20
king gave the **o** for this to be Est 9:14
and whoever **o** his conduct, Ps 50:23
His angels **o** concerning you, Ps 91:11
I will also give **o** to the clouds Is 5:6
Zedekiah gave **o**, and Jeremiah Jr 37:21
of Babylon gave **o** concerning Jr 39:11
So the king gave **o** to summon the Dn 2:2
angry and gave **o** to destroy all Dn 2:12
gave **o** to present an offering Dn 2:46
Nebuchadnezzar gave **o** to bring Dn 3:13
He gave **o** to heat the furnace Dn 3:19
Belshazzar gave **o** to bring in Dn 5:2
and gave **o** to take Daniel out Dn 6:23
He gives **o** to his officers; Nah 2:5
He gave **o** to massacre all the Mt 2:16
give His angels **o** concerning you Mt 4:6
finished giving **o** to His 12 Mt 11:1
So he sent **o** and had John Mt 14:10
the disciples **o** to tell no one Mt 16:20
Therefore give **o** that the tomb Mt 27:64
gave them strict **o** that no one Mk 5:43
had given **o** to arrest John Mk 6:17
His angels **o** concerning you, Lk 4:10
Then He gave **o** that she be given Lk 8:55
I have never disobeyed your **o**, Lk 15:29
had given **o** that if anyone knew Jn 11:57
He had given **o** through the Holy Ac 1:2
and sent ⌊**o**⌋ to the jail to have Ac 5:21
have sent **o** for you to be Ac 16:36

ORDINANCE *(13)*

a statute and **o** for them at Ex 15:25
law and the same **o** will apply to Nm 15:16
to be a statutory **o** for the Nm 27:11
be a statutory **o** for you Nm 35:29
a statute and **o** for them. Jos 24:25
a law and an **o** for Israel ⌊and 1Sm 30:25
specified by **o** for each festival Ezr 3:4
an assembly, according to the **o**. Neh 8:18
an **o** regulating the singers' Neh 11:23
it up as an **o** for Joseph when Ps 81:5
This is an **o** for Israel. Ps 122:4
establish an **o** and enforce Dn 6:7
that no edict or **o** the king Dn 6:15

ORDINANCES *(77)*

These are the **o** that you must Ex 21:1
of the LORD and all the **o**. Ex 24:3
to practice My **o** and you are to Lv 18:4
Keep My statutes and **o**; Lv 18:5
are to keep My statutes and **o**. Lv 18:26
and all My **o** and do them; Lv 19:37
all My statutes and all My **o**, Lv 20:22
My statutes and **o** and carefully Lv 25:18
My statutes and despise My **o**, Lv 26:15
rejected My **o** and abhorred My Lv 26:43
the statutes, **o**, and laws the Lv 26:46
to all its statutes and **o**." Nm 9:3
the Passover statute and its **o**. Nm 9:14
of blood according to these **o**. Nm 35:24
the commands and **o** the LORD Nm 36:13
the statutes and **o** I am teaching Dt 4:1
you statutes and **o** as the LORD Dt 4:5
statutes and **o** like this entire Dt 4:8
you statutes and **o** for you to Dt 4:14
and **o** Moses proclaimed to them Dt 4:45
statutes and **o** I am proclaiming Dt 5:1
the statutes and **o**—you are to Dt 5:31
statutes and **o**—the LORD your Dt 6:1
statutes, and **o**, which the LORD Dt 6:20
the statutes and **o**—that I am Dt 7:11
and are careful to keep these **o**, Dt 7:12
command—the **o** and statutes—I Dt 8:11
His statutes, **o**, and commands. Dt 11:1
statutes and **o** I set before you Dt 11:32
statutes and **o** in the land that Dt 12:1
to follow these statutes and **o**. Dt 26:16
commands, and **o**, and obey Him. Dt 26:17
statutes, and **o**, so that you may Dt 30:16
will teach Your **o** to Jacob and Dt 33:10
justice and His **o** for Israel. Dt 33:21
kept all His **o** in mind and have 2Sm 22:23
execute My **o**, and keep all My 1Kg 6:12
His commands, **o**, and judgments, 1Kg 8:58
to walk in His **o** and to keep His 1Kg 8:61
if you keep My statutes and **o**, 1Kg 9:4
or observe their statutes and **o**, 2Kg 17:34
the statutes, the **o**, the laws, 2Kg 17:37
the statutes and **o** the LORD 1Ch 22:13
and My **o** as ⌊he is⌋ today. 1Ch 28:7
if you keep My statutes and **o**, 2Ch 7:17
According to the **o** of his father 2Ch 8:14
its⌋ statutes and **o** in Israel. Ezr 7:10
and **o** You gave Your servant Neh 1:7

You gave them impartial **o**, Neh 9:13
They sinned against Your **o**, Neh 9:29
the commands, **o**, and statutes Neh 10:29
kept all His **o** in mind and have Ps 18:22
the **o** of the LORD are reliable Ps 19:9
and do not live by My **o**, Ps 89:30
I have set Your **o** ⌊before me⌋. Ps 119:30
rebelled against My **o** with more Ezk 5:6
have rejected My **o** and have not Ezk 5:6
in My statutes or kept My **o**; Ezk 5:7
even kept the **o** of the nations Ezk 5:7
followed and whose **o** you have Ezk 11:12
according to the **o** of the Ezk 11:12
statutes, keep My **o**, and Ezk 11:20
My statutes and keeps My **o**, Ezk 18:9
He practices My **o** and follows My Ezk 18:17
and explained My **o** to them— Ezk 20:11
and they rejected My **o**— Ezk 20:13
because they rejected My **o**, Ezk 20:16
their idols, or keep their **o**. Ezk 20:18
statutes, keep My **o**, and Ezk 20:19
or carefully keep My **o**— Ezk 20:21
not practice My **o** but rejected Ezk 20:24
were not good and **o** that did not Ezk 20:25
and carefully observe My **o**. Ezk 36:27
will follow My **o**, and keep My Ezk 37:24
the case according to My **o**. Ezk 44:24
from Your commandments and **o**. Dn 9:5
statutes and **o** I commanded him Mal 4:4

ORDINARY *(7)*
not be used for ⌊**o**⌋ anointing Ex 30:32
There is no **o** bread on hand. 1Sm 21:4
even on an **o** mission, 1Sm 21:5
and write on it with an **o** pen: Is 8:1
what are you doing out of the **o**? Mt 5:47
and living like **o** people? 1Co 3:3
for special use, some for **o**. 2Tm 2:20

ORDINATION *(12)*
since this is a ram for **o** Ex 29:22
ram of Aaron's **o** and wave it as Ex 29:26
is lifted up from the ram of **o**. Ex 29:27
take the ram of **o** and boil its Ex 29:31
time of⌋ their **o** and Ex 29:33
any of the meat of **o** or any of Ex 29:34
offering, the **o** offering, Lv 7:37
ram, the ram of **o**, and Aaron and Lv 8:22
This was an **o** offering for a Lv 8:28
portion of the **o** ram as the LORD Lv 8:29
basket for the **o** offering as I Lv 8:31
your days of **o** are completed, Lv 8:33

ORE *(2)*
and copper is smelted from **o**. Jb 28:2
recesses for **o** in the gloomy Jb 28:3

OREB *(7)*
They captured **O** and Zeeb, the Jdg 7:25
killed **O** at the rock of Oreb Jdg 7:25
Oreb at the rock of **O** and Zeeb Jdg 7:25
heads of **O** and Zeeb to Gideon Jdg 7:25
handed over to you **O** and Zeeb, Jdg 8:3
their nobles like **O** and Zeeb, Ps 83:11
struck Midian at the rock of **O**; Is 10:26

OREN *(1)*
Bunah, **O**, Ozem, and Ahijah 1Ch 2:25

ORGANIZE *(1)*
O your ancestral houses by your 2Ch 35:4

ORGANIZED *(2)*
The next day Saul **o** the troops 1Sm 11:11
son of Elah **o** a conspiracy 2Kg 15:30

ORGANS *(1)*
as well as its legs and inner **o**. Ex 12:9

ORGIES *(1)*
drunkenness, **o**, carousing, 1Pt 4:3

ORIGIN *(7)*
whose **o** was in ancient times, Is 23:7
Your **o** and your birth were in Ezk 16:3
created, in the land of your **o**. Ezk 21:30
of Pathros, the land of their **o**. Ezk 29:14
His **o** is from antiquity, from Mc 5:2
that they did not know its **o**. Lk 20:7
does not have its **o** here." Jn 18:36

ORIGINAL *(8)*
he bought it from, the **o** owner. Lv 27:24
have it rebuilt on its ⌊**o**⌋ site. Ezr 2:68
be rebuilt on its ⌊**o**⌋ site.' Ezr 5:15
and let its ⌊**o**⌋ foundations be Ezr 6:3
house of God on its ⌊**o**⌋ site. Ezr 6:7
that were on the **o** scroll that Jr 36:28
just as the **o** eyewitnesses and Lk 1:2
have renounced their **o** pledge. 1Tm 5:12

ORIGINATE *(2)*
of them should **o** from the same Ezk 21:19
Did the word of God **o** from you, 1Co 14:36

ORIGINATOR *(1)*
the **O** of God's creation says: Rv 3:14

ORION *(3)*
the Bear, **O**, the Pleiades, and Jb 9:9
or loosen the belt of **O**? Jb 38:31
One who made the Pleiades and **O**, Am 5:8

ORNAMENT *(1)*
a gold ring or an **o** of gold. Pr 25:12

ORNAMENTAL *(4)*
and shaft, its ⌊**o**⌋ cups, and its Ex 25:31
and shaft, its ⌊**o**⌋ cups, and its Ex 37:17
was carved with ⌊**o**⌋ gourds and 1Kg 6:18
⌊**O**⌋ gourds encircled it below 1Kg 7:24

ORNAMENTS *(5)*
took the crescent **o** that were Jdg 8:21
to the crescent **o** and ear Jdg 8:26
your garments with gold **o**. 2Sm 1:24
His beautiful **o** for majesty, Ezk 7:20
of gold **o** or fine clothes 1Pt 3:3

ORNAN *(11)*
(AKA ARAUNAH)
floor of **O** the Jebusite. 1Ch 21:15
floor of **O** the Jebusite. 1Ch 21:18
O was threshing wheat when he 1Ch 21:20
David came to **O**, and when 1Ch 21:21
when **O** looked and saw David, 1Ch 21:21
David said to **O**, "Give me this 1Ch 21:22
O said to David, "Take it! 1Ch 21:23
David answered **O**, "No, I insist 1Ch 21:24
David gave **O** 15 pounds of gold 1Ch 21:25
floor of **O** the Jebusite, 1Ch 21:28
floor of **O** the Jebusite. 2Ch 3:1

ORNATE *(1)*
turban and the **o** headbands of Ex 39:28

ORPAH *(2)*
one was named **O** and the second Ru 1:4
and **O** kissed her mother-in-law, Ru 1:14

ORPHANS *(5)*
as the case of **o**, so they might Jr 5:28
Abandon your **o**; I will preserve Jr 49:11
We have become **o**, fatherless; Lm 5:3
I will not leave you as **o**; Jn 14:18
to look after **o** and widows in Jms 1:27

OSPREY *(2)*
owl, the desert owl, the **o**, Lv 11:18
owl, the **o**, the cormorant, Dt 14:17

OSTRICH *(3)*
the **o**, the short-eared owl, the Lv 11:16
the **o**, the short-eared owl, the Dt 14:15
wings of the **o** flap joyfully, Jb 39:13

OSTRICHES *(7)*
to jackals and a companion of **o**. Jb 30:29
O will dwell there, and wild Is 13:21
for jackals, an abode for **o**. Is 34:13
Me, jackals and **o**, because I Is 43:20
and **o** will also live in her. Jr 50:39
cruel like **o** in the wilderness Lm 4:3
the jackals and mourn like **o**. Mc 1:8

OTHER *(488)*
Adah and the **o** named Zillah. Gn 4:19
said to each **o**, "Come, let us Gn 11:3
and fathered ⌊**o**⌋ sons and Gn 11:11
and fathered ⌊**o**⌋ sons and Gn 11:13
and fathered ⌊**o**⌋ sons and Gn 11:15
and fathered ⌊**o**⌋ sons and Gn 11:17
and fathered ⌊**o**⌋ sons and Gn 11:19
and fathered ⌊**o**⌋ sons and Gn 11:21
and fathered ⌊**o**⌋ sons and Gn 11:23
and fathered ⌊**o**⌋ sons and Gn 11:25
and they separated from each **o**. Gn 13:11
one end of the land to the **o**, Gn 13:17
as the women and the ⌊**o**⌋ people. Gn 14:16
laid the pieces opposite each **o**, Gn 15:10
her struggled with each **o**, Gn 25:22
will be stronger than the **o**, Gn 25:23
and swore an oath to each **o**. Gn 26:31
in addition to his **o** wives, Gn 28:9
This is none **o** than the house of Gn 28:17
her to you than to some **o** man. Gn 29:19
my daughters or take **o** wives, Gn 31:50
Jacob's ⌊**o**⌋ sons came to the Gn 34:27
more than his **o** sons because Gn 37:3
After them, seven **o** cows, sickly Gn 41:3
and the **o** man was hanged." Gn 41:13
them, seven **o** cows—ugly, very Gn 41:19
do you keep looking at each **o**? Gn 42:1
Then they said to each **o**, Gn 42:21
will release your **o** brother and Gn 43:14
at each **o** in astonishment. Gn 43:33
from one end of Egypt to the **o**. Gn 47:21
named Shiphrah and the **o** Puah, Ex 1:15
came near the **o** all night long. Ex 14:20
much as they gather on **o** days." Ex 16:5
and one on the **o** so that his Ex 17:12
and the **o** Eliezer (because ⌊he Ex 18:4
They asked each **o** how they had Ex 18:7
Do not have **o** gods besides Me. Ex 20:3
one strikes the **o** with a stone Ex 21:18
or any ⌊**o**⌋ animal to care for, Ex 22:10
and the **o** man does not have to Ex 22:11
not invoke the names of **o** gods; Ex 23:13
the ⌊**o**⌋ half of the blood he Ex 24:6
onyx along with ⌊**o**⌋ gemstones Ex 25:7
and two rings on the **o** side. Ex 25:12
end and one cherub at the **o** end. Ex 25:19
the lampstand from the **o** side. Ex 25:32
and the ⌊**o**⌋ five curtains joined Ex 26:3
and the ⌊**o**⌋ six curtains by Ex 26:9
yard on the **o** of what is left Ex 26:13
for the planks on the **o** side of Ex 26:27
planks from one end to the **o**. Ex 26:28
hangings on the **o** side 22 and a Ex 27:15
Attach the **o** ends of the two Ex 28:25
Make two ⌊**o**⌋ gold rings and put Ex 28:26
put them at the two **o** corners Ex 28:26
at twilight offer the **o** lamb. Ex 29:39
and all the ⌊**o**⌋ furnishings of Ex 31:7
from all the **o** people on the Ex 33:16
five of the curtains to each **o**, Ex 36:10
and the ⌊**o**⌋ five curtains he Ex 36:10
curtains he joined to each **o**. Ex 36:10
the loops lined up with each **o**. Ex 36:12
joined the curtains to each **o**, Ex 36:13
and ⌊the **o**⌋ six together. Ex 36:16
to each **o** for each plank. Ex 36:22
for the planks on the **o** side of Ex 36:32
planks from one end to the **o**. Ex 36:33
and two rings on the **o** side. Ex 37:3
end and one cherub at the **o** end. Ex 37:8
their wings and facing each **o**. Ex 37:9
the lampstand from the **o** side. Ex 37:18
It was the same for the **o** side. Ex 38:15
attached the **o** ends of the two Ex 39:18
They made two ⌊**o**⌋ gold rings and Ex 39:19
put ⌊them⌋ at the two **o** corners Ex 39:19
offering and the **o** as a burnt Lv 5:7
garments, put on **o** clothes, and Lv 6:11
is clean may eat any ⌊**o**⌋ meat. Lv 7:19
things and ⌊**o**⌋ living creatures Lv 11:10
All ⌊**o**⌋ winged insects that have Lv 11:23
offering and the **o** for a sin Lv 12:8
and the **o** a burnt offering Lv 14:22
offering and the **o** as a burnt Lv 14:31
offering and the **o** as a burnt Lv 15:15
offering and the **o** as a burnt Lv 15:30
the LORD and the **o** for Azazel, Lv 16:8
country look the **o** way when that Lv 20:4
of Levi with the ⌊**o**⌋ Israelites. Nm 1:49
duties and all their ⌊**o**⌋ work, Nm 4:27
and a man **o** than your husband Nm 5:20
offering and the **o** as a burnt Nm 6:11
offering and the **o** as a burnt Nm 8:12
time with the ⌊**o**⌋ Israelites?" Nm 9:7
a strong craving ⌊for **o** food⌋. Nm 11:4
named Eldad and the **o** Medad; Nm 11:26
camped on the **o** side of the Nm 21:13
among the ⌊**o**⌋ Israelites, Nm 26:62
morning and the **o** lamb at Nm 28:4
and all their ⌊**o**⌋ animals. Nm 35:3
to these, give 42 ⌊**o**⌋ cities. Nm 35:6
men from the ⌊**o**⌋ Israelite Nm 36:3
on the **o** side of the Jordan, Dt 3:25
one end of the heavens to the **o**: Dt 4:32
there is no **o** besides Him. Dt 4:35
on earth below; there is no **o**. Dt 4:39
Do not have **o** gods besides Me. Dt 5:7

not follow **o** gods, the gods of Dt 6:14
away from Me to worship **o** gods. Dt 7:4
and go after **o** gods to worship Dt 8:19
worship, and bow down to **o** gods. Dt 11:16
by following **o** gods you have not Dt 11:28
blood of your ⌊**o**⌋ sacrifices is Dt 12:27
Let us follow **o** gods,' which you Dt 13:2
'Let us go and worship **o** gods'— Dt 13:6
one end of the earth to the **o**— Dt 13:7
'Let us go and worship **o** gods,' Dt 13:13
gone to worship **o** gods by bowing Dt 17:3
speaks in the name of **o** gods— Dt 18:20
one loved and the **o** unloved, Dt 21:15
men are fighting with each **o**, Dt 25:11
not go after **o** gods to worship Dt 28:14
there you will worship **o** gods, Dt 28:36
one end of the earth to the **o**, Dt 28:64
you will worship **o** gods of wood Dt 28:64
They began to worship **o** gods, Dt 29:26
bow down to **o** gods and worship Dt 30:17
have done by turning to **o** gods. Dt 31:18
will turn to **o** gods and worship Dt 31:20
to remain on the **o** side of the Jos 7:7
on one side and some on the **o**. Jos 8:22
With the **o** half of the tribe, Jos 13:8
clans of Kohath's **o** descendants. Jos 21:26
given ⌊territory⌋ to the **o** half, Jos 22:7
an altar **o** than the altar Jos 22:19
o than the altar of the LORD our Jos 22:29
and go and worship **o** gods, Jos 23:16
River and worshiped **o** gods. Jos 24:2
the LORD to worship **o** gods! Jos 24:16
They went after **o** gods from the Jdg 2:12
themselves with **o** gods, Jdg 2:17
going after **o** gods to worship Jdg 2:19
said to each **o**, "Who did this?" Jdg 6:29
a torch inside it ⌊in the **o**⌋. Jdg 7:16
man in the army against each **o**. Jdg 7:22
The **o** two units rushed against Jdg 9:44
who were on the **o** side of the Jdg 10:8
Me and worshiped **o** gods. Jdg 10:13
camped on the **o** side of the Jdg 11:18
he had no **o** son or daughter Jdg 11:34
to drink wine or **o** alcoholic Jdg 13:4
not drink wine or **o** alcoholic Jdg 13:7
or drink wine or **o** alcoholic Jdg 13:14
weak and be like any **o** man." Jdg 16:7
weak and be like any **o** man." Jdg 16:11
weak and be like any **o** man." Jdg 16:17
hand and the **o** on his left. Jdg 16:29
Bethel and the **o** to Gibeah Jdg 20:31
against the ⌊**o**⌋ Benjaminites Jdg 20:48
isn't anyone **o** than you to Ru 4:4
⌊it⌋ to the **o** party in order Ru 4:7
same as all the **o** nations have." 1Sm 8:5
Me and worshiping **o** gods. 1Sm 8:8
we'll be like all the **o** nations: 1Sm 8:20
with the prophets asked each **o**, 1Sm 10:11
garrison on the **o** side." 1Sm 14:1
was named Bozez and the **o** Seneh; 1Sm 14:4
Michmash and the **o** to the south 1Sm 14:5
against each **o** in great 1Sm 14:20
Jonathan will be on the **o** side." 1Sm 14:40
a man so we can fight each **o**!" 1Sm 17:10
battle formation facing each **o**. 1Sm 17:21
king desires no **o** bride-price 1Sm 18:25
Saul, he sent **o** agents, and they 1Sm 19:21
kissed each **o** and wept with each 1Sm 20:41
each other and wept with each **o**, 1Sm 20:41
his men went along the **o** side. 1Sm 23:26
crossed to the **o** side and stood 1Sm 26:13
saying, 'Go and worship **o** gods.' 1Sm 26:19
driven ahead of the **o** livestock, 1Sm 30:20
of Israel on the **o** side of the 1Sm 31:7
valley and on the **o** side of the 1Sm 31:7
named Baanah and the **o** Rechab, 2Sm 4:2
city, one rich and the **o** poor. 2Sm 12:1
were whispering to each **o**, 2Sm 12:19
one struck the **o** and killed him. 2Sm 14:6
of the caves or some **o** place. 2Sm 17:9
"No," the **o** woman said. 1Kg 3:22
half to one and half to the **o**." 1Kg 3:25
But the **o** one said, "He will 1Kg 3:26
as far as the **o** side of Jokmeam; 1Kg 4:12
chariot teams and the **o** horses 1Kg 4:28
and the **o** wing was seven and a 1Kg 6:24
wing touched the **o** wall, 1Kg 6:27
facing each **o** in three tiers. 1Kg 7:4

facing each **o** in three tiers. 1Kg 7:5
in the **o** courtyard behind the 1Kg 7:8
the LORD is God. There is no **o**! 1Kg 8:60
go and serve **o** gods and worship 1Kg 9:6
They clung to **o** gods and 1Kg 9:9
ever been made in any **o** kingdom. 1Kg 10:20
seduced him ⌊to follow⌋ **o** gods. 1Kg 11:4
that he would not follow **o** gods, 1Kg 11:10
in Bethel, and put the **o** in Dan. 1Kg 12:29
for yourself **o** gods and cast 1Kg 14:9
went the **o** way by himself. 1Kg 18:6
prepare the **o** bull and place 1Kg 18:23
opposite each **o** for seven days. 1Kg 20:29
swords and killed each **o**. 2Kg 3:23
to any **o** god but Yahweh. 2Kg 5:17
said to each **o**, "Why just sit 2Kg 7:3
The Arameans had said to each **o**, 2Kg 7:6
Then they said to each **o**, 2Kg 7:9
filled from one end to the **o**. 2Kg 10:21
priest and the **o** priests and 2Kg 12:7
they had worshiped **o** gods. 2Kg 17:7
them, "Do not fear **o** gods; 2Kg 17:35
for you; do not fear **o** gods. 2Kg 17:37
with you. Do not fear **o** gods, 2Kg 17:38
incense to **o** gods in order to 2Kg 22:17
⌊David's **o** sons⌋: Ibhar, Elishua, 1Ch 3:6
with their ⌊**o**⌋ relatives. 1Ch 8:32
were exempt from **o** tasks because 1Ch 9:33
with their ⌊**o**⌋ relatives. 1Ch 9:38
O Benjaminites and men from 1Ch 12:16
Eliezer did not have any **o** sons, 1Ch 23:17
its **o** wing was seven and a half 2Ch 3:11
the wing of the **o** cherub. 2Ch 3:11
The wing of the **o** cherub was 2Ch 3:12
its **o** wing was seven and a half 2Ch 3:12
the wing of the **o** cherub. 2Ch 3:12
go and serve **o** gods and worship 2Ch 7:19
They clung to **o** gods and 2Ch 7:22
ever been made in any **o** kingdom. 2Ch 9:19
the peoples of ⌊**o**⌋ lands do? 2Ch 13:9
they helped destroy each **o**. 2Ch 20:23
to offer incense to **o** gods, 2Ch 28:25
towers and the **o** outside wall. 2Ch 32:5
incense to **o** gods in order to 2Ch 34:25
bowls, and 1,000 **o** articles. Ezr 1:10
the **o** Elam's people 1,254 Ezr 2:31
and the **o** leaders of Israel's Ezr 4:3
or ⌊**o**⌋ servants of this house of Ezr 7:24
work while the **o** half held Neh 4:16
and held a weapon with the **o**. Neh 4:17
prophetess and the **o** prophets Neh 6:14
the **o** Nebo's men 52 Neh 7:33
the **o** Elam's people 1,254 Neh 7:34
and ⌊**o**⌋ leafy trees to make Neh 8:15
while the **o** nine-tenths remained Neh 11:1
or of one of the **o** peoples but Neh 13:24
with the **o** captives when King Est 2:6
more than all the **o** women. Est 2:17
than did any of the **o** virgins. Est 2:17
than all the **o** officials. Est 3:1
position over the **o** officials Est 5:11
up quicker than any ⌊**o**⌋ plant. Jb 8:12
we can take each **o** to court. Jb 9:32
and let **o** men sleep with her. Jb 31:10
and circles to their **o** end; Ps 19:6
terror like no **o**—because God Ps 53:5
each **o** in an evil plan; Ps 64:5
men and fall like any **o** ruler." Ps 82:7
inherited what **o** peoples had Ps 105:44
As one dies, so dies the **o**; Ec 3:19
made the one as well as the **o**, Ec 7:14
do not let the **o** slip from your Ec 7:18
whether one or the **o**, or if both Ec 11:6
the sword against ⌊**o**⌋ nations, Is 2:4
will look at each **o**, their faces Is 13:8
o lords than You have ruled over Is 26:13
Each one helps the **o**, and says Is 41:6
and there is no **o** Savior but Me. Is 43:11
There is no ⌊**o**⌋ Rock; I do not Is 44:8
am the LORD, and there is no **o**; Is 45:5
am the LORD, and there is no **o**. Is 45:6
with you, and there is no **o**; Is 45:14
is no other; there is no **o** God. Is 45:14
am the LORD, and there is no **o**. Is 45:18
There is no **o** God but Me, a Is 45:21
For I am God, and there is no **o**. Is 45:22
that we should be like each **o**? Is 46:5
for I am God, and there is no **o**; Is 46:9

Let us confront each **o**. Is 50:8
and all the **o** cities of Judah. Jr 1:15
to burn incense to **o** gods and to Jr 1:16
in this place or follow **o** gods, Jr 7:6
and follow **o** gods that you have Jr 7:9
offerings to **o** gods so that they Jr 7:18
offerings to your **o** sacrifices, Jr 7:21
there will be no **o** burial place. Jr 7:32
will give their wives to **o** men, Jr 8:10
have followed **o** gods to worship Jr 11:10
one end of the earth to the **o**. Jr 12:12
have followed **o** gods to serve Jr 13:10
will smash them against each **o**, Jr 13:14
followed **o** gods, served them, Jr 16:11
you will worship **o** gods both day Jr 16:13
and from all the **o** lands where Jr 16:15
in it to **o** gods that they, Jr 19:4
out drink offerings to **o** gods." Jr 19:13
worshiped and served **o** gods." Jr 22:9
from all the **o** countries where Jr 23:8
who steal My words from each **o**. Jr 23:30
but the **o** basket contained very Jr 24:2
Do not follow **o** gods to serve Jr 25:6
and the ⌊**o**⌋ cities of Judah, Jr 25:18
one end of the earth to the **o**. Jr 25:33
and ⌊certain **o**⌋ men with him Jr 26:22
poured out to **o** gods to provoke Jr 32:29
and all **o** nations were fighting Jr 34:1
Stop following **o** gods to serve Jr 35:15
and all the **o** officials. Jr 36:12
turned to each **o** in fear and Jr 36:16
And many **o** words like them were Jr 36:32
in all the **o** lands also heard Jr 40:11
and all the **o** arrogant men Jr 43:2
incense to serve **o** gods they, Jr 44:3
stop burning incense to **o** gods. Jr 44:5
incense to **o** gods in the land Jr 44:8
were burning incense to **o** gods, Jr 44:15
Indeed, each falls over the **o**. Jr 46:16
against each **o** and the sound Ezk 3:13
forest, compare to any **o** wood? Ezk 15:2
the opposite of **o** women in your Ezk 16:34
the peoples of ⌊**o**⌋ countries, Ezk 20:32
is like all the ⌊**o**⌋ nations, Ezk 25:8
city like ⌊**o**⌋ deserted cities Ezk 26:19
with all the **o** people on board, Ezk 27:27
and so that no ⌊**o**⌋ well-watered Ezk 31:14
of the recesses faced each **o**. Ezk 40:13
all around, like the **o** windows. Ezk 40:25
tables on the **o** side of the Ezk 40:40
offerings and ⌊**o**⌋ sacrifices Ezk 40:42
face turned toward it on the **o**. Ezk 41:19
for one door and two for the **o**. Ezk 41:24
are to put on **o** clothes before Ezk 42:14
offerings and ⌊**o**⌋ sacrifices for Ezk 44:11
and dress in **o** clothes so that Ezk 44:19
those of the **o** young men your Dn 1:10
coverings, and **o** clothes, were Dn 3:21
there is no **o** god who is able Dn 3:29
each different from the **o**. Dn 7:3
and about the **o** horn that came Dn 7:20
from all the **o** kingdoms. Dn 7:23
but one was longer than the **o**, Dn 8:3
or for any **o** god, because he Dn 11:37
of the river and one on the **o**. Dn 12:5
they turn to **o** gods and love Hs 3:1
They do not push each **o**; Jl 2:8
your God, and there is no **o**. Jl 2:27
the sailors said to each **o**. Jnh 1:7
they hunt each **o** with a net. Mc 7:2
wine, oil, or any **o** food, does Hg 2:12
the bowl and the **o** on its left." Zch 4:3
what is written on the **o** side. Zch 5:3
one Favor and the **o** Union, Zch 11:7
eastern sea and the **o** half Zch 14:8
of one will rise against the **o**. Zch 14:13
You, on the **o** hand, have turned Mal 2:8
He saw two **o** brothers, James Mt 4:21
cheek, turn the **o** to him also. Mt 5:39
he will hate one and love the **o**, Mt 6:24
to one and despise the **o**. Mt 6:24
to go to the **o** side ⌊of the sea⌋ Mt 8:18
When He had come to the **o** side, Mt 8:28
the road leading to **o** nations, Mt 10:5
who call out to each **o**: Mt 11:16
was restored, as good as the **o**. Mt 12:13
it seven **o** spirits more evil Mt 12:45
go ahead of Him to the **o** side, Mt 14:22

disciples reached the **o** shore, Mt 16:5
When the **o** slaves saw what had Mt 18:31
right and the **o** on Your left, Mt 20:21
man went to the **o** and said the Mt 21:30
Again, he sent **o** slaves, more Mt 21:36
his vineyard to **o** farmers who Mt 21:41
he sent out **o** slaves, and said, Mt 22:4
one end of the sky to the **o**. Mt 24:31
and the **o** Mary were seated Mt 27:61
and the **o** Mary went to view Mt 28:1
On the **o** hand, no one can enter Mk 3:27
O seed fell on rocky ground Mk 4:5
O seed fell among thorns, and Mk 4:7
the desires for **o** things enter Mk 4:19
over to the **o** side ⌊of the lake Mk 4:35
And **o** boats were with Him. Mk 4:36
came to the **o** side of the sea Mk 5:1
again by boat to the **o** side, Mk 5:21
go ahead of Him to the **o** side, Mk 6:45
there are many **o** customs they Mk 7:4
you do many **o** similar things. Mk 7:13
again, and went to the **o** side. Mk 8:13
the ⌊**o**⌋ 10 ⌊disciples⌋ heard Mk 10:41
is no **o** commandment greater Mk 12:31
Many **o** women had come up with Mk 15:41
along with many **o** exhortations, Lk 3:18
of God to the **o** towns also, Lk 4:43
partners in the **o** boat to come Lk 5:7
on the cheek, offer the **o** also. Lk 6:29
the **o** hand, a bad tree doesn't Lk 6:43
and calling to each **o**: Lk 7:32
owed 500 denarii, and the **o** 50. Lk 7:41
O seed fell on the rock; Lk 8:6
O seed fell among thorns; Lk 8:7
o seed fell on good ground; Lk 8:8
over to the **o** side of the lake. Lk 8:22
he passed by on the **o** side. Lk 10:31
him, passed by on the **o** side. Lk 10:32
and brings seven **o** spirits more Lk 11:26
presence of all the **o** guests. Lk 14:10
while the **o** is still far off, Lk 14:32
he will hate one and love the **o**, Lk 16:13
to one and despise the **o**. Lk 16:13
be taken and the **o** will be left. Lk 17:34
will be taken and the **o** left. Lk 17:35
taken, and the **o** will be left." Lk 17:36
and the **o** a tax collector Lk 18:10
You that I'm not like **o** people— Lk 18:11
justified rather than the **o**; Lk 18:14
were saying many **o** blasphemous Lk 22:65
had been hostile toward each **o**. Lk 23:12
the **o** answered, rebuking him: Lk 23:40
and the **o** women with them were Lk 24:10
having with each **o** as you are Lk 24:17
they said to each **o**, "Weren't Lk 24:32
stayed on the **o** side of the sea Jn 6:22
Him on the **o** side of the sea Jn 6:25
door but climbs in some **o** way, Jn 10:1
But I have **o** sheep that are not Jn 10:16
So the **o** disciple, the one known Jn 18:16
and of the **o** one who had been Jn 19:32
Peter and to the **o** disciple, Jn 20:2
Peter and the **o** disciple went Jn 20:3
but the **o** disciple outran Peter Jn 20:4
The **o** disciple, who had reached Jn 20:8
So the **o** disciples kept telling Jn 20:25
Jesus performed many **o** signs in Jn 20:30
o disciples came in the boat, Jn 21:8
also many **o** things that Jesus Jn 21:25
And with many **o** words he Ac 2:40
for there is no **o** name under Ac 4:12
are you mistreating each **o**?' Ac 7:26
them speaking in ⌊**o**⌋ languages Ac 10:46
to speak with ⌊**o**⌋ languages and Ac 19:6
Sadducees and the **o** part were Ac 23:6
talked with each **o** and said, Ac 26:31
over Paul and some **o** prisoners Ac 27:1
any **o** created thing will have Rm 8:39
if there is any **o** commandment— Rm 13:9
can lay any **o** foundation than 1Co 3:11
wife, like the **o** apostles, the 1Co 9:5
but ⌊the good⌋ of the **o** person. 1Co 10:24
conscience, but the **o** person's. 1Co 10:29
this, we have no **o** custom, nor 1Co 11:16
about the **o** matters whenever I 1Co 11:34
the same concern for each **o**. 1Co 12:25
all of you spoke in **o** languages, 1Co 14:5
you speaking in ⌊**o**⌋ languages, 1Co 14:6
but the **o** person is not being 1Co 14:17
I speak in ⌊**o**⌋ languages more 1Co 14:18
By people of **o** languages and by 1Co 14:21
that speaking in **o** languages is 1Co 14:22
are speaking in ⌊**o**⌋ languages, 1Co 14:23
speaking in ⌊**o**⌋ languages. 1Co 14:39
you nothing **o** than what you can 2Co 1:13
will cheer me **o** than the one 2Co 2:2
measure about **o** people's labors. 2Co 10:15
robbed **o** churches by taking pay 2Co 11:8
Not to mention **o** things, there 2Co 11:28
worse than the **o** churches, 2Co 12:13
to you a gospel **o** than what we Gl 1:8
see any of the **o** apostles except Gl 1:19
slave and the **o** by a free woman Gl 4:22
you will not accept any **o** view. Gl 5:10
these are opposed to each **o**, Gl 5:17
to people in **o** generations as it Eph 3:5
and build each **o** up as you are 1Th 5:11
people not to teach **o** doctrine 1Tm 1:3
anyone teaches **o** doctrine and 1Tm 6:3
But encourage each **o** daily, Heb 3:13
but in the **o** case, ⌊Scripture⌋ Heb 7:8
encouraging each **o**, and all the Heb 10:25
and at **o** times you were Heb 10:33
or by earth or with any **o** oath. Jms 5:12
do not put any **o** burden on you. Rv 2:24
occurred like no **o** since man has Rv 16:18
one is, the **o** has not yet come, Rv 17:10

OTHER'S *(5)*

when we are out of each **o** sight. Gn 31:49
Let's feast on each **o** love! Pr 7:18
will eat each **o** flesh in the Jr 19:9
the rest devour each **o** flesh." Zch 11:9
encouraged by each **o** faith, Rm 1:12

OTHERS *(129)*

but the **o** are not to approach, Ex 24:2
⌊the ability⌋ to teach ⌊**o**⌋. Ex 35:34
and higher in rank than the **o**. Nm 22:15
here overnight as the **o** did, Nm 22:19
Along with the **o** slain by them, Nm 31:8
to Sheol, and He raises ⌊**o**⌋ up. 1Sm 2:6
beside him to **o** in front of him 1Sm 17:30
human rod and with blows from **o**. 2Sm 7:14
and five **o**—Hashubah, Ohel, 1Ch 3:20
O were put in charge of the 1Ch 9:29
and from the power of all **o**. 2Ch 32:22
but many ⌊**o**⌋ shouted joyfully. Ezr 3:12
O were saying, "We are Neh 5:3
Still **o** were saying, "We have Neh 5:4
and vineyards belong to **o**." Neh 5:5
yet **o** will sprout from the dust. Jb 8:19
your babbling put **o** to silence, Jb 11:3
When **o** are humiliated and you Jb 22:29
as **o** do by hiding my Jb 31:33
and sets **o** in their place. Jb 34:24
a chariot, and **o** in horses, but Ps 20:7
they leave their wealth to **o**. Ps 49:10
They are not in trouble like **o**; Ps 73:5
O sat in darkness and gloom— Ps 107:10
O went to sea in ships, Ps 107:23
vitality to **o** and your years Pr 5:9
how to conduct himself before **o**? Ec 6:8
you yourself have cursed **o**. Ec 7:22
to them still **o** besides those Is 56:8
not build and **o** live ⌊in them⌋; Is 65:22
they will not plant and **o** eat. Is 65:22
houses will be turned over to **o**, Jr 6:12
To the **o** He said in my hearing, Ezk 9:5
the same measurements as the **o**. Ezk 40:24
the same measurements as the **o**. Ezk 40:28
the same measurements as the **o**. Ezk 40:29
the same measurements as the **o**. Ezk 40:32
the same measurements as the **o**. Ezk 40:33
the same measurements as the **o**, Ezk 40:35
appointed ⌊**o**⌋ to keep charge Ezk 44:8
will crush and smash all the **o**. Dn 2:40
one different from all the **o**, Dn 7:19
was more visible than the **o**. Dn 7:20
will be far richer than the **o**. Dn 11:2
and will go to **o** besides them. Dn 11:4
but many **o** will join them Dn 11:34
and two **o** were standing there, Dn 12:5
you want **o** to do for you, Mt 7:12
O fell on rocky ground, where Mt 13:5
O fell among thorns, and the Mt 13:7
Still **o** fell on good ground, Mt 13:8
unable to speak, and many **o**. Mt 15:30
the Baptist; **o**, Elijah; still Mt 16:14
still **o**, Jeremiah or one of the Mt 16:14
he saw **o** standing in the Mt 20:3
went and found **o** standing around Mt 20:6
o were cutting branches from the Mt 21:8
And the **o** seized his slaves, Mt 22:6
everything to be observed by **o**: Mt 23:5
done without neglecting the **o**. Mt 23:23
face and beat Him; **o** slapped Him Mt 26:67
He saved **o**, but He cannot save Mt 27:42
Still **o** fell on good ground and Mk 4:8
O are sown among thorns; Mk 4:18
But **o** said, "He's Elijah." Mk 6:15
Still **o** said, "He's a prophet— Mk 6:15
the Baptist; **o**, Elijah; still Mk 8:28
still **o**, one of the prophets." Mk 8:28
and **o** spread leafy branches cut Mk 11:8
⌊He⌋ also ⌊sent⌋ many **o**; Mk 12:5
and give the vineyard to **o**. Mk 12:9
another and saying, "He saved **o**; Mk 15:31
collectors and **o** who were guests Lk 5:29
as you want **o** to do for you, Lk 6:31
and many **o** who were supporting Lk 8:3
and **o** that one of the ancient Lk 9:8
the Baptist; **o**, Elijah; still Lk 9:19
still **o**, that one of the ancient Lk 9:19
appointed 70 **o**, and He sent them Lk 10:1
And **o**, as a test, were demanding Lk 11:16
done without neglecting the **o**. Lk 11:42
yourselves in the sight of **o**, Lk 16:15
and give the vineyard to **o**." Lk 20:16
o—criminals—were also led Lk 23:32
He saved **o**; let Him save Lk 23:35
o have labored, and you have Jn 4:38
O were saying, "No, on the Jn 7:12
O said, "This is the Messiah!" Jn 7:41
"No," **o** were saying, "but he Jn 9:9
But **o** were saying, "How can a Jn 9:16
O were saying, "These aren't the Jn 10:21
O said, "An angel has spoken to Jn 12:29
or have **o** told you about Me?" Jn 18:34
Him and two **o** with Him, Jn 19:18
and two **o** of His disciples were Jn 21:2
and some **o** of them to go up Ac 15:2
along with many **o**, remained in Ac 15:35
bond from Jason and the **o**, Ac 17:9
O replied, "He seems to be a Ac 17:18
But **o** said, "We will hear you Ac 17:32
named Damaris, and **o** with them. Ac 17:34
he said, but **o** did not believe. Ac 28:24
but even applaud **o** who practice Rm 1:32
If I am not an apostle to **o**, 1Co 9:2
If **o** share this authority over 1Co 9:12
so that after preaching to **o**, 1Co 9:27
takes his own supper ahead of **o**, 1Co 11:21
order to teach **o** also, than 1Co 14:19
and the **o** should evaluate. 1Co 14:29
death, but to **o**, a scent of life 2Co 2:16
by means of the diligence of **o**, 2Co 8:8
be relief for **o** and hardship for 2Co 8:13
in sharing with them and with **o**. 2Co 9:13
under wrath, as the **o** were also. Eph 2:3
and strife, but **o** out of good Php 1:15
the **o** proclaim Christ out of Php 1:17
consider **o** as more important Php 2:3
but also for the interests of **o**. Php 2:4
either from you or from **o**. 1Th 2:6
with the work ⌊of **o**⌋. 2Th 3:11
don't share in the sins of **o**. 1Tm 5:22
but ⌊the sins⌋ of **o** follow them. 1Tm 5:24
will be able to teach **o** also. 2Tm 2:2
For **o** became priests without an Heb 7:20
and **o** experienced mockings and Heb 11:36
should use it to serve **o**, 1Pt 4:10
and seven **o**, when He brought a 2Pt 2:5
save **o** by snatching ⌊them⌋ from Jd 23
on **o** have mercy in fear, hating Jd 23

OTHERWISE *(73)*

(See pp. xi-xii.)

OTHNI *(1)*

O, Rephael, Obed, and Elzabad; 1Ch 26:7

OTHNIEL *(9)*

So **O** son of Caleb's brother, Jos 15:17
persuaded **O** to ask her father Jos 15:18
So **O** son of Kenaz, Caleb's Jdg 1:13
persuaded **O** to ask her father Jdg 1:14
LORD raised up **O** son of Kenaz, Jdg 3:9
O went out to battle, and the Jdg 3:10

so that **O** overpowered him. Jdg 3:10
40 years, and **O** son of Kenaz Jdg 3:11
Kenaz's sons: **O** and Seraiah. 1Ch 4:13

OTHNIEL'S *(2)*
and Seraiah. **O** sons: Hathath 1Ch 4:13
the Netophathite, of **O** family; 1Ch 27:15

OUGHT *(12)*
king, "This man **o** to die, Jr 38:4
you also **o** to wash one another's Jn 13:14
It is they who **o** to be here Ac 24:19
tribunal, where I **o** to be tried. Ac 25:10
yet know it as he **o** to know it. 1Co 8:2
he who plows **o** to plow in hope, 1Co 9:10
from those who **o** to give me joy, 2Co 2:3
I **o** to have been recommended by 2Co 12:11
how people **o** to act in God's 1Tm 3:15
farmer who **o** to be the first to 2Tm 2:6
this time you **o** to be teachers, Heb 5:12
Therefore, we **o** to support such 3Jn 8

OUNCE *(2)*
two-fifths of an **o** per man, Ex 38:26
an eighth of an **o** of silver Neh 10:32

OUNCES *(18)*
one gold bowl weighing four **o**, Nm 7:14
one gold bowl weighing four **o**, Nm 7:20
one gold bowl weighing four **o**, Nm 7:26
one gold bowl weighing four **o**, Nm 7:32
one gold bowl weighing four **o**, Nm 7:38
one gold bowl weighing four **o**, Nm 7:44
one gold bowl weighing four **o**, Nm 7:50
one gold bowl weighing four **o**, Nm 7:56
one gold bowl weighing four **o**, Nm 7:62
one gold bowl weighing four **o**, Nm 7:68
one gold bowl weighing four **o**, Nm 7:74
one gold bowl weighing four **o**, Nm 7:80
each ⌊weighed⌋ four **o** ⌊measured⌋ Nm 7:86
give you four **o** of silver a year Jdg 17:10
and the oxen for 50 **o** of silver. 2Sm 24:24
Menahem exacted 20 **o** of silver 2Kg 15:20
of the nails was 20 **o** of gold, 2Ch 3:9
day will be eight **o** by weight; Ezk 4:10

OUR *(1139)*
(See pp. xi-xii.)

OURS *(18)*
(See pp. xi-xii.)

OURSELVES *(59)*
(See pp. xi-xii.)

OUSTED *(1)*
will be **o** from your position. Is 22:19

OUSTS *(1)*
girl when she **o** her lady. Pr 30:23

OUT *(2240)*
(See pp. xi-xii.)

OUTBREAK *(9)*
It is a scaly **o**, a skin disease Lv 13:30
the scaly **o** has not spread and Lv 13:32
has the scaly **o** for another Lv 13:33
the scaly **o** on the seventh Lv 13:34
if the scaly **o** spreads further Lv 13:35
If the scaly **o** has spread on the Lv 13:36
scaly **o** remains unchanged and Lv 13:37
or mildew, for a scaly **o**, Lv 14:54
the oldest, with an **o** of tumors. 1Sm 5:9

OUTBURST *(6)*
Why this great **o** of anger?' Dt 29:24
of the LORD's **o** against Uzzah, 2Sm 6:8
that place an **O** Against Uzzah, 2Sm 6:8
of the LORD's **o** against Uzzah, 1Ch 13:11
that place **O** Against Uzzah, 1Ch 13:11
I know his **o**. ⌊This is⌋ the Jr 48:30

OUTBURSTS *(2)*
jealousy, **o** of anger, selfish 2Co 12:20
jealousy, **o** of anger, selfish Gl 5:20

OUTCAST *(1)*
call you The **O**, that Zion no one Jr 30:17

OUTCOME *(9)*
"What was the **o**? Tell me," David 2Sm 1:4
reflect on it and know the **o**. Is 41:22
to heart or think about their **o**. Is 47:7
will be the **o** of these things? Dn 12:8
only son and its **o** like a bitter Am 8:10
the temple police to see the **o**. Mt 26:58
observe the **o** of their lives, Heb 13:7
have seen the **o** from the Lord: Jms 5:11
what will the **o** be for those who 1Pt 4:17

OUTCRY *(12)*
o against Sodom and Gomorrah Gn 18:20
place because the **o** against its Gn 19:13
Eli heard the **o** and asked, 1Sm 4:14
and the **o** of the city went up to 1Sm 5:12
a widespread **o** from the people Neh 5:1
when I heard their **o** and these Neh 5:6
He heard the **o** of the afflicted Jb 34:28
Let him hear an **o** in the morning Jr 20:16
and your **o** fills the earth, Jr 46:12
Because of the **o** of the king and Dn 5:10
there will be an **o** from the Fish Zph 1:10
and the **o** of the harvesters has Jms 5:4

OUTDO *(1)*
O one another in showing honor. Rm 12:10

OUTDOOR *(1)*
Complete your **o** work, and Pr 24:27

OUTDOORSMAN *(1)*
hunter, an **o**, but Jacob was Gn 25:27

OUTER *(34)*
corners of the **o** garment you Dt 22:12
against the **o** wall of the city 2Sm 20:15
the inner and **o** sanctuaries. 1Kg 6:29
the inner and **o** sanctuaries. 1Kg 6:30
on the inner and **o** surfaces, 1Kg 7:9
he closed⌋ the **o** entrance for 2Kg 16:18
he built the **o** wall of the city 2Ch 33:14
just entering the **o** court of the Est 6:4
can strip off his **o** covering? Jb 41:13
be heard as far as the **o** court; Ezk 10:5
he brought me into the **o** court, Ezk 40:17
the gate of the **o** court facing Ezk 40:20
Its portico faced the **o** court, Ezk 40:31
Its portico faced the **o** court, Ezk 40:34
Its portico faced the **o** court, Ezk 40:37
of the **o** wall of the side Ezk 41:9
and the ⌊**o**⌋ chambers was 35 feet Ezk 41:10
the north gate into the **o** court. Ezk 42:1
belonging to the **o** court, Ezk 42:3
to them, toward the **o** court; Ezk 42:7
chambers on the **o** court were 87 Ezk 42:8
enters them from the **o** court. Ezk 42:9
area to the **o** court until they Ezk 42:14
sanctuary's **o** gate that faced Ezk 44:1
they go out to the **o** court, Ezk 44:19
them⌋ into the **o** court and Ezk 46:20
me into the **o** court and led me Ezk 46:21
corners of the ⌊**o**⌋ court there Ezk 46:22
outside to the **o** gate that faced Ezk 47:2
be thrown into the **o** darkness. Mt 8:12
throw him into the **o** darkness, Mt 22:13
slave into the **o** darkness. Mt 25:30
he tied his **o** garment around him Jn 21:7
though our **o** person is being 2Co 4:16

OUTERMOST *(5)*
on the edge of the **o** curtain in Ex 26:4
curtain, the **o** in the ⌊first⌋ Ex 26:10
on the edge of the **o** curtain in Ex 36:11
on the edge of the **o** curtain in Ex 36:17
These were the **o** cities of the Jos 15:21

OUTLAWS *(2)*
And He was counted among **o**. Mk 15:28
And He was counted among the **o**. Lk 22:37

OUTLET *(1)*
blocked the **o** of the water 2Ch 32:30

OUTLINES *(2)*
line, he **o** it with a stylus; Is 44:13
with chisels and **o** it with a Is 44:13

OUTLIVED *(2)*
of the elders who **o** Joshua, Jos 24:31
of the elders who **o** Joshua. Jdg 2:7

OUTLYING *(3)*
clear it and its **o** areas will be Jos 17:18
cities and the **o** villages. 1Sm 6:18
a place in one of the **o** towns, 1Sm 27:5

OUTNUMBER *(3)*
Israelites who **o** the Levites, Nm 3:46
who are with us **o** those who are 2Kg 6:16
they would **o** the grains of sand; Ps 139:18

OUTPOST *(4)*
servant to the **o** of the troops Jdg 7:11
I come to the **o** of the camp, Jdg 7:17
him went to the **o** of the camp at Jdg 7:19
to its farthest **o**, its densest 2Kg 19:23

OUTPOURED *(2)*
outstretched arm, and **o** wrath. Ezk 20:33
outstretched arm, and **o** wrath. Ezk 20:34

OUTRAGE *(6)*
committed an **o** against Israel Gn 34:7
has committed an **o** in Israel by Dt 22:21
committed an **o** in Israel.' " Jos 7:15
Tell us, how did this **o** occur?" Jdg 20:3
What is this **o** that has occurred Jdg 20:12
have committed an **o** in Israel Jr 29:23

OUTRAGEOUS *(1)*
and he will say **o** things against Dn 11:36

OUTRAGEOUSLY *(2)*
treated them **o** and killed them. Mt 22:6
suffered and been **o** treated in 1Th 2:2

OUTRAN *(2)*
of the plain and **o** the Cushite. 2Sm 18:23
other disciple **o** Peter and got Jn 20:4

OUTSIDE *(148)*
it with pitch inside and **o**. Gn 6:14
and told his two brothers **o**. Gn 9:22
He took him **o** and said, "Look at Gn 15:5
him out and left him **o** the city. Gn 19:16
soon as the angels got them **o**, Gn 19:17
a well of water **o** the town at Gn 24:11
her hand, he escaped and ran **o**. Gn 39:12
garment with her and had run **o**, Gn 39:13
his garment with me and ran **o**." Gn 39:15
his garment with me and ran **o**." Gn 39:18
any of the meat **o** the house, Ex 12:46
and walk around **o** ⌊leaning⌋ on Ex 21:19
Place the table **o** the veil and Ex 26:35
tent of meeting **o** the veil that Ex 27:21
hide, and its dung **o** the camp; Ex 29:14
a tent and set it up **o** the camp, Ex 33:7
of meeting that was **o** the camp. Ex 33:7
of the tabernacle, **o** the veil. Ex 40:22
clean place **o** the camp to the Lv 4:12
bring the bull **o** the camp and Lv 4:21
and bring the ashes **o** the camp Lv 6:11
flesh, and dung **o** the camp, as Lv 8:17
You must not go **o** the entrance Lv 8:33
flesh and the hide **o** the camp. Lv 9:11
to ⌊a place⌋ **o** the camp." Lv 10:4
them in their tunics **o** the camp, Lv 10:5
You must not go **o** the entrance Lv 10:7
alone in a place **o** the camp. Lv 13:46
will go **o** the camp and examine Lv 14:3
he must remain **o** his tent for Lv 14:8
priest is to go **o** the house to Lv 14:38
an unclean place **o** the city. Lv 14:40
in an unclean place **o** the city. Lv 14:41
and taken **o** the city to an Lv 14:45
the open countryside **o** the city. Lv 14:53
must be brought **o** the camp and Lv 16:27
or slaughters ⌊it⌋ **o** the camp, Lv 17:3
No one **o** a priest's family is to Lv 22:10
married to a man **o** a priest's Lv 22:12
before the LORD **o** the veil Lv 24:3
has cursed to the **o** of the camp Lv 24:14
had cursed to the **o** of the camp Lv 24:23
send them **o** the camp, so that Nm 5:3
this, sending them **o** the camp. Nm 5:4
her be confined **o** the camp for Nm 12:14
was confined **o** the camp for Nm 12:15
is to stone him **o** the camp." Nm 15:35
brought him **o** the camp and Nm 15:36
unauthorized person **o** the Nm 16:40
will have it brought **o** the camp Nm 19:3
ashes and deposit them **o** the Nm 19:9
went to meet them **o** the camp. Nm 31:13
You are to remain **o** the camp for Nm 31:19
1,000 yards **o** the city for Nm 35:5
someone ever goes **o** the border Nm 35:26
blood finds him **o** the border of Nm 35:27
night, he must go **o** the camp; Dt 23:10
have a place **o** the camp and go Dt 23:12
You must stand **o** while the man Dt 24:11
marry a stranger **o** ⌊the family⌋. Dt 25:5
O, the sword will take their Dt 32:25
and settled them **o** the camp of Jos 6:23
chased them from **o** the gate to Jos 7:5
in marriage ⌊to men⌋ **o** the tribe Jdg 12:9
for his sons from **o** ⌊the tribe⌋. Jdg 12:9
and took her **o** to them. Jdg 19:25

and both he and Samuel went **o**. 1Sm 9:26
all around the **o** so that nothing 1Kg 6:6
and from the **o** to the great 1Kg 7:9
not seen from **o** ⌊the sanctuary⌋; 1Kg 8:8
So they took him **o** the city and 1Kg 21:13
Now Jehu had stationed 80 men **o**, 2Kg 10:24
burned them **o** Jerusalem in the 2Kg 23:4
the Kidron Valley **o** Jerusalem. 2Kg 23:6
his sons had the **o** duties as 1Ch 26:29
but they were not seen from **o**; 2Ch 5:9
was made and placed **o** the gate 2Ch 24:8
and took them **o** to the Kidron 2Ch 29:16
springs that were **o** the city, 2Ch 32:3
the towers and the other **o** wall. 2Ch 32:5
and he threw them **o** the city. 2Ch 33:15
the work **o** the house of God; Neh 11:16
of goods camped **o** Jerusalem, Neh 13:20
grew silent and would not go **o**? Jb 31:34
slacker says, "There's a lion **o**! Pr 22:13
are besieging you **o** the wall, Jr 21:4
off and thrown **o** the gates of Jr 22:19
O, the sword takes the children; Lm 1:20
The sword is on the **o**; Ezk 7:15
surrounding the **o** of the temple. Ezk 40:5
O, as one approaches the Ezk 40:40
inside the gate and four **o**, Ezk 40:41
O the inner gate, within the Ezk 40:44
the inner temple and on the **o**. Ezk 41:17
the inside and **o**, was a pattern Ezk 41:17
There was a wooden canopy **o**, Ezk 41:25
A wall on the **o** ran in front of Ezk 42:7
must be burned **o** the sanctuary Ezk 43:21
enter from the **o** by way of the Ezk 46:2
me around the **o** to the outer Ezk 47:2
breaks in; a gang pillages **o**. Hs 7:1
when the crowd had been put **o**, Mt 9:25
were standing **o** wanting to speak Mt 12:46
Your brothers are standing **o**, Mt 12:47
You clean the **o** of the cup and Mt 23:25
so the **o** of it may also become Mt 23:26
which appear beautiful on the **o**, Mt 23:27
on the **o** you seem righteous to Mt 23:28
was sitting **o** in the courtyard Mt 26:69
And he went **o** and wept Mt 26:75
and standing **o**, they sent ⌊word Mk 3:31
sisters are **o** asking for You. Mk 3:32
but to those **o**, everything comes Mk 4:11
at Him, but He put them all **o**. Mk 5:40
a person from **o** can defile him, Mk 7:15
a man from the **o** can defile him? Mk 7:18
a young donkey **o** in the street, Mk 11:4
of the people was praying **o**. Lk 1:10
Your brothers are standing **o**, Lk 8:20
clean the **o** of the cup and dish Lk 11:39
who made the **o** make the inside Lk 11:40
Then you will stand **o** and knock Lk 13:25
to perish **o** of Jerusalem! Lk 13:33
And he went **o** and wept bitterly. Lk 22:62
he has brought all his own **o**, Jn 10:4
remained standing **o** by the door. Jn 18:16
Pilate went **o** again and said to Jn 19:4
I'm bringing Him **o** to you to let Jn 19:4
these words, he brought Jesus **o**. Jn 19:13
Mary stood **o** facing the tomb, Jn 20:11
men to be taken **o** for a little Ac 5:34
their infants **o** so they wouldn't Ac 7:19
when he was left **o**, Pharaoh's Ac 7:21
went **o** and passed one street, Ac 12:10
temple was just **o** the town, Ac 14:13
day we went **o** the city gate Ac 16:13
can commit is **o** the body," 1Co 6:18
To those who are **o** the law, 1Co 9:21
law, like one **o** the law—not 1Co 9:21
the law—not being **o** God's law, 1Co 9:21
Christ—to win those **o** the law. 1Co 9:21
on the **o**, fears inside. 2Co 7:5
offering are burned **o** the camp. Heb 13:11
Jesus also suffered **o** the gate, Heb 13:12
us then go to Him **o** the camp, Heb 13:13
the courtyard **o** the sanctuary. Rv 11:2
press was trampled **o** the city, Rv 14:20
O are the dogs, the sorcerers, Rv 22:15

OUTSIDER *(2)*
But no **o** may share it. Lv 22:13
and no **o** shares in its joy. Pr 14:10

OUTSIDERS *(6)*
Are we not regarded by him as **o**? Gn 31:15
For what is it to me to judge **o**? 1Co 5:12
But God judges **o**. Put away the 1Co 5:13
wisdom toward **o**, making the most Col 4:5
in the presence of **o** and not be 1Th 4:12
have a good reputation among **o**, 1Tm 3:7

OUTSKIRTS *(4)*
and consumed the **o** of the camp. Nm 11:1
he saw the **o** of the people's Nm 22:41
only see the **o** of their camp; Nm 23:13
in Migron on the **o** of Gibeah. 1Sm 14:2

OUTSTANDING *(2)*
the land produced **o** harvests. Gn 41:47
They are **o** among the apostles, Rm 16:7

OUTSTRETCHED *(18)*
you with an **o** arm and great acts Ex 6:6
by a strong hand and an **o** arm, Dt 4:34
with a strong hand and an **o** arm. Dt 5:15
the strong hand and **o** arm, Dt 7:19
by Your great power and **o** arm. Dt 9:29
strong hand, and **o** arm; Dt 11:2
with a strong hand and an **o** arm, Dt 26:8
mighty hand, and **o** arm, and will 1Kg 8:42
with great power and an **o** arm. 2Kg 17:36
and Your mighty hand and **o** arm: 2Ch 6:32
with a strong hand and **o** arm. Ps 136:12
hand that is **o**, so who can turn Is 14:27
you with an **o** hand and a mighty Jr 21:5
By My great strength and **o** arm, Jr 27:5
great power and with Your **o** arm. Jr 32:17
with a strong hand and an **o** arm, Jr 32:21
a strong hand, an **o** arm, and Ezk 20:33
a strong hand, an **o** arm, and Ezk 20:34

OUTWARD *(3)*
according to **o** appearances; Jn 7:24
pride in the **o** appearance rather 2Co 5:12
not consist of **o** things ⌊like⌋ 1Pt 3:3

OUTWARDLY *(1)*
is not a Jew who is one **o**, Rm 2:28

OUTWEIGH *(1)*
For then it would **o** the sand of Jb 6:3

OUTWEIGHS *(2)*
from a fool **o** them both. Pr 27:3
a little folly **o** wisdom and Ec 10:1

OUTWITTED *(1)*
he had been **o** by the wise men Mt 2:16

OVEN *(9)*
a grain offering baked in an **o**, Lv 2:4
offering that is baked in an **o**, Lv 7:9
If it is an **o** or stove, it must Lv 11:35
in a single **o** and ration out Lv 26:26
is as hot as an **o** from the Lm 5:10
are⌋ like an **o** heated by a baker Hs 7:4
their hearts like an **o**—draw Hs 7:6
an oven—draw him into their **o**. Hs 7:6
All of them are as hot as an **o**, Hs 7:7

OVEN-FIRED *(1)*
Come, let us make **o** bricks." Gn 11:3

OVENS *(4)*
and into your **o** and kneading Ex 8:3
well as to the Tower of the **O**. Neh 3:11
the Tower of the **O** to the Broad Neh 12:38
with **o** built at the base of the Ezk 46:23

OVER *(1213)*
(See pp. xi-xii.)

OVERALL *(1)*
The **o** length of the wings of the 2Ch 3:11

OVERBOARD *(3)*
the ship's gear **o** with their own Ac 27:19
the grain **o** into the sea. Ac 27:38
swim to jump **o** first and get to Ac 27:43

OVERCAME *(4)*
and the torments of Sheol **o** me; Ps 116:3
friends misled you and **o** you. Jr 38:22
the seas, and the current **o** me. Jnh 2:3
the watery depths **o** me; Jnh 2:5

OVERCAST *(1)*
a day of clouds and dense **o**, Jl 2:2

OVERCOME *(16)*
because he was **o** with emotion Gn 43:30
the people were **o** with grief. Nm 14:39
and the queen was **o** with fear. Est 4:4
you won't **o** him, because your Est 6:13
fear of the Jews had **o** them. Est 8:17
am continually **o** by longing for Ps 119:20
my heart is **o** with dismay. Ps 143:4
when trouble and stress **o** you. Pr 1:27
⌊Woe⌋ to those **o** with wine. Is 28:1
against you but will not **o** you, Jr 15:20
like a man **o** by wine, because Jr 23:9
was **o** and lay sick for days. Dn 8:27
he was startled and **o** with fear. Lk 1:12
yet the darkness did not **o** it. Jn 1:5
When he was **o** by sleep he fell Ac 20:9
I am **o** with joy in all our 2Co 7:4

OVERCOMES *(1)*
No disaster ⌊**o**⌋ the righteous, Pr 12:21

OVERCONFIDENT *(5)*
Edom, and you have become **o**. 2Kg 14:10
you have become **o** that you will 2Ch 25:19
to what I say, you **o** daughters. Is 32:9
than a year you **o** ones will Is 32:10
tremble, you **o** ones! Is 32:11

OVEREXTENDING *(1)*
For we are not **o** ourselves, 2Co 10:14

OVERFLOW *(22)*
as seasonal streams that **o** Jb 6:15
Your ways **o** with plenty. Ps 65:11
The wilderness pastures **o**, Ps 65:12
your vats will **o** with new wine. Pr 3:10
It will **o** its channels and spill Is 8:7
O your land like the Nile, Is 23:10
that our eyes may **o** with tears, Jr 9:18
My eyes will **o** with tears, Jr 13:17
Let my eyes **o** with tears; Jr 14:17
They will **o** the land and Jr 47:2
My eyes **o** unceasingly, without Lm 3:49
the vats will **o** with new wine Jl 2:24
the wine vats **o** because the Jl 3:13
will again **o** with prosperity; Zch 1:17
speaks from the **o** of the heart. Mt 12:34
speaks from the **o** of the heart. Lk 6:45
who receive the **o** of grace and Rm 5:17
so that you may **o** with hope by Rm 15:13
sufferings of Christ **o** to us, 2Co 1:5
to **o** to God's glory. 2Co 4:15
to make every grace **o** to you, 2Co 9:8
to increase and **o** with love for 1Th 3:12

OVERFLOWED *(4)*
out; torrents **o**. But can He also Ps 78:20
God and the gift **o** to the many Rm 5:15
deep poverty **o** into the wealth 2Co 8:2
and the grace of our Lord **o**, 1Tm 1:14

OVERFLOWING *(6)*
when it was **o** all its banks, 1Ch 12:15
and drink in their **o** waters. Ps 73:10
breath is like an **o** torrent that Is 30:28
north and becoming an **o** wadi. Jr 47:2
but is also **o** in many acts of 2Co 9:12
were taught, and **o** with Col 2:7

OVERFLOWS *(5)*
Now the Jordan **o** its banks Jos 3:15
my head with oil; my cup **o**. Ps 23:5
has been decreed; justice **o**. Is 10:22
so our comfort **o** through Christ. 2Co 1:5
righteousness **o** with even more 2Co 3:9

OVERGROWN *(2)*
palaces will be **o** with thorns; Is 34:13
a place **o** with weeds, a salt Zph 2:9

OVERHEARD *(2)*
David said was **o** and reported to 1Sm 17:31
But when Jesus **o** what was said, Mk 5:36

OVERJOYED *(4)*
the ark, they were **o** to see it. 1Sm 6:13
The king was **o** and gave orders Dn 6:23
they were **o** beyond measure. Mt 2:10
Abraham was **o** that he would see Jn 8:56

OVERLAID *(39)*
He **o** them with gold and made Ex 36:34
He also **o** the crossbars with Ex 36:34
wood and **o** them with gold; Ex 36:36
He **o** the tops of the posts and Ex 36:38
o it with pure gold inside and Ex 37:2
wood and **o** them with gold. Ex 37:4
He **o** it with pure gold and made Ex 37:11
wood and **o** them with gold. Ex 37:15
He **o** it, its top, all around its Ex 37:26
wood and **o** them with gold. Ex 37:28
Then he **o** it with bronze. Ex 38:2
acacia wood and **o** them with Ex 38:6
for the posts, **o** their tops, Ex 38:28

a carved image **o** with silver." Jdg 17:3
a carved image **o** with silver, Jdg 17:4
and a carved image **o** with silver Jdg 18:14
the carved image **o** with silver, Jdg 18:17
the carved image **o** with silver, Jdg 18:18
the ceiling he **o** the interior 1Kg 6:15
He also **o** the floor with cypress 1Kg 6:15
he **o** it with pure gold. 1Kg 6:20
He also **o** the cedar altar. 1Kg 6:20
Solomon **o** the interior of the 1Kg 6:21
sanctuary and **o** it with gold. 1Kg 6:21
also **o** the cherubim with gold. 1Kg 6:28
He **o** the temple floor with gold 1Kg 6:30
on them and **o** them with gold, 1Kg 6:32
on them and **o** them with gold 1Kg 6:35
ivory throne and **o** it with fine 1Kg 10:18
doorposts he had **o** and gave it 2Kg 18:16
he **o** its inner surface with pure 2Ch 3:4
cypress wood, **o** with fine gold, 2Ch 3:5
He **o** the temple—the beams, the 2Ch 3:7
He **o** it with 45,000 pounds of 2Ch 3:8
and he **o** the ceiling with gold. 2Ch 3:9
place, and he **o** them with gold. 2Ch 3:10
He **o** the doors with bronze. 2Ch 4:9
ivory throne and **o** it with pure 2Ch 9:17
were **o** with wood on all sides. Ezk 41:16

OVERLAY *(13)*
O it with pure gold; Ex 25:11
o it both inside and out. Ex 25:11
wood and **o** them with gold. Ex 25:13
O it with pure gold and make a Ex 25:24
acacia wood and **o** them with gold Ex 25:28
Then **o** the planks with gold, Ex 26:29
Also **o** the crossbars with gold. Ex 26:29
the screen and **o** them with gold; Ex 26:37
of one piece. **O** it with bronze. Ex 27:2
wood, and **o** them with bronze Ex 27:6
O its top, all around its sides, Ex 30:3
wood and **o** them with gold. Ex 30:5
added the gold **o** to the entire 1Kg 6:22

OVERLAYING *(1)*
refined silver for **o** the walls 1Ch 29:4

OVERLOOK *(4)*
highlands that **o** the wasteland. Nm 21:20
I taken a bribe to **o** something? 1Sm 12:3
has chosen to **o** some of your sin Jb 11:6
his virtue is to **o** an offense. Pr 19:11

OVERLOOKED *(2)*
widows were being **o** in the daily Ac 6:1
having **o** the times of ignorance, Ac 17:30

OVERLOOKING *(3)*
top of the mountain **o** Hebron. Jdg 16:3
to a place **o** the wilderness, 2Ch 20:24
At the heights **o** the road, Pr 8:2

OVERLOOKS *(1)*
of Peor, which **o** the wasteland. Nm 23:28

OVERLY *(2)*
Why then have I been **o** wise?" Ec 2:15
righteous, and don't be **o** wise. Ec 7:16

OVERNIGHT *(4)*
the trip, at an **o** campsite, it Ex 4:24
Please stay here **o** as the others Nm 22:19
on the tree **o** but are to bury Dt 21:23
to stay **o** and enjoy yourself. Jdg 19:6

OVERPOWER *(5)*
They intend to **o** us, seize us, Gn 43:18
so we can **o** him, tie him up Jdg 16:5
enemies had hoped to **o** them, Est 9:1
You completely **o** him, and he Jb 14:20
forces of Hades will not **o** it. Mt 16:18

OVERPOWERED *(5)*
to him, so that Othniel **o** him. Jdg 3:10
o the Ammonites, and that year 2Ch 27:5
The Jews **o** those who hated them. Est 9:1
the lions **o** them and crushed Dn 6:24
leaped on them, **o** them all, Ac 19:16

OVERPOWERS *(2)*
And if somebody **o** one person, Ec 4:12
than he attacks and **o** him, Lk 11:22

OVERRUN *(2)*
Their land was **o** with frogs, Ps 105:30
will never **o** it again. Jl 3:17

OVERSAW *(2)*
those who **o** the LORD's temple. 2Kg 12:11
those who **o** the LORD's temple. 2Ch 34:10

OVERSEE *(2)*
those who **o** the LORD's temple. 2Kg 22:5
those who **o** the LORD's temple." 2Kg 22:9

OVERSEEING *(1)*
not **o** out of compulsion but 1Pt 5:2

OVERSEER *(5)*
So the **o** of the palace, the 2Kg 10:5
the palace, the **o** of the city, 2Kg 10:5
If anyone aspires to be an **o**, 1Tm 3:1
An **o**, therefore, must be above 1Tm 3:2
For an **o**, as God's manager, must Ti 1:7

OVERSEERS *(10)*
Let him appoint **o** over the land Gn 41:34
commanded the **o** of the people as Ex 5:6
So the **o** and foremen of the Ex 5:10
The **o** insisted, "Finish your Ex 5:13
of Manasseh as **o** in every matter 1Ch 26:32
by the Levites to the king's **o**, 2Ch 24:11
Their **o** were Jahath and Obadiah 2Ch 34:12
the hand of the **o** and the hand 2Ch 34:17
Spirit has appointed you as **o**, Ac 20:28
including the **o** and deacons. Php 1:1

OVERSHADOW *(1)*
of the Most High will **o** you. Lk 1:35

OVERSHADOWED *(2)*
How the Lord has **o** Daughter Zion Lm 2:1
a cloud appeared and **o** them. Lk 9:34

OVERSHADOWING *(2)*
cloud appeared, **o** them, and a Mk 9:7
were above it **o** the mercy seat. Heb 9:5

OVERSIGHT *(4)*
had **o** of those responsible for Nm 3:32
priest, has **o** of the lamp oil Nm 4:16
⌊He has⌋ **o** of the entire Nm 4:16
Jehoiada put the **o** of the LORD's 2Ch 23:18

OVERSTEPPED *(1)*
teachings, **o** decrees, and broken Is 24:5

OVERTAKE *(25)*
disaster will **o** me, and I will Gn 19:19
and when you **o** them, say to them Gn 44:4
pursue, I will **o**, I will divide Ex 15:9
o him because the distance is Dt 19:6
blessings will come and **o** you, Dt 28:2
curses will come and **o** you: Dt 28:15
and **o** you until you are Dt 28:45
raiders? Will I **o** them?" The 1Sm 30:8
will certainly **o** ⌊them⌋ and 1Sm 30:8
or he will **o** us, heap disaster 2Sm 15:14
Terrors **o** him like a flood; Jb 27:20
may an enemy pursue and **o** me; Ps 7:5
I pursue my enemies and **o** them; Ps 18:37
let Your burning anger **o** them. Ps 69:24
Joy and gladness will **o** ⌊them⌋, Is 35:10
Joy and gladness will **o** ⌊them⌋, Is 51:11
sword you fear will **o** you there Jr 42:16
the unjust **o** them in Gibeah? Hs 10:9
will never **o** or confront us, Am 9:10
the plowman will **o** the reaper Am 9:13
shame will not **o** us." Mc 2:6
No calamity will **o** us." Mc 3:11
the prophets **o** your ancestors? Zch 1:6
so that darkness doesn't **o** you. Jn 12:35
this day would **o** you like a 1Th 5:4

OVERTAKEN *(7)*
the hardships that have **o** us. Nm 20:14
For the thing I feared has **o** me, Jb 3:25
my sins have **o** me; Ps 40:12
Trouble and distress have **o** me, Ps 119:143
pursuers have **o** her in narrow Lm 1:3
temptation has **o** you except what 1Co 10:13
and wrath has **o** them completely. 1Th 2:16

OVERTAKES *(2)*
of the LORD's anger **o** you, Zph 2:2
day of the LORD's anger **o** you. Zph 2:2

OVERTAKING *(1)*
the sword of your enemy **o** you, 1Ch 21:12

OVERTHREW *(10)*
He **o** these cities, the entire Gn 19:25
when He **o** the cities where Gn 19:29
the LORD **o** them in the sea. Ex 14:27
You **o** Your adversaries by Your Ex 15:7
and Gomorrah when God **o** them. Is 13:19
cities the LORD **o** without Jr 20:16
Just as when God **o** Sodom and Jr 50:40
sacrifice and **o** the place of His Dn 8:11
I **o** some of you as I overthrew Am 4:11
some of you as I **o** Sodom and Am 4:11

OVERTHROW *(6)*
and will not **o** the town you Gn 19:21
the city, spy on it, and **o** it?" 2Sm 10:3
order to scout out, **o**, and spy 1Ch 19:3
to dwell there **o** any king or Ezr 6:12
you will not be able to **o** them. Ac 5:39
they **o** whole households by Ti 1:11

OVERTHROWN *(6)*
The wicked are **o** and perish, Pr 12:7
a desolation **o** by foreigners. Is 1:7
Gomorrah were **o** along with their Jr 49:18
was **o** in an instant without Lm 4:6
"In 40 days Nineveh will be **o**!" Jnh 3:4
work is of men, it will be **o**; Ac 5:38

OVERTHROWS *(3)*
away barefoot and **o** established Jb 12:19
deeds and **o** ⌊them⌋ by night Jb 34:25
but He **o** the words of the Pr 22:12

OVERTOOK *(10)*
and **o** him at Mount Gilead. Gn 31:23
When Laban **o** Jacob, Jacob had Gn 31:25
When he **o** them, he said these Gn 44:6
but the battle **o** them, and those Jdg 20:42
and easily **o** them near Gibeah Jdg 20:43
They **o** them at Gidom and struck Jdg 20:45
The Philistines **o** Saul and his 1Sm 31:2
pursued him and **o** him in the 2Kg 25:5
army pursued them and **o** Zedekiah Jr 39:5
pursued the king and **o** Zedekiah Jr 52:8

OVERTURN *(2)*
I will **o** royal thrones and Hg 2:22
I will **o** chariots and their Hg 2:22

OVERTURNED *(4)*
cease and have **o** his throne. Ps 89:44
He **o** the money changers' tables Mt 21:12
He **o** the money changers' tables Mk 11:15
coins and **o** the tables. Jn 2:15

OVERTURNING *(2)*
their knowledge, **o** them in His Jb 9:5
and are **o** the faith of some. 2Tm 2:18

OVERWHELM *(6)*
grief that would **o** my father." Gn 44:34
Iniquities **o** me; only You can Ps 65:3
their lips cause **o** ⌊them⌋. Ps 140:9
the rivers, they will not **o** you. Is 43:2
and horror will **o** them. Ezk 7:18
against Lebanon will **o** you; Hab 2:17

OVERWHELMED *(9)*
I was **o** with fear Neh 2:2
but Haman, **o**, hurried off for Est 6:12
he will not be **o**, because the Ps 37:24
horror has **o** me. Ps 55:5
You have **o** me with all Your Ps 88:7
vision, I am **o** and powerless. Dn 10:16
and astonishment **o** them. Mk 16:8
were completely **o**—beyond our 2Co 1:8
this one may be **o** by excessive 2Co 2:7

OVERWHELMING *(5)*
o him like a king prepared for Jb 15:24
when the **o** scourge passes Is 28:15
When the **o** scourge passes Is 28:18
out on you an **o** urge to sleep; Is 29:10
destroy Nineveh with an **o** flood, Nah 1:8

OVERWHELMS *(1)*
My anger **o** me because my foes Ps 119:139

OWE *(9)*
him, and said, 'Pay what you **o**!' Mt 18:28
'How much do you **o** my master?' Lk 16:5
another, 'How much do you **o**?' Lk 16:7
taxes to those you **o** taxes, Rm 13:7
tolls to those you **o** tolls, Rm 13:7
respect to those you **o** respect, Rm 13:7
and honor to those you **o** honor. Rm 13:7
Do not **o** anyone anything, except Rm 13:8
to you that you **o** me even your Phm 19

OWED *(6)*
one who **o** 10,000 talents was Mt 18:24
slaves who **o** him 100 denarii. Mt 18:28
until he could pay what was **o**. Mt 18:30
could pay everything that was **o**. Mt 18:34
One **o** 500 denarii, and the other Lk 7:41
as a gift, but as something **o**. Rm 4:4

OWES *(2)*
whatever your brother **o** you. Dt 15:3
in any way, or **o** you anything, Phm 18

OWL *(17)*
the short-eared **o**, the gull, the Lv 11:16
the little **o**, the cormorant, the Lv 11:17
the cormorant, the long-eared **o**, Lv 11:17
the white **o**, the desert owl, the Lv 11:18
owl, the desert **o**, the osprey, Lv 11:18
the short-eared **o**, the gull, the Dt 14:15
little **o**, the long-eared owl, Dt 14:16
the long-eared **o**, the white owl, Dt 14:16
the long-eared owl, the white **o**, Dt 14:16
the desert **o**, the osprey, the Dt 14:17
am like a desert **o**, like an owl Ps 102:6
like an **o** among the ruins. Ps 102:6
The desert **o** and the hedgehog Is 34:11
and the great **o** and the raven Is 34:11
screech **o** will stay there and Is 34:14
the desert **o** and the screech Zph 2:14
owl and the screech **o** will roost Zph 2:14

OWLS *(1)*
and **o** will fill the houses. Is 13:21

OWN *(595)*
God created man in His **o** image; Gn 1:27
Each ⌊group⌋ had its **o** language. Gn 10:5
in their **o** lands and their Gn 10:20
comes from your **o** body will be Gn 15:4
you are my **o** flesh and blood." Gn 29:14
do something for my **o** family?" Gn 30:30
Then he set his **o** stock apart Gn 30:40
is our brother, our ⌊**o**⌋ flesh." Gn 37:27
each dream had its **o** meaning. Gn 40:5
each dream had its **o** meaning. Gn 41:11
each had its **o** interpretation. Gn 41:12
he went out to his **o** people and Ex 2:11
but it is your **o** people who are Ex 5:16
that the Israelites **o** will die." Ex 9:4
livestock you **o** that are males Ex 13:12
and he journeyed to his **o** land. Ex 18:27
you will be My **o** possession out Ex 19:5
the best of his **o** field or Ex 22:5
accept us as Your **o** possession." Ex 34:9
His **o** hands will bring the fire Lv 7:30
Abihu each took his **o** firepan, Lv 10:1
his blood is on his **o** hands. Lv 20:9
their blood is on their **o** hands. Lv 20:11
their blood is on their **o** hands. Lv 20:12
their blood is on their **o** hands. Lv 20:13
their ⌊**o**⌋ blood is on them. Lv 20:16
exposing one's **o** blood relative; Lv 20:19
blood is on their **o** hands." Lv 20:27
a virgin from his **o** people, Lv 21:14
I will go to my **o** land and my Nm 10:30
following your **o** heart and your Nm 15:39
your own heart and your **o** eyes. Nm 15:39
that it was not of my **o** will: Nm 16:28
at the cost of their **o** lives, Nm 16:38
and each man took his **o** staff. Nm 17:9
good or bad of my **o** will? Nm 24:13
he died because of his **o** sin, Nm 27:3
and your servants **o** livestock." Nm 32:4
it Nobah after his **o** name. Nm 32:42
responsibility for⌋ you on my **o**. Dt 1:9
He called Bashan by his **o** name, Dt 3:14
Your **o** eyes have seen everything Dt 3:21
and see ⌊it⌋ with your **o** eyes, Dt 3:27
careful for your **o** good— Dt 4:15
nation as his **o** out of ⌊another Dt 4:34
you to be His **o** possession out Dt 7:6
'My power and my **o** ability have Dt 8:17
you today, for your **o** good. Dt 10:13
Your ⌊**o**⌋ eyes have seen every Dt 11:7
seems right in his **o** eyes. Dt 12:8
me from among your **o** brothers. Dt 18:15
hearts won't melt like his **o**.' Dt 20:8
be put to death for his **o** sin. Dt 24:16
seen with your **o** eyes everything Dt 29:2
saw with your **o** eyes the great Dt 29:3
I follow my ⌊**o**⌋ stubborn heart.' Dt 29:19
Jacob, His **o** inheritance. Dt 32:9
Our **o** hand has prevailed; Dt 32:27
for his cause with his **o** hands, Dt 33:7
let you see it with your **o** eyes, Dt 34:4
his blood will be on his **o** head, Jos 2:19
things⌋ with their **o** belongings. Jos 7:11
home to his **o** city from which he Jos 20:6
cities had its **o** surrounding Jos 21:42
homes in your **o** land that Moses Jos 22:4
to go to their **o** land of Gilead, Jos 22:9
your God for your **o** well-being. Jos 23:11
Your **o** eyes saw what I did to Jos 24:7
each to his **o** inheritance. Jos 24:28
each to his **o** inheritance. Jdg 2:6
gave their **o** daughters to their Jdg 3:6
him plead his **o** case, because Jdg 6:31
70 sons, his **o** offspring, since Jdg 8:30
I am your **o** flesh and blood. Jdg 9:2
also cut his **o** branch and Jdg 9:49
my life in my **o** hands and Jdg 12:3
back to their **o** inheritance, Jdg 21:23
there to his **o** tribe and family Jdg 21:24
from there to his **o** inheritance. Jdg 21:24
I will ruin my ⌊**o**⌋ inheritance. Ru 4:6
not prevail by ⌊his **o**⌋ strength. 1Sm 2:9
to make you His **o** people. 1Sm 12:22
troops away, each to his **o** tent. 1Sm 13:2
returned to their **o** territory. 1Sm 14:46
Saul had his **o** military clothes 1Sm 17:38
weapons in his ⌊**o**⌋ tent. 1Sm 17:54
son to your **o** shame and to 1Sm 20:30
tells me when my **o** son makes a 1Sm 22:8
stirred up my **o** servant to wait 1Sm 22:8
see with your **o** eyes that the 1Sm 24:10
yourself by your **o** hand. 1Sm 25:26
avenging myself by my **o** hand. 1Sm 25:33
evil deeds back on his **o** head." 1Sm 25:39
fell on his **o** sword and died 1Sm 31:5
blood is on your **o** head because 2Sm 1:16
because your **o** mouth testified 2Sm 1:16
man in his **o** house on his own 2Sm 4:11
in his own house on his **o** bed! 2Sm 4:11
we are, your **o** flesh and blood. 2Sm 5:1
people left, each to his **o** home. 2Sm 6:19
Israel Your **o** people forever, 2Sm 7:24
one of his **o** sheep or cattle 2Sm 12:4
took his wife as your **o** wife— 2Sm 12:9
the Hittite to be your **o** wife.' 2Sm 12:10
on you from your **o** family: 2Sm 12:11
he has pronounced his **o** guilt. 2Sm 14:13
brought back his **o** banished one. 2Sm 14:13
Look, my **o** son, my own flesh 2Sm 16:11
own son, my **o** flesh and blood, 2Sm 16:11
If I had jeopardized my **o** life— 2Sm 18:13
I may die in my **o** city near the 2Sm 19:37
the city, each to his **o** tent. 2Sm 20:22
killed him with his **o** spear. 2Sm 23:21
son Solomon ride on my **o** mule, 1Kg 1:33
that blood on his **o** waistband 1Kg 2:5
bring back his **o** blood on his 1Kg 2:32
blood on his **o** head because he 1Kg 2:32
blood will be on your **o** head." 1Kg 2:37
man under his **o** vine and his own 1Kg 4:25
his own vine and his **o** fig tree. 1Kg 4:25
Solomon's **o** palace where he 1Kg 7:8
your son, your **o** offspring, will 1Kg 8:19
has done on his **o** head and 1Kg 8:32
man knowing his **o** afflictions 1Kg 8:38
LORD's temple, his **o** palace, the 1Kg 9:15
I heard in my **o** country about 1Kg 10:6
I came and saw with my **o** eyes. 1Kg 10:7
returned to her **o** country. 1Kg 10:13
the sister of his **o** wife, Queen 1Kg 11:19
so I can go to my **o** country." 1Kg 11:21
to go back to your **o** country?" 1Kg 11:22
now look after your **o** house! 1Kg 12:16
month he had decided on his **o**. 1Kg 12:33
laid the corpse in his **o** grave, 1Kg 13:30
and his **o** consecrated gifts 1Kg 15:15
and laid him on his **o** bed. 1Kg 17:19
each sitting on his **o** throne. 1Kg 22:10
Each man to his **o** city, and each 1Kg 22:36
and each man to his **o** land! 1Kg 22:36
hold of his **o** clothes and tore 2Kg 2:12
"I am living among my **o** people." 2Kg 4:13
in fact see it with your **o** eyes, 2Kg 7:2
in fact see it with your **o** eyes, 2Kg 7:19
and appointed their **o** king. 2Kg 8:20
each in his **o** chariot, and met 2Kg 9:21
along with his **o** consecrated 2Kg 12:18
be put to death for his **o** sin." 2Kg 14:6
men⌋ fled, each to his **o** tent. 2Kg 14:12
making their **o** gods and putting 2Kg 17:29
worshiped their **o** gods according 2Kg 17:33
you to eat their **o** excrement and 2Kg 18:27
and drink their **o** urine?" 2Kg 18:27
eat from his **o** vine and his own 2Kg 18:31
his own vine and his **o** fig tree, 2Kg 18:31
drink water from his **o** cistern 2Kg 18:31
to a land like your **o** land— 2Kg 18:32
return to his **o** land where I 2Kg 19:7
will eat what grows on its **o**, 2Kg 19:29
in the garden of his **o** house, 2Kg 21:18
and killed him in his **o** house. 2Kg 21:23
and buried him in his **o** tomb. 2Kg 23:30
the same, with its **o** grating. 2Kg 25:17
towns on their **o** property again 1Ch 9:2
fell on his **o** sword and died. 1Ch 10:5
we are, your **o** flesh and blood. 1Ch 11:1
killed him with his **o** spear. 1Ch 11:23
from his **o** ancestral house. 1Ch 12:28
who is one of your **o** sons, 1Ch 17:11
Israel Your **o** people forever, 1Ch 17:22
were under their **o** fathers' 1Ch 25:6
what comes from Your **o** hand. 1Ch 29:14
your son, your **o** offspring, will 2Ch 6:9
has done on his **o** head and 2Ch 6:23
man knowing his **o** affliction 2Ch 6:29
and for his **o** palace succeeded. 2Ch 7:11
LORD's temple and his **o** palace— 2Ch 8:1
I heard in my **o** country about 2Ch 9:5
I came and saw with my **o** eyes. 2Ch 9:6
returned to her **o** country. 2Ch 9:12
of them would bring his **o** gift— 2Ch 9:24
look after your **o** house now! 2Ch 10:16
appointed his **o** priests for the 2Ch 11:15
and make your **o** priests like the 2Ch 13:9
and his **o** consecrated gifts 2Ch 15:18
buried in his **o** tomb that he had 2Ch 16:14
each sitting on his **o** throne. 2Ch 18:9
and appointed their **o** king. 2Ch 21:8
one will die for his **o** sin." 2Ch 25:4
deliver their **o** people from your 2Ch 25:15
and each fled to his **o** tent. 2Ch 25:22
and it led to his **o** destruction. 2Ch 26:16
as you see with your **o** eyes. 2Ch 29:8
each to his **o** possession. 2Ch 31:1
from his **o** possessions for 2Ch 31:3
some of his **o** children cut him 2Ch 32:21
he was buried in his **o** house. 2Ch 33:20
put him to death in his **o** house. 2Ch 33:24
bulls from his **o** possessions, 2Ch 35:7
each opposite his **o** house. Neh 3:28
return on their **o** heads and let Neh 4:4
returned to his **o** work on the Neh 4:15
now you sell your **o** countrymen, Neh 5:8
inventing them in your **o** mind." Neh 6:8
returned to his **o** town in Neh 7:6
lived on his **o** property in their Neh 11:3
on his **o** inherited property. Neh 11:20
had gone back to his **o** field. Neh 13:10
province in its **o** script and to Est 1:22
ethnic group in its **o** language, Est 1:22
master of his **o** house and speak Est 1:22
in the language of his **o** people. Est 1:22
adopted her as his **o** daughter. Est 2:7
adopted ⌊her⌋ as his **o** daughter. Est 2:15
province in its **o** script and to Est 3:12
ethnic group in its **o** language. Est 3:12
each province in its **o** script, Est 8:9
ethnic group in its **o** language, Est 8:9
the Jews in their **o** script and Est 8:9
return on his **o** head and that he Est 9:25
my **o** mouth would condemn me; Jb 9:20
and my **o** clothes despise me! Jb 9:31
is not the case; I am on my **o**. Jb 9:35
and take my life in my **o** hands? Jb 13:14
pain of his **o** body and mourns Jb 14:22
Your **o** mouth condemns you, Jb 15:6
your **o** lips testify against you. Jb 15:6
and his **o** schemes trip him up. Jb 18:7
For his **o** feet lead him into a Jb 18:8
if I beg him with my **o** mouth. Jb 19:16
and my **o** children find me Jb 19:17
vanish forever like his **o** dung. Jb 20:7
for his **o** hands must give back Jb 20:10
is not of their **o** doing. Jb 21:16
Let his **o** eyes see his demise; Jb 21:20
I will die in my **o** nest and Jb 29:18
let my **o** wife grind ⌊grain⌋ for Jb 31:10
because my **o** hand has acquired Jb 31:25
he was righteous in his **o** eyes. Jb 32:1
as if ⌊they⌋ were not her **o**, Jb 39:16
you that your **o** right hand can Jb 40:14

them fall by their **o** schemes. Ps 5:10
comes back on his **o** head, Ps 7:16
one boasts about his **o** cravings; Ps 10:3
lips are our **o**—who can be our Ps 12:4
chosen to be His **o** possession! Ps 33:12
for in his **o** eyes he flatters Ps 36:2
will enter their **o** hearts, Ps 37:15
their **o** tongues work against Ps 64:8
not despise His **o** who are Ps 69:33
the tribe for Your **o** possession. Ps 74:2
hearts to follow their **o** plans. Ps 81:12
He abhorred His **o** inheritance. Ps 106:40
wicked fall into their **o** nets, Ps 141:10
they attack their **o** lives. Pr 1:18
be glutted with their **o** schemes. Pr 1:31
rely on your **o** understanding; Pr 3:5
Drink water from your **o** cistern, Pr 5:15
water flowing from your **o** well. Pr 5:15
in the ropes of his **o** sin. Pr 5:22
you are wise for your **o** benefit; Pr 9:12
are trapped by their **o** desires. Pr 11:6
way is right in his **o** eyes, Pr 12:15
his lips invites his **o** ruin. Pr 13:3
tears it down with her **o** hands. Pr 14:1
heart knows its **o** bitterness, Pr 14:10
are thrown down by their **o** sin, Pr 14:32
ways seem right in his **o** eyes, Pr 16:2
fathers a fool to his **o** sorrow; Pr 17:21
A man's **o** foolishness leads him Pr 19:3
a man proclaims his **o** loyalty, Pr 20:6
can anyone understand his **o** way? Pr 20:24
he'll become wise in his **o** eyes. Pr 26:5
cuts off his **o** feet and drinks Pr 26:6
a man who is wise in his **o** eyes? Pr 26:12
his **o** eyes, a slacker is wiser Pr 26:16
you, and not your **o** mouth—a Pr 27:2
a stranger, and not your **o** lips. Pr 27:2
way will fall into his **o** pit, Pr 28:10
rich man is wise in his **o** eyes, Pr 28:11
that is pure in its **o** eyes, Pr 30:12
She makes her **o** bed coverings; Pr 31:22
arms and consumes his **o** flesh. Ec 4:5
I have not kept my **o** vineyard. Sg 1:6
I have my **o** vineyard. The 1,000 Sg 8:12
We will eat our **o** bread and Is 4:1
and provide our **o** clothing. Is 4:1
as ⌊if in⌋ their **o** pastures, Is 5:17
are wise in their **o** opinion and Is 5:21
and clever in their **o** sight. Is 5:21
one eats the flesh of his **o** arm. Is 9:20
done ⌊this⌋ by my **o** strength and Is 10:13
world, and their ⌊**o**⌋ iniquity, Is 13:11
one will turn to his **o** people, Is 13:14
one will flee to his **o** land. Is 13:14
settle them on their **o** land. Is 14:1
in splendor, each in his **o** tomb. Is 14:18
and slaughtered your **o** people. Is 14:20
idols that your **o** hands have Is 31:7
eat from his **o** vine and his own Is 36:16
own vine and his **o** fig tree and Is 36:16
drink water from his **o** cistern Is 36:16
rumor and return to his **o** land, Is 37:7
will eat what grows on its **o**, Is 37:30
it was for ⌊my **o**⌋ welfare that I Is 38:17
for My **o** sake and remember Is 43:25
each wanders on his **o** way; Is 47:15
will act for My **o** sake, indeed, Is 48:11
sake, indeed, My **o**, for how can Is 48:11
My **o** hand founded the earth, Is 48:13
oppressors eat their **o** flesh, Is 49:26
drunk with their **o** blood as with Is 49:26
we all have turned to our **o** way; Is 53:6
all of them turn to their **o** way, Is 56:11
every last one for his **o** gain. Is 56:11
not ignore your **o** flesh ⌊and Is 58:7
not going your **o** ways, seeking Is 58:13
ways, seeking your **o** pleasure, Is 58:13
so His **o** arm brought salvation, Is 59:16
His **o** righteousness supported Is 59:16
following their **o** thoughts. Is 65:2
the works of their **o** hands. Jr 1:16
Your **o** evil will discipline you; Jr 2:19
your **o** apostasies will reprimand Jr 2:19
Your **o** sword has devoured your Jr 2:30
rule by their **o** authority. Jr 5:31
Each will pasture his **o** portion. Jr 6:3
the fruit of their **o** plotting, Jr 6:19
according to their **o** advice and Jr 7:24

according to their **o** stubborn, Jr 7:24
man's way of life is not his **o**; Jr 10:23
walks determines his **o** steps. Jr 10:23
your **o** father's household— Jr 12:6
stubbornness of their **o** hearts, Jr 13:10
the deceit of their **o** minds. Jr 14:14
pour out their **o** evil on them." Jr 14:16
Your **o** father, did he not eat Jr 22:15
except your **o** unjust gain, Jr 22:17
once more in their **o** land." Jr 23:8
visions from their **o** minds, Jr 23:16
of the deceit of their **o** minds? Jr 23:26
who use their **o** tongues to Jr 23:31
have heard with your **o** ears." Jr 26:11
the time for his **o** land comes, Jr 27:7
I will leave it in its **o** land, Jr 27:11
You in your **o** name have sent out Jr 29:25
return to their **o** territory. Jr 31:17
will die for his **o** wrongdoing. Jr 31:30
his **o** teeth will be set on edge. Jr 31:30
you **o** the right of redemption Jr 32:7
for you **o** the right of Jr 32:8
corpses of ⌊their **o**⌋ men I Jr 33:5
return to its **o** land of Egypt. Jr 37:7
he settled among ⌊his **o**⌋ people. Jr 39:14
as you can see with your **o** eyes Jr 42:2
you to return to your **o** soil. Jr 42:12
have led your **o** selves astray Jr 42:20
their wives, your **o** evils, and Jr 44:9
Moab will wallow in his **o** vomit, Jr 48:26
each will turn to his **o** people, Jr 50:16
each will flee to his **o** land. Jr 50:16
Let each of us go to his **o** land, Jr 51:9
women eat their **o** children, Lm 2:20
have cooked their **o** children; Lm 4:10
each over his **o** iniquity. Ezk 7:16
according to their **o** conduct, Ezk 7:27
judge them by their **o** standards. Ezk 7:27
actions down on their **o** heads." Ezk 9:10
of man, your **o** relatives, those Ezk 11:15
actions down on their **o** heads." Ezk 11:21
out of their **o** imagination: Ezk 13:2
follow their **o** spirit and have Ezk 13:3
out of their **o** imagination. Ezk 13:17
My people but preserve your **o**? Ezk 13:18
actions down on your **o** head." Ezk 16:43
die for his **o** iniquity because Ezk 18:18
actions down on their **o** heads." Ezk 22:31
judge you by their **o** standards. Ezk 23:24
they will live in their **o** land, Ezk 28:25
My Nile is my **o**; I made ⌊it⌋ for Ezk 29:3
The Nile is my **o**; I made ⌊it⌋, Ezk 29:9
his blood will be on his **o** head. Ezk 33:4
his blood is on his **o** hands. Ezk 33:5
it is their **o** way that isn't Ezk 33:17
bring them into their **o** land. Ezk 34:13
land as their **o** possession with Ezk 36:5
you will endure their **o** insults. Ezk 36:7
will bring you into your **o** land. Ezk 36:24
will settle you in your **o** land. Ezk 37:14
bring them into their **o** land. Ezk 37:21
to their **o** land after having Ezk 39:28
his sons from his **o** property, Ezk 46:18
displaced from his **o** property." Ezk 46:18
He will **o** ⌊the land⌋ adjacent to Ezk 48:21
any god except their **o** God. Dn 3:28
Your **o** predecessor, the king, Dn 5:11
sealed it with his **o** signet ring Dn 6:17
great, but it will not be his **o**. Dn 8:24
and in his **o** mind he will make Dn 8:25
My God, for Your **o** sake, do not Dn 9:19
and then return to his **o** land. Dn 11:9
ones among your **o** people will Dn 11:14
to the fortresses of his **o** land, Dn 11:19
then return to his **o** land. Dn 11:28
for their **o** destruction. Hs 8:4
wild donkey going off on its **o**. Hs 8:9
trusted in your **o** way and in Hs 10:13
goes on his **o** path, and they Jl 2:7
each man proceeds on his **o** path. Jl 2:8
them far from their **o** territory. Jl 3:6
and invent their **o** musical Am 6:5
ourselves by our **o** strength?" Am 6:13
will return on your **o** head. Ob 15
I was still in my **o** country? Jnh 4:2
child of my body for my **o** sin? Mc 6:7
are the people in his **o** home. Mc 7:6
to seize territories not its **o**. Hab 1:6

and sinning against your **o** self. Hab 2:10
his head with his **o** spears; Hab 3:14
to Him, each in its **o** place. Zph 2:11
of you is busy with his **o** house. Hg 1:9
plunder for their **o** servants. Zch 2:9
now I have seen with My **o** eyes. Zch 9:8
Even their **o** shepherds have no Zch 11:5
Your **o** eyes will see this, Mal 1:5
returned to their **o** country by Mt 2:12
day has enough trouble of its **o**. Mt 6:34
notice the log in your **o** eye? Mt 7:3
let the dead bury their **o** dead." Mt 8:22
over, and came to His **o** town. Mt 9:1
one to his **o** farm, another to Mt 22:5
called his **o** slaves and turned Mt 25:14
each according to his **o** ability. Mt 25:15
everything to His **o** disciples. Mk 4:34
Go back home to your **o** people, Mk 5:19
When Herodias' **o** daughter came Mk 6:22
registered, each to his **o** town. Lk 2:3
sword will pierce your **o** soul— Lk 2:35
to their **o** town of Nazareth. Lk 2:39
notice the log in your **o** eye? Lk 6:41
tree is known by its **o** fruit. Lk 6:44
Let the dead bury their **o** dead, Lk 9:60
Then he put him on his **o** animal, Lk 10:34
not hate his **o** father and mother Lk 14:26
and even his **o** life—he cannot Lk 14:26
not bear his **o** cross and come Lk 14:27
in dealing⌋ with their **o** people. Lk 16:8
will give you what is your **o**? Lk 16:12
He came to His **o**, and His own Jn 1:11
and His **o** people did not receive Jn 1:11
first found his **o** brother Simon Jn 1:41
has no honor in his **o** country. Jn 4:44
even calling God His **o** Father, Jn 5:18
able to do anything on His **o**, Jn 5:19
I can do nothing on My **o**. Jn 5:30
because I do not seek My **o** will, Jn 5:30
else comes in his **o** name, Jn 5:43
God or if I am speaking on My **o**. Jn 7:17
for himself seeks his **o** glory. Jn 7:18
Yet I have not come on My **o**, Jn 7:28
and that I do nothing on My **o**. Jn 8:28
For I didn't come on My **o**, Jn 8:42
he speaks from his **o** nature, Jn 8:44
He calls his **o** sheep by name and Jn 10:3
has brought all his **o** outside, Jn 10:4
and doesn't **o** the sheep, Jn 10:12
I know My **o** sheep, and they know Jn 10:14
but I lay it down on My **o**. Jn 10:18
He did not say this on his **o**, Jn 11:51
For I have not spoken on My **o**, Jn 12:49
Having loved His **o** who were in Jn 13:1
to you I do not speak on My **o**. Jn 14:10
world would love ⌊you as⌋ its **o**. Jn 15:19
For He will not speak on His **o**, Jn 16:13
will be scattered to his **o** home, Jn 16:32
Are you asking this on your **o**, Jn 18:34
Your **o** nation and the chief Jn 18:35
Carrying His **o** cross, He went Jn 19:17
has set by His **o** authority. Ac 1:7
so that in their **o** language that Ac 1:19
left to go to his **o** place." Ac 1:25
them speaking in his **o** language. Ac 2:6
of us, in our **o** native language? Ac 2:8
them speaking in our **o** languages Ac 2:11
as though by our **o** power or Ac 3:12
they went to their **o** fellowship Ac 4:23
of his possessions was his **o**, Ac 4:32
and raised him as her **o** son. Ac 7:21
Get up and make your **o** bed," Ac 9:34
after serving his **o** generation Ac 13:36
the nations to go their **o** way, Ac 14:16
some of your **o** poets have said, Ac 17:28
Your blood is on your **o** heads! Ac 18:6
names, and your **o** law, see to it Ac 18:15
He purchased with His **o** blood. Ac 20:28
tied his **o** feet and hands, Ac 21:11
him about their **o** religion and Ac 25:19
the beginning among my **o** nation Ac 26:4
overboard with their **o** hands. Ac 27:19
years in his **o** rented house. Ac 28:30
and received in their **o** persons Rm 1:27
He considered his **o** body to be Rm 4:19
But God proves His **o** love for us Rm 5:8
by sending His **o** Son in flesh Rm 8:3
He did not even spare His **o** Son, Rm 8:32

establish their **o** righteousness, Rm 10:3
make my **o** people jealous Rm 11:14
grafted into their **o** olive tree? Rm 11:24
be wise in your **o** estimation. Rm 12:16
Before his **o** Lord he stands or Rm 14:4
fully convinced in his **o** mind. Rm 14:5
who risked their **o** necks for my Rm 16:4
Christ but their **o** appetites, Rm 16:18
receive his **o** reward according 1Co 3:8
reward according to his **o** labor. 1Co 3:8
labor, working with our **o** hands. 1Co 4:12
immoral sins against his **o** body. 1Co 6:18
from God? You are not your **o**, 1Co 6:19
each man should have his **o** wife, 1Co 7:2
woman should have her **o** husband. 1Co 7:2
have authority over her **o** body, 1Co 7:4
have authority over his **o** body, 1Co 7:4
each has his **o** gift from God, 1Co 7:7
saying this for your **o** benefit, 1Co 7:35
but has control over his **o** will 1Co 7:37
his heart to keep his **o** virgin, 1Co 7:37
goes to war at his **o** expense? 1Co 9:7
No one should seek his **o** ⌊good⌋, 1Co 10:24
I do not mean your **o** conscience, 1Co 10:29
not seeking my **o** profit, but the 1Co 10:33
one takes his **o** supper ahead 1Co 11:21
ask their **o** husbands at home 1Co 14:35
But each in his **o** order: 1Co 15:23
to each of the seeds its **o** body. 1Co 15:38
This greeting is in my **o** hand— 1Co 16:21
limited by your **o** affections. 2Co 6:12
that, on their **o**, according to 2Co 8:3
went out to you by his **o** choice. 2Co 8:17
from my **o** people, dangers 2Co 11:26
should examine his **o** work, Gl 6:4
will have to carry his **o** load. Gl 6:5
to you in my **o** handwriting. Gl 6:11
do honest work with his **o** hands, Eph 4:28
submit to your **o** husbands as to Eph 5:22
their wives as their **o** bodies. Eph 5:28
no one ever hates his **o** flesh, Eph 5:29
not ⌊only⌋ for his **o** interests, Php 2:4
Make your **o** attitude that of Php 2:5
to be used for His **o** advantage. Php 2:6
work out your **o** salvation with Php 2:12
all seek their **o** interests, Php 2:21
of my **o** from the law, Php 3:9
This greeting is in my **o** hand— Col 4:18
mother nurtures her **o** children. 1Th 2:7
of God but also our **o** lives, 1Th 2:8
a father with his **o** children, 1Th 2:11
you into His **o** kingdom and glory 1Th 2:12
from people of your **o** country, 1Th 2:14
how to possess his **o** vessel in 1Th 4:4
to mind your **o** business, and to 1Th 4:11
and to work with your **o** hands, 1Th 4:11
they may eat their **o** bread. 2Th 3:12
This greeting is in my **o** hand— 2Th 3:17
one who manages his **o** household 1Tm 3:4
how to manage his **o** household, 1Tm 3:5
children and their **o** households 1Tm 3:12
toward their **o** family first and 1Tm 5:4
not provide for his **o** relatives, 1Tm 5:8
must regard their **o** masters to 1Tm 6:1
will bring about in His **o** time. 1Tm 6:15
according to His **o** purpose and 2Tm 1:9
according to their **o** desires, 2Tm 4:3
and has in His **o** time revealed Ti 1:3
of their very **o** prophets said, Ti 1:12
but of your **o** free will. Phm 14
write this with my **o** hand: Phm 19
you owe me even your **o** self. Phm 19
has rested from his **o** works, Heb 4:10
to their **o** harm, they are Heb 6:6
first for their **o** sins, then for Heb 7:27
but by His **o** blood, having Heb 9:12
the people by His **o** blood. Heb 13:12
enticed by his **o** evil desires. Jms 1:14
His **o** choice, He gave us a new Jms 1:18
looking at his **o** face in a Jms 1:23
to your **o** husbands so that, 1Pt 3:1
submitting to their **o** husbands, 1Pt 3:5
called us by His **o** glory and 2Pt 1:3
from one's **o** interpretation, 2Pt 1:20
A dog returns to its **o** vomit, 2Pt 2:22
scoff, following their **o** lusts, 2Pt 3:3
them to their **o** destruction, 2Pt 3:16
and fall from your **o** stability. 2Pt 3:17
not keep their **o** position but Jd 6
people for their **o** advantage. Jd 16
to their **o** ungodly desires." Jd 18

OWNED *(16)*

She **o** an Egyptian slave named Gn 16:1
household who managed all he **o**, Gn 24:2
gave everything he **o** to Isaac. Gn 25:5
placed all that he **o** under his Gn 39:4
household and of all that he **o**, Gn 39:5
blessing was on all that he **o**, Gn 39:5
all that he **o** under Joseph's Gn 39:6
woman who **o** the house became 1Kg 17:17
he **o** remains in his tent. Jb 18:15
away the donkeys ⌊o⌋ by the Jb 24:3
He **o** 14,000 sheep, 6,000 camels, Jb 42:12
also **o** many herds of cattle and Ec 2:7
Solomon **o** a vineyard in Sg 8:11
the poor people who **o** nothing, Jr 39:10
all those who **o** lands or houses Ac 4:34
sold a field he **o**, brought the Ac 4:37

OWNER *(34)*

his abuse, the **o** must be Ex 21:20
the **o** should not be punished Ex 21:21
but the ox's **o** is innocent. Ex 21:28
and its **o** has been warned yet Ex 21:29
and its **o** must also be put to Ex 21:29
the **o** of the pit must give Ex 21:34
he must pay money to its **o**, Ex 21:34
yet its **o** has not restrained it, Ex 21:36
the **o** of the house must present Ex 22:8
Its **o** must accept ⌊the oath⌋, Ex 22:11
must make restitution to its **o**. Ex 22:12
dies while its **o** is not there Ex 22:14
If its **o** is there with it, Ex 22:15
to pay it to its **o** on the day he Lv 6:5
o of the house is to come and Lv 14:35
A foreign **o** is not to rule over Lv 25:53
bought it from, the original **o**. Lv 27:24
man who was the **o** of the house, Jdg 19:22
The **o** of the house went out and Jdg 19:23
name Shemer, the **o** of the hill. 1Kg 16:24
like a magic stone to its **o**; Pr 17:8
profit to the **o**, except to gaze Ec 5:11
kept by its **o** to his harm. Ec 5:13
preserves the life of its **o**. Ec 7:12
ox knows its **o**, and the donkey Is 1:3
the **o** of the vineyard told his Mt 20:8
the **o** of the vineyard comes, Mt 21:40
what will the **o** of the vineyard Mk 12:9
tell the **o** of the house, Mk 14:14
Then the **o** of the vineyard said, Lk 20:13
what will the **o** of the vineyard Lk 20:15
Tell the **o** of the house, 'The Lk 22:11
captain and the **o** of the ship Ac 27:11
he is the **o** of everything. Gl 4:1

OWNER'S *(1)*

because he is his ⌊o⌋ property. Ex 21:21

OWNERS *(3)*

donkey, its **o** said to them, Lk 19:33
profit for her **o** by Ac 16:16
When her **o** saw that their hope Ac 16:19

OWNS *(8)*

has given him everything he **o**. Gn 24:36
put all that he **o** under my Gn 39:8
apart to the LORD from all he **o**, Lv 27:28
household, and everything he **o**? Jb 1:10
hand and strike everything he **o**, Jb 1:11
everything he **o** is in your Jb 1:12
everything he **o** in exchange for Jb 2:4
bind the man who **o** this belt, Ac 21:11

OX *(77)*

female slave, his **o** or donkey, Ex 20:17
When an **o** gores a man or a woman Ex 21:28
to death, the **o** must be stoned, Ex 21:28
if the **o** was in the habit of Ex 21:29
a woman, the **o** must be stoned, Ex 21:29
If the **o** gores a male or female Ex 21:32
and the **o** must be stoned. Ex 21:32
and an **o** or a donkey falls into Ex 21:33
When a man's **o** injures his Ex 21:35
his neighbor's **o** and it dies, Ex 21:35
sell the live **o** and divide its Ex 21:35
known that the **o** was in the Ex 21:36
must compensate fully, **o** for ox; Ex 21:36
must compensate fully, ox for **o**; Ex 21:36
a man steals an **o** or a sheep Ex 22:1
cattle for the **o** or four sheep Ex 22:1
stolen—whether **o**, donkey, or Ex 22:4
of wrongdoing involving an **o**, Ex 22:9
a donkey, an **o**, a sheep, or any Ex 22:10
your enemy's stray **o** or donkey, Ex 23:4
so that your **o** and your donkey Ex 23:12
removed from the **o** of the Lv 4:10
are not to eat any fat of an **o**, Lv 7:23
an **o** and a ram for a fellowship Lv 9:4
slaughtered the **o** and the ram as Lv 9:18
from the **o** and the ram— Lv 9:19
of Israel who slaughters an **o**, Lv 17:3
When an **o**, sheep, or goat is Lv 22:27
leaders and an **o** from each one, Nm 7:3
This is to be done for each **o**, Nm 15:11
redeem the firstborn of an **o**, Nm 18:17
us like an **o** eats up the green Nm 22:4
the horns of a wild **o** for them. Nm 23:22
the horns of a wild **o** for them. Nm 24:8
slave, your **o** or donkey, any Dt 5:14
female slave, his **o** or donkey, Dt 5:21
the **o**, the sheep, the goat, Dt 14:4
LORD your God an **o** or sheep with Dt 17:1
whether it is an **o**, a sheep, or Dt 18:3
your brother's **o** or sheep Dt 22:1
brother's donkey or **o** fallen Dt 22:4
not plow with an **o** and a donkey Dt 22:10
not muzzle an **o** while it treads Dt 25:4
o will be slaughtered before Dt 28:31
horns like those of a wild **o**; Dt 33:17
old, and every **o**, sheep, and Jos 6:21
daughters, his **o**, donkey, and Jos 7:24
well as no sheep, **o** or donkey. Jdg 6:4
be done to the **o** of anyone who 1Sm 11:7
Whose **o** or donkey have I taken? 1Sm 12:3
bring me his **o** or his sheep. 1Sm 14:34
troops brought his **o** that night 1Sm 14:34
sacrificed an **o** and a fattened 2Sm 6:13
and **o** yokes for the wood. 2Sm 24:22
Each day, one **o**, six choice Neh 5:18
fresh grass or an **o** low over its Jb 6:5
the widow's **o** as collateral. Jb 24:3
Would the wild **o** be willing to Jb 39:9
hold the wild **o** by its harness Jb 39:10
trust the wild **o** to harvest your Jb 39:12
you. He eats grass like an **o**. Jb 40:15
and Sirion, like a young wild **o**. Ps 29:6
please the LORD more than an **o**, Ps 69:31
my horn like that of a wild **o**; Ps 92:10
the image of a grass-eating **o**. Ps 106:20
impulsively like an **o** going to Pr 7:22
through the strength of an **o**. Pr 14:4
The **o** knows its owner, and the Is 1:3
lion will eat straw like an **o**. Is 11:7
who let **o** and donkey range Is 32:20
lion will eat straw like the **o**, Is 65:25
slaughters an **o**, one kills a man Is 66:3
the face of an **o** on the left, Ezk 1:10
one of you untie his **o** or donkey Lk 13:15
you whose son or **o** falls into a Lk 14:5
not muzzle an **o** while it treads 1Co 9:9
not muzzle an **o** that is 1Tm 5:18

OX'S *(1)*

but the **o** owner is innocent. Ex 21:28

OX-TEAM *(1)*

will smash the farmer and his **o**. Jr 51:23

OXEN *(53)*

I have **o**, donkeys, flocks, male Gn 32:5
and on a whim they hamstring **o**. Gn 49:6
LORD six covered carts and 12 **o**, Nm 7:3
the carts and **o** and gave them to Nm 7:6
carts and four **o** corresponding Nm 7:7
carts and eight **o** corresponding Nm 7:8
of your **o** to work or shear Dt 15:19
in from the field behind his **o**. 1Sm 11:5
He took a team of **o**, cut them in 1Sm 11:7
and infants, **o** and sheep, camels 1Sm 15:3
and infants, **o**, donkeys, and 1Sm 22:19
because the **o** had stumbled. 2Sm 6:6
Here are the **o** for a burnt 2Sm 24:22
floor and the **o** for 50 ounces of 2Sm 24:24
sacrificed sheep, **o**, and 1Kg 1:9
He has lavishly sacrificed **o**, 1Kg 1:19
down and lavishly sacrificed **o**, 1Kg 1:25
fattened **o**, 20 range oxen, and 1Kg 4:23
oxen, 20 range **o**, and 100 sheep, 1Kg 4:23
It stood on 12 **o**, three facing 1Kg 7:25
were lions, **o**, and cherubim. 1Kg 7:29
the lions and **o** were wreaths 1Kg 7:29

the 12 **o** underneath the 1Kg 7:44
Twelve teams of **o** were in front 1Kg 19:19
Elisha left the **o**, ran to follow 1Kg 19:20
the team of **o**, and slaughtered 1Kg 19:21
sheep and **o**, and male and female 2Kg 5:26
the bronze **o** that were under 2Kg 16:17
camels, mules, and **o**—abundant 1Ch 12:40
wine and oil, **o**, and sheep. 1Ch 12:40
because the **o** had stumbled. 1Ch 13:9
I give the **o** for the burnt 1Ch 21:23
The likeness of **o** was below it, 2Ch 4:3
The **o** were cast in two rows when 2Ch 4:3
It stood on 12 **o**, three facing 2Ch 4:4
and the 12 **o** underneath it, 2Ch 4:15
500 yoke of **o**, 500 female Jb 1:3
While the **o** were plowing and the Jb 1:14
yoke of **o**, and 1,000 female Jb 42:12
all the sheep and **o**, as well as Ps 8:7
me from the horns of the wild **o**. Ps 22:21
I will sacrifice **o** with goats. Ps 66:15
Where there are no **o**, the Pr 14:4
be places for **o** to graze and for Is 7:25
The **o** and donkeys that work the Is 30:24
The wild **o** will be struck down Is 34:7
does someone plow ⌊it⌋ with **o**? Am 6:12
my **o** and fattened cattle have Mt 22:4
'I have bought five yoke of **o**, Lk 14:19
He found people selling **o**, Jn 2:14
complex with their sheep and **o**. Jn 2:15
brought **o** and garlands to the Ac 14:13
Is God really concerned with **o**? 1Co 9:9

OXEN'S *(1)*
the **o** wooden yoke and plow, 1Kg 19:21

OXGOAD *(2)*
down 600 Philistines with an **o**. Jdg 3:31
and for putting a point on an **o**. 1Sm 13:21

OZEM *(2)*
O sixth, and David seventh. 1Ch 2:15
Bunah, Oren, **O**, and Ahijah. 1Ch 2:25

OZNI *(1)*
the Oznite clan from **O**; Nm 26:16

OZNITE *(1)*
the **O** clan from Ozni; Nm 26:16

P

PAARAI *(1)*
(AKA NAARAI)
the Carmelite, **P** the Arbite, 2Sm 23:35

PACE *(2)*
at a **p** suited to the livestock Gn 33:14
don't slow the **p** for me unless I 2Kg 4:24

PACED *(1)*
the house, and **p** back and forth. 2Kg 4:35

PACIFIED *(1)*
of the north have **p** My Spirit Zch 6:8

PACK *(2)*
P your bags for exile, Jr 46:19
p your bags for exile and go Ezk 12:3

PACKED *(1)*
Gehazi and then **p** 150 pounds of 2Kg 5:23

PACKS *(2)*
the land in your **p** and take them Gn 43:11
The food from our **p** is gone, 1Sm 9:7

PADDAN *(1)*
(AKA PADDAN-ARAM)
When I was returning from **P**, Gn 48:7

PADDAN-ARAM *(10)*
(AKA PADDAN)
of Bethuel the Aramean from **P**, Gn 25:20
Go at once to **P**, to the house of Gn 28:2
sent Jacob to **P**, to Laban son Gn 28:5
and sent him to **P** to get a wife Gn 28:6
father and mother and went to **P**. Gn 28:7
he had acquired in **P**, Gn 31:18
Jacob came from **P**, he arrived Gn 33:18
again after he returned from **P**, Gn 35:9
who were born to him in **P**. Gn 35:26
Leah's sons born to Jacob in **P**, Gn 46:15

PADON'S *(2)*
descendants, **P** descendants, Ezr 2:44
descendants, **P** descendants, Neh 7:47

PAGAN *(3)*
He removed the **p** altars and the 2Ch 14:3
You yourself will die on **p** soil, Am 7:17
the names of the **p** priests along Zph 1:4

PAGANS *(3)*
when you were **p**, you were led to 1Co 12:2
in doing the will of the **p**: 1Pt 4:3
name, accepting nothing from **p**. 3Jn 7

PAGIEL *(5)*
P son of Ochran from Asher; Nm 1:13
Asherites is **P** son of Ochran. Nm 2:27
eleventh day **P** son of Ochran, Nm 7:72
the offering of **P** son of Ochran. Nm 7:77
P son of Ochran was over the Nm 10:26

PAHATH-MOAB *(2)*
Hasshub son of **P** made repairs to Neh 3:11
Parosh, **P**, Elam, Zattu, Bani, Neh 10:14

PAHATH-MOAB'S *(4)*
P descendants: Ezr 2:6
of Zerahiah from **P** descendants, Ezr 8:4
P descendants: Ezr 10:30
P descendants: Neh 7:11

PAI *(1)*
(AKA PAU)
city was named **P**, and his wife's 1Ch 1:50

PAID *(46)*
I have **p** close attention to you Ex 3:16
the LORD had **p** attention to them Ex 4:31
the LORD had **p** attention to His Ru 1:6
The LORD **p** attention to Hannah's 1Sm 2:21
yet he **p** me back evil for good. 1Sm 25:21
face to the ground and **p** homage. 1Sm 28:14
fell to the ground and **p** homage. 2Sm 1:2
down to the ground and **p** homage. 2Sm 9:6
The LORD has **p** you back for all 2Sm 16:8
bowed down and **p** homage to the 1Kg 1:16
He came and **p** homage to King 1Kg 1:53
answered, no one **p** attention. 1Kg 18:29
his vassal and **p** him tribute 2Kg 17:3
and had not **p** tribute money to 2Kg 17:4
bowed down and **p** homage to the 1Ch 29:20
Judah came and **p** homage to the 2Ch 24:17
p him the same in the second 2Ch 27:5
of Jerusalem **p** him honor at his 2Ch 32:33
and land tax were **p** to them. Ezr 4:20
cost is to be **p** from the royal Ezr 6:4
cost is to be **p** in full to these Ezr 6:8
down and **p** homage to Haman, Est 3:2
I **p** close attention to you. Jb 32:12
He has **p** attention to the sound Ps 66:19
my hand and no one **p** attention, Pr 1:24
him, but he **p** no attention. Is 42:25
only you had **p** attention to My Is 48:18
for they have **p** no attention to Jr 6:19
I have **p** careful attention. Jr 8:6
Who has **p** attention to His word Jr 23:18
not obeyed or even **p** attention. Jr 25:4
When you **p** a fee instead of one Ezk 16:34
instead of one being **p** to you, Ezk 16:34
fell down, **p** homage to Daniel, Dn 2:46
Ephraim has **p** for love. Hs 8:9
He **p** the fare and went down into Jnh 1:3
until you have **p** the last penny! Mt 5:26
But they **p** no attention and went Mt 22:5
until you have **p** the last cent." Lk 12:59
The crowds **p** attention with one Ac 8:6
They all **p** attention to him, Ac 8:10
Caesarea and **p** a courtesy call Ac 25:13
But the centurion **p** attention to Ac 27:11
will be **p** back for whatever Col 3:25
has **p** tithes through Abraham, Heb 7:9
Pay her back the way she also **p**, Rv 18:6

PAIN *(40)*
when they were still in **p**, Gn 34:25
"I gave birth to him in **p**." 1Ch 4:9
so that I will not cause any **p**." 1Ch 4:10
in unrelenting **p** that I have not Jb 6:10
feels only the **p** of his own body Jb 14:22
man writhes in **p** all his days; Jb 15:20
on his bed with **p** and constant Jb 33:19
my loins are full of burning **p**, Ps 38:7
and my **p** is constantly with me. Ps 38:17
good, and my **p** intensified. Ps 39:2
talk about the **p** of those You Ps 69:26
me—poor and in **p**—let Your Ps 69:29
They struck me, but I feel no **p**! Pr 23:35
and put away **p** from your flesh, Ec 11:10
p and agony will seize ⌊them⌋; Is 13:8
LORD gives you rest from your **p**, Is 14:3
day of disease and incurable **p**. Is 17:11
P grips me, like the pain of a Is 21:3
like the **p** of a woman in labor. Is 21:3
pregnant, we writhed in **p**; Is 26:18
who gave birth to you in **p**. Is 51:2
she was in **p**, she delivered Is 66:7
agony! Oh, the **p** in my heart! My Jr 4:19
struck them, but they felt no **p**. Jr 5:3
has seized us—**p** like a woman Jr 6:24
Why has my **p** become unending, Jr 15:18
injury? Your **p** has no cure! I Jr 30:15
LORD has added misery to my **p**! Jr 45:3
has seized him—**p**, like a woman Jr 50:43
Is there any **p** like mine, which Lm 1:12
look at my **p**. My young men Lm 1:18
pierced ⌊with **p**⌋ because the Lm 4:9
and will writhe in great **p**, Zch 9:5
labor she has **p** because her time Jn 16:21
if I cause you **p**, then who will 2Co 2:2
I wouldn't have **p** from those who 2Co 2:3
anyone has caused **p**, he has not 2Co 2:5
he has not caused **p** to me, 2Co 2:5
gnawed their tongues from **p** Rv 16:10
and **p** will exist no longer, Rv 21:4

PAINFUL *(7)*
it by means of **p** labor all the Gn 3:17
and thighs with **p** and incurable Dt 28:35
How **p** honest words can be! Jb 6:25
briers or **p** thorns from all Ezk 28:24
come to you on another **p** visit. 2Co 2:1
enjoyable at the time, but **p**. Heb 12:11
and severely **p** sores broke out Rv 16:2

PAINS *(21)*
I will intensify your labor **p**; Gn 3:16
because her labor **p** came on her. 1Sm 4:19
have taken great **p** to provide 1Ch 22:14
live in terror of all my **p**. Jb 9:28
and my gnawing **p** never abate. Jb 30:17
Many **p** come to the wicked, Ps 32:10
writhes and cries out in her **p**, Is 26:17
and He carried our **p**; Is 53:4
labor **p** seize you, as ⌊they Jr 13:21
groan when labor **p** come on you, Jr 22:23
and labor **p** have seized her Jr 49:24
Labor **p** come on him. He is not a Hs 13:13
various diseases and intense **p**, Mt 4:24
are the beginning of birth **p**. Mt 24:8
are the beginning of birth **p**. Mk 13:8
up, ending the **p** of death, Ac 2:24
together with labor **p** until now. Rm 8:22
I am in the **p** of childbirth for Gl 4:19
labor **p** on a pregnant woman, 1Th 5:3
pierced themselves with many **p**. 1Tm 6:10
of their **p** and their sores Rv 16:11

PAINT *(1)*
you enlarge your eyes with **p**? Jr 4:30

PAINTED *(3)*
about it, so she **p** her eyes, 2Kg 9:30
with cedar and **p** with vermilion. Jr 22:14
You bathed, **p** your eyes, and Ezk 23:40

PAIR *(16)*
under the ⌊first⌋ **p** of branches Ex 25:35
under the ⌊second⌋ **p** of branches Ex 25:35
under the ⌊third⌋ **p** of branches Ex 25:35
under the first **p** of branches Ex 37:21
under the second **p** of branches Ex 37:21
under the third **p** of branches Ex 37:21
ground ⌊it⌋ on a **p** of grinding Nm 11:8
Do not take a **p** of millstones or Dt 24:6
a torch between each **p** of tails. Jdg 15:4
He had a **p** of saddled donkeys 2Sm 16:1
and two **p** at the storehouses. 1Ch 26:17
Then take a **p** of scales and Ezk 5:1
tree between each **p** of cherubim. Ezk 41:18
needy person for a **p** of sandals. Am 2:6
the needy for a **p** of sandals and Am 8:6
a **p** of turtledoves or two young Lk 2:24

PAIRED *(2)*
They are to be **p** at the bottom, Ex 26:24
They were **p** at the bottom and Ex 36:29

PAIRS *(6)*
are to take with you seven **p**, Gn 7:2
and seven **p**, male and female, of Gn 7:3
he sees riders—**p** of horsemen, Is 21:7
riders come—horsemen in **p**." Is 21:9

send them out in **p** and gave them Mk 6:7
ahead of Him in **p** to every town Lk 10:1

PALACE *(134)*

went into his **p**, and didn't even Ex 7:23
will come up and go into your **p**, Ex 8:3
Pharaoh's **p** and his officials' Ex 8:24
and belonged to Pharaoh's **p**? 1Sm 2:27
he began to rave inside the **p**. 1Sm 18:10
in his **p** holding a spear. 1Sm 19:9
and they built a **p** for David. 2Sm 5:11
into his **p** and the LORD had 2Sm 7:1
around on the roof of the **p**. 2Sm 11:2
So Uriah left the **p**, and a gift 2Sm 11:8
the door of the **p** with all his 2Sm 11:9
sent word to Tamar at the **p**: 2Sm 13:7
to take care of the **p**. 2Sm 15:16
hear from the king's **p** to Zadok 2Sm 15:35
he left to take care of the **p**. 2Sm 16:21
to restore the king to his **p**? 2Sm 19:11
king has come to his **p** safely, 2Sm 19:30
came to his **p** in Jerusalem, 2Sm 20:3
care of the **p** and placed them 2Sm 20:3
he finished building his **p**, 1Kg 3:1
Ahishar, in charge of the **p**; 1Kg 4:6
Solomon's own **p** where he would 1Kg 7:8
LORD, the royal **p**, and all that 1Kg 9:1
LORD's temple and the royal **p**— 1Kg 9:10
temple, his own **p**, the 1Kg 9:15
wisdom, the **p** he had built, 1Kg 10:4
and the king's **p** and into harps 1Kg 10:12
weaned him in Pharaoh's **p**, 1Kg 11:20
the treasuries of the royal **p**. 1Kg 14:26
the entrance to the king's **p**. 1Kg 14:27
of the royal **p** and put it 1Kg 15:18
of the royal **p** and burned down 1Kg 16:18
down the royal **p** over himself. 1Kg 16:18
who was in charge of the **p**. 1Kg 18:3
search your **p** and your servants' 1Kg 20:6
next to the **p** of Ahab king 1Kg 21:1
since it is right next to my **p**. 1Kg 21:2
Ahab went to his **p** resentful and 1Kg 21:4
the ivory **p** he built, and all 1Kg 22:39
overseer of the **p**, the overseer 2Kg 10:5
protection for the king's **p**. 2Kg 11:5
providing protection for the **p**. 2Kg 11:6
Entrance to the king's **p**, 2Kg 11:16
entered the king's **p** by way of 2Kg 11:19
by the sword in the king's **p**. 2Kg 11:20
temple and in the king's **p**, 2Kg 12:18
the treasuries of the king's **p**, 2Kg 14:14
at the citadel of the king's **p**. 2Kg 15:25
of the king's **p** and sent ⌊them⌋ 2Kg 16:8
canopy they had built in the **p**, 2Kg 16:18
the treasuries of the king's **p**. 2Kg 18:15
who was in charge of the **p**, 2Kg 18:18
who was in charge of the **p**, 2Kg 18:37
who was in charge of the **p**, 2Kg 19:2
nothing in his **p** and in all his 2Kg 20:13
"What have they seen in your **p**?" 2Kg 20:15
have seen everything in my **p**. 2Kg 20:15
in your **p** and all that your 2Kg 20:17
eunuchs in the **p** of the king 2Kg 20:18
the treasures of the king's **p**, 2Kg 24:13
temple, the king's **p**, and all 2Kg 25:9
carpenters to build a **p** for him. 1Ch 14:1
David had settled into his **p**, 1Ch 17:1
LORD and a royal **p** for himself, 2Ch 2:1
LORD and a royal **p** for himself. 2Ch 2:12
LORD's temple and the royal **p**. 2Ch 7:11
and for his own **p** succeeded. 2Ch 7:11
LORD's temple and his own **p**— 2Ch 8:1
wisdom, the **p** he had built, 2Ch 9:3
for the king's **p** and into harps 2Ch 9:11
the treasuries of the royal **p**. 2Ch 12:9
the entrance to the king's **p**. 2Ch 12:10
and the royal **p** and sent it to 2Ch 16:2
the king's **p** and also his sons 2Ch 21:17
third are to be at the king's **p**, 2Ch 23:5
Horses' Gate to the king's **p**, 2Ch 23:15
the king's **p** through the upper 2Ch 23:20
the treasures of the king's **p**, 2Ch 25:24
Azrikam governor of the **p**, 2Ch 28:7
temple and the **p** of the king 2Ch 28:21
from the upper **p** of the king, Neh 3:25
of the royal **p** for all the Est 1:5
the women of King Ahasuerus' **p**. Est 1:9
taken to the **p** and placed under Est 2:8
her from the **p** and transferred Est 2:9
her from the harem to the **p**. Est 2:13
in the royal **p** in the tenth Est 2:16
because you are in the king's **p**. Est 4:13
courtyard of the **p** facing it. Est 5:1
court of the **p** to ask the king Est 6:4
wine and ⌊went to⌋ the **p** garden. Est 7:7
returned from the **p** garden to Est 7:8
the queen while I am in the **p**?" Est 7:8
exercised⌋ great power in the **p**, Est 9:4
they enter the king's **p**. Ps 45:15
deceitfully will live in my **p**; Ps 101:7
the beams of His **p** on the waters Ps 104:3
waters the mountains from His **p**; Ps 104:13
that are carved in the **p** style. Ps 144:12
who is in charge of the **p**, Is 22:15
For the **p** will be forsaken, Is 32:14
who was in charge of the **p**, Is 36:3
who was in charge of the **p**, Is 36:22
who was in charge of the **p**, Is 37:2
nothing in his **p** and in all his Is 39:2
"What have they seen in your **p**?" Is 39:4
have seen everything in my **p**. Is 39:4
in your **p** and all that your Is 39:6
be eunuchs in the **p** of the king Is 39:7
Go down to the **p** of the king of Jr 22:1
the gates of this **p** riding on Jr 22:4
the one who builds his **p** through Jr 22:13
I will build myself a massive **p**, Jr 22:14
from the king's **p** to the LORD's Jr 26:10
in the **p** of the king of Judah, Jr 27:18
in the **p** of the king of Judah, Jr 27:21
courtyard in the **p** of the king Jr 32:2
chamber in the king's **p**. Jr 36:12
employed in the king's **p**, Jr 38:7
from the king's **p** and spoke to Jr 38:8
to the king's **p** to a place below Jr 38:11
remain in the **p** of Judah's king Jr 38:22
down the king's **p** and the Jr 39:8
of Pharaoh's **p** at Tahpanhes. Jr 43:9
the king's **p**, all the houses Jr 52:13
of serving in the king's **p**— Dn 1:4
house and flourishing in my **p**. Dn 4:4
roof of the royal **p** in Babylon, Dn 4:29
of the king's **p** wall next to Dn 5:5
king went to his **p** and spent the Dn 6:18
send fire against Hazael's **p**, Am 1:4
opened, and the **p** erodes away. Nah 2:6
assembled in the **p** of the high Mt 26:3
kept under guard in Herod's **p**. Ac 23:35

PALACE-COMPLEX *(1)*

his entire **p** after 13 years 1Kg 7:1

PALACES *(12)*

down all its **p**, and destroyed 2Ch 36:19
ivory **p** harps bring you joy. Ps 45:8
hands, yet it lives in kings' **p**. Pr 30:28
and jackals, in the luxurious **p**. Is 13:22
siege towers and stripped its **p**. Is 23:13
Her **p** will be overgrown with Is 34:13
city and the **p** of Judah's kings Jr 33:4
up all its **p** and destroyed its Lm 2:5
the walls of her **p** over to the Lm 2:7
forgotten his Maker and built **p**; Hs 8:14
soft clothes are in kings' **p**. Mt 11:8
live in luxury are in royal **p**. Lk 7:25

PALAL *(1)*

P son of Uzai ⌊made repairs⌋ Neh 3:25

PALATE *(4)*

test words as the **p** tastes food? Jb 12:11
tongue will form words on my **p**. Jb 33:2
test words as the **p** tastes food? Jb 34:3
honeycomb is sweet to your **p**; Pr 24:13

PALE *(11)*

combers and weavers will turn **p**. Is 19:9
his face will no longer be **p**. Is 29:22
labor and every face turned **p**? Jr 30:6
his face turned **p**, and his Dn 5:6
face turned **p**, and his nobles Dn 5:9
terrify you or your face be **p**. Dn 5:10
and my face turned **p**, but I kept Dn 7:28
face grew deathly **p**, and I was Dn 10:8
before them; all faces turn **p**. Jl 2:6
loins shake, every face grows **p**! Nah 2:10
and there was a **p** green horse. Rv 6:8

PALLBEARERS *(1)*

open coffin, and the **p** stopped. Lk 7:14

PALLETS *(1)*

them on beds and **p** so that when Ac 5:15

PALLU *(5)*

Hanoch, **P**, Hezron, and Carmi. Gn 46:9
Hanoch and **P**, Hezron and Carmi. Ex 6:14
the Palluite clan from **P**; Nm 26:5
The son of **P** was Eliab. Nm 26:8
Hanoch, **P**, Hezron, and Carmi. 1Ch 5:3

PALLUITE *(1)*

the **P** clan from Pallu; Nm 26:5

PALM *(39)*

oil and pour it into his left **p**. Lv 14:15
oil in his left **p** and sprinkle Lv 14:16
in his **p** the priest will Lv 14:17
in the priest's **p** he is to put Lv 14:18
some of the oil into his left **p**. Lv 14:26
oil in his left **p** seven times Lv 14:27
of the oil in his **p** on the right Lv 14:28
in the priest's **p** he is to put Lv 14:29
majestic trees—**p** fronds, Lv 23:40
sit under the **p** tree of Deborah Jdg 4:5
p trees and flower blossoms— 1Kg 6:29
p trees and flower blossoms on 1Kg 6:32
over the cherubim and **p** trees. 1Kg 6:32
p trees and flower blossoms on 1Kg 6:35
and **p** trees on the plates of its 1Kg 7:36
go into his **p** and pierce it. 2Kg 18:21
decorated with **p** trees and 2Ch 3:5
olive, myrtle, **p**, and ⌊other⌋ Neh 8:15
thrive like a **p** tree and grow Ps 92:12
Your stature is like a **p** tree; Sg 7:7
I will climb the **p** tree and take Sg 7:8
p branch and reed in a single Is 9:14
head or tail, **p** or reed, will be Is 19:15
diadem in the **p** of your God. Is 62:3
was decorated with **p** trees. Ezk 40:16
and **p** trees had the same Ezk 40:22
It had **p** trees on its pilasters, Ezk 40:26
were decorated with **p** trees. Ezk 40:31
decorated with **p** trees on each Ezk 40:34
decorated with **p** trees on each Ezk 40:37
with cherubim and **p** trees. Ezk 41:18
There was a **p** tree between each Ezk 41:18
toward the **p** tree on one side Ezk 41:19
Cherubim and **p** trees were carved Ezk 41:20
Cherubim and **p** trees were carved Ezk 41:25
windows and **p** trees on both Ezk 41:26
the date **p**, and the apple—all Jl 1:12
they took **p** branches and went Jn 12:13
white with **p** branches in their Rv 7:9

PALMS *(9)*

springs of water and 70 date **p** Ex 15:27
of water and 70 date **p** at Elim, Nm 33:9
the City of **P**, as far as Zoar. Dt 34:3
from the City of **P** to the Jdg 1:16
possession of the City of **P**. Jdg 3:13
head and the **p** of his hands were 1Sm 5:4
feet, and the **p** of her hands. 2Kg 9:35
the City of **P**, among their 2Ch 28:15
you on the **p** of My hands; Is 49:16

PALTI *(2)*
(AKA PALTIEL)

P son of Raphu from the tribe of Nm 13:9
David's wife, to **P** son of Laish, 1Sm 25:44

PALTIEL *(2)*
(AKA PALTI)

P son of Azzan, a leader from Nm 34:26
her husband, **P** son of Laish. 2Sm 3:15

PALTITE *(1)*
(AKA PELONITE)

Helez the **P**, Ira son of Ikkesh 2Sm 23:26

PAMPERED *(2)*

A slave **p** from his youth will Pr 29:21
longer be called **p** and spoiled. Is 47:1

PAMPHYLIA *(5)*

Phrygia and **P**, Egypt and the Ac 2:10
Paphos and came to Perga in **P**. Ac 13:13
through Pisidia and came to **P**. Ac 14:24
them in **P** and had not gone Ac 15:38
the open sea off Cilicia and **P**, Ac 27:5

PAN *(3)*

offering ⌊prepared⌋ in a **p**, Lv 2:7
prepared in a **p** or on a griddle Lv 7:9
brought the **p** and set it down 2Sm 13:9

PANEL *(1)*
body is an ivory **p** covered with Sg 5:14

PANELED *(8)*
p it with boards and planks of 1Kg 6:9
he **p** the interior temple walls 1Kg 6:15
It was **p** above with cedar at the 1Kg 7:3
It was **p** with cedar from the 1Kg 7:7
larger room he **p** with cypress 2Ch 3:5
and it will be **p** with cedar and Jr 22:14
⌊They were **p**⌋ from the ground to Ezk 41:16
to live in your **p** houses, Hg 1:4

PANELING *(1)*
cedar **p** inside the temple was 1Kg 6:18

PANELS *(3)*
second door had two folding **p**. 1Kg 6:34
of the doors had two swinging **p**. Ezk 41:24
There were two **p** for one door Ezk 41:24

PANIC *(12)*
inhabitants of Canaan will **p**; Ex 15:15
city of Gath, causing a great **p**. 1Sm 5:9
the **p** in the Philistine camp 1Sm 14:19
throw him into a **p**, and all the 2Sm 17:2
P, pit, and trap await you, Jr 48:43
who flees from the **p** will fall Jr 48:44
to run; **p** has gripped her. Jr 49:24
have experienced **p** and pitfall, Lm 3:47
There will be **p** on the mountains Ezk 7:7
at this time their **p** is here. Mc 7:4
every horse with **p** and its rider Zch 12:4
that day a great **p** from the LORD Zch 14:13

PANICKED *(1)*
they **p**. "The gods have entered 1Sm 4:7

PANICKING *(3)*
in the land is **p** because of you. Jos 2:9
land is also **p** because of us." Jos 2:24
they saw the **p** troops scattering 1Sm 14:16

PANS *(1)*
lampstands, the **p**, and the drink Jr 52:19

PANT *(2)*
The thirsty **p** for his children's Jb 5:5
I **p** with open mouth because I Ps 119:131

PANTING *(2)*
p, ⌊it returns⌋ to its place Ec 1:5
barren heights **p** for air like Jr 14:6

PAPER *(1)*
want to do so with **p** and ink. 2Jn 12

PAPERS *(2)*
give divorce **p** and to send her Mt 19:7
divorce **p** and send her away. Mk 10:4

PAPHOS *(2)*
the whole island as far as **P**, Ac 13:6
sail from **P** and came to Perga Ac 13:13

PAPYRUS *(4)*
she got a **p** basket for him and Ex 2:3
Does **p** grow where there is no Jb 8:11
sweep by like boats made of **p**, Jb 9:26
will be grass, reeds, and **p**. Is 35:7

PARABLE *(34)*
understanding a proverb or a **p**, Pr 1:6
riddle and speak a **p** to the Ezk 17:2
Now speak a **p** to the rebellious Ezk 24:3
listen to the **p** of the sower: Mt 13:18
He presented another **p** to them: Mt 13:24
He presented another **p** to them: Mt 13:31
He told them another **p**: Mt 13:33
anything to them without a **p**, Mt 13:34
Explain the **p** of the weeds in Mt 13:36
to Him, "Explain this **p** to us." Mt 15:15
Listen to another **p**: Mt 21:33
Now learn this **p** from the fig Mt 24:32
Do you not understand this **p**? Mk 4:13
or what **p** can we use to describe Mk 4:30
not speak to them without a **p**. Mk 4:34
disciples asked Him about the **p**. Mk 7:17
He had said this **p** against them, Mk 12:12
Learn this **p** from the fig tree: Mk 13:28
He also told them a **p**: Lk 5:36
He also told them a **p**: Lk 6:39
from every town, He said in a **p**: Lk 8:4
Him, "What does this **p** mean?" Lk 8:9
This is the meaning of the **p**: Lk 8:11
Then He told them a **p**: Lk 12:16
You telling this **p** to us or to Lk 12:41
And He told this **p**: Lk 13:6
He told a **p** to those who were Lk 14:7
So He told them this **p**: Lk 15:3
told them a **p** on the need for Lk 18:1
He also told this **p** to some who Lk 18:9
on to tell a **p** because He was Lk 19:11
began to tell the people this **p**: Lk 20:9
He had told this **p** against them, Lk 20:19
Then He told them a **p**: Lk 21:29

PARABLES *(17)*
I gave **p** through the prophets. Hs 12:10
He told them many things in **p**, Mt 13:3
"Why do You speak to them in **p**?" Mt 13:10
reason I speak to them in **p**, Mt 13:13
crowds all these things in **p**, Mt 13:34
I will open My mouth in **p**; Mt 13:35
When Jesus had finished these **p**, Mt 13:53
and the Pharisees heard His **p**, Mt 21:45
more Jesus spoke to them in **p**: Mt 22:1
them and spoke to them in **p**: Mk 3:23
He taught them many things in **p**, Mk 4:2
Him asked Him about the **p**. Mk 4:10
outside, everything comes in **p** Mk 4:11
you understand any of the **p**? Mk 4:13
to them with many **p** like these, Mk 4:33
He began to speak to them in **p**: Mk 12:1
but to the rest it is in **p**, Lk 8:10

PARADE *(1)*
p him on the horse through the Est 6:9

PARADED *(1)*
Mordecai and **p** him through the Est 6:11

PARADISE *(4)*
branches are a **p** of pomegranates Sg 4:13
Today you will be with Me in **p**." Lk 23:43
was caught up into **p**. 2Co 12:4
life, which is in the **p** of God. Rv 2:7

PARAH *(1)*
Avvim, **P**, Ophrah, Jos 18:23

PARALLEL *(1)*
the chambers, **p** to them, toward Ezk 42:7

PARALYTIC *(8)*
brought to Him a **p** lying on a Mt 9:2
Jesus told the **p**, "Have courage, Mt 9:2
He told the **p**, "Get up, pick Mt 9:6
they came to Him bringing a **p**, Mk 2:3
on which the **p** was lying. Mk 2:4
Jesus told the **p**, "Son, your Mk 2:5
to say to the **p**, 'Your sins are Mk 2:9
to forgive sins," He told the **p**, Mk 2:10

PARALYTICS *(1)*
the epileptics, and the **p**. Mt 4:24

PARALYZED *(12)*
he had a seizure and became **p**. 1Sm 25:37
my servant is lying at home **p**, Mt 8:6
He saw a man who had a **p** hand. Mt 12:10
man was there who had a **p** hand. Mk 3:1
He told the man with the **p** hand, Mk 3:3
on a stretcher a man who was **p**. Lk 5:18
He told the **p** man, "I tell you: Lk 5:24
there whose right hand was **p**. Lk 6:6
told the man with the **p** hand, Lk 6:8
blind, lame, and **p**—waiting for Jn 5:3
many who were **p** and lame were Ac 8:7
who was **p** and had been bedridden Ac 9:33

PARAN *(11)*
settled in the Wilderness of **P**, Gn 21:21
stopped in the Wilderness of **P**. Nm 10:12
camped in the Wilderness of **P**. Nm 12:16
Wilderness of **P** at the LORD's Nm 13:3
the Wilderness of **P** at Kadesh. Nm 13:26
Suph, between **P** and Tophel, Dt 1:1
them⌋ from Mount **P** and came with Dt 33:2
down to the Wilderness of **P**. 1Sm 25:1
out from Midian and went to **P**. 1Kg 11:18
with them from **P** and went to 1Kg 11:18
the Holy One from Mount **P**. Hab 3:3

PARAPET *(1)*
we will build a silver **p** on it. Sg 8:9

PARCEL *(1)*
Shechem in the **p** of land Jacob Jos 24:32

PARCHED *(14)*
and a wadi becomes **p** and dry, Jb 14:11
to satisfy the **p** wasteland and Jb 38:27
my throat is **p**. My eyes fail, Ps 69:3
I am like **p** land before You. Ps 143:6
like cold water to a **p** throat. Pr 25:25
the masses are **p** with thirst. Is 5:13
and the river will be **p** and dry. Is 19:5
and Egypt's canals will be **p**. Is 19:6
the **p** ground will become a pool Is 35:7
their tongues are **p** with thirst. Is 41:17
satisfy you in a **p** land, and Is 58:11
comes but dwells in the **p** places Jr 17:6
sit on **p** ground, resident of the Jr 48:18
like a desert and like a **p** land, Hs 2:3

PARCHMENT *(1)*
large piece of **p** and write on it Is 8:1

PARCHMENTS *(1)*
the scrolls, especially the **p**. 2Tm 4:13

PARDON *(5)*
Please **p** the wrongdoing of this Nm 14:19
may the LORD **p** your servant: 2Kg 5:18
may the LORD **p** your servant in 2Kg 5:18
my sin and **p** my transgression? Jb 7:21
I will **p** their bloodguilt, Jl 3:21

PARDONED *(5)*
I have **p** ⌊them⌋ as you Nm 14:20
p King Jehoiachin of Judah ⌊and 2Kg 25:27
iniquity has been **p**, and she has Is 40:2
p King Jehoiachin of Judah and Jr 52:31
which⌋ I have not **p**, for the Jl 3:21

PARENT *(1)*
who loves the **p** also loves his 1Jn 5:1

PARENTS *(23)*
up against their **p** and have them Mt 10:21
rise up against **p** and put them Mk 13:12
When the **p** brought in the child Lk 2:27
Every year His **p** traveled to Lk 2:41
but His **p** did not know it. Lk 2:43
When His **p** saw Him, they were Lk 2:48
Her **p** were astounded, but He Lk 8:56
p or children because of the Lk 18:29
You will even be betrayed by **p**, Lk 21:16
this man or his **p**, that he was Jn 9:2
this man nor his **p** sinned," Jn 9:3
summoned the **p** of the one who Jn 9:18
was born blind," his **p** answered. Jn 9:20
His **p** said these things because Jn 9:22
This is why his **p** said, "He's of Jn 9:23
of evil, disobedient to **p**, Rm 1:30
to save up for their **p**, 2Co 12:14
parents, but **p** for their 2Co 12:14
obey your **p** in the Lord, Eph 6:1
obey your **p** in everything, Col 3:20
first and to repay their **p**, 1Tm 5:4
disobedient to **p**, ungrateful, 2Tm 3:2
hidden by his **p** for three months Heb 11:23

PARKS *(1)*
I made gardens and **p** for myself Ec 2:5

PARMASHTA *(1)*
P, Arisai, Aridai, and Vaizatha. Est 9:9

PARMENAS *(1)*
Nicanor, Timon, **P**, and Nicolaus, Ac 6:5

PARNACH *(1)*
Eli-zaphan son of **P**, a leader Nm 34:25

PAROSH *(2)*
Beside him Pedaiah son of **P**, Neh 3:25
P, Pahath-moab, Elam, Zattu, Neh 10:14

PAROSH'S *(4)*
P descendants 2,172 Ezr 2:3
Zechariah, from **P** descendants, Ezr 8:3
The Israelites: **P** descendants: Ezr 10:25
P descendants 2,172 Neh 7:8

PARSHANDATHA *(1)*
including **P**, Dalphon, Aspatha, Est 9:7

PARSIN *(1)*
MENE, MENE, TEKEL, **P** Dn 5:25

PART *(66)*
and the smooth **p** of his neck. Gn 27:16
there and took **p** of what he had Gn 32:13
in the best **p** of the land. Gn 47:6
in the best **p** of the land, Gn 47:11
on the **p** of the Egyptians. Gn 50:11
burn up any **p** of it that does Ex 12:10
some people left **p** of it until Ex 16:20
the holiest **p** of the fire Lv 2:3
the holiest **p** of the fire Lv 2:10
He will present **p** of the Lv 3:3
then present **p** of the fellowship Lv 3:9
will present **p** of his offering Lv 3:14
on the **p** of the Israelites Lv 24:8

and sells **p** of his property, Lv 25:25
the LORD any **p** of a field that Lv 27:16
that is not **p** of his inherited Lv 27:22
to redeem any **p** of this tenth, Lv 27:31
lived in that ⌊**p** of the⌋ hill Nm 14:45
you must present **p** of it as an Nm 18:26
The best **p** of the tenth is to be Nm 18:29
the best **p** of the tenth, Nm 18:30
have presented the best **p** of it, Nm 18:32
offering that is **p** of the Nm 28:23
p of our allotted inheritance Nm 36:3
chose the best ⌊**p**⌋ for himself, Dt 33:21
from the central **p** of the land, Jdg 9:37
living in a remote **p** of the hill Jdg 19:1
with the best **p** of all of the 1Sm 2:29
Our **p** will be to hand him over 1Sm 23:20
the king had no **p** in the killing 2Sm 3:37
also considered **p** of Benjamin, 2Sm 4:2
wheel axles were **p** of the water 1Kg 7:32
They dedicated **p** of the plunder 1Ch 26:27
You may have no **p** with us in Ezr 4:3
the latter **p** of Job's life more Jb 42:12
me in the lowest **p** of the Pit, Ps 88:6
p Your heavens and come down. Ps 144:5
the land must take **p** in this Ezk 45:16
this choice ⌊**p**⌋ of the land, Ezk 48:14
of the feet were **p** iron and part Dn 2:42
part iron and **p** fired clay— Dn 2:42
p of the kingdom will be strong, Dn 2:42
strong, and **p** will be brittle. Dn 2:42
to the lowest **p** of the vessel Jnh 1:5
wouldn't have taken **p** with them Mt 23:30
with no **p** of it in darkness, Lk 11:36
worthy to take **p** in that age Lk 20:35
would steal **p** of what was put Jn 12:6
you, you have no **p** with Me." Jn 13:8
four parts, a **p** for each soldier Jn 19:23
he kept back **p** of the proceeds Ac 5:2
and keep back **p** of the proceeds Ac 5:3
You have no **p** or share in this Ac 8:21
realized that one **p** of them were Ac 23:6
and the other **p** were Pharisees, Ac 23:6
law in every **p** of us and bore Rm 7:5
on your **p**, live at peace Rm 12:18
you, and in **p** I believe it. 1Co 11:18
the body is not one **p** but many. 1Co 12:14
And if they were all the same **p**, 1Co 12:19
we know in **p**, and we prophesy 1Co 13:9
in part, and we prophesy in **p**. 1Co 13:9
Now I know in **p**, but then I will 1Co 13:12
working of each individual **p**. Eph 4:16
sending him—a **p** of myself— Phm 12
is a small **p** ⌊of the body⌋, Jms 3:5

PARTAKE *(1)*
If I **p** with thanks, why am I 1Co 10:30

PARTED *(6)*
they were not **p** in life or in 2Sm 1:23
He **p** the heavens and came down, 2Sm 22:10
which **p** to the right and left. 2Kg 2:8
and they **p** to the right and the 2Kg 2:14
He **p** the heavens and came down, Ps 18:9
that they **p** company, Ac 15:39

PARTHIANS *(1)*
P, Medes, Elamites; Ac 2:9

PARTIAL *(5)*
Do not be **p** to the poor or give Lv 19:15
will be **p** to no one, and I will Jb 32:21
God is not **p** to princes and does Jb 34:19
a **p** hardening has come to Israel Rm 11:25
the **p** will come to an end. 1Co 13:10

PARTIALITY *(14)*
Do not show **p** when rendering Dt 1:17
no **p** and taking no bribe. Dt 10:17
justice or show **p** ⌊to anyone⌋. Dt 16:19
no injustice or **p** or taking 2Ch 19:7
Would you show **p** to Him or argue Jb 13:8
you if you secretly showed **p**. Jb 13:10
and show **p** to the wicked? Ps 82:2
not good to show **p** to the guilty Pr 18:5
not good to show **p** in judgment. Pr 24:23
It is not good to show **p**— Pr 28:21
ways but are showing **p** in ⌊your⌋ Mal 2:9
to no one, for You don't show **p**. Mt 22:16
for You don't show **p** but teach Mk 12:14
and You don't show **p**, but teach Lk 20:21

PARTIALLY *(1)*
as you have **p** understood us— 2Co 1:14

PARTICIPANT *(1)*
and also a **p** in the glory about 1Pt 5:1

PARTICIPATE *(2)*
circumcised, and then he may **p**; Ex 12:48
Don't **p** in the fruitless works Eph 5:11

PARTICIPATING *(2)*
kept you from **p** in bloodshed 1Sm 25:26
you kept me from **p** in bloodshed 1Sm 25:33

PARTICIPATION *(1)*
pray⌋ that your **p** in the faith Phm 6

PARTICULAR *(3)*
On this **p** day you are not to do Lv 23:28
self-denial on this **p** day, Lv 23:29
a **p** matter may the LORD pardon 2Kg 5:18

PARTIES *(5)*
be an oath between two **p**— Gn 26:28
between the two **p** is to come Ex 22:9
Raiding **p** went out from the 1Sm 13:17
the raiding **p** were terrified. 1Sm 14:15
who were leaders of raiding **p**: 2Sm 4:2

PARTISANS *(2)*
and all his **p** were dispersed and Ac 5:36
and all his **p** were scattered. Ac 5:37

PARTLY *(4)*
its feet were **p** iron and partly Dn 2:33
partly iron and **p** fired clay. Dn 2:33
p of a potter's fired clay and Dn 2:41
fired clay and **p** of iron— Dn 2:41

PARTNER *(10)*
To be a thief's **p** is to hate Pr 29:24
your trading **p** because of ⌊your Ezk 27:12
your trading **p** because of your Ezk 27:16
your trading **p** because of your Ezk 27:18
your marriage **p** and your wife Mal 2:14
may become a **p** in its benefits. 1Co 9:23
he is my **p** and co-worker serving 2Co 8:23
ask you, true **p**, to help these Php 4:3
So if you consider me a **p**, Phm 17
your brother and **p** in the Rv 1:9

PARTNERS *(9)*
the prostitute with many **p**— Jr 3:1
of Kedar were your business **p**, Ezk 27:21
to their **p** in the other boat Lk 5:7
sons, who were Simon's **p**. Lk 5:10
the sacrifices **p** in the altar? 1Co 10:18
want you to be **p** with demons! 1Co 10:20
and **p** of the promise in Christ Eph 3:6
do not become their **p**. Eph 5:7
and you are all **p** with me in Php 1:7

PARTNERSHIP *(2)*
For what **p** is there between 2Co 6:14
because of your **p** in the gospel Php 1:5

PARTRIDGE *(3)*
who pursues a **p** in the mountains 1Sm 26:20
The sand **p** will make her nest Is 34:15
is ⌊like⌋ a **p** that hatches eggs Jr 17:11

PARTS *(33)*
terraces to the surrounding **p**, 1Ch 11:8
The **p** of the burnt offering were 2Ch 4:6
P of his skin are eaten away; Jb 18:13
You who created my inward **p**; Ps 139:13
searching the innermost **p**. Pr 20:27
cleanse the innermost **p**. Pr 20:30
in the remotest **p** of the North. Is 14:13
from the remotest **p** of the north Ezk 38:6
in the remotest **p** of the north— Ezk 38:15
the remotest **p** of the north. Ezk 39:2
the richest **p** of the province Dn 11:24
lose one of the **p** of your body Mt 5:29
lose one of the **p** of your body Mt 5:30
and divided them into four **p**, Jn 19:23
Egypt and the **p** of Libya near Ac 2:10
not offer any **p** of it to sin as Rm 6:13
and all the **p** of yourselves to Rm 6:13
you offered the **p** of yourselves Rm 6:19
law in the **p** of my body, Rm 7:23
law of sin in the **p** of my body. Rm 7:23
as we have many **p** in one body, Rm 12:4
and all the **p** do not have the Rm 12:4
the body is one and has many **p**, 1Co 12:12
and all the **p** of that body, 1Co 12:12
But now God has placed the **p**, 1Co 12:18
there are many **p**, yet one body. 1Co 12:20
those **p** of the body that seem to 1Co 12:22
And those **p** of the body that we 1Co 12:23
unpresentable **p** have a better 1Co 12:23
our presentable **p** have no need 1Co 12:24
to the lower **p** of the earth? Eph 4:9
among the **p** of our ⌊bodies⌋ Jms 3:6
great city split into three **p**, Rv 16:19

PARTY *(9)*
If the guilty **p** deserves to be Dt 25:2
to the other **p** in order to make Ru 4:7
of a raiding **p** when David killed 1Kg 11:24
He was in the traveling **p**, Lk 2:44
belonged to the **p** of the Ac 5:17
from the **p** of the Pharisees Ac 15:5
the Pharisees' **p** got up and Ac 23:9
the strictest **p** of our religion Ac 26:5
those from the circumcision **p**. Gl 2:12

PARUAH *(1)*
son of **P**, in Issachar; 1Kg 4:17

PARVAIM *(1)*
and the gold was the gold of **P**. 2Ch 3:6

PAS-DAMMIM *(1)*
was with David at **P** when the 1Ch 11:13

PASACH *(1)*
P, Bimhal, and Ashvath. 1Ch 7:33

PASEAH *(2)*
Beth-rapha, **P**, and Tehinnah 1Ch 4:12
Joiada son of **P** and Meshullam Neh 3:6

PASEAH'S *(2)*
descendants, **P** descendants, Ezr 2:49
descendants, **P** descendants, Neh 7:51

PASHHUR *(11)*
Jeroham, son of **P**, son of 1Ch 9:12
P, Amariah, Malchijah, Neh 10:3
son of **P**, son of Malchijah Neh 11:12
P the priest, the son of Immer Jr 20:1
So **P** had Jeremiah the prophet Jr 20:2
when **P** released Jeremiah from Jr 20:3
The LORD does not call you **P**, Jr 20:3
As for you, **P**, and all who live Jr 20:6
Zedekiah sent **P** son of Malchijah Jr 21:1
Gedaliah son of **P**, Jucal son of Jr 38:1
and **P** son of Malchijah heard the Jr 38:1

PASHHUR'S *(3)*
P descendants 1,247 Ezr 2:38
and Elasah from **P** descendants. Ezr 10:22
P descendants 1,247 Neh 7:41

PASS *(115)*
a wind to **p** over the earth, Gn 8:1
that I will not **p** beyond this Gn 31:52
and you will not **p** beyond this Gn 31:52
I will **p** through the land of Ex 12:12
the blood, I will **p** over you. Ex 12:13
He will **p** over the door and not Ex 12:23
powerful arm until Your people **p** Ex 15:16
the people whom You purchased **p** Ex 15:16
goodness to **p** in front of you, Ex 33:19
of your children **p** through ⌊the Lv 18:21
no sword will **p** through your Lv 26:6
son or daughter **p** through the Dt 18:10
control of the **p** at Michmash. 1Sm 13:23
sides of the **p** that Jonathan 1Sm 14:4
down a mountain **p** hidden from 1Sm 25:20
would come and **p** along 2Sm 17:17
chariot at Gur **P** near Ibleam, 2Kg 9:27
made his son **p** through the fire 2Kg 16:3
and daughters **p** through the fire 2Kg 17:17
I have now brought it to **p**, 2Kg 19:25
He made his son **p** through the 2Kg 21:6
or his daughter **p** through the 2Kg 23:10
My days **p** more swiftly than a Jb 7:6
You have set limits he cannot **p**, Jb 14:5
a few years will **p** before I go Jb 16:22
way so that I cannot **p** through; Jb 19:8
people shudder, then **p** away. Jb 34:20
that no air can **p** between them. Jb 41:16
and the senseless also **p** away. Ps 49:10
are right when You **p** sentence; Ps 51:4
so that all who **p** by pick its Ps 80:12
As they **p** through the Valley of Ps 84:6
All who **p** by plunder him; Ps 89:41
they **p** quickly and we fly away. Ps 90:10
a garment, and they will **p** away. Ps 102:26
Then none who **p** by will say, Ps 129:8
own nets, while I **p** ⌊safely⌋ Ps 141:10
an order that will never **p** away. Ps 148:6
Turn away from it, and **p** it by. Pr 4:15
calling to those who **p** by, Pr 9:15

storms that **p** over the Negev, Is 21:1
will **p** through every morning— Is 28:19
His rock will **p** away because of Is 31:9
and majestic vessels will not **p**. Is 33:21
no one will **p** through it forever Is 34:10
I have now brought it to **p**, Is 37:26
with you when you **p** through the Is 43:2
and ⌊when you **p**⌋ through the Is 43:2
road for the redeemed to **p** over? Is 51:10
They roar but cannot **p** over it. Jr 5:22
P your hand once more like a Jr 6:9
so no one can **p** through? Jr 9:12
Many nations will **p** by this city Jr 22:8
and daughters **p** through ⌊the Jr 32:35
will again **p** under the hands Jr 33:13
two in order to **p** between its Jr 34:18
you will certainly come to **p**. Jr 44:29
he let the opportune moment **p**. Jr 46:17
nothing to you, all you who **p** Lm 1:12
All who **p** by ⌊scornfully⌋ clap Lm 2:15
so that no prayer can **p** through. Lm 3:44
the cup will **p** to you as well; Lm 4:21
P throughout the city of Ezk 9:4
P through the city after him and Ezk 9:5
a message and bring it to **p**." Ezk 12:25
animals to **p** through the land Ezk 14:15
a sword **p** through it, so that Ezk 14:17
Will you **p** judgment against Ezk 20:4
them, will you **p** judgment, son Ezk 20:4
every firstborn **p** through ⌊the Ezk 20:26
children **p** through the fire, Ezk 20:31
I will make you **p** under the rod Ezk 20:37
son of man, will you **p** judgment? Ezk 22:2
Will you **p** judgment against the Ezk 22:2
will you **p** judgment against Ezk 23:36
they bore to Me **p** through ⌊the Ezk 23:37
No human foot will **p** through it, Ezk 29:11
animal foot will **p** through it. Ezk 29:11
basis to **p** through the land Ezk 39:14
When they **p** through the land and Ezk 39:15
dominion that will not **p** away, Dn 7:14
for I will **p** among you. Am 5:17
will break out, **p** through the Mc 2:13
Their King will **p** through before Mc 2:13
mowed down, and he will **p** away. Nah 1:12
by like the wind and **p** through. Hab 1:11
with no one to **p** through. Zph 3:6
He will **p** through the sea of Zch 10:11
Until heaven and earth **p** away, Mt 5:18
of a letter will **p** from the law Mt 5:18
that no one could **p** that way. Mt 8:28
certainly not **p** away until all Mt 24:34
Heaven and earth will **p** away, Mt 24:35
but My words will never **p** away. Mt 24:35
let this cup **p** from Me. Mt 26:39
if this cannot **p** unless I drink Mt 26:42
the sea and wanted to **p** by them. Mk 6:48
certainly not **p** away until all Mk 13:30
Heaven and earth will **p** away, Mk 13:31
but My words will never **p** away. Mk 13:31
the hour might **p** from Him. Mk 14:35
and earth to **p** away than for one Lk 16:17
who want to **p** over from here to Lk 16:26
He was about to **p** that way. Lk 19:4
certainly not **p** away until all Lk 21:32
Heaven and earth will **p** away, Lk 21:33
but My words will never **p** away. Lk 21:33
Him the right to **p** judgment, Jn 5:27
is necessary to **p** through many Ac 14:22
in the Spirit to **p** through Ac 19:21
to see you when I **p** through, Rm 15:24
to you after I **p** through 1Co 16:5
we may appear to **p** the test, 2Co 13:7
because he will **p** away like a Jms 1:10
heavens will **p** away with a loud 2Pt 3:10

PASSAGE *(8)*

stood in a narrow **p** between the Nm 22:24
grant me ⌊safe⌋ **p** until I reach Neh 2:7
in the **p** about the burning bush, Mk 12:26
indicated ⌊in the **p**⌋ about the Lk 20:37
the Scripture **p** he was reading Ac 8:32
He also says in another **p**, Ac 13:35
Again, in that **p** ⌊He says⌋, They Heb 4:5
said in another **p**, You are a Heb 5:6

PASSAGEWAY *(2)*

with a **p** in front of them, Ezk 42:11
at the beginning of the **p**, Ezk 42:12

PASSED *(84)*

Abram **p** through the land to the Gn 12:6
torch appeared and **p** between the Gn 15:17
is why you have **p** your servant's Gn 18:5
Sarah had **p** the age of Gn 18:11
its cave **p** from the Hittites Gn 23:20
shone on him as he **p** by Penuel— Gn 32:31
When Midianite traders **p** by, Gn 37:28
Seven days **p** after the LORD Ex 7:25
for He **p** over the houses of the Ex 12:27
you with My hand until I have **p** Ex 33:22
Then the LORD **p** in front of him Ex 34:6
a year has **p** after its sale; Lv 25:29
The land we **p** through to explore Nm 13:32
The land we **p** through and Nm 14:7
saw that Aaron had **p** away, Nm 20:29
land of Egypt and **p** through the Dt 29:16
Kadesh-barnea, **p** Hezron, Jos 15:3
and **p** it east of Janoah Jos 16:6
p Zebulun and the valley of Jos 19:27
everyone who **p** by them on the Jdg 9:25
20 years had **p** since the ark had 1Sm 7:2
Some time **p**. David's son Absalom 2Sm 13:1
four years had **p**, Absalom said 2Sm 15:7
"They **p** by toward the water," 2Sm 17:20
all the men **p** by and followed 2Sm 20:13
Sheba **p** through all the tribes 2Sm 20:14
At that moment, the LORD **p** by. 1Kg 19:11
Some time **p** after these events. 1Kg 21:1
So whenever he **p** by, he stopped 2Kg 4:8
was in Lebanon **p** by and trampled 2Kg 14:9
and they **p** sentence on him. 2Kg 25:6
day until two full years **p**. 2Ch 21:19
in Lebanon **p** by and trampled 2Ch 25:18
p his sons through the fire in 2Ch 33:6
A wind **p** by me, and I shuddered Jb 4:15
when no foreigner **p** among them. Jb 15:19
prosperity has **p** by like a cloud Jb 30:15
Then I **p** by and noticed he was Ps 37:36
our fathers have **p** down to us. Ps 78:3
God repeats what has **p**. Ec 3:15
I had just **p** them when I found Sg 3:4
while until the wrath has **p**. Is 26:20
Harvest has **p**, summer has ended, Jr 8:20
of the land who **p** between the Jr 34:19
king **p** sentence on him ⌊there⌋ Jr 39:5
Hamath, and he **p** sentence on him Jr 52:9
I **p** by you and saw you lying in Ezk 16:6
Then I **p** by you and saw you, Ezk 16:8
sexual favors on everyone who **p** Ezk 16:15
them up when you **p** them through Ezk 16:21
to everyone who **p** by and Ezk 16:25
that has been **p** against my lord Dn 4:24
At that time Jesus **p** through the Mt 12:1
p along the Sea of Galilee. Mt 15:29
Those who **p** by were yelling Mt 27:39
Those who **p** by were yelling Mk 15:29
But He **p** right through the crowd Lk 4:30
He **p** through the grainfields. Lk 6:1
he **p** by on the other side. Lk 10:31
and saw him, **p** by on the other Lk 10:32
p between Samaria and Galilee. Lk 17:11
judgment but has **p** from death to Jn 5:24
40 years had **p**, an angel Ac 7:30
many days had **p**, the Jews Ac 9:23
they **p** the first and second Ac 12:10
went outside and **p** one street, Ac 12:10
Then they **p** through Pisidia and Ac 14:24
they **p** through both Phoenicia Ac 15:3
some time had **p**, Paul said to Ac 15:36
And when he had **p** through those Ac 20:2
two years had **p**, Felix received Ac 24:27
some days had **p**, King Agrippa Ac 25:13
much time had **p**, and the voyage Ac 27:9
restraint God **p** over the sins Rm 3:25
cloud, all **p** through the sea, 1Co 10:1
Lord what I also **p** on to you: 1Co 11:23
For I **p** on to you as most 1Co 15:3
things have **p** away, and look, 2Co 5:17
priest who has **p** through the Heb 4:14
know that we have **p** from death 1Jn 3:14
first woe has **p**. There are still Rv 9:12
The second woe has **p**. Rv 11:14
and the first earth had **p** away, Rv 21:1
the previous things have **p** away. Rv 21:4

PASSERBY *(3)*

every **p** will be appalled and 1Kg 9:8
every **p** will be appalled and 2Ch 7:21
A **p** who meddles in a quarrel Pr 26:17

PASSES *(29)*

the LORD **p** through to strike Ex 12:23
when My glory **p** by, I will put Ex 33:22
which **p** under the ⌊shepherd's⌋ Lv 27:32
one who often **p** by here is a 2Kg 4:9
If He **p** by me, I wouldn't see Jb 9:11
If He **p** by and throws ⌊someone⌋ Jb 11:10
conceal me until Your anger **p**, Jb 14:13
overpower him, and he **p** Jb 14:20
of Your wings until danger **p**. Ps 57:1
a wind that **p** and does not Ps 78:39
years are like yesterday that **p** Ps 90:4
when the wind **p** over it, it Ps 103:16
the whirlwind **p**, the wicked are Pr 10:25
overwhelming scourge **p** through, Is 28:15
overwhelming scourge **p** through, Is 28:18
Every time it **p** through, it will Is 28:19
scorched that no one **p** through. Jr 9:10
everyone who **p** by it will be Jr 18:16
Everyone who **p** by it will be Jr 19:8
Everyone who **p** by her will be Jr 49:17
Everyone who **p** through Babylon Jr 50:13
where no human being **p** through. Jr 51:43
in the sight of everyone who **p** Ezk 5:14
in the sight of everyone who **p** Ezk 36:34
and tears as it **p** through, Mc 5:8
effect and the day **p** like chaff, Zph 2:2
Everyone who **p** by her jeers and Zph 2:15
the mouth **p** into the stomach Mt 15:17
because when he **p** the test he Jms 1:12

PASSING *(33)*

leaders were **p** ⌊in review with 1Sm 29:2
and his men were **p** ⌊in review⌋ 1Sm 29:2
There were men **p** by who saw the 1Kg 13:25
As the king was **p** by, he cried 1Kg 20:39
Be careful **p** by this place, 2Kg 6:9
of Israel was **p** by on the wall, 2Kg 6:26
as he was **p** by on the wall, 2Kg 6:30
fish of the sea **p** through the Ps 8:8
his days are like a **p** shadow. Ps 144:4
or who hires those **p** by, is like Pr 26:10
inhabitants of what is **p** away. Is 38:11
with no one **p** through, I will Is 60:15
Woe to us, for the day is **p**; Jr 6:4
The days keep **p** by, and every Ezk 12:22
with no one **p** through ⌊it⌋ for Ezk 14:15
desolate, with no one **p** through. Ezk 33:28
from those who are **p** through Mc 2:8
iniquity and **p** over rebellion Mc 7:18
When they heard that Jesus was **p** Mt 20:30
As He was **p** along by the Sea of Mk 1:16
as they were **p** by, they saw the Mk 11:20
country, who was **p** by, to carry Mk 15:21
a crowd **p** by, he inquired Lk 18:36
"Jesus the Nazarene is **p** by," Lk 18:37
Jericho and was **p** through. Lk 19:1
When he saw Jesus **p** by, he said, Jn 1:36
As He was **p** by, He saw a man Jn 9:1
in Azotus, and **p** through, he was Ac 8:40
For as I was **p** through and Ac 17:23
in its current form is **p** away. 1Co 7:31
want to see you now just in **p**, 1Co 16:7
the darkness is **p** away and the 1Jn 2:8
world with its lust is **p** away, 1Jn 2:17

PASSION *(1)*

Who can control her **p**? Jr 2:24

PASSIONATE *(1)*

you if you are **p** for what is 1Pt 3:13

PASSIONS *(6)*

them over to degrading **p**. Rm 1:26
sinful **p** operated through the Rm 7:5
flesh with its **p** and desires. Gl 5:24
Flee from youthful **p**, and pursue 2Tm 2:22
led along by a variety of **p**, 2Tm 3:6
of various **p** and pleasures, Ti 3:3

PASSOVER *(78)*

it is the LORD's **P**. Ex 12:11
and slaughter the **P** lamb. Ex 12:21
'It is the **P** sacrifice to the Ex 12:27
This is the statute of the **P**: Ex 12:43
or hired hand may not eat the **P**. Ex 12:45
wants to celebrate the LORD's **P**, Ex 12:48
sacrifice of the **P** Festival must Ex 34:25
The **P** to the LORD comes in the Lv 23:5
observe the **P** at its appointed Nm 9:2

the Israelites to observe the **P**, Nm 9:4
not observe the **P** on that day. Nm 9:6
still observe the **P** to the LORD. Nm 9:10
observe the **P** according to all Nm 9:12
observe the **P** is to be cut off Nm 9:13
to observe the **P** to the LORD, Nm 9:14
to the **P** statute and its Nm 9:14
The **P** to the LORD comes in the Nm 28:16
day after the **P** the Israelites Nm 33:3
celebrate the **P** to the LORD your Dt 16:1
LORD your God a **P** animal from Dt 16:2
to sacrifice the **P** animal in any Dt 16:5
only sacrifice the **P** animal at Dt 16:6
they kept the **P** on the evening Jos 5:10
The day after **P** they ate Jos 5:11
Keep the **P** of the LORD your God 2Kg 23:21
such **P** had ever been kept from 2Kg 23:22
this **P** was observed to the LORD 2Kg 23:23
to observe the **P** of the LORD God 2Ch 30:1
to observe the **P** of the LORD 2Ch 30:2
to observe the **P** of the LORD God 2Ch 30:5
They slaughtered the **P** lamb on 2Ch 30:15
slaughtering the **P** ⌊lambs⌋ for 2Ch 30:17
had eaten the **P** contrary to what 2Ch 30:18
the LORD's **P** and slaughtered 2Ch 35:1
and slaughtered the **P** ⌊lambs⌋ on 2Ch 35:1
Slaughter the **P** ⌊lambs⌋, 2Ch 35:6
for the **P** sacrifices for all the 2Ch 35:7
gave 2,600 **P** sacrifices and 300 2Ch 35:8
donated 5,000 **P** sacrifices for 2Ch 35:9
they slaughtered the **P** ⌊lambs⌋, 2Ch 35:11
They roasted the **P** ⌊lambs⌋ with 2Ch 35:13
observing the **P** and for offering 2Ch 35:16
also observed the **P** at that time 2Ch 35:17
P had been observed like it in 2Ch 35:18
ever observed a **P** like the one 2Ch 35:18
reign, this **P** was observed. 2Ch 35:19
observed the **P** on the fourteenth Ezr 6:19
They killed the **P** lamb for Ezr 6:20
you are to celebrate the **P**, Ezk 45:21
know that the **P** takes place Mt 26:2
to prepare the **P** so You may eat Mt 26:17
celebrating the **P** at your place Mt 26:18
them and prepared the **P**. Mt 26:19
days it was the **P** and the Mk 14:1
when they sacrifice the **P** lamb, Mk 14:12
and prepare the **P** so You may eat Mk 14:12
Me to eat the **P** with My Mk 14:14
them, and they prepared the **P**. Mk 14:16
to Jerusalem for the **P** Festival. Lk 2:41
which is called **P**, was drawing Lk 22:1
came when the **P** lamb had to be Lk 22:7
and prepare the **P** meal for us, Lk 22:8
can eat the **P** with My disciples? Lk 22:11
them, and they prepared the **P**. Lk 22:13
to eat this **P** with you before I Lk 22:15
The Jewish **P** was near, so Jesus Jn 2:13
in Jerusalem at the **P** Festival, Jn 2:23
the **P**, a Jewish festival, was Jn 6:4
The Jewish **P** was near, and many Jn 11:55
purify themselves before the **P**. Jn 11:55
days before the **P**, Jesus came to Jn 12:1
Before the **P** Festival, Jesus Jn 13:1
defiled and unable to eat the **P**. Jn 18:28
one ⌊prisoner⌋ to you at the **P**. Jn 18:39
the preparation day for the **P**, Jn 19:14
out to the people after the **P**. Ac 12:4
For Christ our **P** has been 1Co 5:7
he instituted the **P** and the Heb 11:28

PAST *(41)*

do not go on **p** your servant. Gn 18:3
either in the **p** or recently or Ex 4:10
been with you this **p** 40 years, Dt 2:7
consider the years long **p**. Dt 32:7
In the **p** you wanted David to be 2Sm 3:17
all his servants marched **p** him. 2Sm 15:18
from Gath—marched **p** the king. 2Sm 15:18
Gittite marched **p** with all his 2Sm 15:22
all the people were marching **p**. 2Sm 15:23
were marching **p** on the road that 2Sm 15:23
people had finished marching **p**. 2Sm 15:24
In the **p** they used to say, 2Sm 20:18
p the Tower of the Ovens to the Neh 12:38
days of old, years long **p**. Ps 77:5
speak mysteries from the **p**— Ps 78:2
Do not hold **p** sins against us; Ps 79:8
For now the winter is **p**; Sg 2:11
my love gliding **p** my lips and Sg 7:9
will meditate on the ⌊**p**⌋ terror: Is 33:18
Tell us the **p** events, so that we Is 41:22
and from times **p**, so that we Is 41:26
The **p** events have indeed Is 42:9
I have kept silent from ages **p**; Is 42:14
Do not remember the **p** events, Is 43:18
declared the **p** events long ago; Is 48:3
up as in days **p**, as in Is 51:9
them all the days of the **p**. Is 63:9
He remembered the days of the **p**, Is 63:11
the **p** events will not be Is 65:17
like all His ⌊**p**⌋ wonderful works Jr 21:2
children will be as in **p** days; Jr 30:20
and led me **p** its four corners Ezk 46:21
existed in ages **p** and never will Jl 2:2
In **p** generations He allowed all Ac 14:16
decided to sail **p** Ephesus so he Ac 20:16
if she is **p** marriageable age, 1Co 7:36
But in the **p**, when you didn't Gl 4:8
even though she was **p** the age, Heb 11:11
For in the **p**, the holy women who 1Pt 3:5
who in the **p** were disobedient, 1Pt 3:20
the cleansing from his **p** sins. 2Pt 1:9

PASTORS *(1)*

some **p** and teachers, Eph 4:11

PASTRY *(1)*

It tasted like a **p** cooked with Nm 11:8

PASTURE *(31)*

had gone to **p** their father's Gn 37:12
took you from the **p** and from 2Sm 7:8
valley to seek **p** for their 1Ch 4:39
found rich, good **p**, and the land 1Ch 4:40
there was **p** for their flocks 1Ch 4:41
took you from the **p** and from 1Ch 17:7
a flock and provide **p** for ⌊it⌋. Jb 24:2
against the sheep of Your **p**? Ps 74:1
sheep of Your **p**, will thank You Ps 79:13
and we are the people of His **p**, Ps 95:7
His people, the sheep of His **p**. Ps 100:3
Where do you **p** your sheep? Sg 1:7
and **p** your young goats near the Sg 1:8
wild asses, and a **p** for flocks, Is 32:14
a peaceful **p**, a tent that does Is 33:20
Sharon will be a **p** for flocks, Is 65:10
Each will **p** his own portion. Jr 6:3
and scatter the sheep of My **p**!" Jr 23:1
the LORD is destroying their **p**. Jr 25:36
are like stags that find no **p**; Lm 1:6
will make Rabbah a **p** for camels Ezk 25:5
I will tend them with good **p**, Ezk 34:14
feed in rich **p** on the mountains Ezk 34:14
for you to feed on the good **p**? Ezk 34:18
rest of the **p** with your feet? Ezk 34:18
flock of My **p**, and I am your Ezk 34:31
When they had **p**, they became Hs 13:6
confusion since they have no **p**. Jl 1:18
they will find **p** there. Zph 2:7
But they will **p** and lie down, Zph 3:13
come in and go out and find **p**. Jn 10:9

PASTURELAND *(4)*

The open **p** around their cities Lv 25:34
to live in and **p** around the Nm 35:2
roams the mountains for its **p**, Jb 39:8
so that its **p** became plunder. Ezk 36:5

PASTURELANDS *(108)*

and their **p** will be for their Nm 35:3
The **p** of the cities you are to Nm 35:4
to them as **p** for the cities. Nm 35:5
will be 48, along with their **p**. Nm 35:7
along with **p** for their cattle Jos 14:4
with their **p** for our livestock." Jos 21:2
cities with their **p** from their Jos 21:3
with their **p** around them to Jos 21:8
its surrounding **p** in the hill Jos 21:11
with its **p**, Libnah with its Jos 21:13
pasturelands, Libnah with its **p**, Jos 21:13
Jattir with its **p**, Eshtemoa with Jos 21:14
Eshtemoa with its **p**, Jos 21:14
Holon with its **p**, Debir with its Jos 21:15
pasturelands, Debir with its **p**, Jos 21:15
Ain with its **p**, Juttah with its Jos 21:16
Juttah with its **p**, and Jos 21:16
and Beth-shemesh with its **p**— Jos 21:16
Gibeon with its **p**, Geba with its Jos 21:17
pasturelands, Geba with its **p**, Jos 21:17
with its **p**, and Almon with Jos 21:18
Almon with its **p**—four cities. Jos 21:18
cities with their **p** were for the Jos 21:19
with its **p** in the hill country Jos 21:21
of Ephraim, Gezer with its **p**, Jos 21:21
with its **p**, and Beth-horon Jos 21:22
and Beth-horon with its **p**— Jos 21:22
Elteke with its **p**, Gibbethon Jos 21:23
Gibbethon with its **p**, Jos 21:23
with its **p**, and Gath-rimmon Jos 21:24
and Gath-rimmon with its **p**— Jos 21:24
with its **p** and Gath-rimmon Jos 21:25
and Gath-rimmon with its **p**— Jos 21:25
cities with their **p** were for the Jos 21:26
with its **p** in Bashan, Jos 21:27
and Beeshterah with its **p**— Jos 21:27
Kishion with its **p**, Daberath Jos 21:28
Daberath with its **p**, Jos 21:28
with its **p**, and En-gannim Jos 21:29
and En-gannim with its **p**— Jos 21:29
Mishal with its **p**, Abdon with Jos 21:30
pasturelands, Abdon with its **p**, Jos 21:30
with its **p**, and Rehob with Jos 21:31
Rehob with its **p**—four cities. Jos 21:31
with its **p**, Hammoth-dor with its Jos 21:32
with its **p**, and Kartan with its Jos 21:32
with its **p**—three cities. Jos 21:32
13 cities with their **p** were for Jos 21:33
with its **p**, Kartah with its Jos 21:34
pasturelands, Kartah with its **p**, Jos 21:34
Dimnah with its **p**, and Nahalal Jos 21:35
with its **p**—four cities. Jos 21:35
Bezer with its **p**, Jahzah with Jos 21:36
pasturelands, Jahzah with its **p**, Jos 21:36
with its **p**, and Mephaath Jos 21:37
with its **p**—four cities. Jos 21:37
with its **p**, Mahanaim with its Jos 21:38
Mahanaim with its **p**, Jos 21:38
with its **p**, and Jazer with Jos 21:39
Jazer with its **p**—four cities Jos 21:39
all with their **p** for the Levites Jos 21:41
had its own surrounding **p**; Jos 21:42
and throughout the **p** of Sharon. 1Ch 5:16
of Judah and its surrounding **p**, 1Ch 6:55
Libnah and its **p**, Jattir, 1Ch 6:57
Jattir, Eshtemoa and its **p**, 1Ch 6:57
Hilen and its **p**, Debir and its 1Ch 6:58
pasturelands, Debir and its **p**, 1Ch 6:58
and its **p**, and Beth-shemesh 1Ch 6:59
and Beth-shemesh and its **p**. 1Ch 6:59
they were given⌋ Geba and its **p**, 1Ch 6:60
Alemeth and its **p**, and Anathoth 1Ch 6:60
and Anathoth and its **p**. 1Ch 6:60
and their **p** to the Levites. 1Ch 6:64
with its **p** in the hill country 1Ch 6:67
of Ephraim, Gezer and its **p**, 1Ch 6:67
Jokmeam and its **p**, Beth-horon 1Ch 6:68
Beth-horon and its **p**, 1Ch 6:68
Aijalon and its **p**, and 1Ch 6:69
and Gath-rimmon and its **p**. 1Ch 6:69
Aner and its **p**, and Bileam and 1Ch 6:70
Bileam and its **p** ⌊were given⌋ to 1Ch 6:70
Golan in Bashan and its **p**, 1Ch 6:71
and its **p** from the families 1Ch 6:71
they received⌋ Kedesh and its **p**, 1Ch 6:72
Daberath and its **p**, 1Ch 6:72
Ramoth and its **p**, and Anem and 1Ch 6:73
and Anem and its **p**. 1Ch 6:73
they received⌋ Mashal and its **p**, 1Ch 6:74
pasturelands, Abdon and its **p**, 1Ch 6:74
Hukok and its **p**, and Rehob and 1Ch 6:75
and Rehob and its **p**. 1Ch 6:75
Kedesh in Galilee and its **p**, 1Ch 6:76
Hammon and its **p**, and Kiriathaim 1Ch 6:76
and Kiriathaim and its **p**. 1Ch 6:76
Rimmono and its **p** and Tabor and 1Ch 6:77
and Tabor and its **p**. 1Ch 6:77
Bezer in the desert and its **p**, 1Ch 6:78
pasturelands, Jahzah and its **p**, 1Ch 6:78
Kedemoth and its **p**, and Mephaath 1Ch 6:79
and Mephaath and its **p**. 1Ch 6:79
Ramoth in Gilead and its **p**, 1Ch 6:80
Mahanaim and its **p**, 1Ch 6:80
Heshbon and its **p**, and Jazer and 1Ch 6:81
and Jazer and its **p**. 1Ch 6:81
Levites in their cities with **p**, 1Ch 13:2
Levites left their **p** and their 2Ch 11:14
will become **p** with caves for Zph 2:6

PASTURES *(15)*

He lets me lie down in green **p**; Ps 23:2

glory of the **p**, will fade away Ps 37:20
The wilderness **p** overflow, Ps 65:12
The **p** are clothed with flocks, Ps 65:13
us seize God's **p** for ourselves." Ps 83:12
graze as ⌊if in⌋ their own **p**, Is 5:17
p abandoned and forsaken like a Is 27:10
cattle will graze in open **p**. Is 30:23
and their **p** will be on all the Is 49:9
the well-watered **p** of Israel. Ezk 45:15
has consumed the **p** of the Jl 1:19
has consumed the **p** of the Jl 1:20
the wilderness **p** have turned Jl 2:22
the **p** of the shepherds mourn, Am 1:2
in a scrubland, surrounded by **p**. Mc 7:14

PASTURING *(3)*
while he was **p** the donkeys of Gn 36:24
are **p** ⌊the flocks⌋ at Shechem. Gn 37:13
where they are **p** ⌊their flocks⌋? Gn 37:16

PATARA *(1)*
to Rhodes, and from there to **P**. Ac 21:1

PATCH *(7)*
and there is a **p** of raw flesh in Lv 13:10
and the **p** made raw by the burn Lv 13:24
Like scarecrows in a cucumber **p**, Jr 10:5
because the **p** pulls away from Mt 9:16
one sews a **p** of unshrunk cloth Mk 2:21
new **p** pulls away from the old Mk 2:21
No one tears a **p** from a new Lk 5:36

PATCHED *(1)*
p sandals on their feet and Jos 9:5

PATCHES *(1)*
No one **p** an old garment with Mt 9:16

PATH *(72)*
a viper beside the **p**, that bites Gn 49:17
stand on the **p** to oppose him. Nm 22:22
standing on the **p** with a drawn Nm 22:23
she turned off the **p** and went Nm 22:23
hit her to return her to the **p**. Nm 22:23
standing in the **p** with a drawn Nm 22:31
in the **p** to confront me. Nm 22:34
aside from the **p** I command you Dt 11:28
turn from the **p** I have commanded Dt 31:29
As he was walking up the **p**, 2Kg 2:23
to a man whose **p** is hidden, Jb 3:23
waits⌋ for him along the **p**. Jb 18:10
on the ancient **p** that wicked men Jb 22:15
explained ⌊the **p** to⌋ success! Jb 26:3
No bird of prey knows that **p**; Jb 28:7
the rain and a **p** for the Jb 28:26
They tear up my **p**; they Jb 30:13
or take the **p** of sinners, or Ps 1:1
You reveal the **p** of life to me; Ps 16:11
LORD, and lead me on a level **p**. Ps 27:11
himself on a **p** that is not good Ps 36:4
have not strayed from Your **p**. Ps 44:18
and Your **p** through the great Ps 77:19
He cleared a **p** for His anger. Ps 78:50
by the right **p** to go to a city Ps 107:7
me stay on the **p** of Your Ps 119:35
from every evil **p** to follow Your Ps 119:101
for my feet and a light on my **p**. Ps 119:105
a net along the **p** and set snares Ps 140:5
Along this **p** I travel they have Ps 142:3
them or set foot on their **p**, Pr 1:15
and integrity—every good **p**. Pr 2:9
set foot on the **p** of the wicked; Pr 4:14
The **p** of the righteous is like Pr 4:18
consider the **p** for your feet, Pr 4:26
doesn't consider the **p** of life; Pr 5:6
instruction is on the **p** to life, Pr 10:17
of the blameless clears his **p**, Pr 11:5
is life in the **p** of Pr 12:28
but another **p** leads to death. Pr 12:28
for the one who leaves the **p**; Pr 15:10
but the **p** of the upright is a Pr 15:19
walks a straight **p**. Pr 15:21
discerning the **p** of life leads Pr 15:24
snares on the **p** of the crooked; Pr 22:5
don't know the **p** of the wind, Ec 11:5
The **p** of the righteous is level; Is 26:7
clear a straight **p** for the Is 26:7
for You in the **p** of Your Is 26:8
will be for him who walks the **p**. Is 35:8
touching the **p** with his feet. Is 41:3
and a **p** through surging waters, Is 43:16
have not known the **p** of peace, Is 59:8
people who walk in the wrong **p**, Is 65:2
consumes everything ⌊in its **p**⌋. Lm 2:3
of them ⌊had taken⌋ the same **p**. Ezk 23:13
followed the **p** of your sister, Ezk 23:31
lurk like a leopard on the **p**. Hs 13:7
goes on his own **p**, and they do Jl 2:7
each man proceeds on his own **p**. Jl 2:8
and block the **p** of the needy. Am 2:7
His **p** is in the whirlwind and Nah 1:3
some seeds fell along the **p**, Mt 13:4
is the one sown along the **p**. Mt 13:19
Some seed fell along the **p**, Mk 4:4
ones along the **p** where the word Mk 4:15
sowing, some fell along the **p**; Lk 8:5
seeds along the **p** are those who Lk 8:12
came near the **p** down the Mount Lk 19:37
and the **p** of peace they have not Rm 3:17
By abandoning the straight **p**, 2Pt 2:15
have followed the **p** of Balaam, 2Pt 2:15

PATHETIC *(1)*
What are these **p** Jews doing? Neh 4:2

PATHROS *(5)*
Assyria, Egypt, **P**, Cush, Elam, Is 11:11
Memphis, and in the land of **P**: Jr 44:1
land of Egypt at **P** answered Jr 44:15
them back to the land of **P**, Ezk 29:14
I will make **P** desolate, set fire Ezk 30:14

PATHRUSIM *(2)*
P, Casluhim (the Philistines Gn 10:14
P, Casluhim (the Philistines 1Ch 1:12

PATHS *(39)*
and stand watch over all my **p**, Jb 13:27
has veiled my **p** with darkness. Jb 19:8
its ways or stay on its **p**. Jb 24:13
He stands watch over all my **p**." Jb 33:11
familiar with the **p** to its home? Jb 38:20
My steps are on Your **p**; Ps 17:5
along the right **p** for His name's Ps 23:3
to me, LORD; teach me Your **p**. Ps 25:4
Such are the **p** of all who pursue Pr 1:19
He may guard the **p** of justice Pr 2:8
the right **p** to walk in ways Pr 2:13
whose **p** are crooked, and whose Pr 2:15
none reach the **p** of life. Pr 2:19
and keep to the **p** of the Pr 2:20
will guide you on the right **p**. Pr 3:6
and all her **p**, peaceful. Pr 3:17
I am guiding you on straight **p**. Pr 4:11
and He considers all his **p**. Pr 5:21
don't stray onto her **p**. Pr 7:25
along the **p** of justice, Pr 8:20
go straight ahead on their **p**: Pr 9:15
so that we may walk in His **p**." Is 2:3
confuse the direction of your **p**. Is 3:12
and taught Him the **p** of justice? Is 40:14
guide them on **p** they have not Is 42:16
and wretchedness are in their **p**. Is 59:7
Ask about the ancient **p**: Jr 6:16
walk on ⌊new⌋ **p**, not the highway Jr 18:15
like slippery **p** in the gloom. Jr 23:12
He has made my **p** crooked. Lm 3:9
so that she cannot find her **p**. Hs 2:6
ways so we may walk in His **p**." Mc 4:2
the Lord; make His **p** straight!" Mt 3:3
the Lord; make His **p** straight!" Mk 1:3
the Lord; make His **p** straight! Lk 3:4
revealed the **p** of life to me; Ac 2:28
the straight **p** of the Lord? Ac 13:10
and wretchedness are in their **p**, Rm 3:16
make straight **p** for your feet, Heb 12:13

PATHWAY *(1)*
the way! Leave the **p**. Rid us of Is 30:11

PATHWAYS *(2)*
They will feed along the **p**, Is 49:9
sink down. His **p** are ancient. Hab 3:6

PATIENCE *(19)*
P is better than power, and Pr 16:32
A person's insight gives him **p**, Pr 19:11
can be persuaded through **p**, Pr 25:15
for you to try the **p** of men? Is 7:13
you also try the **p** of my God? Is 7:13
In Your **p**, don't take me away. Jr 15:15
restraint, and **p**, not Rm 2:4
we eagerly wait for it with **p**. Rm 8:25
with much **p** objects of wrath Rm 9:22
by knowledge, by **p**, by kindness, 2Co 6:6
love, joy, peace, **p**, kindness, Gl 5:22
gentleness, with **p**, accepting Eph 4:2
all endurance and **p**, with joy Col 1:11
humility, gentleness, and **p**, Col 3:12
the utmost **p** as an example to 1Tm 1:16
purpose, faith, **p**, love, and 2Tm 3:10
with great **p** and teaching. 2Tm 4:2
an example of suffering and **p**. Jms 5:10
regard the **p** of our Lord as ⌊an 2Pt 3:15

PATIENT *(15)*
You were **p** with them for many Neh 9:30
my future, that I should be **p**? Jb 6:11
Be **p** with me a little longer, Jb 36:2
A **p** person ⌊shows⌋ great Pr 14:29
p spirit is better than a proud Ec 7:8
and said, 'Be **p** with me, and I Mt 18:26
begging him, 'Be **p** with me, and Mt 18:29
in hope; be **p** in affliction; be Rm 12:12
Love is **p**; love is kind. Love 1Co 13:4
the weak, be **p** with everyone. 1Th 5:14
everyone, able to teach, and **p**, 2Tm 2:24
be **p** until the Lord's coming. Jms 5:7
earth and is **p** with it until it Jms 5:7
also must be **p**. Strengthen your Jms 5:8
delay, but is **p** with you, not 2Pt 3:9

PATIENTLY *(6)*
I waited **p** for the LORD, and He Ps 40:1
are all who wait **p** for Him. Is 30:18
I beg you to listen to me **p**. Ac 26:3
those who by **p** doing good seek Rm 2:7
after waiting **p**, Abraham Heb 6:15
when God **p** waited in the days of 1Pt 3:20

PATMOS *(1)*
island called **P** because of God's Rv 1:9

PATRIARCH *(2)*
speak to you about the **p** David: Ac 2:29
even Abraham the **p** gave a tenth Heb 7:4

PATRIARCHAL *(3)*
and heads of their **p** families. 1Ch 5:24
them according to **p** family, 2Ch 25:5
to the strict view of our **p** law. Ac 22:3

PATRIARCHS *(2)*
Jacob, and Jacob with the 12 **p**. Ac 7:8
The **p** became jealous of Joseph Ac 7:9

PATROBAS *(1)*
Phlegon, Hermes, **P**, Hermas, and Rm 16:14

PATROL *(3)*
LORD has sent to **p** the earth." Zch 1:10
they wanted to go **p** the earth, Zch 6:7
LORD said, "Go, **p** the earth." Zch 6:7

PATROLLED *(2)*
trees, "We have **p** the earth, and Zch 1:11
So they **p** the earth. Zch 6:7

PATTERN *(8)*
according to the **p** the LORD had Nm 8:4
the inside and outside, was a **p** Ezk 41:17
Let them measure ⌊its⌋ **p**, Ezk 43:10
according to the **p** he had seen. Ac 7:44
the heart that **p** of teaching you Rm 6:17
Hold on to the **p** of sound 2Tm 1:13
into the same **p** of disobedience. Heb 4:11
according to the **p** that was Heb 8:5

PAU *(1)*
(AKA PAI)
His city was **P**, and his wife's Gn 36:39

PAUL *(159)*
(AKA SAUL)
also called **P**—filled with Ac 13:9
P and his companions set sail Ac 13:13
P motioned with his hand and Ac 13:16
followed **P** and Barnabas, Ac 13:43
to oppose what **P** was saying Ac 13:45
Then **P** and Barnabas boldly said: Ac 13:46
against **P** and Barnabas Ac 13:50
and heard **P** speaking. After Ac 14:9
⌊**P**⌋ said in a loud voice, Ac 14:10
the crowds saw what **P** had done, Ac 14:11
Zeus, and **P**, Hermes, because he Ac 14:12
Barnabas and **P** tore their robes Ac 14:14
over the crowds and stoned **P**, Ac 14:19
But after **P** and Barnabas had Ac 15:2
they arranged for **P** and Barnabas Ac 15:2
to Barnabas and **P** describing all Ac 15:12
to Antioch with **P** and Barnabas: Ac 15:22
with our beloved Barnabas and **P**, Ac 15:25
But **P** and Barnabas, along with Ac 15:35

had passed, **P** said to Barnabas Ac 15:36
But **P** did not think it Ac 15:38
Then **P** chose Silas and departed, Ac 15:40
P wanted Timothy to go with him, Ac 16:3
night a vision appeared to **P**: Ac 16:9
to what was spoken by **P**. Ac 16:14
As she followed **P** and us she Ac 16:17
But **P** was greatly aggravated, Ac 16:18
they seized **P** and Silas and Ac 16:19
About midnight **P** and Silas were Ac 16:25
P called out in a loud voice, Ac 16:28
trembling before **P** and Silas. Ac 16:29
reported these words to **P**: Ac 16:36
But **P** said to them, "They beat Ac 16:37
they heard that **P** and Silas were Ac 16:38
As usual, **P** went to them, and on Ac 17:2
and joined **P** and Silas, Ac 17:4
brothers sent **P** and Silas off to Ac 17:10
been proclaimed by **P** at Beroea, Ac 17:13
immediately sent **P** away to go to Ac 17:14
who escorted **P** brought him as Ac 17:15
While **P** was waiting for them in Ac 17:16
Then **P** stood in the middle of Ac 17:22
So **P** went out from their Ac 17:33
to leave Rome. **P** came to them, Ac 18:2
P was occupied with preaching Ac 18:5
the Lord said to **P** in a night Ac 18:9
attack against **P** and brought him Ac 18:12
And as **P** was about to open his Ac 18:14
So **P**, having stayed on for many Ac 18:18
P traveled through the interior Ac 19:1
P said, "John baptized with a Ac 19:4
And when **P** had laid his hands on Ac 19:6
by the Jesus whom **P** preaches!" Ac 19:13
I know, and **P** I recognize— Ac 19:15
P resolved in the Spirit to pass Ac 19:21
this man **P** has persuaded and Ac 19:26
Though **P** wanted to go in before Ac 19:30
the uproar was over, **P** sent for Ac 20:1
P spoke to them, and since he Ac 20:7
a deep sleep as **P** kept on Ac 20:9
But **P** went down, threw himself Ac 20:10
intending to take **P** on board. Ac 20:13
For **P** had decided to sail past Ac 20:16
embracing **P**, they kissed him, Ac 20:37
said to **P** through the Spirit Ac 21:4
Then **P** replied, "What are you Ac 21:13
following day **P** went in with us Ac 21:18
the next day, **P** took the men, Ac 21:26
supposed that **P** had brought him Ac 21:29
They seized **P**, dragged him out Ac 21:30
they stopped beating **P**. Ac 21:32
When **P** got to the steps, he had Ac 21:35
into the barracks, **P** said to the Ac 21:37
P said, "I am a Jewish man from Ac 21:39
P stood on the steps and Ac 21:40
P said to the centurion standing Ac 22:25
was born a citizen," **P** said. Ac 22:28
when he realized **P** was a Roman Ac 22:29
out exactly why **P** was being Ac 22:30
he brought **P** down and placed Ac 22:30
P looked intently at the Ac 23:1
P said to him, "God is going Ac 23:3
know, brothers," **P** said, "that Ac 23:5
When **P** realized that one part of Ac 23:6
feared that **P** might be torn Ac 23:10
drink until they had killed **P**. Ac 23:12
anything until we have killed **P**. Ac 23:14
barracks and reported it to **P**. Ac 23:16
Then **P** called one of the Ac 23:17
The prisoner **P** called me and Ac 23:18
ask you to bring **P** down to the Ac 23:20
so they can put **P** on them and Ac 23:24
soldiers took **P** and brought him Ac 23:31
they also presented **P** to him. Ac 23:33
case against **P** to the governor. Ac 24:1
to him to speak, **P** replied: Ac 24:10
centurion keep **P** under guard, Ac 24:23
sent for **P** and listened to him Ac 24:24
would be given to him by **P**. Ac 24:26
Jews, Felix left **P** in prison. Ac 24:27
their case against **P** to him; Ac 25:2
to do them a favor against **P**, Ac 25:3
answered that **P** should be kept Ac 25:4
he commanded **P** to be brought in. Ac 25:6
while **P** made the defense that, Ac 25:8
Jews, replied to **P**, "Are you Ac 25:9
But **P** said: "I am standing at Ac 25:10
a dead man whom **P** claimed to be Ac 25:19
But when **P** appealed to be held Ac 25:21
gave the command, **P** was brought Ac 25:23
Agrippa said to **P**, "It is Ac 26:1
Then **P** stretched out his hand Ac 26:1
You're out of your mind, **P**! Ac 26:24
But **P** replied, "I'm not out of Ac 26:25
Agrippa said to **P**, "Are you Ac 26:28
God," replied **P**, "that whether Ac 26:29
handed over **P** and some other Ac 27:1
Julius treated **P** kindly and Ac 27:3
already over, **P** gave his advice Ac 27:9
ship rather than to what **P** said. Ac 27:11
P stood up among them and said, Ac 27:21
saying, 'Don't be afraid, **P**. Ac 27:24
P said to the centurion and the Ac 27:31
P urged them all to take food, Ac 27:33
because he wanted to save **P**, Ac 27:43
As **P** gathered a bundle of Ac 28:3
P went to him, and praying and Ac 28:8
When **P** saw them, he thanked God Ac 28:15
P was permitted to stay by Ac 28:16
to leave after **P** made one Ac 28:25
P, a slave of Christ Jesus, Rm 1:1
P, called as an apostle of 1Co 1:1
says, "I'm with **P**," or "I'm with 1Co 1:12
Was it **P** who was crucified for 1Co 1:13
says, "I'm with **P**," and another, 1Co 3:4
And what is **P**? They are servants 1Co 3:5
whether **P** or Apollos or Cephas 1Co 3:22
greeting is in my own hand—**P**. 1Co 16:21
P, an apostle of Christ Jesus by 2Co 1:1
Now I, **P**, make a personal appeal 2Co 10:1
P, an apostle—not from men or Gl 1:1
I, **P**, tell you that if you get Gl 5:2
P, an apostle of Christ Jesus by Eph 1:1
this reason, I, **P**, the prisoner Eph 3:1
P and Timothy, slaves of Christ Php 1:1
P, an apostle of Christ Jesus by Col 1:1
heaven, and I, **P**, have become Col 1:23
greeting is in my own hand—**P**. Col 4:18
P, Silvanus, and Timothy: 1Th 1:1
you—even I, **P**, time and again 1Th 2:18
P, Silvanus, and Timothy: 2Th 1:1
greeting is in my own hand—**P**. 2Th 3:17
P, an apostle of Christ Jesus 1Tm 1:1
P, an apostle of Christ Jesus by 2Tm 1:1
P, a slave of God, and an Ti 1:1
P, a prisoner of Christ Jesus, Phm 1
I, **P**, as an elderly man and now Phm 9
I, **P**, write this with my own Phm 19
just as our dear brother **P**, 2Pt 3:15

PAUL'S *(6)*

miracles by **P** hands, Ac 19:11
who were **P** traveling companions Ac 19:29
came to us, took **P** belt, tied Ac 21:11
But the son of **P** sister, hearing Ac 23:16
presented **P** case to the king Ac 25:14
Or were you baptized in **P** name? 1Co 1:13

PAULUS *(1)*

Sergius **P**, an intelligent Ac 13:7

PAVED *(2)*

chambers and a **p** surface laid Ezk 40:17
and opposite the **p** surface Ezk 42:3

PAVEMENT *(8)*

like a **p** made of sapphire Ex 24:10
it and put it on a stone **p**. 2Kg 16:17
faces to the ground on the **p**. 2Ch 7:3
on a mosaic **p** of red feldspar, Est 1:6
mortar of the brick **p** that is at Jr 43:9
Thirty chambers faced the **p**, Ezk 40:17
⌊this⌋ was the lower **p**. Ezk 40:18
in a place called the Stone **P** Jn 19:13

PAVILION *(2)*

the thunder roars from God's **p**? Jb 36:29
he will pitch his **p** over them. Jr 43:10

PAW *(2)*

rescued me from the **p** of the 1Sm 17:37
lion and the **p** of the bear will 1Sm 17:37

PAWS *(2)*

walk on their **p** are unclean for Lv 11:27
He **p** in the valley and rejoices Jb 39:21

PAY *(168)*

of Lamech, **p** attention to my Gn 4:23
Let me **p** the price of the field. Gn 23:13
your wages, and I will **p** them." Gn 30:28
me, and I will **p** your wages." Ex 2:9
with it and not **p** attention to Ex 5:9
p attention to His commands, Ex 15:26
he must **p** for his lost work time Ex 21:19
and he must **p** according to Ex 21:22
he can **p** a redemption price for Ex 21:30
he must **p** money to its owner, Ex 21:34
must certainly **p** the bridal Ex 22:16
he must **p** an amount in silver Ex 22:17
P strict attention to everything Ex 23:13
of the men must **p** a ransom for Ex 30:12
registered must **p** half a shekel Ex 30:13
will be able to **p** for your sin." Ex 32:30
is to **p** it to its owner on the Lv 6:5
must **p** his redemption price in Lv 25:51
calculate and **p** the price of his Lv 25:52
if they will **p** the penalty for Lv 26:41
while they **p** the penalty for Lv 26:43
is too poor to **p** the valuation, Lv 27:8
the person will **p** the valuation Lv 27:23
He is to **p** full compensation, Nm 5:7
You will **p** the redemption price Nm 18:16
your water, we will **p** its price. Nm 20:19
p attention to what I say! Nm 23:18
requests or **p** attention to you Dt 1:45
to directly **p** back the one who Dt 7:10
You are to **p** him his wages each Dt 24:15
P attention, heavens, and I will Dt 32:1
commanded them: "**P** attention. Jos 8:4
Listen, kings! **P** attention, Jdg 5:3
Samson and **p** him back for what Jdg 15:10
me **p** back the Philistines for Jdg 16:28
and did not **p** attention. 1Sm 4:20
to **p** attention ⌊is better⌋ than 1Sm 15:22
My lord should **p** no attention to 1Sm 25:25
must **p** four lambs for that lamb. 2Sm 12:6
they will not **p** any attention to 2Sm 18:3
they will not **p** any attention to 2Sm 18:3
I will **p** your servants' wages 1Kg 5:6
He used to **p** the king of Israel 2Kg 3:4
Go sell the oil and **p** your debt; 2Kg 4:7
in turn⌋ would **p** it out to those 2Kg 12:11
the money to **p** those doing the 2Kg 12:15
you demand from me, I will **p**." 2Kg 18:14
they will not **p** tribute, duty, Ezr 4:13
treasury to **p** for anything else Ezr 7:20
money to **p** the king's tax Neh 5:4
would not bow down or **p** homage. Est 3:2
and I will **p** 375 tons of silver Est 3:9
had promised to **p** the royal Est 4:7
something⌋ or **P** a bribe for me Jb 6:22
a hired man he waits for his **p**. Jb 7:2
of him and **p** so much attention Jb 7:17
and **p** attention to what their Jb 8:8
believe He would **p** attention to Jb 9:16
P close attention to my words; Jb 13:17
P close attention to my words; Jb 21:2
will certainly **p** attention to me Jb 23:6
But now, Job, **p** attention to my Jb 33:1
P attention, Job, and listen to Jb 33:31
and He does not **p** attention to Jb 35:15
P homage to the Son, or He will Ps 2:12
P attention to the sound of my Ps 5:2
a just cause; **p** attention to my Ps 17:1
Listen, daughter, **p** attention Ps 45:10
a person or **p** his ransom to God Ps 49:7
p your vows to the Most High. Ps 50:14
P attention to me and answer me. Ps 55:2
p attention to my prayer. Ps 61:1
increases, **p** no attention to Ps 62:10
offerings; I will **p** You my vows Ps 66:13
P back sevenfold to our Ps 79:12
of Jacob doesn't **p** attention." Ps 94:7
P attention, you stupid people! Ps 94:8
He will **p** them back for their Ps 94:23
I will **p** attention to the way of Ps 101:2
will **p** attention to the prayer Ps 102:17
whoever is wise **p** attention to Ps 107:43
and **p** attention so that you may Pr 4:1
My son, **p** attention to my words; Pr 4:20
son, **p** attention to my wisdom; Pr 5:1
he must **p** seven times as much; Pr 6:31
and **p** attention to the words of Pr 7:24
instruction will **p** the penalty, Pr 13:13
p attention to the words of the Pr 22:17
If you have no money to **p**, Pr 22:27
and **p** attention to your herds, Pr 27:23
Don't **p** attention to everything Ec 7:21

heavens, and **p** attention, earth, Is 1:2
p attention, all you distant Is 8:9
on camels—**p** close attention." Is 21:7
P attention and hear what I say. Is 28:23
P attention to what I say, Is 32:9
you peoples, **p** attention! Is 34:1
among you will **p** attention to Is 42:23
p no attention to things of old. Is 43:18
distant peoples, **p** attention. Is 49:1
P attention to Me, My people, Is 51:4
P attention and come to Me; Is 55:3
p attention to the word of the Jr 2:31
so they cannot **p** attention. Jr 6:10
didn't listen or **p** attention but Jr 7:24
listen to Me or **p** attention but Jr 7:26
P attention to the word of His Jr 9:20
would not obey or **p** attention; Jr 11:8
Listen and **p** attention. Do not Jr 13:15
wouldn't listen or **p** attention Jr 17:23
him and **p** no attention to Jr 18:18
P attention to me, LORD. Jr 18:19
serve without **p** and will not Jr 22:13
of Hosts says: **P** attention! Jr 25:32
not obey Me or **p** any attention. Jr 34:14
you would not **p** attention or Jr 35:15
Now **p** attention ⌊to what I say⌋. Jr 40:4
did not listen or **p** attention; Jr 44:5
confirm your vows! **P** your vows!' Jr 44:25
He will **p** her what she deserves. Jr 51:6
You will **p** them back what they Lm 3:64
must **p** for the water we drink; Lm 5:4
never again **p** fees for lovers Ezk 16:41
Egypt as the **p** he labored for, Ezk 29:20
and **p** attention to everything I Ezk 40:4
Son of man, **p** attention; Ezk 44:5
P attention, house of Israel! Hs 5:1
p attention, earth and everyone Mc 1:2
P attention to the rod and the Mc 6:9
not listen or **p** attention to Me Zch 1:4
But they refused to **p** attention Zch 7:11
Teacher **p** the double-drachma Mt 17:24
if he doesn't **p** attention even Mt 18:17
he had no way to **p** it back, Mt 18:25
he had be sold to **p** the debt. Mt 18:25
and I will **p** you everything!' Mt 18:26
him, and said, '**P** what you owe!' Mt 18:28
with me, and I will **p** you back.' Mt 18:29
until he could **p** what was owed. Mt 18:30
until he could **p** everything that Mt 18:34
workers and give them their **p**, Mt 20:8
it lawful to **p** taxes to Caesar Mt 22:17
You **p** a tenth of mint, dill, and Mt 23:23
P attention to what you hear. Mk 4:24
it lawful to **p** taxes to Caesar Mk 12:14
we **p**, or should we not pay? Mk 12:15
we pay, or should we not **p**?" Mk 12:15
Since they could not **p** it back, Lk 7:42
I'll **p** back four times as much!" Lk 19:8
for us to **p** taxes to Caesar Lk 20:22
receiving **p** and gathering Jn 4:36
to you and **p** attention to my Ac 2:14
her heart to **p** attention to what Ac 16:14
p for them to get their heads Ac 21:24
p is not considered as a gift, Rm 4:4
And for this reason you **p** taxes, Rm 13:6
P your obligations to everyone: Rm 13:7
by taking **p** ⌊from them⌋ to 2Co 11:8
you will **p** the penalty. Gl 5:10
P careful attention, then, to Eph 5:15
P attention to the ministry you Col 4:17
These will **p** the penalty of 2Th 1:9
or to **p** attention to myths and 1Tm 1:4
may not **p** attention to Jewish Ti 1:14
We must therefore **p** even more Heb 2:1
The **p** that you withheld from the Jms 5:4
do well to **p** attention to it 2Pt 1:19
P her back the way she also paid, Rv 18:6

PAYING *(13)*

a free man without **p** anything. Ex 21:2
have finished **p** all the tenth Dt 26:12
exempt from **p** taxes in Israel." 1Sm 17:25
to the ground, **p** homage to the 1Kg 1:31
I insist on **p** the full price, 1Ch 21:24
not bowing down or **p** him homage, Est 3:5
a time of **p** back ⌊Edom⌋ for its Is 34:8
p back His enemies what they Is 66:6
injustice and **p** attention to Dn 9:13
Are you **p** Me back or trying to Jl 3:4
knees, they were **p** Him homage. Mk 15:19
p attention to deceitful spirits 1Tm 4:1
not **p** back evil for evil or 1Pt 3:9

PAYMENT *(13)*

demanded ⌊**p**⌋ from me for what Gn 31:39
freewill gifts or **p** of vows to Lv 22:18
them as full **p** to the king to 1Sm 18:27
produce without **p** or shown Jb 31:39
be the LORD's **p** to my accusers, Ps 109:20
because you scorned **p**. Ezk 16:31
ivory tusks and ebony as your **p**. Ezk 27:15
teach for **p**, and her prophets Mc 3:11
opposing **p** of taxes to Caesar, Lk 23:2
as a down **p** in our hearts. 2Co 1:22
gave us the Spirit as a down **p**. 2Co 5:5
He is the down **p** of our Eph 1:14
harm as the **p** for 2Pt 2:13

PAYMENTS *(2)*

from tax **p** and gave gifts Est 2:18
not making the **p**⌋ of 10 percent Mal 3:8

PAYS *(6)*

But He directly **p** back and Dt 7:10
yet God **p** no attention to this Jb 24:12
is the one who **p** you back what Ps 137:8
a liar **p** attention to a Pr 17:4
king who no longer **p** attention Ec 4:13
If he **p** no attention to them, Mt 18:17

PEACE *(258)*

your fathers in **p** and be buried Gn 15:15
to you, sending you away in **p**. Gn 26:29
way, and they left him in **p**. Gn 26:31
you can go in **p** to your father. Gn 44:17
Jethro said to Moses, "Go in **p**." Ex 4:18
I will give **p** to the land, Lv 26:6
favor on you and give you **p**. Nm 6:26
I grant him My covenant of **p**. Nm 25:12
with an offer of **p** to Sihon king Dt 2:26
you must make an offer of **p**. Dt 20:10
your offer of **p** and opens ⌊its Dt 20:11
it does not make **p** with you but Dt 20:12
Never seek **p** or friendship with Dt 23:6
You will find no **p** among those Dt 28:65
'I will have **p** even though I Dt 29:19
established **p** with them and made Jos 9:15
of Gibeon had made **p** with Israel Jos 10:1
they have made **p** with Joshua Jos 10:4
No city made **p** with the Jos 11:19
because there was **p** between Jdg 4:17
the LORD said to him, "**P** to you. Jdg 6:23
When I return in **p**, I will tear Jdg 8:9
when I return in **p** from the Jdg 11:31
The priest told them, "Go in **p**. Jdg 18:6
"**P** to you," said the old man. Jdg 19:20
sent a message of **p** to the Jdg 21:13
Go in **p**, and may the God 1Sm 1:17
There was also **p** between Israel 1Sm 7:14
and asked, "Do you come in **p**?" 1Sm 16:4
"In **p**," he replied. "I've come 1Sm 16:5
you away, and you will go in **p**. 1Sm 20:13
to you, and **p** to you, to your 1Sm 25:6
him and said, "Go home in **p**. 1Sm 25:35
Abner, and he went in **p**. 2Sm 3:21
him, and he had gone in **p**. 2Sm 3:22
him, and he went in **p**." 2Sm 3:23
they made **p** with Israel and 2Sm 10:19
"Go in **p**," the king said to him. 2Sm 15:9
to the city in **p** and your two 2Sm 15:27
all the people will be at **p**." 2Sm 17:3
in a time⌋ of **p** to avenge blood 1Kg 2:5
gray head descend to Sheol in **p**. 1Kg 2:6
there will be **p** from the LORD 1Kg 2:33
He had **p** on all his surrounding 1Kg 4:24
There was **p** between Hiram and 1Kg 5:12
If they have marched out in **p**, 1Kg 20:18
let everyone return home in **p**.' 1Kg 22:17
also made **p** with the king 1Kg 22:44
So he said to him, "Go in **p**." 2Kg 5:19
ask, '⌊Do you come in⌋ **p**?' " 2Kg 9:17
'⌊Do you come in⌋ **p**?' " 2Kg 9:18
What do you have to do with **p**? 2Kg 9:18
'⌊Do you come in⌋ **p**?' " 2Kg 9:19
What do you have to do with **p**? 2Kg 9:19
Do you come in⌋ **p**, Jehu?" 2Kg 9:22
What **p** can there be as long as 2Kg 9:22
Do you come in⌋ **p**, Zimri, killer 2Kg 9:31
'Make **p** with me and surrender to 2Kg 18:31
if there will be **p** and security 2Kg 20:19
be gathered to your grave in **p**. 2Kg 22:20
you have come in **p** to help me, 1Ch 12:17
P, peace to you, and peace to 1Ch 12:18
Peace, **p** to you, and peace to 1Ch 12:18
and **p** to him who helps you, 1Ch 12:18
made **p** with David and became 1Ch 19:19
and I will give **p** and quiet to 1Ch 22:9
land experienced **p** for 10 years. 2Ch 14:1
kingdom experienced **p** under him. 2Ch 14:5
Because the land experienced **p**, 2Ch 14:6
there was no **p** for those who 2Ch 15:5
let each return home in **p**.' 2Ch 18:16
to his home in Jerusalem in **p**. 2Ch 19:1
be gathered to your grave in **p**. 2Ch 34:28
seek their **p** or prosperity, Ezr 9:12
messages of **p** and faithfulness Est 9:30
I would have laid down in **p**; Jb 3:13
animals will be at **p** with you. Jb 5:23
he is at **p**, a robber attacks Jb 15:21
and go down to Sheol in **p**. Jb 21:13
to terms with God and be at **p**; Jb 22:21
both lie down and sleep in **p**, Ps 4:8
harm to one at **p** with me or have Ps 7:4
LORD blesses His people with **p**. Ps 29:11
is good; seek **p** and pursue it. Ps 34:14
for the man of **p** will have a Ps 37:37
against those at **p** with him; Ps 55:20
will declare **p** to His people, Ps 85:8
and **p** will embrace. Ps 85:10
Abundant **p** belongs to those who Ps 119:165
too long with those who hate **p**. Ps 120:6
I am for **p**; but when I speak, Ps 120:7
Pray for the **p** of Jerusalem: Ps 122:6
there be **p** within your walls, Ps 122:7
I will say, "**P** be with you." Ps 122:8
the evildoers. **P** be with Israel. Ps 125:5
children! **P** be with Israel. Ps 128:6
those who promote **p** have joy. Pr 12:20
his enemies to be at **p** with him. Pr 16:7
a dry crust with **p** than a house Pr 17:1
a time for war and a time for **p**. Ec 3:8
become like one who finds **p**. Sg 8:10
Eternal Father, Prince of **P**. Is 9:6
keep in perfect **p** the mind ⌊that Is 26:3
You will establish **p** for us, Is 26:12
let it make **p** with Me—make Is 27:5
peace with Me—make **p** with Me. Is 27:5
of righteousness will be **p**; Is 32:17
messengers of **p** weep bitterly. Is 33:7
Make **p** with me and surrender to Is 36:16
There will be **p** and security Is 39:8
Then your **p** would have been like Is 48:18
"There is no **p**," says the LORD, Is 48:22
who proclaims **p**, who brings news Is 52:7
punishment for our **p** was on Him, Is 53:5
My covenant of **p** will not be Is 54:10
will enter into **p**—they will Is 57:2
The LORD says, "**P**, peace to the Is 57:19
p to the one who is far or near, Is 57:19
There is no **p** for the wicked," Is 57:21
have not known the path of **p**, Is 59:8
who walks on them will know **p**. Is 59:8
I will appoint **p** as your guard Is 60:17
I will make **p** flow to her like a Is 66:12
You will have **p**,' while a sword Jr 4:10
P, peace, when there is no peace. Jr 6:14
p, when there is no peace. Jr 6:14
peace, when there is no **p**. Jr 6:14
P, peace, when there is no peace. Jr 8:11
p, when there is no peace. Jr 8:11
peace, when there is no **p**. Jr 8:11
We hoped for **p**, but there was Jr 8:15
to the other. No one has **p**. Jr 12:12
give you true **p** in this place.' Jr 14:13
We hoped for **p**, but there was Jr 14:19
have removed My **p** from these Jr 16:5
You will have **p**. To everyone who Jr 23:17
the prophet who prophesies **p**— Jr 28:9
of dread—there is no **p**. Jr 30:5
the abundance of **p** and truth. Jr 33:6
good and all the **p** I will bring Jr 33:9
My soul has been deprived of **p**; Lm 3:17
They will seek **p**, but there will Ezk 7:25
P, when there is no peace, for Ezk 13:10
when there is no **p**, for when Ezk 13:10
saw a vision of **p** for her when Ezk 13:16
for her when there was no **p**." Ezk 13:16
make a covenant of **p** with them Ezk 34:25

make a covenant of **p** with them; Ezk 37:26
⌊a time of⌋ **p**, he will destroy Dn 8:25
by God⌋. **P** to you; be very Dn 10:19
during a time of **p** and seize the Dn 11:21
During a time of **p**, he will come Dn 11:24
everyone at **p** with you will Ob 7
who proclaim **p** when they have Mc 3:5
There will be **p**. When Assyria Mc 5:5
good news and proclaiming **p**! Nah 1:15
"I will provide **p** in this place" Hg 2:9
For they will sow in **p**: Zch 8:12
Therefore, love truth and **p**." Zch 8:19
will proclaim **p** to the nations. Zch 9:10
with him was one of life and **p**, Mal 2:5
walked with Me in **p** and fairness Mal 2:6
is worthy, let your **p** be on it. Mt 10:13
let your **p** return to you. Mt 10:13
I came to bring **p** on the earth. Mt 10:34
I did not come to bring **p**, Mt 10:34
Go in **p** and be free from your Mk 5:34
and be at **p** with one another." Mk 9:50
our feet into the way of **p**. Lk 1:79
and **p** on earth to people He Lk 2:14
You can dismiss Your slave in **p**, Lk 2:29
faith has saved you. Go in **p**." Lk 7:50
has made you well. Go in **p**." Lk 8:48
first say, '**P** to this household. Lk 10:5
If a son of **p** is there, your Lk 10:6
is there, your **p** will rest on Lk 10:6
here to give **p** to the earth? Lk 12:51
and asks for terms of **p**. Lk 14:32
P in heaven and glory in the Lk 19:38
this day what ⌊would bring⌋ **p**— Lk 19:42
He said to them, "**P** to you!" Lk 24:36
P I leave with you. My peace I Jn 14:27
with you. My **p** I give to you. I Jn 14:27
so that in Me you may have **p**. Jn 16:33
and said to them, "**P** to you!" Jn 20:19
said to them again, "**P** to you! Jn 20:21
among them. He said, "**P** to you!" Jn 20:26
and Samaria had **p**, being built Ac 9:31
the good news of **p** through Jesus Ac 10:36
they asked for **p**, because their Ac 12:20
sent back in **p** by the brothers Ac 15:33
So come out now and go in **p**." Ac 16:36
we enjoy great **p** because of you, Ac 24:2
Grace to you and **p** from God our Rm 1:7
p for everyone who does good, Rm 2:10
and the path of **p** they have not Rm 3:17
we have **p** with God through our Rm 5:1
of the Spirit is life and **p**. Rm 8:6
part, live at **p** with everyone. Rm 12:18
but righteousness, **p**, and joy in Rm 14:17
what promotes **p** and what builds Rm 14:19
with all joy and **p** in believing, Rm 15:13
The God of **p** be with all of you. Rm 15:33
The God of **p** will soon crush Rm 16:20
Grace to you and **p** from God our 1Co 1:3
God has called you to **p**. 1Co 7:15
not a God of disorder but of **p**. 1Co 14:33
on his way in **p** so he can come 1Co 16:11
Grace to you and **p** from God our 2Co 1:2
same mind, be at **p**, and the God 2Co 13:11
God of love and **p** will be with 2Co 13:11
Grace to you and **p** from God the Gl 1:3
is love, joy, **p**, patience, Gl 5:22
May **p** be on all those who follow Gl 6:16
Grace to you and **p** from God our Eph 1:2
For He is our **p**, who made both Eph 2:14
from the two, resulting in **p**. Eph 2:15
good news of **p** to you who were Eph 2:17
far away and **p** to those who were Eph 2:17
Spirit with the **p** that binds Eph 4:3
readiness for the gospel of **p**. Eph 6:15
P to the brothers, and love with Eph 6:23
Grace to you and **p** from God our Php 1:2
the **p** of God, which surpasses Php 4:7
and the God of **p** will be with Php 4:9
Grace to you and **p** from God our Col 1:2
by making **p** through the blood Col 1:20
And let the **p** of the Messiah, Col 3:15
Christ. Grace to you and **p**. 1Th 1:1
When they say, "**P** and security," 1Th 5:3
Be at **p** among yourselves. 1Th 5:13
the God of **p** Himself sanctify 1Th 5:23
Grace to you and **p** from God our 2Th 1:2
May the Lord of **p** Himself give 2Th 3:16
give you **p** always in every 2Th 3:16
and **p** from God the Father and 1Tm 1:2
and **p** from God the Father and 2Tm 1:2
faith, love, and **p**, along with 2Tm 2:22
Grace and **p** from God the Father Ti 1:4
Grace to you and **p** from God our Phm 3
of Salem," meaning "king of **p**"; Heb 7:2
the spies in **p** and didn't perish Heb 11:31
the fruit of **p** and righteousness Heb 12:11
Pursue **p** with everyone, and Heb 12:14
may the God of **p**, who brought Heb 13:20
them, "Go in **p**, keep warm, and Jms 2:16
is sown in **p** by those who make Jms 3:18
in peace by those who make **p**. Jms 3:18
May grace and **p** be multiplied to 1Pt 1:2
He must seek **p** and pursue it, 1Pt 3:11
P to all of you who are in Christ. 1Pt 5:14
May grace and **p** be multiplied to 2Pt 1:2
to be found in **p** without spot 2Pt 3:14
and **p** will be with us from God 2Jn 3
face to face. **P** be with you. 3Jn 14
May mercy, **p**, and love be Jd 2
Grace and **p** to you from the One Rv 1:4
to take **p** from the earth, Rv 6:4

PEACE-LOVING *(1)*
first pure, then **p**, gentle, Jms 3:17

PEACEABLY *(3)*
themselves to speak **p** to him. Gn 37:4
Now restore it **p**." Jdg 11:13
a man speaks **p** with his friend, Jr 9:8

PEACEFUL *(14)*
"These men are **p** toward us," Gn 34:21
Then the land was **p** 40 years. Jdg 3:11
and the land was **p** 80 years. Jdg 3:30
And the land was **p** 40 years. Jdg 5:31
The land was **p** 40 years during Jdg 8:28
I am a **p** person, one of the 2Sm 20:19
land was broad, **p**, and quiet, 1Ch 4:40
pleasant, and all her paths, **p**. Pr 3:17
people will dwell in a **p** place, Is 32:18
Jerusalem, a **p** pasture, a tent Is 33:20
If you stumble in a **p** land, Jr 12:5
P grazing land will become Jr 25:37
there will be **p** counsel between Zch 6:13
honest and **p** judgments in your Zch 8:16

PEACEFULLY *(6)*
She asked, "Do you come **p**?" 1Kg 2:13
"**P**," he replied, 1Kg 2:13
those who live **p** in the land. Ps 35:20
go out with joy and be **p** guided; Is 55:12
you will die **p**. There will be a Jr 34:5
and tried to reconcile them **p**, Ac 7:26

PEACEMAKERS *(1)*
Blessed are the **p**, because they Mt 5:9

PEACOCKS *(2)*
silver, ivory, apes, and **p**. 1Kg 10:22
silver, ivory, apes, and **p**. 2Ch 9:21

PEAK *(1)*
Descend from the **p** of Amana, Sg 4:8

PEAKS *(4)*
of Jordan and the **p** of Hermon, Ps 42:6
Bashan is a mountain of many **p**. Ps 68:15
you mountain **p**, at the mountain Ps 68:16
and the mountain **p** are His. Ps 95:4

PEARL *(2)*
When he found one priceless **p**, Mt 13:46
gate was made of a single **p**. Rv 21:21

PEARLS *(8)*
The price of wisdom is beyond **p**. Jb 28:18
dogs or toss your **p** before pigs, Mt 7:6
a merchant in search of fine **p**. Mt 13:45
hairstyles, gold, **p**, or 1Tm 2:9
gold, precious stones, and **p**. Rv 17:4
silver, precious stones, and **p**; Rv 18:12
gold, precious stones, and **p**; Rv 18:16
The 12 gates are 12 **p**; Rv 21:21

PEBBLE *(2)*
until not even a **p** can be found 2Sm 17:13
but not a **p** will fall to the Am 9:9

PEDAHEL *(1)*
P son of Ammihud, a leader from Nm 34:28

PEDAHZUR *(5)*
Gamaliel son of **P** from Manasseh; Nm 1:10
Manassites is Gamaliel son of **P**. Nm 2:20
eighth day Gamaliel son of **P**, Nm 7:54
offering of Gamaliel son of **P**. Nm 7:59
Gamaliel son of **P** was over the Nm 10:23

PEDAIAH *(7)*
name was Zebidah daughter of **P**; 2Kg 23:36
Malchiram, **P**, Shenazzar, 1Ch 3:18
of Manasseh, Joel son of **P**; 1Ch 27:20
Beside him **P** son of Parosh, Neh 3:25
to his left were **P**, Mishael, Neh 8:4
Joed, son of **P**, son of Kolaiah Neh 11:7
scribe, and **P** of the Levites, Neh 13:13

PEDAIAH'S *(1)*
P sons: Zerubbabel and Shimei. 1Ch 3:19

PEDESTAL *(4)*
there was a **p** above, 1Kg 7:29
made as a **p** 27 inches wide. 1Kg 7:31
who shapes a **p**, choosing wood Is 40:20
will be placed there on its **p**." Zch 5:11

PEDESTALS *(1)*
pillars set on **p** of pure gold. Sg 5:15

PEELED *(2)*
plane wood, and **p** ⌊the bark⌋, Gn 30:37
He set the **p** branches in the Gn 30:38

PEER *(1)*
a man who is my **p**, my companion Ps 55:13

PEERED *(1)*
she ⌊**p**⌋ through the lattice, Jdg 5:28

PEERING *(1)*
the windows, **p** through the Sg 2:9

PEG *(8)*
Heber's wife Jael took a tent **p**, Jdg 4:21
hammered the **p** into his temple Jdg 4:21
dead with a tent **p** through his Jdg 4:22
for a tent **p**, her right hand, Jdg 5:26
drive him, like a **p**, into a firm Is 22:23
the **p** that was driven into a Is 22:25
anyone make a **p** from it to hang Ezk 15:3
from them the tent **p**, from them Zch 10:4

PEGS *(12)*
all its tent **p** as well as all Ex 27:19
as all the tent **p** of the Ex 27:19
tent **p** for the tabernacle and Ex 35:18
the tent **p** for the courtyard, Ex 35:18
the tent **p** for the tabernacle Ex 38:20
all the tent **p** for the Ex 38:31
and all the tent **p** for the Ex 38:31
ropes and tent **p**, and all the Ex 39:40
their bases, tent **p**, and ropes. Nm 3:37
their bases, tent **p**, and ropes, Nm 4:32
its tent **p** will not be pulled up Is 33:20
ropes, and drive your **p** deep. Is 54:2

PEKAH *(11)*
his officer, **P** son of Remaliah, 2Kg 15:25
were 50 Gileadite men with **P**. 2Kg 15:25
P son of Remaliah became king 2Kg 15:27
In the days of **P** king of Israel, 2Kg 15:29
against **P** son of Remaliah. 2Kg 15:30
Israel's King **P** son of Remaliah 2Kg 15:32
of Aram and **P** son of Remaliah 2Kg 15:37
year of **P** son of Remaliah, 2Kg 16:1
Israel's King **P** son of Remaliah 2Kg 16:5
P son of Remaliah killed 120,000 2Ch 28:6
along with **P**, son of Remaliah Is 7:1

PEKAH'S *(1)*
rest of the events of **P** ⌊reign⌋, 2Kg 15:31

PEKAHIAH *(3)*
and his son **P** became king in his 2Kg 15:22
P son of Menahem became king 2Kg 15:23
He killed **P** and became king in 2Kg 15:25

PEKAHIAH'S *(1)*
rest of the events of **P** ⌊reign⌋, 2Kg 15:26

PEKOD *(2)*
and against those living in **P**. Jr 50:21
the Chaldeans; **P**, Shoa, and Koa; Ezk 23:23

PELAIAH *(3)*
Eliashib, **P**, Akkub, Johanan, 1Ch 3:24
Hanan, and **P**, who were Levites, Neh 8:7
Hodiah, Kelita, **P**, Hanan, Neh 10:10

PELALIAH *(1)*
Jeroham, son of **P**, son of Amzi, Neh 11:12

PELATIAH *(5)*
P, Jeshaiah, and the sons of 1Ch 3:21
sons of Simeon went with **P**, 1Ch 4:42
P, Hanan, Anaiah, Neh 10:22

of Azzur, and **P** son of Benaiah, Ezk 11:1
prophesying, **P** son of Benaiah Ezk 11:13

PELEG *(8)*
One was named **P**, for during his Gn 10:25
lived 34 years and fathered **P**. Gn 11:16
he fathered **P**, Eber lived 430 Gn 11:17
P lived 30 years and fathered Gn 11:18
P lived 209 years and fathered Gn 11:19
of them was named **P**, because the 1Ch 1:19
Eber, **P**, Reu, 1Ch 1:25
Reu, ⌊son⌋ of **P**, ⌊son⌋ of Eber, Lk 3:35

PELET *(2)*
Jotham, Geshan, **P**, Ephah, and 1Ch 2:47
Jeziel and **P** sons of Azmaveth; 1Ch 12:3

PELETH *(2)*
and On son of **P**, sons of Reuben, Nm 16:1
sons: **P** and Zaza. These 1Ch 2:33

PELETHITES *(7)*
over⌋ the Cherethites and the **P**; 2Sm 8:18
Cherethites, the **P**, and the 2Sm 15:18
the Cherethites, the **P**, and all 2Sm 20:7
was over the Cherethites and **P**; 2Sm 20:23
and the **P** went down, had 1Kg 1:38
and the **P**, and they have had 1Kg 1:44
over the Cherethites and the **P**; 1Ch 18:17

PELONITE *(3)*
(AKA PALTITE)
the Harorite, Helez the **P**, 1Ch 11:27
the Mecherathite, Ahijah the **P**, 1Ch 11:36
was Helez the **P** from the sons of 1Ch 27:10

PELUSIUM *(2)*
I will pour out My wrath on **P**, Ezk 30:15
P will writhe in anguish, Thebes Ezk 30:16

PEN *(9)*
their calves away and **p** them up. 1Sm 6:7
confined their calves in the **p**. 1Sm 6:10
my tongue is the **p** of a skillful Ps 45:1
write on it with an ordinary **p**: Is 8:1
the lying **p** of scribes has Jr 8:8
them together like sheep in a **p**, Mc 2:12
no sheep in the **p** and no cattle Hab 3:17
enter the sheep **p** by the door Jn 10:1
to write to you with **p** and ink. 3Jn 13

PEN-FED *(1)*
roebucks, and **p** poultry, 1Kg 4:23

PENALTY *(13)*
them bear the **p** of restitution Lv 22:16
will pay the **p** for their sin, Lv 26:41
they pay the **p** for their sin, Lv 26:43
and bear the **p** for your acts Nm 14:33
the death **p** and is executed, Dt 21:22
been summoned—⌊the⌋ death ⌊**p**⌋. Est 4:11
for instruction will pay the **p**, Pr 13:13
with great anger bears the **p**; Pr 19:19
Him no grounds for the death **p**. Lk 23:22
no grounds for the death **p**, Ac 13:28
the appropriate **p** for their Rm 1:27
is troubling you will pay the **p**. Gl 5:10
will pay the **p** of everlasting 2Th 1:9

PENDANTS *(2)*
crescent ornaments and ear **p**, Jdg 8:26
p, bracelets, veils, Is 3:19

PENETRATE *(2)*
its eyes **p** the distance. Jb 39:29
Who can **p** his double layer of Jb 41:13

PENETRATING *(1)*
p as far as to divide soul, Heb 4:12

PENIEL *(1)*
(AKA PENUEL)
Jacob then named the place **P**, Gn 32:30

PENINNAH *(3)*
named Hannah and the second **P**. 1Sm 1:2
P had children, but Hannah was 1Sm 1:2
meat to his wife **P** and to each 1Sm 1:4

PENIS *(1)*
or whose **p** has been cut off Dt 23:1

PENNED *(1)*
who **p** this epistle in the Lord, Rm 16:22

PENNIES *(1)*
five sparrows sold for two **p**? Lk 12:6

PENNY *(2)*
until you have paid the last **p**! Mt 5:26
two sparrows sold for a **p**? Mt 10:29

PENS *(3)*
to the sheep **p** along the road, 1Sm 24:3
of cattle, and **p** for flocks. 2Ch 32:28
or male goats from your **p**, Ps 50:9

PENTECOST *(3)*
(AKA Festival of HARVEST, Festival of WEEKS)
When the day of **P** had arrived, Ac 2:1
if possible, for the day of **P**. Ac 20:16
I will stay in Ephesus until **P**, 1Co 16:8

PENUEL *(8)*
(AKA PENIEL)
shone on him as he passed by **P**— Gn 32:31
from there to **P** and asked the Jdg 8:8
men of **P** answered just as the Jdg 8:8
He also told the men of **P**, Jdg 8:9
down the tower of **P** and killed Jdg 8:17
there he went out and built **P**. 1Kg 12:25
P fathered Gedor, and Ezer 1Ch 4:4
and **P** were Shashak's sons. 1Ch 8:25

PEOPLE *(2119)*
At that time **p** began to call on Gn 4:26
As **p** migrated from the east, Gn 11:2
as one **p** all having the same Gn 11:6
and the **p** he had acquired in Gn 12:5
as the women and the ⌊other⌋ **p**. Gn 14:16
Abram, "Give me the **p**, but take Gn 14:21
man will be cut off from his **p**; Gn 17:14
are 50 righteous **p** in the city? Gn 18:24
50 righteous **p** who are in it? Gn 18:24
find 50 righteous **p** in the city, Gn 18:26
against its **p** is great before Gn 19:13
the Hittites, the **p** of the land. Gn 23:7
to you in the presence of my **p**. Gn 23:11
bowed down to the **p** of the land Gn 23:12
presence of the **p** of the land, Gn 23:13
and he was gathered to his **p**. Gn 25:8
and was gathered to his **p**. Gn 25:17
two **p** will ⌊come⌋ from you and Gn 25:23
One **p** will be stronger than the Gn 25:23
One of the **p** could easily have Gn 26:10
warned all the **p** with these Gn 26:11
he divided the **p** with him into Gn 32:7
me leave some of my **p** with you." Gn 33:15
live with you, and become one **p**. Gn 34:16
us and be one **p** only on this Gn 34:22
and was gathered to his **p**, Gn 35:29
and all the **p** of his household, Gn 36:6
and all my **p** will obey your Gn 41:40
and the **p** cried out to Pharaoh Gn 41:55
he sold grain to all its **p**. Gn 42:6
Joseph moved the **p** to the cities Gn 47:21
Then Joseph said to the **p**, Gn 47:23
Dan will judge his **p** as one of Gn 49:16
am about to be gathered to my **p**. Gn 49:29
He was gathered to his **p**. Gn 49:33
result—the survival of many **p**. Gn 50:20
He said to his **p**, "Look, the Ex 1:9
Israelite **p** are more numerous Ex 1:9
and the **p** multiplied and became Ex 1:20
then commanded all his **p**: Ex 1:22
out to his own **p** and observed Ex 2:11
beating a Hebrew, one of his **p**. Ex 2:11
the misery of My **p** in Egypt, Ex 3:7
so that you may lead My **p**, Ex 3:10
you bring the **p** out of Egypt, Ex 3:12
I will give this **p** such favor Ex 3:21
He will speak to the **p** for you. Ex 4:16
so that he won't let the **p** go. Ex 4:21
the signs before the **p**. Ex 4:30
The **p** believed, and when they Ex 4:31
Let My **p** go, so that they may Ex 5:1
you causing the **p** to neglect Ex 5:4
the **p** of the land are so Ex 5:5
of the **p** as well as their Ex 5:6
to supply the **p** with straw for Ex 5:7
foremen of the **p** went out and Ex 5:10
the **p** scattered throughout the Ex 5:12
drivers had set over the **p**, Ex 5:14
is your own **p** who are at fault. Ex 5:16
You caused trouble for this **p**? Ex 5:22
has caused trouble for this **p**, Ex 5:23
delivered Your **p** at all." Ex 5:23
take you as My **p**, and I will be Ex 6:7
ranks of My **p** the Israelites, Ex 7:4
he refuses to let the **p** go. Ex 7:14
Let My **p** go, so that they may Ex 7:16
Let My **p** go, so that they may Ex 8:1
of your officials and your **p**, Ex 8:3
up on you, your **p**, and all your Ex 8:4
the frogs from me and my **p**. Ex 8:8
I will let the **p** go and they can Ex 8:8
and your **p**, that the frogs be Ex 8:9
your officials, and your **p**. Ex 8:11
gnats were on the **p** and animals. Ex 8:17
remained on the **p** and animals. Ex 8:18
Let My **p** go, so that they may Ex 8:20
But if you will not let My **p** go, Ex 8:21
officials, your **p**, and your Ex 8:21
Goshen, where My **p** are living; Ex 8:22
between My **p** and your people. Ex 8:23
between My people and your **p**. Ex 8:23
his officials, and his **p**. Ex 8:29
to let the **p** go and sacrifice to Ex 8:29
his officials, and his **p**; Ex 8:31
also and did not let the **p** go. Ex 8:32
Let My **p** go, so that they may Ex 9:1
and he did not let the **p** go. Ex 9:7
festering boils on **p** and animals Ex 9:9
Let My **p** go, so that they may Ex 9:13
you, your officials, and your **p**. Ex 9:14
you and your **p** with a plague, Ex 9:15
against My **p** by not letting them Ex 9:17
and I and my **p** are the guilty Ex 9:27
Let My **p** go, that they may Ex 10:3
if you refuse to let My **p** go, Ex 10:4
announce to the **p** that both men Ex 11:2
The LORD gave the **p** favor in the Ex 11:3
Pharaoh's officials and the **p**. Ex 11:3
and all the **p** who follow you. Ex 11:8
on the combined number of **p**; Ex 12:4
preparing what **p** need to eat— Ex 12:16
So the **p** bowed down and Ex 12:27
Get up, leave my **p**, both you Ex 12:31
pressured the **p** in order to send Ex 12:33
So the **p** took their dough before Ex 12:34
the LORD gave the **p** such favor Ex 12:36
The **p** baked the dough they had Ex 12:39
Then Moses said to the **p**, Ex 13:3
When Pharaoh let the **p** go, Ex 13:17
The **p** will change their minds Ex 13:17
He led the **p** around toward the Ex 13:18
its place in front of the **p**. Ex 13:22
was told that the **p** had fled, Ex 14:5
minds about the **p** and said: Ex 14:5
said to the **p**, "Don't be afraid Ex 14:13
the **p** feared the LORD and Ex 14:31
will lead the **p** You have Ex 15:13
powerful arm until Your **p** pass Ex 15:16
until the **p** whom You purchased Ex 15:16
The **p** grumbled to Moses, "What Ex 15:24
The **p** are to go out each day and Ex 16:4
the number of **p** each of you has Ex 16:16
some **p** left part of it until Ex 16:20
day some of the **p** went out to Ex 16:27
So the **p** rested on the seventh Ex 16:30
was no water for the **p** to drink. Ex 17:1
So the **p** complained to Moses: Ex 17:2
But the **p** thirsted there for Ex 17:3
What should I do with these **p**? Ex 17:4
on ahead of the **p** and take some Ex 17:5
out of it and the **p** will drink." Ex 17:6
done for Moses and His **p** Israel, Ex 18:1
snatched the **p** from the power Ex 18:10
Moses sat down to judge the **p**, Ex 18:13
thing you're doing for the **p**? Ex 18:14
while all the **p** stand around you Ex 18:14
Because the **p** come to me to Ex 18:15
and these **p** who are with you, Ex 18:18
represent the **p** before God and Ex 18:19
select from all the **p** able men, Ex 18:21
them⌋ over the **p** as officials Ex 18:21
should judge the **p** at all times. Ex 18:22
also all these **p** will be able to Ex 18:23
over the **p** ⌊as⌋ officials Ex 18:25
They judged the **p** at all times; Ex 18:26
He summoned the elders of the **p**, Ex 19:7
Then all the **p** responded Ex 19:8
so that the **p** will hear when I Ex 19:9
Go to the **p** and purify them Ex 19:10
Sinai in the sight of all the **p**. Ex 19:11
boundaries for the **p** all around Ex 19:12
to the **p** and consecrated Ex 19:14
said to the **p**, "Be prepared by Ex 19:15
so that all the **p** in the camp Ex 19:16
brought the **p** out of the camp Ex 19:17

down and warn the **p** not to break Ex 19:21
The **p** cannot come up Mount Ex 19:23
priests and the **p** must not break Ex 19:24
down to the **p** and told them. Ex 19:25
All the **p** witnessed the thunder Ex 20:18
the **p** saw ⌊it⌋ they trembled Ex 20:18
Moses responded to the **p**, Ex 20:20
And the **p** remained standing at a Ex 20:21
If you lend money to My **p**— Ex 22:25
or curse a leader among your **p**. Ex 22:28
Be My holy **p**. You must not eat Ex 22:31
poor among your **p** may eat ⌊from Ex 23:11
will cause the **p** ahead of you to Ex 23:27
the **p** are not to go up with him. Ex 24:2
and told the **p** all the commands Ex 24:3
Then all the **p** responded with a Ex 24:3
and read ⌊it⌋ aloud to the **p**. Ex 24:7
it on the **p**, and said, "This is Ex 24:8
must be cut off from his **p**." Ex 30:33
must be cut off from his **p**." Ex 30:38
must be cut off from his **p**. Ex 31:14
the **p** saw that Moses delayed Ex 32:1
So all the **p** took off the gold Ex 32:3
The **p** sat down to eat and drink, Ex 32:6
For your **p** you brought up from Ex 32:7
I have seen this **p**, and they are Ex 32:9
are indeed a stiff-necked **p**. Ex 32:9
against Your **p** You brought out Ex 32:11
disaster ⌊planned⌋ for Your **p**. Ex 32:12
He said He would bring on His **p**. Ex 32:14
sound of the **p** as they shouted Ex 32:17
What did this **p** do to you that Ex 32:21
know that the **p** are ⌊intent⌋ on Ex 32:22
Moses saw that the **p** were out of Ex 32:25
fell dead that day among the **p**. Ex 32:28
day Moses said to the **p**, Ex 32:30
p has committed a great sin; Ex 32:31
lead the **p** to the place I told Ex 32:34
a plague on the **p** for what they Ex 32:35
and the **p** you brought up from Ex 33:1
you are a stiff-necked **p**; Ex 33:3
When the **p** heard this bad news, Ex 33:4
You are a stiff-necked **p**. Ex 33:5
tent, all the **p** would stand up, Ex 33:8
As all the **p** saw the pillar of Ex 33:10
me, 'Lead this **p** up,' but You Ex 33:12
that this nation is Your **p**." Ex 33:13
that I and Your **p** have found Ex 33:16
and Your **p** will be distinguished Ex 33:16
from all the other **p** on the face Ex 33:16
though this is a stiff-necked **p**, Ex 34:9
of all your **p** that have never Ex 34:10
the **p** you live among will see Ex 34:10
all the skilled **p** are to work Ex 36:1
p continued to bring freewill Ex 36:3
The **p** are bringing more than is Ex 36:5
sanctuary." So the **p** stopped. Ex 36:6
guilt on the **p**, he is to present Lv 4:3
any of the common **p** sins Lv 4:27
must be cut off from his **p**. Lv 7:20
must be cut off from his **p**." Lv 7:21
it⌋ must be cut off from his **p**. Lv 7:25
must be cut off from his **p**." Lv 7:27
for yourself and the **p**. Lv 9:7
toward the **p** and blessed them Lv 9:22
blessed the **p**, and the glory Lv 9:23
the LORD appeared to all the **p**. Lv 9:23
And when all the **p** saw it, Lv 9:24
My glory before all the **p**." Lv 10:3
for himself and for the **p**. Lv 16:24
and all the **p** of the assembly. Lv 16:33
and must be cut off from his **p**. Lv 17:4
must be cut off from his **p**. Lv 17:9
and cut him off from his **p**. Lv 17:10
must be cut off from his **p**. Lv 18:29
must be cut off from his **p**. Lv 19:8
spreading slander among your **p**; Lv 19:16
p of the country are to stone Lv 20:2
man and cut him off from his **p**, Lv 20:3
But if the **p** of the country look Lv 20:4
from their **p** both him and all Lv 20:5
and cut him off from his **p**. Lv 20:6
cut off publicly from their **p**. Lv 20:17
must be cut off from their **p**. Lv 20:18
both **p** will bear their Lv 20:19
marry a virgin from his own **p**, Lv 21:14
his bloodline among his **p**, Lv 21:15
if the **p** eat their holy Lv 22:16

he must be cut off from his **p**. Lv 23:29
among his **p** anyone who does Lv 23:30
your God, and you will be My **p**. Lv 26:12
by lying desolate without the **p**, Lv 26:43
involves the valuation of **p**, Lv 27:2
will become a curse among her **p**. Nm 5:27
Such **p** are to observe it in the Nm 9:11
is to be cut off from his **p**, Nm 9:13
Now the **p** began complaining Nm 11:1
Then the **p** cried out to Moses, Nm 11:2
Contemptible **p** among them had a Nm 11:4
The **p** walked around and gathered Nm 11:8
Moses heard the **p**, family after Nm 11:10
You burden me with all these **p**? Nm 11:11
Did I conceive all these **p**? Nm 11:12
I get meat to give all these **p**? Nm 11:13
carry all these **p** by myself. Nm 11:14
as elders and officers of the **p**. Nm 11:16
you bear the burden of the **p**, Nm 11:17
Tell the **p**: Purify yourselves Nm 11:18
the middle of a **p** with 600,000 Nm 11:21
out and told the **p** the words of Nm 11:24
the elders of the **p** and had them Nm 11:24
all the LORD's **p** were prophets, Nm 11:29
The **p** were up all that day and Nm 11:32
anger burned against the **p**, Nm 11:33
they buried the **p** who had craved Nm 11:34
the **p** moved on to Hazeroth Nm 11:35
and the **p** did not move on until Nm 12:15
the **p** set out from Hazeroth and Nm 12:16
and whether the **p** who live there Nm 13:18
the **p** living in the land are Nm 13:28
quieted the **p** in the presence Nm 13:30
up against the **p** because they Nm 13:31
and all the **p** we saw in it are Nm 13:32
and the **p** wept that night. Nm 14:1
be afraid of the **p** of the land, Nm 14:9
long will these **p** despise Me? Nm 14:11
You brought up this **p** from them. Nm 14:13
among these **p**, how You, LORD, Nm 14:14
If You kill this **p** with a single Nm 14:15
to bring this **p** into the land He Nm 14:16
of this **p** in keeping with Nm 14:19
the **p** were overcome with grief. Nm 14:39
to all the **p** unintentionally. Nm 15:26
is to be cut off from his **p**. Nm 15:30
die ⌊naturally⌋ as all **p** would, Nm 16:29
all Korah's **p**, and all ⌊their⌋ Nm 16:32
all ⌊the **p** of Israel⌋ who were Nm 16:34
"You have killed the LORD's **p**!" Nm 16:41
plague had begun among the **p**. Nm 16:47
he made atonement for the **p**. Nm 16:47
and the **p** who were there. Nm 19:18
The **p** quarreled with Moses and Nm 20:3
large force of heavily-armed **p**. Nm 20:20
Aaron will be gathered to his **p**; Nm 20:24
⌊to his **p**⌋ and die there. Nm 20:26
deliver this **p** into our hands, Nm 21:2
but the **p** became impatient Nm 21:4
The **p** spoke against God and Nm 21:5
poisonous snakes among the **p**, Nm 21:6
The **p** then came to Moses and Nm 21:7
And Moses interceded for the **p**. Nm 21:7
Gather the **p** so I may give them Nm 21:16
nobles of the **p** hollowed it out Nm 21:18
been destroyed, **p** of Chemosh! Nm 21:29
terrified of the **p** because they Nm 22:3
Euphrates in the land of his **p**. Nm 22:5
a **p** has come out of Egypt; Nm 22:5
curse on these **p** for me because Nm 22:6
a **p** has come out of Egypt, Nm 22:11
You are not to curse this **p**, Nm 22:12
a curse on these **p** for me!' " Nm 22:17
There is a **p** living alone; Nm 23:9
A **p** rise up like a lioness; Nm 23:24
Now I am going back to my **p**, Nm 24:14
you what these **p** will do to your Nm 24:14
do to your **p** in the future." Nm 24:14
the **p** began to have sexual Nm 25:1
and the **p** ate and bowed in Nm 25:2
leaders of the **p** and execute Nm 25:4
will also be gathered to your **p**, Nm 27:13
you will be gathered to your **p**." Nm 31:2
Moses spoke to the **p**, "Equip Nm 31:3
one out of every 50 from the **p**, Nm 31:30
32,000 **p**, all the females who Nm 31:35
from the 16,000 **p**, the tribute Nm 31:40
tribute to the LORD was 32 **p**. Nm 31:40

and 16,000 **p**. Nm 31:46
from the **p** and the livestock Nm 31:47
again leave this **p** in the Nm 32:15
was no water for the **p** to drink. Nm 33:14
The **p** are larger and taller than Dt 1:28
Command the **p**: You are about to Dt 2:4
great and numerous **p** as tall as Dt 2:10
men had died among the **p**, Dt 2:16
great and numerous **p**, tall as Dt 2:21
destroyed the **p** of every city, Dt 2:34
ahead of the **p** and enable them Dt 3:28
a wise and understanding **p**.' Dt 4:6
'Assemble the **p** before Me, Dt 4:10
them for all **p** everywhere under Dt 4:19
furnace to be a **p** for His Dt 4:20
Has a **p** ever heard God's voice Dt 4:33
words that these **p** have spoken Dt 5:28
For you are a holy **p** belonging Dt 7:6
The **p** are strong and tall, Dt 9:2
for you are a stiff-necked **p**. Dt 9:6
For your **p** you brought out of Dt 9:12
I have seen this **p**, and indeed, Dt 9:13
they are a stiff-necked **p**. Dt 9:13
annihilate Your **p**, Your Dt 9:26
they are Your **p**, Your Dt 9:29
your journey ahead of the **p**, Dt 10:11
to Egypt, 70 **p** in all, and now Dt 10:22
and then the hands of all the **p**. Dt 13:9
for you are a holy **p** belonging Dt 14:2
to be His special **p** out of all Dt 14:2
For you are a holy **p** belonging Dt 14:21
cease to be poor **p** in the land; Dt 15:11
to judge the **p** with righteous Dt 16:18
that, the hands of all the **p**. Dt 17:7
Then all the **p** will hear ⌊about Dt 17:13
or one who is not of your **p**. Dt 17:15
or send the **p** back to Egypt to Dt 17:16
share from the **p** who offer a Dt 18:3
the two **p** in the dispute must Dt 19:17
the **p** found in it will become Dt 20:11
cities of these **p** the LORD your Dt 20:16
forgive Your **p** Israel You Dt 21:8
with a few **p** and lived there Dt 26:5
and bless Your **p** Israel and the Dt 26:15
are His special **p** as He promised Dt 26:18
be a holy **p** to the LORD your Dt 26:19
of Israel commanded the **p**, Dt 27:1
have become the **p** of the LORD Dt 27:9
that day Moses commanded the **p**, Dt 27:11
on Mount Gerizim to bless the **p**: Dt 27:12
And all the **p** will reply, 'Amen!' Dt 27:15
And all the **p** will say, 'Amen!' Dt 27:16
And all the **p** will say, 'Amen!' Dt 27:17
And all the **p** will say, 'Amen!' Dt 27:18
And all the **p** will say, 'Amen!' Dt 27:19
And all the **p** will say, 'Amen!' Dt 27:20
And all the **p** will say, 'Amen!' Dt 27:21
And all the **p** will say, 'Amen!' Dt 27:22
And all the **p** will say, 'Amen!' Dt 27:23
And all the **p** will say, 'Amen!' Dt 27:24
And all the **p** will say, 'Amen!' Dt 27:25
And all the **p** will say, 'Amen!' Dt 27:26
establish you as His holy **p**, Dt 28:9
will be given to another **p**, Dt 28:32
A **p** you don't know will eat your Dt 28:33
will be left with only a few **p**, Dt 28:62
you today as His **p** and He may be Dt 29:13
Then **p** will answer, 'It is Dt 29:25
go with this **p** into the land Dt 31:7
Gather the **p**—men, women, Dt 31:12
and this **p** will soon commit Dt 31:16
p have acted corruptly toward Dt 32:5
you foolish and senseless **p**? Dt 32:6
the number of the **p** of Israel. Dt 32:8
But the LORD's portion is His **p**, Dt 32:9
jealousy with an inferior **p**; Dt 32:21
vindicate His **p** and have Dt 32:36
nations, over His **p**, for He will Dt 32:43
will purify His land and His **p**. Dt 32:43
song in the presence of the **p**. Dt 32:44
you will be gathered to your **p**, Dt 32:50
Hor and was gathered to his **p**. Dt 32:50
Indeed He loves the **p**. Dt 33:3
leaders of the **p** gathered with Dt 33:5
not die though his **p** become few. Dt 33:6
cry and bring him to his **p**. Dt 33:7
⌊with⌋ the leaders of the **p**; Dt 33:21
is like you, a **p** saved by the Dt 33:29

you and all the **p** prepare to Jos 1:2
commanded the officers of the **p**: Jos 1:10
the camp and tell the **p**, Jos 1:11
and commanded the **p**: Jos 3:3
Joshua told the **p**, "Consecrate Jos 3:5
and go on ahead of the **p**." Jos 3:6
When the **p** broke camp to cross Jos 3:14
of the covenant ahead of the **p**. Jos 3:14
and the **p** crossed opposite Jos 3:16
Choose 12 men from the **p**, Jos 4:2
commanded Joshua to tell the **p**, Jos 4:10
The **p** hurried across, Jos 4:10
crossed in the sight of the **p**. Jos 4:11
The **p** came up from the Jordan on Jos 4:19
so that all the **p** of the earth Jos 4:24
All the **p** who came out of Egypt Jos 5:4
Though all the **p** who came out Jos 5:5
none of the **p** born in the Jos 5:5
have all the **p** give a mighty Jos 6:5
and the **p** will advance, Jos 6:5
He said to the **p**, "Move forward, Jos 6:7
Joshua had spoken to the **p**, Jos 6:8
But Joshua had commanded the **p**: Jos 6:10
and Joshua said to the **p**, Jos 6:16
So the **p** shouted, and the Jos 6:20
the trumpet, the **p** gave a great Jos 6:20
The **p** advanced into the city, Jos 6:20
send all the **p**, but send about Jos 7:3
Since the **p** of Ai are so few, Jos 7:3
don't wear out all our **p** there." Jos 7:3
ever bring these **p** across the Jos 7:7
Go and consecrate the **p**. Jos 7:13
of Ai, his **p**, city, and land Jos 8:1
I and all the **p** who are with me Jos 8:5
he and all his **p** could engage Jos 8:14
was 12,000—all the **p** of Ai. Jos 8:25
Ebal, to bless the **p** of Israel. Jos 8:33
and his **p** were greatly Jos 10:2
The **p** returned safely to Joshua Jos 10:21
him down along with his **p**, Jos 10:33
have many **p**, because the LORD Jos 17:14
have so many **p**," Joshua replied Jos 17:15
You have many **p** and great Jos 17:17
Joshua said to all the **p**, Jos 24:2
p of Jericho—as well as the Jos 24:11
p replied, "We will certainly Jos 24:16
Joshua told the **p**, "You will not Jos 24:19
the **p** answered Joshua. Jos 24:21
then told the **p**, "You are Jos 24:22
the **p** said to Joshua, "We will Jos 24:24
a covenant for the **p** at Shechem Jos 24:25
And Joshua said to all the **p**, Jos 24:27
Then Joshua sent the **p** away, Jos 24:28
They went to live among the **p**. Jdg 1:16
drive out the **p** who were living Jdg 1:19
because those **p** had iron Jdg 1:19
with the **p** who are living Jdg 2:2
drive out these **p** before you. Jdg 2:3
Israelites, the **p** wept loudly. Jdg 2:4
Joshua sent the **p** away, and the Jdg 2:6
The **p** worshiped the LORD Jdg 2:7
and saved the **p** from the power Jdg 2:18
dismissed the **p** who had carried Jdg 3:18
and all the **p** who were with him Jdg 4:13
Israel, when the **p** volunteer, Jdg 5:2
with the volunteers of the **p**. Jdg 5:9
Then the LORD's **p** went down to Jdg 5:11
LORD's **p** came down to me with Jdg 5:13
came with⌋ your **p** after you. Jdg 5:14
Zebulun was a **p** risking their Jdg 5:18
have too many **p** for Me to hand Jdg 7:2
in the presence of the **p**: Jdg 7:3
So 22,000 of the **p** turned back, Jdg 7:3
There are still too many **p**. Jdg 7:4
he brought the **p** down to the Jdg 7:5
the rest of the **p** knelt to drink Jdg 7:6
of bread to the **p** who are Jdg 8:5
him by putting **p** on the tops Jdg 9:25
only these **p** were in my power, Jdg 9:29
you and the **p** with you are to Jdg 9:32
When he and the **p** who are with Jdg 9:33
and all the **p** with him got up at Jdg 9:34
and the **p** who were with him Jdg 9:35
Gaal saw the **p**, he said to Zebul Jdg 9:36
p are coming down from the Jdg 9:36
p are coming down from the Jdg 9:37
Aren't these the **p** you despised? Jdg 9:38
next day when the **p** went into Jdg 9:42

He took the **p**, divided them into Jdg 9:43
and the **p** were coming out of the Jdg 9:43
and killed the **p** who were in it. Jdg 9:45
and all the **p** who were with him Jdg 9:48
and said to the **p** who were with Jdg 9:48
and set it on fire around the **p**, Jdg 9:49
and all the **p** in the Tower of Jdg 9:49
The **p** put him over themselves as Jdg 11:11
all his **p**, camped at Jahaz Jdg 11:20
Sihon and all his **p** to Israel, Jdg 11:21
Amorites before His **p** Israel, Jdg 11:23
My **p** and I had a serious Jdg 12:2
relatives or among any of our **p**? Jdg 14:3
You told my **p** the riddle, but Jdg 14:16
Then she explained it to her **p**. Jdg 14:17
When the **p** saw him, they praised Jdg 16:24
the leaders and all the **p** in it. Jdg 16:30
saw that the **p** who were there Jdg 18:7
Eshtaol, their **p** asked them, Jdg 18:8
unsuspecting **p** and a wide-open Jdg 18:10
image, and went with the **p**. Jdg 18:20
to a quiet and unsuspecting **p**. Jdg 18:27
leaders of all the **p** and of all Jdg 20:2
in the assembly of God's **p**: Jdg 20:2
Then all the **p** stood united and Jdg 20:8
for the **p** when they go to Jdg 20:10
left-handed among all these **p**; Jdg 20:16
out against the **p** and were drawn Jdg 20:31
began to attack the **p** as before, Jdg 20:31
So the **p** went to Bethel and sat Jdg 21:2
The next day the **p** got up early, Jdg 21:4
For when the **p** were counted, Jdg 21:9
p had compassion on Benjamin, Jdg 21:15
"We will go with you to your **p**." Ru 1:10
back to her **p** and to her god. Ru 1:15
your **p** will be my people, and Ru 1:16
people will be my **p**, and your Ru 1:16
how⌋ you came to a **p** you didn't Ru 2:11
since all the **p** in my town know Ru 3:11
presence of the elders of my **p**. Ru 4:4
to the elders and all the **p**, Ru 4:9
elders and all the **p** who were at Ru 4:11
of the sacrifices⌋ from the **p**. 1Sm 2:13
evil actions from all these **p**. 1Sm 2:23
from the LORD's **p** is not good. 1Sm 2:24
the offerings of My **p** Israel.' 1Sm 2:29
So the **p** sent ⌊men⌋ to Shiloh to 1Sm 4:4
a great slaughter among the **p**. 1Sm 4:17
the **p** of Ashdod got up early 1Sm 5:3
oppressed the **p** of Ashdod, 1Sm 5:6
afflicting the **p** of Ashdod and 1Sm 5:6
God to us to kill us and our **p**!" 1Sm 5:10
so it won't kill us and our **p**!" 1Sm 5:11
The **p** of Beth-shemesh were 1Sm 6:13
The **p** of the city chopped up the 1Sm 6:14
The **p** wept because the LORD 1Sm 6:19
Listen to the **p** and everything 1Sm 8:7
words to the **p** who were asking 1Sm 8:10
The **p** refused to listen to 1Sm 8:19
for the **p** at the high place 1Sm 9:12
The **p** won't eat until he comes 1Sm 9:13
him ruler over My **p** Israel. 1Sm 9:16
seen ⌊the affliction of⌋ My **p**, 1Sm 9:16
he will rule over My **p**." 1Sm 9:17
I said, 'I've invited the **p**.' " 1Sm 9:24
summoned the **p** to the LORD at 1Sm 10:17
When he stood among the **p**, 1Sm 10:23
Samuel said to all the **p**, 1Sm 10:24
And all the **p** shouted, "Long 1Sm 10:24
proclaimed to the **p** the rights 1Sm 10:25
Samuel sent all the **p** away, 1Sm 10:25
and told the terms to the **p**, 1Sm 11:4
What's the matter with the **p**? 1Sm 11:5
of the LORD fell on the **p**, 1Sm 11:7
the **p** said to Samuel, 1Sm 11:12
Then Samuel said to the **p**, 1Sm 11:14
So all the **p** went to Gilgal, 1Sm 11:15
Then Samuel said to the **p**, 1Sm 12:6
the **p** greatly feared the LORD 1Sm 12:18
LORD will not abandon His **p**, 1Sm 12:22
to make you His own **p**. 1Sm 12:22
him as ruler over His **p**, 1Sm 13:14
But the **p** said to Saul, "Must 1Sm 14:45
So the **p** rescued Jonathan, 1Sm 14:45
you as king over His **p** Israel. 1Sm 15:1
rest of the **p** with the sword. 1Sm 15:8
Because I was afraid of the **p**, 1Sm 15:24
the elders of my **p** and before 1Sm 15:30

The **p** told him about the offer, 1Sm 17:27
The **p** gave him the same answer 1Sm 17:30
pleased all the **p** and Saul's 1Sm 18:5
of crazy **p** that you brought 1Sm 21:15
to the words of **p** who say, 1Sm 24:9
comes from wicked **p**. 1Sm 24:13
one of the **p** came to destroy 1Sm 26:15
But if it is **p**, may they be 1Sm 26:19
detestable to his **p** Israel, 1Sm 27:12
them⌋ and rescue ⌊the **p**⌋." 1Sm 30:8
and the **p** shouted, "This is 1Sm 30:20
of their idols and among the **p**. 1Sm 31:9
the LORD's **p**, and the house 2Sm 1:12
David I will save My **p** Israel 2Sm 3:18
Joab and all the **p** who were with 2Sm 3:31
at Abner's tomb. All the **p** wept, 2Sm 3:32
And all the **p** wept over him even 2Sm 3:34
All the **p** took note of this, 2Sm 3:36
will shepherd My **p** Israel and be 2Sm 5:2
for the sake of His **p** Israel. 2Sm 5:12
he blessed the **p** in the name of 2Sm 6:18
multitude of the **p** of Israel, 2Sm 6:19
Then all the **p** left, each to his 2Sm 6:19
ruler over the LORD's **p** Israel. 2Sm 6:21
to shepherd My **p** Israel: 2Sm 7:7
to be ruler over My **p** Israel. 2Sm 7:8
place for My **p** Israel and plant 2Sm 7:10
judges to be over My **p** Israel. 2Sm 7:11
And who is like Your **p** Israel? 2Sm 7:23
order to redeem a **p** for Himself, 2Sm 7:23
before Your **p** You redeemed for 2Sm 7:23
Your **p** Israel Your own 2Sm 7:24
Israel Your own **p** forever, 2Sm 7:24
and righteousness for all his **p**. 2Sm 8:15
strong for our **p** and for the 2Sm 10:12
He removed the **p** who were in 2Sm 12:31
there were many **p** coming from 2Sm 13:34
similar against the **p** of God? 2Sm 14:13
king because the **p** have made me 2Sm 14:15
and the **p** supporting Absalom 2Sm 15:12
and all the **p** followed him. 2Sm 15:17
while all the **p** were marching 2Sm 15:23
all the **p** were marching past on 2Sm 15:23
until the **p** had finished 2Sm 15:24
Each of the **p** with him covered 2Sm 15:30
p and the warriors on David's 2Sm 16:6
and all the **p** with him arrived 2Sm 16:14
the LORD, the **p**, and all the men 2Sm 16:18
and all the **p** with him will 2Sm 17:2
and bring all the **p** back to you. 2Sm 17:3
all the **p** will be at peace." 2Sm 17:3
spend the night with the **p**. 2Sm 17:8
among the **p** who follow Absalom. 2Sm 17:9
and all the **p** with him will be 2Sm 17:16
and all the **p** with him got up 2Sm 17:22
David and the **p** with him to eat 2Sm 17:29
reasoned, "The **p** must be hungry, 2Sm 17:29
not go!" the **p** pleaded. "If we 2Sm 18:3
All the **p** heard the king's 2Sm 18:5
The **p** of Israel were defeated by 2Sm 18:7
claimed more **p** than the sword. 2Sm 18:8
day like **p** come in when they 2Sm 19:3
gate, and all the **p** were told: 2Sm 19:8
All the **p** among all the tribes 2Sm 19:9
So all the **p** crossed the Jordan, 2Sm 19:39
had seen that all the **p** stopped. 2Sm 20:12
went to all the **p** with her wise 2Sm 20:22
You rescue an afflicted **p**, 2Sm 22:28
me from the feuds among my **p**; 2Sm 22:44
a **p** I had not known serve me. 2Sm 22:44
who rules the **p** with justice, 2Sm 23:3
⌊the **p** of⌋ Israel and Judah. 2Sm 24:1
angel who was destroying the **p**, 2Sm 24:16
saw the angel striking the **p**, 2Sm 24:17
plague on the **p** may be halted." 2Sm 24:21
and all the **p** proclaimed, 1Kg 1:39
All the **p** followed him, playing 1Kg 1:40
the **p** were sacrificing on the 1Kg 3:2
is among Your **p** You have chosen, 1Kg 3:8
a **p** too numerous to be numbered 1Kg 3:8
to judge Your **p** and to discern 1Kg 3:9
to judge this great **p** of Yours?" 1Kg 3:9
wisdom of all the **p** of the East, 1Kg 4:30
P came from everywhere, ⌊sent⌋ 1Kg 4:34
son to be over this great **p**!" 1Kg 5:7
ruled over the **p** doing the work. 1Kg 5:16
and not abandon My **p** Israel." 1Kg 6:13
day I brought My **p** Israel out of 1Kg 8:16

David to rule My **p** Israel." 1Kg 8:16
Your servant and Your **p** Israel, 1Kg 8:30
When Your **p** Israel are defeated 1Kg 8:33
the sin of Your **p** Israel. 1Kg 8:34
Your servants and Your **p** Israel, 1Kg 8:36
You gave Your **p** for an 1Kg 8:36
anyone from Your **p** Israel might 1Kg 8:38
is not of Your **p** Israel but has 1Kg 8:41
all the **p** on earth will know 1Kg 8:43
fear You as Your **p** Israel do and 1Kg 8:43
When Your **p** go out to fight 1Kg 8:44
You forgive Your **p** who sinned 1Kg 8:50
For they are Your **p** and Your 1Kg 8:51
the petition of Your **p** Israel, 1Kg 8:52
from all the **p** on earth, 1Kg 8:53
rest to His **p** Israel according 1Kg 8:56
and the cause of His **p** Israel, 1Kg 8:59
day he sent the **p** away. 1Kg 8:66
David and for His **p** Israel. 1Kg 8:66
ruled over the **p** doing the work. 1Kg 9:23
return to me." So the **p** left. 1Kg 12:5
me to respond to these **p**?" 1Kg 12:6
to these **p** and serve them, 1Kg 12:7
to these **p** who said to me, 1Kg 12:9
to these **p** who said to you, 1Kg 12:10
and all the **p** came to Rehoboam 1Kg 12:12
the king answered the **p** harshly. 1Kg 12:13
king did not listen to the **p**, 1Kg 12:15
to them, the **p** answered him: 1Kg 12:16
and to the rest of the **p**, 1Kg 12:23
If these **p** regularly go to offer 1Kg 12:27
heart of these **p** will return to 1Kg 12:27
and he said to the **p**, "Going to 1Kg 12:28
the **p** walked ⌊in procession⌋ 1Kg 12:30
every class of **p** who were not 1Kg 12:31
every class of **p** for the high 1Kg 13:33
me becoming king over this **p**. 1Kg 14:2
raised you up from among the **p**, 1Kg 14:7
you ruler over My **p** Israel, 1Kg 14:7
Israel ⌊and the **p** will shake⌋ as 1Kg 14:15
made you ruler over My **p** Israel, 1Kg 16:2
have caused My **p** Israel to sin, 1Kg 16:2
that time the **p** of Israel were 1Kg 16:21
half the **p** followed Tibni son of 1Kg 16:21
the **p** who followed Omri proved 1Kg 16:22
approached all the **p** and said, 1Kg 18:21
But the **p** didn't answer him a 1Kg 18:21
Then Elijah said to the **p**, 1Kg 18:22
All the **p** answered, "That 1Kg 18:24
Then Elijah said to all the **p**, 1Kg 18:30
So all the **p** approached him. 1Kg 18:30
me so that this **p** will know that 1Kg 18:37
When all the **p** saw it, they fell 1Kg 18:39
the meat and gave it to the **p**, 1Kg 19:21
and all the **p** said to him, 1Kg 20:8
each of the **p** who follow me." 1Kg 20:10
life and your **p** in place of his 1Kg 20:42
people in place of his **p**.' " 1Kg 20:42
Naboth at the head of the **p**. 1Kg 21:9
Naboth at the head of the **p**. 1Kg 21:12
Naboth in the presence of the **p**, 1Kg 21:13
as you are, my **p** as your people, 1Kg 22:4
people as your **p**, my horses as 1Kg 22:4
he said, "Listen, all you **p**!" 1Kg 22:28
p still sacrificed and burned 1Kg 22:43
as you are, my **p** as your people, 2Kg 3:7
people as your **p**, my horses as 2Kg 3:7
"I am living among my own **p**." 2Kg 4:13
"Serve it for the **p** to eat." 2Kg 4:41
"Give it to the **p** to eat." 2Kg 4:42
"Give it to the **p** to eat," 2Kg 4:43
the **p** saw that there was 2Kg 6:30
the **p** went out and plundered 2Kg 7:16
but the **p** trampled him in the 2Kg 7:17
the **p** trampled him in the 2Kg 7:20
you will do to the **p** of Israel. 2Kg 8:12
you king over the LORD's **p**, 2Kg 9:6
said to all the **p**, "You are 2Kg 10:9
brought all the **p** together and 2Kg 10:18
went out to the **p** at the LORD's 2Kg 11:13
and all the **p** of the land were 2Kg 11:14
and the **p** that they would be the 2Kg 11:17
the LORD's **p** and ⌊another one⌋ 2Kg 11:17
one⌋ between the king and the **p**. 2Kg 11:17
So all the **p** of the land went to 2Kg 11:18
and all the **p** of the land, 2Kg 11:19
All the **p** of the land rejoiced, 2Kg 11:20
the **p** continued sacrificing and 2Kg 12:3
money from the **p** and they would 2Kg 12:8
Then the **p** of Israel dwelt in 2Kg 13:5
and the **p** continued sacrificing 2Kg 14:4
Then all the **p** of Judah took 2Kg 14:21
the **p** continued sacrificing and 2Kg 15:4
governing the **p** of the land. 2Kg 15:5
and deported the **p** to Assyria. 2Kg 15:29
the **p** continued sacrificing and 2Kg 15:35
He deported its **p** to Kir but put 2Kg 16:9
of all the **p** of the land, 2Kg 16:15
because the **p** of Israel had 2Kg 17:7
brought ⌊**p**⌋ from Babylon, 2Kg 17:24
them because the **p** don't know 2Kg 17:26
But ⌊the **p** of⌋ each nation, 2Kg 17:29
earshot of the **p** on the wall." 2Kg 18:26
But the **p** kept silent; 2Kg 18:36
When the **p** got up the ⌊next⌋ 2Kg 19:35
leader of My **p**, 'This is what 2Kg 20:5
Then the common **p** executed all 2Kg 21:24
have collected from the **p**. 2Kg 22:4
for me, the **p**, and all Judah 2Kg 22:13
all the **p** from the youngest to 2Kg 23:2
the **p** agreed to the covenant. 2Kg 23:3
on the graves of the common **p**. 2Kg 23:6
The king commanded all the **p**, 2Kg 23:21
the common **p** took Jehoahaz 2Kg 23:30
the gold from the **p** of the land, 2Kg 23:35
for the poorest **p** of the land, 2Kg 24:14
city that the **p** of the land had 2Kg 25:3
the rest of the **p** who were left 2Kg 25:11
enlisted the **p** of the land for 2Kg 25:19
from the common **p** who were 2Kg 25:19
the rest of the **p** he left in the 2Kg 25:22
all the **p**, from the youngest 2Kg 25:26
donkeys—as well as 100,000 **p**. 1Ch 5:21
These **p** from the descendants of 1Ch 9:3
news to their idols and their **p**. 1Ch 10:9
will shepherd My **p** Israel and be 1Ch 11:2
be ruler over My **p** Israel.' " 1Ch 11:2
seemed right to all the **p**, 1Ch 13:4
for the sake of His **p** Israel. 1Ch 14:2
he blessed the **p** in the name of 1Ch 16:2
Then all the **p** said, "Amen" and 1Ch 16:36
Then all the **p** left for their 1Ch 16:43
I commanded to shepherd My **p**, 1Ch 17:6
to be ruler over My **p** Israel. 1Ch 17:7
place for My **p** Israel and plant 1Ch 17:9
judges to be over My **p** Israel. 1Ch 17:10
And who is like Your **p** Israel? 1Ch 17:21
to redeem a **p** for Yourself, 1Ch 17:21
before Your **p** You redeemed 1Ch 17:21
You made Your **p** Israel Your own 1Ch 17:22
Israel Your own **p** forever, 1Ch 17:22
and righteousness for all his **p**. 1Ch 18:14
strong for our **p** and for the 1Ch 19:13
Joab and the **p** with him 1Ch 19:14
brought out the **p** who were in it 1Ch 20:3
to count ⌊the **p** of⌋ Israel. 1Ch 21:1
number of His **p** a hundred times 1Ch 21:3
who was destroying ⌊the **p**⌋, 1Ch 21:15
gave the order to count the **p**? 1Ch 21:17
the plague be against Your **p**." 1Ch 21:17
plague on the **p** may be halted." 1Ch 21:22
and **p** skilled in every kind of 1Ch 22:15
before the LORD and His **p**. 1Ch 22:18
Israel has given rest to His **p**, 1Ch 23:25
to me, my brothers and my **p**. 1Ch 28:2
and all the **p** are at your every 1Ch 28:21
Then the **p** rejoiced because of 1Ch 29:9
and who are my **p**, that we should 1Ch 29:14
have seen Your **p** who are present 1Ch 29:17
of the hearts of Your **p**, 1Ch 29:18
me king over a **p** as numerous as 2Ch 1:9
so that I may lead these **p**, 2Ch 1:10
judge this great **p** of Yours?" 2Ch 1:10
may judge My **p** over whom I have 2Ch 1:11
Because the LORD loves His **p**, 2Ch 2:11
supervisors to make the **p** work. 2Ch 2:18
day I brought My **p** Israel out 2Ch 6:5
to be ruler over My **p** Israel. 2Ch 6:5
David to be over My **p** Israel." 2Ch 6:6
Your servant and Your **p** Israel, 2Ch 6:21
If Your **p** Israel are defeated 2Ch 6:24
the sin of Your **p** Israel. 2Ch 6:25
Your servants and Your **p** Israel, 2Ch 6:27
You gave Your **p** for an 2Ch 6:27
anyone from your **p** Israel might 2Ch 6:29
is not of Your **p** Israel but has 2Ch 6:32
fear You as Your **p** Israel do and 2Ch 6:33
When Your **p** go out to fight 2Ch 6:34
You forgive Your **p** who sinned 2Ch 6:39
and may Your godly **p** rejoice in 2Ch 6:41
king and all the **p** were offering 2Ch 7:4
and all the **p** dedicated God's 2Ch 7:5
and all the **p** were standing. 2Ch 7:6
he sent the **p** away to their 2Ch 7:10
Solomon, and for His **p** Israel. 2Ch 7:10
or if I send pestilence on My **p**, 2Ch 7:13
and My **p** who are called by My 2Ch 7:14
250 who ruled over the **p**. 2Ch 8:10
in three days." So the **p** left. 2Ch 10:5
advise me to respond to this **p**?" 2Ch 10:6
kind to these **p** and please them 2Ch 10:7
back to this **p** who said to me, 2Ch 10:9
say to the **p** who said to you, 2Ch 10:10
and all the **p** came to Rehoboam 2Ch 10:12
listen to the **p** because the turn 2Ch 10:15
them, the **p** answered the king: 2Ch 10:16
and to the rest of the **p**: 2Ch 11:3
countless **p** who came with him 2Ch 12:3
Abijah and his **p** struck them 2Ch 13:17
He told ⌊the **p** of⌋ Judah to seek 2Ch 14:4
So he said to ⌊the **p** of⌋ Judah, 2Ch 14:7
Asa and the **p** who were with 2Ch 14:13
So the **p** of Judah carried off a 2Ch 14:13
some of the **p** at that time. 2Ch 16:10
towns of Judah and taught the **p**. 2Ch 17:9
him and for the **p** who were with 2Ch 18:2
as you are, my **p** as your people; 2Ch 18:3
as you are, my people as your **p**; 2Ch 18:3
he said, "Listen, all you **p**!" 2Ch 18:27
out among the **p** from Beer-sheba 2Ch 19:4
P came and told Jehoshaphat, 2Ch 20:2
land before Your **p** Israel and 2Ch 20:7
with the **p** and appointed some 2Ch 20:21
and his **p** went to gather 2Ch 20:25
the **p** had not yet determined in 2Ch 20:33
is now about to strike your **p**, 2Ch 21:14
But his **p** did not hold a fire in 2Ch 21:19
but all the **p** are to obey the 2Ch 23:6
and all the **p** of the land were 2Ch 23:13
and the **p** that they would be the 2Ch 23:16
that they would be the LORD's **p**. 2Ch 23:16
So all the **p** went to the temple 2Ch 23:17
governors of the **p**, and all the 2Ch 23:20
and all the **p** of the land and 2Ch 23:20
All the **p** of the land rejoiced, 2Ch 23:21
leaders and all the **p** rejoiced, 2Ch 24:10
stood above the **p** and said to 2Ch 24:20
the leaders of the **p** among them 2Ch 24:23
them because the **p** of Judah had 2Ch 24:24
and led his **p** to the Valley 2Ch 25:11
struck down 3,000 of their **p**, 2Ch 25:13
their own **p** from your hand?" 2Ch 25:15
All the **p** of Judah took Uzziah, 2Ch 26:1
governing the **p** of the land. 2Ch 26:21
the **p** still behaved corruptly. 2Ch 27:2
plan to reduce the **p** of Judah 2Ch 28:10
and all the **p** rejoiced over how 2Ch 29:36
over how God had prepared the **p**, 2Ch 29:36
themselves and the **p** hadn't been 2Ch 30:3
large assembly of **p** was gathered 2Ch 30:13
For a large number of the **p**— 2Ch 30:18
heard Hezekiah and healed the **p**. 2Ch 30:20
Levites stood to bless the **p**, 2Ch 30:27
He told the **p** who lived in 2Ch 31:4
the LORD and His **p** Israel. 2Ch 31:8
the LORD has blessed His **p**; 2Ch 31:10
Many **p** gathered and stopped up 2Ch 32:4
over the **p** and gathered 2Ch 32:6
and gathered the **p** in the square 2Ch 32:6
So the **p** relied on the words of 2Ch 32:8
to deliver his **p** from my power, 2Ch 32:14
to deliver his **p** from my power 2Ch 32:15
deliver their **p** from my power, 2Ch 32:17
not deliver His **p** from my power. 2Ch 32:17
Hebrew to the **p** of Jerusalem who 2Ch 32:18
spoke to Manasseh and his **p**, 2Ch 33:10
the **p** still sacrificed at the 2Ch 33:17
Then the common **p** executed all 2Ch 33:25
all the **p** from great to small. 2Ch 34:30
LORD your God and His **p** Israel. 2Ch 35:3
brothers, the lay **p**, and the 2Ch 35:5
for all the lay **p** who were 2Ch 35:7
donated willingly for the **p**, 2Ch 35:8
houses of the lay **p** to offer to 2Ch 35:12

brought ⌊them⌋ to the lay **p**.	2Ch 35:13
Then the common **p** took Jehoahaz	2Ch 36:1
priests and the **p** multiplied	2Ch 36:14
compassion on His **p** and on His	2Ch 36:15
up against His **p** that there was	2Ch 36:16
among you of His **p** may go up,	2Ch 36:23
is among His **p**, may his God be	Ezr 1:3
now are the **p** of the province	Ezr 2:1
Bethlehem's **p** 123	Ezr 2:21
Azmaveth's **p** 42	Ezr 2:24
Chephirah's, and Beeroth's **p** 743	Ezr 2:25
Ramah's and Geba's **p** 621	Ezr 2:26
Nebo's **p** 52	Ezr 2:29
Magbish's **p** 156	Ezr 2:30
the other Elam's **p** 1,254	Ezr 2:31
Harim's **p** 320	Ezr 2:32
Lod's, Hadid's, and Ono's **p** 725	Ezr 2:33
Jericho's **p** 345	Ezr 2:34
Senaah's **p** 3,630	Ezr 2:35
and some of the **p** settled in	Ezr 2:70
and the **p** gathered together in	Ezr 3:1
and oil to the **p** of Sidon and	Ezr 3:7
Then all the **p** gave a great	Ezr 3:11
The **p** could not distinguish the	Ezr 3:13
because the **p** were shouting so	Ezr 3:13
Then the **p** who were already in	Ezr 4:4
discouraged the **p** of Judah and	Ezr 4:4
the **p** who were already in the	Ezr 4:6
Susa (that is, the **p** of Elam),	Ezr 4:9
and deported the **p** to Babylon.	Ezr 5:12
any king or **p** who dares to harm	Ezr 6:12
given by the **p** and the priests	Ezr 7:16
to judge all the **p** in the region	Ezr 7:25
among the **p** and priests,	Ezr 8:15
support the **p** and the house	Ezr 8:36
The **p** of Israel, the priests,	Ezr 9:1
that the holy **p** has become mixed	Ezr 9:2
The **p** also wept bitterly.	Ezr 10:1
all the **p** sat in the square at	Ezr 10:9
But there are many **p**, and it is	Ezr 10:13
are Your servants and Your **p**.	Neh 1:10
for the **p** had the will to keep	Neh 4:6
So I stationed ⌊**p**⌋ behind the	Neh 4:13
the rest of the **p**, "Don't be	Neh 4:14
supported all the **p** of Judah,	Neh 4:16
and the rest of the **p**:	Neh 4:19
said to the **p**, "Let everyone	Neh 4:22
outcry from the **p** and their	Neh 5:1
Then the **p** did as they had	Neh 5:13
me had heavily burdened the **p**,	Neh 5:15
also oppressed the **p**,	Neh 5:15
burden on the **p** was so heavy.	Neh 5:18
all that I have done for this **p**.	Neh 5:19
but there were few **p** in it,	Neh 7:4
and the **p** to be registered by	Neh 7:5
These are the **p** of the province	Neh 7:6
the other Elam's **p** 1,254	Neh 7:34
Harim's **p** 320	Neh 7:35
Jericho's **p** 345	Neh 7:36
Lod's, Hadid's, and Ono's **p** 721	Neh 7:37
Senaah's **p** 3,930	Neh 7:38
The rest of the **p** gave 20,000	Neh 7:72
some of the **p**, temple servants,	Neh 7:73
all the **p** gathered together at	Neh 8:1
All the **p** listened attentively	Neh 8:3
book in full view of all the **p**,	Neh 8:5
opened it, all the **p** stood up.	Neh 8:5
hands uplifted all the **p** said,	Neh 8:6
the law to the **p** as they stood	Neh 8:7
so that the **p** could understand	Neh 8:8
instructing the **p** said to all of	Neh 8:9
For all the **p** were weeping as	Neh 8:9
the Levites quieted all the **p**,	Neh 8:11
Then all the **p** began to eat and	Neh 8:12
the family leaders of all the **p**,	Neh 8:13
The **p** went out, brought back	Neh 8:16
and all the **p** of his land,	Neh 9:10
our ancestors and all Your **p**,	Neh 9:32
The leaders of the **p** were:	Neh 10:14
The rest of the **p**—the priests,	Neh 10:28
and **p** for the donation of wood	Neh 10:34
the leaders of the **p** stayed in	Neh 11:1
the rest of the **p** cast lots for	Neh 11:1
The **p** praised all the men who	Neh 11:2
every matter concerning the **p**.	Neh 11:24
they purified the **p**, the gates,	Neh 12:30
it with half the **p** along the top	Neh 12:38
was read publicly to the **p**.	Neh 13:1
that time I saw **p** in Judah	Neh 13:15
the Sabbath to the **p** of Judah in	Neh 13:16
the royal palace for all the **p**,	Est 1:5
beauty to the **p** and the	Est 1:11
in the language of his own **p**.	Est 1:22
to destroy all of Mordecai's **p**,	Est 3:6
the enemy of the Jewish **p**.	Est 3:10
The money and **p** are given to you	Est 3:11
annihilate all the Jewish **p**—	Est 3:13
among the Jewish **p** in every	Est 4:3
with him personally for her **p**.	Est 4:8
officials and the **p** of the royal	Est 4:11
to the Jewish **p** from another	Est 4:14
and [spare] my **p**—[this is] my	Est 7:3
my **p** and I have been sold out	Est 7:4
evil that would come on my **p**?	Est 8:6
the number of **p** killed in the	Est 9:11
good for his **p** and to speak for	Est 10:3
man among all the **p** of the east.	Jb 1:3
the young **p** so that they died,	Jb 1:19
He knows which **p** are worthless.	Jb 11:11
you are the **p**, and wisdom will	Jb 12:2
me an object of scorn to the **p**;	Jb 17:6
I have become a man **p** spit at.	Jb 17:6
or descendants among his **p**,	Jb 18:19
Suspended far away from **p**,	Jb 28:4
p shouted at them as ⌊if they	Jb 30:5
sleep falls on **p** as they slumber	Jb 33:15
p shudder, then pass away.	Jb 34:20
not rule or ensnare the **p**.	Jb 34:30
P cry out because of severe	Jb 35:9
If **p** are bound with chains and	Jb 36:8
work, which **p** have sung about	Jb 36:24
p have looked at it from a	Jb 36:25
thousands of **p** who have taken	Ps 3:6
may Your blessing be on Your **p**.	Ps 3:8
consume my **p** as they consume	Ps 14:4
the LORD restores His captive **p**,	Ps 14:7
As for the holy **p** who are in the	Ps 16:3
Concerning what **p** do:	Ps 17:4
For You rescue an afflicted **p**,	Ps 18:27
me from the feuds among the **p**;	Ps 18:43
a **p** I had not known serve me.	Ps 18:43
by men and despised by **p**.	Ps 22:6
p look and stare at me.	Ps 22:17
come and tell a **p** yet to be born	Ps 22:31
LORD is the strength of His **p**;	Ps 28:8
Save Your **p**, bless Your	Ps 28:9
The LORD gives His **p** strength;	Ps 29:11
LORD blesses His **p** with peace.	Ps 29:11
p He has chosen to be His own	Ps 33:12
I will exalt You among many **p**.	Ps 35:18
so valuable that **p** take refuge	Ps 36:7
the abundance of many wicked **p**.	Ps 37:16
while all day long **p** say to me,	Ps 42:3
You sell Your **p** for nothing;	Ps 44:12
forget your **p** and your father's	Ps 45:10
the wealthy **p**, will seek your	Ps 45:12
assembled ⌊with⌋ the **p** of the	Ps 47:9
p praise you when you do well	Ps 49:18
earth in order to judge His **p**.	Ps 50:4
Listen, My **p**, and I will speak;	Ps 50:7
the presence of Your faithful **p**,	Ps 52:9
consume My **p** as they consume	Ps 53:4
When God restores His captive **p**,	Ps 53:6
Do you judge **p** fairly?	Ps 58:1
Then **p** will say, "Yes, there is	Ps 58:11
otherwise, my **p** will forget.	Ps 59:11
made Your **p** suffer hardship;	Ps 60:3
in Him at all times, you **p**;	Ps 62:8
way, providing ⌊**p**⌋ with grain.	Ps 65:9
when You went out before Your **p**,	Ps 68:7
Your **p** settled in it;	Ps 68:10
You received gifts from **p**,	Ps 68:18
P have seen Your procession,	Ps 68:24
power and strength to His **p**.	Ps 68:35
will judge Your **p** with	Ps 72:2
bring prosperity to the **p**,	Ps 72:3
the afflicted among the **p**,	Ps 72:4
p flourish in the cities like	Ps 72:16
are not afflicted like most **p**.	Ps 73:5
Therefore His **p** turn to them and	Ps 73:10
I would have betrayed Your **p**.	Ps 73:15
a foolish **p** has insulted Your	Ps 74:18
lives of Your poor **p** forever.	Ps 74:19
P tell about Your wonderful	Ps 75:1
With power You redeemed Your **p**,	Ps 77:15
You led Your **p** like a flock by	Ps 77:20
My **p**, hear my instruction;	Ps 78:1
or furnish meat for His **p**?"	Ps 78:20
P ate the bread of angels.	Ps 78:25
He led His **p** out like sheep and	Ps 78:52
surrendered His **p** to the sword	Ps 78:62
be shepherd over His **p** Jacob—	Ps 78:71
Then we, Your **p**, the sheep of	Ps 79:13
Listen, My **p**, and I will	Ps 81:8
But My **p** did not listen to Me;	Ps 81:11
If only My **p** would listen to Me	Ps 81:13
clever schemes against Your **p**;	Ps 83:3
Happy are the **p** whose strength	Ps 84:5
so that Your **p** may rejoice in	Ps 85:6
will declare peace to His **p**,	Ps 85:8
arrogant **p** have attacked me;	Ps 86:14
Happy are the **p** who know the	Ps 89:15
exalted one chosen from the **p**.	Ps 89:19
LORD, they crush Your **p**;	Ps 94:5
Pay attention, you stupid **p**!	Ps 94:8
not forsake His **p** or abandon His	Ps 94:14
and we are the **p** of His pasture,	Ps 95:7
'They are a **p** whose hearts go	Ps 95:10
we are His—His **p**, the sheep of	Ps 100:3
a newly created **p** will praise	Ps 102:18
His deeds to the **p** of Israel.	Ps 103:7
LORD made His **p** very fruitful;	Ps 105:24
turned to hate His **p** and to deal	Ps 105:25
He brought His **p** out with	Ps 105:43
when You show favor to Your **p**.	Ps 106:4
anger burned against His **p**,	Ps 106:40
Let all the **p** say, "Amen!"	Ps 106:48
assembly of the **p** and praise Him	Ps 107:32
Your **p** will volunteer on Your	Ps 110:3
has shown His **p** the power of His	Ps 111:6
He has sent redemption to His **p**.	Ps 111:9
with the nobles of His **p**.	Ps 113:8
of Jacob from a **p** who spoke a	Ps 114:1
in the presence of all His **p**.	Ps 116:14
the very presence of all His **p**,	Ps 116:18
p persecute me with lies—	Ps 119:86
of tears because **p** do not follow	Ps 119:136
And the LORD surrounds His **p**,	Ps 125:2
may Your godly **p** shout for joy.	Ps 132:9
and its godly **p** will shout for	Ps 132:16
of Egypt, both **p** and animals.	Ps 135:8
an inheritance to His **p** Israel.	Ps 135:12
will judge His **p** and have	Ps 135:14
He led His **p** in the wilderness.	Ps 136:16
the **p** will listen to my words,	Ps 141:6
He subdues my **p** under me.	Ps 144:2
Happy are the **p** with such	Ps 144:15
Happy are the **p** whose God is the	Ps 144:15
informing ⌊all⌋ **p** of Your mighty	Ps 145:12
He gathers Israel's exiled **p**.	Ps 147:2
has raised up a horn for His **p**,	Ps 148:14
Israelites, the **p** close to Him.	Ps 148:14
LORD takes pleasure in His **p**;	Ps 149:4
honor is for all His godly **p**.	Ps 149:9
So follow the way of good **p**,	Pr 2:20
P don't despise the thief if he	Pr 6:30
P, I call out to you;	Pr 8:4
guidance, **p** fall, but with	Pr 11:14
P will curse anyone who hoards	Pr 11:26
but faithful **p** are His delight.	Pr 12:22
but treacherous **p** have an	Pr 13:2
guards **p** of integrity,	Pr 13:6
turning **p** away from the snares	Pr 13:14
turning **p** from the snares of	Pr 14:27
but a shortage of **p** is a ruler's	Pr 14:28
but sin is a disgrace to any **p**.	Pr 14:34
and a mocker is detestable to **p**.	Pr 24:9
innocent"—**p** will curse him,	Pr 24:24
to power, **p** hide themselves.	Pr 28:12
over a helpless **p** is like a	Pr 28:15
come to power, **p** hide, but when	Pr 28:28
flourish, the **p** rejoice, but	Pr 29:2
when the wicked rule, **p** groan.	Pr 29:2
Without revelation **p** run wild,	Pr 29:18
the ants are not a strong **p**,	Pr 30:25
hyraxes are not a mighty **p**,	Pr 30:26
God has given **p** this miserable	Ec 1:13
what is good for **p** to do under	Ec 2:3
God has given **p** to keep them	Ec 3:10
works so that **p** will be in awe	Ec 3:14
This happens concerning **p**,	Ec 3:18
For the fate of **p** and the fate	Ec 3:19
P have no advantage over animals,	Ec 3:19
if the spirit of **p** rises upward	Ec 3:21

to all the **p** who were before Ec 4:16
attention to everything **p** say, Ec 7:21
a thousand ⌊**p**⌋ I have found one Ec 7:28
that God made **p** upright, Ec 7:29
the heart of **p** is filled ⌊with Ec 8:11
will go well with God-fearing **p**, Ec 8:12
are righteous **p** who get what Ec 8:14
there are wicked **p** who get what Ec 8:14
P don't know whether ⌊to expect⌋ Ec 9:1
hearts of **p** are full of evil, Ec 9:3
p are trapped in an evil time, Ec 9:12
taught the **p** knowledge; Ec 12:9
the chariots of my noble **p**. Sg 6:12
My **p** do not understand." Is 1:3
p weighed down with iniquity, Is 1:4
of our God, you **p** of Gomorrah! Is 1:10
For You have abandoned Your **p**, Is 2:6
P will go into caves in the Is 2:19
On that day **p** will throw their Is 2:20
The **p** will oppress one another, Is 3:5
make me the leader of the **p**!" Is 3:7
oppress My **p**, and women rule Is 3:12
My **p**, your leaders mislead you; Is 3:12
case and stands to judge the **p**. Is 3:13
the elders and leaders of His **p**: Is 3:14
do you crush My **p** and grind the Is 3:15
Therefore My **p** go into exile Is 5:13
anger burns against His **p**. Is 5:25
live among a **p** of unclean lips Is 6:5
Say to these **p**: Keep listening Is 6:9
Dull the minds of these **p**; Is 6:10
houses are without **p**, the land Is 6:11
the LORD drives the **p** far away, Is 6:12
hearts of his **p** trembled like Is 7:2
will be too shattered to be a **p** Is 7:8
on you, your **p**, and the house Is 7:17
Because these **p** rejected the Is 8:6
me from going the way of this **p**: Is 8:11
an alliance these **p** say is an Is 8:12
shouldn't a **p** consult their Is 8:19
The **p** walking in darkness have Is 9:2
⌊The **p**⌋ have rejoiced before You Is 9:3
All the **p**—Ephraim and the Is 9:9
The **p** did not turn to Him who Is 9:13
leaders of the **p** mislead ⌊them⌋, Is 9:16
and the **p** are like fuel for the Is 9:19
afflicted among my **p** of justice, Is 10:2
go⌋ against a **p** destined for My Is 10:6
even if your **p** were as numerous Is 10:22
My **p** who dwell in Zion, do not Is 10:24
The **p** of Ramah are trembling; Is 10:29
remnant of His **p** who survive. Is 11:11
will plunder the **p** of the east. Is 11:14
letting **p** walk through on foot. Is 11:15
of His **p** who will survive Is 11:16
like that of a mighty **p**! Is 13:4
each one will turn to his own **p**, Is 13:14
p shout with a ringing cry. Is 14:7
land and slaughtered your own **p**. Is 14:20
and His afflicted **p** find refuge Is 14:32
On that day **p** will look to their Is 17:7
to a **p** feared near and far, Is 18:2
LORD of Hosts from a **p** tall and Is 18:7
smooth-skinned, a **p** feared near Is 18:7
Blessed be Egypt My **p**, Assyria Is 19:25
My downtrodden and threshed **p**, Is 21:10
the destruction of my dear **p**." Is 22:4
p shouting and crying to the Is 22:5
of Chaldeans—a **p** who no longer Is 23:13
p and priest alike, servant and Is 24:2
the exalted **p** of the earth waste Is 24:4
a strong **p** will honor You. Is 25:3
city of violent **p** will fear You. Is 25:3
see ⌊Your⌋ zeal for ⌊Your⌋ **p**, Is 26:11
Go, my **p**, enter your rooms and Is 26:20
they are not a **p** with Is 27:11
to the remnant of His **p**, Is 28:5
speak to this **p** with stammering Is 28:11
who rule this **p** in Jerusalem. Is 28:14
Because these **p** approach Me with Is 29:13
confound these **p** with wonder Is 29:14
and the poor **p** will rejoice in Is 29:19
because of a **p** who can't help. Is 30:5
to a **p** who will not help them. Is 30:6
are a rebellious **p**, deceptive Is 30:9
For you **p** will live on Zion in Is 30:19
ground of my **p** growing thorns Is 32:13
Then my **p** will dwell in a Is 32:18

p will swarm over it like an Is 33:4
a **p** whose speech is difficult to Is 33:19
The **p** who dwell there will be Is 33:24
Edom and on the **p** I have set Is 34:5
of the **p** who are on the wall. Is 36:11
When the **p** got up the ⌊next⌋ Is 37:36
of these ⌊promises⌋ **p** live, Is 38:16
comfort My **p**," says your God. Is 40:1
indeed, the **p** are grass. Is 40:7
breath to the **p** on it and life Is 42:5
for the **p** ⌊and⌋ a light to Is 42:6
But this is a **p** plundered and Is 42:22
Bring out a **p** who are blind, Is 43:8
so that **p** may hear and say, Is 43:9
to give drink to My chosen **p**. Is 43:20
The **p** I formed for Myself will Is 43:21
I have established an ancient **p**. Is 44:7
Such **p** do not comprehend and Is 44:18
I was angry with My **p**; Is 47:6
one abhorred by **p**, to a servant Is 49:7
you to be a covenant for the **p**, Is 49:8
the LORD has comforted His **p**, Is 49:13
to Me, My **p**, and listen to Me, Is 51:4
the **p** in whose heart is My Is 51:7
to say to Zion, "You are My **p**." Is 51:16
cup that ⌊causes **p**⌋ to stagger. Is 51:17
defends His **p**—"Look, I have Is 51:22
At first My **p** went down to Egypt Is 52:4
that My **p** are taken away for Is 52:5
My **p** will know My name; Is 52:6
the LORD has comforted His **p**; Is 52:9
He was like one **p** turned away Is 53:3
will exclude me from His **p**"; Is 56:3
Tell My **p** their transgression, Is 58:1
of streets where **p** live. Is 58:12
Then all your **p** will be Is 60:21
that they are a **p** the LORD has Is 61:9
prepare a way for the **p**! Is 62:10
they will be called the Holy **P**, Is 62:12
are indeed My **p**, children who Is 63:8
⌊the days⌋ of Moses ⌊and⌋ his **p**. Is 63:11
You led Your **p** this way to make Is 63:14
Your holy **p** had a possession for Is 63:18
look—all of us are Your **p**! Is 64:9
long to a rebellious **p** who walk Is 65:2
These **p** continually provoke Me Is 65:3
for My **p** who have sought Me. Is 65:10
and its **p** to be a delight. Is 65:18
Jerusalem and be glad in My **p**. Is 65:19
P will build houses and live ⌊in Is 65:21
for they will be a **p** blessed by Is 65:23
the **p** of Jerusalem went into Jr 1:3
Yet My **p** have exchanged their Jr 2:11
For My **p** have committed a double Jr 2:13
Why do My **p** claim: We will go Jr 2:31
Yet My **p** have forgotten Me for Jr 2:32
deceived this **p** and Jerusalem, Jr 4:10
be said to this **p** and to Jr 4:11
on the way to My dear **p**. Jr 4:11
For My **p** are fools; they do not Jr 4:22
These **p** are the wood, and the Jr 5:14
When **p** ask: For what offense has Jr 5:19
you foolish and senseless **p**. Jr 5:21
But these **p** have stubborn and Jr 5:23
for wicked men live among My **p**. Jr 5:26
My **p** love it like this. Jr 5:31
to bring disaster on these **p**, Jr 6:19
stumbling blocks before these **p**; Jr 6:21
My dear **p**, dress yourselves in Jr 6:26
to be an assayer among My **p**— Jr 6:27
all ⌊you **p**⌋ of Judah who enter Jr 7:2
of the evil of My **p** Israel. Jr 7:12
you, do not pray for these **p**. Jr 7:16
your God, and you will be My **p**. Jr 7:23
of these **p** will become food Jr 7:33
⌊**p**⌋ fall and not get up again? Jr 8:4
Why have these **p** turned away? Jr 8:5
but My **p** do not know the Jr 8:7
the brokenness of My dear **p**, Jr 8:11
cry of my dear **p** from a far away Jr 8:19
by the brokenness of my dear **p**. Jr 8:21
of my dear **p** not come about? Jr 8:22
over the slain of my dear **p**. Jr 9:1
I would abandon my **p** and depart Jr 9:2
assembly of treacherous **p**. Jr 9:2
can I do because of My dear **p**? Jr 9:7
to feed this **p** wormwood and give Jr 9:15
all the wise **p** of the nations Jr 10:7

you will be My **p**, and I will be Jr 11:4
you, do not pray for these **p**. Jr 11:14
concerning the **p** of Anathoth who Jr 11:21
disaster on the **p** of Anathoth Jr 11:23
away, for ⌊the **p**⌋ have said, "He Jr 12:4
that I bequeathed to My **p**, Jr 12:14
learn the ways of My **p**— Jr 12:16
they taught My **p** to swear by Jr 12:16
will be built up among My **p**. Jr 12:16
These evil **p**, who refuse to Jr 13:10
they might be My **p** for My fame, Jr 13:11
⌊Her **p**⌋ are on the ground in Jr 14:2
LORD says concerning these **p**: Jr 14:10
for the well-being of these **p**. Jr 14:11
The **p** they are prophesying to Jr 14:16
daughter of my **p** has been Jr 14:17
not ⌊reach out⌋ to these **p**. Jr 15:1
I destroyed My **p**. They would not Jr 15:7
wall of bronze to this **p**. Jr 15:20
power of evil **p** and redeem you Jr 15:21
removed My peace from these **p**"— Jr 16:5
you tell these **p** all these Jr 16:10
Then ⌊**p**⌋ will come from the Jr 17:26
Yet My **p** have forgotten Me. Jr 18:15
of the elders of the **p** and some Jr 19:1
presence of the **p** traveling with Jr 19:10
shatter these **p** and this city, Jr 19:11
and proclaimed to all the **p**, Jr 19:14
needy from the hand of evil **p**. Jr 20:13
and the **p**—those in this Jr 21:7
But you must say to this **p**, Jr 21:8
your **p** who enter these gates. Jr 22:2
their officers, and their **p**. Jr 22:4
the shepherds who shepherd My **p**: Jr 23:2
Baal and led My **p** Israel astray. Jr 23:13
have enabled My **p** to hear My Jr 23:22
to cause My **p** to forget My name Jr 23:27
and leading My **p** astray with Jr 23:32
no benefit at all to these **p**"— Jr 23:32
Now when these **p** or a prophet or Jr 23:33
prophet, priest, or **p** who say: Jr 23:34
They will be My **p**, and I will be Jr 24:7
concerning all the **p** of Judah in Jr 25:1
all the **p** of Judah and all Jr 25:2
his leaders, all his **p**, Jr 25:19
and all the **p** heard Jeremiah Jr 26:7
him to deliver to all the **p**. Jr 26:8
and all the **p** took hold of him, Jr 26:8
Then all the **p** assembled Jr 26:9
to the officials and all the **p**, Jr 26:11
to all the officials and the **p**, Jr 26:12
and all the **p** told the priests Jr 26:16
and said to all the assembled **p**, Jr 26:17
said to all the **p** of Judah, Jr 26:18
and all ⌊the **p** of⌋ Judah put him Jr 26:19
burial place of the common **p**. Jr 26:23
over to the **p** to be put to death Jr 26:24
earth, and the **p**, and animals Jr 27:5
serve him and his **p**, and live! Jr 27:12
you and your **p** die by the sword, Jr 27:13
to the priests and all these **p**, Jr 27:16
of the priests and all the **p**, Jr 28:1
and all the **p** who were standing Jr 28:5
and in the hearing of all the **p**. Jr 28:7
of all the **p** Hananiah proclaimed Jr 28:11
have led these **p** to trust in a Jr 28:15
and all the **p** Nebuchadnezzar had Jr 29:1
all the **p** living in this Jr 29:16
to all the **p** of Jerusalem, Jr 29:25
living among these **p**, Jr 29:32
that I will bring to My **p**"— Jr 29:32
fortunes of My **p** Israel and Jr 30:3
You will be My **p**, and I will be Jr 30:22
Israel, and they will be My **p**." Jr 31:1
the **p** who survived the sword. Jr 31:2
LORD, save Your **p**, the remnant Jr 31:7
and My **p** will be satisfied with Jr 31:14
God, and they will be My **p**. Jr 31:33
You brought Your **p** Israel out of Jr 32:21
They will be My **p**, and I will be Jr 32:38
this great disaster on these **p**, Jr 32:42
The **p** coming to fight the Jr 33:5
noticed what these **p** have said? Jr 33:24
My **p** are treated with contempt Jr 33:24
with all the **p** who were in Jr 34:8
the officials and **p** who entered Jr 34:10
and all the **p** of the land who Jr 34:19
but these **p** have not obeyed Me. Jr 35:16

hearing of the **p** at the temple Jr 36:6
against this **p** are great." Jr 36:7
all the **p** of Jerusalem and all Jr 36:9
in the hearing of all the **p**, Jr 36:10
scroll in the hearing of the **p**. Jr 36:13
read in the hearing of the **p**, Jr 36:14
and the **p** of the land did Jr 37:2
his daily tasks among the **p**, Jr 37:4
his portion there among the **p**. Jr 37:12
or these **p** that you have put Jr 37:18
was speaking to all the **p**: Jr 38:1
and of all the **p** by speaking to Jr 38:4
the well-being of this **p**, Jr 38:4
to Babylon the rest of the **p**— Jr 39:9
the rest of the **p** who had Jr 39:9
some of the poor **p** who owned Jr 39:10
So he settled among ⌊his own⌋ **p**. Jr 39:14
Because you ⌊**p**⌋ have sinned Jr 40:3
him among the **p** or go wherever Jr 40:5
him among the **p** who remained Jr 40:6
the remnant of the **p** of Mizpah Jr 41:10
When all the **p** with Ishmael saw Jr 41:13
and all the **p** whom Ishmael had Jr 41:14
the remnant of the **p** whom he had Jr 41:16
and all the **p** from the least to Jr 42:1
and all the **p** from the least to Jr 42:8
to all the **p** all the words Jr 43:1
and all the **p** who were living in Jr 44:15
responded to all the **p**— Jr 44:20
and all the **p** who were answering Jr 44:20
and the **p** of the land—did Jr 44:21
Then Jeremiah said to all the **p**, Jr 44:24
return to our **p** and to the land Jr 46:16
handed over to a northern **p**. Jr 46:24
The **p** will cry out, and every Jr 47:2
flutes for the **p** of Kir-heres. Jr 48:36
destroyed as a **p** because he has Jr 48:42
The **p** of Chemosh have perished Jr 48:46
Gad and his **p** settled in their Jr 49:1
devised against the **p** of Teman: Jr 49:20
and destroy the **p** of the east! Jr 49:28
My **p** are lost sheep; their Jr 50:6
each will turn to his own **p**, Jr 50:16
A **p** comes from the north. Jr 50:41
Come out from among her, My **p**! Jr 51:45
city that the **p** of the land had Jr 52:6
some of the poorest of the **p**, Jr 52:15
the rest of the **p** who were left Jr 52:15
some of the poor **p** of the land Jr 52:16
enlisted the **p** of the land for Jr 52:25
from the common **p** who were found Jr 52:25
These are the **p** Nebuchadnezzar Jr 52:28
year, 832 **p** from Jerusalem; Jr 52:29
4,600 **p** ⌊were deported⌋. Jr 52:30
the city ⌊once⌋ crowded with **p**! Lm 1:1
When her **p** fell into the Lm 1:7
her **p** groan while they search Lm 1:11
Listen, all you **p**; look at my Lm 1:18
P have heard me groaning, but Lm 1:21
of the destruction of my dear **p**, Lm 2:11
The hearts of the **p** cry out to Lm 2:18
am a laughingstock to all my **p**, Lm 3:14
of the destruction of my dear **p**. Lm 3:48
Zion's precious **p**—⌊once⌋ worth Lm 4:2
but my dear **p** have become cruel Lm 4:3
of my dear **p** is greater than Lm 4:6
the destruction of my dear **p**. Lm 4:10
p shouted at them. Lm 4:15
being sent to a **p** of Ezk 3:5
Go to your **p**, the exiles, and Ezk 3:11
For her **p** have rejected My Ezk 5:6
One third of your **p** will die by Ezk 5:12
concerning all its **p** will not be Ezk 7:13
hands of the **p** of the land will Ezk 7:27
out killing ⌊**p**⌋ in the city. Ezk 9:7
of Benaiah, leaders of the **p**. Ezk 11:1
they will be My **p**, and I will be Ezk 11:20
Then say to the **p** of the land: Ezk 12:19
this proverb you ⌊**p**⌋ have about Ezk 12:22
fellowship of My **p** or be Ezk 13:9
have led My **p** astray saying: Ezk 13:10
women of your **p** who prophesy Ezk 13:17
the heads of **p** of every height Ezk 13:18
the lives of My **p** but preserve Ezk 13:18
Me in front of My **p** for handfuls Ezk 13:19
you lie to My **p**, who listen to Ezk 13:19
you ensnare **p** with like birds Ezk 13:20
I will free the **p** you have Ezk 13:20

deliver My **p** from your hands, Ezk 13:21
deliver My **p** from your hands Ezk 13:23
cut him off from among My **p**. Ezk 14:8
him from among My **p** Israel. Ezk 14:9
they will be My **p** and I will be Ezk 14:11
strength and many **p** will not be Ezk 17:9
did what was wrong among his **p**. Ezk 18:18
to tear prey, he devoured **p**. Ezk 19:3
to tear prey, he devoured **p**. Ezk 19:6
Then all **p** will see that I, Ezk 20:48
So all the **p** will know that I, Ezk 21:5
of man, for it is against My **p**. Ezk 21:12
over to the sword with My **p**. Ezk 21:12
P who ⌊live⌋ in you eat at the Ezk 22:9
P who ⌊live⌋ in you accept Ezk 22:12
they devour **p**, seize wealth and Ezk 22:25
The **p** of the land have practiced Ezk 22:29
I spoke to the **p** in the morning, Ezk 24:18
Then the **p** asked me, "Won't you Ezk 24:19
give you to the **p** of the east as Ezk 25:4
Ammon to the **p** of the east as Ezk 25:10
on Edom through My **p** Israel, Ezk 25:14
slaughter your **p** with the sword, Ezk 26:11
the Pit, to the **p** of antiquity. Ezk 26:20
with all the other **p** on board, Ezk 27:27
goods and the **p** within you have Ezk 27:34
along with his **p**, ruthless men Ezk 30:11
among the **p** who descend to the Ezk 31:14
speak to your **p** and tell them: Ezk 33:2
and the **p** of that land select a Ezk 33:2
blows his trumpet to warn the **p**. Ezk 33:3
so that the **p** aren't warned, Ezk 33:6
Now, son of man, say to your **p**: Ezk 33:12
But your **p** say: The Lord's way Ezk 33:17
p are talking about you near Ezk 33:30
So My **p** come to you in crowds, Ezk 33:31
the house of Israel, are My **p**." Ezk 34:30
bear your fruit for My **p** Israel, Ezk 36:8
fill you with **p**, with the whole Ezk 36:10
fill you with **p** and animals, Ezk 36:11
will cause **p**, My people Israel, Ezk 36:12
people, My **p** Israel, to walk Ezk 36:12
Because **p** are saying to you: Ezk 36:13
These are the **p** of the LORD, Ezk 36:20
you will be My **p**, and I will be Ezk 36:28
be filled with a flock of **p**, Ezk 36:38
up from them, My **p**, and lead you Ezk 37:12
am the LORD, My **p**, when I open Ezk 37:13
When your **p** ask you: Won't you Ezk 37:18
hand and in full view of the **p**, Ezk 37:20
they will be My **p**, and I will be Ezk 37:23
God, and they will be My **p**. Ezk 37:27
a tranquil **p** who are living Ezk 38:11
and against a **p** gathered Ezk 38:12
that day when My **p** Israel are Ezk 38:14
advance against My **p** Israel like Ezk 38:16
known among My **p** Israel and will Ezk 39:7
All the **p** of the land will bury Ezk 39:13
the rebellious **p**, the house of Ezk 44:6
for the **p** and will stand Ezk 44:11
court, to the **p**, they must take Ezk 44:19
holiness to the **p** through their Ezk 44:19
must teach My **p** the difference Ezk 44:23
longer oppress My **p** but give the Ezk 45:8
end to your evictions of My **p**." Ezk 45:9
to make atonement for the **p**." Ezk 45:15
All the **p** of the land must take Ezk 45:16
and all the **p** of the land. Ezk 45:22
The **p** of the land will also bow Ezk 46:3
When the **p** of the land come Ezk 46:9
the **p** enter, the prince will Ezk 46:10
that none of My **p** will be Ezk 46:18
and transmit holiness to the **p**." Ezk 46:20
Wherever **p** live—or wild Dn 2:38
will not be left to another **p**. Dn 2:44
P of every nation and language, Dn 3:4
when all the **p** heard the sound Dn 3:7
p of every nation and language Dn 3:7
a decree that anyone of any **p**, Dn 3:29
To those of every **p**, nation, and Dn 4:1
driven away from **p** to live with Dn 4:25
driven away from **p** to live with Dn 4:32
He was driven away from **p**. Dn 4:33
He was driven away from **p**, Dn 5:21
wrote to those of every **p**, Dn 6:25
p must tremble in fear before Dn 6:26
that those of every **p**, nation, Dn 7:14
heaven will be given to the **p**, Dn 7:27

powerful along with the holy **p**. Dn 8:24
and all the **p** of the land. Dn 9:6
brought Your **p** out of the land Dn 9:15
Jerusalem and Your **p** have become Dn 9:16
city and Your **p** are called by Dn 9:19
sin and the sin of my **p** Israel, Dn 9:20
about your **p** and your holy city Dn 9:24
The **p** of the coming prince will Dn 9:26
happen to your **p** in the last Dn 10:14
among your own **p** will assert Dn 11:14
the **p** who know their God will Dn 11:32
are wise among the **p** will give Dn 11:33
the prominent **p** of the Ammonites Dn 11:41
watch over your **p** will rise up. Dn 12:1
time all your **p** who are found Dn 12:1
of the holy **p** is shattered, Dn 12:7
Name him Not My **P**, for you are Hs 1:9
you are not My **p**, and I will not Hs 1:9
You are not My **p**, they will be Hs 1:10
My **P** and your sisters: Hs 2:1
will enable the **p** to rest Hs 2:18
I will say to Not My **P**: Hs 2:23
You are My **p**, and he will say: Hs 2:23
the **p** of Israel will return and Hs 3:5
of the LORD, **p** of Israel, for Hs 4:1
My **p** are destroyed for lack of Hs 4:6
They feed on the sin of My **p**; Hs 4:8
happen to both **p** and priests. Hs 4:9
p consult their wooden ⌊idols⌋ Hs 4:12
P without discernment are doomed. Hs 4:14
I return My **p** from captivity, Hs 6:11
the **p** will mourn over it, over Hs 10:5
battle will rise against your **p**, Hs 10:14
p are bent on turning from Me. Hs 11:7
P say about them, "Let the men Hs 13:2
The **p** will return and live Hs 14:7
a great and strong **p** ⌊appears⌋, Jl 2:2
Gather the **p**; sanctify the Jl 2:16
pity on Your **p**, LORD, and do not Jl 2:17
for His land and spared His **p**. Jl 2:18
The LORD answered His **p**: Jl 2:19
My **p** will never again be put to Jl 2:26
My **p** will never again be put to Jl 2:27
with them there because of My **p**, Jl 3:2
They cast lots for My **p**; Jl 3:3
You sold the **p** of Judah and Jl 3:6
the hands of the **p** of Judah, Jl 3:8
LORD will be a refuge for His **p**, Jl 3:16
done⌋ to the **p** of Judah in whose Jl 3:19
The **p** of Aram will be exiled to Am 1:5
in a city, aren't **p** afraid? Am 3:6
The **p** are incapable of doing Am 3:10
the notable **p** in this first of Am 6:1
a plumb line among My **p** Israel; Am 7:8
prophesy to My **p** Israel.'" Am 7:15
end has come for My **p** Israel; Am 8:2
P will stagger from sea to sea Am 8:12
down on the heads of all the **p**. Am 9:1
All the sinners among My **p**, Am 9:10
the fortunes of My **p** Israel. Am 9:14
rejoice over the **p** of Judah in Ob 12
the gate of My **p** in the day of Ob 13
⌊**P** from⌋ the Negev will possess Ob 19
your country and what **p** are you Jnh 1:8
more than 120,000 **p** who cannot Jnh 4:11
has approached the gate of my **p**, Mc 1:9
out the allotted land of my **p**. Mc 2:4
But recently My **p** have risen up Mc 2:8
the women of My **p** out of their Mc 2:9
be just the preacher for this **p**! Mc 2:11
It will be noisy with **p**. Mc 2:12
off the skin of **p** and ⌊strip⌋ Mc 3:2
flesh of my **p** after you strip Mc 3:3
prophets who lead my **p** astray, Mc 3:5
will return to the **p** of Israel. Mc 5:3
LORD has a case against His **p**, Mc 6:2
p, what have I done to you, or Mc 6:3
p, remember what Balak king of Mc 6:5
will bear the scorn of My **p**." Mc 6:16
Godly **p** have vanished from the Mc 7:2
is no one upright among the **p**. Mc 7:2
are the **p** in his own home Mc 7:6
On that day **p** will come to you Mc 7:12
Shepherd Your **p** with Your staff, Mc 7:14
Your **p** are scattered across the Nah 3:18
You come out to save Your **p**, Hab 3:13
come against the **p** invading us. Hab 3:16
have taunted My **p** and threatened Zph 2:8

remnant of My **p** will plunder Zph 2:9
against the **p** of the LORD of Zph 2:10
My dispersed **p**, will bring an Zph 3:10
a meek and humble **p** among you, Zph 3:12
says this: These **p** say: The time Hg 1:2
yields, on the **p** and animals, Hg 1:11
remnant of the **p** obeyed the Hg 1:12
So the **p** feared the LORD. Hg 1:12
the LORD's message to the **p**, Hg 1:13
of all the remnant of the **p**. Hg 1:14
and to the remnant of the **p**: Hg 2:2
strong, all you **p** of the land"— Hg 2:4
So is this **p**, and so is this Hg 2:14
So tell the **p**: This is what the Zch 1:3
of the number of **p** and livestock Zch 2:4
on that day and become My **p**. Zch 2:11
Let all **p** be silent before the Zch 2:13
P who are far off will come and Zch 6:15
Now ⌊the **p** of⌋ Bethel had sent Zch 7:2
Ask all the **p** of the land and Zch 7:5
remnant of this **p** in those days, Zch 8:6
I will save My **p** from the land Zch 8:7
They will be My **p**, and I will be Zch 8:8
remnant of this **p** as in the Zch 8:11
remnant of this **p** all these Zch 8:12
A mongrel **p** will live in Ashdod, Zch 9:6
that day as the flock of His **p**; Zch 9:16
Therefore ⌊the **p**⌋ wander like Zch 10:2
are My **p**, and they will say: Zch 13:9
the rest of the **p** will not be Zch 14:2
P will live there, and never Zch 14:11
And if the **p** of Egypt will not Zch 14:18
country and the **p** the LORD has Mal 1:4
and **p** should seek instruction Mal 2:7
before all the **p** because you are Mal 2:9
will save His **p** from their sins. Mt 1:21
scribes of the **p** and asked them Mt 2:4
who will shepherd My **p** Israel." Mt 2:6
Then ⌊**p** from⌋ Jerusalem, all Mt 3:5
The **p** who live in darkness have Mt 4:16
"and I will make you fish for **p**!" Mt 4:19
and sickness among the **p**. Mt 4:23
and teaches **p** to do so will be Mt 5:19
righteousness in front of **p**, Mt 6:1
streets, to be applauded by **p**. Mt 6:2
street corners to be seen by **p**. Mt 6:5
if you forgive **p** their Mt 6:14
But if you don't forgive **p**, Mt 6:15
their fasting is obvious to **p**. Mt 6:16
your fasting to **p** but to your Mt 6:18
Because **p** will hand you over to Mt 10:17
p will be forgiven every sin and Mt 12:31
day of judgment **p** will have to Mt 12:36
and righteous **p** longed to see Mt 13:17
But while **p** were sleeping, Mt 13:25
separate the evil **p** from the Mt 13:49
p honor Me with their lips, Mt 15:8
do **p** say that the Son of Man is? Mt 16:13
is made up of **p** like this." Mt 19:14
elders of the **p** came up to Him Mt 21:23
and to be called 'Rabbi' by **p**. Mt 23:7
up the kingdom of heaven from **p**. Mt 23:13
Blind **p**! For which is greater, Mt 23:19
outside you seem righteous to **p**, Mt 23:28
the elders of the **p** assembled Mt 26:3
won't be rioting among the **p**." Mt 26:5
priests and elders of the **p**. Mt 26:47
elders of the **p** plotted against Mt 27:1
All the **p** answered, "His blood Mt 27:25
Him, and tell the **p**, 'He has Mt 27:64
among Jewish **p** to this day. Mt 28:15
and all the **p** of Jerusalem were Mk 1:5
"and I will make you fish for **p**!" Mk 1:17
So many **p** gathered together that Mk 2:2
P came and asked Him, "Why do Mk 2:18
P will be forgiven for all sins Mk 3:28
and **p** went to see what had Mk 5:14
Go back home to your own **p**, Mk 5:19
p came from the synagogue Mk 5:35
p weeping and wailing loudly. Mk 5:38
on a few sick **p** and healed them. Mk 6:5
welcome you and **p** refuse to Mk 6:11
preached that **p** should repent. Mk 6:12
anointing many sick **p** with oil, Mk 6:13
For many **p** were coming and Mk 6:31
P ran there by land from all the Mk 6:33
to have all the **p** sit down in Mk 6:39
disciples to set before the **p**. Mk 6:41
p immediately recognized Him. Mk 6:54
p honor Me with their lips, Mk 7:6
He even makes deaf **p** hear, Mk 7:37
hear, and **p** unable to speak Mk 7:37
desolate place to fill these **p**?" Mk 8:4
disciples to set before ⌊the **p**⌋. Mk 8:6
and said, "I see **p**—they look Mk 8:24
Who do **p** say that I am?" Mk 8:27
Some **p** were bringing little Mk 10:13
Many **p** told him to keep quiet, Mk 10:48
Many **p** spread their robes on the Mk 11:8
rich **p** were putting in large Mk 12:41
may be rioting among the **p**." Mk 14:2
release for the **p** a prisoner Mk 15:6
assembly of the **p** was praying Lk 1:10
ready for the Lord a prepared **p**. Lk 1:17
p were waiting for Zechariah, Lk 1:21
away my disgrace among the **p**." Lk 1:25
provided redemption for His **p**. Lk 1:68
to give His **p** knowledge of Lk 1:77
joy that will be for all the **p**: Lk 2:10
peace on earth to **p** He favors! Lk 2:14
and glory to Your **p** Israel. Lk 2:32
in favor with God and with **p**. Lk 2:52
Now the **p** were waiting Lk 3:15
proclaimed good news to the **p**. Lk 3:18
When all the **p** were baptized, Lk 3:21
now on you will be catching **p**!" Lk 5:10
multitude of **p** from all Judea Lk 6:17
Blessed are you when **p** hate you, Lk 6:22
to you when all **p** speak well of Lk 6:26
sayings in the hearing of the **p**, Lk 7:1
and "God has visited His **p**." Lk 7:16
Jesus healed many **p** of diseases, Lk 7:21
granted sight to many blind **p**. Lk 7:21
And when all the **p**, including Lk 7:29
I compare the **p** of this Lk 7:31
and **p** were flocking to Him from Lk 8:4
Then **p** went out to see what had Lk 8:35
Then all the **p** of the Gerasene Lk 8:37
In the presence of all the **p**, Lk 8:47
and buy food for all these **p**." Lk 9:13
a sign to the **p** of Nineveh, Lk 11:30
the **p** who walk over them don't Lk 11:44
You load **p** with burdens that are Lk 11:46
to throw ⌊**p**⌋ into hell after Lk 12:5
You must be like **p** waiting for Lk 12:36
some **p** came and reported to Him Lk 13:1
sinful than all the **p** who live Lk 13:4
99 righteous **p** who don't need Lk 15:7
p will welcome me into their Lk 16:4
in dealing⌋ with their own **p**. Lk 16:8
highly admired by **p** is revolting Lk 16:15
p went on eating, drinking, Lk 17:27
p went on eating, drinking, Lk 17:28
You that I'm not like other **p**— Lk 18:11
p were even bringing infants Lk 18:15
the **p**, when they saw it, gave Lk 18:43
leaders of the **p** were looking Lk 19:47
all the **p** were captivated Lk 19:48
was teaching the **p** in the temple Lk 20:1
all the **p** will stone us, Lk 20:6
to tell the **p** this parable: Lk 20:9
them, but they feared the **p**. Lk 20:19
While all the **p** were listening, Lk 20:45
all these **p** have put in gifts Lk 21:4
land and wrath against this **p**. Lk 21:23
P will faint from fear and Lk 21:26
Then all the **p** would come early Lk 21:38
they were afraid of the **p**. Lk 22:2
elders of the **p**, both the chief Lk 22:66
He stirs up the **p**, teaching Lk 23:5
priests, the leaders, and the **p**, Lk 23:13
man as one who subverts the **p**. Lk 23:14
multitude of the **p** followed Him, Lk 23:27
The **p** stood watching, and even Lk 23:35
speech before God and all the **p**, Lk 24:19
and His own **p** did not receive Jn 1:11
after **p** have drunk freely, Jn 2:10
complex He found **p** selling oxen, Jn 2:14
and **p** loved darkness rather than Jn 3:19
P were coming and being baptized, Jn 3:23
wants such **p** to worship Him. Jn 4:23
Unless you ⌊**p**⌋ see signs and Jn 4:48
so that all **p** will honor the Son Jn 5:23
buy bread so these **p** can eat?" Jn 6:5
said, "Have the **p** sit down." Jn 6:10
When the **p** saw the sign He had Jn 6:14
contrary, He's deceiving the **p**." Jn 7:12
Some of the **p** of Jerusalem were Jn 7:25
all the **p** were coming to Him. Jn 8:2
should die for the **p** rather than Jn 11:50
I will draw all ⌊**p**⌋ to Myself." Jn 12:32
By this all **p** will know that you Jn 13:35
one man should die for the **p**. Jn 18:14
number of **p** who were together Ac 1:15
For these **p** are not drunk, Ac 2:15
you used lawless **p** to nail Him Ac 2:23
day about 3,000 **p** were added to Ac 2:41
and having favor with all the **p**. Ac 2:47
All the **p** saw him walking and Ac 3:9
John, all the **p**, greatly amazed Ac 3:11
saw this, he addressed the **p**: Ac 3:12
completely cut off from the **p**. Ac 3:23
as they were speaking to the **p**, Ac 4:1
teaching the **p** and proclaiming Ac 4:2
Rulers of the **p** and elders: Ac 4:8
you and to all the **p** of Israel, Ac 4:10
heaven given to **p** by which we Ac 4:12
spread any further among the **p**, Ac 4:17
because the **p** were all giving Ac 4:21
done among the **p** through the Ac 5:12
but the **p** praised them highly. Ac 5:13
bringing sick **p** and those who Ac 5:16
tell the **p** all about this life. Ac 5:20
complex and teaching the **p**." Ac 5:25
were afraid the **p** might stone Ac 5:26
who was respected by all the **p**, Ac 5:34
wonders and signs among the **p**. Ac 6:8
stirred up the **p**, the elders, Ac 6:12
all his relatives, 75 **p** in all, Ac 7:14
the **p** flourished and multiplied Ac 7:17
the oppression of My **p** in Egypt; Ac 7:34
You stiff-necked **p** with Ac 7:51
and astounded the Samaritan **p**, Ac 8:9
from many **p** about this man, Ac 9:13
for the ⌊Jewish⌋ **p** and always Ac 10:2
not by all the **p**, but by us, Ac 10:41
commanded us to preach to the **p**, Ac 10:42
large numbers of **p** were added to Ac 11:24
him out to the **p** after the Ac 12:4
all that the Jewish **p** expected." Ac 12:11
of encouragement for the **p**, Ac 13:15
The God of this **p** Israel chose Ac 13:17
exalted the **p** during their stay Ac 13:17
to all the **p** of Israel. Ac 13:24
are now His witnesses to the **p**. Ac 13:31
But the **p** of the city were Ac 14:4
the Gentiles a **p** for His name. Ac 15:14
The **p** here were more open-minded Ac 17:11
now commands all **p** everywhere to Ac 17:30
I have many **p** in this city." Ac 18:10
persuades **p** to worship God Ac 18:13
telling the **p** that they should Ac 19:4
number of **p** by saying that gods Ac 19:26
wanted to go in before the **p**, Ac 19:30
to make his defense to the **p**. Ac 19:33
and the local **p** begged him not Ac 21:12
everywhere against our **p**, Ac 21:28
and the **p** rushed together. Ac 21:30
for the mass of **p** were following Ac 21:36
ask you, let me speak to the **p**." Ac 21:39
motioned with his hand to the **p**. Ac 21:40
Him to all **p** of what you have Ac 22:15
evil of a ruler of your **p**." Ac 23:5
rescue you from the **p** and from Ac 26:17
to our **p** and to the Gentiles. Ac 26:23
The local **p** showed us Ac 28:2
the local **p** saw the creature Ac 28:4
against our **p** or the customs Ac 28:17
He said, Go to this **p** and say: Ac 28:26
unrighteousness of **p** who by Rm 1:18
As a result, **p** are without Rm 1:20
God judges what **p** have kept Rm 2:16
as some **p** slanderously claim Rm 3:8
are not My **p**, there they will Rm 9:26
to a disobedient and defiant **p**. Rm 10:21
then, has God rejected His **p**? Rm 11:1
rejected His **p** whom He foreknew Rm 11:2
make my own **p** jealous and save Rm 11:14
you Gentiles, with His **p**! Rm 15:10
for such **p** do not serve our Lord Rm 16:18
spiritual things to spiritual **p**. 1Co 2:13
you as spiritual **p** but as people 1Co 3:1
people but as **p** of the flesh, 1Co 3:1
and living like ordinary **p**? 1Co 3:3

with sexually immoral **p**— 1Co 5:9
to this world's immoral **p**, 1Co 5:10
sexually immoral **p**, idolaters, 1Co 6:9
thieves, greedy **p**, drunkards, 1Co 6:10
I wish that all **p** were just like 1Co 7:7
But such **p** will have trouble in 1Co 7:28
although I am free from all **p**, 1Co 9:19
to all, in order to win more **p**. 1Co 9:19
have become all things to all **p**, 1Co 9:22
The **p** sat down to eat and drink, 1Co 10:7
a single day 23,000 **p** fell dead. 1Co 10:8
I am speaking as to wise **p**. 1Co 10:15
Look at the **p** of Israel. 1Co 10:18
to please all **p** in all things, 1Co 10:33
speaks to **p** for edification, 1Co 14:3
By **p** of other languages and by 1Co 14:21
I will speak to this **p**; 1Co 14:21
and **p** who are uninformed or 1Co 14:23
at His coming, the **p** of Christ. 1Co 15:23
why are **p** baptized for them? 1Co 15:29
because some **p** are ignorant 1Co 15:34
submit to such **p**, and to 1Co 16:16
Therefore recognize such **p**. 1Co 16:18
through more and more **p**, 2Co 4:15
fear of the Lord, we persuade **p**. 2Co 5:11
God, and they will be My **p**. 2Co 6:16
certain **p** who think we are 2Co 10:2
For such **p** are false apostles, 2Co 11:13
dangers from my own **p**, dangers 2Co 11:26
trying to win the favor of **p**, Gl 1:10
Or am I striving to please **p**? Gl 1:10
I were still trying to please **p**, Gl 1:10
many contemporaries among my **p**, Gl 1:14
to these **p** for even an hour, Gl 2:5
not made known to **p** in other Eph 3:5
captivity; He gave gifts to **p**. Eph 4:8
not as unwise **p** but as wise— Eph 5:15
and we didn't seek glory from **p**, 1Th 2:6
same things from **p** of your own 1Th 2:14
we command and exhort such **p**, 2Th 3:12
command certain **p** not to teach 1Tm 1:3
you will know how **p** ought to act 1Tm 3:15
which plunge **p** into ruin and 1Tm 6:9
some **p** have deviated from the 1Tm 6:21
For **p** will be lovers of self, 2Tm 3:2
its power. Avoid these **p**! 2Tm 3:5
Evil **p** and imposters will become 2Tm 3:13
are also many rebellious **p**, Ti 1:10
with salvation for all **p**, Ti 2:11
cleanse for Himself a special **p**, Ti 2:14
showing gentleness to all **p**. Ti 3:2
And our **p** must also learn to Ti 3:14
for the sins of the **p**. Heb 2:17
remains, therefore, for God's **p**. Heb 4:9
in service to God for the **p**, Heb 5:1
himself as well as for the **p**, Heb 5:3
to collect a tenth from the **p**— Heb 7:5
under it the **p** received the law Heb 7:11
sins, then for those of the **p**. Heb 7:27
But finding fault with His **p**, Heb 8:8
God, and they will be My **p**. Heb 8:10
for the sins of the **p** committed Heb 9:7
a will is valid only when **p** die, Heb 9:17
Moses to all the **p** according to Heb 9:19
the scroll itself and all the **p**, Heb 9:19
is appointed for **p** to die once— Heb 9:27
The Lord will judge His **p**. Heb 10:30
suffer with the **p** of God rather Heb 11:25
of righteous **p** made perfect, Heb 12:23
judge immoral **p** and adulterers. Heb 13:4
sanctify the **p** by His own blood Heb 13:12
your hearts, double-minded **p**! Jms 4:8
Come now, you rich **p**! Jms 5:1
a holy nation, a **p** for His 1Pt 2:9
were not a **p**, but now you are 1Pt 2:10
people, but now you are God's **p**; 1Pt 2:10
the ignorance of foolish **p**. 1Pt 2:15
live⌋ as free **p**, but don't use 1Pt 2:16
that is, eight **p**—were saved 1Pt 3:20
also false prophets among the **p**, 2Pt 2:1
Bold, arrogant **p**! They do not 2Pt 2:10
But these **p**, like irrational 2Pt 2:12
unstable **p**, and with hearts 2Pt 2:14
These **p** are springs without 2Pt 2:17
p who have barely escaped from 2Pt 2:18
since **p** are enslaved to whatever 2Pt 2:19
what sort of **p** you should be 2Pt 3:11
of all saved a **p** out of Egypt, Jd 5
But these **p** blaspheme anything Jd 10
These **p** are discontented Jd 16
flattering **p** for their own Jd 16
These **p** create divisions and are Jd 19
you have a few **p** in Sardis who Rv 3:4
You redeemed ⌊**p**⌋ for God by Your Rv 5:9
and language and **p** and nation. Rv 5:9
so that **p** would slaughter one Rv 6:4
nation, tribe, **p**, and language, Rv 7:9
Who are these **p** robed in white, Rv 7:13
many of the **p** died from the Rv 8:11
but only **p** who do not have God's Rv 9:4
In those days **p** will seek death Rv 9:6
power to harm **p** for five months Rv 9:10
The rest of the **p**, who were not Rv 9:20
and 7,000 **p** were killed in the Rv 11:13
over every tribe, **p**, language, Rv 13:7
from heaven to earth before **p**. Rv 13:13
nation, tribe, language, and **p**. Rv 14:6
out on the **p** who had the mark Rv 16:2
the power to burn **p** with fire, Rv 16:8
and **p** were burned by the intense Rv 16:9
P gnawed their tongues from pain Rv 16:10
fell from heaven on the **p**, Rv 16:21
out of her, My **p**, so that you Rv 18:4
and **p** seated on them who were Rv 20:4
will be His **p**, and God Himself Rv 21:3
and **p** will not need lamplight or Rv 22:5

PEOPLE'S *(38)*

Moses brought the **p** words back Ex 19:8
reported the **p** words to the LORD Ex 19:9
Sacrifice the **p** offering and Lv 9:7
Aaron presented the **p** offering. Lv 9:15
goat for the **p** sin offering, Lv 9:15
and the ram as the **p** fellowship Lv 9:18
male goat for the **p** sin offering Lv 16:15
and the **p** burnt offering; Lv 16:24
an object of your **p** cursing and Nm 5:21
saw the outskirts of the **p** camp. Nm 22:41
Disregard this **p** stubbornness, Dt 9:27
the **p** hearts melted and became Jos 7:5
me caused the **p** hearts to melt Jos 14:8
who took the **p** provisions and Jdg 7:8
attention to His **p** ⌊need⌋ by Ru 1:6
to all the **p** words and then 1Sm 8:21
you sought a **p** gods that could 2Ch 25:15
through the **p** efforts. Ezr 5:8
be angry with Your **p** prayers? Ps 80:4
You took away Your **p** guilt; Ps 85:2
and **p** eyes are never satisfied. Pr 27:20
face and remove His **p** disgrace Is 25:8
LORD bandages His **p** injuries and Is 30:26
because of My **p** rebellion. Is 53:8
every⌋ obstacle from My **p** way." Is 57:14
For My **p** lives will be like the Is 65:22
have treated My **p** brokenness Jr 6:14
Go and stand in the **P** Gate, Jr 17:19
palace and the **p** houses and tore Jr 39:8
and an object of **p** gossip and Ezk 36:3
take any of the **p** inheritance, Ezk 46:18
will cook the **p** sacrifices." Ezk 46:24
For this **p** heart has grown Mt 13:15
and put them on **p** shoulders, Mt 23:4
within, out of **p** hearts, come Mk 7:21
For this **p** heart has grown Ac 28:27
measure about other **p** labors. 2Co 10:15
Some **p** sins are evident, going 1Tm 5:24

PEOPLES *(197)*

The coastland **p** spread out into Gn 10:5
and all the **p** on earth will be Gn 12:3
kings of **p** will come from her." Gn 17:16
May **p** serve you and nations bow Gn 27:29
you become an assembly of **p**. Gn 28:3
All the **p** on earth will be Gn 28:14
of the **p** belongs to Him. Gn 49:10
When the **p** hear, they will Ex 15:14
own possession out of all the **p**, Ex 19:5
who set you apart from the **p**. Lv 20:24
of you on the **p** everywhere under Dt 2:25
in the eyes of the **p**. Dt 4:6
will scatter you among the **p**, Dt 4:27
the gods of the **p** around you, Dt 6:14
out of all the **p** on the face of Dt 7:6
were more numerous than all **p**, Dt 7:7
you were the fewest of all **p**. Dt 7:7
You will be blessed above all **p**; Dt 7:14
destroy all the **p** the LORD your Dt 7:16
the same to all the **p** you fear. Dt 7:19
⌊He chose⌋ you out of all the **p**, Dt 10:15
of the gods of the **p** around you, Dt 13:7
out of all the **p** on the face Dt 14:2
Then all the **p** of the earth will Dt 28:10
among all the **p** where the LORD Dt 28:37
you among all **p** from one end Dt 28:64
from all the **p** where the LORD Dt 30:3
boundaries of the **p** according to Dt 32:8
he gores all the **p** with them to Dt 33:17
They summon the **p** to a mountain; Dt 33:19
among all the **p** whose lands we Jos 24:17
drove out before us all the **p**, Jos 24:18
the surrounding **p** and bowed down Jdg 2:12
and the eastern **p** came and Jdg 6:3
and casts down **p** under me. 2Sm 22:48
so that all the **p** of the earth 1Kg 8:60
and ridicule among all the **p**. 1Kg 9:7
As for all the **p** who remained of 1Kg 9:20
proclaim His deeds among the **p**. 1Ch 16:8
His wonderful works among all **p**. 1Ch 16:24
all the gods of the **p** are idols, 1Ch 16:26
families of the **p**, ascribe to 1Ch 16:28
Then all the **p** of the earth will 2Ch 6:33
and ridicule among all the **p**. 2Ch 7:20
As for all the **p** who remained of 2Ch 8:7
like the **p** of ⌊other⌋ lands 2Ch 13:9
done to all the **p** of the lands? 2Ch 32:13
the gods of the **p** of the land, 2Ch 32:19
they feared the surrounding **p**. Ezr 3:3
the rest of the **p** whom the great Ezr 4:10
the surrounding **p** whose Ezr 9:1
mixed with the surrounding **p**. Ezr 9:2
The surrounding **p** have filled it Ezr 9:11
with the **p** who commit these Ezr 9:14
women from the surrounding **p**, Ezr 10:2
the surrounding **p** and ⌊your⌋ Ezr 10:11
I will scatter you among the **p**. Neh 1:8
kingdoms and **p** and assigned them Neh 9:22
the surrounding **p** over to them, Neh 9:24
them over to the surrounding **p**. Neh 9:30
the surrounding **p** to ⌊obey⌋ the Neh 10:28
the surrounding **p** and will not Neh 10:30
the surrounding **p** bring Neh 10:31
one of the other **p** but could not Neh 13:24
and the **p** who are in every Est 1:16
throughout the **p** in every Est 3:8
to all the **p** so that they might Est 3:14
rebel and the **p** plot in vain? Ps 2:1
the assembly of **p** gather around Ps 7:7
The LORD judges the **p**; Ps 7:8
judgment on the **p** with fairness. Ps 9:8
proclaim His deeds among the **p**. Ps 9:11
and subdues **p** under me. Ps 18:47
He thwarts the plans of the **p**. Ps 33:10
settle them, You crushed the **p**. Ps 44:2
a laughingstock among the **p**. Ps 44:14
the **p** fall under you. Ps 45:5
therefore the **p** will praise you Ps 45:17
Clap your hands, all you **p**; Ps 47:1
subdues **p** under us and nations Ps 47:3
nobles of the **p** have assembled Ps 47:9
Hear this, all you **p**; Ps 49:1
praise You, Lord, among the **p**; Ps 57:9
Praise our God, you **p**; Ps 66:8
Let the **p** praise You, God; Ps 67:3
let all the **p** praise You. Ps 67:3
You judge the **p** with fairness Ps 67:4
Let the **p** praise You, God, let Ps 67:5
God, let all the **p** praise You. Ps 67:5
bulls with the calves of the **p**. Ps 68:30
Scatter the **p** who take pleasure Ps 68:30
Your strength among the **p**. Ps 77:14
registers the **p**, the LORD will Ps 87:6
I carry ⌊abuse⌋ from all the **p**— Ps 89:50
His wonderful works among all **p**. Ps 96:3
all the gods of the **p** are idols, Ps 96:5
you families of the **p**, ascribe Ps 96:7
He judges the **p** fairly." Ps 96:10
and the **p** with His faithfulness Ps 96:13
all the **p** see His glory. Ps 97:6
righteously and the **p** fairly. Ps 98:9
reigns! Let the **p** tremble. He is Ps 99:1
He is exalted above all the **p**. Ps 99:2
p and kingdoms are assembled Ps 102:22
proclaim His deeds among the **p**. Ps 105:1
the ruler of **p** set him free. Ps 105:20
what other **p** had worked for. Ps 105:44
destroy the **p** as the LORD had Ps 106:34

praise You, LORD, among the **p**; Ps 108:3
all nations! Glorify Him, all **p**! Ps 117:1
kings of the earth and all **p**, Ps 148:11
nations and punishment on the **p**, Ps 149:7
and many **p** will come and say, Is 2:3
provide arbitration for many **p**. Is 2:4
Band together, **p**, and be broken; Is 8:9
stand as a banner for the **p**. Is 11:10
Celebrate His deeds among the **p**. Is 12:4
It struck the **p** in anger with Is 14:6
roar of many **p**—they roar like Is 17:12
for all the **p** on this mountain Is 25:6
the shroud over all the **p**, Is 25:7
the jaws of the **p** to lead ⌊them⌋ Is 30:28
The **p** flee at the thunderous Is 33:3
The **p** will be burned to ashes, Is 33:12
you **p**, pay attention! Is 34:1
And let **p** renew their strength. Is 41:1
and **p** in place of your life. Is 43:4
and the **p** are assembled. Is 43:9
distant **p**, pay attention. Is 49:1
and raise My banner to the **p**. Is 49:22
made him a witness to the **p**, Is 55:4
leader and commander for the **p**, Is 55:4
earth, and total darkness the **p**; Is 60:2
and their posterity among the **p**. Is 61:9
Raise a banner for the **p**. Is 62:10
customs of the **p** are worthless. Jr 10:3
and all the mixed **p**; Jr 25:20
of the mixed **p** who have settled Jr 25:24
The **p** will have labored for Jr 51:58
us disgusting filth among the **p**. Lm 3:45
to many **p** of unintelligible Ezk 3:6
you from the **p** and assemble you Ezk 11:17
like the **p** of ⌊other⌋ countries, Ezk 20:32
you from the **p** and gather you Ezk 20:34
wilderness of the **p** and enter Ezk 20:35
you from the **p** and gather you Ezk 20:41
you off from the **p** and eliminate Ezk 25:7
what remains of the coastal **p**. Ezk 25:16
gateway to the **p** is shattered. Ezk 26:2
merchant of the **p** to many coasts Ezk 27:3
the seas, you satisfied many **p**. Ezk 27:33
trade among the **p** hiss at you; Ezk 27:36
Israel from the **p** where they are Ezk 28:25
All the **p** of the earth left its Ezk 31:12
you with an assembly of many **p**, Ezk 32:3
trouble the hearts of many **p**, Ezk 32:9
will bring them out from the **p**, Ezk 34:13
the reproach of the **p** any more; Ezk 36:15
troops—many **p** are with you. Ezk 38:6
from many **p** to the mountains Ezk 38:8
were brought out from the **p**, Ezk 38:8
many **p** with you will advance, Ezk 38:9
you and many **p** with you, who are Ezk 38:15
and the many **p** who are with him. Ezk 38:22
and the **p** who are with you will Ezk 39:4
back from the **p** and gather them Ezk 39:27
the **p** will mix with one another Dn 2:43
He gave him, all **p**, nations, and Dn 5:19
should it be said among the **p**, Jl 2:17
all you **p**; pay attention, Mc 1:2
P will stream to it, Mc 4:1
disputes among many **p** and Mc 4:3
Though all the **p** each walk in Mc 4:5
bronze, so you can crush many **p**. Mc 4:13
will be among many **p** like dew Mc 5:7
among many **p**, like a lion among Mc 5:8
collects all the **p** for himself. Hab 2:5
the **p** who remain will plunder Hab 2:8
by wiping out many **p** and sinning Hab 2:10
that the **p** labor ⌊only⌋ to fuel Hab 2:13
pure speech to the **p** so that all Zph 3:9
among all the **p** of the earth, Zph 3:20
P will yet come, the residents Zch 8:20
Many **p** and strong nations will Zch 8:22
I had made with all the **p**. Zch 11:10
staggering for the **p** who Zch 12:2
a heavy stone for all the **p**; Zch 12:3
consume all the **p** around them Zch 12:6
the LORD strikes all the **p** with, Zch 14:12
and then all the **p** of the earth Mt 24:30
it⌋ in the presence of all **p**— Lk 2:31
and the **p** plot futile things? Ac 4:25
Gentiles and the **p** of Israel, Ac 4:27
all the **p** should praise Him! Rm 15:11
prophesy again about many **p**, Rv 10:11
And representatives from the **p**, Rv 11:9
was seated, are **p**, multitudes, Rv 17:15

PEOR *(9)*
took Balaam to the top of **P**, Nm 23:28
aligned itself with Baal of **P**, Nm 25:3
themselves with Baal of **P**." Nm 25:5
against you in the **P** incident. Nm 25:18
the day the plague came at **P**." Nm 25:18
the LORD in the **P** incident, Nm 31:16
of you who followed Baal of **P**. Dt 4:3
the sin of **P**, which brought Jos 22:17
Baal of **P** and ate sacrifices Ps 106:28

PER *(6)*
one animal **p** household. Ex 12:3
take two quarts **p** individual, Ex 16:16
two-fifths of an ounce **p** man, Ex 38:26
on 45 pillars, fifteen **p** row. 1Kg 7:3
of half a bushel **p** bull and half Ezk 45:24
bull and half a bushel **p** ram, Ezk 45:24

PERAZIM *(1)*
rise up as ⌊He did⌋ at Mount **P**. Is 28:21

PERCEIVE *(8)*
I **p** him, but not near. Nm 24:17
if I go west, I cannot **p** Him. Jb 23:8
do not **p** the LORD's actions, Is 5:12
keep looking, but do not **p**. Is 6:9
then we will be in awe and **p**. Is 41:23
will look and look, yet never **p**. Mt 13:14
may look and look, yet not **p**; Mk 4:12
will look and look, yet never **p**. Ac 28:26

PERCEIVES *(1)*
Who **p** his unintentional sins? Ps 19:12

PERCEIVING *(3)*
p their thoughts, Jesus said, Mt 9:4
But **p** their malice, Jesus said, Mt 22:18
But **p** their thoughts, Jesus Lk 5:22

PERCENT *(3)*
will be one **p** of every cor. Ezk 45:14
the payments⌋ of 10 **p** and the Mal 3:8
Bring the full 10 **p** into the Mal 3:10

PERCENTAGE *(1)*
along with the **p** of the money, Neh 5:11

PERCEPTION *(2)*
no one has the **p** or insight to Is 44:19
knowledge and **p**, and the ability Dn 5:12

PERCEPTIVE *(6)*
All of them are clear to the **p**, Pr 8:9
comes⌋ easily to the **p**. Pr 14:6
cuts into a **p** person more than Pr 17:10
Wisdom is the focus of the **p**, Pr 17:24
of the **p** will be hidden. Is 29:14
knowledgeable, **p**, and capable Dn 1:4

PERENNIALLY *(2)*
Jordan to the **p** watered grazing Jr 49:19
Jordan to the **p** watered grazing Jr 50:44

PERES *(1)*
P ⌊means that⌋ your kingdom has Dn 5:28

PERESH *(1)*
to a son, and she named ⌊him⌋ **P**. 1Ch 7:16

PEREZ *(14)*
out ⌊first⌋!" So he was named **P**. Gn 38:29
Er, Onan, Shelah, **P**, and Zerah; Gn 46:12
the Perezite clan from **P**; Nm 26:20
descendants of **P**: the Hezronite Nm 26:21
become like the house of **P**, Ru 4:12
Now this is the genealogy of **P**: Ru 4:18
of Perez: **P** fathered Hezron. Ru 4:18
Tamar bore him **P** and Zerah. 1Ch 2:4
P, Hezron, Carmi, Hur, and 1Ch 4:1
a descendant of **P** son of Judah; 1Ch 9:4
a descendant of **P** and chief of 1Ch 27:3
Judah fathered **P** and Zerah by Mt 1:3
by Tamar, **P** fathered Hezron Mt 1:3
son⌋ of **P**, ⌊son⌋ of Judah Lk 3:33

PEREZ'S *(4)*
land of Canaan. **P** sons: Hezron Gn 46:12
P sons: Hezron and Hamul. 1Ch 2:5
of Mahalalel, of **P** descendants; Neh 11:4
total number of **P** descendants, Neh 11:6

PEREZITE *(1)*
the **P** clan from Perez; Nm 26:20

PERFECT *(35)*
The Rock—His work is **p**; Dt 32:4
God—His way is **p**; the word of 2Sm 22:31
refuge; He makes my way **p**. 2Sm 22:33
He was a man of **p** integrity, Jb 1:1
him, a man of **p** integrity, who Jb 1:8
him, a man of **p** integrity, who Jb 2:3
profit if you **p** your behavior? Jb 22:3
one who has **p** knowledge is with Jb 36:4
of Him who has **p** knowledge? Jb 37:16
God—His way is **p**; the word of Ps 18:30
strength and makes my way **p**. Ps 18:32
instruction of the LORD is **p**, Ps 19:7
my darling, my dove, my **p** one. Sg 5:2
p to the one who gave her birth. Sg 6:9
long ago, with **p** faithfulness. Is 25:1
will keep in **p** peace the mind Is 26:3
it was **p** through My splendor, Ezk 16:14
you declared: I am **p** in beauty. Ezk 27:3
full of wisdom and **p** in beauty. Ezk 28:12
p, therefore, as your heavenly Mt 5:48
as your heavenly Father is **p**. Mt 5:48
you want to be **p**," Jesus said to Mt 19:21
given him this **p** health in front Ac 3:16
pleasing, and **p** will of God. Rm 12:2
when the **p** comes, the partial 1Co 13:10
on⌋ love—the **p** bond of unity. Col 3:14
their salvation **p** through Heb 2:10
that cannot **p** the worshiper's Heb 9:9
greater and more **p** tabernacle Heb 9:11
it can never **p** the worshipers by Heb 10:1
would not be made **p** without us. Heb 11:40
of righteous people made **p**, Heb 12:23
act and every **p** gift is from Jms 1:17
into the **p** law of freedom Jms 1:25
instead, **p** love drives out fear, 1Jn 4:18

PERFECTED *(12)*
"We have **p** a secret plan." Ps 64:6
your builders **p** your beauty. Ezk 27:4
they **p** your beauty. Ezk 27:11
for power is **p** in weakness." 2Co 12:9
After He was **p**, He became the Heb 5:9
(for the law **p** nothing), but a Heb 7:19
a Son, who has been **p** forever. Heb 7:28
offering He has **p** forever those Heb 10:14
and by works, faith was **p**. Jms 2:22
in him the love of God is **p**. 1Jn 2:5
in us and His love is **p** in us. 1Jn 4:12
love is **p** with us so that we may 1Jn 4:17

PERFECTER *(1)*
the source and **p** of our faith, Heb 12:2

PERFECTION *(6)*
From Zion, the **p** of beauty, God Ps 50:2
I have seen a limit to all **p**, Ps 119:96
that was called the **p** of beauty, Lm 2:15
the seal of **p**, full of wisdom Ezk 28:12
p came through the Levitical Heb 7:11
fears has not reached **p** in love. 1Jn 4:18

PERFECTLY *(3)*
feet from brim to brim, **p** round. 1Kg 7:23
feet from brim to brim, **p** round. 2Ch 4:2
as touched it were made **p** well. Mt 14:36

PERFORM *(42)*
P your duty as her Gn 38:8
My miracles that I will **p** in it. Ex 3:20
that you will **p** the signs with." Ex 4:17
P a miracle, tell Aaron: Ex 7:9
Aaron is to **p** the purification Ex 30:10
he is to **p** the purification Ex 30:10
I will **p** wonders in the presence Ex 34:10
They are to **p** duties for him and Nm 3:7
tent of meeting and **p** duties for Nm 3:8
who is qualified to **p** service, Nm 4:23
that they may **p** the LORD's work Nm 8:11
and his sons to **p** the work for Nm 8:19
to **p** the work at the LORD's Nm 16:9
They are to **p** duties for you and Nm 18:3
to the Levites who **p** the duties Nm 31:30
to the Levites who **p** the duties Nm 31:47
earth who can **p** deeds and mighty Dt 3:24
and **p** the duty of a Dt 25:5
isn't willing to **p** the duty of Dt 25:7
Shiloh come out to **p** the dances, Jdg 21:21
and to **p** for them great and 2Sm 7:23
my petition and **p** my request, Est 5:8
With God we will **p** valiantly; Ps 60:12
For You are great and **p** wonders; Ps 86:10
With God we will **p** valiantly; Ps 108:13
thing or wickedly **p** reckless Ps 141:4
work, and to **p** His task, His Is 28:21

the LORD will **p** for us something Jr 21:2
They failed to **p** all You Jr 32:23
will arise and **p** great signs and Mt 24:24
one who will **p** a miracle in My Mk 9:39
rise up and will **p** signs and Mk 13:22
child Jesus to **p** for Him what Lk 2:27
He did not first **p** the ritual Lk 11:38
no one could **p** these signs You Jn 3:2
can we do to **p** the works of God? Jn 6:28
What are You going to **p**? Jn 6:30
He won't **p** more signs than this Jn 7:31
can a sinful man **p** such signs?" Jn 9:16
promised He was also able to **p**. Rm 4:21
that those who **p** the temple 1Co 9:13
is permitted to **p** on behalf of Rv 13:14

PERFORMED *(33)*

to Moses and **p** the signs before Ex 4:30
Egyptians and **p** miraculous signs Ex 10:2
p the duties of the sanctuary Nm 3:38
the signs I have **p** among them? Nm 14:11
glory and the signs I **p** in Egypt Nm 14:22
deeds that Moses **p** in the sight Dt 34:12
of slavery and **p** these great Jos 24:17
and they **p** their task according 1Ch 6:32
of the men who **p** their service: 1Ch 25:1
the Levites who **p** skillfully 2Ch 30:22
You **p** signs and wonders against Neh 9:10
Your wonders You **p** among them. Neh 9:17
They **p** the service of their God Neh 12:45
the wonderful works He has **p**. Ps 78:4
when He **p** His miraculous signs Ps 78:43
the LORD, for He has **p** wonders; Ps 98:1
p His miraculous signs among Ps 105:27
Who has **p** and done ⌊this⌋, Is 41:4
You **p** signs and wonders in the Jr 32:20
these miracles **p** by His hands? Mk 6:2
to see some miracle **p** by Him. Lk 23:8
Jesus **p** this first sign in Cana Jn 2:11
second sign Jesus **p** after He Jn 4:54
though He had **p** so many signs Jn 12:37
Jesus **p** many other signs in the Jn 20:30
signs were being **p** through the Ac 2:43
this sign of healing had been **p**. Ac 4:22
wonders to be **p** through the name Ac 4:30
led them out and **p** wonders and Ac 7:36
miracles that were being **p**. Ac 8:13
and wonders be **p** through them. Ac 14:3
an apostle were **p** among you in 2Co 12:12
had **p** signs on his authority, Rv 19:20

PERFORMING *(11)*

revered with praises, **p** wonders? Ex 15:11
the singers **p** the service had Neh 13:10
p saving acts on the earth. Ps 74:12
out demons and **p** healings today Lk 13:32
signs that He was **p** on the sick. Jn 6:2
was **p** great wonders and signs Ac 6:8
and saw the signs he was **p**. Ac 8:6
God was **p** extraordinary miracles Ac 19:11
another, the **p** of miracles, to 1Co 12:10
repeatedly, **p** their ministry. Heb 9:6
are spirits of demons **p** signs, Rv 16:14

PERFORMS *(4)*

The priest who **p** the cleansing Lv 14:11
He **p** great and unsearchable Jb 9:10
He **p** signs and wonders in the Dn 6:27
He also **p** great signs, even Rv 13:13

PERFUME *(9)*

cassia ⌊**p**⌋ all your garments; Ps 45:8
good name is better than fine **p**, Ec 7:1
of your **p** is intoxicating; Sg 1:3
your name is **p** poured out. Sg 1:3
my **p** releases its fragrance. Sg 1:12
of your **p** than any balsam. Sg 4:10
like beds of spice, towers of **p**. Sg 5:13
sashes, **p** bottles, amulets Is 3:20
Instead of **p** there will be a Is 3:24

PERFUMED *(2)*

Wash, put on ⌊**p**⌋ oil, and wear Ru 3:3
I've **p** my bed with myrrh, aloes, Pr 7:17

PERFUMER *(2)*

scented blend, the work of a **p**; Ex 30:25
son of the **p** made repairs. Neh 3:8

PERFUMER'S *(1)*

Dead flies make a **p** oil ferment Ec 10:1

PERFUMERS *(1)*

take your daughters to become **p**, 1Sm 8:13

PERFUMES *(3)*

then with **p** and cosmetics for Est 2:12
with oil and multiplied your **p**; Is 57:9
and prepared spices and **p**. Lk 23:56

PERGA *(3)*

and came to **P** in Pamphylia. Ac 13:13
their journey from **P** and reached Ac 13:14
they spoke the message in **P**, Ac 14:25

PERGAMUM *(2)*

Ephesus, Smyrna, **P**, Thyatira, Rv 1:11
angel of the church in **P** write: Rv 2:12

PERHAPS *(41)*

(See pp. xi-xii.)

PERIDA'S *(1)*

(AKA PERUDA'S)
descendants, **P** descendants, Neh 7:57

PERIMETER *(2)*

arrived at the **p** of the camp as 1Sm 17:20
The **p** ⌊of the city⌋ will be six Ezk 48:35

PERIOD *(11)*

I am having my monthly **p**." Gn 31:35
has a discharge beyond her **p**, Lv 15:25
unclean as in her menstrual **p**. Lv 15:26
woman who is in her menstrual **p**; Lv 15:33
so that the time **p** of the seven Lv 25:8
But do not count the previous **p**, Nm 6:12
there for a **p** of four months. Jdg 19:2
At an earlier **p** in Israel, Ru 4:7
me a considerable **p** of time. 1Sm 29:3
to them for a certain **p** of time. Dn 7:12
boldly over a **p** of three months, Ac 19:8

PERIODS *(5)*

an animal for seven **p** of time. Dn 4:16
animals for seven **p** of time.' Dn 4:23
the sky for seven **p** of time, Dn 4:25
like cattle for seven **p** of time, Dn 4:32
know times or **p** that the Father Ac 1:7

PERISH *(68)*

Why should we **p** here in front of Gn 47:19
You will **p** among the nations; Lv 26:38
will die. Will we all **p**?" Nm 17:13
you will quickly **p** from the land Dt 4:26
and those hiding from you **p**. Dt 7:20
you today that you will **p**. Dt 8:19
will **p** if you do not obey the Dt 8:20
and you will **p** quickly from the Dt 11:17
you are destroyed and quickly **p**, Dt 28:20
will pursue you until you **p**. Dt 28:22
until they cause you to **p**. Dt 28:51
to cause you to **p** and to destroy Dt 28:63
will certainly **p** and will not Dt 30:18
your enemies **p** as Sisera did. Jdg 5:31
or he will go into battle and **p**. 1Sm 26:10
The whole house of Ahab will **p**, 2Kg 9:8
the law. If I **p**, I perish." Est 4:16
the law. If I perish, I **p**." Est 4:16
day I was born **p**, and the night Jb 3:3
They **p** at a ⌊single⌋ blast from Jb 4:9
they **p** forever while no one Jb 4:20
go up into the desert, and **p**. Jb 6:18
the hope of the godless will **p**. Jb 8:13
living thing would **p** together Jb 34:15
you will **p** in your rebellion, Ps 2:12
they stumble and **p** before You. Ps 9:3
afflicted will not **p** forever. Ps 9:18
nations will **p** from His land. Ps 10:16
But the wicked will **p**; Ps 37:20
he is like the animals that **p**. Ps 49:12
is like the animals that **p**. Ps 49:20
far from You will certainly **p**; Ps 73:27
they **p** at the rebuke of Your Ps 80:16
let them **p** in disgrace. Ps 83:17
indeed, Your enemies will **p**; Ps 92:9
will **p**, but You will endure; Ps 102:26
The wicked are overthrown and **p**, Pr 12:7
witness will **p**, but the one who Pr 21:28
who abandon the LORD will **p**. Is 1:28
both will **p** together. Is 31:3
become as nothing and will **p**. Is 41:11
that will not serve you will **p**; Is 60:12
and rats, will **p** together." Is 66:17
and neighbors will ⌊also⌋ **p**. Jr 6:21
the earth will **p** from the earth Jr 10:11
will banish you, and you will **p**. Jr 27:10
you, and you will **p**—you and Jr 27:15
the remnant of Judah would **p**?" Jr 40:15
The valley will **p**, and the plain Jr 48:8
faithful love we do not **p**, Lm 3:22
will **p** from the priests Ezk 7:26
of the Philistines will **p**. Am 1:8
consider us, and we won't **p**." Jnh 1:6
don't let us **p** because of this Jnh 1:14
anger so that we will not **p**. Jnh 3:9
that one of these little ones **p**. Mt 18:14
up a sword will **p** by a sword. Mt 26:52
repent, you will all **p** as well! Lk 13:3
repent, you will all **p** as well!" Lk 13:5
for a prophet to **p** outside of Lk 13:33
in Him will not **p** but have Jn 3:16
and they will never **p**—ever! Jn 10:28
rather than the whole nation **p**." Jn 11:50
law will also **p** without the law Rm 2:12
⌊They **p**⌋ because they did not 2Th 2:10
they will **p**, but You remain. Heb 1:11
peace and didn't **p** with those Heb 11:31
wanting any to **p**, but all to 2Pt 3:9

PERISHABLE *(3)*

they do it to receive a **p** crown, 1Co 9:25
fathers, not with **p** things, like 1Pt 1:18
of **p** seed but of imperishable 1Pt 1:23

PERISHED *(26)*

All flesh **p**—creatures that Gn 7:21
If only we had **p** when our Nm 20:3
our brothers **p** before the LORD. Nm 20:3
men had **p** from the camp, Dt 2:14
the camp until they had all **p**. Dt 2:15
only one who **p** because of his Jos 22:20
and the weapons of war have **p**! 2Sm 1:27
who has **p** when he was innocent? Jb 4:7
the very memory of them has **p**. Ps 9:6
Truth has **p**—it has disappeared Jr 7:28
until they have **p** from the land Jr 24:10
the wealth he has gained has **p**. Jr 48:36
of Chemosh have **p** because your Jr 48:46
Has counsel **p** from the prudent? Jr 49:7
and elders **p** in the city while Lm 1:19
How you have **p**, city of renown, Ezk 26:17
dried up, and our hope has **p**; Ezk 37:11
the harvest of the field has **p**. Jl 1:11
in a night and **p** in a night. Jnh 4:10
counselor **p**, so that anguish Mc 4:9
into the sea and **p** in the water. Mt 8:32
who **p** between the altar and the Lk 11:51
That man also **p**, and all his Ac 5:37
asleep in Christ have also **p**. 1Co 15:18
world of that time **p** when it was 2Pt 3:6
and have **p** in Korah's rebellion. Jd 11

PERISHES *(6)*

memory of him **p** from the earth; Jb 18:17
and one who utters lies **p**. Pr 19:9
man who **p** in spite of his Ec 7:15
righteous one **p**, and no one Is 57:1
the food that **p** but for the food Jn 6:27
which **p** though refined by fire— 1Pt 1:7

PERISHING *(5)*

to Moses, "Look, we're **p**! Nm 17:12
to those who are **p** the message 1Co 1:18
saved and among those who are **p**. 2Co 2:15
it is veiled to those who are **p**. 2Co 4:3
deception among those who are **p**. 2Th 2:10

PERIZZITE *(1)*

Amorite, Canaanite, **P**, Hivite, Dt 20:17

PERIZZITES *(22)*

Canaanites and the **P** were living Gn 13:7
Hittites, **P**, Rephaim, Gn 15:20
land, the Canaanites and the **P**. Gn 34:30
Hittites, Amorites, **P**, Hivites, Ex 3:8
Hittites, Amorites, **P**, Hivites, Ex 3:17
Hittites, **P**, Canaanites, Ex 23:23
Amorites, Hittites, **P**, Hivites, Ex 33:2
Hittites, **P**, Hivites, Ex 34:11
Amorites, Canaanites, **P**, Hivites Dt 7:1
Hivites, **P**, Girgashites, Jos 3:10
Canaanites, **P**, Hivites, Jos 9:1
Hittites, **P**, and Jebusites Jos 11:3
Canaanites, **P**, Hivites, Jos 12:8
land of the **P** and the Rephaim Jos 17:15
as the Amorites, **P**, Canaanites, Jos 24:11
Canaanites and **P** over to them. Jdg 1:4
down the Canaanites and **P**. Jdg 1:5
Hittites, Amorites, **P**, Hivites, Jdg 3:5
Amorites, Hittites, **P**, Hivites, 1Kg 9:20
Hittites, Amorites, **P**, Hivites, 2Ch 8:7

Hittites, **P**, Jebusites, Ezr 9:1
Amorites, **P**, Jebusites, Neh 9:8

PERJURER *(1)*
to be a poor man than a **p**. Pr 19:22

PERJURERS *(1)*
liars, **p**, and for whatever 1Tm 1:10

PERJURY *(1)*
do not love **p**, for I hate all Zch 8:17

PERMANENT *(30)*
your generations as a **p** statute. Ex 12:14
your generations as a **p** statute. Ex 12:17
This is to be a **p** statute for Ex 27:21
This is to be a **p** statute for Ex 28:43
is to be theirs by a **p** statute. Ex 29:9
this is to be a **p** statute for Ex 30:21
to inaugurate a **p** priesthood for Ex 40:15
This is a **p** statute throughout Lv 3:17
is a **p** portion throughout your Lv 6:18
burned as a **p** portion for the Lv 6:22
and his sons as a **p** portion Lv 7:34
It is a **p** portion throughout Lv 7:36
this is a **p** statute throughout Lv 10:9
is to be a **p** statute for you Lv 16:29
it is a **p** statute. Lv 16:31
is to be a **p** statute for you Lv 16:34
will be a **p** statute for them Lv 17:7
This is to be a **p** statute Lv 23:14
This is to be a **p** statute Lv 23:21
This is a **p** statute throughout Lv 23:31
This is a **p** statute for you Lv 23:41
This is a **p** statute throughout Lv 24:3
this is a **p** rule." Lv 24:9
man inflicts a **p** injury on his Lv 24:19
for it is their **p** possession. Lv 25:34
use of these is a **p** statute Nm 10:8
resident as a **p** statute Nm 15:15
burned Ai and left it a **p** ruin, Jos 8:28
appoint you as my **p** bodyguard." 1Sm 28:2
⌊This is⌋ a **p** statute ⌊to be Ezk 46:14

PERMANENTLY *(13)*
this command **p** as a statute for Ex 12:24
It will belong **p** to you and your Lv 10:15
is not to be **p** sold because it Lv 25:23
walled city is **p** transferred to Lv 25:30
LORD like a field **p** set apart; Lv 27:21
that a man **p** sets apart to Lv 27:28
Israel that is **p** dedicated ⌊to Nm 18:14
presence and to stay there **p**." 1Sm 1:22
LORD would have **p** established 1Sm 13:13
the land and dwell in it **p**. Ps 37:29
Israel that is **p** dedicated ⌊to Ezk 44:29
that you might get him back **p**, Phm 15
He holds His priesthood **p**. Heb 7:24

PERMEATES *(1)*
a little yeast **p** the whole batch 1Co 5:6

PERMISSIBLE *(4)*
"Everything is **p** for me," but 1Co 6:12
"Everything is **p** for me," but I 1Co 6:12
"Everything is **p**," but not 1Co 10:23
"Everything is **p**," but not 1Co 10:23

PERMISSION *(8)*
but without your **p** no one will Gn 41:44
requested my **p** to quickly go to 1Sm 20:6
asked for my **p** to go to 1Sm 20:28
So he asked **p** from the chief Dn 1:8
And He gave them **p**. Mk 5:13
the pigs, and He gave them **p**. Lk 8:32
Pilate gave him **p**, so he came Jn 19:38
After he had given **p**, Paul stood Ac 21:40

PERMIT *(4)*
But He would not **p** the demons to Mk 1:34
and would not **p** anyone to carry Mk 11:16
begged Him to **p** them to enter Lk 8:32
days and not **p** their bodies to Rv 11:9

PERMITS *(2)*
of the rich **p** him no sleep. Ec 5:12
And we will do this if God **p**. Heb 6:3

PERMITTED *(13)*
God has not **p** you to do this. Dt 18:14
LORD had not **p** them ⌊to worship Dt 29:26
Moses **p** you to divorce your Mt 19:8
Moses **p** us to write divorce Mk 10:4
third day and **p** Him to be seen, Ac 10:40
It is **p** for you to speak for Ac 26:1
Paul was **p** to stay by himself Ac 28:16
for they are not **p** to speak, 1Co 14:34
They were not **p** to kill them, Rv 9:5
And he was **p** to wage war against Rv 13:7
signs that he is **p** to perform on Rv 13:14
He was **p** to give a spirit to the Rv 13:15
She was **p** to wear fine linen, Rv 19:8

PERPETUAL *(13)*
generations as a **p** covenant. Ex 31:16
Sabbath day as a **p** covenant Lv 24:8
as a portion and a **p** statute. Nm 18:8
and daughters as a **p** statute. Nm 18:11
to the LORD as a **p** statute. Nm 18:19
is a **p** covenant of salt before Nm 18:19
this is a **p** statute throughout Nm 18:23
This is a **p** statute for the Nm 19:10
This is a **p** statute for them. Nm 19:21
a covenant of **p** priesthood for Nm 25:13
a horror, a **p** object of scorn Jr 18:16
I will make you a **p** desolation; Ezk 35:9
a salt pit, and a **p** wasteland. Zph 2:9

PERPETUATE *(2)*
to **p** the man's name on his Ru 4:5
to **p** the deceased man's name on Ru 4:10

PERPLEXED *(6)*
I am too **p** to hear, too dismayed Is 21:3
He was **p**, because some said that Lk 9:7
While they were **p** about this, Lk 24:4
they were all astounded and **p**, Ac 2:12
Peter was deeply **p** about what Ac 10:17
we are **p** but not in despair; 2Co 4:8

PERSECUTE *(12)*
your enemies who hate and **p** you. Dt 30:7
Why do you **p** me as God ⌊does⌋? Jb 19:22
they **p** the one You struck and Ps 69:26
people **p** me with lies—help me! Ps 119:86
insult you and **p** you and falsely Mt 5:11
and pray for those who **p** you, Mt 5:44
When they **p** you in one town, Mt 10:23
of them they will kill and **p**,' Lk 11:49
their hands on you and **p** you. Lk 21:12
Me, they will also **p** you. Jn 15:20
prophets did your fathers not **p**? Ac 7:52
Bless those who **p** you; Rm 12:14

PERSECUTED *(16)*
Princes have **p** me without cause, Ps 119:161
those who are **p** for Mt 5:10
is how they **p** the prophets who Mt 5:12
If they **p** Me, they will also Jn 15:20
I **p** this Way to the death, Ac 22:4
when we are **p**, we endure it; 1Co 4:12
because I **p** the church of God. 1Co 15:9
we are **p** but not abandoned; 2Co 4:9
I **p** God's church to an extreme Gl 1:13
who formerly **p** us now preaches Gl 1:23
to the flesh **p** the one born Gl 4:29
circumcision, why am I still **p**? Gl 5:11
to avoid being **p** for the cross Gl 6:12
and the prophets, and **p** us; 1Th 2:15
life in Christ Jesus will be **p**. 2Tm 3:12
he **p** the woman who gave birth to Rv 12:13

PERSECUTING *(8)*
the Jews began **p** Jesus because Jn 5:16
Saul, Saul, why are you **p** Me?" Ac 9:4
whom you are **p**," He replied. Ac 9:5
Saul, Saul, why are you **p** Me?' Ac 22:7
the Nazarene, whom you are **p**!' Ac 22:8
Saul, Saul, why are you **p** Me? Ac 26:14
'I am Jesus, whom you are **p**. Ac 26:15
as to zeal, **p** the church; Php 3:6

PERSECUTION *(11)*
in rage with relentless **p**. Is 14:6
When pressure or **p** comes because Mt 13:21
they will hand you over for **p**, Mt 24:9
affliction or **p** comes because Mk 4:17
day a severe **p** broke out against Ac 8:1
a result of the **p** that started Ac 11:19
They stirred up **p** against Paul Ac 13:50
or anguish or **p** or famine or Rm 8:35
spite of severe **p**, you welcomed 1Th 1:6
that we were going to suffer **p**, 1Th 3:4
in all our distress and **p**, 1Th 3:7

PERSECUTIONS *(6)*
and fields, with **p**—and eternal Mk 10:30
catastrophes, in **p**, and in 2Co 12:10
one will be shaken by these **p**. 1Th 3:3
in all the **p** and afflictions 2Th 1:4
along with the **p** and sufferings 2Tm 3:11
What **p** I endured! 2Tm 3:11

PERSECUTOR *(1)*
a blasphemer, a **p**, and an 1Tm 1:13

PERSECUTORS *(6)*
of my enemies and from my **p**. Ps 31:15
You execute judgment on my **p**? Ps 119:84
My **p** and foes are many. Ps 119:157
Avenge me against my **p**. Jr 15:15
Let my **p** be put to shame, but Jr 17:18
my **p** will stumble and not Jr 20:11

PERSEVERANCE *(3)*
with all **p** and intercession for Eph 6:18
promises through faith and **p**. Heb 6:12
kingdom, and **p** in Jesus, was Rv 1:9

PERSEVERE *(1)*
p in these things, for by doing 1Tm 4:16

PERSEVERED *(1)*
anger, for he **p**, as one who sees Heb 11:27

PERSEVERES *(2)*
forever if he **p** in keeping My 1Ch 28:7
law of freedom and **p** in it, Jms 1:25

PERSIA *(28)*
first year of Cyrus king of **P**, 2Ch 36:22
mind of King Cyrus of **P** to issue 2Ch 36:22
is what King Cyrus of **P** says: 2Ch 36:23
first year of Cyrus king of **P**, Ezr 1:1
is what King Cyrus of **P** says: Ezr 1:2
King Cyrus of **P** had them brought Ezr 1:8
given⌋ them by King Cyrus of **P**. Ezr 3:7
the king of **P** has commanded us." Ezr 4:3
of King Cyrus of **P** and until the Ezr 4:5
the reign of King Darius of **P**. Ezr 4:5
time of ⌊King⌋ Artaxerxes of **P**, Ezr 4:7
Tripolis, **P**, Erech, Babylon, Ezr 4:9
the reign of King Darius of **P**. Ezr 4:24
and King Artaxerxes of **P**. Ezr 6:14
reign of King Artaxerxes of **P**, Ezr 7:1
staff, the army of **P** and Media, Est 1:3
officials of **P** and Media who had Est 1:14
noble women of **P** and Media who Est 1:18
in the laws of **P** and Media, Est 1:19
of the kings of Media and **P**? Est 10:2
⌊Men of⌋ **P**, Lud, and Put were in Ezk 27:10
P, Cush, and Put are with them, Ezk 38:5
the kings of Media and **P**. Dn 8:20
third year of Cyrus king of **P**, Dn 10:1
the kingdom of **P** opposed me for Dn 10:13
left there with the kings of **P**. Dn 10:13
fight against the prince of **P**, Dn 10:20
more kings will arise in **P**, Dn 11:2

PERSIAN *(4)*
until the rise of the **P** kingdom. 2Ch 36:20
in the presence of the **P** kings, Ezr 9:9
while Darius the **P** ruled. Neh 12:22
and the reign of Cyrus the **P**. Dn 6:28

PERSIANS *(4)*
and given to the Medes and **P**." Dn 5:28
as a law of the Medes and **P**, Dn 6:8
As a law of the Medes and **P**, Dn 6:12
of the Medes and **P** that no edict Dn 6:15

PERSIS *(1)*
my dear friend **P**, who has worked Rm 16:12

PERSIST *(2)*
and don't **p** in a bad cause, Ec 8:3
p in it whether convenient or 2Tm 4:2

PERSISTED *(3)*
son of Zadok **p** and said to Joab, 2Sm 18:22
The Israelites **p** in all the sins 2Kg 17:22
When they **p** in questioning Him, Jn 8:7

PERSISTENCE *(1)*
because of his **p**, he will get up Lk 11:8

PERSISTENT *(3)*
seduces him with her **p** pleading; Pr 7:21
wear me out by her **p** coming.'" Lk 18:5
in affliction; be **p** in prayer. Rm 12:12

PERSISTS *(1)*
If he **p** and says, 'I don't want Dt 25:8

PERSON *(370)*
Every **p** and animal that is in Ex 9:19
One **p** could not see another, Ex 10:23
that **p** and the neighbor nearest Ex 12:4
to what each **p** will eat. Ex 12:4
leavened, that **p**, whether a Ex 12:19

no uncircumcised **p** may eat it. Ex 12:48
of it as each **p** needs to eat. Ex 16:16
the **p** who gathered a lot had no Ex 16:18
and the **p** who gathered a little Ex 16:18
strikes a **p** so that he dies Ex 21:12
a **p** willfully acts against his Ex 21:14
kidnaps a **p** must be put to Ex 21:16
him or the **p** is found in his Ex 21:16
to the poor **p** among you, you Ex 22:25
to a poor **p** in his lawsuit. Ex 23:3
An unauthorized **p** must not eat Ex 29:33
unauthorized **p** must be cut off Ex 30:33
that **p** must be cut off from his Ex 31:14
every skilled **p** in whose heart Ex 36:2
anything a **p** may speak rashly Lv 5:4
the sinful things a **p** may do— Lv 6:3
The **p** who eats any of it will be Lv 7:18
that **p** must be cut off from his Lv 7:20
that **p** must be cut off from his Lv 7:21
the **p** who eats ⌊it⌋ must be cut Lv 7:25
that **p** must be cut off from his Lv 7:27
When a **p** has a swelling, scab, Lv 13:2
the infected **p** for seven days. Lv 13:4
The **p** is to wash his clothes and Lv 13:6
a skin disease develops on a **p**, Lv 13:9
of the infected **p** from his head Lv 13:12
pronounce the infected **p** clean. Lv 13:13
pronounce the infected **p** clean; Lv 13:17
p must present himself to the Lv 13:19
must pronounce the **p** unclean. Lv 13:30
quarantine the **p** with the scaly Lv 13:31
the **p** must shave himself but not Lv 13:33
quarantine the **p** who has the Lv 13:33
is to pronounce the **p** clean. Lv 13:34
the priest is to examine the **p**. Lv 13:36
yellow hair; the **p** is unclean. Lv 13:36
is to pronounce the **p** clean. Lv 13:37
out on the skin; the **p** is clean. Lv 13:39
The **p** afflicted with an Lv 13:45
concerning the **p** afflicted with Lv 14:2
from the afflicted **p**, Lv 14:3
will place the **p** who is to be Lv 14:11
the **p** who was touched is to wash Lv 15:11
that **p** will be charged with Lv 17:4
that **p** must be cut off from his Lv 17:9
against that **p** who eats blood Lv 17:10
Every **p**, whether the native or Lv 17:15
a **p** will live if he does them. Lv 18:5
Any **p** who does any of these Lv 18:29
That **p** must be cut off from his Lv 19:8
against that **p** and cut him off Lv 20:6
for a ⌊dead⌋ **p** among his Lv 21:1
near any dead **p** or make himself Lv 21:11
that **p** will be cut off from My Lv 22:3
by a dead **p** or by a man who Lv 22:4
unclean or any **p** who makes him Lv 22:5
his money, that **p** may eat it, Lv 22:11
If any **p** does not practice Lv 23:29
injury he inflicted on the **p**, Lv 24:20
whoever kills a **p** is to be put Lv 24:21
If the **p** is a female, your Lv 27:4
the **p** is from five to 20 years Lv 27:5
If the **p** is from one month to Lv 27:6
If the **p** is 60 years or more, Lv 27:7
must present the **p** before the Lv 27:8
If a **p** consecrates to the LORD a Lv 27:22
and the **p** will pay the valuation Lv 27:23
owns, whether a **p**, an animal, or Lv 27:28
No **p** who has been set apart ⌊for Lv 27:29
unauthorized **p** who comes near Nm 1:51
unauthorized **p** who comes near Nm 3:10
Any unauthorized **p** who came near Nm 3:38
collect five shekels for each **p**, Nm 3:47
that **p** acts unfaithfully toward Nm 5:6
The **p** is to confess the sin he Nm 5:7
atonement for the ⌊guilty⌋ **p**. Nm 5:8
If one **p** sins unintentionally, Nm 15:27
on behalf of the **p** who acts in Nm 15:28
same law for the **p** who acts in Nm 15:29
But the **p** who acts defiantly, Nm 15:30
That **p** is to be cut off from his Nm 15:30
no unauthorized **p** outside the Nm 16:40
no unauthorized **p** may come near Nm 18:4
an unauthorized **p** who comes near Nm 18:7
clean **p** in your house may Nm 18:11
Every clean **p** in your house may Nm 18:13
The **p** who touches any human Nm 19:11
a body of a **p** who has died, Nm 19:13

That **p** will be cut off from Nm 19:13
the law when a **p** dies in a tent: Nm 19:14
who touches a **p** who has been Nm 19:16
purification of⌋ the unclean **p**, Nm 19:17
A **p** who is clean is to take Nm 19:18
or a **p** who had been killed. Nm 19:18
the unclean **p** on the third day Nm 19:19
the unclean **p** on the seventh day Nm 19:19
But a **p** who is unclean and does Nm 19:20
that **p** will be cut off from the Nm 19:20
p who sprinkles the water for Nm 19:21
the unclean **p** touches will Nm 19:22
who have killed a **p** or touched Nm 31:19
so that a **p** who kills someone Nm 35:11
who kills a **p** unintentionally Nm 35:15
anyone strikes a **p** with an iron Nm 35:16
in hatred pushes a **p** or throws Nm 35:20
pushes a **p** without hostility Nm 35:22
that could kill a **p** and he dies, Nm 35:23
who killed a **p** was supposed to Nm 35:28
who has killed a **p** return to the Nm 35:28
anyone kills a **p**, the murderer Nm 35:30
ransom for the **p** who flees to Nm 35:32
the blood of the **p** who shed it. Nm 35:33
seen that God speaks with a **p**, Dt 5:24
If there is a poor **p** among you, Dt 15:7
both the unclean **p** and the clean Dt 15:22
The **p** who acts arrogantly, Dt 17:12
who kills a **p** and flees there to Dt 19:4
that **p** may flee to one of these Dt 19:5
wrongdoing or sin against a **p**, Dt 19:15
whatever that **p** has done. Dt 19:15
each **p** will be put to death for Dt 24:16
'Cursed is the **p** who makes a Dt 27:15
leads a blind **p** astray on the Dt 27:18
a bribe to kill an innocent **p**.' Dt 27:25
will burn against that **p**, Dt 29:20
down every **p** with the sword Jos 11:14
so that a **p** who kills someone Jos 20:3
who kills a **p** unintentionally Jos 20:9
Each **p** also cut his own branch Jdg 9:49
house of one **p** or for you to be Jdg 18:19
transformed into a different **p**. 1Sm 10:6
you, that **p** can play the harp, 1Sm 16:16
did not leave a single **p** alive, 1Sm 27:9
when the **p** told me, 'Look, Saul 2Sm 4:10
a vulgar **p** would expose himself. 2Sm 6:20
When a **p** approached to bow 2Sm 15:5
I am a peaceful **p**, one of the 2Sm 20:19
did this crazy **p** come to you?" 2Kg 9:11
every unclean **p** to consecrate 2Ch 30:17
which a **p** will live if he does Neh 9:29
serve as much as each **p** wanted. Est 1:8
golden scepter will that **p** live. Est 4:11
Not a single **p** could withstand Est 9:2
Can a **p** be more righteous than Jb 4:17
not reject a **p** of integrity, Jb 8:20
but how can a **p** be justified Jb 9:2
for no godless **p** can appear Jb 13:16
Were you the first **p** ever born, Jb 15:7
the righteous **p** will hold to his Jb 17:9
Let God repay the **p** himself, Jb 21:19
One **p** dies in excellent health, Jb 21:23
Yet another **p** dies with a bitter Jb 21:25
How can a **p** be justified before Jb 25:4
or a needy **p** without a cloak, Jb 31:19
not answering anything a **p** asks? Jb 33:13
but a **p** may not notice it. Jb 33:14
order to turn a **p** ⌊from his⌋ Jb 33:17
p may be disciplined on his bed Jb 33:19
tell a **p** what is right for him Jb 33:23
For He repays a **p** ⌊according to⌋ Jb 34:11
need to⌋ examine a **p** further, Jb 34:23
affects⌋ a **p** like yourself, Jb 35:8
on every proud **p** and humiliate Jb 40:11
on every proud **p** and humble him; Jb 40:12
a **p** not collapse at the very Jb 41:9
arm of the wicked and evil **p**; Ps 10:15
Not one **p** who waits for You will Ps 25:3
Who is the **p** who fears the LORD? Ps 25:12
gone from memory like a dead **p**— Ps 31:12
am like a deaf **p**; I do not hear Ps 38:13
a speechless **p** who does not open Ps 38:13
cannot redeem a **p** or pay his Ps 49:7
is the **p** who trusts in You! Ps 84:12
A stupid **p** does not know, a fool Ps 92:6
Set a wicked **p** over him; Ps 109:6
some innocent **p** just for fun! Pr 1:11

A worthless **p**, a wicked man, who Pr 6:12
but the wicked **p** will fall Pr 11:5
One **p** gives freely, yet gains Pr 11:24
A generous **p** will be enriched, Pr 11:25
A shrewd **p** conceals knowledge, Pr 12:23
Every sensible **p** acts Pr 13:16
A patient **p** ⌊shows⌋ great Pr 14:29
but a **p** who heeds correction is Pr 15:5
of the righteous **p** thinks before Pr 15:28
A wicked **p** listens to malicious Pr 17:4
into a perceptive **p** more than a Pr 17:10
not good to fine an innocent **p**, Pr 17:26
The intelligent **p** restrains his Pr 17:27
and a lazy **p** will go hungry. Pr 19:15
A **p** with great anger bears the Pr 19:19
A wicked **p** desires evil; Pr 21:10
and arrogant **p**, named "Mocker," Pr 21:24
of a wicked **p** is detestable— Pr 21:27
A sensible **p** sees danger and Pr 22:3
A generous **p** will be blessed, Pr 22:9
He repay a **p** according to his Pr 24:12
an unreliable **p** in a time of Pr 25:19
A righteous **p** who yields to the Pr 25:26
A hateful **p** disguises himself Pr 26:24
A **p** who is full tramples on a Pr 27:7
but to a hungry **p**, any bitter Pr 27:7
so the heart reflects the **p**. Pr 27:19
discerning and knowledgeable **p**, Pr 28:2
who rebukes a **p** will later find Pr 28:23
A greedy **p** provokes conflict, Pr 28:25
The righteous **p** knows the rights Pr 29:7
men hate an honest **p**, Pr 29:10
better than for a **p** to enjoy his Ec 3:22
is a **p** without a companion, Ec 4:8
how can one **p** alone keep warm Ec 4:11
if somebody overpowers one **p**, Ec 4:12
for the poor **p** who knows how to Ec 6:8
from a wise **p** than to listen to Ec 7:5
turns a wise **p** into a fool, Ec 7:7
like the wise **p**, and who knows Ec 8:1
not curse a rich **p** even in your Ec 10:20
as a sickness consumes a **p**. Is 10:18
the humble **p** in his distress, Is 25:4
accuse a **p** of wrongdoing, Is 29:21
a noble **p** plans noble things; Is 32:8
like a beautiful **p**, to dwell in Is 44:13
A day for a **p** to deny himself, Is 58:5
favorably on this kind of **p**: Is 66:2
find a single **p**, anyone who acts Jr 5:1
the thirsty **p** and feed all those Jr 31:25
to give to each **p** according to Jr 32:19
for Him, to the **p** who seeks Him. Lm 3:25
should ⌊any⌋ living **p** complain, Lm 3:39
If I say to the wicked **p**: Ezk 3:18
that wicked **p** will die for his Ezk 3:18
warn a wicked **p** and he does not Ezk 3:19
if a righteous **p** turns from his Ezk 3:20
the righteous **p** that he should Ezk 3:21
the righteous **p** with lies, Ezk 13:22
the wicked **p** not to turn from Ezk 13:22
The **p** who sins is the one who Ezk 18:4
Such a **p** is righteous; Ezk 18:9
Such a **p** will not die for his Ezk 18:17
The **p** who sins is the one who Ezk 18:20
the righteous **p** will be on him, Ezk 18:20
of the wicked **p** will be on him. Ezk 18:20
if the wicked **p** turns from all Ezk 18:21
when a righteous **p** turns from Ezk 18:24
When a righteous **p** turns from Ezk 18:26
But if a wicked **p** turns from the Ezk 18:27
the **p** who does them will live by Ezk 20:11
the **p** who does them will live by Ezk 20:13
the **p** who does them will live by Ezk 20:21
that wicked **p** will die for his Ezk 33:8
warn a wicked **p** to turn from his Ezk 33:9
that the wicked **p** should turn Ezk 33:11
of the righteous **p** will not save Ezk 33:12
of the wicked **p** cause him to Ezk 33:12
The righteous **p** won't be able to Ezk 33:12
the righteous **p** that he will Ezk 33:13
So when I tell the wicked **p**: Ezk 33:14
When a righteous **p** turns from Ezk 33:18
when a wicked **p** turns from his Ezk 33:19
was only one **p**, yet he received Ezk 33:24
One **p** speaks to another, each Ezk 33:30
near⌋ a dead **p** so that he Ezk 44:25
place a despised **p** will arise; Dn 11:21
sell a righteous **p** for silver Am 2:6

silver and a needy **p** for a pair Am 2:6
the wise **p** will keep silent at Am 5:13
That **p** will reply, "None." Am 6:10
of his home, a **p** of his Mc 2:2
devastated, without a **p**, without Zph 3:6
The **p** who loves father or mother Mt 10:37
the **p** who loves son or daughter Mt 10:37
a righteous **p** because he's Mt 10:41
that **p** is My brother and sister Mt 12:50
hard for a rich **p** to enter the Mt 19:23
than for a rich **p** to enter the Mt 19:24
goes into a **p** from outside can Mk 7:15
come out of a **p** are what defile Mk 7:15
comes out of a **p**—that defiles Mk 7:20
from within and defile a **p**." Mk 7:23
than for a rich **p** to enter the Mk 10:25
distinguished **p** than you may Lk 14:8
than for a rich **p** to enter the Lk 18:25
the eyes of a **p** born blind. Jn 9:32
the joy that a **p** has been born Jn 16:21
proclaiming in the **p** of Jesus Ac 4:2
was not a needy **p** among them, Ac 4:34
to each **p** as anyone had Ac 4:35
about—himself or another **p**?" Ac 8:34
not call any **p** common or unclean Ac 10:28
every nation the **p** who fears Him Ac 10:35
For a **p** named Demetrius, a Ac 19:24
Wipe this **p** off the earth— Ac 22:22
For a **p** is not a Jew who is one Rm 2:28
p is a Jew who is one inwardly, Rm 2:29
will someone die for a just **p**— Rm 5:7
for a good **p** perhaps someone Rm 5:7
since a **p** who has died is freed Rm 6:7
One **p** believes he may eat Rm 14:2
One **p** considers one day to be Rm 14:5
The spiritual **p**, however, can 1Co 2:15
A **p** should consider us in this 1Co 4:1
in favor of one **p** over another. 1Co 4:6
Do not even eat with such a **p**. 1Co 5:11
Put away the evil **p** from among 1Co 5:13
is not one wise **p** among you who 1Co 6:5
Every sin a **p** can commit is 1Co 6:18
but the **p** who is sexually 1Co 6:18
Each **p** should remain in the life 1Co 7:20
each **p** should remain with God in 1Co 7:24
Then the weak **p**, the brother for 1Co 8:11
but ⌊the good⌋ of the other **p**. 1Co 10:24
one **p** is hungry while another 1Co 11:21
given to each **p** to produce what 1Co 12:7
the **p** who speaks in ⌊another⌋ 1Co 14:2
But the **p** who prophesies speaks 1Co 14:3
The **p** who speaks in ⌊another⌋ 1Co 14:4
The **p** who prophesies is greater 1Co 14:5
is greater than the **p** who speaks 1Co 14:5
Therefore the **p** who speaks in 1Co 14:13
the uninformed **p** say "Amen" at 1Co 14:16
but the other **p** is not being 1Co 14:17
unbeliever or uninformed **p** comes 1Co 14:24
If any **p** speaks in ⌊another⌋ 1Co 14:27
that **p** should keep silent in the 1Co 14:28
to another **p** sitting there, 1Co 14:30
is sufficient for such a **p**, 2Co 2:6
but whenever a **p** turns to the 2Co 3:16
though our outer **p** is being 2Co 4:16
our inner **p** is being renewed day 2Co 4:16
The **p** who gathered much did not 2Co 8:15
the **p** who gathered little did 2Co 8:15
the **p** who sows sparingly will 2Co 9:6
and the **p** who sows generously 2Co 9:6
Each **p** should do as he has 2Co 9:7
I who am humble among you in **p**, 2Co 10:1
Such a **p** should consider this: 2Co 10:11
For if a **p** comes and preaches 2Co 11:4
I will boast about this **p**, 2Co 12:5
mediator is not for just one **p**, Gl 3:20
restore such a **p** with a gentle Gl 6:1
each **p** should examine his own Gl 6:4
each **p** will have to carry his Gl 6:5
immoral or impure or greedy **p**, Eph 5:5
all who have not seen me in **p**. Col 2:1
how you should answer each **p**. Col 4:6
short time (in **p**, not in heart) 1Th 2:17
the **p** who rejects this does not 1Th 4:8
letter, take note of that **p**; 2Th 3:14
is not meant for a righteous **p**, 1Tm 1:9
Reject a divisive **p** after a Ti 3:10
that such a **p** is perverted Ti 3:11
For the **p** who has entered His Heb 4:10
instead, a **p** is called by God, Heb 5:4
And each **p** will not teach his Heb 8:11
or irreverent **p** like Esau, Heb 12:16
That **p** should not expect to Jms 1:7
But each **p** is tempted when he is Jms 1:14
this **p** will be blessed in what Jms 1:25
for the **p** who knows to do good Jms 4:17
of faith will save the sick **p**, Jms 5:15
of⌋ the hidden **p** of the heart 1Pt 3:4
The **p** who lacks these things is 2Pt 1:9
For the **p** who does not love his 1Jn 4:20
and free **p** hid in the caves Rv 6:15
Me to repay each **p** according to Rv 22:12

PERSON'S *(14)*
are stolen from that **p** house, Ex 22:7
ordinary⌋ anointing on a **p** body, Ex 30:32
on his behalf for that **p** sin, Lv 4:26
God reserves a **p** punishment for Jb 21:19
A **p** insight gives him patience, Pr 19:11
A **p** breath is the lamp of the Pr 20:27
Don't eat a stingy **p** bread, Pr 23:6
A **p** pride will humble him, Pr 29:23
or suppressing a **p** lawsuit— Lm 3:36
p enemies are the people in his Mc 7:6
receive a righteous **p** reward. Mt 10:41
own conscience, but the other **p**. 1Co 10:29
judged by another **p** conscience? 1Co 10:29
ourselves to every **p** conscience 2Co 4:2

PERSONAL *(11)*
and became his **p** attendant. Gn 39:4
and he became their **p** attendant. Gn 40:4
your tenths and **p** contributions, Dt 12:6
of the tenth, **p** contributions, Dt 12:11
or your **p** contributions. Dt 12:17
Hushai, David's **p** adviser, 2Sm 15:37
now give my **p** treasures of gold 1Ch 29:3
Media who had **p** access to the Est 1:14
The king's **p** attendants Est 2:2
The king's **p** attendants Est 6:3
make a **p** appeal to you by the 2Co 10:1

PERSONALLY *(14)*
p told them all these things; Gn 20:8
You can hold me **p** accountable! Gn 43:9
your servant speak **p** to my lord. Gn 44:18
I **p** consecrate the silver to the Jdg 17:3
and that you **p** go into battle. 2Sm 17:11
seven eunuchs who **p** served him, Est 1:10
should **p** issue a royal decree. Est 1:19
plead with him **p** for her people. Est 4:8
will **p** report the same things Ac 15:27
we **p** had a death sentence within 2Co 1:9
except that I **p** did not burden 2Co 12:13
I remained **p** unknown to the Gl 1:22
And He **p** gave some to be Eph 4:11
Jesus, will **p** restore, establish 1Pt 5:10

PERSONS *(8)*
The total number of **p**: Gn 46:15
that she bore to Jacob: 16 **p**. Gn 46:18
who were born to Jacob: 14 **p**. Gn 46:22
She bore to Jacob: seven **p**. Gn 46:25
total number of **p** belonging to Gn 46:26
him in Egypt: two **p**. All those Gn 46:27
who had come to Egypt: 70 **p**. Gn 46:27
in their own **p** the appropriate Rm 1:27

PERSPECTIVE *(3)*
many are wise from a human **p**, 1Co 1:26
Am I saying this from a human **p**? 1Co 9:8
many boast from a human **p**, 2Co 11:18

PERSUADE *(12)*
P your husband to explain the Jdg 14:15
P him to tell you where his Jdg 16:5
Do not **p** me to leave you or go Ru 1:16
she stopped trying to **p** her. Ru 1:18
let Hezekiah **p** you to trust 2Kg 18:30
let Hezekiah **p** you to trust Is 36:15
I am going to **p** her, lead her to Hs 2:14
and tried to **p** both Jews and Ac 18:4
and trying to **p** them about the Ac 19:8
Don't let them **p** you, because Ac 23:21
Are you going to **p** me to become Ac 26:28
fear of the Lord, we **p** people. 2Co 5:11

PERSUADED *(22)*
she **p** Othniel to ask her father Jos 15:18
she **p** Othniel to ask her father Jdg 1:14
but his father-in-law **p** him, Jdg 19:7
these words David **p** his men, 1Sm 24:7
lived⌋ there **p** him to eat some 2Kg 4:8
Then he **p** him to march up to 2Ch 18:2
sinners entice you, don't be **p**. Pr 1:10
anything or be **p** by lavish gifts Pr 6:35
A ruler can be **p** through Pr 25:15
p the crowds to ask for Barabbas Mt 27:20
will not be **p** if someone rises Lk 16:31
So they were **p** by him. Ac 5:39
stay at my house." And she **p** us. Ac 16:15
of them were **p** and joined Paul Ac 17:4
this man Paul has **p** and misled a Ac 19:26
he would not be **p**, we stopped Ac 21:14
He **p** them concerning Jesus from Ac 28:23
Some were **p** by what he said, Ac 28:24
I am **p** that neither death nor Rm 8:38
know and am **p** by the Lord Jesus Rm 14:14
Since I am **p** of this, I know Php 1:25
believed and am **p** that He is 2Tm 1:12

PERSUADES *(1)*
p people to worship God contrary Ac 18:13

PERSUADING *(1)*
with them and **p** them to continue Ac 13:43

PERSUASION *(1)*
This **p** did not come from Him who Gl 5:8

PERSUASIVE *(2)*
were not with **p** words of wisdom, 1Co 2:4
deceive you with **p** arguments. Col 2:4

PERTAINING *(2)*
speak of things **p** to this life? 1Co 6:3
you have cases **p** to this life, 1Co 6:4

PERTAINS *(1)*
Jesus regarding what **p** to God. Rm 15:17

PERUDA'S *(1)*
(AKA PERIDA'S)
descendants, **P** descendants, Ezr 2:55

PERVADED *(1)*
the fear of death **p** the city; 1Sm 5:11

PERVERSE *(7)*
for they are a **p** generation— Dt 32:20
You son of a **p** and rebellious 1Sm 20:30
from the one who says **p** things, Pr 2:12
none of them are deceptive or **p**. Pr 8:8
evil conduct, and **p** speech. Pr 8:13
but a **p** tongue will be cut out. Pr 10:31
of the wicked, ⌊only⌋ what is **p**. Pr 10:32

PERVERSELY *(1)*
They have acted **p**; Lv 20:12

PERVERSION *(3)*
to mate with it; it is a **p**. Lv 18:23
of the poor and **p** of justice Ec 5:8
appropriate penalty for their **p**. Rm 1:27

PERVERSIONS *(1)*
immorality and practiced **p**, Jd 7

PERVERSITY *(4)*
doing evil and celebrate **p**, Pr 2:14
plots evil with **p** in his heart— Pr 6:14
but the **p** of the treacherous Pr 11:3
and the city full of **p**. Ezk 9:9

PERVERT *(7)*
with a crowd to **p** ⌊justice⌋. Ex 23:2
Does God **p** justice? Does the Jb 8:3
the Almighty **p** what is right? Jb 8:3
the Almighty does not **p** justice. Jb 34:12
and **p** justice for all the Pr 31:5
his burden and you **p** the words Jr 23:36
justice and **p** everything that Mc 3:9

PERVERTED *(8)*
p men of the city surrounded the Jdg 19:22
Hand over the **p** men in Gibeah so Jdg 20:13
took bribes, and **p** justice. 1Sm 8:3
sinned and **p** what was right; Jb 33:27
for they have **p** their way; Jr 3:21
therefore, justice comes out **p**. Hab 1:4
in a crooked and **p** generation, Php 2:15
such a person is **p** and sins, Ti 3:11

PERVERTING *(2)*
the guilty by **p** the justice due Pr 18:5
you ever stop **p** the straight Ac 13:10

PERVERTS *(1)*
but whoever **p** his ways will be Pr 10:9

PESTERING *(1)*
because this widow keeps **p** me, Lk 18:5

PESTILENCE *(10)*
I will send a **p** among you, Lv 26:25
LORD will make **p** cling to you Dt 28:21
ravaged by **p** and bitter plague; Dt 32:24
when there is **p**, when there is 1Kg 8:37
when there is **p**, when there is 2Ch 6:28
or if I send **p** on My people, 2Ch 7:13
or judgment, **p** or famine—we 2Ch 20:9
or the **p** that ravages at noon. Ps 91:6
right hand, the **p** will not reach Ps 91:7
and **p** follows in His steps. Hab 3:5

PESTLE *(1)*
a mortar with a **p** along with Pr 27:22

PETALS *(9)*
cups, and its calyxes and **p**. Ex 25:31
with a calyx and **p**, on the first Ex 25:33
with a calyx and **p**, on the next Ex 25:33
along with its calyxes and **p**. Ex 25:34
cups, and its calyxes and **p**. Ex 37:17
with a calyx and **p**, on the first Ex 37:19
with a calyx and **p**, on the next Ex 37:19
blossoms with its calyxes and **p**. Ex 37:20
from its base to its flower **p**. Nm 8:4

PETER *(155)*
(AKA CEPHAS, SIMEON, SIMON)
was called **P**, and his brother Mt 4:18
who is called **P**, and Andrew his Mt 10:2
if it's You," **P** answered Him, Mt 14:28
P started walking on the water Mt 14:29
Then **P** replied to Him, "Explain Mt 15:15
Simon **P** answered, "You are the Mt 16:16
also say to you that you are **P**, Mt 16:18
Then **P** took Him aside and began Mt 16:22
But He turned and told **P**, Mt 16:23
After six days Jesus took **P**, Mt 17:1
P said to Jesus, "Lord, it's Mt 17:4
tax approached **P** and said, Mt 17:24
Then **P** came to Him and said, Mt 18:21
Then **P** responded to Him, "Look, Mt 19:27
P told Him, "Even if everyone Mt 26:33
die with You," **P** told Him, "I Mt 26:35
Taking along **P** and the two sons Mt 26:37
He asked **P**. "So, couldn't you Mt 26:40
P was following Him at a Mt 26:58
Now **P** was sitting outside in the Mt 26:69
there approached and said to **P**, Mt 26:73
and **P** remembered the words Jesus Mt 26:75
To Simon, He gave the name **P**; Mk 3:16
anyone accompany Him except **P**, Mk 5:37
P answered Him, "You are the Mk 8:29
So **P** took Him aside and began to Mk 8:32
He rebuked **P** and said, "Get Mk 8:33
After six days Jesus took **P**, Mk 9:2
Then **P** said to Jesus, "Rabbi, it Mk 9:5
P began to tell Him, "Look, we Mk 10:28
Then **P** remembered and said to Mk 11:21
temple complex, **P**, James, John, Mk 13:3
P told Him, "Even if everyone Mk 14:29
He took **P**, James, and John with Mk 14:33
He asked **P**. "Couldn't you stay Mk 14:37
P followed Him at a distance, Mk 14:54
While **P** was in the courtyard Mk 14:66
When she saw **P** warming himself, Mk 14:67
standing there said to **P** again, Mk 14:70
and **P** remembered when Jesus had Mk 14:72
tell His disciples and **P**, Mk 16:7
When Simon **P** saw this, he fell Lk 5:8
He also named **P**, and Andrew his Lk 6:14
all denied it, **P** said, "Master, Lk 8:45
no one enter with Him except **P**, Lk 8:51
P answered, "God's Messiah!" Lk 9:20
took along **P**, John, and James, Lk 9:28
P and those with him were in a Lk 9:32
from Him, **P** said to Jesus, Lk 9:33
"Lord," **P** asked, "are You Lk 12:41
Then **P** said, "Look, we have left Lk 18:28
Jesus sent **P** and John, saying, Lk 22:8
"I tell you, **P**," He said, "the Lk 22:34
Meanwhile **P** was following at a Lk 22:54
together, and **P** sat among them. Lk 22:55
too!" "Man, I am not!" **P** said. Lk 22:58
But **P** said, "Man, I don't know Lk 22:60
the Lord turned and looked at **P**. Lk 22:61
So **P** remembered the word of the Lk 22:61
P, however, got up and ran to Lk 24:12
the hometown of Andrew and **P**. Jn 1:44
Simon **P** answered, "Lord, who Jn 6:68
came to Simon **P**, who asked Him, Jn 13:6
my feet—ever!" **P** said. Jesus Jn 13:8
Simon **P** said to Him, "Lord, not Jn 13:9
Simon **P** motioned to him to find Jn 13:24
"Lord," Simon **P** said to Him, Jn 13:36
"Lord," **P** asked, "why can't I Jn 13:37
Then Simon **P**, who had a sword, Jn 18:10
Jesus said to **P**, "Sheathe your Jn 18:11
Meanwhile Simon **P** was following Jn 18:15
But **P** remained standing outside Jn 18:16
was the doorkeeper and brought **P** Jn 18:16
was the doorkeeper said to **P**, Jn 18:17
and **P** was standing with them, Jn 18:18
Now Simon **P** was standing and Jn 18:25
the man whose ear **P** had cut off, Jn 18:26
P then denied it again. Jn 18:27
ran to Simon **P** and to the other Jn 20:2
P and the other disciple went Jn 20:3
disciple outran **P** and got to the Jn 20:4
him, Simon **P** came also. Jn 20:6
Simon **P**, Thomas (called "Twin"), Jn 21:2
fishing," Simon **P** said to them. Jn 21:3
said to **P**, "It is the Lord! Jn 21:7
When Simon **P** heard that it was Jn 21:7
So Simon **P** got up and hauled the Jn 21:11
Jesus asked Simon **P**, "Simon, son Jn 21:15
P was grieved that He asked him Jn 21:17
So **P** turned around and saw the Jn 21:20
P saw him, he said to Jesus, Jn 21:21
P, John, James, Andrew, Philip, Ac 1:13
these days **P** stood up among Ac 1:15
But **P** stood up with the Eleven, Ac 2:14
heart and said to **P** and the rest Ac 2:37
"Repent," **P** said to them, "and Ac 2:38
Now **P** and John were going up Ac 3:1
When he saw **P** and John about to Ac 3:3
P, along with John, looked at Ac 3:4
But **P** said, "I have neither Ac 3:6
he was holding on to **P** and John, Ac 3:11
When **P** saw this, he addressed Ac 3:12
After they had **P** and John stand Ac 4:7
Then **P** was filled with the Holy Ac 4:8
the boldness of **P** and John and Ac 4:13
But **P** and John answered them, Ac 4:19
Then **P** said, "Ananias, why has Ac 5:3
"Tell me," **P** asked her, "did you Ac 5:8
Then **P** said to her, "Why did you Ac 5:9
and pallets so that when **P** came Ac 5:15
But **P** and the apostles replied, Ac 5:29
they sent **P** and John to them. Ac 8:14
Then **P** and John laid their hands Ac 8:17
But **P** told him, "May your silver Ac 8:20
As **P** was traveling from place to Ac 9:32
P said to him, "Aeneas, Jesus Ac 9:34
heard that **P** was there and sent Ac 9:38
So **P** got up and went with them. Ac 9:39
Then **P** sent them all out of the Ac 9:40
her eyes, saw **P**, and sat up. Ac 9:40
And **P** stayed on many days in Ac 9:43
for Simon, who is also named **P**. Ac 10:5
P went up to pray on the Ac 10:9
a voice said to him, "Get up, **P**; Ac 10:13
"No, Lord!" **P** said. "For I have Ac 10:14
While **P** was deeply perplexed Ac 10:17
was also named **P**, was lodging Ac 10:18
While **P** was thinking about the Ac 10:19
Then **P** went down to the men and Ac 10:21
P then invited them in and gave Ac 10:23
When **P** entered, Cornelius met Ac 10:25
But **P** helped him up and said, Ac 10:26
P said to them, "You know it's Ac 10:28
Simon here, who is also named **P**. Ac 10:32
Then **P** began to speak: Ac 10:34
While **P** was still speaking these Ac 10:44
had come with **P** were astounded, Ac 10:45
of God. Then **P** responded, Ac 10:46
When **P** went up to Jerusalem, Ac 11:2
P began to explain to them in an Ac 11:4
a voice telling me, 'Get up, **P**; Ac 11:7
for Simon, who is also named **P**. Ac 11:13
he proceeded to arrest **P** too, Ac 12:3
So **P** was kept in prison, but Ac 12:5
P was sleeping between two Ac 12:6
Striking **P** on the side, he woke Ac 12:7
Then **P** came to himself and said, Ac 12:11
announced that **P** was standing at Ac 12:14
P, however, kept on knocking, Ac 12:16
to what could have become of **P**. Ac 12:18
P stood up and said to them: Ac 15:7
just as **P** was for the Gl 2:7
was at work with **P** in the Gl 2:8
P, an apostle of Jesus Christ: 1Pt 1:1
Simeon **P**, a slave and an apostle 2Pt 1:1

PETER'S *(4)*
When Jesus went into **P** house, Mt 8:14
Andrew, Simon **P** brother, was one Jn 1:40
Andrew, Simon **P** brother, said to Jn 6:8
She recognized **P** voice, and Ac 12:14

PETHAHIAH *(4)*
nineteenth to **P**, the twentieth 1Ch 24:16
that is Kelita), **P**, Judah, and Ezr 10:23
Hodiah, Shebaniah, and **P**—said: Neh 9:5
P son of Meshezabel, of the Neh 11:24

PETHOR *(2)*
to Balaam son of Beor at **P**, Nm 22:5
of Beor from **P** in Aram-naharaim Dt 23:4

PETHUEL *(1)*
LORD that came to Joel son of **P**: Jl 1:1

PETITION *(26)*
grant the **p** you've requested 1Sm 1:17
Your servant's prayer and his **p**, 1Kg 8:28
Hear the **p** of Your servant and 1Kg 8:30
prayer or **p** anyone from Your 1Kg 8:38
their prayer and **p** in heaven and 1Kg 8:45
and repent and **p** You in their 1Kg 8:47
prayer and **p** and uphold their 1Kg 8:49
to Your servant's **p** and to the 1Kg 8:52
and to the **p** of Your people 1Kg 8:52
entire prayer and **p** to the LORD, 1Kg 8:54
I have made my **p** with before the 1Kg 8:59
your prayer and **p** you have made 1Kg 9:3
Your servant's prayer and his **p**, 2Ch 6:19
prayer or **p** anyone from your 2Ch 6:29
their prayer and **p** in heaven and 2Ch 6:35
and repent and **p** You in their 2Ch 6:37
He heard his **p** and granted his 2Ch 33:13
⌊This is⌋ my **p** and my request: Est 5:7
king to grant my **p** and perform Est 5:8
Perhaps their **p** will come before Jr 36:7
May my **p** come before you. Jr 37:20
the king my **p** that he not return Jr 38:26
May our **p** come before you; Jr 42:2
me to bring your **p** before Him: Jr 42:9
presenting my **p** before Yahweh my Dn 9:20
prayer and **p** with thanksgiving Php 4:6

PETITIONING *(1)*
and found Daniel **p** and imploring Dn 6:11

PETITIONS *(10)*
Hear the **p** of Your servant and 2Ch 6:21
prayer and **p** and uphold their 2Ch 6:39
anyone who **p** any god or man Dn 6:7
days any man who **p** any god or Dn 6:12
God to seek Him by prayer and **p**, Dn 9:3
and the **p** of Your servant. Dn 9:17
presenting our **p** before You Dn 9:18
of your **p** an answer went Dn 9:23
then, I urge that **p**, prayers, 1Tm 2:1
and day in her **p** and prayers; 1Tm 5:5

PEULLETHAI *(1)*
seventh, and **P** the eighth, for 1Ch 26:5

PHANUEL *(1)*
a daughter of **P**, of the tribe Lk 2:36

PHARAOH *(206)*
saw her and praised her to **P**, Gn 12:15
the LORD struck **P** and his house Gn 12:17
So **P** sent for Abram and said, Gn 12:18
Then **P** gave ⌊his⌋ men orders Gn 12:20
an officer of **P** and the captain Gn 37:36
an officer of **P** and the captain Gn 39:1
P was angry with his two Gn 40:2
just three days **P** will lift up Gn 40:13
to me by mentioning me to **P**, Gn 40:14
all sorts of baked goods for **P**, Gn 40:17
just three days **P** will lift up Gn 40:19
Two years later **P** had a dream: Gn 41:1
well-fed cows. Then **P** woke up. Gn 41:4
Then **P** woke up, and it was only Gn 41:7
P told them his dreams, but no Gn 41:8
the chief cupbearer said to **P**, Gn 41:9
P had been angry with his Gn 41:10
Then **P** sent for Joseph, and they Gn 41:14
his clothes, and went to **P**. Gn 41:14
P said to Joseph, "I have had a Gn 41:15
not able to," Joseph answered **P**. Gn 41:16
God who will give **P** a favorable Gn 41:16

So **P** said to Joseph: Gn 41:17
Joseph said to **P**, "Pharaoh's Gn 41:25
has revealed to **P** what He is Gn 41:25
It is just as I told **P**: Gn 41:28
God has shown **P** what He is about Gn 41:28
the dream was given twice to **P**, Gn 41:32
let **P** look for a discerning and Gn 41:33
Let **P** do this: Let him appoint Gn 41:34
proposal pleased **P** and all his Gn 41:37
Then **P** said to his servants, Gn 41:38
So **P** said to Joseph, "Since God Gn 41:39
P also said to Joseph, "See, I Gn 41:41
P removed his signet ring from Gn 41:42
P said to Joseph, "I am Pharaoh, Gn 41:44
to Joseph, "I am **P**, but without Gn 41:44
P gave Joseph the name Gn 41:45
the service of **P** king of Egypt. Gn 41:46
people cried out to **P** for food. Gn 41:55
P told all Egypt, "Go to Joseph Gn 41:55
As surely as **P** lives, you will Gn 42:15
then as surely as **P** lives, Gn 42:16
servant, for you are like **P**. Gn 44:18
He has made me a father to **P**, Gn 45:8
P and his servants were Gn 45:16
P said to Joseph, "Tell your Gn 45:17
wagons as **P** had commanded, Gn 45:21
the wagons **P** had sent to carry Gn 46:5
I will go up and inform **P**, Gn 46:31
When **P** addresses you and asks, Gn 46:33
So Joseph went and informed **P**: Gn 47:1
and presented them before **P**. Gn 47:2
Then **P** asked his brothers, Gn 47:3
they said to **P**, "Your servants Gn 47:3
they said to **P**, "We have come to Gn 47:4
Then **P** said to Joseph, "⌊Now Gn 47:5
and presented him before **P**, Gn 47:7
Pharaoh, and Jacob blessed **P**. Gn 47:7
Then **P** said to Jacob, "How many Gn 47:8
Jacob said to **P**, "My pilgrimage Gn 47:9
So Jacob blessed **P** and departed Gn 47:10
of Rameses, as **P** had commanded. Gn 47:11
all the land in Egypt for **P**, Gn 47:20
it was their allotment from **P**. Gn 47:22
the allotment **P** had given them; Gn 47:22
you and your land for **P**. Gn 47:23
are to give a fifth of it to **P**, Gn 47:24
of the produce⌋ belongs to **P**. Gn 47:26
land does not belong to **P**. Gn 47:26
with you, please tell **P** that Gn 50:4
So **P** said, "Go and bury your Gn 50:6
Rameses as supply cities for **P**. Ex 1:11
midwives said to **P**, "The Hebrew Ex 1:19
P then commanded all his people: Ex 1:22
P heard about this, he tried Ex 2:15
Moses fled from **P** and went to Ex 2:15
sending you to **P** so that you may Ex 3:10
I should go to **P** and that I Ex 3:11
do in front of **P** all the wonders Ex 4:21
Then you will say to **P**: Ex 4:22
and Aaron went in and said to **P**, Ex 5:1
P responded, "Who is the LORD Ex 5:2
P also said, "Look, the people Ex 5:5
That day **P** commanded the Ex 5:6
to them, "This is what **P** says: Ex 5:10
went in and cried for help to **P**: Ex 5:15
they left **P**, they confronted Ex 5:20
reek in front of **P** and his Ex 5:21
I went in to **P** to speak in Your Ex 5:23
to see what I will do to **P**: Ex 6:1
Go and tell **P** king of Egypt to Ex 6:11
then how will **P** listen to me, Ex 6:12
Israelites and **P** king of Egypt Ex 6:13
who spoke to **P** king of Egypt Ex 6:27
tell **P** king of Egypt everything Ex 6:29
how will **P** listen to me?" Ex 6:30
I have made you like God to **P**, Ex 7:1
declare it to **P** so that he will Ex 7:2
P will not listen to you, but I Ex 7:4
Aaron 83 when they spoke to **P**. Ex 7:7
When **P** tells you: Perform a Ex 7:9
and throw it down before **P**. Ex 7:9
went in to **P** and did just as Ex 7:10
his staff before **P** and his Ex 7:10
But then **P** called the wise men Ex 7:11
to Moses, "**P** is unresponsive Ex 7:14
Go to **P** in the morning. Ex 7:15
in the sight of **P** and his Ex 7:20
P turned around, went into his Ex 7:23
Moses, "Go in to **P** and tell him: Ex 8:1
P summoned Moses and Aaron and Ex 8:8
said to **P**, "Make the choice Ex 8:9
Moses and Aaron went out from **P**, Ex 8:12
that He had brought against **P**. Ex 8:12
But when **P** saw there was relief, Ex 8:15
the magicians said to **P**. Ex 8:19
yourself to **P** when you see him Ex 8:20
Then **P** summoned Moses and Aaron Ex 8:25
P responded, "I will let you go Ex 8:28
of flies will depart from **P**, Ex 8:29
But **P** must not act deceptively Ex 8:29
the swarms of flies from **P**, Ex 8:31
But **P** hardened his heart this Ex 8:32
Go in to **P** and say to him: Ex 9:1
P sent ⌊messengers⌋ who saw that Ex 9:7
toward heaven in the sight of **P**. Ex 9:8
furnace soot and stood before **P**. Ex 9:10
and present yourself to **P**. Ex 9:13
P sent for Moses and Aaron. Ex 9:27
went out from **P** and the city, Ex 9:33
When **P** saw that the rain, hail, Ex 9:34
to Moses, "Go to **P**, for I have Ex 10:1
Aaron went in to **P** and told him, Ex 10:3
Aaron were brought back to **P**. Ex 10:8
the LORD your God," **P** said. Ex 10:8
P urgently sent for Moses and Ex 10:16
P summoned Moses and said, Ex 10:24
P said to him, "Leave me! Ex 10:28
more plague on **P** and on Egypt. Ex 11:1
firstborn of **P** who sits on his Ex 11:5
P will not listen to you, Ex 11:9
did all these wonders before **P**, Ex 11:10
firstborn of **P** who sat on his Ex 12:29
During the night **P** got up, Ex 12:30
When **P** stubbornly refused to let Ex 13:15
When **P** let the people go, God Ex 13:17
P will say of the Israelites: Ex 14:3
by means of **P** and all his army Ex 14:4
P and his officials changed Ex 14:5
the heart of **P** king of Egypt, Ex 14:8
As **P** approached, the Israelites Ex 14:10
receive glory by means of **P**, Ex 14:17
when I receive glory through **P**, Ex 14:18
entire army of **P**, that had gone Ex 14:28
LORD had done to **P** and the Ex 18:8
rescued you from **P** and the power Ex 18:10
'We were slaves of **P** in Egypt, Dt 6:21
on **P** and all his household, Dt 6:22
the power of **P** king of Egypt. Dt 7:8
your God did to **P** and all Egypt: Dt 7:18
did in Egypt to **P** king of Egypt Dt 11:3
the LORD did in Egypt to **P**, Dt 29:2
land of Egypt—to **P**, to all his Dt 34:11
Egyptians and **P** hardened theirs 1Sm 6:6
an alliance with **P** king of Egypt 1Kg 3:1
P king of Egypt had attacked and 1Kg 9:16
to Egypt, to **P** king of Egypt, 1Kg 11:18
P liked Hadad so much that he 1Kg 11:19
Hadad said to **P**, "Let me leave, 1Kg 11:21
But **P** asked him, "What do you 1Kg 11:22
the power of **P** king of Egypt 2Kg 17:7
This is how **P** king of Egypt is 2Kg 18:21
P Neco king of Egypt marched up 2Kg 23:29
P Neco imprisoned him at Riblah 2Kg 23:33
Then **P** Neco made Eliakim son 2Kg 23:34
the silver and the gold to **P**, 2Kg 23:35
valuation, to give it to **P** Neco. 2Kg 23:35
the daughter of **P** from the city 2Ch 8:11
signs and wonders against **P**, Neh 9:10
against **P** and all his officials. Ps 135:9
but hurled **P** and his army into Ps 136:15
How can you say to **P**, "I am one Is 19:11
This is how **P** king of Egypt is Is 36:6
P king of Egypt, his officers, Jr 25:19
am about to hand over **P** Hophra, Jr 44:30
Egypt and the army of **P** Neco, Jr 46:2
P king of Egypt was all noise; Jr 46:17
along with **P**, Egypt, her gods, Jr 46:25
P and those trusting in him. Jr 46:25
before **P** defeated Gaza. Jr 47:1
P will not help him with ⌊his⌋ Ezk 17:17
your face toward **P** king of Egypt Ezk 29:2
am against you, **P** king of Egypt, Ezk 29:3
the arm of **P** king of Egypt. Ezk 30:21
I am against **P** king of Egypt. Ezk 30:22
But I will break the arms of **P**, Ezk 30:24
to **P** king of Egypt and to his Ezk 31:2
This is **P** and all his hordes"— Ezk 31:18
lament for **P** king of Egypt and Ezk 32:2
P will see them and be comforted Ezk 32:31
his hordes—**P** and all his army Ezk 32:31
so **P** and all his hordes will be Ezk 32:32
and wisdom in the sight of **P**, Ac 7:10
family became known to **P**. Ac 7:13
For the Scripture tells **P**: Rm 9:17

PHARAOH'S *(72)*

P officials saw her and praised Gn 12:15
the woman was taken to **P** house. Gn 12:15
So he asked **P** officers who were Gn 40:7
P cup was in my hand, and I took Gn 40:11
them into **P** cup, and placed Gn 40:11
and placed the cup in **P** hand." Gn 40:11
You will put **P** cup in his hand Gn 40:13
day, which was **P** birthday, he Gn 40:20
and he placed the cup in **P** hand; Gn 40:21
P dreams mean the same thing. Gn 41:25
the grain under **P** authority as Gn 41:35
Joseph left **P** presence and Gn 41:46
and also **P** household heard it. Gn 45:2
When the news reached **P** house, Gn 45:16
and departed from **P** presence. Gn 47:10
he brought the money to **P** house. Gn 47:14
our land will become **P** slaves. Gn 47:19
The land became **P**, Gn 47:20
eyes and will be **P** slaves." Gn 47:25
Joseph said to **P** household, Gn 50:4
his father, and all **P** servants, Gn 50:7
P daughter went down to bathe at Ex 2:5
his sister said to **P** daughter, Ex 2:7
P daughter told her. Ex 2:8
Then **P** daughter said to her, Ex 2:9
she brought him to **P** daughter, Ex 2:10
P slave drivers had set over Ex 5:14
But I will harden **P** heart and Ex 7:3
However, **P** heart hardened, and Ex 7:13
P heart hardened, and he would Ex 7:22
But **P** heart hardened, and he Ex 8:19
flies went into **P** palace and his Ex 8:24
Then Moses left **P** presence and Ex 8:30
But **P** heart was hardened, and he Ex 9:7
LORD hardened **P** heart and he did Ex 9:12
Those among **P** officials who Ex 9:20
So **P** heart hardened, and he did Ex 9:35
he turned and left **P** presence. Ex 10:6
P officials asked him, "How long Ex 10:7
were driven from **P** presence. Ex 10:11
Moses left **P** presence and Ex 10:18
But the LORD hardened **P** heart, Ex 10:20
But the LORD hardened **P** heart, Ex 10:27
by **P** officials and the people. Ex 11:3
And he left **P** presence in Ex 11:8
but the LORD hardened **P** heart, Ex 11:10
I will harden **P** heart so that he Ex 14:4
all **P** horses and chariots, Ex 14:9
in pursuit—all **P** horses, his Ex 14:23
He threw **P** chariots and his army Ex 15:4
When **P** horses with his chariots Ex 15:19
and delivered me from **P** sword" Ex 18:4
Egypt and belonged to **P** palace? 1Sm 2:27
of Egypt by marrying **P** daughter. 1Kg 3:1
like this hall for **P** daughter, 1Kg 7:8
P daughter moved from the city 1Kg 9:24
women in addition to **P** daughter: 1Kg 11:1
herself⌋ weaned him in **P** palace, 1Kg 11:20
lived⌋ there along with **P** sons. 1Kg 11:20
but at **P** command he taxed the 2Kg 23:35
the sons of **P** daughter Bithiah 1Ch 4:18
to a mare among **P** chariots. Sg 1:9
P wisest advisers give stupid Is 19:11
seek shelter under **P** protection Is 30:2
P protection will become your Is 30:3
P army had left Egypt, and when Jr 37:5
P army, which has come out to Jr 37:7
Jerusalem because of **P** army, Jr 37:11
at the opening of **P** palace at Jr 43:9
king, but **P** arms will fall. Ezk 30:25
P daughter adopted and raised Ac 7:21
be called the son of **P** daughter Heb 11:24

PHARISEE *(10)*

Blind **P**! First clean the inside Mt 23:26
When the **P** who had invited Him Lk 7:39
a **P** asked Him to dine with him. Lk 11:37
When the **P** saw this, he was Lk 11:38
one a **P** and the other a tax Lk 18:10
The **P** took his stand and was Lk 18:11

the five rulers of the **P** and all Jdg 3:3
down 600 **P** with an oxgoad. Jdg 3:31
gods of the Ammonites and the **P**. Jdg 10:6
sold them to the **P** and the Jdg 10:7
Amorites, Ammonites, **P**, Jdg 10:11
them over to the **P** 40 years. Jdg 13:1
Israel from the power of the **P**." Jdg 13:5
the uncircumcised **P** for a wife?" Jdg 14:3
an occasion against the **P**. Jdg 14:4
the **P** were ruling over Israel. Jdg 14:4
When the **P** saw him, they brought Jdg 14:11
responsible when I harm the **P**." Jdg 15:3
the standing grain of the **P**. Jdg 15:5
the **P** asked, "Who did this?" Jdg 15:6
So the **P** went to her and her Jdg 15:6
The **P** went up, camped in Judah, Jdg 15:9
realize that the **P** rule over us? Jdg 15:11
you and hand you over to the **P**." Jdg 15:12
the **P** came to meet him shouting. Jdg 15:14
20 years in the days of the **P**. Jdg 15:20
him, "Samson, the **P** are here!" Jdg 16:9
Samson, the **P** are here!" Jdg 16:12
him, "Samson, the **P** are here!" Jdg 16:14
cried, "Samson, the **P** are here!" Jdg 16:20
The **P** seized him and gouged out Jdg 16:21
the leaders of the **P** were there, Jdg 16:27
pay back the **P** for my two eyes. Jdg 16:28
said, "Let me die with the **P**." Jdg 16:30
out to meet the **P** in battle and 1Sm 4:1
while the **P** camped at Aphek. 1Sm 4:1
The **P** lined up in battle 1Sm 4:2
Israel was defeated by the **P**, 1Sm 4:2
us be defeated today by the **P**? 1Sm 4:3
The **P** heard the sound of the war 1Sm 4:6
When the **P** discovered that the 1Sm 4:6
Show some courage and be men, **P**! 1Sm 4:9
So the **P** fought, and Israel was 1Sm 4:10
Israel has fled from the **P**, 1Sm 4:17
After the **P** had captured the ark 1Sm 5:1
the land of the **P** for seven 1Sm 6:1
the **P** summoned the priests and 1Sm 6:2
the **P** had sent back one gold 1Sm 6:17
The **P** have returned the ark of 1Sm 6:21
you from the hand of the **P**." 1Sm 7:3
When the **P** heard that the 1Sm 7:7
were afraid because of the **P**. 1Sm 7:7
save us from the hand of the **P**." 1Sm 7:8
offering as the **P** drew near to 1Sm 7:10
against the **P** that day and threw 1Sm 7:10
and pursued the **P** striking them 1Sm 7:11
the **P** were subdued and did not 1Sm 7:13
against the **P** all of Samuel's 1Sm 7:13
the hand of the **P** because I have 1Sm 9:16
Hazor, to the **P**, and to the king 1Sm 12:9
Geba, and the **P** heard about it. 1Sm 13:3
is now repulsive to the **P**." 1Sm 13:4
The **P** also gathered to fight 1Sm 13:5
days and the **P** were gathering at 1Sm 13:11
The **P** will now descend on me at 1Sm 13:12
and the **P** were camped at 1Sm 13:16
Israel, because the **P** had said, 1Sm 13:19
went to the **P** to sharpen their 1Sm 13:20
garrison, and the **P** said, "Look, 1Sm 14:11
the **P** were fighting against each 1Sm 14:20
into the camp to join the **P**, 1Sm 14:21
heard that the **P** were fleeing, 1Sm 14:22
of the **P** would have been 1Sm 14:30
struck down the **P** that day from 1Sm 14:31
go down after the **P** tonight and 1Sm 14:36
God, "Should I go after the **P**? 1Sm 14:37
gave up the pursuit of the **P**, 1Sm 14:46
and the **P** returned to their own 1Sm 14:46
the kings of Zobah, and the **P**. 1Sm 14:47
with the **P** was fierce all 1Sm 14:52
The **P** gathered their forces for 1Sm 17:1
battle formation to face the **P**. 1Sm 17:2
The **P** were standing on one hill, 1Sm 17:3
of Elah fighting with the **P**." 1Sm 17:19
Israel and the **P** lined up in 1Sm 17:21
When the **P** saw that their hero 1Sm 17:51
and chased the **P** to the entrance 1Sm 17:52
from the pursuit of the **P**, 1Sm 17:53
hand of the **P** be against him. 1Sm 18:17
hand of the **P** will be against 1Sm 18:21
death at the hands of the **P**. 1Sm 18:25
men went out and killed 200 **P**. 1Sm 18:27
out and fought against the **P**. 1Sm 19:8
P are fighting against Keilah 1Sm 23:1

an attack against these **P**?" 1Sm 23:2
against the **P** and rescue Keilah. 1Sm 23:2
I will hand the **P** over to you." 1Sm 23:4
fought against the **P**, drove 1Sm 23:5
the **P** have raided the land! 1Sm 23:27
David and went to engage the **P**. 1Sm 23:28
returned from pursuing the **P**, 1Sm 24:1
to the land of the **P**. 1Sm 27:1
the **P** brought their military 1Sm 28:1
The **P** came together and camped 1Sm 28:4
The **P** are fighting against me 1Sm 28:15
over to the **P** along with you. 1Sm 28:19
Israel's army over to the **P**." 1Sm 28:19
The **P** brought all their military 1Sm 29:1
to return to the land of the **P**. 1Sm 29:11
And the **P** went up to Jezreel. 1Sm 29:11
the land of the **P** and the land 1Sm 30:16
The **P** fought against Israel, 1Sm 31:1
The **P** overtook Saul and his sons 1Sm 31:2
So the **P** came and settled in 1Sm 31:7
day when the **P** came to strip 1Sm 31:8
the land of the **P** to spread the 1Sm 31:9
heard what the **P** had done to 1Sm 31:11
daughters of the **P** will rejoice, 2Sm 1:20
the power of the **P** and the power 2Sm 3:18
When the **P** heard that David had 2Sm 5:17
So the **P** came and spread out in 2Sm 5:18
I go to war against the **P**? 2Sm 5:19
hand the **P** over to you." 2Sm 5:19
The **P** abandoned their idols 2Sm 5:21
The **P** came up again and spread 2Sm 5:22
to attack the camp of the **P**." 2Sm 5:24
he struck down the **P** all the way 2Sm 5:25
defeated the **P**, subdued them, 2Sm 8:1
the **P**, the Amalekites, 2Sm 8:12
us from the grasp of the **P**, 2Sm 19:9
where the **P** had hung them 2Sm 21:12
them the day the **P** killed Saul 2Sm 21:12
The **P** again waged war against 2Sm 21:15
they fought the **P**, but David 2Sm 21:15
battle with the **P** at Gob. 2Sm 21:18
was a battle with the **P** at Gob, 2Sm 21:19
David when they defied the **P**. 2Sm 23:9
attacked the **P** until his hand 2Sm 23:10
The **P** had assembled ⌊in 2Sm 23:11
The troops fled from the **P**, 2Sm 23:11
it, and struck down the **P**. 2Sm 23:12
a company of **P** was camping 2Sm 23:13
the land of the **P** and as far as 1Kg 4:21
Gibbethon of the **P** while Nadab 1Kg 15:27
against Gibbethon of the **P**. 1Kg 16:15
land of the **P** for seven years 2Kg 8:2
the land of the **P** at the end of 2Kg 8:3
He defeated the **P** as far as Gaza 2Kg 18:8
Casluhim (the **P** came from them), 1Ch 1:12
The **P** fought against Israel, 1Ch 10:1
The **P** pursued Saul and his sons 1Ch 10:2
So the **P** came and settled in 1Ch 10:7
day when the **P** came to strip 1Ch 10:8
the land of the **P** to spread the 1Ch 10:9
everything the **P** had done to 1Ch 10:11
when the **P** had gathered there 1Ch 11:13
the troops had fled from the **P**. 1Ch 11:13
They killed the **P**, and the LORD 1Ch 11:14
went with the **P** to fight against 1Ch 12:19
they did not help the **P** because 1Ch 12:19
When the **P** heard that David had 1Ch 14:8
Now the **P** had come and made a 1Ch 14:9
I go to war against the **P**? 1Ch 14:10
and David defeated the **P** there. 1Ch 14:11
The **P** abandoned their idols 1Ch 14:12
Once again the **P** made a raid in 1Ch 14:13
to attack the camp of the **P**." 1Ch 14:15
defeated the **P**, subdued them, 1Ch 18:1
the Ammonites, the **P**, and the 1Ch 18:11
broke out with the **P** at Gezer. 1Ch 20:4
giants, and the **P** were subdued. 1Ch 20:4
there was a battle with the **P**, 1Ch 20:5
the land of the **P** and as far as 2Ch 9:26
Some of the **P** also brought gifts 2Ch 17:11
the mind of the **P** and the Arabs 2Ch 21:16
out to wage war against the **P**, 2Ch 26:6
of⌋ Ashdod and among the **P**. 2Ch 26:6
God helped him against the **P**, 2Ch 26:7
The **P** also raided the cities of 2Ch 28:18
of fortune-tellers like the **P**. Is 2:6
the kings of the land of the **P**— Jr 25:20
about the **P** before Pharaoh Jr 47:1

is coming to destroy all the **P**, Jr 47:4
LORD is about to destroy the **P**, Jr 47:4
and by the daughters of the **P**— Ezk 16:57
Because the **P** acted in vengeance Ezk 25:15
out My hand against the **P**, Ezk 25:16
remainder of the **P** will perish. Am 1:8
then go down to Gath of the **P**. Am 6:2
of Egypt, the **P** from Caphtor, Am 9:7
possess ⌊the land of⌋ the **P**. Ob 19
you, Canaan, land of the **P**: Zph 2:5
will destroy the pride of the **P**. Zch 9:6

PHILOLOGUS *(1)*
Greet **P** and Julia, Nereus and Rm 16:15

PHILOSOPHER *(1)*
Where is the **p**? Where is the 1Co 1:20

PHILOSOPHERS *(1)*
and Stoic **p** argued with him. Ac 17:18

PHILOSOPHY *(1)*
captive through **p** and empty Col 2:8

PHINEHAS *(23)*
of Putiel and she bore him **P**. Ex 6:25
When **P** son of Eleazar, son of Nm 25:7
P son of Eleazar, son of Aaron Nm 25:11
They went with **P** son of Eleazar Nm 31:6
Israelites sent **P** son of Eleazar Jos 22:13
When **P** the priest and the Jos 22:30
P son of Eleazar the priest said Jos 22:31
Then **P** son of Eleazar the priest Jos 22:32
given to his son **P** in the hill Jos 24:33
and **P** son of Eleazar, son of Jdg 20:28
Hophni and **P**, were the LORD's 1Sm 1:3
your two sons Hophni and **P**: 1Sm 2:34
Hophni and **P**, were there with 1Sm 4:4
two sons, Hophni and **P**, died. 1Sm 4:11
Hophni and **P**, are both dead, 1Sm 4:17
the wife of **P**, was pregnant and 1Sm 4:19
the brother of Ichabod son of **P**, 1Sm 14:3
Eleazar fathered **P**; 1Ch 6:4
P fathered Abishua; 1Ch 6:4
his son **P**, his son Abishua 1Ch 6:50
earlier times **P** son of Eleazar 1Ch 9:20
Eleazar son of **P** was with him. Ezr 8:33
But **P** stood up and intervened, Ps 106:30

PHINEHAS'S *(2)*
Abishua's son, **P** son, Eleazar's Ezr 7:5
Gershom, from **P** descendants; Ezr 8:2

PHLEGON *(1)*
Asyncritus, **P**, Hermes, Patrobas Rm 16:14

PHOEBE *(1)*
I commend to you our sister **P**, Rm 16:1

PHOENICIA *(3)*
made their way as far as **P**, Ac 11:19
through both **P** and Samaria, Ac 15:3
a ship crossing over to **P**, Ac 21:2

PHOENIX *(1)*
hoping somehow to reach **P**, Ac 27:12

PHRYGIA *(3)*
P and Pamphylia, Egypt and the Ac 2:10
the region of **P** and Galatia and Ac 16:6
in the Galatian territory and **P**, Ac 18:23

PHYGELUS *(1)*
including **P** and Hermogenes. 2Tm 1:15

PHYLACTERIES *(1)*
enlarge their **p** and lengthen Mt 23:5

PHYSICAL *(14)*
who has a **p** defect is to come Lv 21:17
or all ⌊your⌋ **p** exertion keep Jb 36:19
lament when your **p** body has been Pr 5:11
young men without any **p** defect, Dn 1:4
on Him in a **p** appearance like Lk 3:22
my countrymen by **p** descent. Rm 9:3
from them, by **p** descent, came Rm 9:5
children by **p** descent who are Rm 9:8
but his **p** presence is weak, 2Co 10:10
the gospel to you in **p** weakness, Gl 4:13
and though my **p** condition was a Gl 4:14
you by His **p** body through His Col 1:22
concerning **p** descent but based Heb 7:16
They are **p** regulations and only Heb 9:10

PHYSICALLY *(1)*
A man who is **p** uncircumcised, Rm 2:27

PHYSICIAN *(2)*
Is there no **p** there? Jr 8:22
Luke, the loved **p**, and Demas Col 4:14

PHYSICIANS *(2)*
servants who were **p** to embalm Gn 50:2
didn't seek the LORD but the **p**. 2Ch 16:12

PI-BESETH *(1)*
young men of On and **P** will fall Ezk 30:17

PI-HAHIROTH *(4)*
back and camp in front of **P**, Ex 14:2
they camped by the sea beside **P**, Ex 14:9
from Etham and turned back to **P**, Nm 33:7
They departed from **P** and crossed Nm 33:8

PICK *(22)*
cut off used to **p** up ⌊scraps⌋ Jdg 1:7
David would **p** up his harp and 1Sm 16:23
Elisha said, "**P** up your son." 2Kg 4:36
Then he said, "**P** it up." 2Kg 6:7
P him up and throw him on the 2Kg 9:25
p him up and throw him on the 2Kg 9:26
all who pass by **p** its fruit? Ps 80:12
P up ⌊your⌋ harp, stroll through Is 23:16
do not **p** up a load and bring it Jr 17:21
P up some large stones and set Jr 43:9
fall with no one to **p** him up. Jr 50:32
P me up and throw me into the Jnh 1:12
Get up, **p** up your stretcher, Mt 9:6
and began to **p** and eat some Mt 12:1
to say, 'Get up, **p** up your Mk 2:9
get up, **p** up your stretcher, and Mk 2:11
they will **p** up snakes; if they Mk 16:18
get up, **p** up your stretcher, and Lk 5:24
"**p** up your bedroll and walk!" Jn 5:8
for you to **p** up your bedroll." Jn 5:10
'**P** up your bedroll and walk.' Jn 5:11
'**P** up ⌊your bedroll⌋ and walk?' Jn 5:12

PICKED *(29)*
Jacob **p** out a stone and set it Gn 31:45
p up the branch, put it on his Jdg 9:48
his house, he **p** up a knife, took Jdg 19:29
She **p** up ⌊the grain⌋ and went Ru 2:18
The cook **p** up the thigh and what 1Sm 9:24
young man **p** up the arrow 1Sm 20:38
His nurse **p** him up and fled, 2Sm 4:4
they can never be **p** up by hand. 2Sm 23:6
and the priests **p** up the ark. 1Kg 8:3
Elisha **p** up the mantle that had 2Kg 2:13
So he **p** him up and took him to 2Kg 4:20
she **p** up her son and left. 2Kg 4:37
Then they **p** up the silver, 2Kg 7:8
another tent, **p** ⌊things⌋ up, and 2Kg 7:8
and the Levites **p** up the ark. 2Ch 5:4
emptied the chest, **p** it up, and 2Ch 24:11
for You have **p** me up and thrown Ps 102:10
Then they **p** up Jonah and threw Jnh 1:15
Then they **p** up 12 baskets full Mt 14:20
he got up, **p** up the stretcher, Mk 2:12
Then they **p** up 12 baskets full Mk 6:43
p up what he had been lying on, Lk 5:25
or grapes **p** from a bramble bush. Lk 6:44
Then they **p** up 12 baskets of Lk 9:17
man got well, **p** up his bedroll, Jn 5:9
p up stones to throw at Him. Jn 8:59
Again the Jews **p** up rocks to Jn 10:31
third story, and was **p** up dead. Ac 20:9
a mighty angel **p** up a stone like Rv 18:21

PICKERS *(1)*
If grape **p** came to you, wouldn't Ob 5

PICKING *(3)*
he is only **p** a fight with me. 2Kg 5:7
make their way **p** some heads of Mk 2:23
disciples were **p** heads of grain, Lk 6:1

PICKS *(5)*
saws, iron **p**, and iron axes, 2Sm 12:31
with saws, iron **p**, and axes. 1Ch 20:3
An east wind **p** him up, and he is Jb 27:21
carvings with hatchets and **p**. Ps 74:6
as a shepherd **p** lice off his Jr 43:12

PIECE *(42)*
cherubim of one **p** with the mercy Ex 25:19
It is to be made of one **p**: Ex 25:31
and branches are to be of one **p**. Ex 25:36
single hammered **p** of pure gold. Ex 25:36
the horns are to be of one **p**. Ex 27:2
on the ephod must be of one **p**, Ex 28:8
Its horns must be of one **p**. Ex 30:2
of one **p**⌋ with the mercy Ex 37:8
He made it ⌊all⌋ of one **p**: Ex 37:17
and branches were of one **p**. Ex 37:22
single hammered **p** of pure gold. Ex 37:22
Its horns were of one **p**. Ex 37:25
the horns were of one **p**. Ex 38:2
was of one **p** with the ephod, Ex 39:5
the burnt offering **p** by piece, Lv 9:13
the burnt offering piece by **p**, Lv 9:13
is selling a **p** of land that Ru 4:3
down to him for a **p** of silver or 1Sm 2:36
I can have a **p** of bread to eat. 1Sm 2:36
Here, I have a **p** of silver. 1Sm 9:8
the reserved **p** is set before you 1Sm 9:24
support was one **p** with the water 1Kg 7:34
its frames were one **p** with it. 1Kg 7:35
bring me a **p** of bread in your 1Kg 17:11
ruin every good **p** of land with 2Kg 3:19
to cover every good **p** of land. 2Kg 3:25
Then Job took a **p** of broken Jb 2:8
pinched off from ⌊a **p** of⌋ clay. Jb 33:6
a man may sin for a **p** of bread. Pr 28:21
Take a large **p** of parchment and Is 8:1
in it, every good **p**—thigh and Ezk 24:4
off! Empty it **p** by piece; lots Ezk 24:6
it piece by **p**; lots should not Ezk 24:6
two legs or a **p** of an ear Am 3:12
but also the **p** from the new Lk 5:36
they gave Him a **p** of a broiled Lk 24:42
one I give the **p** of bread to Jn 13:26
⌊Judas ate⌋ the **p** of bread, Jn 13:27
After receiving the **p** of bread, Jn 13:30
woven in one **p** from the top. Jn 19:23
his wife, sold a **p** of property. Ac 5:1
same lump one **p** of pottery for Rm 9:21

PIECES *(90)*
and laid the **p** opposite each Gn 15:10
your brother 1,000 **p** of silver. Gn 20:16
sold him for 20 **p** of silver to Gn 37:28
Joseph has been torn to **p**!" Gn 37:33
he must have been torn to **p**— Gn 44:28
gave Benjamin 300 **p** of silver Gn 45:22
smash their sacred pillars to **p**. Ex 23:24
two shoulder **p** attached to its Ex 28:7
the shoulder **p** of the ephod as Ex 28:12
ephod's shoulder **p** in the front. Ex 28:25
two shoulder **p** on its front, Ex 28:27
Cut the ram into **p**. Wash its Ex 29:17
head and its **p** ⌊on the altar⌋. Ex 29:17
made shoulder **p** for attaching it Ex 39:4
the shoulder **p** of the ephod as Ex 39:7
the ephod's shoulder **p** in front. Ex 39:18
two shoulder **p** on its front, Ex 39:20
offering and cut it into **p**. Lv 1:6
priests are to arrange the **p**, Lv 1:8
will cut it into **p** with its head Lv 1:12
Break it into **p** and pour oil on Lv 2:6
as a grain offering of baked **p**, Lv 6:21
the ram into **p** and burned the Lv 8:20
the head, the **p**, and the suet, Lv 8:20
will cut them to **p** and blot out Dt 32:26
So they gave him 70 **p** of silver Jdg 9:4
give you 1,100 **p** of silver." Jdg 16:5
The 1,100 **p** of silver taken from Jdg 17:2
the 1,100 **p** of silver to his Jdg 17:3
cut her into 12 **p**, limb by limb, Jdg 19:29
my concubine and cut her in **p**, Jdg 20:6
cut them in **p**, and sent them 1Sm 11:7
hacked Agag to **p** before the 1Sm 15:33
you 10 silver **p** and a belt!" 2Sm 18:11
weight of 1,000 **p** of silver in 2Sm 18:12
he had on, tore it into 12 **p**, 1Kg 11:30
Take 10 **p** for yourself, for 1Kg 11:31
cut it in **p**, and place it 1Kg 18:23
and tore them into two **p**. 2Kg 2:12
dash their little ones to **p**. 2Kg 8:12
its altars and images into **p**, 2Kg 11:18
He broke into **p** the bronze snake 2Kg 18:4
broke the sacred pillars into **p**, 2Kg 23:14
and he cut into **p** all the gold 2Kg 24:13
broke into **p** the bronze pillars 2Kg 25:13
and images into **p** and killed 2Ch 23:17
all of them were dashed to **p**. 2Ch 25:12
cut them into **p**, shut the doors 2Ch 28:24
are smashed to **p** from dawn to Jb 4:20
of the neck and smashed me to **p**. Jb 16:12
bows and cuts spears to **p**; Ps 46:9
thousands of gold and silver **p**. Ps 119:72
for his fruit 1,000 **p** of silver. Sg 8:11
worth 1,000 **p** of silver, will Is 7:23
bows will cut young men to **p**. Is 13:18
jar, crushed to **p**, so that not Is 30:14
it You who hacked Rahab to **p**, Is 51:9
will be torn to **p** because their Jr 5:6
in order to pass between its **p**. Jr 34:18
passed between the **p** of the calf Jr 34:19
broke into **p** the bronze pillars Jr 52:17
me off my way and tore me to **p**; Lm 3:11
and cut you to **p** with their Ezk 16:40
then you will gnaw its broken **p**, Ezk 23:34
Place the **p** of meat in it, Ezk 24:4
tear ⌊them⌋ to **p** and depart. Hs 5:14
be dashed to **p** along with ⌊their Hs 10:14
little ones will be dashed to **p**, Hs 13:16
house will be smashed to **p**, Am 6:11
images will be smashed to **p**, Mc 1:7
also dashed to **p** at the head Nah 3:10
my wages, 30 **p** of silver. Zch 11:12
So I took the 30 **p** of silver and Zch 11:13
feet, turn, and tear you to **p**. Mt 7:6
12 baskets full of leftover **p**! Mt 14:20
they collected the leftover **p**— Mt 15:37
this stone will be broken to **p**; Mt 21:44
will cut him to **p** and assign him Mt 24:51
weighed out 30 **p** of silver for Mt 26:15
returned the 30 **p** of silver to Mt 27:3
They took the 30 **p** of silver, Mt 27:9
baskets full of **p** of bread and Mk 6:43
large baskets of leftover **p**. Mk 8:8
baskets full of **p** of bread did Mk 8:19
baskets full of **p** of bread did Mk 8:20
up 12 baskets of leftover **p**. Lk 9:17
will cut him to **p** and assign him Lk 12:46
that stone will be broken to **p**, Lk 20:18
baskets with the **p** from the five Jn 6:13
it to be 50,000 **p** of silver. Ac 19:19

PIERCE *(11)*
His master must **p** his ear with Ex 21:6
take an awl and **p** through his Dt 15:17
will go into his palm and **p** it. 2Kg 18:21
from⌋ a bronze bow will **p** him. Jb 20:24
or **p** his nose with snares? Jb 40:24
his nose or **p** his jaw with a Jb 41:2
Your arrows **p** the hearts of the Ps 45:5
will enter and **p** the hand of Is 36:6
You **p** his head with his own Hab 3:14
who bore him will **p** him through. Zch 13:3
a sword will **p** your own soul— Lk 2:35

PIERCED *(15)*
she shattered and **p** his temple. Jdg 5:26
of the Almighty have **p** me; Jb 6:4
His hand **p** the fleeing serpent. Jb 26:13
they **p** my hands and my feet. Ps 22:16
pieces, who **p** the sea monster? Is 51:9
But He was **p** because of our Is 53:5
those who were **p** through, in her Jr 51:4
He **p** my kidneys with His arrows. Lm 3:13
p ⌊with pain⌋ because the fields Lm 4:9
will look at Me whom they **p**. Zch 12:10
of the soldiers **p** His side with Jn 19:34
will look at the One they **p**. Jn 19:37
were **p** to the heart and said Ac 2:37
the faith and **p** themselves with 1Tm 6:10
including those who **p** Him. Rv 1:7

PIERCES *(4)*
My enemy **p** me with His eyes. Jb 16:9
p my kidneys without mercy and Jb 16:13
Night **p** my bones, and my gnawing Jb 30:17
until an arrow **p** its liver, Pr 7:23

PIERCING *(1)*
speaks rashly, like a **p** sword; Pr 12:18

PIETY *(2)*
Isn't your **p** your confidence, Jb 4:6
you to court because of your **p**? Jb 22:4

PIG *(2)*
the **p**, though it has divided Lv 11:7
and the **p**, though it has hooves, Dt 14:8

PIG'S *(1)*
like a gold ring in a **p** snout. Pr 11:22

PIGEON *(2)*
a turtledove, and a young **p**." Gn 15:9
a young **p** or a turtledove for Lv 12:6

PIGEONS *(10)*
from the turtledoves or young **p**. Lv 1:14
two young **p** as restitution for Lv 5:7
two turtledoves or two young **p**, Lv 5:11
two turtledoves or two young **p**, Lv 12:8

two turtledoves or two young **p**, Lv 14:22
the turtledoves or young **p**, Lv 14:30
two young **p** on the eighth day, Lv 15:14
or two young **p** and bring them to Lv 15:29
or two young **p** to the priest at Nm 6:10
of turtledoves or two young **p** Lk 2:24

PIGS *(14)*
eating meat from **p**, vermin, and Is 66:17
or toss your pearls before **p**, Mt 7:6
a large herd of **p** was feeding. Mt 8:30
"send us into the herd of **p**." Mt 8:31
come out, they entered the **p**. Mt 8:32
Now a large herd of **p** was there, Mk 5:11
us to the **p**, so we may enter Mk 5:12
came out and entered the **p**, Mk 5:13
man and ⌊told⌋ about the **p**. Mk 5:16
A large herd of **p** was there, Lk 8:32
to permit them to enter the **p**, Lk 8:32
of the man and entered the **p**, Lk 8:33
him into his fields to feed **p**. Lk 15:15
carob pods the **p** were eating, Lk 15:16

PILASTER *(3)*
around to the **p** of the court. Ezk 40:14
Each **p** was decorated with palm Ezk 40:16
the width of the **p** was 10 and a Ezk 41:1

PILASTERS *(17)*
and its **p** were three and a half Ezk 40:9
the **p** on either side also had Ezk 40:10
he measured the **p**—105 feet. Ezk 40:14
recesses and their **p** had beveled Ezk 40:16
each side, its **p**, and its Ezk 40:21
He measured its **p** and portico; Ezk 40:24
It had palm trees on its **p**, Ezk 40:26
Its recesses, **p**, and portico had Ezk 40:29
and its **p** were decorated with Ezk 40:31
Its recesses, **p**, and portico had Ezk 40:33
and its **p** were decorated with Ezk 40:34
its recesses, **p**, and portico. Ezk 40:36
and its **p** were decorated with Ezk 40:37
measured the **p** of the portico; Ezk 40:48
There were pillars by the **p**, Ezk 40:49
great hall and measured the **p**; Ezk 41:1
measured the **p** at the entrance Ezk 41:3

PILATE *(57)*
away and handed Him over to **P**, Mt 27:2
Then **P** said to Him, "Don't You Mt 27:13
together, **P** said to them, "Who Mt 27:17
P asked them, "What should I do Mt 27:22
When **P** saw that he was getting Mt 27:24
approached **P** and asked for Mt 27:58
Then **P** ordered that it be Mt 27:58
the Pharisees gathered before **P** Mt 27:62
of soldiers⌋," **P** told them. Mt 27:65
away and handed Him over to **P**. Mk 15:1
P asked Him, "Are You the King Mk 15:2
Then **P** questioned Him again, Mk 15:4
anything, so **P** was amazed. Mk 15:5
began to ask ⌊**P**⌋ to do for them Mk 15:8
So **P** answered them, "Do you want Mk 15:9
P asked them again, "Then what Mk 15:12
Then **P** said to them, "Why? Mk 15:14
P released Barabbas to them. Mk 15:15
boldly went in to **P** and asked Mk 15:43
P was surprised that He was Mk 15:44
while Pontius **P** was governor of Lk 3:1
whose blood **P** had mixed with Lk 13:1
up and brought Him before **P**. Lk 23:1
P asked Him, "Are You the King Lk 23:3
P then told the chief priests Lk 23:4
When **P** heard this, he asked if Lk 23:6
robe, and sent Him back to **P**. Lk 23:11
day Herod and **P** became friends. Lk 23:12
P called together the chief Lk 23:13
P, wanting to release Jesus, Lk 23:20
So **P** decided to grant their Lk 23:24
approached **P** and asked for Lk 23:52
P came out to them and said, Jn 18:29
So **P** told them, "Take Him Jn 18:31
Then **P** went back into the Jn 18:33
a Jew, am I?" **P** replied. "Your Jn 18:35
a king then?" **P** asked. "You say Jn 18:37
is truth?" said **P**. After he had Jn 18:38
Then **P** took Jesus and had Him Jn 19:1
P went outside again and said to Jn 19:4
P said to them, "Here is the man! Jn 19:5
P responded, "Take Him and Jn 19:6
When **P** heard this statement, Jn 19:8
So **P** said to Him, "You're not Jn 19:10
From that moment **P** made every Jn 19:12
When **P** heard these words, he Jn 19:13
P said to them, "Should I Jn 19:15
P also had a sign lettered and Jn 19:19
priests of the Jews said to **P**, Jn 19:21
P replied, "What I have written, Jn 19:22
requested that **P** have the men's Jn 19:31
P that he might remove Jesus' Jn 19:38
P gave him permission, so he Jn 19:38
and denied in the presence of **P**, Ac 3:13
city both Herod and Pontius **P**, Ac 4:27
they asked **P** to have Him killed. Ac 13:28
confession before Pontius **P**, 1Tm 6:13

PILATE'S *(1)*
festival it was **P** custom to Mk 15:6

PILDASH *(1)*
Chesed, Hazo, **P**, Jidlaph, and Gn 22:22

PILE *(15)*
I will **p** disasters on them; Dt 32:23
over him a large **p** of rocks that Jos 7:26
and put a large **p** of rocks over Jos 8:29
at the end of the **p** of barley. Ru 3:7
the needy from the garbage **p**. 1Sm 2:8
P them in two heaps at the 2Kg 10:8
intertwined around a **p** of rocks. Jb 8:17
the needy from the garbage **p** Ps 113:7
the city into a **p** of rubble, Is 25:2
straw is trampled in a dung **p**. Is 25:10
p her up like mounds of grain Jr 50:26
flock and also **p** up the fuel Ezk 24:5
will make the **p** of kindling Ezk 24:9
P on the logs and kindle the Ezk 24:10
the soil or for the manure **p**; Lk 14:35

PILED *(4)*
They **p** them in countless heaps, Ex 8:14
donkey I have **p** them in a heap. Jdg 15:16
p a huge mound of stones over 2Sm 18:17
For her sins are **p** up to heaven, Rv 18:5

PILES *(9)*
He burned up the **p** of grain and Jdg 15:5
cities into **p** of rubble. 2Kg 19:25
gathered ⌊them⌋ into large **p**. 2Ch 31:6
they began building up the **p**, 2Ch 31:7
officials came and viewed the **p**, 2Ch 31:8
priests and Levites about the **p**. 2Ch 31:9
destined to become **p** of rubble. Jb 15:28
Though he **p** up silver like dust Jb 27:16
cities into **p** of rubble. Is 37:26

PILGRIMAGE *(3)*
My **p** has lasted 130 years. Gn 47:9
whose hearts are set on **p**. Ps 84:5
Gilgal or make a **p** to Beth-aven, Hs 4:15

PILGRIMAGES *(1)*
of my fathers during their **p**." Gn 47:9

PILHA *(1)*
Hallohesh, **P**, Shobek, Neh 10:24

PILING *(1)*
against My will, **p** sin on top of Is 30:1

PILLAGED *(1)*
How Esau will be **p**, his hidden Ob 6

PILLAGES *(1)*
breaks in; a gang **p** outside. Hs 7:1

PILLAR *(39)*
back and became a **p** of salt. Gn 19:26
of them in a **p** of cloud to lead Ex 13:21
day and in a **p** of fire to give Ex 13:21
The **p** of cloud by day and the Ex 13:22
day and the **p** of fire by night Ex 13:22
The **p** of cloud moved from in Ex 14:19
forces from the **p** of fire and Ex 14:24
the **p** of cloud would come down Ex 33:9
people saw the **p** of cloud Ex 33:10
or sacred **p** for yourselves, Lv 26:1
LORD descended in a **p** of cloud, Nm 12:5
them in a **p** of cloud by day Nm 14:14
by day and in a **p** of fire by Nm 14:14
and do not set up a sacred **p**; Dt 16:22
at the tent in a **p** of cloud, Dt 31:15
at the oak of the **p** in Shechem. Jdg 9:6
for himself a **p** in the King's 2Sm 18:18
So he gave the **p** his name. 2Sm 18:18
set up the right **p** and named it 1Kg 7:21
set up the left **p** and named it 1Kg 7:21
the sacred **p** of Baal his father 2Kg 3:2
and tore down the **p** of Baal. 2Kg 10:27
standing by the **p** according to 2Kg 11:14
king stood by the **p** and made a 2Kg 23:3
One **p** was 27 feet tall and had a 2Kg 25:17
The second **p** was the same, 2Kg 25:17
by his **p** at the entrance 2Ch 23:13
them with a **p** of cloud by day Neh 9:12
and with a **p** of fire by night, Neh 9:12
the day the **p** of cloud never Neh 9:19
the night the **p** of fire Neh 9:19
spoke to them in a **p** of cloud; Ps 99:7
Egypt and a **p** to the LORD near Is 19:19
city, an iron **p**, and bronze Jr 1:18
One **p** was 27 feet tall, had a Jr 52:21
The second **p** was the same, Jr 52:22
without sacrifice or sacred **p**, Hs 3:4
the **p** and foundation of the 1Tm 3:15
will make him a **p** in the Rv 3:12

PILLARS *(66)*
smash their sacred **p** to pieces. Ex 23:24
an altar and 12 **p** for the 12 Ex 24:4
their sacred **p**, and chop down Ex 34:13
their standing **p**, cut down their Dt 7:5
their sacred **p**, burn up their Dt 12:3
had him stand between the **p**. Jdg 16:25
I can feel the **p** supporting Jdg 16:26
of the two middle **p** supporting Jdg 16:29
The **p** of the doorposts were 1Kg 6:31
high on four rows of cedar **p**, 1Kg 7:2
cedar beams on top of the **p**. 1Kg 7:2
chambers that ⌊rested⌋ on 45 **p**, 1Kg 7:3
made the hall of **p** 75 feet long 1Kg 7:6
A portico was in front of the **p**, 1Kg 7:6
a canopy with **p** were in front 1Kg 7:6
He cast two ⌊hollow⌋ bronze **p**: 1Kg 7:15
bronze to set on top of the **p**; 1Kg 7:16
on top of the **p** had gratings 1Kg 7:17
made the **p** with two encircling 1Kg 7:18
on top of the **p** in the portico 1Kg 7:19
capitals on the two **p** were also 1Kg 7:20
set up the **p** at the portico of 1Kg 7:21
The tops of the **p** were shaped 1Kg 7:22
the work of the **p** was completed. 1Kg 7:22
two **p**; bowls for the capitals 1Kg 7:41
that were on top of the two **p**; 1Kg 7:41
that were on top of the **p**; 1Kg 7:41
capitals' bowls on top of the **p** 1Kg 7:42
places, sacred **p**, and Asherah 1Kg 14:23
brought out the **p** of the temple 2Kg 10:26
sacred **p** and Asherah poles 2Kg 17:10
the sacred **p** and cut down 2Kg 18:4
broke the sacred **p** into pieces, 2Kg 23:14
the bronze **p** of the LORD's 2Kg 25:13
As for the two **p**, the one 2Kg 25:16
reservoir, the **p**, and the bronze 1Ch 18:8
of the temple he made two **p**, 2Ch 3:15
and also put it on top of the **p**. 2Ch 3:16
Then he set up the **p** in front of 2Ch 3:17
p; the bowls and the capitals 2Ch 4:12
capitals on top of the two **p**; 2Ch 4:12
that were on top of the **p**; 2Ch 4:12
capitals' bowls on top of the **p** 2Ch 4:13
their sacred **p** and chopped down 2Ch 14:3
Judah and broke up the sacred **p**, 2Ch 31:1
its place so that its **p** tremble. Jb 9:6
The **p** ⌊that hold up⌋ the sky Jb 26:11
I am the One who steadies its **p**. Ps 75:3
like corner **p** that are carved in Ps 144:12
she has carved out her seven **p**. Pr 9:1
are alabaster **p** set on pedestals Sg 5:15
LORD of Hosts says about the **p**, Jr 27:19
smash the sacred **p** of the sun Jr 43:13
the bronze **p** for the LORD's Jr 52:17
As for the two **p**, the one Jr 52:20
and your mighty **p** will fall to Ezk 26:11
There were **p** by the pilasters, Ezk 40:49
and had no **p** like the pillars Ezk 42:6
like the **p** of the courts; Ezk 42:6
better they made the sacred **p**. Hs 10:1
and demolish their sacred **p**. Hs 10:2
capitals of the **p** so that the Am 9:1
images and sacred **p** from you, Mc 5:13
roost in the capitals of its **p**. Zph 2:14
recognized as **p**, acknowledged Gl 2:9
his legs were like fiery **p**, Rv 10:1

PILLOW *(1)*
I dampen my **p** and drench my bed Ps 6:6

PILOT *(1)*
the will of the **p** directs. Jms 3:4
PILTAI *(1)*
Zichri of Abijah, **P** of Moadiah, Neh 12:17
PIN *(4)*
braids with a **p** and called to Jdg 16:14
his sleep and pulled out the **p**, Jdg 16:14
"I'll **p** David to the wall." 1Sm 18:11
Saul tried to **p** David to the 1Sm 19:10
PINCHED *(1)*
I was also **p** off from ⌊a piece Jb 33:6
PINE *(5)*
makes its home in the **p** trees. Ps 104:17
to you—⌊its⌋ **p**, fir, and Is 60:13
planking with **p** trees from Senir Ezk 27:5
p trees couldn't compare with Ezk 31:8
I am like a flourishing **p** tree; Hs 14:8
PINES *(1)*
the woman with many sons **p** away. 1Sm 2:5
PINIONS *(2)*
and lifts him up on His **p**. Dt 32:11
wings, long **p**, and full plumage Ezk 17:3
PINNACLE *(2)*
stand on the **p** of the temple, Mt 4:5
stand on the **p** of the temple, Lk 4:9
PINON *(2)*
Oholibamah, Elah, **P**, Gn 36:41
Oholibamah, Elah, **P**, 1Ch 1:52
PIPES *(1)*
the playing of **p** for the flocks? Jdg 5:16
PIRAM *(1)*
of Hebron, **P** king of Jarmuth Jos 10:3
PIRATHON *(2)*
who was from **P**, judged Israel. Jdg 12:13
was buried in **P** in the land of Jdg 12:15
PIRATHONITE *(3)*
Benaiah the **P**, Hiddai from the 2Sm 23:30
the Benjaminites, Benaiah the **P**, 1Ch 11:31
was Benaiah the **P** from the sons 1Ch 27:14
PISGAH *(8)*
Moab near the **P** highlands that Nm 21:20
to Lookout Field on top of **P**, Nm 23:14
the slopes of **P** on the east. Dt 3:17
Go to the top of **P** and look to Dt 3:27
Dead Sea below the slopes of **P**. Dt 4:49
to the top of **P**, which faces Dt 34:1
southward below the slopes of **P**. Jos 12:3
the slopes of **P**, and Jos 13:20
PISHON *(1)*
The name of the first is **P**, Gn 2:11
PISIDIA *(2)*
Perga and reached Antioch in **P**. Ac 13:14
they passed through **P** and came Ac 14:24
PISPA *(1)*
Jephunneh, **P**, and Ara. 1Ch 7:38
PISTACHIOS *(1)*
gum and resin, **p** and almonds. Gn 43:11
PIT *(79)*
him into this **p** in the Gn 37:22
him and threw him into the **p**. Gn 37:24
the pit. The **p** was empty; there Gn 37:24
out of the **p** and sold him for Gn 37:28
returned to the **p** and saw that Gn 37:29
man uncovers a **p** or digs a pit, Ex 21:33
man uncovers a pit or digs a **p**, Ex 21:33
the owner of the **p** must give Ex 21:34
into a large **p** in the forest, 2Sm 18:17
went down into a **p** on a snowy 2Sm 23:20
them at the **p** of Beth-eked— 2Kg 10:14
went down into a **p** on a snowy 1Ch 11:22
then You dip me in a **p** ⌊of mud⌋, Jb 9:31
and say to the **P**: You are my Jb 17:14
God spares his soul from the **P**, Jb 33:18
draws near the **P**, and his life Jb 33:22
him from going down to the **P**; Jb 33:24
soul from going down to the **P**, Jb 33:28
to turn him back from the **P**, Jb 33:30
He dug a **p** and hollowed it out, Ps 7:15
fallen into the **p** they made; Ps 9:15
Your Faithful One to see the **P**. Ps 16:10
like those going down to the **P**. Ps 28:1
among those going down to the **P**. Ps 30:3
in my descending to the **P**? Ps 30:9
they dug a **p** for me without Ps 35:7
brought me up from a desolate **p**, Ps 40:2
live forever and not see the **P**. Ps 49:9
down to the **p** of destruction; Ps 55:23
They dug a **p** ahead of me, but Ps 57:6
don't let the **P** close its mouth Ps 69:15
among those going down to the **P**. Ps 88:4
me in the lowest part of the **P**, Ps 88:6
times until a **p** is dug for the Ps 94:13
He redeems your life from the **P**; Ps 103:4
He rescued them from the **P**. Ps 107:20
like those going down to the **P**. Ps 143:7
as they go down to the **P**. Pr 1:12
the forbidden woman is a deep **p**; Pr 22:14
For a prostitute is a deep **p**, Pr 23:27
one who digs a **p** will fall into Pr 26:27
way will fall into his own **p**, Pr 28:10
one who digs a **p** may fall into Ec 10:8
will play beside the cobra's **p**, Is 11:8
the deepest regions of the **P**. Is 14:15
into a rocky **p** like a trampled Is 14:19
Terror, **p**, and snare ⌊await⌋ you Is 24:17
of terror will fall into a **p**, Is 24:18
escapes from the **p** will be Is 24:18
together like prisoners in a **p**. Is 24:22
me from the **P** of destruction, Is 38:17
go down to the **P** cannot hope for Is 38:18
will not die ⌊and go⌋ to the **P**, Is 51:14
Yet they have dug a **p** for me. Jr 18:20
they have dug a **p** to capture me Jr 18:22
Panic, **p**, and trap await you, Jr 48:43
the panic will fall in the **p**, Jr 48:44
climbs from the **p** will be Jr 48:44
me alive into a **p** and threw Lm 3:53
from the depths of the **P**. Lm 3:55
him, he was caught in their **p**. Ezk 19:4
he was caught in their **p**. Ezk 19:8
with those who descend to the **P**, Ezk 26:20
with those who descend to the **P**, Ezk 26:20
will bring you down to the **P**, Ezk 28:8
the people who descend to the **P**. Ezk 31:14
with those who descend to the **P**. Ezk 31:16
with those who descend to the **P**: Ezk 32:18
in the deepest regions of the **P**, Ezk 32:23
with those who descend to the **P**. Ezk 32:24
with those who descend to the **P**. Ezk 32:25
with those who descend to the **P**. Ezk 32:29
with those who descend to the **P**. Ezk 32:30
You raised my life from the **P**, Jnh 2:6
weeds, a salt **p**, and a perpetual Zph 2:9
fell into a **p** on the Sabbath, Mt 12:11
blind, both will fall into a **p**." Mt 15:14
dug out a **p** for a winepress, Mk 12:1
Won't they both fall into a **p**? Lk 6:39
PITCH *(11)*
and cover it with **p** inside and Gn 6:14
coated it with asphalt and **p**. Ex 2:3
nomad will not **p** his tent there Is 13:20
streams will be turned into **p**, Is 34:9
her land will become burning **p**. Is 34:9
they will **p** ⌊their⌋ tents all Jr 6:3
have⌋ no one to **p** my tent again Jr 10:20
and he will **p** his pavilion over Jr 43:10
build a ramp, **p** military camps, Ezk 4:2
encampments and **p** their tents Ezk 25:4
will **p** his royal tents between Dn 11:45
PITCHED *(14)*
east of Bethel and **p** his tent, Gn 12:8
the LORD, and **p** his tent there. Gn 26:25
Jacob had **p** his tent in the hill Gn 31:25
brothers also **p** ⌊their tents⌋ Gn 31:25
where he had **p** his tent. Gn 33:19
out again and **p** his tent beyond Gn 35:21
the camps **p** on the east are to Nm 10:5
the camps **p** on the south are to Nm 10:6
and **p** his tent beside the oak Jdg 4:11
So they **p** a tent for Absalom on 2Sm 16:22
ark of God and **p** a tent for it. 1Ch 15:1
the tent David had **p** for it. 1Ch 16:1
because he had **p** a tent for it 2Ch 1:4
heavens He has **p** a tent for the Ps 19:4
PITCHER *(1)*
hand and an empty **p** with a torch Jdg 7:16
PITCHERS *(6)*
as well as its **p** and bowls for Ex 25:29
as its bowls and **p** for pouring Ex 37:16
as the bowls and **p** for the drink Nm 4:7
and broke the **p** that were in Jdg 7:19
trumpets and shattered their **p**. Jdg 7:20
forks, sprinkling basins, and **p**; 1Ch 28:17
PITCHFORKS *(1)*
of a shekel⌋ for **p** and axes, 1Sm 13:21
PITFALL *(3)*
We have experienced panic and **p**, Lm 3:47
a **p** and a retribution to them. Rm 11:9
block or **p** in your brother's Rm 14:13
PITFALLS *(1)*
dissensions and **p** contrary to Rm 16:17
PITHOM *(1)*
They built **P** and Rameses as Ex 1:11
PITHON *(2)*
P, Melech, Tarea, and Ahaz. 1Ch 8:35
P, Melech, Tahrea, and Ahaz. 1Ch 9:41
PITIED *(2)*
them to be **p** before all their Ps 106:46
we should be **p** more than anyone. 1Co 15:19
PITIFUL *(1)*
are wretched, **p**, poor, blind, Rv 3:17
PITS *(3)*
Siddim contained many asphalt **p**, Gn 14:10
and throw him into one of the **p**. Gn 37:20
The arrogant have dug **p** for me; Ps 119:85
PITY *(24)*
you and not look on them with **p**. Dt 7:16
Show him no **p**, and do not spare Dt 13:8
not look on him with **p** but purge Dt 19:13
must not show **p**: life for life, Dt 19:21
her hand. You must not show **p**. Dt 25:12
was moved to **p** whenever they Jdg 2:18
for you have taken **p** on me. 1Sm 23:21
but I took **p** on you and said: 1Sm 24:10
done this thing and shown no **p**, 2Sm 12:6
He had no **p** on young man and 2Ch 36:17
He will have **p** on the poor and Ps 72:13
but **p** the one who falls without Ec 4:10
not look with **p** on children. Is 13:18
allow no mercy, **p**, or compassion Jr 13:14
Who will have **p** on you, Jr 15:5
them or show **p** or compassion.' Jr 21:7
you⌋ off and show ⌊you⌋ no **p**, Ezk 5:11
on you with **p** or spare ⌊you⌋, Ezk 7:4
on ⌊you⌋ with **p** or spare ⌊you⌋. Ezk 7:9
will not show **p** or spare ⌊them⌋ Ezk 8:18
do not show **p** or spare ⌊them⌋! Ezk 9:5
will not show **p** or spare ⌊them⌋ Ezk 9:10
will not show **p**, and I will not Ezk 24:14
Have **p** on Your people, LORD, and Jl 2:17
PIVOTING *(3)*
without **p** as they moved. Ezk 1:17
without **p** as they moved. Ezk 10:11
without **p** as they went. Ezk 10:11
PLACE *(889)*
the sky be gathered into one **p**, Gn 1:9
and closed the flesh at that **p**. Gn 2:21
me another child in **p** of Abel, Gn 4:25
found no resting **p** for her foot. Gn 8:9
to the **p** between Bethel and Ai Gn 13:3
Look from the **p** where you are. Gn 13:14
of sparing the **p** for the sake of Gn 18:24
the whole **p** for their sake. Gn 18:26
and Abraham returned to his **p**. Gn 18:33
Get them out of this **p**, Gn 19:12
to destroy this **p** because the Gn 19:13
Get out of this **p**, for the LORD Gn 19:14
It is a small **p**. Please let me Gn 19:20
it's only a small **p**, isn't it? Gn 19:20
went to the **p** where he had stood Gn 19:27
no fear of God in this **p**. Gn 20:11
the boy from the **p** where he is. Gn 21:17
Therefore that **p** was called Gn 21:31
to go to the **p** God had told him Gn 22:3
and saw the **p** in the distance. Gn 22:4
arrived at the **p** that God had Gn 22:9
burnt offering in **p** of his son. Gn 22:13
named that **p** The LORD Will Gn 22:14
dead in our finest burial **p**. Gn 23:6
his burial **p** for burying your Gn 23:6
the full price, as a burial **p**." Gn 23:9
to Abraham as a burial **p**. Gn 23:20
P your hand under my thigh, Gn 24:2
and a **p** to spend the night." Gn 24:25
house and a **p** for the camels. Gn 24:31

the men of the **p** asked about his	Gn 26:7
The men of the **p** will kill me on	Gn 26:7
dwelling **p** will be away from	Gn 27:39
reached a certain **p** and spent	Gn 28:11
one of the stones from the **p**,	Gn 28:11
head, and lay down in that **p**.	Gn 28:11
Surely the LORD is in this **p**,	Gn 28:16
What an awesome **p** this is!	Gn 28:17
and named the **p** Bethel, though	Gn 28:19
all the men of the **p** to a feast.	Gn 29:22
the custom in this **p** to give the	Gn 29:26
I in God's **p**, who has withheld	Gn 30:2
Therefore the **p** was called	Gn 31:48
So he called that **p** Mahanaim.	Gn 32:2
Jacob then named the **p** Peniel,	Gn 32:30
that is why the **p** was called	Gn 33:17
and called the **p** God of Bethel	Gn 35:7
from him at the **p** where He had	Gn 35:13
a marker at the **p** where He had	Gn 35:14
Jacob named the **p** where God had	Gn 35:15
from Bozrah ruled in his **p**.	Gn 36:33
of the Temanites ruled in his **p**.	Gn 36:34
son of Bedad ruled in his **p**.	Gn 36:35
from Masrekah ruled in his **p**.	Gn 36:36
ruled in his **p**.	Gn 36:37
son of Achbor ruled in his **p**.	Gn 36:38
died, Hadar ruled in his **p**.	Gn 36:39
He asked the men of the **p**,	Gn 38:21
men of the **p** said, 'There has	Gn 38:22
years of famine will take **p**,	Gn 41:30
that will take **p** in the land of	Gn 41:36
not leave this **p** unless your	Gn 42:15
At the **p** where they lodged for	Gn 42:27
we came to the **p** where we lodged	Gn 43:21
lord's slave, in **p** of the boy.	Gn 44:33
and bury me in their burial **p**."	Gn 47:30
that his resting **p** was good and	Gn 49:15
Therefore the **p** is named	Gn 50:11
be afraid. Am I in the **p** of God?	Gn 50:19
for the **p** where you are standing	Ex 3:5
"This will take **p**," He continued,	Ex 4:5
This sign will take **p** tomorrow."	Ex 8:23
The only **p** it didn't hail was in	Ex 9:26
out of the **p** of slavery, for	Ex 13:3
Egypt, out of the **p** of slavery.	Ex 13:14
my bones with you from this **p**."	Ex 13:19
night never left its **p** in front	Ex 13:22
prepared the **p** for Your dwelling	Ex 15:17
is to leave his **p** on the seventh	Ex 16:29
Then **p** it before the LORD to be	Ex 16:33
moving from one **p** to the next	Ex 17:1
named the **p** Massah and Meribah	Ex 17:7
P ⌊them⌋ over the people as	Ex 18:21
Egypt, out of the **p** of slavery.	Ex 20:2
you in every **p** where I cause My	Ex 20:24
will appoint a **p** for you where	Ex 21:13
you to the **p** I have prepared	Ex 23:20
For I will **p** the inhabitants of	Ex 23:31
rings for it and **p** ⌊them⌋ on its	Ex 25:12
between the holy **p** and the most	Ex 26:33
holy place and the most holy **p**.	Ex 26:33
testimony in the most holy **p**.	Ex 26:34
P the table outside the veil and	Ex 26:35
P a setting of gemstones on it,	Ex 28:17
P the Urim and Thummim in the	Ex 28:30
his head and **p** the holy diadem	Ex 29:6
and **p** ⌊them⌋ with its head and	Ex 29:17
and boil its flesh in a holy **p**.	Ex 29:31
and that **p** will be consecrated	Ex 29:43
You are to **p** the altar in front	Ex 30:6
people to the **p** I told you about	Ex 32:34
LORD said, "Here is a **p** near Me.	Ex 33:21
P the gold altar for incense in	Ex 40:5
P the basin between the tent of	Ex 40:7
of the altar at the **p** for ashes.	Lv 1:16
clean **p** outside the camp	Lv 4:12
it at the **p** where the burnt	Lv 4:24
it at the **p** of the burnt	Lv 4:29
offering at the **p** where the	Lv 4:33
and **p** them beside the altar.	Lv 6:10
camp to a ceremonially clean **p**.	Lv 6:11
as unleavened bread in a holy **p**;	Lv 6:16
will be anointed to take his **p**,	Lv 6:22
LORD at the **p** where the burnt	Lv 6:25
It must be eaten in a holy **p**,	Lv 6:26
wash that garment in a holy **p**.	Lv 6:27
to make atonement in the holy **p**;	Lv 6:30
at the **p** where the burnt	Lv 7:2
It is to be eaten in a holy **p**;	Lv 7:6
sanctuary to ⌊a **p**⌋ outside the	Lv 10:4
eat it in a holy **p** because it is	Lv 10:13
in any ceremonially clean **p**,	Lv 10:14
live alone in a **p** outside the	Lv 13:46
cleansing will **p** the person who	Lv 14:11
lamb at the **p** in the sanctuary	Lv 14:13
on the ⌊same⌋ **p** as the blood of	Lv 14:28
and I **p** a mildew contamination	Lv 14:34
into an unclean **p** outside the	Lv 14:40
an unclean **p** outside the city.	Lv 14:41
the city to an unclean **p**.	Lv 14:45
into the holy **p** behind the veil	Lv 16:2
the ⌊most⌋ holy **p** in this way:	Lv 16:3
the two goats and **p** them before	Lv 16:7
⌊most⌋ holy **p** in this way for	Lv 16:16
⌊most⌋ holy **p** until he leaves	Lv 16:17
purifying the ⌊most⌋ holy **p**,	Lv 16:20
he entered the ⌊most⌋ holy **p**,	Lv 16:23
water in a holy **p** and put on his	Lv 16:24
the ⌊most⌋ holy **p** to make	Lv 16:27
high⌋ priest in **p** of his father	Lv 16:32
and purify the most holy **p**.	Lv 16:33
P pure frankincense near each	Lv 24:7
who are to eat it in a holy **p**,	Lv 24:9
or **p** a sculpted stone in your	Lv 26:1
I will **p** My residence among you,	Lv 26:11
camp, each in his **p**, with their	Nm 2:17
the Israelites in **p** of every	Nm 3:12
p of every firstborn among the	Nm 3:41
cattle in **p** of every firstborn	Nm 3:41
the Levites in **p** of every	Nm 3:45
cattle in **p** of their cattle.	Nm 3:45
They are to **p** over this a	Nm 4:6
Presence and **p** the plates and	Nm 4:7
Then they must **p** it with all its	Nm 4:10
the sanctuary, **p** ⌊them⌋ in a	Nm 4:12
and **p** all the equipment on it	Nm 4:14
down her hair and **p** in her hands	Nm 5:18
for Myself in **p** of all who come	Nm 8:16
the Levites in **p** of every	Nm 8:18
the **p** where the cloud stopped,	Nm 9:17
moving from one **p** to the next	Nm 10:12
out for the **p** the LORD promised	Nm 10:29
to seek a resting **p** for them,	Nm 10:33
So that **p** was named Taberah,	Nm 11:3
the LORD would **p** His Spirit on	Nm 11:29
they named that **p**	Nm 11:34
That **p** was called the Valley of	Nm 13:24
Let's go to the **p** the LORD	Nm 14:40
p fire in them and put incense	Nm 16:7
his firepan, **p** incense on it,	Nm 16:17
p fire from the altar in it,	Nm 16:46
Then **p** them in the tent of	Nm 17:4
camp in a ceremonially clean **p**.	Nm 19:9
to bring us to this evil **p**?	Nm 20:5
It's not a **p** of grain, figs,	Nm 20:5
So they named the **p** Hormah.	Nm 21:3
in a narrow **p** where there was	Nm 22:26
me to another **p** where you can	Nm 23:13
I will take you to another **p**.	Nm 23:27
Your dwelling **p** is enduring;	Nm 24:21
your fathers' **p** adding even more	Nm 32:14
have brought them into their **p**.	Nm 32:17
Whatever **p** the lot indicates for	Nm 33:54
until you reached this **p**.	Dt 1:31
to seek out a **p** for you to camp.	Dt 1:33
and settling in their **p**,	Dt 2:12
them out and settled in their **p**.	Dt 2:21
have lived in their **p** until now.	Dt 2:22
as Gaza, and settled in their **p**.	Dt 2:23
over to you, as has now taken **p**.	Dt 2:30
inheritance, as is now taking **p**.	Dt 4:38
Egypt, out of the **p** of slavery.	Dt 5:6
Egypt, out of the **p** of slavery.	Dt 6:12
you from the **p** of slavery,	Dt 7:8
Egypt, out of the **p** of slavery.	Dt 8:14
Egypt until you reached this **p**.	Dt 9:7
you are to **p** them in the ark.	Dt 10:2
his son became priest in his **p**.	Dt 10:6
until you reached this **p**;	Dt 11:5
Every **p** the sole of your foot	Dt 11:24
out their names from every **p**.	Dt 12:3
must go to the **p** the LORD your	Dt 12:5
into the resting **p** and the	Dt 12:9
will choose the **p** to have His	Dt 12:11
only in the **p** the LORD chooses	Dt 12:14
your God at the **p** the LORD your	Dt 12:18
If the **p** where the LORD your God	Dt 12:21
go to the **p** the LORD chooses.	Dt 12:26
you from the **p** of slavery,	Dt 13:5
Egypt, out of the **p** of slavery.	Dt 13:10
your God at the **p** where He	Dt 14:23
since the **p** where the LORD your	Dt 14:24
go to the **p** the LORD your God	Dt 14:25
your God in the **p** the LORD	Dt 15:20
or flock in the **p** where the LORD	Dt 16:2
animal at the **p** where the LORD	Dt 16:6
eat ⌊it⌋ in the **p** the LORD your	Dt 16:7
your God in the **p** where He	Dt 16:11
your God in the **p** He chooses,	Dt 16:15
your God in the **p** He chooses:	Dt 16:16
go up to the **p** the LORD your God	Dt 17:8
give you at the **p** the LORD	Dt 17:10
to go to the **p** the LORD chooses	Dt 18:6
to a **p** not tilled or sown,	Dt 21:4
You must have a **p** outside the	Dt 23:12
Then go to the **p** where the LORD	Dt 26:2
from your hand and **p** it before	Dt 26:4
led us to this **p** and gave us	Dt 26:9
You will then **p** the container	Dt 26:10
He will **p** an iron yoke on your	Dt 28:48
be no resting **p** for the sole	Dt 28:65
you reached this **p**, Sihon king	Dt 29:7
your God at the **p** He chooses,	Dt 31:11
of the law and **p** it beside the	Dt 31:26
God of old is ⌊your⌋ dwelling **p**,	Dt 33:27
given you every **p** where the sole	Jos 1:3
stones from this **p** in the middle	Jos 4:3
down at the **p** where you spend	Jos 4:3
raised up their sons in their **p**;	Jos 5:7
that **p** has been called Gilgal to	Jos 5:9
for the **p** where you are standing	Jos 5:15
Therefore that **p** has been called	Jos 7:26
at a suitable **p** facing the plain	Jos 8:14
altar at the **p** He would choose.	Jos 9:27
and give him a **p** to live among	Jos 20:4
the **p** of slavery and performed	Jos 24:17
they named that **p** Bochim and	Jdg 2:5
and out of the **p** of slavery.	Jdg 6:8
not leave this **p** until I return	Jdg 6:18
and named that **p** Ramath-lehi.	Jdg 15:17
split a hollow **p** ⌊in the ground⌋	Jdg 15:19
they surrounded the **p** and waited	Jdg 16:2
wherever he could find a **p**.	Jdg 17:8
settle wherever I can find a **p**.	Jdg 17:9
What are you doing in this **p**?	Jdg 18:3
It is a **p** where nothing on earth	Jdg 18:10
This is why the **p** is called the	Jdg 18:12
the men of that **p** were	Jdg 19:16
in the same **p** where they	Jdg 20:22
left the **p** where she had been	Ru 1:7
notice the **p** where he's lying,	Ru 3:4
this woman in **p** of the one she	1Sm 2:20
I require at the **p** of worship?	1Sm 2:29
distress ⌊in the⌋ **p** of worship,	1Sm 2:32
went and lay down in his **p**.	1Sm 3:9
Dagon and returned him to his **p**.	1Sm 5:3
return to its **p** so it won't kill	1Sm 5:11
we can send it back to its **p**."	1Sm 6:2
of the LORD, **p** it on the cart,	1Sm 6:8
the way to a **p** below Beth-car.	1Sm 7:11
the people at the high **p** today.	1Sm 9:12
he goes to the high **p** to eat.	1Sm 9:13
them on his way to the high **p**.	1Sm 9:14
me to the high **p** and eat with me	1Sm 9:19
and gave them a **p** at the head of	1Sm 9:22
from the high **p** to the city,	1Sm 9:25
from the high **p** prophesying.	1Sm 10:5
and went to the high **p**.	1Sm 10:13
and settled them in this **p**.	1Sm 12:8
in a secret **p** and stay there.	1Sm 19:2
and go to the **p** where you hid	1Sm 20:19
sat at his usual **p** on the seat	1Sm 20:25
Abner took his **p** beside Saul,	1Sm 20:25
Saul, but David's **p** was empty.	1Sm 20:25
David's **p** was ⌊still⌋ empty,	1Sm 20:27
my⌋ young men at a certain **p**.	1Sm 21:2
the tamarisk tree at the high **p**.	1Sm 22:6
once and moved from **p** to place.	1Sm 23:13
once and moved from place to **p**.	1Sm 23:13
that **p** was named the Rock of	1Sm 23:28
safely in the **p** where the LORD	1Sm 25:29
went to the **p** where Saul had	1Sm 26:5
saw the **p** where Saul and Abner	1Sm 26:5
me be given a **p** in one of the	1Sm 27:5

return to the **p** you assigned him 1Sm 29:4
this **p**, which is in Gibeon, is 2Sm 2:16
who came to the **p** where Asahel 2Sm 2:23
he named that **p** the Lord Bursts 2Sm 5:20
so he named that **p** an Outburst 2Sm 6:8
set it in its **p** inside the tent 2Sm 6:17
will establish a **p** for My people 2Sm 7:10
son Hanun became king in his **p**. 2Sm 10:1
put Uriah in the **p** where he knew 2Sm 11:16
see both it and its dwelling **p**. 2Sm 15:25
of Saul in whose **p** you rule, 2Sm 16:8
of the caves or some other **p**. 2Sm 17:9
Amasa over the army in Joab's **p**. 2Sm 17:25
which took **p** in the forest of 2Sm 18:6
brought me out to a wide-open **p**; 2Sm 22:20
You widen ⌊a **p**⌋ beneath me for 2Sm 22:37
retreated in the **p** they had 2Sm 23:9
is to sit on my throne in my **p**, 1Kg 1:30
who is to become king in my **p**; 1Kg 1:35
in Joab's **p** over the army, 1Kg 2:35
the priest in Abiathar's **p**. 1Kg 2:35
it was the most famous high **p**. 1Kg 3:4
king in my father David's **p**. 1Kg 3:7
to the required **p** according to 1Kg 4:28
anointed king in his father's **p**, 1Kg 5:1
son on your throne in your **p**, 1Kg 5:5
go by sea to the **p** you indicate. 1Kg 5:9
sanctuary, the most holy **p**. 1Kg 6:16
in front of the most holy **p**, 1Kg 6:17
is, the most holy **p**) and for the 1Kg 7:50
of the LORD's covenant to its **p**, 1Kg 8:6
to the most holy **p** beneath the 1Kg 8:6
wings over the **p** of the ark, 1Kg 8:7
seen from the holy **p** in front of 1Kg 8:8
priests came out of the holy **p**, 1Kg 8:10
a **p** for Your dwelling forever. 1Kg 8:13
I have taken the **p** of my father 1Kg 8:20
have provided a **p** there for the 1Kg 8:21
toward the **p** where You said: 1Kg 8:29
servant prays toward this **p**. 1Kg 8:29
which they pray toward this **p**. 1Kg 8:30
in Your dwelling **p** in heaven. 1Kg 8:30
toward this **p** and praise Your 1Kg 8:35
Your dwelling **p**, and may You 1Kg 8:39
dwelling **p**, and do according 1Kg 8:43
Your dwelling **p**, their prayer 1Kg 8:49
built a high **p** for Chemosh, 1Kg 11:7
Rehoboam became king in his **p**. 1Kg 11:43
bread or drink water in this **p**. 1Kg 13:8
drink water with you in this **p**, 1Kg 13:16
water in the **p** that He said to 1Kg 13:22
son Nadab became king in his **p**. 1Kg 14:20
shields in their **p** and committed 1Kg 14:27
son Abijam became king in his **p**. 1Kg 14:31
son Asa became king in his **p**. 1Kg 15:8
became king in his **p**. 1Kg 15:24
Nadab and reigned in his **p**. 1Kg 15:28
son Elah became king in his **p**. 1Kg 16:6
Then Zimri became king in his **p**. 1Kg 16:10
son Ahab became king in his **p**. 1Kg 16:28
you off to some **p** I don't know. 1Kg 18:12
and **p** it on the wood but not 1Kg 18:23
other bull and **p** it on the wood 1Kg 18:23
as prophet in your **p**. 1Kg 19:16
and appoint captains in their **p**. 1Kg 20:24
the battle took **p**, and the 1Kg 20:29
be your life in **p** of his life, 1Kg 20:39
your life in **p** of his life and 1Kg 20:42
your people in **p** of his people.' 1Kg 20:42
you a better vineyard in its **p**, 1Kg 21:2
give you a vineyard in its **p**. 1Kg 21:6
In the **p** where the dogs licked 1Kg 21:19
Ahaziah became king in his **p**. 1Kg 22:40
Jehoram became king in his **p**. 1Kg 22:50
Joram became king in his **p**. 2Kg 1:17
who was to become king in his **p**, 2Kg 3:27
p my staff on the boy's face. 2Kg 4:29
notice that the **p** where we live 2Kg 6:1
ourselves a **p** to live there." 2Kg 6:2
When he showed him the **p**, 2Kg 6:6
will be at such and such a **p**." 2Kg 6:8
Be careful passing by this **p**, 2Kg 6:9
word⌋ to the **p** the man of God 2Kg 6:10
Ahaziah became king in his **p**. 2Kg 8:24
Jehoahaz became king in his **p**. 2Kg 10:35
Amaziah became king in his **p**. 2Kg 12:21
Jehoash became king in his **p**. 2Kg 13:9
Ben-hadad became king in his **p**. 2Kg 13:24

Jeroboam became king in his **p**. 2Kg 14:16
made him king in **p** of his father 2Kg 14:21
Zechariah became king in his **p**. 2Kg 14:29
son Jotham became king in his **p**. 2Kg 15:7
him, and became king in his **p**. 2Kg 15:10
him and became king in his **p**. 2Kg 15:14
Pekahiah became king in his **p**. 2Kg 15:22
and became king in his **p**. 2Kg 15:25
king in his **p** in the twentieth 2Kg 15:30
son Ahaz became king in his **p**. 2Kg 15:38
Hezekiah became king in his **p**. 2Kg 16:20
settled them in **p** of the 2Kg 17:24
I attacked this **p** to destroy it 2Kg 18:25
became king in his **p**. 2Kg 19:37
Manasseh became king in his **p**. 2Kg 20:21
son Amon became king in his **p**. 2Kg 21:18
his son Josiah king in his **p**. 2Kg 21:24
son Josiah became king in his **p**. 2Kg 21:26
disaster on this **p** and on its 2Kg 22:16
will be kindled against this **p**, 2Kg 22:17
against this **p** and against its 2Kg 22:19
that I am bringing on this **p**.'" 2Kg 22:20
and the high **p** that Jeroboam son 2Kg 23:15
Then he burned the high **p**, 2Kg 23:15
him king in **p** of his father. 2Kg 23:30
Josiah king in **p** of his father 2Kg 23:34
Jehoiachin became king in his **p**. 2Kg 24:6
king in his **p** and changed his 2Kg 24:17
from Bozrah ruled in his **p**. 1Ch 1:44
of the Temanites ruled in his **p**. 1Ch 1:45
country of Moab, ruled in his **p**. 1Ch 1:46
from Masrekah ruled in his **p**. 1Ch 1:47
Euphrates River ruled in his **p**. 1Ch 1:48
son of Achbor ruled in his **p**. 1Ch 1:49
died, Hadad ruled in his **p**. 1Ch 1:50
settled in their **p** because there 1Ch 4:41
the Hagrites' **p** until the exile 1Ch 5:22
all the work of the most holy **p**. 1Ch 6:49
he named that **p** Outburst Against 1Ch 13:11
named that **p** the Lord Bursts 1Ch 14:11
and he prepared a **p** for the ark 1Ch 15:1
LORD to the **p** he had prepared 1Ch 15:3
Israel to ⌊the **p**⌋ I have 1Ch 15:12
strength and joy are in His **p**. 1Ch 16:27
the LORD at the high **p** in Gibeon 1Ch 16:39
will establish a **p** for My people 1Ch 17:9
his son became king in his **p**. 1Ch 19:1
were at the high **p** in Gibeon, 1Ch 21:29
to the holy **p**, and to their 1Ch 23:32
house as a resting **p** for the ark 1Ch 28:2
the room for the **p** of atonement. 1Ch 28:11
as king in **p** of his father 1Ch 29:23
Solomon became king in his **p**. 1Ch 29:28
went to the high **p** that was in 2Ch 1:3
to the **p** he had set up for it 2Ch 1:4
You have made me king in his **p**. 2Ch 1:8
from the high **p** that was in 2Ch 1:13
except as a **p** to burn incense 2Ch 2:6
Then he made the most holy **p**; 2Ch 3:8
the most holy **p**, and he overlaid 2Ch 3:10
inner doors to the most holy **p**, 2Ch 4:22
of the LORD's covenant to its **p**, 2Ch 5:7
to the most holy **p**, beneath the 2Ch 5:7
wings over the **p** of the ark so 2Ch 5:8
seen from the holy **p** in front of 2Ch 5:9
priests came out of the holy **p**— 2Ch 5:11
a **p** for Your residence forever. 2Ch 6:2
I have taken the **p** of my father 2Ch 6:10
toward the **p** where You said You 2Ch 6:20
servant prays toward this **p**. 2Ch 6:20
which they pray toward this **p**. 2Ch 6:21
in Your dwelling **p** in heaven. 2Ch 6:21
toward this **p** and praise Your 2Ch 6:26
Your dwelling **p**, and may You 2Ch 6:30
in heaven in Your dwelling **p**, 2Ch 6:33
in Your dwelling **p**, their prayer 2Ch 6:39
to the prayer of this **p**. 2Ch 6:40
to Your resting **p**, You and the 2Ch 6:41
have chosen this **p** for Myself as 2Ch 7:12
attentive to prayer from this **p**. 2Ch 7:15
Rehoboam became king in his **p**. 2Ch 9:31
shields in their **p** and committed 2Ch 12:10
son Abijah became king in his **p**. 2Ch 12:16
son Asa became king in his **p**. 2Ch 14:1
king in his **p** and strengthened 2Ch 17:1
Judah came to a **p** overlooking 2Ch 20:24
p is still called the Valley 2Ch 20:26
Jehoram became king in his **p**. 2Ch 21:1

son, king in his **p**, because the 2Ch 22:1
it up, and returned it to its **p**. 2Ch 24:11
Amaziah became king in his **p**. 2Ch 24:27
made him king in **p** of his father 2Ch 26:1
son Jotham became king in his **p**. 2Ch 26:23
son Ahaz became king in his **p**. 2Ch 27:9
Hezekiah became king in his **p**. 2Ch 28:27
detestable from the holy **p**. 2Ch 29:5
in the holy **p** of the God of 2Ch 29:7
His holy dwelling **p** in heaven. 2Ch 30:27
Manasseh became king in his **p**. 2Ch 32:33
son Amon became king in his **p**. 2Ch 33:20
his son Josiah king in his **p**. 2Ch 33:25
disaster on this **p** and on its 2Ch 34:24
will be poured out on this **p**, 2Ch 34:25
against this **p** and against its 2Ch 34:27
am bringing on this **p** and on its 2Ch 34:28
in the holy **p** by the divisions 2Ch 35:5
in Jerusalem in **p** of his father. 2Ch 36:1
Jehoiachin became king in his **p**. 2Ch 36:8
people and on His dwelling **p**. 2Ch 36:15
be rebuilt as a **p** for offering Ezr 6:3
you must stay away from that **p**, Ezr 6:6
give us a stake in His holy **p**. Ezr 9:8
them to the **p** where I chose to Neh 1:9
events took **p** during the days Est 1:1
king will reign in **p** of Vashti." Est 2:4
made her queen in **p** of Vashti. Est 2:17
all this took **p**, King Ahasuerus Est 3:1
Jewish people from another **p**, Est 4:14
This would take **p**⌋ on a single Est 8:12
took **p** among the Jews. Est 8:17
If he is uprooted from his **p**, Jb 8:18
the earth from its **p** so that its Jb 9:6
a rock is dislodged from its **p**, Jb 14:18
you were in my **p** I could also Jb 16:4
cry for help find no resting **p**. Jb 16:18
or a rock be removed from its **p**? Jb 18:4
and this is the **p** of the one who Jb 18:21
and **p** His sayings in your heart. Jb 22:22
it carries him away from his **p**. Jb 27:21
him and scorns him from its **p**. Jb 27:23
for silver and a **p** where gold is Jb 28:1
p appointed for all who live. Jb 30:23
and sets others in their **p**. Jb 34:24
to a spacious and unconfined **p**. Jb 36:16
put ⌊its⌋ bars and doors in **p**, Jb 38:10
or assigned the dawn its **p**, Jb 38:12
entered the ⌊**p**⌋ where the snow Jb 38:22
leads to ⌊the **p**⌋ where light is Jb 38:24
I **p** my hand over my mouth. Jb 40:4
the stars, which You set in **p**, Ps 8:3
put in a safe **p** the one who Ps 12:5
He made darkness His hiding **p**, Ps 18:11
brought me out to a wide-open **p**; Ps 18:19
You widen ⌊a **p**⌋ beneath me for Ps 18:36
p a crown of pure gold on his Ps 21:3
Who may stand in His holy **p**? Ps 24:3
the **p** where Your glory resides. Ps 26:8
set my feet in a spacious **p**. Ps 31:8
are my hiding **p**; You protect me Ps 32:7
the earth from His dwelling **p**. Ps 33:14
mountain, to Your dwelling **p**. Ps 43:3
holy dwelling **p** of the Most High Ps 46:4
P no trust in oppression, or Ps 62:10
in the meeting **p** where You met Ps 74:4
the dwelling **p** of Your name. Ps 74:7
burned down every **p** throughout Ps 74:8
Salem, His dwelling **p** in Zion. Ps 76:2
You cleared ⌊a **p**⌋ for it; Ps 80:9
has taken His **p** in the divine Ps 82:1
How lovely is Your dwelling **p**, Ps 84:1
the Most High—your dwelling **p**, Ps 91:9
and its **p** is no longer known. Ps 103:16
to the **p** You established for Ps 104:8
me ⌊and put me⌋ in a spacious **p**. Ps 118:5
in an open **p** because I seek Ps 119:45
until I find a **p** for the LORD, Ps 132:5
Let us go to His dwelling **p**; Ps 132:7
to Your resting **p**, You and the Ps 132:8
This is My resting **p** forever; Ps 132:14
up your hands in the holy **p**, Ps 134:2
She will **p** a garland of grace on Pr 4:9
in his **p**, the wicked goes in. Pr 11:8
stand in the **p** of the great; Pr 25:6
to its **p** where it rises. Ec 1:5
streams are flowing to the **p**, Ec 1:7
wickedness at the **p** of judgment Ec 3:16

at the **p** of righteousness Ec 3:16
All are going to the same **p**; Ec 3:20
do not both go to the same **p**? Ec 6:6
came and went from the holy **p**, Ec 8:10
don't leave your **p**, for calmness Ec 10:4
the **p** where the tree falls, Ec 11:3
of Israel take **p** so that we can Is 5:19
This took **p** during the reign of Is 7:1
that day every **p** where there Is 7:23
and His resting **p** will be Is 11:10
Prepare a **p** of slaughter for his Is 14:21
When Moab appears on the high **p**, Is 16:12
will quietly look out from My **p**, Is 18:4
the **p** of the name of the LORD of Is 18:7
I will **p** the key of the House of Is 22:22
him, like a peg, into a firm **p**. Is 22:23
into a firm **p** will give way, Is 22:25
be trampled in his **p** as straw is Is 25:10
is coming from His **p** to punish Is 26:21
there is no **p** without a stench. Is 28:8
This is the **p** of rest, let the Is 28:12
this is the **p** of repose." Is 28:12
water will flood your hiding **p**. Is 28:17
will dwell in a peaceful **p**, Is 32:18
a **p** of rivers and broad streams, Is 33:21
find a resting **p** for herself. Is 34:14
became king in his **p**. Is 37:38
you, Cush and Seba in your **p**. Is 43:3
give human beings in your **p**, Is 43:4
and peoples in **p** of your life. Is 43:4
things, and what will take **p**. Is 44:7
set it in its **p**, and there it Is 46:7
it does not budge from its **p**. Is 46:7
plan will take **p**, and I will do Is 46:10
This **p** is too small for me; Is 49:20
will lie down in a **p** of torment. Is 50:11
I live in a high and holy **p**, Is 57:15
beautify the **p** of My sanctuary Is 60:13
I will glorify My dwelling **p**. Is 60:13
of Achor a **p** for cattle to lie Is 65:10
And what **p** could be My home? Is 66:1
thing has taken **p** in the land. Jr 5:30
I am going to **p** stumbling blocks Jr 6:21
allow you to live in this **p**. Jr 7:3
blood in this **p** or follow other Jr 7:6
allow you to live in this **p**, Jr 7:7
But return to My **p** that was at Jr 7:12
the **p** that I gave you and your Jr 7:14
to be poured out on this **p**, Jr 7:20
when ⌊this **p**⌋ will no longer be Jr 7:32
there will be no other burial **p**. Jr 7:32
lodging **p** in the wilderness Jr 9:2
a desolation, an uninhabited **p**. Jr 9:11
got it from the **p** where I had Jr 13:7
you true peace in this **p**.'" Jr 14:13
sons or daughters in this **p**. Jr 16:2
born in this **p** as well as Jr 16:3
a mourning feast is taking **p**. Jr 16:5
is taking **p** to sit with them Jr 16:8
about to eliminate from this **p**, Jr 16:9
is the **p** of our sanctuary Jr 17:12
disaster on this **p** that everyone Jr 19:3
Me and made this a foreign **p**. Jr 19:4
filled this **p** with the blood Jr 19:4
when this **p** will no longer be Jr 19:6
Judah and Jerusalem in this **p**. Jr 19:7
there is no **p** left to bury. Jr 19:11
I will do so to this **p**"— Jr 19:12
impure like that **p** Topheth— Jr 19:13
shed innocent blood in this **p**. Jr 22:3
has left this **p**—he will never Jr 22:11
he will die in the **p** where they Jr 22:12
away from this **p** to the land Jr 24:5
into the burial **p** of the common Jr 26:23
and does not **p** its neck under Jr 27:8
and restore them to this **p**.'" Jr 27:22
restore to this **p** all the Jr 28:3
restore to this **p** Jeconiah son Jr 28:4
exiles from Babylon to this **p**! Jr 28:6
but in its **p** you will make an Jr 28:13
you to restore you to this **p**. Jr 29:10
you to the **p** I deported you Jr 29:14
you priest in **p** of Jehoiada the Jr 29:26
I will **p** My law within them and Jr 31:33
them to this **p** and make them Jr 32:37
In this **p** which you say is a Jr 33:10
In this desolate **p**—without man Jr 33:12
Egypt, out of the **p** of slavery, Jr 34:13

land of Judah in **p** of Jehoiachin Jr 37:1
king's palace to a **p** below the Jr 38:11
P these old rags and clothes Jr 38:12
will take **p** before your eyes Jr 39:16
decreed this disaster on this **p**, Jr 40:2
p them in your ⌊storage⌋ jars, Jr 40:10
will never see this **p** again.' Jr 42:18
will die in the **p** where you Jr 42:22
and I will **p** his throne on these Jr 43:10
about to punish you in this **p**, Jr 44:29
on the high **p** and burns incense Jr 48:35
have forgotten their resting **p**. Jr 50:6
set the watchmen in **p**; Jr 51:12
to cut off this **p** so that no one Jr 51:62
nations but finds no **p** to rest. Lm 1:3
destroying His **p** of meeting. Lm 2:6
the glory of the LORD in His **p**! Ezk 3:12
and **p** battering rams against it Ezk 4:2
left side and **p** the iniquity Ezk 4:4
as they profane My treasured **p**. Ezk 7:22
exile from your **p** to another Ezk 12:3
to another **p** while they watch Ezk 12:3
an elevated **p** in every square. Ezk 16:24
built your elevated **p** at the Ezk 16:25
your elevated **p** in every square. Ezk 16:31
is this high **p** you are going to Ezk 20:29
it is called High **P** to this day. Ezk 20:29
judge you in the **p** where you Ezk 21:30
P the pieces of meat in it, Ezk 24:4
She will become a **p** in the sea Ezk 26:5
you will be a **p** to spread nets. Ezk 26:14
king and **p** My sword in his Ezk 30:24
am the LORD when I **p** My sword Ezk 30:25
all around the **p** where the tree Ezk 31:4
is all around her burial **p**. Ezk 32:23
a resting **p** for Elam with all Ezk 32:25
and their grazing **p** will be on Ezk 34:14
lie down in a good grazing **p**; Ezk 34:14
for them a **p** renowned for ⌊its⌋ Ezk 34:29
will **p** My Spirit within you and Ezk 36:27
My dwelling **p** will be with them; Ezk 37:27
come from your **p** in the remotest Ezk 38:15
Gog a burial **p** there in Israel Ezk 39:11
"This is the most holy **p**." Ezk 41:4
offerings—for the **p** is holy. Ezk 42:13
this is the **p** of My throne and Ezk 43:7
throne and the **p** for the soles Ezk 43:7
sanctuary in the **p** appointed for Ezk 43:21
the most holy **p**, will stand. Ezk 45:3
It will be a **p** for their houses, Ezk 45:4
I saw a **p** there at the far Ezk 46:19
This is the **p** where the priests Ezk 46:20
a most holy **p** adjacent to the Ezk 48:12
were set in **p**, and the Ancient Dn 7:9
horns came up in its **p**, Dn 8:8
overthrew the **p** of His sanctuary Dn 8:11
that took the **p** of the shattered Dn 8:22
and to anoint the most holy **p**. Dn 9:24
In the **p** of the king of the Dn 11:7
In his **p** one will arise who will Dn 11:20
In his **p** a despised person will Dn 11:21
And in the **p** where they were Hs 1:10
and return to My **p** until they Hs 5:15
but I will **p** a yoke on her fine Hs 10:11
up from the **p** where you sold Jl 3:7
you⌋ in your **p** as a wagon full Am 2:13
toward Tarshish in the first **p**. Jnh 4:2
is leaving His **p** and coming down Mc 1:3
And what is the high **p** of Judah? Mc 1:5
for this is not your **p** of rest, Mc 2:10
you from that **p** of slavery. Mc 6:4
you a desolate **p** and the city's Mc 6:16
protective shield is set in **p**. Nah 2:5
is taking **p** in your days that Hab 1:5
his house to **p** his nest on high Hab 2:9
off from this **p** every vestige Zph 1:4
Gomorrah—a **p** overgrown with Zph 2:9
to Him, each in its own **p**. Zph 2:11
p for wild animals to lie down! Zph 2:15
her dwelling **p** would not be cut Zph 3:7
will provide peace in this **p**"— Hg 2:9
make crowns and **p** them on the Zch 6:11
branch out from His **p** and build Zch 6:12
and Damascus is its resting **p**— Zch 9:1
Gate to the **p** of the First Gate, Zch 14:10
name in every **p** because My name Mal 1:11
all this took **p** to fulfill what Mt 1:22
above the **p** where the child Mt 2:9

over Judea in **p** of his father Mt 2:22
coming to the **p** of his baptism, Mt 3:7
In that **p** there will be weeping Mt 8:12
of Man has no **p** to lay His head. Mt 8:20
In that **p** there will be weeping Mt 13:50
boat to a remote **p** to be alone. Mt 14:13
said, "This **p** is a wilderness Mt 14:15
men of that **p** recognized Him, Mt 14:35
in this desolate **p** to fill such Mt 15:33
slaves saw what had taken **p**, Mt 18:31
This took **p** so that what was Mt 21:4
came together in the same **p**. Mt 22:34
They love the **p** of honor at Mt 23:6
these things must take **p**, Mt 24:6
in the holy **p**" (let the reader Mt 24:15
that hasn't taken **p** from the Mt 24:21
until all these things take **p**. Mt 24:34
and assign him a **p** with the Mt 24:51
In that **p** there will be weeping Mt 24:51
In that **p** there will be weeping Mt 25:30
Passover takes **p** after two days, Mt 26:2
Passover at your **p** with My Mt 26:18
with them to a **p** called Mt 26:36
sword back in **p** because all who Mt 26:52
living God I **p** You under oath: Mt 26:63
it as a burial **p** for foreigners. Mt 27:7
they came to a **p** called Golgotha Mt 27:33
Golgotha (which means Skull **P**), Mt 27:33
Come and see the **p** where He lay. Mt 28:6
made His way to a deserted **p**. Mk 1:35
entered the **p** where the child Mk 5:40
there until you leave that **p**. Mk 6:10
any **p** does not welcome you and Mk 6:11
to a remote **p** and rest a while." Mk 6:31
by themselves to a remote **p**, Mk 6:32
said, "This **p** is a wilderness Mk 6:35
in this desolate **p** to fill these Mk 8:4
they left that **p** and made their Mk 9:30
things are about to take **p**?" Mk 13:4
must take **p**, but the end is Mk 13:7
until all these things take **p**. Mk 13:30
they came to a **p** named Mk 14:32
Jesus to the **p** called Golgotha Mk 15:22
Golgotha (which means Skull **P**). Mk 15:22
See the **p** where they put Him. Mk 16:6
the day these things take **p**, Lk 1:20
took **p** while Quirinius Lk 2:2
He found the **p** where it was Lk 4:17
heard that took **p** in Capernaum, Lk 4:23
out to every **p** in the vicinity Lk 4:37
made His way to a deserted **p**. Lk 4:42
stood on a level **p** with a large Lk 6:17
we are in a deserted **p** here." Lk 9:12
of Man has no **p** to lay His head. Lk 9:58
every town and **p** where He Lk 10:1
he arrived at the **p** and saw him, Lk 10:32
He was praying in a certain **p**, Lk 11:1
and assign him a **p** with the Lk 12:46
and gnashing of teeth in that **p**, Lk 13:28
don't recline at the best **p**, Lk 14:8
'Give your **p** to this man,' Lk 14:9
proceed to take the lowest **p**. Lk 14:9
go and recline in the lowest **p**, Lk 14:10
also come to this **p** of torment.' Lk 16:28
Jesus came to the **p**, He looked Lk 19:5
at the **p** called the Mount of Lk 19:29
things are about to take **p**?" Lk 21:7
these things must take **p** first, Lk 21:9
these things begin to take **p**, Lk 21:28
away until all things take **p**. Lk 21:32
are going to take **p** and to stand Lk 21:36
He reached the **p**, He told them, Lk 22:40
that had taken **p** in the city, Lk 23:19
arrived at the **p** called The Lk 23:33
when they saw what had taken **p**, Lk 23:48
everything that had taken **p**. Lk 24:14
a wedding took **p** in Cana of Jn 2:1
say that the **p** to worship is Jn 4:20
festival took **p**, and Jesus went Jn 5:1
was plenty of grass in that **p**, Jn 6:10
came near the **p** where they ate Jn 6:23
a division took **p** among the Jews Jn 10:19
Dedication took **p** in Jerusalem, Jn 10:22
Jordan to the **p** where John had Jn 10:40
more days in the **p** where He was. Jn 11:6
still in the **p** where Martha had Jn 11:30
both our **p** and our nation. Jn 11:48
away to prepare a **p** for you. Jn 14:2

go away and prepare a **p** for you, Jn 14:3
do. "Get up; let's leave this **p**. Jn 14:31
also knew the **p**, because Jesus Jn 18:2
bench in a **p** called the Stone Jn 19:13
out to what is called Skull **P**, Jn 19:17
because the **p** where Jesus was Jn 19:20
a garden in the **p** where He was Jn 19:41
They **p** Jesus there because of Jn 19:42
up in a separate **p** by itself. Jn 20:7
to take the **p** in this apostolic Ac 1:25
Judas left to go to his own **p**." Ac 1:25
they were all together in one **p**. Ac 2:1
plan had predestined to take **p**. Ac 4:28
the **p** where they were assembled Ac 4:31
against this holy **p** and the law. Ac 6:13
will destroy this **p** and change Ac 6:14
out and worship Me in this **p**. Ac 7:7
because the **p** where you are Ac 7:33
provide a dwelling **p** for the God Ac 7:46
Lord, or what is My resting **p**? Ac 7:49
was traveling from **p** to place, Ac 9:32
was traveling from place to **p**, Ac 9:32
events that took **p** throughout Ac 10:37
This took **p** during the time of Ac 11:28
that what took **p** through the Ac 12:9
and went to a different **p**. Ac 12:17
thought there was a **p** of prayer. Ac 16:13
through one **p** after another Ac 18:23
our people, our law, and this **p**. Ac 21:28
and has profaned this holy **p**." Ac 21:28
are taking **p** for the benefit Ac 24:2
and Moses said would take **p**— Ac 26:22
and came to a **p** called Fair Ac 27:8
run aground in some rocky **p**, Ac 27:29
area around that **p** was an estate Ac 28:7
will be in the **p** where they were Rm 9:26
all those in every **p** who call on 1Co 1:2
apostles, in last **p**, like men 1Co 4:9
when you come together in one **p**, 1Co 11:20
that is written will take **p**: 1Co 15:54
that took **p** in the province 2Co 1:8
through us in every **p** the scent 2Co 2:14
to have first **p** in everything. Col 1:18
but in every **p** that your faith 1Th 1:8
⌊This will take **p**⌋ at the 2Th 1:7
want the men in every **p** to pray, 1Tm 2:8
has already taken **p**, 2Tm 2:18
he might serve me in your **p**, Phm 13
which is called "the holy **p**," Heb 9:2
death has taken **p** for redemption Heb 9:15
went out to a **p** he was going to Heb 11:8
here in a good **p**," and yet you Jms 2:3
to a lamp shining in a dismal **p**, 2Pt 1:19
to have first **p** among them, 3Jn 9
slaves what must quickly take **p**. Rv 1:1
and what will take **p** after this. Rv 1:19
your lampstand from its **p**— Rv 2:5
taught Balak to **p** a stumbling Rv 2:14
what must take **p** after this." Rv 4:1
and island was moved from its **p**. Rv 6:14
a violent earthquake took **p**, Rv 11:13
she had a **p** prepared by God Rv 12:6
and there was no **p** for them in Rv 12:8
presence to her **p** in the Rv 12:14
them at the **p** called in Hebrew Rv 16:16
and no **p** was found for them. Rv 20:11
what must quickly take **p**." Rv 22:6

PLACED *(127)*

God **p** them in the expanse of the Gn 1:17
and there He **p** the man He had Gn 2:8
took the man and **p** him in the Gn 2:15
And He **p** a mark on Cain so that Gn 4:15
They are **p** under your authority. Gn 9:2
I have **p** My bow in the clouds, Gn 9:13
took a cloak and **p** it over both Gn 9:23
son Isaac and **p** him on the altar Gn 22:9
So the servant **p** his hand under Gn 24:9
stone was then **p** back on the Gn 29:3
and he **p** his sons in charge of Gn 30:35
Jacob **p** the branches in the Gn 30:41
household and **p** all that he Gn 39:4
p the cup in Pharaoh's hand." Gn 40:11
and he **p** the cup in Pharaoh's Gn 40:21
and **p** a gold chain around his Gn 41:42
So he **p** him over all the land Gn 41:43
seven years and **p** it in the Gn 41:48
He **p** the food in every city from Gn 41:48
his father had **p** his right hand Gn 48:17
him and **p** him in a coffin Gn 50:26
She **p** the child in it and set it Ex 2:3
Aaron **p** it before the testimony Ex 16:34
so it can be **p** on the turban; Ex 28:37
I have **p** wisdom within every Ex 31:6
heart the LORD had **p** wisdom, Ex 36:2
testimony and **p** ⌊it⌋ in the ark Ex 40:20
Moses **p** the table in the tent of Ex 40:22
Then he **p** the altar of burnt Ex 40:29
him and **p** the Urim and Thummim Lv 8:8
on his head and **p** the plate of Lv 8:9
and **p** ⌊them⌋ on the fat portions Lv 8:26
and **p** these on the breasts. Lv 9:20
put fire in it, **p** incense on it, Lv 10:1
was on Moses and **p** ⌊the Spirit⌋ Nm 11:25
They **p** him in custody, because Nm 15:34
his firepan, **p** fire in it, put Nm 16:18
Moses **p** the staffs before the Nm 17:7
the mountain and **p** the tablets Dt 10:5
stones were **p** against the mouth Jos 10:27
p the meat in a basket and the Jdg 6:19
the child, **p** him on her lap, Ru 4:16
of Dagon and **p** it next to his 1Sm 5:2
and **p** them on the large rock. 1Sm 6:15
the LORD was **p** is in the field 1Sm 6:18
which he **p** in the presence of 1Sm 10:25
to me and **p** a king over you. 1Sm 12:1
king the LORD has **p** over you. 1Sm 12:13
for Saul had **p** the troops under 1Sm 14:24
p some goats' hair on its head, 1Sm 19:13
your feet not **p** in bronze 2Sm 3:34
Then he **p** garrisons in Aram of 2Sm 8:6
He **p** garrisons throughout Edom, 2Sm 8:14
p the rest of the forces under 2Sm 10:10
and it was ⌊**p**⌋ on David's head. 2Sm 12:30
p it over the mouth of the well, 2Sm 17:19
the palace and **p** them under 2Sm 20:3
had a throne **p** for the king's 1Kg 2:19
the bread of the Presence was **p** 1Kg 7:48
the bull, and **p** it on the wood. 1Kg 18:33
ahead of them and **p** the staff on 2Kg 4:31
deported and **p** in the cities 2Kg 17:26
ark of God and **p** it inside the 1Ch 16:1
Then he **p** garrisons in Aram of 1Ch 18:6
p the rest of the forces under 1Ch 19:11
and it was ⌊**p**⌋ on David's head. 1Ch 20:2
made 10 tables and **p** them in the 2Ch 4:8
was made and **p** outside the gate 2Ch 24:8
He also **p** military commanders in 2Ch 33:14
all that was **p** in their hands. 2Ch 34:16
Jerusalem and had **p** in the house Ezr 1:7
same day men were **p** in charge of Neh 12:44
restraint was **p** on the drinking Est 1:8
the palace and **p** under the care Est 2:8
He **p** the royal crown on her head Est 2:17
You **p** a hedge around him, Jb 1:10
my devastation **p** with it on a Jb 6:2
the time⌋ man was **p** on earth, Jb 20:4
If I **p** my confidence in gold or Jb 31:24
You **p** burdens on our backs. Ps 66:11
thrones for judgment are **p**, Ps 122:5
You have **p** Your hand on me. Ps 139:5
when He **p** the skies above, Pr 8:28
and hope **p** in wealth vanishes. Pr 11:7
crown his mother **p** on him the Sg 3:11
and I **p** them under your control. Is 47:6
have **p** your bed on a high and Is 57:7
baskets of figs **p** before the Jr 24:1
So now I have **p** all these lands Jr 27:6
They have **p** their detestable Jr 32:34
and beat him and **p** him in jail Jr 37:15
Jeremiah was **p** in the guard's Jr 37:21
they have been **p** on my neck, Lm 1:14
They are **p** among the slain. Ezk 32:25
swords were **p** under their heads Ezk 32:27
have been **p** among those slain by Ezk 32:29
sacrifices were **p** on them. Ezk 40:42
Whenever they **p** their threshold Ezk 43:8
⌊**P**⌋ a gold chain around his neck, Dn 5:29
was brought and **p** over the mouth Dn 6:17
one stone was **p** on another Hg 2:15
clean turban was **p** on his head, Zch 3:5
basket⌋ will be **p** there on its Zch 5:11
and **p** a reed in His right hand. Mt 27:29
and **p** it in his new tomb, which Mt 27:60
his corpse and **p** it in a tomb. Mk 6:29
Again Jesus **p** His hands on the Mk 8:25
Then he **p** Him in a tomb cut out Mk 15:46
were watching where He was **p**. Mk 15:47
too am a man **p** under authority, Lk 7:8
fine linen and **p** it in a tomb Lk 23:53
where no one had ever been **p**. Lk 23:53
the tomb and how His body was **p**. Lk 23:55
no one had yet been **p** in it. Jn 19:41
carried there and **p** every day at Ac 3:2
and were **p** in the tomb that Ac 7:16
Then he **p** his hands on him and Ac 9:17
they **p** her in a room upstairs. Ac 9:37
Paul down and **p** him before them. Ac 22:30
an obligation is **p** on me. 1Co 9:16
But now God has **p** the parts, 1Co 12:18
And God has **p** these in the 1Co 12:28
If we have **p** our hope in Christ 1Co 15:19
have **p** our hope in Him that He 2Co 1:10
should be **p** on the official 1Tm 5:9
is **p** among the parts of our Jms 3:6
I have **p** before you an open door Rv 3:8

PLACES *(132)*

I will destroy your high **p**, Lv 26:30
and demolish all their high **p**. Nm 33:52
all the **p** where the nations Dt 12:2
in all the ⌊sacred⌋ **p** you see. Dt 12:13
the singers at the watering **p**. Jdg 5:11
made hiding **p** for themselves Jdg 6:2
reach one of these **p** and spend Jdg 19:13
up from their **p** and took their Jdg 20:33
out of their **p** west of Geba. Jdg 20:33
out all the **p** where he hides. 1Sm 23:23
those in⌋ all the **p** where David 1Sm 30:31
were sacrificing on the high **p**, 1Kg 3:2
burned incense on the high **p**. 1Kg 3:3
on the high **p** and set up priests 1Kg 12:31
for the high **p** he had set up. 1Kg 12:32
of the high **p** who are burning 1Kg 13:2
of the high **p** in the cities 1Kg 13:32
class of people for the high **p**. 1Kg 13:33
became priests of the high **p**. 1Kg 13:33
built for themselves high **p**, 1Kg 14:23
The high **p** were not taken away; 1Kg 15:14
the high **p** were not taken away; 1Kg 22:43
burned incense on the high **p**. 1Kg 22:43
Yet the high **p** were not taken 2Kg 12:3
burning incense on the high **p**. 2Kg 12:3
the high **p** were not taken away, 2Kg 14:4
burning incense on the high **p**. 2Kg 14:4
the high **p** were not taken away; 2Kg 15:4
burning incense on the high **p**. 2Kg 15:4
the high **p** were not taken away; 2Kg 15:35
burning incense on the high **p**. 2Kg 15:35
burned incense on the high **p**, 2Kg 16:4
They built high **p** in all their 2Kg 17:9
all the high **p** just like those 2Kg 17:11
of the high **p** that the 2Kg 17:29
in the shrines of the high **p**. 2Kg 17:32
removed the high **p** and shattered 2Kg 18:4
the One whose high **p** and altars 2Kg 18:22
the high **p** that his father 2Kg 21:3
at the high **p** in the cities 2Kg 23:5
defiled the high **p** from Geba to 2Kg 23:8
down the high **p** of the gates at 2Kg 23:8
The priests of the high **p**, 2Kg 23:9
the high **p** that were across 2Kg 23:13
filled their **p** with human bones 2Kg 23:14
shrines of the high **p** that were 2Kg 23:19
of the high **p** who were there, 2Kg 23:20
These were the **p** assigned to 1Ch 6:54
because the **p** to which the ark 2Ch 8:11
his own priests for the high **p**, 2Ch 11:15
the pagan altars and the high **p**. 2Ch 14:3
the high **p** and the incense 2Ch 14:5
The high **p** were not taken away 2Ch 15:17
removed the high **p** and Asherah 2Ch 17:6
the high **p** were not taken away; 2Ch 20:33
also built high **p** in the hills 2Ch 21:11
fame spread even to distant **p**, 2Ch 26:15
burned incense on the high **p**, 2Ch 28:4
He made high **p** in every city of 2Ch 28:25
tore down the high **p** and altars 2Ch 31:1
remove His high **p** and His altars 2Ch 32:12
the high **p** that his father 2Ch 33:3
still sacrificed at the high **p**, 2Ch 33:17
he built high **p** and set up 2Ch 33:19
and Jerusalem of the high **p**, 2Ch 34:3
people as they stood in their **p**. Neh 8:7
While they stood in their **p**, Neh 9:3
⌊in **p**⌋ unknown to those who walk Jb 28:4

will disappear from their **p**. Jb 36:20
kills the innocent in secret **p**; Ps 10:8
fallen for me in pleasant **p**; Ps 16:6
concealed **p** at the innocent. Ps 64:4
You put them in slippery **p**; Ps 73:18
for the dark **p** of the land are Ps 74:20
with their high **p** and provoked Ps 78:58
herself where she **p** her young— Ps 84:3
in the darkest **p**, in the depths. Ps 88:6
in all the **p** where He rules. Ps 103:22
hills⌋ will be **p** for oxen to Is 7:25
temple to weep at its high **p**. Is 15:2
they will be ⌊**p**⌋ for flocks. Is 17:2
those who live in lofty **p**— Is 26:5
will become barren **p** forever, Is 32:14
the One whose high **p** and altars Is 36:7
smooth, and the rough **p** a plain. Is 40:4
and rough **p** into level ground. Is 42:16
you and level the uneven **p**; Is 45:2
and riches from secret **p**, Is 45:3
and desolate **p** and your land Is 49:19
He will comfort all her waste **p**, Is 51:3
spending nights in secret **p**, Is 65:4
have built the high **p** of Topheth Jr 7:31
of your high **p** within all your Jr 17:3
in the parched **p** in the Jr 17:6
have built high **p** to Baal on Jr 19:5
Who can enter our hiding **p**? Jr 21:13
in secret **p** where I cannot Jr 23:24
the nations and **p** where I Jr 29:14
have built the high **p** of Baal in Jr 32:35
from all the **p** where they had Jr 40:12
I will uncover his secret **p**. Jr 49:10
her from the most distant **p**. Jr 50:26
entered the holy **p** of the LORD's Jr 51:51
have overtaken her in narrow **p**. Lm 1:3
and I will destroy your high **p**. Ezk 6:3
and the high **p** will be desolate Ezk 6:6
p where they offered pleasing Ezk 6:13
their sacred **p** will be profaned Ezk 7:24
colorful high **p** for yourself, Ezk 16:16
These **p** should not have been Ezk 16:16
and tear down your elevated **p**. Ezk 16:39
from all the **p** where they have Ezk 34:12
all the inhabited **p** of the land. Ezk 34:13
of their kings at their high **p**. Ezk 43:7
will become **p** where nets are Ezk 47:10
The high **p** of Aven, the sin of Hs 10:8
Isaac's high **p** will be deserted, Am 7:9
of their hiding **p** like reptiles Mc 7:17
waterless **p** looking for rest Mt 12:43
and earthquakes in various **p**. Mt 24:7
But He was out in deserted **p**, Mk 1:45
and the **p** of honor at banquets. Mk 12:39
be earthquakes in various **p**, Mk 13:8
to deserted **p** and prayed. Lk 5:16
by the demon into deserted **p**. Lk 8:29
waterless **p** looking for rest Lk 11:24
the best **p** for themselves: Lk 14:7
and the **p** of honor at banquets. Lk 20:46
and plagues in various **p**, Lk 21:11
house are many dwelling **p**; Jn 14:2
of the Jews who were in those **p**, Ac 16:3
them always and in all **p**, Ac 24:3

PLACING *(2)*

I am **p** you over all the land of Gn 41:41
coming in and **p** his hands on him Ac 9:12

PLAGUE *(81)*

may strike us with **p** or sword." Ex 5:3
then I will **p** all your territory Ex 8:2
bring a severe **p** against your Ex 9:3
you and your people with a **p**, Ex 9:15
will bring one more **p** on Pharaoh Ex 11:1
p will be among you to destroy Ex 12:13
Then no **p** will come on them as Ex 30:12
LORD inflicted a **p** on the people Ex 32:35
so that no **p** will come against Nm 8:19
them with a very severe **p**. Nm 11:33
them with a **p** and destroy them. Nm 14:12
from the LORD; the **p** has begun." Nm 16:46
saw that the **p** had begun among Nm 16:47
living, and the **p** was halted. Nm 16:48
died from the **p** numbered 14,700 Nm 16:49
since the **p** had been halted. Nm 16:50
Then the **p** on the Israelites was Nm 25:8
died in the **p** numbered 24,000 Nm 25:9
the day the **p** came at Peor." Nm 25:18
After the **p**, the LORD said to Nm 26:1
so that the **p** came against the Nm 31:16
sickness and **p** not recorded Dt 28:61
by pestilence and bitter **p**; Dt 32:24
which brought a **p** on the LORD's Jos 22:17
there was one **p** for both you 1Sm 6:4
to have a **p** in your land three 2Sm 24:13
So the LORD sent a **p** on Israel 2Sm 24:15
p on the people may be halted. 2Sm 24:21
land, and the **p** on Israel ended. 2Sm 24:25
⌊when there is⌋ any **p** or illness, 1Kg 8:37
of the LORD—a **p** on the land, 1Ch 21:12
So the LORD sent a **p** on Israel, 1Ch 21:14
don't let the **p** be against Your 1Ch 21:17
p on the people may be halted. 1Ch 21:22
⌊when there is⌋ any **p** or illness, 2Ch 6:28
him will be buried by the **p**, Jb 27:15
delivered their lives to the **p**. Ps 78:50
net, from the destructive **p**. Ps 91:3
the **p** that stalks in darkness, Ps 91:6
no **p** will come near your tent. Ps 91:10
and a **p** broke out against them. Ps 106:29
and the **p** was stopped. Ps 106:30
off by sword, famine, and **p**." Jr 14:12
They will die in a great **p**. Jr 21:6
in this city who survive the **p**, Jr 21:7
famine, and **p**, but whoever goes Jr 21:9
and **p** against them until they Jr 24:10
sword, famine, and **p**"—⌊this Jr 27:8
or **p** as the LORD has threatened Jr 27:13
and **p** against many lands and Jr 28:8
and **p** and will make them like Jr 29:17
them with sword, famine, and **p**. Jr 29:18
famine, and **p**, has been handed Jr 32:24
through sword, famine, and **p**: Jr 32:36
the sword, to **p**, and to famine! Jr 34:17
sword, famine, and **p**, but Jr 38:2
die by the sword, famine, and **p**. Jr 42:17
and **p** you will die in the place Jr 42:22
by sword, famine, and **p**. Jr 44:13
will die by **p** and be consumed Ezk 5:12
P and bloodshed will sweep Ezk 5:17
by the sword, famine, and **p**. Ezk 6:11
who is far off will die by **p**; Ezk 6:12
p and famine are on the inside. Ezk 7:15
and famine and **p** will devour Ezk 7:15
and **p** so they can tell about all Ezk 12:16
Or if I send a **p** into that land Ezk 14:19
animals, and **p**—in order to Ezk 14:21
I will send a **p** against her and Ezk 28:23
and caves will die by **p**. Ezk 33:27
on him with **p** and bloodshed. Ezk 38:22
P goes before Him, and Hab 3:5
will be the **p** the LORD strikes Zch 14:12
The same **p** as the previous one Zch 14:15
this will be the **p** the LORD Zch 14:18
have found this man to be a **p**, Ac 24:5
kill her children with the **p**. Rv 2:23
by famine, by **p**, and by the wild Rv 6:8
earth with any **p** whenever they Rv 11:6
God for the **p** of hail because Rv 16:21
because that **p** was extremely Rv 16:21

PLAGUED *(1)*

I **p** Egypt by what I did there, Jos 24:5

PLAGUES *(20)*

house with severe **p** because of Gn 12:17
to send all My **p** against you, Ex 9:14
multiply your **p** seven times for Lv 26:21
extraordinary **p** on you and your Dt 28:59
and lasting **p**, and terrible Dt 28:59
will see the **p** of the land Dt 29:22
all kinds of **p** in the wilderness 1Sm 4:8
I sent **p** like those of Egypt; Am 4:10
of diseases, **p**, and evil spirits Lk 7:21
and famines and **p** in various Lk 21:11
was killed by these three **p**— Rv 9:18
who were not killed by these **p**, Rv 9:20
angels with the seven last **p**, Rv 15:1
seven angels with the seven **p**, Rv 15:6
until the seven **p** of the seven Rv 15:8
who had the power over these **p**, Rv 16:9
sins, or receive any of her **p**. Rv 18:4
therefore her **p** will come in one Rv 18:8
filled with the seven last **p**, Rv 21:9
to him the **p** that are written Rv 22:18

PLAIN *(27)*

don't stop anywhere on the **p**! Gn 19:17
cities, the entire **p**, all the Gn 19:25
and all the land of the **p**, Gn 19:28
destroyed the cities of the **p**, Gn 19:29
It is **p** that we are being Gn 42:21
facing the **p** ⌊of the Jordan⌋ Jos 8:14
the **p** south of Chinnereth, Jos 11:2
foothills, the **p**, and the hill Jos 11:16
foothills, the **p**, the slopes, Jos 12:8
was the Jordan and its **p**. Jos 13:23
ran by way of the **p** and outran 2Sm 18:23
should fight with them on the **p**; 1Kg 20:23
let's fight with them on the **p**; 1Kg 20:25
both in the lowlands and the **p**, 2Ch 26:10
demote you in **p** view of a noble Pr 25:7
and the rough places a **p**. Is 40:4
from an arid **p** will ravage them Jr 5:6
and the **p** will be annihilated, Jr 48:8
go out to the **p**, and I will Ezk 3:22
I got up and went out to the **p**. Ezk 3:23
the vision I had seen in the **p**. Ezk 8:4
He set it up on the **p** of Dura in Dn 3:1
Zerubbabel you will become a **p**. Zch 4:7
in the **p** of Megiddo. Zch 12:11
will be changed into a **p**. Zch 14:10
since it is **p** that you are 2Co 3:3
us might be made **p** to you in the 2Co 7:12

PLAINLY *(4)*

You are the Messiah, tell us **p**." Jn 10:24
So Jesus then told them **p**, Jn 11:14
I will tell you **p** about the Jn 16:25
You're speaking **p** and not using Jn 16:29

PLAINS *(18)*

and camped in the **p** of Moab near Nm 22:1
said to them in the **p** of Moab by Nm 26:3
Israelites on the **p** of Moab by Nm 26:63
at the camp on the **p** of Moab by Nm 31:12
and camped on the **p** of Moab by Nm 33:48
Meadows on the **p** of Moab. Nm 33:49
to Moses in the **p** of Moab by the Nm 33:50
to Moses in the **p** of Moab by the Nm 35:1
through Moses in the **p** of Moab Nm 36:13
up from the **p** of Moab to Mount Dt 34:1
Moses in the **p** of Moab 30 days Dt 34:8
war crossed to the **p** of Jericho Jos 4:13
at Gilgal on the **p** of Jericho, Jos 5:10
them⌋ on the **p** of Moab beyond Jos 13:32
him in the **p** of Jericho. 2Kg 25:5
springs in the middle of the **p**. Is 41:18
Zedekiah in the **p** of Jericho, Jr 39:5
Zedekiah in the **p** of Jericho. Jr 52:8

PLAN *(51)*

then nothing they **p** to do will Gn 11:6
to the **p** for it that you Ex 26:30
The **p** seemed good to me, so I Dt 1:23
So I **p** to build a temple for the 1Kg 5:5
all the details of the **p**." 1Ch 28:19
Now you **p** to reduce the people 2Ch 28:10
for you **p** to bring guilt on us 2Ch 28:13
you and the Jews **p** to rebel. Neh 6:6
the evil **p** Haman had devised Est 9:25
that this was Your hidden **p**: Jb 10:13
anything and no **p** of Yours can Jb 42:2
harm you and devise a wicked **p**, Ps 21:11
let those who **p** to harm me be Ps 35:4
about me; they **p** to harm me. Ps 41:7
They only **p** to bring him down Ps 62:4
each other in an evil **p**; Ps 64:5
"We have perfected a secret **p**." Ps 64:6
who **p** evil in their hearts. Ps 140:2
violent men who **p** to make me Ps 140:4
Don't **p** any harm against your Pr 3:29
those who **p** evil go astray? Pr 14:22
those who **p** good find loyalty Pr 14:22
for their hearts **p** violence, Pr 24:2
Let the **p** of the Holy One of Is 5:19
Devise a **p**; it will fail. Make a Is 8:10
This is the **p** prepared for the Is 14:26
carry out a **p**, but not Mine, Is 30:1
My **p** will take place, and I will Is 46:10
disaster that I **p** to do to them Jr 26:3
they **p** harm against her in Jr 48:2
has drawn up a **p** against you; Jr 49:30
Medes because His **p** is aimed at Jr 51:11
are the men who **p** evil and give Ezk 11:2
and you will devise an evil **p**. Ezk 38:10
intentions or understand His **p**, Mc 4:12
the elders and agreed on a **p**, Mt 28:12
they rejected the **p** of God for Lk 7:30
agreed with their **p** and action. Lk 23:51
God's determined **p** and Ac 2:23

hand and Your **p** had predestined Ac 4:28
For if this **p** or this work is of Ac 5:38
his own generation in God's **p**, Ac 13:36
to you the whole **p** of God. Ac 20:27
The soldiers' **p** was to kill the Ac 27:42
out their **p** because he wanted Ac 27:43
Or what I **p**, do I plan in a 2Co 1:17
do I **p** in a purely human way so 2Co 1:17
by which I **p** to challenge 2Co 10:2
rather than God's **p**, 1Tm 1:4
God's hidden **p** will be completed Rv 10:7
to carry out His **p** by having one Rv 17:17

PLANE *(2)*
almond, and **p** wood, and peeled Gn 30:37
nor could the **p** trees match its Ezk 31:8

PLANK *(13)*
length of each **p** is to be 15 Ex 26:16
the width of each **p** 27 inches. Ex 26:16
p must be connected together Ex 26:17
under the first **p** for its two Ex 26:19
under the next **p** for its two Ex 26:19
under the first **p** and two bases Ex 26:21
and two bases under each **p**; Ex 26:21
under the first **p** and two bases Ex 26:25
and two bases under each **p**. Ex 26:25
length of each **p** was 15 feet, Ex 36:21
to each other for each **p**. Ex 36:22
under the first **p** for its two Ex 36:24
under the first **p** and two bases Ex 36:26

PLANKING *(1)*
all your **p** with pine trees Ezk 27:5

PLANKS *(32)*
to make upright **p** of acacia wood Ex 26:15
same for all the **p** of the Ex 26:17
Make the **p** for the tabernacle as Ex 26:18
20 **p** for the south side, Ex 26:18
40 silver bases under the 20 **p**, Ex 26:19
20 **p** for the second side of the Ex 26:20
and make six **p** for the west side Ex 26:22
additional **p** for the two back Ex 26:23
are to be eight **p** with their Ex 26:25
acacia wood for the **p** on one Ex 26:26
for the **p** on the other side Ex 26:27
for the **p** of the back side Ex 26:27
middle of the **p** from one end to Ex 26:28
Then overlay the **p** with gold, Ex 26:29
its clasps and **p**, its crossbars, Ex 35:11
He made upright **p** of acacia wood Ex 36:20
same for all the **p** of the Ex 36:22
He made **p** for the tabernacle as Ex 36:23
bases to put under the 20 **p**, Ex 36:24
of the following **p** for their two Ex 36:24
the north side, he made 20 **p**, Ex 36:25
of the tabernacle he made six **p**. Ex 36:27
additional **p** for the two back Ex 36:28
there were eight **p** with their 16 Ex 36:30
acacia wood for the **p** on one Ex 36:31
for the **p** on the other side Ex 36:32
middle of the **p** from one end to Ex 36:33
clasps, its **p**, its crossbars, Ex 39:33
positioned its **p**, inserted its Ex 40:18
it with boards and **p** of cedar. 1Kg 6:9
we will enclose it with cedar **p**. Sg 8:9
on **p** and some on debris from Ac 27:44

PLANNED *(32)*
You **p** evil against me; Gn 50:20
God **p** it for good to bring about Gn 50:20
this disaster ⌊**p**⌋ for Your Ex 32:12
And what I had **p** to do to them, Nm 33:56
Absalom has **p** this ever since 2Sm 13:32
Then he **p** to attack Jerusalem. 2Kg 12:17
I **p** it in days gone by. 2Kg 19:25
and that he **p** war on Jerusalem 2Ch 32:2
when they **p** to assassinate King Est 6:2
conceal what the Almighty has **p**. Jb 27:11
Your book and **p** before a single Ps 139:16
As I have **p**, so it will be; Is 14:24
LORD of Hosts Himself has **p** it; Is 14:27
of Hosts has **p** against Egypt. Is 19:12
LORD of Hosts has **p** against it. Is 19:17
Who **p** this against Tyre, the Is 23:8
LORD of Hosts **p** it, to desecrate Is 23:9
I **p** it in days gone by. Is 37:26
about. I have **p** it; I will also Is 46:11
For I **p** the day of vengeance, Is 63:4
I have **p**, and I will not relent Jr 4:28
the disaster on it I had **p**. Jr 18:8
LORD has both **p** and accomplished Jr 51:12
The LORD has done what He **p**; Lm 2:17
the king **p** to set him over the Dn 6:3
You have **p** shame for your house Hab 2:10
is it that you **p** this thing in Ac 5:4
They **p** to run the ship ashore if Ac 27:39
that I often **p** to come to you Rm 1:13
confidence, I **p** to come to you 2Co 1:15
So when I **p** this, was I 2Co 1:17
good pleasure that He **p** in Him Eph 1:9

PLANNING *(9)*
himself by **p** to kill you. Gn 27:42
Are you **p** to kill me as you Ex 2:14
Look out—you are **p** evil. Ex 10:10
But they were **p** to harm me. Neh 6:2
king was **p** something terrible Est 7:7
his eyes is **p** deceptions; Pr 16:30
there is no work, **p**, knowledge, Ec 9:10
disaster I am **p** to bring on them Jr 36:3
I am now **p** a disaster against Mc 2:3

PLANS *(44)*
would devise **p** so that the one 2Sm 14:14
altar and complete **p** for its 2Kg 16:10
son Solomon the **p** for the 1Ch 28:11
p contained everything he had 1Ch 28:12
included were **p**⌋ for the 1Ch 28:13
and the **p** for the chariot of the 1Ch 28:18
to frustrate their **p** throughout Ezr 4:5
so that the **p** of the deceptive Jb 5:13
and favor the **p** of the wicked? Jb 10:3
my **p** have been ruined, even the Jb 17:11
the **p** of the afflicted, Ps 14:6
He thwarts the **p** of the peoples. Ps 33:10
the **p** of His heart from Ps 33:11
on his bed he makes malicious **p**. Ps 36:4
the man who carries out evil **p**. Ps 37:7
works and Your **p** for us; Ps 40:5
hearts to follow their own **p**. Ps 81:12
who pursue evil **p** come near; Ps 119:150
on that day his **p** die. Ps 146:4
P fail when there is no counsel, Pr 15:22
detests the **p** of an evil man, Pr 15:26
LORD and your **p** will be achieved Pr 16:3
A man's heart **p** his way, but the Pr 16:9
Many **p** are in a man's heart, Pr 19:21
Finalize **p** through counsel, Pr 20:18
The **p** of the diligent certainly Pr 21:5
this is not what he **p**. Is 10:7
and I will frustrate its **p**. Is 19:3
wonders, **p** ⌊formed⌋ long ago, Is 25:1
to hide their **p** from the LORD. Is 29:15
a noble person **p** noble things; Is 32:8
I say that your **p** and military Is 36:5
to you and make **p** against you. Jr 18:11
will continue to follow our **p**, Jr 18:12
let's make **p** against Jeremiah, Jr 18:18
I will spoil the **p** of Judah and Jr 19:7
they make **p** to cause My people Jr 23:27
For I know the **p** I have for you" Jr 29:11
declaration—"**p** for ⌊your⌋ Jr 29:11
hear the **p** that the LORD has Jr 49:20
hear the **p** that the LORD has Jr 50:45
and he will make **p** against Dn 11:24
prepare evil ⌊**p**⌋ on their beds! Mc 2:1
and make no **p** to satisfy the Rm 13:14

PLANT *(61)*
seed-bearing **p** on the surface Gn 1:29
given⌋ every green **p** for food." Gn 1:30
and no **p** of the field had yet Gn 2:5
was the first to **p** a vineyard. Gn 9:20
beast and every **p** of the field Ex 9:22
beat down every **p** of the field Ex 9:25
it and eat every **p** in the land, Ex 10:12
bring them in and **p** them on the Ex 15:17
the land and **p** any kind of tree Lv 19:23
groves that you did not **p**— Dt 6:11
Do not **p** your vineyard with two Dt 22:9
the crop you **p** and the produce Dt 22:9
You will **p** a vineyard but not Dt 28:30
You will **p** and cultivate Dt 28:39
with no **p** growing on it, Dt 29:23
and olive groves you did not **p**.' Jos 24:13
for My people Israel and **p** them, 2Sm 7:10
p vineyards and eat their fruit. 2Kg 19:29
for My people Israel and **p** them, 1Ch 17:9
up quicker than any ⌊other⌋ **p**. Jb 8:12
amply watered **p** in the sunshine Jb 8:16
to **p** them, You drove out the Ps 44:2
sow fields and **p** vineyards that Ps 107:37
time to **p** and a time to uproot; Ec 3:2
men of Judah, the **p** He delighted Is 5:7
you will **p** beautiful plants Is 17:10
day that you **p**, you will help Is 17:11
plow every day to **p** seed? Is 28:24
p vineyards and eat their fruit. Is 37:30
I will **p** cedars in the desert, Is 41:19
in order to **p** the heavens, Is 51:16
like a young **p** and like a root Is 53:2
they will **p** vineyards and eat Is 65:21
they will not **p** and others eat. Is 65:22
and demolish, to build and **p**. Jr 1:10
I will build and **p** a nation or a Jr 18:9
I will **p** them and not uproot Jr 24:6
P gardens and eat their produce. Jr 29:5
P gardens and eat their produce." Jr 29:28
will **p** vineyards again on the Jr 31:5
planters will **p** and will enjoy Jr 31:5
to build and to **p** them," Jr 31:28
and I will **p** them faithfully in Jr 32:41
or sow seed or **p** a vineyard. Jr 35:7
and I will **p** and not uproot you, Jr 42:10
like⌋ a willow, a **p** by abundant Ezk 17:5
top of the cedar and **p** ⌊it⌋. Ezk 17:22
and I will **p** ⌊it⌋ on a high Ezk 17:22
I will **p** it on Israel's high Ezk 17:23
build houses, and **p** vineyards. Ezk 28:26
p vineyards and drink their wine, Am 9:14
I will **p** them on their land, Am 9:15
Then the LORD God appointed a **p**, Jnh 4:6
was greatly pleased with the **p**. Jnh 4:6
a worm that attacked the **p**. Jnh 4:7
you to be angry about the **p**?" Jnh 4:9
cared about the **p**, which you did Jnh 4:10
p vineyards but never drink Zph 1:13
Every **p** that My heavenly Father Mt 15:13
didn't **p** will be uprooted. Mt 15:13
or any green **p**, or any tree, Rv 9:4

PLANTED *(36)*
The LORD God **p** a garden in Eden, Gn 2:8
Abraham **p** a tamarisk tree in Gn 21:33
like aloes the LORD has **p**, Nm 24:6
Has any man **p** a vineyard and not Dt 20:6
Whenever the Israelites **p** crops, Jdg 6:3
is like a tree **p** beside streams Ps 1:3
drove out the nations and **p** it. Ps 80:8
the root Your right hand has **p**, Ps 80:15
P in the house of the LORD, Ps 92:13
the cedars of Lebanon that He **p**. Ps 104:16
built houses and **p** vineyards for Ec 2:4
for myself and **p** every kind of Ec 2:5
and **p** it with the finest vines. Is 5:2
They are barely **p**, barely sown, Is 40:24
the branch I **p**, the work of My Is 60:21
trees, **p** by the LORD, to Is 61:3
I **p** you, a choice vine from the Jr 2:21
of Hosts who **p** you has decreed Jr 11:17
You **p** them, and they have taken Jr 12:2
will be like a tree **p** by water: Jr 17:8
and what I have **p** I am about to Jr 45:4
It had been **p** in a good field by Ezk 17:8
though it is **p**, will it flourish Ezk 17:10
your vineyard, **p** by the water; Ezk 19:10
Now it is **p** in the wilderness, Ezk 19:13
the tree was **p** and sending their Ezk 31:4
that no trees ⌊**p**⌋ beside water Ezk 31:14
like Tyre, **p** in a meadow, so Hs 9:13
the lush vineyards you have **p**. Am 5:11
You have **p** much but harvested Hg 1:6
landowner, who **p** a vineyard, put Mt 21:33
A man **p** a vineyard, put a fence Mk 12:1
tree that was **p** in his vineyard Lk 13:6
'Be uprooted and **p** in the sea,' Lk 17:6
A man **p** a vineyard, leased it to Lk 20:9
I **p**, Apollos watered, but God 1Co 3:6

PLANTERS *(1)*
the **p** will plant and will enjoy Jr 31:5

PLANTING *(4)*
does not plow during **p** season; Pr 20:4
branches to him from its **p** bed, Ezk 17:7
the countryside, a **p** area for a Mc 1:6
buying, selling, **p**, building. Lk 17:28

PLANTS *(25)*
seed-bearing **p**, and fruit trees Gn 1:11
seed-bearing **p** according to Gn 1:12
you will eat the **p** of the field. Gn 3:18

gave⌋ the green **p**, I have given Gn 9:3
consumed all the **p** on the ground Ex 10:15
the trees or the **p** in the field Ex 10:15
up the green **p** in the field." Nm 22:4
grass and showers on tender **p**. Dt 32:2
They are **p** of the field, tender 2Kg 19:26
He lies under the lotus **p**, Jb 40:21
Lotus **p** cover him with their Jb 40:22
and wilt like tender green **p**. Ps 37:2
will be like **p** nurtured in their Ps 144:12
she **p** a vineyard with her Pr 31:16
plant beautiful **p** and set out Is 17:10
He **p** wheat in rows and barley in Is 28:25
They are **p** of the field, tender Is 37:27
p a laurel, and the rain makes Is 44:14
because there are no green **p**. Jr 14:6
you thrive like **p** of the field. Ezk 16:7
and share the **p** of the earth Dn 4:15
When the **p** sprouted and produced Mt 13:26
the one who **p** nor the one who 1Co 3:7
the one who **p** and the one who 1Co 3:8
p a vineyard and does not eat 1Co 9:7

PLASTER *(10)*
and the **p** that is scraped off Lv 14:41
take additional **p** to replaster Lv 14:42
and all its **p**, and taken outside Lv 14:45
stones and cover them with **p**. Dt 27:2
you are to cover them with **p**. Dt 27:4
a wall they **p** it with whitewash Ezk 13:10
tell those who **p** ⌊it⌋ that it Ezk 13:11
those who **p** it with whitewash Ezk 13:15
prophets **p** with whitewash for Ezk 22:28
writing on the **p** of the king's Dn 5:5

PLASTERED *(3)*
of this law on the ⌊**p**⌋ stones." Dt 27:8
the wall you **p** with whitewash Ezk 13:14
and neither are those who **p** it— Ezk 13:15

PLATE *(5)*
You are to make a **p** of pure gold Ex 28:36
the **p** is to be on the front of Ex 28:37
also made a **p**, the holy diadem Ex 39:30
head and placed the **p** of gold, Lv 8:9
Take an iron **p** and set it up as Ezk 4:3

PLATEAU *(9)*
the cities of the **p**, Gilead, and Dt 3:10
in the wilderness on the **p** land, Dt 4:43
the Medeba **p** as far as Dibon, Jos 13:9
to the whole **p** as far as Medeba, Jos 13:16
and all its cities on the **p**— Jos 13:17
the cities of the **p**, and all the Jos 13:21
the wilderness **p** from Reuben's Jos 20:8
atop⌋ the rocky **p**—⌊this is⌋ Jr 21:13
has come to the land of the **p**— Jr 48:21

PLATED *(1)*
may be **p** with gold and silver, Hab 2:19

PLATES *(5)*
are also to make its **p** and cups, Ex 25:29
its **p** and cups, as well as its Ex 37:16
and place the **p** and cups on it, Nm 4:7
trees on the **p** of its braces 1Kg 7:36
a metalworker **p** with gold and Is 40:19

PLATFORM *(4)*
made a bronze **p** seven and a half 2Ch 6:13
on a high wooden **p** made for this Neh 8:4
stood on the raised **p** ⌊built⌋ Neh 9:4
had a raised **p** surrounding ⌊it⌋; Ezk 41:8

PLATING *(4)*
and the **p** for the tops of the Ex 38:17
as well as the **p** of their tops Ex 38:19
sheets as **p** for the altar, Nm 16:38
hammered into **p** for the altar, Nm 16:39

PLATTER *(4)*
the Baptist's head here on a **p**!" Mt 14:8
was brought on a **p** and given to Mt 14:11
John the Baptist's head on a **p**— Mk 6:25
his head on a **p**, and gave it to Mk 6:28

PLAY *(18)*
the father of all who **p** the lyre Gn 4:21
who knows how to **p** the harp. 1Sm 16:16
that person can **p** the harp, 1Sm 16:16
who knows how to **p** ⌊the harp⌋. 1Sm 16:18
would pick up his harp and **p**, 1Sm 16:23
were to **p** harps according 1Ch 15:20
and cymbals to **p** and musical 1Ch 16:42
sorts of⌋ wild animals **p** there. Jb 40:20
Can you **p** with him like a bird Jb 41:5
p skillfully on the strings, Ps 33:3
up a song—**p** the tambourine, Ps 81:2
which You formed to **p** there. Ps 104:26
I will **p** on a ten-stringed harp Ps 144:9
thanksgiving; **p** the lyre to our Ps 147:7
An infant will **p** beside the Is 11:8
P skillfully, sing many a song, Is 23:16
we will **p** stringed instruments Is 38:20
eat and drink, and got up to **p**. 1Co 10:7

PLAYED *(7)*
the musician **p**, the LORD's hand 2Kg 3:15
and Jeiel **p** the harps and lyres, 1Ch 16:5
You have **p** the prostitute with Jr 3:1
they have **p** the fool. Jr 5:4
We **p** the flute for you, but you Mt 11:17
We **p** the flute for you, but you Lk 7:32
how will what is **p** on the flute 1Co 14:7

PLAYERS *(1)*
He saw the flute **p** and a crowd Mt 9:23

PLAYFULLY *(1)*
will go out and **p** jump like Mal 4:2

PLAYING *(8)*
listening to the **p** of pipes for Jdg 5:16
David was **p** ⌊the harp⌋ as usual, 1Sm 18:10
David was **p** ⌊the harp⌋, 1Sm 19:9
p flutes and rejoicing with such 1Kg 1:40
and the **p** of harps and lyres. 1Ch 15:28
are young women **p** tambourines. Ps 68:25
with boys and girls **p** in them." Zch 8:5
like harpists **p** on their harps. Rv 14:2

PLAYS *(2)*
someone who **p** well and bring 1Sm 16:17
beautiful voice and **p** skillfully Ezk 33:32

PLAZA *(1)*
be rebuilt with a **p** and a moat, Dn 9:25

PLAZAS *(2)*
through the streets and the **p**. Sg 3:2
they rush around in the **p**. Nah 2:4

PLEA *(6)*
LORD has heard my **p** for help; Ps 6:9
and do not ignore my **p** for help. Ps 55:1
listen to my **p** for mercy. Ps 86:6
Let my **p** reach You; rescue me Ps 119:170
faithfulness listen to my **p**, Ps 143:1
You hear my **p**: Do not ignore my Lm 3:56

PLEAD *(23)*
How can we **p**? How can we justify Gn 44:16
Would you **p** Baal's case for him? Jdg 6:31
a god, let him **p** his own case, Jdg 6:31
"Let Baal **p** his case with him," Jdg 6:32
He take notice and **p** my case and 1Sm 24:15
and they pray and **p** with You for 1Kg 8:33
Please **p** for the favor of the 1Kg 13:6
they pray and **p** for mercy before 2Ch 6:24
p with him personally for her Est 4:8
I would **p** my case before Him and Jb 23:4
at daybreak I **p** my case to You Ps 5:3
I **p** aloud to the LORD for mercy. Ps 142:1
yourself, and **p** with your Pr 6:3
the fatherless. **P** the widow's Is 1:17
the LORD and **p** for the LORD's Jr 26:19
will fervently **p** their case so Jr 50:34
I am about to **p** your case and Jr 51:36
when I cry out and **p** for help, Lm 3:8
p ⌊your⌋ case before the Mc 6:1
their men to **p** for the LORD's Zch 7:2
go at once to **p** for the LORD's Zch 8:21
Jerusalem and to **p** for the Zch 8:22
through us, we **p** on Christ's 2Co 5:20

PLEADED *(14)*
deep distress when he **p** with us, Gn 42:21
a vow, she **p**, "LORD of Hosts, 1Sm 1:11
priests and the diviners and **p**, 1Sm 6:2
They **p** with Samuel, "Pray to the 1Sm 12:19
David **p** with God for the boy. 2Sm 12:16
"LORD," David **p**, "please turn 2Sm 15:31
go!" the people **p**. "If we have 2Sm 18:3
the man of God **p** for the favor 1Kg 13:6
So we fasted and **p** with our God Ezr 8:23
they **p** with Him earnestly, Lk 7:4
Jesus' feet and **p** with Him to Lk 8:41
father came out and **p** with him. Lk 15:28
went to Him and **p** with Him to Jn 4:47
I **p** with the Lord three times to 2Co 12:8

PLEADING *(8)*
will we gain by **p** with Him?" Jb 21:15
the sound of my **p** when I cry to Ps 28:2
He has heard the sound of my **p**. Ps 28:6
the sound of my **p** when I cried Ps 31:22
him with her persistent **p**; Pr 7:21
came to Him, **p** with Him, Mt 8:5
man was standing and **p** with him, Ac 16:9
p with him not to take a chance Ac 19:31

PLEADS *(5)*
Whoever **p** his case will be put Jdg 6:31
as a man ⌊**p**⌋ for his friend. Jb 16:21
The poor man **p**, but the rich one Pr 18:23
justly; no one **p** honestly. They Is 59:4
he **p** with God against Israel? Rm 11:2

PLEASANT *(17)*
good and that the land was **p**, Gn 49:15
what is **p** and what is not 2Sm 19:35
have fallen for me in **p** places; Ps 16:6
despised the **p** land and did not Ps 106:24
How good and **p** it is when Ps 133:1
for praise is **p** and lovely. Ps 147:1
Her ways are **p**, and all her Pr 3:17
down, and your sleep will be **p**. Pr 3:24
evil man, but **p** words are pure. Pr 15:26
and **p** speech increases learning. Pr 16:21
P words are a honeycomb: Pr 16:24
eaten and waste your **p** words. Pr 23:8
How beautiful you are and how **p**, Sg 7:6
My sleep had been most **p** to me. Jr 31:26
Whether it is **p** or unpleasant, Jr 42:6
because their shade is **p**. Hs 4:13
They turned a **p** land into a Zch 7:14

PLEASE *(195)*
P say you're my sister so it Gn 12:13
said to Lot, "**P**, let's not have Gn 13:8
p do not go on past your servant. Gn 18:3
Lot said to them, "No, Lord—**p**. Gn 19:18
P let me go there—it's only a Gn 19:20
of the land, "**P** listen to me. Gn 23:13
'**P** lower your water jug so that Gn 24:14
P let me have a little water Gn 24:17
P tell me, is there room in your Gn 24:23
P let me drink a little water Gn 24:43
P let me have a drink. Gn 24:45
P sit up and eat some of my game Gn 27:19
P come closer so I can touch Gn 27:21
P come closer and kiss me, Gn 27:26
P give me some of your son's Gn 30:14
P rescue me from the hand of my Gn 32:11
asked Him, "**P** tell me Your name Gn 32:29
But Jacob said, "No, **p**! Gn 33:10
P take my present that was Gn 33:11
P indulge me, my lord." Gn 33:15
P give her to him as a wife. Gn 34:8
P show kindness to me by Gn 40:14
p let your servant speak Gn 44:18
Now **p** let your servant remain Gn 44:33
his brothers, "**P**, come near me," Gn 45:4
p let your servants settle in Gn 47:4
favor with you, **p** tell Pharaoh Gn 50:4
P forgive your brothers' Gn 50:17
p forgive the transgression of Gn 50:17
Now **p** let us go on a three-day Ex 3:18
to the LORD, "**P**, Lord, I have Ex 4:10
Moses said, "**P**, Lord, send Ex 4:13
P let me return to my relatives Ex 4:18
P let us go on a three-day trip Ex 5:3
P forgive my sin once more and Ex 10:17
p erase me from the book You Ex 32:32
in Your sight, **p** teach me Your Ex 33:13
Moses said, "**P**, let me see Your Ex 33:18
sight, my Lord, **p** go with us. Ex 34:9
"**P** don't leave us," Moses said, Nm 10:31
me like this, **p** kill me right Nm 11:15
p don't hold against us this sin Nm 12:11
P don't let her be like a dead Nm 12:12
to the LORD, "God, **p** heal her!" Nm 12:13
P pardon the wrongdoing of this Nm 14:19
P let us travel through your Nm 20:17
P come and put a curse on these Nm 22:6
So **p** come and put a curse on Nm 22:17
P stay here overnight as the Nm 22:19
P come with me to another place Nm 23:13
Balak said to Balaam, "**P** come. Nm 23:27
P let me cross over and see the Dt 3:25
Now **p** swear to me by the LORD Jos 2:12
P make a treaty with us." Jos 9:6

P make a treaty with us." ' Jos 9:11
if it doesn't **p** you to worship Jos 24:15
P show us how to get into town, Jdg 1:24
P give me a little water to Jdg 4:19
said to Him, "**P** Sir, if the LORD Jdg 6:13
said to Him, "**P**, Lord, how can I Jdg 6:15
P do not leave this place until Jdg 6:18
P allow me to make one more test Jdg 6:39
P give some loaves of bread to Jdg 8:5
P speak in the presence of all Jdg 9:2
P let us travel through your land, Jdg 11:17
'**P** let us travel through your Jdg 11:19
told him, "**P** say Shibboleth. Jdg 12:6
Now **p** be careful not to drink Jdg 13:4
LORD and said, "**P** Lord, let the Jdg 13:8
"**P** stay here," Manoah told Him, Jdg 13:15
to Samson, "**P** tell me, where Jdg 16:6
Won't you **p** tell me how you can Jdg 16:10
Lord GOD, **p** remember me. Jdg 16:28
P inquire of God so we will know Jdg 18:5
P agree to stay overnight and Jdg 19:6
"**P** keep up your strength." Jdg 19:8
is coming. **P** spend the night Jdg 19:9
his master, "**P**, why not let us Jdg 19:11
"**P**, my lord," she said, "as sure 1Sm 1:26
P appoint me to some priestly 1Sm 2:36
Would you **p** tell me where the 1Sm 9:18
p forgive my sin and return with 1Sm 15:25
P honor me now before the elders 1Sm 15:30
'**P** let me go because our clan is 1Sm 20:29
P let my father and mother stay 1Sm 22:3
P don't let the king make an 1Sm 22:15
of Israel, **p** tell Your servant. 1Sm 23:11
P give whatever you can afford 1Sm 25:8
but **p** let your servant speak to 1Sm 25:24
P forgive your servant's offense, 1Sm 25:28
lord the king **p** hear the words 1Sm 26:19
Now **p** listen to your servant. 1Sm 28:22
p bless Your servant's house so 2Sm 7:29
'**P** let my sister Tamar come and 2Sm 13:5
P let my sister Tamar come and 2Sm 13:6
P go to your brother Amnon's 2Sm 13:7
P, speak to the king, for he 2Sm 13:13
his servants **p** come with your 2Sm 13:24
p let my brother Amnon go with 2Sm 13:26
She replied, "**P**, may the king 2Sm 14:11
the woman said, "**P**, may your 2Sm 14:12
P let me go to Hebron to fulfill 2Sm 15:7
p turn the counsel of Ahithophel 2Sm 15:31
P let me run and tell the king 2Sm 18:19
p let me run too behind the 2Sm 18:22
P let your servant return so 2Sm 19:37
P tell Joab to come here and let 2Sm 20:16
p take away Your servant's guilt. 2Sm 24:10
P, let us fall into the LORD's 2Sm 24:14
P, let Your hand be against me 2Sm 24:17
p come and let me advise you. 1Kg 1:12
P speak to King Solomon since he 1Kg 2:17
One woman said, "**P** my lord, this 1Kg 3:17
"but **p** don't have him killed!" 1Kg 3:26
p confirm what You promised to 1Kg 8:26
replied, "but **p** let me leave." 1Kg 11:22
P plead for the favor of the 1Kg 13:6
P bring me a little water in a 1Kg 17:10
P bring me a piece of bread in 1Kg 17:11
p let this boy's life return to 1Kg 17:21
P let me kiss my father and 1Kg 19:20
says, '**P** spare my life.' 1Kg 20:32
p ask what the LORD's will is." 1Kg 22:5
p let my life and the lives of 2Kg 1:13
Elisha answered, "**P**, let there 2Kg 2:9
p let them go and search for 2Kg 2:16
P send me one of the servants 2Kg 4:22
p accept a gift from your servant. 2Kg 5:15
p let two mule-loads of dirt be 2Kg 5:17
P give them 75 pounds of silver 2Kg 5:22
Naaman insisted, "**P**, accept 150 2Kg 5:23
P notice that the place where we 2Kg 6:1
P let us go to the Jordan where 2Kg 6:2
"**P** come with your servants." 2Kg 6:3
p open his eyes and let him see." 2Kg 6:17
P strike this nation with 2Kg 6:18
responded, "**P**, let ⌊messengers⌋ 2Kg 7:13
P speak to your servants in 2Kg 18:26
p save us from his hand so that 2Kg 19:19
P LORD, remember how I have 2Kg 20:3
p take away Your servant's guilt. 1Ch 21:8
P, let me fall into the LORD's 1Ch 21:13
p let Your hand be against me 1Ch 21:17
p confirm what You promised to 2Ch 6:17
p let Your eyes be open and Your 2Ch 6:40
people and **p** them by speaking 2Ch 10:7
p ask what the LORD's will is." 2Ch 18:4
P remember what You commanded Neh 1:8
P, Lord, let Your ear be Neh 1:11
P, let us stop charging this Neh 5:10
and our livestock as they **p**. Neh 9:37
Call out if you **p**. Will anyone Jb 5:1
But now, **p** look at me; Jb 6:28
P remember that You formed me Jb 10:9
That will **p** the LORD more than Ps 69:31
LORD, **p** grant us success! Ps 118:25
p accept my willing offerings of Ps 119:108
When a man's ways **p** the LORD, Pr 16:7
p judge between Me and My Is 5:3
P speak to your servants in Is 36:11
He said, "**P**, LORD, remember how Is 38:3
but it will accomplish what I **p**, Is 55:11
you do as you **p** on the day of Is 58:3
P look—all of us are Your Is 64:9
your sacrifices do not **p** Me. Jr 6:20
I give it to anyone I **p**. Jr 27:5
'**P** buy my field in Anathoth in Jr 32:8
P pray to the LORD our God for us! Jr 37:3
So now **p** listen, my lord the Jr 37:20
P test your servants for 10 Dn 1:12
They **p** the king with their evil, Hs 7:3
their sacrifices will not **p** Him. Hs 9:4
I said, "Lord GOD, **p** forgive! Am 7:2
Then I said, "Lord GOD, **p** stop! Am 7:5
P, Yahweh, don't let us perish Jnh 1:14
P, LORD, isn't this what I said Jnh 4:2
And now, LORD, **p** take my life Jnh 4:3
and Jerusalem will **p** the LORD as Mal 3:4
"**P** pray to the Lord for me," Ac 8:24
the flesh are unable to **p** God. Rm 8:8
and not to **p** ourselves. Rm 15:1
of us must **p** his neighbor for Rm 15:2
the Messiah did not **p** Himself. Rm 15:3
Lord—how he may **p** the Lord. 1Co 7:32
world—how he may **p** his wife— 1Co 7:33
how she may **p** her husband. 1Co 7:34
as I also try to **p** all people in 1Co 10:33
Or am I striving to **p** people? Gl 1:10
I were still trying to **p** people, Gl 1:10
in order to **p** men, but as slaves Eph 6:6
in order to **p** men, but ⌊work⌋ Col 3:22
speak, not to **p** men, but rather 1Th 2:4
us how you must walk and **p** God— 1Th 4:1
To **p** the recruiter, no one 2Tm 2:4
faith it is impossible to **p** God, Heb 11:6

PLEASED *(60)*

The proposal **p** Pharaoh and all Gn 41:37
Pharaoh and his servants were **p**. Gn 45:16
If You are **p** with me, don't let Nm 11:15
the LORD is **p** with us, He will Nm 14:8
saw that it **p** the LORD to bless Nm 24:1
had to say, they were **p**. Jos 22:30
were **p** with the report Jos 22:33
So the priest was **p** and took his Jdg 18:20
service, for I am **p** with him." 1Sm 16:22
p all the people and Saul's 1Sm 18:5
was reported to Saul, it **p** him. 1Sm 18:20
the king is **p** with you, and all 1Sm 18:22
he was **p** to become the king's 1Sm 18:26
now, if you are **p** with me, let 1Sm 20:29
note of this, and it **p** them. 2Sm 3:36
everything the king did **p** them. 2Sm 3:36
Now it **p** the Lord that Solomon 1Kg 3:10
but he was not **p** with them. 1Kg 9:12
You have been **p** to bless Your 1Ch 17:27
was **p** to make me king over all 1Ch 28:4
that You are **p** with uprightness 1Ch 29:17
The proposal **p** the king and the 2Ch 30:4
and it **p** the king to send me. Neh 2:6
to do as they **p** with them. Neh 9:24
This suggestion **p** the king, Est 2:4
The young woman **p** him and gained Est 2:9
The advice **p** Haman, so he had Est 5:14
the king is **p**, spare my life— Est 7:3
did what they **p** to those who Est 9:5
LORD, be **p** to deliver me; Ps 40:13
face, for You were **p** with them. Ps 44:3
You are not **p** with a burnt Ps 51:16
Hezekiah was **p** with them, and Is 39:2
The LORD was **p**, because of His Is 42:21
Yet the LORD was **p** to crush Him, Is 53:10
you repented and did what **p** Me, Jr 34:15
to gather all the lovers you **p**— Ezk 16:37
I am **p** to tell you about the Dn 4:2
have done just as You **p**." Jnh 1:14
was greatly **p** with the plant. Jnh 4:6
the LORD be **p** with thousands Mc 6:7
Then I will be **p** with it and be Hg 1:8
Would he be **p** with you or show Mal 1:8
I am not **p** with you," says the Mal 1:10
sight, and He is **p** with them," Mal 2:17
danced before them and **p** Herod. Mt 14:6
they did whatever they **p** to him. Mt 17:12
she **p** Herod and his guests. Mk 6:22
proposal **p** the whole company. Ac 6:5
When he saw that it **p** the Jews, Ac 12:3
and Achaia were **p** to make a Rm 15:26
Yes, they were **p**, and they are Rm 15:27
God was **p** to save those who 1Co 1:21
But God was not **p** with most of 1Co 10:5
of Christ, I am **p** in weaknesses, 2Co 12:10
called me by His grace, was **p** Gl 1:15
For God was **p** ⌊to have⌋ all His Col 1:19
you that we were **p** to share with 1Th 2:8
he was approved, having **p** God. Heb 11:5
for God is **p** with such Heb 13:16

PLEASES *(19)*

can do with me whatever **p** Him." 2Sm 15:26
if it **p** the king, let a search Ezr 5:17
king, "If it **p** the king, and if Neh 2:5
If it **p** the king, let me have Neh 2:7
young woman who **p** the king will Est 2:4
"If it **p** the king," Esther Est 5:4
of me and if it **p** the king to Est 5:8
said, "If it **p** the king, and I Est 8:5
name whatever **p** you concerning Est 8:8
answered, "If it **p** the king, may Est 9:13
heaven and does whatever He **p**. Ps 115:3
does whatever He **p** in heaven Ps 135:6
The one who **p** God will escape Ec 7:26
and choose what **p** Me, and hold Is 56:4
If it **p** you to come with me to Jr 40:4
The wind blows where it **p**. Jn 3:8
because I always do what **p** Him." Jn 8:29
good, and it **p** God our Savior, 1Tm 2:3
their parents, for this **p** God. 1Tm 5:4

PLEASING *(63)*

every tree **p** in appearance Gn 2:9
the LORD smelled the **p** aroma, Gn 8:21
It is a **p** aroma, a fire offering Ex 29:18
as a **p** aroma before the LORD; Ex 29:25
morning, as a **p** aroma, a fire Ex 29:41
offering of a **p** aroma to the Lv 1:9
offering of a **p** aroma to the Lv 1:13
offering of a **p** aroma to the Lv 1:17
offering of a **p** aroma to the Lv 2:2
offering of a **p** aroma to the Lv 2:9
on the altar as a **p** aroma. Lv 2:12
offering of a **p** aroma to the Lv 3:5
a fire offering for a **p** aroma. Lv 3:16
the altar as a **p** aroma to the Lv 4:31
the altar as a **p** aroma to the Lv 6:15
baked pieces, a **p** aroma to the Lv 6:21
a burnt offering for a **p** aroma, Lv 8:21
offering for a **p** aroma, Lv 8:28
the fat as a **p** aroma to the LORD Lv 17:6
to the LORD, a **p** aroma, and its Lv 23:13
offering of a **p** aroma to the Lv 23:18
not smell the **p** aroma of your Lv 26:31
to produce a **p** aroma for the Nm 15:3
offering as a **p** aroma to the Nm 15:7
fire offering of **p** aroma to the Nm 15:10
offering as a **p** aroma to the Nm 15:13
offering as a **p** aroma to the Nm 15:14
offering as a **p** aroma to the Nm 15:24
offering for a **p** aroma to the Nm 18:17
fire offering, a **p** aroma to Me. Nm 28:2
at Mount Sinai for a **p** aroma, Nm 28:6
fire offering, a **p** aroma to the Nm 28:8
burnt offering, a **p** aroma, a Nm 28:13
fire offering, a **p** aroma to the Nm 28:24
offering for a **p** aroma to the Nm 28:27
offering as a **p** aroma to the Nm 29:2
They are a **p** aroma, a fire Nm 29:6
offering to the LORD, a **p** aroma: Nm 29:8
offering as a **p** aroma to the Nm 29:13
offering as a **p** aroma to the Nm 29:36
was found **p** to the LORD God 1Kg 14:13

sacrifices of **p** aroma to the God Ezr 6:10
king and I am **p** in his sight, Est 8:5
The sacrifice **p** to God is a Ps 51:17
May my meditation be **p** to Him; Ps 104:34
to my words, for they are **p**. Ps 141:6
For it is **p** if you keep them Pr 22:18
the man who is **p** in His sight, Ec 2:26
the one who is **p** in God's sight. Ec 2:26
and it is **p** for the eyes to see Ec 11:7
they offered **p** aromas to all Ezk 6:13
them as a **p** aroma the food I Ezk 16:19
sent up their **p** aromas and Ezk 20:28
I will accept you as a **p** aroma. Ezk 20:41
sacrifice, holy and **p** to God; Rm 12:1
is the good, **p**, and perfect will Rm 12:2
make it our aim to be **p** to Him. 2Co 5:9
what is **p** to the Lord. Eph 5:10
a welcome sacrifice, **p** to God. Php 4:18
the Lord, fully **p** ⌊to Him⌋, Col 1:10
for this is **p** in the Lord. Col 3:20
in us what is **p** in His sight, Heb 13:21
and do what is **p** in His sight. 1Jn 3:22

PLEASURE *(32)*
the LORD take **p** in burnt 1Sm 15:22
him, since He takes **p** in him." Ps 22:8
and He takes **p** in his way. Ps 37:23
In Your good **p**, cause Zion to Ps 51:18
They take **p** in lying; Ps 62:4
the peoples who take **p** in war. Ps 68:30
commands, for I take **p** in it. Ps 119:35
the LORD takes **p** in His people; Ps 149:4
and take **p** in the wife of your Pr 5:18
conduct is **p** for a fool, Pr 10:23
The one who loves **p** will become Pr 21:17
test you with **p** and enjoy what Ec 2:1
and about **p**, "What does this Ec 2:2
I did not refuse myself any **p**, Ec 2:10
I took **p** in all my struggles. Ec 2:10
of fools is in a house of **p**. Ec 7:4
bread with **p**, and drink your Ec 9:7
will fulfill all My **p** and say to Is 44:28
your own **p**, or talking too Is 58:13
to them—they find no **p** in it. Jr 6:10
Do I take any **p** in the death of Ezk 18:23
don't I ⌊take **p**⌋ when he turns Ezk 18:23
I take no **p** in anyone's death. Ezk 18:32
I take no **p** in the death of the Ezk 33:11
because this was Your good **p**. Mt 11:26
because this was Your good **p**. Lk 10:21
to His good **p** that He planned Eph 1:9
lovers of **p** rather than lovers 2Tm 3:4
back, My soul has no **p** in him. Heb 10:38
enjoy the short-lived **p** of sin. Heb 11:25
spend it on your desires for **p**. Jms 4:3
They consider it a **p** to carouse 2Pt 2:13

PLEASURES *(3)*
Your right hand are eternal **p**. Ps 16:11
riches, and **p** of life, and Lk 8:14
of various passions and **p**, Ti 3:3

PLED *(1)*
after day and **p** with him until Jdg 16:16

PLEDGE *(7)*
your vow offerings that you **p**; Dt 12:17
though he gave his hand ⌊in **p**⌋. Ezk 17:18
himself with goods taken in **p**. Hab 2:6
those who bow and **p** loyalty to Zph 1:5
LORD but also **p** loyalty to Zph 1:5
have renounced their original **p**. 1Tm 5:12
but the **p** of a good conscience 1Pt 3:21

PLEDGED *(4)*
the two of us **p** in the name of 1Sm 20:42
p their allegiance to King 1Ch 29:24
They **p** to send their wives away, Ezr 10:19
p Myself to you, entered into a Ezk 16:8

PLEIADES *(3)*
the Bear, Orion, the **P**, and the Jb 9:9
chains of the **P** or loosen the Jb 38:31
One who made the **P** and Orion, Am 5:8

PLENTIFUL *(6)*
the ground, will be rich and **p**. Is 30:23
of branches because of **p** waters. Ezk 19:10
out because of the **p** water. Ezk 31:5
summon the grain and make it **p**, Ezk 36:29
and the produce of the field **p**, Ezk 36:30
is rich and their food **p**. Hab 1:16

PLENTY *(14)*
We have **p** of straw and feed, Gn 24:25
you will have **p** of food to eat Lv 26:5
He gave them **p** of provisions and 2Ch 11:23
and there is **p** left over because 2Ch 31:10
come and find **p** of water?" 2Ch 32:4
Your ways overflow with **p**. Ps 65:11
May there be **p** of grain in the Ps 72:16
his land will have **p** of food, Pr 12:11
his land will have **p** of food, Pr 28:19
and wide, with **p** of fire and Is 30:33
daughters had pride, **p** of food, Ezk 16:49
You will have **p** to eat and be Jl 2:26
there was **p** of water there. Jn 3:23
There was **p** of grass in that Jn 6:10

PLOT *(30)*
Jezebel in the **p** of land at 1Kg 21:23
Jezebel in the **p** of land at 2Kg 9:10
met Jehu at the **p** of land of 2Kg 9:21
throw him on the **p** of ground 2Kg 9:25
I repay you on this **p** of land,' 2Kg 9:26
and throw him on the **p** of land." 2Kg 9:26
'In the **p** of land at Jezreel, 2Kg 9:36
the field in the **p** of land at 2Kg 9:37
A **p** of ground full of barley was 1Ch 11:13
middle of the **p** and defended it 1Ch 11:14
threshing-floor **p** so that I may 1Ch 21:22
15 pounds of gold for the **p**. 1Ch 21:25
When Mordecai learned of the **p**, Est 2:22
and his **p** he had devised against Est 8:3
rebel and the peoples **p** in vain? Ps 2:1
they **p** treachery all day long. Ps 38:12
those who spy on me **p** together, Ps 71:10
the hearts of those who **p** evil, Pr 12:20
they have trampled My **p** of land. Jr 12:10
My desirable **p** into a desolate Jr 12:10
but they **p** evil against Me. Hs 7:15
evil desire, they **p** it together. Mc 7:3
Whatever you **p** against the LORD, Nah 1:9
and do not **p** evil in your hearts Zch 7:10
Do not **p** evil in your hearts Zch 8:17
and the peoples **p** futile things? Ac 4:25
their **p** became known to Saul. Ac 9:24
a **p** was devised against him by Ac 20:3
than 40 who had formed this **p**. Ac 23:13
there was a **p** against the man Ac 23:30

PLOTS *(14)*
p evil with perversity in his Pr 6:14
a heart that **p** wicked schemes, Pr 6:18
one who **p** evil will be called Pr 24:8
wheat in rows and barley in **p**, Is 28:25
and his mind **p** iniquity. Is 32:6
hatches **p** to destroy the needy Is 32:7
murderous **p** and shuts his eyes Is 33:15
they had devised **p** against me: Jr 11:19
all their deadly **p** against me. Jr 18:23
malice, all their **p** against me. Lm 3:60
insults, all their **p** against me. Lm 3:61
because **p** will be made against Dn 11:25
who **p** evil against the LORD, Nah 1:11
me through the **p** of the Jews— Ac 20:19

PLOTTED *(10)*
them, they **p** to kill him. Gn 37:18
us and **p** to exterminate us 2Sm 21:5
They all **p** together to come and Neh 4:8
p against the Jews to destroy Est 9:24
me, they **p** to take my life Ps 31:13
Remaliah, has **p** harm against you Is 7:5
went out and **p** against Him, Mt 12:14
went and **p** how to trap Him Mt 22:15
of the people **p** against Jesus to Mt 27:1
that day on they **p** to kill Him. Jn 11:53

PLOTTING *(3)*
Saul was **p** evil against him, 1Sm 23:9
of their own **p**, for they have Jr 6:19
out and started **p** with the Mk 3:6

PLOW *(11)*
Do not **p** with an ox and a donkey Dt 22:10
to **p** his ground or reap his 1Sm 8:12
the oxen's wooden yoke and **p**, 1Kg 19:21
those who **p** injustice and those Jb 4:8
it **p** the valleys behind you? Jb 39:10
does not **p** during planting Pr 20:4
Does the plowman **p** every day to Is 28:24
Judah will **p**; Jacob will do Hs 10:11
does someone **p** ⌊it⌋ with oxen? Am 6:12
his hand to the **p** and looks back Lk 9:62
he who plows ought to **p** in hope, 1Co 9:10

PLOWED *(5)*
If you hadn't **p** with my young Jdg 14:18
Plowmen **p** over my back; Ps 129:3
Zion will be **p** like a field, Jr 26:18
You have **p** wickedness and reaped Hs 10:13
Zion will be **p** like a field, Mc 3:12

PLOWING *(6)*
years without **p** or harvesting. Gn 45:6
rest during **p** and harvesting Ex 34:21
son of Shaphat as he was **p**. 1Kg 19:19
the oxen were **p** and the donkeys Jb 1:14
Jacob will do the final **p**. Hs 10:11
having a slave **p** or tending Lk 17:7

PLOWMAN *(2)*
Does the **p** plow every day to Is 28:24
when the **p** will overtake the Am 9:13

PLOWMEN *(2)*
P plowed over my back; Ps 129:3
will be your **p** and vinedressers. Is 61:5

PLOWS *(4)*
As when one **p** and breaks up the Ps 141:7
swords into **p** and their spears Is 2:4
will beat their swords into **p**, Mc 4:3
because he who **p** ought to plow 1Co 9:10

PLOWSHARES *(3)*
Philistines to sharpen their **p**, 1Sm 13:20
of a shekel for **p** and mattocks, 1Sm 13:21
Hammer your **p** into swords and Jl 3:10

PLUCK *(3)*
you may **p** heads of grain with Dt 23:25
of the valley **p** it out and young Pr 30:17
I will **p** a tender sprig from its Ezk 17:22

PLUCKED *(4)*
there was a **p** olive leaf in her Gn 8:11
They **p** mallow among the shrubs, Jb 30:4
My dwelling is **p** up and removed Is 38:12
He **p** off its topmost shoot, Ezk 17:4

PLUMAGE *(3)*
feathers and **p** like the stork's Jb 39:13
and full **p** of many colors came Ezk 17:3
with great wings and thick **p**. Ezk 17:7

PLUMB *(5)*
line and a **p** line over her for Is 34:11
wall with a **p** line in His hand. Am 7:7
I replied, "A **p** line." Am 7:8
I am setting a **p** line among My Am 7:8
when they see the **p** line in Zch 4:10

PLUNDER *(89)*
the evening he divides the **p**." Gn 49:27
So you will **p** the Egyptians." Ex 3:22
little children will become **p**. Nm 14:3
would become **p** into the land you Nm 14:31
from the **p** the army had taken Nm 31:32
had taken **p** for himself. Nm 31:53
who you said would be **p**, Dt 1:39
we captured as **p** for ourselves. Dt 2:35
the cities as **p** for ourselves. Dt 3:7
the city—all its spoil—as **p**. Dt 20:14
may **p** its spoil and livestock Jos 8:2
give me an earring from his **p**." Jdg 8:24
an earring from his **p** on it. Jdg 8:25
today from the **p** they took from 1Sm 14:30
rushed to the **p**, took sheep, 1Sm 14:32
and **p** them until morning. 1Sm 14:36
rush on the **p** and do what was 1Sm 15:19
sheep and cattle from the **p**— 1Sm 15:21
great amount of **p** they had taken 1Sm 30:16
of all the **p** the Amalekites had 1Sm 30:19
shouted, "This is David's **p**!" 1Sm 30:20
give any of the **p** we recovered 1Sm 30:22
some of the **p** to his friends, 1Sm 30:26
for you from the **p** of the LORD's 1Sm 30:26
quantity of **p** from the city. 2Sm 12:30
to him, but only to **p** the dead. 2Sm 23:10
will become **p** and spoil to all 2Kg 21:14
quantity of **p** from the city. 1Ch 20:2
part of the **p** from their battles 1Ch 26:27
was a great deal of **p** in them. 2Ch 14:14
from all the **p** they had brought 2Ch 15:11
his people went to gather the **p**. 2Ch 20:25
gathering the **p** for three days 2Ch 20:25
and sent all the **p** to the king 2Ch 24:23
and took a great deal of **p**. 2Ch 25:13

took a great deal of **p** from them 2Ch 28:8
and the **p** in the presence 2Ch 28:14
for their naked ones from the **p**. 2Ch 28:15
rulers and gave the **p** to the 2Ch 28:21
let them be taken as **p** to a land Neh 4:4
and **p** their possessions on a Est 3:13
they did not seize any **p**. Est 9:10
but they did not seize any **p**. Est 9:15
but they did not seize any **p**. Est 9:16
us have taken **p** for themselves. Ps 44:10
All who pass by **p** him; Ps 89:41
let strangers **p** what he has Ps 109:11
and fill our houses with **p**. Pr 1:13
than to divide **p** with the proud. Pr 16:19
and will **p** those who plunder Pr 22:23
will plunder those who **p** them. Pr 22:23
The **p** from the poor is in your Is 3:14
and they can **p** the fatherless. Is 10:2
spoils, to **p**, and to trample Is 10:6
Together they will **p** the people Is 11:14
of those who **p** us and the lot Is 17:14
be divided, the lame will **p** it, Is 33:23
have become **p**, with no one to Is 42:22
your treasures I will give as **p**, Jr 15:13
I will give up as **p** because of Jr 17:3
They will **p** them, seize them, Jr 20:5
and all who **p** you will be Jr 30:16
Their camels will become **p**, Jr 49:32
The Chaldeans will become **p**; Jr 50:10
to foreigners as **p** and to the Ezk 7:21
consign them to terror and **p**. Ezk 23:46
give you as **p** to the nations. Ezk 25:7
will become **p** for the nations Ezk 26:5
as spoil and **p** your merchandise. Ezk 26:12
its spoil and taking its **p**. Ezk 29:19
have become **p** and a mockery to Ezk 36:4
that its pastureland became **p**. Ezk 36:5
to seize spoil and carry off **p**, Ezk 38:12
your hordes to carry off **p**, Ezk 38:13
looted them and **p** those who Ezk 39:10
He will lavish **p**, loot, and Dn 11:24
The wind will **p** the treasury of Hs 13:15
strongholds and **p** your citadels. Am 3:11
"**P** the silver! Plunder the gold!" Nah 2:9
the silver! **P** the gold!" There Nah 2:9
full of **p**, never without Nah 3:1
peoples who remain will **p** you— Hab 2:8
will become **p** and their houses Zph 1:13
of My people will **p** them; Zph 2:9
until the day I rise up for **p**. Zph 3:8
they will become **p** for their own Zch 2:9
when your **p** will be divided Zch 14:1
in, and divides up his **p**. Lk 11:22
patriarch gave a tenth of the **p**! Heb 7:4

PLUNDERED *(25)*
slaughter and **p** the city because Gn 34:27
and **p** everything in the houses. Gn 34:29
this way they **p** the Egyptians. Ex 12:36
and they **p** all their cattle, Nm 31:9
Israel **p** only the cattle and Jos 8:27
The Israelites **p** all the spoils Jos 11:14
the hand of those who **p** them. 1Sm 14:48
Philistines, they **p** their camps. 1Sm 17:53
amount of **p** goods with them 2Sm 3:22
went out and **p** the Aramean camp. 2Kg 7:16
They also **p** all the cities, 2Ch 14:14
Although Ahaz **p** the LORD's 2Ch 28:21
with me or have **p** my adversary Ps 7:4
The brave-hearted have been **p**; Ps 76:5
nations and **p** their treasures; Is 10:13
bare and will be totally **p**, Is 24:3
this is a people **p** and looted, Is 42:22
whoever turns from evil is **p**. Is 59:15
all who plunder you will be **p**. Jr 30:16
you who **p** My inheritance— Jr 50:11
treasuries, and they will be **p**. Jr 50:37
and plunder those who **p** them." Ezk 39:10
be captured and **p** for a time. Dn 11:33
devote what they **p** to the LORD, Mc 4:13
Since you have **p** many nations, Hab 2:8

PLUNDERERS *(3)*
them over to **p** until He had 2Kg 17:20
the robber, and Israel to the **p**? Is 42:24
all her **p** will be fully Jr 50:10

PLUNDERING *(2)*
captivity, **p**, and open shame, Ezr 9:7
the nations who are **p** you, Zch 2:8

PLUNGE *(3)*
and **p** it into the container or 1Sm 2:14
which **p** people into ruin and 1Tm 6:9
that you don't **p** with them into 1Pt 4:4

PLUNGED *(3)*
and **p** it into Eglon's belly. Jdg 3:21
stripped) and **p** into the sea. Jn 21:7
his kingdom was **p** into darkness. Rv 16:10

PLUNGING *(1)*
I will send hailstones **p** down, Ezk 13:11

PLUS *(7)*
p 3,000 bulls from his own 2Ch 35:7
for the Levites, **p** 500 bulls. 2Ch 35:9
p Hashabiah, along with Jeshaiah, Ezr 8:19
p Libya and the men of the Ezk 30:5
standard length **p** three inches. Ezk 40:5
standard length **p** three inches Ezk 43:13
countless thousands, **p** thousands Rv 5:11

POCHERETH-HAZZEBAIM'S *(2)*
descendants, **P** descendants, Ezr 2:57
descendants, **P** descendants, Neh 7:59

PODS *(1)*
from the carob **p** the pigs were Lk 15:16

POEM *(8)*
Balaam proclaimed his **p**: Nm 23:7
Balaam proclaimed his **p**: Nm 23:18
and he proclaimed his **p**: Nm 24:3
Then he proclaimed his **p**: Nm 24:15
saw Amalek and proclaimed his **p**: Nm 24:20
Kenites and proclaimed his **p**: Nm 24:21
Once more he proclaimed his **p**: Nm 24:23
A **p** by Hezekiah king of Judah Is 38:9

POETS *(2)*
Therefore the **p** say: Come to Nm 21:27
some of your own **p** have said, Ac 17:28

POINT *(28)*
p out anything that is yours and Gn 31:32
at this **p** the priest must make Nm 5:21
LORD has helped us to this **p**." 1Sm 7:12
for putting a **p** on an oxgoad. 1Sm 13:21
and the iron **p** of his spear 1Sm 17:7
to the **p** of making himself 2Sm 13:2
him to the **p** of embarrassment 2Kg 2:17
have come to the **p** of birth, 2Kg 19:3
came to the **p** in Jerusalem and 2Kg 24:20
became sick to the **p** of death, 2Ch 32:24
repairs up to ⌊a **p**⌋ opposite the Neh 3:16
section from ⌊a **p**⌋ opposite the Neh 3:27
at the highest **p** of the city, Pr 9:14
children come to the **p** of birth, Is 37:3
a baby to the **p** of birth and not Is 66:9
With a diamond **p** it is engraved Jr 17:1
came to the **p** in Jerusalem and Jr 52:3
border up to a **p** opposite Ezk 47:20
on Jesus began to **p** out to His Mt 16:21
in sorrow—to the **p** of death. Mt 26:38
in sorrow—to the **p** of death. Mk 14:34
not based on a human **p** of view. Gl 1:11
obedient to the **p** of death— Php 2:8
If you **p** these things out to the 1Tm 4:6
to the **p** of being bound like a 2Tm 2:9
Now the main **p** of what is being Heb 8:1
resisted to the **p** of shedding Heb 12:4
yet fails in one **p**, is guilty Jms 2:10

POINTED *(1)*
was a man **p** out to you by God Ac 2:22

POINTING *(1)*
⌊**p**⌋ toward the four winds of Dn 8:8

POINTS *(5)*
the starting **p** for the stages Nm 33:2
listed⌋ by their starting **p**: Nm 33:2
from the highest **p** of the city: Pr 9:3
him ten thousand **p** of My law, Hs 8:12
more boldly on some **p** because of Rm 15:15

POISON *(7)*
venom, the deadly **p** of cobras. Dt 32:33
my spirit drinks their **p**. Jb 6:4
He will suck the **p** of cobras; Jb 20:16
Lethal **p** has been poured into Ps 41:8
the wormwood and the **p**. Lm 3:19
justice into **p** and the fruit Am 6:12
restless evil, full of deadly **p**. Jms 3:8

POISONED *(4)*
has given us **p** water to drink, Jr 8:14
and give them **p** water to drink, Jr 23:15
I see you are **p** by bitterness Ac 8:23
stirred up and **p** the minds Ac 14:2

POISONOUS *(7)*
the LORD sent **p** snakes among Nm 21:6
wilderness with its **p** snakes and Dt 8:15
you bearing **p** and bitter fruit Dt 29:18
Their grapes are **p**; Dt 32:32
p vipers that cannot be charmed. Jr 8:17
and give them **p** waters to drink. Jr 9:15
break out like **p** weeds in the Hs 10:4

POLE *(12)*
was carried on a **p** by two men. Nm 13:23
image⌋ and mount it on a **p**. Nm 21:8
snake and mounted it on a **p**. Nm 21:9
down the Asherah **p** beside it. Jdg 6:25
of the Asherah **p** you cut down." Jdg 6:26
Asherah **p** beside it cut down, Jdg 6:28
down the Asherah **p** beside it." Jdg 6:30
Ahab also made an Asherah **p**. 1Kg 16:33
and the Asherah **p** also remained 2Kg 13:6
two calves—and an Asherah **p**. 2Kg 17:16
the Asherah **p** from the LORD's 2Kg 23:6
a ⌊solitary⌋ **p** on a mountaintop Is 30:17

POLES *(57)*
p of acacia wood and overlay Ex 25:13
Insert the **p** into the rings on Ex 25:14
The **p** are to remain in the rings Ex 25:15
holders for the **p** to carry the Ex 25:27
Make the **p** of acacia wood and Ex 25:28
Then make **p** for the altar, Ex 27:6
for the altar, **p** of acacia wood, Ex 27:6
p are to be inserted into the Ex 27:7
that the **p** are on two sides of Ex 27:7
holders for the **p** to carry it Ex 30:4
Make the **p** of acacia wood and Ex 30:5
and chop down their Asherah **p**. Ex 34:13
ark with its **p**, the mercy seat Ex 35:12
table with its **p**, all its Ex 35:13
the altar of incense with its **p**; Ex 35:15
bronze grate, its **p**, and all its Ex 35:16
He made **p** of acacia wood and Ex 37:4
He inserted the **p** into the rings Ex 37:5
holders for the **p** to carry the Ex 37:14
He made the **p** for carrying the Ex 37:15
holders for the **p** to carry it Ex 37:27
He made the **p** of acacia wood and Ex 37:28
four rings as holders for the **p**. Ex 38:5
also made the **p** of acacia wood Ex 38:6
he inserted the **p** into the rings Ex 38:7
with its **p** and the mercy seat Ex 39:35
bronze grate, its **p**, and all its Ex 39:39
and attached the **p** to the ark. Ex 40:20
cloth on top, and insert its **p**. Nm 4:6
and insert the **p** ⌊in the table⌋. Nm 4:8
manatee skin, and insert its **p**. Nm 4:11
skin over it and insert its **p**. Nm 4:14
their Asherah **p**, and burn up Dt 7:5
up their Asherah **p**, cut down the Dt 12:3
the ark and its **p** from above. 1Kg 8:7
The **p** were so long that their 1Kg 8:8
they made their Asherah **p**, 1Kg 14:15
and Asherah **p** on every high hill 1Kg 14:23
and Asherah **p** on every high hill 2Kg 17:10
and cut down the Asherah ⌊**p**⌋. 2Kg 18:4
down the Asherah **p**, then filled 2Kg 23:14
on their shoulders with the **p**. 1Ch 15:15
a cover above the ark and its **p**. 2Ch 5:8
The **p** were so long that their 2Ch 5:9
chopped down their Asherah **p**. 2Ch 14:3
places and Asherah **p** from Judah. 2Ch 17:6
the Asherah **p** from the land 2Ch 19:3
the Asherah **p** and the idols. 2Ch 24:18
chopped down the Asherah **p**, 2Ch 31:1
He made Asherah **p**, and he 2Ch 33:3
set up Asherah **p** and carved 2Ch 33:19
the Asherah **p**, the carved images 2Ch 34:3
Asherah **p**, the carved images, 2Ch 34:4
the Asherah **p** and the carved 2Ch 34:7
no Asherah **p** or incense altars Is 27:9
altars and their Asherah **p**, Jr 17:2
up the Asherah **p** from among you Mc 5:14

POLICE *(18)*
with the temple **p** to see the Mt 26:58
was sitting with the temple **p**, Mk 14:54
Even the temple **p** took Him and Mk 14:65
and temple **p** how he could hand Lk 22:4
priests, temple **p**, and the Lk 22:52

sent temple **p** to arrest Him. Jn 7:32
Then the temple **p** came to the Jn 7:45
The **p** answered, "No man ever Jn 7:46
and some temple **p** from the chief Jn 18:3
Jewish temple **p** arrested Jesus Jn 18:12
and the temple **p** had made a Jn 18:18
one of the temple **p** standing by Jn 18:22
and the temple **p** saw Him, Jn 19:6
But when the temple **p** got there, Ac 5:22
of the temple **p** and the chief Ac 5:24
with the temple **p** and brought Ac 5:26
magistrates sent the **p** to say, Ac 16:35
Then the **p** reported these words Ac 16:38

POLICIES *(1)*
you have followed their **p**. Mc 6:16

POLICY *(1)*
established ⌊this **p**⌋ as a law 1Sm 30:25

POLISH *(1)*
helmets on! **P** the lances; put Jr 46:4

POLISHED *(8)*
these were made⌋ of **p** bronze. 2Ch 4:16
like the gleam of **p** bronze. Ezk 1:7
A sword is sharpened and also **p**. Ezk 21:9
p to flash like lightning! Ezk 21:10
The sword is given to be **p**, Ezk 21:11
sharpened, and it is **p**, to be Ezk 21:11
for slaughter, **p** to consume, to Ezk 21:28
feet like the gleam of **p** bronze, Dn 10:6

POLLUTED *(7)*
so the land became **p** with blood. Ps 106:38
a muddied spring or a **p** well. Pr 25:26
The earth is **p** by its Is 24:5
acts are like a **p** garment; Is 64:6
and putting **p** broth in their Is 65:4
sin because they have **p** My land. Jr 16:18
abstain from things **p** by idols, Ac 15:20

POLLUTES *(1)*
it **p** the whole body, sets the Jms 3:6

POLLUTING *(1)*
who follow the **p** desires of the 2Pt 2:10

POMEGRANATE *(7)*
a bell and a **p** alternating all Ex 39:26
under the **p** tree in Migron 1Sm 14:2
your brow is like a slice of **p**. Sg 4:3
your brow is like a slice of **p**. Sg 6:7
wine to drink from my **p** juice. Sg 8:2
the **p**, the date palm, and the Jl 1:12
the fig, the **p**, and the olive Hg 2:19

POMEGRANATES *(23)*
Make **p** of blue, purple, and Ex 28:33
bells and **p** alternate around Ex 28:34
They made **p** of finely spun blue, Ex 39:24
the bells between the **p**, Ex 39:25
hem of the robe between the **p**, Ex 39:25
also ⌊took⌋ some **p** and figs. Nm 13:23
vines, and **p**, and there is no Nm 20:5
barley, vines, figs, and **p**; Dt 8:8
rows of **p** on the one grating 1Kg 7:18
200 **p** were in rows encircling 1Kg 7:20
the 400 **p** for the two gratings 1Kg 7:42
two rows of **p** for each grating 1Kg 7:42
by a grating and **p** of bronze, 2Kg 25:17
He made 100 **p** and fastened them 2Ch 3:16
the 400 **p** for the two gratings 2Ch 4:13
two rows of **p** for each grating 2Ch 4:13
a paradise of **p** with choicest Sg 4:13
were budding and the **p** blooming. Sg 6:11
opened, if the **p** are in bloom. Sg 7:12
by bronze latticework and **p**, Jr 52:22
pillar was the same, with **p**. Jr 52:22
capital had⌋ 96 **p** all around it. Jr 52:23
All the **p** around the latticework Jr 52:23

POMP *(1)*
came with great **p** and entered Ac 25:23

PONDERS *(1)*
in my heart, and my spirit **p**. Ps 77:6

PONDS *(2)*
rivers, canals, **p**, and all their Ex 7:19
rivers, canals, and **p**, and cause Ex 8:5

PONTIUS *(3)*
while **P** Pilate was governor of Lk 3:1
city both Herod and **P** Pilate, Ac 4:27
good confession before **P** Pilate, 1Tm 6:13

PONTUS *(3)*
and Cappadocia, **P** and Asia, Ac 2:9
a native of **P**, who had recently Ac 18:2
in the provinces of **P**, 1Pt 1:1

POOL *(23)*
and met them by the **p** of Gibeon. 2Sm 2:13
on opposite sides of the **p**. 2Sm 2:13
bodies⌋ by the **p** in Hebron, 2Sm 4:12
the chariot at the **p** of Samaria. 1Kg 22:38
by the aqueduct of the upper **p**, 2Kg 18:17
how he made the **p** and the tunnel 2Kg 20:20
Fountain Gate and the King's **P**, Neh 2:14
the wall of the **P** of Shelah near Neh 3:15
the artificial **p** and the House Neh 3:16
a desert into a **p** of water, Ps 107:35
the rock into a **p** of water, Ps 114:8
of the conduit of the upper **p**, Is 7:3
water from the lower **p**. Is 22:9
for the waters of the ancient **p**, Is 22:11
ground will become a **p** of water, Is 35:7
near the conduit of the upper **p**, Is 36:2
desert into a **p** of water and dry Is 41:18
him by the great **p** in Gibeon. Jr 41:12
been like a **p** of water from her Nah 2:8
Gate in Jerusalem there is a **p**, Jn 5:2
go down into the **p** from time to Jn 5:4
put me into the **p** when the water Jn 5:7
"wash in the **p** of Siloam" Jn 9:7

POOLS *(1)*
your eyes like **p** in Heshbon by Sg 7:4

POOR *(173)*
eyesight was **p** because of old Gn 48:10
since I am such a **p** speaker?" Ex 6:12
Since I am such a **p** speaker, Ex 6:30
to the **p** person among you, Ex 22:25
favoritism to a **p** person in his Ex 23:3
justice to the **p** among you in Ex 23:6
so that the **p** among your people Ex 23:11
and the **p** may not give less, Ex 30:15
But if he is **p** and cannot afford Lv 14:21
them for the **p** and the foreign Lv 19:10
be partial to the **p** or give Lv 19:15
them for the **p** and the foreign Lv 23:22
But if one is too **p** to pay the Lv 27:8
There will be no **p** among you, Dt 15:4
If there is a **p** person among Dt 15:7
toward your **p** brother. Dt 15:7
toward your **p** brother and give Dt 15:9
never cease to be **p** people in Dt 15:11
afflicted and **p** brother in your Dt 15:11
If he is a **p** man, you must not Dt 24:12
a hired hand who is **p** and needy, Dt 24:14
because he is **p** and depends on Dt 24:15
younger men, whether rich or **p**. Ru 3:10
raises the **p** from the dust and 1Sm 2:8
I am a **p** man who is common." 1Sm 18:23
city, one rich and the other **p**. 2Sm 12:1
but the **p** man had nothing except 2Sm 12:3
he took the **p** man's lamb and 2Sm 12:4
gifts to one another and the **p**. Est 9:22
the **p** have hope, and injustice Jb 5:16
children will beg from the **p**, Jb 20:10
oppressed and abandoned the **p**; Jb 20:19
p of the land are forced into Jb 24:4
the **p** go out to their task of Jb 24:5
child of the **p** is seized as Jb 24:9
at dawn to kill the **p** and needy, Jb 24:14
I rescued the **p** man who cried Jb 29:12
the wishes of the **p** or let the Jb 31:16
not favor the rich over the **p**, Jb 34:19
but caused the **p** to cry out to Jb 34:28
and the groaning of the **p**, Ps 12:5
This **p** man cried, and the LORD Ps 34:6
rescuing the **p** from one too Ps 35:10
the **p** or the needy from one who Ps 35:10
is one who cares for the **p**; Ps 41:1
and high, rich and **p** together. Ps 49:2
goodness You provided for the **p**, Ps 68:10
But as for me—**p** and in pain— Ps 69:29
people, help the **p**, and crush Ps 72:4
he will rescue the **p** who cry out Ps 72:12
have pity on the **p** and helpless Ps 72:13
and save the lives of the **p**. Ps 72:13
lives of Your **p** people forever. Ps 74:19
let the **p** and needy praise Your Ps 74:21
Rescue the **p** and needy; Ps 82:4
answer me, for I am **p** and needy. Ps 86:1
pursued the wretched **p** and the Ps 109:16
For I am **p** and needy; my heart Ps 109:22
He distributes freely to the **p**; Ps 112:9
raises the **p** from the dust and Ps 113:7
upholds the just cause of the **p**, Ps 140:12
hands make one **p**, but diligent Pr 10:4
the poverty of the **p** is their Pr 10:15
what is right, only to become **p**. Pr 11:24
pretends to be **p** but has great Pr 13:7
but a **p** man hears no threat. Pr 13:8
field of the **p** yields abundant Pr 13:23
A **p** man is hated even by his Pr 14:20
kindness to the **p** will be happy. Pr 14:21
oppresses the **p** insults their Pr 14:31
who mocks the **p** insults his Pr 17:5
The **p** man pleads, but the rich Pr 18:23
Better a **p** man who walks in Pr 19:1
a **p** man is separated from his Pr 19:4
brothers of a **p** man hate him; Pr 19:7
Kindness to the **p** is a loan to Pr 19:17
better to be a **p** man than a Pr 19:22
sleep, or you will become **p**; Pr 20:13
who is reckless only becomes **p**. Pr 21:5
the cry of the **p** will himself Pr 21:13
pleasure will become a **p** man; Pr 21:17
The rich and the **p** have this in Pr 22:2
rule over the **p**, and the Pr 22:7
he shares his food with the **p**. Pr 22:9
Oppressing the **p** to enrich Pr 22:16
Don't rob a **p** man because he is Pr 22:22
rob a poor man because he is **p**, Pr 22:22
and the glutton will become **p**, Pr 23:21
oppresses the **p** is like a Pr 28:3
Better a **p** man who lives with Pr 28:6
it for one who is kind to the **p**. Pr 28:8
but a **p** man who has discernment Pr 28:11
who gives to the **p** will not be Pr 28:27
knows the rights of the **p**, Pr 29:7
p and the oppressor have this Pr 29:13
who judges the **p** with fairness— Pr 29:14
Her hands reach out to the **p**, Pr 31:20
Better is a **p** but wise youth Ec 4:13
he was born **p** in his kingdom. Ec 4:14
of the **p** and perversion Ec 5:8
there for the **p** person who knows Ec 6:8
a **p** wise man was found in the Ec 9:15
no one remembered that **p** man. Ec 9:15
wisdom of the **p** man is despised Ec 9:16
plunder from the **p** is in your Is 3:14
and grind the faces of the **p**?" Is 3:15
keep the **p** from getting a fair Is 10:2
He will judge the **p** righteously Is 11:4
of the **p** will be well fed Is 14:30
been a stronghold for the **p**, Is 25:4
the humble, the steps of the **p**. Is 26:6
and the **p** people will rejoice in Is 29:19
by charging the **p** during a Is 32:7
The **p** and the needy seek water, Is 41:17
P ⌊Jerusalem⌋, storm-tossed, and Is 54:11
to bring the **p** and homeless into Is 58:7
Me to bring good news to the **p**. Is 61:1
the blood of the innocent **p**. Jr 2:34
are just the **p**; they have played Jr 5:4
up the case of the **p** and needy, Jr 22:16
some of the **p** people who owned Jr 39:10
But some of the **p** people of the Jr 52:16
didn't support the **p** and needy. Ezk 16:49
he oppresses the **p** and needy, Ezk 18:12
his hand from ⌊harming⌋ the **p**, Ezk 18:17
have oppressed the **p** and needy Ezk 22:29
the heads of the **p** on the dust Am 2:7
who oppress the **p** and crush the Am 4:1
trample on the **p** and exact a Am 5:11
and deprive the **p** of justice at Am 5:12
do away with the **p** of the land, Am 8:4
We can buy the **p** with silver and Am 8:6
stranger or the **p**, and do not Zch 7:10
Blessed are the **p** in spirit, Mt 5:3
So whenever you give to the **p**, Mt 6:2
But when you give to the **p**, Mt 6:3
the **p** are told the good news. Mt 11:5
belongings and give to the **p**, Mt 19:21
great deal and given to the **p**." Mt 26:9
You always have the **p** with you, Mt 26:11
all you have and give to the **p**, Mk 10:21
And a **p** widow came and dropped Mk 12:42
p widow has put in more than Mk 12:43
300 denarii and given to the **p**." Mk 14:5
You always have the **p** with you, Mk 14:7
Me to preach good news to the **p**. Lk 4:18
Blessed are you who are **p**, Lk 6:20

P yourselves, stand still, and 2Ch 20:17
his **p** by killing with 2Ch 21:4
strengthened his **p** and led his 2Ch 25:11
strengthened his **p** by rebuilding 2Ch 32:5
and her royal **p** is to be given Est 1:19
gave him a higher **p** than all the Est 3:1
him a high **p** over the other Est 5:11
mine, they run and take up a **p**. Ps 59:4
bring him down from his high **p**. Ps 62:4
let another take over his **p**. Ps 109:8
He set them in **p** forever and Ps 148:6
you will be ousted from your **p**. Is 22:19
third highest **p** in the kingdom. Dn 5:7
third highest **p** in the kingdom. Dn 5:16
the men of high **p** exercise power Mt 20:25
and Let someone else take his **p**. Ac 1:20
keep their own **p** but deserted Jd 6

POSITIONED *(4)*

he laid its bases, **p** its planks, Ex 40:18
place where they **p** themselves Jdg 20:22
horsemen were **p** at the gates. Is 22:7
right hand is **p** like an Lm 2:4

POSITIONS *(14)*

their battle **p** against Gibeah. Jdg 20:20
their battle **p** in the same place Jdg 20:22
their battle **p** against Gibeah as Jdg 20:30
their battle **p** at Baal-tamar, Jdg 20:33
groups took up **p** on opposite 2Sm 2:13
his servants, "Take ⌊your⌋ **p**." 1Kg 20:12
took ⌊their⌋ **p** against the city 1Kg 20:12
them to their trusted **p**. 1Ch 9:22
took their **p** to praise the LORD, Ezr 3:10
the highest **p** in the kingdom. Est 1:14
but the rich remain in lowly **p**. Ec 10:6
take your **p** with helmets on! Jr 46:4
Say: Take **p**! Prepare yourself, Jr 46:14
men of high **p** exercise power Mk 10:42

POSITIVE *(1)*

that the interpretation was **p**, Gn 40:16

POSSESS *(76)*

to give you this land to **p**." Gn 15:7
can I know that I will **p** it?" Gn 15:8
offspring will **p** the gates of Gn 22:17
your offspring **p** the gates of Gn 24:60
so that you may **p** the land where Gn 28:4
in a house in the land you **p**, Lv 14:34
I will give it to you to **p**, Lv 20:24
houses in the cities they **p**. Lv 25:32
a house sold in a city they **p**— Lv 25:33
I have given you the land to **p**. Nm 33:53
will **p** the inheritance Nm 36:8
has given you this land to **p**. Dt 3:18
the land you are entering to **p**. Dt 4:5
are about to cross into and **p**. Dt 4:14
about to cross the Jordan to **p**. Dt 4:26
the land I am giving them to **p**.' Dt 5:31
life in the land you will **p**. Dt 5:33
you are about to enter and **p**. Dt 6:1
may enter and **p** the good land Dt 6:18
the land you are entering to **p**, Dt 7:1
good land to **p** because of your Dt 9:6
'Go up and **p** the land I have Dt 9:23
may enter and **p** the land I swore Dt 10:11
cross into and **p** the land you Dt 11:8
are entering to **p** is not like Dt 11:10
you are entering to **p** is a land Dt 11:11
the land you are entering to **p**, Dt 11:29
When you **p** it and settle in it, Dt 11:31
given you to **p** all the days you Dt 12:1
is giving you to **p** as an Dt 15:4
will live and **p** the land the Dt 16:20
your God is giving you to **p**. Dt 19:2
your God is giving you to **p**. Dt 19:14
your God is giving you to **p**, Dt 21:1
the land you are entering to **p**. Dt 23:20
is giving you to **p** as an Dt 25:19
the land you are entering to **p**. Dt 28:21
the land you are entering to **p**. Dt 28:63
the land you are entering to **p**. Dt 30:16
are entering to **p** across the Dt 30:18
are crossing the Jordan to **p**." Dt 31:13
are crossing the Jordan to **p**." Dt 32:47
and they too **p** the land the LORD Jos 1:15
could not **p** these cities, Jos 17:12
if the land you **p** is defiled, Jos 22:19
that you may **p** whatever your god Jdg 11:24
we may **p** everything the LORD Jdg 11:24
so that you may **p** this good land 1Ch 28:8
to God's wisdom that you **p**, Ezr 7:25
are entering to **p** is an impure Ezr 9:11
to go in and **p** the land You had Neh 9:15
They will live there and **p** it. Ps 69:35
I **p** good advice and competence; Pr 8:14
of Israel will **p** them as male Is 14:2
never rise up to **p** a land or Is 14:21
owl and the hedgehog will **p** it, Is 34:11
They will **p** it forever; Is 34:17
to make them **p** the desolate Is 49:8
the land and **p** My holy mountain. Is 57:13
they will **p** the land forever; Is 60:21
will **p** double in their land, Is 61:7
chosen ones will **p** it, and My Is 65:9
ancestors and they will **p** it." Jr 30:3
mine, and we will **p** them— Ezk 35:10
they will **p** you, and you will be Ezk 36:12
the kingdom and **p** it forever, Dn 7:18
wilderness in order to **p** the Am 2:10
that they may **p** the remnant of Am 9:12
Negev will **p** the hill country Ob 19
Judean foothills will **p** ⌊the Ob 19
They will **p** the territories of Ob 19
while Benjamin will **p** Gilead. Ob 19
in Sepharad will **p** the cities Ob 20
buy as though they did not **p**, 1Co 7:30
knows how to **p** his own vessel 1Th 4:4
You also **p** endurance and have Rv 2:3

POSSESSED *(12)*

settlements in the land they **p**. Gn 36:43
Everyone who **p** acacia wood Ex 35:24
into the land your fathers **p**, Dt 30:5
of the land remains to be **p**. Jos 13:1
You **p** their land, and I Jos 24:8
who **p** 23 towns in the land of 1Ch 2:22
went in and **p** the land: Neh 9:24
entered and **p** it, but they did Jr 32:23
those **p** fell down before Him and Mk 3:11
has put in everything she **p**— Mk 12:44
Wasn't it yours while you **p** it? Ac 5:4
came out of many who were **p**, Ac 8:7

POSSESSES *(4)*

any part of a field that he **p**, Lv 27:16
person return to the land he **p**. Nm 35:28
daughter who **p** an inheritance Nm 36:8
land the LORD **p** where the LORD's Jos 22:19

POSSESSING *(1)*

having nothing yet **p** everything. 2Co 6:10

POSSESSION *(122)*

as an eternal **p**, and I will be Gn 17:8
Abraham's **p** in the presence of Gn 23:18
in whose **p** the cup was found. Gn 44:16
The man in whose **p** the cup was Gn 44:17
land as an eternal **p** to your Gn 48:4
I will give it to you as a **p**. Ex 6:8
them on the mountain of Your **p**; Ex 15:17
you will be My own **p** out of all Ex 19:5
or the person is found in his **p**. Ex 21:16
actually found alive in his **p**, Ex 22:4
numerous and take **p** of the land. Ex 23:30
and accept us as Your own **p**." Ex 34:9
Everyone who had in his **p** blue, Ex 35:23
that I am giving you as a **p**, Lv 14:34
remain in the **p** of its purchaser Lv 25:28
cities are their **p** among the Lv 25:33
for it is their permanent **p**. Lv 25:34
go up and take **p** of the land Nm 13:30
the sword and took **p** of his land Nm 21:24
and they took **p** of his land. Nm 21:35
Edom will become a **p**; Nm 24:18
will become a **p** of its enemies, Nm 24:18
clan, and he will take **p** of it. Nm 27:11
given to your servants as a **p**. Nm 32:5
has taken **p** of his inheritance. Nm 32:18
to you as a **p** before the LORD. Nm 32:22
them the land of Gilead as a **p**. Nm 32:29
hereditary **p** across the Jordan. Nm 32:32
are to take **p** of the land and Nm 33:53
Enter and take **p** of the land the Dt 1:8
Go up and take **p** of it as the Dt 1:21
and they will take **p** of it. Dt 1:39
hill country of Seir as ⌊his⌋ **p**. Dt 2:5
you any of their land as a **p**, Dt 2:9
given Ar as a **p** to the Dt 2:9
the land of its **p** the LORD gave Dt 2:12
of the Ammonites' land as a **p**; Dt 2:19
given it as a **p** to the Dt 2:19
Begin to take **p** ⌊of it⌋; Dt 2:24
Begin to take **p** of it.' Dt 2:31
time we took **p** of this land. Dt 3:12
and they also take **p** of the land Dt 3:20
return to his **p** that I have Dt 3:20
and take **p** of the land the LORD, Dt 4:1
over and take **p** of this good Dt 4:22
They took **p** of his land and the Dt 4:47
you to be His own **p** out of all Dt 7:6
may enter and take **p** of the land Dt 8:1
me in to take **p** of this land Dt 9:4
going to take **p** of their land Dt 9:5
to enter and take **p** of the land Dt 11:31
which you are entering to take **p** Dt 12:29
giving you, take **p** of it, live Dt 17:14
and you take **p** of it and live in Dt 26:1
will take **p** of all your trees Dt 28:42
and you will take **p** of it. Dt 30:5
enable them to take **p** of it. Dt 31:7
am giving the Israelites as a **p**. Dt 32:49
a **p** for the assembly of Jacob. Dt 33:4
p to the west and the south. Dt 33:23
to go in and take **p** of the land Jos 1:11
and take **p** of what Moses Jos 1:15
land and took **p** of their land Jos 12:1
out to take **p** of the land that Jos 18:3
So they took **p** of it, lived Jos 19:47
Caleb son of Jephunneh as his **p**. Jos 21:12
the Israelite **p** there were 48 Jos 21:41
they took **p** of it and settled Jos 21:43
which they took **p** of according Jos 22:9
and take **p** ⌊of it⌋ among us. Jos 22:19
you can take **p** of their land, Jos 23:5
country of Seir to Esau as a **p**, Jos 24:4
them to take **p** of the hill Jdg 1:19
failed to take **p** of Beth-shean Jdg 1:27
went to take **p** of the land, Jdg 2:6
Israel and took **p** of the City of Jdg 3:13
So Israel took **p** of the entire Jdg 11:21
They took **p** of all the territory Jdg 11:22
invade and take **p** of the land! Jdg 18:9
up and take **p** of the vineyard 1Kg 21:15
the Jezreelite to take **p** of it. 1Kg 21:16
he has gone to take **p** of it. 1Kg 21:18
you murdered and also taken **p**?' 1Kg 21:19
The settlers took **p** of Samaria 2Kg 17:24
out of Your **p** that You gave us 2Ch 20:11
their cities, each to his own **p**. 2Ch 31:1
will not have any **p** west of the Ezr 4:16
of your God, which is in your **p**. Ezr 7:14
They took **p** of the land of Sihon Neh 9:22
to go in and take **p** ⌊of it⌋. Neh 9:23
land and took **p** of well-supplied Neh 9:25
the ends of the earth Your **p**. Ps 2:8
bless Your **p**, shepherd them, Ps 28:9
He has chosen to be His own **p**! Ps 33:12
as the tribe for Your own **p**. Ps 74:2
Israel as His treasured **p**. Ps 135:4
I profaned My **p**, and I placed Is 47:6
holy people had a **p** for a little Is 63:18
to take **p** of their houses Ezk 7:24
has been given to us as a **p**. Ezk 11:15
the people of the east as a **p**. Ezk 25:4
the people of the east as a **p**, Ezk 25:10
yet he received **p** of the land. Ezk 33:24
has been given to us as a **p**. Ezk 33:24
you then receive **p** of the land? Ezk 33:25
you then receive **p** of the land? Ezk 33:26
heights have become our **p**,' Ezk 36:2
that you became a **p** for the rest Ezk 36:3
as their own **p** with wholehearted Ezk 36:5
are to give them no **p** in Israel: Ezk 44:28
in Israel: I am their **p**. Ezk 44:28
it will be their **p** for towns to Ezk 45:5
be his land as a **p** in Israel. Ezk 45:8
holy ones took **p** of the kingdom. Dn 7:22
will take **p** of their precious Hs 9:6
staff, the flock that is Your **p**. Mc 7:14
LORD will take **p** of Judah as His Zch 2:12
a special **p** on the day I am Mal 3:17
to give it to him as a **p**, Ac 7:5
for the redemption of the **p**, Eph 1:14
have a better and enduring **p**. Heb 10:34
people for His **p**, so that you 1Pt 2:9

POSSESSIONS *(55)*

all the **p** they had accumulated, Gn 12:5
had so many **p** that they could Gn 13:6

Abram's nephew Lot and his **p**, Gn 14:12
but take the **p** for yourself." Gn 14:21
they will go out with many **p**. Gn 15:14
livestock and **p** he had acquired Gn 31:18
He fled with all his **p**, crossed Gn 31:21
You've searched all my **p**! Gn 31:37
stream, along with all his **p**. Gn 32:23
herds, their **p**, and all their Gn 34:23
They captured all their **p**, Gn 34:29
For their **p** were too many ⌊for Gn 36:7
their cattle and **p** they had Gn 46:6
people, and all ⌊their⌋ **p**. Nm 16:32
LORD, bless his **p**, and accept Dt 33:11
livestock, and **p** in front of Jdg 18:21
and their **p** and went to Judah 2Ch 11:14
and all your **p** with a horrible 2Ch 21:14
off all the **p** found in the 2Ch 21:17
from his own **p** for the regular 2Ch 31:3
for God gave him abundant **p**. 2Ch 32:29
plus 3,000 bulls from his own **p**, 2Ch 35:7
us, our children, and all our **p**. Ezr 8:21
days would forfeit all his **p**, Ezr 10:8
household **p** out of the room. Neh 13:8
plunder their **p** on a single day Est 3:13
to take their **p** as spoils of war Est 8:11
and his **p** are spread out in the Jb 1:10
His **p** will not spread over the Jb 15:29
The **p** in his house will be Jb 20:28
and doubled his ⌊previous⌋ **p**. Jb 42:10
gathering **p** without knowing who Ps 39:6
man with valuable **p** but without Ps 49:20
ruler over all his **p**— Ps 105:21
LORD with your **p** and with the Pr 3:9
cattle and **p** and who live at Ezk 38:12
cattle and **p**, to seize great Ezk 38:13
appropriate their **p** in the day Ob 13
and steal his **p** unless he first Mt 12:29
grieving, because he had many **p**. Mt 19:22
put him in charge of all his **p**. Mt 24:47
and turned over his **p** to them. Mt 25:14
and rob his **p** unless he first Mk 3:27
grieving, because he had many **p**. Mk 10:22
supporting them from their **p**. Lk 8:3
his estate, his **p** are secure. Lk 11:21
not in the abundance of his **p**." Lk 12:15
your **p** and give to the poor. Lk 12:33
put him in charge of all his **p**. Lk 12:44
to all his **p** cannot be My Lk 14:33
manager was squandering his **p**. Lk 16:1
give half of my **p** to the poor, Lk 19:8
they sold their **p** and property Ac 2:45
that any of his **p** was his own, Ac 4:32
joy the confiscation of your **p**, Heb 10:34

POSSESSOR *(1)*
is a fountain of life for its **p**, Pr 16:22

POSSIBLE *(17)*
them with every **p** distress. 2Ch 15:6
but with God all things are **p**." Mt 19:26
astray, if **p**, even the elect Mt 24:24
If it is **p**, let this cup pass Mt 26:39
Everything is **p** to the one who Mk 9:23
all things are **p** with God." Mk 10:27
to lead astray, if **p**, the elect. Mk 13:22
began to pray that if it were **p**, Mk 14:35
All things are **p** for You. Mk 14:36
it is not **p** for a prophet to Lk 13:33
with men is **p** with God." Lk 18:27
it was not **p** for Him to be held Ac 2:24
to come to him as quickly as **p**, Ac 17:15
in Jerusalem, if **p**, for the day Ac 20:16
p, on your part, live at peace Rm 12:18
you that, if **p**, you would have Gl 4:15
It is not **p** to speak about these Heb 9:5

POSSIBLY *(7)*
You could not **p** do such a thing: Gn 18:25
You could not **p** do that! Gn 18:25
could not **p** do such a thing. Gn 44:7
house could you **p** build for Me? Is 66:1
how could you **p** go unpunished? Jr 25:29
can you **p** remain unpunished? Jr 49:12
how could I **p** hinder God?" Ac 11:17

POST *(5)*
king stood at his **p** and made a 2Ch 34:31
said to me, "Go, **p** a lookout; Is 21:6
and I stay at my **p** all night. Is 21:8
the watch **p**; set the watchmen Jr 51:12
stand at my guard **p** and station Hab 2:1

POSTED *(1)*
I **p** some of my men at the gates, Neh 13:19

POSTERITY *(3)*
husband's name or **p** on earth." 2Sm 14:7
offspring, and **p**"—the LORD's Is 14:22
and their **p** among the peoples. Is 61:9

POSTS *(46)*
gold-plated **p** of acacia wood Ex 26:32
Make five **p** of acacia wood for Ex 26:37
are to be 20 **p** and 20 bronze Ex 27:10
bands of the **p** must be silver. Ex 27:10
are to be 20 **p** and 20 bronze Ex 27:11
bands of the **p** must be silver. Ex 27:11
their 10 **p** and 10 bases. Ex 27:12
their three **p** and their three Ex 27:14
their three **p** and their three Ex 27:15
to have four **p** including their Ex 27:16
All the **p** around the courtyard Ex 27:17
bases of the **p** must be bronze. Ex 27:18
its crossbars, its **p** and bases; Ex 35:11
the courtyard, its **p** and bases, Ex 35:17
it he made four **p** of acacia wood Ex 36:36
four silver bases for the **p**. Ex 36:36
with its five **p** and their hooks. Ex 36:38
tops of the **p** and their bands Ex 36:38
their 20 **p** and 20 bronze Ex 38:10
and bands of the **p** were silver. Ex 38:10
their 20 **p** and 20 bronze Ex 38:11
and bands of the **p** were silver. Ex 38:11
their 10 **p** and 10 bases. Ex 38:12
and bands of the **p** were silver. Ex 38:12
their three **p** and three bases. Ex 38:14
their three **p** and three bases Ex 38:15
The bases for the **p** were bronze; Ex 38:17
and bands of the **p** were silver; Ex 38:17
the tops of the **p** was silver. Ex 38:17
All the **p** of the courtyard were Ex 38:17
It had four **p**, including their Ex 38:19
he made the hooks for the **p**, Ex 38:28
crossbars, and its **p** and bases; Ex 39:33
the courtyard, its **p** and bases, Ex 39:40
its crossbars, and set up its **p**. Ex 40:18
crossbars, **p**, bases, all its Nm 3:36
addition to the **p** of the Nm 3:37
its crossbars, **p**, and bases, Nm 4:31
the **p** of the surrounding Nm 4:32
stood at their prescribed **p**, 2Ch 30:16
stood at their **p** and the Levites 2Ch 35:10
at their **p** and some at their Neh 7:3
and stationed them at their **p**. Neh 13:11
waiting by the **p** of my doorway. Pr 8:34
made its **p** of silver, its back Sg 3:10
the first and second guard **p**, Ac 12:10

POT *(27)*
a smoking fire **p** and a flaming Gn 15:17
A clay **p** in which the sin Lv 6:28
of them falls into any clay **p**, Lv 11:33
over fresh water in a clay **p**. Lv 14:5
over a clay **p** containing fresh Lv 14:50
Any clay **p** that the man with the Lv 15:12
it⌋ in a cooking **p** and shaped it Nm 11:8
a basket and the broth in a **p**. Jdg 6:19
kettle or caldron or cooking **p**. 1Sm 2:14
Put on the large **p** and make stew 2Kg 4:38
cut them up into the **p** of stew, 2Kg 4:39
death in the **p**, man of God!" 2Kg 4:40
He threw it into the **p** and said, 2Kg 4:41
there was nothing bad in the **p**. 2Kg 4:41
as from a boiling **p** or ⌊burning⌋ Jb 41:20
of ⌊burning⌋ thorns under the **p**, Ec 7:6
Maker—one clay **p** among many. Is 45:9
I see a boiling **p**, its mouth Jr 1:13
shattered **p**, a jar no one wants Jr 22:28
city is the **p**, and we are the Ezk 11:3
the city is the **p**, but I will Ezk 11:7
city will not be a **p** for you, Ezk 11:11
Put the **p** on ⌊the fire⌋—put Ezk 24:3
the **p** that has rust inside it, Ezk 24:6
Set the empty **p** on its coals so Ezk 24:11
up like flesh for the cooking **p**, Mc 3:3
p in Jerusalem and in Judah Zch 14:21

POTENCY *(1)*
and the **p** of your spells. Is 47:9

POTIPHAR *(3)*
sold Joseph in Egypt to **P**, Gn 37:36
Egyptian ⌊named⌋ **P**, an officer Gn 39:1
P also put him in charge of his Gn 39:4

POTIPHERA *(3)*
Asenath daughter of **P**, priest at Gn 41:45
daughter of **P**, priest at On, Gn 41:50
to him by Asenath daughter of **P**, Gn 46:20

POTS *(14)*
when we sat by **p** of meat and ate Ex 16:3
Make its **p** for removing ashes, Ex 27:3
the **p**, shovels, basins, meat Ex 38:3
and the **p**, shovels, and 1Kg 7:45
Fill four water **p** with water and 1Kg 18:33
also took the **p**, the shovels, 2Kg 25:14
Huram made the **p**, the shovels, 2Ch 4:11
the **p**, the shovels, the forks, 2Ch 4:16
the holy ⌊sacrifices⌋ in **p**, 2Ch 35:13
Before your **p** can feel the heat Ps 58:9
They took the **p**, the shovels, Jr 52:18
basins, the **p**, the lampstands, Jr 52:19
The **p** in the house of the LORD Zch 14:20
and take some of the **p** to cook Zch 14:21

POTSHERD *(1)*
near the entrance of the **P** Gate. Jr 19:2

POTSHERDS *(1)*
His undersides are jagged **p**, Jb 41:30

POTTER *(7)*
as if the **p** were the same as the Is 29:16
like a **p** who treads the clay. Is 41:25
are the clay, and You are our **p**; Is 64:8
you as this **p** ⌊treats his clay⌋ Jr 18:6
it to the **p**," the LORD said Zch 11:13
the house of the LORD, to the **p**. Zch 11:13
Or has the **p** no right over His Rm 9:21

POTTER'S *(11)*
like the shattering of a **p** jar, Is 30:14
Go down at once to the **p** house; Jr 18:2
So I went down to the **p** house, Jr 18:3
became flawed in the **p** hand, Jr 18:4
Just like clay in the **p** hand, Jr 18:6
Go, buy a **p** clay jug. Jr 19:1
one shatters a **p** jar that can Jr 19:11
jars, the work of a **p** hands! Lm 4:2
partly of a **p** fired clay and Dn 2:41
and bought the **p** field with it Mt 27:7
they gave them for the **p** field, Mt 27:10

POTTERS *(1)*
They were the **p** and residents of 1Ch 4:23

POTTERY *(8)*
beds, basins, and **p** items. 2Sm 17:28
piece of broken **p** to scrape Jb 2:8
You will shatter them like **p**." Ps 2:9
a dead person—like broken **p**. Ps 31:12
a fragment of **p** will be found Is 30:14
the nations like discarded **p**. Hs 8:8
lump one piece of **p** for honor Rm 9:21
He will shatter them like **p**— Rv 2:27

POUCH *(1)*
the wadi and put them in the **p**, 1Sm 17:40

POULTRY *(1)*
roebucks, and pen-fed **p**, 1Kg 4:23

POUND *(2)*
them, as well as a **p** of silver. Neh 5:15
Mary took a **p** of fragrant oil Jn 12:3

POUNDED *(2)*
the winds blew and **p** that house. Mt 7:25
the winds blew and **p** that house, Mt 7:27

POUNDING *(2)*
floods lift up their **p** waves. Ps 93:3
up with the **p** of the waves. Ac 27:41

POUNDS *(86)*
be made from 75 **p** of pure gold. Ex 25:39
12 and a half **p** of liquid myrrh, Ex 30:23
and a quarter **p**) of fragrant Ex 30:23
and a quarter **p** of fragrant cane Ex 30:23
12 and a half **p** of cassia Ex 30:24
utensils of 75 **p** of pure gold. Ex 37:24
was 2,193 **p**, according to Ex 38:24
who were registered was 7,544 **p**, Ex 38:25
were 7,500 **p** of silver ⌊used Ex 38:27
bases from 7,500 **p**, 75 pounds Ex 38:27
pounds, 75 **p** for each base. Ex 38:27
remaining⌋ 44 **p** he made the Ex 38:28
offering totaled 5,310 **p**. Ex 38:29
and a quarter **p** and one silver Nm 7:13
one and three-quarter **p**, Nm 7:13
and a quarter **p** and one silver Nm 7:19
one and three-quarter **p**, Nm 7:19

and a quarter **p** and one silver Nm 7:25
one and three-quarter **p**, Nm 7:25
and a quarter **p** and one silver Nm 7:31
one and three-quarter **p**, Nm 7:31
and a quarter **p** and one silver Nm 7:37
one and three-quarter **p**, Nm 7:37
and a quarter **p** and one silver Nm 7:43
one and three-quarter **p**, Nm 7:43
and a quarter **p** and one silver Nm 7:49
one and three-quarter **p**, Nm 7:49
and a quarter **p** and one silver Nm 7:55
one and three-quarter **p**, Nm 7:55
and a quarter **p** and one silver Nm 7:61
one and three-quarter **p**, Nm 7:61
and a quarter **p** and one silver Nm 7:67
one and three-quarter **p**, Nm 7:67
and a quarter **p** and one silver Nm 7:73
one and three-quarter **p**, Nm 7:73
and a quarter **p** and one silver Nm 7:79
one and three-quarter **p**, Nm 7:79
weighed⌋ three and a quarter **p**, Nm 7:85
basin one and three-quarter **p**. Nm 7:85
articles was 60 **p** ⌊measured⌋ Nm 7:85
of the gold bowls was three **p**. Nm 7:86
and of hundreds, was 420 **p**. Nm 31:52
was about 43 **p** of gold, Jdg 8:26
she took five **p** of silver and Jdg 17:4
scale armor that weighed 125 **p**. 1Sm 17:5
point of his spear weighed 15 **p**. 1Sm 17:7
The crown weighed 75 **p** of gold, 2Sm 12:30
it would be five **p** according to 2Sm 14:26
about eight **p** and who wore new 2Sm 21:16
sent the king 9,000 **p** of gold. 1Kg 9:14
15 **p** of gold went into each 1Kg 10:16
about four **p** of gold went into 1Kg 10:17
from Egypt for 15 **p** ⌊of silver⌋, 1Kg 10:29
and a horse for about four **p**. 1Kg 10:29
from Shemer for 150 **p** of silver, 1Kg 16:24
will weigh out 75 **p** of silver.' 1Kg 20:39
took with him 750 **p** of silver, 2Kg 5:5
of silver, 150 **p** of gold, and 10 2Kg 5:5
give them 75 **p** of silver and two 2Kg 5:22
"Please, accept 150 **p**." 2Kg 5:23
then packed 150 **p** of silver in 2Kg 5:23
gave Pul 75,000 **p** of silver so 2Kg 15:19
a fine of 7,500 **p** of silver and 2Kg 23:33
of silver and 75 **p** of gold. 2Kg 23:33
the crown weighed 75 **p** of gold, 1Ch 20:2
David gave Ornan 15 **p** of gold 1Ch 21:25
from Egypt for 15 **p** ⌊of silver⌋ 2Ch 1:17
and a horse for about four **p**. 2Ch 1:17
it with 45,000 **p** of fine gold. 2Ch 3:8
15 **p** of hammered gold went into 2Ch 9:15
about eight **p** of gold went into 2Ch 9:16
Then for 7,500 **p** of silver he 2Ch 25:6
about the 7,500 **p** of silver I 2Ch 25:9
they gave him 7,500 **p** of silver, 2Ch 27:5
the land 7,500 **p** of silver and 2Ch 36:3
of silver and 75 **p** of gold. 2Ch 36:3
gold coins, 6,250 **p** of silver, Ezr 2:69
up to 7,500 **p** of silver, 500 Ezr 7:22
articles weighing 7,500 **p**, Ezr 8:26
7,500 pounds, 7,500 **p** of gold, Ezr 8:26
heart **p** at this and leaps from Jb 37:1
heart! My heart **p**; I cannot be Jr 4:19
mixed into 50 **p** of flour until Mt 13:33
mixed into 50 **p** of flour until Lk 13:21
of about 75 **p** of myrrh and aloes Jn 19:39
each weighing about 100 **p**, Rv 16:21

POUR *(73)*

from the Nile and **p** it on the Ex 4:9
anointing oil, **p** ⌊it⌋ on his Ex 29:7
then **p** out all the ⌊rest⌋ of the Ex 29:12
are not to **p** a drink offering Ex 30:9
He is to **p** olive oil on it, Lv 2:1
it into pieces and **p** oil on it; Lv 2:6
He must **p** out the rest of the Lv 4:7
He must **p** out the rest of the Lv 4:18
blood he must **p** out at the base Lv 4:25
He must **p** out the rest of its Lv 4:30
He must **p** out the rest of its Lv 4:34
olive oil and **p** it into his left Lv 14:15
priest will **p** some of the oil Lv 14:26
is not to **p** oil over it or put Nm 5:15
P out the offering of beer to Nm 28:7
p it on the ground like water. Dt 12:16
p it on the ground like water. Dt 12:24
p it on the ground like water. Dt 15:23
this stone, and **p** the broth ⌊on Jdg 6:20
with water and **p** it on the 1Kg 18:33
who used to **p** water on Elijah's 2Kg 3:11
and **p** oil into all these 2Kg 4:4
flask of oil, **p** it on his head, 2Kg 9:3
and my groans **p** out like water. Jb 3:24
Did You not **p** me out like milk Jb 10:10
the clouds **p** out and shower Jb 36:28
and flames **p** out of his mouth. Jb 41:21
I will not **p** out their drink Ps 16:4
Day after day they **p** out speech; Ps 19:2
this as I **p** out my heart: Ps 42:4
p out your hearts before Him. Ps 62:8
P out Your rage on them, and let Ps 69:24
P out Your wrath on the nations Ps 79:6
They **p** out arrogant words; Ps 94:4
mountains, and they **p** out smoke. Ps 104:32
My eyes **p** out streams of tears Ps 119:136
My lips **p** out praise, for You Ps 119:171
I **p** out my complaint before Him; Ps 142:2
then I will **p** out my spirit on Pr 1:23
they will **p** out rain on the Ec 11:3
It will **p** into Judah, flood over Is 8:8
I will **p** water on the thirsty Is 44:3
I will **p** out My Spirit on your Is 44:3
Those who **p** out their bags of Is 46:6
P ⌊it⌋ out on the children in Jr 6:11
and they **p** out drink offerings Jr 7:18
P out Your wrath on the nations Jr 10:25
p out their own evil on them. Jr 14:16
and **p** the sword's power on them. Jr 18:21
so will My fury **p** out on you if Jr 42:18
of heaven and to **p** out drink Jr 44:25
to him, who will **p** him out. Jr 48:12
P out your heart like water Lm 2:19
will **p** out My wrath on you very Ezk 7:8
Israel when You **p** out Your wrath Ezk 9:8
that land and **p** out My wrath on Ezk 14:19
I will **p** out My indignation on Ezk 21:31
on, and then **p** water into it! Ezk 24:3
she didn't **p** it on the ground to Ezk 24:7
I will **p** out My wrath on Ezk 30:15
I will **p** out torrential rain, Ezk 38:22
I will **p** out My Spirit on the Ezk 39:29
will **p** out My fury on them like Hs 5:10
They will not **p** out their wine Hs 9:4
this I will **p** out My Spirit Jl 2:28
I will even **p** out My Spirit on Jl 2:29
in order to **p** out My indignation Zph 3:8
Then I will **p** out a spirit of Zch 12:10
of heaven and **p** out a blessing Mal 3:10
that I will **p** out My Spirit on Ac 2:17
will even **p** out My Spirit on My Ac 2:18
Does a spring **p** out sweet and Jms 3:11
Go and **p** out the seven bowls of Rv 16:1

POURED *(76)*

He **p** oil on top of it Gn 28:18
where you **p** oil on the stone Gn 31:13
He **p** a drink offering on it and Gn 35:14
rain no longer **p** down on the Ex 9:33
p some of the anointing oil on Lv 8:12
p out the blood at the base of Lv 8:15
p out the blood at the base of Lv 9:9
the anointing oil **p** on his head Lv 21:10
sacrifices is to be **p** out beside Dt 12:27
the heavens **p** ⌊rain⌋, the clouds Jdg 5:4
rain⌋, the clouds **p** water. Jdg 5:4
they drew water and **p** it out in 1Sm 7:6
flask of oil, **p** it out on Saul's 1Sm 10:1
be like water **p** out on the 2Sm 14:14
the rain **p** down from heaven 2Sm 21:10
he **p** it out to the LORD. 2Sm 23:16
young prophet **p** the oil on his 2Kg 9:6
grain offering, **p** out his drink 2Kg 16:13
he **p** it out to the LORD. 1Ch 11:18
will not be **p** out on Jerusalem 2Ch 12:7
that is **p** out on us because 2Ch 34:21
My wrath will be **p** out on this 2Ch 34:25
and the rock **p** out streams of Jb 29:6
Now my life is **p** out before my Jb 30:16
am **p** out like water, and all my Ps 22:14
poison has been **p** into him, Ps 41:8
and the skies **p** down ⌊rain⌋ Ps 68:8
The clouds **p** down water. Ps 77:17
p out their blood like water Ps 79:3
your name is perfume **p** out. Sg 1:3
they **p** out whispered ⌊prayers Is 26:16
For the LORD has **p** out on you an Is 29:10
from heaven is **p** out on us. Is 32:15
So He **p** out on Jacob His furious Is 42:25
You have even **p** out a drink Is 57:6
My wrath and **p** out their blood Is 63:6
Disaster will be **p** out from the Jr 1:14
is about to be **p** out on this Jr 7:20
heavenly host and **p** out drink Jr 19:13
have been **p** out to other gods Jr 32:29
and fury were **p** out on Jr 42:18
My fierce wrath **p** forth and Jr 44:6
of heaven and **p** out drink Jr 44:19
in her image and **p** out drink Jr 44:19
He hasn't been **p** from one Jr 48:11
My heart is **p** out in grief Lm 2:11
His wrath, **p** out His burning Lm 4:11
your lust was **p** out and your Ezk 16:36
aromas and **p** out their drink Ezk 20:28
have **p** out My wrath on you." Ezk 22:22
I have **p** out My indignation on Ezk 22:31
and **p** out their lust on her. Ezk 23:8
So I **p** out My wrath on them Ezk 36:18
has been **p** out on us because we Dn 9:11
destruction is **p** out on the Dn 9:27
His wrath is **p** out like fire, Nah 1:6
blood will be **p** out like dust Zph 1:17
She **p** it on His head as He was Mt 26:7
the jar and **p** it on His head. Mk 14:3
over—will be **p** into your lap. Lk 6:38
also **p** out the money changers' Jn 2:15
p water into a basin and began Jn 13:5
He has **p** out what you both see Ac 2:33
Spirit had been **p** out on the Ac 10:45
has been **p** out in our hearts Rm 5:5
even if I am **p** out as a drink Php 2:17
already being **p** out as a drink 2Tm 4:6
This ⌊Spirit⌋ He **p** out on us Ti 3:6
first went and **p** out his bowl Rv 16:2
The second **p** out his bowl into Rv 16:3
third **p** out his bowl into the Rv 16:4
Because they **p** out the blood of Rv 16:6
The fourth **p** out his bowl on the Rv 16:8
The fifth **p** out his bowl on the Rv 16:10
The sixth **p** out his bowl on the Rv 16:12
Then the seventh **p** out his bowl Rv 16:17

POURING *(12)*

and bowls for **p** drink offerings. Ex 25:29
pitchers for **p** drink offerings Ex 37:16
I've been **p** out my heart before 1Sm 1:15
⌊containers⌋, and she kept **p**. 2Kg 4:5
or like ⌊**p**⌋ vinegar on soda. Pr 25:20
p out His wrath like fire on the Lm 2:4
I considered **p** out My wrath on Ezk 20:8
I considered **p** out My wrath on Ezk 20:13
I considered **p** out My wrath on Ezk 20:21
p out your wrath and even making Hab 2:15
By **p** this fragrant oil on My Mt 26:12
his wounds, **p** on oil and wine. Lk 10:34

POURS *(8)*

He **p** out contempt on nobles and Jb 12:21
without mercy and **p** my bile on Jb 16:13
with spices, and He **p** from it. Ps 75:8
p contempt on nobles and makes Ps 107:40
water, so she **p** forth her evil. Jr 6:7
of the sea and **p** them out over Am 5:8
of the sea and **p** them out on the Am 9:6
from which golden ⌊oil⌋ **p** out?" Zch 4:12

POVERTY *(18)*

Israel became **p** stricken because Jdg 6:6
The LORD brings **p** and gives 1Sm 2:7
Emaciated from **p** and hunger, Jb 30:3
and your **p** will come like a Pr 6:11
the **p** of the poor is their Pr 10:15
P and disgrace ⌊come to⌋ those Pr 13:18
endless talk leads only to **p**. Pr 14:23
the rich—both lead only to **p**. Pr 22:16
and your **p** will come like a Pr 24:34
will have his fill of **p**. Pr 28:19
know that **p** will come to him Pr 28:22
Give me neither **p** nor wealth; Pr 30:8
can forget his **p** and remember Pr 31:7
but she out of her **p** has put in Mk 12:44
she out of her **p** has put in all Lk 21:4
joy and their deep **p** overflowed 2Co 8:2
that by His **p** you might become 2Co 8:9
I know your tribulation and **p**, Rv 2:9

POWDER *(8)*

of it into a fine **p** and put some Ex 30:36

it⌋ up, and ground ⌊it⌋ to **p**. Ex 32:20
scattered ⌊the **p**⌋ over the Ex 32:20
grinding it to **p** as ⌊fine as⌋ Dt 9:21
and the carved images to **p**. 2Ch 34:7
fragrant **p** of the merchant? Sg 3:6
falls, it will grind him to **p**!" Mt 21:44
anyone, it will grind him to **p**!" Lk 20:18

POWER *(286)*

in prominence, excelling in **p**. Gn 49:3
Joseph, came to **p** in Egypt. Ex 1:8
them from the **p** of the Egyptians Ex 3:8
I have put within your **p**. Ex 4:21
to show you My **p** and to make My Ex 9:16
Israel from the **p** of the Ex 14:30
saw the great **p** that the LORD Ex 14:31
right hand is glorious in **p**. Ex 15:6
Pharaoh and the **p** of the Ex 18:10
people from the **p** of the Ex 18:10
Egypt with great **p** and a strong Ex 32:11
Moses, "Is the LORD's **p** limited? Nm 11:23
My Lord's **p** be magnified just Nm 14:17
greatness and **p** to Your servant, Dt 3:24
by His presence and great **p**, Dt 4:37
from the **p** of Pharaoh king of Dt 7:8
'My **p** and my own ability have Dt 8:17
gives you the **p** to gain wealth, Dt 8:18
by Your great **p** and outstretched Dt 9:29
terrifying **p**, and with signs Dt 26:8
⌊acts of⌋ **p** and terrifying Dt 34:12
Israelites from the LORD's **p**." Jos 22:31
them from the **p** of their Jdg 2:16
people from the **p** of their Jdg 2:18
king of Moab **p** over Israel, Jdg 3:12
p of the Israelites continued Jdg 4:24
you from the **p** of Egypt and the Jdg 6:9
of Egypt and the **p** of all who Jdg 6:9
Israel from the **p** of Midian. Jdg 6:14
now in your **p** that we should Jdg 8:15
us from the **p** of Midian." Jdg 8:22
them from the **p** of the enemies Jdg 8:34
only these people were in my **p**, Jdg 9:29
I not deliver you from their **p**? Jdg 10:12
didn't deliver me from their **p**. Jdg 12:2
from the **p** of the Philistines. Jdg 13:5
He will give **p** to His king; 1Sm 2:10
you from the **p** of the Egyptians 1Sm 10:18
us from the **p** of our enemies, 1Sm 12:10
you from the **p** of the enemies 1Sm 12:11
acquiring more **p** in the house 2Sm 3:6
Israel from the **p** of the 2Sm 3:18
and the **p** of all Israel's 2Sm 3:18
king, I have little **p** today. 2Sm 3:39
⌊the promise⌋ by His **p**. 1Kg 8:15
by Your **p** as it is today. 1Kg 8:24
The **p** of the LORD was on Elijah, 1Kg 18:46
your royal **p** over Israel. 1Kg 21:7
them to the **p** of Hazael king of 2Kg 13:3
from the **p** of the Arameans 2Kg 13:5
and the **p** he had to wage war 2Kg 13:12
and the **p** he had to wage war 2Kg 14:28
save me from the **p** of the king 2Kg 16:7
Egypt from the **p** of Pharaoh king 2Kg 17:7
Egypt with great **p** and an 2Kg 17:36
his land from the **p** of the king 2Kg 18:33
delivered his land from my **p**? 2Kg 18:35
who were defeated by their **p**. 1Ch 5:10
greatness and the **p** and the 1Ch 29:11
In Your hand are **p** and might, 1Ch 29:12
⌊the promise⌋ by His **p**. 2Ch 6:4
Your promise⌋ by Your **p**, 2Ch 6:15
his sovereignty and royal **p**, 2Ch 12:1
his royal **p** in Jerusalem. 2Ch 12:13
retained his **p** during Abijah's 2Ch 13:20
P and might are in Your hand, 2Ch 20:6
one to exercise **p** over the 2Ch 22:9
for God has the **p** to help or to 2Ch 25:8
deliver us from the **p** of the 2Ch 32:11
to deliver their land from my **p**? 2Ch 32:13
to deliver his people from my **p**, 2Ch 32:14
people from my **p** or the power of 2Ch 32:15
my power or the **p** of my fathers. 2Ch 32:15
gods deliver you from my **p**!' " 2Ch 32:15
deliver their people from my **p**, 2Ch 32:17
deliver His people from my **p**. 2Ch 32:17
Jerusalem from the **p** of King 2Ch 32:22
and from the **p** of all others. 2Ch 32:22
us from the **p** of the enemy Ezr 8:31
by Your great **p** and strong hand. Neh 1:10
from the **p** of their enemies. Neh 9:27
them to the **p** of their enemies, Neh 9:28
great **p** in the palace, Est 9:4
everything he owns is in your **p**. Jb 1:12
told Satan, "he is in your **p**; Jb 2:6
battle, from the **p** of the sword. Jb 5:20
to unleash His **p** and cut me off! Jb 6:9
from the enemy's **p** or Redeem me Jb 6:23
Your miraculous **p** against me. Jb 10:16
God's **p** provides this. Jb 12:6
True wisdom and **p** belong to Him. Jb 12:16
drags away the mighty by His **p**; Jb 24:22
By His **p** He stirred the sea, Jb 26:12
I will teach you about God's **p**. Jb 27:11
shows Himself exalted by His **p**. Jb 36:22
reach Him—He is exalted in **p**! Jb 37:23
loins and the **p** in the muscles Jb 40:16
his limbs, his **p**, and his Jb 41:12
Through our tongues we have **p**; Ps 12:4
very life from the **p** of the dog. Ps 22:20
the voice of the LORD in **p**, Ps 29:4
course of my life is in Your **p**; Ps 31:15
me from the **p** of my enemies Ps 31:15
no escape by its great **p**. Ps 33:17
my life from the **p** of Sheol, Ps 49:15
By Your **p**, make them homeless Ps 59:11
over to the **p** of the sword; Ps 63:10
the mountains by Your **p**, Ps 65:6
Ascribe **p** to God. His majesty is Ps 68:34
Israel, His **p** among the clouds Ps 68:34
Israel gives **p** and strength to Ps 68:35
proclaim Your **p** to ⌊another⌋ Ps 71:18
With **p** You redeemed Your people, Ps 77:15
remember His **p** ⌊shown⌋ on the Ps 78:42
according to Your great **p**, Ps 79:11
Your **p** and come to save us. Ps 80:2
I will extend his **p** to the sea Ps 89:25
himself from the **p** of Sheol? Ps 89:48
understands the **p** of Your anger? Ps 90:11
His name, to make His **p** known. Ps 106:8
they were subdued under their **p**. Ps 106:42
His people the **p** of His works Ps 111:6
right hand strikes with **p**! Ps 118:15
right hand strikes with **p**!" Ps 118:16
will proclaim the **p** of Your Ps 145:6
Our Lord is great, vast in **p**; Ps 147:5
does not value the **p** of a man. Ps 147:10
it is in your **p**, don't withhold Pr 3:27
yourself in your neighbor's **p**: Pr 6:3
Patience is better than **p**, Pr 16:32
are in the **p** of the tongue, Pr 18:21
but when the wicked come to **p**, Pr 28:12
When the wicked come to **p**, Pr 28:28
P is with those who oppress them; Ec 4:1
LORD said to me with great **p**, Is 8:11
the branches with terrifying **p**, Is 10:33
will extend their **p** over Edom Is 11:14
For the LORD's **p** will rest on Is 25:10
and His **p** establishes His rule. Is 40:10
of His great **p** and strength, Is 40:26
furious anger and the **p** of war. Is 42:25
from the **p** of the flame. Is 47:14
Or do I have no **p** to deliver? Is 50:2
on the strength of the LORD's **p**. Is 51:9
then the LORD's **p** will be Is 66:14
Your name is great in **p**. Jr 10:6
He made the earth by His **p**, Jr 10:12
you from the **p** of evil people Jr 15:21
them know My **p** and My might; Jr 16:21
and pour the sword's **p** on them. Jr 18:21
and their **p** is not rightly used Jr 23:10
him from the **p** of one stronger Jr 31:11
by Your great **p** and with Your Jr 32:17
He made the earth by His **p**, Jr 51:15
the pride of your **p**, the delight Ezk 24:21
Israelites to the **p** of the sword Ezk 35:5
for wisdom and **p** belong to Him. Dn 2:20
You have given me wisdom and **p**. Dn 2:23
sovereignty, **p**, strength, and Dn 2:37
who can rescue you from my **p**?" Dn 3:15
can rescue us from the **p** of you, Dn 3:17
built by my vast **p** to be a royal Dn 4:30
Daniel from the **p** of the lions." Dn 6:27
there was no rescue from his **p**. Dn 8:4
to rescue the ram from his **p**. Dn 8:7
that nation, but without its **p**. Dn 8:22
His **p** will be great, but it will Dn 8:24
By the **p** he gains through his Dn 11:2
will not retain **p**, and his Dn 11:6
He will rise to **p** with a small Dn 11:23
stir up his **p** and his courage Dn 11:25
these will escape from his **p**: Dn 11:41
He will extend his **p** against the Dn 11:42
When the **p** of the holy people is Dn 12:7
ransom them from the **p** of Sheol. Hs 13:14
it because the **p** is in their Mc 2:1
I am filled with **p** by the Spirit Mc 3:8
you from the **p** of your enemies! Mc 4:10
and be ashamed of all their **p**. Mc 7:16
is slow to anger but great in **p**; Nah 1:3
This is where His **p** is hidden. Hab 3:4
and destroy the **p** of the Gentile Hg 2:22
move against them with My **p**, Zch 2:9
kingdom and the **p** and the glory Mt 6:13
position exercise **p** over them. Mt 20:25
the Scriptures or the **p** of God. Mt 22:29
heaven with **p** and great glory. Mt 24:30
right hand of the **P** and coming Mt 26:64
in Himself that **p** had gone out Mk 5:30
the kingdom of God come in **p**." Mk 9:1
positions exercise **p** over them. Mk 10:42
the Scriptures or the **p** of God? Mk 12:24
clouds with great **p** and glory. Mk 13:26
hand of the **P** and coming with Mk 14:62
in the spirit and **p** of Elijah, Lk 1:17
and the **p** of the Most High will Lk 1:35
Galilee in the **p** of the Spirit, Lk 4:14
spirits with authority and **p**, Lk 4:36
And the Lord's **p** to heal was in Lk 5:17
because **p** was coming out from Lk 6:19
that **p** has gone out from Me. Lk 8:46
gave them **p** and authority over Lk 9:1
the demons, and ⌊**p**⌋ to heal Lk 9:1
and over all the **p** of the enemy; Lk 10:19
a cloud with **p** and great glory Lk 21:27
the right hand of the **P** of God." Lk 22:69
is coming. He has no **p** over Me. Jn 14:30
you will receive **p** when the Holy Ac 1:8
by our own **p** or godliness we Ac 3:12
By what **p** or in what name have Ac 4:7
And with great **p** the apostles Ac 4:33
of grace and **p**, was performing Ac 6:8
is called the Great **P** of God!" Ac 8:10
Give me this **p** too, so that Ac 8:19
with the Holy Spirit and with **p**, Ac 10:38
and from the **p** of Satan to God, Ac 26:18
it is God's **p** for salvation to Rm 1:16
His eternal **p** and divine nature, Rm 1:20
out of flesh, sold into sin's **p**. Rm 7:14
will have the **p** to separate us Rm 8:39
that I may display My **p** in you, Rm 9:17
wrath and to make His **p** known, Rm 9:22
God has the **p** to graft them Rm 11:23
with hope by the **p** of the Holy Rm 15:13
by the **p** of miraculous signs and Rm 15:19
and by the **p** of God's Spirit. Rm 15:19
to Him who has **p** to strengthen Rm 16:25
are being saved it is God's **p**. 1Co 1:18
Christ is God's **p** and God's 1Co 1:24
of the Spirit and **p**, 1Co 2:4
on men's wisdom but on God's **p**. 1Co 2:5
talk but the **p** of those who are 1Co 4:19
of God is not in talk but in **p**. 1Co 4:20
and with the **p** of our Lord Jesus 1Co 5:4
will also raise us up by His **p**. 1Co 6:14
rule and all authority and **p**. 1Co 15:24
sown in weakness, raised in **p**; 1Co 15:43
and the **p** of sin is the law. 1Co 15:56
extraordinary **p** may be from God 2Co 4:7
of truth, by the **p** of God; 2Co 6:7
for **p** is perfected in weakness." 2Co 12:9
that Christ's **p** may reside in me 2Co 12:9
but He lives by God's **p**. 2Co 13:4
will live with Him by God's **p**. 2Co 13:4
everything under sin's **p**, Gl 3:22
greatness of His **p** to us who Eph 1:19
this **p**⌋ in the Messiah Eph 1:20
and authority, **p** and dominion, Eph 1:21
to me by the working of His **p**. Eph 3:7
strengthened with **p** through His Eph 3:16
according to the **p** that works in Eph 3:20
know Him and the **p** of His Php 3:10
by the **p** that enables Him to Php 3:21
you be strengthened with all **p**, Col 1:11
only, but also in **p**, in the Holy 1Th 1:5
will, by His **p**, fulfill every 2Th 1:11

but one of **p**, love, and sound 2Tm 1:7
gospel, relying on the **p** of God, 2Tm 1:8
of religion but denying its **p**. 2Tm 3:5
the one holding the **p** of death— Heb 2:14
but based on the **p** of an Heb 7:16
p to conceive offspring, Heb 11:11
by God's **p** through faith for 1Pt 1:5
glory and the **p** forever and ever 1Pt 4:11
For His divine **p** has given us 2Pt 1:3
known to you the **p** and coming of 2Pt 1:16
who are greater in might and **p**, 2Pt 2:11
glory, majesty, **p**, and authority Jd 25
receive glory and honor and **p**, Rv 4:11
worthy to receive **p** and riches Rv 5:12
and honor and **p** and strength, Rv 7:12
and **p** was given to them like the Rv 9:3
them like the **p** that scorpions Rv 9:3
they had the **p** to harm people Rv 9:10
For the **p** of the horses is in Rv 9:19
men have the **p** to close the sky Rv 11:6
They also have **p** over the waters Rv 11:6
Your great **p** and have begun Rv 11:17
and the **p** and the kingdom Rv 12:10
The dragon gave him his **p**, Rv 13:2
from God's glory and from His **p**, Rv 15:8
was given the **p** to burn people Rv 16:8
God who had the **p** over these Rv 16:9
they give their **p** and authority Rv 17:13
glory, and **p** belong to our God, Rv 19:1
death has no **p** over these, Rv 20:6

POWERFUL *(70)*

They were the **p** men of old, Gn 6:4
was the first **p** man on earth. Gn 10:8
was a **p** hunter in the sight of Gn 10:9
p hunter in the sight of the LORD. Gn 10:9
to become a great and **p** nation, Gn 18:18
for you are much too **p** for us." Gn 26:16
more numerous and **p** than we are. Ex 1:9
⌊back⌋ with a **p** east wind all Ex 14:21
because of Your **p** arm until Your Ex 15:16
they are more **p** than I am. Nm 22:6
more numerous and **p** than you— Dt 7:1
became a great, **p**, and populous Dt 26:5
out great and **p** nations before Jos 23:9
May you be **p** in Ephrathah and Ru 4:11
David became more and more **p**, 2Sm 5:10
rescued me from my **p** enemy and 2Sm 22:18
David steadily grew more **p**, 1Ch 11:9
for ⌊God⌋ made ⌊him⌋ very **p**. 2Ch 26:8
a **p** force to help the king 2Ch 26:13
P kings have also ruled over Ezr 4:20
and all his **p** officers. Ezr 7:28
and the **p** men of Samaria, Neh 4:2
as he became more and more **p**. Est 9:4
All of his **p** and magnificent Est 10:2
Suddenly a **p** wind swept in from Jb 1:19
and from the clutches of the **p**. Jb 5:15
His **p** stride is shortened, Jb 18:7
growing old and becoming **p**? Jb 21:7
land belonged to a **p** man and an Jb 22:8
rescued me from my **p** enemy and Ps 18:17
my enemies are vigorous and **p**; Ps 38:19
P men attack me, but not because Ps 59:3
He thunders with His **p** voice! Ps 68:33
who would destroy me, are **p**. Ps 69:4
Your enemies with Your **p** arm. Ps 89:10
Your hand is **p**; Your right hand Ps 89:13
will be **p** in the land; Ps 112:2
p wind that executes His command, Ps 148:8
Praise Him for His **p** acts; Ps 150:2
and separates **p** opponents. Pr 18:18
a **p** nation with a strange Is 18:2
a **p** nation with a strange Is 18:7
vindication, **p** to save. Is 63:1
I will go to the **p** and speak to Jr 5:5
they have grown **p** and rich. Jr 5:27
who was **p** on the sea, she and Ezk 26:17
great and **p**, has ever asked Dn 2:10
when he became **p**, the large horn Dn 8:8
will destroy the **p** along with Dn 8:24
king of the South will grow **p**, Dn 11:5
will grow more **p** and will rule a Dn 11:5
an extremely large and **p** army, Dn 11:25
invaded My land, **p** and without Jl 1:6
who carry out His command are **p**. Jl 2:11
when the **p** man communicates his Mc 7:3
after me is more **p** than I. Mt 3:11
Someone more **p** than I will come Mk 1:7
is coming who is more **p** than I. Lk 3:16
was a Prophet **p** in action and Lk 24:19
and was **p** in his speech and Ac 7:22
man who was **p** in the Scriptures, Ac 18:24
established as the **p** Son of God Rm 1:4
not many **p**, not many of noble 1Co 1:26
but are **p** through God for the 2Co 10:4
His letters are weighty and **p**, 2Co 10:10
toward you, but **p** among you. 2Co 13:3
from heaven with His **p** angels, 2Th 1:7
all things by His **p** word. Heb 1:3
of the righteous is very **p**. Jms 5:16
the rich, the **p**, and every slave Rv 6:15

POWERFULLY *(2)*

and the LORD's hand was on me **p**. Ezk 3:14
His strength that works **p** in me. Col 1:29

POWERLESS *(9)*

you will be **p** to do anything. Dt 28:32
Their inhabitants have become **p**, 2Kg 19:26
For we are **p** before this vast 2Ch 20:12
but we are **p** because our fields Neh 5:5
have helped the **p** and delivered Jb 26:2
Their inhabitants have become **p**, Is 37:27
the weary and strengthens the **p**. Is 40:29
grew deathly pale, and I was **p**. Dn 10:8
vision, I am overwhelmed and **p**. Dn 10:16

POWERS *(9)*

why supernatural **p** are at work Mt 14:2
the celestial **p** will be shaken. Mt 24:29
why supernatural **p** are at work Mk 6:14
the celestial **p** will be shaken. Mk 13:25
the celestial **p** will be shaken. Lk 21:26
nor things to come, nor **p**, Rm 8:38
the world **p** of this darkness Eph 6:12
word and the **p** of the coming age Heb 6:5
and **p** subjected to Him 1Pt 3:22

PRACTICE *(41)*

month you are to **p** self-denial Lv 16:29
and you must **p** self-denial; Lv 16:31
You are to **p** My ordinances and Lv 18:4
You are not to **p** divination or Lv 19:26
assembly and **p** self-denial; Lv 23:27
person does not **p** self-denial on Lv 23:29
and you must **p** self-denial. Lv 23:32
seventh month and **p** self-denial; Nm 29:7
because they **p** for their gods Dt 12:31
the fire, **p** divination, tell Dt 18:10
interpret omens, **p** sorcery, Dt 18:10
the words of this law into **p**.' Dt 27:26
continue the **p** they had begun, Est 9:23
This was Job's regular **p**. Jb 1:5
you **p** injustice in your hearts; Ps 58:2
Deliver me from those who **p** sin, Ps 59:2
p righteousness at all times. Ps 106:3
This is my ⌊**p**⌋: I obey Your Ps 119:56
as is ⌊Your⌋ **p** toward those who Ps 119:132
terror to those who **p** iniquity. Pr 21:15
the **p** of extortion turns a wise Ec 7:7
allow those who **p** it to escape. Ec 8:8
keep My ordinances, and **p** them. Ezk 11:20
false visions or **p** divination. Ezk 13:23
in their ways and **p** their Ezk 16:47
keep My ordinances, and **p** them. Ezk 20:19
For they did not **p** My ordinances Ezk 20:24
the two roads, to **p** divination: Ezk 21:21
For they **p** fraud; a thief Hs 7:1
her prophets **p** divination for Mc 3:11
Be careful not to **p** your Mt 6:1
they don't **p** what they teach. Mt 23:3
for us as Romans to adopt or **p**." Ac 16:21
that those who **p** such things Rm 1:32
even applaud others who **p** them. Rm 1:32
because I do not **p** what I want Rm 7:15
but I **p** the evil that I do not Rm 7:19
those who **p** such things will Gl 5:21
for the **p** of every kind Eph 4:19
P these things; be committed to 1Tm 4:15
should learn to **p** their religion 1Tm 5:4

PRACTICED *(14)*

customs that were **p** before you, Lv 18:30
that they **p** against Me, Lv 26:40
the fire and **p** divination 2Kg 17:17
p witchcraft and divination, 2Kg 21:6
He **p** witchcraft, divination, and 2Ch 33:6
whose ordinances you have not **p**. Ezk 11:12
own iniquity because he **p** fraud, Ezk 18:18
of the righteousness he has **p**. Ezk 18:22
of the iniquity he has **p**. Ezk 18:26
of the land have **p** extortion and Ezk 22:29
had previously **p** sorcery in that Ac 8:9
those who had **p** magic collected Ac 19:19
and promiscuity they **p**. 2Co 12:21
immorality and **p** perversions, Jd 7

PRACTICES *(35)*

same thing by their occult **p**. Ex 7:11
same thing by their occult **p**. Ex 7:22
by their occult **p** and brought Ex 8:7
gnats using their occult **p**, Ex 8:18
Do not imitate their **p**. Ex 23:24
Do not follow the **p** of the land Lv 18:3
or follow the **p** of the land of Lv 18:3
yourselves by any of these ⌊**p**⌋, Lv 18:24
enraged Him with detestable **p**. Dt 32:16
from their ⌊evil⌋ **p** or their Jdg 2:19
according to the **p** of Israel. 2Ch 17:4
the detestable **p** of the nations 2Ch 28:3
the detestable **p** of the nations 2Ch 33:2
the detestable **p** of the nations, 2Ch 36:14
detestable **p** are like those Ezr 9:1
their impurity and detestable **p**. Ezr 9:11
who commit these detestable **p**? Ezr 9:14
descendants to the **p** of fasting Est 9:31
lives honestly, **p** righteousness, Ps 15:2
p are smoke in My nostrils, Is 65:5
righteousness and **p** iniquity, Ezk 3:20
your detestable **p** and Ezk 5:11
p My ordinances and follows My Ezk 18:17
righteousness and **p** iniquity, Ezk 18:24
righteousness and **p** iniquity, Ezk 18:26
and all the **p** of Ahab's house Mc 6:16
But whoever **p** and teaches ⌊these Mt 5:19
For everyone who **p** wicked things Jn 3:20
and disclosing their **p**, Ac 19:18
on ascetic **p** and the worship Col 2:18
wisdom by promoting ascetic **p**, Col 2:23
put off the old man with his **p** Col 3:9
you hate the **p** of the Rv 2:6
unless they repent of her **p**. Rv 2:22
everyone who loves and **p** lying. Rv 22:15

PRACTICING *(5)*

They are ⌊still⌋ **p** the former 2Kg 17:34
but continued **p** their former 2Kg 17:40
abominations they are **p** here, Ezk 8:17
of life without **p** iniquity— Ezk 33:15
lying and are not **p** the truth. 1Jn 1:6

PRAISE *(275)*

P the LORD, the God of Shem; Gn 9:26
and give **p** to God Most High who Gn 14:20
and said, "**P** the LORD, the God Gn 24:27
"This time I will **p** the LORD." Gn 29:35
Judah, your brothers will **p** you. Gn 49:8
God, and I will **p** Him, my Ex 15:2
consecrated as a **p** offering to Lv 19:24
you will **p** the LORD your God for Dt 8:10
He is your **p** and He is your God, Dt 10:21
the nations He has made in **p**, Dt 26:19
people volunteer, **p** the LORD. Jdg 5:2
I will sing **p** to the LORD God of Jdg 5:3
of the people. **P** the LORD! Jdg 5:9
who travel on the road, give **p**! Jdg 5:10
said to Naomi, "**P** the LORD, who Ru 4:14
P to the LORD God of Israel, 1Sm 25:32
P the LORD who championed my 1Sm 25:39
is worthy of **p**, and I was saved 2Sm 22:4
I will **p** You, LORD, among 2Sm 22:50
return to You and **p** Your name, 1Kg 8:33
this place and **p** Your name, 1Kg 8:35
and to give thanks and **p** to Him. 1Ch 16:4
Sing to Him; sing **p** to Him; tell 1Ch 16:9
holy name and rejoice in Your **p**. 1Ch 16:35
said, "Amen" and "**P** the LORD." 1Ch 16:36
and 4,000 are to **p** the LORD with 1Ch 23:5
give thanks and **p** to the LORD, 1Ch 23:30
giving thanks and **p** to the LORD. 1Ch 25:3
You thanks and **p** Your glorious 1Ch 29:13
assembly, "**P** the LORD your God. 1Ch 29:20
together to **p** and thank the LORD 2Ch 5:13
instruments, in **p** to the LORD: 2Ch 5:13
return ⌊to You⌋ and **p** Your name, 2Ch 6:24
this place and **p** Your name, 2Ch 6:26
David had made to **p** the LORD— 2Ch 7:6
when David offered **p** with them. 2Ch 7:6
offer **p** and to minister before 2Ch 8:14
stood up to **p** the LORD God 2Ch 20:19
LORD and some to **p** the splendor 2Ch 20:21

instruments were leading the **p**. 2Ch 23:13
Levites to sing **p** to the LORD 2Ch 29:30
and for **p** in the gates of the 2Ch 31:2
their positions to **p** the LORD, Ezr 3:10
sang with **p** and thanksgiving Ezr 3:11
a great shout of **p** to the LORD Ezr 3:11
P the LORD God of our fathers, Ezr 7:27
P Your glorious name, and may it Neh 9:5
above all blessing and **p**. Neh 9:5
were in charge of the **p** songs. Neh 12:8
them—gave **p** and thanks, Neh 12:24
and songs of **p** and thanksgiving Neh 12:46
P the name of the LORD. Jb 1:21
that you should **p** His work, Jb 36:24
will **p** the LORD who counsels me Ps 16:7
is worthy of **p**, and I was saved Ps 18:3
I will **p** You, LORD, among Ps 18:49
we will sing and **p** Your might. Ps 21:13
will **p** You in the congregation. Ps 22:22
You who fear the LORD, **p** Him! Ps 22:23
I will give **p** in the great Ps 22:25
who seek the LORD will **p** Him. Ps 22:26
I will **p** the LORD in the Ps 26:12
rejoices, and I **p** Him with my Ps 28:7
ones, and **p** His holy name. Ps 30:4
Pit? Will the dust **p** You? Will Ps 30:9
my God, I will **p** You forever. Ps 30:12
p from the upright is beautiful. Ps 33:1
P the LORD with the lyre; Ps 33:2
I will **p** the LORD at all times; Ps 34:1
His **p** will always be on my lips. Ps 34:1
I will **p** You in the great Ps 35:18
Your **p** all day long. Ps 35:28
mouth, a hymn of **p** to our God. Ps 40:3
I will still **p** Him, my Savior Ps 42:5
I will still **p** Him, my Savior Ps 42:11
I will **p** You with the lyre, Ps 43:4
I will still **p** Him, my Savior Ps 43:5
we will **p** Your name forever. Ps 44:8
the peoples will **p** you forever Ps 45:17
Sing **p** to God, sing praise; Ps 47:6
Sing praise to God, sing **p**; Ps 47:6
sing **p** to our King, sing praise! Ps 47:6
sing praise to our King, sing **p**! Ps 47:6
God, like Your **p**, reaches to the Ps 48:10
people **p** you when you do well Ps 49:18
my mouth will declare Your **p**. Ps 51:15
will **p** You forever for what You Ps 52:9
will **p** Your name, LORD, because Ps 54:6
whose word I **p**, in God I trust; Ps 56:4
whose word I **p**, in the LORD, Ps 56:10
in the LORD, whose word I **p**, Ps 56:10
I will **p** You, Lord, among the Ps 57:9
So I will **p** You as long as I Ps 63:4
my mouth will **p** You with joyful Ps 63:5
the upright in heart offer **p**. Ps 64:10
P is rightfully Yours, God, in Ps 65:1
His name; make His **p** glorious. Ps 66:2
worship You and sing **p** to You. Ps 66:4
They will sing **p** to Your name." Ps 66:4
P our God, you peoples; Ps 66:8
let the sound of His **p** be heard. Ps 66:8
my mouth, and **p** was on my tongue Ps 66:17
Let the peoples **p** You, God; Ps 67:3
let all the peoples **p** You. Ps 67:3
Let the peoples **p** You, God, let Ps 67:5
let all the peoples **p** You. Ps 67:5
P God in the assemblies; Ps 68:26
⌊**P**⌋ the LORD from the fountain Ps 68:26
sing **p** to the Lord, Selah Ps 68:32
will **p** God's name with song and Ps 69:30
Let heaven and earth **p** Him, Ps 69:34
My **p** is always about You. Ps 71:6
is full of **p** and honor to You Ps 71:8
and will **p** You more and more. Ps 71:14
a lute I will **p** You for Your Ps 71:22
for joy when I sing **p** to You, Ps 71:23
the poor and needy **p** Your name. Ps 74:21
I will sing **p** to the God of Ps 75:9
Even human wrath will **p** You; Ps 76:10
declare Your **p** to generation Ps 79:13
house, who **p** You continually Ps 84:4
I will **p** You with all my heart, Ps 86:12
spirits rise up to **p** You? Ps 88:10
the heavens **p** Your wonders— Ps 89:5
is good to **p** the LORD, to sing Ps 92:1
LORD, to sing **p** to Your name, Ps 92:1
Sing to the LORD, **p** His name; Ps 96:2

ones, and **p** His holy name. Ps 97:12
Let them **p** Your great and Ps 99:3
and His courts with **p**. Ps 100:4
thanks to Him and **p** His name. Ps 100:4
I will sing **p** to You, LORD. Ps 101:1
created people will **p** the LORD: Ps 102:18
in Zion and His **p** in Jerusalem, Ps 102:21
soul, **p** the LORD, and all that Ps 103:1
is within me, **p** His holy name. Ps 103:1
My soul, **p** the LORD, and do not Ps 103:2
P the LORD, ⌊all⌋ His angels of Ps 103:20
P the LORD, all His armies, His Ps 103:21
P the LORD, all His works in all Ps 103:22
He rules. My soul, **p** the LORD! Ps 103:22
soul, **p** the LORD! LORD my God, Ps 104:1
I will sing **p** to my God while I Ps 104:33
no more. My soul, **p** the LORD! Ps 104:35
Sing to Him, sing **p** to Him; Ps 105:2
or proclaim all the **p** due Him? Ps 106:2
His promises and sang His **p**. Ps 106:12
holy name and rejoice in Your **p**. Ps 106:47
of the people and **p** Him in the Ps 107:32
I will **p** You, LORD, among the Ps 108:3
God of my **p**, do not be silent. Ps 109:1
I will **p** Him in the presence of Ps 109:30
I will **p** the LORD with all my Ps 111:1
His **p** endures forever. Ps 111:10
Give **p**, servants of the LORD; Ps 113:1
p the name of the LORD. Ps 113:1
is not the dead who **p** the LORD, Ps 115:17
But we will **p** the LORD, both now Ps 115:18
P the LORD, all nations! Ps 117:1
will **p** You with a sincere heart Ps 119:7
my willing offerings of **p**, Ps 119:108
I **p** You seven times a day for Ps 119:164
lips pour out **p**, for You teach Ps 119:171
Let me live, and I will **p** You; Ps 119:175
P the LORD, who has not let us Ps 124:6
Now **p** the LORD, all you servants Ps 134:1
the holy place, and **p** the LORD! Ps 134:2
P the name of the LORD. Ps 135:1
Give **p**, you servants of the LORD Ps 135:1
P the LORD, for the LORD is good; Ps 135:3
sing **p** to His name, for it is Ps 135:3
House of Israel, **p** the LORD! Ps 135:19
House of Aaron, **p** the LORD! Ps 135:19
House of Levi, **p** the LORD! Ps 135:20
who revere the LORD, **p** the LORD! Ps 135:20
I will sing Your **p** before the Ps 138:1
will **p** You, because I have been Ps 139:14
the righteous will **p** Your name; Ps 140:13
so that I can **p** Your name. Ps 142:7
p Your name forever and ever. Ps 145:1
I will **p** You every day; Ps 145:2
All You have made will **p** You, Ps 145:10
mouth will declare the LORD's **p**; Ps 145:21
living thing **p** His holy name Ps 145:21
Hallelujah! My soul, **p** the LORD. Ps 146:1
I will **p** the LORD all my life; Ps 146:2
for **p** is pleasant and lovely. Ps 147:1
Jerusalem; **p** your God, Zion! Ps 147:12
P the LORD from the heavens; Ps 148:1
p Him in the heights. Ps 148:1
P Him, all His angels; Ps 148:2
p Him, all His hosts. Ps 148:2
P Him, sun and moon; praise Him, Ps 148:3
p Him, all you shining stars. Ps 148:3
P Him, highest heavens, and you Ps 148:4
Let them **p** the name of the LORD, Ps 148:5
P the LORD from the earth, Ps 148:7
Let them **p** the name of the LORD, Ps 148:13
p from all His godly ones, Ps 148:14
His **p** in the assembly of the Ps 149:1
Let them **p** His name with dancing Ps 149:3
P God in His sanctuary. Ps 150:1
P Him in His mighty heavens. Ps 150:1
P Him for His powerful acts; Ps 150:2
p Him for His abundant greatness. Ps 150:2
P Him with trumpet blast; Ps 150:3
p Him with harp and lyre. Ps 150:3
P Him with tambourine and dance; Ps 150:4
p Him with flute and strings. Ps 150:4
P Him with resounding cymbals; Ps 150:5
p Him with clashing cymbals. Ps 150:5
that breathes **p** the LORD. Ps 150:6
Let another **p** you, and not your Pr 27:2
and a man, by the **p** he receives. Pr 27:21
who reject the law **p** the wicked, Pr 28:4

let her works **p** her at the city Pr 31:31
we will **p** your love more than Sg 1:4
I will **p** You, LORD, although You Is 12:1
I will **p** Your name, for You have Is 25:1
Death cannot **p** You. Those who go Is 38:18
to another, or My **p** to idols. Is 42:8
⌊sing⌋ His **p** from the ends of Is 42:10
declare His **p** in the islands. Is 42:12
for Myself will declare My **p**. Is 43:21
for your benefit and ⌊for⌋ My **p**, Is 48:9
creating words of **p**." Is 57:19
salvation, and your gates **p**. Is 60:18
righteousness and **p** to spring up Is 61:11
Jerusalem the **p** of the earth. Is 62:7
will eat it and **p** the LORD, Is 62:9
for My fame, **p**, and glory, Jr 13:11
will be saved, for You are my **p**. Jr 17:14
P the LORD, for He rescues the Jr 20:13
Proclaim, **p**, and say: Jr 31:7
a name of joy, **p**, and glory Jr 33:9
of those saying, **P** the LORD of Jr 33:11
There is no longer **p** for Moab; Jr 48:2
can the city of **p** not be Jr 49:25
the **p** of the whole earth seized. Jr 51:41
p the glory of the LORD in His Ezk 3:12
I offer thanks and **p** to You, Dn 2:23
P to the God of Shadrach, Dn 3:28
I, Nebuchadnezzar, **p**, exalt, and Dn 4:37
repay You with **p** from our lips. Hs 14:2
You will **p** the name of Yahweh Jl 2:26
and the earth is full of His **p**. Hab 3:3
the earth receive **p** and fame. Zph 3:19
P the LORD because I have become Zch 11:5
Jesus said, "I **p** You, Father, Mt 11:25
have prepared **p** from the mouths Mt 21:16
P the Lord, the God of Israel, Lk 1:68
and said, "I **p** You, Father, Lord Lk 10:21
when they saw it, gave **p** to God. Lk 18:43
began to **p** God joyfully with Lk 19:37
For they loved **p** from men more Jn 12:43
from men more than **p** from God. Jn 12:43
His **p** is not from men but from Rm 2:29
every tongue will give **p** to God. Rm 14:11
Therefore I will **p** You among the Rm 15:9
P the Lord, all you Gentiles; Rm 15:11
all the peoples should **p** Him! Rm 15:11
And then **p** will come to each one 1Co 4:5
I **p** you because you remember 1Co 11:2
instruction I do not **p** you, 1Co 11:17
to you? Should I **p** you? I do not 1Co 11:22
I do not **p** you for this! 1Co 11:22
to the **p** of His glorious grace Eph 1:6
might bring **p** to His glory. Eph 1:12
to the **p** of His glory. Eph 1:14
to the glory and **p** of God. Php 1:11
and if there is any **p**— Php 4:8
up to God a sacrifice of **p**, Heb 13:15
result in **p**, glory, and honor 1Pt 1:7
do evil and to **p** those who do 1Pt 2:14
P our God, all you His servants, Rv 19:5

PRAISED *(59)*

saw her and **p** her to Pharaoh, Gn 12:15
LORD, and **p** the LORD, the God Gn 24:48
with the report, and they **p** God. Jos 22:33
they **p** their god and said: Jdg 16:24
ground in homage and **p** the king. 2Sm 14:22
and highly **p** as Absalom. 2Sm 14:25
May the LORD your God be **p**! 2Sm 18:28
LORD lives—may my rock be **p**! 2Sm 22:47
'May the LORD God of Israel be **p**! 1Kg 1:48
said, "May the LORD be **p** today! 1Kg 5:7
May the LORD God of Israel be **p**! 1Kg 8:15
May the LORD be **p**! He has given 1Kg 8:56
May the LORD your God be **p**! 1Kg 10:9
LORD is great and is highly **p**; 1Ch 16:25
p from everlasting to everlasting. 1Ch 16:36
Then David **p** the LORD in the 1Ch 29:10
May You be **p**, LORD God of our 1Ch 29:10
whole assembly **p** the LORD God 1Ch 29:20
the heavens and the earth, be **p**! 2Ch 2:12
May the LORD God of Israel be **p**! 2Ch 6:4
They worshiped and **p** the LORD: 2Ch 7:3
May the LORD your God be **p**! 2Ch 9:8
for there they **p** the LORD. 2Ch 20:26
and the priests **p** the LORD day 2Ch 30:21
they **p** the LORD and His people 2Ch 31:8
Amen," and they **p** the LORD. Neh 5:13
The people **p** all the men who Neh 11:2

LORD lives—may my rock be **p**! Ps 18:46
May the LORD be **p**, for He has Ps 28:6
May the LORD be **p**, for He has Ps 31:21
be **p** from everlasting to Ps 41:13
and is highly **p** in the city of Ps 48:1
May God be **p**! He has not turned Ps 66:20
May the Lord be **p**! Day after day Ps 68:19
to His people. May God be **p**! Ps 68:35
of Israel, be **p**, who alone does Ps 72:18
His glorious name be **p** forever; Ps 72:19
May the LORD be **p** forever. Ps 89:52
LORD is great and is highly **p**; Ps 96:4
be **p** from everlasting to Ps 106:48
name of the LORD be **p** both now Ps 113:2
let the name of the LORD be **p**. Ps 113:3
LORD, may You be **p**; teach me Ps 119:12
May the LORD be **p** from Zion; Ps 135:21
May the LORD my rock be **p**, Ps 144:1
Yahweh is great and is highly **p**; Ps 145:3
A man is **p** for his insight, Pr 12:8
who fears the LORD will be **p**. Pr 31:30
they were **p** in the city where Ec 8:10
where our fathers **p** You, has Is 64:11
and Daniel **p** the God of heaven Dn 2:19
name of God be **p** forever and Dn 2:20
Then I **p** the Most High and Dn 4:34
the wine and **p** their gods made Dn 5:4
p the gods made of silver and Dn 5:23
up in his arms, **p** God, and said: Lk 2:28
The master **p** the unrighteous Lk 16:8
but the people **p** them highly. Ac 5:13
the brother who is **p** throughout 2Co 8:18

PRAISES *(19)*

revered with **p**, performing Ex 15:11
they began ⌊their⌋ shouts and **p**, 2Ch 20:22
they sang **p** with rejoicing and 2Ch 29:30
that I may declare all Your **p**. Ps 9:14
enthroned on the **p** of Israel. Ps 22:3
Though he **p** himself during his Ps 49:18
I will sing; I will sing **p**. Ps 57:7
I will sing **p** to You among the Ps 57:9
I sing **p**, because God is Ps 59:17
Sing to God! Sing **p** to His name. Ps 68:4
generation the **p** of the LORD, Ps 78:4
I will sing **p** with the whole of Ps 108:1
I will sing **p** to You among the Ps 108:3
Her husband also **p** her: Pr 31:28
also, and they sing her **p**: Sg 6:9
and proclaim the **p** of the LORD. Is 60:6
incense, one **p** an idol—all Is 66:3
cheerful? He should sing **p**. Jms 5:13
proclaim the **p** of the One who 1Pt 2:9

PRAISEWORTHY *(2)*

love ⌊and⌋ the LORD's **p** acts, Is 63:7
make you famous and **p** among all Zph 3:20

PRAISING *(7)*

guards, and those **p** the king, 2Ch 23:12
and he began to speak, **p** God. Lk 1:64
the angel, **p** God and saying: Lk 2:13
glorifying and **p** God for all Lk 2:20
p God and having favor with all Ac 2:47
walking, leaping, and **p** God. Ac 3:8
saw him walking and **p** God, Ac 3:9

PRANCING *(1)*

along with **p** steps, jingling Is 3:16

PRAY *(108)*

and he will **p** for you and you Gn 20:7
and I will **p** to the LORD on your 1Sm 7:5
P to the LORD your God for your 1Sm 12:19
LORD by ceasing to **p** for you. 1Sm 12:23
the courage to **p** this prayer to 2Sm 7:27
which they **p** toward this place. 1Kg 8:30
they **p** and plead with You for 1Kg 8:33
and they **p** toward this place and 1Kg 8:35
and will come and **p** toward this 1Kg 8:42
and they **p** to the LORD in the 1Kg 8:44
and when they **p** to You in the 1Kg 8:48
your God and **p** for me so that my 1Kg 13:6
courage⌋ to **p** in Your presence. 1Ch 17:25
which they **p** toward this place. 2Ch 6:21
and they **p** and plead for mercy 2Ch 6:24
and they **p** toward this place and 2Ch 6:26
and they **p** to You in the 2Ch 6:34
and when they **p** in the direction 2Ch 6:38
themselves, **p** and seek My face, 2Ch 7:14
God of heaven and **p** for the life Ezr 6:10
prayer that I now **p** to You day Neh 1:6
You will **p** to Him, and He will Jb 22:27
He will **p** to God, and God will Jb 33:26
My servant Job will **p** for you. Jb 42:8
King and my God, for I **p** to You. Ps 5:2
who is faithful **p** to You at a Ps 32:6
accuse me, but I continue to **p**. Ps 109:4
P for the peace of Jerusalem: Ps 122:6
and comes to his sanctuary to **p**, Is 16:12
and **p** to a god who cannot save, Is 45:20
do not **p** for these people. Jr 7:16
do not **p** for these people. Jr 11:14
Do not **p** for the well-being of Jr 14:11
P to the LORD on its behalf, Jr 29:7
call to Me and come and **p** to Me, Jr 29:12
p to the LORD our God for us! Jr 37:3
p to the LORD your God on our Jr 42:2
will now **p** to the LORD your God Jr 42:4
'**P** to the LORD our God on our Jr 42:20
your enemies and **p** for those who Mt 5:44
Whenever you **p**, you must not be Mt 6:5
because they love to **p** standing Mt 6:5
But when you **p**, go into your Mt 6:6
and **p** to your Father who is in Mt 6:6
When you **p**, don't babble like Mt 6:7
you should **p** like this: Mt 6:9
p to the Lord of the harvest to Mt 9:38
on the mountain by Himself to **p**. Mt 14:23
about any matter that you **p** for, Mt 18:19
put His hands on them and **p**. Mt 19:13
P that your escape may not be in Mt 24:20
while I go over there and **p**." Mt 26:36
Stay awake and **p**, so that you Mt 26:41
went away to the mountain to **p**. Mk 6:46
the things you **p** and ask for— Mk 11:24
P it won't happen in winter. Mk 13:18
disciples, "Sit here while I **p**." Mk 14:32
and began to **p** that if it were Mk 14:35
Stay awake and **p** so that you Mk 14:38
the mountain to **p** and spent all Lk 6:12
p for those who mistreat you. Lk 6:28
went up on the mountain to **p**. Lk 9:28
p to the Lord of the harvest to Lk 10:2
Lord, teach us to **p**, just as Lk 11:1
to them, "Whenever you **p**, say: Lk 11:2
need for them to **p** always and Lk 18:1
up to the temple complex to **p**, Lk 18:10
P that you may not enter into Lk 22:40
knelt down, and began to **p**, Lk 22:41
Get up and **p**, so that you won't Lk 22:46
I **p** for them. I am not praying Jn 17:9
I **p** not only for these, but also Jn 17:20
p to the Lord that the intent Ac 8:22
"Please **p** to the Lord for me," Ac 8:24
went up to **p** on the housetop Ac 10:9
kneeling down on the beach to **p**, Ac 21:5
know what to **p** for as we should Rm 8:26
for a woman to **p** to God with her 1Co 11:13
language should **p** that he can 1Co 14:13
if I **p** in ⌊another⌋ language, 1Co 14:14
I will **p** with the spirit, and I 1Co 14:15
and I will also **p** with my 1Co 14:15
Now we **p** to God that you do 2Co 13:7
strong. We also **p** for this: your 2Co 13:9
⌊I **p**⌋ that the God of our Lord Eph 1:17
p⌋ that the eyes of your heart Eph 1:18
⌊I **p**⌋ that He may grant you, Eph 3:16
⌊I **p** that⌋ you, being rooted and Eph 3:17
p at all times in the Spirit, Eph 6:18
P also for me, that the message Eph 6:19
P that I might be bold enough in Eph 6:20
I **p** this: that your love will Php 1:9
Jesus Christ, when we **p** for you, Col 1:3
p also for us that God may open Col 4:3
as we **p** earnestly night and day 1Th 3:10
P constantly. 1Th 5:17
Brothers, **p** for us also. 1Th 5:25
we always **p** for you that our God 2Th 1:11
Finally, **p** for us, brothers, 2Th 3:1
the men in every place to **p**, 1Tm 2:8
⌊I **p**⌋ that your participation in Phm 6
P for us; for we are convinced Heb 13:18
urge you to **p** that I may be Heb 13:19
He should **p**. Is anyone cheerful Jms 5:13
and they should **p** over him after Jms 5:14
another and **p** for one another Jms 5:16
saying he should **p** about that. 1Jn 5:16
p that you may prosper in every 3Jn 2

PRAYED *(52)*

Then Abraham **p** to God, and God Gn 20:17
Abraham," he **p**, "grant me Gn 24:12
when I came to the spring, I **p**: Gn 24:42
Isaac **p** to the LORD on behalf of Gn 25:21
to Moses, and he **p** to the LORD, Nm 11:2
But I **p** for Aaron at that time Dt 9:20
p to the LORD: Lord GOD, do not Dt 9:26
Manoah **p** to the LORD and said, Jdg 13:8
Hannah **p** to the LORD and wept 1Sm 1:10
I **p** for this boy, and since the 1Sm 1:27
Hannah **p**: My heart rejoices in 1Sm 2:1
sinful, so he **p** to the LORD. 1Sm 8:6
a broom tree and **p** that he might 1Kg 19:4
two of them, and **p** to the LORD. 2Kg 4:33
Elisha **p**, "LORD, please open 2Kg 6:17
him, Elisha **p** to the LORD, 2Kg 6:18
Hezekiah **p** before the LORD: 2Kg 19:15
to the wall and **p** to the LORD, 2Kg 20:2
Isaiah son of Amoz **p** about this 2Ch 32:20
of death, so he **p** to the LORD, 2Ch 32:24
He **p** to Him, so He heard his 2Ch 33:13
While Ezra **p** and confessed, Ezr 10:1
So I **p** to the God of heaven Neh 2:4
So we **p** to our God and stationed Neh 4:9
After Job had **p** for his friends, Jb 42:10
Hezekiah **p** to the LORD: Is 37:15
'Because you **p** to Me about Is 37:21
to the wall and **p** to the LORD. Is 38:2
son of Neriah, I **p** to the LORD: Jr 32:16
on his knees, **p**, and gave thanks Dn 6:10
I **p** to the LORD my God and Dn 9:4
Jonah **p** to the LORD his God from Jnh 2:1
He **p** to the LORD: "Please, LORD, Jnh 4:2
fell facedown and **p**, "My Father! Mt 26:39
went away and **p**, "My Father, if Mt 26:42
away again and **p** a third time, Mt 26:44
Once again He went away and **p**, Mk 14:39
to deserted places and **p**. Lk 5:16
But I have **p** for you that your Lk 22:32
in anguish, He **p** more fervently, Lk 22:44
Then they **p**, "You, Lord, know Ac 1:24
When they had **p**, the place where Ac 4:31
who **p** and laid their hands on Ac 6:6
there, they **p** for them, that Ac 8:15
He knelt down, **p**, and turning Ac 9:40
people and always **p** to God. Ac 10:2
had fasted, **p**, and laid hands Ac 13:3
every church and **p** with fasting, Ac 14:23
knelt down and **p** with all of Ac 20:36
the stern and **p** for daylight to Ac 27:29
yet he **p** earnestly that it would Jms 5:17
he **p** again, and the sky gave Jms 5:18

PRAYER *(104)*

LORD heard his **p**, and his wife Gn 25:21
courage to pray this **p** to You. 2Sm 7:27
God answered **p** for the land. 2Sm 21:14
the LORD answered **p** on behalf of 2Sm 24:25
Your servant's **p** and his 1Kg 8:28
the cry and the **p** that Your 1Kg 8:28
You may hear the **p** that Your 1Kg 8:29
whatever **p** or petition anyone 1Kg 8:38
You hear their **p** and petition 1Kg 8:45
their **p** and petition and uphold 1Kg 8:49
this entire **p** and petition to 1Kg 8:54
have heard your **p** and petition 1Kg 9:3
offer a **p** for the surviving 2Kg 19:4
'I have heard your **p** to Me about 2Kg 19:20
have heard your **p**; I have seen 2Kg 20:5
Your servant's **p** and his 2Ch 6:19
the cry and the **p** that Your 2Ch 6:19
You may hear the **p** Your servant 2Ch 6:20
whatever **p** or petition anyone 2Ch 6:29
You hear their **p** and petition 2Ch 6:35
their **p** and petitions and uphold 2Ch 6:39
to the **p** of this place. 2Ch 6:40
heard your **p** and have chosen 2Ch 7:12
attentive to **p** from this place. 2Ch 7:15
and their **p** came into His holy 2Ch 30:27
along with his **p** to his God and 2Ch 33:18
His **p** and how God granted his 2Ch 33:19
Your servant's **p** that I now pray Neh 1:6
to the **p** of Your servant Neh 1:11
who began the thanksgiving in **p**; Neh 11:17
up your hands to Him ⌊in **p**⌋— Jb 11:13
from violence and my **p** is pure. Jb 16:17
accept his ⌊**p**⌋ and not deal with Jb 42:8
and the LORD accepted Job's ⌊**p**⌋. Jb 42:9

be gracious to me and hear my **p**. Ps 4:1
the LORD accepts my **p**. Ps 6:9
listen to my **p**—from lips free Ps 17:1
fasting, and my **p** was genuine. Ps 35:13
Hear my **p**, LORD, and listen to Ps 39:12
a **p** to the God of my life. Ps 42:8
God, hear my **p**; listen to the Ps 54:2
listen to my **p** and do not ignore Ps 55:1
pay attention to my **p**. Ps 61:1
to You, the One who hears **p**. Ps 65:2
attention to the sound of my **p**. Ps 66:19
turned away my **p** or turned His Ps 66:20
my **p** to You is for a time of Ps 69:13
May **p** be offered for him Ps 72:15
LORD God of Hosts, hear my **p**; Ps 84:8
LORD, hear my **p**; listen to my Ps 86:6
May my **p** reach Your presence; Ps 88:2
in the morning my **p** meets You. Ps 88:13
LORD, hear my **p**; let my cry for Ps 102:1
to the **p** of the destitute Ps 102:17
and will not despise their **p**. Ps 102:17
and let his **p** be counted as sin. Ps 109:7
May my **p** be set before You as Ps 141:2
now my **p** is against the evil Ps 141:5
LORD, hear my **p**. In Your Ps 143:1
but the **p** of the upright is His Pr 15:8
He hears the **p** of the righteous Pr 15:29
law—even his **p** is detestable. Pr 28:9
you lift up your hands ⌊in **p**⌋, Is 1:15
offer a **p** for the surviving Is 37:4
have heard your **p**; I have seen Is 38:5
them rejoice in My house of **p**. Is 56:7
a house of **p** for all nations. Is 56:7
a cry or a **p** on their behalf Jr 7:16
up a cry or a **p** on their behalf, Jr 11:14
plead for help, He rejects my **p**. Lm 3:8
so that no **p** can pass through Lm 3:44
to seek Him by **p** and petitions, Dn 9:3
hear the **p** and the petitions of Dn 9:17
My **p** came to You, to Your holy Jnh 2:7
A **p** of Habakkuk the prophet. Hab 3:1
of grace and **p** on the house Zch 12:10
out except by **p** and fasting." Mt 17:21
will be called a house of **p**. Mt 21:13
whatever you ask for in **p**." Mt 21:22
by nothing but **p** and fasting ." Mk 9:29
a house of **p** for all nations? Mk 11:17
because your **p** has been heard. Lk 1:13
and spent all night in **p** to God. Lk 6:12
My house will be a house of **p**, Lk 19:46
When He got up from **p** and came Lk 22:45
were continually united in **p**, Ac 1:14
complex at the hour of **p** at Ac 3:1
devote ourselves to **p** and to the Ac 6:4
your **p** has been heard, Ac 10:31
but **p** was being made earnestly Ac 12:5
thought there was a place of **p**. Ac 16:13
as we were on our way to **p**, Ac 16:16
desire and **p** to God concerning Rm 10:1
affliction; be persistent in **p**. Rm 12:12
to devote yourselves to **p**. 1Co 7:5
join in helping with **p** for us, 2Co 1:11
With every **p** and request, pray Eph 6:18
for all of you in my every **p**, Php 1:4
through **p** and petition with Php 4:6
Devote yourselves to **p**; Col 4:2
by the word of God and by **p**. 1Tm 4:5
p of faith will save the sick Jms 5:15
The intense **p** of the righteous Jms 5:16
and disciplined for **p**. 1Pt 4:7

PRAYERS (32)

The **p** of David son of Jesse are Ps 72:20
be angry with Your people's **p**? Ps 80:4
even if you offer countless **p**, Is 1:15
will hear their **p** and heal them. Is 19:22
out whispered ⌊**p** because⌋ Your Is 26:16
your God, your **p** were heard. Dn 10:12
I have come because of your **p**. Dn 10:12
and make long **p** just for show. Mt 23:14
and say long **p** just for show. Mk 12:40
and day with fastings and **p**. Lk 2:37
disciples fast often and say **p**, Lk 5:33
and say long **p** just for show. Lk 20:47
the breaking of bread, and to **p**. Ac 2:42
Your **p** and your acts of charity Ac 10:4
asking in my **p** that if it is Rm 1:10
with me in your **p** to God on my Rm 15:30
to us through ⌊the **p** of⌋ many. 2Co 1:11
And in their **p** for you they will 2Co 9:14
you as I remember you in my **p**. Eph 1:16
through your **p** and help from the Php 1:19
contending for you in his **p**, Col 4:12
you constantly in our **p**. 1Th 1:2
petitions, **p**, intercessions, 1Tm 2:1
and day in her petitions and **p**; 1Tm 5:5
you in my **p** night and day. 2Tm 1:3
God when I mention you in my **p**, Phm 4
that through your **p** I will be Phm 22
life, He offered **p** and appeals, Heb 5:7
so that your **p** will not be 1Pt 3:7
which are the **p** of the saints. Rv 5:8
offer with the **p** of all the Rv 8:3
with the **p** of the saints, Rv 8:4

PRAYING (30)

I had finished **p** in my heart, Gn 24:45
While she was **p** in the LORD's 1Sm 1:12
I've been **p** from the depth of my 1Sm 1:16
here beside you **p** to the LORD. 1Sm 1:26
Solomon finished **p** this entire 1Kg 8:54
finished **p**, fire descended 2Ch 7:1
fasting and **p** before the God of Neh 1:4
I was speaking, **p**, confessing my Dn 9:20
while I was **p**, Gabriel, the man Dn 9:21
place. And He was **p** there. Mk 1:35
whenever you stand **p**, if you Mk 11:25
of the people was **p** outside. Lk 1:10
As He was **p**, heaven opened, Lk 3:21
While He was **p** in private and Lk 9:18
As He was **p**, the appearance of Lk 9:29
He was **p** in a certain place, Lk 11:1
his stand and was **p** like this: Lk 18:11
p that you may have strength to Lk 21:36
I am not **p** for the world but for Jn 17:9
am not **p** that You take them out Jn 17:15
named Saul, since he is **p** there. Ac 9:11
afternoon, I was **p** in my house. Ac 10:30
I was in the town of Joppa **p**, Ac 11:5
many had assembled and were **p**. Ac 12:12
and Silas were **p** and singing Ac 16:25
Jerusalem and was **p** in the Ac 22:17
and **p** and laying his hands on Ac 28:8
always **p** with joy for all of you Php 1:4
we haven't stopped **p** for you. Col 1:9
holy faith and **p** in the Holy Jd 20

PRAYS (10)

Your servant **p** before You today 1Kg 8:28
Your servant **p** toward this place 1Kg 8:29
that Your servant **p** before You, 2Ch 6:19
Your servant **p** toward this place 2Ch 6:20
when he comes and **p** toward this 2Ch 6:32
p to it, "Save me, for you are Is 44:17
for he **p** three times a day." Dn 6:13
Every man who **p** or prophesies 1Co 11:4
every woman who **p** or prophesies 1Co 11:5
language, my spirit **p**, but my 1Co 14:14

PREACH (33)

face the south and **p** against it. Ezk 20:46
toward Jerusalem and **p** against Ezk 21:2
do not **p** against the house of Am 7:16
of Nineveh and **p** against it, Jnh 1:2
Nineveh and **p** the message that Jnh 3:2
"Stop your preaching," they **p**. Mc 2:6
They should not **p** these things; Mc 2:6
p to you about wine and beer, Mc 2:11
From then on Jesus began to **p**, Mt 4:17
to teach and **p** in their towns. Mt 11:1
so that I may **p** there too. Mk 1:38
with Him, to send them out to **p**, Mk 3:14
all the world and **p** the gospel Mk 16:15
has anointed Me to **p** good news Lk 4:18
them not to **p** or teach at all Ac 4:18
commanded us to **p** to the people, Ac 10:42
I am eager to **p** the good news to Rm 1:15
who **p**, "You must not steal"— Rm 2:21
how can they **p** unless they are Rm 10:15
baptize, but to **p** the gospel— 1Co 1:17
but we **p** Christ crucified, 1Co 1:23
that those who **p** the gospel 1Co 9:14
For if I **p** the gospel, I have no 1Co 9:16
to me if I do not **p** the gospel! 1Co 9:16
p the gospel and offer it free 1Co 9:18
we **p** and so you have believed. 1Co 15:11
so that we may **p** the gospel to 2Co 10:16
we did not **p**, or you receive 2Co 11:4
heaven should **p** to you a gospel Gl 1:8
so that I could **p** Him among the Gl 1:16
them the gospel I **p** among the Gl 2:2
if I still **p** circumcision, Gl 5:11
p Christ out of envy and strife, Php 1:15

PREACHED (20)

for he has **p** rebellion against Jr 29:32
they went out and **p** that people Mk 6:12
they went out and **p** everywhere, Mk 16:20
have the good news **p** to them. Lk 7:22
in Samaria and **p** the Messiah to Ac 8:5
after the baptism that John **p**: Ac 10:37
town where we have **p** the message Ac 15:36
I **p** to those in Damascus first, Ac 26:20
foolishness of the message **p**. 1Co 1:21
if Christ is **p** as raised from 1Co 15:12
who was **p** among you by us— 2Co 1:19
because I **p** the gospel of God to 2Co 11:7
than what we have **p** to you, Gl 1:8
that the gospel **p** by me is not Gl 1:11
previously I **p** the gospel to you Gl 4:13
any of you, we **p** God's gospel to 1Th 2:9
seen by angels, **p** among the 1Tm 3:16
those who **p** the gospel to you 1Pt 1:12
word that was **p** as the gospel to 1Pt 1:25
gospel was also **p** to ⌊those who 1Pt 4:6

PREACHER (4)

be just the **p** for this people! Mc 2:11
He seems to be a **p** of foreign Ac 17:18
how can they hear without a **p**? Rm 10:14
Noah, a **p** of righteousness 2Pt 2:5

PREACHES (4)

you by the Jesus whom Paul **p**!" Ac 19:13
comes and **p** another Jesus, 2Co 11:4
if anyone **p** to you a gospel Gl 1:9
us now **p** the faith he once Gl 1:23

PREACHING (19)

"Stop your **p**," they preach. Mc 2:6
p in the Wilderness of Judea Mt 3:1
p the good news of the kingdom, Mt 4:23
p the good news of the kingdom, Mt 9:35
the wilderness and **p** a baptism Mk 1:4
He was **p**: "Someone more powerful Mk 1:7
went to Galilee, **p** the good news Mk 1:14
p in their synagogues and Mk 1:39
p a baptism of repentance for Lk 3:3
And He was **p** in the synagogues Lk 4:44
p and telling the good news of Lk 8:1
us to give up **p** about God to Ac 6:2
prayer and to the **p** ministry." Ac 6:4
So the **p** about God flourished, Ac 6:7
was occupied with **p** the message Ac 18:5
whom I went about **p** the kingdom, Ac 20:25
so that after **p** to others, 1Co 9:27
our **p** is without foundation, 1Co 15:14
who work hard at **p** and teaching. 1Tm 5:17

PREARRANGED (1)

Israel had a **p** signal with the Jdg 20:38

PRECAUTION (1)

are taking this **p** so no one can 2Co 8:20

PRECEDED (7)

the earlier days that **p** you, Dt 4:32
They will be **p** by harps, 1Sm 10:5
the kings of Israel who **p** him. 2Kg 17:2
Amorites who **p** him had done— 2Kg 21:11
governors who **p** me had heavily Neh 5:15
The prophets who **p** you and me Jr 28:8
the former kings who **p** you. Jr 34:5

PRECEDES (1)

Devouring fire **p** Him, and a Ps 50:3

PRECEPTS (22)

The **p** of the LORD are right, Ps 19:8
that Your **p** be diligently kept Ps 119:4
on Your **p** and think about Ps 119:15
meaning of Your **p** so that I can Ps 119:27
How I long for Your **p**! Ps 119:40
place because I seek Your **p**. Ps 119:45
is my ⌊practice⌋: I obey Your **p**. Ps 119:56
You, to those who keep Your **p**. Ps 119:63
but I obey Your **p** with all my Ps 119:69
I will meditate on Your **p**. Ps 119:78
but I did not abandon Your **p**. Ps 119:87
I will never forget Your **p**, Ps 119:93
me, for I have sought Your **p**. Ps 119:94
elders because I obey Your **p**. Ps 119:100
gain understanding from Your **p**; Ps 119:104
I have not wandered from Your **p**. Ps 119:110
follow all Your **p** and hate every Ps 119:128

and I will keep Your **p**. Ps 119:134
but I do not forget Your **p**. Ps 119:141
Consider how I love Your **p**; Ps 119:159
I obey Your **p** and decrees, Ps 119:168
me, for I have chosen Your **p**. Ps 119:173

PRECINCTS *(1)*
temple in the **p** by the chamber 2Kg 23:11

PRECIOUS *(56)*
He also gave **p** gifts to her Gn 24:53
today you considered my life **p**. 1Sm 26:21
and it had a **p** stone ⌊in it⌋. 2Sm 12:30
great abundance, and **p** stones. 1Kg 10:2
of spices, and **p** stones. 1Kg 10:10
of almug wood and **p** stones. 1Kg 10:11
Whatever is **p** to you, they will 1Kg 20:6
of yours be **p** in your sight. 2Kg 1:13
let my life be **p** in your sight." 2Kg 1:14
spices, and the **p** oil—and his 2Kg 20:13
and there was a **p** stone in it. 1Ch 20:2
all kinds of **p** stones, and a 1Ch 29:2
Whoever had ⌊**p**⌋ stones gave them 1Ch 29:8
the temple with **p** stones for 2Ch 3:6
gold in abundance, and **p** stones. 2Ch 9:1
of spices, and **p** stones. 2Ch 9:9
brought algum wood and **p** stones. 2Ch 9:10
silver, gold, **p** stones, spices, 2Ch 32:27
mother-of-pearl, and **p** stones. Est 1:6
of Ophir, in **p** onyx or sapphire Jb 28:16
like a moth what is **p** to him; Ps 39:11
their lives are **p** in his sight. Ps 72:14
She is more **p** than jewels; Pr 3:15
tender and **p** to my mother, Pr 4:3
wisdom is better than **p** stones, Pr 8:11
a diligent man, his wealth is **p**. Pr 12:27
P treasure and oil are in the Pr 21:20
with every **p** and beautiful Pr 24:4
She is far more **p** than jewels. Pr 31:10
a tested stone, a **p** cornerstone, Is 28:16
spices, and the **p** oil—and all Is 39:2
Because you are **p** in My sight Is 43:4
and all your walls of **p** stones. Is 54:12
become shattered like a **p** vase. Jr 25:34
Isn't Ephraim a **p** son to Me, Jr 31:20
all her **p** belongings that Lm 1:7
has seized all her **p** belongings. Lm 1:10
traded their **p** belongings for Lm 1:11
Zion's **p** people—⌊once⌋ worth Lm 4:2
all kinds of **p** stones for your Ezk 27:22
Every kind of **p** stone covered Ezk 28:13
images and their **p** articles of Dn 11:8
gold, silver, **p** stones, and Dn 11:38
possession of their **p** silver; Hs 9:6
I will kill the **p** offspring of Hs 9:16
the treasury of every **p** item. Hs 13:15
in sorrow for your **p** children; Mc 1:16
an abundance of every **p** thing. Nah 2:9
waits for the **p** fruit of the Jms 5:7
but with the **p** blood of Christ, 1Pt 1:19
us very great and **p** promises, 2Pt 1:4
with gold, **p** stones, and pearls Rv 17:4
of gold, silver, **p** stones, and Rv 18:12
with gold, **p** stones, and pearls Rv 18:16
was like a very **p** stone, Rv 21:11
with every kind of **p** stone: Rv 21:19

PRECISELY *(1)*
P what I've been telling you Jn 8:25

PREDATORY *(1)*
to every kind of **p** bird and to Ezk 39:4

PREDECESSOR *(6)*
that his **p** Nebuchadnezzar Dn 5:2
days of your **p** he was found to Dn 5:11
Your **p**, King Nebuchadnezzar, Dn 5:11
Your own **p**, the king, Dn 5:11
that my **p** the king brought Dn 5:13
to your **p** Nebuchadnezzar. Dn 5:18

PREDECESSORS *(3)*
nations that my **p** destroyed 2Kg 19:12
nations that my **p** destroyed Is 37:12
his fathers and **p** never did. Dn 11:24

PREDESTINED *(6)*
Your plan had **p** to take place. Ac 4:28
He also **p** to be conformed Rm 8:29
And those He **p**, He also called; Rm 8:30
which God **p** before the ages for 1Co 2:7
He **p** us to be adopted through Eph 1:5
p according to the purpose of Eph 1:11

PREDICT *(1)*
who **p** monthly what will happen Is 47:13

PREDICTED *(6)*
man of God had **p** when the king 2Kg 7:17
sanctuary, just as God had **p**. 2Kg 24:13
Who **p** this long ago? Is 45:21
But what God **p** through the mouth Ac 3:18
stood up and **p** by the Spirit Ac 11:28
And just as Isaiah **p**: Rm 9:29

PREDICTION *(3)*
Until the time his **p** came true, Ps 105:19
will fail. Make a **p**; it will not Is 8:10
had a spirit of **p** and made a Ac 16:16

PREFECTS *(7)*
governors and **p**, all of them Ezk 23:6
governors and **p**, warriors Ezk 23:12
all of them governors and **p**, Ezk 23:23
the satraps, **p**, governors, Dn 3:2
So the satraps, **p**, governors, Dn 3:3
When the satraps, **p**, governors, Dn 3:27
the kingdom, the **p**, satraps, Dn 6:7

PREFER *(3)*
or if you **p**, I will give you 1Kg 21:2
so that I **p** strangling, death Jb 7:15
Yet I **p** to speak to the Almighty Jb 13:3

PREFERABLE *(1)*
it is **p** to silver. Pr 16:16

PREFERENCE *(1)*
the poor or give **p** to the rich; Lv 19:15

PREGNANT *(33)*
with Hagar, and she became **p**. Gn 16:4
she realized that she was **p**, Gn 16:4
since she saw that she was **p**, Gn 16:5
became **p** by their father Gn 19:36
Sarah became **p** and bore a son to Gn 21:2
with her, and she got **p** by him. Gn 38:18
a prostitute, and now she is **p**." Gn 38:24
I am **p** by the man to whom these Gn 38:25
woman became **p** and gave birth Ex 2:2
and hit a **p** woman so that her Ex 21:22
woman becomes **p** and gives birth Lv 12:2
was **p** and about to give birth. 1Sm 4:19
word to inform David: "I am **p**." 2Sm 11:5
will rip open their **p** women." 2Kg 8:12
ripped open all the **p** women. 2Kg 15:16
months they are **p** so you can Jb 39:2
See, he is **p** with evil, Ps 7:14
in the womb of a **p** woman, Ec 11:5
As a **p** woman about to give birth Is 26:17
We became **p**, we writhed in pain; Is 26:18
my grave, her womb eternally **p**. Jr 20:17
those who are **p** and those about Jr 31:8
and their **p** women ripped open. Hs 13:16
open the **p** women of Gilead Am 1:13
that she was **p** by the Holy Mt 1:18
will become **p** and give birth to Mt 1:23
Woe to **p** women and nursing Mt 24:19
Woe to **p** women and nursing Mk 13:17
was engaged to him and was **p**. Lk 2:5
Woe to **p** women and nursing Lk 21:23
Rebekah became **p** by Isaac our Rm 9:10
like labor pains on a **p** woman, 1Th 5:3
She was **p** and cried out in labor Rv 12:2

PREJUDICE *(2)*
God, without **p**, He is righteous Dt 32:4
observe these things without **p**, 1Tm 5:21

PREMATURELY *(3)*
that her children are born ⌊**p**⌋, Ex 21:22
inheritance gained **p** will not be Pr 20:21
don't judge anything **p**, 1Co 4:5

PREPARATION *(6)*
followed the **p** day, the chief Mt 27:62
because it was **p** day (that is, Mk 15:42
was **p** day, and the Sabbath was Lk 23:54
It was the **p** day for the Jn 19:14
Since it was the **p** day, the Jews Jn 19:31
of the Jewish **p** and since the Jn 19:42

PREPARATIONS *(10)*
made lavish **p** for it before his 1Ch 22:5
I had made **p** to build, 1Ch 28:2
and make **p** for your brothers to 2Ch 35:6
they made **p** for themselves and 2Ch 35:14
Levites made **p** for themselves 2Ch 35:14
brothers had made **p** for them, 2Ch 35:15
on the day of its ⌊battle⌋ **p**, Nah 2:3
Make the **p** for us there." Mk 14:15
Samaritans to make **p** for Him. Lk 9:52
Make the **p** there." Lk 22:12

PREPARE *(76)*
young man, who hurried to **p** it. Gn 18:7
Slaughter an animal and **p** it, Gn 43:16
to Joseph to **p** for his arrival Gn 46:28
offerings to **p** for the LORD our Ex 10:25
when they **p** what they bring in, Ex 16:5
P from these a holy anointing Ex 30:25
P expertly blended incense from Ex 30:35
the priest will **p** a fire on the Lv 1:7
He must **p** the second ⌊bird⌋ as a Lv 5:10
to take his place, is to **p** it. Lv 6:22
You are also to **p** one male goat Lv 23:19
P a quart of wine as a drink Nm 15:5
If you **p** a grain offering with a Nm 15:6
If you **p** a young bull as a burnt Nm 15:8
is how you must **p** each of them, Nm 15:12
Israelite is to **p** these things Nm 15:13
and wants to **p** a fire offering Nm 15:14
community is to **p** one young bull Nm 15:24
altars here and **p** seven bulls Nm 23:1
altars here and **p** seven bulls Nm 23:29
all the people **p** to cross over Jos 1:2
we will **p** a young goat for You. Jdg 13:15
if you want to **p** a burnt Jdg 13:16
p one new cart and two milk cows 1Sm 6:7
or cattle to **p** for the traveler 2Sm 12:4
Let her **p** food in my presence so 2Sm 13:5
house and **p** a meal for him." 2Sm 13:7
in order to go **p** it for myself 1Kg 17:12
will **p** the other bull and place 1Kg 18:23
one bull and **p** it first. 1Kg 18:25
to **p** logs for me in abundance 2Ch 2:9
Hezekiah told them to **p** chambers 2Ch 31:11
the banquet I will **p** for them. Est 5:8
P your case against me; Jb 33:5
cannot **p** ⌊our case⌋ because of Jb 37:19
You **p** a table before me in the Ps 23:5
for You **p** the earth in this way, Ps 65:9
before Him to **p** the way for His Ps 85:13
outdoor work, and **p** your field; Pr 24:27
p for war, and be broken; Is 8:9
p for war, and be broken. Is 8:9
P a place of slaughter for his Is 14:21
P a table, and spread out a Is 21:5
of Hosts will **p** a feast for all Is 25:6
P the way of the LORD in the Is 40:3
build it up, **p** the way, remove Is 57:14
p a way for the people! Is 62:10
who **p** a table for Fortune and Is 65:11
P yourself, for the sword Jr 46:14
in place; **p** the ambush. For Jr 51:12
the slain they **p** a resting place Ezk 32:25
You must also **p** a grain offering Ezk 46:14
the South will **p** for battle with Dn 11:25
the nations: **P** for holy war; Jl 3:9
to you, Israel, **p** to meet your Am 4:12
up wickedness and **p** evil ⌊plans⌋ Mc 2:1
I will **p** your grave, for you are Nah 1:14
P the way for the Lord; Mt 3:3
he will **p** Your way before You. Mt 11:10
You want us to **p** the Passover so Mt 26:17
of You, who will **p** Your way. Mk 1:2
P the way for the Lord; Mk 1:3
us to go and **p** the Passover so Mk 14:12
before the Lord to **p** His ways, Lk 1:76
P the way for the Lord; Lk 3:4
he will **p** Your way before You. Lk 7:27
will and didn't **p** himself or do Lk 12:47
'**P** something for me to eat, Lk 17:8
your minds not to **p** your defense Lk 21:14
Go and **p** the Passover meal for Lk 22:8
"Where do You want us to **p** it?" Lk 22:9
going away to **p** a place for you Jn 14:2
I go away and **p** a place for you Jn 14:3
sound, who will **p** for battle? 1Co 14:8
also **p** a guest room for me, Phm 22
dried up to **p** the way for the Rv 16:12

PREPARED *(93)*
and the calf that he had **p**, Gn 18:8
p a feast and baked unleavened Gn 19:3
I have **p** the house and a place Gn 24:31
So he **p** a banquet for them, Gn 26:30
they **p** their gift for Joseph's Gn 43:25
and had not **p** any provisions Ex 12:39
You have **p** the place for Your Ex 15:17

and be **p** by the third day, Ex 19:11
the people, "Be **p** by the third Ex 19:15
bring you to the place I have **p**. Ex 23:20
Be **p** by morning. Come up Mount Ex 34:2
grain offering **p** on the griddle Lv 2:5
a grain offering ⌊**p**⌋ in a pan, Lv 2:7
It is to be **p** with oil on a Lv 6:21
or **p** in a pan or on a griddle, Lv 7:9
eat it **p** without yeast beside Lv 10:12
As the men **p** to go, Joshua Jos 18:8
Gideon went and **p** a young goat Jdg 6:19
and Samson **p** a feast there, Jdg 14:10
They **p** to leave, putting their Jdg 18:21
in the morning and **p** to go, Jdg 19:5
daughters-in-law **p** to leave the Ru 1:6
man's lamb and **p** it for his 2Sm 12:4
the stone⌋ and **p** the timber and 1Kg 5:18
He **p** the inner sanctuary inside 1Kg 6:19
he gave them, **p** it, and called 1Kg 18:26
So he **p** a great feast for them. 2Kg 6:23
and he **p** a place for the ark of 1Ch 15:1
to the place he had **p** for it. 1Ch 15:3
to ⌊the place⌋ I have **p** for it. 1Ch 15:12
David had **p** on the threshing 2Ch 3:1
various mixtures of **p** ointments; 2Ch 16:14
over how God had **p** the people, 2Ch 29:36
temple, and they **p** ⌊them⌋. 2Ch 31:11
Josiah had **p** for the temple, 2Ch 35:20
p to go up and rebuild the Ezr 1:5
and some fowl were **p** for me. Neh 5:18
to those who have nothing **p**, Neh 8:10
and had **p** a large room for him Neh 13:5
the banquet I have **p** for them." Est 5:4
to the banquet Esther had **p**. Est 5:5
king at the banquet she had **p**. Est 5:12
on the gallows he had **p** for him. Est 6:4
to the banquet Esther had **p**. Est 6:14
gallows he had **p** for Mordecai. Est 7:10
thinks⌋ it is **p** for those whose Jb 12:5
Now then, I have **p** ⌊my⌋ case; Jb 13:18
him like a king **p** for battle. Jb 15:24
He has **p** His deadly weapons; Ps 7:13
They **p** a net for my steps; Ps 57:6
I have **p** a lamp for My anointed Ps 132:17
She has **p** her meat; Pr 9:2
LORD has **p** everything for His Pr 16:4
Judgments are **p** for mockers, Pr 19:29
A horse is **p** for the day of Pr 21:31
A feast is **p** for laughter, Ec 10:19
This is the plan **p** for the whole Is 14:26
the trumpet and **p** everything, Ezk 7:14
they were **p** on the day you were Ezk 28:13
Be **p** and get yourself ready, Ezk 38:7
feast that I have **p** for you. Ezk 39:19
the LORD has **p** a sacrifice; Zph 1:7
it has been **p** by My Father." Mt 20:23
have **p** praise from the mouths Mt 21:16
Look, I've **p** my dinner; Mt 22:4
inherit the kingdom **p** for you Mt 25:34
the eternal fire **p** for the Devil Mt 25:41
body, she has **p** Me for burial. Mt 26:12
them and **p** the Passover. Mt 26:19
is for those it has been **p** for." Mk 10:40
them, and they **p** the Passover. Mk 14:16
ready for the Lord a **p** people. Lk 1:17
You have **p** ⌊it⌋ in the presence Lk 2:31
And the things you have **p**— Lk 12:20
them, and they **p** the Passover. Lk 22:13
they returned and **p** spices and Lk 23:56
bringing the spices they had **p**. Lk 24:1
mercy that He **p** beforehand for Rm 9:23
is what God has **p** for those who 1Co 2:9
And the One who **p** us for this 2Co 5:5
has been **p** since last year 2Co 9:2
you would be **p** just as I said. 2Co 9:3
which God **p** ahead of time so Eph 2:10
day, and having **p** everything, to Eph 6:13
to the Master, **p** for every good 2Tm 2:21
but You **p** a body for Me. Heb 10:5
for He has **p** a city for them. Heb 11:16
Noah while an ark was being **p**; 1Pt 3:20
seven trumpets **p** to blow them. Rv 8:6
angels who were **p** for the hour, Rv 9:15
where she had a place **p** by God, Rv 12:6
and His wife has **p** herself. Rv 19:7
p like a bride adorned for her Rv 21:2

PREPAREDNESS *(1)*

and military **p** are mere words. Is 36:5

PREPARES *(3)*

their womb **p** deception. Jb 15:35
sky with clouds, **p** rain for the Ps 147:8
it **p** its provisions in summer; Pr 6:8

PREPARING *(7)*

except for **p** what people need Ex 12:16
community for ⌊**p**⌋ the water ⌊to Nm 19:9
were responsible for **p** the rows 1Ch 9:32
possession on the day I am **p**. Mal 3:17
of your feet on the day I am **p**," Mal 4:3
while they were **p** something he Ac 10:10
They were **p** an ambush along the Ac 25:3

PRESCRIBED *(16)*

making your **p** number of bricks Ex 5:14
to the number **p** for them. 1Ch 23:31
hadn't observed it often, as **p**. 2Ch 30:5
They stood at their **p** posts, 2Ch 30:16
the Festival of Booths as **p**, Ezr 3:4
our livestock, as **p** by the law, Neh 10:36
as David the man of God had **p**. Neh 12:24
David and his son Solomon had **p**. Neh 12:45
and oil **p** for the Levites, Neh 13:5
your New Moons and **p** festivals. Is 1:14
and offer the gift that Moses **p**, Mt 8:4
offer what Moses **p** for your Mk 1:44
offer what Moses **p** for your Lk 5:14
to the custom **p** by Moses, Ac 15:1
offering the gifts **p** by the law. Heb 8:4
the royal law **p** in Scripture, Jms 2:8

PRESENCE *(308)*

myself from Your **p** and become a Gn 4:14
out from the LORD's **p** and lived Gn 4:16
Live in My **p** and be devout. Gn 17:1
Ishmael could live in Your **p**!" Gn 17:18
Let him give it to me in your **p**, Gn 23:9
So in the **p** of all the Hittites Gn 23:10
it to you in the **p** of my people. Gn 23:11
to Ephron in the **p** of the people Gn 23:13
possession in the **p** of all the Gn 23:18
in the LORD's **p** before I die.' Gn 27:7
had left the **p** of his father Gn 27:30
I cannot stand up in your **p**; Gn 31:35
left Pharaoh's **p** and traveled Gn 41:46
and departed from Pharaoh's **p**. Gn 47:10
But Moses said in the LORD's **p**: Ex 6:12
Moses replied in the LORD's **p**, Ex 6:30
left Pharaoh's **p** and appealed to Ex 8:30
he turned and left Pharaoh's **p**. Ex 10:6
were driven from Pharaoh's **p**. Ex 10:11
left Pharaoh's **p** and appealed to Ex 10:18
left Pharaoh's **p** in fierce anger Ex 11:8
Moses' father-in-law in God's **p**. Ex 18:12
the bread of the **P** on the table Ex 25:30
He replied, "My **p** will go ⌊with Ex 33:14
"If Your **p** does not go," Moses Ex 33:15
wonders in the **p** of all your Ex 34:10
and the bread of the **P**; Ex 35:13
community left Moses' **p**. Ex 35:20
took from Moses' **p** all the Ex 36:3
and the bread of the **P**; Ex 39:36
the LORD's **p** and burned them Lv 10:2
approached the **p** of the LORD Lv 16:1
to rise in the **p** of the elderly Lv 19:32
will be cut off from My **p**; Lv 22:3
gold⌋ lampstand in the LORD's **p**. Lv 24:4
died in the LORD's **p** when they Nm 3:4
the table of the **P** and place the Nm 4:7
meeting in the **p** of Aaron and Nm 8:22
who hate You flee from Your **p**. Nm 10:35
people in the **p** of Moses and Nm 13:30
from the LORD's **p** to all the Nm 17:9
camp and slaughtered in his **p**. Nm 19:3
went from the **p** of the assembly Nm 20:6
from the LORD's **p** just as He had Nm 20:9
driven His enemies from His **p**, Nm 32:21
Egypt by His **p** and great power Dt 4:37
time in the **p** of the LORD for Dt 9:18
fell down in the **p** of the LORD Dt 9:25
there in the **p** of the LORD your Dt 12:7
eat them in the **p** of the LORD Dt 12:18
in the **p** of the LORD your God at Dt 14:23
there in the **p** of the LORD your Dt 14:26
a scroll in the **p** of the Dt 17:18
there in the **p** of the LORD. Dt 18:7
must stand in the **p** of the LORD Dt 19:17
flogged in his **p** with the number Dt 25:2
saying in the **p** of the LORD your Dt 26:5
will say in the **p** of the LORD Dt 26:13
rejoice in the **p** of the LORD Dt 27:7
today in the **p** of the LORD our Dt 29:15
in the **p** of the LORD your Dt 31:11
song in the **p** of the people. Dt 32:44
to treat Me as holy in their **p**. Dt 32:51
of Jericho in the LORD's **p**. Jos 4:13
spread them out in the LORD's **p**. Jos 7:23
written in the **p** of the Jos 8:32
to the LORD in the **p** of Israel: Jos 10:12
here in the **p** of the LORD our Jos 18:6
in Shiloh in the **p** of the LORD." Jos 18:8
at Shiloh in the **p** of the LORD Jos 18:10
in the LORD's **p** at the entrance Jos 19:51
the LORD in His **p** with our burnt Jos 22:27
in the **p** of the people: Jdg 7:3
speak in the **p** of all the lords Jdg 9:2
him in the **p** of all the lords Jdg 9:3
his terms in the **p** of the LORD Jdg 11:11
Benjamin in the **p** of Israel, Jdg 20:35
back in the **p** of those seated Ru 4:4
here and in the **p** of the elders Ru 4:4
she was praying in the LORD's **p**, 1Sm 1:12
the LORD's **p** and to stay there 1Sm 1:22
the LORD in the **p** of Eli the 1Sm 2:11
severe in the **p** of the LORD, 1Sm 2:17
in the LORD's **p** and wore a linen 1Sm 2:18
grew up in the **p** of the LORD. 1Sm 2:21
and to wear an ephod in My **p**. 1Sm 2:28
served the LORD in Eli's **p**. 1Sm 3:1
to stand in the **p** of this holy 1Sm 6:20
poured it out in the LORD's **p**. 1Sm 7:6
he placed in the **p** of the LORD. 1Sm 10:25
in the LORD's **p** they made Saul 1Sm 11:15
offerings in the LORD's **p**, 1Sm 11:15
him in the **p** of his brothers, 1Sm 16:13
here in your **p** to look for 1Sm 16:16
the bread of the **P** that had been 1Sm 21:6
day from Saul's **p** and went to 1Sm 21:10
to be insane in their **p**. 1Sm 21:13
made a covenant in the LORD's **p**. 1Sm 23:18
be cursed in the **p** of the LORD, 1Sm 26:19
ground far from the LORD's **p**, 1Sm 26:20
them at Hebron in the LORD's **p**, 2Sm 5:3
offerings in the LORD's **p**. 2Sm 6:17
in the LORD's **p**, and said, "Who 2Sm 7:18
food in my **p** so I can watch 2Sm 13:5
of cakes in my **p** so I can eat 2Sm 13:6
cakes in his **p**, and baked them. 2Sm 13:8
As I served in your father's **p**, 2Sm 16:19
they all came into the king's **p**. 2Sm 19:8
hang them in the **p** of the LORD 2Sm 21:6
the hill in the **p** of the LORD; 2Sm 21:9
From the radiance of His **p**, 2Sm 22:13
left the king's **p** to register 2Sm 24:4
into the king's **p** and bowed to 1Kg 1:23
eating and drinking in his **p**, 1Kg 1:25
into the king's **p** and stood 1Kg 1:28
So they came into the king's **p**. 1Kg 1:32
Lord GOD in the **p** of my father 1Kg 2:26
the bread of the **P** was placed 1Kg 7:48
in the **p** of King Solomon 1Kg 8:2
sacrifices in the LORD's **p**. 1Kg 8:62
time in the **p** of the LORD our 1Kg 8:65
with them in the LORD's **p**. 1Kg 9:25
stand in your **p** hearing your 1Kg 10:8
had fled from King Solomon's **p**, 1Kg 12:2
the mountain in the LORD's **p**." 1Kg 19:11
Naboth in the **p** of the people, 1Kg 21:13
went out from his **p** diseased— 2Kg 5:27
not banished them from His **p**. 2Kg 13:23
and He removed them from His **p**. 2Kg 17:18
He had banished them from His **p**. 2Kg 17:20
Israel from His **p** just as He had 2Kg 17:23
read it in the **p** of the king. 2Kg 22:10
covenant in the **p** of the LORD to 2Kg 23:3
banished them from His **p**. 2Kg 24:20
regularly in the **p** of the king 2Kg 25:29
bread ⌊of the **P**⌋ every Sabbath. 1Ch 9:32
them at Hebron in the LORD's **p**, 1Ch 11:3
do such a thing in the **p** of God! 1Ch 11:19
banned from the **p** of Saul son of 1Ch 12:1
he died there in the **p** of God. 1Ch 13:10
fellowship offerings in God's **p**. 1Ch 16:1
in the LORD's **p**, and said, "Who 1Ch 17:16
courage⌋ to pray in Your **p**. 1Ch 17:25
incense in the **p** of the LORD, 1Ch 23:13
rows ⌊of the bread of the **P**⌋, 1Ch 23:29
in the LORD's **p** according to the 1Ch 23:31

them in the **p** of the king 1Ch 24:6
did in the **p** of King David, 1Ch 24:31
bread of the **P**⌋ and the silver 1Ch 28:16
in Your **p** as were all our 1Ch 29:15
joy in the LORD's **p** that day. 1Ch 29:22
in the LORD's **p** on the bronze 2Ch 1:6
bread of the **P**⌋ continuously, 2Ch 2:4
to put⌋ the bread of the **P**; 2Ch 4:19
in the king's **p** at the festival; 2Ch 5:3
sacrifices in the LORD's **p**. 2Ch 7:4
My name I will banish from My **p**; 2Ch 7:20
stand in your **p** hearing your 2Ch 9:7
had fled from King Solomon's **p**— 2Ch 10:2
the bread ⌊of the **P**⌋ on the 2Ch 13:11
Levites are officers in your **p**. 2Ch 19:11
in the **p** of the priests in the 2Ch 26:19
plunder in the **p** of the officers 2Ch 28:14
chosen you to stand in His **p**, 2Ch 29:11
the bread of the **P**⌋ and all its 2Ch 29:18
right into the **p** of the king 2Ch 29:23
mercy in the **p** of their captors 2Ch 30:9
Then in his **p** the altars of the 2Ch 34:4
read it in the **p** of the king. 2Ch 34:18
they read in the **p** of the king 2Ch 34:24
in the LORD's **p** to follow the 2Ch 34:31
translated and read in my **p**. Ezr 4:18
to us in the **p** of the Persian Ezr 9:9
stand in Your **p** because of this Ezr 9:15
on him in the **p** of this man. Neh 1:11
I had never been sad in his **p**, Neh 2:1
said in the **p** of the king and Est 1:16
not to enter King Ahasuerus' **p**, Est 1:19
of daily events in the king's **p**. Est 2:23
or tremble in fear at his **p**, Est 5:9
the king's **p** because Esther had Est 8:1
from the king's **p** clothed in Est 8:15
went out from the LORD'S **p**. Jb 1:12
left the LORD's **p** and infected Jb 2:7
not have to hide from Your **p**: Jb 13:20
I am terrified in His **p**; Jb 23:15
have cast off restraint in my **p**. Jb 30:11
he ⌊scornfully⌋ claps in our **p**, Jb 34:37
The thunder declares His **p**; Jb 36:33
boastful cannot stand in Your **p**; Ps 5:5
the nations be judged in Your **p**. Ps 9:19
in Your **p** is abundant joy; Ps 16:11
I will be satisfied with Your **p**. Ps 17:15
From the radiance of His **p**, Ps 18:12
cheer him with joy in Your **p**. Ps 21:6
me in the **p** of my enemies; Ps 23:5
in the protection of Your **p**; Ps 31:20
be insane in the **p** of Abimelech, Ps 34:1
long as the wicked are in my **p**." Ps 39:1
and set me in Your **p** forever. Ps 41:12
me from Your **p** or take Your Holy Ps 51:11
the **p** of Your faithful people, Ps 52:9
who hate Him flee from His **p**. Ps 68:1
as for me, God's **p** is my good. Ps 73:28
May my prayer reach Your **p**; Ps 88:2
walk in the light of Your **p**. Ps 89:15
sins in the light of Your **p**. Ps 90:8
Let us enter His **p** with Ps 95:2
like wax at the **p** of the LORD— Ps 97:5
at the **p** of the Lord of all the Ps 97:5
in the **p** of the LORD, Ps 98:6
tells lies will remain in my **p**. Ps 101:7
praise Him in the **p** of many. Ps 109:30
earth, at the **p** of the Lord, at Ps 114:7
at the **p** of the God of Jacob, Ps 114:7
the LORD in the **p** of all His Ps 116:14
in the very **p** of all His people, Ps 116:18
Where can I flee from Your **p**? Ps 139:7
the upright will live in Your **p**. Ps 140:13
He will stand in the **p** of kings. Pr 22:29
stand in the **p** of unknown men. Pr 22:29
the wicked from the king's **p**, Pr 25:5
not say in the **p** of the Ec 5:6
Leave his **p**, and don't persist Ec 8:3
from the **p** of the ruler: Ec 10:5
His **p** is like Lebanon, as Sg 5:15
LORD, defying His glorious **p**. Is 3:8
those who live in the LORD's **p**, Is 23:18
glory in the **p** of His elders. Is 24:23
tablet in their **p** and inscribe Is 30:8
cut off or eliminated from My **p**. Is 48:19
swept away from the **p** of evil. Is 57:1
the Angel of His **P** saved them. Is 63:9
would quake at Your **p**— Is 64:1
nations will tremble at Your **p**! Is 64:2
the mountains quaked at Your **p**. Is 64:3
from My **p** and do not waver, Jr 4:1
I will drive you from My **p**, Jr 7:15
them from My **p**, and let them go Jr 15:1
sword in the **p** of their enemies. Jr 15:9
you will stand in My **p**. Jr 15:19
my words were spoken in Your **p**. Jr 17:16
the jug in the **p** of the people Jr 19:10
throw away from My **p** both you Jr 23:39
the LORD in the **p** of the priests Jr 28:1
Hananiah in the **p** of the priests Jr 28:5
In the **p** of all the people Jr 28:11
will be established in My **p**. Jr 30:20
fixed order departs from My **p**— Jr 31:36
therefore remove it from My **p**, Jr 32:31
banished them from His **p**. Jr 52:3
regularly in the **p** of the king Jr 52:33
hand in the **p** of the enemy. Lm 2:3
like water before the Lord's **p**. Lm 2:19
to a man in the **p** of the Most Lm 3:35
in the **p** of those who kill you? Ezk 28:9
and drank wine in their **p**. Dn 5:1
flowing, coming out from His **p**. Dn 7:10
us up so we can live in His **p**. Hs 6:2
His voice in the **p** of His army. Jl 2:11
to Tarshish from the LORD's **p**. Jnh 1:3
to Tarshish, from the LORD's **p**. Jnh 1:3
was fleeing from the LORD's **p**, Jnh 1:10
the earth trembles at His **p**— Nah 1:5
on earth be silent in His **p**. Hab 2:20
silent in the **p** of the Lord GOD Zph 1:7
will be divided in your **p**. Zch 14:1
who stands in the **p** of God, Lk 1:19
in His **p** all our days. Lk 1:75
it⌋ in the **p** of all peoples— Lk 2:31
In the **p** of all the people, Lk 8:47
'We ate and drank in Your **p**, Lk 13:26
honored in the **p** of all the Lk 14:10
is joy in the **p** of God's angels Lk 15:10
and slaughter them in my **p**.' " Lk 19:27
after examining Him in your **p**, Lk 23:14
He took it and ate in their **p**. Lk 24:43
seen in the **p** of the Father, Jn 8:38
so many signs in their **p**, Jn 12:37
Me in Your **p** with that glory I Jn 17:5
signs in the **p** of His disciples Jn 20:30
fill me with gladness in Your **p**. Ac 2:28
and denied in the **p** of Pilate, Ac 3:13
may come from the **p** of the Lord, Ac 3:19
out from the **p** of the Sanhedrin Ac 5:41
So Paul went out from their **p**. Ac 17:33
case against him in your **p**. Ac 23:30
to God in the **p** of them all, Ac 27:35
that no one can boast in His **p**. 1Co 1:29
over the **p** of Stephanas, 1Co 16:17
is for you in the **p** of Christ, 2Co 2:10
but his physical **p** is weak, 2Co 10:10
again humiliate me in your **p**, 2Co 12:21
not only in my **p**, but now even Php 2:12
in the **p** of our God and Father, 1Th 1:3
boasting in the **p** of our Lord 1Th 2:19
properly in the **p** of outsiders 1Th 4:12
from the Lord's **p** and from His 2Th 1:9
In the **p** of God, who gives life 1Tm 6:13
from me in the **p** of many 2Tm 2:2
appear in the **p** of God for us. Heb 9:24
convince our hearts in His **p**, 1Jn 3:19
you stand in the **p** of His glory, Jd 24
who stand in the **p** of God; Rv 8:2
went up in the **p** of God from the Rv 8:4
the serpent's **p** to her place Rv 12:14
Great was remembered in God's **p**; Rv 16:19
and heaven fled from His **p**, Rv 20:11

PRESENT *(180)*

Ephron was **p** with the Hittites. Gn 23:10
take my **p** that was brought Gn 33:11
to bring about the **p** result— Gn 50:20
in the morning and **p** yourself to Ex 8:20
in the morning and **p** yourself to Ex 9:13
you are to **p** to the LORD every Ex 13:12
of the house must **p** himself to Ex 22:8
Do not **p** the blood for My Ex 34:25
the priests are to **p** the blood Lv 1:5
he is to **p** an unblemished male. Lv 1:10
priest will then **p** all of it and Lv 1:13
he is to **p** his offering from the Lv 1:14
When you **p** a grain offering Lv 2:4
that you **p** to the LORD is to Lv 2:11
You may **p** them to the LORD as an Lv 2:12
You are to **p** salt with each of Lv 2:13
If you **p** a grain offering of Lv 2:14
you must **p** fresh heads of grain, Lv 2:14
he must **p** one without blemish Lv 3:1
He will **p** part of the fellowship Lv 3:3
he must **p** a male or female Lv 3:6
he is to **p** it before the LORD. Lv 3:7
He will then **p** part of the Lv 3:9
he is to **p** it before the LORD. Lv 3:12
will **p** part of his offering as Lv 3:14
he is to **p** to the LORD a young, Lv 4:3
assembly must **p** a young bull as Lv 4:14
who will first **p** the one for the Lv 5:8
Aaron's sons will **p** it before Lv 6:14
and his sons must **p** to the LORD Lv 6:20
must **p** it as a grain offering Lv 6:21
The offerer must **p** all the fat Lv 7:3
that someone may **p** to the LORD: Lv 7:11
is to **p** unleavened cakes mixed Lv 7:12
He is to **p** as his offering cakes Lv 7:13
cakes he must **p** one ⌊portion⌋ Lv 7:14
Israelites to **p** their offerings Lv 7:38
and **p** ⌊them⌋ before the LORD. Lv 9:2
He will **p** them before the LORD Lv 12:7
he must **p** himself again to the Lv 13:7
the person must **p** himself to the Lv 13:19
one male lamb and **p** it as a Lv 14:12
Aaron will **p** the bull for his Lv 16:6
is to **p** the goat chosen by lot Lv 16:9
he is to **p** the live male goat. Lv 16:20
tent of meeting to **p** ⌊it⌋ as an Lv 17:4
woman is not to **p** herself to an Lv 18:23
they **p** the fire offerings Lv 21:6
come near to **p** the food of his Lv 21:17
to come near to **p** the fire Lv 21:21
come near to **p** the food of his Lv 21:21
whether they **p** freewill gifts or Lv 22:18
You are not to **p** anything that Lv 22:20
You are not to **p** any ⌊animal⌋ to Lv 22:22
You are not to **p** to the LORD Lv 22:24
are to **p** food to your God Lv 22:25
You are to **p** a fire offering to Lv 23:8
Sabbath and then **p** an offering Lv 23:16
are to **p** with the bread seven Lv 23:18
but you must **p** a fire offering Lv 23:25
you are to **p** a fire offering to Lv 23:27
You are to **p** a fire offering to Lv 23:36
assembly and **p** a fire offering Lv 23:36
he must **p** the person before the Lv 27:8
of Levi near and **p** them to Aaron Nm 3:6
the Israelites **p** to the priest Nm 5:9
He is to **p** an offering to the Nm 6:14
priest is to **p** ⌊these⌋ before Nm 6:16
have one leader **p** his offering Nm 7:11
Then **p** the Levites before the Nm 8:10
Aaron is to **p** the Levites before Nm 8:11
and you are to **p** them before the Nm 8:13
because he did not **p** the LORD's Nm 9:13
must also **p** a grain offering Nm 15:4
Also **p** a third of a gallon of Nm 15:7
Also **p** two quarts of wine as a Nm 15:10
is to **p** a year-old female goat Nm 15:27
p his firepan before the LORD Nm 16:17
are⌋ each ⌊to **p**⌋ your firepan Nm 16:17
the Israelites **p** to the LORD as Nm 18:19
the Israelites **p** to the LORD as Nm 18:24
you must **p** part of it as an Nm 18:26
You are to **p** an offering to the Nm 18:28
You must **p** the entire offering Nm 18:29
Be sure to **p** to Me at its Nm 28:2
you are to **p** to the LORD: Nm 28:3
Each day ⌊**p**⌋ two unblemished Nm 28:3
Sabbath day ⌊**p**⌋ two unblemished Nm 28:9
your months **p** a burnt offering Nm 28:11
P a fire offering, a burnt Nm 28:19
assembly when you **p** an offering Nm 28:26
P a burnt offering for a Nm 28:27
P a burnt offering to the LORD, Nm 29:8
P a burnt offering, a fire Nm 29:13
second day ⌊**p**⌋ 12 young bulls Nm 29:17
On the third day ⌊**p**⌋ 11 bulls, Nm 29:20
On the fourth day ⌊**p**⌋ 10 bulls, Nm 29:23
On the fifth day ⌊**p**⌋ nine bulls, Nm 29:26
the sixth day ⌊**p**⌋ eight bulls, Nm 29:29
the seventh day ⌊**p**⌋ seven bulls, Nm 29:32

P a burnt offering, a fire Nm 29:36
P the meat and blood of your Dt 12:27
Call Joshua and **p** yourselves at Dt 31:14
you must **p** yourselves tribe Jos 7:14
Now therefore **p** yourselves 1Sm 10:19
Now **p** yourselves, so I may judge 1Sm 12:7
p yourselves and see this great 1Sm 12:16
I've come to **p** this matter to my 2Sm 14:15
Go and **p** yourself to Ahab. 1Kg 18:1
Elijah went to **p** himself to Ahab 1Kg 18:2
today I will **p** myself to Ahab." 1Kg 18:15
people who are **p** here giving 1Ch 29:17
who were **p** had consecrated 2Ch 5:11
and all those **p** with him bowed 2Ch 29:29
who were **p** in Jerusalem 2Ch 30:21
he had all those **p** in Jerusalem 2Ch 34:32
who were **p** in Israel to serve 2Ch 34:33
all the lay people who were **p**. 2Ch 35:7
who were **p** ⌊in Judah⌋ also 2Ch 35:17
who were **p** ⌊in Judah⌋, 2Ch 35:18
who were **p** had offered. Ezr 8:25
days of our fathers until the **p**. Ezr 9:7
who were **p** in the fortress of Est 1:5
of God came to **p** themselves Jb 1:6
came again to **p** themselves Jb 2:1
with them to **p** himself before Jb 2:1
God and would **p** my case to Him. Jb 5:8
"**P** your arguments," says Jacob's Is 41:21
Let them **p** their witnesses to Is 43:9
Speak up and **p** ⌊your case⌋— Is 45:21
The LORD's glory was **p** there, Ezk 3:23
They will not be **p** in the Ezk 13:9
day you are to **p** an unblemished Ezk 43:22
are to **p** a young, unblemished Ezk 43:23
You must **p** them before the LORD; Ezk 43:24
he must **p** his sin offering." Ezk 44:27
the king had said to **p** them, Dn 1:18
and gave orders to **p** an offering Dn 2:46
know that I am **p** in Israel and Jl 2:27
and My Spirit is **p** among you; Hg 2:5
When you **p** a blind ⌊animal⌋ for Mal 1:8
And when you **p** a lame or sick Mal 1:8
even if they **p** an offering to Mal 2:12
Then they will **p** offerings to Mal 3:3
Jerusalem to **p** Him to the Lord Lk 2:22
them when the crowd was not **p**. Lk 22:6
So we are all **p** before God, Ac 10:33
and all the elders were **p**. Ac 21:18
Agrippa and all men **p** with us, Ac 25:24
His righteousness at the **p** time, Rm 3:26
of this **p** time are not worth Rm 8:18
nor things **p**, nor things to Rm 8:38
is also at the **p** time a remnant Rm 11:5
I urge you to **p** your bodies as a Rm 12:1
death or things **p** or things to 1Co 3:22
Up to the **p** hour we are both 1Co 4:11
absent in body but **p** in spirit, 1Co 5:3
this thing as though I were **p**. 1Co 5:3
good because of the **p** distress: 1Co 7:26
most of whom remain to the **p**, 1Co 15:6
with Jesus, and **p** us with you. 2Co 4:14
at the **p** time your surplus is 2Co 8:14
that when I am **p** I will not need 2Co 10:2
we will be in actions when **p**. 2Co 10:11
to **p** a pure virgin to Christ. 2Co 11:2
When I was **p** with you and in 2Co 11:9
as when I was **p** the second time, 2Co 13:2
rescue us from this **p** evil age, Gl 1:4
corresponds to the **p** Jerusalem, Gl 4:25
He did this to **p** the church to Eph 5:27
His death, to **p** you holy, Col 1:22
so that we may **p** everyone mature Col 1:28
promise for the **p** life and also 1Tm 4:8
are rich in the **p** age not to be 1Tm 6:17
Be diligent to **p** yourself 2Tm 2:15
because he loved this **p** world, 2Tm 4:10
and godly way in the **p** age, Ti 2:12
This is a symbol for the **p** time, Heb 9:9
same word the **p** heavens and 2Pt 3:7
is not, and will be **p** ⌊again⌋. Rv 17:8

PRESENTABLE *(1)*

But our **p** parts have no need ⌊of 1Co 12:24

PRESENTATION *(29)*

wave them as a **p** offering before Ex 29:24
wave it as a **p** offering before Ex 29:26
breast of the **p** offering that is Ex 29:27
who waved a **p** offering of gold Ex 35:22
the gold of the **p** offering that Ex 38:24
bronze of the **p** offering totaled Ex 38:29
be waved as a **p** offering before Lv 7:30
the breast of the **p** offering and Lv 7:34
before the LORD as a **p** offering. Lv 8:27
before the LORD as a **p** offering; Lv 8:29
thigh as a **p** offering before Lv 9:21
eat the breast of the **p** offering Lv 10:14
the breast of the **p** offering, Lv 10:15
to wave as a **p** offering before Lv 10:15
wave them as a **p** offering before Lv 14:12
wave them as a **p** offering before Lv 14:24
the sheaf of the **p** offering. Lv 23:15
settlements as a **p** offering, Lv 23:17
as a **p** offering before Lv 23:20
wave them as a **p** offering before Nm 6:20
to the breast of the **p** offering Nm 6:20
before the LORD as a **p** offering Nm 8:11
before the LORD as a **p** offering. Nm 8:13
presented them as a **p** offering. Nm 8:15
before the LORD as a **p** offering. Nm 8:21
the Israelites' **p** offerings to Nm 18:11
the breast of the **p** offering and Nm 18:18
parts have a better **p**. 1Co 12:23
the table, and the **p** loaves. Heb 9:2

PRESENTED *(83)*

of time Cain **p** some of the Gn 4:3
And Abel also **p** ⌊an offering⌋— Gn 4:4
Joseph **p** himself to him, threw Gn 46:29
his brothers and **p** them before Gn 47:2
father Jacob and **p** him before Gn 47:7
and **p** fellowship offerings. Ex 32:6
it is to be **p** to the priest, Lv 2:8
he has **p** belongs to him; Lv 7:8
a fire offering **p** to the LORD, Lv 7:25
day they were **p** to serve the Lv 7:35
Then Moses **p** Aaron and his sons Lv 8:6
Then Moses **p** Aaron's sons, Lv 8:13
Then he **p** the ram for the burnt Lv 8:18
Next he **p** the second ram, the Lv 8:22
Moses also **p** Aaron's sons and Lv 8:24
Aaron **p** the people's offering. Lv 9:15
He **p** the burnt offering and Lv 9:16
Next he **p** the grain offering, Lv 9:17
and **p** unauthorized fire before Lv 10:1
today they **p** their sin offering Lv 10:19
skin after he has **p** himself to Lv 13:7
Azazel is to be **p** alive before Lv 16:10
animal must be **p** before the Lv 27:11
when they **p** unauthorized fire Nm 3:4
houses, **p** ⌊an offering⌋. Nm 7:2
and **p** them in front of the Nm 7:3
leaders also **p** the dedication Nm 7:10
The leaders **p** their offerings in Nm 7:10
one who **p** his offering on the Nm 7:12
of Issachar, **p** ⌊an offering⌋. Nm 7:18
he **p** one silver dish weighing Nm 7:19
Zebulunites, ⌊**p** an offering⌋. Nm 7:24
the Reubenites, ⌊**p** an offering⌋. Nm 7:30
the Simeonites, ⌊**p** an offering⌋. Nm 7:36
of the Gadites, ⌊**p** an offering⌋. Nm 7:42
Ephraimites, ⌊**p** an offering⌋. Nm 7:48
the Manassites, ⌊**p** an offering⌋. Nm 7:54
Benjaminites, ⌊**p** an offering⌋. Nm 7:60
of the Danites, ⌊**p** an offering⌋. Nm 7:66
the Asherites, ⌊**p** an offering⌋. Nm 7:72
Naphtalites, ⌊**p** an offering⌋. Nm 7:78
cleansed them and **p** them as a Nm 8:15
Aaron **p** them before the LORD Nm 8:21
of oil must be **p** with the bull. Nm 15:9
for they **p** them before the LORD, Nm 16:38
those who were burned had **p**, Nm 16:39
p to the LORD belongs to you. Nm 18:15
Once you have **p** the best part of Nm 18:30
it once you have **p** the best part Nm 18:32
died when they **p** unauthorized Nm 26:61
So we have **p** to the LORD an Nm 31:50
Joshua went and **p** themselves at Dt 31:14
they **p** themselves before God. Jos 24:1
tribes of Israel **p** themselves Jdg 20:2
Abinadab and **p** him to Samuel. 1Sm 16:8
Jesse **p** Shammah, but Samuel 1Sm 16:9
After Jesse **p** seven of his sons 1Sm 16:10
foreskins and **p** them as full 1Sm 18:27
p the offerings on the altar 1Ch 6:49
they **p** the rest of the money to 2Ch 24:14
for I have **p** my case to You. Jr 11:20
for I have **p** my case to You. Jr 20:12
sacrifices and **p** their offensive Ezk 20:28
the chief official **p** them to Dn 1:18
offerings that you **p** to Me Am 5:25
offerings will be **p** in My name Mal 1:11
treasures and **p** Him with gifts: Mt 2:11
He **p** another parable to them: Mt 13:24
He **p** another parable to them: Mt 13:31
approached, **p** five more talents Mt 25:20
He also **p** Himself alive to them Ac 1:3
They also **p** false witnesses who Ac 6:13
and widows and **p** her alive. Ac 9:41
Together they **p** themselves Ac 12:20
these matters be **p** to them the Ac 13:42
they also **p** Paul to him. Ac 23:33
These men **p** their case against Ac 24:1
of the Jews **p** their case against Ac 25:2
p Paul's case to the king, Ac 25:14
elders of the Jews **p** their case Ac 25:15
God **p** Him as a propitiation Rm 3:25
He **p** Him to demonstrate His Rm 3:26
a revelation and **p** to them the Gl 2:2

PRESENTING *(12)*

and he is **p** ⌊an animal⌋ from the Lv 3:1
If he is **p** a lamb for his Lv 3:7
assemblies for **p** fire offerings Lv 23:37
be excluded from **p** the LORD's Nm 9:7
the one **p** his offering to the Nm 15:4
250 men who were **p** the incense. Nm 16:35
Ehud had finished **p** the tribute, Jdg 3:18
am **p** to you the way of life and Jr 21:8
For we are not **p** our petitions Dn 9:18
and **p** my petition before Yahweh Dn 9:20
going out after **p** themselves to Zch 6:5
"By **p** defiled food on My altar." Mal 1:7

PRESENTS *(14)*

When anyone **p** a grain offering Lv 2:1
the priest who **p** someone's burnt Lv 7:8
belongs to the priest who **p** it; Lv 7:9
If he **p** it for thanksgiving, Lv 7:12
on the day he **p** his sacrifice, Lv 7:16
be credited to the one who **p** it; Lv 7:18
The one who **p** a fellowship Lv 7:29
The son of Aaron who **p** the blood Lv 7:33
When Aaron **p** the bull for his Lv 16:11
holy since he **p** the food of your Lv 21:8
in Israel who **p** his offering— Lv 22:18
When a man **p** a fellowship Lv 22:21
way when he **p** a fire offering Nm 15:13
that the prince **p** to the LORD Ezk 46:4

PRESERVATION *(1)*

prosperity always and for our **p**, Dt 6:24

PRESERVE *(19)*

with him and **p** our father's line Gn 19:32
him and we can **p** our father's Gn 19:34
food in the cities, and **p** ⌊it⌋. Gn 41:35
sent me ahead of you to **p** life. Gn 45:5
refuses to **p** his brother's name Dt 25:7
have no son to **p** the memory of 2Sm 18:18
LORD our God to **p** a remnant for Ezr 9:8
the one who cannot **p** his life. Ps 22:29
LORD, You **p** man and beast. Ps 36:6
LORD will keep him and **p** him; Ps 41:2
great power, **p** those condemned Ps 79:11
I will always **p** My faithful love Ps 89:28
will **p** my life from the anger Ps 138:7
P justice and do what is right, Is 56:1
orphans; I will **p** them; let your Jr 49:11
of them will **p** his life because Ezk 7:13
of My people but **p** your own? Ezk 13:18
and right, he will **p** his life. Ezk 18:27
loses his life will **p** it. Lk 17:33

PRESERVED *(5)*

it are to be **p** throughout your Ex 16:32
the LORD to be **p** throughout your Ex 16:33
it before the testimony to be **p**. Ex 16:34
Ephraim's guilt is **p**; Hs 13:12
wineskins, and both are **p**." Mt 9:17

PRESERVES *(2)*

who keeps commands **p** himself; Pr 19:16
is that wisdom **p** the life of its Ec 7:12

PRESERVING *(1)*

ember by not **p** my husband's 2Sm 14:7

PRESIDED *(1)*

their course and **p** as chief. Jb 29:25

PRESIDES *(1)*

to the judge who **p** at that time. Dt 17:9

PRESS *(3)*
you will **p** olives but not anoint Mc 6:15
Then the **p** was trampled outside Rv 14:20
out of the **p** up to the horses' Rv 14:20

PRESSED *(6)*
the LORD and **p** herself against Nm 22:25
200 cakes of **p** figs, and loaded 1Sm 25:18
they gave him some **p** figs and 1Sm 30:12
said, "Bring a lump of **p** figs." 2Kg 20:7
and Your hand has **p** down on me. Ps 38:2
a good measure—**p** down, shaken Lk 6:38

PRESSES *(2)*
treading wine **p** on the Sabbath. Neh 13:15
They crush olives in their **p**; Jb 24:11

PRESSING *(5)*
had diseases were **p** toward Him Mk 3:10
was following and **p** against Him. Mk 5:24
You see the crowd **p** against You, Mk 5:31
the crowd was **p** in on Jesus to Lk 5:1
You in and **p** against You." Lk 8:45

PRESSURE *(6)*
They put **p** on Lot and came up Gn 19:9
the **p** I exert against you will Jb 33:7
because of the **p** of the wicked. Ps 55:3
When **p** or persecution comes Mt 13:21
kept up the **p**, demanding with Lk 23:23
there is the daily **p** on me: 2Co 11:28

PRESSURED *(3)*
Now the Egyptians **p** the people Ex 12:33
We are **p** in every way but not 2Co 4:8
am **p** by both. I have the desire Php 1:23

PRESSURES *(2)*
afflictions, by hardship, by **p**, 2Co 6:4
in persecutions, and in **p**. 2Co 12:10

PRESUME *(1)*
don't **p** to say to yourselves, Mt 3:9

PRESUMPTUOUS *(2)*
your **p** heart has deceived you. Jr 49:16
Your **p** heart has deceived you, Ob 3

PRESUMPTUOUSLY *(1)*
The prophet has spoken it **p**. Dt 18:22

PRETEND *(4)*
on your bed and **p** you're sick. 2Sm 13:5
He told her, "**P** to be in 2Sm 14:2
the LORD would **p** submission to Ps 81:15
Who do You **p** to be?" Jn 8:53

PRETENDED *(5)*
and all Israel **p** to be beaten Jos 8:15
so he **p** to be insane in their 1Sm 21:13
Amnon lay down and **p** to be sick. 2Sm 13:6
when he **p** to be insane in the Ps 34:1
spies who **p** to be righteous, Lk 20:20

PRETENDING *(1)*
p that they were going to put Ac 27:30

PRETENDS *(2)*
One man **p** to be rich but has Pr 13:7
another **p** to be poor but has Pr 13:7

PRETENSE *(1)*
with all her heart—only in **p**." Jr 3:10

PRETENTIOUS *(1)*
its eyes and **p** its looks. Pr 30:13

PREVAIL *(16)*
a man does not **p** by ⌊his own⌋ 1Sm 2:9
great things and will also **p**." 1Sm 26:25
will certainly entice him and **p**. 1Kg 22:22
'You will entice him and also **p**. 2Ch 18:21
not let man **p**; let the nations Ps 9:19
a wicked plan, they will not **p**. Ps 21:11
but the LORD's decree will **p**. Pr 19:21
no counsel ⌊will **p**⌋ against the Pr 21:30
you but never **p** over you, Jr 1:19
waves surge, but they cannot **p**. Jr 5:22
not faithfulness **p** in the land, Jr 9:3
holding it in, and I cannot **p**. Jr 20:9
so that we might **p** against him Jr 20:10
will stumble and not **p**. Jr 20:11
one will not **p** by his strength, Am 2:14
he could not **p**, and there was Rv 12:8

PREVAILED *(12)*
God and with men and have **p**." Gn 32:28
hand, Israel **p**, but whenever he Ex 17:11
he put his hand down, Amalek **p**. Ex 17:11
Our own hand has **p**; Dt 32:27
Yet the king's order **p** over Joab 2Sm 24:4
the king's order **p** over Joab. 1Ch 21:4
but they have not **p** against me. Ps 129:2
You seized me and **p**. Jr 20:7
because the enemy has **p**. Lm 1:16
struggled with the Angel and **p**; Hs 12:4
them all, and **p** against them, so Ac 19:16
Lord's message flourished and **p**. Ac 19:20

PREVAILING *(1)*
holy ones and was **p** over them Dn 7:21

PREVAILS *(1)*
roars aloud, He **p** over His Is 42:13

PREVENT *(4)*
Can holy meat **p** your disaster so Jr 11:15
flock from them and **p** them from Ezk 34:10
water and **p** these from being Ac 10:47
he should not **p** any of his Ac 24:23

PREVENTED *(8)*
the LORD has **p** me from bearing Gn 16:2
who **p** me from harming you, 1Sm 25:34
But they were **p** from recognizing Lk 24:16
Galatia and were **p** by the Holy Ac 16:6
to you (but was **p** until now) in Rm 1:13
is why I have been **p** many times Rm 15:22
p you from obeying the truth? Gl 5:7
since they are **p** by death from Heb 7:23

PREVIOUS *(11)*
be eating from the **p** harvest. Lv 25:22
old grain of the **p** year and will Lv 26:10
But do not count the **p** period, Nm 6:12
to seek omens as on **p** occasions, Nm 24:1
king of Assyria as in **p** years. 2Kg 17:4
ask the **p** generation, and pay Jb 8:8
and doubled his ⌊**p**⌋ possessions. Jb 42:10
different from the **p** ones, Dn 7:24
plague as the **p** one will strike Zch 14:15
So the **p** commandment is annulled Heb 7:18
because the **p** things have passed Rv 21:4

PREVIOUSLY *(36)*
though **p** the city was named Luz. Gn 28:19
Didn't I **p** tell the messengers Nm 24:12
the Anakim, had **p** lived there. Dt 2:10
The Horites had **p** lived in Seir, Dt 2:12
The Rephaim lived there **p**, Dt 2:20
without **p** hating him. Dt 4:42
tablets what had been written **p**, Dt 10:4
without **p** hating him: Dt 19:4
since he did not **p** hate his Dt 19:6
to a people you didn't **p** know. Ru 2:11
who knew him **p** and saw him 1Sm 10:11
P, an Israelite man had declared, 1Sm 17:25
P, I was your father's servant, 2Sm 15:34
some Hamites had lived there **p**. 1Ch 4:40
he was **p** stationed at the King's 1Ch 9:18
they had **p** stored the grain Neh 13:5
that the LORD **p** announced about Is 16:13
P, they had been hostile toward Lk 23:12
the one who came to Him **p**, Jn 7:50
who had **p** come to Him at night Jn 19:39
named Simon had **p** practiced Ac 8:9
John had **p** proclaimed a baptism Ac 13:24
they had **p** seen Trophimus the Ac 21:29
They had **p** known me for quite Ac 26:5
For we have **p** charged that both Rm 3:9
over the sins **p** committed. Rm 3:25
that was **p** ratified by God, Gl 3:17
you know that **p** I preached the Gl 4:13
in which you **p** walked according Eph 2:2
We too all **p** lived among them in Eph 2:3
after we had **p** suffered and been 1Th 2:2
we told you **p** that we were going 1Th 3:4
we also **p** told and warned you. 1Th 4:6
the prophecies **p** made about you, 1Tm 1:18
such a long time, as **p** stated: Heb 4:7
the words **p** spoken by the holy 2Pt 3:2

PREY *(37)*
Birds of **p** came down on the Gn 15:11
he tears ⌊his **p**.⌋ In the morning Gn 49:27
In the morning he devours the **p**, Gn 49:27
they devour the **p** and drink the Nm 23:24
so that they will become easy **p**. Dt 31:17
lion dies if ⌊it catches⌋ no **p**, Jb 4:11
eagle swooping down on ⌊its⌋ **p**. Jb 9:26
They **p** on the barren, childless Jb 24:21
No bird of **p** knows that path; Jb 28:7
snatched the **p** from his teeth. Jb 29:17
Can you hunt **p** for a lioness or Jb 38:39
From there it searches for **p**; Jb 39:29
they will become the jackals' **p**. Ps 63:10
down⌋ from the mountains of **p**. Ps 76:4
roar for their **p** and seek their Ps 104:21
and seize their **p** and carry ⌊it⌋ Is 5:29
for the birds of **p** on the hills Is 18:6
growls over its **p** when a band Is 31:4
birds of **p** will gather there, Is 34:15
call a bird of **p** from the east, Is 46:11
Can the **p** be taken from the Is 49:24
and the **p** of a tyrant will be Is 49:25
Why else has he become a **p**? Jr 2:14
Are birds of **p** circling her? Jr 12:9
no longer be **p** in your hands. Ezk 13:21
After he learned to tear **p**, Ezk 19:3
After he learned to tear **p**, Ezk 19:6
a roaring lion tearing ⌊its⌋ **p**: Ezk 22:25
like wolves tearing ⌊their⌋ **p**, Ezk 22:27
flock has become ⌊**p** and⌋ food Ezk 34:8
will no longer be **p** for you. Ezk 34:22
no longer be **p** for the nations, Ezk 34:28
in the forest when it has no **p**? Am 3:4
and strangled ⌊**p**⌋ for its Nah 2:12
and its lairs with mauled **p**. Nah 2:12
cut off your **p** from the earth, Nah 2:13
of plunder, never without **p**. Nah 3:1

PRICE *(45)*
the full **p**, as a burial place. Gn 23:9
Let me pay the **p** of the field. Gn 23:13
pay a redemption **p** for his life Ex 21:30
loss is covered by its rental **p**. Ex 22:15
pay the bridal **p** for her to be Ex 22:16
to the bridal **p** for virgins. Ex 22:17
to increase its **p** in proportion Lv 25:16
decrease its **p** in proportion to Lv 25:16
The **p** of his sale will be Lv 25:50
his redemption **p** in proportion Lv 25:51
to them based on his purchase **p**. Lv 25:51
and pay the **p** of his redemption Lv 25:52
the **p** will be set as the priest Lv 27:12
The **p** will stand just as the Lv 27:14
add a fifth to the valuation **p**, Lv 27:15
the **p** will stand according to Lv 27:17
will calculate the **p** for him in Lv 27:18
add a fifth to the valuation **p**, Lv 27:19
As the redemption **p** for the 273 Nm 3:46
the redemption **p** for those who Nm 3:48
the redemption **p** for a month-old Nm 18:16
your water, we will pay its **p**. Nm 20:19
The **p** was two-thirds of a shekel 1Sm 13:21
to her for the **p** of 100 2Sm 3:14
on buying it from you for a **p**, 2Sm 24:24
them from Kue at the going **p**. 1Kg 10:28
Give it to me for the full **p**, 1Ch 21:22
I insist on paying the full **p**, 1Ch 21:24
them from Kue at the going **p**. 2Ch 1:16
and negotiate a **p** to ⌊sell⌋ your Jb 6:27
informs on his friends for a **p**, Jb 17:5
cannot be weighed out for its **p**. Jb 28:15
p of wisdom is beyond pearls. Jb 28:18
since the **p** of redeeming him is Ps 49:8
and goats, the **p** of a field; Pr 27:26
free, not for a **p** or a bribe," Is 45:13
our wood comes at a **p**. Lm 5:4
increasing the **p** and cheat with Am 8:5
this magnificent **p** I was valued Zch 11:13
the **p** of Him whose price was set Mt 27:9
price of Him whose **p** was set by Mt 27:9
you sell the field for this **p**?" Ac 5:8
"Yes," she said, "for that **p**." Ac 5:8
for you were bought at a **p**; 1Co 6:20
You were bought at a **p**; 1Co 7:23

PRICELESS *(1)*
When he found one **p** pearl, Mt 13:46

PRICKLING *(1)*
be hurt by **p** briers or painful Ezk 28:24

PRIDE *(59)*
I will break down your strong **p**. Lv 26:19
voice and lifted your eyes in **p**? 2Kg 19:22
himself for the **p** of his heart— 2Ch 32:26
his⌋ actions and suppress his **p**. Jb 33:17
because of the **p** of evil men. Jb 35:12
⌊His⌋ **p** is in ⌊his⌋ rows of Jb 41:15
Some take **p** in a chariot, and Ps 20:7
but we take **p** in the name of the Ps 20:7
righteous with **p** and contempt. Ps 31:18
the **p** of Jacob, whom He Ps 47:4

let them be caught in their **p**. Ps 59:12
Therefore, **p** is their necklace, Ps 73:6
I hate arrogant **p**, evil conduct, Pr 8:13
When **p** comes, disgrace follows, Pr 11:2
P comes before destruction, Pr 16:18
and the **p** of sons is their Pr 17:6
Mocker," acts with excessive **p**. Pr 21:24
A person's **p** will humble him, Pr 29:23
Human **p** will be humbled, and the Is 2:11
So human **p** will be brought low, Is 2:17
the land will be the **p** and glory Is 4:2
will say with **p** and arrogance: Is 9:9
an end to the **p** of the arrogant Is 13:11
glory of the **p** of the Chaldeans Is 13:19
We have heard of Moab's **p**— Is 16:6
his **p**, his arrogance, Is 16:6
His **p** will be brought low, Is 25:11
and lifted your eyes in **p**? Is 37:23
make you an object of eternal **p**, Is 60:15
by Him and will **p** themselves in Jr 4:2
ruin the great **p** of both Judah Jr 13:9
in secret because of your **p**. Jr 13:17
the sheep ⌊that were⌋ your **p**? Jr 13:20
We have heard of Moab's **p**, Jr 48:29
pride, great **p**, indeed—his Jr 48:29
arrogance, **p**, and haughty heart. Jr 48:29
an end to the **p** of the strong, Ezk 7:24
she and her daughters had **p**, Ezk 16:49
sanctuary, the **p** of your power, Ezk 24:21
from them, their **p** and joy, the Ezk 24:25
cities, the **p** of the land: Ezk 25:9
They will ravage Egypt's **p**, Ezk 32:12
to humble those who walk in **p**. Dn 4:37
I loathe Jacob's **p** and hate his Am 6:8
has sworn by the **P** of Jacob: Am 8:7
is what they get for their **p**, Zph 2:10
will destroy the **p** of the Zch 9:6
The **p** of Assyria will be brought Zch 10:11
blasphemy, **p**, and foolishness. Mk 7:22
inflated with **p** in favor of one 1Co 4:6
Now some are inflated with **p**, 1Co 4:18
those who are inflated with **p**. 1Co 4:19
And you are inflated with **p**, 1Co 5:2
Knowledge inflates with **p**, 1Co 8:1
I affirm by the **p** in you that I 1Co 15:31
that we are your reason for **p**, 2Co 1:14
those who take **p** in the outward 2Co 5:12
I have great **p** in you. 2Co 7:4
and the **p** in one's lifestyle— 1Jn 2:16

PRIEST *(492)*

he was a **p** to God Most High. Gn 14:18
daughter of Potiphera, **p** at Gn 41:45
of Potiphera, **p** at On, bore Gn 41:50
daughter of Potiphera, a **p** at Gn 46:20
Now the **p** of Midian had seven Ex 2:16
Jethro, the **p** of Midian. Ex 3:1
Jethro, the **p** of Midian, heard Ex 18:1
Israelites to serve Me as **p**— Ex 28:1
him to serve Me as **p**. Ex 28:3
Any **p** who is one of his sons and Ex 29:30
for Aaron the **p** and the garments Ex 31:10
for Aaron the **p** and the garments Ex 35:19
of Ithamar son of Aaron the **p**. Ex 38:21
for Aaron the **p** and the garments Ex 39:41
so that he can serve Me as a **p**. Ex 40:13
sons of Aaron the **p** will prepare Lv 1:7
Then the **p** will burn all of it Lv 1:9
and the **p** will arrange them on Lv 1:12
The **p** will then present all of Lv 1:13
Then the **p** must bring it to the Lv 1:15
Then the **p** is to burn it on the Lv 1:17
p will take a handful of fine Lv 2:2
it is to be presented to the **p**, Lv 2:8
The **p** will remove the memorial Lv 2:9
The **p** will then burn some of its Lv 2:16
Then the **p** will burn it on the Lv 3:11
Then the **p** will burn them on the Lv 3:16
If the anointed **p** sins, bringing Lv 4:3
The anointed **p** must then take Lv 4:5
p is to dip his finger in the Lv 4:6
The **p** must apply some of the Lv 4:7
The **p** is to burn them on the Lv 4:10
The anointed **p** will bring some Lv 4:16
p is to dip his finger in the Lv 4:17
So the **p** will make atonement on Lv 4:20
Then the **p** must take some of the Lv 4:25
In this way the **p** will make Lv 4:26
Then the **p** must take some of its Lv 4:30
The **p** is to burn ⌊it⌋ on the Lv 4:31
In this way the **p** will make Lv 4:31
Then the **p** must take some of the Lv 4:34
The **p** will burn it on the altar Lv 4:35
In this way the **p** will make Lv 4:35
In this way the **p** will make Lv 5:6
He is to bring them to the **p**, Lv 5:8
In this way the **p** will make Lv 5:10
He is to bring it to the **p**, Lv 5:12
In this way the **p** will make Lv 5:13
The rest will belong to the **p**, Lv 5:13
to it, and give it to the **p**. Lv 5:16
Then the **p** will make atonement Lv 5:16
a restitution offering to the **p**. Lv 5:18
Then the **p** will make atonement Lv 5:18
a restitution offering to the **p**. Lv 6:6
In this way the **p** will make Lv 6:7
p is to put on his linen robe Lv 6:10
morning the **p** will burn wood Lv 6:12
The **p** is to remove a handful of Lv 6:15
p, who is of Aaron's sons and Lv 6:22
offering for a **p** will be a whole Lv 6:23
The **p** who offers it as a sin Lv 6:26
and the **p** is to sprinkle its Lv 7:2
p will burn them on the altar Lv 7:5
It belongs to the **p** who makes Lv 7:7
As for the **p** who presents Lv 7:8
to the **p** who presents it; Lv 7:9
belong to the **p** who sprinkles Lv 7:14
The **p** is to burn the fat on the Lv 7:31
thigh to the **p** as a contribution Lv 7:32
to Aaron the **p** and his sons as Lv 7:34
bring to the **p** at the entrance Lv 12:6
Then the **p** will make atonement Lv 12:8
to Aaron the **p** or to one of his Lv 13:2
The **p** will examine the infection Lv 13:3
After the **p** examines him, he Lv 13:3
the **p** must quarantine the Lv 13:4
The **p** will then reexamine him on Lv 13:5
the **p** must quarantine him for Lv 13:5
The **p** will examine him again on Lv 13:6
the **p** is to pronounce him clean; Lv 13:6
himself to the **p** for his Lv 13:7
present himself again to the **p**. Lv 13:7
The **p** will examine him, and if Lv 13:8
then the **p** must pronounce him Lv 13:8
he is to be brought to the **p**. Lv 13:9
The **p** will examine him. Lv 13:10
and the **p** must pronounce him Lv 13:11
feet so far as the **p** can see, Lv 13:12
the **p** will look, and if the skin Lv 13:13
When the **p** examines the raw Lv 13:15
white, he must go to the **p**. Lv 13:16
The **p** will examine him, and if Lv 13:17
p must pronounce the infected Lv 13:17
must present himself to the **p**. Lv 13:19
The **p** will make an examination, Lv 13:20
p must pronounce him unclean; Lv 13:20
But when the **p** examines it, Lv 13:21
the **p** must quarantine him seven Lv 13:21
p must pronounce him unclean; Lv 13:22
The **p** is to pronounce him clean. Lv 13:23
the **p** is to examine it. Lv 13:25
p must pronounce him unclean; Lv 13:25
But when the **p** examines it, Lv 13:26
the **p** must quarantine him seven Lv 13:26
The **p** will reexamine him on the Lv 13:27
p must pronounce him unclean; Lv 13:27
The **p** is to pronounce him clean, Lv 13:28
p must examine the infection. Lv 13:30
the **p** must pronounce the person Lv 13:30
When the **p** examines the scaly Lv 13:31
the **p** must quarantine the person Lv 13:31
The **p** will reexamine the Lv 13:32
Then the **p** must quarantine the Lv 13:33
The **p** will examine the scaly Lv 13:34
the **p** is to pronounce the person Lv 13:34
the **p** is to examine the person. Lv 13:36
the **p** does not need to look for Lv 13:36
The **p** is to pronounce the person Lv 13:37
the **p** is to make an examination. Lv 13:39
The **p** is to examine him, and if Lv 13:43
p must pronounce him unclean; Lv 13:44
and is to be shown to the **p**. Lv 13:49
The **p** is to examine the Lv 13:50
The **p** is to reexamine the Lv 13:51
When the **p** examines ⌊it⌋, Lv 13:53
the **p** is to order whatever is Lv 13:54
the **p** is to reexamine the Lv 13:55
If the **p** examines ⌊it⌋, and the Lv 13:56
He is to be brought to the **p**, Lv 14:2
the **p** will order that two live Lv 14:4
Then the **p** will order that one Lv 14:5
The **p** who performs the cleansing Lv 14:11
The **p** is to take one male lamb Lv 14:12
offering belongs to the **p**; Lv 14:13
The **p** is to take some of the Lv 14:14
Then the **p** will take some of the Lv 14:15
The **p** will dip his right finger Lv 14:16
in his palm the **p** will put some Lv 14:17
In this way the **p** will make Lv 14:18
The **p** must sacrifice the sin Lv 14:19
The **p** is to offer the burnt Lv 14:20
The **p** will make atonement for Lv 14:20
to the **p** at the entrance Lv 14:23
p will take the male lamb for Lv 14:24
the **p** is to take some of the Lv 14:25
Then the **p** will pour some of the Lv 14:26
right finger the **p** will sprinkle Lv 14:27
The **p** will also put some of the Lv 14:28
In this way the **p** will make Lv 14:31
house is to come and tell the **p**: Lv 14:35
The **p** must order them to clear Lv 14:36
Afterwards the **p** will come to Lv 14:36
the **p** is to go outside the house Lv 14:38
p is to return on the seventh Lv 14:39
the **p** must order that the stones Lv 14:40
the **p** must come and examine it. Lv 14:44
of the days the **p** quarantines it Lv 14:46
But when the **p** comes and Lv 14:48
meeting, and give them to the **p**. Lv 15:14
The **p** is to sacrifice them, Lv 15:15
In this way the **p** will make Lv 15:15
them to the **p** at the entrance Lv 15:29
The **p** is to sacrifice one as a Lv 15:30
In this way the **p** will make Lv 15:30
The **p** who is anointed and Lv 16:32
serve as ⌊high⌋ **p** in place of Lv 16:32
them to the **p** at the entrance Lv 17:5
The **p** will then sprinkle the Lv 17:6
The **p** will make atonement on his Lv 19:22
A **p** is not to make himself Lv 21:1
for the **p** is holy to his God. Lv 21:7
The **p** who is highest among his Lv 21:10
of Aaron the **p** who has a defect Lv 21:21
staying with a **p** or a hired hand Lv 22:10
if a **p** purchases someone with Lv 22:11
give the holy offering to the **p**. Lv 22:14
sheaf of your harvest to the **p**. Lv 23:10
the **p** is to wave it on the day Lv 23:11
The **p** will wave the lambs with Lv 23:20
be holy to the LORD for the **p**. Lv 23:20
before the **p** and the priest Lv 27:8
priest and the **p** will set a Lv 27:8
The **p** will set a value for him Lv 27:8
must be presented before the **p**. Lv 27:11
p will set its value, whether Lv 27:12
will be set as the **p** makes the Lv 27:12
the **p** will assess its value, Lv 27:14
stand just as the **p** assesses it. Lv 27:14
the **p** will calculate the price Lv 27:18
then the **p** will calculate for Lv 27:23
to Aaron the **p** to assist him. Nm 3:6
was Eleazar son of Aaron the **p**; Nm 3:32
of Aaron the **p**, has oversight Nm 4:16
of Ithamar son of Aaron the **p**. Nm 4:28
of Ithamar son of Aaron the **p**." Nm 4:33
goes to the LORD for the **p**, Nm 5:8
ram by which the **p** will make Nm 5:8
present to the **p** will be his. Nm 5:9
one gives to the **p** will be his." Nm 5:10
is to bring his wife to the **p**. Nm 5:15
The **p** is to bring her forward Nm 5:16
Then the **p** is to take holy water Nm 5:17
After the **p** has the woman stand Nm 5:18
p is to hold the bitter water Nm 5:18
The **p** will require the woman to Nm 5:19
this point the **p** must make the Nm 5:21
Then the **p** is to write these Nm 5:23
The **p** is to take the grain Nm 5:25
p is to take a handful of the Nm 5:26
and the **p** will apply this entire Nm 5:30
pigeons to the **p** at the entrance Nm 6:10
The **p** is to offer one as a sin Nm 6:11
The **p** is to present ⌊these⌋ Nm 6:16
Then the **p** will offer the Nm 6:17

The **p** is to take the boiled Nm 6:19
The **p** is to wave them as a Nm 6:20
It is a holy portion for the **p**, Nm 6:20
of Ithamar son of Aaron the **p**. Nm 7:8
The **p** must then make atonement Nm 15:25
The **p** must then make atonement Nm 15:28
son of Aaron the **p** to remove the Nm 16:37
So Eleazar the **p** took the bronze Nm 16:39
it to Aaron the **p** as an offering Nm 18:28
to Eleazar the **p**, and he will Nm 19:3
Eleazar the **p** is to take some of Nm 19:4
The **p** is to take cedar wood, Nm 19:6
Then the **p** must wash his clothes Nm 19:7
of Aaron the **p**, saw ⌊this⌋, he Nm 25:7
of Aaron the **p**, has turned back Nm 25:11
and Eleazar son of Aaron the **p**, Nm 26:1
and Eleazar the **p** said to them Nm 26:3
and Eleazar the **p** when they Nm 26:63
Moses and Aaron the **p** when they Nm 26:64
Eleazar the **p**, the leaders, Nm 27:2
Eleazar the **p** and the whole Nm 27:19
Eleazar the **p** and the entire Nm 27:22
Phinehas son of Eleazar the **p**, Nm 31:6
Eleazar the **p**, and the Israelite Nm 31:12
Moses, Eleazar the **p**, and all Nm 31:13
Then Eleazar the **p** said to the Nm 31:21
Eleazar the **p**, and the family Nm 31:26
to Eleazar the **p** as a Nm 31:29
Eleazar the **p** did as the LORD Nm 31:31
to Eleazar the **p** as a Nm 31:41
and Eleazar the **p** received from Nm 31:51
and Eleazar the **p** received the Nm 31:54
Eleazar the **p**, and the leaders Nm 32:2
about them to Eleazar the **p**, Nm 32:28
Aaron the **p** climbed Mount Hor Nm 33:38
Eleazar the **p** and Joshua son of Nm 34:17
of the high **p** who was anointed Nm 35:25
until the death of the high **p**. Nm 35:28
of the high **p** may the one who Nm 35:28
the death of the ⌊high⌋ **p**. Nm 35:32
his son became **p** in his place. Dt 10:6
either to the **p** who stands there Dt 17:12
the **p** is to come forward and Dt 20:2
come before the **p** who is serving Dt 26:3
Then the **p** will take the Dt 26:4
portions that Eleazar the **p**, Jos 14:1
They came before Eleazar the **p**, Jos 17:4
the portions that Eleazar the **p**, Jos 19:51
of the high **p** serving at that Jos 20:6
approached Eleazar the **p**, Jos 21:1
Aaron the **p** received 13 cities Jos 21:4
the descendants of Aaron the **p**: Jos 21:13
of Eleazar the **p** to the Jos 22:13
Phinehas the **p** and the community Jos 22:30
son of Eleazar the **p** said to the Jos 22:31
of Eleazar the **p** and the leaders Jos 22:32
one of his sons to be his **p**. Jdg 17:5
with me and be my father and **p**, Jdg 17:10
man became his **p** and lived in Jdg 17:12
a Levite has become my **p**." Jdg 17:13
that he had hired him as his **p**. Jdg 18:4
The **p** told them, "Go in peace. Jdg 18:6
while the **p** was standing by the Jdg 18:17
idols, the **p** said to them, "What Jdg 18:18
and be a father and a **p** to us. Jdg 18:19
for you to be a **p** for the house Jdg 18:19
or for you to be a **p** for a tribe Jdg 18:19
the **p** was pleased and took his Jdg 18:20
the gods I had made and the **p**, Jdg 18:24
made and the **p** that belonged to Jdg 18:27
Eli the **p** was sitting on a chair 1Sm 1:9
in the presence of Eli the **p**. 1Sm 2:11
The **p** would claim for himself 1Sm 2:14
Give the **p** ⌊some⌋ meat to roast, 1Sm 2:15
up a faithful **p** for Myself. 1Sm 2:35
of Eli the LORD's **p** at Shiloh. 1Sm 14:3
While Saul spoke to the **p**, 1Sm 14:19
Saul said to the **p**, "Stop what 1Sm 14:19
But the **p** said, "We must consult 1Sm 14:36
went to Ahimelech the **p** at Nob. 1Sm 21:1
David answered Ahimelech the **p**, 1Sm 21:2
The **p** told him, "There is no 1Sm 21:4
the **p** gave him the consecrated 1Sm 21:6
The **p** replied, "The sword of 1Sm 21:9
to summon Ahimelech the **p**, 1Sm 22:11
he said to Abiathar the **p**, 1Sm 23:9
David said to Abiathar the **p**, 1Sm 30:7
king also said to Zadok the **p**, 2Sm 15:27
Ira the Jairite was David's **p**. 2Sm 20:26
Zeruiah and with Abiathar the **p**. 1Kg 1:7
but Zadok the **p**, Benaiah son of 1Kg 1:8
sons, Abiathar the **p**, and Joab 1Kg 1:19
of the army, and Abiathar the **p**. 1Kg 1:25
or Zadok the **p** or Benaiah son of 1Kg 1:26
Call in Zadok the **p**, Nathan the 1Kg 1:32
Zadok the **p** and Nathan the 1Kg 1:34
Then Zadok the **p**, Nathan the 1Kg 1:38
Zadok the **p** took the horn of oil 1Kg 1:39
Jonathan son of Abiathar the **p**, 1Kg 1:42
the king has sent Zadok the **p**, 1Kg 1:44
Zadok the **p** and Nathan the 1Kg 1:45
for Abiathar the **p**, and for Joab 1Kg 2:22
The king said to Abiathar the **p**, 1Kg 2:26
from being the LORD's **p**, 1Kg 2:27
Zadok the **p** in Abiathar's place 1Kg 2:35
Azariah son of Zadok, **p**; 1Kg 4:2
a **p** and adviser to the king; 1Kg 4:5
Jehoiada the **p** commanded. 2Kg 11:9
and went to Jehoiada the **p**. 2Kg 11:9
The **p** gave to the commanders of 2Kg 11:10
Then Jehoiada the **p** ordered the 2Kg 11:15
sword," for the **p** had said, "She 2Kg 11:15
killed Mattan, the **p** of Baal, at 2Kg 11:18
Jehoiada⌋ the **p** appointed guards 2Kg 11:18
Jehoiada the **p** instructed him, 2Kg 12:2
each **p** is to take from his 2Kg 12:5
Jehoiada the **p** and the other 2Kg 12:7
Jehoiada the **p** took a chest, 2Kg 12:9
and the high **p** would go to the 2Kg 12:10
its construction to Uriah the **p**. 2Kg 16:10
Uriah the **p** had made it. 2Kg 16:11
Ahaz commanded Uriah the **p**, 2Kg 16:15
Uriah the **p** did everything King 2Kg 16:16
Hilkiah the high **p** so that he 2Kg 22:4
Hilkiah the high **p** told Shaphan 2Kg 22:8
the **p** has given me a book, 2Kg 22:10
he commanded Hilkiah the **p**, 2Kg 22:12
Hilkiah the **p**, Ahikam, Achbor, 2Kg 22:14
the high **p** and the priests 2Kg 23:4
that Hilkiah the **p** found in the 2Kg 23:24
took away Seraiah the chief **p**, 2Kg 25:18
Zephaniah the **p** of the second 2Kg 25:18
who served as **p** in the temple 1Ch 6:10
left⌋ Zadok the **p** and his fellow 1Ch 16:39
Zadok the **p**, Ahimelech son 1Ch 24:6
Benaiah son of Jehoiada the **p**; 1Ch 27:5
ruler, and Zadok as the **p**. 1Ch 29:22
may become a **p** of what are not 2Ch 13:9
a teaching **p**, and without law, 2Ch 15:3
Amariah, the chief **p**, is over 2Ch 19:11
and the wife of Jehoiada the **p**. 2Ch 22:11
Jehoiada the **p** commanded. 2Ch 23:8
Jehoiada the **p** did not release 2Ch 23:8
Jehoiada the **p** gave to the 2Ch 23:9
Then Jehoiada the **p** sent out the 2Ch 23:14
sword," for the **p** had said, 2Ch 23:14
killed Mattan, the **p** of Baal, at 2Ch 23:17
the time of Jehoiada the **p**, 2Ch 24:2
Jehoiada the high ⌊**p**⌋ and said, 2Ch 24:6
Zechariah son of Jehoiada the **p**. 2Ch 24:20
of the sons of Jehoiada the **p**. 2Ch 24:25
Azariah the **p**, along with 80 2Ch 26:17
Azariah the chief **p** and all the 2Ch 26:20
the chief **p** of the household of 2Ch 31:10
they went to Hilkiah the high **p**, 2Ch 34:9
Hilkiah the **p** found the book of 2Ch 34:14
"Hilkiah the **p** gave me a book," 2Ch 34:18
there was a **p** who could consult Ezr 2:63
gave to Ezra the **p** and scribe, Ezr 7:11
kings, to Ezra the **p**, an expert Ezr 7:12
Whatever Ezra the **p** and expert Ezr 7:21
into the care of Meremoth the **p**, Ezr 8:33
Ezra the **p** stood up and said Ezr 10:10
Ezra the **p** selected men who were Ezr 10:16
the high **p** and his fellow Neh 3:1
house of Eliashib the high **p**. Neh 3:20
there was a **p** who could consult Neh 7:65
the **p** brought the law before Neh 8:2
governor, Ezra the **p** and scribe, Neh 8:9
A **p** of Aaronic descent must Neh 10:38
and Ezra the **p** and scribe. Neh 12:26
Eliashib the **p** had been put in Neh 13:4
the storehouses Shelemiah the **p**, Neh 13:13
son of Eliashib the high **p**, Neh 13:28
You are a **p** like Melchizedek." Ps 110:4
Uriah the **p** and Zechariah son of Is 8:2
people and **p** alike, servant and Is 24:2
p and prophet stagger because of Is 28:7
prophet to **p**, everyone deals Jr 6:13
prophet to **p**, everyone deals Jr 8:10
prophet and **p** travel to a land Jr 14:18
will never be lost from the **p**, Jr 18:18
Pashhur the **p**, the son of Immer Jr 20:1
Malchijah and the **p** Zephaniah Jr 21:1
both prophet and **p** are ungodly, Jr 23:11
or a prophet or a **p** asks you: Jr 23:33
the prophet, **p**, or people who Jr 23:34
to the **p** Zephaniah son of Jr 29:25
has appointed you **p** in place of Jr 29:26
Jehoiada the **p** to be the chief Jr 29:26
Zephaniah the **p** read this letter Jr 29:29
of Maaseiah, the **p**, to Jeremiah Jr 37:3
took away Seraiah the chief **p**, Jr 52:24
Zephaniah the **p** of the second Jr 52:24
despised king and **p** in His Lm 2:6
came directly to Ezekiel the **p**, Ezk 1:3
No **p** may drink wine before he Ezk 44:21
a widow who is the widow of a **p**. Ezk 44:22
A **p** may not come ⌊near⌋ a dead Ezk 44:25
of dough to the **p** so that a Ezk 44:30
p must take some of the blood Ezk 45:19
reject you from serving as My **p**. Hs 4:6
Amaziah the **p** of Bethel sent Am 7:10
son of Jehozadak, the high **p**: Hg 1:1
the high **p** Joshua son of Hg 1:12
spirit of the high **p** Joshua son Hg 1:14
to the high **p** Joshua son of Hg 2:2
Joshua son of Jehozadak, high **p**. Hg 2:4
the high **p** standing before Zch 3:1
Joshua the high **p**, you and your Zch 3:8
son of Jehozadak, the high **p**. Zch 6:11
will also be a **p** on His throne, Zch 6:13
For the lips of a **p** should guard Mal 2:7
yourself to the **p**, and offer the Mt 8:4
in the palace of the high **p**, Mt 26:3
Him away to Caiaphas the high **p**, Mt 26:57
high **p** then stood up and said Mt 26:62
Then the high **p** said to Him, Mt 26:63
Then the high **p** tore his robes Mt 26:65
go and show yourself to the **p**, Mk 1:44
Abiathar the high **p** and ate the Mk 2:26
led Jesus away to the high **p**, Mk 14:53
Then the high **p** stood up before Mk 14:60
Again the high **p** questioned Him, Mk 14:61
Then the high **p** tore his robes Mk 14:63
there was a **p** of Abijah's Lk 1:5
he was serving as **p** before God, Lk 1:8
go and show yourself to the **p**, Lk 5:14
A **p** happened to be going down Lk 10:31
who was high **p** that year, said Jn 11:49
but being high **p** that year he Jn 11:51
who was high **p** that year. Jn 18:13
an acquaintance of the high **p**; Jn 18:15
the one known to the high **p**, Jn 18:16
high **p** questioned Jesus about Jn 18:19
the way you answer the high **p**?" Jn 18:22
bound to Caiaphas the high **p**. Jn 18:24
Annas the high **p**, Caiaphas, John Ac 4:6
Then the high **p** took action. Ac 5:17
When the high **p** and those who Ac 5:21
Sanhedrin, and the high **p** asked, Ac 5:27
"Is this true?" the high **p** asked. Ac 7:1
of the Lord, went to the high **p** Ac 9:1
Then the **p** of Zeus, whose temple Ac 14:13
a Jewish chief **p**, were doing Ac 19:14
as both the high **p** and the whole Ac 22:5
But the high **p** Ananias ordered Ac 23:2
you dare revile God's high **p**?" Ac 23:4
said, "that it was the high **p**. Ac 23:5
Ananias the high **p** came down Ac 24:1
serving as a **p** of God's good Rm 15:16
faithful high **p** in service to Heb 2:17
apostle and high **p** of our Heb 3:1
a great high **p** who has passed Heb 4:14
not have a high **p** who is unable Heb 4:15
For every high **p** taken from men Heb 5:1
Himself to become a high **p**, Heb 5:5
You are a **p** forever in the order Heb 5:6
by God a high **p** "in the order Heb 5:10
has become a "high **p** forever in Heb 6:20
of Salem, **p** of the Most High Heb 7:1
of God—remains a **p** forever. Heb 7:3
there for another **p** to arise in Heb 7:11
if another **p** like Melchizedek Heb 7:15

become a ⌊**p**⌋ based on a legal Heb 7:16
You are a **p** forever in the order Heb 7:17
His mind, You are a **p** forever. Heb 7:21
is the kind of high **p** we need: Heb 7:26
we have this kind of high **p**, Heb 8:1
For every high **p** is appointed to Heb 8:3
for this ⌊**p**⌋ also to have Heb 8:3
wouldn't be a **p**, since there are Heb 8:4
But the high **p** alone enters the Heb 9:7
high **p** of the good things that Heb 9:11
as the high **p** enters the Heb 9:25
Now every **p** stands day after day Heb 10:11
a great high **p** over the house Heb 10:21
by the high **p** as a sin offering Heb 13:11

PRIEST'S *(23)*

belongs to him; it is the **p**. Lv 7:8
the oil in the **p** palm he is to Lv 14:18
the oil in the **p** palm he is to Lv 14:29
If a **p** daughter defiles herself Lv 21:9
one outside a **p** family is to eat Lv 22:10
If the **p** daughter is married to Lv 22:12
to a man outside a **p** family, Lv 22:12
But if the **p** daughter becomes Lv 22:13
it becomes the **p** property. Lv 27:21
the **p** servant would come with a 1Sm 2:13
the **p** servant would come and say 1Sm 2:15
and the high **p** deputy came 2Ch 24:11
son, Aaron the chief **p** son Ezr 7:5
struck the high **p** slave and cut Mt 26:51
right to the high **p** courtyard. Mt 26:58
struck the high **p** slave, and cut Mk 14:47
right into the high **p** courtyard. Mk 14:54
one of the high **p** servants came. Mk 14:66
struck the high **p** slave and cut Lk 22:50
Him into the high **p** house. Lk 22:54
struck the high **p** slave, and cut Jn 18:10
Jesus into the high **p** courtyard. Jn 18:15
One of the high **p** slaves, a Jn 18:26

PRIESTHOOD *(18)*

The **p** is to be theirs by a Ex 29:9
permanent **p** for them throughout Ex 40:15
you are seeking the **p** as well. Nm 16:10
for sin involving your **p**. Nm 18:1
you the work of the **p** as a gift, Nm 18:7
of perpetual **p** for him and his Nm 25:13
is the **p** of the LORD. Jos 18:7
were disqualified from the **p**. Ezr 2:62
were disqualified from the **p**. Neh 7:64
defiling the **p** as well as the Neh 13:29
of the **p** and the Levites Neh 13:29
to the custom of the **p**, Lk 1:9
during the high **p** of Annas and Lk 3:2
came through the Levitical **p** Heb 7:11
when there is a change of the **p**, Heb 7:12
He holds His **p** permanently. Heb 7:24
house for a holy **p** to offer 1Pt 2:5
race, a royal **p**, a holy nation, 1Pt 2:9

PRIESTLY *(9)*

carry out their **p** Nm 3:10
out your **p** responsibilities Nm 18:7
me to some **p** office so I can 1Sm 2:36
and 100 **p** garments to the Ezr 2:69
their **p** brothers, and all Ezr 6:20
and 530 **p** garments to the Neh 7:70
silver minas, and 67 **p** garments. Neh 7:72
leaders of the **p** families were: Neh 12:12
who receive the **p** office have Heb 7:5

PRIESTS *(410)*

acquire was that of the **p**, Gn 47:22
be My kingdom of **p** and My holy Ex 19:6
the **p** who come near the LORD Ex 19:22
the **p** and the people must not Ex 19:24
so that they may serve Me as **p**. Ex 28:4
so that they may serve Me as **p**. Ex 28:41
them to serve Me as **p**. Ex 29:1
and his sons to serve Me as **p**. Ex 29:44
them to serve Me as **p**. Ex 30:30
for his sons to serve as **p**, Ex 31:10
for his sons to serve as **p**." Ex 35:19
for his sons to serve as **p**. Ex 39:41
they may also serve Me as **p**. Ex 40:15
sons the **p** are to present Lv 1:5
sons the **p** are to arrange Lv 1:8
Aaron's sons the **p** will sprinkle Lv 1:11
bring it to Aaron's sons the **p**. Lv 2:2
Aaron's sons the **p** will sprinkle Lv 3:2
Any male among the **p** may eat it; Lv 6:29
Any male among the **p** may eat it. Lv 7:6
to serve the LORD as **p**. Lv 7:35
or to one of his sons, the **p**. Lv 13:2
atonement for the **p** and all the Lv 16:33
sons, the **p**, and tell them: Lv 21:1
P may not make bald spots on Lv 21:5
The **p** must not profane the holy Lv 22:15
the anointed **p**, who were Nm 3:3
who were ordained to serve as **p**. Nm 3:3
Ithamar served as **p** under the Nm 3:4
of Aaron, the **p**, are to sound Nm 10:8
the Levitical **p** and to the judge Dt 17:9
the presence of the Levitical **p**. Dt 17:18
The Levitical **p**, the whole tribe Dt 18:1
the **p** are to be given the Dt 18:3
the LORD before the **p** and judges Dt 19:17
Then the **p**, the sons of Levi, Dt 21:5
the Levitical **p** instruct you to Dt 24:8
and the Levitical **p** spoke to all Dt 27:9
this law and gave it to the **p**, Dt 31:9
God carried by the Levitical **p**, Jos 3:3
he said to the **p**, "Take the ark Jos 3:6
Command the **p** carrying the ark Jos 3:8
the feet of the **p** who carry the Jos 3:13
the **p** carried the ark of the Jos 3:14
soon as the **p** carrying the ark Jos 3:15
The **p** carrying the ark of the Jos 3:17
Jordan where the **p** who carried Jos 4:9
The **p** carrying the ark continued Jos 4:10
the **p** with the ark of the LORD Jos 4:11
Command the **p** who carry the ark Jos 4:16
So Joshua commanded the **p**, Jos 4:17
When the **p** carrying the ark of Jos 4:18
Have seven **p** carry seven Jos 6:4
while the **p** blow the trumpets. Jos 6:4
summoned the **p** and said to them Jos 6:6
and have seven **p** carry seven Jos 6:6
seven **p** carrying seven trumpets Jos 6:8
went in front of the **p** who blew Jos 6:9
The **p** took the ark of the LORD, Jos 6:12
and the seven **p** carrying seven Jos 6:13
time, the **p** blew the trumpets Jos 6:16
the Levitical **p** who carried it. Jos 8:33
pasturelands were for the **p**, Jos 21:19
his sons were **p** for the Danite Jdg 18:30
and Phinehas, were the LORD's **p**. 1Sm 1:3
the tribes of Israel to be **p**, 1Sm 2:28
the **p** of Dagon and everyone who 1Sm 5:5
summoned the **p** and the diviners 1Sm 6:2
whole family, who were **p** in Nob. 1Sm 22:11
Turn and kill the **p** of the LORD 1Sm 22:17
to execute the **p** of the LORD. 1Sm 22:17
to Doeg, "Go and execute the **p**!" 1Sm 22:18
went and executed the **p** himself. 1Sm 22:18
city of the **p**, with the sword 1Sm 22:19
had killed the **p** of the LORD. 1Sm 22:21
son of Abiathar were **p**; 2Sm 8:17
and Abiathar the **p** be there with 2Sm 15:35
to Zadok and Abiathar the **p**. 2Sm 15:35
then told the **p** Zadok and 2Sm 17:15
King David sent word to the **p**, 2Sm 19:11
Zadok and Abiathar were **p**; 2Sm 20:25
Zadok and Abiathar, **p**; 1Kg 4:4
and the **p** picked up the ark. 1Kg 8:3
p and the Levites brought the 1Kg 8:4
The **p** brought the ark of the 1Kg 8:6
When the **p** came out of the holy 1Kg 8:10
the **p** were not able to continue 1Kg 8:11
and set up **p** from every class 1Kg 12:31
in Bethel the **p** for the high 1Kg 12:32
on you the **p** of the high places 1Kg 13:2
again set up **p** from every class 1Kg 13:33
and they became **p** of the high 1Kg 13:33
friends, and **p**—leaving him no 2Kg 10:11
all his servants, and all his **p**. 2Kg 10:19
Then Joash said to the **p**, 2Kg 12:4
p had not repaired the damage 2Kg 12:6
priest and the other **p** and said, 2Kg 12:7
So the **p** agreed they would not 2Kg 12:8
in it the **p** who guarded the 2Kg 12:9
since it belonged to the **p**. 2Kg 12:16
back one of the **p** you deported. 2Kg 17:27
one of the **p** they had deported 2Kg 17:28
p to serve them in the shrines 2Kg 17:32
elders of the **p**, covered with 2Kg 19:2
well as the **p** and the prophets 2Kg 23:2
priest and the **p** of the second 2Kg 23:4
the idolatrous **p** the kings of 2Kg 23:5
brought all the **p** from the 2Kg 23:8
where the **p** had burned incense. 2Kg 23:8
The **p** of the high places, 2Kg 23:9
bread with their fellow **p**. 2Kg 23:9
altars all the **p** of the high 2Kg 23:20
were Israelites, **p**, Levites, and 1Ch 9:2
The **p**: Jedaiah; Jehoiarib; 1Ch 9:10
including the **p** and Levites in 1Ch 13:2
summoned the **p** Zadok and 1Ch 15:11
So the **p** and the Levites 1Ch 15:14
The **p**, Shebaniah, Joshaphat, 1Ch 15:24
and the **p** Benaiah and Jahaziel 1Ch 16:6
and his fellow **p** before the 1Ch 16:39
son of Abiathar were **p**; 1Ch 18:16
of Israel, the **p**, and the 1Ch 23:2
Eleazar and Ithamar served as **p**. 1Ch 24:2
of the **p** and the Levites 1Ch 24:6
families of the **p** and Levites— 1Ch 24:31
of the **p** and the Levites 1Ch 28:13
of the **p** and the Levites 1Ch 28:21
was used by the **p** for washing. 2Ch 4:6
courtyard of the **p** and the large 2Ch 4:9
The **p** and the Levites brought 2Ch 5:5
The **p** brought the ark of the 2Ch 5:7
When the **p** came out of the holy 2Ch 5:11
for all the **p** who were present 2Ch 5:11
them were 120 **p** blowing trumpets 2Ch 5:12
the **p** were not able to continue 2Ch 5:14
May Your **p**, LORD God, be clothed 2Ch 6:41
The **p** were not able to enter the 2Ch 7:2
The **p** were standing at their 2Ch 7:6
the **p** were blowing trumpets, 2Ch 7:6
divisions of the **p** over their 2Ch 8:14
before the **p** following the daily 2Ch 8:14
regarding the **p** and the Levites 2Ch 8:15
The **p** and Levites from all their 2Ch 11:13
let them serve as **p** of the LORD. 2Ch 11:14
appointed his own **p** for the high 2Ch 11:15
you banish the **p** of the LORD, 2Ch 13:9
make your own **p** like the peoples 2Ch 13:9
p ministering to the LORD are 2Ch 13:10
God and His **p** are with us at our 2Ch 13:12
Then the **p** blew the trumpets, 2Ch 13:14
p, Elishama and Jehoram, were 2Ch 17:8
of the Levites and **p** and some of 2Ch 19:8
p and Levites who are coming on 2Ch 23:4
temple but the **p** and those 2Ch 23:6
the hands of the Levitical **p**, 2Ch 23:18
So he gathered the **p** and Levites 2Ch 24:5
with 80 brave **p** of the LORD, 2Ch 26:17
the consecrated **p**, the 2Ch 26:18
he became enraged with the **p**, 2Ch 26:19
presence of the **p** in the LORD's 2Ch 26:19
and all the **p** turned to him 2Ch 26:20
he brought in the **p** and Levites 2Ch 29:4
p went to the entrance of the 2Ch 29:16
of Aaron, the **p**, to offer them 2Ch 29:21
and the **p** received the blood and 2Ch 29:22
The **p** slaughtered the goats and 2Ch 29:24
and the **p** with the trumpets. 2Ch 29:26
since there were not enough **p**, 2Ch 29:34
and until the **p** consecrated 2Ch 29:34
themselves than the **p** were. 2Ch 29:34
enough of the **p** had consecrated 2Ch 30:3
The **p** and Levites were ashamed, 2Ch 30:15
The **p** sprinkled the blood 2Ch 30:16
Levites and the **p** praised the 2Ch 30:21
and many **p** consecrated 2Ch 30:24
of Judah with the **p** and Levites, 2Ch 30:25
Then the **p** and the Levites stood 2Ch 30:27
of the **p** and Levites for 2Ch 31:2
service among the **p** and Levites. 2Ch 31:2
for the **p** and Levites so that 2Ch 31:4
asked the **p** and Levites about 2Ch 31:9
the cities of the **p** were to 2Ch 31:15
genealogy of the **p** by their 2Ch 31:17
of Aaron, the **p**, in the common 2Ch 31:19
male among the **p** and to every 2Ch 31:19
bones of the **p** on their altars 2Ch 34:5
as well as the **p** and the Levites 2Ch 34:30
He appointed the **p** to their 2Ch 35:2
the people, the **p**, and the 2Ch 35:8
and 300 bulls for the **p**. 2Ch 35:8
the **p** stood at their posts and 2Ch 35:10
the **p** sprinkled the blood they 2Ch 35:11
for themselves and for the **p**, 2Ch 35:14
since the **p**, the descendants 2Ch 35:14
for themselves and for the **p**, 2Ch 35:14

that Josiah observed with the **p**, 2Ch 35:18
leaders of the **p** and the people 2Ch 36:14
along with the **p** and Levites— Ezr 1:5
The **p** ⌊included⌋: Jedaiah's Ezr 2:36
from the descendants of the **p**: Ezr 2:61
The **p**, Levites, singers, Ezr 2:70
his brothers the **p** along with Ezr 3:2
including the **p**, the Levites, Ezr 3:8
temple, the **p**, dressed in their Ezr 3:10
many of the older **p**, Levites, Ezr 3:12
by the **p** in Jerusalem— Ezr 6:9
including the **p**, the Levites, Ezr 6:16
appointed the **p** by their Ezr 6:18
All of the **p** and Levites were Ezr 6:20
the Israelites, **p**, Levites, Ezr 7:7
including their **p** and Levites, Ezr 7:13
people and the **p** to the house Ezr 7:16
must not be imposed on any **p**, Ezr 7:24
searched among the people and **p**, Ezr 8:15
I selected 12 of the leading **p**, Ezr 8:24
house before the leading **p**, Ezr 8:29
So the **p** and Levites took charge Ezr 8:30
Israel, the **p**, and the Levites Ezr 9:1
along with our kings and **p**, Ezr 9:7
got up and made the leading **p**, Ezr 10:5
from the descendants of the **p**: Ezr 10:18
told the Jews, **p**, nobles, Neh 2:16
his fellow **p** began rebuilding Neh 3:1
And next to him the **p** from the Neh 3:22
Each of the **p** made repairs above Neh 3:28
I summoned the **p** and made Neh 5:12
The **p** ⌊included⌋: Jedaiah's Neh 7:39
and from the **p**: the descendants Neh 7:63
So the **p**, Levites, gatekeepers, Neh 7:73
along with the **p** and Levites, Neh 8:13
and leaders, our **p** and prophets, Neh 9:32
kings, leaders, **p**, and ancestors Neh 9:34
of⌋ our leaders, Levites, and **p**. Neh 9:38
and Shemaiah. These were the **p**. Neh 10:8
the people—the **p**, Levites, Neh 10:28
We have cast lots among the **p**, Neh 10:34
to the **p** who serve in our God's Neh 10:36
of dough to the **p** at the Neh 10:37
are kept and where the **p**, Neh 10:39
the Israelites, **p**, Levites, Neh 11:3
The **p**: Jedaiah son of Joiarib, Neh 11:10
Israel, the **p**, and the Levites Neh 11:20
These are the **p** and Levites who Neh 12:1
the leaders of the **p** and their Neh 12:7
the Levites and **p** were recorded Neh 12:22
After the **p** and Levites had Neh 12:30
the **p**: Eliakim, Maaseiah, Neh 12:41
for the **p** and Levites were Neh 12:44
grateful to the **p** and Levites Neh 12:44
the contributions for the **p**. Neh 13:5
to each of the **p** and Levites. Neh 13:30
He leads **p** away barefoot and Jb 12:19
His **p** fell by the sword, but the Ps 78:64
and Aaron were among His **p**; Ps 99:6
May Your **p** be clothed with Ps 132:9
clothe its **p** with salvation, Ps 132:16
and the older **p**, wearing Is 37:2
you will be called the LORD's **p**; Is 61:6
some of them as **p** and Levites," Is 66:21
one of the **p** living in Anathoth Jr 1:1
its officials, its **p**, and the Jr 1:18
The **p** quit asking: Where is the Jr 2:8
officials, their **p**, and their Jr 2:26
The **p** will tremble in fear, Jr 4:9
and the **p** rule by their own Jr 5:31
the bones of the **p**, the bones of Jr 8:1
his throne, the **p**, the prophets Jr 13:13
and some of the elders of the **p** Jr 19:1
The **p**, the prophets, and all the Jr 26:7
Then the **p**, the prophets, and Jr 26:8
Then the **p** and prophets said to Jr 26:11
people told the **p** and prophets, Jr 26:16
I spoke to the **p** and all these Jr 27:16
presence of the **p** and all the Jr 28:1
presence of the **p** and all the Jr 28:5
the exiles, the **p**, the prophets, Jr 29:1
and to all the **p**, saying: Jr 29:25
will give the **p** their fill with Jr 31:14
officials, their **p**, and their Jr 32:32
The Levitical **p** will never fail Jr 33:18
the Levitical **p** will not be My Jr 33:21
officials, the **p**, and all the Jr 34:19
exile with his **p** and officials. Jr 48:7
with his **p** and officials. Jr 49:3
her **p** groan, her young women Lm 1:4
My **p** and elders perished in the Lm 1:19
Should **p** and prophets be killed Lm 2:20
prophets and the guilt of her **p**, Lm 4:13
The **p** are not respected; Lm 4:16
perish from the **p** and counsel Ezk 7:26
Her **p** do violence to My law and Ezk 22:26
is for the **p** who keep charge Ezk 40:45
is for the **p** who keep charge Ezk 40:46
where the **p** who approach Ezk 42:13
Once the **p** have entered, they Ezk 42:14
to the Levitical **p** who are Ezk 43:19
p will throw salt on them and Ezk 43:24
For seven days the **p** are to make Ezk 43:26
the **p** will offer your burnt Ezk 43:27
to serve Me as **p** or come near Ezk 44:13
But the Levitical **p** descended Ezk 44:15
your gifts will belong to the **p**. Ezk 44:30
The **p** may not eat any bird or Ezk 44:31
to be used by the **p** who minister Ezk 45:4
gate while the **p** sacrifice his Ezk 46:2
the place where the **p** will boil Ezk 46:20
be set apart for the **p** ⌊alone⌋. Ezk 48:10
It is for the consecrated **p**, Ezk 48:11
Next to the territory of the **p**, Ezk 48:13
for My case is against you **p**. Hs 4:4
happen to both people and **p**. Hs 4:9
Hear this, **p**! Pay attention, Hs 5:1
a band of **p** murders on the road Hs 6:9
its idolatrous **p** rejoiced over Hs 10:5
the **p**, who are ministers of the Jl 1:9
in sackcloth⌋ and lament, you **p**; Jl 1:13
Let the **p**, the LORD's ministers, Jl 2:17
for a bribe, her **p** teach for Mc 3:11
names of the pagan **p** along with Zph 1:4
pagan priests along with the **p**; Zph 1:4
Her **p** profane the sanctuary; Zph 3:4
Ask the **p** for a ruling. Hg 2:11
The **p** answered, "No." Hg 2:12
The **p** answered, "It becomes Hg 2:13
by asking the **p** who were at the Zch 7:3
people of the land and the **p**: Zch 7:5
says the LORD of Hosts to you **p**, Mal 1:6
this decree is for you **p**: Mal 2:1
all the chief **p** and scribes Mt 2:4
him to eat, but only for the **p**? Mt 12:4
Sabbath days the **p** in the temple Mt 12:5
elders, chief **p**, and scribes, be Mt 16:21
over to the chief **p** and scribes, Mt 20:18
When the chief **p** and the scribes Mt 21:15
chief **p** and the elders of the Mt 21:23
When the chief **p** and the Mt 21:45
Then the chief **p** and the elders Mt 26:3
Iscariot—went to the chief **p** Mt 26:14
him from the chief **p** and elders Mt 26:47
The chief **p** and the whole Mt 26:59
all the chief **p** and the elders Mt 27:1
to the chief **p** and elders. Mt 27:3
The chief **p** took the silver and Mt 27:6
by the chief **p** and elders, Mt 27:12
The chief **p** and the elders, Mt 27:20
In the same way the chief **p**, Mt 27:41
the chief **p** and the Pharisees Mt 27:62
to the chief **p** everything that Mt 28:11
After the **p** had assembled with Mt 28:12
for anyone to eat except the **p**— Mk 2:26
the chief **p**, and the scribes Mk 8:31
to the chief **p** and the scribes, Mk 10:33
Then the chief **p** and the scribes Mk 11:18
the chief **p**, the scribes, Mk 11:27
The chief **p** and the scribes were Mk 14:1
to the chief **p** to hand Him over Mk 14:10
from the chief **p**, the scribes, Mk 14:43
and all the chief **p**, the elders, Mk 14:53
The chief **p** and the whole Mk 14:55
the chief **p** had a meeting with Mk 15:1
And the chief **p** began to accuse Mk 15:3
that the chief **p** had handed Him Mk 15:10
But the chief **p** stirred up the Mk 15:11
chief **p** with the scribes were Mk 15:31
lawful for any but the **p** to eat? Lk 6:4
elders, chief **p**, and scribes, be Lk 9:22
and show yourselves to the **p**." Lk 17:14
chief **p**, the scribes, and the Lk 19:47
the chief **p** and the scribes, Lk 20:1
and the chief **p** looked for a way Lk 20:19
The chief **p** and the scribes were Lk 22:2
with the chief **p** and temple Lk 22:4
Then Jesus said to the chief **p**, Lk 22:52
the chief **p** and the scribes, Lk 22:66
told the chief **p** and the crowds, Lk 23:4
chief **p** and the scribes stood Lk 23:10
called together the chief **p**, Lk 23:13
and how our chief **p** and leaders Lk 24:20
Jerusalem sent **p** and Levites to Jn 1:19
so the chief **p** and the Pharisees Jn 7:32
to the chief **p** and Pharisees, Jn 7:45
So the chief **p** and the Pharisees Jn 11:47
chief **p** and the Pharisees had Jn 11:57
the chief **p** decided to also Jn 12:10
from the chief **p** and the Jn 18:3
and the chief **p** handed You over Jn 18:35
When the chief **p** and the temple Jn 19:6
the chief **p** answered. Jn 19:15
So the chief **p** of the Jews said Jn 19:21
the people, the **p**, the commander Ac 4:1
that the chief **p** and the elders Ac 4:23
and the chief **p** heard these Ac 5:24
large group of **p** became obedient Ac 6:7
from the chief **p** to arrest all Ac 9:14
as prisoners to the chief **p**?" Ac 9:21
instructed the chief **p** and all Ac 22:30
went to the chief **p** and elders Ac 23:14
Then the chief **p** and the leaders Ac 25:2
chief **p** and the elders of the Ac 25:15
for that from the chief **p**. Ac 26:10
a commission from the chief **p**. Ac 26:12
Moses said nothing concerning **p**. Heb 7:14
others became **p** without an oath Heb 7:20
many have become ⌊Levitical⌋ **p**, Heb 7:23
day, as high **p** do—first for Heb 7:27
as high **p** men who are weak Heb 7:28
the **p** enter the first room Heb 9:6
made us a kingdom, **p** to His God Rv 1:6
them a kingdom and **p** to our God, Rv 5:10
they will be **p** of God and the Rv 20:6

PRIESTS' *(7)*

Only the **p** land does not belong Gn 47:26
This is the **p** share from the Dt 18:3
Jordan where the **p** feet are Jos 4:3
or for the **p** share ⌊of the 1Sm 2:13
But some of the **p** sons mixed the 1Ch 9:30
Some of the **p** sons had trumpets: Neh 12:35
gate, into the **p** holy chambers, Ezk 46:19

PRIME *(2)*

youth and the **p** of life are Ec 11:10
In the **p** of my life I must go to Is 38:10

PRINCE *(43)*

the Hivite, a **p** of the region, Gn 34:2
crown of the **p** of his brothers Gn 49:26
crown of the **p** of his brothers Dt 33:16
to Sheshbazzar the **p** of Judah. Ezr 1:8
I would approach Him like a **p**. Jb 31:37
God, Eternal Father, **P** of Peace. Is 9:6
the **p** will be clothed in grief; Ezk 7:27
is about the **p** in Jerusalem Ezk 12:10
p who is among them will lift Ezk 12:12
profane and wicked **p** of Israel, Ezk 21:25
every **p** of Israel within you has Ezk 22:6
no longer be a **p** from the land Ezk 30:13
David will be a **p** among them. Ezk 34:24
David will be their **p** forever. Ezk 37:25
chief **p** of Meshech and Tubal. Ezk 38:2
chief **p** of Meshech and Tubal. Ezk 38:3
chief **p** of Meshech and Tubal. Ezk 39:1
The **p** himself will sit in the Ezk 44:3
And the **p** will have the area on Ezk 45:7
for the **p** in Israel. Ezk 45:16
On that day the **p** will provide a Ezk 45:22
The **p** should enter from the Ezk 46:2
offering that the **p** presents to Ezk 46:4
When the **p** enters, he must go in Ezk 46:8
the **p** will enter with them, Ezk 46:10
When the **p** makes a freewill Ezk 46:12
If the **p** gives a gift to each of Ezk 46:16
when it will revert to the **p**. Ezk 46:17
The **p** must not take any of the Ezk 46:18
property will belong to the **p**. Ezk 48:21
of the area belonging to the **p**, Ezk 48:22
Benjamin will belong to the **p**. Ezk 48:22
even up to the **P** of the host; Dn 8:11
stand against the **P** of princes. Dn 8:25
Messiah the **P** will be seven Dn 9:25
of the coming **p** will destroy Dn 9:26
But the **p** of the kingdom of Dn 10:13

fight against the **p** of Persia, Dn 10:20
the **p** of Greece will come. Dn 10:20
them except Michael, your **p**. Dn 10:21
as well as the covenant **p**. Dn 11:22
the great **p** who stands watch Dn 12:1
many days without king or **p**, Hs 3:4

PRINCE'S *(1)*
will be the **p** responsibility. Ezk 45:17

PRINCES *(47)*
The **p** dug the well; The nobles Nm 21:18
the **p** of Sihon who lived in the Jos 13:21
Pay attention, **p**! I will sing to Jdg 5:3
The **p** of Issachar were with Jdg 5:15
and Zeeb, the two **p** of Midian; Jdg 7:25
and Zeeb, the two **p** of Midian. Jdg 8:3
But the **p** of Succoth asked, Jdg 8:6
names of the⌋ 77 **p** and elders of Jdg 8:14
well as some of the **p** of Israel. 2Ch 21:4
or with **p** who had gold, who Jb 3:15
is not partial to **p** and does not Jb 34:19
you will make them **p** throughout Ps 45:16
Though **p** sit together speaking Ps 119:23
P have persecuted me without Ps 119:161
p and all judges of the earth, Ps 148:11
me, **p** lead, as do nobles ⌊and⌋ Pr 8:16
less for a slave to rule over **p**! Pr 19:10
but **p** walking on the ground like Ec 10:7
and your **p** feast in the morning. Ec 10:16
nobles and your **p** feast at the Ec 10:17
p of Zoan are complete fools; Is 19:11
The **p** of Zoan have been fools; Is 19:13
the **p** of Memphis are deceived. Is 19:13
Rise up, you **p**, and oil the Is 21:5
traders are **p**, whose merchants Is 23:8
For though his **p** are at Zoan and Is 30:4
and all her **p** will come to Is 34:12
reduces **p** to nothing and makes Is 40:23
stand up, and **p** will bow down, Is 49:7
kings and **p** will enter through Jr 17:25
will make her **p** and sages drunk Jr 51:57
P are hung up by their hands; Lm 5:12
lament for the **p** of Israel Ezk 19:1
is against all the **p** of Israel! Ezk 21:12
the **p** of the sea will descend Ezk 26:16
and all the **p** of Kedar were your Ezk 27:21
and all her **p**, who, despite Ezk 32:29
the blood of the earth's **p**: Ezk 39:18
My **p** will no longer oppress My Ezk 45:8
have gone too far, **p** of Israel! Ezk 45:9
stand against the Prince of **p**. Dn 8:25
of the chief **p**, came to help me Dn 10:13
p of Judah are like those who Hs 5:10
evil, the **p** with their lies Hs 7:3
the **p** are sick with the heat of Hs 7:5
king and his **p** will go into Am 1:15
The **p** within her are roaring Zph 3:3

PRINCESS *(2)*
are your sandaled feet, **p**! Sg 7:1
The **p** among the provinces has Lm 1:1

PRINCESSES *(2)*
Her wisest **p** answer her; Jdg 5:29
wives who were **p** and 300 1Kg 11:3

PRINCIPLE *(1)*
So I discover this **p**: Rm 7:21

PRINCIPLES *(1)*
again the basic **p** of God's Heb 5:12

PRIOR *(3)*
were in the land **p** to you have Lv 18:27
For **p** to those days neither man Zch 8:10
For **p** to his transformation he Heb 11:5

PRISCA *(2)*
my greetings to **P** and Aquila, Rm 16:3
Greet **P** and Aquila, and the 2Tm 4:19

PRISCILLA *(4)*
with his wife **P** because Claudius Ac 18:2
P and Aquila were with him. Ac 18:18
After **P** and Aquila heard him, Ac 18:26
Aquila and **P** greet you heartily 1Co 16:19

PRISON *(57)*
and had him thrown into **p**, Gn 39:20
So Joseph was there in **p**. Gn 39:20
in the eyes of the **p** warden. Gn 39:21
who were in the **p** under Joseph's Gn 39:22
in the **p** where Joseph was Gn 40:3
who were confined in the **p**, Gn 40:5
and get me out of this **p**. Gn 40:14
forced to grind grain in the **p**. Jdg 16:21
So they brought Samson from **p**, Jdg 16:25
Put this guy in **p** and feed him 1Kg 22:27
arrested him and put him in **p**. 2Kg 17:4
Judah ⌊and released him⌋ from **p**. 2Kg 25:27
changed his **p** clothes, 2Kg 25:29
and put him in **p** because of his 2Ch 16:10
Put this guy in **p** and feed him 2Ch 18:26
someone⌋ in **p** or convenes a Jb 11:10
Free me from **p** so that I can Ps 142:7
For he came from **p** to be king, Ec 4:14
in darkness from the **p** house. Is 42:7
not ⌊yet⌋ put him into the **p**. Jr 37:4
for it had been made into a **p**. Jr 37:15
that you have put me in **p**? Jr 37:18
and released him from the **p**. Jr 52:31
changed his **p** clothes, Jr 52:33
earth with its **p** bars closed Jnh 2:6
and you will be thrown into **p**. Mt 5:25
John heard in **p** what the Messiah Mt 11:2
and put him in **p** on account of Mt 14:3
and had John beheaded in the **p**. Mt 14:10
threw him into **p** until he could Mt 18:30
I was in **p** and you visited Me.' Mt 25:36
sick, or in **p**, and visit You? Mt 25:39
and in **p** and you didn't take Mt 25:43
or sick, or in **p**, and not help Mt 25:44
and to chain him in **p** on account Mk 6:17
he went and beheaded him in **p**, Mk 6:27
who was in **p** with rebels who had Mk 15:7
else—he locked John up in **p**. Lk 3:20
the bailiff throw you into **p**. Lk 12:58
You both to **p** and to death!" Lk 22:33
thrown into **p** for a rebellion Lk 23:19
been thrown into **p** for rebellion Lk 23:25
had not yet been thrown into **p**. Jn 3:24
and women, and put them in **p**. Ac 8:3
put him in **p** and assigned four Ac 12:4
was kept in **p**, but prayer was Ac 12:5
front of the door guarded the **p**. Ac 12:6
had brought him out of the **p**. Ac 12:17
into the inner **p** and secured Ac 16:24
and saw the doors of the **p** open, Ac 16:27
the Jews, Felix left Paul in **p**. Ac 24:27
up many of the saints in **p**, Ac 26:10
Messiah—for which I am in **p**— Col 4:3
though you were in **p** with them, Heb 13:3
proclamation to the spirits in **p** 1Pt 3:19
some of you into **p** to test you, Rv 2:10
will be released from his **p** Rv 20:7

PRISONER *(24)*
his relative had been taken **p**, Gn 14:14
the firstborn of the **p** who was Ex 12:29
you and you take some of them **p**, Dt 21:10
wearing when she was taken **p**, Dt 21:13
because they will be taken **p**. Dt 28:41
The **p** is soon to be set free; Is 51:14
will burn them and take them **p**. Jr 43:12
to the crowd a **p** they wanted. Mt 27:15
a notorious **p** called Barabbas Mt 27:16
the people a **p** they requested. Mk 15:6
that I release one ⌊**p**⌋ to you at Jn 18:39
The **p** Paul called me and asked Ac 23:18
who was left as a **p** by Felix. Ac 25:14
to me to send a **p** and not to Ac 25:27
delivered as a **p** from Jerusalem Ac 28:17
and taking me **p** to the law of Rm 7:23
the **p** of Christ Jesus on behalf Eph 3:1
therefore, the **p** in the Lord, Eph 4:1
my fellow **p**, greets you, as does Col 4:10
about our Lord, or of me His **p**. 2Tm 1:8
Paul, a **p** of Christ Jesus, and Phm 1
now also as a **p** of Christ Jesus Phm 9
my fellow **p** in Christ Jesus, Phm 23
But the beast was taken **p**, Rv 19:20

PRISONER'S *(1)*
hear a **p** groaning, to set free Ps 102:20

PRISONERS *(32)*
my daughters away like **p** of war! Gn 31:26
the king's **p** were confined. Gn 39:20
warden put all the **p** who were in Gn 39:22
Israel and captured some **p**. Nm 21:1
They brought the **p**, animals, and Nm 31:12
you and your **p** who have killed Nm 31:19
leads out the **p** to prosperity, Ps 68:6
not despise His own who are **p**. Ps 69:33
the groans of the **p** reach You; Ps 79:11
and gloom—**p** in cruel chains— Ps 107:10
to the hungry. The LORD frees **p**. Ps 146:7
crouch among the **p** or fall among Is 10:4
release the **p** to return home? Is 14:17
together like **p** in a pit. Is 24:22
to bring out **p** from the dungeon, Is 42:7
saying to the **p**: Come out, and Is 49:9
captives, and freedom to the **p**; Is 61:1
Crushing all the **p** of the land Lm 3:34
They gather **p** like sand. Hab 1:9
will release your **p** from the Zch 9:11
stronghold, you **p** who have hope; Zch 9:12
bring them as **p** to Jerusalem. Ac 9:2
of taking them as **p** to the chief Ac 9:21
the **p** were listening to them. Ac 16:25
he thought the **p** had escaped. Ac 16:27
those who were **p** there to be Ac 22:5
and some other **p** to a centurion Ac 27:1
was to kill the **p** so that no one Ac 27:42
fellow countrymen and fellow **p**. Rm 16:7
high, He took **p** into captivity; Eph 4:8
with the **p** and accepted with Heb 10:34
Remember the **p**, as though you Heb 13:3

PRISONS *(1)*
over to the synagogues and **p**, Lk 21:12

PRIVATE *(8)*
to David in **p** and tell him, 1Sm 18:22
Zedekiah swore to Jeremiah in **p**, Jr 38:16
to Gedaliah in **p** at Mizpah, Jr 40:15
go into your **p** room, shut your Mt 6:6
you, go and rebuke him in **p**. Mt 18:15
was praying in **p** and His Lk 9:18
in an ear in **p** rooms will be Lk 12:3
Mary, saying in **p**, "The Teacher Jn 11:28

PRIVATELY *(13)*
speak to him **p**, and there Joab 2Sm 3:27
and in his house **p** asked him, Jr 37:17
approached Jesus **p** and said, Mt 17:19
disciples aside **p** and said to Mt 20:17
approached Him **p** and said, Mt 24:3
P, however, He would explain Mk 4:34
took him away from the crowd **p**. Mk 7:33
His disciples asked Him **p**, Mk 9:28
John, and Andrew asked Him **p**, Mk 13:3
and withdrew **p** to a town called Lk 9:10
to His disciples He said **p**, Lk 10:23
and inquired **p**, "What is it you Ac 23:19
but **p** to those recognized ⌊as Gl 2:2

PRIVILEGE *(3)*
He has given us the **p**, Lk 1:73
insistently for the **p** of sharing 2Co 8:4
a faith of equal **p** with ours 2Pt 1:1

PRIZE *(2)*
but only one receives the **p**? 1Co 9:24
as my goal the **p** promised by Php 3:14

PROBABLY *(2)*
He's **p** already hiding in one of 2Sm 17:9
This man is **p** a murderer, Ac 28:4

PROBES *(1)*
p the deepest recesses for ore Jb 28:3

PROBLEM *(3)*
There will be no **p**; only let us Nm 20:19
safe for you and there is no **p**. 1Sm 20:21
root of the **p** lies with him?" Jb 19:28

PROBLEMS *(2)*
explain riddles, and solve **p**. Dn 5:12
interpretations and solve **p**. Dn 5:16

PROCEDURE *(3)*
was his normal **p** to confer with Est 1:13
knows the right time and **p**. Ec 8:5
there is a right time and **p**, Ec 8:6

PROCEDURES *(1)*
of Him about the proper **p**." 1Ch 15:13

PROCEED *(7)*
I will **p** to discipline you seven Lv 26:18
of Akrabbim, **p** to Zin, and end Nm 34:4
to Hazar-addar and **p** to Azmon. Nm 34:4
You will **p** from there until you 1Sm 10:3
don't **p** in the way of evil ones. Pr 4:14
for they **p** from one evil to Jr 9:3
you will **p** to take the lowest Lk 14:9

PROCEEDED *(22)*
time Joshua **p** to exterminate Jos 11:21
of Akrabbim, **p** to Zin, ascended Jos 15:3
p to Azmon and to the Brook of Jos 15:4
to Beth-hoglah, **p** north of Jos 15:6

The border **p** to the waters of Jos 15:7
Beth-shemesh, and **p** to Timnah. Jos 15:10
to Shikkeron, **p** to Mount Baalah, Jos 15:11
went to Luz and **p** to the border Jos 16:2
Valley and **p** into the valley. Jos 18:18
together and **p** to make Abimelech Jdg 9:6
and his men **p** along the road as 2Sm 16:13
and then ⌊**p**⌋ toward Gad and 2Sm 24:5
you have **p** to make for yourself 1Kg 14:9
and then **p** to serve Baal and 1Kg 16:31
So she **p** to do according to the 1Kg 17:15
p to annihilate all the royal 2Kg 11:1
p to annihilate all the royal 2Ch 22:10
They **p** to take away the altars 2Ch 30:14
Then He **p** to denounce the towns Mt 11:20
So Philip **p** to tell him the good Ac 8:35
the Jews, he **p** to arrest Peter Ac 12:3
against them, they **p** to Iconium. Ac 13:51

PROCEEDING *(1)*
an error **p** from the presence of Ec 10:5

PROCEEDS *(7)*
the live ox and divide its **p**; Ex 21:35
each man **p** on his own path. Jl 2:8
of truth who **p** from the Father— Jn 15:26
and distributed the **p** to all, Ac 2:45
brought the **p** of the things that Ac 4:34
part of the **p** with his wife's Ac 5:2
part of the **p** from the field? Ac 5:3

PROCESS *(1)*
accelerated the **p** of the beauty Est 2:9

PROCESSION *(9)*
you mean by this whole **p** I met?" Gn 33:8
it was a very impressive **p**. Gn 50:9
walked behind the funeral **p**. 2Sm 3:31
people walked ⌊in **p**⌋ before one 1Kg 12:30
thanksgiving **p** went to the left, Neh 12:38
the festive **p** to the house of Ps 42:4
have seen Your **p**, God, the Ps 68:24
God, the **p** of my God, my King, Ps 68:24
their kings being led ⌊in **p**⌋. Is 60:11

PROCESSIONS *(2)*
two large **p** that gave thanks. Neh 12:31
two thanksgiving **p** stood in the Neh 12:40

PROCHORUS *(1)*
and Philip, **P**, Nicanor, Timon, Ac 6:5

PROCLAIM *(96)*
and I will **p** the name Yahweh Ex 33:19
LORD that you will **p** as sacred Lv 23:2
you are to **p** at their appointed Lv 23:4
that you are to **p** as sacred Lv 23:37
fiftieth year and **p** freedom in Lv 25:10
you are to **p** the blessing at Dt 11:29
Levites will **p** in a loud voice Dt 27:14
and **p** it to us so that we may Dt 30:12
and **p** it to us so that we may Dt 30:13
For I will **p** the LORD's name. Dt 32:3
P a fast and seat Naboth at the 1Kg 21:9
p His deeds among the peoples. 1Ch 16:8
P His salvation from day to day. 1Ch 16:23
Jerusalem to **p** on your behalf: Neh 6:7
city square, and **p** before him, Est 6:9
p His deeds among the peoples. Ps 9:11
I will **p** Your name to my Ps 22:22
Will it **p** Your truth? Ps 30:9
P with me the LORD's greatness; Ps 34:3
my tongue will **p** Your Ps 35:28
I **p** righteousness in the great Ps 40:9
The heavens **p** His righteousness, Ps 50:6
will joyfully **p** Your faithful Ps 59:16
I will **p** Your righteousness, Ps 71:16
and I still **p** Your wonderful Ps 71:17
Then I will **p** Your power to Ps 71:18
my tongue will **p** Your Ps 71:24
my mouth I will **p** Your Ps 89:1
p His salvation from day to day. Ps 96:2
The heavens **p** His righteousness; Ps 97:6
p His deeds among the peoples. Ps 105:1
mighty acts or **p** all the praise Ps 106:2
of the LORD **p** that He has Ps 107:2
I will live and **p** what the LORD Ps 118:17
With my lips I **p** all the Ps 119:13
next and will **p** Your mighty acts Ps 145:4
They will **p** the power of Your Ps 145:6
to the LORD; **p** His name! Is 12:4
they **p** in the west the majesty Is 24:14
nobles will be left to **p** a king, Is 34:12
shout of joy, **p** this, let it go Is 48:20
frankincense and **p** the praises Is 60:6
to **p** liberty to the captives, Is 61:1
to **p** the year of the LORD's Is 61:2
And they will **p** My glory among Is 66:19
p these words to the north, Jr 3:12
in Judah, **p** in Jerusalem, Jr 4:5
nations: Look! **P** to Jerusalem: Jr 4:16
p it in Judah, saying: Jr 5:20
P all these words in the cities Jr 11:6
P there the words I speak to you. Jr 19:2
and you are to **p** to them: Jr 19:11
I speak, I cry out—I **p**: Jr 20:8
P, praise, and say: Jr 31:7
Jerusalem to **p** freedom to them Jr 34:8
I hereby **p** freedom for you"— Jr 34:17
are to **p** concerning Jehoiakim Jr 36:29
it in Egypt, and **p** it in Migdol! Jr 46:14
P it in Memphis and in Tahpanhes! Jr 46:14
p and raise up a signal flag; Jr 50:2
p, and hide nothing. Jr 50:2
says! You are to **p**: A sword! A Ezk 21:9
You are to **p**: Sword, sword! ⌊You Ezk 21:28
horses, and we will no longer **p**: Hs 14:3
a sacred fast; **p** an assembly! Jl 1:14
a sacred fast; **p** an assembly. Jl 2:15
P this among the nations: Jl 3:9
P on the citadels in Ashdod and Am 3:9
and loudly **p** your freewill Am 4:5
p peace when they have ⌊food⌋ Mc 3:5
to **p** to Jacob his rebellion and Mc 3:8
was speaking with me said, "**P**: Zch 1:14
P further: This is what the LORD Zch 1:17
and He will **p** peace to the Zch 9:10
in a whisper, **p** on the housetops Mt 10:27
and He will **p** justice to the Mt 12:18
and began to **p** it widely and to Mk 1:45
and began to **p** in the Decapolis Mk 5:20
them, the more they would **p** it. Mk 7:36
p to you good news of great joy Lk 2:10
He has sent Me to **p** freedom to Lk 4:18
to **p** the year of the Lord's Lk 4:19
I must **p** the good news about the Lk 4:43
He sent them to **p** the kingdom of Lk 9:2
we ourselves **p** to you the good Ac 13:32
in every city those who **p** him, Ac 15:21
in ignorance, this I **p** to you. Ac 17:23
He would **p** light to our people Ac 26:23
the message of faith that we **p**: Rm 10:8
you **p** the Lord's death until He 1Co 11:26
to **p** to the Gentiles the Eph 3:8
the others **p** Christ out of Php 1:17
We **p** Him, warning and teaching Col 1:28
p the message; persist in it 2Tm 4:2
I will **p** Your name to My Heb 2:12
so that you may **p** the praises of 1Pt 2:9

PROCLAIMED *(56)*
him there, and **p** ⌊His⌋ name Ex 34:5
passed in front of him and **p**: Ex 34:6
Balaam **p** his poem: Nm 23:7
Balaam **p** his poem: Nm 23:18
and he **p** his poem: Nm 24:3
Then he **p** his poem: Nm 24:15
saw Amalek and **p** his poem: Nm 24:20
saw the Kenites and **p** his poem: Nm 24:21
Once more he **p** his poem: Nm 24:23
ordinances Moses **p** to them after Dt 4:45
release of debts has been **p**. Dt 15:2
p to the people the rights 1Sm 10:25
the people **p**, "Long live King 1Kg 1:39
They **p** a fast and seated Naboth 1Kg 21:12
They blew the ram's horn and **p**, 2Kg 9:13
word of the LORD **p** by the man of 2Kg 23:16
man of God who **p** these things. 2Kg 23:16
from Judah and **p** these things 2Kg 23:17
So he **p** a fast for all Judah, 2Ch 20:3
I **p** a fast by the Ahava River, Ezr 8:21
So they **p** and spread this news Neh 8:15
saved, and **p**—and not some Is 43:12
of My mouth; I **p** them. Suddenly Is 48:3
the LORD has **p** to the end of the Is 62:11
temple, and **p** to all the people Jr 19:14
of all the people Hananiah **p**, Jr 28:11
into Jerusalem **p** a fast before Jr 36:9
the report is **p** in the land, Jr 51:46
a lying divination when you **p**: Ezk 13:7
A herald loudly **p**, "People of Dn 3:4
of his walk in the city and **p**, Jnh 3:4
They **p** a fast and dressed in Jnh 3:5
the earlier prophets **p** to them: Zch 1:4
that the LORD **p** through the Zch 7:7
kingdom will be **p** in all the Mt 24:14
this gospel is **p** in the whole Mt 26:13
must first be **p** to all nations. Mk 13:10
the gospel is **p** in the whole Mk 14:9
he **p** good news to the people. Lk 3:18
will be **p** on the housetops. Lk 12:3
the kingdom of God has been **p**, Lk 16:16
sins would be **p** in His name to Lk 24:47
raised his voice, and **p** to them: Ac 2:14
as he **p** the good news about the Ac 8:12
they **p** God's message in the Ac 13:5
John had previously **p** a baptism Ac 13:24
of sins is being **p** to you, Ac 13:38
message had been **p** by Paul at Ac 17:13
My name may be **p** in all the Rm 9:17
I have fully **p** the good news Rm 15:19
for you the gospel I **p** to you; 1Co 15:1
hold to the message I **p** to you— 1Co 15:2
He **p** the good news of peace to Eph 2:17
motives or true, Christ is **p**. Php 1:18
has been **p** in all creation Col 1:23
had been **p** by Moses to all Heb 9:19

PROCLAIMING *(25)*
ordinances I am **p** as you hear Dt 5:1
It is I, **p** vindication, powerful Is 63:1
p malice from Mount Ephraim. Jr 4:15
each of you **p** freedom for his Jr 34:15
have not obeyed Me by **p** freedom, Jr 34:17
all My servants the prophets, **p**: Jr 35:15
bringing good news and **p** peace! Nah 1:15
p throughout the town all that Lk 8:39
p the good news and healing Lk 9:6
complex and **p** the good news, Lk 20:1
the people and **p** in the person Ac 4:2
teaching and **p** the good news Ac 5:42
went on their way **p** the message Ac 8:4
Immediately he began **p** Jesus in Ac 9:20
p the good news of peace through Ac 10:36
p the good news about the Lord Ac 11:20
and we are **p** good news to you, Ac 14:15
teaching and **p** the message Ac 15:35
who are **p** to you the way of Ac 16:17
Jesus, whom I am **p** to you." Ac 17:3
back from **p** to you anything Ac 20:20
p the kingdom of God and Ac 28:31
worship God, **p**, "God is really 1Co 14:25
For we are not **p** ourselves but 2Co 4:5
mighty angel **p** in a loud voice, Rv 5:2

PROCLAIMS *(6)*
among you and **p** a sign or wonder Dt 13:1
and the sky **p** the work of His Ps 19:1
Many a man **p** his own loyalty, Pr 20:6
the herald, who **p** peace, who Is 52:7
good things, who **p** salvation, Is 52:7
My soul **p** the greatness of the Lk 1:46

PROCLAMATION *(16)*
they sent a **p** throughout the Ex 36:6
are to make a **p** and hold a Lv 23:21
The **p** of David son of Jesse, 2Sm 23:1
the **p** of the man raised on high, 2Sm 23:1
Then a **p** was issued in Judah and 2Ch 24:9
to issue a **p** throughout his 2Ch 36:22
Cyrus to issue a **p** throughout Ezr 1:1
circulated a **p** throughout Judah Ezr 10:7
and issued a **p** concerning him Dn 5:29
they repented at Jonah's **p**; Mt 12:41
they repented at Jonah's **p**, Lk 11:32
gospel and the **p** of Jesus Christ Rm 16:25
My speech and my **p** were not with 1Co 2:4
that the **p** might be fully made 2Tm 4:17
His message in the **p** that I was Ti 1:3
went and made a **p** to the spirits 1Pt 3:19

PROCONSUL *(4)*
was with the **p**, Sergius Paulus Ac 13:7
tried to turn the **p** away from Ac 13:8
the **p**, seeing what happened, Ac 13:12
While Gallio was **p** of Achaia, Ac 18:12

PROCONSULS *(1)*
are in session, and there are **p**. Ac 19:38

PRODUCE *(95)*
Let the earth **p** vegetation: Gn 1:11
Let the earth **p** living creatures Gn 1:24
will **p** thorns and thistles for Gn 3:18
of the land's **p** as an offering Gn 4:3

her, and she will **p** nations; Gn 17:16
and **p** offspring for your Gn 38:8
he would not **p** offspring for his Gn 38:9
a fifth ⌊of the **p**⌋ belongs to Gn 47:26
and he will **p** royal delicacies. Gn 49:20
but you must **p** the same quantity Ex 5:18
tried to **p** gnats using their Ex 8:18
for six years and gather its **p**. Ex 23:10
of your **p** from what you sow Ex 23:16
gather your **p** from the field. Ex 23:16
have gathered the **p** of the land. Lv 23:39
and gather its **p** for six years. Lv 25:3
may ⌊only⌋ eat its **p** ⌊directly⌋ Lv 25:12
we don't sow or gather our **p**?' Lv 25:20
so that it will **p** a crop Lv 25:21
and the land will yield its **p**, Lv 26:4
Your land will not yield its **p**, Lv 26:20
Every tenth of the land's **p**, Lv 27:30
to **p** a pleasing aroma for the Nm 15:3
as the **p** of the threshing Nm 18:30
and the **p** of your soil—your Dt 7:13
the land will not yield its **p**, Dt 11:17
tenth of all the **p** grown in your Dt 14:22
tenth of all your **p** for that Dt 14:28
you in all your **p** and in all the Dt 16:15
that you know do not **p** food. Dt 20:20
plant and the **p** of the vineyard Dt 22:9
all the soil's **p** that you Dt 26:2
first of the land's **p** that You, Dt 26:10
tenth of your **p** in the third Dt 26:12
and your soil's **p**, and the Dt 28:4
your soil's **p** in the land the Dt 28:11
and your soil's **p**, the young of Dt 28:18
eat your soil's **p** and everything Dt 28:33
your trees and your land's **p**. Dt 28:42
and your soil's **p** until you are Dt 28:51
livestock, and your soil's **p**. Dt 30:9
land and eat the **p** of the field. Dt 32:13
it devours the land and its **p**, Dt 32:22
grain from the **p** of the land. Jos 5:11
they ate from the **p** of the land, Jos 5:12
and destroyed the **p** of the land, Jdg 6:4
charge of the **p** of the vineyards 1Ch 27:27
and of all the **p** of the field, 2Ch 31:5
of our land's ⌊**p**⌋ from our lands Neh 10:37
You **p** new witnesses against me Jb 10:17
Who can **p** something pure from Jb 14:4
makes it thrive and **p** twigs like Jb 14:9
consumed its **p** without payment Jb 31:39
consumed the **p** of their soil. Ps 105:35
full, supplying all kinds of **p**; Ps 144:13
with the first **p** of your entire Pr 3:9
the food, the **p** of the ground, Is 30:23
I will **p** descendants from Jacob, Is 65:9
Plant gardens and eat their **p**. Jr 29:5
Plant gardens and eat their **p**." Jr 29:28
pain⌋ because the fields lack **p**. Lm 4:9
waters in order to **p** branches, Ezk 17:8
bear branches, **p** fruit, and Ezk 17:23
and the land will yield its **p**; Ezk 34:27
the trees and the **p** of the field Ezk 36:30
Its **p** will be food for the Ezk 48:18
make gardens and eat their **p**. Am 9:14
fails and the fields **p** no food, Hab 3:17
and on all that your hands **p**." Hg 1:11
the land will yield its **p**, Zch 8:12
not ruin the **p** of your ground, Mal 3:11
Therefore **p** fruit consistent Mt 3:8
that doesn't **p** good fruit will Mt 3:10
A good tree can't **p** bad fruit; Mt 7:18
can a bad tree **p** good fruit. Mt 7:18
that doesn't **p** good fruit is cut Mt 7:19
give him his **p** at the harvest." Mt 21:41
it, and it didn't **p** a crop. Mk 4:7
word, welcome it, and **p** a crop: Mk 4:20
the wife and **p** offspring for his Mk 12:19
Therefore **p** fruit consistent Lk 3:8
that doesn't **p** good fruit will Lk 3:9
A good tree doesn't **p** bad fruit; Lk 6:43
a bad tree doesn't **p** good fruit. Lk 6:43
of life, and **p** no mature fruit. Lk 8:14
the wife and **p** offspring for his Lk 20:28
that does not **p** fruit He removes Jn 15:2
so that it will **p** more fruit. Jn 15:2
is unable to **p** fruit by itself Jn 15:4
that you **p** much fruit and prove Jn 15:8
go out and **p** fruit and that Jn 15:16
to each person to **p** what is 1Co 12:7
for this will **p** an even greater 2Tm 2:16
Can a fig tree **p** olives, my Jms 3:12
or a grapevine ⌊**p**⌋ figs? Jms 3:12

PRODUCED *(21)*
abundance the land **p** outstanding Gn 41:47
skin of one's body **p** by fire, Lv 13:24
to eat anything **p** by the Nm 6:4
buds, blossomed, and **p** almonds! Nm 17:8
firstborn male **p** by your herd Dt 15:19
The earth has **p** its harvest; Ps 67:6
a vessel will be **p** for a Pr 25:4
pen of scribes has **p** falsehood. Jr 8:8
They have grown and **p** fruit. Jr 12:2
became a vine, **p** branches, and Ezk 17:6
better his land **p**, the better Hs 10:1
the olive tree have not yet **p**. Hg 2:19
on good ground, and **p** a crop: Mt 13:8
the plants sprouted and **p** grain, Mt 13:26
on good ground and **p** a crop that Mk 4:8
when it sprang up, it **p** a crop: Lk 8:8
And what fruit was **p** then from Rm 6:21
p in me coveting of every kind. Rm 7:8
Christ's letter, **p** by us, not 2Co 3:3
as God wills—has **p** in you: 2Co 7:11
rain and the land **p** its fruit. Jms 5:18

PRODUCES *(33)*
the land ⌊**p** during⌋ the Sabbath Lv 25:6
for it **p** reverence for You. Ps 119:38
mouth of the righteous **p** wisdom, Pr 10:31
root of the righteous **p** ⌊fruit⌋. Pr 12:12
of fools **p** foolishness. Pr 14:24
a sad heart ⌊**p**⌋ a broken spirit Pr 15:13
The north wind **p** rain, and a Pr 25:23
the churning of milk **p** butter, Pr 30:33
and stirring up anger **p** strife. Pr 30:33
if it **p** thorns and briers for Is 27:4
fire and **p** a weapon suitable Is 54:16
every good tree **p** good fruit, Mt 7:17
but a bad tree **p** bad fruit. Mt 7:17
good man **p** good things from his Mt 12:35
and an evil man **p** evil things Mt 12:35
The soil **p** a crop by itself— Mk 4:28
and **p** large branches, Mk 4:32
good man **p** good out of the good Lk 6:45
An evil man **p** evil out of the Lk 6:45
if it dies, it **p** a large crop. Jn 12:24
branch that **p** fruit so that it Jn 15:2
in Me and I in him **p** much fruit, Jn 15:5
For the law **p** wrath; Rm 4:15
that affliction **p** endurance, Rm 5:3
endurance **p** proven character, Rm 5:4
and proven character **p** hope. Rm 5:4
kills, but the Spirit **p** life. 2Co 3:6
For godly grief **p** a repentance 2Co 7:10
but worldly grief **p** death. 2Co 7:10
which **p** thanksgiving to God 2Co 9:11
and that **p** vegetation useful to Heb 6:7
But if it **p** thorns and thistles, Heb 6:8
of your faith **p** endurance. Jms 1:3

PRODUCING *(8)*
salt, unsown, **p** nothing, with no Dt 29:23
to cultivate, **p** food from the Ps 104:14
of drought or cease **p** fruit. Jr 17:8
given to a nation **p** its fruit. Mt 21:43
was **p** death in me through what Rm 7:13
Even inanimate things **p** sounds— 1Co 14:7
light affliction is **p** for us an 2Co 4:17
of fruit, **p** its fruit every Rv 22:2

PRODUCT *(3)*
are to take the **p** of majestic Lv 23:40
filled with the **p** of his lips. Pr 18:20
defiled, and its **p**, its food, is Mal 1:12

PRODUCTIVE *(1)*
A rich man's land was very **p**. Lk 12:16

PRODUCTS *(8)*
some of the best **p** of the land Gn 43:11
carrying the best **p** of Egypt, Gn 45:23
with the best **p** of the ancient Dt 33:15
The **p** of Egypt and the Is 45:14
city, all its **p** and valuables. Jr 20:5
because of your numerous **p**. Ezk 27:16
your numerous **p** and your great Ezk 27:18
all kinds of fragrant wood **p**; Rv 18:12

PROFANE *(18)*
Do not **p** the name of your God; Lv 18:21
God and not **p** the name of their Lv 21:6
so they do not **p** My holy name; Lv 22:2
and die because they **p** it; Lv 22:9
priests must not **p** the holy Lv 22:15
You must not **p** My holy name; Lv 22:32
as spoil, and they will **p** them. Ezk 7:21
wicked as they **p** My treasured Ezk 7:22
men will enter it and **p** it. Ezk 7:22
You **p** Me in front of My people Ezk 13:19
p and wicked prince of Israel, Ezk 21:25
the necks of the **p** wicked ones; Ezk 21:29
holy things and **p** My Sabbaths. Ezk 22:8
to My law and **p** My holy things. Ezk 22:26
entered My sanctuary to **p** it. Ezk 23:39
Her priests **p** the sanctuary; Zph 3:4
regarded as **p** the blood of the Heb 10:29
Nothing **p** will ever enter it: Rv 21:27

PROFANED *(23)*
for he has **p** what is holy to the Lv 19:8
I **p** My possession, and I placed Is 47:6
your minds and **p** My name. Jr 34:16
their sacred places will be **p**. Ezk 7:24
it would not be **p** in the eyes Ezk 20:9
also completely **p** My Sabbaths. Ezk 20:13
it would not be **p** in the eyes Ezk 20:14
ordinances, **p** My Sabbaths, and Ezk 20:16
They also **p** My Sabbaths. Ezk 20:21
it would not be **p** in the eyes Ezk 20:22
My statutes and **p** My Sabbaths, Ezk 20:24
will be **p** in the sight of the Ezk 22:16
Sabbaths, and I am **p** among them. Ezk 22:26
that same day and **p** My Sabbaths. Ezk 23:38
You **p** your sanctuaries by the Ezk 28:18
they went, they **p** My holy name, Ezk 36:20
house of Israel **p** among the Ezk 36:21
which you **p** among the nations Ezk 36:22
which has been **p** among the Ezk 36:23
the name you have **p** among them. Ezk 36:23
will no longer allow it to be **p**. Ezk 39:7
For Judah has **p** the LORD's Mal 2:11
and has **p** this holy place. Ac 21:28

PROFANES *(1)*
Whoever **p** it must be put to Ex 31:14

PROFANING *(8)*
by My name, **p** the name of your Lv 19:12
My sanctuary and **p** My holy name. Lv 20:3
are doing—**p** the Sabbath day Neh 13:17
Israel by **p** the Sabbath!" Neh 13:18
and steal, **p** the name of my God Pr 30:9
the same girl, **p** My holy name. Am 2:7
But you are **p** it when you say: Mal 1:12
p the covenant of our fathers? Mal 2:10

PROFESS *(1)*
p to know God, but they deny Ti 1:16

PROFESSED *(1)*
of the land **p** themselves to be Est 8:17

PROFESSING *(1)*
By **p** it, some people have 1Tm 6:21

PROFESSIONAL *(1)*
to mourn, and **p** mourners to wail Am 5:16

PROFIT *(30)*
Do not **p** or take interest from Lv 25:36
or sell ⌊him⌋ your food for **p**. Lv 25:37
that can't **p** or deliver you; 1Sm 12:21
Does He **p** if you perfect your Jb 22:3
What does it **p** You, and what Jb 35:3
You make no **p** from selling them. Ps 44:12
lives of those who **p** from it. Pr 1:19
Ill-gotten gains do not **p** anyone, Pr 10:2
There is **p** in all hard work, Pr 14:23
diligent certainly lead to **p**, Pr 21:5
The **p** from the land is taken by Ec 5:9
then, is the **p** to the owner, Ec 5:11
for her **p** will go to those who Is 23:18
what they treasure does not **p**. Is 44:9
or casts a metal image for no **p**? Is 44:10
works—they will not **p** you. Is 57:12
everyone is gaining **p** unjustly. Jr 6:13
everyone is gaining **p** unjustly. Jr 8:10
themselves but have no **p**. Jr 12:13
interest or for **p** but keeps his Ezk 18:8
and lends at interest or for **p**, Ezk 18:13
interest or **p** ⌊on a loan⌋. Ezk 18:17
take interest and **p** ⌊on a loan⌋ Ezk 22:12
made a large **p** for her owners Ac 16:16
that their hope of **p** was gone, Ac 16:19
seeking my own **p**, but the profit 1Co 10:33

profit, but the **p** of many, that 1Co 10:33
trade in God's message ⌊for **p**⌋, 2Co 2:17
and do business and make a **p**." Jms 4:13
to the error of Balaam for **p**, Jd 11

PROFITABLE *(7)*
for she is more **p** than silver, Pr 3:14
Wealth is not **p** on a day of Pr 11:4
to you anything that was **p**, Ac 20:20
on this because it is **p** for you, 2Co 8:10
this is in no way **p** and leads to 2Tm 2:14
by God and is **p** for teaching, 2Tm 3:16
are good and **p** for everyone. Ti 3:8

PROFITS *(4)*
enjoy the **p** from his trading Jb 20:18
The one who **p** dishonestly Pr 15:27
She sees that her **p** are good, Pr 31:18
But her **p** and wages will be Is 23:18

PROFOUND *(2)*
LORD, how **p** Your thoughts! Ps 92:5
This mystery is **p**, but I am Eph 5:32

PROGENY *(2)*
the first **p** of the tents of Ham. Ps 78:51
their land, all their first **p**. Ps 105:36

PROGRESS *(2)*
so that your **p** may be evident to 1Tm 4:15
they will not make further **p**, 2Tm 3:9

PROGRESSED *(1)*
and through them the repairs **p**. 2Ch 24:13

PROGRESSING *(1)*
of Jerusalem was **p** and that the Neh 4:7

PROHIBIT *(1)*
and does not **p** her, all her vows Nm 30:11

PROHIBITED *(7)*
and does anything **p** by them— Lv 4:2
incur guilt by doing what is **p**, Lv 4:13
LORD his God by doing what is **p**, Lv 4:22
what is **p**, and incurs guilt, Lv 4:27
commands concerning anything **p**, Lv 5:17
because her father has **p** her. Nm 30:5
since ⌊the law⌋ **p** anyone wearing Est 4:2

PROHIBITS *(2)*
if her father **p** her on the day Nm 30:5
if her husband **p** her when he Nm 30:8

PROJECT *(5)*
used for the **p** in all the work Ex 38:24
to the treasury for the **p**. Ezr 2:69
family leaders gave to the **p**. Neh 7:70
minas to the treasury for the **p**. Neh 7:71
and four horns **p** upward from the Ezk 43:15

PROJECTED *(2)*
the Most High **p** His voice. 2Sm 22:14
the Most High **p** His voice. Ps 18:13

PROLONG *(3)*
and He will **p** your life in the Dt 30:20
Will You **p** Your anger for all Ps 85:5
His⌋ seed, He will **p** His days, Is 53:10

PROLONGED *(2)*
When there is a **p** blast of the Jos 6:5
engaging in a **p** debate among Ac 28:29

PROLONGS *(3)*
The fear of the LORD **p** life, Pr 10:27
hates unjust gain **p** his life. Pr 28:16
a hundred times and **p** his life, Ec 8:12

PROMINENCE *(1)*
excelling in **p**, excelling in Gn 49:3

PROMINENT *(8)*
250 **p** Israelite men who were Nm 16:2
was a **p** man of noble character Ru 2:1
A **p** woman who ⌊lived⌋ there 2Kg 4:8
cared for by the city's **p** men. 2Kg 10:6
and the **p** people of the Dn 11:41
a **p** member of the Sanhedrin who Mk 15:43
a number of the **p** Greek women as Ac 17:12
and **p** men of the city. Ac 25:23

PROMISCUITY *(19)*
daughter defiles herself by **p**, Lv 21:9
didn't give up her **p** that began Ezk 23:8
increased her **p** when she saw Ezk 23:14
flaunted her **p** and exposed her Ezk 23:18
she multiplied her acts of **p**, Ezk 23:19
both your indecency and **p**. Ezk 23:29
of your indecency and **p**." Ezk 23:35
wife and ⌊have⌋ children of **p**, Hs 1:2
they are the children of **p**. Hs 2:4
P, wine, and new wine take away Hs 4:11
For a spirit of **p** leads them Hs 4:12
is over, they turn to **p**. Hs 4:18
for a spirit of **p** is among them, Hs 5:4
Ephraim's **p** is there; Hs 6:10
not in sexual impurity and **p**; Rm 13:13
and **p** they practiced. 2Co 12:21
immorality, moral impurity, **p**, Gl 5:19
over to **p** for the practice Eph 4:19
our God into **p** and denying our Jd 4

PROMISCUOUS *(10)*
by being **p** in her father's Dt 22:21
crushed by their **p** hearts that Ezk 6:9
You engaged in **p** acts with Ezk 16:26
and made her **p** acts worse than Ezk 23:11
Go and marry a **p** wife and ⌊have⌋ Hs 1:2
land has been **p** by abandoning Hs 1:2
her remove the **p** look from her Hs 2:2
For their mother is **p**; Hs 2:5
Don't be **p** or belong to any man, Hs 3:3
they will be **p** but not multiply; Hs 4:10

PROMISCUOUSLY *(7)*
behaving **p** in their youth. Ezk 23:3
they act **p** in disobedience to Hs 4:12
so your daughters act **p** and your Hs 4:13
daughters when they act **p** or Hs 4:14
if you act **p**, don't let Judah Hs 4:15
now, Ephraim, you have acted **p**; Hs 5:3
you have acted **p**, leaving your Hs 9:1

PROMISE *(72)*
thigh ⌊and **p** me⌋ that you will Gn 47:29
not act, or **p** and not fulfill Nm 23:19
to keep the **p** He swore to your Dt 9:5
not one **p** has failed. Jos 23:14
fulfill the **p** forever that You 2Sm 7:25
carry out His **p** that He made to 1Kg 2:4
I will fulfill My **p** to you, 1Kg 6:12
fulfilled ⌊the **p**⌋ by His power. 1Kg 8:15
fulfilled ⌊Your **p**⌋ by Your power 1Kg 8:24
the **p** He ordained for a thousand 1Ch 16:15
Your **p** to my father David now 2Ch 1:9
fulfilled ⌊the **p**⌋ by His power. 2Ch 6:4
⌊Your **p**⌋ by Your power, 2Ch 6:15
who doesn't keep this **p**. Neh 5:13
have kept Your **p**, for You are Neh 9:8
Is ⌊His⌋ **p** at an end for all Ps 77:8
the **p** He ordained for a thousand Ps 105:8
His holy **p** to Abraham His Ps 105:42
land and did not believe His **p**. Ps 106:24
Your **p** has given me life. Ps 119:50
to me according to Your **p**. Ps 119:58
and for Your righteous **p**. Ps 119:123
my steps steady through Your **p**; Ps 119:133
the night to meditate on Your **p**. Ps 119:148
rejoice over Your **p** like one who Ps 119:162
rescue me according to Your **p**. Ps 119:170
My tongue sings about Your **p**, Ps 119:172
oath to David, a **p** He will not Ps 132:11
name and Your **p** above everything Ps 138:2
will confirm My **p** concerning you Jr 29:10
⌊This is⌋ the **p** I made to you Hg 2:5
"**P**," she said to Him, "that Mt 20:21
but to wait for the Father's **p**. Ac 1:4
the **p** is for you and for your Ac 2:39
to fulfill the **p** that God had Ac 7:17
according to the **p**, God brought Ac 13:23
news of the **p** that was made to Ac 13:32
the hope of the **p** made by God to Ac 26:6
⌊the **p**⌋ our 12 tribes hope to Ac 26:7
For the **p** to Abraham or to his Rm 4:13
empty and the **p** is canceled. Rm 4:14
This is why the **p** is by faith, Rm 4:16
waver in unbelief at God's **p**, Rm 4:20
children of the **p** are considered Rm 9:8
this is the statement of the **p**: Rm 9:9
receive the **p** of the Spirit Gl 3:14
by God, so as to cancel the **p**. Gl 3:17
it is no longer from the **p**; Gl 3:18
it to Abraham through the **p**. Gl 3:18
to whom the **p** was made would Gl 3:19
so that the **p** by faith in Jesus Gl 3:22
seed, heirs according to the **p**. Gl 3:29
was born as the result of a **p**. Gl 4:23
like Isaac, are children of **p**. Gl 4:28
to the covenants of the **p**, Eph 2:12
partners of the **p** in Christ Eph 3:6
the first commandment with a **p**— Eph 6:2
since it holds **p** for the present 1Tm 4:8
for the **p** of life in Christ 2Tm 1:1
while the **p** remains of entering Heb 4:1
when God made a **p** to Abraham, Heb 6:13
Abraham obtained the **p**. Heb 6:15
clearly to the heirs of the **p**, Heb 6:17
are weak, but the **p** of the oath, Heb 7:28
receive the **p** of the eternal Heb 9:15
as a foreigner in the land of **p**, Heb 11:9
Jacob, co-heirs of the same **p**. Heb 11:9
They **p** them freedom, but they 2Pt 2:19
Where is the **p** of His coming? 2Pt 3:4
The Lord does not delay His **p**, 2Pt 3:9
based on His **p**, we wait for new 2Pt 3:13
this is the **p** that He Himself 1Jn 2:25

PROMISED *(111)*
to Abraham what He **p** him." Gn 18:19
did for Sarah what He had **p**. Gn 21:1
I have done what I have **p** you." Gn 28:15
land to the land He **p** Abraham, Gn 50:24
And I have **p** you that I will Ex 3:17
the LORD will give you as He **p**, Ex 12:25
who was not **p** in marriage, Ex 22:16
all this land that I have **p**, Ex 32:13
to the land I **p** to Abraham, Ex 33:1
And I **p** you: You will inherit Lv 20:24
out for the place the LORD **p**: Nm 10:29
for the LORD has **p** good things Nm 10:29
not what I have **p** will happen to Nm 11:23
enter the land I **p** to settle you Nm 14:30
go to the place the LORD **p**, Nm 14:40
he must do whatever he has **p**. Nm 30:2
flocks, but do what you have **p**." Nm 32:24
and bless you as He **p** you. Dt 1:11
has **p** you a land flowing with Dt 6:3
into the land He had **p** them, Dt 9:28
you set foot, as He has **p** you. Dt 11:25
your territory as He has **p** you, Dt 12:20
wonder he has **p** you comes about Dt 13:2
God blesses you as He has **p** you, Dt 15:6
is his inheritance, as He **p** him. Dt 18:2
all the land He **p** to give them— Dt 19:8
vowed what you **p** to the LORD Dt 23:23
His special people as He **p** you, Dt 26:18
to the LORD your God as He **p**." Dt 26:19
God of your fathers, has **p** you. Dt 27:3
your God as He **p** you and as He Dt 29:13
This is the land I **p** Abraham, Dt 34:4
foot treads, just as I **p** Moses. Jos 1:3
with her, just as you **p** her." Jos 6:22
as the leaders had **p** them. Jos 9:21
inheritance, just as He had **p**: Jos 13:14
just as He had **p** them. Jos 13:33
what the LORD **p** Moses the man Jos 14:6
that day Moses **p** me, 'The land Jos 14:9
alive ⌊these⌋ 45 years as He **p**, Jos 14:10
the LORD **p** ⌊me⌋ on that day Jos 14:12
drive them out as the LORD **p**." Jos 14:12
just as He **p** them, return to Jos 22:4
as the LORD your God **p** you. Jos 23:5
was fighting for you, as He **p**. Jos 23:10
LORD your God **p** you has come Jos 23:15
to Caleb, just as Moses had **p**. Jdg 1:20
land I had **p** to your fathers. Jdg 2:1
just as He had **p** and sworn to Jdg 2:15
all the good He **p** and appoints 1Sm 25:30
and his house. Do as You have **p**, 2Sm 7:25
You have **p** this grace to Your 2Sm 7:28
and made me a dynasty as He **p**— 1Kg 2:24
what the LORD **p** my father David 1Kg 5:5
Solomon wisdom, as He had **p** 1Kg 5:12
LORD has fulfilled what He **p**. 1Kg 8:20
throne of Israel, as the LORD **p**. 1Kg 8:20
kept what You **p** to Your servant, 1Kg 8:24
keep what You **p** to Your servant, 1Kg 8:25
what You **p** to Your servant 1Kg 8:26
forever, as I **p** your father 1Kg 9:5
year, as Elisha had **p** her. 2Kg 4:17
as the LORD had **p**, they ate and 2Kg 4:44
since He had **p** to give a lamp to 2Kg 8:19
has done what He **p** through His 2Kg 10:10
that He will do what He has **p**: 2Kg 20:9
forever, and do as You have **p**. 1Ch 17:23
and You have **p** this good thing 1Ch 17:26
and wine to his servants as **p**. 2Ch 2:15
LORD has fulfilled what He **p**. 2Ch 6:10
throne of Israel, as the LORD **p**. 2Ch 6:10
kept what You **p** to Your servant, 2Ch 6:15
keep what You **p** to Your servant, 2Ch 6:16

what You **p** to Your servant 2Ch 6:17
throne, as I **p** your father David 2Ch 7:18
the LORD had **p** to give a lamp to 2Ch 21:7
just as the LORD **p** concerning 2Ch 23:3
the people did as they had **p**. Neh 5:13
money Haman had **p** to pay the Est 4:7
my lips **p** and my mouth spoke Ps 66:14
LORD, Your salvation, as You **p**. Ps 119:41
I have **p** to keep Your words. Ps 119:57
servant well, just as You **p**. Ps 119:65
me, as You **p** Your servant. Ps 119:76
looking⌋ for what You have **p**; Ps 119:82
me as You **p**, and I will live Ps 119:116
give me life, as You **p**. Ps 119:154
when they hear what You have **p**. Ps 138:4
the LORD will do what He has **p**: Is 38:7
The **p** curse written in the law Dn 9:11
as the LORD **p**, among the Jl 2:32
the LORD of Hosts has **p** ⌊this⌋. Mc 4:4
So he **p** with an oath to give her Mt 14:7
were glad and **p** to give him Mk 14:11
am sending you what My Father **p**. Lk 24:49
the Father the **p** Holy Spirit, Ac 2:33
but He **p** to give it to him as a Ac 7:5
which He **p** long ago through His Rm 1:2
what He had **p** He was also able Rm 4:21
advance the generous gift you **p**, 2Co 9:5
because I have **p** you in marriage 2Co 11:2
sealed with the **p** Holy Spirit. Eph 1:13
goal the prize **p** by God's Php 3:14
who cannot lie, **p** before time Ti 1:2
for He who **p** is faithful. Heb 10:23
you may receive what was **p**. Heb 10:36
the One who had **p** was faithful. Heb 11:11
they did not receive what was **p**, Heb 11:39
but now He has **p**, Yet once more Heb 12:26
life that He has **p** to those who Jms 1:12
that He has **p** to those who love Jms 2:5

PROMISES *(22)*
None of the good **p** the LORD had Jos 21:45
none of the good **p** the LORD your Jos 23:14
all the good **p** He made through 1Kg 8:56
these great ⌊**p**⌋ because of Your 1Ch 17:19
given⌋ by the **p** of God to exalt 1Ch 25:5
they believed His **p** and sang His Ps 106:12
of these ⌊**p**⌋ people live, Is 38:16
you, the **p** assured to David. Is 55:3
fulfill the good **p** that I have Jr 33:14
the temple service, and the **p**. Rm 9:4
to confirm the **p** to the fathers, Rm 15:8
one of God's **p** is "Yes" in Him. 2Co 1:20
we have such **p**, we should wash 2Co 7:1
Now the **p** were spoken to Abraham Gl 3:16
therefore contrary to God's **p**? Gl 3:21
who inherit the **p** through faith Heb 6:12
blessed the one who had the **p**. Heb 7:6
legally enacted on better **p**. Heb 8:6
without having received the **p**, Heb 11:13
received the **p** was offering up Heb 11:17
obtained **p**, shut the mouths Heb 11:33
us very great and precious **p**, 2Pt 1:4

PROMISING *(2)*
deceive you by **p** that Jerusalem 2Kg 19:10
them all the good I am **p** them. Jr 32:42

PROMOTE *(3)*
but those who **p** peace have joy. Pr 12:20
p empty speculations rather 1Tm 1:4
in order to **p** love and good Heb 10:24

PROMOTED *(4)*
He **p** him in rank and gave him a Est 3:1
how the king had **p** him in rank Est 5:11
to which the king had **p** him, Est 10:2
Then the king **p** Daniel and gave Dn 2:48

PROMOTER *(1)*
is Christ then a **p** of sin? Gl 2:17

PROMOTES *(5)*
quick-tempered one **p** foolishness. Pr 14:29
conceals an offense **p** love, Pr 17:9
pursue what **p** peace and what Rm 14:19
p the growth of the body for Eph 4:16
the teaching that **p** godliness, 1Tm 6:3

PROMOTING *(2)*
and are **p** customs that are not Ac 16:21
wisdom by **p** ascetic practices, Col 2:23

PROMPTED *(3)*
and whose spirit **p** him came and Ex 35:21
whose hearts **p** them to bring Ex 35:29
And **p** by her mother, she Mt 14:8

PROMPTLY *(1)*
asks of you must be provided **p**, Ezr 7:21

PRONE *(1)*
I know what they are **p** to do, Dt 31:21

PRONOUNCE *(26)*
him, he must **p** him unclean. Lv 13:3
the priest is to **p** him clean; Lv 13:6
the priest must **p** him unclean; Lv 13:8
the priest must **p** him unclean. Lv 13:11
he is to **p** the infected person Lv 13:13
flesh, he must **p** him unclean. Lv 13:15
the priest must **p** the infected Lv 13:17
the priest must **p** him unclean; Lv 13:20
the priest must **p** him unclean; Lv 13:22
The priest is to **p** him clean. Lv 13:23
The priest must **p** him unclean; Lv 13:25
the priest must **p** him unclean; Lv 13:27
The priest is to **p** him clean, Lv 13:28
the priest must **p** the person Lv 13:30
priest is to **p** the person clean Lv 13:34
priest is to **p** the person clean Lv 13:37
The priest must **p** him unclean; Lv 13:44
order to **p** it clean or unclean. Lv 13:59
He is to **p** him clean and release Lv 14:7
he is to **p** the house clean Lv 14:48
to serve Him and **p** blessings Dt 21:5
he could not **p** it correctly, Jdg 12:6
and to **p** blessings in His name 1Ch 23:13
I will **p** My judgments against Jr 1:16
Now I will also **p** judgments Jr 4:12
attempted to **p** the name of the Ac 19:13

PRONOUNCED *(13)*
the LORD has **p** ⌊judgment⌋ on me Ru 1:21
matter, he has **p** his own guilt. 2Sm 14:13
the LORD has **p** disaster against 1Kg 22:23
and the judgments He has **p**, 1Ch 16:12
the LORD has **p** disaster against 2Ch 18:22
decree has been **p** by me. Ezr 4:21
I immediately **p** a curse on his Jb 5:3
From heaven You **p** judgment. Ps 76:8
and the judgments He has **p**, Ps 105:5
disaster He had **p** against them? Jr 26:19
disaster I have **p** against them Jr 35:17
that the LORD has **p** against this Jr 36:7
condemnation, ⌊**p**⌋ long ago, is 2Pt 2:3

PROOF *(5)*
He has provided **p** of this to Ac 17:31
show them the **p** of your love and 2Co 8:24
Through the **p** of this service, 2Co 9:13
since you seek **p** of Christ 2Co 13:3
the **p** of what is not seen. Heb 11:1

PROOFS *(1)*
to them by many convincing **p**, Ac 1:3

PROPER *(18)*
you have said is **p**, but only the Gn 44:10
of Him about the **p** procedures." 1Ch 15:13
of Purim at their **p** time just as Est 9:31
does not even have a **p** burial, Ec 6:3
princes feast at the **p** time— Ec 10:17
will stand on its **p** site. Jr 30:18
to give them food at the **p** time? Mt 24:45
be fulfilled in their **p** time." Lk 1:20
allotted food at the **p** time? Lk 12:42
of what is **p**, and so that you 1Co 7:35
Is it **p** for a woman to pray to 1Co 11:13
reap at the **p** time if we don't Gl 6:9
in love by the **p** working of each Eph 4:16
among you, as is **p** for saints. Eph 5:3
a testimony at the **p** time. 1Tm 2:6
is **p** for women who affirm that 1Tm 2:10
grace to help us at the **p** time. Heb 4:16
but deserted their **p** dwelling. Jd 6

PROPERLY *(2)*
If we were **p** evaluating 1Co 11:31
you may walk **p** in the presence 1Th 4:12

PROPERTY *(50)*
about, and acquire **p** in it." Gn 34:10
and all the **p** he had acquired in Gn 36:6
and gave them **p** in the best part Gn 47:11
They acquired **p** in it and became Gn 47:27
because he is his ⌊owner's⌋ **p**. Ex 21:21
he has taken his neighbor's **p**. Ex 22:8
he has taken his neighbor's **p**. Ex 22:11
return to his **p** and each of you Lv 25:10
of you will return to his **p**. Lv 25:13
and sells part of his **p**, Lv 25:25
sold it to, and return to his **p**. Lv 25:27
so that he may return to his **p**. Lv 25:28
Whatever ⌊**p**⌋ one of the Levites Lv 25:33
to his clan and his ancestral **p**. Lv 25:41
These may become your **p**. Lv 25:45
sons after you to inherit as **p**; Lv 25:46
it becomes the priest's **p**. Lv 27:21
give us **p** among our father's Nm 27:4
them hereditary **p** among their Nm 27:7
all their cattle, flocks, and **p**. Nm 31:9
hereditary **p** for the Levites Nm 35:2
on the same **p** and one of them Dt 25:5
the man's name on his **p**." Ru 4:5
redemption or the exchange of **p**. Ru 4:7
"Buy back ⌊the **p**⌋ yourself." Ru 4:8
deceased man's name on his **p**, Ru 4:10
towns on their own **p** again were 1Ch 9:2
in charge of King David's **p**. 1Ch 27:31
charge of all the **p** and cattle 1Ch 28:1
confiscation of **p**, or Ezr 7:26
from his house and **p** everyone Neh 5:13
on his own **p** in their towns Neh 11:3
each on his own inherited **p**. Neh 11:20
kinds of valuable **p** and fill our Pr 1:13
move an ancient **p** line that your Pr 22:28
Don't move an ancient **p** line, Pr 23:10
As the **p** of the city, you must Ezk 45:6
of land⌋ and the city's **p**, Ezk 45:7
holy donation and the city's **p**, Ezk 45:7
become their **p** by inheritance. Ezk 46:16
evicting them from their **p**. Ezk 46:18
for his sons from his own **p**, Ezk 46:18
be displaced from his own **p**." Ezk 46:18
the city **p** as a square ⌊area⌋ Ezk 48:20
and the city **p** will belong to Ezk 48:21
for the Levitical **p** and the city Ezk 48:22
and the city **p** in the middle Ezk 48:22
Sychar near the **p** that Jacob had Jn 4:5
and **p** and distributed Ac 2:45
his wife, sold a piece of **p**. Ac 5:1

PROPHECIES *(6)*
P Against the Nations Jr 45:5
P Against the Nations Ezk 24:27
living and give ⌊your⌋ **p** there, Am 7:12
But as for **p**, they will come to 1Co 13:8
Don't despise **p**, 1Th 5:20
with the **p** previously made 1Tm 1:18

PROPHECY *(17)*
the LORD's **p** He had spoken at 1Kg 2:27
the **P** of Ahijah the Shilonite, 2Ch 9:29
words and the **p** of ⌊Azariah son 2Ch 15:8
of the **p** he spoke against Neh 6:12
up vision and **p**, and to anoint Dn 9:24
Isaiah's **p** is fulfilled in them, Mt 13:14
If **p**, use it according to the Rm 12:6
to another, **p**, to another, 1Co 12:10
If I have ⌊the gift of⌋ **p**, 1Co 13:2
or knowledge or **p** or teaching? 1Co 14:6
But **p** is not for unbelievers but 1Co 14:22
it was given to you through **p**, 1Tm 4:14
no **p** of Scripture comes from 2Pt 1:20
because no **p** ever came by the 2Pt 1:21
words of this **p** and keep what is Rv 1:3
rain during the days of their **p**. Rv 11:6
about Jesus is the spirit of **p**." Rv 19:10

PROPHESIED *(33)*
on them, they **p**, but they never Nm 11:25
tent—and they **p** in the camp. Nm 11:26
him, and he **p** along with them. 1Sm 10:10
he **p** until he entered Naioth in 1Sm 19:23
and also **p** before Samuel; 1Sm 19:24
who **p** under the authority of the 1Ch 25:2
of Mareshah **p** against 2Ch 20:37
son of Iddo **p** to the Jews who Ezr 5:1
The prophets **p** by Baal and Jr 2:8
that you **p** falsely to.' " Jr 20:6
They **p** by Baal and led My people Jr 23:13
not speak to them, yet they **p**. Jr 23:21
book that Jeremiah **p** against all Jr 25:13
because he has **p** against this Jr 26:11
Micah the Moreshite **p** in the Jr 26:18
He **p** against this city and Jr 26:20
words you have **p** come true and Jr 28:6
and me from ancient times **p** war, Jr 28:8
Because Shemaiah **p** to you, Jr 29:31
are your prophets who **p** to you, Jr 37:19

rael who **p** to Jerusalem and Ezk 13:16
I **p** as I had been commanded. Ezk 37:7
o I **p** as He commanded me; Ezk 37:10
who for years **p** in those times Ezk 38:17
and the law **p** until John; Mt 11:13
Isaiah **p** correctly about you Mt 15:7
Isaiah **p** correctly about you Mk 7:6
with the Holy Spirit and **p**: Lk 1:67
that year he **p** that Jesus was Jn 11:51
had four virgin daughters who **p**. Ac 21:9
but even more that you **p**. 1Co 14:5
prophets who **p** about the grace 1Pt 1:10
from Adam, **p** about them: Jd 14

PROPHESIES *(14)*

he never **p** good about me, 1Kg 22:8
you he never **p** good about me, 1Kg 22:18
he never **p** good about me, 2Ch 18:7
you he never **p** good about me, 2Ch 18:17
As for the prophet who **p** peace— Jr 28:9
he **p** about distant times. Ezk 12:27
If a man still **p**, his father and Zch 13:3
When he **p**, his father and his Zch 13:3
ashamed of his vision when he **p**; Zch 13:4
who prays or **p** with something 1Co 11:4
who prays or **p** with her head 1Co 11:5
person who **p** speaks to people 1Co 14:3
but he who **p** builds up the 1Co 14:4
The person who **p** is greater than 1Co 14:5

PROPHESY *(65)*

you, you will **p** with them, and 1Sm 10:6
and saw him **p** with the prophets 1Sm 10:11
who were to **p** accompanied by 1Ch 25:1
Do not **p** the truth to us. Is 30:10
flattering things. **P** illusions. Is 30:10
The prophets **p** falsely, and the Jr 5:31
You must not **p** in the name of Jr 11:21
the prophets who **p** in My name, Jr 14:15
the LORD had sent him to **p**, Jr 19:14
of the prophets who **p** to you. Jr 23:16
prophets who **p** a lie in My name Jr 23:25
those who **p** false dreams"— Jr 23:32
you are to **p** all these things to Jr 25:30
dare you **p** in the name of the Jr 26:9
LORD sent me to **p** all the words Jr 26:12
for they **p** a lie to you so that Jr 27:10
arm bared, and **p** against it. Ezk 4:7
of Israel and **p** against them. Ezk 6:2
Therefore, **p** against them. Ezk 11:4
against them. **P**, son of man!" Ezk 11:4
p against the prophets of Israel Ezk 13:2
to those who **p** out of their own Ezk 13:2
your people who **p** out of their Ezk 13:17
own imagination. **P** against them Ezk 13:17
P against the forest land in the Ezk 20:46
P against the land of Israel, Ezk 21:2
Son of man, **p**: This is what the Ezk 21:9
p and clap ⌊your⌋ hands together. Ezk 21:14
Now **p**, son of man, and say: Ezk 21:28
Ammonites and **p** against them. Ezk 25:2
toward Sidon and **p** against it. Ezk 28:21
king of Egypt and **p** against him Ezk 29:2
Son of man, **p** and say: Ezk 30:2
p against the shepherds of Ezk 34:2
P, and say to them: Ezk 34:2
Mount Seir and **p** against it. Ezk 35:2
p to the mountains of Israel and Ezk 36:1
therefore, **p** and say: Ezk 36:3
p concerning the land of Israel Ezk 36:6
P concerning these bones and say Ezk 37:4
He said to me, "**P** to the breath, Ezk 37:9
to the breath, **p**, son of man. Ezk 37:9
Therefore, **p** and say to them: Ezk 37:12
Meshech and Tubal. **P** against him Ezk 38:2
Therefore **p**, son of man, and say Ezk 38:14
you, son of man, **p** against Gog Ezk 39:1
sons and your daughters will **p**, Jl 2:28
the prophets: Do not **p**. Am 2:12
GOD has spoken; who will not **p**? Am 3:8
don't ever **p** at Bethel again, Am 7:13
p to My people Israel.' " Am 7:15
Do not **p** against Israel; Am 7:16
Lord, didn't we **p** in Your name, Mt 7:22
and said, "**P** to us, Messiah! Mt 26:68
and to beat Him, saying, "**P**!" Mk 14:65
Him, they kept asking, "**P**! Lk 22:64
sons and your daughters will **p**, Ac 2:17
in those days, and they will **p**. Ac 2:18
with ⌊other⌋ languages and to **p**. Ac 19:6
know in part, and we **p** in part. 1Co 13:9
and above all that you may **p**. 1Co 14:1
For you can all **p** one by one, 1Co 14:31
be eager to **p**, and do not forbid 1Co 14:39
You must **p** again about many Rv 10:11
and they will **p** for 1,260 days, Rv 11:3

PROPHESYING *(31)*

and Medad are **p** in the camp." Nm 11:27
down from the high place **p**. 1Sm 10:5
Then Saul finished **p** and went to 1Sm 10:13
group of prophets **p** with Samuel 1Sm 19:20
agents, and they also started **p**. 1Sm 19:20
agents, and they also began **p**. 1Sm 19:21
agents, and even they began **p**. 1Sm 19:21
prophets were **p** in front of them 1Kg 22:10
the prophets were **p** the same: 1Kg 22:12
p to the accompaniment of lyres, 1Ch 25:3
prophets were **p** in front of them 2Ch 18:9
the prophets were **p** the same, 2Ch 18:11
building under the **p** of Haggai Ezr 6:14
prophets are **p** a lie in My name Jr 14:14
are **p** to you a false vision, Jr 14:14
people they are **p** to will be Jr 14:16
heard Jeremiah **p** these things. Jr 20:1
minds of the prophets **p** lies, Jr 23:26
man was also **p** in the name Jr 26:20
for they are **p** a lie to you. Jr 27:14
'and they are **p** falsely in My Jr 27:15
prophets who are **p** to you.' " Jr 27:15
They are **p** to you, claiming: Jr 27:16
They are **p** a lie to you. Jr 27:16
for they are **p** falsely to you in Jr 29:9
the ones **p** a lie to you in My Jr 29:21
Why are you **p**, 'This is what the Jr 32:3
Now while I was **p**, Pelatiah son Ezk 11:13
prophets of Israel who are **p**. Ezk 13:2
I was **p**, there was a noise, Ezk 37:7
But if all are **p**, and some 1Co 14:24

PROPHET *(245)*

for he is a **p**, and he will pray Gn 20:7
your brother will be your **p**. Ex 7:1
If there is a **p** among you from Nm 12:6
If a **p** or someone who has dreams Dt 13:1
That **p** or dreamer must be put to Dt 13:5
up for you a **p** like me from Dt 18:15
up for them a **p** like you from Dt 18:18
But the **p** who dares to speak in Dt 18:20
other gods—that **p** must die.' Dt 18:20
When a **p** speaks in the LORD's Dt 18:22
The **p** has spoken it Dt 18:22
No **p** has arisen again in Israel Dt 34:10
a woman who was a **p** and the wife Jdg 4:4
the LORD sent a **p** to them. Jdg 6:8
was a confirmed **p** of the LORD. 1Sm 3:20
for the **p** of today was formerly 1Sm 9:9
Then the **p** Gad said to David, 1Sm 22:5
the king said to Nathan the **p**, 2Sm 7:2
a message⌋ through Nathan the **p**, 2Sm 12:25
the LORD had come to the **p** Gad, 2Sm 24:11
Nathan the **p**, Shimei, Rei, 1Kg 1:8
he did not invite Nathan the **p**, 1Kg 1:10
the king, Nathan the **p** arrived, 1Kg 1:22
king, "Nathan the **p** is here." 1Kg 1:23
Nathan the **p**, and Benaiah son 1Kg 1:32
and Nathan the **p** are to anoint 1Kg 1:34
priest, Nathan the **p**, Benaiah 1Kg 1:38
priest, Nathan the **p**, Benaiah 1Kg 1:44
and Nathan the **p** have anointed 1Kg 1:45
the **p** Ahijah the Shilonite met 1Kg 11:29
Now a certain old **p** was living 1Kg 13:11
to him, "I am also a **p** like you. 1Kg 13:18
The old **p** deceived him, 1Kg 13:18
came to the **p** who had brought 1Kg 13:20
and the **p** cried out to the man 1Kg 13:21
the old **p** saddled the donkey for 1Kg 13:23
donkey for the **p** he had brought 1Kg 13:23
the city where the old **p** lived. 1Kg 13:25
When the **p** who had brought him 1Kg 13:26
Then the old **p** instructed his 1Kg 13:27
the **p** lifted the corpse of the 1Kg 13:29
The old **p** came into to the city 1Kg 13:29
Ahijah the **p** is there; 1Kg 14:2
His servant Ahijah the **p**. 1Kg 14:18
Through the **p** Jehu son of Hanani 1Kg 16:7
Baasha through Jehu the **p**, 1Kg 16:12
only remaining **p** of the LORD, 1Kg 18:22
Elijah the **p** approached ⌊the 1Kg 18:36
Abel-meholah as **p** in your place. 1Kg 19:16
A **p** came to Ahab king of Israel 1Kg 20:13
And the **p** said, "This is what 1Kg 20:14
The **p** approached the king of 1Kg 20:22
said to his fellow **p** by the word 1Kg 20:35
The **p** found another man and said 1Kg 20:37
Then the **p** went and waited for 1Kg 20:38
The **p** said to him, "This is what 1Kg 20:42
Isn't there a **p** of Yahweh here 1Kg 22:7
Isn't there a **p** of the LORD 2Kg 3:11
would go to the **p** who is in 2Kg 5:3
know there is a **p** in Israel." 2Kg 5:8
if the **p** had told you to do some 2Kg 5:13
Elisha, the **p** in Israel, tells 2Kg 6:12
The **p** Elisha called one of the 2Kg 9:1
So the young **p** went to 2Kg 9:4
young **p** poured the oil on his 2Kg 9:6
Then the young **p** opened the door 2Kg 9:10
the **p** Jonah son of Amittai from 2Kg 14:25
through every **p** and every seer, 2Kg 17:13
to the **p** Isaiah son of Amoz. 2Kg 19:2
p Isaiah son of Amoz came and 2Kg 20:1
Isaiah the **p** called out to the 2Kg 20:11
Then the **p** Isaiah came to King 2Kg 20:14
the bones of the **p** who came from 2Kg 23:18
he said to Nathan the **p**, "Look! 1Ch 17:1
the Events of Nathan the **P**, 1Ch 29:29
in the Events of Nathan the **P**, 2Ch 9:29
Shemaiah the **p** went to Rehoboam 2Ch 12:5
Shemaiah the **P** and of Iddo the 2Ch 12:15
in the Writing of the **P** Iddo. 2Ch 13:22
of ⌊Azariah son of⌋ Oded the **p**, 2Ch 15:8
Isn't there a **p** of Yahweh here 2Ch 18:6
to Jehoram from Elijah the **p**, 2Ch 21:12
He sent a **p** to him, who said, 2Ch 25:15
So the **p** stopped, but he said, 2Ch 25:16
Now the **p** Isaiah son of Amoz 2Ch 26:22
A **p** of the LORD named Oded was 2Ch 28:9
king's seer, and Nathan the **p**. 2Ch 29:25
Hezekiah and the **p** Isaiah son of 2Ch 32:20
Visions of the **P** Isaiah son of 2Ch 32:32
since the days of Samuel the **p**. 2Ch 35:18
Jeremiah the **p** at the LORD's 2Ch 36:12
Haggai the **p** and Zechariah son Ezr 6:14
There is no longer a **p**. Ps 74:9
the judge and **p**, the Is 3:2
the tail is the **p**, the lying Is 9:15
priest and **p** stagger because of Is 28:7
to the **p** Isaiah son of Amoz. Is 37:2
p Isaiah son of Amoz came and Is 38:1
Then Isaiah the **p** came to King Is 39:3
you a **p** to the nations. Jr 1:5
From **p** to priest, everyone deals Jr 6:13
From **p** to priest, everyone deals Jr 8:10
For both **p** and priest travel to Jr 14:18
wise, or an oracle from the **p**. Jr 18:18
Jeremiah the **p** beaten and put Jr 20:2
because both **p** and priest are Jr 23:11
The **p** who has ⌊only⌋ a dream Jr 23:28
people or a **p** or a priest asks Jr 23:33
As for the **p**, priest, or people Jr 23:34
You must say to the **p**: Jr 23:37
The **p** Jeremiah spoke concerning Jr 25:2
the **p** Hananiah son of Azzur from Jr 28:1
The **p** Jeremiah replied to the Jr 28:5
replied to the **p** Hananiah Jr 28:5
The **p** Jeremiah said, "Amen! Jr 28:6
for the **p** who prophesies peace Jr 28:9
word of the **p** comes true will Jr 28:9
true will the **p** be recognized as Jr 28:9
p Hananiah then took the yoke Jr 28:10
of Jeremiah the **p** and broke it. Jr 28:10
Jeremiah the **p** then went on his Jr 28:11
after Hananiah the **p** had broken Jr 28:12
from the neck of Jeremiah the **p**: Jr 28:12
The **p** Jeremiah said to the Jr 28:15
Jeremiah said to the **p** Hananiah, Jr 28:15
the **p** Hananiah died that year Jr 28:17
that Jeremiah the **p** sent from Jr 29:1
every madman who acts like a **p**. Jr 29:26
been acting like a **p** among you? Jr 29:27
the hearing of Jeremiah the **p**. Jr 29:29
Jeremiah the **p** was imprisoned Jr 32:2
So Jeremiah the **p** related all Jr 34:6
the **p** had commanded him. Jr 36:8
the scribe and Jeremiah the **p**, Jr 36:26
He spoke through Jeremiah the **p**. Jr 37:2
to Jeremiah the **p**, requesting, Jr 37:3
the LORD came to Jeremiah the **p**: Jr 37:6

he apprehended Jeremiah the **p**, Jr 37:13
have done to Jeremiah the **p**. Jr 38:9
pull Jeremiah the **p** up from the Jr 38:10
Jeremiah the **p** and received him Jr 38:14
Jeremiah the **p** and said, "May Jr 42:2
So Jeremiah the **p** said to them, Jr 42:4
Jeremiah the **p** and Baruch son Jr 43:6
Jeremiah the **p** spoke to Baruch Jr 45:1
to Jeremiah the **p** about the Jr 46:1
to Jeremiah the **p** about the Jr 46:13
came to Jeremiah the **p** about the Jr 47:1
to Jeremiah the **p** about Elam at Jr 49:34
through Jeremiah the **p**: Jr 50:1
Jeremiah the **p** commanded Seraiah Jr 51:59
know that a **p** has been among Ezk 2:5
will seek a vision from a **p**, Ezk 7:26
comes to the **p**, I, the LORD, Ezk 14:4
comes to the **p** to inquire of Me Ezk 14:7
But if the **p** is deceived and Ezk 14:9
the LORD, who deceived that **p**. Ezk 14:9
be the same as that of the **p**— Ezk 14:10
know that a **p** has been among Ezk 33:33
Jeremiah the **p** that the number Dn 9:2
the **p** will also stumble with you Hs 4:5
p is a fool, and the inspired Hs 9:7
The **p** ⌊encounters⌋ a fowler's Hs 9:8
Israel from Egypt by a **p**, Hs 12:13
and Israel was tended by a **p**. Hs 12:13
I was not a **p** or the son of a Am 7:14
not a prophet or the son of a **p**; Am 7:14
oracle that Habakkuk the **p** saw. Hab 1:1
A prayer of Habakkuk the **p**. Hab 3:1
Haggai the **p** to Zerubbabel son Hg 1:1
LORD came through Haggai the **p**: Hg 1:3
and the words of the **p** Haggai, Hg 1:12
LORD came through Haggai the **p**: Hg 2:1
the LORD came to Haggai the **p**: Hg 2:10
LORD came to the **p** Zechariah son Zch 1:1
LORD came to the **p** Zechariah son Zch 1:7
that day every **p** will be ashamed Zch 13:4
say: I am not a **p**; I am a tiller Zch 13:5
Elijah the **p** before the great Mal 4:5
by the Lord through the **p**: Mt 1:22
is what was written by the **p**: Mt 2:5
Lord through the **p** might be Mt 2:15
Jeremiah the **p** was fulfilled: Mt 2:17
spoken of through the **p** Isaiah, Mt 3:3
was spoken through the **p** Isaiah: Mt 4:14
through the **p** Isaiah might be Mt 8:17
who welcomes a **p** because he is Mt 10:41
because he is a **p** will receive Mt 10:41
out to see? A **p**? Yes, I tell you Mt 11:9
tell you, and far more than a **p**. Mt 11:9
through the **p** Isaiah might be Mt 12:17
except the sign of the **p** Jonah. Mt 12:39
through the **p** might be fulfilled Mt 13:35
A **p** is not without honor except Mt 13:57
since they regarded him as a **p**. Mt 14:5
through the **p** might be fulfilled Mt 21:4
This is the **p** Jesus from Mt 21:11
everyone thought John was a **p**." Mt 21:26
they regarded Him as a **p**. Mt 21:46
spoken of by the **p** Daniel, Mt 24:15
spoken through the **p** Jeremiah Mt 27:9
it is written in Isaiah the **p**: Mk 1:2
A **p** is not without honor except Mk 6:4
others said, "He's a **p**—like Mk 6:15
that John was a genuine **p**. Mk 11:32
be called a **p** of the Most High Lk 1:76
of the words of the **p** Isaiah: Lk 3:4
scroll of the **p** Isaiah was given Lk 4:17
p is accepted in his hometown. Lk 4:24
And in the **p** Elisha's time, Lk 4:27
"A great **p** has risen among us," Lk 7:16
out to see? A **p**? Yes, I tell you Lk 7:26
tell you, and far more than a **p**. Lk 7:26
if He were a **p**, would know who Lk 7:39
possible for a **p** to perish Lk 13:33
convinced that John was a **p**." Lk 20:6
who was a **P** powerful in action Lk 24:19
said. "Are you the **P**?" "No," he Jn 1:21
just as Isaiah the **p** said." Jn 1:23
Messiah, or Elijah, or the **P**?" Jn 1:25
"I see that You are a **p**. Jn 4:19
testified that a **p** has no honor Jn 4:44
really is the **P** who was to come Jn 6:14
said, "This really is the **P**!" Jn 7:40
will see that no **p** arises from Jn 7:52
"He's a **p**," he said. Jn 9:17
the word of Isaiah the **p**, Jn 12:38
was spoken through the **p** Joel: Ac 2:16
Since he was a **p**, he knew that Ac 2:30
up for you a **P** like me from Ac 3:22
listen to that **P** will be Ac 3:23
up for you a **P** like me from Ac 7:37
made with hands, as the **p** says: Ac 7:48
reading the **p** Isaiah aloud. Ac 8:28
heard him reading the **p** Isaiah, Ac 8:30
who is the **p** saying this about— Ac 8:34
Jewish false **p** named Bar-Jesus. Ac 13:6
them judges until Samuel the **p**. Ac 13:20
p named Agabus came down from Ac 21:10
through the **p** Isaiah to your Ac 28:25
the first **p** should be silent. 1Co 14:30
thinks he is a **p** or spiritual, 1Co 14:37
from the mouth of the false **p**. Rv 16:13
and along with him the false **p**, Rv 19:20
the beast and the false **p** are, Rv 20:10

PROPHET'S *(3)*

listen to that **p** words or to Dt 13:3
prophet will receive a **p** reward. Mt 10:41
and restrained the **p** madness. 2Pt 2:16

PROPHETESS *(7)*

Miriam the **p**, Aaron's sister Ex 15:20
and Asaiah went to the **p** Huldah, 2Kg 22:14
designated went to the **p** Huldah, 2Ch 34:22
also Noadiah the **p** and the other Neh 6:14
I was then intimate with the **p**, Is 8:3
There was also a **p**, Anna, a Lk 2:36
calls herself a **p**, and teaches Rv 2:20

PROPHETIC *(8)*

was rare and **p** visions were not 1Sm 3:1
so that the **p** Scriptures would Mt 26:56
known through the **p** Scriptures, Rm 16:26
So we have the **p** word strongly 2Pt 1:19
who keeps the **p** words of this Rv 22:7
Don't seal the **p** words of this Rv 22:10
who hears the **p** words of this Rv 22:18
from the words of this **p** book, Rv 22:19

PROPHETICALLY *(1)*

is called, **p**, Sodom and Egypt Rv 11:8

PROPHETS *(235)*

all the LORD's people were **p**, Nm 11:29
meet a group of **p** coming down 1Sm 10:5
at Gibeah, a group of **p** met him. 1Sm 10:10
with the **p** asked each other 1Sm 10:11
Is Saul also among the **p**?" 1Sm 10:11
"Is Saul also among the **p**?" 1Sm 10:12
the group of **p** prophesying with 1Sm 19:20
"Is Saul also among the **p**?" 1Sm 19:24
or by the Urim or by the **p**. 1Sm 28:6
through the **p** or in dreams. 1Sm 28:15
and took 100 **p** and hid them, 1Kg 18:4
slaughtered the LORD's **p**. 1Kg 18:4
slaughtered the LORD's **p**? 1Kg 18:13
I hid 100 of the **p** of the LORD, 1Kg 18:13
along with the 450 **p** of Baal and 1Kg 18:19
Baal and the 400 **p** of Asherah 1Kg 18:19
gathered the **p** at Mount Carmel 1Kg 18:20
LORD, but Baal's **p** are 450 men. 1Kg 18:22
Elijah said to the **p** of Baal, 1Kg 18:25
them, "Seize the **p** of Baal! 1Kg 18:40
killed all the **p** with the sword. 1Kg 19:1
killed Your **p** with the sword. 1Kg 19:10
killed Your **p** with the sword. 1Kg 19:14
the sons of the **p** said to his 1Kg 20:35
that he was one of the **p**. 1Kg 20:41
king of Israel gathered the **p**, 1Kg 22:6
and all the **p** were prophesying 1Kg 22:10
And all the **p** were prophesying 1Kg 22:12
words of the **p** are unanimously 1Kg 22:13
in the mouth of all his **p**.' 1Kg 22:22
mouth of all these **p** of yours, 1Kg 22:23
the sons of the **p** who were at 2Kg 2:3
the sons of the **p** who were in 2Kg 2:5
the sons of the **p** came and stood 2Kg 2:7
the sons of the **p** from Jericho, 2Kg 2:15
sons of the **p** said to Elisha, 2Kg 2:16
Go to the **p** of your father and 2Kg 3:13
the sons of the **p** cried out to 2Kg 4:1
the sons of the **p** were sitting 2Kg 4:38
stew for the sons of the **p**." 2Kg 4:38
the sons of the **p** have come to 2Kg 5:22
sons of the **p** said to Elisha, 2Kg 6:1
of the sons of the **p** and said, 2Kg 9:1
of My servants the **p** and of all 2Kg 9:7
summon to me all the **p** of Baal, 2Kg 10:19
you through My servants the **p**." 2Kg 17:13
through all His servants the **p**. 2Kg 17:23
through His servants the **p**, 2Kg 21:10
well as the priests and the **p**— 2Kg 23:2
through His servants the **p**. 2Kg 24:2
My anointed ones or harm My **p**." 1Ch 16:22
king of Israel gathered the **p**, 2Ch 18:5
and all the **p** were prophesying 2Ch 18:9
And all the **p** were prophesying 2Ch 18:11
words of the **p** are unanimously 2Ch 18:12
in the mouth of all his **p**.' 2Ch 18:21
the mouth of these **p** of yours, 2Ch 18:22
believe in His **p**, and you will 2Ch 20:20
sent them **p** to bring them back 2Ch 24:19
was from the LORD through His **p**. 2Ch 29:25
scoffing at His **p**, until the 2Ch 36:16
But when the **p** Haggai and Ezr 5:1
The **p** of God were with them, Ezr 5:2
through Your servants the **p**, Ezr 9:11
even set up the **p** in Jerusalem Neh 6:7
and the other **p** who wanted to Neh 6:14
killed Your **p** who warned them Neh 9:26
warned them through Your **p**, Neh 9:30
our priests and **p**, our ancestors Neh 9:32
My anointed ones, or harm My **p**." Ps 105:15
your eyes—the **p**, and covered Is 29:10
see," and to the **p**, "Do not Is 30:10
of the false **p** and makes fools Is 44:25
The **p** prophesied by Baal and Jr 2:8
their priests, and their **p** Jr 2:26
devoured your **p** like a ravaging Jr 2:30
the **p** will be scared speechless. Jr 4:9
p become ⌊only⌋ wind, for the Jr 5:13
The **p** prophesy falsely, and the Jr 5:31
My servants the **p** to you time Jr 7:25
bones of the **p**, and the bones Jr 8:1
the **p** and all the residents of Jr 13:13
The **p** are telling them, 'You Jr 14:13
These **p** are prophesying a lie in Jr 14:14
concerning the **p** who prophesy in Jr 14:15
famine these **p** will meet their Jr 14:15
Concerning the **p**: My heart is Jr 23:9
Among the **p** of Samaria I saw Jr 23:13
Among the **p** of Jerusalem also I Jr 23:14
of Hosts says concerning the **p**: Jr 23:15
for from the **p** of Jerusalem Jr 23:15
words of the **p** who prophesy to Jr 23:16
not send these **p**, yet they ran Jr 23:21
heard what the **p** who prophesy a Jr 23:25
minds of the **p** prophesying lies Jr 23:26
p of the deceit of their own Jr 23:26
I am against the **p**"—the LORD's Jr 23:30
I am against the **p**"—the LORD's Jr 23:31
His servants the **p** to you time Jr 25:4
of My servants the **p** I have been Jr 26:5
The priests, the **p**, and all the Jr 26:7
the priests, the **p**, and all the Jr 26:8
Then the priests and **p** said to Jr 26:11
people told the priests and **p**, Jr 26:16
listen to your **p**, your diviners, Jr 27:9
words of the **p** who are telling Jr 27:14
and the **p** who are prophesying Jr 27:15
listen to the words of your **p**. Jr 27:16
are indeed **p** and if the word Jr 27:18
The **p** who preceded you and me Jr 28:8
the priests, the **p**, and all the Jr 29:1
Don't let your **p** who are among Jr 29:8
has raised up **p** for us in Jr 29:15
My servants the **p** time and time Jr 29:19
and their **p**, the men of Judah Jr 32:32
sent you all My servants the **p**, Jr 35:15
Where are your **p** who prophesied Jr 37:19
My servants the **p** time and time Jr 44:4
and even her **p** receive no vision Lm 2:9
Your **p** saw visions for you that Lm 2:14
Should priests and **p** be killed Lm 2:20
the sins of her **p** and the guilt Lm 4:13
against the **p** of Israel who are Ezk 13:2
the foolish **p** who follow their Ezk 13:3
Your **p**, Israel, are like jackals Ezk 13:4
be against the **p** who see false Ezk 13:9
those **p** of Israel who prophesied Ezk 13:16
conspiracy of her **p** within her Ezk 22:25
Her **p** plaster with whitewash for Ezk 22:28
servants, the **p** of Israel, who Ezk 38:17
listened to Your servants the **p**, Dn 9:6

us through His servants the **p**. Dn 9:10
I have used the **p** to cut them Hs 6:5
through the **p** and granted many Hs 12:10
I gave parables through the **p**. Hs 12:10
of your sons as **p** and some of Am 2:11
drink wine and commanded the **p**: Am 2:12
counsel to His servants the **p**. Am 3:7
concerning the **p** who lead my Mc 3:5
The sun will set on these **p**, Mc 3:6
her **p** practice divination for Mc 3:11
Her **p** are reckless—treacherous Zph 3:4
earlier **p** proclaimed to them: Zch 1:4
And do the **p** live forever? Zch 1:5
My servants the **p** overtake your Zch 1:6
LORD of Hosts as well as the **p**, Zch 7:3
the earlier **p** when Jerusalem was Zch 7:7
Spirit through the earlier **p**. Zch 7:12
these words that the **p** spoke Zch 8:9
remove the **p** and the unclean Zch 13:2
what was spoken through the **p**, Mt 2:23
persecuted the **p** who were before Mt 5:12
to destroy the Law or the **P**. Mt 5:17
this is the Law and the **P**. Mt 7:12
of false **p** who come to you Mt 7:15
For all the **p** and the law Mt 11:13
Many **p** and righteous people Mt 13:17
Jeremiah or one of the **p**.” Mt 16:14
Law and the **P** depend on these Mt 22:40
the tombs of the **p** and decorate Mt 23:29
of those who murdered the **p**. Mt 23:31
This is why I am sending you **p**, Mt 23:34
who kills the **p** and stones those Mt 23:37
Many false **p** will rise up and Mt 24:11
messiahs and false **p** will arise Mt 24:24
a prophet—like one of the **p**.” Mk 6:15
still others, one of the **p**.” Mk 8:28
messiahs and false **p** will rise Mk 13:22
of His holy **p** in ancient times Lk 1:70
ancestors used to treat the **p**. Lk 6:23
used to treat the false **p**. Lk 6:26
one of the ancient **p** had risen. Lk 9:8
of the ancient **p** has come back.” Lk 9:19
you that many **p** and kings wanted Lk 10:24
You build monuments to the **p**, Lk 11:47
‘I will send them **p** and apostles, Lk 11:49
blood of all the **p** shed since Lk 11:50
and all the **p** in the kingdom of Lk 13:28
who kills the **p** and stones those Lk 13:34
Law and the **P** were until John Lk 16:16
‘They have Moses and the **p**; Lk 16:29
don’t listen to Moses and the **p**, Lk 16:31
through the **p** about the Son Lk 18:31
all that the **p** have spoken! Lk 24:25
with Moses and all the **P**, Lk 24:27
of Moses, the **P**, and the Psalms Lk 24:44
in the law (and so did the **p**): Jn 1:45
It is written in the **P**: Jn 6:45
Abraham died and so did the **p**. Jn 8:52
died? Even the **p** died. Who do Jn 8:53
through the mouth of all the **p**— Ac 3:18
mouth of His holy **p** from the Ac 3:21
all the **p** who have spoken, Ac 3:24
the sons of the **p** and of the Ac 3:25
is written in the book of the **p**: Ac 7:42
Which of the **p** did your fathers Ac 7:52
All the **p** testify about Him that Ac 10:43
In those days some **p** came down Ac 11:27
there were **p** and teachers: Ac 13:1
reading of the Law and the **P**, Ac 13:15
voices of the **p** that are read Ac 13:27
is said in the **p** does not happen Ac 13:40
words of the **p** agree with this Ac 15:15
who were also **p** themselves, Ac 15:32
written in the Law and in the **P**. Ac 24:14
than what the **p** and Moses said Ac 26:22
Agrippa, do you believe the **p**? Ac 26:27
both the Law of Moses and the **P**. Ac 28:23
ago through His **p** in the Holy Rm 1:2
attested by the Law and the **P** Rm 3:21
killed Your **p**, torn down Your Rm 11:3
second **p**, third teachers 1Co 12:28
Are all **p**? Are all teachers 1Co 12:29
Two or three **p** should speak, 1Co 14:29
are under the control of the **p**, 1Co 14:32
of the apostles and **p**, Eph 2:20
apostles and **p** by the Spirit: Eph 3:5
apostles, some **p**, some Eph 4:11
both the Lord Jesus and the **p**, 1Th 2:15
One of their very own **p** said, Ti 1:12
fathers by the **p** at different Heb 1:1
of David and Samuel and the **p**, Heb 11:32
take the **p** who spoke in the Jms 5:10
the **p** who prophesied about the 1Pt 1:10
were also false **p** among the 2Pt 2:1
previously spoken by the holy **p**, 2Pt 3:2
many false **p** have gone out 1Jn 4:1
to His servants the **p**.” Rv 10:7
these two **p** tormented those Rv 11:10
reward to Your servants the **p**, Rv 11:18
blood of the saints and the **p**, Rv 16:6
apostles, and **p**, because God has Rv 18:20
and the blood of **p** and saints, Rv 18:24
the God of the spirits of the **p**, Rv 22:6
brothers the **p**, and those who Rv 22:9

PROPHETS’ *(2)*
them in shedding the **p** blood.’ Mt 23:30
And the **p** spirits are under the 1Co 14:32

PROPITIATION *(4)*
Him as a **p** through faith Rm 3:25
to make **p** for the sins of the Heb 2:17
Himself is the **p** for our sins, 1Jn 2:2
Son to be the **p** for our sins. 1Jn 4:10

PROPORTION *(14)*
its price in **p** to a greater Lv 25:16
price in **p** to a lesser amount Lv 25:16
price in **p** to them based Lv 25:51
redemption in **p** to his Lv 25:52
price for him in **p** to the years Lv 27:18
and lambs, in **p** to their number. Nm 29:18
and lambs, in **p** to their number. Nm 29:21
and lambs, in **p** to their number. Nm 29:24
and lambs, in **p** to their number. Nm 29:27
and lambs, in **p** to their number. Nm 29:30
and lambs, in **p** to their number. Nm 29:33
and lambs, in **p** to their number. Nm 29:37
to the Levites in **p** to the Nm 35:8
you give in **p** to how the LORD Dt 16:10

PROPORTIONAL *(1)*
valuation will be **p** to the seed Lv 27:16

PROPORTIONS *(1)*
his power, and his graceful **p**. Jb 41:12

PROPOSAL *(11)*
p pleased Pharaoh and all his Gn 41:37
Who can agree to your **p**? 1Sm 30:24
This **p** seemed good to Absalom 2Sm 17:4
Ahithophel offered this **p**. 2Sm 17:6
Should we carry out his **p**? 2Sm 17:6
Since the **p** seemed right to all 1Ch 13:4
The **p** pleased the king and the 2Ch 30:4
they affirmed the **p** and spread 2Ch 30:5
times they sent me the same **p**, Neh 6:4
his counselors approved the **p**, Est 1:21
The **p** pleased the whole company. Ac 6:5

PROPOSE *(1)*
‘What you **p** to do is good.’ Dt 1:14

PROPOSED *(4)*
The exiles did what had been **p**. Ezr 10:16
Hurry, and do just as you **p**. Est 6:10
what Balak king of Moab **p**, Mc 6:5
So they **p** two: Joseph, called Ac 1:23

PROPPED *(2)*
and the king was **p** up in his 1Kg 22:35
king of Israel **p** himself up in 2Ch 18:34

PROPRIETY *(1)*
with all **p**, the younger women 1Tm 5:2

PROSECUTE *(2)*
Let me know why You **p** me. Jb 10:2
Would He **p** me forcefully? Jb 23:6

PROSELYTE *(2)*
over land and sea to make one **p**, Mt 23:15
and Nicolaus, a **p** from Antioch. Ac 6:5

PROSELYTES *(2)*
from Rome, both Jews and **p**, Ac 2:10
Jews and devout **p** followed Paul Ac 13:43

PROSPER *(32)*
and I will cause you to **p**,’ Gn 32:9
cause you to **p**, and I will make Gn 32:12
after you may **p** and so that you Dt 4:40
so that you may **p** in the land Dt 5:16
their children will **p** forever. Dt 5:29
you may live, **p**, and have a long Dt 5:33
so that you may **p** and multiply Dt 6:3
that you may **p** and so that you Dt 6:18
the end He might cause you to **p**. Dt 8:16
your children after you will **p**, Dt 12:25
after you may **p** forever, Dt 12:28
innocent blood, and you will **p**. Dt 19:13
so that you may **p** and live long. Dt 22:7
will make you **p** abundantly with Dt 28:11
cause you to **p** and to multiply Dt 28:63
cause you to **p** and multiply you Dt 30:5
will make you **p** abundantly in Dt 30:9
they will eat their fill and **p**. Dt 31:20
For then you will **p** and succeed Jos 1:8
commands and you do not **p**? 2Ch 24:20
All who **p** on earth will eat and Ps 22:29
good pleasure, cause Zion to **p**; Ps 51:18
May those who love you **p**; Ps 122:6
conceals his sins will not **p**, Pr 28:13
trusts in the LORD will **p**. Pr 28:25
and will **p** in what I send it ⌊to Is 55:11
so they might **p**, and they have Jr 5:28
does the way of the wicked **p**? Jr 12:1
it has prosperity, you will **p**.” Jr 29:7
cause deceit to **p** through his Dn 8:25
those who commit wickedness **p**, Mal 3:15
pray that you may **p** in every way 3Jn 2

PROSPERED *(5)*
him, and wherever he went, he **p**. 2Kg 18:7
He **p**, and all Israel obeyed him. 1Ch 29:23
order to seek his God, and he **p**. 2Ch 31:21
Therefore they have not **p**, Jr 10:21
So Daniel **p** during the reign of Dn 6:28

PROSPERITY *(32)*
our God for our **p** always and for Dt 6:24
will again delight in your **p**, Dt 30:9
have set before you life and **p**, Dt 30:15
Your wisdom and **p** far exceed the 1Kg 10:7
Never seek their peace or **p**, Ezr 9:12
final days will be full of **p**. Jb 8:7
therefore, his **p** will not last. Jb 20:21
their days in **p** and go down to Jb 21:13
But their **p** is not of their own Jb 21:16
soul, having never tasted **p**. Jb 21:25
and my **p** has passed by like a Jb 30:15
their days in **p** and their years Jb 36:11
restored his **p** and doubled his Jb 42:10
land and will enjoy abundant **p**. Ps 37:11
He leads out the prisoners to **p**, Ps 68:6
mountains bring **p** to the people, Ps 72:3
and **p** abound until the moon is Ps 72:7
I saw the **p** of the wicked. Ps 73:3
You restored Jacob’s **p**. Ps 85:1
I may enjoy the **p** of Your chosen Ps 106:5
p within your fortresses.” Ps 122:7
will see the **p** of Jerusalem all Ps 128:5
He endows your territory with **p**; Ps 147:14
In the day of **p** be joyful, Ec 7:14
vast, and its **p** will never end. Is 9:7
the LORD, their **p** will be great, Is 54:13
for when it has **p**, you will Jr 29:7
May your **p** increase. Dn 4:1
will be an extension of your **p**.” Dn 4:27
May your **p** abound. Dn 6:25
will again overflow with **p**; Zch 1:17
you know that our **p** is derived Ac 19:25

PROSPEROUS *(1)*
filled, became **p**, and delighted Neh 9:25

PROSPERS *(7)*
but he **p** and obtains enough to Lv 25:26
resident ⌊living⌋ among you **p**, Lv 25:47
If he **p**, he may redeem himself. Lv 25:49
Whatever he does **p**. Ps 1:3
by one who **p** in his way, Ps 37:7
save to the extent that he **p**, 1Co 16:2
health, just as your soul **p**. 3Jn 2

PROSTITUTE *(51)*
treated our sister like a **p**?” Gn 34:31
thought she was a **p**, for she had Gn 38:15
is the cult **p** who was beside Gn 38:21
There has been no cult **p** here,” Gn 38:21
has been no cult **p** here.’ ” Gn 38:22
has been acting like a **p**, Gn 38:24
else when they **p** themselves with Ex 34:15
daughters will **p** themselves with Ex 34:16
your sons to **p** themselves with Ex 34:16
your daughter by making her a **p**, Lv 19:29
woman is to be a cult **p**, Dt 23:17
Israelite man is to be a cult **p**. Dt 23:17
of a woman, a **p** named Rahab, Jos 2:1

Only Rahab the **p** and everyone Jos 6:17
But Joshua spared Rahab the **p**, Jos 6:25
but he was the son of a **p**, Jdg 11:1
where he saw a **p** and went to bed Jdg 16:1
of Jerusalem to **p** themselves, 2Ch 21:11
Jerusalem to **p** themselves like 2Ch 21:13
dressed like a **p**, having a Pr 7:10
For a **p** is a deep pit, and a Pr 23:27
says⌋ about the **p** will happen to Is 23:15
the city, **p** forgotten ⌊by men Is 23:16
of an adulterer and a **p**! Is 57:3
tree you lie down ⌊like⌋ a **p**. Jr 2:20
have played the **p** with many Jr 3:1
look of a **p** and refuse to be Jr 3:3
green tree to **p** herself there. Jr 3:6
acted like a **p** because of your Ezk 16:15
things, the acts of a brazen **p**, Ezk 16:30
you were unlike a **p** because you Ezk 16:31
Therefore, you **p**, hear the word Ezk 16:35
I will stop you from being a **p**, Ezk 16:41
acted like a **p** even though she Ezk 23:5
she acted like a **p** in the land Ezk 23:19
acted like a **p** with the nations Ezk 23:30
with her as one does with a **p**. Ezk 23:44
loved the wages of a **p** on every Hs 9:1
a boy for a **p** and sold a girl Jl 3:3
wife will be a **p** in the city, Am 7:17
she collected the wages of a **p**, Mc 1:7
they will be used again for a **p**. Mc 1:7
continual prostitution of the **p**, Nah 3:4
and make them members of a **p**? 1Co 6:15
joined to a **p** is one body with 1Co 6:16
faith Rahab the **p** received the Heb 11:31
Rahab the **p** also justified Jms 2:25
the notorious **p** who sits on many Rv 17:1
saw, where the **p** was seated, are Rv 17:15
and the beast, will hate the **p**. Rv 17:16
the notorious **p** who corrupted Rv 19:2

PROSTITUTE'S *(5)*
bring a female **p** wages or a male Dt 23:18
wages or a male **p** earnings into Dt 23:18
Go to the **p** house and bring the Jos 6:22
For a **p** fee is only a loaf of Pr 6:26
themselves at the **p** house. Jr 5:7

PROSTITUTED *(9)*
they have **p** themselves with. Lv 17:7
land will be **p** and filled with Lv 19:29
they **p** themselves with other Jdg 2:17
all Israel **p** themselves with Jdg 8:27
turned and **p** themselves with Jdg 8:33
They **p** themselves with the gods 1Ch 5:25
like the house of Ahab **p** itself, 2Ch 21:13
their actions and **p** themselves Ps 106:39
but also went and **p** herself. Jr 3:8

PROSTITUTES *(18)*
spiritists and **p** himself with Lv 20:6
women who were **p** came to the 1Kg 3:16
even male shrine **p** in the land. 1Kg 14:24
the male shrine **p** from the land 1Kg 15:12
blood, and the **p** bathed ⌊in it⌋, 1Kg 22:38
the male shrine **p** who were left 1Kg 22:46
the male shrine **p** that were in 2Kg 23:7
life ⌊ends⌋ among male cult **p**. Jb 36:14
who consorts with **p** destroys his Pr 29:3
gifts to all **p**, but you gave Ezk 16:33
who acted like **p** in Egypt, Ezk 23:3
off with **p** and make sacrifices Hs 4:14
and make sacrifices with cult **p**. Hs 4:14
collectors and **p** are entering Mt 21:31
and **p** did believe him, Mt 21:32
has devoured your assets with **p**, Lk 15:30
adulterers, male **p**, homosexuals, 1Co 6:9
MOTHER OF **P** AND OF THE Rv 17:5

PROSTITUTING *(3)*
follow him, **p** themselves with Lv 20:5
p herself with all the kingdoms Is 23:17
and **p** yourselves with their Ezk 20:30

PROSTITUTION *(21)*
woman defiled by **p** or divorced Lv 21:7
woman, or one defiled by **p**. Lv 21:14
is so much **p** and witchcraft 2Kg 9:22
land with your **p** and wickedness. Jr 3:2
Indifferent to her **p**, she Jr 3:9
your heinous **p** on the hills, Jr 13:27
and you engaged in **p** on them. Ezk 16:16
you could engage in **p** with them. Ezk 16:17
Wasn't your **p** enough? Ezk 16:20
your abominations and acts of **p**, Ezk 16:22
passed by and increased your **p**. Ezk 16:25
increased your **p** to provoke Me Ezk 16:26
you engaged in **p** with the Ezk 16:28
you extended your **p** to Chaldea, Ezk 16:29
other women in your acts of **p**; Ezk 16:34
by your acts of **p** with your Ezk 16:36
their ⌊religious⌋ **p** and by the Ezk 43:7
remove their **p** and the corpses Ezk 43:9
of the continual **p** of the Nah 3:4
nations by her **p** and clans by Nah 3:4
with the impurities of her **p**. Rv 17:4

PROTECT *(33)*
before you to **p** you on the way Ex 23:20
The LORD bless you and **p** you; Nm 6:24
assembly is to **p** the one who Nm 35:25
your camp to **p** you and deliver Dt 23:14
why didn't you **p** your lord the 1Sm 26:15
since you didn't **p** your lord, 1Sm 26:16
P the young man Absalom for me 2Sm 18:12
and cavalry to **p** us from enemies Ezr 8:22
You will **p** us from this Ps 12:7
P me, God, for I take refuge in Ps 16:1
the name of Jacob's God **p** you. Ps 20:1
You **p** me from trouble. Ps 32:7
p me from those who rise up Ps 59:1
P my life from the terror of the Ps 64:1
let Your salvation **p** me, God. Ps 69:29
P my life, for I am faithful. Ps 86:2
to **p** you in all your ways. Ps 91:11
The LORD will **p** you from all Ps 121:7
He will **p** your life. Ps 121:7
The LORD will **p** your coming and Ps 121:8
P me, LORD, from the clutches of Ps 140:4
P me from the trap they have set Ps 141:9
of justice and **p** the way of His Pr 2:8
They will **p** you from an evil Pr 6:24
p my teachings as you would the Pr 7:2
but the lips of the wise **p** them. Pr 14:3
and higher officials ⌊**p**⌋ them. Ec 5:8
LORD of Hosts will **p** Jerusalem— Is 31:5
up to strengthen and **p** him. Dn 11:1
orders concerning you, to **p** you, Lk 4:10
p them by Your name that You Jn 17:11
but that You **p** them from the Jn 17:15
who is able to **p** you from Jd 24

PROTECTED *(9)*
also **p** us all along the way we Jos 24:17
p us and handed over to us the 1Sm 30:23
He **p** us from the power of the Ezr 8:31
who hates such agreements is **p**. Pr 11:15
righteous run to it and are **p**. Pr 18:10
one who trusts in the LORD is **p**. Pr 29:25
restoring the **p** ones of Israel. Is 49:6
who are being **p** by God's power 1Pt 1:5
world, but **p** Noah, a preacher 2Pt 2:5

PROTECTING *(3)*
Jerusalem—by **p** ⌊it⌋, He will Is 31:5
in awe of John and was **p** him, Mk 6:20
I was **p** them by Your name that Jn 17:12

PROTECTION *(16)*
come under the **p** of my roof." Gn 19:8
Their **p** has been removed from Nm 14:9
are to provide **p** for the king's 2Kg 11:5
providing **p** for the palace. 2Kg 11:6
are to provide **p** for the LORD's 2Kg 11:7
hiding in the **p** of marshy reeds. Jb 40:21
them in the **p** of Your presence Ps 31:20
lives under the **p** of the Most Ps 91:1
my God is the rock of my **p**. Ps 94:22
I come to You for **p**. Ps 143:9
For wisdom is **p** as money is Ec 7:12
is protection as money is **p**, Ec 7:12
Pharaoh's **p** and take refuge Is 30:2
But Pharaoh's **p** will become your Is 30:3
live under his **p** among the Lm 4:20
for me and is a **p** for you. Php 3:1

PROTECTIVE *(2)*
faithfulness will be a **p** shield. Ps 91:4
the **p** shield is set in place. Nah 2:5

PROTECTOR *(2)*
your **P** will not slumber. Ps 121:3
the **P** of Israel does not slumber Ps 121:4

PROTECTS *(13)*
He is the shield that **p** you, Dt 33:29
the LORD your God **p** the living. 1Sm 25:29
The LORD **p** the loyal, but fully Ps 31:23
He **p** all his bones; Ps 34:20
p the lives of His godly ones; Ps 97:10
The LORD **p** you; the LORD is a Ps 121:5
The LORD **p** foreigners and helps Ps 146:9
who guards his mouth **p** his life; Pr 13:3
but He **p** the widow's territory. Pr 15:25
who guards his way **p** his life. Pr 16:17
Won't He who **p** your life know? Pr 24:12
one official **p** another official, Ec 5:8
He **p** His flock like a shepherd; Is 40:11

PROTEST *(2)*
or brothers come to us and **p**, Jdg 21:22
How can you **p**: I am not defiled; Jr 2:23

PROTESTED *(5)*
I done now?" **p** David. "It was 1Sm 17:29
Joab **p**: "Never! I do not want to 2Sm 20:20
But I **p**, "Oh no, Lord GOD! Jr 1:6
But they **p**: We won't! Jr 6:16
horn. But they **p**: We won't Jr 6:17

PROTOTYPE *(1)*
He is a **p** of the Coming One. Rm 5:14

PROUD *(44)*
doesn't become **p** and you forget Dt 8:14
eyes are set against the **p**— 2Sm 22:28
his heart was **p**, Hezekiah didn't 2Ch 32:25
If I am **p**, You hunt me like a Jb 10:16
P beasts have never walked on it; Jb 28:8
your **p** waves stop here"? Jb 38:11
His **p** snorting ⌊fills one with⌋ Jb 39:20
look on every **p** person and Jb 40:11
on every **p** person and humble Jb 40:12
is king over all the **p** beasts. Jb 41:34
turned to the **p** or to those who Ps 40:4
repay the **p** what they deserve. Ps 94:2
You rebuke the **p**, the accursed, Ps 119:21
and⌋ contempt from the **p**. Ps 123:4
LORD, my heart is not **p**; Ps 131:1
The **p** hide a trap with ropes for Ps 140:5
⌊Otherwise,⌋ they will become **p**. Ps 140:8
The **p** speech of a fool ⌊brings⌋ Pr 14:3
destroys the house of the **p**, Pr 15:25
Everyone with a **p** heart is Pr 16:5
to divide plunder with the **p**. Pr 16:19
his downfall a man's heart is **p**, Pr 18:12
The **p** and arrogant person, Pr 21:24
is better than a **p** spirit. Ec 7:8
against all that is **p** and lofty, Is 2:12
and the **p** look in his eyes." Is 10:12
pride—how very **p** he is—his Is 16:6
Do not be **p**, for the LORD has Jr 13:15
object of scorn when you were **p**, Ezk 16:56
Your heart is **p**, and you have Ezk 28:2
has become **p** because of your Ezk 28:5
heart became **p** because of your Ezk 28:17
its **p** strength will collapse. Ezk 30:6
there and its **p** strength comes Ezk 30:18
and it grew **p** on account of its Ezk 31:10
and its **p** strength will come to Ezk 33:28
and their hearts became **p**. Hs 13:6
has scattered the **p** because of Lk 1:51
arrogant, **p**, boastful, inventors Rm 1:30
another. Do not be **p**; instead, Rm 12:16
an opportunity to be **p** of us, 2Co 5:12
money, boastful, **p**, blasphemers, 2Tm 3:2
God resists the **p**, but gives Jms 4:6
because God resists the **p**, 1Pt 5:5

PROUDLY *(4)*
Do not boast so **p**, or let 1Sm 2:3
When she **p** spreads her wings, Jb 39:18
rising up **p** in His great might? Is 63:1
not walk so **p** because it will Mc 2:3

PROVE *(20)*
and let nothing he said **p** false. 1Sm 3:19
We must **p** ourselves strong for 2Sm 10:12
the faithful You **p** Yourself 2Sm 22:26
blameless man You **p** Yourself 2Sm 22:26
the pure You **p** Yourself pure, 2Sm 22:27
crooked You **p** Yourself shrewd 2Sm 22:27
We must **p** ourselves strong for 1Ch 19:13
but were unable to **p** that their Ezr 2:59
but were unable to **p** that their Neh 7:61
But what does your rebuke **p**? Jb 6:25
in exchange will **p** worthless. Jb 15:31
who can **p** me a liar and show Jb 24:25
the faithful You **p** Yourself Ps 18:25
blameless man You **p** Yourself Ps 18:25

… pure You **p** Yourself pure, Ps 18:26
…rooked You **p** Yourself shrewd Ps 18:26
much fruit and **p** to be My Jn 15:8
that they were not able to **p**, Ac 25:7
in the matter would not **p** empty, 2Co 9:3
if they **p** blameless, then they 1Tm 3:10

PROVED *(4)*
followed Omri **p** stronger than 1Kg 16:22
Yet no one **p** Job wrong; Jb 32:12
you, and you will be **p** a liar. Pr 30:6
do you think **p** to be a neighbor Lk 10:36

PROVEN *(4)*
endurance produces **p** character, Rm 5:4
and **p** character produces hope. Rm 5:4
so I may know your **p** character, 2Co 2:9
But you know his **p** character, Php 2:22

PROVERB *(13)*
As the old **p** says, 'Wickedness 1Sm 24:13
I turn my ear to a **p**; Ps 49:4
understanding a **p** or a parable, Pr 1:6
A **p** in the mouth of a fool is Pr 26:7
A **p** in the mouth of a fool is Pr 26:9
what is this **p** you ⌊people⌋ have Ezk 12:22
I will put a stop to this **p**, Ezk 12:23
one and make him a sign and a **p**; Ezk 14:8
will say this **p** about you: Ezk 16:44
mean by using this **p** concerning Ezk 18:2
no longer use this **p** in Israel. Ezk 18:3
you will quote this **p** to Me: Lk 4:23
to them according to the true **p**: 2Pt 2:22

PROVERBS *(7)*
composed 3,000 **p**, and his songs 1Kg 4:32
memorable sayings are **p** of ash; Jb 13:12
The **p** of Solomon son of David, Pr 1:1
Solomon's **p**: A wise son brings Pr 10:1
These too are **p** of Solomon, Pr 25:1
explored, and arranged many **p**. Ec 12:9
everyone who uses **p** will say Ezk 16:44

PROVES *(2)*
hope of ⌊capturing⌋ him **p** false. Jb 41:9
But God **p** His own love for us in Rm 5:8

PROVIDE *(47)*
the sky to **p** light on the earth. Gn 1:15
of the sky to **p** light on the Gn 1:17
God Himself will **p** the lamb for Gn 22:8
that place The LORD Will **P**, Gn 22:14
He will **p** for you today; Ex 14:13
work time and **p** for ⌊his⌋ Ex 21:19
from the rock and **p** drink for Nm 20:8
which you must **p** so that the one Nm 35:6
I will **p** rain for your land in Dt 11:14
will **p** grass in your fields for Dt 11:15
and I'll **p** for you at my side in 2Sm 19:33
the ravens to **p** for you there." 1Kg 17:4
is a widow to **p** for you there." 1Kg 17:9
Sabbath are to **p** protection for 2Kg 11:5
Sabbath are to **p** protection for 2Kg 11:7
great pains to **p** for the house 1Ch 22:14
May the good LORD **p** atonement 2Ch 30:18
and God would **p** what I hope for: Jb 6:8
a flock and **p** pasture for ⌊it⌋ Jb 24:2
Is God able to **p** food in the Ps 78:19
But can He also **p** bread or Ps 78:20
P justice for the needy and the Ps 82:3
the LORD will **p** what is good, Ps 85:12
lambs will **p** your clothing, Pr 27:26
nations and **p** arbitration for Is 2:4
own bread and **p** our own clothing Is 4:1
to **p** them with ample food and Is 23:18
because I **p** water in the Is 43:20
p for those who mourn in Zion; Is 61:3
I will **p** their corpses as food Jr 19:7
He will **p** the sin offerings, Ezk 45:17
prince will **p** a bull as a sin Ezk 45:22
he will **p** seven bulls and seven Ezk 45:23
He will also **p** a grain offering Ezk 45:24
he will **p** the same things for Ezk 45:25
He will **p** a grain offering of Ezk 46:7
is to **p** an inheritance for his Ezk 46:18
and it grew up to **p** shade over Jnh 4:6
peoples and **p** arbitration for Mc 4:3
"I will **p** peace in this place"— Hg 2:9
and He will **p** Me at once with Mt 26:53
that he might **p** a dwelling place Ac 7:46
Also **p** mounts so they can put Ac 23:24
can they **p** evidence to you Ac 24:13
He will also **p** a way of escape, 1Co 10:13
food will **p** and multiply your 2Co 9:10
if anyone does not **p** for his own 1Tm 5:8

PROVIDED *(44)*
It will be **p** on the LORD's Gn 22:14
And Joseph **p** his father, his Gn 47:12
That year he **p** them with food in Gn 47:17
⌊you did⌋ when straw was ⌊**p**⌋." Ex 5:13
anyone they like **p** they marry Nm 36:6
LORD your God has **p** them for all Dt 4:19
p you keep every one of these Dt 19:9
today the LORD has **p** deliverance 1Sm 11:13
he had **p** for the needs of the 2Sm 19:32
He **p** for them, but he was not 2Sm 20:3
Today He has **p** one to sit on my 1Kg 1:48
They **p** food for the king and his 1Kg 4:7
a month in turn **p** food for King 1Kg 4:27
So Hiram **p** Solomon with all the 1Kg 5:10
Solomon **p** Hiram with 100,000 1Kg 5:11
He also **p** offset ledges for the 1Kg 6:6
I have **p** a place there for the 1Kg 8:21
and **p** them with food and water 1Kg 18:4
I **p** them with food and water. 1Kg 18:13
their relatives had **p** for them. 1Ch 12:39
I have also **p** timber and stone, 1Ch 22:14
all that I've **p** for the holy 1Ch 29:3
that we've **p** for building You 1Ch 29:16
Uzziah **p** the entire army with 2Ch 26:14
the captives and **p** clothes for 2Ch 28:15
p donkeys for all the feeble. 2Ch 28:15
asks of you must be **p** promptly, Ezr 7:21
of wine was ⌊**p**⌋ every 10 days. Neh 5:18
p bread from heaven for their Neh 9:15
You **p** for them in the wilderness Neh 9:21
goodness You **p** for the poor, Ps 68:10
He has **p** food for those who fear Ps 111:5
his food **p**, his water assured. Is 33:16
Food won't be **p** for the mourner Jr 16:7
cloth and **p** you with leather Ezk 16:10
these things will be **p** for you. Mt 6:33
has visited and **p** redemption for Lk 1:68
these things will be **p** for you. Lk 12:31
He has **p** proof of this to Ac 17:31
p a great deal of business for Ac 19:24
these hands have **p** for my needs, Ac 20:34
from Epaphroditus what you **p**— Php 4:18
p one uses it legitimately. 1Tm 1:8
since God had **p** something better Heb 11:40

PROVIDES *(14)*
if He **p** me with food to eat and Gn 28:20
God's power **p** this. Jb 12:6
the wilderness **p** nourishment for Jb 24:5
who **p** ⌊us⌋ with songs in the Jb 35:10
Who **p** the raven's food when its Jb 38:41
it **p** no escape by its great Ps 33:17
God **p** homes for those who are Ps 68:6
livestock and ⌊**p**⌋ crops for man Ps 104:14
p the animals with their food, Ps 147:9
still night and **p** food for her Pr 31:15
Now the One who **p** seed for the 2Co 9:10
own flesh, but **p** and cares for Eph 5:29
who richly **p** us with all things 1Tm 6:17
be⌋ from the strength God **p**, 1Pt 4:11

PROVIDING *(9)*
people's ⌊need⌋ by **p** them food. Ru 1:6
meet my needs by **p** my household 1Kg 5:9
his own head and **p** justice for 1Kg 8:32
to take turns **p** protection for 2Kg 11:6
his own head and **p** justice for 2Ch 6:23
behalf of Tobiah by **p** him a room Neh 13:7
in this way, **p** ⌊people⌋ with Ps 65:9
and **p** seed to sow and food to Is 55:10
kinds of⌋ trees **p** food will grow Ezk 47:12

PROVINCE *(39)*
people of the **p** who came from Ezr 2:1
the great God in the **p** of Judah. Ezr 5:8
Ecbatana in the **p** of Media that Ezr 6:2
throughout the **p** of Babylon, Ezr 7:16
survivors in the **p**, who returned Neh 1:3
the people of the **p** who went up Neh 7:6
the heads of the **p** who stayed Neh 11:3
to each **p** in its own script and Est 1:22
in each **p** of his kingdom, Est 2:3
in every **p** of your kingdom Est 3:8
written for each **p** in its own Est 3:12
as law throughout every **p**, Est 3:14
people in every **p** where the Est 4:3
for each **p** in its own script Est 8:9
to be issued as law in every **p**. Est 8:13
In every **p** and every city, Est 8:17
family, **p**, and city, so that Est 9:28
and righteousness in the **p**, Ec 5:8
over the entire **p** of Babylon and Dn 2:48
to manage the **p** of Babylon. Dn 2:49
of Dura in the **p** of Babylon. Dn 3:1
to manage the **p** of Babylon: Dn 3:12
Abednego in the **p** of Babylon. Dn 3:30
city of Susa, in the **p** of Elam. Dn 8:2
parts of the **p** and do what his Dn 11:24
the message in the **p** of Asia. Ac 16:6
inhabitants of the **p** of Asia, Ac 19:10
stayed in the **p** of Asia for a Ac 19:22
in almost the whole **p** of Asia, Ac 19:26
one whom the whole **p** of Asia and Ac 19:27
to spend time in the **p** of Asia, Ac 20:16
Jews from the **p** of Asia saw him Ac 21:27
he asked what **p** he was from. Ac 23:34
Jews from the **p** of Asia found me Ac 24:18
after Festus arrived in the **p**, Ac 25:1
the coast of the **p** of Asia. Ac 27:2
of the Asian **p** greet you. 1Co 16:19
took place in the **p** of Asia: 2Co 1:8
seven churches in the **p** of Asia. Rv 1:4

PROVINCES *(26)*
city, harmful to kings and **p**. Ezr 4:15
who ruled 127 **p** from India to Est 1:1
and the officials from the **p**. Est 1:3
every one of King Ahasuerus' **p**. Est 1:16
sent letters to all the royal **p**, Est 1:22
He freed his **p** from tax payments Est 2:18
the governors of each of the **p**, Est 3:12
to each of the royal **p** ⌊telling Est 3:13
of the royal **p** know that one law Est 4:11
⌊reside⌋ in all the king's **p**. Est 8:5
of the 127 **p** from India to Cush Est 8:9
all the **p** of King Ahasuerus Est 8:12
King Ahasuerus' **p** the Jews Est 9:2
All the officials of the **p**, Est 9:3
throughout the **p** as he became Est 9:4
done in the rest of the royal **p**? Est 9:12
Jews in the royal **p** assembled, Est 9:16
in all of King Ahasuerus' **p**, Est 9:20
were in the 127 **p** of the kingdom Est 9:30
and the treasure of kings and **p**. Ec 2:8
among the **p** has become a slave Lm 1:1
surrounding **p** set out against Ezk 19:8
the rulers of the **p** to attend Dn 3:2
rulers of the **p** assembled for Dn 3:3
have any work to do in these **p**, Rm 15:23
Dispersion in the **p** of Pontus, 1Pt 1:1

PROVINCIAL *(6)*
young men of the **p** leaders.'" 1Kg 20:14
the young men of the **p** leaders, 1Kg 20:15
men of the **p** leaders marched 1Kg 20:17
young men of the **p** leaders and 1Kg 20:19
ethnic and **p** army hostile to Est 8:11
Even some of the **p** officials of Ac 19:31

PROVING *(1)*
Damascus by **p** that this One is Ac 9:22

PROVISION *(6)*
Their entire **p** of bread was dry Jos 9:5
each one made **p** for one month 1Kg 4:7
I must make **p** for it." 1Ch 22:5
ability I've made **p** for the 1Ch 29:2
temple for which I have made **p**." 1Ch 29:19
For we are making **p** for what is 2Co 8:21

PROVISIONS *(19)*
and give them **p** for their Gn 42:25
he gave them **p** for the journey Gn 45:21
and **p** for his father on the Gn 45:23
prepared any **p** for themselves. Ex 12:39
'Get **p** ready for yourselves, Jos 1:11
gathered **p** and took worn-out Jos 9:4
'Take **p** with you for the journey; Jos 9:11
of Israel⌋ took some of their **p**, Jos 9:14
took the people's **p** and their Jdg 7:8
along with your clothing and **p**." Jdg 17:10
10,000 to get **p** for the people Jdg 20:10
the LORD for him and gave him **p**. 1Sm 22:10
Solomon's **p** for one day were 150 1Kg 4:22
oxen—abundant **p** of flour, fig 1Ch 12:40
them plenty of **p** and sought many 2Ch 11:23
it prepares its **p** in summer; Pr 6:8
against you and reduced your **p**. Ezk 16:27

them daily **p** from the royal food Dn 1:5
who eat his **p** will destroy him Dn 11:26

PROVOCATION *(1)*
commit in the **p** he had provoked 1Kg 15:30

PROVOCATIONS *(1)*
because of all the **p** Manasseh 2Kg 23:26

PROVOKE *(20)*
and do not **p** them to battle, Dt 2:9
You continued to **p** the LORD at Dt 9:22
So I will **p** their jealousy with Dt 32:21
her severely just to **p** her, 1Sm 1:6
In order to **p** Me, you have 1Kg 14:9
Ahab did more to **p** the LORD 1Kg 16:33
gods in order to **p** Me with all 2Kg 22:17
Israel had made to **p** ⌊the LORD⌋. 2Kg 23:19
gods in order to **p** Me with all 2Ch 34:25
and those who **p** God are secure; Jb 12:6
I will **p** Egypt against Egypt; Is 19:2
continually **p** Me to My face, Is 65:3
gods so that they **p** Me to anger. Jr 7:18
and do not **p** Me to anger by the Jr 25:6
that you might **p** Me to anger Jr 25:7
to other gods to **p** Me to anger. Jr 32:29
done nothing but **p** Me to anger Jr 32:30
have done to **p** Me to anger— Jr 32:32
and repeatedly **p** Me to anger, Ezk 8:17
prostitution to **p** Me to anger. Ezk 16:26

PROVOKED *(27)*
very angry; Moses was also **p**. Nm 11:10
forget how you **p** the LORD your Dt 9:7
You **p** the LORD at Horeb, and He Dt 9:8
They **p** His jealousy with foreign Dt 32:16
p ⌊to anger⌋ by His sons and Dt 32:19
They have **p** My jealousy with Dt 32:21
They **p** Him to jealous anger more 1Kg 14:22
provocation he had **p** the LORD 1Kg 15:30
because you have **p** ⌊My⌋ anger 1Kg 21:22
He **p** the LORD God of Israel just 1Kg 22:53
in the LORD's sight and **p** Him. 2Kg 17:17
sight and have **p** Me from the day 2Kg 21:15
Manasseh had **p** Him with. 2Kg 23:26
and he **p** the God of his 2Ch 28:25
they have **p** the builders. Neh 4:5
tested God and **p** the Holy One of Ps 78:41
high places and **p** His jealousy Ps 78:58
p the LORD with their deeds, Ps 106:29
being **p**⌋ to disgrace?" Jr 7:19
Why have they **p** Me to anger with Jr 8:19
evil ways that **p** Me to anger, Jr 44:3
Ephraim has **p** bitter anger, Hs 12:14
when your fathers **p** Me to anger, Zch 8:14
they were **p** that they were Ac 4:2
selfish; is not **p**; does not keep 1Co 13:5
Therefore I was **p** with this Heb 3:10
whom was He "**p** for 40 years"? Heb 3:17

PROVOKES *(5)*
What **p** you that you continue Jb 16:3
and his mouth **p** a beating. Pr 18:6
anyone who **p** him endangers Pr 20:2
A greedy person **p** conflict, Pr 28:25
statue that **p** jealousy was Ezk 8:3

PROVOKING *(15)*
LORD your God, **p** Him to anger, Dt 4:25
LORD's sight and **p** Him to anger. Dt 9:18
their Asherah poles, **p** the LORD. 1Kg 14:15
Israel to sin, **p** Me with their 1Kg 16:2
p Him with the work of his hands 1Kg 16:7
p the LORD God of Israel with 1Kg 16:13
p the LORD God of Israel with 1Kg 16:26
did evil things, **p** the LORD. 2Kg 17:11
in the LORD's sight, **p** ⌊Him⌋. 2Kg 21:6
evil in the LORD's sight, **p** Him. 2Ch 33:6
But are they really **p** Me?" Jr 7:19
p Me to anger by burning incense Jr 11:17
are **p** Me to anger by the work Jr 44:8
are we **p** the Lord to jealousy? 1Co 10:22
become conceited, **p** one another, Gl 5:26

PROWLED *(3)*
no lion has ever **p** over it. Jb 28:8
He **p** among the lions, and he Ezk 19:6
where the lion and lioness **p**, Nah 2:11

PROWLING *(4)*
like dogs and **p** around the city. Ps 59:6
like dogs and **p** around the city. Ps 59:14
and has⌋ jackals **p** in it. Lm 5:18
the Devil is **p** around like a 1Pt 5:8

PRUDENT *(2)*
who gathers during summer is **p**; Pr 10:5
Has counsel perished from the **p**? Jr 49:7

PRUNE *(3)*
and you may **p** your vineyard and Lv 25:3
your field or **p** your vineyard. Lv 25:4
P away her shoots, for they do Jr 5:10

PRUNED *(1)*
It will not be **p** or weeded; Is 5:6

PRUNES *(1)*
and He **p** every branch that Jn 15:2

PRUNING *(4)*
and their spears into **p** knives. Is 2:4
off the shoots with a **p** knife, Is 18:5
swords and your **p** knives into Jl 3:10
and their spears into **p** knives. Mc 4:3

PSALM *(2)*
it is written in the second **P**: Ac 13:33
each one has a **p**, a teaching, 1Co 14:26

PSALMS *(8)*
After singing **p**, they went out Mt 26:30
After singing **p**, they went out Mk 14:26
himself says in the Book of **P**: Lk 20:42
and the **P** must be fulfilled." Lk 24:44
it is written in the Book of **P**: Ac 1:20
and I will sing **p** to Your name. Rm 15:9
speaking to one another in **p**, Eph 5:19
wisdom, and singing **p**, hymns, Col 3:16

PSEUDO-INTELLECTUAL *(1)*
"What is this **p** trying to say?" Ac 17:18

PTOLEMAIS *(1)*
Tyre, we reached **P**, where we Ac 21:7

PUAH *(3)*
named Shiphrah and the other **P**, Ex 1:15
Tola son of **P**, son of Dodo Jdg 10:1
Tola, **P**, Jashub, and Shimron— 1Ch 7:1

PUBLIC *(34)*
respond to a **p** call to testify Lv 5:1
them from the **p** square of 2Sm 21:12
them in the eastern **p** square. 2Ch 29:4
will become **p** knowledge to all Est 1:17
and edict became **p** knowledge, Est 2:8
view of the **p**, He strikes them Jb 34:26
cry of lament in our **p** squares. Ps 144:14
her voice in the **p** squares. Pr 1:20
of water in the **p** squares? Pr 5:16
road—a lion in the **p** square!" Pr 26:13
find you in **p** and kiss you, Sg 8:1
and in its **p** squares everyone Is 15:3
has stumbled in the **p** square, Is 59:14
of Moab and in her **p** squares, Jr 48:38
men will fall in her **p** squares; Jr 49:26
men will fall in her **p** squares; Jr 50:30
they approach the **p** area." Ezk 42:14
but this day **p** shame belongs to Dn 9:7
LORD, **p** shame belongs to us, our Dn 9:8
be wailing in all the **p** squares; Am 5:16
the day of his **p** appearance to Lk 1:80
catch Him in what He said in **p**, Lk 20:26
he's seeking **p** recognition. Jn 7:4
delivered a **p** address to them. Ac 12:21
Before He came to **p** attention, Ac 13:24
beat us in **p** without a trial Ac 16:37
them out to the **p** assembly. Ac 17:5
refuted the Jews in **p**, Ac 18:28
it to you in **p** and from house to Ac 20:20
are God's **p** servants, Rm 13:6
his **p** speaking is despicable. 2Co 10:10
Though untrained in **p** speaking, 2Co 11:6
your attention to **p** reading, 1Tm 4:13
will lie in the **p** square of the Rv 11:8

PUBLICIZES *(1)*
but a foolish heart **p** stupidity. Pr 12:23

PUBLICIZING *(1)*
sanctuary, **p** that he himself 2Th 2:4

PUBLICLY *(10)*
must be cut off **p** from their Lv 20:17
and he will sleep with them **p**. 2Sm 12:11
struck him down **p**, killed him, 2Kg 15:10
Moses was read **p** to the people. Neh 13:1
not wanting to disgrace her **p**, Mt 1:19
was talking **p** about Him because Jn 7:13
He's speaking **p** and they're Jn 7:26
and disgraced them **p**; Col 2:15
P rebuke those who sin, so that 1Tm 5:20
you were **p** exposed to taunts Heb 10:33

PUBLISHED *(1)*
It was to be **p** for every ethnic Est 8:13

PUBLIUS *(1)*
island, named **P**, who welcomed us Ac 28:7

PUBLIUS' *(1)*
It happened that **P** father was in Ac 28:8

PUDENS *(1)*
you, as do **P**, Linus, Claudia, 2Tm 4:21

PUL *(4)*
(AKA TIGLATH-PILESER)
P king of Assyria invaded the 2Kg 15:19
Menahem gave **P** 75,000 pounds 2Kg 15:19
silver so that **P** would support 2Kg 15:19
Israel put it into the mind of **P** 1Ch 5:26

PULL *(11)*
P out ⌊some⌋ stalks from the Ru 2:16
and he could not **p** it back to 1Kg 13:4
Can you **p** in Leviathan with a Jb 41:1
for He will **p** my feet out of the Ps 25:15
of deceit and ⌊**p**⌋ sin along with Is 5:18
will **p** your skirts up over your Jr 13:26
your authority and **p** Jeremiah Jr 38:10
not be needed to **p** it from its Ezk 17:9
I will **p** up the Asherah poles Mc 5:14
The Chaldeans **p** them all up with Hab 1:15
will not immediately **p** him out Lk 14:5

PULLED *(18)*
they **p** Joseph out of the pit and Gn 37:28
But then he **p** his hand back, Gn 38:29
contamination be **p** out and Lv 14:40
the stones have been **p** out, Lv 14:43
gateposts, and **p** them out, bar Jdg 16:3
his sleep and **p** out the pin, Jdg 16:14
sword, **p** it from its sheath 1Sm 17:51
Joab **p** him aside to the middle 2Sm 3:27
He **p** me out of deep waters. 2Sm 22:17
and Jehu **p** him up into the 2Kg 10:15
p out some of the hair from my Ezr 9:3
their men, and **p** out their hair. Neh 13:25
Are their tent cords not **p** up? Jb 4:21
and my arm be **p** from its socket. Jb 31:22
He **p** me out of deep waters. Ps 18:16
will not be **p** up nor will any Is 33:20
and they **p** him up with the ropes Jr 38:13
twice dead, **p** out by the roots; Jd 12

PULLS *(3)*
He **p** it out of his back, the Jb 20:25
because the patch **p** away from Mt 9:16
new patch **p** away from the old Mk 2:21

PULVERIZE *(3)*
I **p** them like dust of the earth; 2Sm 22:43
I **p** them like dust before the Ps 18:42
thresh mountains and **p** ⌊them⌋, Is 41:15

PULVERIZES *(1)*
like a sledgehammer that **p** rock? Jr 23:29

PUNISH *(68)*
the LORD will **p** anyone who Ex 20:7
the LORD will **p** anyone who Dt 5:11
will take the man and **p** him. Dt 22:18
in Benjamin to **p** them for all Jdg 20:10
May God **p** you and do so severely 1Sm 3:17
May God **p** me severely if you do 1Sm 14:44
then may God **p** Jonathan and do 1Sm 20:13
May God **p** me, and even more if 1Sm 25:22
May God **p** Abner and do so 2Sm 3:9
May God **p** me and do so severely 2Sm 3:35
God **p** me and do so severely 2Sm 19:13
May God **p** me and do so severely 1Kg 2:23
May the gods **p** me and do so 1Kg 19:2
May the gods **p** me and do so 1Kg 20:10
May God **p** me and do so severely 2Kg 6:31
anger does not **p** and He does not Jb 35:15
P them, God; let them fall by Ps 5:10
do not **p** me in Your anger or Ps 38:1
rise up to **p** all the nations; Ps 59:5
I will **p** the king of Assyria Is 10:12
day the LORD will **p** the host of Is 24:21
His place to **p** the inhabitants Is 26:21
Should I not **p** them for these Jr 5:9
Should I not **p** them for these Jr 5:29
When I **p** them, they will Jr 6:15
When I **p** them, they will Jr 8:12
Should I not **p** them for these Jr 9:9

when I will **p** all the Jr 9:25
I am about to **p** them. Jr 11:22
their guilt and **p** their sins. Jr 14:10
I will **p** you according to what Jr 21:14
I will **p** that man and his Jr 23:34
I will **p** the king of Babylon and Jr 25:12
that nation I will **p** by sword, Jr 27:8
I am about to **p** Shemaiah the Jr 29:32
I will **p** all his oppressors. Jr 30:20
I will **p** him, his descendants, Jr 36:31
will **p** those living in the land Jr 44:13
I am about to **p** you in this Jr 44:29
I am about to **p** Amon, ⌊god⌋ of Jr 46:25
on him at the time I **p** him. Jr 49:8
I am about to **p** the king of Jr 50:18
the time when I will **p** you. Jr 50:31
I will **p** Bel in Babylon. Jr 51:44
when I will **p** Babylon's carved Jr 51:47
when I will **p** her carved images, Jr 51:52
But He will **p** your iniquity, Lm 4:22
I will **p** you for all your Ezk 7:3
but I will **p** you for your ways Ezk 7:4
I will **p** you for all your Ezk 7:8
I will **p** you for your ways and Ezk 7:9
And I will **p** her for the days of Hs 2:13
I will **p** them for their ways and Hs 4:9
I will not **p** your daughters when Hs 4:14
their guilt and **p** their sins; Hs 8:13
He will **p** their sins. Hs 9:9
He is about to **p** Jacob according Hs 12:2
I will **p** you for all your Am 3:2
I will **p** the altars of Bethel on Am 3:14
on the day I **p** Israel for its Am 3:14
You destined them to **p** ⌊us⌋. Hab 1:12
I will **p** the officials, Zph 1:8
that day I will **p** all who skip Zph 1:9
with lamps and **p** the men who Zph 1:12
so I will **p** the leaders. Zch 10:3
They found no way to **p** them, Ac 4:21
we are ready to **p** any 2Co 10:6
out by him to **p** those who do 1Pt 2:14

PUNISHED *(22)*

we are being **p** for what we did Gn 42:21
his abuse, the owner must be **p**. Ex 21:20
should not be **p** because he is Ex 21:21
it was not His hand that **p** us— 1Sm 6:9
morning light, we will be **p**. 2Kg 7:9
have **p** ⌊us⌋ less than our sins Ezr 9:13
hate the righteous will be **p**. Ps 34:21
refuge in Him will not be **p**. Ps 34:22
day long, and **p** every morning. Ps 73:14
them, but **p** their misdeeds. Ps 99:8
When a mocker is **p**, the Pr 21:11
keep going and are **p**. Pr 22:3
foolish keep going and are **p**. Pr 27:12
after many days they will be **p**. Is 24:22
and the LORD has **p** Him for the Is 53:6
This city must be **p**. Jr 6:6
Egypt just as I **p** Jerusalem by Jr 44:13
his land just as I **p** the king of Jr 50:18
in me that I can be **p** for!" Hs 12:8
slaughter them but are not **p**. Zch 11:5
We are **p** justly, because we're Lk 23:41
there to be **p** in Jerusalem. Ac 22:5

PUNISHES *(1)*

p every son whom He receives. Heb 12:6

PUNISHING *(12)*

p the children for the fathers' Ex 20:5
so I am **p** it for its sin, Lv 18:25
p the children for the fathers' Dt 5:9
not relent from **p** Damascus for Am 1:3
not relent from **p** Gaza for three Am 1:6
not relent from **p** Tyre for three Am 1:9
not relent from **p** Edom for three Am 1:11
not relent from **p** the Ammonites Am 1:13
not relent from **p** Moab for three Am 2:1
relent from **p** Judah for three Am 2:4
not relent from **p** Israel for Am 2:6
make them blaspheme by **p** them. Ac 26:11

PUNISHMENT *(61)*

My **p** is too great to bear! Gn 4:13
away in the **p** of the city." Gn 19:15
him⌋ will be exempt from **p**. Ex 21:19
himself, he will bear his **p**." Lv 17:16
who eats it will bear his **p**, Lv 19:8
her freedom, there must be **p**. Lv 19:20
he will bear his **p**. Lv 20:17
both people will bear their **p**. Lv 20:19
wrath ⌊brings⌋ **p** by the sword, Jb 19:29
a person's **p** for his children. Jb 21:19
it would be a crime deserving **p**. Jb 31:11
also be a crime deserving **p**, Jb 31:28
to God, "I have endured ⌊my **p**⌋; Jb 34:31
He causes this to happen for **p**, Jb 37:13
discipline a man with **p** for sin, Ps 39:11
and witness the **p** of the wicked. Ps 91:8
nations and **p** on the peoples, Ps 149:7
on the day of **p** when devastation Is 10:3
p for our peace was on Him, Is 53:5
choose their **p**, and I will bring Is 66:4
you. This is your **p**. It is very Jr 4:18
the time of their **p** they will be Jr 10:15
in⌋ the year of their **p**." Jr 11:23
on them, the year of their **p**. Jr 23:12
on them, the time of their **p**. Jr 46:21
Moab the year of their **p**. Jr 48:44
has come, the time of their **p**. Jr 50:27
the time of their **p** they will be Jr 51:18
because of the **p** for his sins? Lm 3:39
The **p** of my dear people is Lm 4:6
Zion, your **p** is complete; Lm 4:22
exist, but we bear their **p**. Lm 5:7
will bear their **p**—the Ezk 14:10
the **p** of the one who inquires Ezk 14:10
son suffer **p** for the father's Ezk 18:19
won't suffer **p** for the father's Ezk 18:20
won't suffer **p** for the son's Ezk 18:20
block that causes your **p**. Ezk 18:30
the day has come for your **p**." Ezk 21:25
the day has come for your **p**. Ezk 21:29
have come to your years ⌊of **p**⌋. Ezk 22:4
The **p** for their sins rested on Ezk 32:27
disaster, the time of final **p**, Ezk 35:5
I will be a **p** for all of them. Hs 5:2
a desolation on the day of **p**; Hs 5:9
The days of **p** have come; Hs 9:7
the flocks of sheep suffer **p**. Jl 1:18
the day of⌋ your **p**, is coming; Mc 7:4
The LORD has removed your **p**; Zph 3:15
will be the **p** of Egypt and all Zch 14:19
you will receive a harsher **p**. Mt 23:14
will go away into eternal **p**, Mt 25:46
These will receive harsher **p**." Mk 12:40
These will receive greater **p**." Lk 20:47
you are undergoing the same **p**? Lk 23:40
The **p** by the majority is 2Co 2:6
disobedience received a just **p**, Heb 2:2
How much worse **p**, do you think Heb 10:29
unrighteous under **p** until the 2Pt 2:9
fear, because fear involves **p**. 1Jn 4:18
undergoing the **p** of eternal fire Jd 7

PUNITE *(1)*

the **P** clan from Puvah; Nm 26:23

PUNON *(2)*

from Zalmonah and camped at **P**. Nm 33:42
departed from **P** and camped at Nm 33:43

PUPIL *(4)*

guarded him as the **p** of His eye. Dt 32:10
the teacher along with the **p**. 1Ch 25:8
as you would the **p** of your eye. Pr 7:2
you touches the **p** of His eye. Zch 2:8

PUR *(3)*

twelfth year, **P** (that is, the Est 3:7
He cast the **P** (that is, the lot) Est 9:24
called Purim, from the word **P**. Est 9:26

PURAH *(2)*

camp, go with **P** your servant. Jdg 7:10
So he went with **P** his servant to Jdg 7:11

PURCHASE *(11)*

your neighbor or a **p** from him, Lv 25:14
are to make the **p** from your Lv 25:15
may **p** male and female slaves. Lv 25:44
You may also **p** them from the Lv 25:45
to them based on his **p** price. Lv 25:51
You may **p** food from them with Dt 2:6
I took the **p** agreement—the Jr 32:11
and gave the **p** agreement to Jr 32:12
were signing the **p** agreement, Jr 32:12
this **p** agreement with the sealed Jr 32:14
I had given the **p** agreement to Jr 32:16

PURCHASED *(17)*

your house and one **p** with money Gn 17:12
as well as one **p** with money, Gn 17:13
in his house or **p** with his money Gn 17:23
his house and those **p** with money Gn 17:27
He **p** a section of the field from Gn 33:19
the field Abraham **p** from Ephron Gn 49:30
cave in it ⌊were **p**⌋ from the Gn 49:32
Abraham had **p** as a burial site Gn 50:13
slave a man has **p** may eat it, Ex 12:44
until the people whom You **p** pass Ex 15:16
one who **p** him is to calculate Lv 25:50
field he has **p** that is not part Lv 27:22
land Jacob had **p** from the sons Jos 24:32
You **p** long ago and redeemed Ps 74:2
Fields will be **p** with silver, Jr 32:44
a man **p** me as a servant since Zch 13:5
which He **p** with His own blood. Ac 20:28

PURCHASER *(2)*

of its **p** until the Year Lv 25:28
to its **p** throughout his Lv 25:30

PURCHASES *(1)*

But if a priest **p** someone with Lv 22:11

PURCHASING *(1)*

for the grain they were **p**, Gn 47:14

PURE *(116)*

Gold from that land is **p**; Gn 2:12
Overlay it with **p** gold; Ex 25:11
Make a mercy seat of **p** gold, Ex 25:17
Overlay it with **p** gold and make Ex 25:24
Make them out of **p** gold. Ex 25:29
to make a lampstand out of **p**, Ex 25:31
single hammered piece of **p** gold. Ex 25:36
and firepans must be of **p** gold. Ex 25:38
made from 75 pounds of **p** gold. Ex 25:39
to bring you **p** oil from crushed Ex 27:20
and two chains of **p** gold; Ex 28:14
chains of **p** gold cord work Ex 28:22
make a plate of **p** gold and Ex 28:36
and its horns with **p** gold; Ex 30:3
spices and **p** frankincense are Ex 30:34
seasoned with salt, **p** and holy. Ex 30:35
the **p** ⌊gold⌋ lampstand with all Ex 31:8
overlaid it with **p** gold inside Ex 37:2
He made a mercy seat of **p** gold, Ex 37:6
overlaid it with **p** gold and made Ex 37:11
be on the table out of **p** gold: Ex 37:16
out of **p** hammered gold. Ex 37:17
single hammered piece of **p** gold. Ex 37:22
and firepans of **p** gold. Ex 37:23
utensils of 75 pounds of **p** gold. Ex 37:24
and its horns with **p** gold. Ex 37:26
holy anointing oil and the **p**, Ex 37:29
braided chains of **p** gold cord Ex 39:15
made bells of **p** gold and Ex 39:25
diadem, out of **p** gold, and wrote Ex 39:30
the **p** ⌊gold⌋ lampstand, with its Ex 39:37
to bring you **p** oil of beaten Lv 24:2
lamps on the **p** ⌊gold⌋ lampstand Lv 24:4
on the **p** ⌊gold⌋ table before the Lv 24:6
Place **p** frankincense near each Lv 24:7
not defiled herself and is **p**, Nm 5:28
with the **p** You prove Yourself 2Sm 22:27
the pure You prove Yourself **p**, 2Sm 22:27
the word of the LORD is **p**. 2Sm 22:31
he overlaid it with **p** gold. 1Kg 6:20
of the temple with **p** gold, 1Kg 6:21
the **p** gold lampstands in front 1Kg 7:49
the **p** gold ceremonial bowls, 1Kg 7:50
Forest of Lebanon were **p** gold. 1Kg 10:21
the **p** gold for the forks, 1Ch 28:17
its inner surface with **p** gold. 2Ch 3:4
their lamps of **p** gold to burn 2Ch 4:20
and overlaid it with **p** gold. 2Ch 9:17
Forest of Lebanon were **p** gold. 2Ch 9:20
or a man more **p**" than his Maker?" Jb 4:17
you are **p** and upright, then He Jb 8:6
and I am **p** in Your sight." Jb 11:4
produce something **p** from what is Jb 14:4
that he should be **p**, or one born Jb 15:14
heavens are not **p** in His sight, Jb 15:15
violence and my prayer is **p**. Jb 16:17
me, I will emerge as **p** gold. Jb 23:10
How can one born of woman be **p**? Jb 25:4
stars are not **p** in His sight, Jb 25:5
it cannot be valued in **p** gold. Jb 28:19
I am **p**, without transgression; Jb 33:9
words of the LORD are **p** words, Ps 12:6
with the **p** You prove Yourself Ps 18:26
the pure You prove Yourself **p**, Ps 18:26

the word of the LORD is **p**. Ps 18:30
The fear of the LORD is **p**, Ps 19:9
than an abundance of **p** gold; Ps 19:10
a crown of **p** gold on his head Ps 21:3
has clean hands and a **p** heart, Ps 24:4
to Israel, to the **p** in heart. Ps 73:1
them with a **p** heart and guided Ps 78:72
can a young man keep his way **p**? Ps 119:9
Your word is completely **p**, Ps 119:140
knowledge rather than **p** gold. Pr 8:10
and my harvest than **p** silver. Pr 8:19
of the righteous is **p** silver; Pr 10:20
man, but pleasant words are **p**. Pr 15:26
say, "I have kept my heart **p**; Pr 20:9
his behavior is **p** and upright. Pr 20:11
one who loves a **p** heart and Pr 22:11
Every word of God is **p**; Pr 30:5
that is **p** in its own eyes, Pr 30:12
set on pedestals of **p** gold. Sg 5:15
worth their weight in **p** gold— Lm 4:2
you will not be **p** again until I Ezk 24:13
head of the statue was **p** gold, Dn 2:32
eyes are too **p** to look on evil, Hab 1:13
I will then restore **p** speech to Zph 3:9
Incense and **p** offerings will be Mal 1:11
Blessed are the **p** in heart, Mt 5:8
alabaster jar of **p** and expensive Mk 14:3
fragrant oil—**p** and expensive Jn 12:3
to be **p** in this matter. 2Co 7:11
to present a **p** virgin to Christ. 2Co 11:2
a complete and **p** devotion to 2Co 11:3
and can be **p** and blameless Php 1:10
that you may be blameless and **p**, Php 2:15
just, whatever is **p**, whatever is Php 4:8
is love from a **p** heart, 1Tm 1:5
sins of others. Keep yourself **p**. 1Tm 5:22
call on the Lord from a **p** heart. 2Tm 2:22
the **p**, everything is pure, but Ti 1:15
everything is **p**, but to those Ti 1:15
and unbelieving nothing is **p**; Ti 1:15
to be sensible, **p**, good Ti 2:5
our bodies washed in **p** water. Heb 10:22
P and undefiled religion before Jms 1:27
wisdom from above is first **p**, Jms 3:17
earnestly from a **p** heart, 1Pt 1:22
observe your **p**, reverent lives. 1Pt 3:2
I awaken your **p** understanding 2Pt 3:1
himself just as He is **p**. 1Jn 3:3
wear fine linen, bright and **p**. Rv 19:8
horses, wearing **p** white linen. Rv 19:14
the city was **p** gold like clear Rv 21:18
street of the city was **p** gold, Rv 21:21

PURELY *(3)*
do I plan in a **p** human way so 2Co 1:17
know anyone in a **p** human way. 2Co 5:16
known Christ in a **p** human way, 2Co 5:16

PUREST *(4)*
and gold tongs—of **p** gold; 2Ch 4:21
and firepans—of **p** gold; 2Ch 4:22
more than gold, even the **p** gold, Ps 119:127
His head is **p** gold. His hair is Sg 5:11

PURGE *(14)*
You must **p** the evil from you. Dt 13:5
You must **p** the evil from you. Dt 17:7
You must **p** the evil from Israel. Dt 17:12
him with pity but **p** from Israel Dt 19:13
You must **p** the evil from you. Dt 19:19
You must **p** from yourselves the Dt 21:9
You must **p** the evil from you, Dt 21:21
You must **p** the evil from you. Dt 22:21
You must **p** the evil from Israel. Dt 22:22
You must **p** the evil from you. Dt 22:24
You must **p** the evil from you. Dt 24:7
Lashes and wounds **p** away evil, Pr 20:30
And I will also **p** you of those Ezk 20:38
I will **p** your uncleanness. Ezk 22:15

PURGED *(1)*
iniquity will be **p** in this way, Is 27:9

PURIFICATION *(23)*
to perform the **p** rite on the Ex 30:10
to perform the **p** rite for it Ex 30:10
will continue in **p** from her Lv 12:4
until completing her days of **p**. Lv 12:4
will continue in **p** from her Lv 12:5
When her days of **p** are complete, Lv 12:6
the LORD to make **p** with it by Lv 16:10
his head on the day of his **p**; Nm 6:9
you must do to them for their **p**: Nm 8:7
Sprinkle them with the **p** water. Nm 8:7
For ⌊the **p** of⌋ the unclean Nm 19:17
be purified with the **p** water. Nm 31:23
the **p** of all the holy things, 1Ch 23:28
not according to the **p** ⌊rules⌋ 2Ch 30:19
their God and the service of **p**, Neh 12:45
When you have finished the **p**, Ezk 43:23
and complete the days ⌊of **p**⌋. Ezk 43:27
the days of their **p** according to Lk 2:22
had been set there for Jewish **p**. Jn 2:6
disciples and a Jew about **p**. Jn 3:25
completion of the **p** days when Ac 21:26
After making **p** for sins, He sat Heb 1:3
sanctify for the **p** of the flesh, Heb 9:13

PURIFIED *(20)*
for the one to be **p** from his Lv 14:19
The Levites **p** themselves and Nm 8:21
the one being **p** must wash his Nm 19:19
It must still be **p** with the Nm 31:23
because they had **p** themselves. Ezr 6:20
and Levites had **p** themselves, Neh 12:30
themselves, they **p** the people, Neh 12:30
I ordered that the rooms be **p**, Neh 13:9
So I **p** them from everything Neh 13:30
earthen furnace, **p** seven times. Ps 12:6
but you would not be **p** from your Ezk 24:13
may be refined, **p**, and cleansed Dn 11:35
Many will be **p**, cleansed, and Dn 12:10
p himself along with them, Ac 21:26
me ritually **p** in the temple, Ac 24:18
everything is **p** with blood, Heb 9:22
the heavens to be **p** with these Heb 9:23
themselves ⌊to be **p**⌋ with better Heb 9:23
once **p**, would no longer Heb 10:2
having **p** yourselves for sincere 1Pt 1:22

PURIFIER *(1)*
like a refiner and **p** of silver; Mal 3:3

PURIFIES *(3)*
After he **p** the unclean person on Nm 19:19
if anyone **p** himself from these 2Tm 2:21
hope in Him **p** himself just as 1Jn 3:3

PURIFY *(33)*
P yourselves and change your Gn 35:2
to the people and **p** them today Ex 19:10
near the LORD must **p** themselves Ex 19:22
P the altar when you make Ex 29:36
and hyssop to **p** the house, Lv 14:49
He will **p** the house with the Lv 14:52
He will **p** the ⌊most⌋ holy place Lv 16:16
and **p** the most holy place. Lv 16:33
will **p** the tent of meeting and Lv 16:33
clothes, and so **p** themselves. Nm 8:7
P yourselves ⌊in readiness⌋ for Nm 11:18
is to **p** himself with the water Nm 19:12
But if he does not **p** himself on Nm 19:12
and does not **p** himself, defiles Nm 19:13
unclean and does not **p** himself, Nm 19:20
the dead are to **p** yourselves on Nm 31:19
Also **p** everything: garments, Nm 31:20
He will **p** His land and His Dt 32:43
the Levites to **p** themselves and Neh 13:22
for his children⌋ and **p** them, Jb 1:5
P me with hyssop, and I will be Ps 51:7
Did I **p** my heart and wash my Ps 73:13
out from her, **p** yourselves, you Is 52:11
who dedicate and **p** themselves to Is 66:17
will **p** them from all the wrongs Jr 33:8
since I tried to **p** you, but you Ezk 24:13
this way you will **p** the altar Ezk 43:20
They will **p** the altar just as Ezk 43:22
bull and **p** the sanctuary. Ezk 45:18
He will **p** the sons of Levi and Mal 3:3
the country to **p** themselves Jn 11:55
p yourself along with them, Ac 21:24
sinners, and **p** your hearts, Jms 4:8

PURIFYING *(3)*
altar on all sides, **p** the altar. Lv 8:15
has finished **p** the ⌊most⌋ holy Lv 16:20
had just been **p** herself from her 2Sm 11:4

PURIM *(5)*
reason these days are called **P**, Est 9:26
these days of **P** will not lose Est 9:28
to confirm the letter about **P**. Est 9:29
these days of **P** at their proper Est 9:31
confirmed these customs of **P**, Est 9:32

PURITY *(5)*
rescued by the **p** of your hands. Jb 22:30
with God-given sincerity and **p**, 2Co 1:12
by **p**, by knowledge, by patience, 2Co 6:6
and **p** of the truth. Eph 4:24
in love, in faith, in **p**. 1Tm 4:12

PURPLE *(53)*
blue, **p**, and scarlet yarn; Ex 25:4
linen, and blue, **p**, and scarlet Ex 26:1
a veil of blue, **p**, and scarlet Ex 26:31
with blue, **p**, and scarlet yarn, Ex 26:36
with blue, **p**, and scarlet yarn, Ex 27:16
blue, **p**, and scarlet yarn; Ex 28:5
and with blue, **p**, and scarlet Ex 28:6
gold, of blue, **p**, and scarlet Ex 28:8
gold, of blue, **p**, and scarlet Ex 28:15
of blue, **p**, and scarlet yarn Ex 28:33
blue, **p**, and scarlet yarn; Ex 35:6
blue, **p**, or scarlet yarn Ex 35:23
blue, **p**, and scarlet yarn, and Ex 35:25
in blue, **p**, and scarlet yarn Ex 35:35
as well as blue, **p**, and scarlet Ex 36:8
veil with blue, **p**, and scarlet Ex 36:35
with blue, **p**, and scarlet yarn, Ex 36:37
with blue, **p**, and scarlet yarn, Ex 38:18
with blue, **p**, and scarlet yarn, Ex 38:23
from the blue, **p**, and scarlet Ex 39:1
gold, of blue, **p**, and scarlet Ex 39:2
with the blue, **p**, and scarlet Ex 39:3
gold, of blue, **p**, and scarlet Ex 39:5
gold, of blue, **p**, and scarlet Ex 39:8
spun blue, **p**, and scarlet yarn Ex 39:24
blue, **p**, and scarlet yarn Ex 39:29
altar, spread a **p** cloth over it, Nm 4:13
the **p** garments on the kings of Jdg 8:26
iron, and with **p**, crimson, and 2Ch 2:7
and wood, with **p**, blue, crimson 2Ch 2:14
veil of blue, **p**, and crimson 2Ch 3:14
fine white and **p** linen cords to Est 1:6
clothed in royal **p** and white, Est 8:15
crown and a **p** robe of fine linen Est 8:15
clothing is fine linen and **p**. Pr 31:22
back of gold, and its seat of **p**. Sg 3:10
hair of your head like **p** cloth— Sg 7:5
Their clothing is blue and **p**, Jr 10:9
were reared in **p** ⌊garments⌋ Lm 4:5
of blue and **p** fabric from the Ezk 27:7
turquoise, **p** and embroidered Ezk 27:16
will be clothed in **p**, Dn 5:7
be clothed in **p**, have a gold Dn 5:16
and they clothed Daniel in **p**, Dn 5:29
They dressed Him in a **p** robe, Mk 15:17
they stripped Him of the **p** robe, Mk 15:20
would dress in **p** and fine linen, Lk 16:19
and threw a **p** robe around Him. Jn 19:2
crown of thorns and the **p** robe. Jn 19:5
dealer in **p** cloth from the city Ac 16:14
was dressed in **p** and scarlet, Rv 17:4
fabrics of linen, **p**, silk, and Rv 18:12
in fine linen, **p**, and scarlet, Rv 18:16

PURPOSE *(34)*
I have let you live for this **p**: Ex 9:16
beasts may be used for any **p**, Lv 7:24
of it for the **p** of their Jos 18:4
singleness of **p** to help David. 1Ch 12:33
wooden platform made for this **p**. Neh 8:4
with words that serve no good **p**? Jb 15:3
and fulfill your whole **p**. Ps 20:4
God who fulfills ⌊His **p**⌋ for me. Ps 57:2
will fulfill ⌊His **p**⌋ for me. Ps 138:8
prepared everything for His **p**— Pr 16:4
called you for a righteous ⌊**p**⌋, Is 42:6
a man for My **p** from a far Is 46:11
and serve Him with a single **p**. Zph 3:9
because I was sent for this **p**." Lk 4:43
here for the **p** of taking them as Ac 9:21
have appeared to you for this **p**, Ac 26:16
they had achieved their **p**; Ac 27:13
are called according to His **p**. Rm 8:28
so that God's **p** according to Rm 9:11
My **p** is that the offering of the Rm 15:16
The **p** is that none of you will 1Co 4:6
unless you believed to no **p**. 1Co 15:2
It was for this **p** I wrote: 2Co 2:9
The **p** was that the blessing of Gl 3:14
according to the **p** of the One Eph 1:11
according to the **p** of the ages, Eph 3:11
will and to act for His good **p**. Php 2:13

sent him to you for this very **p**, Col 4:8
to His own **p** and grace, 2Tm 1:9
conduct, **p**, faith, patience, 2Tm 3:10
His unchangeable **p** even more Heb 6:17
of God was revealed for this **p**: 1Jn 3:8
These have one **p**, and they give Rv 17:13
out His plan by having one **p**, Rv 17:17

PURPOSED *(3)*
as I have **p** it, so it will Is 14:24
day that you **p** to understand Dn 10:12
LORD of Hosts **p** to deal with us Zch 1:6

PURPOSES *(3)*
fulfilled the **p** of His heart. Jr 23:20
fulfilled the **p** of His heart. Jr 30:24
the LORD's **p** against Babylon Jr 51:29

PURSES *(1)*
festive robes, capes, cloaks, **p**, Is 3:22

PURSUE *(60)*
and they did not **p** Jacob's sons. Gn 35:5
P the men, and when you overtake Gn 44:4
heart so that he will **p** them. Ex 14:4
I will **p**, I will overtake, I Ex 15:9
will **p** your enemies, and they Lv 26:7
Five of you will **p** 100, and 100 Lv 26:8
and 100 of you will **p** 10,000; Lv 26:8
P justice and justice alone, Dt 16:20
of his anger might **p** the one who Dt 19:6
these will **p** you until you Dt 28:22
will come, **p**, and overtake you Dt 28:45
How could one man **p** a thousand, Dt 32:30
as soon as they left to **p** them, Jos 2:7
of Ai were summoned to **p** them, Jos 8:16
P your enemies and attack them Jos 10:19
Should I **p** these raiders? 1Sm 30:8
to him, "**P** ⌊them⌋, for you 1Sm 30:8
your lord's soldiers and **p** him, 2Sm 20:6
left Jerusalem to **p** Sheba son of 2Sm 20:7
followed Joab to **p** Sheba son of 2Sm 20:13
I **p** my enemies and destroy them; 2Sm 22:38
three months while they **p** you, 2Sm 24:13
him, "Do not **p** them directly. 1Ch 14:14
say, "How will we **p** him, since Jb 19:28
what is worthless and **p** a lie? Ps 4:2
may an enemy **p** and overtake me; Ps 7:5
relentlessly **p** the afflicted; Ps 10:2
p my enemies and overtake them; Ps 18:37
love will **p** me all the days Ps 23:6
is good; seek peace and **p** it. Ps 34:14
so **p** them with Your tempest and Ps 83:15
I **p** the way of Your commands, Ps 119:32
who **p** evil plans come near; Ps 119:150
Rescue me from those who **p** me, Ps 142:6
of all who **p** gain dishonestly Pr 1:19
p the way of understanding. Pr 9:6
He may **p** ⌊them with⌋ words, Pr 19:7
but those who **p** you will be Is 30:16
to Me, you who **p** righteousness, Is 51:1
How skillfully you **p** love; Jr 2:33
will **p** them with sword, famine, Jr 29:18
the sword will **p** you. Jr 48:2
You will **p** ⌊them⌋ in anger and Lm 3:66
whose hearts **p** their desire for Ezk 11:21
their hearts **p** unjust gain. Ezk 33:31
bloodshed, and it will **p** you. Ezk 35:6
hate bloodshed, it will **p** you. Ezk 35:6
She will **p** her lovers but not Hs 2:7
is good; an enemy will **p** him. Hs 8:3
who did not **p** righteousness, Rm 9:30
they did not **p** it by faith, Rm 9:32
in their needs; **p** hospitality. Rm 12:13
must **p** what promotes peace and Rm 14:19
P love and desire spiritual 1Co 14:1
p as my goal the prize promised Php 3:14
always **p** what is good for one 1Th 5:15
but **p** righteousness, godliness, 1Tm 6:11
passions, and **p** righteousness, 2Tm 2:22
P peace with everyone, and Heb 12:14
He must seek peace and **p** it, 1Pt 3:11

PURSUED *(41)*
p them as far as Hobah to the Gn 14:15
with him, **p** Jacob for seven Gn 31:23
is my sin, that you have **p** me? Gn 31:36
Egypt, and he **p** the Israelites, Ex 14:8
flow over them as they **p** you, Dt 11:4
The men **p** them along the road to Jos 2:7
and they **p** Joshua and were drawn Jos 8:16
exposed while they **p** Israel. Jos 8:17
in Ai who had **p** them into the Jos 8:24
Egyptians **p** your fathers with Jos 24:6
fled, they **p** him, seized him, Jdg 1:6
Barak **p** the chariots and the Jdg 4:16
and they **p** the Midianites. Jdg 7:23
Zalmunna fled, and he **p** them. Jdg 8:12
but Abimelech **p** him, and Gaal Jdg 9:40
Benjaminites, **p** them, and easily Jdg 20:43
you have not **p** younger men, Ru 3:10
of Mizpah and **p** the Philistines 1Sm 7:11
heard of this and **p** David there. 1Sm 23:25
but Joab and Abishai **p** Abner. 2Sm 2:24
they no longer **p** Israel or 2Sm 2:28
brother Abishai **p** Sheba son of 2Sm 20:10
Arameans fled and Israel **p** them, 1Kg 20:20
Gehazi **p** Naaman. When Naaman 2Kg 5:21
Jehu **p** him, shouting, "Shoot him 2Kg 9:27
p worthless idols and became 2Kg 17:15
Chaldean army **p** him and overtook 2Kg 25:5
The Philistines **p** Saul and his 1Ch 10:2
Abijah **p** Jeroboam and captured 2Ch 13:19
were with him **p** them as far as 2Ch 14:13
but **p** the wretched poor and the Ps 109:16
the enemy has **p** me, crushing me Ps 143:3
but they **p** many schemes." Ec 7:29
followed, **p**, and worshiped. Jr 8:2
Chaldean army **p** them and Jr 39:5
The Chaldean army **p** the king and Jr 52:8
Yourself in anger and **p** us; Lm 3:43
they relentlessly **p** us over the Lm 4:19
We are closely **p**; we are tired, Lm 5:5
because he **p** his brother with Am 1:11
I even **p** them to foreign cities. Ac 26:11

PURSUERS *(6)*
days until the **p** had returned. Jos 2:22
the wilderness now became the **p**. Jos 8:20
hurled their **p** into the depths Neh 9:11
me from all my **p** and rescue me, Ps 7:1
spear and javelin against my **p**, Ps 35:3
All her **p** have overtaken her in Lm 1:3

PURSUES *(9)*
if the avenger of blood **p** him, Jos 20:5
When someone **p** you and 1Sm 25:29
like one who **p** a partridge in 1Sm 26:20
Disaster **p** sinners, but good Pr 13:21
the one who **p** righteousness. Pr 15:9
isolates himself **p** ⌊selfish⌋ Pr 18:1
The one who **p** righteousness and Pr 21:21
He **p** them, going on safely, Is 41:3
the wind and **p** the east wind. Hs 12:1

PURSUING *(20)*
even though no one is **p** you. Lv 26:17
fall though no one is **p** ⌊them⌋. Lv 26:36
sword though no one is **p** ⌊them⌋. Lv 26:37
so that the men **p** you won't find Jos 2:16
p them as far as Great Sidon and Jos 11:8
they were **p** the Midianites. Jdg 7:25
for I am **p** Zebah and Zalmunna, Jdg 8:5
returned from **p** the Philistines, 1Sm 24:1
Why is my lord **p** his servant? 1Sm 26:18
to stop **p** their brothers?" 2Sm 2:26
have stopped **p** their brothers 2Sm 2:27
had turned back from **p** Abner, 2Sm 2:30
they turned back from **p** him. 1Kg 22:33
they turned back from **p** him. 2Ch 18:32
the angel of the LORD **p** them. Ps 35:6
for good attack me for **p** good. Ps 38:20
but **p** evil ⌊leads⌋ to death. Pr 11:19
flee when no one is **p** ⌊them⌋, Pr 28:1
p the law for righteousness, Rm 9:31
away while **p** his activities. Jms 1:11

PURSUIT *(22)*
they went in **p** as far as Dan. Gn 14:14
The Egyptians set out in **p**— Ex 14:23
Barak arrived in **p** of Sisera, Jdg 4:22
were exhausted, but still in **p**. Jdg 8:4
Saul gave up the **p** of the 1Sm 14:46
returned from the **p** of the 1Sm 17:53
broke off his **p** of David and 1Sm 23:28
400 of the men continued in **p**. 1Sm 30:10
or the left in his **p** of him. 2Sm 2:19
will set out in **p** of David 2Sm 17:1
broke off their **p** of Israel 2Sm 18:16
a vanishing mist, a **p** of death. Pr 21:6
to be futile, a **p** of the wind. Ec 1:14
this too is a **p** of the wind. Ec 1:17
be futile and a **p** of the wind. Ec 2:11
is futile and a **p** of the wind. Ec 2:17
is futile and a **p** of the wind. Ec 2:26
is futile and a **p** of the wind. Ec 4:4
with effort and **p** of the wind. Ec 4:6
is futile and a **p** of the wind. Ec 4:16
is futile and a **p** of the wind. Ec 6:9
in the morning in **p** of beer, Is 5:11

PUSH *(3)*
Gehazi came to **p** her away, 2Kg 4:27
They **p** the needy off the road; Jb 24:4
They do not **p** each other; Jl 2:8

PUSHED *(7)*
He **p** with all his might, Jdg 16:30
You **p** me hard to make me fall, Ps 118:13
Since you have **p** with flank and Ezk 34:21
the basket and **p** the lead weight Zch 5:8
his neighbor **p** him away, Ac 7:27
to obey him, but **p** him away, and Ac 7:39
the Jews **p** him to the front. Ac 19:33

PUSHES *(2)*
anyone in hatred **p** a person or Nm 35:20
anyone suddenly **p** a person Nm 35:22

PUT *(802)*
(See also PUT proper noun.)
I will **p** hostility between you Gn 3:15
have decided to **p** an end to all Gn 6:13
You are to **p** a door in the side Gn 6:16
I **p** my slave in your arms, Gn 16:5
They **p** pressure on Lot and came Gn 19:9
⌊**p** them⌋ on Hagar's shoulders, Gn 21:14
master **p** me under this oath: Gn 24:37
So I **p** the ring on her nose Gn 24:47
She **p** the goatskins on his hands Gn 27:16
from the place, **p** it there at Gn 28:11
He **p** a three-day journey between Gn 30:36
apart and didn't **p** them with Gn 30:40
he did not **p** out the branches. Gn 30:42
Jacob got up and **p** his children Gn 31:17
p them in the saddlebag of the Gn 31:34
P it here before my relatives Gn 31:37
He **p** the female slaves first, Gn 33:2
p sackcloth around his waist, Gn 37:34
and the LORD **p** him to death. Gn 38:7
so He **p** him to death also. Gn 38:10
her veil and **p** her widow's Gn 38:19
one of them **p** out his hand, Gn 38:28
Potiphar also **p** him in charge of Gn 39:4
the time that he **p** him in charge Gn 39:5
and he has **p** all that he owns Gn 39:8
p Joseph's garment beside her Gn 39:16
The warden **p** all the prisoners Gn 39:22
and **p** them in custody in the Gn 40:3
You will **p** Pharaoh's cup in his Gn 40:13
they should **p** me in the dungeon. Gn 40:15
and he **p** me and the chief baker Gn 41:10
his hand and **p** it on Joseph's Gn 41:42
P him in my care, and I will Gn 42:37
P some of the best products of Gn 43:11
We don't know who **p** our money Gn 43:22
must have **p** treasure in your Gn 43:23
p each one's money at the top Gn 44:1
P my cup, the silver one, at the Gn 44:2
will **p** his hands on your eyes. Gn 46:4
p them in charge of my livestock. Gn 47:6
p your hand under my thigh ⌊and Gn 47:29
right hand and **p** it on the head Gn 48:14
p his left on Manasseh's head, Gn 48:14
P your right hand on his head." Gn 48:18
and you will **p** them on your sons Ex 3:22
"**P** your hand inside your cloak." Ex 4:6
So he **p** his hand inside his Ex 4:6
P your hand back inside your Ex 4:7
He **p** his hand back inside his Ex 4:7
wife and sons, **p** them on a Ex 4:20
wonders I have **p** within your Ex 4:21
and sought to **p** him to death. Ex 4:24
I will **p** My hand on Egypt and Ex 7:4
of the blood and **p** it on the two Ex 12:7
a container and **p** two quarts of Ex 16:33
but whenever he **p** his hand down, Ex 17:11
a stone and **p** ⌊it⌋ under him, Ex 17:12
p before them all these words Ex 19:7
P boundaries for the people all Ex 19:12
the mountain will be **p** to death. Ex 19:12
P a boundary around the mountain Ex 19:23
that he dies must be **p** to death. Ex 21:12
from My altar to be **p** to death. Ex 21:14

his mother must be **p** to death.	Ex 21:15
a person must be **p** to death,	Ex 21:16
his mother must be **p** to death.	Ex 21:17
owner must also be **p** to death.	Ex 21:29
an animal must be **p** to death.	Ex 22:19
P the ⌊tablets of the⌋ testimony	Ex 25:16
of the ark and **p** the testimony	Ex 25:21
P the bread of the Presence on	Ex 25:30
p the clasps through the loops	Ex 26:11
P the mercy seat on the ark of	Ex 26:34
p the table on the north side.	Ex 26:35
gold rings and **p** them at the two	Ex 28:26
P gold bells between them all	Ex 28:33
P these on your brother Aaron	Ex 28:41
p them in a basket, and bring	Ex 29:3
P the turban on his head and	Ex 29:6
and **p** it on Aaron's right	Ex 29:20
and **p** all of them in the hands	Ex 29:24
p these on opposite sides of it	Ex 30:4
the altar, and **p** water in it.	Ex 30:18
fine powder and **p** some in front	Ex 30:36
profanes it must be **p** to death.	Ex 31:14
Sabbath day must be **p** to death.	Ex 31:15
and didn't **p** on their jewelry.	Ex 33:4
I will **p** you in the crevice of	Ex 33:22
he **p** a veil over his face.	Ex 34:33
Then Moses would **p** the veil over	Ex 34:35
silver bases to **p** under the 20	Ex 36:24
⌊he **p** these⌋ on opposite sides	Ex 37:27
gold rings and **p** ⌊them⌋ at the	Ex 39:19
P the ark of the testimony there,	Ex 40:3
P up the screen for the entrance	Ex 40:5
the altar, and **p** water in it.	Ex 40:7
tabernacle and **p** the covering	Ex 40:19
p up the veil for the screen,	Ex 40:21
He also **p** the lampstand in the	Ex 40:24
He **p** up the screen at the	Ex 40:28
the altar and **p** water in it for	Ex 40:30
olive oil on it, **p** frankincense	Lv 2:1
are to **p** oil and frankincense	Lv 2:15
He must not **p** olive oil or	Lv 5:11
The priest is to **p** on his linen	Lv 6:10
his garments, **p** on other clothes	Lv 6:11
He **p** the tunic on Aaron, wrapped	Lv 8:7
the robe, and **p** the ephod on him	Lv 8:7
He **p** the woven band of the ephod	Lv 8:7
Then he **p** the breastpiece on him	Lv 8:8
He also **p** the turban on his head	Lv 8:9
and **p** ⌊it⌋ on Aaron's right	Lv 8:23
Aaron's sons and **p** some of the	Lv 8:24
He **p** all ⌊these⌋ in the hands of	Lv 8:27
his own firepan, **p** fire in it,	Lv 10:1
if water has been **p** on the seed	Lv 11:38
offering and **p** ⌊it⌋ on the lobe	Lv 14:14
the priest will **p** some on the	Lv 14:17
palm he is to **p** on the head of	Lv 14:18
offering and **p** ⌊it⌋ on the right	Lv 14:25
will also **p** some of the oil	Lv 14:28
palm he is to **p** on the head of	Lv 14:29
He is to **p** the incense on the	Lv 16:13
goat's blood and **p** ⌊it⌋ on the	Lv 16:18
He is to **p** them on the goat's	Lv 16:21
holy place and **p** on his clothes	Lv 16:24
He will **p** on the linen garments,	Lv 16:32
the deaf or **p** a stumbling block	Lv 19:14
or **p** on a garment made of two	Lv 19:19
They are not to be **p** to death,	Lv 19:20
for the dead or **p** tattoo marks	Lv 19:28
to Molech must be **p** to death;	Lv 20:2
and do not **p** him to death,	Lv 20:4
mother, he must be **p** to death.	Lv 20:9
adulteress must be **p** to death.	Lv 20:10
Both of them must be **p** to death;	Lv 20:11
both of them must be **p** to death.	Lv 20:12
They must be **p** to death;	Lv 20:13
animal, he must be **p** to death;	Lv 20:15
They must be **p** to death;	Lv 20:16
a spiritist must be **p** to death.	Lv 20:27
you may not **p** any of them on the	Lv 22:22
They **p** him in custody until the	Lv 24:12
of the LORD is to be **p** to death;	Lv 24:16
he is to be **p** to death, whether	Lv 24:16
anyone, he must be **p** to death.	Lv 24:17
a person is to be **p** to death.	Lv 24:21
I will **p** anxiety in the hearts	Lv 26:36
leaf will **p** them to flight,	Lv 26:36
ransomed; he must be **p** to death.	Lv 27:29
near ⌊it⌋ must be **p** to death.	Nm 1:51
sanctuary⌋ must be **p** to death."	Nm 3:10
near ⌊it⌋ was to be **p** to death.	Nm 3:38
of manatee skin and **p** ⌊them⌋ on	Nm 4:10
p ⌊them⌋ on a carrying frame.	Nm 4:12
oil over it or **p** frankincense on	Nm 5:15
floor and **p** ⌊it⌋ in the water.	Nm 5:17
and **p** ⌊it⌋ on the fire under the	Nm 6:18
and **p** ⌊them⌋ into the hands of	Nm 6:19
In this way they will **p** My name	Nm 6:27
who is on you and **p** ⌊the Spirit⌋	Nm 11:17
The man is to be **p** to death.	Nm 15:35
p a blue cord on the tassel at	Nm 15:38
in them and **p** incense on them	Nm 16:7
fire in it, **p** incense on it,	Nm 16:18
P Aaron's rod back in front of	Nm 17:10
that you may **p** an end to their	Nm 17:10
sanctuary⌋ will be **p** to death."	Nm 18:7
I have **p** you in charge of the	Nm 18:8
sin offering, ⌊**p** them⌋ in a jar,	Nm 19:17
garments and **p** them on his son	Nm 20:26
garments and **p** them on his son	Nm 20:28
Please come and **p** a curse on	Nm 22:6
Now come and **p** a curse on them	Nm 22:11
please come and **p** a curse on	Nm 22:17
Then the LORD **p** a message in	Nm 23:5
p a curse on Jacob for me;	Nm 23:7
p a curse on them for me."	Nm 23:13
with Balaam and **p** a message in	Nm 23:16
that you can **p** a curse on them	Nm 23:27
summoned you to **p** a curse on my	Nm 24:10
swears an oath to **p** himself	Nm 30:2
obligation she **p** herself under,	Nm 30:4
obligation she **p** herself under	Nm 30:4
obligations she **p** herself under	Nm 30:5
obligations she **p** herself under	Nm 30:7
or divorcée **p** herself under is	Nm 30:9
made a vow or **p** herself under	Nm 30:10
obligation she **p** herself under	Nm 30:11
withstand fire—**p** through fire,	Nm 31:23
withstand fire, **p** through the	Nm 31:23
the murderer must be **p** to death.	Nm 35:16
the murderer must be **p** to death.	Nm 35:17
the murderer must be **p** to death.	Nm 35:18
struck him must be **p** to death;	Nm 35:21
is to be **p** to death based	Nm 35:30
no one is to be **p** to death based	Nm 35:30
someone; he must be **p** to death.	Nm 35:31
each of you **p** on his weapons	Dt 1:41
I will begin to **p** the fear and	Dt 2:25
He will not **p** on you all the	Dt 7:15
your God will **p** fear and dread	Dt 11:25
your tribes to **p** His name for	Dt 12:5
God chooses to **p** His name is too	Dt 12:21
or dreamer must be **p** to death,	Dt 13:5
against him to **p** him to death,	Dt 13:9
God chooses to **p** His name is too	Dt 14:24
You are not to **p** the firstborn	Dt 15:19
is first ⌊**p**⌋ to the standing	Dt 16:9
I will **p** My words in his mouth,	Dt 18:18
a man is not to **p** on a woman's	Dt 22:5
but you must not **p** ⌊any⌋ in your	Dt 23:24
you must not **p** a sickle to your	Dt 23:25
are not to be **p** to death for	Dt 24:16
person will be **p** to death for	Dt 24:16
is giving you and **p** ⌊it⌋ in a	Dt 26:2
that He will **p** you far above all	Dt 26:19
who does not **p** the words of this	Dt 27:26
your God will **p** you far above	Dt 28:1
your God will **p** all these curses	Dt 30:7
or two **p** ten thousand to flight,	Dt 32:30
command him, will be **p** to death.	Jos 1:18
but they **p** the silver and gold	Jos 6:24
they all **p** dust on their heads.	Jos 7:6
p ⌊the things⌋ with their own	Jos 7:11
the city gate and **p** a large pile	Jos 8:29
Come here and **p** your feet on the	Jos 10:24
came forward and **p** their feet on	Jos 10:24
those the Israelites **p** to death,	Jos 13:22
so He **p** darkness between you and	Jos 24:7
They **p** the city to the sword and	Jdg 1:8
they **p** the town to the sword but	Jdg 1:25
bread, **p** it on this stone	Jdg 6:20
his case will be **p** to death by	Jdg 6:31
will **p** a fleece of wool here on	Jdg 6:37
all this and **p** it in Ophrah,	Jdg 8:27
up the branch, **p** it on his	Jdg 9:48
They **p** the branches against the	Jdg 9:49
The people **p** him over themselves	Jdg 11:11
and **p** a torch between each pair	Jdg 15:4
He **p** them on his shoulders and	Jdg 16:3
So the man **p** her on his donkey	Jdg 19:28
Gibeah so we can **p** them to death	Jdg 20:13
advanced and **p** the whole city to	Jdg 20:37
would certainly be **p** to death.	Jdg 21:5
Wash, **p** on ⌊perfumed⌋ oil, and	Ru 3:3
and **p** the gold objects in a box	1Sm 6:8
Then they **p** the ark of the LORD	1Sm 6:11
your sons and **p** them to his use	1Sm 8:11
own military clothes **p** on David.	1Sm 17:38
He **p** a bronze helmet on David's	1Sm 17:38
head and had him **p** on armor.	1Sm 17:38
the wadi and **p** them in the pouch	1Sm 17:40
David **p** his hand in the bag,	1Sm 17:49
he **p** Goliath's weapons in his	1Sm 17:54
Saul **p** him in command of the	1Sm 18:5
idol and **p** it on the bed,	1Sm 19:13
All of you, **p** on your swords!"	1Sm 25:13
all his men **p** on their swords	1Sm 25:13
Then they **p** his armor in the	1Sm 31:10
because he had **p** their brother	2Sm 3:30
your clothes, **p** on sackcloth,	2Sm 3:31
seized him and **p** him to death at	2Sm 4:10
of those⌋ to be **p** to death and	2Sm 8:2
P Uriah at the front of the	2Sm 11:15
he **p** Uriah in the place where he	2Sm 11:16
in the city and **p** ⌊them to work⌋	2Sm 12:31
Tamar **p** ashes on her head and	2Sm 13:19
She **p** her hand on her head and	2Sm 13:19
clothes and don't **p** on any oil.	2Sm 14:2
so we may **p** him to death for	2Sm 14:7
"Did Joab **p** you up to all this?"	2Sm 14:19
Shimei be **p** to death for this,	2Sm 19:21
and we cannot **p** anyone to death	2Sm 21:4
David **p** him in charge of his	2Sm 23:23
will be **p** to death today!	1Kg 2:24
I will not **p** you to death today,	1Kg 2:26
down Joab, and **p** him to death.	1Kg 2:34
and she **p** her dead son in my	1Kg 3:20
until the LORD **p** his enemies	1Kg 5:3
'I will **p** your son on your	1Kg 5:5
inside the temple to **p** the ark	1Kg 6:19
Then he **p** the cherubim inside	1Kg 6:27
p the reservoir near the right	1Kg 7:39
and **p** them in the treasuries of	1Kg 7:51
that Moses had **p** there at Horeb,	1Kg 8:9
to **p** My name there forever;	1Kg 9:3
King Solomon **p** together a fleet	1Kg 9:26
in you and **p** you on the throne	1Kg 10:9
The king **p** them in the House of	1Kg 10:17
that God had **p** in his heart.	1Kg 10:24
for Myself to **p** My name there.	1Kg 11:36
and the heavy yoke he **p** on us,	1Kg 12:4
the yoke your father **p** on us'?"	1Kg 12:9
in Bethel, and **p** the other in	1Kg 12:29
tribes of Israel to **p** His name.	1Kg 14:21
royal palace and **p** it into the	1Kg 15:18
over to Ahab to **p** me to death?	1Kg 18:9
the ground and **p** his face	1Kg 18:42
Jehu will **p** to death whoever	1Kg 19:17
and Elisha will **p** to death	1Kg 19:17
So let's **p** sackcloth around our	1Kg 20:31
p sackcloth over his body,	1Kg 21:27
the LORD has **p** a lying spirit	1Kg 22:23
P this guy in prison and feed	1Kg 22:27
carried him away and **p** him on	2Kg 2:16
me a new bowl and **p** salt in it."	2Kg 2:20
small room upstairs and **p** a bed,	2Kg 4:10
he **p** mouth to mouth, eye to eye,	2Kg 4:34
P on the large pot and make stew	2Kg 4:38
his garment and **p** it under Jehu	2Kg 9:13
slaughtered all 70, **p** their	2Kg 10:7
being killed and ⌊**p**⌋ him and his	2Kg 11:2
with them and **p** them under oath.	2Kg 11:4
the ranks is to be **p** to death.	2Kg 11:8
the king's son, **p** the crown on	2Kg 11:12
and **p** anyone who follows her to	2Kg 11:15
She is not to be **p** to death in	2Kg 11:15
where she was **p** to death.	2Kg 11:16
for they had **p** Athaliah to death	2Kg 11:20
the threshold **p** all the money	2Kg 12:9
Then they would **p** the counted	2Kg 12:11
king of Israel, "**P** your hand on	2Kg 13:16
So the king **p** his hand on it,	2Kg 13:16
and Elisha **p** his hands on the	2Kg 13:16
you have **p** an end to them."	2Kg 13:17
until you had **p** an end to them,	2Kg 13:19

he did not **p** the children of the 2Kg 14:6
must not be **p** to death because 2Kg 14:6
must not be **p** to death because 2Kg 14:6
one will be **p** to death for his 2Kg 14:6
and they **p** him to death there. 2Kg 14:19
to Kir but **p** Rezin to death. 2Kg 16:9
and **p** it on the north side of 2Kg 16:14
under it and **p** it on a stone 2Kg 16:17
him and **p** him in prison. 2Kg 17:4
to Assyria and **p** them in Halah 2Kg 18:11
I am about to **p** a spirit in him, 2Kg 19:7
will **p** My hook in your nose and 2Kg 19:28
'**P** your affairs in order, for 2Kg 20:1
is where I will **p** My name." 2Kg 21:4
It is to be **p** into the hands of 2Kg 22:5
for the money **p** into their hands 2Kg 22:7
temple and have **p** it into the 2Kg 22:9
king of Babylon **p** them to death 2Kg 25:21
sight, so He **p** him to death. 1Ch 2:3
God of Israel **p** it into the mind 1Ch 5:26
are the men David **p** in charge of 1Ch 6:31
Others were **p** in charge of the 1Ch 9:29
Then they **p** his armor in the 1Ch 10:10
So the LORD **p** him to death and 1Ch 10:14
David **p** him in charge of his 1Ch 11:25
and **p** to flight all ⌊those in⌋ 1Ch 12:15
He **p** garrisons in Edom, and all 1Ch 18:13
were in it and **p** them to work 1Ch 20:3
and he **p** his sword back into its 1Ch 21:27
but he **p** the bronze altar, 2Ch 1:5
sanctuary and also **p** it on top 2Ch 3:16
washing and he **p** five on the 2Ch 4:6
specifications and **p** them in the 2Ch 4:7
He **p** the reservoir on the right 2Ch 4:10
tables on which ⌊to **p**⌋ the bread 2Ch 4:19
and **p** them in the treasuries of 2Ch 5:1
that Moses had **p** ⌊in it⌋ at 2Ch 5:10
have **p** the ark there, where the 2Ch 6:11
feet high and **p** it in the court. 2Ch 6:13
You said You would **p** Your name; 2Ch 6:20
in you and **p** you on his throne 2Ch 9:8
The king **p** them in the House of 2Ch 9:16
wisdom God had **p** in his heart. 2Ch 9:23
and the heavy yoke he **p** on us, 2Ch 10:4
the yoke your father **p** on us'?" 2Ch 10:9
and **p** leaders in them 2Ch 11:11
He also **p** large shields and 2Ch 11:12
tribes of Israel to **p** His name. 2Ch 12:13
of Israel would be **p** to death, 2Ch 15:13
the seer and **p** him in prison 2Ch 16:10
the LORD has **p** a lying spirit 2Ch 18:22
P this guy in prison and feed 2Ch 18:26
The LORD **p** it into the mind of 2Ch 21:16
being killed and **p** him and his 2Ch 22:11
the temple is to be **p** to death. 2Ch 23:7
the king's son, **p** the crown on 2Ch 23:11
and **p** anyone who follows her to 2Ch 23:14
Don't **p** her to death in the 2Ch 23:14
where they **p** her to death. 2Ch 23:15
Then Jehoiada **p** the oversight of 2Ch 23:18
for they had **p** Athaliah to death 2Ch 23:21
and **p** it in the chest until it 2Ch 24:10
he did not **p** their children to 2Ch 25:4
and they **p** him to death there. 2Ch 25:27
the goats and **p** their blood on 2Ch 29:24
against him and **p** him to death 2Ch 33:24
p it into the hands of those 2Ch 34:10
temple and have **p** it into the 2Ch 34:17
P the holy ark in the temple 2Ch 35:3
to Babylon and **p** them in his 2Ch 36:7
The LORD **p** it into the mind of 2Ch 36:22
and also ⌊to **p** it⌋ in writing: 2Ch 36:22
The LORD **p** it into the mind of Ezr 1:1
and ⌊to **p** it⌋ in writing: Ezr 1:1
p them in the temple in Ezr 5:15
and **p** into the house of God. Ezr 6:5
has **p** it into the king's mind Ezr 7:27
Then I **p** my brother Hanani in Neh 7:2
Then my God **p** it into my mind to Neh 7:5
⌊and had **p**⌋ dust on their heads. Neh 9:1
the priest had been **p** in charge Neh 13:4
⌊**P** them⌋ under the care of Hegai, Est 2:3
tore his clothes, **p** on sackcloth Est 4:1
P the garment and the horse Est 6:9
and Esther **p** him in charge of Est 8:2
The Jews **p** all their enemies to Est 9:5
sigh when food is ⌊**p**⌋ before me, Jb 3:24
and **p** him to the test every Jb 7:18

your babbling **p** others to Jb 11:3
releases the bonds **p** on by kings Jb 12:18
Why do I **p** myself at risk and Jb 13:14
You **p** my feet in the stocks and Jb 13:27
Let him not **p** trust in worthless Jb 15:31
arrangements! **P** up security for Jb 17:3
the lamp beside him is **p** out. Jb 18:6
p ⌊your⌋ hand over ⌊your⌋ mouth. Jb 21:5
is the lamp of the wicked **p** out? Jb 21:17
have refused to **p** with my sheep Jb 30:1
p Him in charge of the entire Jb 34:13
If He **p** His mind to it and Jb 34:14
its boundaries and **p** ⌊its⌋ bars Jb 38:10
p wisdom in the heart or gave Jb 38:36
you **p** a cord through his nose Jb 41:2
like a bird or **p** him on a leash Jb 41:5
You have **p** more joy in my heart Ps 4:7
You **p** everything under his feet: Ps 8:6
P terror in them, LORD; let the Ps 9:20
p the arrow on the bowstring Ps 11:2
I will **p** in a safe place the one Ps 12:5
you will **p** them to flight when Ps 21:12
You **p** me into the dust of death. Ps 22:15
do not let me be **p** to shame, Ps 25:20
all you who **p** your hope in the Ps 31:24
LORD, for we **p** our hope in You Ps 33:22
those who **p** their hope in the Ps 37:9
I **p** my hope in You, LORD; Ps 38:15
He **p** a new song in my mouth, Ps 40:3
and **p** their trust in the LORD. Ps 40:3
the man who has **p** his trust in Ps 40:4
P your hope in God, for I will Ps 42:5
P your hope in God, for I will Ps 42:11
P your hope in God, for I will Ps 43:5
I will **p** my hope in Your name, Ps 52:9
will **p** them to shame, for God Ps 53:5
P my tears in Your bottle. Ps 56:8
let those who **p** their hope in Ps 69:6
Indeed You **p** them in slippery Ps 73:18
that they might **p** their Ps 78:7
Let them be **p** to shame and Ps 83:17
will see and be **p** to shame Ps 86:17
You have **p** me in the lowest part Ps 88:6
in idols, will be **p** to shame. Ps 97:7
neck was **p** in an iron collar. Ps 105:18
in order to **p** them to death. Ps 109:16
up, they will be **p** to shame, but Ps 109:28
answered me ⌊and **p** me⌋ in a Ps 118:5
LORD, do not **p** me to shame. Ps 119:31
for I **p** my hope in Your word. Ps 119:74
the arrogant be **p** to shame for Ps 119:78
that I will not be **p** to shame. Ps 119:80
I **p** my hope in Your word. Ps 119:81
I **p** my hope in Your word. Ps 119:114
I **p** my hope in Your word. Ps 119:147
will never be **p** to shame when Ps 127:5
and **p** my hope in His word. Ps 130:5
Israel, **p** your hope in the LORD. Ps 130:7
Israel, **p** your hope in the LORD, Ps 131:3
those who **p** their hope in His Ps 147:11
if you have **p** up security for Pr 6:1
for you have **p** yourself in your Pr 6:3
for he has **p** up security for a Pr 20:16
who **p** up security for loans. Pr 22:26
of the wicked will be **p** out. Pr 24:20
for he has **p** up security for a Pr 27:13
p your hand over your mouth. Pr 30:32
He has also **p** eternity in their Ec 3:11
and **p** away pain from your flesh, Ec 11:10
How can I **p** it back on? I have Sg 5:3
my desire **p** me ⌊among⌋ the Sg 6:12
P no more trust in man, who has Is 2:22
the Lord will **p** scabs on the Is 3:17
and a toddler will **p** his hand Is 11:8
I will **p** an end to the pride of Is 13:11
I have **p** an end to the shouting. Is 16:10
p an end to all her groaning. Is 21:2
I will **p** your authority into his Is 22:21
The moon will be **p** to shame and Is 24:23
and they will be **p** to shame. Is 26:11
destruction and to **p** a bridle on Is 30:28
men will be **p** to forced labor. Is 31:8
bare and **p** ⌊sackcloth⌋ about Is 32:11
if you can **p** riders on them! Is 36:8
his clothes, **p** on sackcloth, Is 37:1
will **p** My hook in your nose and Is 37:29
'**P** your affairs in order, for Is 38:1
I will **p** cypress trees in the Is 41:19

I have **p** My Spirit on Him; Is 42:1
and He will not **p** out a Is 42:3
so they will be **p** to shame. Is 44:9
worshipers will be **p** to shame, Is 44:11
will be startled and **p** to shame. Is 44:11
All of them are **p** to shame, Is 45:16
you will not be **p** to shame or Is 45:17
come to Him and be **p** to shame. Is 45:24
I will **p** salvation in Zion, Is 46:13
and **p** them on as a bride does. Is 49:18
those who **p** their hope in Me Is 49:23
in Me will not be **p** to shame. Is 49:23
your mother was **p** away because Is 50:1
I know I will not be **p** to shame. Is 50:7
coastlands will **p** their hope in Is 51:5
P on the strength of the LORD's Is 51:9
I have **p** My words in your mouth, Is 51:16
I will **p** it into the hands of Is 51:23
p on your strength, Zion! Is 52:1
P on your beautiful garments, Is 52:1
for you will not be **p** to shame; Is 54:4
He **p** on righteousness like a Is 59:17
p on garments of vengeance for Is 59:17
that I have **p** in your mouth, Is 59:21
is He who **p** His Holy Spirit Is 63:11
but you will be **p** to shame. Is 65:13
But they will be **p** to shame." Is 66:5
to Tarshish, **P**, Lud (who are Is 66:19
of Israel has been **p** to shame. Jr 2:26
You will be **p** to shame by Egypt Jr 2:36
just as you were **p** to shame by Jr 2:36
Because of this, **p** on sackcloth; Jr 4:8
The wise will be **p** to shame; Jr 8:9
goldsmith is **p** to shame by ⌊his Jr 10:14
Be **p** to shame by your harvests Jr 12:13
yourself linen underwear and **p** Jr 13:1
the LORD instructed me and **p** it Jr 13:2
We therefore **p** our hope in You, Jr 14:22
abandon You will be **p** to shame. Jr 17:13
my persecutors be **p** to shame, Jr 17:18
but don't let me be **p** to shame. Jr 17:18
beaten and **p** him in the stocks Jr 20:2
to Babylon and **p** them to the Jr 20:4
He will **p** them to the sword; Jr 21:7
that if you **p** me to death, Jr 26:15
people of⌋ Judah **p** him to death? Jr 26:19
king tried to **p** him to death. Jr 26:21
to the people to be **p** to death. Jr 26:24
for yourself and **p** them on your Jr 27:2
nation that will **p** its neck Jr 27:11
P your necks under the yoke of Jr 27:12
have **p** an iron yoke on the neck Jr 28:14
I have also **p** the wild animals Jr 28:14
and **p** them in an earthen storage Jr 32:14
and I will **p** fear of Me in their Jr 32:40
they had not ⌊yet⌋ **p** him into Jr 37:4
that you have **p** me in prison? Jr 37:18
had been **p** into the cistern Jr 38:7
Zedekiah and **p** him in bronze Jr 39:7
and that he had **p** him in charge Jr 40:7
the Chaldeans to **p** us to death Jr 43:3
Polish the lances; **p** on armor! Jr 46:4
Egypt will be **p** to shame, Jr 46:24
Kiriathaim will be **p** to shame; Jr 48:1
The fortress will be **p** to shame Jr 48:1
Moab will be **p** to shame because Jr 48:13
of Israel was **p** to shame because Jr 48:13
Moab is **p** to shame, indeed Jr 48:20
Hamath and Arpad are **p** to shame, Jr 49:23
Bel is **p** to shame; Marduk Jr 50:2
her idols are **p** to shame; Jr 50:2
who bore you will be **p** to shame. Jr 50:12
living in Pekod. **P** them to the Jr 50:21
P all her young bulls to the Jr 50:27
don't let him **p** on his armor. Jr 51:3
The LORD has **p** it into the mind Jr 51:11
goldsmith is **p** to shame by ⌊his Jr 51:17
king of Babylon **p** them to death Jr 52:27
their heads and **p** on sackcloth. Lm 2:10
I will **p** my hope in Him. Lm 3:24
him **p** his mouth in the dust— Lm 3:29
and I **p** a stumbling block in Ezk 3:20
will **p** ropes on you and bind Ezk 3:25
that I will **p** cords on you so Ezk 4:8
P them in a single container and Ezk 4:9
They will **p** on sackcloth, and Ezk 7:18
I will **p** an end to the pride of Ezk 7:24
and **p** a mark on the foreheads of Ezk 9:4

and **p** ⌊it⌋ into the hands of the Ezk 10:7
slain you have **p** within it are Ezk 11:7
one heart and **p** a new spirit Ezk 11:19
I will **p** a stop to this proverb, Ezk 12:23
of whitewash that you **p** on ⌊it⌋? Ezk 13:12
hearts and have **p** sinful Ezk 14:3
it is **p** into the fire as fuel. Ezk 15:4
p a ring in your nose, earrings Ezk 16:12
seed and **p** it in a fertile Ezk 17:5
of the king who **p** him on the Ezk 17:16
They **p** a wooden yoke on him with Ezk 19:9
wilderness to **p** an end to them. Ezk 20:13
to be **p** in the hand of the Ezk 21:11
has come to **p** you to the necks Ezk 21:29
anger and wrath, **p** you ⌊inside⌋, Ezk 22:20
So I will **p** an end to your Ezk 23:27
I will **p** her cup in your hand. Ezk 23:31
They **p** bracelets on the women's Ezk 23:42
So I will **p** an end to indecency Ezk 23:48
P the pot on ⌊the fire⌋—put Ezk 24:3
on ⌊the fire⌋—**p** ⌊it⌋ on, and Ezk 24:3
She **p** it out on the bare rock; Ezk 24:7
I have **p** her blood on the bare Ezk 24:8
P on your turban and strap your Ezk 24:17
I will **p** an end to the noise of Ezk 26:13
I will **p** hooks in your jaws and Ezk 29:4
I will **p** an end to the hordes of Ezk 30:10
the idols and **p** an end to the Ezk 30:13
and no splint **p** on to bandage it Ezk 30:21
I will **p** your flesh on the Ezk 32:5
will **p** forth your branches and Ezk 36:8
a new heart and **p** a new spirit Ezk 36:26
I will **p** tendons on you, make Ezk 37:6
I will **p** breath in you so that Ezk 37:6
I will **p** My Spirit in you, Ezk 37:14
and **p** them together with the Ezk 37:19
turn you around, **p** hooks in your Ezk 38:4
They are to **p** on other clothes Ezk 42:14
They are not to **p** on ⌊anything Ezk 44:18
P away violence and oppression Ezk 45:9
P an end to your evictions of My Ezk 45:9
p the vessels in the treasury Dn 1:2
an end, to **p** a stop to sin, to Dn 9:24
the week he will **p** a stop to Dn 9:27
and I didn't **p** any oil ⌊on my Dn 10:3
a commander will **p** an end to his Dn 11:18
house of Jehu and **p** an end to Hs 1:4
I will **p** an end to all her Hs 2:11
p on her rings and jewelry, Hs 2:13
⌊**P**⌋ the horn to your mouth! Hs 8:1
them to **p** them in bondage Hs 10:10
and always **p** your hope in God. Hs 12:6
will never again be **p** to shame. Jl 2:26
will never again be **p** to shame. Jl 2:27
his royal robe, **p** on sackcloth, Jnh 3:6
They will **p** ⌊their⌋ hands over Mc 7:16
you will not be **p** to shame Zph 3:11
You **p** on clothes but never have Hg 1:6
Let them **p** a clean turban on his Zch 3:5
and they will **p** horsemen to Zch 10:5
they will not **p** on a hairy cloak Zch 13:4
I will **p** this third through the Zch 13:9
when you fast, **p** oil on your Mt 6:17
But they **p** new wine into fresh Mt 9:17
the crowd had been **p** outside, Mt 9:25
and have them **p** to death. Mt 10:21
I will **p** My Spirit on Him, Mt 12:18
and He will not **p** out a Mt 12:20
The nations will **p** their hope in Mt 12:21
vacant, swept, and **p** in order. Mt 12:44
and **p** him in prison on account Mt 14:3
or mother must be **p** to death. Mt 15:4
They **p** them at His feet, and He Mt 15:30
How long must I **p** up with you? Mt 17:17
Him so He might **p** His hands on Mt 19:13
'These last men **p** in one hour, Mt 20:12
a vineyard, **p** a fence around it Mt 21:33
hand until I **p** Your enemies Mt 22:44
to carry and **p** them on people's Mt 23:4
master has **p** in charge of his Mt 24:45
He will **p** him in charge of all Mt 24:47
talents went, **p** them to work, Mt 25:16
I will **p** you in charge of many Mt 25:21
I will **p** you in charge of many Mt 25:23
will **p** the sheep on His right, Mt 25:33
P your sword back in place Mt 26:52
so they could **p** Him to death. Mt 26:59
against Jesus to **p** Him to death. Mt 27:1

not lawful to **p** it into the Mt 27:6
of thorns, **p** it on His head, Mt 27:29
Him of the robe, **p** His clothes Mt 27:31
His head they **p** up the charge Mt 27:37
He has **p** His trust in God; Mt 27:43
brought in to be **p** under a Mk 4:21
Isn't it to be **p** on a lampstand? Mk 4:21
but He **p** them all outside. Mk 5:40
but not **p** on an extra shirt. Mk 6:9
or mother must be **p** to death. Mk 7:10
How long must I **p** up with you? Mk 9:19
a vineyard, **p** a fence around it Mk 12:1
hand until I **p** Your enemies Mk 12:36
poor widow has **p** in more than Mk 12:43
her poverty has **p** in everything Mk 12:44
parents and **p** them to death. Mk 13:12
against Jesus to **p** Him to death, Mk 14:55
of thorns, and **p** it on Him. Mk 15:17
the purple robe, **p** His clothes Mk 15:20
See the place where they **p** Him. Mk 16:6
and asked him to **p** out a little Lk 5:3
P out into deep water and let Lk 5:4
new wine should be **p** into fresh Lk 5:38
I be with you and **p** up with you? Lk 9:41
Then he **p** him on his own animal, Lk 10:34
the house⌋ swept and **p** in order. Lk 11:25
his master will **p** in charge of Lk 12:42
he will **p** him in charge of all Lk 12:44
the best robe and **p** it on him; Lk 15:22
p a ring on his finger and Lk 15:22
why didn't you **p** my money in the Lk 19:23
poor widow has **p** in more than Lk 21:3
these people have **p** in gifts out Lk 21:4
her poverty has **p** in all she had Lk 21:4
As soon as they **p** out ⌊leaves⌋ Lk 21:30
for a way to **p** Him to death, Lk 22:2
have a man to **p** me into the pool Jn 5:7
"He **p** mud on my eyes," he told Jn 9:15
"Where have you **p** him?" He asked Jn 11:34
steal part of what was **p** in it. Jn 12:6
had already **p** it into the heart Jn 13:2
their feet and **p** on His robe, Jn 13:12
for us to **p** anyone to death, Jn 18:31
of thorns, **p** it on His head, Jn 19:2
lettered and **p** on the cross. Jn 19:19
know where they have **p** Him!" Jn 20:2
don't know where they've **p** Him." Jn 20:13
tell me where you've **p** Him, Jn 20:15
p my finger into the mark of the Jn 20:25
and **p** my hand into His side, Jn 20:25
P your finger here and observe Jn 20:27
your hand and **p** it into My side Jn 20:27
them and **p** them in custody Ac 4:3
apostles and **p** them in the city Ac 5:18
The men you **p** in jail are Ac 5:25
and women, and **p** them in prison. Ac 8:3
he **p** him in prison and assigned Ac 12:4
him, "and **p** on your sandals. Ac 12:8
about 40 years He **p** up with them Ac 13:18
the tree and **p** Him in a tomb. Ac 13:29
to **p** no greater burden on you Ac 15:28
he **p** them into the inner prison Ac 16:24
for me to **p** up with you Jews. Ac 18:14
mounts so they can **p** Paul on Ac 23:24
When they were **p** to death, Ac 26:10
Adramyttium, we **p** to sea, Ac 27:2
The next day we **p** in at Sidon, Ac 27:3
When we had **p** out to sea from Ac 27:4
for Italy and **p** us on board. Ac 27:6
they were going to **p** out anchors Ac 27:30
brushwood and **p** it on the fire, Ac 28:3
you also were **p** to death in Rm 7:4
by the Spirit you **p** to death the Rm 8:13
on Him will not be **p** to shame. Rm 9:33
on Him will be **p** to shame, Rm 10:11
darkness and **p** on the armor of Rm 13:12
But **p** on the Lord Jesus Christ, Rm 13:14
decide not to **p** a stumbling Rm 14:13
P away the evil person from 1Co 5:13
Why not rather **p** up with 1Co 6:7
not to **p** a restraint on you, 1Co 7:35
God has **p** the body together, 1Co 12:24
I **p** aside childish things. 1Co 13:11
He has **p** everything under His 1Co 15:27
"everything" is **p** under Him, 1Co 15:27
who used to **p** a veil over his 2Co 3:13
longing to **p** on our house from 2Co 5:2
be to God who **p** the same 2Co 8:16

wish you would **p** up with a 2Co 11:1
from me. Yes, do **p** up with me. 2Co 11:1
you **p** up with it splendidly! 2Co 11:4
For you gladly **p** up with fools 2Co 11:19
you **p** up with it if someone 2Co 11:20
into Christ have **p** on Christ. Gl 3:27
we who had already **p** our hope in Eph 1:12
And He **p** everything under His Eph 1:22
the cross and **p** the hostility to Eph 2:16
you **p** on the new man, the one Eph 4:24
Since you **p** away lying, Speak Eph 4:25
P on the full armor of God so Eph 6:11
and do not **p** confidence in the Php 3:3
p to death whatever in you is Col 3:5
But now you must also **p** away all Col 3:8
since you have **p** off the old man Col 3:9
and have **p** on the new man, Col 3:10
p on heartfelt compassion, Col 3:12
Above all, ⌊**p** on⌋ love—the Col 3:14
must be sober and **p** the armor of 1Th 5:8
and **p** on a helmet of the hope of 1Th 5:8
because we have **p** our hope in 1Tm 4:10
has **p** her hope in God and 1Tm 5:5
I will **p** My laws into their Heb 8:10
will **p** My laws on their hearts, Heb 10:16
and **p** foreign armies to flight. Heb 11:34
Now when we **p** bits into the Jms 3:3
in Him will never be **p** to shame! 1Pt 2:6
life will be **p** to shame. 1Pt 3:16
after being **p** to death in the 1Pt 3:18
I do not **p** any other burden on Rv 2:24
He **p** his right foot on the sea, Rv 10:2
bodies to be **p** into a tomb. Rv 11:9
For God has **p** it into their Rv 17:17
and **p** a seal on it so that he Rv 20:3

PUT (proper noun) *(7)*
Cush, Egypt, **P**, and Canaan. Gn 10:6
Cush, Mizraim, **P**, and Canaan. 1Ch 1:8
Cush and **P**, who are able to Jr 46:9
Persia, Lud, and **P** were in your Ezk 27:10
Cush, **P**, and Lud, and all the Ezk 30:5
Cush, and **P** are with them, Ezk 38:5
P and Libya were among her Nah 3:9

PUTEOLI *(1)*
and the second day we came to **P**. Ac 28:13

PUTHITES *(1)*
Ithrites, **P**, Shumathites, and 1Ch 2:53

PUTIEL *(1)*
daughters of **P** and she bore him Ex 6:25

PUTS *(32)*
something like it or **p** some of Ex 30:33
the message God **p** in my mouth." Nm 22:38
what the LORD **p** in my mouth?" Nm 23:12
to the LORD or **p** ⌊herself⌋ under Nm 30:3
and she **p** out her hand and grabs Dt 25:11
'Let not him who **p** on his armor 1Kg 20:11
when He **p** you in charge 1Ch 22:12
God **p** no trust in His servants Jb 4:18
If God **p** no trust in His holy Jb 15:15
miner **p** an end to the darkness; Jb 28:3
He **p** my feet in the stocks; Jb 33:11
p the depths into storehouses. Ps 33:7
If someone **p** up security for a Pr 11:15
agreement and **p** up security for Pr 17:18
A wicked man **p** on a bold face, Pr 21:29
for calmness **p** great offenses to Ec 10:4
p a sinful stumbling block Ezk 14:4
the one who **p** nothing in their Mc 3:5
The wage earner ⌊**p** his⌋ wages Hg 1:6
a lamp and **p** it under a basket Mt 5:15
And no one **p** new wine into old Mt 9:17
And no one **p** new wine into old Mk 2:22
a new garment and **p** it on an old Lk 5:36
And no one **p** new wine into old Lk 5:37
a basket or **p** it under a bed, Lk 8:16
but **p** it on a lampstand so that Lk 8:16
No one who **p** his hand to the Lk 9:62
a lamp and **p** it in the cellar Lk 11:33
he joyfully **p** it on his Lk 15:5
reign until He **p** all His enemies 1Co 15:25
that He who **p** everything under 1Co 15:27
who always **p** us on display in 2Co 2:14

PUTTING *(29)*
p Ephraim before Manasseh. Gn 48:20
p a sword in their hand to kill Ex 5:21
be the first in **p** him to death, Dt 17:7
its trees by **p** an ax to them, Dt 20:19

p everyone in it to the sword, Jos 10:30
p everyone in it to the sword, Jos 10:32
p everyone in it to the sword. Jos 10:35
them down, p them to death. Jos 11:17
against him by p people on the Jdg 9:25
prepared to leave, p their small Jdg 18:21
and for p a point on an oxgoad. 1Sm 13:21
himself by p on different 1Sm 28:8
their own gods and p them in the 2Kg 17:29
I am tired of p up with ⌊them⌋. Is 1:14
I am p a spirit in him and he Is 37:7
and p polluted broth in their Is 65:4
even p the branch to their nose? Ezk 8:17
in his heart and p a sinful Ezk 14:7
p bracelets on your wrists and a Ezk 16:11
with him, p him under oath. Ezk 17:13
After p His hands on them, Mt 19:15
After p His fingers in the man's Mk 7:33
people were p in large sums. Mk 12:41
Saul agreed with p him to death. Ac 8:1
God by p on the disciples' Ac 15:10
binding and p both men and women Ac 22:4
P in at Syracuse, we stayed Ac 28:12
am p a stone in Zion to stumble Rm 9:33
by p off the body of flesh, Col 2:11

PUVAH *(2)*
Tola, P, Jashub, and Shimron. Gn 46:13
the Punite clan from P; Nm 26:23

PUZZLES *(1)*
gods and that no mystery p you, Dn 4:9

PYRE *(1)*
His funeral p is deep and wide, Is 30:33

PYRRHUS *(1)*
Sopater, son of P, from Beroea, Ac 20:4

Q

QEDEMITES *(3)*
Amalekites, and Q gathered Jdg 6:33
and all the Q had settled down Jdg 7:12
of the entire army of the Q. Jdg 8:10

QESITAH *(1)*
one gave him a q , and a gold Jb 42:11

QESITAHS *(2)*
father, for 100 q, where he had Gn 33:19
Shechem's father, for 100 q . Jos 24:32

QUAIL *(4)*
So at evening q came and covered Ex 16:13
up and blew q in from the sea Nm 11:31
the next day gathering the q— Nm 11:32
and He brought q and satisfied Ps 105:40

QUAKE *(10)*
the mountains q with its turmoil Ps 46:3
the cherubim. Let the earth q. Ps 99:1
mountains would q at Your Is 64:1
of their fall the earth will q; Jr 49:21
conquest the earth will q; Jr 50:46
coasts and islands q at the Ezk 26:15
made the nations q at the sound Ezk 31:16
won't the land q and all who Am 8:8
The mountains q before Him, Nah 1:5
the earth—so great was the q. Rv 16:18

QUAKED *(6)*
Then the earth shook and q; 2Sm 22:8
Then the earth shook and q; Ps 18:7
The earth shook and q. Ps 77:18
the mountains q, and their Is 5:25
the mountains q at Your presence Is 64:3
the earth q and the rocks were Mt 27:51

QUAKES *(4)*
mighty steeds, the whole land q. Jr 8:16
earth q at His wrath, and the Jr 10:10
earth q and trembles, because Jr 51:29
The earth q before them; Jl 2:10

QUAKING *(1)*
the mountains, and they were q; Jr 4:24

QUALIFIED *(8)*
everyone who is q to do work at Nm 4:3
everyone who is q to perform Nm 4:23
everyone who is q to do the work Nm 4:30
everyone who was q for work at Nm 4:35
everyone who was q for work at Nm 4:39
everyone who was q for work at Nm 4:43
everyone who was q to do the Nm 4:47
select the most q of your 2Kg 10:3

QUALITIES *(1)*
For if these q are yours and are 2Pt 1:8

QUALITY *(2)*
will test the q of each one's 1Co 3:13
the imperishable q of a gentle 1Pt 3:4

QUANTITIES *(2)*
also took huge q of bronze from 2Sm 8:8
also took huge q of bronze, 1Ch 18:8

QUANTITY *(11)*
produce the same q of bricks." Ex 5:18
and a large q of clothing. Jos 22:8
took away a large q of plunder 2Sm 12:30
of gold, a great q of spices, 1Kg 10:10
did such a q of spices arrive 1Kg 10:10
Ophir a large q of almug wood 1Kg 10:11
took away a large q of plunder 1Ch 20:2
an immeasurable q of bronze, 1Ch 22:3
brought a large q of cedar logs 1Ch 22:4
stones, and a great q of marble. 1Ch 29:2
of gold, a great q of spices, 2Ch 9:9

QUARANTINE *(10)*
the priest must q the infected Lv 13:4
priest must q him for another Lv 13:5
He need not q him, for he is Lv 13:11
priest must q him seven days. Lv 13:21
priest must q him seven days. Lv 13:26
priest must q the person with Lv 13:31
the priest must q the person who Lv 13:33
and q the contaminated Lv 13:50
its doorway and q the house for Lv 14:38
lived in q with a serious skin 2Ch 26:21

QUARANTINED *(1)*
to be washed and q for another Lv 13:54

QUARANTINES *(1)*
days the priest q it will be Lv 14:46

QUARREL *(6)*
he named the well Q because they Gn 26:20
and they did not q over it. Gn 26:22
When men q and one strikes the Ex 21:18
fool can get himself into a q. Pr 20:3
meddles in a q that's not his Pr 26:17
The Lord's slave must not q, 2Tm 2:24

QUARRELED *(6)*
herdsmen of Gerar q with Isaac's Gn 26:20
Quarrel because they q with him. Gn 26:20
another well and q over that one Gn 26:21
people q with Moses and said, Nm 20:3
the Israelites q with the LORD, Nm 20:13
the community q in the Nm 27:14

QUARRELING *(5)*
and there was q between the Gn 13:7
let's not have q between you and Gn 13:8
not in q and jealousy. Rm 13:13
there may be q, jealousy, 2Co 12:20
come envy, q, slanders, evil 1Tm 6:4

QUARRELS *(5)*
the lot ends q and separates Pr 18:18
and q are like the bars of a Pr 18:19
that there are q among you. 1Co 1:11
knowing that they breed q. 2Tm 2:23
genealogies, q, and disputes Ti 3:9

QUARRELSOME *(3)*
schemes of men, from q tongues. Ps 31:20
so is a q man for kindling Pr 26:21
but gentle, not q, not greedy— 1Tm 3:3

QUARRIED *(4)*
q ⌊the stone⌋ and prepared the 1Kg 5:18
buy timber and q stone to repair 2Kg 12:12
buy timber and q stone to repair 2Kg 22:6
used it⌋ to buy q stone and 2Ch 34:11

QUARRIES *(2)*
from outside the gate to the q, Jos 7:5
The one who q stones may be hurt Ec 10:9

QUARRY *(3)*
king commanded them to q large, 1Kg 5:17
cut at the q so that no hammer 1Kg 6:7
and to the q from which you were Is 51:1

QUART *(14)*
with one q of crushed olive Ex 29:40
drink offering of one q of wine. Ex 29:40
one-third of a q of olive oil. Lv 14:10
the one-third q of olive oil, Lv 14:12
one-third of a q of olive oil Lv 14:15
one-third of a q of olive oil, Lv 14:21
one-third of a q of olive oil, Lv 14:24
offering will be one q of wine. Lv 23:13
flour mixed with a q of oil. Nm 15:4
Prepare a q of wine as a drink Nm 15:5
mixed with a q of beaten olive Nm 28:5
is to be a q with each lamb. Nm 28:7
and one q with each male lamb. Nm 28:14
A q of wheat for a denarius, Rv 6:6

QUARTER *(18)*
as much (six and a q pounds) of Ex 30:23
six and a q pounds of fragrant Ex 30:23
three and a q pounds and one Nm 7:13
three and a q pounds and one Nm 7:19
three and a q pounds and one Nm 7:25
three and a q pounds and one Nm 7:31
three and a q pounds and one Nm 7:37
three and a q pounds and one Nm 7:43
three and a q pounds and one Nm 7:49
three and a q pounds and one Nm 7:55
three and a q pounds and one Nm 7:61
three and a q pounds and one Nm 7:67
three and a q pounds and one Nm 7:73
three and a q pounds and one Nm 7:79
weighed⌋ three and a q pounds, Nm 7:85
were five and a q feet ⌊wide⌋ on Ezk 40:48
each side was 12 and a q feet. Ezk 41:3
five and a q feet high and three Ezk 41:22

QUARTERMASTER *(2)*
in the care of the q and ran to 1Sm 17:22
Mahseiah, the q, when he went to Jr 51:59

QUARTERS *(2)*
servants to the harem's best q. Est 2:9
in his winter q with a fire Jr 36:22

QUARTS *(53)*
may take two q per individual, Ex 16:16
When they measured it by q, Ex 16:18
much food, four q apiece, and Ex 16:22
'Two q of it are to be preserved Ex 16:32
and put two q of manna in it. Ex 16:33
Two q are a tenth of an ephah. Ex 16:36
lamb offer two q of fine flour Ex 29:40
may bring two q of fine flour as Lv 5:11
two q of fine flour as a regular Lv 6:20
offering of three q of fine Lv 14:10
along with two q of fine flour Lv 14:21
is to be four q of fine flour Lv 23:13
made from four q of fine flour, Lv 23:17
loaf is to be made with four q. Lv 24:5
her of two q of barley flour. Nm 5:15
offering of two q of fine flour Nm 15:4
it must be four q of fine flour Nm 15:6
offering of six q of fine flour Nm 15:9
mixed with two q of oil must be Nm 15:9
Also present two q of wine as a Nm 15:10
along with two q of fine flour Nm 28:5
four q of fine flour mixed with Nm 28:9
with six q of fine flour mixed Nm 28:12
four q of fine flour mixed with Nm 28:12
and two q of fine flour mixed Nm 28:13
to be two q of wine with each Nm 28:14
one and a third q with the ram, Nm 28:14
offer six q with each bull and Nm 28:20
bull and four q with the ram. Nm 28:20
Offer two q with each of the Nm 28:21
with oil, six q with each bull, Nm 28:28
each bull, four q with the ram, Nm 28:28
and two q with each of the seven Nm 28:29
with oil, six q with the bull, Nm 29:3
the bull, four q with the ram, Nm 29:3
and two q with each of the seven Nm 29:4
with oil, six q with the bull, Nm 29:9
the bull, four q with the ram, Nm 29:9
and two q with each of the seven Nm 29:10
six q with each of the 13 bulls, Nm 29:14
q with each of the two rams, Nm 29:14
and two q with each of the 14 Nm 29:15
and it was about 26 q of barley. Ru 2:17
six q of fine meal ⌊will sell⌋ 2Kg 7:1
shekel and 12 q of barley ⌊will 2Kg 7:1
was then that six q of fine meal 2Kg 7:16
shekel and 12 q of barley ⌊sold 2Kg 7:16
tomorrow 12 q of barley ⌊will 2Kg 7:18
a shekel and six q of fine meal 2Kg 7:18
Three q from five bushels of Ezk 45:13
wheat and three q from five Ezk 45:13
three q, with one-third of a Ezk 46:14
and three q of barley for a Rv 6:6

QUARTUS *(1)*
and our brother **Q** greet you. Rm 16:23
QUARTZ *(1)*
Coral and **q** are not worth Jb 28:18
QUEEN *(50)*
The **q** of Sheba heard about 1Kg 10:1
When the **q** of Sheba observed all 1Kg 10:4
as those the **q** of Sheba gave to 1Kg 10:10
Solomon gave the **q** of Sheba her 1Kg 10:13
of his own wife, **Q** Tahpenes. 1Kg 11:19
from being **q** mother because 1Kg 15:13
sons and the **q** mother's sons." 2Kg 10:13
q of Sheba heard of Solomon's 2Ch 9:1
When the **q** of Sheba observed 2Ch 9:3
as those the **q** of Sheba gave to 2Ch 9:9
Solomon gave the **q** of Sheba her 2Ch 9:12
from being **q** mother because she 2Ch 15:16
with the **q** seated beside him, Neh 2:6
Q Vashti also gave a feast for Est 1:9
bring **Q** Vashti before him with Est 1:11
But **Q** Vashti refused to come at Est 1:12
should be done with **Q** Vashti, Est 1:15
Q Vashti has defied not only the Est 1:16
ordered **Q** Vashti brought Est 1:17
head and made her **q** in place of Est 2:17
he reported it to **Q** Esther, Est 2:22
the **q** was overcome with fear. Est 4:4
the king saw **Q** Esther standing Est 5:2
"What is it, **Q** Esther?" Est 5:3
Q Esther invited no one but me Est 5:12
came to feast with Esther the **q**. Est 7:1
Esther, "**Q** Esther, whatever Est 7:2
Q Esther answered, "If I have Est 7:3
spoke up and asked **Q** Esther, Est 7:5
terrified before the king and **q**. Est 7:6
remained to beg **Q** Esther for his Est 7:7
actually violate the **q** while I Est 7:8
awarded **Q** Esther the estate Est 8:1
to Esther the **Q** and to Mordecai Est 8:7
The king said to **Q** Esther, Est 9:12
Q Esther daughter of Abihail, Est 9:29
Mordecai the Jew and **Q** Esther Est 9:31
the **q**, adorned with gold from Ps 45:9
make cakes for the **q** of heaven, Jr 7:18
to the king and the **q** mother: Jr 13:18
Jeconiah, the **q** mother, the Jr 29:2
incense to the **q** of heaven and Jr 44:17
incense to the **q** of heaven and Jr 44:18
incense to the **q** of heaven and Jr 44:19
incense to the **q** of heaven and Jr 44:25
the **q** came to the banquet hall. Dn 5:10
The **q** of the south will rise up Mt 12:42
The **q** of the south will rise up Lk 11:31
of Candace, **q** of the Ethiopians, Ac 8:27
says in her heart, 'I sit as **q**; Rv 18:7
QUEEN'S *(2)*
For the **q** action will become Est 1:17
hear about the **q** act will say Est 1:18
QUEENS *(3)*
There are 60 **q** and 80 concubines Sg 6:8
q and concubines also, and they Sg 6:9
their **q** your nursing mothers. Is 49:23
QUENCH *(2)*
the wild donkeys **q** their thirst. Ps 104:11
with no one to **q** ⌊the flames⌋. Is 1:31
QUENCHED *(8)*
place, and it will not be **q**. 2Kg 22:17
place, and it will not be **q**.' 2Ch 34:25
extinguished, **q** like a wick)— Is 43:17
wrath will burn and not be **q**." Jr 7:20
not die, and the fire is not **q**. Mk 9:44
not die, and the fire is not **q**. Mk 9:46
not die, and the fire is not **q**. Mk 9:48
q the raging of fire, escaped Heb 11:34
QUESTION *(22)*
David. "It was just a **q**." 1Sm 17:29
I **q** you, you will inform Me. Jb 38:3
I **q** you, you will inform Me. Jb 40:7
I **q** you, you will inform Me. Jb 42:4
they **q** me about things I do not Ps 35:11
without **q**, God has made the one Ec 7:14
to give you an answer to this **q**. Dn 3:16
I will also ask you one **q**, Mt 21:24
the law, asked a **q** to test Him: Mt 22:35
no one dared to **q** Him any more. Mt 22:46
Then they began to **q** Him, Mk 9:11
to them, "I will ask you one **q**; Mk 11:29
one dared to **q** Him any longer. Mk 12:34
Jesus asked this **q** as He taught Mk 12:35
Jesus took up ⌊the **q**⌋ and said: Lk 10:30
them, "I will also ask you a **q**. Lk 20:3
Jesus knew they wanted to **q** Him, Jn 16:19
and don't need anyone to **q** You. Jn 16:30
Why do you **q** Me? Question those Jn 18:21
Q those who heard what I told Jn 18:21
before them, they asked the **q**: Ac 4:7
but it is a **q** of equality— 2Co 8:13
QUESTIONED *(22)*
David **q** him, "How is it that you 2Sm 1:14
Ish-bosheth **q** Abner, "Why did 2Sm 3:7
home," David **q** Uriah, "Haven't 2Sm 11:10
But Elisha **q** him, "Wasn't my 2Kg 5:26
So we **q** the elders and asked, Ezr 5:9
and I **q** them about Jerusalem and Neh 1:2
came to Jeremiah and **q** him, Jr 38:27
And I **q** him further, "What are Zch 4:12
the disciples **q** Him, "Why then Mt 17:10
came up to Him and **q** Him: Mt 22:23
were together, Jesus **q** them, Mt 22:41
the disciples **q** Him again about Mk 10:10
came to Him and **q** Him: Mk 12:18
up before them all and **q** Jesus, Mk 14:60
Again the high priest **q** Him, Mk 14:61
Then Pilate **q** Him again, "Are Mk 15:4
Some soldiers also **q** him: Lk 3:14
They **q** Him, "Teacher, we know Lk 20:21
resurrection, came up and **q** Him: Lk 20:27
You?" they **q**. "Precisely what Jn 8:25
His disciples **q** Him: Jn 9:2
high priest **q** Jesus about His Jn 18:19
QUESTIONING *(1)*
When they persisted in **q** Him, Jn 8:7
QUESTIONS *(9)*
to test him with difficult **q**. 1Kg 10:1
So Solomon answered all her **q**; 1Kg 10:3
with difficult **q** at Jerusalem 2Ch 9:1
So Solomon answered all her **q**; 2Ch 9:2
to them and asking them **q**. Lk 2:46
kept asking Him **q**, but Jesus did Lk 23:9
But if these are **q** about words, Ac 18:15
no **q** for conscience' sake, 1Co 10:25
without raising **q** of conscience. 1Co 10:27
QUICK *(7)*
the tent and said to Sarah, "**Q**! Gn 18:6
is right and is **q** to execute Is 16:5
the father told his slaves, '**Q**! Lk 15:22
him up and said, "**Q**, get up!" Ac 12:7
Don't be too **q** to lay hands on 1Tm 5:22
arrogant, not **q** tempered, not Ti 1:7
everyone must be **q** to hear, Jms 1:19
QUICK-TEMPERED *(2)*
q man acts foolishly, and a man Pr 14:17
a **q** one promotes foolishness. Pr 14:29
QUICKER *(1)*
would dry up **q** than any ⌊other⌋ Jb 8:12
QUICKLY *(87)*
She **q** lowered her jug to her Gn 24:18
She **q** emptied her jug into the Gn 24:20
She **q** lowered her jug from her Gn 24:46
How did you ever find it so **q**, Gn 27:20
and they **q** brought him from the Gn 41:14
each one **q** lowered his sack to Gn 44:11
Return **q** to my father and say to Gn 45:9
And bring my father here **q**." Gn 45:13
have you come back so **q** today?" Ex 2:18
to send them **q** out of the Ex 12:33
They have **q** turned from the way Ex 32:8
Go **q** to the community and make Nm 16:46
today that you will **q** perish Dt 4:26
They have **q** turned from the way Dt 9:12
had **q** turned from the way the Dt 9:16
you will perish **q** from the good Dt 11:17
you are destroyed and **q** perish, Dt 28:20
and their doom is coming **q**." Dt 32:35
Chase after them **q**, and you can Jos 2:5
men in ambush rose **q** from their Jos 8:19
servants. Come **q** and save us! Jos 10:6
and you will **q** disappear from Jos 23:16
They **q** turned from the way of Jdg 2:17
He **q** called his armor-bearer and Jdg 9:54
The woman ran **q** to her husband Jdg 13:10
had rushed **q** against Gibeah; Jdg 20:37
The man **q** came and reported to 1Sm 4:14
If you go **q**, you can catch up 1Sm 9:13
David ran **q** to the battle line 1Sm 17:48
permission to **q** go to his town 1Sm 20:6
to Saul saying, "Come **q**, because 1Sm 23:27
q got off the donkey and fell 1Sm 25:23
you had not come **q** to meet me, 1Sm 25:34
Abigail got up **q**, and with her 1Sm 25:42
house, and she **q** slaughtered it. 1Sm 28:24
Leave **q**, or he will overtake us, 2Sm 15:14
send someone **q** and tell David, 2Sm 17:16
the two left **q** and came to the 2Sm 17:18
so they **q** latched onto the hint 1Kg 20:33
q removed the bandage from his 1Kg 20:41
Each man **q** took his garment and 2Kg 9:13
year by year, and do it **q**." 2Ch 24:5
and they **q** brought ⌊them⌋ to the 2Ch 35:13
deceptive are **q** brought to an Jb 5:13
My strength, come **q** to help me. Ps 22:19
to me; rescue me **q**. Be a rock of Ps 31:2
For they wither **q** like grass and Ps 37:2
I am in distress. Answer me **q**! Ps 69:17
Your compassion come to us **q**, Ps 79:8
I would **q** subdue their enemies Ps 81:14
they pass **q** and we fly away. Ps 90:10
answer me **q** when I call. Ps 102:2
Answer me **q**, LORD; my spirit Ps 143:7
act is not carried out **q**, Ec 8:11
and do His work **q** so that we can Is 5:19
how **q** and swiftly they come! Is 5:26
I will bring it about **q**. Is 51:4
and your recovery will come **q**. Is 58:8
accomplish it **q** in its time. Is 60:22
them come **q** to raise a lament Jr 9:18
Run! Escape **q**! Lie low, Jr 49:30
Then Arioch **q** brought Daniel Dn 2:25
I will **q** bring retribution on Jl 3:4
Come **q**, all you surrounding Jl 3:11
Reach a settlement **q** with your Mt 5:25
they sprang up **q** since the soil Mt 13:5
did the fig tree wither so **q**?" Mt 21:20
go **q** and tell His disciples, Mt 28:7
departing **q** from the tomb with Mt 28:8
'Go out **q** into the streets and Lk 14:21
him, 'sit down **q**, and write 50.' Lk 16:6
So he **q** came down and welcomed Lk 19:6
she got up **q** and went to Him. Jn 11:29
that Mary got up **q** and went out. Jn 11:31
him, "What you're doing, do **q**." Jn 13:27
to come to him as **q** as possible, Ac 17:15
and get out of Jerusalem **q**, Ac 22:18
that you are so **q** turning away Gl 1:6
that I myself will also come **q**. Php 2:24
slaves what must **q** take place. Rv 1:1
will come to you **q** and fight Rv 2:16
I am coming **q**. Hold on to what Rv 3:11
the third woe is coming **q**! Rv 11:14
what must **q** take place." Rv 22:6
Look, I am coming **q**! Rv 22:7
I am coming **q**, and My reward is Rv 22:12
says, "Yes, I am coming **q**." Rv 22:20
QUIET *(39)*
but Jacob was a **q** man who stayed Gn 25:27
fight for you; you must be **q**." Ex 14:14
the Sidonians, **q** and Jdg 18:7
told him, "Be **q**. Keep your mouth Jdg 18:19
to a **q** and unsuspecting people. Jdg 18:27
Be **q** for now, my sister. 2Sm 13:20
He said, "Yes, I know. Be **q**." 2Kg 2:3
He said, "Yes, I know. Be **q**." 2Kg 2:5
and the city was **q**, for they had 2Kg 11:20
peaceful, and **q**, for some 1Ch 4:40
peace and **q** to Israel during 1Ch 22:9
Jehoshaphat's kingdom was **q**, 2Ch 20:30
and the city was **q**, for they had 2Ch 23:21
my eyes. I heard a **q** voice: Jb 4:16
Be **q**, and I will speak. Jb 13:13
Be **q**, and I will speak. Jb 33:31
be **q**, and I will teach you Jb 33:33
He leads me beside **q** waters. Ps 23:2
I was speechless and **q**; Ps 39:2
The earth feared and grew **q** Ps 76:8
rejoiced when the waves grew **q**. Ps 107:30
down and be **q**. Don't be afraid Is 7:4
and how the raging has become **q**! Is 14:4
will lie in **q** confidence. Is 30:15
will be **q** confidence forever. Is 32:17
I have been **q** and restrained Is 42:14

have calm and **q** with no one to Jr 30:10
have calm and **q** with no one to Jr 46:27
has been left **q** since his youth, Jr 48:11
sea so it may **q** down for you, Jnh 1:12
the whole earth is calm and **q**." Zch 1:11
The crowd told them to keep **q**, Mt 20:31
and said, "Be **q**, and come out Mk 1:25
Many people told him to keep **q**, Mk 10:48
"Be **q** and come out of him!" Lk 4:35
in front told him to keep **q**, Lk 18:39
seek to lead a **q** life, to mind 1Th 4:11
lead a tranquil and **q** life in 1Tm 2:2
of a gentle and **q** spirit, 1Pt 3:4

QUIETED *(5)*
Then Caleb **q** the people in the Nm 13:30
the Levites **q** all the people, Neh 8:11
Let lying lips be **q**; Ps 31:18
have calmed and **q** myself like a Ps 131:2
How the oppressor has **q** down, Is 14:4

QUIETER *(1)*
language, they became even **q**. Ac 22:2

QUIETLY *(8)*
While they were waiting **q**, Jdg 16:2
Now go back **q** and you won't be 1Sm 29:7
to the city **q** that day like 2Sm 19:3
I will **q** look out from My place, Is 18:4
good to wait **q** for deliverance Lm 3:26
Groan **q**; do not observe mourning Ezk 24:17
Now I must **q** wait for the day of Hab 3:16
Christ, that **q** working, they may 2Th 3:12

QUIETNESS *(1)*
bring ⌊you⌋ **q** with His love. Zph 3:17

QUIRINIUS *(1)*
took place while **Q** was governing Lk 2:2

QUIT *(5)*
q building Ramah and stayed in 1Kg 15:21
he **q** building Ramah and stopped 2Ch 16:5
these three men **q** answering Job, Jb 32:1
The priests **q** asking: Where is Jr 2:8
and they **q** speaking with him Jr 38:27

QUITE *(3)*
he was **q** handsome and was born 1Kg 1:6
he sent for him **q** often and Ac 24:26
known me for **q** some time, Ac 26:5

QUIVER *(6)*
gear, your **q** and bow, and go out Gn 27:3
A **q** rattles at his side, along Jb 39:23
who has filled his **q** with them. Ps 127:5
Elam took up a **q** with chariots Is 22:6
arrow; He hid me in His **q**. Is 49:2
Their **q** is like an open grave; Jr 5:16

QUIVERED *(1)*
my lips **q** at the sound. Hab 3:16

QUIVERS *(2)*
and **q** that were in God's temple. 2Ch 23:9
arrows! Fill the **q**! The LORD has Jr 51:11

QUOTA *(4)*
require the same **q** of bricks Ex 5:8
reduce your daily **q** of bricks." Ex 5:19
The **q** of oil in liquid measures Ezk 45:14
⌊the **q**⌋ from the flock is one Ezk 45:15

QUOTE *(1)*
doubt you will **q** this proverb to Lk 4:23

R

RAAMA *(1)*
Havilah, Sabta, **R**, and Sabteca. 1Ch 1:9

RAAMA'S *(1)*
Raama, and Sabteca. **R** sons: 1Ch 1:9

RAAMAH *(2)*
Havilah, Sabtah, **R**, and Sabteca. Gn 10:7
of Sheba and **R** traded with you. Ezk 27:22

RAAMAH'S *(1)*
and Sabteca. And **R** sons: Sheba Gn 10:7

RAAMIAH *(1)*
(AKA REELAIAH)
Nehemiah, Azariah, **R**, Nahamani, Neh 7:7

RAB-MAG *(2)*
the **R**, and all the rest Jr 39:3
Nergal-sharezer the **R**, and all Jr 39:13

RAB-SARIS *(3)*
the Tartan, the **R**, and the 2Kg 18:17
Sarsechim the **R**, Nergal-sharezer Jr 39:3
Nebushazban the **R**, Jr 39:13

RABBAH *(15)*
Isn't it in **R** of the Ammonites? Dt 3:11
the Ammonites to Aroer, near **R**; Jos 13:25
and **R**—two cities, with Jos 15:60
the Ammonites and besieged **R**, 2Sm 11:1
against **R** of the Ammonites 2Sm 12:26
fought against **R** and have also 2Sm 12:27
all the troops and went to **R**; 2Sm 12:29
of Nahash from **R** of the 2Sm 17:27
He came to **R** and besieged it, 1Ch 20:1
Joab attacked **R** and demolished 1Ch 20:1
against **R** of the Ammonites. Jr 49:2
cry out, daughters of **R**! Jr 49:3
can take to **R** of the Ammonites Ezk 21:20
I will make **R** a pasture for Ezk 25:5
will set fire to the walls of **R**, Am 1:14

RABBI *(15)*
and to be called '**R**' by people. Mt 23:7
not be called '**R**,' because you Mt 23:8
replied, "Surely not I, **R**?" Mt 26:25
Jesus and said, "Greetings, **R**!" Mt 26:49
said to Jesus, "**R**, it is good Mk 9:5
and said to Him, "**R**, look! Mk 11:21
right up to Him and said, "**R**!" Mk 14:45
said to Him, "**R**" (which means Jn 1:38
"**R**," Nathanael replied, "You are Jn 1:49
night and said, "**R**, we know that Jn 3:2
and told him, "**R**, the One you Jn 3:26
urging Him, "**R**, eat something." Jn 4:31
said to Him, "**R**, when did You Jn 6:25
R, who sinned, this man or his Jn 9:2
"**R**," the disciples told Him, Jn 11:8

RABBITH *(1)*
R, Kishion, Ebez, Jos 19:20

RABBLE *(1)*
The **r** rise up at my right; Jb 30:12

RABBOUNI *(2)*
"**R**," the blind man told Him, "I Mk 10:51
she said to Him in Hebrew, "**R**!" Jn 20:16

RABSHAKEH *(16)*
Rab-saris, and the **R**, along with 2Kg 18:17
Then the **R** said to them, "Tell 2Kg 18:19
said to the **R**, "Please speak 2Kg 18:26
But the **R** said to them, "Has my 2Kg 18:27
R stood and called out loudly 2Kg 18:28
to him the words of the **R**. 2Kg 18:37
hear all the words of the **R**, 2Kg 19:4
When the **R** heard that the king 2Kg 19:8
the king of Assyria sent the **R**, Is 36:2
The **R** said to them, "Tell Is 36:4
said to the **R**, "Please speak Is 36:11
the **R** replied, "Has my master Is 36:12
Then the **R** stood and called out Is 36:13
to him the words of the **R**. Is 36:22
will hear the words of the **R**, Is 37:4
When the **R** heard that the king Is 37:8

RACAL *(1)*
to those in **R**, in the towns of 1Sm 30:29

RACE *(25)*
and divided the human **r**, Dt 32:8
disappeared from the human **r**. Ps 12:1
is exalted by the human **r**. Ps 12:8
on the human **r** to see if there Ps 14:2
offspring from the human **r**. Ps 21:10
on the human **r** to see if there Ps 53:2
wonderful works for the human **r**. Ps 107:8
wonderful works for the human **r**. Ps 107:15
wonderful works for the human **r**. Ps 107:21
wonderful works for the human **r**. Ps 107:31
He has given to the human **r**. Ps 115:16
delighting in the human **r**. Pr 8:31
the sun that the **r** is not to the Ec 9:11
children, you **r** of liars, Is 57:4
R furiously, you chariots! Jr 46:9
advance. They **r** to its wall; Nah 2:5
with our **r** and oppressed our Ac 7:19
of Abraham's **r**, and those among Ac 13:26
the runners in a stadium all **r**, 1Co 9:24
have finished the **r**, I have kept 2Tm 4:7
endurance the **r** that lies before Heb 12:1
you are a chosen **r**, a royal 1Pt 2:9
to kill a third of the human **r**. Rv 9:15
third of the human **r** was killed Rv 9:18
from the human **r** as the Rv 14:4

RACED *(1)*
If you have **r** with runners and Jr 12:5

RACES *(2)*
My heart **r**, my strength leaves Ps 38:10
Messenger **r** to meet messenger, Jr 51:31

RACHEL *(41)*
and here is his daughter **R**, Gn 29:6
R came with her father's sheep, Gn 29:9
daughter **R** with his sheep, Gn 29:10
Jacob kissed **R** and wept loudly. Gn 29:11
He told **R** that he was her Gn 29:12
and the younger was named **R**. Gn 29:16
but **R** was shapely and beautiful. Gn 29:17
Jacob loved **R**, so he answered Gn 29:18
for your younger daughter **R**." Gn 29:18
Jacob worked seven years for **R**, Gn 29:20
Wasn't it for **R** that I worked Gn 29:25
him his daughter **R** as his wife. Gn 29:28
to his daughter **R** as her slave. Gn 29:29
slept with **R** also, and indeed Gn 29:30
he loved **R** more than Leah. Gn 29:30
her womb; but **R** was barren. Gn 29:31
When **R** saw that she was not Gn 30:1
became angry with **R** and said, Gn 30:2
So **R** gave her slave Bilhah to Gn 30:4
R said, "God has vindicated me; Gn 30:6
R said, "In ⌊my⌋ wrestlings with Gn 30:8
mother Leah, **R** asked, "Please Gn 30:14
"Well," **R** said, "you can sleep Gn 30:15
Then God remembered **R**. Gn 30:22
After **R** gave birth to Joseph, Gn 30:25
Jacob had **R** and Leah called to Gn 31:4
Then **R** and Leah answered him, Gn 31:14
R stole her father's household Gn 31:19
did not know that **R** had stolen Gn 31:32
R had taken Laban's household Gn 31:34
among Leah, **R**, and the two Gn 33:1
next, and **R** and Joseph last. Gn 33:2
and then Joseph and **R** approached Gn 33:7
from Ephrath, **R** began to give Gn 35:16
So **R** died and was buried on the Gn 35:19
The sons of Jacob's wife **R**: Gn 46:19
Laban gave to his daughter **R**. Gn 46:25
to my sorrow **R** died along the Gn 48:7
your house like **R** and Leah, Ru 4:11
R weeping for her children, Jr 31:15
R weeping for her children; Mt 2:18

RACHEL'S *(7)*
R slave Bilhah conceived again Gn 30:7
left Leah's tent and entered **R**. Gn 31:33
is the marker at **R** grave to this Gn 35:20
R sons were Joseph and Benjamin. Gn 35:24
The sons of **R** slave Bilhah were Gn 35:25
These were **R** sons who were born Gn 46:22
two men at **R** Grave at Zelzah 1Sm 10:2

RACING *(1)*
bred from the royal **r** mares. Est 8:10

RADDAI *(1)*
Nethanel fourth, **R** fifth, 1Ch 2:14

RADIANCE *(6)*
From the **r** of His presence, 2Sm 22:13
From the **r** of His presence, Ps 18:12
of beauty, God appears in **r**. Ps 50:2
to the brightness of your **r**. Is 60:3
He is the **r** of His glory, the Heb 1:3
Her **r** was like a very precious Rv 21:11

RADIANT *(5)*
see that Moses' face was **r**. Ex 34:35
commandment of the LORD is **r**, Ps 19:8
who look to Him are **r** with joy; Ps 34:5
Then you will see and be **r**, Is 60:5
they will be **r** with joy because Jr 31:12

RAFTERS *(3)*
cedar from the floor to the **r**. 1Kg 7:7
cedars, and our **r** are cypresses. Sg 1:17
and the **r** will answer them from Hab 2:11

RAFTS *(2)*
make them into **r** to go by sea to 1Kg 5:9
to you as **r** by sea to Joppa. 2Ch 2:16

RAGE *(38)*
your brother's **r** turns away from Gn 27:45
In a **r**, Samson returned to his Jdg 14:19
So he turned and left in a **r**. 2Kg 5:12
and returned home in a fierce **r**. 2Ch 25:10
them in a **r** that has reached 2Ch 28:9
Ahasuerus' **r** had cooled down Est 2:1

homage, he was filled with **r**. Est 3:5
filled with **r** toward Mordecai Est 5:9
charges ahead with trembling **r**; Jb 39:24
from anger and give up ⌊your⌋ **r**; Ps 37:8
Nations **r**, kingdoms topple; Ps 46:6
them⌋ in **r**; consume ⌊them⌋ Ps 59:13
Pour out Your **r** on them, and let Ps 69:24
R seizes me because of the Ps 119:53
king's **r** is like a lion's roar, Pr 19:12
and a covert bribe, fierce **r**. Pr 21:14
a people destined for My **r**, Is 10:6
with **r** and burning anger— Is 13:9
the nations in **r** with relentless Is 14:6
they **r** like the raging of mighty Is 17:12
The nations **r** like the raging of Is 17:13
the nations cannot endure His **r**. Jr 10:10
with anger, **r**, and great wrath Jr 21:5
in My wrath, **r**, and great fury, Jr 32:37
I strike down in My wrath and **r**. Jr 33:5
When I vent My jealous **r** on you, Ezk 23:25
I swear in My zeal and fiery **r**: Ezk 38:19
in a furious **r** Nebuchadnezzar Dn 3:13
was filled with **r**, Dn 3:19
Then he will **r** against the holy Dn 11:30
among you; I will not come in **r**. Hs 11:9
he harbored his **r** incessantly. Am 1:11
the LORD's **r** until He argues Mc 7:9
is Your **r** against the sea when Hab 3:8
by the wise men, flew into a **r**. Mt 2:16
were filled with **r** and started Lk 6:11
the Gentiles **r**, and the peoples Ac 4:25
filled with **r** and began to cry Ac 19:28

RAGED *(2)*
battle **r** throughout that day, 1Kg 22:35
battle **r** throughout that day, 2Ch 18:34

RAGES *(3)*
Though the river **r**, Behemoth is Jb 40:23
Him, and a storm **r** around Him. Ps 50:3
his heart **r** against the LORD. Pr 19:3

RAGING *(18)*
in, and your **r** against Me. 2Kg 19:27
Because your **r** against Me and 2Kg 19:28
Unleash your **r** anger; Jb 40:11
shelter from the **r** wind and the Ps 55:8
You rule the **r** sea; when its Ps 89:9
the **r** waters would have swept Ps 124:5
and how the **r** has become quiet! Is 14:4
The **r** of the nations—they rage Is 17:12
rage like the **r** of mighty waters Is 17:12
rage like the **r** of many waters. Is 17:13
in, and your **r** against Me. Is 37:28
Because your **r** against Me and Is 37:29
r flames killed those men who Dn 3:22
the sea was **r** against them more Jnh 1:13
and the sea stopped its **r**. Jnh 1:15
the wind and the **r** waves. Lk 8:24
and the severe storm kept **r**; Ac 27:20
quenched the **r** of fire, escaped Heb 11:34

RAGS *(3)*
will clothe ⌊them⌋ in **r**. Pr 23:21
there he took old **r** and worn-out Jr 38:11
Place these old **r** and clothes Jr 38:12

RAHAB *(13)*
(AKA EGYPT)
prostitute named **R**, and stayed Jos 2:1
sent ⌊word⌋ to **R** and said, Jos 2:3
Only **R** the prostitute and Jos 6:17
brought out **R** and her father, Jos 6:23
Joshua spared **R** the prostitute, Jos 6:25
His understanding He crushed **R**. Jb 26:12
R, Babylon, Philistia, Tyre, and Ps 87:4
You crushed **R** like one who is Ps 89:10
I call her: **R** Who Just Sits. Is 30:7
it You who hacked **R** to pieces, Is 51:9
Salmon fathered Boaz by **R**, Mt 1:5
By faith **R** the prostitute Heb 11:31
wasn't **R** the prostitute also Jms 2:25

RAHAB'S *(1)*
R assistants cringe in fear Jb 9:13

RAHAM *(1)*
Shema fathered **R**, who fathered 1Ch 2:44

RAID *(6)*
Where did you **r** today?" 1Sm 27:10
returned from a **r** and brought a 2Sm 3:22
went down to **r** their cattle. 1Ch 7:21
come and made a **r** in the Valley 1Ch 14:9
made a **r** in the valley. 1Ch 14:13
bands, made a **r** on the camels, Jb 1:17

RAIDED *(8)*
over to marauders who **r** them. Jdg 2:14
up, camped in Judah, and **r** Lehi. Jdg 15:9
Philistines have **r** the land!" 1Sm 23:27
went up and **r** the Geshurites, 1Sm 27:8
The Amalekites had **r** the Negev 1Sm 30:1
We **r** the south country of the 1Sm 30:14
they **r** the cities of Judah from 2Ch 25:13
Philistines also **r** the cities 2Ch 28:18

RAIDERS *(6)*
Should I pursue these **r**? 1Sm 30:8
"Will you lead me to these **r**?" 1Sm 30:15
to us the **r** who came against 1Sm 30:23
The Aramean **r** did not come into 2Kg 6:23
Ammonite **r** against Jehoiakim. 2Kg 24:2
suddenly bring **r** against them, Jr 18:22

RAIDING *(5)*
R parties went out from the 1Sm 13:17
garrison and the **r** parties were 1Sm 14:15
Keilah and **r** the threshing 1Sm 23:1
who were leaders of **r** parties: 2Sm 4:2
captain of a **r** party when David 1Kg 11:24

RAIDS *(1)*
had gone on **r** and brought back 2Kg 5:2

RAILING *(1)*
make a **r** around your roof, Dt 22:8

RAIN *(102)*
had not made it **r** on the land, Gn 2:5
I will make it **r** on the earth 40 Gn 7:4
and the **r** fell on the earth 40 Gn 7:12
and the **r** from the sky stopped. Gn 8:2
time I will **r** down the worst Ex 9:18
and **r** no longer poured down on Ex 9:33
When Pharaoh saw that the **r**, Ex 9:34
I am going to **r** bread from Ex 16:4
I will give you **r** at the right Lv 26:4
watered by **r** from the sky. Dt 11:11
will provide **r** for your land in Dt 11:14
the sky, and there will be no **r**; Dt 11:17
give your land **r** in its season Dt 28:12
will turn the **r** of your land Dt 28:24
fall like **r** and my word settle Dt 32:2
like gentle **r** on new grass and Dt 32:2
heavens poured ⌊**r**⌋, the clouds Jdg 5:4
and He will send thunder and **r**, 1Sm 12:17
day the LORD sent thunder and **r**. 1Sm 12:18
let no dew or **r** be on you, 2Sm 1:21
harvest until the **r** poured down 2Sm 21:10
glisten of **r** on sprouting grass. 2Sm 23:4
are shut and there is no **r**, 1Kg 8:35
May You send **r** on Your land that 1Kg 8:36
will be no dew or **r** during these 1Kg 17:1
there had been no **r** in the land. 1Kg 17:7
the LORD sends **r** on the surface 1Kg 17:14
I will send **r** on the surface of 1Kg 18:1
down so the **r** doesn't stop you. 1Kg 18:44
'You will not see wind or **r**, 2Kg 3:17
and there is no **r** because they 2Ch 6:26
May You send **r** on Your land that 2Ch 6:27
close the sky so there is no **r**, 2Ch 7:13
and because of the heavy **r**. Ezr 10:9
gives **r** to the earth and sends Jb 5:10
a limit for the **r** and a path for Jb 28:26
me as for the **r** and opened their Jb 29:23
distill the **r** into its mist, Jb 36:27
for the flooding **r** or clears the Jb 38:25
to bring **r** on an uninhabited Jb 38:26
Does the **r** have a father? Jb 38:28
He will **r** burning coals and Ps 11:6
poured down ⌊**r**⌋ before God, Ps 68:8
You, God, showered abundant **r**; Ps 68:9
May he be like **r** that falls on Ps 72:6
even the autumn **r** will cover it Ps 84:6
them hail for **r**, and lightning Ps 105:32
lightning for the **r** and brings Ps 135:7
prepares **r** for the earth, Ps 147:8
is like a cloud with spring **r**. Pr 16:15
like clouds and wind without **r**. Pr 25:14
The north wind produces **r**, Pr 25:23
snow in summer and **r** at harvest, Pr 26:1
like a driving **r** that leaves no Pr 28:3
will pour out **r** on the earth; Ec 11:3
the clouds return after the **r**; Ec 12:2
the **r** has ended and gone away. Sg 2:11
and shelter from storm and **r**. Is 4:6
clouds that **r** should not fall Is 5:6
like a **r** cloud in harvest heat. Is 18:4
refuge from the **r**, a shade from Is 25:4
violent is like **r** ⌊against⌋ a Is 25:4
He will send **r** for your seed Is 30:23
fire, in driving **r**, a torrent, Is 30:30
refuge from the **r**, like streams Is 32:2
laurel, and the **r** makes it grow. Is 44:14
For just as **r** and snow fall from Is 55:10
why there has been no spring **r**. Jr 3:3
God, who gives the **r**, both early Jr 5:24
lightning for the **r** and brings Jr 10:13
cracked since no **r** ⌊has fallen⌋ Jr 14:4
idols of the nations bring **r**? Jr 14:22
lightning for the **r** and brings Jr 51:16
Torrential **r** will come, and I Ezk 13:11
Torrential **r** will come in My Ezk 13:13
has not received **r** in the day Ezk 22:24
I will pour out torrential **r**, Ezk 38:22
He will come to us like the **r**, Hs 6:3
righteousness on you like the **r**. Hs 10:12
you the autumn **r** for your Jl 2:23
autumn and spring **r** as before. Jl 2:23
withheld the **r** from you while Am 4:7
I sent **r** on one city but no rain Am 4:7
on one city but no **r** on another. Am 4:7
field received **r** while a field Am 4:7
a field with no **r** withered. Am 4:7
Ask the LORD for **r** in the season Zch 10:1
rain in the season of spring **r**. Zch 10:1
The LORD makes the **r** clouds, Zch 10:1
give them showers of **r** and crops Zch 10:1
LORD of Hosts, **r** will not fall Zch 14:17
then **r** will not fall on them; Zch 14:18
and sends **r** on the righteous and Mt 5:45
The **r** fell, the rivers rose, and Mt 7:25
The **r** fell, the rivers rose, the Mt 7:27
giving you **r** from heaven and Ac 14:17
since **r** was falling and it was Ac 28:2
has drunk the **r** that has often Heb 6:7
earnestly that it would not **r**, Jms 5:17
months it did not **r** on the land. Jms 5:17
and the sky gave **r** and the land Jms 5:18
it does not **r** during the days Rv 11:6

RAINBOW *(3)*
was like that of a **r** in a cloud Ezk 1:28
A **r** that looked like an emerald Rv 4:3
a cloud, with a **r** over his head. Rv 10:1

RAINED *(5)*
Then the LORD **r** burning sulfur Gn 19:24
and the LORD **r** hail on the land Ex 9:23
He **r** manna for them to eat; Ps 78:24
He **r** meat on them like dust, Ps 78:27
fire and sulfur **r** from heaven Lk 17:29

RAINING *(1)*
r ⌊it⌋ down on him while he is Jb 20:23

RAINS *(5)*
early and late **r**, and you will Dt 11:14
by mountain **r**, they huddle Jb 24:8
and the torrential **r**, His mighty Jb 37:6
rains, His mighty torrential **r**, Jb 37:6
the early and the late **r**. Jms 5:7

RAINSTORM *(1)*
for there is the sound of a **r**." 1Kg 18:41

RAINY *(3)*
people, and it is the **r** season. Ezr 10:13
dripping on a **r** day and a Pr 27:15
a rainbow in a cloud on a **r** day. Ezk 1:28

RAISE *(78)*
will be able to **r** his hand or Gn 41:44
indeed they **r** livestock. Gn 46:32
LORD your God will **r** up for you Dt 18:15
I will **r** up for them a prophet Dt 18:18
I **r** My hand to heaven and Dt 32:40
Don't **r** your voice against us, Jdg 18:25
Then I will **r** up a faithful 1Sm 2:35
I will **r** up after you your 2Sm 7:12
would not **r** my hand against the 2Sm 18:12
The LORD will **r** up for Himself a 1Kg 14:14
in Jerusalem to **r** up his son 1Kg 15:4
R another army for yourself like 1Kg 20:25
and to have them **r** their voices 1Ch 15:16
I will **r** up after you your 1Ch 17:11
be gracious to me and **r** me up; Ps 41:10
r my eyes toward the mountains. Ps 121:1
day a man will **r** a young cow and Is 7:21

and He will **r** His staff over the Is 10:26
they **r** a cry of destruction on Is 15:5
They **r** their voices, they sing Is 24:14
of good news, **r** your voice Is 40:9
R it, do not be afraid! Is 40:9
and **r** My banner to the peoples. Is 49:22
R your voice like a trumpet. Is 58:1
R your eyes and look around: Is 60:4
R a banner for the peoples. Is 62:10
they **r** their voices against the Jr 4:16
r a smoke signal over Jr 6:1
r a siege ramp against Jerusalem. Jr 6:6
R up a dirge on the barren Jr 7:29
I will **r** weeping and a lament Jr 9:10
come quickly to **r** a lament over Jr 9:18
Do not **r** up a cry or a prayer on Jr 11:14
r your voice in Bashan; Jr 22:20
I will **r** up shepherds over them Jr 23:4
when I will **r** up a righteous Jr 23:5
God and I will **r** up David their Jr 30:9
they **r** their voices as far as Jr 48:34
proclaim and **r** up a signal flag; Jr 50:2
R a war cry against her on every Jr 50:15
R up a signal flag against the Jr 51:12
R a signal flag in the land; Jr 51:27
shrines⌋ or **r** his eyes to the Ezk 18:6
shrines⌋ or **r** his eyes to the Ezk 18:15
slaughter, **r** a battle cry, set Ezk 21:22
I will **r** up many nations against Ezk 26:3
build a ramp and **r** a wall of Ezk 26:8
when I **r** up the deep against you Ezk 26:19
They **r** their voices over you and Ezk 27:30
r your eyes to your idols, Ezk 33:25
who will **r** a great multitude, Dn 11:11
North will again **r** a multitude Dn 11:13
r the war cry in Beth-aven: Hs 5:8
day He will **r** us up so we can Hs 6:2
Even if they **r** children, I will Hs 9:12
roar from Zion and **r** His voice Jl 3:16
land, with no one to **r** her up. Am 5:2
we will **r** against it seven Mc 5:5
so no one could **r** his head. Zch 1:21
I am about to **r** up a shepherd in Zch 11:16
God is able to **r** up children for Mt 3:9
Heal the sick, **r** the dead, Mt 10:8
his wife and **r** up offspring for Mt 22:24
God is able to **r** up children for Lk 3:8
would not even **r** his eyes to Lk 18:13
I will **r** it up in three days. Jn 2:19
will You **r** it up in three days? Jn 2:20
Me but should **r** them up on the Jn 6:39
I will **r** him up on the last day. Jn 6:40
and I will **r** him up on the last Jn 6:44
and I will **r** him up on the last Jn 6:54
Lord your God will **r** up for you Ac 3:22
God will **r** up for you a Prophet Ac 7:37
and will also **r** us up by His 1Co 6:14
whom He did not **r** up if in fact 1Co 15:15
Lord Jesus will **r** us also with 2Co 4:14
be able even to **r** someone from Heb 11:19
and the Lord will **r** him up; Jms 5:15

RAISED *(149)*

I have **r** my hand in an oath to Gn 14:22
have **r** livestock from our youth Gn 46:34
he **r** the staff and struck the Ex 7:20
Then Moses **r** his hand and struck Nm 20:11
Joshua **r** up their sons in their Jos 5:7
and **r** over him a large pile of Jos 7:26
The LORD **r** up judges, who saved Jdg 2:16
the LORD **r** up a judge for Jdg 2:18
So the LORD **r** up Othniel son of Jdg 3:9
and He **r** up Ehud son of Gera, Jdg 3:15
of Mount Gerizim, **r** his voice, Jdg 9:7
the Israelites **r** such a loud 1Sm 4:5
of the man **r** on high, 2Sm 23:1
He **r** his spear against 300 ⌊men⌋ 2Sm 23:18
So the LORD **r** up Hadad the 1Kg 11:14
God **r** up Rezon son of Eliada as 1Kg 11:23
r you up from among the people, 1Kg 14:7
Because I **r** you up from the dust 1Kg 16:2
whom have you **r** ⌊your⌋ voice 2Kg 19:22
He **r** his spear against 300 ⌊men⌋ 1Ch 11:20
They **r** ⌊their⌋ voices, 2Ch 5:13
men of Judah **r** the battle cry. 2Ch 13:15
men of Judah **r** the battle cry, 2Ch 13:15
be torn from his house and **r** up; Ezr 6:11
stood on the **r** platform ⌊built⌋ Neh 9:4
she always had while he **r** her. Est 2:20
from my youth, I **r** him as ⌊his⌋ Jb 31:18
and the arm **r** ⌊in violence⌋ is Jb 38:15
So He **r** His hand against them Ps 106:26
He spoke and **r** a tempest that Ps 107:25
The LORD's right hand is **r**! Ps 118:16
He has **r** up a horn for His Ps 148:14
I have **r** children and brought Is 1:2
and will be **r** above the hills. Is 2:2
He **r** His hand against them and Is 5:25
His hand is still **r** ⌊to strike⌋. Is 5:25
The LORD has **r** up Rezin's Is 9:11
His hand is still **r** ⌊to strike⌋. Is 9:12
His hand is still **r** ⌊to strike⌋. Is 9:17
His hand is still **r** ⌊to strike⌋. Is 9:21
His hand is still **r** ⌊to strike⌋. Is 10:4
a banner is **r** on the mountains Is 18:3
I have not **r** young men ⌊or⌋ Is 23:4
and every **r** hill on the day Is 30:25
Who have you **r** ⌊your⌋ voice Is 37:23
I have **r** up one from the north, Is 41:25
have **r** him up in righteousness, Is 45:13
and My highways will be **r** up. Is 49:11
all the children she has **r**; Is 51:18
He will be **r** and lifted up and Is 52:13
any accusation **r** against you in Is 54:17
The LORD has **r** up prophets for Jr 29:15
They have **r** a shout in the house Lm 2:7
the temple had a **r** platform Ezk 41:8
It was **r** up on one side, with Dn 7:5
touched me and **r** me to my hands Dn 10:10
r both his hands toward heaven Dn 12:7
I **r** up some of your sons as Am 2:11
But You **r** my life from the Pit, Jnh 2:6
and will be **r** above the hills. Mc 4:1
the nations that **r** ⌊their⌋ horns Zch 1:21
will be **r** up and will remain Zch 14:10
the dead are **r**, and the poor are Mt 11:5
He has been **r** from the dead, Mt 14:2
killed, and be **r** the third day. Mt 16:21
Son of Man is **r** from the dead." Mt 17:9
the third day He will be **r** up." Mt 17:23
had gone to their rest were **r**. Mt 27:52
'He has been **r** from the dead.' Mt 27:64
'He has been **r** from the dead. Mt 28:7
her by the hand, and **r** her up. Mk 1:31
has been **r** from the dead, Mk 6:14
the one I beheaded, has been **r**!" Mk 6:16
him by the hand, **r** him, and he Mk 9:27
concerning the dead being **r**— Mk 12:26
He has **r** up a horn of salvation Lk 1:69
the dead are **r**, and the poor Lk 7:22
John had been **r** from the dead, Lk 9:7
killed, and be **r** the third day." Lk 9:22
from the crowd **r** her voice and Lk 11:27
and **r** their voices, saying, Lk 17:13
bush that the dead are **r**, Lk 20:37
Nation will be **r** up against Lk 21:10
The Lord has certainly been **r**, Lk 24:34
So when He was **r** from the dead, Jn 2:22
Then Jesus **r** His eyes and said, Jn 11:41
one Jesus had **r** from the dead. Jn 12:1
the one He had **r** from the dead. Jn 12:9
of the tomb and **r** him from the Jn 12:17
My bread has **r** his heel against Jn 13:18
after He was **r** from the dead. Jn 21:14
up with the Eleven, **r** his voice, Ac 2:14
God **r** Him up, ending the pains Ac 2:24
by the right hand he **r** him up, Ac 3:7
life, whom God **r** from the dead; Ac 3:15
r up His Servant and sent Him Ac 3:26
and whom God **r** from the dead— Ac 4:10
they **r** their voices to God Ac 4:24
God of our fathers **r** up Jesus, Ac 5:30
adopted and **r** him as her own son Ac 7:21
God **r** up this man on the third Ac 10:40
He **r** up David as their king, Ac 13:22
But God **r** Him from the dead, Ac 13:30
Since He **r** Him from the dead, Ac 13:34
One whom God **r** up did not decay Ac 13:37
had done, they **r** their voices, Ac 14:11
Egyptian who **r** a rebellion some Ac 21:38
Then they **r** their voices, Ac 22:22
in Him who **r** Jesus our Lord Rm 4:24
our trespasses and **r** for our Rm 4:25
as Christ was **r** from the dead Rm 6:4
having been **r** from the dead, Rm 6:9
to Him who was **r** from the dead— Rm 7:4
Spirit of Him who **r** Jesus from Rm 8:11
then He who **r** Christ from the Rm 8:11
died, but even more, has been **r**; Rm 8:34
For this reason I **r** you up: Rm 9:17
heart that God **r** Him from the Rm 10:9
God **r** up the Lord and will also 1Co 6:14
that He was **r** on the third day 1Co 15:4
is preached as **r** from the dead, 1Co 15:12
then Christ has not been **r**; 1Co 15:13
and if Christ has not been **r**, 1Co 15:14
about God that He **r** up Christ— 1Co 15:15
if in fact the dead are not **r**. 1Co 15:15
For if the dead are not **r**, 1Co 15:16
raised, Christ has not been **r**. 1Co 15:16
And if Christ has not been **r**, 1Co 15:17
Christ has been **r** from the dead, 1Co 15:20
If the dead are not **r** at all, 1Co 15:29
the dead are not **r**, Let us eat 1Co 15:32
will say, "How are the dead **r**? 1Co 15:35
corruption, **r** in incorruption; 1Co 15:42
sown in dishonor, **r** in glory; 1Co 15:43
sown in weakness, **r** in power; 1Co 15:43
a natural body, **r** a spiritual 1Co 15:44
dead will be **r** incorruptible, 1Co 15:52
the One who **r** the Lord Jesus 2Co 4:14
One who died for them and was **r**. 2Co 5:15
thing that is **r** up against the 2Co 10:5
the Father who **r** Him from the Gl 1:1
He also **r** us up with Him and Eph 2:6
you were also **r** with Him through Col 2:12
of God, who **r** Him from the dead Col 2:12
you have been **r** with the Messiah Col 3:1
whom He **r** from the dead— 1Th 1:10
their dead **r** to life again. Heb 11:35
who **r** Him from the dead and gave 1Pt 1:21
and on the land **r** his right hand Rv 10:5

RAISES *(18)*

to Sheol, and He **r** ⌊others⌋ up. 1Sm 2:6
He **r** the poor from the dust and 1Sm 2:8
He **r** the poor from the dust and Ps 113:7
He **r** up all who are oppressed. Ps 145:14
The LORD **r** up those who are Ps 146:8
she **r** her voice in the public Pr 1:20
He **r** a signal flag for the Is 5:26
with a rod and **r** his staff over Is 10:24
Hosts when He **r** it against her. Is 19:16
When the LORD **r** His hand ⌊to Is 31:3
He **r** His voice from His holy Jr 25:30
and ⌊when⌋ he **r** his eyes to the Ezk 18:12
just as the sea **r** its waves. Ezk 26:3
The LORD **r** His voice in the Jl 2:11
roars from Zion and **r** His voice Am 1:2
as the Father **r** the dead and Jn 5:21
any of you that God **r** the dead? Ac 26:8
but in God who **r** the dead. 2Co 1:9

RAISIN *(4)*

and a **r** cake to each one of the 2Sm 6:19
a date cake, and a **r** cake. 1Ch 16:3
for the **r** cakes of Kir-hareseth. Is 16:7
to other gods and love **r** cakes." Hs 3:1

RAISING *(10)*

that you are **r** against Him. Ex 16:8
r my voice in thanksgiving and Ps 26:7
the **r** of my hands as the evening Ps 141:2
to be My servant **r** up the tribes Is 49:6
I am **r** up a nation against you, Am 6:14
I am **r** up the Chaldeans, that Hab 1:6
us their children by **r** up Jesus, Ac 13:33
everyone by **r** Him from the dead. Ac 17:31
without **r** questions of 1Co 10:27
the Messiah by **r** Him from the Eph 1:20

RAISINS *(6)*

juice or eat fresh grapes or **r**. Nm 6:3
100 clusters of **r**, and 200 cakes 1Sm 25:18
figs and two clusters of **r**. 1Sm 30:12
100 clusters of **r**, 100 ⌊bunches⌋ 2Sm 16:1
fig cakes, **r**, wine and oil, 1Ch 12:40
Sustain me with **r**; refresh me Sg 2:5

RAKED *(1)*

wicked are like thorns **r** aside; 2Sm 23:6

RAKKATH *(1)*

Zer, Hammath, **R**, Chinnereth, Jos 19:35

RAKKON *(1)*

Me-jarkon, and **R**, with the Jos 19:46

RALLIED *(10)*

and the Abiezrites **r** behind him. Jdg 6:34
of Manasseh, who **r** behind him. Jdg 6:35

Benjaminites **r** 26,000 armed men Jdg 20:15
700 choice men **r** by the Jdg 20:15
from Benjamin, **r** 400,000 armed Jdg 20:17
Israelite army **r** and again took Jdg 20:22
The men of Israel and Judah **r**, 1Sm 17:52
or discontented **r** around him, 1Sm 22:2
The Benjaminites **r** to Abner; 2Sm 2:25
group of about 400 men **r** to him. Ac 5:36

RALLY *(2)*
trumpet sound, **r** to us there. Neh 4:20
R Your power and come to save us. Ps 80:2

RAM *(92)*
(See also RAM proper noun.)
three-year-old **r**, a turtledove, Gn 15:9
up and saw a **r** caught by its Gn 22:13
and took the **r** and offered it as Gn 22:13
r skins dyed red and manatee Ex 25:5
the tent from **r** skins dyed red, Ex 26:14
Take one **r**, and Aaron and his Ex 29:15
You are to slaughter the **r**, Ex 29:16
Cut the **r** into pieces. Wash its Ex 29:17
burn the whole **r** on the altar; Ex 29:18
You are to take the second **r**, Ex 29:19
Slaughter the **r**, take some of Ex 29:20
fat from the **r**, the fat tail, Ex 29:22
since this is a **r** for ordination Ex 29:22
the breast from the **r** of Aaron's Ex 29:26
up from the **r** of ordination. Ex 29:27
are to take the **r** of ordination Ex 29:31
the meat of the **r** and the bread Ex 29:32
r skins dyed red and manatee Ex 35:7
r skins dyed red or manatee Ex 35:23
the tent from **r** skins dyed red Ex 36:19
the covering of **r** skins dyed red Ex 39:34
an unblemished **r** from the flock Lv 5:15
behalf with the **r** of the Lv 5:16
an unblemished **r** from the flock Lv 5:18
an unblemished **r** from the flock, Lv 6:6
he presented the **r** for the burnt Lv 8:18
hands on the head of the **r**. Lv 8:18
Moses cut the **r** into pieces and Lv 8:20
the entire **r** on the altar. Lv 8:21
Next he presented the second **r**, Lv 8:22
second ram, the **r** of ordination, Lv 8:22
hands on the head of the **r**. Lv 8:22
the ordination **r** as the LORD had Lv 8:29
sin offering and a **r** for a burnt Lv 9:2
an ox and a **r** for a fellowship Lv 9:4
the ox and the **r** as the people's Lv 9:18
portions from the ox and the **r**— Lv 9:19
sin offering and a **r** for a burnt Lv 16:3
offering and one **r** for a burnt Lv 16:5
must bring his **r** as a Lv 19:21
the LORD with the **r** of the Lv 19:22
with the atonement **r** by which Nm 5:8
unblemished **r** as a fellowship Nm 6:14
also offer the **r** as a fellowship Nm 6:17
the boiled shoulder from the **r**, Nm 6:19
young bull, one **r**, and one male Nm 7:15
young bull, one **r**, and one male Nm 7:21
young bull, one **r**, and one male Nm 7:27
young bull, one **r**, and one male Nm 7:33
young bull, one **r**, and one male Nm 7:39
young bull, one **r**, and one male Nm 7:45
young bull, one **r**, and one male Nm 7:51
young bull, one **r**, and one male Nm 7:57
young bull, one **r**, and one male Nm 7:63
young bull, one **r**, and one male Nm 7:69
young bull, one **r**, and one male Nm 7:75
young bull, one **r**, and one male Nm 7:81
a grain offering with a **r**, Nm 15:6
for each ox, **r**, lamb, or goat. Nm 15:11
a bull and a **r** on each altar. Nm 23:2
a bull and a **r** on each altar." Nm 23:4
a bull and a **r** on each altar. Nm 23:14
a bull and a **r** on each altar. Nm 23:30
young bulls, one **r**, seven male Nm 28:11
as a grain offering for the **r**, Nm 28:12
and a third quarts with the **r**, Nm 28:14
bulls, one **r**, and seven male Nm 28:19
bull and four quarts with the **r**. Nm 28:20
bulls, one **r**, and seven male Nm 28:27
bull, four quarts with the **r**, Nm 28:28
young bull, one **r**, seven male Nm 29:2
bull, four quarts with the **r**, Nm 29:3
young bull, one **r**, and seven Nm 29:8
bull, four quarts with the **r**, Nm 29:9
bull, one **r**, seven male lambs Nm 29:36
offered⌋ a **r** from the flock Ezr 10:19
an unblemished **r** from the flock. Ezk 43:23
bull and a **r** from the flock, Ezk 43:25
bull and half a bushel per **r**, Ezk 45:24
lambs and an unblemished **r**. Ezk 46:4
be half a bushel with the **r**, Ezk 46:5
lambs and a **r** without blemish Ezk 46:6
bushel with the **r**, and whatever Ezk 46:7
bushel with the **r**, and whatever Ezk 46:11
there was a **r** standing beside Dn 8:3
saw the **r** charging to the west, Dn 8:4
the two-horned **r** I had seen Dn 8:6
I saw him approaching the **r**, Dn 8:7
he struck the **r**, shattering his Dn 8:7
and the **r** was not strong enough Dn 8:7
to rescue the **r** from his power. Dn 8:7
The two-horned **r** that you saw Dn 8:20

RAM (proper noun) *(7)*
(AKA ARAM)
Hezron fathered **R**, who fathered Ru 4:19
Jerahmeel, **R**, and Chelubai. 1Ch 2:9
R fathered Amminadab, and 1Ch 2:10
R, his firstborn, Bunah, Oren, 1Ch 2:25
The sons of **R**, Jerahmeel's 1Ch 2:27
the family of **R** became angry. Jb 32:2
son⌋ of **R**, ⌊son⌋ of Hezron, Lk 3:33

RAM'S *(27)*
When the **r** horn sounds a long Ex 19:13
lay their hands on the **r** head. Ex 29:15
lay their hands on the **r** head. Ex 29:19
he sounded the **r** horn throughout Jdg 3:27
and he blew the **r** horn and the Jdg 6:34
Saul blew the **r** horn throughout 1Sm 13:3
Then Joab blew the **r** horn, 2Sm 2:28
and the sound of the **r** horn. 2Sm 6:15
hear the sound of the **r** horn, 2Sm 15:10
Joab blew the **r** horn, and the 2Sm 18:16
He blew the **r** horn and shouted: 2Sm 20:1
So he blew the **r** horn, and they 2Sm 20:22
to blow the **r** horn and say, 1Kg 1:34
Then they blew the **r** horn, 1Kg 1:39
sound of the **r** horn and said, 1Kg 1:41
They blew the **r** horn and 2Kg 9:13
sound of the **r** horn, trumpets, 1Ch 15:28
the blast of the **r** horn shout Ps 98:6
Blow the **r** horn throughout the Jr 4:5
heard the sound of the **r** horn— Jr 4:19
hear the sound of the **r** horn? Jr 4:21
Sound the **r** horn in Tekoa; Jr 6:1
for the sound of the **r** horn. Jr 6:17
sound of the **r** horn or hunger Jr 42:14
blow a **r** horn among the nations; Jr 51:27
and the sound of the **r** horn. Am 2:2
If a **r** horn is blown in a city, Am 3:6

RAM'S-HORN *(1)*
carry seven **r** trumpets in front Jos 6:4

RAMAH *(33)*
(AKA RAMOTH-GILEAD, RAMATHAIM-ZOPHIM)
Gibeon, **R**, Beeroth, Jos 18:25
Baalath-beer (**R** of the south). Jos 19:8
then turned to **R** as far as the Jos 19:29
Adamah, **R**, Hazor, Jos 19:36
of Deborah between **R** and Bethel Jdg 4:5
spend the night in Gibeah or **R**." Jdg 19:13
they returned home to **R**. 1Sm 1:19
went home to **R**, but the boy 1Sm 2:11
would return to **R** because his 1Sm 7:17
and went to Samuel at **R**. 1Sm 8:4
Samuel went to **R**, and Saul went 1Sm 15:34
Samuel set out and went to **R**. 1Sm 16:13
went to Samuel at **R** and told him 1Sm 19:18
that David was at Naioth in **R**, 1Sm 19:19
Then Saul himself went to **R**. 1Sm 19:22
"At Naioth in **R**," someone said. 1Sm 19:22
So he went to Naioth in **R**. 1Sm 19:23
until he entered Naioth in **R**. 1Sm 19:23
fled from Naioth in **R** and came 1Sm 20:1
buried him by his home in **R**. 1Sm 25:1
for him and buried him in **R**, 1Sm 28:3
He built **R** in order to deny 1Kg 15:17
he quit building **R** and stayed in 1Kg 15:21
the stones of **R** and the timbers 1Kg 15:22
He built **R** in order to deny 2Ch 16:1
quit building **R** and stopped his 2Ch 16:5
the stones of **R** and the timbers 2Ch 16:6
Hazor, **R**, Gittaim, Neh 11:33
The people of **R** are trembling; Is 10:29
was heard in **R**, a lament with Jr 31:15
released him at **R** when he had Jr 40:1
in Gibeah, the trumpet in **R**; Hs 5:8
voice was heard in **R**, weeping, Mt 2:18

RAMAH'S *(2)*
R and Geba's people 621 Ezr 2:26
R and Geba's men 621 Neh 7:30

RAMATH-LEHI *(1)*
jawbone and named that place **R**. Jdg 15:17

RAMATH-MIZPEH *(1)*
from Heshbon to **R** and Betonim, Jos 13:26

RAMATHAIM-ZOPHIM *(1)*
(AKA RAMAH)
was a man from **R** in the hill 1Sm 1:1

RAMATHITE *(1)*
Shimei the **R** was in charge of 1Ch 27:27

RAMESES *(5)*
the land of **R**, as Pharaoh had Gn 47:11
Pithom and **R** as supply cities Ex 1:11
traveled from **R** to Succoth, Ex 12:37
departed from **R** in the first Nm 33:3
departed from **R** and camped at Nm 33:5

RAMIAH *(1)*
R, Izziah, Malchijah, Mijamin, Ezr 10:25

RAMOTH *(6)*
R in Gilead, belonging to the Dt 4:43
R in Gilead from Gad's tribe, Jos 20:8
R in Gilead, the city of refuge Jos 21:38
in Bethel, in **R** of the Negev, 1Sm 30:27
R and its pasturelands, and Anem 1Ch 6:73
they received⌋ **R** in Gilead and 1Ch 6:80

RAMOTH-GILEAD *(22)*
(AKA RAMAH)
Ben-geber, in **R** (he had the 1Kg 4:13
Don't you know that **R** is ours, 1Kg 22:3
"Will you go with me to fight **R**?" 1Kg 22:4
I go against **R** for war or should 1Kg 22:6
March up to **R** and succeed, 1Kg 22:12
should we go to **R** for war, 1Kg 22:15
to march up and fall at **R**?' 1Kg 22:20
King Jehoshaphat went up to **R**. 1Kg 22:29
Hazael king of Aram in **R**, 2Kg 8:28
on him in **R** when he fought 2Kg 8:29
of oil with you, and go to **R**. 2Kg 9:1
So the young prophet went to **R**. 2Kg 9:4
had been at **R** on guard against 2Kg 9:14
persuaded him to march up to **R**, 2Ch 18:2
"Will you go with me to **R**?" 2Ch 18:3
Should we go to **R** for war or 2Ch 18:5
March up to **R** and succeed, 2Ch 18:11
should we go to **R** for war, 2Ch 18:14
to march up and fall at **R**?' 2Ch 18:19
King Jehoshaphat went up to **R**. 2Ch 18:28
Hazael, king of Aram, in **R**. 2Ch 22:5
on him in **R** when he fought 2Ch 22:6

RAMP *(10)*
built an assault **r** against the 2Sm 20:15
up an assault **r** against it. 2Kg 19:32
they construct a **r** against me Jb 19:12
their siege **r** against me. Jb 30:12
up an assault **r** against it. Is 37:33
raise a siege **r** against Jr 6:6
wall, build a **r**, pitch military Ezk 4:2
gates, build a **r**, and construct Ezk 21:22
will build a **r** and raise a wall Ezk 26:8
up an assault **r**, and capture Dn 11:15

RAMPANT *(1)*
stealing, and adultery are **r**; Hs 4:2

RAMPART *(1)*
her, whose **r** was the sea, the Nah 3:8

RAMPARTS *(3)*
note its **r**; tour its citadels so Ps 48:13
is established as walls and **r**. Is 26:1
He made the **r** and walls grieve; Lm 2:8

RAMPS *(5)*
I will besiege you with earth **r**, Is 29:3
Siege **r** have come against the Jr 32:24
the siege **r** and the sword: Jr 33:4
when **r** are built and siege walls Ezk 17:17
and build siege **r** to capture it. Hab 1:10

RAMS *(70)*
not eaten the **r** from your flock. Gn 31:38
20 male goats, 200 ewes, 20 **r**, Gn 32:14

bull and two unblemished **r**, Ex 29:1
along with the bull and two **r**. Ex 29:3
the two **r**, and the basket Lv 8:2
old, one young bull, and two **r**. Lv 23:18
two bulls, five **r**, five male Nm 7:17
two bulls, five **r**, five male Nm 7:23
two bulls, five **r**, five male Nm 7:29
two bulls, five **r**, five male Nm 7:35
two bulls, five **r**, five male Nm 7:41
two bulls, five **r**, five male Nm 7:47
two bulls, five **r**, five male Nm 7:53
two bulls, five **r**, five male Nm 7:59
two bulls, five **r**, five male Nm 7:65
two bulls, five **r**, five male Nm 7:71
two bulls, five **r**, five male Nm 7:77
two bulls, five **r**, five male Nm 7:83
bulls, 12 **r**, and 12 male lambs Nm 7:87
24 bulls, 60 **r**, 60 male breeding Nm 7:88
seven bulls and seven **r** for me." Nm 23:1
seven bulls and seven **r** for me." Nm 23:29
young bulls, two **r**, and 14 male Nm 29:13
quarts with each of the two **r**, Nm 29:14
young bulls, two **r**, and 14 male Nm 29:17
for the bulls, **r**, and lambs, Nm 29:18
11 bulls, two **r**, 14 male lambs a Nm 29:20
for the bulls, **r**, and lambs, Nm 29:21
10 bulls, two **r**, 14 male lambs a Nm 29:23
for the bulls, **r**, and lambs, Nm 29:24
nine bulls, two **r**, 14 male lambs Nm 29:26
for the bulls, **r**, and lambs, Nm 29:27
bulls, two **r**, 14 male lambs Nm 29:29
for the bulls, **r**, and lambs, Nm 29:30
seven bulls, two **r**, and 14 male Nm 29:32
for the bulls, **r**, and lambs, Nm 29:33
for the bulls, **r**, and lambs, Nm 29:37
the fat of lambs, **r** from Bashan, Dt 32:14
well as the young **r** and the best 1Sm 15:9
is better⌋ than the fat of **r**. 1Sm 15:22
lambs and the wool of 100,000 **r**, 2Kg 3:4
seven bulls and seven **r**. 1Ch 15:26
bulls, 1,000 **r**, and 1,000 lambs 1Ch 29:21
bull and seven **r** may become a 2Ch 13:9
7,700 **r** and 7,700 male goats. 2Ch 17:11
bulls, seven **r**, seven lambs, 2Ch 29:21
slaughtered the **r** and sprinkled 2Ch 29:22
70 bulls, 100 **r**, and 200 lambs; 2Ch 29:32
young bulls, **r**, and lambs for Ezr 6:9
100 bulls, 200 **r**, and 400 lambs, Ezr 6:17
as many bulls, **r**, and lambs as Ezr 7:17
all Israel, 96 **r**, and 77 lambs, Ezr 8:35
take seven bulls and seven **r**, Jb 42:8
with the fragrant smoke of **r**; Ps 66:15
The mountains skipped like **r**, Ps 114:4
that you skipped like **r**? Ps 114:6
burnt offerings and **r** and the Is 1:11
the fat of the kidneys of **r**. Is 34:6
the **r** of Nebaioth will serve you Is 60:7
Be like the **r** that lead the Jr 50:8
like **r** together with male goats. Jr 51:40
place battering **r** against it on Ezk 4:2
he should set up battering **r**, Ezk 21:22
set battering **r** against the Ezk 21:22
of his battering **r** against your Ezk 26:9
with you in lambs, **r**, and goats. Ezk 27:21
between the **r** and male goats. Ezk 34:17
r, lambs, male goats, and bulls, Ezk 39:18
and seven **r** without blemish Ezk 45:23
be pleased with thousands of **r**, Mc 6:7

RAMS' *(1)*
with trumpets, and with **r** horns. 2Ch 15:14

RAN *(63)*
much that she **r** away from her. Gn 16:6
he **r** from the entrance of the Gn 18:2
Abraham **r** to the herd and got a Gn 18:7
Then the servant **r** to meet her Gn 24:17
The girl **r** and told her mother's Gn 24:28
Laban **r** out to the man at the Gn 24:29
She **r** and told her father. Gn 29:12
son Jacob, he **r** to meet him, Gn 29:13
But Esau **r** to meet him, hugged Gn 33:4
hand, he escaped and **r** outside. Gn 39:12
garment with me and **r** outside." Gn 39:15
garment with me and **r** outside." Gn 39:18
became a snake. Moses **r** from it, Ex 4:3
A young man **r** and reported to Nm 11:27
r into the middle of the Nm 16:47
messengers who **r** to the tent, Jos 7:22
They **r**, entered the city, Jos 8:19
a few survivors **r** away to the Jos 10:20
It **r** down the Valley of Hinnom Jos 18:16
fled, and cried out as they **r**. Jdg 7:21
The woman **r** quickly to her Jdg 13:10
r to Eli and said, "Here I am; 1Sm 3:5
Benjaminite man **r** from the 1Sm 4:12
They **r** and got him from there. 1Sm 10:23
quartermaster and **r** to the 1Sm 17:22
David **r** quickly to the battle 1Sm 17:48
David **r** and stood over him. 1Sm 17:51
their hero was dead, they **r**. 1Sm 17:51
escaped. That night he **r** away. 1Sm 19:10
the young man **r**, Jonathan shot 1Sm 20:36
So Ahimaaz **r** by way of the plain 2Sm 18:23
Shimei's slaves **r** away to Achish 1Kg 2:39
So the water **r** all around the 1Kg 18:35
his belt and **r** ahead of Ahab to 1Kg 18:46
and immediately **r** for his life. 1Kg 19:3
left the oxen, **r** to follow 1Kg 19:20
yet they **r** ⌊with a message⌋. Jr 23:21
near; our time **r** out. Our end Lm 4:18
A wall on the outside **r** in front Ezk 42:7
on them, and they **r** and hid. Dn 10:7
deserted Him and **r** away. Mt 26:56
one of them **r** and got a sponge, Mt 27:48
they **r** to tell His disciples the Mt 28:8
he **r** and knelt down before Him. Mk 5:6
who tended them **r** off and Mk 5:14
People **r** there by land from all Mk 6:33
were amazed and **r** to greet Him. Mk 9:15
journey, a man **r** up, knelt down Mk 10:17
all deserted Him and **r** away. Mk 14:50
cloth behind and **r** away naked. Mk 14:52
Someone **r** and filled a sponge Mk 15:36
they **r** off and reported it in Lk 8:34
He **r**, threw his arms around his Lk 15:20
got up and **r** to the tomb. Lk 24:12
When the wine **r** out, Jesus' Jn 2:3
So she **r** to Simon Peter and to Jn 20:2
r toward them in what is called Ac 3:11
When Philip **r** up to it, he heard Ac 8:30
r in and announced that Peter Ac 12:14
we **r** a straight course to Ac 16:11
so that they **r** out of that house Ac 19:16
he immediately **r** down to them. Ac 21:32
sandbar and **r** the ship aground. Ac 27:41

RANG *(2)*
Then the cry **r** out in the army 1Kg 22:36
Lord's message **r** out from you, 1Th 1:8

RANGE *(7)*
of the Abarim ⌊**r**⌋ and see the Nm 27:12
in the Abarim ⌊**r**⌋ facing Nebo. Nm 33:47
from the Abarim ⌊**r**⌋ and camped Nm 33:48
in the Abarim ⌊**r**⌋ in the land Dt 32:49
fattened oxen, 20 **r** oxen, and 1Kg 4:23
eyes of the LORD **r** throughout 2Ch 16:9
who let ox and donkey **r** freely. Is 32:20

RANK *(9)*
and higher in **r** than the others. Nm 22:15
of the second **r** and the 2Kg 23:4
the priest of the second **r**, 2Kg 25:18
their relatives second in **r**: 1Ch 15:18
promoted him in **r** and gave him Est 3:1
promoted him in **r** and given him Est 5:11
Mordecai's great **r** to which the Est 10:2
the priest of the second **r**, Jr 52:24
higher in **r** than the angels Heb 1:4

RANKS *(10)*
and bring out the **r** of My people Ex 7:4
I brought your **r** out of the land Ex 12:17
I defy the **r** of Israel today. 1Sm 17:10
approaches the **r** is to be put to 2Kg 11:8
Take her out between the **r**, 2Kg 11:15
Take her out between the **r**, 2Ch 23:14
yet all of them march in **r**; Pr 30:27
missing from ⌊the invader's⌋ **r**. Is 14:31
his front **r** into the Dead Sea, Jl 2:20
they sat down in **r** of hundreds Mk 6:40

RANSOM *(15)*
If instead a **r** is demanded of Ex 21:30
men must pay a **r** for himself to Ex 30:12
not to accept a **r** for the life Nm 35:31
you accept a **r** for the person Nm 35:32
to the Pit; I have found a **r**," Jb 33:24
let a large **r** lead you astray Jb 36:18
a person or pay his **r** to God— Ps 49:7
r me because of my enemies. Ps 69:18
Riches are a **r** for a man's life, Pr 13:8
The wicked are a **r** for the Pr 21:18
give Egypt as a **r** for you, Is 43:3
I will **r** them from the power of Hs 13:14
give His life—a **r** for many." Mt 20:28
give His life—a **r** for many." Mk 10:45
gave Himself—a **r** for all, a 1Tm 2:6

RANSOMED *(5)*
it must be **r** according to your Lv 27:27
for destruction⌋ is to be **r**; Lv 27:29
the **r** of the LORD will return Is 35:10
the **r** of the LORD will return Is 51:11
for the LORD has **r** Jacob and Jr 31:11

RANTING *(2)*
"You know the sort and their **r**." 2Kg 9:11
there will be **r** and raving but Pr 29:9

RAPE *(1)*
but another man will **r** her. Dt 28:30

RAPED *(9)*
saw her, he took her and **r** her. Gn 34:2
only the man who **r** her must die. Dt 22:25
the man who **r** her must give the Dt 22:29
They **r** her and abused her all Jdg 19:25
me, but they **r** my concubine, Jdg 20:5
stronger than she was, he **r** her. 2Sm 13:14
be looted, and their wives **r**. Is 13:16
Women are **r** in Zion, virgins in Lm 5:11
houses looted, and the women **r**. Zch 14:2

RAPES *(2)*
he seizes and **r** her, only the Dt 22:25
takes hold of her and **r** her, Dt 22:28

RAPHA *(1)*
(AKA NAAMAN)
Nohah fourth, and **R** fifth. 1Ch 8:2

RAPHAH *(1)*
His son was **R**, his son Eleasah, 1Ch 8:37

RAPHU *(1)*
Palti son of **R** from the tribe of Nm 13:9

RAPIDLY *(4)*
increased **r**, multiplied, Ex 1:7
is near, near and **r** approaching. Zph 1:14
a crowd was **r** coming together Mk 9:25
may spread **r** and be honored, 2Th 3:1

RARE *(3)*
of the LORD was **r** and prophetic 1Sm 3:1
lips are a **r** treasure. Pr 20:15
and mankind more **r** than the gold Is 13:12

RARELY *(1)*
r will someone die for a just Rm 5:7

RASH *(8)*
it is ⌊only⌋ a **r** that has broken Lv 13:39
defect, a festering **r**, scabs, or Lv 21:20
sore, festering **r**, or scabs; Lv 22:22
her vows or the **r** commitment she Nm 30:6
binding or the **r** commitment she Nm 30:8
a festering **r**, and scabies, Dt 28:27
That is why my words are **r**. Jb 6:3
keep calm and not do anything **r**. Ac 19:36

RASHLY *(5)*
someone swears **r** to do what is Lv 5:4
person may speak **r** in an oath— Lv 5:4
and he spoke **r** with his lips. Ps 106:33
There is one who speaks **r**, Pr 12:18
dedicate something **r** and later Pr 20:25

RATE *(2)*
at the current commercial **r**. Gn 23:16
the **r** of 50 silver shekels for Lv 27:16

RATHER *(47)*
(See pp. xi-xii.)

RATIFIED *(2)*
human covenant that has been **r**, Gl 3:15
that was previously **r** by God, Gl 3:17

RATION *(2)*
single oven and **r** out your bread Lv 26:26
guard gave him a **r** and a gift Jr 40:5

RATIONED *(1)*
anxiously eat bread ⌊**r**⌋ by Ezk 4:16

RATS *(1)*
pigs, vermin, and **r**, will perish Is 66:17

RATTLES *(1)*
A quiver **r** at his side, along Jb 39:23

RATTLING *(1)*
was a noise, a **r** sound, and the Ezk 37:7

RAVAGE *(5)*
your children, **r** your livestock, Lv 26:22
against them to **r** the land where Jos 22:33
and the lot of those who **r** us. Is 17:14
from an arid plain will **r** them. Jr 5:6
They will **r** Egypt's pride, Ezk 32:12

RAVAGED *(3)*
r by pestilence and bitter Dt 32:24
by night—how **r** you will be! Ob 5
ravagers have **r** them and ruined Nah 2:2

RAVAGERS *(1)*
though **r** have ravaged them and Nah 2:2

RAVAGES *(3)*
Rescue my life from their **r**, Ps 35:17
the pestilence that **r** at noon. Ps 91:6
as an oven from the **r** of hunger. Lm 5:10

RAVAGING *(3)*
your prophets like a **r** lion. Jr 2:30
but inwardly are **r** wolves. Mt 7:15
however, was **r** the church, and Ac 8:3

RAVE *(1)*
and he began to **r** inside the 1Sm 18:10

RAVEN *(5)*
he sent out a **r**. It went back Gn 8:7
every kind of **r**, Lv 11:15
every kind of **r**, Dt 14:14
hair is wavy and black as a **r**. Sg 5:11
owl and the **r** will dwell there Is 34:11

RAVEN'S *(1)*
Who provides the **r** food when its Jb 38:41

RAVENS *(5)*
commanded the **r** to provide for 1Kg 17:4
r kept bringing him bread and 1Kg 17:6
and the young **r**, what they cry Ps 147:9
may **r** of the valley pluck it out Pr 30:17
Consider the **r**: they don't sow Lk 12:24

RAVINE *(2)*
which is south of the **r**. Jos 15:7
hill with a **r** between them. 1Sm 17:3

RAVINES *(11)*
Suphah and the **r** of the Arnon, Nm 21:14
slopes of the **r** that extend to Nm 21:15
come and settle in the steep **r**, Is 7:19
through a land of deserts and **r**, Jr 2:6
hills, to the **r** and the valleys Ezk 6:3
lay broken in all the earth's **r**. Ezk 31:12
the **r** will be filled with your Ezk 32:6
of Israel, in the **r**, and in all Ezk 34:13
your valleys, and in all your **r**. Ezk 35:8
hills, to the **r** and valleys, to Ezk 36:4
and hills, to the **r** and valleys: Ezk 36:6

RAVING *(2)*
kept on **r** until the offering 1Kg 18:29
be ranting and **r** but no Pr 29:9

RAVISHED *(2)*
rejoice any more, **r** young woman, Is 23:12
been stripped off, your body **r**. Jr 13:22

RAW *(8)*
not eat any of it **r** or cooked in Ex 12:9
there is a patch of **r** flesh in Lv 13:10
But whenever **r** flesh appears on Lv 13:14
the priest examines the **r** flesh, Lv 13:15
him unclean. **R** flesh is unclean; Lv 13:15
But if the **r** flesh changes and Lv 13:16
and the patch made **r** by the burn Lv 13:24
boiled meat from you—only **r**." 1Sm 2:15

RAYS *(2)*
his eyes are like the **r** of dawn. Jb 41:18
r are flashing from His hand. Hab 3:4

RAZOR *(3)*
Like a sharpened **r**, your tongue Ps 52:2
Lord will use a **r** hired from Is 7:20
it as you would a barber's **r**, Ezk 5:1

REACH *(40)*
evil, he must not **r** out, and Gn 3:22
and the border will **r** Zedad. Nm 34:8
down and **r** the eastern slope Nm 34:11
too difficult or beyond your **r**. Dt 30:11
'When you **r** the edge of the Jos 3:8
let's try to **r** one of these Jdg 19:13
in your family will **r** old age. 1Sm 2:31
will ever again **r** old age. 1Sm 2:32
to cross to **r** the Philistine 1Sm 14:4
Wait until we **r** you,' then we 1Sm 14:9
water shaft to **r** the lame and 2Sm 5:8
will never **r** the grave of your 1Kg 13:22
safe⌋ passage until I **r** Judah. Neh 2:7
are glad when they **r** the grave? Jb 3:22
we cannot **r** Him—He is exalted Jb 37:23
come, they will not **r** him. Ps 32:6
groans of the prisoners **r** You; Ps 79:11
May my prayer **r** Your presence; Ps 88:2
the pestilence will not **r** you. Ps 91:7
Let my cry **r** You, LORD; Ps 119:169
Let my plea **r** You; rescue me Ps 119:170
I am unable to ⌊**r**⌋ it. Ps 139:6
R down from on high; rescue me Ps 144:7
none **r** the paths of life. Pr 2:19
⌊harder to **r**⌋ than a fortified Pr 18:19
Her hands **r** out to the poor, Pr 31:20
is beyond ⌊**r**⌋ and very deep. Ec 7:24
messengers **r** as far as Hanes, Is 30:4
and righteousness does not **r** us. Is 59:9
would not ⌊**r** out⌋ to these Jr 15:1
trees would **r** them in height. Ezk 31:14
kingdom and will **r** an agreement Dn 11:17
escape from the **r** of disaster! Hab 2:9
R a settlement quickly with your Mt 5:25
R out your hand and put it into Jn 20:27
they might **r** out and find Him, Ac 17:27
hoping somehow to **r** Phoenix, Ac 27:12
we all **r** unity in the faith Eph 4:13
will somehow **r** the resurrection Php 3:11
that He does not **r** out to help Heb 2:16

REACHED *(91)*
r out and brought her into the Gn 8:9
has not yet **r** its full measure." Gn 15:16
the angels **r** out, brought Lot Gn 19:10
over the land when Lot **r** Zoar. Gn 19:23
Then Abraham **r** out and took the Gn 22:10
He **r** a certain place and spent Gn 28:11
and before he had **r** them, they Gn 37:18
When they **r** their father Jacob Gn 42:29
his brothers **r** Joseph's house, Gn 44:14
When the news **r** Pharaoh's house, Gn 45:16
When they **r** the threshing floor Gn 50:10
manna until they **r** the border Ex 16:35
When we **r** Kadesh-barnea, Dt 1:19
You have **r** the hill country of Dt 1:20
traveled until you **r** this place. Dt 1:31
of Egypt until you **r** this place. Dt 9:7
until you **r** this place; Dt 11:5
you **r** this place, Sihon king Dt 29:7
carrying the ark **r** the Jordan, Jos 3:15
set out and **r** the Gibeonite Jos 9:17
Then the border **r** to the slope Jos 15:11
and then **r** Jericho and went to Jos 16:7
They **r** Asher on the north and Jos 17:10
to Maralah, **r** Dabbesheth, and Jos 19:11
The border **r** Tabor, Shahazumah, Jos 19:22
and Mishal and **r** westward to Jos 19:26
of Egypt and you **r** the Red Sea, Jos 24:6
Ehud **r** with his left hand, Jdg 3:21
the carved images and **r** Seirah. Jdg 3:26
She **r** for a tent peg, her right Jdg 5:26
a donkey, **r** out his hand, took Jdg 15:15
He **r** out with the end of the 1Sm 14:27
all night and **r** Hebron at dawn. 2Sm 2:32
Uzzah **r** out to the ark of God 2Sm 6:6
on the way, a report **r** David: 2Sm 13:30
to him, Absalom **r** out his hand, 2Sm 15:5
all Israel has **r** the king at his 2Sm 19:11
my cry for help ⌊**r**⌋ His ears. 2Sm 22:7
He **r** down from on high and took 2Sm 22:17
The news **r** Joab. Since he had 1Kg 2:28
So he **r** out and took it. 2Kg 6:7
The messenger **r** them but hasn't 2Kg 9:18
He **r** them but hasn't started 2Kg 9:20
your arrogance have **r** My ears, 2Kg 19:28
Uzzah **r** out to hold the ark, 1Ch 13:9
because he had **r** out to the ark. 1Ch 13:10
in a rage that has **r** heaven. 2Ch 28:9
king's command and his law **r**, Est 8:17
and my cry to Him **r** His ears. Ps 18:6
He **r** down from on high and took Ps 18:16
My hand has **r** out, as if into a Is 10:14
vines that **r** as far as Jazer Is 16:8
spread out and **r** the Dead Sea. Is 16:8
Word has **r** them from the land of Is 23:1
your arrogance has **r** My ears, Is 37:29
Then the LORD **r** out His hand, Jr 1:9
because it has **r** your heart! Jr 4:18
they have **r** to the sea ⌊and to⌋ Jr 48:32
the cherubim **r** out his hand to Ezk 10:7
its top **r** to the sky, and it was Dn 4:11
whose top **r** to the sky and was Dn 4:20
When he **r** the den, he cried out Dn 6:20
They had not **r** the bottom of the Dn 6:24
the rebels have **r** the full Dn 8:23
When word **r** the king of Nineveh, Jnh 3:6
incurable and has **r** even Judah; Mc 1:9
Jesus **r** out His hand, Mt 14:31
The disciples **r** the other shore, Mt 16:5
When they **r** the crowd, a man Mt 17:14
those with Jesus **r** out his hand Mt 26:51
Jesus **r** out His hand and touched Mk 1:41
of your greeting **r** my ears, Lk 1:44
When they **r** Jesus, they pleaded Lk 7:4
When the men **r** Him, they said, Lk 7:20
When He **r** the place, He told Lk 22:40
who had **r** the tomb first, Jn 20:8
the report about them **r** the ears Ac 11:22
from Perga and **r** Antioch in Ac 13:14
the decisions **r** by the apostles Ac 16:4
When they **r** Ephesus he left them Ac 18:19
In five days we **r** them at Troas, Ac 20:6
from Tyre, we **r** Ptolemais, where Ac 21:7
we **r** Jerusalem, the brothers Ac 21:17
Pamphylia, we **r** Myra in Lycia. Ac 27:5
along the coast, we **r** Rhegium. Ac 28:13
your obedience has **r** everyone. Rm 16:19
since we have **r** this conclusion: 2Co 5:14
as if we had not **r** you, since we 2Co 10:14
have already **r** ⌊the goal⌋ or am Php 3:12
the harvesters has **r** the ears of Jms 5:4
who fears has not **r** perfection 1Jn 4:18

REACHES *(19)*
Nophah, which **r** as far as Medeba Nm 21:30
Though his arrogance **r** heaven, Jb 20:6
The sword that **r** him will have Jb 41:26
faithful love ⌊**r**⌋ to heaven, Ps 36:5
r to the ends of the earth; Ps 48:10
He **r** down from heaven and saves Ps 57:3
faithfulness **r** to the clouds. Ps 57:10
Your righteousness **r** heaven, Ps 71:19
Your faithfulness **r** the clouds. Ps 108:4
Their wailing **r** Eglaim; Is 15:8
their wailing **r** Beer-elim. Is 15:8
When the news **r** Egypt, they will Is 23:5
The tumult **r** to the ends of the Jr 25:31
to the sky and **r** as far as the Jr 51:9
has grown and even **r** the sky, Dn 4:22
who waits for and **r** 1,335 days. Dn 12:12
the news that **r** their assembly. Hs 7:12
If this **r** the governor's ears, Mt 28:14
to us, ⌊which⌋ **r** even to you. 2Co 10:13

REACHING *(9)*
ground with its top **r** heaven, Gn 28:12
there to Hukkok, **r** Zebulun on Jos 19:34
r the wing of the other cherub. 2Ch 3:12
sweep through, **r** up to the neck; Is 8:8
and saw a hand **r** out to me, Ezk 2:9
r to the top of the entrance, Ezk 41:17
R out His hand He touched him, Mt 8:3
R out His hand, He touched him, Lk 5:13
is behind and **r** forward to what Php 3:13

READ *(75)*
scroll and **r** ⌊it⌋ aloud to Ex 24:7
and he is to **r** from it all the Dt 17:19
you are to **r** this law aloud Dt 31:11
Joshua **r** aloud all the words of Jos 8:34
Joshua did not **r** before the Jos 8:35
to the king of Israel, and it **r**: 2Kg 5:6
the king of Israel **r** the letter, 2Kg 5:7
the messengers, **r** it, then went 2Kg 19:14
the book to Shaphan, who **r** it. 2Kg 22:8
and Shaphan **r** it in the 2Kg 22:10
that the king of Judah has **r**, 2Kg 22:16
r all the words of the book of 2Kg 23:2
and Shaphan **r** it in the 2Ch 34:18
book that they **r** in the presence 2Ch 34:24
He **r** in their hearing all the 2Ch 34:30
translated and **r** in my presence. Ezr 4:18
letter was **r** to Rehum, Ezr 4:23
he **r** out of it from daybreak Neh 8:3
They **r** the book of the law of Neh 8:8
could understand what was **r**. Neh 8:8
Ezra **r** out of the book of the Neh 8:18
they **r** from the book of the law Neh 9:3
book of Moses was **r** publicly to Neh 13:1

to be brought and **r** to the king. Est 6:1
to one who can **r** and he is asked Is 29:11
read and he is asked to **r** it, Is 29:11
say, "I can't **r** it, because it Is 29:11
one who cannot **r** and he is asked Is 29:12
read and he is asked to **r** it, Is 29:12
it, he will say, "I can't **r**." Is 29:12
Search and **r** the scroll of the Is 34:16
the messengers, **r** it, then went Is 37:14
the priest **r** this letter Jr 29:29
must go and **r** from the scroll Jr 36:6
You must also **r** them in the Jr 36:6
temple he **r** the LORD's words Jr 36:8
Baruch **r** Jeremiah's words from Jr 36:10
when Baruch **r** from the scroll Jr 36:13
scroll that you **r** in the hearing Jr 36:14
Sit down and **r** ⌊it⌋ in our Jr 36:15
So Baruch **r** ⌊it⌋ in their Jr 36:15
Jehudi then **r** it in the hearing Jr 36:21
as Jehudi would **r** three or four Jr 36:23
see that you **r** all these words Jr 51:61
but none could **r** the inscription Dn 5:8
before me to **r** this inscription Dn 5:15
you can **r** this inscription and Dn 5:16
I will **r** the inscription for the Dn 5:17
tablets so one may easily **r** it. Hab 2:2
Haven't you **r** what David did Mt 12:3
Or haven't you **r** in the Law that Mt 12:5
You know how to **r** the appearance Mt 16:3
but you can't **r** the signs of the Mt 16:3
"Haven't you **r**," He replied, Mt 19:4
Have you never **r**: You have Mt 21:16
Have you never **r** in the Mt 21:42
haven't you **r** what was spoken to Mt 22:31
Have you never **r** what David and Mk 2:25
Haven't you **r** this Scripture: Mk 12:10
haven't you **r** in the book of Mk 12:26
Sabbath day and stood up to **r**. Lk 4:16
Haven't you **r** what David and Lk 6:3
He asked him. "How do you **r** it?" Lk 10:26
Many of the Jews **r** this sign, Jn 19:20
that are **r** every Sabbath, Ac 13:27
and he is **r** aloud in the Ac 15:21
When they **r** it, they rejoiced Ac 15:31
After he **r** it, he asked what Ac 23:34
than what you can **r** and also 2Co 1:13
recognized and **r** by everyone, 2Co 3:2
Moses is **r**, a veil lies over 2Co 3:15
letter has been **r** among you, Col 4:16
have it **r** also in the church of Col 4:16
see that you also **r** the letter Col 4:16
this letter be **r** to all the 1Th 5:27

READER *(2)*
place" (let the **r** understand), Mt 24:15
not" (let the **r** understand), Mk 13:14

READINESS *(2)*
yourselves ⌊in **r**⌋ for tomorrow, Nm 11:18
sandaled with **r** for the gospel Eph 6:15

READING *(9)*
you have finished **r** this scroll, Jr 51:63
r the prophet Isaiah aloud. Ac 8:28
he heard him **r** the prophet Ac 8:30
you understand what you're **r**?" Ac 8:30
passage he was **r** was this: Ac 8:32
After the **r** of the Law and the Ac 13:15
at the **r** of the old covenant, 2Co 3:14
By **r** this you are able to Eph 3:4
give your attention to public **r**, 1Tm 4:13

READS *(2)*
Whoever **r** this inscription and Dn 5:7
is the one who **r** and blessed are Rv 1:3

READY *(62)*
at Shechem. Get **r**. I'm sending Gn 37:13
"I'm **r**," Joseph replied. Gn 37:13
stand **r** to meet him by the bank Ex 7:15
got his chariot **r** and took his Ex 14:6
ourselves and be **r** ⌊to go⌋ ahead Nm 32:17
'Get provisions **r** for yourselves, Jos 1:11
from it, and all of you be **r**. Jos 8:4
I was carrying. I am **r** to die!" 1Sm 14:43
your chariot⌋ **r** and go down so 1Kg 18:44
to life, "Get **r**, you and your 2Kg 8:1
So the woman got **r** and did what 2Kg 8:2
7,100 brave warriors **r** for war. 1Ch 12:25
The trumpets are **r** to sound the 2Ch 13:12
they might get **r** for that day. Est 3:14
the Jews could be **r** to avenge Est 8:13
disaster lies **r** for him to Jb 18:12
Get **r** to answer Me like a man; Jb 38:3
Get **r** to answer Me like a man; Jb 40:7
strung His bow and made it **r**. Ps 7:12
are kind and **r** to forgive, Ps 86:5
May Your hand be **r** to help me, Ps 119:173
has been **r** for the king for Is 30:33
Now, get **r**. Stand up and tell Jr 1:17
mighty men ⌊**r**⌋ for battle? Jr 48:14
It is **r** to flash like lightning; Ezk 21:15
Be prepared and get yourself **r**, Ezk 38:7
Now if you're **r**, when you hear Dn 3:15
the arrows are **r** to be used with Hab 3:9
gloating as if **r** to secretly Hab 3:14
When that is **r**, ⌊the basket⌋ Zch 5:11
and I will be **r** to witness Mal 3:5
now the ax is **r** to strike the Mt 3:10
and everything is **r**. Mt 22:4
The banquet is **r**, but those who Mt 22:8
This is why you also must be **r**, Mt 24:44
those who were **r** went in with Mt 25:10
to have a small boat **r** for Him, Mk 3:9
But as soon as the crop is **r**, Mk 4:29
room upstairs, furnished and **r**. Mk 14:15
make **r** for the Lord a prepared Lk 1:17
now the ax is **r** to strike the Lk 3:9
Be **r** for service and have your Lk 12:35
He will get **r**, have them recline Lk 12:37
You also be **r**, because the Son Lk 12:40
because everything is now **r**.' Lk 14:17
me to eat, get **r**, and serve me Lk 17:8
I'm **r** to go with You both to Lk 22:33
for they are **r** for harvest. Jn 4:35
For I am **r** not only to be bound, Ac 21:13
days we got **r** and went up to Ac 21:15
near, we are **r** to kill him." Ac 23:15
Now they are **r**, waiting for a Ac 23:21
200 soldiers **r** with 70 cavalry Ac 23:23
of wrath **r** for destruction Rm 9:22
that it will be **r** as a gift and 2Co 9:5
And we are **r** to punish any 2Co 10:6
I am **r** to come to you this third 2Co 12:14
to be **r** for every good work, Ti 3:1
that is **r** to be revealed 1Pt 1:5
get your minds **r** for action, 1Pt 1:13
always be **r** to give a defense 1Pt 3:15
One who stands **r** to judge the 1Pt 4:5

REAIAH *(2)*
R son of Shobal fathered Jahath, 1Ch 4:2
Micah, his son **R**, his son Baal, 1Ch 5:5

REAIAH'S *(2)*
descendants, **R** descendants, Ezr 2:47
R descendants, Rezin's Neh 7:50

REAL *(6)*
gives you the **r** bread from Jn 6:32
My flesh is **r** food and My blood Jn 6:55
food and My blood is **r** drink. Jn 6:55
place through the angel was **r**, Ac 12:9
The **r** widow, left all alone, has 1Tm 5:5
may take hold of life that is **r**. 1Tm 6:19

REALITIES *(1)*
not the actual form of those **r**, Heb 10:1

REALITY *(2)*
the end the **r** that we had at Heb 3:14
faith is the **r** of what is hoped Heb 11:1

REALIZATION *(1)*
for the final **r** of your hope, Heb 6:11

REALIZE *(11)*
They did not **r** that Joseph Gn 42:23
Don't you **r** yet that Egypt is Ex 10:7
did not **r** that the skin of his Ex 34:29
Don't you **r** that the Philistines Jdg 15:11
Don't you **r** this will only end 2Sm 2:26
Didn't you **r** they would shoot 2Sm 11:20
R now that the LORD has chosen 1Ch 28:10
r that wisdom is the same for Pr 24:14
him, "Don't you **r** that Baalis, Jr 40:14
Don't you **r** that whatever goes Mt 15:17
Don't you **r** that nothing going Mk 7:18

REALIZED *(29)*
she **r** that she was pregnant, Gn 16:4
Esau **r** that his father Isaac Gn 28:8
When she **r** that he had left his Gn 39:13
When Gideon **r** that He was the Jdg 6:22
Then Manoah **r** that it was the Jdg 13:21
When Delilah **r** that he had told Jdg 16:18
the Benjaminites **r** they had been Jdg 20:36
when they **r** that disaster had Jdg 20:41
Saul **r** that the LORD was with 1Sm 18:28
the Ammonites **r** they had become 2Sm 10:6
Ahithophel **r** that his advice 2Sm 17:23
him because he **r** that all those 2Sm 20:12
woke up and **r** it had been a 1Kg 3:15
at him I **r** that he was not 1Kg 3:21
the Ammonites **r** they had made 1Ch 19:6
When the Arameans **r** that they 1Ch 19:16
When our enemies **r** that we knew Neh 4:15
I **r** that God had not sent him, Neh 6:12
for they **r** that this task had Neh 6:16
life because he **r** the king was Est 7:7
And I **r** that there is an Ec 2:13
At once Jesus **r** in Himself that Mk 5:30
Then they **r** that he had seen a Lk 1:22
The father **r** this was the very Jn 4:53
and John and **r** that they were Ac 4:13
When he **r** this, he went to the Ac 12:12
alarmed when he **r** Paul was a Ac 22:29
Paul **r** that one part of them Ac 23:6
Now I **r** that he had not done Ac 25:25

REALIZING *(1)*
with no one **r** that the righteous Is 57:1

REALLY *(49)*
(See pp. xi-xii.)

REALM *(12)*
and in all his **r** that Hezekiah 2Kg 20:13
fall on the **r** of the king and Ezr 7:23
and in all his **r** that Hezekiah Is 39:2
Your **r** was in the heart of the Ezk 27:4
stationed throughout the **r**, Dn 6:1
to set him over the whole **r**. Dn 6:3
rule a vast **r** and do whatever Dn 11:3
to a visionary **r** and inflated Col 2:18
in the fleshly **r** but made alive 1Pt 3:18
made alive in the spiritual **r**. 1Pt 3:18
judged by men in the fleshly **r**, 1Pt 4:6
live by God in the spiritual **r**. 1Pt 4:6

REAP *(32)*
When you **r** the harvest of your Lv 19:9
are not to **r** to the very edge Lv 19:9
am giving you and **r** its harvest, Lv 23:10
When you **r** the harvest of your Lv 23:22
you are not to **r** all the way to Lv 23:22
You are not to **r** what grows by Lv 25:5
you are not to sow, **r** what grows Lv 25:11
When you **r** the harvest in your Dt 24:19
his ground or **r** his harvest, 1Sm 8:12
But in the third year sow and **r**, 2Kg 19:29
who sow trouble **r** the same. Jb 4:8
sow in tears will **r** with shouts Ps 126:5
sows injustice will **r** disaster, Pr 22:8
looks at the clouds will not **r**. Ec 11:4
But in the third year sow and **r**, Is 37:30
the wind and **r** the whirlwind. Hs 8:7
yourselves and **r** faithful love; Hs 10:12
You will sow but not **r**; Mc 6:15
they don't sow or **r** or gather Mt 6:26
knew that I **r** where I haven't Mt 25:26
don't sow or **r**; they don't have Lk 12:24
deposit and **r** what you didn't Lk 19:21
I sent you to **r** what you didn't Jn 4:38
too much if we **r** material things 1Co 9:11
sparingly will also **r** sparingly, 2Co 9:6
will also **r** generously. 2Co 9:6
a man sows he will also **r**, Gl 6:7
to his flesh will **r** corruption Gl 6:8
the Spirit will **r** eternal life Gl 6:8
for we will **r** at the proper time Gl 6:9
your sickle and **r**, for the time Rv 14:15
for the time to **r** has come, Rv 14:15

REAPED *(3)*
that year he **r** a hundred times Gn 26:12
wickedness and **r** injustice; Hs 10:13
the workers who **r** your fields Jms 5:4

REAPER *(6)*
the hands of the **r** or the arms Ps 129:7
will be as if a **r** had gathered Is 17:5
grain after the **r** with no one to Jr 9:22
overtake the **r** and the one who Am 9:13
The **r** is already receiving pay Jn 4:36
so the sower and **r** can rejoice Jn 4:36

REAPERS *(1)*
At harvest time I'll tell the **r**: Mt 13:30

REAPING *(2)*
r where you haven't sown and Mt 25:24
deposit and **r** what I didn't sow Lk 19:22

REAPPEARS *(2)*
But if it **r** in the fabric, Lv 13:57
the contamination **r** in the house Lv 14:43

REAPS *(1)*
'One sows and another **r**.' Jn 4:37

REAR *(7)*
and the **r** guard went behind the Jos 6:9
and the **r** guard went behind the Jos 6:13
the city and its **r** guard to the Jos 8:13
30 feet of the **r** of the temple 1Kg 6:16
God of Israel is your **r** guard. Is 52:12
glory will be your **r** guard. Is 58:8
and his **r** guard into the Jl 2:20

REARED *(4)*
If it **r** up against me, I would 1Sm 17:35
those I nurtured and **r**. Lm 2:22
those who were **r** in purple Lm 4:5
she **r** her cubs among the young Ezk 19:2

REARGUARD *(1)*
serving as **r** for all the camps, Nm 10:25

REASON *(60)*
For this **r** you stayed in Kadesh Dt 1:46
For this **r**, Levi does not have a Dt 10:9
This is the **r** for Joshua circumcised Jos 5:4
Then the **r** His hand hasn't been 1Sm 6:3
by killing David for no **r**?" 1Sm 19:5
For this **r** it is said, "The 2Sm 5:8
and this is the **r** he rebelled 1Kg 11:27
unclean could enter for any **r**. 2Ch 23:19
This is the **r** you are building Neh 6:6
For this **r** these days are called Est 9:26
the world's leaders of **r**, Jb 12:24
an upright man could **r** with Him, Jb 23:7
many hate me for no **r**. Ps 38:19
Who has wounds for no **r**? Pr 23:29
For no ⌊apparent⌋ **r**, my enemies Lm 3:52
disaster on them without a **r**. Ezk 6:10
This was the **r** for the temple's Ezk 41:7
For this **r** the land mourns, Hs 4:3
Yet you ask, "For what **r**?" Mal 2:14
For this **r** they will be your Mt 12:27
For this **r** I speak to them in Mt 13:13
this **r**, the kingdom of heaven Mt 18:23
For this **r** a man will leave his Mt 19:5
For this **r** a man will leave his Mk 10:7
and the Pharisees began to **r**: Lk 5:21
declared the **r** she had touched Lk 8:47
For this **r** they will be your Lk 11:19
he was the **r** many of the Jews Jn 12:11
They hated Me for no **r**. Jn 15:25
What is the **r** you're here?" Ac 10:21
we can give as a **r** for this Ac 19:40
discover the **r** they were Ac 22:24
For this **r** he sent for him quite Ac 24:26
For this **r** the Jews seized me in Ac 26:21
for this **r** I've asked to see you Ac 28:20
For this **r** I raised you up: Rm 9:17
not carry the sword for no **r**. Rm 13:4
And for this **r** you pay taxes, Rm 13:6
Therefore I have **r** to boast in Rm 15:17
I have no **r** to boast, because 1Co 9:16
that we are your **r** for pride, 2Co 1:14
For this **r** we have been 2Co 7:13
he will have a **r** for boasting Gl 6:4
this **r**, I, Paul, the prisoner Eph 3:1
For this **r** I bow my knees before Eph 3:14
For this **r** a man will leave his Eph 5:31
him to you for this very **r**, Eph 6:22
For this **r** God also highly Php 2:9
For this **r**, I am very eager to Php 2:28
For this **r** also, since the day Col 1:9
For this **r**, when I could no 1Th 3:5
For this **r** God sends them a 2Th 2:11
The **r** I left you in Crete was to Ti 1:5
this **r**, although I have great Phm 8
it's without **r** the Scripture Jms 4:5
asks you for a **r** for the hope 1Pt 3:15
For this **r** the gospel was also 1Pt 4:6
For this very **r**, make every 2Pt 1:5
The **r** the world does not know us 1Jn 3:1
For this **r** they are before the Rv 7:15

REASONABLE *(2)*
R men will say to me, along with Jb 34:34
it would be **r** for me to put up Ac 18:14

REASONED *(6)*
They had **r**, "The people must be 2Sm 17:29
they were terrified and **r**, 2Kg 10:4
three Sabbath days **r** with them Ac 17:2
he **r** in the synagogue with the Ac 17:17
He **r** in the synagogue every Ac 18:4
like a child, I **r** like a child. 1Co 13:11

REASONING *(3)*
they were **r** like this within Mk 2:8
Why are you **r** these things in Mk 2:8
Why are you **r** this in your Lk 5:22

REASONINGS *(1)*
Lord knows the **r** of the wise, 1Co 3:20

REASONS *(1)*
But He finds **r** to oppose me; Jb 33:10

REASSIGNED *(1)*
Saul **r** David and made him 1Sm 18:13

REBA *(2)*
Zur, Hur, and **R**, the five kings Nm 31:8
Zur, Hur, and **R**—the princes Jos 13:21

REBEKAH *(28)*
And Bethuel fathered **R**. Gn 22:23
speaking, there was **R**—daughter Gn 24:15
R had a brother named Laban, Gn 24:29
there was **R** coming with her jug Gn 24:45
R is here in front of you. Gn 24:51
garments, and gave ⌊them⌋ to **R**. Gn 24:53
They called **R** and said to her, Gn 24:58
their sister **R** and her nurse, Gn 24:59
They blessed **R**, saying to her: Gn 24:60
Then **R** and her young women got Gn 24:61
So the servant took **R** and left. Gn 24:61
R looked up, and when she saw Gn 24:64
Sarah and took **R** to be his wife. Gn 24:67
took as his wife **R** daughter of Gn 25:20
and his wife **R** conceived. Gn 25:21
wild game, but **R** loved Jacob. Gn 25:28
will kill me on account of **R**, Gn 26:7
see Isaac caressing his wife **R**. Gn 26:8
life bitter for Isaac and **R**. Gn 26:35
R was listening to what Isaac Gn 27:5
R said to her son Jacob, "Listen! Gn 27:6
Jacob answered **R** his mother, Gn 27:11
Then **R** took the best clothes of Gn 27:15
son Esau were reported to **R**, Gn 27:42
So **R** said to Isaac, "I'm sick of Gn 27:46
the brother of **R**, the mother of Gn 28:5
and his wife **R** are buried there Gn 49:31
but also when **R** became pregnant Rm 9:10

REBEKAH'S *(3)*
had heard his sister **R** words— Gn 24:30
her father's relative, **R** son. Gn 29:12
Deborah, **R** nurse, died and was Gn 35:8

REBEL *(21)*
But when you **r**, you will break Gn 27:40
Only don't **r** against the LORD, Nm 14:9
more ⌊will you **r**⌋ after I am Dt 31:27
If you **r** against the LORD today, Jos 22:18
But don't **r** against the LORD or Jos 22:19
would never **r** against the LORD Jos 22:29
and if you don't **r** against the 1Sm 12:14
the LORD and **r** against His 1Sm 12:15
that you and the Jews plan to **r**. Neh 6:6
are those who **r** against the Jb 24:13
do the nations **r** and the peoples Ps 2:1
crimes, for they **r** against You. Ps 5:10
from those who **r** against Your Ps 17:7
they continued to **r** deliberately Ps 106:43
detest those who **r** against You? Ps 139:21
if you refuse and **r**, you will be Is 1:20
were known as a **r** from birth. Is 48:8
of those who **r** and transgress Ezk 20:38
covenant and **r** against My law. Hs 8:1
to Bethel and **r**; rebel even more Am 4:4
r even more at Gilgal! Am 4:4

REBELLED *(54)*
in the thirteenth year they **r**. Gn 14:4
and they **r** against Moses. Nm 16:2
because you both **r** against My Nm 20:24
of you **r** against My command Nm 27:14
You **r** against the LORD's command Dt 1:43
you **r** against the command of the Dt 9:23
Then Jeshurun became fat and **r**— Dt 32:15
lords of Shechem **r** against him Jdg 9:25
up the men who **r** against my lord 2Sm 18:28
who has **r** against King David. 2Sm 20:21
Jeroboam **r** against Solomon, 1Kg 11:26
the reason he **r** against the king 1Kg 11:27
'Because you **r** against the 1Kg 13:21
of Ahab, Moab **r** against Israel. 2Kg 1:1
king of Moab **r** against the king 2Kg 3:5
king of Moab has **r** against me. 2Kg 3:7
Edom **r** against Judah's control 2Kg 8:20
Libnah also **r** at that time. 2Kg 8:22
He **r** against the king of Assyria 2Kg 18:7
so that you have **r** against me? 2Kg 18:20
he turned and **r** against him. 2Kg 24:1
Zedekiah **r** against the king of 2Kg 24:20
rose up and **r** against his lord. 2Ch 13:6
r against Judah's domination 2Ch 21:8
Libnah also **r** at that time 2Ch 21:10
He also **r** against King 2Ch 36:13
for we have **r** terribly in this Ezr 10:13
disobedient and **r** against You. Neh 9:26
How often they **r** against Him in Ps 78:40
instead, they **r** by the sea—the Ps 106:7
because they **r** against God's Ps 107:11
but they have **r** against Me. Is 1:2
have greatly **r** against. Is 31:6
in that you have **r** against me? Is 36:5
mediators have **r** against Me. Is 43:27
But they **r**, and grieved His Holy Is 63:10
the men who have **r** against Me; Is 66:24
and the rulers **r** against Me. Jr 2:8
All of you have **r** against Me. Jr 2:29
you have **r** against the LORD your Jr 3:13
because she has **r** against Me. Jr 4:17
Zedekiah **r** against the king of Jr 52:3
I have **r** against His command. Lm 1:18
We have sinned and **r**; Lm 3:42
nations who have **r** against Me. Ezk 2:3
But she has **r** against My Ezk 5:6
But they **r** against Me and were Ezk 20:8
the house of Israel **r** against Me Ezk 20:13
But the children **r** against Me. Ezk 20:21
acted wickedly, **r**, and turned Dn 9:5
though we have **r** against Him Dn 9:9
to them, for they **r** against Me! Hs 7:13
she has **r** against her God Hs 13:16
For who heard and **r**? Heb 3:16

REBELLING *(9)*
r against the command of the Dt 1:26
You have been **r** against the LORD Dt 9:7
You have been **r** against the LORD Dt 9:24
If you are **r** against the LORD Dt 31:27
Are you **r** against the king?" Neh 2:19
r in the desert against the Most Ps 78:17
Why do you keep on **r**? Is 1:5
against Me, **r** against Me. Jr 33:8
you have done in **r** against Me. Zph 3:11

REBELLION *(47)*
will not forgive your acts of **r**, Ex 23:21
wrongdoing, **r**, and sin. Ex 34:7
forgiving wrongdoing and **r**. Nm 14:18
he has urged **r** against the LORD Dt 13:5
that you are in **r** against the Jos 22:16
if ⌊it was⌋ in **r** or treachery Jos 22:22
For **r** is like the sin of 1Sm 15:23
there is no evil or **r** in me. 1Sm 24:11
Israel is in **r** against the house 1Kg 12:19
is still in **r** against Judah's 2Kg 8:22
Israel is in **r** against the house 2Ch 10:19
is still in **r** against Judah's 2Ch 21:10
He gave them over to their **r**. Jb 8:4
r would be sealed up in a bag, Jb 14:17
my eyes must gaze at their **r**. Jb 17:2
For he adds **r** to his sin; Jb 34:37
and you will perish in your **r**, Ps 2:12
and cleansed from blatant **r**. Ps 19:13
of my youth or my acts of **r**; Ps 25:7
compassion, blot out my **r**. Ps 51:1
For I am conscious of my **r**, Ps 51:3
because of any sin or **r** of mine. Ps 59:3
call their **r** to account with Ps 89:32
An evil man seeks only **r**; Pr 17:11
When a land is in **r**, it has many Pr 28:2
wicked increase, **r** increases, Pr 29:16
a hot-tempered man increases **r**. Pr 29:22
Earth's **r** weighs it down, and it Is 24:20
struck because of My people's **r**. Is 53:8
you have spoken **r** against the Jr 28:16

He **r** them, and they flee far Is 17:13
in anger, wrath, and furious **r**. Ezk 5:15
against them with furious **r**. Ezk 25:17
r the sea so that it dries up, Nah 1:4

REBUKING *(2)*
But the other answered, **r** him: Lk 23:40
teaching, for **r**, for correcting 2Tm 3:16

REBURIED *(1)*
a field, that a man found and **r**. Mt 13:44

RECAH *(1)*
These were the men of **R**. 1Ch 4:12

RECALL *(2)*
We **r**, in the presence of our God 1Th 1:3
may be able to **r** these things at 2Pt 1:15

RECALLING *(2)*
r ⌊it only⌋ as waters that have Jb 11:16
clearly **r** your sincere faith 2Tm 1:5

RECEDE *(1)*
continued to **r** until the tenth Gn 8:5

RECEDED *(1)*
water steadily **r** from the earth, Gn 8:3

RECEIVE *(120)*
its mouth to **r** your brother's Gn 4:11
Then I will **r** glory by means of Ex 14:4
and I will **r** glory by means of Ex 14:17
the LORD when I **r** glory through Ex 14:18
offering you are to **r** from them: Ex 25:3
no relative to **r** compensation, Nm 5:8
will not **r** an inheritance Nm 18:23
they would not **r** an inheritance Nm 18:24
When you **r** from the Israelites Nm 18:26
every tenth you **r** from the Nm 18:28
they will **r** an inheritance Nm 26:55
You are to **r** the land as an Nm 33:54
You will **r** an inheritance Nm 33:54
the land you are to **r** by lot as Nm 34:13
the mountain to **r** the stone Dt 9:9
you will **r** in the land the LORD Dt 19:14
but you will **r** no honor on the Jdg 4:9
and may you **r** a full reward from Ru 2:12
You will not **r** honor from the 2Ch 26:18
and your sons ⌊will **r**⌋ mercy in 2Ch 30:9
so that they could **r** written Ezr 5:5
silver and gold you **r** throughout Ezr 7:16
required her to **r** beauty Est 2:12
did the knees **r** me, and why were Jb 3:12
man should **r** loyalty from his Jb 6:14
If his sons **r** honor, he does not Jb 14:21
R instruction from His mouth, Jb 22:22
ruthless **r** from the Almighty. Jb 27:13
what does He **r** from your hand? Jb 35:7
r instruction, you judges of the Ps 2:10
will **r** blessing from the LORD, Ps 24:5
a drink of water will **r** water. Pr 11:25
to counsel and **r** instruction so Pr 19:20
eyes away will **r** many curses. Pr 28:27
and He will **r** the mighty as Is 53:12
do not listen and **r** discipline. Jr 32:33
even her prophets **r** no vision Lm 2:9
be ashamed when you **r** your older Ezk 16:61
Should you then **r** possession of Ezk 33:25
Should you then **r** possession of Ezk 33:26
Joseph will **r** two shares. Ezk 47:13
to me, you'll **r** gifts, a reward, Dn 2:6
the Most High will **r** the kingdom Dn 7:18
the earth **r** praise and fame. Zph 3:19
is a prophet will **r** a prophet's Mt 10:41
righteous will **r** a righteous Mt 10:41
of My name will **r** 100 times more Mt 19:29
you will **r** whatever you ask for Mt 21:22
is why you will **r** a harsher Mt 23:14
immediately they **r** it with joy. Mk 4:16
who will not **r** 100 times more, Mk 10:30
will **r** harsher punishment." Mk 12:40
those from whom you expect to **r**, Lk 6:34
blind **r** their sight, the lame Lk 7:22
who will not **r** many times more Lk 18:30
"**R** your sight!" Jesus told him. Lk 18:42
a far country to **r** for himself Lk 19:12
will **r** greater punishment." Lk 20:47
His own people did not **r** Him. Jn 1:11
to all who did **r** Him, He gave Jn 1:12
No one can **r** a single thing Jn 3:27
I don't **r** man's testimony, Jn 5:34
believed in Him were going to **r**, Jn 7:39
come back and **r** you to Myself, Jn 14:3
is unable to **r** Him because it Jn 14:17
and you will **r**, that your joy Jn 16:24
and said, "**R** the Holy Spirit Jn 20:22
But you will **r** power when the Ac 1:8
and you will **r** the gift of the Ac 2:38
"Lord Jesus, **r** my spirit!" Ac 7:59
they might **r** the Holy Spirit Ac 8:15
hands on may **r** the Holy Spirit. Ac 8:19
in Him will **r** forgiveness of Ac 10:43
Did you **r** the Holy Spirit when Ac 19:2
blessed to give than to **r**.'" Ac 20:35
we gratefully **r** them always and Ac 24:3
that they may **r** forgiveness of Ac 26:18
to his friends to **r** their care. Ac 27:3
will those who **r** the overflow Rm 5:17
For you did not **r** a spirit of Rm 8:15
that they also now may **r** mercy. Rm 11:31
you were not yet able to **r** it. 1Co 3:2
and each will **r** his own reward 1Co 3:8
survives, he will **r** a reward. 1Co 3:14
do you have that you didn't **r**? 1Co 4:7
fact, you did **r** it, why do you 1Co 4:7
they do it to **r** a perishable 1Co 9:25
comfort we ourselves **r** from God. 2Co 1:4
"Don't **r** God's grace in vain." 2Co 6:1
or you **r** a different spirit, 2Co 11:4
For I did not **r** it from a human Gl 1:12
you **r** the Spirit by the works Gl 3:2
that we could **r** the promise of Gl 3:14
that we might **r** adoption as sons Gl 4:5
he will **r** this back from the Eph 6:8
that you will **r** the reward Col 3:24
will therefore **r** condemnation 1Tm 5:12
so that we may **r** mercy and find Heb 4:16
sons of Levi who **r** the priestly Heb 7:5
men who will die **r** tithes; Heb 7:8
are called might **r** the promise Heb 9:15
you may **r** what was promised. Heb 10:36
he was going to **r** as an Heb 11:8
but they did not **r** what was Heb 11:39
which all **r**—then you are Heb 12:8
I urge you to **r** this word of Heb 13:22
should not expect to **r** anything Jms 1:7
the test he will **r** the crown of Jms 1:12
humbly **r** the implanted word, Jms 1:21
that we will **r** a stricter Jms 3:1
ask and don't **r** because you ask Jms 4:3
you will **r** the unfading crown of 1Pt 5:4
and can **r** whatever we ask from 1Jn 3:22
but you may **r** a full reward. 2Jn 8
do not **r** him into your home, 2Jn 10
place among them, does not **r** us. 3Jn 9
are worthy to **r** glory and honor Rv 4:11
is worthy to **r** power and riches Rv 5:12
but they will **r** authority as Rv 17:12
in her sins, or **r** any of her Rv 18:4

RECEIVED *(139)*
in your bags. I **r** your money." Gn 43:23
I have indeed **r** ⌊a command⌋ to Nm 23:20
the priest **r** from them all Nm 31:51
Eleazar the priest **r** the gold Nm 31:54
the Gadites have **r** ⌊their Nm 34:14
Manasseh has **r** its inheritance Nm 34:14
half tribes have **r** their Nm 34:15
what he has **r** from the sale Dt 18:8
Gadites had **r** the inheritance Jos 13:8
The Israelites **r** these portions Jos 14:1
sons of Joseph, **r** their Jos 16:4
daughters **r** an inheritance among Jos 17:6
descendants **r** an inheritance Jos 19:9
the priest **r** 13 cities by lot Jos 21:4
of Kohath **r** 10 cities by lot Jos 21:5
descendants **r** 13 cities by lot Jos 21:6
descendants **r** 12 cities for Jos 21:7
because they **r** the first lot. Jos 21:10
I would make sure he **r** justice." 2Sm 15:4
the men who **r** the money to pay 2Kg 12:15
They **r** help against these 1Ch 5:20
The Gershomites ⌊**r**⌋: 1Ch 6:71
Issachar ⌊they **r**⌋ Kedesh and its 1Ch 6:72
of Asher ⌊they **r**⌋ Mashal and its 1Ch 6:74
of Naphtali ⌊they **r**⌋ Kedesh in 1Ch 6:76
The rest of the Merarites ⌊**r**⌋: 1Ch 6:77
⌊they **r**⌋ Rimmono and its 1Ch 6:77
⌊they **r**⌋ Bezer in the desert and 1Ch 6:78
of Gad ⌊they **r**⌋ Ramoth in Gilead 1Ch 6:80
So David **r** them and made them 1Ch 12:18
house ⌊and **r**⌋ a single 1Ch 23:11
which they **r** from their ancestor 1Ch 24:19
Then the Levites **r** them and took 2Ch 29:16
and the priests **r** the blood and 2Ch 29:22
the blood ⌊**r**⌋ from the hand 2Ch 30:16
and the special diet that she **r**. Est 2:9
You **r** gifts from people, even Ps 68:18
I looked, and **r** instruction: Pr 24:32
and she has **r** from the LORD's Is 40:2
later sent ⌊for him⌋ and **r** him, Jr 37:17
the prophet and **r** him at the Jr 38:14
that has not **r** rain in the day Ezk 22:24
and his army **r** no compensation Ezk 29:18
yet he **r** possession of the land. Ezk 33:24
Darius the Mede **r** the kingdom at Dn 5:31
One field **r** rain while a field Am 4:7
The wounds I **r** in the house of Zch 13:6
You have **r** free of charge; Mt 10:8
might have **r** from me is a gift Mt 15:5
came, they each **r** one denarius. Mt 20:9
but they also **r** a denarius each. Mt 20:10
When they **r** it, they began to Mt 20:11
the man who had **r** five talents Mt 25:16
man who had **r** one talent went Mt 25:18
The man who had **r** five talents Mt 25:20
man who had **r** one talent also Mt 25:24
would have **r** my money back with Mt 25:27
customs they have **r** and keep, Mk 7:4
you might have **r** from me is Mk 7:11
believe that you have **r** them, Mk 11:24
because you have **r** your comfort. Lk 6:24
a rich man who **r** an accusation Lk 16:1
life you **r** your good things, Lk 16:25
just as Lazarus **r** bad things, Lk 16:25
having **r** the authority to be Lk 19:15
we have all **r** grace after grace Jn 1:16
the Spirit had not yet been **r**, Jn 7:39
I went and washed I **r** my sight." Jn 9:11
asked him how he **r** his sight. Jn 9:15
that he was blind and **r** sight— Jn 9:18
of the one who had **r** his sight. Jn 9:18
r this command from My Father. Jn 10:18
They have **r** them and have known Jn 17:8
When Jesus had **r** the sour wine, Jn 19:30
and a cloud **r** Him out of their Ac 1:9
of God and has **r** from the Father Ac 2:33
He **r** living oracles to give to Ac 7:38
in turn **r** it and with Joshua Ac 7:45
r the law under the direction Ac 7:53
and they **r** the Holy Spirit. Ac 8:17
who have **r** the Holy Spirit just Ac 10:47
and Jason has **r** them as guests! Ac 17:7
the ministry I **r** from the Lord Ac 20:24
Having **r** letters from them to Ac 22:5
had passed, Felix **r** a successor, Ac 24:27
since I had **r** authority for that Ac 26:10
We haven't **r** any letters about Ac 28:21
We have **r** grace and apostleship Rm 1:5
with males and **r** in their own Rm 1:27
he **r** the sign of circumcision Rm 4:11
we have now **r** reconciliation. Rm 5:11
you **r** the Spirit of adoption, Rm 8:15
but now have **r** mercy through Rm 11:30
Now we have not **r** the spirit of 1Co 2:12
you boast as if you hadn't **r** it? 1Co 4:7
I **r** from the Lord what I also 1Co 11:23
you **r** it and have taken your 1Co 15:1
as most important what I also **r**: 1Co 15:3
as we have **r** mercy, we do not 2Co 4:1
by the comfort he **r** from you. 2Co 7:7
and how you **r** him with fear and 2Co 7:15
you had not **r**, or a different 2Co 11:4
Five times I **r** from the Jews 40 2Co 11:24
a gospel contrary to what you **r**, Gl 1:9
you **r** me as an angel of God, Gl 4:14
of the calling you have **r**, Eph 4:1
have learned and **r** and heard and Php 4:9
But I have **r** everything in full, Php 4:18
having **r** from Epaphroditus what Php 4:18
as you have **r** Christ Jesus the Col 2:6
whom you have **r** instructions: Col 4:10
ministry you have **r** in the Lord, Col 4:17
because when you **r** the message 1Th 2:13
as you have **r** from us how you 1Th 4:1
to the tradition **r** from us. 2Th 3:6
acted in unbelief, I **r** mercy, 1Tm 1:13
But I **r** mercy because of this, 1Tm 1:16
created to be **r** with gratitude 1Tm 4:3
if it is **r** with thanksgiving 1Tm 4:4

and disobedience **r** a just Heb 2:2
For we also have **r** the good news Heb 4:2
who formerly **r** the good news did Heb 4:6
under it the people **r** the law Heb 7:11
r power to conceive offspring, Heb 11:11
without having **r** the promises, Heb 11:13
he who had **r** the promises was Heb 11:17
the prostitute **r** the spies in Heb 11:31
Women **r** their dead raised to Heb 11:35
works when she **r** the messengers Jms 2:25
you had not **r** mercy, but now you 1Pt 2:10
mercy, but now you have **r** mercy. 1Pt 2:10
Based on the gift they have **r**, 1Pt 4:10
For when He **r** honor and glory 2Pt 1:17
but **r** a rebuke for his 2Pt 2:16
anointing you **r** from Him remains 1Jn 2:27
we have **r** from the Father 2Jn 4
just as I have **r** ⌊this⌋ from My Rv 2:27
what you have **r** and heard; Rv 3:3
who have not yet **r** a kingdom, Rv 17:12

RECEIVES *(23)*

to the inheritance it **r**." Nm 35:8
at Your feet. Each **r** Your words. Dt 33:3
and a man, by the praise he **r**. Pr 27:21
but a man **r** justice from the Pr 29:26
who **r** strangers instead of her Ezk 16:32
the fatherless **r** compassion in Hs 14:3
offerings or **r** ⌊them⌋ gladly Mal 2:13
who asks **r**, and the one who Mt 7:8
and immediately **r** it with joy. Mt 13:20
who asks **r**, and the one who Lk 11:10
If a man **r** circumcision on the Jn 7:23
The one who **r** whomever I send Jn 13:20
receives whomever I send **r** Me, Jn 13:20
the one who **r** Me receives Him Jn 13:20
receives Me **r** Him who sent Me. Jn 13:20
race, but only one **r** the prize? 1Co 9:24
is cultivated for, **r** a blessing Heb 6:7
himself, who **r** tithes, has paid Heb 7:9
punishes every son whom He **r**. Heb 12:6
with it until it **r** the early and Jms 5:7
knows except the one who **r** it. Rv 2:17
his image and **r** a mark on his Rv 14:9
or anyone who **r** the mark of his Rv 14:11

RECEIVING *(9)*

for **r** wise instruction ⌊in⌋ Pr 1:3
is already **r** pay and gathering Jn 4:36
After **r** the piece of bread, Jn 13:30
R such an order, he put them Ac 16:24
and after **r** instructions for Ac 17:15
giving and **r** except you alone. Php 4:15
sin after **r** the knowledge Heb 10:26
since we are **r** a kingdom that Heb 12:28
because you are **r** the goal of 1Pt 1:9

RECENTLY *(3)*

in the past or **r** or since You Ex 4:10
But **r** My people have risen up Mc 2:8
who had **r** come from Italy with Ac 18:2

RECEPTION *(1)*

what kind of **r** we had from you 1Th 1:9

RECEPTIVE *(1)*

correction to a **r** ear is like a Pr 25:12

RECESS *(2)*

Each **r** was about 10 feet long Ezk 40:7
the roof of one **r** to the roof Ezk 40:13

RECESSES *(14)*

to the far **r** of Lebanon. 2Kg 19:23
probes the deepest **r** for ore in Jb 28:3
to the far **r** of Lebanon. Is 37:24
feet between the **r**. Ezk 40:7
There were three **r** on each side Ezk 40:10
in front of the **r** on both sides, Ezk 40:12
and the **r** on each side were 10 Ezk 40:12
openings of the **r** faced each Ezk 40:13
The **r** and their pilasters had Ezk 40:16
Its three **r** on each side, its Ezk 40:21
r, pilasters, and portico had Ezk 40:29
r, pilasters, and portico had Ezk 40:33
⌊as did⌋ its **r**, pilasters, and Ezk 40:36
in the inner **r** of the house, Am 6:10

RECHAB *(13)*

named Baanah and the other **R**, 2Sm 4:2
R and Baanah, the sons of Rimmon 2Sm 4:5
Then **R** and his brother Baanah 2Sm 4:6
David answered **R** and his brother 2Sm 4:9
and they killed **R** and Baanah. 2Sm 4:12
son of **R** ⌊coming⌋ to meet 2Kg 10:15
Jehonadab son of **R** entered the 2Kg 10:23
Malchijah son of **R**, ruler over Neh 3:14
of our ancestor **R**, commanded: Jr 35:6
son of our ancestor **R**, in all he Jr 35:8
Jonadab, son of **R**, have been Jr 35:14
Jonadab son of **R** carried out Jr 35:16
Jonadab son of **R** will never fail Jr 35:19

RECHAB'S *(1)*

Hammath, the father of **R** family. 1Ch 2:55

RECHABITES *(4)*

Go to the house of the **R**, Jr 35:2
the entire house of the **R**— Jr 35:3
house of the **R** and said to them Jr 35:5
said to the house of the **R**: Jr 35:18

RECITE *(5)*

a reminder and **r** it to Joshua: Ex 17:14
them **r** it, so that this song Dt 31:19
you are to **r** it day and night, Jos 1:8
noble theme as I **r** my verses to Ps 45:1
do you have to **r** My statutes and Ps 50:16

RECITED *(3)*

Then Moses **r** aloud every single Dt 31:30
son of Nun and **r** all the words Dt 32:44
He **r** all these words to me while Jr 36:18

RECITING *(1)*

Moses finished **r** all these words Dt 32:45

RECKLESS *(7)*

worthless and **r** men with this Jdg 9:4
wickedly perform **r** acts with men Ps 141:4
anyone who is **r** only becomes Pr 21:5
The **r** mind will gain knowledge, Is 32:4
Her prophets are **r**—treacherous Zph 3:4
which ⌊leads to⌋ **r** actions, Eph 5:18
traitors, **r**, conceited, lovers 2Tm 3:4

RECLAIM *(1)*

May darkness and gloom **r** it, Jb 3:5

RECLINE *(5)*

and **r** at the table with Abraham, Mt 8:11
ready, have them **r** at the table, Lk 12:37
r at the table in the kingdom Lk 13:29
don't **r** at the best place, Lk 14:8
go and **r** in the lowest place, Lk 14:10

RECLINED *(6)*

house and **r** at the table. Lk 7:36
He went in and **r** at the table. Lk 11:37
one of those who **r** at the table Lk 14:15
hour came, He **r** at the table, Lk 22:14
It was as He **r** at the table with Lk 24:30
He **r** again and said to them, Jn 13:12

RECLINING *(12)*

on the couch where Esther was **r**. Est 7:8
While He was **r** at the table in Mt 9:10
head as He was **r** at the table. Mt 26:7
He was **r** at the table with the Mt 26:20
While He was **r** at the table in Mk 2:15
as He was **r** at the table, Mk 14:3
While they were **r** and eating, Mk 14:18
as they were **r** at the table. Mk 16:14
that Jesus was **r** at the table Lk 7:37
was one of those **r** at the table Jn 12:2
Jesus loved, was **r** close beside Jn 13:23
of those **r** at the table knew Jn 13:28

RECOGNITION *(3)*

and special **r** have been given Est 6:3
while he's seeking public **r**. Jn 7:4
to give **r** to those who labor 1Th 5:12

RECOGNIZE *(38)*

He did not **r** him, because his Gn 27:23
brothers, they did not **r** him. Gn 42:8
r and keep in mind that the LORD Dt 4:39
'How can we **r** a message the LORD Dt 18:21
Look and **r** that there is no evil 1Sm 24:11
that they may **r** ⌊the difference 2Ch 12:8
they could ⌊barely⌋ **r** him. Jb 2:12
I could not **r** its appearance; Jb 4:16
Am I lying, or can I not **r** lies? Jb 6:30
goes right by, I wouldn't **r** Him. Jb 9:11
They do not **r** its ways or stay Jb 24:13
and He will **r** my integrity. Jb 31:6
see them will **r** that they are Is 61:9
know us and Israel doesn't **r** us. Is 63:16
the nations that don't **r** You and Jr 10:25
She does not **r** that it is I who Hs 2:8
place until they **r** their guilt Hs 5:15
Let Israel **r** it! The prophet Hs 9:7
whoever is insightful **r** them. Hs 14:9
You'll **r** them by their fruit. Mt 7:16
So you'll **r** them by their fruit. Mt 7:20
come, and they didn't **r** him. Mt 17:12
these things, **r** that He is near Mt 24:33
you did not **r** the time of your Lk 19:44
then **r** that its desolation has Lk 21:20
yourselves and **r** that summer is Lk 21:30
r that the kingdom of God is Lk 21:31
yet the world did not **r** Him. Jn 1:10
him because they **r** his voice. Jn 10:4
because they don't **r** the voice Jn 10:5
they did not **r** Him or the voices Ac 13:27
know, and Paul I **r**—but who are Ac 19:15
came, they did not **r** the land, Ac 27:39
he should **r** that what I write to 1Co 14:37
Therefore **r** such people. 1Co 16:18
Or do you not **r** for yourselves 2Co 13:5
hope you will **r** that we are not 2Co 13:6
For know and **r** this: Eph 5:5

RECOGNIZED *(29)*

His father **r** it. Gn 37:33
Judah **r** ⌊them⌋ and said, "She is Gn 38:26
his brothers, he **r** them, but he Gn 42:7
Although Joseph **r** his brothers, Gn 42:8
son Machir were **r** by Joseph. Gn 50:23
they **r** the speech of the young Jdg 18:3
Saul **r** David's voice and asked, 1Sm 26:17
When Obadiah **r** him, he fell with 1Kg 18:7
king of Israel **r** that he was one 1Kg 20:41
the prophet be **r** as one whom Jr 28:9
they are not **r** in the streets. Lm 4:8
and I **r** that they were cherubim. Ezk 10:20
the men of that place **r** Him, Mt 14:35
saw them leaving and **r** them. Mk 6:33
boat, people immediately **r** Him. Mk 6:54
opened, and they **r** Him, but He Lk 24:31
and they **r** that he was the one Ac 3:10
She **r** Peter's voice, and because Ac 12:14
But when they **r** that he was a Ac 19:34
sin, in order to be **r** as sin, Rm 7:13
approved among you may be **r**. 1Co 11:19
on the flute or harp be **r**? 1Co 14:7
on our hearts, **r** and read by 2Co 3:2
as unknown yet **r**; 2Co 6:9
to those **r** ⌊as leaders⌋— Gl 2:2
But from those **r** as important Gl 2:6
those **r** as important added Gl 2:6
Cephas, and John, **r** as pillars, Gl 2:9
you heard it and **r** God's grace Col 1:6

RECOGNIZES *(3)*

it, but ⌊later⌋ **r** ⌊it⌋, he is Lv 5:3
it, but ⌊later⌋ **r** it, he incurs Lv 5:4
He **r** their deeds and overthrows Jb 34:25

RECOGNIZING *(3)*

they were prevented from **r** Him. Lk 24:16
not **r** that God's kindness is Rm 2:4
and drinks without **r** the body, 1Co 11:29

RECOIL *(1)*

all who see you will **r** from you, Nah 3:7

RECOMMEND *(1)*

those whom you **r** by letter to 1Co 16:3

RECOMMENDATION *(1)*

need letters of **r** to you or from 2Co 3:1

RECOMMENDED *(1)*

I ought to have been **r** by you, 2Co 12:11

RECOMPENSE *(1)*

Him, and His **r** is before Him." Is 62:11

RECONCILE *(3)*

and tried to **r** them peacefully, Ac 7:26
so⌋ that He might **r** both to God Eph 2:16
through Him to **r** everything to Col 1:20

RECONCILED *(7)*

First go and be **r** with your Mt 5:24
we were **r** to God through the Rm 5:10
having been **r**, will we be saved Rm 5:10
unmarried or be **r** to her husband 1Co 7:11
who **r** us to Himself through 2Co 5:18
Christ's behalf, "Be **r** to God." 2Co 5:20
But now He has **r** you by His Col 1:22

RECONCILIATION *(4)*

whom we have now received **r**. Rm 5:11
their being rejected is world **r**, Rm 11:15

and gave us the ministry of **r**: 2Co 5:18
the message of **r** to us. 2Co 5:19

RECONCILING *(1)*
God was **r** the world to Himself, 2Co 5:19

RECONSIDER *(3)*
R; don't be unjust. Reconsider; Jb 6:29
don't be unjust. **R**; my Jb 6:29
rashly and later to **r** his vows. Pr 20:25

RECORD *(48)*
the Historical **R** of Israel's 1Kg 14:19
the Historical **R** of Judah's 1Kg 14:29
the Historical **R** of Judah's 1Kg 15:7
the Historical **R** of Judah's 1Kg 15:23
the Historical **R** of Israel's 1Kg 15:31
the Historical **R** of Israel's 1Kg 16:5
the Historical **R** of Israel's 1Kg 16:14
the Historical **R** of Israel's 1Kg 16:20
the Historical **R** of Israel's 1Kg 16:27
the Historical **R** of Israel's 1Kg 22:39
the Historical **R** of Judah's 1Kg 22:45
the Historical **R** of Israel's 2Kg 1:18
the Historical **R** of Israel's 2Kg 8:23
the Historical **R** of Israel's 2Kg 10:34
the Historical **R** of Judah's 2Kg 12:19
the Historical **R** of Israel's 2Kg 13:8
the Historical **R** of Israel's 2Kg 13:12
the Historical **R** of Israel's 2Kg 14:15
the Historical **R** of Judah's 2Kg 14:18
the Historical **R** of Israel's 2Kg 14:28
the Historical **R** of Judah's 2Kg 15:6
the Historical **R** of Israel's 2Kg 15:11
the Historical **R** of Israel's 2Kg 15:15
the Historical **R** of Israel's 2Kg 15:21
the Historical **R** of Israel's 2Kg 15:26
the Historical **R** of Israel's 2Kg 15:31
the Historical **R** of Judah's 2Kg 15:36
the Historical **R** of Judah's 2Kg 16:19
the Historical **R** of Judah's 2Kg 20:20
the Historical **R** of Judah's 2Kg 21:17
the Historical **R** of Judah's 2Kg 21:25
the Historical **R** of Judah's 2Kg 23:28
the Historical **R** of Judah's 2Kg 24:5
a genealogical **r** for themselves. 1Ch 4:33
the Historical **R** of King David. 1Ch 27:24
made in your fathers' **r** books. Ezr 4:15
In these **r** books you will Ezr 4:15
found with this **r** written on it: Ezr 6:2
the genealogical **r** of those who Neh 7:5
were then written into the **r**. Est 9:32
in the court **r** of daily events Est 10:2
For You **r** bitter accusations Jb 13:26
the LORD will **r**, "This one was Ps 87:6
of Asaph, the **r** keeper, came out Is 36:3
of Asaph, the **r** keeper, came to Is 36:22
R this man as childless, a man Jr 22:30
historical **r** of Jesus Christ, Mt 1:1
does not keep a **r** of wrongs; 1Co 13:5

RECORDED *(27)*
and will be **r** under the names Gn 48:6
that was **r** at Moses' command. Ex 38:21
They **r** their ancestry by their Nm 1:18
and plague not **r** in the book of Dt 28:61
Joshua **r** these things in the Jos 24:26
These who were **r** by name came in 1Ch 4:41
as they are **r** in their genealogy 1Ch 5:7
of Tola were **r** as warriors in 1Ch 7:2
genealogies were **r** according to 1Ch 7:9
r them in the presence of the 1Ch 24:6
which is **r** in the Book of 2Ch 20:34
they are **r** in the Writing of the 2Ch 24:27
r by Jeiel the court secretary 2Ch 26:11
also⌋ to those **r** by genealogy 2Ch 31:17
to every Levite **r** by genealogy. 2Ch 31:19
total weight was **r** at that time. Ezr 8:34
and priests were **r** while Darius Neh 12:22
were **r** in the Book of the Neh 12:23
it be **r** in the laws of Persia Est 1:19
This event was **r** in the court Est 2:23
Mordecai **r** these events and sent Est 9:20
that they were **r** on a scroll Jb 19:23
Yourself have **r** my wanderings. Ps 56:8
life and not be **r** with the Ps 69:28
I **r** it on a scroll, sealed it, Jr 32:10
people or be **r** in the register Ezk 13:9
tell you what is **r** in the book Dn 10:21

RECORDER *(1)*
the city and the **r** Joah son of 2Ch 34:8

RECORDING *(1)*
the book **r** daily events to Est 6:1

RECORDS *(38)*
These are the **r** of the heavens Gn 2:4
are the family **r** of the Gn 5:1
These are the family **r** of Noah. Gn 6:9
are the family **r** of Noah's sons, Gn 10:1
according to their family **r**, Gn 10:32
These are the family **r** of Shem. Gn 11:10
These are the family **r** of Terah. Gn 11:27
the family **r** of Abraham's son Gn 25:12
according to the family **r** are: Gn 25:13
are the family **r** of Isaac son Gn 25:19
These are the family **r** of Esau Gn 36:1
These are the family **r** of Esau, Gn 36:9
These are the family **r** of Jacob. Gn 37:2
to their family **r** by their clans Nm 1:20
to their family **r** by their clans Nm 1:22
to their family **r** by their clans Nm 1:24
to their family **r** by their clans Nm 1:26
to their family **r** by their clans Nm 1:28
to their family **r** by their clans Nm 1:30
to their family **r** by their clans Nm 1:32
to their family **r** by their clans Nm 1:34
to their family **r** by their clans Nm 1:36
to their family **r** by their clans Nm 1:38
to their family **r** by their clans Nm 1:40
to their family **r** by their clans Nm 1:42
are the family **r** of Aaron and Nm 3:1
These are their family **r**: 1Ch 1:29
⌊names⌋ are from ancient **r**. 1Ch 4:22
the genealogical **r** of their 1Ch 7:4
to their genealogical **r**. 1Ch 9:9
genealogical **r** of his ancestors 1Ch 26:31
written about in the **R** of Hozai. 2Ch 33:19
entries in the genealogical **r**, Ezr 2:62
the genealogical **r** of those who Ezr 8:1
entries in the genealogical **r**, Neh 7:64
the Historical **R** during the days Neh 12:23
in the court **r** of daily events Est 2:23
Are they not in Your **r**? Ps 56:8

RECOUNT *(1)*
a dream should **r** the dream, Jr 23:28

RECOUNTED *(2)*
Moses **r** to his father-in-law all Ex 18:8
Nathan **r** all these words and 1Ch 17:15

RECOVER *(13)*
bitten looks at it, he will **r**. Nm 21:8
if I will **r** from this injury." 2Kg 1:2
'Will I **r** from this sickness?' " 2Kg 8:8
'Will I **r** from this sickness?' " 2Kg 8:9
say to him, 'You are sure to **r**.' 2Kg 8:10
"He told me you are sure to **r**." 2Kg 8:14
to Jezreel to **r** from the wounds 2Kg 8:29
to Jezreel to **r** from the wounds 2Kg 9:15
to die; you will not **r**.' " 2Kg 20:1
to Jezreel to **r** from the wounds 2Ch 22:6
His hand a second time to **r**— Is 11:11
about to die; you will not **r**.' " Is 38:1
skin, so that he may **r**." Is 38:21

RECOVERED *(14)*
at the bronze snake, he **r**. Nm 21:9
were in the camp until they **r**. Jos 5:8
r everything the Amalekites 1Sm 30:18
the plunder we **r** to them except 1Sm 30:22
on the ground, which can't be **r**. 2Sm 14:14
three times and **r** the cities of 2Kg 13:25
war and how he **r** for Israel 2Kg 14:28
king of Aram **r** Elath for Aram 2Kg 16:6
to his infected skin, and he **r**. 2Kg 20:7
signet ring he had **r** from Haman Est 8:2
sick and had **r** from his illness Is 38:9
that he had been sick and had **r**. Is 39:1
whom he had **r** from Ishmael son Jr 41:16
was stirred up **r** from whatever Jn 5:4

RECOVERY *(4)*
provide for ⌊his⌋ complete **r**. Ex 21:19
shattered instantly—beyond **r**. Pr 6:15
and your **r** will come quickly. Is 58:8
the captives and **r** of sight to Lk 4:18

RECRUCIFYING *(1)*
they are **r** the Son of God and Heb 6:6

RECRUITED *(1)*
So 1,000 were **r** from each Nm 31:5

RECRUITER *(1)*
To please the **r**, no one serving 2Tm 2:4

RECTANGULAR *(1)*
and doorposts had **r** frames, 1Kg 7:5

RECUR *(1)*
after year; let the festivals **r**. Is 29:1

RED *(52)*
Let me eat some of that **r** stuff, Gn 25:30
and blew them into the **R** Sea. Ex 10:19
around toward the **R** Sea along Ex 13:18
were drowned in the **R** Sea. Ex 15:4
led Israel on from the **R** Sea, Ex 15:22
your borders from the **R** Sea to Ex 23:31
ram skins dyed **r** and manatee Ex 25:5
the tent from ram skins dyed **r**, Ex 26:14
ram skins dyed **r** and manatee Ex 35:7
ram skins dyed **r** or manatee Ex 35:23
ram skins dyed **r** and a covering Ex 36:19
ram skins dyed **r** and the Ex 39:34
is green or **r** in the fabric, Lv 13:49
of green or **r** indentations that Lv 14:37
in the direction of the **R** Sea." Nm 14:25
an unblemished **r** cow that has no Nm 19:2
by way of the **R** Sea to bypass Nm 21:4
Elim and camped by the **R** Sea. Nm 33:10
from the **R** Sea and camped Nm 33:11
by way of the **R** Sea.' Dt 1:40
wilderness by way of the **R** Sea, Dt 2:1
waters of the **R** Sea flow over Dt 11:4
waters of the **R** Sea before you Jos 2:10
LORD your God did to the **R** Sea, Jos 4:23
Egypt and you reached the **R** Sea, Jos 24:6
to the **R** Sea and came to Jdg 11:16
shore of the **R** Sea in the land 1Kg 9:26
from them was **r** like blood. 2Kg 3:22
heard their cry at the **R** Sea. Neh 9:9
a mosaic pavement of **r** feldspar, Est 1:6
face has grown **r** with weeping, Jb 16:16
rebelled by the sea—the **R** Sea. Ps 106:7
He rebuked the **R** Sea, and it Ps 106:9
awe-inspiring deeds at the **R** Sea. Ps 106:22
He divided the **R** Sea His love is Ps 136:13
and his army into the **R** Sea. Ps 136:15
for no reason? Who has **r** eyes? Pr 23:29
Don't gaze at wine when it is **r**, Pr 23:31
though they are as **r** as crimson, Is 1:18
is Your clothing **r**, and Your Is 63:2
cry will be heard at the **R** Sea. Jr 49:21
of his warriors are dyed **r**; Nah 2:3
saw a man riding on a **r** horse. Zch 1:8
Behind him were **r**, sorrel, and Zch 1:8
The first chariot had **r** horses, Zch 6:2
weather because the sky is **r**.' Mt 16:2
the sky is **r** and threatening.' Mt 16:3
land of Egypt, at the **R** Sea, and Ac 7:36
they crossed the **R** Sea as though Heb 11:29
went out, a fiery **r** one, and its Rv 6:4
breastplates that were fiery **r**, Rv 9:17
a great fiery **r** dragon having Rv 12:3

REDDISH *(1)*
one came out **r**, covered with Gn 25:25

REDDISH-WHITE *(4)*
swelling or a **r** spot develops Lv 13:19
burn becomes a **r** or white spot, Lv 13:24
But if there is a **r** infection on Lv 13:42
his bald head or forehead is **r**, Lv 13:43

REDEDICATE *(1)*
He is to **r** his time of Nm 6:12

REDEEM *(59)*
will **r** you with an outstretched Ex 6:6
You must **r** every firstborn of a Ex 13:13
if you do not **r** it, break its Ex 13:13
you must **r** every firstborn among Ex 13:13
r all the firstborn of my sons. Ex 13:15
You must **r** the firstborn of a Ex 34:20
if you do not **r** ⌊it⌋, break its Ex 34:20
You must **r** all the firstborn of Ex 34:20
may come and **r** what his brother Lv 25:25
obtains enough to **r** his land, Lv 25:26
The right to **r** ⌊such⌋ houses Lv 25:31
have the right to **r** houses in Lv 25:32
one of the Levites can **r**— Lv 25:33
One of his brothers may **r** him. Lv 25:48
His uncle or cousin may **r** him, Lv 25:49
from his clan may **r** him. Lv 25:49
he prospers, he may **r** himself. Lv 25:49
who brought it decides to **r** it, Lv 27:13
the field decides to **r** it, Lv 27:19
if he does not **r** the field or if Lv 27:20

man decides to **r** any part of Lv 27:31
must certainly **r** the firstborn Nm 18:15
r the firstborn of an unclean Nm 18:15
you must not **r** the firstborn of Nm 18:17
if he wants to **r** you, ⌊that's⌋ Ru 3:13
good. Let him **r** ⌊you⌋. But if he Ru 3:13
But if he doesn't want to **r** you, Ru 3:13
If you want to **r** ⌊it⌋, do so. Ru 4:4
if you do not want to **r** ⌊it⌋, Ru 4:4
anyone other than you to **r** ⌊it⌋, Ru 4:4
"I want to **r** ⌊it⌋," he Ru 4:4
I can't **r** ⌊it⌋ myself, or I Ru 4:6
because I can't **r** it." Ru 4:6
earth in order to **r** a people for 2Sm 7:23
nation on earth to **r** a people 1Ch 17:21
famine He will **r** you from death, Jb 5:20
enemy's power or **R** me from the Jb 6:23
God, **r** Israel, from all its Ps 25:22
r me and be gracious to me. Ps 26:11
You **r** me, LORD, God of truth. Ps 31:5
R us because of Your faithful Ps 44:26
these cannot **r** a person or pay Ps 49:7
But God will **r** my life from the Ps 49:15
He will **r** me from my battle Ps 55:18
Draw near to me and **r** me; Ps 69:18
He will **r** them from oppression Ps 72:14
R me from human oppression, Ps 119:134
Defend my cause, and **r** me; Ps 119:154
He will **r** Israel from all its Ps 130:8
Is My hand too short to **r**? Is 50:2
evil people and **r** you from the Jr 15:21
my cause, Lord; You **r** my life. Lm 3:58
who have the right to **r** you, Ezk 11:15
Though I want to **r** ⌊them⌋, Hs 7:13
I will **r** them from death. Hs 13:14
the LORD will **r** you from the Mc 4:10
One who was about to **r** Israel. Lk 24:21
r those under the law, so that Gl 4:5
Himself for us to **r** us from all Ti 2:14

REDEEMABLE (1)
another man, it is no longer **r**. Lv 27:20

REDEEMED (49)
Angel who has **r** me from all harm Gn 48:16
people You have **r** with Your Ex 15:13
then he must let her be **r**. Ex 21:8
she has not been **r** or given her Lv 19:20
If it is not **r** by the end of a Lv 25:30
If he is not **r** in any of these Lv 25:54
If it is not **r**, it can be sold Lv 27:27
landholding, can be sold or **r**; Lv 27:28
will be holy; they cannot be **r**." Lv 27:33
of the ones **r** by the Levites. Nm 3:49
a strong hand and **r** you from the Dt 7:8
You **r** through Your greatness Dt 9:26
land of Egypt and **r** you from the Dt 13:5
and the LORD your God **r** you; Dt 15:15
Your people Israel You **r**, Dt 21:8
LORD your God **r** you from there. Dt 24:18
⌊the One⌋ who has **r** my life from 2Sm 4:9
Your people You **r** for Yourself 2Sm 7:23
who has **r** my life from every 1Kg 1:29
Your people You **r** from Egypt. 1Ch 17:21
You **r** ⌊them⌋ by Your great power Neh 1:10
He **r** my soul from going down to Jb 33:28
to You, because You have **r** me. Ps 71:23
long ago and **r** as the tribe for Ps 74:2
With power You **r** Your people, Ps 77:15
on the day He **r** them from the Ps 78:42
He **r** them from the hand of the Ps 106:10
Let the **r** of the LORD proclaim Ps 107:2
that He has **r** them from the hand Ps 107:2
Zion will be **r** by justice, Is 1:27
the LORD who **r** Abraham says this Is 29:22
But the **r** will walk ⌊on it⌋, Is 35:9
Do not fear, for I have **r** you; Is 43:1
Return to Me, for I have **r** you. Is 44:22
For the LORD has **r** Jacob, and Is 44:23
LORD has **r** His servant Jacob! Is 48:20
a road for the **r** to pass over? Is 51:10
you will be **r** without silver. Is 52:3
He has **r** Jerusalem. Is 52:9
the Holy People, the LORD's **R**; Is 62:12
r them because of His love and Is 63:9
Jacob and **r** him from the power Jr 31:11
of Egypt and **r** you from that Mc 6:4
them because I have **r** them; Zch 10:8
Christ has **r** us from the curse Gl 3:13
that you were **r** from your empty 1Pt 1:18
and You **r** ⌊people⌋ for God by Rv 5:9
who had been **r** from the earth. Rv 14:3
They were **r** from the human race Rv 14:4

REDEEMER (28)
has no family **r**, but he prospers Lv 25:26
me, for you are a family **r**." Ru 3:9
it is true that I am a family **r**, Ru 3:12
but there is a **r** closer than I Ru 3:12
the family **r** Boaz had spoken Ru 4:1
said to the **r**, "Naomi, who has Ru 4:3
The **r** replied, "I can't redeem Ru 4:6
So the **r** removed his sandal and Ru 4:8
you without a family **r** today. Ru 4:14
I know my living **R**, and He will Jb 19:25
to You, LORD, my rock and my **R**. Ps 19:14
the Most High God, their **R**. Ps 78:35
for their **R** is strong, and He Pr 23:11
R is the Holy One of Israel. Is 41:14
the LORD, your **R**, the Holy One Is 43:14
the King of Israel and its **R**, Is 44:6
your **R** who formed you from the Is 44:24
The Holy One of Israel is our **R**; Is 47:4
the LORD, your **R**, the Holy One Is 48:17
the LORD, the **R** of Israel, his Is 49:7
and your **R**, the Mighty One Is 49:26
Holy One of Israel is your **R**; Is 54:5
love," says the LORD your **R**. Is 54:8
The **R** will come to Zion, and to Is 59:20
your Savior and **R**, the Mighty Is 60:16
times, Your name is our **R**. Is 63:16
Their **R** is strong; the LORD of Jr 50:34
as a ruler and a **r** by means of Ac 7:35

REDEEMERS (1)
He is one of our family **r**." Ru 2:20

REDEEMING (1)
the price of **r** him is too costly Ps 49:8

REDEEMS (3)
consecrated his house **r** ⌊it⌋, Lv 27:15
The LORD **r** the life of His Ps 34:22
He **r** your life from the Pit; Ps 103:4

REDEMPTION (31)
can pay a **r** price for his life Ex 21:30
to allow the **r** of any land you Lv 25:24
his right of **r** will last until a Lv 25:29
his right of **r** will last a year. Lv 25:29
has the right of **r** after he has Lv 25:48
he must pay his **r** price in Lv 25:51
price of his **r** in proportion to Lv 25:52
As the **r** price for the 273 Nm 3:46
sons as the **r** price for those Nm 3:48
collected the **r** money from those Nm 3:49
He gave the **r** money to Aaron and Nm 3:51
You will pay the **r** price for a Nm 18:16
my right of **r**, because I can't Ru 4:6
the right of **r** or the exchange Ru 4:7
He has sent **r** to His people. Ps 111:9
and with Him is **r** in abundance. Ps 130:7
and the year of My **r** came. Is 63:4
own the right of **r** to buy it.' Jr 32:7
the right of inheritance and **r**. Jr 32:8
and provided **r** for His people. Lk 1:68
forward to the **r** of Jerusalem. Lk 2:38
heads, because your **r** is near!" Lk 21:28
through the **r** that is in Christ Rm 3:24
adoption, the **r** of our bodies. Rm 8:23
sanctification, and **r**, 1Co 1:30
In Him we have **r** through His Eph 1:7
for the **r** of the possession, Eph 1:14
who sealed you for the day of **r**. Eph 4:30
in whom we have **r**, the Col 1:14
having obtained eternal **r**. Heb 9:12
has taken place for **r** from the Heb 9:15

REDIRECT (1)
if you **r** your heart and lift up Jb 11:13

REDUCE (9)
before; do not **r** it. For they Ex 5:8
You cannot **r** your daily quota of Ex 5:19
wife, he must not **r** the food, Ex 21:10
and **r** your numbers until your Lv 26:22
will **r** your cities to ruins and Lv 26:31
the LORD began to **r** the size of 2Kg 10:32
Now you plan to **r** the people of 2Ch 28:10
or You will **r** me to nothing. Jr 10:24
We can **r** the measure while Am 8:5

REDUCED (7)
that your valuation will be **r**. Lv 27:18
and you will be **r** to a few Dt 4:27
You have **r** his fortified cities Ps 89:40
cities will be **r** to uninhabited Jr 4:7
you and **r** your provisions Ezk 16:27
r you to ashes on the ground in Ezk 28:18
and if He **r** the cities of Sodom 2Pt 2:6

REDUCES (1)
r princes to nothing and makes Is 40:23

REDUCTION (1)
there will be no **r** at all in Ex 5:11

REED (19)
shake⌋ as a **r** shakes in water 1Kg 14:15
the stalk of this splintered **r**, 2Kg 18:21
branch and **r** in a single day Is 9:14
in **r** vessels on the waters. Is 18:2
will be parched. **R** and rush will Is 19:6
tail, palm or **r**, will be able to Is 19:15
that splintered **r** of a staff, Is 36:6
He will not break a bruised **r**, Is 42:3
his head like a **r**, and to spread Is 58:5
a staff ⌊made⌋ of **r** to the house Ezk 29:6
A **r** swaying in the wind? Mt 11:7
He will not break a bruised **r**, Mt 12:20
placed a **r** in His right hand. Mt 27:29
at Him, took the **r**, and kept Mt 27:30
fixed it on a **r**, and offered Him Mt 27:48
the head with a **r** and spitting Mk 15:19
fixed it on a **r**, offered Him Mk 15:36
A **r** swaying in the wind? Lk 7:24
given a measuring **r** like a rod, Rv 11:1

REEDS (10)
and began to graze among the **r**. Gn 41:2
and began to graze among the **r**. Gn 41:18
set it among the **r** by the bank Ex 2:3
Seeing the basket among the **r**, Ex 2:5
Do **r** flourish without water? Jb 8:11
in the protection of marshy **r**. Jb 40:21
a boiling pot or ⌊burning⌋ **r**. Jb 41:20
Rebuke the beast in the **r**, Ps 68:30
The **r** by the Nile, by the mouth Is 19:7
will be grass, **r**, and papyrus. Is 35:7

REEFS (1)
like dangerous **r** at your love Jd 12

REEK (1)
you have made us **r** in front of Ex 5:21

REELAIAH (1)
(AKA RAAMIAH)
Seraiah, **R**, Mordecai, Bilshan Ezr 2:2

REELED (1)
r and staggered like drunken Ps 107:27

REENTER (2)
afterwards he may **r** the camp. Lv 16:26
afterwards he may **r** the camp. Lv 16:28

REESTABLISHED (4)
destroyed and **r** the altars for 2Kg 21:3
Hezekiah **r** the divisions of the 2Ch 31:2
torn down and **r** the altars for 2Ch 33:3
me out, I was **r** over my kingdom, Dn 4:36

REEXAMINE (5)
priest will then **r** him on the Lv 13:5
The priest will **r** him on the Lv 13:27
The priest will **r** the infection Lv 13:32
The priest is to **r** the Lv 13:51
the priest is to **r** the Lv 13:55

REFER (2)
But no longer **r** to the burden of Jr 23:36
these ⌊regulations⌋ **r** to what is Col 2:22

REFERRING (6)
of blood," **r** to the circumcision Ex 4:26
r to the capture of the ark of 1Sm 4:21
He was **r** to Judas, Simon Jn 6:71
by no means **r** to this world's 1Co 5:10
seeds," as though **r** to many, but Gl 3:16
to your seed, **r** to one, who is Gl 3:16

REFERS (4)
that the vision **r** to the time of Dn 8:17
because it **r** to the appointed Dn 8:19
vision because it **r** to many days Dn 8:26
for the vision **r** to those days." Dn 10:14

REFINE (3)
I am about to **r** them and test Jr 9:7
I will **r** them as silver is Zch 13:9
of Levi and **r** them like gold Mal 3:3

REFINED *(14)*
- sensitive and **r** man among you Dt 28:54
- sensitive and **r** woman among you, Dt 28:56
- the weight of **r** gold for the 1Ch 28:18
- and 250 tons of **r** silver for 1Ch 29:4
- and a place where gold is **r**. Jb 28:1
- like silver **r** in an earthen Ps 12:6
- You **r** us as silver is refined. Ps 66:10
- You refined us as silver is **r**. Ps 66:10
- Look, I have **r** you, but not as Is 48:10
- will fall so that they may be **r**, Dn 11:35
- cleansed, and **r**, but the wicked Dn 12:10
- as silver is **r** and test them as Zch 13:9
- perishes though **r** by fire— 1Pt 1:7
- buy from Me gold **r** in the fire Rv 3:18

REFINEMENT *(1)*
- of her **r** and sensitivity, Dt 28:56

REFINER *(2)*
- people—a **r**—so you may know Jr 6:27
- He will be like a **r** and purifier Mal 3:3

REFINER'S *(1)*
- will be like a **r** fire and like Mal 3:2

REFINING *(1)*
- The **r** is completely in vain; Jr 6:29

REFLECT *(5)*
- **r** in your heart and be still. Ps 4:4
- will **r** on all You have done and Ps 77:12
- I **r** on the work of Your hands. Ps 143:5
- so that we may **r** on it and know Is 41:22
- Now, **r** back from this day: Hg 2:15

REFLECTING *(1)*
- are **r** the glory of the Lord and 2Co 3:18

REFLECTIONS *(1)*
- **r** of the heart belong to man, Pr 16:1

REFLECTS *(3)*
- As the water **r** the face, so the Pr 27:19
- so the heart **r** the person. Pr 27:19
- No one **r**, no one has the Is 44:19

REFORMS *(1)*
- and **r** are taking place for the Ac 24:2

REFRAIN *(9)*
- you want to **r** from helping it Ex 23:5
- But if you **r** from making a vow, Dt 23:22
- for war or should I **r**?" 1Kg 22:6
- for war, or should we **r**?" 1Kg 22:15
- for war or should I **r**?" 2Ch 18:5
- for war, or should I **r**?" 2Ch 18:14
- **R** from anger and give up ⌊your⌋ Ps 37:8
- I will not **r**, I will not show Ezk 24:14
- have no right to **r** from working? 1Co 9:6

REFRESH *(3)*
- home with me, **r** yourself, and 1Kg 13:7
- **r** me with apricots, for I am Sg 2:5
- **r** my heart in Christ. Phm 20

REFRESHED *(8)*
- the foreign resident may be **r**. Ex 23:12
- day He rested and was **r**." Ex 31:17
- My strength will be **r** within me, Jb 29:20
- with joy and be **r** together with Rm 15:32
- For they have **r** my spirit and 1Co 16:18
- his spirit was **r** by all of you. 2Co 7:13
- because he often **r** me and was 2Tm 1:16
- saints have been **r** through you, Phm 7

REFRESHES *(1)*
- he **r** the life of his masters. Pr 25:13

REFRESHING *(2)*
- them drink from Your **r** stream, Ps 36:8
- so that seasons of **r** may come Ac 3:19

REFUGE *(97)*
- will include six cities of **r**, Nm 35:6
- to serve as cities of **r** for you, Nm 35:11
- the cities as a **r** from the Nm 35:12
- will be your six cities of **r**. Nm 35:13
- of Canaan to be cities of **r**. Nm 35:14
- will serve as a **r** for the Nm 35:15
- him to the city of **r** he fled to, Nm 35:25
- of the city of **r** he fled to, Nm 35:26
- of his city of **r** and kills him, Nm 35:27
- in his city of **r** until the death Nm 35:28
- who flees to his city of **r**, Nm 35:32
- the 'rock' they found **r** in? Dt 32:37
- cities of **r**, as I instructed Jos 20:2
- will be your **r** from the avenger Jos 20:3
- the city of **r** for the one who Jos 21:13
- the city of **r** for the one who Jos 21:21
- the city of **r** for the one who Jos 21:27
- the city of **r** for the one who Jos 21:32
- the city of **r** for the one who Jos 21:38
- come and find **r** in my shade. Jdg 9:15
- wings you have come for **r**." Ru 2:12
- left Gath and took **r** in the cave 1Sm 22:1
- my mountain where I seek **r**. 2Sm 22:3
- stronghold, my **r**, and my Savior, 2Sm 22:3
- shield to all who take **r** in Him. 2Sm 22:31
- is my strong **r**; He makes my way 2Sm 22:33
- a city of **r**), Libnah and its 1Ch 6:57
- Shechem (a city of **r**) with its 1Ch 6:67
- those who take **r** in Him are Ps 2:12
- all who take **r** in You rejoice; Ps 5:11
- LORD my God, I seek **r** in You; Ps 7:1
- The LORD is a **r** for the Ps 9:9
- the oppressed, a **r** in times of Ps 9:9
- I have taken **r** in the LORD. Ps 11:1
- but the LORD is his **r**. Ps 14:6
- me, God, for I take **r** in You. Ps 16:1
- of all who seek **r** from those who Ps 17:7
- my mountain where I seek **r**, Ps 18:2
- shield to all who take **r** in Him. Ps 18:30
- to shame, for I take **r** in You. Ps 25:20
- LORD, I seek **r** in You; Ps 31:1
- a rock of **r** for me, a mountain Ps 31:2
- set for me, for You are my **r**. Ps 31:4
- for those who take **r** in You. Ps 31:19
- is the man who takes **r** in Him! Ps 34:8
- all who take **r** in Him will not Ps 34:22
- that people take **r** in the shadow Ps 36:7
- their **r** in a time of distress. Ps 37:39
- them because they take **r** in Him. Ps 37:40
- For You are the God of my **r**. Ps 43:2
- God is our **r** and strength, Ps 46:1
- who would not make God his **r**, Ps 52:7
- **r** in his destructive behavior. Ps 52:7
- to me, for I take **r** in You. Ps 57:1
- I will seek **r** in the shadow of Ps 57:1
- for me, a **r** in my day of trouble Ps 59:16
- for You have been a **r** for me, Ps 61:3
- forever and take **r** under the Ps 61:4
- my strong rock, my **r**, is in God. Ps 62:7
- before Him. God is our **r**. Selah Ps 62:8
- in the LORD and take **r** in Him; Ps 64:10
- LORD, I seek **r** in You; Ps 71:1
- Be a rock of **r** for me, where I Ps 71:3
- many, but You are my strong **r**. Ps 71:7
- I have made the Lord GOD my **r**, Ps 73:28
- You have been our **r** in every Ps 90:1
- the LORD, "My **r** and my fortress Ps 91:2
- you will take **r** under His wings. Ps 91:4
- the LORD—my **r**, the Most High— Ps 91:9
- But the LORD is my **r**; Ps 94:22
- the cliffs are a **r** for hyraxes. Ps 104:18
- better to take **r** in the LORD Ps 118:8
- better to take **r** in the LORD Ps 118:9
- Lord GOD. I seek **r** in You; do Ps 141:8
- there is no **r** for me; Ps 142:4
- my shield, and I take **r** in Him; Ps 144:2
- and his children have a **r**. Pr 14:26
- have a **r** when they die. Pr 14:32
- to those who take **r** in Him. Pr 30:5
- and a **r** and shelter from storm Is 4:6
- of Gebim have sought **r**. Is 10:31
- afflicted people find **r** in her. Is 14:32
- be a **r** for Moab from the Is 16:4
- his distress, a **r** from the rain, Is 25:4
- falsehood our **r** and have hidden Is 28:15
- will sweep away the false **r**, Is 28:17
- and take **r** in Egypt's shadow. Is 30:2
- and **r** in Egypt's shadow your Is 30:3
- the wind, a **r** from the rain, Is 32:2
- his **r** will be the rocky Is 33:16
- But whoever takes **r** in Me will Is 57:13
- my **r** in a time of distress, Jr 16:19
- You are my **r** in the day of Jr 17:17
- LORD will be a **r** for His people, Jl 3:16
- for those who take **r** in Him. Nah 1:7
- also will seek **r** from the enemy. Nah 3:11
- have fled for **r** might have Heb 6:18

REFUGEE *(1)*
- night. Hide the **r**; do not betray Is 16:3

REFUGEES *(3)*
- up his sons as **r**, and his Nm 21:29
- Let my **r** stay with you; Is 16:4
- of Tema meet the **r** with food. Is 21:14

REFUSE *(29)*
- But if you **r** to let them go, Ex 8:2
- if you **r** to let ⌊them⌋ go and Ex 9:2
- How long will you **r** to humble Ex 10:3
- if you **r** to let My people go, Ex 10:4
- How long will you **r** to keep My Ex 16:28
- you so upset that you **r** to eat?" 1Kg 21:5
- I **r** to touch ⌊them⌋; they are Jb 6:7
- let me not **r** it. Even now my Ps 141:5
- because they **r** to act justly. Pr 21:7
- him because his hands **r** to work. Pr 21:25
- I did not **r** myself any pleasure, Ec 2:10
- I will **r** to look at you; Is 1:15
- But if you **r** and rebel, you will Is 1:20
- prostitute and **r** to be ashamed. Jr 3:3
- of deceit; they **r** to return. Jr 8:5
- deception they **r** to know Me. Jr 9:6
- people, who **r** to listen to Me Jr 13:10
- If they **r** to take the cup from Jr 25:28
- But if you **r** to surrender, Jr 38:21
- they **r** to release them. Jr 50:33
- they listen or **r** ⌊to listen⌋— Ezk 2:5
- they listen or **r** ⌊to listen⌋, Ezk 2:7
- they listen or **r** ⌊to listen⌋." Ezk 3:11
- who refuses, **r**—for they are Ezk 3:27
- you and people **r** to listen to Mk 6:11
- guests he did not want to **r** her. Mk 6:26
- He did not **r** to answer, but he Jn 1:20
- death, I do not **r** to die, but if Ac 25:11
- But **r** to enroll younger widows; 1Tm 5:11

REFUSED *(42)*
- but he **r** to be comforted. Gn 37:35
- he **r** and said to his master's Gn 39:8
- he **r** to go to bed with her. Gn 39:10
- But his father **r** and said, Gn 48:19
- Me, but you **r** to let him go. Ex 4:23
- stubbornly **r** to let us go, Ex 13:15
- Edom **r** to allow Israel to travel Nm 20:21
- the LORD has **r** to let me go with Nm 22:13
- "Balaam **r** to come with us." Nm 22:14
- the Canaanites **r** to leave this Jdg 1:27
- The Amorites **r** to leave Jdg 1:35
- to the king of Moab, but he **r**. Jdg 11:17
- people **r** to listen to Samuel. 1Sm 8:19
- He **r**, saying, "I won't eat," but 1Sm 28:23
- But Asahel **r** to turn away, 2Sm 2:23
- front of him, but he **r** to eat. 2Sm 13:9
- But he **r** to listen to her, 2Sm 13:14
- But he **r** to listen to her. 2Sm 13:16
- to David, but he **r** to drink it. 2Sm 23:16
- So he **r** to drink it. 2Sm 23:17
- But the man **r** to strike him. 1Kg 20:35
- Jezreelite who **r** to give it to 1Kg 21:15
- him to accept it, but he **r**. 2Kg 5:16
- to David, but he **r** to drink it. 1Ch 11:18
- and his sons **r** to let them serve 2Ch 11:14
- They **r** to listen and did not Neh 9:17
- Queen Vashti **r** to come at the Est 1:12
- she **r** to obey King Ahasuerus' Est 1:15
- I would have **r** to put with my Jb 30:1
- If I have **r** the wishes of the Jb 31:16
- I **r** to be comforted. Ps 77:2
- covenant and **r** to live by His Ps 78:10
- Since I called out and you **r**, Pr 1:24
- but they **r** to accept discipline. Jr 5:3
- than rock, and they **r** to return. Jr 5:3
- ancestors who **r** to obey My words Jr 11:10
- for a nation that **r** to help. Lm 4:17
- king, because they **r** to repent. Hs 11:5
- But they **r** to pay attention and Zch 7:11
- she **r** to be consoled, because Mt 2:18
- But the Jews who **r** to believe Ac 14:2
- **r** to be called the son of Heb 11:24

REFUSES *(7)*
- he **r** to let the people go. Ex 7:14
- absolutely **r** to give her to Ex 22:17
- brother-in-law **r** to preserve his Dt 25:7
- who **r** gain from extortion, Is 33:15
- let the one who **r**, refuse—for Ezk 3:27
- but the one who **r** to believe in Jn 3:36
- He not only **r** to welcome the 3Jn 10

REFUSING *(6)*
- again by **r** to let the people go Ex 8:29
- **r** to listen either to the priest Dt 17:12
- **r** to share with any of them his Dt 28:55
- wound incurable, **r** to be healed? Jr 15:18
- **r** to be comforted for her Jr 31:15
- and turned away, **r** to obey You. Dn 9:11

REFUTE *(4)*
they had failed to **r** ⌊him⌋, Jb 32:3
R me if you can. Prepare your Jb 33:5
and you will **r** any accusation Is 54:17
teaching and to **r** those who Ti 1:9

REFUTED *(2)*
not one of you **r** his arguments. Jb 32:12
For he vigorously **r** the Jews in Ac 18:28

REGAIN *(4)*
way could he **r** his master's 1Sm 29:4
on him so he may **r** his sight." Ac 9:12
me so you may **r** your sight and Ac 9:17
Brother Saul, **r** your sight.' Ac 22:13

REGAINED *(2)*
his eyes, and he **r** his sight. Ac 9:18
some food, he **r** his strength. Ac 9:19

REGAINING *(1)*
R his composure, he said, "Serve Gn 43:31

REGARD *(32)*
The LORD had **r** for Abel and his Gn 4:4
He did not have **r** for Cain and Gn 4:5
Only with **r** to the throne will I Gn 41:40
their brothers with **r** to their Gn 48:6
committed in **r** to the command Lv 4:14
unintentionally in **r** to any of Lv 5:15
his neighbor in **r** to a deposit, Lv 6:2
You must **r** the foreigner who Lv 19:34
In **r** to the Levites: Nm 8:24
Do not **r** it as a hardship when Dt 15:18
and mother, "I do not **r** them." Dt 33:9
they had no **r** for the LORD 1Sm 2:12
such was the **r** that both David 2Sm 16:23
r me as a man of distinction, 1Ch 17:17
female servants **r** me as a Jb 19:15
They have no **r** for God. Ps 54:3
They have no **r** for You. Ps 86:14
favor and high **r** in the sight of Pr 3:4
You are to **r** only the LORD of Is 8:13
so I **r** as good the exiles from Jr 24:5
Because you **r** your heart as that Ezk 28:6
nothing in **r** to Daniel could Dn 6:17
He will not show **r** for the gods Dn 11:37
I will have no **r** for your Am 5:22
and had high **r** for His name. Mal 3:16
With **r** to the Gentiles who have Ac 21:25
In this **r**, it is expected of 1Co 4:2
judge you in **r** to food and drink Col 2:16
as slaves must **r** their own 1Tm 6:1
worthless in **r** to the faith. 2Tm 3:8
In **r** to this, they are surprised 1Pt 4:4
r the patience of our Lord as 2Pt 3:15

REGARDED *(18)*
we not **r** by him as outsiders? Gn 31:15
is to be **r** by you as sacred to Ex 30:37
They were also **r** as Rephaim, Dt 2:11
too used to be **r** as the land Dt 2:20
Solomon will be **r** as criminals." 1Kg 1:21
and highly **r** because through 2Kg 5:1
are we **r** as cattle, as stupid Jb 18:3
A club is **r** as stubble, and he Jb 41:29
but we in turn **r** Him stricken, Is 53:4
no longer **r** as a nation among Jr 33:24
how they are **r** as clay jars, Lm 4:2
though you have **r** your heart as Ezk 28:2
they would be **r** as something Hs 8:12
since they **r** him as a prophet. Mt 14:5
because they **r** Him as a prophet. Mt 21:46
that those who are **r** as rulers Mk 10:42
to be **r** just as we are 2Co 11:12
r as profane the blood of the Heb 10:29

REGARDING *(25)*
(See pp. xi-xii.)

REGARDLESS *(2)*
or the leather, **r** of how it is Lv 13:51
themselves **r** of their tour of 2Ch 5:11

REGARDS *(5)*
whether it **r** differences of 2Ch 19:10
and He **r** me as ⌊one of⌋ His Jb 19:11
He **r** me as his enemy. Jb 33:10
r iron as straw, and bronze as Jb 41:27
them; He **r** them no more. Lm 4:16

REGATHER *(1)*
their God when I **r** them to their Ezk 39:28

REGATHERED *(1)*
from war and **r** from many peoples Ezk 38:8

REGEM *(1)*
R, Jotham, Geshan, Pelet, Ephah, 1Ch 2:47

REGEM-MELECH *(1)*
sent Sharezer, **R**, and their men Zch 7:2

REGENERATION *(1)*
the washing of **r** and renewal Ti 3:5

REGIMENT *(3)*
what was called the Italian **R**. Ac 10:1
commander of the **r** that all Ac 21:31
named Julius, of the Imperial **R**. Ac 27:1

REGION *(75)*
traveled to the **r** of the Negev Gn 20:1
he was living in the Negev **r**. Gn 24:62
a prince of the **r**, saw her, he Gn 34:2
the **r** is large enough for them. Gn 34:21
Israel was living in that **r**, Gn 35:22
was no food in that entire **r**, Gn 47:13
of Egypt, in the **r** of Goshen. Gn 47:27
saw that the **r** was a ⌊good⌋ one Nm 32:1
cities, the entire **r** of Argob, Dt 3:4
The entire **r** of Argob, the whole Dt 3:13
over the entire **r** of Argob as Dt 3:14
and the **r** from the Valley of Dt 34:3
Joshua conquered the whole **r**— Jos 10:40
clans was in the southernmost **r**, Jos 15:1
The **r** of Tappuah belonged to Jos 17:8
they came to the **r** of the Jordan Jos 22:10
Canaan at the **r** of the Jordan, Jos 22:11
Abraham from the **r** beyond the Jos 24:3
then through the **r** of Shalishah, 1Sm 9:4
went through the **r** of Shaalim— 1Sm 9:4
the Benjaminite **r** but still 1Sm 9:4
turns out he really is in the **r**, 1Sm 23:23
of the **r** through Shur as 1Sm 27:8
battle spread over the entire **r**, 2Sm 18:8
and he had the **r** of Argob, 1Kg 4:13
them in the **r** of their fortified 1Kg 8:37
throughout the **r** east of Gilead. 1Ch 5:10
them in the **r** of their fortified 2Ch 6:28
the men of that **r** with silver, Ezr 1:4
of Samaria and the **r** west of the Ezr 4:10
the men from the **r** west of the Ezr 4:11
and elsewhere in the **r** west of Ezr 4:17
authority over the whole **r**, Ezr 4:20
governor of the **r** west of the Ezr 5:3
governor of the **r** west of the Ezr 5:6
officials in the **r**, sent to King Ezr 5:6
governor of the **r** west of the Ezr 6:6
the officials in the **r**. Ezr 6:6
the taxes of the **r** west of the Ezr 6:8
governor of the **r** west of the Ezr 6:13
treasurers in the **r** west of the Ezr 7:21
the people in the **r** west of the Ezr 7:25
and governors of the **r** west of Ezr 8:36
the governors of the **r** west of Neh 2:7
the governors of the **r** west of Neh 2:9
governor of the **r** west of the Neh 3:7
from the **r** around Jerusalem Neh 12:28
land of Egypt, the **r** of Zoan. Ps 78:12
His marvels in the **r** of Zoan. Ps 78:43
swampland and a **r** for wild Is 14:23
the eastern **r** and goes down to Ezk 47:8
the southern **r** and the Judean Zch 7:7
he withdrew to the **r** of Galilee. Mt 2:22
the **r** of Zebulun and Naphtali. Mt 4:13
to the **r** of the Gadarenes, Mt 8:28
begged Him to leave their **r**. Mt 8:34
woman from that **r** came and kept Mt 15:22
and went to the **r** of Magadan. Mt 15:39
Jesus came to the **r** of Caesarea Mt 16:13
went to the **r** of Judea across Mt 19:1
to the **r** of the Gerasenes. Mk 5:1
not to send them out of the **r**. Mk 5:10
to beg Him to leave their **r**. Mk 5:17
there to the **r** of Tyre and Sidon Mk 7:24
leaving the **r** of Tyre, He went Mk 7:31
through the **r** of the Decapolis. Mk 7:31
and went to the **r** of Judea and Mk 10:1
In the same **r**, shepherds were Lk 2:8
tetrarch of the **r** of Iturea Lk 3:1
sailed to the **r** of the Gerasenes Lk 8:26
of the Gerasene **r** asked Him to Lk 8:37
Lord spread through the whole **r**. Ac 13:49
went through the **r** of Phrygia Ac 16:6
and in all the **r** of Judea, Ac 26:20
in the entire **r** of Macedonia. 1Th 4:10

REGIONS *(12)*
as an inheritance into three **r**, Dt 19:3
from all their **r** throughout 2Ch 11:13
his sons to all the **r** of Judah 2Ch 11:23
into the deepest **r** of the Pit. Is 14:15
from the remote **r** of the earth. Jr 6:22
from remote **r** of the earth— Jr 31:8
from the remote **r** of the earth. Jr 50:41
set in the deepest **r** of the Pit, Ezk 32:23
the interior **r** and came to Ac 19:1
the gospel to the **r** beyond you, 2Co 10:16
be stopped in the **r** of Achaia. 2Co 11:10
I went to the **r** of Syria and Gl 1:21

REGISTER *(12)*
of the Israelites to **r** them, Ex 30:12
Aaron are to **r** those who are 20 Nm 1:3
Do not **r** or take a census of the Nm 1:49
R the Levites by their ancestral Nm 3:15
are to **r** every male one month Nm 3:15
R every firstborn male of the Nm 3:40
R men from 30 years old to 50 Nm 4:23
you are to **r** them by their clans Nm 4:29
R men from 30 years old to 50 Nm 4:30
Beer-sheba and **r** the troops so I 2Sm 24:2
king's presence to **r** the troops 2Sm 24:4
recorded in the **r** of the house Ezk 13:9

REGISTERED *(79)*
to the LORD as they are **r**. Ex 30:12
will come on them as they are **r**. Ex 30:12
Everyone who is **r** must pay half Ex 30:13
Each man who is **r**, 20 years old Ex 30:14
who were **r** was 7,544 pounds, Ex 38:25
had crossed over to the **r** group, Ex 38:26
He **r** them in the Wilderness of Nm 1:19
those **r** for the tribe of Reuben Nm 1:21
those **r** counting one by one the Nm 1:22
those **r** for the tribe of Simeon Nm 1:23
those **r** for the tribe of Gad Nm 1:25
those **r** for the tribe of Judah Nm 1:27
r for the tribe of Issachar Nm 1:29
those **r** for the tribe of Zebulun Nm 1:31
those **r** for the tribe of Ephraim Nm 1:33
r for the tribe of Manasseh Nm 1:35
r for the tribe of Benjamin Nm 1:37
those **r** for the tribe of Dan Nm 1:39
those **r** for the tribe of Asher Nm 1:41
r for the tribe of Naphtali Nm 1:43
are the men Moses and Aaron **r**, Nm 1:44
r by their ancestral houses. Nm 1:45
All those **r** numbered 603,550. Nm 1:46
Levites were not **r** with them by Nm 1:47
the Israelites **r** by their Nm 2:32
Levites were not **r** among the Nm 2:33
So Moses **r** them in obedience to Nm 3:16
Those **r**, counting every male one Nm 3:22
Those **r**, counting every male one Nm 3:34
Moses and Aaron **r** by their clans Nm 3:39
So Moses **r** every firstborn among Nm 3:42
the community **r** the Kohathites Nm 4:34
men **r** by their clans numbered Nm 4:36
These were the **r** men of the Nm 4:37
Moses and Aaron **r** them at the Nm 4:37
Gershonites were **r** by their Nm 4:38
The men **r** by their clans and Nm 4:40
These were the **r** men of the Nm 4:41
Moses and Aaron **r** everyone who Nm 4:41
clans were **r** by their clans Nm 4:42
men **r** by their clans numbered Nm 4:44
These were the **r** men of the Nm 4:45
Moses and Aaron **r** them at the Nm 4:45
of Israel **r** all the Levites Nm 4:46
Their **r** men numbered 8,580. Nm 4:48
command they were **r** under the Nm 4:49
you who were **r** ⌊in the census⌋ Nm 14:29
and their **r** men numbered 43,730. Nm 26:7
clans ⌊numbered⌋ by their **r** men: Nm 26:18
clans ⌊numbered⌋ by their **r** men: Nm 26:22
clans ⌊numbered⌋ by their **r** men: Nm 26:25
clans ⌊numbered⌋ by their **r** men: Nm 26:27
clans, numbered by their **r** men: Nm 26:34
clans ⌊numbered⌋ by their **r** men: Nm 26:37
clans numbered by their **r** men: Nm 26:41
by their **r** men were 64,400. Nm 26:43
clans ⌊numbered⌋ by their **r** men: Nm 26:47
clans numbered by their **r** men: Nm 26:50
These **r** Israelite men numbered Nm 26:51
to those who were **r** in it. Nm 26:54
the Levites **r** by their clans: Nm 26:57

Those **r** were 23,000, every male Nm 26:62
were not **r** among the ⌊other⌋ Nm 26:62
These were the ones **r** by Moses Nm 26:63
when they **r** the Israelites Nm 26:63
who had been **r** by Moses and Nm 26:64
when they **r** the Israelites Nm 26:64
Saul **r** the troops who were with 1Sm 13:15
All of them were **r** in the 1Ch 5:17
All Israel was **r** in the 1Ch 9:1
were **r** by genealogy in their 1Ch 9:22
to males **r** by genealogy three 2Ch 31:16
to those **r** by genealogy—with 2Ch 31:18
were⌋ men who were **r** by name to 2Ch 31:19
him who were **r** by genealogy; Ezr 8:3
the people to be **r** by genealogy. Neh 7:5
the whole empire should be **r**. Lk 2:1
went to be **r**, each to his own Lk 2:3
to be **r** along with Mary, who was Lk 2:5

REGISTERS *(1)*
When He **r** the peoples, the LORD Ps 87:6

REGISTRATION *(5)*
leaders who supervised the **r**. Nm 7:2
total of the **r** of the troops. 2Sm 24:9
total of the **r** of the troops. 1Ch 21:5
according to their **r** by name in 1Ch 23:24
This first **r** took place while Lk 2:2

REGRET *(6)*
for I **r** that I made them." Gn 6:7
I **r** that I made Saul king, 1Sm 15:11
to no one's **r** and was buried 2Ch 21:20
I do not **r** it—even though 2Co 7:8
though I did **r** it since I saw 2Co 7:8
out of **r** or out of necessity, 2Co 9:7

REGRETS *(1)*
No one **r** his evil, asking: Jr 8:6

REGRETTED *(4)*
the LORD **r** that He had made man Gn 6:6
the LORD **r** He had made Saul 1Sm 15:35
the king **r** it, he commanded Mt 14:9
not to be **r** and leading to 2Co 7:10

REGROUPED *(1)*
been defeated by Israel, they **r**. 2Sm 10:15

REGULAR *(31)*
and his sons as a **r** portion Ex 29:28
This will be a **r** burnt offering Ex 29:42
flour as a **r** grain offering, Lv 6:20
The **r** bread ⌊offering⌋ is to be Nm 4:7
lambs as a **r** burnt offering. Nm 28:3
It is a **r** burnt offering Nm 28:6
addition to the **r** burnt offering Nm 28:10
addition to the **r** burnt offering Nm 28:15
is part of the **r** burnt offering. Nm 28:23
and the **r** burnt offering. Nm 28:24
addition to the **r** burnt offering Nm 28:31
monthly and **r** burnt offerings Nm 29:6
The **r** burnt offering with its Nm 29:11
addition to the **r** burnt offering Nm 29:16
addition to the **r** burnt offering Nm 29:19
addition to the **r** burnt offering Nm 29:22
addition to the **r** burnt offering Nm 29:25
addition to the **r** burnt offering Nm 29:28
addition to the **r** burnt offering Nm 29:31
addition to the **r** burnt offering Nm 29:34
addition to the **r** burnt offering Nm 29:38
r allowance was given to him by 2Kg 25:30
Benjamin bearing **r** shields and 2Ch 14:8
for the **r** morning and evening 2Ch 31:3
offered⌋ the **r** burnt offering Ezr 3:5
offering, the **r** burnt offering, Neh 10:33
This was Job's **r** practice. Jb 1:5
cease to come at their **r** time, Jr 33:20
r allowance was given to him by Jr 52:34
and islands were your **r** markets. Ezk 27:15
morning as a **r** burnt offering. Ezk 46:15

REGULARLY *(14)*
you are to offer **r** on the altar Ex 29:38
so that the lamp will burn **r**. Lv 24:2
is to tend it **r** from evening Lv 24:3
He must **r** tend the lamps on the Lv 24:4
If these people **r** go to offer 1Kg 12:27
and he dined **r** in the presence 2Kg 25:29
the trumpets **r** before the ark 1Ch 16:6
to minister **r** before the ark 1Ch 16:37
to offer burnt offerings **r**, 1Ch 16:40
are to do so **r** in the LORD's 1Ch 23:31
They **r** offered burnt offerings 2Ch 24:14
it; I water it **r**. I guard it Is 27:3
and he dined **r** in the presence Jr 52:33
statute ⌊to be observed⌋ **r**. Ezk 46:14

REGULATING *(1)*
and an ordinance **r** the singers' Neh 11:23

REGULATION *(5)*
offering according to the **r**. Lv 5:10
it according to the **r**. Lv 9:16
offering according to the **r**, Nm 15:24
lambs⌋ with fire according to **r**. 2Ch 35:13
the harem **r** required her to Est 2:12

REGULATIONS *(7)*
to the **r** ⌊given⌋ to them 1Ch 6:32
according to their **r**, which they 1Ch 24:19
law of the commandments in **r**, Eph 2:15
Why do you submit to **r**: Col 2:20
All these ⌊**r**⌋ refer to what is Col 2:22
covenant⌋ also had **r** for Heb 9:1
are physical **r** and only deal Heb 9:10

REHABIAH *(3)*
Eliezer's sons were **R**, first; 1Ch 23:17
From **R**: from Rehabiah's sons: 1Ch 24:21
his son **R**, his son Jeshaiah, his 1Ch 26:25

REHABIAH'S *(2)*
but **R** sons were very numerous. 1Ch 23:17
Rehabiah: from **R** sons: Isshiah 1Ch 24:21

REHOB *(10)*
of Zin as far as **R** near the Nm 13:21
Ebron, **R**, Hammon, and Kanah, Jos 19:28
Aphek, and **R**—22 cities, with Jos 19:30
and **R** with its pasturelands— Jos 21:31
Achzib, Helbah, Aphik, or **R**. Jdg 1:31
defeated Hadadezer son of **R**, 2Sm 8:3
the spoil of Hadadezer son of **R**, 2Sm 8:12
Zobah and **R** and the men of Tob 2Sm 10:8
and **R** and its pasturelands. 1Ch 6:75
Mica, **R**, Hashabiah, Neh 10:11

REHOBOAM *(55)*
His son **R** became king in his 1Kg 11:43
Then **R** went to Shechem, for all 1Kg 12:1
of Israel came and spoke to **R**: 1Kg 12:3
R replied, "Go home for three 1Kg 12:5
Then King **R** consulted with the 1Kg 12:6
people came to **R** on the third 1Kg 12:12
R reigned over the Israelites 1Kg 12:17
Then King **R** sent Adoram, who 1Kg 12:18
King **R** managed to get into the 1Kg 12:18
When **R** arrived in Jerusalem, 1Kg 12:21
kingdom to **R** son of Solomon. 1Kg 12:21
Say to **R** son of Solomon, king of 1Kg 12:23
to their lord, **R** king of Judah. 1Kg 12:27
Now **R**, Solomon's son, reigned 1Kg 14:21
R was 41 years old when he 1Kg 14:21
In the fifth year of King **R**, 1Kg 14:25
King **R** made bronze shields in 1Kg 14:27
was war between **R** and Jeroboam 1Kg 14:30
R rested with his fathers and 1Kg 14:31
war between **R** and Jeroboam all 1Kg 15:6
Solomon's son was **R**; 1Ch 3:10
His son **R** became king in his 2Ch 9:31
Then **R** went to Shechem, for all 2Ch 10:1
all Israel came and spoke to **R**: 2Ch 10:3
R replied, "Return to me in 2Ch 10:5
Then King **R** consulted with the 2Ch 10:6
people came to **R** on the third 2Ch 10:12
King **R** rejected the elders' 2Ch 10:13
cities of Judah, **R** reigned over 2Ch 10:17
Then King **R** sent Hadoram, who 2Ch 10:18
King **R** managed to get up into 2Ch 10:18
When **R** arrived in Jerusalem, 2Ch 11:1
to restore the reign to **R**. 2Ch 11:1
Say to **R** son of Solomon, king of 2Ch 11:3
R stayed in Jerusalem, and he 2Ch 11:5
Israel took their stand with **R**, 2Ch 11:13
and supported **R** son of Solomon 2Ch 11:17
R married Mahalath, daughter of 2Ch 11:18
R loved Maacah daughter of 2Ch 11:21
R appointed Abijah son of 2Ch 11:22
R also showed discernment by 2Ch 11:23
When **R** had established his 2Ch 12:1
in the fifth year of King **R**, 2Ch 12:2
went to **R** and the leaders 2Ch 12:5
King **R** made bronze shields in 2Ch 12:10
When **R** humbled himself, the 2Ch 12:12
King **R** established his royal 2Ch 12:13
R was 41 years old when he 2Ch 12:13
R did what was evil, because he 2Ch 12:14
was war between **R** and Jeroboam 2Ch 12:15
R rested with his fathers and 2Ch 12:16
him to resist **R** son of Solomon 2Ch 13:7
of Solomon when **R** was young, 2Ch 13:7
Solomon fathered **R**, Rehoboam Mt 1:7
Rehoboam, **R** fathered Abijah, Mt 1:7

REHOBOAM'S *(5)*
R mother's name was Naamah the 1Kg 14:21
rest of the events of **R** ⌊reign⌋, 1Kg 14:29
Jeroboam all the days of **R** life. 1Kg 15:6
R mother's name was Naamah the 2Ch 12:13
The events of **R** ⌊reign⌋, from 2Ch 12:15

REHOBOTH *(1)*
Shaul from **R** on the Euphrates 1Ch 1:48

REHOBOTH-IR *(1)*
and built Nineveh, **R**, Calah, Gn 10:11

REHOBOTH-ON-THE-RIVER *(1)*
Shaul from **R** ruled in his place. Gn 36:37

REHUM *(8)*
(AKA NEHUM)
Mispar, Bigvai, **R**, and Baanah. Ezr 2:2
R the chief deputy and Shimshai Ezr 4:8
⌊From⌋ **R** the chief deputy, Ezr 4:9
a reply to his chief deputy **R**, Ezr 4:17
letter was read to **R**, Ezr 4:23
repairs ⌊under⌋ **R** son of Bani. Neh 3:17
R, Hashabnah, Maaseiah, Neh 10:25
Shecaniah, **R**, Meremoth, Neh 12:3

REI *(1)*
prophet, Shimei, **R**, and David's 1Kg 1:8

REIGN *(149)*
you really going to **r** over us?" Gn 37:8
LORD will **r** forever and ever! Ex 15:18
to the olive tree, "**R** over us." Jdg 9:8
fig tree, "Come and **r** over us." Jdg 9:10
grapevine, "Come and **r** over us." Jdg 9:12
bramble, "Come and **r** over us." Jdg 9:14
that Saul should not **r** over us? 1Sm 11:12
established your **r** over Israel, 1Sm 13:13
but now your **r** will not endure. 1Sm 13:14
during Saul's **r** was ⌊already⌋ 1Sm 17:12
when he began his **r** over Israel; 2Sm 2:10
years old when he began his **r**; 2Sm 5:4
During David's **r** there was a 2Sm 21:1
Solomon's ⌊**r**⌋, Judah and Israel 1Kg 4:25
year of his **r** over Israel, 1Kg 6:1
enemy throughout Solomon's **r**, 1Kg 11:25
and you will **r** as king over all 1Kg 11:37
of the events of Solomon's ⌊**r**⌋, 1Kg 11:41
of Solomon's **r** in Jerusalem over 1Kg 11:42
of the events of Jeroboam's ⌊**r**⌋, 1Kg 14:19
of Jeroboam's **r** was 22 years. 1Kg 14:20
of the events of Rehoboam's ⌊**r**⌋, 1Kg 14:29
of the events of Abijam's ⌊**r**⌋, 1Kg 15:7
of all the events of Asa's ⌊**r**⌋, 1Kg 15:23
of the events of Nadab's ⌊**r**⌋, 1Kg 15:31
of the events of Baasha's ⌊**r**⌋, 1Kg 16:5
of the events of Elah's ⌊**r**⌋, 1Kg 16:14
of the events of Zimri's ⌊**r**⌋, 1Kg 16:20
of the events of Omri's ⌊**r**⌋, 1Kg 16:27
During his **r**, Hiel the Bethelite 1Kg 16:34
of the events of Ahab's ⌊**r**⌋, 1Kg 22:39
the events of Jehoshaphat's ⌊**r**⌋, 1Kg 22:45
of the events of Ahaziah's ⌊**r**⌋, 2Kg 1:18
Jehoram's **r**, Edom rebelled 2Kg 8:20
of the events of Jehoram's ⌊**r**⌋, 2Kg 8:23
of the events of Jehu's ⌊**r**⌋, 2Kg 10:34
length of Jehu's **r** over Israel 2Kg 10:36
year ⌊of the **r**⌋ of King Joash, 2Kg 12:6
of the events of Joash's ⌊**r**⌋, 2Kg 12:19
of the events of Jehoahaz's ⌊**r**⌋, 2Kg 13:8
of the events of Jehoash's ⌊**r**⌋, 2Kg 13:12
throughout the **r** of Jehoahaz, 2Kg 13:22
of the events of Jehoash's ⌊**r**⌋, 2Kg 14:15
of Amaziah's ⌊**r**⌋ are written 2Kg 14:18
the events of Jeroboam's ⌊**r**⌋— 2Kg 14:28
of the events of Azariah's ⌊**r**⌋, 2Kg 15:6
the events of Zechariah's ⌊**r**⌋, 2Kg 15:11
of the events of Shallum's ⌊**r**⌋, 2Kg 15:15
Throughout his **r**, he did not 2Kg 15:18
of the events of Menahem's ⌊**r**⌋, 2Kg 15:21
of the events of Pekahiah's ⌊**r**⌋, 2Kg 15:26
of the events of Pekah's ⌊**r**⌋, 2Kg 15:31
of the events of Jotham's ⌊**r**⌋, 2Kg 15:36
of the events of Ahaz's ⌊**r**⌋, 2Kg 16:19
of the events of Hezekiah's ⌊**r**⌋, 2Kg 20:20

of the events of Manasseh's ⌊**r**⌋, 2Kg 21:17
of the events of Amon's ⌊**r**⌋, 2Kg 21:25
of the events of Josiah's ⌊**r**⌋, 2Kg 23:28
During his **r**, Pharaoh Neco king 2Kg 23:29
During his **r**, Nebuchadnezzar 2Kg 24:1
the events of Jehoiakim's ⌊**r**⌋, 2Kg 24:5
in the eighth year of his **r**. 2Kg 24:12
the ninth year of Zedekiah's **r**, 2Kg 25:1
During Saul's **r** they waged war 1Ch 5:10
During David's **r**, 22,600 1Ch 7:2
him in his **r** to make him king 1Ch 11:10
quiet to Israel during his **r**. 1Ch 22:9
year of David's **r** a search was 1Ch 26:31
length of his **r** over Israel was 1Ch 29:27
the events of King David's ⌊**r**⌋, 1Ch 29:29
along with all his **r**, his might, 1Ch 29:30
in the fourth year of his **r**. 2Ch 3:2
events of Solomon's ⌊**r**⌋, 2Ch 9:29
to restore the **r** to Rehoboam. 2Ch 11:1
The events of Rehoboam's ⌊**r**⌋, 2Ch 12:15
his power during Abijah's **r**; 2Ch 13:20
of the events of Abijah's ⌊**r**⌋, 2Ch 13:22
his **r** the land experienced 2Ch 14:1
the fifteenth year of Asa's **r**. 2Ch 15:10
thirty-fifth year of Asa's **r**. 2Ch 15:19
that the events of Asa's ⌊**r**⌋, 2Ch 16:11
the thirty-ninth year of his **r**, 2Ch 16:12
year of his **r** and rested with 2Ch 16:13
In the third year of his **r**, 2Ch 17:7
Jehoshaphat's ⌊**r**⌋ from beginning 2Ch 20:34
Jehoram's **r**, Edom rebelled 2Ch 21:8
He must **r**, just as the LORD 2Ch 23:3
of the events of Amaziah's ⌊**r**⌋, 2Ch 25:26
of the events of Uzziah's ⌊**r**⌋, 2Ch 26:22
of the events of Jotham's ⌊**r**⌋, 2Ch 27:7
In the first year of his **r**, 2Ch 29:3
during his **r** when he became 2Ch 29:19
of Hezekiah's ⌊**r**⌋ and his deeds 2Ch 32:32
of the events of Manasseh's ⌊**r**⌋, 2Ch 33:18
In the eighth year of his **r**, 2Ch 34:3
In the eighteenth year of his **r**, 2Ch 34:8
Throughout his **r** they did not 2Ch 34:33
eighteenth year of Josiah's **r**, 2Ch 35:19
of the events of Josiah's ⌊**r**⌋, 2Ch 35:26
throughout the **r** of King Cyrus Ezr 4:5
and until the **r** of King Darius Ezr 4:5
beginning of the **r** of Ahasuerus, Ezr 4:6
year of the **r** of King Darius Ezr 4:24
year of the **r** of King Darius. Ezr 6:15
during the **r** of King Artaxerxes Ezr 7:1
during the **r** of King Artaxerxes Ezr 8:1
thirty-second year of his ⌊**r**⌋. Neh 13:6
third year of his **r** for all his Est 1:3
king will **r** in place of Vashti. Est 2:4
in the seventh year of his **r**. Est 2:16
me that kings **r** and rulers enact Pr 8:15
took place during the **r** of Ahaz, Is 7:1
He will **r** on the throne of David Is 9:7
of Hosts will **r** as king on Mount Is 24:23
a king will **r** righteously, Is 32:1
year of the **r** of Josiah son of Jr 1:2
the kings who **r** for David on his Jr 13:13
He will **r** wisely as king and Jr 23:5
of the **r** of Jehoiakim son Jr 26:1
of the **r** of Zedekiah son Jr 27:1
of the **r** of Zedekiah king Jr 28:1
during Josiah's **r** until today. Jr 36:2
of the **r** of Zedekiah king Jr 49:34
the fourth year of Zedekiah's **r**. Jr 51:59
the ninth year of Zedekiah's **r**, Jr 52:4
in the ⌊first⌋ year of his **r**, Jr 52:31
year of the **r** of Jehoiakim king Dn 1:1
In the second year of his **r**, Dn 2:1
prospered during the **r** of Darius Dn 6:28
of Darius and the **r** of Cyrus the Dn 6:28
year of King Belshazzar's **r**, Dn 8:1
in the first year of his **r**, Dn 9:2
and bring in a **r** of violence. Am 6:3
will **r** over the house of Jacob Lk 1:33
of the **r** of Tiberius Caesar, Lk 3:1
righteousness **r** in life through Rm 5:17
so also grace will **r** through Rm 5:21
do not let sin **r** in your mortal Rm 6:12
have begun to **r** as kings without 1Co 4:8
wish you did **r**, so that we also 1Co 4:8
that we also could **r** with you! 1Co 4:8
For He must **r** until He puts all 1Co 15:25
endure, we will also **r** with Him; 2Tm 2:12
and they will **r** on the earth. Rv 5:10
and He will **r** forever and ever! Rv 11:15
great power and have begun to **r**. Rv 11:17
the Almighty, has begun to **r**! Rv 19:6
and they will **r** with Him for Rv 20:6
they will **r** forever and ever. Rv 22:5

REIGNED (83)

Amorites, who **r** in Heshbon, to Jos 13:10
who **r** in Ashtaroth and Edrei; Jos 13:12
the Amorites, who **r** in Heshbon. Jos 13:21
king of Canaan, who **r** in Hazor. Jdg 4:2
and he **r** 42 years over Israel. 1Sm 13:1
began his reign; he **r** 40 years. 2Sm 5:4
In Hebron he **r** over Judah seven 2Sm 5:5
in Jerusalem he **r** 33 years over 2Sm 5:5
So David **r** over all Israel, 2Sm 8:15
of⌊ time David **r** over Israel was 1Kg 2:11
r seven years in Hebron and 33 1Kg 2:11
but Rehoboam **r** over the 1Kg 12:17
how he waged war and how he **r**, 1Kg 14:19
Solomon's son, **r** in Judah. 1Kg 14:21
he **r** 17 years in Jerusalem, 1Kg 14:21
he **r** three years in Jerusalem. 1Kg 15:2
he **r** 41 years in Jerusalem. 1Kg 15:10
he **r** over Israel two years. 1Kg 15:25
killed Nadab and **r** in his place. 1Kg 15:28
at Tirzah; ⌊he **r**⌋ 24 years. 1Kg 15:33
in Tirzah; ⌊he **r**⌋ two years. 1Kg 16:8
over Israel; ⌊he **r**⌋ 12 years. He 1Kg 16:23
He **r** six years in Tirzah, 1Kg 16:23
Ahab son of Omri **r** over Israel 1Kg 16:29
he **r** 25 years in Jerusalem. 1Kg 22:42
he **r** over Israel two years. 1Kg 22:51
King Jehoshaphat; he **r** 12 years. 2Kg 3:1
and Hazael **r** instead of him. 2Kg 8:15
he **r** eight years in Jerusalem. 2Kg 8:17
he **r** one year in Jerusalem. 2Kg 8:26
he **r** 40 years in Jerusalem. 2Kg 12:1
in Samaria; ⌊he **r**⌋ 17 years. 2Kg 13:1
in Samaria; ⌊he **r**⌋ 16 years. 2Kg 13:10
he **r** 29 years in Jerusalem. 2Kg 14:2
in Samaria; he **r** 41 years. 2Kg 14:23
he **r** 52 years in Jerusalem. 2Kg 15:2
he **r** in Samaria a full month. 2Kg 15:13
⌊he **r**⌋ 10 years in Samaria. 2Kg 15:17
in Samaria; ⌊he **r**⌋ two years. 2Kg 15:23
in Samaria; ⌊he **r**⌋ 20 years. 2Kg 15:27
he **r** 16 years in Jerusalem. 2Kg 15:33
he **r** 16 years in Jerusalem. 2Kg 16:2
in Samaria; ⌊he **r**⌋ nine years. 2Kg 17:1
he **r** 29 years in Jerusalem. 2Kg 18:2
he **r** 55 years in Jerusalem. 2Kg 21:1
he **r** two years in Jerusalem. 2Kg 21:19
he **r** 31 years in Jerusalem. 2Kg 22:1
he **r** three months in Jerusalem. 2Kg 23:31
he **r** 11 years in Jerusalem. 2Kg 23:36
he **r** three months in Jerusalem. 2Kg 24:8
he **r** 11 years in Jerusalem. 2Kg 24:18
So David **r** over all Israel, 1Ch 18:14
he **r** in Hebron for seven years 1Ch 29:27
meeting, and he **r** over Israel. 2Ch 1:13
Solomon **r** in Jerusalem over all 2Ch 9:30
of Judah, Rehoboam **r** over them. 2Ch 10:17
he **r** 17 years in Jerusalem, 2Ch 12:13
he **r** three years in Jerusalem. 2Ch 13:2
he **r** 25 years in Jerusalem. 2Ch 20:31
he **r** eight years in Jerusalem. 2Ch 21:5
he **r** eight years in Jerusalem. 2Ch 21:20
he **r** one year in Jerusalem. 2Ch 22:2
he **r** 40 years in Jerusalem. 2Ch 24:1
he **r** 29 years in Jerusalem. 2Ch 25:1
he **r** 52 years in Jerusalem. 2Ch 26:3
he **r** 16 years in Jerusalem. 2Ch 27:1
he **r** 16 years in Jerusalem. 2Ch 27:8
he **r** 16 years in Jerusalem. 2Ch 28:1
he **r** 29 years in Jerusalem. 2Ch 29:1
he **r** 55 years in Jerusalem. 2Ch 33:1
he **r** two years in Jerusalem. 2Ch 33:21
he **r** 31 years in Jerusalem. 2Ch 34:1
he **r** three months in Jerusalem. 2Ch 36:2
he **r** 11 years in Jerusalem. 2Ch 36:5
he **r** three months and 10 days in 2Ch 36:9
he **r** 11 years in Jerusalem. 2Ch 36:11
King Ahasuerus **r** from his royal Est 1:2
son of Josiah **r** as king in the Jr 37:1
he **r** 11 years in Jerusalem. Jr 52:1
death **r** from Adam to Moses, Rm 5:14
death **r** through that one man, Rm 5:17
just as sin **r** in death, so also Rm 5:21
to life and **r** with the Messiah Rv 20:4

REIGNING (2)

to keep him from **r** in Jerusalem, 2Kg 23:33
not have a son **r** on his throne, Jr 33:21

REIGNS (16)

and Jeroboam throughout their **r**. 1Kg 14:30
of Israel throughout their **r**. 1Kg 15:16
of Israel throughout their **r**. 1Kg 15:32
son Ben-hadad during their **r**. 2Kg 13:3
during the **r** of Judah's King 1Ch 5:17
and Jeroboam throughout their **r**. 2Ch 12:15
God **r** over the nations; Ps 47:8
The LORD **r**! He is robed in Ps 93:1
The LORD **r**. The world is Ps 96:10
The LORD **r**! Let the earth Ps 97:1
The LORD **r**! Let the peoples Ps 99:1
The LORD **r** forever; Zion, your Ps 146:10
God ⌊**r**⌋ for all generations. Ps 146:10
Amoz saw during the **r** of Uzziah, Is 1:1
who says to Zion, "Your God **r**!" Is 52:7
of Beeri during the **r** of Uzziah, Hs 1:1

REIMBURSE (1)

come back I'll **r** you for Lk 10:35

REINFORCED (1)

to its specifications and **r** it. 2Ch 24:13

REJECT (37)

among you, and I will not **r** you. Lv 26:11
if you **r** My statutes and despise Lv 26:15
of your idols; I will **r** you. Lv 26:30
I will not **r** or abhor them so as Lv 26:44
and I will **r** the temple I have 1Kg 9:7
I will **r** this city Jerusalem, 2Kg 23:27
Him, He will **r** you forever. 1Ch 28:9
do not **r** Your anointed one; 2Ch 6:42
do not **r** the discipline of the Jb 5:17
God does not **r** a person of Jb 8:20
to **r** the work of Your hands, Jb 10:3
is not good and does not **r** evil. Ps 36:4
Get up! Don't **r** us forever! Ps 44:23
Will the Lord **r** forever and Ps 77:7
LORD, why do You **r** me? Ps 88:14
the wicked who **r** Your Ps 119:53
You **r** all who stray from Your Ps 119:118
do not **r** Your anointed one. Ps 132:10
and don't **r** your mother's Pr 1:8
and don't **r** your mother's Pr 6:20
Those who **r** the law praise the Pr 28:4
time he learns to **r** what is bad Is 7:15
the boy knows to **r** what is bad Is 7:16
each one will **r** the silver and Is 31:7
Your lovers **r** you; they want to Jr 4:30
I will **r** all of Israel's Jr 31:37
I might also **r** the seed of Jacob Jr 33:26
Lord will not **r** ⌊us⌋ forever. Lm 3:31
I will **r** you from serving as My Hs 4:6
My God will **r** them because they Hs 9:17
But since you **r** it, and consider Ac 13:46
you did not despise or **r** me. Gl 4:14
who rejects this does not **r** man, 1Th 4:8
But **r** foolish and ignorant 2Tm 2:23
of men who **r** the truth. Ti 1:14
R a divisive person after a Ti 3:10
that you do not **r** the One who Heb 12:25

REJECTED (76)

because they **r** My ordinances and Lv 26:43
you have **r** the LORD who is Nm 11:20
plunder into the land you **r**, Nm 14:31
you. They have **r** you; they have 1Sm 8:7
they have **r** Me as their king. 1Sm 8:7
But today you have **r** your God, 1Sm 10:19
Because you have **r** the word of 1Sm 15:23
the LORD, He has **r** you as king. 1Sm 15:23
Because you **r** the word of the 1Sm 15:26
the LORD has **r** you from being 1Sm 15:26
since I have **r** him as king over 1Sm 16:1
stature, because I have **r** him. 1Sm 16:7
he **r** the advice of the elders 1Kg 12:8
He **r** the advice the elders had 1Kg 12:13
They **r** His statutes and His 2Kg 17:15
the LORD **r** all the descendants 2Kg 17:20
he **r** the advice of the elders 2Ch 10:8
King Rehoboam **r** the elders' 2Ch 10:13
King Ahaz **r** during his reign 2Ch 29:19
terms when you have **r** ⌊His⌋? Jb 34:33
despises the one **r** by the LORD, Ps 15:4
Why have You **r** me? Why must I go Ps 43:2

You have **r** and humiliated us; Ps 44:9
to shame, for God has **r** them. Ps 53:5
God, You have **r** us; Ps 60:1
it not You, God, who have **r** us? Ps 60:10
Why have You **r** ⌊us⌋ forever, Ps 74:1
He completely **r** Israel. Ps 78:59
He **r** the tent of Joseph and did Ps 78:67
But You have spurned and **r** him; Ps 89:38
Have You not **r** us, God? Ps 108:11
that the builders **r** has become Ps 118:22
my counsel, and **r** all my Pr 1:30
for they have **r** the instruction Is 5:24
people **r** the slowly flowing Is 8:6
Because you have **r** this message Is 30:12
I have chosen you and not **r** you. Is 41:9
He was despised and **r** by men, Is 53:3
of one's youth when she is **r**," Is 54:6
the LORD has **r** those you trust; Jr 2:37
They have **r** My law. Jr 6:19
They are called **r** silver, for Jr 6:30
silver, for the LORD has **r** them. Jr 6:30
for the LORD has **r** and abandoned Jr 7:29
have **r** the word of the LORD, Jr 8:9
Have You completely **r** Judah? Jr 14:19
The LORD has **r** the two families Jr 33:24
Lord has **r** all the mighty men Lm 1:15
The Lord has **r** His altar, Lm 2:7
You have completely **r** us and are Lm 5:22
her people have **r** My ordinances Ezk 5:6
and they **r** My ordinances— Ezk 20:13
because they **r** My ordinances, Ezk 20:16
My ordinances but **r** My statutes Ezk 20:24
Because you have **r** knowledge, Hs 4:6
Israel has **r** what is good; Hs 8:3
Your calf-idol is **r**, Samaria. Hs 8:5
because they have **r** the law of Am 2:4
be as though I had never **r** them. Zch 10:6
that the builders **r** has become Mt 21:42
things, and be **r** by the elders, Mk 8:31
The stone that the builders **r**— Mk 12:10
they **r** the plan of God for Lk 7:30
things and be **r** by the elders, Lk 9:22
things and be **r** by this Lk 17:25
The stone that the builders **r**— Lk 20:17
whom they **r** when they said, Ac 7:35
ask, then, has God **r** His people? Rm 11:1
God has not **r** His people whom He Rm 11:2
For if their being **r** is world Rm 11:15
Some have **r** these and have 1Tm 1:19
should be **r** if it is received 1Tm 4:4
he was **r** because he didn't find Heb 12:17
when they **r** Him who warned Heb 12:25
r by men but chosen and valuable 1Pt 2:4
The stone that the builders **r**— 1Pt 2:7

REJECTS *(9)*

the one who **r** correction goes Pr 10:17
woman who **r** good sense is like Pr 11:22
plead for help, He **r** my prayer. Lm 3:8
Whoever **r** you rejects Me. Lk 10:16
Whoever rejects you **r** Me. Lk 10:16
And whoever **r** Me rejects the One Lk 10:16
rejects Me **r** the One who sent Lk 10:16
The one who **r** Me and doesn't Jn 12:48
the person who **r** this does not 1Th 4:8

REJOICE *(176)*

he sees you, his heart will **r**. Ex 4:14
and **r** before the LORD your God Lv 23:40
LORD your God and **r** with your Dt 12:7
You will **r** before the LORD your Dt 12:12
R before the LORD your God in Dt 12:18
your God and **r** with your family Dt 14:26
R before the LORD your God in Dt 16:11
R during your festival—you, Dt 16:14
among you will **r** in all the good Dt 26:11
r in the presence of the LORD Dt 27:7
R, you nations, over His people, Dt 32:43
R, Zebulun, in your journeys, Dt 33:18
r in Abimelech and may he also Jdg 9:19
and may he also **r** in you. Jdg 9:19
because I **r** in Your salvation. 1Sm 2:1
of the Philistines will **r**, 2Sm 1:20
of those who seek the LORD **r**. 1Ch 16:10
heavens be glad and the earth **r**, 1Ch 16:31
holy name and **r** in Your praise. 1Ch 16:35
Your godly people **r** in goodness. 2Ch 6:41
enabled them to **r** over their 2Ch 20:27
The righteous see ⌊this⌋ and **r**; Jb 22:19
and I made the widow's heart **r**. Jb 29:13
awe, and **r** with trembling. Ps 2:11
all who take refuge in You **r**; Ps 5:11
I will **r** and boast about You; Ps 9:2
will **r** in Your salvation within Ps 9:14
and my foes will **r** because I am Ps 13:4
my heart will **r** in Your Ps 13:5
captive people, Jacob will **r**; Ps 14:7
I will **r** and be glad in Your Ps 31:7
Be glad in the LORD and **r**, Ps 32:11
R in the LORD, you righteous Ps 33:1
For our hearts **r** in Him, because Ps 33:21
Then I will **r** in the LORD; Ps 35:9
my deceitful enemies **r** over me; Ps 35:19
and do not let them **r** over me. Ps 35:24
Let those who **r** at my misfortune Ps 35:26
Don't let them **r** over me— Ps 38:16
all who seek You **r** and be glad Ps 40:16
towns of Judah **r** because of Your Ps 48:11
the bones You have crushed **r**. Ps 51:8
captive people, Jacob will **r**; Ps 53:6
righteous will **r** when he sees Ps 58:10
I will **r** in the shadow of Your Ps 63:7
But the king will **r** in God; Ps 63:11
The righteous **r** in the LORD and Ps 64:10
Let the nations **r** and shout for Ps 67:4
they **r** before God and celebrate Ps 68:3
is Yahweh—and **r** before Him. Ps 68:4
The humble will see it and **r**. Ps 69:32
all who seek You **r** and be glad Ps 70:4
that Your people may **r** in You? Ps 85:6
r in Your name all day long, Ps 89:16
You have made all his enemies **r**. Ps 89:42
Make us **r** for as many days as Ps 90:15
have made me **r**, LORD, by what Ps 92:4
heavens be glad and the earth **r**; Ps 96:11
Let the earth **r**; let the many Ps 97:1
towns of Judah **r** because of Your Ps 97:8
may the LORD **r** in His works. Ps 104:31
I will **r** in the LORD. Ps 104:34
of those who seek the LORD **r**. Ps 105:3
r in the joy of Your nation, Ps 106:5
holy name and **r** in Your praise. Ps 106:47
see it and **r**, and all injustice Ps 107:42
shame, but Your servant will **r**. Ps 109:28
let us **r** and be glad in it. Ps 118:24
r in the way ⌊revealed by⌋ Your Ps 119:14
who fear You will see me and **r**, Ps 119:74
I **r** over Your promise like one Ps 119:162
of Zion **r** in their King. Ps 149:2
is wise, my heart will indeed **r**. Pr 23:15
a righteous son will **r** greatly, Pr 23:24
let her who gave birth to you **r**. Pr 23:25
let your heart **r** when he Pr 24:17
the people **r**, but when the Pr 29:2
for them than to **r** and enjoy the Ec 3:12
come later will not **r** in him. Ec 4:16
his reward, and **r** in his labor. Ec 5:19
years, let him **r** in them all, Ec 11:8
R, young man, while you are Ec 11:9
We will **r** and be glad for you; Sg 1:4
You as they **r** at harvest time Is 9:3
time and as they **r** when dividing Is 9:3
Lord does not **r** over Israel's Is 9:17
cedars of Lebanon **r** over you: Is 14:8
Don't **r**, all of you ⌊in⌋ Is 14:29
You will not **r** any more, Is 23:12
Let us **r** and be glad in His Is 25:9
people will **r** in the Holy One Is 29:19
your⌋ heart will **r** like one who Is 30:29
the desert will **r** and blossom Is 35:1
and will also **r** with joy and Is 35:2
But you will **r** in the LORD; Is 41:16
in the ships in which they **r**. Is 43:14
R, heavens, for the LORD has Is 44:23
heavens! Earth, **r**! Mountains Is 49:13
Be joyful, **r** together, you ruins Is 52:9
R, barren one, who did not give Is 54:1
and let them **r** in My house of Is 56:7
your heart will tremble and **r**, Is 60:5
I greatly **r** in the LORD, I exult Is 61:10
so your God will **r** over you. Is 62:5
servants will **r**, but you will be Is 65:13
be glad and **r** forever in what Is 65:18
will **r** in Jerusalem and be glad Is 65:19
for Jerusalem and **r** over her, Is 66:10
R greatly with her, all who Is 66:10
see, you will **r**, and you will Is 66:14
your disaster so you can **r**? Jr 11:15
the virgin will **r** with dancing, Jr 31:13
young and old men ⌊**r**⌋ together. Jr 31:13
I will **r** over them to do what is Jr 32:41
Because you **r**, because you sing Jr 50:11
So **r** and be glad, Daughter Edom, Lm 4:21
the buyer not **r** and the seller Ezk 7:12
Should we **r**? The scepter of My Ezk 21:10
do not **r** jubilantly as the Hs 9:1
r and be glad, for the LORD has Jl 2:21
r and be glad in the LORD your Jl 2:23
you who **r** over Lo-debar and say, Am 6:13
not **r** over the people of Judah Ob 12
Do not **r** over me, my enemy! Mc 7:8
that is why they are glad and **r**. Hab 1:15
I will **r** in the God of my Hab 3:18
Be glad and **r** with all ⌊your⌋ Zph 3:14
will **r** over you with gladness. Zph 3:17
will **r** when they see the plumb Zch 4:10
R greatly, Daughter Zion! Zch 9:9
their hearts will **r** in the LORD. Zch 10:7
Be glad and **r**, because your Mt 5:12
and many will **r** at his birth. Lk 1:14
her and said, "**R**, favored woman! Lk 1:28
R in that day and leap for joy! Lk 6:23
don't **r** that the spirits submit Lk 10:20
r that your names are written Lk 10:20
to them, '**R** with me, because Lk 15:6
saying, '**R** with me, because I Lk 15:9
But we had to celebrate and **r**, Lk 15:32
sower and reaper can **r** together. Jn 4:36
and wail, but the world will **r**. Jn 16:20
hearts will **r**, and no one will Jn 16:22
we **r** in the hope of the glory Rm 5:2
we also **r** in our afflictions, Rm 5:3
but we also **r** in God through our Rm 5:11
R in hope; be patient in Rm 12:12
R with those who rejoice; Rm 12:15
Rejoice with those who **r**; Rm 12:15
R, you Gentiles, with His people! Rm 15:10
Therefore I **r** over you. Rm 16:19
those who **r** as though they did 1Co 7:30
as though they did not **r**, 1Co 7:30
all the members **r** with it. 1Co 12:26
we were made to **r** even more over 2Co 7:13
I **r** that I have complete 2Co 7:16
r when we are weak and you are 2Co 13:9
Finally, brothers, **r**. 2Co 13:11
R, O barren woman who does not Gl 4:27
And in this I **r**. Yes, and I will Php 1:18
I rejoice. Yes, and I will **r** Php 1:18
I am glad and **r** with all of you. Php 2:17
you also should **r** and share your Php 2:18
so that you may **r** when you see Php 2:28
my brothers, **r** in the Lord. Php 3:1
R in the Lord always. Php 4:4
always. I will say it again: **R**! Php 4:4
I **r** in my sufferings for you, Col 1:24
R always! 1Th 5:16
You **r** in this, though now for a 1Pt 1:6
in Him and **r** with inexpressible 1Pt 1:8
the sufferings of the Messiah **r**, 1Pt 4:13
you may also **r** with great joy at 1Pt 4:13
Therefore **r**, O heavens, and you Rv 12:12
R over her, heaven, and you Rv 18:20
Let us be glad, **r**, and give Him Rv 19:7

REJOICED *(40)*

r over all the good things Ex 18:9
god Dagon. They **r** and said: Our Jdg 16:23
the men of Jabesh, and they **r**. 1Sm 11:9
all the men of Israel greatly **r**. 1Sm 11:15
You saw it and **r**, so why would 1Sm 19:5
he greatly **r** and said, "May 1Kg 5:7
All the people of the land **r**, 2Kg 11:20
Then the people **r** because of 1Ch 29:9
King David also **r** greatly. 1Ch 29:9
All Judah **r** over the oath, 2Ch 15:15
His mind **r** in the LORD's ways, 2Ch 17:6
All the people of the land **r**, 2Ch 23:21
leaders and all the people **r**, 2Ch 24:10
the people **r** over how God had 2Ch 29:36
who were living in Judah, **r**. 2Ch 30:25
sacrifices and **r** because God had Neh 12:43
The city of Susa shouted and **r**, Est 8:15
if I have **r** because my wealth is Jb 31:25
Have I **r** over my enemy's Jb 31:29
on foot. There we **r** in Him. Ps 66:6
r when the waves grew quiet. Ps 107:30
I **r** with those who said to me, Ps 122:1

of Shiloah and **r** with Rezin Is 8:6
⌊The people⌋ have **r** before You Is 9:3
of the army with him, they **r**, Jr 41:13
and **r** over the land of Israel Ezk 25:6
Just as you **r** over the Ezk 35:15
idolatrous priests **r** over it; Hs 10:5
my spirit has **r** in God my Savior Lk 1:47
mercy, and they **r** with her. Lk 1:58
that same hour He **r** in the Holy Lk 10:21
see My day; he saw it and **r**." Jn 8:56
you would have **r** that I am going Jn 14:28
So the disciples **r** when they saw Jn 20:20
heart was glad, and my tongue **r**. Ac 2:26
they **r** and glorified the message Ac 13:48
they **r** because of its Ac 15:31
r because he had believed God Ac 16:34
for me, so that I **r** even more. 2Co 7:7
I **r** in the Lord greatly that now Php 4:10

REJOICES *(14)*
My heart **r** in the LORD; 1Sm 2:1
the valley and **r** in his strength Jb 39:21
heart is glad, and my spirit **r**; Ps 16:9
it **r** like an athlete running a Ps 19:5
greatly he **r** in Your victory! Ps 21:1
my heart **r**, and I praise Him Ps 28:7
thrive, a city **r**, and when the Pr 11:10
and one who **r** over disaster will Pr 17:5
the righteous one sings and **r**. Pr 29:6
as a bridegroom **r** over ⌊his⌋ Is 62:5
the whole world **r**, I will make Ezk 35:14
He **r** over that sheep more than Mt 18:13
r greatly at the groom's voice. Jn 3:29
but **r** in the truth; 1Co 13:6

REJOICING *(38)*
and there is **r** over the King Nm 23:21
to the city of David with **r**. 2Sm 6:12
flutes and **r** with such a great 1Kg 1:40
They have gone from there **r**. 1Kg 1:45
were⌋ eating, drinking, and **r**. 1Kg 4:20
to their tents **r** and with joyful 1Kg 8:66
of the land were **r** and blowing 2Kg 11:14
went with **r** to bring the ark 1Ch 15:25
r and with happy hearts for the 2Ch 7:10
of the land were **r** and blowing 2Ch 23:13
with **r** and song ordained by 2Ch 23:18
praises with **r** and bowed down 2Ch 29:30
Such **r** had not been seen in 2Ch 30:26
comes from⌋ **r** in the LORD." Neh 8:10
and Jerusalem's **r** was heard far Neh 12:43
r and jubilation took place Est 8:17
became a day of feasting and **r**. Est 9:17
became a day of feasting and **r**. Est 9:18
as ⌊a time of⌋ **r** and feasting. Est 9:19
was turned into **r** and their Est 9:22
of feasting, **r**, and of sending Est 9:22
and lyre and **r** at the sound Jb 21:12
are led in with gladness and **r**; Ps 45:15
brought His people out with **r**, Ps 105:43
and our tormentors, for **r**: Ps 137:3
every day, always **r** before Him. Pr 8:30
I was **r** in His inhabited world, Pr 8:31
there is great **r**, but when the Pr 28:12
the day of his heart's **r**. Sg 3:11
Joy and **r** have been removed from Is 16:10
earth's **r** goes into exile. Is 24:11
with wholehearted **r** and utter Ezk 36:5
the whole crowd was **r** over all Lk 13:17
r that they were counted worthy Ac 5:41
But he went on his way **r**. Ac 8:39
as grieving yet always **r**; 2Co 6:10
Now I am **r**, not because you were 2Co 7:9
r to see your good order and the Col 2:5

REJOINED *(1)*
turned around and **r** Johanan son Jr 41:14

REKEM *(6)*
kings—Evi, **R**, Zur, Hur, and Nm 31:8
Midian—Evi, **R**, Zur, Hur, and Jos 13:21
R, Irpeel, Taralah, Jos 18:27
Korah, Tappuah, **R**, and Shema. 1Ch 2:43
Jorkeam, and **R** fathered Shammai. 1Ch 2:44
and his sons were Ulam and **R**. 1Ch 7:16

REKINDLING *(1)*
And now you are **r** ⌊His⌋ anger Neh 13:18

RELATE *(1)*
they **r** empty dreams and offer Zch 10:2

RELATED *(9)*
unclean for those **r** to him by Lv 21:4
and all the work **r** to these, Nm 3:36
and all the work **r** to them. Nm 4:32
service **r** to the holy objects Nm 7:9
in all matters **r** to the LORD, 2Ch 19:11
in all matters **r** to the king, 2Ch 19:11
the prophet **r** all these words to Jr 34:6
the things **r** to the kingdom Ac 19:8
he **r** one by one what God did Ac 21:19

RELATING *(3)*
ropes—all the work **r** to these. Nm 3:26
and all the work **r** to them. Nm 3:31
in every matter **r** to God and the 1Ch 26:32

RELATION *(1)*
put to death in **r** to the law Rm 7:4

RELATIONS *(15)*
haven't had sexual **r** with a man. Gn 19:8
not have sexual **r** with women." Ex 19:15
and he has sexual **r** with her, Ex 22:16
they have sexual **r**, it is a Lv 20:17
to have sexual **r** with the women Nm 25:1
who has had sexual **r** with a man, Nm 31:17
who have not had sexual **r**. Nm 31:18
had not had sexual **r** with a man. Nm 31:35
may have sexual **r** with her and Dt 21:13
woman, has sexual **r** with her, Dt 22:13
having sexual **r** with ⌊another⌋ Dt 22:22
wife, have sexual **r** with her, Dt 25:5
had not had sexual **r** with a man, Jdg 21:12
have sexual **r** with the same girl Am 2:7
man not to have **r** with a woman." 1Co 7:1

RELATIONSHIP *(4)*
concerning ⌊the **r**⌋ between a man Nm 30:16
'What **r** do you have with the Jos 22:24
had revealed her **r** to Mordecai. Est 8:1
If the **r** of a man with his wife Mt 19:10

RELATIVE *(22)*
heard that his **r** had been taken Gn 14:14
and also his **r** Lot and his goods Gn 14:16
that he was her father's **r**, Gn 29:12
Just because you're my **r**, Gn 29:15
come near any close **r** for sexual Lv 18:6
she is your father's close **r**. Lv 18:12
she is your mother's close **r**. Lv 18:13
is exposing one's own blood **r**; Lv 20:19
nearest **r** may come and redeem Lv 25:25
individual has no **r** to receive Nm 5:8
to the nearest **r** of his clan, Nm 27:11
Now Naomi had a **r** on her Ru 2:1
"The man is a close **r**. Ru 2:20
Now isn't Boaz our **r**? Ru 3:2
Because the king is our **r**. 2Sm 19:42
Heman's **r** was Asaph, who stood 1Ch 6:39
His **r** through Eliezer: 1Ch 26:25
He was a **r** of Tobiah Neh 13:4
and call understanding ⌊your⌋ **r**. Pr 7:4
A close **r** and a burner, will Am 6:10
And consider your **r** Elizabeth— Lk 1:36
a **r** of the man whose ear Peter Jn 18:26

RELATIVES *(89)*
your land, your **r**, and your Gn 12:1
and my herdsmen, since we are **r**. Gn 13:8
to the house of my master's **r**." Gn 24:27
all of his **r** as his servants, Gn 27:37
So he took his **r** with him, Gn 31:23
Before our **r**, point out anything Gn 31:32
it here before my **r** and yours, Gn 31:37
Then Jacob said to his **r**, Gn 31:46
and invited his **r** to eat a meal. Gn 31:54
me return to my **r** in Egypt and Ex 4:18
and carry your **r** away from the Lv 10:4
are close **r**; it is depraved. Lv 18:17
for a ⌊dead⌋ person among his **r**, Lv 21:1
any of his close **r** from his clan Lv 25:49
go to my own land and my **r**." Nm 10:30
woman to his **r** in the sight of Nm 25:6
inheritance among our male **r**." Jos 17:4
His mother's **r** spoke all these Jdg 9:3
woman among your **r** or among any Jdg 14:3
among his **r** or from the gate Ru 4:10
Jehu met the **r** of Ahaziah king 2Kg 10:13
answered, "We're Ahaziah's **r**. 2Kg 10:13
His **r** by their families as they 1Ch 5:7
Their **r** according to their 1Ch 5:13
their **r** were Merari's sons: 1Ch 6:44
r the Levites were assigned 1Ch 6:48
and his **r** came to comfort him. 1Ch 7:22
opposite their **r** in Jerusalem, 1Ch 8:32
Jerusalem, with their ⌊other⌋ **r**. 1Ch 8:32
Jeuel and 690 of their **r**. 1Ch 9:6
and 956 of their **r** according to 1Ch 9:9
and 1,760 of their **r**, the heads 1Ch 9:13
Talmon, Ahiman, and their **r**. 1Ch 9:17
of Korah and his **r** from his 1Ch 9:19
Their **r** came from their villages 1Ch 9:25
the Kohathites' **r** were 1Ch 9:32
opposite their **r** in Jerusalem 1Ch 9:38
Jerusalem with their ⌊other⌋ **r**. 1Ch 9:38
were Saul's **r** from Benjamin: 1Ch 12:2
the Benjaminites, the **r** of Saul: 1Ch 12:29
with all their **r** under their 1Ch 12:32
for their **r** had provided for 1Ch 12:39
to the rest of our **r** in all the 1Ch 13:2
the leader and 120 of his **r**; 1Ch 15:5
the leader and 220 of his **r**; 1Ch 15:6
the leader and 130 of his **r**; 1Ch 15:7
the leader and 200 of his **r**; 1Ch 15:8
the leader and 80 of his **r**; 1Ch 15:9
the leader and 112 of his **r**. 1Ch 15:10
You and your **r** must consecrate 1Ch 15:12
appoint their **r** as singers and 1Ch 15:16
from his **r**, Asaph son of 1Ch 15:17
and from their **r** the Merarites, 1Ch 15:17
were their **r** second in rank: 1Ch 15:18
to the LORD by Asaph and his **r**: 1Ch 16:7
Asaph and his **r** there before 1Ch 16:37
left⌋ Obed-edom and his 68 **r**. 1Ch 16:38
and to their **r**, the sons of 1Ch 23:32
lots the same way as their **r**, 1Ch 24:31
with their **r** who were all 1Ch 25:7
and his **r**, 1,700 capable 1Ch 26:30
There were among Jerijah's **r**, 1Ch 26:32
and of their sons and their **r**, 2Ch 5:12
and their **r** who did the work at Neh 11:12
and his **r**, the leaders of Neh 11:13
and their **r**, capable men: Neh 11:14
Bakbukiah, second among his **r**; Neh 11:17
Talmon, and their **r**, who guarded Neh 11:19
priests and their **r** in the days Neh 12:7
he and his **r** were in charge of Neh 12:8
their **r** ⌊stood⌋ opposite them Neh 12:9
with their **r** opposite them— Neh 12:24
and his **r**: Shemaiah, Azarel, Neh 12:36
to see the destruction of my **r**?" Est 8:6
popular with many of his **r**. Est 10:3
r stop coming by, and my close Jb 19:14
and my **r** stand at a distance. Ps 38:11
along with his **r** and neighbors. Jr 49:10
man, your own **r**, those who have Ezk 11:15
hometown, among his **r**, and in Mk 6:4
her neighbors and **r** heard that Lk 1:58
"None of your **r** has that name." Lk 1:61
Him among their **r** and friends. Lk 2:44
brothers, your **r**, or your rich Lk 14:12
brothers, **r**, and friends. Lk 21:16
country and away from your **r**, Ac 7:3
his father Jacob and all his **r**, Ac 7:14
together his **r** and close friends Ac 10:24
does not provide for his own **r**, 1Tm 5:8

RELAX *(1)*
I cannot **r** or be still; Jb 3:26

RELEASE *(33)*
so that he will **r** your other Gn 43:14
him clean and **r** the live bird Lv 14:7
Then he is to **r** the live bird Lv 14:53
land, and he will **r** it there. Lv 16:22
the LORD's **r** of debts has been Dt 15:2
basis of this treaty, I **r** you." 1Kg 20:34
priest did not **r** the divisions. 2Ch 23:8
a conflict is to **r** a flood; Pr 17:14
and would not **r** the prisoners to Is 14:17
they refuse to **r** them. Jr 50:33
will **r** a windstorm in My wrath. Ezk 13:13
I will **r** your prisoners from the Zch 9:11
custom was to **r** to the crowd a Mt 27:15
is it you want me to **r** for you— Mt 27:17
do you want me to **r** for you?" Mt 27:21
custom to **r** for the people Mk 15:6
Do you want me to **r** the King of Mk 15:9
that he would **r** Barabbas to them Mk 15:11
Him whipped and ⌊then⌋ **r** Him." Lk 23:16
he had to **r** someone to them. Lk 23:17
man away! **R** Barabbas to us!" Lk 23:18
wanting to **r** Jesus, addressed Lk 23:20

Him whipped and ⌊then⌋ **r** Him." Lk 23:22
a custom that I **r** one ⌊prisoner⌋ Jn 18:39
you want me to **r** to you the King Jn 18:39
the authority to **r** You and the Jn 19:10
made every effort to **r** Him. Jn 19:12
shouted, "If you **r** this man, you Jn 19:12
when he had decided to **r** Him. Ac 3:13
police to say, "**R** those men!" Ac 16:35
me, wanted to **r** me, since I had Ac 28:18
not accepting **r**, so that they Heb 11:35
R the four angels bound at the Rv 9:14

RELEASED *(44)*
he **r** his semen on the ground so Gn 38:9
have **r** Israel from serving us. Ex 14:5
man who **r** the goat for Azazel Lv 16:26
It is to be **r** at the Jubilee, Lv 25:28
is not to be **r** on the Jubilee. Lv 25:30
they are to be **r** at the Jubilee. Lv 25:31
must be **r** at the Jubilee, Lv 25:33
children are to be **r** from you, Lv 25:41
children are to be **r** at the Year Lv 25:54
the field is **r** in the Jubilee, Lv 27:21
the sword but **r** the man and his Jdg 1:25
the torches and **r** the foxes Jdg 15:5
a treaty with him and **r** him. 1Kg 20:34
'Because you **r** from your hand 1Kg 20:42
Judah ⌊and **r** him⌋ from prison. 2Kg 25:27
So Amaziah **r** the division that 2Ch 25:10
He **r** them from the temple in Ezr 5:14
He imprisons cannot be **r**. Jb 12:14
Who **r** the swift donkey from its Jb 39:5
king sent ⌊for him⌋ and **r** him; Ps 105:20
suddenly **r** on her agitation and Jr 15:8
when Pashhur **r** Jeremiah from the Jr 20:3
r him at Ramah when he had been Jr 40:1
a ration and a gift and **r** him. Jr 40:5
of Judah and **r** him from the Jr 52:31
and a windstorm will be **r**. Ezk 13:11
had compassion, **r** him, and Mt 18:27
Then he **r** Barabbas to them. Mt 27:26
Pilate ordered that it be **r**. Mt 27:58
Pilate **r** Barabbas to them. Mk 15:15
and **r** the one they were asking Lk 23:25
them further, they **r** them. Ac 4:21
After they were **r**, they went to Ac 4:23
in the name of Jesus and **r** them. Ac 5:40
sent orders for you to be **r**. Ac 16:36
and the others, they **r** them. Ac 17:9
r him and instructed the chief Ac 22:30
could have been **r** if he had not Ac 26:32
she is **r** from the law regarding Rm 7:2
now we have been **r** from the law, Rm 7:6
our brother Timothy has been **r**. Heb 13:23
and year were **r** to kill a third Rv 9:15
he must be **r** for a short time. Rv 20:3
Satan will be **r** from his prison Rv 20:7

RELEASES *(3)*
up, and when He **r** them, they Jb 12:15
He **r** the bonds put on by kings Jb 12:18
my perfume **r** its fragrance. Sg 1:12

RELENT *(17)*
and I will not **r** or turn back Jr 4:28
so that I might **r** concerning the Jr 26:3
so that He might **r** concerning Jr 26:13
did not the LORD **r** concerning Jr 26:19
because I **r** concerning the Jr 42:10
not show pity, and I will not **r**. Ezk 24:14
He may turn and **r** and leave a Jl 2:14
I will not **r** from punishing Am 1:3
I will not **r** from punishing Gaza Am 1:6
I will not **r** from punishing Tyre Am 1:9
I will not **r** from punishing Edom Am 1:11
I will not **r** from punishing the Am 1:13
I will not **r** from punishing Moab Am 2:1
will not **r** from punishing Judah Am 2:4
I will not **r** from punishing Am 2:6
God may turn and **r**; He may turn Jnh 3:9
and would not **r**," says the LORD Zch 8:14

RELENTED *(6)*
but the LORD **r** concerning the 2Sm 24:16
r concerning the destruction, 1Ch 21:15
and **r** according to the abundance Ps 106:45
The LORD **r** concerning this. Am 7:3
The LORD **r** concerning this. Am 7:6
God **r** from the disaster He had Jnh 3:10

RELENTLESS *(1)*
in rage with **r** persecution. Is 14:6

RELENTLESSLY *(4)*
the wicked **r** pursue the Ps 10:2
hearts, "Let us oppress them **r**." Ps 74:8
Let evil **r** hunt down a violent Ps 140:11
they **r** pursued us over the Lm 4:19

RELENTS *(2)*
and He **r** from sending disaster. Jl 2:13
and One who **r** from ⌊sending⌋ Jnh 4:2

RELIABLE *(9)*
leaders don't think you are **r**. 1Sm 29:6
that you are as **r** as an angel of 1Sm 29:9
ordinances, **r** instructions, Neh 9:13
is nothing **r** in what they say Ps 5:9
of the LORD are **r** and altogether Ps 19:9
testimonies are completely **r**; Ps 93:5
to teach you true and **r** words, Pr 22:21
to me—water that is not **r**. Jr 15:18
not able to get **r** information Ac 21:34

RELIANCE *(1)*
boldly, in **r** on the Lord, who Ac 14:3

RELIED *(3)*
So the people **r** on the words of 2Ch 32:8
to those we **r** on and fled to for Is 20:6
You have **r** on your swords, Ezk 33:26

RELIEF *(13)*
one will bring us **r** from the Gn 5:29
when Pharaoh saw there was **r**, Ex 8:15
of my lord the king bring **r**, 2Sm 14:17
But as soon as they had **r**, Neh 9:28
of my struggle until my **r** comes. Jb 14:14
from my lips would bring **r**. Jb 16:5
must speak so that I can find **r**; Jb 32:20
give him **r** from troubled times Ps 94:13
yourself no **r** and your eyes no Lm 2:18
Do not ignore my cry for **r**. Lm 3:56
to send **r** to the brothers Ac 11:29
had completed their **r** mission, Ac 12:25
that there may be **r** for others 2Co 8:13

RELIES *(2)*
For the king **r** on the LORD; Ps 21:7
He **r** on the LORD; let Him rescue Ps 22:8

RELIEVE *(5)*
and take grain ⌊to **r**⌋ the hunger Gn 42:19
take ⌊food to **r**⌋ the hunger of Gn 42:33
and go there ⌊to **r** yourself⌋. Dt 23:12
when you **r** yourself, dig a hole Dt 23:13
and he went in to **r** himself. 1Sm 24:3

RELIEVED *(3)*
would then be **r**, feel better, 1Sm 16:23
suffering is not **r**, and if I Jb 16:6
I **r** his shoulder from the Ps 81:6

RELIEVING *(1)*
and thought he was **r** himself in Jdg 3:24

RELIGION *(6)*
about their own **r** and about a Ac 25:19
party of our **r** I lived as a Ac 26:5
practice their **r** toward their 1Tm 5:4
to the form of **r** but denying its 2Tm 3:5
his heart, his **r** is useless. Jms 1:26
and undefiled **r** before our God Jms 1:27

RELIGIOUS *(5)*
name by their ⌊**r**⌋ prostitution Ezk 43:7
intend to change **r** festivals and Dn 7:25
Jews incited the **r** women of high Ac 13:50
are extremely **r** in every respect Ac 17:22
anyone thinks he is **r**, without Jms 1:26

RELINQUISH *(1)*
r your inheritance that I gave Jr 17:4

RELY *(6)*
so they can **r** ⌊on it⌋, but His Jb 24:23
believe God or **r** on His Ps 78:22
for I **r** on Your commands. Ps 119:66
and do not **r** on your own Pr 3:5
not **r** on a friend; don't trust Mc 7:5
For all who ⌊**r** on⌋ the works of Gl 3:10

RELYING *(3)*
Assyria, says: 'What are you **r** 2Kg 18:19
What are you now **r** on so that 2Kg 18:20
for the gospel, **r** on the power 2Tm 1:8

REMAIN *(157)*
Spirit will not **r** with mankind Gn 6:3
R a widow in your father's house Gn 38:11
let your servant **r** here as my Gn 44:33
houses, and **r** only in the Nile. Ex 8:9
frogs will **r** only in the Nile. Ex 8:11
let any of it **r** until morning; Ex 12:10
of it that does **r** until morning. Ex 12:10
let any of it **r** until morning." Ex 16:19
must not **r** until morning. Ex 23:18
They must not **r** in your land, Ex 23:33
The poles are to **r** in the rings Ex 25:15
come down and **r** at the entrance Ex 33:9
must not **r** until morning. Ex 34:25
itself must **r** on the altar's Lv 6:9
must **r** at the entrance to the Lv 8:35
They are to **r** detestable to you; Lv 11:11
water and will **r** unclean until Lv 11:32
and will **r** unclean for you Lv 11:35
containing water will **r** clean, Lv 11:36
He will **r** unclean as long as he Lv 13:46
but he must **r** outside his tent Lv 14:8
and he will **r** unclean until Lv 15:5
and he will **r** unclean until Lv 15:6
and he will **r** unclean until Lv 15:7
and he will **r** unclean until Lv 15:8
and he will **r** unclean until Lv 15:10
and he will **r** unclean until Lv 15:11
and he will **r** unclean until Lv 15:16
and it will **r** unclean until Lv 15:17
and they will **r** unclean until Lv 15:18
and he will **r** unclean until Lv 15:21
and he will **r** unclean until Lv 15:22
and he will **r** unclean until Lv 15:27
and he will **r** unclean until Lv 17:15
hand must not **r** with you until Lv 19:13
of these will **r** unclean until Lv 22:6
it must **r** with its mother for Lv 22:27
let any of it **r** until morning; Lv 22:30
he sold will **r** in the possession Lv 25:28
a few years **r** until the Year Lv 25:52
wouldn't she **r** in disgrace for Nm 12:14
but he will **r** ceremonially Nm 19:7
and he will **r** unclean until Nm 19:8
and he will **r** unclean until Nm 19:10
You are to **r** outside the camp Nm 31:19
dependents will **r** in the Nm 32:17
our animals will **r** here in the Nm 32:26
you allow to **r** will become Nm 33:55
r in the cities I have given Dt 3:19
R faithful to Him and take oaths Dt 10:20
His ways, and **r** faithful to Him Dt 11:22
Him and **r** faithful to Him Dt 13:4
The city must **r** a mound of ruins Dt 13:16
is to **r** in your hand, Dt 13:17
first day is to **r** until morning. Dt 16:4
is to **r** with him, and he is to Dt 17:19
to your home to **r** with you until Dt 22:2
bad name. She will **r** his wife; Dt 22:19
but they will not **r** yours, Dt 28:41
obey Him, and **r** faithful to Him. Dt 30:20
so that it may **r** there as a Dt 31:26
livestock may **r** in the land Jos 1:14
been content to **r** on the other Jos 7:7
Judah is to **r** in its territory Jos 18:5
His commands, **r** faithful to Him, Jos 22:5
r faithful to the LORD your God, Jos 23:8
Let it **r** dry, and the dew be all Jdg 6:39
Don't let even one **r**!" 1Sm 14:36
Let David **r** in my service, 1Sm 16:22
200 who were to **r** behind would 1Sm 30:9
from Him does not **r** banished. 2Sm 14:14
not a man will **r** with you 2Sm 19:7
throne will **r** established before 1Kg 2:45
one tribe will **r** his because of 1Kg 11:32
return to those of you who **r**, 2Ch 30:6
you who **r** under the siege of 2Ch 32:10
where My name will **r** forever." 2Ch 33:4
If You **r** silent to me, I will be Ps 28:1
lies will **r** in my presence. Ps 101:7
sins always **r** before the LORD, Ps 109:15
wicked will not **r** over the land Ps 125:3
those of integrity will **r** in it; Pr 2:21
wicked will not **r** on the earth. Pr 10:30
but the rich **r** in lowly Ec 10:6
a tenth will **r** in the land, Is 6:13
incense altars will **r** standing. Is 27:9
until you alone **r** like a Is 30:17
we will **r** in Your ways and be Is 64:5
those who **r** wherever I have Jr 8:3
articles that **r** in the LORD's Jr 27:18
that still **r** in this city, Jr 27:19
articles that **r** in the temple Jr 27:21

Babylon and will **r** there until I Jr 27:22
the warriors who **r** in this city Jr 38:4
the women who **r** in the palace Jr 38:22
for few of us **r** out of the many, Jr 42:2
had allowed to **r** with Gedaliah Jr 43:6
can you possibly **r** unpunished? Jr 49:12
You will not **r** unpunished, Jr 49:12
it will **r** desolate forever.' Jr 51:62
none of them ⌊will **r**⌋: Ezk 7:11
as he and the buyer **r** alive. Ezk 7:13
Things will not **r** as they are; Ezk 21:26
turbans will **r** on your heads Ezk 24:23
nations that **r** around you will Ezk 36:36
invaders who **r** on the surface Ezk 39:14
This gate will **r** closed. Ezk 44:2
Therefore it will **r** closed. Ezk 44:2
no survivor will **r** of the house Ob 18
the peoples who **r** will plunder Hab 2:8
You cannot **r** alive because you Zch 13:3
raised up and will **r** on its site Zch 14:10
R here and stay awake with Me." Mt 26:38
R here and stay awake." Mk 14:34
R in the same house, eating and Lk 10:7
slave does not **r** in the Jn 8:35
but a son does **r** forever. Jn 8:35
that the Messiah will **r** forever. Jn 12:34
in Me would not **r** in darkness. Jn 12:46
to you while I **r** with you. Jn 14:25
R in Me, and I in you. Jn 15:4
can you unless you **r** in Me. Jn 15:4
If anyone does not **r** in Me, Jn 15:6
If you **r** in Me and My words Jn 15:7
in Me and My words **r** in you, Jn 15:7
also loved you. **R** in My love. Jn 15:9
commands you will **r** in My love, Jn 15:10
commands and **r** in His love. Jn 15:10
and that your fruit should **r**, Jn 15:16
the bodies to **r** on the cross Jn 19:31
I want him to **r** until I come," Jn 21:22
If I want him to **r** until I come, Jn 21:23
of them to **r** true to the Lord Ac 11:23
you—if you **r** in His kindness. Rm 11:22
if they do not **r** in unbelief, Rm 11:23
good for them if they **r** as I am. 1Co 7:8
she must **r** unmarried or be 1Co 7:11
Each person should **r** in the life 1Co 7:20
each person should **r** with God in 1Co 7:24
Now these three **r**: faith, hope, 1Co 13:13
most of whom **r** to the present, 1Co 15:6
and perhaps I will **r** with you, 1Co 16:6
of the gospel would **r** for you. Gl 2:5
but to **r** in the flesh is more Php 1:24
know that I will **r** and continue Php 1:25
if indeed you **r** grounded and Col 1:23
r in Ephesus so that you may 1Tm 1:3
not ⌊obvious⌋ cannot **r** hidden. 1Tm 5:25
they will perish, but You **r**. Heb 1:11
that what is not shaken might **r**. Heb 12:27
the beginning must **r** in you. 1Jn 2:24
then you will **r** in the Son and 1Jn 2:24
as it has taught you, **r** in Him. 1Jn 2:27
children, **r** in Him, so that 1Jn 2:28
we know that we **r** in Him and He 1Jn 4:13
who does not **r** in the teaching 2Jn 9
he must **r** for a little while. Rv 17:10

REMAINDER *(4)*

will eat the **r** left to you that Ex 10:5
The **r** of the length alongside Ezk 48:18
the **r** of the Philistines will Am 1:8
the **r** of My nation will Zph 2:9

REMAINED *(81)*

while Abraham **r** standing before Gn 18:22
of him while he **r** in the camp Gn 32:21
he **r** silent until they returned. Gn 34:5
Yet his bow **r** steady, and his Gn 49:24
father's household **r** in Egypt. Gn 50:22
The gnats **r** on the people and Ex 8:18
so that his hands **r** steady until Ex 17:12
And the people **r** standing at a Ex 20:21
and he **r** on the mountain 40 days Ex 24:18
the Israelites ⌊**r**⌋ stripped of Ex 33:6
But Aaron **r** silent. Lv 10:3
if the spot has **r** where it was Lv 13:28
It **r** that way continuously: Nm 9:16
the cloud **r** over the tabernacle Nm 9:20
the cloud **r** ⌊only⌋ from evening Nm 9:21
Or if it **r** a day and a night, Nm 9:21
Two men had **r** in the camp, Nm 11:26
on to Hazeroth and **r** there. Nm 11:35
of Jephunneh **r** alive of those Nm 14:38
inheritance **r** within the tribe Nm 36:12
But you who have **r** faithful to Dt 4:4
And they have **r** there, as the Dt 10:5
until no survivor or fugitive **r**, Jos 8:22
I **r** loyal to the LORD my God. Jos 14:8
because you have **r** loyal to the Jos 14:9
because he **r** loyal to the LORD, Jos 14:14
Gilead **r** beyond the Jordan. Jdg 5:17
Asher **r** at the seashore and Jdg 5:17
turned back, but 10,000 **r**. Jdg 7:3
of⌋ his strength **r** unknown. Jdg 16:9
animals, and everything that **r**. Jdg 20:48
down all the cities that **r**. Jdg 20:48
She came and has **r** from early Ru 2:7
Only Dagon's torso **r**. 1Sm 5:4
David **r** in Horesh, while 1Sm 23:18
they all **r** asleep because a deep 1Sm 26:12
ark of the LORD **r** in his house 2Sm 6:11
but David **r** in Jerusalem. 2Sm 11:1
to Jerusalem **r** loyal to their 2Sm 20:2
peoples who **r** of the Amorites 1Kg 9:20
descendants who **r** in the land 1Kg 9:21
all Israel had **r** there six 1Kg 11:16
he **r** until Solomon's death. 1Kg 11:40
gold that **r** in the treasuries 1Kg 15:18
severe until no breath **r** in him. 1Kg 17:17
ones who **r** fled into the city 1Kg 20:30
killed all who **r** of the house 2Kg 10:11
down all who **r** from ⌊the house 2Kg 10:17
Asherah pole also **r** standing in 2Kg 13:6
Only the tribe of Judah **r**. 2Kg 17:18
people of the land, nobody **r**. 2Kg 24:14
ark of God **r** with Obed-edom's 1Ch 13:14
it, but David **r** in Jerusalem. 1Ch 20:1
peoples who **r** of the Hittites 2Ch 8:7
descendants who **r** in the land 2Ch 8:8
stopped and **r** at a standstill Ezr 4:24
They **r** silent and could not say Neh 5:8
nine-tenths **r** in their towns. Neh 11:1
Haman **r** to beg Queen Esther for Est 7:7
their foes; not one of them **r**. Ps 106:11
my wisdom also **r** with me. Ec 2:9
and there **r** among them only the Jr 37:10
So Jeremiah **r** in the guard's Jr 37:21
Jeremiah **r** in the guard's Jr 38:28
those who had **r** in the city and Jr 39:9
rest of the people who had **r**. Jr 39:9
the people who **r** in the land. Jr 40:6
all those who **r** in Mizpah over Jr 41:10
So his taste has **r** the same, Jr 48:11
Daniel **r** there until the first Dn 1:21
Daniel **r** at the king's court. Dn 2:49
it would have **r** until today. Mt 11:23
signs to them and **r** speechless. Lk 1:22
earlier, and He **r** there. Jn 10:40
But Mary **r** seated in the house. Jn 11:20
But Peter **r** standing outside by Jn 18:16
r in Antioch teaching and Ac 15:35
bow jammed fast and **r** immovable, Ac 27:41
I **r** personally unknown to the Gl 1:22
Erastus has **r** at Corinth; 2Tm 4:20
they would have **r** with us. 1Jn 2:19

REMAINING *(37)*

it, the **r** one can escape. Gn 32:8
first stone and the **r** six names Ex 28:10
Sprinkle the ⌊**r**⌋ blood on all Ex 29:20
of cloud **r** at the entrance Ex 33:10
With the ⌊**r**⌋ 44 pounds he made Ex 38:28
spoke to Aaron and his **r** sons, Lv 10:12
From the oil **r** in his palm the Lv 14:17
the number of ⌊**r**⌋ harvest years. Lv 25:15
in proportion to his ⌊**r**⌋ years. Lv 25:52
The captives **r** from the plunder Nm 31:32
except for some **r** in Gaza, Jos 11:22
he was one of the **r** Rephaim. Jos 13:12
The **r** descendants of Kohath Jos 21:5
to the **r** clans of Kohath's Jos 21:20
Merari, who were the **r** Levites: Jos 21:34
descendants, the **r** Levite clans. Jos 21:40
allotted these **r** nations to you Jos 23:4
with these nations **r** among you. Jos 23:7
of these nations **r** among you, Jos 23:12
Is there anyone **r** from Saul's 2Sm 9:1
extinguish my one **r** ember by not 2Sm 14:7
I am the only **r** prophet of the 1Kg 18:22
wall fell on those 27,000 **r** men. 1Kg 20:30
r events of Solomon's ⌊reign⌋ 2Ch 9:29
me and for those **r** in Israel and 2Ch 34:21
Yourself with their **r** wrath. Ps 76:10
The **r** trees of its forest will Is 10:19
The **r** Kedarite archers will be Is 21:17
those **r** in this land and those Jr 24:8
and all of Judah's **r** cities— Jr 34:7
Tyre and Sidon every **r** ally. Jr 47:4
The **r** ⌊area⌋, one and two-thirds Ezk 48:15
The **r** ⌊area⌋ on both sides of Ezk 48:21
all the **r** families, every family Zch 12:14
by death from **r** in office. Heb 7:23
to live the **r** time in the flesh 1Pt 4:2
because of the **r** trumpet blasts Rv 8:13

REMAINS *(69)*

But what **r** of the sacrificial Lv 7:17
must burn up what **r** of the meat Lv 8:32
the infection **r** unchanged in his Lv 13:5
if the spot **r** where it is and Lv 13:23
the scaly outbreak **r** unchanged Lv 13:37
of meeting that **r** among them, Lv 16:16
but what **r** on the third day must Lv 19:6
his guilt **r** on him." Nm 15:31
He **r** unclean because the water Nm 19:13
What **r** will be for the foreign Dt 24:20
What **r** will be for the foreign Dt 24:21
of rocks that **r** to this day. Jos 7:26
over it, which **r** to this day. Jos 8:29
of the land **r** to be possessed Jos 13:1
This is the land that **r**: Jos 13:2
of the one who **r** with the 1Sm 30:24
the water **r** healthy to this very 2Kg 2:22
of Shaphat **r** on his shoulders 2Kg 6:31
Nothing he owned **r** in his tent. Jb 18:15
from God **r** in my nostrils, Jb 27:3
he **r** confident, even if the Jb 40:23
account until nothing **r** of it. Ps 10:15
LORD, for no faithful one **r**; Ps 12:1
cannot be shaken; it **r** forever. Ps 125:1
He **r** faithful forever, Ps 146:6
comes, but the earth **r** forever. Ec 1:4
Whoever **r** in Zion and whoever is Is 4:3
Only desolation **r** in the city; Is 24:12
come in—one that **r** faithful. Is 26:2
be found among its shattered **r**— Is 30:14
the word of our God **r** forever." Is 40:8
comes, and its foliage **r** green. Jr 17:8
and the one who **r** and is spared Ezk 6:12
wiping out what **r** of the coastal Ezk 25:16
the wrath of God **r** on him. Jn 3:36
you say, 'We see'—your sin **r**. Jn 9:41
ground and dies, it **r** by itself. Jn 12:24
because He **r** with you and will Jn 14:17
itself unless it **r** on the vine, Jn 15:4
The one who **r** in Me and I in him Jn 15:5
is happier if she **r** as she is, 1Co 7:40
old covenant, the same veil **r**; 2Co 3:14
faithless, He **r** faithful, for He 2Tm 2:13
the promise **r** of entering His Heb 4:1
Since it **r** for some to enter it, Heb 4:6
A Sabbath rest **r**, therefore, for Heb 4:9
Son of God—**r** a priest forever Heb 7:3
But because He **r** forever, He Heb 7:24
there no longer **r** a sacrifice Heb 10:26
one who says he **r** in Him should 1Jn 2:6
his brother **r** in the light, 1Jn 2:10
God's word **r** in you, and you 1Jn 2:14
who does God's will **r** forever. 1Jn 2:17
from the beginning **r** in you, 1Jn 2:24
you received from Him **r** in you, 1Jn 2:27
Everyone who **r** in Him does not 1Jn 3:6
because His seed **r** in him; 1Jn 3:9
who does not love **r** in death. 1Jn 3:14
who keeps His commands **r** in Him, 1Jn 3:24
way we know that He **r** in us is 1Jn 3:24
God **r** in us and His love is 1Jn 4:12
God **r** in him and he in God. 1Jn 4:15
the one who **r** in love remains 1Jn 4:16
who remains in love **r** in God, 1Jn 4:16
in God, and God **r** in him. 1Jn 4:16
the truth that **r** in us and will 2Jn 2
The one who **r** in that teaching, 2Jn 9
Be alert and strengthen what **r**, Rv 3:2
is alert and **r** clothed so that Rv 16:15

REMALIAH *(13)*

son of **R**, conspired against 2Kg 15:25
Pekah son of **R** became king over 2Kg 15:27
against Pekah son of **R**. 2Kg 15:30

of Israel's King Pekah son of **R**, 2Kg 15:32
Pekah son of **R** against Judah. 2Kg 15:37
year of Pekah son of **R**, 2Kg 16:1
Pekah son of **R** came to wage war 2Kg 16:5
Pekah son of **R** killed 120,000 in 2Ch 28:6
Pekah, son of **R**, king of Israel, Is 7:1
Rezin of Aram, and the son of **R**. Is 7:4
with Ephraim and the son of **R**, Is 7:5
head of Samaria is the son of **R**. Is 7:9
with Rezin and the son of **R**, Is 8:6

REMARK *(1)*
What is this **r** He made: Jn 7:36

REMARKABLE *(2)*
over and look at this **r** sight. Ex 3:3
the great and **r** day of the Lord Ac 2:20

REMARKABLY *(1)*
I have been **r** and wonderfully Ps 139:14

REMARRYING *(1)*
you restrain yourselves from **r**? Ru 1:13

REMEDIES *(1)*
You have multiplied **r** in vain; Jr 46:11

REMEDY *(3)*
His people that there was no **r**. 2Ch 36:16
suddenly—and without a **r**. Pr 29:1
There is no **r** for your injury; Nah 3:19

REMEMBER *(162)*
I will **r** My covenant between Me Gn 9:15
look at it and **r** the everlasting Gn 9:16
well for you, **r** that I was with Gn 40:14
cupbearer did not **r** Joseph; Gn 40:23
Pharaoh, "Today I **r** my faults. Gn 41:9
R this day when you came out of Ex 13:3
R to dedicate the Sabbath day: Ex 20:8
R that You swore to Your Ex 32:13
then I will **r** My covenant with Lv 26:42
I will also **r** My covenant with Lv 26:42
Abraham, and I will **r** the land. Lv 26:42
sake I will **r** the covenant with Lv 26:45
We **r** the free fish we ate in Nm 11:5
so that you may **r** all the LORD's Nm 15:39
way you will **r** and obey all My Nm 15:40
R that you were a slave in the Dt 5:15
Be sure to **r** what the LORD your Dt 7:18
R that the LORD your God led you Dt 8:2
but **r** that the LORD your God Dt 8:18
R and do not forget how you Dt 9:7
R Your servants Abraham, Isaac, Dt 9:27
R that you were a slave in the Dt 15:15
that you may **r** for the rest of Dt 16:3
R that you were slaves in Egypt; Dt 16:12
R what the LORD your God did to Dt 24:9
R that you were a slave in Egypt, Dt 24:18
R that you were a slave in the Dt 24:22
R what the Amalekites did to you Dt 25:17
R the days of old; consider the Dt 32:7
R what Moses the LORD's servant Jos 1:13
did not **r** the LORD their God Jdg 8:34
R that I am your own flesh and Jdg 9:2
Lord GOD, please **r** me. Jdg 16:28
affliction, **r** and not forget me, 1Sm 1:11
may you **r** ⌊me⌋ your servant." 1Sm 25:31
R, I'll wait at the fords of the 2Sm 15:28
and don't **r** your servant's 2Sm 19:19
For **r** when you and I were riding 2Kg 9:25
r how I have walked before You 2Kg 20:3
R the wonderful works He has 1Ch 16:12
R His covenant forever—the 1Ch 16:15
r the loyalty of Your servant 2Ch 6:42
Joash didn't **r** the kindness that 2Ch 24:22
Please **r** what You commanded Your Neh 1:8
R the great and awe-inspiring Neh 4:14
R me favorably, my God, for all Neh 5:19
r Tobiah and Sanballat for what Neh 6:14
and did not **r** Your wonders You Neh 9:17
R me for this, my God, and don't Neh 13:14
R me for this also, my God, and Neh 13:22
R them, my God, for defiling the Neh 13:29
R me, my God, with favor. Neh 13:31
R that my life is ⌊but⌋ a breath. Jb 7:7
hometown will no longer **r** him. Jb 7:10
Please **r** that You formed me like Jb 10:9
a time for me and then **r** me. Jb 14:13
R that you should praise His Jb 36:24
You will **r** the battle and never Jb 41:8
what is man that You **r** him, Ps 8:4
May He **r** all your offerings and Ps 20:3
of the earth will **r** and turn to Ps 22:27
R, LORD, Your compassion and Ps 25:6
Do not **r** the sins of my youth or Ps 25:7
r me because of Your goodness, Ps 25:7
I **r** this as I pour out my heart: Ps 42:4
therefore I **r** You from the land Ps 42:6
R Your congregation, which You Ps 74:2
⌊**R**⌋ Mount Zion where You dwell. Ps 74:2
R this: the enemy has mocked the Ps 74:18
R the insults that fools bring Ps 74:22
At night I **r** my music; Ps 77:6
I will **r** the LORD's works; Ps 77:11
I will **r** Your ancient wonders. Ps 77:11
They did not **r** His power ⌊shown⌋ Ps 78:42
You no longer **r**, and who are cut Ps 88:5
R how short my life is. Ps 89:47
R, Lord, the ridicule against Ps 89:50
who **r** to observe His Ps 103:18
R the wonderful works He has Ps 105:5
R me, LORD, when You show favor Ps 106:4
works or **r** Your many acts Ps 106:7
R ⌊Your⌋ word to Your servant; Ps 119:49
I **r** Your judgments from long ago Ps 119:52
I **r** Your name in the night, Ps 119:55
r David and all the hardships he Ps 132:1
of my mouth if I do not **r** you, Ps 137:6
R, LORD, ⌊what⌋ the Edomites Ps 137:7
I **r** the days of old; Ps 143:5
his poverty and **r** his trouble no Pr 31:7
and let him **r** the days of Ec 11:8
So **r** your Creator in the days of Ec 12:1
failed to **r** the rock of your Is 17:10
us, but we **r** Your name alone Is 26:13
r how I have walked before You Is 38:3
Do not **r** the past events, Is 43:18
My own sake and **r** your sins no Is 43:25
R these things, Jacob, and Is 44:21
R this and be brave; Is 46:8
R what happened long ago, for I Is 46:9
will no longer **r** the disgrace Is 54:4
lied and didn't **r** Me or take it Is 57:11
they **r** You in Your ways. Is 64:5
angry or **r** ⌊our⌋ iniquity Is 64:9
I **r** the loyalty of your youth, Jr 2:2
and no one will **r** or miss it. Jr 3:16
Now He will **r** their guilt and Jr 14:10
R Your covenant with us; Jr 14:21
r me and take note of me. Jr 15:15
their children **r** their altars Jr 17:2
R how I stood before You to Jr 18:20
and never again **r** their sin." Jr 31:34
land—did the LORD not **r** them? Jr 44:21
R the LORD from far away, and Jr 51:50
R my affliction and my Lm 3:19
I continually **r** ⌊them⌋ and have Lm 3:20
r what has happened to us. Lm 5:1
your survivors will **r** Me among Ezk 6:9
you did not **r** the days of your Ezk 16:22
you did not **r** the days of your Ezk 16:43
But I will **r** the covenant I made Ezk 16:60
Then you will **r** your ways and be Ezk 16:61
you will **r** and be ashamed, Ezk 16:63
There you will **r** your ways and Ezk 20:43
at them or **r** Egypt any more. Ezk 23:27
Then you will **r** your evil ways Ezk 36:31
that I **r** all their evil. Hs 7:2
Now He will **r** their guilt and Hs 8:13
He will **r** their guilt; Hs 9:9
r what Balak king of Moab Mc 6:5
In ⌊Your⌋ wrath **r** mercy! Hab 3:2
they will **r** Me in the distant Zch 10:9
R the instruction of Moses My Mal 4:4
there you **r** that your brother Mt 5:23
Don't you **r** the five loaves for Mt 16:9
r that while this deceiver was Mt 27:63
And **r**, I am with you always, to Mt 28:20
and not hear? And do you not **r**? Mk 8:18
'**r** that during your life you Lk 16:25
R Lot's wife! Lk 17:32
r me when You come into Your Lk 23:42
R how He spoke to you when He Lk 24:6
R the word I spoke to you: Jn 15:20
comes you may **r** I told them to Jn 16:4
you because you **r** me in all 1Co 11:2
R this: the person who sows 2Co 9:6
only that we would **r** the poor, Gl 2:10
for you as I **r** you in my prayers Eph 1:16
r that at one time you were Eph 2:11
hand—Paul. **R** my imprisonment Col 4:18
you **r** our labor and hardship, 1Th 2:9
you **r** that when I was still 2Th 2:5
I constantly **r** you in my prayers 2Tm 1:3
man, that You **r** him, or the son Heb 2:6
will never again **r** their sins." Heb 8:12
I will never again **r** their sins Heb 10:17
R the earlier days when, after Heb 10:32
R the prisoners, as though you Heb 13:3
R your leaders who have spoken Heb 13:7
so that you can **r** the words 2Pt 3:2
r the words foretold by the Jd 17
R then how far you have fallen; Rv 2:5
R therefore what you have Rv 3:3

REMEMBERED *(52)*
God **r** Noah, as well as all the Gn 8:1
He **r** Abraham and brought Lot out Gn 19:29
Then God **r** Rachel. Gn 30:22
the land will not be **r** because Gn 41:31
Joseph **r** his dreams about them Gn 42:9
and He **r** His covenant with Ex 2:24
is how I am to be **r** in every Ex 3:15
and I have **r** My covenant. Ex 6:5
where I cause My name to be **r**. Ex 20:24
you will be **r** before the LORD Nm 10:9
wife Hannah, and the LORD **r** her. 1Sm 1:19
cooled down, he **r** Vashti, what Est 2:1
These days are **r** and celebrated Est 9:28
they are **r** no more. Jb 24:20
your name to be **r** for all Ps 45:17
They **r** that God was their rock, Ps 78:35
r that they were ⌊only⌋ flesh, Ps 78:39
name will no longer be **r**." Ps 83:4
He has **r** His love and Ps 98:3
For He **r** His holy promise to Ps 105:42
r His covenant with them, and Ps 106:45
guilt be **r** before the LORD, Ps 109:14
His wonderful works to be **r**. Ps 111:4
The righteous will be **r** forever. Ps 112:6
He **r** us in our humiliation His Ps 136:23
down and wept when we **r** Zion. Ps 137:1
Yet no one **r** that poor man. Ec 9:15
of evildoers will never be **r**. Is 14:20
Then He **r** the days of the past, Is 63:11
will not be **r** or come to mind. Is 65:17
his name will no longer be **r**." Jr 11:19
acts he did will not be **r**. Ezk 3:20
righteous acts he did will be **r**. Ezk 18:24
You will not be **r**, for I, the Ezk 21:32
will not be **r** among the nations Ezk 25:10
of his righteousness will be **r**, Ezk 33:13
no longer be **r** by their names. Hs 2:17
was fading away, I **r** the LORD. Jnh 2:7
and they will no longer be **r**. Zch 13:2
and Peter **r** the words Jesus had Mt 26:75
Then Peter **r** and said to Him, Mk 11:21
Peter **r** when Jesus had spoken Mk 14:72
our fathers and **r** His holy Lk 1:72
So Peter **r** the word of the Lord, Lk 22:61
And they **r** His words. Lk 24:8
And His disciples **r** that it is Jn 2:17
His disciples **r** that He had said Jn 2:22
then they **r** that these things Jn 12:16
have been **r** in God's sight. Ac 10:31
Then I **r** the word of the Lord, Ac 11:16
the Great was **r** in God's Rv 16:19
and God has **r** her crimes. Rv 18:5

REMEMBERING *(6)*
we are made of, **r** that we are Ps 103:14
r the days of her youth when she Ezk 23:19
r that night and day for three Ac 20:31
r you constantly in our prayers. 1Th 1:2
R your tears, I long to see you 2Tm 1:4
they had been **r** that land they Heb 11:15

REMEMBERS *(7)*
accounting for bloodshed **r** them; Ps 9:12
He forever **r** His covenant, Ps 105:8
He **r** His covenant forever. Ps 111:5
LORD **r** us and will bless ⌊us⌋ Ps 115:12
Jerusalem **r** all her precious Lm 1:7
she no longer **r** the suffering Jn 16:21
greater as he **r** the obedience 2Co 7:15

REMEMBRANCE *(10)*
offering for **r** that brings sin Nm 5:15
hands the grain offering for **r**, Nm 5:18
there is no **r** of You in death Ps 6:5
The **r** of the righteous is a Pr 10:7

is no lasting **r** of the wise man, Ec 2:16
a book of **r** was written before Mal 3:16
Do this in **r** of Me." Lk 22:19
Do this in **r** of Me." 1Co 11:24
as you drink it, in **r** of Me." 1Co 11:25
to my God for every **r** of you, Php 1:3

REMETH *(1)*
R, En-gannim, En-haddah, Jos 19:21

REMIND *(12)*
you come to **r** me of my guilt 1Kg 17:18
You, who **r** the LORD, no rest for Is 62:6
all things and **r** you of Jn 14:26
Nevertheless, to **r** you, I have Rm 15:15
He will **r** you about my ways in 1Co 4:17
he should **r** himself of this: 2Co 10:7
I **r** you to keep ablaze the gift 2Tm 1:6
R them of these things, charging 2Tm 2:14
R them to be submissive to Ti 3:1
I will always **r** you about these 2Pt 1:12
I will **r** him of the works he is 3Jn 10
Now I want to **r** you, though you Jd 5

REMINDER *(10)*
hand and as a **r** on your forehead Ex 13:9
a scroll as a **r** and recite it to Ex 17:14
before the LORD as a **r**. Ex 28:12
a continual **r** before the LORD. Ex 28:29
will serve as a **r** for the Ex 30:16
will serve as a **r** for you before Nm 10:10
It was to be a **r** for the Nm 16:40
there is a **r** of sins every year. Heb 10:3
tent, to wake you up with a **r**, 2Pt 1:13
pure understanding with a **r**, 2Pt 3:1

REMNANT *(71)*
you as a **r** within the land Gn 45:7
left of the **r** of the Rephaim. Dt 3:11
Bashan, of the **r** of the Rephaim, Jos 12:4
but rather a **r** of the Amorites. 2Sm 21:2
prayer for the surviving **r**.'" 2Kg 19:4
The surviving **r** of the house of 2Kg 19:30
For a **r** will go out from 2Kg 19:31
will abandon the **r** of My 2Kg 21:14
struck down the **r** of the 1Ch 4:43
and from the entire **r** of Israel, 2Ch 34:9
to preserve a **r** for us and give Ezr 9:8
for we survive as a **r** today. Ezr 9:15
and the Jewish **r** that had Neh 1:2
On that day the **r** of Israel and Is 10:20
The **r** will return, the remnant Is 10:21
will return, the **r** of Jacob, to Is 10:21
⌊only⌋ a **r** of them will return. Is 10:22
the **r** of His people who survive. Is 11:11
highway for the **r** of His people Is 11:16
her reputation, **r**, offspring, Is 14:22
and your **r** will be slain. Is 14:30
The **r** of Aram will be like the Is 17:3
splendor to the **r** of His people, Is 28:5
prayer for the surviving **r**.'" Is 37:4
The surviving **r** of the house of Is 37:31
For a **r** will go out from Is 37:32
the **r** of the house of Israel, Is 46:3
as a vine the **r** of Israel. Jr 6:9
will have no **r**, for I will bring Jr 11:23
I will gather the **r** of My flock Jr 23:3
and the **r** of Jerusalem— Jr 24:8
Ekron, and the **r** of Ashdod; Jr 25:20
Your people, the **r** of Israel! Jr 31:7
had left a **r** in Judah and had Jr 40:11
you so that the **r** of Judah would Jr 40:15
captive all the **r** of the people Jr 41:10
Mizpah all the **r** of the people Jr 41:16
on behalf of this entire **r** Jr 42:2
word of the LORD, **r** of Judah! Jr 42:15
concerning you, **r** of Judah: Jr 42:19
took the whole **r** of Judah, Jr 43:5
leaving yourselves without a **r**. Jr 44:7
I will take away the **r** of Judah, Jr 44:12
the **r** of Judah—those going Jr 44:14
and the whole **r** of Judah, the Jr 44:28
the **r** of the islands of Caphtor. Jr 47:4
silent, a **r** of their valley Jr 47:5
forgive those I leave as a **r**. Jr 50:20
I will leave a **r** when you are Ezk 6:8
the entire **r** of Israel when You Ezk 9:8
to an end the **r** of Israel?" Ezk 11:13
be gracious to the **r** of Joseph. Am 5:15
possess the **r** of Edom and all Am 9:12
I will collect the **r** of Israel. Mc 2:12
I will make the lame into a **r**, Mc 4:7
the **r** of Jacob will be among Mc 5:7
the **r** of Jacob will be among Mc 5:8
rebellion for the **r** of His Mc 7:18
belong to the **r** of the house Zph 2:7
The **r** of My people will plunder Zph 2:9
The **r** of Israel will no longer Zph 3:13
and the entire **r** of the people Hg 1:12
of all the **r** of the people. Hg 1:14
and to the **r** of the people: Hg 2:2
to the **r** of this people Zch 8:6
not treat the **r** of this people Zch 8:11
I will give the **r** of this people Zch 8:12
too will become a **r** for our God; Zch 9:7
make ⌊us⌋ with a **r** of His Mal 2:15
sea, only the **r** will be saved; Rm 9:27
time a **r** chosen by grace. Rm 11:5

REMORSE *(3)*
will not be **r** or a troubled 1Sm 25:31
They will feel **r** for their Ezk 39:26
was full of **r** and returned the Mt 27:3

REMOTE *(8)*
living in a **r** part of the hill Jdg 19:1
Judah to the **r** hill country of Jdg 19:18
awakened from the **r** regions of Jr 6:22
gather them from **r** regions of Jr 31:8
stirred up from the **r** regions of Jr 50:41
by boat to a **r** place to be alone Mt 14:13
yourselves to a **r** place and rest Mk 6:31
boat by themselves to a **r** place, Mk 6:32

REMOTEST *(5)*
in the **r** parts of the North. Is 14:13
I came to its **r** heights, its Is 37:24
from the **r** parts of the north Ezk 38:6
your place in the **r** parts of the Ezk 38:15
you up from the **r** parts of the Ezk 39:2

REMOVAL *(4)*
result of the **r** of his sin will Is 27:9
the **r** of sin by the sacrifice Heb 9:26
indicates the **r** of what can be Heb 12:27
not the **r** of the filth of the 1Pt 3:21

REMOVE *(86)*
sheep today and **r** every sheep Gn 30:32
LORD that He **r** the frogs from Ex 8:8
day you must **r** yeast from your Ex 12:15
would **r** the veil until he came Ex 34:34
He will **r** its digestive tract, Lv 1:16
The priest will **r** the memorial Lv 2:9
he will also **r** the fatty lobe of Lv 3:4
which he is to **r** close to the Lv 3:9
He will also **r** the fat Lv 3:9
he will also **r** the fatty lobe of Lv 3:15
He is to **r** all the fat from the Lv 4:8
He will also **r** the fatty lobe of Lv 4:9
He is to **r** all the fat from it Lv 4:19
He is to **r** all its fat just as Lv 4:31
He is to **r** all its fat just as Lv 4:35
is to **r** the ashes of the burnt Lv 6:10
The priest is to **r** a handful of Lv 6:15
he will also **r** the fatty lobe of Lv 7:4
I will **r** dangerous animals from Lv 26:6
They are to **r** the ashes from the Nm 4:13
the priest to **r** the firepans Nm 16:37
the water ⌊to **r**⌋ impurity; Nm 19:9
R Aaron's garments and put them Nm 20:26
LORD will **r** all sickness from Dt 7:15
r the clothes she was wearing Dt 21:13
r his sandal from his foot, Dt 25:9
R the sandals from your feet, Jos 5:15
you unless you **r** from you what Jos 7:12
until you **r** what is set apart Jos 7:13
will not **r** your transgressions Jos 24:19
my power, I would **r** Abimelech." Jdg 9:29
him in order to **r** from me and 1Kg 2:31
r each king from his position 1Kg 20:24
I will also **r** Judah from My 2Kg 23:27
LORD's command to **r** them from 2Kg 24:3
R everything detestable from the 2Ch 29:5
himself **r** His high places 2Ch 32:12
I will never again **r** the feet of 2Ch 33:8
in your hand, **r** it, and don't Jb 11:14
r Your hand from me, and do not Jb 13:21
my Maker would **r** me in an Jb 32:22
He does not **r** His gaze from the Jb 36:7
R Your torment from me; Ps 39:10
You **r** all the wicked on earth as Ps 119:119
R impurities from silver, and a Pr 25:4
R the wicked from the king's Pr 25:5
R sorrow from your heart, and Ec 11:10
R your evil deeds from My sight. Is 1:16
I will **r** all your impurities. Is 1:25
is about to **r** from Jerusalem Is 3:1
I will **r** its hedge, and it will Is 5:5
and to **r** the beard as well. Is 7:20
tear away and **r** the branches. Is 18:5
your sackcloth and **r** the sandals Is 20:2
I will **r** you from your office; Is 22:19
every face and **r** His people's Is 25:8
r your veil, strip off ⌊your⌋ Is 47:2
R the bonds from your neck, Is 52:2
r ⌊every⌋ obstacle from My Is 57:14
if you **r** your detestable idols Jr 4:1
r the foreskin of your hearts, Jr 4:4
will **r** from the cities of Judah Jr 7:34
I will therefore **r** it from My Jr 32:31
pot, but I will **r** you from it. Ezk 11:7
they will **r** all its detestable Ezk 11:18
I will **r** their heart of stone Ezk 11:19
R the turban, and take off the Ezk 21:26
their thrones, **r** their robes, Ezk 26:16
I will **r** your heart of stone and Ezk 36:26
let them **r** their prostitution Ezk 43:9
guard continued to **r** their food Dn 1:16
Let her **r** the promiscuous look Hs 2:2
For I will **r** the names of the Hs 2:17
to the Greeks to **r** them far from Jl 3:6
r his corpse from the house. Am 6:10
will **r** your horses from you and Mc 5:10
I will **r** the cities of your land Mc 5:11
I will **r** sorceries from your Mc 5:12
I will **r** your carved images and Mc 5:13
For then I will **r** your boastful Zph 3:11
I will **r** the blood from their Zch 9:7
I will **r** the prophets and the Zch 13:2
"**R** the stone," Jesus said. Jn 11:39
will come and **r** both our place Jn 11:48
that he might **r** Jesus' body. Jn 19:38
come to you and **r** your lampstand Rv 2:5

REMOVED *(101)*
Then Noah **r** the ark's cover and Gn 8:13
That day Laban **r** the streaked Gn 30:35
then **r** her veil and put her Gn 38:19
Pharaoh **r** his signet ring from Gn 41:42
He **r** the swarms of flies from Ex 8:31
they must not be **r** from it. Ex 25:15
just as the fat is **r** from the ox Lv 4:10
just as the fat is **r** from the Lv 4:31
fat of the lamb is **r** from the Lv 4:35
protection has been **r** from them, Nm 14:9
After Moses **r** Aaron's garments Nm 20:28
of the man whose sandal was **r**.' Dt 25:10
or **r** any of it while unclean, Dt 26:14
a man **r** his sandal and gave ⌊it⌋ Ru 4:7
So the redeemer **r** his sandal and Ru 4:8
hasn't been **r** from you will be 1Sm 6:3
The Levites **r** the ark of the 1Sm 6:15
the Israelites **r** the Baals and 1Sm 7:4
Then Jonathan **r** the robe he was 1Sm 18:4
Saul then **r** his clothes and also 1Sm 19:24
that had been **r** from before the 1Sm 21:6
the bread was **r**, it had been 1Sm 21:6
and Saul had **r** the mediums and 1Sm 28:3
leave him as I **r** it from Saul; 2Sm 7:15
I **r** him from your way. 2Sm 7:15
He **r** the people who were in the 2Sm 12:31
When he was **r** from the highway, 2Sm 20:13
the land and **r** all of the idols 1Kg 15:12
also **r** his grandmother Maacah 1Kg 15:13
quickly **r** the bandage from his 1Kg 20:41
He **r** from the land the rest of 1Kg 22:46
for he **r** the sacred pillar of 2Kg 3:2
water carts and **r** the bronze 2Kg 16:17
he **r** from the LORD's temple the 2Kg 16:18
and He **r** them from His presence. 2Kg 17:18
the LORD **r** Israel from His 2Kg 17:23
He **r** the high places and 2Kg 18:4
and altars Hezekiah has **r**, 2Kg 18:22
Josiah also **r** all the shrines of 2Kg 23:19
addition, Josiah **r** the mediums, 2Kg 23:24
sight just as I have **r** Israel. 2Kg 23:27
He **r** the pagan altars and the 2Ch 14:3
also **r** the high places and the 2Ch 14:5
courage and **r** the detestable 2Ch 15:8
King Asa also **r** Maacah, his 2Ch 15:16
and he again **r** the high places 2Ch 17:6

for you have **r** the Asherah poles 2Ch 19:3
He **r** the foreign gods and the 2Ch 33:15
So Josiah **r** everything that was 2Ch 34:33
They **r** the burnt offerings so 2Ch 35:12
The king **r** his signet ring from Est 3:10
king **r** his signet ring he had Est 8:2
or a rock be **r** from its place? Jb 18:4
of my honor and **r** the crown from Jb 19:9
He has **r** my brothers from me; Jb 19:13
in his house will be **r**, Jb 20:28
the mighty are **r** without effort. Jb 34:20
You **r** my sackcloth and clothed Ps 30:11
so far has He **r** our Ps 103:12
his disgrace will never be **r**. Pr 6:33
When hay is **r** and new growth Pr 27:25
anger is not **r**, and His hand is Is 5:25
wickedness is **r**, and your sin is Is 6:7
anger is not **r**, and His hand is Is 9:12
anger is not **r**, and His hand is Is 9:17
anger is not **r**, and His hand is Is 9:21
anger is not **r**, and His hand is Is 10:4
his burden will be **r** from their Is 14:25
have been **r** from the orchard; Is 16:10
He **r** the defenses of Judah. Is 22:8
He **r** ⌊her⌋ with His severe storm Is 27:8
Babies **r** from the breast? Is 28:9
and altars Hezekiah has **r**, Is 36:7
is plucked up and **r** from me like Is 38:12
hardhearted, far **r** from justice: Is 46:12
I have **r** the cup of staggering Is 51:22
will not be **r** from you and My Is 54:10
for I have **r** My peace from these Jr 16:5
you will be **r** from your land. Jr 27:10
so I **r** them when I saw ⌊this⌋. Ezk 16:50
until they have **r** the clothes Ezk 42:14
their authority to rule was **r**, Dn 7:12
it **r** His daily sacrifice and Dn 8:11
far **r** into a strong nation. Mc 4:7
The LORD has **r** your punishment; Zph 3:15
I have **r** your guilt from you, Zch 3:4
thief will be **r** according to Zch 5:3
falsely⌋ will be **r** according to Zch 5:3
of war will be **r**, and He will Zch 9:10
will not be **r** from the city. Zch 14:2
disciples came, **r** the corpse, Mt 14:12
they **r** the roof above where He Mk 2:4
they came and **r** his corpse and Mk 6:29
his speech difficulty was **r**, Mk 7:35
that when I'm **r** from management Lk 16:4
So they **r** the stone. Jn 11:41
stone had been **r** from the tomb. Jn 20:1
Sir, if you've **r** Him, tell me Jn 20:15
act might be **r** from among you. 1Co 5:2
to the Lord, the veil is **r**. 2Co 3:16
and slander must be **r** from you, Eph 4:31

REMOVES *(5)*
Philistine and **r** this disgrace 1Sm 17:26
He **r** mountains without their Jb 9:5
r kings and establishes kings. Dn 2:21
How He **r** ⌊it⌋ from me! Mc 2:4
does not produce fruit He **r**, Jn 15:2

REMOVING *(3)*
Make its pots for **r** ashes, Ex 27:3
r iniquity and passing over Mc 7:18
After **r** him, He raised up David Ac 13:22

RENAMED *(4)*
and Moses **r** Hoshea son of Nun, Nm 13:16
which he **r** Jair's Villages. Nm 32:41
r Leshem after their ancestor Jos 19:47
of Jacob; He **r** him Israel. 2Kg 17:34

RENDER *(3)*
Hosts says this: **R** true justice. Zch 7:9
r honest and peaceful judgments Zch 8:16
R service with a good attitude, Eph 6:7

RENDERED *(1)*
In this way, she **r** him helpless, Jdg 16:19

RENDERING *(3)*
act unjustly when **r** judgment. Lv 19:15
show partiality when **r** judgment; Dt 1:17
families for ⌊**r**⌋ the LORD's 2Ch 19:8

RENEW *(9)*
He will **r** your life and sustain Ru 4:15
so we can **r** the kingship there." 1Sm 11:14
heart for me and **r** a steadfast Ps 51:10
and You **r** the face of the earth. Ps 104:30
the LORD will **r** their strength; Is 40:31
let peoples **r** their strength. Is 41:1
they will **r** the ruined cities, Is 61:4
r our days as in former times, Lm 5:21
is impossible to **r** to repentance Heb 6:4

RENEWAL *(2)*
You found a **r** of your strength; Is 57:10
regeneration and **r** by the Holy Ti 3:5

RENEWED *(9)*
ate the honey, he had **r** energy. 1Sm 14:27
at how I have **r** energy because I 1Sm 14:29
to the Almighty, you will be **r**. Jb 22:23
and my bow will be **r** in my hand. Jb 29:20
your youth is **r** like the eagle. Ps 103:5
person is being **r** day by day. 2Co 4:16
you are being **r** in the spirit of Eph 4:23
last you have **r** your care for me Php 4:10
who is being **r** in knowledge Col 3:10

RENEWING *(1)*
by the **r** of your mind, Rm 12:2

RENEWS *(1)*
He **r** my life; He leads me along Ps 23:3

RENOUNCE *(1)*
care about myself; I **r** my life. Jb 9:21

RENOUNCED *(2)*
have **r** shameful secret things, 2Co 4:2
they have **r** their original 1Tm 5:12

RENOUNCES *(1)*
confesses and **r** them will find Pr 28:13

RENOVATE *(2)*
it to heart to **r** the LORD's 2Ch 24:4
carpenters to **r** the LORD's 2Ch 24:12

RENOVATED *(1)*
He **r** the altar of the LORD that 2Ch 15:8

RENOWN *(3)*
desire is for Your name and **r**. Is 26:8
perished, city of **r**, you who Ezk 26:17
His **r** will be like the wine of Hs 14:7

RENOWNED *(2)*
for them a place **r** for ⌊its⌋ Ezk 34:29
made Your name ⌊**r**⌋ as it is this Dn 9:15

RENTAL *(1)*
loss is covered by its **r** price. Ex 22:15

RENTED *(2)*
If it was **r**, the loss is covered Ex 22:15
whole years in his own **r** house. Ac 28:30

REOPENED *(1)*
Isaac **r** the water wells that had Gn 26:18

REPAID *(14)*
'Why have you **r** evil for good? Gn 44:4
has **r** me for what I have done. Jdg 1:7
He **r** me according to the 2Sm 22:21
the LORD **r** me according to my 2Sm 22:25
He **r** me according to the Ps 18:20
So the LORD **r** me according to my Ps 18:24
sins deserve or **r** us according Ps 103:10
righteous will be **r** on earth, Pr 11:31
Should good be **r** with evil? Jr 18:20
lend to sinners to be **r** in full. Lk 6:34
you back, and you would be **r**. Lk 14:12
for you will be **r** at the Lk 14:14
given to Him, and has to be **r**? Rm 11:35
each may be **r** for what he has 2Co 5:10

REPAIR *(16)*
assessor and **r** whatever damage 2Kg 12:5
over for the **r** of the temple." 2Kg 12:7
they would not **r** the temple's 2Kg 12:8
quarried stone to **r** the damage 2Kg 12:12
LORD's temple to **r** the damage. 2Kg 22:5
quarried stone to **r** the temple. 2Kg 22:6
battles for the **r** of the LORD's 1Ch 26:27
all Israel to **r** the temple of 2Ch 24:5
coppersmiths to **r** the LORD's 2Ch 24:12
to **r** the temple of the LORD his 2Ch 34:8
to **r** and restore the temple; 2Ch 34:10
of our God and **r** its ruins, Ezr 9:9
heard that the **r** to the walls of Neh 4:7
them who would **r** the wall and Ezk 22:30
those who **r** your leaks, those Ezk 27:27
I will **r** its gaps, restore its Am 9:11

REPAIRED *(13)*
terraces ⌊and⌋ **r** the opening in 1Kg 11:27
Then he **r** the LORD's altar that 1Kg 18:30
priests had not **r** the damage to 2Kg 12:6
Why haven't you **r** the temple's 2Kg 12:7
they **r** the LORD's temple with 2Kg 12:14
of the LORD's temple and **r** them. 2Ch 29:3
He **r** the supporting terraces of 2Ch 32:5
son of Besodeiah **r** the Old Gate. Neh 3:6
of Zanoah **r** the Valley Gate. Neh 3:13
and **r** 500 yards of the wall to Neh 3:13
Beth-haccherem, **r** the Dung Gate. Neh 3:14
of Mizpah, **r** the Fountain Gate. Neh 3:15
diligently **r** another section, Neh 3:20

REPAIRER *(1)*
be called the **r** of broken walls, Is 58:12

REPAIRING *(2)*
walls, and **r** its foundations. Ezr 4:12
were within you, **r** your leaks. Ezk 27:9

REPAIRS *(34)*
for all spending for temple **r**. 2Kg 12:12
through them the **r** progressed. 2Ch 24:13
of Uriah, son of Hakkoz, made **r**. Neh 3:4
son of Meshezabel, made **r**. Neh 3:4
them Zadok son of Baana made **r**. Neh 3:4
Beside them the Tekoites made **r**, Neh 3:5
goldsmith, made **r**, and next to Neh 3:8
son of the perfumer made **r**. Neh 3:8
district of Jerusalem, made **r**. Neh 3:9
Harumaph made **r** across from his Neh 3:10
the son of Hashabneiah made **r**. Neh 3:10
Pahath-moab made **r** to another Neh 3:11
Jerusalem, made **r**—he and his Neh 3:12
also made **r** to the wall of the Neh 3:15
made **r** up to ⌊a point⌋ opposite Neh 3:16
the Levites made **r** ⌊under⌋ Rehum Neh 3:17
of Keilah, made **r** for his Neh 3:17
Levites⌋ made **r** ⌊under⌋ Binnui Neh 3:18
made **r** to another section Neh 3:19
made **r** to another section, Neh 3:21
the surrounding area made **r**. Neh 3:22
Hasshub made **r** opposite their Neh 3:23
Ananiah, made **r** beside his house Neh 3:23
of Henadad made **r** to another Neh 3:24
of Uzai ⌊made **r**⌋ opposite the Neh 3:25
on Ophel ⌊made **r**⌋ opposite the Neh 3:26
the Tekoites made **r** to another Neh 3:27
priests made **r** above the Horse Neh 3:28
son of Immer made **r** opposite his Neh 3:29
guard of the East Gate, made **r**. Neh 3:29
of Zalaph made **r** to another Neh 3:30
Berechiah made **r** opposite his Neh 3:30
r to the house of the temple Neh 3:31
merchants made **r** between the Neh 3:32

REPAY *(62)*
he will certainly **r** us for all Gn 50:15
he must **r** five cattle for the ox Ex 22:1
possession, he must **r** double. Ex 22:4
he must **r** with the best of his Ex 22:5
thief, if caught, must **r** double. Ex 22:7
condemn must **r** double to his Ex 22:9
r the balance to the man he sold Lv 25:27
cannot obtain enough to **r** him, Lv 25:28
Is this how you **r** the LORD, Dt 32:6
to Me; I will **r**. In time their Dt 32:35
adversaries and **r** those who hate Dt 32:41
May the LORD **r** you with good 1Sm 24:19
May the LORD **r** every man for 1Sm 26:23
May the LORD **r** the evildoer 2Sm 3:39
should the king **r** me with such 2Sm 19:36
forgive, act, and **r** the man, 1Kg 8:39
'so will I **r** you on this plot of 2Kg 9:26
You forgive and **r** the man 2Ch 6:30
Look how they **r** us by coming to 2Ch 20:11
Let God **r** the person himself, Jb 21:19
Who would **r** him for what he has Jb 21:31
Should God **r** ⌊you⌋ on your terms Jb 34:33
Me, that I should **r** him? Jb 41:11
R them according to what they Ps 28:4
R them according to the work of Ps 28:4
They **r** me evil for good, making Ps 35:12
wicked borrows and does not **r**, Ps 37:21
Those who **r** evil for good attack Ps 38:20
raise me up; then I will **r** them. Ps 41:10
He will **r** my adversaries for Ps 54:5
For You **r** each according to his Ps 62:12
I did not steal, I must **r**. Ps 69:4
r the proud what they deserve. Ps 94:2
They **r** me evil for good, and Ps 109:5
can I **r** the LORD all the good Ps 116:12
Won't He **r** a person according to Pr 24:12
r the man for what he has done. Pr 24:29

LORD **r** to Moses, “Take Joshua Nm 27:18
Moses **r** to them, “If you do this Nm 32:20
The Gadites and Reubenites **r**, Nm 32:31
You **r** to me, ‘What you propose Dt 1:14
as you say,” she **r**, and she sent Jos 2:21
“Neither,” He **r**. “I have now Jos 5:14
Achan **r** to Joshua, “It is true. Jos 7:20
men of Israel **r** to the Hivites, Jos 9:7
They **r** to him, “Your servants Jos 9:9
She **r**, “Give me a blessing. Jos 15:19
people,” Joshua **r** to them, “go Jos 17:15
So Joshua **r** to Joseph’s family Jos 17:17
The people **r**, “We will certainly Jos 24:16
Gideon **r**, “Very well, when the Jdg 8:7
Zebul **r**, “Where is your mouthing Jdg 9:38
Jephthah **r** to the elders of Jdg 11:7
“Tell us your riddle,” they **r**. Jdg 14:13
They **r**, “We have come to arrest Jdg 15:10
Micah **r**, “Stay with me and be my Jdg 17:10
his master **r** to him, “We will Jdg 19:12
But Naomi **r**, “Return home, my Ru 1:11
But Ruth **r**: Do not persuade me Ru 1:16
“The LORD bless you,” they **r**. Ru 2:4
I am Ruth, your slave,” she **r**. Ru 3:9
The redeemer **r**, “I can’t redeem Ru 4:6
“No, my lord,” Hannah **r**. 1Sm 1:15
find favor with you,” she **r**. 1Sm 1:18
husband Elkanah **r**, “Do what you 1Sm 1:23
“I didn’t call,” Eli **r**. 1Sm 3:5
“I didn’t call, my son,” he **r**. 1Sm 3:6
be moved to Gath,” they **r**. 1Sm 5:8
They **r**, “If you send the ark of 1Sm 6:3
Saul **r** to his attendant. 1Sm 9:10
The LORD **r**, “There he is, 1Sm 10:22
the Ammonite **r**, “I’ll make one 1Sm 11:2
Samuel **r**, “Don’t be afraid. 1Sm 12:20
right,” Jonathan **r**, “we’ll cross 1Sm 14:8
Jonathan **r**, “My father has 1Sm 14:29
you want,” the troops **r**. 1Sm 14:36
And the troops **r**, “Do whatever 1Sm 14:40
Samuel **r**, “Then what is this 1Sm 15:14
me last night.” “Tell me,” he **r**. 1Sm 15:16
Samuel **r** to Saul, “I will not 1Sm 15:26
“In peace,” he **r**. “I’ve come to 1Sm 16:5
But Saul **r**, “You can’t go fight 1Sm 17:33
live, I don’t know,” Abner **r**. 1Sm 17:55
David, but he **r**, “Is it trivial 1Sm 18:23
Then Saul **r**, “Say this to David: 1Sm 18:25
The priest **r**, “The sword of 1Sm 21:9
Ahimelech **r** to the king: 1Sm 22:14
by the LORD,” **r** Saul, “for you 1Sm 23:21
to him, Saul **r**, “Is that your 1Sm 24:16
David **r**, “The south country of 1Sm 27:10
David **r** to Achish, “Good, you 1Sm 28:2
His servants **r**, “There is a 1Sm 28:7
An old man is coming up,” she **r**. 1Sm 28:14
I’m in serious trouble,” **r** Saul. 1Sm 28:15
David **r** to Achish. 1Sm 29:8
The LORD **r** to him, “Pursue 1Sm 30:8
He **r** to him, “I’ve escaped from 2Sm 1:3
Gilboa,” he **r**, “and there was 2Sm 1:6
“To Hebron,” the LORD **r**. 2Sm 2:1
“Let them get up,” Joab **r**. 2Sm 2:14
“Yes it is,” Asahel **r**. 2Sm 2:20
lives,” Joab **r**, “if you had not 2Sm 2:27
David **r**, “Good, I will make a 2Sm 3:13
The LORD **r** to David, “Go, for I 2Sm 5:19
r to Michal, “I was dancing 2Sm 6:21
“⌊I am⌋ your servant,” he **r**. 2Sm 9:2
“I am your servant,” he **r**. 2Sm 9:6
Nathan **r** to David, “You are the 2Sm 12:7
Then Nathan **r** to David, 2Sm 12:13
“He is dead,” they **r**. 2Sm 12:19
Amnon **r**, “I’m in love with 2Sm 13:4
The king **r** to Absalom, “No, my 2Sm 13:25
She **r**, “Please, may the king 2Sm 14:11
lord the king?” “Speak,” he **r**. 2Sm 14:12
the king speak,” the woman **r**. 2Sm 14:18
If he **r**, “Your servant is from 2Sm 15:2
“March on,” David **r** to Ittai. 2Sm 15:22
Jerusalem,” Ziba **r** to the king, 2Sm 16:3
The king **r**, “Sons of Zeruiah, do 2Sm 16:10
Ahithophel **r** to Absalom, “Sleep 2Sm 16:21
Hushai **r** to Absalom, “The advice 2Sm 17:7
the water,” the woman **r** to them. 2Sm 17:20
is best,” the king **r** to them. 2Sm 18:4
man **r** to Joab, “Even if I had 2Sm 18:12
Joab **r** to him, “You are not the 2Sm 18:20

Joab **r**, “My son, why do you 2Sm 18:22
Ahimaaz **r**, “When Joab sent the 2Sm 18:29
The Cushite **r**, “May what has 2Sm 18:32
the king,” he **r**, “my servant 2Sm 19:26
Barzillai **r** to the king, “How 2Sm 19:34
The king **r**, “Chimham will cross 2Sm 19:38
Joab?” “I am,” he **r**. “Listen to 2Sm 20:17
The woman **r** to Joab, “All 2Sm 20:21
They **r** to the king, “As for the 2Sm 21:5
r to the king, “May the LORD 2Sm 24:3
David **r**, “To buy the threshing 2Sm 24:21
She **r**, “My lord, you swore to 1Kg 1:17
son of Jehoiada **r** to the king. 1Kg 1:36
“Peacefully,” he **r**, 1Kg 2:13
He **r**, “Please speak to King 1Kg 2:17
“Very well,” Bathsheba **r**. 1Kg 2:18
mother,” the king **r**, “for I 1Kg 2:20
And Solomon **r**, “You have shown 1Kg 3:6
The king **r**, “This woman says, 1Kg 3:23
“Nothing,” he **r**, “but please 1Kg 11:22
Rehoboam **r**, “Go home for three 1Kg 12:5
They **r**, “Today if you will be a 1Kg 12:7
the man of God **r**, “If you were 1Kg 13:8
“It is I,” he **r**. “Go tell your 1Kg 18:8
He **r**, “I have not destroyed 1Kg 18:18
He **r**, “I have been very zealous 1Kg 19:10
God of Hosts,” he **r**, “but the 1Kg 19:14
on back,” he **r**, “for what have 1Kg 19:20
to Naboth the Jezreelite,” he **r**. 1Kg 21:6
He **r**, “I have caught you 1Kg 21:20
Jehoshaphat **r** to the king of 1Kg 22:4
They **r**, “March up, and the Lord 1Kg 22:6
say that!” Jehoshaphat **r**. 1Kg 22:8
Micaiah **r**, “You will soon see 1Kg 22:25
They **r**, “A man came to meet us 2Kg 1:6
They **r**, “A hairy man with a 2Kg 1:8
But Elisha **r**, “As the LORD 2Kg 2:2
Elijah **r**, “You have asked for 2Kg 2:10
He **r**, “Bring me a new bowl and 2Kg 2:20
Joram **r**, “The route of the 2Kg 3:8
But the king of Israel **r**, 2Kg 3:13
But he **r**, “There aren’t any 2Kg 4:6
She **r**, “Everything is all right. 2Kg 4:23
didn’t go anywhere,” he **r**. 2Kg 5:25
Elisha **r**, “Don’t kill them. 2Kg 6:22
He **r**, “Because I know the evil 2Kg 8:12
But they **r**, “⌊That’s⌋ a lie! 2Kg 9:12
Jehu **r**, “What do you have to 2Kg 9:18
“It is,” Jehonadab **r**. 2Kg 10:15
Hezekiah **r**, “They came from a 2Kg 20:14
The LORD **r**, “Go, and I will 1Ch 14:10
Joab **r**, “May the LORD multiply 1Ch 21:3
Rehoboam **r**, “Return to me in 2Ch 10:5
They **r**, “If you will be kind to 2Ch 10:7
He **r** to him, “I am as you are, 2Ch 18:3
They **r**, “March up, and God will 2Ch 18:5
say that,” Jehoshaphat **r**. 2Ch 18:7
Micaiah **r**, “You will soon see 2Ch 18:24
The man of God **r**, “The LORD is 2Ch 25:9
and **r** to the king, “May the king Neh 2:3
Then I **r** to him, “There is Neh 6:8
king,” Esther **r**, “may the king Est 5:4
king’s personal attendants **r**, Est 6:3
Then Eliphaz the Temanite **r**: Jb 4:1
Then Bildad the Shuhite **r**: Jb 8:1
Then Zophar the Naamathite **r**: Jb 11:1
Then Eliphaz the Temanite **r**: Jb 15:1
Then Bildad the Shuhite **r**: Jb 18:1
Then Zophar the Naamathite **r**: Jb 20:1
Then Eliphaz the Temanite **r**: Jb 22:1
Then Bildad the Shuhite **r**: Jb 25:1
son of Barachel the Buzite **r**: Jb 32:6
Then Job **r** to the LORD: Jb 42:1
And He **r**: Go! Say to these Is 6:9
Lord?” And He **r**: Until cities Is 6:11
But Ahaz **r**, “I will not ask. Is 7:12
the Rabshakeh **r**, “Has my master Is 36:12
Hezekiah **r**, “They came to me Is 39:3
I **r**, “I see a branch of an Jr 1:11
And I **r**, “I see a boiling pot, Jr 1:13
And I **r**, “Oh no, Lord GOD! Jr 14:13
Jeremiah **r** to the prophet Jr 28:5
Jeremiah **r**, “The word of the Jr 32:6
But they **r**, “We do not drink Jr 35:6
“⌊That’s⌋ a lie,” Jeremiah **r**. Jr 37:14
Jeremiah **r** to Zedekiah, “If I Jr 38:15
not hand you over,” Jeremiah **r**. Jr 38:20
r to me, “Look, I will let you Ezk 4:15

I **r**, “Lord GOD, ⌊only⌋ You know. Ezk 37:3
The king **r** to the Chaldeans, Dn 2:5
The king **r**, “I know for certain Dn 2:8
and Abednego **r** to the king, Dn 3:16
Majesty,” they **r** to the king. Dn 3:24
they **r** to the king, “Daniel, Dn 6:13
I **r**, “A plumb line.” Am 7:8
I **r**, “A basket of summer fruit. Am 8:2
Yes,⌋” he **r**. “It is right. I’m Jnh 4:9
Then Haggai **r**, “So is this Hg 2:14
angel who was talking to me **r**, Zch 1:9
The LORD **r** with kind and Zch 1:13
He **r**, “These are the horns that Zch 1:21
I **r**, “I see a solid gold Zch 4:2
r the angel who was speaking Zch 4:5
“No, my lord,” I **r**. Zch 4:13
scroll,” I **r**, “30 feet long Zch 5:2
centurion **r**, “I am not worthy Mt 8:8
Jesus **r** to them, “Go and report Mt 11:4
He **r** to the one who told Him, Mt 12:48
He **r**: “The One who sows the good Mt 13:37
He **r**, “Every plant that My Mt 15:13
Then Peter **r** to Him, “Explain Mt 15:15
He **r**, “I was sent only to the Mt 15:24
Jesus **r** to her, “Woman, your Mt 15:28
will restore everything,” He **r**. Mt 17:11
Jesus **r**, “You unbelieving and Mt 17:17
you read,” He **r**, “that He who Mt 19:4
He **r** to one of them, ‘Friend, Mt 20:13
Then He **r** to them, “Don’t you Mt 24:2
Then Jesus **r** to them: Mt 24:4
But he **r**, ‘I assure you: Mt 25:12
But his master **r** to him, Mt 25:26
He **r**, “The one who dipped his Mt 26:23
His betrayer, **r**, “Surely not I, Mt 26:25
He **r** to them, “Who are My mother Mk 3:33
she **r** to Him, “Lord, even the Mk 7:28
and restores everything,” He **r**. Mk 9:12
He **r** to them, “You unbelieving Mk 9:19
He **r** to them, “What did Moses Mk 10:3
Jesus **r** to them, “Have faith in Mk 11:22
The angel **r** to her: The Holy Lk 1:35
He **r** to them, “The one who has Lk 3:11
“Master,” Simon **r**, “we’ve worked Lk 5:5
thoughts, Jesus **r** to them, “Why Lk 5:22
Jesus **r** to them, “The healthy Lk 5:31
He **r** to them, “Go and report to Lk 7:22
Jesus **r** to him, “Simon, I have Lk 7:40
But He **r** to them, “My mother and Lk 8:21
Jesus **r**, “You unbelieving and Lk 9:41
But he **r** to him, ‘Sir, leave it Lk 13:8
But he **r** to his father, ‘Look, I Lk 15:29
He **r**, “What is impossible with Lk 18:27
“Come and you’ll see,” He **r**. Jn 1:39
Nathanael **r**, “You are the Son Jn 1:49
So the Jews **r** to Him, “What sign Jn 2:18
Jesus **r**, “I assure you: Jn 3:3
know these things?” Jesus **r**. Jn 3:10
Sir,” the woman **r**, “I see that Jn 4:19
He **r**, “The man who made me well Jn 5:11
Then Jesus **r**, “I assure you: Jn 5:19
Jesus **r**, “This is the work of Jn 6:29
r to them, “Didn’t I choose Jn 6:70
are you?” they **r**. “Investigate Jn 7:52
Myself,” Jesus **r**, “My testimony Jn 8:14
Abraham!” they **r**. “If you were Jn 8:39
The Jews **r**, “You aren’t 50 years Jn 8:57
in sin,” they **r**, “and are you Jn 9:34
Jesus **r**, “I have shown you many Jn 10:32
Jesus **r** to them, “The hour has Jn 12:23
the crowd **r** to Him, “We have Jn 12:34
Jesus **r**, “If I don’t wash you, Jn 13:8
Jesus **r**, “He’s the one I give Jn 13:26
Jesus **r**, “Will you lay down your Jn 13:38
“I told you I am ⌊He⌋,” Jesus **r**. Jn 18:8
am I?” Pilate **r**. “Your own Jn 18:35
say that I’m a king,” Jesus **r**. Jn 18:37
have a law,” the Jews **r** to him, Jn 19:7
Pilate **r**, “What I have written, Jn 19:22
gardener, she **r**, “Sir, if you’ve Jn 20:15
But Peter and the apostles **r**, Ac 5:29
for me,” Simon **r**, “so that Ac 8:24
The eunuch **r** to Philip, “I ask Ac 8:34
And he **r**, “I believe that Jesus Ac 8:37
whom you are persecuting,” He **r**. Ac 9:5
Cornelius **r**, “Four days ago at Ac 10:30
Others **r**, “He seems to be a Ac 17:18
“With John’s baptism,” they **r**. Ac 19:3

Paul **r**, "What are you doing, Ac 21:13
He **r**, "Do you know Greek? Ac 21:37
The commander **r**, "I bought this Ac 22:28
to him to speak, Paul **r**: Ac 24:10
Felix became afraid and **r**, Ac 24:25
the Jews, **r** to Paul, "Are you Ac 25:9
his council, he **r**, "You have Ac 25:12
the Lord **r**: 'I am Jesus, whom Ac 26:15
But Paul **r**, "I'm not out of my Ac 26:25
wish before God," **r** Paul, "that Ac 26:29

REPLY *(20)*

are to **r**, 'It is the Passover Ex 12:27
the woman must **r**, 'Amen, Amen.' Nm 5:22
And all the people will **r**, Dt 27:15
in the future, we would **r**: Jos 22:28
servant would **r**, "No, I insist 1Sm 2:16
Hiram sent ⌊a **r**⌋ to Solomon, 1Kg 5:8
The king sent a **r** to his chief Ezr 4:17
This is the **r** they gave us: Ezr 5:11
I gave them this **r**, "The God of Neh 2:20
and I gave them the same **r**. Neh 6:4
the messenger⌋ to **r** to Esther, Est 4:13
Esther sent this **r** to Mordecai: Est 4:15
and my understanding makes me **r**. Jb 20:3
spoken once, and I will not **r**; Jb 40:5
The king said in **r** to Daniel, Dn 2:26
That person will **r**, "None." Am 6:10
and what I should **r** about my Hab 2:1
Because of this **r**, you may go. Mk 7:29
But what was God's **r** to him? Rm 11:4
you may have a **r** for those who 2Co 5:12

REPORT *(74)*

You didn't **r** anything to me, Gn 21:26
he brought a bad **r** about them to Gn 37:2
You must not spread a false **r**. Ex 23:1
They brought back a **r** for them Nm 13:26
gave a negative **r** to the Nm 13:32
spreading a bad **r** about the land Nm 14:36
who spread the **r** about the land Nm 14:37
us back a **r** about the route Dt 1:22
us, and brought us back a **r**: Dt 1:25
They will hear the **r** about you, Dt 2:25
the LORD and you to **r** the word Dt 5:5
If the **r** turns out to be true Dt 13:14
If the **r** turns out to be true Dt 17:4
If you don't **r** our mission, Jos 2:14
And if you **r** our mission, we are Jos 2:20
and I brought back an honest **r**. Jos 14:7
and brought back a **r** to them. Jos 22:32
were pleased with the **r**, Jos 22:33
the **r** I hear from the LORD's 1Sm 2:24
entered the city to give a **r**, 1Sm 4:13
that he was sure to **r** to Saul. 1Sm 22:22
man who had brought him the **r**, 2Sm 1:5
man who had brought him the **r**, 2Sm 1:13
years old when the **r** about Saul 2Sm 4:4
sent someone to **r** to David all 2Sm 11:18
on the way, a **r** reached David: 2Sm 13:30
seriously the **r** that says all 2Sm 13:33
R everything you hear from the 2Sm 15:35
The **r** I heard in my own country 1Kg 10:6
far exceed the **r** I heard. 1Kg 10:7
Then when I go **r** to Ahab and he 1Kg 18:12
went to meet Ahab and **r** to him. 1Kg 18:16
King Hezekiah heard ⌊their **r**⌋, 2Kg 19:1
and bring ⌊a **r**⌋ to me so I can 1Ch 21:2
The **r** I heard in my own country 2Ch 9:5
You far exceed the **r** I heard. 2Ch 9:6
stop them until a **r** was sent to Ezr 5:5
They sent him a **r**, written as Ezr 5:7
I heard this **r**, I tore my tunic Ezr 9:3
When the **r** was investigated and Est 2:23
the written **r** of how Mordecai Est 6:2
gave⌋ the **r** that saved the king. Est 7:9
go? Do they **r** to you: "Here we Jb 38:35
I were to **r** and speak ⌊of them⌋ Ps 40:5
a dependable **r** to those who sent Pr 22:21
creature may **r** the matter. Ec 10:20
let him **r** what he sees. Is 21:6
King Hezekiah heard ⌊their **r**⌋, Is 37:1
is on every side! **R** ⌊him⌋; let's Jr 20:10
him⌋; let's **r** him!" Everyone I Jr 20:10
heard the **r**, they withdrew Jr 37:5
heard a bad **r** and are agitated Jr 49:23
fearful when the **r** is proclaimed Jr 51:46
for the **r** will come one year, Jr 51:46
will come to you and **r** the news. Ezk 24:26
R everything you see to the Ezk 40:4
I have heard the **r** about You; Hab 3:2
r back to me so that I too can Mt 2:8
Go and **r** to John what you hear Mt 11:4
heard the **r** about Jesus. Mt 14:1
and **r** to them how much the Lord Mk 5:19
This **r** about Him went throughout Lk 7:17
Go and **r** to John the things you Lk 7:22
he should **r** it so they could Jn 11:57
So this **r** spread to the brothers Jn 21:23
Then the **r** about them reached Ac 11:22
R these things to James and the Ac 12:17
personally **r** the same things Ac 15:27
he has something to **r** to him." Ac 23:17
"What is it you have to **r** to me?" Ac 23:19
who had no **r** of Him will see Rm 15:21
The **r** of your obedience has Rm 16:19
through slander and good **r**; 2Co 6:8
they themselves **r** about us what 1Th 1:9

REPORTED *(112)*

son Esau were **r** to Rebekah, Gn 27:42
We **r** your words to him. Gn 44:24
came and **r** ⌊this⌋ to Moses. Ex 16:22
Then Moses **r** the people's words Ex 19:9
A young man ran and **r** to Moses, Nm 11:27
They **r** to Moses: "We went into Nm 13:27
When Moses **r** these words to all Nm 14:39
to Balaam and **r** Balak's words to Nm 22:7
to Balak, and **r**, "Balaam refused Nm 22:14
son of Nun and **r** everything that Jos 2:23
to Joshua they **r** to him, Jos 7:3
It was clearly **r** to your Jos 9:24
It was **r** to Joshua: Jos 10:17
was **r** to Sisera that Barak son Jdg 4:12
So this was **r** to Abimelech. Jdg 9:25
this was **r** to Abimelech. Jdg 9:42
Then it was **r** to Abimelech that Jdg 9:47
death has been fully **r** to me: Ru 2:11
man quickly came and **r** to Eli. 1Sm 4:14
r to Saul: "Look, the troops 1Sm 14:33
but it was **r** to Samuel, "Saul 1Sm 15:12
was overheard and **r** to Saul, 1Sm 17:31
and when it was **r** to Saul, 1Sm 18:20
Saul's servants **r** these words 1Sm 18:23
The servants **r** back to Saul, 1Sm 18:24
the servants **r** these terms to 1Sm 18:26
When it was **r** to Saul that David 1Sm 19:19
When they **r** to Saul, he sent 1Sm 19:21
It was **r** to David: 1Sm 23:1
When it was **r** to Saul that David 1Sm 23:7
When it was **r** to Saul that David 1Sm 23:13
to him, they **r** all these words. 1Sm 25:12
When it was **r** to Saul that David 1Sm 27:4
It was **r** to King David: 2Sm 6:12
this was **r** to David, he sent 2Sm 10:5
When this was **r** to David, he 2Sm 10:17
about her, and he **r**, "This is 2Sm 11:3
When it was **r** to David, "Uriah 2Sm 11:10
he **r** to David all that Joab had 2Sm 11:22
The messenger **r** to David, 2Sm 11:23
an informer came to David and **r**, 2Sm 15:13
Then someone **r** to David: 2Sm 15:31
It was **r** to Joab, "The king is 2Sm 19:1
When it was **r** to David what 2Sm 21:11
It was **r** to Solomon: 1Kg 1:51
It was **r** to King Solomon: 1Kg 2:29
It was **r** to Solomon that Shimei 1Kg 2:41
Wasn't it **r** to my lord what I 1Kg 18:13
seventh time, he **r**, "There's a 1Kg 18:44
and they **r** to him, saying, 1Kg 20:17
the news⌋ was **r** to the king's 2Kg 7:11
The watchman **r**, "The messenger 2Kg 9:18
the watchman **r**, "He reached them 2Kg 9:20
torn and **r** to him the words 2Kg 18:37
went to the king and **r**, 2Kg 22:9
Then they **r** to the king. 2Kg 22:20
Someone came and **r** to David 1Ch 19:5
When this was **r** to David, he 1Ch 19:17
king, and also **r**, "Your servants 2Ch 34:16
Then they **r** to the king. 2Ch 34:28
It is **r** among the nations— Neh 6:6
and they **r** my words to him. Neh 6:19
of the plot, he **r** it to Queen Est 2:22
came and **r** the news to her Est 4:4
response was **r** to Mordecai. Est 4:12
of Susa was **r** to the king. Est 9:11
a messenger came to Job and **r**: Jb 1:14
another ⌊messenger⌋ came and **r**: Jb 1:16
when ⌊yet⌋ another came and **r**: Jb 1:17
another ⌊messenger⌋ came and **r**: Jb 1:18
the lookout **r**, "Lord, I stand Is 21:8
and they **r** to him the words of Is 36:22
Disaster after disaster is **r**, Jr 4:20
Micaiah **r** to them all the words Jr 36:13
and **r** everything in the hearing Jr 36:20
he **r** the exact words to them the Jr 38:27
equipment at his side **r** back, Ezk 9:11
from Jerusalem came to me and **r**, Ezk 33:21
They **r** to the Angel of the LORD Zch 1:11
into the city and **r** everything— Mt 8:33
it, and went and **r** to Jesus. Mt 14:12
and went and **r** to their master Mt 18:31
into the city and **r** to the chief Mt 28:11
it was **r** that He was at home. Mk 2:1
ran off and **r** it in the town Mk 5:14
Jesus and **r** to Him all that Mk 6:30
She went and **r** to those who had Mk 16:10
they went and **r** it to the rest, Mk 16:13
r the message they were told Lk 2:17
ran off and **r** it in the town Lk 8:34
the eyewitnesses **r** to them how Lk 8:36
they **r** to Jesus all that they Lk 9:10
people came and **r** to Him about Lk 13:1
came back and **r** these things to Lk 14:21
they **r** all these things to the Lk 24:9
they came and **r** that they had Lk 24:23
man went and **r** to the Jews that Jn 5:15
fellowship and **r** all that the Ac 4:23
jail, so they returned and **r**, Ac 5:22
Someone came and **r** to them, Ac 5:25
He **r** to us how he had seen the Ac 11:13
they **r** everything God had done Ac 14:27
and they **r** all that God had done Ac 15:4
Simeon has **r** how God first Ac 15:14
jailer **r** these words to Paul: Ac 16:36
Then the police **r** these words to Ac 16:38
he went and **r** to the commander, Ac 22:26
the barracks and **r** it to Paul. Ac 23:16
come and **r** or spoken anything Ac 28:21
faith is being **r** in all the Rm 1:8
it has been **r** to me about you 1Co 1:11
It is widely **r** that there is 1Co 5:1

REPORTS *(6)*

didn't believe the **r** until I 1Kg 10:7
believe their **r** until I came and 2Ch 9:6
to these **r**, you are to become Neh 6:6
Don't you accept their **r**? Jb 21:29
Babylon has heard **r** about them, Jr 50:43
r from the east and the north Dn 11:44

REPOSE *(1)*

this is the place of **r**." Is 28:12

REPRESENT *(6)*

be the one to **r** the people Ex 18:19
Let our leaders **r** the entire Ezr 10:14
to **r** their ancestral houses. Ezr 10:16
live in Mizpah to **r** ⌊you⌋ before Jr 40:10
shattered horn **r** four kingdoms. Dn 8:22
for the women **r** the two Gl 4:24

REPRESENTATIVE *(1)*

Jerusalem as the **r** of the king Jr 52:12

REPRESENTATIVES *(3)*

community and **r** in the assembly Nm 16:2
as his **r** to say to David, 2Sm 3:12
And **r** from the peoples, tribes, Rv 11:9

REPRESENTED *(1)*

each **r** his ancestral house. Nm 1:44

REPRESENTING *(1)*

Aaron's staff, **r** the house of Nm 17:8

REPRESENTS *(6)*

Oholah **r** Samaria and Oholibah Ezk 23:4
and Oholibah **r** Jerusalem. Ezk 23:4
ram that you saw **r** the kings of Dn 8:20
The shaggy goat **r** the king of Dn 8:21
his eyes **r** the first king. Dn 8:21
the fine linen **r** the righteous Rv 19:8

REPRIMAND *(2)*

Better an open **r** than concealed Pr 27:5
your own apostasies will **r** you. Jr 2:19

REPRIMANDED *(1)*

had never once **r** him by saying, 1Kg 1:6

REPRIMANDS *(1)*

after many **r** will be broken Pr 29:1

REPROACH *(12)*

not invite⌋ the **r** of our foreign Neh 5:9

me be clothed with shame and **r**. Ps 35:26
us an object of **r** to our Ps 44:13
an object of **r** to our neighbors, Ps 79:4
neighbors the **r** they have hurled Ps 79:12
for nothing but shame and **r**. Is 30:5
to endure the **r** of the peoples Ezk 36:15
experience **r** among the nations Ezk 36:30
from you, and **r** ⌊on her⌋. Zph 3:18
must be above **r**, the husband of 1Tm 3:2
message is to be sound beyond **r**, Ti 2:8
For he considered **r** for the sake Heb 11:26

REPROACHED *(1)*
mountains and **r** Me on the hills Is 65:7

REPROVED *(1)*
or faint when you are **r** by Him; Heb 12:5

REPTILE *(1)*
animal or bird, **r** or fish—is Jms 3:7

REPTILES *(5)*
animals, birds, **r**, and fish. 1Kg 4:33
hiding places like **r** slithering Mc 7:17
animals and **r** of the earth, Ac 10:12
beasts, the **r**, and the birds Ac 11:6
four-footed animals, and **r**. Rm 1:23

REPUDIATED *(2)*
have **r** the covenant with Your Ps 89:39
His altar, **r** His sanctuary; Lm 2:7

REPULSIVE *(8)*
it; it is **r**. The person who Lv 7:18
the third day, it is a **r** thing; Lv 19:7
and Israel is now **r** to the 1Sm 13:4
they had become **r** to David, 2Sm 10:6
have become **r** to your father, 2Sm 16:21
had made themselves **r** to David, 1Ch 19:6
and my own children find me **r**. Jb 19:17
You have made me **r** to them. Ps 88:8

REPUTATION *(16)*
because of the **r** of the LORD Jos 9:9
David made a **r** for himself when 2Sm 8:13
gaining a **r** among the Three. 2Sm 23:18
who had a **r** among the three 2Sm 23:22
His **r** extended to all the 1Kg 4:31
gaining a **r** among the Three. 1Ch 11:20
who had a **r** among the three 1Ch 11:24
and get a bad **r**, in order that Neh 6:13
forever, Your **r**, LORD, through Ps 135:13
will cut off from Babylon her **r**, Is 14:22
among you seven men of good **r**, Ac 6:3
who has a good **r** with the whole Ac 10:22
having a good **r** with all the Ac 22:12
Although these have a **r** of Col 2:23
have a good **r** among outsiders 1Tm 3:7
you have a **r** for being alive, Rv 3:1

REQUEST *(25)*
I'll grant your **r** about this Gn 19:21
The LORD listened to Israel's **r**, Nm 21:3
them, "Let me make a **r** of you: Jdg 8:24
said and have granted your **r**." 1Sm 25:35
king will grant his servant's **r**. 2Sm 14:15
to Joab, "I hereby grant this **r**. 2Sm 14:21
granted the **r** of your servant. 2Sm 14:22
So now I have just one **r** of you; 1Kg 2:16
I have just one small **r** of you. 1Kg 2:20
has not made this **r** at the cost 1Kg 2:23
And God granted his **r**. 1Ch 4:10
He granted their **r** because they 1Ch 5:20
his petition and granted his **r**, 2Ch 33:13
and how God granted his **r**, 2Ch 33:19
this, and He granted our **r**. Ezr 8:23
king asked me, "What is your **r**?" Neh 2:4
⌊This is⌋ my petition and my **r**: Est 5:7
my petition and perform my **r**, Est 5:8
spare my life—[this is] my **r**; Est 7:3
only my **r** would be granted and Jb 6:8
not denied the **r** of his lips. Ps 21:2
Daniel's **r**, the king appointed Dn 2:49
make a **r** to the commander that Ac 23:15
every prayer and **r**, pray at all Eph 6:18
His ears are open to their **r**. 1Pt 3:12

REQUESTED *(24)*
that they gave them what they **r**. Ex 12:36
I have pardoned ⌊them⌋ as you **r**. Nm 14:20
This is what you **r** from the LORD Dt 18:16
country of Ephraim, which he **r**. Jos 19:50
night God did ⌊as Gideon **r**⌋: Jdg 6:40
gold earrings he **r** was about 43 Jdg 8:26
the petition you've **r** from Him." 1Sm 1:17
said⌋, "I **r** him from the LORD. 1Sm 1:20
you've chosen, the one you **r**. 1Sm 12:13
'David urgently **r** my permission 1Sm 20:6
he went home and **r** ⌊something to 2Sm 12:20
Lord that Solomon had **r** this. 1Kg 3:10
you have **r** this and did not 1Kg 3:11
and you have not **r** riches, 2Ch 1:11
you have not even **r** long life, 2Ch 1:11
but you have **r** for yourself 2Ch 1:11
as **r** by the priests in Jerusalem Ezr 6:9
everything he **r** because the hand Ezr 7:6
whatever she **r** to take with her Est 2:13
so we can do as Esther has **r**." Est 5:5
the people a prisoner they **r**. Mk 15:6
in Galilee, and **r** of him, "Sir, Jn 12:21
r that Pilate have the men's Jn 19:31
and **r** letters from him to the Ac 9:2

REQUESTING *(5)*
the LORD's sight by **r** a king for 1Sm 12:17
sins the evil of **r** a king for 1Sm 12:19
Why are you **r** Abishag the 1Kg 2:22
the prophet, **r**, "Please pray to Jr 37:3
r Him to come and save the life Lk 7:3

REQUESTS *(6)*
to your **r** or pay attention Dt 1:45
The king granted my ⌊**r**⌋, Neh 2:8
May the LORD fulfill all your **r**. Ps 20:5
can make known what the king **r**. Dn 2:10
that I will make **r** to the Father Jn 16:26
let your **r** be made known to God. Php 4:6

REQUIRE *(14)*
will **r** the life of every animal Gn 9:5
I will **r** the life of each man's Gn 9:5
But **r** the same quota of bricks Ex 5:8
The priest will **r** the woman to Nm 5:19
He will **r** the woman to drink the Nm 5:24
he will **r** the woman to drink Nm 5:26
because He will **r** it of you, Dt 23:21
offerings that I **r** at the place 1Sm 2:29
circumstances **r** because God is 1Sm 10:7
there's one thing I **r** of you: 2Sm 3:13
should I not **r** his blood from 2Sm 4:11
these things⌋ and **r** nothing more Neh 5:12
them and will **r** your Ezk 20:40
matter she may **r** your help. Rm 16:2

REQUIRED *(11)*
horses to the **r** place according 1Kg 4:28
accounting was **r** from the men 2Kg 12:15
is to be **r** from them for 2Kg 22:7
Why haven't you **r** the Levites to 2Ch 24:6
and he **r** all who were present in 2Ch 34:33
The legally **r** portions for the Neh 12:44
give them the **r** beauty Est 2:3
regulation **r** her to receive Est 2:12
Much will be **r** of everyone who Lk 12:48
reveal it as I am **r** to speak. Col 4:4
given us everything **r** for life 2Pt 1:3

REQUIREMENT *(7)*
out the LORD's **r** and did not set Nm 9:19
the LORD's **r** according to His Nm 9:23
carried out the **r** of the command Jos 22:3
the daily **r** for offerings 2Ch 8:13
priests following the daily **r**, 2Ch 8:14
are to obey the **r** of the LORD. 2Ch 23:6
order that the law's **r** would be Rm 8:4

REQUIREMENTS *(6)*
ark according to the daily **r**. 1Ch 16:37
out the **r** of the LORD our 2Ch 13:11
do not know the **r** of the LORD. Jr 8:7
by keeping His **r** and walking Mal 3:14
commandments and **r** of the Lord. Lk 1:6
man keeps the law's **r**, Rm 2:26

REQUIRES *(4)*
people Israel, as each day **r**, 1Kg 8:59
before Me, who **r** this from you— Is 1:12
what it is the LORD **r** of you: Mc 6:8
And he **r** everyone—small and Rv 13:16

RESCUE *(86)*
Please **r** me from the hand of my Gn 32:11
intending to **r** him from their Gn 37:22
to their **r** and watered their Ex 2:17
have come down to **r** them from Ex 3:8
but there was no one to **r** her. Dt 22:27
of one steps in to **r** her husband Dt 25:11
No one can **r** ⌊anyone⌋ from My Dt 32:39
who will **r** us from the hand of 1Sm 4:8
Then He will **r** you from the hand 1Sm 7:3
the bear will **r** me from the hand 1Sm 17:37
the Philistines and **r** Keilah." 1Sm 23:2
life valuable and **r** me from all 1Sm 26:24
them⌋ and **r** ⌊the people⌋." 1Sm 30:8
listen in order to **r** his servant 2Sm 14:16
You **r** an afflicted people, 2Sm 22:28
You **r** me from violent men. 2Sm 22:49
predecessors destroyed **r** them— 2Kg 19:12
this city and **r** it for My sake 2Kg 19:34
gather us and **r** us from the 1Ch 16:35
He will **r** you from six Jb 5:19
He will ⌊even⌋ **r** the guilty one, Jb 22:30
Turn, LORD! **R** me; save me Ps 6:4
from all my pursuers and **r** me, Ps 7:1
me apart, with no one to **r** me. Ps 7:2
For You **r** an afflicted people, Ps 18:27
You **r** me from violent men. Ps 18:48
LORD; let Him **r** him; let the Ps 22:8
closely to me; **r** me quickly. Be Ps 31:2
R my life from their ravages, Ps 35:17
r me from the deceitful and Ps 43:1
I will **r** you, and you will honor Ps 50:15
R me from the miry mud; Ps 69:14
Your justice, **r** and deliver me; Ps 71:2
for there is no one to **r** ⌊him⌋." Ps 71:11
For he will **r** the poor who cry Ps 72:12
R the poor and needy; Ps 82:4
I will **r** him and give him honor. Ps 91:15
Consider my affliction and **r** me, Ps 119:153
r me according to Your promise. Ps 119:170
R me, LORD, from evil men. Ps 140:1
R me from those who pursue me, Ps 142:6
R me from my enemies, LORD; Ps 143:9
r me from deep water, and set me Ps 144:7
Set me free and **r** me from the Ps 144:11
It will **r** you from a forbidden Pr 2:16
if you **r** him, you'll have to do Pr 19:19
on the LORD, and He will **r** you. Pr 20:22
and you will **r** his life from Pr 23:14
R those being taken off to death, Pr 24:11
it⌋ off, and no one can **r** ⌊it⌋. Is 5:29
and leader, and he will **r** them. Is 19:20
to for help to **r** ⌊us⌋ from the Is 20:6
it⌋, He will **r** ⌊it⌋, by sparing Is 31:5
predecessors destroyed **r** them— Is 37:12
will defend this city and **r** it, Is 37:35
with no one to **r** them, and loot, Is 42:22
are not able to **r** the burden, Is 46:2
since I am with you to **r** you." Jr 1:19
and **r** the victim of robbery from Jr 21:12
R the victim of robbery from the Jr 22:3
But I will **r** you on that day"— Jr 39:17
for I will **r** My flock from their Ezk 34:10
will **r** them from all the places Ezk 34:12
their yoke and **r** them from the Ezk 34:27
the god who can **r** you from my Dn 3:15
He can **r** us from the furnace Dn 3:17
and He can **r** us from the power Dn 3:17
But even if He does not **r** us, Dn 3:18
you serve continually, **r** you!" Dn 6:16
able to **r** you from the lions? Dn 6:20
there was no **r** from his power. Dn 8:4
was no one to **r** the ram from his Dn 8:7
and no one will **r** her from My Hs 2:10
off, and no one can **r** ⌊them⌋. Hs 5:14
He will **r** us from Assyria when Mc 5:6
and there is no one to **r** ⌊them⌋. Mc 5:8
not be able to **r** them on the day Zph 1:18
let God **r** Him now—if He wants Mt 27:43
he came to his **r** and avenged the Ac 7:24
and have come down to **r** them. Ac 7:34
to go down, **r** him from them, Ac 23:10
I will **r** you from the people and Ac 26:17
Who will **r** me from this body of Rm 7:24
for our sins to **r** us from this Gl 1:4
The Lord will **r** me from every 2Tm 4:18
Lord knows how to **r** the godly 2Pt 2:9

RESCUED *(53)*
An Egyptian **r** us from the Ex 2:19
for Israel when He **r** them from Ex 18:9
who **r** you from Pharaoh and the Ex 18:10
Israel even **r** their surrounding 1Sm 7:14
I **r** you from the power of the 1Sm 10:18
He **r** you from the power of the 1Sm 12:11
So the people **r** Jonathan, 1Sm 14:45
and **r** ⌊the lamb⌋ from its mouth. 1Sm 17:35
LORD who **r** me from the paw 1Sm 17:37

So David **r** the inhabitants of 1Sm 23:5
he also **r** his two wives. 1Sm 30:18
those who **r** your life and the 2Sm 19:5
he **r** us from the grasp of the 2Sm 19:9
the day the LORD **r** him from the 2Sm 22:1
r me from my powerful enemy 2Sm 22:18
He **r** me because He delighted in 2Sm 22:20
secretly **r** Joash son of Ahaziah 2Kg 11:2
them completely. Will you be **r**? 2Kg 19:11
r Joash son of Ahaziah from the 2Ch 22:11
who **r** them from the power of Neh 9:27
heaven and **r** them many times Neh 9:28
day of disaster, **r** from the day Jb 21:30
who will be **r** by the purity of Jb 22:30
For I **r** the poor man who cried Jb 29:12
He **r** me from my powerful enemy Ps 18:17
He **r** me because He delighted in Ps 18:19
they trusted, and You **r** them. Ps 22:4
You have **r** me from the horns of Ps 22:21
so that those You love may be **r**. Ps 60:5
Let me be **r** from those who hate Ps 69:14
out in distress, and I **r** you; Ps 81:7
He **r** them many times, but they Ps 106:43
He **r** them from their distress. Ps 107:6
He **r** them from the Pit. Ps 107:20
so that those You love may be **r**. Ps 108:6
You, ⌊LORD,⌋ **r** me from death, Ps 116:8
and **r** us from our foes. Ps 136:24
The righteous is **r** from trouble; Pr 11:8
knowledge the righteous are **r**. Pr 11:9
them completely. Will you be **r**? Is 37:11
His angel and **r** His servants who Dn 3:28
for He has **r** Daniel from the Dn 6:27
in Samaria will be **r** with ⌊only⌋ Am 3:12
there you will be **r**; Mc 4:10
we have been **r** from our enemies' Lk 1:74
and **r** him out of all his Ac 7:10
His angel and **r** me from Herod's Ac 12:11
my troops and **r** him because I Ac 23:27
that I may be **r** from the Rm 15:31
He has **r** us from the domain of Col 1:13
Yet the Lord **r** me from them all. 2Tm 3:11
I was **r** from the lion's mouth. 2Tm 4:17
and if He **r** righteous Lot, 2Pt 2:7

RESCUER *(1)*
apart, and there will be no **r**. Ps 50:22

RESCUES *(12)*
r the afflicted by afflicting Jb 36:15
those who fear Him, and **r** them. Ps 34:7
He **r** them from the hand of the Ps 97:10
but righteousness **r** from death. Pr 10:2
but righteousness **r** from death. Pr 11:4
of the upright **r** them, Pr 11:6
speech of the upright **r** them. Pr 12:6
A truthful witness **r** lives, Pr 14:25
for He **r** the life of the needy Jr 20:13
no one **r** ⌊us⌋ from their hands. Lm 5:8
He **r** and delivers; He performs Dn 6:27
who **r** us from the coming wrath. 1Th 1:10

RESCUING *(3)*
r the poor from one too strong Ps 35:10
r you from the way of evil— Pr 2:12
his mind on **r** Daniel and made Dn 6:14

RESEMBLE *(2)*
like Sodom, we would **r** Gomorrah. Is 1:9
form did not **r** a human being— Is 52:14

RESEMBLED *(5)*
It **r** coriander seed, was white, Ex 16:31
The manna **r** coriander seed, Nm 11:7
"Each **r** the son of a king." Jdg 8:18
coming down that **r** a large sheet Ac 10:11
coming down that **r** a large sheet Ac 11:5

RESEMBLING *(4)*
like sapphire stone **r** the shape Ezk 10:1
slope⌋ was a structure **r** a city. Ezk 40:2
God for images **r** mortal man, Rm 1:23
of life, but **r** the Son of God Heb 7:3

RESEN *(1)*
and **R**, between Nineveh and the Gn 10:12

RESENTED *(1)*
was furious and **r** this song. 1Sm 18:8

RESENTFUL *(2)*
left for home **r** and angry, 1Kg 20:43
went to his palace **r** and angry, 1Kg 21:4

RESENTMENT *(1)*
the depth of my anguish and **r**." 1Sm 1:16

RESERVE *(3)*
food will be a **r** for the land Gn 41:36
the Almighty not **r** times for Jb 24:1
which I hold in **r** for times of Jb 38:23

RESERVED *(6)*
Notice that the **r** piece is set 1Sm 9:24
darkness is **r** for his treasures Jb 20:26
of the hope **r** for you in heaven Col 1:5
there is **r** for me the crown of 2Tm 4:8
of darkness has been **r** for them. 2Pt 2:17
for whom is **r** the blackness Jd 13

RESERVES *(1)*
God **r** a person's punishment for Jb 21:19

RESERVOIR *(23)*
He made the cast ⌊metal⌋ **r**, 1Kg 7:23
completely encircling the **r**. 1Kg 7:24
in two rows when the **r** was cast. 1Kg 7:24
The **r** was on top of them and all 1Kg 7:25
The **r** was three inches thick, 1Kg 7:26
He put the **r** near the right side 1Kg 7:39
r; the 12 oxen underneath the 1Kg 7:44
the 12 oxen underneath the **r**; 1Kg 7:44
He took the **r** from the bronze 2Kg 16:17
and the bronze **r**, which were 2Kg 25:13
pillars, the one **r**, and the 2Kg 25:16
which Solomon made the bronze **r**, 1Ch 18:8
Then he made the cast ⌊metal⌋ **r**, 2Ch 4:2
completely surrounding the **r**. 2Ch 4:3
in two rows when the **r** was cast. 2Ch 4:3
The **r** was on top of them and all 2Ch 4:4
The **r** was three inches thick, 2Ch 4:5
the **r** was used by the priests 2Ch 4:6
He put the **r** on the right side, 2Ch 4:10
The one **r** and the 12 oxen 2Ch 4:15
You made a **r** between the walls Is 22:11
carts and the bronze **r** that were Jr 52:17
pillars, the one **r**, and the 12 Jr 52:20

RESERVOIRS *(2)*
their water **r**—and they will Ex 7:19
I constructed **r** of water for Ec 2:6

RESHEPH *(1)*
his son **R**, his son Telah, 1Ch 7:25

RESIDE *(11)*
where you live and where I **r**; Nm 35:34
for I, the LORD, **r** among the Nm 35:34
the Jews who ⌊**r**⌋ in all the Est 8:5
are those who **r** in Your house, Ps 84:4
temples and **r** in the wilderness Jr 9:26
will till it and **r** in it." Jr 27:11
You who **r** by many waters, rich Jr 51:13
the foreigners who **r** in Israel Ezk 14:7
The crown will **r** in the LORD's Zch 6:14
that Christ's power may **r** in me. 2Co 12:9
how can God's love **r** in him? 1Jn 3:17

RESIDED *(3)*
who **r** within the clan of Judah. Jdg 17:7
Absalom **r** in Jerusalem two years 2Sm 14:28
the tent where He **r** among men. Ps 78:60

RESIDENCE *(11)*
a man sells a **r** in a walled city Lv 25:29
I will place My **r** among you, Lv 26:11
David took up **r** in the 2Sm 5:9
his servants' **r**, his attendants' 1Kg 10:5
David took up **r** in the 1Ch 11:7
a place for Your **r** forever. 2Ch 6:2
his servants' **r**, his attendants' 2Ch 9:4
be a royal **r** and to display my Dn 4:30
stand still in ⌊their⌋ lofty **r**, Hab 3:11
flesh and took up **r** among us. Jn 1:14
during this time of temporary **r**. 1Pt 1:17

RESIDENT *(44)*
where you are a **r** alien." Gn 21:23
I am a **r** alien among you. Gn 23:4
whether a foreign **r** or native of Ex 12:19
A temporary **r** or hired hand may Ex 12:45
a foreign **r** or oppress him, Ex 22:21
must not oppress a foreign **r**; Ex 23:9
as the foreign **r** may be Ex 23:12
for the poor and the foreign **r**; Lv 19:10
for the poor and the foreign **r**; Lv 23:22
the foreign **r** or the native. Lv 24:16
the foreign **r** and the native, Lv 24:22
as a foreigner or temporary **r**, Lv 25:35
as a hired hand or temporary **r**; Lv 25:40
temporary **r** ⌊living⌋ among you Lv 25:47
the foreign **r** and the native Nm 9:14
and the foreign **r** as a permanent Nm 15:15
whether native or foreign **r**, Nm 15:30
or temporary **r** among them, Nm 35:15
and his brother or a foreign **r**. Dt 1:16
the foreign **r**, giving him food Dt 10:18
may give it to a **r** alien within Dt 14:21
you, the foreign **r**, fatherless, Dt 14:29
the foreign **r**, the fatherless, Dt 16:11
the foreign **r**, the fatherless, Dt 16:14
were a foreign **r** in his land. Dt 23:7
to a foreign **r** ⌊or⌋ fatherless Dt 24:17
is to be left for the foreign **r**, Dt 24:19
will be for the foreign **r**, Dt 24:20
will be for the foreign **r**, Dt 24:21
and the foreign **r** among you will Dt 26:11
the foreign **r**, the fatherless, Dt 26:12
the foreign **r**, the fatherless, Dt 26:13
denies justice to a foreign **r**, Dt 27:19
foreign **r** among you will rise Dt 28:43
where you stay as a **r** alien.' Jr 35:7
r of the daughter of Dibon, Jr 48:18
highway and look, **r** of Aroer! Jr 48:19
and trap await you, **r** of Moab. Jr 48:43
even stay in it as a **r** alien. Jr 49:18
even stay in it as a **r** alien. Jr 49:33
even stay in it as a **r** alien. Jr 50:40
Edom, you **r** of the land of Uz Lm 4:21
and the foreign **r** is exploited Ezk 22:7
exploited the foreign **r**. Ezk 22:29

RESIDENTIAL *(1)*
for ⌊both⌋ **r** and open space. Ezk 48:15

RESIDENTS *(82)*
of the foreign **r** in Israel who Lv 22:18
and temporary **r** on My land. Lv 25:23
marched against the **r** of Debir Jdg 1:11
the **r** of Dor and its villages, Jdg 1:27
or the **r** of Ibleam and its Jdg 1:27
or the **r** of Megiddo and its Jdg 1:27
to drive out the **r** of Kitron Jdg 1:30
of Kitron or the **r** of Nahalol, Jdg 1:30
to drive out the **r** of Acco or of Jdg 1:31
drive out the **r** of Beth-shemesh Jdg 1:33
or the **r** of Beth-anath. Jdg 1:33
but the **r** of Beth-shemesh and Jdg 1:33
to the **r** of Kiriath-jearim 1Sm 6:21
the **r** of Jabesh-gilead heard 1Sm 31:11
were the potters and **r** of Netaim 1Ch 4:23
of Aijalon's **r** and who drove out 1Ch 8:13
and who drove out the **r** of Gath, 1Ch 8:13
indeed, and temporary **r** in 1Ch 16:19
because the **r** of the lands had 2Ch 15:5
disputes of the **r** of Jerusalem. 2Ch 19:8
against the **r** of Judah and Ezr 4:6
and temporary **r** in Canaan, Ps 105:12
r of Jerusalem and men of Judah, Is 5:3
men of Judah and **r** of Jerusalem. Jr 4:4
hand against the **r** of the land. Jr 6:12
the bones of the **r** of Jerusalem Jr 8:1
in it, the city and all its **r**. Jr 8:16
out the land's **r** at this time Jr 10:18
of Judah and the **r** of Jerusalem. Jr 11:2
of Judah and the **r** of Jerusalem. Jr 11:9
of Judah and the **r** of Jerusalem Jr 11:12
Because of the evil of its **r**, Jr 12:4
and all the **r** of Jerusalem— Jr 13:13
and all the **r** of Jerusalem who Jr 17:20
Judah, and the **r** of Jerusalem. Jr 17:25
Judah and to the **r** of Jerusalem: Jr 18:11
of Judah and **r** of Jerusalem. Jr 19:3
and to its **r**, making this city Jr 19:12
will strike the **r** of this city, Jr 21:6
You **r** of Lebanon, nestled among Jr 22:23
Jerusalem's **r** are like Gomorrah. Jr 23:14
and all the **r** of Jerusalem as Jr 25:2
against its **r**, and against all Jr 25:9
city, and on its **r**, for it is Jr 26:15
Judah, and the **r** of Jerusalem. Jr 32:32
of Judah and the **r** of Jerusalem: Jr 35:13
to all the **r** of Jerusalem all Jr 35:17
on them, on the **r** of Jerusalem, Jr 36:31
poured out on Jerusalem's **r**, Jr 42:18
destroy cities with their **r**. Jr 46:8
Live in the cliffs, **r** of Moab! Jr 48:28
Lie low, **r** of Dedan, for I will Jr 49:8
Lie low, **r** of Hazor—⌊this is⌋ Jr 49:30
and all the **r** of Chaldea for all Jr 51:24
those the **r** of Jerusalem have Ezk 11:15
says about the **r** of Jerusalem Ezk 12:19

will give up the **r** of Jerusalem. Ezk 15:6
where they live as foreign **r**, Ezk 20:38
of Judah, the **r** of Jerusalem, Dn 9:7
The **r** of Samaria will have Hs 10:5
and all the **r** of the land at Jl 1:14
Let all the **r** of the land Jl 2:1
nakedness, you **r** of Shaphir; Mc 1:11
the **r** of Zaanan will not come Mc 1:11
Though the **r** of Maroth anxiously Mc 1:12
the chariot, you **r** of Lachish. Mc 1:13
violence, and its **r** speak lies; Mc 6:12
place and the city's **r** an object Mc 6:16
against all the **r** of Jerusalem. Zph 1:4
Wail, you **r** of the Hollow, for Zph 1:11
yet come, the **r** of many cities; Zch 8:20
the **r** of one city will go to Zch 8:21
The **r** of Jerusalem are my Zch 12:5
of Jerusalem's **r** may not be Zch 12:7
of David and the **r** of Jerusalem, Zch 12:10
and for the **r** of Jerusalem, Zch 13:1
known to all the **r** of Jerusalem, Ac 1:19
men and all you **r** of Jerusalem, Ac 2:14
For the **r** of Jerusalem and their Ac 13:27
and temporary **r** on the earth. Heb 11:13
To the temporary **r** of the 1Pt 1:1
and temporary **r** to abstain 1Pt 2:11

RESIDES *(12)*

If a foreigner **r** with you and Ex 12:48
the foreigner who **r** among you." Ex 12:49
the foreigner who **r** among you. Lv 16:29
If a foreigner **r** with you and Nm 9:14
When a foreigner **r** with you or Nm 15:14
the foreigner who **r** with you." Nm 15:16
foreigner who **r** among them will Nm 15:26
the foreigner who **r** among them. Nm 19:10
Strength **r** in his neck, and Jb 41:22
the place where Your glory **r**. Ps 26:8
Your instruction **r** within me." Ps 40:8
Wisdom **r** in the heart of the Pr 14:33

RESIDING *(7)*

give the land where you are **r**— Gn 17:8
the foreigners **r** within a town Dt 24:14
of Ephraim but was **r** in Gibeah, Jdg 19:16
For I am a foreigner **r** with You, Ps 39:12
the foreigners **r** there spent Ac 17:21
with all the Jews **r** there, Ac 22:12
has eternal life **r** in him. 1Jn 3:15

RESIN *(2)*

gum, balsam, and **r**, going down Gn 37:25
aromatic gum and **r**, pistachios Gn 43:11

RESIST *(12)*

could no longer **r** their enemies. Jdg 2:14
around him to **r** Rehoboam son 2Ch 13:7
one person, two can **r** him. Ec 4:12
troops will not be able to **r**. Dn 11:15
I tell you, don't **r** an evildoer. Mt 5:39
will be able to **r** or contradict. Lk 21:15
For who can **r** His will?" Rm 9:19
be able to **r** in the evil day, Eph 6:13
so these also **r** the truth, 2Tm 3:8
r the Devil, and he will flee Jms 4:7
man; he does not **r** you. Jms 5:6
R him, firm in the faith, 1Pt 5:9

RESISTED *(4)*

They stubbornly **r**, stiffened Neh 9:29
But when they **r** and blasphemed, Ac 18:6
as Jannes and Jambres **r** Moses, 2Tm 3:8
you have not yet **r** to the point Heb 12:4

RESISTING *(1)*

are always **r** the Holy Spirit; Ac 7:51

RESISTS *(3)*

the one who **r** the authority is Rm 13:2
God **r** the proud, but gives grace Jms 4:6
because God **r** the proud, but 1Pt 5:5

RESOLUTION *(1)*

be ranting and raving but no **r**. Pr 29:9

RESOLVE *(5)*

for a man to **r** a dispute, Pr 20:3
All who **r** to go to Egypt to live Jr 42:17
He will **r** to come with the force Dn 11:17
with a firm **r** of the heart— Ac 11:23
also with the same **r**— 1Pt 4:1

RESOLVED *(8)*

afraid, so he **r** to seek the LORD 2Ch 20:3
I am **r** to obey Your statutes to Ps 119:112
r, "I will be wise," but it was Ec 7:23
you are firmly **r** to go to Egypt Jr 42:15
those who have **r** to go to the Jr 44:12
As I **r** to treat you badly when Zch 8:14
so I have **r** again in these days Zch 8:15
Paul **r** in the Spirit to pass Ac 19:21

RESOLVES *(1)*

rest unless he **r** this today." Ru 3:18

RESOUND *(4)*

the sea and everything in it **r**; 1Ch 16:32
the sea and all that fills it **r**. Ps 96:11
and those who live in it, **r**. Ps 98:7
and destruction **r** in her. Jr 6:7

RESOUNDING *(1)*

Praise Him with **r** cymbals; Ps 150:5

RESOUNDS *(1)*

the tumult of their voice **r**, Jr 51:55

RESOURCES *(1)*

strangers will drain your **r**, Pr 5:10

RESPECT *(25)*

Each of you is to **r** his mother Lv 19:3
LORD, "Don't **r** their offering. Nm 16:15
showing no **r** for the old and not Dt 28:50
he's showing **r** for your father? 2Sm 10:3
If I did not have **r** for King 2Kg 3:14
he's showing **r** for your father? 1Ch 19:3
divisions with **r** to each gate, 2Ch 8:14
in Israel with **r** to God and His 2Ch 24:16
elders are shown no **r**. Lm 5:12
'They will **r** my son,' he said. Mt 21:37
saying, 'They will **r** my son.' Mk 12:6
who didn't fear God or **r** man. Lk 18:2
I don't fear God or **r** man, Lk 18:4
Perhaps they will **r** him.' Lk 20:13
extremely religious in every **r**. Ac 17:22
r to those you owe respect, Rm 13:7
respect to those you owe **r**, Rm 13:7
and not in **r** to someone else. Gl 6:4
the wife is to **r** her husband. Eph 5:33
be worthy of **r**, not hypocritical 1Tm 3:8
be worthy of **r**, not slanderers, 1Tm 3:11
masters to be worthy of all **r**, 1Tm 6:1
worthy of **r**, sensible, and sound Ti 2:2
to your masters with all **r**, 1Pt 2:18
do this with gentleness and **r**, 1Pt 3:16

RESPECTABLE *(1)*

sensible, **r**, hospitable, an able 1Tm 3:2

RESPECTED *(7)*

and **r** men from each of your Dt 1:13
tribes, wise and **r** men, and set Dt 1:15
in this city who is highly **r**; 1Sm 9:6
The priests are not **r**; Lm 4:16
the law who was **r** by all the Ac 5:34
discipline us, and we **r** them. Heb 12:9
Marriage must be **r** by all, Heb 13:4

RESPECTFULLY *(1)*

his sons to deal **r** with the holy Lv 22:2

RESPECTIVE *(1)*

under their **r** banners beside Nm 2:2

RESPECTS *(2)*

but the one who **r** a command will Pr 13:13
He no longer **r** your offerings Mal 2:13

RESPLENDENT *(1)*

You are **r** and majestic ⌊coming Ps 76:4

RESPOND *(24)*

and will not **r** to the evidence Ex 4:8
and did not **r** to a public call Lv 5:1
You are to **r** by saying in the Dt 26:5
But she did not **r**, and did not 1Sm 4:20
advise me to **r** to these people? 1Kg 12:6
and if you **r** to them by speaking 1Kg 12:7
advise me to **r** to this people? 2Ch 10:6
Hezekiah didn't **r** according to 2Ch 32:25
will speak, and You can **r** to me. Jb 13:22
I will not **r** to him with your Jb 32:14
I must open my lips and **r**. Jb 32:20
he understands, he doesn't **r**. Pr 29:19
They all **r** to you, saying: Is 14:10
to us? You will **r** to them: Just Jr 5:19
Then they will **r** to you: Jr 13:12
LORD? you will **r** to them: What Jr 23:33
Therefore I will **r** with wrath. Ezk 8:18
I will **r** to the house of Israel Ezk 36:37
There she will **r** as ⌊she did⌋ in Hs 2:15
that day I will **r**—the LORD's Hs 2:21
I will **r** to the sky, and it will Hs 2:21
and it will **r** to the earth. Hs 2:21
The earth will **r** to the grain, Hs 2:22
and they will **r** to Jezreel. Hs 2:22

RESPONDED *(73)*

She **r**, 'The daughter of Bethuel Gn 24:47
But he **r** to them, "Do not delay Gn 24:56
But Pharaoh **r**, "Who is the LORD Ex 5:2
Pharaoh **r**, "I will let you go Ex 8:28
Moses **r**, "You must also let us Ex 10:25
Then all the people **r** together, Ex 19:8
But Moses **r** to the LORD, "The Ex 19:23
Moses **r** to the people, "Don't be Ex 20:20
all the people **r** with a single Ex 24:3
They **r**, "We will do and obey Ex 24:7
not go," Moses **r** to Him, "don't Ex 33:15
And the LORD **r**: "Look, I am Ex 34:10
his youth, **r**, "Moses, my lord Nm 11:28
men who had gone up with him **r**, Nm 13:31
The LORD **r**, "I have pardoned Nm 14:20
But Moses **r**, "Why are you going Nm 14:41
But Balaam **r** to the servants of Nm 22:18
Eli **r**, "Go in peace, and may the 1Sm 1:17
Samuel **r**, "Speak, for Your 1Sm 3:10
Eli **r**, "He is the LORD. 1Sm 3:18
Saul **r**, "Am I not a Benjaminite 1Sm 9:21
from anyone's hand," they **r**. 1Sm 12:4
His armor-bearer **r**, "Do what is 1Sm 14:7
David **r**, "Who am I, and what 1Sm 18:18
"No!" Jonathan **r**. "If I ever 1Sm 20:9
"They will," the LORD **r**. 1Sm 23:12
Saul **r**, "I have sinned. 1Sm 26:21
r to Nathan, "I have sinned 2Sm 12:13
the men of Judah **r** to the men of 2Sm 19:42
King David **r** by saying, "Call in 1Kg 1:28
king **r**, "Give the living baby 1Kg 3:27
Then the king **r** to the man of 1Kg 13:6
⌊Ahab **r**⌋,"On the basis of this 1Kg 20:34
Elijah **r** to the captain of the 2Kg 1:10
Elijah **r**, "If I am a man of God, 2Kg 1:12
Elisha **r**, "As the LORD of Hosts 2Kg 3:14
Naaman **r**, "If not, please let 2Kg 5:17
right-hand man, **r** to the man of 2Kg 7:2
But one of his servants **r**, 2Kg 7:13
He **r**, "He told me you are sure 2Kg 8:14
Joram **r**, "Choose a rider and 2Kg 9:17
r, "Take a bow and arrows. 2Kg 13:15
Jehiel, an Elamite, **r** to Ezra: Ezr 10:2
all the assembly **r** with a loud Ezr 10:12
They **r**: "We will return ⌊these Neh 5:12
is," Jeremiah **r**, and he Jr 37:17
son of Ahikam **r** to Johanan son Jr 40:16
arrogant men **r** to Jeremiah, Jr 43:2
But Jeremiah **r** to all the people Jr 44:20
Then Daniel **r** with tact and Dn 2:14
Then the Angel of the LORD **r**, Zch 1:12
He **r**, "It's a measuring basket Zch 5:6
Jesus **r**, "Simon son of Jonah, Mt 16:17
Then Peter **r** to Him, "Look, we Mt 19:27
them something to eat," He **r**. Mk 6:37
But his mother **r**, "No! Lk 1:60
John **r**, "Master, we saw someone Lk 9:49
And He **r** to them, "Do you think Lk 13:2
on the Sabbath, **r** by telling the Lk 13:14
But Jesus **r**, "No more of this!" Lk 22:51
Jesus **r** to him, "Do you believe Jn 1:50
John **r**, "No one can receive a Jn 3:27
But Jesus **r** to them, "My Father Jn 5:17
the crowd **r**. "Who wants to Jn 7:20
Then the Pharisees **r** to them: Jn 7:47
Jesus **r**, "I assure you: Jn 8:34
The Jews **r** to Him, "Aren't we Jn 8:48
Jesus **r**, "This voice came, not Jn 12:30
Jesus **r** to them, "Do you now Jn 16:31
Pilate **r**, "Take Him and crucify Jn 19:6
Thomas **r** to Him, "My Lord and Jn 20:28
greatness of God. Then Peter **r**, Ac 10:46
they stopped speaking, James **r**: Ac 15:13

RESPONDS *(2)*

drink,' and who **r**, 'Drink, and Gn 24:14
who **r** to me, 'Drink, and I'll Gn 24:44

RESPONSE *(10)*

But there was no **r**. Jdg 19:28
In **r** the king stood up, tore his 2Sm 13:31
But in **r**, Ittai vowed to the 2Sm 15:21
When Ben-hadad heard this **r**, 1Kg 20:12
repeated Mordecai's **r** to Esther. Est 4:9
Esther's **r** was reported to Est 4:12
but get no **r**; I call for help, Jb 19:7

r, Jesus asked the law experts Lk 14:3
they had nothing to say in **r**. Ac 4:14
Now in like **r**—I speak as to 2Co 6:13

RESPONSIBILITIES (9)

to carry out their priestly **r**, Nm 3:10
brothers to fulfill **r** at the Nm 8:26
your priestly **r** for everything Nm 18:7
the boy's **r** and mission be?" Jdg 13:12
to carry out their **r** to the tent 1Ch 23:32
over their **r** to offer praise 2Ch 8:14
service in their **r** according to 2Ch 31:16
by their **r** in their divisions; 2Ch 31:17
to their **r** and encouraged 2Ch 35:2

RESPONSIBILITY (5)

their **r** was service related Nm 7:9
can't bear ⌊the **r** for⌋ you on my Dt 1:9
be absolved of **r** for bloodshed. Dt 21:8
for this matter is your **r**, Ezr 10:4
Israel—will be the prince's **r**. Ezk 45:17

RESPONSIBLE (23)

You are **r** for my suffering! Gn 16:5
and he was **r** for everything that Gn 39:22
I will be **r** for him. Gn 43:9
were 8,600 **r** for the duties Nm 3:28
of those **r** for the duties Nm 3:32
all that they are **r** to carry. Nm 4:27
is what they are **r** to carry as Nm 4:31
items that they are **r** to carry. Nm 4:32
house will be **r** for sin against Nm 18:1
sons will be **r** for sin involving Nm 18:1
will be **r** for her commitment." Nm 30:15
time I won't be **r** when I harm Jdg 15:3
I myself am **r** for the lives of 1Sm 22:22
relatives were **r** for preparing 1Ch 9:32
being **r** for the courts and the 1Ch 23:28
They were **r** for the distribution Neh 13:13
r for every madman who acts like Jr 29:26
I will hold you **r** for his blood. Ezk 3:18
I will hold you **r** for his blood. Ezk 3:20
I will hold you **r** for his blood. Ezk 33:8
will make them **r** for the duties Ezk 44:14
may be held **r** for the blood of Lk 11:50
this generation will be held **r**. Lk 11:51

REST (305)

The ark came to **r** in the seventh Gn 8:4
but the **r** fled to the mountains. Gn 14:10
your feet and **r** yourselves under Gn 18:4
shepherding the **r** of Laban's Gn 30:36
The **r** of you will be imprisoned Gn 42:16
while the **r** of you go and take Gn 42:19
the **r** of you will be blameless. Gn 44:10
The **r** of you can go in peace to Gn 44:17
they **r** on the head of Joseph, Gn 49:26
become like the **r** of his skin. Ex 4:7
and all the **r** of the chariots Ex 14:7
'Tomorrow is a day of complete **r**, Ex 16:23
you are to let it **r** and leave it Ex 23:11
six days but **r** on the seventh Ex 23:12
your ox and your donkey may **r**, Ex 23:12
out all the ⌊**r**⌋ of the blood at Ex 29:12
must be a Sabbath of complete **r**, Ex 31:15
you⌋, and I will give you **r**." Ex 33:14
but you must **r** on the seventh Ex 34:21
you must even **r** during plowing Ex 34:21
of complete **r** to the LORD. Ex 35:2
But the **r** of the grain offering Lv 2:3
But the **r** of the grain offering Lv 2:10
pour out the **r** of the bull's Lv 4:7
⌊the **r**⌋ of the bull—he must Lv 4:12
pour out the **r** of the blood at Lv 4:18
The **r** of its blood he must pour Lv 4:25
pour out the **r** of its blood at Lv 4:30
pour out the **r** of its blood at Lv 4:34
while the **r** of the blood is to Lv 5:9
The **r** will belong to the priest, Lv 5:13
his sons may eat the **r** of it. Lv 6:16
eyebrows, and the **r** of his hair. Lv 14:9
a Sabbath of complete **r** for you, Lv 16:31
must be a Sabbath of complete **r**, Lv 23:3
are to have a day of complete **r**, Lv 23:24
a Sabbath of complete **r** for you, Lv 23:32
be complete **r** on the first day Lv 23:39
day and complete **r** on the eighth Lv 23:39
of complete **r** for the land Lv 25:4
year of complete **r** for the land. Lv 25:5
the land will **r** and make up for Lv 26:34
will have the **r** it did not have Lv 26:35
Levites from the **r** of the Nm 8:14
When it came to **r**, he would say: Nm 10:36
of Manasseh the **r** of Gilead and Dt 3:13
LORD gives **r** to your brothers Dt 3:20
female slaves may **r** as you do. Dt 5:14
and He gives you **r** from all the Dt 12:10
remember for the **r** of your life Dt 16:3
your God gives you **r** from all Dt 25:19
and the **r** of his children, Dt 28:54
You are about to **r** with your Dt 31:16
May these **r** on the head of Dt 33:16
LORD your God will give you **r**, Jos 1:13
the LORD gives our brothers **r**, Jos 1:15
to **r** in the Jordan's waters, Jos 3:13
But as for the **r** of you, don't Jos 10:19
this, the land had **r** from war. Jos 11:23
the **r** of the kingdom of Sihon Jos 13:27
this, the land had **r** from war. Jos 14:15
was for the **r** of Manasseh's Jos 17:2
belonged to the **r** of Manasseh's Jos 17:6
LORD gave them **r** on every side Jos 21:44
He has given your brothers **r**, Jos 22:4
had given Israel **r** from all the Jos 23:1
cling to the **r** of these nations Jos 23:12
all the **r** of the people knelt Jdg 7:6
that I won't **r** until I have Jdg 15:7
he won't **r** unless he resolves Ru 3:18
sent the **r** of the troops away, 1Sm 13:2
destroyed all the **r** of the 1Sm 15:8
God, but the **r** we destroyed." 1Sm 15:15
had given him **r** on every side 2Sm 7:1
I will give you **r** from all your 2Sm 7:11
comes and you **r** with your 2Sm 7:12
He placed the **r** of the forces 2Sm 10:10
assemble the **r** of the troops, 2Sm 12:28
Then all ⌊the **r** of⌋ the king's 2Sm 13:29
has now given me **r** all around; 1Kg 5:4
He has given **r** to His people 1Kg 8:56
The **r** of the events of Solomon's 1Kg 11:41
and to the **r** of the people, 1Kg 12:23
As for the **r** of the events of 1Kg 14:19
r of the events of Rehoboam's 1Kg 14:29
The **r** of the events of Abijam's 1Kg 15:7
The **r** of all the events of Asa's 1Kg 15:23
The **r** of the events of Nadab's 1Kg 15:31
The **r** of the events of Baasha's 1Kg 16:5
The **r** of the events of Elah's 1Kg 16:14
The **r** of the events of Zimri's 1Kg 16:20
The **r** of the events of Omri's 1Kg 16:27
The **r** of the events of Ahab's 1Kg 22:39
The **r** of the events of 1Kg 22:45
from the land the **r** of the male 1Kg 22:46
The **r** of the events of Ahaziah's 2Kg 1:18
your sons can live on the **r**." 2Kg 4:7
The **r** of the events of Jehoram's 2Kg 8:23
the **r** of the events of Jehu's 2Kg 10:34
The **r** of the events of Joash's 2Kg 12:19
r of the events of Jehoahaz's 2Kg 13:8
The **r** of the events of Jehoash's 2Kg 13:12
The **r** of the events of Jehoash's 2Kg 14:15
The **r** of the events of Amaziah's 2Kg 14:18
r of the events of Jeroboam's 2Kg 14:28
The **r** of the events of Azariah's 2Kg 15:6
As for the **r** of the events of 2Kg 15:11
As for the **r** of the events of 2Kg 15:15
The **r** of the events of Menahem's 2Kg 15:21
As for the **r** of the events of 2Kg 15:26
As for the **r** of the events of 2Kg 15:31
The **r** of the events of Jotham's 2Kg 15:36
The **r** of the events of Ahaz's 2Kg 16:19
r of the events of Hezekiah's 2Kg 20:20
r of the events of Manasseh's 2Kg 21:17
The **r** of the events of Amon's 2Kg 21:25
So he said, "Let him **r**. 2Kg 23:18
The **r** of the events of Josiah's 2Kg 23:28
The **r** of the events of 2Kg 24:5
deported the **r** of the people who 2Kg 25:11
and the **r** of the population. 2Kg 25:11
over the **r** of the people he left 2Kg 25:22
Babylon for the **r** of his life. 2Kg 25:29
each day, for the **r** of his life. 2Kg 25:30
after the ark came to **r** there. 1Ch 6:31
To the **r** of the Kohathites, 1Ch 6:61
given⌋ to the **r** of the families 1Ch 6:70
r of the Merarites ⌊received⌋ 1Ch 6:77
Joab restored the **r** of the city. 1Ch 11:8
All the **r** of Israel was also of 1Ch 12:38
to the **r** of our relatives 1Ch 13:2
and the **r** who were chosen and 1Ch 16:41
He placed the **r** of the forces 1Ch 19:11
be a man of **r**. I will give him 1Ch 22:9
I will give him **r** from all his 1Ch 22:9
He given you **r** on every side? 1Ch 22:18
has given **r** to His people, 1Ch 23:25
As for the **r** of Levi's sons: 1Ch 24:20
and to the **r** of the people: 2Ch 11:3
The **r** of the events of Abijah's 2Ch 13:22
because the LORD gave him **r**. 2Ch 14:6
and He gave us **r** on every side." 2Ch 14:7
LORD gave them **r** on every side. 2Ch 15:15
God gave him **r** on every side. 2Ch 20:30
The **r** of the events of 2Ch 20:34
presented the **r** of the money to 2Ch 24:14
The **r** of the events of Amaziah's 2Ch 25:26
wrote about the **r** of the events 2Ch 26:22
As for the **r** of the events of 2Ch 27:7
for the **r** of his deeds and all 2Ch 28:26
He gave them **r** on every side. 2Ch 32:22
As for the **r** of the events of 2Ch 32:32
r of the events of Manasseh's 2Ch 33:18
The **r** of the events of Josiah's 2Ch 35:26
The **r** of the deeds of Jehoiakim, 2Ch 36:8
its Sabbath **r** all the days 2Ch 36:21
and ⌊the **r** of⌋ Israel ⌊settled⌋ Ezr 2:70
and the **r** of their brothers, Ezr 3:8
Tabeel and the **r** of his Ezr 4:7
and the **r** of their colleagues— Ezr 4:9
the **r** of the peoples whom the Ezr 4:10
and the **r** of their colleagues Ezr 4:17
and the **r** of the exiles, Ezr 6:16
brothers with the **r** of the Ezr 7:18
or the **r** of those who would be Neh 2:16
and the **r** of the people, Neh 4:14
and the **r** of the people: Neh 4:19
and the **r** of our enemies heard Neh 6:1
The **r** of the people gave 20,000 Neh 7:72
The **r** of the people—the Neh 10:28
the **r** of the people cast lots Neh 11:1
r of Israel, the priests, and Neh 11:20
they done in the **r** of the royal Est 9:12
The **r** of the Jews in the royal Est 9:16
be asleep. Then I would be at **r** Jb 3:13
and there the weary find **r**. Jb 3:17
I have no **r**, for trouble comes. Jb 3:26
him and let him **r** so that he can Jb 14:6
the dew will **r** on my branches Jb 29:19
am churning within and cannot **r**; Jb 30:27
by night, yet I have no **r**. Ps 22:2
May Your faithful love **r** on us, Ps 33:22
I would fly away and find **r**. Ps 55:6
I am at **r** in God alone; Ps 62:1
R in God alone, my soul, for my Ps 62:5
⌊the **r**⌋ began to seek Him; Ps 78:34
would soon **r** in the silence ⌊of Ps 94:17
'They will not enter My **r**.' " Ps 95:11
Return to your **r**, my soul, for Ps 116:7
You observe my travels and my **r**; Ps 139:3
little folding of the arms to **r**, Pr 6:10
will come to **r** in the assembly Pr 21:16
little folding of the arms to **r**, Pr 24:33
at night, his mind does not **r**. Ec 2:23
Better one handful with **r**, Ec 4:6
it has more **r** than he. Ec 6:5
puts great offenses to **r**. Ec 10:4
evening do not let your hand **r**, Ec 11:6
Where do you let them **r** at noon? Sg 1:7
of the LORD will **r** on Him— Is 11:2
not let ⌊their flocks⌋ **r** there. Is 13:20
LORD gives you **r** from your pain, Is 14:3
All the earth is calm and at **r**; Is 14:7
even there you will have no **r**!" Is 23:12
power will **r** on this mountain Is 25:10
is the place of **r**, let the weary Is 28:12
place of rest, let the weary **r**; Is 28:12
deprived of the **r** of my years. Is 38:10
or his idol with the **r** of it. Is 44:17
detestable with the **r** of it, Is 44:19
they will **r** on their beds— Is 57:2
remind the LORD, no **r** for you! Is 62:6
Do not give Him **r** until He Is 62:7
Spirit of the LORD gave them **r**. Is 63:14
it and find **r** for yourselves. Jr 6:16
they never **r** their feet. Jr 14:10
The **r** of them I will give over Jr 15:9
and the **r** of the articles that Jr 27:19
Jerusalem to the **r** of the elders Jr 29:1

⌊When⌋ Israel went to find **r**, Jr 31:2
where shepherds may **r** flocks. Jr 33:12
and all the **r** of the officials Jr 39:3
to Babylon the **r** of the people— Jr 39:9
along with the **r** of the people Jr 39:9
groaning and have found no **r**. Jr 45:3
How can it **r** when the LORD has Jr 47:7
He might bring **r** to the earth Jr 50:34
as well as the **r** of the people Jr 52:15
and the **r** of the craftsmen. Jr 52:15
Babylon for the **r** of his life. Jr 52:33
death, for the **r** of his life. Jr 52:34
nations but finds no place to **r**. Lm 1:3
no relief and your eyes no **r**. Lm 2:18
tired, and no one offers us **r**. Lm 5:5
down and be laid to **r** with the Ezk 32:19
hordes will be laid to **r** among Ezk 32:32
trample the **r** of the pasture Ezk 34:18
also muddy the **r** with your feet? Ezk 34:18
for the **r** of the nations Ezk 36:3
mockery to the **r** of the nations Ezk 36:4
against the **r** of the nations Ezk 36:5
a blessing may **r** on your homes. Ezk 44:30
but give the ⌊**r** of the⌋ land to Ezk 45:8
As for the **r** of the tribes: Ezk 48:23
killed with the **r** of Babylon's Dn 2:18
As for the **r** of the beasts, Dn 7:12
you will **r**, then rise to your Dn 12:13
enable the people to **r** securely. Hs 2:18
I will kill the **r** of them with Am 9:1
for this is not your place of **r**, Mc 2:10
then the **r** of His brothers will Mc 5:3
an arrogant man is never at **r**. Hab 2:5
let the **r** devour each other's Zch 11:9
but the **r** of the people will not Zch 14:2
burdened, and I will give you **r**. Mt 11:28
you will find **r** for yourselves. Mt 11:29
looking for **r** but doesn't find Mt 12:43
Later the **r** of the virgins also Mt 25:11
But the **r** said, "Let's see if Mt 27:49
had gone to their **r** were raised. Mt 27:52
a remote place and **r** a while." Mk 6:31
went and reported it to the **r**, Mk 16:13
but to the **r** it is in parables, Lk 8:10
there, your peace will **r** on him; Lk 10:6
waterless places looking for **r**, Lk 11:24
not finding **r**, it then says, Lk 11:24
thing, why worry about the **r**? Lk 12:26
to the Eleven and to all the **r**. Lk 24:9
my flesh will **r** in hope, Ac 2:26
Peter and the **r** of the apostles Ac 2:37
of the **r** dared to join them, Ac 5:13
The **r** were to follow, some on Ac 27:44
the **r** of those on the island who Ac 28:9
as among the **r** of the Gentiles. Rm 1:13
a Jew, and **r** in the law, Rm 2:17
find it. The **r** were hardened, Rm 11:7
But to the **r** I, not the Lord, 1Co 7:12
had no **r** in my spirit because I 2Co 2:13
into Macedonia, we had no **r**. 2Co 7:5
sinned before and to all the **r**: 2Co 13:2
Then the **r** of the Jews joined Gl 2:13
Clement and the **r** of my Php 4:3
you will not grieve like the **r**, 1Th 4:13
sleep, like the **r**, but we must 1Th 5:6
to reward⌋ with **r** you who are 2Th 1:7
so that the **r** will also be 1Tm 5:20
"They will not enter My **r**." Heb 3:11
they would not enter His **r**," Heb 3:18
remains of entering His **r**, Heb 4:1
we who have believed enter the **r** Heb 4:3
anger, they will not enter My **r**. Heb 4:3
They will never enter My **r**. Heb 4:5
For if Joshua had given them **r**, Heb 4:8
A Sabbath **r** remains, therefore, Heb 4:9
entered His **r** has rested from Heb 4:10
every effort to enter that **r**, Heb 4:11
also do with the **r** of the 2Pt 3:16
I say to the **r** of you in Rv 2:24
were told to **r** a little while Rv 6:11
r of the people, who were not Rv 9:20
war against the **r** of her Rv 12:17
There is no **r** day or night for Rv 14:11
let them **r** from their labors, Rv 14:13
The **r** were killed with the sword Rv 19:21
The **r** of the dead did not come Rv 20:5

RESTED *(57)*

and He **r** on the seventh day from Gn 2:2
for on it He **r** from His work of Gn 2:3
So the people **r** on the seventh Ex 16:30
then He **r** on the seventh day. Ex 20:11
seventh day He **r** and was Ex 31:17
because the cloud **r** on it, Ex 40:35
As the Spirit **r** on them, they Nm 11:25
the Spirit **r** on them—they were Nm 11:26
except that she **r** a little in Ru 2:7
exhausted, so they **r** there. 2Sm 16:14
Then David **r** with his fathers 1Kg 2:10
chambers that ⌊**r**⌋ on 45 pillars, 1Kg 7:3
that David **r** with his fathers 1Kg 11:21
Solomon **r** with his fathers and 1Kg 11:43
He **r** with his fathers, and his 1Kg 14:20
Rehoboam **r** with his fathers and 1Kg 14:31
Abijam **r** with his fathers and 1Kg 15:8
Then Asa **r** with his fathers and 1Kg 15:24
Baasha **r** with his fathers and 1Kg 16:6
Omri **r** with his fathers and was 1Kg 16:28
Ahab **r** with his fathers, and his 1Kg 22:40
Jehoshaphat **r** with his fathers 1Kg 22:50
Jehoram **r** with his fathers and 2Kg 8:24
Jehu **r** with his fathers, and he 2Kg 10:35
Jehoahaz **r** with his fathers, 2Kg 13:9
Jehoash **r** with his fathers, 2Kg 13:13
Jehoash **r** with his fathers, 2Kg 14:16
the king **r** with his fathers 2Kg 14:22
Jeroboam **r** with his fathers, 2Kg 14:29
Azariah **r** with his fathers, 2Kg 15:7
Menahem **r** with his fathers, 2Kg 15:22
Jotham **r** with his fathers, 2Kg 15:38
Ahaz **r** with his fathers and was 2Kg 16:20
Hezekiah **r** with his fathers, 2Kg 20:21
Manasseh **r** with his fathers and 2Kg 21:18
Jehoiakim **r** with his fathers, 2Kg 24:6
Solomon **r** with his fathers and 2Ch 9:31
Rehoboam **r** with his fathers and 2Ch 12:16
Abijah **r** with his fathers and 2Ch 14:1
his reign and **r** with his fathers 2Ch 16:13
Jehoshaphat **r** with his fathers 2Ch 21:1
the king **r** with his fathers 2Ch 26:2
Uzziah **r** with his fathers, 2Ch 26:23
Jotham **r** with his fathers and 2Ch 27:9
Ahaz **r** with his fathers and was 2Ch 28:27
Hezekiah **r** with his fathers and 2Ch 32:33
Manasseh **r** with his fathers, 2Ch 33:20
Jerusalem and **r** there for three Ezr 8:32
of Adar and **r** on the fourteenth Est 9:17
They **r** on the fifteenth day of Est 9:18
God's friendship **r** on my tent, Jb 29:4
for their sins **r** on their bones, Ezk 32:27
And they **r** on the Sabbath Lk 23:56
like a dove, and He **r** on Him. Jn 1:32
to them and **r** on each one of Ac 2:3
seventh day God **r** from all His Heb 4:4
His rest has **r** from his own Heb 4:10

RESTFUL *(1)*

and in safe and **r** dwellings. Is 32:18

RESTING *(20)*

dove found no **r** place for her Gn 8:9
He saw that his **r** place was good Gn 49:15
to seek a **r** place for them, Nm 10:33
yet come into the **r** place and Dt 12:9
there will be no **r** place for the Dt 28:65
a house as a **r** place for the ark 1Ch 28:2
God, ⌊come⌋ to Your **r** place, You 2Ch 6:41
my cry for help find no **r** place. Jb 16:18
LORD, come to Your **r** place, You Ps 132:8
This is My **r** place forever; Ps 132:14
His **r** place will be glorious. Is 11:10
be delivered by returning and **r**; Is 30:15
and will find a **r** place for Is 34:14
have forgotten their **r** place. Jr 50:6
they prepare a **r** place for Elam Ezk 32:25
and Damascus is its **r** place— Zch 9:1
Are you still sleeping and **r**? Mt 26:45
Are you still sleeping and **r**? Mk 14:41
see the Spirit descending and **r** Jn 1:33
the Lord, or what is My **r** place? Ac 7:49

RESTITUTION *(48)*

A thief must make full **r**. Ex 22:3
must make full **r** for what was Ex 22:6
man does not have to make **r**. Ex 22:11
he must make **r** to its owner. Ex 22:12
not have to make **r** for the torn Ex 22:13
it, the man must make full **r**. Ex 22:14
the man does not have to make **r**. Ex 22:15
must bring his **r** for the sin he Lv 5:6
young pigeons as **r** for his sin— Lv 5:7
he must bring his **r** offering to Lv 5:15
shekel, as a **r** offering. Lv 5:15
He must make **r** for his sin Lv 5:16
with the ram of the **r** offering, Lv 5:16
your valuation as a **r** offering Lv 5:18
It is a **r** offering; Lv 5:19
must make full **r** for it and add Lv 6:5
he must bring his **r** offering to Lv 6:6
as a **r** offering to the priest. Lv 6:6
sin offering and the **r** offering. Lv 6:17
is the law of the **r** offering; Lv 7:1
The **r** offering must be Lv 7:2
it is a **r** offering. Lv 7:5
The **r** offering is like the sin Lv 7:7
sin offering, the **r** offering, Lv 7:37
and present it as a **r** offering, Lv 14:12
the **r** offering belongs to the Lv 14:13
blood from the **r** offering and Lv 14:14
of the blood of the **r** offering. Lv 14:17
male lamb for a **r** offering to be Lv 14:21
the male lamb for the **r** offering Lv 14:24
male lamb for the **r** offering, Lv 14:25
blood of the **r** offering and put Lv 14:25
as the blood of the **r** offering. Lv 14:28
bring his ram as a **r** offering to Lv 19:21
the ram of the **r** offering for Lv 19:22
the penalty of **r** if the people Lv 22:16
an animal is to make **r** for it, Lv 24:18
an animal is to make **r** for it, Lv 24:21
male lamb as a **r** offering. Nm 6:12
or **r** offering will be most holy Nm 18:9
money from the **r** offering and 2Kg 12:16
mock at making **r**, but there is Pr 14:9
When You make Him a **r** offering, Is 53:10
makes **r** for what he has stolen, Ezk 33:15
sin offering, and **r** offering. Ezk 40:39
offerings, and **r** offerings—for Ezk 42:13
offering, and the **r** offering. Ezk 44:29
will boil the **r** offering and the Ezk 46:20

RESTLESS *(5)*

You will be a **r** wanderer on the Gn 4:12
and become a **r** wanderer on the Gn 4:14
I am **r** and in turmoil with my Ps 55:2
How long will you be **r**? Jr 47:6
It is a **r** evil, full of deadly Jms 3:8

RESTORATION *(3)*

and the **r** of the LORD's temple, 2Ch 24:27
times of the **r** of all things, Ac 3:21
imposed until the time of **r**. Heb 9:10

RESTORE *(73)*

up your head and **r** you to your Gn 40:13
then He will **r** your fortunes, Dt 30:3
Now **r** it peaceably." Jdg 11:13
who went to **r** his control at the 2Sm 8:3
I will **r** to you all your 2Sm 9:7
of Israel will **r** my father's 2Sm 16:3
affliction and **r** goodness to me 2Sm 16:12
be the last to **r** the king to his 2Sm 19:11
you be the last to **r** the king?' 2Sm 19:12
May You **r** them to the land You 1Kg 8:34
of Israel to **r** the kingdom to 1Kg 12:21
from your father I **r** to you, 1Kg 20:34
her, saying, "**R** all that was 2Kg 8:6
May You **r** them to the land You 2Ch 6:25
against Israel to **r** the reign to 2Ch 11:1
to repair and **r** the temple; 2Ch 34:10
Can they **r** ⌊it⌋ by themselves? Neh 4:2
your behalf and **r** the home where Jb 8:6
and God will **r** his righteousness Jb 33:26
R brightness to my eyes; Ps 13:3
R the joy of Your salvation to Ps 51:12
us; You have been angry. **R** us! Ps 60:1
R us, God; look ⌊on us⌋ with Ps 80:3
R us, God of Hosts; look ⌊on us⌋ Ps 80:7
R us, LORD God of Hosts; Ps 80:19
R our fortunes, LORD, like Ps 126:4
will **r** your judges to what they Is 1:26
LORD will **r** Tyre and she will Is 23:17
rebuilt, and I will **r** her ruins; Is 44:26
the people, to **r** the land, to Is 49:8
you will **r** the foundations laid Is 58:12
they will **r** the former Is 61:4
If you return, I will **r** you; Jr 15:19
bring them up and **r** them to this Jr 27:22
two years I will **r** to this place Jr 28:3
And I will **r** to this place Jr 28:4
true and may He **r** the articles Jr 28:6

you to **r** you to this place Jr 29:10
and I will **r** your fortunes and Jr 29:14
I will **r** you to the place I Jr 29:14
when I will **r** the fortunes of My Jr 30:3
I will **r** them to the land I gave Jr 30:3
I will certainly **r** the fortunes Jr 30:18
R me, and I will return, for you, Jr 31:18
When I **r** their fortunes, they Jr 31:23
I will **r** their fortunes." Jr 32:44
I will **r** the fortunes of Judah Jr 33:7
For I will **r** the fortunes of the Jr 33:11
I will **r** their fortunes and have Jr 33:26
I will **r** the fortunes of Moab in Jr 48:47
I will **r** the fortunes of the Jr 49:6
I will **r** the fortunes of Elam. Jr 49:39
guilt and so **r** your fortunes. Lm 2:14
LORD, **r** us to Yourself, so we Lm 5:21
to the gaps or **r** the wall around Ezk 13:5
I will **r** their fortunes, the Ezk 16:53
will also **r** your fortunes among Ezk 16:53
I will **r** the fortunes of Egypt Ezk 29:14
Now I will **r** the fortunes of Ezk 39:25
of the decree to **r** and rebuild Dn 9:25
when I **r** the fortunes of Judah Jl 3:1
that day I will **r** the fallen Am 9:11
repair its gaps, **r** its ruins, Am 9:11
I will **r** the fortunes of My Am 9:14
For the LORD will **r** the majesty Nah 2:2
to them and **r** their fortunes. Zph 2:7
For I will then **r** pure speech to Zph 3:9
when I **r** your fortunes before Zph 3:20
that I will **r** double to you. Zch 9:12
I will **r** them because I have Zch 10:6
coming and will **r** everything," Mt 17:11
spiritual should **r** such a person Gl 6:1
will personally **r**, establish, 1Pt 5:10

RESTORED *(34)*

he **r** the chief cupbearer to his Gn 40:21
I was **r** to my position, and the Gn 41:13
let the city of Sihon be **r**. Nm 21:27
had taken from Israel, were **r**; 1Sm 7:14
so that my hand may be **r** to me." 1Kg 13:6
king's hand was **r** to him and 1Kg 13:6
flesh will be **r** and you will be 2Kg 5:10
his skin was **r** ⌊and became⌋ like 2Kg 5:14
whose son he had **r** to life, 2Kg 8:1
king how Elisha **r** the dead ⌊son⌋ 2Kg 8:5
son he had **r** to life came to 2Kg 8:5
is the son Elisha **r** to life." 2Kg 8:5
Elath and **r** it to Judah after 2Kg 14:22
It was he who **r** Israel's border 2Kg 14:25
and Joab **r** the rest of the city. 1Ch 11:8
They **r** God's temple to its 2Ch 24:13
Eloth and **r** it to Judah after 2Ch 26:2
They **r** Jerusalem as far as the Neh 3:8
of the house of God **r** there, Neh 13:9
the LORD **r** his prosperity and Jb 42:10
You **r** Jacob's prosperity. Ps 85:1
When the LORD **r** the fortunes of Ps 126:1
You have **r** me to health and let Is 38:16
a land that has been **r** from war Ezk 38:8
kingdom will be **r** to you as soon Dn 4:26
then the sanctuary will be **r**." Dn 8:14
it out, and it was **r**, as good as Mt 12:13
deformed **r**, the lame walking, Mt 15:31
it out, and his hand was **r**. Mk 3:5
He did so, and his hand was **r**. Lk 6:10
instantly she was **r** and began to Lk 13:13
Be **r**, be encouraged, be of the 2Co 13:11
your prayers I will be **r** to you. Phm 22
that I may be **r** to you very soon Heb 13:19

RESTORER *(1)*

the **r** of streets where people Is 58:12

RESTORES *(3)*

When the LORD **r** His captive Ps 14:7
When God **r** His captive people, Ps 53:6
come first and **r** everything," Mk 9:12

RESTORING *(4)*

say nothing about **r** the king?" 2Sm 19:10
first to speak of **r** our king?" 2Sm 19:43
of Jacob and **r** the protected Is 49:6
time are You **r** the kingdom to Ac 1:6

RESTRAIN *(11)*

been warned yet does not **r** it, Ex 21:29
Would you **r** yourselves from Ru 1:13
Therefore I will not **r** my mouth. Jb 7:11
He does not **r** the lightning when Jb 37:4
authority over the wind to **r** it, Ec 8:8
no longer anything to **r** ⌊you⌋. Is 23:10
and I will **r** Myself for your Is 48:9
all this, will You **r** Yourself? Is 64:12
line and did not **r** Himself from Lm 2:8
they set out to **r** Him, because Mk 3:21
one was able to **r** him any more— Mk 5:3

RESTRAINED *(6)*

yet its owner has not **r** it, Ex 21:36
insults and **r** His servant 1Sm 25:39
of Israel because Joab **r** them. 2Sm 18:16
I have been quiet and **r** Myself. Is 42:14
⌊its⌋ abundant waters were **r**. Ezk 31:15
human voice and **r** the prophet's 2Pt 2:16

RESTRAINING *(2)*

but the one now **r** will do so 2Th 2:7
r the four winds of the earth so Rv 7:1

RESTRAINS *(2)*

intelligent person **r** his words, Pr 17:27
you know what currently **r** ⌊him⌋, 2Th 2:6

RESTRAINT *(6)*

who threw off **r** in Judah and was 2Ch 28:19
and no **r** was placed on the Est 1:8
have cast off **r** in my presence. Jb 30:11
His kindness, **r**, and patience, Rm 2:4
because in His **r** God passed over Rm 3:25
not to put a **r** on you, but 1Co 7:35

RESTRAINTS *(2)*

free ourselves from their **r**." Ps 2:3
would snap the **r** and be driven Lk 8:29

RESTRICT *(1)*

For the wicked **r** the righteous; Hab 1:4

RESTRICTED *(2)*

who was **r** ⌊to his house⌋. Neh 6:10
commanded Baruch, "I am **r**; Jr 36:5

RESTS *(8)*

beloved **r** securely on Him. Dt 33:12
and he **r** on His shoulders. Dt 33:12
lord the king **r** with his fathers 1Kg 1:21
spirit of Elijah **r** on Elisha." 2Kg 2:15
my body also **r** securely. Ps 16:9
His compassion ⌊**r**⌋ on all He has Ps 145:9
goes home and **r** his hand against Am 5:19
of glory and of God **r** on you. 1Pt 4:14

RESULT *(38)*

to bring about the present **r**— Gn 50:20
shone as a **r** of his speaking Ex 34:29
As a **r**, the people's hearts Jos 7:5
As a **r**, 10 tracts fell to Jos 17:5
As a **r**, you have delivered the Jos 22:31
As a **r**, "Is Saul also among the 1Sm 10:12
As a **r**, the terror of the LORD 1Sm 11:7
As a **r**, all the people greatly 1Sm 12:18
As a **r**, Saul was David's enemy 1Sm 18:29
or unfruitfulness **r** from it.' " 2Kg 2:21
this will **r** in my deliverance, Jb 13:16
The **r** of humility is fear of the Pr 22:4
For dreams **r** from much work and Ec 5:3
and the **r** of the removal of his Is 27:9
The **r** of righteousness will be Is 32:17
As a **r**, you are free to continue Jr 7:10
as a **r** of the sword I am sending Jr 25:27
his ways and the **r** of his deeds. Jr 32:19
the city, as a **r** of the sword, Jr 32:24
As a **r**, you will be cut off and Jr 44:8
As a **r**, fathers will eat ⌊their⌋ Ezk 5:10
As a **r**, I have begun to strike Mc 6:13
and as a **r** of their actions. Mc 7:13
a **r**, that man's last condition Mt 12:45
with the **r** that Jesus could no Mk 1:45
As a **r**, they were all astounded Mk 2:12
As a **r**, He made all foods Mk 7:19
a **r**, that man's last condition Lk 11:26
a **r**, they would carry the sick Ac 5:15
scattered as a **r** of the Ac 11:19
As a **r**, people are without Rm 1:20
As a **r**, I have fully proclaimed Rm 15:19
and as a **r** he will fall down on 1Co 14:25
was born as the **r** of a promise. Gl 4:23
As a **r**, you became an example to 1Th 1:7
with you was not without **r**. 1Th 2:1
a **r**, they are always adding to 1Th 2:16
fire—may **r** in praise, glory, 1Pt 1:7

RESULTED *(2)*

for life **r** in death for me. Rm 7:10
me has actually **r** in the Php 1:12

RESULTING *(9)*

r in more contempt and fury. Est 1:18
repentance **r** in life to even Ac 11:18
the judgment, **r** in condemnation, Rm 5:16
came the gift, **r** in Rm 5:16
r in eternal life through Jesus Rm 5:21
believes, **r** in righteousness, Rm 10:10
one confesses, **r** in salvation. Rm 10:10
now disobeyed, ⌊**r**⌋ in mercy to Rm 11:31
man from the two, **r** in peace. Eph 2:15

RESULTS *(4)*

with an iron object and death **r**, Nm 35:16
which **r** in sanctification. Rm 6:19
which **r** in sanctification— Rm 6:22
the light ⌊**r**⌋ in all goodness, Eph 5:9

RESUME *(1)*

R your journey and go to the Dt 1:7

RESUMED *(2)*

Jacob **r** his journey and went to Gn 29:1
of the Jordan **r** their course, Jos 4:18

RESURRECTED *(8)*

He will be **r** on the third day. Mt 20:19
I have been **r**, I will go ahead Mt 26:32
For He has been **r**, just as He Mt 28:6
I have been **r**, I will go ahead Mk 14:28
He has been **r**! He is not here! Mk 16:6
who saw Him after He had been **r**. Mk 16:14
is not here, but He has been **r**! Lk 24:6
God has **r** this Jesus. Ac 2:32

RESURRECTION *(41)*

there is no **r**, came up to Him Mt 22:23
in the **r**, whose wife will Mt 22:28
For in the **r** they neither marry Mt 22:30
concerning the **r** of the dead, Mt 22:31
out of the tombs after His **r**, Mt 27:53
say there is no **r**, came to Him Mk 12:18
In the **r**, when they rise, whose Mk 12:23
at the **r** of the righteous. Lk 14:14
who say there is no **r**, came up Lk 20:27
in the **r**, whose wife will Lk 20:33
age and in the **r** from the dead Lk 20:35
since they are sons of the **r**. Lk 20:36
things, to the **r** of life, but Jn 5:29
things, to the **r** of judgment. Jn 5:29
again in the **r** at the last day. Jn 11:24
her, "I am the **r** and the life. Jn 11:25
a witness with us of His **r**." Ac 1:22
concerning the **r** of the Messiah: Ac 2:31
of Jesus the **r** from the dead. Ac 4:2
testimony to the **r** of the Lord Ac 4:33
good news about Jesus and the **r**. Ac 17:18
they heard about **r** of the dead, Ac 17:32
the hope of the **r** of the dead!" Ac 23:6
the Sadducees say there is no **r**, Ac 23:8
that there is going to be a **r**, Ac 24:15
concerning the **r** of the dead.' " Ac 24:21
of God by the **r** from the dead Rm 1:4
be in the likeness of His **r**. Rm 6:5
"There is no **r** of the dead"? 1Co 15:12
if there is no **r** of the dead, 1Co 15:13
the **r** of the dead also comes 1Co 15:21
So it is with the **r** of the dead: 1Co 15:42
the power of His **r** and the Php 3:10
somehow reach the **r** from among Php 3:11
saying that the **r** has already 2Tm 2:18
on of hands, the **r** of the dead, Heb 6:2
that they might gain a better **r**, Heb 11:35
through the **r** of Jesus Christ 1Pt 1:3
through the **r** of Jesus Christ. 1Pt 3:21
This is the first **r**. Rv 20:5
one who shares in the first **r**! Rv 20:6

RETAIN *(6)*

is to **r** the inheritance Nm 36:7
tribes is to **r** its inheritance." Nm 36:9
Do you still **r** your integrity? Jb 2:9
live and will **r** his life like Jr 21:9
She will not **r** power, and his Dn 11:6
if you **r** ⌊the sins of⌋ any, Jn 20:23

RETAINED *(3)*

no longer **r** his power during 2Ch 13:20
its ⌊original⌋ foundations be **r**. Ezr 6:3
the sins of⌋ any, they are **r**." Jn 20:23

RETAINS *(3)*

secretes the discharge or **r** it, Lv 15:3
secretes or **r** anything because Lv 15:3
He still **r** his integrity, even Jb 2:3

RETINUE *(2)*
Jerusalem with a very large **r**, 1Kg 10:2
Jerusalem with a very large **r**, 2Ch 9:1

RETIRE *(1)*
old he is to **r** from his service Nm 8:25

RETORTED *(1)*
those who had gone with David **r**, 1Sm 30:22

RETRACED *(1)*
David's men **r** their steps. 1Sm 25:12

RETREAT *(8)*
turn their backs to you in **r**. Ex 23:27
made my enemies **r** before me; 2Sm 22:41
When my enemies **r**, they stumble Ps 9:3
made my enemies **r** before me; Ps 18:40
You make us **r** from the foe, Ps 44:10
enemies will **r** on the day when Ps 56:9
r because of their shame. Ps 70:3
and doesn't **r** before anything, Pr 30:30

RETREATED *(5)*
of Israel had **r** before Benjamin Jdg 20:36
They **r** before the men of Israel Jdg 20:42
they **r** from him terrified. 1Sm 17:24
bow never **r**, Saul's sword never 2Sm 1:22
men of Israel **r** in the place 2Sm 23:9

RETREATING *(1)*
they are **r**, their warriors are Jr 46:5

RETREATS *(1)*
If he **r** to some city, all Israel 2Sm 17:13

RETRIBUTION *(8)*
will rejoice when he sees the **r**; Ps 58:10
God's **r** is coming; Is 35:4
to His enemies, **r** to His foes, Is 59:18
for the LORD is a God of **r**; Jr 51:56
the days of **r** have come. Hs 9:7
quickly bring **r** on your heads. Jl 3:4
I will bring **r** on your heads. Jl 3:7
a pitfall and a **r** to them. Rm 11:9

RETRIEVE *(1)*
will be able to **r** a cornerstone Jr 51:26

RETRIEVED *(2)*
and **r** the body of Saul and the 1Sm 31:12
men set out and **r** the body of 1Ch 10:12

RETURN *(274)*
brow until you **r** to the ground, Gn 3:19
dust, and you will **r** to dust." Gn 3:19
but she did not **r** to him again. Gn 8:12
generation they will **r** here, Gn 15:16
Now **r** the man's wife, for he is Gn 20:7
if you do not **r** her, know that Gn 20:7
and if I **r** safely to my father's Gn 28:21
younger⌋ one in **r** for working Gn 29:27
so that I can **r** to my homeland. Gn 30:25
and **r** to your native land.'" Gn 31:13
Then Laban left to **r** home. Gn 31:55
their hands and **r** him to his Gn 37:22
r each man's money to his sack, Gn 42:25
care, and I will **r** him to you." Gn 42:37
R the money that was returned Gn 43:12
'If I do not **r** him to you, Gn 44:32
R quickly to my father and say Gn 45:9
my son, you **r** from the kill—he Gn 49:9
bury my father. Then I will **r**." Gn 50:5
Please let me **r** to my relatives Ex 4:18
told Moses, "**R** to Egypt, for all Ex 4:19
their minds and **r** to Egypt if Ex 13:17
r it to him before sunset. Ex 22:26
or donkey, you must **r** it to him. Ex 23:4
here for us until we **r** to you. Ex 24:14
Then Moses would **r** to the camp, Ex 33:11
he must **r** what he stole or Lv 6:4
priest is to **r** on the seventh Lv 14:39
of you are to **r** to his property Lv 25:10
of you will **r** to his property Lv 25:13
it to, and **r** to his property Lv 25:27
that he may **r** to his property. Lv 25:28
and he may **r** to his clan and his Lv 25:41
the field will **r** to the one he Lv 27:24
R, LORD, to the countless Nm 10:36
inheritance in **r** for the work Nm 18:21
is your wage in **r** for your work Nm 18:31
hit her to **r** her to the path. Nm 22:23
R to Balak and say what I tell Nm 23:5
R to Balak and say what I tell Nm 23:16
We will not **r** to our homes until Nm 32:18
afterwards you may **r** and be free Nm 32:22
assembly will **r** him to the city Nm 35:25
killed a person **r** to the land he Nm 35:28
allowing him to **r** and live in Nm 35:32
each of you may **r** to his Dt 3:20
you will **r** to the LORD your God Dt 4:30
and tell them: **R** to your tents. Dt 5:30
and you are to **r** to your tents Dt 16:7
Let him leave and **r** home. Dt 20:5
Let him leave and **r** home. Dt 20:6
Let him leave and **r** home. Dt 20:7
him leave and **r** home, so that Dt 20:8
make sure you **r** it to your Dt 22:1
then you can **r** it to him. Dt 22:2
Do not **r** a slave to his master Dt 23:15
sure to **r** it to him at sunset. Dt 24:13
your children **r** to the LORD your Dt 30:2
of the law and **r** to Him with all Dt 30:10
You may then **r** to the land of Jos 1:15
for three days until they **r**; Jos 2:16
their inheritance, and **r** to me. Jos 18:4
description of it, and **r** to me. Jos 18:8
may **r** home to his own Jos 20:6
r to your homes in your own land Jos 22:4
R to your homes with great Jos 22:8
this place until I **r** to You. Jdg 6:18
"I will stay until you **r**." Jdg 6:18
Penuel, "When I **r** in peace, I Jdg 8:9
to greet me when I **r** in peace Jdg 11:31
So now I **r** it to you." Jdg 17:2
to his tent or **r** to his house. Jdg 20:8
of Israel would **r** to the battle. Jdg 20:39
Naomi replied, "**R** home, my Ru 1:11
R home, my daughters. Ru 1:12
It must **r** to its place so it 1Sm 5:11
You must **r** it with a guilt 1Sm 6:3
Then he would **r** to Ramah 1Sm 7:17
something? I will **r** it to you." 1Sm 12:3
my sin and **r** with me so I can 1Sm 15:25
to Saul, "I will not **r** with you. 1Sm 15:26
not let him **r** to his father's 1Sm 18:2
and **r** to the land of Judah. 1Sm 22:5
and let him **r** to the place you 1Sm 29:4
in the morning to **r** to the land 1Sm 29:11
your beards grow back; then **r**." 2Sm 10:5
but he will never **r** to me." 2Sm 12:23
added, "He may **r** to his house, 2Sm 14:24
R the ark of God to the city. 2Sm 15:25
r to the city in peace and your 2Sm 15:27
if you **r** to the city and tell 2Sm 15:34
let your servant **r** so that I may 2Sm 19:37
they **r** to You and praise Your 1Kg 8:33
when they **r** to You with their 1Kg 8:48
three days and then **r** to me." 1Kg 12:5
"**R** to me on the third day." 1Kg 12:12
Israel, **r** to your tents; 1Kg 12:16
of you must **r** home, for I have 1Kg 12:24
the kingdom might **r** to the house 1Kg 12:26
people will **r** to their lord, 1Kg 12:27
let this boy's life **r** to him!" 1Kg 17:21
Go and **r** by the way you came to 1Kg 19:15
let everyone **r** home in peace.' 1Kg 22:17
Take Micaiah and **r** him to Amon, 1Kg 22:26
If you ever **r** safely, the LORD 1Kg 22:28
a rumor and **r** to his own land 2Kg 19:7
your beards grow back; then **r**." 1Ch 19:5
and they **r** ⌊to You⌋ and praise 2Ch 6:24
when they **r** to You with their 2Ch 6:38
replied, "**R** to me in three 2Ch 10:5
"**R** to me on the third day." 2Ch 10:12
of you must **r** home, for this 2Ch 11:4
let each **r** home in peace.' 2Ch 18:16
Take Micaiah and **r** him to Amon, 2Ch 18:25
If you ever **r** safely, the LORD 2Ch 18:27
to me and **r** the captives you 2Ch 28:11
r to the LORD God of Abraham, 2Ch 30:6
so that He may **r** to those of you 2Ch 30:6
for when you **r** to the LORD, 2Ch 30:9
captors and will **r** to this land. 2Ch 30:9
away from you if you **r** to Him." 2Ch 30:9
Israelite leaders to **r** with me. Ezr 7:28
But if you **r** to Me and carefully Neh 1:9
take, and when will you **r**?" Neh 2:6
their insults **r** on their own Neh 4:4
R their fields, vineyards, olive Neh 5:11
We will **r** ⌊these things⌋ and Neh 5:12
a leader to **r** to their slavery Neh 9:17
so I could **r** to Jerusalem. Neh 13:7
she would **r** to a second harem Est 2:14
the Jews **r** on his own head Est 9:25
He will never **r** to his house; Jb 7:10
Will You now **r** me to dust? Jb 10:9
darkness and gloom, never to **r**. Jb 10:21
believe he will **r** from darkness; Jb 15:22
before I go the way of no **r**. Jb 16:22
He must **r** the fruit of his labor Jb 20:18
If you **r** to the Almighty, you Jb 22:23
and he will **r** to the days of his Jb 33:25
and mankind would **r** to the dust. Jb 34:15
They leave and do not **r**. Jb 39:4
The wicked will **r** to Sheol— Ps 9:17
and sinners will **r** to You. Ps 51:13
They **r** at evening, snarling like Ps 59:6
And they **r** at evening, snarling Ps 59:14
wind that passes and does not **r**. Ps 78:39
R, God of Hosts. Look down from Ps 80:14
R to us, God of our salvation, Ps 85:4
You **r** mankind to the dust, Ps 90:3
dust, saying, "**R**, descendants Ps 90:3
they die and **r** to the dust. Ps 104:29
In **r** for my love they accuse me, Ps 109:4
R to your rest, my soul, for the Ps 116:7
None **r** who go to her; Pr 2:19
from dust, and all **r** to dust. Ec 3:20
and the clouds **r** after the rain; Ec 12:2
The remnant will **r**, the remnant Is 10:21
⌊only⌋ a remnant of them will **r**. Is 10:22
the prisoners to **r** home?" Is 14:17
Then they will **r** to the LORD and Is 19:22
R to the One the Israelites have Is 31:6
the LORD will **r** and come to Zion Is 35:10
a rumor and **r** to his own land Is 37:7
Ahaz's stairway **r** by 10 steps." Is 38:8
R to Me, for I have redeemed you. Is 44:22
the LORD will **r** and come to Zion Is 51:11
let him **r** to the LORD, so He may Is 55:7
and do not **r** there without Is 55:10
My mouth will not **r** to Me empty, Is 55:11
R, because of Your servants, the Is 63:17
another, can he ever **r** to her? Jr 3:1
many partners—can you **r** to Me? Jr 3:1
these things, she will **r** to Me. Jr 3:7
But she didn't **r**, and her Jr 3:7
Judah didn't **r** to Me with all Jr 3:10
R, unfaithful Israel. Jr 3:12
"**R**, you faithless children"— Jr 3:14
R, you faithless children. Jr 3:22
If you **r**, Israel—⌊this is⌋ the Jr 4:1
if⌋ you **r** to Me, if you remove Jr 4:1
rock, and they refused to **r**. Jr 5:3
But **r** to My place that was at Jr 7:12
they turn away, do they not **r**? Jr 8:4
of deceit; they refuse to **r**. Jr 8:5
on them and **r** each one to his Jr 12:15
their containers **r** empty. Jr 14:3
If you **r**, I will restore you; Jr 15:19
It is they who must **r** to you; Jr 15:19
you must not **r** to them. Jr 15:19
For I will **r** them to their land Jr 16:15
he will never **r** again and see Jr 22:10
he will never **r** here again, Jr 22:11
They will never **r** to the land Jr 22:27
to the land they long to **r** to." Jr 22:27
and I will **r** them to their Jr 23:3
good and will **r** them to this Jr 24:6
they will **r** to Me with all Jr 24:7
Perhaps they will listen and **r**— Jr 26:3
Jacob will **r** and have calm and Jr 30:10
They will **r** here as a great Jr 31:8
children will **r** from the enemy's Jr 31:16
your children will **r** to their Jr 31:17
me, and I will **r**, for you, LORD, Jr 31:18
have traveled. **R**, Virgin Israel! Jr 31:21
R to these cities of yours. Jr 31:21
and I will **r** them to this place Jr 32:37
is going to **r** to its own land of Jr 37:7
will then **r** and fight against Jr 37:8
that he not **r** me to the house Jr 38:26
R to Gedaliah son of Ahikam, Jr 40:5
allow you to **r** to your own soil Jr 42:12
or survivor to **r** to the land of Jr 44:14
they are longing to **r** to live, Jr 44:14
they will not **r** except ⌊for a Jr 44:14
the sword will **r** from the land Jr 44:28
Let's **r** to our people and to the Jr 46:16
Jacob will **r** and have calm and Jr 46:27
who does not **r** empty-handed. Jr 50:9

I will **r** Israel to his grazing Jr 50:19
us to Yourself, so we may **r**; Lm 5:21
certainly not **r** to what was sold Ezk 7:13
daughters will **r** to their former Ezk 16:55
will also **r** to your former Ezk 16:55
and does not **r** collateral, Ezk 18:12
R ⌊it⌋ to its sheath! Ezk 21:30
one must **r** through the gate by Ezk 46:9
must **r** at once to fight against Dn 10:20
and then **r** to his own land. Dn 11:9
the North will **r** to his land Dn 11:28
action, then **r** to his own land. Dn 11:28
his **r**, he will favor those who Dn 11:30
of Israel will **r** and seek the Hs 3:5
allow ⌊them⌋ to **r** to their God, Hs 5:4
will depart and **r** to My place Hs 5:15
Come, let us **r** to the LORD. Hs 6:1
When I **r** My people from Hs 6:11
yet they do not **r** to the LORD Hs 7:10
they will **r** to Egypt. Hs 8:13
Ephraim will **r** to Egypt, and Hs 9:3
Israel will not **r** to the land of Hs 11:5
But you must **r** to your God. Hs 12:6
Israel, **r** to the LORD your God, Hs 14:1
with you and **r** to the LORD. Hs 14:2
The people will **r** and live Hs 14:7
and **r** to the LORD your God. Jl 2:13
yet you did not **r** to Me—the Am 4:6
yet you did not **r** to Me—the Am 4:8
yet you did not **r** to Me—the Am 4:9
yet you did not **r** to Me—the Am 4:10
yet you did not **r** to Me—the Am 4:11
deserve will **r** on your own head Ob 15
brothers will **r** to the people Mc 5:3
their God will **r** to them and Zph 2:7
R to Me"—⌊this is⌋ the Zch 1:3
and I will **r** to you, says Zch 1:3
I will **r** to Zion and live in Zch 8:3
R to a stronghold, you prisoners Zch 9:12
their children will live and **r**. Zch 10:9
R to Me, and I will return to you, Mal 3:7
Me, and I will **r** to you," says Mal 3:7
But you ask: "How can we **r**?" Mal 3:7
let your peace **r** to you. Mt 10:13
lend, expecting nothing in **r**. Lk 6:35
but if not, it will **r** to you. Lk 10:6
their master to **r** from the Lk 12:36
Didn't any **r** to give glory to Lk 17:18
authority to be king and then **r**. Lk 19:12
At his **r**, having received the Lk 19:15
dead, never to **r** to decay, He Ac 13:34
things I will **r** and will rebuild Ac 15:16
every effort to **r** and see you 1Th 2:17
God for you in **r** for all the joy 1Th 3:9
would have had opportunity to **r**. Heb 11:15
reviled, He did not revile in **r**; 1Pt 2:23

RETURNED *(177)*

She **r** to him in the ark because Gn 8:9
After Abram **r** from defeating Gn 14:17
and Abraham **r** to his place. Gn 18:33
and **r** his wife Sarah to him. Gn 20:14
left and **r** to the land of the Gn 21:32
When the messengers **r** to Jacob, Gn 32:6
he remained silent until they **r**. Gn 34:5
Jacob's sons **r** from the field Gn 34:7
again after he **r** from Gn 35:9
When Reuben **r** to the pit and saw Gn 37:29
So the Adullamite **r** to Judah, Gn 38:22
brothers, "My money has been **r**! Gn 42:28
the money that was **r** ⌊to you⌋ in Gn 43:12
the money that was **r** in our bags Gn 43:18
his donkey and **r** to the city. Gn 44:13
he **r** to Egypt with his brothers Gn 50:14
they **r** to their father Reuel Ex 2:18
daybreak the sea **r** to its normal Ex 14:27
So Moses **r** to the LORD and said, Ex 32:31
of the community **r** to him, Ex 34:31
Then Moses **r** to the camp along Nm 11:30
of 40 days they **r** from scouting Nm 13:25
and who **r** and incited the entire Nm 14:36
Aaron then **r** to Moses at the Nm 16:50
of Moab arose, **r** to Balak, and Nm 22:14
So he **r** to Balak, who was Nm 23:6
So he **r** to Balak, who was Nm 23:17
When you **r**, you wept before the Dt 1:45
away from you and not **r** to you. Dt 28:31
days until the pursuers had **r**. Jos 2:22
Then the men **r**, came down from Jos 2:23
They **r** to the camp and spent the Jos 6:11
the city once and **r** to the camp. Jos 6:14
all Israel **r** to Ai and struck it Jos 8:24
Israel with him **r** to the camp at Jos 10:15
The people **r** safely to Joshua in Jos 10:21
Then Joshua **r** with all Israel to Jos 10:43
They **r** to Joshua at the camp in Jos 18:9
and the leaders **r** from the Jos 22:32
near Gilgal he **r** and said, Jdg 3:19
He **r** to Israel's camp and said, Jdg 7:15
son of Joash **r** from the battle Jdg 8:13
And God also **r** all the evil of Jdg 9:57
two months, she **r** to her father, Jdg 11:39
time, when he **r** to get her, he Jdg 14:8
When he **r** to his father and Jdg 14:9
Samson **r** to his father's house, Jdg 14:19
his strength **r**, and he revived. Jdg 15:19
He **r** the 1,100 pieces of silver Jdg 17:3
he **r** the silver to his mother, Jdg 17:4
the men of Israel **r**, and the men Jdg 20:41
Benjamin **r** at that time, and Jdg 21:14
the Israelites **r** from there to Jdg 21:24
Each **r** from there to his own Jdg 21:24
Moabite woman who **r** with Naomi Ru 2:6
who has **r** from the land of Moab, Ru 4:3
they **r** home to Ramah. 1Sm 1:19
When the troops **r** to the camp, 1Sm 4:3
took Dagon and **r** him to his 1Sm 5:3
they **r** to Ekron that same day. 1Sm 6:16
Philistines have **r** the ark of 1Sm 6:21
the Philistines **r** to their own 1Sm 14:46
Israelites **r** from the pursuit 1Sm 17:53
When David **r** from killing the 1Sm 17:57
the arrow and **r** to his master. 1Sm 20:38
When Saul **r** from pursuing the 1Sm 24:1
they **r** to him, they reported 1Sm 25:12
on his way, and Saul **r** home. 1Sm 26:25
David **r** from defeating the 2Sm 1:1
Saul's sword never **r** unstained, 2Sm 1:22
soldiers and Joab **r** from a raid 2Sm 3:22
When Abner **r** to Hebron, Joab 2Sm 3:27
When David **r** ⌊home⌋ to bless his 2Sm 6:20
himself when he **r** from striking 2Sm 8:13
Afterwards, she **r** home. 2Sm 11:4
all his troops **r** to Jerusalem. 2Sm 12:31
So Absalom **r** to his house, 2Sm 14:24
and Abiathar **r** the ark of God to 2Sm 15:29
them⌋, so they **r** to Jerusalem. 2Sm 17:20
So they **r** to the city quietly 2Sm 19:3
Then the king **r**. When he arrived 2Sm 19:15
left until the day he **r** safely. 2Sm 19:24
and Barzillai **r** to his home. 2Sm 19:39
Joab **r** to the king in Jerusalem. 2Sm 20:22
they **r** to Jerusalem at the end 2Sm 24:8
Jerusalem to Gath and had **r**. 1Kg 2:41
her servants, **r** to her own 1Kg 10:13
and the boy's life **r** to him, 1Kg 17:22
angel of the LORD **r** a second 1Kg 19:7
The messengers then **r** and said, 1Kg 20:5
The messengers **r** to the king, 2Kg 1:5
When they **r** to him in Jericho 2Kg 2:18
and then he **r** to Samaria. 2Kg 2:25
from him and **r** to their land. 2Kg 3:27
When Elisha **r** to Gilgal, there 2Kg 4:38
The messengers **r** and told the 2Kg 7:15
When the woman **r** from the land 2Kg 8:3
So King Joram **r** to Jezreel to 2Kg 8:29
King Joram had **r** to Jezreel to 2Kg 9:15
Then he **r** to Samaria. 2Kg 14:14
he **r** and found him fighting 2Kg 19:8
r ⌊home⌋ and lived in Nineveh. 2Kg 19:36
Then he **r** to Jerusalem. 2Kg 23:20
married Moabites and **r** to Lehem. 1Ch 4:22
and David **r** ⌊home⌋ to bless his 1Ch 16:43
all his troops **r** to Jerusalem. 1Ch 20:3
Israel and then **r** to Jerusalem. 1Ch 21:4
her servants, **r** to her own 2Ch 9:12
—Jeroboam **r** from Egypt. 2Ch 10:2
Then they **r** to Jerusalem. 2Ch 14:15
king of Judah **r** to his home in 2Ch 19:1
so he **r** to Jezreel to recover 2Ch 22:6
it up, and **r** it to its place. 2Ch 24:11
Judah and **r** home in a fierce 2Ch 25:10
Then he **r** to Samaria. 2Ch 25:24
Then they **r** to Samaria. 2Ch 28:15
Israelites **r** to their cities, 2Ch 31:1
king of Assyria **r** with shame to 2Ch 32:21
of Israel and **r** to Jerusalem. 2Ch 34:7
Each of them **r** to his hometown Ezr 2:1
and all who had **r** to Jerusalem Ezr 3:8
heard that the **r** exiles were Ezr 4:1
from you have **r** to us at Ezr 4:12
to Babylon must also be **r**. Ezr 6:5
who had **r** from exile ate ⌊it Ezr 6:21
of those who **r** with me from Ezr 8:1
exiles who had **r** from the Ezr 8:35
remnant that had **r** from exile. Neh 1:2
province, who **r** from the exile, Neh 1:3
through the Valley Gate and **r**. Neh 2:15
every one of us **r** to his own Neh 4:15
Each of them **r** to his own town Neh 7:6
that had **r** from exile made Neh 8:17
because I had **r** to King Neh 13:6
Then Mordecai **r** to the King's Est 6:12
as the king **r** from the palace Est 7:8
r and discovered that the king Is 37:8
r ⌊home⌋ and lived in Nineveh. Is 37:37
They have **r** to the sins of their Jr 11:10
After I **r**, I repented; Jr 31:19
they all **r** from all the places Jr 40:12
those who had **r** from all the Jr 43:5
When I had **r**, I saw a very large Ezk 47:7
heaven, and my sanity **r** to me. Dn 4:34
At that time my sanity **r** to me, Dn 4:36
and splendor **r** to me for the Dn 4:36
have graciously **r** to Jerusalem; Zch 1:16
with me then **r** and roused me as Zch 4:1
they **r** to their own country by Mt 2:12
And when I **r** I would have Mt 25:27
of remorse and **r** the 30 pieces Mt 27:3
then she **r** to her home. Lk 1:56
had left them and **r** to heaven, Lk 2:15
The shepherds **r**, glorifying and Lk 2:20
the Lord, they **r** to Galilee, to Lk 2:39
they **r** to Jerusalem to search Lk 2:45
Then Jesus **r** from the Jordan, Lk 4:1
Then Jesus **r** to Galilee in the Lk 4:14
had been sent **r** to the house, Lk 7:10
So getting into the boat, He **r**. Lk 8:37
When Jesus **r**, the crowd welcomed Lk 8:40
Her spirit **r**, and she got up at Lk 8:55
the apostles **r**, they reported to Lk 9:10
The Seventy **r** with joy, saying, Lk 10:17
was healed, **r** and, with a loud Lk 17:15
And when I **r**, I would have Lk 19:23
Then they **r** and prepared spices Lk 23:56
they got up and **r** to Jerusalem. Lk 24:33
they **r** to Jerusalem with great Lk 24:52
Then they **r** to Jerusalem from Ac 1:12
jail, so they **r** and reported, Ac 5:22
Barnabas and Saul **r** to Jerusalem Ac 12:25
disciples, they **r** to Lystra, to Ac 14:21
the ship, and they **r** home. Ac 21:6
day, they **r** to the barracks, Ac 23:32
him as he **r** from defeating Heb 7:1
you have now **r** to the shepherd 1Pt 2:25

RETURNING *(14)*

Now Isaac was **r** from Gn 24:62
When I was **r** from Paddan, to my Gn 48:7
who were **r** from the military Nm 31:14
After **r** to Joshua they reported Jos 7:3
If you are **r** to the LORD with 1Sm 7:3
As David was **r** from killing the 1Sm 18:6
at their head, **r** joyfully to 2Ch 20:27
heart against **r** to the LORD God 2Ch 36:13
be delivered by **r** and resting; Is 30:15
like those **r** from war. Mc 2:8
as He was **r** to the city, He Mt 21:18
as they were **r**, the boy Jesus Lk 2:43
r, it finds ⌊the house⌋ swept Lk 11:25
R from the tomb, they reported Lk 24:9

RETURNS *(13)*

and **r** to her father's house as Lv 22:13
When everyone **r** ⌊except⌋ the man 2Sm 17:3
leaves him, he **r** to the ground; Ps 146:4
If anyone **r** evil for good, Pr 17:13
As a dog **r** to its vomit, so a Pr 26:11
⌊it **r**⌋ to its place where it Ec 1:5
and the wind **r** in its cycles. Ec 1:6
and the dust **r** to the earth as Ec 12:7
and the spirit **r** to God who gave Ec 12:7
see when the LORD **r** to Zion. Is 52:8
anyone but **r** his collateral to Ezk 18:7
he **r** collateral, makes Ezk 33:15
dog **r** to its own vomit, and, "a 2Pt 2:22

REU *(6)*
lived 30 years and fathered **R**. Gn 11:18
he fathered **R**, Peleg lived 209 Gn 11:19
R lived 32 years and fathered Gn 11:20
R lived 207 years and fathered Gn 11:21
Eber, Peleg, **R**, 1Ch 1:25
son⌋ of **R**, ⌊son⌋ of Peleg Lk 3:35

REUBEN *(44)*
and named him **R**, for she said, Gn 29:32
R went out during the wheat Gn 30:14
R went in and slept with his Gn 35:22
Leah's sons were **R** (Jacob's Gn 35:23
When **R** heard this, he tried to Gn 37:21
R also said to them, "Don't shed Gn 37:22
When **R** returned to the pit and Gn 37:29
R replied: "Didn't I tell you Gn 42:22
Then **R** said to his father, Gn 42:37
to Egypt: Jacob's firstborn: **R**. Gn 46:8
to me just as **R** and Simeon do. Gn 48:5
R, you are my firstborn, my Gn 49:3
R, Simeon, Levi, and Judah; Ex 1:2
The sons of **R**, the firstborn of Ex 6:14
These are the clans of **R**. Ex 6:14
Elizur son of Shedeur from **R**; Nm 1:5
descendants of **R**, the firstborn Nm 1:20
the tribe of **R** numbered 46,500 Nm 1:21
of the camp of **R** with their Nm 10:18
of Zaccur from the tribe of **R**; Nm 13:4
son of Peleth, sons of **R**, took Nm 16:1
R was the firstborn of Israel. Nm 26:5
R, Gad, Asher, Zebulun, Dan, and Dt 27:13
R live and not die though his Dt 33:6
to the stone of Bohan son of **R**. Jos 15:6
Gad, **R**, and half the tribe of Jos 18:7
clans from the tribes of **R**, Jos 21:7
the tribe of **R**, ⌊they gave⌋: Jos 21:36
you descendants of **R** and Gad. Jos 22:25
heard what the descendants of **R**, Jos 22:30
said to the descendants of **R**, Jos 22:31
of heart among the clans of **R**. Jdg 5:15
of heart among the clans of **R**. Jdg 5:16
R, Simeon, Levi, Judah, Issachar, 1Ch 2:1
the sons of **R** the firstborn 1Ch 5:1
because **R** defiled his father's 1Ch 5:1
The sons of **R**, Israel's 1Ch 5:3
The sons of **R** and Gad and half 1Ch 5:18
12 towns from the tribes of **R**, 1Ch 6:63
the tribe of **R** across the Jordan 1Ch 6:78
west, will be **R**—one ⌊portion⌋ Ezk 48:6
Next to the territory of **R**, Ezk 48:7
one, the gate of **R**; one, the Ezk 48:31
12,000 from the tribe of **R**, Rv 7:5

REUBEN'S *(7)*
R sons: Hanoch, Pallu, Hezron, Gn 46:9
R military divisions will camp Nm 2:10
who belong to **R** encampment is Nm 2:16
of Shedeur was over **R** division. Nm 10:18
of Israel. **R** descendants: Nm 26:5
to the Stone of Bohan, **R** son. Jos 18:17
wilderness plateau from **R** tribe, Jos 20:8

REUBENITE *(3)*
were the **R** clans, and their Nm 26:7
sons of Eliab the **R**, when in the Dt 11:6
Adina son of Shiza the **R**, chief 1Ch 11:42

REUBENITES *(39)*
leader of the **R** is Elizur son Nm 2:10
leader of the **R**, ⌊presented Nm 7:30
The **R** and Gadites had a very Nm 32:1
the Gadites and **R** came to Moses, Nm 32:2
Moses asked the Gadites and **R**, Nm 32:6
Gadites and **R** answered Moses, Nm 32:25
the Gadites and **R** cross the Nm 32:29
The Gadites and **R** replied, Nm 32:31
the Gadites, **R**, and half the Nm 32:33
The **R** rebuilt Heshbon, Elealeh, Nm 32:37
the tribe of the **R** and the tribe Nm 34:14
I gave to the **R** and Gadites ⌊the Dt 3:12
and I gave to the **R** and Gadites Dt 3:16
land, belonging to the **R**; Dt 4:43
it as an inheritance to the **R**, Dt 29:8
said to the **R**, the Gadites, Jos 1:12
The **R**, Gadites, and half the Jos 4:12
land as an inheritance to the **R**, Jos 12:6
the **R** and Gadites had received Jos 13:8
tribe of the **R** by their clans, Jos 13:15
border of the **R** was the Jordan Jos 13:23
of the **R** by their clans, Jos 13:23
summoned the **R**, Gadites, and Jos 22:1
The **R**, Gadites, and half the Jos 22:9
of Canaan, the **R**, Gadites, and Jos 22:10
said, "Look, the **R**, Gadites, and Jos 22:11
of Eleazar the priest to the **R**, Jos 22:13
They went to the **R**, Gadites, and Jos 22:15
The **R**, Gadites, and half the Jos 22:21
returned from the **R** and Gadites Jos 22:32
land where the **R** and Gadites Jos 22:33
So the **R** and Gadites named the Jos 22:34
the Gadites, the **R**, and the 2Kg 10:33
Beerah was a leader of the **R**, 1Ch 5:6
king of Assyria to take the **R**, 1Ch 5:26
chief of the **R**, and 30 with him, 1Ch 11:42
Jordan—from the **R**, Gadites, 1Ch 12:37
David appointed them over the **R**, 1Ch 26:32
For the **R**, Eliezer son of Zichri 1Ch 27:16

REUEL *(8)*
(AKA DEUEL, HOBAB, JETHRO)
to Esau, Basemath bore **R**, Gn 36:4
and **R** son of Esau's wife Gn 36:10
are the sons of **R**, Esau's son: Gn 36:17
are the chiefs of **R** in the land Gn 36:17
to their father **R** he asked, Ex 2:18
father-in-law **R** the Midianite: Nm 10:29
Eliphaz, **R**, Jeush, Jalam, and 1Ch 1:35
son of **R**, son of Ibnijah; 1Ch 9:8

REUEL'S *(2)*
These are **R** sons: Nahath, Zerah, Gn 36:13
R sons: Nahath, Zerah, Shammah, 1Ch 1:37

REUMAH *(1)*
whose name was **R**, also bore Gn 22:24

REVEAL *(27)*
and I will **r** My glory before all Lv 10:3
the LORD will **r** who belongs to Nm 16:5
'Didn't I **r** Myself to your 1Sm 2:27
I'll **r** the word of God to you. 1Sm 9:27
Esther did not **r** her ethnic Est 2:10
R to me my transgression and sin. Jb 13:23
You **r** the path of life to me; Ps 16:11
r to me the end of my life and Ps 39:4
I **r** my trouble to Him. Ps 142:2
R to me the way I should go, Ps 143:8
tell you and **r** what the LORD Is 19:12
The earth will **r** the blood shed Is 26:21
voice heard and **r** His arm Is 30:30
there I will **r** My words to you." Jr 18:2
they did not **r** your guilt and so Lm 2:14
and will **r** Myself in the sight Ezk 38:23
R the design of the temple to Ezk 43:11
were able to **r** this mystery." Dn 2:47
whom the Son desires to **r** Him. Mt 11:27
and blood did not **r** this to you, Mt 16:17
whom the Son desires to **r** Him." Lk 10:22
him and will **r** Myself to him." Jn 14:21
You're going to **r** Yourself to us Jn 14:22
in darkness and **r** the intentions 1Co 4:5
to **r** His Son in me, so that I Gl 1:16
God will **r** this to you also. Php 3:15
so that I may **r** it as I am Col 4:4

REVEALED *(77)*
that God had **r** Himself to him Gn 35:7
God has **r** to Pharaoh what He is Gn 41:25
him when he **r** his identity to Gn 45:1
the **r** things belong to us and Dt 29:29
LORD had not yet been **r** to him. 1Sm 3:7
because there He **r** Himself to 1Sm 3:21
removed from you will be **r**." 1Sm 6:3
have **r** all these great things 2Sm 7:21
have **r** this to Your servant when 2Sm 7:27
have **r** to Your servant that You 1Ch 17:25
You **r** Your holy Sabbath to them, Neh 9:14
still had not **r** her birthplace Est 2:20
Esther had **r** her relationship Est 8:1
gates of death been **r** to you? Jb 38:17
The LORD has **r** Himself; Ps 9:16
You **r** Your strength among the Ps 77:14
has **r** His righteousness in the Ps 98:2
r His ways to Moses, His deeds Ps 103:7
in the way ⌊**r** by⌋ Your decrees Ps 119:14
evil will be **r** in the assembly Pr 26:26
LORD of Hosts has **r** ⌊this⌋ in my Is 22:14
the arm of the LORD been **r** to? Is 53:1
and My righteousness will be **r**. Is 56:1
power will be **r** to His servants, Is 66:14
that your sins are **r** in all your Ezk 21:24
The mystery was then **r** to Daniel Dn 2:19
this mystery has been **r** to me, Dn 2:30
a message was **r** to Daniel, Dn 10:1
learned and **r** them to infants Mt 11:25
is concealed except to be **r**, Mk 4:22
It had been **r** to him by the Holy Lk 2:26
of many hearts may be **r**." Lk 2:35
is concealed that won't be **r**, Lk 8:17
and have **r** them to infants Lk 10:21
on the day the Son of Man is **r**. Lk 17:30
Father's side—He has **r** Him. Jn 1:18
so He might be **r** to Israel." Jn 1:31
the arm of the Lord been **r** to? Jn 12:38
have **r** Your name to the men You Jn 17:6
Jesus **r** Himself again to His Jn 21:1
He **r** Himself in this way: Jn 21:1
You have **r** the paths of life to Ac 2:28
Joseph was **r** to his brothers, Ac 7:13
righteousness is **r** from faith to Rm 1:17
For God's wrath is **r** from heaven Rm 1:18
God's righteous judgment is **r**. Rm 2:5
God's righteousness has been **r**— Rm 3:21
that is going to be **r** to us. Rm 8:18
for God's sons to be **r**. Rm 8:19
I **r** Myself to those who were not Rm 10:20
but now **r** and made known Rm 16:26
Now God has **r** them to us by the 1Co 2:10
because it will be **r** by fire; 1Co 3:13
secrets of his heart will be **r**, 1Co 14:25
has been **r** to another person 1Co 14:30
Jesus may also be **r** in our body. 2Co 4:10
life may also be **r** in our mortal 2Co 4:11
until the coming faith was **r**. Gl 3:23
as it is now **r** to His holy Eph 3:5
but now **r** to His saints. Col 1:26
your life, is **r**, then you also Col 3:4
you also will be **r** with Him in Col 3:4
and the man of lawlessness is **r**, 2Th 2:3
that he will be **r** in his time. 2Th 2:6
then the lawless one will be **r**. 2Th 2:8
in His own time **r** His message Ti 1:3
is ready to be **r** in the last 1Pt 1:5
It was **r** to them that they were 1Pt 1:12
was **r** at the end of the times 1Pt 1:20
in the glory about to be **r**, 1Pt 5:1
life was **r**, and we have seen 1Jn 1:2
the Father and was **r** to us— 1Jn 1:2
we will be has not yet been **r**. 1Jn 3:2
that He was **r** so that He might 1Jn 3:5
Son of God was **r** for this 1Jn 3:8
God's love was **r** among us in 1Jn 4:9
Your righteous acts have been **r**. Rv 15:4

REVEALER *(2)*
The **r** of mysteries has let you Dn 2:29
of kings, and a **r** of mysteries, Dn 2:47

REVEALING *(3)*
A gossip goes around **r** a secret, Pr 11:13
without **r** another's secret Pr 25:9
nothing without **r** His counsel to Am 3:7

REVEALS *(8)*
tell you whatever He **r** to me." Nm 23:3
He **r** mysteries from the darkness Jb 12:22
and He **r** His covenant to them. Ps 25:14
The one who **r** secrets is a Pr 20:19
her strength and **r** that her arms Pr 31:17
He **r** the deep and hidden things; Dn 2:22
a God in heaven who **r** mysteries, Dn 2:28
and **r** His thoughts to man, Am 4:13

REVEL *(2)*
eat and drink, then got up to **r**. Ex 32:6
make them drunk so that they **r**. Jr 51:39

REVELATION *(25)*
And this is a **r** for mankind, 2Sm 7:19
r from the LORD had come to the 2Sm 24:11
But a **r** from God came to 1Kg 12:22
to Bethel by a **r** from the LORD 1Kg 13:1
the altar by a **r** from the LORD: 1Kg 13:2
cried out by a **r** from the LORD 1Kg 13:32
Then a **r** from the LORD came to 1Kg 17:2
The **r** of Your words brings light Ps 119:130
Without **r** people run wild, Pr 29:18
light for **r** to the Gentiles and Lk 2:32
according to the **r** of the sacred Rm 16:25
wait for the **r** of our Lord Jesus 1Co 1:7
to you with a **r** or knowledge 1Co 14:6
a teaching, a **r**, ⌊another⌋ 1Co 14:26
but it came by a **r** from Jesus Gl 1:12
up because of a **r** and presented Gl 2:2

of wisdom and **r** in the knowledge Eph 1:17
was made known to me by **r**, Eph 3:3
to you by a **r** from the Lord: 1Th 4:15
place⌋ at the **r** of the Lord 2Th 1:7
the basic principles of God's **r**. Heb 5:12
honor at the **r** of Jesus Christ 1Pt 1:7
to you at the **r** of Jesus Christ. 1Pt 1:13
great joy at the **r** of His glory. 1Pt 4:13
The **r** of Jesus Christ that God Rv 1:1

REVELATIONS *(2)*
on to visions and **r** of the Lord. 2Co 12:1
because of the extraordinary **r**. 2Co 12:7

REVELERS *(1)*
I never sat with the band of **r**, Jr 15:17

REVELRY *(1)*
jubilant town, is filled with **r**. Is 22:2

REVENGE *(9)*
Do not take **r** or bear a grudge Lv 19:18
to take **r** on his enemies.' " 1Sm 18:25
bloodshed or my lord's **r**. 1Sm 25:31
So Abner died in **r** for the death 2Sm 3:27
show no mercy when he takes **r**. Pr 6:34
will take **r** against My enemies. Is 1:24
I not take My **r** against a nation Jr 9:9
guilt by taking **r** on them, Ezk 25:12
and took **r** with deep contempt Ezk 25:15

REVENUE *(3)*
and the royal **r** will suffer. Ezr 4:13
and her **r** is better than gold. Pr 3:14
Tyre's **r** was the grain from Is 23:3

REVENUES *(1)*
of the royal **r** from the taxes Ezr 6:8

REVERE *(4)*
My Sabbaths and **r** My sanctuary; Lv 19:30
who delight to **r** Your name. Neh 1:11
descendants of Israel, **r** Him! Ps 22:23
You who **r** the LORD, praise the Ps 135:20

REVERED *(5)*
in holiness, **r** with praises, Ex 15:11
and they **r** him throughout his Jos 4:14
his life, as they had **r** Moses. Jos 4:14
so that You may be **r**. Ps 130:4
and he **r** Me and stood in awe of Mal 2:5

REVERENCE *(6)*
for it produces **r** for You. Ps 119:38
it called for **r**, and he revered Mal 2:5
He was heard because of His **r**. Heb 5:7
in **r** built an ark to deliver his Heb 11:7
God acceptably, with **r** and awe; Heb 12:28
yourselves in **r** during this time 1Pt 1:17

REVERENT *(5)*
is the one who is always **r**, Pr 28:14
for they are **r** before Him. Ec 8:12
for they are not **r** before God. Ec 8:13
women are to be **r** in behavior, Ti 2:3
they observe your pure, **r** lives. 1Pt 3:2

REVERENTIAL *(2)*
Serve the LORD with **r** awe, Ps 2:11
holy temple in **r** awe of You. Ps 5:7

REVERSE *(1)*
I act, and who can **r** it?" Is 43:13

REVERT *(1)*
when it will **r** to the prince. Ezk 46:17

REVIEW *(2)*
passing ⌊in **r** with their units 1Sm 29:2
were passing ⌊in **r**⌋ behind them 1Sm 29:2

REVIEWED *(1)*
David **r** his troops and appointed 2Sm 18:1

REVILE *(2)*
Do you dare **r** God's high priest? Ac 23:4
reviled, He did not **r** in return; 1Pt 2:23

REVILED *(3)*
all who **r** you will fall down on Is 60:14
When we are **r**, we bless; 1Co 4:12
when **r**, He did not revile in 1Pt 2:23

REVILER *(2)*
the voice of the scorner and **r**, Ps 44:16
an idolater or a **r**, a drunkard 1Co 5:11

REVILERS *(1)*
drunkards, **r**, or swindlers will 1Co 6:10

REVISITED *(1)*
So you **r** the indecency of your Ezk 23:21

REVIVE *(7)*
but You will **r** me again. Ps 71:20
r us, and we will call on Your Ps 80:18
Will You not **r** us again so that Ps 85:6
to **r** the spirit of the lowly and Is 57:15
of the lowly and **r** the heart Is 57:15
He will **r** us after two days, Hs 6:2
R ⌊Your work⌋ in these years; Hab 3:2

REVIVED *(5)*
spirit of their father Jacob **r**. Gn 45:27
his strength returned, and he **r**. Jdg 15:19
After he ate he **r**, for he hadn't 1Sm 30:12
bones, the man **r** and stood up! 2Kg 13:21
You **r** Your inheritance when it Ps 68:9

REVIVING *(1)*
the LORD is perfect, **r** the soul; Ps 19:7

REVOKE *(4)*
begged him to **r** the evil of Est 8:3
Let it **r** the documents the Est 8:5
You **r** God's word by your Mk 7:13
does not **r** a covenant that was Gl 3:17

REVOKED *(5)*
Media, so that it cannot be **r**: Est 1:19
royal signet ring cannot be **r**." Est 8:8
a word that will not be **r**: Is 45:23
all its people will not be **r**, Ezk 7:13
you have **r** God's word because of Mt 15:6

REVOLT *(1)*
speaking oppression and **r**, Is 59:13

REVOLTED *(1)*
this king **r** against him by Ezk 17:15

REVOLTING *(3)*
less one who is **r** and corrupt, Jb 15:16
their actions are **r**. Ps 14:1
by people is **r** in God's sight. Lk 16:15

REVOLTS *(2)*
There have been **r** in it since Ezr 4:15
been rebellions and **r** in it. Ezr 4:19

REVOLUTIONARY *(1)*
Now Barabbas was a **r**. Jn 18:40

REWARD *(60)*
your **r** will be very great. Gn 15:1
Am I really not able to **r** you?" Nm 22:37
I said I would **r** you richly, Nm 24:11
the LORD has denied you a **r**." Nm 24:11
May the LORD **r** you for what you Ru 2:12
receive a full **r** from the LORD Ru 2:12
That was my **r** to him for his 2Sm 4:10
to run since you won't get a **r**?" 2Sm 18:22
the king repay me with such a **r**? 2Sm 19:36
and I'll give you a **r**." 1Kg 13:7
for your work has a **r**." 2Ch 15:7
is great **r** in keeping them. Ps 19:11
there is a **r** for the righteous! Ps 58:11
from the LORD, children, a **r**. Ps 127:3
sows righteousness, a true **r**. Pr 11:18
of a man's hands will **r** him. Pr 12:14
He will give a **r** to the lender. Pr 19:17
head, and the LORD will **r** you. Pr 25:22
Give her the **r** of her labor, Pr 31:31
This was my **r** for all my Ec 2:10
because that is his **r**. Ec 3:22
they have a good **r** for their Ec 4:9
him, because that is his **r**. Ec 5:18
them, take his **r**, and rejoice in Ec 5:19
no longer a **r** for them because Ec 9:5
His **r** is with Him, and His gifts Is 40:10
LORD, and my **r** is with my God. Is 49:4
will faithfully **r** them and make Is 61:8
coming, His **r** is with Him, and Is 62:11
I will **r** them fully for their Is 65:7
the **r** for your work will come Jr 31:16
gifts, a **r**, and great honor Dn 2:6
and distributing land as a **r**. Dn 11:39
because your **r** is great in Mt 5:12
love you, what **r** will you have? Mt 5:46
will have no **r** from your Father Mt 6:1
assure you: They've got their **r**! Mt 6:2
who sees in secret will **r** you. Mt 6:4
assure you: They've got their **r**! Mt 6:5
who sees in secret will **r** you. Mt 6:6
assure you: They've got their **r**! Mt 6:16
who sees in secret will **r** you. Mt 6:18
will receive a prophet's **r**. Mt 10:41
receive a righteous person's **r**. Mt 10:41
He will never lose his **r**!" Mt 10:42
then He will **r** each according Mt 16:27
He will never lose his **r**. Mk 9:41
your **r** is great in heaven, Lk 6:23
Then your **r** will be great, Lk 6:35
receive his own **r** according to 1Co 3:8
survives, he will receive a **r**. 1Co 3:14
I do this willingly, I have a **r**; 1Co 9:17
What then is my **r**? To preach the 1Co 9:18
will receive the **r** of an Col 3:24
and ⌊to **r**⌋ with rest you who are 2Th 1:7
confidence, which has a great **r**. Heb 10:35
his attention was on the **r**. Heb 11:26
but you may receive a full **r**. 2Jn 8
and to give the **r** to Your Rv 11:18
My **r** is with Me to repay each Rv 22:12

REWARDED *(8)*
God has **r** me for giving my slave Gn 30:18
and if you have **r** him Jdg 9:16
The LORD **r** me according to my 2Sm 22:21
The LORD **r** me according to my Ps 18:20
respects a command will be **r**. Pr 13:13
Then the king **r** Shadrach, Dn 3:30
working when he comes will be **r**. Mt 24:46
working when he comes will be **r**. Lk 12:43

REWARDING *(2)*
righteous by **r** him according to 1Kg 8:32
righteous by **r** him according to 2Ch 6:23

REWARDS *(4)*
but good **r** the righteous. Pr 13:21
She **r** him with good, not evil, Pr 31:12
and give your **r** to someone else; Dn 5:17
He exists and **r** those who seek Heb 11:6

REZEPH *(2)*
Gozan, Haran, **R**, and the 2Kg 19:12
Gozan, Haran, **R**, and the Is 37:12

REZIN *(8)*
began sending **R** king of Aram 2Kg 15:37
Then Aram's King **R** and Israel's 2Kg 16:5
At that time **R** king of Aram 2Kg 16:6
to Kir but put **R** to death. 2Kg 16:9
R king of Aram, along with Pekah, Is 7:1
firebrands, **R** of Aram, and the Is 7:4
the head of Damascus is **R** Is 7:8
and rejoiced with **R** and the son Is 8:6

REZIN'S *(3)*
R descendants, Nekoda's Ezr 2:48
descendants, **R** descendants, Neh 7:50
LORD has raised up **R** adversaries Is 9:11

REZON *(3)*
God raised up **R** son of Eliada as 1Kg 11:23
R had fled from his master 1Kg 11:23
R was Israel's enemy throughout 1Kg 11:25

RHEGIUM *(1)*
along the coast, we reached **R**. Ac 28:13

RHESA *(1)*
of Joanan, ⌊son⌋ of **R**, ⌊son⌋ of Lk 3:27

RHODA *(1)*
servant named **R** came to answer. Ac 12:13

RHODES *(1)*
next day to **R**, and from there Ac 21:1

RIB *(2)*
LORD God made the **r** He had taken Gn 2:22
tear open the **r** cage over their Hs 13:8

RIBAI *(2)*
Ittai son of **R** from Gibeah of 2Sm 23:29
Ithai son of **R** from Gibeah of 1Ch 11:31

RIBLAH *(11)*
from Shepham to **R** east of Ain. Nm 34:11
imprisoned him at **R** in the land 2Kg 23:33
up to the king of Babylon at **R**, 2Kg 25:6
to the king of Babylon at **R**. 2Kg 25:20
them to death at **R** in the land 2Kg 25:21
at **R** in the land of Hamath. Jr 39:5
At **R** the king of Babylon Jr 39:6
king of Babylon at **R** in the land Jr 52:9
At **R** the king of Babylon Jr 52:10
to the king of Babylon at **R**. Jr 52:26
them to death at **R** in the land Jr 52:27

RIBS *(2)*
God took one of his **r** and closed Gn 2:21
three **r** in its mouth between Dn 7:5

RICH *(95)*
Abram was very **r** in livestock, Gn 13:2
can never say, 'I made Abram **r**.' Gn 14:23

my master, and he has become **r**. Gn 24:35
man became **r** and kept getting Gn 26:13
And the man became very **r**. Gn 30:43
food will be **r**, and he will Gn 49:20
to anger and **r** in faithful love Ex 34:6
or give preference to the **r**; Lv 19:15
to anger and **r** in faithful love Nm 14:18
younger men, whether **r** or poor. Ru 3:10
kills him very **r** and will give 1Sm 17:25
he was a very **r** man with 3,000 1Sm 25:2
certain city, one **r** and the 2Sm 12:1
The **r** man had a large number of 2Sm 12:2
a traveler came to the **r** man, 2Sm 12:4
but the **r** man could not bring 2Sm 12:4
They found **r**, good pasture, and 1Ch 4:40
and eat what is **r**, drink what is Neh 8:10
to anger and **r** in faithful love Neh 9:17
He will no longer be **r**; Jb 15:29
not favor the **r** over the poor, Jb 34:19
You meet him with **r** blessings; Ps 21:3
low and high, **r** and poor Ps 49:2
not be afraid when a man gets **r**, Ps 49:16
You satisfy me as with **r** food; Ps 63:5
r man's wealth is his fortified Pr 10:15
to be **r** but has nothing; Pr 13:7
there are many who love the **r**. Pr 14:20
r man's wealth is his fortified Pr 18:11
but the **r** one answers roughly. Pr 18:23
wine and oil will not get **r**. Pr 21:17
The **r** and the poor have this in Pr 22:2
r rule over the poor, and the Pr 22:7
giving to the **r**—both lead only Pr 22:16
wear yourself out to get **r**; Pr 23:4
than a **r** man who distorts Pr 28:6
A **r** man is wise in his own eyes, Pr 28:11
in a hurry to get **r** will not go Pr 28:20
abundance of the **r** permits him Ec 5:12
but the **r** remain in lowly Ec 10:6
and do not curse a **r** person even Ec 10:20
eat ⌊among⌋ the ruins of the **r**. Is 5:17
the summit above the **r** valley. Is 28:1
the summit above the **r** valley, Is 28:4
ground, will be **r** and plentiful. Is 30:23
and with a **r** man at His death, Is 53:9
they have grown powerful and **r**. Jr 5:27
the **r** must not boast in his Jr 9:23
by many waters, **r** in treasures, Jr 51:13
they will feed in **r** pasture on Ezk 34:14
I didn't eat any **r** food, no meat Dn 10:3
says: "How **r** I have become; I Hs 12:8
slow to anger, **r** in faithful Jl 2:13
become angry, **r** in faithful love Jnh 4:2
their portion is **r** and their Hab 1:16
LORD because I have become **r**! Zch 11:5
be hard for a **r** person to enter Mt 19:23
than for a **r** person to enter Mt 19:24
a **r** man from Arimathea named Mt 27:57
than for a **r** person to enter Mk 10:25
Many **r** people were putting in Mk 12:41
and sent the **r** away empty. Lk 1:53
to you who are **r**, because you Lk 6:24
A **r** man's land was very Lk 12:16
and is not **r** toward God." Lk 12:21
or your **r** neighbors, because Lk 14:12
There was a **r** man who received Lk 16:1
There was a **r** man who would Lk 16:19
fell from the **r** man's table, Lk 16:21
The **r** man also died and was Lk 16:22
sad, because he was very **r**. Lk 18:23
than for a **r** person to enter Lk 18:25
tax collector, and he was **r**. Lk 19:2
up and saw the **r** dropping their Lk 21:1
Lord of all is **r** to all who call Rm 10:12
come to share in the **r** root of Rm 11:17
you were made **r** in everything— 1Co 1:5
Already you are **r**! You have 1Co 4:8
although He was **r**, for your sake 2Co 8:9
His poverty you might become **r**. 2Co 8:9
who want to be **r** fall into 1Tm 6:9
those who are **r** in the present 1Tm 6:17
do good, to be **r** in good works, 1Tm 6:18
the one who is **r** ⌊should boast⌋ Jms 1:10
the **r** man will wither away while Jms 1:11
this world to be **r** in faith and Jms 2:5
Don't the **r** oppress you and drag Jms 2:6
Come now, you **r** people! Jms 5:1
and poverty, yet you are **r**. Rv 2:9
Because you say, 'I'm **r**; Rv 3:17
the fire so that you may be **r**, Rv 3:18
commanders, the **r**, the powerful, Rv 6:15
small and great, **r** and poor, Rv 13:16
who became **r** from her, will Rv 18:15
the sea became **r** from her wealth Rv 18:19

RICHER *(2)*
and kept getting **r** until he was Gn 26:13
will be far **r** than the others. Dn 11:2

RICHES *(49)*
for long life or **r** for yourself, 1Kg 3:11
both **r** and honor, so that no man 1Kg 3:13
of the world in **r** and in wisdom. 1Kg 10:23
R and honor come from You, 1Ch 29:12
age, full of days, **r**, and honor, 1Ch 29:28
and you have not requested **r**, 2Ch 1:11
also give you **r**, wealth, and 2Ch 1:12
of the world in **r** and wisdom. 2Ch 9:22
and he had **r** and honor in 2Ch 17:5
Now Jehoshaphat had **r** and honor 2Ch 18:1
had abundant **r** and glory, 2Ch 32:27
that no one lures you with **r**; Jb 36:18
and boast of their abundant **r**. Ps 49:6
in the abundance of his **r**, Ps 52:7
Wealth and **r** are in his house, Ps 112:3
decrees as much as in all **r**. Ps 119:14
in her left, **r** and honor. Pr 3:16
With me are **r** and honor, lasting Pr 8:18
but diligent hands bring **r**. Pr 10:4
but violent men gain ⌊only⌋ **r**. Pr 11:16
trusting in his **r** will fall, Pr 11:28
R are a ransom for a man's life, Pr 13:8
are still not content with **r**. Ec 4:8
has also given **r** and wealth to Ec 5:19
God gives a man **r**, wealth, and Ec 6:2
to the wise, or **r** to the Ec 9:11
of darkness and **r** from secret Is 45:3
because the **r** of the sea will Is 60:5
and you will boast in their **r**. Is 61:6
rich must not boast in his **r**. Jr 9:23
of his days ⌊his **r**⌋ will abandon Jr 17:11
power he gains through his **r**, Dn 11:2
silver, precious stones, and **r**. Dn 11:38
and over all the **r** of Egypt. Dn 11:43
and grapevine yield their **r**. Jl 2:22
with worries, **r**, and pleasures Lk 8:14
despise the **r** of His kindness Rm 2:4
to make known the **r** of His glory Rm 9:23
brings **r** for the world, Rm 11:12
their failure **r** for the Gentiles Rm 11:12
the depth of the **r** both of the Rm 11:33
according to the **r** of His grace Eph 1:7
are the glorious **r** of His Eph 1:18
the immeasurable **r** of His grace Eph 2:7
incalculable **r** of the Messiah, Eph 3:8
according to the **r** of His glory, Eph 3:16
according to His **r** in glory in Php 4:19
may have all the **r** of assured Col 2:2
receive power and **r** and wisdom Rv 5:12

RICHEST *(1)*
will come into the **r** parts of Dn 11:24

RICHLY *(5)*
I said I would reward you **r**, Nm 24:11
r colored linen from Egypt. Pr 7:16
the Messiah dwell **r** among you, Col 3:16
r provides us with all things 1Tm 6:17
will be **r** supplied to you. 2Pt 1:11

RICHNESS *(3)*
sky and from the **r** of the land— Gn 27:28
be away from the **r** of the land, Gn 27:39
can eat from the **r** of the land.' Gn 45:18

RID *(13)*
Get **r** of the foreign gods that Gn 35:2
and I will **r** Myself of the Nm 17:5
Get **r** of the gods your ancestors Jos 24:14
Then get **r** of the foreign gods Jos 24:23
they got **r** of the foreign gods Jdg 10:16
be drunk? Get **r** of your wine!" 1Sm 1:14
r of the foreign gods and the 1Sm 7:3
and got **r** of their enemies. Est 9:16
the Jews got **r** of their enemies Est 9:22
R us of the Holy One of Israel." Is 30:11
If you get **r** of the yoke from Is 58:9
one month I got **r** of three Zch 11:8
So **r** yourselves of all 1Pt 2:1

RIDDEN *(2)*
donkey you've **r** all your life Nm 22:30
a horse the king himself has **r**, Est 6:8

RIDDING *(1)*
r yourselves of all moral filth Jms 1:21

RIDDLE *(9)*
me tell you a **r**," Samson said to Jdg 14:12
"Tell us your **r**," they replied. Jdg 14:13
were unable to explain the **r**. Jdg 14:14
husband to explain the **r** to us, Jdg 14:15
my people the **r**, but haven't Jdg 14:16
you wouldn't know my **r** now! Jdg 14:18
those who had explained the **r**. Jdg 14:19
I explain my **r** with a lyre. Ps 49:4
pose a **r** and speak a parable to Ezk 17:2

RIDDLES *(5)*
directly, openly, and not in **r**; Nm 12:8
words of the wise, and their **r**. Pr 1:6
Isn't he ⌊just⌋ posing **r**?" Ezk 20:49
dreams, explain **r**, and solve Dn 5:12
with mockery and **r** about him? Hab 2:6

RIDE *(18)*
He had Joseph **r** in his second Gn 41:43
He made him **r** on the heights of Dt 32:13
You who **r** on white donkeys, Jdg 5:10
for the king's household to **r**, 2Sm 16:2
so that I may **r** it and go with 2Sm 19:26
son Solomon **r** on my own mule, 1Kg 1:33
had Solomon **r** on King David's 1Kg 1:38
have had him **r** on the king's 1Kg 1:44
So he let him **r** with him in his 2Kg 10:16
on the wind and make me **r** ⌊it⌋; Jb 30:22
in your splendor **r** triumphantly Ps 45:4
You let men **r** over our heads; Ps 66:12
"We will **r** on fast horses"— Is 30:16
I will make you **r** over the Is 58:14
sea, and they **r** on horses, lined Jr 6:23
sea, and they **r** on horses, lined Jr 50:42
us, we will not **r** on horses, and Hs 14:3
sea when You **r** on Your horses, Hab 3:8

RIDER *(11)*
so that its **r** falls backwards. Gn 49:17
horse and its **r** into the sea. Ex 15:1
horse and its **r** into the sea. Ex 15:21
Choose a **r** and send him to meet 2Kg 9:17
laughs at the horse and its **r**. Jb 39:18
will smash the horse and its **r**; Jr 51:21
smash the chariot and its **r**. Jr 51:21
panic and its **r** with madness. Zch 12:4
Its **r** is called Faithful and Rv 19:11
war against the **r** on the horse Rv 19:19
the mouth of the **r** on the horse, Rv 19:21

RIDERS *(11)*
able to supply **r** for them! 2Kg 18:23
When he sees **r**—pairs of Is 21:7
of horsemen, **r** on donkeys, Is 21:7
on donkeys, **r** on camels—pay Is 21:7
r come—horsemen in pairs. Is 21:9
horses if you can put **r** on them! Is 36:8
horses and **r**, who are all Ezk 38:4
eat your fill of horses and **r**, Ezk 39:20
overturn chariots and their **r**. Hg 2:22
Horses and their **r** will fall, Hg 2:22
flesh of horses and of their **r**, Rv 19:18

RIDES *(5)*
the discharge **r** on will be Lv 15:9
who **r** the heavens to your aid on Dt 33:26
Exalt Him who **r** on the clouds— Ps 68:4
to Him who **r** in the ancient, Ps 68:33
the LORD **r** on a swift cloud and Is 19:1

RIDGE *(3)*
and went up the **r** of the hill Nm 14:40
dared to go up the **r** of the hill Nm 14:44
going along the **r** of the hill 2Sm 16:13

RIDGES *(1)*
its furrows and leveling its **r**. Ps 65:10

RIDICULE *(15)*
r among all the peoples where Dt 28:37
object of scorn and **r** among all 1Kg 9:7
object of scorn and **r** among all 2Ch 7:20
of mockery and **r** to those around Ps 44:13
look on with awe and will **r** him: Ps 52:6
You **r** all the nations. Ps 59:8
of mockery and **r** to those around Ps 79:4
the **r** against Your servants— Ps 89:50
they **r** and curse me. Ps 102:8

an object of **r** to my accusers; Ps 109:25
The arrogant constantly **r** me, Ps 119:51
object of scorn, **r**, and cursing, Jr 24:9
be an object of **r** and scorn, Ezk 23:32
an object of **r** to all those Dn 9:16
the dead, some began to **r** him. Ac 17:32

RIDICULED *(7)*

he **r** the LORD's anointed? 2Sm 19:21
I am **r** by all my adversaries and Ps 31:11
enemies have **r**, LORD, how they Ps 89:51
how they have **r** every step of Ps 89:51
They will be **r** for this in the Hs 7:16
They **r** him: "You're that man's Jn 9:28
If you are **r** for the name of 1Pt 4:14

RIDICULES *(3)*

heaven laughs; the Lord **r** them. Ps 2:4
As for the eye that **r** a father Pr 30:17
all the time; everyone **r** me. Jr 20:7

RIDICULING *(2)*

they kept **r** God's messengers, 2Ch 36:16
you can keep on **r** with no one to Jb 11:3

RIDING *(14)*

Balaam was **r** his donkey, and his Nm 22:22
Absalom was **r** on his mule when 2Sm 18:9
you and I were **r** side by side 2Kg 9:25
I took was the one I was **r**. Neh 2:12
r in chariots and on horses with Jr 17:25
of this palace **r** on chariots Jr 22:4
young men, horsemen **r** on steeds. Ezk 23:6
horsemen **r** on steeds, all Ezk 23:12
all of them **r** on horses. Ezk 23:23
merchant in saddlecloths for **r**. Ezk 27:20
you, who are all **r** horses—a Ezk 38:15
and the one **r** a horse will not Am 2:15
and saw a man **r** on a red horse. Zch 1:8
humble and **r** on a donkey, on a Zch 9:9

RIGHT *(444)*

If you do **r**, won't you be Gn 4:7
if you do not do **r**, sin is Gn 4:7
to the left, I will go to the **r**; Gn 13:9
you go⌋ to the **r**, I will go to Gn 13:9
by doing what is **r** and just. Gn 18:19
to him, "All **r**, I'll grant your Gn 19:21
guided me on the **r** way to take Gn 24:48
servant Jacob is **r** behind us.' " Gn 32:20
She is more in the **r** than I, Gn 38:26
with his **r** hand Ephraim toward Gn 48:13
Manasseh toward Israel's **r**— Gn 48:13
out his **r** hand and put it Gn 48:14
had placed his **r** hand on Gn 48:17
Put your **r** hand on his head." Gn 48:18
until He whose **r** it is comes and Gn 49:10
It would not be **r** to do that, Ex 8:26
them on their **r** and their left. Ex 14:22
them on their **r** and their left. Ex 14:29
r hand is glorious in power. Ex 15:6
Your **r** hand shattered the enemy. Ex 15:6
You stretched out Your **r** hand, Ex 15:12
God, do what is **r** in His eyes, Ex 15:26
He has no **r** to sell her to Ex 21:8
and put it on Aaron's **r** earlobe, Ex 29:20
on his sons' **r** earlobes, Ex 29:20
on the thumbs of their **r** hands, Ex 29:20
on the big toes of their **r** feet. Ex 29:20
on them, and the **r** thigh (since Ex 29:22
are to give the **r** thigh to the Lv 7:32
fat will have the **r** thigh as a Lv 7:33
put ⌊it⌋ on Aaron's **r** earlobe, Lv 8:23
on the thumb of his **r** hand, Lv 8:23
on the big toe of his **r** foot. Lv 8:23
the blood on their **r** earlobes, Lv 8:24
on the thumbs of their **r** hands, Lv 8:24
on the big toes of their **r** feet. Lv 8:24
fat—as well as the **r** thigh. Lv 8:25
fat portions and the **r** thigh. Lv 8:26
the breasts and the **r** thigh as a Lv 9:21
the lobe of the **r** ear of the one Lv 14:14
on the thumb of his **r** hand, Lv 14:14
on the big toe of his **r** foot. Lv 14:14
will dip his **r** finger into the Lv 14:16
the lobe of the **r** ear of the one Lv 14:17
on the thumb of his **r** hand, Lv 14:17
on the big toe of his **r** foot, Lv 14:17
put ⌊it⌋ on the **r** earlobe of the Lv 14:25
on the thumb of his **r** hand, Lv 14:25
on the big toe of his **r** foot. Lv 14:25
his **r** finger the priest will Lv 14:27
his palm on the **r** earlobe of the Lv 14:28
on the thumb of his **r** hand, Lv 14:28
on the big toe of his **r** foot, Lv 14:28
his **r** of redemption will last Lv 25:29
his **r** of redemption will last a Lv 25:29
The **r** to redeem ⌊such⌋ houses Lv 25:31
always have the **r** to redeem Lv 25:32
he has the **r** of redemption after Lv 25:48
give you rain at the **r** time, Lv 26:4
like this, please kill me **r** now. Nm 11:15
are **r** in front of you, Nm 14:43
offering and the **r** thigh. Nm 18:18
turn to the **r** or the left until Nm 20:17
and are living **r** across from me. Nm 22:5
to turn to the **r** or the left. Nm 22:26
Joseph's descendants says is **r**. Nm 36:5
not turn to the **r** or the left. Dt 2:27
Everything they have said is **r**. Dt 5:28
turn aside to the **r** or the left. Dt 5:32
Do what is **r** and good in the Dt 6:18
seems **r** in his own eyes. Dt 12:8
be doing what is **r** in the LORD's Dt 12:25
what is good and **r** in the sight Dt 12:28
doing what is **r** in the sight of Dt 13:18
Do not turn to the **r** or the left Dt 17:11
command to the **r** or the left, Dt 17:20
be doing what is **r** in the LORD's Dt 21:9
turn aside to the **r** or the left Dt 28:14
from His **r** hand for them. Dt 33:2
from it to the **r** or the left, Jos 1:7
to us whatever you think is **r**." Jos 9:25
turn from it to the **r** or left Jos 23:6
it to his **r** thigh under his Jdg 3:16
took the sword from his **r** thigh, Jdg 3:21
for a tent peg, her **r** hand, for Jdg 5:26
their trumpets in their **r** hands, Jdg 7:20
one on his **r** hand and the other Jdg 16:29
Take my **r** of redemption, because Ru 4:6
concerning the **r** of redemption Ru 4:7
that you hand it over **r** now. 1Sm 2:16
strayed to the **r** or to the left. 1Sm 6:12
out everyone's **r** eye and 1Sm 11:2
teach you the good and **r** way. 1Sm 12:23
I'm **r** here with you whatever you 1Sm 14:7
"All **r**," Jonathan replied, "we'll 1Sm 14:8
give us the **r** ⌊decision⌋." 1Sm 14:41
r now he's tending the sheep. 1Sm 16:11
I will be **r** behind you." 1Sm 25:19
not turn to the **r** or the left in 2Sm 2:19
Turn to your **r** or left, seize 2Sm 2:21
and he fell and died **r** there. 2Sm 2:23
counterattacked **r** up to the 2Sm 11:23
can turn to the **r** or left from 2Sm 14:19
Joab has a field **r** next to mine, 2Sm 14:30
your claims are good and **r**, 2Sm 15:3
was **r** there to meet him. 2Sm 16:1
warriors on David's **r** and left. 2Sm 16:6
him to the ground **r** there? 2Sm 18:11
Is the young man Absalom all **r**? 2Sm 18:29
Is the young man Absalom all **r**? 2Sm 18:32
So what further **r** do I have to 2Sm 19:28
Then with his **r** hand Joab 2Sm 20:9
woman replied to Joab, "All **r**. 2Sm 20:21
So she sat down at his **r** hand. 1Kg 2:19
was on the **r** side of the temple 1Kg 6:8
he set up the **r** pillar and named 1Kg 7:21
carts on the **r** side of the 1Kg 7:39
near the **r** side of the temple 1Kg 7:39
five on the **r** and five on the 1Kg 7:49
My ways to do **r** in My eyes and 1Kg 11:33
and do what is **r** in My sight in 1Kg 11:38
doing only what is **r** in My eyes. 1Kg 14:8
did what was **r** in the LORD's 1Kg 15:5
Asa did what was **r** in the LORD's 1Kg 15:11
since it is **r** next to my palace. 1Kg 21:2
by Him at His **r** hand and at His 1Kg 22:19
but did what was **r** in the LORD's 1Kg 22:43
which parted to the **r** and left. 2Kg 2:8
parted to the **r** and the left, 2Kg 2:14
replied, "Everything is all **r**." 2Kg 4:23
her and ask, 'Are you all **r**? 2Kg 4:26
Is your husband all **r**? 2Kg 4:26
Is your son all **r**?' " And she 2Kg 4:26
answered, "Everything's all **r**." 2Kg 4:26
asked, "Is everything all **r**?" 2Kg 5:21
Gehazi said, "It's all **r**. 2Kg 5:22
We're not doing what is **r**. 2Kg 7:9
asked, "Is everything all **r**? 2Kg 9:11
Do whatever you think is **r**." 2Kg 10:5
out what is **r** in My sight and 2Kg 10:30
from the **r** side of the temple to 2Kg 11:11
did what was **r** in the LORD's 2Kg 12:2
the altar on the **r** side as one 2Kg 12:9
He did what was **r** in the LORD's 2Kg 14:3
did what was **r** in the LORD's 2Kg 15:3
He did what was **r** in the LORD's 2Kg 15:34
not do what was **r** in the sight 2Kg 16:2
what was not **r** against the LORD 2Kg 17:9
He did what was **r** in the LORD's 2Kg 18:3
He did what was **r** in the LORD's 2Kg 22:2
not turn to the **r** or the left. 2Kg 22:2
Asaph, who stood at his **r** hand: 1Ch 6:39
either their **r** or left hand, 1Ch 12:2
proposal seemed **r** to all the 1Ch 13:4
on the **r** and one on the left. 2Ch 3:17
the one on the **r** Jachin and the 2Ch 3:17
he put five on the **r** and five on 2Ch 4:6
five on the **r** and five on the 2Ch 4:7
five on the **r** and five on the 2Ch 4:8
put the reservoir on the **r** side, 2Ch 4:10
what was good and **r** in the sight 2Ch 14:2
standing at His **r** hand and at 2Ch 18:18
but did what was **r** in the LORD's 2Ch 20:32
from the **r** side of the temple to 2Ch 23:10
did what was **r** in the LORD's 2Ch 24:2
He did what was **r** in the LORD's 2Ch 25:2
He did what was **r** in the LORD's 2Ch 26:4
you have no **r** to offer incense 2Ch 26:18
have the **r** to offer incense. 2Ch 26:18
He did what was **r** in the LORD's 2Ch 27:2
not do what was **r** in the LORD's 2Ch 28:1
He did what was **r** in the LORD's 2Ch 29:2
offering goats **r** into the 2Ch 29:23
He did what was **r** in the LORD's 2Ch 34:2
turn aside to the **r** or the left. 2Ch 34:2
it is not **r** for us to witness Ezr 4:14
have no share, **r**, or historic Neh 2:20
What you are doing isn't **r**. Neh 5:9
stood beside him on his **r**; Neh 8:4
One went to the **r** on the wall, Neh 12:31
the matter seems **r** to the king Est 8:5
and every city the **r** to assemble Est 8:11
the Almighty pervert what is **r**? Jb 8:3
⌊if⌋ He goes **r** by, I wouldn't Jb 9:11
if I were in the **r**, I could not Jb 9:15
if I were in the **r**, my own mouth Jb 9:20
my⌋ case; I know that I am **r**. Jb 13:18
never affirm that you are **r**. Jb 27:5
The rabble rise up at my **r**; Jb 30:12
tell a person what is **r** for him Jb 33:23
sinned and perverted what was **r**; Jb 33:27
judge for ourselves what is **r**; Jb 34:4
that your own **r** hand can deliver Jb 40:14
Because He is at my **r** hand, Ps 16:8
in Your **r** hand are eternal Ps 16:11
You, ⌊for⌋ You see what is **r**. Ps 17:2
who rebel against Your **r** hand. Ps 17:7
Your **r** hand upholds me, and Your Ps 18:35
The precepts of the LORD are **r**, Ps 19:8
victories from His **r** hand. Ps 20:6
your **r** hand will seize those who Ps 21:8
me along the **r** paths for His Ps 23:3
in what is **r** and teaches them Ps 25:9
whose **r** hands are filled with Ps 26:10
For the word of the LORD is **r**, Ps 33:4
but by Your **r** hand, Your arm, Ps 44:3
May your **r** hand show your Ps 45:4
Ophir, stands at your **r** hand. Ps 45:9
Your **r** hand is filled with Ps 48:10
What **r** do you have to recite My Ps 50:16
So You are **r** when You pass Ps 51:4
with Your **r** hand, and answer Ps 60:5
Your **r** hand holds on to me. Ps 63:8
with You; You hold my **r** hand. Ps 73:23
out Your **r** hand and destroy Ps 74:11
sorrow that the **r** hand of the Ps 77:10
mountain His **r** hand acquired. Ps 78:54
root Your **r** hand has planted, Ps 80:15
be with the man at Your **r** hand, Ps 80:17
Your **r** hand is lifted high. Ps 89:13
the sea and his **r** hand to the Ps 89:25
lifted high the **r** hand of his Ps 89:42
and ten thousand at your **r** hand, Ps 91:7
His **r** hand and holy arm have won Ps 98:1
them their food at the **r** time. Ps 104:27
led them by the **r** path to go to Ps 107:7

Save with Your **r** hand and answer Ps 108:6
an accuser stand at his **r** hand. Ps 109:6
He stands at the **r** hand of the Ps 109:31
Sit at My **r** hand until I make Ps 110:1
The Lord is at Your **r** hand; Ps 110:5
The LORD's **r** hand strikes with Ps 118:15
The LORD's **r** hand is raised! Ps 118:16
r hand strikes with power! Ps 118:16
I have done what is just and **r**; Ps 119:121
is a shelter **r** by your side. Ps 121:5
my **r** hand forget ⌊its skill⌋. Ps 137:5
Your **r** hand will save me. Ps 138:7
Your **r** hand will hold on to me. Ps 139:10
Look to the **r** and see: Ps 142:4
whose **r** hands are deceptive. Ps 144:8
whose **r** hands are deceptive. Ps 144:11
who abandon the **r** paths to walk Pr 2:13
will guide you on the **r** paths. Pr 3:6
Long life is in her **r** hand; Pr 3:16
turn to the **r** or to the left; Pr 4:27
and what my lips say is **r**. Pr 8:6
and **r** to those who discover Pr 8:9
another withholds what is **r**, Pr 11:24
fool's way is **r** in his own eyes Pr 12:15
the truth declares what is **r**, Pr 12:17
is a way that seems **r** to a man, Pr 14:12
ways seem **r** in his own eyes Pr 16:2
is a way that seems **r** to a man, Pr 16:25
his case seems **r** until another Pr 18:17
the ways of a man seem **r** to him, Pr 21:2
when your lips say what is **r**. Pr 23:16
keep your mind on the **r** course. Pr 23:19
spoken at the **r** time is like Pr 25:11
and grasps oil with his **r** hand. Pr 27:16
man who distorts **r** and wrong. Pr 28:6
who distorts **r** and wrong will Pr 28:18
heart knows the **r** time and Ec 8:5
there is a **r** time and procedure Ec 8:6
man's heart ⌊goes⌋ to the **r**, Ec 10:2
is only **r** that they adore you. Sg 1:4
and his **r** hand embraces me. Sg 2:6
and his **r** hand embraces me. Sg 8:3
They carve ⌊meat⌋ on the **r**, Is 9:20
seeks what is **r** and is quick to Is 16:5
turn to the **r** or to the left, Is 30:21
to you with My righteous **r** hand. Is 41:10
hold your **r** hand and say to you: Is 41:13
might say: He is **r**? No one Is 41:26
"Isn't there a lie in my **r** hand?" Is 44:20
whose **r** hand I have grasped to Is 45:1
truthfully; I say what is **r**. Is 45:19
and My **r** hand spread out the Is 48:13
out to the **r** and to the left, Is 54:3
justice and do what is **r**, Is 56:1
that does what is **r** and does not Is 58:2
sworn with His **r** hand and His Is 62:8
glorious arm at Moses' **r** hand, Is 63:12
one who joyfully does what is **r**; Is 64:5
They do not speak what is **r**. Jr 8:6
What ⌊**r**⌋ does My beloved have to Jr 11:15
as it seemed **r** for him to do. Jr 18:4
were a signet ring on My **r** hand, Jr 22:24
me what you think is good and **r**. Jr 26:14
for you own the **r** of redemption Jr 32:7
for you own the **r** of inheritance Jr 32:8
seems good and **r** for you to go, Jr 40:4
The LORD is in the **r**, for I have Lm 1:18
and withdrawn His **r** hand in the Lm 2:3
His **r** hand is positioned like an Lm 2:4
had the face of a lion on the **r**, Ezk 1:10
but on your **r** side, and bear Ezk 4:6
from the earth **r** before my eyes; Ezk 10:19
who have the **r** to redeem you, Ezk 11:15
and does what is just and **r**: Ezk 18:5
son has done what is just and **r**, Ezk 18:19
and does what is just and **r**, Ezk 18:21
and does what is just and **r**, Ezk 18:27
a broken heart **r** before their Ezk 21:6
Slash to the **r**; turn to the left Ezk 21:16
Jerusalem appears in his **r** hand, Ezk 21:22
and does what is just and **r**— Ezk 33:14
He has done what is just and **r**; Ezk 33:16
and does what is just and **r**, Ezk 33:19
arrows drop from your **r** hand. Ezk 39:3
and do what is just and **r**. Ezk 45:9
your sins by doing what is **r**, Dn 4:27
they are **r** in front of My face. Hs 7:2
For the ways of the LORD are **r**, Hs 14:9
are incapable of doing **r**— Am 3:10
against you ⌊**r** here⌋ in the Am 7:10
"Is it **r** for you to be angry?" Jnh 4:4
Is it **r** for you to be angry Jnh 4:9
replied. "It is **r**. I'm angry Jnh 4:9
between their **r** and their left, Jnh 4:11
pervert everything that is **r**, Mc 3:9
r into the mouth of the eater! Nah 3:12
violence are **r** in front of me. Hab 1:3
in the LORD's **r** hand will come Hab 2:16
r now the whole earth is calm Zch 1:11
standing at his **r** side to accuse Zch 3:1
one on the **r** of the bowl and the Zch 4:3
olive trees on the **r** and left Zch 4:11
If it seems **r** to you, give me my Zch 11:12
strike his arm and his **r** eye! Zch 11:17
away and his **r** eye go completely Zch 11:17
them on the **r** and the left, Zch 12:6
If your **r** eye causes you to sin, Mt 5:29
And if your **r** hand causes you to Mt 5:30
slaps you on your **r** cheek, Mt 5:39
know what your **r** hand is doing, Mt 6:3
R away a man with a serious skin Mt 8:2
It isn't **r** to take the Mt 15:26
I'll give you whatever is **r**.' Mt 20:4
Don't I have the **r** to do what I Mt 20:15
one on Your **r** and the other on Mt 20:21
to sit at My **r** and left is not Mt 20:23
'Sit at My **r** hand until I put Mt 22:44
He will put the sheep on His **r**, Mt 25:33
will say to those on His **r**, Mt 25:34
So he went **r** up to Jesus and Mt 26:49
Him at a distance **r** to the high Mt 26:58
seated at the **r** hand of the Mt 26:64
and placed a reed in His **r** hand. Mt 27:29
on the **r** and one on the left. Mt 27:38
and **r** away He entered the Mk 1:21
R away Jesus understood in His Mk 2:8
and it sprang up **r** away, since Mk 4:5
dressed and in his **r** mind; Mk 5:15
head on a platter—**r** now!" Mk 6:25
because it isn't **r** to take the Mk 7:27
to sit at Your **r** and at Your Mk 10:37
to sit at My **r** or left is not Mk 10:40
send it back here **r** away.'" Mk 11:3
to Him, "You are **r**, Teacher! Mk 12:32
'Sit at My **r** hand until I put Mk 12:36
he went **r** up to Him and said, Mk 14:45
r into the high priest's Mk 14:54
seated at the **r** hand of the Mk 14:62
on His **r** and one on His left. Mk 15:27
robe sitting on the **r** side; Mk 16:5
sat down at the **r** hand of God. Mk 16:19
standing to the **r** of the altar Lk 1:11
He passed **r** through the crowd Lk 4:30
was there whose **r** hand was Lk 6:6
dressed and in his **r** mind. Lk 8:35
Mary has made the **r** choice, Lk 10:42
in the west, **r** away you say, Lk 12:54
judge for yourselves what is **r**? Lk 12:57
God was going to appear **r** away. Lk 19:11
to my Lord, 'Sit at My **r** hand Lk 20:42
but the end won't come **r** away." Lk 21:9
slave and cut off his **r** ear. Lk 22:50
be seated at the **r** hand of the Lk 22:69
on the **r** and one on the left. Lk 23:33
gave them the **r** to be children Jn 1:12
granted Him the **r** to pass Jn 5:27
Aren't we **r** in saying that Jn 8:48
I have the **r** to lay it down, Jn 10:18
and I have the **r** to take it up Jn 10:18
slave, and cut off his **r** ear. Jn 18:10
net on the **r** side of the boat, Jn 21:6
because He is at my **r** hand, Ac 2:25
exalted to the **r** hand of God and Ac 2:33
to my Lord, 'Sit at My **r** hand Ac 2:34
him by the **r** hand he raised Ac 3:7
it's **r** in the sight of God Ac 4:19
this man to His **r** hand as ruler Ac 5:31
It would not be **r** for us to give Ac 6:2
standing at the **r** hand of God, Ac 7:55
standing at the **r** hand of God!" Ac 7:56
your heart is not **r** before God. Ac 8:21
you did the **r** thing in coming Ac 10:33
And it came out **r** away. Ac 16:18
R away he and all his family Ac 16:33
man, I sent him to you **r** away. Ac 23:30
He also is at the **r** hand of God Rm 8:34
the potter no **r** over His clay, Rm 9:21
that this **r** of yours in no 1Co 8:9
we have the **r** to eat and drink 1Co 9:4
we have the **r** to be accompanied 1Co 9:5
and I who have no **r** to refrain 1Co 9:6
on the **r** hand and the left, 2Co 6:7
but that you may do what is **r**, 2Co 13:7
they gave the **r** hand of Gl 2:9
to be with you **r** now and change Gl 4:20
seating Him at His **r** hand in the Eph 1:20
in the Lord, because this is **r**. Eph 6:1
It is **r** for me to think this way Php 1:7
seated at the **r** hand of God. Col 3:1
slaves with what is **r** and fair, Col 4:1
don't have the **r** ⌊to support⌋, 2Th 3:9
Crete was to set **r** what was left Ti 1:5
to command you to do what is **r**, Phm 8
He sat down at the **r** hand of the Heb 1:3
Sit at My **r** hand until I make Heb 1:13
sat down at the **r** hand of the Heb 8:1
these things in detail **r** now. Heb 9:5
sat down at the **r** hand of God. Heb 10:12
sat down at the **r** hand of God's Heb 12:2
do not have a **r** to eat. Heb 13:10
and **r** away forgets what kind of Jms 1:24
He is at God's **r** hand, with 1Pt 3:22
I consider it **r**, as long as I am 2Pt 1:13
who does what is **r** has been born 1Jn 2:29
who does what is **r** is righteous, 1Jn 3:7
not do what is **r** is not of God, 1Jn 3:10
His **r** hand He had seven stars; Rv 1:16
He laid His **r** hand on me, and Rv 1:17
stars you saw in My **r** hand, Rv 1:20
stars in His **r** hand and who Rv 2:1
the victor the **r** to eat from Rv 2:7
give him the **r** to sit with Me Rv 3:21
I saw in the **r** hand of the One Rv 5:1
out of the **r** hand of the One Rv 5:7
He put his **r** foot on the sea, Rv 10:2
raised his **r** hand to heaven. Rv 10:5
a mark on his **r** hand or on his Rv 13:16
they may have the **r** to the tree Rv 22:14

RIGHT-HAND *(3)*

worship and I, as his **r** man, bow 2Kg 5:18
the king's **r** man, responded to 2Kg 7:2
the captain, his **r** man, to be in 2Kg 7:17

RIGHT-MINDED *(1)*

Become **r** and stop sinning, 1Co 15:34

RIGHTEOUS *(319)*

was a **r** man, blameless among Gn 6:9
you ⌊alone⌋ are **r** before Me in Gn 7:1
away the **r** with the wicked? Gn 18:23
if there are 50 **r** people in the Gn 18:24
sake of the 50 **r** people who are Gn 18:24
to kill the **r** with the wicked, Gn 18:25
treating the **r** and the wicked Gn 18:25
Sodom I find 50 **r** people in the Gn 18:26
suppose the 50 **r** lack five. Gn 18:28
The LORD is the **R** One, and I and Ex 9:27
and corrupts the words of the **r**. Ex 23:8
what great nation has **r** statutes Dt 4:8
the people with **r** judgment. Dt 16:18
and twists the words of the **r**. Dt 16:19
prejudice, He is **r** and true. Dt 32:4
them tell the **r** acts of the LORD Jdg 5:11
the **r** deeds of His warriors in Jdg 5:11
about all the **r** acts He has done 1Sm 12:7
You are more **r** than I, for you 1Sm 24:17
men kill a **r** man in his own 2Sm 4:11
two men more **r** and better than 1Kg 2:32
justice for the **r** by rewarding 1Kg 8:32
justice for the **r** by rewarding 2Ch 6:23
and said, "The LORD is **r**." 2Ch 12:6
Israel, You are **r**, for we Ezr 9:15
Your promise, for You are **r**. Neh 9:8
are **r** concerning all that has Neh 9:33
Can a person be more **r** than God, Jb 4:17
even if I am **r**, I cannot lift Jb 10:15
The **r** and upright man is a Jb 12:4
of woman, that he should be **r**? Jb 15:14
the **r** person will hold to his Jb 17:9
the Almighty if you are **r**? Jb 22:3
The **r** see ⌊this⌋ and rejoice; Jb 22:19
up, but the **r** will wear ⌊it⌋, Jb 27:17
he was **r** in his own eyes. Jb 32:1
declared, "I am **r**, yet God has Jb 34:5
you condemn the mighty **R** One, Jb 34:17
you say, "I am **r** before God"? Jb 35:2

If you are **r**, what do you give Jb 35:7
not remove His gaze from the **r**, Jb 36:7
be in the community of the **r**. Ps 1:5
watches over the way of the **r**, Ps 1:6
For You, LORD, bless the **r** one; Ps 5:12
to an end, but establish the **r**. Ps 7:9
and emotions is a **r** God. Ps 7:9
God is a **r** judge, and a God who Ps 7:11
on Your throne as a **r** judge. Ps 9:4
destroyed, what can the **r** do?" Ps 11:3
examines the **r** and the wicked. Ps 11:5
For the LORD is **r**; Ps 11:7
He loves **r** deeds. The upright Ps 11:7
for God is with those who are **r**. Ps 14:5
are reliable and altogether **r**. Ps 19:9
against the **r** with pride Ps 31:18
LORD and rejoice, you **r** ones; Ps 32:11
Rejoice in the LORD, you **r** ones; Ps 33:1
eyes of the LORD are on the **r**, Ps 34:15
The **r** cry out, and the LORD Ps 34:17
come to the one who is **r**, Ps 34:19
who hate the **r** will be punished Ps 34:21
against the **r** and gnashes his Ps 37:12
little that the **r** man has than Ps 37:16
but the LORD supports the **r**. Ps 37:17
the **r** is gracious and giving. Ps 37:21
not seen the **r** abandoned or his Ps 37:25
The **r** will inherit the land and Ps 37:29
mouth of the **r** utters wisdom; Ps 37:30
in wait for the **r** and seeks to Ps 37:32
of the **r** is from the LORD Ps 37:39
will delight in **r** sacrifices, Ps 51:19
The **r** will look on with awe and Ps 52:6
never allow the **r** to be shaken. Ps 55:22
The **r** will rejoice when he sees Ps 58:10
there is a reward for the **r**! Ps 58:11
The **r** rejoice in the LORD and Ps 64:10
But the **r** are glad; Ps 68:3
and not be recorded with the **r**. Ps 69:28
May the **r** flourish in his days, Ps 72:7
of the **r** will be lifted up. Ps 75:10
r thrive like a palm tree and Ps 92:12
for justice will again be **r**, Ps 94:15
the life of the **r** and condemn Ps 94:21
dawns for the **r**, gladness for Ps 97:11
the LORD, you **r** ones, and praise Ps 97:12
gracious, compassionate, and **r**. Ps 112:4
r will be remembered forever. Ps 112:6
The LORD is gracious and **r**; Ps 116:5
victory in the tents of the **r**: Ps 118:15
the **r** will enter through it. Ps 118:20
when I learn Your **r** judgments. Ps 119:7
thank You for Your **r** judgments. Ps 119:62
sworn to keep Your **r** judgments. Ps 119:106
and for Your **r** promise. Ps 119:123
You are **r**, LORD, and Your Ps 119:137
You issue are **r** and altogether Ps 119:138
Your decrees are **r** forever. Ps 119:144
and all Your **r** judgments endure Ps 119:160
a day for Your **r** judgments. Ps 119:164
for all Your commandments are **r**. Ps 119:172
over the land allotted to the **r**, Ps 125:3
so that the **r** will not apply Ps 125:3
The LORD is **r**; He has cut the Ps 129:4
Surely the **r** will praise Your Ps 140:13
Let the **r** one strike me—it is Ps 141:5
The **r** will gather around me Ps 142:7
no one alive is **r** in Your sight. Ps 143:2
LORD is **r** in all His ways and Ps 145:17
The LORD loves the **r**. Ps 146:8
and keep to the paths of the **r**. Pr 2:20
He blesses the home of the **r**; Pr 3:33
The path of the **r** is like the Pr 4:18
All the words of my mouth are **r**; Pr 8:8
as do nobles ⌊and⌋ all **r** judges. Pr 8:16
teach a **r** man, and he will learn Pr 9:9
will not let the **r** go hungry, Pr 10:3
are on the head of the **r**, Pr 10:6
of the **r** is a blessing, Pr 10:7
The mouth of the **r** is a fountain Pr 10:11
labor of the **r** leads to life; Pr 10:16
tongue of the **r** is pure silver; Pr 10:20
The lips of the **r** feed many, Pr 10:21
but what the **r** desires will be Pr 10:24
but the **r** are secure forever. Pr 10:25
hope of the **r** is joy, but the Pr 10:28
The **r** will never be shaken, Pr 10:30
mouth of the **r** produces wisdom Pr 10:31

The lips of the **r** know what is Pr 10:32
The **r** is rescued from trouble; Pr 11:8
knowledge the **r** are rescued. Pr 11:9
When the **r** thrive, a city Pr 11:10
offspring of the **r** will escape. Pr 11:21
desire of the **r** ⌊turns out⌋ well Pr 11:23
but the **r** will flourish like Pr 11:28
The fruit of the **r** is a tree of Pr 11:30
the **r** will be repaid on earth, Pr 11:31
the root of the **r** is immovable. Pr 12:3
thoughts of the **r** ⌊are⌋ just, Pr 12:5
the house of the **r** will stand. Pr 12:7
A **r** man cares about his animal's Pr 12:10
root of the **r** produces ⌊fruit⌋ Pr 12:12
but the **r** escapes from trouble. Pr 12:13
No disaster ⌊overcomes⌋ the **r**, Pr 12:21
A **r** man is careful in dealing Pr 12:26
The **r** hate lying, but the wicked Pr 13:5
light of the **r** shines brightly Pr 13:9
sinners, but good rewards the **r**. Pr 13:21
wealth is stored up for the **r**. Pr 13:22
A **r** man eats until he is Pr 13:25
wicked, at the gates of the **r**. Pr 14:19
the **r** have a refuge when they Pr 14:32
house of the **r** has great wealth Pr 15:6
The mind of the **r** person thinks Pr 15:28
He hears the prayer of the **r**. Pr 15:29
R lips are a king's delight, Pr 16:13
the **r** run to it and are Pr 18:10
who lives with integrity is **r**; Pr 20:7
Doing what is **r** and just is more Pr 21:3
The **R** One considers the house of Pr 21:12
a joy to the **r** but a terror to Pr 21:15
wicked are a ransom for the **r**, Pr 21:18
but the **r** give and don't hold Pr 21:26
The father of a **r** son will Pr 23:24
man, at the camp of the **r** man; Pr 24:15
a **r** man falls seven times, Pr 24:16
A **r** person who yields to the Pr 25:26
but the **r** are as bold as a lion. Pr 28:1
When the **r** triumph, there is Pr 28:12
are destroyed, the **r** flourish. Pr 28:28
When the **r** flourish, the people Pr 29:2
the **r** one sings and rejoices. Pr 29:6
The **r** person knows the rights of Pr 29:7
but the **r** will see their Pr 29:16
man is detestable to the **r**, Pr 29:27
will judge the **r** and the wicked, Ec 3:17
there is a **r** man who perishes in Ec 7:15
be excessively **r**, and don't be Ec 7:16
is certainly no **r** man on the Ec 7:20
there are **r** people who get what Ec 8:14
the actions of the **r** deserve. Ec 8:14
the **r**, the wise, and their works Ec 9:1
fate for the **r** and the wicked, Ec 9:2
you will be called the **R** City, Is 1:26
Tell the **r** that it will go well Is 3:10
The Splendor of the **R** One. Is 24:16
the gates so a **r** nation can come Is 26:2
The path of the **r** is level; Is 26:7
clear a straight path for the **r**. Is 26:7
In a **r** land he acts unjustly and Is 26:10
cause deprive the **r** of justice. Is 29:21
on to you with My **r** right hand. Is 41:10
called you for a **r** ⌊purpose⌋, Is 42:6
God but Me, a **r** God and Savior; Is 45:21
captives of the **r** be delivered? Is 49:24
My **r** servant will justify many, Is 53:11
The **r** one perishes, and no one Is 57:1
that the **r** one is swept away Is 57:1
They ask Me for **r** judgments; Is 58:2
Then all your people will be **r**; Is 60:21
And they will be called **r** trees, Is 61:3
and all our **r** acts are like a Is 64:6
herself more **r** than treacherous Jr 3:11
You will be **r**, LORD, even if I Jr 12:1
testing the **r** and seeing the Jr 20:12
raise up a **r** Branch of David Jr 23:5
LORD bless you, **r** settlement, Jr 31:23
the LORD, their **r** grazing land, Jr 50:7
the blood of the **r** within her. Lm 4:13
Now if a **r** person turns from his Ezk 3:20
his sin and the **r** acts he did Ezk 3:20
if you warn the **r** person that he Ezk 3:21
the **r** person with lies Ezk 13:22
your sisters appear **r** by all the Ezk 16:51
appear more **r** than you because Ezk 16:52
have made your sisters appear **r**. Ezk 16:52

a man is **r** and does what is Ezk 18:5
Such a person is **r**; Ezk 18:9
of the **r** person will be Ezk 18:20
But when a **r** person turns from Ezk 18:24
None of the **r** acts he did will Ezk 18:24
When a **r** person turns from his Ezk 18:26
off both the **r** and the wicked Ezk 21:3
off ⌊both⌋ the **r** and the wicked, Ezk 21:4
r men will judge them the way Ezk 23:45
of the **r** person will not save Ezk 33:12
The **r** person won't be able to Ezk 33:12
When I tell the **r** person that he Ezk 33:13
When a **r** person turns from his Ezk 33:18
LORD our God is **r** in all He has Dn 9:14
in keeping with all Your **r** acts, Dn 9:16
before You based on our **r** acts, Dn 9:18
right, and the **r** walk in them, Hs 14:9
they sell a **r** person for silver Am 2:6
oppress the **r**, take a bribe, Am 5:12
acknowledge the LORD's **r** acts. Mc 6:5
For the wicked restrict the **r**; Hab 1:4
one who is more **r** than himself? Hab 1:13
But the **r** one will live by his Hab 2:4
The **r** LORD is in her; Zph 3:5
be their faithful and **r** God." Zch 8:8
He is **r** and victorious, humble Zch 9:9
between the **r** and the wicked, Mal 3:18
Joseph, being a **r** man, and not Mt 1:19
sends rain on the **r** and the Mt 5:45
For I didn't come to call the **r**, Mt 9:13
who welcomes a **r** person because Mt 10:41
because he's **r** will receive Mt 10:41
receive a **r** person's reward. Mt 10:41
prophets and **r** people longed to Mt 13:17
Then the **r** will shine like the Mt 13:43
the evil people from the **r**, Mt 13:49
outside you seem **r** to people, Mt 23:28
decorate the monuments of the **r**, Mt 23:29
So all the **r** blood shed on the Mt 23:35
the blood of **r** Abel to the blood Mt 23:35
Then the **r** will answer Him, Mt 25:37
but the **r** into eternal life." Mt 25:46
nothing to do with that **r** man, Mt 27:19
I didn't come to call the **r**, Mk 2:17
knowing he was a **r** and holy man. Mk 6:20
Both were **r** in God's sight, Lk 1:6
to the understanding of the **r**, Lk 1:17
This man was **r** and devout, Lk 2:25
I have not come to call the **r**, Lk 5:32
at the resurrection of the **r**." Lk 14:14
than over 99 **r** people who don't Lk 15:7
that they were **r** and looked down Lk 18:9
spies who pretended to be **r**, Lk 20:20
saying, "This man really was **r**!" Lk 23:47
was a good and **r** man named Lk 23:50
My judgment is **r**, because I do Jn 5:30
judge according to **r** judgment." Jn 7:24
R Father! The world has not Jn 17:25
you denied the Holy and **R** One, Ac 3:14
the coming of the **R** One, Ac 7:52
to see the **R** One, and to hear Ac 22:14
both of the **r** and the Ac 24:15
The **r** will live by faith. Rm 1:17
when God's **r** judgment is Rm 2:5
of the law are not **r** before God, Rm 2:13
of the law will be declared **r**. Rm 2:13
There is no one **r**, not even one; Rm 3:10
that He would be **r** and declare Rm 3:26
and declare **r** the one who has Rm 3:26
Him who declares **r** the ungodly, Rm 4:5
have been declared **r** by faith, Rm 5:1
been declared **r** by His blood, Rm 5:9
also through one **r** act there is Rm 5:18
the many will be made **r**. Rm 5:19
the **r** will live by faith. Gl 3:11
of God's **r** judgment that you 2Th 1:5
since it is **r** for God to repay 2Th 1:6
law is not meant for a **r** person, 1Tm 1:9
the Lord, the **r** Judge, will give 2Tm 4:8
is good, sensible, **r**, holy, Ti 1:8
in a sensible, **r**, and godly way Ti 2:12
But My **r** one will live by faith; Heb 10:38
this he was approved as a **r** man, Heb 11:4
to the spirits of **r** people made Heb 12:23
you have murdered—the **r** man; Jms 5:6
of the **r** is very powerful. Jms 5:16
Lord are on the **r** and His ears 1Pt 3:12
the **r** for the unrighteous, 1Pt 3:18

And if the **r** is saved with 1Pt 4:18
if He rescued **r** Lot, distressed 2Pt 2:7
that **r** man tormented himself day 2Pt 2:8
is faithful and **r** to forgive us 1Jn 1:9
Father—Jesus Christ the **r** One. 1Jn 2:1
know that He is **r**, you know this 1Jn 2:29
one who does what is right is **r**, 1Jn 3:7
is righteous, just as He is **r**. 1Jn 3:7
evil, and his brother's were **r**. 1Jn 3:12
r and true are Your ways, King Rv 15:3
because Your **r** acts have been Rv 15:4
You are **r**, who is and who was, Rv 16:5
true and **r** are Your judgments. Rv 16:7
His judgments are true and **r**, Rv 19:2
represents the **r** acts of the Rv 19:8
the **r** go on in righteousness; Rv 22:11

RIGHTEOUSLY *(8)*

really speak **r**, you mighty ones Ps 58:1
the world **r** and the peoples Ps 98:9
Speak up, judge **r**, and defend Pr 31:9
judge the poor **r** and execute Is 11:4
king will reign **r**, and rulers Is 32:1
The one who lives **r** and speaks Is 33:15
who judges **r**, who tests heart Jr 11:20
how devoutly, **r**, and blamelessly 1Th 2:10

RIGHTEOUSNESS *(267)*

and He credited it to him as **r**. Gn 15:6
R will be ours if we are careful Dt 6:25
of this land because of my **r**.' Dt 9:4
because of your **r** or your Dt 9:5
to possess because of your **r**, Dt 9:6
be counted as **r** to you before Dt 24:13
man for his **r** and his loyalty. 1Sm 26:23
and **r** for all his people. 2Sm 8:15
rewarded me according to my **r**; 2Sm 22:21
repaid me according to my **r**, 2Sm 22:25
faithfulness, **r**, and integrity. 1Kg 3:6
him according to his **r**. 1Kg 8:32
to carry out justice and **r**." 1Kg 10:9
and **r** for all his people. 1Ch 18:14
him according to his **r**. 2Ch 6:23
to carry out justice and **r**." 2Ch 9:8
my **r** is still the issue. Jb 6:29
the home where your **r** dwells. Jb 8:6
cling to my **r** and never let it Jb 27:6
myself in **r**, and it enveloped Jb 29:14
God will restore his **r** to him. Jb 33:26
your **r** ⌊another⌋ human being. Jb 35:8
afar and ascribe **r** to my Maker. Jb 36:3
His justice and **r**, He will not Jb 37:23
Offer sacrifices in **r** and trust Ps 4:5
lead me in Your **r**, because of my Ps 5:8
according to my **r** and my Ps 7:8
I will thank the LORD for His **r**; Ps 7:17
He judges the world with **r**; Ps 9:8
practices **r**, and acknowledges Ps 15:2
But I will see Your face in **r**; Ps 17:15
rewarded me according to my **r**; Ps 18:20
repaid me according to my **r**, Ps 18:24
yet to be born about His **r**— Ps 22:31
and **r** from the God of his Ps 24:5
Save me by Your **r**. Ps 31:1
He loves **r** and justice; Ps 33:5
with Your **r**, and do not let Ps 35:24
my tongue will proclaim Your **r**, Ps 35:28
Your **r** is like the highest Ps 36:6
and Your **r** over the upright in Ps 36:10
making your **r** shine like the Ps 37:6
I proclaim **r** in the great Ps 40:9
did not hide Your **r** in my heart; Ps 40:10
You love **r** and hate wickedness; Ps 45:7
The heavens proclaim His **r**, Ps 50:6
my tongue will sing of Your **r**. Ps 51:14
You answer us in **r**, with Ps 65:5
do not let them share in Your **r**. Ps 69:27
tell about Your **r** and Your Ps 71:15
proclaim Your **r**, Yours alone. Ps 71:16
Your **r** reaches heaven, God, You Ps 71:19
proclaim Your **r** all day long, Ps 71:24
king and Your **r** to the king's Ps 72:1
Your people with **r** and Your Ps 72:2
to the people, and the hills, **r**. Ps 72:3
r and peace will embrace. Ps 85:10
r will look down from heaven. Ps 85:11
R will go before Him to prepare Ps 85:13
or Your **r** in the land of Ps 88:12
R and justice are the foundation Ps 89:14
and they are exalted by Your **r**. Ps 89:16
the world with **r** and the peoples Ps 96:13
r and justice are the foundation Ps 97:2
The heavens proclaim His **r**; Ps 97:6
has revealed His **r** in the sight Ps 98:2
justice and **r** in Jacob. Ps 99:4
acts of **r** and justice for Ps 103:6
and His **r** toward the Ps 103:17
who practice **r** at all times. Ps 106:3
to him as **r** throughout all Ps 106:31
His **r** endures forever. Ps 111:3
and his **r** endures forever. Ps 112:3
his **r** endures forever. Ps 112:9
Open the gates of **r** for me; Ps 118:19
Give me life through Your **r**. Ps 119:40
Your **r** is an everlasting Ps 119:142
is an everlasting **r**, Ps 119:142
Your priests be clothed with **r**, Ps 132:9
plea, and in Your **r** answer me. Ps 143:1
In Your **r** deliver me from Ps 143:11
will joyfully sing of Your **r**. Ps 145:7
wise instruction ⌊in⌋ **r**, Pr 1:3
Then you will understand **r**, Pr 2:9
and honor, lasting wealth and **r**. Pr 8:18
in the way of **r**, along the paths Pr 8:20
anyone, but **r** rescues from death Pr 10:2
day of wrath, but **r** rescues from Pr 11:4
r of the blameless clears his Pr 11:5
The **r** of the upright rescues Pr 11:6
one who sows **r**, a true reward. Pr 11:18
Genuine **r** ⌊leads⌋ to life, Pr 11:19
There is life in the path of **r**, Pr 12:28
R guards people of integrity, Pr 13:6
R exalts a nation, but sin is a Pr 14:34
He loves the one who pursues **r**. Pr 15:9
little with **r** than great income Pr 16:8
throne is established through **r**. Pr 16:12
it is found in the way of **r**. Pr 16:31
one who pursues **r** and faithful Pr 21:21
will find life, **r**, and honor. Pr 21:21
throne will be established in **r**. Pr 25:5
is wickedness at the place of **r**. Ec 3:16
justice and **r** in the province, Ec 5:8
who perishes in spite of his **r**, Ec 7:15
R once dwelt in her—but now, Is 1:21
her repentant ones by **r**. Is 1:27
injustice, for **r**, but heard Is 5:7
holy God is distinguished by **r**. Is 5:16
with justice and **r** from now on Is 9:7
R and faithfulness will be a Is 11:5
of the world will learn **r**. Is 26:9
favor, he does not learn **r**. Is 26:10
line and **r** the mason's level. Is 28:17
and **r** will dwell in the orchard. Is 32:16
The result of **r** will be peace; Is 32:17
the effect of **r** will be quiet Is 32:17
filled Zion with justice and **r**. Is 33:5
He calls **r** to his feet. Is 41:2
because of His **r**, to magnify Is 42:21
and let the skies shower **r**. Is 45:8
sprout and **r** spring up with it. Is 45:8
I have raised him up in **r**, Is 45:13
in the LORD is **r** and strength." Is 45:24
Israel, ⌊but⌋ not in truth or **r**. Is 48:1
and your **r** like the waves of the Is 48:18
you who pursue **r**, you who seek Is 51:1
My **r** is near, My salvation Is 51:5
My **r** will never be shattered. Is 51:6
Me, you who know **r**, the people Is 51:7
But My **r** will last forever, Is 51:8
on ⌊a foundation of⌋ **r**. Is 54:14
and their **r** is from Me." Is 54:17
and My **r** will be revealed. Is 56:1
expose your **r**, and your works Is 57:12
Your **r** will go before you, Is 58:8
from us, and **r** does not reach Is 59:9
back, and **r** stands far off. Is 59:14
and His own **r** supported Him. Is 59:16
He put on **r** like a breastplate, Is 59:17
your guard and **r** as your ruler. Is 60:17
and wrapped me in a robe of **r**, Is 61:10
GOD will cause **r** and praise to Is 61:11
Jerusalem until her **r** shines Is 62:1
will see your **r**, and all kings Is 62:2
justice, and in **r**, then the Jr 4:2
justice, and **r** on the earth, for Jr 9:24
Administer justice and **r**. Jr 22:3
He administered justice and **r**, Jr 22:15
justice and **r** in the land. Jr 23:5
The LORD Is Our **R**. Jr 23:6
a Branch of **r** to sprout up for Jr 33:15
justice and **r** in the land. Jr 33:15
The LORD Is Our **R**. Jr 33:16
turns from his **r** and practices Ezk 3:20
only⌋ themselves by their **r**." Ezk 14:14
only⌋ themselves by their **r**. Ezk 14:20
The **r** of the righteous person Ezk 18:20
because of the **r** he has Ezk 18:22
turns from his **r** and practices Ezk 18:24
turns from his **r** and practices Ezk 18:26
The **r** of the righteous person Ezk 33:12
survive by his **r** on the day he Ezk 33:12
he trusts in his **r** and commits Ezk 33:13
then none of his **r** will be Ezk 33:13
turns from his **r** and commits Ezk 33:18
Lord, **r** belongs to You, but this Dn 9:7
to bring in everlasting **r**, Dn 9:24
and those who lead many to **r**, Dn 12:3
take you to be My wife in **r**, Hs 2:19
Sow **r** for yourselves and reap Hs 10:12
He comes and sends **r** on you like Hs 10:12
wormwood throw **r** to the ground. Am 5:7
like water, and **r**, like an Am 5:24
the fruit of **r** into wormwood— Am 6:12
Seek **r**, seek humility; Zph 2:3
offerings to the LORD in **r**. Mal 3:3
the sun of **r** will rise with Mal 4:2
way for us to fulfill all **r**." Mt 3:15
who hunger and thirst for **r**, Mt 5:6
those who are persecuted for **r**, Mt 5:10
unless your **r** surpasses that of Mt 5:20
to practice your **r** in front of Mt 6:1
the kingdom of God and His **r**, Mt 6:33
came to you in the way of **r**, Mt 21:32
holiness and **r** in His presence Lk 1:75
acknowledged God's way of **r**, Lk 7:29
about sin, **r**, and judgment: Jn 16:8
about **r**, because I am going to Jn 16:10
Him and does **r** is acceptable to Ac 10:35
and all fraud, enemy of all **r**! Ac 13:10
the world in **r** by the Man He has Ac 17:31
he spoke about **r**, self-control, Ac 24:25
For in it God's **r** is revealed Rm 1:17
highlights God's **r**, Rm 3:5
God's **r** has been revealed— Rm 3:21
God's **r** through faith in Jesus Rm 3:22
demonstrate His **r**, because in Rm 3:25
demonstrate His **r** at the present Rm 3:26
it was credited to him for **r**. Rm 4:3
his faith is credited for **r**. Rm 4:5
God credits **r** apart from works Rm 4:6
was credited to Abraham for **r**. Rm 4:9
a seal of the **r** that he had by Rm 4:11
that **r** may be credited to them Rm 4:11
but through the **r** that comes by Rm 4:13
it was credited to him for **r**. Rm 4:22
and the gift of **r** reign in life Rm 5:17
also grace will reign through **r**, Rm 5:21
to God as weapons for **r**. Rm 6:13
or of obedience leading to **r**? Rm 6:16
sin, you became enslaved to **r**. Rm 6:18
now offer them as slaves to **r**, Rm 6:19
were free from allegiance to **r**. Rm 6:20
the Spirit is life because of **r**. Rm 8:10
did not pursue **r**, have obtained Rm 9:30
have obtained **r**—namely the Rm 9:30
namely the **r** that comes from Rm 9:30
the law for **r**, has not achieved Rm 9:31
they disregarded the **r** from God Rm 10:3
to establish their own **r**, Rm 10:3
have not submitted to God's **r**. Rm 10:3
of the law for **r** to everyone who Rm 10:4
writes about the **r** that is from Rm 10:5
But the **r** that comes from faith Rm 10:6
resulting in **r**, and with the Rm 10:10
drinking, but **r**, peace, and joy Rm 14:17
as well as **r**, sanctification 1Co 1:30
the ministry of **r** overflows with 2Co 3:9
become the **r** of God in Him. 2Co 5:21
weapons of **r** on the right hand 2Co 6:7
there between **r** and lawlessness 2Co 6:14
His **r** endures forever. 2Co 9:9
increase the harvest of your **r**, 2Co 9:10
themselves as servants of **r**. 2Co 11:15
for if **r** comes through the law, Gl 2:21
it was credited to him for **r**, Gl 3:6
then **r** would certainly be by the Gl 3:21

for the hope of **r** from faith. Gl 5:5
God's ⌊likeness⌋ in **r** and purity Eph 4:24
in all goodness, **r**, and truth— Eph 5:9
r like armor on your chest, Eph 6:14
with the fruit of **r** that ⌊comes⌋ Php 1:11
as to the **r** that is in the law, Php 3:6
having a **r** of my own from the Php 3:9
the **r** from God based on faith. Php 3:9
but pursue **r**, godliness, faith, 1Tm 6:11
and pursue **r**, faith, love, 2Tm 2:22
correcting, for training in **r**, 2Tm 3:16
reserved for me the crown of **r**, 2Tm 4:8
not by works of **r** that we had Ti 3:5
You have loved **r** and hated Heb 1:9
with the message about **r**, Heb 5:13
his name means "king of **r**," Heb 7:2
an heir of the **r** that comes by Heb 11:7
of peace and **r** to those who have Heb 12:11
does not accomplish God's **r**. Jms 1:20
it was credited to him for **r**, Jms 2:23
the fruit of **r** is sown in peace Jms 3:18
to sins, we might live for **r**; 1Pt 2:24
even if you should suffer for **r**, 1Pt 3:14
ours through the **r** of our God 2Pt 1:1
a preacher of **r**, and seven 2Pt 2:5
to have known the way of **r** than, 2Pt 2:21
a new earth, where **r** will dwell. 2Pt 3:13
in **r** He judges and makes war. Rv 19:11
let the righteous go on in **r**; Rv 22:11

RIGHTFULLY *(1)*
Praise is **r** Yours, God, in Zion; Ps 65:1

RIGHTLY *(5)*
said, "Isn't he **r** named Jacob? Gn 27:36
judge **r** between a man and his Dt 1:16
lives righteously and speaks **r**, Is 33:15
and their power is not **r** used Jr 23:10
but if **r**, why do you hit Me?" Jn 18:23

RIGHTS *(11)*
or marital **r** of the first wife. Ex 21:10
he has the **r** of the firstborn. Dt 21:17
them about the **r** of the king who 1Sm 8:9
These are the **r** of the king who 1Sm 8:11
to the people the **r** of kingship. 1Sm 10:25
uphold the **r** of the oppressed Ps 82:3
person knows the **r** of the poor, Pr 29:7
Defend the **r** of the fatherless. Is 1:17
not defend the **r** of the Is 1:23
not defended the **r** of the needy. Jr 5:28
But I have used none of these **r**, 1Co 9:15

RIGID *(1)*
grinds his teeth, and becomes **r**. Mk 9:18

RIM *(10)*
from Aroer on the **r** of the Arnon Dt 2:36
from Aroer on the **r** of the Arnon Dt 4:48
from Aroer on the **r** of the Arnon Jos 12:2
From Aroer on the **r** of the Arnon Jos 13:9
From Aroer on the **r** of the Arnon Jos 13:16
and its **r** was fashioned like the 1Kg 7:26
and its **r** was fashioned like the 2Ch 4:5
with a **r** of nine inches around Ezk 43:13
The **r** all around it is 10 and a Ezk 43:17
the ledge, and all around the **r**. Ezk 43:20

RIMMON *(14)*
(AKA DIMNAH, HADAD, RIMMONO)
Shilhim, Ain, and **R**—29 cities Jos 15:32
Ain, **R**, Ether, and Ashan—four Jos 19:7
it extended to **R**, curving around Jos 19:13
the wilderness to the rock of **R**, Jdg 20:45
the rock of **R** and stayed there Jdg 20:47
who were at the rock of **R**. Jdg 21:13
sons of **R** the Beerothite of the 2Sm 4:2
the sons of **R** the Beerothite, 2Sm 4:5
sons of **R** the Beerothite, 2Sm 4:9
the temple of **R** to worship and I 2Kg 5:18
in the temple of **R**—when I bow 2Kg 5:18
when I bow in the temple of **R**, 2Kg 5:18
were Etam, Ain, **R**, Tochen, and 1Ch 4:32
land from Geba to **R** south of Zch 14:10

RIMMON-PEREZ *(2)*
from Rithmah and camped at **R**. Nm 33:19
departed from **R** and camped at Nm 33:20

RIMMONO *(1)*
(AKA RIMMON)
⌊they received⌋ **R** and its 1Ch 6:77

RIMS *(3)*
their axles, **r**, spokes, and hubs 1Kg 7:33

Their **r** were large and Ezk 1:18
of their four **r** were full of Ezk 1:18

RING *(23)*
man took a gold **r** weighing half Gn 24:22
As soon as he had seen the **r**, Gn 24:30
So I put the **r** on her nose and Gn 24:47
Your signet **r**, your cord, Gn 38:18
Whose signet **r**, cord, and staff Gn 38:25
his signet **r** from his hand Gn 41:42
at the top in a single **r**. Ex 26:24
at the top in a single **r**. Ex 36:29
his signet **r** from his finger Est 3:10
sealed with the royal signet **r**. Est 3:12
his signet **r** he had recovered Est 8:2
seal it with the royal signet **r**. Est 8:8
signet **r** cannot be revoked. Est 8:8
edicts⌋ with the royal signet **r**. Est 8:10
my declaration ⌊**r**⌋ in your ears. Jb 13:17
is like a gold **r** in a pig's Pr 11:22
is like a gold **r** or an ornament Pr 25:12
a signet **r** on My right hand, Jr 22:24
I put a **r** in your nose, earrings Ezk 16:12
his own signet **r** and with the Dn 6:17
and make you like My signet **r**, Hg 2:23
a **r** on his finger and sandals Lk 15:22
your meeting wearing a gold **r**, Jms 2:2

RINGING *(1)*
people shout with a **r** cry. Is 14:7

RINGLEADER *(1)*
and a **r** of the sect of the Ac 24:5

RINGS *(44)*
four gold **r** for it and place Ex 25:12
two **r** on one side and two rings Ex 25:12
one side and two **r** on the other Ex 25:12
poles into the **r** on the sides Ex 25:14
to remain in the **r** of the ark; Ex 25:15
Make four gold **r** for it, and Ex 25:26
and attach the **r** to the four Ex 25:26
r should be next to the frame Ex 25:27
and make their **r** of gold as the Ex 26:29
make four bronze **r** on the mesh Ex 27:4
are to be inserted into the **r**, Ex 27:7
Fashion two gold **r** for the Ex 28:23
to the two gold **r** at the corners Ex 28:24
other⌋ gold **r** and put them at Ex 28:26
⌊more⌋ gold **r** and attach them Ex 28:27
from its **r** to the rings Ex 28:28
its rings to the **r** of the ephod Ex 28:28
Make two gold **r** for it under the Ex 30:4
Take off the gold **r** that are on Ex 32:2
took off the gold **r** that were on Ex 32:3
earrings, **r**, necklaces, and all Ex 35:22
and made their **r** and holders for Ex 36:34
He cast four gold **r** for it to be Ex 37:3
two **r** on one side and two rings Ex 37:3
one side and two **r** on the other Ex 37:3
poles into the **r** on the sides Ex 37:5
He cast four gold **r** for it and Ex 37:13
and attached the **r** to the four Ex 37:13
The **r** were next to the frame as Ex 37:14
He made two gold **r** for it under Ex 37:27
he cast four **r** as holders for Ex 38:5
poles into the **r** on the sides Ex 38:7
and two gold **r** and attached the Ex 39:16
attached the two **r** to its two Ex 39:16
to the two gold **r** on the corners Ex 39:17
⌊other⌋ gold **r** and put ⌊them⌋ Ex 39:19
two ⌊more⌋ gold **r** and attached Ex 39:20
from its **r** to the rings Ex 39:21
its rings to the **r** of the ephod Ex 39:21
armlets, bracelets, **r**, earrings, Nm 31:50
signet **r**, nose rings, Is 3:21
signet rings, nose **r**, Is 3:21
with the signet **r** of his nobles, Dn 6:17
them, put on her **r** and jewelry, Hs 2:13

RINNAH *(1)*
Amnon, **R**, Ben-hanan, and Tilon. 1Ch 4:20

RINSED *(5)*
be scoured and **r** with water. Lv 6:28
is to be **r** with water and will Lv 11:32
utensil must be **r** with water. Lv 15:12
burnt offering were **r** in them, 2Ch 4:6
with water, **r** off your blood, Ezk 16:9

RINSING *(1)*
without ⌊first⌋ **r** his hands in Lv 15:11

RIOT *(1)*
but that a **r** was starting Mt 27:24

RIOTING *(3)*
there won't be **r** among the Mt 26:5
there may be **r** among the people. Mk 14:2
charged with **r** for what happened Ac 19:40

RIOTS *(1)*
imprisonments, by **r**, by labors, 2Co 6:5

RIP *(2)*
r open their pregnant women. 2Kg 8:12
beast that would **r** them open. Hs 13:8

RIPE *(9)*
and be buried at a **r** old age. Gn 15:15
breath and died at a **r** old age, Gn 25:8
barley was **r** and the flax was Ex 9:31
season for the first **r** grapes. Nm 13:20
Joash died at a **r** old age and Jdg 8:32
will be like a **r** fig before the Is 28:4
sickle because the harvest is **r**. Jl 3:13
then the **r** grain on the head. Mk 4:28
the harvest of the earth is **r**." Rv 14:15

RIPENED *(3)*
and its clusters **r** into grapes. Gn 40:10
trees with figs that **r** first; Nah 3:12
because its grapes have **r**." Rv 14:18

RIPENING *(1)*
the blossom becomes a **r** grape, Is 18:5

RIPENS *(1)*
The fig tree **r** its figs; Sg 2:13

RIPHATH *(2)*
Ashkenaz, **R**, and Togarmah. Gn 10:3
Ashkenaz, **R**, and Togarmah. 1Ch 1:6

RIPPED *(7)*
'The altar will now be **r** apart, 1Kg 13:3
The altar was **r** apart, and the 1Kg 13:5
he attacked ⌊it and⌋ **r** open all 2Kg 15:16
He is **r** from the security of his Jb 18:14
not let us be **r** apart by their Ps 124:6
and their pregnant women **r** open. Hs 13:16
because they **r** open the pregnant Am 1:13

RIPPING *(2)*
me like a lion, **r** me apart, with Ps 7:2
will take you, **r** you out of your Ps 52:5

RISE *(125)*
You are to **r** in the presence of Lv 19:32
A people **r** up like a lioness; Nm 23:24
the enemies who **r** up against you Dt 28:7
among you will **r** higher and Dt 28:43
Let them **r** up and help you; Dt 32:38
so that they cannot **r** again. Dt 33:11
so he could **r** up against me and 1Sm 22:13
not let them **r** up against Saul 1Sm 24:7
and to all who **r** up against you 2Sm 18:32
crush them, and they do not **r**; 2Sm 22:39
sons until the **r** of the Persian 2Ch 36:20
Mordecai didn't **r** or tremble in Est 5:9
to Sheol will never **r** again. Jb 7:9
man lies down never to **r** again. Jb 14:12
the earth will **r** up against him. Jb 20:27
The rabble **r** up at my right; Jb 30:12
R up, LORD! Save me, my God! You Ps 3:7
R up, LORD, in Your anger; Ps 7:6
R up, LORD! Do not let man Ps 9:19
R up, LORD God! Lift up Your Ps 10:12
poor, I will now **r** up," says the Ps 12:5
R up, LORD! Confront him; bring Ps 17:13
fall, but we **r** and stand firm. Ps 20:8
you gates! **R** up, ancient doors Ps 24:7
you gates! **R** up, ancient doors Ps 24:9
false witnesses **r** up against me, Ps 27:12
Wake up and **r** to my defense, Ps 35:23
been thrown down and cannot **r**. Ps 36:12
and he won't **r** again from where Ps 41:8
R up! Help us! Redeem us because Ps 44:26
For strangers **r** up against me, Ps 54:3
from those who **r** up against me. Ps 59:1
r up to punish all the nations; Ps 59:5
They were to **r** and tell their Ps 78:6
enthroned ⌊on⌋ the cherubim, **r** Ps 80:1
R up, God, judge the earth, for Ps 82:8
spirits **r** up to praise You Ps 88:10
R up, Judge of the earth; Ps 94:2
When they **r** up, they will be put Ps 109:28
I **r** at midnight to thank You for Ps 119:62
I **r** before dawn and cry out for Ps 119:147

the clouds to **r** from the ends Ps 135:7
the abyss, never again to **r**. Ps 140:10
Her sons **r** up and call her Pr 31:28
Woe to those who **r** early in the Is 5:11
of the nations **r** from their Is 14:9
never **r** up to possess a land Is 14:21
"I will **r** up against them"— Is 14:22
R up, you princes, and oil the Is 21:5
and it falls, never to **r** again. Is 24:20
departed spirits do not **r** up. Is 26:14
bodies will **r**. Awake and sing, Is 26:19
the LORD will **r** up as ⌊He did⌋ Is 28:21
He will **r** in wrath, as at the Is 28:21
will **r** up against the house of Is 31:2
when You **r** in Your majesty Is 33:3
"Now I will **r** up," says the LORD. Is 33:10
stench of their corpses will **r**; Is 34:3
lie down, they do not **r** again; Is 43:17
they beg: **R** up and save us! Jr 2:27
Let them **r** up and save you in Jr 2:28
r up, let's attack at noon. Jr 6:4
R up, let's attack by night. Jr 6:5
the clouds to **r** from the ends Jr 10:13
R up, you cavalry! Race Jr 46:9
come against her. **R** up for war! Jr 49:14
R up, go against Kedar, and Jr 49:28
R up, go up against a nation at Jr 49:31
the clouds to **r** from the ends Jr 51:16
sink and never **r** again because Jr 51:64
When they sit and when they **r**, Lm 3:63
their wings to **r** from the earth, Ezk 10:16
kings who will **r** from the earth. Dn 7:17
kings who will **r** from this Dn 7:24
will **r** after them and subdue Dn 7:24
They will **r** from that nation, Dn 8:22
one from her family will **r** up, Dn 11:7
times many will **r** up against the Dn 11:14
He will **r** to power with a small Dn 11:23
His forces will **r** up and Dn 11:31
over your people will **r** up. Dn 12:1
then **r** to your destiny at the Dn 12:13
of battle will **r** against your Hs 10:14
His stench will **r**; yes, his Jl 2:20
smell will **r**, for he has done Jl 2:20
Israel will never **r** again. Am 5:2
I will **r** up against the house of Am 7:9
All of it will **r** like the Nile; Am 8:8
will fall, never to **r** again. Am 8:14
R up, and let us go to war Ob 1
R and thresh, Daughter Zion, for Mc 4:13
R, plead ⌊your⌋ case before the Mc 6:1
will not **r** up a second time. Nah 1:9
the day I **r** up for plunder. Zph 3:8
hand of one will **r** against the Zch 14:13
righteousness will **r** with Mal 4:2
causes His sun to **r** on the evil Mt 5:45
will even **r** up against their Mt 10:21
of the south will **r** up at the Mt 12:42
For nation will **r** up against Mt 24:7
prophets will **r** up and deceive Mt 24:11
three days I will **r** again.' Mt 27:63
be killed, and **r** after three Mk 8:31
He will **r** three days later." Mk 9:31
and He will **r** after three days." Mk 10:34
when they **r**, whose wife will she Mk 12:23
For when they **r** from the dead, Mk 12:25
For nation will **r** up against Mk 13:8
Children will **r** up against Mk 13:12
prophets will **r** up and will Mk 13:22
the fall and **r** of many in Israel Lk 2:34
of the south will **r** up at the Lk 11:31
of Nineveh will **r** up at the Lk 11:32
and He will **r** on the third day." Lk 18:33
crucified, and **r** on the third Lk 24:7
would suffer and **r** from the dead Lk 24:46
"Your brother will **r** again," Jn 11:23
I know that he will **r** again in Jn 11:24
that He must **r** from the dead. Jn 20:9
to suffer and **r** from the dead, Ac 17:3
yourselves will **r** up with Ac 20:30
as the first to **r** from the dead, Ac 26:23
sleeper, and **r** up from the dead Eph 5:14
the dead in Christ will **r** first. 1Th 4:16
another angel **r** up from the east Rv 7:2

RISEN *(11)*
The sun had **r** over the land when Gn 19:23
whole clan has **r** up against your 2Sm 14:7
for the water has **r** to my neck. Ps 69:1
The sea has **r** over Babylon; Jr 51:42
For the water had **r**; it was deep Ezk 47:5
My people have **r** up like an Mc 2:8
Son of Man had **r** from the dead. Mk 9:9
after He had **r**, He appeared Mk 16:9
"A great prophet has **r** among us," Lk 7:16
of the ancient prophets had **r**. Lk 9:8
Jesus Christ, **r** from the dead, 2Tm 2:8

RISES *(27)*
when the sun **r** on a cloudless 2Sm 23:4
My frailty **r** up against me and Jb 16:8
The murderer **r** at dawn to kill Jb 24:14
when He **r** up, they have no Jb 24:22
When Leviathan **r**, the mighty are Jb 41:25
It **r** from one end of the heavens Ps 19:6
not a foe who **r** up against me— Ps 55:12
The sun **r**; they go back and lie Ps 104:22
r while it is still night and Pr 31:15
The sun **r** and the sun sets; Ec 1:5
to its place where it **r**. Ec 1:5
spirit of people **r** upward and Ec 3:21
the ruler's anger **r** against you, Ec 10:4
when one **r** at the sound of a Ec 12:4
when He **r** to terrify the earth. Is 2:19
when He **r** to terrify the earth. Is 2:21
The LORD **r** to argue the case and Is 3:13
The sun will be dark when it **r**, Is 13:10
torrent that **r** to the neck. Is 30:28
mourning; Jerusalem's cry **r** up. Jr 14:2
Egypt **r** like the Nile, and its Jr 46:8
all of it **r** like the Nile and Am 9:5
when the sun **r**, they take off, Nah 3:17
he sleeps and **r**—night and day, Mk 4:27
if someone **r** from the dead.'" Lk 16:31
the One who **r** to rule the Rm 15:12
For the sun **r** with its scorching Jms 1:11

RISING *(21)*
r up ⌊in⌋ a mass that extended Jos 3:16
from the city was **r** to the sky! Jos 8:20
and that smoke was **r** from it, Jos 8:21
Him be like the **r** of the sun in Jdg 5:31
all those **r** up against you!" 2Sm 18:31
who are **r** up against me." 2Kg 16:7
r early in the morning to offer Jb 1:5
r splendidly, is the joy of the Ps 48:2
R up to the sky, sinking down to Ps 107:26
From the **r** of the sun to its Ps 113:3
and is **r** up to show you Is 30:18
know from the **r** of the sun to Is 45:6
r up proudly in His great might? Is 63:1
Who is this, **r** like the Nile, Jr 46:7
waters are **r** from the north and Jr 47:2
cloud of incense was **r** up. Ezk 8:11
from the LORD **r** up from the Hs 13:15
As the sun was **r**, God appointed Jnh 4:8
from the **r** of the sun to its Mal 1:11
what "**r** from the dead" Mk 9:10
you see a cloud **r** in the west, Lk 12:54

RISK *(6)*
it at the **r** of their lives. 1Ch 11:19
I put myself at **r** and take my Jb 13:14
who would otherwise **r** his life Jr 30:21
our food at the **r** of our lives Lm 5:9
only do we run a **r** that our Ac 19:27
we run a **r** of being charged with Ac 19:40

RISKED *(6)*
fought for you, **r** his life, Jdg 9:17
blood of men who **r** their lives?" 2Sm 23:17
of these men who **r** their lives?" 1Ch 11:19
command and **r** their lives rather Dn 3:28
who have **r** their lives for the Ac 15:26
who **r** their own necks for my Rm 16:4

RISKING *(2)*
was a people **r** their lives, Jdg 5:18
r his life to make up what was Php 2:30

RISSAH *(2)*
from Libnah and camped at **R**. Nm 33:21
departed from **R** and camped at Nm 33:22

RITE *(2)*
the purification **r** on the horns Ex 30:10
the purification **r** for it once a Ex 30:10

RITES *(1)*
observe mourning **r** for the dead. Ezk 24:17

RITHMAH *(2)*
from Hazeroth and camped at **R**. Nm 33:18
departed from **R** and camped at Nm 33:19

RITUAL *(8)*
you are to observe this **r**. Ex 12:25
'What does this **r** mean to you?' Ex 12:26
carry out this **r** in this month. Ex 13:5
will apply this entire **r** to her. Nm 5:30
This is the **r** of the Nazirite Nm 6:21
in keeping with the **r** for his Nm 6:21
perform the **r** washing before Lk 11:38
teaching about **r** washings, Heb 6:2

RITUALLY *(3)*
unless they wash their hands **r**, Mk 7:3
bread with **r** unclean hands?" Mk 7:5
of Asia found me **r** purified in Ac 24:18

RIVAL *(5)*
not make gods of silver to **r** Me; Ex 20:23
a woman as a **r** to her sister Lv 18:18
Her **r** would taunt her severely 1Sm 1:6
her **r** taunted her in this way 1Sm 1:7
in God's garden could not **r** it; Ezk 31:8

RIVALRY *(2)*
others proclaim Christ out of **r**, Php 1:17
Do nothing out of **r** or conceit, Php 2:3

RIVER *(102)*
A **r** went out from Eden to water Gn 2:10
name of the second **r** is Gihon, Gn 2:13
of the third **r** is the Tigris, Gn 2:14
And the fourth **r** is the Gn 2:14
of Egypt to the Euphrates **R**: Gn 15:18
Nile will die, the **r** will stink, Ex 7:18
and the **r** smelled so bad the Ex 7:21
not drink the water from the **r**. Ex 7:24
wilderness to the Euphrates **R**. Ex 23:31
the other side of the Arnon ⌊**R**⌋, Nm 21:13
they stretch out like **r** valleys, Nm 24:6
as far as the Euphrates **R**. Dt 1:7
of the Jabbok **R** and the cities Dt 2:37
up to the Jabbok **R**, the border Dt 3:16
from the Euphrates **R** to the Dt 11:24
to the great Euphrates **R**— Jos 1:4
of Gilead up to the Jabbok **R** Jos 12:2
the Euphrates **R** and worshiped Jos 24:2
region beyond the Euphrates **R**, Jos 24:3
the Euphrates **R** and in Egypt, Jos 24:14
beyond the Euphrates **R**, Jos 24:15
The **r** Kishon swept them away, Jdg 5:21
the ancient **r**, the river Kishon Jdg 5:21
the ancient river, the **r** Kishon. Jdg 5:21
his control at the Euphrates **R**. 2Sm 8:3
who were across the Euphrates **R**, 2Sm 10:16
up and immediately ford the **r**, 2Sm 17:21
to the Jordan **R** to see him off 2Sm 19:31
down to meet me at the Jordan **R**, 1Kg 2:8
from the Euphrates **R** to the land 1Kg 4:21
Habor, Gozan's **r**, and in the 2Kg 17:6
Habor, Gozan's **r**, and in the 2Kg 18:11
of Assyria at the Euphrates **r**. 2Kg 23:29
of Egypt to the Euphrates **R**. 2Kg 24:7
on the Euphrates **R** ruled in his 1Ch 1:48
that extends to the Euphrates **R**, 1Ch 5:9
and Gozan's **r**, ⌊where they are 1Ch 5:26
his control at the Euphrates **R**. 1Ch 18:3
from the Euphrates **R** to the land 2Ch 9:26
region west of the Euphrates **R**. Ezr 4:10
region west of the Euphrates **R**: Ezr 4:11
region west of the Euphrates **R**: Ezr 4:17
region west of the Euphrates **R**, Ezr 5:3
region west of the Euphrates **R**, Ezr 5:6
region west of the Euphrates **R**, Ezr 6:6
region west of the Euphrates **R**, Ezr 6:8
region west of the Euphrates **R**, Ezr 6:13
region west of the Euphrates **R**: Ezr 7:21
them at the **r** that flows to Ezr 8:15
a fast by the Ahava **R**, Ezr 8:21
from the Ahava **R** on the twelfth Ezr 8:31
region west of the Euphrates **R**, Neh 2:7
region west of the Euphrates **R**. Neh 3:7
were washed away by a **r**. Jb 22:16
from crossing the **r** ⌊of death⌋. Jb 33:18
will cross the **r** ⌊of death⌋ and Jb 36:12
Though the **r** rages, Behemoth is Jb 40:23
⌊There is⌋ a **r**—its streams Ps 46:4
and they crossed the **r** on foot. Ps 66:6
the Sea and shoots toward the **R**. Ps 80:11
and Jabin at the Kishon **R**. Ps 83:9
waters, a flowing **r**, a fountain Pr 18:4
from beyond the Euphrates **R**— Is 7:20
waters of the Euphrates **R**— Is 8:7

and the **r** will be parched and Is 19:5
by the mouth of the **r**, and all Is 19:7
the Euphrates **R** as far as the Is 27:12
peace would have been like a **r**, Is 48:18
make peace flow to her like a **r**, Is 66:12
to the Euphrates **R** and hide it Jr 13:4
on the Euphrates **R** by Jr 46:2
by the bank of the Euphrates **R**, Jr 46:6
land by the Euphrates **R**. Jr 46:10
the middle of the Euphrates **R**. Jr 51:63
run down like a **r** day and night. Lm 2:18
and it was a **r** that I could not Ezk 47:5
r that could not be crossed ⌊on Ezk 47:5
me back to the bank of the **r**. Ezk 47:6
will live wherever the **r** flows, Ezk 47:9
be life everywhere the **r** goes. Ezk 47:9
grow along both banks of the **r**. Ezk 47:12
A **r** of fire was flowing, coming Dn 7:10
on the bank of the great **r**, Dn 10:4
on this bank of the **r** and one on Dn 12:5
was above the waters of the **r**, Dn 12:6
was above the waters of the **r**. Dn 12:7
for the **r** beds are dried up, Jl 1:20
the Euphrates **R** and from sea to Mc 7:12
The **r** gates are opened, and the Nah 2:6
was the sea, the **r** her wall? Nah 3:8
from the Euphrates **R** to the ends Zch 9:10
in the Jordan **R** as they Mt 3:6
in the Jordan **R** as they Mk 1:5
the **r** crashed against that house Lk 6:48
The **r** crashed against it, and Lk 6:49
outside the city gate by the **r**, Ac 16:13
bound at the great **r** Euphrates." Rv 9:14
water like a **r** after the woman, Rv 12:15
up the **r** that the dragon Rv 12:16
bowl on the great **r** Euphrates, Rv 16:12
showed me the **r** of living water Rv 22:1
both sides of the **r** was the tree Rv 22:2

RIVERBANK *(2)*

girls walked along the **r**. Ex 2:5
trees along both sides of the **r**. Ezk 47:7

RIVERS *(43)*

and became the source of four **r**. Gn 2:10
over their **r**, canals, ponds, Ex 7:19
hand with your staff over the **r**, Ex 8:5
king of Aram of the Two **R**, Jdg 3:8
and Pharpar, the **r** of Damascus, 2Kg 5:12
the **r** flowing with honey and Jb 20:17
and established it on the **r**. Ps 24:2
You dried up ever-flowing **r**. Ps 74:15
and made water flow down like **r**. Ps 78:16
He turned their **r** into blood, Ps 78:44
sea and his right hand to the **r**. Ps 89:25
Let the **r** clap their hands; Ps 98:8
He turns **r** into desert, springs Ps 107:33
By the **r** of Babylon—there we Ps 137:1
r cannot sweep it away. Sg 8:7
insect wings beyond the **r** of Is 18:1
whose land is divided by **r**. Is 18:2
whose land is divided by **r**— Is 18:7
a place of **r** and broad streams, Is 33:21
I will open **r** on the barren Is 41:18
I will turn **r** into islands, Is 42:15
when you pass⌋ through the **r**, Is 43:2
the wilderness, **r** in the desert. Is 43:19
wilderness, and **r** in the desert, Is 43:20
dry, and I will dry up your **r**; Is 44:27
I turn the **r** into a wilderness; Is 50:2
like **r** whose waters churn? Jr 46:7
and its waters churn like **r**. Jr 46:8
directing their **r** all around the Ezk 31:4
I held back the **r** of the deep, Ezk 31:15
You thrash about in your **r**, Ezk 32:2
your feet, and muddy the **r**." Ezk 32:2
will make their **r** flow like oil. Ezk 32:14
and He makes all the **r** run dry. Nah 1:4
Are You angry at the **r**, LORD? Hab 3:8
Is Your wrath against the **r**? Hab 3:8
You split the earth with **r**. Hab 3:9
From beyond the **r** of Cush My Zph 3:10
The rain fell, the **r** rose, and Mt 7:25
rain fell, the **r** rose, the winds Mt 7:27
faced⌋ dangers from **r**, dangers 2Co 11:26
on a third of the **r** and springs Rv 8:10
bowl into the **r** and the springs Rv 16:4

RIZIA *(1)*

sons: Arah, Hanniel, and **R**. 1Ch 7:39

RIZPAH *(4)*

whose name was **R** daughter of 2Sm 3:7
sons whom **R** daughter of Aiah 2Sm 21:8
R, Aiah's daughter, took 2Sm 21:10
David what Saul's concubine **R**, 2Sm 21:11

ROAD *(102)*

who was beside the **r** at Enaim?" Gn 38:21
He will be a snake by the **r**, Gn 49:17
them along the **r** to the land Ex 13:17
Sea along the **r** of the Ex 13:18
"We will go on the main **r**," Nm 20:19
was coming on the Atharim **r**, Nm 21:1
and went up the **r** to Bashan, Nm 21:33
guide you on the **r** you were to Dt 1:33
from the Arabah **r** and from Elath Dt 2:8
along the **r** to the Wilderness Dt 2:8
and went up the **r** to Bashan, Dt 3:1
and when you walk along the **r**, Dt 6:7
and when you walk along the **r**, Dt 11:19
beyond the western **r** in the land Dt 11:30
or ox fallen down on the **r**, Dt 22:4
or on the ground along the **r**, Dt 22:6
a blind person astray on the **r**.' Dt 27:18
them along the **r** to the fords Jos 2:7
no honor on the **r** you are about Jdg 4:9
travel on the **r**, give praise! Jdg 5:10
who passed by them on the **r**. Jdg 9:25
left ⌊the **r**⌋ to see the lion's Jdg 14:8
along the **r** leading back to Ru 1:7
his chair beside the **r** watching, 1Sm 4:13
it goes up the **r** to its homeland 1Sm 6:9
up the **r** to Beth-shemesh 1Sm 6:12
toward the Ophrah **r** leading to 1Sm 13:17
headed toward the Beth-horon **r**, 1Sm 13:18
down the border **r** that looks out 1Sm 13:18
the Shaaraim **r** to Gath and Ekron 1Sm 17:52
to the sheep pens along the **r**, 1Sm 24:3
camped beside the **r** at the hill 1Sm 26:3
coming from the **r** west of him 2Sm 13:34
stand beside the **r** leading to 2Sm 15:2
past on the **r** that leads to 2Sm 15:23
along the **r** as Shimei was going 2Sm 16:13
Jeroboam on the **r** as Jeroboam 1Kg 11:29
His corpse was thrown on the **r**, 1Kg 13:24
thrown on the **r** and the lion 1Kg 13:25
thrown on the **r** with the donkey 1Kg 13:28
was ⌊walking⌋ along the **r**, 1Kg 18:7
or maybe he's on the **r**. 1Kg 18:27
waited for the king on the **r**. 1Kg 20:38
he fled up the **r** toward 2Kg 9:27
on the **r** that⌋ goes down to 2Kg 12:20
back on the **r** that he came and 2Kg 19:33
They push the needy off the **r**; Jb 24:4
Where is the **r** to the home of Jb 38:19
r leads to ⌊the place⌋ where Jb 38:24
drink from the brook by the **r**; Ps 110:7
travel that **r** with them or set Pr 1:15
strolled down the **r** to her house Pr 7:8
Her house is the **r** to Sheol, Pr 7:27
the heights overlooking the **r**, Pr 8:2
There's a lion in the **r**— Pr 26:13
when the fool walks along the **r**, Ec 10:3
of heights and dangers on the **r**; Ec 12:5
by the **r** to the Fuller's Field. Is 7:3
on the **r** to Horonaim. Is 15:5
A **r** will be there and a way; Is 35:8
by the **r** to the Fuller's Field. Is 36:2
back on the **r** that he came and Is 37:34
make all My mountains into a **r**, Is 49:11
into a **r** for the redeemed Is 51:10
walk on the **r**. For the enemy Jr 6:25
Set up **r** markers for yourself; Jr 31:21
⌊turning⌋ their faces to this **r**. Jr 50:5
fork in the **r** to ⌊each⌋ city. Ezk 21:19
Mark out a **r** that the sword can Ezk 21:20
stands at the split in the **r**, Ezk 21:21
end, along the **r** of Hethlon, to Ezk 48:1
murders on the **r** to Shechem. Hs 6:9
Watch the **r**! Brace yourself! Nah 2:1
along the sea **r**, beyond the Mt 4:15
is wide and the **r** is broad that Mt 7:13
and difficult the **r** that leads Mt 7:14
Don't take the **r** leading to Mt 10:5
take a traveling bag for the **r**, Mt 10:10
two blind men sitting by the **r**. Mt 20:30
spread their robes on the **r**; Mt 21:8
and spreading them on the **r**. Mt 21:8
Seeing a lone fig tree by the **r**, Mt 21:19
nothing for the **r** except a Mk 6:8
And on the **r** He asked His Mk 8:27
They were on the **r**, going up to Mk 10:32
beggar, was sitting by the **r**. Mk 10:46
began to follow Him on the **r**. Mk 10:52
spread their robes on the **r**, Mk 11:8
for the **r**," He told them, Lk 9:3
on the **r** someone said to Lk 9:57
don't greet anyone along the **r**. Lk 10:4
to be going down that **r**. Lk 10:31
was sitting by the **r** begging. Lk 18:35
spreading their robes on the **r**. Lk 19:36
with us on the **r** and explaining Lk 24:32
happened on the **r** and how He was Lk 24:35
go south to the **r** that goes down Ac 8:26
they were traveling down the **r**, Ac 8:36
to you on the **r** you were Ac 9:17
how, on the **r**, Saul had seen Ac 9:27
ambush along the **r** to kill him. Ac 25:3
while on the **r**, O king, I saw Ac 26:13

ROADS *(11)*

until your **r** are deserted. Lv 26:22
travelers kept to the side **r**. Jdg 5:6
those who travel the **r**? Jb 21:29
and will level all **r** for him. Is 45:13
They have made their **r** crooked; Is 59:8
in the ancient **r**—to walk on Jr 18:15
The **r** to Zion mourn, for no one Lm 1:4
mark out two **r** that the sword of Ezk 21:19
fork of the two **r**, to practice Ezk 21:21
go to where the **r** exit the city Mt 22:9
went out on the **r** and gathered Mt 22:10

ROADWAYS *(1)*

Stand by the **r** and look. Jr 6:16

ROAM *(4)*

but a fool's eyes **r** to the ends Pr 17:24
R through the streets of Jr 5:1
Many will **r** about, and knowledge Dn 12:4
sea to sea and **r** from north to Am 8:12

ROAMED *(1)*

where David and his men had **r**. 1Sm 30:31

ROAMING *(2)*

"From **r** through the earth," Jb 1:7
"From **r** through the earth," Jb 2:2

ROAMS *(3)*

It **r** the mountains for its Jb 39:8
it **r** through waterless places Mt 12:43
it **r** through waterless places Lk 11:24

ROAR *(25)*

The lion may **r** and the fierce Jb 4:10
to deep in the **r** of Your Ps 42:7
though its waters **r** and foam and Ps 46:3
You silence the **r** of the seas, Ps 65:7
the seas, the **r** of their waves, Ps 65:7
Greater than the **r** of many Ps 93:4
The young lions **r** for their prey Ps 104:21
king's rage is like a lion's **r**, Pr 19:12
they **r** like young lions; Is 5:29
On that day they will **r** over it, Is 5:30
r of many peoples—they roar Is 17:12
they **r** like the roaring of the Is 17:12
up the sea so that its waves **r**— Is 51:15
They **r** but cannot pass over it. Jr 5:22
the sea and makes its waves **r**— Jr 31:35
They will **r** together like young Jr 51:38
Their waves **r** like abundant Jr 51:55
wings like the **r** of mighty Ezk 1:24
so his **r** could no longer Ezk 19:9
like the **r** of mighty waters Ezk 43:2
r of battle will rise against Hs 10:14
LORD; He will **r** like a lion. Hs 11:10
The LORD will **r** from Zion and Jl 3:16
Does a lion **r** in the forest when Am 3:4
Listen to the **r** of young lions, Zch 11:3

ROARED *(5)*

adversaries **r** in the meeting Ps 74:4
The young lions have **r** at him; Jr 2:15
him; they have **r** loudly. They Jr 2:15
She has **r** against Me. Jr 12:8
A lion has **r**; who will not fear? Am 3:8

ROARING *(15)*

a young lion came **r** at him, Jdg 14:5
Then there comes a **r** sound; Jb 37:4
me—lions, mauling and **r**. Ps 22:13
wrath is like the **r** of a lion; Pr 20:2
people is like a **r** lion or a Pr 28:15

- Their **r** is like a lion's; Is 5:29
- over it, like the **r** of the sea. Is 5:30
- roar like the **r** of the seas. Is 17:12
- consumed with a great **r** sound. Jr 11:16
- shuddered at the sound of his **r**. Ezk 19:7
- her is like a **r** lion tearing Ezk 22:25
- princes within her are **r** lions; Zph 3:3
- by the **r** sea and waves. Lk 21:25
- prowling around like a **r** lion, 1Pt 5:8
- with a loud voice like a **r** lion. Rv 10:3

ROARS *(9)*

- or how the thunder **r** from God's Jb 36:29
- He shouts, He **r** aloud, He Is 42:13
- Their voice **r** like the sea, Jr 6:23
- The LORD **r** from on high; Jr 25:30
- He **r** loudly over His grazing Jr 25:30
- Their voice **r** like the sea, Jr 50:42
- He **r**, His children will come Hs 11:10
- The LORD **r** from Zion and raises Am 1:2
- The deep **r** with its voice and Hab 3:10

ROAST *(3)*

- the priest ⌊some⌋ meat to **r**, 1Sm 2:15
- A lazy man doesn't **r** his game, Pr 12:27
- He eats the **r** and is satisfied. Is 44:16

ROASTED *(12)*

- **r** over the fire along with Ex 12:8
- water, but only **r** over fire— Ex 12:9
- kernels, **r** on the fire, for Lv 2:14
- not eat bread, **r** grain, or ⌊any⌋ Lv 23:14
- unleavened bread and **r** grain Jos 5:11
- and he offered her **r** grain. Ru 2:14
- half-bushel of **r** grain along 1Sm 17:17
- sheep, a bushel of **r** grain, 100 1Sm 25:18
- barley, flour, **r** grain, beans, 2Sm 17:28
- They **r** the Passover ⌊lambs⌋ with 2Ch 35:13
- on its coals, I **r** meat and ate. Is 44:19
- king of Babylon **r** in the fire! Jr 29:22

ROASTS *(1)*

- and he **r** meat on that half. Is 44:16

ROB *(11)*

- your neighbor or **r** ⌊him⌋. Lv 19:13
- to ambush and **r** everyone who Jdg 9:25
- Did you invite us here to **r** us?" Jdg 14:15
- Don't **r** a poor man because he is Pr 22:22
- Will a man **r** God? Yet you are Mal 3:8
- ask: "How do we **r** You?" "⌊By not Mal 3:8
- Then he can **r** his house. Mt 12:29
- house and **r** his possessions Mk 3:27
- Then he will **r** his house. Mk 3:27
- no one will **r** you of your joy Jn 16:22
- idols, do you **r** their temples? Rm 2:22

ROBBED *(7)*

- be oppressed and **r** continually, Dt 28:29
- like a wild bear **r** of her cubs. 2Sm 17:8
- they are **r** of sleep unless they Pr 4:16
- meet a bear **r** of her cubs than Pr 17:12
- fraud, **r** ⌊his⌋ brother, Ezk 18:18
- them like a bear **r** of her cubs Hs 13:8
- I **r** other churches by taking pay 2Co 11:8

ROBBER *(6)*

- he is at peace, a **r** attacks him. Jb 15:21
- your poverty will come like a **r**, Pr 6:11
- an ambush like a **r** and increases Pr 23:28
- your poverty will come like a **r**, Pr 24:34
- Jacob to the **r**, and Israel to Is 42:24
- other way, is a thief and a **r**. Jn 10:1

ROBBERS *(8)*

- The tents of **r** are safe, and Jb 12:6
- become a den of **r** in your view? Jr 7:11
- Like **r** who wait in ambush for Hs 6:9
- and fell into the hands of **r**. Lk 10:30
- fell into the hands of the **r**?" Lk 10:36
- before Me are thieves and **r**, Jn 10:8
- are not temple **r** or blasphemers Ac 19:37
- dangers from **r**, dangers from my 2Co 11:26

ROBBERY *(9)*

- a deposit, a security, or a **r**; Lv 6:2
- oppression, or false hope in **r**. Ps 62:10
- I hate **r** and injustice; Is 61:8
- the victim of **r** from the hand of Jr 21:12
- the victim of **r** from the hand of Jr 22:3
- does not commit **r**, but gives his Ezk 18:7
- needy, commits **r**, and does not Ezk 18:12
- hold collateral, or commit **r**. Ezk 18:16
- extortion and committed **r**. Ezk 22:29

ROBBING *(2)*

- God? Yet you are **r** Me!" You ask: Mal 3:8
- whole nation—are ⌊still⌋ **r** Me. Mal 3:9

ROBE *(70)*

- and he made a **r** of many colors Gn 37:3
- stripped off his **r**, the robe of Gn 37:23
- the **r** of many colors that he had Gn 37:23
- took Joseph's **r**, slaughtered Gn 37:31
- and dipped the **r** in its blood. Gn 37:31
- They sent the **r** of many colors Gn 37:32
- Is it your son's **r** or not?" Gn 37:32
- "It is my son's **r**," he said. Gn 37:33
- an ephod, a **r**, a specially woven Ex 28:4
- are to make the **r** of the ephod Ex 28:31
- around the lower hem of the **r**. Ex 28:34
- The **r** must be ⌊worn by⌋ Aaron Ex 28:35
- the tunic, the **r** for the ephod, Ex 29:5
- made the woven **r** of the ephod Ex 39:22
- center of the **r** like that for Ex 39:23
- yarn on the lower hem of the **r**. Ex 39:24
- around the hem of the **r** between Ex 39:25
- around the lower hem of the **r**. Ex 39:26
- to put on his linen **r** and linen Lv 6:10
- with the **r**, and put the ephod Lv 8:7
- him a little **r** and took it to 1Sm 2:19
- Saul grabbed the hem of his **r**, 1Sm 15:27
- removed the **r** he was wearing 1Sm 18:4
- cut off the corner of Saul's **r**. 1Sm 24:4
- cut off the corner of Saul's **r**. 1Sm 24:5
- the corner of your **r** in my hand, 1Sm 24:11
- wearing a **r**." Then Saul knew 1Sm 28:14
- Archite with his **r** torn and dust 2Sm 15:32
- dressed in a **r** of fine linen, 1Ch 15:27
- my tunic and **r**, pulled out some Ezr 9:3
- with my tunic and **r** torn. Ezr 9:5
- the folds of my **r** and said, Neh 5:13
- and a purple **r** of fine linen. Est 8:15
- tore his **r** and shaved his head. Jb 1:20
- man tore his **r** and threw dust Jb 2:12
- were like a **r** and a turban. Jb 29:14
- in light as if it were a **r**, Ps 104:2
- it be like a **r** he wraps around Ps 109:19
- and His **r** filled the temple. Is 6:1
- with your **r** and tie your sash Is 22:21
- wrapped me in a **r** of Is 61:10
- them in the folds of your ⌊**r**⌋. Ezk 5:3
- off his royal **r**, put on Jnh 3:6
- the splendid **r** from those who Mc 2:8
- will grab the **r** of a Jewish man Zch 8:23
- and touched the tassel on His **r**, Mt 9:20
- If I can just touch His **r**, Mt 9:21
- only touch the tassel on His **r**. Mt 14:36
- and dressed Him in a scarlet **r**. Mt 27:28
- they stripped Him of the **r**, Mt 27:31
- and his **r** was as white as snow. Mt 28:3
- in the crowd and touched His **r**. Mk 5:27
- touch just the tassel of His **r**. Mk 6:56
- They dressed Him in a purple **r**, Mk 15:17
- stripped Him of the purple **r**, Mk 15:20
- in a long white **r** sitting on the Mk 16:5
- and touched the tassel of His **r**. Lk 8:44
- out the best **r** and put it on him Lk 15:22
- should sell his **r** and buy one. Lk 22:36
- dressed Him in a brilliant **r**, Lk 23:11
- laid aside His **r**, took a towel, Jn 13:4
- their feet and put on His **r**, Jn 13:12
- and threw a purple **r** around Him. Jn 19:2
- of thorns and the purple **r**. Jn 19:5
- in a dazzling **r** stood before me Ac 10:30
- they will be changed like a **r**. Heb 1:12
- in a long **r**, and with a gold Rv 1:13
- a white **r** was given to each of Rv 6:11
- He wore a **r** stained with blood, Rv 19:13
- And on His **r** and on His thigh He Rv 19:16

ROBED *(6)*

- by Your power, **r** with strength; Ps 65:6
- and the hills are **r** with joy. Ps 65:12
- LORD reigns! He is **r** in majesty; Ps 93:1
- The LORD is **r**, enveloped in Ps 93:1
- They were **r** in white with palm Rv 7:9
- Who are these people **r** in white, Rv 7:13

ROBES *(28)*

- his **r** in the blood of grapes. Gn 49:11
- dressed in their **r** and holding Ezr 3:10
- down Aaron's beard, on his **r**. Ps 133:2
- **r**, capes, cloaks, purses, Is 3:22
- remove their **r**, and strip off Ezk 26:16
- trousers, **r**, head coverings Dn 3:21
- singed, their **r** were unaffected Dn 3:27
- clothe you with splendid **r**." Zch 3:4
- then they laid their **r** on them, Mt 21:7
- spread their **r** on the road; Mt 21:8
- high priest tore his **r** and said, Mt 26:65
- If I can just touch His **r**, Mk 5:28
- and said, "Who touched My **r**?" Mk 5:30
- Jesus and threw their **r** on it, Mk 11:7
- spread their **r** on the road, Mk 11:8
- who want to go around in long **r**, Mk 12:38
- high priest tore his **r** and said, Mk 14:63
- A man dressed in soft **r**? Lk 7:25
- throwing their **r** on the donkey, Lk 19:35
- spreading their **r** on the road. Lk 19:36
- go around in long **r** and who love Lk 20:46
- laid their **r** at the feet Ac 7:58
- showing him the **r** and clothes Ac 9:39
- dressed in royal **r** and seated on Ac 12:21
- tore their **r** when they heard Ac 14:14
- aside their **r** and throwing dust Ac 22:23
- washed their **r** and made them Rv 7:14
- are those who wash their **r**, Rv 22:14

ROBS *(2)*

- the needy from one who **r** him?" Ps 35:10
- The one who **r** his father or Pr 28:24

ROCK *(115)*

- the Shepherd, the **R** of Israel, Gn 49:24
- front of you on the **r** at Horeb; Ex 17:6
- you hit the **r**, water will come Ex 17:6
- You are to stand on the **r**, Ex 33:21
- crevice of the **r** and cover you Ex 33:22
- to speak to the **r** while they Nm 20:8
- them from the **r** and provide Nm 20:8
- the assembly in front of the **r**, Nm 20:10
- water out of this **r** for you?" Nm 20:10
- and struck the **r** twice with his Nm 20:11
- out of the flintlike **r** for you. Dt 8:15
- The **R**—His work is perfect; Dt 32:4
- with honey from the **r** and oil Dt 32:13
- rock and oil from flintlike **r**, Dt 32:13
- and scorned the **R** of his Dt 32:15
- You ignored the **R** who gave you Dt 32:18
- unless their **R** had sold them, Dt 32:30
- But their "**r**" is not like our Dt 32:31
- their "rock" is not like our **R**; Dt 32:31
- the '**r**' they found refuge in? Dt 32:37
- came up from the **r** and consumed Jdg 6:21
- your God on the top of this **r**. Jdg 6:26
- Oreb at the **r** of Oreb and Zeeb Jdg 7:25
- offered them on a **r** to the LORD, Jdg 13:19
- in the cave at the **r** of Etam. Jdg 15:8
- to the cave at the **r** of Etam, Jdg 15:11
- and led him away from the **r**. Jdg 15:13
- wilderness to the **r** of Rimmon, Jdg 20:45
- wilderness to the **r** of Rimmon Jdg 20:47
- who were at the **r** of Rimmon. Jdg 21:13
- And there is no **r** like our God. 1Sm 2:2
- stopped there near a large **r**. 1Sm 6:14
- and placed them on the large **r**. 1Sm 6:15
- The large **r** on which the ark of 1Sm 6:18
- sharp columns of **r** on both sides 1Sm 14:4
- and stay beside the **r** Ezel. 1Sm 20:19
- he went down to the **r** and stayed 1Sm 23:25
- was named the **R** of Separation. 1Sm 23:28
- herself on the **r** from the 2Sm 21:10
- The LORD is my **r**, my fortress, 2Sm 22:2
- And who is a **r**? Only our God. 2Sm 22:32
- lives—may my **r** be praised! 2Sm 22:47
- God, the **r** of my salvation, is 2Sm 22:47
- the **R** of Israel said to me, 2Sm 23:3
- to the **r** at the cave of Adullam, 1Ch 11:15
- water from the **r** for their Neh 9:15
- crumbles and a **r** is dislodged Jb 14:18
- a **r** be removed from its place? Jb 18:4
- in cream and the **r** poured out Jb 29:6
- His heart is as hard as a **r**, Jb 41:24
- The LORD is my **r**, my fortress, Ps 18:2
- And who is a **r**? Only our God. Ps 18:31
- lives—may my **r** be praised! Ps 18:46
- You, LORD, my **r** and my Redeemer Ps 19:14
- He will set me high on a **r**. Ps 27:5
- my **r**, do not be deaf to me. Ps 28:1
- Be a **r** of refuge for me, a Ps 31:2
- You are my **r** and my fortress; Ps 31:3
- my feet on a **r**, making my steps Ps 40:2
- say to God, my **r**, "Why have You Ps 42:9
- me to a **r** that is high above Ps 61:2
- He alone is my **r** and my Ps 62:2

He alone is my **r** and my Ps 62:6
my strong **r**, my refuge, is in Ps 62:7
Be a **r** of refuge for me, where I Ps 71:3
for You are my **r** and fortress. Ps 71:3
He struck the **r** and water gushed Ps 78:20
remembered that God was their **r**, Ps 78:35
you with honey from the **r**." Ps 81:16
my God, the **r** of my salvation. Ps 89:26
He is my **r**, and there is no Ps 92:15
God is the **r** of my protection. Ps 94:22
to the **r** of our salvation! Ps 95:1
He opened a **r**, and water gushed Ps 105:41
who turned the **r** into a pool of Ps 114:8
May the LORD my **r** be praised, Ps 144:1
the way of a snake on a **r**, Pr 30:19
clefts of the **r**, in the crevices Sg 2:14
over and a **r** to trip over, Is 8:14
struck Midian at the **r** of Oreb; Is 10:26
to remember the **r** of your Is 17:10
a crypt for yourself out of **r**? Is 22:16
the LORD, is an everlasting **r**! Is 26:4
of the LORD, to the **R** of Israel. Is 30:29
His **r** will pass away because of Is 31:9
of a massive **r** in an arid land. Is 32:2
is no ⌊other⌋ **R**; I do not know Is 44:8
water flow for them from the **r**; Is 48:21
He split the **r**, and water gushed Is 48:21
to the **r** from which you were Is 51:1
made their faces harder than **r**, Jr 5:3
sledgehammer that pulverizes **r**? Jr 23:29
who live in the clefts of the **r**, Jr 49:16
She put it out on the bare **r**; Ezk 24:7
put her blood on the bare **r**, Ezk 24:8
her and turn her into a bare **r**. Ezk 26:4
I will turn you into a bare **r**, Ezk 26:14
horses run on **r**, or does someone Am 6:12
in clefts of the **r** in your home Ob 3
⌊my⌋ **R**, You destined them to Hab 1:12
hearts like a **r** so as not to Zch 7:12
who built his house on the **r**. Mt 7:24
its foundation was on the **r**. Mt 7:25
and on this **r** I will build My Mt 16:18
which he had cut into the **r**. Mt 27:60
Him in a tomb cut out of the **r**, Mk 15:46
laid the foundation on the **r**. Lk 6:48
Other seed fell on the **r**; Lk 8:6
seeds on the **r** are those who, Lk 8:13
it in a tomb cut into the **r**, Lk 23:53
Cephas" (which means "**R**"). Jn 1:42
over, and a **r** to trip over, yet Rm 9:33
from a spiritual **r** that followed 1Co 10:4
them, and that **r** was Christ. 1Co 10:4
and a **r** that trips them up. 1Pt 2:8

ROCK-HEWN *(1)*
houses, **r** cisterns, vineyards, Neh 9:25

ROCKS *(26)*
a land whose **r** are iron and from Dt 8:9
large pile of **r** that remains to Jos 7:26
put a large pile of **r** over it, Jos 8:29
thickets, among **r**, and in holes 1Sm 13:6
in front of the **R** of the Wild 1Sm 24:2
intertwined around a pile of **r**. Jb 8:17
they huddle against the **r**, Jb 24:8
Its **r** are a source of sapphire, Jb 28:6
He cuts out channels in the **r**, Jb 28:10
among the **r** and in holes in the Jb 30:6
He split **r** in the wilderness and Ps 78:15
and dashes them against the **r**. Ps 137:9
turning up **r**⌋, so our bones Ps 141:7
Go into the **r** and hide in the Is 2:10
go into caves in the **r** and holes Is 2:19
caves of the **r** and the crevices Is 2:21
in the clefts of the **r**, in all Is 7:19
wadis below the clefts of the **r**? Is 57:5
thickets and climb among the **r**. Jr 4:29
and out of the clefts of the **r**, Jr 16:16
like heaps of **r** on the furrows Hs 12:11
even **r** are shattered before Him. Nah 1:6
quaked and the **r** were split. Mt 27:51
Jews picked up **r** to stone Him. Jn 10:31
among the **r** of the mountains. Rv 6:15
to the mountains and to the **r**, Rv 6:16

ROCKY *(11)*
them from the top of **r** cliffs, Nm 23:9
its stronghold is on a **r** crag. Jb 39:28
and dumped into a **r** pit like a Is 14:19
refuge will be the **r** fortresses, Is 33:16
and hide it in a **r** crevice." Jr 13:4
⌊you atop⌋ the **r** plateau— Jr 21:13
Others fell on **r** ground, where Mt 13:5
And the one sown on **r** ground— Mt 13:20
seed fell on **r** ground where it Mk 4:5
are the ones sown on **r** ground: Mk 4:16
run aground in some **r** place, Ac 27:29

ROD *(44)*
Take the **r** you struck the Nile Ex 17:5
male or female slave with a **r**, Ex 21:20
passes under the ⌊shepherd's⌋ **r**, Lv 27:32
Put Aaron's **r** back in front of Nm 17:10
with a human **r** and with blows 2Sm 7:14
Him take His **r** away from me so Jb 9:34
no **r** from God ⌊strikes⌋ them. Jb 21:9
break them with a **r** of iron; Ps 2:9
Your **r** and Your staff—they Ps 23:4
rebellion to account with the **r**, Ps 89:32
but a **r** is for the back of the Pr 10:13
not use the **r** hates his son, Pr 13:24
⌊brings⌋ a **r** ⌊of discipline⌋ Pr 14:3
and the **r** of his fury will be Pr 22:8
the **r** of discipline will drive Pr 22:15
beat him with a **r**, he will not Pr 23:13
Strike him with a **r**, and you Pr 23:14
and a **r** for the backs of fools. Pr 26:3
r of correction imparts wisdom, Pr 29:15
yoke and the **r** on their Is 9:4
to Assyria, the **r** of My anger— Is 10:5
As if a **r** could lift what isn't Is 10:15
you with a **r** and raises his Is 10:24
because the **r** of the one who Is 14:29
a stick, and cumin with a **r**. Is 28:27
He will strike with a **r**. Is 30:31
under the **r** of God's wrath. Lm 3:1
gone out. The **r** has blossomed; Ezk 7:10
grown into a **r** of wickedness; Ezk 7:11
pass under the **r** and will bring Ezk 20:37
and a measuring **r** in his hand. Ezk 40:3
measuring **r** in the man's hand Ezk 40:5
east side with a measuring **r**; Ezk 42:16
was 875 feet by the measuring **r**. Ezk 42:16
was 875 feet by the measuring **r**. Ezk 42:17
was 875 feet by the measuring **r**. Ezk 42:18
875 feet by the measuring **r**. Ezk 42:19
of Israel on the cheek with a **r**. Mc 5:1
to the **r** and the One who Mc 6:9
Should I come to you with a **r**, 1Co 4:21
manna, Aaron's **r** that budded, Heb 9:4
given a measuring reed like a **r**, Rv 11:1
gold measuring **r** to measure the Rv 21:15
city with the **r** at 12,000 stadia Rv 21:16

RODANIM *(1)*
(AKA DODANIM)
Tarshish, Kittim, and **R**. 1Ch 1:7

RODE *(9)*
He had 30 sons who **r** on 30 young Jdg 10:4
grandsons, who **r** on 70 donkeys. Jdg 12:14
As she **r** the donkey down a 1Sm 25:20
r on the donkey following 1Sm 25:42
He **r** on a cherub and flew, 2Sm 22:11
the horses, and Jehu **r** over her. 2Kg 9:33
who **r** fast horses bred from the Est 8:10
the couriers **r** out in haste, Est 8:14
He **r** on a cherub and flew, Ps 18:10

RODS *(6)*
cords to silver **r** on marble Est 1:6
his limbs are like iron **r**. Jb 40:18
His arms are **r** of gold set with Sg 5:14
their divining **r** inform them. Hs 4:12
them to be beaten with **r**. Ac 16:22
Three times I was beaten with **r**. 2Co 11:25

ROE *(1)*
gazelle, the **r** deer, the wild Dt 14:5

ROEBUCKS *(1)*
deer, gazelles, **r**, and pen-fed 1Kg 4:23

ROGELIM *(2)*
Barzillai the Gileadite from **R** 2Sm 17:27
down from **R** and accompanied 2Sm 19:31

ROHGAH *(1)*
Ahi, **R**, Hubbah, and Aram. 1Ch 7:34

ROLE *(1)*
and each has the **r** the Lord has 1Co 3:5

ROLL *(14)*
⌊shepherds⌋ would **r** the stone Gn 29:3
R large stones against the mouth Jos 10:18
Call the **r** and determine who has 1Sm 14:17
They called the **r** and saw that 1Sm 14:17
R a large stone over here at once. 1Sm 14:33
The skies will **r** up like a Is 34:4
in sackcloth and **r** in the dust. Jr 6:26
R ⌊in the dust⌋, you leaders of Jr 25:34
r you down from the cliffs, Jr 51:25
on their heads; they **r** in ashes. Ezk 27:30
I will **r** her stones into the Mc 1:6
In Beth-leaphrah **r** in the dust. Mc 1:10
Who will **r** away the stone from Mk 16:3
You will **r** them up like a cloak, Heb 1:12

ROLLED *(13)*
the stone is **r** from the well's Gn 29:8
he went up and **r** the stone from Gn 29:10
Today I have **r** away the disgrace Jos 5:9
took his mantle, **r** it up, and 2Kg 2:8
wheel is not **r** over the cumin. Is 28:27
I have **r** up my life like a Is 38:12
He **r** back the stone and was Mt 28:2
fell to the ground and **r** around, Mk 9:20
and **r** a stone against the Mk 15:46
very large—had been **r** away. Mk 16:4
He then **r** up the scroll, gave it Lk 4:20
found the stone **r** away from the Lk 24:2
like a scroll being **r** up; Rv 6:14

ROLLING *(2)*
keep **r** in through the ruins. Jb 30:14
He left after **r** a great stone Mt 27:60

ROLLS *(1)*
it, and whoever **r** a stone—it Pr 26:27

ROMAMTI-EZER *(2)*
Giddalti, **R**, Joshbekashah, 1Ch 25:4
and the twenty-fourth to **R**, 1Ch 25:31

ROMAN *(10)*
famine throughout the **R** world. Ac 11:28
Philippi, a **R** colony, which is Ac 16:12
although we are **R** citizens, Ac 16:37
Paul and Silas were **R** citizens. Ac 16:38
a man who is a **R** citizen and is Ac 22:25
For this man is a **R** citizen." Ac 22:26
Tell me—are you a **R** citizen?" Ac 22:27
Paul was a **R** citizen and he had Ac 22:29
learned that he is a **R** citizen. Ac 23:27
the Jews throughout the **R** world, Ac 24:5

ROMANS *(3)*
Then the **R** will come and remove Jn 11:48
not legal for us as **R** to adopt Ac 16:21
into the hands of the **R** Ac 28:17

ROMANS' *(1)*
it's not the **R** custom to give Ac 25:16

ROME *(9)*
visitors from **R**, both Jews and Ac 2:10
ordered all the Jews to leave **R**. Ac 18:2
he said, "I must see **R** as well!" Ac 19:21
so you must also testify in **R**." Ac 23:11
seven days. And so we came to **R**. Ac 28:14
when we entered **R**, Paul was Ac 28:16
all who are in **R**, loved by God, Rm 1:7
news to you also who are in **R**. Rm 1:15
when he was in **R**, he diligently 2Tm 1:17

ROOF *(33)*
You are to make a **r**, finishing Gn 6:16
to within 18 inches ⌊of the **r**.⌋ Gn 6:16
under the protection of my **r**." Gn 19:8
make a railing around your **r**, Dt 22:8
them up to the **r** and hidden them Jos 2:6
that she had arranged on the **r**. Jos 2:6
asleep, she went up on the **r** Jos 2:8
went up to the **r** of the tower. Jdg 9:51
were on the **r** watching Samson Jdg 16:27
spoke with Saul on ⌊the⌋ **r**. 1Sm 9:25
Samuel called to Saul on the **r**, 1Sm 9:26
around on the **r** of the palace. 2Sm 11:2
the **r** he saw a woman bathing 2Sm 11:2
a tent for Absalom on the **r**, 2Sm 16:22
went up to the **r** of the gate and 2Sm 18:24
the altars that were on the **r**— 2Kg 23:12
stuck to the **r** of their mouths. Jb 29:10
sticks to the **r** of my mouth. Ps 22:15
am like a solitary bird on a **r**. Ps 102:7
stick to the **r** of my mouth if I Ps 137:6
the corner of a **r** than to share Pr 21:9
corner of a **r** than in a house Pr 25:24
Because of laziness the **r** caves Ec 10:18
clings to the **r** of his mouth Lm 4:4
stick to the **r** of your mouth, Ezk 3:26

from the **r** of one recess to Ezk 40:13
recess to the **r** of the ⌊opposite Ezk 40:13
walking on the **r** of the royal Dn 4:29
to have You come under my **r**. Mt 8:8
they removed the **r** above where Mk 2:4
went up on the **r** and lowered him Lk 5:19
through the **r** tiles into the Lk 5:19
to have You come under my **r**. Lk 7:6

ROOFED (1)
He rebuilt it and **r** it. Neh 3:15

ROOFTOPS (10)
grass, grass on the **r**, blasted 2Kg 19:26
themselves on each of their **r**, Neh 8:16
Let them be like grass on the **r**, Ps 129:6
on its **r** and in its public Is 15:3
all of you gone up to the **r**? Is 22:1
grass, grass on the **r**, blasted Is 37:27
houses on whose **r** they have Jr 19:13
Baal on their **r** and where drink Jr 32:29
On all the **r** of Moab and in her Jr 48:38
worship on the **r** to the heavenly Zph 1:5

ROOM (57)
there **r** in your father's house Gn 24:23
now the LORD has made **r** for us, Gn 26:22
He went into an inner **r** to weep. Gn 43:30
the old to make **r** for the new. Lv 26:10
where there was no **r** to turn to Nm 22:26
alone in his **r** upstairs ⌊where Jdg 3:20
of the upstairs **r** behind him. Jdg 3:23
of the upstairs **r** locked and Jdg 3:24
relieving himself in the cool **r**. Jdg 3:24
the doors of the upstairs **r**. Jdg 3:25
want to go to my wife in her **r**," Jdg 15:1
in ambush were waiting in her **r**, Jdg 16:9
in ambush were waiting in her **r**, Jdg 16:12
was failing, was lying in his **r**. 1Sm 3:2
up to the upper **r** where he was 1Kg 17:19
from the upper **r** into the house, 1Kg 17:23
into an inner **r** in the city. 1Kg 20:30
of his upper **r** in Samaria and 2Kg 1:2
make a small **r** upstairs and put 2Kg 4:10
went to the **r** upstairs to lie 2Kg 4:11
and take him to an inner **r**. 2Kg 9:2
into the inner **r** of the temple 2Kg 10:25
and the **r** for the place of 1Ch 28:11
The larger **r** he paneled with 2Ch 3:5
touching the wall of the **r**; 2Ch 3:11
touching the wall of the **r**; 2Ch 3:12
feet and faced the larger **r**. 2Ch 3:13
made repairs opposite his **r**. Neh 3:30
as the upper **r** of the corner. Neh 3:31
between the upper **r** of the Neh 3:32
prepared a large **r** for him where Neh 13:5
providing him a **r** in the courts Neh 13:7
possessions out of the **r**. Neh 13:8
there is no more **r** and you alone Is 5:8
make **r** for me so that I may Is 49:20
all around the inside of the **r**, Ezk 40:43
inside ⌊the next **r**⌋ and measured Ezk 41:3
the length of the **r** adjacent to Ezk 41:4
in its upper **r** opened toward Dn 6:10
your private **r**, shut your door, Mt 6:6
that there was no more **r**, Mk 2:2
is the guest **r** for Me to eat Mk 14:14
show you a large **r** upstairs, Mk 14:15
there was no **r** for them at the Lk 2:7
been done, and there's still **r**.' Lk 14:22
is the guest **r** where I can eat Lk 22:11
a large, furnished **r** upstairs. Lk 22:12
went to the **r** upstairs where Ac 1:13
they placed her in a **r** upstairs. Ac 9:37
they led him to the **r** upstairs. Ac 9:39
sent them all out of the **r**. Ac 9:40
lamps in the **r** upstairs where we Ac 20:8
instead, leave **r** for His wrath. Rm 12:19
also prepare a guest **r** for me, Phm 22
in the first **r**, which is called Heb 9:2
enter the first **r** repeatedly, Heb 9:6
alone enters the second **r**, Heb 9:7

ROOMS (22)
Make **r** in the ark, and cover it Gn 6:14
with the **r** and the treasuries 1Ch 9:26
upper **r**, inner rooms, 1Ch 28:11
rooms, inner **r**, and the room for 1Ch 28:11
in charge of the **r** ⌊that housed⌋ Neh 12:44
ordered that the **r** be purified, Neh 13:9
knowledge the **r** are filled with Pr 24:4
your **r** and close your doors Is 26:20
his upper **r** through injustice, Jr 22:13
palace, with spacious upper **r**. Jr 22:14
width of the side **r** all around Ezk 41:5
The side **r** were arranged one Ezk 41:6
in three stories of 30 **r** each. Ezk 41:6
as supports for the side **r**, Ezk 41:6
The side **r** surrounding ⌊the Ezk 41:7
for the side **r** was 10 and a half Ezk 41:8
wall of the side **r** was eight Ezk 41:9
between the side **r** of the temple Ezk 41:9
The side **r** opened into the free Ezk 41:11
the side **r** of the temple, Ezk 41:26
'Look, he's in the inner **r**!' Mt 24:26
an ear in private **r** will be Lk 12:3

ROOST (1)
owl will **r** in the capitals Zph 2:14

ROOSTER (14)
strutting **r**, a goat, and a king Pr 30:31
before the **r** crows, you will Mt 26:34
Immediately a **r** crowed, Mt 26:74
Before the **r** crows, you will Mt 26:75
at the crowing of the **r** or early Mk 13:35
before the **r** crows twice, you Mk 14:30
to the entryway, and a **r** crowed. Mk 14:68
Immediately a **r** crowed a second Mk 14:72
Before the **r** crows twice, Mk 14:72
the **r** will not crow today until Lk 22:34
was still speaking, a **r** crowed. Lk 22:60
Before the **r** crows today, Lk 22:61
A **r** will not crow until you have Jn 13:38
Immediately a **r** crowed. Jn 18:27

ROOT (34)
sure there is no **r** among you Dt 29:18
will again take **r** downward and 2Kg 19:30
I have seen a fool taking **r**, Jb 5:3
since the **r** of the problem lies Jb 19:28
it took **r** and filled the land. Ps 80:9
the **r** Your right hand has Ps 80:15
but the **r** of the righteous is Pr 12:3
the **r** of the righteous produces Pr 12:12
On that day the **r** of Jesse will Is 11:10
come out of the **r** of a snake, Is 14:29
I will kill your **r** with hunger, Is 14:30
days to come, Jacob will take **r**. Is 27:6
will again take **r** downward and Is 37:31
hardly takes **r** in the ground Is 40:24
plant and like a **r** out of dry Is 53:2
them, and they have taken **r**. Jr 12:2
lily and take **r** like ⌊the cedars Hs 14:5
not leaving them **r** or branches. Mal 4:1
to strike the **r** of the trees! Mt 3:10
they had no **r**, they withered. Mt 13:6
Yet he has no **r** in himself, Mt 13:21
and since it didn't have a **r**, Mk 4:6
they have no **r** in themselves; Mk 4:17
to strike the **r** of the trees! Lk 3:9
Having no **r**, these believe for a Lk 8:13
And if the **r** is holy, so are the Rm 11:16
in the rich **r** of the cultivated Rm 11:17
not sustain the **r**, but the root Rm 11:18
root, but the **r** sustains you. Rm 11:18
The **r** of Jesse will appear, Rm 15:12
of money is a **r** of all kinds 1Tm 6:10
God and that no **r** of bitterness Heb 12:15
of Judah, the **R** of David, has Rv 5:5
I am the **R** and the Offspring of Rv 22:16

ROOTED (2)
being **r** and firmly established Eph 3:17
r and built up in Him and Col 2:7

ROOTS (21)
with their **r** in Amalek ⌊came Jdg 5:14
His **r** are intertwined around a Jb 8:17
If its **r** grow old in the ground Jb 14:8
His **r** below dry up, and his Jb 18:16
My **r** will have access to water, Jb 29:19
and the **r** of the broom tree were Jb 30:4
so their **r** will become like Is 5:24
from his **r** will bear fruit Is 11:1
it sends its **r** out toward a Jr 17:8
yet its **r** stayed under it. Ezk 17:6
this vine bent its **r** toward him! Ezk 17:7
not tear out its **r** and strip off Ezk 17:9
be needed to pull it from its **r**. Ezk 17:9
for its **r** extended to abundant Ezk 31:7
stump with its **r** in the ground, Dn 4:15
stump with its **r** in the ground Dn 4:23
the tree's stump with its **r**, Dn 4:26
blighted; their **r** are withered; Hs 9:16
fruit above and his **r** beneath. Am 2:9
fig tree withered from the **r** up. Mk 11:20
twice dead, pulled out by the **r**; Jd 12

ROPE (4)
them down by a **r** through the Jos 2:15
A **r** lies hidden for him on the Jb 18:10
or tie his tongue down with a **r**? Jb 41:1
instead of a belt, a **r**; Is 3:24

ROPES (35)
courtyard, along with their **r**; Ex 35:18
courtyard, its **r** and tent pegs, Ex 39:40
and the tent **r**—all the work Nm 3:26
their bases, tent pegs, and **r**. Nm 3:37
along with their **r** and all the Nm 4:26
tent pegs, and **r**, including all Nm 4:32
up with two new **r** and led him Jdg 15:13
and the **r** that were on his arms Jdg 15:14
me up with new **r** that have never Jdg 16:11
Delilah took new **r**, tied him up Jdg 16:12
he snapped the **r** off his arms Jdg 16:12
will bring **r** to that city, 2Sm 17:13
The **r** of Sheol entangled me; 2Sm 22:6
our waists and **r** around our 1Kg 20:31
their waists and **r** around their 1Kg 20:32
The **r** of death were wrapped Ps 18:4
The **r** of Sheol entangled me; Ps 18:5
The **r** of death were wrapped Ps 116:3
Though the **r** of the wicked were Ps 119:61
He has cut the **r** of the wicked. Ps 129:4
proud hide a trap with **r** for me; Ps 140:5
in the **r** of his own sin. Pr 5:22
⌊pull⌋ sin along with cart **r**, Is 5:18
Your **r** are slack; they cannot Is 33:23
lengthen your **r**, and drive your Is 54:2
to untie the **r** of the yoke, Is 58:6
lowering Jeremiah with **r**. Jr 38:6
lowered them by **r** to Jeremiah Jr 38:11
between your armpits and the **r**." Jr 38:12
him up with the **r** and lifted him Jr 38:13
they will put **r** on you and bind Ezk 3:25
human cords, with **r** of kindness. Hs 11:4
used **r** and tackle and girded Ac 27:17
soldiers cut the **r** holding the Ac 27:32
time loosening the **r** that held Ac 27:40

ROSE (31)
so that it **r** above the earth. Gn 7:17
Then Abraham **r** and bowed down to Gn 23:7
He **r** early the next morning and Ex 24:4
the men in ambush **r** quickly from Jos 8:19
generation **r** up who did not Jdg 2:10
Smoke **r** from His nostrils, 2Sm 22:9
Then King David **r** to his feet 1Ch 28:2
r up and rebelled against his 2Ch 13:6
Smoke **r** from His nostrils, Ps 18:8
when God **r** up to judge and to Ps 76:9
mountains **r** and valleys sank— Ps 104:8
am a **r** of Sharon, a lily of the Sg 2:1
I **r** to open for my love. Sg 5:5
rejoice and blossom like a **r**. Is 35:1
the creatures **r** from the earth, Ezk 1:19
the earth, the wheels also **r**. Ezk 1:19
The wheels **r** alongside them, Ezk 1:20
the creatures **r** from the earth, Ezk 1:21
the wheels **r** alongside them, Ezk 1:21
the God of Israel **r** from above Ezk 9:3
glory of the LORD **r** from above Ezk 10:4
of the LORD **r** up from within Ezk 11:23
the temple's broadness as it **r**. Ezk 41:7
⌊the structure **r**⌋ gallery by Ezk 42:3
fell, the rivers **r**, and the Mt 7:25
the rivers **r**, the winds blew Mt 7:27
whole assembly **r** up and brought Lk 23:1
Not long ago Theudas **r** up, Ac 5:36
the Galilean **r** up in the days Ac 5:37
Him after He **r** from the dead. Ac 10:41
that Jesus died and **r** again, 1Th 4:14

ROSH (1)
Ehi, **R**, Muppim, Huppim, Gn 46:21

ROT (7)
the name of the wicked will **r**. Pr 10:7
choosing wood that does not **r**? Is 40:20
their fish **r** because of lack of Is 50:2
So I am like **r** to Ephraim and Hs 5:12
flesh will **r** while they stand Zch 14:12

their eyes will **r** in their Zch 14:12
tongues will **r** in their mouths. Zch 14:12

ROTATED *(1)*
were on **r** military duty each 1Ch 27:1

ROTE *(1)*
man-made rules learned ⌊by **r**⌋— Is 29:13

ROTTED *(1)*
Has their wisdom **r** away? Jr 49:7

ROTTEN *(7)*
Man wears out like something **r**, Jb 13:28
as straw, and bronze as **r** wood. Jb 41:27
trouble is like a **r** tooth or a Pr 25:19
like something **r** and their Is 5:24
make them like **r** figs that are Jr 29:17
yes, his **r** smell will rise, for Jl 2:20
No **r** talk should come from your Eph 4:29

ROTTENNESS *(3)*
shame is like **r** in his bones. Pr 12:4
but jealousy is **r** to the bones. Pr 14:30
R entered my bones; Hab 3:16

ROUGH *(3)*
and the **r** places a plain. Is 40:4
and **r** places into level ground. Is 42:16
straight, the **r** ways smooth, Lk 3:5

ROUGHLY *(2)*
but the rich one answers **r**. Pr 18:23
poorly clothed, **r** treated, 1Co 4:11

ROUND *(8)*
from brim to brim, perfectly **r**. 1Kg 7:23
The opening was **r**, made as a 1Kg 7:31
their frames were square, not **r**. 1Kg 7:31
from brim to brim, perfectly **r**. 2Ch 4:2
Whenever a **r** of banqueting was Jb 1:5
turning **r** and round at His Jb 37:12
round and **r** at His direction Jb 37:12
I will now **r** them up, and they Hs 8:10

ROUNDED *(3)*
above the **r** surface next to 1Kg 7:20
there was a **r** top at the back of 1Kg 10:19
Your navel is a **r** bowl; Sg 7:2

ROUNDS *(1)*
they make the **r** on its walls. Ps 55:10

ROUSE *(7)*
a lioness—who wants to **r** him? Gn 49:9
They **r** themselves like a lion. Nm 23:24
a lioness—who dares to **r** him? Nm 24:9
enough⌋ to **r** Leviathan; Jb 41:10
I am about to **r** them up from the Jl 3:7
holy war; **r** the warriors; let Jl 3:9
will **r** your sons, Zion, against Zch 9:13

ROUSED *(4)*
the innocent are **r** against the Jb 17:8
They will be **r** like birds from Hs 11:11
Let the nations be **r** and come to Jl 3:12
then returned and **r** me as one Zch 4:1

ROUSING *(1)*
who are skilled in **r** Leviathan. Jb 3:8

ROUT *(1)*
shoot Your arrows and **r** them. Ps 144:6

ROUTE *(12)*
about the **r** we should go up Dt 1:22
to Egypt by a **r** that I said you Dt 28:68
traveled on the caravan **r**, Jdg 8:11
asked, "Which **r** should we take? 2Kg 3:8
The **r** of the wilderness of Edom. 2Kg 3:8
their indirect **r** for seven days, 2Kg 3:9
way along the **r** to the Arabah, 2Kg 25:4
left along the **r** to the Arabah. Jr 39:4
way along the **r** to the Arabah. Jr 52:7
their own country by another **r**. Mt 2:12
we came by a direct **r** to Cos, Ac 21:1
sent them out by a different **r**? Jms 2:25

ROUTED *(10)*
and **r** them as far as Hormah. Nm 14:45
They **r** you from Seir as far as Dt 1:44
One of you **r** a thousand, because Jos 23:10
of Midian and **r** the entire army. Jdg 8:12
lightning bolts and **r** them. 2Sm 22:15
Judah was **r** before Israel, 2Kg 14:12
God **r** Jeroboam and all Israel 2Ch 13:15
the LORD **r** the Cushites before 2Ch 14:12
Judah was **r** before Israel, 2Ch 25:22
lightning bolts and **r** them. Ps 18:14

ROUTES *(1)*
Caravans turn away from their **r**, Jb 6:18

ROW *(15)*
The first **r** should be a row of Ex 28:17
row should be a **r** of carnelian, Ex 28:17
the second **r**, a turquoise, a Ex 28:18
third **r**, a jacinth, an agate, Ex 28:19
and the fourth **r**, a beryl, an Ex 28:20
The first **r** was a row of Ex 39:10
first row was a **r** of carnelian, Ex 39:10
the second **r**, a turquoise, a Ex 39:11
third **r**, a jacinth, an agate, Ex 39:12
and the fourth **r**, a beryl, an Ex 39:13
rows, six to a **r**, on the pure Lv 24:6
pure frankincense near each **r**, Lv 24:7
stone and a **r** of trimmed cedar 1Kg 6:36
on 45 pillars, fifteen per **r**. 1Kg 7:3
stone and a **r** of trimmed cedar 1Kg 7:12

ROWDY *(2)*
Folly is **r**; she is gullible Pr 9:13
drink and be **r** as if with wine. Zch 9:15

ROWED *(4)*
ships that are **r** will not go, Is 33:21
men **r** hard to get back to dry Jnh 1:13
them being battered as they **r**, Mk 6:48
After they had **r** about three or Jn 6:19

ROWERS *(2)*
of Sidon and Arvad were your **r**. Ezk 27:8
Your **r** have brought you onto the Ezk 27:26

ROWS *(21)*
on it, four **r** of stones: Ex 28:17
They mounted four **r** of gemstones Ex 39:10
them in two **r**, six to a row, Lv 24:6
with three **r** of dressed stone 1Kg 6:36
high on four **r** of cedar pillars 1Kg 7:2
were three **r** of window frames 1Kg 7:4
were three **r** of dressed stone 1Kg 7:12
two encircling **r** of pomegranates 1Kg 7:18
were in **r** encircling each 1Kg 7:20
were cast in two **r** when the 1Kg 7:24
two **r** of pomegranates for each 1Kg 7:42
for preparing the **r** of the bread 1Ch 9:32
well as the **r** ⌊of the bread of 1Ch 23:29
table for the **r** ⌊of the bread 1Ch 28:16
displaying⌋ the **r** ⌊of the bread 2Ch 2:4
were cast in two **r** when the 2Ch 4:3
two **r** of pomegranates for each 2Ch 4:13
they set⌋ the **r** of the bread 2Ch 13:11
table for the **r** ⌊of the bread 2Ch 29:18
pride is in ⌊his⌋ **r** of scales, Jb 41:15
He plants wheat in **r** and barley Is 28:25

ROYAL *(112)*
he will produce **r** delicacies. Gn 49:20
he is seated on his **r** throne, Dt 17:18
city like one of the **r** cities; Jos 10:2
and Og's **r** cities in Bashan— Jos 13:31
live in the **r** city with you?" 1Sm 27:5
and captured the **r** fortress. 2Sm 12:26
according to the **r** standard. 2Sm 14:26
David and at all the **r** servants, 2Sm 16:6
invited all his **r** brothers and 1Kg 1:9
taken his seat on the **r** throne. 1Kg 1:46
the LORD, the **r** palace, and all 1Kg 9:1
establish your **r** throne over 1Kg 9:5
LORD's temple and the **r** palace— 1Kg 9:10
given her out of his **r** bounty. 1Kg 10:13
He was of the **r** family in Edom. 1Kg 11:14
the treasuries of the **r** palace. 1Kg 14:26
captains of the **r** escorts who 1Kg 14:27
the **r** escorts would carry the 1Kg 14:28
back to the **r** escorts' armory 1Kg 14:28
of the **r** palace and put it 1Kg 15:18
citadel of the **r** palace and 1Kg 16:18
burned down the **r** palace over 1Kg 16:18
exercise your **r** power over 1Kg 21:7
clothed in **r** attire, were each 1Kg 22:10
but you wear your **r** attire." 1Kg 22:30
to annihilate all the **r** heirs. 2Kg 11:1
five trusted **r** aides found in 2Kg 25:19
Elishama, of the **r** family, came 2Kg 25:25
on him such **r** majesty as had not 1Ch 29:25
of the LORD and a **r** palace for 2Ch 2:1
the LORD and a **r** palace for 2Ch 2:12
LORD's temple and the **r** palace. 2Ch 7:11
I will establish your **r** throne, 2Ch 7:18
his sovereignty and **r** power, 2Ch 12:1
the treasuries of the **r** palace. 2Ch 12:9
captains of the **r** escorts who 2Ch 12:10
the **r** escorts would carry the 2Ch 12:11
back to the **r** escorts' armory 2Ch 12:11
established his **r** power in 2Ch 12:13
temple and the **r** palace and sent 2Ch 16:2
clothed in **r** attire, were each 2Ch 18:9
but you wear your **r** attire." 2Ch 18:29
all the **r** heirs of the house 2Ch 22:10
and the **r** revenue will suffer. Ezr 4:13
increase and the **r** interests Ezr 4:22
a search of the **r** archives in Ezr 5:17
to be paid from the **r** treasury. Ezr 6:4
these men out of the **r** revenues Ezr 6:8
may use the **r** treasury to pay Ezr 7:20
king's edicts to the **r** satraps Ezr 8:36
reigned from his **r** throne in the Est 1:2
courtyard of the **r** palace for Est 1:5
R wine flowed freely, according Est 1:7
before him with her **r** crown. Est 1:11
personally issue a **r** decree. Est 1:19
her **r** position is to be given Est 1:19
letters to all the **r** provinces, Est 1:22
Ahasuerus in the **r** palace in the Est 2:16
placed the **r** crown on her head Est 2:17
The entire **r** staff at the King's Est 3:2
members of the **r** staff at the Est 3:3
for deposit in the **r** treasury." Est 3:9
The **r** scribes were summoned on Est 3:12
was intended for⌋ the **r** satraps, Est 3:12
sealed with the **r** signet ring. Est 3:12
to each of the **r** provinces Est 3:13
left, spurred on by **r** command, Est 3:15
to pay the **r** treasury for Est 4:7
All the **r** officials and the Est 4:11
people of the **r** provinces know Est 4:11
dressed up in her **r** clothing and Est 5:1
was sitting on his **r** throne in Est 5:1
royal throne in the **r** courtroom, Est 5:1
other officials and the **r** staff. Est 5:11
Have them bring a **r** garment that Est 6:8
has a **r** diadem on its head. Est 6:8
one of the **r** eunuchs, said: Est 7:9
let ⌊a **r** edict⌋ be written. Est 8:5
seal it with the **r** signet ring. Est 8:8
sealed with the **r** signet ring Est 8:8
the **r** scribes were summoned. Est 8:9
edicts⌋ with the **r** signet ring. Est 8:10
bred from the **r** racing mares. Est 8:10
On their **r** horses, the couriers Est 8:14
clothed in **r** purple and white, Est 8:15
and the **r** civil administrators Est 9:3
in the rest of the **r** provinces? Est 9:12
of the Jews in the **r** provinces Est 9:16
the **r** daughter is all glorious, Ps 45:13
It is Solomon's **r** litter Sg 3:7
and a **r** diadem in the palm of Is 62:3
of the **r** family and one of the Jr 41:1
seven trusted **r** aides found in Jr 52:25
one of the **r** family and made Ezk 17:13
the Israelites from the **r** family Dn 1:3
provisions from the **r** food and Dn 1:5
the roof of the **r** palace in Dn 4:29
power to be a **r** residence and to Dn 4:30
deposed from his **r** throne and Dn 5:20
that in all my **r** dominion, Dn 6:26
r honors will not be given to Dn 11:21
will pitch his **r** tents between Dn 11:45
of Israel! Listen, **r** house! For Hs 5:1
sanctuary and a **r** temple." Am 7:13
throne, took off his **r** robe, put Jnh 3:6
I will overturn **r** thrones and Hg 2:22
of Hananel to the **r** winepresses. Zch 14:10
live in luxury are in **r** palaces. Lk 7:25
was a certain **r** official whose Jn 4:46
dressed in **r** robes and seated on Ac 12:21
carry out the **r** law prescribed Jms 2:8
a chosen race, a **r** priesthood, a 1Pt 2:9

ROYALTY *(1)*
beautiful and attained **r**. Ezk 16:13

RUBBED *(1)*
You were not **r** with salt or Ezk 16:4

RUBBING *(1)*
heads of grain, **r** them in their Lk 6:1

RUBBLE *(10)*
cities into piles of **r**. 2Kg 19:25
to life from the mounds of **r**?" Neh 4:2
fails, since there is so much **r**. Neh 4:10

destined to become piles of **r**. Jb 15:28
heap of **r** will be under your Is 3:6
the city into a pile of **r**, Is 25:2
cities into piles of **r**. Is 37:26
will make Jerusalem a heap of **r**, Jr 9:11
Babylon will become a heap of **r**, Jr 51:37
and the small house to **r**. Am 6:11

RUBIES *(2)*
will make your battlements of **r**, Is 54:12
and **r** for your merchandise. Ezk 27:16

RUDDER *(1)*
by a very small **r** wherever the Jms 3:4

RUDDERS *(1)*
the ropes that held the **r**. Ac 27:40

RUDDY *(1)*
bodies were more **r** than coral, Lm 4:7

RUE *(1)*
tenth of mint, **r**, and every kind Lk 11:42

RUFUS *(2)*
the father of Alexander and **R**. Mk 15:21
Greet **R**, chosen in the Lord; Rm 16:13

RUG *(1)*
and she covered him with a **r**. Jdg 4:18

RUIN *(55)*
Ai and left it a permanent **r**, Jos 8:28
I will **r** my ⌊own⌋ inheritance. Ru 4:6
to bring about Absalom's **r**, 2Sm 17:14
LORD brought all this **r** on them. 1Kg 9:9
You must **r** every good piece of 2Kg 3:19
He brought all this **r** on them. 2Ch 7:22
way of the wicked leads to **r**. Ps 1:6
The enemy has come to eternal **r**; Ps 9:6
Let **r** come on him unexpectedly, Ps 35:8
let him fall into it—to his **r**. Ps 35:8
You make them fall into **r**. Ps 73:18
danger or the **r** of the wicked Pr 3:25
of complete **r** before the entire Pr 5:14
who brings **r** on his household Pr 11:29
his lips invites his own **r**. Pr 13:3
speech will fall into **r**. Pr 17:20
A foolish son is his father's **r**, Pr 19:13
He brings the wicked to **r**. Pr 21:12
the wicked will stumble into **r**. Pr 24:16
and a flattering mouth causes **r**. Pr 26:28
foxes that **r** the vineyards— Sg 2:15
its palaces. They made it a **r**. Is 23:13
a fortified city, into a **r**; Is 25:2
r and wretchedness are in their Is 59:7
this I will **r** the great pride Jr 13:9
this house will become a **r**." Jr 22:5
land will become a desolate **r**, Jr 25:11
and I will make it a **r** forever. Jr 25:12
to make them a desolate **r**, Jr 25:18
will become an uninhabited **r**'!" Jr 26:9
Why should this city become a **r**? Jr 27:17
this place which you say is a **r**, Jr 33:10
they are a **r** today without an Jr 44:2
the desolate **r** they are today. Jr 44:6
disgrace, a **r**, and a curse, and Jr 49:13
you I will bring kingdoms to **r**. Jr 51:20
your **r** is as vast as the sea. Lm 2:13
will make you a **r** and a disgrace Ezk 5:14
A **r**, a ruin, I will make it a Ezk 21:27
A ruin, a **r**, I will make it a Ezk 21:27
a ruin, I will make it a **r**! Ezk 21:27
of Egypt will be a desolate **r**. Ezk 29:9
Israel, which had long been a **r**. Ezk 38:8
are in **r**, and the granaries Jl 1:17
not grieve over the **r** of Joseph. Am 6:6
plunder and their houses a **r**. Zph 1:13
and Ashkelon will become a **r**. Zph 2:4
will make Nineveh a desolate **r**, Zph 2:13
that it will not **r** the produce Mal 3:11
come to the verge of **r**— Ac 19:27
r and wretchedness are in their Rm 3:16
God's sanctuary, God will **r** him; 1Co 3:17
people into **r** and destruction. 1Tm 6:9
leads to the **r** of the hearers. 2Tm 2:14
ashes and condemned them to **r**, 2Pt 2:6

RUINED *(26)*
Egypt the land was **r** because of Ex 8:24
who rebuilt **r** cities for Jb 3:14
he will dwell in **r** cities, Jb 15:28
plans have been **r**, even the Jb 17:11
on every side so that I am **r**. Jb 19:10
hand against a **r** man when he Jb 30:24
and the stone wall was **r**. Pr 24:31
is me, for I am **r**, because I am Is 6:5
the land is **r** and desolate, Is 6:11
It has become a **r** heap. Is 17:1
they will renew the **r** cities, Is 61:4
Woe to us, for we are **r**! Jr 4:13
it, but it was **r**—of no use Jr 13:7
I make you a **r** city like ⌊other Ezk 26:19
desolation among **r** cities for 40 Ezk 29:12
cities will lie among **r** cities. Ezk 30:7
The cities that were once **r**, Ezk 36:35
So the **r** cities will be filled Ezk 36:38
rebuild and occupy **r** cities, Am 9:14
are totally **r**! He measures out Mc 2:4
ravaged them and **r** their vine Nah 2:2
harvest⌋ to your house, I **r** it. Hg 1:9
spills out, and the skins are **r**. Mt 9:17
spill, and the skins will be **r**. Lk 5:37
Christ died, is **r** by your 1Co 8:11
Your wealth is **r**: your clothes Jms 5:2

RUINS *(49)*
your cities to **r** and devastate Lv 26:31
and your cities will become **r**. Lv 26:33
remain a mound of **r** forever; Dt 13:16
of our God and repair its **r**, Ezr 9:9
buried lies in **r** and its gates Neh 2:3
Jerusalem lies in **r** and its Neh 2:17
keep rolling in through the **r**. Jb 30:14
Your way to the everlasting **r**, Ps 74:3
and turned Jerusalem into **r**. Ps 79:1
his fortified cities to **r**. Ps 89:40
owl, like an owl among the **r**. Ps 102:6
eat ⌊among⌋ the **r** of the rich. Is 5:17
cities lie in **r** without Is 6:11
its gate has collapsed in **r**. Is 24:12
and I will restore her **r**; Is 44:26
and your land marked by **r**— Is 49:19
together, you **r** of Jerusalem! Is 52:9
you will rebuild the ancient **r**; Is 58:12
They will rebuild the ancient **r**; Is 61:4
that was dear to us lies in **r**. Is 64:11
His cities are in **r**, without Jr 2:15
be reduced to uninhabited **r**. Jr 4:7
a derision, and **r** forever. Jr 25:9
will become **r**, and the temple Jr 26:18
a desolation, uninhabited **r**. Jr 46:19
cities will become **r** forever." Jr 49:13
cities will be in **r** and the high Ezk 6:6
will lie in **r** and be desecrated Ezk 6:6
are like jackals among **r**. Ezk 13:4
filled ⌊now that⌋ she lies in **r**, Ezk 26:2
underworld like the ancient **r**, Ezk 26:20
turn the land of Egypt into **r**, Ezk 29:10
who live in the **r** in the land of Ezk 33:24
those who are in the **r** will fall Ezk 33:27
I will turn your cities into **r**, Ezk 35:4
to the desolate **r** and abandoned Ezk 36:4
be inhabited and the **r** rebuilt. Ezk 36:10
and the **r** will be rebuilt. Ezk 36:33
hand against **r** now inhabited Ezk 38:12
sanctuaries will be in **r**; Am 7:9
restore its **r**, and rebuild it Am 9:11
Samaria a heap of **r** in the Mc 1:6
will become **r**, and the hill Mc 3:12
and the **r** along with the wicked. Zph 1:3
while this house lies in **r**?" Hg 1:4
My house still lies in **r**, Hg 1:9
but we will rebuild the **r**," Mal 1:4
rebuild its **r** and will set it Ac 15:16
If anyone **r** God's sanctuary, 1Co 3:17

RULE *(74)*
They will **r** the fish of the sea, Gn 1:26
R the fish of the sea, the birds Gn 1:28
"Are you really going to **r** us?" Gn 37:8
this is a permanent **r**." Lv 24:9
You are not to **r** over them Lv 25:43
you must not **r** over one another Lv 25:46
owner is not to **r** over him Lv 25:53
who hate you will **r** over you, Lv 26:17
One who comes from Jacob will **r**; Nm 24:19
you will **r** over many nations, Dt 15:6
but they will not **r** over you. Dt 15:6
to Gideon, "**R** over us, you as Jdg 8:22
I will not **r** over you, and my Jdg 8:23
and my son will not **r** over you; Jdg 8:23
the LORD will **r** over you." Jdg 8:23
r over you or that one man rule Jdg 9:2
you or that one man **r** over you?' Jdg 9:2
and man, and **r** over the trees? Jdg 9:9
good fruit, and **r** over trees?" Jdg 9:11
God and man, and **r** over trees?" Jdg 9:13
that the Philistines **r** over us? Jdg 15:11
the king who will **r** over them." 1Sm 8:9
of the king who will **r** over you: 1Sm 8:11
he will **r** over My people." 1Sm 9:17
we must have a king **r** over us'— 1Sm 12:12
you will **r** over all you desire. 2Sm 3:21
of Saul in whose place you **r**, 2Sm 16:8
David to **r** My people Israel. 1Kg 8:16
and do You not **r** over all the 2Ch 20:6
They **r** over our bodies and our Neh 9:37
men should not **r** or ensnare the Jb 34:30
do not let them **r** over me. Ps 19:13
The upright will **r** over them in Ps 49:14
And may he **r** from sea to sea and Ps 72:8
You **r** the raging sea; when its Ps 89:9
R over Your surrounding enemies. Ps 110:2
the sun to **r** by day, His love is Ps 136:8
moon and stars to **r** by night. Ps 136:9
Your **r** is for all generations. Ps 145:13
hand will **r**, but laziness will Pr 12:24
wise servant will **r** over a Pr 17:2
for a slave to **r** over princes! Pr 19:10
rich **r** over the poor, and the Pr 22:7
when the wicked **r**, people groan. Pr 29:2
people, and women **r** over them. Is 3:12
captors and will **r** over their Is 14:2
and a strong king will **r** it. Is 19:4
you mockers who **r** this people in Is 28:14
and rulers will **r** justly. Is 32:1
and His power establishes His **r**. Is 40:10
and the priests **r** by their own Jr 5:31
and all the lands they **r**. Jr 51:28
Slaves **r** over us; no one rescues Lm 5:8
I will **r** over you with a strong Ezk 20:33
they cannot **r** over the nations Ezk 29:15
one king will **r** over all of them Ezk 37:22
which will **r** the whole earth. Dn 2:39
and was given authority to **r**. Dn 7:6
authority to **r** was removed, Dn 7:12
He was given authority to **r**, Dn 7:14
he will **r** a vast realm and do Dn 11:3
and will **r** a kingdom greater Dn 11:5
Mount Zion to **r** over the hill Ob 21
the LORD will **r** over them in Mc 4:7
the former **r** will come to you, Mc 4:8
will both **r** My house and take Zch 3:7
will sit on His throne and **r**. Zch 6:13
want this man to **r** over us!' Lk 19:14
did not want me to **r** over them, Lk 19:27
the governor's **r** and authority. Lk 20:20
For sin will not **r** over you, Rm 6:14
that He might **r** over both the Rm 14:9
One who rises to **r** the Gentiles; Rm 15:12
He abolishes all **r** and all 1Co 15:24

RULED *(44)*
are the kings who **r** in the land Gn 36:31
before any king **r** over the Gn 36:31
Bela son of Beor **r** in Edom; Gn 36:32
from Bozrah **r** in his place. Gn 36:33
of the Temanites **r** in his place. Gn 36:34
son of Bedad **r** in his place. Gn 36:35
from Masrekah **r** in his place. Gn 36:36
r in his place. Gn 36:37
son of Achbor **r** in his place. Gn 36:38
died, Hadar **r** in his place. Gn 36:39
He **r** ⌊over the territory⌋ from Jos 12:2
He **r** over Mount Hermon, Salecah, Jos 12:5
Abimelech had **r** over Israel Jdg 9:22
over Israel; he **r** for two years. 2Sm 2:10
King Solomon **r** over Israel, 1Kg 4:1
Solomon **r** over all the kingdoms 1Kg 4:21
They **r** over the people doing the 1Kg 5:16
550 who **r** over the people doing 1Kg 9:23
He **r** over Aram, but he loathed 1Kg 11:25
while Athaliah **r** over the land. 2Kg 11:3
were the kings who **r** in the land 1Ch 1:43
before any king **r** over the 1Ch 1:43
from Bozrah **r** in his place. 1Ch 1:44
of the Temanites **r** in his place. 1Ch 1:45
country of Moab, **r** in his place. 1Ch 1:46
from Masrekah **r** in his place. 1Ch 1:47
Euphrates River **r** in his place. 1Ch 1:48
son of Achbor **r** in his place. 1Ch 1:49
died, Hadad **r** in his place. 1Ch 1:50
where he **r** seven years and six 1Ch 3:4

and he **r** in Jerusalem 33 years. 1Ch 3:4
were born sons who **r** over their 1Ch 26:6
250 who **r** over the people. 2Ch 8:10
He **r** over all the kings from the 2Ch 9:26
While Athaliah **r** over the land, 2Ch 22:12
kings have also **r** over Jerusalem Ezr 4:20
while Darius the Persian **r**. Neh 12:22
who **r** 127 provinces from India Est 1:1
those who hated them **r** them. Ps 106:41
lords than You have **r** over us, Is 26:13
like those You never **r** over, Is 63:19
have **r** them with violence and Ezk 34:4
be the same kingdom that he **r**, Dn 11:4
different king **r** over Egypt who Ac 7:18

RULER *(84)*

r over all the land of Egypt. Gn 45:8
and he is **r** over all the land of Gn 45:26
appoint yourself as **r** over us? Nm 16:13
When Zebul, the **r** of the city, Jdg 9:30
in the land and no oppressive **r**. Jdg 18:7
Anoint him **r** over My people 1Sm 9:16
LORD anointed you **r** over His 1Sm 10:1
him as **r** over His people 1Sm 13:14
and appoints you **r** over Israel, 1Sm 25:30
Israel and be **r** over Israel.' " 2Sm 5:2
to appoint me **r** over the LORD's 2Sm 6:21
the sheep to be **r** over My people 2Sm 7:8
commanded to be **r** over Israel 1Kg 1:35
will let him be **r** all the days 1Kg 11:34
appointed you **r** over My people 1Kg 14:7
and made you **r** over My people 1Kg 16:2
brothers and a **r** came from him, 1Ch 5:2
Israel and be **r** over My people 1Ch 11:2
to be **r** over My people Israel. 1Ch 17:7
and You are the **r** of everything. 1Ch 29:12
anointed him as the LORD's **r**, 1Ch 29:22
a man to be **r** over My people 2Ch 6:5
the **r** of the house of Judah, 2Ch 19:11
Azariah the **r** of God's temple. 2Ch 31:13
r over half the district of Neh 3:9
r over half the district of Neh 3:12
r over the district of Neh 3:14
r over the district of Mizpah, Neh 3:15
r over half the district of Neh 3:16
r over half the district of Neh 3:17
r over half the district of Neh 3:18
son of Jeshua, **r** over Mizpah, Neh 3:19
men and fall like any other **r**." Ps 82:7
the **r** of peoples set him free. Ps 105:20
r over all his possessions— Ps 105:21
leader, administrator, or **r**, Pr 6:7
how much worse are lies for a **r**. Pr 17:7
Many seek the favor of a **r**, Pr 19:6
you sit down to dine with a **r**, Pr 23:1
A **r** can be persuaded through Pr 25:15
wicked **r** over a helpless people Pr 28:15
If a **r** listens to lies, all his Pr 29:12
the shouts of a **r** over fools. Ec 9:17
from the presence of the **r**: Ec 10:5
Send lambs to the **r** of the land, Is 16:1
and righteousness as your **r**. Is 60:17
his **r** will issue from him. Jr 30:21
the land with **r** against ruler. Jr 51:46
the land with ruler against **r**. Jr 51:46
of man, say to the **r** of Tyre: Ezk 28:2
hand it over to a **r** of nations; Ezk 31:11
and made you **r** over them all. Dn 2:38
He made him **r** over the entire Dn 2:48
Most High is **r** over the kingdom Dn 4:17
Most High is **r** over the kingdom Dn 4:25
Most High is **r** over the kingdom Dn 4:32
High God is **r** over the kingdom Dn 5:21
be the third **r** in the kingdom. Dn 5:29
was **r** over the kingdom of the Dn 9:1
for themselves a single **r**, Hs 1:11
cut off the **r** from the Valley Am 1:5
will cut off the **r** from Ashdod, Am 1:8
from you to be **r** over Israel for Mc 5:2
marine creatures that have no **r**. Hab 1:14
battle bow, from them every **r**. Zch 10:4
demons by the **r** of the demons!" Mt 9:34
Beelzebul, the **r** of the demons." Mt 12:24
demons by the **r** of the demons!" Mk 3:22
Beelzebul, the **r** of the demons!" Lk 11:15
with your adversary to the **r**, Lk 12:58
A **r** asked Him, "Good Teacher, Lk 18:18
Nicodemus, a **r** of the Jews. Jn 3:1
Now the **r** of this world will be Jn 12:31
because the **r** of the world is Jn 14:30
because the **r** of this world has Jn 16:11
His right hand as **r** and Savior, Ac 5:31
appointed you a **r** and a judge Ac 7:27
appointed you a **r** and a judge? Ac 7:35
God sent as a **r** and a redeemer Ac 7:35
evil of a **r** of your people. Ac 23:5
far above every **r** and authority, Eph 1:21
according to the **r** of the Eph 2:2
head over every **r** and authority. Col 2:10
the dead and the **r** of the kings Rv 1:5

RULER'S *(4)*

because a **r** portion was assigned Dt 33:21
of people is a **r** devastation. Pr 14:28
Many seek a **r** favor, but a man Pr 29:26
the **r** anger rises against you, Ec 10:4

RULERS *(69)*

the five Philistine **r** of Gaza, Jos 13:3
the five **r** of the Philistines Jdg 3:3
The **r** of Gilead said to one Jdg 10:18
the Philistine **r** together and 1Sm 5:8
all the Philistine **r** together. 1Sm 5:11
to⌋ the number of Philistine **r**, 1Sm 6:4
plague for both you and your **r**. 1Sm 6:4
The Philistine **r** were walking 1Sm 6:12
Philistine **r** observed ⌊this⌋ 1Sm 6:16
Philistine cities of the five **r**, 1Sm 6:18
r marched up toward Israel. 1Sm 7:7
to Samaria to the **r** of Jezreel, 2Kg 10:1
because the Philistine **r**, 1Ch 12:19
he found the **r** of Judah and the 2Ch 22:8
the **r** of Judah came and paid 2Ch 24:17
the king and of the **r** and gave 2Ch 28:21
of Babylon's **r** were sent to him 2Ch 32:31
and the **r** conspire together Ps 2:2
r of Judah in their assembly, Ps 68:27
assembly, the **r** of Zebulun, Ps 68:27
of Zebulun, the **r** of Naphtali. Ps 68:27
When their **r** will be thrown off Ps 141:6
reign and **r** enact just law; Pr 8:15
it has many **r**, but with a Pr 28:2
wine or for **r** ⌊to desire⌋ beer Pr 31:4
stronger than ten **r** of a city. Ec 7:19
of the LORD, you **r** of Sodom! Is 1:10
Your **r** are rebels, friends of Is 1:23
wicked, the scepter of the **r**. Is 14:5
you—all the **r** of the earth. Is 14:9
The **r** of the nations have Is 16:8
All your **r** have fled together, Is 22:3
and **r** will rule justly Is 32:1
march over **r** as if they were Is 41:25
by people, to a servant of **r**: Is 49:7
Its **r** wail"—the LORD's Is 52:5
and the **r** rebelled against Me. Jr 2:8
his descendants **r** over the Jr 33:26
⌊fit⌋ for the scepters of **r**; Ezk 19:11
with all its **r** will ask you: Ezk 38:13
and all the **r** of the provinces Dn 3:2
and all the **r** of the provinces Dn 3:3
all **r** will serve and obey Him. Dn 7:27
and against our **r** by bringing on Dn 9:12
making them **r** over many and Dn 11:39
oven, and they consume their **r**. Hs 7:7
cities, and the **r** you demanded, Hs 13:10
you **r** of the house of Israel. Mc 3:1
you **r** of the house of Israel, Mc 3:9
mock kings, and **r** are a joke to Hab 1:10
know that the **r** of the Gentiles Mt 20:25
regarded as **r** of the Gentiles Mk 10:42
and **r** and authorities, Lk 12:11
any of the **r** believed in Him Jn 7:48
believe in Him even among the **r**, Jn 12:42
The next day, their **r**, elders, Ac 4:5
R of the people and elders: Ac 4:8
and the **r** assembled together Ac 4:26
of Jerusalem and their **r**, Ac 13:27
Jews, with their **r**, to assault Ac 14:5
nor angels nor **r**, nor things Rm 8:38
For **r** are not a terror to good Rm 13:3
age, or of the **r** of this age, 1Co 2:6
None of the **r** of this age knew 1Co 2:8
church to the **r** and authorities Eph 3:10
blood, but against the **r**, Eph 6:12
or dominions or **r** or authorities Col 1:16
disarmed the **r** and authorities Col 2:15
submissive to **r** and authorities Ti 3:1

RULES *(13)*

and the king who **r** over you will 1Sm 12:14
The one who **r** the people with 2Sm 23:3
with justice, who **r** in the fear 2Sm 23:3
purification ⌊**r**⌋ of the 2Ch 30:19
He **r** over the nations. Ps 22:28
the earth that God **r** over Jacob. Ps 59:13
He **r** forever by His might; Ps 66:7
and His kingdom **r** over all. Ps 103:19
in all the places where He **r**. Ps 103:22
of⌋ man-made **r** learned ⌊by rote⌋ Is 29:13
you acknowledge that Heaven **r**. Dn 4:26
Death no longer **r** over Him. Rm 6:9
he competes according to the **r**. 2Tm 2:5

RULING *(7)*

will continue **r** many years over Dt 17:20
are to give a **r** in every dispute Dt 21:5
Philistines were **r** over Israel. Jdg 14:4
of David or **r** again in Judah. Jr 22:30
strong branch, a scepter for **r**. Ezk 19:14
Ask the priests for a **r**. Hg 2:11
that Archelaus was **r** over Judea Mt 2:22

RULINGS *(1)*

Her leaders issue **r** for a bribe, Mc 3:11

RUMAH *(1)*

of Pedaiah; ⌊she was⌋ from **R**. 2Kg 23:36

RUMBLE *(1)*

of the whip and **r** of the wheel, Nah 3:2

RUMBLES *(1)*

wheel of ⌊the farmer's⌋ cart **r**, Is 28:28

RUMBLING *(7)*

voice and the **r** that comes from Jb 37:2
when His ⌊**r**⌋ voice is heard. Jb 37:4
the **r** of his chariots, Jr 47:3
heard a great **r** sound behind me Ezk 3:12
beside them, a great **r** sound. Ezk 3:13
and like the **r** of loud thunder. Rv 14:2
and like the **r** of loud thunder, Rv 19:6

RUMBLINGS *(4)*

of lightning, **r**, and thunder. Rv 4:5
were thunders, **r**, lightnings, Rv 8:5
were lightnings, **r**, thunders, Rv 11:19
lightnings, **r**, and thunders. Rv 16:18

RUMOR *(4)*

he will hear a **r** and return to 2Kg 19:7
he will hear a **r** and return to Is 37:7
and there will be **r** after rumor. Ezk 7:26
and there will be rumor after **r**. Ezk 7:26

RUMORS *(5)*

These **r** will be heard by the Neh 6:7
nothing to these **r** you are Neh 6:8
I had heard **r** about You, but now Jb 42:5
to hear of wars and **r** of wars. Mt 24:6
you hear of wars and **r** of wars, Mk 13:7

RUN *(83)*

of them said, "**R** for your lives! Gn 19:17
R to the mountains, or you will Gn 19:17
But I can't **r** to the mountains; Gn 19:19
is close enough for me to **r** to. Gn 19:20
R there, for I cannot do Gn 19:22
with her and had **r** outside, Gn 39:13
crossbar is to **r** through the Ex 26:28
central crossbar **r** through the Ex 36:33
its back ⌊and **r**⌋ from its Jos 7:8
their backs ⌊and **r**⌋ from their Jos 7:12
R and find the arrows I'm 1Sm 20:36
letting saliva **r** down his beard. 1Sm 21:13
your sword and **r** me through with 1Sm 31:4
men will come and **r** me through 1Sm 31:4
Israel's men had **r** away and that 1Sm 31:7
and 50 men to **r** before him. 2Sm 15:1
Please let me **r** and tell the 2Sm 18:19
please let me **r** too behind the 2Sm 18:22
do you want to **r** since you won't 2Sm 18:22
"No matter what I want to **r**!" 2Sm 18:23
to run!" "Then **r**!" Joab said to 2Sm 18:23
and 50 men to **r** ahead of him. 1Kg 1:5
oil jug will not **r** dry until the 1Kg 17:14
and the oil jug did not **r** dry, 1Kg 17:16
R out to meet her and ask, 2Kg 4:26
I will **r** after him and get 2Kg 5:20
your sword and **r** me through with 1Ch 10:4
the army had **r** away and that 1Ch 10:7
Should a man like me **r** away? Neh 6:11
little ones **r** around like lambs Jb 21:11
number of his months has **r** out? Jb 21:21
he does not **r** from the sword. Jb 39:22
see me in the street **r** from me. Ps 31:11

or to those who **r** after lies! Ps 40:4
they **r** and take up a position. Ps 59:4
of their hearts **r** wild. Ps 73:7
their feet **r** toward trouble Pr 1:16
you **r**, you will not stumble. Pr 4:12
feet eager to **r** to evil, Pr 6:18
the righteous **r** to it and are Pr 18:10
revelation people **r** wild, Pr 29:18
Who will you **r** to for help? Is 10:3
they will **r** and not grow weary; Is 40:31
do not know you will **r** to you. Is 55:5
spring whose waters never **r** dry. Is 58:11
Their feet **r** after evil, and Is 59:7
toward Zion. **R** for cover! Don't Jr 4:6
R for cover, Benjaminites, out Jr 6:1
But I have not **r** away from being Jr 17:16
salt marsh, for she will **r** away; Jr 48:9
r back and forth within your Jr 49:3
R! Turn back! Lie low, residents Jr 49:8
she has turned to **r**; panic has Jr 49:24
R! Escape quickly! Lie low, Jr 49:30
sea and make her fountain **r** dry. Jr 51:36
let ⌊your⌋ tears **r** down like a Lm 2:18
the border will **r** from the sea Ezk 47:17
side it will **r** between Hauran Ezk 47:18
side it will **r** from Tamar to Ezk 47:19
It will **r** alongside the holy Ezk 48:18
the border will **r** from Tamar to Ezk 48:28
and his spring will **r** dry. Hs 13:15
the city; they **r** on the wall; Jl 2:9
Do horses **r** on rock, or does Am 6:12
He makes all the rivers **r** dry. Nah 1:4
R and tell this young man: Zch 2:4
all of you will **r** away because Mt 26:31
of You, I will never **r** away!" Mt 26:33
All of you will **r** away, because Mk 14:27
Don't follow or **r** after them. Lk 17:23
they will **r** away from him, Jn 10:5
not only do we **r** a risk that our Ac 19:27
r a risk of being charged with Ac 19:40
fearing they would **r** aground on Ac 27:17
we must **r** aground on a certain Ac 27:26
we might **r** aground in some Ac 27:29
planned to **r** the ship ashore Ac 27:39
R in such a way that you may win. 1Co 9:24
I do not **r** like one who runs 1Co 9:26
be running, or have **r**, in vain. Gl 2:2
that I didn't **r** in vain or labor Php 2:16
you, man of God, **r** from these 1Tm 6:11
and **r** with endurance the race Heb 12:1

RUNNER *(3)*
Asahel was a fast **r**, like one of 2Sm 2:18
As the first **r** came closer, 2Sm 18:25
My days fly by faster than a **r**; Jb 9:25

RUNNERS *(2)*
have raced with **r** and they have Jr 12:5
know that the **r** in a stadium all 1Co 9:24

RUNNING *(19)*
r away from my mistress Sarai. Gn 16:8
or has a **r** sore, festering Lv 22:22
or **r** in front of his chariots. 1Sm 8:11
these days are **r** away from their 1Sm 25:10
bowed to Joab and took off **r**. 2Sm 18:21
out and saw a man **r** alone. 2Sm 18:24
the watchman saw another man **r**. 2Sm 18:26
Another man is **r** alone!" 2Sm 18:26
Naaman saw someone **r** after him, 2Kg 5:21
like an athlete **r** a course. Ps 19:5
oil on the head, **r** down on the Ps 133:2
on the beard, **r** down Aaron's Ps 133:2
out and started **r** from the tomb, Mk 16:8
together, and **r** over—will be Lk 6:38
So **r** ahead, he climbed up a Lk 19:4
The two were **r** together, but the Jn 20:4
After **r** under the shelter of a Ac 27:16
I might not be **r**, or have run, Gl 2:2
You were **r** well. Who prevented Gl 5:7

RUNS *(7)*
the first man **r** looks to me like 2Sm 18:27
the way Ahimaaz son of Zadok **r**. 2Sm 18:27
the earth; His word **r** swiftly. Ps 147:15
Even if everyone **r** away because Mt 26:33
Even if everyone **r** away, I will Mk 14:29
leaves them and **r** away when he Jn 10:12
run like one who **r** aimlessly, 1Co 9:26

RURAL *(2)*
a large number of **r** villages. Dt 3:5
explains why the **r** Jews who live Est 9:19

RUSH *(6)*
Why did you **r** on the plunder and 1Sm 15:19
frantically **r** around in vain, Ps 39:6
let your spirit **r** to be angry, Ec 7:9
be parched. Reed and **r** will die. Is 19:6
and they **r** to shed innocent Is 59:7
they **r** around in the plazas. Nah 2:4

RUSHED *(18)*
were with him **r** forward and took Jdg 9:44
other two units **r** against all Jdg 9:44
in ambush had **r** quickly against Jdg 20:37
they **r** to the plunder, took 1Sm 14:32
20 servants also **r** down to the 2Sm 19:17
They **r** him out of there. 2Ch 26:20
king arrived and **r** Haman to the Est 6:14
or my foot has **r** to deceit, Jb 31:5
the canal and **r** at him with Dn 8:6
the whole herd **r** down the steep Mt 8:32
of about 2,000 **r** down the steep Mk 5:13
and the herd **r** down the steep Lk 8:33
and **r** together against him. Ac 7:57
heard this and **r** into the crowd, Ac 14:14
for lights, **r** in, and fell down Ac 16:29
and they **r** all together into the Ac 19:29
and the people **r** together. Ac 21:30
"northeaster" **r** down from the Ac 27:14

RUSHES *(1)*
He **r** headlong at Him with his Jb 15:26

RUSHING *(6)*
them the mighty **r** waters of the Is 8:7
will come like a **r** stream driven Is 59:19
like a horse **r** into battle. Jr 8:6
his disaster is **r** swiftly. Jr 48:16
that of a violent **r** wind came Ac 2:2
with many horses **r** into battle; Rv 9:9

RUST *(7)*
the pot that has **r** inside it, Ezk 24:6
and whose **r** will not come off! Ezk 24:6
its **r** will be consumed. Ezk 24:11
its thick **r** will not come off. Ezk 24:12
Into the fire with its **r**! Ezk 24:12
where moth and **r** destroy and Mt 6:19
neither moth nor **r** destroys, Mt 6:20

RUTH *(21)*
and the second was named **R**. Ru 1:4
but **R** clung to her. Ru 1:14
But **R** replied: Do not persuade Ru 1:16
Naomi saw that **R** was determined Ru 1:18
daughter-in-law **R** the Moabitess. Ru 1:22
R the Moabitess asked Naomi, Ru 2:2
So **R** left and entered the field Ru 2:3
Then Boaz said to **R**, "Listen, my Ru 2:8
So **R** gathered ⌊grain⌋ in the Ru 2:17
R told her mother-in-law about Ru 2:19
R the Moabitess said, "He also Ru 2:21
said to her daughter-in-law **R**, Ru 2:22
R stayed close to Boaz's young Ru 2:23
So ⌊**R**⌋ said to her, "I will do Ru 3:5
"I am **R**, your slave," she Ru 3:9
he told ⌊**R**⌋, "Bring the shawl Ru 3:15
Then **R** told her everything the Ru 3:16
also acquire **R** the Moabitess, Ru 4:5
also acquire **R** the Moabitess, Ru 4:10
Boaz took **R** and she became his Ru 4:13
Obed by **R**, Obed fathered Mt 1:5

RUTH'S *(1)*
R mother-in-law Naomi said to Ru 3:1

RUTHLESS *(12)*
a **r** nation, showing no respect Dt 28:50
me from the grasp of the **r**? Jb 6:23
years are stored up for the **r**. Jb 15:20
the inheritance the **r** receive Jb 27:13
a gang of **r** men seeks my life. Ps 86:14
and the multitude of the **r**, Is 29:5
For the **r** one will vanish, Is 29:20
you from the control of the **r**. Jr 15:21
against you, **r** men from the Ezk 28:7
with his people, **r** men from the Ezk 30:11
Foreigners, **r** men from the Ezk 31:12
all of them **r** men from the Ezk 32:12

RUTHLESSLY *(2)*
They worked the Israelites **r** Ex 1:13
They **r** imposed all this work on Ex 1:14

S

SABACHTHÁNI *(2)*
loud voice, "Elí, Elí, lemá **s**?" Mt 27:46
voice, "Eloi, Eloi, lemá **s**?" Mk 15:34

SABBATH *(134)*
rest, a holy **S** to the LORD. Ex 16:23
today is a **S** to the LORD. Ex 16:25
seventh day, the **S**, there will Ex 16:26
the LORD has given you the **S**; Ex 16:29
Remember to dedicate the **S** day: Ex 20:8
day is a **S** to the LORD your Ex 20:10
blessed the **S** day and declared Ex 20:11
Observe the **S**, for it is holy to Ex 31:14
there must be a **S** of complete Ex 31:15
work on the **S** day must be put Ex 31:15
Israelites must observe the **S**, Ex 31:16
S of complete rest to the LORD. Ex 35:2
any of your homes on the **S** day." Ex 35:3
It is a **S** of complete rest for Lv 16:31
there must be a **S** of complete Lv 23:3
it is a **S** to the LORD wherever Lv 23:3
wave it on the day after the **S**. Lv 23:11
from the day after the **S**, Lv 23:15
the seventh **S** and then present Lv 23:16
It will be a **S** of complete rest Lv 23:32
to observe your **S** from the Lv 23:32
the LORD every **S** day as a Lv 24:8
will observe a **S** to the LORD. Lv 25:2
there will be a **S** of complete Lv 25:4
seventh year, a **S** to the LORD: Lv 25:4
during⌋ the **S** year can be food Lv 25:6
make up for its **S** ⌊years⌋ during Lv 26:34
man gathering wood on the **S** day. Nm 15:32
On the **S** day ⌊present⌋ two Nm 28:9
the burnt offering for every **S**, Nm 28:10
careful to dedicate the **S** day, Dt 5:12
day is a **S** to the LORD your Dt 5:14
commanded you to keep the **S** day. Dt 5:15
It's neither New Moon or **S**." 2Kg 4:23
on duty on the **S** are to provide 2Kg 11:5
off duty on the **S** are to provide 2Kg 11:7
on duty on the **S** and those going 2Kg 11:9
temple the **S** canopy they had 2Kg 16:18
bread ⌊of the Presence⌋ every **S**. 1Ch 9:32
who are coming on duty on the **S**, 2Ch 23:4
on duty on the **S** and those going 2Ch 23:8
those going off duty on the **S**— 2Ch 23:8
land enjoyed its **S** rest all the 2Ch 36:21
revealed Your holy **S** to them, Neh 9:14
of grain to sell on the **S** day, Neh 10:31
them on the **S** or a holy day. Neh 10:31
the **S** and New Moon offerings, Neh 10:33
treading wine presses on the **S**. Neh 13:15
to Jerusalem on the **S** day. Neh 13:15
them on the **S** to the people Neh 13:16
are doing—profaning the **S** day? Neh 13:17
Israel by profaning the **S**!" Neh 13:18
of Jerusalem just before the **S**, Neh 13:19
not opened until after the **S**. Neh 13:19
could enter during the **S** day. Neh 13:19
did not come again on the **S**. Neh 13:21
in order to keep the **S** day holy. Neh 13:22
who keeps the **S** without Is 56:2
all who keep the **S** without Is 56:6
you keep from desecrating the **S**, Is 58:13
if you call the **S** a delight, Is 58:13
and from one **S** to another," Is 66:23
gates of Jerusalem on the **S** day. Jr 17:21
houses on the **S** day or do any Jr 17:22
you must consecrate the **S** day, Jr 17:22
this city on the **S** day and Jr 17:24
consecrate the **S** day and do no Jr 17:24
to consecrate the **S** day by not Jr 17:27
gates of Jerusalem on the **S** day, Jr 17:27
opened on the **S** day and opened Ezk 46:1
the LORD on the **S** day is to be Ezk 46:4
just as he does on the **S** day. Ezk 46:12
grain, and the **S**, so we may Am 8:5
the grainfields on the **S**. Mt 12:1
is not lawful to do on the **S**!" Mt 12:2
the Law that on **S** days the Mt 12:5
violate the **S** and are innocent? Mt 12:5
Son of Man is Lord of the **S**." Mt 12:8
"Is it lawful to heal on the **S**?" Mt 12:10
that fell into a pit on the **S**, Mt 12:11
is lawful to do good on the **S**." Mt 12:12
may not be in winter or on a **S**. Mt 24:20

After the S, as the first day of Mt 28:1
synagogue on the S and began to Mk 1:21
the S He was going through the Mk 2:23
what is not lawful on the S?" Mk 2:24
The S was made for man and not Mk 2:27
for man and not man for the S. Mk 2:27
of Man is Lord even of the S." Mk 2:28
He would heal him on the S. Mk 3:2
lawful on the S to do good or to Mk 3:4
When the S came, He began to Mk 6:2
that is, the day before the S), Mk 15:42
When the S was over, Mary Mk 16:1
on the S day and stood up Lk 4:16
and was teaching them on the S. Lk 4:31
On a S, He passed through the Lk 6:1
what is not lawful on the S?" Lk 6:2
Son of Man is Lord of the S." Lk 6:5
On another S He entered the Lk 6:6
see if He would heal on the S, Lk 6:7
lawful on the S to do good or to Lk 6:9
one of the synagogues on the S, Lk 13:10
Jesus had healed on the S, Lk 13:14
be healed and not on the S day." Lk 13:14
the feeding trough on the S, Lk 13:15
from this bondage on the S day?" Lk 13:16
S, when He went to eat at the Lk 14:1
lawful to heal on the S or not?" Lk 14:3
pull him out on the S day?" Lk 14:5
and the S was about to begin. Lk 23:54
they rested on the S according Lk 23:56
Now that day was the S, Jn 5:9
had been healed, "This is the S! Jn 5:10
was doing these things on the S. Jn 5:16
not only was He breaking the S, Jn 5:18
you circumcise a man on the S. Jn 7:22
on the S so that the law Jn 7:23
a man entirely well on the S? Jn 7:23
mud and opened his eyes was a S. Jn 9:14
for He doesn't keep the S!" Jn 9:16
to remain on the cross on the S Jn 19:31
for that S was a special day Jn 19:31
Jerusalem—a S day's journey Ac 1:12
On the S day they went into the Ac 13:14
prophets that are read every S, Ac 13:27
to them the following S. Ac 13:42
The following S almost the whole Ac 13:44
in the synagogues every S day." Ac 15:21
On the S day we went outside the Ac 16:13
on three S days reasoned with Ac 17:2
synagogue every S and tried to Ac 18:4
or a new moon or a s day. Col 2:16
A S rest remains, therefore, for Heb 4:9

SABBATHS *(28)*

must observe My S, for it is a Ex 31:13
You are to keep My S; Lv 19:3
You must keep My S and revere Lv 19:30
the offerings for the LORD's S, Lv 23:38
You must keep My S and honor My Lv 26:2
will rest and make up for its S. Lv 26:34
during your S when you lived Lv 26:35
make up for its S by lying Lv 26:43
offered to the LORD on the S, 1Ch 23:31
the morning, the S and the New 2Ch 2:4
the commandment of Moses for S, 2Ch 8:13
the burnt offerings of the S, 2Ch 31:3
New Moons and S, and the calling Is 1:13
For the eunuchs who keep My S, Is 56:4
festivals and S in Zion. Lm 2:6
also gave them My S to serve as Ezk 20:12
also completely profaned My S. Ezk 20:13
profaned My S, and did not Ezk 20:16
Keep My S holy, and they will be Ezk 20:20
They also profaned My S. Ezk 20:21
My statutes and profaned My S, Ezk 20:24
My holy things and profane My S. Ezk 22:8
They disregard My S, and I am Ezk 22:26
that same day and profaned My S. Ezk 23:38
festivals, and keep My S holy. Ezk 44:24
New Moons, and S—for all the Ezk 45:17
gate on the S and New Moons. Ezk 46:3
New Moons, and S—all her Hs 2:11

SABBATIC *(2)*

You are to count seven s years, Lv 25:8
of the seven s years amounts to Lv 25:8

SABEANS *(3)*

the S swooped down and took them Jb 1:15
merchandise of Cush and the S, Is 45:14
they will sell them to the S, Jl 3:8

SABTA *(1)*

Seba, Havilah, S, Raama, and 1Ch 1:9

SABTAH *(1)*

Seba, Havilah, S, Raamah, and Gn 10:7

SABTECA *(2)*

Havilah, Sabtah, Raamah, and S. Gn 10:7
Havilah, Sabta, Raama, and S. 1Ch 1:9

SACHAR *(2)*
(AKA SHARAR)

Ahiam son of S the Hararite, 1Ch 11:35
Joah the third, S the fourth, 1Ch 26:4

SACHET *(1)*

My love is a s of myrrh to me, Sg 1:13

SACHIA *(1)*

Jeuz, S, and Mirmah. These were 1Ch 8:10

SACK *(6)*

each man's money to his s, Gn 42:25
them opened his s to get feed Gn 42:27
there in each man's s was his Gn 42:35
lowered his s to the ground Gn 44:11
cup was found in Benjamin's s. Gn 44:12
of God with his s full of 20 2Kg 4:42

SACKCLOTH *(49)*

clothes, put s around his waist Gn 37:34
leather, s, or any implement Lv 11:32
clothes, put on s, and mourn 2Sm 3:31
took s and spread it out for 2Sm 21:10
So let's put s around our waists 1Kg 20:31
they dressed with s around their 1Kg 20:32
clothes, put s over his body, 1Kg 21:27
He lay down in s and walked 1Kg 21:27
that there was s under his 2Kg 6:30
covered himself with s, and went 2Kg 19:1
covered with s, to the prophet 2Kg 19:2
clothed in s, fell down with 1Ch 21:16
wearing⌋ s, ⌊and had put⌋ Neh 9:1
clothes, put on s and ashes, Est 4:1
anyone wearing s from entering Est 4:2
and many lay on s and ashes. Est 4:3
wear so he could take off his s, Est 4:4
I have sewn s over my skin; Jb 16:15
You removed my s and clothed me Ps 30:11
were sick, my clothing was s; Ps 35:13
I wore s as my clothing, and I Ps 69:11
instead of fine clothes, s; Is 3:24
In its streets they wear s; Is 15:3
take off your s and remove the Is 20:2
heads, and for the wearing of s. Is 22:12
bare and put ⌊s⌋ about your Is 32:11
clothes, put on s, and went to Is 37:1
wearing s, to the prophet Is 37:2
black and make s their clothing. Is 50:3
and to spread out s and ashes? Is 58:5
Because of this, put on s; Jr 4:8
dress yourselves in s and roll Jr 6:26
is a gash and s around the waist Jr 48:37
yourselves with s, and lament; Jr 49:3
on their heads and put on s. Lm 2:10
will put on s, and horror will Ezk 7:18
of you and wrap themselves in s. Ezk 27:31
with fasting, s, and ashes. Dn 9:3
like a young woman dressed in s, Jl 1:8
Dress ⌊in s⌋ and lament, you Jl 1:13
Come and spend the night in s, Jl 1:13
everyone to wear s and every Am 8:10
a fast and dressed in s— Jnh 3:5
robe, put on s, and sat in ashes Jnh 3:6
beast must be covered with s, Jnh 3:8
repented in s and ashes long Mt 11:21
ago, sitting in s and ashes! Lk 10:13
black like s made of goat hair Rv 6:12
for 1,260 days, dressed in s." Rv 11:3

SACKS *(2)*

As they began emptying their s, Gn 42:35
took worn-out s on their donkeys Jos 9:4

SACRED *(52)*

You are to hold a s assembly on Ex 12:16
first day and another s assembly Ex 12:16
and smash their s pillars to Ex 23:24
by you as s to the LORD. Ex 30:37
smash their s pillars, and chop Ex 34:13
will proclaim as s assemblies. Lv 23:2
of complete rest, a s assembly. Lv 23:3
the s assemblies you are to Lv 23:4
you are to hold a s assembly; Lv 23:7
day there will be a s assembly; Lv 23:8
and hold a s assembly. Lv 23:21
and jubilation—a s assembly. Lv 23:24
You are to hold a s assembly and Lv 23:27
There is to be a s assembly on Lv 23:35
you are to hold a s assembly and Lv 23:36
to proclaim as s assemblies for Lv 23:37
a carved image or s pillar for Lv 26:1
day there is to be a s assembly; Nm 28:18
you are to hold a s assembly; Nm 28:25
are to hold a s assembly when Nm 28:26
You are to hold a s assembly in Nm 29:1
You are to hold a s assembly on Nm 29:7
You are to hold a s assembly on Nm 29:12
smash their s pillars, burn up Dt 12:3
in all the ⌊s⌋ places you see, Dt 12:13
and do not set up a s pillar; Dt 16:22
high places, s pillars, and 1Kg 14:23
he removed the s pillar of Baal 2Kg 3:2
up for themselves s pillars and 2Kg 17:10
shattered the s pillars and cut 2Kg 18:4
He broke the s pillars into 2Kg 23:14
day they held a s assembly, 2Ch 7:9
He shattered their s pillars and 2Ch 14:3
even used the s things of the 2Ch 24:7
and broke up the s pillars, 2Ch 31:1
have anointed him with My s oil. Ps 89:20
ashamed of the s trees you Is 1:29
with ample food and s clothing. Is 23:18
hair of your s vow and throw it Jr 7:29
He will smash the s pillars of Jr 43:13
and their s places will be Ezk 7:24
without sacrifice or s pillar, Hs 3:4
better they made the s pillars. Hs 10:1
and demolish their s pillars. Hs 10:2
Announce a s fast; proclaim an Jl 1:14
Zion! Announce a s fast; Jl 2:15
images and s pillars from you Mc 5:13
they ate the s bread, which is Mt 12:4
priest and ate the s bread— Mk 2:26
and took and ate the s bread, Lk 6:4
revelation of the s secret kept Rm 16:25
you have known the s Scriptures, 2Tm 3:15

SACRIFICE *(185)*

offered a s on the mountain Gn 31:54
so that we may s to the LORD our Ex 3:18
so that we may s to the LORD our Ex 5:3
'Let us go and s to our God.' Ex 5:8
'Let us go s to the LORD.' Ex 5:17
go and they can s to the LORD." Ex 8:8
s to your God within the country. Ex 8:25
what we will s to the LORD our Ex 8:26
we s what the Egyptians detest Ex 8:26
wilderness and s to the LORD our Ex 8:27
you go and s to the LORD your Ex 8:28
people go and s to the LORD." Ex 8:29
is the Passover s to the LORD, Ex 12:27
That is why I s to the LORD all Ex 13:15
for Me and s on it your burnt Ex 20:24
S a bull as a sin offering each Ex 29:36
their gods and s to their gods, Ex 34:15
and you will eat of their s. Ex 34:15
the blood for My s with anything Ex 34:25
The s of the Passover Festival Ex 34:25
his offering is a fellowship s, Lv 3:1
of the fellowship s as a fire Lv 3:3
as a fellowship s to the LORD is Lv 3:6
of the fellowship s as a fire Lv 3:9
from the ox of the fellowship s. Lv 4:10
the fat of the fellowship s. Lv 4:26
removed from the fellowship s. Lv 4:31
removed from the fellowship s. Lv 4:35
the fellowship s that someone Lv 7:11
addition to the thanksgiving s, Lv 7:12
thanksgiving s of fellowship. Lv 7:13
his thanksgiving s of fellowship Lv 7:15
If the s he offers is a vow or a Lv 7:16
on the day he presents his s, Lv 7:16
of his fellowship s is eaten on Lv 7:18
LORD's fellowship s while he is Lv 7:20
from the LORD's fellowship s, Lv 7:21
a fellowship s to the LORD must Lv 7:29
offering to the LORD from his s. Lv 7:29
offering, and the fellowship s, Lv 7:37
offering to s before the LORD; Lv 9:4
altar and s your sin offering Lv 9:7
S the people's offering and make Lv 9:7
as the people's fellowship s. Lv 9:18
The priest must s the sin Lv 14:19

He must then s one type of what Lv 14:30
The priest is to s them, one as Lv 15:15
The priest is to s one as a sin Lv 15:30
for the LORD and s it as a sin Lv 16:9
must go out and s his burnt Lv 16:24
offers a burnt offering or a s Lv 17:8
of meeting to s it to the LORD, Lv 17:9
a fellowship s to the LORD, Lv 19:5
s it that you may be accepted. Lv 19:5
on the day you s ⌊it⌋ or on the Lv 19:6
a fellowship s to the LORD to Lv 22:21
You may s as a freewill offering Lv 22:23
you must not s ⌊them⌋ in your Lv 22:24
When you s a thank offering to Lv 22:29
s it so that you may be accepted. Lv 22:29
a year old as a fellowship s. Lv 23:19
the LORD and s the Nazirite's Nm 6:16
as a fellowship s to the LORD, Nm 6:17
the fire under the fellowship s. Nm 6:18
year old, for the fellowship s. Nm 7:17
year old, for the fellowship s. Nm 7:23
year old, for the fellowship s. Nm 7:29
year old, for the fellowship s. Nm 7:35
year old, for the fellowship s. Nm 7:41
year old, for the fellowship s. Nm 7:47
year old, for the fellowship s. Nm 7:53
year old, for the fellowship s. Nm 7:59
year old, for the fellowship s. Nm 7:65
year old, for the fellowship s. Nm 7:71
year old, for the fellowship s. Nm 7:77
year old, for the fellowship s. Nm 7:83
the fellowship s totaled 24 Nm 7:88
S one as a sin offering and the Nm 8:12
either a burnt offering or a s, Nm 15:3
offering or s of each lamb. Nm 15:5
as a burnt offering or as a s, Nm 15:8
you must not s it to the LORD Dt 15:21
S to the LORD your God a Dt 16:2
of the meat you s in the evening Dt 16:4
You are not to s the Passover Dt 16:5
You must only s the Passover Dt 16:6
You must not s to the LORD your Dt 17:1
from the people who offer a s, Dt 18:3
There you are to s fellowship Dt 27:7
or to s fellowship offerings on Jos 22:23
but not for burnt offering or s. Jos 22:26
not for burnt offering or s, Jos 22:28
grain offering, or s, other than Jos 22:29
to offer a great s to their god Jdg 16:23
to worship and to s to the LORD 1Sm 1:3
Whenever Elkanah offered a s, 1Sm 1:4
to make the annual s and his vow 1Sm 1:21
man offered a s, the priest's 1Sm 2:13
husband to offer the annual s. 1Sm 2:19
out by either s or offering." 1Sm 3:14
there's a s for the people at 1Sm 9:12
because he must bless the s; 1Sm 9:13
offerings and to s fellowship 1Sm 10:8
to offer a s to the LORD your 1Sm 15:15
s to the LORD your God at Gilgal. 1Sm 15:21
is better than s, to pay 1Sm 15:22
'I have come to s to the LORD.' 1Sm 16:2
Then invite Jesse to the s, 1Sm 16:3
I've come to s to the LORD. 1Sm 16:5
and come with me to the s." 1Sm 16:5
sons and invited them to the s. 1Sm 16:5
for an annual s there involving 1Sm 20:6
clan is holding a s in the town, 1Sm 20:29
to Gibeon to s there because it 1Kg 3:4
offered a s of fellowship 1Kg 8:63
in Bethel to s to the calves he 1Kg 12:32
and he will s on you the priests 1Kg 13:2
the offering of the evening s, 1Kg 18:29
for offering the ⌊evening⌋ s, 1Kg 18:36
offering or a s to any other god 2Kg 5:17
for I have a great s for Baal. 2Kg 10:19
offering and all the blood of s. 2Kg 16:15
serve them; do not s to them. 2Kg 17:35
to Him, and you are to s to Him. 2Kg 17:36
offered a s of 22,000 cattle 2Ch 7:5
for Myself as a temple of s. 2Ch 7:12
Jerusalem to s to the LORD God 2Ch 11:16
I will s to them so that they 2Ch 28:23
not delight in s and offering; Ps 40:6
made a covenant with Me by s." Ps 50:5
S a thank offering to God, Ps 50:14
do not want a s, or I would give Ps 51:16
s pleasing to God is a broken Ps 51:17
I will s a freewill offering to Ps 54:6
I will s oxen with goats. Ps 66:15
offer You a s of thanksgiving Ps 116:17
Bind the festival s with cords Ps 118:27
s of the wicked is detestable Pr 15:8
acceptable to the LORD than s. Pr 21:3
The s of a wicked person is Pr 21:27
than to offer the s as fools do, Ec 5:1
and the one who does not s. Ec 9:2
For the LORD has a s in Bozrah, Is 34:6
also went up there to offer s. Is 57:7
My altar as an acceptable ⌊s⌋. Is 60:7
concerning burnt offering and s. Jr 7:22
bringing burnt offerings and s, Jr 17:26
it will be a s to the Lord, Jr 46:10
flock of sheep for s is filled Ezk 36:38
on them and s them as a burnt Ezk 43:24
while the priests s his burnt Ezk 46:2
His daily s and overthrew Dn 8:11
together with the daily s, Dn 8:12
—the daily s, the rebellion Dn 8:13
put a stop to s and offering. Dn 9:27
abolish the daily s and set up Dn 11:31
time the daily s is abolished Dn 12:11
without s or sacred pillar, Hs 3:4
They s on the mountaintops, Hs 4:13
For I desire loyalty and not s, Hs 6:6
They s bulls in Gilgal; Hs 12:11
the men who s kiss the calves Hs 13:2
and they offered a s to the LORD Jnh 1:16
I will s to You with a voice of Jnh 2:9
is why they s to their dragnet Hab 1:16
the LORD has prepared a s; Zph 1:7
of the LORD's s I will punish Zph 1:8
present a blind ⌊animal⌋ for s, Mal 1:8
I desire mercy and not s. Mt 9:13
mercy and not s, you would not Mt 12:7
when they s the Passover lamb, Mk 14:12
and to offer a s (according to Lk 2:24
days, offered s to the idol, Ac 7:41
the crowds, intended to offer s. Ac 14:13
your bodies as a living s, Rm 12:1
but I do say that what they s, 1Co 10:20
they s to demons and not to God. 1Co 10:20
offering on the s and service of Php 2:17
a welcome s, pleasing to God. Php 4:18
of sin by the s of Himself. Heb 9:26
You did not want s and offering, Heb 10:5
offering one s for sins forever Heb 10:12
no longer remains a s for sins, Heb 10:26
God a better s than Cain ⌊did⌋ Heb 11:4
offer up to God a s of praise, Heb 13:15

SACRIFICED *(31)*

offerings and s bulls as Ex 24:5
down to it, s to it, and said, Ex 32:8
offering and s it according to Lv 9:16
Balak s cattle and sheep, and Nm 22:40
They s to demons, not God, to Dt 32:17
to the LORD and s fellowship Jos 8:31
they s fellowship offerings 1Sm 11:15
he s an ox and a fattened calf. 2Sm 6:13
Adonijah s sheep, oxen, and 1Kg 1:9
He has lavishly s oxen, fattened 1Kg 1:19
went down and lavishly s oxen, 1Kg 1:25
but he also s and burned incense 1Kg 3:3
the people still s and burned 1Kg 22:43
He s and burned incense on the 2Kg 16:4
they s seven bulls and seven 1Ch 15:26
that time they s to the LORD 700 2Ch 15:11
Ahab s many sheep and cattle for 2Ch 18:2
He s and burned incense on the 2Ch 28:4
He s to the gods of Damascus 2Ch 28:23
the people still s at the high 2Ch 33:17
Amon s to all the carved images 2Ch 33:22
of those who had s to them. 2Ch 34:4
They s their sons and daughters Ps 106:37
whom they s to the idols Ps 106:38
bore to Me and s them to these Ezk 16:20
may be s on it and blood Ezk 43:18
the Passover lamb had to be s. Lk 22:7
themselves from food s to idols, Ac 21:25
Christ our Passover has been s. 1Co 5:7
to eat meat s to idols and to Rv 2:14
and to eat meat s to idols. Rv 2:20

SACRIFICES *(99)*

and he offered s to the God of Gn 46:1
also let us have s and burnt Ex 10:25
a burnt offering and s to God, Ex 18:12
Whoever s to any gods, except Ex 22:20
the blood of My s with anything Ex 23:18
from their fellowship s, Ex 29:28
from your fellowship s, Lv 7:32
from their fellowship s, Lv 7:34
the Israelites' fellowship s. Lv 10:14
to the LORD the s they have been Lv 17:5
as fellowship s to the LORD. Lv 17:5
offer their s to the goat-demons Lv 17:7
grain offerings, s and drink Lv 23:37
the pleasing aroma of your ⌊s⌋. Lv 26:31
your fellowship s and on your Nm 10:10
them to the s for their gods, Nm 25:2
your burnt offerings and s, Dt 12:6
burnt offerings, s, offerings Dt 12:11
your ⌊other⌋ s is to be poured Dt 12:27
the fat of their s and drank the Dt 32:38
there they offer acceptable s. Dt 33:19
offerings, s, and fellowship Jos 22:27
and offered s there to the LORD Jdg 2:5
⌊of the s⌋ from the people. 1Sm 2:13
to offer s on My altar, to 1Sm 2:28
you despise My s and offerings 1Sm 2:29
and made s to the LORD. 1Sm 6:15
burnt offerings and s as much as 1Sm 15:22
While he was offering the s, 2Sm 15:12
offered ⌊s⌋ until the people 2Sm 15:24
were offering s in the LORD's 1Kg 8:62
and offering s to their gods. 1Kg 11:8
go to offer s in the LORD's 1Kg 12:27
He offered s on the altar; 1Kg 12:32
He offered s on the altar he had 1Kg 12:33
offered s on the altar, 1Kg 12:33
went in to offer s and burnt 2Kg 10:24
Jebusite, he offered s there. 1Ch 21:28
day they offered s to the LORD 1Ch 29:21
and s in abundance for all 1Ch 29:21
Solomon offered s there in the 2Ch 1:6
the burnt offering and the s, 2Ch 7:1
were offering s in the LORD's 2Ch 7:4
near and bring s and thank 2Ch 29:31
brought s and thank offerings 2Ch 29:31
the Passover s for all the lay 2Ch 35:7
2,600 Passover s and 300 bulls 2Ch 35:8
Passover s for the Levites, 2Ch 35:9
boiled the holy ⌊s⌋ in pots, 2Ch 35:13
as a place for offering s, Ezr 6:3
they can offer s of pleasing Ezr 6:10
Will they offer s? Neh 4:2
offered great s and rejoiced Neh 12:43
Offer s in righteousness and Ps 4:5
I will offer s in His tent with Ps 27:6
you for your s or for your burnt Ps 50:8
Whoever s a thank offering Ps 50:23
You will delight in righteous s, Ps 51:19
of Peor and ate s offered to Ps 106:28
Let them offer s of thanksgiving Ps 107:22
the one who s and the one who Ec 9:2
"What are all your s to Me?" Is 1:11
They will offer s and offerings; Is 19:21
or honored Me with your s. Is 43:23
Me with the fat of your s. Is 43:24
offerings and s will be Is 56:7
one s a lamb, one breaks a dog's Is 66:3
your s do not please Me. Jr 6:20
burnt offerings to your other s, Jr 7:21
grain offerings, and to make s." Jr 33:18
one who offers s on the high Jr 48:35
offered their s and presented Ezk 20:28
and ⌊other⌋ s were placed on Ezk 40:42
and ⌊other⌋ s for the people Ezk 44:11
will cook the people's s." Ezk 46:24
prostitutes and make s with cult Hs 4:14
they will be ashamed of their s. Hs 4:19
and their s will not please Him. Hs 9:4
Bring your s every morning, Am 4:4
it s and grain offerings that Am 5:25
Everyone who s will come and Zch 14:21
makes a vow but s a defective Mal 1:14
the waste from your festival s, Mal 2:3
all the burnt offerings and s." Mk 12:33
Pilate had mixed with their s. Lk 13:1
Me offerings and s for 40 years Ac 7:42
those who eat the s partners in 1Co 10:18
offer both gifts and s for sins. Heb 5:1
need to offer s every day, Heb 7:27
appointed to offer gifts and s; Heb 8:3
which gifts and s are offered Heb 9:9

to be purified with these ⌊s⌋, Heb 9:23
with better s than these. Heb 9:23
by the same s they continually Heb 10:1
But in the s there is a reminder Heb 10:3
or delight in s and offerings, Heb 10:8
time after time the same s, Heb 10:11
for God is pleased with such s. Heb 13:16
offer spiritual s acceptable to 1Pt 2:5

SACRIFICIAL *(7)*
took the fire and the s knife, Gn 22:6
remains of the s meat by the Lv 7:17
we made s cakes in her image Jr 44:19
around to My s feast that I am Ezk 39:17
at My s feast that I have Ezk 39:19
Though they offer s gifts and Hs 8:13
s and fragrant offering to God. Eph 5:2

SACRIFICING *(16)*
came down after s the sin Lv 9:22
⌊s⌋ what he can afford together Lv 14:31
and say to the man who was s, 1Sm 2:15
the people were s on the high 1Kg 3:2
were s sheep and cattle that 1Kg 8:5
people continued s and burning 2Kg 12:3
people continued s and burning 2Kg 14:4
people continued s and burning 2Kg 15:4
people continued s and burning 2Kg 15:35
and for ⌊s⌋ burnt offerings for 2Ch 2:4
of the ark s sheep and cattle 2Ch 5:6
s fellowship offerings and 2Ch 30:22
God and have been s to Him since Ezr 4:2
Me to My face, s in gardens, Is 65:3
They kept s to the Baals and Hs 11:2
the crowds from s to them. Ac 14:18

SAD *(11)*
"Why are your faces s today?" Gn 40:7
had never been s in his presence Neh 2:1
Why are you s, when you aren't Neh 2:2
should I not be s when the city Neh 2:3
in laughter a heart may be s, Pr 14:13
a s heart ⌊produces⌋ a broken Pr 15:13
when a face is s, a heart may be Ec 7:3
How s for me! For I am like one Mc 7:1
guests be s while the groom Mt 9:15
extremely s, because he was Lk 18:23
that he became s, Jesus said, Lk 18:24

SAD-FACED *(1)*
don't be s like the hypocrites. Mt 6:16

SADDLE *(5)*
Any s the man with the discharge Lv 15:9
who sit on s blankets, and who Jdg 5:10
'I'll s the donkey for myself so 2Sm 19:26
to his sons, "S the donkey for 1Kg 13:13
his sons, "S the donkey for me." 1Kg 13:27

SADDLEBAG *(1)*
put them in the s of the camel, Gn 31:34

SADDLEBAGS *(1)*
donkey lying down between the s. Gn 49:14

SADDLECLOTHS *(1)*
your merchant in s for riding. Ezk 27:20

SADDLED *(10)*
Abraham got up, s his donkey, Gn 22:3
Balaam s his donkey and went Nm 22:21
had his two s donkeys and his Jdg 19:10
had a pair of s donkeys loaded 2Sm 16:1
he s his donkey and set out for 2Sm 17:23
So Shimei s his donkey and set 1Kg 2:40
So they s the donkey for him, 1Kg 13:13
the old prophet s the donkey for 1Kg 13:23
the donkey for me." They s it, 1Kg 13:27
Then she s the donkey and said 2Kg 4:24

SADDUCEES *(14)*
Pharisees and S coming to the Mt 3:7
The Pharisees and S approached, Mt 16:1
yeast of the Pharisees and S." Mt 16:6
yeast of the Pharisees and S,' Mt 16:11
teaching of the Pharisees and S. Mt 16:12
same day some S, who say there Mt 22:23
that He had silenced the S, Mt 22:34
Some S, who say there is no Mk 12:18
Some of the S, who say there is Lk 20:27
and the S confronted them, Ac 4:1
belonged to the party of the S, Ac 5:17
of them were S and the other Ac 23:6
between the Pharisees and the S, Ac 23:7
For the S say there is no Ac 23:8

SADNESS *(2)*
will bring grief and s to you. 1Sm 2:33
This is nothing but s of heart." Neh 2:2

SAFE *(16)*
your servant is s, but if he 1Sm 20:7
it is s for you and there is no 1Sm 20:21
You will be s with me." 1Sm 22:23
ask Him for a s journey for us, Ezr 8:21
will grant me ⌊s⌋ passage until Neh 2:7
You will be s from slander and Jb 5:21
The tents of robbers are s, Jb 12:6
I will put in a s place the one Ps 12:5
They are kept s forever, but the Ps 37:28
that I can be s and be concerned Ps 119:117
Keep me s from violent men Ps 140:1
Keep me s from violent men who Ps 140:4
who walks in wisdom will be s. Pr 28:26
and in s and restful dwellings. Is 32:18
insist: We are s? As a result, Jr 7:10
he has him back s and sound.' Lk 15:27

SAFEGUARD *(1)*
and your lips s knowledge. Pr 5:2

SAFEGUARDS *(1)*
one who s understanding finds Pr 19:8

SAFELY *(19)*
and if I return s to my father's Gn 28:21
he arrived s at the Canaanite Gn 33:18
The people returned s to Joshua Jos 10:21
will be tucked s in the place 1Sm 25:29
until the day he returned s. 2Sm 19:24
king has come to his palace s, 2Sm 19:30
water until I come back s.'" 1Kg 22:27
you ever return s, the LORD has 1Kg 22:28
water until I come back s.'" 2Ch 18:26
you ever return s, the LORD has 2Ch 18:27
He led them s, and they were not Ps 78:53
their own nets, while I pass ⌊s⌋ Ps 141:10
Then you will go s on your way; Pr 3:23
them, going on s, hardly Is 41:3
them and bring him s to Felix Ac 23:24
In this way, all got s to land. Ac 27:44
S ashore, we then learned that Ac 28:1
finished this and s delivered Rm 15:28
will bring me s into His 2Tm 4:18

SAFETY *(9)*
and Israel lived in s from Dan 1Kg 4:25
His children are far from s. Jb 5:4
and mourners are lifted to s. Jb 5:11
about and lie down in s. Jb 11:18
alone, LORD, make me live in s. Ps 4:8
The horse is a false hope for s; Ps 33:17
impoverished will lie down in s, Is 14:30
place and make them live in s. Jr 32:37
There was no s from the enemy Zch 8:10

SAFFRON *(1)*
and s, calamus and cinnamon, Sg 4:14

SAGES *(3)*
officials, and against her s. Jr 50:35
make her princes and s drunk, Jr 51:57
you prophets, s, and scribes. Mt 23:34

SAID *(2855)*
(See pp. xi-xii.)

SAIL *(13)*
Your s was ⌊made of⌋ fine Ezk 27:7
his companions set s from Paphos Ac 13:13
Then, setting s from Troas, we Ac 16:11
Then he set s from Ephesus. Ac 18:21
he was about to set s for Syria, Ac 20:3
had decided to s past Ephesus so Ac 20:16
away from them and set s, Ac 21:1
Phoenicia, we boarded and set s. Ac 21:2
that we were to s to Italy, Ac 27:1
intending to s to ports along Ac 27:2
decided to set s from there, Ac 27:12
advice not to s from Crete and Ac 27:21
we set s in an Alexandrian Ac 28:11

SAILED *(14)*
Then they s to the region of the Lk 8:26
and from there they s to Cyprus. Ac 13:4
there they s back to Antioch Ac 14:26
with him and s off to Cyprus. Ac 15:39
brothers and s away to Syria. Ac 18:18
we s away from Philippi after Ac 20:6
to the ship and s for Assos, Ac 20:13
we s on to Syria and arrived at Ac 21:3
we s along the northern coast of Ac 27:4
we s along the south side of Ac 27:7
difficulty we s along the coast, Ac 27:8
anchor and s along the shore Ac 27:13
when they had s a little farther Ac 27:28
us, and when we s, they gave us Ac 28:10

SAILING *(6)*
as they were s He fell asleep. Lk 8:23
S from there, the next day we Ac 20:15
After s through the open sea off Ac 27:5
Alexandrian ship s for Italy and Ac 27:6
S slowly for many days, we came Ac 27:7
all those who are s with you.' Ac 27:24

SAILORS *(8)*
sea and their s came to you to Ezk 27:9
and goods, your s and helmsmen, Ezk 27:27
s and all the helmsmen of the Ezk 27:29
s were afraid, and each cried Jnh 1:5
the s said to each other, Jnh 1:7
of the night the s thought they Ac 27:27
Some s tried to escape from the Ac 27:30
seafarer, the s, and all who do Rv 18:17

SAILORS' *(1)*
at the sound of your s cries. Ezk 27:28

SAINT *(1)*
Greet every s in Christ Jesus. Php 4:21

SAINTS *(60)*
LORD, you His s, for those who Ps 34:9
bodies of the s who had gone to Mt 27:52
has done to Your s in Jerusalem. Ac 9:13
came down to the s who lived in Ac 9:32
Then he called the s and widows Ac 9:41
up many of the s in prison, Ac 26:10
Rome, loved by God, called as s. Rm 1:7
intercedes for the s according Rm 8:27
Share with the s in their needs; Rm 12:13
to Jerusalem to serve the s; Rm 15:25
poor among the s in Jerusalem. Rm 15:26
may be acceptable to the s, Rm 15:31
in a manner worthy of the s, Rm 16:2
and all the s who are with them. Rm 16:15
in Christ Jesus and called as s, 1Co 1:2
and not before the s? 1Co 6:1
not know that the s will judge 1Co 6:2
As in all the churches of the s, 1Co 14:33
about the collection for the s: 1Co 16:1
themselves to serving the s. 1Co 16:15
all the s who are throughout 2Co 1:1
in the ministry to the s, 2Co 8:4
the ministry to the s, 2Co 9:1
supplying the needs of the s, 2Co 9:12
holy kiss. All the s greet you. 2Co 13:12
To the s and believers in Christ Eph 1:1
and your love for all the s, Eph 1:15
of His inheritance among the s, Eph 1:18
but fellow citizens with the s, Eph 2:19
to me—the least of all the s! Eph 3:8
all the s what is the length Eph 3:18
training of the s in the work Eph 4:12
among you, as is proper for s. Eph 5:3
and intercession for all the s. Eph 6:18
To all the s in Christ Jesus who Php 1:1
All the s greet you, but Php 4:22
the s and faithful brothers in Col 1:2
the love you have for all the s Col 1:4
but now revealed to His s. Col 1:26
our Lord Jesus with all His s. 1Th 3:13
glorified by His s and to be 2Th 1:10
Lord Jesus and for all the s. Phm 5
the hearts of the s have been Phm 7
His name when you served the s— Heb 6:10
all your leaders and all the s. Heb 13:24
delivered to the s once for all. Jd 3
which are the prayers of the s. Rv 5:8
of all the s on the gold altar Rv 8:3
with the prayers of the s, Rv 8:4
prophets, to the s, and to those Rv 11:18
war against the s and to conquer Rv 13:7
and the faith of the s. Rv 13:10
Here is the endurance of the s, Rv 14:12
blood of the s and the prophets Rv 16:6
blood of the s and on the blood Rv 17:6
heaven, and you s, apostles, Rv 18:20
and the blood of prophets and s, Rv 18:24
the righteous acts of the s. Rv 19:8
the encampment of the s, Rv 20:9
Lord Jesus be with all the s. Rv 22:21

SAINTS' *(2)*
to share in the **s** inheritance Col 1:12
washed the **s** feet, helped 1Tm 5:10

SAKE *(26)*
the place for the **s** of the 50 Gn 18:24
the whole place for their **s**." Gn 18:26
the Egyptians for Israel's **s**, Ex 18:8
For their **s** I will remember the Lv 26:45
kingdom for the **s** of His people 2Sm 5:12
man Absalom gently for my **s**." 2Sm 18:5
it for My **s** and for the sake 2Kg 19:34
sake and for the **s** of My servant 2Kg 19:34
city for My **s** and for the sake 2Kg 20:6
sake and for the **s** of My servant 2Kg 20:6
exalted for the **s** of His people 1Ch 14:2
right paths for His name's **s**. Ps 23:3
for My own **s** and remember your Is 43:25
for My own **s**, indeed, My own, Is 48:11
us, LORD, act for Your name's **s**. Jr 14:7
I acted for the **s** of My name, Ezk 20:9
For the **s** of your splendor you Ezk 28:17
not for your **s** that I will act Ezk 36:22
not for your **s** that I will act Ezk 36:32
sanctuary for the Lord's **s**. Dn 9:17
for Your own **s**, do not delay, Dn 9:19
no questions for conscience' **s**, 1Co 10:25
told you, and for conscience' **s**. 1Co 10:28
for your **s** He became poor, 2Co 8:9
reproach for the **s** of the Heb 11:26
set out for the **s** of the name, 3Jn 7

SAKKUTH *(1)*
have taken up **S** your king and Am 5:26

SALAMIS *(1)*
Arriving in **S**, they proclaimed Ac 13:5

SALATHIEL *(2)*
to Babylon Jechoniah fathered **S**, Mt 1:12
Salathiel, **S** fathered Zerubbabel Mt 1:12

SALE *(5)*
If you make a **s** to your neighbor Lv 25:14
calculate the years since its **s**, Lv 25:27
a year has passed after its **s**; Lv 25:29
The price of his **s** will be Lv 25:50
received from the **s** of the Dt 18:8

SALECAH *(4)*
Bashan as far as **S** and Edrei, Dt 3:10
Mount Hermon, **S**, all Bashan up Jos 12:5
Hermon, and all Bashan to **S**— Jos 13:11
the land of Bashan as far as **S**: 1Ch 5:11

SALEM *(4)*
(AKA JERUSALEM)
king of **S**, brought out bread Gn 14:18
His tent is in **S**, His dwelling Ps 76:2
King of **S**, priest of the Most Heb 7:1
also, "king of **S**," meaning "king Heb 7:2

SALIM *(1)*
was baptizing in Aenon near **S**, Jn 3:23

SALIVA *(3)*
gate and letting **s** run down his 1Sm 21:13
me alone until I swallow my **s**? Jb 7:19
some mud from the **s**, and spread Jn 9:6

SALLAI *(2)*
(AKA SALLU)
and after him Gabbai ⌊and⌋ **S**: Neh 11:8
Kallai of **S**, Eber of Amok, Neh 12:20

SALLU *(3)*
(AKA SALLAI)
S son of Meshullam, son of 1Ch 9:7
S son of Meshullam, son of Joed, Neh 11:7
S, Amok, Hilkiah, Jedaiah. Neh 12:7

SALMA *(3)*
(AKA SALMON)
Nahshon fathered **S**, and Salma 1Ch 2:11
Salma, and **S** fathered Boaz. 1Ch 2:11
S fathered Bethlehem, and Hareph 1Ch 2:51

SALMA'S *(1)*
S sons: Bethlehem, the 1Ch 2:54

SALMON *(5)*
(AKA SALMA)
Nahshon, who fathered **S**. Ru 4:20
S fathered Boaz, who fathered Ru 4:21
Nahshon, Nahshon fathered **S**, Mt 1:4
S fathered Boaz by Rahab, Boaz Mt 1:5
Boaz, ⌊son⌋ of **S**, ⌊son⌋ of Lk 3:32

SALMONE *(1)*
the south side of Crete off **S**. Ac 27:7

SALOME *(2)*
the younger and of Joses, and **S**. Mk 15:40
James, and **S** bought spices, so Mk 16:1

SALT *(33)*
back and became a pillar of **s**. Gn 19:26
it is to be seasoned with **s**, Ex 30:35
of your grain offerings with **s**; Lv 2:13
offering the **s** of the covenant Lv 2:13
are to present **s** with each of Lv 2:13
covenant of **s** before the LORD Nm 18:19
a burning waste of sulfur and **s**, Dt 29:23
the City of **S**, and En-gedi—six Jos 15:62
the city and sowed it with **s**. Jdg 9:45
Edomites in the Valley of **S**. 2Sm 8:13
me a new bowl and put **s** in it." 2Kg 2:20
water, threw **s** in it, and said 2Kg 2:21
Edomites in the Valley of **S**. 2Kg 14:7
Edomites in the Valley of **S**. 1Ch 18:12
forever by a covenant of **s**? 2Ch 13:5
his people to the Valley of **S**. 2Ch 25:11
or wheat, **s**, wine, and oil, Ezr 6:9
of oil, and **s** without limit. Ezr 7:22
Is bland food eaten without **s**? Jb 6:6
in a **s** land where no one lives. Jr 17:6
Moab a **s** marsh, for she will Jr 48:9
not rubbed with **s** or wrapped in Ezk 16:4
priests will throw **s** on them and Ezk 43:24
they will be left for **s**. Ezk 47:11
with weeds, a **s** pit, and a Zph 2:9
You are the **s** of the earth. Mt 5:13
But if the **s** should lose its Mt 5:13
S is good, but if the salt Mk 9:50
but if the **s** should lose its Mk 9:50
Have **s** among yourselves and be Mk 9:50
Now, **s** is good, but if salt Lk 14:34
but if **s** should lose its taste, Lk 14:34
seasoned with **s**, so that you may Col 4:6

SALTED *(2)*
ground will eat **s** fodder Is 30:24
everyone will be **s** with fire. Mk 9:49

SALTWATER *(1)*
Neither can a **s** spring yield Jms 3:12

SALTY *(5)*
the **s** wasteland its dwelling. Jb 39:6
fruitful land into **s** wasteland, Ps 107:34
its taste, how can it be made **s**? Mt 5:13
flavor, how can you make it **s**? Mk 9:50
taste, how will it be made **s**? Lk 14:34

SALU *(1)*
was Zimri son of **S**, the leader Nm 25:14

SALUTE *(1)*
they began to **s** Him, "Hail, King Mk 15:18

SALVATION *(140)*
I wait for Your **s**, LORD. Gn 49:18
see the LORD's **s** He will provide Ex 14:13
He has become my **s**. Ex 15:2
and scorned the Rock of his **s**. Dt 32:15
because I rejoice in Your **s**. 1Sm 2:1
the horn of my **s**, my stronghold, 2Sm 22:3
given me the shield of Your **s**; 2Sm 22:36
the rock of my **s**, is exalted. 2Sm 22:47
He is a tower of **s** for His king; 2Sm 22:51
about my whole **s** and ⌊my⌋ every 2Sm 23:5
Proclaim His **s** from day to day. 1Ch 16:23
Save us, God of our **s**; 1Ch 16:35
be clothed with **s**, and may Your 2Ch 6:41
and see the **s** of the LORD. 2Ch 20:17
S belongs to the LORD; Ps 3:8
rejoice in Your **s** within the Ps 9:14
my shield and the horn of my **s**, Ps 18:2
given me the shield of Your **s**; Ps 18:35
The God of my **s** is exalted. Ps 18:46
from the God of his **s**. Ps 24:5
for You are the God of my **s**; Ps 25:5
The LORD is my light and my **s**— Ps 27:1
me or abandon me, God of my **s**. Ps 27:9
a stronghold of **s** for His Ps 28:8
The **s** of the righteous is from Ps 37:39
about Your faithfulness and **s**; Ps 40:10
who love Your **s** continually say, Ps 40:16
I will show him the **s** of God." Ps 50:23
Restore the joy of Your **s** to me, Ps 51:12
the God of my **s**, and my tongue Ps 51:14
my **s** comes from Him. Ps 62:1
He alone is my rock and my **s**, Ps 62:2
He alone is my rock and my **s**, Ps 62:6
My **s** and glory depend on God; Ps 62:7
God of our **s**, the hope of all Ps 65:5
on earth, Your **s** among all Ps 67:2
our burdens; God is our **s**. Selah Ps 68:19
God is a God of **s**, and escape Ps 68:20
answer me with Your sure **s**. Ps 69:13
let Your **s** protect me, God Ps 69:29
who love Your **s** continually say, Ps 70:4
and Your **s** all day long, Ps 71:15
believe God or rely on His **s**. Ps 78:22
God of our **s**, help us—for the Ps 79:9
us, God of our **s**, and abandon Ps 85:4
love, LORD, and give us Your **s**. Ps 85:7
s is very near those who fear Ps 85:9
LORD, God of my **s**, I cry out Ps 88:1
my God, the rock of my **s**.' Ps 89:26
a long life and show him My **s**. Ps 91:16
to the rock of our **s**! Ps 95:1
proclaim His **s** from day to day. Ps 96:2
Come to me with Your **s** Ps 106:4
take the cup of **s** and worship Ps 116:13
He has become my **s**. Ps 118:14
me and have become my **s**. Ps 118:21
me, LORD, Your **s**, as You Ps 119:41
I long for Your **s**; Ps 119:81
looking for⌋ Your **s** and for Your Ps 119:123
S is far from the wicked because Ps 119:155
I hope for Your **s** and carry out Ps 119:166
long for Your **s**, LORD, and Your Ps 119:174
will clothe its priests with **s**, Ps 132:16
He adorns the humble with **s**. Ps 149:4
Indeed, God is my **s**. Is 12:2
my song, He has become my **s**." Is 12:2
water from the springs of **s**, Is 12:3
forgotten the God of your **s**, Is 17:10
rejoice and be glad in His **s**." Is 25:9
S is established as walls and Is 26:1
and our **s** in time of trouble. Is 33:2
you—a storehouse of **s**, wisdom, Is 33:6
the earth open up that **s** sprout Is 45:8
the LORD with an everlasting **s**; Is 45:17
away, and My **s** will not delay. Is 46:13
will put **s** in Zion, My splendor Is 46:13
My **s** to the ends of the earth. Is 49:6
I will help you in the day of **s**. Is 49:8
is near, My **s** appears, and My Is 51:5
But My **s** will last forever, Is 51:6
and My **s** for all generations. Is 51:8
who proclaims **s**, who says to Is 52:7
earth will see the **s** of our God. Is 52:10
right, for My **s** is coming soon, Is 56:1
for **s**, ⌊but⌋ it is far from us. Is 59:11
own arm brought **s**, and His own Is 59:16
and a helmet of **s** on His head; Is 59:17
But you will name your walls **s**, Is 60:18
the garments of **s** and wrapped me Is 61:10
and her **s** like a flaming torch. Is 62:1
Look, your **s** is coming, His Is 62:11
but the **s** of Israel is only in Jr 3:23
S is from the LORD! Jnh 2:9
I will wait for the God of my **s**. Mc 7:7
the light; I will see His **s**. Mc 7:9
will rejoice in the God of my **s**! Hab 3:18
up a horn of **s** for us in the Lk 1:69
s from our enemies and from the Lk 1:71
people knowledge of **s** through Lk 1:77
For my eyes have seen Your **s**. Lk 2:30
everyone will see the **s** of God." Lk 3:6
"Today **s** has come to this house," Lk 19:9
because **s** is from the Jews. Jn 4:22
There is **s** in no one else, Ac 4:12
message of this **s** has been sent Ac 13:26
s to the ends of the earth. Ac 13:47
to you the way of **s**." Ac 16:17
God's power for **s** to everyone Rm 1:16
concerning them is for their **s**! Rm 10:1
one confesses, resulting in **s**. Rm 10:10
s has come to the Gentiles to Rm 11:11
now our **s** is nearer than when Rm 13:11
it is for your comfort and **s**; 2Co 1:6
in the day of **s**, I helped you. 2Co 6:2
look, now is the day of **s**. 2Co 6:2
be regretted and leading to **s**, 2Co 7:10
gospel of your **s**—in Him when Eph 1:13
the helmet of **s**, and the sword Eph 6:17
work out your own **s** with fear Php 2:12

on a helmet of the hope of s. 1Th 5:8
but to obtain s through our Lord 1Th 5:9
has chosen you for s through 2Th 2:13
so that they also may obtain s, 2Tm 2:10
instruct you for s through faith 2Tm 3:15
appeared, with s for all people, Ti 2:11
who are going to inherit s? Heb 1:14
if we neglect such a great s? Heb 2:3
of their s perfect through Heb 2:10
of eternal s to all who obey Heb 5:9
better things connected with s. Heb 6:9
but to bring s to those who are Heb 9:28
faith for a s that is ready to 1Pt 1:5
your faith, the s of your souls. 1Pt 1:9
Concerning this s, the prophets 1Pt 1:10
you may grow by it in ⌊your⌋ s, 1Pt 2:2
Lord as ⌊an opportunity for⌋ s, 2Pt 3:15
to write you about our common s, Jd 3
S belongs to our God, who is Rv 7:10
The s and the power and the Rv 12:10
S, glory, and power belong to Rv 19:1

SAMARIA *(115)*

in the cities of S is certain to 1Kg 13:32
the hill of S from Shemer for 1Kg 16:24
city he built S based on the 1Kg 16:24
his fathers and was buried in S. 1Kg 16:28
over Israel in S 22 years. 1Kg 16:29
of Baal that he had built in S. 1Kg 16:32
The famine was severe in S. 1Kg 18:2
up, besieged S, and fought 1Kg 20:1
"Men are marching out of S." 1Kg 20:17
like my father set up in S." 1Kg 20:34
and angry, and he entered S. 1Kg 20:43
to the palace of Ahab king of S. 1Kg 21:1
king of Israel, who is in S. 1Kg 21:18
king died and was brought to S. 1Kg 22:37
They buried the king in S. 1Kg 22:37
the chariot at the pool of S. 1Kg 22:38
over Israel in S in the 1Kg 22:51
upper room in S and was injured 2Kg 1:2
of the king of S and ask them, 2Kg 1:3
and then he returned to S. 2Kg 2:25
king over Israel in S during the 2Kg 3:1
marched out from S at that time 2Kg 3:6
go to the prophet who is in S, 2Kg 5:3
And he led them to S. 2Kg 6:19
they entered S, Elisha said, 2Kg 6:20
and discovered ⌊they were⌋ in S. 2Kg 6:20
and marched up to besiege S. 2Kg 6:24
there was a great famine in S, 2Kg 6:25
time tomorrow at the gate of S, 2Kg 7:1
for a shekel at the gate of S," 2Kg 7:18
Since Ahab had 70 sons in S, 2Kg 10:1
and sent them to S to the rulers 2Kg 10:1
out and went on his way to S. 2Kg 10:12
Jehu came to S, he struck down 2Kg 10:17
house of⌋ Ahab in S until he had 2Kg 10:17
fathers, and he was buried in S. 2Kg 10:35
over Israel in S was 28 years. 2Kg 10:36
became king over Israel in S; 2Kg 13:1
also remained standing in S. 2Kg 13:6
fathers, and he was buried in S. 2Kg 13:9
became king over Israel in S; 2Kg 13:10
was buried in S with the kings 2Kg 13:13
Then he returned to S. 2Kg 14:14
was buried in S with the kings 2Kg 14:16
became king of Israel in S; 2Kg 14:23
over Israel in S for six months. 2Kg 15:8
he reigned in S a full month. 2Kg 15:13
from Tirzah to S and struck down 2Kg 15:14
⌊he reigned⌋ 10 years in S. 2Kg 15:17
became king over Israel in S; 2Kg 15:23
S at the citadel of the king's 2Kg 15:25
became king over Israel in S; 2Kg 15:27
became king over Israel in S; 2Kg 17:1
marched up to S, and besieged it 2Kg 17:5
the king of Assyria captured S. 2Kg 17:6
Israelites in the cities of S. 2Kg 17:24
possession of S and lived in its 2Kg 17:24
in the cities of S do not know 2Kg 17:26
against S and besieged it 2Kg 18:9
King Hoshea, S was captured. 2Kg 18:10
they delivered S from my hand? 2Kg 18:34
line ⌊used on⌋ S and the mason's 2Kg 21:13
of the prophet who came from S. 2Kg 23:18
that were in the cities of S, 2Kg 23:19
he went down to visit Ahab in S. 2Ch 18:2
him (he was hiding in S). 2Ch 22:9
of Judah from S to Beth-horon, 2Ch 25:13
Then he returned to S. 2Ch 25:24
from them and brought it to S. 2Ch 28:8
that came to S and said to them 2Ch 28:9
Then they returned to S. 2Ch 28:15
the cities of S and the region Ezr 4:10
living in S and elsewhere Ezr 4:17
and the powerful men of S, Neh 4:2
of Ephraim is S, and the head Is 7:9
and the head of S is the son of Is 7:9
the spoils of S will be carried Is 8:4
and the inhabitants of S— Is 9:9
Isn't S like Damascus? Is 10:9
those of Jerusalem and S, Is 10:10
and as I did to S and its idols Is 10:11
they delivered S from my hand? Is 36:19
prophets of S I saw something Jr 23:13
again on the mountains of S; Jr 31:5
and S who had shaved their Jr 41:5
sister was S, who lived with Ezk 16:46
But S did not commit ⌊even⌋ half Ezk 16:51
those of S and her daughters. Ezk 16:53
daughters and S and her Ezk 16:55
Oholah represents S and Oholibah Ezk 23:4
the cup of your sister S. Ezk 23:33
the crimes of S will be exposed Hs 7:1
Your calf-idol is rejected, S. Hs 8:5
The calf of S will be smashed to Hs 8:6
The residents of S will have Hs 10:5
S will bear her guilt because Hs 13:16
the mountains of S and see the Am 3:9
who live in S will be rescued Am 3:12
Bashan who are on the hill of S, Am 4:1
feel secure on the hill of S— Am 6:1
swear by the guilt of S and say, Am 8:14
territories of Ephraim and S, Ob 19
he saw regarding S and Jerusalem Mc 1:1
Jacob? Isn't it S? And what is Mc 1:5
I will make S a heap of ruins in Mc 1:6
He passed between S and Galilee. Lk 17:11
He had to travel through S, Jn 4:4
to a town of S called Sychar Jn 4:5
A woman of S came to draw water. Jn 4:7
all Judea and S, and to the ends Ac 1:8
the land of Judea and S. Ac 8:1
down to a city in S and preached Ac 8:5
heard that S had welcomed God's Ac 8:14
Galilee, and S had peace, being Ac 9:31
through both Phoenicia and S, Ac 15:3

SAMARIA'S *(4)*

so severely if S dust amounts to 1Kg 20:10
floor at the entrance to S gate, 1Kg 22:10
floor at the entrance to S gate, 2Ch 18:9
S king will disappear like foam Hs 10:7

SAMARITAN *(6)*

and don't enter any S town. Mt 10:5
But a S on his journey came up Lk 10:33
thanking Him. And he was a S. Lk 17:16
for a drink from me, a S woman?" Jn 4:9
You're a S and have a demon? Jn 8:48
city and astounded the S people, Ac 8:9

SAMARITANS *(7)*

high places that the S had made. 2Kg 17:29
a village of the S to make Lk 9:52
Jews do not associate with S. Jn 4:9
You S worship what you do not Jn 4:22
Now many S from that town Jn 4:39
when the S came to Him, they Jn 4:40
many villages of the S. Ac 8:25

SAME *(313)*

that s day Noah along with his Gn 7:13
whole earth had the s language Gn 11:1
all having the s language, Gn 11:6
that s day Abraham and his son Gn 17:26
gave them the s names his father Gn 26:18
that s day Isaac's slaves came Gn 26:32
toward him was not the s. Gn 31:2
attitude toward me is not the s, Gn 31:5
Say the s thing to Esau when you Gn 32:19
Then she told him the s story: Gn 39:17
Both had a dream on the s night, Gn 40:5
and I had dreams on the s night; Gn 41:11
dreams mean the s thing. Gn 41:25
The dreams mean the s thing. Gn 41:26
brothers, sons of the s father. Gn 42:32
require the s quota of bricks Ex 5:8
must produce the s quantity of Ex 5:18
also did the s thing by their Ex 7:11
Egypt did the s thing by their Ex 7:22
did the s thing by their Ex 8:7
of 430 years, on that s day, all Ex 12:41
This s night is in honor of the Ex 12:42
The s law will apply to both the Ex 12:49
On that s day the LORD brought Ex 12:51
on the s day ⌊of the month⌋ that Ex 19:1
with according to this s law. Ex 21:31
Do the s with your cattle and Ex 22:30
Do the s with your vineyard and Ex 23:11
are to have the s measurements. Ex 26:2
and do the s on the edge of the Ex 26:4
are to have the s measurements. Ex 26:8
Do the s for all the planks of Ex 26:17
according to the s workmanship Ex 28:8
Make it with the s workmanship Ex 28:15
curtains had the s measurements. Ex 36:9
set and did the s on the edge Ex 36:11
curtains had the s measurements. Ex 36:15
He did the s for all the planks Ex 36:22
It was the s for the other side. Ex 38:15
according to the s workmanship Ex 39:5
with the s workmanship as Ex 39:8
he will offer it the s way. Lv 4:20
the law is the s for both. Lv 7:7
on the ⌊s⌋ place as the blood of Lv 14:28
he must do the s with its blood Lv 16:15
He will do the s for the tent of Lv 16:16
or flock on the s day as its Lv 22:28
It is to be eaten on the s day. Lv 22:30
fifteenth day of the s month. Lv 23:6
On that s day you are to make a Lv 23:21
who does any work on this s day. Lv 23:30
the s is to be inflicted on him. Lv 24:20
are to have the s law for the Lv 24:22
way and moved out the s way, Nm 2:34
before Moses and Aaron the s day Nm 9:6
to apply the s statute to both Nm 9:14
must have seemed the s to them." Nm 13:33
to have the s statute for both Nm 15:15
The s law and the same ordinance Nm 15:16
law and the s ordinance will Nm 15:16
are to have the s law for the Nm 15:29
They did the s in the case Nm 25:18
along with the s kind of grain Nm 28:8
are to offer the s food each day Nm 28:24
LORD will do the s to all the Dt 3:21
God will do the s to all the Dt 7:19
their gods? I'll also do the s.' Dt 12:30
must not do the s to the LORD Dt 12:31
your female slave the s way. Dt 15:17
sets at the ⌊s⌋ time ⌊of day⌋ Dt 16:6
Do the s for his donkey, his Dt 22:3
live on the s property and one Dt 25:5
On that s day the LORD spoke to Dt 32:48
city seven times in the s way. Jos 6:15
At the s time the Benjaminites Jdg 1:21
the s with everyone who kneels Jdg 7:5
me," he said, "and do the s. Jdg 7:17
and asked the s thing from them. Jdg 8:8
years ⌊they did the s to⌋ all Jdg 10:8
in the s way as the Sidonians, Jdg 18:7
in the s place where they Jdg 20:22
That s day the Benjaminites came Jdg 20:25
of them will die on the s day. 1Sm 2:34
That s day, a Benjaminite man 1Sm 4:12
returned to Ekron that s day. 1Sm 6:16
to judge us the s as all the 1Sm 8:5
are doing the s thing to you 1Sm 8:8
That s day Saul's son Jonathan 1Sm 14:1
gave him the s answer as before. 1Sm 17:30
is to be the s as the share 1Sm 30:24
all the men with him did the s. 2Sm 1:11
also show the s goodness to you 2Sm 2:6
He did the s to all the Ammonite 2Sm 12:31
woman and I live in the s house, 1Kg 3:17
had the s size and shape. 1Kg 6:25
In the s way, he made four-sided 1Kg 6:33
he did the s for the second 1Kg 7:18
water carts using the s casting, 1Kg 7:37
On the s day, the king 1Kg 8:64
In the s way, they exported them 1Kg 10:29
He did the s for all his foreign 1Kg 11:8
prophets were prophesying the s: 1Kg 22:12
to a son at the s time the 2Kg 4:17
Josiah did the s things to them 2Kg 23:19
The second pillar was the s, 2Kg 25:17

David did the **s** to all the 1Ch 20:3
cast lots the **s** way as their 1Ch 24:31
In the **s** way, they exported them 2Ch 1:17
prophets were prophesying the **s**, 2Ch 18:11
paid him the **s** in the second 2Ch 27:5
be able to do the **s** for you? 2Ch 32:14
This **s** Hezekiah blocked the 2Ch 32:30
⌊He did the **s**⌋ in the cities of 2Ch 34:6
⌊they did⌋ the **s** with the bulls. 2Ch 35:12
Then this **s** Sheshbazzar came and Ezr 5:16
they sent me the **s** proposal, Neh 6:4
and I gave them the **s** reply. Neh 6:4
sent me this **s** message a fifth Neh 6:5
On that **s** day men were placed in Neh 12:44
Didn't your ancestors do the **s**, Neh 13:18
will say ⌊the **s** thing⌋ to all Est 1:18
will also fast in the **s** way. Est 4:16
s day King Ahasuerus awarded Est 8:1
who sow trouble reap the **s**. Jb 4:8
is all the **s**. Therefore I say, Jb 9:22
Did not the **s** God form us both Jb 31:15
You are the **s**, and Your years Ps 102:27
that wisdom is the **s** for you. Pr 24:14
the fate of animals is the **s**. Ec 3:19
they all have the **s** breath. Ec 3:19
All are going to the **s** place; Ec 3:20
do not both go to the **s** place? Ec 6:6
is the **s** for everyone: Ec 9:2
potter were the **s** as the clay. Is 29:16
I will be the **s** until ⌊your⌋ old Is 46:4
king of Judah in the **s** way: Jr 27:12
In that **s** year, at the beginning Jr 28:1
So his taste has remained the **s**, Jr 48:11
she has done, do the **s** to her. Jr 50:15
done, do the **s** to her, for she Jr 50:29
say, 'In the **s** way, Babylon will Jr 51:64
The second pillar was the **s**, Jr 52:22
and all four had the **s** form. Ezk 1:16
all four had the **s** form, like a Ezk 10:10
looked like the **s** faces I had Ezk 10:22
inquires will be the **s** as that Ezk 14:10
committing the **s** abominations Ezk 18:24
originate from the **s** land. Ezk 21:19
daughters of the **s** mother, Ezk 23:2
of them ⌊had taken⌋ the **s** path. Ezk 23:13
on that **s** day and profaned Ezk 23:38
On the **s** day they slaughtered Ezk 23:39
feet, and its height was the **s**. Ezk 40:5
each with the **s** measurements. Ezk 40:10
also had the **s** measurements. Ezk 40:10
portico had the **s** measurements Ezk 40:21
trees had the **s** measurements as Ezk 40:22
they had the **s** measurements as Ezk 40:24
it had the **s** measurements as the Ezk 40:28
portico had the **s** measurements Ezk 40:29
it had the **s** measurements as the Ezk 40:32
portico had the **s** measurements Ezk 40:33
it had the **s** measurements as the Ezk 40:35
sanctuary had the **s** appearance. Ezk 41:21
the gate and go out the **s** way." Ezk 44:3
You must do the **s** thing on the Ezk 45:20
provide the **s** things for seven Ezk 45:25
days—the **s** sin offerings, Ezk 45:25
portico and go out the **s** way. Ezk 46:8
areas had the **s** dimensions. Ezk 46:22
will not be the **s** kingdom that Dn 11:4
lies at the **s** table but to no Dn 11:27
will act the **s** way toward you." Hs 3:3
⌊The **s** judgment⌋ will happen to Hs 4:9
relations with the **s** girl, Am 2:7
and go that **s** day to the house Zch 6:10
The **s** plague as the previous one Zch 14:15
In the **s** way, let your light Mt 5:16
the tax collectors do the **s**? Mt 5:46
even the Gentiles do the **s**? Mt 5:47
do also the **s** for them—this Mt 7:12
In the **s** way, every good tree Mt 7:17
In the **s** way the Son of Man is Mt 17:12
In the **s** way, it is not the will Mt 18:14
out again and did the **s** thing. Mt 20:5
last man the **s** as I gave you. Mt 20:14
other and said the **s** thing. Mt 21:30
and they did the **s** to them. Mt 21:36
s day some Sadducees, who say Mt 22:23
The **s** happened to the second Mt 22:26
came together in the **s** place. Mt 22:34
In the **s** way, on the outside you Mt 23:28
In the **s** way, when you see all Mt 24:33
In the **s** way the man with two Mt 25:17
the disciples said the **s** thing. Mt 26:35
saying the **s** thing once more. Mt 26:44
In the **s** way the chief priests, Mt 27:41
In the **s** way even the criminals Mt 27:44
In the **s** way, when you see these Mk 13:29
And they all said the **s** thing. Mk 14:31
and prayed, saying the **s** thing. Mk 14:39
In the **s** way, the chief priests Mk 15:31
In the **s** region, shepherds were Lk 2:8
one who has food must do the **s**." Lk 3:11
those of the Pharisees do the **s**, Lk 5:33
do for you, do the **s** for them. Lk 6:31
Remain in the **s** house, eating Lk 10:7
that **s** hour He rejoiced in the Lk 10:21
In the **s** way, a Levite, when he Lk 10:32
told him, "Go and do the **s**." Lk 10:37
In the **s** way, therefore, every Lk 14:33
you, in the **s** way, there will Lk 15:7
tell you, in the **s** way, there is Lk 15:10
In the **s** way, when you have done Lk 17:10
will be the **s** as it was in the Lk 17:28
In the **s** way, all seven died and Lk 20:31
In the **s** way, when you see these Lk 21:31
the **s** way He also took the cup Lk 22:20
are undergoing the **s** punishment? Lk 23:40
Now that **s** day two of them were Lk 24:13
does these things in the **s** way. Jn 5:19
He did the **s** with the fish. Jn 21:13
will come in the **s** way that you Ac 1:11
Isaac did the **s** with Jacob, Ac 7:8
s way you killed the Egyptian Ac 7:28
gave them the **s** gift that He Ac 11:17
The **s** thing happened in Iconium; Ac 14:1
also, with the **s** nature as you, Ac 14:15
Jesus, in the **s** way they are." Ac 15:11
report the **s** things by word Ac 15:27
He took them the **s** hour of the Ac 16:33
and being of the **s** occupation, Ac 18:3
At the **s** time he was also hoping Ac 24:26
the **s** time loosening the ropes Ac 27:40
The males in the **s** way also left Rm 1:27
you, the judge, do the **s** things. Rm 2:1
do such things yet do the **s**— Rm 2:3
In the **s** way the Spirit also Rm 8:26
make from the **s** lump one piece Rm 9:21
since the **s** Lord of all is rich Rm 10:12
the **s** way, then, there is also Rm 11:5
do not have the **s** function, Rm 12:4
in the **s** way we who are many are Rm 12:5
considers every day to be the **s**. Rm 14:5
that you all say the **s** thing, 1Co 1:10
united with the **s** understanding 1Co 1:10
and the **s** conviction. 1Co 1:10
In the **s** way, no one knows the 1Co 2:11
the law also say the **s** thing? 1Co 9:8
In the **s** way, the Lord has 1Co 9:14
all ate the **s** spiritual food, 1Co 10:3
all drank the **s** spiritual drink 1Co 10:4
is one and the **s** as having her 1Co 11:5
the **s** way ⌊He⌋ also ⌊took⌋ the 1Co 11:25
gifts, but the **s** Spirit. 1Co 12:4
ministries, but the **s** Lord. 1Co 12:5
but the **s** God is active in 1Co 12:6
of knowledge by the **s** Spirit, 1Co 12:8
faith by the **s** Spirit, to 1Co 12:9
But one and the **s** Spirit is 1Co 12:11
And if they were all the **s** part, 1Co 12:19
would have the **s** concern for 1Co 12:25
the **s** way, unless you use your 1Co 14:9
Not all flesh is the **s** flesh; 1Co 15:39
should do the **s** as I instructed 1Co 16:1
of the **s** sufferings that 2Co 1:6
covenant, the **s** veil remains; 2Co 3:14
into the **s** image from glory to 2Co 3:18
we have the **s** spirit of faith 2Co 4:13
God who put the **s** diligence for 2Co 8:16
Didn't we walk in the **s** spirit 2Co 12:18
spirit and in the **s** footsteps? 2Co 12:18
be of the **s** mind, be at peace, 2Co 13:11
In the **s** way we also, when we Gl 4:3
members of the **s** body, and Eph 3:6
descended is the **s** as the One Eph 4:10
In the **s** way, husbands should Eph 5:28
treat them the **s** way, without Eph 6:9
having the **s** struggle that you Php 1:30
my joy by thinking the **s** way, Php 2:2
way, having the **s** love, sharing Php 2:2
love, sharing the **s** feelings, Php 2:2
In the **s** way you also should Php 2:18
At the **s** time, pray also for us Col 4:3
also suffered the **s** things from 1Th 2:14
in the **s** way God will bring with 1Th 4:14
the **s** time, they also learn to 1Tm 5:13
In the **s** way, older women are to Ti 2:3
You are the **s**, and Your years Heb 1:12
the **s** time, God also testified Heb 2:4
one will fall into the **s** pattern Heb 4:11
the **s** way, the Messiah did not Heb 5:5
demonstrate the **s** diligence for Heb 6:11
In the **s** way, he sprinkled the Heb 9:21
by the **s** sacrifices they Heb 10:1
after time the **s** sacrifices, Heb 10:11
co-heirs of the **s** promise. Heb 11:9
Jesus Christ is the **s** yesterday, Heb 13:8
In the **s** way, the rich man will Jms 1:11
the **s** way faith, if it doesn't Jms 2:17
And in the **s** way, wasn't Rahab Jms 2:25
Out of the **s** mouth come blessing Jms 3:10
bitter water from the **s** opening? Jms 3:11
Wives, in the **s** way, submit 1Pt 3:1
Husbands, in the **s** way, live 1Pt 3:7
also with the **s** resolve— 1Pt 4:1
with them into the **s** flood of 1Pt 4:4
knowing that the **s** sufferings 1Pt 5:9
But by the **s** word the present 2Pt 3:7
In the **s** way, Sodom and Gomorrah Jd 7
the **s** way, you also have those Rv 2:15
In the **s** way, the victor will be Rv 3:5
its length and width are the **s**. Rv 21:16

SAMGAR-NEBO *(1)*

Nergal-sharezer, **S**, Sarsechim Jr 39:3

SAMLAH *(4)*

S from Masrekah ruled in his Gn 36:36
When **S** died, Shaul from Gn 36:37
S from Masrekah ruled in his 1Ch 1:47
When **S** died, Shaul from Rehoboth 1Ch 1:48

SAMOS *(1)*

day we crossed over to **S**, Ac 20:15

SAMOTHRACE *(1)*

we ran a straight course to **S**, Ac 16:11

SAMSON *(36)*

birth to a son and named him **S**. Jdg 13:24
S went down to Timnah and saw a Jdg 14:1
But **S** told his father, "Get her Jdg 14:3
S went down to Timnah with his Jdg 14:5
the woman, because **S** wanted her. Jdg 14:7
and **S** prepared a feast there, Jdg 14:10
you a riddle," **S** said to them. Jdg 14:12
S returned to his father's house, Jdg 14:19
S ⌊took⌋ a young goat ⌊as a Jdg 15:1
S said to them, "This time I Jdg 15:3
told, "⌊It was⌋ **S**, the Timnite's Jdg 15:6
Then **S** told them, "Because you Jdg 15:7
to arrest **S** and pay him back Jdg 15:10
and they asked **S**, "Don't you Jdg 15:11
Then **S** told them, "Swear to me Jdg 15:12
Then **S** said: With the jawbone of Jdg 15:16
After **S** drank, his strength Jdg 15:19
S went to Gaza, where he saw a Jdg 16:1
⌊heard⌋ that **S** was there, Jdg 16:2
But **S** stayed in bed until Jdg 16:3
Delilah said to **S**, "Please tell Jdg 16:6
S told her, "If they tie me up Jdg 16:7
out to him, "**S**, the Philistines Jdg 16:9
Delilah said to **S**, "You have Jdg 16:10
and shouted, "**S**, the Philistines Jdg 16:12
Delilah said to **S**, "You have Jdg 16:13
called to him, "**S**, the Jdg 16:14
she cried, "**S**, the Philistines Jdg 16:20
handed over our enemy **S** to us. Jdg 16:23
"Bring **S** here to entertain us." Jdg 16:25
So they brought **S** from prison, Jdg 16:25
S said to the young man who was Jdg 16:26
roof watching **S** entertain ⌊them⌋ Jdg 16:27
S took hold of the two middle Jdg 16:29
S said, "Let me die with the Jdg 16:30
Gideon, Barak, **S**, Jephthah, of Heb 11:32

SAMSON'S *(3)*

fourth day they said to **S** wife, Jdg 14:15
So **S** wife came to him, weeping, Jdg 14:16
has taken **S** wife and given her Jdg 15:6

SAMUEL *(135)*

She named him **S**, because ⌊she 1Sm 1:20

The boy **S** served in the LORD's 1Sm 2:18
boy **S** grew up in the presence 1Sm 2:21
the boy **S** grew in stature and in 1Sm 2:26
The boy **S** served the LORD in 1Sm 3:1
S was lying down in the 1Sm 3:3
the LORD called **S**, and he 1Sm 3:4
Once again the LORD called, "**S**!" 1Sm 3:6
S got up, went to Eli, and 1Sm 3:6
S had not yet experienced the 1Sm 3:7
third time, the LORD called **S**. 1Sm 3:8
He told **S**, "Go and lie down. 1Sm 3:9
So **S** went and lay down in his 1Sm 3:9
called as before, "**S**, Samuel!" 1Sm 3:10
called as before, "Samuel, **S**!" 1Sm 3:10
S responded, "Speak, for Your 1Sm 3:10
LORD said to **S**, "I am about to 1Sm 3:11
S lay down until the morning; 1Sm 3:15
him and said, "**S**, my son." 1Sm 3:16
"Here I am," answered **S**. 1Sm 3:16
So **S** told him everything and did 1Sm 3:18
S grew, and the LORD was with 1Sm 3:19
knew that **S** was a confirmed 1Sm 3:20
Himself to **S** by His word. 1Sm 3:21
S told them, "If you are 1Sm 7:3
S said, "Gather all Israel at 1Sm 7:5
And **S** ⌊began to lead⌋ the 1Sm 7:6
The Israelites said to **S**, 1Sm 7:8
Then **S** took a young lamb and 1Sm 7:9
S was offering the burnt 1Sm 7:10
S took a stone and set it 1Sm 7:12
S judged Israel throughout his 1Sm 7:15
When **S** grew old, he appointed 1Sm 8:1
together and went to **S** at Ramah. 1Sm 8:4
S considered their demand 1Sm 8:6
S told all the LORD's words to 1Sm 8:10
people refused to listen to **S**. 1Sm 8:19
S listened to all the people's 1Sm 8:21
to them," the LORD told **S**. 1Sm 8:22
Then **S** told the men of Israel, 1Sm 8:22
when they saw **S** coming toward 1Sm 9:14
the LORD had informed **S**, 1Sm 9:15
When **S** saw Saul, the LORD told 1Sm 9:17
Saul approached **S** in the gate 1Sm 9:18
"I am the seer," **S** answered. 1Sm 9:19
S took Saul and his attendant, 1Sm 9:22
Then **S** said to the cook, "Get 1Sm 9:23
Then **S** said, "Notice that the 1Sm 9:24
So Saul ate with **S** that day. 1Sm 9:24
and **S** spoke with Saul on ⌊the⌋ 1Sm 9:25
S called to Saul on the roof, 1Sm 9:26
and both he and **S** went outside. 1Sm 9:26
of the city, **S** said to Saul, 1Sm 9:27
S took the flask of oil, poured 1Sm 10:1
Saul turned around to leave **S**, 1Sm 10:9
weren't there, we went to **S**." 1Sm 10:14
asked, "what did **S** say to you?" 1Sm 10:15
tell him what **S** had said about 1Sm 10:16
S summoned the people to the 1Sm 10:17
S had all the tribes of Israel 1Sm 10:20
S said to all the people, 1Sm 10:24
S proclaimed to the people the 1Sm 10:25
S sent all the people away, 1Sm 10:25
march behind Saul and **S**." 1Sm 11:7
people said to **S**, "Who said that 1Sm 11:12
Then **S** said to the people, 1Sm 11:14
Then **S** said to all Israel, 1Sm 12:1
Then **S** said to the people, 1Sm 12:6
Barak, Jephthah, and **S**. 1Sm 12:11
S called on the LORD, and on 1Sm 12:18
greatly feared the LORD and **S**. 1Sm 12:18
They pleaded with **S**, "Pray to 1Sm 12:19
S replied, "Don't be afraid. 1Sm 12:20
appointed time that **S** had set, 1Sm 13:8
but **S** didn't come to Gilgal, 1Sm 13:8
the burnt offering, **S** arrived. 1Sm 13:10
S asked, "What have you done? 1Sm 13:11
S said to Saul, "You have been 1Sm 13:13
S went from Gilgal to Gibeah 1Sm 13:15
S told Saul, "The LORD sent me 1Sm 15:1
the word of the LORD came to **S**: 1Sm 15:10
So **S** became angry and cried out 1Sm 15:11
in the morning **S** got up to 1Sm 15:12
but it was reported to **S**, 1Sm 15:12
When **S** came to him, Saul said, 1Sm 15:13
S replied, "Then what is this 1Sm 15:14
Stop!" exclaimed **S**. "Let me tell 1Sm 15:16
S continued, "Although you once 1Sm 15:17
Then **S** said: Does the LORD take 1Sm 15:22
Saul answered **S**, "I have sinned. 1Sm 15:24
S replied to Saul, "I will not 1Sm 15:26
S turned to go, Saul grabbed 1Sm 15:27
S said to him, "The LORD has 1Sm 15:28
S went back, following Saul, 1Sm 15:31
S said, "Bring me Agag king of 1Sm 15:32
S declared: As your sword has 1Sm 15:33
S went to Ramah, and Saul went 1Sm 15:34
S never again visited Saul. 1Sm 15:35
S mourned for Saul, and the 1Sm 15:35
LORD said to **S**, "How long are 1Sm 16:1
S asked, "How can I go? 1Sm 16:2
S did what the LORD directed and 1Sm 16:4
they arrived, **S** saw Eliab and 1Sm 16:6
LORD said to **S**, "Do not look at 1Sm 16:7
Abinadab and presented him to **S**. 1Sm 16:8
chosen this one either," **S** said. 1Sm 16:8
Shammah, but **S** said, "The LORD 1Sm 16:9
his sons to him, **S** told Jesse, 1Sm 16:10
S asked him, "Are these all the 1Sm 16:11
S told Jesse, "Send for him. 1Sm 16:11
So **S** took the horn of oil, 1Sm 16:13
S set out and went to Ramah. 1Sm 16:13
and went to **S** at Ramah and told 1Sm 19:18
Then he and **S** left and stayed at 1Sm 19:18
prophesying with **S** leading them, 1Sm 19:20
asked, "Where are **S** and David?" 1Sm 19:22
and also prophesied before **S**; 1Sm 19:24
S died, and all Israel assembled 1Sm 25:1
By this time **S** had died, and all 1Sm 28:3
"Bring up **S** for me," he answered 1Sm 28:11
the woman saw **S**, she screamed, 1Sm 28:12
Then Saul knew that it was **S**, 1Sm 28:14
me up?" **S** asked Saul. "I'm 1Sm 28:15
S answered, "Since the LORD has 1Sm 28:16
singer, son of Joel, son of **S**, 1Ch 6:33
David and **S** the seer had 1Ch 9:22
with the LORD's word through **S**. 1Ch 11:3
All that **S** the seer, Saul son of 1Ch 26:28
in the Events of **S** the Seer, 1Ch 29:29
since the days of **S** the prophet. 2Ch 35:18
S also was among those calling Ps 99:6
Even if Moses and **S** should stand Jr 15:1
from **S** and those after him, Ac 3:24
them judges until **S** the prophet. Ac 13:20
of David and **S** and the prophets, Heb 11:32

SAMUEL'S *(4)*

And **S** words came to all Israel. 1Sm 4:1
the Philistines all of **S** life. 1Sm 7:13
was terrified by **S** words and was 1Sm 28:20
S sons: his firstborn Joel, and 1Ch 6:28

SANBALLAT *(10)*

When **S** the Horonite and Tobiah Neh 2:10
When **S** the Horonite, Tobiah the Neh 2:19
When **S** heard that we were Neh 4:1
When **S**, Tobiah, and the Arabs, Neh 4:7
When **S**, Tobiah, Geshem the Arab, Neh 6:1
S and Geshem sent me a message: Neh 6:2
S sent me this same message a Neh 6:5
Tobiah and **S** had hired him. Neh 6:12
Tobiah and **S** for what they have Neh 6:14
a son-in-law to **S** the Horonite. Neh 13:28

SANCTIFICATION *(8)*

which results in **s**. Rm 6:19
results in **s**—and the end is Rm 6:22
righteousness, **s**, and redemption 1Co 1:30
making our **s** complete in the 2Co 7:1
For this is God's will, your **s**: 1Th 4:3
his own vessel in **s** and honor, 1Th 4:4
called us to impurity, but to **s**. 1Th 4:7
salvation through **s** by the 2Th 2:13

SANCTIFIED *(16)*

the temple I have **s** for My name. 1Kg 9:7
that I have **s** for My name I will 2Ch 7:20
the sanctuary that **s** the gold? Mt 23:17
they also may be **s** by the truth. Jn 17:19
inheritance among all who are **s**. Ac 20:32
who are **s** by faith in Me.' Ac 26:18
be acceptable, **s** by the Holy Rm 15:16
those who are **s** in Christ Jesus 1Co 1:2
washed, you were **s**, you were 1Co 6:11
husband is **s** by the wife, 1Co 7:14
wife is **s** by the Christian 1Co 7:14
since it is **s** by the word of God 1Tm 4:5
and those who are **s** all have one Heb 2:11
we have been **s** through the Heb 10:10
forever those who are **s**. Heb 10:14
the covenant by which he was **s**, Heb 10:29

SANCTIFIES *(2)*

or the altar that **s** the gift? Mt 23:19
For the One who **s** and those who Heb 2:11

SANCTIFY *(7)*

that I, the LORD, **s** Israel." Ezk 37:28
s the congregation; Jl 2:16
S them by the truth; Jn 17:17
s Myself for them, so they also Jn 17:19
peace Himself **s** you completely. 1Th 5:23
s for the purification of the Heb 9:13
so that He might **s** the people by Heb 13:12

SANCTUARIES *(9)*

He is not to desecrate My **s**, Lv 21:23
to ruins and devastate your **s**. Lv 26:31
in both the inner and outer **s**. 1Kg 6:29
in both the inner and outer **s**. 1Kg 6:30
You are awe-inspiring in Your **s**. Ps 68:35
and preach against the **s**. Ezk 21:2
profaned your **s** by the magnitude Ezk 28:18
and Israel's **s** will be in ruins; Am 7:9
not dwell in **s** made with hands, Ac 7:48

SANCTUARY *(222)*

hands have established the **s**. Ex 15:17
are to make a **s** for Me so that I Ex 25:8
Whenever he enters the **s**, Ex 28:29
he enters the **s** before the LORD Ex 28:35
to minister in the **s** ⌊area⌋, Ex 28:43
minister in the **s** must wear them Ex 29:30
shekel according to the **s** shekel Ex 30:13
cassia (by the **s** shekel), and Ex 30:24
the fragrant incense for the **s**. Ex 31:11
for ministering in the **s**— Ex 35:19
the work of constructing the **s**." Ex 36:1
for the task of making the **s**. Ex 36:3
work for the **s** came one by one Ex 36:4
else as an offering for the **s**." Ex 36:6
in all the work on the **s**, Ex 38:24
according to the **s** shekel. Ex 38:24
according to the **s** shekel— Ex 38:25
according to the **s** shekel, Ex 38:26
the bases of the **s** and the bases Ex 38:27
garments for ministry in the **s**, Ex 39:1
for ministering in the **s**, Ex 39:41
in front of the veil of the **s**. Lv 4:6
according to the **s** shekel, Lv 5:15
the front of the **s** to ⌊a place⌋ Lv 10:4
the sin offering in the **s** area? Lv 10:17
was not brought inside the **s**, Lv 10:18
have eaten it in the **s** ⌊area⌋, Lv 10:18
go into the **s** until completing Lv 12:4
place in the **s** area where the Lv 14:13
My Sabbaths and revere My **s**; Lv 19:30
defiling My **s** and profaning My Lv 20:3
must not leave the **s** or he will Lv 21:12
will desecrate the **s** of his God, Lv 21:12
keep My Sabbaths and honor My **s**; Lv 26:2
by the standard **s** shekel. Lv 27:3
by the standard **s** shekel, Lv 27:25
comes near ⌊the **s**⌋ must be put Nm 3:10
for the duties of the **s**. Nm 3:28
the **s** utensils that were used Nm 3:31
for the duties of the **s**. Nm 3:32
the duties of the **s** as a service Nm 3:38
to the standard **s** shekel— Nm 3:47
by the standard **s** shekel. Nm 3:50
utensils they use in the **s**, Nm 4:12
by the standard **s** shekel, Nm 7:13
by the standard **s** shekel, Nm 7:19
by the standard **s** shekel, Nm 7:25
by the standard **s** shekel, Nm 7:31
by the standard **s** shekel, Nm 7:37
by the standard **s** shekel, Nm 7:43
by the standard **s** shekel, Nm 7:49
by the standard **s** shekel, Nm 7:55
by the standard **s** shekel, Nm 7:61
by the standard **s** shekel, Nm 7:67
by the standard **s** shekel, Nm 7:73
by the standard **s** shekel, Nm 7:79
by the standard **s** shekel. Nm 7:85
by the standard **s** shekel. Nm 7:86
when they approach the **s**." Nm 8:19
for sin against the **s**. Nm 18:1
not come near the **s** equipment or Nm 18:3
to guard the **s** and the altar so Nm 18:5
comes near ⌊the **s**⌋ will be put Nm 18:7

silver by the standard s shekel, Nm 18:16
has defiled the s of the LORD. Nm 19:20
beer to the LORD in the s area. Nm 28:7
oak next to the s of the LORD. Jos 24:26
his sons are defiling the s, 1Sm 3:13
of the temple s was 30 feet long 1Kg 6:3
the s and the inner sanctuary. 1Kg 6:5
the sanctuary and the inner s. 1Kg 6:5
the interior as an inner s, 1Kg 6:16
the s in front of the most holy 1Kg 6:17
the inner s inside the temple 1Kg 6:19
interior of the s was 30 feet 1Kg 6:20
of the inner s and overlaid it 1Kg 6:21
that belongs in the inner s. 1Kg 6:22
In the inner s he made two 1Kg 6:23
For the entrance of the inner s, 1Kg 6:31
doorposts for the s entrance. 1Kg 6:33
pillars at the portico of the s: 1Kg 7:21
in front of the inner s, 1Kg 7:49
for the doors of the temple s. 1Kg 7:50
into the inner s of the temple, 1Kg 8:6
place in front of the inner s, 1Kg 8:8
not seen from outside ⌊the s⌋; 1Kg 8:8
doors of the LORD's s and from 2Kg 18:16
had made for the LORD's s, 2Kg 24:13
and all the utensils of the s, 1Ch 9:29
the LORD God's s so that you may 1Ch 22:19
officers of the s and officers 1Ch 24:5
you to build a house for the s. 1Ch 28:10
the inner s and also put it on 2Ch 3:16
the pillars in front of the s, 2Ch 3:17
and put them in the s, 2Ch 4:7
tables and placed them in the s, 2Ch 4:8
front of the inner s according 2Ch 4:20
and the doors of the temple s— 2Ch 4:22
into the inner s of the temple, 2Ch 5:7
place in front of the inner s, 2Ch 5:9
built You a s in it for Your 2Ch 20:8
the LORD's s to burn incense 2Ch 26:16
Leave the s, for you have acted 2Ch 26:18
he didn't enter the LORD's s. 2Ch 27:2
in the LORD's s to the courtyard 2Ch 29:16
for the s, and for Judah. 2Ch 29:21
and come to His s that He has 2Ch 30:8
purification ⌊rules⌋ of the s." 2Ch 30:19
sword in the house of their s. 2Ch 36:17
articles of the s are kept and Neh 10:39
help from the s and sustain you Ps 20:2
up my hands toward Your holy s. Ps 28:2
God has spoken in His s: Ps 60:6
gaze on You in the s to see Your Ps 63:2
among them in the s as He was at Ps 68:17
of my God, my King, in the s. Ps 68:24
until I entered God's s. Ps 73:17
enemy has destroyed in the s. Ps 74:3
They set Your s on fire; Ps 74:7
He built His s like the heights, Ps 78:69
and beauty are in His s. Ps 96:6
God has spoken in His s: Ps 108:7
Judah became His s, Israel, His Ps 114:2
Praise God in His s. Ps 150:1
He will be a s; but for the two Is 8:14
out and comes to his s to pray, Is 16:12
I defiled the officers of the s, Is 43:28
to beautify the place of My s, Is 60:13
have trampled down Your s. Is 63:18
beginning is the place of our s, Jr 17:12
seen the nations enter her s— Lm 1:10
His altar, repudiated His s; Lm 2:7
be killed in the Lord's s? Lm 2:20
have defiled My s with all your Ezk 5:11
so that I must depart from My s? Ezk 8:6
Now begin at My s." Ezk 9:6
while I have been a s for them Ezk 11:16
they defiled My s on that same Ezk 23:38
they entered My s to profane it. Ezk 23:39
I am about to desecrate My s, Ezk 24:21
about My s when it was Ezk 25:3
and will set My s among them Ezk 37:26
When My s is among them forever Ezk 37:28
the front of the s had the same Ezk 41:21
hall and the s each had a double Ezk 41:23
burned outside the s in the Ezk 43:21
with all the exits of the s. Ezk 44:5
to occupy My s, you defiled My Ezk 44:7
to keep charge of My s for you. Ezk 44:8
flesh, may enter My s, not even Ezk 44:9
Yet they will occupy My s, Ezk 44:11
kept charge of My s when the Ezk 44:15
may enter My s and draw near to Ezk 44:16
On the day he goes into the s, Ezk 44:27
court to minister in the s, Ezk 44:27
be a square ⌊section⌋ for the s, Ezk 45:2
in which the s, the most holy Ezk 45:3
priests who minister in the s, Ezk 45:4
well as a holy area for the s. Ezk 45:4
bull and purify the s. Ezk 45:18
the water ⌊comes⌋ from the s. Ezk 47:12
The s will be in the middle of Ezk 48:8
The LORD's s will be in the Ezk 48:10
donation and the s of the temple Ezk 48:21
overthrew the place of His s. Dn 8:11
over of the s and of the host to Dn 8:13
then the s will be restored." Dn 8:14
Your desolate s for the Lord's Dn 9:17
will destroy the city and the s. Dn 9:26
it is the king's s and a royal Am 7:13
Her priests profane the s; Zph 3:4
Judah has profaned the LORD's s, Mal 2:11
'Whoever takes an oath by the s, Mt 23:16
gold of the s is bound by his Mt 23:16
gold or the s that sanctified Mt 23:17
oath by the s takes an oath by Mt 23:21
between the s and the altar. Mt 23:35
demolish God's s and rebuild it Mt 26:61
silver into the s and departed. Mt 27:5
demolish the s and rebuild it Mt 27:40
curtain of the s was split in Mt 27:51
demolish this s made by ⌊human⌋ Mk 14:58
would demolish the s and build Mk 15:29
curtain of the s was split in Mk 15:38
to enter the s of the Lord and Lk 1:9
that he stayed so long in the s. Lk 1:21
he had seen a vision in the s. Lk 1:22
between the altar and the s. Lk 11:51
curtain of the s was split down Lk 23:45
Destroy this s, and I will raise Jn 2:19
This s took 46 years to build, Jn 2:20
about the s of His body. Jn 2:21
that you are God's s and that 1Co 3:16
ruins God's s, God will ruin him 1Co 3:17
for God's s is holy, and that is 1Co 3:17
your body is a s of the Holy 1Co 6:19
does God's s have with idols? 2Co 6:16
For we are the s of the living 2Co 6:16
into a holy s in the Lord, Eph 2:21
so that he sits in God's s, 2Th 2:4
enters the inner s behind the Heb 6:19
a minister of the s and the true Heb 8:2
for ministry and an earthly s. Heb 9:1
not enter a s made with hands Heb 9:24
priest enters the s yearly with Heb 9:25
to enter the s through the blood Heb 10:19
him a pillar in the s of My God, Rv 3:12
Him day and night in His s. Rv 7:15
measure God's s and the altar, Rv 11:1
the courtyard outside the s. Rv 11:2
God's s in heaven was opened, Rv 11:19
His covenant appeared in His s. Rv 11:19
Another angel came out of the s, Rv 14:15
came out of the s in heaven. Rv 14:17
the heavenly s—the tabernacle Rv 15:5
Out of the s came the seven Rv 15:6
Then the s was filled with smoke Rv 15:8
enter the s until the seven Rv 15:8
voice from the s saying to the Rv 16:1
a loud voice came out of the s, Rv 16:17
I did not see a s in it, because Rv 21:22
Almighty and the Lamb are its s. Rv 21:22

SANCTUARY'S *(1)*

toward the s outer gate that Ezk 44:1

SAND *(30)*

sky and the s on the seashore Gn 22:17
offspring like the s of the sea, Gn 32:12
like the s of the sea—that he Gn 41:49
dead and hid him in the s. Ex 2:12
the hidden treasures of the s. Dt 33:19
as the s on the seashore Jos 11:4
as the s on the seashore. Jdg 7:12
as the s on the seashore 1Sm 13:5
numerous as the s by the sea— 2Sm 17:11
as numerous as the s by the sea; 1Kg 4:20
vast⌋ as the s on the seashore 1Kg 4:29
outweigh the s of the seas! Jb 6:3
and multiply ⌊my⌋ days as the s. Jb 29:18
lets them be warmed in the s. Jb 39:14
birds like the s of the seas. Ps 78:27
would outnumber the grains of s; Ps 139:18
stone is heavy and s, a burden, Pr 27:3
as numerous as the s of the sea, Is 10:22
The s partridge will make her Is 34:15
been as ⌊countless⌋ as the s, Is 48:19
who set the s as the boundary Jr 5:22
numerous than the s of the seas. Jr 15:8
the s of the sea cannot be Jr 33:22
will be like the s of the sea, Hs 1:10
They gather prisoners like s. Hab 1:9
who built his house on the s. Mt 7:26
sons is like the s of the sea, Rm 9:27
the grains of s by the seashore Heb 11:12
He stood on the s of the sea. Rv 12:18
number is like the s of the sea. Rv 20:8

SANDAL *(9)*

take a thread or s strap or Gn 14:23
remove his s from his foot, Dt 25:9
the man whose s was removed.' Dt 25:10
man removed his s and gave ⌊it⌋ Ru 4:7
removed his s and said to Boaz, Ru 4:8
on Edom I throw My s. Ps 60:8
on Edom I throw My s. Ps 108:9
is loose, and no s strap broken. Is 5:27
whose s strap I'm not worthy to Jn 1:27

SANDALED *(2)*

How beautiful are your s feet, Sg 7:1
and your feet s with readiness Eph 6:15

SANDALS *(25)*

Take your s off your feet, Ex 3:5
for travel, your s on your feet, Ex 12:11
clothes and the s on your feet Dt 29:5
Remove the s from your feet, Jos 5:15
patched s on their feet and Jos 9:5
clothes and s of ours are worn Jos 9:13
and on the s of his feet. 1Kg 2:5
gave them s, food and drink 2Ch 28:15
remove the s from your feet," Is 20:2
and provided you with leather s. Ezk 16:10
and strap your s on your feet; Ezk 24:17
heads and your s on your feet. Ezk 24:23
a needy person for a pair of s. Am 2:6
for a pair of s and even sell Am 8:6
am not worthy to take off His s. Mt 3:11
an extra shirt, s, or a walking Mt 10:10
and untie the strap of His s. Mk 1:7
They were to wear s, but not put Mk 6:9
to untie the strap of His s. Lk 3:16
money-bag, traveling bag, or s; Lk 10:4
on his finger and s on his feet. Lk 15:22
traveling bag, or s, did you Lk 22:35
the s off your feet, because Ac 7:33
told him, "and put on your s." Ac 12:8
to untie the s on His feet.' Ac 13:25

SANDBAR *(1)*

they struck a s and ran the ship Ac 27:41

SANG *(17)*

and the Israelites s this song Ex 15:1
Miriam s to them: Sing to the Ex 15:21
Then Israel s this song: Nm 21:17
and Barak son of Abinoam s: Jdg 5:1
As they celebrated, the women s: 1Sm 18:7
David s the following lament for 2Sm 1:17
and the king s a lament for 2Sm 3:33
So they s praises with rejoicing 2Ch 29:30
They s with praise and Ezr 3:11
the singers s, with Jezrahiah Neh 12:42
morning stars s together and all Jb 38:7
His promises and s His praise. Ps 106:12
we s a lament, but you didn't Mt 11:17
we s a lament, but you didn't Lk 7:32
And they s a new song: You are Rv 5:9
They s a new song before the Rv 14:3
They s the song of God's servant Rv 15:3

SANHEDRIN *(22)*

will be subject to the S. Mt 5:22
and the whole S were looking for Mt 26:59
and the whole S were looking for Mk 14:55
scribes, and the whole S. Mk 15:1
member of the S who was himself Mk 15:43
and brought Him before their S. Lk 22:66
named Joseph, a member of the S, Lk 23:50
convened the S and said, Jn 11:47
had ordered them to leave the S, Ac 4:15
convened the S—the full Senate Ac 5:21
had them stand before the S, Ac 5:27

stood up in the S and ordered Ac 5:34
out from the presence of the S, Ac 5:41
him off, and took him to the S. Ac 6:12
sitting in the S looked intently Ac 6:15
and all the S to convene. Ac 22:30
intently at the S and said, Ac 23:1
out in the S, "Brothers, I am Ac 23:6
along with the S, make a request Ac 23:15
Paul down to the S tomorrow, Ac 23:20
brought him down before their S. Ac 23:28
in me when I stood before the S, Ac 24:20

SANHEDRINS *(2)*
hand you over to s and flog you Mt 10:17
They will hand you over to s, Mk 13:9

SANITY *(2)*
heaven, and my s returned to me. Dn 4:34
that time my s returned to me, Dn 4:36

SANK *(9)*
Their hearts s. Trembling, they Gn 42:28
they s to the depths like a Ex 15:5
They s like lead in the mighty Ex 15:10
The stone s into his forehead, 1Sm 17:49
mountains rose and valleys s— Ps 104:8
and Jeremiah s in the mud. Jr 38:6
Your feet s into the mire, Jr 38:22
I s to the foundations of the Jnh 2:6
window sill and s into a deep Ac 20:9

SANSANNAH *(1)*
Ziklag, Madmannah, S, Jos 15:31

SAPH *(1)*
(AKA SIPPAI)
the Hushathite killed S, 2Sm 21:18

SAPLING *(1)*
and produce twigs like a s. Jb 14:9

SAPPHIRA *(1)*
Ananias, with S his wife, sold Ac 5:1

SAPPHIRE *(10)*
like a pavement made of s stone, Ex 24:10
a turquoise, a s, and a diamond; Ex 28:18
a turquoise, a s, and a diamond; Ex 39:11
Its rocks are a source of s, Jb 28:6
of Ophir, in precious onyx or s. Jb 28:16
their appearance ⌊like⌋ s. Lm 4:7
appearance of s stone was above Ezk 1:26
like s stone resembling Ezk 10:1
onyx, and jasper, s, turquoise Ezk 28:13
jasper, the second s, the third Rv 21:19

SAPPHIRES *(2)*
an ivory panel covered with s. Sg 5:14
and lay your foundations in s. Is 54:11

SARAH *(37)*
(AKA SARAI)
her Sarai, for S will be her Gn 17:15
Can S, a ninety-year-old woman, Gn 17:17
Your wife S will bear you a son, Gn 17:19
whom S will bear to you at this Gn 17:21
into the tent and said to S, Gn 18:6
"Where is your wife S?" Gn 18:9
your wife S will have a son!" Gn 18:10
Now S was listening at the Gn 18:10
Abraham and S were old and Gn 18:11
S had passed the age of Gn 18:11
Why did S laugh, saying, Gn 18:13
S denied it. "I did not laugh," Gn 18:15
Abraham said about his wife S, Gn 20:2
of Gerar had S brought to him. Gn 20:2
and returned his wife S to him. Gn 20:14
And to S he said, "Look, I am Gn 20:16
household on account of S, Gn 20:18
LORD came to S as He had said, Gn 21:1
the LORD did for S what He had Gn 21:1
S became pregnant and bore a son Gn 21:2
to him—the one S bore to him— Gn 21:3
S said, "God has made me laugh, Gn 21:6
told Abraham that S would nurse Gn 21:7
But S saw the son mocking— Gn 21:9
Whatever S says to you, listen Gn 21:12
Now S lived 127 years; Gn 23:1
S died in Kiriath-arba (that is, Gn 23:2
to mourn for S and to weep for Gn 23:2
buried his wife S in the cave Gn 23:19
S, my master's wife, bore a son Gn 24:36
of his mother S and took Rebekah Gn 24:67
buried there with his wife S. Gn 25:10
and his wife S are buried there, Gn 49:31
and to S who gave birth to you Is 51:2
will come, and S will have a son Rm 9:9
faith even S herself, when she Heb 11:11
as S obeyed Abraham, calling 1Pt 3:6

SARAH'S *(2)*
the Egyptian, S slave, bore to Gn 25:12
and the deadness of S womb, Rm 4:19

SARAI *(17)*
(AKA SARAH)
wife was named S, and Nahor's Gn 11:29
S was barren; she had no child. Gn 11:30
and his daughter-in-law S, Gn 11:31
took his wife S, his nephew Lot Gn 12:5
to his wife S, "Look, I know Gn 12:11
because of Abram's wife S. Gn 12:17
Abram's wife S had not borne him Gn 16:1
S said to Abram, "Since the LORD Gn 16:2
And Abram agreed to what S said. Gn 16:2
So Abram's wife S took Hagar, Gn 16:3
Then S said to Abram, "You are Gn 16:5
Abram replied to S, "Here, your Gn 16:6
Then S mistreated her so much Gn 16:6
Hagar, slave of S, where have Gn 16:8
away from my mistress S." Gn 16:8
for your wife S, do not call her Gn 17:15
not call her S, for Sarah will Gn 17:15

SARAPH *(1)*
and Joash and S, who married 1Ch 4:22

SARDIS *(3)*
Thyatira, S, Philadelphia, Rv 1:11
angel of the church in S write: Rv 3:1
a few people in S who have not Rv 3:4

SARDONYX *(1)*
fifth s, the sixth carnelian, Rv 21:20

SARGON *(1)*
sent by S king of Assyria, Is 20:1

SARID *(2)*
stretched as far as S; Jos 19:10
From S, it turned east toward Jos 19:12

SARSECHIM *(1)*
Samgar-nebo, S the Rab-saris, Jr 39:3

SASH *(8)*
woven tunic, a turban, and a s. Ex 28:4
and make an embroidered s. Ex 28:39
and the s of finely spun linen Ex 39:29
Aaron, wrapped the s around him, Lv 8:7
must tie a linen s ⌊around him⌋ Lv 16:4
robe and tie your s around him. Is 22:21
or a bride her wedding s? Jr 2:32
and with a gold s wrapped around Rv 1:13

SASHES *(5)*
Make tunics, s, and headbands Ex 28:40
and tie s around both Aaron and Ex 29:9
tunics, wrapped s around them, Lv 8:13
ankle jewelry, s, perfume Is 3:20
with gold s wrapped around their Rv 15:6

SAT *(97)*
Then she went and s down nearby, Gn 21:16
So as she s nearby, she wept Gn 21:16
of the camel, and s on them. Gn 31:34
Then they s down to eat a meal. Gn 37:25
and s at the entrance to Enaim, Gn 38:14
his strength and s up in bed. Gn 48:2
of Midian, and s down by a well. Ex 2:15
Pharaoh who s on his throne to Ex 12:29
when we s by pots of meat and Ex 16:3
under him, and he s down on it. Ex 17:12
next day Moses s down to judge Ex 18:13
The people s down to eat and Ex 32:6
and He s under the oak that was Jdg 6:11
So they s down and the two of Jdg 19:6
went in and s down in the city Jdg 19:15
they wept and s before the LORD. Jdg 20:26
to Bethel and s there before God Jdg 21:2
So she s beside the harvesters, Ru 2:14
of the town⌋ and s down there. Ru 4:1
So he went over and s down. Ru 4:1
Sit here." And they s down. Ru 4:2
the king s down to eat the meal. 1Sm 20:24
He s at his usual place on the 1Sm 20:25
Jonathan s facing him and Abner 1Sm 20:25
off the ground and s on the bed. 1Sm 28:23
David went in, s in the LORD's 2Sm 7:18
king got up and s in the gate, 2Sm 19:8
Solomon s on the throne of his 1Kg 2:12
bowed to her, s down on his 1Kg 2:19
So she s down at his right hand. 1Kg 2:19
He s down under a broom tree and 1Kg 19:4
men came in and s opposite him. 1Kg 21:13
child s on her lap until noon 2Kg 4:20
Then Joash s on the throne of 2Kg 11:19
and Jeroboam s on his throne. 2Kg 13:13
David went in, s in the LORD's 1Ch 17:16
Solomon s on the LORD's throne 1Ch 29:23
beard, and s down devastated. Ezr 9:3
while I s devastated until the Ezr 9:4
all the people s in the square Ezr 10:9
these words, I s down and wept. Neh 1:4
king and Haman s down to drink, Est 3:15
while he s among the ashes Jb 2:8
Then they s on the ground with Jb 2:13
The LORD s enthroned at the Ps 29:10
Others s in darkness and gloom— Ps 107:10
there we s down and wept when we Ps 137:1
s waiting for them beside the Jr 3:2
I never s with the band of Jr 15:17
was ⌊on me⌋, I s alone, for You Jr 15:17
temple and s at the entrance Jr 26:10
entered and s at the Middle Gate Jr 39:3
and I s there stunned for seven Ezk 3:15
came to me and s down in front Ezk 14:1
and they s down in front of me. Ezk 20:1
You s on a luxurious couch with Ezk 23:41
on sackcloth, and s in ashes. Jnh 3:6
the city and s down east of it. Jnh 4:5
there and s in its shade to Jnh 4:5
Thebes that s along the Nile Nah 3:8
and after He s down, His Mt 5:1
He got into a boat and s down, Mt 13:2
it ashore, s down, and gathered Mt 13:48
up on a mountain and s there, Mt 15:29
robes on them, and He s on them. Mt 21:7
Then they s down and were Mt 27:36
a boat on the sea and s down, Mk 4:1
So they s down in ranks of Mk 6:40
on which no one has ever s. Mk 11:2
robes on it, and He s on it. Mk 11:7
into heaven and s down at the Mk 16:19
to the attendant, and s down. Lk 4:20
Then He s down and was teaching Lk 5:3
The dead man s up and began to Lk 7:15
also s at the Lord's feet and Lk 10:39
on which no one has ever s. Lk 19:30
courtyard and s down together, Lk 22:55
and Peter s among them. Lk 22:55
His journey, s down at the well Jn 4:6
a mountain and s down there with Jn 6:3
in that place, so they s down. Jn 6:10
He s down and began to teach Jn 8:2
this the man who s begging?" Jn 9:8
a young donkey and s on it, Jn 12:14
s down on the judge's bench in Jn 19:13
her eyes, saw Peter, and s up. Ac 9:40
into the synagogue and s down. Ac 13:14
and who had never walked, s Ac 14:8
We s down and spoke to the women Ac 16:13
The next day I s at the judge's Ac 25:17
The people s down to eat and 1Co 10:7
He s down at the right hand of Heb 1:3
who s down at the right hand of Heb 8:1
s down at the right hand of God. Heb 10:12
and has s down at the right hand Heb 12:2
the victory and s down with My Rv 3:21
on the thrones s 24 elders Rv 4:4

SATAN *(52)*
(AKA BAAL-ZEBUB, BEELZEBUL, DEVIL)
S stood up against Israel and 1Ch 21:1
and S also came with them. Jb 1:6
LORD asked S, "Where have you Jb 1:7
the earth," S answered Him, Jb 1:7
the LORD said to S, "Have you Jb 1:8
S answered the LORD, "Does Job Jb 1:9
the LORD told S, "everything he Jb 1:12
So S went out from the LORD'S Jb 1:12
and S also came with them to Jb 2:1
LORD asked S, "Where have you Jb 2:2
the earth," S answered Him, Jb 2:2
the LORD said to S, "Have you Jb 2:3
S answered the LORD. Jb 2:4
the LORD told S, "he is in your Jb 2:6
S left the LORD's presence and Jb 2:7
S standing at his right side Zch 3:1
The LORD said to S: "The LORD Zch 3:2
The LORD rebuke you, S! Zch 3:2

Jesus told him, "Go away, **S**! Mt 4:10
If **S** drives out Satan, he is Mt 12:26
drives out **S**, he is divided Mt 12:26
told Peter, "Get behind Me, **S**! Mt 16:23
40 days, being tempted by **S**. Mk 1:13
How can **S** drive out Satan? Mk 3:23
How can Satan drive out **S**? Mk 3:23
And if **S** rebels against himself Mk 3:26
immediately **S** comes and takes Mk 4:15
Get behind Me, **S**, because you're Mk 8:33
I watched **S** fall from heaven Lk 10:18
If **S** also is divided against Lk 11:18
S has bound this woman, a Lk 13:16
Then **S** entered Judas, called Lk 22:3
S has asked to sift you like Lk 22:31
piece of bread, **S** entered him. Jn 13:27
why has **S** filled your heart to Ac 5:3
and from the power of **S** to God, Ac 26:18
soon crush **S** under your feet Rm 16:20
that one over to **S** for the 1Co 5:5
S may tempt you because of your 1Co 7:5
not be taken advantage of by **S**; 2Co 2:11
For **S** himself is disguised as an 2Co 11:14
messenger of **S** to torment me so 2Co 12:7
and again—but **S** hindered us. 1Th 2:18
and I have delivered them to **S**, 1Tm 1:20
already turned away to follow **S**. 1Tm 5:15
not, but are a synagogue of **S**. Rv 2:9
killed among you, where **S** lives. Rv 2:13
known the deep things of **S**— Rv 2:24
those from the synagogue of **S**, Rv 3:9
who is called the Devil and **S**, Rv 12:9
serpent who is the Devil and **S**, Rv 20:2
S will be released from his Rv 20:7

SATAN'S *(2)*

one⌋ is based on **S** working, 2Th 2:9
you live—where **S** throne is! Rv 2:13

SATED *(1)*

bitterness, **s** me with wormwood Lm 3:15

SATIATED *(1)*

You will be **s** with them, and I Jl 2:19

SATISFACTION *(1)*

I will gain **s** against My foes; Is 1:24

SATISFIED *(67)*

will be able to go home **s**." Ex 18:23
you can eat, be **s**, and live Lv 25:19
that you will eat but not be **s**. Lv 26:26
and when you eat and are **s**, Dt 6:11
You will eat and be **s**. Dt 11:15
gates may come, eat, and be **s**. Dt 14:29
Then if you are not **s** with her, Dt 21:14
may eat in your towns and be **s**. Dt 26:12
She ate and was **s** and had ⌊some⌋ Ru 2:14
we eat and are **s** and there is 2Ch 31:10
Because his appetite is never **s**, Jb 20:20
their sons are **s**, and they leave Ps 17:14
I will be **s** with Your presence. Ps 17:15
The humble will eat and be **s**; Ps 22:26
will be **s** in days of hunger. Ps 37:19
they growl if they are not **s**. Ps 59:15
will be **s** with the goodness of Ps 65:4
They ate and were completely **s**, Ps 78:29
Before they had **s** their desire, Ps 78:30
the earth is **s** by the fruit of Ps 104:13
they are **s** with good things. Ps 104:28
quail and **s** them with bread Ps 105:40
For He has **s** the thirsty and Ps 107:9
A man will be **s** with good by the Pr 12:14
but the diligent is fully **s**. Pr 13:4
man eats until he is **s**, Pr 13:25
his mouth a man's stomach is **s**; Pr 18:20
Sheol and Abaddon are never **s**, Pr 27:20
and people's eyes are never **s**. Pr 27:20
Three things are never **s**; Pr 30:15
which is never **s** with water; Pr 30:16
eye is not **s** by seeing or the Ec 1:8
money is never **s** with money, Ec 5:10
is⌋ never ⌊**s**⌋ with income. Ec 5:10
he is not **s** by good things and Ec 6:3
yet the appetite is never **s**. Ec 6:7
but they are ⌊still⌋ not **s**. Is 9:20
or **s** Me with the fat of your Is 43:24
He eats the roast and is **s**. Is 44:16
and He will be **s** with His Is 53:11
should I be **s** with these? Is 57:6
may nurse and be **s** from her Is 66:11
I **s** their needs, yet they Jr 5:7
people will be **s** with My Jr 31:14
The sword will devour and be **s**; Jr 46:10
her plunderers will be fully **s**. Jr 50:10
he will be **s** in the hill country Jr 50:19
men because you were not **s**. Ezk 16:28
with them, you were still not **s**. Ezk 16:28
you were not even **s** with this! Ezk 16:29
until I have **s** My wrath on you. Ezk 24:13
the seas, you **s** many peoples. Ezk 27:33
until you are **s** and drink blood Ezk 39:19
They will eat but not be **s**; Hs 4:10
they had pasture, they became **s**; Hs 13:6
they were **s**, and their hearts Hs 13:6
have plenty to eat and be **s**. Jl 2:26
to drink water but were not **s**, Am 4:8
You will eat but not be **s**, Mc 6:14
and like Death he is never **s**. Hab 2:5
but never have enough to be **s**. Hg 1:6
the children to be **s** first, Mk 7:27
He has **s** the hungry with good Lk 1:53
be **s** with your wages." Lk 3:14
we are confident and **s** to be out 2Co 5:8
Be **s** with what you have, for He Heb 13:5
And he is not **s** with that! 3Jn 10

SATISFIES *(3)*

none of this **s** me since I see Est 5:13
He **s** you with goodness; Ps 103:5
He **s** you with the finest wheat. Ps 147:14

SATISFY *(19)*

To **s** the king of Assyria, he 2Kg 16:18
to **s** the parched wasteland and Jb 38:27
for a lioness or **s** the appetite Jb 38:39
You **s** me as with rich food; Ps 63:5
I would **s** you with honey from Ps 81:16
S us in the morning with Your Ps 90:14
will **s** him with a long life and Ps 91:16
I will **s** its needy with bread. Ps 132:15
open Your hand and **s** the desire Ps 145:16
let her breasts always **s** you; Pr 5:19
he steals to **s** himself when he Pr 6:30
your wages on what does not **s**? Is 55:2
the hungry, and **s** the afflicted Is 58:10
lead you, **s** you in a parched Is 58:11
for I **s** the thirsty person and Jr 31:25
They will not **s** their appetites Ezk 7:19
I will **s** My wrath against you, Ezk 16:42
together, and I will **s** My wrath. Ezk 21:17
make no plans to **s** the fleshly Rm 13:14

SATISFYING *(1)*

and **s** your hearts with food and Ac 14:17

SATRAPS *(13)*

to the royal **s** and governors Ezr 8:36
was intended for⌋ the royal **s**, Est 3:12
Jews, to the **s**, the governors, Est 8:9
provinces, the **s**, the governors, Est 9:3
sent word to assemble the **s**, Dn 3:2
So the **s**, prefects, governors, Dn 3:3
When the **s**, prefects, governors, Dn 3:27
to appoint 120 **s** over the Dn 6:1
These **s** would be accountable to Dn 6:2
and **s** because he had Dn 6:3
and **s**, therefore, kept Dn 6:4
and **s** went together to Dn 6:6
the prefects, **s**, advisers, Dn 6:7

SATURATED *(1)*

their soil will be **s** with fat. Is 34:7

SATURATES *(1)*

He **s** clouds with moisture; Jb 37:11

SATURATING *(1)*

there without **s** the earth, Is 55:10

SAUCE *(1)*

and dip it in the vinegar **s**." Ru 2:14

SAUL *(361)*

(AKA PAUL)

had a son named **S**, an impressive 1Sm 9:2
Kish said to his son **S**, "Take 1Sm 9:3
S and his attendant went through 1Sm 9:4
S said to the attendant who was 1Sm 9:5
S said to his attendant, 1Sm 9:7
The attendant answered **S**: 1Sm 9:8
S replied to his attendant. 1Sm 9:10
S and his attendant were 1Sm 9:14
When Samuel saw **S**, the LORD 1Sm 9:17
S approached Samuel in the gate 1Sm 9:18
S responded, "Am I not a 1Sm 9:21
Samuel took **S** and his attendant, 1Sm 9:22
to it and set it before **S**. 1Sm 9:24
So **S** ate with Samuel that 1Sm 9:24
spoke with **S** on ⌊the⌋ roof. 1Sm 9:25
Samuel called to **S** on the roof, 1Sm 9:26
S got up, and both he and 1Sm 9:26
Samuel said to **S**, "Tell the 1Sm 9:27
When **S** turned around to leave 1Sm 10:9
When **S** and his attendant arrived 1Sm 10:10
Is **S** also among the prophets?" 1Sm 10:11
"Is **S** also among the prophets?" 1Sm 10:12
Then **S** finished prophesying and 1Sm 10:13
for the donkeys," **S** answered. 1Sm 10:14
S told him, "He assured us the 1Sm 10:16
S did not tell him what Samuel 1Sm 10:16
S son of Kish was selected. 1Sm 10:21
S also went to his home in 1Sm 10:26
him a gift, but **S** said nothing. 1Sm 10:27
Just then **S** was coming in from 1Sm 11:5
S inquired, and they repeated 1Sm 11:5
When **S** heard these words, the 1Sm 11:6
march behind **S** and Samuel." 1Sm 11:7
S counted them at Bezek. 1Sm 11:8
The next day **S** organized the 1Sm 11:11
Who said that **S** should not reign 1Sm 11:12
But **S** ordered, "No one will be 1Sm 11:13
presence they made **S** king. 1Sm 11:15
and **S** and all the men of Israel 1Sm 11:15
S was 30 years old when he 1Sm 13:1
2,000 were with **S** at Michmash 1Sm 13:2
So **S** blew the ram's horn 1Sm 13:3
S has attacked the Philistine 1Sm 13:4
summoned to join **S** at Gilgal. 1Sm 13:4
S, however, was still at Gilgal, 1Sm 13:7
So **S** said, "Bring me the burnt 1Sm 13:9
So **S** went out to greet him, 1Sm 13:10
S answered, "When I saw that 1Sm 13:11
Samuel said to **S**, "You have been 1Sm 13:13
S registered the troops who were 1Sm 13:15
S, his son Jonathan, and the 1Sm 13:16
who were with **S** and Jonathan; 1Sm 13:22
only **S** and his son Jonathan had 1Sm 13:22
S was staying under the 1Sm 14:2
S said to the troops with him, 1Sm 14:17
S told Ahijah, "Bring the ark of 1Sm 14:18
While **S** spoke to the priest, 1Sm 14:19
So **S** said to the priest, "Stop 1Sm 14:19
S and all the troops with him 1Sm 14:20
who were with **S** and Jonathan. 1Sm 14:21
they also joined **S** and Jonathan 1Sm 14:22
S had placed the troops under 1Sm 14:24
Some reported to **S**: "Look, the 1Sm 14:33
S said, "You have been 1Sm 14:33
Then **S** built an altar to the 1Sm 14:35
S said, "Let's go down after the 1Sm 14:36
So **S** inquired of God, "Should I 1Sm 14:37
S said, "All you leaders of the 1Sm 14:38
So **S** said to the LORD, "God of 1Sm 14:41
Jonathan and **S** were selected, 1Sm 14:41
Then **S** said, "Cast ⌊the lot⌋ 1Sm 14:42
S commanded him, "Tell me what 1Sm 14:43
S declared to him, "May God 1Sm 14:44
But the people said to **S**, 1Sm 14:45
Then **S** gave up the pursuit of 1Sm 14:46
When **S** assumed the kingship 1Sm 14:47
so whenever **S** noticed any strong 1Sm 14:52
Samuel told **S**, "The LORD sent me 1Sm 15:1
Then **S** summoned the troops and 1Sm 15:4
S came to the city of Amalek and 1Sm 15:5
S struck down the Amalekites 1Sm 15:7
S and the troops spared Agag, 1Sm 15:9
I regret that I made **S** king, 1Sm 15:11
Samuel got up to confront **S**, 1Sm 15:12
S went to Carmel where he set up 1Sm 15:12
came to him, **S** said, "May the 1Sm 15:13
S answered, "The troops brought 1Sm 15:15
obey the LORD!" **S** answered. "I 1Sm 15:20
S answered Samuel, "I have 1Sm 15:24
Samuel replied to **S**, "I will not 1Sm 15:26
S grabbed the hem of his robe, 1Sm 15:27
S said, "I have sinned. 1Sm 15:30
back, following **S**, and Saul 1Sm 15:31
and **S** bowed down to the LORD. 1Sm 15:31
and **S** went up to his home in 1Sm 15:34
up to his home in Gibeah of **S**. 1Sm 15:34
Samuel never again visited **S**. 1Sm 15:35
mourned for **S**, and the LORD 1Sm 15:35
He had made **S** king over Israel. 1Sm 15:35
are you going to mourn for **S**, 1Sm 16:1

S will hear ⌊about it⌋ and kill 1Sm 16:2
Spirit of the LORD had left S, 1Sm 16:14
Then S commanded his servants, 1Sm 16:17
Then S dispatched messengers to 1Sm 16:19
sent them by his son David to S. 1Sm 16:20
David came to S and entered his 1Sm 16:21
his service, S admired him 1Sm 16:21
Then S sent word to Jesse: 1Sm 16:22
spirit from God ⌊troubled⌋ S, 1Sm 16:23
and S would then be relieved, 1Sm 16:23
S and the men of Israel gathered 1Sm 17:2
and are you not servants of S? 1Sm 17:8
S and all Israel heard these 1Sm 17:11
sons had followed S to the war, 1Sm 17:13
The three oldest had followed S, 1Sm 17:14
back and forth from S to tend 1Sm 17:15
They are with S and all the men 1Sm 17:19
was overheard and reported to S, 1Sm 17:31
David said to S, "Don't let 1Sm 17:32
But S replied, "You can't go 1Sm 17:33
David answered S, "Your servant 1Sm 17:34
S said to David, "Go, and may 1Sm 17:37
Then S had his own military 1Sm 17:38
David said to S, "I'm not used 1Sm 17:39
When S had seen David going out 1Sm 17:55
brought him before S with the 1Sm 17:57
S said to him, "Whose son are 1Sm 17:58
had finished speaking with S, 1Sm 18:1
S kept David with him from that 1Sm 18:2
in everything S sent him to do. 1Sm 18:5
S put him in command of the 1Sm 18:5
cities of Israel to meet King S, 1Sm 18:6
S has killed his thousands, 1Sm 18:7
S was furious and resented this 1Sm 18:8
S watched David jealously from 1Sm 18:9
from God took control of S, 1Sm 18:10
but S was holding a spear, 1Sm 18:10
S was afraid of David, because 1Sm 18:12
with David but had left from S. 1Sm 18:12
S reassigned David and made him 1Sm 18:13
When S observed that David was 1Sm 18:15
S told David, "Here is my oldest 1Sm 18:17
But S was thinking, "My hand 1Sm 18:17
and when it was reported to S, 1Sm 18:20
give her to him," S thought. 1Sm 18:21
So S said to David a second 1Sm 18:21
S then ordered his servants, 1Sm 18:22
The servants reported back to S, 1Sm 18:24
Then S replied, "Say this to 1Sm 18:25
S intended to cause David's 1Sm 18:25
Then S gave his daughter Michal 1Sm 18:27
S realized that the LORD was 1Sm 18:28
S was David's enemy from then 1Sm 18:29
S ordered his son Jonathan and 1Sm 19:1
My father S intends to kill you. 1Sm 19:2
well of David to his father S. 1Sm 19:4
S listened to Jonathan's advice 1Sm 19:6
Jonathan brought David to S, 1Sm 19:7
the LORD came on S as he was 1Sm 19:9
and S tried to pin David to the 1Sm 19:10
David eluded S and escaped. 1Sm 19:10
S sent agents to David's house 1Sm 19:11
When S sent agents to seize 1Sm 19:14
S sent the agents ⌊back⌋ to see 1Sm 19:15
S asked Michal, "Why did you 1Sm 19:17
everything S had done to him. 1Sm 19:18
was reported to S that David was 1Sm 19:19
S sent agents to seize David. 1Sm 19:20
reported to S, he sent other 1Sm 19:21
S tried again and sent a third 1Sm 19:21
Then S himself went to Ramah. 1Sm 19:22
S then removed his clothes and 1Sm 19:24
"Is S also among the prophets?" 1Sm 19:24
Abner took his place beside S, 1Sm 20:25
S did not say anything that day 1Sm 20:26
and S asked his son Jonathan, 1Sm 20:27
S became angry with Jonathan 1Sm 20:30
Then S threw his spear at 1Sm 20:33
S has killed his thousands, 1Sm 21:11
S heard that David and his men 1Sm 22:6
At that time S was in Gibeah, 1Sm 22:6
S said to his servants, "Listen, 1Sm 22:7
Then S said, "Listen, son of 1Sm 22:12
S asked him, "Why did you and 1Sm 22:13
told David that S had killed the 1Sm 22:21
that he was sure to report to S. 1Sm 22:22
was reported to S that David had 1Sm 23:7
Then S summoned all the troops 1Sm 23:8
learned that S was plotting evil 1Sm 23:9
has heard that S intends to come 1Sm 23:10
Will S come down as Your 1Sm 23:11
hand me and my men over to S?" 1Sm 23:12
was reported to S that David had 1Sm 23:13
S searched for him every day, 1Sm 23:14
he saw that S had come out to 1Sm 23:15
for my father S will never lay a 1Sm 23:17
my father S knows it is true. 1Sm 23:17
came up to S at Gibeah and said 1Sm 23:19
LORD," replied S, "for you have 1Sm 23:21
So they went to Ziph ahead of S. 1Sm 23:24
S and his men went to look for 1Sm 23:25
S heard of this and pursued 1Sm 23:25
S went along one side of the 1Sm 23:26
was hurrying to get away from S, 1Sm 23:26
S and his men were closing in on 1Sm 23:26
a messenger came to S saying, 1Sm 23:27
So S broke off his pursuit of 1Sm 23:28
When S returned from pursuing 1Sm 24:1
So S took 3,000 of Israel's 1Sm 24:2
When S came to the sheep pens 1Sm 24:3
not let them rise up against S. 1Sm 24:7
Then S left the cave and went on 1Sm 24:7
and called to S, "My lord the 1Sm 24:8
When S looked behind him, 1Sm 24:8
David said to S, "Why do you 1Sm 24:9
things to him, S replied, "Is 1Sm 24:16
David my son?" Then S wept 1Sm 24:16
David swore to S. Then Saul went 1Sm 24:22
S went back home, and David 1Sm 24:22
But S gave his daughter Michal, 1Sm 25:44
came to S at Gibeah saying 1Sm 26:1
S, accompanied by 3,000 of the 1Sm 26:2
S camped beside the road at the 1Sm 26:3
and discovered S had come there 1Sm 26:3
for certain that S had come. 1Sm 26:4
to the place where S had camped. 1Sm 26:5
the place where S and Abner son 1Sm 26:5
S was lying inside the inner 1Sm 26:5
go with me into the camp to S?" 1Sm 26:6
and S was lying there asleep in 1Sm 26:7
S recognized David's voice and 1Sm 26:17
S responded, "I have sinned. 1Sm 26:21
S said to him, "You are blessed, 1Sm 26:25
on his way, and S returned home. 1Sm 26:25
days I'll be swept away by S. 1Sm 27:1
Then S will stop searching for 1Sm 27:1
was reported to S that David had 1Sm 27:4
S had removed the mediums and 1Sm 28:3
So S gathered all Israel, and 1Sm 28:4
When S saw the Philistine camp, 1Sm 28:5
S then said to his servants, 1Sm 28:7
S disguised himself by putting 1Sm 28:8
at night, and S said, "Consult 1Sm 28:8
You surely know what S has done, 1Sm 28:9
Then S swore to her by the LORD: 1Sm 28:10
then she asked S, "Why did you 1Sm 28:12
did you deceive me? You are S!" 1Sm 28:12
Then S asked her, "What does he 1Sm 28:14
Then S knew that it was Samuel, 1Sm 28:14
Samuel asked S. "I'm in serious 1Sm 28:15
in serious trouble," replied S. 1Sm 28:15
S fell flat on the ground. 1Sm 28:20
came over to S, and she saw that 1Sm 28:21
served it to S and his servants 1Sm 28:25
servant of King S of Israel. 1Sm 29:3
S has killed his thousands, 1Sm 29:5
overtook S and his sons 1Sm 31:2
battle intensified against S, 1Sm 31:3
Then S said to his armor-bearer, 1Sm 31:4
Then S took his sword and fell 1Sm 31:4
saw that S was dead, 1Sm 31:5
S died together with his three 1Sm 31:6
away and that S and his sons 1Sm 31:7
they found S and his three sons 1Sm 31:8
the Philistines had done to S, 1Sm 31:11
the body of S and the bodies of 1Sm 31:12
the death of S, David returned 2Sm 1:1
S and his son Jonathan are dead." 2Sm 1:4
How do you know S and his son 2Sm 1:5
and there was S, leaning on his 2Sm 1:6
the sword—for S, his son 2Sm 1:12
lament for S and his son 2Sm 1:17
the shield of S, no longer 2Sm 1:21
S and Jonathan, loved and 2Sm 1:23
weep for S, who clothed you 2Sm 1:24
of Jabesh-gilead who buried S." 2Sm 2:4
kindness to S your lord when you 2Sm 2:5
for though S your lord is dead, 2Sm 2:7
Ish-bosheth son of S marched out 2Sm 2:12
and Ish-bosheth son of S, 2Sm 2:15
the house of S and the house 2Sm 3:1
the house of S becoming weaker 2Sm 3:1
the house of S and the house 2Sm 3:6
more power in the house of S. 2Sm 3:6
S had a concubine whose name 2Sm 3:7
to the house of your father S, 2Sm 3:8
the house of S and establish 2Sm 3:10
to say to Ish-bosheth son of S, 2Sm 3:14
the report about S and Jonathan 2Sm 4:4
head of Ish-bosheth son of S, 2Sm 4:8
against S and his offspring. 2Sm 4:8
told me, 'Look, S is dead,' he 2Sm 4:10
Even while S was king over us, 2Sm 5:2
him as I removed it from S; 2Sm 7:15
Jonathan son of S came to David, 2Sm 9:6
belonged to S and his family. 2Sm 9:9
you from the hand of S. 2Sm 12:7
the house of S was just coming 2Sm 16:5
of the house of S in whose place 2Sm 16:8
attendant from the house of S, 2Sm 19:17
blood shed by S and his family 2Sm 21:1
but S had tried to kill them in 2Sm 21:2
for money from S or his family, 2Sm 21:4
of the LORD at Gibeah of S, 2Sm 21:6
daughter of Aiah had borne to S, 2Sm 21:8
Merab daughter of S had borne to 2Sm 21:8
got the bones of S and his son 2Sm 21:12
Philistines killed S at Gilboa. 2Sm 21:12
buried the bones of S and his 2Sm 21:14
enemies and from the hand of S. 2Sm 22:1
Kish fathered S, and Saul 1Ch 8:33
Saul, and S fathered Jonathan 1Ch 8:33
Kish fathered S, and Saul 1Ch 9:39
Saul, and S fathered Jonathan 1Ch 9:39
pursued S and his sons 1Ch 10:2
battle intensified against S, 1Ch 10:3
Then S said to his armor-bearer, 1Ch 10:4
Then S took his sword and fell 1Ch 10:4
saw that S was dead, 1Ch 10:5
So S and his three sons died— 1Ch 10:6
away and that S and his sons 1Ch 10:7
they found S and his sons dead 1Ch 10:8
They stripped S, cut off his 1Ch 10:9
the Philistines had done to S, 1Ch 10:11
the body of S and the bodies of 1Ch 10:12
S died for his unfaithfulness to 1Ch 10:13
Even when S was king, you led us 1Ch 11:2
the presence of S son of Kish. 1Ch 12:1
Philistines to fight against S. 1Ch 12:19
if he defects to his master S." 1Ch 12:19
the relatives of S: 1Ch 12:29
allegiance to the house of S 1Ch 12:29
Samuel the seer, S son of Kish, 1Ch 26:28
those at Gibeah of S have fled. Is 10:29
the feet of a young man named S. Ac 7:58
S agreed with putting him to Ac 8:1
S, however, was ravaging the Ac 8:3
Meanwhile S, still breathing Ac 9:1
saying to him, "S, Saul, why are Ac 9:4
to him, "Saul, S, why are you Ac 9:4
Then S got up from the ground, Ac 9:8
for a man from Tarsus named S, Ac 9:11
"Brother S, the Lord Jesus, Ac 9:17
S was with the disciples in Ac 9:19
S grew more capable, and kept Ac 9:22
their plot became known to S. Ac 9:24
on the road, S had seen the Lord Ac 9:27
S was coming and going with them Ac 9:28
went to Tarsus to search for S, Ac 11:25
by means of Barnabas and S. Ac 11:30
And Barnabas and S returned to Ac 12:25
of Herod the tetrarch, and S. Ac 13:1
Me Barnabas and S for the work Ac 13:2
Barnabas and S and desired to Ac 13:7
Then S—also called Paul— Ac 13:9
God gave them S the son of Kish Ac 13:21
saying to me, 'S, Saul, why are Ac 22:7
to me, 'Saul, S, why are you Ac 22:7
said, 'Brother S, regain your Ac 22:13
language, 'S, Saul, why are Ac 26:14
language, 'Saul, S, why are you Ac 26:14

SAUL'S *(60)*

day the donkeys of S father Kish 1Sm 9:3
Now the day before S arrival, 1Sm 9:15

it out on S head, kissed him 1Sm 10:1
S uncle asked him and his 1Sm 10:14
"Tell me," S uncle asked, "what 1Sm 10:15
came to Gibeah, S ⌊hometown⌋, 1Sm 11:4
same day S son Jonathan said 1Sm 14:1
When S watchmen in Gibeah of 1Sm 14:16
S sons were Jonathan, Ishvi, and 1Sm 14:49
The name of S wife was Ahinoam 1Sm 14:50
was Abner son of S uncle Ner. 1Sm 14:50
S father was Kish. Abner's 1Sm 14:51
was fierce all of S days, 1Sm 14:52
so S servants said to him, 1Sm 16:15
and during S reign was ⌊already⌋ 1Sm 17:12
the people and S servants as 1Sm 18:5
time to give S daughter Merab 1Sm 18:19
Now S daughter Michal loved 1Sm 18:20
S servants reported these words 1Sm 18:23
than all of S officers. 1Sm 18:30
But S son Jonathan liked David 1Sm 19:1
Spirit of God came on S agents, 1Sm 19:20
One of S servants, detained 1Sm 21:7
Edomite, chief of S shepherds. 1Sm 21:7
that day from S presence and 1Sm 21:10
who was in charge of S servants, 1Sm 22:9
S son Jonathan came to David 1Sm 23:16
cut off the corner of S robe. 1Sm 24:4
cut off the corner of S robe. 1Sm 24:5
and the water jug by S head, 1Sm 26:12
They cut off S head, stripped 1Sm 31:9
on his head came from S camp. 2Sm 1:2
S sword never returned unstained, 2Sm 1:22
commander of S army, took Saul's 2Sm 2:8
took S son Ish-bosheth and moved 2Sm 2:8
S son Ish-bosheth was 40 years 2Sm 2:10
you bring S daughter Michal 2Sm 3:13
When S son ⌊Ish-bosheth⌋ heard 2Sm 4:1
S son had two men who were 2Sm 4:2
S son Jonathan had a son whose 2Sm 4:4
S daughter Michal looked down 2Sm 6:16
S daughter Michal came out to 2Sm 6:20
And S daughter Michal had no 2Sm 6:23
remaining from S family I can 2Sm 9:1
was a servant of S family named 2Sm 9:2
anyone left of S family I can 2Sm 9:3
all your grandfather S fields, 2Sm 9:7
king summoned S attendant Ziba 2Sm 9:9
Mephibosheth, S grandson, also 2Sm 19:24
the son of S son Jonathan, 2Sm 21:7
David and Jonathan, S son. 2Sm 21:7
David what S concubine Rizpah, 2Sm 21:11
up the bones of S family who had 2Sm 21:13
in the tomb of S father Kish. 2Sm 21:14
During S reign they waged war 1Ch 5:10
sons and killed S sons Jonathan, 1Ch 10:2
They were S relatives from 1Ch 12:2
Hebron to turn S kingdom over to 1Ch 12:23
not inquire of Him in S days." 1Ch 13:3
S daughter Michal looked down 1Ch 15:29

SAVAGE *(2)*

and rushed at him with **s** fury. Dn 8:6
my departure **s** wolves will come Ac 20:29

SAVE *(149)*

he tried to **s** him from them. Gn 37:21
and flees there to **s** his life, Dt 19:4
to them, and **s** us from death." Jos 2:13
quickly and **s** us! Help us, for Jos 10:6
a deliverer to **s** the Israelites. Jdg 3:9
him? Would you **s** him? Whoever Jdg 6:31
and he will begin to **s** Israel Jdg 13:5
There was no one to **s** them, Jdg 18:28
with us and **s** us from the hand 1Sm 4:3
so that He will **s** us from the 1Sm 7:8
He will **s** them from the hand of 1Sm 9:16
said, "How can this guy **s** us?" 1Sm 10:27
David I will **s** My people Israel 2Sm 3:18
my Savior, You **s** me from 2Sm 22:3
there is no one to **s** ⌊them⌋— 2Sm 22:42
S your life and the life of your 1Kg 1:12
March up and **s** me from the power 2Kg 16:7
please **s** us from his hand so 2Kg 19:19
S us, God of our salvation; 1Ch 16:35
up," God will **s** the humble. Jb 22:29
Rise up, LORD! **S** me, my God! You Ps 3:7
s me because of Your faithful Ps 6:4
s me from all my pursuers and Ps 7:1
With Your sword, **s** me from the Ps 17:13
hand, LORD, ⌊**s** me⌋ from men, Ps 17:14
there is no one to **s** ⌊them⌋— Ps 18:41
S me from the mouth of the lion! Ps 22:21
S Your people, bless Your Ps 28:9
S me by Your righteousness. Ps 31:1
a mountain fortress to **s** me. Ps 31:2
s me by Your faithful love. Ps 31:16
wicked and will **s** them because Ps 37:40
the LORD will **s** him in a day of Ps 41:1
S me from the guilt of bloodshed, Ps 51:14
God, **s** me by Your name, and Ps 54:1
to God, and the LORD will **s** me. Ps 55:16
and **s** me from men of bloodshed. Ps 59:2
S with Your right hand, and Ps 60:5
S me, God, for the water has Ps 69:1
for God will **s** Zion and build up Ps 69:35
listen closely to me and **s** me. Ps 71:2
the command to **s** me, for You are Ps 71:3
and helpless and **s** the lives of Ps 72:13
to judge and to **s** all the lowly Ps 76:9
Your power and come to **s** us. Ps 80:2
s them from the hand of the Ps 82:4
s Your servant who trusts in You. Ps 86:2
s the son of Your female servant. Ps 86:16
Who can **s** himself from the power Ps 89:48
S us, LORD our God, and gather Ps 106:47
S with Your right hand and Ps 108:6
s me according to Your faithful Ps 109:26
to **s** him from those who would Ps 109:31
name of the LORD: "LORD, **s** me!" Ps 116:4
LORD, **s** us! LORD, please grant Ps 118:25
s me, for I have sought Your Ps 119:94
s me, and I will keep Your Ps 119:146
Your right hand will **s** me. Ps 138:7
in nobles, in man, who cannot **s**. Ps 146:3
and **s** those stumbling toward Pr 24:11
LORD is our King. He will **s** us. Is 33:22
is coming; He will **s** you." Is 35:4
s us from his hand so that all Is 37:20
The LORD will **s** me; we will play Is 38:20
prays to it, "**S** me, for you are Is 44:17
and pray to a god who cannot **s**, Is 45:20
I will bear and **s** ⌊you⌋. Is 46:4
So let them stand and **s** you— Is 47:13
his own way; no one can **s** you. Is 47:15
and I will **s** your children. Is 49:25
hand is not too short to **s**, Is 59:1
vindication, powerful to **s**. Is 63:1
they beg: Rise up and **s** us! Jr 2:27
rise up and **s** you in your time Jr 2:28
will not **s** them in their time Jr 11:12
like a warrior unable to **s**? Jr 14:9
am with you to **s** you and deliver Jr 15:20
s me, and I will be saved, for Jr 17:14
without fail **s** you from far away Jr 30:10
LORD's declaration—to **s** you! Jr 30:11
LORD, **s** Your people, the remnant Jr 31:7
am with you to **s** you and deliver Jr 42:11
fail I will **s** you from far away Jr 46:27
Flee! **S** your lives! Be like a Jr 48:6
s your lives, each of you! Jr 51:6
S your lives, each of you, from Jr 51:45
way in order to **s** his life— Ezk 3:18
be unable to **s** them in the day Ezk 7:19
from his evil way to **s** his life, Ezk 13:22
person will not **s** him on the day Ezk 33:12
I will **s** My flock, and they will Ezk 34:22
I will **s** you from all your Ezk 36:29
I will **s** them from all their Ezk 37:23
that he may **s** you in all your Hs 13:10
will not **s** us, we will not Hs 14:3
the brave will not **s** his life. Am 2:14
of foot will not **s** himself, Am 2:15
a horse will not **s** his life. Am 2:15
you cannot **s**, and what you do Mc 6:14
and what you do **s**, I will give Mc 6:14
about violence and You do not **s**? Hab 1:2
You come out to **s** Your people, Hab 3:13
Your people, to **s** Your anointed. Hab 3:13
I will **s** the lame and gather the Zph 3:19
I will **s** My people from the land Zch 8:7
so I will **s** you, and you will Zch 8:13
their God will **s** them on that Zch 9:16
The LORD will **s** the tents of Zch 12:7
because He will **s** His people Mt 1:21
Him up, saying, "Lord, **s** ⌊us⌋! Mt 8:25
sink he cried out, "Lord, **s** me!" Mt 14:30
whoever wants to **s** his life will Mt 16:25
of Man has come to **s** the lost. Mt 18:11
it in three days, **s** Yourself! Mt 27:40
others, but He cannot **s** Himself! Mt 27:42
see if Elijah comes to **s** Him!" Mt 27:49
do evil, to **s** life or to kill? Mk 3:4
whoever wants to **s** his life will Mk 8:35
of Me and the gospel will **s** it. Mk 8:35
s Yourself by coming down from Mk 15:30
others; He cannot **s** Himself! Mk 15:31
to **s** life or to destroy it?" Lk 6:9
to come and **s** the life of his Lk 7:3
whoever wants to **s** his life will Lk 9:24
life because of Me will **s** it. Lk 9:24
come to seek and to **s** the lost." Lk 19:10
let Him **s** Himself if this is Lk 23:35
King of the Jews, **s** Yourself!" Lk 23:37
the Messiah? **S** Yourself and us! Lk 23:39
I say—Father, **s** Me from this Jn 12:27
the world but to **s** the world. Jn 12:47
because he wanted to **s** Paul, Ac 27:43
jealous and **s** some of them. Rm 11:14
was pleased to **s** those who 1Co 1:21
whether you will **s** your husband? 1Co 7:16
whether you will **s** your wife? 1Co 7:16
that I may by all means **s** some. 1Co 9:22
aside and **s** to the extent that 1Co 16:2
not obligated to **s** up for their 2Co 12:14
into the world to **s** sinners"— 1Tm 1:15
this you will **s** both yourself 1Tm 4:16
was able to **s** Him from death, Heb 5:7
always able to **s** those who come Heb 7:25
word, which is able to **s** you. Jms 1:21
have works? Can his faith **s** him? Jms 2:14
who is able to **s** and to destroy. Jms 4:12
of faith will **s** the sick person, Jms 5:15
of his way will **s** his life from Jms 5:20
s others by snatching ⌊them⌋ Jd 23

SAVED *(86)*

Haven't you **s** a blessing for me? Gn 27:36
said, "You have **s** our lives. Gn 47:25
That day the LORD **s** Israel from Ex 14:30
you, a people **s** by the LORD? Dt 33:29
who **s** them from the power of Jdg 2:16
was with him and **s** the people Jdg 2:18
because it was **s** for you for 1Sm 9:24
So the LORD **s** Israel that day. 1Sm 14:23
and I was **s** from my enemies. 2Sm 22:4
So the LORD **s** Hezekiah and the 2Ch 32:22
the report that **s** the king." Est 7:9
and I was **s** from my enemies. Ps 18:3
A king is not **s** by a large army; Ps 33:16
heard ⌊him⌋ and **s** him from all Ps 34:6
with favor, and we will be **s**. Ps 80:3
with favor, and we will be **s**. Ps 80:7
with favor, and we will be **s**. Ps 80:19
Yet He **s** them because of His Ps 106:8
He **s** them from the hand of the Ps 106:10
He **s** them from their distress. Ps 107:13
He **s** them from their distress. Ps 107:19
I was helpless, and He **s** me. Ps 116:6
They will not be stored or **s**, Is 23:18
waited for Him, and He has **s** us. Is 25:9
declared, **s**, and proclaimed Is 43:12
Israel will be **s** by the LORD Is 45:17
to Me and be **s**, all the ends Is 45:22
Angel of His Presence **s** them. Is 63:9
remain in Your ways and be **s**. Is 64:5
ended, but we have not been **s**. Jr 8:20
and I will be **s**, for You are my Jr 17:14
In His days Judah will be **s**, Jr 23:6
In those days Judah will be **s**, Jr 33:16
but you will have **s** your life. Ezk 3:19
and you will have **s** your life." Ezk 3:21
he would have **s** his life. Ezk 33:5
but you will have **s** your life. Ezk 33:9
on the name of Yahweh will be **s**, Jl 2:32
and asked, "Then who can be **s**?" Mt 19:25
He **s** others, but He cannot save Mt 27:42
another, "Then who can be **s**?" Mk 10:26
and saying, "He **s** others; Mk 15:31
and is baptized will be **s**, Mk 16:16
woman, "Your faith has **s** you. Lk 7:50
they may not believe and be **s**. Lk 8:12
Him, "are there few being **s**?" Lk 13:23
this asked, "Then who can be **s**?" Lk 18:26
scoffing: "He **s** others; let Him Lk 23:35
world might be **s** through Him. Jn 3:17
things so that you may be **s**. Jn 5:34
will be **s** and will come in and Jn 10:9
the name of the Lord will be **s**. Ac 2:21

s from this corrupt generation! Ac 2:40
to them those who were being s. Ac 2:47
people by which we must be s." Ac 4:12
all your household will be s.' Ac 11:14
by Moses, you cannot be s!" Ac 15:1
believe we are s through the Ac 15:11
Sirs, what must I do to be s?" Ac 16:30
and you will be s—you and your Ac 16:31
we would be s was disappearing Ac 27:20
in the ship, you cannot be s." Ac 27:31
we will be s through Him from Rm 5:9
will we be s by His life! Rm 5:10
Now in this hope we were s, Rm 8:24
only the remnant will be s; Rm 9:27
from the dead, you will be s. Rm 10:9
the name of the Lord will be s. Rm 10:13
this way all Israel will be s, Rm 11:26
us who are being s it is God's 1Co 1:18
will be lost, but he will be s; 1Co 3:15
his spirit may be s in the Day 1Co 5:5
of many, that they may be s. 1Co 10:33
are also s by it, if you hold 1Co 15:2
who are being s and among those 2Co 2:15
trespasses. By grace you are s! Eph 2:5
grace you are s through faith, Eph 2:8
Gentiles so that they may be s. 1Th 2:16
of the truth in order to be s. 2Th 2:10
everyone to be s and to come to 1Tm 2:4
But she will be s through 1Tm 2:15
who has s us and called us with 2Tm 1:9
He s us—not by works of Ti 3:5
people—were s through water. 1Pt 3:20
righteous is s with difficulty 1Pt 4:18
first of all s a people out Jd 5

SAVES *(12)*

who s you from all your troubles 1Sm 10:19
no one s us, we will surrender 1Sm 11:3
as the LORD lives who s Israel, 1Sm 14:39
or by spear that the LORD s, 1Sm 17:47
He s the needy from their sharp Jb 5:15
who s the upright in heart. Ps 7:10
He s those crushed in spirit. Ps 34:18
down from heaven and s me, Ps 57:3
their cry for help and s them. Ps 145:19
it s no one from his trouble. Is 46:7
is among you, a warrior who s. Zph 3:17
to this, now s you (not the 1Pt 3:21

SAVING *(4)*

me great kindness by s my life. Gn 19:19
can keep the LORD from s, 1Sm 14:6
performing s acts on the earth. Ps 74:12
you that this s work of God has Ac 28:28

SAVIOR *(42)*

my refuge, and my S, You save me 2Sm 22:3
S of all who seek refuge from Ps 17:7
Hurry to help me, Lord, my S. Ps 38:22
praise Him, my S and my God. Ps 42:5
praise Him, my S and my God. Ps 42:11
praise Him, my S and my God. Ps 43:5
forgot God their S, who did Ps 106:21
GOD, my strong S, You shield my Ps 140:7
will send them a s and leader, Is 19:20
Israel, and your S, give Egypt Is 43:3
and there is no other S but Me. Is 43:11
hides Himself, God of Israel, S. Is 45:15
but Me, a righteous God and S; Is 45:21
the LORD, am your S, and your Is 49:26
LORD, am your S and Redeemer, Is 60:16
and He became their S. Is 63:8
its S in time of distress, Jr 14:8
and no S exists besides Me. Hs 13:4
spirit has rejoiced in God my S, Lk 1:47
today a S, who is Messiah the Lk 2:11
really is the S of the world." Jn 4:42
His right hand as ruler and S, Ac 5:31
God brought the S, Jesus, to Ac 13:23
He is the S of the body. Eph 5:23
we also eagerly wait for a S, Php 3:20
of God our S and of Christ 1Tm 1:1
good, and it pleases God our S, 1Tm 2:3
God, who is the S of everyone, 1Tm 4:10
appearing of our S Christ Jesus, 2Tm 1:10
by the command of God our S: Ti 1:3
Father and Christ Jesus our S. Ti 1:4
of God our S in everything. Ti 2:10
glory of our great God and S, Ti 2:13
for man appeared from God our S, Ti 3:4
through Jesus Christ our S, Ti 3:6
of our God and S Jesus Christ. 2Pt 1:1
of our Lord and S Jesus Christ. 2Pt 1:11
of our Lord and S Jesus Christ, 2Pt 2:20
our Lord and S ⌊given⌋ through 2Pt 3:2
of our Lord and S Jesus Christ. 2Pt 3:18
sent the Son as S of the world. 1Jn 4:14
only God our S, through Jesus Jd 25

SAVIORS *(1)*

S will ascend Mount Zion to rule Ob 21

SAW *(577)*

God s that the light was good, Gn 1:4
And God s that it was good. Gn 1:10
And God s that it was good. Gn 1:12
And God s that it was good. Gn 1:18
And God s that it was good. Gn 1:21
And God s that it was good. Gn 1:25
God s all that He had made, Gn 1:31
Then the woman s that the tree Gn 3:6
the sons of God s that the Gn 6:2
When the LORD s that man's Gn 6:5
God s how corrupt the earth was, Gn 6:12
ark's cover and s that the Gn 8:13
s his father naked and told his Gn 9:22
the Egyptians s that the woman Gn 12:14
officials s her and praised her Gn 12:15
looked out and s that the entire Gn 13:10
ever since she s that she was Gn 16:5
and he s three men standing near Gn 18:2
When he s them, he ran from the Gn 18:2
When Lot s ⌊them⌋, he got up to Gn 19:1
and he s that smoke was going up Gn 19:28
But Sarah s the son mocking— Gn 21:9
and she s a well of water. Gn 21:19
Abraham looked up and s the Gn 22:4
looked up and s a ram caught by Gn 22:13
looking up, he s camels coming. Gn 24:63
up, and when she s Isaac, she Gn 24:64
He looked and s a well in a Gn 29:2
As soon as Jacob s his uncle Gn 29:10
When the LORD s that Leah was Gn 29:31
When Rachel s that she was not Gn 30:1
When Leah s that she had stopped Gn 30:9
And Jacob s from Laban's face Gn 31:2
s in a dream that the streaked, Gn 31:10
he s them, Jacob said, "This Gn 32:2
When the man s that He could not Gn 32:25
looked up and s Esau coming Gn 33:1
Esau looked up and s the women Gn 33:5
the region, s her, he took her Gn 34:2
his brothers s that their father Gn 37:4
They s him in the distance, Gn 37:18
to the pit and s that Joseph was Gn 37:29
There Judah s the daughter of a Gn 38:2
she s that, though Shelah had Gn 38:14
When Judah s her, he thought she Gn 38:15
When his master s that the LORD Gn 39:3
s that they looked distraught. Gn 40:6
When the chief baker s that the Gn 40:16
When Joseph s his brothers, Gn 42:7
We s his deep distress when he Gn 42:21
and he s his money there at the Gn 42:27
and their father s their bags of Gn 42:35
Joseph s Benjamin with them, Gn 43:16
he looked up and s his brother Gn 43:29
and when he s the wagons that Gn 45:27
When Israel s Joseph's sons, Gn 48:8
When Joseph s that his father Gn 48:17
He s that his resting place was Gn 49:15
of the land s the mourning at Gn 50:11
brothers s that their father Gn 50:15
He s Ephraim's sons to the third Gn 50:23
she s that he was beautiful, Ex 2:2
she opened it, she s the child— Ex 2:6
He s an Egyptian beating a Ex 2:11
he went out and s two Hebrews Ex 2:13
s the Israelites, and He took Ex 2:25
he s that the bush was on fire Ex 3:2
When the LORD s that he had gone Ex 3:4
foremen s that they were Ex 5:19
when Pharaoh s there was relief Ex 8:15
messengers⌋ who s that not a Ex 9:7
When Pharaoh s that the rain, Ex 9:34
ancestors never s since the time Ex 10:6
looked up and s the Egyptians Ex 14:10
and Israel s the Egyptians dead Ex 14:30
When Israel s the great power Ex 14:31
the Israelites s it, they asked Ex 16:15
father-in-law s everything he Ex 18:14
When the people s ⌊it⌋ they Ex 20:18
and they s the God of Israel. Ex 24:10
they s Him, and they ate and Ex 24:11
When the people s that Moses Ex 32:1
When Aaron s ⌊this⌋, he built an Ex 32:5
the camp and s the calf Ex 32:19
Moses s that the people were out Ex 32:25
all the people s the pillar of Ex 33:10
and all the Israelites s Moses, Ex 34:30
And when all the people s it, Lv 9:24
he s that she was diseased Nm 12:10
also s the descendants of Anak Nm 13:28
the people we s in it are men Nm 13:32
We even s the Nephilim there." Nm 13:33
and s that the plague had begun Nm 16:47
the testimony and s that Aaron's Nm 17:8
They s ⌊them⌋, and each man took Nm 17:9
whole community s that Aaron had Nm 20:29
son of Zippor s all that Israel Nm 22:2
When the donkey s the Angel of Nm 22:23
The donkey s the Angel of the Nm 22:25
When the donkey s the Angel of Nm 22:27
and he s the Angel of the LORD Nm 22:31
The donkey s Me and turned away Nm 22:33
From there he s the outskirts of Nm 22:41
Since Balaam s that it pleased Nm 24:1
looked up and s Israel encamped Nm 24:2
Then Balaam s Amalek and Nm 24:20
Next he s the Kenites and Nm 24:21
the priest, s ⌊this⌋, he got up Nm 25:7
they s that the region was a Nm 32:1
as Eshcol Valley and s the land, Nm 32:9
wilderness you s on the way to Dt 1:19
We also s the descendants of the Dt 1:28
just as you s Him do for you in Dt 1:30
And you s in the wilderness how Dt 1:31
the great trials that you s, Dt 7:19
I s how you had sinned against Dt 9:16
experienced or s the discipline Dt 11:2
heard our cry and s our misery, Dt 26:7
You s with your own eyes the Dt 29:3
s their detestable images and Dt 29:17
When the LORD s ⌊this⌋, He Dt 32:19
looked up and s a man standing Jos 5:13
When I s among the spoils a Jos 7:21
king of Ai s ⌊the Israelites⌋ Jos 8:14
and all Israel s that the ⌊men Jos 8:21
Your own eyes s what I did to Jos 24:7
The spies s a man coming out of Jdg 1:24
worried and s that he had still Jdg 3:25
When Gaal s the people, he said Jdg 9:36
the Israelites s that Abimelech Jdg 9:55
When he s her, he tore his Jdg 11:35
When I s that you weren't going Jdg 12:3
Manoah and his wife s ⌊this⌋, Jdg 13:20
to Timnah and s a young Jdg 14:1
When the Philistines s him, Jdg 14:11
where he s a prostitute and went Jdg 16:1
When the people s him, they Jdg 16:24
They s that the people who were Jdg 18:7
because he s that they were Jdg 18:26
when the girl's father s him, Jdg 19:3
he looked up and s the traveler Jdg 19:17
Everyone who s it said, "Nothing Jdg 19:30
When Naomi s that Ruth was Ru 1:18
her mother-in-law s what she had Ru 2:18
the men of Ashdod s what was 1Sm 5:7
they looked up and s the ark, 1Sm 6:13
city when they s Samuel coming 1Sm 9:14
Samuel s Saul, the LORD told 1Sm 9:17
previously and s him prophesy 1Sm 10:11
When we s they weren't there, 1Sm 10:14
But when you s that Nahash king 1Sm 12:12
men of Israel s that they were 1Sm 13:6
When I s that the troops were 1Sm 13:11
they s the panicking troops 1Sm 14:16
the roll and s that Jonathan 1Sm 14:17
the forest, they s the flow of 1Sm 14:26
Samuel s Eliab and said, 1Sm 16:6
all the Israelite men s Goliath, 1Sm 17:24
Philistine looked and s David, 1Sm 17:42
Philistines s that their hero 1Sm 17:51
You s it and rejoiced, so why 1Sm 19:5
they s the group of prophets 1Sm 19:20
I s Jesse's son come to 1Sm 22:9
Horesh when he s that Saul had 1Sm 23:15
she s David and his men coming 1Sm 25:20
Abigail s David, she quickly 1Sm 25:23

He **s** the place where Saul and 1Sm 26:5
No one **s** them, no one knew, and 1Sm 26:12
When Saul **s** the Philistine camp, 1Sm 28:5
When the woman **s** Samuel, she 1Sm 28:12
and she **s** that he was terrified 1Sm 28:21
his armor-bearer **s** that Saul was 1Sm 31:5
of the Jordan **s** that Israel's 1Sm 31:7
When he turned around and **s** me, 2Sm 1:7
the window and **s** King David 2Sm 6:16
When Joab **s** that there was a 2Sm 10:9
the Ammonites **s** that the 2Sm 10:14
When the Arameans **s** that they 2Sm 10:15
subjects **s** that they had been 2Sm 10:19
the roof he **s** a woman bathing 2Sm 11:2
When David **s** that his servants 2Sm 12:19
two years but never **s** the king. 2Sm 14:28
One of the men **s** ⌊him⌋ and 2Sm 18:10
I just **s** Absalom hanging in an 2Sm 18:10
"You just **s** ⌊him⌋!" Joab 2Sm 18:11
looked out and **s** a man running 2Sm 18:24
the watchman **s** another man 2Sm 18:26
your servant, I **s** a big 2Sm 18:29
When David **s** the angel striking 2Sm 24:17
looked down and **s** the king and 2Sm 24:20
because they **s** that God's wisdom 1Kg 3:28
I came and **s** with my own eyes 1Kg 10:7
When all Israel **s** that the king 1Kg 12:16
passing by who **s** the corpse 1Kg 13:25
When Zimri **s** that the city was 1Kg 16:18
When Ahab **s** Elijah, Ahab said to 1Kg 18:17
all the people **s** it, they fell 1Kg 18:39
I **s** all Israel scattered on the 1Kg 22:17
I **s** the LORD sitting on His 1Kg 22:19
commanders **s** Jehoshaphat, 1Kg 22:32
commanders **s** that he was not 1Kg 22:33
Then he never **s** Elijah again. 2Kg 2:12
facing him, **s** him, they said, 2Kg 2:15
the Moabites **s** that the water 2Kg 3:22
king of Moab **s** that the battle 2Kg 3:26
the man of God **s** her at a 2Kg 4:25
When Naaman **s** someone running 2Kg 5:21
looked and **s** that the mountain 2Kg 6:17
When the king of Israel **s** them, 2Kg 6:21
the people **s** that there was 2Kg 6:30
They **s** that the whole way was 2Kg 7:15
He **s** Jehu's troops approaching 2Kg 9:17
When Joram **s** Jehu he asked, 2Kg 9:22
'As surely as I **s** the blood of 2Kg 9:26
Ahaziah of Judah **s** ⌊what was 2Kg 9:27
mother, **s** that her son was 2Kg 11:1
Whenever they **s** there was a 2Kg 12:10
for He **s** the oppression the king 2Kg 13:4
they **s** a marauding band, 2Kg 13:21
For the LORD **s** that the 2Kg 14:26
When he **s** the altar that was in 2Kg 16:10
from Damascus, he **s** the altar. 2Kg 16:12
he **s** the tombs there on the 2Kg 23:16
when Neco **s** him he killed him 2Kg 23:29
his armor-bearer **s** that Saul was 1Ch 10:5
the valley **s** that the army had 1Ch 10:7
the window and **s** King David 1Ch 15:29
When Joab **s** that there was a 1Ch 19:10
the Ammonites **s** that the 1Ch 19:15
subjects **s** that they had been 1Ch 19:19
David looked up and **s** the angel 1Ch 21:16
when he turned and **s** the angel. 1Ch 21:20
when Ornan looked and **s** David, 1Ch 21:21
when David **s** that the LORD 1Ch 21:28
I came and **s** with my own eyes 2Ch 9:6
When all Israel **s** that the king 2Ch 10:16
When the LORD **s** that they had 2Ch 12:7
when they **s** that the LORD his 2Ch 15:9
I **s** all Israel scattered on the 2Ch 18:16
I **s** the LORD sitting on His 2Ch 18:18
commanders **s** Jehoshaphat, 2Ch 18:31
commanders **s** that he was not 2Ch 18:32
mother, **s** that her son was 2Ch 22:10
and when they **s** that there was a 2Ch 24:11
the Arameans **s** that Joash had 2Ch 24:25
turned to him and **s** that he was 2Ch 26:20
Hezekiah **s** that Sennacherib had 2Ch 32:2
when they **s** the foundation Ezr 3:12
You **s** the oppression of our Neh 9:9
At that time I **s** people in Judah Neh 13:15
those days I also **s** Jews who had Neh 13:23
the sight of everyone who **s** her. Est 2:15
When Haman **s** that Mordecai was Est 3:5
soon as the king **s** Queen Esther Est 5:2

But when Haman **s** Mordecai at the Est 5:9
him because they **s** that his Jb 2:13
him, saying, "I never **s** you." Jb 8:18
eye that **s** him will see ⌊him⌋ Jb 20:9
the young men **s** me and withdrew, Jb 29:8
and when they **s** me, they spoke Jb 29:11
when I **s** that I had support Jb 31:21
But when he **s** that the three men Jb 32:5
after this and **s** his children Jb 42:16
me and say, "Aha, aha! We **s** it!" Ps 35:21
s it, LORD; do not be silent. Ps 35:22
s the prosperity of the wicked. Ps 73:3
waters **s** You, God. The waters Ps 77:16
God. The waters **s** You; they Ps 77:16
They **s** the LORD's works, His Ps 107:24
Your eyes **s** me when I was Ps 139:16
I **s** among the inexperienced, Pr 7:7
I **s**, and took it to heart; Pr 24:32
I **s** that all labor and all Ec 4:4
I **s** futility under the sun: Ec 4:7
s all the living who move about Ec 4:15
circumstances, I **s** the wicked Ec 8:10
Again I **s** under the sun that the Ec 9:11
son of Amoz **s** during the reigns Is 1:1
son of Amoz **s** concerning Judah Is 2:1
for justice but **s** injustice, Is 5:7
s the Lord seated on a high and Is 6:1
Does a **s** magnify itself above Is 10:15
that Isaiah son of Amoz **s**: Is 13:1
You **s** that there were many Is 22:9
The LORD **s** that there was no Is 59:15
He **s** that there was no man— Is 59:16
treacherous sister Judah **s** it. Jr 3:7
of Samaria I **s** something Jr 23:13
also I **s** a horrible thing Jr 23:14
When he **s** them, Zedekiah king of Jr 39:4
people with Ishmael **s** Johanan Jr 41:13
good things and **s** no disaster, Jr 44:17
Your prophets **s** visions for you Lm 2:14
They **s** oracles for you that were Lm 2:14
opened and I **s** visions of God. Ezk 1:1
His waist up, I **s** a gleam like Ezk 1:27
I also **s** what looked like fire. Ezk 1:27
When I **s** ⌊it⌋, I fell facedown Ezk 1:28
I looked and **s** a hand reaching Ezk 2:9
I **s** the glory of the God of Ezk 8:4
and I **s** women sitting there Ezk 8:14
And I **s** six men coming from the Ezk 9:2
Among them I **s** Jaazaniah son of Ezk 11:1
to Jerusalem and **s** a vision of Ezk 13:16
by you and **s** you lying in your Ezk 16:6
Then I passed by you and **s** you, Ezk 16:8
I removed them when I **s** ⌊this⌋. Ezk 16:50
When she **s** that she waited ⌊in Ezk 19:5
them and they **s** any high hill Ezk 20:28
her sister Oholibah **s** ⌊this⌋, Ezk 23:11
And I **s** that she had defiled Ezk 23:13
when she **s** male figures carved Ezk 23:14
and I **s** a man whose appearance Ezk 40:3
I **s** that the temple had a raised Ezk 41:8
and I **s** the glory of the God of Ezk 43:2
The vision I **s** was like the one Ezk 43:3
I **s** a place there at the far Ezk 46:19
I **s** a very large number of trees Ezk 47:7
happen⌋ if he **s** your faces Dn 1:10
You **s** the feet and toes, partly Dn 2:41
You **s** the iron mixed with clay, Dn 2:41
You **s** the iron mixed with clay— Dn 2:43
You **s** a stone break off from the Dn 2:45
they **s** that the fire had no Dn 3:27
visions of my dream that I **s**, Dn 4:9
as I was lying in bed, I **s** this: Dn 4:10
I also **s** in the visions of my Dn 4:13
The tree you **s**, which grew large Dn 4:20
The king **s** an observer, a holy Dn 4:23
and I **s** One like a son of man Dn 7:13
s the vision, and as I watched, Dn 8:2
I **s** in the vision that I was Dn 8:2
s the ram charging to the west, Dn 8:4
I **s** him approaching the ram, Dn 8:7
ram that you **s** represents the Dn 8:20
Only I, Daniel, **s** the vision. Dn 10:7
When Ephraim **s** his sickness and Hs 5:13
I **s** your fathers like the first Hs 9:10
what he **s** regarding Israel in Am 1:1
I **s** the LORD standing beside the Am 9:1
Then God **s** their actions— Jnh 3:10
what he **s** regarding Samaria and Mc 1:1

that Habakkuk the prophet **s**. Hab 1:1
among you who **s** this house in Hg 2:3
in the night and **s** a man riding Zch 1:8
I looked up and **s** four horns. Zch 1:18
I looked up and **s** a man with a Zch 2:1
up again and **s** a flying scroll. Zch 5:1
Then I looked up and **s** two women Zch 5:9
up again and **s** four chariots Zch 6:1
we **s** His star in the east and Mt 2:2
When they **s** the star, they were Mt 2:10
they **s** the child with Mary His Mt 2:11
when he **s** that he had been Mt 2:16
When he **s** many of the Pharisees Mt 3:7
and He **s** the Spirit of God Mt 3:16
of Galilee, He **s** two brothers, Mt 4:18
on from there, He **s** two other Mt 4:21
When He **s** the crowds, He went up Mt 5:1
He **s** his mother-in-law lying in Mt 8:14
When Jesus **s** large crowds around Mt 8:18
When they **s** Him, they begged Him Mt 8:34
the crowds **s** this, they were Mt 9:8
He **s** a man named Matthew sitting Mt 9:9
When the Pharisees **s** this, Mt 9:11
But Jesus turned and **s** her. Mt 9:22
He **s** the flute players and a Mt 9:23
When He **s** the crowds, He felt Mt 9:36
But when the Pharisees **s** it, Mt 12:2
There He **s** a man who had a Mt 12:10
ashore, He **s** a huge crowd, felt Mt 14:14
When the disciples **s** Him walking Mt 14:26
when he **s** the strength of the Mt 14:30
when they **s** those unable to Mt 15:31
looked up they **s** no one except Mt 17:8
other slaves **s** what had taken Mt 18:31
he **s** others standing in the Mt 20:3
and the scribes **s** the wonders Mt 21:15
the disciples **s** it, they were Mt 21:20
you, when you **s** it, didn't even Mt 21:32
the tenant farmers **s** the son, Mt 21:38
he **s** a man there who was not Mt 22:11
the disciples **s** it, they were Mt 26:8
another woman **s** him and told Mt 26:71
Pilate **s** that he was getting Mt 27:24
s the earthquake and the things Mt 27:54
When they **s** Him, they worshiped, Mt 28:17
He **s** the heavens being torn open Mk 1:10
of Galilee, He **s** Simon and Mk 1:16
s James the son of Zebedee and Mk 1:19
He **s** Levi the son of Alphaeus Mk 2:14
of the Pharisees **s** that He was Mk 2:16
the unclean spirits **s** Him, Mk 3:11
When he **s** Jesus from a distance, Mk 5:6
to Jesus and **s** the man who had Mk 5:15
and when he **s** Jesus, he fell at Mk 5:22
house, and He **s** a commotion— Mk 5:38
but many **s** them leaving and Mk 6:33
He **s** a huge crowd and had Mk 6:34
He **s** them being battered as they Mk 6:48
When they **s** Him walking on the Mk 6:49
for they all **s** Him and were Mk 6:50
man's eyes, and he **s** distinctly. Mk 8:25
no longer **s** anyone with them Mk 9:8
they **s** a large crowd around them Mk 9:14
when the whole crowd **s** Him, Mk 9:15
When the spirit **s** Him, it Mk 9:20
When Jesus **s** that a crowd was Mk 9:25
we **s** someone driving out demons Mk 9:38
Jesus **s** it, He was indignant Mk 10:14
s the fig tree withered from Mk 11:20
them debating and **s** that Jesus Mk 12:28
When Jesus **s** that he answered Mk 12:34
she **s** Peter warming himself, Mk 14:67
When the servant **s** him again she Mk 14:69
s the way He breathed His last, Mk 15:39
they **s** a young man dressed in a Mk 16:5
those who **s** Him after He had Mk 16:14
When Zechariah **s** him, he was Lk 1:12
death before he **s** the Lord's Lk 2:26
His parents **s** Him, they were Lk 2:48
s two boats at the edge of the Lk 5:2
Simon Peter **s** this, he fell at Lk 5:8
He **s** Jesus, fell facedown, and Lk 5:12
went out and **s** a tax collector Lk 5:27
When the Lord **s** her, He had Lk 7:13
who had invited Him **s** this, Lk 7:39
When he **s** Jesus, he cried out, Lk 8:28
who tended them **s** what had Lk 8:34
When the woman **s** that she was Lk 8:47

they **s** His glory and the two men Lk 9:32
we **s** someone driving out demons Lk 9:49
disciples James and John **s** this, Lk 9:54
When he **s** him, he passed by on Lk 10:31
arrived at the place and **s** him, Lk 10:32
him, and when he **s** ⌊the man⌋, he Lk 10:33
When the Pharisee **s** this, he was Lk 11:38
When Jesus **s** her, He called out Lk 13:12
his father **s** him and was filled Lk 15:20
looked up and **s** Abraham a long Lk 16:23
He **s** them, He told them, "Go Lk 17:14
but when the disciples **s** it, Lk 18:15
when they **s** it, gave praise Lk 18:43
All who **s** it began to complain, Lk 19:7
As He approached and **s** the city, Lk 19:41
when the tenant farmers **s** him, Lk 20:14
He looked up and **s** the rich Lk 21:1
He also **s** a poor widow dropping Lk 21:2
around Him **s** what was going Lk 22:49
When a servant **s** him sitting in Lk 22:56
someone else **s** him and said, Lk 22:58
the centurion **s** what happened, Lk 23:47
they **s** what had taken place, Lk 23:48
he **s** only the linen cloths. Lk 24:12
The next day John **s** Jesus coming Jn 1:29
When he **s** Jesus passing by, Jn 1:36
So they went and **s** where He was Jn 1:39
When Jesus **s** him, He said, "You Jn 1:42
Then Jesus **s** Nathanael coming Jn 1:47
the fig tree, I **s** you," Jesus Jn 1:48
I told you I **s** you under the fig Jn 1:50
name when they **s** the signs He Jn 2:23
When Jesus **s** him lying there and Jn 5:6
because they **s** the signs that Jn 6:2
When the people **s** the sign He Jn 6:14
they **s** Jesus walking on the sea. Jn 6:19
When the crowd **s** that neither Jn 6:24
not because you **s** the signs, Jn 6:26
My day; he **s** it and rejoiced. Jn 8:56
He **s** a man blind from birth. Jn 9:1
consoling her **s** that Mary got up Jn 11:31
to where Jesus was and **s** Him, Jn 11:32
When Jesus **s** her crying, and the Jn 11:33
came to Mary and **s** what He did Jn 11:45
things because he **s** His glory Jn 12:41
and the temple police **s** Him, Jn 19:6
When Jesus **s** His mother and the Jn 19:26
legs since they **s** that He was Jn 19:33
He who **s** this has testified so Jn 19:35
She **s** that the stone had been Jn 20:1
he **s** the linen cloths lying Jn 20:5
the tomb and **s** the linen cloths Jn 20:6
the tomb, **s**, and believed. Jn 20:8
s two angels in white sitting Jn 20:12
around and **s** Jesus standing Jn 20:14
rejoiced when they **s** the Lord. Jn 20:20
they **s** a charcoal fire there, Jn 21:9
turned around and **s** the disciple Jn 21:20
When Peter **s** him, he said to Jn 21:21
I **s** the Lord ever before me; Ac 2:25
When he **s** Peter and John about Ac 3:3
All the people **s** him walking and Ac 3:9
When Peter **s** this, he addressed Ac 3:12
And since they **s** the man who had Ac 4:14
at him and **s** that his face was Ac 6:15
When he **s** one of them being Ac 7:24
When Moses **s** it, he was amazed Ac 7:31
He **s** God's glory, with Jesus Ac 7:55
they heard and **s** the signs he Ac 8:6
Simon **s** that the Holy Spirit Ac 8:18
and Sharon **s** him and turned Ac 9:35
opened her eyes, **s** Peter, and Ac 9:40
he distinctly **s** in a vision an Ac 10:3
He **s** heaven opened and an object Ac 10:11
praying, and I **s**, in a visionary Ac 11:5
I **s** the four-footed animals of Ac 11:6
he arrived and **s** the grace of Ac 11:23
When he **s** that it pleased the Ac 12:3
they opened the door and **s** him, Ac 12:16
But when the Jews **s** the crowds, Ac 13:45
When the crowds **s** what Paul had Ac 14:11
her owners **s** that their hope Ac 16:19
jailer woke up and **s** the doors Ac 16:27
where they **s** and encouraged Ac 16:40
him when he **s** that the city was Ac 17:16
province of Asia **s** him in the Ac 21:27
who were with me **s** the light, Ac 22:9
very hour I looked up and **s** him. Ac 22:13
and **s** Him telling me, 'Hurry and Ac 22:18
I **s** a light from heaven brighter Ac 26:13
the local people **s** the creature Ac 28:4
long time and **s** nothing unusual Ac 28:6
When Paul **s** them, he thanked God Ac 28:15
it since I **s** that the letter 2Co 7:8
they **s** that I had been entrusted Gl 2:7
But when I **s** that they were Gl 2:14
struggle that you **s** I had and Php 1:30
Me, tried ⌊Me⌋, and **s** My works Heb 3:9
but they **s** them from a distance, Heb 11:13
because they **s** that the child Heb 11:23
lawless deeds he **s** and heard 2Pt 2:8
about Jesus Christ, in all he **s**. Rv 1:2
When I turned I **s** seven gold Rv 1:12
When I **s** Him, I fell at His feet Rv 1:17
seven stars you **s** in My right Rv 1:20
Then I **s** in the right hand of Rv 5:1
I also **s** a mighty angel Rv 5:2
Then I **s** one like a slaughtered Rv 5:6
Then I **s** the Lamb open one of Rv 6:1
I **s** under the altar the souls of Rv 6:9
I **s** Him open the sixth seal. Rv 6:12
After this I **s** four angels Rv 7:1
Then I **s** another angel rise up Rv 7:2
Then I **s** the seven angels who Rv 8:2
and I **s** a star that had fallen Rv 9:1
This is how I **s** the horses in my Rv 9:17
Then I **s** another mighty angel Rv 10:1
fear fell on those who **s** them. Rv 11:11
When the dragon **s** that he had Rv 12:13
And I **s** a beast coming up out of Rv 13:1
beast I **s** was like a leopard, Rv 13:2
Then I **s** another beast coming up Rv 13:11
Then I **s** another angel flying in Rv 14:6
Then I **s** another great and Rv 15:1
I also **s** something like a sea of Rv 15:2
Then I **s** three unclean spirits Rv 16:13
I **s** a woman sitting on a scarlet Rv 17:3
I **s** that the woman was drunk Rv 17:6
When I **s** her, I was utterly Rv 17:6
that you **s** was, and is not, Rv 17:8
10 horns you **s** are 10 kings who Rv 17:12
me, "The waters you **s**, where the Rv 17:15
10 horns you **s**, and the beast, Rv 17:16
the woman you **s** is the great Rv 17:18
After this I **s** another angel Rv 18:1
I **s** heaven opened, and there Rv 19:11
Then I **s** an angel standing in Rv 19:17
Then I **s** the beast, the kings of Rv 19:19
Then I **s** an angel coming down Rv 20:1
Then I **s** thrones, and people Rv 20:4
⌊I⌋ also ⌊**s**⌋ the souls of those Rv 20:4
Then I **s** a great white throne Rv 20:11
I also **s** the dead, the great and Rv 20:12
Then I **s** a new heaven and a new Rv 21:1
I also **s** the Holy City, new Rv 21:2
who heard and **s** these things. Rv 22:8
When I heard and **s** them, I fell Rv 22:8

SAWED *(2)*
cut to size and **s** with saws on 1Kg 7:9
they were **s** in two, they died Heb 11:37

SAWS *(4)*
and put ⌊them to work⌋ with **s**, 2Sm 12:31
and sawed with **s** on the inner 1Kg 7:9
it and put them to work with **s**, 1Ch 20:3
above the one who **s** with it? Is 10:15

SAY *(788)*
(See pp. xi-xii.)

SAYING *(371)*
(See pp. xi-xii.)

SAYING (noun, *proverb*) *(12)*
became a popular **s**. 1Sm 10:12
magnified forever in the **s**, 1Ch 17:24
Not everyone can accept this **s**, Mt 19:11
This **s** was hidden from them, Lk 18:34
in this case the **s** is true: Jn 4:37
you may learn from us the **s**: 1Co 4:6
then the **s** that is written will 1Co 15:54
This **s** is trustworthy and 1Tm 1:15
This **s** is trustworthy: 1Tm 3:1
This **s** is trustworthy and 1Tm 4:9
This **s** is trustworthy: 2Tm 2:11
This **s** is trustworthy. Ti 3:8

SAYINGS *(15)*
of one who hears the **s** of God, Nm 24:4
who hears the **s** of God and has Nm 24:16
along with his ways and his **s**, 2Ch 13:22
Your memorable **s** are proverbs of Jb 13:12
and place His **s** in your heart. Jb 22:22
I will declare wise **s**; Ps 78:2
for understanding insightful **s**; Pr 1:2
listen closely to my **s**. Pr 4:20
for you thirty **s** about counsel Pr 22:20
These ⌊**s**⌋ also belong to the Pr 24:23
find delightful **s** and to Ec 12:10
s of the wise are like goads, Ec 12:11
The **s** are given by one Shepherd. Ec 12:11
all His **s** in the hearing Lk 7:1
accept My **s** has this as his Jn 12:48

SAYS *(696)*
(See pp. xi-xii.)

SCAB *(5)*
a swelling, **s**, or spot on the Lv 13:2
clean; it is a **s**. The person is Lv 13:6
But if the **s** spreads further on Lv 13:7
and if the **s** has spread on the Lv 13:8
and for a swelling, **s**, or spot, Lv 14:56

SCABBARD *(1)*
Go back to your **s**; be still; be Jr 47:6

SCABIES *(1)*
rash, and **s**, from which you Dt 28:27

SCABS *(4)*
festering rash, **s**, or a crushed Lv 21:20
sore, festering rash, or **s**; Lv 22:22
My skin forms **s** and then oozes. Jb 7:5
the Lord will put **s** on the heads Is 3:17

SCALE *(7)*
helmet and bronze **s** armor that 1Sm 17:5
placed with it on a **s**. Jb 6:2
s is so close to another that Jb 41:16
On a balance **s**, they go up; Ps 62:9
weighed out the silver on a **s**. Jr 32:10
they **s** walls as men of war ⌊do⌋. Jl 2:7
it had a balance **s** in his hand. Rv 6:5

SCALES *(19)*
the water that has fins and **s**, Lv 11:9
not have fins and **s** in the seas Lv 11:10
not have fins and **s** will be Lv 11:12
the water that has fins and **s**, Dt 14:9
that does not have fins and **s**— Dt 14:10
pride is in ⌊his⌋ rows of **s**, Jb 41:15
Dishonest **s** are detestable to Pr 11:1
balances and **s** are the LORD's; Pr 16:11
and dishonest **s** are unfair. Pr 20:23
in a balance and the hills in **s**? Is 40:12
as a speck of dust on the **s**; Is 40:15
and weigh out silver on a **s**— Is 46:6
take a pair of **s** and divide the Ezk 5:1
of your streams cling to your **s**. Ezk 29:4
streams will cling to your **s**. Ezk 29:4
with dishonest **s** in his hands. Hs 12:7
and cheat with dishonest **s**. Am 8:5
Can I excuse wicked **s** or bags of Mc 6:11
something like **s** fell from his Ac 9:18

SCALY *(11)*
It is a **s** outbreak, a skin Lv 13:30
priest examines the **s** infection, Lv 13:31
person with the **s** infection for Lv 13:31
If the **s** outbreak has not spread Lv 13:32
but not shave the **s** area. Lv 13:33
person who has the **s** outbreak Lv 13:33
will examine the **s** outbreak on Lv 13:34
But if the **s** outbreak spreads Lv 13:35
If the **s** outbreak has spread on Lv 13:36
the **s** outbreak remains unchanged Lv 13:37
or mildew, for a **s** outbreak, Lv 14:54

SCAN *(1)*
which **s** throughout the whole Zch 4:10

SCAR *(2)*
is ⌊only⌋ the **s** from the boil. Lv 13:23
is ⌊only⌋ the **s** from the burn. Lv 13:28

SCARCER *(1)*
I will make man **s** than gold, Is 13:12

SCARE *(2)*
and no one will **s** them away. Dt 28:26
with no one to **s** them off. Jr 7:33

SCARECROWS *(1)*
Like **s** in a cucumber patch, Jr 10:5

SCARED *(1)*
prophets will be **s** speechless." Jr 4:9

SCARLET *(47)*
it and tied a s ⌊thread⌋ around Gn 38:28
who had the s ⌊thread⌋ tied to Gn 38:30
blue, purple, and s yarn; Ex 25:4
blue, purple, and s yarn, with a Ex 26:1
purple, and s yarn, and finely Ex 26:31
purple, and s yarn, and finely Ex 26:36
purple, and s yarn, and finely Ex 27:16
blue, purple, and s yarn; Ex 28:5
with blue, purple, and s yarn. Ex 28:6
blue, purple, and s yarn, and of Ex 28:8
blue, purple, and s yarn, and of Ex 28:15
and s yarn on its lower hem and Ex 28:33
blue, purple, and s yarn; Ex 35:6
purple, or s yarn, fine linen Ex 35:23
purple, and s yarn, and fine Ex 35:25
and s yarn and fine linen; Ex 35:35
blue, purple, and s yarn, with a Ex 36:8
purple, and s yarn, and finely Ex 36:35
purple, and s yarn, and finely Ex 36:37
purple, and s yarn, and finely Ex 38:18
purple, and s yarn, and fine Ex 38:23
blue, purple, and s yarn, just Ex 39:1
blue, purple, and s yarn, and of Ex 39:2
blue, purple, and s yarn, and Ex 39:3
blue, purple, and s yarn, and of Ex 39:5
blue, purple, and s yarn, and of Ex 39:8
and s yarn on the lower hem of Ex 39:24
blue, purple, and s yarn. Ex 39:29
cedar wood, s yarn, and hyssop Lv 14:4
the cedar wood, s yarn, and Lv 14:6
cedar wood, s yarn, and hyssop Lv 14:49
the hyssop, the s yarn, and the Lv 14:51
the hyssop, and the s yarn. Lv 14:52
to spread a s cloth over them Nm 4:8
tie this s cord to the window Jos 2:18
she tied the s cord to the Jos 2:21
clothed you in s, with luxurious 2Sm 1:24
Your lips are like a s cord, Sg 4:3
Though your sins are like s, Is 1:18
that you dress yourself in s, Jr 4:30
valiant men are dressed in s. Nah 2:3
Him and dressed Him in a s robe. Mt 27:28
with water, s wool, and hyssop Heb 9:19
sitting on a s beast that was Rv 17:3
was dressed in purple and s, Rv 17:4
of linen, purple, silk, and s; Rv 18:12
purple, and s, adorned with gold Rv 18:16

SCATTER *(41)*
Jacob and s them throughout Gn 49:7
But I will s you among the Lv 26:33
are holy, and s the fire far Nm 16:37
The LORD will s you among the Dt 4:27
the LORD will s you among all Dt 28:64
all the people with him will s. 2Sm 17:2
He will s them beyond the 1Kg 14:15
I will s you among the peoples. Neh 1:8
You s me in the storm. Jb 30:22
like sheep and s us among the Ps 44:11
because God will s the bones of Ps 53:5
enemies s, and those who hate Ps 68:1
S the peoples who take pleasure Ps 68:30
Your⌋ lightning and s the foe; Ps 144:6
surface and s its inhabitants Is 24:1
does he not then s cumin and sow Is 28:25
the nations s when You rise in Is 33:3
away, and a gale will s them. Is 41:16
I will s them among nations that Jr 9:16
I will s you like drifting chaff Jr 13:24
I will s them before the enemy Jr 18:17
who destroy and s the sheep of Jr 23:1
you down and s all of Judah that Jr 40:15
I will s them to the wind in Jr 49:32
and I will s them to all these Jr 49:36
Babylon who will s her and strip Jr 51:2
you are to s one third to the Ezk 5:2
against you and s all your Ezk 5:10
and I will s one third to every Ezk 5:12
their idols and s your bones Ezk 6:5
the cherubim and s ⌊them⌋ over Ezk 10:2
I will also s all the attendants Ezk 12:14
the nations and s them among Ezk 12:15
the nations and s them among Ezk 20:23
the nations and s you among Ezk 22:15
the nations and s them across Ezk 29:12
the nations and s them among Ezk 30:23
the nations and s them among Ezk 30:26
off its leaves and s its fruit. Dn 4:14
his warriors storm out to s us, Hab 3:14
the land of Judah to s it." Zch 1:21

SCATTERED *(70)*
the Canaanite clans s. Gn 10:18
will be s over the face of the Gn 11:4
So the LORD s them from there Gn 11:8
there the LORD s them over the Gn 11:9
So the people s throughout the Ex 5:12
He s ⌊the powder⌋ over the Ex 32:20
Your enemies be s, and those who Nm 10:35
your corpses lie ⌊s⌋ in the Nm 14:33
the LORD your God has s you. Dt 30:3
but they were so s that no two 1Sm 11:11
s grain on it so nobody would 2Sm 17:19
He shot arrows and s them; 2Sm 22:15
I saw all Israel s on the hills 1Kg 22:17
entire army was s from him. 2Kg 25:5
I saw all Israel s on the hills 2Ch 18:16
and s over the graves of those 2Ch 34:4
s throughout the peoples in Est 3:8
the cubs of the lioness are s. Jb 4:11
sulfur is s over his home. Jb 18:15
He shot His arrows and s them; Ps 18:14
the Almighty s kings in the land Ps 68:14
You s Your enemies with Your Ps 89:10
all evildoers will be s. Ps 92:9
bones have been s at the mouth Ps 141:7
He will collect the s of Judah Is 11:12
salted fodder s with winnowing Is 30:24
You have s your favors to Jr 3:13
and their whole flock is s. Jr 10:21
s them with a winnowing fork at Jr 15:7
You have s My flock, banished Jr 23:2
the nations where I have s you; Jr 30:11
The One who s Israel will gather Jr 31:10
entire army was s from him. Jr 52:8
the temple lie s at the corner Lm 4:1
The LORD Himself has s them; Lm 4:16
you are s among the nations, Ezk 6:8
the nations and s them among Ezk 11:16
countries where you have been s, Ezk 11:17
survive will be s to every Ezk 17:21
the countries where you were s, Ezk 20:34
countries where you have been s, Ezk 20:41
where they are s and demonstrate Ezk 28:25
They were s for lack of a Ezk 34:5
wild animals when they were s. Ezk 34:5
They were s over the whole face Ezk 34:6
the day he is among his s flock, Ezk 34:12
they have been s on a cloudy and Ezk 34:12
horns until you s them all over, Ezk 34:21
and they were s among the Ezk 36:19
nations have s the Israelites Jl 3:2
the lame and gather the s, Mc 4:6
Your people are s across the Nah 3:18
save the lame and gather the s; Zph 3:19
are the horns that s Judah, Zch 1:19
the horns that s Judah so no one Zch 1:21
for I have s you like the four Zch 2:6
I s them with a windstorm over Zch 7:14
and the sheep will be s; Zch 13:7
where you haven't s seed. Mt 25:24
and gather where I haven't s, Mt 25:26
sheep of the flock will be s. Mt 26:31
and the sheep will be s. Mk 14:27
has s the proud because of the Lk 1:51
to unite the s children of God. Jn 11:52
you will be s to his own home, Jn 16:32
and all his partisans were s. Ac 5:37
the apostles were s throughout Ac 8:1
those who were s went on their Ac 8:4
Those who had been s as a result Ac 11:19
written: He has s; He has given 2Co 9:9

SCATTERING *(2)*
panicking troops s in every 1Sm 14:16
s them throughout the lands. Ps 106:27

SCATTERS *(7)*
He s His lightning through them. Jb 37:11
He s frost like ashes; Ps 147:16
One who s is coming up against Nah 2:1
who does not gather with Me s. Mt 12:30
A man s seed on the ground; Mk 4:26
who does not gather with Me s. Lk 11:23
wolf then snatches and s them. Jn 10:12

SCAVENGE *(1)*
They s for food; they growl if Ps 59:15

SCENT *(3)*
place the s of knowing Him. 2Co 2:14
some we are a s of death leading 2Co 2:16
a s of life leading to life. 2Co 2:16

SCENTED *(2)*
oil, a s blend, the work Ex 30:25
s with myrrh and frankincense Sg 3:6

SCEPTER *(27)*
s will not depart from Judah, Gn 49:10
it out with a s and with their Nm 21:18
and a s will arise from Israel. Nm 24:17
the golden s will that person Est 4:11
the golden s in his hand toward Est 5:2
and touched the tip of the s. Est 5:2
the golden s toward Esther, Est 8:4
the s of Your kingdom is a Ps 45:6
Your kingdom is a s of justice. Ps 45:6
is My helmet; Judah is My s. Ps 60:7
is My helmet; Judah is My s. Ps 108:8
extend Your mighty s from Zion. Ps 110:2
The s of the wicked will not Ps 125:3
the wicked, the s of the rulers. Is 14:5
How the mighty s is shattered, Jr 48:17
a strong branch, a s for ruling. Ezk 19:14
The s of My son, the sword Ezk 21:10
the sword despises even the s? Ezk 21:13
The s will not continue. Ezk 21:13
who wields the s from Beth-eden. Am 1:5
who wields the s from Ashkelon. Am 1:8
and the s of Egypt will come to Zch 10:11
and the s of Your kingdom is a Heb 1:8
Your kingdom is a s of justice. Heb 1:8
shepherd them with an iron s; Rv 2:27
all nations with an iron s— Rv 12:5
shepherd them with an iron s. Rv 19:15

SCEPTERS *(1)*
⌊fit⌋ for the s of rulers; Ezk 19:11

SCEVA *(1)*
Seven sons of S, a Jewish chief Ac 19:14

SCHEME *(4)*
that every s his mind thought Gn 6:5
we knew their s and that God had Neh 4:15
one who would devise such a s?" Est 7:5
A foolish s is sin, and a mocker Pr 24:9

SCHEMER *(1)*
plots evil will be called a s. Pr 24:8

SCHEMES *(17)*
frustrates the s of the crafty Jb 5:12
and his own s trip him up. Jb 18:7
the s you would wrong me with. Jb 21:27
let them fall by their own s. Ps 5:10
be caught in the s they have Ps 10:2
in whose hands are evil s, Ps 26:10
in a shelter from the s of men, Ps 31:20
deceitful s against those who Ps 35:20
The wicked s against the Ps 37:12
devise clever s against Your Ps 83:3
and be glutted with their own s. Pr 1:31
a heart that plots wicked s, Pr 6:18
but He condemns a man who s. Pr 12:2
and a man who s is hated. Pr 14:17
but they pursued many s." Ec 7:29
carried out so many evil s? Jr 11:15
his gates, because of their s. Hs 11:6

SCHEMING *(5)*
his neighbor to murder him by s, Ex 21:14
the documents the s Haman son of Est 8:5
In all his s, the wicked Ps 10:4
me from the s of the wicked, Ps 64:2
if you've been s, put your hand Pr 30:32

SCHOLAR *(1)*
Where is the s? Where is the 1Co 1:20

SCOFF *(5)*
My friends s at me as I weep Jb 16:20
horrified and s because of all Jr 19:8
horrified and s because of all Jr 49:17
horrified and s because of all Jr 50:13
will come in the last days to s, 2Pt 3:3

SCOFFERS *(3)*
Look, you s, marvel and vanish Ac 13:41
s will come in the last days to 2Pt 3:3
there will be s walking Jd 18

SCOFFING *(3)*
words, and s at His prophets, 2Ch 36:16

all these things and **s** at Him. Lk 16:14
and even the leaders kept **s**: Lk 23:35

SCOFFS *(2)*
It **s** at the noise of the village Jb 39:7
he **s** at all his adversaries. Ps 10:5

SCOLD *(1)*
And they began to **s** her. Mk 14:5

SCOLDED *(1)*
and **s** her, "How long are you 1Sm 1:14

SCOOP *(1)*
from a hearth or **s** water from a Is 30:14

SCOOPED *(2)*
He **s** ⌊some honey⌋ into his hands Jdg 14:9
them that he had **s** the honey Jdg 14:9

SCORCHED *(11)*
thin and **s** by the east wind, Gn 41:6
thin, and **s** by the east wind— Gn 41:23
s heads of grain are seven years Gn 41:27
the rebellious live in a **s** land. Ps 68:6
land is **s** by the wrath of the Is 9:19
You will not be **s** when you walk Is 43:2
they have been so **s** that no one Jr 9:10
destroyed and **s** like a Jr 9:12
to the north will be **s** by it. Ezk 20:47
the sun came up they were **s**, Mt 13:6
came up, it was **s**, and since it Mk 4:6

SCORCHER *(1)*
you say, 'It's going to be a **s**!' Lk 12:55

SCORCHES *(1)*
and **s** the foundations of the Dt 32:22

SCORCHING *(6)*
a **s** wind will be their portion. Ps 11:6
on coals without **s** his feet? Pr 6:28
and his speech is like a **s** fire. Pr 16:27
s heat or sun will not strike Is 49:10
God appointed a **s** east wind. Jnh 4:8
rises with its **s** heat and dries Jms 1:11

SCORN *(24)*
of horror, **s**, and ridicule Dt 28:37
an object of **s** and ridicule 1Kg 9:7
it an object of **s** and ridicule 2Ch 7:20
me an object of **s** to the people; Jb 17:6
Even young boys **s** me. When I Jb 19:18
become an object of **s** to them. Jb 30:9
they shake their heads ⌊in **s**⌋. Ps 109:25
more than enough **s** from the Ps 123:4
kiss you, and no one would **s** me. Sg 8:1
My face from **s** and spitting. Is 50:6
horror, a perpetual object of **s**; Jr 18:16
city desolate, an object of **s**. Jr 19:8
an object of **s**, ridicule, and Jr 24:9
an object of **s** and cursing— Jr 25:18
an object of **s** and a disgrace Jr 29:18
of execration, **s**, cursing, Jr 42:18
of execration, of **s**, of cursing, Jr 44:12
a desolation and an object of **s**, Jr 51:37
she has become an object of **s**. Lm 1:8
as an object of **s** when you were Ezk 16:56
be an object of ridicule and **s**, Ezk 23:32
object of **s** among the nations. Jl 2:17
will bear the **s** of My people." Mc 6:16
"And you **s** it," says the LORD Mal 1:13

SCORNED *(5)*
made him and **s** the Rock of his Dt 32:15
s by men and despised by people. Ps 22:6
for love, it would be utterly **s**. Sg 8:7
because you **s** payment. Ezk 16:31
time you were **s** by the daughters Ezk 16:57

SCORNER *(2)*
the voice of the **s** and reviler, Ps 44:16
vanish, the **s** will disappear, Is 29:20

SCORNFULLY *(2)*
he ⌊**s**⌋ claps in our presence, Jb 34:37
All who pass by ⌊**s**⌋ clap their Lm 2:15

SCORNS *(4)*
Zion, despises you and **s** you: 2Kg 19:21
hands at him and **s** him from its Jb 27:23
Zion, despises you and **s** you: Is 37:22
For who **s** the day of small Zch 4:10

SCORPION *(2)*
for an egg, will give him a **s**? Lk 11:12
caused by a **s** when it strikes Rv 9:5

SCORPIONS *(5)*
with its poisonous snakes and **s**, Dt 8:15
beside you and you live among **s**. Ezk 2:6
on snakes and **s** and over all Lk 10:19
the power that **s** have on the Rv 9:3
stingers, like **s**, so that with Rv 9:10

SCOUNDREL *(1)*
nor a **s** said to be important. Is 32:5

SCOUNDREL'S *(1)*
The **s** weapons are destructive; Is 32:7

SCOUNDRELS *(1)*
together some **s** from the Ac 17:5

SCOURED *(1)*
it must be **s** and rinsed with Lv 6:28

SCOURGE *(5)*
a **s** for your sides and thorns in Jos 23:13
overwhelming **s** passes through, Is 28:15
overwhelming **s** passes through, Is 28:18
that he be examined with the **s**, Ac 22:24
legal for you to **s** a man who is Ac 22:25

SCOURGINGS *(1)*
experienced mockings and **s**, Heb 11:36

SCOUT *(10)*
Send men to **s** out the land of Nm 13:2
Moses sent to **s** out the land, Nm 13:16
Moses sent them to **s** out the Nm 13:17
Moses sent to **s** out the land, Nm 14:36
men who went to **s** out the land. Nm 14:38
saying, "Go and **s** the land, Jos 2:1
them, "Go up and **s** the land." Jos 7:2
Kadesh-barnea to **s** the land, Jos 14:7
in order to **s** out the city, 2Sm 10:3
emissaries in order to **s** out, 1Ch 19:3

SCOUTED *(7)*
they went up and **s** out the land Nm 13:21
about the land they had **s**: Nm 13:32
among those who **s** out the land, Nm 14:6
the 40 days that you **s** the land, Nm 14:34
the two men who had **s** the land, Jos 6:22
young men who had **s** went in and Jos 6:23
So the men went up and **s** Ai. Jos 7:2

SCOUTING *(2)*
returned from **s** out the land. Nm 13:25
Valley of Eshcol, **s** the land. Dt 1:24

SCOUTS *(1)*
Then Ben-hadad sent out **s**, 1Kg 20:17

SCRAPE *(2)*
pottery to **s** himself while he Jb 2:8
I will **s** the soil from her and Ezk 26:4

SCRAPED *(3)*
of the house completely **s**, Lv 14:41
plaster that is **s** off must be Lv 14:41
has been **s** and replastered, Lv 14:43

SCRAPS *(2)*
to pick up ⌊**s**⌋ under my table Jdg 1:7
of barley and **s** of bread; Ezk 13:19

SCREAMED *(6)*
and I **s** as loud as I could. Gn 39:14
but when I **s** for help, he left Gn 39:18
saw Samuel, she **s**, and then she 1Sm 28:12
tore her clothes and **s** "Treason! 2Kg 11:14
Athaliah tore her clothes and **s**, 2Ch 23:13
Then they **s** at the top of their Ac 7:57

SCREAMING *(1)*
When he heard me **s** for help, Gn 39:15

SCREECH *(2)*
the **s** owl will stay there and Is 34:14
owl and the **s** owl will roost Zph 2:14

SCREEN *(22)*
are to make a **s** embroidered with Ex 26:36
wood for the **s** and overlay them Ex 26:37
a thirty-foot **s** embroidered with Ex 27:16
seat, and the veil for the **s**; Ex 35:12
the entryway **s** for the entrance Ex 35:15
and the **s** for the gate of the Ex 35:17
He made a **s** embroidered with Ex 36:37
The **s** for the gate of the Ex 38:18
skins; the veil for the **s**; Ex 39:34
the **s** for the entrance to the Ex 39:38
the **s** for the gate of the Ex 39:40
and **s** off the ark with the veil. Ex 40:3
Put up the **s** for the entrance to Ex 40:5
and hang the **s** for the gate Ex 40:8
put up the veil for the **s**, Ex 40:21
He put up the **s** at the entrance Ex 40:28
altar and hung a **s** for the gate Ex 40:33
the **s** for the entrance to the Nm 3:25
the **s** for the entrance to the Nm 3:26
these, and the **s**—and all the Nm 3:31
the **s** for the entrance to the Nm 4:25
the **s** for the entrance at the Nm 4:26

SCREENED *(1)*
and **s** off the ark of the Ex 40:21

SCREENING *(1)*
take down the **s** veil, and cover Nm 4:5

SCRIBBLING *(1)*
s on the doors of the gate and 1Sm 21:13

SCRIBE *(27)*
a man of understanding and a **s**. 1Ch 27:32
Shimshai the **s** wrote a letter Ezr 4:8
Shimshai the **s**, and the rest Ezr 4:9
Shimshai the **s**, and the rest Ezr 4:17
Rehum, Shimshai the **s**, and their Ezr 4:23
He was a **s** skilled in the law of Ezr 7:6
gave to Ezra the priest and **s**, Ezr 7:11
asked Ezra the **s** to bring the Neh 8:1
the **s** stood on a high wooden Neh 8:4
priest and **s**, and the Levites Neh 8:9
before Ezra the **s** to study the Neh 8:13
and Ezra the priest and **s**. Neh 12:26
the **s** went in front of them. Neh 12:36
priest, Zadok the **s**, and Pedaiah Neh 13:13
Shebna the **s**, and Joah son Is 36:3
Shebna the **s**, and Joah son Is 36:22
Shebna the **s**, and the older Is 37:2
Gemariah son of Shaphan the **s**, Jr 36:10
Elishama the **s**, Delaiah son Jr 36:12
the chamber of Elishama the **s**, Jr 36:20
the chamber of Elishama the **s**. Jr 36:21
seize Baruch the **s** and Jeremiah Jr 36:26
of Neriah, the **s**, and he wrote Jr 36:32
in the house of Jonathan the **s**, Jr 37:15
to the house of Jonathan the **s**, Jr 37:20
A **s** approached Him and said, Mt 8:19
Then the **s** said to Him, "You are Mk 12:32

SCRIBE'S *(2)*
he went down to the **s** chamber in Jr 36:12
scroll with a **s** knife and throw Jr 36:23

SCRIBES *(64)*
the families of **s** who lived in 1Ch 2:55
The royal **s** were summoned on the Est 3:12
the royal **s** were summoned. Est 8:9
the lying pen of **s** has produced Jr 8:8
and your **s** like clouds of Nah 3:17
priests and **s** of the people Mt 2:4
that of the **s** and Pharisees, Mt 5:20
authority, and not like their **s**. Mt 7:29
some of the **s** said among Mt 9:3
Then some of the **s** and Pharisees Mt 12:38
Then Pharisees and **s** came from Mt 15:1
priests, and **s**, be killed, and Mt 16:21
then do the **s** say that Elijah Mt 17:10
over to the chief priests and **s**, Mt 20:18
and the **s** saw the wonders Mt 21:15
The **s** and the Pharisees are Mt 23:2
But woe to you, **s** and Pharisees, Mt 23:13
Woe to you, **s** and Pharisees, Mt 23:14
Woe to you, **s** and Pharisees, Mt 23:15
Woe to you, **s** and Pharisees, Mt 23:23
Woe to you, **s** and Pharisees, Mt 23:25
Woe to you, **s** and Pharisees, Mt 23:27
Woe to you, **s** and Pharisees, Mt 23:29
you prophets, sages, and **s**. Mt 23:34
where the **s** and the elders had Mt 26:57
priests, with the **s** and elders, Mt 27:41
unlike the **s**, He was teaching Mk 1:22
But some of the **s** were sitting Mk 2:6
When the **s** of the Pharisees saw Mk 2:16
The **s** who had come down from Mk 3:22
and some of the **s** who had come Mk 7:1
Pharisees and the **s** asked Him, Mk 7:5
priests, and the **s**, be killed, Mk 8:31
Why do the **s** say that Elijah Mk 9:11
around them and **s** disputing with Mk 9:14
to the chief priests and the **s**, Mk 10:33
priests and the **s** heard it and Mk 11:18
priests, the **s**, and the elders Mk 11:27
One of the **s** approached. Mk 12:28
How can the **s** say that the Mk 12:35
Beware of the **s**, who want to go Mk 12:38
priests and the **s** were looking Mk 14:1
priests, the **s**, and the elders. Mk 14:43
the elders, and the **s** convened. Mk 14:53

the elders, s, and the whole Mk 15:1
with the s were mocking Him Mk 15:31
Then the s and the Pharisees Lk 5:21
and their s were complaining to Lk 5:30
s and Pharisees were watching Lk 6:7
priests, and s, be killed, and Lk 9:22
the s and the Pharisees began to Lk 11:53
Pharisees and s were complaining Lk 15:2
priests, the s, and the leaders Lk 19:47
the chief priests and the s, Lk 20:1
Then the s and the chief priests Lk 20:19
of the s answered, "Teacher, Lk 20:39
Beware of the s, who want to go Lk 20:46
priests and the s were looking Lk 22:2
the chief priests and the s, Lk 22:66
chief priests and the s stood Lk 23:10
Then the s and the Pharisees Jn 8:3
and s assembled in Jerusalem Ac 4:5
people, the elders, and the s; Ac 6:12
and some of the s of the Ac 23:9

SCRIPT *(4)*
in its own s and to each ethnic Est 1:22
in its own s and to each ethnic Est 3:12
for each province in its own s, Est 8:9
in their own s and language. Est 8:9

SCRIPTURE *(34)*
every student of S instructed in Mt 13:52
Haven't you read this S: Mk 12:10
the S was fulfilled that says: Mk 15:28
this S has been fulfilled." Lk 4:21
what is the meaning of this S: Lk 20:17
believed the S and the statement Jn 2:22
in Me, as the S has said, will Jn 7:38
Doesn't the S say that the Jn 7:42
and the S cannot be broken— Jn 10:35
But the S must be fulfilled: Jn 13:18
so that the S may be fulfilled. Jn 17:12
to fulfill the S that says: Jn 19:24
that the S might be fulfilled, Jn 19:28
so that the S would be fulfilled Jn 19:36
Also, another S says: Jn 19:37
understand the S that He must Jn 20:9
the S had to be fulfilled that Ac 1:16
Now the S passage he was reading Ac 8:32
Jesus, beginning from that S. Ac 8:35
For what does the S say? Rm 4:3
For the S tells Pharaoh: Rm 9:17
Now the S says, No one who Rm 10:11
not know what the S says in the Rm 11:2
Now the S foresaw that God would Gl 3:8
But the S has imprisoned Gl 3:22
But what does the S say? Gl 4:30
For the S says: You must not 1Tm 5:18
All S is inspired by God and is 2Tm 3:16
⌊S⌋ testifies that he lives. Heb 7:8
the royal law prescribed in S, Jms 2:8
the S was fulfilled that says, Jms 2:23
without reason the S says that Jms 4:5
For it stands in S: 1Pt 2:6
prophecy of S comes from one's 2Pt 1:20

SCRIPTURES *(22)*
Have you never read in the S: Mt 21:42
don't know the S or the power Mt 22:29
would the S be fulfilled that Mt 26:54
the prophetic S would be Mt 26:56
don't know the S or the power Mk 12:24
But the S must be fulfilled." Mk 14:49
concerning Himself in all the S. Lk 24:27
and explaining the S to us?" Lk 24:32
their minds to understand the S. Lk 24:45
pore over the S because you Jn 5:39
He know the S, since He hasn't Jn 7:15
reasoned with them from the S, Ac 17:2
examined the S daily to see if Ac 17:11
man who was powerful in the S, Ac 18:24
through the S that Jesus is the Ac 18:28
His prophets in the Holy S— Rm 1:2
of the S we may have hope. Rm 15:4
known through the prophetic S, Rm 16:26
for our sins according to the S, 1Co 15:3
third day according to the S, 1Co 15:4
you have known the sacred S, 2Tm 3:15
also do with the rest of the S. 2Pt 3:16

SCROLL *(66)*
this down on a s as a reminder Ex 17:14
the covenant s and read ⌊it⌋ Ex 24:7
curses on a s and wash ⌊them⌋ Nm 5:23
himself on a s in the presence Dt 17:18
which are written in this s, Dt 28:58
written in this s will descend Dt 29:20
down on a s every single word Dt 31:24
wrote them on a s, which he 1Sm 10:25
of Media that a s was found with Ezr 6:2
that they were recorded on a s Jb 19:23
about me in the volume of the s. Ps 40:7
presence and inscribe it on a s; Is 30:8
The skies will roll up like a s, Is 34:4
and read the s of the LORD: Is 34:16
Write down on a s all the words Jr 30:2
recorded it on a s, sealed it, Jr 32:10
written on a s and sealed, Jr 32:44
Take a s, and write on it all Jr 36:2
Baruch wrote on a s all the Jr 36:4
must go and read from the s— Jr 36:6
the LORD's words from the s. Jr 36:8
Jeremiah's words from the s. Jr 36:10
words of the LORD from the s, Jr 36:11
read from the s in the hearing Jr 36:13
Bring the s that you read in the Jr 36:14
Neriah took the s and went to Jr 36:14
I was writing on the s in ink." Jr 36:18
deposited the s in the chamber Jr 36:20
king sent Jehudi to get the s, Jr 36:21
would cut the s with a scribe's Jr 36:23
until the entire s was consumed Jr 36:23
the king not to burn the s, Jr 36:25
had burned the s with the words Jr 36:27
Take another s, and once again Jr 36:28
on the original s that Jehoiakim Jr 36:28
You have burned the s, saying: Jr 36:29
took another s and gave it to Jr 36:32
words of the s that Jehoiakim, Jr 36:32
these words on a s at Jeremiah's Jr 45:1
Jeremiah wrote on one s about Jr 51:60
have finished reading this s, Jr 51:63
and there was a written s in it. Ezk 2:9
Eat this s, then go and speak to Ezk 3:1
my mouth, and He fed me the s. Ezk 3:2
with this s I am giving you. Ezk 3:3
up again and saw a flying s. Zch 5:1
"I see a flying s," I replied, Zch 5:2
The s of the prophet Isaiah was Lk 4:17
unrolling the s, He found the Lk 4:17
rolled up the s, gave it back to Lk 4:20
sprinkled the s itself and all Heb 9:19
Me in the volume of the s— Heb 10:7
Write on a s what you see and Rv 1:11
on the throne a s with writing Rv 5:1
to open the s and break its Rv 5:2
to open the s or even to look Rv 5:3
to open the s or even to look Rv 5:4
He may open the s and its seven Rv 5:5
and took ⌊the s⌋ out of the Rv 5:7
He took the s, the four living Rv 5:8
to take the s and to open its Rv 5:9
like a s being rolled up Rv 6:14
he had a little s opened in his Rv 10:2
take the s that lies open in the Rv 10:8
him to give me the little s. Rv 10:9
took the little s from the Rv 10:10

SCROLLS *(2)*
Take these s—this purchase Jr 32:14
as well as the s, especially 2Tm 4:13

SCRUBLAND *(1)*
live alone in a s, surrounded Mc 7:14

SCRUBLANDS *(1)*
night in the s of the desert, Is 21:13

SCRUFF *(1)*
seized ⌊me⌋ by the s of the neck Jb 16:12

SCULPTED *(1)*
or place a s stone in your land Lv 26:1

SCULPTURED *(1)*
He made two cherubim of s work, 2Ch 3:10

SCYTHIAN *(1)*
barbarian, S, slave and free; Col 3:11

SEA *(368)*
will rule the fish of the s, Gn 1:26
the fish of the s, the birds Gn 1:28
and all the fish of the s. Gn 9:2
Siddim (that is, the Dead S). Gn 14:3
like the sand of the s, Gn 32:12
the sand of the s—that he Gn 41:49
and blew them into the Red S. Ex 10:19
toward the Red S along the road Ex 13:18
between Migdol and the s; Ex 14:2
Baal-zephon, facing it by the s. Ex 14:2
camped by the s beside Ex 14:9
out your hand over the s, Ex 14:16
go through the s on dry ground. Ex 14:16
out his hand over the s. Ex 14:21
The LORD drove the s ⌊back⌋ with Ex 14:21
and turned the s into dry land. Ex 14:21
through the s on dry ground, Ex 14:22
and went into the s after them. Ex 14:23
hand over the s so that the Ex 14:26
out his hand over the s, Ex 14:27
daybreak the s returned to its Ex 14:27
LORD overthrew them in the s. Ex 14:27
had gone after them into the s. Ex 14:28
through the s on dry ground, Ex 14:29
horse and its rider into the s. Ex 15:1
and his army into the s; Ex 15:4
were drowned in the Red S. Ex 15:4
congealed in the heart of the s. Ex 15:8
breath, and the s covered them. Ex 15:10
and horsemen went into the s, Ex 15:19
waters of the s back over them. Ex 15:19
through the s on dry ground. Ex 15:19
horse and its rider into the s. Ex 15:21
led Israel on from the Red S, Ex 15:22
the earth, the s, and everything Ex 20:11
from the Red S to the Ex 23:31
Red Sea to the Mediterranean S, Ex 23:31
fish in the s were caught for Nm 11:22
up and blew quail in from the s; Nm 11:31
by the s and along the Jordan. Nm 13:29
in the direction of the Red S." Nm 14:25
way of the Red S to bypass the Nm 21:4
the middle of the s into the Nm 33:8
Elim and camped by the Red S. Nm 33:10
from the Red S and camped Nm 33:11
at the east end of the Dead S. Nm 34:3
will end at the Mediterranean S. Nm 34:5
of the Mediterranean S; Nm 34:6
Mediterranean S draw a line to Nm 34:7
slope of the S of Chinnereth. Nm 34:11
Jordan and end at the Dead S. Nm 34:12
the Negev and the s coast— Dt 1:7
by way of the Red S.' Dt 1:40
wilderness by way of the Red S, Dt 2:1
as far as the S of the Arabah, Dt 3:17
Arabah, the Dead S, under the Dt 3:17
far as the Dead S below the Dt 4:49
of the Red S flow over them as Dt 11:4
River to the Mediterranean S. Dt 11:24
And it is not across the s, Dt 30:13
will cross the s, get it for us, Dt 30:13
as far as the Mediterranean S, Dt 34:2
and west to the Mediterranean S. Jos 1:4
of the Red S before you when Jos 2:10
into the S of the Arabah Jos 3:16
the Dead S) was completely Jos 3:16
LORD your God did to the Red S, Jos 4:23
kings near the s heard how the Jos 5:1
Mediterranean S toward Lebanon Jos 9:1
east of the S of Chinnereth to Jos 12:3
to the S of the Arabah Jos 12:3
that is, the Dead S), eastward Jos 12:3
the edge of the S of Chinnereth Jos 13:27
tip of the Dead S on the south Jos 15:2
ended at the Mediterranean S. Jos 15:4
along the Dead S to the mouth Jos 15:5
the bay of the s at the mouth Jos 15:5
ended at the Mediterranean S. Jos 15:11
of the Mediterranean S. Jos 15:12
Ekron to the s, all ⌊the cities Jos 15:46
of the Mediterranean S. Jos 15:47
ended at the Mediterranean S. Jos 16:3
ended at the Mediterranean S. Jos 16:8
ended at the Mediterranean S. Jos 17:9
north, with the S as its border. Jos 17:10
the northern bay of the Dead S, Jos 18:19
to Hosah and ended at the s, Jos 19:29
westward to the Mediterranean S. Jos 23:4
Egypt and you reached the Red S, Jos 24:6
and horsemen as far as the s. Jos 24:6
and brought the s over them, Jos 24:7
to the Red S and came to Kadesh. Jdg 11:16
numerous as the sand by the s— 2Sm 17:11
depths of the s became visible, 2Sm 22:16
numerous as the sand by the s; 1Kg 4:20

down from Lebanon to the s, 1Kg 5:9
rafts to go by s to the place 1Kg 5:9
shore of the Red S in the land 1Kg 9:26
of Tarshish at s with Hiram's 1Kg 10:22
"Go up and look toward the s." 1Kg 18:43
a man's hand coming from the s." 1Kg 18:44
as far as the S of the Arabah, 2Kg 14:25
Let the s and everything in it 1Ch 16:32
to you as rafts by s to Joppa. 2Ch 2:16
beyond the Dead S and from Edom 2Ch 20:2
wood from Lebanon to Joppa by s, Ezr 3:7
heard their cry at the Red S. Neh 9:9
You divided the s before them, Neh 9:11
Am I the s or a sea monster, Jb 7:12
Am I the sea or a s monster, Jb 7:12
treads on the waves of the s. Jb 9:8
the earth and wider than the s. Jb 11:9
the fish of the s inform you. Jb 12:8
from the s and a wadi becomes Jb 14:11
By His power He stirred the s, Jb 26:12
in me," while the s declares, "I Jb 28:14
and covers the depths of the s. Jb 36:30
Who enclosed the s behind doors Jb 38:8
the sources of the s or walked Jb 38:16
he makes the s like an ointment Jb 41:31
fish of the s passing through Ps 8:8
depths of the s became visible, Ps 18:15
the waters of the s into a heap; Ps 33:7
judgments, like the deepest s. Ps 36:6
He turned the s into dry land, Ps 66:6
back from the depths of the s Ps 68:22
may he rule from s to sea and Ps 72:8
he rule from sea to s and from Ps 72:8
You divided the s with Your Ps 74:13
the heads of the s monsters in Ps 74:13
Your way went through the s, Ps 77:19
He split the s and brought them Ps 78:13
but the s covered their enemies. Ps 78:53
toward the S and shoots toward Ps 80:11
the raging s; when its waves Ps 89:9
his power to the s and his right Ps 89:25
the mighty breakers of the s— Ps 93:4
The s is His; He made it. His Ps 95:5
let the s and all that fills it Ps 96:11
Let the s and all that fills it, Ps 98:7
Here is the s, vast and wide, Ps 104:25
rebelled by the s—the Red Sea. Ps 106:7
rebelled by the sea—the Red S. Ps 106:7
rebuked the Red S, and it dried Ps 106:9
awe-inspiring deeds at the Red S. Ps 106:22
Others went to s in ships, Ps 107:23
stirred up the waves of the s. Ps 107:25
the waves of the s were hushed. Ps 107:29
s looked and fled; the Jordan Ps 114:3
Why was it, s, that you fled? Ps 114:5
He divided the Red S His love is Ps 136:13
and his army into the Red S. Ps 136:15
the s and everything in them. Ps 146:6
all s monsters and ocean depths, Ps 148:7
a limit for the s so that the Pr 8:29
sleeping out at s or lying down Pr 23:34
way of a ship at s, and the way Pr 30:19
All the streams flow to the s, Ec 1:7
sea, yet the s is never full. Ec 1:7
against every splendid s vessel. Is 2:16
like the roaring of the s. Is 5:30
bring honor to the Way of the S, Is 9:1
numerous as the sand of the s, Is 10:22
His staff over the s as ⌊He did⌋ Is 10:26
the LORD as the s is filled with Is 11:9
out and reached the Dead S. Is 16:8
sends envoys by s, in reed Is 18:2
The waters of the s will dry up, Is 19:5
against the desert by the s: Is 21:1
your agents have crossed the s Is 23:2
of the s, for the sea has Is 23:4
the sea, for the s has spoken: Is 23:4
out His hand over the s; Is 23:11
the monster that is in the s. Is 27:1
go down to the s with all that Is 42:10
makes a way in the s, and a path Is 43:16
who says to the depths of the s: Is 44:27
like the waves of the s. Is 48:18
I dry up the s by My rebuke; Is 50:2
who pierced the s monster? Is 51:9
it You who dried up the s, Is 51:10
who stirs up the s so that its Is 51:15
are like the storm-tossed s, Is 57:20

riches of the s will become Is 60:5
up out of the s with the Is 63:11
sand as the boundary of the s, Jr 5:22
Their voice roars like the s, Jr 6:23
of the coastlands across the s; Jr 25:22
pillars, the s, the water carts Jr 27:19
who stirs up the s and makes its Jr 31:35
the sand of the s cannot be Jr 33:22
and like Carmel by the s. Jr 46:18
Ashkelon and the shore of the s. Jr 47:7
tendrils have extended to the s; Jr 48:32
reached to the s ⌊and to⌋ Jazer. Jr 48:32
cry will be heard at the Red S. Jr 49:21
in the s there is anxiety that Jr 49:23
Their voice roars like the s, Jr 50:42
swallowed me like a s monster; Jr 51:34
I will dry up her s and make her Jr 51:36
The s has risen over Babylon; Jr 51:42
your ruin is as vast as the s. Lm 2:13
just as the s raises its waves. Ezk 26:3
a place in the s to spread nets, Ezk 26:5
princes of the s will descend Ezk 26:16
She who was powerful on the s, Ezk 26:17
the islands in the s are alarmed Ezk 26:18
at the entrance of the s, Ezk 27:3
realm was in the heart of the s; Ezk 27:4
the ships of the s and their Ezk 27:9
loaded in the heart of the s. Ezk 27:25
you in the heart of the s. Ezk 27:26
the heart of the s on the day of Ezk 27:27
helmsmen of the s stand on the Ezk 27:29
silenced in the middle of the s? Ezk 27:32
shattered by the s in the depths Ezk 27:34
of gods in the heart of the s. Ezk 28:2
death in the heart of the s. Ezk 28:8
The fish of the s, the birds of Ezk 38:20
of the Travelers east of the S. Ezk 39:11
it enters the s, the sea of foul Ezk 47:8
the sea, the s of foul water, Ezk 47:8
water ⌊of the s⌋ becomes fresh. Ezk 47:8
the fish of the Mediterranean S. Ezk 47:10
Mediterranean S by way of Ezk 47:15
run from the s to Hazar-enon at Ezk 47:17
border to the eastern s. Ezk 47:18
as far as the Mediterranean S. Ezk 47:19
the Mediterranean S will be the Ezk 47:20
from the eastern side to the s, Ezk 48:1
and out to the Mediterranean S. Ezk 48:28
heaven stirred up the great s. Dn 7:2
huge beasts came up from the s, Dn 7:3
between the s and the beautiful Dn 11:45
will be like the sand of the s, Hs 1:10
the fish of the s disappear. Hs 4:3
his front ranks into the Dead S, Jl 2:20
guard into the Mediterranean S. Jl 2:20
waters of the s and pours them Am 5:8
stagger from s to sea and roam Am 8:12
from sea to s and roam from Am 8:12
from My sight on the s floor, Am 9:3
command the ⌊s⌋ serpent to bite Am 9:3
waters of the s and pours them Am 9:6
hurled a violent wind on the s, Jnh 1:4
arose on the s that the ship Jnh 1:4
cargo into the s to lighten the Jnh 1:5
made the s and the dry land." Jnh 1:9
to calm this s that's against Jnh 1:11
For the s was getting worse and Jnh 1:11
me into the s so it may quiet Jnh 1:12
not because the s was raging Jnh 1:13
Jonah and threw him into the s, Jnh 1:15
and the s stopped its raging. Jnh 1:15
River and from s to sea and Mc 7:12
and from sea to s and mountain Mc 7:12
sins into the depths of the s. Mc 7:19
rebukes the s so that it dries Nah 1:4
rampart was the s, the river her Nah 3:8
mankind like the fish of the s, Hab 1:14
as the waters cover the s. Hab 2:14
rage against the s when You ride Hab 3:8
tread the s with Your horses, Hab 3:15
the sky and the fish of the s, Zph 1:3
the earth, the s and the dry Hg 2:6
and cast her wealth into the s; Zch 9:4
will extend from s to sea, Zch 9:10
will extend from sea to s, Zch 9:10
pass through the s of distress Zch 10:11
and strike the waves of the s; Zch 10:11
the eastern s and the other half Zch 14:8

other half toward the western s, Zch 14:8
to live in Capernaum by the s, Mt 4:13
along the s road, beyond Mt 4:15
walking along the S of Galilee, Mt 4:18
were casting a net into the s, Mt 4:18
go to the other side ⌊of the s⌋. Mt 8:18
a violent storm arose on the s, Mt 8:24
and rebuked the winds and the s. Mt 8:26
the winds and the s obey Him!" Mt 8:27
bank into the s and perished Mt 8:32
house and was sitting by the s. Mt 13:1
a large net thrown into the s. Mt 13:47
toward them walking on the s. Mt 14:25
saw Him walking on the s, Mt 14:26
passed along the S of Galilee. Mt 15:29
them, go to the s, cast in a Mt 17:27
drowned in the depths of the s! Mt 18:6
up and thrown into the s,' Mt 21:21
over land and s to make one Mt 23:15
along by the S of Galilee, Mk 1:16
were casting a net into the s, Mk 1:16
went out again beside the s. Mk 2:13
with His disciples to the s, Mk 3:7
He began to teach by the s, Mk 4:1
a boat on the s and sat down, Mk 4:1
was on the shore facing the s. Mk 4:1
and said to the s, "Silence! Mk 4:39
the wind and the s obey Him!" Mk 4:41
came to the other side of the s, Mk 5:1
bank into the s and drowned Mk 5:13
Him while He was by the s. Mk 5:21
boat was in the middle of the s, Mk 6:47
walking on the s and wanted to Mk 6:48
they saw Him walking on the s, Mk 6:49
of Sidon to the S of Galilee, Mk 7:31
and he were thrown into the s. Mk 9:42
up and thrown into the s,' Mk 11:23
thrown into the s than for him Lk 17:2
uprooted and planted in the s,' Lk 17:6
by the roaring s and waves. Lk 21:25
Jesus crossed the S of Galilee Jn 6:1
disciples went down to the s, Jn 6:16
across the s to Capernaum. Jn 6:17
arose, and the s began to churn. Jn 6:18
they saw Jesus walking on the s. Jn 6:19
side of the s knew there had Jn 6:22
Him on the other side of the s, Jn 6:25
disciples by the S of Tiberias. Jn 21:1
) and plunged into the s. Jn 21:7
earth, and the s, and everything Ac 4:24
Egypt, at the Red S, and in the Ac 7:36
whose house is by the s." Ac 10:6
the tanner's house by the s.' Ac 10:32
the earth, the s, and everything Ac 14:15
sent Paul away to go to the s, Ac 17:14
we put to s, intending to sail Ac 27:2
we had put out to s from there, Ac 27:4
through the open s off Cilicia Ac 27:5
were drifting in the Adriatic S, Ac 27:27
let down the skiff into the s, Ac 27:30
the grain overboard into the s. Ac 27:38
left them in the s, at the same Ac 27:40
and though he has escaped the s, Ac 28:4
sons is like the sand of the s, Rm 9:27
cloud, all passed through the s, 1Co 10:1
Moses in the cloud and in the s. 1Co 10:2
a day in the depths of the s. 2Co 11:25
dangers on the s, and dangers 2Co 11:26
crossed the Red S as though they Heb 11:29
doubter is like the surging s, Jms 1:6
waves of the s, foaming up their Jd 13
was something like a s of glass, Rv 4:6
earth, on the s, and everything Rv 5:13
or on the s or on any tree. Rv 7:1
to harm the earth and the s: Rv 7:2
the earth or the s or the trees Rv 7:3
with fire was hurled into the s. Rv 8:8
a third of the s became blood, Rv 8:8
living creatures in the s died, Rv 8:9
He put his right foot on the s, Rv 10:2
standing on the s and on the Rv 10:5
and the s and what is in it: Rv 10:6
on the s and on the land. Rv 10:8
Woe to the earth and the s, Rv 12:12
He stood on the sand of the s. Rv 12:18
a beast coming up out of the s. Rv 13:1
the s and springs of water." Rv 14:7
something like a s of glass Rv 15:2

standing on the s of glass with Rv 15:2
poured out his bowl into the s. Rv 16:3
and all life in the s died. Rv 16:3
and all who do business by s, Rv 18:17
have ships on the s became rich Rv 18:19
and threw it into the s, Rv 18:21
is like the sand of the s. Rv 20:8
Then the s gave up its dead, Rv 20:13
and the s existed no longer. Rv 21:1

SEA-BED *(1)*
who made the s into a road for Is 51:10

SEA-CREATURES *(1)*
the large s and every living Gn 1:21

SEACOAST *(3)*
Woe, inhabitants of the s, Zph 2:5
The s will become pasturelands Zph 2:6
from the s of Tyre and Sidon. Lk 6:17

SEAFARER *(1)*
shipmaster, s, the sailors, Rv 18:17

SEAL *(33)*
as a gem cutter engraves a s. Ex 28:11
stone must be engraved like a s, Ex 28:21
like the engraving of a s: Ex 28:36
as a gem cutter engraves a s. Ex 39:6
was engraved like a s with one Ex 39:14
like the engraving on a s: Ex 39:30
name and sealed them with his s. 1Kg 21:8
and s it with the royal signet Est 8:8
is changed as clay is by a s; Jb 38:14
Set me as a s on your heart, Sg 8:6
your heart, as a s on your arm. Sg 8:6
S up the instruction among my Is 8:16
You were the s of perfection, Ezk 28:12
Now you must s up the vision Dn 8:26
to s up vision and prophecy, Dn 9:24
of the North to s the agreement. Dn 11:6
secret and s the book until Dn 12:4
S your mouth from the woman who Mc 7:5
has set His s of approval on Him Jn 6:27
circumcision as a s of the Rm 4:11
for you are the s of my 1Co 9:2
When He opened the second s, Rv 6:3
When He opened the third s, Rv 6:5
When He opened the fourth s, Rv 6:7
When He opened the fifth s, Rv 6:9
Then I saw Him open the sixth s. Rv 6:12
who had the s of the living God. Rv 7:2
trees until we s the slaves of Rv 7:3
When He opened the seventh s, Rv 8:1
do not have God's s on their Rv 9:4
S up what the seven thunders Rv 10:4
and put a s on it so that he Rv 20:3
Don't s the prophetic words of Rv 22:10

SEALED *(25)*
up with Me, s up in My vaults? Dt 32:34
Ahab's name and s them with his 1Kg 21:8
in writing on a s document Neh 9:38
Ahasuerus and s with the royal Est 3:12
king's name and s with the royal Est 8:8
name and s ⌊the edicts⌋ with Est 8:10
would be s up in a bag, Jb 14:17
of scales, closely s together. Jb 41:15
a locked garden and a s spring. Sg 4:12
like the words of a s document. Is 29:11
can't read it, because it is s." Is 29:11
it on a scroll, s it, called in Jr 32:10
the s copy with its terms and Jr 32:11
with the s copy and this open Jr 32:14
written on a scroll and s, Jr 32:44
king s it with his own signet Dn 6:17
are secret and s until the time Dn 12:9
has also s us and given us the 2Co 1:22
were s with the promised Holy Eph 1:13
who s you for the day of Eph 4:30
on the back, s with seven seals Rv 5:1
the number of those who were s: Rv 7:4
144,000 s from every tribe of Rv 7:4
s from the tribe of Judah, Rv 7:5
12,000 s from the tribe of Rv 7:8

SEALING *(1)*
the tomb secure by s the stone Mt 27:66

SEALS *(8)*
Those whose s were ⌊on the Neh 10:1
to shine and s off the stars. Jb 9:7
discerning, when he s his lips. Pr 17:28
the back, sealed with seven s. Rv 5:1
the scroll and break its s?" Rv 5:2
the scroll and its seven s." Rv 5:5
the scroll and to open its s; Rv 5:9
Lamb open one of the seven s, Rv 6:1

SEAM *(2)*
front, close to its s, and above Ex 28:27
close to its s, above the Ex 39:20

SEAMEN *(2)*
experienced s, along with 1Kg 9:27
with crews of experienced s. 2Ch 8:18

SEAMLESS *(1)*
tunic, which was s, woven in one Jn 19:23

SEARCH *(44)*
will s for the LORD your God, Dt 4:29
I'll s for him among all the 1Sm 23:23
of Ziph to s for David there. 1Sm 26:2
has come out to s for a flea, 1Sm 26:20
they all went in s of David, 2Sm 5:17
Let us s for a young virgin for 1Kg 1:2
at Gath to s for his slaves. 1Kg 2:40
not sent someone to s for you. 1Kg 18:10
and they will s your palace and 1Kg 20:6
them go and s for your master 2Kg 2:16
they all went in s of David; 1Ch 14:8
S for the LORD and for His 1Ch 16:11
of David's reign a s was made, 1Ch 26:31
that a s should be made in your Ezr 4:15
a decree and a s was conducted. Ezr 4:19
let a s of the royal archives in Ezr 5:17
Let a s be made for beautiful Est 2:2
s for it more than for hidden Jb 3:21
my wrongdoing and s for my sin, Jb 10:6
S for the LORD and for His Ps 105:4
S me, God, and know my heart; Ps 139:23
they will s for me, but won't Pr 1:28
like silver and s for it like Pr 2:4
to meet you, to s for you, and Pr 7:15
and those who s for me find me. Pr 8:17
a time to s and a time to count Ec 3:6
S and read the scroll of the Is 34:16
and take note; s in her squares. Jr 5:1
Me when you s for Me with all Jr 29:13
one will s for Israel's guilt, Jr 50:20
groan while they s for bread. Lm 1:11
Let us s out and examine our Lm 3:40
shepherds do not s for My flock, Ezk 34:8
I Myself will s for My flock and Ezk 34:11
will make ⌊their⌋ s at the end Ezk 39:14
they will s for Me in their Hs 5:15
time I will s Jerusalem with Zph 1:12
Go and s carefully for the Mt 2:8
is about to s for the child to Mt 2:13
a merchant in s of fine pearls. Mt 13:45
and go and s for the stray? Mt 18:12
to Jerusalem to s for Him. Lk 2:45
and s carefully until she finds Lk 15:8
he went to Tarsus to s for Saul, Ac 11:25

SEARCHED *(25)*
Laban s the whole tent but found Gn 31:34
So Laban s, but could not find Gn 31:35
You've s all my possessions! Gn 31:37
steward s, beginning with the Gn 44:12
They s all along the way, but Jos 2:22
But when they s for him, they 1Sm 10:21
Saul s for him every day, but 1Sm 23:14
to Gath, he no longer s for him. 1Sm 27:4
men s but did not find ⌊them⌋ 2Sm 17:20
They s for a beautiful girl 1Kg 1:3
These s for their entries in the Ezr 2:62
and they s in the library of Ezr 6:1
s among the people and priests, Ezr 8:15
These s for their entries in the Neh 7:64
I s for him, but he could not be Ps 37:36
they repented and s for God. Ps 78:34
You have s me and known me. Ps 139:1
a land I had s out for them, Ezk 20:6
I s for a man among them who Ezk 22:30
and they s for Daniel and his Dn 2:13
his hidden treasures s out! Ob 6
After Herod had s and did not Ac 12:19
they s for them to bring them Ac 17:5
he diligently s for me and found 2Tm 1:17
come to you s and carefully 1Pt 1:10

SEARCHES *(8)*
for the LORD s every heart and 1Ch 28:9
From there it s for prey; Jb 39:29
The one who s for what is good Pr 11:27
continually s for but does not Ec 7:28
and the one who s finds, and to Mt 7:8
and the one who s finds, and to Lk 11:10
He who s the hearts knows the Rm 8:27
for the Spirit s everything, 1Co 2:10

SEARCHING *(14)*
There was great s of heart among Jdg 5:15
There was great s of heart among Jdg 5:16
Saul will stop s for me 1Sm 27:1
its pastureland, s for anything Jb 39:8
s ⌊for food⌋ far from their Ps 109:10
of the LORD, s the innermost Pr 20:27
the city while s for food to Lm 1:19
was no one s or seeking ⌊for Ezk 34:6
Keep s, and you will find. Mt 7:7
his companions went s for Him. Mk 1:36
have been anxiously s for You." Lk 2:48
"Why were you s for Me?" Lk 2:49
But the crowds were s for Him. Lk 4:42
Keep s, and you will find. Lk 11:9

SEARED *(1)*
liars whose consciences are s. 1Tm 4:2

SEARING *(1)*
A s wind ⌊blows⌋ from the barren Jr 4:11

SEAS *(22)*
the gathering of the water "s." Gn 1:10
and fill the waters of the s, Gn 1:22
whether in the s or streams. Lv 11:9
and scales in the s or streams, Lv 11:10
wealth of the s and the hidden Dt 33:19
the s and all that is in them. Neh 9:6
outweigh the sand of the s! Jb 6:3
through the currents of the s. Ps 8:8
on the s and established Ps 24:2
topple into the depths of the s, Ps 46:2
the earth and of the distant s; Ps 65:5
You silence the roar of the s, Ps 65:7
the s and everything that moves Ps 69:34
birds like the sand of the s. Ps 78:27
in the s and all the depths. Ps 135:6
roar like the roaring of the s. Is 17:12
numerous than the sand of the s. Jr 15:8
who were populated from the s! Ezk 26:17
brought you onto the high s, Ezk 27:26
was unloaded from the s, Ezk 27:33
you are like a monster in the s. Ezk 32:2
heart of the s, and the current Jnh 2:3

SEASHORE *(10)*
the sky and the sand on the s. Gn 22:17
will live by the s and will be a Gn 49:13
saw the Egyptians dead on the s. Ex 14:30
numerous as the sand on the s— Jos 11:4
remained at the s and stayed in Jdg 5:17
as the sand on the s. Jdg 7:12
numerous as the sand on the s. 1Sm 13:5
as ⌊vast⌋ as the sand on the s. 1Kg 4:29
to Eloth on the s in the land of 2Ch 8:17
as the grains of sand by the s. Heb 11:12

SEASON *(17)*
You are to s each of your grain Lv 2:13
It was the s for the first ripe Nm 13:20
provide rain for your land in s, Dt 11:14
rain in its s and to bless all Dt 28:12
banks throughout the harvest s. Jos 3:15
people, and it is the rainy s. Ezr 10:13
of sheaves is gathered in its s. Jb 5:26
in their s and lead the Bear Jb 38:32
its fruit in s and whose leaf Ps 1:3
does not plow during planting s; Pr 20:4
will find her in her mating s. Jr 2:24
late, in its s, who guarantees Jr 5:24
send down showers in their s— Ezk 34:26
time and My new wine in its s; Hs 2:9
of the fig tree in its first s. Hs 9:10
rain in the s of spring rain. Zch 10:1
it was not the s for figs. Mk 11:13

SEASONAL *(1)*
as s streams that overflow Jb 6:15

SEASONED *(2)*
is to be s with salt, pure and Ex 30:35
be gracious, s with salt, so Col 4:6

SEASONS *(8)*
and the abundant yield of the s; Dt 33:14
He made the moon to mark the s; Ps 104:19
stork in the sky knows her s. Jr 8:7
He changes the times and s; Dn 2:21

out so that s of refreshing may Ac 3:19
rain from heaven and fruitful s, Ac 14:17
days, months, s, and years. Gl 4:10
About the times and the s: 1Th 5:1

SEAT *(46)*

Make a mercy s of pure gold, Ex 25:17
at the two ends of the mercy s. Ex 25:18
the mercy s at its two ends. Ex 25:19
the mercy s with their wings, Ex 25:20
should be toward the mercy s. Ex 25:20
the mercy s on top of the ark Ex 25:21
you there above the mercy s, Ex 25:22
the mercy s on the ark of the Ex 26:34
front of the mercy s that is Ex 30:6
mercy s that is on top of it, Ex 31:7
poles, the mercy s, and the veil Ex 35:12
He made a mercy s of pure gold, Ex 37:6
at the two ends of the mercy s, Ex 37:7
of one piece⌋ with the mercy s, Ex 37:8
the mercy s with their wings Ex 37:9
were looking toward the mercy s. Ex 37:9
with its poles and the mercy s; Ex 39:35
He set the mercy s on top of the Ex 40:20
of the mercy s on the ark or Lv 16:2
in the cloud above the mercy s. Lv 16:2
covers the mercy s that is over Lv 16:13
the east side of the mercy s; Lv 16:14
before the mercy s seven times. Lv 16:14
against the mercy s and in front Lv 16:15
above the mercy s that was on Nm 7:89
because your s will be empty. 1Sm 20:18
place on the s by the wall. 1Sm 20:25
even taken his s on the royal 1Kg 1:46
on either side of the s, 1Kg 10:19
a fast and s Naboth at the head 1Kg 21:9
Then s two wicked men opposite 1Kg 21:10
on either side of the s, 2Ch 9:18
gate and took my s in the town Jb 29:7
take Your s on high over it. Ps 7:7
in order to s them with nobles— Ps 113:8
on a s at the highest point of Pr 9:14
of gold, and its s of purple. Sg 3:10
Take your s, Jerusalem. Is 52:2
Take a humble s, for your Jr 13:18
I sit in the s of gods in the Ezk 28:2
the Ancient of Days took His s. Dn 7:9
love the front s in the Lk 11:43
an oath to him to s one of his Ac 2:30
before the judgment s of God. Rm 14:10
before the judgment s of Christ, 2Co 5:10
it overshadowing the mercy s. Heb 9:5

SEATED *(42)*

They were s before him in order Gn 43:33
he is s on his royal throne, Dt 17:18
the presence of those s here and Ru 4:4
s me on the throne of my father 1Kg 2:24
soon as he was s on his throne, 1Kg 16:11
a fast and s Naboth at the head 1Kg 21:12
the upper ⌊gate⌋ and s the king 2Ch 23:20
with the queen s beside him, Neh 2:6
You are s on Your throne as a Ps 9:4
God is s on His holy throne. Ps 47:8
I saw the Lord s on a high and Is 6:1
the Pharisees are s in the chair Mt 23:2
the Son of Man s at the right Mt 26:64
and the other Mary were s there, Mt 27:61
the Son of Man s at the right Mk 14:62
of Man will be s at the right Lk 22:69
them to those who were s— Jn 6:11
Mary remained s in the house. Jn 11:20
royal robes and s on the throne, Ac 12:21
The next day, s at the judge's Ac 25:6
us up with Him and s us with Him Eph 2:6
s at the right hand of God. Col 3:1
One was s on the throne, Rv 4:2
and the One s looked like jasper Rv 4:3
to the One s on the throne, Rv 4:9
before the One s on the throne, Rv 4:10
hand of the One s on the throne Rv 5:1
hand of the One s on the throne. Rv 5:7
to the One s on the throne, Rv 5:13
face of the One s on the throne Rv 6:16
our God, who is s on the throne, Rv 7:10
The One s on the throne will Rv 7:15
who were s before God on their Rv 11:16
Son of Man was s on the cloud, Rv 14:14
the One who was s on the cloud, Rv 14:15
So the One s on the cloud swung Rv 14:16
on which the woman is s. Rv 17:9
where the prostitute was s, Rv 17:15
God, who is s on the throne, Rv 19:4
and people s on them who were Rv 20:4
white throne and One s on it. Rv 20:11
Then the One s on the throne Rv 21:5

SEATING *(1)*

the dead and s Him at His right Eph 1:20

SEATS *(5)*

s them with noblemen and gives 1Sm 2:8
but He s them forever with Jb 36:7
the front s in the synagogues, Mt 23:6
the front s in the synagogues, Mk 12:39
the front s in the synagogues, Lk 20:46

SEAWEED *(1)*

s was wrapped around my head. Jnh 2:5

SEBA *(4)*

S, Havilah, Sabtah, Raamah, and Gn 10:7
S, Havilah, Sabta, Raama, and 1Ch 1:9
of Sheba and S offer gifts. Ps 72:10
you, Cush and S in your place. Is 43:3

SEBAM *(1)*

Elealeh, S, Nebo, and Beon, Nm 32:3

SECACAH *(1)*

Beth-arabah, Middin, S, Jos 15:61

SECLUSION *(1)*

herself in s for five months Lk 1:24

SECOND *(194)*

and then morning: the s day. Gn 1:8
name of the s river is Gihon, Gn 2:13
of Noah's life, in the s month, Gn 7:11
day of the s month, Gn 8:14
to Abraham a s time from heaven Gn 22:15
again and bore Jacob a s son. Gn 30:7
slave Zilpah bore Jacob a s son, Gn 30:12
also told the s one, the third, Gn 32:19
asleep and dreamed a s time: Gn 41:5
Joseph ride in his s chariot, Gn 41:43
And the s son he named Ephraim, Gn 41:52
the evidence of the s sign. Ex 4:8
day of the s month after they Ex 16:1
calyx under the ⌊s⌋ pair of Ex 25:35
outermost curtain in the s set. Ex 26:4
of the curtain in the s set, Ex 26:5
curtain of the s set. Ex 26:10
20 planks for the s side of the Ex 26:20
six names on the s stone, Ex 28:10
the s row, a turquoise, a Ex 28:18
You are to take the s ram, Ex 29:19
to offer the s lamb at twilight Ex 29:41
outermost curtain in the s set. Ex 36:11
of the curtain in the s set, Ex 36:12
curtain in the s set. Ex 36:17
the s side of the tabernacle, Ex 36:25
calyx under the s pair of Ex 37:21
the s row, a turquoise, a Ex 39:11
the first month of the s year, Ex 40:17
must prepare the s ⌊bird⌋ as a Lv 5:10
Next he presented the s ram, Lv 8:22
first ⌊day⌋ of the s month of Nm 1:1
month of the s year after Nm 1:1
on the first day of the s month. Nm 1:18
they will move out s. Nm 2:16
On the s day Nethanel son of Nm 7:18
are to take a s young bull for Nm 8:8
month of the s year after their Nm 9:1
to observe it in the s month, Nm 9:11
you sound short blasts a s time, Nm 10:6
During the s year, in the second Nm 10:11
in the s month on the twentieth Nm 10:11
Offer the s lamb at twilight, Nm 28:8
On the s day ⌊present⌋ 12 young Nm 29:17
and the s man hates her, writes Dt 24:3
On the s day they marched around Jos 6:14
Joshua captured it on the s day. Jos 10:32
The s lot came out for Simeon, Jos 19:1
bull and a s bull seven years Jdg 6:25
Take the s bull and offer it as Jdg 6:26
and the s bull offered up on the Jdg 6:28
On the s day the Israelites Jdg 20:24
Orpah and the s was named Ruth. Ru 1:4
named Hannah and the s Peninnah. 1Sm 1:2
was Joel and his s was Abijah. 1Sm 8:2
So Saul said to David a s time, 1Sm 18:21
the New Moon, the s day, David's 1Sm 20:27
any food that s day of the New 1Sm 20:34
his s was Chileab, by Abigail, 2Sm 3:3
he sent again, a s time, but he 2Sm 14:29
Israel, in the s month, in the 1Kg 6:1
The s cherub also was 15 feet; 1Kg 6:25
feet and so was the s cherub's. 1Kg 6:26
wall while the s cherub's wing 1Kg 6:27
and the s door had two folding 1Kg 6:34
the height of the s capital. 1Kg 7:16
capital and seven for the s. 1Kg 7:17
did the same for the s capital. 1Kg 7:18
to Solomon a s time just as He 1Kg 9:2
Israel in the s year of Judah's 1Kg 15:25
Then he said, "A s time!" 1Kg 18:34
and they did it a s time. 1Kg 18:34
LORD returned a s time and 1Kg 19:7
in the s year of Judah's 2Kg 1:17
So he sent out a s horseman, 2Kg 9:19
Then Jehu wrote them a s letter, 2Kg 10:6
In the s year of Israel's King 2Kg 14:1
In the s year of Israel's King 2Kg 15:32
in the s year what grows from 2Kg 19:29
in Jerusalem in the S District. 2Kg 22:14
the priests of the s rank and 2Kg 23:4
The s pillar was the same, 2Kg 25:17
the priest of the s rank, 2Kg 25:18
was ⌊born⌋ s, Shimea third, 1Ch 2:13
Mareshah, his s son, fathered 1Ch 2:42
Daniel was ⌊born⌋ s, by Abigail 1Ch 3:1
Jehoiakim s, Zedekiah third, 1Ch 3:15
Shapham the s ⌊in command⌋, 1Ch 5:12
Joel, and his s son Abijah. 1Ch 6:28
was ⌊born⌋ s, Aharah third, 1Ch 8:1
firstborn, Jeush s, and 1Ch 8:39
chief, Obadiah s, Eliab third, 1Ch 12:9
were their relatives s in rank: 1Ch 15:18
and Zechariah was s to him. 1Ch 16:5
the first and Zizah was the s; 1Ch 23:11
Amariah s, Jahaziel third, 1Ch 23:19
Micah was first, and Isshiah s. 1Ch 23:20
to Jehoiarib, the s to Jedaiah, 1Ch 24:7
Amariah the s, Jahaziel the 1Ch 24:23
12 ⌊to⌋ Gedaliah the s: 1Ch 25:9
Jediael the s, Zebadiah the 1Ch 26:2
Jehozabad the s, Joah the third, 1Ch 26:4
Hilkiah the s, Tebaliah the 1Ch 26:11
of the division for the s month, 1Ch 27:4
Then, for a s time, they made 1Ch 29:22
to build on the s ⌊day⌋ of the 2Ch 3:2
day⌋ of the s month in the 2Ch 3:2
same in the s and third years 2Ch 27:5
Elkanah who was s to the king. 2Ch 28:7
of the LORD in the s month 2Ch 30:2
Unleavened Bread in the s month. 2Ch 30:13
fourteenth day of the s month. 2Ch 30:15
and his brother Shimei was s. 2Ch 31:12
in Jerusalem in the S District. 2Ch 34:22
carried him in his s chariot, 2Ch 35:24
the s month of the second year Ezr 3:8
month of the s year after they Ezr 3:8
until the s year of the reign Ezr 4:24
On the s day, the family leaders Neh 8:13
Hassenuah was s in command over Neh 11:9
s among his relatives; Neh 11:17
The s thanksgiving procession Neh 12:38
would return to a s harem under Est 2:14
assembled together for a s time, Est 2:19
the s day while drinking wine, Est 7:2
wrote this s letter with full Est 9:29
the Jew was s only to King Est 10:3
only for himself. S Series of Jb 14:22
Jemimah, his s Keziah, and his Jb 42:14
the sun follow a s youth who Ec 4:15
His hand a s time to recover— Is 11:11
in the s year what grows from Is 37:30
of the LORD came to me a s time: Jr 13:3
LORD came to Jeremiah a s time: Jr 33:1
On the s day after he had killed Jr 41:4
The s pillar was the same, Jr 52:22
the priest of the s rank, Jr 52:24
a cherub, the s that of a man, Ezk 10:14
On the s day you are to present Ezk 43:22
In the s year of his reign, Dn 2:1
They answered a s time, "May the Dn 2:7
appeared, a s one, that looked Dn 7:5
the LORD came to Jonah a s time: Jnh 3:1
will not rise up a s time. Nah 1:9
a wailing from the S District, Zph 1:10
In the s year of King Darius, Hg 1:1

in the **s** year of King Darius. Hg 1:15
month⌋, in the **s** year of Darius, Hg 2:10
LORD came to Haggai a **s** time on Hg 2:20
month, in the **s** year of Darius, Zch 1:1
Shebat, in the **s** year of Darius, Zch 1:7
the **s** chariot black horses, Zch 6:2
Then I cut in two my **s** staff, Zch 11:14
The same happened to the **s** also, Mt 22:26
The **s** is like it: Love your Mt 22:39
Again, a **s** time, He went away Mt 26:42
s also took her, and he died, Mk 12:21
The **s** is: Love your neighbor as Mk 12:31
a rooster crowed a **s** time, Mk 14:72
The **s** came and said, 'Master, Lk 19:18
Also the **s** Lk 20:30
womb a **s** time and be born? Jn 3:4
therefore was the **s** sign Jesus Jn 4:54
a **s** time they summoned the man Jn 9:24
A **s** time He asked him, "Simon, Jn 21:16
The **s** time, Joseph was revealed Ac 7:13
Again, a **s** time, a voice said to Ac 10:15
answered from heaven a **s** time, Ac 11:9
the first and **s** guard posts, Ac 12:10
as it is written in the **s** Psalm: Ac 13:33
the **s** day we came to Puteoli. Ac 28:13
apostles, **s** prophets, third 1Co 12:28
the **s** man is from heaven. 1Co 15:47
when I was present the **s** time, 2Co 13:2
after a first and **s** warning, Ti 3:10
have been sought for a **s** one. Heb 8:7
Behind the **s** curtain, the Heb 9:3
priest alone enters the **s** room, Heb 9:7
appear a **s** time, not to bear Heb 9:28
the first to establish the **s**. Heb 10:9
this is now the **s** letter I've 2Pt 3:1
never be harmed by the **s** death. Rv 2:11
the **s** living creature was like a Rv 4:7
When He opened the **s** seal, Rv 6:3
I heard the **s** living creature Rv 6:3
The **s** angel blew his trumpet, Rv 8:8
The **s** woe has passed. Rv 11:14
A **s** angel followed, saying: Rv 14:8
The **s** poured out his bowl into Rv 16:3
A **s** time they said: Hallelujah! Rv 19:3
The **s** death has no power over Rv 20:6
This is the **s** death, the lake of Rv 20:14
sulfur, which is the **s** death." Rv 21:8
jasper, the **s** sapphire, the Rv 21:19

SECOND-IN-COMMAND *(1)*
over Israel, and I'll be your **s**. 1Sm 23:17

SECRET *(43)*
and sets ⌊it⌋ up in **s**.' Dt 27:15
who kills his neighbor in **s**.' Dt 27:24
I have a **s** message for you." Jdg 3:19
⌊The **s** of⌋ his strength remained Jdg 16:9
and hide in a **s** place and stay 1Sm 19:2
You acted in **s**, but I will do 2Sm 12:12
A word was brought to me in **s**; Jb 4:12
kills the innocent in **s** places; Ps 10:8
He lurks in **s** like a lion in a Ps 10:9
The **s** counsel of the LORD is for Ps 25:14
"We have perfected a **s** plan." Ps 64:6
our **s** sins in the light of Your Ps 90:8
from You when I was made in **s**, Ps 139:15
goes around revealing a **s**, Pr 11:13
A **s** gift soothes anger, and a Pr 21:14
without revealing another's **s**; Pr 25:9
and riches from **s** places, Is 45:3
have not spoken in **s**, somewhere Is 45:19
I have not spoken in **s**; Is 48:16
spending nights in **s** places, Is 65:4
will weep in **s** because of your Jr 13:17
hide himself in **s** places where I Jr 23:24
I will uncover his **s** places. Jr 49:10
no **s** is hidden from you! Ezk 28:3
keep these words **s** and seal the Dn 12:4
the words are **s** and sealed until Dn 12:9
so that your giving may be in **s**. Mt 6:4
who sees in **s** will reward you. Mt 6:4
pray to your Father who is in **s**. Mt 6:6
who sees in **s** will reward you. Mt 6:6
but to your Father who is in **s**. Mt 6:18
who sees in **s** will reward you. Mt 6:18
things kept **s** from the Mt 13:35
The **s** of the kingdom of God has Mk 4:11
does anything in **s** while he's Jn 7:4
I haven't spoken anything in **s**. Jn 18:20
judges what people have kept **s**, Rm 2:16
of the sacred **s** kept silent for Rm 16:25
renounced shameful **s** things, 2Co 4:2
what is done by them in **s**. Eph 5:12
have learned the **s** ⌊of being Php 4:12
The **s** of the seven stars you saw Rv 1:20
I will tell you the **s** meaning of Rv 17:7

SECRETARIES *(2)*
Ahijah the sons of Shisha, **s**; 1Kg 4:3
Some of the Levites were **s**, 2Ch 34:13

SECRETARY *(20)*
Seraiah was court **s**; 2Sm 8:17
Sheva was court **s**; 2Sm 20:25
the king's **s** and the high priest 2Kg 12:10
Shebnah the court **s**, and Joah 2Kg 18:18
Shebna the court **s**, and Joah son 2Kg 18:37
the court **s**, and the elders 2Kg 19:2
king sent the court **s** Shaphan 2Kg 22:3
priest told Shaphan the court **s**, 2Kg 22:8
the court **s** went to the king 2Kg 22:9
the court **s** told the king, 2Kg 22:10
the court **s**, and the king's 2Kg 22:12
the **s** of the commander of the 2Kg 25:19
Shavsha was court **s**; 1Ch 18:16
The **s**, Shemaiah son of Nethanel, 1Ch 24:6
the king's **s** and the high 2Ch 24:11
Jeiel the court **s** and Maaseiah 2Ch 26:11
told Shaphan the court **s**, 2Ch 34:15
the court **s** told the king, 2Ch 34:18
the court **s**, and the king's 2Ch 34:20
the **s** of the commander of the Jr 52:25

SECRETES *(2)*
Whether his body **s** the discharge Lv 15:3
days that his body **s** or retains Lv 15:3

SECRETLY *(24)*
Why did you **s** flee from me, Gn 31:27
closest friend **s** entices you, Dt 13:6
because she will **s** eat them for Dt 28:57
son of Nun **s** sent two men as Jos 2:1
sent messengers **s** to Abimelech, Jdg 9:31
Then she went in **s**, uncovered Ru 3:7
David got up and **s** cut off the 1Sm 24:4
take you away **s** and transport 2Sm 19:41
s rescued Joash son of Ahaziah 2Kg 11:2
Israelites **s** did what was not 2Kg 17:9
you if you **s** showed partiality Jb 13:10
that my heart was **s** enticed and Jb 31:27
the net that is **s** set for me, Ps 31:4
destroy anyone who **s** slanders Ps 101:5
and bread ⌊eaten⌋ **s** is tasty!" Pr 9:17
A wicked man **s** takes a bribe to Pr 17:23
if ready to **s** devour the weak. Hab 3:14
decided to divorce her **s**. Mt 1:19
Then Herod **s** summoned the wise Mt 2:7
also went up, not openly but **s**. Jn 7:10
but **s** because of his fear of the Jn 19:38
they going to smuggle us out **s**? Ac 16:37
who came in **s** to spy on our Gl 2:4
They will **s** bring in destructive 2Pt 2:1

SECRETS *(6)*
would show you the **s** of wisdom, Jb 11:6
He knows the **s** of the heart? Ps 44:21
one who reveals **s** is a constant Pr 20:19
Because the **s** of the kingdom of Mt 13:11
The **s** of the kingdom of God have Lk 8:10
The **s** of his heart will be 1Co 14:25

SECT *(3)*
of the **s** of the Nazarenes Ac 24:5
they call a **s**, so I worship my Ac 24:14
concerning this **s**, we are aware Ac 28:22

SECTION *(12)*
He purchased a **s** of the field Gn 33:19
the contaminated **s** out of the Lv 13:56
made repairs to another **s**, Neh 3:11
repairs to another **s** opposite Neh 3:19
diligently repaired another **s**, Neh 3:20
made repairs to another **s**, Neh 3:21
made repairs to another **s**, Neh 3:24
to another **s** from ⌊a point⌋ Neh 3:27
made repairs to another **s**. Neh 3:30
Their **s** of the land is cursed, Jb 24:18
will be a square ⌊**s**⌋ for the Ezk 45:2
Scripture says in the Elijah **s**— Rm 11:2

SECTIONS *(2)*
towns in a document of seven **s**. Jos 18:9
behind the lowest **s** of the wall, Neh 4:13

SECU *(1)*
came to the large cistern at S, 1Sm 19:22

SECUNDUS *(1)*
Aristarchus and S from Ac 20:4

SECURE *(23)*
you and your kingship are not **s**. 1Sm 20:31
will know that your tent is **s**, Jb 5:24
and those who provoke God are **s**; Jb 12:6
Their homes are **s** and free of Jb 21:9
completely **s** and at ease. Jb 21:23
His ways are always **s**; Ps 10:5
making me **s** while at my mother's Ps 22:9
When I was **s**, I said, "I will Ps 30:6
on a rock, making my steps **s**. Ps 40:2
but the righteous are **s** forever. Pr 10:25
cannot be made **s** by wickedness, Pr 12:3
You were **s** in your wickedness; Is 47:10
I spoke to you when you were **s**. Jr 22:21
We **s** our food at the risk of our Lm 5:9
the hair and **s** them in the folds Ezk 5:3
flock will be **s** in their land. Ezk 34:27
to those who feel **s** on the hill Am 6:1
Jerusalem was inhabited and **s**, Zch 7:7
tomb be made **s** until the third Mt 27:64
make it as **s** as you know how. Mt 27:65
and made the tomb **s** by sealing Mt 27:66
estate, his possessions are **s**. Lk 11:21
to make his life **s** will lose it, Lk 17:33

SECURED *(3)*
ordered and **s** in every ⌊detail⌋. 2Sm 23:5
were bound and **s** with cords in Ezk 27:24
inner prison and **s** their feet Ac 16:24

SECURELY *(32)*
that you may live **s** in the land. Lv 25:18
and live **s** in the land. Lv 25:19
to eat and live **s** in your land. Lv 26:5
LORD's beloved rests **s** on Him. Dt 33:12
So Israel dwells **s**; Dt 33:28
will tie you up **s** and hand you Jdg 15:13
who were there were living **s**, Jdg 18:7
around you, and you lived **s**. 1Sm 12:11
and sets me **s** on the heights. 2Sm 22:34
be shut and **s** fastened while Neh 7:3
my body also rests **s**. Ps 16:9
and sets me **s** on the heights. Ps 18:33
dwell in the land and live **s**. Ps 37:3
children will dwell ⌊**s**⌋, Ps 102:28
to me will live **s** and be free Pr 1:33
lives with integrity lives **s**, Pr 10:9
luxury, who sits **s**, who says to Is 47:8
saved, and Israel will dwell **s**. Jr 23:6
and Jerusalem will dwell **s**, Jr 33:16
will live there **s**, build houses, Ezk 28:26
They will live **s** when I execute Ezk 28:26
they may live **s** in the Ezk 34:25
will live **s**, and no one will Ezk 34:28
and all of them ⌊now⌋ live **s**. Ezk 38:8
people who are living **s**, Ezk 38:11
My people Israel are dwelling **s**, Ezk 38:14
those who live **s** on the coasts Ezk 39:6
when they live **s** in their land Ezk 39:26
enable the people to rest **s**. Hs 2:18
They will live **s**, for then His Mc 5:4
We found the jail **s** locked, Ac 5:23
jailer to keep them **s** guarded. Ac 16:23

SECURITY *(29)*
to a deposit, a **s**, or a robbery; Lv 6:2
around you and you live in **s**, Dt 12:10
upper millstone as **s** for a debt, Dt 24:6
that is like taking a life as **s**. Dt 24:6
to collect what he offers as **s**. Dt 24:10
loan to brings the **s** out to you. Dt 24:11
the garment⌋ he has given as **s**. Dt 24:12
not take a widow's garment as **s**. Dt 24:17
of you to find **s** in the house Ru 1:9
shouldn't I find **s** for you, Ru 3:1
will be peace and **s** during my 2Kg 20:19
Put up **s** for me. Who ⌊else⌋ Jb 17:3
is ripped from the **s** of his tent Jb 18:14
He gives them a sense of **s**, Jb 24:23
you have put up **s** for your Pr 6:1
puts up **s** for a stranger, Pr 11:15
and puts up **s** for his friend. Pr 17:18
he has put up **s** for a stranger; Pr 20:16
who put up **s** for loans. Pr 22:26
he has put up **s** for a stranger; Pr 27:13
and from Judah every kind of **s**: Is 3:1

will be times of s for you— Is 33:6
will be peace and s during my Is 39:8
nation at ease, one living in s. Jr 49:31
and comfortable s, but didn't Ezk 16:49
city that lives in s, Zph 2:15
So Jerusalem will dwell in s. Zch 14:11
taking a s bond from Jason and Ac 17:9
say, "Peace and s," then sudden 1Th 5:3

SEDAN *(1)*
Solomon made a s chair for Sg 3:9

SEDUCE *(1)*
empty words, they s, by fleshly 2Pt 2:18

SEDUCED *(2)*
wives s him ⌊to follow⌋ other 1Kg 11:4
heart has been s by ⌊my Jb 31:9

SEDUCES *(2)*
When a man s a virgin who was Ex 22:16
She s him with her persistent Pr 7:21

SEDUCING *(1)*
for sin, s unstable people 2Pt 2:14

SEDUCTION *(2)*
age and the s of wealth choke Mt 13:22
of this age, the s of wealth, Mk 4:19

SEDUCTIVE *(1)*
with heads held high and s eyes, Is 3:16

SEE *(692)*
to the man to s what he would Gn 2:19
out a dove to s whether the Gn 8:8
and they did not s their father Gn 9:23
the Egyptians s you, they will Gn 12:12
forever all the land that you s. Gn 13:15
walking with them to s them off. Gn 18:16
will go down to s if what they Gn 18:21
watched her to s whether or not Gn 24:21
surprised to s Isaac caressing Gn 26:8
so weak that he could not s, Gn 27:1
I can s from your father's face Gn 31:5
And He said, 'Look up and s: Gn 31:12
Everything you s is mine! Gn 31:43
went out to s some of the young Gn 34:1
Go and s how your brothers and Gn 37:14
Then we'll s what becomes of his Gn 37:20
said to Joseph, "S, I am placing Gn 41:41
You have come to s the weakness Gn 42:9
You have come to s the weakness Gn 42:12
be tested to s if they are true Gn 42:16
'You will not s me again unless Gn 43:3
'You will not s me again unless Gn 43:5
him to me so that I can s him.' Gn 44:21
you will not s me again.' Gn 44:23
with us, we cannot s the man.' Gn 44:26
not bear to s the grief that Gn 44:34
eyes can s that it is I⌊, Gn 45:12
will go to s him before I die." Gn 45:28
could hardly s. Joseph brought Gn 48:10
expected to s your face ⌊again⌋ Gn 48:11
even let me s your offspring. Gn 48:11
in order to s what would happen Ex 2:4
in Egypt and s if they are still Ex 4:18
you are going to s what I will Ex 6:1
Moses, "S, I have made you Ex 7:1
When you s him walking out to Ex 7:15
when you s him going out to Ex 8:20
one will be able to s the land. Ex 10:5
One person could not s another, Ex 10:23
sure you never s my face again, Ex 10:28
for on the day you s my face, Ex 10:28
"I will never s your face again." Ex 10:29
when I s the blood, I will pass Ex 12:13
Stand firm and s the LORD's Ex 14:13
for the Egyptians you s today, Ex 14:13
today, you will never s again. Ex 14:13
test them to s whether or not Ex 16:4
you will s the LORD's glory Ex 16:7
that they may s the bread I fed Ex 16:32
to break through to s the LORD; Ex 19:21
If you s the donkey of someone Ex 23:5
s, My angel will go before you. Ex 32:34
Please, let me s Your glory." Ex 33:18
You cannot s My face, for no one Ex 33:20
for no one can s Me and live." Ex 33:20
and you will s My back, but My Ex 33:23
among will s the LORD's work Ex 34:10
would s that Moses' face Ex 34:35
replied to Moses, "S, today they Lv 10:19
feet so far as the priest can s, Lv 13:12
But if as far as he can s, Lv 13:37
S, I have taken the Levites from Nm 3:12
don't let me s my misery ⌊any Nm 11:15
You will s whether or not what I Nm 11:23
S what the land is like, and Nm 13:18
will ever s the land I swore to Nm 14:23
who have despised Me will s it. Nm 14:23
I s them from the top of rocky Nm 23:9
place where you can s them. Nm 23:13
You will only s the outskirts of Nm 23:13
you won't s all of them. Nm 23:13
I s him, but not now; I perceive Nm 24:17
range⌋ and s the land that I Nm 27:12
Kadesh-barnea to s the land. Nm 32:8
from Egypt will s the land I Nm 32:11
S, I have set the land before Dt 1:8
S, the LORD your God has set the Dt 1:21
generation will s the good land Dt 1:35
will s it, and I will give him Dt 1:36
S, I have handed Sihon the Dt 2:24
said to me, 'S, I have begun to Dt 2:31
cross over and s the beautiful Dt 3:25
and s ⌊it⌋ with your own eyes, Dt 3:27
this land that you will s.' Dt 3:28
the words, but didn't s a form; Dt 4:12
you did not s any form on the Dt 4:15
to the heavens and s the sun, Dt 4:19
which cannot s, hear, eat, Dt 4:28
all the ⌊sacred⌋ places you s. Dt 12:13
our God or s this great fire Dt 18:16
your enemies and s horses, Dt 20:1
our eyes did not s ⌊it⌋. Dt 21:7
if you s a beautiful woman among Dt 21:11
If you s your brother's ox or Dt 22:1
you s your brother's donkey or Dt 22:4
He must not s anything improper Dt 23:14
of the earth will s that you are Dt 28:10
be driven mad by what you s. Dt 28:34
and because of what you will s. Dt 28:67
I said you would never s again. Dt 28:68
eyes to s, or ears to hear. Dt 29:4
country will s the plagues Dt 29:22
S, today I have set before you Dt 30:15
I will s what will become of Dt 32:20
S now that I alone am He; Dt 32:39
I have let you s it with your Dt 34:4
When you s the ark of the Jos 3:3
so that you can s the way to go, Jos 3:4
to let them s the land He had Jos 5:6
them. You can s for yourself. Jos 7:21
s ⌊that you do⌋ as I have Jos 8:8
As you s, the LORD has kept me Jos 14:10
S, I have allotted these Jos 23:4
people, "You s this stone—it Jos 24:27
Israel and to s whether they Jdg 2:22
Deal with us as You s fit; Jdg 10:15
the road⌋ to s the lion's Jdg 14:8
S, the day is almost over. Jdg 19:9
and when you s the young women Jdg 21:21
S which field they are Ru 2:9
You will s distress ⌊in the⌋ 1Sm 2:32
was fixed because he couldn't s. 1Sm 4:15
they were overjoyed to s it. 1Sm 6:13
Do you s the one the LORD has 1Sm 10:24
you can s that the king is 1Sm 12:2
yourselves and s this great 1Sm 12:16
will know and s what a great 1Sm 12:17
the men and then let them s us. 1Sm 14:8
Man does not s what the LORD 1Sm 16:7
You s that an evil spirit from 1Sm 16:15
Do you s this man who keeps 1Sm 17:25
you came down to s the battle!" 1Sm 17:28
When I s what ⌊he says⌋, I'll 1Sm 19:3
back⌋ to s David and said, 1Sm 19:15
me go so I can s my brothers.' 1Sm 20:29
You can s the man is crazy," 1Sm 21:14
can s with your own eyes that 1Sm 24:10
S, my father! Look at the corner 1Sm 24:11
didn't s my lord's young men 1Sm 25:25
S, I have heard what you said 1Sm 25:35
What do you s?" "I see a spirit 1Sm 28:13
I s a spirit form coming up 1Sm 28:13
here when you come to s me." 2Sm 3:13
son of Ner came to s the king, 2Sm 3:23
When your father comes to s you, 2Sm 13:5
When the king came to s him, 2Sm 13:6
but he may not s my face." 2Sm 14:24
but he did not s the king. 2Sm 14:24
his servants, "S, Joab has a 2Sm 14:30
So now, let me s the king. 2Sm 14:32
allow me to s both it and its 2Sm 15:25
the LORD will s my affliction 2Sm 16:12
a young man did s them and 2Sm 17:18
the Jordan River to s him off at 2Sm 19:31
Ahijah could not s; his gaze was 1Kg 14:4
and you will s that this one is 1Kg 20:7
'Do you s this entire immense 1Kg 20:13
You s, the LORD has put a lying 1Kg 22:23
You will soon s when you go to 1Kg 22:25
you s me being taken from you, 2Kg 2:10
our lord can s that the city's 2Kg 2:19
'You will not s wind or rain, 2Kg 3:17
and you will s that he is only 2Kg 5:7
said, "Go and s where he is, so 2Kg 6:13
open his eyes and let him s." 2Kg 6:17
men's eyes and let them s." 2Kg 6:20
Do you s how this murderer has 2Kg 6:32
will in fact s it with your own 2Kg 7:2
so let's send them and s." 2Kg 7:13
army, saying, "Go and s." 2Kg 7:14
will in fact s it with your own 2Kg 7:19
and shouted, "I s troops!" 2Kg 9:17
Come with me and s my zeal for 2Kg 10:16
carefully to s that there are no 2Kg 10:23
open Your eyes, LORD, and s; 2Kg 19:16
eyes will not s all the disaster 2Kg 22:20
"What is this monument I s?" 2Kg 23:17
S, I give the oxen for the burnt 1Ch 21:23
Now, you s, the LORD has put a 2Ch 18:22
You will soon s when you go to 2Ch 18:24
You will s them coming up the 2Ch 20:16
and s the salvation of the LORD. 2Ch 20:17
May the LORD s and demand an 2Ch 24:22
as you s with your own eyes. 2Ch 29:8
of horror as you yourselves s. 2Ch 30:7
eyes will not s all the disaster 2Ch 34:28
S that you not neglect this Ezr 4:22
conducted ⌊to s⌋ if it is true Ezr 5:17
You s the trouble we are in. Neh 2:17
won't know or s anything until Neh 4:11
was doing and to s what was Est 2:11
told Haman to s if Mordecai's Est 3:4
to you to do with as you s fit." Est 3:11
me since I s Mordecai the Jew Est 5:13
answered him, "S, Haman is Est 6:5
could I bear to s the evil that Est 8:6
I bear to s the destruction Est 8:6
may it not s the breaking of Jb 3:9
infants who never s daylight? Jb 3:16
S how happy the man is God Jb 5:17
When you s something dreadful, Jb 6:21
never again s anything good. Jb 7:7
looks on me will no longer s me. Jb 7:8
passes by me, I wouldn't s Him; Jb 9:11
or do You s as a human sees? Jb 10:4
Who can s ⌊any⌋ hope for me? Jb 17:15
yet I will s God in my flesh. Jb 19:26
will s Him myself; my eyes will Jb 19:27
saw him will s ⌊him⌋ no more, Jb 20:9
household will no longer s him. Jb 20:9
Let his own eyes s his demise; Jb 21:20
so you cannot s, and a flood of Jb 22:11
veil Him so that He cannot s, Jb 22:14
The righteous s ⌊this⌋ and Jb 22:19
to the north, I cannot s Him; Jb 23:9
who know Him never s His days? Jb 24:1
eye will s me, he covers ⌊his⌋ Jb 24:15
Does He not s my ways and number Jb 31:4
I will continue to s the light." Jb 33:28
hides ⌊His⌋ face, who can s Him? Jb 34:29
Teach me what I cannot s; Jb 34:32
Look at the heavens and s; Jb 35:5
complain that you do not s Him, Jb 35:14
S, he is pregnant with evil, Ps 7:14
His face and will never s." Ps 10:11
The upright will s His face. Ps 11:7
human race to s if there is one Ps 14:2
Your Faithful One to s the Pit. Ps 16:10
⌊for⌋ You s what is right. Ps 17:2
But I will s Your face in Ps 17:15
that I will s the LORD's Ps 27:13
those who s me in the street run Ps 31:11
Taste and s that the LORD is Ps 34:8
In Your light we will s light. Ps 36:9
Many will s and fear, and put Ps 40:3
Then I said, "S, I have come; Ps 40:7

You s the crowd pressing against Mk 5:31
around to s who had done this Mk 5:32
eyes, and not s, and do you have Mk 8:18
asked him, "Do you s anything?" Mk 8:23
up and said, "I s people—they Mk 8:24
cured and could s everything Mk 8:25
death until they s the kingdom Mk 9:1
man told Him, "I want to s!" Mk 10:51
he could s and began to follow Mk 10:52
Do you s these great buildings? Mk 13:2
When you s the abomination that Mk 13:14
Then they will s the Son of Man Mk 13:26
when you s these things Mk 13:29
S—My betrayer is near." Mk 14:42
all of you will s the Son of Man Mk 14:62
so that we may s and believe." Mk 15:32
Let's s if Elijah comes to take Mk 15:36
S the place where they put Him. Mk 16:6
you will s Him there just as He Mk 16:7
you s, when the sound of your Lk 1:44
to Bethlehem and s what has Lk 2:15
he would not s death before he Lk 2:26
everyone will s the salvation Lk 3:6
to s if He would heal on the Lk 6:7
yourself don't s the log in your Lk 6:42
then you will s clearly to take Lk 6:42
go out into the wilderness to s? Lk 7:24
What then did you go out to s? Lk 7:25
What then did you go out to s? Lk 7:26
to Simon, "Do you s this woman? Lk 7:44
so that Looking they may not s, Lk 8:10
who come in may s the light. Lk 8:16
outside, wanting to s You." Lk 8:20
went out to s what had happened Lk 8:35
And he wanted to s Him. Lk 9:9
death until they s the kingdom Lk 9:27
The eyes that s the things you Lk 10:23
the things you s are blessed! Lk 10:23
kings wanted to s the things you Lk 10:24
the things you s yet didn't see Lk 10:24
you see yet didn't s them; Lk 10:24
who come in may s its light. Lk 11:33
When you s a cloud rising in the Lk 12:54
when you s Abraham, Isaac, Lk 13:28
S, your house is abandoned to Lk 13:35
you will not s Me until the time Lk 13:35
and I must go out and s it. Lk 14:18
the cost to s if he has enough Lk 14:28
For you s, the kingdom of God Lk 17:21
will long to s one of the days Lk 17:22
Son of Man, but you won't s it. Lk 17:22
"Lord," he said, "I want to s!" Lk 18:41
he could s, and he began to Lk 18:43
was trying to s who Jesus was, Lk 19:3
up a sycamore tree to s Jesus, Lk 19:4
These things that you s— Lk 21:6
When you s Jerusalem surrounded Lk 21:20
Then they will s the Son of Man Lk 21:27
leaves⌋ you can s for yourselves Lk 21:30
when you s these things Lk 21:31
Herod was very glad to s Jesus; Lk 23:8
time he had wanted to s Him, Lk 23:8
and was hoping to s some miracle Lk 23:8
said, but they didn't s Him." Lk 24:24
Touch Me and s, because a ghost Lk 24:39
and bones as you can s I have." Lk 24:39
'The One you s the Spirit Jn 1:33
"Come and you'll s," He replied. Jn 1:39
"Come and s," Philip answered. Jn 1:46
will s greater things than this. Jn 1:50
You will s heaven opened and the Jn 1:51
he cannot s the kingdom of God." Jn 3:3
in the Son will not s life; Jn 3:36
I s that You are a prophet. Jn 4:19
s a man who told me everything I Jn 4:29
you ⌊people⌋ s signs and wonders Jn 4:48
said to him, "S, you are well. Jn 5:14
do so we may s and believe You? Jn 6:30
disciples can s Your works that Jn 7:3
and you will s that no prophet Jn 7:52
he will never s death—ever!" Jn 8:51
that he would s My day; Jn 8:56
them. "I washed and I can s." Jn 9:15
How then does he now s?" Jn 9:19
I was blind, and now I can s!" Jn 9:25
those who do not s will see and Jn 9:39
do not see will s and those who Jn 9:39
who do s will become blind. Jn 9:39
that you say, 'We s'—your sin Jn 9:41
they told Him, "come and s." Jn 11:34
Jews said, "S how He loved him! Jn 11:36
you would s the glory of God? Jn 11:40
but also to s Lazarus the one He Jn 12:9
said to one another, "You s? Jn 12:19
him, "Sir, we want to s Jesus." Jn 12:21
they would not s with their eyes Jn 12:40
it doesn't s Him or know Him. Jn 14:17
the world will s Me no longer, Jn 14:19
Me no longer, but you will s Me. Jn 14:19
and you will no longer s Me; Jn 16:10
and you will no longer s Me; Jn 16:16
little while and you will s Me." Jn 16:16
while and you will not s Me; Jn 16:17
little while and you will s Me'; Jn 16:17
while and you will not s Me; Jn 16:19
little while and you will s Me'? Jn 16:19
now. But I will s you again. Jn 16:22
Then they will s My glory, Jn 17:24
Didn't I s you with Him in the Jn 18:26
toss for it, to s who gets it." Jn 19:24
If I don't s the mark of the Jn 20:25
your young men will s visions, Ac 2:17
allow Your Holy One to s decay. Ac 2:27
out what you both s and hear. Ac 2:33
man strong, whom you s and know. Ac 3:16
I s the heavens opened and the Ac 7:56
For I s you are poisoned by Ac 8:23
eunuch did not s him any longer. Ac 8:39
were open, he could s nothing. Ac 9:8
was unable to s for three days, Ac 9:9
will not s the sun for a time. Ac 13:11
allow Your Holy One to s decay. Ac 13:35
of the Lord, and s how they're Ac 15:36
daily to s if these things Ac 17:11
I s that you are extremely Ac 17:22
your own law, s to it yourselves Ac 18:15
said, "I must s Rome as well!" Ac 19:21
both s and hear that not only Ac 19:26
will ever s my face again. Ac 20:25
would never s his face again. Ac 20:38
and said, "You s, brother, how Ac 21:20
Since I couldn't s because of Ac 22:11
His will, to s the Righteous One Ac 22:14
as even you can s very well. Ac 25:10
you s this man about whom the Ac 25:24
I can s that this voyage is Ac 27:10
I've asked to s you and speak to Ac 28:20
they might s with their eyes Ac 28:27
For I want very much to s you, Rm 1:11
But I s a different law in the Rm 7:23
if we hope for what we do not s, Rm 8:25
eyes that cannot s and ears that Rm 11:8
be darkened so they cannot s, Rm 11:10
who had no report of Him will s, Rm 15:21
I do hope to s you when I pass Rm 15:24
For now we s indistinctly, 1Co 13:12
don't want to s you now just in 1Co 16:7
s that he has nothing to fear 1Co 16:10
they cannot s the light of the 2Co 4:4
Test yourselves ⌊to s⌋ if you 2Co 13:5
But I didn't s any of the other Gl 1:19
I come and s you or am absent, Php 1:27
him as soon as I s how things go Php 2:23
when you s him again and I Php 2:28
rejoicing to s your good order Col 2:5
and s that you also read the Col 4:16
return and s you face to face. 1Th 2:17
us, wanting to s us, as we also 1Th 3:6
us, as we also want to s you. 1Th 3:6
and day to s you face to face 1Th 3:10
S to it that no one repays evil 1Th 5:15
of mankind has seen or can s, 1Tm 6:16
I long to s you so that I may be 2Tm 1:4
we do not yet s everything Heb 2:8
But we do s Jesus—made lower Heb 2:9
So we s that they were unable to Heb 3:19
Then I said, "S, I have come— Heb 10:7
He then says, S, I have come to Heb 10:9
more as you s the day drawing Heb 10:25
it no one will s the Lord. Heb 12:14
S to it that no one falls short Heb 12:15
And s that there isn't any Heb 12:16
S that you do not reject the One Heb 12:25
he will be with me when I s you. Heb 13:23
You s that faith was active Jms 2:22
You s that a man is justified by Jms 2:24
S how the farmer waits for the Jms 5:7
S, we count as blessed those who Jms 5:11
life and to s good days must 1Pt 3:10
because we will s Him as He is. 1Jn 3:2
hope to s you soon, and we will 3Jn 14
every eye will s Him, including Rv 1:7
scroll what you s and send it to Rv 1:11
I turned to s the voice that was Rv 1:12
on your eyes so that you may s. Rv 3:18
not able to s, hear, or walk. Rv 9:20
go naked, and they s his shame." Rv 16:15
when they s the beast that was Rv 17:8
and I will never s grief,' Rv 18:7
her when they s the smoke of her Rv 18:9
I did not s a sanctuary in it, Rv 21:22
They will s His face, and His Rv 22:4

SEED *(77)*

bearing fruit with s in it, Gn 1:11
bearing fruit with s in it, Gn 1:12
tree whose fruit contains s. Gn 1:29
and between your s and her seed. Gn 3:15
and between your seed and her s. Gn 3:15
Isaac sowed s in that land, Gn 26:12
Give us s so that we can live Gn 47:19
Here is s for you. Sow it Gn 47:23
will be yours as s for the field Gn 47:24
coriander s, was white, Ex 16:31
falls on any s that is to be Lv 11:37
been put on the s and one of Lv 11:38
your fields with two kinds of s, Lv 19:19
will sow your s in vain because Lv 26:16
to the s needed to sow it, Lv 27:16
every⌋ five bushels of barley s. Lv 27:16
The manna resembled coriander s, Nm 11:7
and his s will be by abundant Nm 24:7
you sowed your s and irrigated Dt 11:10
vineyard with two types of s; Dt 22:9
You will sow much s in the field Dt 28:38
the bag of s, he will surely Ps 126:6
In the morning sow your s, Ec 11:6
10 bushels of s will yield only Is 5:10
felled, the holy s is the stump. Is 6:13
you will help your s to sprout, Is 17:11
plow every day to plant s? Is 28:24
rain for your s that you have Is 30:23
you who sow s beside abundant Is 32:20
will see ⌊His⌋ s, He will Is 53:10
and providing s to sow and food Is 55:10
vine from the very best s. Jr 2:21
of Judah with the s of man and Jr 31:27
seed of man and the s of beast. Jr 31:27
also reject the s of Jacob and Jr 33:26
a house or sow s or plant a Jr 35:7
not have vineyard, field, or s. Jr 35:9
some of the land's s and put it Ezk 17:5
treads grapes, the sower of s. Am 9:13
Is there still s left in the Hg 2:19
who sowed good s in his field. Mt 13:24
you sow good s in your field? Mt 13:27
like a mustard s that a man took Mt 13:31
sows the good s is the Son of Mt 13:37
and the good s—these are the Mt 13:38
faith the size of a mustard s, Mt 17:20
where you haven't scattered s. Mt 25:24
Some s fell along the path, Mk 4:4
Other s fell on rocky ground Mk 4:5
Other s fell among thorns, Mk 4:7
A man scatters s on the ground; Mk 4:26
and the s sprouts and grows— Mk 4:27
It's like a mustard s that, Mk 4:31
A sower went out to sow his s. Lk 8:5
Other s fell on the rock; Lk 8:6
Other s fell among thorns; Lk 8:7
Still other s fell on good Lk 8:8
The s is the word of God. Lk 8:11
As for the s that fell among Lk 8:14
But the s in the good ground— Lk 8:15
like a mustard s that a man took Lk 13:19
faith the size of a mustard s," Lk 17:6
And in your s all the families Ac 3:25
in Isaac your s will be called. Rm 9:7
of the promise are considered s. Rm 9:8
of Hosts had not left us a s, Rm 9:29
body, but only a s, perhaps of 1Co 15:37
One who provides s for the sower 2Co 9:10
and multiply your s and increase 2Co 9:10
Are they the s of Abraham? 2Co 11:22
spoken to Abraham and to his s. Gl 3:16

but and to your s, referring to Gl 3:16
until the S to whom the promise Gl 3:19
are Abraham's s, heirs according Gl 3:29
In Isaac your s will be called. Heb 11:18
not of perishable s but of 1Pt 1:23
because His s remains in him; 1Jn 3:9

SEED-BEARING *(3)*

s plants, and fruit trees on the Gn 1:11
s plants according to their Gn 1:12
given you every s plant on the Gn 1:29

SEEDS *(9)*

grapevine, from s to skin, Nm 6:4
The s lie shriveled in their Jl 1:17
some s fell along the path, Mt 13:4
It's the smallest of all the s, Mt 13:32
than all the s on the ground. Mk 4:31
The s along the path are those Lk 8:12
And the s on the rock are those Lk 8:13
to each of the s its own body. 1Co 15:38
He does not say "and to s," Gl 3:16

SEEDTIME *(1)*

earth endures, s and harvest, Gn 8:22

SEEING *(32)*

⌊and it is⌋ like s God's face, Gn 33:10
S the basket among the reeds, Ex 2:5
Looking all around and s no one, Ex 2:12
him mute or deaf, s or blind? Ex 4:11
they flee without s any good. Jb 9:25
The hearing ear and the s eye— Pr 20:12
not satisfied by s or the ear Ec 1:8
Though s many things, you do not Is 42:20
righteous and s the heart and Jr 20:12
him, never s this land again." Jr 22:12
for them by s false visions Ezk 22:28
S their faith, Jesus told the Mt 9:2
lame walking, and the blind s. Mt 15:31
S a lone fig tree by the road, Mt 21:19
s that He had been condemned, Mt 27:3
S their faith, Jesus told the Mk 2:5
After s in the distance a fig Mk 11:13
After s ⌊them⌋, they reported Lk 2:17
S their faith He said, "Friend, Lk 5:20
But one of them, s that he was Lk 17:15
S that he became sad, Jesus said, Lk 18:24
and thought they were s a ghost. Lk 24:37
left, washed, and came back s. Jn 9:7
believe without s are blessed." Jn 20:29
S this in advance, he spoke Ac 2:31
hearing the sound but s no one. Ac 9:7
but thought he was s a vision. Ac 12:9
the proconsul, s what happened, Ac 13:12
him closely and s that he had Ac 14:9
S the commander and the soldiers, Ac 21:32
s that we suffer with Him so Rm 8:17
And though not s Him now, you 1Pt 1:8

SEEK *(158)*

in order to s your favor.'" Gn 32:5
journey to s a resting place for Nm 10:33
while I s ⌊the LORD⌋ over Nm 23:15
he did not go to s omens as on Nm 24:1
the journey to s out a place for Dt 1:33
when you s Him with all your Dt 4:29
Never s peace or friendship with Dt 23:6
did not s the LORD's counsel. Jos 9:14
of Israel began to s the LORD. 1Sm 7:2
used to say, 'S counsel in Abel, 2Sm 20:18
my mountain where I s refuge. 2Sm 22:3
will be for me to s guidance." 2Kg 16:15
of the valley to s pasture for 1Ch 4:39
of those who s the LORD rejoice. 1Ch 16:10
His strength; s His face always 1Ch 16:11
and heart to s the LORD your God 1Ch 22:19
observe and s after all the 1Ch 28:8
you s Him, He will be found by 1Ch 28:9
pray and s My face, and turn 2Ch 7:14
their hearts to s the LORD their 2Ch 11:16
in his heart to s the LORD. 2Ch 12:14
of⌋ Judah to s the LORD God 2Ch 14:4
you s Him, He will be found by 2Ch 15:2
into a covenant to s the LORD 2Ch 15:12
Whoever would not s the LORD 2Ch 15:13
his disease he didn't s the LORD 2Ch 16:12
David. He did not s the Baals 2Ch 17:3
land and have decided to s God." 2Ch 19:3
so he resolved to s the LORD. 2Ch 20:3
who gathered to s the LORD. 2Ch 20:4
the cities of Judah to s Him. 2Ch 20:4
in order to s his God, and he 2Ch 31:21
Josiah began to s the God of his 2Ch 34:3
is gracious to all who s Him, Ezr 8:22
Never s their peace or Ezr 9:12
had come to s the well-being Neh 2:10
Whatever you s, even to half the Est 7:2
you s will also be done. Est 9:12
He continued to s good for his Est 10:3
will eagerly s me, but I will Jb 7:21
if you earnestly s God and ask Jb 8:5
and many will s your favor. Jb 11:19
LORD my God, I s refuge in You; Ps 7:1
not abandoned those who s You, Ps 9:10
of all who s refuge from those Ps 17:7
my mountain where I s refuge, Ps 18:2
those who s the LORD will praise Ps 22:26
generation of those who s Him, Ps 24:6
who s the face of the God of Ps 24:6
my heart says, "S My face." Ps 27:8
LORD, I will s Your face. Ps 27:8
LORD, I s refuge in You; Ps 31:1
those who s the LORD will not Ps 34:10
what is good; s peace and pursue Ps 34:14
Let those who s to kill me be Ps 35:4
Those who s my life set traps, Ps 38:12
Let those who s to take my life Ps 40:14
Let all who s You rejoice and be Ps 40:16
will s your favor with gifts. Ps 45:12
and violent men s my life. Ps 54:3
I will s refuge in the shadow of Ps 57:1
God; I eagerly s You. I thirst Ps 63:1
But those who s to destroy my Ps 63:9
let those who s You be Ps 69:6
You who s God, take heart! Ps 69:32
Let those who s my life be Ps 70:2
Let all who s You rejoice and be Ps 70:4
LORD, I s refuge in You; Ps 71:1
may those who s my harm be Ps 71:13
for those who s my harm will be Ps 71:24
⌊the rest⌋ began to s Him; Ps 78:34
so that they will s Your name, Ps 83:16
for their prey and s their food Ps 104:21
of those who s the LORD rejoice. Ps 105:3
His strength; s His face always Ps 105:4
His decrees and s Him with all Ps 119:2
place because I s Your precepts. Ps 119:45
they do not s Your statutes. Ps 119:155
s Your servant, for I do not Ps 119:176
our God, I will s your good. Ps 122:9
Lord GOD. I s refuge in You; Ps 141:8
if you s it like silver and Pr 2:4
Many s the favor of a ruler, Pr 19:6
or to s glory after glory. Pr 25:27
but those who s the LORD Pr 28:5
Many s a ruler's favor, but a Pr 29:26
applied my mind to s and explore Ec 1:13
and s wisdom and an explanation Ec 7:25
I will s the one I love. Sg 3:2
We will s him with you. Sg 6:1
what is good. S justice. Correct Is 1:17
did not s the LORD of Hosts. Is 9:13
The nations will s Him, and His Is 11:10
Then they will s idols, ghosts, Is 19:3
in order to s shelter under Is 30:2
they do not s the LORD's help Is 31:1
The poor and the needy s water, Is 41:17
of Jacob: S Me in a wasteland. I Is 45:19
you who s the LORD: Is 51:1
S the LORD while He may be found; Is 55:6
They s Me day after day and Is 58:2
found by those who did not s Me. Is 65:1
stupid: they don't s the LORD. Jr 10:21
S the welfare of the city I have Jr 29:7
You will s Me and find Me when Jr 29:13
do you s great things for Jr 45:5
and will s the LORD their God. Jr 50:4
will s peace, but there will Ezk 7:25
Then they will s a vision from a Ezk 7:26
I will s the lost, bring back Ezk 34:16
the Lord God to s Him by prayer Dn 9:3
she will s them but not find Hs 2:7
will return and s the LORD their Hs 3:5
and herds to s the LORD but do Hs 5:6
their guilt and s My face; Hs 5:15
for all this, they do not s Him. Hs 7:10
is time to s the LORD until He Hs 10:12
house of Israel: S Me and live! Am 5:4
Do not s Bethel or go to Gilgal Am 5:5
S Yahweh and live, or He will Am 5:6
S good and not evil so that you Am 5:14
You also will s refuge from the Nah 3:11
who do not s the LORD or inquire Zph 1:6
S the LORD, all you humble of Zph 2:3
S righteousness, seek humility; Zph 2:3
Seek righteousness, s humility; Zph 2:3
favor and to s the LORD of Hosts Zch 8:21
will come to s the LORD of Hosts Zch 8:22
and he will not s the lost or Zch 11:16
and people should s instruction Mal 2:7
And what does the One s? Mal 2:15
the Lord you s will suddenly Mal 3:1
eagerly s all these things Mt 6:32
But s first the kingdom of God Mt 6:33
But s His kingdom, and these Lk 12:31
of Man has come to s and to save Lk 19:10
because I do not s My own will, Jn 5:30
you don't s the glory that comes Jn 5:44
I do not s My glory; the One who Jn 8:50
left of mankind may s the Lord— Ac 15:17
that they might s God, and Ac 17:27
doing good s for glory, Rm 2:7
signs and the Greeks s wisdom, 1Co 1:22
a wife? Do not s to be loosed. 1Co 7:27
from a wife? Do not s a wife. 1Co 7:27
No one should s his own ⌊good⌋, 1Co 10:24
s to excel in building up the 1Co 14:12
since you s proof of Christ 2Co 13:3
all s their own interests, Php 2:21
that I s the gift, but I seek Php 4:17
but I s the fruit that is Php 4:17
the Messiah, s what is above, Col 3:1
and we didn't s glory from 1Th 2:6
to s to lead a quiet life, 1Th 4:11
and rewards those who s Him. Heb 11:6
instead, we s the one to come. Heb 13:14
He must s peace and pursue it, 1Pt 3:11
people will s death and will Rv 9:6

SEEKING *(17)*

but you are s the priesthood as Nm 16:10
was s an occasion against the Jdg 14:4
except⌋ the man you're s, 2Sm 17:3
sets his whole heart on s God, 2Ch 30:19
of the LORD and s ⌊Him⌋ in His Ps 27:4
your own ways, s your own Is 58:13
This man is not s the well-being Jr 38:4
yourself? Stop s! For I am about Jr 45:5
one searching or s ⌊for them⌋. Ezk 34:6
from north to east, s the word Am 8:12
secret while he's s public Jn 7:4
he went around s someone to lead Ac 13:11
all things, not s my own profit, 1Co 10:33
for I am not s what is yours, 2Co 12:14
while s to be justified by Gl 2:17
s to cause ⌊me⌋ trouble in my Php 1:17
that they are s a homeland. Heb 11:14

SEEKS *(18)*

For the One who s an accounting Ps 9:12
one who is wise, one who s God. Ps 14:2
the righteous and s to kill him; Ps 37:32
one who is wise and who s God. Ps 53:2
gang of ruthless men s my life. Ps 86:14
A mocker s wisdom and doesn't Pr 14:6
A discerning mind s knowledge, Pr 15:14
An evil man s only rebellion; Pr 17:11
and the ear of the wise s it. Pr 18:15
A judge who s what is right and Is 16:5
within me diligently s You, Is 26:9
justly, who s to be faithful, Jr 5:1
Him, to the person who s Him. Lm 3:25
eagerly s all these things, Lk 12:30
for himself s his own glory. Jn 7:18
He who s the glory of the One Jn 7:18
the One who s it also judges. Jn 8:50
there is no one who s God. Rm 3:11

SEEM *(16)*

Then I will s to be deceiving Gn 27:12
made⌋ light ⌊s⌋ near in the face Jb 17:12
a man's ways s right in his own Pr 16:2
ways of a man s right to him, Pr 21:2
orchard will s like a forest? Is 29:17
orchard will s like a forest. Is 32:15
their gold will s like something Ezk 7:19
It will s like false divination Ezk 21:23
may my advice s good to you my Dn 4:27
Though you s to soar like an Ob 4
it s like nothing to you? Hg 2:3

Though it may s incredible to Zch 8:6
it also s incredible to Me? Zch 8:6
the outside you s righteous to Mt 23:28
the body that s to be weaker are 1Co 12:22
I don't want to s as though I am 2Co 10:9

SEEMED *(16)*

and they s like only a few days Gn 29:20
Their words s good in the eyes Gn 34:18
To ourselves we s like Nm 13:33
we must have s the same to them. Nm 13:33
The plan s good to me, so I Dt 1:23
but it s impossible to do 2Sm 13:2
This proposal s good to Absalom 2Sm 17:4
Since the proposal s right to 1Ch 13:4
all this, it s hopeless Ps 73:16
as it s right for him to do. Jr 18:4
From what s to be His waist up, Ezk 1:27
what s to be His waist down, Ezk 1:27
From what s to be His waist down Ezk 8:2
It also s good to me, since I Lk 1:3
But these words s like nonsense Lk 24:11
based on what s good to them, Heb 12:10

SEEMS *(17)*

and if the spot s to be beneath Lv 13:20
doing⌋ whatever s right in his Dt 12:8
Do for him what s good to you." 2Sm 19:37
do for him what s good to you, 2Sm 19:38
of Israel, "If it s good to you, 1Ch 13:2
may do whatever s best to you Ezr 7:18
the matter s right to the king Est 8:5
is a way that s right to a man, Pr 14:12
is a way that s right to a man, Pr 16:25
A bribe s like a magic stone to Pr 17:8
to state his case s right until Pr 18:17
But if it s wrong to you to come Jr 40:4
Wherever it s good and right for Jr 40:4
to them, "If it s right to you, Zch 11:12
He s to be a preacher of foreign Ac 17:18
For it s unreasonable to me to Ac 25:27
No discipline s enjoyable at the Heb 12:11

SEEN *(210)*

I have s that you ⌊alone⌋ are Gn 7:1
Have I really s here the One who Gn 16:13
As soon as he had s the ring, Gn 24:30
We have clearly s how the LORD Gn 26:28
The LORD has s my affliction; Gn 29:32
for I have s all that Laban has Gn 31:12
But God has s my affliction and Gn 31:42
I have s God face to face, Gn 32:30
indeed, I have s your face, ⌊and Gn 33:10
I've never s such ugly ones as Gn 41:19
dream I had also s seven heads Gn 41:22
and I have never s him again. Gn 44:28
Egypt and about all you have s. Gn 45:13
now that I have s your face ⌊and Gn 46:30
and I have also s the way the Ex 3:9
and that He had s their misery, Ex 4:31
You have s what I did to the Ex 19:4
You have s that I have spoken to Ex 20:22
I have s this people, and they Ex 32:9
but My face will not be s." Ex 33:23
no one must be s anywhere on the Ex 34:3
⌊If⌋ he has s, heard, or known Lv 5:1
You, LORD, are s face to face, Nm 14:14
of the men who have s My glory Nm 14:22
After you have s it, you will Nm 27:13
Your own eyes have s everything Dt 3:21
Your eyes have s what the LORD Dt 4:3
eyes have s and so that they Dt 4:9
Today we have s that God speaks Dt 5:24
to me, 'I have s this people, Dt 9:13
awesome works your eyes have s. Dt 10:21
eyes have s every great work Dt 11:7
You have s with your own eyes Dt 29:2
and you have s for yourselves Jos 23:3
They had s all the LORD's great Jdg 2:7
or spear was s among 40,000 Jdg 5:8
I have s the Angel of the LORD Jdg 6:22
and do what you have s me do." Jdg 9:48
wife, "because we have s God!" Jdg 13:22
I have s a young Philistine Jdg 14:2
for we have s the land, and it Jdg 18:9
happened or been s since the day Jdg 19:30
because I have s ⌊the affliction 1Sm 9:16
themselves be s by the 1Sm 14:11
I have s a son of Jesse of 1Sm 16:18
When Saul had s David going out 1Sm 17:55
he goes and who has s him there; 1Sm 23:22
dared not be s entering the city 2Sm 17:17
tell the king what you have s." 2Sm 18:21
and the man had s that all the 2Sm 20:12
not a stone could be s. 1Kg 6:18
their ends were s from the holy 1Kg 8:8
but they were not s from outside 1Kg 8:8
has not been s ⌊again⌋ even to 1Kg 10:12
His sons had s the way taken by 1Kg 13:12
you s how Ahab has humbled 1Kg 21:29
prayer; I have s your tears. 2Kg 20:5
What have they s in your palace? 2Kg 20:15
They have s everything in my 2Kg 20:15
things that were s in the land 2Kg 23:24
and now I have s Your people who 1Ch 29:17
their ends were s from the holy 2Ch 5:9
they were not s from outside; 2Ch 5:9
like them been s in the land of 2Ch 9:11
not been s in Jerusalem since 2Ch 30:26
who had s the first temple, Ezr 3:12
I have s a fool taking root, Jb 5:3
have died and never been s. Jb 10:18
Look, my eyes have s all this; Jb 13:1
I will describe what I have s, Jb 15:17
All of you have s ⌊this⌋ for Jb 27:12
no falcon's eye has s it. Jb 28:7
I have s anyone dying for lack Jb 31:19
mankind has s it; people have Jb 36:25
Have you s the gates of death's Jb 38:17
Or have you s the storehouses of Jb 38:22
but now my eyes have s You. Jb 42:5
Yourself have s trouble and Ps 10:14
You have s my affliction. Ps 31:7
yet I have not s the righteous Ps 37:25
I have s a wicked, violent man Ps 37:35
so we have s in the city of the Ps 48:8
People have s Your procession, Ps 68:24
years as we have s adversity. Ps 90:15
Your work be s by Your servants Ps 90:16
though they had s what I did. Ps 95:9
the earth have s our God's Ps 98:3
I have s a limit to all Ps 119:96
I have s the disloyal and feel Ps 119:158
I have s all the things that are Ec 1:14
I have s that even this is from Ec 2:24
I have s the task that God has Ec 3:10
I have s that there is nothing Ec 3:22
who has not s the evil activity Ec 4:3
tragedy I have s under the sun: Ec 5:13
is what I have s to be good: Ec 5:18
futile life I have s everything: Ec 7:15
All this I have s, applying my Ec 8:9
an evil I have s under the sun, Ec 10:5
I have s slaves on horses, Ec 10:7
"Have you s the one I love?" Sg 3:3
because my eyes have s the King, Is 6:5
darkness have s a great light; Is 9:2
prayer; I have s your tears. Is 38:5
What have they s in your palace? Is 39:4
They have s everything in my Is 39:4
I have s his ways, but I will Is 57:18
we fasted, but You have not s? Is 58:3
no eye has s any God except You, Is 64:4
thing? Who has s such things? Is 66:8
heard of My fame or s My glory. Is 66:19
me, "You have s correctly, for I Jr 1:12
Have you s what unfaithful Jr 3:6
Yes, I too have s ⌊it⌋." Jr 7:11
so that your shame might be s. Jr 13:26
I have s your detestable acts. Jr 13:27
You have s all the disaster I Jr 44:2
Why have I s ⌊this⌋? They are Jr 46:5
for they have s her nakedness. Lm 1:8
She has even s the nations enter Lm 1:10
the man who has s affliction Lm 3:1
the glory I had s by the Chebar Ezk 3:23
the vision I had s in the plain. Ezk 8:4
creatures I had s by the Chebar Ezk 10:15
creatures I had s beneath the Ezk 10:20
same faces I had s by the Chebar Ezk 10:22
the vision I had s left me, Ezk 11:24
own spirit and have s nothing. Ezk 13:3
the one I had s when He came to Ezk 43:3
the ones I had s by the Chebar Ezk 43:3
ram I had s standing beside Dn 8:6
the man I had s in the first Dn 9:21
I have s something horrible in Hs 6:10
I have s Ephraim like Tyre, Hs 9:13
for now I have s with My own Zch 9:8
the star they had s in the east! Mt 2:9
darkness have s a great light, Mt 4:16
of people, to be s by them. Mt 6:1
corners to be s by people. Mt 6:5
this has ever been s in Israel!" Mt 9:33
have never s anything like this! Mk 2:12
what they had s until the Son Mk 9:9
was alive and had been s by her, Mk 16:11
realized that he had s a vision Lk 1:22
for all they had s and heard, Lk 2:20
my eyes have s Your salvation. Lk 2:30
have s incredible things today! Lk 5:26
the things you have s and heard: Lk 7:22
told no one what they had s. Lk 9:36
for all the miracles they had s: Lk 19:37
that they had s a vision of Lk 24:23
No one has ever s God. The One Jn 1:18
have s and testified that He is Jn 1:34
We testify to what We have s, Jn 3:11
to what He has s and heard, Jn 3:32
because they had s everything He Jn 4:45
and you haven't s His form. Jn 5:37
you, you've s Me, and yet you Jn 6:36
that anyone has s the Father Jn 6:46
from God. He has s the Father. Jn 6:46
what I have s in the presence Jn 8:38
old yet, and You've s Abraham?" Jn 8:57
formerly had s him as a beggar Jn 9:8
Jesus answered, "You have s Him; Jn 9:37
you do know Him and have s Him." Jn 14:7
one who has s Me has seen the Jn 14:9
has seen Me has s the Father. Jn 14:9
Now they have s and hated both Jn 15:24
disciples, "I have s the Lord!" Jn 20:18
him, "We have s the Lord!" Jn 20:25
Because you have s Me, you have Jn 20:29
way that you have s Him going Ac 1:11
about what we have s and heard." Ac 4:20
have certainly s the oppression Ac 7:34
to the pattern he had s. Ac 7:44
In a vision he has s a man named Ac 9:12
road, Saul had s the Lord, and Ac 9:27
the vision he had s might mean, Ac 10:17
day and permitted Him to be s, Ac 10:40
to us how he had s the angel Ac 11:13
After he had s the vision, Ac 16:10
they had previously s Trophimus Ac 21:29
of what you have s and heard. Ac 22:15
a witness of things you have s, Ac 26:16
been clearly s, being understood Rm 1:20
yet hope that is s is not hope, Rm 8:24
What no eye has s and no ear has 1Co 2:9
Have I not s Jesus our Lord? 1Co 9:1
So we do not focus on what is s, 2Co 4:18
for what is s is temporary, 2Co 4:18
received and heard and s in me, Php 4:9
all who have not s me in person. Col 2:1
in the Spirit, s by angels, 1Tm 3:16
of mankind has s or can see, 1Tm 6:16
the proof of what is not s. Heb 11:1
so that what is s has been made Heb 11:3
warned about what was not yet s, Heb 11:7
endurance and have s the outcome Jms 5:11
though you have not s Him. 1Pt 1:8
what we have s with our eyes, 1Jn 1:1
and we have s it and we testify 1Jn 1:2
what we have s and heard we also 1Jn 1:3
sins has not s Him or known Him 1Jn 3:6
one has ever s God. If we love 1Jn 4:12
we have s and we testify that 1Jn 4:14
whom he has s cannot love God 1Jn 4:20
love God whom he has not s. 1Jn 4:20
one who does evil has not s God. 3Jn 11
Therefore write what you have s, Rv 1:19
angel that I had s standing on Rv 10:5

SEER *(21)*

let's go to the s," for the 1Sm 9:9
today was formerly called the s. 1Sm 9:9
and asked, "Is the s here?" 1Sm 9:11
"I am the s," Samuel answered. 1Sm 9:19
to the prophet Gad, David's s: 2Sm 24:11
every prophet and every s, 2Kg 17:13
and Samuel the s had appointed 1Ch 9:22
LORD instructed Gad, David's s, 1Ch 21:9
Heman, the king's s, were 1Ch 25:5
that Samuel the s, Saul son of 1Ch 26:28
in the Events of Samuel the S, 1Ch 29:29
and the Events of Gad the S, 1Ch 29:29

of Iddo the S concerning 2Ch 9:29
and of Iddo the S concerning 2Ch 12:15
Hanani the s came to King Asa of 2Ch 16:7
was angry with the s and put him 2Ch 16:10
son of Hanani the s went out to 2Ch 19:2
Gad the king's s, and Nathan 2Ch 29:25
of David and of Asaph the s. 2Ch 29:30
and Jeduthun the king's s. 2Ch 35:15
said to Amos, "Go away, you s! Am 7:12

SEER'S *(1)*
tell me where the s house is?" 1Sm 9:18

SEERS *(4)*
words of the s who spoke to him 2Ch 33:18
and covered your heads—the s. Is 29:10
They say to the s, "Do not see," Is 30:10
Then the s will be ashamed and Mc 3:7

SEES *(54)*
The God Who S, for she said, Gn 16:13
seen here the One who s me?" Gn 16:13
of the Living One Who S Me." Gn 16:14
when he s that the boy is not Gn 44:31
When he s you, his heart will Ex 4:14
to strike Egypt and s the blood Ex 12:23
he s the form of the LORD. Nm 12:8
He s no trouble for Israel. Nm 23:21
s a vision from the Almighty, Nm 24:4
s a vision from the Almighty, Nm 24:16
servants when He s that ⌊their⌋ Dt 32:36
does not see what the LORD s, 1Sm 16:7
for man s what is visible, 1Sm 16:7
but the LORD s the heart." 1Sm 16:7
or do You see as a human s? Jb 10:4
If He s iniquity, will He not Jb 11:11
the earth and s everything under Jb 28:24
Everyone who s me mocks me; Ps 22:7
him because He s that his day is Ps 37:13
when he s the retribution Ps 58:10
the earth s and trembles. Ps 97:4
sensible person s danger and Pr 22:3
has discernment s through him. Pr 28:11
She s that her profits are good, Pr 31:18
by what He s with His eyes, Is 11:3
let him report what he s. Is 21:6
When he s riders—pairs of Is 21:7
Whoever s it will swallow it Is 28:4
in darkness, and say, "Who s us? Is 29:15
For when he s his children, Is 29:23
said: No one s me. Your wisdom Is 47:10
looks down from heaven and s. Lm 3:50
vision that he s concerns many Ezk 12:27
has a son who s all the sins his Ezk 18:14
though he s them, he does not Ezk 18:14
he s the sword coming against Ezk 33:3
if the watchman s the sword Ezk 33:6
and one of them s a human bone, Ezk 39:15
your Father who s in secret will Mt 6:4
your Father who s in secret will Mt 6:6
your Father who s in secret will Mt 6:18
only what He s the Father doing Jn 5:19
that everyone who s the Son and Jn 6:40
But we don't know how he now s, Jn 9:21
away when he s a wolf coming. Jn 10:12
because he s the light of this Jn 11:9
the one who s Me sees Him who Jn 12:45
who sees Me s Him who sent Me Jn 12:45
because who hopes for what he s? Rm 8:24
For if somebody s you, the one 1Co 8:10
beyond what he s in me or hears 2Co 12:6
as one who s Him who is Heb 11:27
world's goods and s his brother 1Jn 3:17
If anyone s his brother 1Jn 5:16

SEETHE *(1)*
the depths s like a caldron; Jb 41:31

SEGUB *(3)*
at the cost of S his youngest, 1Kg 16:34
years old, and she bore him S. 1Ch 2:21
S fathered Jair, who possessed 1Ch 2:22

SEIR *(36)*
(AKA EDOM, IDUMEA)
Horites in the mountains of S, Gn 14:6
brother Esau in the land of S, Gn 32:3
until I come to my lord at S." Gn 33:14
started on his way back to S, Gn 33:16
lived in the mountains of S. Gn 36:8
Edomites in the mountains of S. Gn 36:9
are the sons of S the Horite, Gn 36:20
the sons of S, in the land of Gn 36:21
divisions, in the land of S. Gn 36:30
S will become a possession of Nm 24:18
Kadesh-barnea by way of Mount S. Dt 1:2
routed you from S as far as Dt 1:44
hill country of S for many days. Dt 2:1
of Esau, who live in S. Dt 2:4
hill country of S as ⌊his⌋ Dt 2:5
of Esau, who live in S. Dt 2:8
had previously lived in S, Dt 2:12
of Esau who lived in S, Dt 2:22
Esau who live in S did for us, Dt 2:29
and appeared to them from S; Dt 33:2
which ascends to S, as far as Jos 11:17
ascends toward S (Joshua gave Jos 12:7
westward from Baalah to Mount S, Jos 15:10
the hill country of S to Esau as Jos 24:4
You came from S, when You Jdg 5:4
as their leaders to Mount S. 1Ch 4:42
⌊the inhabitants of⌋ Mount S. 2Ch 20:10
of⌋ Mount S who came ⌊to fight⌋ 2Ch 20:22
of Mount S and completely 2Ch 20:23
with the inhabitants of S, 2Ch 20:23
to me from S, "Watchman, what Is 21:11
Because Moab and S said: Ezk 25:8
face toward Mount S and prophesy Ezk 35:2
I am against you, Mount S. Ezk 35:3
will make Mount S a desolate Ezk 35:7
Mount S, and ⌊so will⌋ Ezk 35:15

SEIR'S *(1)*
S sons: Lotan, Shobal, Zibeon, 1Ch 1:38

SEIRAH *(1)*
the carved images and reached S. Jdg 3:26

SEIRITES *(2)*
He struck down 10,000 S, 2Ch 25:11
the gods of the S and set them 2Ch 25:14

SEIZE *(38)*
to overpower us, s us, make us Gn 43:18
anguish will s the inhabitants Ex 15:14
trembling will s the leaders of Ex 15:15
of your ambush and s the city, Jos 8:7
Saul sent agents to s David, 1Sm 19:14
Saul sent agents to s David. 1Sm 19:20
s one of the young soldiers, 2Sm 2:21
ordered them, "S the prophets of 1Kg 18:40
they did not s any plunder. Est 9:10
but they did not s any plunder. Est 9:15
but they did not s any plunder. Est 9:16
so it may s the edges of the Jb 38:13
in order to s the afflicted. Ps 10:9
right hand will s those who hate Ps 21:8
Let us s God's pastures for Ps 83:12
Let a creditor s all he has; Ps 109:11
A man will even s his brother in Is 3:6
day seven women will s one man, Is 4:1
they growl and s their prey and Is 5:29
to s the wealth of the nations. Is 10:14
pain and agony will s ⌊them⌋; Is 13:8
labor pains s you, as ⌊they do Jr 13:21
plunder them, s them, and carry Jr 20:5
son of Abdeel to s Baruch the Jr 36:26
they devour people, s wealth and Ezk 22:25
They will s your sons and Ezk 23:25
order to s spoil and carry off Ezk 38:12
Have you come to s spoil? Ezk 38:13
possessions, to s great spoil? Ezk 38:13
time of peace and s the kingdom Dn 11:21
will track them down and s them; Am 9:3
They covet fields and s them; Mc 2:2
open spaces to s territories not Hab 1:6
so that each will s the hand of Zch 14:13
Then they tried to s Him. Jn 7:30
Some of them wanted to s Him, Jn 7:44
they were trying again to s Him, Jn 10:39
encouragement to s the hope set Heb 6:18

SEIZED *(46)*
that Abimelech's servants had s. Gn 21:25
pursued him, s him, and cut off Jdg 1:6
they s my land from the Arnon to Jdg 11:13
they s him and killed him at the Jdg 12:6
The Philistines s him and gouged Jdg 16:21
so the man s his concubine and Jdg 19:25
but I s him and put him to death 2Sm 4:10
s the treasuries of the LORD's 1Kg 14:26
So they s them, and Elijah 1Kg 18:40
The Chaldeans s the king and 2Kg 25:6
went to Hamath-zobah and s it. 2Ch 8:3
s the treasuries of the LORD's 2Ch 12:9
He s ⌊me⌋ by the scruff of the Jb 16:12
he s a house he did not build. Jb 20:19
of the poor is s as collateral. Jb 24:9
and days of suffering have s me. Jb 30:16
judgment and justice have s you. Jb 36:17
Trembling s them there, agony Ps 48:6
They were s with craving in the Ps 106:14
As my hand s the idolatrous Is 10:10
Distress has s us—pain like a Jr 6:24
You s me and prevailed. Jr 20:7
for you will be s by the king of Jr 38:23
captured, and the strongholds s. Jr 48:41
pains have s her like a woman Jr 49:24
Distress has s him—pain, like Jr 50:43
fords have been s, the marshes Jr 51:32
the praise of the whole earth s. Jr 51:41
The Chaldeans s the king and Jr 52:9
adversary has s all her precious Lm 1:10
her nakedness, s her sons and Ezk 23:10
So they s him and threw him out Mt 21:39
And the others s his slaves, Mt 22:6
So they s him, killed him, and Mk 12:8
times it had s him, and although Lk 8:29
They s Him, led Him away, and Lk 22:54
Him away, they s Simon, a Lk 23:26
But no one s Him, because His Jn 8:20
So they s them and put them in Ac 4:3
s Paul and Silas and dragged Ac 16:19
Then they all s Sosthenes, Ac 18:17
up the whole crowd, and s him, Ac 21:27
They s Paul, dragged him out of Ac 21:30
this man had been s by the Jews Ac 23:27
reason the Jews s me in the Ac 26:21
He s the dragon, that ancient Rv 20:2

SEIZES *(7)*
country, and he s and rapes her, Dt 22:25
him⌋ by the heel; a noose s him. Jb 18:9
He s the afflicted and drags him Ps 10:9
Rage s me because of the wicked Ps 119:53
trembling s the ungodly: Is 33:14
Wherever it s him, it throws him Mk 9:18
Often a spirit s him; Lk 9:39

SEIZING *(4)*
s its spoil and taking its Ezk 29:19
violent have been s it by force. Mt 11:12
s an opportunity through the Rm 7:8
s an opportunity through the Rm 7:11

SEIZURE *(1)*
Then he had a s and became 1Sm 25:37

SEIZURES *(1)*
because he has s and suffers Mt 17:15

SELA *(4)*
Akrabbim, that is from S upward. Jdg 1:36
took S in battle and called it 2Kg 14:7
from S in the desert to the Is 16:1
inhabitants of S sing for joy; Is 42:11

SELAH *(74)*
is no help for him in God." S Ps 3:2
me from His holy mountain. S Ps 3:4
blessing be on Your people. S Ps 3:8
is worthless and pursue a lie? S Ps 4:2
in your heart and be still. S Ps 4:4
leave my honor in the dust. S Ps 7:5
work of their hands. Higgaion. S Ps 9:16
know they are only men. S Ps 9:20
accept your burnt offering. S Ps 20:3
the request of his lips. S Ps 21:2
the face of the God of Jacob. S Ps 24:6
Hosts, He is the King of glory. S Ps 24:10
as in the summer's heat. S Ps 32:4
took away the guilt of my sin. S Ps 32:5
joyful shouts of deliverance. S Ps 32:7
mortal man is only a vapor. S Ps 39:5
him; every man is a mere vapor. S Ps 39:11
will praise Your name forever. S Ps 44:8
quake with its turmoil. S Ps 46:3
of Jacob is our stronghold. S Ps 46:7
of Jacob is our stronghold. S Ps 46:11
pride of Jacob, whom He loves. S Ps 47:4
God will establish it forever. S Ps 48:8
who approve of their words. S Ps 49:13
of Sheol, for He will take me. S Ps 49:15
for God is the judge. S Ps 50:6
of speaking truthfully. S Ps 52:3
from the land of the living. S Ps 52:5
They have no regard for God. S Ps 54:3
would stay in the wilderness. S Ps 55:7

humiliate them **S** because they do Ps 55:19
S God sends His faithful love Ps 57:3
of me, but they fell into it! **S** Ps 57:6
grace to any wicked traitors. **S** Ps 59:5
that God rules over Jacob. **S** Ps 59:13
can flee before the archers. **S** Ps 60:4
the shelter of Your wings. **S** Ps 61:4
but they curse inwardly. **S** Ps 62:4
before Him. God is our refuge. **S** Ps 62:8
sing praise to Your name." **S** Ps 66:4
should not exalt themselves. **S** Ps 66:7
sacrifice oxen with goats. **S** Ps 66:15
look on us with favor **S** Ps 67:1
and lead the nations on earth. **S** Ps 67:4
marched through the desert, **S** Ps 68:7
burdens; God is our salvation. **S** Ps 68:19
sing praise to the Lord, **S** Ps 68:32
One who steadies its pillars. **S** Ps 75:3
sword, and the weapons of war. **S** Ps 76:3
all the lowly of the earth. **S** Ps 76:9
my spirit becomes weak. **S** Ps 77:3
withheld His compassion?" **S** Ps 77:9
of Jacob and Joseph. **S** Ps 77:15
you at the waters of Meribah. **S** Ps 81:7
show partiality to the wicked? **S** Ps 82:2
support to the sons of Lot. **S** Ps 83:8
who praise You continually. **S** Ps 84:4
prayer; listen, God of Jacob. **S** Ps 84:8
You covered all their sin. **S** Ps 85:2
said about you, city of God. **S** Ps 87:3
This one was born there." **S** Ps 87:6
me with all Your waves. **S** Ps 88:7
spirits rise up to praise You? **S** Ps 88:10
for all generations.' " **S** Ps 89:4
faithful witness in the sky." **S** Ps 89:37
have covered him with shame. **S** Ps 89:45
from the power of Sheol? **S** Ps 89:48
venom is under their lips. **S** Ps 140:3
path and set snares for me. **S** Ps 140:5
they will become proud. **S** Ps 140:8
like parched land before You. **S** Ps 143:6
S His splendor covers the Hab 3:3
S You split the earth with Hab 3:9
strip ⌊him⌋ from foot to neck. **S** Hab 3:13

SELDOM *(1)*
S set foot in your neighbor's Pr 25:17

SELECT *(15)*
month they must each **s** an animal Ex 12:3
his house are to **s** one based Ex 12:4
s an animal from the flock Ex 12:21
to Joshua, "**S** some men for us Ex 17:9
But you should **s** from all the Ex 18:21
cities you **s** will be your six Nm 35:13
S three cities across the Jordan Nm 35:14
'**S** your cities of refuge, as I Jos 20:2
s the most qualified of your 2Kg 10:3
of that land **s** a man from among Ezk 33:2
even their **s** troops will not be Dn 11:15
s from among you seven men of Ac 6:3
decided to **s** men from among them Ac 15:22
decided to **s** men and send them Ac 15:25
do you **s** those who have no 1Co 6:4

SELECTED *(21)*
I have also **s** Oholiab son of Ex 31:6
have **s** your fellow Levites from Nm 18:6
s from the people and the Nm 31:47
so I **s** 12 men from among you, Dt 1:23
But the LORD **s** you and brought Dt 4:20
the 12 men **s** from the Israelites Jos 4:4
and the tribe of Judah was **s**. Jos 7:16
and the Zerahite clan was **s**. Jos 7:17
of families, and Zabdi was **s**. Jos 7:17
of the tribe of Judah, was **s**. Jos 7:18
Joshua **s** 30,000 fighting men and Jos 8:3
they **s** Bezer on the wilderness Jos 20:8
s your house from the tribes of 1Sm 2:28
and the tribe of Benjamin was **s**. 1Sm 10:20
and the Matrite clan was **s**. 1Sm 10:21
Finally, Saul son of Kish was **s**. 1Sm 10:21
Jonathan and Saul were **s**, 1Sm 14:41
Jonathan," and Jonathan was **s**. 1Sm 14:42
because I have **s** a king from his 1Sm 16:1
I **s** 12 of the leading priests, Ezr 8:24
Ezra the priest **s** men who were Ezr 10:16

SELECTS *(4)*
tribe the LORD **s** is to come Jos 7:14
The clan the LORD **s** is to come Jos 7:14
family the LORD **s** is to come Jos 7:14
She **s** wool and flax and works Pr 31:13

SELED *(2)*
Nadab's sons: **S** and Appaim. 1Ch 2:30
S died without children. 1Ch 2:30

SELEUCIA *(1)*
came down to **S**, and from there Ac 13:4

SELF *(6)*
desire integrity in the inner **s**, Ps 51:6
and sinning against your own **s**. Hab 2:10
that our old **s** was crucified Rm 6:6
For in my inner **s** I joyfully Rm 7:22
For people will be lovers of **s**, 2Tm 3:2
that you owe me even your own **s**. Phm 19

SELF-ASSURED *(1)*
This is the **s** city that lives in Zph 2:15

SELF-CONDEMNED *(1)*
is perverted and sins, being **s**. Ti 3:11

SELF-CONTROL *(8)*
righteousness, **s**, and the Ac 24:25
you because of your lack of **s**. 1Co 7:5
But if they do not have **s**, 1Co 7:9
exercises **s** in everything. 1Co 9:25
gentleness, **s**. Against such Gl 5:23
without **s**, brutal, without 2Tm 3:3
knowledge with **s**, self-control 2Pt 1:6
self-control, **s** with endurance, 2Pt 1:6

SELF-CONTROLLED *(4)*
of one wife, **s**, sensible, 1Tm 3:2
not slanderers, **s**, faithful in 1Tm 3:11
sensible, righteous, holy, **s**, Ti 1:8
men are to be **s**, worthy of Ti 2:2

SELF-COUNSEL *(1)*
of a friend is better than **s**. Pr 27:9

SELF-DENIAL *(6)*
to practice **s** and do no work, Lv 16:29
you, and you must practice **s**; Lv 16:31
sacred assembly and practice **s**; Lv 23:27
does not practice **s** on this Lv 23:29
you, and you must practice **s**. Lv 23:32
seventh month and practice **s**; Nm 29:7

SELF-DISCIPLINED *(1)*
action, being **s**, and set your 1Pt 1:13

SELF-INDULGENCE *(1)*
they are full of greed and **s**! Mt 23:25

SELF-INDULGENT *(1)*
she who is **s** is dead even while 1Tm 5:6

SELF-SEEKING *(1)*
to those who are **s** and disobey Rm 2:8

SELFISH *(6)*
himself pursues ⌊**s**⌋ desires; Pr 18:1
is not **s**; is not provoked; 1Co 13:5
of anger, **s** ambitions, slander 2Co 12:20
outbursts of anger, **s** ambitions, Gl 5:20
bitter envy and **s** ambition in Jms 3:14
where envy and **s** ambition exist, Jms 3:16

SELL *(39)*
"First **s** me your birthright." Gn 25:31
let's **s** him to the Ishmaelites Gn 37:27
they did not **s** their land. Gn 47:22
has no right to **s** her to Ex 21:8
they must **s** the live ox and Ex 21:35
He is to **s** to you based on the Lv 25:15
interest or **s** ⌊him⌋ your food Lv 25:37
can **s** us food in exchange for Dt 2:28
or you may **s** it to a foreigner. Dt 14:21
but you must not **s** her for money Dt 21:14
There you will **s** yourselves to Dt 28:68
the LORD will **s** Sisera into a Jdg 4:9
Go **s** the oil and pay your debt; 2Kg 4:7
fine meal ⌊will **s**⌋ for a shekel 2Kg 7:1
of barley ⌊will **s**⌋ for a shekel. 2Kg 7:1
of barley ⌊will **s**⌋ for a shekel 2Kg 7:18
fine meal ⌊will **s**⌋ for a shekel 2Kg 7:18
but now you **s** your own Neh 5:8
of grain to **s** on the Sabbath Neh 10:31
and those who **s** all kinds of Neh 13:20
a price to ⌊**s**⌋ your friend. Jb 6:27
You **s** Your people for nothing; Ps 44:12
and do not **s**—truth, wisdom Pr 23:23
the streams dry and **s** the land Ezk 30:12
They must not **s** or exchange any Ezk 48:14
I will **s** your sons and daughters Jl 3:8
and they will **s** them to the Jl 3:8
because they **s** a righteous Am 2:6
Moon be over so we may **s** grain, Am 8:5
and even **s** the wheat husks! Am 8:6
Those who **s** them say: Praise Zch 11:5
s your belongings and give to Mt 19:21
Go instead to those who **s**, Mt 25:9
s all you have and give to the Mk 10:21
S your possessions and give to Lk 12:33
s all that you have and Lk 18:22
sword should **s** his robe and buy Lk 22:36
you **s** the field for this price? Ac 5:8
one can buy or **s** unless he has Rv 13:17

SELLER *(3)*
mistress, buyer and **s**, lender Is 24:2
not rejoice and the **s** not mourn, Ezk 7:12
The **s** will certainly not return Ezk 7:13

SELLING *(14)*
with yourselves for **s** me here, Gn 45:5
what he is **s** to you is a number Lv 25:16
is **s** a piece of land that Ru 4:3
against **s** food on that day. Neh 13:15
of merchandise and **s** them on the Neh 13:16
You make no profit from **s** them. Ps 44:12
buying and **s** in the temple. Mt 21:12
and the chairs of those **s** doves. Mt 21:12
buying and **s** in the temple. Mk 11:15
and the chairs of those **s** doves, Mk 11:15
drinking, buying, **s**, planting, Lk 17:28
to throw out those who were **s**, Lk 19:45
complex He found people **s** oxen, Jn 2:14
He told those who were **s** doves, Jn 2:16

SELLS *(11)*
When a man **s** his daughter as a Ex 21:7
whether he **s** him or the person Ex 21:16
a sheep and butchers it or **s** it, Ex 22:1
destitute and **s** part of his Lv 25:25
If a man **s** a residence in a Lv 25:29
destitute and **s** himself to you, Lv 25:39
destitute and **s** himself to Lv 25:47
treats him as a slave or **s** him, Dt 24:7
will come to the one who **s** it. Pr 11:26
She makes and **s** linen garments; Pr 31:24
joy he goes and **s** everything he Mt 13:44

SELVES *(1)*
led your own **s** astray because Jr 42:20

SEMACHIAH *(1)*
Elihu and **S** were also capable 1Ch 26:7

SEMEIN *(1)*
son⌋ of **S**, ⌊son⌋ of Josech, Lk 3:26

SEMEN *(6)*
he released his **s** on the ground Gn 38:9
When a man has an emission of **s**, Lv 15:16
an emission of **s** must be washed Lv 15:17
woman and has an emission of **s**, Lv 15:18
a man who has an emission of **s**, Lv 15:32
a man who has an emission of **s**, Lv 22:4

SENAAH'S *(2)*
(AKA HASSENAAH)
S people 3,630 Ezr 2:35
S people 3,930 Neh 7:38

SENATE *(1)*
the full **S** of the sons of Israel Ac 5:21

SEND *(236)*
S them out to us so we can have Gn 19:5
He will **s** His angel before you, Gn 24:7
walked will **s** His angel with Gn 24:40
he said, "**S** me to my master." Gn 24:54
S me away so that I may go to my Gn 24:56
Then I will **s** for you and bring Gn 27:45
S me on my way so that I can Gn 30:25
I will **s** you a young goat from Gn 38:17
with me⌋ until you **s** it." Gn 38:17
all, I did **s** this young goat Gn 38:23
Jacob did not **s** Joseph's brother Gn 42:4
S one of your number to get your Gn 42:16
If you will **s** our brother with Gn 43:4
But if you will not **s** him, Gn 43:5
Israel, "**S** the boy with me Gn 43:8
"**S** everyone away from me!" Gn 45:1
Please, Lord, **s** someone else." Ex 4:13
And why did You ever **s** me? Ex 5:22
then I will **s** swarms of flies Ex 8:21
I am going to **s** all My plagues Ex 9:14
in order to **s** them quickly out Ex 12:33
I am going to **s** an Angel before Ex 23:20
I will **s** the hornet in front of Ex 23:28

I will **s** an angel ahead of you Ex 33:2
know whom You will **s** with me. Ex 33:12
the goat's head and **s** ⌊it⌋ away Lv 16:21
will **s** wild animals against you Lv 26:22
I will **s** a pestilence among you, Lv 26:25
the Israelites to **s** away anyone Nm 5:2
You must **s** away both male or Nm 5:3
s them outside the camp, so that Nm 5:3
S men to scout out the land of Nm 13:2
S one man who is a leader among Nm 13:2
Did I not **s** you an urgent Nm 22:37
S 1,000 men to war from each Nm 31:4
said, 'Let's **s** men ahead of us Dt 1:22
God will also **s** the hornet Dt 7:20
do not **s** him away empty-handed. Dt 15:13
for himself or **s** the people back Dt 17:16
of his city must **s** ⌊for him⌋, Dt 19:12
and **s** her away from his house. Dt 24:1
The LORD will **s** against you Dt 28:20
the LORD will **s** against you, Dt 28:48
everywhere you **s** us we will go. Jos 1:16
to him, "Don't **s** all the people, Jos 7:3
but **s** about 2,000 or 3,000 men Jos 7:3
tribe, and I will **s** them out. Jos 18:4
S the ark of Israel's God away. 1Sm 5:11
us how we can **s** it back to its 1Sm 6:2
If you **s** the ark of Israel's God 1Sm 6:3
you must not **s** it without ⌊an 1Sm 6:3
should we **s** back to Him?" 1Sm 6:4
didn't they **s** Israel away, 1Sm 6:6
S it off and let it go its way. 1Sm 6:8
time tomorrow I will **s** you a man 1Sm 9:16
When I **s** you off in the morning, 1Sm 9:19
and I'll **s** you on your way!" 1Sm 9:26
and let us **s** messengers 1Sm 11:3
and He will **s** thunder and rain 1Sm 12:17
Samuel told Jesse, "**S** for him. 1Sm 16:11
Jesse and said, "**S** me your son 1Sm 16:19
S me a man so we can fight each 1Sm 17:10
and if I do not **s** for you and 1Sm 20:12
you, and I will **s** you away, and 1Sm 20:13
Then I will **s** the young man ⌊and 1Sm 20:21
Now **s** for him and bring him to 1Sm 20:31
S that man back and let him 1Sm 29:4
"**S** me Uriah the Hittite." 2Sm 11:6
"and tomorrow I will **s** you back." 2Sm 11:12
in order to **s** him to the king 2Sm 14:29
I want to **s** you to the king to 2Sm 14:32
S me everything you hear through 2Sm 15:36
Now **s** someone quickly and tell 2Sm 17:16
May You **s** rain on Your land that 1Kg 8:36
wherever You **s** them, and they 1Kg 8:44
advise that we **s** back to these 1Kg 12:9
I will **s** rain on the surface of 1Kg 18:1
tomorrow I will **s** my servants to 1Kg 20:6
He answered, "Don't **s** ⌊them⌋." 2Kg 2:16
so he said, "**S** ⌊them⌋." 2Kg 2:17
Please **s** me one of the servants 2Kg 4:22
Go and I will **s** a letter ⌊with 2Kg 5:5
I can **s** ⌊men⌋ to capture him." 2Kg 6:13
die, so let's **s** them and see." 2Kg 7:13
a rider and **s** him to meet them 2Kg 9:17
S back one of the priests you 2Kg 17:27
spread out and **s** the message to 1Ch 13:2
s me a craftsman who is skilled 2Ch 2:7
Also, **s** me cedar, cypress, and 2Ch 2:8
Now, let my lord **s** the wheat, 2Ch 2:15
May You **s** rain on Your land that 2Ch 6:27
wherever You **s** them, and they 2Ch 6:34
or if I **s** pestilence on My 2Ch 7:13
do you advise we **s** back to this 2Ch 10:9
before our God to **s** away all the Ezr 10:3
They pledged to **s** their wives Ezr 10:19
s me to Judah and to the city Neh 2:5
and it pleased the king to **s** me. Neh 2:6
and **s** portions to those who have Neh 8:10
eat and drink, **s** portions, and Neh 8:12
holiday when they **s** gifts to one Est 9:19
They would **s** an invitation to Jb 1:4
Job would **s** ⌊for his children⌋ Jb 1:5
his appearance and **s** him away. Jb 14:20
God will **s** His burning anger Jb 20:23
Can you **s** out lightning bolts, Jb 38:35
May He **s** you help from the Ps 20:2
LORD will **s** His faithful love Ps 42:8
S Your light and Your truth; Ps 43:3
When You **s** Your breath, they are Ps 104:30
those who **s** him, a trustworthy Pr 25:13
S your bread on the surface of Ec 11:1
Who should I **s**? Who will go for Is 6:8
for Us? I said: Here I am. **S** me. Is 6:8
I will **s** him against a godless Is 10:6
S lambs to the ruler of the land, Is 16:1
He will **s** them a savior and Is 19:20
He will **s** rain for your seed Is 30:23
will **s** to Babylon and bring all Is 43:14
that I used to **s** her away? Is 50:1
prosper in what I **s** it ⌊to do⌋." Is 55:11
and I will **s** survivors from them Is 66:19
to everyone I **s** you to and speak Jr 1:7
S ⌊someone⌋ to Kedar and Jr 2:10
am about to **s** snakes among you, Jr 8:17
will **s** a sword after them until Jr 9:16
s for the skillful women. Jr 9:17
Their nobles **s** their servants Jr 14:3
I did not **s** them, nor did I Jr 14:14
though I did not **s** them, and who Jr 14:15
S them from My presence, and let Jr 15:1
I am about to **s** for many Jr 16:16
Then I will **s** for many hunters, Jr 16:16
I did not **s** these prophets, Jr 23:21
I will **s** the sword, famine, and Jr 24:10
I am going to **s** for all the Jr 25:9
and ⌊**s** for⌋ My servant Jr 25:9
S ⌊word⌋ to the king of Edom, Jr 27:3
The LORD did not **s** you, but you Jr 28:15
'I am about to **s** you off the Jr 28:16
I am about to **s** against them Jr 29:17
S ⌊a message⌋ to all the exiles, Jr 29:31
though I did not **s** him, and made Jr 29:31
but then you must **s** him out free Jr 34:14
Don't **s** me back to the house of Jr 37:20
I will **s** for My servant Jr 43:10
when I will **s** those to him, Jr 48:12
I will **s** the sword after them Jr 49:37
will **s** strangers to Babylon who Jr 51:2
that I will **s** to destroy you, Ezk 5:16
I will **s** famine and dangerous Ezk 5:17
will **s** My anger against you and Ezk 7:3
when the LORD did not **s** them, Ezk 13:6
and I will **s** hailstones plunging Ezk 13:11
of bread, to **s** famine through it Ezk 14:13
Or if I **s** a plague into that Ezk 14:19
will it be when I **s** My four Ezk 14:21
will **s** a plague against her and Ezk 28:23
I will **s** down showers in their Ezk 34:26
I will **s** fire against Magog and Ezk 39:6
arise who will **s** out a tax Dn 11:20
I will **s** fire on their cities, Hs 8:14
I am about to **s** you grain, Jl 2:19
I will **s** fire against Hazael's Am 1:4
I will **s** fire against the walls Am 1:7
I will **s** fire against the walls Am 1:10
I will **s** fire against Teman, Am 1:12
I will **s** fire against Moab, Am 2:2
I will **s** fire against Judah, Am 2:5
I will **s** you into exile beyond Am 5:27
when I will **s** a famine through Am 8:11
s farewell gifts to Mc 1:14
I will **s** it out,"—the Zch 5:4
I will **s** a curse among you, Mal 2:2
I am going to **s** My messenger, Mal 3:1
I am going to **s** you Elijah the Mal 4:5
"**s** us into the herd of pigs." Mt 8:31
of the harvest to **s** out workers Mt 9:38
of Man will **s** out His angels, Mt 13:41
S the crowds away so they can go Mt 14:15
S her away because she cries out Mt 15:23
I don't want to **s** them away Mt 15:32
papers and to **s** her away?" Mt 19:7
and immediately he will **s** them." Mt 21:3
He will **s** out His angels with a Mt 24:31
be with Him, to **s** them out to Mk 3:14
begging Him not to **s** them out of Mk 5:10
begged Him, "**S** us to the pigs, Mk 5:12
and began to **s** them out in pairs Mk 6:7
S them away, so they can go into Mk 6:36
If I **s** them home famished, Mk 8:3
divorce papers and **s** her away." Mk 10:4
needs it and will **s** it back here Mk 11:3
had one to **s**, a beloved son. Mk 12:6
He will **s** out the angels and Mk 13:27
said to Him, "**S** the crowd away, Lk 9:12
of the harvest to **s** out workers Lk 10:2
'I will **s** them prophets and Lk 11:49
mercy on me and **s** Lazarus to dip Lk 16:24
then I beg you to **s** him to my Lk 16:27
I will **s** my beloved son. Lk 20:13
For God did not **s** His Son into Jn 3:17
whomever I **s** receives Me, Jn 13:20
the Father will **s** Him in My name Jn 14:26
the One I will **s** to you from the Jn 15:26
If I go, I will **s** Him to you. Jn 16:7
has sent Me, I also **s** you." Jn 20:21
and He may **s** Jesus, who has been Ac 3:20
come, I will **s** you to Egypt. Ac 7:34
Now **s** men to Joppa and call for Ac 10:5
I ask, 'Why did you **s** for me?' " Ac 10:29
Therefore **s** someone to Joppa and Ac 10:32
and saying, '**S** to Joppa, and Ac 11:13
determined to **s** relief to the Ac 11:29
them and to **s** them to Antioch Ac 15:22
select men and **s** them to you Ac 15:25
because I will **s** you far away to Ac 22:21
until I could **s** him to Caesar." Ac 25:21
the Emperor, I decided to **s** him. Ac 25:25
to me to **s** a prisoner and not to Ac 25:27
Gentiles, to whom I now **s** you, Ac 26:17
of Christ **s** you greetings. Rm 16:16
Christ did not **s** me to baptize, 1Co 1:17
will **s** those whom you recommend 1Co 16:3
that you may **s** me on my way 1Co 16:6
but you should **s** him on his way 1Co 16:11
Lord Jesus to **s** Timothy to you Php 2:19
I hope to **s** him as soon as I see Php 2:23
it necessary to **s** you Php 2:25
very eager to **s** him so that you Php 2:28
When I **s** Artemas to you, or Ti 3:12
elect sister **s** you greetings. 2Jn 13
will do well to **s** them on their 3Jn 6
The friends **s** you greetings. 3Jn 14
you see and **s** it to the seven Rv 1:11
and celebrate and **s** gifts to one Rv 11:10

SENDING *(43)*

was good to you, **s** you away in Gn 26:29
I'm **s** you to them." Gn 37:13
am **s** you to Pharaoh so that you Ex 3:10
with it by **s** it into the Lv 16:10
did this, **s** them outside Nm 5:4
of Midian. Am I not **s** you?" Jdg 6:14
which you're **s** Him as a guilt 1Sm 6:8
I am **s** you to Jesse of Bethlehem 1Sm 16:1
for the LORD is **s** you away. 1Sm 20:22
the mission I'm **s** you on or what 1Sm 21:2
s me away is much worse than the 2Sm 13:16
that you're **s** ⌊these men⌋ to 2Kg 1:6
the LORD is **s** me on to Bethel." 2Kg 2:2
the LORD is **s** me to Jericho." 2Kg 2:4
the LORD is **s** me to the Jordan." 2Kg 2:6
the LORD began **s** Rezin king of 2Kg 15:37
s them time and time again, 2Ch 36:15
of **s** gifts to one another and Est 9:22
deaf like My messenger I am **s**? Is 42:19
the nations I am **s** you to drink Jr 25:15
of the sword I am **s** among them." Jr 25:16
of the sword I am **s** among you. Jr 25:27
I have been **s** you time and time Jr 26:5
who is **s** you to inquire of Me: Jr 37:7
to whom we are **s** you so that it Jr 42:6
I am **s** you to the Israelites Ezk 2:3
I am **s** you to them, and you must Ezk 2:4
against him by **s** his ambassadors Ezk 17:15
was planted and **s** their channels Ezk 31:4
and He relents from **s** disaster. Jl 2:13
who relents from ⌊**s**⌋ disaster. Jnh 4:2
I'm **s** you out like sheep among Mt 10:16
am **s** My messenger ahead of You; Mt 11:10
This is why I am **s** you prophets, Mt 23:34
am **s** My messenger ahead of You, Mk 1:2
am **s** My messenger ahead of You; Lk 7:27
I'm **s** you out like lambs among Lk 10:3
I am **s** you what My Father Lk 24:49
s it to the elders by means of Ac 11:30
So after **s** two of those who Ac 19:22
in the flesh by **s** His own Son Rm 8:3
I am **s** him to you for this very Eph 6:22
I am **s** him—a part of myself— Phm 12

SENDS *(19)*

and **s** her away from his house or Dt 24:3
He **s** ⌊some⌋ to Sheol, and He 1Sm 2:6
the day the LORD **s** rain on the 1Kg 17:14
to the earth and **s** water to the Jb 5:10
Selah God **s** His faithful love Ps 57:3
He **s** His command throughout the Ps 147:15

He s His word and melts them; Ps 147:18
to the one who s him ⌊on an Pr 10:26
The one who s a message by a Pr 26:6
s envoys by sea, in reed vessels Is 18:2
it s its roots out toward a Jr 17:8
LORD your God s you to ⌊tell⌋ us Jr 42:5
He comes and s righteousness Hs 10:12
s showers for you, both autumn Jl 2:23
and s rain on the righteous and Mt 5:45
is ready, he s for the sickle, Mk 4:29
he s a delegation and asks for Lk 14:32
this reason God s them a strong 2Th 2:11
also chosen, s you greetings, as 1Pt 5:13

SENEH *(1)*
was named Bozez and the other S; 1Sm 14:4

SENIR *(4)*
(AKA BAAL-HERMON, HERMAN, SION, SIRION)
Sirion, but the Amorites call S, Dt 3:9
that is, S or Mount Hermon). 1Ch 5:23
from the summit of S and Hermon, Sg 4:8
planking with pine trees from S. Ezk 27:5

SENNACHERIB *(13)*
S king of Assyria attacked all 2Kg 18:13
words that S has sent to mock 2Kg 19:16
to Me about S king of Assyria. 2Kg 19:20
So S king of Assyria broke camp 2Kg 19:36
S king of Assyria came and 2Ch 32:1
saw that S had come and that 2Ch 32:2
while S king of Assyria with all 2Ch 32:9
is what King S of Assyria says: 2Ch 32:10
the power of King S of Assyria 2Ch 32:22
S king of Assyria advanced Is 36:1
words that S has sent to mock Is 37:17
to Me about S king of Assyria, Is 37:21
So S king of Assyria broke camp Is 37:37

SENSE *(24)*
is a nation lacking s with no Dt 32:28
Show some s, and then we can Jb 18:2
He gives them a s of security, Jb 24:23
who commits adultery lacks s; Pr 6:32
youths, a young man lacking s. Pr 7:7
develop common s, you who are Pr 8:5
the one who lacks s, she says, Pr 9:4
the one who lacks s, she says, Pr 9:16
the back of the one who lacks s. Pr 10:13
but fools die for lack of s. Pr 10:21
for his neighbor lacks s, Pr 11:12
rejects good s is like a gold Pr 11:22
chases fantasies lacks s. Pr 12:11
Good s wins favor, but the way Pr 13:15
brings joy to one without s, Pr 15:21
to correction acquires good s. Pr 15:32
without s enters an agreement Pr 17:18
acquires good s loves himself; Pr 19:8
the vineyard of a man lacking s. Pr 24:30
his heart lacks s, and he shows Ec 10:3
where would be the s of smell? 1Co 12:17
with decency and good s; 1Tm 2:9
love, and holiness, with good s. 1Tm 2:15
And in a s Levi himself, who Heb 7:9

SENSED *(1)*
and she s in her body that she Mk 5:29

SENSELESS *(6)*
LORD, you foolish and s people? Dt 32:6
and the s also pass away. Ps 49:10
this, you foolish and s people. Jr 5:21
They are both s and foolish, Jr 10:8
has become like a silly, s dove; Hs 7:11
and their s minds were darkened. Rm 1:21

SENSES *(6)*
come to your s ⌊while you are⌋ Dt 30:1
come to their s in the land 1Kg 8:47
come to their s in the land 2Ch 6:37
he came to his s, he said, 'How Lk 15:17
may come to their s and escape 2Tm 2:26
for those whose s have been Heb 5:14

SENSIBLE *(22)*
whoever ignores an insult is s. Pr 12:16
Every s person acts Pr 13:16
s man's wisdom is to consider Pr 14:8
but the s watch their steps. Pr 14:15
but the s are crowned with Pr 14:18
who heeds correction is s. Pr 15:5
but a s wife is from the LORD. Pr 19:14
A s person sees danger and takes Pr 22:3
The s see danger and take cover; Pr 27:12
will be like a s man who built Mt 7:24
then is a faithful and s slave, Mt 24:45
were foolish and five were s. Mt 25:2
But the s ones took oil in their Mt 25:4
ones said to the s ones, Mt 25:8
The s ones answered, 'No, there Mt 25:9
the faithful and s manager his Lk 12:42
self-controlled, s, respectable, 1Tm 3:2
is good, s, righteous, holy, Ti 1:8
worthy of respect, s, and sound Ti 2:2
to be s, pure, good homemakers, Ti 2:5
encourage the young men to be s Ti 2:6
lusts and to live in a s, Ti 2:12

SENSIBLY *(2)*
than seven men who can answer s. Pr 26:16
Instead, think s, as God has Rm 12:3

SENSITIVE *(2)*
The most s and refined man among Dt 28:54
The most s and refined woman Dt 28:56

SENSITIVITY *(1)*
because of her refinement and s, Dt 28:56

SENSUAL *(1)*
but is earthly, s, demonic. Jms 3:15

SENT *(641)*
So the LORD God s him away from Gn 3:23
and he s out a raven. It went Gn 8:7
Then he s out a dove to see Gn 8:8
more days and s out the dove Gn 8:10
seven days, he s out the dove, Gn 8:12
So Pharaoh s for Abram and said, Gn 12:18
him, and they s him away, with Gn 12:20
the LORD has s us to destroy it. Gn 19:13
and s her and the boy away. Gn 21:14
So they s away their sister Gn 24:59
still alive he s them eastward, Gn 25:6
Abimelech s for Isaac and said, Gn 26:9
hated me and s me away from you. Gn 26:27
Then Isaac s them on their way, Gn 26:31
So Isaac s Jacob to Paddan-aram, Gn 28:5
blessed Jacob and s him to Gn 28:6
I would have s you away with joy Gn 31:27
now you would have s me off Gn 31:42
Jacob s messengers ahead of him Gn 32:3
have s ⌊this message⌋ to inform Gn 32:5
are a gift s to my lord Esau Gn 32:18
the gift was s on ahead of him Gn 32:21
So he s him from the valley of Gn 37:14
They s the robe of many colors Gn 37:32
When Judah s the young goat by Gn 38:20
she s her father-in-law ⌊this Gn 38:25
Then Pharaoh s for Joseph, Gn 41:14
the men were s off with their Gn 44:3
because God s me ahead of you to Gn 45:5
God s me ahead of you to Gn 45:7
it was not you who s me here, Gn 45:8
He s his father the following: Gn 45:23
Joseph s his brothers on their Gn 45:24
that Joseph had s to transport Gn 45:27
Pharaoh had s to carry him, Gn 46:5
Now Jacob had s Judah ahead of Gn 46:28
they s this message to Joseph, Gn 50:16
she s her slave girl to get it. Ex 2:5
sign to you that I have s you: Ex 3:12
of your fathers has s me to you, Ex 3:13
I AM has s me to you." Ex 3:14
God of Jacob, has s me to you. Ex 3:15
the LORD had s him to say, Ex 4:28
Hebrews, has s me to tell you: Ex 7:16
Pharaoh s ⌊messengers⌋ who saw Ex 9:7
and the LORD s thunder and hail. Ex 9:23
Pharaoh s for Moses and Aaron. Ex 9:27
and the LORD s an east wind over Ex 10:13
Pharaoh urgently s for Moses and Ex 10:16
wife, after he had s her back, Ex 18:2
He s word to Moses, "I, your Ex 18:6
Then he s out young Israelite Ex 24:5
they s a proclamation throughout Ex 36:6
when the LORD s the fire. Lv 10:6
A wind s by the LORD came up Nm 11:31
Moses s them from the Wilderness Nm 13:3
of the men Moses s to scout out Nm 13:16
When Moses s them to scout out Nm 13:17
into the land where you s us. Nm 13:27
So the men Moses s to scout out Nm 14:36
Moses s for Dathan and Abiram, Nm 16:12
that the LORD s me to do all Nm 16:28
then the LORD has not s me. Nm 16:29
Moses s messengers from Kadesh Nm 20:14
He heard our voice, s an Angel, Nm 20:16
Then the LORD s poisonous snakes Nm 21:6
Israel s messengers to say to Nm 21:21
After Moses s spies to Jazer, Nm 21:32
he s messengers to Balaam son of Nm 22:5
king of Moab, s ⌊this message⌋ Nm 22:10
Balak s officials again who were Nm 22:15
and s for Balaam and the Nm 22:40
tell the messengers you s me: Nm 24:12
Moses s 1,000 from each tribe to Nm 31:6
fathers did when I s them from Nm 32:8
So I s messengers with an offer Dt 2:26
When the LORD s you from Dt 9:23
husband who s her away may not Dt 24:4
wonders the LORD s him to do Dt 34:11
of Nun secretly s two men as Jos 2:1
of Jericho s ⌊word⌋ to Rahab Jos 2:3
replied, and she s them away. Jos 2:21
because she hid the men we s. Jos 6:17
men Joshua had s to spy on Jos 6:25
Joshua s men from Jericho to Ai, Jos 7:2
Joshua s messengers who ran to Jos 7:22
fighting men and s them out at Jos 8:3
So Joshua s them out, and they Jos 8:9
of Jerusalem s ⌊word⌋ to Hoham Jos 10:3
men of Gibeon s ⌊word⌋ to Joshua Jos 10:6
this news⌋, he s ⌊a message⌋ to: Jos 11:1
the LORD's servant s me from Jos 14:7
as I was the day Moses s me out. Jos 14:11
blessed them and s them on their Jos 22:6
Joshua s them to their homes Jos 22:7
The Israelites s Phinehas son of Jos 22:13
⌊They s⌋ 10 leaders with him— Jos 22:14
Then I s Moses and Aaron, Jos 24:5
He s for Balaam son of Beor to Jos 24:9
I s the hornet ahead of you, Jos 24:12
Then Joshua s the people away, Jos 24:28
They s spies to Bethel (the town Jdg 1:23
Joshua s the people away, and Jdg 2:6
The Israelites s him to Eglon Jdg 3:15
the LORD s a prophet to them. Jdg 6:8
s messengers throughout all of Jdg 6:35
He also s messengers throughout Jdg 6:35
Gideon s all the Israelites to Jdg 7:8
Gideon s messengers throughout Jdg 7:24
God s an evil spirit between Jdg 9:23
So he s messengers secretly to Jdg 9:31
Jephthah s messengers to the Jdg 11:12
Jephthah again s messengers to Jdg 11:14
Israel s messengers to the king Jdg 11:17
They also s ⌊messengers⌋ to the Jdg 11:17
Then Israel s messengers to Jdg 11:19
message that he s him. Jdg 11:28
And he s her away two months. Jdg 11:38
man of God you s come again to Jdg 13:8
she s this message to the Jdg 16:18
So the Danites s out five brave Jdg 18:2
and s her throughout the Jdg 19:29
and s her throughout Israel's Jdg 20:6
of Israel s men throughout Jdg 20:12
when they s up a great cloud of Jdg 20:38
The congregation s 12,000 brave Jdg 21:10
congregation s a message of Jdg 21:13
So the people s ⌊men⌋ to Shiloh 1Sm 4:4
Gathites then s the ark of God 1Sm 5:10
Philistines had s back one gold 1Sm 6:17
They s messengers to the 1Sm 6:21
Samuel s all the people away, 1Sm 10:25
and s them throughout the land 1Sm 11:7
and He s them Moses and Aaron, 1Sm 12:8
So the LORD s Jerubbaal, Barak, 1Sm 12:11
day the LORD s thunder and rain 1Sm 12:18
s the rest of the troops away, 1Sm 13:2
The LORD s me to anoint you as 1Sm 15:1
and then s you on a mission and 1Sm 15:18
So Jesse s for him. He had 1Sm 16:12
young goat and s them by his son 1Sm 16:20
Then Saul s word to Jesse: 1Sm 16:22
in everything Saul s him to do. 1Sm 18:5
Saul s agents to David's house 1Sm 19:11
When Saul s agents to seize 1Sm 19:14
Saul s the agents ⌊back⌋ to see 1Sm 19:15
You s my enemy away, and he 1Sm 19:17
Saul s agents to seize David. 1Sm 19:20
to Saul, he s other agents, 1Sm 19:21
tried again and s a third group 1Sm 19:21

king **s** ⌊messengers⌋ to summon 1Sm 22:11
so David **s** 10 young men 1Sm 25:5
David **s** messengers from the 1Sm 25:14
lord's young men whom you **s**. 1Sm 25:25
who **s** you to meet me today! 1Sm 25:32
Then David **s** messengers to 1Sm 25:39
David **s** us to bring you to him 1Sm 25:40
David **s** out spies and knew for 1Sm 26:4
he **s** some of the plunder to his 1Sm 30:26
⌊He **s** gifts⌋ to those in Bethel, 1Sm 30:27
and **s** messengers throughout the 1Sm 31:9
David **s** messengers to the men of 2Sm 2:5
Abner **s** messengers as his 2Sm 3:12
Then David **s** messengers to say 2Sm 3:14
So Ish-bosheth **s** someone to take 2Sm 3:15
David and **s** messengers after 2Sm 3:26
Hiram of Tyre **s** envoys to David; 2Sm 5:11
⌊he also **s**⌋ cedar logs, 2Sm 5:11
he **s** his son Joram to King David 2Sm 8:10
So David **s** his emissaries to 2Sm 10:2
because David has **s** men with 2Sm 10:3
hasn't David **s** his emissaries in 2Sm 10:3
at the hips, and **s** them away. 2Sm 10:4
he **s** ⌊someone⌋ to meet them, 2Sm 10:5
heard about it and **s** Joab and 2Sm 10:7
Hadadezer **s** ⌊messengers⌋ to 2Sm 10:16
David **s** Joab with his officers 2Sm 11:1
So David **s** someone to inquire 2Sm 11:3
David **s** messengers to get her, 2Sm 11:4
conceived and **s** word to inform 2Sm 11:5
David **s** orders to Joab: 2Sm 11:6
So Joab **s** Uriah to David. 2Sm 11:6
to Joab and **s** it with Uriah. 2Sm 11:14
s someone to report to David 2Sm 11:18
that Joab had **s** him ⌊to tell⌋. 2Sm 11:22
So the LORD **s** Nathan to David. 2Sm 12:1
and He **s** ⌊a message⌋ through 2Sm 12:25
Then Joab **s** messengers to David 2Sm 12:27
David **s** word to Tamar at the 2Sm 13:7
so he **s** Amnon and all the king's 2Sm 13:27
So Joab **s** someone to Tekoa to 2Sm 14:2
Then Absalom **s** for Joab in order 2Sm 14:29
he **s** again, a second time, but 2Sm 14:29
to Joab, "I **s** for you and said, 2Sm 14:32
Then Absalom **s** messengers 2Sm 15:10
Absalom **s** for David's adviser 2Sm 15:12
He then **s** out the troops, one 2Sm 18:2
When Joab **s** the king's servant 2Sm 18:29
David **s** word to the priests, 2Sm 19:11
and they **s** word to the king: 2Sm 19:14
take back to the One who **s** me." 2Sm 24:13
So the LORD **s** a plague on Israel 2Sm 24:15
the king has **s** Zadok the priest, 1Kg 1:44
So King Solomon **s** for him, 1Kg 1:53
Then Solomon **s** Benaiah son of 1Kg 2:29
⌊**s**⌋ by every king on earth who 1Kg 4:34
king of Tyre **s** his servants to 1Kg 5:1
Solomon **s** ⌊this message⌋ to 1Kg 5:2
Then Hiram **s** ⌊a reply⌋ to 1Kg 5:8
s 10,000 to Lebanon each month 1Kg 5:14
day he **s** the people away 1Kg 8:66
Now Hiram had **s** the king 9,000 1Kg 9:14
the fleet, Hiram **s** his servants, 1Kg 9:27
Then King Rehoboam **s** Adoram, 1Kg 12:18
King Asa **s** them to Ben-hadad 1Kg 15:18
have **s** you a gift of silver and 1Kg 15:19
King Asa and **s** the commanders 1Kg 15:20
my lord has not **s** someone to 1Kg 18:10
So Jezebel **s** a messenger to 1Kg 19:2
He **s** messengers into the city to 1Kg 20:2
I have **s** ⌊messengers⌋ to you, 1Kg 20:5
Then Ben-hadad **s** ⌊messengers⌋ to 1Kg 20:10
Then Ben-hadad **s** out scouts, 1Kg 20:17
She **s** the letters to the elders 1Kg 21:8
in the letters she had **s** them. 1Kg 21:11
Then they **s** ⌊word⌋ to Jezebel, 1Kg 21:14
So he **s** messengers instructing 2Kg 1:2
the king who **s** you and declare 2Kg 1:6
King Ahaziah **s** a captain of 50 2Kg 1:9
So the king **s** another captain of 2Kg 1:11
Then the king **s** a third captain 2Kg 1:13
'Because you have **s** messengers 2Kg 1:16
They **s** 50 men, who looked for 2Kg 2:17
Then he **s** ⌊a message⌋ to King 2Kg 3:7
that I have **s** you my servant 2Kg 5:6
he **s** ⌊a message⌋ to the king, 2Kg 5:8
Then Elisha **s** him a messenger, 2Kg 5:10
My master has **s** me to say, 2Kg 5:22

the man of God **s** ⌊word⌋ to the 2Kg 6:9
the king of Israel **s** ⌊word⌋ to 2Kg 6:10
he **s** horses, chariots, and a 2Kg 6:14
and drunk, he **s** them away, and 2Kg 6:23
The king **s** a man ahead of him, 2Kg 6:32
murderer has **s** ⌊someone⌋ to cut 2Kg 6:32
and the king **s** them after the 2Kg 7:14
of Aram, has **s** me to ask you, 2Kg 8:9
So he **s** out a second horseman, 2Kg 9:19
letters and **s** them to Samaria 2Kg 10:1
the guardians **s** ⌊a message⌋ to 2Kg 10:5
and **s** them to Jehu at Jezreel. 2Kg 10:7
Then Jehu **s** ⌊messengers⌋ 2Kg 10:21
Jehoiada **s** ⌊messengers⌋ and 2Kg 11:4
and he **s** ⌊them⌋ to Hazael king 2Kg 12:18
Amaziah then **s** messengers to 2Kg 14:8
of Israel **s** ⌊word⌋ to Amaziah 2Kg 14:9
in Lebanon once **s** ⌊a message⌋ to 2Kg 14:9
⌊men⌋ were **s** after him to 2Kg 14:19
So Ahaz **s** messengers to 2Kg 16:7
king's palace and **s** ⌊them⌋ to 2Kg 16:8
King Ahaz **s** a model of the altar 2Kg 16:10
King Ahaz **s** from Damascus. 2Kg 16:11
he had **s** envoys to So king of 2Kg 17:4
ancestors and **s** to you through 2Kg 17:13
So the LORD **s** lions among them, 2Kg 17:25
He has **s** lions among them, 2Kg 17:26
king of Judah **s** word to the king 2Kg 18:14
king of Assyria **s** the Tartan, 2Kg 18:17
Has my master **s** me only to your 2Kg 18:27
he⌋ also ⌊**s** me⌋ to the men 2Kg 18:27
Then he **s** Eliakim, who was in 2Kg 19:2
king of Assyria **s** to mock the 2Kg 19:4
So he again **s** messengers to 2Kg 19:9
Sennacherib has **s** to mock the 2Kg 19:16
son of Amoz **s** ⌊a message⌋ to 2Kg 19:20
s letters and a gift to Hezekiah 2Kg 20:12
the king **s** the court secretary 2Kg 22:3
'Say to the man who **s** you to Me: 2Kg 22:15
of Judah who **s** you to inquire 2Kg 22:18
So the king **s** ⌊messengers⌋, 2Kg 23:1
He **s** ⌊someone⌋ to take the bones 2Kg 23:16
The LORD **s** Chaldean, Aramean, 2Kg 24:2
He **s** them against Judah to 2Kg 24:2
when the LORD **s** Judah and 1Ch 6:15
and **s** messengers throughout the 1Ch 10:9
consultation, **s** David away. 1Ch 12:19
Hiram of Tyre **s** envoys to David, 1Ch 14:1
he **s** his son Hadoram to King 1Ch 18:10
So David **s** messengers to 1Ch 19:2
because David has **s** men with 1Ch 19:3
hasn't David **s** his emissaries in 1Ch 19:3
at the hips, and **s** them away. 1Ch 19:4
so he **s** ⌊someone⌋ to meet them, 1Ch 19:5
the Ammonites **s** 38 tons of 1Ch 19:6
about this and **s** Joab and the 1Ch 19:8
they **s** messengers to bring out 1Ch 19:16
take back to the One who **s** me." 1Ch 21:12
the LORD **s** a plague on Israel, 1Ch 21:14
Then God **s** an angel to Jerusalem 1Ch 21:15
Then Solomon **s** ⌊word⌋ to King 2Ch 2:3
You **s** him cedars to build him a 2Ch 2:3
a letter and **s** ⌊it⌋ to Solomon: 2Ch 2:11
I have now **s** Huram-abi, a 2Ch 2:13
I have **s** him to be with your 2Ch 2:14
month he **s** the people away 2Ch 7:10
Hiram **s** him ships with crews of 2Ch 8:18
Then King Rehoboam **s** Hadoram, 2Ch 10:18
Jeroboam had **s** an ambush around 2Ch 13:13
royal palace and **s** it to Aram's 2Ch 16:2
I have **s** you silver and gold. 2Ch 16:3
to King Asa and **s** the commanders 2Ch 16:4
Jehoshaphat **s** his officials— 2Ch 17:7
the priest **s** out the commanders 2Ch 23:14
He **s** them prophets to bring them 2Ch 24:19
among them and **s** all the plunder 2Ch 24:23
Amaziah **s** back so they would 2Ch 25:13
and He **s** a prophet to him, 2Ch 25:15
took counsel and **s** ⌊word⌋ to 2Ch 25:17
of Israel **s** ⌊word⌋ to King 2Ch 25:18
was in Lebanon **s** ⌊a message⌋ to 2Ch 25:18
⌊men⌋ were **s** after him to 2Ch 25:27
Hezekiah **s** ⌊word⌋ throughout 2Ch 30:1
he **s** his servants to Jerusalem 2Ch 32:9
and the LORD **s** an angel who 2Ch 32:21
rulers were **s** to him to inquire 2Ch 32:31
Josiah **s** Shaphan son of Azaliah, 2Ch 34:8
Say to the man who **s** you to Me, 2Ch 34:23

of Judah who **s** you to inquire 2Ch 34:26
So the king **s** ⌊messengers⌋ and 2Ch 34:29
But Neco **s** messengers to him, 2Ch 35:21
Nebuchadnezzar **s** ⌊for him⌋ and 2Ch 36:10
their ancestors **s** word against 2Ch 36:15
of the letter they **s** to him: Ezr 4:11
we have **s** to inform the king Ezr 4:14
The king **s** a reply to his chief Ezr 4:17
The letter you **s** us has been Ezr 4:18
until a report was **s** to Darius, Ezr 5:5
in the region, **s** to King Darius. Ezr 5:6
They **s** him a report, written as Ezr 5:7
this matter⌋ be **s** to us. Ezr 5:17
You are **s** by the king and his Ezr 7:14
I **s** them to Iddo, the leader at Ezr 8:17
The king had also **s** officers of Neh 2:9
and Geshem **s** me a message: Neh 6:2
So I **s** messengers to them, Neh 6:3
Four times they **s** me the same Neh 6:4
Sanballat **s** me this same message Neh 6:5
realized that God had not **s** him, Neh 6:12
nobles of Judah **s** many letters Neh 6:17
And Tobiah **s** letters to Neh 6:19
You **s** Your good Spirit to Neh 9:20
they **s** for the Levites wherever Neh 12:27
He **s** letters to all the royal Est 1:22
Letters were **s** by couriers to Est 3:13
She **s** clothes for Mordecai to Est 4:4
Esther **s** this reply to Mordecai: Est 4:15
s for his friends and his wife Est 5:10
He **s** the documents by mounted Est 8:10
these events and **s** letters to Est 9:20
He **s** letters with messages of Est 9:30
You **s** widows away empty-handed, Jb 22:9
He **s** them an abundant supply of Ps 78:25
He **s** among them swarms of flies, Ps 78:45
He **s** His burning anger against Ps 78:49
It **s** out sprouts toward the Sea Ps 80:11
He had **s** a man ahead of them— Ps 105:17
king **s** ⌊for him⌋ and released Ps 105:20
He **s** Moses His servant, and Ps 105:26
s darkness, and it became dark Ps 105:28
but **s** a wasting disease among Ps 106:15
He **s** His word and healed them; Ps 107:20
He has **s** redemption to His Ps 111:9
He **s** signs and wonders against Ps 135:9
She has **s** out her servants; Pr 9:3
messenger will be **s** against him. Pr 17:11
report to those who **s** you? Pr 22:21
The Lord **s** a message against Is 9:8
s by Sargon king of Assyria, Is 20:1
king of Assyria **s** the Rabshakeh, Is 36:2
Has my master **s** me to speak Is 36:12
Then he **s** Eliakim, who was in Is 37:2
king of Assyria, **s** to mock the Is 37:4
he **s** messengers to Hezekiah, Is 37:9
Sennacherib has **s** to mock the Is 37:17
son of Amoz **s** ⌊a message⌋ to Is 37:21
s letters and a gift to Hezekiah Is 39:1
the Lord GOD has **s** me and His Is 48:16
s your envoys far away and sent Is 57:9
far away and **s** ⌊them⌋ down even Is 57:9
He has **s** Me to heal the Is 61:1
He **s** His glorious arm at Moses' Is 63:12
that I had **s** her away and had Jr 3:8
I have **s** all My servants the Jr 7:25
the LORD had **s** him to prophesy, Jr 19:14
when King Zedekiah **s** Pashhur son Jr 21:1
It was not I who **s** or commanded Jr 23:32
from Judah I **s** away from this Jr 24:5
The LORD **s** all His servants the Jr 25:4
everyone the LORD **s** me to. Jr 25:17
The LORD **s** me to prophesy all Jr 26:12
the LORD has **s** me to speak all Jr 26:15
King Jehoiakim **s** men to Egypt: Jr 26:22
I have not **s** them'—⌊this is⌋ Jr 27:15
one whom the LORD has truly **s**." Jr 28:9
the prophet **s** from Jerusalem to Jr 29:1
⌊The letter was **s**⌋ by Elasah son Jr 29:3
king of Judah had **s** to Babylon Jr 29:3
I have not **s** them." ⌊This is Jr 29:9
that I **s** to them with My Jr 29:19
exiles I have **s** from Jerusalem Jr 29:20
own name have **s** out letters to Jr 29:25
For he has **s** ⌊word⌋ to us in Jr 29:28
time again I have **s** you all My Jr 35:15
the officials **s** ⌊word⌋ to Baruch Jr 36:14
The king **s** Jehudi to get the Jr 36:21

King Zedekiah **s** Jehucal son of Jr 37:3
King Zedekiah later **s** ⌊for him⌋ Jr 37:17
King Zedekiah **s** for Jeremiah the Jr 38:14
has **s** Ishmael son of Nethaniah Jr 40:14
to whom you **s** me to bring your Jr 42:9
the ones who **s** me to the LORD Jr 42:20
He has **s** me to ⌊tell⌋ you Jr 42:21
their God had **s** him to give them Jr 43:1
our God has not **s** you to say, Jr 43:2
So I **s** you all My servants the Jr 44:4
envoy has been **s** among the Jr 49:14
He **s** fire from on high into my Lm 1:13
you are not being **s** to a people Ezk 3:5
are⌋ not ⌊being **s**⌋ to many Ezk 3:6
No doubt, if I **s** you to them, Ezk 3:6
Though I **s** them far away among Ezk 11:16
branches, and **s** forth shoots. Ezk 17:6
They also **s** up their pleasing Ezk 20:28
after them and **s** messengers to Ezk 23:16
they **s** for men who came from far Ezk 23:40
So I **s** out fire from within you, Ezk 28:18
Nebuchadnezzar **s** word to Dn 3:2
He **s** His angel and rescued His Dn 3:28
Therefore, He **s** the hand, and Dn 5:24
My God **s** His angel and shut the Dn 6:22
for I have now been **s** to you." Dn 10:11
to Assyria and **s** ⌊a delegation⌋ Hs 5:13
great army that I **s** against you. Jl 2:25
I **s** rain on one city but no rain Am 4:7
I **s** plagues like those of Egypt; Am 4:10
priest of Bethel **s** ⌊word⌋ to Am 7:10
envoy has been **s** among the Ob 1
I **s** Moses, Aaron, and Miriam Mc 6:4
the LORD their God had **s** him. Hg 1:12
ones the LORD has **s** to patrol Zch 1:10
He has **s** Me for ⌊His⌋ glory Zch 2:8
that the LORD of Hosts has **s** Me. Zch 2:9
LORD of Hosts has **s** Me to you. Zch 2:11
LORD of Hosts has **s** me to you. Zch 4:9
LORD of Hosts has **s** Me to you. Zch 6:15
of⌋ Bethel had **s** Sharezer, Zch 7:2
of Hosts had **s** by His Spirit Zch 7:12
know that I **s** you this decree Mal 2:4
He **s** them to Bethlehem and said, Mt 2:8
s out these 12 after giving Mt 10:5
Me welcomes Him who **s** Me. Mt 10:40
s ⌊a message⌋ by his disciples Mt 11:2
So he **s** orders and had John Mt 14:10
I was **s** only to the lost sheep Mt 15:24
he **s** them into his vineyard. Mt 20:2
Jesus then **s** two disciples, Mt 21:1
s his slaves to the farmers to Mt 21:34
Again, he **s** other slaves, more Mt 21:36
Finally, he **s** his son to them. Mt 21:37
He **s** out his slaves to summon Mt 22:3
Again, he **s** out other slaves, Mt 22:4
enraged, so he **s** out his troops, Mt 22:7
They **s** their disciples to Him, Mt 22:16
stones those who are **s** to her. Mt 23:37
bench, his wife **s** word to him, Mt 27:19
warned him and **s** him away at Mk 1:43
they **s** ⌊word⌋ to Him and called Mk 3:31
king immediately **s** for an Mk 6:27
Then He **s** him home, saying, Mk 8:26
welcome Me, but Him who **s** Me." Mk 9:37
Mount of Olives, He **s** two of His Mk 11:1
At harvest time he **s** a slave to Mk 12:2
and **s** him away empty-handed. Mk 12:3
he **s** another slave to them, Mk 12:4
Then he **s** another, and they Mk 12:5
⌊He⌋ also ⌊**s**⌋ many others; Mk 12:5
he **s** him to them, saying, Mk 12:6
they **s** some of the Pharisees Mk 12:13
So He **s** two of His disciples and Mk 14:13
and I was **s** to speak to you and Lk 1:19
Gabriel was **s** by God to a town Lk 1:26
good things and **s** the rich away Lk 1:53
He has **s** Me to proclaim freedom Lk 4:18
was not **s** to any of them— Lk 4:26
I was **s** for this purpose. Lk 4:43
he **s** some Jewish elders to Him, Lk 7:3
the centurion **s** friends to tell Lk 7:6
those who had been **s** returned to Lk 7:10
and **s** them to the Lord, asking, Lk 7:19
the Baptist **s** us to ask You, Lk 7:20
But He **s** him away and said, Lk 8:38
Then He **s** them to proclaim the Lk 9:2
Me welcomes Him who **s** Me. Lk 9:48
He **s** messengers ahead of Him, Lk 9:52
and He **s** them ahead of Him in Lk 10:1
Me rejects the One who **s** Me." Lk 10:16
stones those who are **s** to her. Lk 13:34
man, healed him, and **s** him away. Lk 14:4
he **s** his slave to tell those who Lk 14:17
s him into his fields to feed Lk 15:15
hated him and **s** a delegation Lk 19:14
Mount of Olives, He **s** two of the Lk 19:29
those who were **s** left and found Lk 19:32
At harvest time he **s** a slave to Lk 20:10
farmers beat him and **s** him away Lk 20:10
He **s** yet another slave, but they Lk 20:11
and **s** him away empty-handed. Lk 20:11
And he **s** yet a third, but they Lk 20:12
closely and **s** spies who Lk 20:20
Jesus **s** Peter and John, saying, Lk 22:8
When I **s** you out without Lk 22:35
jurisdiction, he **s** Him to Herod, Lk 23:7
robe, and **s** Him back to Pilate Lk 23:11
because he **s** Him back to us. Lk 23:15
named John who was **s** from God. Jn 1:6
from Jerusalem **s** priests and Jn 1:19
an answer to those who **s** us. Jn 1:22
Now they had been **s** from the Jn 1:24
but He who **s** me to baptize with Jn 1:33
but I've been **s** ahead of Him.' Jn 3:28
For God **s** Him, and He speaks Jn 3:34
will of Him who **s** Me and to Jn 4:34
I **s** you to reap what you didn't Jn 4:38
not honor the Father who **s** Him. Jn 5:23
believes Him who **s** Me has Jn 5:24
but the will of Him who **s** Me. Jn 5:30
You have **s** ⌊messengers⌋ to John, Jn 5:33
Me that the Father has **s** Me. Jn 5:36
The Father who **s** Me has Himself Jn 5:37
you don't believe the One He **s**. Jn 5:38
believe in the One He has **s**." Jn 6:29
but the will of Him who **s** Me. Jn 6:38
is the will of Him who **s** Me: Jn 6:39
the Father who **s** Me draws him, Jn 6:44
living Father **s** Me and I live Jn 6:57
but is from the One who **s** Me. Jn 7:16
of the One who **s** Him is true, Jn 7:18
but the One who **s** Me is true. Jn 7:28
I am from Him, and He **s** Me." Jn 7:29
the Pharisees **s** temple police to Jn 7:32
I'm going to the One who **s** Me. Jn 7:33
the Father who **s** Me ⌊judge⌋ Jn 8:16
the Father who **s** Me testifies Jn 8:18
but the One who **s** Me is true, Jn 8:26
The One who **s** Me is with Me. Jn 8:29
come on my own, but He **s** Me. Jn 8:42
works of Him who **s** Me while it Jn 9:4
of Siloam" (which means "S"). Jn 9:7
set apart and **s** into the world, Jn 10:36
So the sisters **s** a message to Jn 11:3
so they may believe You **s** Me." Jn 11:42
not in Me, but in Him who **s** Me. Jn 12:44
who sees Me sees Him who **s** Me. Jn 12:45
Himself who **s** Me has given Me Jn 12:49
greater than the one who **s** him. Jn 13:16
Me receives Him who **s** Me." Jn 13:20
but is from the Father who **s** Me. Jn 14:24
don't know the One who **s** Me. Jn 15:21
I am going away to Him who **s** Me, Jn 16:5
One You have **s**—Jesus Christ. Jn 17:3
have believed that You **s** Me. Jn 17:8
As You **s** Me into the world, Jn 17:18
I also have **s** them into the Jn 17:18
the world may believe You **s** Me. Jn 17:21
know You have **s** Me and have Jn 17:23
these have known that You **s** Me. Jn 17:25
Then Annas **s** Him bound to Jn 18:24
the Father has **s** Me, I also send Jn 20:21
His Servant and **s** Him first to Ac 3:26
and **s** ⌊orders⌋ to the jail to Ac 5:21
he **s** our forefathers the first Ac 7:12
this one God **s** as a ruler and a Ac 7:35
they **s** Peter and John to them. Ac 8:14
has **s** me so you may regain your Ac 9:17
to Caesarea and **s** him off to Ac 9:30
was there and **s** two men to him Ac 9:38
Then Peter **s** them all out of the Ac 9:40
to them, he **s** them to Joppa. Ac 10:8
men who had been **s** by Cornelius, Ac 10:17
at all, because I have **s** them." Ac 10:20
any objection when I was **s** for. Ac 10:29
I immediately **s** for you, Ac 10:33
He **s** the message to the sons of Ac 10:36
men who had been **s** to me from Ac 11:11
they **s** out Barnabas to travel Ac 11:22
that the Lord has **s** His angel Ac 12:11
hands on them, they **s** them off. Ac 13:3
Being **s** out by the Holy Spirit, Ac 13:4
the synagogue **s** ⌊word⌋ to them, Ac 13:15
this salvation has been **s** to us. Ac 13:26
When they had been **s** on their Ac 15:3
we have **s** Judas and Silas, Ac 15:27
Then, being **s** off, they went Ac 15:30
they were **s** back in peace by the Ac 15:33
to those who had **s** them. Ac 15:33
magistrates **s** the police to say Ac 16:35
magistrates have **s** orders for Ac 16:36
brothers **s** Paul and Silas off Ac 17:10
immediately **s** Paul away to go to Ac 17:14
were his friends, **s** word to him, Ac 19:31
was over, Paul **s** for the Ac 20:1
he **s** to Ephesus and called for Ac 20:17
I **s** him to you right away. Ac 23:30
s for Paul and listened to him Ac 24:24
this reason he **s** for him quite Ac 24:26
God has been **s** to the Gentiles Ac 28:28
they preach unless they are **s**? Rm 10:15
and to be **s** on my way there by Rm 15:24
is why I have **s** to you Timothy, 1Co 4:17
him we have **s** the brother who 2Co 8:18
We have also **s** with them our 2Co 8:22
But I **s** the brothers so our 2Co 9:3
of you by anyone I **s** you? 2Co 12:17
and I **s** the brother with him. 2Co 12:18
time came, God **s** His Son, born Gl 4:4
God has **s** the Spirit of His Son Gl 4:6
Thessalonica you **s** ⌊gifts⌋ for Php 4:16
have **s** him to you for this very Col 4:8
we **s** Timothy, our brother and 1Th 3:2
I also **s** to find out about your 1Th 3:5
I have **s** Tychicus to Ephesus. 2Tm 4:12
spirits **s** out to serve those Heb 1:14
the messengers and **s** them out by Jms 2:25
the Holy Spirit **s** from heaven. 1Pt 1:12
as those **s** out by him to 1Pt 2:14
God **s** His One and Only Son into 1Jn 4:9
He loved us and **s** His Son to be 1Jn 4:10
the Father has **s** the Son as 1Jn 4:14
He **s** it and signified it through Rv 1:1
spirits of God **s** into all the Rv 5:6
has **s** His angel to show His Rv 22:6
have **s** My angel to attest these Rv 22:16

SENTENCE *(15)*

to the king, "The **s** is fair; 1Kg 2:38
you said to me, 'The **s** is fair; 1Kg 2:42
to him, "That will be your **s**; 1Kg 20:40
and they passed **s** on him. 2Kg 25:6
You are right when You pass **s**; Ps 51:4
Because the **s** against a criminal Ec 8:11
the death **s** because he has Jr 26:11
man doesn't deserve the death **s**, Jr 26:16
king passed **s** on him ⌊there⌋. Jr 39:5
Hamath, and he passed **s** on him. Jr 52:9
and this is the **s** of the Most Dn 4:24
At that moment the **s** against Dn 4:33
know full well God's just **s**— Rm 1:32
will execute His **s** completely Rm 9:28
had a death **s** within ourselves 2Co 1:9

SENTENCED *(1)*

Him over to be **s** to death, Lk 24:20

SENTRIES *(2)*

watch after the **s** had been Jdg 7:19
while the **s** in front of the door Ac 12:6

SEORIM *(1)*

third to Harim, the fourth to S, 1Ch 24:8

SEPARATE *(23)*

expanse of the sky to **s** the day Gn 1:14
and to **s** light from darkness. Gn 1:18
before you? S from me: if ⌊you Gn 13:9
his slaves as **s** herds and said Gn 32:16
way you are to **s** the Levites Nm 8:14
S yourselves from this community Nm 16:21
S everyone who laps water with Jdg 7:5
the field with no one to **s** them, 2Sm 14:6
trembling and went their **s** ways. 1Kg 1:49
He lived in a **s** house, while 2Kg 15:5
S yourselves from the Ezr 10:11
you will not **s** his foolishness Pr 27:22

to s the holy from the common. Ezk 42:20
There was a ⌊s⌋ court in each of Ezk 46:21
S yourself from your sins by Dn 4:27
s the evil people from the Mt 13:49
together, man must not s." Mt 19:6
and He will s them one from Mt 25:32
together, man must not s." Mk 10:9
up in a s place by itself. Jn 20:7
Who can s us from the love of Rm 8:35
the power to s us from the love Rm 8:39
out from among them and be s, 2Co 6:17

SEPARATED *(23)*
and God s the light from the Gn 1:4
expanse and s the water under Gn 1:7
and they s from each other. Gn 13:11
After Lot had s from him, the Gn 13:14
will ⌊come⌋ from you and be s. Gn 25:23
Jacob s the lambs and made the Gn 30:40
the God of Israel has s you from Nm 16:9
which Moses s from the men who Nm 31:42
appeared and s the two of them. 2Kg 2:11
with all who had s themselves Ezr 6:21
Levites have not s themselves Ezr 9:1
we are s far from one another Neh 4:19
Israelite descent s themselves Neh 9:2
and who has s themselves Neh 10:28
s all those of mixed descent Neh 13:3
connected they cannot be s. Jb 41:17
a poor man is s from his friend Pr 19:4
since Ephraim s from Judah— Is 7:17
the evil ones are not s out. Jr 6:29
he withdrew and s himself, Gl 2:12
is why he was s ⌊from you⌋ for Phm 15
undefiled, s from sinners, Heb 7:26
the sky s like a scroll being Rv 6:14

SEPARATELY *(1)*
from them and met s with the Ac 19:9

SEPARATES *(7)*
anything but death s you and me. Ru 1:17
and a gossip s friends. Pr 16:28
gossips about it s friends. Pr 17:9
ends quarrels and s powerful Pr 18:18
A wise king s out the wicked and Pr 20:26
in Israel s himself from Me Ezk 14:7
just as a shepherd s the sheep Mt 25:32

SEPARATING *(1)*
the waters, s water from water. Gn 1:6

SEPARATION *(2)*
will make a s for you between Ex 26:33
place was named the Rock of S. 1Sm 23:28

SEPHAR *(1)*
extended from Mesha to S, Gn 10:30

SEPHARAD *(1)*
who are in S will possess Ob 20

SEPHARVAIM *(6)*
and S and settled them in place 2Kg 17:24
Anammelech, the gods of the S. 2Kg 17:31
are the gods of S, Hena, and 2Kg 18:34
the king of the city of S, 2Kg 19:13
Where are the gods of S? Is 36:19
the king of the city of S, Is 37:13

SEPHARVITES *(1)*
and the S burned their children 2Kg 17:31

SEQUENCE *(2)*
to write to you in orderly s, Lk 1:3
explain to them in an orderly s, Ac 11:4

SERAH *(3)*
Beriah, and their sister S. Gn 46:17
name of Asher's daughter was S. Nm 26:46
and Beriah, with their sister S. 1Ch 7:30

SERAIAH *(18)*
(AKA AZARIAH, SHAVSHA, SHEVA, SHISHA)
S was court secretary; 2Sm 8:17
also took away S the chief 2Kg 25:18
S son of Tanhumeth the 2Kg 25:23
Othniel and S. Othniel's sons: 1Ch 4:13
Ophrah, and S fathered Joab, 1Ch 4:14
son of S, son of Asiel, 1Ch 4:35
Azariah fathered S; and Seraiah 1Ch 6:14
and S fathered Jehozadak. 1Ch 6:14
Jeshua, Nehemiah, S, Reelaiah, Ezr 2:2
S, Azariah, Jeremiah, Neh 10:2
S son of Hilkiah, son of Neh 11:11
with Jeshua: S, Jeremiah, Ezra Neh 12:1
Meraiah of S, Hananiah of Neh 12:12
the king's son, S son of Azriel, Jr 36:26
sons of Kareah, S son of Jr 40:8
commanded S son of Neriah son Jr 51:59
Jeremiah told S, "When you get Jr 51:61
also took away S the chief Jr 52:24

SERAIAH'S *(1)*
Persia, Ezra—S son, Azariah's Ezr 7:1

SERAPHIM *(2)*
S were standing above Him; Is 6:2
Then one of the s flew to me, Is 6:6

SERED *(2)*
Zebulun's sons: S, Elon, and Gn 46:14
the Seredite clan from S; Nm 26:26

SEREDITE *(1)*
the S clan from Sered; Nm 26:26

SERGIUS *(1)*
with the proconsul, S Paulus, an Ac 13:7

SERIES *(3)*
comes. First S of Speeches Jb 3:26
himself. Second S of Speeches Jb 14:22
deceptive. Third S of Speeches Jb 21:34

SERIOUS *(16)*
and their sin is extremely s. Gn 18:20
or blind or has any s defect, Dt 15:21
with a defect or any s flaw, Dt 17:1
and I had a s conflict with Jdg 12:2
"I'm in s trouble," replied Saul. 1Sm 28:15
he had a s skin disease until 2Kg 15:5
quarantine with a s skin disease 2Ch 26:21
a man with a s skin disease came Mt 8:2
a man who had a s skin disease, Mt 26:6
a man with a s skin disease came Mk 1:40
Simon who had a s skin disease, Mk 14:3
Israel who had s skin diseases, Lk 4:27
there who had a s skin disease Lk 5:12
10 men with s skin diseases met Lk 17:12
engaged them in s argument and Ac 15:2
and brought many s charges that Ac 25:7

SERIOUSLY *(4)*
the LORD's word s left their Ex 9:21
don't take s the report that 2Sm 13:33
After s considering the matter, Neh 5:7
These men are s disturbing our Ac 16:20

SERMON *(2)*
the Jordan. The S on the Mount Mt 4:25
When Jesus had finished this s, Mt 7:28

SERPENT *(19)*
Now the s was the most cunning Gn 3:1
woman said to the s, "We may eat Gn 3:2
the s said to the woman. Gn 3:4
the woman said, "It was the s. Gn 3:13
Then the LORD God said to the s: Gn 3:14
It will become a s." Ex 7:9
officials, and it became a s. Ex 7:10
his staff, and it became a s. Ex 7:12
His hand pierced the fleeing s. Jb 26:13
the young lion and the s. Ps 91:13
from its egg comes a flying s. Is 14:29
the fleeing s—Leviathan, Is 27:1
Leviathan, the twisting s. Is 27:1
viper and flying s, they carry Is 30:6
the ⌊sea⌋ s to bite them. Am 9:3
as the s deceived Eve by his 2Co 11:3
the ancient s, who is called Rv 12:9
his mouth the s spewed water Rv 12:15
that ancient s who is the Devil Rv 20:2

SERPENT'S *(3)*
Gate toward the S Well and the Neh 2:13
but the s food will be dust! Is 65:25
fly from the s presence to her Rv 12:14

SERPENTS *(1)*
as shrewd as s and as harmless Mt 10:16

SERPENTS' *(1)*
wine is s venom, the deadly Dt 32:33

SERUG *(6)*
lived 32 years and fathered S. Gn 11:20
he fathered S, Reu lived 207 Gn 11:21
S lived 30 years and fathered Gn 11:22
S lived 200 years and fathered Gn 11:23
S, Nahor, Terah, 1Ch 1:26
⌊son⌋ of S, ⌊son⌋ of Reu, ⌊son⌋ Lk 3:35

SERVANT *(406)*
please do not go on past your s. Gn 18:3
Your s has indeed found favor in Gn 19:19
said to his s, the elder of his Gn 24:2
The s said to him, "Suppose the Gn 24:5
So the s placed his hand under Gn 24:9
The s took 10 of his master's Gn 24:10
have appointed for Your s Isaac. Gn 24:14
Then the s ran to meet her and Gn 24:17
"I am Abraham's s," he said. Gn 24:34
When Abraham's s heard their Gn 24:52
and Abraham's s and his men. Gn 24:59
So the s took Rebekah and left. Gn 24:61
asked the s, "Who is that man Gn 24:65
The s answered, "It is my Gn 24:65
Then the s told Isaac everything Gn 24:66
because of My s Abraham." Gn 26:24
'This is what your s Jacob says. Gn 32:4
You have shown Your s. Gn 32:10
'They belong to your s Jacob. Gn 32:18
s Jacob is right behind us.' Gn 32:20
has graciously given your s." Gn 33:5
Let my lord go ahead of his s. Gn 33:14
Your s our father is well. Gn 43:28
please let your s speak Gn 44:18
Do not be angry with your s, Gn 44:18
went back to your s my father: Gn 44:24
Your s my father said to us, Gn 44:27
I come to your s my father and Gn 44:30
hairs of your s our father down Gn 44:31
Your s became accountable to my Gn 44:32
please let your s remain here as Gn 44:33
Nile while her s girls walked Ex 2:5
have been speaking to Your s— Ex 4:10
firstborn of the s girl who is Ex 11:5
in Him and in His s Moses. Ex 14:31
brought such trouble on Your s? Nm 11:11
Not so with My s Moses; Nm 12:7
to speak against My s Moses?" Nm 12:8
But since My s Caleb has a Nm 14:24
greatness and power to Your s, Dt 3:24
So Moses the s of the LORD died Dt 34:5
the death of Moses the LORD's s, Jos 1:1
Moses My s is dead. Jos 1:2
instruction My s Moses commanded Jos 1:7
Moses the LORD's s commanded Jos 1:13
Moses the LORD's s gave you on Jos 1:15
my Lord want to say to His s?" Jos 5:14
the LORD's s had commanded Jos 8:31
the LORD's s had commanded Jos 8:33
commanded His s Moses to give Jos 9:24
the LORD's s had commanded. Jos 11:12
LORD had commanded His s Moses Jos 11:15
Moses the LORD's s and the Jos 12:6
the LORD's s gave their land Jos 12:6
the LORD's s had given them: Jos 13:8
when Moses the LORD's s sent me Jos 14:7
Moses the LORD's s gave them." Jos 18:7
Moses the LORD's s commanded Jos 22:2
the LORD's s gave you across Jos 22:4
Moses the LORD's s gave you: Jos 22:5
the LORD's s, Joshua son of Nun Jos 24:29
son of Nun, the s of the LORD, Jdg 2:8
the camp, go with Purah your s. Jdg 7:10
with Purah his s to the outpost Jdg 7:11
great victory through Your s. Jdg 15:18
His s and a couple of donkeys Jdg 19:3
go with his concubine and his s, Jdg 19:9
the s said to his master, Jdg 19:11
me, your female s, and the young Jdg 19:19
and the young man with your s. Jdg 19:19
Boaz asked his s who was in Ru 2:5
s answered, "She is the young Ru 2:6
me, and give Your s a son, I 1Sm 1:11
"May your s find favor with you," 1Sm 1:18
the priest's s would come with a 1Sm 2:13
priest's s would come and say 1Sm 2:15
yourself," the s would reply, 1Sm 2:16
for Your s is listening.' " 1Sm 3:9
Speak, for Your s is listening." 1Sm 3:10
your s will go and fight this 1Sm 17:32
Your s has been tending his 1Sm 17:34
Your s has killed lions and 1Sm 17:36
The son of your s Jesse of 1Sm 17:58
not sin against his s David. 1Sm 19:4
then your s is safe, but if 1Sm 20:7
Deal faithfully with your s, 1Sm 20:8
up my own s to wait in ambush 1Sm 22:8
against your s or any of my 1Sm 22:15
for your s didn't have any idea 1Sm 22:15

Your s has heard that Saul 1Sm 23:10
come down as Your s has heard? 1Sm 23:11
of Israel, please tell Your s." 1Sm 23:11
please let your s speak to you 1Sm 25:24
Listen to the words of your s. 1Sm 25:24
I, your s, didn't see my lord's 1Sm 25:25
this gift your s has brought to 1Sm 25:27
may you remember ⌊me⌋ your s." 1Sm 25:31
His s from doing evil. 1Sm 25:39
Here I am, your s, to wash the 1Sm 25:41
Why is my lord pursuing his s? 1Sm 26:18
please hear the words of his s: 1Sm 26:19
Why should your s live in the 1Sm 27:5
he will be my s forever." 1Sm 27:12
find out what your s can do." 1Sm 28:2
Look, your s has obeyed you. 1Sm 28:21
Now please listen to your s. 1Sm 28:22
That is David, s of King Saul of 1Sm 29:3
found against your s to keep me 1Sm 29:8
The s struck him, and he died. 2Sm 1:15
'Through My s David I will save 2Sm 3:18
Go to My s David and say, 2Sm 7:5
you are to say to My s David: 2Sm 7:8
You know Your s, Lord GOD. 2Sm 7:20
these great things to Your s. 2Sm 7:21
made to Your s and his house. 2Sm 7:25
The house of Your s David will 2Sm 7:26
this to Your s when You said, 2Sm 7:27
Your s has found the courage to 2Sm 7:27
promised this grace to Your s. 2Sm 7:28
There was a s of Saul's family 2Sm 9:2
"⌊I am⌋ your s," he replied. 2Sm 9:2
"I am your s," he replied. 2Sm 9:6
What is your s that you take an 2Sm 9:8
Your s will do all my lord the 2Sm 9:11
'Your s Uriah the Hittite is 2Sm 11:21
Your s Uriah the Hittite is also 2Sm 11:24
he called to the s who waited on 2Sm 13:17
Amnon's s threw her out and 2Sm 13:18
Your s has just hired 2Sm 13:24
please come with your s?" 2Sm 13:24
It's exactly like your s said." 2Sm 13:35
Your s had two sons. 2Sm 14:6
up against your s and said, 2Sm 14:7
may your s speak a word to my 2Sm 14:12
afraid. Your s thought: I must 2Sm 14:15
to rescue his s from the hand 2Sm 14:16
Your s thought: May the word of 2Sm 14:17
your s Joab is the one who gave 2Sm 14:19
he told your s exactly what to 2Sm 14:19
Joab your s has done this to 2Sm 14:20
your s knows I have found favor 2Sm 14:22
granted the request of your s." 2Sm 14:22
Your s is from one of the tribes 2Sm 15:2
For your s made a vow when I 2Sm 15:8
or death, your s will be there!" 2Sm 15:21
I will be your s, my king! 2Sm 15:34
your father's s, but now I will 2Sm 15:34
but now I will be your s,' 2Sm 15:34
Mephibosheth's s, was right 2Sm 16:1
where a s girl would come and 2Sm 17:17
sent the king's s and your 2Sm 18:29
the king's servant and your s, 2Sm 18:29
For your s knows that I have 2Sm 19:20
replied, "my s ⌊Ziba⌋ betrayed 2Sm 19:26
Actually your s said: 2Sm 19:26
the king'—for your s is lame. 2Sm 19:26
slandered your s to my lord the 2Sm 19:27
you set your s among those who 2Sm 19:28
Can your s taste what he eats or 2Sm 19:35
Why should your s be an added 2Sm 19:35
Since your s is only going with 2Sm 19:36
Please let your s return so that 2Sm 19:37
But here is your s Chimham: 2Sm 19:37
"Listen to the words of your s," 2Sm 20:17
my lord the king come to his s?" 2Sm 24:21
did you not swear to your s: 1Kg 1:13
swore to your s by the LORD your 1Kg 1:17
did not invite your s Solomon. 1Kg 1:19
invite me—me, your s—or 1Kg 1:26
of Jehoiada or your s Solomon. 1Kg 1:26
letting your s know who will sit 1Kg 1:27
not kill his s with the sword.' 1Kg 1:51
your s will do as my lord the 1Kg 2:38
and faithful love to Your s, 1Kg 3:6
now made Your s king in my 1Kg 3:7
Your s is among Your people You 1Kg 3:8
So give Your s an obedient heart 1Kg 3:9
my side while your s was asleep. 1Kg 3:20
what You promised to Your s, 1Kg 8:24
what You promised to Your s, 1Kg 8:25
what You promised to Your s, 1Kg 8:26
that Your s prays before You 1Kg 8:28
prayer that Your s prays toward 1Kg 8:29
of Your s and Your people 1Kg 8:30
through Your s Moses when You 1Kg 8:53
through His s Moses has failed 1Kg 8:56
had done for His s David and for 1Kg 8:66
from you and give it to your s. 1Kg 11:11
because of my s David and 1Kg 11:13
Now Solomon's s, Jeroboam son 1Kg 11:26
because of my s David and 1Kg 11:32
his life because of My s David, 1Kg 11:34
so that My s David will always 1Kg 11:36
commandments as My s David 1Kg 11:38
you will be a s to these people 1Kg 12:7
you were not like My s David, 1Kg 14:8
through His s Ahijah the prophet 1Kg 14:18
spoken through His s Ahijah the 1Kg 15:29
His s Zimri, commander of half 1Kg 16:9
handing your s over to Ahab to 1Kg 18:9
But ⌊I⌋, your s, have feared the 1Kg 18:12
God in Israel and I am Your s, 1Kg 18:36
said to his s, "Go up and look 1Kg 18:43
to Judah, he left his s there, 1Kg 19:3
of your s the first time, 1Kg 20:9
said, "Your s Ben-hadad says, 1Kg 20:32
Your s marched out into the 1Kg 20:39
But while your s was busy here 1Kg 20:40
Elisha, "Your s, my husband, has 2Kg 4:1
that your s feared the LORD. 2Kg 4:1
Your s has nothing in the house 2Kg 4:2
of God, do not deceive your s." 2Kg 4:16
father told his s, "Carry him to 2Kg 4:19
the donkey and said to her s, 2Kg 4:24
have sent you my s Naaman for 2Kg 5:6
accept a gift from your s." 2Kg 5:15
of dirt be given to your s, 2Kg 5:17
for your s will no longer offer 2Kg 5:17
may the LORD pardon your s: 2Kg 5:18
pardon your s in this matter. 2Kg 5:18
"Your s didn't go anywhere," 2Kg 5:25
When the s of the man of God got 2Kg 6:15
to Gehazi, the s of the man of 2Kg 8:4
How could your s, a mere dog, do 2Kg 8:13
Judah because of His s David, 2Kg 8:19
spoke through His s Elijah the 2Kg 9:36
promised through His s Elijah." 2Kg 10:10
through His s, the prophet Jonah 2Kg 14:25
I am your s and your son. 2Kg 16:7
Moses the s of the LORD. 2Kg 18:12
and for the sake of My s David. 2Kg 19:34
for the sake of My s David.'" 2Kg 20:6
law that My s Moses commanded 2Kg 21:8
and the king's s Asaiah: 2Kg 22:12
a s of the king of Babylon, 2Kg 25:8
have an Egyptian s whose name 1Ch 2:34
in marriage to his s Jarha, 1Ch 2:35
all that Moses the s of God had 1Ch 6:49
you offspring of Israel His s, 1Ch 16:13
Go to David My s and say, 1Ch 17:4
you will say to My s David: 1Ch 17:7
say to You for honoring Your s? 1Ch 17:18
Your servant? You know Your s. 1Ch 17:18
because of Your s and according 1Ch 17:19
concerning Your s and his house 1Ch 17:23
the house of Your s David be 1Ch 17:24
revealed to Your s that You will 1Ch 17:25
Your s has found ⌊courage⌋ to 1Ch 17:25
this good thing to Your s. 1Ch 17:26
which the LORD's s Moses had 2Ch 1:3
what You promised to Your s, 2Ch 6:15
what You promised to Your s, 2Ch 6:16
You promised to Your s David. 2Ch 6:17
that Your s prays before You 2Ch 6:19
the prayer Your s prays toward 2Ch 6:20
of Your s and Your people 2Ch 6:21
the loyalty of Your s David. 2Ch 6:42
a s of Solomon son of David, 2Ch 13:6
by⌋ the LORD's s Moses and the 2Ch 24:6
the tax God's s Moses ⌊imposed⌋ 2Ch 24:9
God and against His s Hezekiah. 2Ch 32:16
and the king's s Asaiah, 2Ch 34:20
You gave Your s Moses. Neh 1:7
You commanded Your s Moses: Neh 1:8
the prayer of Your s and to that Neh 1:11
Give Your s success today, Neh 1:11
and if your s has found favor Neh 2:5
and his s spend the night Neh 4:22
and a law through Your s Moses. Neh 9:14
through God's s Moses and to Neh 10:29
Have you considered My s Job? Jb 1:8
Have you considered My s Job? Jb 2:3
I call for my s, but he does not Jb 19:16
truth about Me, as My s Job has. Jb 42:7
rams, go to My s Job, and offer Jb 42:8
Then My s Job will pray for you. Jb 42:8
about Me, as My s Job has." Jb 42:8
addition, Your s is warned by Ps 19:11
keep Your s from willful sins; Ps 19:13
not turn Your s away in anger. Ps 27:9
Show Your favor to Your s; Ps 31:16
hide Your face from Your s, Ps 69:17
chose David His s and took him Ps 78:70
save Your s who trusts in You. Ps 86:2
Give Your strength to Your s; Ps 86:16
save the son of Your female s. Ps 86:16
sworn an oath to David My s: Ps 89:3
I have found David My s; Ps 89:20
the covenant with Your s; Ps 89:39
You offspring of Abraham His s, Ps 105:6
sent Moses His s, and Aaron, Ps 105:26
holy promise to Abraham His s. Ps 105:42
shame, but Your s will rejoice. Ps 109:28
LORD, I am indeed Your s; Ps 116:16
I am Your s, the son of Your Ps 116:16
the son of Your female s. Ps 116:16
with Your s so that I might live Ps 119:17
Your s will think about Your Ps 119:23
Confirm what You said to Your s, Ps 119:38
Remember ⌊Your⌋ word to Your s; Ps 119:49
You have treated Your s well, Ps 119:65
me, as You promised Your s. Ps 119:76
many days ⌊must⌋ Your s ⌊wait⌋? Ps 119:84
Deal with Your s based on Your Ps 119:124
I am Your s; give me Ps 119:125
favor to Your s, and teach me Ps 119:135
pure, and Your s loves it. Ps 119:140
seek Your s, for I do not forget Ps 119:176
like a s girl's eyes on her Ps 123:2
Because of Your s David, do not Ps 132:10
an inheritance to Israel His s. Ps 136:22
not bring Your s into judgment, Ps 143:2
who attack me, for I am Your s. Ps 143:12
who frees His s David from the Ps 144:10
yet have a s, than to act Pr 12:9
favors a wise s, but his anger Pr 14:35
A wise s will rule over a Pr 17:2
A s cannot be disciplined by Pr 29:19
Don't slander a s to his master, Pr 30:10
a s when he becomes king, a fool Pr 30:22
you may hear your s cursing you; Ec 7:21
when your king is a household s, Ec 10:16
As My s Isaiah has gone naked Is 20:3
that day I will call for my s, Is 22:20
and priest alike, s and master, Is 24:2
master, female s and mistress, Is 24:2
and because of My s David.'" Is 37:35
you, Israel, My s, Jacob, whom I Is 41:8
you: You are My s; I have chosen Is 41:9
This is My S; I strengthen Him, Is 42:1
is blind but My s, or deaf like Is 42:19
or blind like the s of the LORD? Is 42:19
and My s whom I have chosen, Is 43:10
listen, Jacob My s, Israel whom Is 44:1
Jacob is My s; I have chosen Is 44:2
and Israel, for you are My s; Is 44:21
I formed you, you are My s; Is 44:21
message of His s and fulfills Is 44:26
of Jacob My s and Israel My Is 45:4
LORD has redeemed His s Jacob!" Is 48:20
to me, "You are My s, Israel; Is 49:3
me from the womb to be His s, Is 49:5
you to be My s raising up the Is 49:6
by people, to a s of rulers: Is 49:7
listening to the voice of His s? Is 50:10
See, My s will act wisely; Is 52:13
righteous s will justify many, Is 53:11
send for⌋ My s Nebuchadnezzar Jr 25:9
of My s Nebuchadnezzar, Jr 27:6
for you, My s Jacob, do not be Jr 30:10
covenant with My s David may be Jr 33:21
descendants of My s David and Jr 33:22
of Jacob and of My s David— Jr 33:26

send for My s Nebuchadnezzar Jr 43:10
But you, My s Jacob, do not be Jr 46:27
And you, My s Jacob, do not be Jr 46:28
which I gave to My s Jacob. Ezk 28:25
shepherd, My s David, and he Ezk 34:23
and My s David will be a prince Ezk 34:24
My s David will be king over Ezk 37:24
land that I gave to My s Jacob, Ezk 37:25
and My s David will be their Ezk 37:25
belong to that s until the year Ezk 46:17
"Daniel, s of the living God," Dn 6:20
of Moses, the s of God, has been Dn 9:11
and the petitions of Your s. Dn 9:17
like me, your s, speak with Dn 10:17
of Shealtiel, My s"—the LORD's Hg 2:23
that I am about to bring My s, Zch 3:8
me as a s since my youth. Zch 13:5
his⌋ father, and a s his master. Mal 1:6
the instruction of Moses My s, Mal 4:4
my s is lying at home paralyzed, Mt 8:6
word, and my s will be cured. Mt 8:8
And his s was cured that very Mt 8:13
Here is My S whom I have chosen, Mt 12:18
great among you must be your s, Mt 20:26
among you will be your s. Mt 23:11
A s approached him and she said, Mt 26:69
be last of all and s of all." Mk 9:35
great among you must be your s, Mk 10:43
When the s saw him again she Mk 14:69
He has helped His s Israel, Lk 1:54
us in the house of His s David, Lk 1:69
word, and my s will be cured. Lk 7:7
When a s saw him sitting in the Lk 22:56
out and take it to the chief s." Jn 2:8
the chief s tasted the water Jn 2:9
I am, there My s also will be. Jn 12:26
has glorified His S Jesus, Ac 3:13
God raised up His S and sent Him Ac 3:26
of our father David Your s: Ac 4:25
against Your holy S Jesus, Ac 4:27
the name of Your holy S Jesus." Ac 4:30
and a s named Rhoda came to Ac 12:13
appoint you as a s and a witness Ac 26:16
is God's s to you for good. Rm 13:4
For government is God's s, Rm 13:4
has become a s of the Rm 15:8
who is a s of the church in Rm 16:1
I was made a s of this ⌊gospel⌋ Eph 3:7
and faithful s in the Lord, Eph 6:21
a faithful s, and a fellow slave Col 4:7
be a good s of Christ Jesus, 1Tm 4:6
was faithful as a s in all God's Heb 3:5
sang the song of God's s Moses, Rv 15:3

SERVANT'S *(23)*

you have passed your s ⌊way⌋. Gn 18:5
turn aside to your s house, Gn 19:2
notice of Your s affliction, 1Sm 1:11
Please forgive your s offense, 1Sm 25:28
spoken about Your s house in the 2Sm 7:19
bless Your s house so that it 2Sm 7:29
blessing Your s house will be 2Sm 7:29
king will grant his s request. 2Sm 14:15
remember your s wrongdoing 2Sm 19:19
please take away Your s guilt." 2Sm 24:10
Listen to Your s prayer and his 1Kg 8:28
open to Your s petition and to 1Kg 8:52
may uphold His s cause and the 1Kg 8:59
So the LORD opened the s eyes. 2Kg 6:17
spoken about Your s house in the 1Ch 17:17
bless Your s house that it may 1Ch 17:27
please take away Your s guilt." 1Ch 21:8
Listen to Your s prayer and his 2Ch 6:19
to hear Your s prayer that I now Neh 1:6
who wants His s well-being." Ps 35:27
joy to Your s life, since I set Ps 86:4
Guarantee Your s well-being; Ps 119:122
Like a s eyes on His master's Ps 123:2

SERVANTS *(331)*

he and his s deployed against Gn 14:15
except what the s have eaten. Gn 14:24
called all his s together, Gn 20:8
that Abimelech's s had seized. Gn 21:25
all of his relatives as his s, Gn 27:37
of the household s was there. Gn 39:11
she called the household s. Gn 39:14
he gave a feast for all his s. Gn 40:20
had been angry with his s, Gn 41:10
pleased Pharaoh and all his s. Gn 41:37
Then Pharaoh said to his s, Gn 41:38
and ⌊s⌋ called out before him, Gn 41:43
Your s have come to buy food," Gn 42:10
your s are not spies." Gn 42:11
We, your s, were 12 brothers Gn 42:13
s could not possibly do such Gn 44:7
lord asked his s, 'Do you have Gn 44:19
you said to your s, 'Bring him Gn 44:21
you said to your s, 'If your Gn 44:23
Then your s will have brought Gn 44:31
Pharaoh and his s were pleased. Gn 45:16
to say, 'Your s, both we and our Gn 46:34
Pharaoh, "Your s, both we and Gn 47:3
please let your s settle in the Gn 47:4
He commanded his s who were Gn 50:2
and all Pharaoh's s, the elders Gn 50:7
of the s of the God of your Gn 50:17
you treating your s this way? Ex 5:15
straw has been given to your s, Ex 5:16
Look, your s are being beaten, Ex 5:16
LORD made their s and livestock Ex 9:20
left their s and livestock Ex 9:21
You swore to Your s Abraham, Ex 32:13
responded to the s of Balak, Nm 22:18
and his two s were with him. Nm 22:22
Your s have taken a census of Nm 31:49
and your s own livestock." Nm 32:4
given to your s as a possession Nm 32:5
Your s will do just as my lord Nm 32:25
but your s are equipped for war Nm 32:27
spoken to your s is what we will Nm 32:31
Remember Your s Abraham, Isaac, Dt 9:27
on His s when He sees that Dt 32:36
will avenge the blood of His s. Dt 32:43
said to Joshua, "We are your s." Jos 9:8
Your s have come from a far away Jos 9:9
them and say, "We are your s. Jos 9:11
reported to your s that the LORD Jos 9:24
Don't abandon your s. Jos 10:6
was gone when Eglon's s came Jdg 3:24
The s waited until they became Jdg 3:25
Ehud escaped while the s waited. Jdg 3:26
10 of his male s and did as the Jdg 6:27
not like one of your female s." Ru 2:13
orchards and give them to his s. 1Sm 8:14
them to his officials and s. 1Sm 8:15
take your male s, your female 1Sm 8:16
your female s, your best young 1Sm 8:16
you yourselves can become his s. 1Sm 8:17
to the LORD your God for your s, 1Sm 12:19
Saul's s said to him, "You see 1Sm 16:15
lord command your s here in your 1Sm 16:16
Then Saul commanded his s, 1Sm 16:17
and are you not s of Saul? 1Sm 17:8
and kills me, we will be your s. 1Sm 17:9
you will be our s and serve us." 1Sm 17:9
the people and Saul's s as well. 1Sm 18:5
ordered his s, "Speak to David 1Sm 18:22
you, and all his s love you. 1Sm 18:22
Saul's s reported these words 1Sm 18:23
The s reported back to Saul, 1Sm 18:24
When the s reported these terms 1Sm 18:26
and all his s to kill David. 1Sm 19:1
One of Saul's s, detained before 1Sm 21:7
But Achish's s said to him, 1Sm 21:11
is crazy," Achish said to his s. 1Sm 21:14
and all his s were standing 1Sm 22:6
Saul said to his s, "Listen, men 1Sm 22:7
who was in charge of Saul's s, 1Sm 22:9
among all your s is as faithful 1Sm 22:14
But the king's s would not lift 1Sm 22:17
afford to your s and to your son 1Sm 25:8
Then she said to her male s, 1Sm 25:19
When David's s came to Abigail 1Sm 25:40
wash the feet of my lord's s." 1Sm 25:41
her five female s accompanying 1Sm 25:42
then said to his s, "Find me a 1Sm 28:7
His s replied, "There is a 1Sm 28:7
but when his s and the woman 1Sm 28:23
She served it to Saul and his s, 1Sm 28:25
your masters' s who came with 1Sm 29:10
summoned one of his s and said, 2Sm 1:15
your s are to work the ground 2Sm 9:10
Now Ziba had 15 sons and 20 s. 2Sm 9:10
house were Mephibosheth's s. 2Sm 9:12
palace with all his master's s; 2Sm 11:9
on his cot with his master's s, 2Sm 11:13
David's s were afraid to tell 2Sm 12:18
saw that his s were whispering 2Sm 12:19
So he asked his s, "Is the baby 2Sm 12:19
His s asked him, "What did you 2Sm 12:21
king and his s please come with 2Sm 13:24
all his s stood by with their 2Sm 13:31
king and all his s also wept 2Sm 13:36
Then Absalom said to his s, 2Sm 14:30
So Absalom's s set the field on 2Sm 14:30
did your s set my field on fire? 2Sm 14:31
said to all the s with him in 2Sm 15:14
The king's s said to him, 2Sm 15:15
king decides, we are your s." 2Sm 15:15
all his s marched past him. 2Sm 15:18
at David and at all the royal s, 2Sm 16:6
said to Abishai and all his s, 2Sm 16:11
Absalom's s came to the woman 2Sm 17:20
"Come back, you and all your s." 2Sm 19:14
sons and 20 s also rushed down 2Sm 19:17
the king and his s coming toward 2Sm 24:20
So his s said to him: 1Kg 1:2
men of Judah, the s of the king, 1Kg 1:9
them, "Take my s with you, have 1Kg 1:33
The king's s have also gone to 1Kg 1:47
he held a feast for all his s. 1Kg 3:15
Tyre sent his s to Solomon when 1Kg 5:1
My s will be with your servants, 1Kg 5:6
My servants will be with your s, 1Kg 5:6
My s will bring ⌊the logs⌋ down 1Kg 5:9
with Your s who walk before 1Kg 8:23
May You judge Your s, 1Kg 8:32
sin of Your s and Your people 1Kg 8:36
soldiers, his s, his commanders, 1Kg 9:22
Hiram sent his s, experienced 1Kg 9:27
seamen, along with Solomon's s. 1Kg 9:27
How happy are these s of yours, 1Kg 10:8
along with her s, returned to 1Kg 10:13
Edomites from his father's s. 1Kg 11:17
they will be your s forever." 1Kg 12:7
put it into the hands of his s. 1Kg 15:18
I will send my s to you, 1Kg 20:6
he said to his s, "Take ⌊your⌋ 1Kg 20:12
king of Aram's s said to him, 1Kg 20:23
His s said to him, "Consider 1Kg 20:31
of Israel had said to his s, 1Kg 22:3
Let my s go with your servants 1Kg 22:49
go with your s in the ships," 1Kg 22:49
lives of these 50 s of yours be 2Kg 1:13
50 strong men here with your s, 2Kg 2:16
One of the s of the king of 2Kg 3:11
send me one of the s and one of 2Kg 4:22
But his s approached and said to 2Kg 5:13
"Please come with your s." 2Kg 6:3
with his s, "My camp will be 2Kg 6:8
and he called his s and demanded 2Kg 6:11
One of his s said, "No one, my 2Kg 6:12
in the night and said to his s, 2Kg 7:12
But one of his s responded, 2Kg 7:13
the blood of My s the prophets 2Kg 9:7
and of all the s of the LORD. 2Kg 9:7
Jehu came out to his master's s, 2Kg 9:11
Then his s carried him to 2Kg 9:28
We are your s, and we will do 2Kg 10:5
of Baal, all his s, and all his 2Kg 10:19
order to destroy the s of Baal. 2Kg 10:19
and all the s of Baal came; 2Kg 10:21
garments for all the s of Baal." 2Kg 10:22
and Jehu said to the s of Baal, 2Kg 10:23
there are no s of the LORD here 2Kg 10:23
among you—only s of Baal." 2Kg 10:23
Joash's s conspired against him 2Kg 12:20
s Jozabad son of Shimeath and 2Kg 12:21
killed his s who had murdered 2Kg 14:5
you through My s the prophets." 2Kg 17:13
through all His s the prophets. 2Kg 17:23
of my master's s and trust in 2Kg 18:24
speak to your s in Aramaic, 2Kg 18:26
the s of King Hezekiah went to 2Kg 19:5
through His s the prophets, 2Kg 21:10
Amon's s conspired against the 2Kg 21:23
Your s have emptied out the 2Kg 22:9
Megiddo his s carried his dead 2Kg 23:30
through His s the prophets. 2Kg 24:2
At that time the s of 2Kg 24:10
city while his s were besieging 2Kg 24:11
mother, his s, his commanders 2Kg 24:12
afraid of the s of the Chaldeans 2Kg 25:24
priests, Levites, and temple s. 1Ch 9:2
aren't they all my lord's s? 1Ch 21:3

know that your s know how to cut 2Ch 2:8
Note that my s will be with your 2Ch 2:8
my servants will be with your s 2Ch 2:8
will give your s, the 2Ch 2:10
and wine to his s as promised. 2Ch 2:15
with Your s who walk before 2Ch 6:14
May You judge Your s, 2Ch 6:23
sin of Your s and Your people 2Ch 6:27
So through his s, Hiram sent him 2Ch 8:18
went with Solomon's s to Ophir, 2Ch 8:18
How happy are these s of yours, 2Ch 9:7
Hiram's s and Solomon's servants 2Ch 9:10
and Solomon's s who brought gold 2Ch 9:10
along with her s, returned to 2Ch 9:12
to Tarshish with Hiram's s, 2Ch 9:21
they will be your s forever." 2Ch 10:7
will become his s so that they 2Ch 12:8
His s conspired against him, 2Ch 24:25
he executed his s who had 2Ch 25:3
he sent his s to Jerusalem 2Ch 32:9
His s said more against the LORD 2Ch 32:16
So his s conspired against him 2Ch 33:24
Your s are doing all that was 2Ch 34:16
he said to his s, "Take me away, 2Ch 35:23
So his s took him out of the war 2Ch 35:24
and they became s to him and his 2Ch 36:20
The temple s ⌊included⌋: Ezr 2:43
of Solomon's s ⌊included⌋: Ezr 2:55
All the temple s and the Ezr 2:58
descendants of Solomon's s 392 Ezr 2:58
gatekeepers, temple s, and some Ezr 2:70
To King Artaxerxes from your s, Ezr 4:11
are the s of the God of heaven Ezr 5:11
and temple s accompanied ⌊him⌋ Ezr 7:7
doorkeepers, temple s, or Ezr 7:24
or ⌊other⌋ s of this house of Ezr 7:24
the temple s at Casiphia, that Ezr 8:17
were also 220 of the temple s, Ezr 8:20
through Your s the prophets, Ezr 9:11
to You day and night for Your s, Neh 1:6
They are Your s and Your people. Neh 1:10
to that of Your s who delight to Neh 1:11
We, His s, will start building, Neh 2:20
and the temple s living on Ophel Neh 3:26
of the temple s and the Neh 3:31
as well as my brothers and my s, Neh 5:10
The temple s ⌊included⌋: Neh 7:46
of Solomon's s ⌊included⌋: Neh 7:57
All the temple s and the Neh 7:60
descendants of Solomon's s 392 Neh 7:60
people, temple s, and all Israel Neh 7:73
and temple s, along with their Neh 10:28
Levites, temple s, and Neh 11:3
and descendants of Solomon's s— Neh 11:3
The temple s lived on Ophel; Neh 11:21
Gishpa supervised the temple s. Neh 11:21
hand-picked female s to her from Est 2:9
and her s to the harem's best Est 2:9
Esther's female s and her Est 4:4
I and my female s will also fast Est 4:16
and a very large number of s. Jb 1:3
down the s with the sword, Jb 1:15
burned up the sheep and the s, Jb 1:16
down the s with the sword, Jb 1:17
no trust in His s and He charges Jb 4:18
guests and female s regard me as Jb 19:15
male or female s when they made Jb 31:13
LORD redeems the life of His s, Ps 34:22
of His s will inherit it, Ps 69:36
corpses of Your s to the birds Ps 79:2
blood of Your s be known among Ps 79:10
the ridicule against Your s— Ps 89:50
and have compassion on Your s. Ps 90:13
Let Your work be seen by Your s, Ps 90:16
For Your s take delight in its Ps 102:14
armies, His s who do His will Ps 103:21
flames of fire His s. Ps 104:4
to deal deceptively with His s. Ps 105:25
Give praise, s of the LORD; Ps 113:1
for all things are Your s. Ps 119:91
all you s of the LORD who stand Ps 134:1
Give praise, you s of the LORD Ps 135:1
and have compassion on His s. Ps 135:14
She has sent out her s; Pr 9:3
and nourishment for your s. Pr 27:27
lies, all his s will be wicked. Pr 29:12
and portions for her s. Pr 31:15
male and female s and had slaves Ec 2:7
speak to your s in Aramaic, Is 36:11
Hezekiah's s came to Isaiah, Is 37:5
mocked the LORD through your s. Is 37:24
is the heritage of the LORD's s, Is 54:17
name, and are His s, all who Is 56:6
because of Your s, the tribes of Is 63:17
because of My s and not destroy Is 65:8
and My s will dwell there. Is 65:9
My s will eat, but you will be Is 65:13
My s will drink, but you will be Is 65:13
My s will rejoice, but you will Is 65:13
My s will shout for joy from a Is 65:14
He will give His s another name. Is 65:15
power will be revealed to His s, Is 66:14
sent all My s the prophets to Jr 7:25
nobles send their s for water. Jr 14:3
sent all His s the prophets to Jr 25:4
the words of My s the prophets I Jr 26:5
to them with My s the prophets Jr 29:19
sent you all My s the prophets, Jr 35:15
and all of his s did not become Jr 36:24
you or your s or these people Jr 37:18
sent you all My s the prophets Jr 44:4
in former times through My s, Ezk 38:17
his inheritance to one of his s, Ezk 46:17
Please test your s for 10 days. Dn 1:12
deal with your s based on what Dn 1:13
Tell your s the dream, and we Dn 2:4
king tell the dream to his s, Dn 2:7
you s of the Most High God— Dn 3:26
and rescued His s who trusted in Dn 3:28
listened to Your s the prophets, Dn 9:6
us through His s the prophets. Dn 9:10
counsel to His s the prophets. Am 3:7
I commanded My s the prophets Zch 1:6
become plunder for their own s. Zch 2:9
he told his s. "He has been Mt 14:2
one of the high priest's s came. Mk 14:66
eyewitnesses and s of the word Lk 1:2
of his household s to give them Lk 12:42
one of the s and asked what Lk 15:26
you," His mother told the s. Jn 2:5
though the s who had drawn the Jn 2:9
this world, My s would fight, so Jn 18:36
authorities⌋ are God's public s, Rm 13:6
They are s through whom you 1Co 3:5
as s of Christ and managers of 1Co 4:1
thing if his s also disguise 2Co 11:15
as s of righteousness. 2Co 11:15
Are they s of Christ? 2Co 11:23
winds, and His s a fiery flame; Heb 1:7
to His s the prophets." Rv 10:7
reward to Your s the prophets, Rv 11:18
blood of His s that was on her Rv 19:2
God, all you His s, you who fear Rv 19:5
city, and His s will serve Him. Rv 22:3
to show His s what must quickly Rv 22:6

SERVANTS' *(8)*

God has exposed your s iniquity. Gn 44:16
grazing land for your s sheep, Gn 47:4
So the s sin was very severe in 1Sm 2:17
will pay your s wages according 1Kg 5:6
his table, his s residence, his 1Kg 10:5
your palace and your s houses. 1Kg 20:6
his table, his s residence, his 2Ch 9:4
Your s children will dwell Ps 102:28

SERVE *(221)*

They will s as signs for Gn 1:14
I will judge the nation they s, Gn 15:14
of your foreskin to s as a sign Gn 17:11
this act will s as my witness Gn 21:30
the older will s the younger. Gn 25:23
Then he said, "S me, and let me Gn 27:25
peoples s you and nations bow Gn 27:29
and you will s your brother. Gn 27:40
he said, "S the meal." Gn 43:31
and you will s as God to him. Ex 4:16
Let it s as a sign for you on Ex 13:9
so that we may s the Egyptians? Ex 14:12
better for us to s the Egyptians Ex 14:12
slave, he is to s for six years; Ex 21:2
and he will s his master for Ex 21:6
they will s as the two corners. Ex 26:24
Israelites to s Me as priest— Ex 28:1
him to s Me as priest. Ex 28:3
that they may s Me as priests. Ex 28:4
that they may s Me as priests. Ex 28:41
them to s Me as priests. Ex 29:1
and his sons to s Me as priests. Ex 29:44
It will s as a reminder for the Ex 30:16
them to s Me as priests. Ex 30:30
for his sons to s as priests, Ex 31:10
for his sons to s as priests." Ex 35:19
for his sons to s as priests. Ex 39:41
so that he can s Me as a priest. Ex 40:13
they may also s Me as priests. Ex 40:15
anointing will s to inaugurate Ex 40:15
were presented to s the LORD as Lv 7:35
and ordained to s as ⌊high⌋ Lv 16:32
so that it may s as a memorial Lv 24:7
its growth may s as food for Lv 25:7
who can s in Israel's army Nm 1:3
who could s in the army, Nm 1:20
who could s in the army, Nm 1:22
who could s in the army, Nm 1:24
who could s in the army, Nm 1:26
who could s in the army, Nm 1:28
who could s in the army, Nm 1:30
who could s in the army, Nm 1:32
who could s in the army, Nm 1:34
who could s in the army, Nm 1:36
who could s in the army, Nm 1:38
who could s in the army, Nm 1:40
who could s in the army, Nm 1:42
who could s in Israel's army, Nm 1:45
were ordained to s as priests. Nm 3:3
everyone who could s at the tent Nm 4:37
everyone who could s at the tent Nm 4:41
may come to s ⌊at⌋ the tent Nm 8:15
in the work and no longer s. Nm 8:25
They will s as a reminder for Nm 10:10
and you can s as our eyes. Nm 10:31
These will s as tassels for you Nm 15:39
may join you and s with you and Nm 18:2
or more who can s in Israel's Nm 26:2
They ⌊s as⌋ a warning sign. Nm 26:10
cities to s as cities of refuge Nm 35:11
cities will s as a refuge for Nm 35:15
stand before the LORD to s Him, Dt 10:8
he may s in the name of the LORD Dt 18:7
laborers for you and s you. Dt 20:11
chosen them to s Him and Dt 21:5
you didn't s the LORD your God Dt 28:47
you will s your enemies the LORD Dt 28:48
s Him with all your heart and Jos 22:5
the Canaanites s as forced labor Jdg 1:28
were made to s as forced labor. Jdg 1:35
is Shechem that we should s him? Jdg 9:28
You are to s the men of Hamor, Jdg 9:28
Why should we s Abimelech? Jdg 9:28
Abimelech that we should s him?' Jdg 9:38
you'll s the Hebrews just like 1Sm 4:9
with us, and we will s you." 1Sm 11:1
our enemies, and we will s You.' 1Sm 12:10
will be our servants and s us." 1Sm 17:9
whom will I s if not his son? 2Sm 16:19
I will also s in yours." 2Sm 16:19
a people I had not known s me. 2Sm 22:44
and if you go and s other gods 1Kg 9:6
put on us, and we will s you." 1Kg 12:4
to these people and s them, 1Kg 12:7
proceeded to s Baal and worship 1Kg 16:31
"S it for the people to eat." 2Kg 4:41
but Jehu will s him a lot. 2Kg 10:18
priests to s them in the shrines 2Kg 17:32
to them; do not s them; do not 2Kg 17:35
of Assyria and did not s him. 2Kg 18:7
in the land and s the king of 2Kg 25:24
who could s in the army— 1Ch 5:18
17,200 who could s in the army. 1Ch 7:11
50,000 who could s in the army, 1Ch 12:33
40,000 who could s in the army, 1Ch 12:36
and s Him with a whole heart and 1Ch 28:9
and if you go and s other gods 2Ch 7:19
put on us, and we will s you." 2Ch 10:4
refused to let them s as priests 2Ch 11:14
the Levites ⌊s⌋ at their tasks 2Ch 13:10
priests and those Levites who s; 2Ch 23:6
men who could s in the army, 2Ch 25:5
His presence, to s Him, and to 2Ch 29:11
S the LORD your God so that He 2Ch 30:8
he told Judah to s the LORD God 2Ch 33:16
in Israel to s the LORD their 2Ch 34:33
them to s in the LORD's 2Ch 35:2
now s the LORD your God and His 2Ch 35:3
S in the holy place by the 2Ch 35:5

would not **s** You or turn from Neh 9:35
the priests who **s** in our God's Neh 10:36
gatekeepers, and singers **s**. Neh 10:39
household to **s** as much as each Est 1:8
words that **s** no good purpose Jb 15:3
that we should **s** Him, and what Jb 21:15
If they **s** Him obediently, they Jb 36:11
s as His signature to all Jb 37:7
the wild ox be willing to **s** you? Jb 39:9
S the LORD with reverential awe, Ps 2:11
a people I had not known **s** me. Ps 18:43
Descendants will **s** Him; Ps 22:30
down to him, all nations **s** him. Ps 72:11
All who **s** carved images, those Ps 97:7
S the LORD with gladness; Ps 100:2
the way of integrity may **s** me. Ps 101:6
are assembled to **s** the LORD. Ps 102:22
of Nebaioth will **s** you and go up Is 60:7
and their kings will **s** you. Is 60:10
that will not **s** you will perish; Is 60:12
I will not **s**! On every high hill Jr 2:20
will you **s** strangers in a land Jr 5:19
other gods to **s** and worship— Jr 13:10
I will make you **s** your enemies Jr 15:14
will make you **s** your enemies in Jr 17:4
his fellow man **s** without pay and Jr 22:13
other gods to **s** them and to Jr 25:6
these nations will **s** the king of Jr 25:11
him the wild animals to **s** him. Jr 27:6
All nations will **s** him, his son, Jr 27:7
that does not **s** Nebuchadnezzar Jr 27:8
Don't **s** the king of Babylon! Jr 27:9
the king of Babylon and **s** him, Jr 27:11
king of Babylon, **s** him and his Jr 27:12
that does not **s** the king of Jr 27:13
must not **s** the king of Babylon, Jr 27:14
S the king of Babylon and live! Jr 27:17
that they might **s** Nebuchadnezzar Jr 28:14
of Babylon, and they will **s** him. Jr 28:14
They will **s** the LORD their God Jr 30:9
He may **s** you six years, but then Jr 34:14
following other gods to **s** them. Jr 35:15
be afraid to **s** the Chaldeans. Jr 40:9
in the land and **s** the king of Jr 40:9
incense to **s** other gods they, Jr 44:3
heat, I will **s** them a feast, Jr 51:39
My Sabbaths to **s** as a sign Ezk 20:12
and **s** your idols, each of you. Ezk 20:39
of them, will **s** Me in the land. Ezk 20:40
may approach the LORD to **s** Him. Ezk 40:46
all around to **s** as supports for Ezk 41:6
approach Me in order to **s** Me." Ezk 43:19
stand before them to **s** them. Ezk 44:11
approach Me to **s** Me as priests Ezk 44:13
Me, will approach Me to **s** Me. Ezk 44:15
draw near to My table to **s** Me. Ezk 44:16
who draw near to **s** the LORD. Ezk 45:4
they were to **s** in the king's Dn 1:5
So they began to **s** in the king's Dn 1:19
they do not **s** your gods or Dn 3:12
that you don't **s** my gods or Dn 3:14
If the God we **s** exists, then He Dn 3:17
that we will not **s** your gods or Dn 3:18
rather than **s** or worship any Dn 3:28
God, whom you **s** continually, Dn 6:16
God whom you **s** continually been Dn 6:20
and language should **s** Him. Dn 7:14
all rulers will **s** and obey Him.' Dn 7:27
of Yahweh and **s** Him with a Zph 3:9
It is useless to **s** God. Mal 3:14
God and one who does not **s** Him. Mal 3:18
Lord your God, and **s** only Him." Mt 4:10
angels came and began to **s** Him. Mt 4:11
she got up and began to **s** Him. Mt 8:15
served, but to **s**, and to give Mt 20:28
and the angels began to **s** Him. Mk 1:13
her, and she began to **s** them. Mk 1:31
served, but to **s**, and to give Mk 10:45
clutches, to **s** Him without fear Lk 1:74
Lord your God, and **s** Him only." Lk 4:8
immediately and began to **s** them. Lk 4:39
sister has left me to **s** alone? Lk 10:40
the table, then come and **s** them. Lk 12:37
and **s** me while I eat and drink; Lk 17:8
that they will **s** as slaves, Ac 7:7
they earnestly **s** Him night and Ac 26:7
I belong to and **s** stood by me, Ac 27:23
whom I **s** with my spirit in Rm 1:9
so that we may **s** in the new way Rm 7:6
The older will **s** the younger. Rm 9:12
fervent in spirit; **s** the Lord. Rm 12:11
to Jerusalem to **s** the saints; Rm 15:25
people do not **s** our Lord Christ Rm 16:18
and those who **s** at the altar 1Co 9:13
but **s** one another through love. Gl 5:13
the ones who **s** by the Spirit of Php 3:3
Lord—you **s** the Lord Christ. Col 3:24
God from idols to **s** the living 1Th 1:9
then they can **s** as deacons. 1Tm 3:10
but should **s** them better, since 1Tm 6:2
whom I **s** with a clear conscience 2Tm 1:3
gospel he might **s** me in your Phm 13
sent out to **s** those who are Heb 1:14
and you continue to **s** them. Heb 6:10
These **s** as a copy and shadow of Heb 8:5
dead works to **s** the living God? Heb 9:14
By it, we may **s** God acceptably, Heb 12:28
which those who **s** the tabernacle Heb 13:10
should use it to **s** others, 1Pt 4:10
s as an example by undergoing Jd 7
and they **s** Him day and night in Rv 7:15
and His servants will **s** Him. Rv 22:3

SERVED *(67)*

He **s** them as they ate under the Gn 18:8
They **s** him by himself, his Gn 43:32
Portions were **s** to them from Gn 43:34
the women who **s** at the entrance Ex 38:8
and Ithamar **s** as priests under Nm 3:4
son of Nun, who had **s** Moses: Jos 1:1
them and **s** as forced labor. Jdg 1:30
and Beth-anath **s** as their forced Jdg 1:33
Israelites **s** him eight years. Jdg 3:8
The Israelites **s** Eglon king of Jdg 3:14
but the boy **s** the LORD in the 1Sm 2:11
The boy Samuel **s** in the LORD's 1Sm 2:18
the women who **s** at the entrance 1Sm 2:22
The boy Samuel **s** the LORD in 1Sm 3:1
Hebrews just like they **s** you. 1Sm 4:9
and he **s** him as ⌊he did⌋ before. 1Sm 19:7
She **s** it to Saul and his 1Sm 28:25
So they **s** him food, and he ate. 2Sm 12:20
I **s** in your father's presence, 2Sm 16:19
She **s** him, but he was not 1Kg 1:4
offered tribute and **s** Solomon 1Kg 4:21
gods and worshiped and **s** them. 1Kg 9:9
elders who had **s** his father 1Kg 12:6
had grown up with him and **s** him. 1Kg 12:8
followed Elijah, and **s** him. 1Kg 19:21
in Edom; a deputy **s** as king. 1Kg 22:47
He **s** Baal and worshiped him. 1Kg 22:53
They **s** some for the men to eat, 2Kg 4:40
young girl who **s** Naaman's wife. 2Kg 5:2
to them, "Ahab **s** Baal a little, 2Kg 10:18
They **s** idols, although the LORD 2Kg 17:12
whole heavenly host and **s** Baal. 2Kg 17:16
the LORD but also **s** their idols. 2Kg 17:41
whole heavenly host and **s** them. 2Kg 21:3
he **s** the idols his father had 2Kg 21:21
the idols his father had **s**, 2Kg 21:21
who **s** as priest in the temple 1Ch 6:10
the men who **s** with their sons 1Ch 6:33
and Ithamar **s** as priests. 1Ch 24:2
officers who **s** the king in every 1Ch 27:1
gods and worshiped and **s** them. 2Ch 7:22
elders who had **s** his father 2Ch 10:6
were the ones who **s** the king, 2Ch 17:19
ancestors and **s** the Asherah 2Ch 24:18
whole heavenly host and **s** them. 2Ch 33:3
had made, and he **s** them. 2Ch 33:22
These ⌊**s**⌋ in the days of Joiakim Neh 12:26
Beverages were **s** in an array of Est 1:7
eunuchs who personally **s** him, Est 1:10
They **s** their idols, which became Ps 106:36
the king is **s** by the field. Ec 5:9
abandoned Me and **s** foreign gods Jr 5:19
they have loved, **s**, followed, Jr 8:2
other gods, **s** them, and Jr 16:11
and worshiped and **s** other gods." Jr 22:9
Egypt, and **s** as your banner. Ezk 27:7
Thousands upon thousands **s** Him; Dn 7:10
Son of Man did not come to be **s**, Mt 20:28
So they **s** the ⌊loaves⌋ to the Mk 8:6
said these were to be **s** as well. Mk 8:7
Son of Man did not come to be **s**, Mk 10:45
Neither is He **s** by human hands, Ac 17:25
worshiped and **s** something Rm 1:25
because he has **s** with me in the Php 2:22
those who have **s** well as deacons 1Tm 3:13
His name when you **s** the saints— Heb 6:10
which no one has **s** at the altar. Heb 7:13

SERVES *(9)*

sold to you and **s** you six years, Dt 15:12
It **s** as fuel for man. Is 44:15
compassion on his son who **s** him. Mal 3:17
between one who **s** God and one Mal 3:18
I am among you as the One who **s**. Lk 22:27
If anyone **s** Me, he must follow Jn 12:26
If anyone **s** Me, the Father will Jn 12:26
Whoever **s** the Messiah in this Rm 14:18
if anyone **s**, ⌊his service should 1Pt 4:11

SERVICE *(83)*

he entered the **s** of Pharaoh king Gn 41:46
and use it for the **s** of the tent Ex 30:16
for the **s** of the tabernacle Ex 39:40
attending to the **s** of the Nm 3:7
attending to the **s** of the Nm 3:8
the sanctuary as a **s** on behalf Nm 3:38
The **s** of the Kohathites at the Nm 4:4
jars of oil by which they **s** it. Nm 4:9
who is qualified to perform **s**, Nm 4:23
This is the **s** of the Gershonite Nm 4:24
all the equipment for their **s**. Nm 4:26
All the **s** of the Gershonites, Nm 4:27
This is the **s** of the Gershonite Nm 4:28
the whole of their **s** at the tent Nm 4:31
This is the **s** of the Merarite Nm 4:33
division⌋ according to their **s**." Nm 7:5
oxen corresponding to their **s**, Nm 7:7
oxen corresponding to their **s**, Nm 7:8
responsibility was **s** related to Nm 7:9
man enters the **s** in the work at Nm 8:24
retire from his **s** in the work Nm 8:25
came to Saul and entered his **s**, 1Sm 16:21
Let David remain in my **s**, 1Sm 16:22
"I'm at your **s**, my lord," he 1Sm 22:12
so I answered: I'm at your **s**. 2Sm 1:7
his attendants' **s** and their 1Kg 10:5
father's harsh **s** and the heavy 1Kg 12:4
articles used in ⌊temple⌋ **s**. 2Kg 25:14
there in the **s** of the king. 1Ch 4:23
to all the **s** of the tabernacle, 1Ch 6:48
for military **s** was 26,000. 1Ch 7:40
worked in the **s** of the LORD's 1Ch 23:24
of the equipment for its **s**"— 1Ch 23:26
Aaron with the **s** of the LORD's 1Ch 23:28
work of the **s** of God's temple 1Ch 23:28
in the **s** of the LORD's temple." 1Ch 23:32
the assigned duties of their **s**. 1Ch 24:3
duties for **s** when they entered 1Ch 24:19
the men who performed their **s**: 1Ch 25:1
lyres for the **s** of God's temple 1Ch 25:6
LORD and for the **s** of the king. 1Ch 26:30
the divisions in the king's **s**, 1Ch 28:1
all the work of **s** in the LORD's 1Ch 28:13
the articles of **s** of the LORD's 1Ch 28:13
articles for every kind of **s**; 1Ch 28:14
articles for every kind of **s**; 1Ch 28:14
according to the **s** of each 1Ch 28:15
the work for the **s** of the LORD's 1Ch 28:20
for all the **s** of God's house. 1Ch 28:21
For the **s** of God's house they 1Ch 29:7
of the priests over their **s**, 2Ch 8:14
his attendants' **s** and their 2Ch 9:4
father's harsh **s** and the heavy 2Ch 10:4
the **s** of the LORD's temple was 2Ch 29:35
to his **s** among the priests 2Ch 31:2
for their **s** in their 2Ch 31:16
began in the **s** of God's temple 2Ch 31:21
So the **s** was established; 2Ch 35:10
So all the **s** of the LORD was 2Ch 35:16
groups to the **s** of God in Ezr 6:18
to you for the **s** of the house of Ezr 7:19
yearly for the **s** of the house of Neh 10:32
for the **s** of God's house. Neh 11:22
They performed the **s** of their Neh 12:45
God and the **s** of purification, Neh 12:45
performing the **s** had gone back Neh 13:10
articles used in ⌊temple⌋ **s**. Jr 52:18
Be ready for **s** and have your Lk 12:35
think he is offering **s** to God. Jn 16:2
this apostolic **s** that Judas left Ac 1:25
law, the temple **s**, and the Rm 9:4
s, in service; if teaching, in Rm 12:7
service, in **s**; if teaching, in Rm 12:7

that my **s** for Jerusalem may be Rm 15:31
ministry of this **s** is not only 2Co 9:12
Through the proof of this **s**, 2Co 9:13
Render **s** with a good attitude, Eph 6:7
sacrifice and **s** of your faith, Php 2:17
from their **s** are believers 1Tm 6:2
high priest in **s** to God, Heb 2:17
men is appointed in **s** to God for Heb 5:1
⌊his **s** should be⌋ from the 1Pt 4:11
faithfulness, **s**, and endurance. Rv 2:19

SERVICES *(3)*

stood⌋ opposite them in the **s**. Neh 12:9
house of my God and for its **s**. Neh 13:14
perform the temple **s** eat the 1Co 9:13

SERVING *(34)*

s in the household of his Gn 39:2
have released Israel from **s** us." Ex 14:5
to take all the **s** utensils they Nm 4:12
on it that they use in **s**: Nm 4:14
to do the work of **s** at the tent Nm 4:47
s as rearguard for all the camps, Nm 10:25
who stands there **s** the LORD your Dt 17:12
priest who is **s** at that time, Dt 26:3
the high priest **s** at that time. Jos 20:6
son of Aaron, was **s** before it. Jdg 20:28
the Shunammite was **s** him. 1Kg 1:15
up with him, the ones **s** him. 2Ch 10:8
between⌋ **s** Me and serving 2Ch 12:8
serving Me and **s** the kingdoms 2Ch 12:8
brothers who were **s** Ahaziah, 2Ch 22:8
priests and Levites who were **s**. Neh 12:44
and a **s** girl when she ousts her Pr 30:23
in your army, ⌊**s**⌋ as your Ezk 27:10
s as guards at the temple gates Ezk 44:11
and capable of **s** in the king's Dn 1:4
reject you from **s** as My priest. Hs 4:6
duty and he was **s** as priest Lk 1:8
s God night and day with Lk 2:37
whoever leads, like the one **s**. Lk 22:26
one at the table or the one **s**? Lk 22:27
Martha was **s** them, and Lazarus Jn 12:2
after **s** his own generation in Ac 13:36
s the Lord with all humility, Ac 20:19
any of his friends from **s** him. Ac 24:23
s as a priest of God's good news. Rm 15:16
themselves to **s** the saints. 1Co 16:15
my partner and co-worker **s** you; 2Co 8:23
no one **s** as a soldier gets 2Tm 2:4
they were not **s** themselves but 1Pt 1:12

SERVITUDE *(1)*

her that her time of **s** is over, Is 40:2

SESSION *(1)*

courts are in **s**, and there are Ac 19:38

SET *(537)*

and they **s** out together from Ur Gn 11:31
and they **s** out for the land of Gn 12:5
the valley and **s** up his tent Gn 13:12
the sun had **s** and it was dark Gn 15:17
and **s** ⌊them⌋ before the men. Gn 18:8
Abraham had **s** apart seven ewe Gn 21:28
Why have you **s** apart these seven Gn 21:29
burnt offering and **s** out to go Gn 22:3
Then he **s** out for the town of Gn 24:10
A meal was **s** before him, but he Gn 24:33
there because the sun had **s**. Gn 28:11
A stairway was **s** on the ground Gn 28:12
his head and **s** it up as a marker Gn 28:18
that I have **s** up as a marker Gn 28:22
He **s** the peeled branches in the Gn 30:38
Then he **s** his own stock apart Gn 30:40
out a stone and **s** it up as a Gn 31:45
marker I have **s** up between you Gn 31:51
And he **s** up an altar there and Gn 33:20
S for me the compensation and Gn 34:12
When they **s** out, a terror from Gn 35:5
Jacob **s** up a marker at the place Gn 35:14
s out from Bethel. When they Gn 35:16
s up a marker on her grave; Gn 35:20
Israel **s** out again and pitched Gn 35:21
So Joseph **s** out after his Gn 37:17
and wise man and **s** him over the Gn 41:33
to you and **s** him before you, Gn 43:9
Israel **s** out with all that he Gn 46:1
So he **s** out with his two sons, Gn 48:1
is a doe **s** free that bears Gn 49:21
child in it and **s** it among the Ex 2:3
and **s** out for the land of Egypt. Ex 4:20
drivers had **s** over the people, Ex 5:14
And the LORD **s** a time, saying, Ex 9:5
They **s** out from Succoth and Ex 13:20
The Egyptians **s** out in pursuit— Ex 14:23
left over **s** aside to be kept Ex 16:23
So they **s** it aside until morning Ex 16:24
that you must **s** before them: Ex 21:1
to be **s** apart for destruction. Ex 22:20
I will **s** your borders from the Ex 23:31
next morning and **s** up an altar Ex 24:4
the blood and **s** it in basins; Ex 24:6
S the mercy seat on top of the Ex 25:21
Its lamps are to be **s** up so they Ex 25:37
last curtain in the ⌊first⌋ **s**, Ex 26:4
curtain in the second **s**. Ex 26:4
of the curtain in the second **s**, Ex 26:5
the outermost in the ⌊first⌋ **s**, Ex 26:10
curtain of the second **s**. Ex 26:10
You are to **s** up the tabernacle Ex 26:30
S it below, under the altar's Ex 27:5
S it between the tent of meeting Ex 30:18
took a tent and **s** it up outside Ex 33:7
in the first **s** and did the same Ex 36:11
curtain in the second **s**. Ex 36:11
of the curtain in the second **s**, Ex 36:12
in the ⌊first⌋ **s** and 50 loops Ex 36:17
curtain in the second **s**. Ex 36:17
You are to **s** up the tabernacle, Ex 40:2
lampstand and **s** up its lamps. Ex 40:4
tabernacle was **s** up in the first Ex 40:17
Moses **s** up the tabernacle: Ex 40:18
crossbars, and **s** up its posts. Ex 40:18
s the mercy seat on top of the Ex 40:20
and **s** up the lamps before the Ex 40:25
He **s** the basin between the tent Ex 40:30
Next Moses **s** up the surrounding Ex 40:33
Israelites **s** out whenever the Ex 40:36
they did not **s** out until the day Ex 40:37
times to cleanse and **s** it apart Lv 16:19
LORD your God who **s** you apart Lv 20:24
I have **s** these apart as unclean Lv 20:25
and I have **s** you apart from the Lv 20:26
the sun has **s**, he will become Lv 22:7
The bread is to be **s** out before Lv 24:8
It will be ⌊**s**⌋ for him like the Lv 25:50
s up a carved image or sacred Lv 26:1
priest will **s** a value for him Lv 27:8
priest will **s** a value for him Lv 27:8
The priest will **s** its value, Lv 27:12
price will be **s** as the priest Lv 27:12
a field permanently **s** apart; Lv 27:21
everything **s** apart is especially Lv 27:28
person who has been **s** apart ⌊for Lv 27:29
the Levites are to **s** it up. Nm 1:51
When you **s** up the lamps, the Nm 8:2
s up its lamps ⌊to give light⌋ Nm 8:3
the day the tabernacle was **s** up, Nm 9:15
the Israelites would **s** out; Nm 9:17
command the Israelites **s** out, Nm 9:18
requirement and did not **s** out. Nm 9:19
command and **s** out at the LORD's Nm 9:20
in the morning, they **s** out. Nm 9:21
and did not **s** out as long as Nm 9:22
when it was lifted, they **s** out. Nm 9:22
and they **s** out at the LORD's Nm 9:23
and have the camps **s** out. Nm 10:2
on the east are to **s** out. Nm 10:5
on the south are to **s** out. Nm 10:6
to be sounded for them to **s** out. Nm 10:6
They **s** out for the first time Nm 10:13
with their banner **s** out first, Nm 10:14
and the Merarites **s** out, Nm 10:17
Reuben with their banner **s** out, Nm 10:18
The Kohathites then **s** out, Nm 10:21
was to be **s** up before their Nm 10:21
Ephraim with their banner **s** out, Nm 10:22
of Dan with their banner **s** out, Nm 10:25
divisions as they **s** out. Nm 10:28
They **s** out from the mountain of Nm 10:33
by day when they **s** out from the Nm 10:34
the ark **s** out, Moses would Nm 10:35
the people **s** out from Hazeroth Nm 12:16
to Him, who is **s** apart, and ⌊the Nm 16:5
will be the one who is **s** apart. Nm 16:7
After they **s** out from Kadesh, Nm 20:22
Then they **s** out from Mount Hor Nm 21:4
The Israelites **s** out and camped Nm 21:10
They **s** out from Oboth and Nm 21:11
They **s** out from there and camped Nm 21:13
your nest is **s** in the cliffs. Nm 24:21
S aside a tribute for the LORD Nm 31:28
I have **s** the land before you. Dt 1:8
and **s** them over you as leaders: Dt 1:15
We then **s** out from Horeb and Dt 1:19
your God has **s** the land before Dt 1:21
the land on which he has **s** foot, Dt 1:36
entire law I **s** before you today Dt 4:8
Then Moses **s** apart three cities Dt 4:41
or you will be **s** apart for Dt 7:26
because it is **s** apart for Dt 7:26
time the LORD **s** apart the tribe Dt 10:8
all the land where you **s** foot, Dt 11:25
today I **s** before you a blessing Dt 11:26
ordinances I **s** before you today Dt 11:32
Nothing **s** apart for destruction Dt 13:17
year you are to **s** aside a tenth Dt 14:22
you must **s** him free in the Dt 15:12
When you **s** him free, do not send Dt 15:13
a hardship when you **s** him free, Dt 15:18
Do not **s** up an Asherah of any Dt 16:21
and do not **s** up a sacred pillar; Dt 16:22
are not to **s** a foreigner over Dt 17:15
you are to **s** apart three cities Dt 19:2
commanding you to **s** apart three Dt 19:7
you must **s** up large stones and Dt 27:2
you are to **s** up these stones on Dt 27:4
not venture to **s** the sole of her Dt 28:56
and curses I have **s** before you— Dt 30:1
today I have **s** before you life Dt 30:15
that I have **s** before you life Dt 30:19
He **s** the boundaries of the Dt 32:8
they will **s** incense before You Dt 33:10
and **s** them down at the place Jos 4:3
the camp and **s** them down there Jos 4:8
Joshua also **s** up 12 stones in Jos 4:9
Then Joshua **s** up in Gilgal the Jos 4:20
in it are **s** apart to the LORD Jos 6:17
from the things **s** apart, Jos 6:18
or you will be **s** apart for Jos 6:18
you will **s** apart the camp of Jos 6:18
He will **s** up its gates ⌊at the Jos 6:26
regarding the things **s** apart for Jos 7:1
took some of what was **s** apart, Jos 7:1
taken some of what was **s** apart. Jos 7:11
they have been **s** apart for Jos 7:12
remove from you what is **s** apart. Jos 7:12
you, Israel, things **s** apart. Jos 7:13
you remove what is **s** apart. Jos 7:13
with the things **s** apart must be Jos 7:15
S an ambush behind the city." Jos 8:2
military force **s** out to attack Jos 8:3
taking the city, **s** it on fire. Jos 8:8
5,000 men and **s** them in ambush Jos 8:12
and immediately **s** it on fire. Jos 8:19
the Israelites **s** out and reached Jos 9:17
where you have **s** foot will be Jos 14:9
the cities **s** apart for the Jos 16:9
at Shiloh where it **s** up the tent Jos 18:1
regarding what was **s** apart for Jos 22:20
s out to fight against Israel. Jos 24:9
large stone and **s** it up there Jos 24:26
to the sword and **s** it on fire. Jdg 1:8
They **s** out at his heels in the Jdg 5:15
my gift and **s** it before You." Jdg 6:18
LORD **s** the swords of each man Jdg 7:22
The trees **s** out to anoint a king Jdg 9:8
chamber and **s** it on fire around Jdg 9:49
its entrance to **s** it on fire. Jdg 9:52
Danites **s** up the carved image Jdg 18:30
So they **s** up for themselves Jdg 18:31
and the sun **s** as they neared Jdg 19:14
his donkey and **s** out for home. Jdg 19:28
They **s** out, went to Bethel, and Jdg 20:18
the Israelites **s** out and camped Jdg 20:19
So Israel **s** up an ambush around Jdg 20:29
they had **s** against Gibeah. Jdg 20:36
He has **s** the world on them. 1Sm 2:8
took a stone and **s** it upright 1Sm 7:12
you and told you to **s** aside." 1Sm 9:23
to it and **s** it before Saul. 1Sm 9:24
reserved piece is **s** before you. 1Sm 9:24
'You must **s** a king over us.' 1Sm 10:19
time that Samuel had **s**, 1Sm 13:8
of Amalek and **s** up an ambush 1Sm 15:5
where he **s** up a monument 1Sm 15:12
the best of what was **s** apart for 1Sm 15:21

Then Samuel s out and went to 1Sm 16:13
s out as Jesse had instructed 1Sm 17:20
So David s out with his 600 men 1Sm 27:2
clothes and s out with two of 1Sm 28:8
Let me s some food in front of 1Sm 28:22
all their brave men s out, 1Sm 31:12
s out and arrived at 2Sm 4:5
all his troops s out to bring 2Sm 6:2
They s the ark of God on a new 2Sm 6:3
the LORD and s it in its place 2Sm 6:17
the tent David had s up for it. 2Sm 6:17
the pan and s it down in front 2Sm 13:9
there. Go and s fire to it!" So 2Sm 14:30
servants s the field on fire 2Sm 14:30
your servants s my field on fire 2Sm 14:31
Then the king s out, and his 2Sm 15:16
So the king s out, and all the 2Sm 15:17
They s the ark of God down, 2Sm 15:24
and I will s out in pursuit of 2Sm 17:1
his donkey and s out for his 2Sm 17:23
He s his affairs in order and 2Sm 17:23
but you s your servant among 2Sm 19:28
coals were s ablaze by it. 2Sm 22:9
Your eyes are s against the 2Sm 22:28
Go up and s up an altar to the 2Sm 24:18
his donkey and s out to Achish 1Kg 2:40
cast bronze to s on top of the 1Kg 7:16
He s up the pillars at the 1Kg 7:21
he s up the right pillar and 1Kg 7:21
then he s up the left pillar and 1Kg 7:21
He s five water carts on the 1Kg 7:39
have s them apart as Your 1Kg 8:53
that I have s before you— 1Kg 9:6
and his men s out from Midian 1Kg 11:18
He s up one in Bethel, and put 1Kg 12:29
the high places and s up priests 1Kg 12:31
to the calves he had s up. 1Kg 12:32
for the high places he had s up. 1Kg 12:32
the altar he had s up in Bethel 1Kg 12:33
evil way but again s up priests 1Kg 13:33
He s up an altar for Baal in the 1Kg 16:32
his youngest, he s up its gates, 1Kg 16:34
you may s up marketplaces for 1Kg 20:34
like my father s up in Samaria." 1Kg 20:34
out in the army as the sun s, 1Kg 22:36
and the king of Edom s out. 2Kg 3:9
S the full ones to one side." 2Kg 4:4
So she s out and went to the man 2Kg 4:25
I to s 20 loaves before 100 men? 2Kg 4:43
S food and water in front of 2Kg 6:22
You will s their fortresses on 2Kg 8:12
Then at night he s out to attack 2Kg 8:21
and Ahaziah king of Judah s out, 2Kg 9:21
s him on his father's throne, 2Kg 10:3
Then he s out and went on his 2Kg 10:12
and s it beside the altar on the 2Kg 12:9
They s up for themselves sacred 2Kg 17:10
has s out to fight against you. 2Kg 19:9
Manasseh s up the carved image 2Kg 21:7
to him and s his throne over 2Kg 25:28
s them apart for destruction, 1Ch 4:41
their brave men s out and 1Ch 10:12
they s the ark of God on a new 1Ch 13:7
David to go and s up an altar to 1Ch 21:18
s apart forever to consecrate 1Ch 23:13
of the army also s apart some of 1Ch 25:1
to the place he had s up for it, 2Ch 1:4
He s you over them as king. 2Ch 2:11
he s up the pillars in front 2Ch 3:17
that I have s before you and if 2Ch 7:19
has s you over them as king to 2Ch 9:8
Abijah s his army of warriors in 2Ch 13:3
and ⌊they s⌋ the rows of the 2Ch 13:11
city of Judah and s garrisons in 2Ch 17:2
the LORD s an ambush against the 2Ch 20:22
Then at night he s out to attack 2Ch 21:9
Seirites and s them up as his 2Ch 25:14
we have s up and consecrated 2Ch 29:19
s military commanders over the 2Ch 32:6
Manasseh s up a carved image of 2Ch 33:7
high places and s up Asherah 2Ch 33:19
They s up the altar on its Ezr 3:3
beams are being s in the walls. Ezr 5:8
We s out from the Ahava River on Ezr 8:31
when wine was s before him, Neh 2:1
and have even s up the prophets Neh 6:7
fertile land You s before them, Neh 9:35
to the kings You have s over us, Neh 9:37

They also s aside daily portions Neh 12:47
and the Levites s aside daily Neh 12:47
He s out to destroy all of Est 3:6
and the slave is s free from his Jb 3:19
since⌋ You have s limits he Jb 14:5
He s me up as His target; Jb 16:12
or a booth s up by a watchman. Jb 27:18
Who s the wild donkey free? Jb 39:5
that the LORD has s apart the Ps 4:3
the stars, which You s in place, Ps 8:3
coals were s ablaze by it. Ps 18:8
cried to You and were s free; Ps 22:5
who has not s his mind on what Ps 24:4
He will s me high on a rock. Ps 27:5
net that is secretly s for me, Ps 31:4
You have s my feet in a spacious Ps 31:8
of the LORD is s against those Ps 34:16
Those who seek my life s traps, Ps 38:12
muddy clay, and s my feet on a Ps 40:2
my integrity and s me in Your Ps 41:12
They s an ambush for me. Ps 59:3
Let their table s before them be Ps 69:22
They s their mouths against Ps 73:9
s up their emblems as signs. Ps 74:4
They s Your sanctuary on fire; Ps 74:7
You s all the boundaries of the Ps 74:17
in Jacob and s up a law in Ps 78:5
You s us at strife with our Ps 80:6
He s it up as an ordinance for Ps 81:5
hearts are s on pilgrimage. Ps 84:5
life, since I s my hope on You, Ps 86:4
have s our unjust ways before Ps 90:8
I will not s anything godless Ps 101:3
s free those condemned to die, Ps 102:20
You s a boundary they cannot Ps 104:9
the sun knows when to s. Ps 104:19
the ruler of peoples s him free. Ps 105:20
S a wicked person over him; Ps 109:6
I have s Your ordinances ⌊before Ps 119:30
The wicked have s a trap for me, Ps 119:110
I will s one of your descendants Ps 132:11
the path and s snares for me. Ps 140:5
May my prayer be s before You as Ps 141:2
s up a guard for my mouth; Ps 141:3
the trap they have s for me, Ps 141:9
and s me free from the grasp of Ps 144:7
S me free and rescue me from the Ps 144:11
s them in position forever and Ps 148:6
Let's s an ambush and kill Pr 1:11
with them or s foot on their Pr 1:15
but they s an ambush to kill Pr 1:18
Don't s foot on the path of the Pr 4:14
when He s a limit for the sea so Pr 8:29
she has also s her table. Pr 9:2
line that your fathers s up. Pr 22:28
Don't s an ambush, wicked man, Pr 24:15
Seldom s foot in your neighbor's Pr 25:17
in milk and s like jewels. Sg 5:12
are rods of gold s with topaz. Sg 5:14
alabaster pillars s on pedestals Sg 5:15
S me as a seal on your heart, Sg 8:6
I will s up my throne above the Is 14:13
plants and s out cuttings Is 17:10
They s up their siege towers and Is 23:13
and I will s up my siege towers Is 29:3
who s a trap at the gate for the Is 29:21
They s out to go down to Egypt Is 30:2
He will s them apart for Is 34:2
on the people I have s apart for Is 34:5
has s out to fight against you. Is 37:9
craftsman to s up an idol that Is 40:20
My city, and s My exiles free, Is 45:13
s it in its place, and there Is 46:7
therefore I have s My face like Is 50:7
who has s himself to destroy. Is 51:13
prisoner is soon to be s free; Is 51:14
I will s your stones in black Is 54:11
You have s up your memorial Is 57:8
of the yoke, to s the oppressed Is 58:6
Your sun will no longer s, Is 60:20
I s you apart before you were Jr 1:5
today I have s you over nations Jr 1:10
king⌋ will s up his throne at Jr 1:15
destroyer of nations has s out. Jr 4:7
the One who s the sand as the Jr 5:22
in wait. They s a trap; they Jr 5:26
S ⌊them⌋ apart for war against Jr 6:4
They have s up their detestable Jr 7:30

My law I s in front of them Jr 9:13
altars you have s up to Shame— Jr 11:13
He has s fire to it, and its Jr 11:16
and s them apart for the day of Jr 12:3
sun s while it was still day; Jr 15:9
I will s you free and care for Jr 15:11
for you have s My anger on fire; Jr 17:4
I will s fire to its gates, Jr 17:27
to My law that I s before you Jr 26:4
S up road markers for yourself; Jr 31:21
children's teeth are s on edge. Jr 31:29
his own teeth will be s on edge. Jr 31:30
city will come, s this city on Jr 32:29
I s jars filled with wine and Jr 35:5
them captive and s off to cross Jr 41:10
large stones and s them in the Jr 43:9
My statutes that I s before you Jr 44:10
I will s fire to the wall of Jr 49:27
I will s My throne in Elam, Jr 49:38
I will s fire to his cities, Jr 50:32
s the watchmen in place; Jr 51:12
s apart the nations against her. Jr 51:27
S apart the nations for battle Jr 51:28
homes have been s ablaze, Jr 51:30
seized, the marshes s on fire, Jr 51:32
He has s me aside like an empty Jr 51:34
to him and s his throne above Jr 52:32
His bow and s me as the target Lm 3:12
entered me and s me on my feet, Ezk 2:2
entered me and s me on my feet. Ezk 3:24
take a brick, s it in front of Ezk 4:1
iron plate and s it up as an Ezk 4:3
I have s this Jerusalem in the Ezk 5:5
these men have s up idols in Ezk 14:3
and s My oil and incense before Ezk 16:18
You also s before them as a Ezk 16:19
and s it in a city of traders. Ezk 17:4
he s it ⌊like⌋ a willow, a plant Ezk 17:5
children's teeth are s on edge? Ezk 18:2
provinces s out against him. Ezk 19:8
that he should s up battering Ezk 21:22
s battering rams against the Ezk 21:22
They will s themselves against Ezk 23:24
which you had s My incense and Ezk 23:41
S the empty pot on its coals so Ezk 24:11
They will s up their encampments Ezk 25:4
He will s up siege works against Ezk 26:8
the LORD when I s fire to Egypt Ezk 30:8
desolate, s fire to Zoan, Ezk 30:14
I will s fire to Egypt; Pelusium Ezk 30:16
in height and s its top among Ezk 31:10
in height and s their tops among Ezk 31:14
Her graves are s in the deepest Ezk 32:23
by His Spirit and s me down in Ezk 37:1
and will s My sanctuary among Ezk 37:26
of Israel and s me down on a Ezk 40:2
upper chambers were s back from Ezk 42:6
you must s aside a donation to Ezk 45:1
you must s aside an area one and Ezk 45:6
donation will be s apart for the Ezk 48:10
you are to s apart the holy Ezk 48:20
of heaven will s up a kingdom Dn 2:44
He s it up on the plain of Dura Dn 3:1
King Nebuchadnezzar had s up. Dn 3:2
of the statue the king had s up. Dn 3:3
statue Nebuchadnezzar had s up. Dn 3:3
King Nebuchadnezzar has s up. Dn 3:5
King Nebuchadnezzar had s up. Dn 3:7
the gold statue you have s up." Dn 3:12
the gold statue I have s up? Dn 3:14
the gold statue you s up." Dn 3:18
king planned to s him over the Dn 6:3
he s his mind on rescuing Daniel Dn 6:14
the ground, s on its feet like Dn 7:4
thrones were s in place, Dn 7:9
that He s before us through Dn 9:10
heart will be s against the holy Dn 11:28
sacrifice and s up the Dn 11:31
of desolation is s up, Dn 12:11
I will s fire to the walls of Am 1:14
bread will s a trap for you. Ob 7
they will s them on fire and Ob 18
Jonah s out on the first day of Jnh 3:4
sun will s on these prophets, Mc 3:6
a siege is s against us! Mc 5:1
protective shield is s in place. Nah 2:5
their faces are s in Hab 1:9
stone I have s before Joshua; Zch 3:9

I will s up camp at My house Zch 9:8
that day I will s out to destroy Zch 12:9
whose price was s by the sons Mt 27:9
after the sun had s, they began Mk 1:32
they s out to restrain Him, Mk 3:21
His disciples to s before the Mk 6:41
His disciples to s before ⌊the Mk 8:6
He s out from there and went to Mk 10:1
days Mary s out and hurried Lk 1:39
opened and his tongue ⌊s free⌋, Lk 1:64
to the blind, to s free the Lk 4:18
him in and s him down before Lk 5:18
of the lake." So they s out, Lk 8:22
disciples to s before the crowd Lk 9:16
eat the things s before you. Lk 10:8
I wish it were already s ablaze! Lk 12:49
jars had been s there for Jewish Jn 2:6
on whom you have s your hope. Jn 5:45
Darkness had already s in, Jn 6:17
God the Father has s His seal of Jn 6:27
and the truth will s you free." Jn 8:32
One the Father s apart and sent Jn 10:36
that the Father has s by His own Ac 1:7
he got up and s out with them, Ac 10:23
S apart for Me Barnabas and Saul Ac 13:2
companions s sail from Paphos Ac 13:13
ruins and will s it up again, Ac 15:16
made efforts to s out for Ac 16:10
into his house, s a meal before Ac 16:34
they s the city in an uproar. Ac 17:5
because He has s a day on which Ac 17:31
Then he s sail from Ephesus. Ac 18:21
He s out, traveling through one Ac 18:23
was about to s sail for Syria, Ac 20:3
the first day I s foot in Asia, Ac 20:18
away from them and s sail, Ac 21:1
we boarded and s sail. Ac 21:2
decided to s sail from there, Ac 27:12
After three months we s sail in Ac 28:11
in Christ Jesus has s you free Rm 8:2
itself will also be s free from Rm 8:21
and I will s aside the 1Co 1:19
everything that is s before you, 1Co 10:27
of you is to s something aside 1Co 16:2
because it is s aside ⌊only⌋ in 2Co 3:14
my mother's womb s me apart and Gl 1:15
I do not s aside the grace of Gl 2:21
until the time s by his father. Gl 4:2
S your minds on what is above, Col 3:2
be arrogant or to s their hope 1Tm 6:17
instrument, s apart, useful to 2Tm 2:21
in Crete was to s right what was Ti 1:5
S an example of good works Ti 2:7
to seize the hope s before us. Heb 6:18
the Lord s up, and not man. Heb 8:2
For a tabernacle was s up; Heb 9:2
having been s up this way, Heb 9:6
fire, and is s on fire by hell Jms 3:6
the Father and s apart by the 1Pt 1:2
s your hope completely on the 1Pt 1:13
but s apart the Messiah as Lord 1Pt 3:15
since they s out for the sake of 3Jn 7
us and has s us free from our Rv 1:5
there in heaven a throne was s. Rv 4:2

SETH *(8)*

birth to a son and named him S, Gn 4:25
A son was born to S also, and he Gn 4:26
to his image, and named him S. Gn 5:3
800 years after the birth of S, Gn 5:4
S was 105 years old when he Gn 5:6
S lived 807 years after the Gn 5:7
Adam, S, Enosh, 1Ch 1:1
Enos, ⌊son⌋ of S, ⌊son⌋ of Adam, Lk 3:38

SETH'S *(1)*

So S life lasted 912 years; Gn 5:8

SETHUR *(1)*

S son of Michael from the tribe Nm 13:13

SETS *(32)*

When Aaron s up the lamps at Ex 30:8
I am the LORD who s you apart. Ex 31:13
I am the LORD who s you apart. Lv 20:8
I, the LORD who s you apart, am Lv 21:8
I am the LORD who s him apart." Lv 21:15
I am the LORD who s them apart." Lv 21:23
I am the LORD who s them apart. Lv 22:9
I am the LORD who s them apart." Lv 22:16
I am the LORD who s you apart, Lv 22:32
man permanently s apart to the Lv 27:28
as the sun s at the ⌊same⌋ time Dt 16:6
and when the sun s he may come Dt 23:11
wages each day before the sun s, Dt 24:15
a craftsman, and s ⌊it⌋ up in Dt 27:15
of⌋ a deer and s me securely 2Sm 22:34
whoever s his whole heart on 2Ch 30:19
He s the lowly on high, and Jb 5:11
and s others in their Jb 34:24
His breath s coals ablaze, Jb 41:21
feet of a deer and s me securely Ps 18:33
He s himself on a path that is Ps 36:4
s an ambush like a robber and Pr 23:28
The sun rises and the sun s; Ec 1:5
but inwardly he s up an ambush. Jr 9:8
house of Israel s up idols in Ezk 14:4
am the LORD who s them apart as Ezk 20:12
anyone He wants and s over it Dn 4:17
of men and s anyone He wants Dn 5:21
Everybody s out the fine wine Jn 2:10
Therefore if the Son s you free, Jn 8:36
No one s aside even a human Gl 3:15
s the course of life on fire, Jms 3:6

SETTING *(17)*

As the sun was s, a deep sleep Gn 15:12
Place a s of gemstones on it, Ex 28:17
Moses finished s up the Nm 7:1
We're s out for the place the Nm 10:29
and delayed its s almost a full Jos 10:13
Why are you s a trap for me to 1Sm 28:9
s a limit for the soles of my Jb 13:27
the rising of the sun to its s, Ps 113:3
the sun to its s that there is Is 45:6
Today I am s you free from the Jr 40:4
s up idols in his heart and Ezk 14:7
I am s a plumb line among My Am 7:8
the rising of the sun to its s. Mal 1:11
the stone and s the guard. Mt 27:66
As He was s out on a journey, Mk 10:17
When the sun was s, all those Lk 4:40
Then, s sail from Troas, we ran Ac 16:11

SETTINGS *(10)*

surrounded with gold filigree s. Ex 28:11
Fashion gold filigree s Ex 28:13
attach the cord chains to the s. Ex 28:14
with gold filigree in their s. Ex 28:20
two filigree s and in this way Ex 28:25
surrounded with gold filigree s, Ex 39:6
with gold filigree in their s. Ex 39:13
two gold filigree s and two gold Ex 39:16
two cords to the two filigree s Ex 39:18
mountings and s were crafted Ezk 28:13

SETTLE *(37)*

S wherever you want." Gn 20:15
S here, move about, and acquire Gn 34:10
Go to Bethel and s there. Gn 35:1
You can s in the land of Goshen Gn 45:10
will be allowed to s in the land Gn 46:34
let your servants s in the land Gn 47:4
s your father and brothers in Gn 47:6
But on the day I s accounts, Ex 32:34
the land I promised to s you Nm 14:30
the land I am giving you to s Nm 15:2
of the land and s in it because Nm 33:53
When you possess it and s in it, Dt 11:31
rain and my word s like dew, Dt 32:2
in Judah to s wherever he could Jdg 17:8
I'm going to s wherever I can Jdg 17:9
it, and a cloud s over it. Jb 3:5
to s them, You crushed the Ps 44:2
He causes the hungry to s there, Ps 107:36
horizon ⌊or⌋ s at the western Ps 139:9
He will s disputes among the Is 2:4
will come and s in the steep Is 7:19
will s them on their own land. Is 14:1
have taken her to s far away? Is 23:7
room for me so that I may s. Is 49:20
Build houses and s down. Jr 29:28
of the sky to s on you and let Ezk 32:4
let their waters s and will make Ezk 32:14
and I will s you in your own Ezk 37:14
Then I will s them in their Hs 11:11
He will s disputes among many Mc 4:3
which s on the walls on a cold Nah 3:17
the men who s down comfortably, Zph 1:12
and they enter and s down there. Mt 12:45
who wanted to s accounts with Mt 18:23
When he began to s accounts, Mt 18:24
and they enter and s down there. Lk 11:26
make an effort to s with him on Lk 12:58

SETTLED *(59)*

the land of Shinar and s there. Gn 11:2
came to Haran, they s there. Gn 11:31
the Negev and s between Kadesh Gn 20:1
s in the wilderness and became Gn 21:20
He s in the Wilderness of Paran, Gn 21:21
And Abraham s in Beer-sheba. Gn 22:19
And they s from Havilah to Shur, Gn 25:18
So Isaac s in Gerar. Gn 26:6
his brothers and s near an Gn 38:1
Then Joseph s his father and Gn 47:11
Israel s in the land of Egypt, Gn 47:27
land of Egypt and s on the whole Ex 10:14
of the LORD s on Mount Sinai, Ex 24:16
month, and they s in Kadesh. Nm 20:1
of Manasseh, and they s in it. Nm 32:40
them out and s in their place. Dt 2:21
as Gaza, and s in their place. Dt 2:23
whole family and s them outside Jos 6:23
possession of it and s there. Jos 21:43
But they s among the Canaanites, Jdg 3:5
the Qedemites had s down in the Jdg 7:12
the land of Moab and ⌊s⌋ there. Ru 1:2
out of Egypt and s them in this 1Sm 12:8
Philistines came and s in them. 1Sm 31:7
and they s in the towns near 2Sm 2:3
the king had s into his palace 2Sm 7:1
that's how they s ⌊disputes⌋. 2Sm 20:18
to Assyria and s them in Halah 2Kg 17:6
Sepharvaim and s them in place 2Kg 17:24
Then they s in their place 1Ch 4:41
They s in Aroer as far as Nebo 1Ch 5:8
They also s in the east as far 1Ch 5:9
tribe of Manasseh s in the land 1Ch 5:23
and Manasseh s in Jerusalem: 1Ch 9:3
Philistines came and s in them. 1Ch 10:7
David had s into his palace, 1Ch 17:1
him and having s the Israelites 2Ch 8:2
Simeon who had s among them, 2Ch 15:9
of the people s in their towns, Ezr 2:70
of⌋ Israel ⌊s⌋ in their towns Ezr 2:70
Israelites had s in their towns, Ezr 3:1
deported and s in the cities of Ezr 4:10
and all Israel s in their towns. Neh 7:73
Israelites had s in their towns, Neh 8:1
and Benjamin s in Jerusalem Neh 11:4
descendants, who s in Jerusalem, Neh 11:6
So they s from Beer-sheba to the Neh 11:30
my speech s on them ⌊like dew⌋. Jb 29:22
Your people s in it; Ps 68:10
lot and s the tribes of Israel Ps 78:55
away; grief has s on me. My Jr 8:18
who have s in the desert; Jr 25:24
So he s among ⌊his own⌋ people. Jr 39:14
s ⌊like wine⌋ on its dregs. Jr 48:11
his people s in their cities? Jr 49:1
he went and s in a town called Mt 2:23
slaves came and s accounts with Mt 25:19
before he s in Haran, Ac 7:2
of the Chaldeans and s in Haran. Ac 7:4

SETTLEMENT *(4)*

to bring before the king for s, 2Sm 15:2
who came to the king for a s. 2Sm 15:6
you, righteous s, holy mountain. Jr 31:23
Reach a s quickly with your Mt 5:25

SETTLEMENTS *(8)*

Their s extended from Mesha to Gn 10:30
to their s in the land they Gn 36:43
bread from your s as a Lv 23:17
These were their s, and they 1Ch 4:33
family for their s in their 1Ch 6:54
Their holdings and s were Bethel 1Ch 7:28
for the farming s with their Neh 11:25
the s where Kedar dwells ⌊cry Is 42:11

SETTLERS *(3)*

from the Gilead s, said to Ahab, 1Kg 17:1
The s took possession of Samaria 2Kg 17:24
The s spoke to the king of 2Kg 17:26

SETTLING *(2)*

completely and s in their place, Dt 2:12
judgments and for ⌊s⌋ disputes 2Ch 19:8

SEVEN *(396)*

suffer vengeance s times over." Gn 4:15
is to be avenged s times over, Gn 4:24
are to take with you s pairs, Gn 7:2

and **s** pairs, male and female, of Gn 7:3
S days from now I will make it Gn 7:4
S days later the waters of the Gn 7:10
So Noah waited **s** more days and Gn 8:10
he had waited another **s** days, Gn 8:12
Abraham had set apart **s** ewe Gn 21:28
set apart these **s** ewe lambs?" Gn 21:29
to accept the **s** ewe lambs from Gn 21:30
work for you **s** years for your Gn 29:18
So Jacob worked **s** years for Gn 29:20
yet another **s** years for me." Gn 29:27
for Laban another **s** years. Gn 29:30
pursued Jacob for **s** days, and Gn 31:23
to the ground **s** times until he Gn 33:3
when **s** healthy-looking, well-fed Gn 41:2
After them, **s** other cows, sickly Gn 41:3
S heads of grain, full and good, Gn 41:5
After them, **s** heads of grain, Gn 41:6
grain swallowed up the **s** full, Gn 41:7
when **s** well-fed, healthy-looking Gn 41:18
After them, **s** other cows—ugly, Gn 41:19
ate the first **s** well-fed cows. Gn 41:20
had also seen **s** heads of grain, Gn 41:22
After them, **s** heads of grain— Gn 41:23
grain swallowed the **s** full ones. Gn 41:24
The **s** good cows are seven years, Gn 41:26
The seven good cows are **s** years, Gn 41:26
and the **s** good heads are seven Gn 41:26
seven good heads are **s** years. Gn 41:26
The **s** thin, ugly cows that came Gn 41:27
came up after them are **s** years, Gn 41:27
years, and the **s** worthless, Gn 41:27
of grain are **s** years of famine. Gn 41:27
S years of great abundance are Gn 41:29
s years of famine will take Gn 41:30
Egypt during the **s** years of Gn 41:34
during the **s** years of famine Gn 41:36
During the **s** years of abundance Gn 41:47
during the **s** years and placed Gn 41:48
Then the **s** years of abundance in Gn 41:53
and the **s** years of famine began, Gn 41:54
She bore to Jacob: **s** persons. Gn 46:25
Joseph mourned **s** days for his Gn 50:10
of Midian had **s** daughters. Ex 2:16
S days passed after the LORD Ex 7:25
eat unleavened bread for **s** days. Ex 12:15
found in your houses for **s** days. Ex 12:19
For **s** days you must eat Ex 13:6
is to be eaten for those **s** days. Ex 13:7
with their mothers for **s** days, Ex 22:30
unleavened bread for **s** days at Ex 23:15
Make **s** lamps on it. Its lamps Ex 25:37
be square, **s** and a half feet Ex 27:1
and **s** and a half feet wide; Ex 27:1
the height **s** and a half feet, Ex 27:18
must wear them for **s** days. Ex 29:30
Ordain them for **s** days. Ex 29:35
For **s** days you must make Ex 29:37
unleavened bread for **s** days at Ex 34:18
also made its **s** lamps, snuffers Ex 37:23
s and a half feet long and seven Ex 38:1
feet long and **s** and a half feet Ex 38:1
the courtyard, **s** and a half feet Ex 38:18
some of it **s** times before Lv 4:6
and sprinkle ⌊it⌋ **s** times before Lv 4:17
of the oil on the altar **s** times, Lv 8:11
the tent of meeting for **s** days, Lv 8:33
it will take **s** days to ordain Lv 8:33
and night for **s** days and keep Lv 8:35
she will be unclean **s** days, Lv 12:2
the infected person for **s** days. Lv 13:4
him for another **s** days. Lv 13:5
must quarantine him **s** days. Lv 13:21
must quarantine him **s** days. Lv 13:26
the scaly infection for **s** days. Lv 13:31
outbreak for another **s** days. Lv 13:33
contaminated fabric for **s** days. Lv 13:50
quarantined for another **s** days. Lv 13:54
the blood⌋ **s** times on the one Lv 14:7
outside his tent for **s** days. Lv 14:8
with his finger **s** times before Lv 14:16
in his left palm **s** times before Lv 14:27
quarantine the house for **s** days. Lv 14:38
and sprinkle the house **s** times. Lv 14:51
he is to count **s** days for his Lv 15:13
of her menstruation for **s** days. Lv 15:19
he will be unclean for **s** days, Lv 15:24
is to count **s** days, and after Lv 15:28
before the mercy seat **s** times. Lv 16:14
with his finger **s** times to Lv 16:19
with its mother for **s** days; Lv 22:27
For **s** days you must eat Lv 23:6
offering to the LORD for **s** days. Lv 23:8
are to count **s** complete weeks Lv 23:15
the bread **s** unblemished male Lv 23:18
month and continues for **s** days. Lv 23:34
offering to the LORD for **s** days. Lv 23:36
month for **s** days after you Lv 23:39
the LORD your God for **s** days. Lv 23:40
to the LORD **s** days each year. Lv 23:41
to live in booths for **s** days. Lv 23:42
are to count **s** sabbatic years, Lv 25:8
sabbatic years, **s** times seven Lv 25:8
seven times **s** years, so that Lv 25:8
period of the **s** sabbatic years Lv 25:8
discipline you **s** times for your Lv 26:18
your plagues **s** times for your Lv 26:21
will strike you **s** times for your Lv 26:24
discipline you **s** times for your Lv 26:28
the **s** lamps are to give light in Nm 8:2
remain in disgrace for **s** days? Nm 12:14
outside the camp for **s** days; Nm 12:14
outside the camp for **s** days, Nm 12:15
Hebron was built **s** years before Nm 13:22
and sprinkle it **s** times toward Nm 19:4
will be unclean for **s** days. Nm 19:11
tent will be unclean for **s** days, Nm 19:14
will be unclean for **s** days. Nm 19:16
Build me **s** altars here and Nm 23:1
and prepare **s** bulls and seven Nm 23:1
seven bulls and **s** rams for me." Nm 23:1
I have arranged **s** altars and Nm 23:4
of Pisgah, built **s** altars, and Nm 23:14
Build me **s** altars here and Nm 23:29
and prepare **s** bulls and seven Nm 23:29
seven bulls and **s** rams for me." Nm 23:29
s male lambs a year old— Nm 28:11
bread is to be eaten for **s** days. Nm 28:17
and **s** male lambs a year old. Nm 28:19
quarts with each of the **s** lambs Nm 28:21
each day for **s** days as a fire Nm 28:24
and **s** male lambs a year old, Nm 28:27
quarts with each of the **s** lambs Nm 28:29
s male lambs a year old— Nm 29:2
with each of the **s** male lambs. Nm 29:4
and **s** male lambs a year old. Nm 29:8
quarts with each of the **s** lambs. Nm 29:10
seventh day ⌊present⌋ **s** bulls, Nm 29:32
s male lambs a year old— Nm 29:36
outside the camp for **s** days. Nm 31:19
s nations more numerous and Dt 7:1
end of ⌊every⌋ **s** years you must Dt 15:1
For **s** days you are to eat Dt 16:3
in your territory for **s** days, Dt 16:4
You are to count **s** weeks, Dt 16:9
of Booths for **s** days when you Dt 16:13
flee from you in **s** directions. Dt 28:7
flee from them in **s** directions. Dt 28:25
At the end of ⌊every⌋ **s** years, Dt 31:10
Have **s** priests carry seven Jos 6:4
priests carry **s** ram's-horn Jos 6:4
march around the city **s** times, Jos 6:4
covenant and have **s** priests Jos 6:6
priests carry **s** trumpets in Jos 6:6
s priests carrying seven Jos 6:8
carrying **s** trumpets before Jos 6:8
and the **s** priests carrying seven Jos 6:13
carrying **s** trumpets marched Jos 6:13
around the city **s** times in the Jos 6:15
marched around the city **s** times. Jos 6:15
S tribes among the Israelites Jos 18:2
to divide it into **s** portions. Jos 18:5
of the **s** portions of land Jos 18:6
in a document of **s** sections. Jos 18:9
them over to Midian **s** years, Jdg 6:1
and a second bull **s** years old. Jdg 6:25
Ibzan judged Israel **s** years, Jdg 12:9
to me during the **s** days of the Jdg 14:12
wept the whole **s** days of the Jdg 14:17
me up with **s** fresh bowstrings Jdg 16:7
brought her **s** fresh bowstrings Jdg 16:8
If you weave the **s** braids on my Jdg 16:13
to shave off the **s** braids on his Jdg 16:19
is better to you than **s** sons, Ru 4:15
barren woman gives birth to **s**, 1Sm 2:5
of the Philistines for **s** months, 1Sm 6:1
Wait **s** days until I come to you 1Sm 10:8
do anything to us for **s** days," 1Sm 11:3
He waited **s** days for the 1Sm 13:8
Jesse presented **s** of his sons to 1Sm 16:10
in Jabesh and fasted **s** days. 1Sm 31:13
of Judah was **s** years and six 2Sm 2:11
over Judah **s** years and six 2Sm 5:5
let **s** of his male descendants be 2Sm 21:6
the **s** of them died together. 2Sm 21:9
he reigned **s** years in Hebron and 1Kg 2:11
chamber was **s** and a half feet 1Kg 6:6
story was⌋ **s** and a half feet 1Kg 6:10
cherub was **s** and a half feet 1Kg 6:24
other wing was **s** and a half feet 1Kg 6:24
So he built it in **s** years. 1Kg 6:38
s and a half feet was the height 1Kg 7:16
and **s** and a half feet was also 1Kg 7:16
s for the first capital and 1Kg 7:17
capital and **s** for the second. 1Kg 7:17
was **s** and a half feet high and 1Kg 7:23
LORD our God, **s** days, and seven 1Kg 8:65
seven days, and **s** ⌊more⌋ days— 1Kg 8:65
king for **s** days in Tirzah. 1Kg 16:15
S times Elijah said, "Go back." 1Kg 18:43
opposite each other for **s** days. 1Kg 20:29
their indirect route for **s** days, 2Kg 3:9
The boy sneezed **s** times and 2Kg 4:35
Go wash **s** times in the Jordan 2Kg 5:10
himself in the Jordan **s** times, 2Kg 5:14
of the Philistines for **s** years. 2Kg 8:2
at the end of **s** years, 2Kg 8:3
Joash was **s** years old when he 2Kg 12:21
where he ruled **s** years and six 1Ch 3:4
Johanan, Delaiah, and Anani—**s**. 1Ch 3:24
Jorai, Jacan, Zia, and Eber—**s**. 1Ch 5:13
times to be with them **s** days, 1Ch 9:25
oak in Jabesh and fasted **s** days. 1Ch 10:12
who was **s** and a half feet 1Ch 11:23
sacrificed **s** bulls and seven 1Ch 15:26
seven bulls and **s** rams. 1Ch 15:26
reigned in Hebron for **s** years 1Ch 29:27
of one was **s** and a half feet 2Ch 3:11
wing was **s** and a half feet, 2Ch 3:11
cherub was **s** and a half feet 2Ch 3:12
wing was **s** and a half feet, 2Ch 3:12
top of each was **s** and half feet 2Ch 3:15
It was **s** and a half feet high, 2Ch 4:2
bronze platform **s** and a half 2Ch 6:13
feet long, **s** and a half feet 2Ch 6:13
at that time for **s** days. 2Ch 7:8
of the altar lasted **s** days and 2Ch 7:9
days and the festival **s** days. 2Ch 7:9
young bull and **s** rams may become 2Ch 13:9
Joash was **s** years old when he 2Ch 24:1
brought **s** bulls, seven rams, 2Ch 29:21
bulls, **s** rams, seven lambs, 2Ch 29:21
seven rams, **s** lambs, and seven 2Ch 29:21
and **s** male goats as a sin 2Ch 29:21
Bread **s** days with great 2Ch 30:21
the appointed feast for **s** days, 2Ch 30:22
decided to observe **s** more days, 2Ch 30:23
they observed **s** days with joy, 2Ch 30:23
of Unleavened Bread for **s** days. 2Ch 35:17
Bread for **s** days with joy, Ezr 6:22
the king and his **s** counselors to Ezr 7:14
celebrated the feast for **s** days, Neh 8:18
the **s** eunuchs who personally Est 1:10
They were the **s** officials of Est 1:14
He assigned **s** hand-picked female Est 2:9
He had **s** sons and three Jb 1:2
with him **s** days and nights Jb 2:13
no harm will touch you in **s**. Jb 5:19
Now take **s** bulls and seven rams, Jb 42:8
Now take seven bulls and **s** rams, Jb 42:8
He also had **s** sons and three Jb 42:13
furnace, purified **s** times. Ps 12:6
I praise You **s** times a day for Ps 119:164
fact, **s** are detestable to Him: Pr 6:16
he must pay **s** times as much; Pr 6:31
has carved out her **s** pillars. Pr 9:1
a righteous man falls **s** times, Pr 24:16
is wiser than **s** men who can Pr 26:16
for there are **s** abominations in Pr 26:25
a portion to **s** or even to eight Ec 11:2
On that day **s** women will seize Is 4:1
will split it into **s** streams, Is 11:15
will be **s** times brighter Is 30:26
like the light of **s** days— Is 30:26

The mother of **s** grew faint; Jr 15:9
At the end of **s** years, each of Jr 34:14
stood **s** and a half feet high. Jr 52:22
s trusted royal aides found in Jr 52:25
I sat there stunned for **s** days. Ezk 3:15
at the end of **s** days the word Ezk 3:16
For **s** years they will use them Ezk 39:9
will spend **s** months burying Ezk 39:12
at the end of the **s** months. Ezk 39:14
S steps led up to the gate, Ezk 40:22
stairway had **s** steps, and its Ezk 40:26
around the temple was **s** feet. Ezk 41:5
There are **s** feet from the small Ezk 43:14
altar hearth is **s** feet ⌊high⌋, Ezk 43:15
offering each day for **s** days. Ezk 43:25
For **s** days the priests are to Ezk 43:26
is to count off **s** days for Ezk 44:26
a festival of **s** days ⌊during Ezk 45:21
During the **s** days of the Ezk 45:23
will provide **s** bulls and seven Ezk 45:23
seven bulls and **s** rams without Ezk 45:23
the LORD on each of the **s** days, Ezk 45:23
the same things for **s** days— Ezk 45:25
the furnace **s** times more than Dn 3:19
an animal for **s** periods of time Dn 4:16
animals for **s** periods of time. Dn 4:23
the sky for **s** periods of time Dn 4:25
cattle for **s** periods of time Dn 4:32
Prince will be **s** weeks and 62 Dn 9:25
raise against it **s** shepherds, Mc 5:5
on ⌊that⌋ one stone are **s** eyes. Zch 3:9
It has **s** lamps on it and seven Zch 4:2
lamps on it and **s** channels for Zch 4:2
These **s** eyes of the LORD, which Zch 4:10
brings with it **s** other spirits Mt 12:45
"**S**," they said, "and a few small Mt 15:34
He took the **s** loaves and the Mt 15:36
leftover pieces—**s** large Mt 15:37
the **s** loaves for the 4,000 and Mt 16:10
him? As many as **s** times?" Mt 18:21
not as many as **s**," Jesus said to Mt 18:22
said to him, "but 70 times **s**. Mt 18:22
Now there were **s** brothers among Mt 22:25
and the third, and so to all **s**. Mt 22:26
whose wife will she be of the **s**? Mt 22:28
He asked them. "**S**," they said. Mk 8:5
Taking the **s** loaves, He gave Mk 8:6
they collected **s** large baskets Mk 8:8
When I broke the **s** loaves for Mk 8:20
you collect?" "**S**," they said. Mk 8:20
There were **s** brothers. Mk 12:20
The **s** also left no offspring. Mk 12:22
since the **s** had married her?" Mk 12:23
of whom He had driven **s** demons. Mk 16:9
her husband **s** years after her Lk 2:36
s demons had come out of her Lk 8:2
goes and brings **s** other spirits Lk 11:26
against you **s** times in a day, Lk 17:4
and comes back to you **s** times, Lk 17:4
Now there were **s** brothers. Lk 20:29
all **s** died and left no children. Lk 20:31
For all **s** had married her." Lk 20:33
which was about **s** miles from Lk 24:13
Yesterday at **s** in the morning Jn 4:52
from among you **s** men of good Ac 6:3
after destroying **s** nations in Ac 13:19
S sons of Sceva, a Jewish chief Ac 19:14
at Troas, where we spent **s** days. Ac 20:6
and stayed there **s** days. Ac 21:4
one of the **S**, and stayed with Ac 21:8
As the **s** days were about to end, Ac 21:27
to stay with them for **s** days. Ac 28:14
being encircled for **s** days. Heb 11:30
and **s** others, when He 2Pt 2:5
the **s** churches in the province Rv 1:4
from the **s** spirits before His Rv 1:4
and send it to the **s** churches: Rv 1:11
turned I saw **s** gold lampstands, Rv 1:12
His right hand He had **s** stars; Rv 1:16
secret of the **s** stars you saw Rv 1:20
and of the **s** gold lampstands, Rv 1:20
s stars are the angels of the Rv 1:20
the angels of the **s** churches, Rv 1:20
and the **s** lampstands are the Rv 1:20
lampstands are the **s** churches. Rv 1:20
The Letters to the **S** Churches Rv 1:20
One who holds the **s** stars in His Rv 2:1
among the **s** gold lampstands Rv 2:1
One who has the **s** spirits of God Rv 3:1
of God and the **s** stars says: Rv 3:1
the throne were **s** fiery torches, Rv 4:5
which are the **s** spirits of God. Rv 4:5
the back, sealed with **s** seals. Rv 5:1
the scroll and its **s** seals." Rv 5:5
He had **s** horns and seven eyes, Rv 5:6
He had seven horns and **s** eyes, Rv 5:6
which are the **s** spirits of God Rv 5:6
Lamb open one of the **s** seals, Rv 6:1
I saw the **s** angels who stand Rv 8:2
s trumpets were given to them. Rv 8:2
And the **s** angels who had the Rv 8:6
who had the **s** trumpets prepared Rv 8:6
the **s** thunders spoke with their Rv 10:3
And when the **s** thunders spoke, Rv 10:4
up what the **s** thunders said, Rv 10:4
red dragon having **s** heads and 10 Rv 12:3
and on his heads were **s** diadems. Rv 12:3
He had 10 horns and **s** heads. Rv 13:1
s angels with the seven last Rv 15:1
angels with the **s** last plagues, Rv 15:1
sanctuary came the **s** angels with Rv 15:6
seven angels with the **s** plagues, Rv 15:6
gave the **s** angels seven gold Rv 15:7
the seven angels **s** gold bowls Rv 15:7
sanctuary until the **s** plagues of Rv 15:8
plagues of the **s** angels were Rv 15:8
saying to the **s** angels, Rv 16:1
pour out the **s** bowls of God's Rv 16:1
Then one of the **s** angels who had Rv 17:1
angels who had the **s** bowls came Rv 17:1
having **s** heads and 10 horns. Rv 17:3
with the **s** heads and the 10 Rv 17:7
the **s** heads are seven mountains Rv 17:9
seven heads are **s** mountains on Rv 17:9
They are also **s** kings: Rv 17:10
yet is of the **s** and goes to Rv 17:11
Then one of the **s** angels, who Rv 21:9
who had held the **s** bowls filled Rv 21:9
filled with the **s** last plagues, Rv 21:9

SEVEN-DAY *(2)*

to celebrate a **s** festival for Nm 29:12
You are to hold a **s** festival for Dt 16:15

SEVEN-YEAR *(1)*

LORD has announced a **s** famine, 2Kg 8:1

SEVENFOLD *(1)*

Pay back **s** to our neighbors the Ps 79:12

SEVENTEENTH *(6)*

on the **s** day of the month, Gn 7:11
on the **s** day of the month, Gn 8:4
Samaria in the **s** year of Judah's 1Kg 22:51
In the **s** year of Pekah son of 2Kg 16:1
the **s** to Hezir, the eighteenth 1Ch 24:15
the **s** to Joshbekashah, his sons, 1Ch 25:24

SEVENTH *(113)*

By the **s** day, God completed His Gn 2:2
rested on the **s** day from all His Gn 2:2
God blessed the **s** day and Gn 2:3
ark came to rest in the **s** month, Gn 8:4
through the **s** day must be cut Ex 12:15
sacred assembly on the **s** day. Ex 12:16
and on the **s** day there is to be Ex 13:6
it, but on the **s** day, the Ex 16:26
Yet on the **s** day some of the Ex 16:27
leave his place on the **s** day." Ex 16:29
the people rested on the **s** day. Ex 16:30
the **s** day is a Sabbath to the Ex 20:10
then He rested on the **s** day. Ex 20:11
then in the **s** he is to leave as Ex 21:2
But during the **s** year you are to Ex 23:11
but rest on the **s** day so that Ex 23:12
On the **s** day He called to Moses Ex 24:16
but on the **s** day there must be a Ex 31:15
but on the **s** day He rested and Ex 31:17
but you must rest on the **s** day; Ex 34:21
but on the **s** day you are to have Ex 35:2
then reexamine him on the **s** day. Lv 13:5
examine him again on the **s** day. Lv 13:6
will reexamine him on the **s** day. Lv 13:27
the infection on the **s** day. Lv 13:32
the scaly outbreak on the **s** day, Lv 13:34
the contamination on the **s** day. Lv 13:51
his hair ⌊again⌋ on the **s** day: Lv 14:9
return on the **s** day and examine Lv 14:39
In the **s** month, on the tenth Lv 16:29
but on the **s** day there must be a Lv 23:3
On the **s** day there will be a Lv 23:8
day after the **s** Sabbath and then Lv 23:16
In the **s** month, on the first Lv 23:24
day⌋ of this **s** month is the Day Lv 23:27
of this **s** month and continues Lv 23:34
day of the **s** month for seven Lv 23:39
celebrate it in the **s** month. Lv 23:41
rest for the land in the **s** year, Lv 25:4
a trumpet loudly in the **s** month, Lv 25:9
we eat in the **s** year if we don't Lv 25:20
he is to shave it on the **s** day. Nm 6:9
On the **s** day Elishama son of Nm 7:48
on the third day and the **s** day; Nm 19:12
himself on the third and **s** days, Nm 19:12
on the third day and the **s** day. Nm 19:19
the unclean person on the **s** day, Nm 19:19
On the **s** day you are to hold a Nm 28:25
sacred assembly in the **s** month, Nm 29:1
day⌋ of this **s** month and Nm 29:7
fifteenth day of the **s** month; Nm 29:12
On the **s** day ⌊present⌋ seven Nm 29:32
on the third day and the **s** day. Nm 31:19
On the **s** day wash your clothes, Nm 31:24
the **s** day is a Sabbath to the Dt 5:14
heart, 'The **s** year, the year Dt 15:9
must set him free in the **s** year. Dt 15:12
On the **s** day there is to be a Dt 16:8
But on the **s** day, march around Jos 6:4
Early on the **s** day, they started Jos 6:15
After the **s** time, the priests Jos 6:16
s lot came out for the Danite Jos 19:40
at last, on the **s** day, he Jdg 14:17
On the **s** day before sunset, Jdg 14:18
On the **s** day the baby died. 2Sm 12:18
of King Solomon in the **s** month, 1Kg 8:2
On the **s** time, he reported, 1Kg 18:44
On the **s** day, the battle took 1Kg 20:29
Then, in the **s** year, Jehoiada 2Kg 11:4
In the **s** year of Jehu, Joash 2Kg 12:1
which was the **s** year of Israel's 2Kg 18:9
On the **s** day of the fifth month, 2Kg 25:8
In the **s** month, however, Ishmael 2Kg 25:25
Ozem sixth, and David **s**. 1Ch 2:15
Attai sixth, Eliel **s**, 1Ch 12:11
the **s** to Hakkoz, the eighth to 1Ch 24:10
the **s** ⌊to⌋ Jesarelah, his sons, 1Ch 25:14
the sixth, and Eliehoenai the **s**. 1Ch 26:3
Issachar the **s**, and Peullethai 1Ch 26:5
s, for the seventh month, was 1Ch 27:10
for the **s** month, was Helez 1Ch 27:10
this was in the **s** month. 2Ch 5:3
day of the **s** month he sent 2Ch 7:10
Then, in the **s** year, Jehoiada 2Ch 23:1
they finished in the **s** month. 2Ch 31:7
By the **s** month, the Israelites Ezr 3:1
day of the **s** month they began Ezr 3:6
Jerusalem in the **s** year of King Ezr 7:7
during the **s** year of the king. Ezr 7:8
When the **s** month came and the Neh 8:1
On the first day of the **s** month, Neh 8:2
the festival of the **s** month. Neh 8:14
in the **s** year and will Neh 10:31
On the **s** day, when the king was Est 1:10
in the **s** year of his reign. Est 2:16
died that year in the **s** month. Jr 28:17
In the **s** month, Ishmael son of Jr 41:1
in the **s** year, 3,023 Jews; Jr 52:28
In the **s** year, in the fifth Ezk 20:1
on the **s** ⌊day⌋ of the month, Ezk 30:20
same thing on the **s** ⌊day⌋ of the Ezk 45:20
fifteenth day of the **s** month, Ezk 45:25
twenty-first day of the **s** month, Hg 2:1
fifth and in the **s** ⌊months⌋ for Zch 7:5
the fast of the **s**, and the fast Zch 8:19
about the **s** day in this way Heb 4:4
And on the **s** day God rested from Heb 4:4
in the **s** ⌊generation⌋ from Adam, Jd 14
When He opened the **s** seal, Rv 8:1
of the sound of the **s** angel, Rv 10:7
The **s** angel blew his trumpet, Rv 11:15
Then the **s** poured out his bowl Rv 16:17
carnelian, the **s** chrysolite, Rv 21:20

SEVENTY *(5)*

S kings with their thumbs and Jdg 1:7
Our lives last **s** years or, Ps 90:10
S elders from the house of Ezk 8:11
S weeks are decreed about your Dn 9:24
The **S** returned with joy, saying, Lk 10:17

SEVENTY-SEVEN *(1)*
for Lamech it will be s times! Gn 4:24

SEVERAL *(1)*
⌊gifts⌋ for my need s times. Php 4:16

SEVERE *(39)*
the famine in the land was s. Gn 12:10
his house with s plagues because Gn 12:17
for the famine will be very s. Gn 41:31
for the famine was s in the land Gn 41:56
the famine was s all over the Gn 41:57
the famine in the land was s. Gn 43:1
the land of Canaan has been s. Gn 47:4
for the famine was very s. Gn 47:13
the famine was so s for them. Gn 47:20
will bring a s plague against Ex 9:3
so s that nothing like it had Ex 9:24
them with a very s plague. Nm 11:33
your descendants, s and lasting Dt 28:59
sin was very s in the presence 1Sm 2:17
The slaughter was s—30,000 of 1Sm 4:10
His hand is s against us and our 1Sm 5:7
became very s until no breath 1Kg 17:17
The famine was s in Samaria. 1Kg 18:2
alone—she is in s anguish, and 2Kg 4:27
famine was so s in the city that 2Kg 25:3
disease became increasingly s. 2Ch 16:12
and he died from s illnesses. 2Ch 21:19
cry out because of s oppression; Jb 35:9
her⌋ with His s storm on the day Is 27:8
disaster, an extremely s wound. Jr 14:17
is incurable; your wound most s. Jr 30:12
famine was so s in the city that Jr 52:6
your wound is s. All who hear Nah 3:19
threw him into s convulsions. Lk 9:42
a s famine struck that country, Lk 15:14
that day a s persecution broke Ac 8:1
there would be a s famine Ac 11:28
and the s storm kept raging; Ac 27:20
a s testing by affliction, 2Co 8:2
and s treatment of the body, Col 2:23
in spite of s persecution, 1Th 1:6
an earthquake, and s hail. Rv 11:19
And a s earthquake occurred like Rv 16:18
that plague was extremely s. Rv 16:21

SEVERED *(1)*
crushed, torn, or s ⌊testicles⌋; Lv 22:24

SEVERELY *(28)*
and grandson how s I dealt with Ex 10:2
taunt her s just to provoke 1Sm 1:6
you and do so s if you hide 1Sm 3:17
The LORD s oppressed the people 1Sm 5:6
God punish me s if you do not 1Sm 14:44
God punish Jonathan and do so s. 1Sm 20:13
up with him and s wounded him. 1Sm 31:3
Abner and do so s if I don't do 2Sm 3:9
me and do so s if I taste bread 2Sm 3:35
me and do so s if you don't 2Sm 19:13
me and do so s if Adonijah has 1Kg 2:23
me and do so s if I don't make 1Kg 19:2
me and do so s if Samaria's dust 1Kg 20:10
punish me and do so s if the 2Kg 6:31
found him and s wounded him. 1Ch 10:3
me away, for I am s wounded!" 2Ch 35:23
I am faint and s crushed; Ps 38:8
when I said, "I am s afflicted." Ps 116:10
disciplined me s but did not Ps 118:18
I am s afflicted; LORD, give me Ps 119:107
You keep silent and afflict s? Is 64:12
my brokenness—I am s wounded! Jr 10:19
I have begun to strike you s, Mc 6:13
injure themselves s when all the Zch 12:3
he has seizures and suffers s. Mt 17:15
or do it will be s beaten. Lk 12:47
we were being s battered by the Ac 27:18
and s painful sores broke out on Rv 16:2

SEVERING *(1)*
back of the neck without s ⌊it⌋. Lv 5:8

SEVERITY *(3)*
consider God's kindness and s: Rm 11:22
s toward those who have fallen, Rm 11:22
I am there I will not use s, 2Co 13:10

SEW *(2)*
a time to tear and a time to s; Ec 3:7
to the women who s ⌊magic⌋ bands Ezk 13:18

SEWED *(1)*
they s fig leaves together and Gn 3:7

SEWN *(1)*
I have s sackcloth over my skin; Jb 16:15

SEWS *(1)*
No one s a patch of unshrunk Mk 2:21

SEX *(12)*
us so we can have s with them!" Gn 19:5
by having s with your mother Lv 18:7
are not to have s with your Lv 18:8
You are not to have s with her. Lv 18:9
you are not to have s with her. Lv 18:15
daughter and have s with her. Lv 18:17
the man who had s with the woman Dt 22:22
in the city and has s with her, Dt 22:23
so we can have s with him!" Jdg 19:22
now have illicit s with her, Ezk 23:43
Yet they had s with her as one Ezk 23:44
is how they had s with Oholah Ezk 23:44

SEXUAL *(77)*
who haven't had s relations with Gn 19:8
not have s relations with women. Ex 19:15
and he has s relations with her, Ex 22:16
Whoever has s intercourse with Ex 22:19
relative for s intercourse; Lv 18:6
must not have s intercourse with Lv 18:7
are not to have s intercourse Lv 18:9
are not to have s intercourse Lv 18:10
are not to have s intercourse Lv 18:11
are not to have s intercourse Lv 18:12
are not to have s intercourse Lv 18:13
his wife to have s intercourse; Lv 18:14
are not to have s intercourse Lv 18:15
are not to have s intercourse Lv 18:16
are not to have s intercourse Lv 18:17
sister and have s intercourse Lv 18:18
to have s intercourse with Lv 18:19
are not to have s intercourse Lv 18:20
are not to have s intercourse Lv 18:23
If a man has s intercourse with Lv 19:20
If a man has s intercourse with Lv 20:15
and they have s relations, Lv 20:17
has had s intercourse with his Lv 20:17
woman and has s intercourse with Lv 20:18
must not have s intercourse with Lv 20:19
began to have s relations with Nm 25:1
who has had s relations with Nm 31:17
who have not had s relations. Nm 31:18
who had not had s relations with Nm 31:35
may have s relations with her Dt 21:13
a woman, has s relations with Dt 22:13
having s relations with Dt 22:22
have s relations with her, Dt 25:5
the one who has s intercourse Dt 27:21
who had not had s relations with Jdg 21:12
You lavished your s favors on Ezk 16:15
all around for your s favors. Ezk 16:33
you have s intercourse with Ezk 22:10
offered her s favors to them; Ezk 23:7
whose s members were like those Ezk 23:20
your indecency and s immorality, Ezk 23:27
his father have s relations with Am 2:7
in a case of s immorality, Mt 5:32
adulteries, s immoralities, Mt 15:19
wife, except for s immorality, Mt 19:9
evil thoughts, s immoralities, Mk 7:21
weren't born of s immorality," Jn 8:41
idols, from s immorality, from Ac 15:20
and from s immorality. Ac 15:29
and from s immorality." Ac 21:25
of their hearts to s impurity, Rm 1:24
natural s intercourse for Rm 1:26
left natural s intercourse with Rm 1:27
not in s impurity and Rm 13:13
that there is s immorality among 1Co 5:1
the kind of s immorality that 1Co 5:1
body is not for s immorality but 1Co 6:13
Flee from s immorality! 1Co 6:18
But because of s immorality, 1Co 7:2
Let us not commit s immorality 1Co 10:8
the uncleanness, s immorality, 2Co 12:21
s immorality, moral impurity, Gl 5:19
s immorality and any impurity Eph 5:3
s immorality, impurity, lust, Col 3:5
you abstain from s immorality, 1Th 4:3
them committed s immorality Jd 7
and to commit s immorality. Rv 2:14
slaves to commit s immorality Rv 2:20
to repent of her s immorality. Rv 2:21
sorceries, their s immorality, Rv 9:21
the wine of her s immorality, Rv 14:8
earth committed s immorality Rv 17:2
the wine of her s immorality." Rv 17:2
the wine of her s immorality, Rv 18:3
have committed s immorality with Rv 18:3
who have committed s immorality Rv 18:9
the earth with her s immorality; Rv 19:2

SEXUALLY *(8)*
associate with s immoral people 1Co 5:9
brother who is s immoral or 1Co 5:11
no s immoral people, idolaters, 1Co 6:9
the person who is s immoral sins 1Co 6:18
no s immoral or impure or greedy Eph 5:5
for the s immoral and 1Tm 1:10
vile, murderers, s immoral, Rv 21:8
sorcerers, the s immoral, the Rv 22:15

SHAALABBIN *(1)*
(AKA SHAALBIM)
S, Aijalon, Ithlah, Jos 19:42

SHAALBIM *(2)*
(AKA SHAALABBIN)
leave Har-heres, Aijalon, and S. Jdg 1:35
in Makaz, S, Beth-shemesh, 1Kg 4:9

SHAALBONITE *(2)*
Eliahba the S, the sons of 2Sm 23:32
the Baharumite, Eliahba the S, 1Ch 11:33

SHAALIM *(1)*
went through the region of S— 1Sm 9:4

SHAAPH *(2)*
Geshan, Pelet, Ephah, and S. 1Ch 2:47
She was also the mother of S, 1Ch 2:49

SHAARAIM *(3)*
(AKA SHARUHEN, SHILHIM)
S, Adithaim, Gederah, and Jos 15:36
all along the S road to Gath 1Sm 17:52
Hazar-susim, Beth-biri, and S. 1Ch 4:31

SHAASHGAZ *(1)*
under the supervision of S, Est 2:14

SHABBETHAI *(3)*
with Meshullam and S the Levite Ezr 10:15
Jamin, Akkub, S, Hodiah, Neh 8:7
and S and Jozabad, from the Neh 11:16

SHACK *(1)*
like a s in a cucumber field, Is 1:8

SHACKLES *(11)*
and bound him with bronze s, Jdg 16:21
feet not placed in bronze ⌊s⌋. 2Sm 3:34
bound him with bronze ⌊s⌋, 2Ch 33:11
him in bronze ⌊s⌋ to take him to 2Ch 36:6
They hurt his feet with s; Ps 105:18
their dignitaries with iron s, Ps 149:8
or your s will become stronger. Is 28:22
from you and tear off your s. Nah 1:13
been bound with s and chains, Mk 5:4
the chains and smashed the s. Mk 5:4
by chains and s, he would snap Lk 8:29

SHADE *(19)*
come and find refuge in my s. Jdg 9:15
Like a slave he longs for s; Jb 7:2
plants cover him with their s; Jb 40:22
mountains were covered by its s, Ps 80:10
I delight to sit in his s, Sg 2:3
be a booth for s from heat by Is 4:6
noonday with s that is as dark Is 16:3
the rain, a s from the heat. Is 25:4
As the s of a cloud ⌊cools⌋ the Is 25:5
dry land and the s of a massive Is 32:2
in the s of its branches. Ezk 17:23
great nations lived in its s. Ezk 31:6
earth left its s and abandoned Ezk 31:12
had lived in its s among the Ezk 31:17
because their s is pleasant. Hs 4:13
return and live beneath his s. Hs 14:7
and sat in its s to see what Jnh 4:5
up to provide s over Jonah's Jnh 4:6
of the sky can nest in its s." Mk 4:32

SHADOW *(37)*
Should the s go ahead 10 steps 2Kg 20:9
easy for the s to lengthen 10 2Kg 20:10
let the s go back 10 steps." 2Kg 20:10
He brought the s back the 10 2Kg 20:11
Our days on earth are like a s, 1Ch 29:15
Our days on earth are but a s. Jb 8:9
he flees like a s and does not Jb 14:2
and the s of death covers my Jb 16:16

whole body has become but a **s**. Jb 17:7
is like death's **s** to them. Jb 24:17
with the terrors of death's **s**! Jb 24:17
you seen the gates of death's **s**? Jb 38:17
hide me in the **s** of Your wings Ps 17:8
refuge in the **s** of Your wings. Ps 36:7
man walks about like a mere **s**. Ps 39:6
refuge in the **s** of Your wings Ps 57:1
rejoice in the **s** of Your wings. Ps 63:7
dwells in the **s** of the Almighty. Ps 91:1
days are like a lengthening **s**, Ps 102:11
fade away like a lengthening **s**; Ps 109:23
his days are like a passing **s**. Ps 144:4
life that he spends like a **s**? Ec 6:12
lengthen their days like a **s**, Ec 8:13
and take refuge in Egypt's **s**. Is 30:2
in Egypt's **s** your disgrace. Is 30:3
gather ⌊her brood⌋ under her **s**. Is 34:15
make the sun's **s** that goes down Is 38:8
So the sun's **s** went back the 10 Is 38:8
He hid me in the **s** of His hand. Is 49:2
covered you in the **s** of My hand, Is 51:16
in Heshbon's **s** because fire has Jr 48:45
in darkness and the **s** of death, Lk 1:79
least his **s** might fall on some Ac 5:15
These are a **s** of what was to Col 2:17
as a copy and **s** of the heavenly Heb 8:5
law has ⌊only⌋ a **s** of the good Heb 10:1
variation or **s** cast by turning Jms 1:17

SHADOWLAND *(1)*
those living in the **s** of death, Mt 4:16

SHADOWS *(6)*
The **s** of the mountains look like Jdg 9:36
s began to fall on the gates Neh 13:19
shoot from the **s** at the upright Ps 11:2
the day breaks and the **s** flee, Sg 2:17
the day breaks and the **s** flee, Sg 4:6
the evening **s** grow long. Jr 6:4

SHADRACH *(15)*
(AKA HANANIAH)
to Hananiah, S; to Mishael, Dn 1:7
the king appointed S, Meshach, Dn 2:49
S, Meshach, and Abednego. Dn 3:12
gave orders to bring in S, Dn 3:13
asked them, "S, Meshach, and Dn 3:14
S, Meshach, and Abednego replied Dn 3:16
on his face changed toward S, Dn 3:19
in his army to tie up S, Dn 3:20
killed those men who carried S, Dn 3:22
And these three men, S, Meshach, Dn 3:23
S, Meshach, and Abednego, you Dn 3:26
So S, Meshach, and Abednego Dn 3:26
Praise to the God of S, Meshach, Dn 3:28
offensive against the God of S, Dn 3:29
king rewarded S, Meshach, and Dn 3:30

SHADY *(1)*
branches and **s** foliage, Ezk 31:3

SHAFT *(14)*
its base and **s**, its ⌊ornamental⌋ Ex 25:31
the lampstand ⌊**s**⌋ along with its Ex 25:34
its base and **s**, its ⌊ornamental⌋ Ex 37:17
the lampstand **s** there were four Ex 37:20
His spear **s** was like a weaver's 1Sm 17:7
the water **s** to reach the lame 2Sm 5:8
The **s** of his spear was like a 2Sm 21:19
with iron and the **s** of a spear. 2Sm 23:7
The **s** of his spear was like a 1Ch 20:5
He cuts a **s** far from human Jb 28:4
key to the **s** of the abyss was Rv 9:1
He opened the **s** of the abyss, Rv 9:2
came up out of the **s** like smoke Rv 9:2
by the smoke from the **s**. Rv 9:2

SHAGEE *(1)*
Jonathan son of S the Hararite, 1Ch 11:34

SHAGGY *(1)*
The **s** goat represents the king Dn 8:21

SHAHARAIM *(1)*
S had sons in the country of 1Ch 8:8

SHAHAZUMAH *(1)*
reached Tabor, S, and Jos 19:22

SHAKE *(33)*
I did before and **s** myself free." Jdg 16:20
the people will **s**⌋ as a reed 1Kg 14:15
God likewise **s** from his house Neh 5:13
over me and made all my bones **s**. Jb 4:14
you and **s** my head at you, Jb 16:4
the earth and **s** the wicked out Jb 38:13
be ashamed and **s** with terror; Ps 6:10
they sneer and **s** their heads: Ps 22:7
who see them will **s** their heads. Ps 64:8
let their loins continually **s**. Ps 69:23
earth and all its inhabitants **s**, Ps 75:3
they **s** their heads ⌊in scorn⌋. Ps 109:25
and the earth will **s** from its Is 13:13
is about to **s** you violently. Is 22:17
Bashan and Carmel **s** off ⌊their⌋ Is 33:9
Stand up, **s** the dust off Is 52:2
mountains move and the hills **s**, Is 54:10
be horrified and **s** his head. Jr 18:16
speak of him you **s** ⌊your head⌋." Jr 48:27
They hiss and **s** their heads at Lm 2:15
your walls will **s** from the noise Ezk 26:10
heaven and earth will **s**. Jl 3:16
so that the thresholds **s**; Am 9:1
and I will **s** the house of Israel Am 9:9
tremble, loins **s**, every face Nah 2:10
I am going to **s** the heavens and Hg 2:6
I will **s** all the nations so that Hg 2:7
I am going to **s** the heavens and Hg 2:21
s the dust off your feet when Mt 10:14
s the dust off your feet as a Mk 6:11
that house and couldn't **s** it, Lk 6:48
s off the dust from your feet as Lk 9:5
once more I will **s** not only the Heb 12:26

SHAKEN *(37)*
established; it cannot be **s**. 1Ch 16:30
he be **s** out and have nothing! Neh 5:13
my whole being is **s** with terror. Ps 6:3
will rejoice because I am **s**. Ps 13:4
my right hand, I will not be **s**. Ps 16:8
of the Most High he is not **s**. Ps 21:7
I said, "I will never be **s**." Ps 30:6
allow the righteous to be **s**. Ps 55:22
You have **s** the land and split it Ps 60:2
stronghold; I will never be **s**. Ps 62:2
my stronghold; I will not be **s**. Ps 62:6
foundations of the earth are **s**. Ps 82:5
established; it cannot be **s**. Ps 93:1
it cannot be **s**. He judges the Ps 96:10
foundations; it will never be **s**. Ps 104:5
I am **s** off like a locust. Ps 109:23
will never be **s**. The righteous Ps 112:6
Zion. It cannot be **s**; it remains Ps 125:1
The righteous will never be **s**, Pr 10:30
foundations of the earth are **s**. Is 24:18
the earth is violently **s**. Is 24:19
of peace will not be **s**," Is 54:10
when **s**, they fall—right into Nah 3:12
whole city was **s**, saying, "Who Mt 21:10
the celestial powers will be **s**. Mt 24:29
guards were so **s** from fear of Mt 28:4
the celestial powers will be **s**. Mk 13:25
pressed down, **s** together, and Lk 6:38
the celestial powers will be **s**. Lk 21:26
my right hand, I will not be **s**. Ac 2:25
where they were assembled was **s**, Ac 4:31
foundations of the jail were **s**, Ac 16:26
that no one will be **s** by these 1Th 3:3
the removal of what can be **s**— Heb 12:27
that what is not **s** might remain. Heb 12:27
a kingdom that cannot be **s**, Heb 12:28
figs when **s** by a high wind; Rv 6:13

SHAKES *(12)*
shake⌋ as a reed **s** in water. 1Kg 14:15
Jerusalem **s** ⌊her⌋ head behind 2Kg 19:21
He **s** the earth from its place so Jb 9:6
of the LORD **s** the wilderness; Ps 29:8
the LORD **s** the wilderness of Ps 29:8
Jerusalem **s** ⌊her⌋ head behind Is 37:22
he **s** the arrows, consults the Ezk 21:21
The countryside **s** at the sound Ezk 27:28
them; the sky **s**. The sun and Jl 2:10
nations, as one **s** a sieve, but Am 9:9
He stands and **s** the earth; Hab 3:6
by her jeers and **s** his fist. Zph 2:15

SHAKING *(8)*
me, LORD, for my bones are **s**; Ps 6:2
trees of a forest **s** in a wind. Is 7:2
s his fist at the mountain of Is 10:32
weak hands, steady the **s** knees! Is 35:3
your water with **s** and anxiety. Ezk 12:18
insults at Him, **s** their heads Mt 27:39
insults at Him, **s** their heads, Mk 15:29
But **s** the dust off their feet Ac 13:51

SHALISHAH *(1)*
then through the region of S, 1Sm 9:4

SHALL *(9)*
(See pp. xi-xii.)

SHALLECHETH *(1)*
and the gate of S on the 1Ch 26:16

SHALLUM *(23)*
(AKA JEHOAHAZ, MESHULLAM)
S son of Jabesh conspired 2Kg 15:10
S son of Jabesh became king; 2Kg 15:13
and struck down S son of Jabesh 2Kg 15:14
Huldah, wife of S son of Tikvah, 2Kg 22:14
Sismai, and Sismai fathered S. 1Ch 2:40
S fathered Jekamiah, and 1Ch 2:41
Zedekiah third, and S fourth. 1Ch 3:15
his son S, his son Mibsam, and 1Ch 4:25
Zadok; Zadok fathered S; 1Ch 6:12
S fathered Hilkiah; Hilkiah 1Ch 6:13
Jezer, and S—Bilhah's sons 1Ch 7:13
S, Akkub, Talmon, Ahiman, and 1Ch 9:17
relatives. S was their chief 1Ch 9:17
S son of Kore, son of Ebiasaph, 1Ch 9:19
the firstborn of S the Korahite, 1Ch 9:31
Jehizkiah son of S, and Amasa 2Ch 28:12
the wife of S son of Tokhath, 2Ch 34:22
gatekeepers: S, Telem, and Uri Ezr 10:24
S, Amariah, and Joseph; Ezr 10:42
Beside him S son of Hallohesh, Neh 3:12
says concerning S son of Josiah, Jr 22:11
of your uncle S, is coming to Jr 32:7
son of S the doorkeeper. Jr 35:4

SHALLUM'S *(4)*
rest of the events of S ⌊reign⌋, 2Kg 15:15
S descendants, Ater's Ezr 2:42
S son, Zadok's son, Ahitub's son, Ezr 7:2
S descendants, Ater's Neh 7:45

SHALLUN *(1)*
S son of Col-hozeh, ruler over Neh 3:15

SHALMAI'S *(2)*
descendants, S descendants, Ezr 2:46
descendants, S descendants, Neh 7:48

SHALMAN'S *(1)*
S destruction of Beth-arbel. Hs 10:14

SHALMANESER *(2)*
S king of Assyria attacked him, 2Kg 17:3
S king of Assyria marched 2Kg 18:9

SHALOM *(1)*
there and called it Yahweh S. Jdg 6:24

SHAMA *(1)*
S and Jeiel the sons of Hotham 1Ch 11:44

SHAME *(117)*
wife were naked, yet felt no **s**. Gn 2:25
"God has taken away my **s**." Gn 30:23
You are not to **s** your father by Lv 18:7
it will **s** your father. Lv 18:8
because it will **s** your family. Lv 18:10
You are not to **s** your father's Lv 18:14
it will **s** your brother. Lv 18:16
a horrible **s** in Israel. Jdg 20:6
son to your own **s** and to the 1Sm 20:30
returned with **s** to his land. 2Ch 32:21
and open **s**, as it is today. Ezr 9:7
enemies will be clothed with **s**; Jb 8:22
am filled with **s** and aware of my Jb 10:15
and you mistreat me without **s**. Jb 19:3
do not let me be put to **s**, Ps 25:20
be clothed with **s** and reproach. Ps 35:26
be horrified because of their **s**. Ps 40:15
and **s** has covered my face, Ps 44:15
will put them to **s**, for God has Ps 53:5
and **s** has covered my face. Ps 69:7
I endure—my **s** and disgrace. Ps 69:19
retreat because of their **s**. Ps 70:3
the oppressed turn away in **s**; Ps 74:21
He gave them lasting **s**. Ps 78:66
their faces with **s** so that they Ps 83:16
them be put to **s** and terrified Ps 83:17
see and be put to **s** because You, Ps 86:17
You have covered him with **s**. Ps 89:45
in idols, will be put to **s**. Ps 97:7
will be put to **s**, but Your Ps 109:28
will wear their **s** like a cloak. Ps 109:29
LORD, do not put me to **s**. Ps 119:31
be put to **s** for slandering me Ps 119:78
so that I will not be put to **s**. Ps 119:80

be put to s when they speak Ps 127:5
will clothe his enemies with s, Ps 132:18
a wife who causes s is like Pr 12:4
a wicked man comes, s does also, Pr 18:3
bared buttocks, to Egypt's s. Is 20:4
moon will be put to s and the Is 24:23
and they will be put to s. Is 26:11
protection will become your s, Is 30:3
for nothing but s and reproach. Is 30:5
so they will be put to s. Is 44:9
its worshipers will be put to s, Is 44:11
will be startled and put to s. Is 44:11
them are put to s, even Is 45:16
not be put to s or humiliated Is 45:17
come to Him and be put to s. Is 45:24
and your s will be exposed. Is 47:3
hope in Me will not be put to s. Is 49:23
I know I will not be put to s. Is 50:7
for you will not be put to s; Is 54:4
will forget the s of your youth, Is 54:4
Because your s was double, Is 61:7
but you will be put to s. Is 65:13
But they will be put to s." Is 66:5
Like the s of a thief when he is Jr 2:26
of Israel has been put to s. Jr 2:26
will be put to s by Egypt just Jr 2:36
as you were put to s by Assyria. Jr 2:36
Let us lie down in our s; Jr 3:25
The wise will be put to s; Jr 8:9
is put to s by ⌊his⌋ carved Jr 10:14
altars you have set up to S— Jr 11:13
Be put to s by your harvests Jr 12:13
so that your s might be seen. Jr 13:26
abandon You will be put to s. Jr 17:13
Let my persecutors be put to s, Jr 17:18
but don't let me be put to s. Jr 17:18
and sorrow, to end my life in s? Jr 20:18
everlasting s and humiliation Jr 23:40
Daughter Egypt will be put to s, Jr 46:24
Kiriathaim will be put to s; Jr 48:1
will be put to s and dismayed! Jr 48:1
will be put to s because of Jr 48:13
was put to s because of Bethel Jr 48:13
Moab is put to s, indeed Jr 48:20
Hamath and Arpad are put to s, Jr 49:23
Bel is put to s; Marduk is Jr 50:2
her idols are put to s; Jr 50:2
who bore you will be put to s. Jr 50:12
is put to s by ⌊his⌋ carved Jr 51:17
Her entire land will suffer s, Jr 51:47
let him be filled with s. Lm 3:30
S will cover all ⌊their⌋ faces, Ezk 7:18
so that the s of your debauchery Ezk 23:29
went down in s with the slain, Ezk 32:30
this day public s belongs to us: Dn 9:7
LORD, public s belongs to us, Dn 9:8
and some to s and eternal Dn 12:2
I will expose her s in the sight Hs 2:10
consecrated themselves to S, Hs 9:10
Ephraim will experience s; Hs 10:6
will never again be put to s. Jl 2:26
will never again be put to s. Jl 2:27
be covered with s and destroyed Ob 10
s will not overtake us." Mc 2:6
and she will be covered with s, Mc 7:10
to nations, your s to kingdoms. Nah 3:5
have planned s for your house Hab 2:10
one who does wrong knows no s. Zph 3:5
will not be put to s because of Zph 3:11
and they will put horsemen to s. Zch 10:5
on Him will not be put to s. Rm 9:33
on Him will be put to s, Rm 10:11
foolish things to s the wise, 1Co 1:27
weak things to s the strong. 1Co 1:27
I'm not writing this to s you, 1Co 4:14
this to your s! Can it be that 1Co 6:5
about God. I say this to your s. 1Co 15:34
I say this to ⌊our⌋ s: 2Co 11:21
their glory is in their s. Php 3:19
a cross and despised the s, Heb 12:2
in Him will never be put to s! 1Pt 2:6
Christian life will be put to s. 1Pt 3:16
go naked, and they see his s." Rv 16:15

SHAMED *(5)*
wife, he has s his father. Lv 20:11
his aunt, he has s his uncle; Lv 20:20
He has s his brother; Lv 20:21
Today you have s all your 2Sm 19:5
be utterly s, an everlasting Jr 20:11

SHAMEFUL *(11)*
and accuses ⌊her⌋ of s conduct, Dt 22:14
He has accused her of s conduct, Dt 22:17
his father's s behavior toward 1Sm 20:34
As s conduct is pleasure for a Pr 10:23
is a disgraceful and s son. Pr 19:26
our youth the s one has consumed Jr 3:24
Depart in s nakedness, you Mc 1:11
have renounced s secret things, 2Co 4:2
For it is s even to mention what Eph 5:12
sea, foaming up their s deeds; Jd 13
and your s nakedness not be Rv 3:18

SHAMEFULLY *(3)*
she conceived them and acted s. Hs 2:5
on the head and treated him s. Mk 12:4
too, treated him s, and sent him Lk 20:11

SHAMELESS *(1)*
committed s acts with males Rm 1:27

SHAMGAR *(2)*
S son of Anath ⌊became judge⌋. Jdg 3:31
In the days of S son of Anath, Jdg 5:6

SHAMHUTH *(1)*
(AKA SHAMMAH, SHAMMOTH)
the commander S the Izrahite; 1Ch 27:8

SHAMIR *(4)*
hill country: S, Jattir, Socoh, Jos 15:48
and lived in S in the hill Jdg 10:1
when he died, was buried in S. Jdg 10:2
Micah; from Micah's sons: S. 1Ch 24:24

SHAMMA *(1)*
Bezer, Hod, S, Shilshah, Ithran, 1Ch 7:37

SHAMMAH *(9)*
(AKA SHAMHUTH, SHAMMOTH)
Nahath, Zerah, S, and Mizzah. Gn 36:13
Nahath, Zerah, S, and Mizzah. Gn 36:17
Jesse presented S, but Samuel 1Sm 16:9
the next, and S, the third, 1Sm 17:13
After him was S son of Agee the 2Sm 23:11
but S took his stand in the 2Sm 23:12
S the Harodite, Elika the 2Sm 23:25
S the Hararite, Ahiam son of 2Sm 23:33
Nahath, Zerah, S, and Mizzah. 1Ch 1:37

SHAMMAI *(4)*
Onam's sons: S and Jada. 1Ch 2:28
The sons of Jada brother of S: 1Ch 2:32
Jorkeam, and Rekem fathered S. 1Ch 2:44
birth to Miriam, S, and Ishbah 1Ch 4:17

SHAMMAI'S *(2)*
Shammai and Jada. S sons: Nadab 1Ch 2:28
S son was Maon, and Maon 1Ch 2:45

SHAMMOTH *(1)*
(AKA SHAMHUTH, SHAMMAH)
S the Harorite, Helez the 1Ch 11:27

SHAMMUA *(5)*
(AKA SHEMAIAH, SHIMEA)
S son of Zaccur from the tribe Nm 13:4
S, Shobab, Nathan, Solomon, 2Sm 5:14
S, Shobab, Nathan, Solomon, 1Ch 14:4
and Abda son of S, son of Galal, Neh 11:17
S of Bilgah, Jehonathan of Neh 12:18

SHAMSHERAI *(1)*
S, Shehariah, Athaliah, 1Ch 8:26

SHANKS *(6)*
entrails and s, and place ⌊them Ex 29:17
its entrails and s with water. Lv 1:9
the entrails and s with water. Lv 1:13
its head and s, and its entrails Lv 4:11
the entrails and s with water. Lv 8:21
and the s and burned them Lv 9:14

SHAPE *(10)*
whether in the s of anything in Ex 20:4
in the s of any figure: Dt 4:16
in the s of anything He Dt 4:23
yourself in the s of anything Dt 5:8
had the same size and s. 1Kg 6:25
and s for all of them 1Kg 7:37
s of an expanse, with a gleam Ezk 1:22
The s of a throne with the Ezk 1:26
resembling the s of a throne Ezk 10:1
one who crafts its s trusts in Hab 2:18

SHAPED *(12)*
to be three cups s like almond Ex 25:33
and three cups s like almond Ex 25:33
to be four cups s like almond Ex 25:34
were three cups s like almond Ex 37:19
and three cups s like almond Ex 37:19
were four cups s like almond Ex 37:20
cooking pot and s it into cakes. Nm 11:8
the portico were s like lilies, 1Kg 7:19
the pillars were s like lilies. 1Kg 7:22
Your hands s me and formed me. Jb 10:8
Can the One who s the ear not Ps 94:9
your Maker who s you from birth; Is 44:2

SHAPELY *(1)*
but Rachel was s and beautiful. Gn 29:17

SHAPES *(3)*
one who s a pedestal, choosing Is 40:20
over the coals, s the idol with Is 44:12
s it with chisels and outlines Is 44:13

SHAPHAM *(1)*
S the second ⌊in command⌋, 1Ch 5:12

SHAPHAN *(30)*
secretary S son of Azaliah, 2Kg 22:3
high priest told S the court 2Kg 22:8
and he gave the book to S, 2Kg 22:8
Then S the court secretary went 2Kg 22:9
Then S the court secretary told 2Kg 22:10
and S read it in the presence 2Kg 22:10
Ahikam son of S, Achbor son 2Kg 22:12
son of Micaiah, S the court 2Kg 22:12
Ahikam, Achbor, S, and Asaiah 2Kg 22:14
Ahikam, son of S, over the rest 2Kg 25:22
Josiah sent S son of Azaliah, 2Ch 34:8
Hilkiah told S the court 2Ch 34:15
and he gave the book to S. 2Ch 34:15
S took the book to the king, 2Ch 34:16
Then S the court secretary told 2Ch 34:18
and S read it in the presence 2Ch 34:18
Ahikam son of S, Abdon son of 2Ch 34:20
son of Micah, S the court 2Ch 34:20
But Ahikam son of S supported Jr 26:24
Elasah son of S and Gemariah son Jr 29:3
of Gemariah son of S the scribe, Jr 36:10
of Gemariah, son of S, heard all Jr 36:11
Gemariah son of S, Zedekiah son Jr 36:12
Ahikam, son of S, to take him Jr 39:14
Ahikam, son of S, whom the king Jr 40:5
Ahikam, son of S, swore an oath Jr 40:9
of Ahikam, son of S, over them, Jr 40:11
Ahikam, son of S, with the sword Jr 41:2
Gedaliah son of Ahikam son of S, Jr 43:6
Jaazaniah son of S standing Ezk 8:11

SHAPHAT *(8)*
S son of Hori from the tribe of Nm 13:5
Elisha son of S from 1Kg 19:16
Elisha son of S as he was 1Kg 19:19
Elisha son of S, who used to 2Kg 3:11
Elisha son of S remains on his 2Kg 6:31
Bariah, Neariah, and S—six. 1Ch 3:22
Janai, and S in Bashan. 1Ch 5:12
while S son of Adlai was in 1Ch 27:29

SHAPHIR *(1)*
nakedness, you residents of S; Mc 1:11

SHARAI *(1)*
Machnadebai, Shashai, S, Ezr 10:40

SHARAR *(1)*
(AKA SACHAR)
Ahiam son of S the Hararite, 2Sm 23:33

SHARE *(59)*
But as for the s of the men who Gn 14:24
Mamre—they can take their s." Gn 14:24
she may s her father's food. Lv 22:13
But no outsider may s it. Lv 22:13
the priests' s from the people Dt 18:3
refusing to s with any of them Dt 28:55
because the s for Judah's Jos 19:9
S the spoil of your enemies with Jos 22:8
You have no s in the LORD!' Jos 22:25
'You have no s in the LORD!' Jos 22:27
much too bitter for you ⌊to s⌋, Ru 1:13
for the priests' s ⌊of the 1Sm 2:13
The s of the one who goes into 1Sm 30:24
the same as the s of the one who 1Sm 30:24
supplies. They will s equally." 1Sm 30:24
but you have no s, right, or Neh 2:20
have their s from the enemies. Ps 68:23
do not let them s in Your Ps 69:27
and we'll all s our money"— Pr 1:14

for you ⌊to s⌋ with strangers Pr 5:17
s a home with shrewdness and Pr 8:12
son and s an inheritance Pr 17:2
of a roof than to s a house with Pr 21:9
Is it not to s your bread with Is 58:7
from the sky and s the plants Dn 4:15
and s ⌊food⌋ with the wild Dn 4:23
S your master's joy!' Mt 25:21
of many things. S your master's Mt 25:23
two shirts must s with someone Lk 3:11
give me the s of the estate I Lk 15:12
Take this and s it among Lk 22:17
allotted a s in this ministry. Ac 1:17
no part or s in this matter, Ac 8:21
of sins and a s among those who Ac 26:18
have come to s in the rich root Rm 11:17
S with the saints in their needs; Rm 12:13
If others s this authority over 1Co 9:12
at the altar s in the offerings 1Co 9:13
for all of us s that one bread. 1Co 10:17
You cannot s in the Lord's table 1Co 10:21
know that as you s in the 2Co 1:7
so you will s in the comfort. 2Co 1:7
message must s his goods with Gl 6:6
has something to s with anyone Eph 4:28
rejoice and s your joy with me. Php 2:18
enabled you to s in the saints' Col 1:12
were pleased to s with you not 1Th 2:8
and don't s in the sins of 1Tm 5:22
to be generous, willing to s, 1Tm 6:18
s in suffering for the gospel, 2Tm 1:8
S in suffering as a good soldier 2Tm 2:3
first to get a s of the crops. 2Tm 2:6
so that we can s His holiness. Heb 12:10
neglect to do good and to s, Heb 13:16
you s in the sufferings of the 1Pt 4:13
them you may s in the divine 2Pt 1:4
that you will not s in her sins, Rv 18:4
their s will be in the lake that Rv 21:8
will take away his s of the tree Rv 22:19

SHARED *(5)*
It s his meager food and drank 2Sm 12:3
than in a house s with a nagging Pr 25:24
the Gentiles have s in their Rm 15:27
church s with me in the matter Php 4:15
common, He also s in these, so Heb 2:14

SHARES *(6)*
We have 10 s in the king, 2Sm 19:43
and no outsider s in its joy. Pr 14:10
for he s his food with the poor. Pr 22:9
Joseph will receive two s. Ezk 47:13
to him s in his evil works. 2Jn 11
is the one who s in the first Rv 20:6

SHAREZER *(3)*
Adrammelech and S struck him 2Kg 19:37
Adrammelech and S struck him Is 37:38
people of⌋ Bethel had sent S, Zch 7:2

SHARING *(8)*
me away from s in the 1Sm 26:19
do so in hope of s the crop. 1Co 9:10
is it not a s in the blood of 1Co 10:16
is it not a s in the body of 1Co 10:16
privilege of s in the ministry 2Co 8:4
generosity in s with them and 2Co 9:13
the same love, s the same Php 2:2
you did well by s with me in my Php 4:14

SHARON *(7)*
the pasturelands of S. 1Ch 5:16
of the herds that grazed in S, 1Ch 27:29
I am a rose of S, a lily of the Sg 2:1
and decayed. S is like a desert; Is 33:9
the splendor of Carmel and S. Is 35:2
S will be a pasture for flocks, Is 65:10
in Lydda and S saw him and Ac 9:35

SHARONITE *(1)*
Shitrai the S was in charge of 1Ch 27:29

SHARP *(20)*
There were s columns of rock on 1Sm 14:4
the needy from their s words Jb 5:15
their tongues are s swords. Ps 57:4
mouths—s words from their Ps 59:7
turned back his s sword and have Ps 89:43
A warrior's s arrows, with Ps 120:4
their tongues as s as a snake's Ps 140:3
wormwood and as s as a Pr 5:4
a club, a sword, or a s arrow. Pr 25:18
you into a s threshing board Is 41:15
He made my words like a s sword; Is 49:2
man, take a s sword, use it as Ezk 5:1
There was such a s disagreement Ac 15:39
mouth came a s two-edged sword Rv 1:16
One who has the s, two-edged Rv 2:12
His head and a s sickle in His Rv 14:14
who also had a s sickle came out Rv 14:17
to the one who had the s sickle, Rv 14:18
Use your s sickle and gather the Rv 14:18
From His mouth came a s sword, Rv 19:15

SHARPEN *(6)*
when I s My flashing sword, Dt 32:41
Philistines to s their 1Sm 13:20
repent, God will s His sword; Ps 7:12
who s their tongues like swords Ps 64:3
and one does not s its edge, Ec 10:10
S the arrows! Fill the quivers! Jr 51:11

SHARPENED *(6)*
Like a s razor, your tongue Ps 52:2
arrows are s, and all their Is 5:28
He made me like a s arrow; Is 49:2
A sword is s and also polished. Ezk 21:9
It is s for slaughter, polished Ezk 21:10
It is s, and it is polished, to Ezk 21:11

SHARPENS *(2)*
s iron, and one man sharpens Pr 27:17
iron, and one man s another. Pr 27:17

SHARPER *(1)*
and effective and s than any Heb 4:12

SHARPLY *(1)*
So, rebuke them s, that they may Ti 1:13

SHARUHEN *(1)*
(AKA SHAARAIM, SHILHIM)
and S—13 cities, with Jos 19:6

SHASHAI *(1)*
Machnadebai, S, Sharai, Ezr 10:40

SHASHAK *(1)*
Ahio, S, and Jeremoth. 1Ch 8:14

SHASHAK'S *(1)*
and Penuel were S sons. 1Ch 8:25

SHATTER *(8)*
You will s them like pottery." Ps 2:9
will s the bronze doors and cut Is 45:2
s them with total destruction. Jr 17:18
Then you are to s the jug in the Jr 19:10
I will s these people and this Jr 19:11
I am about to s Elam's bow, Jr 49:35
I will s bow, sword, and weapons Hs 2:18
He will s them like pottery— Rv 2:27

SHATTERED *(47)*
of the field and s every tree Ex 9:25
Your right hand s the enemy. Ex 15:6
she s and pierced his temple. Jdg 5:26
trumpets and s their pitchers. Jdg 7:20
s and crushed the Israelites Jdg 10:8
who oppose the LORD will be s; 1Sm 2:10
high places and s the sacred 2Kg 18:4
He s their sacred pillars and 2Ch 14:3
cast images he s, crushed to 2Ch 34:4
I was at ease, but He s me; Jb 16:12
I s the fangs of the unjust and Jb 29:17
and fig trees and s the trees of Ps 105:33
he will be s instantly—beyond Pr 6:15
and the jar is s at the spring, Ec 12:6
will be too s to be a people Is 7:8
For You have s their burdensome Is 9:4
gods have been s on the ground." Is 21:9
The city of chaos is s; Is 24:10
be found among its s remains— Is 30:14
Assyria will be s by the voice Is 30:31
righteousness will never be s. Is 51:6
and do not be s by their taunts. Is 51:7
a despised, s pot, a jar no one Jr 22:28
and become s like a precious Jr 25:34
Moab will be s; her little ones Jr 48:4
How the mighty scepter is s, Jr 48:17
off; his arm is s." ⌊This is⌋ Jr 48:25
because I have s Moab like a jar Jr 48:38
Suddenly Babylon fell and was s. Jr 51:8
set ablaze, her gate bars are s. Jr 51:30
their bows s, for the LORD is Jr 51:56
destroyed and s the bars on her Lm 2:9
He has s my bones. Lm 3:4
The gateway to the peoples is s. Ezk 26:2
east wind has s you in the heart Ezk 27:26
Now you are s by the sea in the Ezk 27:34
you s and made all their hips Ezk 29:7
Egypt and all its allies are s. Ezk 30:8
But you will be s and will lie Ezk 32:28
the gold were s and became like Dn 2:35
powerful, the large horn was s. Dn 8:8
place of the s horn represent Dn 8:22
But he will be s, not by human Dn 8:25
within a few days he will be s, Dn 11:20
they will be s, as well as the Dn 11:22
power of the holy people is s, Dn 12:7
even rocks are s before Him. Nah 1:6

SHATTERING *(4)*
my hands, s them before your Dt 9:17
mountains and was s cliffs 1Kg 19:11
will be like the s of a potter's Is 30:14
struck the ram, s his two horns, Dn 8:7

SHATTERS *(6)*
He s the mighty without an Jb 34:24
LORD s the cedars of Lebanon. Ps 29:5
He s bows and cuts spears to Ps 46:9
There He s the bow's flaming Ps 76:3
like one s a potter's jar that Jr 19:11
iron crushes and s everything, Dn 2:40

SHAUL *(9)*
S from Rehoboth-on-the-River Gn 36:37
When S died, Baal-hanan son of Gn 36:38
Jachin, Zohar, and S, the son of Gn 46:10
Jachin, Zohar, and S, the son of Ex 6:15
the Shaulite clan from S. Nm 26:13
S from Rehoboth on the Euphrates 1Ch 1:48
When S died, Baal-hanan son of 1Ch 1:49
Jamin, Jarib, Zerah, and S; 1Ch 4:24
his son Uzziah, and his son S. 1Ch 6:24

SHAUL'S *(1)*
⌊S sons:⌋ his son Shallum, his 1Ch 4:25

SHAULITE *(1)*
the S clan from Shaul. Nm 26:13

SHAVE *(21)*
person must s himself but not Lv 13:33
but not s the scaly area. Lv 13:33
his clothes, s off all his hair Lv 14:8
He is to s off all his hair Lv 14:9
s the edge of their beards, Lv 21:5
he must s his head on the day of Nm 6:9
is to s it on the seventh day. Nm 6:9
Nazirite is to s his consecrated Nm 6:18
Have them s their entire bodies Nm 8:7
She must s her head, trim her Dt 21:12
called a man to s off the seven Jdg 16:19
him that he had to s it off— 2Sm 14:26
the LORD will s their foreheads Is 3:17
of Assyria—to s the head, the Is 7:20
cut himself or s his head for Jr 16:6
all those who s their temples; Jr 25:23
those who s their temples; Jr 49:32
and s your head and beard. Ezk 5:1
They s their heads because of Ezk 27:31
They may not s their heads or Ezk 44:20
S yourselves bald and cut off Mc 1:16

SHAVED *(16)*
He s, changed his clothes, and Gn 41:14
after he has s his consecrated Nm 6:19
I am s, my strength will leave Jdg 16:17
grow back after it had been s. Jdg 16:22
emissaries, s off half their 2Sm 10:4
When he s his head—he shaved 2Sm 14:26
s ⌊it⌋ every year because ⌊his 2Sm 14:26
emissaries, s them, cut their 1Ch 19:4
tore his robe and s his head. Jb 1:20
Every head is s; every beard is Is 15:2
Samaria who had s their beards, Jr 41:5
and every head to be s. Am 8:10
He s his head at Cenchreae, Ac 18:18
for them to get their heads s. Ac 21:24
the same as having her head s. 1Co 11:5
her hair cut off or her head s, 1Co 11:6

SHAVEH *(1)*
to meet him in the Valley of S Gn 14:17

SHAVEH-KIRIATHAIM *(1)*
the Zuzim in Ham, the Emim in S, Gn 14:5

SHAVEN *(1)*
wailing, for s heads, and for Is 22:12

SHAVSHA *(1)*
(AKA SERAIAH, SHEVA, SHISHA)
S was court secretary; 1Ch 18:16
SHAWL *(2)*
Bring the s you're wearing and Ru 3:15
measures⌋ of barley into her s, Ru 3:15
SHE *(976)*
(See pp. xi-xii.)
SHE'LL *(2)*
(See pp. xi-xii.)
SHE'S *(5)*
(See pp. xi-xii.)
SHEAF *(7)*
Suddenly my s stood up, and your Gn 37:7
it and bowed down to my s." Gn 37:7
the first s of your harvest Lv 23:10
will wave the s before the LORD Lv 23:11
On the day you wave the s, Lv 23:12
you brought the s of the Lv 23:15
and you forget a s in the field, Dt 24:19
SHEAL *(1)*
Adaiah, Jashub, S, and Jeremoth; Ezr 10:29
SHEALTIEL *(11)*
the captive: his sons S, 1Ch 3:17
son of S and his brothers Ezr 3:2
Zerubbabel son of S, Jeshua son Ezr 3:8
son of S and Jeshua son Ezr 5:2
son of S and with Jeshua: Neh 12:1
prophet to Zerubbabel son of S, Hg 1:1
son of S, the high priest Hg 1:12
spirit of Zerubbabel son of S, Hg 1:14
Speak to Zerubbabel son of S, Hg 2:2
son of S, My servant"— Hg 2:23
son⌋ of S, ⌊son⌋ of Neri, Lk 3:27
SHEAR *(3)*
Laban had gone to s his sheep, Gn 31:19
up to Timnah to s his sheep." Gn 38:13
oxen to work or s the firstborn Dt 15:19
SHEAR-JASHUB *(1)*
with your son S to meet Ahaz at Is 7:3
SHEARED *(1)*
and the first s⌊wool⌋ of your Dt 18:4
SHEARER *(1)*
a lamb is silent before its s, Ac 8:32
SHEARERS *(2)*
for my s and give them to 1Sm 25:11
a sheep silent before her s, Is 53:7
SHEARIAH *(2)*
Bocheru, Ishmael, S, Obadiah, 1Ch 8:38
Bocheru, Ishmael, S, Obadiah, 1Ch 9:44
SHEARING *(3)*
goats and was s his sheep in 1Sm 25:2
he heard that Nabal was s sheep, 1Sm 25:4
I hear that you are s. 1Sm 25:7
SHEATH *(8)*
it from its s, and used it to 1Sm 17:51
his waist with a sword in its s. 2Sm 20:8
put his sword back into its s. 1Ch 21:27
sword from its s and cut off Ezk 21:3
come out of its s against Ezk 21:4
have taken My sword from its s— Ezk 21:5
Return ⌊it⌋ to its s! Ezk 21:30
You took the s from Your bow; Hab 3:9
SHEATHE *(1)*
said to Peter, "S your sword! Jn 18:11
SHEATHED *(1)*
sheath—it will not be s again. Ezk 21:5
SHEAVES *(9)*
binding s of grain in the field. Gn 37:7
your s gathered around it and Gn 37:7
as a stack of s is gathered in Jb 5:26
They carry s but go hungry. Jb 24:10
shouts of joy, carrying his s. Ps 126:6
the arms of the one who binds s. Ps 129:7
wagon full of s crushes ⌊grain⌋ Am 2:13
them like s to the threshing Mc 4:12
like a flaming torch among s; Zch 12:6
SHEBA *(34)*
(AKA BEER-SHEBA)
And Raamah's sons: S and Dedan. Gn 10:7
Obal, Abimael, S, Gn 10:28
Jokshan fathered S and Dedan. Gn 25:3
Beer-sheba (or S), Moladah, Jos 19:2
named S son of Bichri, 2Sm 20:1
and followed S son of Bichri, 2Sm 20:2
S son of Bichri will do more 2Sm 20:6
to pursue S son of Bichri. 2Sm 20:7
Abishai pursued S son of Bichri. 2Sm 20:10
Joab to pursue S son of Bichri. 2Sm 20:13
S passed through all the tribes 2Sm 20:14
came and besieged S in Abel of 2Sm 20:15
is a man named S son of Bichri, 2Sm 20:21
off the head of S son of Bichri 2Sm 20:22
The queen of S heard about 1Kg 10:1
When the queen of S observed all 1Kg 10:4
those the queen of S gave to 1Kg 10:10
the queen of S her every desire 1Kg 10:13
Raama's sons: S and Dedan. 1Ch 1:9
Ebal, Abimael, S, 1Ch 1:22
Jokshan's sons: S and Dedan. 1Ch 1:32
Meshullam, S, Jorai, Jacan, Zia 1Ch 5:13
queen of S heard of Solomon's 2Ch 9:1
When the queen of S observed 2Ch 9:3
those the queen of S gave to 2Ch 9:9
the queen of S her every desire 2Ch 9:12
merchants of S hope for them. Jb 6:19
the kings of S and Seba offer Ps 72:10
May gold from S be given to him. Ps 72:15
all of them will come from S. Is 60:6
frankincense from S or sweet Jr 6:20
The merchants of S and Raamah Ezk 27:22
the merchants of S, Asshur, and Ezk 27:23
S and Dedan and the merchants of Ezk 38:13
SHEBANIAH *(7)*
The priests, S, Joshaphat, 1Ch 15:24
Bani, Kadmiel, S, Bunni, Neh 9:4
Hodiah, S, and Pethahiah— Neh 9:5
Hattush, S, Malluch, Neh 10:4
brothers S, Hodiah, Kelita, Neh 10:10
Zaccur, Sherebiah, S, Neh 10:12
of Malluchi, Joseph of S, Neh 12:14
SHEBAT *(1)*
is the month of S, in the second Zch 1:7
SHEBER *(1)*
the mother of S and Tirhanah. 1Ch 2:48
SHEBNA *(7)*
of the palace, S the court 2Kg 18:37
of the palace, S the court 2Kg 19:2
Go to S, that steward who is in Is 22:15
of the palace, S the scribe, and Is 36:3
Then Eliakim, S, and Joah said Is 36:11
of the palace, S the scribe, and Is 36:22
of the palace, S the scribe, Is 37:2
SHEBNAH *(2)*
of the palace, S the court 2Kg 18:18
son of Hilkiah, S, and Joah said 2Kg 18:26
SHEBUEL *(3)*
(AKA SHUBAEL)
Gershom's sons: S first. 1Ch 23:16
Mattaniah, Uzziel, S, Jerimoth, 1Ch 25:4
S, a descendant of Moses' son 1Ch 26:24
SHECANIAH *(9)*
Rephaiah, Arnan, Obadiah, and S. 1Ch 3:21
The son of S: Shemaiah. 1Ch 3:22
ninth to Jeshua, the tenth to S, 1Ch 24:11
and S in the cities of the 2Ch 31:15
S son of Jahaziel from Zattu's Ezr 8:5
S son of Jehiel, an Elamite, Ezr 10:2
beside him Shemaiah son of S, Neh 3:29
a son-in-law of S son of Arah, Neh 6:18
S, Rehum, Meremoth, Neh 12:3
SHECANIAH'S *(1)*
who was of S descendants; Ezr 8:3
SHECHEM *(64)*
the land to the site of S, Gn 12:6
Canaanite city of S and camped Gn 33:18
When S son of Hamor the Hivite, Gn 34:2
heard that S had defiled his Gn 34:5
For S had committed an outrage Gn 34:7
My son S is strongly attracted Gn 34:8
Then S said to Dinah's father Gn 34:11
sons answered S and his father Gn 34:13
the eyes of Hamor and his son S. Gn 34:18
and his son S went to the gate Gn 34:20
listened to Hamor and his son S, Gn 34:24
and his son S with their swords Gn 34:26
hid them under the oak near S. Gn 35:4
their father's flocks at S. Gn 37:12
are pasturing ⌊the flocks⌋ at S. Gn 37:13
of Hebron, and he went to S. Gn 37:14
the Shechemite clan ⌊from⌋ S; Nm 26:31
Helek, Asriel, S, Hepher, and Jos 17:2
Asher to Michmethath near S. Jos 17:7
S in the hill country of Ephraim, Jos 20:7
S, the city of refuge for the Jos 21:21
of Israel at S and summoned Jos 24:1
the people at S and established Jos 24:25
were buried at S in the parcel Jos 24:32
who was in S also bore him a son Jdg 8:31
brothers at S and spoke to them Jdg 9:1
of all the lords of S, Jdg 9:2
presence of all the lords of S, Jdg 9:3
all the lords of S and of Jdg 9:6
at the oak of the pillar in S. Jdg 9:6
to me, lords of S, and may God Jdg 9:7
the lords of S 'because he is Jdg 9:18
the lords of S and Beth-millo, Jdg 9:20
the lords of S and Beth-millo Jdg 9:20
Abimelech and the lords of S. Jdg 9:23
the lords of S, who had helped Jdg 9:24
The lords of S rebelled against Jdg 9:25
his brothers and crossed into S, Jdg 9:26
and the lords of S trusted him. Jdg 9:26
and who is S that we should Jdg 9:28
men of Hamor, the father of S. Jdg 9:28
have come to S and are turning Jdg 9:31
in ambush for S in four units. Jdg 9:34
lords of S and fought against Jdg 9:39
Gaal and his brothers from S. Jdg 9:41
lords of the Tower of S heard, Jdg 9:46
of the Tower of S had gathered Jdg 9:47
people in the Tower of S died— Jdg 9:49
of the men of S on their heads. Jdg 9:57
that goes up from Bethel to S, Jdg 21:19
went to S, for all Israel 1Kg 12:1
had gone to S to make him king. 1Kg 12:1
Jeroboam built S in the hill 1Kg 12:25
S (a city of refuge) with its 1Ch 6:67
Ahian, S, Likhi, and Aniam. 1Ch 7:19
and S and its villages as far as 1Ch 7:28
went to S, for all Israel 2Ch 10:1
had gone to S to make him king. 2Ch 10:1
I will divide up S. I will Ps 60:6
I will divide up S. I will Ps 108:7
80 men came from S, Shiloh, and Jr 41:5
murders on the road to S. Hs 6:9
carried back to S, and were Ac 7:16
from the sons of Hamor in S. Ac 7:16
SHECHEM'S *(4)*
sons of Hamor, S father, for 100 Gn 33:19
S father Hamor came to speak Gn 34:6
Dinah from S house, and went Gn 34:26
sons of Hamor, S father, for 100 Jos 24:32
SHECHEMITE *(1)*
the S clan ⌊from⌋ Shechem; Nm 26:31
SHED *(48)*
your brother's blood you have s. Gn 4:11
his blood will be s by man, Gn 9:6
said to them, "Don't s blood. Gn 37:22
He has s blood and must be cut Lv 17:4
of the blood that is s on it, Nm 35:33
blood of the person who s it. Nm 35:33
innocent blood will not be s, Dt 19:10
'Our hands did not s this blood; Dt 21:7
of the blood s by Saul and his 2Sm 21:1
peace to avenge blood s in war. 1Kg 2:5
blood that Joab s without just 1Kg 2:31
avenge the blood s by the hand 2Kg 9:7
Manasseh also s so much innocent 2Kg 21:16
all the innocent blood he had s. 2Kg 24:4
'You have s much blood and waged 1Ch 22:8
because you have s so much blood 1Ch 22:8
a man of war and have s blood.' 1Ch 28:3
because he had s the blood of 2Ch 24:25
vengeance for the s blood of Ps 79:10
s innocent blood—the blood Ps 106:38
hands that s innocent blood, Pr 6:17
reveal the blood s on it and Is 26:21
they rush to s innocent blood. Is 59:7
and no longer s innocent blood Jr 7:6
Don't s innocent blood in this Jr 22:3
who s the blood of the righteous Lm 4:13
those who s blood are judged. Ezk 16:38
guilty of the blood you have s, Ezk 22:4
used his strength to s blood. Ezk 22:6
who slander in order to s blood. Ezk 22:9
bribes in order to s blood. Ezk 22:12

against the blood **s** among you. Ezk 22:13
those who **s** blood are judged, Ezk 23:45
the blood she **s** is in her midst Ezk 24:7
eyes to your idols, and **s** blood. Ezk 33:25
blood they had **s** on the land, Ezk 36:18
land they **s** innocent blood. Jl 3:19
them wait in ambush to **s** blood; Mc 7:2
righteous blood **s** on the earth Mt 23:35
the moon will not **s** its light; Mt 24:29
it is **s** for many for the Mt 26:28
the moon will not **s** its light; Mk 13:24
the covenant; it is **s** for many. Mk 14:24
of all the prophets **s** since the Lk 11:50
by⌋ My blood; it is **s** for you. Lk 22:20
witness Stephen was being **s**, Ac 22:20
Their feet are swift to **s** blood; Rm 3:15
and to **s** light for all about the Eph 3:9

SHEDDING *(8)*

the guilt of **s** innocent blood, Dt 19:13
do not hold the **s** of innocent Dt 21:8
the guilt of **s** innocent blood, Dt 21:9
s innocent blood and committing Jr 22:17
their⌋ prey, **s** blood, and Ezk 22:27
with them in **s** the prophets' Mt 23:30
and without the **s** of blood there Heb 9:22
to the point of **s** your blood. Heb 12:4

SHEDEUR *(5)*

Elizur son of **S** from Reuben; Nm 1:5
Reubenites is Elizur son of **S**. Nm 2:10
the fourth day Elizur son of **S**, Nm 7:30
the offering of Elizur son of **S**. Nm 7:35
Elizur son of **S** was over Nm 10:18

SHEDS *(4)*

Whoever **s** man's blood, his blood Gn 9:6
olive tree that **s** its blossoms. Jb 15:33
s blood and does any of these Ezk 18:10
A city that **s** blood within her Ezk 22:3

SHEEP *(208)*

Abimelech took **s** and cattle and Gn 20:14
Then Abraham took **s** and cattle Gn 21:27
He has given him **s** and cattle, Gn 24:35
had flocks of **s**, herds of cattle Gn 26:14
Three flocks of **s** were lying Gn 29:2
it because the **s** were watered Gn 29:2
of the well and water the **s**. Gn 29:3
Rachel, coming with his **s**." Gn 29:6
Then we will water the **s**." Gn 29:8
Rachel came with her father's **s**, Gn 29:9
daughter Rachel with his **s**, Gn 29:10
and watered his uncle Laban's **s**. Gn 29:10
all your **s** today and remove Gn 30:32
remove every **s** that is speckled Gn 30:32
dark-colored **s** among the lambs, Gn 30:32
dark-colored **s** among the lambs, Gn 30:35
the troughs in front of the **s**— Gn 30:38
where the **s** came to drink. Gn 30:38
And the **s** bred when they came to Gn 30:38
completely dark **s** in Laban's Gn 30:40
didn't put them with Laban's **s**. Gn 30:40
that the weak **s** belonged to Gn 30:42
'The spotted **s** will be your wages, Gn 31:8
then all the **s** were born Gn 31:8
streaked **s** will be your wages, Gn 31:8
then all the **s** were born Gn 31:8
Laban had gone to shear his **s**, Gn 31:19
and I have nursing **s** and cattle. Gn 33:13
They took their **s**, cattle, Gn 34:28
Joseph tended **s** with his Gn 37:2
up to Timnah to shear his **s**." Gn 38:13
your **s**, cattle, and all Gn 45:10
brought their **s** and cattle and Gn 46:32
with their **s** and cattle and all Gn 47:1
land for your servants' **s**, Gn 47:4
the herds of **s**, the herds of Gn 47:17
children, their **s**, and their Gn 50:8
from either the **s** or the goats. Ex 12:5
offerings, your **s** and goats, as Ex 20:24
an ox or a **s** and butchers it Ex 22:1
the ox or four **s** for the sheep. Ex 22:1
the ox or four sheep for the **s**. Ex 22:1
ox, donkey, or **s**—is actually Ex 22:4
an ox, a donkey, a **s**, a garment, Ex 22:9
an ox, a **s**, or any ⌊other⌋ Ex 22:10
the firstborn of cattle or **s**. Ex 34:19
firstborn of a donkey with a **s**, Ex 34:20
the flock, from **s** or goats, he Lv 1:10
fat of an ox, a **s**, or a goat. Lv 7:23
have sufficient means for a **s**, Lv 12:8
slaughters an ox, **s**, or goat in Lv 17:3
from the cattle, **s**, or goats in Lv 22:19
When an ox, **s**, or goat is born, Lv 22:27
of an ox, a **s**, or a goat; Nm 18:17
Balak sacrificed cattle and **s**, Nm 22:40
be like **s** without a shepherd. Nm 27:17
cattle, donkeys, **s**, and goats. Nm 31:28
donkeys, **s**, and goats, all Nm 31:30
totaled: 675,000 **s** and goats, Nm 31:32
numbered: 337,500 **s** and goats, Nm 31:36
was 675 from the **s** and goats; Nm 31:37
half was: 337,500 **s** and goats, Nm 31:43
the ox, the **s**, the goat, Dt 14:4
antelope, and the mountain **s**. Dt 14:5
cattle, **s**, wine, beer, or Dt 14:26
God an ox or **s** with a defect Dt 17:1
it is an ox, a **s**, or a goat; Dt 18:3
your brother's ox or **s** straying, Dt 22:1
and every ox, **s**, and donkey. Jos 6:21
ox, donkey, and **s**, his tent, and Jos 7:24
as well as no **s**, ox or donkey. Jdg 6:4
the plunder, took **s**, cattle, and 1Sm 14:32
must bring me his ox or his **s**. 1Sm 14:34
infants, oxen and **s**, camels and 1Sm 15:3
and the best of the **s**, cattle, 1Sm 15:9
sound of **s** and cattle I hear? 1Sm 15:14
spared the best **s** and cattle in 1Sm 15:15
troops took **s** and cattle from 1Sm 15:21
right now he's tending the **s**." 1Sm 16:11
son David, who is with the **s**." 1Sm 16:19
leave those few **s** with in the 1Sm 17:28
has been tending his father's **s**. 1Sm 17:34
infants, oxen, donkeys, and **s**. 1Sm 22:19
Saul came to the **s** pens along 1Sm 24:3
man with 3,000 **s** and 1,000 goats 1Sm 25:2
was shearing his **s** in Carmel. 1Sm 25:2
heard that Nabal was shearing **s**, 1Sm 25:4
time we were herding the **s**. 1Sm 25:16
five butchered **s**, a bushel of 1Sm 25:18
He took all the **s** and cattle, 1Sm 30:20
following the **s** to be ruler over 2Sm 7:8
a large number of **s** and cattle, 2Sm 12:2
one of his own **s** or cattle to 2Sm 12:4
honey, curds, **s**, and cheese from 2Sm 17:29
these **s**, what have they done? 2Sm 24:17
sacrificed **s**, oxen, and fattened 1Kg 1:9
oxen, fattened cattle, and **s**. 1Kg 1:19
oxen, fattened cattle, and **s**. 1Kg 1:25
oxen, and 100 **s**, besides deer, 1Kg 4:23
sacrificing **s** and cattle that 1Kg 8:5
22,000 cattle and 120,000 **s**. 1Kg 8:63
on the hills like **s** without a 1Kg 22:17
Mesha of Moab was a **s** breeder. 2Kg 3:4
and vineyards, **s** and oxen, and 2Kg 5:26
camels, 250,000 **s**, and 2,000 1Ch 5:21
wine and oil, oxen, and **s**. 1Ch 12:40
and from following the **s**, 1Ch 17:7
these **s**, what have they done? 1Ch 21:17
sacrificing **s** and cattle that 2Ch 5:6
of 22,000 cattle and 120,000 **s**. 2Ch 7:5
and captured many **s** and camels. 2Ch 14:15
cattle and 7,000 **s** from all the 2Ch 15:11
sacrificed many **s** and cattle for 2Ch 18:2
on the hills like **s** without a 2Ch 18:16
bulls and 3,000 **s** were 2Ch 29:33
bulls and 7,000 **s** for the 2Ch 30:24
bulls and 10,000 **s** for the 2Ch 30:24
a tenth of the cattle and **s**, 2Ch 31:6
acquired herds of **s** and cattle 2Ch 32:29
Then Josiah donated 30,000 **s**, 2Ch 35:7
began rebuilding the **S** Gate. Neh 3:1
of the corner and the **S** Gate. Neh 3:32
ox, six choice **s**, and some fowl Neh 5:18
of the Hundred, to the **S** Gate. Neh 12:39
His estate included 7,000 **s**, Jb 1:3
burned up the **s** and the servants Jb 1:16
refused to put with my **s** dogs. Jb 30:1
with the fleece from my **s**, Jb 31:20
He owned 14,000 **s**, 6,000 camels, Jb 42:12
all the **s** and oxen, as well as Ps 8:7
be eaten like **s** and scatter us Ps 44:11
are counted as **s** to be Ps 44:22
s they are headed for Sheol; Ps 49:14
You fattened **s** as burnt Ps 66:15
against the **s** of Your pasture Ps 74:1
people out like **s** and guided Ps 78:52
people, the **s** of Your pasture Ps 79:13
pasture, the **s** under His care. Ps 95:7
people, the **s** of His pasture. Ps 100:3
I wander like a lost **s**; Ps 119:176
Where do you pasture your **s**? Sg 1:7
of newly shorn ⌊**s**⌋ coming up Sg 4:2
raise a young cow and two **s**, Is 7:21
to graze and for **s** to trample. Is 7:25
gazelles and like **s** without a Is 13:14
of **s**, eating of meat Is 22:13
brought Me your **s** for burnt Is 43:23
We all went astray like **s**; Is 53:6
and like a **s** silent before her Is 53:7
wicked away like **s** to slaughter, Jr 12:3
the **s** ⌊that were⌋ your pride? Jr 13:20
scatter the **s** of My pasture!" Jr 23:1
people are lost **s**; their Jr 50:6
looks for his **s** on the day he is Ezk 34:12
judge between one **s** and another, Ezk 34:17
between the fat **s** and the lean Ezk 34:20
the fat sheep and the lean **s**. Ezk 34:20
judge between one **s** and another. Ezk 34:22
as the flock of **s** for sacrifice Ezk 36:38
the flocks of **s** suffer Jl 1:18
who was one of the **s** breeders Am 1:1
them together like **s** in a pen, Mc 2:12
a young lion among flocks of **s**, Mc 5:8
there are no **s** in the pen and no Hab 3:17
for shepherds and folds for **s**. Zph 2:6
the people⌋ wander like **s**; Zch 10:2
flesh of the fat ⌊**s**⌋ and tear Zch 11:16
and the **s** will be scattered; Zch 13:7
like **s** without a shepherd. Mt 9:36
go to the lost **s** of the house of Mt 10:6
you out like **s** among wolves. Mt 10:16
if he had a **s** that fell into a Mt 12:11
man is worth far more than a **s**, Mt 12:12
only to the lost **s** of the house Mt 15:24
a man has 100 **s**, and one of them Mt 18:12
over that **s** more than over Mt 18:13
separates the **s** from the goats. Mt 25:32
He will put the **s** on His right, Mt 25:33
and the **s** of the flock will be Mt 26:31
they were like **s** without a Mk 6:34
and the **s** will be scattered. Mk 14:27
who has 100 **s** and loses one of Lk 15:4
because I have found my lost **s**!' Lk 15:6
a slave plowing or tending **s**, Lk 17:7
selling oxen, **s**, and doves, and Jn 2:14
complex with their **s** and oxen. Jn 2:15
By the **S** Gate in Jerusalem there Jn 5:2
enter the **s** pen by the door Jn 10:1
door is the shepherd of the **s**. Jn 10:2
him, and the **s** hear his voice. Jn 10:3
He calls his own **s** by name and Jn 10:3
The **s** follow him because they Jn 10:4
I am the door of the **s**. Jn 10:7
but the **s** didn't listen to them. Jn 10:8
lays down his life for the **s**. Jn 10:11
shepherd and doesn't own the **s**, Jn 10:12
and doesn't care about the **s**. Jn 10:13
I know My own **s**, and they know Jn 10:14
I lay down My life for the **s**. Jn 10:15
But I have other **s** that are not Jn 10:16
because you are not My **s**. Jn 10:26
My **s** hear My voice, I know them, Jn 10:27
"Shepherd My **s**," He told him. Jn 21:16
"Feed My **s**," Jesus said. Jn 21:17
was led like a **s** to the Ac 8:32
the great Shepherd of the **s**— Heb 13:20
you were like **s** going astray, 1Pt 2:25
grain; cattle and **s**; horses and Rv 18:13

SHEEP'S *(1)*

come to you in **s** clothing but Mt 7:15

SHEEPFOLD *(1)*

for camels and Ammon a **s**. Ezk 25:5

SHEEPFOLDS *(5)*

We want to build **s** here for our Nm 32:16
fortified cities, and ⌊built⌋ **s**. Nm 32:36
you sit among the **s** listening to Jdg 5:16
While you lie among the **s**, Ps 68:13
servant and took him from the **s**; Ps 78:70

SHEEPSHEARERS *(3)*

went up to Timnah to the **s**. Gn 38:12
Absalom's **s** were at Baal-hazor 2Sm 13:23
Your servant has just hired **s**. 2Sm 13:24

SHEEPSKINS *(1)*

about in **s**, in goatskins, Heb 11:37

SHEER *(1)*
glimmer of hope into s terror. Is 21:4

SHEERAH *(1)*
daughter was S, who built Lower 1Ch 7:24

SHEET *(3)*
the s covering all the nations; Is 25:7
a large s being lowered to Ac 10:11
resembled a large s being Ac 11:5

SHEETS *(2)*
hammered out thin s of gold, Ex 39:3
into hammered s as plating for Nm 16:38

SHEHARIAH *(1)*
Shamsherai, S, Athaliah, 1Ch 8:26

SHEKEL *(42)*
a gold ring weighing half a s, Gn 24:22
must pay half a s according to Ex 30:13
according to the sanctuary s Ex 30:13
shekel (20 gerahs to the s). Ex 30:13
This half s is a contribution to Ex 30:13
than half a s when giving the Ex 30:15
the sanctuary s), and one gallon Ex 30:24
according to the sanctuary s. Ex 38:24
according to the sanctuary s— Ex 38:25
half a s according to the Ex 38:26
according to the sanctuary s, Ex 38:26
according to the sanctuary s, Lv 5:15
by the standard sanctuary s. Lv 27:3
by the standard sanctuary s, Lv 27:25
shekel, 20 gerahs to the s. Lv 27:25
to the standard sanctuary s— Nm 3:47
shekel—20 gerahs to the s. Nm 3:47
by the standard sanctuary s. Nm 3:50
by the standard sanctuary s, Nm 7:13
by the standard sanctuary s, Nm 7:19
by the standard sanctuary s, Nm 7:25
by the standard sanctuary s, Nm 7:31
by the standard sanctuary s, Nm 7:37
by the standard sanctuary s, Nm 7:43
by the standard sanctuary s, Nm 7:49
by the standard sanctuary s, Nm 7:55
by the standard sanctuary s, Nm 7:61
by the standard sanctuary s, Nm 7:67
by the standard sanctuary s, Nm 7:73
by the standard sanctuary s, Nm 7:79
by the standard sanctuary s. Nm 7:85
by the standard sanctuary s. Nm 7:86
by the standard sanctuary s, Nm 18:16
two-thirds of a s for plowshares 1Sm 13:21
⌊of a s⌋ for pitchforks 1Sm 13:21
will sell⌋ for a s and 12 quarts 2Kg 7:1
barley ⌊will sell⌋ for a s.'" 2Kg 7:1
⌊sold⌋ for a s and 12 quarts 2Kg 7:16
quarts of barley ⌊sold⌋ for a s, 2Kg 7:16
sell⌋ for a s and six quarts 2Kg 7:18
will sell⌋ for a s at the gate 2Kg 7:18
The s will weigh 20 gerahs. Ezk 45:12

SHEKELS *(26)*
Land worth 400 s of silver— Gn 23:15
400 s of silver at the current Gn 23:16
bracelets weighing 10 s of gold. Gn 24:22
he must give 30 s of silver to Ex 21:32
by your valuation in silver s, Lv 5:15
is 50 silver s ⌊measured⌋ Lv 27:3
female, your valuation is 30 s. Lv 27:4
a male is 20 s and for a female Lv 27:5
shekels and for a female 10 s. Lv 27:5
for a male is five silver s, Lv 27:6
valuation is three s of silver. Lv 27:6
valuation is 15 s for a male and Lv 27:7
a male and 10 s for a female. Lv 27:7
of 50 silver s for ⌊every⌋ five Lv 27:16
collect five s for each person, Nm 3:47
1,365 ⌊s measured⌋ by the Nm 3:50
five s of silver by the standard Nm 18:16
100 silver ⌊s⌋ and give ⌊them Dt 22:19
woman's father 50 silver ⌊s⌋, Dt 22:29
200 silver s, and a bar of gold Jos 7:21
and a bar of gold weighing 50 s, Jos 7:21
head ⌊sold for⌋ 80 silver ⌊s⌋, 2Kg 6:25
dung ⌊sold for⌋ five silver ⌊s⌋. 2Kg 6:25
him the money—17 s of silver. Jr 32:9
Your mina will equal 60 s. Ezk 45:12
bought her for 15 s of silver Hs 3:2

SHELAH *(19)*
Arpachshad fathered S, and Gn 10:24
Shelah, and S fathered Eber. Gn 10:24
lived 35 years and fathered S. Gn 11:12
he fathered S, Arpachshad lived Gn 11:13
S lived 30 years and fathered Gn 11:14
S lived 403 years and fathered Gn 11:15
to another son and named him S. Gn 38:5
house until my son S grows up." Gn 38:11
saw that, though S had grown up, Gn 38:14
I did not give her to my son S." Gn 38:26
Er, Onan, S, Perez, and Zerah; Gn 46:12
the Shelanite clan from S; Nm 26:20
Arpachshad fathered S, and 1Ch 1:18
Shelah, and S fathered Eber. 1Ch 1:18
Shem, Arpachshad, S, 1Ch 1:24
Er, Onan, and S. ⌊These⌋ three 1Ch 2:3
The sons of S son of Judah: 1Ch 4:21
of the Pool of S near the king's Neh 3:15
⌊son⌋ of Eber, ⌊son⌋ of S, Lk 3:35

SHELANITE *(1)*
the S clan from Shelah; Nm 26:20

SHELEMIAH *(10)*
(AKA MESHELEMIAH)
for the east ⌊gate⌋ fell to S. 1Ch 26:14
S, Nathan, Adaiah, Ezr 10:39
Azarel, S, Shemariah, Ezr 10:41
Hananiah son of S and Hanun the Neh 3:30
the storehouses S the priest, Neh 13:13
son of S, son of Cushi, Jr 36:14
and S son of Abdeel to seize Jr 36:26
Jehucal son of S and Zephaniah Jr 37:3
whose name was Irijah son of S, Jr 37:13
Jucal son of S, and Pashhur son Jr 38:1

SHELEPH *(2)*
Almodad, S, Hazarmaveth, Gn 10:26
Almodad, S, Hazarmaveth, 1Ch 1:20

SHELESH *(1)*
Zophah, Imna, S, and Amal. 1Ch 7:35

SHELOMI *(1)*
Ahihud son of S, a leader from Nm 34:27

SHELOMITH *(8)*
(AKA SHELOMOTH)
mother's name was S, a daughter Lv 24:11
Hananiah, with their sister S; 1Ch 3:19
Izhar's sons: S was first. 1Ch 23:18
his son Zichri, and his son S. 1Ch 26:25
This S and his brothers were in 1Ch 26:26
in the care of S and his 1Ch 26:28
him Abijah, Attai, Ziza, and S. 2Ch 11:20
S son of Josiphiah from Bani's Ezr 8:10

SHELOMOTH *(2)*
(AKA SHELOMITH)
S, Haziel, and Haran—three. 1Ch 23:9
the Izharites: S; from 1Ch 24:22

SHELOMOTH'S *(1)*
Shelomoth; from S sons: Jahath. 1Ch 24:22

SHELTER *(21)*
let it be a s for you. Dt 32:38
she rested a little in the s." Ru 2:7
You s them, and may those who Ps 5:11
conceal me in His s in the day Ps 27:5
them in a s from the schemes Ps 31:20
hurry to my s from the raging Ps 55:8
under the s of Your wings. Ps 61:4
You are my s and my shield; Ps 119:114
the LORD is a s right by your Ps 121:5
I say, "You are my s, my portion Ps 142:5
like a s in a vineyard, Is 1:8
a refuge and s from storm and Is 4:6
⌊S us⌋ at noonday with shade Is 16:3
order to seek s under Pharaoh's Is 30:2
will be like a s from the wind, Is 32:2
land—a female will s a man. Jr 31:22
taking s in the shade of its Ezk 17:23
Wild animals found s under it, Dn 4:12
made himself a s there and sat Jnh 4:5
running under the s of a little Ac 27:16
on the throne will s them: Rv 7:15

SHELTERLESS *(1)*
huddle against the rocks, s. Jb 24:8

SHELTERS *(3)*
you have in the field into s. Ex 9:19
and livestock flee to s, Ex 9:20
a cloud, like doves to their s? Is 60:8

SHELUMIEL *(5)*
S son of Zurishaddai from Simeon; Nm 1:6
the Simeonites is S son of Nm 2:12
On the fifth day S son of Nm 7:36
the offering of S son of Nm 7:41
S son of Zurishaddai was over Nm 10:19

SHEM *(16)*
and he fathered S, Ham, and Gn 5:32
three sons: S, Ham, and Japheth. Gn 6:10
day Noah along with his sons S, Gn 7:13
who came out of the ark were S, Gn 9:18
Then S and Japheth took a cloak Gn 9:23
Praise the LORD, the God of S; Gn 9:26
he will dwell in the tents of S; Gn 9:27
of Noah's sons, S, Ham, and Gn 10:1
And S, Japheth's older brother, Gn 10:21
S was the father of all the Gn 10:21
are the family records of S. Gn 11:10
S lived 100 years and fathered Gn 11:10
S lived 500 years and fathered Gn 11:11
Noah's sons: S, Ham, and Japheth 1Ch 1:4
S, Arpachshad, Shelah, 1Ch 1:24
son⌋ of S, ⌊son⌋ of Noah, Lk 3:36

SHEM'S *(3)*
S sons were Elam, Asshur, Gn 10:22
These are S sons by their clans, Gn 10:31
S sons: Elam, Asshur, Arpachshad, 1Ch 1:17

SHEMA *(6)*
Amam, S, Moladah, Jos 15:26
Korah, Tappuah, Rekem, and S. 1Ch 2:43
S fathered Raham, who fathered 1Ch 2:44
of Azaz, son of S, son of Joel. 1Ch 5:8
Beriah and S, who were the heads 1Ch 8:13
Mattithiah, S, Anaiah, Uriah, Neh 8:4

SHEMAAH *(1)*
Ahiezer son of S the Gibeathite. 1Ch 12:3

SHEMAIAH *(39)*
(AKA SHAMMUA)
a revelation from God came to S, 1Kg 12:22
of Shecaniah: S. Shemaiah's sons 1Ch 3:22
son of Shimri, son of S— 1Ch 4:37
his son S, his son Gog, his son 1Ch 5:4
S son of Hasshub, son of Azrikam, 1Ch 9:14
Obadiah son of S, son of Galal, 1Ch 9:16
S the leader and 200 of his 1Ch 15:8
Uriel, Asaiah, Joel, S, Eliel, 1Ch 15:11
secretary, S son of Nethanel, 1Ch 24:6
S the firstborn, Jehozabad the 1Ch 26:4
to his son S were born sons who 1Ch 26:6
the word of the LORD came to S, 2Ch 11:2
Then S the prophet went to 2Ch 12:5
the LORD's message came to S: 2Ch 12:7
in the Events of S the Prophet 2Ch 12:15
The Levites with them were S, 2Ch 17:8
S and Uzziel from the 2Ch 29:14
Miniamin, Jeshua, S, Amariah, 2Ch 31:15
and his brothers S and Nethanel, 2Ch 35:9
Jeuel, and S, and 60 men with Ezr 8:13
Eliezer, Ariel, S, Elnathan, Ezr 8:16
Maaseiah, Elijah, S, Jehiel, and Ezr 10:21
Isshijah, Malchijah, S, Shimeon, Ezr 10:31
And beside him S son of Neh 3:29
the house of S son of Delaiah, Neh 6:10
Maaziah, Bilgai, and S. Neh 10:8
S son of Hasshub, son of Azrikam, Neh 11:15
S, Joiarib, Jedaiah, Neh 12:6
of Bilgah, Jehonathan of S, Neh 12:18
Benjamin, S, and Jeremiah. Neh 12:34
Jonathan, son of S, son of Neh 12:35
S, Azarel, Milalai, Gilalai, Neh 12:36
and Maaseiah, S, Eleazar, Uzzi, Neh 12:42
Uriah son of S from Jr 26:20
To S the Nehelamite you are to Jr 29:24
concerning S the Nehelamite. Jr 29:31
Because S prophesied to you, Jr 29:31
about to punish S the Nehelamite Jr 29:32
Delaiah son of S, Elnathan son Jr 36:12

SHEMAIAH'S *(2)*
Shemaiah. S sons: Hattush, Igal 1Ch 3:22
S sons: Othni, Rephael, Obed, 1Ch 26:7

SHEMARIAH *(4)*
Jerimoth, Bealiah, S, Shephatiah 1Ch 12:5
Jeush, S, and Zaham. 2Ch 11:19
Benjamin, Malluch, and S; Ezr 10:32
Azarel, Shelemiah, S, Ezr 10:41

SHEMEBER *(1)*
of Admah, and S king of Zeboiim, Gn 14:2

SHEMED *(1)*
and S who built Ono and Lod and 1Ch 8:12

SHEMER *(3)*
(AKA SHOMER)
of Samaria from **S** for 150 pounds 1Kg 16:24
Samaria based on the name **S**, 1Kg 16:24
of Amzi, son of Bani, son of **S**, 1Ch 6:46

SHEMER'S *(1)*
S sons: Ahi, Rohgah, Hubbah, and 1Ch 7:34

SHEMIDA *(2)*
the Shemidaite clan ⌊from⌋ **S**; Nm 26:32
Asriel, Shechem, Hepher, and **S**. Jos 17:2

SHEMIDA'S *(1)*
S sons: Ahian, Shechem, Likhi, 1Ch 7:19

SHEMIDAITE *(1)*
the **S** clan ⌊from⌋ Shemida; Nm 26:32

SHEMINITH *(1)*
with lyres according to the **S**. 1Ch 15:21

SHEMIRAMOTH *(4)*
Jaaziel, **S**, Jehiel, Unni, 1Ch 15:18
Aziel, **S**, Jehiel, Unni, 1Ch 15:20
Jeiel, **S**, Jehiel, Mattithiah, 1Ch 16:5
Zebadiah, Asahel, **S**, Jehonathan, 2Ch 17:8

SHEMUEL *(2)*
S son of Ammihud from the tribe Nm 34:20
Jahmai, Ibsam, and **S**, the heads 1Ch 7:2

SHEN *(1)*
it upright between Mizpah and **S**. 1Sm 7:12

SHENAZZAR *(1)*
Pedaiah, **S**, Jekamiah, Hoshama 1Ch 3:18

SHEOL *(66)*
I will go down to **S** to my son, Gn 37:35
gray hairs down to **S** in sorrow." Gn 42:38
hairs down to **S** in sorrow.' Gn 44:29
our father down to **S** in sorrow. Gn 44:31
that they go down alive into **S**, Nm 16:30
down alive into **S** with all that Nm 16:33
and burns to the depths of **S**; Dt 32:22
sends ⌊some⌋ to **S**, and He raises 1Sm 2:6
The ropes of **S** entangled me; 2Sm 22:6
gray head descend to **S** in peace. 1Kg 2:6
gray head down to **S** with blood." 1Kg 2:9
goes down to **S** will never rise Jb 7:9
⌊They are⌋ deeper than **S**— Jb 11:8
would hide me in **S** and conceal Jb 14:13
If I await **S** as my home, spread Jb 17:13
it go down to the gates of **S**, Jb 17:16
and go down to **S** in peace. Jb 21:13
so **S** ⌊steals⌋ those who have Jb 24:19
S is naked before God, and Jb 26:6
who can thank You in **S**? Ps 6:5
The wicked will return to **S**— Ps 9:17
You will not abandon me to **S**; Ps 16:10
The ropes of **S** entangled me; Ps 18:5
LORD, You brought me up from **S**; Ps 30:3
let them be silent in **S**. Ps 31:17
sheep they are headed for **S**; Ps 49:14
their form will waste away in **S**, Ps 49:14
my life from the power of **S**, Ps 49:15
let them go down to **S** alive, Ps 55:15
my life from the depths of **S**. Ps 86:13
troubles, and my life is near **S**. Ps 88:3
himself from the power of **S**? Ps 89:48
the torments of **S** overcame me; Ps 116:3
make my bed in **S**, You are there Ps 139:8
scattered at the mouth of **S**. Ps 141:7
alive, like **S**, still healthy Pr 1:12
her steps head straight for **S**. Pr 5:5
Her house is the road to **S**, Pr 7:27
guests are in the depths of **S**. Pr 9:18
S and Abaddon lie open before Pr 15:11
he may avoid going down to **S**. Pr 15:24
you will rescue his life from **S**. Pr 23:14
S and Abaddon are never Pr 27:20
S; a barren womb; earth, which Pr 30:16
or wisdom in **S** where you are Ec 9:10
love is as unrelenting as **S**. Sg 8:6
Therefore **S** enlarges its throat Is 5:14
the depths of **S** to the heights Is 7:11
S below is eager to greet your Is 14:9
has been brought down to **S**, Is 14:11
brought down to **S** into the Is 14:15
have made an agreement with **S**; Is 28:15
agreement with **S** will not last. Is 28:18
I must go to the gates of **S**; Is 38:10
For **S** cannot thank You; Is 38:18
and sent ⌊them⌋ down even to **S**. Is 57:9
day the cedar went down to **S**. Ezk 31:15
threw it down to **S** ⌊to be⌋ with Ezk 31:16
They too descended with it to **S**, Ezk 31:17
the middle of **S** about him and Ezk 32:21
who went down to **S** with their Ezk 32:27
ransom them from the power of **S**. Hs 13:14
S, where is your sting? Hs 13:14
they dig down to **S**, from there Am 9:2
out for help in the belly of **S**; Jnh 2:2
He enlarges his appetite like **S**, Hab 2:5

SHEPHAM *(2)*
a line from Hazar-enan to **S**. Nm 34:10
go down from **S** to Riblah east Nm 34:11

SHEPHATIAH *(8)*
the fifth was **S**, son of Abital; 2Sm 3:4
S, by Abital, was fifth; 1Ch 3:3
son of **S**, son of Reuel, 1Ch 9:8
Shemariah, **S** the Haruphite; 1Ch 12:5
the Simeonites, **S** son of Maacah; 1Ch 27:16
Azariah, Michael, and **S**; 2Ch 21:2
Amariah, son of **S**, son of Neh 11:4
S son of Mattan, Gedaliah son Jr 38:1

SHEPHATIAH'S *(5)*
S descendants 372 Ezr 2:4
S descendants, Hattil's Ezr 2:57
of Michael from **S** descendants, Ezr 8:8
S descendants 372 Neh 7:9
S descendants, Hattil's Neh 7:59

SHEPHELAH *(1)*
and sycamore trees in the **S**. 1Ch 27:28

SHEPHER *(2)*
and camped at Mount **S**. Nm 33:23
from Mount **S** and camped at Nm 33:24

SHEPHERD *(73)*
Now Abel became a **s** of a flock, Gn 4:2
will continue to **s** and keep your Gn 30:31
who has been my **s** all my life to Gn 48:15
the name of the **S**, the Rock of Gn 49:24
be like sheep without a **s**." Nm 27:17
'You will **s** My people Israel and 2Sm 5:2
I commanded to **s** My people 2Sm 7:7
hills like sheep without a **s**. 1Kg 22:17
'You will **s** My people Israel and 1Ch 11:2
I commanded to **s** My people, 1Ch 17:6
hills like sheep without a **s**. 2Ch 18:16
The LORD is my **s**; there is Ps 23:1
possession, **s** them, and carry Ps 28:9
Death will **s** them. The upright Ps 49:14
ewes to be **s** over His people Ps 78:71
Listen, **S** of Israel, who guides Ps 80:1
The sayings are given by one **S**. Ec 12:11
and like sheep without a **s**, Is 13:14
He protects His flock like a **s**; Is 40:11
My **s**, he will fulfill all My Is 44:28
and they will **s** you with Jr 3:15
not run away from being Your **s**, Jr 17:16
the shepherds who **s** My people: Jr 23:2
over them who will **s** them. Jr 23:4
over him as a **s** ⌊guards⌋ his Jr 31:10
of Egypt as a **s** picks lice off Jr 43:12
Who is the **s** who can stand Jr 49:19
Who is the **s** who can stand Jr 50:44
will smash the **s** and his flock; Jr 51:23
were scattered for lack of a **s**; Ezk 34:5
animal since ⌊they⌋ lack a **s**, Ezk 34:8
a **s** looks for his sheep on the Ezk 34:12
will **s** them on the mountains of Ezk 34:13
I will **s** them with justice. Ezk 34:16
appoint over them a single **s**, Ezk 34:23
David, and he will **s** them. Ezk 34:23
himself and will be their **s**. Ezk 34:23
will be one **s** for all of them. Ezk 37:24
the LORD now **s** them like a lamb Hs 4:16
As the **s** snatches two legs or a Am 3:12
will stand and **s** ⌊them⌋ in the Mc 5:4
They will **s** the land of Assyria Mc 5:6
S Your people with Your staff, Mc 7:14
because there is no **s**. Zch 10:2
S the flock intended for Zch 11:4
I said, "I will no longer **s** you. Zch 11:9
the equipment of a foolish **s**. Zch 11:15
to raise up a **s** in the land who Zch 11:16
to the worthless **s** who deserts Zch 11:17
against My **s**, against the man Zch 13:7
Strike the **s**, and the sheep will Zch 13:7
leader who will **s** My people Mt 2:6
out, like sheep without a **s**. Mt 9:36
just as a **s** separates the sheep Mt 25:32
will strike the **s**, and the sheep Mt 26:31
were like sheep without a **s**. Mk 6:34
will strike the **s**, and the sheep Mk 14:27
the door is the **s** of the sheep. Jn 10:2
I am the good **s**. The good Jn 10:11
good **s** lays down his life for Jn 10:11
he is not the **s** and doesn't own Jn 10:12
I am the good **s**. I know My own Jn 10:14
there will be one flock, one **s**. Jn 10:16
"**S** My sheep," He told him. Jn 21:16
as overseers, to **s** the church of Ac 20:28
the great **S** of the sheep— Heb 13:20
returned to the **s** and guardian 1Pt 2:25
s God's flock among you, not 1Pt 5:2
And when the chief **S** appears, 1Pt 5:4
and He will **s** them with an iron Rv 2:27
of the throne will **s** them; Rv 7:17
who is going to **s** all nations Rv 12:5
He will **s** them with an iron Rv 19:15

SHEPHERD'S *(3)*
which passes under the ⌊**s**⌋ rod, Lv 27:32
them in the pouch, in his **s** bag. 1Sm 17:40
removed from me like a **s** tent. Is 38:12

SHEPHERDED *(3)*
He **s** them with a pure heart and Ps 78:72
So I **s** the flock intended for Zch 11:7
other Union, and I **s** the flock. Zch 11:7

SHEPHERDESS *(1)*
father's sheep, for she was a **s**. Gn 29:9

SHEPHERDING *(3)*
was **s** the rest of Laban's flock. Gn 30:36
Moses was **s** the flock of his Ex 3:1
prevent them from **s** the flock. Ezk 34:10

SHEPHERDS *(49)*
⌊**s**⌋ would roll the stone from Gn 29:3
The men are **s**; indeed they raise Gn 46:32
since all **s** are abhorrent to Gn 46:34
both we and our fathers, are **s**." Gn 47:3
Then some **s** arrived and drove Ex 2:17
Egyptian rescued us from the **s**. Ex 2:19
children will be **s** in the Nm 14:33
the Edomite, chief of Saul's **s**. 1Sm 21:7
When your **s** were with us, we did 1Sm 25:7
he was at Beth-eked of the **S**, 2Kg 10:12
s will not let ⌊their flocks⌋ Is 13:20
when a band of **s** is called out Is 31:4
And they are **s** who have no Is 56:11
the sea with the **s** of His flock? Is 63:11
I will give you **s** who are loyal Jr 3:15
S and their flocks will come Jr 6:3
For the **s** are stupid: Jr 10:21
Many **s** have destroyed My Jr 12:10
will take charge of all your **s**, Jr 22:22
Woe to the **s** who destroy and Jr 23:1
says about the **s** who shepherd My Jr 23:2
I will raise up **s** over them who Jr 23:4
Wail, you **s**, and cry out. Jr 25:34
will be impossible for the **s**, Jr 25:35
land where **s** may rest flocks. Jr 33:12
their **s** have led them astray, Jr 50:6
against the **s** of Israel. Ezk 34:2
what the Lord GOD says to the **s**: Ezk 34:2
Woe to the **s** of Israel, who have Ezk 34:2
the **s** feed their flock? Ezk 34:2
Therefore, you **s**, hear the word Ezk 34:7
for My **s** do not search for My Ezk 34:8
because⌋ the **s** feed themselves Ezk 34:8
therefore, you **s**, hear the word Ezk 34:9
Look, I am against the **s**. Ezk 34:10
The **s** will no longer feed Ezk 34:10
the pastures of the **s** mourn, Am 1:2
will raise against it seven **s**, Mc 5:5
King of Assyria, your **s** slumber; Nah 3:18
with caves for **s** and folds for Zph 2:6
My anger burns against the **s**, Zch 10:3
Listen to the wail of the **s**, Zch 11:3
Even their own **s** have no Zch 11:5
one month I got rid of three **s**. Zch 11:8
s were staying out in the fields Lk 2:8
the **s** said to one another, Lk 2:15
at what the **s** said to them. Lk 2:18
The **s** returned, glorifying and Lk 2:20
Or who **s** a flock and does not 1Co 9:7

SHEPHERDS' *(2)*
young goats near the **s** tents. Sg 1:8
⌊Hear⌋ the sound of the **s** cry, Jr 25:36

SHEPHI *(1)*
Manahath, Ebal, S, and Onam. 1Ch 1:40

SHEPHO *(1)*
Manahath, Ebal, S, and Onam. Gn 36:23

SHEPHUPHAN *(1)*
Gera, S, and Huram. 1Ch 8:5

SHEREBIAH *(8)*
they brought us S—a man of Ezr 8:18
along with S, Hashabiah, and 10 Ezr 8:24
Jeshua, Bani, S, Jamin, Akkub, Neh 8:7
Shebaniah, Bunni, S, Bani, and Neh 9:4
Hashabneiah, S, Hodiah, Neh 9:5
Zaccur, S, Shebaniah, Neh 10:12
Binnui, Kadmiel, S, Judah, and Neh 12:8
Hashabiah, S, and Jeshua son Neh 12:24

SHERESH *(1)*
brother was named S, and his 1Ch 7:16

SHESHACH *(2)*
(AKA BABYLON, SHINAR)
the king of S will drink after Jr 25:26
How S has been captured, the Jr 51:41

SHESHAI *(3)*
where Ahiman, S, and Talmai, Nm 13:22
S, Ahiman, and Talmai, Jos 15:14
They struck down S, Ahiman, and Jdg 1:10

SHESHAN *(3)*
Ishi. Ishi's son: S. Sheshan's 1Ch 2:31
S had no sons, only daughters, 1Ch 2:34
S gave his daughter in marriage 1Ch 2:35

SHESHAN'S *(1)*
son: Sheshan. S descendant: 1Ch 2:31

SHESHBAZZAR *(4)*
them out to S the prince of Ezr 1:8
S brought all of them when the Ezr 1:11
in Babylon to a man named S, Ezr 5:14
Then this same S came and laid Ezr 5:16

SHETHAR *(1)*
were Carshena, S, Admatha, Est 1:14

SHETHAR-BOZENAI *(4)*
Euphrates River, S, and their Ezr 5:3
Euphrates River, S, and their Ezr 5:6
Euphrates River, S, and your Ezr 6:6
Euphrates River, S, and their Ezr 6:13

SHETHITES *(1)*
Moab and strike down all the S. Nm 24:17

SHEVA *(2)*
(AKA SERAIAH, SHAVSHA, SHISHA)
S was court secretary; 2Sm 20:25
father, and of S, the father of 1Ch 2:49

SHIBBOLETH *(1)*
they told him, "Please say S." Jdg 12:6

SHIELD *(45)*
Abram. I am your s; your reward Gn 15:1
and do not spare ⌊him⌋ or s him. Dt 13:8
He is the s that protects you, Dt 33:29
Not a s or spear was seen among Jdg 5:8
there the s of the mighty was 2Sm 1:21
was defiled—the s of Saul, no 2Sm 1:21
My s, the horn of my salvation, 2Sm 22:3
He is a s to all who take refuge 2Sm 22:31
given me the s of Your salvation 2Sm 22:36
pounds of gold went into each s. 1Kg 10:16
pounds of gold went into each s. 1Kg 10:17
before it with a s or build up 2Kg 19:32
men who carried s and sword, 1Ch 5:18
battle, expert with s and spear. 1Ch 12:8
by 37,000 men with s and spear. 1Ch 12:34
hammered gold went into each s. 2Ch 9:15
pounds of gold went into each s. 2Ch 9:16
with him armed with bow and s; 2Ch 17:17
the army, bearing spear and s. 2Ch 25:5
You, LORD, are a s around me, my Ps 3:3
him with favor like a s. Ps 5:12
My s is with God, who saves the Ps 7:10
my s and the horn of my Ps 18:2
He is a s to all who take refuge Ps 18:30
given me the s of Your salvation Ps 18:35
LORD is my strength and my s; Ps 28:7
He is our help and s. Ps 33:20
bring them down, Lord, our s. Ps 59:11
arrows, the s, the sword, Ps 76:3
Consider our s, God; look on the Ps 84:9
For the LORD God is a sun and s. Ps 84:11
our s belongs to the LORD, Ps 89:18
will be a protective s. Ps 91:4
He is their help and s. Ps 115:9
He is their help and s. Ps 115:10
He is their help and s. Ps 115:11
You are my shelter and my s; Ps 119:114
You s my head on the day of Ps 140:7
He is my s, and I take refuge in Ps 144:2
is a s for those who live with Pr 2:7
He is a s to those who take Pr 30:5
and Kir uncovered the s. Is 22:6
before it with a s or build up Is 37:33
protective s is set in place. Nah 2:5
situation take the s of faith, Eph 6:16

SHIELD-BEARER *(2)*
a s was walking in front of him. 1Sm 17:7
with the s in front of him. 1Sm 17:41

SHIELDS *(37)*
He s him all day long, and he Dt 33:12
took the gold s of Hadadezer's 2Sm 8:7
made 200 large s of hammered 1Kg 10:16
made 300 small s of hammered 1Kg 10:17
all the gold s that Solomon had 1Kg 14:26
made bronze s in their place 1Kg 14:27
royal escorts would carry the s, 1Kg 14:28
David's spears and s that were 2Kg 11:10
troops bearing s and spears. 1Ch 12:24
David took the gold s carried by 1Ch 18:7
made 200 large s of hammered 2Ch 9:15
made 300 small s of hammered 2Ch 9:16
also put large s and spears in 2Ch 11:12
took the gold s that Solomon had 2Ch 12:9
made bronze s in their place 2Ch 12:10
would carry the s and take them 2Ch 12:11
bearing large s and spears, 2Ch 14:8
bearing regular s and drawing 2Ch 14:8
David's spears, s, and quivers 2Ch 23:9
provided the entire army with s, 2Ch 26:14
an abundance of weapons and s. 2Ch 32:5
stones, spices, s, and every 2Ch 32:27
held spears, s, bows, and armor Neh 4:16
Him with his thick, studded s. Jb 15:26
Take Your s—large and small— Ps 35:2
all of them s of warriors. Sg 4:4
up, you princes, and oil the s! Is 21:5
Deploy small s and large; Jr 46:3
able to handle s, and the Ludim, Jr 46:9
you on every side with s, Ezk 23:24
raise a wall of s against you. Ezk 26:8
They hung s and helmets in you; Ezk 27:10
hung their s all around your Ezk 27:11
armed with s and bucklers, Ezk 38:4
all of them with s and helmets; Ezk 38:5
the bucklers and s, the bows and Ezk 39:9
The s of his warriors are dyed Nah 2:3

SHIFTED *(1)*
and are not s away from the hope Col 1:23

SHIFTS *(1)*
to Lebanon each month in s; 1Kg 5:14

SHIGIONOTH *(1)*
the prophet. According to S . Hab 3:1

SHIHOR *(3)*
from the S east of Egypt to the Jos 13:3
from the S of Egypt to the 1Ch 13:5
revenue was the grain from S— Is 23:3

SHIHOR-LIBNATH *(1)*
westward to Carmel and S. Jos 19:26

SHIKKERON *(1)*
Ekron, curved to S, proceeded to Jos 15:11

SHILHI *(2)*
name was Azubah daughter of S. 1Kg 22:42
name was Azubah daughter of S. 2Ch 20:31

SHILHIM *(1)*
(AKA SHAARAIM, SHARUHEN)
Lebaoth, S, Ain, and Rimmon—29 Jos 15:32

SHILLEM *(2)*
Jahzeel, Guni, Jezer, and S. Gn 46:24
the Shillemite clan from S. Nm 26:49

SHILLEMITE *(1)*
the S clan from Shillem. Nm 26:49

SHILOAH *(1)*
waters of S and rejoiced with Is 8:6

SHILOH *(32)*
assembled at S where it set up Jos 18:1
you here in S in the presence Jos 18:8
to Joshua at the camp in S. Jos 18:9
for them at S in the presence Jos 18:10
tribes by lot at S in the LORD's Jos 19:51
They told them at S in the land Jos 21:2
the Israelites at S in the land Jos 22:9
assembled at S to go to war Jos 22:12
as the house of God was in S. Jdg 18:31
to the camp at S in the land Jdg 21:12
festival to the LORD in S, Jdg 21:19
the young women of S come out to Jdg 21:21
from the young women of S, Jdg 21:21
to the LORD of Hosts at S, 1Sm 1:3
after they ate and drank at S, 1Sm 1:9
she took him with her to S, 1Sm 1:24
him to the LORD's house at S. 1Sm 1:24
Israelites who came there to S. 1Sm 2:14
LORD continued to appear in S, 1Sm 3:21
of the LORD's covenant from S. 1Sm 4:3
sent ⌊men⌋ to S to bring back 1Sm 4:4
from the battle and came to S. 1Sm 4:12
of Eli the LORD's priest at S. 1Sm 14:3
He had spoken at S against Eli's 1Kg 2:27
Jeroboam's wife, and go to S. 1Kg 14:2
she went to S and arrived at 1Kg 14:4
abandoned the tabernacle at S, Ps 78:60
to My place that was at S, Jr 7:12
what I did to S I will do to the Jr 7:14
I will make this temple like S. Jr 26:6
will become like S and this city Jr 26:9
from Shechem, S, and Samaria who Jr 41:5

SHILONITE *(6)*
Ahijah the S met Jeroboam 1Kg 11:29
Ahijah the S to Jeroboam son 1Kg 12:15
His servant Ahijah the S. 1Kg 15:29
the Prophecy of Ahijah the S, 2Ch 9:29
Ahijah the S to Jeroboam son 2Ch 10:15
a descendant of the S. Neh 11:5

SHILONITES *(1)*
from the S: Asaiah the firstborn 1Ch 9:5

SHILSHAH *(1)*
Hod, Shamma, S, Ithran, and 1Ch 7:37

SHIMEA *(4)*
(AKA SHAMMUA, SHAMMAH, SHIMEAH, SHIMEI)
was ⌊born⌋ second, S third, 1Ch 2:13
S, Shobab, Nathan, and Solomon. 1Ch 3:5
his son S, his son Haggiah, and 1Ch 6:30
son of Berechiah, son of S, 1Ch 6:39

SHIMEAH *(3)*
(AKA SHAMMAH, SHIMEA, SHIMEAM, SHIMEI)
a son of David's brother S. 2Sm 13:3
of David's brother S, spoke up: 2Sm 13:32
and Mikloth who fathered S. 1Ch 8:32

SHIMEAM *(1)*
(AKA SHIMEAH)
Mikloth fathered S. These also 1Ch 9:38

SHIMEATH *(2)*
Jozabad son of S and Jehozabad 2Kg 12:21
son of the Ammonite woman S, 2Ch 24:26

SHIMEATHITES *(1)*
Tirathites, S, and Sucathites 1Ch 2:55

SHIMEI *(42)*
(AKA SHAMMAH, SHIMEA, SHIMEAH)
Libni and S, by their clans. Ex 6:17
by their clans: Libni and S. Nm 3:18
His name was S son of Gera, 2Sm 16:5
S said as he cursed: 2Sm 16:7
the road as S was going along 2Sm 16:13
S went, he cursed ⌊David⌋, and 2Sm 16:13
S son of Gera, a Benjaminite 2Sm 19:16
When S son of Gera crossed the 2Sm 19:18
Shouldn't S be put to death for 2Sm 19:21
king said to S, "You will not 2Sm 19:23
David's brother S, killed him. 2Sm 21:21
the prophet, S, Rei, and David's 1Kg 1:8
Keep an eye on S son of Gera, 1Kg 2:8
king summoned S and said to him 1Kg 2:36
S said to the king, "The 1Kg 2:38
And S lived in Jerusalem for a 1Kg 2:38
S was informed, "Look, your 1Kg 2:39
So S saddled his donkey and set 1Kg 2:40
to Solomon that S had gone from 1Kg 2:41
king summoned S and said to him 1Kg 2:42
he went out and struck S down, 1Kg 2:46
S son of Ela, in Benjamin; 1Kg 4:18
Zerubbabel and S. Zerubbabel's 1Ch 3:19

his son Zaccur, and his son S. 1Ch 4:26
S had 16 sons and six daughters, 1Ch 4:27
his son Gog, his son S, 1Ch 5:4
of Gershom's sons: Libni and S. 1Ch 6:17
Libni, his son S, his son Uzzah, 1Ch 6:29
Ethan, son of Zimmah, son of S, 1Ch 6:42
David's brother S, killed him. 1Ch 20:7
The Gershomites: Ladan and S. 1Ch 23:7
Zeri, Jeshaiah, S, Hashabiah, 1Ch 25:3
the tenth ⌊to⌋ S, his sons, and 1Ch 25:17
S the Ramathite was in charge of 1Ch 27:27
Jehiel and S from the Hemanites; 2Ch 29:14
and his brother S was second. 2Ch 31:12
and his brother S by appointment 2Ch 31:13
Jozabad, S, Kelaiah (that is Ezr 10:23
Jeremai, Manasseh, and S; Ezr 10:33
Bani, Binnui, S, Ezr 10:38
of Jair, son of S, son of Kish, Est 2:5
the family of S by itself and Zch 12:13

SHIMEI'S *(6)*
me instead of S curses today." 2Sm 16:12
two of S slaves ran away to 1Kg 2:39
and Shimrath were S sons. 1Ch 8:21
S sons: Shelomoth, Haziel, and 1Ch 23:9
S sons: Jahath, Zizah, Jeush, 1Ch 23:10
Those were S sons—four. 1Ch 23:10

SHIMEITE *(1)*
Libnite clan and the S clan came Nm 3:21

SHIMEON *(1)*
Malchijah, Shemaiah, S, Ezr 10:31

SHIMMERING *(1)*
My place, like s heat in Is 18:4

SHIMON'S *(1)*
S sons: Amnon, Rinnah, 1Ch 4:20

SHIMRATH *(1)*
Beraiah, and S were Shimei's 1Ch 8:21

SHIMRI *(4)*
Jedaiah, son of S, son of 1Ch 4:37
Jediael son of S and his brother 1Ch 11:45
S the first (although he was not 1Ch 26:10
S and Jeuel from the 2Ch 29:13

SHIMRITH *(1)*
son of the Moabite woman S. 2Ch 24:26

SHIMRON *(5)*
Tola, Puvah, Jashub, and S. Gn 46:13
the Shimronite clan from S. Nm 26:24
the kings of S and Achshaph, Jos 11:1
Kattath, Nahalal, S, Idalah, and Jos 19:15
Puah, Jashub, and S—four. 1Ch 7:1

SHIMRON-MERON *(1)*
the king of S one the king of Jos 12:20

SHIMRONITE *(1)*
the S clan from Shimron. Nm 26:24

SHIMSHAI *(4)*
deputy and S the scribe wrote Ezr 4:8
the chief deputy, S the scribe, Ezr 4:9
deputy Rehum, S the scribe, Ezr 4:17
was read to Rehum, S the scribe, Ezr 4:23

SHINAB *(1)*
of Gomorrah, S king of Admah, Gn 14:2

SHINAR *(6)*
and Calneh, in the land of S. Gn 10:10
in the land of S and settled Gn 11:2
those days Amraphel king of S, Gn 14:1
king of S, and Arioch king Gn 14:9
Pathros, Cush, Elam, S, Hamath, Is 11:11
shrine for it in the land of S," Zch 5:11

SHINE *(23)*
the LORD make His face s on you, Nm 6:25
care about it, or light s on it. Jb 3:4
the sun not to s and seals off Jb 9:7
and light will s on your ways. Jb 22:28
His light not s on everyone? Jb 25:3
moon does not s and the stars Jb 25:5
so he may s with the light of Jb 33:30
righteousness s like the dawn, Ps 37:6
making his face s with oil— Ps 104:15
rises, and the moon will not s. Is 13:10
light will s in the darkness Is 58:10
Arise, s, for your light has Is 60:1
but the LORD will s over you, Is 60:2
of the moon will not s on you; Is 60:19
are wise will s like the bright Dn 12:3
let your light s before men, Mt 5:16
righteous will s like the sun Mt 13:43
to s on those who live in Lk 1:79
"Light shall s out of darkness"— 2Co 4:6
and the Messiah will s on you. Eph 5:14
among whom you s like stars in Php 2:15
lamp will never s in you again; Rv 18:23
the sun or the moon to s on it, Rv 21:23

SHINES *(9)*
long as the sun s, may his fame Ps 72:17
Light s in the darkness for the Ps 112:4
The night s like the day; Ps 139:12
of the righteous s brightly, Pr 13:9
is this who s like the dawn— Sg 6:10
glory of the LORD s over you. Is 60:1
righteousness s like a bright Is 62:1
when a lamp s its light on you. Lk 11:36
That light s in the darkness, Jn 1:5

SHINING *(16)*
the sun was s on the water, 2Kg 3:22
sun when it was s or at the moon Jb 31:26
He leaves a s wake behind him; Jb 41:32
praise Him, all you s stars. Ps 148:3
s brighter and brighter until Pr 4:18
S morning star, how you have Is 14:12
will darken all the s lights in Ezk 32:8
and the stars cease their s. Jl 2:10
the stars will cease their s. Jl 3:15
flashing sword, s spear; Nah 3:3
the brightness of Your s spear. Hab 3:11
John was a burning and s lamp, Jn 5:35
s around me and those traveling Ac 26:13
to a lamp s in a dismal place, 2Pt 1:19
and the true light is already s. 1Jn 2:8
His face was s like the sun at Rv 1:16

SHINS *(1)*
There was bronze armor on his s, 1Sm 17:6

SHION *(1)*
Hapharaim, S, Anaharath, Jos 19:19

SHIP *(24)*
rock, the way of a s at sea, and Pr 30:19
against every s of Tarshish, Is 2:16
and found a s going to Tarshish Jnh 1:3
the sea that the s threatened to Jnh 1:4
on ahead to the s and sailed for Ac 20:13
Then they escorted him to the s. Ac 20:38
Finding a s crossing over to Ac 21:2
because the s was to unload its Ac 21:3
we boarded the s, and they Ac 21:6
had boarded a s of Adramyttium, Ac 27:2
an Alexandrian s sailing for Ac 27:6
not only of the cargo and the s, Ac 27:10
the owner of the s rather than Ac 27:11
Since the s was caught and was Ac 27:15
and tackle and girded the s. Ac 27:17
your lives, but only of the s. Ac 27:22
tried to escape from the s; Ac 27:30
Unless these men stay in the s, Ac 27:31
there were 276 of us on the s. Ac 27:37
to lighten the s by throwing Ac 27:38
to run the s ashore if they Ac 27:39
a sandbar and ran the s aground. Ac 27:41
and some on debris from the s. Ac 27:44
an Alexandrian s that had Ac 28:11

SHIP'S *(3)*
down on the top of a s mast. Pr 23:34
They threw the s cargo into the Jnh 1:5
they threw the s gear overboard Ac 27:19

SHIPHI *(1)*
and Ziza son of S, son of Allon, 1Ch 4:37

SHIPHMITE *(1)*
Zabdi the S was in charge of the 1Ch 27:27

SHIPHRAH *(1)*
whom was named S and the other Ex 1:15

SHIPHTAN *(1)*
Kemuel son of S, a leader from Nm 34:24

SHIPMASTER *(1)*
And every s, seafarer, the Rv 18:17

SHIPS *(34)*
and will be a harbor for s, Gn 49:13
S will come from the coast of Nm 24:24
take you back in s to Egypt by a Dt 28:68
why did you linger at the s? Jdg 5:17
a fleet of s at Ezion-geber, 1Kg 9:26
for the king had s of Tarshish 1Kg 10:22
three years the s of Tarshish 1Kg 10:22
Jehoshaphat made s of Tarshish 1Kg 22:48
go because the s were wrecked at 1Kg 22:48
go with your servants in the s," 1Kg 22:49
Hiram sent him s with crews of 2Ch 8:18
for the king's s kept going to 2Ch 9:21
three years the s of Tarshish 2Ch 9:21
with him to make s to go to 2Ch 20:36
they made the s in Ezion-geber. 2Ch 20:36
So the s were wrecked and were 2Ch 20:37
You wrecked the s of Tarshish Ps 48:7
There the s move about, and Ps 104:26
went to sea in s, conducting Ps 107:23
She is like the merchant s, Pr 31:14
Wail, s of Tarshish, for your Is 23:1
Wail, s of Tarshish, because Is 23:14
where s that are rowed will not Is 33:21
Chaldeans in the s in which they Is 43:14
for Me with the s of Tarshish Is 60:9
All the s of the sea and their Ezk 27:9
S of Tarshish were the carriers Ezk 27:25
an oar disembark from their s. Ezk 27:29
go out from Me in s to terrify Ezk 30:9
S of Kittim will come against Dn 11:30
chariots, horsemen, and many s. Dn 11:40
consider s: though very large Jms 3:4
a third of the s were destroyed. Rv 8:9
those who have s on the sea Rv 18:19

SHIPWRECK *(1)*
suffered the s of their faith. 1Tm 1:19

SHIPWRECKED *(1)*
Three times I was s. 2Co 11:25

SHIRT *(5)*
to sue you and take away your s, Mt 5:40
road, or an extra s, sandals, Mt 10:10
but not put on an extra s. Mk 6:9
don't hold back your s either. Lk 6:29
and don't take an extra s. Lk 9:3

SHIRTS *(1)*
who has two s must share with Lk 3:11

SHISHA *(1)*
(AKA SERAIAH, SHAVSHA, SHEVA)
and Ahijah the sons of S, 1Kg 4:3

SHISHAK *(7)*
to Egypt, to S king of Egypt, 1Kg 11:40
S king of Egypt went to war 1Kg 14:25
S king of Egypt went to war 2Ch 12:2
at Jerusalem because of S. 2Ch 12:5
you into the hand of S.'" 2Ch 12:5
out on Jerusalem through S. 2Ch 12:7
So King S of Egypt went to war 2Ch 12:9

SHITRAI *(1)*
S the Sharonite was in charge of 1Ch 27:29

SHIZA *(1)*
Adina son of S the Reubenite, 1Ch 11:42

SHOA *(1)*
Pekod, S, and Koa; and all Ezk 23:23

SHOBAB *(4)*
Shammua, S, Nathan, Solomon, 2Sm 5:14
Jesher, S, and Ardon. 1Ch 2:18
Shimea, S, Nathan, and Solomon. 1Ch 3:5
Shammua, S, Nathan, Solomon, 1Ch 14:4

SHOBACH *(2)*
(AKA SHOPHACH)
and they came to Helam with S, 2Sm 10:16
also struck down S commander of 2Sm 10:18

SHOBAI'S *(2)*
descendants, S descendants, in Ezr 2:42
descendants, S descendants 138 Neh 7:45

SHOBAL *(7)*
Lotan, S, Zibeon, Anah, Gn 36:20
Chiefs Lotan, S, Zibeon, Anah, Gn 36:29
Lotan, S, Zibeon, Anah, Dishon, 1Ch 1:38
S fathered Kiriath-jearim; 1Ch 2:50
the descendants of S the father 1Ch 2:52
Hezron, Carmi, Hur, and S. 1Ch 4:1
Reaiah son of S fathered Jahath, 1Ch 4:2

SHOBAL'S *(2)*
These are S sons: Alvan, Gn 36:23
S sons: Alian, Manahath, Ebal, 1Ch 1:40

SHOBEK *(1)*
Hallohesh, Pilha, S, Neh 10:24

SHOBI *(1)*
S son of Nahash from Rabbah of 2Sm 17:27

SHOCK *(1)*
and a s to all those around Jr 48:39

SHOCKED *(1)*
be s and utterly appalled. Jr 2:12

SHOHAM *(1)*
his son Jaaziah: S, Zaccur, and 1Ch 24:27

SHOMER *(2)*
(AKA SHEMER)
son of S struck him down 2Kg 12:21
Japhlet, S, and Hotham, with 1Ch 7:32

SHONE *(10)*
The sun s on him as he passed by Gn 32:31
skin of his face s as a result Ex 34:29
Moses, the skin of his face s! Ex 34:30
He s ⌊on them⌋ from Mount Paran Dt 33:2
when His lamp s above my head, Jb 29:3
and the earth s with His glory. Ezk 43:2
and His face s like the sun. Mt 17:2
glory of the Lord s around them, Lk 2:9
and a light s in the cell. Ac 12:7
He has s in our hearts to give 2Co 4:6

SHOOK *(17)*
the whole mountain s violently. Ex 19:18
a loud shout that the ground s. 1Sm 4:5
The earth s, and terror from God 1Sm 14:15
Then the earth s and quaked; 2Sm 22:8
they s because He burned with 2Sm 22:8
also s the folds of my robe and Neh 5:13
Then the earth s and quaked; Ps 18:7
they s because He burned with Ps 18:7
trembled. Even the depths s. Ps 77:16
The earth s and quaked. Ps 77:18
the doorways s at the sound of Is 6:4
to tremble, who s the kingdoms, Is 14:16
were quaking; all the hills s. Jr 4:24
his hip joints s and his knees Dn 5:6
he s out his clothes and told Ac 18:6
he s the creature off into the Ac 28:5
His voice s the earth at that Heb 12:26

SHOOT *(18)*
I will s three arrows beside it 1Sm 20:20
realize they would s from the 2Sm 11:20
him, shouting, "S him too!" 2Kg 9:27
Elisha said, "S!" So he shot. 2Kg 13:17
this city or s an arrow there 2Kg 19:32
with a sling⌋ or ⌊s⌋ arrows with 1Ch 12:2
in Jerusalem to s arrows and 2Ch 26:15
torches s from his mouth; Jb 41:19
bowstring to s from the shadows Ps 11:2
They s at him suddenly and are Ps 64:4
But God will s them with arrows; Ps 64:7
the s that You made strong for Ps 80:15
s Your arrows and rout them. Ps 144:6
a s will grow from the stump Is 11:1
this city or s an arrow there Is 37:33
you archers! S at her! Do not Jr 50:14
When I s deadly arrows of famine Ezk 5:16
He plucked off its topmost s, Ezk 17:4

SHOOTING *(2)*
"Run and find the arrows I'm s." 1Sm 20:36
s from concealed places at the Ps 64:4

SHOOTS *(10)*
still uncut s, they would dry Jb 8:12
s spread out over his garden. Jb 8:16
again, and its s will not die. Jb 14:7
will wither his s, and he will Jb 15:30
the Sea and s toward the River. Ps 80:11
Their s spread out and reached Is 16:8
cut off the s with a pruning Is 18:5
Prune away her s, for they do Jr 5:10
branches, and sent forth s. Ezk 17:6
tender sprig from its topmost s, Ezk 17:22

SHOPHACH *(2)*
(AKA SHOBACH)
across the Euphrates with S, 1Ch 19:16
He also killed S, commander of 1Ch 19:18

SHORE *(9)*
Eloth on the s of the Red Sea 1Kg 9:26
Ashkelon and the s of the sea. Jr 47:7
of the sea stand on the s. Ezk 27:29
the whole crowd stood on the s. Mt 13:2
disciples reached the other s, Mt 16:5
was on the s facing the sea. Mk 4:1
was at the s where they were Jn 6:21
came, Jesus stood on the s. Jn 21:4
and sailed along the s of Crete. Ac 27:13

SHORES *(1)*
the land even to the farthest s. Est 10:1

SHORN *(1)*
flock of newly s ⌊sheep⌋ coming Sg 4:2

SHORT *(27)*
When you sound s blasts, the Nm 10:5
When you sound s blasts a second Nm 10:6
S blasts are to be sounded for Nm 10:6
sound long blasts, not s ones. Nm 10:7
sound s blasts on the trumpets, Nm 10:9
had traveled a s distance from 2Kg 5:19
of woman is s of days and full Jb 14:1
have made my days s in length, Ps 39:5
Remember how s my life is. Ps 89:47
years of the wicked are cut s. Pr 10:27
the bed is too s to stretch out Is 28:20
Is My hand too s to redeem? Is 50:2
hand is not too s to save, Is 59:1
It was only a s time before you Ezk 16:47
the accursed s measure in the Mc 6:10
the crowd, since he was a s man. Lk 19:3
I am only with you for a s time. Jn 7:33
sinned and fall s of the glory Rm 3:23
forced to leave you for a s time 1Th 2:17
than the angels for a s time; Heb 2:7
the angels for a s time so that Heb 2:9
Time is too s for me to tell Heb 11:32
us for a s time based on what Heb 12:10
that no one falls s of the grace Heb 12:15
though now for a s time you have 1Pt 1:6
he knows he has a s time. Rv 12:12
must be released for a s time. Rv 20:3

SHORT-EARED *(2)*
ostrich, the s owl, the gull, Lv 11:16
ostrich, the s owl, the gull, Dt 14:15

SHORT-LIVED *(3)*
no root in himself, but is s. Mt 13:21
they are s. When affliction Mk 4:17
to enjoy the s pleasure of sin. Heb 11:25

SHORTAGE *(5)*
who gathered a little had no s. Ex 16:18
you will eat food without s, Dt 8:9
I have such a s of crazy people 1Sm 21:15
but a s of people is a ruler's Pr 14:28
a s of food in all your Am 4:6

SHORTENED *(3)*
powerful stride is s, and his Jb 18:7
have s the days of his youth; Ps 89:45
in midcourse; He has s my days. Ps 102:23

SHORTLY *(1)*
himself was about to go there s. Ac 25:4

SHORTSIGHTED *(1)*
these things is blind and s, 2Pt 1:9

SHOT *(11)*
attacked him, s at him, and were Gn 49:23
be stoned or s ⌊with arrows⌋, Ex 19:13
Jonathan s an arrow beyond him. 1Sm 20:36
the arrow that Jonathan had s, 1Sm 20:37
the archers s down on your 2Sm 11:24
He s arrows and scattered them; 2Sm 22:15
drew his bow and s Joram between 2Kg 9:24
So they s him in his chariot at 2Kg 9:27
Shoot!" So he s. Then Elisha 2Kg 13:17
The archers s King Josiah, 2Ch 35:23
He s His arrows and scattered Ps 18:14

SHOULD *(535)*
(See pp. xi-xii.)

SHOULDER *(29)*
coming with a jug on her s. Gn 24:15
coming with her jug on her s, Gn 24:45
her jug from her ⌊s⌋ and said, Gn 24:46
and Benjamin wept on his s. Gn 45:14
he leaned his s to bear a load Gn 49:15
must have two s pieces attached Ex 28:7
both stones on the s pieces of Ex 28:12
to the ephod's s pieces in the Ex 28:25
the ephod's two s pieces on its Ex 28:27
They made s pieces for attaching Ex 39:4
them on the s pieces of the Ex 39:7
the ephod's s pieces in front. Ex 39:18
the ephod's two s pieces on its Ex 39:20
take the boiled s from the ram, Nm 6:19
priests are to be given the s, Dt 18:3
of you lift a stone onto his s, Jos 4:5
put it on his s, and said to Jdg 9:48
then let my s blade fall from my Jb 31:22
carry it on my s and wear it Jb 31:36
I relieved his s from the burden Ps 81:6
of the House of David on his s; Is 22:22
lift it to their s and bear it Is 46:7
to ⌊your⌋ s and take ⌊them⌋ Ezk 12:6
them⌋ on my s in their sight. Ezk 12:7
his bags⌋ to his s in the dark Ezk 12:12
every good piece—thigh and s. Ezk 24:4
made bald and every s chafed, Ezk 29:18
with flank and s and butted all Ezk 34:21
and turned a stubborn s; Zch 7:11

SHOULDERS *(20)*
and placed it over both their s, Gn 9:23
them⌋ on Hagar's s, and sent her Gn 21:14
up in their clothes on their s. Ex 12:34
on his two s before the LORD Ex 28:12
holy objects carried on their s. Nm 7:9
day long, and he rests on His s. Dt 33:12
put them on his s and took them Jdg 16:3
sword was slung between his s. 1Sm 17:6
Shaphat remains on his s today." 2Kg 6:31
and shot Joram between the s. 2Kg 9:24
on their s with the poles. 1Ch 15:15
not have to carry it on your s, 2Ch 35:3
yoke and the rod on their s, Is 9:4
the government will be on His s. Is 9:6
burden will fall from your s, Is 10:27
will be removed from their s. Is 14:25
will be carried on their s. Is 49:22
splintered, tearing all their s; Ezk 29:7
and put them on people's s, Mt 23:4
he joyfully puts it on his s, Lk 15:5

SHOULDN'T *(14)*
(See pp. xi-xii.)

SHOUT *(70)*
all the people give a mighty s. Jos 6:5
Do not s or let your voice be Jos 6:10
mouth until the time I say, 'S!' Jos 6:10
'Shout!' Then you are to s." Jos 6:10
Joshua said to the people, "S! Jos 6:16
the people gave a great s, Jos 6:20
such a loud s that the ground 1Sm 4:5
this loud s in the Hebrews' 1Sm 4:6
He said, "S loudly, for he's a 1Kg 18:27
the forest will s for joy before 1Ch 16:33
gave a great s of praise to Ezr 3:11
may no joyful s be heard in it. Jb 3:7
and your lips with a s of joy. Jb 8:21
behold His face with a s of joy, Jb 33:26
they s for help from the arm of Jb 35:9
let them s for joy forever. Ps 5:11
Let us s for joy at your victory Ps 20:5
s for joy, all you upright in Ps 32:11
on the strings, with a joyful s. Ps 33:3
my vindication s for joy and be Ps 35:27
enemy does not s in triumph over Ps 41:11
s to God with a jubilant cry. Ps 47:1
Over Philistia I s in triumph." Ps 60:8
make east and west s for joy. Ps 65:8
with grain. They s in triumph; Ps 65:13
S joyfully to God, all the earth! Ps 66:1
nations rejoice and s for joy, Ps 67:4
My lips will s for joy when I Ps 71:23
s in triumph to the God of Jacob. Ps 81:1
and Hermon s for joy at Your Ps 89:12
people who know the joyful s; Ps 89:15
so that we may s with joy and be Ps 90:14
I will s for joy because of the Ps 92:4
let us s joyfully to the LORD, Ps 95:1
s triumphantly to the rock of Ps 95:1
let us s triumphantly to Him in Ps 95:2
of the forest will s for joy Ps 96:12
S to the LORD, all the earth; Ps 98:4
jubilant, s for joy, and sing. Ps 98:4
of the ram's horn s triumphantly Ps 98:6
the mountains s together for joy Ps 98:8
S triumphantly to the LORD, Ps 100:1
Over Philistia I s in triumph." Ps 108:9
may Your godly people s for joy. Ps 132:9
its godly people will s for joy. Ps 132:16
them s for joy on their beds. Ps 149:5
people s with a ringing cry. Is 14:7
not cry out or s or make His Is 42:2
Let the desert and its cities s, Is 42:11
s, depths of the earth. Is 44:23
with a s of joy, proclaim Is 48:20
S for joy, you heavens! Is 49:13

into song and s, you who have Is 54:1
My servants will s for joy from Is 65:14
ram's horn—the s of battle. Jr 4:19
out with a s, like those who Jr 25:30
s for the chief of the nations! Jr 31:7
They will come and s for joy on Jr 31:12
The shouting is not a s of joy. Jr 48:33
will make the s of battle heard Jr 49:2
in them will s for joy over Jr 51:48
have raised a s in the house Lm 2:7
Daughter Zion; s loudly, Israel! Zph 3:14
Daughter Zion, s for joy and be Zch 2:10
S in triumph, Daughter Jerusalem! Zch 9:9
not argue or s, and no one will Mt 12:19
of the night there was a s: Mt 25:6
began to s, "It's the voice Ac 12:22
Break forth and s, you who are Gl 4:27
descend from heaven with a s, 1Th 4:16

SHOUTED *(32)*

sound of the people as they s, Ex 32:17
they s and fell facedown ⌊on the Lv 9:24
the people s, and the trumpets Jos 6:20
right hands, and s, "The sword Jdg 7:20
up with them, and s, "Samson, Jdg 16:12
And all the people s, "Long live 1Sm 10:24
He stood and s to the battle 1Sm 17:8
line and s his usual words 1Sm 17:23
angry with Jonathan and s, 1Sm 20:30
Then David s to the troops and 1Sm 26:14
and the people s, "This is 1Sm 30:20
He blew the ram's horn and s: 2Sm 20:1
s loudly, and cut themselves 1Kg 18:28
Jehoshaphat, they s, "He must be 1Kg 22:32
Jehu's troops approaching and s, 2Kg 9:17
Joram s, and they harnessed his 2Kg 9:21
Jehoshaphat, they s, "He must be 2Ch 18:31
but many ⌊others⌋ s joyfully. Ezr 3:12
The city of Susa s and rejoiced, Est 8:15
people s at them as ⌊if they Jb 30:5
all the sons of God s for joy? Jb 38:7
people s at them. Lm 4:15
Suddenly they s, "What do You Mt 8:29
Jesus s again with a loud voice Mt 27:50
convulsed him, s with a loud Mk 1:26
Again they s, "Crucify Him!" Mk 15:13
But they s, "Crucify Him!" Mk 15:14
He said this, He s with a loud Jn 11:43
They s back, "Not this man, but Jn 18:40
saw Him, they s, "Crucify! Jn 19:6
But the Jews s, "If you release Jn 19:12
But they s, "Take Him away! Jn 19:15

SHOUTING *(35)*

Philistines came to meet him s. Jdg 15:14
formation s their battle cry 1Sm 17:20
Judah rallied, s their battle 1Sm 17:52
around and fled, s to Ahaziah, 2Kg 9:23
pursued him, s, "Shoot him too! 2Kg 9:27
voice, with s, with trumpets, 2Ch 15:14
God of Israel s in a loud voice. 2Ch 20:19
sound of the joyful s from that Ezr 3:13
the people were s so loudly. Ezr 3:13
wicked die, there is joyful s. Pr 11:10
one is singing or s for joy in Is 16:10
I have put an end to the s. Is 16:10
people s and crying to the Is 22:5
terrified by their s or subdued Is 31:4
their voices, s for joy together Is 52:8
The s is not a shout of joy. Jr 48:33
There will be s on the day of Am 1:14
s and the sound of the ram's Am 2:2
Now, why are you s loudly? Mc 4:9
men followed Him, s, "Have mercy Mt 9:27
and those who followed kept s: Mt 21:9
But they kept s, "Crucify Him!" Mt 27:23
and those who followed kept s: Mk 11:9
out of many, s and saying, "You Lk 4:41
but they kept s, "Crucify! Lk 23:21
Him. They kept s: "Hosanna ! Jn 12:13
and rushed into the crowd, s: Ac 14:14
city officials, s, "These men Ac 17:6
some were s one thing and some Ac 19:32
s, "Men of Israel, help! Ac 21:28
in the mob were s one thing and Ac 21:34
their voices, s, "Wipe this Ac 22:22
they were s against him like Ac 22:24
The s grew loud, and some of the Ac 23:9
s that he should not live any Ac 25:24

SHOUTS *(23)*

with s of joy, and with 1Sm 18:6
of the LORD with s and the sound 2Sm 6:15
covenant of the LORD up with s, 1Ch 15:28
began ⌊their⌋ s and praises, 2Ch 20:22
never hears the s of a driver. Jb 39:7
the officers' s and the battle Jb 39:25
in His tent with s of joy. Ps 27:6
me with joyful s of deliverance. Ps 32:7
with joyful and thankful s. Ps 42:4
God ascends amid s of joy, Ps 47:5
His chosen ones with s of joy. Ps 105:43
His works with s of joy. Ps 107:22
There are s of joy and victory Ps 118:15
and our tongues with s of joy. Ps 126:2
tears will reap with s of joy. Ps 126:5
surely come back with s of joy, Ps 126:6
more than the s of a ruler over Ec 9:17
Triumphant s have fallen silent Is 16:9
s, He roars aloud, He prevails Is 42:13
Mountains break into joyful s! Is 49:13
no one will tread with s of joy. Jr 48:33
delight in you with s of joy." Zph 3:17
the capstone accompanied by s Zch 4:7

SHOVED *(1)*

s her down into the basket and Zch 5:8

SHOVEL *(3)*

with winnowing s and fork. Is 30:24
His winnowing s is in His hand, Mt 3:12
His winnowing s is in His hand Lk 3:17

SHOVELED *(1)*

he s six ⌊measures⌋ of barley Ru 3:15

SHOVELS *(9)*

ashes, and its s, basins, meat Ex 27:3
the pots, s, basins, meat forks, Ex 38:3
meatforks, s, and basins—all Nm 4:14
the basins, the s, and the 1Kg 7:40
and the pots, s, and sprinkling 1Kg 7:45
the pots, the s, the wick 2Kg 25:14
the pots, the s, and the bowls. 2Ch 4:11
the pots, the s, the forks, and 2Ch 4:16
the pots, the s, the wick Jr 52:18

SHOW *(161)*

to the land that I will s you. Gn 12:1
S your loyalty to me wherever we Gn 20:13
and s kindness to my master Gn 24:12
if you are going to s kindness Gn 24:49
Please s kindness to me by Gn 40:14
to s you My power and to make My Ex 9:16
Do not s favoritism to a poor Ex 23:3
according to all that I s you— Ex 25:9
will s My holiness to those who Lv 10:3
not trust Me to s My holiness Nm 20:12
My command to s My holiness in Nm 27:14
Do not s partiality when Dt 1:17
'S no hostility toward Moab, Dt 2:9
don't s any hostility to them or Dt 2:19
have begun to s Your greatness Dt 3:24
this will ⌊s⌋ your wisdom and Dt 4:6
with them and s them no mercy. Dt 7:2
S him no pity, and do not spare Dt 13:8
you mercy, s you compassion, Dt 13:17
deny justice or s partiality ⌊to Dt 16:19
You must not s pity: life for Dt 19:21
he is not to s favoritism to the Dt 21:16
her hand. You must not s pity. Dt 25:12
you will also s kindness to my Jos 2:12
we will s kindness and Jos 2:14
Please s us how to get into Jdg 1:24
and I will s you the man you Jdg 4:22
They did not s kindness to the Jdg 8:35
tell them, 'S favor to them, Jdg 21:22
May the LORD s faithful love to Ru 1:8
S some courage and be men, 1Sm 4:9
to you and s you what to do. 1Sm 10:8
may the LORD s special kindness 2Sm 2:6
and I will also s the same 2Sm 2:6
family I can s kindness to 2Sm 9:1
family I can s the kindness of 2Sm 9:3
since I intend to s you kindness 2Sm 9:7
I'll s kindness to Hanun son of 2Sm 10:2
May the LORD s you kindness and 2Sm 15:20
S loyalty to the sons of 1Kg 2:7
are kings ⌊who s⌋ special 1Kg 20:31
that Hezekiah did not s them. 2Kg 20:13
that I didn't s them." 2Kg 20:15
I'll s kindness to Hanun son of 1Ch 19:2
earth to s Himself strong for 2Ch 16:9
⌊He wanted⌋ to s off her beauty Est 1:11
Hathach might s it to Esther, Est 4:8
He would s you the secrets of Jb 11:6
Would you s partiality to Him or Jb 13:8
S some sense, and then we can Jb 18:2
a liar and s that my speech is Jb 24:25
"Who can s us anything good?" Ps 4:6
LORD's ways ⌊s⌋ faithful love Ps 25:10
He will s him the way he should Ps 25:12
my adversaries, s me Your way, Ps 27:11
S Your favor to Your servant; Ps 31:16
instruct you and s you the way Ps 32:8
your right hand s your Ps 45:4
will s him the salvation of God. Ps 50:23
do not s grace to any wicked Ps 59:5
S Your strength, God, You who Ps 68:28
forever and never again s favor? Ps 77:7
unjustly and s partiality to Ps 82:2
S us Your faithful love, LORD, Ps 85:7
S me a sign of Your goodness; Ps 86:17
a long life and s him My Ps 91:16
it is time to s favor to her— Ps 102:13
when You s favor to Your people. Ps 106:4
Let no one s him kindness, Ps 109:12
he did not think to s kindness, Ps 109:16
S favor to Your servant, and Ps 119:135
S us favor, LORD, show us favor, Ps 123:3
us favor, LORD, s us favor, for Ps 123:3
and he will s no mercy when he Pr 6:34
only wants to s off his opinions Pr 18:2
is not good to s partiality to Pr 18:5
is not good to s partiality in Pr 24:23
It is not good to s partiality— Pr 28:21
LORD is waiting to s you mercy, Is 30:18
rising up to s you compassion, Is 30:18
He will s favor to you at the Is 30:19
that Hezekiah did not s them. Is 39:2
that I didn't s them." Is 39:4
in darkness: S yourselves. They Is 49:9
yet I will s mercy to you with Is 60:10
but He will s His wrath against Is 66:14
They are cruel and s no mercy. Jr 6:23
Who will s sympathy toward you? Jr 15:5
I will s them ⌊My⌋ back and not Jr 18:17
spare them or s pity or Jr 21:7
tents and s compassion on his Jr 30:18
You s faithful love to thousands Jr 32:18
They are cruel and s no mercy. Jr 50:42
will s compassion according to Lm 3:32
you⌋ off and s ⌊you⌋ no pity, Ezk 5:11
will not s pity or spare ⌊them⌋ Ezk 8:18
do not s pity or spare ⌊them⌋! Ezk 9:5
will not s pity or spare ⌊them⌋ Ezk 9:10
I will not s pity, and I will Ezk 24:14
when I s Myself holy through you Ezk 38:16
everything I am going to s you, Ezk 40:4
so that I might s ⌊it⌋ to you. Ezk 40:4
S Your favor to Your desolate Dn 9:17
will not s regard for the gods Dn 11:37
s love to a woman who is loved Hs 3:1
I will s them wondrous deeds as Mc 7:15
You will s loyalty to Jacob and Mc 7:20
who will s sympathy to her? Nah 3:7
"I will s you what they are." Zch 1:9
S faithful love and compassion Zch 7:9
with you or s you favor?" Mal 1:8
will He s any of you favor?" Mal 1:9
that you don't s your fasting to Mt 6:18
go, s yourself to the priest, Mt 8:4
asked Him to s them a sign from Mt 16:1
for You don't s partiality. Mt 22:16
S Me the coin used for the tax." Mt 22:19
make long prayers just for s. Mt 23:14
but go and s yourself to the Mk 1:44
for You don't s partiality but Mk 12:14
and say long prayers just for s. Mk 12:40
He will s you a large room Mk 14:15
But go and s yourself to the Lk 5:14
will s you what someone is like Lk 6:47
I will s you the One to fear: Lk 12:5
and s yourselves to the priests. Lk 17:14
and You don't s partiality, Lk 20:21
S Me a denarius. Whose image and Lk 20:24
and say long prayers just for s. Lk 20:47
Then he will s you a large, Lk 22:12
will You s us for doing these Jn 2:18
and He will s Him greater works Jn 5:20

do these things, **s** Yourself to Jn 7:4
said Philip, "**s** us the Father, Jn 14:8
can you say, '**S** us the Father'? Jn 14:9
s which of these two You have Ac 1:24
to the land that I will **s** you. Ac 7:3
will certainly **s** him how much he Ac 9:16
that God doesn't **s** favoritism, Ac 10:34
Him as God or **s** gratitude. Rm 1:21
They **s** that the work of the law Rm 2:15
I will **s** mercy to whom I show Rm 9:15
show mercy to whom I **s** mercy, Rm 9:15
S family affection to one Rm 12:10
And I will **s** you an even better 1Co 12:31
Himself and to **s** our eagerness 2Co 8:19
s them the proof of your love 2Co 8:24
God does not **s** favoritism Gl 2:6
I **s** myself to be a lawbreaker. Gl 2:18
the opportunity ⌊to **s** it⌋. Php 4:10
God wanted to **s** His unchangeable Heb 6:17
Don't neglect to **s** hospitality, Heb 13:2
But if you **s** favoritism, you Jms 2:9
S me your faith without works, Jms 2:18
and I will **s** you faith from my Jms 2:18
He should **s** his works by good Jms 3:13
gave Him to **s** His slaves what Rv 1:1
and I will **s** you what must take Rv 4:1
I will **s** you the judgment of the Rv 17:1
Come, I will **s** you the bride, Rv 21:9
His angel to **s** His servants what Rv 22:6

SHOWED *(38)*

and the LORD **s** him a tree. Ex 15:25
and they **s** them the fruit of the Nm 13:26
and He **s** His holiness to them. Nm 20:13
s you His great fire on earth, Dt 4:36
and the LORD **s** him all the land: Dt 34:1
because I **s** kindness to you. Jos 2:12
When he **s** them the way into the Jdg 1:25
Since you **s** kindness to all the 1Sm 15:6
as his father **s** kindness to me." 2Sm 10:2
When he **s** him the place, 2Kg 6:6
He **s** them the king's son 2Kg 11:4
a hearing and **s** them his whole 2Kg 20:13
his father **s** kindness to me." 1Ch 19:2
Rehoboam also **s** discernment by 2Ch 11:23
if you secretly **s** partiality. Jb 13:10
LORD, when You **s** Your favor, You Ps 30:7
LORD, You **s** favor to Your land; Ps 85:1
and **s** them his treasure house— Is 39:2
Him knowledge and **s** Him the way Is 40:14
control. You **s** them no mercy; Is 47:6
LORD **s** me two baskets of figs Jr 24:1
jealousy you **s** in your hatred Ezk 35:11
The Lord GOD **s** me this: Am 7:1
The Lord GOD **s** me this: Am 7:4
He **s** me this: The Lord was Am 7:7
The Lord GOD **s** me this: Am 8:1
Then the LORD **s** me four Zch 1:20
Then he **s** me Joshua the high Zch 3:1
high mountain and **s** Him all the Mt 4:8
he took Him up and **s** Him all the Lk 4:5
"The one who **s** mercy to him," Lk 10:37
He **s** them His hands and feet. Lk 24:40
s them His hands and His side. Jn 20:20
The next day he **s** up while they Ac 7:26
local people **s** us extraordinary Ac 28:2
and the love you **s** for His name Heb 6:10
mountain and **s** me the holy city Rv 21:10
Then he **s** me the river of living Rv 22:1

SHOWER *(2)*

clouds pour out and **s** abundantly Jb 36:28
let the skies **s** righteousness. Is 45:8

SHOWERED *(1)*

You, God, **s** abundant rain; Ps 68:9

SHOWERS *(12)*

new grass and **s** on tender plants Dt 32:2
their mouths as for spring **s**. Jb 29:23
soften it with **s** and bless its Ps 65:10
like spring **s** that water the Ps 72:6
This is why the **s** haven't come— Jr 3:3
Or can the skies alone give **s**? Jr 14:22
will send down **s** in their season Ezk 34:26
in their season—**s** of blessing. Ezk 34:26
like the spring **s** that water the Hs 6:3
He sends **s** for you, both autumn Jl 2:23
the LORD, like **s** on the grass, Mc 5:7
will give them **s** of rain and Zch 10:1

SHOWING *(19)*

s faithful love to a thousand Ex 20:6
s faithful love to a thousand Dt 5:10
s no partiality and taking no Dt 10:17
s no respect for the old and not Dt 28:50
believe he's **s** respect for your 2Sm 10:3
believe he's **s** respect for your 1Ch 19:3
I am the LORD, **s** faithful love, Jr 9:24
I am tired of **s** compassion. Jr 15:6
injustices by **s** mercy to the Dn 4:27
My ways but are **s** partiality in Mal 2:9
weeping and **s** him the robes and Ac 9:39
explaining and **s** that the Ac 17:3
s mercy, with cheerfulness. Rm 12:8
Outdo one another in **s** honor. Rm 12:10
make a good **s** in the flesh are Gl 6:12
always **s** gentleness to all Ti 3:2
Christ without **s** favoritism. Jms 2:1
weaker nature yet **s** them honor 1Pt 3:7
you are **s** your faith by whatever 3Jn 5

SHOWN *(45)*

and You have **s** me great kindness Gn 19:19
that You have **s** kindness to my Gn 24:14
You have **s** Your servant. Gn 32:10
God has **s** Pharaoh what He is Gn 41:28
you have been **s** on the mountain. Ex 25:40
you have been **s** on the mountain. Ex 26:30
just as it was **s** to you on the Ex 27:8
and is to be **s** to the priest. Lv 13:49
pattern the LORD had **s** Moses. Nm 8:4
were **s** ⌊these things⌋ so that Dt 4:35
LORD our God has **s** us His glory Dt 5:24
He would not have **s** us all these Jdg 13:23
as you have **s** to the dead and Ru 1:8
have **s** more kindness now than Ru 3:10
because you have **s** this special 2Sm 2:5
done this thing and **s** no pity, 2Sm 12:6
You have **s** great and faithful 1Kg 3:6
But the LORD has **s** me that he is 2Kg 8:10
The LORD has **s** me that you will 2Kg 8:13
You have **s** great faithful love 2Ch 1:8
and who has **s** favor to me before Ezr 7:28
payment or **s** contempt for its Jb 31:39
has wonderfully **s** His faithful Ps 31:21
wonderful works He had **s** them. Ps 78:11
His power ⌊**s**⌋ on the day He Ps 78:42
He has **s** His people the power of Ps 111:6
⌊But if⌋ the wicked is **s** favor, Is 26:10
Israel has **s** herself more Jr 3:11
verdict that the LORD has **s** me: Jr 38:21
elders are **s** no respect. Lm 5:12
the things the LORD had **s** me. Ezk 11:25
Yet you will be ⌊**s** to be⌋ a man, Ezk 28:9
they have **s** toward You. Dn 9:7
because they will be **s** mercy. Mt 5:7
the Lord had **s** her His great Lk 1:58
his works may be **s** to be Jn 3:21
I have **s** you many good works Jn 10:32
But God has **s** me that I must not Ac 10:28
In every way I've **s** you that by Ac 20:35
because God has **s** it to them. Rm 1:19
up children, **s** hospitality, 1Tm 5:10
the pattern that was **s** to you on Heb 8:5
to the one who hasn't **s** mercy. Jms 2:13
Lord Jesus Christ has also **s** me. 2Pt 1:14
the angel who had **s** them to me. Rv 22:8

SHOWS *(14)*

He **s** loyalty to His anointed, 2Sm 22:51
the ark ⌊that **s**⌋ Your strength. 2Ch 6:41
God **s** Himself exalted by His Jb 36:22
He **s** loyalty to His anointed, Ps 18:50
therefore He **s** sinners the way. Ps 25:8
our God until He **s** us favor. Ps 123:2
the ark ⌊that **s**⌋ Your strength. Ps 132:8
Whoever **s** contempt for his Pr 11:12
but whoever **s** kindness to the Pr 14:21
A patient person ⌊**s**⌋ great Pr 14:29
and he **s** everyone he is a fool. Ec 10:3
the Son and **s** Him everything He Jn 5:20
effort, but on God who **s** mercy. Rm 9:16
He **s** mercy to whom He wills, Rm 9:18

SHREWD *(7)*

Jonadab was a very **s** man, 2Sm 13:3
crooked You prove Yourself **s**. 2Sm 22:27
crooked You prove Yourself **s**. Ps 18:26
Learn to be **s**, you who are Pr 8:5
A **s** person conceals knowledge, Pr 12:23
Sidon, though they are very **s**. Zch 9:2
Therefore be as **s** as serpents Mt 10:16

SHREWDLY *(1)*

Let us deal **s** with them; Ex 1:10

SHREWDNESS *(2)*

for teaching **s** to the Pr 1:4
share a home with **s** and have Pr 8:12

SHRIEKING *(1)*

s and convulsing him violently. Mk 9:26

SHRIEKS *(1)*

suddenly he **s**, and it throws him Lk 9:39

SHRINE *(7)*

man Micah had a **s**, and he made Jdg 17:5
were even male **s** prostitutes 1Kg 14:24
banished the male **s** prostitutes 1Kg 15:12
of the male **s** prostitutes who 1Kg 22:46
of the male **s** prostitutes that 2Kg 23:7
each at the **s** of his idol? Ezk 8:12
To build a **s** for it in the land Zch 5:11

SHRINES *(12)*

also built **s** on the high places 1Kg 12:31
against all the **s** of the high 1Kg 13:32
them in the **s** of the high places 2Kg 17:29
serve them in the **s** of the high 2Kg 17:32
removed all the **s** of the high 2Kg 23:19
on their surrounding mountain **s**. 2Ch 34:6
at the mountain ⌊**s**⌋ or raise his Ezk 18:6
the mountain ⌊**s**⌋ and defiles his Ezk 18:11
at the mountain ⌊**s**⌋ or raise his Ezk 18:15
in you eat at the mountain ⌊**s**⌋; Ezk 22:9
not live in **s** made by hands. Ac 17:24
who made silver **s** of Artemis, Ac 19:24

SHRINK *(2)*

and that I did not **s** back from Ac 20:20
for I did not **s** back from Ac 20:27

SHRIVEL *(5)*

your thigh **s** and your belly Nm 5:21
to swell and ⌊your⌋ thigh to **s**.' Nm 5:22
swell, and her thigh will **s**. Nm 5:27
brought low and **s** up like Jb 24:24
nets on the water will **s** up. Is 19:8

SHRIVELED *(4)*

have become **s** up and my lord is Gn 18:12
You have **s** me up—it has become Jb 16:8
Their skin has **s** on their bones; Lm 4:8
seeds lie **s** in their casings. Jl 1:17

SHRIVELS *(2)*

and as dry grass **s** in the flame, Is 5:24
off its fruit so that it **s**? Ezk 17:9

SHROUD *(2)*

He⌋ will destroy the ⌊burial⌋ **s**, Is 25:7
the **s** over all the peoples, Is 25:7

SHROUDED *(2)*

north He comes, ⌊**s**⌋ in a golden Jb 37:22
and his name is **s** in darkness. Ec 6:4

SHRUB *(1)*

s of the field had yet ⌊grown⌋ Gn 2:5

SHRUBS *(2)*

They plucked mallow among the **s**, Jb 30:4
They bray among the **s**; Jb 30:7

SHUA *(3)*

daughter of a Canaanite named **S**; Gn 38:2
wife, the daughter of **S**, died. Gn 38:12
and Hotham, with their sister **S**. 1Ch 7:32

SHUAH *(2)*

Medan, Midian, Ishbak, and **S**. Gn 25:2
Medan, Midian, Ishbak, and **S**. 1Ch 1:32

SHUAL *(2)*

road leading to the land of **S**. 1Sm 13:17
Suah, Harnepher, **S**, Beri, Imrah, 1Ch 7:36

SHUBAEL *(2)*

(AKA SHEBUEL)

Amram's sons: **S**; from Shubael's 1Ch 24:20
thirteenth ⌊to⌋ **S**, his sons, and 1Ch 25:20

SHUBAEL'S *(1)*

Shubael; from **S** sons: Jehdeiah. 1Ch 24:20

SHUDDER *(12)*

the peoples hear, they will **s**; Ex 15:14
who hears about it will **s**. 1Sm 3:11
who hears about it will **s**. 2Kg 21:12
at me and **s**; put ⌊your⌋ hand Jb 21:5
people **s**, then pass away. Jb 34:20
you overconfident ones will **s**, Is 32:10

S, you complacent ones; Is 32:11
who hears about it will s Jr 19:3
Their kings s with fear; Ezk 27:35
their kings will s with fear Ezk 32:10
The mountains see You and s; Hab 3:10
also believe—and they s. Jms 2:19

SHUDDERED *(3)*
all the people in the camp s. Ex 19:16
passed by me, and I s with fear. Jb 4:15
everything in it s at the sound Ezk 19:7

SHUDDERS *(2)*
My heart s within me; Ps 55:4
Heal its fissures, for it s. Ps 60:2

SHUHAH *(1)*
brother of S fathered Mehir, 1Ch 4:11

SHUHAM *(1)*
the Shuhamite clan from S. Nm 26:42

SHUHAMITE *(2)*
the S clan from Shuham. Nm 26:42
All the S clans ⌊numbered⌋ by Nm 26:43

SHUHITE *(5)*
Bildad the S, and Zophar Jb 2:11
Then Bildad the S replied: Jb 8:1
Then Bildad the S replied: Jb 18:1
Then Bildad the S replied: Jb 25:1
Bildad the S, and Zophar Jb 42:9

SHULAMMITE *(2)*
Come back, come back, S! Sg 6:13
Why are you looking at the S, Sg 6:13

SHUMATHITES *(1)*
Puthites, S, and Mishraites. 1Ch 2:53

SHUNAMMITE *(8)*
Abishag the S and brought her 1Kg 1:3
Abishag the S was serving him. 1Kg 1:15
me Abishag the S as a wife." 1Kg 2:17
Let Abishag the S be given to 1Kg 2:21
Abishag the S for Adonijah? 1Kg 2:22
Gehazi, "Call this S woman." 2Kg 4:12
Look, there's the S woman. 2Kg 4:25
and said, "Call the S woman." 2Kg 4:36

SHUNEM *(3)*
and ⌊included⌋ Chesulloth, S, Jos 19:18
came together and camped at S. 1Sm 28:4
One day Elisha went to S. 2Kg 4:8

SHUNI *(2)*
Ziphion, Haggi, S, Ezbon, Eri, Gn 46:16
the Shunite clan from S; Nm 26:15

SHUNITE *(1)*
the S clan from Shuni; Nm 26:15

SHUPHAM *(1)*
(AKA MUPPIM)
the Shuphamite clan from S; Nm 26:39

SHUPHAMITE *(1)*
the S clan from Shupham; Nm 26:39

SHUPPIM *(3)*
S and Huppim were sons of Ir, 1Ch 7:12
took wives from Huppim and S. 1Ch 7:15
for S and Hosah it was the west 1Ch 26:16

SHUR *(6)*
the spring on the way to S. Gn 16:7
settled between Kadesh and S. Gn 20:1
they settled from Havilah to S, Gn 25:18
went out to the Wilderness of S. Ex 15:22
from Havilah all the way to S, 1Sm 15:7
region through S as far as the 1Sm 27:8

SHUT *(36)*
Then the LORD s him in. Gn 7:16
entrance and s the door behind Gn 19:6
house with them, and s the door. Gn 19:10
to pursue them, the gate was s. Jos 2:7
Keep your mouth s. Come with us Jdg 18:19
the skies are s and there is no 1Kg 8:35
Then go in and s the door behind 2Kg 4:4
After she had s the door behind 2Kg 4:5
the man of God, s him in, and 2Kg 4:21
s the door to keep him out. 2Kg 6:32
the skies are s and there is no 2Ch 6:26
s the doors of the LORD's temple, 2Ch 28:24
us s the temple doors because Neh 6:10
let the doors be s and securely Neh 7:3
night did not s the doors of my Jb 3:10
only you would s up and let that Jb 13:5
the mouths of liars will be s. Ps 63:11
I am s in and cannot go out. Ps 88:8
the street are s while the sound Ec 12:4
He has s your eyes—the Is 29:10
for He has s their eyes so they Is 44:18
him and the gates will not be s: Is 45:1
will s their mouths because Is 52:15
will never be s day or night so Is 60:11
in my heart, s up in my bones. Jr 20:9
s yourself inside your house. Ezk 3:24
His angel and s the lions' Dn 6:22
one of you would s the ⌊temple⌋ Mal 1:10
your private room, s your door, Mt 6:6
and they have s their eyes; Mt 13:15
banquet, and the door was s. Mt 25:10
when the sky was s up for three Lk 4:25
and at once the gates were s. Ac 21:30
and they have s their eyes; Ac 28:27
mouth may be s and the whole Rm 3:19
obtained promises, s the mouths Heb 11:33

SHUTHELAH *(3)*
the Shuthelahite clan from S; Nm 26:35
S, and his son Bered, his son 1Ch 7:20
Zabad, his son S, Ezer, and 1Ch 7:21

SHUTHELAH'S *(1)*
These were S descendants: Nm 26:36

SHUTHELAHITE *(1)*
the S clan from Shuthelah; Nm 26:35

SHUTS *(6)*
and injustice s its mouth. Jb 5:16
and all injustice s its mouth. Ps 107:42
one who s his ears to the cry Pr 21:13
plots and s his eyes to avoid Is 33:15
gets up and s the door. Lk 13:25
in need but s off his compassion 1Jn 3:17

SHUTTLE *(1)*
more swiftly than a weaver's s; Jb 7:6

SIA'S *(1)*
(AKA SIAHA'S)
descendants, S descendants, Neh 7:47

SIAHA'S *(1)*
(AKA SIA'S)
descendants, S descendants, Ezr 2:44

SIBBECAI *(4)*
(AKA MEBUNNAI)
At that time S the Hushathite 2Sm 21:18
S the Hushathite, Ilai the 1Ch 11:29
At that time S the Hushathite 1Ch 20:4
month, was S the Hushathite, 1Ch 27:11

SIBBOLETH *(1)*
If he said, "S," because he Jdg 12:6

SIBMAH *(5)*
names were changed), and S. Nm 32:38
Kiriathaim, S, Zereth-shahar on Jos 13:19
grapevines of S have withered. Is 16:8
to weep for the vines of S; Is 16:9
you, vine of S, with more than Jr 48:32

SIBRAIM *(1)*
Berothah, and S (which is Ezk 47:16

SICK *(73)*
I'm s of my life because of Gn 27:46
David, Michal said, "He's s." 1Sm 19:14
me when I got s three days ago. 1Sm 30:13
making himself s over his sister 2Sm 13:2
your bed and pretend you're s. 2Sm 13:5
lay down and pretended to be s. 2Sm 13:6
Abijah son of Jeroboam became s. 1Kg 14:1
you about her son, for he is s. 1Kg 14:5
Ben-hadad king of Aram was s, 2Kg 8:7
Elisha became s with the illness 2Kg 13:14
heard that Hezekiah had been s. 2Kg 20:12
Hezekiah became s to the point 2Ch 32:24
are you sad, when you aren't s? Neh 2:2
when they were s, my clothing Ps 35:13
Delayed hope makes the heart s, Pr 13:12
you'll get s from it and vomit. Pr 25:16
he'll get s of you and hate you. Pr 25:17
hurt, and the whole heart is s. Is 1:5
none there will say, "I am s." Is 33:24
he had been s and had recovered Is 38:9
that he had been s and had Is 39:1
to crush Him, and He made Him s. Is 53:10
settled on me. My heart is s. Jr 8:18
else and desperately s— Jr 17:9
me desolate, s all day long. Lm 1:13
are many, and I am s at heart. Lm 1:22
Because of this, our heart is s; Lm 5:17
the weak, healed the s, bandaged Ezk 34:4
was overcome and lay s for days. Dn 8:27
the princes are s with the heat Hs 7:5
present a lame or s ⌊animal⌋, Mal 1:8
stolen, lame, or s animals. Mal 1:13
word and healed all who were s, Mt 8:16
need a doctor, but the s do. Mt 9:12
Heal the s, raise the dead, Mt 10:8
for them, and healed their s. Mt 14:14
brought to Him all who were s. Mt 14:35
I was s and you took care of Me; Mt 25:36
did we see You s, or in prison, Mt 25:39
s and in prison and you didn't Mt 25:43
clothes, or s, or in prison, Mt 25:44
those who were s and those who Mk 1:32
many who were s with various Mk 1:34
doctor, but the s ⌊do need one⌋. Mk 2:17
hands on a few s people and Mk 6:5
many s people with oil, Mk 6:13
to carry the s on stretchers to Mk 6:55
they laid the s in the Mk 6:56
they will lay hands on the s, Mk 16:18
who had anyone s with various Lk 4:40
need a doctor, but the s do. Lk 5:31
by him, was s and about to die. Lk 7:2
of God and to heal the s. Lk 9:2
Heal the s who are there, and Lk 10:9
these lay a multitude of the s— Jn 5:3
who had been s for 38 years. Jn 5:5
"Sir," the s man answered, "I Jn 5:7
that He was performing on the s. Jn 6:2
Now a man was s, Lazarus, from Jn 11:1
her brother Lazarus who was s. Jn 11:2
"Lord, the one You love is s." Jn 11:3
So when He heard that he was s, Jn 11:6
would carry the s out into the Ac 5:15
bringing s people and those who Ac 5:16
days she became s and died. Ac 9:37
his skin were brought to the s, Ac 19:12
is why many are s and ill among 1Co 11:30
because you heard that he was s. Php 2:26
he was so s that he nearly died. Php 2:27
but having a s interest in 1Tm 6:4
Trophimus I left s at Miletus. 2Tm 4:20
among you s? He should call Jms 5:14
of faith will save the s person, Jms 5:15

SICKBED *(5)*
will not get up from your s— 2Kg 1:4
will not get up from your s— 2Kg 1:6
You will not get up from your s; 2Kg 1:16
LORD will sustain him on his s; Ps 41:3
I will throw her into a s, Rv 2:22

SICKENING *(3)*
There is a s tragedy I have seen Ec 5:13
This too is a s tragedy: Ec 5:16
This is futile and a s tragedy. Ec 6:2

SICKLE *(12)*
the time the s is first ⌊put⌋ to Dt 16:9
must not put a s to your Dt 23:25
wields the s at harvest time. Jr 50:16
Swing the s because the harvest Jl 3:13
sends for the s, because harvest Mk 4:29
head and a sharp s in His hand. Rv 14:14
cloud, "Use your s and reap, for Rv 14:15
swung His s over the earth, Rv 14:16
who also had a sharp s came out Rv 14:17
to the one who had the sharp s, Rv 14:18
Use your sharp s and gather the Rv 14:18
angel swung his s toward earth Rv 14:19

SICKLES *(1)*
mattocks, axes, and s. 1Sm 13:20

SICKLY *(3)*
other cows, s and thin, came up Gn 41:3
s, thin cows ate the healthy, Gn 41:4
ugly, very s, and thin—came Gn 41:19

SICKNESS *(14)*
LORD will remove all s from you; Dt 7:15
you with every s and plague not Dt 28:61
'Will I recover from this s?' " 2Kg 8:8
'Will I recover from this s?' " 2Kg 8:9
A man's spirit can endure s, Pr 18:14
with much sorrow, s, and anger. Ec 5:17
orchards as a s consumes a Is 10:18
suffering who knew what s was. Is 53:3
S and wounds keep coming to My Jr 6:7
Ephraim saw his s and Judah his Hs 5:13
disease and s among the people Mt 4:23

every disease and every **s**. Mt 9:35
and to heal every disease and **s**. Mt 10:1
This **s** will not end in death but Jn 11:4

SICKNESSES *(5)*

and terrible and chronic **s**. Dt 28:59
the land and the **s** the LORD has Dt 29:22
Yet He Himself bore our **s**, Is 53:4
Him and to be healed of their **s**. Lk 5:15
healed of evil spirits and **s**: Lk 8:2

SIDDIM *(3)*

as allies to the Valley of **S** Gn 14:3
up for battle in the Valley of **S** Gn 14:8
the Valley of **S** contained many Gn 14:10

SIDE *(283)*

put a door in the **s** of the ark. Gn 6:16
flock to the far **s** of the Ex 3:1
on one **s** and one on the other Ex 17:12
two rings on one **s** and two rings Ex 25:12
and two rings on the other **s**. Ex 25:12
from one **s** and three branches Ex 25:32
the lampstand from the other **s**. Ex 25:32
half yard on one **s** and the half Ex 26:13
on either **s** to cover it. Ex 26:13
20 planks for the south **s**, Ex 26:18
for the second **s** of the Ex 26:20
of the tabernacle, the north **s**, Ex 26:20
for the west **s** of the tabernacle Ex 26:22
planks on one **s** of the Ex 26:26
on the other **s** of the tabernacle Ex 26:27
of the back **s** of the tabernacle Ex 26:27
the south **s** of the tabernacle, Ex 26:35
put the table on the north **s**. Ex 26:35
linen, 150 feet long on that **s**. Ex 27:9
on the north **s** 150 ⌊feet⌋ long. Ex 27:11
on the west **s** 75 feet long, Ex 27:12
on the east **s** toward the sunrise Ex 27:13
hangings on one **s** ⌊of the gate⌋ Ex 27:14
on the other **s** 22 and a half Ex 27:15
man fasten his sword to his **s**; Ex 32:27
as follows: 20 for the south **s**, Ex 36:23
for the second **s** of the Ex 36:25
the north **s**, he made 20 planks, Ex 36:25
and for the west **s** of the Ex 36:27
planks on one **s** of the Ex 36:31
on the other **s** of the tabernacle Ex 36:32
two rings on one **s** and two rings Ex 37:3
and two rings on the other **s**. Ex 37:3
from one **s** and three branches Ex 37:18
the lampstand from the other **s**. Ex 37:18
on the south **s** of the courtyard Ex 38:9
the north **s** were also 150 feet Ex 38:11
on the west **s** were 75 feet Ex 38:12
hangings on one **s** ⌊of the gate⌋ Ex 38:14
It was the same for the other **s**. Ex 38:15
the north **s** of the tabernacle, Ex 40:22
on the south **s** of the tabernacle Ex 40:24
it on the north **s** of the altar Lv 1:11
drained at the **s** of the altar. Lv 1:15
it on the east **s** of the altar at Lv 1:16
offering on the **s** of the altar, Lv 5:9
against the east **s** of the mercy Lv 16:14
camp on the east **s** toward the Nm 2:3
camp on the south **s** under their Nm 2:10
camp on the west **s** under their Nm 2:18
camp on the north **s** under their Nm 2:25
the tabernacle on the west **s**, Nm 3:23
on the south **s** of the tabernacle Nm 3:29
on the north **s** of the tabernacle Nm 3:35
on the other **s** of the Arnon Nm 21:13
with a stone wall on either **s**. Nm 22:24
Your southern **s** will be from the Nm 34:3
city wall 500 yards on every **s**. Nm 35:4
outside the city for the east **s**, Nm 35:5
1,000 yards for the south **s**, Nm 35:5
1,000 yards for the west **s**, Nm 35:5
and 1,000 yards for the north **s**, Nm 35:5
cousins on their father's **s**. Nm 36:11
on the other **s** of the Jordan, Dt 3:25
on the east **s** of the Jordan as Dt 4:49
you on this **s** of the Jordan. Jos 1:14
on the east **s** of the Jordan." Jos 1:15
on the other **s** of the Jordan! Jos 7:7
some on one **s** and some on the Jos 8:22
stood on either **s** of the ark of Jos 8:33
on the east **s** of the Jordan. Jos 13:27
on the north **s** was from the bay Jos 15:5
was on the north **s** of the brook Jos 17:9
on the north **s** began at the Jos 18:12
On the west **s**, from the hill Jos 18:14
was the west **s** ⌊of their border⌋ Jos 18:14
The south **s** began at the edge of Jos 18:15
formed the border on the east **s**. Jos 18:20
rest on every **s** according to all Jos 21:44
on the west **s** of the Jordan. Jos 22:7
the Jordan, on the Israelite **s**." Jos 22:11
travelers kept to the **s** roads. Jdg 5:6
on the other **s** of the Jordan Jdg 10:8
came to the east **s** of the land Jdg 11:18
on the other **s** of the Arnon Jdg 11:18
on her husband's **s** named Boaz. Ru 2:1
garrison on the other **s**." 1Sm 14:1
will be on one **s**, and I and my 1Sm 14:40
will be on the other **s**." 1Sm 14:40
arrows are on this **s** of you— 1Sm 20:21
from the south **s** of the stone 1Sm 20:41
went along one **s** of the mountain 1Sm 23:26
his men went along the other **s**. 1Sm 23:26
to the other **s** and stood on top 1Sm 26:13
on the other **s** of the valley 1Sm 31:7
and on the other **s** of the Jordan 1Sm 31:7
opponent's **s** so that they all 2Sm 2:16
am on your **s** to hand all Israel 2Sm 3:12
him rest on every **s** from all his 2Sm 7:1
him from the **s** of the mountain 2Sm 13:34
I am on the **s** of the one that 2Sm 16:18
So he stood to one **s**. 2Sm 18:30
for you at my **s** in Jerusalem." 2Sm 19:33
to lie by your **s** so that my lord 1Kg 1:2
did not **s** with Adonijah. 1Kg 1:8
my son from my **s** while your 1Kg 3:20
far as the other **s** of Jokmeam; 1Kg 4:12
And he made **s** chambers all 1Kg 6:5
door for the lowest **s** chamber 1Kg 6:8
on the right **s** of the temple. 1Kg 6:8
on the right **s** of the temple 1Kg 7:39
temple and five on the left **s**. 1Kg 7:39
near the right **s** of the temple 1Kg 7:39
on either **s** of the seat, 1Kg 10:19
Set the full ones to one **s**." 2Kg 4:4
I were riding **s** by side behind 2Kg 9:25
riding side by **s** behind his 2Kg 9:25
and said, "Who is on my **s**? 2Kg 9:32
you are on my **s**, and if you will 2Kg 10:6
from the right **s** of the temple 2Kg 11:11
of the temple to the left **s**, 2Kg 11:11
on the right **s** as one enters 2Kg 12:9
on the north **s** of ⌊his⌋ altar. 2Kg 16:14
to the east **s** of the valley to 1Ch 4:39
the King's Gate on the east **s**. 1Ch 9:18
chief officials at the king's **s**. 1Ch 18:17
He given you rest on every **s**? 1Ch 22:18
the reservoir on the right **s**, 2Ch 4:10
on either **s** of the seat, 2Ch 9:18
and He gave us rest on every **s**." 2Ch 14:7
LORD gave them rest on every **s**. 2Ch 15:15
God gave him rest on every **s**. 2Ch 20:30
from the right **s** of the temple 2Ch 23:10
of the temple to the left **s**, 2Ch 23:10
He gave them rest on every **s**. 2Ch 32:22
him on every **s** and harass him at Jb 18:11
me down on every **s** so that I am Jb 19:10
If there is an angel on his **s**, Jb 33:23
A quiver rattles at his **s**, Jb 39:23
stand against me on every **s**. Ps 3:6
terror is on every **s**. When they Ps 31:13
strap your sword at your **s**. Ps 45:3
close in on me from every **s**. Ps 88:17
fall at your **s** and ten thousand Ps 91:7
burns up His foes on every **s**. Ps 97:3
is a shelter right by your **s**. Ps 121:5
the LORD had not been on our **s**— Ps 124:1
not been on our **s** when men Ps 124:2
his sword at his **s** ⌊to guard⌋ Sg 3:8
a sword; terror is on every **s**. Jr 6:25
Terror is on every **s**! Jr 20:10
look back, terror is on every **s**! Jr 46:5
to them: Terror is on every **s**! Jr 49:29
war cry against her on every **s**! Jr 50:15
her from every **s** in the day of Jr 51:2
my attackers on every **s**, Lm 2:22
down on your left **s** and place Ezk 4:4
of days you lie on your **s**. Ezk 4:4
on your right **s**, and bear the Ezk 4:6
cannot turn from **s** to side until Ezk 4:8
from side to **s** until you have Ezk 4:8
of days you lie on your **s**, Ezk 4:9
with writing equipment at his **s**. Ezk 9:2
the writing equipment at his **s**. Ezk 9:3
at his **s** reported back, Ezk 9:11
you with contempt from every **s**. Ezk 16:57
them against you from every **s**: Ezk 23:22
you on every **s** with shields, Ezk 23:24
sword is against her on every **s**. Ezk 28:23
have trampled you from every **s**, Ezk 36:3
Look! I am on your **s**; I will Ezk 36:9
on the temple **s** next to the Ezk 40:7
of the gate was on the temple **s**. Ezk 40:9
on each **s** of the east gate Ezk 40:10
on either **s** also had the same Ezk 40:10
recesses on each **s** were 10 and a Ezk 40:12
Its three recesses on each **s**, Ezk 40:21
He brought me to the south **s**, Ezk 40:24
on its pilasters, one on each **s**. Ezk 40:26
the inner court on the east **s**. Ezk 40:32
with palm trees on each **s**. Ezk 40:34
with palm trees on each **s**. Ezk 40:37
there were two tables on each **s**, Ezk 40:39
tables on one **s** and two ⌊more⌋ Ezk 40:40
on the other **s** of the gate's Ezk 40:40
feet ⌊thick⌋ on each **s**. Ezk 40:48
a quarter feet ⌊wide⌋ on each **s**. Ezk 40:48
by the pilasters, one on each **s**. Ezk 40:49
on each **s** the width of the Ezk 41:1
feet ⌊wide⌋ on each **s**. Ezk 41:2
sidewalls on each **s** was 12 and a Ezk 41:3
width of the **s** rooms all around Ezk 41:5
The **s** rooms were arranged one Ezk 41:6
as supports for the **s** rooms, Ezk 41:6
The **s** rooms surrounding ⌊the Ezk 41:7
foundation for the **s** rooms was Ezk 41:8
wall of the **s** rooms was eight Ezk 41:9
space between the **s** rooms of the Ezk 41:9
The **s** rooms opened into the free Ezk 41:11
with its galleries on each **s**; Ezk 41:15
toward the palm tree on one **s**, Ezk 41:19
the **s** rooms of the temple, Ezk 41:26
on the east **s** as one enters them Ezk 42:9
as one enters on the east **s**, Ezk 42:12
that were on the south **s**. Ezk 42:12
the east **s** with a measuring Ezk 42:16
He measured the north **s**; Ezk 42:17
He measured the south **s**; Ezk 42:18
to the west **s** and measured 875 Ezk 42:19
the area on each **s** of the holy Ezk 45:7
on the west **s** and to the east Ezk 45:7
and to the east on the east **s**. Ezk 45:7
that was at the **s** of the gate, Ezk 46:19
under the south **s** ⌊of the Ezk 47:1
was trickling from the south **s**. Ezk 47:2
On the north **s** it will extend Ezk 47:15
This will be the northern **s**. Ezk 47:17
the east **s** it will run between Ezk 47:18
This will be the eastern **s**. Ezk 47:18
On the south **s** it will run from Ezk 47:19
This will be the southern **s**. Ezk 47:19
On the west **s** the Mediterranean Ezk 47:20
This will be the western **s**. Ezk 47:20
from the eastern **s** to the sea, Ezk 48:1
from the east **s** to the west, Ezk 48:2
from the east **s** to the west, Ezk 48:3
from the east **s** to the west, Ezk 48:4
from the east **s** to the west, Ezk 48:5
from the east **s** to the west, Ezk 48:6
from the east **s** to the west, Ezk 48:7
from the east **s** to the west, Ezk 48:8
from the east **s** to the west. Ezk 48:8
miles long⌋ on the northern **s**, Ezk 48:10
miles⌋ wide on the western **s**, Ezk 48:10
miles⌋ wide on the eastern **s**, Ezk 48:10
miles⌋ long on the southern **s**. Ezk 48:10
a half ⌊miles⌋ on the north **s**; Ezk 48:16
a half ⌊miles⌋ on the south **s**; Ezk 48:16
a half ⌊miles⌋ on the east **s**; Ezk 48:16
a half ⌊miles⌋ on the west **s**. Ezk 48:16
From the east **s** to the west, Ezk 48:23
from the east **s** to the west, Ezk 48:24
from the east **s** to the west, Ezk 48:25
from the east **s** to the west, Ezk 48:26
from the east **s** to the west, Ezk 48:27
of Gad toward the south **s**, Ezk 48:28
On the north **s**, which measures Ezk 48:30
On the east **s**, which is one and Ezk 48:32
On the south **s**, which measures Ezk 48:33
On the west **s**, which is one and Ezk 48:34

It was raised up on one s, Dn 7:5
at his right s to accuse him. Zch 3:1
to what is written on one s, Zch 5:3
what is written on the other s. Zch 5:3
go to the other s ⌊of the sea⌋. Mt 8:18
When He had come to the other s, Mt 8:28
go ahead of Him to the other s, Mt 14:22
to the other s ⌊of the lake⌋." Mk 4:35
came to the other s of the sea, Mk 5:1
again by boat to the other s, Mk 5:21
go ahead of Him to the other s, Mk 6:45
again, and went to the other s. Mk 8:13
robe sitting on the right s; Mk 16:5
to the other s of the lake." Lk 8:22
he passed by on the other s. Lk 10:31
him, passed by on the other s. Lk 10:32
by the angels to Abraham's s. Lk 16:22
way off, with Lazarus at his s. Lk 16:23
and hem you in on every s. Lk 19:43
One who is at the Father's s— Jn 1:18
on the other s of the sea knew Jn 6:22
Him on the other s of the sea, Jn 6:25
Him, one on either s, with Jesus Jn 19:18
pierced His s with a spear, Jn 19:34
showed them His hands and His s. Jn 20:20
and put my hand into His s, Jn 20:25
your hand and put it into My s. Jn 20:27
net on the right s of the boat," Jn 21:6
Peter on the s, he woke him up Ac 12:7
along the south s of Crete off Ac 27:7
working s by side for the faith Php 1:27
working side by s for the faith Php 1:27
for the gospel at my s, Php 4:3

SIDED *(1)*
LORD because they s with David. 1Sm 22:17

SIDES *(56)*
finishing ⌊the s of the ark⌋ to Gn 6:16
the rings on the s of the ark in Ex 25:14
are to extend from its s, Ex 25:32
over the s of the tabernacle Ex 26:13
poles are on two s of the altar Ex 27:7
it⌋ on all s of the altar. Ex 29:16
blood on all s of the altar. Ex 29:20
all around its s, and its horns Ex 30:3
the molding on two of its s; Ex 30:4
these on opposite s of it to be Ex 30:4
They were inscribed on both s— Ex 32:15
rings on the s of the ark for Ex 37:5
branches extended from its s, Ex 37:18
all around its s, and its horns Ex 37:26
the molding on two of its s; Ex 37:27
these⌋ on opposite s of it to be Ex 37:27
the rings on the s of the altar Ex 38:7
bases on both s of the courtyard Ex 38:15
it on all s of the altar that Lv 1:5
against the altar on all s. Lv 1:11
the blood on all s of the altar. Lv 3:2
its blood on all s of the altar. Lv 3:8
its blood on all s of the altar. Lv 3:13
its blood on all s of the altar. Lv 7:2
the horns of the altar on all s, Lv 8:15
the blood on all s of the altar. Lv 8:19
the blood on all s of the altar. Lv 8:24
it on all s of the altar. Lv 9:12
it on all s of the altar. Lv 9:18
the horns on all s of the altar. Lv 16:18
the hair at the s of your head Lv 19:27
in your eyes and in your s; Nm 33:55
by its borders on all s." Nm 34:12
scourge for your s and thorns in Jos 23:13
They will be thorns in your s, Jdg 2:3
of rock on both s of the pass 1Sm 14:4
on opposite s of the pool. 2Sm 2:13
first door had two folding s, 1Kg 6:34
gatekeepers were on the four s: 1Ch 9:24
for true wisdom has two s. Jb 11:6
be thrown off the s of a cliff, Ps 141:6
their wings on their four s. Ezk 1:8
rams against it on all s. Ezk 4:2
front of the recesses on both s, Ezk 40:12
feet thick on all s, Ezk 41:12
overlaid with wood on all s. Ezk 41:16
throughout the temple on all s. Ezk 41:19
its length and s were of wood. Ezk 41:22
and palm trees on both s, Ezk 41:26
temple complex on all four s. Ezk 42:20
feet wide, with four equal s. Ezk 43:17
the base of the walls on all s. Ezk 46:23
along both s of the riverbank Ezk 47:7
area⌋ on both s of the holy Ezk 48:21
covered with gold on all s, Heb 9:4
On both s of the river was the Rv 22:2

SIDEWALLS *(4)*
and the s of the gate were five Ezk 40:48
and the s of the entrance were Ezk 41:2
the entrance's s on each side Ezk 41:3
sides, on the s of the portico, Ezk 41:26

SIDING *(2)*
that you are s with Jesse's son 1Sm 20:30
some s with the Jews and some Ac 14:4

SIDON *(34)*
Canaan fathered S his firstborn, Gn 10:15
border went from S going toward Gn 10:19
his territory will be next to S. Gn 49:13
as far as Great S and Jos 11:8
and Kanah, as far as Great S. Jos 19:28
the residents of Acco or of S, Jdg 1:31
the gods of Aram, S, and Moab, Jdg 10:6
was far from S and they had no Jdg 18:28
on to Dan-jaan and around to S. 2Sm 24:6
to Zarephath that belongs to S, 1Kg 17:9
fathered S, his firstborn, 1Ch 1:13
oil to the people of S and Tyre, Ezr 3:7
coastland, you merchants of S; Is 23:2
Be ashamed S, the stronghold of Is 23:4
young woman, daughter of S. Is 23:12
the kings of S, and the kings Jr 25:22
and the king of S through Jr 27:3
from Tyre and S every remaining Jr 47:4
inhabitants of S and Arvad were Ezk 27:8
your face toward S and prophesy Ezk 28:21
I am against you, S, and I will Ezk 28:22
Tyre, S, and all the territories Jl 3:4
as Tyre and S, though they are Zch 9:2
you had been done in Tyre and S, Mt 11:21
for Tyre and S on the day of Mt 11:22
to the area of Tyre and S. Mt 15:21
Jordan, and around Tyre and S. Mk 3:8
to the region of Tyre and S. Mk 7:24
went by way of S to the Sea of Mk 7:31
to a widow at Zarephath in S. Lk 4:26
from the seacoast of Tyre and S. Lk 6:17
you had been done in Tyre and S, Lk 10:13
for Tyre and S at the judgment Lk 10:14
The next day we put in at S, Ac 27:3

SIDONIAN *(1)*
Edomite, S, and Hittite women 1Kg 11:1

SIDONIANS *(15)*
which the S call Sirion, but the Dt 3:9
Arah of the S to Aphek and as Jos 13:4
to Misrephoth-maim, all the S. Jos 13:6
Canaanites, the S, and the Jdg 3:3
S, Amalekites, and Maonites Jdg 10:12
in the same way as the S, quiet Jdg 18:7
were far from the S, having no Jdg 18:7
how to cut timber like the S." 1Kg 5:6
goddess of the S, and Milcom, 1Kg 11:5
goddess of the S, to Chemosh, 1Kg 11:33
of Ethbaal king of the S, 1Kg 16:31
the detestable idol of the S; 2Kg 23:13
because the S and Tyrians had 1Ch 22:4
north and all the S are there. Ezk 32:30
angry with the Tyrians and S. Ac 12:20

SIEGE *(50)*
war against you, lay s to it. Dt 20:12
When you lay s to a city for a Dt 20:19
human, to come under s by you? Dt 20:19
down to build s works against Dt 20:20
you during the s and hardship Dt 28:53
left during the s and hardship Dt 28:55
else⌋ during the s and hardship Dt 28:57
They laid s to it and attacked Jos 10:31
They laid s to it and attacked Jos 10:34
up and laid s to Jabesh-gilead 1Sm 11:1
the troops, lay s to the city, 2Sm 12:28
continued the s against it until 2Kg 6:25
and the city came under s. 2Kg 24:10
laid s to the city and built 2Kg 25:1
and built a s wall against it 2Kg 25:1
The city was under s until King 2Kg 25:2
laid s to the fortified cities 2Ch 32:1
remain under the s of Jerusalem? 2Ch 32:10
their s ramp against me Jb 30:12
love to me in a city under s. Ps 31:21
and built large s works against Ec 9:14
Elam! Lay s, you Medes! I will Is 21:2
They set up their s towers and Is 23:13
will set up my s towers against Is 29:3
a s ramp against Jerusalem. Jr 6:6
ground, you who live under s. Jr 10:17
cities of the Negev are under s; Jr 13:19
flesh in the s and distress that Jr 19:9
S ramps have come against the Jr 32:24
against the s ramps and the Jr 33:4
entire army and laid s to it. Jr 39:1
laid s to the city and built Jr 52:4
and built a s wall all around Jr 52:4
The city was under s until King Jr 52:5
He has laid s against me, Lm 3:5
Then lay s against it: Ezk 4:2
a s wall, build a ramp, Ezk 4:2
toward it so that it is under s, Ezk 4:3
face toward the s of Jerusalem Ezk 4:7
finished the days of your s. Ezk 4:8
the days of the s have ended; Ezk 5:2
built and s walls constructed Ezk 17:17
a ramp, and construct a s wall. Ezk 21:22
Babylon has laid s to Jerusalem Ezk 24:2
He will set up s works against Ezk 26:8
to Jerusalem and laid s to it. Dn 1:1
a s is set against us! Mc 5:1
water for the s; strengthen your Nah 3:14
and build s ramps to capture Hab 1:10
s against Jerusalem will also Zch 12:2

SIEGE-WORKS *(1)*
attackers, the s against her, Is 29:7

SIEVE *(2)*
nations in a s of destruction Is 30:28
as one shakes a s, but not a Am 9:9

SIFT *(3)*
⌊He comes⌋ to s the nations in a Is 30:28
⌊It comes⌋ not to winnow or to s; Jr 4:11
has asked to s you like wheat. Lk 22:31

SIFTS *(1)*
throne to judge s out all evil Pr 20:8

SIGH *(3)*
s when food is ⌊put⌋ before me, Jb 3:24
we end our years like a s. Ps 90:9
of the men who s and groan over Ezk 9:4

SIGHED *(1)*
He s deeply and said to him, Mk 7:34

SIGHING *(5)*
my words, LORD; consider my s. Ps 5:1
my s is not hidden from You. Ps 38:9
and sorrow and s will flee. Is 35:10
and sorrow and s will flee. Is 51:11
But s deeply in His spirit, Mk 8:12

SIGHT *(250)*
earth was corrupt in God's s, Gn 6:11
hunter in the s of the LORD. Gn 10:9
hunter in the s of the LORD." Gn 10:9
if I have found favor in your s, Gn 18:3
indeed found favor in Your s, Gn 19:19
If I have found favor in your s, Gn 30:27
we are out of each other's s. Gn 31:49
in the LORD's s, and the LORD Gn 38:7
he did was evil in the LORD's s, Gn 38:10
in his master's s and became his Gn 39:4
and look at this remarkable s. Ex 3:3
favor in the s of the Egyptians Ex 3:21
in the s of Pharaoh and his Ex 7:20
heaven in the s of Pharaoh. Ex 9:8
favor in the s of the Egyptians. Ex 11:3
the Egyptians' s that they gave Ex 12:36
did this in the s of the elders Ex 17:6
Sinai in the s of all the people Ex 19:11
have also found favor in My s.' Ex 33:12
indeed found favor in Your s, Ex 33:13
You and find favor in Your s. Ex 33:13
favor in Your s unless You go Ex 33:16
you have found favor in My s, Ex 33:17
indeed found favor in Your s, Ex 34:9
acceptable in the LORD's s?" Lv 10:19
unchanged in his s and has not Lv 13:5
rule over him harshly in your s. Lv 25:53
of Egypt in the s of the nations Lv 26:45
The cow must be burned in his s. Nm 19:5
holiness in the s of the Nm 20:12
Mount Hor in the s of the whole Nm 20:27
you are doing is evil in My s. Nm 22:32
evil in Your s, I will go back. Nm 22:34

his relatives in the s of Moses Nm 25:6
in their s at the waters." Nm 27:14
and commission him in their s. Nm 27:19
we have found favor in your s, Nm 32:5
evil in the LORD's s was gone. Nm 32:13
triumphantly in the s of all the Nm 33:3
evil in the s of the LORD your Dt 4:25
right and good in the LORD's s, Dt 6:18
in the LORD's s and provoking Dt 9:18
what is right in the LORD's s. Dt 12:25
right in the s of the LORD your Dt 12:28
is right in the s of the LORD Dt 13:18
evil in the s of the LORD your Dt 17:2
what is right in the LORD's s. Dt 21:9
will be degraded in your s. Dt 25:3
to him in the s of the elders, Dt 25:9
to him in the s of all Israel, Dt 31:7
do what is evil in the LORD's s, Dt 31:29
in the s of all Israel. Dt 34:12
you in the s of all Israel, Jos 3:7
crossed in the s of the people. Jos 4:11
Joshua in the s of all Israel, Jos 4:14
what was evil in the LORD's s. Jdg 2:11
what was evil in the LORD's s; Jdg 3:7
what was evil in the LORD's s. Jdg 3:12
what was evil in the LORD's s. Jdg 3:12
was evil in the s of the LORD Jdg 4:1
was evil in the s of the LORD. Jdg 6:1
If I have found favor in Your s, Jdg 6:17
of the LORD vanished from his s. Jdg 6:21
was evil in the s of the LORD. Jdg 10:6
what was evil in the LORD's s, Jdg 13:1
in the LORD's s by requesting a 1Sm 12:17
what was evil in the LORD's s?" 1Sm 15:19
it trivial in your s to become 1Sm 18:23
in the s of the slave girls 2Sm 6:20
in the s of all Israel. 2Sm 16:22
to my cleanness in His s. 2Sm 22:25
what was evil in the LORD's s, 1Kg 11:6
right in My s in order to keep 1Kg 11:38
in the LORD's s and followed 1Kg 15:26
in the LORD's s and followed 1Kg 15:34
he had done in the LORD's s, 1Kg 16:7
in the LORD's s and by following 1Kg 16:19
what was evil in the LORD's s; 1Kg 16:25
in the LORD's s more than all 1Kg 16:30
do what is evil in the LORD's s. 1Kg 21:20
what was evil in the LORD's s, 1Kg 21:25
what was right in the LORD's s, 1Kg 22:43
what was evil in the LORD's s. 1Kg 22:52
of yours be precious in your s. 2Kg 1:13
my life be precious in your s." 2Kg 1:14
what was evil in the LORD's s, 2Kg 3:2
This is easy in the LORD's s. 2Kg 3:18
in his master's s and highly 2Kg 5:1
what was evil in the LORD's s. 2Kg 8:18
in the LORD's s like the house 2Kg 8:27
right in My s and have done to 2Kg 10:30
what was right in the LORD's s. 2Kg 12:2
in the LORD's s and followed 2Kg 13:2
what was evil in the LORD's s. 2Kg 13:11
what was right in the LORD's s, 2Kg 14:3
what was evil in the LORD's s. 2Kg 14:24
in the LORD's s just as his 2Kg 15:3
in the LORD's s as his fathers 2Kg 15:9
what was evil in the LORD's s. 2Kg 15:18
in the LORD's s and did not turn 2Kg 15:24
what was evil in the LORD's s. 2Kg 15:28
in the LORD's s just as his 2Kg 15:34
right in the s of the LORD his 2Kg 16:2
what was evil in the LORD's s, 2Kg 17:2
in the LORD's s and provoked 2Kg 17:17
right in the LORD's s just as 2Kg 18:3
done what is good in Your s." 2Kg 20:3
what was evil in the LORD's s, 2Kg 21:2
amount of evil in the LORD's s, 2Kg 21:6
is evil in My s and have 2Kg 21:15
what was evil in the LORD's s. 2Kg 21:16
in the LORD's s as his father 2Kg 21:20
the LORD's s and walked in all 2Kg 22:2
Judah from My s just as I have 2Kg 23:27
evil in the LORD's s just as his 2Kg 23:32
evil in the LORD's s just as his 2Kg 23:37
to remove them from His s. 2Kg 24:3
in the LORD's s as his father 2Kg 24:9
in the LORD's s just as 2Kg 24:19
in the LORD's s, so He put him 1Ch 2:3
was also evil in God's s, 1Ch 21:7

So now in the s of all Israel, 1Ch 28:8
the LORD in the s of all the 1Ch 29:10
Solomon in the s of all Israel 1Ch 29:25
right in the s of the LORD his 2Ch 14:2
what was right in the LORD's s. 2Ch 20:32
what was evil in the LORD's s, 2Ch 21:6
in the LORD's s like the house 2Ch 22:4
what was right in the LORD's s. 2Ch 24:2
in the LORD's s but not 2Ch 25:2
in the LORD's s as his father 2Ch 26:4
in the LORD's s as his father 2Ch 27:2
in the LORD's s like his 2Ch 28:1
right in the LORD's s just as 2Ch 29:2
is evil in the s of the LORD our 2Ch 29:6
what was evil in the LORD's s, 2Ch 33:2
deal of evil in the LORD's s, 2Ch 33:6
in the LORD's s just as his 2Ch 33:22
right in the LORD's s and walked 2Ch 34:2
evil in the s of the LORD his 2Ch 36:5
what was evil in the LORD's s. 2Ch 36:9
evil in the s of the LORD his 2Ch 36:12
their sin be erased from Your s, Neh 4:5
his heart faithful in Your s, Neh 9:8
did what was evil in Your s. Neh 9:28
approval in the s of everyone Est 2:15
king and I am pleasing in his s, Est 8:5
sound, and I am pure in Your s." Jb 11:4
But the s of the wicked will Jb 11:20
heavens are not pure in His s, Jb 15:15
as cattle, as stupid in your s? Jb 18:3
I am a foreigner in their s. Jb 19:15
the stars are not pure in His s, Jb 25:5
collapse at the very s of him? Jb 41:9
judgments are beyond his s; Ps 10:5
cleanness of my hands in His s. Ps 18:24
in the s of everyone for Ps 31:19
"I am cut off from Your s." Ps 31:22
life span as nothing in Your s. Ps 39:5
and done this evil in Your s. Ps 51:4
lives are precious in his s. Ps 72:14
wonders in the s of their Ps 78:12
For in Your s a thousand years Ps 90:4
in the s of the nations. Ps 98:2
is valuable in the LORD's s. Ps 116:15
alive is righteous in Your s. Ps 143:2
regard in the s of God and man. Pr 3:4
My son, don't lose s of them. Pr 3:21
Don't lose s of them; keep them Pr 4:21
man who is pleasing in His s, Ec 2:26
one who is pleasing in God's s. Ec 2:26
your evil deeds from My s. Is 1:16
and clever in their own s. Is 5:21
done what is good in Your s." Is 38:3
precious in My s and honored, Is 43:4
am honored in the s of the LORD, Is 49:5
holy arm in the s of all the Is 52:10
was evil in My s and chose what Is 65:12
forgotten and hidden from My s. Is 65:16
is evil in My s and chose what I Is 66:4
have done what is evil in My s." Jr 7:30
guilt is not hidden from My s. Jr 16:17
is evil in My s by not listening Jr 18:10
did this⌋ in the s of my cousin Jr 32:12
I instructed Baruch in their s, Jr 32:13
but what is evil in My s! Jr 32:30
⌊Do this⌋ in the s of the Judean Jr 43:9
in the LORD's s just as Jr 52:2
human excrement in their s." Ezk 4:12
you in the s of the nations. Ezk 5:8
in the s of everyone who passes Ezk 5:14
exile in their s during the day. Ezk 12:3
go out in their s like those Ezk 12:4
them⌋ on my shoulder in their s. Ezk 12:7
you in the s of many women. Ezk 16:41
in whose s I had made Myself Ezk 20:9
nations in whose s I had brought Ezk 20:14
nations in whose s I brought Ezk 20:22
you in the s of the nations. Ezk 20:41
in the s of the nations. Ezk 22:16
the s of them she lusted after Ezk 23:16
the ground in the s of everyone Ezk 28:18
them in the s of the nations, Ezk 28:25
holiness through you in their s. Ezk 36:23
desolate in the s of everyone Ezk 36:34
holy through you in their s. Ezk 38:16
Myself in the s of many nations. Ezk 38:23
them in the s of many nations. Ezk 39:27
down in their s so that they may Ezk 43:11

shame in the s of her lovers, Hs 2:10
from My s on the sea floor, Am 9:3
have been banished from Your s, Jnh 2:4
evil is good in the LORD's s, Mal 2:17
Both were righteous in God's s, Lk 1:6
great in the s of the Lord and Lk 1:15
and recovery of s to the blind, Lk 4:18
and He granted s to many blind Lk 7:21
The blind receive their s, Lk 7:22
of them is forgotten in God's s. Lk 12:6
against heaven and in your s. Lk 15:18
against heaven and in your s. Lk 15:21
yourselves in the s of others, Lk 16:15
people is revolting in God's s. Lk 16:15
"Receive your s!" Jesus told him. Lk 18:42
but He disappeared from their s. Lk 24:31
and washed I received my s." Jn 9:11
asked him how he received his s. Jn 9:15
he was blind and received s— Jn 9:18
the one who had received his s. Jn 9:18
received Him out of their s. Ac 1:9
right in the s of God ⌊for us⌋ Ac 4:19
and wisdom in the s of Pharaoh, Ac 7:10
saw it, he was amazed at the s. Ac 7:31
favor in God's s and asked that Ac 7:46
on him so he may regain his s." Ac 9:12
may regain your s and be filled Ac 9:17
his eyes, and he regained his s. Ac 9:18
have been remembered in God's s. Ac 10:31
Brother Saul, regain your s.' Ac 22:13
justified in His s by the works Rm 3:20
in God's s. As it is written: I Rm 4:17
but in God's s we commend 2Co 4:2
for we walk by faith, not by s— 2Co 5:7
plain to you in the s of God. 2Co 7:12
in the s of God we are speaking 2Co 12:19
be holy and blameless in His s. Eph 1:4
in us what is pleasing in His s, Heb 13:21
do what is pleasing in His s. 1Jn 3:22
and sulfur in the s of the holy Rv 14:10
angels and in the s of the Lamb, Rv 14:10

SIGHTED *(2)*

After we s Cyprus, leaving it on Ac 21:3
the land, but s a bay with a Ac 27:39

SIGHTS *(2)*

heart and in the s of your eyes; Ec 11:9
be terrifying s and great signs Lk 21:11

SIGN *(98)*

This is the s of the covenant I Gn 9:12
it will be a s of the covenant Gn 9:13
This is the s of the covenant Gn 9:17
to serve as a s of the covenant Gn 17:11
this will be the s to you that I Ex 3:12
to the evidence of the first s, Ex 4:8
the evidence of the second s. Ex 4:8
s will take place tomorrow." Ex 8:23
it serve as a s for you on your Ex 13:9
let it be a s on your hand and Ex 13:16
for it is a s between Me and you Ex 31:13
It is a s forever between Me and Ex 31:17
will be a s to the Israelites. Nm 16:38
be kept as a s for the rebels, Nm 17:10
They ⌊serve as⌋ a warning s. Nm 26:10
Bind them as a s on your hand Dt 6:8
bind them as a s on your hands, Dt 11:18
and proclaims a s or wonder to Dt 13:1
and that s or wonder he has Dt 13:2
curses will be a s and a wonder Dt 28:46
to you. Give me a sure s Jos 2:12
that this will be a s among you. Jos 4:6
me a s that You are speaking Jdg 6:17
will be the s that will come 1Sm 2:34
to us—that will be our s." 1Sm 14:10
He gave a s that day. He said, 1Kg 13:3
This is the s that the LORD has 1Kg 13:3
according to the s that the man 1Kg 13:5
were looking for a s of hope, 1Kg 20:33
there was no sound or s of life, 2Kg 4:31
This will be the s for you: 2Kg 19:29
What is the s that the LORD will 2Kg 20:8
This is the s to you from the 2Kg 20:9
him and gave him a miraculous s. 2Ch 32:24
the miraculous s that happened 2Ch 32:31
become an ominous s to many, Ps 71:7
Show me a s of Your goodness; Ps 86:17
Ask for a s from the LORD your Is 7:11
Lord Himself will give you a s: Is 7:14
will be a s and witness to the Is 19:20

years as a **s** and omen against Is 20:3
This will be the **s** for you: Is 37:30
This is the **s** to you from the Is 38:7
What is the **s** that I will go up Is 38:22
an everlasting **s** that will not Is 55:13
I will establish a **s** among them, Is 66:19
This will be a **s** to you'— Jr 44:29
This will be a **s** for the house Ezk 4:3
I have made you a **s** to the house Ezk 12:6
say: I am a **s** for you. Just as Ezk 12:11
and make him a **s** and a proverb; Ezk 14:8
to serve as a **s** between Me and Ezk 20:12
they will be a **s** between Me and Ezk 20:20
Now Ezekiel will be a **s** for you. Ezk 24:24
So you will be a **s** for them, Ezk 24:27
the edict and **s** the document so Dn 6:8
Didn't you **s** an edict that for Dn 6:12
men are a **s** that I am about Zch 3:8
we want to see a **s** from You." Mt 12:38
generation demands a **s**, Mt 12:39
but no **s** will be given to it Mt 12:39
it except the **s** of the prophet Mt 12:39
to show them a **s** from heaven. Mt 16:1
adulterous generation wants a **s**, Mt 16:4
but no **s** will be given to it Mt 16:4
to it except the **s** of Jonah." Mt 16:4
And what is the **s** of Your coming Mt 24:3
Then the **s** of the Son of Man Mt 24:30
His betrayer had given them a **s**: Mt 26:48
of Him a **s** from heaven to Mk 8:11
does this generation demand a **s**? Mk 8:12
No **s** will be given to this Mk 8:12
will be the **s** when all these Mk 13:4
This will be the **s** for you: Lk 2:12
Israel and to be a **s** that will Lk 2:34
of Him a **s** from heaven. Lk 11:16
It demands a **s**, but no sign will Lk 11:29
but no **s** will be given to it Lk 11:29
to it except the **s** of Jonah. Lk 11:29
Jonah became a **s** to the people Lk 11:30
what will be the **s** when these Lk 21:7
this first **s** in Cana of Galilee Jn 2:11
What **s** ⌊of authority⌋ will You Jn 2:18
was the second **s** Jesus performed Jn 4:54
people saw the **s** He had done, Jn 6:14
What **s** then are You going to do Jn 6:30
never did a **s**, but everything Jn 10:41
they heard He had done this **s**. Jn 12:18
also had a **s** lettered and put Jn 19:19
Many of the Jews read this **s**, Jn 19:20
For an obvious **s**, evident to all Ac 4:16
on whom this **s** of healing had Ac 4:22
received the **s** of circumcision Rm 4:11
languages is intended as a **s**, 1Co 14:22
This is a **s** in every letter; 2Th 3:17
A great **s** appeared in heaven: Rv 12:1
Then another **s** appeared in Rv 12:3
and awe-inspiring **s** in heaven: Rv 15:1

SIGNAL *(12)*

the holy objects and **s** trumpets. Nm 31:6
had a prearranged **s** with the men Jdg 20:38
You have given a **s** flag to those Ps 60:4
He raises a **s** flag for the Is 5:26
be afraid because of the **s** flag. Is 31:9
Lift up a **s** flag toward Zion. Jr 4:6
must I see the **s** flag and hear Jr 4:21
raise a smoke **s** over Jr 6:1
proclaim and raise up a **s** flag; Jr 50:2
Raise up a **s** flag against the Jr 51:12
Raise a **s** flag in the land; Jr 51:27
His betrayer had given them a **s**. Mk 14:44

SIGNALED *(1)*

So they **s** to their partners in Lk 5:7

SIGNALS *(1)*

winks his eyes, **s** with his feet, Pr 6:13

SIGNATURE *(2)*

Here is my **s**; let the Almighty Jb 31:35
serve as His **s** to all mankind, Jb 37:7

SIGNED *(3)*

So King Darius **s** the document. Dn 6:9
that the document had been **s**, Dn 6:10
the edict you **s**, for he prays Dn 6:13

SIGNET *(14)*

Your **s** ring, your cord Gn 38:18
Whose **s** ring, cord, and staff Gn 38:25
removed his **s** ring from his hand Gn 41:42
king removed his **s** ring from his Est 3:10
sealed with the royal **s** ring. Est 3:12
king removed his **s** ring he had Est 8:2
seal it with the royal **s** ring. Est 8:8
with the royal **s** ring cannot be Est 8:8
edicts⌋ with the royal **s** ring. Est 8:10
s rings, nose rings, Is 3:21
were a **s** ring on My right hand, Jr 22:24
it with his own **s** ring and with Dn 6:17
ring and with the **s** rings of his Dn 6:17
and make you like My **s** ring, Hg 2:23

SIGNIFICANCE *(2)*

not lose their **s** in Jewish life Est 9:28
not grasp ⌊the **s** of⌋ Your Ps 106:7

SIGNIFICANT *(1)*

the sun, and it is **s** to me: Ec 9:13

SIGNIFICANTLY *(1)*

days the waters had decreased **s**. Gn 8:3

SIGNIFIED *(1)*

He sent it and **s** it through His Rv 1:1

SIGNIFY *(2)*

He said this to **s** what kind of Jn 12:33
said this to **s** by what kind of Jn 21:19

SIGNIFYING *(1)*

be fulfilled **s** what sort of Jn 18:32

SIGNING *(1)*

witnesses who were **s** the Jr 32:12

SIGNPOST *(1)*

And make a **s** at the fork in the Ezk 21:19

SIGNPOSTS *(1)*

establish **s**! Keep the highway Jr 31:21

SIGNS *(71)*

will serve as **s** for festivals Gn 1:14
even these two **s** or listen to Ex 4:9
you will perform the **s** with." Ex 4:17
about all the **s** He had commanded Ex 4:28
performed the **s** before the Ex 4:30
and multiply My **s** and wonders Ex 7:3
these miraculous **s** of Mine among Ex 10:1
miraculous **s** among them, Ex 10:2
despite all the **s** I have Nm 14:11
glory and the **s** I performed in Nm 14:22
by trials, **s**, wonders, and war Dt 4:34
and devastating **s** and wonders on Dt 6:22
that you saw, the **s** and wonders, Dt 7:19
His **s** and the works He did in Dt 11:3
power, and with **s** and wonders. Dt 26:8
and those great **s** and wonders. Dt 29:3
for all the **s** and wonders the Dt 34:11
these great **s** before our eyes. Jos 24:17
When these **s** have happened to 1Sm 10:7
and all the **s** came about that 1Sm 10:9
You performed **s** and wonders Neh 9:10
far away are awed by Your **s**; Ps 65:8
They set up their emblems as **s**. Ps 74:4
We don't see any **s** for us. Ps 74:9
miraculous **s** in Egypt and His Ps 78:43
His miraculous **s** among them, Ps 105:27
He sent **s** and wonders against Ps 135:9
has given me to be **s** and wonders Is 8:18
terrified by **s** in the heavens, Jr 10:2
You performed **s** and wonders in Jr 32:20
out of Egypt with **s** and wonders, Jr 32:21
He performs **s** and wonders in the Dn 6:27
can't read the **s** of the times. Mt 16:3
perform great **s** and wonders to Mt 24:24
and will perform **s** and wonders Mk 13:22
And these **s** will accompany those Mk 16:17
the word by the accompanying **s**. Mk 16:20
He kept making **s** to them and Lk 1:22
sights and great **s** from heaven. Lk 21:11
Then there will be **s** in the sun, Lk 21:25
they saw the **s** He was doing. Jn 2:23
perform these **s** You do unless Jn 3:2
you ⌊people⌋ see **s** and wonders, Jn 4:48
they saw the **s** that He was Jn 6:2
not because you saw the **s**, Jn 6:26
perform more **s** than this man has Jn 7:31
a sinful man perform such **s**?" Jn 9:16
do since this man does many **s**? Jn 11:47
so many **s** in their presence Jn 12:37
many other **s** in the presence Jn 20:30
heaven above and **s** on the earth Ac 2:19
and **s** that God did among you Ac 2:22
many wonders and **s** were being Ac 2:43
for healing, **s**, and wonders to Ac 4:30
Many **s** and wonders were being Ac 5:12
wonders and **s** among the people Ac 6:8
wonders and **s** in the land of Ac 7:36
and saw the **s** he was performing Ac 8:6
he observed the **s** and great Ac 8:13
granting that **s** and wonders be Ac 14:3
all the **s** and wonders God Ac 15:12
of miraculous **s** and wonders, Rm 15:19
Jews ask for **s** and the Greeks 1Co 1:22
The **s** of an apostle were 2Co 12:12
not only **s** but also wonders and 2Co 12:12
false miracles, **s**, and wonders, 2Th 2:9
also testified by **s** and wonders, Heb 2:4
performs great **s**, even causing Rv 13:13
because of the **s** that he is Rv 13:14
spirits of demons performing **s**, Rv 16:14
had performed **s** on his authority Rv 19:20

SIHON *(36)*

to say to **S** king of the Amorites Nm 21:21
S would not let Israel travel Nm 21:23
was the city of **S** king of the Nm 21:26
let the city of **S** be restored. Nm 21:27
a flame from the city of **S**. Nm 21:28
captivity to **S** the Amorite king Nm 21:29
him as you did to **S** king of the Nm 21:34
the kingdom of **S** king of the Nm 32:33
he had defeated **S** king of the Dt 1:4
I have handed **S** the Amorite, Dt 2:24
of peace to **S** king of Heshbon Dt 2:26
But **S** king of Heshbon would not Dt 2:30
begun to give **S** and his land to Dt 2:31
So **S** and his whole army came out Dt 2:32
him as you did to **S** king of the Dt 3:2
we had done to **S** king of Heshbon Dt 3:6
in the land of **S** king of the Dt 4:46
S king of Heshbon and Og king of Dt 29:7
with them as He did **S** and Og, Dt 31:4
and what you did to **S** and Og, Jos 2:10
S king of Heshbon and Og king of Jos 9:10
S king of the Amorites lived in Jos 12:2
of Gilead to the border of **S**, Jos 12:5
all the cities of **S** king of the Jos 13:10
all the kingdom of **S** king of the Jos 13:21
princes of **S** who lived in the Jos 13:21
the kingdom of **S** king of Heshbon Jos 13:27
sent messengers to **S** king of the Jdg 11:19
but **S** did not trust Israel. Jdg 11:20
S gathered all his people, Jdg 11:20
handed over **S** and all his people Jdg 11:21
the country of **S** king of the 1Kg 4:19
of the land of **S** king of Heshbon Neh 9:22
S king of the Amorites, Og king Ps 135:11
S king of the Amorites His love Ps 136:19
and a flame from within **S**. Jr 48:45

SILAS *(13)*

Barsabbas, and **S**, both leading Ac 15:22
we have sent Judas and **S**, Ac 15:27
Both Judas and **S**, who were also Ac 15:32
Then Paul chose **S** and departed, Ac 15:40
seized Paul and **S** and dragged Ac 16:19
midnight Paul and **S** were praying Ac 16:25
trembling before Paul and **S**. Ac 16:29
that Paul and **S** were Roman Ac 16:38
persuaded and joined Paul and **S**, Ac 17:4
sent Paul and **S** off to Beroea. Ac 17:10
but **S** and Timothy stayed on Ac 17:14
instructions for **S** and Timothy Ac 17:15
S and Timothy came down from Ac 18:5

SILENCE *(16)*

king called for **s**, and all his Jdg 3:19
your babbling put others to **s**, Jb 11:3
to **s** the enemy and the avenger. Ps 8:2
You **s** the roar of the seas, Ps 65:7
soon rest in the **s** ⌊of death⌋. Ps 94:17
into the **s** ⌊of death⌋. Ps 115:17
sit in **s** and go into darkness. Is 47:5
He will **s** her mighty voice. Jr 51:55
Zion sit on the ground in **s**. Lm 2:10
he will say, "**S**, because Am 6:10
bodies, thrown everywhere! **S**!" Am 8:3
wind, and said to the sea, "**S**! Mk 4:39
should learn in **s** with full 1Tm 2:11
It is necessary to **s** them; Ti 1:11
s the ignorance of foolish 1Pt 2:15
there was **s** in heaven for about Rv 8:1

SILENCED *(8)*

the wicked are **s** in darkness, 1Sm 2:9
You madmen will also be **s**; Jr 48:2

warriors will be s in that day. Jr 49:26
warriors will be s in that day. Jr 50:30
Don't be s by her guilt. Jr 51:6
s in the middle of the sea? Ezk 27:32
for all the merchants will be s; Zph 1:11
that He had s the Sadducees, Mt 22:34

SILENT *(68)*

he remained s until they Gn 34:5
But Aaron remained s. Lv 10:3
all Israel, "Be s, Israel, and Dt 27:9
If we are s and wait until 2Kg 7:9
But the people kept s; 2Kg 18:36
They remained s and could not Neh 5:8
If you keep s at this time, Est 4:14
slaves, I would have kept s. Est 7:4
Teach me, and I will be s. Jb 6:24
If so, I will be s and die. Jb 13:19
so I grew s and would not go Jb 31:34
to wait now that they are s, Jb 32:16
But when God is s, who can Jb 34:29
I cannot be s about his limbs, Jb 41:12
If You remain s to me, I will be Ps 28:1
I can sing to You and not be s. Ps 30:12
let them be s in Sheol. Ps 31:17
When I kept s, my bones became Ps 32:3
LORD; do not be s. Lord, do not Ps 35:22
Be s before the LORD and wait Ps 37:7
I kept s, even from ⌊speaking⌋ Ps 39:2
do not be s at my tears. Ps 39:12
He will not be s! Devouring fire Ps 50:3
done these things, and I kept s; Ps 50:21
do not keep s. Do not be deaf Ps 83:1
God of my praise, do not be s. Ps 109:1
man with understanding keeps s. Pr 11:12
considered wise when he keeps s, Pr 17:28
a time to be s and a time to Ec 3:7
have fallen s over your summer Is 16:9
But they were s and did not Is 36:21
Be s before Me, islands! Is 41:1
I have kept s from ages past; Is 42:14
and like a sheep s before her Is 53:7
I not kept s for such a long Is 57:11
will not keep s because of Zion Is 62:1
will never be s, day or night. Is 62:6
Will You keep s and afflict Is 64:12
I will not keep s, but I will Is 65:6
I cannot be s. For you, my soul Jr 4:19
will become s, a remnant of Jr 47:5
your scabbard; be still; be s! Jr 47:6
Let him sit alone and be s, Lm 3:28
Then I will be s and no longer Ezk 16:42
will keep s at such a time, Am 5:13
Why are You s while one who is Hab 1:13
on earth be s in His presence. Hab 2:20
Be s in the presence of the Lord Zph 1:7
all people be s before the LORD Zch 2:13
But Jesus kept s. Then the high Mt 26:63
or to kill?" But they were s. Mk 3:4
But they were s, because on the Mk 9:34
But He kept s and did not answer Mk 14:61
You will become s and unable to Lk 1:20
They kept s, and in those days Lk 9:36
they kept s. He took the man, Lk 14:4
were to keep s, the stones would Lk 19:40
at His answer, they became s. Lk 20:26
and as a lamb is s before its Ac 8:32
they heard this they became s. Ac 11:18
to them with his hand to be s, Ac 12:17
assembly fell s and listened to Ac 15:12
keep on speaking and don't be s. Ac 18:9
secret kept s for long ages, Rm 16:25
should keep s in the church 1Co 14:28
the first prophet should be s. 1Co 14:30
should be s in the churches 1Co 14:34
instead, she is to be s. 1Tm 2:12

SILENTLY *(3)*

while the man s watched her to Gn 24:21
a hammer, and went s to Sisera. Jdg 4:21
waiting s for my advice. Jb 29:21

SILK *(3)*

linen and covered you with s. Ezk 16:10
fine linen, s, and embroidered Ezk 16:13
linen, purple, s, and scarlet; Rv 18:12

SILL *(1)*

sitting on a window s and sank Ac 20:9

SILLA *(1)*

the road that⌋ goes down to S. 2Kg 12:20

SILLY *(2)*

So Ephraim has become like a s, Hs 7:11
do with irreverent and s myths. 1Tm 4:7

SILOAM *(3)*

that the tower in S fell on and Lk 13:4
in the pool of S" (which means Jn 9:7
and told me, 'Go to S and wash.' Jn 9:11

SILVANUS *(4)*

us—by me and S and Timothy— 2Co 1:19
Paul, S, and Timothy: 1Th 1:1
Paul, S, and Timothy: 2Th 1:1
Through S, whom I consider a 1Pt 5:12

SILVER *(336)*

rich in livestock, s, and gold. Gn 13:2
your brother 1,000 pieces of s. Gn 20:16
Land worth 400 shekels of s— Gn 23:15
out to Ephron the s that he had Gn 23:16
400 shekels of s at the current Gn 23:16
and cattle, s and gold, male Gn 24:35
out objects of s and gold, Gn 24:53
for 20 pieces of s to the Gn 37:28
my cup, the s one, at the top Gn 44:2
we steal gold and s from your Gn 44:8
300 pieces of s and five changes Gn 45:22
her house for s and gold jewelry Ex 3:22
for gold and s jewelry." Ex 11:2
Egyptians for s and gold jewelry Ex 12:35
not make gods of s to rival Me; Ex 20:23
30 shekels of s to the slave's Ex 21:32
pay an amount in s equal to the Ex 22:17
from them: gold, s, and bronze; Ex 25:3
and make 40 s bases under the 20 Ex 26:19
along with their 40 s bases, Ex 26:21
eight planks with their s bases: Ex 26:25
and that stand⌋ on four s bases. Ex 26:32
bands of the posts must be s Ex 27:10
bands of the posts must be s. Ex 27:11
be banded with s and have silver Ex 27:17
silver and have s hooks and Ex 27:17
works in gold, s, and bronze, Ex 31:4
offering: gold, s, and bronze; Ex 35:5
contribution of s or bronze Ex 35:24
works in gold, s, and bronze, Ex 35:32
and he made 40 s bases to put Ex 36:24
with their 40 s bases, two bases Ex 36:26
planks with their 16 s bases, Ex 36:30
And he cast four s bases for the Ex 36:36
and bands of the posts were s. Ex 38:10
and bands of the posts were s. Ex 38:11
and bands of the posts were s. Ex 38:12
and bands of the posts were s; Ex 38:17
for the tops of the posts was s. Ex 38:17
courtyard were banded with s. Ex 38:17
hooks were s, and the bands Ex 38:19
plating of their tops were s. Ex 38:19
s from those of the community Ex 38:25
7,500 pounds of s ⌊used⌋ to cast Ex 38:27
by your valuation in s shekels, Lv 5:15
to lend him your s with interest Lv 25:37
valuation is 50 s shekels Lv 27:3
for a male is five s shekels, Lv 27:6
valuation is three shekels of s. Lv 27:6
at the rate of 50 s shekels for Lv 27:16
offering was one s dish weighing Nm 7:13
pounds and one s basin weighing Nm 7:13
he presented one s dish weighing Nm 7:19
pounds and one s basin weighing Nm 7:19
offering was one s dish weighing Nm 7:25
pounds and one s basin weighing Nm 7:25
offering was one s dish weighing Nm 7:31
pounds and one s basin weighing Nm 7:31
offering was one s dish weighing Nm 7:37
pounds and one s basin weighing Nm 7:37
offering was one s dish weighing Nm 7:43
pounds and one s basin weighing Nm 7:43
offering was one s dish weighing Nm 7:49
pounds and one s basin weighing Nm 7:49
offering was one s dish weighing Nm 7:55
pounds and one s basin weighing Nm 7:55
offering was one s dish weighing Nm 7:61
pounds and one s basin weighing Nm 7:61
offering was one s dish weighing Nm 7:67
pounds and one s basin weighing Nm 7:67
offering was one s dish weighing Nm 7:73
pounds and one s basin weighing Nm 7:73
offering was one s dish weighing Nm 7:79
pounds and one s basin weighing Nm 7:79
12 s dishes, 12 silver basins, Nm 7:84
dishes, 12 s basins, and 12 Nm 7:84
Each s dish ⌊weighed⌋ three and Nm 7:85
weight⌋ of the s articles was 60 Nm 7:85
trumpets of hammered s to summon Nm 10:2
shekels of s by the standard Nm 18:16
me his house full of s and gold, Nm 22:18
me his house full of s and gold, Nm 24:13
Only the gold, s, bronze, iron, Nm 31:22
purchase food from them with s, Dt 2:6
in exchange for s so we may eat, Dt 2:28
us water for s so we may drink. Dt 2:28
Don't covet the s and gold on Dt 7:25
and your s and gold multiply, Dt 8:13
large amounts of s and gold for Dt 17:17
also fine him 100 s ⌊shekels⌋ Dt 22:19
woman's father 50 s ⌊shekels⌋, Dt 22:29
of wood, stone, s, and gold, Dt 29:17
For all the s and gold, and the Jos 6:19
but they put the s and gold and Jos 6:24
from Babylon, 200 s shekels, and Jos 7:21
son of Zerah, the s, the cloak, Jos 7:24
of cattle, and s, gold, bronze, Jos 22:8
but they took no spoil of s. Jdg 5:19
70 pieces of s from the temple Jdg 9:4
give you 1,100 pieces of s." Jdg 16:5
pieces of s taken from you, Jdg 17:2
here, I have the s with me. Jdg 17:2
1,100 pieces of s to his mother, Jdg 17:3
consecrate the s to the LORD for Jdg 17:3
a carved image overlaid with s." Jdg 17:3
he returned the s to his mother, Jdg 17:4
five pounds of s and gave it to Jdg 17:4
a carved image overlaid with s, Jdg 17:4
you four ounces of s a year, Jdg 17:10
overlaid with s in these houses? Jdg 18:14
carved image overlaid with s, Jdg 18:17
carved image overlaid with s, Jdg 18:18
for a piece of s or a loaf of 1Sm 2:36
Here, I have a piece of s. 1Sm 9:8
had items of s, gold, and bronze 2Sm 8:10
along with the s and gold he had 2Sm 8:11
given you 10 s pieces and a belt 2Sm 18:11
of 1,000 pieces of s in my hand, 2Sm 18:12
and the oxen for 50 ounces of s. 2Sm 24:24
father David—the s, the gold, 1Kg 7:51
There was no s, since it was 1Kg 10:21
bearing gold, s, ivory, apes, 1Kg 10:22
items of s and gold, clothing, 1Kg 10:25
The king made s as common in 1Kg 10:27
from Egypt for 15 pounds ⌊of s⌋, 1Kg 10:29
s, gold, and utensils. 1Kg 15:15
withdrew all the s and gold that 1Kg 15:18
sent you a gift of s and gold. 1Kg 15:19
from Shemer for 150 pounds of s, 1Kg 16:24
'Your s and your gold are mine! 1Kg 20:3
Your s, your gold, your wives, 1Kg 20:5
my children, my s, and my gold, 1Kg 20:7
will weigh out 75 pounds of s.' 1Kg 20:39
I will give you its value in s." 1Kg 21:2
Give me your vineyard for s, 1Kg 21:6
refused to give it to you for s, 1Kg 21:15
took with him 750 pounds of s, 2Kg 5:5
75 pounds of s and two changes 2Kg 5:22
150 pounds of s in two bags with 2Kg 5:23
head ⌊sold for⌋ 80 s ⌊shekels⌋, 2Kg 6:25
⌊sold for⌋ five s ⌊shekels⌋. 2Kg 6:25
Then they picked up the s, 2Kg 7:8
However, no s bowls, wick 2Kg 12:13
of gold or s were made for 2Kg 12:13
all the gold and s and all the 2Kg 14:14
75,000 pounds of s so that Pul 2Kg 15:19
exacted 20 ounces of s from each 2Kg 15:20
also took the s and gold found 2Kg 16:8
Judah 11 tons of s and one ton 2Kg 18:14
gave ⌊him⌋ all the s found in 2Kg 18:15
house—the s, the gold, 2Kg 20:13
7,500 pounds of s and 75 pounds 2Kg 23:33
gave the s and the gold to 2Kg 23:35
He exacted the s and the gold 2Kg 23:35
basins—whatever was gold or s. 2Kg 25:15
of items of gold, s, and bronze. 1Ch 18:10
along with the s and gold he had 1Ch 18:11
sent 38 tons of s to hire 1Ch 19:6
37,750 tons of s, and bronze and 1Ch 22:14
in gold, s, bronze, and iron— 1Ch 22:16
weight of all the s articles for 1Ch 28:14
weight of each s lampstand and 1Ch 28:15
and the s for the silver 1Ch 28:16

and the silver for the s tables; 1Ch 28:16
the weight of each s bowl; 1Ch 28:17
articles⌋, s for the silver, 1Ch 29:2
silver for the s, bronze for the 1Ch 29:2
gold and s for the house of my 1Ch 29:3
tons of refined s for overlaying 1Ch 29:4
work⌋ and s for the silver, 1Ch 29:5
work⌋ and the silver for the s, 1Ch 29:5
375 tons of s, 675 tons of 1Ch 29:7
The king made s and gold as 2Ch 1:15
15 pounds ⌊of s⌋ and a horse for 2Ch 1:17
work with gold, s, bronze, and 2Ch 2:7
work with gold, s, bronze, iron, 2Ch 2:14
David—the s, the gold, and all 2Ch 5:1
brought gold and s to Solomon. 2Ch 9:14
There was no s, since it was 2Ch 9:20
bearing gold, s, ivory, apes, 2Ch 9:21
gift—items of s and gold, 2Ch 9:24
The king made s as common in 2Ch 9:27
s, gold, and utensils. 2Ch 15:18
Asa brought out the s and gold 2Ch 16:2
I have sent you s and gold. 2Ch 16:3
brought gifts and s as tribute 2Ch 17:11
had given them many gifts of s, 2Ch 21:3
and articles of gold and s. 2Ch 24:14
7,500 pounds of s he hired 2Ch 25:6
7,500 pounds of s I gave to 2Ch 25:9
all the gold, s, all the 2Ch 25:24
they gave him 7,500 pounds of s, 2Ch 27:5
made himself treasuries for s, 2Ch 32:27
7,500 pounds of s and 75 pounds 2Ch 36:3
the men of that region with s, Ezr 1:4
supported them with s articles, Ezr 1:6
basins, 1,000 s basins, 29 Ezr 1:9
silver basins, 29 s knives, Ezr 1:9
410 various s bowls, and 1,000 Ezr 1:10
The gold and s articles totaled Ezr 1:11
6,250 pounds of s, and 100 Ezr 2:69
the gold and s articles of God's Ezr 5:14
The gold and s articles of God's Ezr 6:5
to bring the s and gold the king Ezr 7:15
and all the s and gold you Ezr 7:16
with the rest of the s and gold, Ezr 7:18
7,500 pounds of s, 500 bushels Ezr 7:22
I weighed out to them the s, Ezr 8:25
out to them 24 tons of s, Ezr 8:26
s articles weighing 7,500 pounds, Ezr 8:26
The s and gold are a freewill Ezr 8:28
Levites took charge of the s, Ezr 8:30
the fourth day the s, the gold, Ezr 8:33
them, as well as a pound of s. Neh 5:15
drachmas and 2,200 s minas to Neh 7:71
drachmas, 2,000 s minas, and 67 Neh 7:72
of an ounce of s yearly for Neh 10:32
linen cords to s rods on marble Est 1:6
Gold and s couches ⌊were Est 1:6
pay 375 tons of s to the Est 3:9
who filled their houses with s. Jb 3:15
be your gold and your finest s. Jb 22:25
Though he piles up s like dust Jb 27:16
innocent will divide up his s. Jb 27:17
a mine for s and a place where Jb 28:1
and s cannot be weighed out for Jb 28:15
like s refined in an earthen Ps 12:6
You refined us as s is refined. Ps 66:10
of a dove are covered with s, Ps 68:13
underfoot those with bars of s. Ps 68:30
Israel out with s and gold, Ps 105:37
Their idols are s and gold, Ps 115:4
thousands of gold and s pieces. Ps 119:72
the nations are of s and gold, Ps 135:15
seek it like s and search for Pr 2:4
she is more profitable than s, Pr 3:14
my instruction instead of s, Pr 8:10
and my harvest than pure s. Pr 8:19
of the righteous is pure s; Pr 10:20
it is preferable to s. Pr 16:16
crucible is for s and a smelter Pr 17:3
favor is better than s and gold. Pr 22:1
impurities from s, and a vessel Pr 25:4
like golden apples on a s tray. Pr 25:11
S is ⌊tested⌋ in a crucible, Pr 27:21
I also amassed s and gold for Ec 2:8
before the s cord is snapped, Ec 12:6
for you, accented with s. Sg 1:11
its posts of s, its back of gold Sg 3:10
we will build a s parapet on it. Sg 8:9
for his fruit 1,000 pieces of s. Sg 8:11

Your s has become dross, your Is 1:22
land is full of s and gold, Is 2:7
throw their s and gold idols, Is 2:20
1,000 pieces of s, will become Is 7:23
bought off with s and who have Is 13:17
will reject the s and gold idols Is 31:7
house—the s, the gold, Is 39:2
gold and makes s welds ⌊for it⌋? Is 40:19
bought Me aromatic cane with s, Is 43:24
and weigh out s on a scales— Is 46:6
have refined you, but not as s; Is 48:10
you will be redeemed without s." Is 52:3
their s and gold with them, Is 60:9
I will bring s instead of iron, Is 60:17
They are called rejected s, Jr 6:30
He decorates it with s and gold. Jr 10:4
Beaten s is brought from Jr 10:9
him the money—17 shekels of s. Jr 32:9
weighed out the s on a scale. Jr 32:10
Buy the field with s and call in Jr 32:25
Fields will be purchased with s, Jr 32:44
bowls—whatever was gold or s. Jr 52:19
throw their s into the streets Ezk 7:19
Their s and gold will be unable Ezk 7:19
were adorned with gold and s, Ezk 16:13
the gold and s I had given you, Ezk 16:17
they are the dross of s. Ezk 22:18
as one gathers s, copper, iron, Ezk 22:20
As s is melted inside a furnace, Ezk 22:22
They exchanged s, iron, tin, and Ezk 27:12
acquired gold and s for your Ezk 28:4
to make off with s and gold, Ezk 38:13
its chest and arms were s, Dn 2:32
the bronze, the s, and the gold Dn 2:35
bronze, fired clay, s, and gold. Dn 2:45
in the gold and s vessels that Dn 5:2
their gods made of gold and s, Dn 5:4
the gods made of s and gold, Dn 5:23
precious articles of s and gold. Dn 11:8
with gold, s, precious stones Dn 11:38
of gold and s and over all Dn 11:43
I lavished s and gold on her, Hs 2:8
15 shekels of s and five bushels Hs 3:2
They make their s and gold into Hs 8:4
possession of their precious s; Hs 9:6
skillfully made from their s, Hs 13:2
For you took My s and gold and Jl 3:5
person for s and a needy person Am 2:6
the poor with s and the needy Am 8:6
Plunder the s! Plunder the gold! Nah 2:9
may be plated with gold and s, Hab 2:19
loaded with s will be cut off. Zph 1:11
Their s and their gold will not Zph 1:18
"The s and gold belong to Me"— Hg 2:8
Take s and gold, make crowns and Zch 6:11
has heaped up s like dust and Zch 9:3
my wages, 30 pieces of s. Zch 11:12
the 30 pieces of s and threw it Zch 11:13
refine them as s is refined and Zch 13:9
gold, s, and clothing in great Zch 14:14
a refiner and purifier of s; Mal 3:3
and refine them like gold and s. Mal 3:3
take along gold, s, or copper Mt 10:9
out 30 pieces of s for him. Mt 26:15
the 30 pieces of s to the chief Mt 27:3
So he threw the s into the Mt 27:5
priests took the s and said, Mt 27:6
They took the 30 pieces of s, Mt 27:9
glad and promised to give him s. Mk 14:11
what woman who has 10 s coins, Lk 15:8
I have found the s coin I lost!' Lk 15:9
glad and agreed to give him s. Lk 22:5
I have neither s nor gold, Ac 3:6
for a sum of s from the sons Ac 7:16
May your s be destroyed with Ac 8:20
is like gold or s or stone, Ac 17:29
it to be 50,000 pieces of s. Ac 19:19
who made s shrines of Artemis, Ac 19:24
coveted anyone's s or gold or Ac 20:33
with gold, s, costly stones, 1Co 3:12
are not only gold and s bowls, 2Tm 2:20
your s and gold are corroded, Jms 5:3
things, like s or gold, 1Pt 1:18
idols of gold, s, bronze, stone, Rv 9:20
of gold, s, precious stones, Rv 18:12

SILVER-PLATED *(1)*
defile your s idols and your Is 30:22

SILVERSMITH *(3)*
of silver and gave it to a s. Jdg 17:4
vessel will be produced for a s. Pr 25:4
a s who made silver shrines of Ac 19:24

SIMEON *(40)*
(AKA CEPHAS, NIGER, PETER, SIMON)
So she named him S. Gn 29:33
of Jacob's sons, S and Levi, Gn 34:25
Then Jacob said to S and Levi, Gn 34:30
firstborn), S, Levi, Judah, Gn 35:23
He took S from them and had him Gn 42:24
Joseph is gone and S is gone. Gn 42:36
Then he brought S out to them. Gn 43:23
to me just as Reuben and S do. Gn 48:5
S and Levi are brothers; Gn 49:5
Reuben, S, Levi, and Judah; Ex 1:2
The sons of S: Jemuel, Jamin, Ex 6:15
These are the clans of S. Ex 6:15
son of Zurishaddai from S; Nm 1:6
The descendants of S: Nm 1:22
the tribe of S numbered 59,300 Nm 1:23
The tribe of S will camp next to Nm 2:12
son of Hori from the tribe of S; Nm 13:5
of Ammihud from the tribe of S; Nm 34:20
S, Levi, Judah, Issachar, Joseph, Dt 27:12
The second lot came out for S, Jos 19:1
of Judah, S, and Benjamin. Jos 21:4
the descendants of Judah and S Jos 21:9
Judah said to his brother S, Jdg 1:3
So S went with him. Jdg 1:3
Judah went with his brother S, Jdg 1:17
S, Levi, Judah, Issachar, 1Ch 2:1
these sons of S went with 1Ch 4:42
S who had settled among them, 2Ch 15:9
Ephraim, and S, and as far as 2Ch 34:6
west, will be S—one ⌊portion⌋ Ezk 48:24
Next to the territory of S, Ezk 48:25
one, the gate of S; one, the Ezk 48:33
in Jerusalem whose name was S. Lk 2:25
S took Him up in his arms, Lk 2:28
Then S blessed them and told His Lk 2:34
of S, ⌊son⌋ of Judah, ⌊son⌋ Lk 3:30
S who was called Niger, Ac 13:1
S has reported how God first Ac 15:14
S Peter, a slave and an apostle 2Pt 1:1
12,000 from the tribe of S, Rv 7:7

SIMEON'S *(7)*
S sons: Jemuel, Jamin, Ohad, Gn 46:10
over the division of S tribe, Nm 10:19
S descendants by their clans: Nm 26:12
of the tribe of S descendants by Jos 19:8
inheritance of S descendants was Jos 19:9
So S descendants received an Jos 19:9
S sons: Nemuel, Jamin, Jarib, 1Ch 4:24

SIMEONITE *(2)*
leader of a S ancestral house Nm 25:14
were the S clans, numbering Nm 26:14

SIMEONITES *(5)*
leader of the S is Shelumiel son Nm 2:12
leader of the S, ⌊presented an Nm 7:36
the Judahites, S, and 1Ch 6:65
From the S: 7,100 brave warriors 1Ch 12:25
for the S, Shephatiah son of 1Ch 27:16

SIMILAR *(7)*
devised something s against the 2Sm 14:13
the hall, was of s construction. 1Kg 7:8
design was s to that of chariot 1Kg 7:33
was s to the entrances of the Ezk 42:12
And you do many other s things." Mk 7:13
and anything s, about which I Gl 5:21
a sea of glass, s to crystal. Rv 4:6

SIMON *(70)*
(AKA CEPHAS, PETER, SIMEON)
two brothers, S, who was called Mt 4:18
First, S, who is called Peter, Mt 10:2
S the Zealot, and Judas Iscariot, Mt 10:4
James, Joseph, S, and Judas? Mt 13:55
S Peter answered, "You are the Mt 16:16
responded, "S son of Jonah, you Mt 16:17
first, "What do you think, S? Mt 17:25
in Bethany at the house of S, Mt 26:6
found a Cyrenian man named S. Mt 27:32
of Galilee, He saw S and Andrew, Mk 1:16
they went into S and Andrew's Mk 1:29
S and his companions went Mk 1:36
To S, He gave the name Peter; Mk 3:16
and Thaddaeus; S the Zealot, Mk 3:18

of James, Joses, Judas, and S? Mk 6:3
at the house of S who had a Mk 14:3
"S, are you sleeping?" Mk 14:37
He was S, a Cyrenian, the father Mk 15:21
belonged to S, and asked him to Lk 5:3
He said to S, "Put out into deep Lk 5:4
"Master," S replied, "we've Lk 5:5
When S Peter saw this, he fell Lk 5:8
"Don't be afraid," Jesus told S. Lk 5:10
S, whom He also named Peter, and Lk 6:14
of Alphaeus, and S called the Lk 6:15
replied to him, "S, I have Lk 7:40
S answered, "I suppose the one Lk 7:43
He said to S, "Do you see this Lk 7:44
S, Simon, look out! Satan has Lk 22:31
Simon, S, look out! Satan has Lk 22:31
they seized S, a Cyrenian, who Lk 23:26
raised, and has appeared to S!" Lk 24:34
Andrew, S Peter's brother, was Jn 1:40
his own brother S and told him, Jn 1:41
and he brought ⌊S⌋ to Jesus. Jn 1:42
said, "You are S, son of John. Jn 1:42
Andrew, S Peter's brother, Jn 6:8
S Peter answered, "Lord, who Jn 6:68
to Judas, S Iscariot's son, one Jn 6:71
of Judas, S Iscariot's son, Jn 13:2
He came to S Peter, who asked Jn 13:6
S Peter said to Him, "Lord, not Jn 13:9
S Peter motioned to him to find Jn 13:24
it to Judas, S Iscariot's son. Jn 13:26
"Lord," S Peter said to Him, Jn 13:36
Then S Peter, who had a sword, Jn 18:10
Meanwhile S Peter was following Jn 18:15
Now S Peter was standing and Jn 18:25
So she ran to S Peter and to the Jn 20:2
him, S Peter came also. Jn 20:6
S Peter, Thomas (called "Twin"), Jn 21:2
going fishing," S Peter said to Jn 21:3
When S Peter heard that it was Jn 21:7
So S Peter got up and hauled the Jn 21:11
Jesus asked S Peter, "Simon, son Jn 21:15
Simon Peter, "S, son of John, do Jn 21:15
asked him, "S, son of John, do Jn 21:16
third time, "S, son of John, do Jn 21:17
son of Alphaeus, S the Zealot, Ac 1:13
A man named S had previously Ac 8:9
Then even S himself believed. Ac 8:13
When S saw that the Holy Spirit Ac 8:18
Lord for me," S replied, "so Ac 8:24
on many days in Joppa with S, Ac 9:43
men to Joppa and call for S, Ac 10:5
is lodging with S, a tanner, Ac 10:6
out, asking if S, who was also Ac 10:18
to Joppa and invite S here, Ac 10:32
He is lodging in S the tanner's Ac 10:32
and call for S, who is also Ac 11:13

SIMON'S *(6)*

saw Simon and Andrew, S brother. Mk 1:16
S mother-in-law was lying in bed Mk 1:30
synagogue, He entered S house. Lk 4:38
S mother-in-law was suffering Lk 4:38
sons, who were S partners. Lk 5:10
asked directions to S house, Ac 10:17

SIMPLICITY *(1)*

with gladness and s of heart, Ac 2:46

SIMPLY *(3)*

and drink ⌊s⌋ for yourselves? Zch 7:6
we stopped talking and s said, Ac 21:14
they s kept hearing: Gl 1:23

SIMULTANEOUSLY *(1)*

say "Yes, yes" and "No, no" ⌊s⌋? 2Co 1:17

SIN *(440)*

(See also SIN proper noun.)
s is crouching at the door. Gn 4:7
their s is extremely serious. Gn 18:20
How did I s against you that you Gn 20:9
What is my s, that you have Gn 31:36
a great evil and s against God?" Gn 39:9
transgression and their s— Gn 50:17
Please forgive my s once more Ex 10:17
the children for the fathers' s, Ex 20:5
will fear Him and will not s." Ex 20:20
they will make you s against Me. Ex 23:33
the camp; it is a s offering. Ex 29:14
a bull as a s offering each day Ex 29:36
the blood of the s offering for Ex 30:10
led them into ⌊such⌋ a grave s?" Ex 32:21
You have committed a great s. Ex 32:30
will be able to pay for your s." Ex 32:30
people has committed a great s; Ex 32:31
You would only forgive their s. Ex 32:32
them accountable for their s." Ex 32:34
wrongdoing, rebellion, and s. Ex 34:7
forgive our wrongdoing and s, Ex 34:9
bull as a s offering for the sin Lv 4:3
for the s he has committed Lv 4:3
from the bull of the s offering: Lv 4:8
a young bull as a s offering. Lv 4:14
When the s they have committed Lv 4:14
with the bull in the s offering; Lv 4:20
It is the s offering for the Lv 4:21
about the s he has committed, Lv 4:23
the LORD. It is a s offering. Lv 4:24
blood from the s offering with Lv 4:25
his behalf for that person's s, Lv 4:26
about the s he has committed, Lv 4:28
offering for the s that he has Lv 4:28
the head of the s offering and Lv 4:29
he brings as a s offering is a Lv 4:32
the head of the s offering and Lv 4:33
slaughter it as a s offering at Lv 4:33
the blood of the s offering with Lv 4:34
behalf for the s he has Lv 4:35
confess he has committed that s. Lv 5:5
for the s he has committed to Lv 5:6
from the flock as a s offering. Lv 5:6
on his behalf for his s. Lv 5:6
as restitution for his s— Lv 5:7
as a s offering and the other Lv 5:7
the one for the s offering. Lv 5:8
the blood of the s offering on Lv 5:9
the altar; it is a s offering. Lv 5:9
behalf for the s he has Lv 5:10
flour as an offering for his s. Lv 5:11
on it, for it is a s offering. Lv 5:11
to the LORD; it is a s offering. Lv 5:12
concerning the s he has Lv 5:13
for his s regarding any holy Lv 5:16
like the s offering and the Lv 6:17
is the law of the s offering. Lv 6:25
The s offering is most holy and Lv 6:25
offers it as a s offering is to Lv 6:26
pot in which the s offering is Lv 6:28
But no s offering may be eaten Lv 6:30
offering is like the s offering; Lv 7:7
grain offering, the s offering, Lv 7:37
the bull of the s offering, Lv 8:2
bull near for the s offering, Lv 8:14
of the bull for the s offering. Lv 8:14
young bull for a s offering and Lv 9:2
a male goat for a s offering; Lv 9:3
sacrifice your s offering and Lv 9:7
the calf as a s offering for Lv 9:8
the liver from the s offering on Lv 9:10
for the people's s offering, Lv 9:15
and made a s offering with it as Lv 9:15
sacrificing the s offering, Lv 9:22
the male goat of the s offering, Lv 10:16
didn't you eat the s offering Lv 10:17
presented their s offering and Lv 10:19
had eaten the s offering today, Lv 10:19
a turtledove for a s offering. Lv 12:6
and the other for a s offering. Lv 12:8
area where the s offering and Lv 14:13
for like the s offering, the Lv 14:13
sacrifice the s offering and Lv 14:19
one to be a s offering and the Lv 14:22
as a s offering and the other Lv 14:31
as a s offering and the other Lv 15:15
to sacrifice one as a s offering Lv 15:30
young bull for a s offering and Lv 16:3
goats for a s offering and one Lv 16:5
the bull for his s offering and Lv 16:6
sacrifice it as a s offering. Lv 16:9
the bull for his s offering and Lv 16:11
the bull for his s offering. Lv 16:11
for the people's s offering and Lv 16:15
burn the fat of the s offering Lv 16:25
The bull for the s offering and Lv 16:27
and the goat for the s offering, Lv 16:27
so I am punishing it for its s, Lv 18:25
for the s he has committed Lv 19:22
forgiven for the s he committed. Lv 19:22
one male goat as a s offering, Lv 23:19
bear the consequences of his s. Lv 24:15
waste away because of their s; Lv 26:39
will confess their s and the sin Lv 26:40
sin and the s of their fathers Lv 26:40
pay the penalty for their s, Lv 26:41
pay the penalty for their s, Lv 26:43
commits any s against another, Nm 5:6
to confess the s he has Nm 5:7
that brings s to mind. Nm 5:15
is to offer one as a s offering Nm 6:11
female lamb as a s offering, Nm 6:14
the Nazirite's s offering and Nm 6:16
one male goat for a s offering; Nm 7:16
one male goat for a s offering; Nm 7:22
one male goat for a s offering; Nm 7:28
one male goat for a s offering; Nm 7:34
one male goat for a s offering; Nm 7:40
one male goat for a s offering; Nm 7:46
one male goat for a s offering; Nm 7:52
one male goat for a s offering; Nm 7:58
one male goat for a s offering; Nm 7:64
one male goat for a s offering; Nm 7:70
one male goat for a s offering; Nm 7:76
one male goat for a s offering; Nm 7:82
male goats for the s offering. Nm 7:87
young bull for a s offering. Nm 8:8
Sacrifice one as a s offering Nm 8:12
bear the consequences of his s. Nm 9:13
against us this s we have so Nm 12:11
When you s unintentionally and Nm 15:22
one male goat as a s offering. Nm 15:24
for the s was unintentional. Nm 15:25
and their s offering before the Nm 15:25
LORD for their unintentional s. Nm 15:25
female goat as a s offering. Nm 15:27
be responsible for s against the Nm 18:1
responsible for s involving your Nm 18:1
the grain offering, s offering, Nm 18:9
the ⌊consequences⌋ of their s. Nm 18:23
impurity; it is a s offering. Nm 19:9
ashes of the burnt s offering, Nm 19:17
he died because of his own s, Nm 27:3
to be offered as a s offering to Nm 28:15
male goat for a s offering to Nm 28:22
goat as a s offering to make Nm 29:5
one male goat for a s offering. Nm 29:11
in addition to the s offering of Nm 29:11
one male goat as a s offering. Nm 29:16
one male goat as a s offering. Nm 29:19
one male goat as a s offering. Nm 29:22
one male goat as a s offering. Nm 29:25
one male goat as a s offering. Nm 29:28
one male goat as a s offering. Nm 29:31
one male goat as a s offering. Nm 29:34
one male goat as a s offering. Nm 29:38
will certainly s against the Nm 32:23
sure your s will catch up with Nm 32:23
for the fathers' s to the third Dt 5:9
of all the s you committed, Dt 9:18
and their wickedness and s. Dt 9:27
wrongdoing or s against a person Dt 19:15
and you s against the LORD your Dt 20:18
be counted against you as s. Dt 23:21
not be counted against you as s. Dt 23:22
be put to death for his own s. Dt 24:16
Wasn't the s of Peor, which Jos 22:17
perished because of his s.' " Jos 22:20
the servants' s was very severe 1Sm 2:17
that I will not s against the 1Sm 12:23
s against the LORD by eating 1Sm 14:34
how this s has occurred today. 1Sm 14:38
is like the s of divination, 1Sm 15:23
forgive my s and return with 1Sm 15:25
king should not s against his 1Sm 19:4
why would you s against innocent 1Sm 19:5
The LORD has taken away your s; 2Sm 12:13
and forgive the s of Your people 1Kg 8:34
and forgive the s of Your 1Kg 8:36
When they s against You—for 1Kg 8:46
there is no one who does not s— 1Kg 8:46
This led to s; the people walked 1Kg 12:30
this was the s that caused it to 1Kg 13:34
father and the s he had caused 1Kg 15:26
Jeroboam and the s he had caused 1Kg 15:34
caused My people Israel to s, 1Kg 16:2
because of his s he committed by 1Kg 16:19
and the s he caused Israel 1Kg 16:19
following the s of Jeroboam son 1Kg 16:31
said, "What s have I committed, 1Kg 18:9

anger and caused Israel to s.	1Kg 21:22
who had caused Israel to s.	1Kg 22:52
and the s offering was not	2Kg 12:16
be put to death for his own s."	2Kg 14:6
caused them to commit great s.	2Kg 17:21
has also caused Judah to s,	2Kg 21:11
addition to his s he caused	2Kg 21:16
and the s that he committed,	2Kg 21:17
caused Israel to s, had made.	2Kg 23:15
and forgive the s of Your people	2Ch 6:25
and forgive the s of Your	2Ch 6:27
When they s against You—for	2Ch 6:36
there is no one who does not s—	2Ch 6:36
forgive their s, and heal their	2Ch 7:14
one will die for his own s."	2Ch 25:4
male goats as a s offering for	2Ch 29:21
brought the s offering goats	2Ch 29:23
on the altar for a s offering,	2Ch 29:24
offering and s offering were for	2Ch 29:24
and all his s and unfaithfulness	2Ch 33:19
male goats as a s offering for	Ezr 6:17
12 male goats as a s offering.	Ezr 8:35
guilt or let their s be erased	Neh 4:5
he suggested, s, and get a bad	Neh 6:13
the s offerings to atone for	Neh 10:33
of Israel s in matters like	Neh 13:26
foreign women drew him into s.	Neh 13:26
Job did not s or blame God for	Jb 1:22
Job did not s in what he said	Jb 2:10
not forgive my s and pardon my	Jb 7:21
wrongdoing and search for my s,	Jb 10:6
if I s, You would notice, and	Jb 10:14
to overlook some of your s.	Jb 11:6
to me my transgression and s.	Jb 13:23
but would not take note of my s.	Jb 14:16
my mouth to s by asking for his	Jb 31:30
For he adds rebellion to his s;	Jb 34:37
comes to me, if I do not s?"	Jb 35:3
you s, how does it affect God?	Jb 35:6
angry and do not s; on your bed,	Ps 4:4
that my mouth will not s.	Ps 17:3
forgive my s, for it is great	Ps 25:11
is forgiven, whose s is covered!	Ps 32:1
the LORD does not charge with s,	Ps 32:2
acknowledged my s to You and did	Ps 32:5
You took away the guilt of my s.	Ps 32:5
to discover and hate his s.	Ps 36:2
in my bones because of my s.	Ps 38:3
I am anxious because of my s.	Ps 38:18
that I may not s with my tongue;	Ps 39:1
a man with punishment for s,	Ps 39:11
burnt offering or a s offering.	Ps 40:6
guilt, and cleanse me from my s.	Ps 51:2
and my s is always before me.	Ps 51:3
they escape in spite of such s?	Ps 56:7
me from those who practice s,	Ps 59:2
because of any s or rebellion	Ps 59:3
s of their mouths is the word	Ps 59:12
they continued to s against Him,	Ps 78:17
You covered all their s.	Ps 85:2
the rod, their s with blows.	Ps 89:32
forgives all your s; He heals	Ps 103:3
and were beaten down by their s.	Ps 106:43
let his prayer be counted as s.	Ps 109:7
his mother's s be blotted out.	Ps 109:14
so that I may not s against You.	Ps 119:11
don't let s dominate me.	Ps 119:133
acts with men who commit s.	Ps 141:4
in the ropes of his own s.	Pr 5:22
of the wicked leads to s.	Pr 10:16
many words, s is unavoidable,	Pr 10:19
are thrown down by their own s,	Pr 14:32
but s is a disgrace to any	Pr 14:34
I am cleansed from my s"?	Pr 20:9
and an arrogant heart—is s.	Pr 21:4
scheme is s, and a mocker is	Pr 24:9
yet a man may s for a piece of	Pr 28:21
That's no s," is a companion	Pr 28:24
An evil man is caught by s,	Pr 29:6
like Sodom, they flaunt their s.	Is 3:9
and ⌊pull⌋ s along with cart	Is 5:18
and your s is atoned for.	Is 6:7
This s of yours will never be	Is 22:14
removal of his s will be this:	Is 27:9
My will, piling s on top of sin.	Is 30:1
My will, piling sin on top of s.	Is 30:1
yet He bore the s of many and	Is 53:12
What is our s that we have	Jr 16:10
their guilt and s because they	Jr 16:18
The s of Judah is written with	Jr 17:1
because of the s of your high	Jr 17:3
not blot out their s before You.	Jr 18:23
never again remember their s."	Jr 31:34
act causing Judah to s!	Jr 32:35
forgive their wrongdoing and s."	Jr 36:3
because of his s and the	Ezk 3:20
person that he should not s,	Ezk 3:21
he does not s, he will indeed	Ezk 3:21
in and the s he has committed.	Ezk 18:24
to their s of turning to	Ezk 29:16
repents of his s and does what	Ezk 33:14
the burnt offering, s offering,	Ezk 40:39
grain offerings, s offerings,	Ezk 42:13
from the herd as a s offering to	Ezk 43:19
the bull for the s offering,	Ezk 43:21
male goat as a s offering.	Ezk 43:22
a goat for a s offering each day	Ezk 43:25
the consequences of their s.	Ezk 44:10
the consequences of their s.	Ezk 44:12
he must present his s offering."	Ezk 44:27
grain offering, the s offering,	Ezk 44:29
He will provide the s offerings,	Ezk 45:17
blood from the s offering and	Ezk 45:19
a bull as a s offering on behalf	Ezk 45:22
goat each day for a s offering.	Ezk 45:23
days—the same s offerings,	Ezk 45:25
offering and the s offering,	Ezk 46:20
the full measure of their s,	Dn 8:23
confessing my s and the sin of	Dn 9:20
my sin and the s of my people	Dn 9:20
to put a stop to s, to wipe away	Dn 9:24
They feed on the s of My people;	Hs 4:8
multiplied his altars for s,	Hs 8:11
of Aven, the s of Israel, will	Hs 10:8
they continue to s and make	Hs 13:2
preserved; his s is stored up.	Hs 13:12
for you have stumbled in your s.	Hs 14:1
all ⌊our⌋ s and accept what	Hs 14:2
the beginning of s for Daughter	Mc 1:13
rebellion and to Israel his s.	Mc 3:8
child of my body for my own s?	Mc 6:7
⌊to wash away⌋ s and impurity.	Zch 13:1
fairness and turned many from s.	Mal 2:6
your right eye causes you to s,	Mt 5:29
your right hand causes you to s,	Mt 5:30
forgiven every s and blasphemy,	Mt 12:31
that causes s and those guilty	Mt 13:41
my brother s against me and I	Mt 18:21
but is guilty of an eternal s"—	Mk 3:29
takes away the s of the world!	Jn 1:29
Do not s any more, so that	Jn 5:14
The one without s among you	Jn 8:7
from now on do not s any more."	Jn 8:11
and you will die in your s.	Jn 8:21
who commits s is a slave of sin.	Jn 8:34
who commits sin is a slave of s.	Jn 8:34
among you can convict Me of s?	Jn 8:46
"You were born entirely in s,"	Jn 9:34
told them, "you wouldn't have s.	Jn 9:41
say, 'We see'—your s remains.	Jn 9:41
to them, they would not have s.	Jn 15:22
they have no excuse for their s.	Jn 15:22
has done, they would not have s.	Jn 15:24
will convict the world about s,	Jn 16:8
about s, because they do not	Jn 16:9
over to you has the greater s."	Jn 19:11
do not charge them with this s!"	Ac 7:60
and Gentiles are all under s,	Rm 3:9
law ⌊comes⌋ the knowledge of s.	Rm 3:20
Lord will never charge with s!	Rm 4:8
just as s entered the world	Rm 5:12
and death through s, in this way	Rm 5:12
s was in the world before the	Rm 5:13
but s is not charged to one's	Rm 5:13
who did not s in the likeness	Rm 5:14
is not like the one man's s,	Rm 5:16
because from one s came the	Rm 5:16
But where s multiplied, grace	Rm 5:20
just as s reigned in death,	Rm 5:21
we continue in s in order that	Rm 6:1
we who died to s still live in	Rm 6:2
may no longer be enslaved to s,	Rm 6:6
He died to s once for all;	Rm 6:10
consider yourselves dead to s,	Rm 6:11
do not let s reign in your	Rm 6:12
parts of it to s as weapons for	Rm 6:13
For s will not rule over you,	Rm 6:14
Should we s because we are not	Rm 6:15
either of s leading to death or	Rm 6:16
you used to be slaves of s,	Rm 6:17
having been liberated from s,	Rm 6:18
For when you were slaves of s,	Rm 6:20
liberated from s and become	Rm 6:22
For the wages of s is death,	Rm 6:23
Is the law s? Absolutely not	Rm 7:7
not have known s if it were not	Rm 7:7
And s, seizing an opportunity	Rm 7:8
apart from the law s is dead.	Rm 7:8
came, s sprang to life	Rm 7:9
For s, seizing an opportunity	Rm 7:11
the contrary, s, in order to be	Rm 7:13
in order to be recognized as s,	Rm 7:13
the commandment s might become	Rm 7:13
it, but it is s living in me.	Rm 7:17
it is the s that lives in me.	Rm 7:20
to the law of s in the parts of	Rm 7:23
with my flesh, to the law of s.	Rm 7:25
from the law of s and of death.	Rm 8:2
He condemned s in the flesh by	Rm 8:3
domain, and as a s offering,	Rm 8:3
the body is dead because of s,	Rm 8:10
that is not from faith is s.	Rm 14:23
Every s a person can commit is	1Co 6:18
Now when you s like this against	1Co 8:12
be guilty of s against the body	1Co 11:27
Now the sting of death is s,	1Co 15:56
and the power of s is the law.	1Co 15:56
did not know s to be sin for us	2Co 5:21
did not know sin to be s for us,	2Co 5:21
Or did I commit a s by humbling	2Co 11:7
is Christ then a promoter of s?	Gl 2:17
angry and do not s. Don't let	Eph 4:26
Publicly rebuke those who s,	1Tm 5:20
way as we are, yet without s.	Heb 4:15
he must make a s offering for	Heb 5:3
removal of s by the sacrifice	Heb 9:26
time, not to bear s, but to	Heb 9:28
burnt offerings and s offerings.	Heb 10:6
burnt offerings and s offerings,	Heb 10:8
is no longer an offering for s.	Heb 10:18
deliberately s after receiving	Heb 10:26
the short-lived pleasure of s.	Heb 11:25
weight and the s that so easily	Heb 12:1
against s, you have not yet	Heb 12:4
high priest as a s offering are	Heb 13:11
gives birth to s, and when sin	Jms 1:15
and when s is fully grown,	Jms 1:15
you commit s and are convicted	Jms 2:9
and doesn't do it, it is a s.	Jms 4:17
when you s and are beaten?	1Pt 2:20
did not commit s, and no deceit	1Pt 2:22
the flesh has finished with s—	1Pt 4:1
and always looking for s,	2Pt 2:14
His Son cleanses us from all s.	1Jn 1:7
say, "We have no s," we are	1Jn 1:8
things so that you may not s.	1Jn 2:1
But if anyone does s, we have an	1Jn 2:1
who commits s also breaks the	1Jn 3:4
s is the breaking of law.	1Jn 3:4
sins, and there is no s in Him.	1Jn 3:5
who remains in Him does not s;	1Jn 3:6
who commits s is of the Devil	1Jn 3:8
has been born of God does not s,	1Jn 3:9
is not able to s, because he has	1Jn 3:9
committing a s that does not	1Jn 5:16
those who commit s that doesn't	1Jn 5:16
There is s that brings death.	1Jn 5:16
is s, and there is sin	1Jn 5:17
and there is s that does not	1Jn 5:17
has been born of God does not s,	1Jn 5:18

SIN (proper noun) *(4)*

and came to the Wilderness of S,	Ex 16:1
left the Wilderness of S,	Ex 17:1
camped in the Wilderness of S.	Nm 33:11
the Wilderness of S and camped	Nm 33:12

SIN'S *(6)*

in order that s dominion over	Rm 6:6
has died is freed from s claims.	Rm 6:7
out of flesh, sold into s power.	Rm 7:14
flesh like ours under s domain,	Rm 8:3
everything under s power,	Gl 3:22
you is hardened by s deception.	Heb 3:13

SINAI *(39)*
(AKA HOREB)
which is between Elim and S, Ex 16:1
entered the Wilderness of S. Ex 19:1
the Wilderness of S and camped Ex 19:2
down on Mount S in the sight Ex 19:11
Mount S was completely enveloped Ex 19:18
The LORD came down on Mount S, Ex 19:20
people cannot come up Mount S, Ex 19:23
of the LORD settled on Mount S, Ex 24:16
speaking with Moses on Mount S, Ex 31:18
Come up Mount S in the morning Ex 34:2
he climbed Mount S, just as the Ex 34:4
Moses descended from Mount S— Ex 34:29
LORD had told him on Mount S. Ex 34:32
Moses on Mount S on the day He Lv 7:38
the LORD in the Wilderness of S. Lv 7:38
LORD spoke to Moses on Mount S: Lv 25:1
through Moses on Mount S. Lv 26:46
for the Israelites on Mount S. Lv 27:34
meeting in the Wilderness of S, Nm 1:1
them in the Wilderness of S: Nm 1:19
spoke with Moses on Mount S. Nm 3:1
the LORD in the Wilderness of S, Nm 3:4
to Moses in the Wilderness of S: Nm 3:14
Moses in the Wilderness of S: Nm 9:1
twilight in the Wilderness of S. Nm 9:5
on from the Wilderness of S, Nm 10:12
in the Wilderness of S. Nm 26:64
at Mount S for a pleasing aroma Nm 28:6
camped in the Wilderness of S. Nm 33:15
the Wilderness of S and camped Nm 33:16
LORD came from S and appeared to Dt 33:2
LORD, even S before the LORD, Jdg 5:5
down on Mount S, and spoke to Neh 9:13
God, the God of S, before God, Ps 68:8
in the sanctuary as He was at S. Ps 68:17
to him in the desert of Mount S, Ac 7:30
who spoke to him on Mount S, Ac 7:38
One is from Mount S and bears Gl 4:24
Now Hagar is Mount S in Arabia Gl 4:25

SINCE *(486)*
(See pp. xi-xii.)

SINCERE *(5)*
praise You with a s heart when I Ps 119:7
by the Holy Spirit, by s love, 2Co 6:6
good conscience, and a s faith. 1Tm 1:5
recalling your s faith that 2Tm 1:5
yourselves for s love of the 1Pt 1:22

SINCERELY *(1)*
of rivalry, not s, seeking to Php 1:17

SINCERITY *(6)*
and worship Him in s and truth. Jos 24:14
speak what they know with s. Jb 33:3
unleavened bread of s and truth. 1Co 5:8
with God-given s and purity, 2Co 1:12
but as those with s, we speak in 2Co 2:17
in the s of your heart, as Eph 6:5

SINFUL *(26)*
any of the s things a person Lv 6:3
I took the s calf you had made, Dt 9:21
considered their demand s, 1Sm 8:6
destroy the s Amalekites. 1Sm 15:18
I was s when my mother conceived Ps 51:5
how much more the wicked and s. Pr 11:31
Oh—s nation, people weighed Is 1:4
and the s one his thoughts; Is 55:7
Because of his s greed I was Is 57:17
Their works are s works, and Is 59:6
Their thoughts are s thoughts; Is 59:7
and have put s stumbling blocks Ezk 14:3
puts a s stumbling block before Ezk 14:4
and putting a s stumbling block Ezk 14:7
and became a s stumbling block Ezk 44:12
Lord GOD are on the s kingdom, Am 9:8
adulterous and s generation, Mk 8:38
me, because I'm a s man, Lord!" Lk 5:8
were more s than all Galileans Lk 13:2
they were more s than all the Lk 13:4
gone to lodge with a s man!" Lk 19:7
into the hands of s men, Lk 24:7
can a s man perform such signs? Jn 9:16
the s passions operated through Rm 7:5
might become s beyond measure. Rm 7:13
ungodly and s, for the unholy 1Tm 1:9

SINFULLY *(1)*
that your own hands have s made. Is 31:7

SINFULNESS *(1)*
has failed because of my s, Ps 31:10

SING *(101)*
I will s to the LORD, for He is Ex 15:1
S to the LORD, for He is highly Ex 15:21
Spring up, well—s to it! Nm 21:17
princes! I will s to the LORD; I Jdg 5:3
I will s praise to the LORD God Jdg 5:3
Awake! Awake, s a song! Arise Jdg 5:12
Don't they s about him during 1Sm 21:11
the David they s about during 1Sm 29:5
I will s about Your name. 2Sm 22:50
S to Him; sing praise to Him; 1Ch 16:9
Sing to Him; s praise to Him; 1Ch 16:9
S to the LORD, all the earth. 1Ch 16:23
appointed some to s for the LORD 2Ch 20:21
the Levites to s praise to the 2Ch 29:30
I will s about the name of the Ps 7:17
I will s about Your name, Most Ps 9:2
S to the LORD, who dwells in Ps 9:11
I will s to the LORD because He Ps 13:6
I will s about Your name. Ps 18:49
we will s and praise Your might. Ps 21:13
I will s and make music to the Ps 27:6
S to the LORD, you His faithful Ps 30:4
that I can s to You and not be Ps 30:12
S a new song to Him; play Ps 33:3
S praise to God, sing praise; Ps 47:6
Sing praise to God, s praise; Ps 47:6
s praise to our King, sing Ps 47:6
praise to our King, s praise! Ps 47:6
S a song of instruction, for God Ps 47:7
and my tongue will s of Your Ps 51:14
confident. I will s; I will sing Ps 57:7
I will sing; I will s praises. Ps 57:7
will s praises to You among the Ps 57:9
I will s of Your strength and Ps 59:16
strength, I s praises, because Ps 59:17
will continually s of Your name, Ps 61:8
in triumph; indeed, they s. Ps 65:13
S the glory of His name; Ps 66:2
worship You and s praise to You. Ps 66:4
will s praise to Your name." Ps 66:4
S to God! Sing praises to His Ps 68:4
Sing to God! S praises to His Ps 68:4
S to God, you kingdoms of the Ps 68:32
s praise to the Lord, Selah Ps 68:32
I will s to You with a harp, Ps 71:22
for joy when I s praise to You, Ps 71:23
I will s praise to the God of Ps 75:9
S for joy to God our strength; Ps 81:1
I will s about the LORD's Ps 89:1
the LORD, to s praise to Your Ps 92:1
S a new song to the LORD; Ps 96:1
s to the LORD, all the earth. Ps 96:1
S to the LORD, praise His name; Ps 96:2
S a new song to the LORD, for He Ps 98:1
jubilant, shout for joy, and s. Ps 98:4
S to the LORD with the lyre, Ps 98:5
I will s of faithful love and Ps 101:1
I will s praise to You, LORD. Ps 101:1
they s among the foliage. Ps 104:12
will s to the LORD all my life; Ps 104:33
will s praise to my God while I Ps 104:33
S to Him, sing praise to Him; Ps 105:2
Sing to Him, s praise to Him; Ps 105:2
God; I will s; I will sing Ps 108:1
I will s praises with the whole Ps 108:1
I will s praises to You among the Ps 108:3
s praise to His name, for it is Ps 135:3
"S us one of the songs of Zion." Ps 137:3
How can we s the LORD's song on Ps 137:4
I will s Your praise before the Ps 138:1
They will s of the LORD's ways, Ps 138:5
I will s a new song to You; Ps 144:9
and will joyfully s of Your Ps 145:7
will s to the LORD as long as I Ps 146:2
How good it is to s to our God, Ps 147:1
S to the LORD with thanksgiving; Ps 147:7
S to the LORD a new song, His Ps 149:1
also, and they s her praises: Sg 6:9
I will s about the one I love, Is 5:1
S to the LORD, for He has done Is 12:5
Cry out and s, citizen of Zion, Is 12:6
you will s this song ⌊of Is 14:4
Play skillfully, s many a song, Is 23:16
They no longer s and drink wine; Is 24:9
raise their voices, they s out; Is 24:14
Awake and s, you who dwell in Is 26:19
On that day s about a desirable Is 27:2
of the mute will s for joy, Is 35:6
S a new song to the LORD; Is 42:10
⌊s⌋ His praise from the ends of Is 42:10
inhabitants of Sela s for joy; Is 42:11
S to the LORD! Praise the LORD, Jr 20:13
the LORD says: S with joy for Jr 31:7
because you s in triumph— Jr 50:11
and they will s the victory song Jr 51:14
S for joy, Daughter Zion; Zph 3:14
I will s psalms to Your name. Rm 15:9
I will s with the spirit, and I 1Co 14:15
and I will also s with my 1Co 14:15
I will s hymns to You in the Heb 2:12
cheerful? He should s praises. Jms 5:13

SINGED *(1)*
not a hair of their heads was s, Dn 3:27

SINGER *(3)*
Jacob, the favorite s of Israel: 2Sm 23:1
Heman the s, son of Joel, son of 1Ch 6:33
you are like a s of love songs Ezk 33:32

SINGERS *(39)*
voices of the s at the watering Jdg 5:11
the voice of male and female s? 2Sm 19:35
into harps and lyres for the s. 1Kg 10:12
The s, the heads of Levite 1Ch 9:33
relatives as s and to have them 1Ch 15:16
The s Heman, Asaph, and Ethan 1Ch 15:19
as well as the s and Chenaniah, 1Ch 15:27
the music leader of the s. 1Ch 15:27
the Levitical s of Asaph, of 2Ch 5:12
trumpeters and s joined together 2Ch 5:13
into harps and lyres for the s. 2Ch 9:11
trumpets while the s with 2Ch 23:13
The s, the descendants of Asaph, 2Ch 35:15
The s ⌊included⌋: Asaph's Ezr 2:41
and their 200 male and female s. Ezr 2:65
Levites, s, gatekeepers, Ezr 2:70
Levites, s, gatekeepers, Ezr 7:7
Levites, s, doorkeepers, Ezr 7:24
s: Eliashib. The gatekeepers: Ezr 10:24
the gatekeepers, s, and Levites Neh 7:1
The s ⌊included⌋: Asaph's Neh 7:44
as their 245 male and female s. Neh 7:67
temple s, some of the people Neh 7:73
Levites, s, gatekeepers, Neh 10:28
gatekeepers, and s serve. Neh 10:39
who were s for the service of Neh 11:22
regulating the s' daily tasks. Neh 11:23
The s gathered from the region Neh 12:28
Then the s sang, with Jezrahiah Neh 12:42
with the s and gatekeepers, Neh 12:45
leaders of the s and songs of Neh 12:46
for the s and gatekeepers Neh 12:47
the Levites, s, and gatekeepers Neh 13:5
the Levites and the s performing Neh 13:10
the Levites and s together and Neh 13:11
S lead the way, with musicians Ps 68:25
S and dancers alike ⌊will say⌋, Ps 87:7
male and female s for myself, Ec 2:8
there were chambers for the s: Ezk 40:44

SINGING *(24)*
sent you away with joy and s, Gn 31:27
I hear the sound of s! Ex 32:18
s and dancing with tambourines, 1Sm 18:6
the armed forces, they kept s: 2Ch 20:21
was worshiping, s the song, and 2Ch 29:28
and all the s men and singing 2Ch 35:25
singing men and s women still 2Ch 35:25
thanksgiving and s accompanied Neh 12:27
s to the tambourine and lyre and Jb 21:12
S songs to a troubled heart is Pr 25:20
The time of s has come, and the Sg 2:12
no one is s or shouting for joy Is 16:10
Your s will be like that on the Is 30:29
also rejoice with joy and s. Is 35:2
return and come to Zion with s, Is 35:10
Break out into s, mountains, Is 44:23
return and come to Zion with s, Is 51:11
will break into s before you, Is 55:12
message that I am s for you, Am 5:1
After s psalms, they went out to Mt 26:30
After s psalms, they went out to Mk 14:26
were praying and s hymns to God, Ac 16:25
s and making music to the Lord Eph 5:19
all wisdom, and s psalms, hymns, Col 3:16

SINGLE (53)

who saw that not a s one of the Ex 9:7
Not a s locust was left in all Ex 10:19
out ahead of you in a s year; Ex 23:29
people responded with a s voice, Ex 24:3
it is to be a s hammered piece Ex 25:36
the tabernacle may be a s unit. Ex 26:6
together so that it is a s unit. Ex 26:11
together at the top in a s ring. Ex 26:24
I went with you for a s moment, Ex 33:5
the tabernacle became a s unit. Ex 36:13
the tent together as a s unit. Ex 36:18
together at the top in a s ring. Ex 36:29
All of it was a s hammered piece Ex 37:22
bread in a s oven and ration Lv 26:26
a branch with a s cluster of Nm 13:23
kill this people with a s blow, Nm 14:15
or mistreated a s one of them." Nm 16:15
on the testimony of a s witness. Dt 17:6
and s him out for harm from all Dt 29:21
a scroll every s word of this Dt 31:24
aloud every s word of this song Dt 31:30
not a s man was left. Jdg 4:16
did not leave a s person alive, 1Sm 27:9
they formed a s unit and took 2Sm 2:25
head, he did not have a s flaw. 2Sm 14:25
then not a s hair of his will 1Kg 1:52
He did not leave him a s male, 1Kg 16:11
there was not a ⌊s⌋ man there, 2Kg 7:5
you drive back a s officer among 2Kg 18:24
and received⌋ a s assignment. 1Ch 23:11
their possessions on a s day, Est 3:13
place⌋ on a s day throughout Est 8:12
Not a s person could withstand Est 9:2
perish at a ⌊s⌋ blast from God Jb 4:9
planned before a s one of them Ps 139:16
palm branch and reed in a s day. Is 9:14
If you find a s person, anyone Jr 5:1
Put them in a s container and Ezk 4:9
appoint over them a s shepherd, Ezk 34:23
take a s stick and write on it: Ezk 37:16
together into a s stick so that Ezk 37:17
make them into a s stick so that Ezk 37:19
for themselves a s ruler, Hs 1:11
and serve Him with a s purpose. Zph 3:9
guilt of this land in a s day. Zch 3:9
you cannot make a s hair white Mt 5:36
any of you add a s cubit to his Mt 6:27
can receive a s thing unless Jn 3:27
in a s day 23,000 people fell 1Co 10:8
in a s hour your judgment has Rv 18:10
in a s hour such fabulous Rv 18:17
because in a s hour she was Rv 18:19
gate was made of a s pearl. Rv 21:21

SINGLED (2)

lots, and the lot s out Jonah. Jnh 1:7
an apostle and s out for God's Rm 1:1

SINGLENESS (1)

with s of purpose to help David. 1Ch 12:33

SINGS (2)

My tongue s about Your promise, Ps 119:172
righteous one s and rejoices. Pr 29:6

SINIM (1)

west, and from the land of S. Is 49:12

SINITES (2)

the Hivites, the Arkites, the S, Gn 10:17
Hivites, Arkites, S, 1Ch 1:15

SINK (10)

while you s lower and lower. Dt 28:43
mud; don't let me s. Let me be Ps 69:14
the city will s into the depths Is 32:19
Babylon will s and never rise Jr 51:64
s into the heart of the sea on Ezk 27:27
have ⌊food⌋ to s their teeth Mc 3:5
the ancient hills s down. Hab 3:6
And beginning to s he cried out, Mt 14:30
so full that they began to s. Lk 5:7
Let these words s in: the Son of Lk 9:44

SINKING (1)

up to the sky, s down to the Ps 107:26

SINKS (1)

her house s down to death and Pr 2:18

SINNED (95)

"I have s this time," he said to Ex 9:27
he s again and hardened his Ex 9:34
I have s against the LORD your Ex 10:16
Whoever has s against Me I will Ex 32:33
once he has s and acknowledged Lv 6:4
he s because of the corpse. Nm 6:11
of those who s at the cost of Nm 16:38
We have s by speaking against Nm 21:7
LORD, "I have s, for I did not Nm 22:34
'We have s against the LORD. Dt 1:41
saw how you had s against the Dt 9:16
Israel has s. They have violated Jos 7:11
I have s against the LORD, Jos 7:20
saying, "We have s against You. Jdg 10:10
the Israelites said, "We have s. Jdg 10:15
have not s against you, but you Jdg 11:27
"We have s against the LORD." 1Sm 7:6
said, 'We have s, for we 1Sm 12:10
Saul answered Samuel, "I have s. 1Sm 15:24
Saul said, "I have s. 1Sm 15:30
He hasn't s against you; 1Sm 19:4
How have I s against your father 1Sm 20:1
I haven't s against you even 1Sm 24:11
Saul responded, "I have s. 1Sm 26:21
"I have s against the LORD." 2Sm 12:13
servant knows that I have s. 2Sm 19:20
I have s greatly in what I've 2Sm 24:10
Look, I am the one who has s; 2Sm 24:17
because they have s against You, 1Kg 8:33
because they have s against You, 1Kg 8:35
We have s and done wrong; 1Kg 8:47
Your people who s against You 1Kg 8:50
of Israel had s against the LORD 2Kg 17:7
I have s greatly because I have 1Ch 21:8
the one who has s and acted very 1Ch 21:17
because they have s against You, 2Ch 6:24
because they have s against You, 2Ch 6:26
We have s and done wrong; 2Ch 6:37
Your people who s against You. 2Ch 6:39
I and my father's house have s. Neh 1:6
They s against Your ordinances, Neh 9:29
Perhaps my children have s, Jb 1:5
⌊If⌋ I have s, what have I done Jb 7:20
your children s against Him, Jb 8:4
if it is true that I have s, Jb 19:4
Sheol ⌊steals⌋ those who have s. Jb 24:19
I have s and perverted what was Jb 33:27
for I have s against You." Ps 41:4
I have s and done this evil in Ps 51:4
Both we and our fathers have s; Ps 106:6
Have we not s against Him? Is 42:24
Your first father s, and your Is 43:27
But we have s, and You were Is 64:5
you have said: I have not s. Jr 2:35
We have s against the LORD our Jr 3:25
because we have s against the Jr 8:14
we have s against You. Jr 14:7
indeed, we have s against You. Jr 14:20
How have I s against you or your Jr 37:18
people⌋ have s against the LORD Jr 40:3
incense and s against the LORD Jr 44:23
they have s against the LORD, Jr 50:7
for she has s against the LORD. Jr 50:14
Jerusalem has s grievously; Lm 1:8
We have s and rebelled; Lm 3:42
Our fathers s; they no longer Lm 5:7
Woe to us, for we have s. Lm 5:16
filled with violence, and you s. Ezk 28:16
apostasies by which they s, Ezk 37:23
we have s, done wrong, acted Dn 9:5
because we have s against You. Dn 9:8
because we have s against Him. Dn 9:11
day, we have s, we have acted Dn 9:15
the more they s against Me. Hs 4:7
you have s since the days of Hs 10:9
Because I have s against Him, Mc 7:9
they have s against the LORD Zph 1:17
I have s by betraying innocent Mt 27:4
I have s against heaven and in Lk 15:18
I have s against heaven and in Lk 15:21
Rabbi, who s, this man or his Jn 9:2
this man nor his parents s," Jn 9:3
against Caesar have I s at all." Ac 25:8
All those who s without the law Rm 2:12
all those who s under the law Rm 2:12
For all have s and fall short of Rm 3:23
to all men, because all s. Rm 5:12
you have not s, and if a virgin 1Co 7:28
a virgin marries, she has not s. 1Co 7:28
for many who s before and have 2Co 12:21
to those who s before and to all 2Co 13:2
Was it not with those who s, Heb 3:17
didn't spare the angels who s, 2Pt 2:4
say, "We have not s," we make 1Jn 1:10
for the Devil has s from the 1Jn 3:8

SINNER (17)

Evil brings death to the s, Ps 34:21
but wickedness undermines the s. Pr 13:6
but to the s He gives the task Ec 2:26
but the s will be captured by Ec 7:26
Although a s commits crime a Ec 8:12
it is for the s, as for the one Ec 9:2
but one s can destroy much good. Ec 9:18
town who was a s found out that Lk 7:37
is touching Him—she's a s!" Lk 7:39
heaven over one s who repents Lk 15:7
angels over one s who repents." Lk 15:10
turn Your wrath from me—a s!' Lk 18:13
We know that this man is a s!" Jn 9:24
or not He's a s, I don't know. Jn 9:25
am I also still judged as a s? Rm 3:7
whoever turns a s from the error Jms 5:20
become of the ungodly and the s? 1Pt 4:18

SINNER'S (1)

the s wealth is stored up for Pr 13:22

SINNERS (44)

you, a brood of s, stand in your Nm 32:14
the path of s, or join a group Ps 1:1
and s will not be in the Ps 1:5
You ⌊s⌋ frustrate the plans of Ps 14:6
therefore He shows s the way. Ps 25:8
Do not destroy me along with s, Ps 26:9
Your ways, and s will return to Ps 51:13
May s vanish from the earth and Ps 104:35
son, if s entice you, don't be Pr 1:10
Disaster pursues s, but good Pr 13:21
Don't be jealous of s; Pr 23:17
both rebels and s will be Is 1:28
and to destroy the s on it. Is 13:9
The s in Zion are afraid; Is 33:14
All the s among My people, Am 9:10
collectors and s came as guests Mt 9:10
eat with tax collectors and s?" Mt 9:11
to call the righteous, but s." Mt 9:13
of tax collectors and s!' Mt 11:19
betrayed into the hands of s. Mt 26:45
collectors and s were also Mk 2:15
was eating with s and tax Mk 2:16
eat with tax collectors and s?" Mk 2:16
to call the righteous, but s." Mk 2:17
betrayed into the hands of s. Mk 14:41
with tax collectors and s?" Lk 5:30
righteous, but s to repentance." Lk 5:32
Even s love those who love them. Lk 6:32
is that to you? Even s do that. Lk 6:33
Even s lend to sinners to be Lk 6:34
sinners lend to s to be repaid Lk 6:34
of tax collectors and s!' Lk 7:34
and s were approaching Lk 15:1
man welcomes s and eats with Lk 15:2
that God doesn't listen to s, Jn 9:31
we were still s Christ died for Rm 5:8
the many were made s, Rm 5:19
by birth and not "Gentile s"; Gl 2:15
are also found to be s, Gl 2:17
came into the world to save s"— 1Tm 1:15
separated from s, and exalted Heb 7:26
from s against Himself, Heb 12:3
your hands, s, and purify your Jms 4:8
things ungodly s have said Jd 15

SINNING (14)

s greatly against the LORD. Gn 13:13
also kept you from s against Me. Gn 20:6
the guilt for s against ⌊you,⌋ Gn 44:32
offends by s unintentionally Lv 5:15
acts in error s unintentionally Nm 15:28
troops are s against the LORD 1Sm 14:33
Him and kept myself from s. 2Sm 22:24
Him and kept myself from s. Ps 18:23
they kept s and did not believe Ps 78:32
they became his altars for s. Hs 8:11
peoples and s against your own Hab 2:10
wants. He is not s; they can get 1Co 7:36
you are s against Christ. 1Co 8:12
Become right-minded and stop s, 1Co 15:34

SINS (207)

When someone s unintentionally Lv 4:2
If the anointed priest s, Lv 4:3

When a leader s and Lv 4:22
common people s unintentionally Lv 4:27
When someone s ⌊in any of these Lv 5:1
If someone s and without knowing Lv 5:17
When someone s and offends the Lv 6:2
this way for all their s because Lv 16:16
rebellious acts—all their s. Lv 16:21
from all your s before the LORD. Lv 16:30
a year because of all their s." Lv 16:34
you seven times for your s. Lv 26:18
plagues seven times for your s. Lv 26:21
you seven times for your s. Lv 26:24
you seven times for your s. Lv 26:28
their fathers' s along with Lv 26:39
of your s 40 years based Nm 14:34
If one person s unintentionally, Nm 15:27
when one man s, will you vent Nm 16:22
away because of all their s." Nm 16:26
your transgressions and s. Jos 24:19
If a man s against another man, 1Sm 2:25
but if a man s against the LORD, 1Sm 2:25
have added to all our s the evil 1Sm 12:19
a man s against his neighbor 1Kg 8:31
turn from their s because You 1Kg 8:35
Jeroboam's s that he committed 1Kg 14:16
done with the s they committed. 1Kg 14:22
in all the s his father had 1Kg 15:3
of Jeroboam's s he had committed 1Kg 15:30
provoking Me with their s, 1Kg 16:2
because of all the s of Baasha 1Kg 16:13
Baasha and the s of his son Elah 1Kg 16:13
Nebat and the s he caused Israel 1Kg 16:26
clung to the s that Jeroboam son 2Kg 3:3
away from the s that Jeroboam 2Kg 10:29
turn from the s that Jeroboam 2Kg 10:31
and followed the s that Jeroboam 2Kg 13:2
away from the s that the house 2Kg 13:6
from all the s that Jeroboam son 2Kg 13:11
away from all the s Jeroboam son 2Kg 14:24
turn away from the s Jeroboam 2Kg 15:9
turn away from the s Jeroboam 2Kg 15:18
turn away from the s Jeroboam 2Kg 15:24
turn away from the s Jeroboam 2Kg 15:28
in all the s that Jeroboam 2Kg 17:22
because of the s of Manasseh, 2Kg 24:3
If a man s against his neighbor 2Ch 6:22
turn from their s because You 2Ch 6:26
to add to our s and our guilt. 2Ch 28:13
less than our s ⌊deserve⌋ and Ezr 9:13
confess the s we have committed Neh 1:6
confessed their s and the guilt Neh 9:2
set over us, because of our s. Neh 9:37
iniquities and s have I Jb 13:23
perceives his unintentional s? Ps 19:12
Your servant from willful s; Ps 19:13
not remember the s of my youth Ps 25:7
trouble, and take away all my s. Ps 25:18
For my s have flooded over my Ps 38:4
my s have overtaken me; Ps 40:12
away from my s and blot out all Ps 51:9
Do not hold past s against us; Ps 79:8
Deliver us and atone for our s, Ps 79:9
secret s in the light of Your Ps 90:8
for their s and destroy them Ps 94:23
with us as our s deserve or Ps 103:10
rebellious ways and their s. Ps 107:17
Let their s always remain before Ps 109:15
You considered s, Lord, who Ps 130:3
redeem Israel from all its s. Ps 130:8
but the one who s against me Pr 8:36
one who despises his neighbor s, Pr 14:21
and the one who acts hastily s. Pr 19:2
conceals his s will not prosper Pr 28:13
earth who does good and never s. Ec 7:20
Though your s are like scarlet, Is 1:18
thrown all my s behind Your back Is 38:17
hand double for all her s. Is 40:2
have burdened Me with your s; Is 43:24
and remember your s no more. Is 43:25
a cloud, and your s like a mist. Is 44:22
and the house of Jacob their s. Is 58:1
and your s have made Him hide Is 59:2
and our s testify against us. Is 59:12
Your s have withheld ⌊My⌋ bounty Jr 5:25
returned to the s of their Jr 11:10
their guilt and punish their s. Jr 14:10
for all your s, and within all Jr 15:13
guilt and your innumerable s. Jr 30:14
guilt and your innumerable s. Jr 30:15
the fathers' s on their sons' Jr 32:18
and for Judah's s, but they will Jr 50:20
of the punishment for his s? Lm 3:39
because of the s of her prophets Lm 4:13
Edom, and will expose your s. Lm 4:22
if a land s against Me by acting Ezk 14:13
not commit ⌊even⌋ half your s. Ezk 16:51
than you because of your s, Ezk 16:52
The person who s is the one who Ezk 18:4
sees all the s his father has Ezk 18:14
The person who s is the one who Ezk 18:20
from all the s he has committed Ezk 18:21
so that your s are revealed in Ezk 21:24
for your s of idolatry. Ezk 23:49
because of your s and will groan Ezk 24:23
for their s rested on their Ezk 32:27
and our s are ⌊heavy⌋ on us, Ezk 33:10
righteousness on the day he s. Ezk 33:12
None of the s he committed will Ezk 33:16
everyone who s unintentionally Ezk 45:20
from your s by doing what is Dn 4:27
because of our s and the Dn 9:16
the s of Ephraim and the crimes Hs 7:1
Now their s are all around them; Hs 7:2
their guilt and punish their s; Hs 8:13
He will punish their s. Hs 9:9
are many and your s innumerable. Am 5:12
rebellion and the s of the house Mc 1:5
desolation because of your s. Mc 6:13
cast all our s into the depths Mc 7:19
save His people from their s." Mt 1:21
River as they confessed their s. Mt 3:6
son, your s are forgiven." Mt 9:2
say, 'Your s are forgiven,' or Mt 9:5
on earth to forgive s"— Mt 9:6
If your brother s against you, Mt 18:15
the measure of your fathers' s! Mt 23:32
many for the forgiveness of s. Mt 26:28
for the forgiveness of s. Mk 1:4
River as they confessed their s. Mk 1:5
Son, your s are forgiven." Mk 2:5
can forgive s but God alone?" Mk 2:7
'Your s are forgiven,' Mk 2:9
on earth to forgive s," Mk 2:10
forgiven for all s and whatever Mk 3:28
the forgiveness of their s. Lk 1:77
for the forgiveness of s, Lk 3:3
Friend, your s are forgiven you. Lk 5:20
can forgive s but God alone?" Lk 5:21
'Your s are forgiven you,' Lk 5:23
on earth to forgive s"— Lk 5:24
her many s have been forgiven; Lk 7:47
to her, "Your s are forgiven." Lk 7:48
this man who even forgives s?" Lk 7:49
forgive us our s, for we Lk 11:4
If your brother s, rebuke him, Lk 17:3
And if he s against you seven Lk 17:4
for forgiveness of s would be Lk 24:47
you that you will die in your s. Jn 8:24
⌊He⌋, you will die in your s." Jn 8:24
If you forgive the s of any, Jn 20:23
if you retain ⌊the s of⌋ any, Jn 20:23
for the forgiveness of your s, Ac 2:38
that your s may be wiped out so Ac 3:19
to Israel, and forgiveness of s. Ac 5:31
will receive forgiveness of s." Ac 10:43
man forgiveness of s is being Ac 13:38
wash away your s by calling on Ac 22:16
forgiveness of s and a share Ac 26:18
God passed over the s previously Rm 3:25
and whose s are covered! Rm 4:7
them, when I take away their s. Rm 11:27
immoral s against his own 1Co 6:18
died for our s according to 1Co 15:3
you are still in your s. 1Co 15:17
Himself for our s to rescue us Gl 1:4
dead in your trespasses and s Eph 2:1
the forgiveness of s. Col 1:14
adding to the number of their s, 1Th 2:16
don't share in the s of others. 1Tm 5:22
Some people's s are evident, 1Tm 5:24
but ⌊the s⌋ of others follow 1Tm 5:24
idle women burdened down with s, 2Tm 3:6
a person is perverted and s, Ti 3:11
After making purification for s, Heb 1:3
for the s of the people. Heb 2:17
both gifts and sacrifices for s. Heb 5:1
for their own s, then for those Heb 7:27
never again remember their s." Heb 8:12
and for the s of the people Heb 9:7
once to bear the s of many, Heb 9:28
have any consciousness of s? Heb 10:2
is a reminder of s every year. Heb 10:3
bulls and goats to take away s. Heb 10:4
which can never take away s. Heb 10:11
one sacrifice for s forever, Heb 10:12
remember their s and their Heb 10:17
remains a sacrifice for s, Heb 10:26
and if he has committed s, Jms 5:15
confess your s to one another Jms 5:16
and cover a multitude of s. Jms 5:20
Himself bore our s in His body 1Pt 2:24
having died to s, we might live 1Pt 2:24
suffered for s once for all, 1Pt 3:18
love covers a multitude of s. 1Pt 4:8
the cleansing from his past s. 2Pt 1:9
we confess our s, He is faithful 1Jn 1:9
forgive us our s and to cleanse 1Jn 1:9
is the propitiation for our s, 1Jn 2:2
your s have been forgiven 1Jn 2:12
so that He might take away s, 1Jn 3:5
everyone who s has not seen Him 1Jn 3:6
be the propitiation for our s. 1Jn 4:10
us free from our s by His blood, Rv 1:5
you will not share in her s, Rv 18:4
her s are piled up to heaven, Rv 18:5

SION *(1)*
(AKA BAAL-HERMON, HERMAN, SENIR, SIRION)
Arnon Valley as far as Mount S Dt 4:48

SIPHMOTH *(1)*
in Aroer, in S, and in Eshtemoa 1Sm 30:28

SIPPAI *(1)*
(AKA SAPH)
the Hushathite killed S, 1Ch 20:4

SIR *(17)*
her father, "S, don't be angry Gn 31:35
said, "S, we really did come Gn 43:20
and said, "S, please let your Gn 44:18
Him, "Please S, if the LORD is Jdg 6:13
'I will, s,' he answered. Mt 21:30
and said, "S, we remember that Mt 27:63
replied to him, 'S, leave it Lk 13:8
"S," said the woman, "You don't Jn 4:11
"S," the woman said to Him, "give Jn 4:15
"S," the woman replied, "I see Jn 4:19
"S," the official said to Him, Jn 4:49
"S," the sick man answered, "I Jn 5:7
Then they said, "S, give us this Jn 6:34
Who is He, S, that I may believe Jn 9:36
of him, "S, we want to see Jn 12:21
she replied, "S, if you've Jn 20:15
I said to him, "S, you know." Rv 7:14

SIRAH *(1)*
him back from the well of S, 2Sm 3:26

SIRION *(2)*
(AKA BAAL-HERMON, HERMAN, SENIR, SION)
which the Sidonians call S, Dt 3:9
like a calf, and S, like a young Ps 29:6

SIRS *(1)*
out and said, "S, what must I do Ac 16:30

SISERA *(20)*
of his forces was S who lived in Jdg 4:2
Then I will lure S commander of Jdg 4:7
LORD will sell S into a woman's Jdg 4:9
was reported to S that Barak son Jdg 4:12
S summoned all his 900 iron Jdg 4:13
LORD has handed S over to you. Jdg 4:14
The LORD threw S, all his Jdg 4:15
S left his chariot and fled on Jdg 4:15
whole army of S fell by the Jdg 4:16
S had fled on foot to the tent Jdg 4:17
out to greet S and said to him, Jdg 4:18
hammer, and went silently to S. Jdg 4:21
Barak arrived in pursuit of S, Jdg 4:22
and there was S lying dead with Jdg 4:22
stars fought with S from their Jdg 5:20
she hammered S—she crushed his Jdg 5:26
spoil of colored garments for S, Jdg 5:30
your enemies perish as S did. Jdg 5:31
handed them over to S commander 1Sm 12:9
as ⌊You did⌋ with S and Jabin at Ps 83:9

SISERA'S *(3)*
S mother looked through the Jdg 5:28
descendants, S descendants, Ezr 2:53
descendants, S descendants, Neh 7:55

SISMAI *(2)*
Eleasah fathered S, and Sismai 1Ch 2:40
Sismai, and S fathered Shallum. 1Ch 2:40

SISTER *(108)*
Tubal-cain's s was Naamah. Gn 4:22
say you're my s so it will go Gn 12:13
say, 'She's my s,' so that I Gn 12:19
his wife Sarah, "She is my s." Gn 20:2
say to me, 'She is my s'? Gn 20:5
she really is my s, the daughter Gn 20:12
had heard his s Rebekah's words Gn 24:30
sent away their s Rebekah and Gn 24:59
Our s, may you become thousands Gn 24:60
and s of Laban the Aramean. Gn 25:20
said, "She is my s," for he was Gn 26:7
could you say, 'She's my s'?" Gn 26:9
She was the s of Nebaioth. Gn 28:9
any children⌋, she envied her s. Gn 30:1
wrestled with my s and won," Gn 30:8
he had defiled their s Dinah. Gn 34:13
Giving our s to an uncircumcised Gn 34:14
because their s had been defiled Gn 34:27
treated our s like a prostitute? Gn 34:31
of Ishmael and s of Nebaioth. Gn 36:3
and Heman. Timna was Lotan's s. Gn 36:22
Beriah, and their s Serah. Gn 46:17
Then his s stood at a distance Ex 2:4
Then his s said to Pharaoh's Ex 2:7
married his father's s Jochebed, Ex 6:20
of Amminadab and s of Nahshon. Ex 6:23
Aaron's s, took a tambourine Ex 15:20
sexual intercourse with your s, Lv 18:9
by your father; she is your s. Lv 18:11
with your father's s; Lv 18:12
with your mother's s, Lv 18:13
a rival to her s and have sexual Lv 18:18
a man marries his s, whether his Lv 20:17
sexual intercourse with his s; Lv 20:17
your mother's s or your father's Lv 20:19
sister or your father's s, Lv 20:19
young unmarried s in his Lv 21:3
his brother or s, when they die, Nm 6:7
case involving their s Cozbi, Nm 25:18
Moses, and their s Miriam. Nm 26:59
the one who sleeps with his s, Dt 27:22
her younger s more beautiful Jdg 15:2
had a beautiful s named Tamar, 2Sm 13:1
sick over his s Tamar because 2Sm 13:2
Tamar, my brother Absalom's s." 2Sm 13:4
'Please let my s Tamar come and 2Sm 13:5
Please let my s Tamar come and 2Sm 13:6
"Come sleep with me, my s!" 2Sm 13:11
Be quiet for now, my s. 2Sm 13:20
since he disgraced his s Tamar. 2Sm 13:22
Amnon disgraced his s Tamar. 2Sm 13:32
Abigail was a s to Zeruiah, 2Sm 17:25
a wife, the s of his own wife 1Kg 11:19
Tahpenes' s gave birth to 1Kg 11:20
daughter and Ahaziah's s, 2Kg 11:2
and Homam. Timna was Lotan's s. 1Ch 1:39
sons, with their s Tamar, in 1Ch 3:9
with their s Shelomith; 1Ch 3:19
and their s was named 1Ch 4:3
Hodiah's wife, the s of Naham: 1Ch 4:19
The name of his s was Maacah. 1Ch 7:15
His s Hammolecheth gave birth to 1Ch 7:18
and Beriah, with their s Serah. 1Ch 7:30
and Hotham, with their s Shua. 1Ch 7:32
Since she was Ahaziah's s, 2Ch 22:11
to the worm: My mother or my s, Jb 17:14
wisdom, "You are my s," and call Pr 7:4
my heart, my s, my bride. Sg 4:9
your love is, my s, my bride. Sg 4:10
My s, my bride, ⌊you are⌋ a Sg 4:12
to my garden—my s, my bride. Sg 5:1
Open to me, my s, my darling, my Sg 5:2
Our s is young; she has no Sg 8:8
we do for our s on the day she Sg 8:8
her treacherous s Judah saw it. Jr 3:7
her treacherous s Judah was not Jr 3:8
her treacherous s Judah didn't Jr 3:10
or Woe, ⌊my⌋ s! They will not Jr 22:18
You are the s of your sisters, Ezk 16:45
Your older s was Samaria, who Ezk 16:46
and your younger s was Sodom, Ezk 16:46
your s Sodom and her daughters Ezk 16:48
the iniquity of your s Sodom: Ezk 16:49
you treat your s Sodom as an Ezk 16:56
⌊yet⌋ another violates his s, Ezk 22:11
Oholah, and her s was Oholibah. Ezk 23:4
Now her s Oholibah saw ⌊this⌋, Ezk 23:11
acts worse than those of her s. Ezk 23:11
as I turned away from her s. Ezk 23:18
followed the path of your s, Ezk 23:31
the cup of your s Samaria. Ezk 23:33
a brother, or an unmarried s. Ezk 44:25
is My brother and s and mother." Mt 12:50
is My brother and s and mother." Mk 3:35
She had a s named Mary, who also Lk 10:39
You care that my s has left me Lk 10:40
of Mary and her s Martha. Jn 11:1
Martha, her s, and Lazarus. Jn 11:5
went back and called her s Mary, Jn 11:28
the dead man's s, told Him, Jn 11:39
His mother's s, Mary the wife Jn 19:25
son of Paul's s, hearing about Ac 23:16
I commend to you our s Phoebe, Rm 16:1
Nereus and his s, and Olympas, Rm 16:15
A brother or a s is not bound in 1Co 7:15
Apphia our s, to Archippus our Phm 2
If a brother or s is without Jms 2:15
your elect s send you greetings. 2Jn 13

SISTER'S *(4)*
the bracelets on his s wrists, Gn 24:30
the news about his s son Jacob, Gn 29:13
her during her ⌊s⌋ lifetime. Lv 18:18
You will drink your s cup, Ezk 23:32

SISTER-IN-LAW *(4)*
man doesn't want to marry his s, Dt 25:7
then his s will go up to him in Dt 25:9
your s has gone back to her Ru 1:15
Follow your s." Ru 1:15

SISTERS *(20)*
mother, brothers, s, and all who Jos 2:13
s were Zeruiah and Abigail. 1Ch 2:16
their three s to eat and drink Jb 1:4
All his brothers, s, and former Jb 42:11
You are the sister of your s, Ezk 16:45
and made your s appear righteous Ezk 16:51
been an advocate for your s. Ezk 16:52
have made your s appear Ezk 16:52
As for your s, Sodom and her Ezk 16:55
your older and younger s. Ezk 16:61
My People and your s: Hs 2:1
And His s, aren't they all with Mt 13:56
brothers or s, father or mother Mt 19:29
Your s are outside asking for Mk 3:32
And aren't His s here with us?" Mk 6:3
brothers or s, mother or father Mk 10:29
houses, brothers and s, mothers Mk 10:30
brothers and s—yes, and even Lk 14:26
So the s sent a message to Him: Jn 11:3
the younger women as s. 1Tm 5:2

SISTRUMS *(1)*
tambourines, s, and cymbals. 2Sm 6:5

SIT *(103)*
Please s up and eat some of my Gn 27:19
them when you s in your house Dt 6:7
them when you s in your house Dt 11:19
her custom to s under the palm Jdg 4:5
donkeys, who s on saddle Jdg 5:10
Why did you s among the Jdg 5:16
"Come over here and s down." Ru 4:1
elders and said, "S here." Ru 4:2
We won't s down to eat until he 1Sm 16:11
I'm supposed to s down and eat 1Sm 20:5
one who is to s on my throne? 1Kg 1:13
one who is to s on my throne.' 1Kg 1:17
them who will s on the throne 1Kg 1:20
one who is to s on my throne?' 1Kg 1:24
know who will s on my lord the 1Kg 1:27
the one who is to s on my throne 1Kg 1:30
to come in and s on my throne. 1Kg 1:35
provided one to s on my throne, 1Kg 1:48
him a son to s on his throne, 1Kg 3:6
and I s on the throne of Israel, 1Kg 8:20
fail to have a man to s before 1Kg 8:25
Why just s here until we die? 2Kg 7:3
city, but if we s here, we will 2Kg 7:4
your sons will s on the throne 2Kg 10:30
your sons will s on the throne 2Kg 15:12
to the men who s on the wall, 2Kg 18:27
son Solomon to s on the throne 1Ch 28:5
David and I s on the throne 2Ch 6:10
fail to have a man to s before 2Ch 6:16
I do not s with the worthless or Ps 26:4
and I do not s with the wicked. Ps 26:5
You s, maligning your brother, Ps 50:20
May he s enthroned before God Ps 61:7
Those who s at the city gate Ps 69:12
You who s enthroned ⌊on⌋ the Ps 80:1
so that they may s down with me. Ps 101:6
S at My right hand until I make Ps 110:1
Though princes s together Ps 119:23
sons will also s on your throne, Ps 132:12
You know when I s down and when Ps 139:2
When you s down to dine with a Pr 23:1
I delight to s in his shade, Sg 2:3
she will s on the ground. Is 3:26
I will s on the mount of the Is 14:13
justice will s on the throne Is 16:5
to the men who s on the wall, Is 36:12
Go down and s in the dust, Is 47:1
S on the ground without a throne, Is 47:1
s in silence and go into Is 47:5
or a fire to s beside! Is 47:14
taking place to s with them to Jr 16:8
They will s on the throne of Jr 17:25
you who s above the valley, Jr 21:13
you who s on the throne of David Jr 22:2
S down and read ⌊it⌋ in our Jr 36:15
have no one to s on David's Jr 36:30
s on parched ground, resident of Jr 48:18
they s in their strongholds. Jr 51:30
of Daughter Zion s on the ground Lm 2:10
Let him s alone and be silent, Lm 3:28
When they s and when they rise, Lm 3:63
they will s on the ground, Ezk 26:16
I s in the seat of gods in the Ezk 28:2
you in crowds, s in front of you Ezk 33:31
himself will s in the gateway to Ezk 44:3
for there I will s down to judge Jl 3:12
But each man will s under his Mc 4:4
though I s in darkness, the LORD Mc 7:8
his neighbor to ⌊s⌋ under ⌊his⌋ Zch 3:10
splendor and will s on His Zch 6:13
women will again s along the Zch 8:4
the crowds to s down on the Mt 14:19
the crowd to s down on the Mt 15:35
Me will also s on 12 thrones, Mt 19:28
these two sons of mine may s, Mt 20:21
But to s at My right and left is Mt 20:23
'S at My right hand until I put Mt 22:44
then He will s on the throne of Mt 25:31
S here while I go over there and Mt 26:36
Every day I used to s, teaching Mt 26:55
all the people s down in groups Mk 6:39
the crowd to s down on the Mk 8:6
Allow us to s at Your right and Mk 10:37
But to s at My right or left is Mk 10:40
'S at My right hand until I put Mk 12:36
disciples, "S here while I pray. Mk 14:32
Have them s down in groups of Lk 9:14
did so, and had them all s down. Lk 9:15
doesn't first s down and Lk 14:28
will not first s down and decide Lk 14:31
told him, 's down quickly, and Lk 16:6
'Come at once and s down to eat'? Lk 17:7
to my Lord, 'S at My right hand Lk 20:42
you will s on thrones judging Lk 22:30
said, "Have the people s down." Jn 6:10
to my Lord, 'S at My right hand Ac 2:34
the one who used to s and beg at Ac 3:10
to come up and s with him. Ac 8:31
S at My right hand until I make Heb 1:13
that you say, "S here in a good Jms 2:3
S here on the floor by my Jms 2:3
him the right to s with Me on My Rv 3:21
in her heart, 'I s as queen; Rv 18:7

SITE *(16)*
the land to the s of Shechem, Gn 12:6
to the s where he had built the Gn 13:4
Give me a burial s among you so Gn 23:4
the Hittite as a burial s. Gn 49:30
as a burial s from Ephron Gn 50:13
extend to the s of Ar and lie Nm 21:15
to the ambush s and waited Jos 8:9
at the s David had prepared on 2Ch 3:1
it rebuilt on its ⌊original⌋ s. Ezr 2:68

rebuilt on its ⌊original⌋ **s**.' Ezr 5:15
of God on its ⌊original⌋ **s**. Ezr 6:7
over the entire **s** of Mount Zion Is 4:5
Enlarge the **s** of your tent, Is 54:2
will stand on its proper **s**. Jr 30:18
to be inhabited on its **s**, Zch 12:6
remain on its **s** from the Zch 14:10

SITES *(1)*
and the **s** where he built high 2Ch 33:19

SITHRI *(1)*
Mishael, Elzaphan, and S. Ex 6:22

SITS *(18)*
Pharaoh who **s** on his throne to Ex 11:5
any furniture he **s** on will be Lv 15:4
Whoever **s** on furniture that the Lv 15:6
anything she **s** on will become Lv 15:20
any furniture she **s** on will be Lv 15:26
the ark of God **s** inside tent 2Sm 7:2
the LORD **s** enthroned forever; Ps 9:7
the LORD **s** enthroned, King Ps 29:10
She **s** by the doorway of her Pr 9:14
where he **s** among the elders of Pr 31:23
to the one who **s** in judgment, Is 28:6
I call her: Rahab Who Just S. Is 30:7
of luxury, who **s** securely, who Is 47:8
How she **s** alone, the city ⌊once⌋ Lm 1:1
the Son of Man **s** on His glorious Mt 19:28
throne and by Him who **s** on it. Mt 23:22
so that he **s** in God's sanctuary, 2Th 2:4
prostitute who **s** on many waters. Rv 17:1

SITTING *(90)*
while he was **s** in the entrance Gn 18:1
as Lot was **s** at Sodom's gate. Gn 19:1
Why are you alone **s** as judge, Ex 18:14
discharge was **s** on is to wash Lv 15:6
she was **s** on is to wash his Lv 15:22
bed or the furniture she was **s** Lv 15:23
the mother is **s** on the chicks Dt 22:6
him while he was **s** alone in his Jdg 3:20
She was **s** in the field, and her Jdg 13:9
Eli the priest was **s** on a chair 1Sm 1:9
there was Eli **s** on his chair 1Sm 4:13
Saul as he was **s** in his palace 1Sm 19:9
s under the tamarisk tree at the 1Sm 22:6
was **s** between the two gates 2Sm 18:24
the king is **s** in the gate." 2Sm 19:8
and found him **s** under an oak 1Kg 13:14
While they were **s** at the table, 1Kg 13:20
were each **s** on his own throne. 1Kg 22:10
I saw the LORD **s** on His throne, 1Kg 22:19
he was **s** on top of the hill. 2Kg 1:9
the prophets were **s** at his feet. 2Kg 4:38
Elisha was **s** in his house, 2Kg 6:32
and the elders were **s** with him. 2Kg 6:32
army commanders were **s** there, 2Kg 9:5
But I know your **s** down, your 2Kg 19:27
were each **s** on his own throne. 2Ch 18:9
They were **s** on the threshing 2Ch 18:9
I saw the LORD **s** on His throne, 2Ch 18:18
Mordecai was **s** at the King's Est 2:19
Mordecai was **s** at the King's Est 2:21
The king was **s** on his royal Est 5:1
Mordecai the Jew **s** at the King's Est 5:13
who is **s** at the King's Gate. Est 6:10
A king **s** on a throne to judge Pr 20:8
But I know your **s** down, your Is 37:28
⌊and⌋ those **s** in darkness from Is 42:7
s among the graves, spending Is 65:4
Why are we just **s** here? Jr 8:14
then kings **s** on David's throne Jr 22:4
will succeed in **s** on the throne Jr 22:30
the king **s** on David's throne Jr 29:16
all the Judeans **s** in the guard's Jr 32:12
to have a man **s** on the throne Jr 33:17
All the officials were **s** there— Jr 36:12
the king was **s** in his winter Jr 36:22
the king was **s** at the Benjamin Jr 38:7
I was **s** in my house and the Ezk 8:1
of Judah were **s** in front of me, Ezk 8:1
and I saw women **s** there weeping Ezk 8:14
your colleagues **s** before you; Zch 3:8
was a woman **s** inside the basket Zch 5:7
named Matthew **s** at the tax Mt 9:9
It's like children **s** in the Mt 11:16
the house and was **s** by the sea. Mt 13:1
two blind men **s** by the road. Mt 20:30
While He was **s** on the Mount of Mt 24:3
in and was **s** with the temple Mt 26:58
Now Peter was **s** outside in the Mt 26:69
While he was **s** on the judge's Mt 27:19
back the stone and was **s** on it. Mt 28:2
of the scribes were **s** there, Mk 2:6
son of Alphaeus **s** at the tax Mk 2:14
crowd was **s** around Him and told Mk 3:32
at those who were **s** in a circle Mk 3:34
by the legion, **s** there, dressed Mk 5:15
S down, He called the Twelve and Mk 9:35
blind beggar, was **s** by the road. Mk 10:46
S across from the temple Mk 12:41
While He was **s** on the Mount of Mk 13:3
He was **s** with the temple police, Mk 14:54
long white robe **s** on the right Mk 16:5
temple complex **s** among the Lk 2:46
of the law were **s** there who had Lk 5:17
named Levi **s** at the tax office, Lk 5:27
are like children **s** in the Lk 7:32
departed from, **s** at Jesus' feet, Lk 8:35
long ago, **s** in sackcloth Lk 10:13
a blind man was **s** by the road Lk 18:35
servant saw him **s** in the Lk 22:56
the money changers **s** there. Jn 2:14
King is coming, **s** on a donkey's Jn 12:15
full of sour wine was **s** there; Jn 19:29
saw two angels in white **s** there, Jn 20:12
all who were **s** in the Sanhedrin Ac 6:15
and was **s** in his chariot on his Ac 8:28
Eutychus was **s** on a window sill Ac 20:9
You are **s** there judging me Ac 23:3
and those **s** with them got up, Ac 26:30
to another person **s** there, 1Co 14:30
I saw a woman **s** on a scarlet Rv 17:3

SITUATED *(1)*
A city **s** on a hill cannot be Mt 5:14

SITUATION *(10)*
troops were in a difficult **s**. 1Sm 13:6
He took in the **s** and announced, 2Kg 1:11
don't be astonished at the **s**, Ec 5:8
fraudulent until the **s** changes. Dn 2:9
explained the **s** to Daniel. Dn 2:15
his life in the **s** the Lord 1Co 7:17
in the life **s** in which he was 1Co 7:20
God in whatever **s** he was called. 1Co 7:24
would be embarrassed in that **s**. 2Co 9:4
In every **s** take the shield of Eph 6:16

SIVAN *(1)*
that is, the month S), the royal Est 8:9

SIX *(122)*
the **s** hundredth year of Noah's Gn 7:11
In the **s** hundred and first year, Gn 8:13
I have borne him **s** sons," Gn 30:20
daughters and **s** years for your Gn 31:41
For **s** days you may gather it, Ex 16:26
are to labor **s** days and do all Ex 20:9
everything in them in **s** days; Ex 20:11
he is to serve for **s** years; Ex 21:2
your land for **s** years and gather Ex 23:10
Do your work for **s** days but rest Ex 23:12
the cloud covered it for **s** days. Ex 24:16
S branches are to extend from Ex 25:32
this way for the **s** branches that Ex 25:33
For the **s** branches that extend Ex 25:35
width of each curtain **s** feet; Ex 26:2
width of each curtain **s** feet. Ex 26:8
and the ⌊other⌋ **s** curtains by Ex 26:9
and make **s** planks for the west Ex 26:22
s of their names on the first Ex 28:10
and the remaining **s** names on the Ex 28:10
half as much (**s** and a quarter Ex 30:23
s and a quarter pounds of Ex 30:23
For **s** days work may be done, Ex 31:15
for in **s** days the LORD made the Ex 31:17
You are to labor **s** days but you Ex 34:21
For **s** days work is to be done, Ex 35:2
width of each curtain **s** feet; Ex 36:9
width of each curtain **s** feet. Ex 36:15
and ⌊the other⌋ **s** together. Ex 36:16
the tabernacle he made **s** planks. Ex 36:27
S branches extended from its Ex 37:18
this way for the **s** branches that Ex 37:19
For the **s** branches that extended Ex 37:21
For **s** days work may be done, Lv 23:3
them in two rows, **s** to a row, on Lv 24:6
may sow your field for **s** years, Lv 25:3
gather its produce for **s** years. Lv 25:3
before the LORD **s** covered carts Nm 7:3
offering of **s** quarts of fine Nm 15:9
s quarts of fine flour mixed Nm 28:12
offer **s** quarts with each bull Nm 28:20
mixed with oil, **s** quarts with Nm 28:28
mixed with oil, **s** quarts with Nm 29:3
mixed with oil, **s** quarts with Nm 29:9
s quarts with each of the 13 Nm 29:14
will include **s** cities of refuge, Nm 35:6
will be your **s** cities of refuge. Nm 35:13
These **s** cities will serve as a Nm 35:15
It is 13 feet **s** inches long and Dt 3:11
six inches long and **s** feet wide Dt 3:11
are to labor **s** days and do all Dt 5:13
to you and serves you **s** years, Dt 15:12
he worked for you **s** years— Dt 15:18
eat unleavened bread for **s** days. Dt 16:8
one time. Do this for **s** days. Jos 6:3
They did this for **s** days. Jos 6:14
and Eltekon—**s** cities, with Jos 15:59
and En-gedi—**s** cities, with Jos 15:62
Jephthah judged Israel **s** years, Jdg 12:7
S hundred Danites departed from Jdg 18:11
he shoveled **s** ⌊measures⌋ of Ru 3:15
He gave me these **s** ⌊measures⌋ of Ru 3:17
was seven years and **s** months. 2Sm 2:11
Judah seven years and **s** months, 2Sm 5:5
of the LORD advanced **s** steps, 2Sm 6:13
was there with **s** fingers on each 2Sm 21:20
on each hand and **s** toes on each 2Sm 21:20
like lilies, **s** feet ⌊high⌋. 1Kg 7:19
Each water cart was **s** feet long, 1Kg 7:27
was six feet long, **s** feet wide, 1Kg 7:27
and each was **s** feet wide— 1Kg 7:38
throne had **s** steps; there was 1Kg 10:19
standing there on the **s** steps, 1Kg 10:20
had remained there **s** months, 1Kg 11:16
He reigned **s** years in Tirzah, 1Kg 16:23
s quarts of fine meal ⌊will 2Kg 7:1
was then that **s** quarts of fine 2Kg 7:16
a shekel and **s** quarts of fine 2Kg 7:18
the LORD's temple **s** years while 2Kg 11:3
the ground five or **s** times. 2Kg 13:19
Israel in Samaria for **s** months. 2Kg 15:8
S sons were born to David in 1Ch 3:4
ruled seven years and **s** months, 1Ch 3:4
Neariah, and Shaphat—**s**. 1Ch 3:22
had 16 sons and **s** daughters, 1Ch 4:27
Azel had **s** sons, and these were 1Ch 8:38
Azel had **s** sons, and these were 1Ch 9:44
stature with **s** fingers ⌊on each 1Ch 20:6
each hand⌋ and **s** toes ⌊on each 1Ch 20:6
and Mattithiah—**s**—under the 1Ch 25:3
There were **s** Levites each day on 1Ch 26:17
throne had **s** steps; there was 2Ch 9:18
standing there on the **s** steps, 2Ch 9:19
them in God's temple **s** years. 2Ch 22:12
S hundred bulls and 3,000 sheep 2Ch 29:33
day, one ox, **s** choice sheep, Neh 5:18
of myrrh for **s** months and then Est 2:12
for ⌊another⌋ **s** months. Est 2:12
rescue you from **s** calamities; Jb 5:19
S things the LORD hates; Pr 6:16
will yield only **s** gallons, Is 5:10
each one had **s** wings: with two Is 6:2
may serve you **s** years, but then Jr 34:14
And I saw **s** men coming from the Ezk 9:2
man's hand was **s** units of 21 Ezk 40:5
miles⌋ long and **s** and two-thirds Ezk 45:1
during the **s** days of work, Ezk 46:1
day is to be **s** unblemished lambs Ezk 46:4
as well as **s** lambs and a ram Ezk 46:6
of the city⌋ will be **s** ⌊miles⌋. Ezk 48:35
After **s** days Jesus took Peter, Mt 17:1
After **s** days Jesus took Peter, Mk 9:2
three years and **s** months while Lk 4:25
There are **s** days when work Lk 13:14
Now **s** stone water jars had been Jn 2:6
It was about **s** in the evening. Jn 4:6
S days before the Passover, Jn 12:1
it was about **s** in the morning. Jn 19:14
These **s** brothers accompanied me, Ac 11:12
there a year and **s** months, Ac 18:11
three years and **s** months it did Jms 5:17
living creatures had **s** wings; Rv 4:8

SIXTEENTH *(3)*
to Bilgah, the **s** to Immer, 1Ch 24:14

the s to Hananiah, his sons, and 1Ch 25:23
and on the s day of the first 2Ch 29:17

SIXTH *(34)*
and then morning: the s day. Gn 1:31
again and bore Jacob a s son. Gn 30:19
On the s day, when they prepare Ex 16:5
On the s day they gathered twice Ex 16:22
on the s day He will give Ex 16:29
Then fold the s curtain double Ex 26:9
blessing for you in the s year, Lv 25:21
On the s day Eliasaph son of Nm 7:42
On the s day ⌊present⌋ eight Nm 29:29
s lot came out for Naphtali's Jos 19:32
the s was Ithream, by David's 2Sm 3:5
In the s year of Hezekiah, 2Kg 18:10
Ozem s, and David seventh. 1Ch 2:15
by David's wife Eglah, was s. 1Ch 3:3
Attai s, Eliel seventh, 1Ch 12:11
to Malchijah, the s to Mijamin, 1Ch 24:9
s ⌊to⌋ Bukkiah, his sons, and 1Ch 25:13
Jehohanan the s, and Eliehoenai 1Ch 26:3
Ammiel the s, Issachar the 1Ch 26:5
The s, for the sixth month, was 1Ch 27:9
sixth, for the s month, was Ira 1Ch 27:9
of Adar in the s year of the Ezr 6:15
and Hanun the s son of Zalaph Neh 3:30
In the s year, in the sixth Ezk 8:1
sixth year, in the s ⌊month⌋, on Ezk 8:1
on the first day of the s month, Hg 1:1
twenty-fourth day of the s month, Hg 1:15
the s month, the angel Gabriel Lk 1:26
and this is the s month for her Lk 1:36
Then I saw Him open the s seal. Rv 6:12
The s angel blew his trumpet. Rv 9:13
say to the s angel who had the Rv 9:14
The s poured out his bowl on the Rv 16:12
fifth sardonyx, the s carnelian, Rv 21:20

SIZE *(7)*
we saw in it are men of great s. Nm 13:32
had the same s and shape. 1Kg 6:25
cut to s and sawed with saws on 1Kg 7:9
stones, cut to s, as well as 1Kg 7:11
began to reduce the s of Israel. 2Kg 10:32
have faith the s of a mustard Mt 17:20
have faith the s of a mustard Lk 17:6

SKIES *(17)*
even his s drip with dew. Dt 33:28
When the s are shut and there is 1Kg 8:35
When the s are shut and there is 2Ch 6:26
the northern ⌊s⌋ over empty Jb 26:7
spread out the s as hard as a Jb 37:18
at the sun when it is in the s, Jb 37:21
Your faithfulness to the s. Ps 36:5
and the s poured down ⌊rain⌋ Ps 68:8
wind blow in the s and drove the Ps 78:26
who in the s can compare with Ps 89:6
when He placed the s above, Pr 8:28
s will roll up like a scroll, Is 34:4
and let the s shower Is 45:8
the s above will grow dark. Jr 4:28
Or can the s alone give showers? Jr 14:22
the s have withheld the dew and Hg 1:10
and the s will yield their dew. Zch 8:12

SKIFF *(3)*
able to get control of the s. Ac 27:16
had let down the s into the sea, Ac 27:30
holding the s and let it drop Ac 27:32

SKILL *(9)*
hair by virtue of ⌊their⌋ s. Ex 35:26
filled them with s to do all the Ex 35:35
had great s, understanding, 1Kg 7:14
man of any s will be at your 1Ch 28:21
and all their s was useless. Ps 107:27
my right hand forget ⌊its s⌋. Ps 137:5
knowledge, and s, but he must Ec 2:21
you with knowledge and s. Jr 3:15
By your great s in trading you Ezk 28:5

SKILLED *(22)*
to instruct all the s craftsmen, Ex 28:3
within every s craftsman in Ex 31:6
Let all the s craftsmen among Ex 35:10
Every s woman spun ⌊yarn⌋ with Ex 35:25
and all the s people are to work Ex 36:1
every s person in whose heart Ex 36:2
All the s craftsmen among those Ex 36:8
and people s in every kind of 1Ch 22:15
who is s in engraving to 2Ch 2:7
Levites were all s on musical 2Ch 34:12
He was a scribe s in the law of Ezr 7:6
those who are s in rousing Jb 3:8
I was a s craftsman beside Him. Pr 8:30
Do you see a man s in his work? Pr 22:29
of them are s with swords and Sg 3:8
looks for a s craftsman to set Is 40:20
are s in doing what is evil, Jr 4:22
all the work of s artisans. Jr 10:9
like those of a s warrior who Jr 50:9
to brutal men, s at destruction. Ezk 21:31
insolent king, s in intrigue, Dn 8:23
a s master builder I have laid 1Co 3:10

SKILLFUL *(9)*
the fine linen in a s design. Ex 39:3
the music because he was s. 1Ch 15:22
all trained and s in music for 1Ch 25:7
a s man who has understanding. 2Ch 2:13
tongue is the pen of a s writer. Ps 45:1
guided them with his s hands. Ps 78:72
labor and all s work is due to Ec 4:4
discerning, or favor to the s; Ec 9:11
send for the s women. Jr 9:17

SKILLFULLY *(10)*
He made s designed devices in 2Ch 26:15
who performed s before the LORD. 2Ch 30:22
play s on the strings, with a Ps 33:3
the charmers who s weave spells. Ps 58:5
He made the heavens s. Ps 136:5
I labored at s under the sun. Ec 2:19
Play s, sing many a song, and Is 23:16
How s you pursue love; Jr 2:33
voice and plays s on an Ezk 33:32
idols s made from their silver, Hs 13:2

SKIN *(121)*
the water in the s was gone, Gn 21:15
but I am a man with smooth s. Gn 27:11
become like the rest of his s. Ex 4:7
realize that the s of his face Ex 34:29
saw Moses, the s of his face Ex 34:30
he must s the burnt offering Lv 1:6
or spot on the s of his body, Lv 13:2
a disease on the s of his body, Lv 13:2
infection on the s of his body. Lv 13:3
deeper than the s of his body, Lv 13:3
of his body, it is a s disease. Lv 13:3
the spot on the s of his body is Lv 13:4
appear to be deeper than the s, Lv 13:4
and has not spread on the s, Lv 13:5
and has not spread on the s, Lv 13:6
further on his s after he has Lv 13:7
if the scab has spread on the s, Lv 13:8
him unclean; he has a s disease. Lv 13:8
When a s disease develops on a Lv 13:9
swelling on the s that has Lv 13:10
disease on the s of his body, Lv 13:11
But if the s disease breaks out Lv 13:12
over the s so that it covers Lv 13:12
covers all the s of the infected Lv 13:12
and if the s disease has covered Lv 13:13
is unclean; it is a s disease. Lv 13:15
appears on the s of one's body Lv 13:18
to be beneath the s and the hair Lv 13:20
is a s disease that has broken Lv 13:20
not beneath the s but is faded, Lv 13:21
If it spreads further on the s, Lv 13:22
is a burn on the s of one's body Lv 13:24
appears to be deeper than the s, Lv 13:25
is a s disease that has broken Lv 13:25
him unclean; it is a s disease. Lv 13:25
not beneath the s but is faded, Lv 13:26
it has spread further on the s, Lv 13:27
him unclean; it is a s disease. Lv 13:27
spread on the s but is faded, Lv 13:28
appears to be deeper than the s, Lv 13:30
a s disease of the head or chin. Lv 13:30
appear to be deeper than the s, Lv 13:31
appear to be deeper than the s, Lv 13:32
not spread on the s and does not Lv 13:34
appear to be deeper than the s, Lv 13:34
further on the s after his Lv 13:35
outbreak has spread on the s, Lv 13:36
spots on the s of the body, Lv 13:38
spots on the s of the body are Lv 13:39
that has broken out on the s; Lv 13:39
is a s disease breaking out on Lv 13:42
appearance of a s disease on his Lv 13:43
is afflicted with a s disease; Lv 13:44
an infectious s disease is to Lv 13:45
afflicted with a s disease on Lv 14:2
If the s disease has disappeared Lv 14:3
be cleansed from the s disease. Lv 14:7
someone who has a s disease and Lv 14:32
the law for any s disease or Lv 14:54
the law regarding s disease and Lv 14:57
descendants who has a s disease Lv 22:4
a covering made of manatee s, Nm 4:6
a covering made of manatee s, Nm 4:8
made of manatee s and put ⌊them⌋ Nm 4:10
a covering made of manatee s, Nm 4:11
a covering made of manatee s, Nm 4:12
made of manatee s over it and Nm 4:14
made of manatee s on top of it, Nm 4:25
is afflicted with a s disease, Nm 5:2
from seeds to s, during his vow. Nm 6:4
Miriam's ⌊s⌋ suddenly became Nm 12:10
a case of infectious s disease, Dt 24:8
and one bringing a s of wine. 1Sm 10:3
with bread, a s of wine, and one 1Sm 16:20
summer fruit, and a s of wine. 2Sm 16:1
warrior, but he had a s disease. 2Kg 5:1
cure him of his s disease." 2Kg 5:3
to cure him of his s disease. 2Kg 5:6
to cure a man of his s disease? 2Kg 5:7
the spot and cure the s disease. 2Kg 5:11
Then his s was restored ⌊and 2Kg 5:14
like the s of a small boy, 2Kg 5:14
Naaman's s disease will cling to 2Kg 5:27
under his clothes next to his s. 2Kg 6:30
Four men with s diseases were at 2Kg 7:3
he had a serious s disease until 2Kg 15:5
applied it to his infected s, 2Kg 20:7
a s disease broke out on his 2Ch 26:19
with a serious s disease and was 2Ch 26:21
they said, "He has a s disease." 2Ch 26:23
weren't able to s all the burnt 2Ch 29:34
"S for skin!" Satan answered the Jb 2:4
"Skin for s!" Satan answered the Jb 2:4
My s forms scabs and then oozes. Jb 7:5
You clothed me with s and flesh, Jb 10:11
I have sewn sackcloth over my s; Jb 16:15
Parts of his s are eaten away; Jb 18:13
My s and my flesh cling to my Jb 19:20
escaped by the s of my teeth. Jb 19:20
Even after my s has been Jb 19:26
My s blackens and flakes off, Jb 30:30
and apply it to his infected s, Is 38:21
Can the Cushite change his s, Jr 13:23
He has worn away my flesh and s; Lm 3:4
Their s has shriveled on their Lm 4:8
Our s is as hot as an oven from Lm 5:10
on you, and cover you with s. Ezk 37:6
flesh grew, and s covered them, Ezk 37:8
You tear off the s of people and Mc 3:2
you strip their s from them and Mc 3:3
with a serious s disease came up Mt 8:2
cleanse those with s diseases, Mt 10:8
with s diseases are healed, Mt 11:5
man who had a serious s disease, Mt 26:6
with a serious s disease came to Mk 1:40
who had a serious s disease, Mk 14:3
who had serious s diseases, Lk 4:27
had a serious s disease all over Lk 5:12
with s diseases are healed, Lk 7:22
with serious s diseases met Him Lk 17:12
had touched his s were brought Ac 19:12

SKINK *(1)*
lizard, the s, and the chameleon Lv 11:30

SKINNING *(1)*
Levites were s the ⌊animals⌋, 2Ch 35:11

SKINS *(20)*
clothing out of s for Adam and Gn 3:21
s dyed red and manatee skins; Ex 25:5
skins dyed red and manatee s; Ex 25:5
the tent from ram s dyed red, Ex 26:14
of manatee s on top of that. Ex 26:14
s dyed red and manatee skins; Ex 35:7
skins dyed red and manatee s; Ex 35:7
ram s dyed red or manatee skins, Ex 35:23
ram skins dyed red or manatee s, Ex 35:23
for the tent from ram s dyed red Ex 36:19
of manatee s on top of it. Ex 36:19
the covering of ram s dyed red Ex 39:34
and the covering of manatee s; Ex 39:34
of bread, two s of wine, five 1Sm 25:18
Otherwise, the s burst, the wine Mt 9:17

SLANDERED *(5)*
Ziba s your servant to my lord 2Sm 19:27
do not let your good be s, Rm 14:16
when we are s, we entreat. 1Co 4:13
why am I s because of something 1Co 10:30
God's message will not be s. Ti 2:5

SLANDERER *(1)*
Do not let a s stay in the land. Ps 140:11

SLANDERERS *(4)*
s, God-haters, arrogant, proud, Rm 1:30
of respect, not s, 1Tm 3:11
irreconcilable, s, without 2Tm 3:3
behavior, not s, not addicted to Ti 2:3

SLANDERING *(4)*
your brother, s your mother's Ps 50:20
put to shame for s me with lies; Ps 119:78
s the Way in front of the crowd, Ac 19:9
s us with malicious words. 3Jn 10

SLANDEROUS *(1)*
do not bring a s charge against 2Pt 2:11

SLANDEROUSLY *(1)*
as some people s claim we say, Rm 3:8

SLANDERS *(2)*
who secretly s his neighbor; Ps 101:5
quarreling, s, evil suspicions 1Tm 6:4

SLAPPED *(3)*
face and beat Him; others s Him Mt 26:67
police took Him and s Him. Mk 14:65
police standing by s Jesus, Jn 18:22

SLAPPING *(1)*
and were s His face. Jn 19:3

SLAPS *(1)*
if anyone s you on your right Mt 5:39

SLASH *(4)*
take one third and s ⌊it⌋ with Ezk 5:2
S to the right; turn to the left Ezk 21:16
They s themselves for grain and Hs 7:14
you s yourself ⌊in grief⌋; Mc 5:1

SLAUGHTER *(78)*
and took the knife to s his son. Gn 22:10
sons came to the s and plundered Gn 34:27
S an animal and prepare it, Gn 43:16
of Israel will s the animals at Ex 12:6
families, and s the Passover Ex 12:21
S the bull before the LORD at Ex 29:11
You are to s the ram, take its Ex 29:16
S the ram, take some of its Ex 29:20
He is to s the bull before the Lv 1:5
will s it on the north side of Lv 1:11
his offering and s it at the Lv 3:2
then s it before the tent of Lv 3:8
on its head and s it before the Lv 3:13
bull's head, and s it before the Lv 4:4
the goat and s it at the place Lv 4:24
offering and s it at the place Lv 4:29
sin offering and s it as a sin Lv 4:33
He is to s the male lamb at the Lv 14:13
he will s the burnt offering Lv 14:19
and he is to s one of the birds Lv 14:50
he will s the bull for his sin Lv 16:11
But you are not to s an animal Lv 22:28
may s and eat meat within any Dt 12:15
you may s any of your herd or Dt 12:21
them in a great s at Gibeon, Jos 10:10
a terrible s on them until they Jos 10:20
with a great s from Aroer all Jdg 11:33
limb from limb with a great s, Jdg 15:8
The s was severe—30,000 of the 1Sm 4:10
was a great s among the people 1Sm 4:17
LORD struck them with a great s. 1Sm 6:19
Then the s of the Philistines 1Sm 14:30
'There's been a s among the 2Sm 17:9
the s there was vast that day 2Sm 18:7
He inflicted a great s on Aram. 1Kg 20:21
S the Passover ⌊lambs⌋, 2Ch 35:6
treasury for the s of the Jews. Est 4:7
needy and to s those whose way Ps 37:14
like an ox going to the s, Pr 7:22
save those stumbling toward s. Pr 24:11
a place of s for his sons, Is 14:21
day of great s when the towers Is 30:25
giving them over to s. Is 34:2
a great s in the land of Edom. Is 34:6
lamb led to the s and like a Is 53:7
s children in the wadis below Is 57:5
of Hinnom, but the Valley of S. Jr 7:32
was like a docile lamb led to s. Jr 11:19
the wicked away like sheep to s, Jr 12:3
of Hinnom, but the Valley of S. Jr 19:6
the days of your s have come, Jr 25:34
young men have gone down to s. Jr 48:15
let them go down to the s. Jr 50:27
them down like lambs to the s, Jr 51:40
S the old men, the young men and Ezk 9:6
is sharpened for s, polished to Ezk 21:10
sword for s at all their gates, Ezk 21:15
it is drawn for s. Ezk 21:15
the order to s, raise a battle Ezk 21:22
You are⌋ drawn for s, polished Ezk 21:28
He will s your villages on the Ezk 26:8
He will s your people with the Ezk 26:11
groan and s occurs within you Ezk 26:15
I will s all its cattle that are Ezk 32:13
which to s the burnt offering, Ezk 40:39
utensils used to s the burnt Ezk 40:42
They will s the burnt offerings Ezk 44:11
Rebels are deeply involved in s; Hs 5:2
of Esau will be destroyed by s. Ob 9
continually s nations without Hab 1:17
the flock intended for s. Zch 11:4
who buy them s them but are not Zch 11:5
the flock intended for s, Zch 11:7
the fattened calf and s it, Lk 15:23
and s them in my presence.'" Lk 19:27
was led like a sheep to the s, Ac 8:32
your hearts for the day of s. Jms 5:5
that people would s one another. Rv 6:4

SLAUGHTERED *(72)*
Joseph's robe, s a young goat, Gn 37:31
it is to be s before the LORD Lv 4:15
offering is s before the LORD. Lv 4:24
where the burnt offering is s. Lv 4:33
and must be s before the LORD Lv 6:25
where the burnt offering is s. Lv 6:25
offering must be s at the place Lv 7:2
where the burnt offering is s, Lv 7:2
Then Moses s ⌊it⌋, took the Lv 8:15
Moses s it and sprinkled the Lv 8:19
Moses s ⌊it⌋, took some of its Lv 8:23
altar and s the calf as a sin Lv 9:8
Then he s the burnt offering. Lv 9:12
sin offering, s it, and made a Lv 9:15
he s the ox and the ram as the Lv 9:18
of the birds be s over fresh Lv 14:5
bird that was s over the fresh Lv 14:6
and burnt offering are s, Lv 14:13
the blood of the s bird and the Lv 14:51
and herds were s for them, Nm 11:22
He has s them in the wilderness. Nm 14:16
the camp and s in his presence. Nm 19:3
Your ox will be s before your Dt 28:31
out of Gibeah and s 22,000 men Jdg 20:21
to meet them and s an additional Jdg 20:25
day the Israelites s 25,100 men Jdg 20:35
of the cities s those between Jdg 20:42
Then they s the bull and brought 1Sm 1:25
the gods that s the Egyptians 1Sm 4:8
Ammonite camp and s them until 1Sm 11:11
and calves, s them on the ground 1Sm 14:32
ox that night and s it there. 1Sm 14:34
her house, and she quickly s it. 1Sm 28:24
David s them from twilight until 1Sm 30:17
water when Jezebel s the LORD's 1Kg 18:4
I did when Jezebel s the LORD's 1Kg 18:13
Wadi Kishon and s them there. 1Kg 18:40
the team of oxen, and s them. 1Kg 19:21
the king's sons and s all 70, 2Kg 10:7
alive and then s them at the pit 2Kg 10:14
He s on the altars all the 2Kg 23:20
They s Zedekiah's sons before 2Kg 25:7
you s them in a rage that has 2Ch 28:9
So they s the bulls, and the 2Ch 29:22
They s the rams and sprinkled 2Ch 29:22
They s the lambs and sprinkled 2Ch 29:22
The priests s the goats and put 2Ch 29:24
They s the Passover lamb on the 2Ch 30:15
Passover and s the Passover 2Ch 35:1
they s the Passover ⌊lambs⌋, 2Ch 35:11
we are counted as sheep to be s. Ps 44:22
many nations and s mighty kings: Ps 135:10
and s famous kings—His love is Ps 136:18
your land and s your own people. Is 14:20
of you will kneel down to be s, Is 65:12
of Babylon s Zedekiah's sons Jr 39:6
and he ⌊also⌋ s all Judah's Jr 39:6
men with him s them and threw Jr 41:7
of Babylon s Zedekiah's sons Jr 52:10
his eyes and also s the Judean Jr 52:10
You s My children and gave them Ezk 16:21
same day they s their children Ezk 23:39
mainland will be s by the sword. Ezk 26:6
and fattened cattle have been s, Mt 22:4
your father has s the fattened Lk 15:27
s the fattened calf for him.' Lk 15:30
I saw one like a s lamb standing Rv 5:6
because You were s, and You Rv 5:9
The Lamb who was s is worthy to Rv 5:12
of those s because of God's Rv 6:9
of life of the Lamb who was s. Rv 13:8
and all those s on earth, was Rv 18:24

SLAUGHTERING *(6)*
Do the s here and then you can 1Sm 14:34
were in charge of s the Passover 2Ch 30:17
of cattle, s of sheep, eating Is 22:13
of Your anger, s without Lm 2:21
feast that I am s for you, Ezk 39:17
on which the s was to be done. Ezk 40:41

SLAUGHTERS *(5)*
After he s the male lamb for the Lv 14:25
When he s the male goat for the Lv 16:15
the house of Israel who s an ox, Lv 17:3
or s ⌊it⌋ outside the camp, Lv 17:3
One s an ox, one kills a man; Is 66:3

SLAVE *(178)*
of Shem; Canaan will be his s. Gn 9:26
of Shem; Canaan will be his s. Gn 9:27
so a s born in my house will be Gn 15:3
owned an Egyptian s named Hagar. Gn 16:1
bearing children, go to my s; Gn 16:2
her Egyptian s, and gave her to Gn 16:3
put my s in your arms, and ever Gn 16:5
Here, your s is in your hands; Gn 16:6
said, "Hagar, s of Sarai, where Gn 16:8
This includes a s born in your Gn 17:12
a s born in your house, as well Gn 17:13
Drive out this s with her son, Gn 21:10
for the son of this s will not Gn 21:10
about the boy and your s. Gn 21:12
Sarah's s, bore to Abraham Gn 25:12
Laban gave his s Zilpah to his Gn 29:24
to his daughter Leah as her s. Gn 29:24
Laban gave his s Bilhah to his Gn 29:29
to his daughter Rachel as her s. Gn 29:29
she said, "Here is my s Bilhah. Gn 30:3
Rachel gave her s Bilhah to Gn 30:4
Rachel's s Bilhah conceived Gn 30:7
she took her s Zilpah and gave Gn 30:9
s Zilpah bore Jacob a son. Gn 30:10
When Leah's s Zilpah bore Jacob Gn 30:12
for giving my s to my husband," Gn 30:18
of Rachel's s Bilhah were Dan Gn 35:25
sons of Leah's s Zilpah were Gad Gn 35:26
The Hebrew s you brought to us Gn 39:17
the things your s did to me"— Gn 39:19
s of the captain of the guards, Gn 41:12
found to have it will be my s, Gn 44:10
the cup was found will be my s. Gn 44:17
remain here as my lord's s, Gn 44:33
she sent her s girl to get it. Ex 2:5
whom Pharaoh's s drivers had set Ex 5:14
any s a man has purchased may Ex 12:44
or female s, your livestock, Ex 20:10
male or female s, his ox or Ex 20:17
buy a Hebrew s, he is to serve Ex 21:2
But if the s declares: Ex 21:5
a man sells his daughter as a s, Ex 21:7
his male or female s with a rod, Ex 21:20
and the s dies under his abuse, Ex 21:20
the s can stand up after a day Ex 21:21
or female s and destroys it, Ex 21:26
he must let the s go free in Ex 21:26
tooth of his male or female s, Ex 21:27
he must let the s go free in Ex 21:27
the ox gores a male or female s, Ex 21:32
son of your female s as well as Ex 23:12
woman who is a s designated for Lv 19:20
male or female s, and the hired Lv 25:6
not force him to do s labor. Lv 25:39
male or female s, your ox or Dt 5:14
that you were a s in the land of Dt 5:15
male or female s, his ox or Dt 5:21

and female s, and the Levite Dt 12:18
that you were a s in the land of Dt 15:15
But if your s says to you, Dt 15:16
he will become your s for life. Dt 15:17
your female s the same way. Dt 15:17
male and female s, the Levite Dt 16:11
male and female s, as well as Dt 16:14
Do not return a s to his master Dt 23:15
treats him as a s or sells him, Dt 24:7
that you were a s in Egypt, Dt 24:18
that you were a s in the land of Dt 24:22
and no one is left—s or free. Dt 32:36
the son of his s, king over the Jdg 9:18
comforted and encouraged your s, Ru 2:13
I am Ruth, your s," she replied. Ru 3:9
the s of an Amalekite man," 1Sm 30:13
the sight of the s girls of his 2Sm 6:20
honored by the s girls you spoke 2Sm 6:22
males, both s and free, in 1Kg 14:10
Ahab's males, both s and free, 1Kg 21:21
Ahab's males, both s and free, 2Kg 9:8
and the s is set free from his Jb 3:19
Like a s he longs for shade; Jb 7:2
you can take him as a s forever? Jb 41:4
Joseph, who was sold as a s. Ps 105:17
fool will be a s to someone Pr 11:29
much less for a s to rule over Pr 19:10
borrower is a s to the lender. Pr 22:7
A s pampered from his youth will Pr 29:21
Is Israel a s? Was he born into Jr 2:14
the provinces has become a s. Lm 1:1
No one can be a s of two masters Mt 6:24
and to my s, 'Do this!' Mt 8:9
teacher, or a s above his master Mt 10:24
teacher and a s like his master Mt 10:25
the s fell facedown before him Mt 18:26
master of that s had compassion, Mt 18:27
But that s went out and found Mt 18:28
his fellow s fell down and began Mt 18:29
said to him, 'You wicked s! Mt 18:32
have had mercy on your fellow s, Mt 18:33
first among you must be your s; Mt 20:27
is a faithful and sensible s, Mt 24:45
That s whose master finds him Mt 24:46
if that wicked s says in his Mt 24:48
Well done, good and faithful s! Mt 25:21
Well done, good and faithful s! Mt 25:23
to him, 'You evil, lazy s! Mt 25:26
good-for-nothing s into the Mt 25:30
high priest's s and cut off his Mt 26:51
among you must be a s to all. Mk 10:44
time he sent a s to the farmers Mk 12:2
Again he sent another s to them, Mk 12:4
struck the high priest's s, Mk 14:47
"I am the Lord's s," said Mary. Lk 1:38
the humble condition of His s. Lk 1:48
You can dismiss Your s in peace, Lk 2:29
A centurion's s, who was highly Lk 7:2
come and save the life of his s. Lk 7:3
and to my s, 'Do this!' Lk 7:8
they found the s in good health. Lk 7:10
That s whose master finds him Lk 12:43
if that s says in his heart, Lk 12:45
And that s who knew his master's Lk 12:47
he sent his s to tell those who Lk 14:17
So the s came back and reported Lk 14:21
of the house told his s, Lk 14:21
'Master,' the s said, 'what you Lk 14:22
Then the master told the s, Lk 14:23
No household s can be the slave Lk 16:13
can be the s of two masters, Lk 16:13
of you having a s plowing or Lk 17:7
he thank that s because he did Lk 17:9
'Well done, good s!' Lk 19:17
what you have said, you evil s! Lk 19:22
time he sent a s to the farmers Lk 20:10
yet another s, but they beat Lk 20:11
high priest's s and cut off his Lk 22:50
who commits sin is a s of sin. Jn 8:34
A s does not remain in the Jn 8:35
A s is not greater than his Jn 13:16
because a s doesn't know what Jn 15:15
'A s is not greater than his Jn 15:20
struck the high priest's s, Jn 18:10
Then the s girl who was the Jn 18:17
a s girl met us who had a spirit Ac 16:16
Paul, a s of Christ Jesus, Rm 1:1
I myself am a s to the law of Rm 7:25
criticize another's household s? Rm 14:4
Were you called while a s? 1Co 7:21
by the Lord as a s is the Lord's 1Co 7:22
as a free man is Christ's s. 1Co 7:22
I have made myself a s to all, 1Co 9:19
I would not be a s of Christ. Gl 1:10
no Jew or Greek, s or free, male Gl 3:28
he differs in no way from a s, Gl 4:1
are no longer a s, but a son; Gl 4:7
one by a s and the other by a Gl 4:22
the one by the s was born Gl 4:23
Throw out the s and her son, Gl 4:30
the son of the s will never Gl 4:30
children of the s but of the Gl 4:31
one does, s or free, he will Eph 6:8
by assuming the form of a s, Php 2:7
our much loved fellow s. Col 1:7
barbarian, Scythian, s and free; Col 3:11
and a fellow s in the Lord, Col 4:7
one of you, a s of Christ Jesus Col 4:12
The Lord's s must not quarrel, 2Tm 2:24
Paul, a s of God, and an apostle Ti 1:1
no longer as a s, but more than Phm 16
but more than a s—as a dearly Phm 16
a s of God and of the Lord Jesus Jms 1:1
a s and an apostle of Jesus 2Pt 1:1
Jude, a s of Jesus Christ, and a Jd 1
through His angel to His s John, Rv 1:1
and every s and free person hid Rv 6:15
poor, free and s—to be given Rv 13:16
am a fellow s with you and your Rv 19:10
free and s, small and great. Rv 19:18
I am a fellow s with you, your Rv 22:9

SLAVE'S (5)

a nation of the s son because he Gn 21:13
of silver to the s master, Ex 21:32
that s master will come on a day Mt 24:50
that s master will come on a day Lk 12:46
The s name was Malchus. Jn 18:10

SLAVERY (28)

and free you from s to them. Ex 6:6
of the place of s, for the LORD Ex 13:3
of Egypt, out of the place of s. Ex 13:14
of Egypt, out of the place of s. Ex 20:2
of Egypt, out of the place of s. Dt 5:6
of Egypt, out of the place of s. Dt 6:12
you from the place of s, Dt 7:8
of Egypt, out of the place of s. Dt 8:14
you from the place of s, Dt 13:5
of Egypt, out of the place of s. Dt 13:10
the place of s and performed Jos 24:17
Egypt and out of the place of s. Jdg 6:8
not consign the Israelites to s; 1Kg 9:22
male and female, to s. 2Ch 28:10
Even in our s, God has given us Ezr 9:8
has not abandoned us in our s. Ezr 9:9
our sons and daughters to s. Neh 5:5
to return to their s in Egypt. Neh 9:17
he born into s? Why else has he Jr 2:14
out of the place of s, saying: Jr 34:13
affliction and harsh s; Lm 1:3
you from that place of s. Mc 6:4
a spirit of s to fall back Rm 8:15
were in s under the elemental Gl 4:3
and bears children into s— Gl 4:24
for she is in s with her Gl 4:25
submit again to a yoke of s. Gl 5:1
were held in s all their lives Heb 2:15

SLAVES (126)

the lowest of s to his brothers Gn 9:25
male and female s, and camels. Gn 12:16
and all the s born in his house Gn 17:23
both s born in his house and Gn 17:27
cattle and male and female s, Gn 20:14
and his female s so that they Gn 20:17
male and female s, and camels Gn 24:35
of cattle, and many s, and the Gn 26:14
that his father's s had dug in Gn 26:15
Isaac's s dug in the valley and Gn 26:19
Isaac's s also dug a well there. Gn 26:25
day Isaac's s came to tell him Gn 26:32
male and female s, and camels Gn 30:43
the tents of the two female s, Gn 31:33
flocks, male and female s. Gn 32:5
them to his s as separate herds Gn 32:16
his two female s, and his 11 Gn 32:22
Rachel, and the two female s. Gn 33:1
He put the female s first, Gn 33:2
Then the female s and their Gn 33:6
seize us, make us s, and take Gn 43:18
also will become my lord's s." Gn 44:9
We are now my lord's s—both we Gn 44:16
land will become Pharaoh's s. Gn 47:19
eyes and will be Pharaoh's s." Gn 47:25
him, and said, "We are your s!" Gn 50:18
are forcing to work as s, Ex 6:5
not to leave as the male s do. Ex 21:7
They are not to be sold as s, Lv 25:42
they are My s I brought out Lv 25:42
Your male and female s are to be Lv 25:44
may purchase male and female s. Lv 25:44
you can make them s for life. Lv 25:46
For the Israelites are My s. Lv 25:55
They are My s I brought out of Lv 25:55
you would no longer be their s. Lv 26:13
male and female s may rest as Dt 5:14
'We were s of Pharaoh in Egypt, Dt 6:21
and female s, and the Levite Dt 12:12
that you were s in Egypt; Dt 16:12
enemies as male and female s, Dt 28:68
cursed and will always be s— Jos 9:23
Many s these days are running 1Sm 25:10
two of Shimei's s ran away to 1Kg 2:39
Look, your s are in Gath." 1Kg 2:39
at Gath to search for his s. 1Kg 2:40
take my two children as his s." 2Kg 4:1
and oxen, and male and female s? 2Kg 5:26
Israelites to be s for his work; 2Ch 8:9
their 7,337 male and female s, Ezr 2:65
Though we are s, our God has not Ezr 9:9
their 7,337 male and female s, Neh 7:67
s in the land You gave our Neh 9:36
Here we are—s in it! Neh 9:36
been sold as male and female s, Est 7:4
servants and had s who were born Ec 2:7
I have seen s on horses, but Ec 10:7
walking on the ground like s. Ec 10:7
male and female s in the LORD's Is 14:2
and female Hebrew s and no one Jr 34:9
free their male and female s— Jr 34:10
male and female s they had freed Jr 34:11
forced them to become s ⌊again⌋. Jr 34:11
male and female s who had been Jr 34:16
subjugated them to be your s. Jr 34:16
S rule over us; no one rescues Lm 5:8
They exchanged s and bronze Ezk 27:13
male and female s in those days. Jl 2:29
You cannot be s of God and of Mt 6:24
landowner's s came to him and Mt 13:27
them up?' the s asked him. Mt 13:28
to settle accounts with his s. Mt 18:23
of his fellow s who owed him 100 Mt 18:28
When the other s saw what had Mt 18:31
he sent his s to the farmers to Mt 21:34
But the farmers took his s, Mt 21:35
he sent other s, more than the Mt 21:36
sent out his s to summon those Mt 22:3
sent out other s, and said, Mt 22:4
And the others seized his s, Mt 22:6
he told his s, 'The banquet is Mt 22:8
So those s went out on the roads Mt 22:10
and starts to beat his fellow s, Mt 24:49
called his own s and turned over Mt 25:14
master of those s came and Mt 25:19
authority to his s, gave each Mk 13:34
Those s the master will find Lk 12:37
them alert, those s are blessed. Lk 12:38
to beat the male and female s, Lk 12:45
But the father told his s, Lk 15:22
be s to both God and money. Lk 16:13
'We are good-for-nothing s; Lk 17:10
called 10 of his s, gave them 10 Lk 19:13
he summoned those s he had given Lk 19:15
s met him saying that his boy Jn 4:51
I do not call you s anymore, Jn 15:15
Now the s and the temple police Jn 18:18
One of the high priest's s, Jn 18:26
male and female s in those days, Ac 2:18
grant that Your s may speak Your Ac 4:29
that they will serve as s, Ac 7:7
of his household s and a devout Ac 10:7
men are the s of the Most High Ac 16:17
to someone as obedient s, Rm 6:16
you are s of that one you obey— Rm 6:16
you used to be s of sin, Rm 6:17
of yourselves as s to moral Rm 6:19

offer them as s to righteousness Rm 6:19
For when you were s of sin, Rm 6:20
do not become s of men. 1Co 7:23
Greeks, whether s or free—and 1Co 12:13
as your s because of Jesus 2Co 4:5
S, obey your human masters with Eph 6:5
men, but as s of Christ, do Eph 6:6
and Timothy, s of Christ Jesus: Php 1:1
S, obey your human masters in Col 3:22
supply your s with what is right Col 4:1
the yoke as s must regard their 1Tm 6:1
S are to be submissive to their Ti 2:9
As God's s, ⌊live⌋ as free 1Pt 2:16
Household s, submit yourselves 1Pt 2:18
themselves are s of corruption, 2Pt 2:19
Him to show His s what must Rv 1:1
and deceives My s to commit Rv 2:20
of⌋ their fellow s and their Rv 6:11
until we seal the s of our God Rv 7:3

SLAVING *(1)*
have been s many years for you, Lk 15:29

SLAY *(1)*
He will s the monster that is in Is 27:1

SLAYER *(2)*
between the s and the avenger Nm 35:24
to be put in the hand of the s. Ezk 21:11

SLAYS *(1)*
and jealousy s the gullible. Jb 5:2

SLEDGE *(1)*
the mud like a threshing s. Jb 41:30

SLEDGEHAMMER *(1)*
and like a s that pulverizes Jr 23:29

SLEDGES *(3)*
the threshing s and ox yokes for 2Sm 24:22
the threshing s for the wood, 1Ch 21:23
threshed Gilead with iron s. Am 1:3

SLEEK *(1)*
They have become fat and s. Jr 5:28

SLEEP *(76)*
God caused a deep s to come over Gn 2:21
setting, a deep s fell on Abram, Gn 15:12
in the land to s with us ⌊as is⌋ Gn 19:31
wine so that we can s with him Gn 19:32
so you can go s with him and we Gn 19:34
When Jacob awoke from his s, Gn 28:16
I want to s with her." Gn 29:21
Go s with her, and she'll bear Gn 30:3
you can s with him tonight in Gn 30:15
by night, and s fled from my Gn 31:40
S with your brother's wife. Gn 38:8
Come, let me s with you," for he Gn 38:16
at Joseph and said, "S with me." Gn 39:7
garment and said, "S with me!" Gn 39:12
to me so he could s with me, Gn 39:14
What will he s in? And if he Ex 22:27
You are not to s with a man as Lv 18:22
you must not s in ⌊the garment⌋ Dt 24:12
Then he will s in it and bless Dt 24:13
awoke from his s and pulled out Jdg 16:14
When he awoke from his s, Jdg 16:20
because a deep s from the LORD 1Sm 26:12
Why did you s with my father's 2Sm 3:7
and drink and s with my wife? 2Sm 11:11
he will s with them publicly. 2Sm 12:11
and said, "Come s with me, my 2Sm 13:11
S with your father's concubines 2Sm 16:21
That night s escaped the king, Est 6:1
when deep s descends on men, Jb 4:13
they will not stir from their s. Jb 14:12
and let other men s with her. Jb 31:10
when deep s falls on people as Jb 33:15
I lie down and s; I wake again Ps 3:5
both lie down and s in peace, Ps 4:8
otherwise, I will s in death, Ps 13:3
slipped into their ⌊final⌋ s. Ps 76:5
the Lord awoke as if from s, Ps 78:65
their life; they s. They are Ps 90:5
of Israel does not slumber or s. Ps 121:4
He gives s to the one He Ps 127:2
my eyes to s or my eyelids to Ps 132:4
and your s will be pleasant. Pr 3:24
they can't s unless they have Pr 4:16
are robbed of s unless they make Pr 4:16
Don't give s to your eyes or Pr 6:4
will you get up from your s? Pr 6:9
A little s, a little slumber, a Pr 6:10
induces deep s, and a lazy Pr 19:15
one will s at night without Pr 19:23
Don't love s, or you will become Pr 20:13
a little s, a little slumber, a Pr 24:33
The s of the worker is sweet, Ec 5:12
of the rich permits him no s. Ec 5:12
do not close in s day or night Ec 8:16
I s, but my heart is awake. Sg 5:2
you an overwhelming urge to s; Is 29:10
dream, lie down, and love to s. Is 56:10
My s had been most pleasant to Jr 31:26
wilderness and s in the forest. Ezk 34:25
him, and s deserted him. Dn 2:1
to him, and he could not s. Dn 6:18
fell into a deep s, with my face Dn 8:18
heard them I fell into a deep s, Dn 10:9
Many of those who s in the dust Dn 12:2
out and fallen into a deep s. Jnh 1:5
your officers s. Your people are Nah 3:18
me as one awakened out of s. Zch 4:1
those with him were in a deep s, Lk 9:32
He was speaking about natural s. Jn 11:13
sank into a deep s as Paul kept Ac 20:9
was overcome by s he fell down Ac 20:9
hour for you to wake up from s, Rm 13:11
we must not s, like the rest, 1Th 5:6
For those who s, sleep at night, 1Th 5:7
those who sleep, s at night, and 1Th 5:7
their destruction does not s. 2Pt 2:3

SLEEPER *(1)*
Get up, s, and rise up from the Eph 5:14

SLEEPING *(25)*
the land that you are now s Gn 28:13
against Israel by s with Jacob's Gn 34:7
will you give me for s with me?" Gn 38:16
While he was s from exhaustion, Jdg 4:21
how they were s with the women 1Sm 2:22
he's s and will wake up!" 1Kg 18:27
Why are You s? Get up! Don't Ps 44:23
be like someone s out at sea or Pr 23:34
When Joseph got up from s, Mt 1:24
by the waves. But He was s. Mt 8:24
the girl isn't dead, but s." Mt 9:24
people were s, his enemy came, Mt 13:25
the disciples and found them s. Mt 26:40
He came again and found them s, Mt 26:43
Are you still s and resting? Mt 26:45
and stole Him while we were s.' Mt 28:13
in the stern, s on the cushion. Mk 4:38
come suddenly and find you s. Mk 13:36
Then He came and found them s. Mk 14:37
"Simon, are you s?" Mk 14:37
He came again and found them s, Mk 14:40
Are you still s and resting? Mk 14:41
He found them s, exhausted from Lk 22:45
"Why are you s?" He asked them. Lk 22:46
was s between two soldiers, Ac 12:6

SLEEPLESS *(2)*
by labors, by s nights, by times 2Co 6:5
hardship, many s nights, hunger 2Co 11:27

SLEEPS *(16)*
If a man s with a woman and has Lv 15:18
If a man s with her, and ⌊blood Lv 15:24
and a man who s with an unclean Lv 15:33
If a man s with his father's Lv 20:11
If a man s with his Lv 20:12
If a man s with a man as with a Lv 20:13
If a man s with a menstruating Lv 20:18
If a man s with his aunt, he has Lv 20:20
and s with another, but it is Nm 5:13
is the one who s with his Dt 27:20
the one who s with his sister, Dt 27:22
'Cursed is the one who s with Dt 27:23
with the one who s with another Pr 6:29
the son who s during harvest is Pr 10:5
no one slumbers or s. Is 5:27
he s and rises—night and day, Mk 4:27

SLEPT *(26)*
to come over the man, and he s. Gn 2:21
He s with Hagar, and she became Gn 16:4
came and s with her father; Gn 19:33
I s with my father last night. Gn 19:34
the younger went and s with him; Gn 19:35
easily have s with your wife, Gn 26:10
her to Jacob, and he s with her. Gn 29:23
Jacob s with Rachel also, and Gn 29:30
as a wife, and he s with her. Gn 30:4
So Jacob s with her that night. Gn 30:16
went in and s with his father's Gn 35:22
her as a wife and s with her. Gn 38:2
so whenever he s with his Gn 38:9
gave them to her and s with her, Gn 38:18
'If no man has s with you, Nm 5:19
your husband has s with you'— Nm 5:20
female who has s with a man." Jdg 21:11
she came to him, he s with her. 2Sm 11:4
But Uriah s at the door of the 2Sm 11:9
s in his arms, and it was like 2Sm 12:3
he went and s with her. 2Sm 12:24
and he s with his father's 2Sm 16:22
lay down and s under the broom 1Kg 19:5
Hezron s with the daughter of 1Ch 2:21
He s with his wife, and she 1Ch 7:23
men s with her in her youth, Ezk 23:8

SLICE *(2)*
brow is like a s of pomegranate. Sg 4:3
brow is like a s of pomegranate. Sg 6:7

SLIME *(1)*
a slug that moves along in s, Ps 58:8

SLING *(7)*
could s a stone at a hair and Jdg 20:16
Then, with his s in his hand, he 1Sm 17:40
Philistine with a s and a stone. 1Sm 17:50
lives like ⌊stones⌋ from a s. 1Sm 25:29
stones ⌊with a s⌋ or ⌊shoot⌋ 1Ch 12:2
is like binding a stone in a s. Pr 26:8
and s you into a wide land. Is 22:18

SLINGING *(1)*
I am s out the land's residents Jr 10:18

SLINGS *(1)*
Then men with s surrounded ⌊the 2Kg 3:25

SLINGSTONES *(3)*
helmets, armor, bows and s. 2Ch 26:14
s become like stubble to him. Jb 41:28
will consume and conquer with s; Zch 9:15

SLIP *(5)*
that they don't s from your mind Dt 4:9
In time their foot will s, Dt 32:35
does not allow our feet to s. Ps 66:9
will not allow your foot to s; Ps 121:3
let the other s from your hand. Ec 7:18

SLIPPED *(6)*
of the Danites s out of their Jos 19:47
My days have s by; my plans have Jb 17:11
Your paths; my feet have not s. Ps 17:5
But as for me, my feet almost s; Ps 73:2
they have s into their ⌊final⌋ Ps 76:5
because Jesus had s away into Jn 5:13

SLIPPERY *(3)*
Let their way be dark and s, Ps 35:6
Indeed You put them in s places; Ps 73:18
be to them like s paths in the Jr 23:12

SLIPPING *(2)*
for those whose feet are s. Jb 12:5
My foot is s," Your faithful Ps 94:18

SLITHER *(1)*
snakes that s in the dust. Dt 32:24

SLITHERING *(2)*
Egypt will hiss like a s snake, Jr 46:22
like reptiles s on the ground. Mc 7:17

SLOPE *(13)*
the one mountain s that I took Gn 48:22
reach the eastern s of the Sea Nm 34:11
to the southern Jebusite s Jos 15:8
the northern s of Mount Jearim Jos 15:10
reached to the s north of Ekron, Jos 15:11
ascended to the s of Jericho on Jos 18:12
the southern s of Luz (that is Jos 18:13
south Jebusite s and downward to Jos 18:16
went north to the s opposite the Jos 18:18
to the north s of Beth-hoglah Jos 18:19
was climbing the s of the Mount 2Sm 15:30
they go up the s of Luhith Is 15:5
its southern ⌊s⌋ was a structure Ezk 40:2

SLOPES *(10)*
even the s of the ravines that Nm 21:15
under the s of Pisgah on the Dt 3:17
Dead Sea below the s of Pisgah. Dt 4:49
and the s—with all their Jos 10:40
and the S of Dor to the west, Jos 11:2
southward below the s of Pisgah. Jos 12:3
the plain, the s, the desert, Jos 12:8

Beth-peor, the s of Pisgah, and Jos 13:20
living on the s of the wadis, Jb 30:6
Zion on the s of the north is Ps 48:2

SLOW *(17)*
because I am s and hesitant in Ex 4:10
s to anger and rich in faithful Ex 34:6
The LORD is s to anger and rich Nm 14:18
God, do not be s to keep it, Dt 23:21
don't s the pace for me unless I 2Kg 4:24
s to anger and rich in faithful Neh 9:17
s to anger and abundant in Ps 86:15
s to anger and full of faithful Ps 103:8
s to anger and great in faithful Ps 145:8
but a man s to anger calms Pr 15:18
compassionate, s to anger, rich Jl 2:13
God, s to become angry, Jnh 4:2
The LORD is s to anger but great Nah 1:3
How unwise and s you are to Lk 24:25
you have become s to understand. Heb 5:11
quick to hear, s to speak, and Jms 1:19
slow to speak, and s to anger, Jms 1:19

SLOWLY *(4)*
will continue on s, at a pace Gn 33:14
rejected the s flowing waters Is 8:6
I walk along s all my years Is 38:15
Sailing s for many days, we came Ac 27:7

SLUG *(1)*
Like a s that moves along in Ps 58:8

SLUMBER *(8)*
people as they s on ⌊their⌋ beds Jb 33:15
your Protector will not s. Ps 121:3
of Israel does not s or sleep. Ps 121:4
eyes to sleep or my eyelids to s Ps 132:4
your eyes or s to your eyelids Pr 6:4
sleep, a little s, a little Pr 6:10
sleep, a little s, a little Pr 24:33
of Assyria, your shepherds s; Nah 3:18

SLUMBERS *(1)*
no one s or sleeps. Is 5:27

SLUMPED *(1)*
and he s down in his chariot. 2Kg 9:24

SLUNG *(2)*
a bronze sword was s between his 1Sm 17:6
took out a stone, s ⌊it⌋, and 1Sm 17:49

SLY *(2)*
s wink of the eye causes grief, Pr 10:10
yet s as I am, I took you in by 2Co 12:16

SMALL *(60)*
run to. It is a s place. Please Gn 19:20
it's only a s place, isn't it? Gn 19:20
household is too s for a ⌊whole⌋ Ex 12:4
God to do ⌊anything⌋ s or great. Nm 22:18
and decrease it for a s one. Nm 26:54
and decrease it for a s one. Nm 33:54
listen to s and great alike. Dt 1:17
hill country is too s for you." Jos 17:15
putting their s children, Jdg 18:21
great or s, without telling 1Sm 20:2
A s young man was with him. 1Sm 20:35
except one s ewe lamb that he 2Sm 12:3
I have just one s request of you 1Kg 2:20
LORD was too s to accommodate 1Kg 8:64
made 300 s shields of hammered 1Kg 10:17
At the time Hadad was a s boy. 1Kg 11:17
Only make me a s loaf from it 1Kg 17:13
a cloud as s as a man's hand 1Kg 18:44
some s boys came out of the city 2Kg 2:23
so let's make a s room upstairs 2Kg 4:10
like the skin of a s boy, 2Kg 5:14
supervision is too s for us. 2Kg 6:1
made 300 s shields of hammered 2Ch 9:16
with anyone, s or great, except 2Ch 18:30
divisions, whether large or s. 2Ch 31:15
all the people from great to s. 2Ch 34:30
large and s, the treasures 2Ch 36:18
Both the s and the great are Jb 3:19
large and s—and come to my Ps 35:2
living things both large and s. Ps 104:25
the LORD—s and great alike Ps 115:13
Four things on earth are s, Pr 30:24
There was a s city with few men Ec 9:14
all the s vessels, from bowls Is 22:24
and its cover too s to wrap up Is 28:20
now be indeed too s for the Is 49:19
This place is too s for me; Is 49:20
great and s will die in this Jr 16:6
Deploy s shields and large; Jr 46:3
make them so s they cannot rule Ezk 29:15
feet from the s ledge to the Ezk 43:14
rise to power with a s nation. Dn 11:23
and the s house to rubble. Am 6:11
Jacob survive since he is so s?" Am 7:2
Jacob survive since he is so s?" Am 7:5
you are s among the clans of Mc 5:2
who scorns the day of s things? Zch 4:10
they said, "and a few s fish." Mt 15:34
to have a s boat ready for Him Mk 3:9
They also had a few s fish, Mk 8:7
faithful in a very s matter, Lk 19:17
and testify to both s and great, Ac 26:22
by a very s rudder wherever Jms 3:4
the tongue is a s part ⌊of the Jms 3:5
large a forest a s fire ignites. Jms 3:5
Your name, both s and great, Rv 11:18
everyone—s and great, rich Rv 13:16
who fear Him, both s and great! Rv 19:5
free and slave, s and great." Rv 19:18
great and the s, standing before Rv 20:12

SMALLER *(4)*
the larger and s ⌊tribes⌋." Nm 26:56
tribe⌋ and less from a s one. Nm 35:8
in your house, a larger and a s. Dt 25:14
is s than all the seeds on the Mk 4:31

SMALLEST *(5)*
from the s of Israel's tribes 1Sm 9:21
thousand, the s a mighty nation Is 60:22
not the s letter or one stroke Mt 5:18
It's the s of all the seeds, Mt 13:32
unworthy to judge the s cases? 1Co 6:2

SMART *(1)*
with fools since you are so s! 2Co 11:19

SMASH *(20)*
demolish them and s their sacred Ex 23:24
their altars, s their sacred Ex 34:13
He will s the forehead of Moab Nm 24:17
their altars, s their standing Dt 7:5
their altars, s their sacred Dt 12:3
S the loins of his adversaries Dt 33:11
will s them against each other, Jr 13:14
Can anyone s iron, iron from the Jr 15:12
He will s the sacred pillars of Jr 43:13
his containers and s his jars. Jr 48:12
With you I will s nations; Jr 51:20
With you I will s the horse and Jr 51:21
with you I will s the chariot Jr 51:21
With you I will s man and woman; Jr 51:22
with you I will s the old man Jr 51:22
with you I will s the young man Jr 51:22
With you I will s the shepherd Jr 51:23
with you I will s the farmer and Jr 51:23
With you I will s governors and Jr 51:23
will crush and s all the others. Dn 2:40

SMASHED *(14)*
an oven or stove, it must be s; Lv 11:35
Then he s them there and threw 2Kg 23:12
and he s the Asherah poles and 2Ch 34:7
They are s to pieces from dawn Jb 4:20
of the neck and s me to pieces. Jb 16:12
You s the heads of the sea Ps 74:13
children will be s ⌊to death⌋ Is 13:16
whole earth is cut down and s! Jr 50:23
and your incense altars s. Ezk 6:4
your idols s and obliterated, Ezk 6:6
of Samaria will be s to bits! Hs 8:6
large house will be s to pieces, Am 6:11
images will be s to pieces, Mc 1:7
the chains and s the shackles. Mk 5:4

SMASHES *(1)*
like iron that s, it will crush Dn 2:40

SMASHING *(2)*
s them at the base of the Ex 32:19
then s all the carvings with Ps 74:6

SMEARED *(1)*
arrogant have s me with lies, Ps 119:69

SMELL *(11)*
s of my son is like the smell Gn 27:27
is like the s of a field that Gn 27:27
and it didn't s or have any Ex 16:24
like it to s its fragrance must Ex 30:38
I will not s the pleasing aroma Lv 26:31
cannot see, hear, eat, or s. Dt 4:28
the s of water makes it thrive Jb 14:9
hear, noses, but cannot s. Ps 115:6
there was no s of fire on them Dn 3:27
yes, his rotten s will rise, for Jl 2:20
where would be the sense of s? 1Co 12:17

SMELLED *(4)*
When the LORD s the pleasing Gn 8:21
When Isaac s his clothes, he Gn 27:27
and the river s so bad the Ex 7:21
and it bred worms and s. Ex 16:20

SMELLS *(1)*
He s the battle from a distance; Jb 39:25

SMELTED *(1)*
and copper is s from ore. Jb 28:2

SMELTER *(3)*
is for silver and a s for gold, Pr 17:3
gold in a s, and a man, Pr 27:21
⌊something that⌋ a s casts, Is 40:19

SMILE *(2)*
change my expression, and s," Jb 9:27
alone, so that I can s a little Jb 10:20

SMILED *(1)*
If I s at them, they couldn't Jb 29:24

SMOKE *(48)*
and he saw that s was going up Gn 19:28
land like the s of a furnace. Gn 19:28
enveloped in s because the LORD Ex 19:18
Its s went up like the smoke of Ex 19:18
went up like the s of a furnace, Ex 19:18
the mountain ⌊surrounded by⌋ s. Ex 20:18
and s from the city was rising Jos 8:20
the city and that s was rising Jos 8:21
great cloud of s from the city, Jdg 20:38
the column of s began to go up Jdg 20:40
whole city was going up in s. Jdg 20:40
S rose from His nostrils, and 2Sm 22:9
S billows from his nostrils as Jb 41:20
S rose from His nostrils, and Ps 18:8
they will fade away like s. Ps 37:20
with the fragrant s of rams; Ps 66:15
As s is blown away, so You blow Ps 68:2
For my days vanish like s, Ps 102:3
mountains, and they pour out s. Ps 104:32
like a wineskin ⌊dried⌋ by s, Ps 119:83
the mountains, and they will s. Ps 144:5
to the teeth and s to the eyes, Pr 10:26
wilderness like columns of s, Sg 3:6
create a cloud of s by day and a Is 4:5
the temple was filled with s. Is 6:4
they go up in a column of s. Is 9:18
anger burning and heavy with s. Is 30:27
Its s will go up forever. Is 34:10
the heavens will vanish like s, Is 51:6
practices are s in My nostrils, Is 65:5
raise a s signal over Jr 6:1
floor, or like s from a window. Hs 13:3
blood, fire, and columns of s. Jl 2:30
chariots go up in s and the Nah 2:13
blood and fire and a cloud of s. Ac 2:19
are a bit of s that appears for Jms 4:14
The s of the incense, with the Rv 8:4
and s came up out of the shaft Rv 9:2
of the shaft like s from a great Rv 9:2
by the s from the shaft. Rv 9:2
Then out of the s locusts came Rv 9:3
mouths came fire, s, and sulfur. Rv 9:17
the fire, the s, and the sulfur Rv 9:18
and the s of their torment will Rv 14:11
was filled with s from God's Rv 15:8
they see the s of her burning. Rv 18:9
watched the s from her burning Rv 18:18
Her s ascends forever and ever! Rv 19:3

SMOKING *(1)*
a s fire pot and a flaming torch Gn 15:17

SMOLDERING *(3)*
of these two s stubs of Is 7:4
He will not put out a s wick; Is 42:3
He will not put out a s wick, Mt 12:20

SMOLDERS *(1)*
Their anger s all night; Hs 7:6

SMOOTH *(10)*
but I am a man with s skin. Gn 27:11
hands and the s part of his neck Gn 27:16
and chose five s stones from 1Sm 17:40
buttery words are s, but war is Ps 55:21
S lips with an evil heart are Pr 26:23

the uneven ground will become **s**, Is 40:4
is among the **s** ⌊stones⌋ of the Is 57:6
with water by a **s** way where they Jr 31:9
straight, the rough ways **s**, Lk 3:5
and by **s** talk and flattering Rm 16:18

SMOOTH-SKINNED *(2)*
a nation tall and **s**, to a people Is 18:2
Hosts from a people tall and **s**, Is 18:7

SMOOTHER *(1)*
and her words are **s** than oil, Pr 5:3

SMOOTHLY *(3)*
and channeled it **s** downward and 2Ch 32:30
in the cup and goes down **s**. Pr 23:31
flowing **s** for my love gliding Sg 7:9

SMUGGLE *(1)*
they going to **s** us out secretly Ac 16:37

SMUGGLED *(1)*
because of false brothers **s** Gl 2:4

SMYRNA *(2)*
Ephesus, **S**, Pergamum, Thyatira, Rv 1:11
angel of the church in **S** write: Rv 2:8

SNAKE *(19)*
He will be a **s** by the road, Gn 49:17
the ground, and it became a **s**. Ex 4:3
the staff that turned into a **s**. Ex 7:15
Make a **s** ⌊image⌋ and mount it on Nm 21:8
made a bronze **s** and mounted it Nm 21:9
and he looked at the bronze **s**, Nm 21:9
the bronze **s** that Moses made, 2Kg 18:4
venom like the venom of a **s**, Ps 58:4
bites like a **s** and stings like Pr 23:32
sky, the way of a **s** on a rock, Pr 30:19
a wall may be bitten by a **s**. Ec 10:8
If the **s** bites before it is Ec 10:11
come out of the root of a **s**, Is 14:29
will hiss like a slithering **s**, Jr 46:22
wall only to have a **s** bite him. Am 5:19
will lick the dust like a **s**; Mc 7:17
for a fish, will give him a **s**? Mt 7:10
will give him a **s** instead of a Lk 11:11
lifted up the **s** in the Jn 3:14

SNAKE'S *(2)*
tongues as sharp as a **s** bite; Ps 140:3
will put his hand into a **s** den. Is 11:8

SNAKES *(10)*
sent poisonous **s** among the Nm 21:6
will take the **s** away from us." Nm 21:7
its poisonous **s** and scorpions, Dt 8:15
well as venomous **s** that slither Dt 32:24
I am about to send **s** among you, Jr 8:17
S! Brood of vipers! How can you Mt 23:33
will pick up **s**; if they should Mk 16:18
trample on **s** and scorpions and Lk 10:19
did, and were destroyed by **s**. 1Co 10:9
their tails, like **s**, have heads, Rv 9:19

SNAP *(2)*
your neck and **s** your fetters so Jr 30:8
he would **s** the restraints and be Lk 8:29

SNAPPED *(5)*
But he **s** the bowstrings as a Jdg 16:9
he **s** the ropes off his arms like Jdg 16:12
before the silver cord is **s**, Ec 12:6
all my tent cords are **s**. Jr 10:20
but had **s** off the chains and Mk 5:4

SNAPS *(1)*
strand of yarn **s** when it touches Jdg 16:9

SNARE *(21)*
long must this man be a **s** to us? Ex 10:7
gods, it will be a **s** for you." Ex 23:33
they will become a **s** among you. Ex 34:12
for that will be a **s** to you. Dt 7:16
will become a **s** and a trap for Jos 23:13
and it became a **s** to Gideon and Jdg 8:27
a **s** ⌊waits⌋ for him along the Jb 18:10
table set before them be a **s**, Ps 69:22
idols, which became a **s** to them. Ps 106:36
will keep your foot from a **s**. Pr 3:26
like a bird darting into a **s**— Pr 7:23
and entangle yourself in a **s**. Pr 22:25
of man is a **s**, but the one who Pr 29:25
and a trap and a **s** to the Is 8:14
and **s** ⌊await⌋ you who dwell on Is 24:17
the pit will be caught in a **s**. Is 24:18
and he will be caught in My **s**. Ezk 12:13
and he will be captured in My **s**. Ezk 17:20
you have been a **s** at Mizpah and Hs 5:1
a fowler's **s** on all his ways. Hs 9:8
feasting become a **s** and a trap, Rm 11:9

SNARED *(2)*
they will be **s** and captured. Is 8:15
they will be dismayed and **s**. Jr 8:9

SNARES *(10)*
the **s** of death confronted me. 2Sm 22:6
Therefore **s** surround you, and Jb 22:10
or pierce his nose with **s**? Jb 40:24
the **s** of death confronted me. Ps 18:5
along the path and set **s** for me. Ps 140:5
and from the **s** of evildoers. Ps 141:9
people away from the **s** of death. Pr 13:14
people from the **s** of death. Pr 14:27
are thorns and **s** on the path Pr 22:5
and have hidden **s** for my feet. Jr 18:22

SNARL *(1)*
a dog will **s**, so that you may Ex 11:7

SNARLING *(2)*
s like dogs and prowling around Ps 59:6
s like dogs and prowling around Ps 59:14

SNATCH *(3)*
and heat **s** away the melted Jb 24:19
No one will **s** them out of My Jn 10:28
No one is able to **s** them out of Jn 10:29

SNATCHED *(8)*
and **s** the people from the power Ex 18:10
s the spear out of the 2Sm 23:21
s the spear out of the 1Ch 11:23
They were **s** away before their Jb 22:16
infant is **s** from the breast; Jb 24:9
the unjust and **s** the prey from Jb 29:17
a burning stick **s** from a fire, Am 4:11
burning stick **s** from the fire?" Zch 3:2

SNATCHES *(4)*
He **s** ⌊something⌋, who can stop Jb 9:12
As the shepherd **s** two legs or a Am 3:12
one comes and **s** away what was Mt 13:19
The wolf then **s** and scatters Jn 10:12

SNATCHING *(1)*
save others by **s** ⌊them⌋ from the Jd 23

SNEER *(1)*
they **s** and shake their heads: Ps 22:7

SNEERED *(1)*
But some **s** and said, "They're Ac 2:13

SNEEZED *(1)*
The boy **s** seven times and opened 2Kg 4:35

SNIFFS *(1)*
s the wind in the heat of her Jr 2:24

SNORTING *(3)*
His proud **s** ⌊fills one with⌋ Jb 39:20
His **s** flashes with light, while Jb 41:18
Dan is heard the **s** of horses. Jr 8:16

SNORTS *(1)*
trumpet blasts, he **s** defiantly. Jb 39:25

SNOUT *(1)*
like a gold ring in a pig's **s**. Pr 11:22

SNOW *(20)*
his hand was diseased, like **s**. Ex 4:6
diseased, as ⌊white⌋ as **s**. Nm 12:10
diseased—⌊white⌋ as **s**. 2Kg 5:27
and the **s** melts into them. Jb 6:16
myself with **s**, and cleanse my Jb 9:30
heat snatch away the melted **s**, Jb 24:19
For He says to the **s**, "Fall to Jb 37:6
place⌋ where the **s** is stored? Jb 38:22
and I will be whiter than **s**. Ps 51:7
He spreads **s** like wool; Ps 147:16
and hail, **s** and cloud, powerful Ps 148:8
the coolness of **s** on a harvest Pr 25:13
Like **s** in summer and rain at Pr 26:1
they will be as white as **s**; Is 1:18
as rain and **s** fall from heaven Is 55:10
Does the **s** of Lebanon ever leave Jr 18:14
were brighter than **s**, Lm 4:7
His clothing was white like **s**, Dn 7:9
and his robe was as white as **s**. Mt 28:3
wool—white as **s**, His eyes like Rv 1:14

SNOWED *(1)*
in the land, it **s** on Zalmon. Ps 68:14

SNOWS *(1)*
for her household when it **s**, Pr 31:21

SNOWY *(2)*
into a pit on a **s** day and killed 2Sm 23:20
into a pit on a **s** day and killed 1Ch 11:22

SNUFF *(1)*
When I **s** you out, I will cover Ezk 32:7

SNUFFERS *(3)*
Its **s** and firepans must be of Ex 25:38
its seven lamps, **s**, and firepans Ex 37:23
with its lamps, **s**, and firepans, Nm 4:9

SNUGLY *(2)*
she wrapped Him **s** in cloth and Lk 2:7
a baby wrapped **s** in cloth and Lk 2:12

SO *(3329)*
(See pp. xi-xii.)

SO (proper noun) *(1)*
sent envoys to **S** king of Egypt 2Kg 17:4

SO-CALLED *(3)*
My jealousy with ⌊their⌋ **s** gods; Dt 32:21
For even if there are **s** gods, 1Co 8:5
above every **s** god or object 2Th 2:4

SOAKED *(2)*
Their land will be **s** with blood, Is 34:7
our eyelids **s** with weeping. Jr 9:18

SOAKING *(1)*
s its furrows and leveling its Ps 65:10

SOAKS *(1)*
my breath but **s** me with bitter Jb 9:18

SOAP *(1)*
lye and use a great amount of **s**, Jr 2:22

SOAR *(3)*
Does the eagle **s** at your command Jb 39:27
will **s** on wings like eagles; Is 40:31
you seem to **s** like an eagle Ob 4

SOARING *(3)*
s on the wings of the wind. 2Sm 22:11
s on the wings of the wind. Ps 18:10
will be like an eagle **s** upward, Jr 49:22

SOBER *(3)*
but we must stay awake and be **s**. 1Th 5:6
must be **s** and put the armor of 1Th 5:8
Be **s**! Be on the alert! Your 1Pt 5:8

SOBERED *(1)*
In the morning when Nabal **s** up, 1Sm 25:37

SOCIETY *(1)*
They were expelled from human **s**; Jb 30:5

SOCKET *(4)*
and dislocated his hip **s**. Gn 32:25
muscle that is at the hip **s**: Gn 32:32
struck Jacob's hip **s** at the Gn 32:32
and my arm be pulled from its **s**. Jb 31:22

SOCKETS *(1)*
their eyes will rot in their **s**, Zch 14:12

SOCO *(3)*
the father of **S**, and Jekuthiel 1Ch 4:18
Beth-zur, **S**, Adullam, 2Ch 11:7
Gederoth, **S** and its villages, 2Ch 28:18

SOCOH *(5)*
Jarmuth, Adullam, **S**, Azekah, Jos 15:35
hill country: Shamir, Jattir, **S**, Jos 15:48
forces for war at **S** in Judah and 1Sm 17:1
and camped between **S** and Azekah 1Sm 17:1
he had **S** and the whole land of 1Kg 4:10

SODA *(1)*
or like ⌊pouring⌋ vinegar on **s**. Pr 25:20

SODI *(1)*
Gaddiel son of **S** from the tribe Nm 13:10

SODOM *(47)*
going toward **S**, Gomorrah, Admah Gn 10:19
God destroyed **S** and Gomorrah. Gn 13:10
and set up his tent near **S**. Gn 13:12
Now the men of **S** were evil, Gn 13:13
war against Bera king of **S**, Gn 14:2
Then the king of **S**, the king of Gn 14:8
as⌋ the kings of **S** and Gomorrah Gn 14:10
all the goods of **S** and Gomorrah Gn 14:11
was living in **S**, and they went Gn 14:12
the king of **S** went out to meet Gn 14:17
the king of **S** said to Abram, Gn 14:21
But Abram said to the king of **S**, Gn 14:22
there and looked out over **S**, Gn 18:16
outcry against **S** and Gomorrah is Gn 18:20
and went toward **S** while Abraham Gn 18:22

If at **S** I find 50 righteous Gn 18:26
angels entered **S** in the evening Gn 19:1
men of the city of **S**, both young Gn 19:4
burning sulfur on **S** and Gomorrah Gn 19:24
down toward **S** and Gomorrah Gn 19:28
like the fall of **S** and Gomorrah, Dt 29:23
from the vine of **S** and from the Dt 32:32
we would be like **S**, we would Is 1:9
of the LORD, you rulers of **S**! Is 1:10
them, and like **S**, they flaunt Is 3:9
will be like **S** and Gomorrah when Is 13:19
They are all like **S** to Me; Jr 23:14
As when **S** and Gomorrah were Jr 49:18
God overthrew **S** and Gomorrah Jr 50:40
is greater than that of **S**, Lm 4:6
and your younger sister was **S**, Ezk 16:46
your sister **S** and her daughters Ezk 16:48
the iniquity of your sister **S**: Ezk 16:49
the fortunes of **S** and her Ezk 16:53
S and her daughters and Samaria Ezk 16:55
treat your sister **S** as an object Ezk 16:56
as I overthrew **S** and Gomorrah, Am 4:11
will be like **S** and the Ammonites Zph 2:9
for the land of **S** and Gomorrah Mt 10:15
done in you had been done in **S**, Mt 11:23
for the land of **S** on the day of Mt 11:24
tolerable for **S** than for that Lk 10:12
But on the day Lot left **S**, Lk 17:29
we would have become like **S**, Rm 9:29
the cities of **S** and Gomorrah to 2Pt 2:6
S and Gomorrah and the cities Jd 7
prophetically, **S** and Egypt, Rv 11:8

SODOM'S *(1)*
as Lot was sitting at **S** gate. Gn 19:1

SOFT *(4)*
there was a voice, a **s** whisper. 1Kg 19:12
A man dressed in **s** clothes? Mt 11:8
those who wear **s** clothes are in Mt 11:8
A man dressed in **s** robes? Lk 7:25

SOFTEN *(1)*
You **s** it with showers and bless Ps 65:10

SOFTER *(1)*
His words are **s** than oil, but Ps 55:21

SOFTLY *(1)*
you for mercy or speak **s** to you? Jb 41:3

SOIL *(35)*
banishing me today from the **s**, Gn 4:14
a man of the **s**, was the first to Gn 9:20
grain from the **s** or fruit from Lv 27:30
and the produce of your **s**— Dt 7:13
its **s** will be a burning waste Dt 29:23
from this good **s** that He gave to 1Kg 14:15
in the fields tilling the **s**. 1Ch 27:26
Israel from the **s** that I gave 2Ch 7:20
since he was a lover of the **s**, 2Ch 26:10
does not grow out of the **s**, Jb 5:6
stump starts to die in the **s**, Jb 14:8
wash away the **s** from the land, Jb 14:19
consumed the produce of their **s**. Ps 105:35
the LORD's song on foreign **s**? Ps 137:4
one plows and breaks up the **s**, Ps 141:7
fields, or the first **s** on earth. Pr 8:26
He broke up the **s**, cleared it of Is 5:2
break up and cultivate the **s**? Is 28:24
and their **s** will be saturated Is 34:7
into pitch, her **s** into sulfur; Is 34:9
manure on the surface of the **s**. Jr 8:2
time on the **s** where you stay Jr 35:7
you to return to your own **s**. Jr 42:12
will scrape the **s** from her and Ezk 26:4
timber, and **s** into the water. Ezk 26:12
yourself will die on pagan **s**, Am 7:17
am a tiller of the **s**, for a man Zch 13:5
where there wasn't much **s**, Mt 13:5
quickly since the **s** wasn't deep. Mt 13:5
where it didn't have much **s**, Mk 4:5
since it didn't have deep **s**. Mk 4:5
s produces a crop by itself— Mk 4:28
sown in the **s**, is smaller than Mk 4:31
should it even waste the **s**?' Lk 13:7
fit for the **s** or for the manure Lk 14:35

SOIL'S *(7)*
of all the **s** produce that you Dt 26:2
be blessed, and your **s** produce, Dt 28:4
and your **s** produce in the land Dt 28:11
cursed, and your **s** produce, the Dt 28:18
know will eat your **s** produce and Dt 28:33
and your **s** produce until you Dt 28:51
livestock, and your **s** produce. Dt 30:9

SOJOURNER *(1)*
with You, a **s** like all my Ps 39:12

SOJOURNERS *(1)*
foreigners and **s** in Your 1Ch 29:15

SOLD *(60)*
to Jacob and **s** his birthright to Gn 25:33
he has **s** us and has certainly Gn 31:15
of the pit and **s** him for 20 Gn 37:28
the Midianites **s** Joseph in Egypt Gn 37:36
the storehouses⌋ and **s** grain to Gn 41:56
he **s** grain to all its people. Gn 42:6
the one you **s** into Egypt. Gn 45:4
every Egyptian **s** his field since Gn 47:20
he is to be **s** because of his Ex 22:3
be permanently **s** because it is Lv 25:23
redeem what his brother has **s**. Lv 25:25
balance to the man he **s** it to, Lv 25:27
what he **s** will remain in the Lv 25:28
a house **s** in a city they possess Lv 25:33
their cities may not be **s**, Lv 25:34
They are not to be **s** as slaves, Lv 25:42
redemption after he has been **s**. Lv 25:48
from the year he **s** himself to Lv 25:50
or if he has **s** it to another man Lv 27:20
it can be **s** according to your Lv 27:27
can be **s** or redeemed; Lv 27:28
is **s** to you and serves you six Dt 15:12
unless their Rock had **s** them, Dt 32:30
He **s** them to the enemies around Jdg 2:14
and He **s** them to Jdg 3:8
So the LORD **s** them into the hand Jdg 4:2
and He **s** them to the Philistines Jdg 10:7
donkey's head ⌊**s** for⌋ 80 silver 2Kg 6:25
of dove's dung ⌊**s** for⌋ five 2Kg 6:25
fine meal ⌊**s**⌋ for a shekel and 2Kg 7:16
of barley ⌊**s**⌋ for a shekel, 2Kg 7:16
who were **s** to foreigners, Neh 5:8
and I have been **s** out to Est 7:4
had merely been **s** as male and Est 7:4
Joseph, who was **s** as a slave. Ps 105:17
My creditors that I **s** you to? Is 50:1
you were **s** for your iniquities, Is 50:1
You were **s** for nothing, and you Is 52:3
brother who **s** himself to you. Jr 34:14
to what was **s** as long as he Ezk 7:13
prostitute and **s** a girl for wine Jl 3:3
You **s** the people of Judah and Jl 3:6
from the place where you **s** them; Jl 3:7
two sparrows **s** for a penny? Mt 10:29
he went and **s** everything he had, Mt 13:46
he had be **s** to pay the debt. Mt 18:25
might have been **s** for a great Mt 26:9
might have been **s** for more than Mk 14:5
five sparrows **s** for two pennies? Lk 12:6
fragrant oil **s** for 300 denarii Jn 12:5
So they **s** their possessions and Ac 2:45
owned lands or houses **s** them, Ac 4:34
of the things that were **s**, Ac 4:34
s a field he owned, brought the Ac 4:37
Sapphira his wife, **s** a piece of Ac 5:1
And after it was **s**, wasn't it at Ac 5:4
of Joseph and **s** him into Egypt, Ac 7:9
out of flesh, **s** into sin's power Rm 7:14
that is **s** in the meat market 1Co 10:25
who **s** his birthright in exchange Heb 12:16

SOLDERING *(1)*
saying of the **s**, "It is good." Is 41:7

SOLDIER *(9)*
an experienced **s** who won't spend 2Sm 17:8
He stirs up His zeal like a **s**. Is 42:13
four parts, a part for each **s**. Jn 19:23
household slaves and a devout **s**, Ac 10:7
with the **s** who guarded him Ac 28:16
and fellow **s**, as well as your Php 2:25
as a good **s** of Christ Jesus. 2Tm 2:3
serving as a **s** gets entangled 2Tm 2:4
to Archippus our fellow **s**, Phm 2

SOLDIERS *(73)*
about 600,000 **s** on foot, besides Ex 12:37
of a people with 600,000 foot **s**, Nm 11:21
said to the **s** who had gone to Nm 31:21
Each of the **s** had taken plunder Nm 31:53
400,000 armed foot **s**. Jdg 20:2
of the Israelite foot **s** fell. 1Sm 4:10
200,000 foot **s** and 10,000 men 1Sm 15:4
put him in command of the **s**, 1Sm 18:5
son of Ner and **s** of Ish-bosheth 2Sm 2:12
and David's **s** marched out and 2Sm 2:13
of Saul, and 12 from David's **s**. 2Sm 2:15
were defeated by David's **s**. 2Sm 2:17
one of the young **s**, and take 2Sm 2:21
19 of David's **s** were missing, 2Sm 2:30
then David's **s** and Joab returned 2Sm 3:22
Then the king said to his **s**, 2Sm 3:38
and 20,000 foot **s** from him, 2Sm 8:4
20,000 foot **s** from the Arameans 2Sm 10:6
charioteers and 40,000 foot **s**. 2Sm 10:18
Joab and his **s** are camping 2Sm 11:11
he knew the best ⌊enemy⌋ **s** were, 2Sm 11:16
from David's **s** fell ⌊in battle⌋ 2Sm 11:17
shot down on your **s** from the top 2Sm 11:24
and some of the king's **s** died. 2Sm 11:24
were defeated by David's **s**, 2Sm 18:7
he happened to meet David's **s**. 2Sm 18:9
you have shamed all your **s**— 2Sm 19:5
commanders and **s** mean nothing to 2Sm 19:6
Go out and encourage your **s**, 2Sm 19:7
your lord's **s** and pursue him, 2Sm 20:6
David went down with his **s**, 2Sm 21:15
were killed by David and his **s**. 2Sm 21:22
they were **s**, his servants, his 1Kg 9:22
100,000 foot **s** in one day. 1Kg 20:29
and 10,000 foot **s**, because the 2Kg 13:7
and 20,000 foot **s** from him and 1Ch 18:4
charioteers and 40,000 foot **s**. 1Ch 19:18
Gath killed by David and his **s**. 1Ch 20:8
they were **s**, commanders of his 2Ch 8:9
and Jehu's **s** captured him 2Ch 22:9
Therefore the **s** of Moab cry out, Is 15:4
of Judah and all the **s** fled. Jr 39:4
the Chaldean **s** who were there. Jr 41:3
Ahikam—men, **s**, women, children Jr 41:16
fire, and the **s** are terrified. Jr 51:32
the strongest **s** in his army to Dn 3:20
and in your large number of **s**, Hs 10:13
having **s** under my command. Mt 8:9
Then the governor's **s** took Jesus Mt 27:27
"You have a guard ⌊of **s**⌋." Mt 27:65
they gave the **s** a large sum of Mt 28:12
Then the **s** led Him away into the Mk 15:16
Some **s** also questioned him: Lk 3:14
having **s** under my command. Lk 7:8
Herod, with his **s**, treated Him Lk 23:11
The **s** also mocked Him. Lk 23:36
a company of **s** and some temple Jn 18:3
the company of **s**, the commander, Jn 18:12
The **s** also twisted together a Jn 19:2
When the **s** crucified Jesus, Jn 19:23
And this is what the **s** did. Jn 19:24
So the **s** came and broke the legs Jn 19:32
one of the **s** pierced His side Jn 19:34
squads of four **s** each to guard Ac 12:4
was sleeping between two **s**, Ac 12:6
among the **s** as to what could Ac 12:18
Taking along **s** and centurions, Ac 21:32
Seeing the commander and the **s**, Ac 21:32
be carried by the **s** because of Ac 21:35
Get 200 **s** ready with 70 cavalry Ac 23:23
the **s** took Paul and brought him Ac 23:31
said to the centurion and the **s**, Ac 27:31
Then the **s** cut the ropes holding Ac 27:32

SOLDIERS' *(1)*
The **s** plan was to kill the Ac 27:42

SOLE *(8)*
Every place the **s** of your foot Dt 11:24
boils from the **s** of your foot to Dt 28:35
venture to set the **s** of her foot Dt 28:56
place for the **s** of your foot. Dt 28:65
place where the **s** of your foot Jos 1:3
From the **s** of his foot to the 2Sm 14:25
boils from the **s** of his foot to Jb 2:7
From the **s** of the foot even to Is 1:6

SOLEMN *(12)*
marker and made a **s** vow to Me. Gn 31:13
This is a **s** mourning on the part Gn 50:11
the Israelites swear a **s** oath, Ex 13:19
LORD. It is a **s** gathering; you Lv 23:36
you are to hold a **s** assembly; Nm 29:35
there is to be a **s** assembly to Dt 16:8
for you for this **s** event at the 1Sm 9:24
a **s** assembly for Baal. 2Kg 10:20
the calling of **s** assemblies— Is 1:13

a s assembly of treacherous Jr 9:2
the stench of your s assemblies. Am 5:21
ourselves under a s curse that Ac 23:14

SOLEMNLY *(7)*
you must s warn them and tell 1Sm 8:9
made the troops s swear, 1Sm 14:28
I have s sworn to keep Your Ps 119:106
and to s testify that He is the Ac 10:42
the message and s testified to Ac 18:5
I s charge you, before God and 1Tm 5:21
and His kingdom, I s charge you: 2Tm 4:1

SOLES *(6)*
of Egypt with the s of my feet. 2Kg 19:24
a limit for the s of my feet. Jb 13:27
of Egypt with the s of my feet. Is 37:25
the s of their feet were like Ezk 1:7
the place for the s of My feet, Ezk 43:7
ashes under the s of your feet Mal 4:3

SOLICITED *(1)*
no one s you. When you paid Ezk 16:34

SOLID *(9)*
spread a s blue cloth on top, Nm 4:6
feet stepped out on s ground, Jos 4:18
are joined together, s as metal Jb 41:23
My fruit is better than s gold, Pr 8:19
I see a s gold lampstand there Zch 4:2
you milk, not s food, because 1Co 3:2
God's s foundation stands firm, 2Tm 2:19
You need milk, not s food. Heb 5:12
But s food is for the mature— Heb 5:14

SOLIDLY *(1)*
should be⌋, s joined together, Ps 122:3

SOLITARY *(2)*
I am like a s bird on a roof. Ps 102:7
alone remain like a ⌊s⌋ pole on Is 30:17

SOLOMON *(253)*
(AKA JEDIDIAH)
Shammua, Shobab, Nathan, S, 2Sm 5:14
birth to a son and named him S. 2Sm 12:24
the warriors, or his brother S. 1Kg 1:10
life and the life of your son S. 1Kg 1:12
Your son S is to become king 1Kg 1:13
'Your son S is to become king 1Kg 1:17
did not invite your servant S. 1Kg 1:19
I and my son S will be regarded 1Kg 1:21
of Jehoiada or your servant S. 1Kg 1:26
Your son S is to become king 1Kg 1:30
have my son S ride on my own 1Kg 1:33
and say, 'Long live King S!' 1Kg 1:34
so may He be with S and make his 1Kg 1:37
had S ride on King David's mule, 1Kg 1:38
the tabernacle and anointed S. 1Kg 1:39
proclaimed, "Long live King S!" 1Kg 1:39
lord King David has made S king. 1Kg 1:43
And with S, the king has sent 1Kg 1:44
S has even taken his seat on the 1Kg 1:46
the name of S more famous than 1Kg 1:47
afraid of S, so he got up and 1Kg 1:50
It was reported to S: 1Kg 1:51
fears King S, and he has taken 1Kg 1:51
'Let King S first swear to me 1Kg 1:51
Then S said, "If he is a man of 1Kg 1:52
So King S sent for him, and they 1Kg 1:53
came and paid homage to King S, 1Kg 1:53
Solomon, and S said to him, "Go 1Kg 1:53
to die, he instructed his son S, 1Kg 2:1
S sat on the throne of his 1Kg 2:12
speak to King S since he won't 1Kg 2:17
went to King S to speak to him 1Kg 2:19
King S answered his mother, 1Kg 2:22
Then S took an oath by the LORD: 1Kg 2:23
Then King S gave the order to 1Kg 2:25
S banished Abiathar from being 1Kg 2:27
It was reported to King S: 1Kg 2:29
Then S sent Benaiah son of 1Kg 2:29
reported to S that Shimei had 1Kg 2:41
but King S will be blessed, 1Kg 2:45
S made an alliance with Pharaoh 1Kg 3:1
S brought her to the city of 1Kg 3:1
S loved the LORD by walking in 1Kg 3:3
LORD appeared to S in a dream at 1Kg 3:5
And S replied, "You have shown 1Kg 3:6
the Lord that S had requested 1Kg 3:10
Then S woke up and realized it 1Kg 3:15
S said, "Cut the living boy in 1Kg 3:25
King S ruled over Israel, 1Kg 4:1
S had 12 deputies for all Israel. 1Kg 4:7
daughter of S was his wife 1Kg 4:11
had married a daughter of S— 1Kg 4:15
S ruled over all the kingdoms 1Kg 4:21
tribute and served S all the 1Kg 4:21
S had 40,000 stalls of horses 1Kg 4:26
food for King S and for everyone 1Kg 4:27
God gave S wisdom, very great 1Kg 4:29
S composed 3,000 proverbs, 1Kg 4:32
his servants to S when he heard 1Kg 5:1
S sent ⌊this message⌋ to Hiram: 1Kg 5:2
Then Hiram sent ⌊a reply⌋ to S, 1Kg 5:8
So Hiram provided S with all the 1Kg 5:10
S provided Hiram with 100,000 1Kg 5:11
S did this for Hiram year after 1Kg 5:11
LORD gave S wisdom, as He had 1Kg 5:12
was peace between Hiram and S, 1Kg 5:12
Then King S drafted forced 1Kg 5:13
S had 70,000 porters and 80,000 1Kg 5:15
S ⌊began to⌋ build the temple 1Kg 6:1
temple that King S built for the 1Kg 6:2
The word of the LORD came to S: 1Kg 6:11
When S finished building the 1Kg 6:14
S overlaid the interior of the 1Kg 6:21
S completed his entire 1Kg 7:1
King S had Hiram brought from 1Kg 7:13
came to King S and carried out 1Kg 7:14
doing for King S on the LORD's 1Kg 7:40
made for King S at the LORD's 1Kg 7:45
S left all the utensils 1Kg 7:47
S also made all the equipment in 1Kg 7:48
the work King S did in the 1Kg 7:51
S brought in the consecrated 1Kg 7:51
At that time S assembled the 1Kg 8:1
presence of King S in the 1Kg 8:2
King S and the entire 1Kg 8:5
Then S said: The LORD said that 1Kg 8:12
Then S stood before the altar of 1Kg 8:22
When S finished praying this 1Kg 8:54
S offered a sacrifice of 1Kg 8:63
S and all Israel with him— 1Kg 8:65
When S finished building the 1Kg 9:1
and all that S desired to do, 1Kg 9:1
LORD appeared to S a second time 1Kg 9:2
during which S had built the two 1Kg 9:10
King S gave Hiram 20 towns in 1Kg 9:11
the towns that S had given him, 1Kg 9:12
labor that King S had imposed to 1Kg 9:15
Then S rebuilt Gezer, Lower 1Kg 9:17
cities that belonged to S, 1Kg 9:19
and whatever S desired to build 1Kg 9:19
S imposed forced labor on them; 1Kg 9:21
But S did not consign the 1Kg 9:22
the house that S had built for 1Kg 9:24
times a year S offered burnt 1Kg 9:25
King S put together a fleet of 1Kg 9:26
16 tons—and delivered it to S. 1Kg 9:28
She came to S and spoke to him 1Kg 10:2
So S answered all her questions; 1Kg 10:3
queen of Sheba gave to King S. 1Kg 10:10
King S gave the queen of Sheba 1Kg 10:13
that came to S annually was 25 1Kg 10:14
King S made 200 large shields of 1Kg 10:16
King S surpassed all the kings 1Kg 10:23
an audience with S to hear the 1Kg 10:24
S accumulated 1,400 chariots and 1Kg 10:26
King S loved many foreign women 1Kg 11:1
S was deeply attached to these 1Kg 11:2
S was old, his wives seduced 1Kg 11:4
S followed Ashtoreth, the 1Kg 11:5
S did what was evil in the 1Kg 11:6
S built a high place for Chemosh, 1Kg 11:7
The LORD was angry with S, 1Kg 11:9
but S did not do what the LORD 1Kg 11:10
LORD said to S, "Since you have 1Kg 11:11
Edomite as an enemy against S. 1Kg 11:14
of Eliada as an enemy against S. 1Kg 11:23
Jeroboam rebelled against S, 1Kg 11:26
S had built the supporting 1Kg 11:27
and S noticed the young man 1Kg 11:28
Therefore, S tried to kill 1Kg 11:40
S rested with his fathers and 1Kg 11:43
his father S when he was alive 1Kg 12:6
kingdom to Rehoboam son of S. 1Kg 12:21
Say to Rehoboam son of S, 1Kg 12:23
gold shields that S had made. 1Kg 14:26
about to David and his son S, 2Kg 21:7
which S king of Israel had built 2Kg 23:13
articles that S king of Israel 2Kg 24:13
water carts that S had made for 2Kg 25:16
Shimea, Shobab, Nathan, and S. 1Ch 3:5
the temple that S built in 1Ch 6:10
until S built the LORD's temple 1Ch 6:32
Shammua, Shobab, Nathan, S, 1Ch 14:4
from which S made the bronze 1Ch 18:8
My son S is young and 1Ch 22:5
his son S and instructed 1Ch 22:6
David said to S, "It was in my 1Ch 22:7
name will be S, and I will give 1Ch 22:9
of Israel to help his son S: 1Ch 22:17
installed his son S as king over 1Ch 23:1
chosen my son S to sit on the 1Ch 28:5
'Your son S is the one who is to 1Ch 28:6
As for you, S my son, know the 1Ch 28:9
gave his son S the plans for 1Ch 28:11
Then David said to his son S, 1Ch 28:20
My son S—God has chosen 1Ch 29:1
Give my son S a whole heart to 1Ch 29:19
they made David's son S king; 1Ch 29:22
S sat on the LORD's throne as 1Ch 29:23
their allegiance to King S. 1Ch 29:24
highly exalted S in the sight of 1Ch 29:25
and his son S became king in his 1Ch 29:28
S son of David strengthened his 2Ch 1:1
Then S spoke to all Israel, 2Ch 1:2
S and the whole assembly with 2Ch 1:3
S and the assembly inquired of 2Ch 1:5
S offered sacrifices there in 2Ch 1:6
appeared to S and said to him 2Ch 1:7
And S said to God: "You have 2Ch 1:8
God said to S, "Because this was 2Ch 1:11
So S went to Jerusalem from the 2Ch 1:13
S accumulated 1,400 chariots and 2Ch 1:14
S decided to build a temple for 2Ch 2:1
Then S sent ⌊word⌋ to King Hiram 2Ch 2:3
a letter and sent ⌊it⌋ to S: 2Ch 2:11
S took a census of all the 2Ch 2:17
S made 70,000 of them porters, 2Ch 2:18
Then S began to build the LORD's 2Ch 3:1
for King S in God's temple: 2Ch 4:11
them for King S for the LORD's 2Ch 4:16
S made all these utensils in 2Ch 4:18
S also made all the equipment in 2Ch 4:19
So all the work S did for the 2Ch 5:1
Then S brought the consecrated 2Ch 5:1
At that time S assembled at 2Ch 5:2
King S and the entire 2Ch 5:6
Then S said: The LORD said He 2Ch 6:1
Then S stood before the altar of 2Ch 6:12
For S had made a bronze platform 2Ch 6:13
When S finished praying, fire 2Ch 7:1
King S offered a sacrifice of 2Ch 7:5
S consecrated the middle of the 2Ch 7:7
altar that S had made could 2Ch 7:7
So S and all Israel with him— 2Ch 7:8
for David, for S, and for His 2Ch 7:10
So S finished the LORD's temple 2Ch 7:11
LORD appeared to S at night and 2Ch 7:12
years during which S had built 2Ch 8:1
S having rebuilt the cities 2Ch 8:2
S went to Hamath-zobah and 2Ch 8:3
cities that belonged to S, 2Ch 8:6
everything S desired to build 2Ch 8:6
S imposed forced labor on them; 2Ch 8:8
But S did not consign the 2Ch 8:9
S brought the daughter of 2Ch 8:11
At that time S offered burnt 2Ch 8:12
At that time S went to 2Ch 8:17
and delivered it to King S. 2Ch 8:18
came to test S with difficult 2Ch 9:1
She came to S and spoke with him 2Ch 9:1
So S answered all her questions; 2Ch 9:2
difficult for S to explain to 2Ch 9:2
queen of Sheba gave to King S. 2Ch 9:9
King S gave the queen of Sheba 2Ch 9:12
that came to S annually was 25 2Ch 9:13
brought gold and silver to S. 2Ch 9:14
King S made 200 large shields of 2Ch 9:15
King S surpassed all the kings 2Ch 9:22
an audience with S to hear the 2Ch 9:23
S had 4,000 stalls for horses 2Ch 9:25
bringing horses for S from Egypt 2Ch 9:28
S reigned in Jerusalem over all 2Ch 9:30
S rested with his fathers and 2Ch 9:31
his father S when he was alive 2Ch 10:6
Say to Rehoboam son of S, 2Ch 11:3
son of S for three years 2Ch 11:17

of David and S for three years 2Ch 11:17
gold shields that S had made. 2Ch 12:9
a servant of S son of David, 2Ch 13:6
Rehoboam son of S when 2Ch 13:7
the days of S son of David, 2Ch 30:26
had said to David and his son S: 2Ch 33:7
temple built by S son of David 2Ch 35:3
of Israel and that of his son S. 2Ch 35:4
and his son S had prescribed. Neh 12:45
Didn't King S of Israel sin in Neh 13:26
The proverbs of S son of David, Pr 1:1
These too are proverbs of S, Pr 25:1
lovely like the curtains of S. Sg 1:5
King S made a sedan chair for Sg 3:9
and gaze at King S, wearing the Sg 3:11
S owned a vineyard in Baal-hamon. Sg 8:11
are for you, S, but 200 for Sg 8:12
carts that King S had made for Jr 52:20
fathered S by Uriah's wife, Mt 1:6
S fathered Rehoboam, Rehoboam Mt 1:7
you that not even S in all his Mt 6:29
earth to hear the wisdom of S; Mt 12:42
greater than S is here! Mt 12:42
earth to hear the wisdom of S, Lk 11:31
greater than S is here! Lk 11:31
not even S in all his splendor Lk 12:27
But it was S who built Him a Ac 7:47

SOLOMON'S *(54)*

to Bathsheba, S mother, "Have 1Kg 1:11
came to Bathsheba, S mother. 1Kg 2:13
was established in S hand. 1Kg 2:46
S provisions for one day were 1Kg 4:22
Throughout S ⌊reign⌋, Judah and 1Kg 4:25
who came to King S table. 1Kg 4:27
S wisdom was greater than the 1Kg 4:30
wisdom, to listen to S wisdom. 1Kg 4:34
When Hiram heard S words, he 1Kg 5:7
So S builders and Hiram's 1Kg 5:18
was laid in ⌊S⌋ fourth year 1Kg 6:37
S own palace where he would live, 1Kg 7:8
a dowry to his daughter, S wife. 1Kg 9:16
deputies who were over S work: 1Kg 9:23
seamen, along with S servants. 1Kg 9:27
heard about S fame connected 1Kg 10:1
Sheba observed all of S wisdom, 1Kg 10:4
All of King S drinking cups were 1Kg 10:21
considered as nothing in S time, 1Kg 10:21
S horses were imported from 1Kg 10:28
enemy throughout S reign, 1Kg 11:25
Now S servant, Jeroboam son of 1Kg 11:26
tear the kingdom out of S hand. 1Kg 11:31
where he remained until S death. 1Kg 11:40
rest of the events of S ⌊reign⌋, 1Kg 11:41
about in the Book of S Events. 1Kg 11:41
The length of S reign in 1Kg 11:42
had fled from King S presence, 1Kg 12:2
Now Rehoboam, S son, reigned in 1Kg 14:21
S son was Rehoboam; 1Ch 3:10
S horses came from Egypt and Kue 2Ch 1:16
These are S foundations for 2Ch 3:3
had entered S heart to do for 2Ch 7:11
These were King S deputies: 2Ch 8:10
All of S work was carried out 2Ch 8:16
They went with S servants to 2Ch 8:18
queen of Sheba heard of S fame, 2Ch 9:1
of Sheba observed S wisdom, 2Ch 9:3
servants and S servants who 2Ch 9:10
All of King S drinking cups were 2Ch 9:20
considered as nothing in S time, 2Ch 9:20
remaining events of S ⌊reign⌋, 2Ch 9:29
had fled from King S presence— 2Ch 10:2
descendants of S servants Ezr 2:55
descendants of S servants 392 Ezr 2:58
descendants of S servants Neh 7:57
descendants of S servants 392 Neh 7:60
and descendants of S servants— Neh 11:3
S proverbs: A wise son brings Pr 10:1
S Finest Song Sg 1:1
It is S royal litter surrounded Sg 3:7
temple complex in S Colonnade. Jn 10:23
in what is called S Colonnade. Ac 3:11
would all meet in S Colonnade. Ac 5:12

SOLVE *(2)*

explain riddles, and s problems. Dn 5:12
interpretations and s problems. Dn 5:16

SOME *(475)*

she took s of its fruit and ate Gn 3:6
also gave ⌊s⌋ to her husband, Gn 3:6
she gave me ⌊s fruit⌋ from the Gn 3:12
Cain presented s of the land's Gn 4:3
s of the firstborn of his flock Gn 4:4
He took s of every kind of clean Gn 8:20
He drank s of the wine, became Gn 9:21
fled, ⌊s⌋ fell into them Gn 14:10
Let me eat s of that red stuff, Gn 25:30
Isaac had been there for s time, Gn 26:8
the field to hunt s game for me. Gn 27:3
field to hunt s game to bring Gn 27:5
'Bring me s game and make some Gn 27:7
game and make s delicious food Gn 27:7
sit up and eat s of my game so Gn 27:19
let me eat s of my son's game Gn 27:25
had also made s delicious food Gn 27:31
get up and eat s of his son's Gn 27:31
her to you than to s other man. Gn 29:19
harvest and found s mandrakes in Gn 30:14
Please give me s of your son's Gn 30:14
and leave s distance between the Gn 32:16
Let me leave s of my people with Gn 33:15
went out to see s of the young Gn 34:1
When they were still s distance Gn 35:16
After s time his master's wife Gn 39:7
they were in custody for s time. Gn 40:4
there and buy s for us so that Gn 42:2
"Go back and buy us s food." Gn 43:2
s of the best products of the Gn 43:11
as a gift—s balsam and some Gn 43:11
balsam and s honey, aromatic Gn 43:11
Go again, and buy us s food.' Gn 44:25
S time after this, Joseph was Gn 48:1
s distance from Ephrath in the Gn 48:7
Then s shepherds arrived and Ex 2:17
take s water from the Nile and Ex 4:9
will take s of them to worship Ex 10:26
They must take s of the blood Ex 12:7
doorposts with s of the blood Ex 12:22
S gathered a lot, some a little. Ex 16:17
Some gathered a lot, s a little. Ex 16:17
s people left part of it until Ex 16:20
the seventh day s of the people Ex 16:27
people and take s of the elders Ex 17:5
Joshua, "Select s men for us, Ex 17:9
will give you s advice, and God Ex 18:19
Take s of the bull's blood and Ex 29:12
ram, take s of its blood, and Ex 29:20
Take s of the blood that is on Ex 29:21
the altar and s of the anointing Ex 29:21
like it or puts s of it on an Ex 30:33
Grind s of it into a fine powder Ex 30:36
a fine powder and put s in front Ex 30:36
you will take s of their Ex 34:16
will then burn s of its crushed Lv 2:16
must then take s of the bull's Lv 4:5
and sprinkle s of it seven times Lv 4:6
must apply s of the blood to Lv 4:7
will bring s of the bull's Lv 4:16
He is to apply s of the blood to Lv 4:18
priest must take s of the blood Lv 4:25
priest must take s of its blood Lv 4:30
priest must take s of the blood Lv 4:34
he will sprinkle s of the blood Lv 5:9
He sprinkled s of the oil on the Lv 8:11
He poured s of the anointing oil Lv 8:12
it⌋, took s of its blood, and Lv 8:23
sons and put s of the blood Lv 8:24
Then Moses took s of the Lv 8:30
oil and s of the blood that Lv 8:30
Anyone who eats s of its carcass Lv 11:40
priest is to take s of the blood Lv 14:14
will take s of the one-third Lv 14:15
and sprinkle s of the oil with Lv 14:16
priest will put s on the lobe Lv 14:17
priest is to take s of the blood Lv 14:25
priest will pour s of the oil Lv 14:26
will sprinkle s of the oil in Lv 14:27
will also put s of the oil in Lv 14:28
He is to take s of the bull's Lv 16:14
he will sprinkle s of the blood Lv 16:14
He is to take s of the bull's Lv 16:18
bull's blood and s of the goat's Lv 16:18
He is to sprinkle s of the blood Lv 16:19
and take s of the dust from the Nm 5:17
But there were ⌊s⌋ men who were Nm 9:6
I will take s of the Spirit who Nm 11:17
He took s of the Spirit that was Nm 11:25
back s fruit from the land. Nm 13:20
also ⌊took⌋ s pomegranates Nm 13:23
and here is s of its fruit. Nm 13:27
Give s of it to Aaron the priest Nm 18:28
is to take s of its blood with Nm 19:4
they are to take s of the ashes Nm 19:17
Israel and captured s prisoners. Nm 21:1
Confer s of your authority on Nm 27:20
Equip s of your men for war. Nm 31:3
is to give s of its cities to Nm 35:8
They took s of the fruit from Dt 1:25
and you take s of them prisoner Dt 21:10
you must take s of the first of Dt 26:2
s of the Israelite men have come Jos 2:2
took s of what was set apart, Jos 7:1
They have taken s of what was Jos 7:11
s on one side and some on the Jos 8:22
on one side and s on the other. Jos 8:22
of Israel⌋ took s of their Jos 9:14
except for s remaining in Gaza, Jos 11:22
Please give s loaves of bread to Jdg 8:5
as well as s thorns and briers Jdg 8:16
Then s lawless men joined Jdg 11:3
S time later, the Ammonites Jdg 11:4
After s time, when he returned Jdg 14:8
He scooped ⌊s honey⌋ into his Jdg 14:9
he gave ⌊s⌋ to them and they ate Jdg 14:9
S time later, he fell in love Jdg 16:4
After they were s distance from Jdg 18:22
here and have s bread and dip it Ru 2:14
satisfied and had ⌊s⌋ left over. Ru 2:14
Pull out ⌊s⌋ stalks from the Ru 2:16
After s time, Hannah conceived 1Sm 1:20
He sends ⌊s⌋ to Sheol, and He 1Sm 2:6
the priest ⌊s⌋ meat to roast, 1Sm 2:15
appoint me to s priestly office 1Sm 2:36
Show s courage and be men, 1Sm 4:9
they found s young women coming 1Sm 9:11
But s wicked men said, "How can 1Sm 10:27
S Hebrews even crossed the 1Sm 13:7
S reported to Saul: "Look, the 1Sm 14:33
s goats' hair on its head, 1Sm 19:13
on the bed with s goats' hair on 1Sm 19:16
S Ziphites came up to Saul at 1Sm 23:19
Let me set s food in front of 1Sm 28:22
They gave him s bread to eat and 1Sm 30:11
they gave him s pressed figs 1Sm 30:12
he sent s of the plunder to his 1Sm 30:26
S time later, David inquired of 2Sm 2:1
S time later the king of the 2Sm 10:1
he chose s men out of all the 2Sm 10:9
and s of the men from David's 2Sm 11:17
and s of the king's soldiers 2Sm 11:24
S time passed. David's son 2Sm 13:1
of the caves or s other place. 2Sm 17:9
If s of our troops fall first, 2Sm 17:9
he retreats to s city, all 2Sm 17:13
along with s Edomites from his 1Kg 11:17
of bread, s cakes, and a jar 1Kg 14:3
you may make s for yourself and 1Kg 17:13
carry you off to s place I don't 1Kg 18:12
S time passed after these events. 1Kg 21:1
up, eat s food, and be happy. 1Kg 21:7
s small boys came out of the 2Kg 2:23
persuaded him to eat s food. 2Kg 4:8
served s for the men to eat, 2Kg 4:40
Then Elisha said, "Get s meal." 2Kg 4:41
they will have s left over.' " 2Kg 4:43
they ate and had s left over. 2Kg 4:44
told you to do s great thing, 2Kg 5:13
S time later, King Ben-hadad of 2Kg 6:24
and s of her blood splattered on 2Kg 9:33
them, which killed s of them. 2Kg 17:25
'S of your descendants who come 2Kg 20:18
the guards left s of the poorest 2Kg 25:12
for s Hamites had lived there 1Ch 4:40
S of the families of the 1Ch 6:66
S of them were in charge of the 1Ch 9:28
But s of the priests' sons mixed 1Ch 9:30
S of the Kohathites' relatives 1Ch 9:32
S Gadites defected to David at 1Ch 12:8
S Manassites defected to David 1Ch 12:19
s men from Manasseh defected to 1Ch 12:20
David appointed s of the Levites 1Ch 16:4
S time later, King Nahash of the 1Ch 19:1
he chose s men out of all the 1Ch 19:10
also set apart s of the sons 1Ch 25:1
by dispersing s of his sons to 2Ch 11:23
captured ⌊s⌋ cities from him: 2Ch 13:19

Asa mistreated **s** of the people 2Ch 16:10
S of the Philistines also 2Ch 17:11
Then after **s** years, he went down 2Ch 18:2
However, **s** good is found in you, 2Ch 19:3
in Jerusalem **s** of the Levites 2Ch 19:8
and priests and **s** of the heads 2Ch 19:8
together with **s** of the Meunites, 2Ch 20:1
and appointed **s** to sing for the 2Ch 20:21
for the LORD and **s** to praise 2Ch 20:21
as well as **s** of the princes 2Ch 21:4
So **s** men who were leaders of the 2Ch 28:12
But **s** from Asher, Manasseh, and 2Ch 30:11
and there **s** of his own children 2Ch 32:21
S of the Levites were 2Ch 34:13
took **s** of the utensils 2Ch 36:7
s of the family leaders gave Ezr 2:68
and **s** of the people settled in Ezr 2:70
S of the Israelites, priests, Ezr 7:7
they have taken **s** of their Ezr 9:2
pulled out **s** of the hair from my Ezr 9:3
and **s** of the wives had borne Ezr 10:44
S were saying, "We, our sons, Neh 5:2
S of our daughters are already Neh 5:5
and **s** fowl were prepared for me. Neh 5:18
s at their posts and some at Neh 7:3
posts and **s** at their homes. Neh 7:3
S of the family leaders gave to Neh 7:70
S of the family leaders gave Neh 7:71
temple singers, **s** of the people, Neh 7:73
while **s** of the descendants of Neh 11:4
S of Judah's descendants lived Neh 11:25
S of the Judean divisions of Neh 11:36
S of the priests' sons had Neh 12:35
I posted **s** of my men at the Neh 13:19
them, beat **s** of their men, Neh 13:25
S time later, when King Est 2:1
to overlook **s** of your sin. Jb 11:6
Show **s** sense, and then we can Jb 18:2
them or that **s** wild animal may Jb 39:15
S take pride in a chariot, Ps 20:7
and He killed **s** of their best Ps 78:31
When He killed ⌊**s** of⌋ them, Ps 78:34
S wandered in the desolate Ps 107:4
Let's attack **s** innocent person Pr 1:11
'**S** of your descendants who come Is 39:7
and not **s** foreign god among you. Is 43:12
He takes **s** of it and warms Is 44:15
Come, let me get ⌊**s**⌋ wine, let's Is 56:12
wine, let's guzzle ⌊**s**⌋ beer; Is 56:12
S of you will rebuild the Is 58:12
it, for there's **s** good in it, so Is 65:8
I will also take **s** of them as Is 66:21
Take **s** of the elders of the Jr 19:1
the people and **s** of the elders Jr 19:1
S of the elders of the land Jr 26:17
with wine and **s** cups before the Jr 35:5
the land of Judah **s** of the poor Jr 39:10
Pick up **s** large stones and set Jr 43:9
wouldn't they leave **s** gleanings? Jr 49:9
deported **s** of the poorest of the Jr 52:15
But **s** of the poor people of the Jr 52:16
Take **s** more of them, throw them Ezk 5:4
there will be **s** of you who will Ezk 6:8
He took ⌊**s**⌋, and put ⌊it⌋ into Ezk 10:7
S of the elders of Israel came Ezk 14:1
You took **s** of your garments and Ezk 16:16
he took **s** of the land's seed Ezk 17:5
s of Israel's elders came to Ezk 20:1
You must take **s** of its blood and Ezk 43:20
priest must take **s** of the blood Ezk 45:19
along with **s** of the vessels from Dn 1:2
bring **s** of the Israelites from Dn 1:3
you are trying to gain **s** time, Dn 2:8
the king to give him **s** time, Dn 2:16
though **s** of the strength of iron Dn 2:41
S Chaldeans took this occasion Dn 3:8
There are **s** Jews you have Dn 3:12
he commanded **s** of the strongest Dn 3:20
made **s** of the stars and some of Dn 8:10
the stars and **s** of the host fall Dn 8:10
After **s** years they will form an Dn 11:6
For **s** years he will stay away Dn 11:8
After **s** years he will advance Dn 11:13
be helped by **s**, but many others Dn 11:34
S of the wise will fall so that Dn 11:35
will awake, **s** to eternal life, Dn 12:2
and **s** to shame and eternal Dn 12:2
I raised up **s** of your sons as Am 2:11

as prophets and **s** of your young Am 2:11
I overthrew **s** of you as I Am 4:11
wouldn't they leave **s** grapes? Ob 5
come and take **s** of the pots to Zch 14:21
Just then **s** men brought to Him a Mt 9:2
s of the scribes said among Mt 9:3
pick and eat **s** heads of grain. Mt 12:1
Then **s** of the scribes and Mt 12:38
s seeds fell along the path, Mt 13:4
s 100, some 60, and some 30 Mt 13:8
100, **s** 60, and some 30 times Mt 13:8
and **s** 30 times ⌊what was sown⌋. Mt 13:8
s 100, some 60, some 30 times Mt 13:23
some 100, **s** 60, some 30 times Mt 13:23
s 30 times ⌊what was sown⌋." Mt 13:23
And they said, "**S** say John the Mt 16:14
There are **s** standing here who Mt 16:28
S Pharisees approached Him to Mt 19:3
same day **s** Sadducees, who say Mt 22:23
S of them you will kill and Mt 23:34
and **s** of them you will flog in Mt 23:34
ones, 'Give us **s** of your oil, Mt 25:8
When they had gone to buy **s**, Mt 25:10
instead, he took **s** water, washed Mt 27:24
When **s** of those standing there Mt 27:47
s of the guard came into the Mt 28:11
they worshiped, but **s** doubted. Mt 28:17
Capernaum again after **s** days, Mk 2:1
s of the scribes were sitting Mk 2:6
way picking **s** heads of grain. Mk 2:23
also gave **s** to his companions? Mk 2:26
S seed fell along the path, Mk 4:4
S said, "John the Baptist has Mk 6:14
Pharisees and **s** of the scribes Mk 7:1
observed that **s** of His disciples Mk 7:2
and **s** of them have come a long Mk 8:3
There are **s** standing here who Mk 9:1
S Pharisees approached Him to Mk 10:2
S people were bringing little Mk 10:13
and **s** of those standing there Mk 11:5
farmers to collect **s** of the Mk 12:2
beat **s** and they killed some. Mk 12:5
beat some and they killed **s**. Mk 12:5
they sent **s** of the Pharisees Mk 12:13
S Sadducees, who say there is no Mk 12:18
s were expressing indignation Mk 14:4
S stood up and were giving false Mk 14:57
Then **s** began to spit on Him, Mk 14:65
When **s** of those standing there Mk 15:35
After he bought **s** fine linen, Mk 15:46
S soldiers also questioned him: Lk 3:14
Just then **s** men came, carrying Lk 5:18
But **s** of the Pharisees said, Lk 6:2
He even gave **s** to those who were Lk 6:4
he sent **s** Jewish elders to Him, Lk 7:3
and also **s** women who had been Lk 8:2
As he was sowing, **s** fell along Lk 8:5
because **s** said that John had Lk 9:7
s that Elijah had appeared, Lk 9:8
there are **s** standing here who Lk 9:27
But **s** of them said, "He drives Lk 11:15
and **s** of them they will kill and Lk 11:49
s people came and reported to Lk 13:1
s are last who will be first, Lk 13:30
s are first who will be last. Lk 13:30
that time **s** Pharisees came and Lk 13:31
this parable to **s** who trusted Lk 18:9
S people were even bringing Lk 18:15
S of the Pharisees from the Lk 19:39
they might give him **s** fruit from Lk 20:10
S of the Sadducees, who say Lk 20:27
S of the scribes answered, Lk 20:39
As **s** were talking about the Lk 21:5
They will kill **s** of you. Lk 21:16
hoping to see **s** miracle Lk 23:8
s women from our group astounded Lk 24:22
S of those who were with us went Lk 24:24
Now draw **s** out and take it to Jn 2:8
S boats from Tiberias came near Jn 6:23
But there are **s** among you who Jn 6:64
S were saying, "He's a good man." Jn 7:12
S of the people of Jerusalem Jn 7:25
s from the crowd heard these Jn 7:40
But **s** said, "Surely the Messiah Jn 7:41
S of them wanted to seize Him, Jn 7:44
made **s** mud from the saliva, Jn 9:6
S said, "He's the one." Jn 9:9
Therefore **s** of the Pharisees Jn 9:16

S of the Pharisees who were with Jn 9:40
door but climbs in **s** other way, Jn 10:1
But **s** of them said, "Couldn't He Jn 11:37
But **s** of them went to the Jn 11:46
s Greeks were among those who Jn 12:20
s thought that Jesus was telling Jn 13:29
Therefore **s** of His disciples Jn 16:17
of soldiers and **s** temple police Jn 18:3
told them, "and you'll find **s**." Jn 21:6
Bring **s** of the fish you've just Jn 21:10
But **s** sneered and said, "They're Ac 2:13
shadow might fall on **s** of them. Ac 5:15
Then **s** from what is called the Ac 6:9
and **s** from Cilicia and Asia, Ac 6:9
the road, they came to **s** water. Ac 8:36
And after taking **s** food, he Ac 9:19
in Damascus for **s** days. Ac 9:19
and **s** of the brothers from Joppa Ac 10:23
there were **s** of them, Cypriot Ac 11:20
In those days **s** prophets came Ac 11:27
attacked **s** who belonged to Ac 12:1
stayed there for **s** time and Ac 14:3
s siding with the Jews and some Ac 14:4
the Jews and **s** with the apostles Ac 14:4
Then **s** Jews came from Antioch Ac 14:19
S men came down from Judea and Ac 15:1
Barnabas and **s** others of them Ac 15:2
But **s** of the believers from the Ac 15:5
heard that **s** to whom we gave Ac 15:24
After spending **s** time there, Ac 15:33
After **s** time had passed, Paul Ac 15:36
Then **s** of them were persuaded Ac 17:4
brought together **s** scoundrels Ac 17:5
Jason and **s** of the brothers Ac 17:6
s of the Epicurean and Stoic Ac 17:18
S said, "What is this Ac 17:18
as even **s** of your own poets have Ac 17:28
of the dead, **s** began to ridicule Ac 17:32
s men joined him and believed, Ac 17:34
to Ephesus. He found **s** disciples Ac 19:1
But when **s** became hardened and Ac 19:9
Then **s** of the itinerant Jewish Ac 19:13
Even **s** of the provincial Ac 19:31
s were shouting one thing and Ac 19:32
one thing and **s** another, Ac 19:32
Then **s** of the crowd gave Ac 19:33
So we found **s** disciples and Ac 21:4
S of the disciples from Caesarea Ac 21:16
S in the mob were shouting one Ac 21:34
one thing and **s** another. Ac 21:34
a rebellion **s** time ago and led Ac 21:38
and **s** of the scribes of the Ac 23:9
came down with **s** elders and a Ac 24:1
s Jews from the province of Asia Ac 24:18
though he could have **s** freedom, Ac 24:23
After **s** days, when Felix came Ac 24:24
After **s** days had passed, King Ac 25:13
Instead they had **s** disagreements Ac 25:19
known me for quite **s** time, Ac 26:5
over Paul and **s** other prisoners Ac 27:1
run aground in **s** rocky place, Ac 27:29
S sailors tried to escape from Ac 27:30
I urge you to take **s** food. Ac 27:34
things and had taken **s** bread, Ac 27:35
s on planks and some on debris Ac 27:44
some on planks and **s** on debris Ac 27:44
S were persuaded by what he said, Ac 28:24
impart to you **s** spiritual gift Rm 1:11
If **s** did not believe, will their Rm 3:3
just as **s** people slanderously Rm 3:8
jealous and save **s** of them. Rm 11:14
Now if **s** of the branches were Rm 11:17
more boldly on **s** points because Rm 15:15
Now **s** are inflated with pride, 1Co 4:18
S of you were like this; 1Co 6:11
s have been so used to idolatry 1Co 8:7
that I may by all means save **s**. 1Co 9:22
idolaters as **s** of them were; 1Co 10:7
immorality as **s** of them did, 1Co 10:8
tempt Christ as **s** of them did, 1Co 10:9
we complain as **s** of them did, 1Co 10:10
and **s** unbeliever or uninformed 1Co 14:24
the present, but **s** have fallen 1Co 15:6
the dead, how can **s** of you say, 1Co 15:12
because **s** people are ignorant 1Co 15:34
I hope to spend **s** time with you, 1Co 16:7
to me, but in **s** degree—not to 2Co 2:5
To **s** we are a scent of death 2Co 2:16

Or like s, do we need letters of 2Co 3:1
For if I boast s more about our 2Co 10:8
ourselves with s who commend 2Co 10:12
there are s who are troubling Gl 1:7
gave s to be apostles, Eph 4:11
to be apostles, s prophets, some Eph 4:11
some prophets, s evangelists, Eph 4:11
some evangelists, s pastors and Eph 4:11
S, to be sure, preach Christ out Php 1:15
that there are s among you who 2Th 3:11
S have deviated from these and 1Tm 1:6
S have rejected these and have 1Tm 1:19
the latter times s will depart 1Tm 4:1
For s have already turned away 1Tm 5:15
S people's sins are evident, 1Tm 5:24
s have wandered away from the 1Tm 6:10
s people have deviated from the 1Tm 6:21
are overturning the faith of s. 2Tm 2:18
earthenware, s for special use 2Tm 2:20
for special use, s for ordinary. 2Tm 2:20
it remains for s to enter it, Heb 4:6
meetings, as s habitually do, Heb 10:25
S men were tortured, not Heb 11:35
by doing this s have welcomed Heb 13:2
if s disobey the ⌊Christian⌋ 1Pt 3:1
His promise, as s understand 2Pt 3:9
which there are s matters that 2Pt 3:16
glad to find s of your children 2Jn 4
very glad when s brothers came 3Jn 3
Have mercy on s who doubt; Jd 22
is about to throw s of you into Rv 2:10
You have s there who hold to the Rv 2:14
give the victor s of the hidden Rv 2:17

SOMEBODY *(5)*
And if s overpowers one person, Ec 4:12
"S did touch Me," said Jesus. Lk 8:46
up, claiming to be s, and a Ac 5:36
while claiming to be s great. Ac 8:9
For if s sees you, the one who 1Co 8:10

SOMEHOW *(4)*
hoping s to reach Phoenix, Ac 27:12
that if it is s in God's will, Rm 1:10
if I can s make my own people Rm 11:14
assuming that I will s reach the Php 3:11

SOMEONE *(176)*
(See pp. xi-xii.)

SOMEONE'S *(1)*
(See pp. xi-xii.)

SOMETHING *(132)*
(See pp. xi-xii.)

SOMETIMES *(3)*
S the cloud remained over the Nm 9:20
S the cloud remained ⌊only⌋ from Nm 9:21
S you were publicly exposed to Heb 10:33

SOMEWHAT *(1)*
going to hold a s more careful Ac 23:20

SOMEWHERE *(3)*
spoken in secret, s in a land of Is 45:19
But one has s testified: Heb 2:6
for s He has spoken about the Heb 4:4

SON *(2310)*
the city Enoch after his s. Gn 4:17
gave birth to a s and named him Gn 4:25
A s was born to Seth also, Gn 4:26
years old when he fathered a s. Gn 5:28
his youngest s had done to him, Gn 9:24
Terah took his s Abram, his Gn 11:31
grandson Lot (Haran's s), and Gn 11:31
Sarai, his s Abram's wife, and Gn 11:31
conceived and will have a s. Gn 16:11
Hagar gave birth to Abram's s, Gn 16:15
name Ishmael to the s Hagar had. Gn 16:15
I will give you a s by her. Gn 17:16
wife Sarah will bear you a s, Gn 17:19
took his s Ishmael and all Gn 17:23
and his s Ishmael was 13 years Gn 17:25
Abraham and his s Ishmael were Gn 17:26
your wife Sarah will have a s!" Gn 18:10
about a year she will have a s." Gn 18:14
gave birth to a s and named him Gn 19:37
younger also gave birth to a s, Gn 19:38
and bore a s to Abraham in his Gn 21:2
named his s who was born to Gn 21:3
When his s Isaac was eight days Gn 21:4
old when his s Isaac was born to Gn 21:5
borne him a s in his old age. Gn 21:7
But Sarah saw the s mocking— Gn 21:9
Drive out this slave with her s, Gn 21:10
for the s of this slave will not Gn 21:10
be a co-heir with my s Isaac!" Gn 21:10
for Abraham because of his s. Gn 21:11
of the slave's s because he is Gn 21:13
"Take your s," He said, "your Gn 22:2
your only ⌊s⌋ Isaac, whom you Gn 22:2
his young men and his s Isaac. Gn 22:3
and laid it on his s Isaac. Gn 22:6
he replied, "Here I am, my s." Gn 22:7
for the burnt offering, my s." Gn 22:8
He bound his s Isaac and placed Gn 22:9
the knife to slaughter his s. Gn 22:10
withheld your only s from Me." Gn 22:12
offering in place of his s. Gn 22:13
have not withheld your only s, Gn 22:16
and ask Ephron s of Zohar on my Gn 23:8
a wife for my s from the Gn 24:3
to take a wife for my s Isaac." Gn 24:4
Should I have your s go back to Gn 24:5
you don't take my s back there. Gn 24:6
take a wife for my s from there. Gn 24:7
don't let my s go back there." Gn 24:8
daughter of Bethuel s of Milcah, Gn 24:15
daughter of Bethuel s of Milcah, Gn 24:24
bore a s to my master in her old Gn 24:36
a wife for my s from the Gn 24:37
family to take a wife for my s.' Gn 24:38
a wife for my s from my family Gn 24:40
has appointed for my master's s. Gn 24:44
daughter of Bethuel s of Nahor, Gn 24:47
my master's brother for his s. Gn 24:48
be a wife for your master's s, Gn 24:51
away from his s Isaac, to the Gn 25:6
the field of Ephron s of Zohar Gn 25:9
God blessed his s Isaac, who Gn 25:11
records of Abraham's s Ishmael, Gn 25:12
records of Isaac s of Abraham. Gn 25:19
his older s Esau and said to Gn 27:1
Esau and said to him, "My s." Gn 27:1
what Isaac said to his s Esau. Gn 27:5
Rebekah said to her s Jacob, Gn 27:6
every order I give you, my s. Gn 27:8
him, "Your curse be on me, my s. Gn 27:13
clothes of her older s Esau, Gn 27:15
her younger s Jacob wear them Gn 27:15
she had made to her s Jacob. Gn 27:17
Here I am. Who are you, my s?" Gn 27:18
Isaac said to his s, "How did Gn 27:20
ever find it so quickly, my s?" Gn 27:20
closer so I can touch you, my s. Gn 27:21
you really my s Esau, or not?" Gn 27:21
"Are you really my s Esau?" Gn 27:24
come closer and kiss me, my s." Gn 27:26
the smell of my s is like the Gn 27:27
"I am Esau your firstborn s." Gn 27:32
then can I do for you, my s?" Gn 27:37
of her older s Esau were Gn 27:42
her younger s Jacob and said to Gn 27:42
So now, my s, listen to me. Gn 27:43
to Laban s of Bethuel the Gn 28:5
of Ishmael, Abraham's s. Gn 28:9
"Do you know Laban s of Nahor?" Gn 29:5
father's relative, Rebekah's s. Gn 29:12
news about his sister's s Jacob, Gn 29:13
gave birth to a s, and named him Gn 29:32
birth to a s, and said, "The Gn 29:33
and has given me this ⌊s⌋ also." Gn 29:33
gave birth to a s, and said, "At Gn 29:34
gave birth to a s, and said, Gn 29:35
conceived and bore Jacob a s. Gn 30:5
has heard me and given me a s," Gn 30:6
again and bore Jacob a second s. Gn 30:7
slave Zilpah bore Jacob a s. Gn 30:10
Zilpah bore Jacob a second s, Gn 30:12
and bore Jacob a fifth s. Gn 30:17
again and bore Jacob a sixth s. Gn 30:19
She conceived and bore a s, Gn 30:23
the LORD add another s to me." Gn 30:24
When Shechem s of Hamor the Gn 34:2
My s Shechem is strongly Gn 34:8
eyes of Hamor and his s Shechem. Gn 34:18
Hamor and his s Shechem went to Gn 34:20
to Hamor and his s Shechem, Gn 34:24
Hamor and his s Shechem with Gn 34:26
for this is another s for you." Gn 35:17
Eliphaz s of Esau's wife Adah, Gn 36:10
and Reuel s of Esau's wife Gn 36:10
a concubine of Esau's s Eliphaz, Gn 36:12
are the sons of Reuel, Esau's s: Gn 36:17
Bela s of Beor ruled in Edom; Gn 36:32
Jobab s of Zerah from Bozrah Gn 36:33
Hadad s of Bedad ruled in his Gn 36:35
Baal-hanan s of Achbor ruled in Gn 36:38
Baal-hanan s of Achbor died, Gn 36:39
Joseph was a s ⌊born to him⌋ in Gn 37:3
and mourned for his s many days. Gn 37:34
I will go down to Sheol to my s, Gn 37:35
conceived and gave birth to a s, Gn 38:3
gave birth to a s, and named him Gn 38:4
birth to another s and named him Gn 38:5
until my s Shelah grows up. Gn 38:11
not give her to my s Shelah." Gn 38:26
And the second s he named Gn 41:52
My s will not go down with you, Gn 42:38
his mother's s, he asked, "Is Gn 43:29
God be gracious to you, my s." Gn 43:29
This is what your s Joseph says: Gn 45:9
My s Joseph is still alive. Gn 45:28
the s of a Canaanite woman. Gn 46:10
Dan's s: Hashum. Gn 46:23
he called his s Joseph and said Gn 47:29
"Your s Joseph has come to you," Gn 48:2
and said, "I know, my s, I know! Gn 48:19
a young lion—my s, you return Gn 49:9
sons of Manasseh's s Machir were Gn 50:23
the child is a s, kill him, but Ex 1:16
must throw every s born to the Ex 1:22
pregnant and gave birth to a s; Ex 2:2
daughter, and he became her s. Ex 2:10
gave birth to a s whom he named Ex 2:22
Israel is My firstborn s. Ex 4:22
Let My s go so that he may Ex 4:23
I will kill your firstborn s!" Ex 4:23
the s of a Canaanite woman. Ex 6:15
Aaron's s Eleazar married one of Ex 6:25
may tell your s and grandson how Ex 10:2
On that day explain to your s, Ex 13:8
when your s asks you, 'What Ex 13:14
work—you, your s or daughter, Ex 20:10
Or if he chooses her for his s, Ex 21:9
If it gores a s or a daughter, Ex 21:31
and the s of your female slave Ex 23:12
by name Bezalel s of Uri, Ex 31:2
Bezalel son of Uri, s of Hur, of Ex 31:2
selected Oholiab s of Ahisamach, Ex 31:6
against his s and his brother Ex 32:29
the young man Joshua s of Nun, Ex 33:11
by name Bezalel s of Uri, Ex 35:30
Bezalel son of Uri, s of Hur, of Ex 35:30
him and Oholiab s of Ahisamach, Ex 35:34
of Ithamar s of Aaron the priest Ex 38:21
Bezalel s of Uri, son of Hur, of Ex 38:22
Bezalel son of Uri, s of Hur, of Ex 38:22
him was Oholiab s of Ahisamach, Ex 38:23
The s of Aaron who presents the Lv 7:33
whether for a s or daughter, Lv 12:6
his mother, father, s, daughter, Lv 21:2
Now the s of an Israelite mother Lv 24:10
woman's s and an Israelite Lv 24:10
Her s cursed and blasphemed the Lv 24:11
Elizur s of Shedeur from Reuben; Nm 1:5
Shelumiel s of Zurishaddai from Nm 1:6
Nahshon s of Amminadab from Nm 1:7
s of Zuar from Issachar; Nm 1:8
Eliab s of Helon from Zebulun; Nm 1:9
Elishama s of Ammihud from Nm 1:10
Gamaliel s of Pedahzur from Nm 1:10
Abidan s of Gideoni from Nm 1:11
Ahiezer s of Ammishaddai from Nm 1:12
Pagiel s of Ochran from Asher; Nm 1:13
Eliasaph s of Deuel from Gad; Nm 1:14
Ahira s of Enan from Naphtali. Nm 1:15
Judah is Nahshon s of Amminadab. Nm 2:3
is Nethanel s of Zuar. Nm 2:5
Zebulunites is Eliab s of Helon. Nm 2:7
is Elizur s of Shedeur. Nm 2:10
is Shelumiel s of Zurishaddai. Nm 2:12
Gadites is Eliasaph s of Deuel. Nm 2:14
is Elishama s of Ammihud. Nm 2:18
is Gamaliel s of Pedahzur. Nm 2:20
is Abidan s of Gideoni. Nm 2:22
is Ahiezer s of Ammishaddai. Nm 2:25
Asherites is Pagiel s of Ochran. Nm 2:27
Naphtalites is Ahira s of Enan. Nm 2:29

He was the **s** of Ahitub, the 1Sm 14:3
of Ichabod **s** of Phinehas, 1Sm 14:3
s of Eli the LORD's priest at 1Sm 14:3
it is because of my **s** Jonathan, 1Sm 14:39
and I and my **s** Jonathan will be 1Sm 14:40
between me and my **s** Jonathan," 1Sm 14:42
army was Abner **s** of Saul's uncle 1Sm 14:50
father was Ner **s** of Abiel. 1Sm 14:51
I have seen a **s** of Jesse of 1Sm 16:18
Send me your **s** David, who is 1Sm 16:19
them by his **s** David to Saul. 1Sm 16:20
David was the **s** of the 1Sm 17:12
Jesse had told his **s** David, 1Sm 17:17
army, "Whose **s** is this youth, 1Sm 17:55
out whose **s** this young man is! 1Sm 17:56
to him, "Whose **s** are you, young 1Sm 17:58
The **s** of your servant Jesse of 1Sm 17:58
ordered his **s** Jonathan and all 1Sm 19:1
Saul's **s** Jonathan liked David 1Sm 19:1
and Saul asked his **s** Jonathan, 1Sm 20:27
didn't Jesse's **s** come to the 1Sm 20:27
You **s** of a perverse and 1Sm 20:30
with Jesse's **s** to your own shame 1Sm 20:30
day Jesse's **s** lives on earth 1Sm 20:31
Jesse's **s** going to give all of 1Sm 22:7
when my own **s** makes a covenant 1Sm 22:8
makes a covenant with Jesse's **s**. 1Sm 22:8
tells me that my **s** has stirred 1Sm 22:8
I saw Jesse's **s** come to 1Sm 22:9
to Ahimelech **s** of Ahitub at Nob 1Sm 22:9
the priest, **s** of Ahitub, and his 1Sm 22:11
said, "Listen, **s** of Ahitub!" 1Sm 22:12
you and Jesse's **s** conspire 1Sm 22:13
of Ahimelech **s** of Ahitub escaped 1Sm 22:20
Abiathar **s** of Ahimelech fled to 1Sm 23:6
Then Saul's **s** Jonathan came to 1Sm 23:16
Is that your voice, David my **s**?" 1Sm 24:16
servants and to your **s** David.' " 1Sm 25:8
Who is Jesse's **s**? Many slaves 1Sm 25:10
wife, to Palti **s** of Laish, who 1Sm 25:44
where Saul and Abner **s** of Ner, 1Sm 26:5
brother Abishai **s** of Zeruiah, 1Sm 26:6
troops and to Abner **s** of Ner: 1Sm 26:14
Is that your voice, my **s** David?" 1Sm 26:17
Come back, my **s** David, I will 1Sm 26:21
You are blessed, my **s** David. 1Sm 26:25
and went to Achish **s** of Maoch, 1Sm 27:2
the priest, **s** of Ahimelech, 1Sm 30:7
and his **s** Jonathan are dead. 2Sm 1:4
Saul and his **s** Jonathan are dead 2Sm 1:5
for Saul, his **s** Jonathan, the 2Sm 1:12
"I'm the **s** of a foreigner" he 2Sm 1:13
for Saul and his **s** Jonathan, 2Sm 1:17
Abner **s** of Ner, commander of 2Sm 2:8
took Saul's **s** Ish-bosheth and 2Sm 2:8
Saul's **s** Ish-bosheth was 40 2Sm 2:10
Abner **s** of Ner and soldiers of 2Sm 2:12
of Ish-bosheth **s** of Saul marched 2Sm 2:12
So Joab **s** of Zeruiah and David's 2Sm 2:13
and Ish-bosheth **s** of Saul, 2Sm 2:15
s of Maacah the daughter of King 2Sm 3:3
was Adonijah, **s** of Haggith; 2Sm 3:4
was Shephatiah, **s** of Abital; 2Sm 3:4
to say to Ish-bosheth **s** of Saul, 2Sm 3:14
her husband, Paltiel **s** of Laish. 2Sm 3:15
Abner **s** of Ner came to see the 2Sm 3:23
know that Abner **s** of Ner came to 2Sm 3:25
the blood of Abner **s** of Ner. 2Sm 3:28
the killing of Abner **s** of Ner. 2Sm 3:37
Saul's **s** ⌊Ish-bosheth⌋ heard 2Sm 4:1
Saul's **s** had two men who were 2Sm 4:2
Saul's **s** Jonathan had a son 2Sm 4:4
Jonathan had a **s** whose feet were 2Sm 4:4
head of Ish-bosheth **s** of Saul, 2Sm 4:8
him, and he will be a **s** to Me. 2Sm 7:14
defeated Hadadezer **s** of Rehob, 2Sm 8:3
sent his **s** Joram to King David 2Sm 8:10
spoil of Hadadezer **s** of Rehob, 2Sm 8:12
Joab **s** of Zeruiah was over the 2Sm 8:16
Jehoshaphat **s** of Ahilud was 2Sm 8:16
Zadok **s** of Ahitub and Ahimelech 2Sm 8:17
and Ahimelech **s** of Abiathar were 2Sm 8:17
Benaiah **s** of Jehoiada ⌊was over⌋ 2Sm 8:18
still Jonathan's **s** who is lame 2Sm 9:3
house of Machir **s** of Ammiel." 2Sm 9:4
the house of Machir **s** of Ammiel 2Sm 9:5
Mephibosheth **s** of Jonathan son 2Sm 9:6
son of Jonathan **s** of Saul came 2Sm 9:6

had a young **s** whose name was 2Sm 9:12
and his **s** Hanun became king in 2Sm 10:1
kindness to Hanun **s** of Nahash, 2Sm 10:2
Abimelech **s** of Jerubbesheth 2Sm 11:21
his wife and bore him a **s**. 2Sm 11:27
the **s** born to you will die." 2Sm 12:14
gave birth to a **s** and named him 2Sm 12:24
s Absalom had a beautiful 2Sm 13:1
and David's **s** Amnon was 2Sm 13:1
a **s** of David's brother Shimeah. 2Sm 13:3
you, the king's **s**, so miserable 2Sm 13:4
Absalom, "No, my **s**, we should 2Sm 13:25
s of David's brother Shimeah, 2Sm 13:32
went to Talmai **s** of Ammihud, 2Sm 13:37
mourned for his **s** every day. 2Sm 13:37
Joab **s** of Zeruiah observed that 2Sm 14:1
they will not eliminate my **s**!" 2Sm 14:11
not a hair of your **s** will fall 2Sm 14:11
both me and my **s** from God's 2Sm 14:16
your **s** Ahimaaz and Abiathar's 2Sm 15:27
and Abiathar's **s** Jonathan. 2Sm 15:27
Zadok's **s** Ahimaaz and 2Sm 15:36
and Abiathar's **s** Jonathan, 2Sm 15:36
"Where is your master's **s**?" 2Sm 16:3
His name was Shimei **s** of Gera, 2Sm 16:5
kingdom over to your **s** Absalom. 2Sm 16:8
Then Abishai **s** of Zeruiah said 2Sm 16:9
Look, my own **s**, my own flesh 2Sm 16:11
whom will I serve if not his **s**? 2Sm 16:19
Amasa was the **s** of a man named 2Sm 17:25
Shobi **s** of Nahash from Rabbah 2Sm 17:27
s of Ammiel from Lo-debar, 2Sm 17:27
brother Abishai **s** of Zeruiah, 2Sm 18:2
my hand against the king's **s**. 2Sm 18:12
I have no **s** to preserve the 2Sm 18:18
Ahimaaz **s** of Zadok said, "Please 2Sm 18:19
because the king's **s** is dead." 2Sm 18:20
Ahimaaz **s** of Zadok persisted and 2Sm 18:22
replied, "My **s**, why do you want 2Sm 18:22
way Ahimaaz **s** of Zadok runs." 2Sm 18:27
walked, he cried, "My **s** Absalom! 2Sm 18:33
Absalom! My **s**, my son Absalom 2Sm 18:33
My son, my **s** Absalom! If only I 2Sm 18:33
of you, Absalom, my **s**, my son!" 2Sm 18:33
of you, Absalom, my son, my **s**!" 2Sm 18:33
king is grieving over his **s**." 2Sm 19:2
top of his voice, "My **s** Absalom! 2Sm 19:4
Absalom! Absalom, my **s**, my son! 2Sm 19:4
Absalom! Absalom, my son, my **s**! 2Sm 19:4
Shimei **s** of Gera, a Benjaminite 2Sm 19:16
When Shimei **s** of Gera crossed 2Sm 19:18
Abishai **s** of Zeruiah asked, 2Sm 19:21
named Sheba **s** of Bichri, 2Sm 20:1
no inheritance in Jesse's **s**. 2Sm 20:1
and followed Sheba **s** of Bichri, 2Sm 20:2
Sheba **s** of Bichri will do more 2Sm 20:6
to pursue Sheba **s** of Bichri. 2Sm 20:7
pursued Sheba **s** of Bichri. 2Sm 20:10
to pursue Sheba **s** of Bichri. 2Sm 20:13
a man named Sheba **s** of Bichri, 2Sm 20:21
head of Sheba **s** of Bichri and 2Sm 20:22
Benaiah **s** of Jehoiada was over 2Sm 20:23
Jehoshaphat **s** of Ahilud was 2Sm 20:24
the **s** of Saul's son Jonathan, 2Sm 21:7
the son of Saul's **s** Jonathan, 2Sm 21:7
David and Jonathan, Saul's **s**. 2Sm 21:7
borne to Adriel **s** of Barzillai 2Sm 21:8
bones of Saul and his **s** Jonathan 2Sm 21:12
of Saul and his **s** Jonathan at 2Sm 21:14
But Abishai **s** of Zeruiah came to 2Sm 21:17
Elhanan **s** of Jaare-oregim the 2Sm 21:19
s of David's brother Shimei, 2Sm 21:21
of David **s** of Jesse, 2Sm 23:1
Eleazar **s** of Dodo son of Ahohi 2Sm 23:9
son of Dodo **s** of Ahohi was among 2Sm 23:9
him was Shammah **s** of Agee the 2Sm 23:11
Joab's brother and **s** of Zeruiah, 2Sm 23:18
Benaiah **s** of Jehoiada was the 2Sm 23:20
Jehoiada was the **s** of a brave 2Sm 23:20
of Benaiah **s** of Jehoiada, 2Sm 23:22
Elhanan **s** of Dodo of Bethlehem, 2Sm 23:24
Ira **s** of Ikkesh the Tekoite, 2Sm 23:26
Heleb **s** of Baanah the 2Sm 23:29
Ittai **s** of Ribai from Gibeah of 2Sm 23:29
the sons of Jashen, Jonathan **s** 2Sm 23:32
Ahiam **s** of Sharar the Hararite, 2Sm 23:33
Eliphelet **s** of Ahasbai son of 2Sm 23:34
son of Ahasbai **s** of the 2Sm 23:34

Eliam **s** of Ahithophel the 2Sm 23:34
Igal **s** of Nathan from Zobah, 2Sm 23:36
for Joab **s** of Zeruiah, 2Sm 23:37
Adonijah **s** of Haggith kept 1Kg 1:5
with Joab **s** of Zeruiah and with 1Kg 1:7
priest, Benaiah **s** of Jehoiada, 1Kg 1:8
that Adonijah **s** of Haggith has 1Kg 1:11
and the life of your **s** Solomon. 1Kg 1:12
Your **s** Solomon is to become king 1Kg 1:13
'Your **s** Solomon is to become 1Kg 1:17
I and my **s** Solomon will be 1Kg 1:21
priest or Benaiah **s** of Jehoiada 1Kg 1:26
Your **s** Solomon is to become king 1Kg 1:30
Benaiah **s** of Jehoiada for me. 1Kg 1:32
have my **s** Solomon ride on my 1Kg 1:33
Benaiah **s** of Jehoiada replied 1Kg 1:36
prophet, Benaiah **s** of Jehoiada, 1Kg 1:38
when Jonathan **s** of Abiathar the 1Kg 1:42
prophet, Benaiah **s** of Jehoiada, 1Kg 1:44
he instructed his **s** Solomon, 1Kg 2:1
know what Joab **s** of Zeruiah did 1Kg 2:5
Abner **s** of Ner and Amasa son of 1Kg 2:5
of Ner and Amasa **s** of Jether. 1Kg 2:5
Keep an eye on Shimei **s** of Gera, 1Kg 2:8
Now Adonijah **s** of Haggith came 1Kg 2:13
and for Joab **s** of Zeruiah." 1Kg 2:22
order to Benaiah **s** of Jehoiada, 1Kg 2:25
sent Benaiah **s** of Jehoiada and 1Kg 2:29
Joab murdered Abner **s** of Ner, 1Kg 2:32
army, and Amasa **s** of Jether, 1Kg 2:32
Benaiah **s** of Jehoiada went up, 1Kg 2:34
appointed Benaiah **s** of Jehoiada 1Kg 2:35
ran away to Achish **s** of Maacah, 1Kg 2:39
commanded Benaiah **s** of Jehoiada, 1Kg 2:46
by giving him a **s** to sit on his 1Kg 3:6
this woman's **s** died because she 1Kg 3:19
night and took my **s** from my side 1Kg 3:20
she put her dead **s** in my arms. 1Kg 3:20
up in the morning to nurse my **s**, 1Kg 3:21
was not the **s** I gave birth to. 1Kg 3:21
My **s** is the living one; 1Kg 3:22
your **s** is the dead one." 1Kg 3:22
No, your **s** is the dead one 1Kg 3:22
my **s** is the living one." 1Kg 3:22
'This is my **s** who is alive, 1Kg 3:23
alive, and your **s** is dead,' but 1Kg 3:23
says, 'No, your **s** is dead, and 1Kg 3:23
is dead, and my **s** is alive.' " 1Kg 3:23
woman whose **s** was alive spoke 1Kg 3:26
felt great compassion for her **s**. 1Kg 3:26
Azariah **s** of Zadok, priest; 1Kg 4:2
Jehoshaphat **s** of Ahilud, 1Kg 4:3
Benaiah **s** of Jehoiada, in charge 1Kg 4:4
Azariah **s** of Nathan, in charge 1Kg 4:5
Zabud **s** of Nathan, a priest and 1Kg 4:5
Adoniram **s** of Abda, in charge 1Kg 4:6
Baana **s** of Ahilud, in Taanach, 1Kg 4:12
villages of Jair **s** of Manasseh, 1Kg 4:13
Ahinadab **s** of Iddo, ⌊in⌋ 1Kg 4:14
Baana **s** of Hushai, in Asher and 1Kg 4:16
Jehoshaphat **s** of Paruah, in 1Kg 4:17
Shimei **s** of Ela, in Benjamin; 1Kg 4:18
Geber **s** of Uri, in the land of 1Kg 4:19
'I will put your **s** on your 1Kg 5:5
David a wise **s** to be over this 1Kg 5:7
was a widow's **s** from the tribe 1Kg 7:14
instead, your **s**, your own 1Kg 8:19
one tribe to your **s** because of 1Kg 11:13
birth to Hadad's **s** Genubath. 1Kg 11:20
raised up Rezon **s** of Eliada as 1Kg 11:23
servant, Jeroboam **s** of Nebat, 1Kg 11:26
I will give one tribe to his **s**, 1Kg 11:36
s Rehoboam became king in his 1Kg 11:43
When Jeroboam **s** of Nebat heard 1Kg 12:2
to Jeroboam **s** of Nebat. 1Kg 12:15
inheritance in the **s** of Jesse. 1Kg 12:16
to Rehoboam **s** of Solomon. 1Kg 12:21
Say to Rehoboam **s** of Solomon, 1Kg 12:23
'A **s** will be born to the house 1Kg 13:2
His **s** came and told him all the 1Kg 13:11
that time Abijah **s** of Jeroboam 1Kg 14:1
soon to ask you about her **s**, 1Kg 14:5
and his **s** Nadab became king in 1Kg 14:20
Solomon's **s**, reigned in Judah. 1Kg 14:21
His **s** Abijam became king in his 1Kg 14:31
King Jeroboam **s** of Nebat, 1Kg 15:1
to raise up his **s** after him and 1Kg 15:4
His **s** Asa became king in his 1Kg 15:8

to Ben-hadad s of Tabrimmon son 1Kg 15:18
of Tabrimmon s of Hezion king 1Kg 15:18
His s Jehoshaphat became king in 1Kg 15:24
Nadab s of Jeroboam became king 1Kg 15:25
Then Baasha s of Ahijah of the 1Kg 15:27
Baasha s of Ahijah became king 1Kg 15:33
came to Jehu s of Hanani against 1Kg 16:1
house of Jeroboam s of Nebat: 1Kg 16:3
His s Elah became king in his 1Kg 16:6
the prophet Jehu s of Hanani the 1Kg 16:7
s of Baasha became king over 1Kg 16:8
and the sins of his s Elah, 1Kg 16:13
followed Tibni s of Ginath, 1Kg 16:21
who followed Tibni s of Ginath. 1Kg 16:22
example of Jeroboam s of Nebat 1Kg 16:26
His s Ahab became king in his 1Kg 16:28
Ahab s of Omri became king over 1Kg 16:29
Ahab s of Omri reigned over 1Kg 16:29
But Ahab s of Omri did what was 1Kg 16:30
sin of Jeroboam s of Nebat were 1Kg 16:31
spoken through Joshua s of Nun. 1Kg 16:34
myself and my s so we can eat it 1Kg 17:12
some for yourself and your s, 1Kg 17:13
the s of the woman who owned 1Kg 17:17
of my guilt and to kill my s?" 1Kg 17:18
said to her, "Give me your s." 1Kg 17:19
staying with by killing her s?" 1Kg 17:20
said, "Look, your s is alive." 1Kg 17:23
to anoint Jehu s of Nimshi as 1Kg 19:16
Israel and Elisha s of Shaphat 1Kg 19:16
found Elisha s of Shaphat as he 1Kg 19:19
of Jeroboam s of Nebat and like 1Kg 21:22
the house of Baasha s of Ahijah, 1Kg 21:22
He is Micaiah s of Imlah." 1Kg 22:8
and get⌋ Micaiah s of Imlah!" 1Kg 22:9
Zedekiah s of Chenaanah made 1Kg 22:11
Zedekiah s of Chenaanah came 1Kg 22:24
and to Joash, the king's s, 1Kg 22:26
and his s Ahaziah became king in 1Kg 22:40
Jehoshaphat s of Asa became king 1Kg 22:41
Ahaziah s of Ahab said to 1Kg 22:49
His s Jehoram became king in his 1Kg 22:50
Ahaziah s of Ahab became king 1Kg 22:51
the way of Jeroboam s of Nebat, 1Kg 22:52
Since he had no s, Joram became 2Kg 1:17
King Jehoram s of Jehoshaphat. 2Kg 1:17
Joram s of Ahab became king over 2Kg 3:1
sins that Jeroboam s of Nebat 2Kg 3:3
Elisha s of Shaphat, who 2Kg 3:11
So he took his firstborn s, 2Kg 3:27
she said to her s, "Bring me 2Kg 4:6
she has no s, and her husband 2Kg 4:14
you will have a s in your arms." 2Kg 4:16
gave birth to a s at the same 2Kg 4:17
right? Is your s all right?' " 2Kg 4:26
Did I ask my lord for a s? 2Kg 4:28
Elisha said, "Pick up your s." 2Kg 4:36
she picked up her s and left. 2Kg 4:37
Give up your s, and we will eat 2Kg 6:28
Then we will eat my s tomorrow.' 2Kg 6:28
So we boiled my s and ate him, 2Kg 6:29
Give up your s, and we will eat 2Kg 6:29
but she has hidden her s." 2Kg 6:29
head of Elisha s of Shaphat 2Kg 6:31
woman whose s he had restored 2Kg 8:1
restored the dead ⌊s⌋ to life, 2Kg 8:5
woman whose s he had restored 2Kg 8:5
this is the s Elisha restored 2Kg 8:5
he said, "Your s, Ben-hadad king 2Kg 8:9
Israel's King Joram s of Ahab, 2Kg 8:16
Jehoram s of Jehoshaphat became 2Kg 8:16
and his s Ahaziah became king in 2Kg 8:24
Israel's King Joram s of Ahab, 2Kg 8:25
Ahaziah s of Jehoram became king 2Kg 8:25
went with Joram s of Ahab to 2Kg 8:28
King Ahaziah s of Jehoram went 2Kg 8:29
to visit Joram s of Ahab since 2Kg 8:29
look for Jehu s of Jehoshaphat, 2Kg 9:2
son of Jehoshaphat, s of Nimshi. 2Kg 9:2
of Jeroboam s of Nebat and like 2Kg 9:9
the house of Baasha s of Ahijah. 2Kg 9:9
Then Jehu s of Jehoshaphat, 2Kg 9:14
son of Jehoshaphat, s of Nimshi, 2Kg 9:14
like that of Jehu s of Nimshi— 2Kg 9:20
year of Joram s of Ahab that 2Kg 9:29
found Jehonadab s of Rechab 2Kg 10:15
and Jehonadab s of Rechab 2Kg 10:23
sins that Jeroboam s of Nebat 2Kg 10:29
s Jehoahaz became king in his 2Kg 10:35
saw that her s was dead, she 2Kg 11:1
rescued Joash s of Ahaziah 2Kg 11:2
He showed them the king's s 2Kg 11:4
He brought out the king's s, 2Kg 11:12
servants Jozabad s of Shimeath 2Kg 12:21
and Jehozabad s of Shomer struck 2Kg 12:21
and his s Amaziah became king in 2Kg 12:21
Judah's King Joash s of Ahaziah, 2Kg 13:1
Jehoahaz s of Jehu became king 2Kg 13:1
sins that Jeroboam s of Nebat 2Kg 13:2
of Aram and his s Ben-hadad 2Kg 13:3
His s Jehoash became king in his 2Kg 13:9
Jehoash s of Jehoahaz became 2Kg 13:10
sins that Jeroboam s of Nebat 2Kg 13:11
and his s Ben-hadad became king 2Kg 13:24
Then Jehoash s of Jehoahaz took 2Kg 13:25
back from Ben-hadad s of Hazael 2Kg 13:25
King Jehoash s of Jehoahaz, 2Kg 14:1
Amaziah s of Joash became king 2Kg 14:1
to Jehoash s of Jehoahaz, 2Kg 14:8
son of Jehoahaz, s of Jehu, king 2Kg 14:8
daughter to my s as a wife.' 2Kg 14:9
Judah's King Amaziah s of Joash, 2Kg 14:13
son of Joash, s of Ahaziah, at 2Kg 14:13
s Jeroboam became king in his 2Kg 14:16
King Amaziah s of Joash lived 15 2Kg 14:17
King Jehoash s of Jehoahaz. 2Kg 14:17
Judah's King Amaziah s of Joash, 2Kg 14:23
Jeroboam s of Jehoash became 2Kg 14:23
the sins Jeroboam s of Nebat had 2Kg 14:24
the prophet Jonah s of Amittai 2Kg 14:25
hand of Jeroboam s of Jehoash. 2Kg 14:27
His s Zechariah became king in 2Kg 14:29
Azariah s of Amaziah became king 2Kg 15:1
Jotham, the king's s, was over 2Kg 15:5
His s Jotham became king in his 2Kg 15:7
Zechariah s of Jeroboam became 2Kg 15:8
the sins Jeroboam s of Nebat had 2Kg 15:9
Shallum s of Jabesh conspired 2Kg 15:10
Shallum s of Jabesh became king; 2Kg 15:13
Menahem s of Gadi came up 2Kg 15:14
down Shallum s of Jabesh there. 2Kg 15:14
Menahem s of Gadi became king 2Kg 15:17
the sins Jeroboam s of Nebat had 2Kg 15:18
and his s Pekahiah became king 2Kg 15:22
Pekahiah s of Menahem became 2Kg 15:23
the sins Jeroboam s of Nebat had 2Kg 15:24
officer, Pekah s of Remaliah, 2Kg 15:25
Pekah s of Remaliah became king 2Kg 15:27
the sins Jeroboam s of Nebat had 2Kg 15:28
Then Hoshea s of Elah organized 2Kg 15:30
against Pekah s of Remaliah. 2Kg 15:30
year of Jotham s of Uzziah. 2Kg 15:30
King Pekah s of Remaliah, 2Kg 15:32
Jotham s of Uzziah became king 2Kg 15:32
of Aram and Pekah s of Remaliah 2Kg 15:37
His s Ahaz became king in his 2Kg 15:38
year of Pekah s of Remaliah, 2Kg 16:1
Ahaz s of Jotham became king of 2Kg 16:1
He even made his s pass through 2Kg 16:3
King Pekah s of Remaliah came to 2Kg 16:5
I am your servant and your s. 2Kg 16:7
and his s Hezekiah became king 2Kg 16:20
Hoshea s of Elah became king 2Kg 17:1
made Jeroboam s of Nebat king. 2Kg 17:21
Israel's King Hoshea s of Elah, 2Kg 18:1
Hezekiah s of Ahaz became king 2Kg 18:1
Israel's King Hoshea s of Elah, 2Kg 18:9
but Eliakim s of Hilkiah, who 2Kg 18:18
and Joah s of Asaph, the court 2Kg 18:18
Then Eliakim s of Hilkiah, 2Kg 18:26
Then Eliakim s of Hilkiah, 2Kg 18:37
and Joah s of Asaph, the court 2Kg 18:37
to the prophet Isaiah s of Amoz. 2Kg 19:2
Then Isaiah s of Amoz sent ⌊a 2Kg 19:20
Then his s Esar-haddon became 2Kg 19:37
prophet Isaiah s of Amoz came 2Kg 20:1
Merodach-baladan s of Baladan, 2Kg 20:12
and his s Manasseh became king 2Kg 20:21
He made his s pass through the 2Kg 21:6
to David and his s Solomon, 2Kg 21:7
His s Amon became king in his 2Kg 21:18
Amon and made his s Josiah king 2Kg 21:24
and his s Josiah became king in 2Kg 21:26
secretary Shaphan s of Azaliah, 2Kg 22:3
son of Azaliah, s of Meshullam, 2Kg 22:3
priest, Ahikam s of Shaphan, 2Kg 22:12
of Shaphan, Achbor s of Micaiah, 2Kg 22:12
wife of Shallum s of Tikvah, 2Kg 22:14
son of Tikvah, s of Harhas, 2Kg 22:14
could make his s or his daughter 2Kg 23:10
place that Jeroboam s of Nebat, 2Kg 23:15
took Jehoahaz s of Josiah, 2Kg 23:30
made Eliakim s of Josiah king 2Kg 23:34
and his s Jehoiachin became king 2Kg 24:6
appointed Gedaliah s of Ahikam, 2Kg 25:22
of Ahikam, s of Shaphan, over 2Kg 25:22
Ishmael s of Nethaniah, 2Kg 25:23
Johanan s of Kareah, Seraiah 2Kg 25:23
Seraiah s of Tanhumeth the 2Kg 25:23
Jaazaniah s of the Maacathite 2Kg 25:23
however, Ishmael s of Nethaniah, 2Kg 25:25
son of Nethaniah, s of Elishama, 2Kg 25:25
Anah's s: Dishon. Dishon's sons: 1Ch 1:41
Bela s of Beor. Bela's 1Ch 1:43
Jobab s of Zerah from Bozrah 1Ch 1:44
died, Hadad s of Bedad, who 1Ch 1:46
Baal-hanan s of Achbor ruled in 1Ch 1:49
Carmi's s: Achar, who brought 1Ch 2:7
Ethan's s: Azariah. 1Ch 2:8
Caleb s of Hezron had children 1Ch 2:18
Appaim's s: Ishi. Ishi's son: 1Ch 2:31
son: Ishi. Ishi's s: Sheshan. 1Ch 2:31
his second s, fathered Hebron. 1Ch 2:42
Shammai's s was Maon, and Maon 1Ch 2:45
Absalom s of Maacah, daughter of 1Ch 3:2
s of Haggith was fourth; 1Ch 3:2
Solomon's s was Rehoboam; 1Ch 3:10
his s was Abijah, his son Asa, 1Ch 3:10
was Abijah, his s Asa, his son 1Ch 3:10
his son Asa, his s Jehoshaphat, 1Ch 3:10
his s Jehoram, his son Ahaziah, 1Ch 3:11
Jehoram, his s Ahaziah, his son 1Ch 3:11
his son Ahaziah, his s Joash, 1Ch 3:11
his s Amaziah, his son Azariah, 1Ch 3:12
Amaziah, his s Azariah, his son 1Ch 3:12
his son Azariah, his s Jotham, 1Ch 3:12
s Ahaz, his son Hezekiah, his 1Ch 3:13
son Ahaz, his s Hezekiah, his 1Ch 3:13
son Hezekiah, his s Manasseh, 1Ch 3:13
his s Amon, and his son Josiah. 1Ch 3:14
his son Amon, and his s Josiah. 1Ch 3:14
The s of Shecaniah: Shemaiah. 1Ch 3:22
Reaiah s of Shobal fathered 1Ch 4:2
families of Aharhel s of Harum. 1Ch 4:8
sons of Caleb s of Jephunneh: 1Ch 4:15
Elah, and Naam. Elah's s: Kenaz. 1Ch 4:15
The sons of Shelah s of Judah: 1Ch 4:21
his s Shallum, his son Mibsam, 1Ch 4:25
Shallum, his s Mibsam, and his 1Ch 4:25
son Mibsam, and his s Mishma. 1Ch 4:25
his s Hammuel, his son Zaccur, 1Ch 4:26
Hammuel, his s Zaccur, and his 1Ch 4:26
son Zaccur, and his s Shimei. 1Ch 4:26
Jamlech, Joshah s of Amaziah, 1Ch 4:34
Joel, Jehu s of Joshibiah, son 1Ch 4:35
of Joshibiah, s of Seraiah, son 1Ch 4:35
son of Seraiah, s of Asiel, 1Ch 4:35
and Ziza s of Shiphi, son of 1Ch 4:37
son of Shiphi, s of Allon, son 1Ch 4:37
son of Allon, s of Jedaiah, son 1Ch 4:37
son of Jedaiah, s of Shimri, son 1Ch 4:37
son of Shimri, s of Shemaiah— 1Ch 4:37
the sons of Joseph s of Israel, 1Ch 5:1
his s Shemaiah, his son Gog, his 1Ch 5:4
son Shemaiah, his s Gog, his son 1Ch 5:4
his son Gog, his s Shimei, 1Ch 5:4
his s Micah, his son Reaiah, his 1Ch 5:5
son Micah, his s Reaiah, his son 1Ch 5:5
his son Reaiah, his s Baal, 1Ch 5:5
and his s Beerah. Beerah was a 1Ch 5:6
Bela s of Azaz, son of Shema, 1Ch 5:8
Bela son of Azaz, s of Shema, 1Ch 5:8
Azaz, son of Shema, s of Joel. 1Ch 5:8
the sons of Abihail s of Huri, 1Ch 5:14
son of Huri, s of Jaroah, son 1Ch 5:14
son of Jaroah, s of Gilead, son 1Ch 5:14
son of Gilead, s of Michael, son 1Ch 5:14
son of Michael, s of Jeshishai, 1Ch 5:14
of Jeshishai, s of Jahdo, son 1Ch 5:14
son of Jahdo, s of Buz. 1Ch 5:14
s of Abdiel, son of Guni, was 1Ch 5:15
son of Abdiel, s of Guni, was 1Ch 5:15
his s Libni, his son Jahath, his 1Ch 6:20
son Libni, his s Jahath, his son 1Ch 6:20

his son Jahath, his s Zimmah, 1Ch 6:20
s Joah, his son Iddo, his son 1Ch 6:21
son Joah, his s Iddo, his son 1Ch 6:21
son Iddo, his s Zerah, and his 1Ch 6:21
son Zerah, and his s Jeatherai. 1Ch 6:21
his s Amminadab, his son Korah, 1Ch 6:22
Amminadab, his s Korah, his son 1Ch 6:22
his son Korah, his s Assir, 1Ch 6:22
his s Elkanah, his son Ebiasaph, 1Ch 6:23
son Elkanah, his s Ebiasaph, his 1Ch 6:23
his son Ebiasaph, his s Assir, 1Ch 6:23
his s Tahath, his son Uriel, his 1Ch 6:24
son Tahath, his s Uriel, his son 1Ch 6:24
son Uriel, his s Uzziah, and his 1Ch 6:24
his son Uzziah, and his s Shaul. 1Ch 6:24
his s Elkanah, his son Zophai, 1Ch 6:26
Elkanah, his s Zophai, his son 1Ch 6:26
his son Zophai, his s Nahath, 1Ch 6:26
s Eliab, his son Jeroham, and 1Ch 6:27
Eliab, his s Jeroham, and his 1Ch 6:27
son Jeroham, and his s Elkanah. 1Ch 6:27
Joel, and his second s Abijah. 1Ch 6:28
Mahli, his s Libni, his son 1Ch 6:29
son Libni, his s Shimei, his son 1Ch 6:29
his son Shimei, his s Uzzah, 1Ch 6:29
his s Shimea, his son Haggiah, 1Ch 6:30
son Shimea, his s Haggiah, and 1Ch 6:30
son Haggiah, and his s Asaiah. 1Ch 6:30
Heman the singer, s of Joel, son 1Ch 6:33
son of Joel, s of Samuel, 1Ch 6:33
s of Elkanah, son of Jeroham, 1Ch 6:34
of Elkanah, s of Jeroham, son 1Ch 6:34
son of Jeroham, s of Eliel, son 1Ch 6:34
son of Eliel, s of Toah, 1Ch 6:34
s of Zuph, son of Elkanah, son 1Ch 6:35
son of Zuph, s of Elkanah, son 1Ch 6:35
son of Elkanah, s of Mahath, son 1Ch 6:35
son of Mahath, s of Amasai, 1Ch 6:35
s of Elkanah, son of Joel, son 1Ch 6:36
son of Elkanah, s of Joel, son 1Ch 6:36
son of Joel, s of Azariah, son 1Ch 6:36
son of Azariah, s of Zephaniah, 1Ch 6:36
s of Tahath, son of Assir, son 1Ch 6:37
son of Tahath, s of Assir, son 1Ch 6:37
son of Assir, s of Ebiasaph, son 1Ch 6:37
son of Ebiasaph, s of Korah, 1Ch 6:37
s of Izhar, son of Kohath, son 1Ch 6:38
son of Izhar, s of Kohath, son 1Ch 6:38
son of Kohath, s of Levi, son 1Ch 6:38
son of Levi, s of Israel. 1Ch 6:38
Asaph s of Berechiah, son of 1Ch 6:39
son of Berechiah, s of Shimea, 1Ch 6:39
s of Michael, son of Baaseiah, 1Ch 6:40
son of Michael, s of Baaseiah, 1Ch 6:40
son of Baaseiah, s of Malchijah, 1Ch 6:40
s of Ethni, son of Zerah, son of 1Ch 6:41
son of Ethni, s of Zerah, son of 1Ch 6:41
son of Zerah, s of Adaiah, 1Ch 6:41
s of Ethan, son of Zimmah, son 1Ch 6:42
son of Ethan, s of Zimmah, son 1Ch 6:42
son of Zimmah, s of Shimei, 1Ch 6:42
s of Jahath, son of Gershom, son 1Ch 6:43
son of Jahath, s of Gershom, son 1Ch 6:43
son of Gershom, s of Levi. 1Ch 6:43
Ethan s of Kishi, son of Abdi, 1Ch 6:44
son of Kishi, s of Abdi, son 1Ch 6:44
son of Abdi, s of Malluch, 1Ch 6:44
s of Hashabiah, son of Amaziah, 1Ch 6:45
of Hashabiah, s of Amaziah, son 1Ch 6:45
son of Amaziah, s of Hilkiah, 1Ch 6:45
s of Amzi, son of Bani, son of 1Ch 6:46
son of Amzi, s of Bani, son of 1Ch 6:46
Amzi, son of Bani, s of Shemer, 1Ch 6:46
s of Mahli, son of Mushi, son of 1Ch 6:47
son of Mahli, s of Mushi, son of 1Ch 6:47
son of Mushi, s of Merari, son 1Ch 6:47
Mushi, son of Merari, s of Levi. 1Ch 6:47
his s Eleazar, his son Phinehas, 1Ch 6:50
son Eleazar, his s Phinehas, his 1Ch 6:50
his son Phinehas, his s Abishua, 1Ch 6:50
his s Bukki, his son Uzzi, his 1Ch 6:51
son Bukki, his s Uzzi, his son 1Ch 6:51
his son Uzzi, his s Zerahiah, 1Ch 6:51
his s Meraioth, his son Amariah, 1Ch 6:52
Meraioth, his s Amariah, his son 1Ch 6:52
his son Amariah, his s Ahitub, 1Ch 6:52
s Zadok, and his son Ahimaaz. 1Ch 6:53
son Zadok, and his s Ahimaaz. 1Ch 6:53
given to Caleb s of Jephunneh. 1Ch 6:56
Uzzi's s: Izrahiah. Izrahiah's 1Ch 7:3
Jediael's s: Bilhan. Bilhan's 1Ch 7:10
wife Maacah gave birth to a s, 1Ch 7:16
Ulam's s: Bedan. These were the 1Ch 7:17
the sons of Gilead s of Machir, 1Ch 7:17
son of Machir, s of Manasseh. 1Ch 7:17
and his s Bered, his son 1Ch 7:20
son Bered, his s Tahath, his son 1Ch 7:20
son Tahath, his s Eleadah, his 1Ch 7:20
his son Eleadah, his s Tahath, 1Ch 7:20
his s Zabad, his son Shuthelah, 1Ch 7:21
Zabad, his s Shuthelah, Ezer, 1Ch 7:21
conceived and gave birth to a s. 1Ch 7:23
his s Rephah, his son Resheph, 1Ch 7:25
son Rephah, his s Resheph, his 1Ch 7:25
Resheph, his s Telah, his son 1Ch 7:25
his son Telah, his s Tahan, 1Ch 7:25
s Ladan, his son Ammihud, his 1Ch 7:26
Ladan, his s Ammihud, his son 1Ch 7:26
his son Ammihud, his s Elishama, 1Ch 7:26
his s Nun, and his son Joshua. 1Ch 7:27
his son Nun, and his s Joshua. 1Ch 7:27
sons of Joseph s of Israel lived 1Ch 7:29
Abdon was his firstborn s, 1Ch 8:30
Jonathan's s was Merib-baal, 1Ch 8:34
His s was Raphah, his son 1Ch 8:37
was Raphah, his s Eleasah, and 1Ch 8:37
his son Eleasah, and his s Azel. 1Ch 8:37
Uthai s of Ammihud, son of Omri, 1Ch 9:4
son of Ammihud, s of Omri, son 1Ch 9:4
son of Omri, s of Imri, son of 1Ch 9:4
Omri, son of Imri, s of Bani, a 1Ch 9:4
descendant of Perez s of Judah; 1Ch 9:4
Sallu s of Meshullam, son of 1Ch 9:7
of Meshullam, s of Hodaviah, son 1Ch 9:7
son of Hodaviah, s of Hassenuah; 1Ch 9:7
Ibneiah s of Jeroham; Elah son 1Ch 9:8
Elah s of Uzzi, son of Michri; 1Ch 9:8
Elah son of Uzzi, s of Michri; 1Ch 9:8
Meshullam s of Shephatiah, 1Ch 9:8
of Shephatiah, s of Reuel, son 1Ch 9:8
son of Reuel, s of Ibnijah; 1Ch 9:8
Azariah s of Hilkiah, son of 1Ch 9:11
son of Hilkiah, s of Meshullam, 1Ch 9:11
of Meshullam, s of Zadok, son 1Ch 9:11
son of Zadok, s of Meraioth, son 1Ch 9:11
of Meraioth, s of Ahitub, the 1Ch 9:11
Adaiah s of Jeroham, son of 1Ch 9:12
of Jeroham, s of Pashhur, son 1Ch 9:12
son of Pashhur, s of Malchijah; 1Ch 9:12
Maasai s of Adiel, son of 1Ch 9:12
son of Adiel, s of Jahzerah, son 1Ch 9:12
son of Jahzerah, s of Meshullam, 1Ch 9:12
of Meshullam, s of Meshillemith 1Ch 9:12
son of Meshillemith, s of Immer; 1Ch 9:12
Shemaiah s of Hasshub, son of 1Ch 9:14
of Hasshub, s of Azrikam, son 1Ch 9:14
s of Hashabiah of the Merarites; 1Ch 9:14
and Mattaniah, s of Mica, son 1Ch 9:15
son of Mica, s of Zichri, son of 1Ch 9:15
Mica, son of Zichri, s of Asaph; 1Ch 9:15
Obadiah s of Shemaiah, son of 1Ch 9:16
son of Shemaiah, s of Galal, son 1Ch 9:16
son of Galal, s of Jeduthun; 1Ch 9:16
and Berechiah s of Asa, son of 1Ch 9:16
s of Elkanah who lived in the 1Ch 9:16
Shallum s of Kore, son of 1Ch 9:19
son of Kore, s of Ebiasaph, son 1Ch 9:19
s of Korah and his relatives 1Ch 9:19
times Phinehas s of Eleazar had 1Ch 9:20
Zechariah s of Meshelemiah was 1Ch 9:21
Abdon was his firstborn s, 1Ch 9:36
Jonathan's s was Merib-baal, 1Ch 9:40
His s was Rephaiah, his son 1Ch 9:43
Rephaiah, his s Eleasah, and his 1Ch 9:43
his son Eleasah, and his s Azel. 1Ch 9:43
over to David s of Jesse. 1Ch 10:14
Joab s of Zeruiah went up 1Ch 11:6
Jashobeam s of Hachmoni was 1Ch 11:11
Eleazar s of Dodo the Ahohite 1Ch 11:12
Benaiah s of Jehoiada was the 1Ch 11:22
Jehoiada was the s of a brave 1Ch 11:22
of Benaiah s of Jehoiada, 1Ch 11:24
Elhanan s of Dodo of Bethlehem, 1Ch 11:26
Ira s of Ikkesh the Tekoite, 1Ch 11:28
Heled s of Baanah the 1Ch 11:30
Ithai s of Ribai from Gibeah of 1Ch 11:31
Jonathan s of Shagee the 1Ch 11:34
Ahiam s of Sachar the Hararite, 1Ch 11:35
the Hararite, Eliphal s of Ur, 1Ch 11:35
Carmelite, Naarai s of Ezbai, 1Ch 11:37
of Nathan, Mibhar s of Hagri, 1Ch 11:38
for Joab s of Zeruiah, 1Ch 11:39
the Hittite, Zabad s of Ahlai, 1Ch 11:41
Adina s of Shiza the Reubenite, 1Ch 11:42
Hanan s of Maacah, Joshaphat the 1Ch 11:43
Jediael s of Shimri and his 1Ch 11:45
the presence of Saul s of Kish. 1Ch 12:1
chief was Ahiezer s of Shemaah 1Ch 12:3
we are⌋ with you, s of Jesse! 1Ch 12:18
appointed Heman s of Joel; 1Ch 15:17
relatives, Asaph s of Berechiah; 1Ch 15:17
Merarites, Ethan s of Kushaiah. 1Ch 15:17
Obed-edom s of Jeduthun and 1Ch 16:38
him, and he will be a s to Me. 1Ch 17:13
he sent his s Hadoram to King 1Ch 18:10
Abishai s of Zeruiah struck down 1Ch 18:12
Joab s of Zeruiah was over the 1Ch 18:15
Jehoshaphat s of Ahilud was 1Ch 18:15
Zadok s of Ahitub and Ahimelech 1Ch 18:16
and Ahimelech s of Abiathar were 1Ch 18:16
Benaiah s of Jehoiada was over 1Ch 18:17
and his s became king in his 1Ch 19:1
kindness to Hanun s of Nahash, 1Ch 19:2
and Elhanan s of Jair killed 1Ch 20:5
s of David's brother Shimei, 1Ch 20:7
My s Solomon is young and 1Ch 22:5
Then he summoned his s Solomon 1Ch 22:6
"My s," David said to Solomon, 1Ch 22:7
But a s will be born to you; 1Ch 22:9
He will be My s, and I will be 1Ch 22:10
Now, my s, may the LORD be with 1Ch 22:11
of Israel to help his s Solomon: 1Ch 22:17
installed his s Solomon as king 1Ch 23:1
Shemaiah s of Nethanel, 1Ch 24:6
priest, Ahimelech s of Abiathar, 1Ch 24:6
from⌋ his sons, Jaaziah his s. 1Ch 24:26
Merari's sons, by his s Jaaziah: 1Ch 24:27
Meshelemiah s of Kore, one of 1Ch 26:1
to his s Shemaiah were born sons 1Ch 26:6
cast lots for his s Zechariah, 1Ch 26:14
descendant of Moses' s Gershom, 1Ch 26:24
s Rehabiah, his son Jeshaiah, 1Ch 26:25
Rehabiah, his s Jeshaiah, his 1Ch 26:25
Jeshaiah, his s Joram, his son 1Ch 26:25
son Joram, his s Zichri, and his 1Ch 26:25
son Zichri, and his s Shelomith. 1Ch 26:25
the seer, Saul s of Kish, Abner 1Ch 26:28
Kish, Abner s of Ner, and Joab 1Ch 26:28
and Joab s of Zeruiah had 1Ch 26:28
Jashobeam s of Zabdiel was in 1Ch 27:2
was Benaiah s of Jehoiada the 1Ch 27:5
his s Ammizabad was in charge 1Ch 27:6
and his s Zebadiah ⌊was 1Ch 27:7
was Ira s of Ikkesh the Tekoite; 1Ch 27:9
Eliezer s of Zichri was the 1Ch 27:16
Shephatiah s of Maacah; 1Ch 27:16
Levites, Hashabiah s of Kemuel; 1Ch 27:17
for Issachar, Omri s of Michael; 1Ch 27:18
Zebulun, Ishmaiah s of Obadiah; 1Ch 27:19
Naphtali, Jerimoth s of Azriel; 1Ch 27:19
Hoshea s of Azaziah; 1Ch 27:20
of Manasseh, Joel s of Pedaiah; 1Ch 27:20
in Gilead, Iddo s of Zechariah; 1Ch 27:21
Benjamin, Jaasiel s of Abner; 1Ch 27:21
for Dan, Azarel s of Jeroham. 1Ch 27:22
Joab s of Zeruiah began to count 1Ch 27:24
Azmaveth s of Adiel was in 1Ch 27:25
Jonathan s of Uzziah was in 1Ch 27:25
Ezri s of Chelub was in charge 1Ch 27:26
while Shaphat s of Adlai was in 1Ch 27:29
Jehiel s of Hachmoni attended 1Ch 27:32
came Jehoiada s of Benaiah, 1Ch 27:34
has chosen my s Solomon to sit 1Ch 28:5
'Your s Solomon is the one who 1Ch 28:6
I have chosen him to be My s, 1Ch 28:6
you, Solomon my s, know the God 1Ch 28:9
David gave his s Solomon the 1Ch 28:11
David said to his s Solomon, 1Ch 28:20
assembly, "My s Solomon—God 1Ch 29:1
Give my s Solomon a whole heart 1Ch 29:19
made David's s Solomon king; 1Ch 29:22
David s of Jesse was king over 1Ch 29:26
and his s Solomon became king in 1Ch 29:28
Solomon s of David strengthened 2Ch 1:1

which Bezalel **s** of Uri, son of	2Ch 1:5
son of Uri, **s** of Hur, had made,	2Ch 1:5
King David a wise **s** with insight	2Ch 2:12
He is the **s** of a woman from the	2Ch 2:14
temple, but your **s**, your own	2Ch 6:9
concerning Jeroboam **s** of Nebat.	2Ch 9:29
s Rehoboam became king in his	2Ch 9:31
When Jeroboam **s** of Nebat heard	2Ch 10:2
to Jeroboam **s** of Nebat.	2Ch 10:15
inheritance in the **s** of Jesse.	2Ch 10:16
Say to Rehoboam **s** of Solomon,	2Ch 11:3
Rehoboam **s** of Solomon for	2Ch 11:17
daughter of David's **s** Jerimoth	2Ch 11:18
daughter of Jesse's **s** Eliab.	2Ch 11:18
appointed Abijah **s** of Maacah as	2Ch 11:22
His **s** Abijah became king in his	2Ch 12:16
But Jeroboam **s** of Nebat, a	2Ch 13:6
a servant of Solomon **s** of David,	2Ch 13:6
resist Rehoboam **s** of Solomon	2Ch 13:7
His **s** Asa became king in his	2Ch 14:1
God came on Azariah **s** of Oded.	2Ch 15:1
of ⌊Azariah **s** of⌋ Oded the	2Ch 15:8
His **s** Jehoshaphat became king in	2Ch 17:1
to him, Amasiah **s** of Zichri,	2Ch 17:16
He is Micaiah **s** of Imlah."	2Ch 18:7
and get⌋ Micaiah **s** of Imlah!"	2Ch 18:8
Zedekiah **s** of Chenaanah made	2Ch 18:10
Zedekiah **s** of Chenaanah came	2Ch 18:23
and to Joash, the king's **s**,	2Ch 18:25
Then Jehu **s** of Hanani the seer	2Ch 19:2
and Zebadiah **s** of Ishmael,	2Ch 19:11
on Jahaziel (**s** of Zechariah, son	2Ch 20:14
of Zechariah, **s** of Benaiah, son	2Ch 20:14
son of Benaiah, **s** of Jeiel, son	2Ch 20:14
son of Jeiel, **s** of Mattaniah, a	2Ch 20:14
the Events of Jehu **s** of Hanani,	2Ch 20:34
Then Eliezer **s** of Dodavahu of	2Ch 20:37
His **s** Jehoram became king in his	2Ch 21:1
not a **s** was left to him except	2Ch 21:17
except Jehoahaz, his youngest **s**.	2Ch 21:17
his youngest **s**, king in his	2Ch 22:1
So Ahaziah **s** of Jehoram became	2Ch 22:1
went with Joram **s** of Israel's	2Ch 22:5
King Ahaziah **s** of Jehoram went	2Ch 22:6
to visit Joram **s** of Ahab since	2Ch 22:6
Joram to meet Jehu **s** of Nimshi,	2Ch 22:7
saw that her **s** was dead, she	2Ch 22:10
rescued Joash **s** of Ahaziah from	2Ch 22:11
Azariah **s** of Jeroham, Ishmael	2Ch 23:1
Jeroham, Ishmael **s** of Jehohanan,	2Ch 23:1
Azariah **s** of Obed, Maaseiah	2Ch 23:1
of Obed, Maaseiah **s** of Adaiah,	2Ch 23:1
and Elishaphat **s** of Zichri.	2Ch 23:1
to them, "Here is the king's **s**!	2Ch 23:3
They brought out the king's **s**,	2Ch 23:11
of Zechariah **s** of Jehoiada	2Ch 24:20
to him, but killed his **s**.	2Ch 24:22
s of the Ammonite woman	2Ch 24:26
s of the Moabite woman Shimrith.	2Ch 24:26
His **s** Amaziah became king in his	2Ch 24:27
word⌋ to Jehoash **s** of Jehoahaz,	2Ch 25:17
son of Jehoahaz, **s** of Jehu, king	2Ch 25:17
daughter to my **s** as a wife.'	2Ch 25:18
Judah's King Amaziah **s** of Joash,	2Ch 25:23
son of Joash, **s** of Jehoahaz, at	2Ch 25:23
King Amaziah **s** of Joash lived 15	2Ch 25:25
King Jehoash **s** of Jehoahaz.	2Ch 25:25
while his **s** Jotham was over the	2Ch 26:21
prophet Isaiah **s** of Amoz wrote	2Ch 26:22
His **s** Jotham became king in his	2Ch 26:23
His **s** Ahaz became king in his	2Ch 27:9
Pekah **s** of Remaliah killed	2Ch 28:6
killed the king's **s** Maaseiah,	2Ch 28:7
Azariah **s** of Johanan, Berechiah	2Ch 28:12
Berechiah **s** of Meshillemoth,	2Ch 28:12
Jehizkiah **s** of Shallum, and	2Ch 28:12
and Amasa **s** of Hadlai—stood	2Ch 28:12
and his **s** Hezekiah became king	2Ch 28:27
Mahath **s** of Amasai and Joel son	2Ch 29:12
of Amasai and Joel **s** of Azariah	2Ch 29:12
Kish **s** of Abdi and Azariah son	2Ch 29:12
Abdi and Azariah **s** of Jehallelel	2Ch 29:12
Joah **s** of Zimmah and Eden son	2Ch 29:12
of Zimmah and Eden **s** of Joah	2Ch 29:12
the days of Solomon **s** of David,	2Ch 30:26
Kore **s** of Imnah the Levite,	2Ch 31:14
prophet Isaiah **s** of Amoz prayed	2Ch 32:20
of the Prophet Isaiah **s** of Amoz,	2Ch 32:32
s Manasseh became king in his	2Ch 32:33
said to David and his **s** Solomon:	2Ch 33:7
His **s** Amon became king in his	2Ch 33:20
Amon and made his **s** Josiah king	2Ch 33:25
sent Shaphan **s** of Azaliah,	2Ch 34:8
the recorder Joah **s** of Joahaz,	2Ch 34:8
Hilkiah, Ahikam **s** of Shaphan,	2Ch 34:20
Shaphan, Abdon **s** of Micah,	2Ch 34:20
wife of Shallum **s** of Tokhath,	2Ch 34:22
son of Tokhath, **s** of Hasrah,	2Ch 34:22
built by Solomon **s** of David king	2Ch 35:3
and that of his **s** Solomon.	2Ch 35:4
took Jehoahaz **s** of Josiah and	2Ch 36:1
Jeshua **s** of Jozadak and his	Ezr 3:2
with Zerubbabel **s** of Shealtiel	Ezr 3:2
Zerubbabel **s** of Shealtiel,	Ezr 3:8
Shealtiel, Jeshua **s** of Jozadak,	Ezr 3:8
and Zechariah **s** of Iddo	Ezr 5:1
Zerubbabel **s** of Shealtiel and	Ezr 5:2
and Jeshua **s** of Jozadak began to	Ezr 5:2
prophet and Zechariah **s** of Iddo.	Ezr 6:14
Seraiah's **s**, Azariah's son,	Ezr 7:1
son, Azariah's **s**, Hilkiah's son,	Ezr 7:1
son, Azariah's son, Hilkiah's **s**,	Ezr 7:1
Shallum's **s**, Zadok's son,	Ezr 7:2
son, Zadok's **s**, Ahitub's son,	Ezr 7:2
son, Zadok's son, Ahitub's **s**,	Ezr 7:2
Amariah's **s**, Azariah's son,	Ezr 7:3
Azariah's **s**, Meraioth's son,	Ezr 7:3
Azariah's son, Meraioth's **s**,	Ezr 7:3
Zerahiah's **s**, Uzzi's son,	Ezr 7:4
son, Uzzi's **s**, Bukki's son,	Ezr 7:4
son, Uzzi's son, Bukki's **s**,	Ezr 7:4
Abishua's **s**, Phinehas's son,	Ezr 7:5
Phinehas's **s**, Eleazar's son,	Ezr 7:5
son, Eleazar's **s**, Aaron the	Ezr 7:5
Aaron the chief priest's **s**	Ezr 7:5
Eliehoenai **s** of Zerahiah from	Ezr 8:4
Shecaniah **s** of Jahaziel from	Ezr 8:5
Ebed **s** of Jonathan from Adin's	Ezr 8:6
Jeshaiah **s** of Athaliah from	Ezr 8:7
Zebadiah **s** of Michael from	Ezr 8:8
Obadiah **s** of Jehiel from Joab's	Ezr 8:9
Shelomith **s** of Josiphiah from	Ezr 8:10
Zechariah **s** of Bebai from	Ezr 8:11
Johanan **s** of Hakkatan from	Ezr 8:12
descendant of Levi **s** of Israel—	Ezr 8:18
Meremoth the priest, **s** of Uriah.	Ezr 8:33
Eleazar **s** of Phinehas was with	Ezr 8:33
The Levites Jozabad **s** of Jeshua	Ezr 8:33
and Noadiah **s** of Binnui were	Ezr 8:33
Then Shecaniah **s** of Jehiel,	Ezr 10:2
of Jehohanan **s** of Eliashib,	Ezr 10:6
Only Jonathan **s** of Asahel and	Ezr 10:15
and Jahzeiah **s** of Tikvah opposed	Ezr 10:15
of Jeshua **s** of Jozadak and his	Ezr 10:18
words of Nehemiah **s** of Hacaliah:	Neh 1:1
to them Zaccur **s** of Imri built.	Neh 3:2
to them Meremoth **s** of Uriah,	Neh 3:4
son of Uriah, **s** of Hakkoz, made	Neh 3:4
them Meshullam **s** of Berechiah,	Neh 3:4
of Berechiah, **s** of Meshezabel,	Neh 3:4
to them Zadok **s** of Baana made	Neh 3:4
Joiada **s** of Paseah and Meshullam	Neh 3:6
and Meshullam **s** of Besodeiah	Neh 3:6
After him Uzziel **s** of Harhaiah,	Neh 3:8
him Hananiah **s** of the perfumer	Neh 3:8
Next to them Rephaiah **s** of Hur,	Neh 3:9
them Jedaiah **s** of Harumaph made	Neh 3:10
him Hattush the **s** of Hashabneiah	Neh 3:10
Malchijah **s** of Harim and Hasshub	Neh 3:11
and Hasshub **s** of Pahath-moab	Neh 3:11
him Shallum **s** of Hallohesh,	Neh 3:12
Malchijah **s** of Rechab, ruler	Neh 3:14
Shallun **s** of Col-hozeh, ruler	Neh 3:15
After him Nehemiah **s** of Azbuk,	Neh 3:16
repairs ⌊under⌋ Rehum **s** of Bani.	Neh 3:17
under⌋ Binnui **s** of Henadad,	Neh 3:18
Next to him Ezer **s** of Jeshua,	Neh 3:19
After him Baruch **s** of Zabbai	Neh 3:20
Beside him Meremoth **s** of Uriah,	Neh 3:21
son of Uriah, **s** of Hakkoz, made	Neh 3:21
them Azariah **s** of Maaseiah,	Neh 3:23
of Maaseiah, **s** of Ananiah, made	Neh 3:23
him Binnui **s** of Henadad made	Neh 3:24
Palal **s** of Uzai ⌊made repairs⌋	Neh 3:25
Beside him Pedaiah **s** of Parosh,	Neh 3:25
After them Zadok **s** of Immer made	Neh 3:29
him Shemaiah **s** of Shecaniah,	Neh 3:29
to him Hananiah **s** of Shelemiah	Neh 3:30
Hanun the sixth **s** of Zalaph made	Neh 3:30
them Meshullam **s** of Berechiah	Neh 3:30
house of Shemaiah **s** of Delaiah,	Neh 6:10
son of Delaiah, **s** of Mehetabel,	Neh 6:10
of Shecaniah **s** of Arah,	Neh 6:18
and his **s** Jehohanan had married	Neh 6:18
of Meshullam **s** of Berechiah.	Neh 6:18
days of Joshua **s** of Nun until	Neh 8:17
the governor, **s** of Hacaliah,	Neh 10:1
Jeshua **s** of Azaniah, Binnui of	Neh 10:9
Athaiah **s** of Uzziah, son of	Neh 11:4
son of Uzziah, **s** of Zechariah,	Neh 11:4
of Zechariah, **s** of Amariah, son	Neh 11:4
son of Amariah, **s** of Shephatiah,	Neh 11:4
of Shephatiah, **s** of Mahalalel,	Neh 11:4
and Maaseiah **s** of Baruch, son of	Neh 11:5
son of Baruch, **s** of Col-hozeh,	Neh 11:5
of Col-hozeh, **s** of Hazaiah, son	Neh 11:5
son of Hazaiah, **s** of Adaiah, son	Neh 11:5
son of Adaiah, **s** of Joiarib, son	Neh 11:5
son of Joiarib, **s** of Zechariah,	Neh 11:5
Sallu **s** of Meshullam, son of	Neh 11:7
son of Meshullam, **s** of Joed, son	Neh 11:7
son of Joed, **s** of Pedaiah, son	Neh 11:7
of Pedaiah, **s** of Kolaiah, son	Neh 11:7
son of Kolaiah, **s** of Maaseiah,	Neh 11:7
of Maaseiah, **s** of Ithiel, son	Neh 11:7
son of Ithiel, **s** of Jeshaiah,	Neh 11:7
Joel **s** of Zichri was the officer	Neh 11:9
and Judah **s** of Hassenuah was	Neh 11:9
Jedaiah **s** of Joiarib, Jachin,	Neh 11:10
Seraiah **s** of Hilkiah, son of	Neh 11:11
son of Hilkiah, **s** of Meshullam,	Neh 11:11
of Meshullam, **s** of Zadok, son	Neh 11:11
son of Zadok, **s** of Meraioth, son	Neh 11:11
of Meraioth, **s** of Ahitub, the	Neh 11:11
Adaiah **s** of Jeroham, son of	Neh 11:12
son of Jeroham, **s** of Pelaliah,	Neh 11:12
son of Pelaliah, **s** of Amzi, son	Neh 11:12
son of Amzi, **s** of Zechariah, son	Neh 11:12
of Zechariah, **s** of Pashhur, son	Neh 11:12
son of Pashhur, **s** of Malchijah	Neh 11:12
Amashsai **s** of Azarel, son of	Neh 11:13
son of Azarel, **s** of Ahzai, son	Neh 11:13
son of Ahzai, **s** of Meshillemoth,	Neh 11:13
son of Meshillemoth, **s** of Immer,	Neh 11:13
Zabdiel **s** of Haggedolim, was	Neh 11:14
Shemaiah **s** of Hasshub, son of	Neh 11:15
of Hasshub, **s** of Azrikam, son	Neh 11:15
son of Azrikam, **s** of Hashabiah,	Neh 11:15
son of Hashabiah, **s** of Bunni;	Neh 11:15
Mattaniah **s** of Mica, son of	Neh 11:17
son of Mica, **s** of Zabdi, son of	Neh 11:17
Mica, son of Zabdi, **s** of Asaph,	Neh 11:17
and Abda **s** of Shammua, son of	Neh 11:17
son of Shammua, **s** of Galal, son	Neh 11:17
son of Galal, **s** of Jeduthun.	Neh 11:17
in Jerusalem was Uzzi **s** of Bani,	Neh 11:22
son of Bani, **s** of Hashabiah, son	Neh 11:22
of Hashabiah, **s** of Mattaniah,	Neh 11:22
son of Mattaniah, **s** of Mica, of	Neh 11:22
Pethahiah **s** of Meshezabel,	Neh 11:24
descendants of Zerah **s** of Judah,	Neh 11:24
with Zerubbabel **s** of Shealtiel	Neh 12:1
days of Johanan **s** of Eliashib.	Neh 12:23
and Jeshua **s** of Kadmiel, along	Neh 12:24
the days of Joiakim **s** of Jeshua,	Neh 12:26
son of Jeshua, **s** of Jozadak,	Neh 12:26
Zechariah **s** of Jonathan, son of	Neh 12:35
of Jonathan, **s** of Shemaiah, son	Neh 12:35
son of Shemaiah, **s** of Mattaniah,	Neh 12:35
of Mattaniah, **s** of Micaiah, son	Neh 12:35
son of Micaiah, **s** of Zaccur, son	Neh 12:35
son of Zaccur, **s** of Asaph,	Neh 12:35
as David and his **s** Solomon had	Neh 12:45
with Hanan **s** of Zaccur, son	Neh 13:13
s of Mattaniah to assist them,	Neh 13:13
s of Eliashib the high priest,	Neh 13:28
Susa named Mordecai **s** of Jair,	Est 2:5
son of Jair, **s** of Shimei, son	Est 2:5
Jair, son of Shimei, **s** of Kish,	Est 2:5
s of Hammedatha the Agagite.	Est 3:1
gave it to Haman **s** of Hammedatha	Est 3:10
scheming Haman **s** of Hammedatha	Est 8:5
sons of Haman **s** of Hammedatha,	Est 9:10
For Haman **s** of Hammedatha the	Est 9:24

S of man, these men have set up	Ezk 14:3
S of man, if a land sins against	Ezk 14:13
deliver ⌊their⌋ **s** or daughter.	Ezk 14:20
S of man, how does the wood of	Ezk 15:2
S of man, explain Jerusalem's	Ezk 16:2
S of man, pose a riddle and	Ezk 17:2
is like the life of the **s**—	Ezk 18:4
suppose the man has a violent **s**,	Ezk 18:10
when the **s** eats at the mountain	Ezk 18:11
suppose he has a **s** who sees all	Ezk 18:14
Why doesn't the **s** suffer	Ezk 18:19
Since the **s** has done what is	Ezk 18:19
A **s** won't suffer punishment for	Ezk 18:20
S of man, speak with the elders	Ezk 20:3
you pass judgment, **s** of man?	Ezk 20:4
Therefore, **s** of man, speak to	Ezk 20:27
S of man, face the south and	Ezk 20:46
S of man, turn your face toward	Ezk 21:2
But you, **s** of man, groan!	Ezk 21:6
S of man, prophesy: This is what	Ezk 21:9
The scepter of My **s**, the sword	Ezk 21:10
out and wail, **s** of man, for it	Ezk 21:12
Therefore, **s** of man, prophesy	Ezk 21:14
Now you, **s** of man, mark out two	Ezk 21:19
Now prophesy, **s** of man, and say:	Ezk 21:28
Now, **s** of man, will you pass	Ezk 22:2
S of man, the house of Israel	Ezk 22:18
S of man, say to her: You are a	Ezk 22:24
S of man, there were two women,	Ezk 23:2
S of man, will you pass judgment	Ezk 23:36
S of man, write down today's	Ezk 24:2
S of man, I am about to take the	Ezk 24:16
S of man, know that on the day	Ezk 24:25
S of man, turn your face toward	Ezk 25:2
S of man, because Tyre said	Ezk 26:2
Now, **s** of man, lament for Tyre.	Ezk 27:2
S of man, say to the ruler of	Ezk 28:2
S of man, lament for the king of	Ezk 28:12
S of man, turn your face toward	Ezk 28:21
S of man, turn your face toward	Ezk 29:2
S of man, Nebuchadnezzar king of	Ezk 29:18
S of man, prophesy and say:	Ezk 30:2
S of man, I have broken the arm	Ezk 30:21
S of man, say to Pharaoh king of	Ezk 31:2
S of man, lament for Pharaoh	Ezk 32:2
S of man, wail over the hordes	Ezk 32:18
S of man, speak to your people	Ezk 33:2
As for you, **s** of man, I have	Ezk 33:7
Now as for you, **s** of man, say to	Ezk 33:10
Now, **s** of man, say to your	Ezk 33:12
S of man, those who live in the	Ezk 33:24
Now, **s** of man, your people are	Ezk 33:30
S of man, prophesy against the	Ezk 34:2
S of man, turn your face toward	Ezk 35:2
S of man, prophesy to the	Ezk 36:1
S of man, while the house of	Ezk 36:17
He said to me, "**S** of man, can	Ezk 37:3
the breath, prophesy, **s** of man.	Ezk 37:9
He said to me, "**S** of man, these	Ezk 37:11
S of man, take a single stick	Ezk 37:16
S of man, turn your face toward	Ezk 38:2
prophesy, **s** of man, and say to	Ezk 38:14
As for you, **s** of man, prophesy	Ezk 39:1
S of man, this is what the Lord	Ezk 39:17
S of man, look with your eyes,	Ezk 40:4
S of man, this is the place of	Ezk 43:7
As for you, **s** of man, describe	Ezk 43:10
S of man, this is what the Lord	Ezk 43:18
S of man, pay attention;	Ezk 44:5
a mother, a **s**, a daughter,	Ezk 44:25
Do you see ⌊this⌋, **s** of man?"	Ezk 47:6
looks like a **s** of the gods."	Dn 3:25
I saw One like a **s** of man coming	Dn 7:13
"**S** of man," he said to me,	Dn 8:17
who was the **s** of Ahasuerus,	Dn 9:1
came to Hosea **s** of Beeri during	Hs 1:1
and of Jeroboam **s** of Joash,	Hs 1:1
she conceived and bore him a **s**.	Hs 1:3
conceived and gave birth to a **s**.	Hs 1:8
and out of Egypt I called My **s**.	Hs 11:1
is not a wise **s**; when the time	Hs 13:13
that came to Joel **s** of Pethuel:	Jl 1:1
and Jeroboam **s** of Joash, king	Am 1:1
a prophet or the **s** of a prophet;	Am 7:14
for an only **s** and its outcome	Am 8:10
LORD came to Jonah **s** of Amittai:	Jnh 1:1
what Balaam **s** of Beor answered	Mc 6:5
For a **s** considers his father a	Mc 7:6
came to Zephaniah **s** of Cushi,	Zph 1:1
son of Cushi, **s** of Gedaliah, son	Zph 1:1
of Gedaliah, **s** of Amariah, son	Zph 1:1
son of Amariah, **s** of Hezekiah,	Zph 1:1
in the days of Josiah **s** of Amon,	Zph 1:1
to Zerubbabel **s** of Shealtiel,	Hg 1:1
and to Joshua **s** of Jehozadak,	Hg 1:1
Then Zerubbabel **s** of Shealtiel,	Hg 1:12
priest Joshua **s** of Jehozadak,	Hg 1:12
of Zerubbabel **s** of Shealtiel,	Hg 1:14
priest Joshua **s** of Jehozadak,	Hg 1:14
to Zerubbabel **s** of Shealtiel,	Hg 2:2
priest Joshua **s** of Jehozadak,	Hg 2:2
strong, Joshua **s** of Jehozadak,	Hg 2:4
Zerubbabel **s** of Shealtiel,	Hg 2:23
Zechariah **s** of Berechiah,	Zch 1:1
son of Berechiah, **s** of Iddo:	Zch 1:1
Zechariah **s** of Berechiah,	Zch 1:7
son of Berechiah, **s** of Iddo:	Zch 1:7
house of Josiah **s** of Zephaniah.	Zch 6:10
head of Joshua **s** of Jehozadak,	Zch 6:11
Jedaiah, and Hen **s** of Zephaniah.	Zch 6:14
A **s** honors ⌊his⌋ father, and a	Mal 1:6
on his **s** who serves him.	Mal 3:17
Christ, the **S** of David, the Son	Mt 1:1
Son of David, the **S** of Abraham:	Mt 1:1
Joseph, **s** of David, don't	Mt 1:20
She will give birth to a **s**,	Mt 1:21
pregnant and give birth to a **s**,	Mt 1:23
until she gave birth to a **s**.	Mt 1:25
Out of Egypt I called My **S**.	Mt 2:15
is My beloved **S**. I take delight	Mt 3:17
If You are the **S** of God, tell	Mt 4:3
If You are the **S** of God, throw	Mt 4:6
James the **s** of Zebedee, and his	Mt 4:21
if his **s** asks him for bread,	Mt 7:9
but the **S** of Man has no place to	Mt 8:20
have to do with us, **S** of God?	Mt 8:29
Have courage, **s**, your sins are	Mt 9:2
may know that the **S** of Man has	Mt 9:6
Have mercy on us, **S** of David!"	Mt 9:27
James the **s** of Zebedee, and John	Mt 10:2
James the **s** of Alphaeus, and	Mt 10:3
before the **S** of Man comes.	Mt 10:23
who loves **s** or daughter more	Mt 10:37
The **S** of Man came eating and	Mt 11:19
No one knows the **S** except the	Mt 11:27
Father except the **S** and anyone	Mt 11:27
to whom the **S** desires to reveal	Mt 11:27
For the **S** of Man is Lord of the	Mt 12:8
"Perhaps this is the **S** of David!"	Mt 12:23
a word against the **S** of Man,	Mt 12:32
so the **S** of Man will be in the	Mt 12:40
the good seed is the **S** of Man;	Mt 13:37
The **S** of Man will send out His	Mt 13:41
Isn't this the carpenter's **s**?	Mt 13:55
"Truly You are the **S** of God!"	Mt 14:33
mercy on me, Lord, **S** of David!	Mt 15:22
say that the **S** of Man is?"	Mt 16:13
the **S** of the living God!	Mt 16:16
Simon **s** of Jonah, you are	Mt 16:17
the **S** of Man is going to come	Mt 16:27
they see the **S** of Man coming	Mt 16:28
is My beloved **S**. I take delight	Mt 17:5
until the **S** of Man is raised	Mt 17:9
same way the **S** of Man is going	Mt 17:12
mercy on my **s**, because he has	Mt 17:15
The **S** of Man is about to be	Mt 17:22
the **S** of Man has come to save	Mt 18:11
when the **S** of Man sits on His	Mt 19:28
The **S** of Man will be handed over	Mt 20:18
as the **S** of Man did not come	Mt 20:28
have mercy on us, **S** of David!"	Mt 20:30
have mercy on us, **S** of David!"	Mt 20:31
Hosanna to the **S** of David!	Mt 21:9
"Hosanna to the **S** of David!"	Mt 21:15
first and said, 'My **s**, go, work	Mt 21:28
he sent his **s** to them.	Mt 21:37
will respect my **s**,' he said.	Mt 21:37
the tenant farmers saw the **s**,	Mt 21:38
a wedding banquet for his **s**.	Mt 22:2
Whose **S** is He?" "David's,	Mt 22:42
then can the Messiah be his **S**"	Mt 22:45
of Zechariah, **s** of Berechiah,	Mt 23:35
be the coming of the **S** of Man.	Mt 24:27
the sign of the **S** of Man will	Mt 24:30
will see the **S** of Man coming	Mt 24:30
heaven, nor the **S**—except the	Mt 24:36
coming of the **S** of Man will be.	Mt 24:37
coming of the **S** of Man will be:	Mt 24:39
because the **S** of Man is coming	Mt 24:44
When the **S** of Man comes in His	Mt 25:31
and the **S** of Man will be handed	Mt 26:2
The **S** of Man will go just as it	Mt 26:24
man by whom the **S** of Man is	Mt 26:24
The **S** of Man is being betrayed	Mt 26:45
are the Messiah, the **S** of God!"	Mt 26:63
will see the **S** of Man seated at	Mt 26:64
If You are the **S** of God, come	Mt 27:40
For He said, 'I am God's **S**.' "	Mt 27:43
"This man really was God's **S**!"	Mt 27:54
and of the **S** and of the Holy	Mt 28:19
of Jesus Christ, the **S** of God.	Mk 1:1
are My beloved **S**; I take delight	Mk 1:11
saw James the **s** of Zebedee and	Mk 1:19
the paralytic, "**S**, your sins are	Mk 2:5
may know that the **S** of Man has	Mk 2:10
He saw Levi the **s** of Alphaeus	Mk 2:14
Therefore the **S** of Man is Lord	Mk 2:28
out, "You are the **S** of God!"	Mk 3:11
and to James the **s** of Zebedee,	Mk 3:17
James the **s** of Alphaeus, and	Mk 3:18
with me, Jesus, **S** of the Most	Mk 5:7
the carpenter, the **s** of Mary,	Mk 6:3
them that the **S** of Man must	Mk 8:31
S of Man will also be ashamed	Mk 8:38
is My beloved **S**; listen to Him!	Mk 9:7
until the **S** of Man had risen	Mk 9:9
about the **S** of Man that He	Mk 9:12
Teacher, I brought my **s** to You.	Mk 9:17
The **S** of Man is being betrayed	Mk 9:31
The **S** of Man will be handed over	Mk 10:33
For even the **S** of Man did not	Mk 10:45
Bartimaeus (the **s** of Timaeus), a	Mk 10:46
to cry out, "**S** of David, Jesus,	Mk 10:47
Have mercy on me, **S** of David!"	Mk 10:48
had one to send, a beloved **s**.	Mk 12:6
'They will respect my **s**.'	Mk 12:6
the Messiah is the **S** of David?	Mk 12:35
then can the Messiah be his **S**?"	Mk 12:37
will see the **S** of Man coming	Mk 13:26
the angels in heaven nor the **S**—	Mk 13:32
For the **S** of Man will go just as	Mk 14:21
man by whom the **S** of Man is	Mk 14:21
the **S** of Man is being betrayed	Mk 14:41
the **S** of the Blessed One?"	Mk 14:61
will see the **S** of Man seated at	Mk 14:62
"This man really was God's **S**!"	Mk 15:39
Elizabeth will bear you a **s**,	Lk 1:13
conceive and give birth to a **s**,	Lk 1:31
be called the **S** of the Most High	Lk 1:32
will be called the **S** of God.	Lk 1:35
conceived a **s** in her old age,	Lk 1:36
to give birth, and she had a **s**.	Lk 1:57
gave birth to her firstborn **S**,	Lk 2:7
said to Him, "**S**, why have You	Lk 2:48
came to John the **s** of Zechariah	Lk 3:2
are My beloved **S**. I take delight	Lk 3:22
thought to be the **s** of Joseph,	Lk 3:23
the son of Joseph, ⌊**s**⌋ of Heli,	Lk 3:23
⌊**s**⌋ of Matthat, ⌊son⌋ of Levi,	Lk 3:24
of Matthat, ⌊**s**⌋ of Levi, ⌊son⌋	Lk 3:24
son⌋ of Levi, ⌊**s**⌋ of Melchi,	Lk 3:24
of Melchi, ⌊**s**⌋ of Jannai, ⌊son	Lk 3:24
son⌋ of Jannai, ⌊**s**⌋ of Joseph,	Lk 3:24
⌊**s**⌋ of Mattathias, ⌊son⌋ of Amos,	Lk 3:25
Mattathias, ⌊**s**⌋ of Amos, ⌊son⌋	Lk 3:25
of Amos, ⌊**s**⌋ of Nahum, ⌊son⌋	Lk 3:25
of Nahum, ⌊**s**⌋ of Esli, ⌊son⌋	Lk 3:25
son⌋ of Esli, ⌊**s**⌋ of Naggai,	Lk 3:25
⌊**s**⌋ of Maath, ⌊son⌋ of	Lk 3:26
son⌋ of Maath, ⌊**s**⌋ of Mattathias	Lk 3:26
of Mattathias, ⌊**s**⌋ of Semein,	Lk 3:26
of Semein, ⌊**s**⌋ of Josech, ⌊son	Lk 3:26
son⌋ of Josech, ⌊**s**⌋ of Joda,	Lk 3:26
⌊**s**⌋ of Joanan, ⌊son⌋ of Rhesa,	Lk 3:27
of Joanan, ⌊**s**⌋ of Rhesa, ⌊son	Lk 3:27
of Rhesa, ⌊**s**⌋ of Zerubbabel,	Lk 3:27
of Zerubbabel, ⌊**s**⌋ of Shealtiel,	Lk 3:27
son⌋ of Shealtiel, ⌊**s**⌋ of Neri,	Lk 3:27
⌊**s**⌋ of Melchi, ⌊son⌋ of Addi,	Lk 3:28
of Melchi, ⌊**s**⌋ of Addi, ⌊son⌋	Lk 3:28
of Addi, ⌊**s**⌋ of Cosam, ⌊son⌋	Lk 3:28
son⌋ of Cosam, ⌊**s**⌋ of Elmadam,	Lk 3:28
son⌋ of Elmadam, ⌊**s**⌋ of Er,	Lk 3:28
⌊**s**⌋ of Joshua, ⌊son⌋ of Eliezer,	Lk 3:29

son⌋ of Joshua, ⌊s⌋ of Eliezer, Lk 3:29
of Eliezer, ⌊s⌋ of Jorim, ⌊son⌋ Lk 3:29
son⌋ of Jorim, ⌊s⌋ of Matthat, Lk 3:29
son⌋ of Matthat, ⌊s⌋ of Levi, Lk 3:29
⌊s⌋ of Simeon, ⌊son⌋ of Judah, Lk 3:30
of Simeon, ⌊s⌋ of Judah, ⌊son Lk 3:30
son⌋ of Judah, ⌊s⌋ of Joseph, Lk 3:30
of Joseph, ⌊s⌋ of Jonam, ⌊son Lk 3:30
son⌋ of Jonam, ⌊s⌋ of Eliakim, Lk 3:30
⌊s⌋ of Melea, ⌊son⌋ of Menna, Lk 3:31
of Melea, ⌊s⌋ of Menna, ⌊son Lk 3:31
son⌋ of Menna, ⌊s⌋ of Mattatha, Lk 3:31
of Mattatha, ⌊s⌋ of Nathan, ⌊son Lk 3:31
son⌋ of Nathan, ⌊s⌋ of David, Lk 3:31
⌊s⌋ of Jesse, ⌊son⌋ of Obed, Lk 3:32
son⌋ of Jesse, ⌊s⌋ of Obed, ⌊son Lk 3:32
son⌋ of Obed, ⌊s⌋ of Boaz, ⌊son⌋ Lk 3:32
son⌋ of Boaz, ⌊s⌋ of Salmon, Lk 3:32
son⌋ of Salmon, ⌊s⌋ of Nahshon, Lk 3:32
⌊s⌋ of Amminadab, ⌊son⌋ of Ram, Lk 3:33
of Amminadab, ⌊s⌋ of Ram, ⌊son⌋ Lk 3:33
of Ram, ⌊s⌋ of Hezron, ⌊son⌋ Lk 3:33
of Hezron, ⌊s⌋ of Perez, ⌊son Lk 3:33
son⌋ of Perez, ⌊s⌋ of Judah, Lk 3:33
⌊s⌋ of Jacob, ⌊son⌋ of Isaac, Lk 3:34
of Jacob, ⌊s⌋ of Isaac, ⌊son Lk 3:34
son⌋ of Isaac, ⌊s⌋ of Abraham, Lk 3:34
of Abraham, ⌊s⌋ of Terah, ⌊son⌋ Lk 3:34
son⌋ of Terah, ⌊s⌋ of Nahor, Lk 3:34
⌊s⌋ of Serug, ⌊son⌋ of Reu, Lk 3:35
of Serug, ⌊s⌋ of Reu, ⌊son⌋ Lk 3:35
son⌋ of Reu, ⌊s⌋ of Peleg, ⌊son⌋ Lk 3:35
of Peleg, ⌊s⌋ of Eber, ⌊son⌋ Lk 3:35
son⌋ of Eber, ⌊s⌋ of Shelah, Lk 3:35
⌊s⌋ of Cainan, ⌊son⌋ of Arphaxad, Lk 3:36
son⌋ of Cainan, ⌊s⌋ of Arphaxad, Lk 3:36
of Arphaxad, ⌊s⌋ of Shem, ⌊son⌋ Lk 3:36
son⌋ of Shem, ⌊s⌋ of Noah, ⌊son⌋ Lk 3:36
son⌋ of Noah, ⌊s⌋ of Lamech, Lk 3:36
⌊s⌋ of Methuselah, ⌊son⌋ of Lk 3:37
Methuselah, ⌊s⌋ of Enoch, ⌊son Lk 3:37
of Enoch, ⌊s⌋ of Jared, ⌊son Lk 3:37
of Jared, ⌊s⌋ of Mahalaleel, Lk 3:37
of Mahalaleel, ⌊s⌋ of Cainan, Lk 3:37
⌊s⌋ of Enos, ⌊son⌋ of Seth, Lk 3:38
of Enos, ⌊s⌋ of Seth, ⌊son⌋ Lk 3:38
son⌋ of Seth, ⌊s⌋ of Adam, ⌊son⌋ Lk 3:38
Seth, ⌊son⌋ of Adam, ⌊s⌋ of God. Lk 3:38
If You are the S of God, tell Lk 4:3
If You are the S of God, throw Lk 4:9
said, "Isn't this Joseph's s?" Lk 4:22
saying, "You are the S of God!" Lk 4:41
may know that the S of Man has Lk 5:24
S of Man is Lord of the Sabbath. Lk 6:5
James the s of Alphaeus, and Lk 6:15
Judas the s of James, and Judas Lk 6:16
evil, because of the S of Man. Lk 6:22
He was his mother's only s, Lk 7:12
The S of Man has come eating and Lk 7:34
You S of the Most High God? Lk 8:28
The S of Man must suffer many Lk 9:22
the S of Man will be ashamed of Lk 9:26
This is My S, the Chosen One; Lk 9:35
I beg You to look at my s, Lk 9:38
up with you? Bring your s here." Lk 9:41
the S of Man is about to be Lk 9:44
but the S of Man has no place to Lk 9:58
If a s of peace is there, your Lk 10:6
knows who the S is except the Lk 10:22
who the Father is except the S, Lk 10:22
to whom the S desires to reveal Lk 10:22
you, if his s asks for a fish, Lk 11:11
so also the S of Man will be to Lk 11:30
the S of Man will also Lk 12:8
word against the S of Man will Lk 12:10
because the S of Man is coming Lk 12:40
father against s, son against Lk 12:53
against son, s against father, Lk 12:53
Which of you whose s or ox falls Lk 14:5
the younger s gathered together Lk 15:13
worthy to be called your s. Lk 15:19
But while the s was still a long Lk 15:20
The s said to him, 'Father, I Lk 15:21
worthy to be called your s.' Lk 15:21
because this s of mine was dead Lk 15:24
Now his older s was in the Lk 15:25
But when this s of yours came, Lk 15:30
'S,' he said to him, 'you are Lk 15:31
'S,' Abraham said, 'remember Lk 16:25
one of the days of the S of Man, Lk 17:22
so the S of Man will be in His Lk 17:24
be in the days of the S of Man: Lk 17:26
on the day the S of Man is Lk 17:30
when the S of Man comes, will He Lk 18:8
about the S of Man will be Lk 18:31
out, "Jesus, S of David, have Lk 18:38
all the more, "S of David, have Lk 18:39
he too is a s of Abraham. Lk 19:9
the S of Man has come to seek Lk 19:10
I will send my beloved s. Lk 20:13
the Messiah is the S of David? Lk 20:41
then can the Messiah be his S?" Lk 20:44
will see the S of Man coming Lk 21:27
to stand before the S of Man." Lk 21:36
For the S of Man will go away as Lk 22:22
you betraying the S of Man with Lk 22:48
the S of Man will be seated at Lk 22:69
Are You, then, the S of God?" Lk 22:70
'The S of Man must be betrayed Lk 24:7
One and Only S from the Father Jn 1:14
One and Only S—the One who is Jn 1:18
that He is the S of God!" Jn 1:34
said, "You are Simon, s of John. Jn 1:42
Jesus the s of Joseph, from Jn 1:45
replied, "You are the S of God! Jn 1:49
and descending on the S of Man." Jn 1:51
from heaven—the S of Man. Jn 3:13
so the S of Man must be lifted Jn 3:14
He gave His One and Only S, Jn 3:16
not send His S into the world Jn 3:17
of the One and Only S of God. Jn 3:18
Father loves the S and has given Jn 3:35
believes in the S has eternal Jn 3:36
believe in the S will not see Jn 3:36
Jacob had given his s Joseph. Jn 4:5
official whose s was ill at Jn 4:46
Him to come down and heal his s, Jn 4:47
told him, "your s will live." Jn 4:50
told him, "Your s will live." Jn 4:53
The S is not able to do anything Jn 5:19
the S also does these things in Jn 5:19
Father loves the S and shows Him Jn 5:20
so the S also gives life to Jn 5:21
has given all judgment to the S, Jn 5:22
will honor the S just as they Jn 5:23
not honor the S does not honor Jn 5:23
hear the voice of the S of God, Jn 5:25
granted to the S to have life Jn 5:26
because He is the S of Man. Jn 5:27
the S of Man will give you, Jn 6:27
who sees the S and believes in Jn 6:40
this Jesus the s of Joseph, Jn 6:42
flesh of the S of Man and drink Jn 6:53
observe the S of Man ascending Jn 6:62
Simon Iscariot's s, one of the Jn 6:71
When you lift up the S of Man, Jn 8:28
but a s does remain forever. Jn 8:35
if the S sets you free, Jn 8:36
Is this your s, ⌊the one⌋ you Jn 9:19
this is our s and that he was Jn 9:20
"Do you believe in the S of Man?" Jn 9:35
I said: I am the S of God? Jn 10:36
so that the S of God may be Jn 11:4
Messiah, the S of God, who was Jn 11:27
has come for the S of Man to be Jn 12:23
'The S of Man must be lifted up'? Jn 12:34
up'? Who is this S of Man?" Jn 12:34
Iscariot's s, to betray Him. Jn 13:2
it to Judas, Simon Iscariot's s. Jn 13:26
Now the S of Man is glorified, Jn 13:31
may be glorified in the S. Jn 14:13
Glorify Your S so that the Son Jn 17:1
so that the S may glorify You Jn 17:1
except the s of destruction, Jn 17:12
He made Himself the S of God." Jn 19:7
mother, "Woman, here is your s." Jn 19:26
the Messiah, the S of God, and Jn 20:31
Peter, "Simon, s of John, do you Jn 21:15
him, "Simon, s of John, do you Jn 21:16
time, "Simon, s of John, do you Jn 21:17
James the s of Alphaeus, Simon Ac 1:13
and Judas the s of James. Ac 1:13
translated S of Encouragement, Ac 4:36
and raised him as her own s. Ac 7:21
opened and the S of Man standing Ac 7:56
Jesus Christ is the S of God." Ac 8:37
"He is the S of God." Ac 9:20
and said, "You s of the Devil, Ac 13:10
gave them Saul the s of Kish, Ac 13:21
have found David the s of Jesse, Ac 13:22
Psalm: You are My S; today I Ac 13:33
the s of a believing Jewish Ac 16:1
by Sopater, s of Pyrrhus, from Ac 20:4
am a Pharisee, a s of Pharisees! Ac 23:6
But the s of Paul's sister, Ac 23:16
concerning His S, Jesus Christ Rm 1:3
as the powerful S of God by the Rm 1:4
the good news about His S, Rm 1:9
God through the death of His S, Rm 5:10
sending His own S in flesh like Rm 8:3
conformed to the image of His S, Rm 8:29
He did not even spare His own S, Rm 8:32
come, and Sarah will have a s. Rm 9:9
into fellowship with His S, 1Co 1:9
then the S Himself will also be 1Co 15:28
For the S of God, Jesus Christ, 2Co 1:19
to reveal His S in me, so that I Gl 1:16
I live by faith in the S of God, Gl 2:20
God sent His S, born of a woman Gl 4:4
Spirit of His S into our hearts Gl 4:6
are no longer a slave, but a s; Gl 4:7
and if a s, then an heir through Gl 4:7
Throw out the slave and her s, Gl 4:30
the s of the slave will never Gl 4:30
inherit with the s of the free Gl 4:30
and in the knowledge of God's S, Eph 4:13
ministry like a s with a father. Php 2:22
the kingdom of the S He loves, Col 1:13
to wait for His S from heaven, 1Th 1:10
revealed, the s of destruction. 2Th 2:3
He has spoken to us by ⌊His⌋ S, Heb 1:2
did He ever say, You are My S; Heb 1:5
His Father, and He will be My S? Heb 1:5
but about the S: Your throne, O Heb 1:8
him, or the s of man, that You Heb 2:6
was faithful as a S over His Heb 3:6
Jesus the S of God—let us Heb 4:14
who said to Him, You are My S; Heb 5:5
Though a S, He learned obedience Heb 5:8
recrucifying the S of God and Heb 6:6
but resembling the S of God— Heb 7:3
law, ⌊appoints⌋ a S, who has Heb 7:28
has trampled on the S of God, Heb 10:29
was offering up his unique s, Heb 11:17
to be called the s of Pharaoh's Heb 11:24
My s, do not take the Lord's Heb 12:5
punishes every s whom He Heb 12:6
what s is there whom a father Heb 12:7
Isaac his s on the altar? Jms 2:21
greetings, as does Mark, my s. 1Pt 5:13
is My beloved S. I take delight 2Pt 1:17
of Balaam, the s of Bosor, who 2Pt 2:15
and with His S Jesus Christ. 1Jn 1:3
blood of Jesus His S cleanses us 1Jn 1:7
who denies the Father and the S. 1Jn 2:22
who denies the S can have the 1Jn 2:23
confesses the S has the Father 1Jn 2:23
remain in the S and in the 1Jn 2:24
The S of God was revealed for 1Jn 3:8
the name of His S Jesus Christ, 1Jn 3:23
One and Only S into the world 1Jn 4:9
loved us and sent His S to be 1Jn 4:10
Father has sent the S as Savior 1Jn 4:14
that Jesus is the S of God— 1Jn 4:15
that Jesus is the S of God? 1Jn 5:5
that He has given about His S. 1Jn 5:9
who believes in the S of God has 1Jn 5:10
that God has given about His S. 1Jn 5:10
and this life is in His S. 1Jn 5:11
The one who has the S has life. 1Jn 5:12
have the S of God does not 1Jn 5:12
in the name of the S of God, 1Jn 5:13
know that the S of God has come 1Jn 5:20
that is, in His S Jesus Christ. 1Jn 5:20
Christ, the S of the Father, 2Jn 3
has both the Father and the S. 2Jn 9
was One like the S of Man, Rv 1:13
The S of God, the One whose eyes Rv 2:18
But she gave birth to a S— Rv 12:5
and One like the S of Man was Rv 14:14
be his God, and he will be My s. Rv 21:7

SON'S *(18)*

eat some of my s game so that I Gn 27:25
up and eat some of his s game, Gn 27:31

me some of your **s** mandrakes." Gn 30:14
want to take my **s** mandrakes?" Gn 30:15
exchange for your **s** mandrakes." Gn 30:15
hired you with my **s** mandrakes." Gn 30:16
Is it your **s** robe or not?" Gn 37:32
"It is my **s** robe," he said. Gn 37:33
flint, cut off her **s** foreskin, Ex 4:25
with your **s** daughter or your Lv 18:10
She is your **s** wife; you are not Lv 18:15
to marry her **s** daughter or her Lv 18:17
LORD for my **s** benefit to make Jdg 17:3
firstborn **s** name was Joel and 1Sm 8:2
will tear it out of your **s** hand. 1Kg 11:12
kingdom from his **s** hand and give 1Kg 11:35
house during his **s** lifetime." 1Kg 21:29
punishment for the **s** iniquity. Ezk 18:20

SON-IN-LAW *(13)*

a **s**, your sons and daughters, or Gn 19:12
the Timnite's **s**, because he has Jdg 15:6
the girl's father said to his **s**, Jdg 19:5
I should become the king's **s**?" 1Sm 18:18
time, "You can now be my **s**." 1Sm 18:21
should become the king's **s**.' " 1Sm 18:22
sight to become the king's **s**? 1Sm 18:23
pleased to become the king's **s**. 1Sm 18:26
to the king to become his **s**. 1Sm 18:27
is the king's **s**, captain of your 1Sm 22:14
for he was a **s** to Ahab's family. 2Kg 8:27
since he was a **s** of Shecaniah Neh 6:18
had become a **s** to Sanballat the Neh 13:28

SONG *(52)*

sang this **s** to the LORD. Ex 15:1
LORD is my strength and my **s**; Ex 15:2
Then Israel sang this **s**: Nm 21:17
write down this **s** for yourselves Dt 31:19
so that this **s** may be a witness Dt 31:19
s will testify against them, Dt 31:21
wrote down this **s** on that day Dt 31:22
word of this **s** to the entire Dt 31:30
words of this **s** in the presence Dt 32:44
Awake, sing a **s**! Arise Barak, Jdg 5:12
was furious and resented this **s**. 1Sm 18:8
be taught ⌊The S of⌋ the Bow. 2Sm 1:18
the words of this **s** to the LORD 2Sm 22:1
They ministered with **s** in front 1Ch 6:32
rejoicing and **s** ordained by 2Ch 23:18
the **s** of the LORD and the 2Ch 29:27
singing the **s**, and blowing 2Ch 29:28
and I praise Him with my **s**. Ps 28:7
Sing a new **s** to Him; play Ps 33:3
He put a new **s** in my mouth, Ps 40:3
His **s** will be with me in the Ps 42:8
Sing a **s** of instruction, for God Ps 47:7
God's name with **s** and exalt Him Ps 69:30
Lift up a **s**—play the Ps 81:2
shout triumphantly to Him in **s**. Ps 95:2
Sing a new **s** to the LORD; Ps 96:1
Sing a new **s** to the LORD, for He Ps 98:1
with the lyre and melodious **s**. Ps 98:5
LORD is my strength and my **s**; Ps 118:14
the theme of⌋ my **s** during my Ps 119:54
the LORD's **s** on foreign soil Ps 137:4
I will sing a new **s** to You; Ps 144:9
to the LORD a new **s**, His praise Ps 149:1
to listen to the **s** of fools. Ec 7:5
the daughters of **s** grow faint. Ec 12:4
Solomon's Finest **S** Sg 1:1
a **s** about my loved one's Is 5:1
strength and my **s**, He has become Is 12:2
will sing this **s** ⌊of contempt⌋ Is 14:4
what the **s** ⌊says⌋ about the Is 23:15
sing many a **s**, and you will be Is 23:16
He stills the **s** of the violent. Is 25:5
On that day this **s** will be sung Is 26:1
Sing a new **s** to the LORD; Is 42:10
thanksgiving and melodious **s**. Is 51:3
burst into **s** and shout, you who Is 54:1
sing the victory **s** over you. Jr 51:14
sang a new **s**: You are worthy Rv 5:9
They sang a new **s** before the Rv 14:3
could learn the **s** except the Rv 14:3
They sang the **s** of God's servant Rv 15:3
Moses, and the **s** of the Lamb: Rv 15:3

SONGS *(23)*

and his **s** numbered 1,005. 1Kg 4:32
God with **s** and with lyres, 1Ch 13:8
were in charge of the praise **s**. Neh 12:8
of the singers and **s** of praise Neh 12:46
Now I am mocked by their **s**; Jb 30:9
us⌋ with **s** in the night, Jb 35:10
drunkards make up **s** about me. Ps 69:12
young women had no wedding **s**. Ps 78:63
come before Him with joyful **s**. Ps 100:2
captors there asked us for **s**, Ps 137:3
"Sing us one of the **s** of Zion." Ps 137:3
Singing **s** to a troubled heart is Pr 25:20
the ends of the earth we hear **s**: Is 24:16
mocked by their **s** all day long. Lm 3:14
look, I am mocked by their **s**. Lm 3:63
an end to the noise of your **s**, Ezk 26:13
a singer of love **s** who has a Ezk 33:32
from Me the noise of your **s**! Am 5:23
They improvise **s** to the sound of Am 6:5
day the temple **s** will become Am 8:3
and all your **s** into lamentation; Am 8:10
and spiritual **s**, singing and Eph 5:19
and spiritual **s**, with gratitude Col 3:16

SONS *(1000)*

and he fathered **s** and daughters. Gn 5:4
and he fathered **s** and daughters. Gn 5:7
and he fathered **s** and daughters. Gn 5:10
and he fathered **s** and daughters. Gn 5:13
and he fathered **s** and daughters. Gn 5:16
and he fathered **s** and daughters. Gn 5:19
and fathered **s** and daughters. Gn 5:22
and he fathered **s** and daughters. Gn 5:26
and he fathered **s** and daughters. Gn 5:30
the **s** of God saw that the Gn 6:2
when the **s** of God came to the Gn 6:4
And Noah fathered three **s**: Gn 6:10
will enter the ark with your **s**, Gn 6:18
Noah, his **s**, his wife, and his Gn 7:7
day Noah along with his **s** Shem, Gn 7:13
wife, your **s**, and your sons' Gn 8:16
along with his **s**, his wife, and Gn 8:18
Noah and his **s** and said to them, Gn 9:1
said to Noah and his **s** with him, Gn 9:8
Noah's **s** who came out of the ark Gn 9:18
These three were Noah's **s**, Gn 9:19
the family records of Noah's **s**, Gn 10:1
also had **s** after the deluge. Gn 10:1
s: Gomer, Magog, Madai, Gn 10:2
Gomer's **s**: Ashkenaz, Riphath, Gn 10:3
Javan's **s**: Elishah, Tarshish, Gn 10:4
⌊Japheth's **s**⌋ by their clans, Gn 10:5
Ham's **s**: Cush, Egypt, Put, and Gn 10:6
Cush's **s**: Seba, Havilah, Sabtah, Gn 10:7
And Raamah's **s**: Sheba and Dedan. Gn 10:7
are Ham's **s**, by their clans Gn 10:20
Shem's **s** were Elam, Asshur, Gn 10:22
Aram's **s**: Uz, Hul, Gether, and Gn 10:23
Eber had two **s**. One was named Gn 10:25
All these were Joktan's **s**. Gn 10:29
are Shem's **s** by their clans, Gn 10:31
These are the clans of Noah's **s**, Gn 10:32
⌊other⌋ **s** and daughters. Gn 11:11
⌊other⌋ **s** and daughters. Gn 11:13
⌊other⌋ **s** and daughters. Gn 11:15
⌊other⌋ **s** and daughters. Gn 11:17
⌊other⌋ **s** and daughters. Gn 11:19
⌊other⌋ **s** and daughters. Gn 11:21
⌊other⌋ **s** and daughters. Gn 11:23
⌊other⌋ **s** and daughters. Gn 11:25
your **s** and daughters, Gn 19:12
also has borne **s** to your brother Gn 22:20
Dedan's **s** were the Asshurim, Gn 25:3
And Midian's **s** were Ephah, Gn 25:4
All these were **s** of Keturah. Gn 25:4
gifts to the **s** of his concubines Gn 25:6
His **s** Isaac and Ishmael buried Gn 25:9
are the names of Ishmael's **s**; Gn 25:13
are Ishmael's **s**, and these are Gn 25:16
your mother's **s** bow down to you Gn 27:29
I have borne him three **s**." Gn 29:34
"Give me **s**, or I will die!" Gn 30:1
because I have borne him six **s**," Gn 30:20
he placed his **s** in charge of Gn 30:35
what Laban's **s** were saying: Gn 31:1
my daughters; the **s**, my sons; Gn 31:43
the sons, my **s**; and the flocks, Gn 31:43
slaves, and his 11 **s**, and Gn 32:22
Leah and her **s** next, and Rachel Gn 33:2
the field from the **s** of Hamor, Gn 33:19
but since his **s** were with his Gn 34:5
Jacob's **s** returned from the Gn 34:7
said to Jacob's **s**, "My son Gn 34:8
But Jacob's **s** answered Shechem Gn 34:13
two of Jacob's **s**, Simeon and Gn 34:25
Jacob's ⌊other⌋ **s** came to the Gn 34:27
they did not pursue Jacob's **s**. Gn 35:5
heard about it. Jacob had 12 **s**: Gn 35:22
Leah's **s** were Reuben (Jacob's Gn 35:23
Rachel's **s** were Joseph and Gn 35:24
The **s** of Rachel's slave Bilhah Gn 35:25
s of Leah's slave Zilpah were Gn 35:26
These are the **s** of Jacob, who Gn 35:26
His **s** Esau and Jacob buried him. Gn 35:29
were Esau's **s**, who were born to Gn 36:5
took his wives, **s**, daughters, Gn 36:6
These are the names of Esau's **s**: Gn 36:10
The **s** of Eliphaz were Teman, Gn 36:11
These were the **s** of Esau's wife Gn 36:12
are Reuel's **s**: Nahath, Zerah, Gn 36:13
These were the **s** of Esau's wife Gn 36:13
These were the **s** of Esau's wife Gn 36:14
are the chiefs of Esau's **s**: Gn 36:15
the **s** of Eliphaz, Esau's Gn 36:15
These are the **s** of Adah. Gn 36:16
These are the **s** of Reuel, Esau's Gn 36:17
These are the **s** of Esau's wife Gn 36:17
These are the **s** of Esau's wife Gn 36:18
are the **s** of Esau (that is, Gn 36:19
These are the **s** of Seir the Gn 36:20
the Horites, the **s** of Seir, in Gn 36:21
The **s** of Lotan were Hori and Gn 36:22
are Shobal's **s**: Alvan, Manahath Gn 36:23
are Zibeon's **s**: Aiah and Anah. Gn 36:24
are Dishon's **s**: Hemdan, Eshban, Gn 36:26
are Ezer's **s**: Bilhan, Zaavan Gn 36:27
are Dishan's **s**: Uz and Aran. Gn 36:28
working⌋ with the **s** of Bilhah Gn 37:2
than his other **s** because Joseph Gn 37:3
All his **s** and daughters tried to Gn 37:35
Two **s** were born to Joseph before Gn 41:50
he said to his **s**, "Why do you Gn 42:1
The **s** of Israel were among those Gn 42:5
We are all **s** of one man. Gn 42:11
the **s** of one man in the land of Gn 42:13
were 12 brothers, **s** of the same Gn 42:32
You have deprived me of my **s**. Gn 42:36
can kill my two **s** if I don't Gn 42:37
am deprived of my **s**, then I am Gn 43:14
only one of his mother's **s** left, Gn 44:20
know that my wife bore me two **s**. Gn 44:27
The **s** of Israel did this. Gn 45:21
s of Israel took their father Gn 46:5
His **s** and grandsons, his Gn 46:7
Reuben's **s**: Hanoch, Pallu, Gn 46:9
Simeon's **s**: Jemuel, Jamin, Ohad, Gn 46:10
Levi's **s**: Gershon, Kohath, and Gn 46:11
Judah's **s**: Er, Onan, Shelah, Gn 46:12
Canaan. Perez's **s**: Hezron and Gn 46:12
Issachar's **s**: Tola, Puvah, Gn 46:13
Zebulun's **s**: Sered, Elon, and Gn 46:14
were Leah's **s** born to Jacob Gn 46:15
Gad's **s**: Ziphion, Haggi, Shuni, Gn 46:16
Asher's **s**: Imnah, Ishvah, Ishvi, Gn 46:17
Beriah's **s** were Heber and Gn 46:17
These were the **s** of Zilpah— Gn 46:18
The **s** of Jacob's wife Rachel: Gn 46:19
Benjamin's **s**: Bela, Becher, Gn 46:21
were Rachel's **s** who were born to Gn 46:22
Naphtali's **s**: Jahzeel, Guni, Gn 46:24
These were the **s** of Bilhah, Gn 46:25
the wives of Jacob's **s**— Gn 46:26
And Joseph's **s** who were born to Gn 46:27
So he set out with his two **s**, Gn 48:1
Your two **s** born to you in the Gn 48:5
When Israel saw Joseph's **s**, Gn 48:8
are my **s** God has given me here. Gn 48:9
Jacob called his **s** and said, Gn 49:1
together and listen, **s** of Jacob; Gn 49:2
your father's **s** will bow down to Gn 49:8
had finished instructing his **s**, Gn 49:33
So Jacob's **s** did for him what he Gn 50:12
He saw Ephraim's **s** to the third Gn 50:23
the **s** of Manasseh's son Machir Gn 50:23
the names of the **s** of Israel who Ex 1:1
them on your **s** and daughters. Ex 3:22
So Moses took his wife and **s**, Ex 4:20
The **s** of Reuben, the firstborn Ex 6:14
The **s** of Simeon: Jemuel, Jamin, Ex 6:15
the names of the **s** of Levi Ex 6:16
The **s** of Gershon: Libni and Ex 6:17

The s of Kohath: Amram, Izhar, Ex 6:18
s of Merari: Mahli and Mushi. Ex 6:19
The s of Izhar: Korah, Nepheg, Ex 6:21
The s of Uzziel: Mishael, Ex 6:22
The s of Korah: Assir, Elkanah, Ex 6:24
will go with our s and daughters Ex 10:9
every firstborn among your s. Ex 13:13
all the firstborn of my s.' Ex 13:15
with her two s, one of whom was Ex 18:3
along with Moses' wife and s, Ex 18:5
with your wife and her two s." Ex 18:6
she bears him s or daughters, Ex 21:4
Give Me the firstborn of your s. Ex 22:29
Aaron and his s are to tend the Ex 27:21
Aaron, with his s, come to you Ex 28:1
Aaron, his s Nadab and Abihu, Ex 28:1
Aaron and his s so that they may Ex 28:4
on them the names of Israel's s: Ex 28:9
of Israel's s as a gem cutter Ex 28:11
to the names of Israel's s. Ex 28:21
of Israel's s over his heart Ex 28:29
for Aaron's s to ⌊give them⌋ Ex 28:40
on your brother Aaron and his s; Ex 28:41
Aaron and his s whenever they Ex 28:43
Aaron and his s to the entrance Ex 29:4
You must also bring his s, Ex 29:8
around both Aaron and his s. Ex 29:9
you will ordain Aaron and his s. Ex 29:9
Aaron and his s must lay their Ex 29:10
Aaron and his s are to lay their Ex 29:15
Aaron and his s must lay their Ex 29:19
as well as on his s and their Ex 29:21
as well as his s and their Ex 29:21
Aaron and his s and wave them as Ex 29:24
for Aaron and his s the breast Ex 29:27
to Aaron and his s as a regular Ex 29:28
to belong to his s after him, Ex 29:29
is one of his s and who succeeds Ex 29:30
Aaron and his s are to eat the Ex 29:32
Aaron and his s based on all I Ex 29:35
Aaron and his s to serve Me as Ex 29:44
Aaron and his s must wash their Ex 30:19
Aaron and his s and consecrate Ex 30:30
garments for his s to serve as Ex 31:10
your wives, your s, and your Ex 32:2
⌊as brides⌋ for your s. Ex 34:16
and cause your s to prostitute Ex 34:16
all the firstborn of your s. Ex 34:20
garments for his s to serve as Ex 35:19
of Israel's s as a gem cutter Ex 39:6
to the names of Israel's s. Ex 39:14
woven linen for Aaron and his s. Ex 39:27
garments for his s to serve as Ex 39:41
Aaron and his s to the entrance Ex 40:12
Have his s come forward and Ex 40:14
and his s washed their hands and Ex 40:31
Aaron's s the priests are to Lv 1:5
The s of Aaron the priest will Lv 1:7
Aaron's s the priests are to Lv 1:8
Aaron's s the priests will Lv 1:11
it to Aaron's s the priests. Lv 2:2
will belong to Aaron and his s, Lv 2:3
will belong to Aaron and his s, Lv 2:10
Then Aaron's s the priests will Lv 3:2
Aaron's s will burn it on the Lv 3:5
Aaron's s will sprinkle its Lv 3:8
Aaron's s will sprinkle its Lv 3:13
Command Aaron and his s: Lv 6:9
Aaron's s will present it before Lv 6:14
Aaron and his s may eat the rest Lv 6:16
Aaron and his s must present to Lv 6:20
who is of Aaron's s and will be Lv 6:22
Aaron and his s: This is the law Lv 6:25
equally to all of Aaron's s. Lv 7:10
belongs to Aaron and his s. Lv 7:31
priest and his s as a permanent Lv 7:34
Aaron and his s since the day Lv 7:35
Take Aaron, his s with him, the Lv 8:2
Aaron and his s and washed them Lv 8:6
Then Moses presented Aaron's s, Lv 8:13
Aaron and his s laid their hands Lv 8:14
Aaron and his s laid their hands Lv 8:18
Aaron and his s laid their hands Lv 8:22
presented Aaron's s and put some Lv 8:24
Aaron and his s and waved them Lv 8:27
as well as on his s and their Lv 8:30
as well as his s and their Lv 8:30
Moses said to Aaron and his s, Lv 8:31

Aaron and his s are to eat it. Lv 8:31
Aaron and his s did everything Lv 8:36
Aaron, his s, and the elders Lv 9:1
Aaron's s brought the blood to Lv 9:9
Aaron's s brought him the blood, Lv 9:12
Aaron's s brought him the blood, Lv 9:18
Aaron's s Nadab and Abihu each Lv 10:1
s of Aaron's uncle Uzziel, Lv 10:4
to Aaron and his s Eleazar and Lv 10:6
You and your s are not to drink Lv 10:9
to Aaron and his remaining s, Lv 10:12
But you and your s and your Lv 10:14
Aaron's surviving s, and asked, Lv 10:16
the priest or to one of his s, Lv 13:2
of two of Aaron's s when they Lv 16:1
Speak to Aaron, his s, and all Lv 17:2
Speak to Aaron's s, the priests, Lv 21:1
to Aaron and his s and to all Lv 21:24
Tell Aaron and his s to deal Lv 22:2
Speak to Aaron, his s, and all Lv 22:18
It belongs to Aaron and his s, Lv 24:9
leave them to your s after you Lv 25:46
will eat the flesh of your s; Lv 26:29
from the s of Joseph: Elishama Nm 1:10
are the names of Aaron's s: Nm 3:2
are the names of Aaron's s, Nm 3:3
of Sinai, and they had no s. Nm 3:4
the Levites to Aaron and his s; Nm 3:9
Aaron and his s to carry out Nm 3:10
These were Levi's s by name: Nm 3:17
of Gershon's s by their clans: Nm 3:18
Kohath's s by their clans were Nm 3:19
Merari's s by their clans were Nm 3:20
Aaron, and his s, who performed Nm 3:38
to Aaron and his s as the Nm 3:48
Aaron and his s in obedience to Nm 3:51
Aaron and his s are to go in, Nm 4:5
Aaron and his s are to finish Nm 4:15
Aaron and his s are to go in and Nm 4:19
the command of Aaron and his s; Nm 4:27
Aaron and his s how you are to Nm 6:23
stand before Aaron and his s, Nm 8:13
Aaron and his s to perform the Nm 8:19
the presence of Aaron and his s. Nm 8:22
The s of Aaron, the priests, are Nm 10:8
Dathan and Abiram, s of Eliab, Nm 16:1
son of Peleth, s of Reuben, took Nm 16:1
and Abiram, the s of Eliab, but Nm 16:12
Aaron, "You, your s, and your Nm 18:1
You and your s will be Nm 18:1
with you and your s in front of Nm 18:2
you and your s will carry out Nm 18:7
to you and your s as a portion Nm 18:8
be most holy for you and your s. Nm 18:9
you and to your s and daughters Nm 18:11
you and to your s and daughters Nm 18:19
He gave up his s as refugees, Nm 21:29
struck him, his s, and his whole Nm 21:35
The s of Eliab were Nemuel, Nm 26:9
The s of Korah, however, did not Nm 26:11
Judah's s included Er and Onan, Nm 26:19
son of Hepher had no s— Nm 26:33
of his own sin, and he had no s. Nm 27:3
from the s of Joseph: Hanniel Nm 34:23
of the clans of the s of Joseph Nm 36:1
your s who don't know good from Dt 1:39
him, his s, and his whole Dt 2:33
to their s or take their Dt 7:3
take their daughters for your s, Dt 7:3
will turn your s away from Me to Dt 7:4
can stand up to the s of Anak?' Dt 9:2
the s of Eliab the Reubenite, Dt 11:6
God—you, your s and daughters, Dt 12:12
even burn their s and daughters Dt 12:31
You are s of the LORD your God; Dt 14:1
and he and his s will continue Dt 17:20
him and his s from all your Dt 18:5
the priests, the s of Levi, will Dt 21:5
and the unloved bear him s, Dt 21:15
he has to his s as an Dt 21:16
Your s and daughters will be Dt 28:32
You will father s and daughters, Dt 28:41
flesh of your s and daughters Dt 28:53
the priests, the s of Levi, who Dt 31:9
anger⌋ by His s and daughters. Dt 32:19
and didn't acknowledge his s, Dt 33:9
be the most blessed of the s; Dt 33:24
up their s in their place; Jos 5:7

of gold, his s and daughters, Jos 7:24
from there the three s of Anak: Jos 15:14
and Manasseh, the s of Joseph, Jos 16:4
clans, for the s of Abiezer, Jos 17:2
had no s, only daughters Jos 17:3
an inheritance among his s. Jos 17:6
to the rest of Manasseh's s. Jos 17:6
but Jacob and his s went down to Jos 24:4
purchased from the s of Hamor, Jos 24:32
the three s of Anak who lived Jdg 1:20
their own daughters to their s, Jdg 3:6
Kenites, the s of Hobab, Moses' Jdg 4:11
my brothers, the s of my mother! Jdg 8:19
as well as your s and your Jdg 8:22
Gideon had 70 s, his own Jdg 8:30
70 men, all the s of Jerubbaal, Jdg 9:2
70 brothers, the s of Jerubbaal, Jdg 9:5
killed his 70 s on top of a Jdg 9:18
against the 70 s of Jerubbaal Jdg 9:24
He had 30 s who rode on 30 young Jdg 10:4
wife bore him s, and when they Jdg 11:2
and had 30 s. He gave his 30 Jdg 12:9
30 wives for his s from outside Jdg 12:9
He had 40 s and 30 grandsons, Jdg 12:14
one of his s to be his priest. Jdg 17:5
man became like one of his s. Jdg 17:11
and his s were priests for the Jdg 18:30
wife and two s to live in the Ru 1:1
names of his two s were Mahlon Ru 1:2
and she was left with her two s. Ru 1:3
s took Moabite women as their Ru 1:4
have any more s who could become Ru 1:11
a husband tonight and to bear s, Ru 1:12
is better to you than seven s, Ru 4:15
where Eli's two s, Hophni and 1Sm 1:3
to each of her s and daughters. 1Sm 1:4
I not better to you than 10 s?" 1Sm 1:8
woman with many s pines away. 1Sm 2:5
Eli's s were wicked men; 1Sm 2:12
birth to three s and two 1Sm 2:21
everything his s were doing to 1Sm 2:22
No, my s, the report I hear from 1Sm 2:24
honored your s more than Me, 1Sm 2:29
your two s Hophni and Phinehas 1Sm 2:34
s are defiling the sanctuary, 1Sm 3:13
two s, Hophni and Phinehas, 1Sm 4:4
and Eli's two s, Hophni and 1Sm 4:11
Your two s, Hophni and Phinehas, 1Sm 4:17
appointed his s as judges over 1Sm 8:1
his s did not walk in his ways— 1Sm 8:3
and your s do not follow your 1Sm 8:5
can take your s and put them to 1Sm 8:11
and my s are here with you. 1Sm 12:2
Saul's s were Jonathan, Ishvi, 1Sm 14:49
selected a king from his s." 1Sm 16:1
Jesse and his s and invited them 1Sm 16:5
presented seven of his s to him, 1Sm 16:10
"Are these all the s you have?" 1Sm 16:11
Jesse had eight s, and during 1Sm 17:12
three oldest s had followed Saul 1Sm 17:13
one of the s of Ahimelech son of 1Sm 22:20
you and your s will be with me, 1Sm 28:19
Their wives, s, and daughters 1Sm 30:3
loss of⌋ their s and daughters. 1Sm 30:6
including the s and daughters, 1Sm 30:19
Saul and his s and killed his 1Sm 31:2
and his sons and killed his s, 1Sm 31:2
died together with his three s, 1Sm 31:6
that Saul and his s were dead, 1Sm 31:7
and his three s dead on Mount 1Sm 31:8
bodies of his s from the wall 1Sm 31:12
The three s of Zeruiah were 2Sm 2:18
S were born to David in Hebron: 2Sm 3:2
These men, the s of Zeruiah, are 2Sm 3:39
s of Rimmon the Beerothite of 2Sm 4:2
the s of Rimmon the Beerothite, 2Sm 4:5
s of Rimmon the Beerothite, 2Sm 4:9
and more s and daughters were 2Sm 5:13
Uzzah and Ahio, s of Abinadab, 2Sm 6:3
and David's s were chief 2Sm 8:18
You, your s, and your servants 2Sm 9:10
Ziba had 15 s and 20 servants 2Sm 9:10
just like one of the king's s. 2Sm 9:11
invited all the king's s. 2Sm 13:23
sent Amnon and all the king's s. 2Sm 13:27
rest of⌋ the king's s got up, 2Sm 13:29
struck down all the king's s; 2Sm 13:30
men, the king's s, because only 2Sm 13:32

says all the king's s are dead. 2Sm 13:33
Look, the king's s have come! 2Sm 13:35
the king's s entered and wept 2Sm 13:36
Your servant had two s. 2Sm 14:6
Three s were born to Absalom, 2Sm 14:27
peace and your two s with you: 2Sm 15:27
their two s, Zadok's son Ahimaaz 2Sm 15:36
king replied, "S of Zeruiah, do 2Sm 16:10
lives of your s and daughters, 2Sm 19:5
with his 15 s and 20 servants 2Sm 19:17
David answered, "S of Zeruiah, 2Sm 19:22
who were the two s whom Rizpah 2Sm 21:8
and the five s whom Merab 2Sm 21:8
killed two s of Ariel of Moab, 2Sm 23:20
Shaalbonite, the s of Jashen, 2Sm 23:32
He invited all the king's s, 1Kg 1:19
invited all the s of the king, 1Kg 1:25
'If your s are careful to walk 1Kg 2:4
loyalty to the s of Barzillai 1Kg 2:7
and Ahijah the s of Shisha, 1Kg 4:3
Calcol, and Darda, s of Mahol. 1Kg 4:31
if only your s guard their walk 1Kg 8:25
If you or your s turn away from 1Kg 9:6
there along with Pharaoh's s. 1Kg 11:20
His s also told their father the 1Kg 13:11
His s had seen the way taken by 1Kg 13:12
he said to his s, "Saddle the 1Kg 13:13
old prophet instructed his s, 1Kg 13:27
he said to his s, "When I die, 1Kg 13:31
of Jeroboam's ⌊s⌋ will come to 1Kg 14:13
of the tribes of the s of Jacob, 1Kg 18:31
of the s of the prophets said 1Kg 20:35
Then the s of the prophets who 2Kg 2:3
Then the s of the prophets who 2Kg 2:5
men from the s of the prophets 2Kg 2:7
When the s of the prophets from 2Kg 2:15
Then the s of the prophets said 2Kg 2:16
wives of the s of the prophets 2Kg 4:1
the door behind you and your s, 2Kg 4:4
the door behind her and her s, 2Kg 4:5
and your s can live on the rest. 2Kg 4:7
The s of the prophets were 2Kg 4:38
stew for the s of the prophets. 2Kg 4:38
men from the s of the prophets 2Kg 5:22
The s of the prophets said to 2Kg 6:1
to David and to his s forever. 2Kg 8:19
one of the s of the prophets 2Kg 9:1
the blood of his s yesterday,' 2Kg 9:26
Since Ahab had 70 s in Samaria, 2Kg 10:1
to the guardians of Ahab's s, 2Kg 10:1
your master's s are with you 2Kg 10:2
qualified of your master's s, 2Kg 10:3
of your master's s at this time 2Kg 10:6
of the king's s were being cared 2Kg 10:6
the king's s and slaughtered 2Kg 10:7
the heads of the king's s," 2Kg 10:8
greet the king's s and the queen 2Kg 10:13
sons and the queen mother's s." 2Kg 10:13
generations of your s will sit 2Kg 10:30
from the king's s who were being 2Kg 11:2
generations of your s will sit 2Kg 15:12
They made their s and daughters 2Kg 17:17
his s Adrammelech and Sharezer 2Kg 19:37
Zedekiah's s before his eyes. 2Kg 25:7
Noah, Noah's s: Shem, Ham, and 1Ch 1:4
s: Gomer, Magog, Madai, 1Ch 1:5
Gomer's s: Ashkenaz, Riphath, 1Ch 1:6
Javan's s: Elishah, Tarshish, 1Ch 1:7
Ham's s: Cush, Mizraim, Put, and 1Ch 1:8
Cush's s: Seba, Havilah, Sabta, 1Ch 1:9
Raama's s: Sheba and Dedan 1Ch 1:9
Shem's s: Elam, Asshur, 1Ch 1:17
Two s were born to Eber. 1Ch 1:19
All of these were Joktan's s. 1Ch 1:23
Abraham's s: Isaac and Ishmael. 1Ch 1:28
These were Ishmael's s. 1Ch 1:31
The s born to Keturah, Abraham's 1Ch 1:32
Jokshan's s: Sheba and Dedan 1Ch 1:32
s: Ephah, Epher, Hanoch, 1Ch 1:33
All of these were Keturah's s. 1Ch 1:33
Isaac. Isaac's s: Esau and 1Ch 1:34
Esau's s: Eliphaz, Reuel, Jeush, 1Ch 1:35
Eliphaz's s: Teman, Omar, Zephi, 1Ch 1:36
Reuel's s: Nahath, Zerah, 1Ch 1:37
Seir's s: Lotan, Shobal, Zibeon, 1Ch 1:38
Lotan's s: Hori and Homam. Timna 1Ch 1:39
Shobal's s: Alian, Manahath, 1Ch 1:40
Onam. Zibeon's s: Aiah and Anah. 1Ch 1:40
Dishon's s: Hamran, Eshban 1Ch 1:41
Ezer's s: Bilhan, Zaavan, and 1Ch 1:42
Jaakan. Dishan's s: Uz and Aran. 1Ch 1:42
were Israel's s: Reuben, Simeon, 1Ch 2:1
Judah's s: Er, Onan, and Shelah. 1Ch 2:3
Judah had five s in all. 1Ch 2:4
Perez's s: Hezron and Hamul. 1Ch 2:5
Zerah's s: Zimri, Ethan, Heman, 1Ch 2:6
s, who were born to him: 1Ch 2:9
three s: Abishai, Joab, 1Ch 2:16
were Azubah's s: Jesher, Shobab, 1Ch 2:18
were the s of Machir father 1Ch 2:23
The s of Jerahmeel, Hezron's 1Ch 2:25
The s of Ram, Jerahmeel's 1Ch 2:27
Onam's s: Shammai and Jada. 1Ch 2:28
Jada. Shammai's s: Nadab and 1Ch 2:28
Nadab's s: Seled and Appaim. 1Ch 2:30
s of Jada brother of Shammai: 1Ch 2:32
Jonathan's s: Peleth and Zaza. 1Ch 2:33
had no s, only daughters, 1Ch 2:34
The s of Caleb brother of 1Ch 2:42
Hebron's s: Korah, Tappuah, 1Ch 2:43
Jahdai's s: Regem, Jotham, 1Ch 2:47
The s of Hur, Ephrathah's 1Ch 2:50
Salma's s: Bethlehem, the 1Ch 2:54
were David's s who were born to 1Ch 3:1
Six s were born to David in 1Ch 3:4
These ⌊s⌋ were born to him in 1Ch 3:5
⌊David's other s⌋: Ibhar, 1Ch 3:6
Eliada, and Eliphelet—nine s. 1Ch 3:8
⌊These⌋ were all David's s, 1Ch 3:9
addition to the s by his 1Ch 3:9
Josiah's s: Johanan was the 1Ch 3:15
Jehoiakim's s: his sons Jeconiah 1Ch 3:16
his s Jeconiah and Zedekiah. 1Ch 3:16
The s of Jeconiah the captive: 1Ch 3:17
the captive: his s Shealtiel, 1Ch 3:17
Pedaiah's s: Zerubbabel and 1Ch 3:19
Shimei. Zerubbabel's s: 1Ch 3:19
Jeshaiah, and the s of Rephaiah, 1Ch 3:21
Shemaiah's s: Hattush, Igal, 1Ch 3:22
Neariah's s: Elioenai, Hizkiah, 1Ch 3:23
s: Hodaviah, Eliashib, 1Ch 3:24
Judah's s: Perez, Hezron, Carmi, 1Ch 4:1
were Etam's s: Jezreel, Ishma, 1Ch 4:3
These were the s of Hur, 1Ch 4:4
These were Naarah's s. 1Ch 4:6
Helah's s: Zereth, Zohar, and 1Ch 4:7
Kenaz's s: Othniel and Seraiah. 1Ch 4:13
Seraiah. Othniel's s: Hathath 1Ch 4:13
The s of Caleb son of Jephunneh: 1Ch 4:15
Jehallelel's s: Ziph, Ziphah, 1Ch 4:16
Ezrah's s: Jether, Mered, Epher, 1Ch 4:17
These were the s of Pharaoh's 1Ch 4:18
The s of Hodiah's wife, the 1Ch 4:19
Shimon's s: Amnon, Rinnah, 1Ch 4:20
and Tilon. Ishi's s: Zoheth and 1Ch 4:20
The s of Shelah son of Judah: 1Ch 4:21
s: Nemuel, Jamin, Jarib, 1Ch 4:24
⌊Shaul's s:⌋ his son Shallum, 1Ch 4:25
Mishma's s: his son Hammuel, his 1Ch 4:26
Shimei had 16 s and six 1Ch 4:27
men from these s of Simeon went 1Ch 4:42
and Uzziel, the s of Ishi, as 1Ch 4:42
⌊These were⌋ the s of Reuben the 1Ch 5:1
was given to the s of Joseph son 1Ch 5:1
The s of Reuben, Israel's 1Ch 5:3
Joel's s: his son Shemaiah, his 1Ch 5:4
The s of Gad lived next to them 1Ch 5:11
These were the s of Abihail son 1Ch 5:14
The s of Reuben and Gad and half 1Ch 5:18
The s of half the tribe of 1Ch 5:23
Levi's s: Gershom, Kohath, and 1Ch 6:1
s: Amram, Izhar, Hebron, 1Ch 6:2
Miriam. Aaron's s: Nadab, Abihu, 1Ch 6:3
Levi's s: Gershom, Kohath, and 1Ch 6:16
are the names of Gershom's s: 1Ch 6:17
Kohath's s: Amram, Izhar, Hebron 1Ch 6:18
Merari's s: Mahli and Mushi. 1Ch 6:19
Kohath's s: his son Amminadab, 1Ch 6:22
Elkanah's s: Amasai and Ahimoth, 1Ch 6:25
Samuel's s: his firstborn Joel, 1Ch 6:28
s: Mahli, his son Libni, 1Ch 6:29
the men who served with their s. 1Ch 6:33
their relatives were Merari's s: 1Ch 6:44
Aaron and his s did all the work 1Ch 6:49
are Aaron's s: his son Eleazar 1Ch 6:50
to Aaron's s from the Kohathite 1Ch 6:54
Aaron's s were given: Hebron (a 1Ch 6:57
s: Tola, Puah, Jashub, 1Ch 7:1
s: Uzzi, Rephaiah, Jeriel, 1Ch 7:2
Izrahiah's s: Michael, Obadiah, 1Ch 7:3
Three of Benjamin's ⌊s⌋: 1Ch 7:6
Bela's s: Ezbon, Uzzi, Uzziel, 1Ch 7:7
Becher's s: Zemirah, Joash, 1Ch 7:8
all these were Becher's s. 1Ch 7:8
Bilhan's s: Jeush, Benjamin 1Ch 7:10
All these s of Jediael listed by 1Ch 7:11
Shuppim and Huppim were s of Ir, 1Ch 7:12
the Hushim were the s of Aher. 1Ch 7:12
Naphtali's s: Jahziel, Guni, 1Ch 7:13
Jezer, and Shallum—Bilhah's s. 1Ch 7:13
Manasseh's s through his Aramean 1Ch 7:14
and his s were Ulam and Rekem. 1Ch 7:16
These were the s of Gilead son 1Ch 7:17
Shemida's s: Ahian, Shechem, 1Ch 7:19
Ephraim's s: Shuthelah, and his 1Ch 7:20
borders of the s of Manasseh, 1Ch 7:29
The s of Joseph son of Israel 1Ch 7:29
Asher's s: Imnah, Ishvah, Ishvi, 1Ch 7:30
Beriah's s: Heber, and Malchiel, 1Ch 7:31
Japhlet's s: Pasach, Bimhal, and 1Ch 7:33
These were Japhlet's s. 1Ch 7:33
Shemer's s: Ahi, Rohgah, Hubbah, 1Ch 7:34
brother Helem's s: Zophah, Imna, 1Ch 7:35
Zophah's s: Suah, Harnepher, 1Ch 7:36
Jether's s: Jephunneh, Pispa, 1Ch 7:38
Ulla's s: Arah, Hanniel, and 1Ch 7:39
All these were Asher's s. 1Ch 7:40
Bela's s: Addar, Gera, Abihud, 1Ch 8:3
These were Ehud's s, who were 1Ch 8:6
Shaharaim had s in the country 1Ch 8:8
His s by his wife Hodesh: 1Ch 8:9
These were his s, heads of 1Ch 8:10
He also had s by Hushim: 1Ch 8:11
Elpaal's s: Eber, Misham, and 1Ch 8:12
and Joha were Beriah's s. 1Ch 8:16
and Jobab were Elpaal's s. 1Ch 8:18
and Shimrath were Shimei's s. 1Ch 8:21
and Penuel were Shashak's s. 1Ch 8:25
and Zichri were Jeroham's s. 1Ch 8:27
s: Pithon, Melech, Tarea, 1Ch 8:35
Azel had six s, and these were 1Ch 8:38
All these were Azel's s. 1Ch 8:38
brother Eshek's s: Ulam was his 1Ch 8:39
Ulam's s were warriors and 1Ch 8:40
They had many s and grandsons— 1Ch 8:40
these were among Benjamin's s. 1Ch 8:40
Asaiah the firstborn and his s; 1Ch 9:5
and from the s of Zerah: 1Ch 9:6
they and their s were assigned 1Ch 9:23
of the priests' s mixed the 1Ch 9:30
Micah's s: Pithon, Melech, 1Ch 9:41
Azel had six s, and these were 1Ch 9:44
and Hanan. These were Azel's s. 1Ch 9:44
Saul and his s and killed Saul's 1Ch 10:2
and killed Saul's s Jonathan, 1Ch 10:2
So Saul and his three s died— 1Ch 10:6
that Saul and his s were dead, 1Ch 10:7
Saul and his s dead on Mount 1Ch 10:8
bodies of his s and brought them 1Ch 10:12
killed two ⌊s of⌋ Ariel of Moab 1Ch 11:22
the s of Hashem the Gizonite, 1Ch 11:34
Shama and Jeiel the s of Hotham 1Ch 11:44
Joshaviah, the s of Elnaam, 1Ch 11:46
Jeziel and Pelet s of Azmaveth; 1Ch 12:3
the s of Jeroham from Gedor. 1Ch 12:7
father of more s and daughters. 1Ch 14:3
Jeduthun's s were at the gate. 1Ch 16:42
is one of your own s, and I will 1Ch 17:11
and David's s were the chief 1Ch 18:17
His four s, who were with him, 1Ch 21:20
divisions according to Levi's s: 1Ch 23:6
Ladan's s: Jehiel was the first, 1Ch 23:8
Shimei's s: Shelomoth, Haziel, 1Ch 23:9
s: Jahath, Zizah, Jeush, 1Ch 23:10
Those were Shimei's s—four. 1Ch 23:10
and Beriah did not have many s, 1Ch 23:11
s: Amram, Izhar, Hebron, 1Ch 23:12
Amram's s: Aaron and Moses. 1Ch 23:13
his s were named among the tribe 1Ch 23:14
Moses' s: Gershom and Eliezer. 1Ch 23:15
Gershom's s: Shebuel first. 1Ch 23:16
Eliezer's s were Rehabiah, 1Ch 23:17
did not have any other s, 1Ch 23:17
but Rehabiah's s were very 1Ch 23:17

Izhar's **s**: Shelomith was first. 1Ch 23:18
Hebron's **s**: Jeriah was first, 1Ch 23:19
Uzziel's **s**: Micah was first, and 1Ch 23:20
Merari's **s**: Mahli and Mushi. 1Ch 23:21
Mushi. Mahli's **s**: Eleazar and 1Ch 23:21
having no **s**, only daughters. 1Ch 23:22
cousins, the **s** of Kish, married 1Ch 23:22
Mushi's **s**: Mahli, Eder, and 1Ch 23:23
were the **s** of Levi by their 1Ch 23:24
be to assist the **s** of Aaron with 1Ch 23:28
their relatives, the **s** of Aaron, 1Ch 23:32
Aaron's **s** were Nadab, Abihu, 1Ch 24:1
they had no **s**, so Eleazar and 1Ch 24:2
with Zadok from the **s** of Eleazar 1Ch 24:3
Ahimelech from the **s** of Ithamar, 1Ch 24:3
As for the rest of Levi's **s**: 1Ch 24:20
sons: from Amram's **s**: Shubael; 1Ch 24:20
from Shubael's **s**: Jehdeiah. 1Ch 24:20
from Rehabiah's **s**: Isshiah was 1Ch 24:21
from Shelomoth's **s**: Jahath. 1Ch 24:22
Hebron's **s**: Jeriah ⌊the first⌋, 1Ch 24:23
⌊From⌋ Uzziel's **s**: Micah; from 1Ch 24:24
Micah; from Micah's **s**: Shamir. 1Ch 24:24
from Isshiah's **s**: Zechariah. 1Ch 24:25
Merari's **s**: Mahli and Mushi, 1Ch 24:26
from⌋ his **s**, Jaaziah his son. 1Ch 24:26
Merari's **s**, by his son Jaaziah: 1Ch 24:27
Mahli: Eleazar, who had no **s**. 1Ch 24:28
From Kish, ⌊from⌋ Kish's **s**: 1Ch 24:29
Mushi's **s**: Mahli, Eder, and 1Ch 24:30
Those were the **s** of the Levites 1Ch 24:30
the **s** of Aaron did in the 1Ch 24:31
apart some of the **s** of Asaph, 1Ch 25:1
From Asaph's **s**: Zaccur, Joseph, 1Ch 25:2
and Asarelah, **s** of Asaph, under 1Ch 25:2
Jeduthun's **s**: Gedaliah, Zeri, 1Ch 25:3
Heman: Heman's **s**: Bukkiah, 1Ch 25:4
All these **s** of Heman, the king's 1Ch 25:5
Heman fourteen **s** and three 1Ch 25:5
to Joseph, ⌊his **s**, and his 1Ch 25:9
him, his brothers, and his **s**— 1Ch 25:9
to⌋ Zaccur, his **s**, and his 1Ch 25:10
to Izri, his **s**, and his brothers 1Ch 25:11
Nethaniah, his **s**, and his 1Ch 25:12
to⌋ Bukkiah, his **s**, and his 1Ch 25:13
Jesarelah, his **s**, and his 1Ch 25:14
Jeshaiah, his **s**, and his 1Ch 25:15
Mattaniah, his **s**, and his 1Ch 25:16
to⌋ Shimei, his **s**, and his 1Ch 25:17
to⌋ Azarel, his **s**, and his 1Ch 25:18
Hashabiah, his **s**, and his 1Ch 25:19
to⌋ Shubael, his **s**, and his 1Ch 25:20
Mattithiah, his **s**, and his 1Ch 25:21
to Jeremoth, his **s**, and his 1Ch 25:22
to Hananiah, his **s**, and his 1Ch 25:23
his **s**, and his brothers 1Ch 25:24
to Hanani, his **s**, and his 1Ch 25:25
to Mallothi, his **s**, and his 1Ch 25:26
to Eliathah, his **s**, and his 1Ch 25:27
to Hothir, his **s**, and his 1Ch 25:28
to Giddalti, his **s**, and his 1Ch 25:29
Mahazioth, his **s**, and his 1Ch 25:30
his **s**, and his brothers 1Ch 25:31
of Kore, one of the **s** of Asaph. 1Ch 26:1
Meshelemiah had **s**: Zechariah the 1Ch 26:2
Obed-edom also had **s**: Shemaiah 1Ch 26:4
were born **s** who ruled over 1Ch 26:6
Shemaiah's **s**: Othni, Rephael, 1Ch 26:7
were among the **s** of Obed-edom 1Ch 26:8
with their **s** and brothers; 1Ch 26:8
also had **s** and brothers who 1Ch 26:9
from the Merarites, also had **s**: 1Ch 26:10
The **s** and brothers of Hosah were 1Ch 26:11
from the **s** of the Korahites 1Ch 26:19
From the **s** of Ladan, who were 1Ch 26:21
were the **s** of the Gershonites 1Ch 26:21
The **s** of Jehieli, Zetham and his 1Ch 26:22
and his **s** had the outside 1Ch 26:29
Pelonite from the **s** of Ephraim; 1Ch 27:10
from the **s** of Ephraim; 1Ch 27:14
Hachmoni attended the king's **s**. 1Ch 27:32
cattle of the king and his **s**, 1Ch 28:1
my father's **s**, He was pleased 1Ch 28:4
out of all my **s**—for the LORD 1Ch 28:5
the LORD has given me many **s**— 1Ch 28:5
all of King David's **s** as well, 1Ch 29:24
and of their **s** and their 2Ch 5:12
only your **s** guard their way to 2Ch 6:16
Jeroboam and his **s** refused to 2Ch 11:14
bore him **s**: Jeush, Shemariah, 2Ch 11:19
father of 28 **s** and 60 daughters 2Ch 11:21
some of his **s** to all the regions 2Ch 11:23
the hand of ⌊one of⌋ David's **s**. 2Ch 13:8
and fathered 22 **s** and 16 2Ch 13:21
Levites from the **s** of the 2Ch 20:19
had brothers, **s** of Jehoshaphat: 2Ch 21:2
these were the **s** of Jehoshaphat, 2Ch 21:2
to David and to his **s** forever. 2Ch 21:7
your people, your **s**, your wives, 2Ch 21:14
palace and also his **s** and wives; 2Ch 21:17
camp had killed all the older **s**. 2Ch 22:1
of Judah and the **s** of Ahaziah's 2Ch 22:8
from the king's **s** who were being 2Ch 22:11
promised concerning David's **s**. 2Ch 23:3
Jehoiada and his **s** anointed him 2Ch 23:11
the father of **s** and daughters. 2Ch 24:3
the **s** of that wicked Athaliah 2Ch 24:7
the blood of the **s** of Jehoiada 2Ch 24:25
Concerning his **s**, the many 2Ch 24:27
women, **s**, and daughters. 2Ch 28:8
sword, and our **s**, our daughters, 2Ch 29:9
s, don't be negligent now, for 2Ch 29:11
and your **s** ⌊will receive⌋ 2Ch 30:9
infants, wives, **s**, and daughters 2Ch 31:18
He passed his **s** through the fire 2Ch 33:6
to him and his **s** until the rise 2Ch 36:20
Jeshua with his **s** and brothers, Ezr 3:9
Kadmiel with his **s**, and the sons Ezr 3:9
and the **s** of Judah and of Ezr 3:9
with their **s** and brothers, Ezr 3:9
the life of the king and his **s**. Ezr 6:10
the realm of the king and his **s**. Ezr 7:23
along with his **s** and brothers, Ezr 8:18
and his brothers and their **s**, Ezr 8:19
for themselves and their **s**, Ezr 9:2
daughters to their **s** in marriage Ezr 9:12
take their daughters for your **s**. Ezr 9:12
inheritance to your **s** forever." Ezr 9:12
s of Hassenaah built the Fish Neh 3:3
your **s** and daughters, Neh 4:14
saying, "We, our **s**, and our Neh 5:2
subjecting our **s** and daughters Neh 5:5
Binnui of the **s** of Henadad, Neh 10:9
their wives, **s**, and daughters, Neh 10:28
daughters as wives for our **s**. Neh 10:30
firstborn of our **s** and our Neh 10:36
of the priests' **s** had trumpets: Neh 12:35
marriage to their **s** or take Neh 13:25
wives for your **s** or yourselves! Neh 13:25
Even one of the **s** of Jehoiada, Neh 13:28
glorious wealth and his many **s**. Est 5:11
killed these 10 **s** of Haman son Est 9:10
500 men, including Haman's 10 **s**. Est 9:12
bodies of⌋ Haman's 10 **s** be hung Est 9:13
the bodies of⌋ Haman's 10 **s**. Est 9:14
with his **s** on the gallows. Est 9:25
He had seven **s** and three Jb 1:2
His **s** used to have banquets, Jb 1:4
One day the **s** of God came to Jb 1:6
day when Job's **s** and daughters Jb 1:13
Your **s** and daughters were eating Jb 1:18
One day the **s** of God came again Jb 2:1
If his **s** receive honor, he does Jb 14:21
and all the **s** of God shouted for Jb 38:7
He also had seven **s** and three Jb 42:13
in store, their **s** are satisfied, Ps 17:14
Your **s** will succeed your Ps 45:16
and a foreigner to my mother's **s** Ps 69:8
you are all **s** of the Most High. Ps 82:6
lend support to the **s** of Lot. Ps 83:8
If his **s** forsake My instruction Ps 89:30
their **s** and daughters to Ps 106:37
blood of their **s** and daughters Ps 106:38
S are indeed a heritage from the Ps 127:3
warrior are the **s** born in one's Ps 127:4
your house, your **s**, like young Ps 128:3
your **s** keep My covenant and My Ps 132:12
their **s** will also sit on your Ps 132:12
Then our **s** will be like plants Ps 144:12
Listen, ⌊my⌋ **s**, to a father's Pr 4:1
now, ⌊my⌋ **s**, listen to me, and Pr 5:7
Now, ⌊my⌋ **s**, listen to me, and Pr 7:24
And now, ⌊my⌋ **s**, listen to me; Pr 8:32
the pride of **s** is their fathers Pr 17:6
Her **s** rise up and call her Pr 31:28
mother's **s** were angry with me; Sg 1:6
a place of slaughter for his **s**, Is 14:21
his **s** Adrammelech and Sharezer Is 37:38
Bring My **s** from far away, and My Is 43:6
Me what is to happen to My **s**, Is 45:11
will bring your **s** in their arms, Is 49:22
better than **s** and daughters. Is 56:5
come here, you **s** of a sorceress, Is 57:3
your **s** will come from far away, Is 60:4
The **s** of your oppressors will Is 60:14
so your **s** will marry you; Is 62:5
labor, she gave birth to her **s**. Is 66:8
to make you ⌊My⌋ **s** and give you Jr 3:19
their **s** and their daughters. Jr 3:24
will consume your **s** and your Jr 5:17
fathers and **s** together will Jr 6:21
The **s** gather wood, the fathers Jr 7:18
to burn their **s** and daughters Jr 7:31
My **s** have departed from me and Jr 10:20
their **s** and daughters will die Jr 11:22
other, fathers and **s** alike"— Jr 13:14
their wives, their **s**, and their Jr 14:16
not marry or have **s** or daughters Jr 16:2
says concerning **s** and daughters Jr 16:3
the flesh of their **s** and their Jr 19:9
wives and have **s** and daughters. Jr 29:6
wives for your **s** and give your Jr 29:6
they may bear **s** and daughters. Jr 29:6
ways of the **s** of men in order Jr 32:19
to make their **s** and daughters Jr 32:35
and his brothers and all his **s**— Jr 35:3
occupied by⌋ the **s** of Hanan son Jr 35:4
cups before the **s** of the house Jr 35:5
'You and your **s** must never drink Jr 35:6
our wives, our **s**, and our Jr 35:8
He commanded his **s** not to drink Jr 35:14
the **s** of Jonadab son of Rechab Jr 35:16
your wives and **s** will be brought Jr 38:23
Zedekiah's **s** before his eyes, Jr 39:6
and Jonathan the **s** of Kareah, Jr 40:8
the **s** of Ephai the Netophathite, Jr 40:8
will not turn back for their **s**, Jr 47:3
because your **s** have been taken Jr 48:46
Israel have no **s**? Is he without Jr 49:1
Zedekiah's **s** before his eyes Jr 52:10
eat ⌊their⌋ **s** within Jerusalem Ezk 5:10
and **s** will eat their fathers. Ezk 5:10
deliver ⌊their⌋ **s** or daughters. Ezk 14:16
deliver ⌊their⌋ **s** or daughters, Ezk 14:18
s and daughters who will be Ezk 14:22
even took your **s** and daughters Ezk 16:20
gave birth to **s** and daughters. Ezk 23:4
seized her **s** and daughters, Ezk 23:10
will seize your **s** and daughters, Ezk 23:25
will kill their **s** and daughters Ezk 23:47
the **s** and daughters you left Ezk 24:21
well as⌋ their **s** and daughters, Ezk 24:25
These are the **s** of Zadok, the Ezk 40:46
ones from the **s** of Levi who may Ezk 40:46
gift to each of his **s** as their Ezk 46:16
it will belong to his **s**. Ezk 46:16
belongs only to his **s**; Ezk 46:17
for his **s** from his own Ezk 46:18
priests, the **s** of Zadok, who Ezk 48:11
His **s** will mobilize for war and Dn 11:10
will be called: **S** of the living Hs 1:10
I will also forget your **s**. Hs 4:6
then your **s** and your daughters Jl 2:28
I will sell your **s** and daughters Jl 3:8
some of your **s** as prophets and Am 2:11
your **s** and daughters will fall Am 7:17
the king's **s**, and all who are Zph 1:8
will rouse your **s**, Zion, against Zch 9:13
Zion, against your **s**, Greece. Zch 9:13
will purify the **s** of Levi and Mal 3:3
they will be called **s** of God. Mt 5:9
that you may be **s** of your Father Mt 5:45
But the **s** of the kingdom will be Mt 8:12
who is it your **s** drive them out Mt 12:27
these are the **s** of the kingdom. Mt 13:38
weeds are the **s** of the evil one Mt 13:38
From their **s** or from strangers?" Mt 17:25
"Then the **s** are free," Jesus Mt 17:26
of Zebedee's **s** approached Him Mt 20:20
sons approached Him with her **s**. Mt 20:20
that these two **s** of mine may sit Mt 20:21
A man had two **s**. He went to Mt 21:28
that you are **s** of those who Mt 23:31
Peter and the two **s** of Zebedee, Mt 26:37

was set by the s of Israel, Mt 27:9
and the mother of Zebedee's s. Mt 27:56
that is, "S of Thunder"); Mk 3:17
and John, the s of Zebedee, Mk 10:35
turn many of the s of Israel to Lk 1:16
John, Zebedee's s, who were Lk 5:10
and you will be s of the Most Lk 6:35
who is it your s drive them out Lk 11:19
He also said: "A man had two s. Lk 15:11
For the s of this age are more Lk 16:8
astute than the s of light ⌊in Lk 16:8
The s of this age marry and are Lk 20:34
like angels and are s of God, Lk 20:36
since they are s of the Lk 20:36
as did his s and livestock." Jn 4:12
that you may become s of light." Jn 12:36
Zebedee's s, and two others Jn 21:2
then your s and your daughters Ac 2:17
are the s of the prophets and Ac 3:25
full Senate of the s of Israel— Ac 5:21
of silver from the s of Hamor in Ac 7:16
his brothers, the s of Israel. Ac 7:23
Midian, where he fathered two s. Ac 7:29
who said to the s of Israel, Ac 7:37
kings, and the s of Israel. Ac 9:15
the message to the s of Israel, Ac 10:36
Brothers, s of Abraham's race, Ac 13:26
Seven s of Sceva, a Jewish chief Ac 19:14
led by God's Spirit are God's s. Rm 8:14
for God's s to be revealed. Rm 8:19
will be called s of the living Rm 9:26
of Israel's s is like the sand Rm 9:27
so that the s of Israel were not 2Co 3:7
so that the s of Israel could 2Co 3:13
and you will be s and daughters 2Co 6:18
who have faith are Abraham's s. Gl 3:7
for you are all s of God through Gl 3:26
we might receive adoption as s. Gl 4:5
because you are s, God has sent Gl 4:6
written that Abraham had two s, Gl 4:22
For you are all s of light and 1Th 5:5
sons of light and s of the day. 1Th 5:5
in bringing many s to glory, Heb 2:10
The s of Levi who receive the Heb 7:5
blessed each of the s of Joseph, Heb 11:21
exodus of the s of Israel and Heb 11:22
that addresses you as s: Heb 12:5
God is dealing with you as s. Heb 12:7
illegitimate children and not s. Heb 12:8
in front of the s of Israel: Rv 2:14
every tribe of the s of Israel: Rv 7:4
12 tribes of the s of Israel. Rv 21:12

SONS' *(9)*
your wife, and your s wives. Gn 6:18
and his s wives entered the ark Gn 7:7
his three s wives entered the Gn 7:13
and your s wives with you. Gn 8:16
wife, and his s wives, came out Gn 8:18
on his s right earlobes, Ex 29:20
portion and your s from the fire Lv 10:13
and his s ⌊lot⌋ was the 1Ch 26:15
sins on their s laps after them, Jr 32:18

SONS-IN-LAW *(2)*
Lot went out and spoke to his s, Gn 19:14
But his s thought he was Gn 19:14

SOON *(65)*
(See pp. xi-xii.)

SOOT *(3)*
Take handfuls of furnace s, Ex 9:8
took furnace s and stood before Ex 9:10
⌊Now⌋ they appear darker than s; Lm 4:8

SOOTHED *(1)*
bandaged, or s with oil. Is 1:6

SOOTHES *(1)*
A secret gift s anger, and a Pr 21:14

SOPATER *(1)*
by S, son of Pyrrhus, Ac 20:4

SOPHERETH'S *(1)*
(AKA HASSOPHERETH'S)
descendants, S descendants, Neh 7:57

SORCERER *(3)*
came across a s, a Jewish false Ac 13:6
But Elymas, the s, which is how Ac 13:8
Spirit, stared straight at the s Ac 13:9

SORCERERS *(6)*
called the wise men and s— Ex 7:11
or your s who say to you: Jr 27:9
mediums, s, and Chaldeans to Dn 2:2
against s and adulterers; Mal 3:5
sexually immoral, s, idolaters, Rv 21:8
the dogs, the s, the sexually Rv 22:15

SORCERESS *(2)*
You must not allow a s to live. Ex 22:18
here, you sons of a s, offspring Is 57:3

SORCERIES *(5)*
of your many s and the potency Is 47:9
your spells and your many s, Is 47:12
I will remove s from your hands, Mc 5:12
them with his s for a long time. Ac 8:11
murders, their s, their sexual Rv 9:21

SORCERY *(7)*
not to practice divination or s. Lv 19:26
interpret omens, practice s, Dt 18:10
divination, and s, and consulted 2Ch 33:6
the attractive mistress of s, Nah 3:4
practiced s in that city Ac 8:9
idolatry, s, hatreds, strife, Gl 5:20
nations were deceived by your s, Rv 18:23

SORE *(1)*
has a running s, festering rash Lv 22:22

SOREK *(1)*
who lived in the S Valley. Jdg 16:4

SORES *(6)*
and festering s not cleansed, Is 1:6
takes up the case for your s. Jr 30:13
covered with s, was left at his Lk 16:20
dogs would come and lick his s. Lk 16:21
and severely painful s broke out Rv 16:2
of their pains and their s, Rv 16:11

SORREL *(1)*
him were red, s, and white Zch 1:8

SORROW *(32)*
gray hairs down to Sheol in s." Gn 42:38
gray hairs down to Sheol in s.' Gn 44:29
our father down to Sheol in s. Gn 44:31
to my s Rachel died along the Gn 48:7
month when their s was turned Est 9:22
womb, and hide s from my eyes. Jb 3:10
eyes are worn out from angry s— Ps 31:9
must I go about in s because of Ps 42:9
must I go about in s because of Ps 43:2
It is my s that the right hand Ps 77:10
best of them are struggle and s; Ps 90:10
by cruel oppression and s, Ps 107:39
I encountered trouble and s. Ps 116:3
man fathers a fool to his own s; Pr 17:21
has woe? Who has s? Who has Pr 23:29
For with much wisdom is much s; Ec 1:18
his days, with much s, sickness, Ec 5:17
Remove s from your heart, and Ec 11:10
and s and sighing will flee. Is 35:10
and s and sighing will flee. Is 51:11
the days of your s will be over. Is 60:20
to see ⌊only⌋ struggle and s, Jr 20:18
off your hair in s for your Mc 1:16
My soul is swallowed up in s— Mt 26:38
with anger and s at the hardness Mk 3:5
My soul is swallowed up in s— Mk 14:34
things to you, s has filled your Jn 16:6
but your s will turn to joy. Jn 16:20
So you also have s now. Jn 16:22
I have intense s and continual Rm 9:2
longing, your s, your zeal for 2Co 7:7
to mourning and your joy to s. Jms 4:9

SORROWFUL *(3)*
grief, and his occupation is s; Ec 2:23
He began to be s and deeply Mt 26:37
You will become s, but your Jn 16:20

SORROWS *(1)*
The s of those who take another Ps 16:4

SORRY *(1)*
She felt s for him and said, Ex 2:6

SORT *(6)*
What s of man came up to meet 2Kg 1:7
know the s and their ranting. 2Kg 9:11
signifying what s of death He Jn 18:32
What s of house will you build Ac 7:49
charge of the s I was expecting Ac 25:18
is clear⌋ what s of people you 2Pt 3:11

SORTS *(2)*
basket were all s of baked goods Gn 40:17
while all ⌊s of⌋ wild animals Jb 40:20

SOSIPATER *(1)*
Lucius, Jason, and S, my fellow Rm 16:21

SOSTHENES *(2)*
they all seized S, the leader Ac 18:17
God's will, and our brother S: 1Co 1:1

SOTAI'S *(2)*
S descendants, Hassophereth's Ezr 2:55
S descendants, Sophereth's Neh 7:57

SOUGHT *(37)*
him and s to put him to Ex 4:24
I haven't s the LORD's favor. 1Sm 13:12
So the king s advice. 1Kg 12:28
Jehoahaz s the LORD's favor, 2Kg 13:4
provisions and s many wives for 2Ch 11:23
ours because we s the LORD our 2Ch 14:7
We s Him and He gave us rest on 2Ch 14:7
in their distress and s Him, 2Ch 15:4
They had s Him with all their 2Ch 15:15
but s the God of his father and 2Ch 17:4
Jehoshaphat who s the LORD with 2Ch 22:9
Why have you s a people's gods 2Ch 25:15
He s God throughout the lifetime 2Ch 26:5
the time that he s the LORD, 2Ch 26:5
he s the favor of the LORD his 2Ch 33:12
insights as you s for words. Jb 32:11
I s favor from my Lord: Ps 30:8
I s the LORD, and He answered me Ps 34:4
my day of trouble I s the Lord. Ps 77:2
I have s You with all my heart; Ps 119:10
I have s Your favor with all my Ps 119:58
for I have s Your precepts. Ps 119:94
The Teacher s to find delightful Ec 12:10
bed at night I s the one I love; Sg 3:1
I s him, but did not find him. Sg 3:1
I s him, but did not find him. Sg 3:2
I s him, but did not find him. Sg 5:6
of Gebim have s refuge. Is 10:31
I was s by those who did not Is 65:1
for My people who have s Me. Is 65:10
You will be s but will never be Ezk 26:21
back the strays, or s the lost. Ezk 34:4
advisers and my nobles s me out, Dn 4:36
he wept and s His favor. Hs 12:4
those who s the child's life Mt 2:20
would have been s for a second Heb 8:7
though he s it with tears. Heb 12:17

SOUL *(52)*
all your heart and all your s. Dt 4:29
with all your s, and with all Dt 6:5
all your heart and all your s? Dt 10:12
all your heart and all your s, Dt 11:13
all your heart and all your s. Dt 13:3
all your heart and all your s. Dt 26:16
heart and all your s by doing Dt 30:2
all your heart and all your s, Dt 30:6
all your heart and all your s. Dt 30:10
all your heart and all your s." Jos 22:5
heart and all your s that none Jos 23:14
March on, my s, in strength! Jdg 5:21
and with all his s in order to 2Ch 34:31
in the bitterness of my s. Jb 7:11
speak in the bitterness of my s. Jb 10:1
person dies with a bitter s, Jb 21:25
Has my s not grieved for the Jb 30:25
God spares his s from the Pit, Jb 33:18
his s ⌊despises his⌋ favorite Jb 33:20
He redeemed my s from going Jb 33:28
LORD is perfect, reviving the s; Ps 19:7
Wake up, my s! Wake up, harp and Ps 57:8
in God alone, my s, for my hope Ps 62:5
My s, praise the LORD, and all Ps 103:1
s, praise the LORD, and do not Ps 103:2
He rules. My s, praise the LORD Ps 103:22
My s, praise the LORD! LORD my Ps 104:1
be no more. My s, praise the Ps 104:35
to your rest, my s, for the LORD Ps 116:7
Hallelujah! My s, praise the Ps 146:1
which my s continually searches Ec 7:28
of the bitterness of my s, Is 38:15
For you, my s, have heard the Jr 4:19
My s has been deprived of peace; Lm 3:17
but are not able to kill the s; Mt 10:28
to destroy both s and body in Mt 10:28
beloved in whom My s delights; Mt 12:18

with all your s, and with all Mt 22:37
My s is swallowed up in sorrow— Mt 26:38
with all your s, with all your Mk 12:30
My s is swallowed up in sorrow— Mk 14:34
My s proclaims the greatness of Lk 1:46
a sword will pierce your own s— Lk 2:35
with all your s, with all your Lk 10:27
Now My s is troubled. What Jn 12:27
will not leave my s in Hades, Ac 2:27
were of one heart and s, Ac 4:32
may your spirit, s, and body be 1Th 5:23
as far as to divide s, Heb 4:12
sure and firm anchor of the s— Heb 6:19
My s has no pleasure in him. Heb 10:38
health, just as your s prospers. 3Jn 2

SOULS *(7)*
of Mine on your hearts and s, Dt 11:18
watch over your s as those who Heb 13:17
faith, the salvation of your s. 1Pt 1:9
shepherd and guardian of your s. 1Pt 2:25
under the altar the s of those Rv 6:9
and human bodies and s. Rv 18:13
also ⌊saw⌋ the s of those who Rv 20:4

SOUND *(168)*
wife heard the s of the LORD God Gn 3:8
a loud trumpet s, so that all Ex 19:16
As the s of the trumpet grew Ex 19:19
lightning, the s of the trumpet, Ex 20:18
and its s will be heard when he Ex 28:35
heard the s of the people as Ex 32:17
There is a s of war in the camp. Ex 32:17
It's not the s of a victory cry Ex 32:18
cry and not the s of a cry of Ex 32:18
I hear the s of singing! Ex 32:18
Then you are to s a trumpet Lv 25:9
you will s it throughout your Lv 25:9
The s of a wind-driven leaf will Lv 26:36
When you s short blasts, the Nm 10:5
When you s short blasts a second Nm 10:6
you are to s long blasts, not Nm 10:7
priests, are to s the trumpets. Nm 10:8
s short blasts on the trumpets, Nm 10:9
You are to s the trumpets over Nm 10:10
kept hearing the s of the words, Dt 4:12
of the horn and you hear its s, Jos 6:5
heard the s of the war cry 1Sm 4:6
Then what is this s of sheep and 1Sm 15:14
I s out my father by this time 1Sm 20:12
When you hear the s of marching 2Sm 5:24
shouts and the s of the ram's 2Sm 6:15
you hear the s of the ram's horn 2Sm 15:10
the earth split open from the s. 1Kg 1:40
Joab heard the s of the ram's 1Kg 1:41
Ahijah heard the s of her feet 1Kg 14:6
there was no s; no one answered 1Kg 18:26
there was no s, no one answered 1Kg 18:29
there is the s of a rainstorm. 1Kg 18:41
there was no s or sign of life 2Kg 4:31
Isn't the s of his master's feet 2Kg 6:32
camp to hear the s of chariots, 2Kg 7:6
When you hear the s of marching 1Ch 14:15
and Ethan were to s the bronze 1Ch 15:19
with shouts, the s of the ram's 1Ch 15:28
ready to s the charge against 2Ch 13:12
distinguish the s of the joyful Ezr 3:13
And the s was heard far away. Ezr 3:13
Wherever you hear the trumpet s, Neh 4:20
My teaching is s, and I am pure Jb 11:4
rejoicing at the s of the flute. Jb 21:12
my flute for the s of weeping. Jb 30:31
Then there comes a roaring s; Jb 37:4
stand still at the trumpet's s. Jb 39:24
attention to the s of my cry, Ps 5:2
has heard the s of my weeping. Ps 6:8
Listen to the s of my pleading Ps 28:2
has heard the s of my pleading. Ps 28:6
You heard the s of my pleading Ps 31:22
LORD, amid the s of trumpets. Ps 47:5
listen to the s of the charmers Ps 58:5
the s of His praise be heard. Ps 66:8
attention to the s of my prayer. Ps 66:19
The s of Your thunder was in the Ps 77:18
Because of the s of my groaning, Ps 102:5
at the s of Your thunder they Ps 104:7
cannot make a s with their Ps 115:7
rebels against all s judgment. Pr 18:1
and wage war with s guidance. Pr 20:18
wage war with s guidance— Pr 24:6
shut while the s of the mill Ec 12:4
one rises at the s of a bird, Ec 12:4
heart is awake. A s! My love is Sg 5:2
shook at the s of their voices, Is 6:4
moan like ⌊the s of⌋ a lyre for Is 16:11
flees at the s of terror will Is 24:18
to you at the s of your cry; Is 30:19
be ⌊to the s⌋ of tambourines Is 30:32
The s of weeping and crying will Is 65:19
A s of uproar from the city! Is 66:6
A s is heard on the barren Jr 3:21
have heard the s of the ram's Jr 4:19
and hear the s of the ram's horn Jr 4:21
flees at the s of the horseman Jr 4:29
S the ram's horn in Tekoa; Jr 6:1
Listen for the s of the ram's Jr 6:17
of Jerusalem the s of joy and Jr 7:34
At the s of the neighing of Jr 8:16
The s of cattle is no longer Jr 9:10
For a s of lamentation is heard Jr 9:19
consumed with a great roaring s. Jr 11:16
the s of joy and gladness, Jr 16:9
will eliminate the s of joy and Jr 25:10
the s of the millstones and the Jr 25:10
⌊Hear⌋ the s of the shepherds' Jr 25:36
out of them, a s of celebration. Jr 30:19
a s of joy and gladness, the Jr 33:11
war or hear the s of the ram's Jr 42:14
At the s of the stomping hooves Jr 47:3
At the s of their fall the earth Jr 49:21
the s of her cry will be heard Jr 49:21
The s of war is in the land— Jr 50:22
At the s of Babylon's conquest Jr 50:46
The s of a cry from Babylon! Jr 51:54
The s of great destruction from Jr 51:54
heard the s of their wings like Ezk 1:24
and a s of commotion like the Ezk 1:24
a great rumbling s behind me— Ezk 3:12
the s of the living creatures' Ezk 3:13
other and the s of the wheels Ezk 3:13
beside them, a great rumbling s. Ezk 3:13
The s of the cherubim's wings Ezk 10:5
at the s of his roaring. Ezk 19:7
The s of a carefree crowd was Ezk 23:42
and the s of your lyres will no Ezk 26:13
quake at the s of your downfall, Ezk 26:15
shakes at the s of your sailors' Ezk 27:28
quake at the s of its downfall, Ezk 31:16
hears the s of the trumpet Ezk 33:4
he heard the s of the trumpet Ezk 33:5
a rattling s, and the bones Ezk 37:7
When you hear the s of the horn, Dn 3:5
people heard the s of the horn, Dn 3:7
who hears the s of the horn, Dn 3:10
when you hear the s of the horn, Dn 3:15
because of the s of the arrogant Dn 7:11
and the s of his words like the Dn 10:6
words like the s of a multitude. Dn 10:6
s the alarm on My holy mountain! Jl 2:1
Their s is like the sound of Jl 2:5
sound is like the s of chariots, Jl 2:5
like the s of fiery flames Jl 2:5
shouting and the s of the ram's Am 2:2
songs to the s of the harp and Am 6:5
What are you doing s asleep? Jnh 1:6
moan like the s of doves, Nah 2:7
the s of your messengers will Nah 2:13
my lips quivered at the s. Hab 3:16
calls will s from the window, Zph 2:14
The Lord GOD will s the trumpet Zch 9:14
don't s a trumpet before you, Mt 6:2
when the s of your greeting Lk 1:44
he has him back safe and s.' Lk 15:27
you hear its s, but you don't Jn 3:8
Suddenly a s like that of a Ac 2:2
When this s occurred, the Ac 2:6
hearing the s but seeing no one. Ac 9:7
and to hear the s of His voice. Ac 22:14
the trumpet makes an unclear s, 1Co 14:8
the trumpet will s, and the dead 1Co 15:52
if we have a s mind, it is for 2Co 5:13
and body be kept s and blameless 1Th 5:23
is contrary to the s teaching 1Tm 1:10
agree with the s teaching of our 1Tm 6:3
of power, love, and s judgment. 2Tm 1:7
the pattern of s teaching that 2Tm 1:13
will not tolerate s doctrine, 2Tm 4:3
encourage with s teaching and to Ti 1:9
that they may be s in the faith Ti 1:13
is consistent with s teaching. Ti 2:1
sensible, and s in faith, love, Ti 2:2
is to be s beyond reproach Ti 2:8
a trumpet, and the s of words. Heb 12:19
voice like the s of cascading Rv 1:15
three angels are about to s!" Rv 8:13
s of their wings was like the Rv 9:9
was like the s of chariots with Rv 9:9
the days of the s of the seventh Rv 10:7
I heard a s from heaven like the Rv 14:2
heaven like the s of cascading Rv 14:2
The s I heard was also like Rv 14:2
The s of harpists, musicians, Rv 18:22
the s of a mill will never be Rv 18:22
like the s of cascading waters, Rv 19:6

SOUNDED *(9)*
When both are s in long blasts, Nm 10:3
if one is s, only the leaders Nm 10:4
are to be s for them to set Nm 10:6
shouted, and the trumpets s. Jos 6:20
he s the ram's horn throughout Jdg 3:27
while Asaph ⌊s⌋ the cymbals 1Ch 16:5
His voice s like the roar of Ezk 43:2
a little farther and s again, Ac 27:28
a lamb, but he s like a dragon. Rv 13:11

SOUNDING *(2)*
They took a s and found it to be Ac 27:28
I am a s gong or a clanging 1Co 13:1

SOUNDNESS *(1)*
There is no s in my body because Ps 38:3

SOUNDS *(7)*
the ram's horn s a long blast, Ex 19:13
answered, "That ⌊s⌋ good." 1Kg 18:24
no one was there—no human s. 2Kg 7:10
Dreadful s fill his ears; Jb 15:21
When a trumpet s, listen! Is 18:3
what you say s strange to us, Ac 17:20
inanimate things producing s— 1Co 14:7

SOUR *(9)*
The fathers have eaten s grapes, Jr 31:29
Anyone who eats s grapes— Jr 31:30
fathers eat s grapes, and the Ezk 18:2
filled it with s wine, fixed it Mt 27:48
and filled a sponge with s wine, Mk 15:36
They came offering Him s wine Lk 23:36
A jar full of s wine was sitting Jn 19:29
sponge full of s wine on hyssop Jn 19:29
Jesus had received the s wine, Jn 19:30

SOURCE *(19)*
and became the s of four rivers. Gn 2:10
has exposed the s of her ⌊flow⌋, Lv 20:18
uncovered the s of her blood. Lv 20:18
His s of confidence is fragile; Jb 8:14
Its rocks are a s of sapphire, Jb 28:6
⌊Where is the s of⌋ the east Jb 38:24
a s of mockery and ridicule to Ps 44:13
a s of mockery and ridicule to Ps 79:4
they make it a s of springwater; Ps 84:6
else, for it is the s of life. Pr 4:23
bow, the s of their might. Jr 49:35
His water s will fail, and his Hs 13:15
were her endless s of strength; Nah 3:9
And you killed the s of life, Ac 3:15
it from a human s and I was not Gl 1:12
should make the s of their Heb 2:10
He became the s of eternal Heb 5:9
s and perfecter of our faith, Heb 12:2
What is the s of the wars and Jms 4:1

SOURCES *(4)*
that day all the s of the watery Gn 7:11
The s of the watery depths and Gn 8:2
deep water s, flowing in both Dt 8:7
you traveled to the s of the sea Jb 38:16

SOUTH *(114)*
Look north and s, east and west, Gn 13:14
the east, the north, and the s. Gn 28:14
under the oak s of Bethel. Gn 35:8
20 planks for the s side, Ex 26:18
the lampstand on the s side of Ex 26:35
on the s of the courtyard Ex 27:9
as follows: 20 for the s side, Ex 36:23
hangings on the s side of the Ex 38:9
the table on the s side of the Ex 40:24
camp on the s side under their Nm 2:10
camped on the s side of the Nm 3:29

pitched on the **s** are to set out. Nm 10:6
border will turn **s** of the Ascent Nm 34:4
and end **s** of Kadesh-barnea. Nm 34:4
1,000 yards for the **s** side, Nm 35:5
west, north, **s**, and east, and Dt 3:27
to the west and the **s**. Dt 33:23
the plain **s** of Chinnereth, Jos 11:2
in the **s**; all the land of the Jos 13:4
s of the wilderness of Zin to Jos 15:1
tip of the Dead Sea on the **s** bay Jos 15:2
and went **s** of the ascent of Jos 15:3
ascended to the **s** of Jos 15:3
which is **s** of the ravine. Jos 15:7
s of the brook, cities belonged Jos 17:9
was to the **s** and Manasseh's to Jos 17:10
in its territory in the **s**, Jos 18:5
over the hill **s** of Lower Jos 18:13
hill facing Beth-horon on the **s**, Jos 18:14
The **s** side began at the edge of Jos 18:15
toward the **s** Jebusite slope Jos 18:16
Baalath-beer (Ramah of the **s**). Jos 19:8
reaching Zebulun on the **s**, Jos 19:34
to Shechem, and **s** of Lebonah." Jdg 21:19
other to the **s** in front of Geba 1Sm 14:5
got up from the **s** side of the 1Sm 20:41
hill of Hachilah **s** of Jeshimon. 1Sm 23:19
in the Arabah **s** of Jeshimon, 1Sm 23:24
"The **s** country of Judah," 1Sm 27:10
The **s** country of the 1Sm 27:10
or "Against the **s** country of 1Sm 27:10
We raided the **s** country of the 1Sm 30:14
and the **s** country of Caleb, 1Sm 30:14
s of the town in the middle of 2Sm 24:5
three facing **s**, and three facing 1Kg 7:25
to the **s** of the Mount of 2Kg 23:13
east, west, north, and **s**. 1Ch 9:24
Obed-edom's was the **s** ⌊gate⌋, 1Ch 26:15
each day on the **s**, and two pair 1Ch 26:17
three facing **s**, and three facing 2Ch 4:4
when He turns **s**, I cannot find Jb 23:9
hot when the **s** wind brings calm Jb 37:17
and spread its wings to the **s**? Jb 39:26
and drove the **s** wind by His Ps 78:26
North and **s**—You created them. Ps 89:12
west, from the north and the **s**. Ps 107:3
Gusting to the **s**, turning to the Ec 1:6
falls to the **s** or the north, Ec 11:3
north wind—come, **s** wind. Sg 4:16
up! and to the **s**: Do not hold Is 43:6
from the north ⌊to the **s**⌋." Jr 1:13
standing to the **s** of the temple Ezk 10:3
her daughters to the **s** of you. Ezk 16:46
the **s** and preach against it. Ezk 20:46
from the **s** to the north will Ezk 20:47
from the **s** to the north. Ezk 21:4
He brought me to the **s** side, Ezk 40:24
there was also a gate on the **s**. Ezk 40:24
inner court had a gate on the **s**. Ezk 40:27
from gate to gate on the **s**; Ezk 40:27
inner court through the **s** gate. Ezk 40:28
When he measured the **s** gate, Ezk 40:28
gate, facing **s**, and another Ezk 40:44
and another beside the **s** gate, Ezk 40:44
that faces **s** is for the priests Ezk 40:45
the north and another to the **s**. Ezk 41:11
wall of the court toward the **s**, Ezk 42:10
that were on the **s** side. Ezk 42:12
He measured the **s** side; Ezk 42:18
go out by way of the **s** gate, Ezk 46:9
by way of the **s** gate must go out Ezk 46:9
down from under the **s** side ⌊of Ezk 47:1
of the temple, **s** of the altar. Ezk 47:1
was trickling from the **s** side. Ezk 47:2
On the **s** side it will run from Ezk 47:19
a half ⌊miles⌋ on the **s** side; Ezk 48:16
feet⌋ to the **s**, 425 ⌊feet⌋ to Ezk 48:17
of Gad toward the **s** side, Ezk 48:28
the **s** side, which measures one Ezk 48:33
the west, the north, and the **s**. Dn 8:4
toward the **s** and the east Dn 8:9
The king of the **S** will grow Dn 11:5
of the king of the **S** will go to Dn 11:6
the place of the king of the **S**, Dn 11:7
king of the **S** and then return Dn 11:9
the king of the **S** will march out Dn 11:11
up against the king of the **S**. Dn 11:14
forces of the **S** will not stand; Dn 11:15
against the king of the **S**. Dn 11:25
The king of the **S** will prepare Dn 11:25
he will come again to the **S**, Dn 11:29
king of the **S** will engage him Dn 11:40
are going to the land of the **s**." Zch 6:6
to the north and half to the **s**. Zch 14:4
Geba to Rimmon **s** of Jerusalem Zch 14:10
queen of the **s** will rise up at Mt 12:42
queen of the **s** will rise up at Lk 11:31
And when the **s** wind is blowing, Lk 12:55
from north and **s**, and recline at Lk 13:29
Get up and go **s** to the road that Ac 8:26
sailed along the **s** side of Crete Ac 27:7
When a gentle **s** wind sprang up, Ac 27:13
one day a **s** wind sprang up, Ac 28:13
gates on the **s**, and three gates Rv 21:13

SOUTHEAST *(2)*

side of the temple toward the **s**. 1Kg 7:39
on the right side, toward the **s**. 2Ch 4:10

SOUTHERN *(16)*

Your **s** side will be from the Nm 34:3
Your **s** border on the east will Nm 34:3
Their **s** border began at the tip Jos 15:2
This is your **s** border. Jos 15:4
Hinnom to the **s** Jebusite slope Jos 15:8
Luz, to the **s** slope of Luz (that Jos 18:13
at the **s** end of the Jordan. Jos 18:19
This was the **s** border. Jos 18:19
the constellations of the **s** sky. Jb 9:9
On its **s** ⌊slope⌋ was a structure Ezk 40:2
The northern and **s** chambers that Ezk 42:13
This will be the **s** side. Ezk 47:19
the ⌊**s**⌋ border up to a point Ezk 47:20
miles⌋ long on the **s** side. Ezk 48:10
and when the **s** region and the Zch 7:7
and advance with the **s** storms. Zch 9:14

SOUTHERNMOST *(1)*

their clans was in the **s** region, Jos 15:1

SOUTHWARD *(3)*

and **s** below the slopes Jos 12:3
It then went **s** toward the Jos 17:7
curved, turning **s**, and ended at Jos 18:14

SOUTHWEST *(1)*

open to the **s** and northwest, Ac 27:12

SOVEREIGN *(1)*

⌊He is⌋ the blessed and only **S**, 1Tm 6:15

SOVEREIGNTY *(5)*

his **s** and royal power 2Ch 12:1
God of heaven has given you **s**, Dn 2:37
High God gave **s**, greatness, Dn 5:18
s will come to Daughter Mc 4:8
of justice and **s** stem from Hab 1:7

SOW *(42)*

seed for you. **S** it in the land. Gn 47:23
S your land for six years and Ex 23:10
from what you **s** in the field, Ex 23:16
s your fields with two kinds of Lv 19:19
You may **s** your field for six Lv 25:3
you are not to **s** your field or Lv 25:4
are not to **s**, reap what grows Lv 25:11
year if we don't **s** or gather our Lv 25:20
When you **s** in the eighth year, Lv 25:22
You will **s** your seed in vain Lv 26:16
to the seed needed to **s** it, Lv 27:16
You will **s** much seed in the Dt 28:38
in the third year **s** and reap, 2Kg 19:29
and those who **s** trouble reap the Jb 4:8
s fields and plant vineyards Ps 107:37
Those who **s** in tears will reap Ps 126:5
who watches the wind will not **s**, Ec 11:4
In the morning **s** your seed, Ec 11:6
scatter cumin and **s** black cumin? Is 28:25
Happy are you who **s** seed beside Is 32:20
in the third year **s** and reap, Is 37:30
seed to **s** and food to eat, Is 55:10
do not **s** among the thorns. Jr 4:3
when I will **s** the house of Jr 31:27
build a house or **s** seed or plant Jr 35:7
I will **s** her in the land for Hs 2:23
they **s** the wind and reap the Hs 8:7
S righteousness for yourselves Hs 10:12
You will **s** but not reap; Mc 6:15
For they will **s** in peace: Zch 8:12
Though I **s** them among the Zch 10:9
they don't **s** or reap or gather Mt 6:26
the sower who went out to **s**. Mt 13:3
didn't you **s** good seed in your Mt 13:27
the sower who went out to **s**. Mk 4:3
A sower went out to **s** his seed. Lk 8:5
they don't **s** or reap; they Lk 12:24
and reap what you didn't **s**.' Lk 19:21
and reaping what I didn't **s**, Lk 19:22
What you **s** does not come to life 1Co 15:36
as for what you **s**—you are not 1Co 15:37
vomit, and, "a **s**, after washing 2Pt 2:22

SOWED *(9)*

Isaac **s** seed in that land, Gn 26:12
where you **s** your seed and Dt 11:10
the city and **s** it with salt. Jdg 9:45
to a man who **s** good seed in his Mt 13:24
enemy came, **s** weeds among the Mt 13:25
a man took and **s** in his field. Mt 13:31
the enemy who **s** them is the Mt 13:39
As he **s**, this occurred: Mk 4:4
a man took and **s** in his garden. Lk 13:19

SOWER *(9)*

Cut off the **s** from Babylon as Jr 50:16
treads grapes, the **s** of seed. Am 9:13
Consider the **s** who went out to Mt 13:3
listen to the parable of the **s**: Mt 13:18
Consider the **s** who went out to Mk 4:3
The **s** sows the word. Mk 4:14
A **s** went out to sow his seed. Lk 8:5
so the **s** and reaper can rejoice Jn 4:36
for the **s** and bread for food 2Co 9:10

SOWING *(4)*

will continue until **s** time; Lv 26:5
As he was **s**, some seeds fell Mt 13:4
As he was **s**, some fell along the Lk 8:5
you are not **s** the future body, 1Co 15:37

SOWN *(35)*

a hundred times ⌊what was **s**⌋. Gn 26:12
on any seed that is to be **s**, Lv 11:37
to a place not tilled or **s**, Dt 21:4
someone else eat what I have **s**, Jb 31:8
that you have **s** in the ground, Is 30:23
planted, barely **s**, their stem Is 40:24
enables what is **s** to spring up, Is 61:11
the wilderness, in a land not **s**. Jr 2:2
They have **s** wheat but harvested Jr 12:13
and you will be tilled and **s**. Ezk 36:9
and some 30 times ⌊what was **s**⌋. Mt 13:8
away what was **s** in his heart. Mt 13:19
is the one **s** along the path. Mt 13:19
And the one **s** on rocky ground— Mt 13:20
Now the one **s** among the thorns— Mt 13:22
But the one **s** on the good ground Mt 13:23
some 30 times ⌊what was **s**⌋." Mt 13:23
you haven't **s** and gathering Mt 25:24
where I haven't **s** and gather Mt 25:26
and 100 times ⌊what was **s**⌋." Mk 4:8
the path where the word is **s**: Mk 4:15
takes away the word **s** in them. Mk 4:15
are the ones **s** on rocky ground: Mk 4:16
Others are **s** among thorns; Mk 4:18
the ones **s** on good ground are Mk 4:20
and 100 times ⌊what was **s**⌋." Mk 4:20
seed that, when **s** in the soil, Mk 4:31
when **s**, it comes up and grows Mk 4:32
100 times ⌊what was **s**⌋." Lk 8:8
we have **s** spiritual things for 1Co 9:11
S in corruption, raised in 1Co 15:42
s in dishonor, raised in glory; 1Co 15:43
s in weakness, raised in power; 1Co 15:43
s a natural body, raised a 1Co 15:44
righteousness is **s** in peace by Jms 3:18

SOWS *(10)*

but the one who **s** righteousness, Pr 11:18
one who **s** injustice will reap Pr 22:8
The One who **s** the good seed is Mt 13:37
The sower **s** the word. Mk 4:14
'One **s** and another reaps.' Jn 4:37
the person who **s** sparingly will 2Co 9:6
the person who **s** generously will 2Co 9:6
whatever a man **s** he will also Gl 6:7
the one who **s** to his flesh will Gl 6:8
but the one who **s** to the Spirit Gl 6:8

SPACE *(12)*

a considerable **s** between them. 1Sm 26:13
each had **s**, with encircling 1Kg 7:36
northern ⌊skies⌋ over empty **s**; Jb 26:7
and there was ⌊a **s** of⌋ eight and Ezk 40:7
free **s** between the side rooms Ezk 41:9
rooms opened into the free **s**, Ezk 41:11

The area of free s was eight and Ezk 41:11
the 35 ⌊foot s⌋ belonging to Ezk 42:3
took away more s from them than Ezk 42:5
feet of open s all around it. Ezk 45:2
both⌋ residential and open s. Ezk 48:15
The city's open s will extend: Ezk 48:17

SPACES *(2)*
He named it Open S and said, Gn 26:22
the earth's open s to seize Hab 1:6

SPACIOUS *(7)*
that land to a good and s land, Ex 3:8
was large and s, but there were Neh 7:4
in the s and fertile land You Neh 9:35
distress to a s and unconfined Jb 36:16
have set my feet in a s place. Ps 31:8
me ⌊and put me⌋ in a s place. Ps 118:5
palace, with s upper rooms. Jr 22:14

SPAIN *(2)*
whenever I travel to S. Rm 15:24
I will go by way of you to S. Rm 15:28

SPAN *(5)*
and his life s was 147 years. Gn 47:28
and my life s as nothing in Your Ps 39:5
his years s many generations. Ps 61:6
years—the life s of one king. Is 23:15
with the s ⌊of his hand⌋? Is 40:12

SPARE *(35)*
I will s the whole place for Gn 18:26
do not s ⌊him⌋ or shield him. Dt 13:8
that you will s the lives of my Jos 2:13
not s us today, if ⌊it was⌋ in Jos 22:22
have. Do not s them. Kill men 1Sm 15:3
Perhaps he will s your life." 1Kg 20:31
says, 'Please s my life.' " 1Kg 20:32
He didn't s any of them. 2Kg 10:14
is pleased, s my life—[this Est 7:3
and [s] my people—[this is] my Est 7:3
in your power; only s his life." Jb 2:6
S him from going down to the Jb 33:24
He did not s them from death, Ps 78:50
take vengeance; I will s no one. Is 47:3
he won't s them or show pity or Jr 21:7
Do not s an arrow, for she has Jr 50:14
Don't s her young men; Jr 51:3
Yes, I will not s ⌊you⌋. Ezk 5:11
on you with pity or s ⌊you⌋, Ezk 7:4
on ⌊you⌋ with pity or s ⌊you⌋. Ezk 7:9
will not show pity or s ⌊them⌋. Ezk 8:18
do not show pity or s ⌊them⌋! Ezk 9:5
will not show pity or s ⌊them⌋. Ezk 9:10
But I will s a few of them from Ezk 12:16
not die and s those who should Ezk 13:19
I will no longer s them: Am 7:8
I will no longer s them. Am 8:2
He did not even s His own Son, Rm 8:32
For if God did not s the natural Rm 11:21
He will not s you either. Rm 11:21
life, and I am trying to s you. 1Co 7:28
it was to s you that I did not 2Co 1:23
But I will s you, so that no one 2Co 12:6
if God didn't s the angels who 2Pt 2:4
and if He didn't s the ancient 2Pt 2:5

SPARED *(11)*
life will be s on your account. Gn 12:13
Egyptians and s our homes.' " Ex 12:27
But Joshua s Rahab the Jos 6:25
Saul and the troops s Agag, 1Sm 15:9
Amalekites and s the best sheep 1Sm 15:15
David s Mephibosheth, the son of 2Sm 21:7
the evil man is s from the day Jb 21:30
You s me from among those going Ps 30:3
remains and is s will die of Ezk 6:12
I s them from destruction and Ezk 20:17
for His land and s His people. Jl 2:18

SPARES *(1)*
God s his soul from the Pit, Jb 33:18

SPARING *(4)*
away instead of s the place for Gn 18:24
for the old and not s the young. Dt 28:50
rescue ⌊it⌋, by s ⌊it⌋, He will Is 31:5
in among you, not s the flock. Ac 20:29

SPARINGLY *(2)*
person who sows s will also reap 2Co 9:6
sows sparingly will also reap s, 2Co 9:6

SPARK *(1)*
become tinder, and his work a s; Is 1:31

SPARKLING *(4)*
your gates of s stones, and all Is 54:12
s like the gleam of polished Ezk 1:7
in a crown, s over His land. Zch 9:16
of living water, s like crystal, Rv 22:1

SPARKS *(2)*
as surely as s fly upward. Jb 5:7
from his mouth; fiery s fly out! Jb 41:19

SPARROW *(2)*
Even a s finds a home, and a Ps 84:3
a flitting s or a fluttering Pr 26:2

SPARROWS *(4)*
Aren't two s sold for a penny? Mt 10:29
you are worth more than many s. Mt 10:31
Aren't five s sold for two Lk 12:6
you are worth more than many s! Lk 12:7

SPARSE *(1)*
the hair in it is yellow and s, Lv 13:30

SPATTERED *(1)*
their blood s My garments, Is 63:3

SPATTERS *(1)*
any of its blood s on a garment, Lv 6:27

SPEAK *(343)*
have ventured to s to the Lord— Gn 18:27
be angry, and I will s further. Gn 18:30
have ventured to s to the Lord, Gn 18:31
and I will s one more time. Gn 18:32
So Laban said, "S on." Gn 24:33
Hamor came to s with Jacob. Gn 34:6
to s peaceably to him. Gn 37:4
your servant s personally to my Gn 44:18
I will help you s and I will Ex 4:12
I know that he can s well. Ex 4:14
You will s with him and tell him Ex 4:15
help both you and him ⌊to s⌋, Ex 4:15
He will s to the people for you. Ex 4:16
to Pharaoh to s in Your name he Ex 5:23
will hear when I s with you and Ex 19:9
You s to us, and we will listen, Ex 20:19
but don't let God s to us, Ex 20:19
I will s with you from there Ex 25:22
I will meet you to s with you. Ex 29:42
the LORD⌋ would s with Moses. Ex 33:9
before the LORD to s with Him, Ex 34:34
he went to s with the LORD. Ex 34:35
S to the Israelites and tell Lv 1:2
a person may s rashly in an oath Lv 5:4
S to the Israelites and tell Lv 15:2
S to Aaron, his sons, and all Lv 17:2
S to the Israelites and tell Lv 18:2
S to the entire Israelite Lv 19:2
S to Aaron's sons, the priests, Lv 21:1
S to Aaron, his sons, and all Lv 22:18
S to the Israelites and tell Lv 23:2
S to the Israelites and tell Lv 23:10
S to the Israelites and tell Lv 25:2
S to the Israelites and tell Lv 27:2
S to the Israelites and tell Nm 5:12
S to the Israelites and tell Nm 6:2
of meeting to s with the LORD, Nm 7:89
S to Aaron and tell him: Nm 8:2
come down and s with you there. Nm 11:17
Does the LORD s only through Nm 12:2
Does He not also s through us?" Nm 12:2
I s with him in a dream. Nm 12:6
I s with him directly, openly, Nm 12:8
you not afraid to s against My Nm 12:8
S to the Israelites and tell Nm 15:2
S to the Israelites and tell Nm 15:18
S to the Israelites and tell Nm 15:38
S to the Israelites and take one Nm 17:2
S to the Levites and tell them: Nm 18:26
Aaron are to s to the rock while Nm 20:8
I must s only the message God Nm 22:38
He s and not act, or promise Nm 23:19
S to the Israelites and tell Nm 35:10
Do not s to Me again about this Dt 3:26
who dares to s in My name a Dt 18:20
I have not commanded him to s, Dt 18:20
will summon him and s with him. Dt 25:8
continued to s these words to Dt 31:1
so that I may s these words Dt 31:28
heavens, and I will s; Dt 32:1
let me s one more time. Jdg 6:39
Please s in the presence of all Jdg 9:2
went after her to s kindly to Jdg 19:3
it over, discuss it, and s up!" Jdg 19:30
you, say, 'S, LORD, for Your 1Sm 3:9
responded, "S, for Your servant 1Sm 3:10
S to David in private and tell 1Sm 18:22
your servant s to you directly 1Sm 25:24
messengers to s to Abigail about 1Sm 25:39
as if to s to him privately, 2Sm 3:27
Please, s to the king, for he 2Sm 13:13
to the king and s these words to 2Sm 14:3
may your servant s a word to my 2Sm 14:12
lord the king?" "S," he replied. 2Sm 14:12
thought: I must s to the king. 2Sm 14:15
"Let my lord the king s," 2Sm 14:18
we the first to s of restoring 2Sm 19:43
here and let me s with him." 2Sm 20:16
Please s to King Solomon since 1Kg 2:17
"I will s to the king for you." 1Kg 2:18
King Solomon to s to him about 1Kg 2:19
like theirs, and s favorably." 1Kg 22:13
the LORD leave me to s to you?" 1Kg 22:24
Can ⌊we⌋ s on your behalf to the 2Kg 4:13
the words you s in your bedroom. 2Kg 6:12
Please s to your servants in 2Kg 18:26
Don't s with us in Hebrew within 2Kg 18:26
and to you to s these words? 2Kg 18:27
like theirs, and s favorably." 2Ch 18:12
the LORD leave me to s to you?" 2Ch 18:23
women still s of Josiah in their 2Ch 35:25
peoples but could not s Hebrew. Neh 13:24
own house and s in the language Est 1:22
people and to s for the welfare Est 10:3
You s as a foolish woman speaks, Jb 2:10
this Job began to s and cursed Jb 3:1
anyone try to s with you when Jb 4:2
I will s in the anguish of my Jb 7:11
and tell you and s from their Jb 8:10
Then I would s and not fear Him. Jb 9:35
my complaint and s in the Jb 10:1
only God would s and declare His Jb 11:5
Or s to the earth, and it will Jb 12:8
I prefer to s to the Almighty Jb 13:3
God's behalf or s deceitfully Jb 13:7
Be quiet, and I will s. Jb 13:13
answer, or I will s, and You can Jb 13:22
Even if I s, my suffering is not Jb 16:6
Bear with me while I s; Jb 21:3
Who did you s these words to? Jb 26:4
my lips will not s unjustly, Jb 27:4
from me they did not s again; Jb 29:22
had waited to s to Job because Jb 32:4
that age should s and maturity Jb 32:7
and my spirit compels me ⌊to s⌋. Jb 32:18
I must s so that I can find Jb 32:20
my lips s what they know with Jb 33:3
Be quiet, and I will s. Jb 33:31
s, for I would like to justify Jb 33:32
He be told that I want to s? Jb 37:20
Can a man s when he is confused? Jb 37:20
for mercy or s softly to you? Jb 41:3
"Listen now, and I will s. Jb 42:4
they s with flattering lips and Ps 12:2
I will not s their names with Ps 16:4
their mouths s arrogantly. Ps 17:10
s in friendly ways with their Ps 28:3
they s arrogantly against the Ps 31:18
For they do not s in friendly Ps 35:20
were to report and s ⌊of them⌋, Ps 40:5
My enemies s maliciously about Ps 41:5
Listen, My people, and I will s; Ps 50:7
Do you really s righteously, Ps 58:1
mock, and they s maliciously; Ps 73:8
heaven or s arrogantly.' " Ps 75:5
I am troubled and cannot s. Ps 77:4
I will s mysteries from the past Ps 78:2
they s against me with lying Ps 109:2
to those who s evil against me. Ps 109:20
but cannot s, eyes, but cannot Ps 115:5
I will s of Your decrees before Ps 119:46
but when I s, they are for war. Ps 120:7
shame when they s with ⌊their⌋ Ps 127:5
but cannot s, eyes, but cannot Ps 135:16
whose mouths s lies, whose right Ps 144:8
foreigners whose mouths s lies, Ps 144:11
I will s of Your glorious Ps 145:5
They will s of the glory of Your Ps 145:11
let your mouth s dishonestly, Pr 4:24
Listen, for I s of noble things, Pr 8:6
who listens will s successfully. Pr 21:28

Don't **s** to a fool, for he will Pr 23:9
S up for those who have no voice, Pr 31:8
S up, judge righteously, and Pr 31:9
is unable to **s**. The eye is not Ec 1:8
to be silent and a time to **s**; Ec 3:7
not be hasty to **s**, and do not be Ec 5:2
If they do not **s** according to Is 8:20
of Egypt will **s** the language Is 19:18
So He will **s** to this people with Is 28:11
you will **s** from the ground, Is 29:4
tongue will **s** clearly and Is 32:4
Please **s** to your servants in Is 36:11
don't **s** to us in Hebrew within Is 36:11
sent me to **s** these words to Is 36:12
S tenderly to Jerusalem, and Is 40:2
I, the LORD, **s** truthfully; Is 45:19
S up and present ⌊your case⌋— Is 45:21
they will **s** of you as ministers Is 61:6
know how to **s** since I am ⌊only Jr 1:6
you to and **s** whatever I tell Jr 1:7
to the powerful and **s** to them. Jr 5:5
Who can I **s** to and give such a Jr 6:10
I did not **s** with them or command Jr 7:22
When you **s** all these things to Jr 7:27
They do not **s** what is right. Jr 8:6
taught their tongues to **s** lies; Jr 9:5
arrows—they **s** deception. Jr 9:8
S as follows: This is what the Jr 9:22
patch, their idols cannot **s**. Jr 10:5
though they **s** well of you. Jr 12:6
did I command them or **s** to them. Jr 14:14
You are to **s** this word to them: Jr 14:17
And if you **s** noble ⌊words⌋, Jr 15:19
before You to **s** good on their Jr 18:20
there the words I **s** to you. Jr 19:2
For whenever I **s**, I cry out—I Jr 20:8
mention Him or **s** any longer in Jr 20:9
They **s** visions from their own Jr 23:16
I did not **s** to them, yet they Jr 23:21
My word should **s** My word Jr 23:28
temple and **s** all the words I Jr 26:2
commanded you to **s** to all Jr 26:2
sent me to **s** all these things Jr 26:15
Whenever I **s** against him, I Jr 31:20
they will once again **s** this word Jr 31:23
will **s** face to face and meet Jr 32:4
s to Zedekiah, king of Judah, Jr 34:2
eye to eye and **s** face to face; Jr 34:3
the Rechabites, **s** to them, and Jr 35:2
whenever you **s** of him you shake Jr 48:27
feet and I will **s** with you." Ezk 2:1
But **s** My words to them whether Ezk 2:7
go and **s** to the house of Israel. Ezk 3:1
Israel and **s** My words to them. Ezk 3:4
words that I **s** to you and take Ezk 3:10
the exiles, and **s** to them. Ezk 3:11
don't **s** out to warn him about Ezk 3:18
and I will **s** with you there." Ezk 3:22
But when I **s** with you, I will Ezk 3:27
will **s** whatever message I will Ezk 12:25
speak whatever message I will **s**, Ezk 12:25
I will **s** a message and bring it Ezk 12:25
message I **s** will be fulfilled. Ezk 12:28
visions and **s** lying divinations Ezk 13:6
false vision and **s** a lying Ezk 13:7
visions and **s** lying divinations Ezk 13:9
Therefore, **s** to them and tell Ezk 14:4
pose a riddle and **s** a parable to Ezk 17:2
s with the elders of Israel and Ezk 20:3
son of man, **s** to the house of Ezk 20:27
s a parable to the rebellious Ezk 24:3
will **s** and no longer be mute. Ezk 24:27
S ⌊to him⌋ and say: This is what Ezk 29:3
enable you to **s** out among them. Ezk 29:21
leaders will **s** from the middle Ezk 32:21
s to your people and tell them: Ezk 33:2
but you do not **s** out to warn him Ezk 33:8
burning zeal I **s** against the Ezk 36:5
I **s** in My burning zeal because Ezk 36:6
He will **s** words against the Most Dn 7:25
your servant, **s** with someone Dn 10:17
Let my lord **s**, for you have Dn 10:19
will **s** lies at the same table Dn 11:27
and **s** tenderly to her Hs 2:14
them⌋, they **s** lies against Me. Hs 7:13
s ⌊mere⌋ words, taking false Hs 10:4
and its residents **s** lies; Mc 6:12
and makes idols that cannot **s**. Hab 2:18
S to Zerubbabel son of Hg 2:2
S to Zerubbabel, governor of Hg 2:21
S truth to one another; Zch 8:16
For the idols **s** falsehood, Zch 10:2
was unable to **s** was brought to Mt 9:32
about how or what you should **s**. Mt 10:19
you in the dark, **s** in the light. Mt 10:27
Jesus began to **s** to the crowds Mt 11:7
and unable to **s** was brought to Mt 12:22
the man could both **s** and see. Mt 12:22
How can you **s** good things when Mt 12:34
for every careless word they **s**. Mt 12:36
outside wanting to **s** to Him. Mt 12:46
outside, wanting to **s** to You." Mt 12:47
do You **s** to them in parables? Mt 13:10
For this reason I **s** to them in Mt 13:13
He would not **s** anything to them Mt 13:34
those unable to **s**, and many Mt 15:30
saw those unable to **s** talking, Mt 15:31
not permit the demons to **s**, Mk 1:34
Why does He **s** like this? Mk 2:7
He would **s** the word to them with Mk 4:33
And He did not **s** to them without Mk 4:34
and he began to **s** clearly. Mk 7:35
and people unable to **s**, talk!" Mk 7:37
that makes him unable to **s**. Mk 9:17
soon afterwards **s** evil of Me. Mk 9:39
Then He began to **s** to them in Mk 12:1
they will **s** in new languages; Mk 16:17
I was sent to **s** to you and tell Lk 1:19
and unable to **s** until the day Lk 1:20
out, he could not **s** to them. Lk 1:22
and he began to **s**, praising God. Lk 1:64
God and to **s** about Him to all Lk 2:38
and would not allow Him to **s**, Lk 4:41
when all people **s** well of you, Lk 6:26
dead man sat up and began to **s**, Lk 7:15
began to **s** to the crowds about Lk 7:24
we know that You **s** and teach Lk 20:21
We **s** what We know and We testify Jn 3:11
I **s** what I have seen in the Jn 8:38
He will **s** for himself." Jn 9:21
should say and what I should **s**. Jn 12:49
things that I **s**, I speak just as Jn 12:50
s just as the Father has told Me. Jn 12:50
The words I **s** to you I do not Jn 14:10
to you I do not **s** on My own. Jn 14:10
For He will not **s** on His own, Jn 16:13
but He will **s** whatever He hears. Jn 16:13
I will no longer **s** to you in Jn 16:25
I **s** these things in the world Jn 17:13
and began to **s** in different Ac 2:4
I can confidently **s** to you about Ac 2:29
Your slaves may **s** Your message Ac 4:29
and began to **s** God's message Ac 4:31
ordered them not to **s** in the Ac 5:40
Then Peter began to **s**: Ac 10:34
He will **s** words to you by which Ac 11:14
As I began to **s**, the Holy Spirit Ac 11:15
for the people, you can **s**." Ac 13:15
He began to **s** boldly in the Ac 18:26
and they began to **s** with ⌊other⌋ Ac 19:6
you, let me **s** to the people." Ac 21:39
You must not **s** evil of a ruler Ac 23:5
governor motioned to him to **s**, Ac 24:10
for you to **s** for yourself." Ac 26:1
asked to see you and **s** to you. Ac 28:20
I **s** the truth in Christ—I am Rm 9:1
the mature we do **s** a wisdom, 1Co 2:6
we **s** God's hidden wisdom in a 1Co 2:7
We also **s** these things, not in 1Co 2:13
I was not able to **s** to you as 1Co 3:1
not to **s** of things pertaining to 1Co 6:3
Do all **s** in languages? 1Co 12:30
If I **s** the languages of men and 1Co 13:1
you unless I **s** to you with 1Co 14:6
I thank God that I **s** in ⌊other⌋ 1Co 14:18
I would rather **s** five words with 1Co 14:19
I will **s** to this people; 1Co 14:21
the church and **s** to himself and 1Co 14:28
Two or three prophets should **s**, 1Co 14:29
for they are not permitted to **s**, 1Co 14:34
for a woman to **s** in the church 1Co 14:35
sincerity, we **s** in Christ, as 2Co 2:17
also believe, and therefore **s**, 2Co 4:13
response—I **s** as to children— 2Co 6:13
I don't **s** as the Lord would, 2Co 11:17
which a man is not allowed to **s**. 2Co 12:4
away lying, **S** the truth, each Eph 4:25
enough in Him to **s** as I should. Eph 6:20
dare even more to **s** the message Php 1:14
s the mystery of the Messiah— Col 4:3
reveal it as I am required to **s**. Col 4:4
our God to **s** the gospel of God 1Th 2:2
gospel, so we **s**, not to please 1Th 2:4
you must **s** what is consistent Ti 2:1
not possible to **s** about these Heb 9:5
to hear, slow to **s**, and slow to Jms 1:19
S and act as those who will be Jms 2:12
case where they **s** against you as 1Pt 2:12
s blasphemies about things they 2Pt 2:12
was given to him to **s** boasts and Rv 13:5
began to **s** blasphemies against Rv 13:6
beast could both **s** and cause Rv 13:15

SPEAKER *(6)*

since I am such a poor **s**?" Ex 6:12
Since I am such a poor **s**, Ex 6:30
another holy one said to the **s**, Dn 8:13
because he was the main **s**. Ac 14:12
I will be a foreigner to the **s**, 1Co 14:11
and the **s** will be a foreigner to 1Co 14:11

SPEAKING *(146)*

had finished **s** with Abraham, Gn 18:33
he had finished **s**, there was Gn 24:15
While he was still **s** with them, Gn 29:9
I ⌊, Joseph,⌋ who am **s** to you. Gn 45:12
have been **s** to Your servant— Ex 4:10
As Aaron was **s** to the entire Ex 16:10
When He finished **s** with Moses on Ex 31:18
a result of his **s** with the LORD. Ex 34:29
Moses had finished **s** with them, Ex 34:33
heard the voice **s** to him from Nm 7:89
he finished **s** all these words, Nm 16:31
have sinned by **s** against the Nm 21:7
God's voice **s** from the fire as Dt 4:33
the living God **s** from the fire, Dt 5:26
a sign that You are **s** with me. Jdg 6:17
he finished **s**, he threw away Jdg 15:17
Hannah was **s** to herself, and 1Sm 1:13
While he was **s** with them, 1Sm 17:23
David had finished **s** with Saul, 1Sm 18:1
he finished **s**, the king's sons 2Sm 13:36
Why keep on **s** about ⌊these⌋ 2Sm 19:29
are still there **s** with the king, 1Kg 1:14
she was still **s** with the king, 1Kg 1:22
He was still **s** when Jonathan son 1Kg 1:42
to them by **s** kind words to them 1Kg 12:7
Elisha was still **s** with them, 2Kg 6:33
The king had been **s** to Gehazi, 2Kg 8:4
please them by **s** kind words to 2Ch 10:7
While he was still **s** to him, 2Ch 25:16
heard'—this is the LORD's. 2Ch 34:27
they were still **s** with him, Est 6:14
He was still **s** when another Jb 1:16
was still **s** when ⌊yet⌋ another Jb 1:17
He was still **s** when another Jb 1:18
Yet who can keep from **s**? Jb 4:2
the LORD had finished **s** to Job, Jb 42:7
even from ⌊**s**⌋ good, and my pain Ps 39:2
lying instead of **s** truthfully. Ps 52:3
sit together **s** against me, Ps 119:23
who goes around **s** dishonestly, Pr 6:12
end of his **s** is evil madness. Ec 10:13
finger-pointing and malicious **s**, Is 58:9
following our God, **s** oppression Is 59:13
they are still **s**, I will hear. Is 65:24
heard Jeremiah **s** these words Jr 26:7
message I am **s** in your hearing Jr 28:7
Jeremiah was **s** to all the people Jr 38:1
the people by **s** to them in this Jr 38:4
and they quit **s** with him because Jr 38:27
⌊**S**⌋ through Nebuzaradan, captain Jr 39:11
had finished **s** to all the people Jr 43:1
to Jeremiah, "You are **s** a lie! Jr 43:2
facedown and heard a voice **s**. Ezk 1:28
to the One who was **s** to me. Ezk 2:2
I heard someone **s** to me from the Ezk 43:6
arrogant words the horn was **s**. Dn 7:11
Then I heard a holy one **s**, Dn 8:13
While he was **s** to me, I fell Dn 8:18
While I was **s**, praying, Dn 9:20
to the angel who was **s** with me. Zch 1:13
angel who was **s** with me said, Zch 1:14
the angel who was **s** with me, Zch 1:19
angel who was **s** with me went out Zch 2:3
The angel who was **s** with me then Zch 4:1

the angel who was s with me, Zch 4:4
the angel who was s with me. Zch 4:5
the angel who was s with me came Zch 5:5
the angel who was s with me, Zch 5:10
of the angel who was s with me, Zch 6:4
you are not s, but the Spirit Mt 10:20
of your Father is s through you. Mt 10:20
was still s to the crowds when Mt 12:46
he was still s, suddenly a Mt 17:5
they knew He was s about them. Mt 21:45
While He was still s, Judas, one Mt 26:47
He was s the message to them. Mk 2:2
While He was still s, people Mk 5:35
For it isn't you s, but the Holy Mk 13:11
While He was still s, Judas, one Mk 14:43
Then after s to them, the Lord Mk 16:19
They were all s well of Him and Lk 4:22
He had finished s, He said to Lk 5:4
He was still s, someone came Lk 8:49
glory and were s of His death, Lk 9:31
He was s, a Pharisee asked Him Lk 11:37
He was still s, suddenly a mob Lk 22:47
he was still s, a rooster crowed Lk 22:60
But He was s about the sanctuary Jn 2:21
told her, "The One s to you." Jn 4:26
from God or if I am s on My own. Jn 7:17
He's s publicly and they're Jn 7:26
not know He was s to them about Jn 8:27
He is the One s with you." Jn 9:37
however, was s about his death, Jn 11:13
thought He was s about natural Jn 11:13
I'm not s about all of you; Jn 13:18
which one He was s about. Jn 13:22
Now You're s plainly and not Jn 16:29
40 days and s about the kingdom Ac 1:3
one heard them s in his own Ac 2:6
all these who are s Galileans? Ac 2:7
we hear them s in our own Ac 2:11
as they were s to the people, Ac 4:1
them against s to anyone in this Ac 4:17
unable to stop s about what we Ac 4:20
We heard him s blasphemous words Ac 6:11
does not stop s blasphemous Ac 6:13
s boldly in the name of the Lord. Ac 9:28
Peter was still s these words, Ac 10:44
For they heard them s in ⌊other⌋ Ac 10:46
s the message to no one except Ac 11:19
and began s to the Hellenists Ac 11:20
who were s with them and Ac 13:43
heard Paul s. After observing Ac 14:9
they stopped s, James responded Ac 15:13
Holy Spirit from s the message Ac 16:6
about this new teaching you're s Ac 17:19
but keep on s and don't be Ac 18:9
a deep sleep as Paul kept on s. Ac 20:9
of the One who was s to me. Ac 22:9
I heard a voice s to me in the Ac 26:14
I'm s words of truth and good Ac 26:25
to him I am actually s boldly. Ac 26:26
Since I am s to those who Rm 7:1
Now I am s to you Gentiles. Rm 11:13
in all s and all knowledge— 1Co 1:5
I am s as to wise people. 1Co 10:15
you that no one s by the Spirit 1Co 12:3
language is not s to men but to 1Co 14:2
if I come to you s in ⌊other⌋ 1Co 14:6
For you will be s into the air. 1Co 14:9
It follows that s in other 1Co 14:22
and all are s in ⌊other⌋ 1Co 14:23
and do not forbid s in ⌊other⌋ 1Co 14:39
and his public s is despicable." 2Co 10:10
Though untrained in public s, 2Co 11:6
sight of God we are s in Christ, 2Co 12:19
seek proof of Christ s in me. 2Co 13:3
But s the truth in love, let us Eph 4:15
s to one another in psalms, Eph 5:19
us from s to the Gentiles 1Th 2:16
s through David after such a Heb 4:7
Even though we are s this way, Heb 6:9
evil and his lips from s deceit, 1Pt 3:10
see the voice that was s to me. Rv 1:12
that I had heard s to me like a Rv 4:1

SPEAKS *(58)*

just as a man s with his friend. Ex 33:11
seen that God s with a person, Dt 5:24
My words that he s in My name. Dt 18:19
or who s in the name of other Dt 18:20
When a prophet s in the LORD's Dt 18:22
"Whoever s to you," the king 2Sm 14:10
The LORD also s of Jezebel: 1Kg 21:23
"You speak as a foolish woman s," Jb 2:10
For God s time and again, but a Jb 33:14
Job s without knowledge; Jb 34:35
Then He s to them in His anger Ps 2:5
the tongue that s boastfully. Ps 12:3
his tongue s what is just. Ps 37:30
to visit, he s deceitfully; Ps 41:6
My mouth s wisdom; my heart's Ps 49:3
God, the LORD God s; He summons Ps 50:1
s at the entrance of the city Pr 1:21
Whoever s the truth declares Pr 12:17
There is one who s rashly, Pr 12:18
and he loves one who s honestly. Pr 16:13
When he s graciously, don't Pr 26:25
Do you see a man who s too soon? Pr 29:20
and every mouth s folly. Is 9:17
For a fool s foolishness and his Is 32:6
godless way and s falsely about Is 32:6
lives righteously and s rightly, Is 33:15
his mouth a man s peaceably with Jr 9:8
is there who s and it happens, Lm 3:37
voice of God Almighty when He s. Ezk 10:5
is deceived and s a message, Ezk 14:9
One person s to another, each Ezk 33:30
the one who s with integrity. Am 5:10
Whoever s a word against the Son Mt 12:32
But whoever s against the Holy Mt 12:32
the mouth s from the overflow Mt 12:34
The one who s evil of father or Mt 15:4
Whoever s evil of father or Mk 7:10
is this man who s blasphemies? Lk 5:21
his mouth s from the overflow Lk 6:45
Anyone who s a word against the Lk 12:10
is earthly and s in earthly Jn 3:31
sent Him, and He s God's words, Jn 3:34
The one who s for himself seeks Jn 7:18
tells a lie, he s from his own Jn 8:44
the law says s to those who are Rm 3:19
David also s of the blessing of Rm 4:6
comes from faith s like this: Rm 10:6
the person who s in ⌊another⌋ 1Co 14:2
he s mysteries in the Spirit. 1Co 14:2
who prophesies s to people for 1Co 14:3
The person who s in ⌊another⌋ 1Co 14:4
the person who s in languages, 1Co 14:5
the person who s in ⌊another⌋ 1Co 14:13
If any person s in ⌊another⌋ 1Co 14:27
dead, he still s through this. Heb 11:4
you do not reject the One who s; Heb 12:25
If anyone s, ⌊his speech should 1Pt 4:11
He s about these things in all 2Pt 3:16

SPEAR *(46)*

assembly, took a s in his hand, Nm 25:7
Not a shield or s was seen among Jdg 5:8
not a sword or s could be found 1Sm 13:22
His s shaft was like a weaver's 1Sm 17:7
point of his s weighed 15 pounds 1Sm 17:7
with a dagger, s, and sword, but 1Sm 17:45
by sword or by s that the LORD 1Sm 17:47
usual, but Saul was holding a s, 1Sm 18:10
in his palace holding a s. 1Sm 19:9
David to the wall with the s. 1Sm 19:10
As the s struck the wall, David 1Sm 19:10
Saul threw his s at Jonathan to 1Sm 20:33
Do you have a s or sword on 1Sm 21:8
His s was in his hand, and all 1Sm 22:6
the camp with his s stuck in the 1Sm 26:7
Let me thrust the s through him 1Sm 26:8
take the s and the water jug by 1Sm 26:11
David took the s and the water 1Sm 26:12
are the king's s and water jug 1Sm 26:16
answered, "Here is the king's s; 1Sm 26:22
was Saul, leaning on his s. 2Sm 1:6
stomach with the end of his s. 2Sm 2:23
The s went through his body, 2Sm 2:23
whose bronze s weighed about 2Sm 21:16
The shaft of his s was like a 2Sm 21:19
with iron and the shaft of a s. 2Sm 23:7
He wielded his s against 800 2Sm 23:8
raised his s against 300 ⌊men⌋ 2Sm 23:18
Egyptian had a s in his hand, 2Sm 23:21
snatched the s out of the 2Sm 23:21
then killed him with his own s. 2Sm 23:21
he wielded his s against 300 and 1Ch 11:11
raised his s against 300 ⌊men⌋ 1Ch 11:20
Egyptian had a s in his hand 1Ch 11:23
snatched the s out of the 1Ch 11:23
then killed him with his own s. 1Ch 11:23
expert with shield and s. 1Ch 12:8
by 37,000 men with shield and s. 1Ch 12:34
The shaft of his s was like a 1Ch 20:5
the army, bearing s and shield. 2Ch 25:5
with a flashing s and a lance. Jb 39:23
nor will a s, dart, or arrow. Jb 41:26
Draw the s and javelin against Ps 35:3
flashing sword, shining s; Nah 3:3
brightness of Your shining s. Hab 3:11
pierced His side with a s, Jn 19:34

SPEARMEN *(1)*

cavalry and 200 s to go to Ac 23:23

SPEARS *(21)*

Hebrews will make swords or s." 1Sm 13:19
He then took three s in his hand 2Sm 18:14
themselves with knives and s, 1Kg 18:28
King David's s and shields that 2Kg 11:10
troops bearing shields and s. 1Ch 12:24
shields and s in each and every 2Ch 11:12
bearing large shields and s, 2Ch 14:8
of hundreds King David's s, 2Ch 23:9
with shields, s, helmets, armor, 2Ch 26:14
with their swords, s, and bows. Neh 4:13
while the other half held s, Neh 4:16
men were holding s from daybreak Neh 4:21
or his head with fishing s? Jb 41:7
bows and cuts s to pieces; Ps 46:9
Their teeth are s and arrows; Ps 57:4
plows and their s into pruning Is 2:4
and arrows, the clubs and s. Ezk 39:9
and your pruning knives into s. Jl 3:10
and their s into pruning knives. Mc 4:3
and the s are brandished. Nah 2:3
pierce his head with his own s; Hab 3:14

SPECIAL *(20)*

day I will give s treatment to Ex 8:22
someone makes a s vow to the Lv 27:2
a man or woman makes a s vow, Nm 6:2
to be His s people out of all Dt 14:2
that you are His s people as He Dt 26:18
have shown this s kindness to 2Sm 2:5
may the LORD show s kindness and 2Sm 2:6
are kings ⌊who show⌋ s kindness. 1Kg 20:31
without taking s aim and struck 1Kg 22:34
without taking s aim and struck 2Ch 18:33
and the s diet that she Est 2:9
What honor and s recognition Est 6:3
The ⌊s⌋ portion you donate to Ezk 48:9
It will be a s donation for them Ezk 48:12
a s possession on the day I am Mal 3:17
for that Sabbath was a s day Jn 19:31
You observe ⌊s⌋ days, months, Gl 4:10
some for s use, some for 2Tm 2:20
he will be a s instrument, 2Tm 2:21
cleanse for Himself a s people, Ti 2:14

SPECIALLY *(5)*

ephod, a robe, a s woven tunic, Ex 28:4
the s woven garments, both the Ex 31:10
and the s woven garments for Ex 35:19
They made s woven garments for Ex 39:1
and the s woven garments for Ex 39:41

SPECIFIC *(2)*

did this from a s concern that Jos 22:24
and assigned s duties to each Neh 13:30

SPECIFICALLY *(2)*

to him, "The man s warned us: Gn 43:3
and I s told you not to say, Jr 23:38

SPECIFICATION *(1)*

detail and according to every s. 1Kg 6:38

SPECIFICATIONS *(4)*

according to their s and put 2Ch 4:7
inner sanctuary according to s; 2Ch 4:20
temple to its s and reinforced 2Ch 24:13
statutes, design s, and laws. Ezk 43:11

SPECIFIED *(1)*

on the number s by ordinance for Ezr 3:4

SPECIFIES *(1)*

again, He s a certain day— Heb 4:7

SPECK *(7)*

are considered as a s of dust on Is 40:15
you look at the s in your Mt 7:3
me take the s out of your eye Mt 7:4
clearly to take the s out of Mt 7:5

- you look at the s in your Lk 6:41
- take out the s that is in your Lk 6:42
- to take out the s in your Lk 6:42

SPECKLED (7)
- sheep that is s or spotted, Gn 30:32
- the spotted and s among the Gn 30:32
- goats that are not s or spotted, Gn 30:33
- goats and all the s and spotted Gn 30:35
- bore streaked, s, and spotted Gn 30:39
- and s males were mating with the Gn 31:10
- spotted, and s, for I have seen Gn 31:12

SPECTACLE (4)
- I made a s of you before kings. Ezk 28:17
- I will make a s of you. Nah 3:6
- that had gathered for this s, Lk 23:48
- we have become a s to the world 1Co 4:9

SPECULATIONS (1)
- promote empty s rather than 1Tm 1:4

SPEECH (48)
- not understand one another's s." Gn 11:7
- I am slow and hesitant in s." Ex 4:10
- recognized the s of the young Jdg 18:3
- advisers of s and takes away Jb 12:20
- and show that my s is worthless? Jb 24:25
- my s settled on them ⌊like dew⌋. Jb 29:22
- attention to my s, and listen to Jb 33:1
- Day after day they pour out s; Ps 19:2
- There is no s; there are no Ps 19:3
- and your lips from deceitful s. Ps 34:13
- confuse and confound their s, Ps 55:9
- evil conduct, and perverse s. Pr 8:13
- but the s of the upright rescues Pr 12:6
- trapped by ⌊his⌋ rebellious s, Pr 12:13
- The proud s of a fool ⌊brings⌋ a Pr 14:3
- gain no knowledge from his s. Pr 14:7
- and pleasant s increases Pr 16:21
- increases learning with its s. Pr 16:23
- and his s is like a scorching Pr 16:27
- Excessive s is not appropriate Pr 17:7
- one with deceitful s will fall Pr 17:20
- himself with his s and harbors Pr 26:24
- to make a s before God. Ec 5:2
- with stammering s and in a Is 28:11
- your s will whisper from the Is 29:4
- with ⌊their⌋ s, accuse a person Is 29:21
- a people whose s is difficult to Is 33:19
- not know and whose s you do not Jr 5:15
- of unintelligible s or difficult Ezk 3:5
- of unintelligible s or difficult Ezk 3:6
- restore pure s to the peoples so Zph 3:9
- man who also had a s difficulty, Mk 7:32
- his s difficulty was removed, Mk 7:35
- in action and s before God and Lk 24:19
- things to you in figures of s. Jn 16:25
- Spirit gave them ability for s. Ac 2:4
- powerful in his s and actions. Ac 7:22
- with brilliance of s or wisdom. 1Co 2:1
- s and my proclamation were not 1Co 2:4
- your tongue for intelligible s, 1Co 14:9
- in faith, in s, in knowledge, in 2Co 8:7
- s should always be gracious, Col 4:6
- For we never used flattering s, 1Th 2:5
- example to the believers in s, 1Tm 4:12
- empty s and contradictions from 1Tm 6:20
- empty s, for this will 2Tm 2:16
- ⌊his s should be⌋ like the 1Pt 4:11
- we must not love in word or s, 1Jn 3:18

SPEECHES (3)
- trouble comes. First Series of S Jb 3:26
- for himself. Second Series of S Jb 14:22
- are deceptive. Third Series of S Jb 21:34

SPEECHLESS (9)
- am like a s person who does not Ps 38:13
- I was s and quiet; Ps 39:2
- I am s; I do not open my mouth Ps 39:9
- the prophets will be scared s." Jr 4:9
- toward the ground and was s. Dn 10:15
- wedding clothes?' The man was s. Mt 22:12
- signs to them and remained s. Lk 1:22
- were traveling with him stood s, Ac 9:7
- a s donkey spoke with a human 2Pt 2:16

SPELL (1)
- certain⌋ days cast a s on it, Jb 3:8

SPELLS (4)
- cast s, consult a medium or a Dt 18:11
- charmers who skillfully weave s. Ps 58:5
- and the potency of your s. Is 47:9
- stand with your s and your many Is 47:12

SPELT (3)
- the wheat and the s were not Ex 9:32
- plots, with s as their border. Is 28:25
- beans, lentils, millet, and s. Ezk 4:9

SPEND (40)
- wash your feet, and s the night. Gn 19:2
- We would rather s the night in Gn 19:2
- house for us to s the night?" Gn 24:23
- and a place to s the night." Gn 24:25
- said to them, "S the night here, Nm 22:8
- You may s the money on anything Dt 14:26
- place where you s the night.' " Jos 4:3
- coming. Please s the night. See, Jdg 19:9
- S the night here, enjoy yourself, Jdg 19:9
- was unwilling to s the night. Jdg 19:10
- city and s the night here?" Jdg 19:11
- these places and s the night in Jdg 19:13
- to go in and s the night in Jdg 19:15
- into their home to s the night. Jdg 19:15
- don't s the night in the square. Jdg 19:20
- my concubine to s the night. Jdg 20:4
- who won't s the night with 2Sm 17:8
- 'Don't s the night at the 2Sm 17:16
- and his servant s the night Neh 4:22
- They s their days in prosperity Jb 21:13
- they s the night naked, Jb 24:7
- stranger had to s the night on Jb 31:32
- Would it s the night by your Jb 39:9
- Weeping may s the night, but Ps 30:5
- Don't s your energy on women or Pr 31:3
- s the night among the henna Sg 7:11
- "We will s the night at Geba." Is 10:29
- The birds will s the summer on Is 18:6
- do you s money on what is not Is 55:2
- of Israel will s seven months Ezk 39:12
- Come and s the night in Jl 1:13
- you for whatever extra you s.' Lk 10:35
- would go out and s the night on Lk 21:37
- would not have to s time in the Ac 20:16
- you, or even s the winter, that 1Co 16:6
- for I hope to s some time with 1Co 16:7
- most gladly s and be spent for 2Co 12:15
- have decided to s the winter Ti 3:12
- so that you may s it on your Jms 4:3
- such a city and s a year there Jms 4:13

SPENDING (4)
- and for all s for temple repairs 2Kg 12:12
- s the night between my breasts. Sg 1:13
- s nights in secret places, Is 65:4
- After s some time there, they Ac 15:33

SPENDS (2)
- on a cliff where it s the night; Jb 39:28
- life that he s like a shadow? Ec 6:12

SPENT (35)
- ate and drank and s the night. Gn 24:54
- place and s the night there Gn 28:11
- and has certainly s our money. Gn 31:15
- they ate a meal and s the night Gn 31:54
- He s the night there and took Gn 32:13
- The time we s traveling from Dt 2:14
- the camp and s the night there Jos 6:11
- But he s that night with the Jos 8:9
- of Micah and s the night there. Jdg 18:2
- ate, drank, and s the nights Jdg 19:4
- he stayed and s the night there Jdg 19:7
- and s the night lying on the 2Sm 12:16
- a cave there and s the night. 1Kg 19:9
- They s the night in the vicinity 1Ch 9:27
- Eliashib, where he s the night. Ezr 10:6
- the day and ⌊s⌋ another fourth Neh 9:3
- My wrath will be s and My anger Is 10:25
- I have s my strength for nothing Is 49:4
- When My anger is s and I have Ezk 5:13
- after I have s My wrath on them, Ezk 5:13
- his palace and s the night Dn 6:18
- Bethany, and s the night there Mt 21:17
- She had s everything she had and Mk 5:26
- to pray and s all night in Lk 6:12
- who had s all she had on doctors Lk 8:43
- After he had s everything, Lk 15:14
- where He s time with them and Jn 3:22
- And they s a considerable time Ac 14:28
- residing there s their time on Ac 17:21
- at Troas, where we s seven days. Ac 20:6
- he had s not more than eight Ac 25:6
- which was s from the beginning Ac 26:4
- have s a night and a day in the 2Co 11:25
- gladly spend and be s for you. 2Co 12:15
- been enough time s in doing the 1Pt 4:3

SPEW (1)
- they s from their mouths— Ps 59:7

SPEWED (2)
- mouth the serpent s water like a Rv 12:15
- the dragon had s from his mouth. Rv 12:16

SPICE (4)
- as well as the s and oil for the Ex 35:28
- His cheeks are like beds of s, Sg 5:13
- garden, to beds of s, to feed Sg 6:2
- cinnamon, s, incense, myrrh, and Rv 18:13

SPICED (1)
- I would give you s wine to drink Sg 8:2

SPICES (30)
- s for the anointing oil and for Ex 25:6
- Take for yourself the finest s: Ex 30:23
- Take fragrant s: stacte, onycha, Ex 30:34
- the s and pure frankincense are Ex 30:34
- s for the anointing oil and for Ex 35:8
- camels bearing s, gold in great 1Kg 10:2
- quantity of s, and precious 1Kg 10:10
- a quantity of s arrive as those 1Kg 10:10
- clothing, weapons, s, and horses 1Kg 10:25
- gold, the s, and the precious 2Kg 20:13
- wine, oil, incense, and s. 1Ch 9:29
- the priests' sons mixed the s. 1Ch 9:30
- camels bearing s, gold in 2Ch 9:1
- quantity of s, and precious 2Ch 9:9
- never were such s as those the 2Ch 9:9
- clothing, weapons, s, and horses 2Ch 9:24
- that was full of s and various 2Ch 16:14
- precious stones, s, shields, and 2Ch 32:27
- full of wine blended with s, Ps 75:8
- and aloes, with all the best s. Sg 4:14
- spread the fragrance of its s. Sg 4:16
- I gather my myrrh with my s. Sg 5:1
- stag on the mountains of s. Sg 8:14
- gold, the s, and the precious Is 39:2
- the meat well and mix in the s! Ezk 24:10
- the best of all s, and all kinds Ezk 27:22
- Salome bought s, so they could Mk 16:1
- and prepared s and perfumes. Lk 23:56
- the s they had prepared. Lk 24:1
- cloths with the aromatic s, Jn 19:40

SPIDER'S (2)
- what he trusts in is a s web. Jb 8:14
- viper's eggs and weave s webs. Is 59:5

SPIED (1)
- the one who s out our defenses? Is 33:18

SPIES (13)
- and said to them, "You are s. Gn 42:9
- your servants are not s." Gn 42:11
- I have spoken: 'You are s!' Gn 42:14
- as Pharaoh lives, you are s!" Gn 42:16
- We are honest men and not s. Gn 42:31
- you are not s but honest men. Gn 42:34
- After Moses sent s to Jazer, Nm 21:32
- sent two men as s from Acacia Jos 2:1
- They sent s to Bethel (the town Jdg 1:23
- s saw a man coming out of the Jdg 1:24
- So David sent out s and knew for 1Sm 26:4
- and sent s who pretended to Lk 20:20
- received the s in peace and Heb 11:31

SPILL (2)
- its channels and s over all its Is 8:7
- skins, it will s, and the skins Lk 5:37

SPILLED (6)
- with it and s his intestines out 2Sm 20:10
- He s that blood on his own 1Kg 2:5
- are on it will be s out.'" 1Kg 13:3
- and the ashes s off the altar, 1Kg 13:5
- blood will be ⌊s⌋ in the land. Ezk 21:32
- and all his insides s out. Ac 1:18

SPILLS (1)
- burst, the wine s out, and the Mt 9:17

SPIN (2)
- they don't labor or s thread. Mt 6:28
- they don't labor or s thread. Lk 12:27

SPINDLE (2)
- can only work a s or someone who 2Sm 3:29
- staff, and her hands hold the s. Pr 31:19

SPINNING *(1)*

her hands to the s staff, Pr 31:19

SPIRIT *(530)*

and the S of God was hovering Gn 1:2
My S will not remain with Gn 6:3
breath of the s of life in its Gn 7:22
who has the s of God in him?" Gn 41:38
the s of their father Jacob Gn 45:27
their broken s and hard labor. Ex 6:9
have filled with a s of wisdom, Ex 28:3
I have filled him with God's S, Ex 31:3
moved and whose s prompted him Ex 35:21
He has filled him with God's S, Ex 35:31
take some of the S who is on you Nm 11:17
on you and put ⌊the S⌋ on them. Nm 11:17
took some of the S that was on Nm 11:25
and placed ⌊the S⌋ on the 70 Nm 11:25
As the S rested on them, they Nm 11:25
the S rested on them—they were Nm 11:26
LORD would place His S on them." Nm 11:29
has a different s and has Nm 14:24
the S of God descended on him, Nm 24:2
a man who has the S in him, Nm 27:18
God made his s stubborn and his Dt 2:30
a medium or a familiar s, Dt 18:11
eyes, and a despondent s. Dt 28:65
was filled with the s of wisdom, Dt 34:9
The S of the LORD was on him, Jdg 3:10
The S of the LORD enveloped Jdg 6:34
God sent an evil s between Jdg 9:23
The S of the LORD came on Jdg 11:29
Then the S of the LORD began to Jdg 13:25
the S of the LORD took control Jdg 14:6
The S of the LORD took control Jdg 14:19
The S of the LORD took control Jdg 15:14
The S of the LORD will control 1Sm 10:6
Then the S of God took control 1Sm 10:10
the S of God suddenly took 1Sm 11:6
and the S of the LORD took 1Sm 16:13
Now the S of the LORD had left 1Sm 16:14
an evil s from the LORD began 1Sm 16:14
see that an evil s from God is 1Sm 16:15
Whenever the evil s from God 1Sm 16:16
Whenever the s from God 1Sm 16:23
and the evil s would leave him. 1Sm 16:23
next day an evil s from God took 1Sm 18:10
Now an evil s from the LORD came 1Sm 19:9
the S of God came on Saul's 1Sm 19:20
The S of God also came on him, 1Sm 19:23
Saul said, "Consult a s for me. 1Sm 28:8
I see a s form coming up out 1Sm 28:13
The S of the LORD spoke through 2Sm 23:2
the S of the LORD may carry you 1Kg 18:12
Then a s came forward, stood 1Kg 22:21
become a lying s in the mouth 1Kg 22:22
has put a lying s into the mouth 1Kg 22:23
Did the S of the LORD leave me 1Kg 22:24
double portion of your s on me." 2Kg 2:9
The s of Elijah rests on Elisha. 2Kg 2:15
Maybe the S of the LORD has 2Kg 2:16
Wasn't my s there when the man 2Kg 5:26
I am about to put a s in him, 2Kg 19:7
Then the S took control of 1Ch 12:18
The S of God came on Azariah son 2Ch 15:1
Then a s came forward, stood 2Ch 18:20
become a lying s in the mouth 2Ch 18:21
has put a lying s into the mouth 2Ch 18:22
Did the S of the LORD leave me 2Ch 18:23
S of the LORD came on Jahaziel 2Ch 20:14
The S of God took control of 2Ch 24:20
sent Your good S to instruct Neh 9:20
and Your S warned them through Neh 9:30
my s drinks their poison. Jb 6:4
speak in the anguish of my s; Jb 7:11
My s is broken. My days are Jb 17:1
But it is a s in man and the Jb 32:8
and my s compels me ⌊to speak⌋. Jb 32:18
S of God has made me, and the Jb 33:4
and withdrew the s and breath He Jb 34:14
is glad, and my s rejoices; Ps 16:9
Into Your hand I entrust my s; Ps 31:5
and in whose s is no deceit! Ps 32:2
He saves those crushed in s. Ps 34:18
renew a steadfast s within me. Ps 51:10
or take Your Holy S from me. Ps 51:11
to me, and give me a willing s. Ps 51:12
pleasing to God is a broken s. Ps 51:17
He humbles the s of leaders; Ps 76:12
I meditate; my s becomes weak. Ps 77:3
in my heart, and my s ponders. Ps 77:6
loyal and whose s was not Ps 78:8
for they embittered his s, Ps 106:33
Where can I go to escape Your S? Ps 139:7
Although my s is weak within me, Ps 142:3
My s is weak within me; Ps 143:4
LORD; my s fails. Don't hide Ps 143:7
Your gracious S lead me on level Ps 143:10
pour out my s on you and teach Pr 1:23
a devious tongue breaks the s. Pr 15:4
sad heart ⌊produces⌋ a broken s. Pr 15:13
and an arrogant s before a fall. Pr 16:18
to be lowly of s with the humble Pr 16:19
but a broken s dries up the Pr 17:22
A man's s can endure sickness, Pr 18:14
but who can survive a broken s? Pr 18:14
but a humble s will gain honor. Pr 29:23
knows if the s of people rises Ec 3:21
upward and the s of animals goes Ec 3:21
a patient s is better than a Ec 7:8
spirit is better than a proud s. Ec 7:8
Don't let your s rush to be Ec 7:9
the s returns to God who gave Ec 12:7
of Jerusalem by a s of judgment Is 4:4
of judgment and a s of burning. Is 4:4
The S of the LORD will rest on Is 11:2
a S of wisdom and understanding, Is 11:2
a S of counsel and strength, Is 11:2
a S of knowledge and of the fear Is 11:2
Egypt's s will be disturbed Is 19:3
within her a s of confusion. Is 19:14
my s within me diligently seeks Is 26:9
a s of justice to the one who Is 28:6
like that of a s from the ground Is 29:4
their horses are flesh, not s. Is 31:3
the S from heaven is poured Is 32:15
He will gather them by His S. Is 34:16
I am putting a s in him and he Is 37:7
is the life of my s as well; Is 38:16
has directed the S of the LORD, Is 40:13
I have put My S on Him; Is 42:1
I will pour out My S on your Is 44:3
Lord GOD has sent me and His S. Is 48:16
wife deserted and wounded in s, Is 54:6
the oppressed and lowly of s, Is 57:15
to revive the s of the lowly and Is 57:15
for then the s would grow weak Is 57:16
My S who is on you, and My words Is 59:21
The S of the Lord GOD is on Me, Is 61:1
and grieved His Holy S. Is 63:10
put His Holy S among the flock Is 63:11
S of the LORD gave them rest. Is 63:14
will lament out of a broken s. Is 65:14
submissive in s, and who Is 66:2
Wherever the S wanted to go, Ezk 1:12
Wherever the S wanted to go, Ezk 1:20
the direction the S was moving. Ezk 1:20
the s of the living creatures Ezk 1:20
the s of the living creatures Ezk 1:21
the S entered me and set me on Ezk 2:2
The S then lifted me up, and I Ezk 3:12
the S lifted me up and took me Ezk 3:14
in bitterness and in an angry s, Ezk 3:14
The S entered me and set me on Ezk 3:24
Then the S lifted me up between Ezk 8:3
the s of the living creatures Ezk 10:17
The S then lifted me up and Ezk 11:1
Then the S of the LORD came on Ezk 11:5
and put a new s within them; Ezk 11:19
The S lifted me up and brought Ezk 11:24
in a vision from the S of God. Ezk 11:24
follow their own s and have seen Ezk 13:3
a new heart and a new s. Ezk 18:31
Every s will be discouraged, Ezk 21:7
and put a new s within you; Ezk 36:26
I will place My S within you and Ezk 36:27
me out by His S and set me down Ezk 37:1
I will put My S in you, and you Ezk 37:14
will pour out My S on the house Ezk 39:29
Then the S lifted me up and Ezk 43:5
and the s of the holy gods is in Dn 4:8
that you have a s of the holy Dn 4:9
you have the s of the holy gods. Dn 4:18
who has the s of the holy gods Dn 5:11
to have an extraordinary s, Dn 5:12
that you have the s of the gods Dn 5:14
and his s became arrogant Dn 5:20
he had an extraordinary s, Dn 6:3
s was deeply distressed within Dn 7:15
a s of promiscuity leads them Hs 4:12
for a s of promiscuity is among Hs 5:4
pour out My S on all humanity Jl 2:28
even pour out My S on the male Jl 2:29
Is the S of the LORD impatient? Mc 2:7
If a man of s comes and invents Mc 2:11
with power by the S of the LORD, Mc 3:8
stirred up the s of Zerubbabel Hg 1:14
the s of the high priest Joshua Hg 1:14
and the s of all the remnant of Hg 1:14
and My S is present among you; Hg 2:5
but by My S,' says the LORD Zch 4:6
pacified My S in the northern Zch 6:8
had sent by His S through the Zch 7:12
and formed the s of man within Zch 12:1
I will pour out a s of grace and Zch 12:10
and the unclean s from the land. Zch 13:2
she was pregnant by the Holy S. Mt 1:18
in her is by the Holy S. Mt 1:20
you with the Holy S and fire. Mt 3:11
and He saw the S of God Mt 3:16
was led up by the S into the Mt 4:1
Blessed are the poor in s, Mt 5:3
but the S of your Father is Mt 10:20
I will put My S on Him, and He Mt 12:18
out demons by the S of God, Mt 12:28
against the S will not be Mt 12:31
speaks against the Holy S, Mt 12:32
When an unclean s comes out of a Mt 12:43
inspired by the S, calls Him Mt 22:43
The s is willing, but the flesh Mt 26:41
a loud voice and gave up His s. Mt 27:50
of the Son and of the Holy S, Mt 28:19
baptize you with the Holy S." Mk 1:8
open and the S descending to Him Mk 1:10
Immediately the S drove Him into Mk 1:12
with an unclean s was in their Mk 1:23
And the unclean s convulsed him, Mk 1:26
in His s that they were Mk 2:8
against the Holy S never has Mk 3:29
saying, "He has an unclean s." Mk 3:30
man with an unclean s came out Mk 5:2
out of the man, you unclean s!" Mk 5:8
had an unclean s came and fell Mk 7:25
But sighing deeply in His s, Mk 8:12
He has a s that makes him unable Mk 9:17
When the s saw Him, it Mk 9:20
the unclean s, saying to it, Mk 9:25
mute and deaf s, I command you: Mk 9:25
himself says by the Holy S: Mk 12:36
you speaking, but the Holy S. Mk 13:11
The s is willing, but the flesh Mk 14:38
with the Holy S while still in Lk 1:15
before Him in the s and power of Lk 1:17
The Holy S will come upon you, Lk 1:35
was filled with the Holy S. Lk 1:41
and my s has rejoiced in God my Lk 1:47
with the Holy S and prophesied: Lk 1:67
and the Holy S was on him. Lk 2:25
him by the Holy S that he would Lk 2:26
Guided by the S, he entered the Lk 2:27
you with the Holy S and fire. Lk 3:16
and the Holy S descended on Him Lk 3:22
full of the Holy S, and was led Lk 4:1
was led by the S in the Lk 4:1
Galilee in the power of the S, Lk 4:14
The S of the Lord is on Me, Lk 4:18
unclean demonic s who cried out Lk 4:33
the unclean s to come out Lk 8:29
Her s returned, and she got up Lk 8:55
Often a s seizes him; Lk 9:39
But Jesus rebuked the unclean s, Lk 9:42
rejoiced in the Holy S and said, Lk 10:21
give the Holy S to those who ask Lk 11:13
When an unclean s comes out of a Lk 11:24
against the Holy S will not be Lk 12:10
For the Holy S will teach you at Lk 12:12
disabled by a s for over 18 Lk 13:11
into Your hands I entrust My s." Lk 23:46
I watched the S descending from Jn 1:32
'The One you see the S Jn 1:33
who baptizes with the Holy S.' Jn 1:33
is born of water and the S, Jn 3:5
is born of the S is spirit. Jn 3:6
is born of the Spirit is s. Jn 3:6
is with everyone born of the S." Jn 3:8

He gives the S without measure.	Jn 3:34
the Father in s and truth.	Jn 4:23
God is s, and those who worship	Jn 4:24
must worship in s and truth."	Jn 4:24
The S is the One who gives life.	Jn 6:63
to you are s and are life.	Jn 6:63
this about the S, whom those who	Jn 7:39
for the S had not yet been	Jn 7:39
angry in His s and deeply moved	Jn 11:33
troubled in His s and testified,	Jn 13:21
He is the S of truth.	Jn 14:17
the Holy S—the Father will	Jn 14:26
the S of truth who proceeds from	Jn 15:26
When the S of truth comes,	Jn 16:13
His head, He gave up His s.	Jn 19:30
and said, "Receive the Holy S.	Jn 20:22
the Holy S to the apostles	Ac 1:2
with the Holy S not many days	Ac 1:5
when the Holy S has come upon	Ac 1:8
the Holy S through the mouth	Ac 1:16
with the Holy S and began to	Ac 2:4
as the S gave them ability for	Ac 2:4
pour out My S on all humanity	Ac 2:17
even pour out My S on My male	Ac 2:18
the Father the promised Holy S,	Ac 2:33
receive the gift of the Holy S.	Ac 2:38
the Holy S and said to them,	Ac 4:8
You said through the Holy S,	Ac 4:25
with the Holy S and began to	Ac 4:31
lie to the Holy S and keep back	Ac 5:3
agree to test the S of the Lord?	Ac 5:9
so is the Holy S whom God has	Ac 5:32
full of the S and wisdom, whom	Ac 6:3
full of faith and the Holy S,	Ac 6:5
wisdom and the S by whom he	Ac 6:10
are always resisting the Holy S;	Ac 7:51
by the Holy S, gazed into heaven	Ac 7:55
"Lord Jesus, receive my s!"	Ac 7:59
they might receive the Holy S.	Ac 8:15
and they received the Holy S.	Ac 8:17
that the Holy S was given	Ac 8:18
on may receive the Holy S."	Ac 8:19
The S told Philip, "Go and join	Ac 8:29
the S of the Lord carried Philip	Ac 8:39
and be filled with the Holy S."	Ac 9:17
the encouragement of the Holy S,	Ac 9:31
the vision, the S told him,	Ac 10:19
with the Holy S and with power,	Ac 10:38
Holy S came down on all those	Ac 10:44
of the Holy S had been poured	Ac 10:45
the Holy S just as we have?	Ac 10:47
Then the S told me to go with	Ac 11:12
the Holy S came down on them,	Ac 11:15
be baptized with the Holy S.'	Ac 11:16
of the Holy S and of faith—	Ac 11:24
by the S that there would	Ac 11:28
the Holy S said, "Set apart	Ac 13:2
Being sent out by the Holy S,	Ac 13:4
with the Holy S, stared straight	Ac 13:9
filled with joy and the Holy S.	Ac 13:52
to them by giving the Holy S,	Ac 15:8
by the Holy S from speaking	Ac 16:6
but the S of Jesus did not allow	Ac 16:7
met us who had a s of prediction	Ac 16:16
turning to the s, said, "I	Ac 16:18
his s was troubled within him	Ac 17:16
being fervent in s, he spoke and	Ac 18:25
the Holy S when you believed?	Ac 19:2
heard that there is a Holy S."	Ac 19:2
them, the Holy S came on them,	Ac 19:6
The evil s answered them,	Ac 19:15
had the evil s leaped on them,	Ac 19:16
resolved in the S to pass	Ac 19:21
bound in my s, not knowing what	Ac 20:22
town the Holy S testifies to me	Ac 20:23
whom the Holy S has appointed	Ac 20:28
Paul through the S not to go to	Ac 21:4
This is what the Holy S says:	Ac 21:11
and no angel or s, but the	Ac 23:8
What if a s or an angel has	Ac 23:9
The Holy S correctly spoke	Ac 28:25
according to the S of holiness.	Rm 1:4
I serve with my s in ⌊telling⌋	Rm 1:9
—by the S, not the letter.	Rm 2:29
the Holy S who was given to	Rm 5:5
new way of the S and not in the	Rm 7:6
flesh but according to the S.	Rm 8:4
lives are according to the S,	Rm 8:5
about the things of the S.	Rm 8:5
mind-set of the S is life and	Rm 8:6
but in the S, since the Spirit	Rm 8:9
since the S of God lives in you.	Rm 8:9
does not have the S of Christ,	Rm 8:9
but the S is life because of	Rm 8:10
And if the S of Him who raised	Rm 8:11
through His S who lives in you	Rm 8:11
But if by the S you put to death	Rm 8:13
led by God's S are God's sons.	Rm 8:14
did not receive a s of slavery	Rm 8:15
you received the S of adoption,	Rm 8:15
The S Himself testifies together	Rm 8:16
with our s that we are God's	Rm 8:16
have the S as the firstfruits	Rm 8:23
the same way the S also joins to	Rm 8:26
but the S Himself intercedes for	Rm 8:26
to me with the Holy S—	Rm 9:1
God gave them a s of stupor,	Rm 11:8
be fervent in s; serve the Lord.	Rm 12:11
peace, and joy in the Holy S.	Rm 14:17
hope by the power of the Holy S.	Rm 15:13
sanctified by the Holy S.	Rm 15:16
and by the power of God's S.	Rm 15:19
and through the love of the S,	Rm 15:30
of the S and power,	1Co 2:4
revealed them to us by the S,	1Co 2:10
for the S searches everything,	1Co 2:10
man except the s of the man that	1Co 2:11
of God except the S of God.	1Co 2:11
not received the s of the world,	1Co 2:12
but the S who is from God,	1Co 2:12
but in those taught by the S,	1Co 2:13
what comes from God's S,	1Co 2:14
and that the S of God lives in	1Co 3:16
in love and a s of gentleness?	1Co 4:21
absent in body but present in s,	1Co 5:3
along with my s and with the	1Co 5:4
that his s may be saved in the	1Co 5:5
Christ and by the S of our God.	1Co 6:11
to the Lord is one s with Him.	1Co 6:17
of the Holy S who is in you,	1Co 6:19
be holy both in body and in s.	1Co 7:34
that I also have the S of God.	1Co 7:40
About matters of the s:	1Co 12:1
speaking by the S of God says,	1Co 12:3
is Lord," except by the Holy S.	1Co 12:3
different gifts, but the same S.	1Co 12:4
of the S is given to each	1Co 12:7
message of wisdom through the S,	1Co 12:8
of knowledge by the same S,	1Co 12:8
faith by the same S, to another,	1Co 12:9
gifts of healing by the one S,	1Co 12:9
and the same S is active in all	1Co 12:11
by one S into one body—	1Co 12:13
were all made to drink of one S.	1Co 12:13
he speaks mysteries in the S.	1Co 14:2
are zealous in matters of the s,	1Co 14:12
language, my s prays, but my	1Co 14:14
pray with the s, and I will also	1Co 14:15
sing with the s, and I will also	1Co 14:15
you bless with the s, how will	1Co 14:16
Adam became a life-giving S.	1Co 15:45
have refreshed my s and yours.	1Co 16:18
and given us the S as a down	2Co 1:22
no rest in my s because I did	2Co 2:13
ink but with the S of the living	2Co 3:3
not of the letter, but of the S;	2Co 3:6
kills, but the S produces life.	2Co 3:6
ministry of the S not be more	2Co 3:8
Now the Lord is the S;	2Co 3:17
and where the S of the Lord is,	2Co 3:17
is from the Lord who is the S.	2Co 3:18
we have the same s of faith in	2Co 4:13
who gave us the S as a down	2Co 5:5
by the Holy S, by sincere love,	2Co 6:6
impurity of the flesh and s,	2Co 7:1
because his s was refreshed by	2Co 7:13
or you receive a different s,	2Co 11:4
in the same s and in the same	2Co 12:18
the Holy S be with all of you.	2Co 13:13
you receive the S by the works	Gl 3:2
After beginning with the S,	Gl 3:3
you with the S and work miracles	Gl 3:5
promise of the S through faith.	Gl 3:14
God has sent the S of His Son	Gl 4:6
the one born according to the S,	Gl 4:29
For by the S we eagerly wait for	Gl 5:5
walk by the S and you will not	Gl 5:16
desires what is against the S,	Gl 5:17
the S desires what is against	Gl 5:17
But if you are led by the S,	Gl 5:18
But the fruit of the S is love,	Gl 5:22
we live by the S, we must also	Gl 5:25
we must also follow the S.	Gl 5:25
such a person with a gentle s,	Gl 6:1
who sows to the S will reap	Gl 6:8
reap eternal life from the S.	Gl 6:8
Jesus Christ be with your s.	Gl 6:18
sealed with the promised Holy S.	Eph 1:13
would give you a s of wisdom and	Eph 1:17
the s now working in the	Eph 2:2
access by one S to the Father.	Eph 2:18
for God's dwelling in the S.	Eph 2:22
apostles and prophets by the S:	Eph 3:5
through His S in the inner man	Eph 3:16
unity of the S with the peace	Eph 4:3
There is one body and one S,	Eph 4:4
renewed in the s of your minds;	Eph 4:23
And don't grieve God's Holy S,	Eph 4:30
but be filled with the S:	Eph 5:18
sword of the S, which is God's	Eph 6:17
pray at all times in the S,	Eph 6:18
help from the S of Jesus Christ	Php 1:19
you are standing firm in one s,	Php 1:27
if any fellowship with the S,	Php 2:1
ones who serve by the S of God,	Php 3:3
Jesus Christ be with your s.	Php 4:23
us about your love in the S.	Col 1:8
I am with you in s, rejoicing to	Col 2:5
in the Holy S, and with much	1Th 1:5
with the joy from the Holy S.	1Th 1:6
who also gives you His Holy S.	1Th 4:8
Don't stifle the S.	1Th 5:19
And may your s, soul, and body	1Th 5:23
either by a s or by a message or	2Th 2:2
by the S and through belief	2Th 2:13
in the S, seen by angels	1Tm 3:16
Now the S explicitly says that	1Tm 4:1
not given us a s of fearfulness,	2Tm 1:7
the Holy S who lives in us	2Tm 1:14
The Lord be with your s.	2Tm 4:22
and renewal by the Holy S.	Ti 3:5
This ⌊S⌋ He poured out on us	Ti 3:6
Jesus Christ be with your s.	Phm 25
from the Holy S according to His	Heb 2:4
Therefore, as the Holy S says:	Heb 3:7
to divide soul, s, joints, and	Heb 4:12
companions with the Holy S,	Heb 6:4
The Holy S was making it clear	Heb 9:8
the eternal S offered Himself	Heb 9:14
The Holy S also testifies to us	Heb 10:15
and insulted the S of grace?	Heb 10:29
the body without the s is dead,	Jms 2:26
says that the S He has caused to	Jms 4:5
set apart by the S for obedience	1Pt 1:2
the S of Christ within	1Pt 1:11
you by the Holy S sent from	1Pt 1:12
quality of a gentle and quiet s,	1Pt 3:4
because the S of glory and of	1Pt 4:14
moved by the Holy S, men spoke	2Pt 1:21
us is from the S He has given us	1Jn 3:24
do not believe every s, but test	1Jn 4:1
is how you know the S of God:	1Jn 4:2
Every s who confesses that Jesus	1Jn 4:2
But every s who does not confess	1Jn 4:3
This is the s of the antichrist;	1Jn 4:3
From this we know the S of truth	1Jn 4:6
of truth and the s of deception.	1Jn 4:6
He has given to us from His S.	1Jn 4:13
And the S is the One who	1Jn 5:6
because the S is the truth.	1Jn 5:6
S, the water, and the blood—	1Jn 5:8
natural, not having the S.	Jd 19
faith and praying in the Holy S,	Jd 20
was in the S on the Lord's day,	Rv 1:10
listen to what the S says to the	Rv 2:7
listen to what the S says to the	Rv 2:11
listen to what the S says to the	Rv 2:17
listen to what the S says to the	Rv 2:29
listen to what the S says to the	Rv 3:6
listen to what the S says to the	Rv 3:13
listen to what the S says to the	Rv 3:22
Immediately I was in the S,	Rv 4:2
to give a s to the image	Rv 13:15
Yes," says the S, "let them rest	Rv 14:13

me away in the **S** to a desert. Rv 17:3
a haunt for every unclean **s**, Rv 18:2
Jesus is the **s** of prophecy." Rv 19:10
me away in the **S** to a great and Rv 21:10
Both the **S** and the bride say, Rv 22:17

SPIRIT'S *(3)*
For it was the Holy **S** decision— Ac 15:28
because the **S** law of life in Rm 8:2
the hearts knows the **S** mind-set, Rm 8:27

SPIRITIST *(1)*
a medium or a **s** must be put to Lv 20:27

SPIRITISTS *(9)*
turn to mediums or consult **s**, Lv 19:31
to mediums or **s** and prostitutes Lv 20:6
the mediums and **s** from the land. 1Sm 28:3
the mediums and **s** in the land. 1Sm 28:9
and consulted mediums and **s**. 2Kg 21:6
mediums, the **s**, household idols 2Kg 23:24
and consulted mediums and **s**. 2Ch 33:6
of the dead and the **s** who chirp Is 8:19
spirits of the dead, and **s**. Is 19:3

SPIRITS *(49)*
God of the **s** of all flesh, Nm 16:22
the God of the **s** of all flesh, Nm 27:16
was in good **s**, he went to lie Ru 3:7
left full of joy and in good **s**. Est 5:9
The departed **s** tremble beneath Jb 26:5
Do departed **s** rise up to praise Ps 88:10
their **s** failed within them. Ps 107:5
broke their **s** with hard labor; Ps 107:12
to the land of the departed **s**. Pr 2:18
that the departed **s** are there, Pr 9:18
the assembly of the departed **s**. Pr 21:16
Consult the **s** of the dead and Is 8:19
stirs up the **s** of the departed Is 14:9
idols, ghosts, **s** of the dead, Is 19:3
departed **s** do not rise up. Is 26:14
will bring forth the departed **s**. Is 26:19
are the four **s** of heaven going Zch 6:5
He drove out the **s** with a word Mt 8:16
them authority over unclean **s**, Mt 10:1
it seven other **s** more evil than Mt 12:45
He commands even the unclean **s**, Mk 1:27
Whenever the unclean **s** saw Him, Mk 3:11
Then the unclean **s** came out and Mk 5:13
them authority over unclean **s**. Mk 6:7
the unclean **s** with authority Lk 4:36
by unclean **s** were made well. Lk 6:18
and evil **s**, and He granted Lk 7:21
healed of evil **s** and sicknesses: Lk 8:2
that the **s** submit to you, Lk 10:20
seven other **s** more evil than Lk 11:26
who were tormented by unclean **s**, Ac 5:16
For unclean **s**, crying out with a Ac 8:7
and the evil **s** came out of them. Ac 19:12
Jesus over those who had evil **s**, Ac 19:13
between **s**, to another, different 1Co 12:10
the prophets' **s** are under the 1Co 14:32
to deceitful **s** and the teachings 1Tm 4:1
all ministering **s** sent out to Heb 1:14
to the Father of **s** and live? Heb 12:9
the **s** of righteous people made Heb 12:23
proclamation to the **s** in prison 1Pt 3:19
but test the **s** to determine if 1Jn 4:1
from the seven **s** before His Rv 1:4
who has the seven **s** of God and Rv 3:1
which are the seven **s** of God. Rv 4:5
which are the seven **s** of God Rv 5:6
saw three unclean **s** like frogs Rv 16:13
For they are **s** of demons Rv 16:14
God of the **s** of the prophets, Rv 22:6

SPIRITUAL *(30)*
to you some **s** gift to strengthen Rm 1:11
For we know that the law is **s**; Rm 7:14
this is your **s** worship. Rm 12:1
have shared in their **s** benefits, Rm 15:27
do not lack any **s** gift as you 1Co 1:7
explaining **s** things to spiritual 1Co 2:13
spiritual things to **s** people. 1Co 2:13
The **s** person, however, can 1Co 2:15
speak to you as **s** people but as 1Co 3:1
we have sown **s** things for you, 1Co 9:11
They all ate the same **s** food, 1Co 10:3
and all drank the same **s** drink. 1Co 10:4
they drank from a **s** rock that 1Co 10:4
Pursue love and desire **s** gifts, 1Co 14:1
thinks he is a prophet or **s**, 1Co 14:37
a natural body, raised a **s** body. 1Co 15:44
body, there is also a **s** body. 1Co 15:44
However, the **s** is not first, but 1Co 15:46
but the natural; then the **s**. 1Co 15:46
who are **s** should restore such Gl 6:1
blessed us with every **s** blessing Eph 1:3
hymns, and **s** songs, singing Eph 5:19
against the **s** forces of evil in Eph 6:12
all wisdom and **s** understanding, Col 1:9
psalms, hymns, and **s** songs, with Col 3:16
desire the unadulterated **s** milk, 1Pt 2:2
built into a **s** house for a holy 1Pt 2:5
priesthood to offer **s** sacrifices 1Pt 2:5
but made alive in the **s** realm. 1Pt 3:18
live by God in the **s** realm. 1Pt 4:6

SPIRITUALLY *(2)*
grew up and became **s** strong, Lk 1:80
know it since it is evaluated **s**. 1Co 2:14

SPIT *(10)*
father had merely **s** in her face, Nm 12:14
his foot, and **s** in his face. Dt 25:9
I have become a man people **s** at. Jb 17:6
do not hesitate to **s** in my face. Jb 30:10
Then they **s** in His face and beat Mt 26:67
Then they **s** at Him, took the Mt 27:30
will mock Him, **s** on Him, flog Mk 10:34
Then some began to **s** on Him, Mk 14:65
He will be mocked, insulted, **s** Lk 18:32
these things He **s** on the ground, Jn 9:6

SPITE *(19)*
If in **s** of these things you do Lv 26:23
And if in **s** of this you do not Lv 26:27
Yet in **s** of this, while they are Lv 26:44
But in **s** of this you did not Dt 1:32
in **s** of all that is good in 1Sm 2:32
In **s** of all that, the LORD did 2Kg 23:26
hope for Israel in **s** of this. Ezr 10:2
they escape in **s** of such sin? Ps 56:7
man who perishes in **s** of his Ec 7:15
who lives long in **s** of his evil. Ec 7:15
in **s** of a very large population. Is 16:14
in **s** of your many sorceries and Is 47:9
But in **s** of all these things Jr 2:34
Yet in **s** of all this, her Jr 3:10
are a lawbreaker in **s** of having Rm 2:27
in **s** of this it still belongs 1Co 12:15
in **s** of this it still belongs 1Co 12:16
in **s** of severe persecution, 1Th 1:6
of God to you in **s** of great 1Th 2:2

SPITS *(1)*
the discharge **s** on anyone who is Lv 15:8

SPITTING *(4)*
hide My face from scorn and **s**. Is 50:6
fingers in the man's ears and **s**, Mk 7:33
S on his eyes and laying His Mk 8:23
head with a reed and **s** on Him. Mk 15:19

SPLATTERED *(1)*
some of her blood **s** on the wall 2Kg 9:33

SPLENDID *(8)*
that He does is **s** and majestic; Ps 111:3
and against every **s** sea vessel. Is 2:16
s clothes instead of despair. Is 61:3
One who is **s** in His apparel, Is 63:1
bear fruit, and become a **s** vine. Ezk 17:8
strip off the **s** robe from those Mc 2:8
I will clothe you with **s** robes." Zch 3:4
All your **s** and glamorous things Rv 18:14

SPLENDIDLY *(5)*
rising **s**, is the joy of the Ps 48:2
warriors **s** dressed, horsemen Ezk 23:12
who are all **s** dressed, a huge Ezk 38:4
those who are **s** dressed and live Lk 7:25
accepted, you put up with it **s**! 2Co 11:4

SPLENDOR *(62)*
bull has **s**, and horns like Dt 33:17
The **s** of Israel lies slain on 2Sm 1:19
S and majesty are before Him; 1Ch 16:27
the LORD in the **s** of ⌊His⌋ 1Ch 16:29
glory and the **s** and the majesty 1Ch 29:11
to praise the **s** of ⌊His⌋ 2Ch 20:21
the magnificent **s** of his Est 1:4
or at the moon moving in **s**, Jb 31:26
yourself with majesty and **s**, Jb 40:10
You confer majesty and **s** on him. Ps 21:5
the LORD in the **s** of ⌊His⌋ Ps 29:2
the voice of the LORD in **s**. Ps 29:4
In your majesty and **s**— Ps 45:3
in your **s** ride triumphantly in Ps 45:4
captivity and His **s** to the hand Ps 78:61
have made his **s** cease and have Ps 89:44
and Your **s** by their children. Ps 90:16
S and majesty are before Him; Ps 96:6
the LORD in the **s** of ⌊His⌋ Ps 96:9
are clothed with majesty and **s**. Ps 104:1
In holy **s**, from the womb of the Ps 110:3
of Your glorious **s** and Your Ps 145:5
the glorious **s** of Your kingdom Ps 145:12
large population is a king's **s**, Pr 14:28
and the **s** of old men is gray Pr 20:29
LORD and from His majestic **s**. Is 2:10
LORD and from His majestic **s**, Is 2:19
LORD and from His majestic **s**, Is 2:21
Your **s** has been brought down to Is 14:11
kings of the nations lie in **s**, Is 14:18
Moab's **s** will become an object Is 16:14
will be like the **s** of the Is 17:3
On that day the **s** of Jacob will Is 17:4
The **S** of the Righteous One. Is 24:16
flower of its beautiful **s**, Is 28:1
flower of his beautiful **s**, Is 28:4
and a diadem of **s** to the remnant Is 28:5
will make the **s** of His voice Is 30:30
the **s** of Carmel and Sharon. Is 35:2
of the LORD, the **s** of our God. Is 35:2
in Zion, My **s** in Israel. Is 46:13
had no form or **s** that we should Is 53:2
and your God will be your **s**. Is 60:19
All her **s** has vanished from Lm 1:6
for it was perfect through My **s**, Ezk 16:14
or display ⌊your⌋ **s** in the land Ezk 26:20
helmets in you; they gave you **s**. Ezk 27:10
wisdom and will defile your **s**. Ezk 28:7
the sake of your **s** you corrupted Ezk 28:17
my majesty and **s** returned to me Dn 4:36
and his **s** will be like the olive Hs 14:6
Selah His **s** covers the heavens, Hab 3:3
will be clothed in **s** and will Zch 6:13
of the world and their **s**. Mt 4:8
in all his **s** was adorned like Mt 6:29
give You their **s** and all this Lk 4:6
in all his **s** was adorned like Lk 12:27
but the **s** of the heavenly bodies 1Co 15:40
There is a **s** of the sun, another 1Co 15:41
for star differs from star in **s**. 1Co 15:41
the church to Himself in **s**, Eph 5:27
earth was illuminated by his **s**. Rv 18:1

SPLINT *(1)*
applied and no **s** put on to Ezk 30:21

SPLINTERED *(4)*
stalk of this **s** reed, which if 2Kg 18:21
Egypt, that **s** reed of a staff, Is 36:6
by the hand, you **s**, tearing all Ezk 29:7
My grapevine and **s** My fig tree. Jl 1:7

SPLIT *(21)*
these to Him, **s** them down the Gn 15:10
He **s** wood for a burnt offering Gn 22:3
the ground beneath them **s** open. Nm 16:31
So God **s** a hollow place ⌊in the Jdg 15:19
joy that the earth **s** open from 1Kg 1:40
people of Israel were **s** in half: 1Kg 16:21
shaken the land and **s** it open. Ps 60:2
He **s** the sea and brought them Ps 78:13
He **s** rocks in the wilderness and Ps 78:15
wind and will **s** it into seven Is 11:15
the earth is **s** open; the earth Is 24:19
He **s** the rock, and water gushed Is 48:21
stands at the **s** in the road, Ezk 21:21
and the valleys will **s** apart, Mc 1:4
Selah You **s** the earth with Hab 3:9
Olives will be **s** in half from Zch 14:4
sanctuary was **s** in two from top Mt 27:51
quaked and the rocks were **s**. Mt 27:51
sanctuary was **s** in two from top Mk 15:38
sanctuary was **s** down the middle Lk 23:45
The great city **s** into three Rv 16:19

SPLITS *(1)*
the one who **s** trees may be Ec 10:9

SPOIL *(32)*
overtake, I will divide the **s**. Ex 15:9
and the **s** from the cities Dt 2:35
and the **s** from the cities Dt 3:7
gather all its **s** in the middle Dt 13:16
city and all its **s** for the LORD Dt 13:16

city—all its **s**—as plunder. Dt 20:14
may enjoy the **s** of your enemies Dt 20:14
may plunder its **s** and livestock Jos 8:2
cattle and **s** of that city for Jos 8:27
Share the **s** of your enemies with Jos 22:8
but they took no **s** of silver. Jdg 5:19
not finding and dividing the **s**— Jdg 5:30
the **s** of colored garments for Jdg 5:30
the **s** of an embroidered garment Jdg 5:30
and the **s** of Hadadezer son of 2Sm 8:12
each other. So, to the **s**, Moab!" 2Kg 3:23
become plunder and **s** to all 2Kg 21:14
who stays at home divides the **s**. Ps 68:12
can be their **s** and they can Is 10:2
Your **s** will be gathered as Is 33:4
Then abundant **s** will be divided, Is 33:23
He will receive the mighty as **s**, Is 53:12
I will **s** the plans of Judah and Jr 19:7
Your despoilers will become **s**, Jr 30:16
herds of cattle will become **s**. Jr 49:32
to the wicked of the earth as **s**, Ezk 7:21
wealth as **s** and plunder your Ezk 26:12
seizing its **s** and taking its Ezk 29:19
order to seize **s** and carry off Ezk 38:12
Have you come to seize **s**? Ezk 38:13
possessions, to seize great **s**? Ezk 38:13
Then you will become **s** for them. Hab 2:7

SPOILED *(1)*

longer be called pampered and **s**. Is 47:1

SPOILS *(12)*

and took away all the **s** of war Nm 31:11
animals, and **s** of war to Moses, Nm 31:12
I saw among the **s** a beautiful Jos 7:21
plundered all the **s** and cattle Jos 11:14
their possessions as **s** of war. Est 8:11
and the **s** of Samaria will Is 8:4
as they rejoice when dividing **s**. Is 9:3
My rage, to take **s**, to plunder, Is 10:6
his life like the **s** ⌊of war⌋. Jr 21:9
life like the **s** ⌊of war⌋ and Jr 38:2
your life like the **s** ⌊of war⌋." Jr 39:18
life like the **s** ⌊of war⌋ Jr 45:5

SPOKE *(306)*

Then God **s** to Noah, Gn 8:15
she named the LORD who **s** to her: Gn 16:13
the ground, and God **s** with him: Gn 17:3
Then he **s** to Him again, "Suppose Gn 18:29
So Lot went out and **s** to his Gn 19:14
Then Isaac **s** to his father Gn 22:7
wife⌋ and **s** to the Hittites Gn 23:3
who **s** to me and swore to me, Gn 24:7
girl and **s** tenderly to her. Gn 34:3
their city and **s** to the men Gn 34:20
Although she **s** to Joseph day Gn 39:10
strangers and **s** harshly to them. Gn 42:7
he turned back and **s** to them. Gn 42:24
of the country **s** harshly to us Gn 42:30
Joseph's steward and **s** to him at Gn 43:19
That night God **s** to Israel in a Gn 46:2
them and **s** kindly to them. Gn 50:21
God **s** to Moses, telling him, Ex 6:2
Then the LORD **s** to Moses, Ex 6:10
Then the LORD **s** to Moses and Ex 6:13
the ones who **s** to Pharaoh king Ex 6:27
the day the LORD **s** to Moses in Ex 6:28
Aaron 83 when they **s** to Pharaoh. Ex 7:7
The LORD **s** to Moses: Ex 13:1
Then the LORD **s** to Moses: Ex 14:1
The LORD **s** to Moses, Ex 16:11
Moses **s** and God answered him in Ex 19:19
Then God **s** all these words: Ex 20:1
The LORD **s** to Moses: Ex 25:1
The LORD **s** to Moses: Ex 30:11
The LORD **s** to Moses: Ex 30:17
The LORD **s** to Moses: Ex 30:22
The LORD also **s** to Moses: Ex 31:1
The LORD **s** to Moses: "Go down at Ex 32:7
The LORD **s** to Moses: "Go, leave Ex 33:1
The LORD **s** with Moses face to Ex 33:11
to him, and Moses **s** to them. Ex 34:31
The LORD **s** to Moses: Ex 40:1
summoned Moses and **s** to him from Lv 1:1
Then the LORD **s** to Moses: Lv 4:1
Then the LORD **s** to Moses: Lv 5:14
The LORD **s** to Moses: Lv 6:1
The LORD **s** to Moses: Lv 6:8
The LORD **s** to Moses: Lv 6:19
The LORD **s** to Moses: Lv 6:24
The LORD **s** to Moses: Lv 7:22
The LORD **s** to Moses: Lv 7:28
The LORD **s** to Moses: Lv 8:1
The LORD **s** to Aaron: Lv 10:8
Moses **s** to Aaron and his Lv 10:12
The LORD **s** to Moses and Aaron: Lv 11:1
The LORD **s** to Moses: Lv 12:1
The LORD **s** to Moses and Aaron: Lv 13:1
The LORD **s** to Moses: Lv 14:1
The LORD **s** to Moses and Aaron: Lv 14:33
The LORD **s** to Moses and Aaron: Lv 15:1
The LORD **s** to Moses after the Lv 16:1
The LORD **s** to Moses: Lv 17:1
The LORD **s** to Moses: Lv 18:1
The LORD **s** to Moses: Lv 19:1
The LORD **s** to Moses: Lv 20:1
The LORD **s** to Moses: Lv 21:16
The LORD **s** to Moses: Lv 22:1
The LORD **s** to Moses: Lv 22:17
The LORD **s** to Moses: Lv 22:26
The LORD **s** to Moses: Lv 23:1
The LORD **s** to Moses: Lv 23:9
The LORD **s** to Moses: Lv 23:23
The LORD again **s** to Moses: Lv 23:26
The LORD **s** to Moses: Lv 23:33
The LORD **s** to Moses: Lv 24:1
Then the LORD **s** to Moses: Lv 24:13
After Moses **s** to the Israelites, Lv 24:23
The LORD **s** to Moses on Mount Lv 25:1
The LORD **s** to Moses: Lv 27:1
The LORD **s** to Moses in the tent Nm 1:1
The LORD **s** to Moses and Aaron: Nm 2:1
the time the LORD **s** with Moses Nm 3:1
The LORD **s** to Moses: Nm 3:5
The LORD **s** to Moses: Nm 3:11
The LORD **s** to Moses in the Nm 3:14
The LORD **s** to Moses again: Nm 3:44
The LORD **s** to Moses and Aaron: Nm 4:1
Then the LORD **s** to Moses and Nm 4:17
The LORD **s** to Moses: Nm 4:21
The LORD **s** to Moses: Nm 5:5
The LORD **s** to Moses: Nm 5:11
The LORD **s** to Moses: Nm 6:22
He **s** to him ⌊that way⌋. Nm 7:89
The LORD **s** to Moses: Nm 8:1
The LORD **s** to Moses: Nm 8:5
The LORD **s** to Moses: Nm 8:23
Then the LORD **s** to Moses: Nm 9:9
The LORD **s** to Moses: Nm 10:1
in the cloud and **s** to him. Nm 11:25
The LORD **s** to Moses: Nm 13:1
Then the LORD **s** to Moses and Nm 14:26
that the LORD **s** to Moses— Nm 15:22
The LORD **s** to Moses and Aaron, Nm 16:20
Then the LORD **s** to Moses: Nm 16:36
So Moses **s** to the Israelites, Nm 17:6
Then the LORD **s** to Aaron, Nm 18:8
The LORD **s** to Moses and Aaron, Nm 19:1
The LORD **s** to Moses, Nm 20:7
The people **s** against God and Nm 21:5
The LORD **s** to Moses, Nm 25:10
The LORD **s** to Moses, Nm 26:52
The LORD **s** to Moses, Nm 28:1
The LORD **s** to Moses, Nm 31:1
So Moses **s** to the people, Nm 31:3
LORD **s** to Moses in the plains Nm 33:50
The LORD **s** to Moses, Nm 34:1
The LORD **s** to Moses, Nm 34:16
The LORD again **s** to Moses in the Nm 35:1
the words Moses **s** to all Israel Dt 1:1
LORD our God **s** to us at Horeb, Dt 1:6
So I **s** to you, but you didn't Dt 1:43
the LORD **s** to me, Dt 2:17
Then the LORD **s** to you from the Dt 4:12
day the LORD **s** to you at Horeb Dt 4:15
The LORD **s** to you face to face Dt 5:4
The LORD **s** these commands in a Dt 5:22
your words when you **s** to me. Dt 5:28
which the LORD **s** to you from the Dt 9:10
priests **s** to all Israel, Dt 27:9
same day the LORD **s** to Moses, Dt 32:48
the LORD **s** to Joshua son of Nun, Jos 1:1
The LORD **s** to Joshua: Jos 3:7
Jordan, the LORD **s** to Joshua, Jos 4:1
Joshua **s** to the LORD in the Jos 10:12
since the LORD **s** this word to Jos 14:10
Then the LORD **s** to Joshua, Jos 20:1
They **s** no more about going to Jos 22:33
at Shechem and **s** to them and to Jdg 9:1
relatives **s** all these words Jdg 9:3
Then Gaal **s** again: "Look, people Jdg 9:37
You the man who **s** to my wife?" Jdg 13:11
Then he went and **s** to the woman, Jdg 14:7
and Samuel **s** with Saul on ⌊the⌋ 1Sm 9:25
While Saul **s** to the priest, 1Sm 14:19
David **s** to the men who were 1Sm 17:26
listened as he **s** to the men, 1Sm 17:28
"These are the words David **s**." 1Sm 18:24
Jonathan **s** well of David to his 1Sm 19:4
by the slave girls you **s** about." 2Sm 6:22
Nathan **s** all these words and 2Sm 7:17
was alive, we **s** to him, and he 2Sm 12:18
David's brother Shimeah, **s** up: 2Sm 13:32
When the king **s** as he did about 2Sm 14:13
the Gibeonites and **s** to them. 2Sm 21:2
David **s** the words of this song 2Sm 22:1
Spirit of the LORD **s** through me, 2Sm 23:2
The God of Israel **s**; the Rock of 2Sm 23:3
son was alive **s** to the king 1Kg 3:26
s directly to my father David, 1Kg 8:15
You **s** directly ⌊to him⌋ and You 1Kg 8:24
as You **s** through Your servant 1Kg 8:53
to Solomon and **s** to him about 1Kg 10:2
Israel came and **s** to Rehoboam: 1Kg 12:3
and **s** to them according to the 1Kg 12:14
An angel **s** to me by the word of 1Kg 13:18
and they went and **s** ⌊about it⌋ 1Kg 13:25
of the LORD that He **s** to him." 1Kg 13:26
So Ahab **s** to Naboth, saying, 1Kg 21:2
Because I **s** to Naboth the 1Kg 21:6
to meet you and **s** those words to 2Kg 1:7
to the word that Elisha **s**. 2Kg 2:22
word that He **s** through His 2Kg 9:36
a word the LORD **s** against the 2Kg 10:10
the LORD that He **s** to Jehu was, 2Kg 15:12
The settlers **s** to the king of 2Kg 17:26
Hebrew. Then he **s**: "Hear the 2Kg 18:28
The LORD **s** through His servants 2Kg 21:10
District. They **s** with her. 2Kg 22:14
you heard what I **s** against this 2Kg 22:19
He **s** kindly to him and set his 2Kg 25:28
Then the LORD **s** to the angel, 1Ch 21:27
Then Solomon **s** to all Israel, 2Ch 1:2
s directly to my father David, 2Ch 6:4
You **s** directly ⌊to him⌋, and You 2Ch 6:15
to Solomon and **s** with him about 2Ch 9:1
Israel came and **s** to Rehoboam: 2Ch 10:3
and **s** to them according to the 2Ch 10:14
They **s** against the God of 2Ch 32:19
and He **s** to him and gave him a 2Ch 32:24
The LORD **s** to Manasseh and his 2Ch 33:10
of the seers who **s** to him in the 2Ch 33:18
They **s** with her about this. 2Ch 34:22
of the prophecy he **s** against me. Neh 6:12
and **s** to them from heaven. Neh 9:13
of their children **s** the language Neh 13:24
s to Hathach and commanded Est 4:10
King Ahasuerus **s** up and asked Est 7:5
but no one **s** a word to him Jb 2:13
they saw me, they **s** well of me. Jb 29:11
Surely I **s** about things I did Jb 42:3
He **s**, and it came into being; Ps 33:9
fire burned. I **s** with my tongue Ps 39:3
I **s** about Your faithfulness and Ps 40:10
and my mouth **s** during my Ps 66:14
They **s** against God, saying, "Is Ps 78:19
You once **s** in a vision to Your Ps 89:19
He **s** to them in a pillar of Ps 99:7
He **s**, and insects came—gnats Ps 105:31
He **s** and locusts came—young Ps 105:34
and he **s** rashly with his lips. Ps 106:33
He **s** and raised a tempest that Ps 107:25
from a people who **s** a foreign Ps 114:1
Then the LORD **s** again to Ahaz: Is 7:10
The LORD **s** to me again: Is 8:5
not answer, I **s** and you did not Is 65:12
I **s** and they didn't hear; Is 66:4
disaster that I **s** against it, Jr 19:15
I **s** to you when you were secure. Jr 22:21
prophet Jeremiah **s** concerning Jr 25:2
I **s** to Zedekiah king of Judah in Jr 27:12
Then I **s** to the priests and all Jr 27:16
the words the LORD **s** to Israel Jr 30:4
time I ⌊first⌋ **s** to you during Jr 36:2
LORD that He **s** through Jeremiah Jr 37:2
king's palace and **s** to the king: Jr 38:8

for the word you s to us in the Jr 44:16
the prophet s to Baruch son Jr 45:1
the word the LORD s to Jeremiah Jr 46:13
word the LORD s about Babylon, Jr 50:1
He s kindly to him and set his Jr 52:32
He s to me, the Spirit entered Ezk 2:2
He s with me and said: Ezk 3:24
The LORD s to the man clothed in Ezk 10:2
I s to the exiles about all the Ezk 11:25
s to the people in the morning, Ezk 24:18
and s many words against Me. Ezk 35:13
you the one I s about in former Ezk 38:17
He s to me: "Son of man, look Ezk 40:4
The Chaldeans s to the king Dn 2:4
Then Daniel s with the king: Dn 6:21
had a mouth that s arrogantly. Dn 7:8
and a mouth that s arrogantly, Dn 7:20
who s in Your name to our kings, Dn 9:6
His words that He s against us Dn 9:12
As he s to me, I was Dn 10:19
When the LORD first s to Hosea, Hs 1:2
Bethel, and there He s with him. Hs 12:4
I s through the prophets and Hs 12:10
When Ephraim s, there was Hs 13:1
So He s to those standing before Zch 3:4
that the prophets s when the Zch 8:9
the LORD s to one another. Mal 3:16
had been driven out, the man s. Mt 9:33
Immediately Jesus s to them. Mt 14:27
that He s to them about John Mt 17:13
the house, Jesus s to him first, Mt 17:25
Once more Jesus s to them in Mt 22:1
Then Jesus s to the crowds and Mt 23:1
summoned them and s to them in Mk 3:23
Immediately He s with them and Mk 6:50
burning bush, how God s to him: Mk 12:26
just as He s to our ancestors, Lk 1:55
just as He s by the mouth of His Lk 1:70
s to them about the kingdom of Lk 9:11
had been mute, s, and the crowds Lk 11:14
Remember how He s to you when Lk 24:6
My words that I s to you while I Lk 24:44
"No man ever s like this!" Jn 7:46
Then Jesus s to them again: Jn 8:12
s these words by the treasury, Jn 8:20
saw His glory and s about Him. Jn 12:41
Remember the word I s to you: Jn 15:20
Jesus s these things, looked up Jn 17:1
went out and s to the girl who Jn 18:16
of David s in advance about Ac 1:16
he s concerning the resurrection Ac 2:31
which God s about by the mouth Ac 3:21
and the Spirit by whom he s. Ac 6:10
God s in this way: His Ac 7:6
the angel who s to him on Mount Ac 7:38
just as He who s to Moses Ac 7:44
angel of the Lord s to Philip: Ac 8:26
the angel who s to him had gone, Ac 10:7
motioned with his hand and s: Ac 13:16
synagogue and s in such a way Ac 14:1
for some time and s boldly, Ac 14:3
After they s the message in Ac 14:25
and Iconium s highly of him. Ac 16:2
We sat down and s to the women Ac 16:13
Then they s the message of the Ac 16:32
he s and taught the things about Ac 18:25
the synagogue and s boldly over Ac 19:8
Paul s to them, and since he was Ac 20:7
Now as he s about righteousness, Ac 24:25
Spirit correctly s through the Ac 28:25
was a child, I s like a child, I 1Co 13:11
I wish all of you s in other 1Co 14:5
therefore I s, we also believe, 2Co 4:13
Long ago God s to the fathers by Heb 1:1
the prophets who s in the Lord's Jms 5:10
the Holy Spirit, men s from God. 2Pt 1:21
speechless donkey s with a human 2Pt 2:16
seven thunders s with their Rv 10:3
And when the seven thunders s, Rv 10:4
heard from heaven s to me again Rv 10:8
He s with a loud voice: Rv 14:7
them and s with a loud voice Rv 14:9
seven bowls came and s with me: Rv 17:1
plagues, came and s with me: Rv 21:9
The one who s with me had a gold Rv 21:15

SPOKEN *(205)*

son, just as the LORD has s." Gn 24:51
the place where He had s to him. Gn 35:13
place where He had s to him— Gn 35:14
where God had s with him Bethel. Gn 35:15
Joseph said to them, "I have s: Gn 42:14
do all that the LORD has s." Ex 19:8
seen that I have s to you from Ex 20:22
be magnified just as You have s: Nm 14:17
the LORD, have s. I swear that I Nm 14:35
as the LORD had s through Moses. Nm 27:23
the LORD has s to your servants Nm 32:31
that these people have s to you. Dt 5:28
that He had s to you on the Dt 10:4
said to me, 'They have s well. Dt 18:17
a message the LORD has not s?' Dt 18:21
is a message the LORD has not s. Dt 18:22
The prophet has s it Dt 18:22
Joshua had s to the people, Jos 6:8
of the LORD had s these words to Jdg 2:4
these things or s to us now like Jdg 13:23
redeemer Boaz had s about came Ru 4:1
matter you and I have s about, 1Sm 20:23
if you had not s up, the troops 2Sm 2:27
LORD has s concerning David: 2Sm 3:18
for You have also s about Your 2Sm 7:19
Lord GOD, have s, and with Your 2Sm 7:29
prophecy He had s at Shiloh 1Kg 2:27
do as my lord the king has s." 1Kg 2:38
the LORD had s through Ahijah 1Kg 12:15
the sign that the LORD has s: 1Kg 13:3
words that he had s to the king. 1Kg 13:11
of the LORD He had s through His 1Kg 14:18
of the LORD He had s through His 1Kg 15:29
the LORD He had s against Baasha 1Kg 16:12
LORD He had s through Joshua 1Kg 16:34
LORD He had s through Elijah. 1Kg 17:16
the LORD has not s through me." 1Kg 22:28
word of the LORD that He had s. 1Kg 22:38
of the LORD that Elijah had s. 2Kg 1:17
word of the LORD s to Elijah. 2Kg 10:17
had s through His servant, 2Kg 14:25
word the LORD has s against him: 2Kg 19:21
LORD that you have s is good," 2Kg 20:19
the LORD had s about to David 2Kg 21:7
of the LORD He had s through His 2Kg 24:2
have I ever s a word to even one 1Ch 17:6
for You have s about Your 1Ch 17:17
that You have s concerning Your 1Ch 17:23
at Gad's command s in the name 1Ch 21:19
that He had s through Ahijah 2Ch 10:15
the LORD has not s through me." 2Ch 18:27
like they had s against the gods 2Ch 32:19
of the LORD s through Jeremiah 2Ch 36:22
of the LORD s through Jeremiah Ezr 1:1
after I have s, you may continue Jb 21:3
Surely you have s in my hearing, Jb 33:8
I have s once, and I will not Jb 40:5
you have not s the truth about Jb 42:7
you have not s the truth about Jb 42:8
God has s in His sanctuary: Ps 60:6
has s once; I have heard this Ps 62:11
God has s in His sanctuary: Ps 108:7
will obey the decree You have s. Ps 119:88
A word s at the right time is Pr 25:11
sister on the day she is s for? Sg 8:8
earth, for the LORD has s: Is 1:2
For the mouth of the LORD has s. Is 1:20
they have s and acted against Is 3:8
the LORD had s through Isaiah Is 20:2
LORD, the God of Israel, has s. Is 21:17
The Lord GOD of Hosts has s. Is 22:14
Indeed, the LORD has s. Is 22:25
of the sea, for the sea has s: Is 23:4
for the LORD has s this message. Is 24:3
whole earth, for the LORD has s. Is 25:8
word the LORD has s against him: Is 37:22
He has s to me, and He Himself Is 38:15
LORD that you have s is good." Is 39:8
for the mouth of the LORD has s. Is 40:5
have not s in secret, somewhere Is 45:19
Yes, I have s; so I will also Is 46:11
I—I have s; yes, I have called Is 48:15
I have not s in secret; Is 48:16
and had not s deceitfully. Is 53:9
For the mouth of the LORD has s. Is 58:14
your lips have s lies, and you Is 59:3
is what you have s and done, Jr 3:5
dark. I have s; I have planned, Jr 4:28
Because you have s this word, Jr 5:14
and because I have s to you time Jr 7:13
has the LORD s to, that he may Jr 9:12
word that the LORD has s to you, Jr 10:1
be proud, for the LORD has s. Jr 13:15
my words were s in Your presence Jr 17:16
or What has the LORD s? Jr 23:35
and What has the LORD s? Jr 23:37
I have s to you time and time Jr 25:3
My words I have s against it, Jr 25:13
for he has s to us in the name Jr 26:16
because you have s rebellion Jr 28:16
wives and have s a lie in My Jr 29:23
the words that I have s to you, Jr 30:2
What You have s has happened. Jr 32:24
that I have s concerning the Jr 33:14
for I have s ⌊this⌋ word." Jr 34:5
I have s to you time and time Jr 35:14
them because I have s to them, Jr 35:17
the words I have s to you Jr 36:2
the LORD had s to Jeremiah. Jr 36:4
hear that I have s with you and Jr 38:25
The LORD has s concerning you, Jr 42:19
you women have s with your Jr 44:25
the LORD, have s in My jealousy. Ezk 5:13
rebukes. I, the LORD, have s. Ezk 5:15
I, the LORD, have s." Ezk 5:17
even though I had not s? Ezk 13:7
you have s falsely and had Ezk 13:8
know that I, Yahweh, have s." Ezk 17:21
have s and I will do ⌊it⌋. Ezk 17:24
I, the LORD, have s." Ezk 21:17
for I, the LORD, have s." Ezk 21:32
the LORD, have s, and I will act Ezk 22:14
says, when the LORD has not s. Ezk 22:28
breasts. For I have s. ⌊This is⌋ Ezk 23:34
the LORD, have s. It is coming, Ezk 24:14
to spread nets, for I have s." Ezk 26:5
for I, the LORD, have s." Ezk 26:14
For I have s. ⌊This is⌋ Ezk 28:10
foreigners. I, the LORD, have s. Ezk 30:12
among them. I, the LORD, have s. Ezk 34:24
have s and I will do ⌊it⌋. Ezk 36:36
I have s, and I will do ⌊it⌋." Ezk 37:14
the open field, for I have s." Ezk 39:5
This is the day I have s about. Ezk 39:8
nation, for the LORD has s. Jl 3:8
exiled to Kir. The LORD has s. Am 1:5
will perish. The Lord GOD has s. Am 1:8
exile together. The LORD has s. Am 1:15
with him. The LORD has s. Am 2:3
that the LORD has s against you, Am 3:1
The Lord GOD has s; who will not Am 3:8
pass among you. The LORD has s. Am 5:17
of Hosts, is His name. He has s. Am 5:27
Yahweh your God has s. Am 9:15
of Esau, for the LORD has s. Ob 18
before your eyes. Yahweh has s. Zph 3:20
because you have s falsely in Zch 13:3
"What have we s against You?" Mal 3:13
fulfill what was s by the Lord Mt 1:22
so that what was s by the Lord Mt 2:15
Then what was s through Jeremiah Mt 2:17
fulfill what was s through the Mt 2:23
For he is the one s of through Mt 3:3
fulfill what was s through the Mt 4:14
so that what was s through the Mt 8:17
so that what was s through the Mt 12:17
so that what was s through the Mt 13:35
so that what was s through the Mt 21:4
read what was s to you by God: Mt 22:31
s of by the prophet Daniel, Mt 24:15
the words Jesus had s, Mt 26:75
Then what was s through the Mt 27:9
Jesus had s the word to him, Mk 14:72
because what was s to her by the Lk 1:45
the voice had s, only Jesus was Lk 9:36
Teacher, You have s well." Lk 20:39
all that the prophets have s! Lk 24:25
that I have s to you are spirit Jn 6:63
We know that God has s to Moses. Jn 9:29
said, "An angel has s to Him!" Jn 12:29
the word I have s will judge him Jn 12:48
For I have not s on My own, Jn 12:49
I have s these things to you Jn 14:25
of the word I have s to you. Jn 15:3
I have s these things to you so Jn 15:11
If I had not come and s to them, Jn 15:22
because I have s these things to Jn 16:6
I have s these things to you in Jn 16:25

"I have s openly to the world," Jn 18:20
and I haven't s anything in Jn 18:20
"If I have s wrongly," Jesus Jn 18:23
this is what was s through the Ac 2:16
all the prophets who have s, Ac 3:24
had testified and s the message Ac 8:25
Damascus he had s boldly in the Ac 9:27
to decay, He has s in this way, Ac 13:34
God's message be s to you first. Ac 13:46
attention to what was s by Paul. Ac 16:14
or an angel has s to him?" Ac 23:9
and reported or s anything evil Ac 28:21
aware that it is s against Ac 28:22
with the s words of God. Rm 3:2
according to what had been s: Rm 4:18
how will what is s be known? 1Co 14:9
We have s openly to you, 2Co 6:11
as I have s everything to you 2Co 7:14
promises were s to Abraham and Gl 3:16
He has s to us by ⌊His⌋ Son, Heb 1:2
if the message s through angels Heb 2:2
It was first s by the Lord and Heb 2:3
somewhere He has s about the Heb 4:4
He would not have s later about Heb 4:8
not another word be s to them, Heb 12:19
leaders who have s God's word to Heb 13:7
words previously s by the holy 2Pt 3:2

SPOKES *(1)*
axles, rims, s, and hubs were 1Kg 7:33

SPOKESMAN *(2)*
He will be your s, and you will Ex 4:16
ones, you will be My s. Jr 15:19

SPONGE *(3)*
one of them ran and got a s, Mt 27:48
and filled a s with sour wine, Mk 15:36
so they fixed a s full of sour Jn 19:29

SPONSOR *(1)*
Who ⌊else⌋ will be my s? Jb 17:3

SPOT *(20)*
or s on the skin of his body, Lv 13:2
But if the s on the skin of his Lv 13:4
a reddish-white s develops where Lv 13:19
and if the s seems to be beneath Lv 13:20
But if the s remains where it is Lv 13:23
a reddish-white or white s, Lv 13:24
the hair in the s has turned Lv 13:25
white and the s appears to be Lv 13:25
white hair in the s and it is Lv 13:26
But if the s has remained where Lv 13:28
and for a swelling, scab, or s, Lv 14:56
or make a bald s on your head on Dt 14:1
him dead on the s for his 2Sm 6:7
completely burned up on the s. 2Sm 23:7
hand over the s and cure the 2Kg 5:11
and his eyes s every treasure. Jb 28:10
to the head, no s is uninjured— Is 1:6
without s or wrinkle or any such Eph 5:27
without s or blame until 1Tm 6:14
in peace without s or blemish 2Pt 3:14

SPOTS *(4)*
a woman has white s on the skin Lv 13:38
If the s on the skin of the body Lv 13:39
not make bald s on their heads, Lv 21:5
his skin, or a leopard his s? Jr 13:23

SPOTTED *(10)*
sheep that is speckled or s, Gn 30:32
and the s and speckled among the Gn 30:32
that are not speckled or s, Gn 30:33
streaked and s male goats and Gn 30:35
speckled and s female goats— Gn 30:35
streaked, speckled, and s young. Gn 30:39
'The s sheep will be your wages,' Gn 31:8
then all the sheep were born s. Gn 31:8
the streaked, s, and speckled Gn 31:10
are streaked, s, and speckled, Gn 31:12

SPRANG *(8)*
and they s up quickly since the Mt 13:5
soil, and it s up right away, Mk 4:5
when it s up, it withered, since Lk 8:6
the thorns s up with it and Lk 8:7
it s up, it produced a crop: Lk 8:8
When a gentle south wind s up, Ac 27:13
After one day a south wind s up, Ac 28:13
commandment came, sin s to life Rm 7:9

SPRAWL *(1)*
of those who s out will come to Am 6:7

SPRAWLED *(1)*
with⌋ ivory, s out on their Am 6:4

SPREAD *(157)*
and they will s over the earth Gn 8:17
s out over the earth and Gn 9:7
peoples s out into their Gn 10:5
nations on earth s out from Gn 10:32
and you will s out toward the Gn 28:14
famine had s across the whole Gn 41:56
they multiplied and s so that Ex 1:12
You must not s a false report. Ex 23:1
are to have wings s out above, Ex 25:20
They had wings s out, covering Ex 37:9
Then he s the tent over the Ex 40:19
sight and has not s on the skin, Lv 13:5
faded and has not s on the skin, Lv 13:6
if the scab has s on the skin, Lv 13:8
where it is and does not s, Lv 13:23
If it has s further on the skin, Lv 13:27
and has not s on the skin but Lv 13:28
has not s and there is no Lv 13:32
and if it has not s on the skin Lv 13:34
outbreak has s on the skin, Lv 13:36
If it has s in the fabric, Lv 13:51
has not s in the fabric, Lv 13:53
the contamination has not s, Lv 13:55
contamination has s on the walls Lv 14:39
has s in the house, Lv 14:44
has not s in the house after it Lv 14:48
s a solid blue cloth on top, Nm 4:6
They are to s a blue cloth over Nm 4:7
They are to s a scarlet cloth Nm 4:8
They are to s a blue cloth over Nm 4:11
bronze⌋ altar, s a purple cloth Nm 4:13
They are to s a covering made of Nm 4:14
and they s them out all around Nm 11:32
those men who s the report about Nm 14:37
They will s out the cloth Dt 22:17
and his fame s throughout the Jos 6:27
and s them out in the LORD's Jos 7:23
So they s out a mantle, and Jdg 8:25
S your cloak over me, for you Ru 3:9
s through the ⌊Philistine⌋ 1Sm 14:15
shook, and terror from God s. 1Sm 14:15
s out over the entire area, 1Sm 30:16
Philistines to s the good news 1Sm 31:9
came and s out in the Valley 2Sm 5:18
up again and s out in the Valley 2Sm 5:22
The battle s over the entire 2Sm 18:8
sackcloth and s it out for 2Sm 21:10
Since their wings were s out, 1Kg 6:27
of Israel and s out his hands 1Kg 8:22
with his hands s out toward 1Kg 8:54
and s it over the king's face. 2Kg 8:15
and s it out before the LORD. 2Kg 19:14
Philistines to s the good news 1Ch 10:9
us s out and send the message 1Ch 13:2
Then David's fame s throughout 1Ch 14:17
cherubim that s out ⌊their wings 1Ch 28:18
the cherubim s their wings over 2Ch 5:8
of Israel and s out his hands. 2Ch 6:12
and s out his hands toward 2Ch 6:13
and his fame s as far as the 2Ch 26:8
So his fame s even to distant 2Ch 26:15
the proposal and s the message 2Ch 30:5
When the word s, the Israelites 2Ch 31:5
my knees and s out my hands to Ezr 9:5
The work is enormous and s out, Neh 4:19
they proclaimed and s this news Neh 8:15
and his fame s throughout the Est 9:4
are s out in the land Jb 1:10
shoots s out over his garden. Jb 8:16
will not s over the land. Jb 15:29
Sheol as my home, s out my bed Jb 17:13
Your table was s with choice Jb 36:16
how the clouds s out or how the Jb 36:29
you help God s out the skies as Jb 37:18
understanding and s its wings to Jb 39:26
S Your faithful love over those Ps 36:10
our God and s out our hands to Ps 44:20
I s out my hands to You. Ps 88:9
He s a cloud as a covering and Ps 105:39
He s the land on the waters. Ps 136:6
they s a net along the path and Ps 140:5
I s out my hands to You; Ps 143:6
is foolish to s a net where any Pr 1:17
I've s coverings on my bed— Pr 7:16
and s the fragrance of its Sg 4:16
Maggots are s out under you, Is 14:11
as Jazer and s to the desert. Is 16:8
Their shoots s out and reached Is 16:8
those who s nets on the water Is 19:8
a table, and s out a carpet! Is 21:5
He will s out his arms in the Is 25:11
there they will s out and strip Is 27:10
of the mast or s out the flag. Is 33:23
LORD's house and s it out before Is 37:14
who s out the earth and what Is 42:5
who alone s out the earth; Is 44:24
My right hand s out the heavens Is 48:13
For you will s out to the right Is 54:3
to s out sackcloth and ashes? Is 58:5
I s out My hands all day long to Is 65:2
and every friend s slander. Jr 9:4
and s out the heavens by His Jr 10:12
ungodliness has s throughout the Jr 23:15
that day will be ⌊s⌋ from one Jr 25:33
an eagle and s his wings against Jr 48:40
and s out the heavens by His Jr 51:15
s a net for my feet and turned Lm 1:13
Their wings were s upward; Ezk 1:11
was s out over the heads of the Ezk 1:22
A fire will s from it to the Ezk 5:4
But I will s My net over him, Ezk 12:13
So I s the edge of My garment Ezk 16:8
Your fame s among the nations Ezk 16:14
You s your legs to everyone who Ezk 16:25
I will s My net over him, and he Ezk 17:20
They s their net over him; Ezk 19:8
couch with a table s before it, Ezk 23:41
a place in the sea to s nets, Ezk 26:5
you will be a place to s nets. Ezk 26:14
grew long as it s ⌊them⌋ out Ezk 31:5
I will s My net over you with an Ezk 32:3
they who ⌊once⌋ s terror in the Ezk 32:23
who ⌊once⌋ s their terror in the Ezk 32:24
terror was ⌊once⌋ s in the land Ezk 32:25
terror was ⌊once⌋ s in the land Ezk 32:26
For I will s My terror in the Ezk 32:32
their fame will s on the day I Ezk 39:13
where nets are s out to dry. Ezk 47:10
Mizpah and a net s out on Tabor. Hs 5:1
I will s My net over them; Hs 7:12
branches will s, and his Hs 14:6
or He will s like fire Am 5:6
and I will s animal waste over Mal 2:3
news about Him s throughout Mt 4:24
And this news s throughout that Mt 9:26
went out and s the news about Mt 9:31
flour until it s through all of Mt 13:33
A very large crowd s their robes Mt 21:8
story has been s among Jewish Mt 28:15
His fame then s throughout the Mk 1:28
it widely and to s the news, Mk 1:45
Many people s their robes on the Mk 11:8
and others s leafy branches cut Mk 11:8
and news about Him s throughout Lk 4:14
the news about Him s even more, Lk 5:15
but you go and s the news of the Lk 9:60
of flour until it s through the Lk 13:21
and s the mud on his eyes. Jn 9:6
Jesus made mud, s it on my eyes, Jn 9:11
So this report s to the brothers Jn 21:23
so this does not s any further Ac 4:17
of the Lord s through the whole Ac 13:49
in this way death s to all men, Rm 5:12
day long I have s out My hands Rm 10:21
message may s rapidly and be 2Th 3:1
their word will s like gangrene, 2Tm 2:17
and ointment to s on your eyes Rv 3:18

SPREADING *(17)*
not go about s slander among Lv 19:16
him by s a bad report about Nm 14:36
cherubim were s their wings over 1Kg 8:7
afflictions and s out his hands 1Kg 8:38
and s out his hands toward this 2Ch 6:29
to these rumors you are s; Neh 6:8
⌊His⌋ throne, s His cloud over Jb 26:9
s the mud like a threshing Jb 41:30
s out the sky like a canopy, Ps 104:2
and its s streams will fill your Is 8:8
yours will be like a s breach, Is 30:13
are stubborn rebels s slander. Jr 6:28
down and s its wings over Jr 49:22
It sprouted and became a s vine, Ezk 17:6
like the dawn s over the Jl 2:2

the trees and s them on the road Mt 21:8
they were s their robes on the Lk 19:36

SPREADS *(15)*
of control, s to thornbushes, Ex 22:6
But if the scab s further on his Lv 13:7
If it s further on the skin, Lv 13:22
the scaly outbreak s further on Lv 13:35
He s His wings, catches him, and Dt 32:11
s His lightning around Him and Jb 36:30
east wind that s across the Jb 38:24
When she proudly s her wings, Jb 39:18
He s snow like wool; Ps 147:16
and whoever s slander is a fool. Pr 10:18
A contrary man s conflict, Pr 16:28
his neighbor s a net for his Pr 29:5
as a swimmer s out ⌊his arms⌋ to Is 25:11
thin cloth and s them out like Is 40:22
and s through us in every place 2Co 2:14

SPRIG *(2)*
I will take ⌊a s⌋ from the lofty Ezk 17:22
a tender s from its topmost Ezk 17:22

SPRING *(53)*
LORD found her by a s of water Gn 16:7
wilderness, the s on the way to Gn 16:7
That is why she named the s, Gn 16:14
here at the s where the Gn 24:13
down to the s, filled her jug Gn 24:16
ran out to the man at the s. Gn 24:29
there by the camels at the s. Gn 24:30
Today when I came to the s, Gn 24:42
I am standing here at a s. Gn 24:43
down to the s and drew water. Gn 24:45
found a well of s water there. Gn 26:19
a fruitful vine beside a s; Gn 49:22
A s or cistern containing water Lv 11:36
S up, well—sing to it! Nm 21:17
curved to the s of the Waters Jos 15:9
went to the s at the Waters of Jos 18:15
camped beside the s of Harod. Jdg 7:1
was camped by the s in Jezreel. 1Sm 29:1
the s when kings march out ⌊to 2Sm 11:1
land to every s of water and to 1Kg 18:5
for in the s the king of Aram 1Kg 20:22
the s, Ben-hadad mobilized the 1Kg 20:26
went out to the s of water, 2Kg 2:21
and stop up every s of water. 2Kg 3:19
up every s of water and cut 2Kg 3:25
the land in the s of the year. 2Kg 13:20
the s when kings march out ⌊to 1Ch 20:1
the s Nebuchadnezzar sent ⌊for 2Ch 36:10
their mouths as for s showers. Jb 29:23
like s showers that water the Ps 72:6
Truth will s up from the earth, Ps 85:11
the flint into a s of water. Ps 114:8
is like a cloud with s rain. Pr 16:15
like a muddied s or a polluted Pr 25:26
the grasshopper loses its s, Ec 12:5
the jar is shattered at the s, Ec 12:6
a locked garden and a sealed s. Sg 4:12
You are⌋ a garden s, a well of Sg 4:15
and righteousness s up with it. Is 45:8
garden and like a s whose waters Is 58:11
enables what is sown to s up, Is 61:11
praise to s up before all the Is 61:11
why there has been no s rain. Jr 3:3
like the s showers that water Hs 6:3
fail, and his s will run dry. Hs 13:15
autumn and s rain as before. Jl 2:23
and a s will issue from the Jl 3:18
Does a trap s from the ground Am 3:5
at the time the s crop first Am 7:1
rain in the season of s rain. Zch 10:1
Does a s pour out sweet and Jms 3:11
can a saltwater s yield fresh Jms 3:12
from the s of living water Rv 21:6

SPRINGING *(1)*
a well of water s up within him Jn 4:14

SPRINGS *(30)*
found the hot s in the Gn 36:24
there were 12 s of water and 70 Ex 15:27
There were 12 s of water and 70 Nm 33:9
of water, s, and deep water Dt 8:7
give me the s of water also." Jos 15:19
gave her the upper and lower s. Jos 15:19
Negev, give me s of water also." Jdg 1:15
her both the upper and lower s. Jdg 1:15
waters of the s that were 2Ch 32:3
up all the s and the stream 2Ch 32:4
You opened up s and streams; Ps 74:15
say⌋, "All my s are in you." Ps 87:7
He causes the s to gush into the Ps 104:10
of the sky live beside ⌊the s⌋; Ps 104:12
s of water into thirsty ground, Ps 107:33
water, dry land into s of water. Ps 107:35
Should your s flow in the Pr 5:16
depths and no s filled with Pr 8:24
water from the s of salvation, Is 12:3
and the thirsty land s of water. Is 35:7
and s in the middle of the Is 41:18
and dry land into s of water. Is 41:18
and lead them to s of water. Is 49:10
the underground s made it tall, Ezk 31:4
that no root of bitterness s up, Heb 12:15
people are s without water, 2Pt 2:17
guide them to s of living waters Rv 7:17
of the rivers and s of water. Rv 8:10
earth, the sea and s of water." Rv 14:7
the rivers and the s of water, Rv 16:4

SPRINGWATER *(1)*
they make it a source of s; Ps 84:6

SPRINKLE *(31)*
and s ⌊it⌋ on all sides of the Ex 29:16
S the ⌊remaining⌋ blood on all Ex 29:20
and s ⌊them⌋ on Aaron and his Ex 29:21
the blood and s it on all sides Lv 1:5
the priests will s its blood Lv 1:11
priests will s the blood on all Lv 3:2
sons will s its blood on all Lv 3:8
sons will s its blood on all Lv 3:13
the blood and s some of it seven Lv 4:6
the blood and s ⌊it⌋ seven times Lv 4:17
Then he will s some of the blood Lv 5:9
priest is to s its blood on all Lv 7:2
He will then s ⌊the blood⌋ seven Lv 14:7
left palm and s some of the oil Lv 14:16
priest will s some of the oil Lv 14:27
and s the house seven times. Lv 14:51
bull's blood and s ⌊it⌋ with his Lv 16:14
then he will s some of the blood Lv 16:14
he is to s it against the mercy Lv 16:15
He is to s some of the blood on Lv 16:19
The priest will then s the blood Lv 17:6
S them with the purification Nm 8:7
You are to s their blood on the Nm 18:17
his finger and s it seven times Nm 19:4
the water, and s the tent, all Nm 19:18
He is also to s the one who Nm 19:18
is clean is to s the unclean Nm 19:19
S on the altar all the blood of 2Kg 16:15
Heavens, s from above, and let Is 45:8
so He will s many nations. Is 52:15
will also s clean water on you, Ezk 36:25

SPRINKLED *(21)*
of the blood he s on the altar. Ex 24:6
took the blood, s it on the Ex 24:8
s some of the oil on the altar Lv 8:11
it and s the blood on all Lv 8:19
Then Moses s the blood on all Lv 8:24
the altar and s ⌊them⌋ on Aaron Lv 8:30
and he s it on all sides of the Lv 9:12
and he s it on all sides of the Lv 9:18
impurity has not been s on him, Nm 19:13
impurity has not been s on him; Nm 19:20
s the blood of his fellowship 2Kg 16:13
the blood and s it on the altar. 2Ch 29:22
the rams and s the blood on the 2Ch 29:22
the lambs and s the blood on the 2Ch 29:22
The priests s the blood 2Ch 30:16
the priests s the blood they had 2Ch 35:11
on it and blood may be s on it: Ezk 43:18
and s the scroll itself and all Heb 9:19
he s the tabernacle and all the Heb 9:21
hearts s ⌊clean⌋ from an evil Heb 10:22
and to the s blood, which says Heb 12:24

SPRINKLES *(2)*
to the priest who s the blood Lv 7:14
The person who s the water for Nm 19:21

SPRINKLING *(14)*
the shovels, and the s basins. 1Kg 7:40
the pots, shovels, and s basins. 1Kg 7:45
wick trimmers, s basins, ladles, 1Kg 7:50
wick trimmers, s basins, 2Kg 12:13
the firepans and the s basins— 2Kg 25:15
gold for the forks, s basins, 1Ch 28:17
wick trimmers, s basins, ladles, 2Ch 4:22
trimmers, the s basins, the Jr 52:18
firepans, the s basins, the pots Jr 52:19
will be as full as the s basin, Zch 9:15
will be like the s basins before Zch 14:20
ashes of a heifer s those who Heb 9:13
Passover and the s of the blood, Heb 11:28
and ⌊for the⌋ s with the blood 1Pt 1:2

SPROUT *(13)*
of the man I choose will s, Nm 17:5
does not s from the ground Jb 5:6
yet others will s from the dust. Jb 8:19
down, it will s again, and its Jb 14:7
and cause the grass to s? Jb 38:27
though the wicked s like grass Ps 92:7
you will help your seed to s, Is 17:11
They will s among the grass like Is 44:4
that salvation s and Is 45:8
and making it germinate and s, Is 55:10
righteousness to s up for David, Jr 33:15
cause a horn to s for the house Ezk 29:21
spring crop first began to s— Am 7:1

SPROUTED *(7)*
no plant of the field had yet s, Gn 2:5
scorched by the east wind, s up. Gn 41:6
by the east wind—s up. Gn 41:23
of Levi, had s, formed buds, Nm 17:8
s and became a spreading vine, Ezk 17:6
wither on the bed where it s." Ezk 17:10
When the plants s and produced Mt 13:26

SPROUTING *(1)*
the glisten of rain on s grass." 2Sm 23:4

SPROUTS *(6)*
It sent out s toward the Sea and Ps 80:11
in the morning it s and grows; Ps 90:6
what s fails to yield flour. Hs 8:7
becomes tender and s leaves, Mt 24:32
and the seed s and grows— Mk 4:27
becomes tender and s leaves, Mk 13:28

SPRUNG *(1)*
wicked men have s up among you, Dt 13:13

SPUN *(22)*
make them of finely s linen, Ex 26:1
and finely s linen with a design Ex 26:31
yarn, and finely s linen. Ex 26:36
courtyard out of finely s linen, Ex 27:9
yarn, and finely s linen. Ex 27:16
of it made⌋ of finely s linen. Ex 27:18
ephod of finely s linen Ex 28:6
yarn, and of finely s linen. Ex 28:8
yarn, and of finely s linen. Ex 28:15
skilled woman s ⌊yarn⌋ with her Ex 35:25
hearts were moved s the goat Ex 35:26
made them of finely s linen, Ex 36:8
yarn, and finely s linen. Ex 36:35
and finely s linen for the Ex 36:37
were of finely s linen, Ex 38:9
were of finely s linen. Ex 38:16
yarn, and finely s linen. Ex 38:18
yarn, and of finely s linen. Ex 39:2
and of finely s linen, just as Ex 39:5
yarn, and of finely s linen. Ex 39:8
pomegranates of finely s blue, Ex 39:24
the sash of finely s linen of Ex 39:29

SPURNED *(1)*
But You have s and rejected him; Ps 89:38

SPURRED *(1)*
The couriers left, s on by royal Est 3:15

SPY *(8)*
Joshua had sent to s on Jericho, Jos 6:25
s out the land and explore it. Jdg 18:2
who had gone to s out the land Jdg 18:14
who had gone to s out the land Jdg 18:17
scout out the city, s on it, and 2Sm 10:3
overthrow, and s on the land?" 1Ch 19:3
and those who s on me plot Ps 71:10
in secretly to s on our freedom Gl 2:4

SPYING *(1)*
accused us of s on the country. Gn 42:30

SQUADS *(1)*
assigned four s of four soldiers Ac 12:4

SQUANDERED *(1)*
where he s his estate in foolish Lk 15:13

SQUANDERING *(1)*
manager was s his possessions Lk 16:1

SQUARE *(36)*
spend the night in the s." Gn 19:2
altar must be s, seven and a Ex 27:1
It must be s and folded double, Ex 28:16
It must be s, 18 inches long and Ex 30:2
It was s, 18 inches long and 18 Ex 37:25
It was s, seven and a half feet Ex 38:1
the breastpiece s and folded Ex 39:9
of the city s and completely Dt 13:16
in and sat down in the city s, Jdg 19:15
saw the traveler in the city s, Jdg 19:17
don't spend the night in the s." Jdg 19:20
from the public s of Beth-shan 2Sm 21:12
their frames were s, not round. 1Kg 7:31
them in the eastern public s. 2Ch 29:4
people in the s of the city gate 2Ch 32:6
people sat in the s at the house Ezr 10:9
together at the s in front of Neh 8:1
he was facing the s in front of Neh 8:3
of God, the s by the Water Gate Neh 8:16
the s by the Gate of Ephraim. Neh 8:16
Mordecai in the city s in front Est 4:6
on the horse through the city s, Est 6:9
paraded him through the city s, Est 6:11
and took my seat in the town s, Jb 29:7
road—a lion in the public s!" Pr 26:13
has stumbled in the public s, Is 59:14
an elevated place in every s. Ezk 16:24
your elevated place in every s. Ezk 16:31
side were 10 and a half feet s. Ezk 40:12
It was s, 175 feet long and 175 Ezk 40:47
of the great hall were s, Ezk 41:21
The hearth is s, 21 feet long by Ezk 43:16
there will be a s ⌊section⌋ for Ezk 45:2
the city property as a s ⌊area⌋. Ezk 48:20
in the public s of the great Rv 11:8
The city is laid out in a s; Rv 21:16

SQUARES *(11)*
cry of lament in our public s. Ps 144:14
her voice in the public s. Pr 1:20
of water in the public s? Pr 5:16
now in the s, she lurks at Pr 7:12
in its public s everyone wails, Is 15:3
search in her s. If you find Jr 5:1
streets, young men from the s. Jr 9:21
of Moab and in her public s, Jr 48:38
men will fall in her public s; Jr 49:26
men will fall in her public s; Jr 50:30
be wailing in all the public s; Am 5:16

SQUEEZED *(2)*
s them into Pharaoh's cup, Gn 40:11
s the fleece and wrung dew out Jdg 6:38

SQUEEZING *(1)*
s Balaam's foot against it. Nm 22:25

STAB *(1)*
Joab did not s him again for 2Sm 20:10

STABBED *(5)*
and there Joab s him in the 2Sm 3:27
to get wheat and s him in the 2Sm 4:6
bedroom and s and killed him. 2Sm 4:7
and Joab s him in the stomach 2Sm 20:10
Whoever is found will be s, Is 13:15

STABILITY *(2)*
a king brings s to a land, Pr 29:4
and fall from your own s. 2Pt 3:17

STACHYS *(1)*
in Christ, and my dear friend S. Rm 16:9

STACK *(1)*
as a s of sheaves is gathered in Jb 5:26

STACKS *(1)*
and consumes s of cut grain, Ex 22:6

STACTE *(1)*
s, onycha, and galbanum; Ex 30:34

STADIA *(1)*
city with the rod at 12,000 s. Rv 21:16

STADIUM *(1)*
the runners in a s all race, 1Co 9:24

STAFF *(67)*
over this Jordan with my s, Gn 32:10
cord, and the s in your hand." Gn 38:18
ring, cord, and s are these?" Gn 38:25
or the s from between his feet, Gn 49:10
your hand?" "A s," he replied. Ex 4:2
and it became a s in his hand. Ex 4:4
take this s in your hand that Ex 4:17
Moses took God's s in his hand. Ex 4:20
Take your s and throw it down Ex 7:9
threw down his s before Pharaoh Ex 7:10
Each one threw down his s, Ex 7:12
But Aaron's s swallowed their Ex 7:12
in your hand the s that turned Ex 7:15
the Nile with the s in my hand, Ex 7:17
Take your s and stretch out your Ex 7:19
he raised the s and struck the Ex 7:20
with your s over the rivers, Ex 8:5
Stretch out your s and strike Ex 8:16
out his hand with his s, Ex 8:17
out his s toward heaven, Ex 9:23
stretched out his s over the Ex 10:13
feet, and your s in your hand. Ex 12:11
lift up your s, stretch out your Ex 14:16
with God's s in my hand." Ex 17:9
outside ⌊leaning⌋ on his s, Ex 21:19
take one s from them for each Nm 17:2
Write each man's name on his s. Nm 17:2
Write Aaron's name on Levi's s, Nm 17:3
there must be one s for the head Nm 17:3
The s of the man I choose will Nm 17:5
of their leaders gave him a s, Nm 17:6
Aaron's s was among them. Nm 17:6
and saw that Aaron's s, Nm 17:8
and each man took his own s. Nm 17:9
Take the s and assemble the Nm 20:8
Moses took the s from the LORD's Nm 20:9
the rock twice with his s, Nm 20:11
carry a marshal's s ⌊came⌋ from Jdg 5:14
the tip of the s that was in His Jdg 6:21
the end of the s he was carrying 1Sm 14:27
the end of the s I was carrying. 1Sm 14:43
he took his s in his hand and 1Sm 17:40
belt, take my s with you, and go 2Kg 4:29
place my s on the boy's face. 2Kg 4:29
and placed the s on the boy's 2Kg 4:31
for all his officials and s, Est 1:3
for all his officials and s, Est 2:18
The entire royal s at the King's Est 3:2
the royal s at the King's Gate Est 3:3
other officials and the royal s. Est 5:11
rod and Your s—they comfort me Ps 23:4
her hands to the spinning s, Pr 31:19
shoulders, the s of their Is 9:4
s in their hands is My wrath. Is 10:5
As if a s could wave those who Is 10:15
rod and raises his s over you as Is 10:24
will raise His s over the sea as Is 10:26
has broken the s of the wicked, Is 14:5
of the appointed s that the LORD Is 30:32
that splintered reed of a s, Is 36:6
is shattered, the glorious s! Jr 48:17
have been a s ⌊made⌋ of reed Ezk 29:6
Your people with Your s, Mc 7:14
each with a s in hand because of Zch 8:4
Next I took my s called Favor Zch 11:10
Then I cut in two my second s, Zch 11:14
leaning on the top of his s. Heb 11:21

STAFFS *(7)*
Aaron's staff swallowed their s. Ex 7:12
12 s from all the leaders of Nm 17:2
ancestral houses, 12 s ⌊in all⌋. Nm 17:6
placed the s before the LORD Nm 17:7
out all the s from the LORD's Nm 17:9
with a scepter and with their s. Nm 21:18
I took two s, calling one Favor Zch 11:7

STAG *(3)*
is like a gazelle or a young s. Sg 2:9
or a young s on the divided Sg 2:17
or a young s on the mountains Sg 8:14

STAGES *(8)*
journeyed by s to the Negev. Gn 12:9
He went by s from the Negev to Gn 13:3
all the s of their journey. Ex 40:36
all the s of their journey. Ex 40:38
were the s of the Israelites' Nm 33:1
points for the s of their Nm 33:2
are the s ⌊listed⌋ by their Nm 33:2
the temple ⌊went up⌋ by s. Ezk 41:7

STAGGER *(9)*
makes them s like drunken men. Jb 12:25
a wine to drink that made us s. Ps 60:3
made Egypt s in all she does Is 19:14
These also s because of wine and Is 28:7
and prophet s because of beer, Is 28:7
they s, but not with beer. Is 29:9
cup that ⌊causes people⌋ to s. Is 51:17
They will drink, s, and go out Jr 25:16
People will s from sea to sea Am 8:12

STAGGERED *(2)*
they reeled and s like drunken Ps 107:27
three cities s to another city Am 4:8

STAGGERING *(2)*
the cup of s from your hand; Is 51:22
that causes s for the peoples Zch 12:2

STAGGERS *(4)*
and whoever s because of them is Pr 20:1
as a drunkard s in his vomit. Is 19:14
My heart s; horror terrifies me. Is 21:4
The earth s like a drunkard and Is 24:20

STAGS *(1)*
leaders are like s that find no Lm 1:6

STAIN *(1)*
the s of your guilt is still in Jr 2:22

STAINED *(4)*
or impurity has s my hands, Jb 31:7
and all My clothes were s. Is 63:3
your skirts are s with the blood Jr 2:34
He wore a robe s with blood, Rv 19:13

STAINS *(1)*
Her uncleanness ⌊s⌋ her skirts. Lm 1:9

STAIRS *(1)*
far as the s that descend from Neh 3:15

STAIRWAY *(8)*
A s was set on the ground with Gn 28:12
They went up a s to the middle 1Kg 6:8
it had descended on Ahaz's s. 2Kg 20:11
down on Ahaz's s return by 10 Is 38:8
Its s had seven steps, and its Ezk 40:26
Its s had eight steps. Ezk 40:31
Its s had eight steps. Ezk 40:34
Its s had eight steps. Ezk 40:37

STAKE *(1)*
us and give us a s in His holy Ezr 9:8

STALK *(3)*
full and good, came up on one s. Gn 41:5
and good, coming up on one s. Gn 41:22
the s of this splintered reed, 2Kg 18:21

STALKS *(3)*
them among the s of flax that Jos 2:6
Pull out ⌊some⌋ s from the Ru 2:16
the plague that s in darkness, Ps 91:6

STALL *(2)*
the flock and calves from the s. Am 6:4
jump like calves from the s. Mal 4:2

STALL-FED *(1)*
among her are like s calves. Jr 46:21

STALLIONS *(5)*
galloping, galloping of his s. Jdg 5:22
well-fed, eager s, each neighing Jr 5:8
of the stomping hooves of his s, Jr 47:3
treading grain and neigh like s, Jr 50:11
emission was like that of s. Ezk 23:20

STALLS *(5)*
himself and s for his cattle; Gn 33:17
had 40,000 s of horses for his 1Kg 4:26
Solomon had 4,000 s for horses 2Ch 9:25
and s for all kinds of cattle, 2Ch 32:28
the pen and no cattle in the s, Hab 3:17

STAMINA *(1)*
We don't have the s to stay out Ezr 10:13

STAMMER *(1)*
who s in a language that is not Is 33:19

STAMMERING *(2)*
to this people with s speech and Is 28:11
and the s tongue will speak Is 32:4

STAMP *(1)*
Clap your hands, s your feet, Ezk 6:11

STAMPED *(1)*
your⌋ hands, s ⌊your⌋ feet, Ezk 25:6

STAND *(253)*
that I cannot s up in your Gn 31:35
s ready to meet him by the bank Ex 7:15
could not s before Moses Ex 9:11
S firm and see the LORD's Ex 14:13
am going to s there in front of Ex 17:6
Tomorrow I will s on the hilltop Ex 17:9

while all the people s around Ex 18:14
the slave can s up after a day Ex 21:21
⌊and that s⌋ on four silver Ex 26:32
washing and a bronze s for it. Ex 30:18
and the basin with its s. Ex 30:28
utensils, the basin with its s— Ex 31:9
all the people would s up, Ex 33:8
tent, they would s up, then bow Ex 33:10
You are to s on the rock, Ex 33:21
in the morning and s before Me Ex 34:2
utensils; the basin with its s; Ex 35:16
and its s from the ⌊bronze⌋ Ex 38:8
utensils; the basin with its s; Ex 39:39
Anoint the basin and its s, Ex 40:11
basin with its s, to consecrate Lv 8:11
not be able to s against your Lv 26:37
The price will s just as the Lv 27:14
the price will s according to Lv 27:17
and have her s before the LORD. Nm 5:16
has the woman s before the LORD, Nm 5:18
have the woman s before the LORD Nm 5:30
have the Levites s before Aaron Nm 8:13
and have them s there with you. Nm 11:16
and had them s around the tent. Nm 11:24
and to s before the community to Nm 16:9
LORD took His s on the path to Nm 22:22
Have him s before Eleazar the Nm 27:19
will s before Eleazar who will Nm 27:21
had him s before Eleazar the Nm 27:22
s in your fathers' place adding Nm 32:14
But you s here with Me, and I Dt 5:31
will be able to s against you; Dt 7:24
'Who can s up to the sons of Dt 9:2
to s before the LORD to serve Dt 10:8
will be able to s against you; Dt 11:25
your tribes to s and minister Dt 18:5
dispute must s in the presence Dt 19:17
You must s outside while the man Dt 24:11
tribes⌋ will s on Mount Gerizim Dt 27:12
tribes⌋ will s on Mount Ebal to Dt 27:13
and they will s in awe of you. Dt 28:10
will be able to s against you as Jos 1:5
of the waters, s in the Jordan.' Jos 3:8
will s up ⌊in⌋ a mass. Jos 3:13
LORD then said to Joshua, "S up! Jos 7:10
Israelites cannot s against Jos 7:12
not be able to s against your Jos 7:13
will be able to s against you." Jos 10:8
Sun, s still over Gibeon, and Jos 10:12
were able to s against them, Jos 21:44
has been able to s against you Jos 23:9
S at the entrance to the tent. Jdg 4:20
and took their s at the entrance Jdg 9:44
They had him s between the Jdg 16:25
Who is able to s in the presence 1Sm 6:20
came forward and took his s. 1Sm 17:16
I'll go out and s beside my 1Sm 19:3
begged me, 'S over me and kill 2Sm 1:9
and took their s on top of a 2Sm 2:25
up early and s beside the road 2Sm 15:2
said, "Move aside and s here." 2Sm 18:30
Shammah took his s in the middle 2Sm 23:12
who always s in your presence 1Kg 10:8
of Israel lives, I s before Him, 1Kg 17:1
before whom I s, today I will 1Kg 18:15
Go out and s on the mountain in 1Kg 19:11
of Hosts lives, I s before Him. 2Kg 3:14
and took their s at the border. 2Kg 3:21
s and call on the name of Yahweh 2Kg 5:11
the LORD lives, I s before Him. 2Kg 5:16
kings couldn't s against him; 2Kg 10:4
David took their s in the middle 1Ch 11:14
are also to s every morning to 1Ch 23:30
who always s in your presence 2Ch 9:7
took their s with Rehoboam, 2Ch 11:13
and no one can s against You. 2Ch 20:6
we will s before this temple and 2Ch 20:9
yourselves, s still, and see 2Ch 20:17
They took their s against King 2Ch 26:18
chosen you to s in His presence 2Ch 29:11
no one can s in Your presence Ezr 9:15
that they can s guard by night Neh 4:22
Pethahiah—said: S up. Bless Neh 9:5
his web, but it doesn't s firm. Jb 8:15
the stocks and s watch over all Jb 13:27
When I s up, they mock me. Jb 19:18
and He will s on the dust at Jb 19:25
when I s up, You ⌊merely⌋ look Jb 30:20
now that they s ⌊there⌋ and no Jb 32:16
case against me; take your s. Jb 33:5
hills⌋ s out like ⌊the folds Jb 38:14
he cannot s still at the Jb 39:24
trample the wicked where they s. Jb 40:12
who then can s against Me? Jb 41:10
take their s and the rulers Ps 2:2
have taken their s against me on Ps 3:6
boastful cannot s in Your Ps 5:5
LORD, why do You s so far away? Ps 10:1
fall, but we rise and s firm. Ps 20:8
Who may s in His holy place? Ps 24:3
You made me s like a strong Ps 30:7
of the world s in awe of Him. Ps 33:8
ones and friends s back from my Ps 38:11
my relatives s at a distance. Ps 38:11
are angry, who can s before You? Ps 76:7
have not let him s in battle. Ps 89:43
Who takes a s for me against Ps 94:16
let an accuser s at his right Ps 109:6
They s today in accordance with Ps 119:91
sins, Lord, who could s? Ps 130:3
of the LORD who s in the LORD's Ps 134:1
who s in the house of the LORD, Ps 135:2
when I sit down and when I s up; Ps 139:2
the crossroads, she takes her s. Pr 8:2
house of the righteous will s. Pr 12:7
the tent of the upright will s. Pr 14:11
He will s in the presence of Pr 22:29
He will not s in the presence of Pr 22:29
and don't s in the place of the Pr 25:6
I cannot s iniquity with a Is 1:13
If you do not s firm in your Is 7:9
then you will not s at all. Is 7:9
Today he will s at Nob, shaking Is 10:32
of Jesse will s as a banner for Is 11:10
therefore, who can s in its way? Is 14:27
I s on the watchtower all day, Is 21:8
One of Jacob and s in awe of the Is 29:23
S up, you complacent women; Is 32:9
They all will assemble and s; Is 44:11
So take your s with your spells Is 47:12
So let them s and save you— Is 47:13
will see and s up, and princes Is 49:7
S up, Jerusalem, you who have Is 51:17
S up, shake the dust off Is 52:2
Strangers will s and feed your Is 61:5
S up and tell them everything Jr 1:17
cover! Don't s still! For I am Jr 4:6
S by the roadways and look. Jr 6:16
S in the gate of the house of Jr 7:2
do you come and s before Me in Jr 7:10
Wild donkeys s on the barren Jr 14:6
and Samuel should s before Me, Jr 15:1
you will s in My presence. Jr 15:19
Go and s in the People's Gate, Jr 17:19
S in the courtyard of the LORD's Jr 26:2
citadel will s on its proper Jr 30:18
a man to always s before Me.'" Jr 35:19
they will not take their s, Jr 46:21
S by the highway and look, Jr 48:19
Those who flee will s exhausted Jr 48:45
shepherd who can s against Me?" Jr 49:19
shepherd who can s against Me?" Jr 50:44
purposes against Babylon s: Jr 51:29
sword, go and do not s still! Jr 51:50
s up on your feet and I will Ezk 2:1
so that it might s in battle on Ezk 13:5
the wall and s in the gap before Ezk 22:30
of the sea s on the shore. Ezk 27:29
people and will s before them to Ezk 44:11
They will s before Me to offer Ezk 44:15
the most holy place, will s. Ezk 45:3
portico and s at the doorpost Ezk 46:2
Fishermen will s beside it from Ezk 47:10
No animal could s against him, Dn 8:4
strong enough to s against him. Dn 8:7
he touched me, made me s up, Dn 8:18
will even s against the Prince Dn 8:25
S on your feet, for I have now Dn 10:11
forces of the South will not s; Dn 11:15
but she will not s with him or Dn 11:17
they have taken their s there. Hs 10:9
archer will not s ⌊his ground⌋, Am 2:15
I can't s the stench of your Am 5:21
not s at the crossroads to cut Ob 14
He will s and shepherd ⌊them⌋ in Mc 5:4
I have fallen, I will s up; Mc 7:8
they will s in awe of You. Mc 7:17
I will s at my guard post and Hab 2:1
LORD, I s in awe of Your deeds. Hab 3:2
Sun and moon s still in ⌊their⌋ Hab 3:11
who s by the Lord of the whole Zch 4:14
day His feet will s on the Mount Zch 14:4
rot while they s on their feet, Zch 14:12
be able to s when He appears Mal 3:2
had Him s on the pinnacle of the Mt 4:5
divided against itself will s. Mt 12:25
How then will his kingdom s? Mt 12:26
of Nineveh will s up at the Mt 12:41
to Him and had him s among them. Mt 18:2
paralyzed hand, "S before us." Mk 3:3
itself, that kingdom cannot s. Mk 3:24
itself, that house cannot s. Mk 3:25
he cannot s but is finished! Mk 3:26
a child, had him s among them, Mk 9:36
And whenever you s praying, Mk 11:25
You will s before governors and Mk 13:9
had Him s on the pinnacle of the Lk 4:9
hand, "Get up and s here." Lk 6:8
child and had him s next to Him. Lk 9:47
himself, how will his kingdom s? Lk 11:18
you will s outside and knock Lk 13:25
took his s and was praying Lk 18:11
s up and lift up your heads, Lk 21:28
place and to s before the Son Lk 21:36
making her s in the center. Jn 8:3
why do you s looking up into Ac 1:11
Peter and John s before them, Ac 4:7
kings of the earth took their s, Ac 4:26
Go and s in the temple complex, Ac 5:20
they had them s before the Ac 5:27
They had them s before the Ac 6:6
they were unable to s up against Ac 6:10
his hand and helped her s up. Ac 9:41
helped him up and said, "S up! Ac 10:26
"S up straight on your feet!" Ac 14:10
now I s on trial for the hope Ac 26:6
But get up and s on your feet. Ac 26:16
to this day I s and testify to Ac 26:22
You must s before Caesar. Ac 27:24
into this grace in which we s, Rm 5:2
according to election might s, Rm 9:11
by unbelief, but you s by faith. Rm 11:20
or falls. And s he will! For Rm 14:4
the Lord is able to make him s. Rm 14:4
For we will all s before the Rm 14:10
it and have taken your s on it. 1Co 15:1
alert, s firm in the faith, be 1Co 16:13
joy, because you s by faith. 2Co 1:24
Therefore s firm and don't Gl 5:1
so that you can s against the Eph 6:11
everything, to take your s. Eph 6:13
S, therefore, with truth like a Eph 6:14
joy and crown, s firm in the Php 4:1
so that you can s mature and Col 4:12
when we could no longer s it, 1Th 3:1
when I could no longer s it, 1Th 3:5
if you s firm in the Lord. 1Th 3:8
s firm and hold to the 2Th 2:15
to the poor man, "S over there," Jms 2:3
grace of God. Take your s in it! 1Pt 5:12
to make you s in the presence Jd 24
I s at the door and knock. Rv 3:20
And who is able to s?" Rv 6:17
angels who s in the presence Rv 8:2
lampstands that s before the Rv 11:4
They s far off in fear of her Rv 18:10
will s far off in fear of her Rv 18:15

STANDARD *(28)*

by the s sanctuary shekel Lv 27:3
by the s sanctuary shekel Lv 27:25
to the s sanctuary shekel Nm 3:47
by the s sanctuary shekel Nm 3:50
by the s sanctuary shekel Nm 7:13
by the s sanctuary shekel Nm 7:19
by the s sanctuary shekel Nm 7:25
by the s sanctuary shekel Nm 7:31
by the s sanctuary shekel Nm 7:37
by the s sanctuary shekel Nm 7:43
by the s sanctuary shekel Nm 7:49
by the s sanctuary shekel Nm 7:55
by the s sanctuary shekel Nm 7:61
by the s sanctuary shekel Nm 7:67
by the s sanctuary shekel Nm 7:73
by the s sanctuary shekel Nm 7:79

by the s sanctuary shekel Nm 7:85
by the s sanctuary shekel Nm 7:86
silver by the s sanctuary shekel Nm 18:16
six feet wide by a s measure. Dt 3:11
pounds according to the royal s. 2Sm 14:26
unit was the s length plus three Ezk 40:5
unit being the s length plus Ezk 43:13
of the s larger capacity Ezk 45:11
or⌋ one s larger capacity Ezk 45:14
equal one s larger capacity Ezk 45:14
it according to the s of faith; Rm 12:6
on all those who follow this s, Gl 6:16

STANDARDS *(3)*

will judge them by their own s. Ezk 7:27
will judge you by their own s. Ezk 23:24
You judge by human s. Jn 8:15

STANDING *(162)*

and he saw three men s near him. Gn 18:2
remained s before the LORD Gn 18:22
I am s here at the spring where Gn 24:13
He was s there by the camels at Gn 24:30
Why are you s out here? Gn 24:31
I am s here at a spring. Gn 24:43
The LORD was s there beside him, Gn 28:13
He was s beside the Nile, Gn 41:1
In my dream I was s on the bank Gn 41:17
where you are s is holy ground." Ex 3:5
people remained s at a distance Ex 20:21
of cut grain, s grain, or a Ex 22:6
of the LORD s on the path with Nm 22:23
of the LORD s in the path with Nm 22:31
that You were s in the path to Nm 22:34
who was s there by his burnt Nm 23:6
who was s there by his burnt Nm 23:17
that time I was s between the Dt 5:5
smash their s pillars, cut down Dt 7:5
is first ⌊put⌋ to the s grain. Dt 16:9
enter your neighbor's s grain, Dt 23:25
All of you are s today before Dt 29:10
those who are s here with us Dt 29:15
where the priests' feet are s, Jos 4:3
the ark of the covenant were s. Jos 4:9
ark continued s in the middle Jos 4:10
and saw a man s in front of him Jos 5:13
place where you are s is holy." Jos 5:15
foxes into the s grain of the Jdg 15:5
grain and the s grain as well as Jdg 15:5
men were s by the entrance Jdg 18:16
the priest was s by the entrance Jdg 18:17
Philistines were s on one hill, 1Sm 17:3
Israelites were s on another 1Sm 17:3
to the men who were s with him: 1Sm 17:26
his servants were s around him. 1Sm 22:6
ordered the guards s by him, 1Sm 22:17
man who was s watch looked up, 2Sm 13:34
of Israel while they were s. 1Kg 8:14
and two lions s beside the 1Kg 10:19
lions were s there on the six 1Kg 10:20
Jeroboam was s beside the altar 1Kg 13:1
and the donkey was s beside it; 1Kg 13:24
the lion was s beside the corpse 1Kg 13:24
road and the lion s beside it, 1Kg 13:25
and the lion s beside the corpse 1Kg 13:28
heavenly host was s by Him at 1Kg 22:19
the watchman was s on the tower 2Kg 9:17
was the king s by the pillar 2Kg 11:14
pole also remained s in Samaria. 2Kg 13:6
LORD was then s at the threshing 1Ch 21:15
of the LORD s between earth 1Ch 21:16
and lyres, were s east of the 2Ch 5:12
of Israel while they were s. 2Ch 6:3
The priests were s at their 2Ch 7:6
and all the people were s. 2Ch 7:6
and two lions s beside the 2Ch 9:18
lions were s there on the six 2Ch 9:19
host was s at His right hand 2Ch 18:18
All Judah was s before the LORD 2Ch 20:13
was the king s by his pillar at 2Ch 23:13
Queen Esther s in the courtyard Est 5:2
Haman is s in the court." Est 6:5
feet are s within your gates, Ps 122:2
Look, he is s behind our wall, Sg 2:9
Seraphim were s above Him; Is 6:2
a reaper had gathered s grain— Is 17:5
or incense altars will remain s. Is 27:9
people who were s in the temple Jr 28:5
who were s by the king. Jr 36:21
all the women s by—a great Jr 44:15
of Israel were s before them, Ezk 8:11
son of Shaphan s among them. Ezk 8:11
the cherubim were s to the south Ezk 10:3
He was s by the gate. Ezk 40:3
While the man was s beside me, Ezk 43:6
dazzling, was s in front of you Dn 2:31
those who were s by and asked Dn 7:16
there was a ram s beside the Dn 8:3
I had seen s beside the canal Dn 8:6
So he approached where I was s; Dn 8:17
as I was s on the bank of the Dn 10:4
to the one s in front of me, Dn 10:16
and two others were s there, Dn 12:5
There is no s grain; Hs 8:7
The Lord was s there by a Am 7:7
I saw the LORD s beside the Am 9:1
He was s among the myrtle trees Zch 1:8
Then the man s among the myrtle Zch 1:10
of the LORD s among the myrtle Zch 1:11
the high priest s before the Zch 3:1
with Satan s at his right side Zch 3:1
He spoke to those s before Him, Zch 3:4
Angel of the LORD was s nearby. Zch 3:5
among these who are s here. Zch 3:7
love to pray s in the synagogues Mt 6:5
brothers were s outside wanting Mt 12:46
and Your brothers are s outside, Mt 12:47
There are some s here who will Mt 16:28
he saw others s in the Mt 20:3
went and found others s around, Mt 20:6
Why have you been s here all day Mt 20:6
prophet Daniel, s in the holy Mt 24:15
while those s there approached Mt 26:73
some of those s there heard this Mt 27:47
came, and s outside, they sent Mk 3:31
There are some s here who will Mk 9:1
and some of those s there said Mk 11:5
desolation s where it should Mk 13:14
began to tell those s nearby, Mk 14:69
while those s there said to Mk 14:70
some of those s there heard this Mk 15:35
who was s opposite Him, saw Mk 15:39
s to the right of the altar of Lk 1:11
He was s by Lake Gennesaret. Lk 5:1
and Your brothers are s outside, Lk 8:20
there are some s here who will Lk 9:27
the two men who were s with Him. Lk 9:32
tax collector, s far off, would Lk 18:13
So he said to those s there, Lk 19:24
John was s with two of his Jn 1:35
of the crowd s here I said this, Jn 11:42
The crowd s there heard it and Jn 12:29
Him, was also s with them. Jn 18:5
But Peter remained s outside by Jn 18:16
They were s there warming Jn 18:18
and Peter was s with them, Jn 18:18
temple police s by slapped Jesus Jn 18:22
Simon Peter was s and warming Jn 18:25
S by the cross of Jesus were His Jn 19:25
the disciple He loved s there, Jn 19:26
around and saw Jesus s there, Jn 20:14
this man is s here before you Ac 4:10
who had been healed s with them, Ac 4:14
with the guards s in front of Ac 5:23
put in jail are s in the temple Ac 5:25
where you are s is holy ground. Ac 7:33
with Jesus s at the right hand Ac 7:55
the Son of Man s at the right Ac 7:56
seen the angel s in his house Ac 11:13
that Peter was s at the gateway. Ac 12:14
Then s up, Paul motioned with Ac 13:16
women of high s and the leading Ac 13:50
man was s and pleading with Ac 16:9
I myself was s by and approving, Ac 22:20
Paul said to the centurion s by, Ac 22:25
those who were s next to him to Ac 23:2
And those s nearby said, "Do you Ac 23:4
cried out while s among them, Ac 24:21
I am s at Caesar's tribunal, Ac 25:10
who have no s in the church to 1Co 6:4
you that you are s firm in one Php 1:27
acquire a good s for themselves, 1Tm 3:13
first tabernacle was still s. Heb 9:8
slaughtered lamb s between the Rv 5:6
I saw four angels s at the four Rv 7:1
s before the throne and before Rv 7:9
that I had seen s on the sea Rv 10:5
of the angel who is s on the sea Rv 10:8
were s on the sea of glass with Rv 15:2
I saw an angel s in the sun, Rv 19:17
and the small, s before the Rv 20:12

STANDS *(38)*

how Your cloud s over them, Nm 14:14
not die until he s trial before Nm 35:12
the priest who s there serving Dt 17:12
s at the entrance of the city Jos 20:4
city until he s trial before Jos 20:6
of blood until he s before the Jos 20:9
where the LORD's tabernacle s, Jos 22:19
I do when God s up ⌊to judge⌋? Jb 31:14
He s watch over all my paths." Jb 33:11
My foot s on level ground; Ps 26:12
counsel of the LORD s forever, Ps 33:11
gold from Ophir, s at your right Ps 45:9
Who s up for me against the Ps 94:16
He s at the right hand of the Ps 109:31
the earth, and it s firm. Ps 119:90
and see: no one s up for me; Ps 142:4
argue the case and s to judge Is 3:13
he s up for noble causes. Is 32:8
it in its place, and there it s; Is 46:7
and righteousness s far off. Is 59:14
whose word s, Mine or theirs Jr 44:28
king of Babylon s at the split Ezk 21:21
table that s before the LORD. Ezk 41:22
the order s and is irrevocable." Dn 6:12
prince who s watch over your Dn 12:1
He s and shakes the earth; Hab 3:6
who s in the presence of God, Lk 1:19
Someone s among you, but you Jn 1:26
who s by and listens for him, Jn 3:29
his own Lord he s or falls. Rm 14:4
whoever doubts s condemned if he Rm 14:23
But he who s firm in his heart 1Co 7:37
thinks he s must be careful 1Co 10:12
God's solid foundation s firm, 2Tm 2:19
Now every priest s day after day Heb 10:11
Look, the judge s at the door! Jms 5:9
For it s in Scripture: 1Pt 2:6
to the One who s ready to judge 1Pt 4:5

STANDSTILL *(1)*

remained at a s until the second Ezr 4:24

STAR *(16)*

A s will come from Jacob, and a Nm 24:17
Shining morning s, how you have Is 14:12
your king and Kaiwan your s god, Am 5:26
For we saw His s in the east and Mt 2:2
the exact time the s appeared. Mt 2:7
the s they had seen in the east! Mt 2:9
When they saw the s, they were Mt 2:10
of Moloch and the s of your god Ac 7:43
for s differs from star in 1Co 15:41
star differs from s in splendor. 1Co 15:41
and the morning s arises in your 2Pt 1:19
also give him the morning s. Rv 2:28
and a great s, blazing like Rv 8:10
The name of the s is Wormwood, Rv 8:11
and I saw a s that had fallen Rv 9:1
of David, the Bright Morning S." Rv 22:16

STARE *(4)*

people look and s at me. Ps 22:17
not s at me because I am dark, Sg 1:6
Those who see you will s at you; Is 14:16
Or why do you s at us, as though Ac 3:12

STARED *(2)*

Then Elisha s steadily at him 2Kg 8:11
s straight at the sorcerer Ac 13:9

STARK *(4)*

hair grew, but you were s naked. Ezk 16:7
when you were s naked and lying Ezk 16:22
jewelry, and leave you s naked. Ezk 16:39
and leave you s naked, so that Ezk 23:29

STARRY *(1)*

brings out the s host by number; Is 40:26

STARS *(57)*

the night—as well as the s. Gn 1:16
Look at the sky and count the s, Gn 15:5
as numerous as the s in the sky Gn 22:17
as numerous as the s of the sky, Gn 26:4
11 s were bowing down to me." Gn 37:9
as numerous as the s of the sky Ex 32:13
as numerous as the s of the sky. Dt 1:10
sun, moon, and s—all the array Dt 4:19
as numerous as the s of the sky. Dt 10:22

moon, or all the **s** in the sky— Dt 17:3
as numerous as the **s** of the sky, Dt 28:62
The **s** fought from the heavens; Jdg 5:20
the **s** fought with Sisera from Jdg 5:20
as numerous as the **s** of heaven. 1Ch 27:23
daybreak until the **s** came out. Neh 4:21
descendants like the **s** of heaven Neh 9:23
May its morning **s** grow dark. Jb 3:9
to shine and seals off the **s**. Jb 9:7
He makes ⌊the **s**⌋: the Bear, Jb 9:9
And look at the highest **s**— Jb 22:12
not shine and the **s** are not pure Jb 25:5
the morning **s** sang together Jb 38:7
moon and the **s**, which You set Ps 8:3
and all the **s**, by the breath Ps 33:6
the moon and **s** to rule by night. Ps 136:9
He counts the number of the **s**; Ps 147:4
praise Him, all you shining **s**. Ps 148:3
moon and the **s**, and the clouds Ec 12:2
the **s** of the sky and its Is 13:10
up my throne above the **s** of God. Is 14:13
and their **s** will all wither as Is 34:4
who observe the **s**, who predict Is 47:13
order of moon and **s** for light by Jr 31:35
the heavens and darken their **s**. Ezk 32:7
made some of the **s** and some of Dn 8:10
like the **s** forever and ever. Dn 12:3
and the **s** cease their shining. Jl 2:10
and the **s** will cease their Jl 3:15
and make your nest among the **s**, Ob 4
numerous than the **s** of the sky. Nah 3:16
the **s** will fall from the sky, Mt 24:29
the **s** will be falling from the Mk 13:25
signs in the sun, moon, and **s**; Lk 21:25
days neither sun nor **s** appeared, Ac 27:20
the moon, and another of the **s**; 1Co 15:41
you shine like **s** in the world. Php 2:15
numerous as the **s** of heaven and Heb 11:12
wandering **s** for whom is reserved Jd 13
His right hand He had seven **s**; Rv 1:16
of the seven **s** you saw in My Rv 1:20
seven **s** are the angels of the Rv 1:20
holds the seven **s** in His right Rv 2:1
of God and the seven **s** says: Rv 3:1
s of heaven fell to the earth Rv 6:13
third of the **s**, so that a third Rv 8:12
and a crown of 12 **s** on her head. Rv 12:1
away a third of the **s** in heaven Rv 12:4

START *(10)*
at the **s** in the inheritance Dt 19:14
donkeys and **s** worrying about us. 1Sm 9:5
asked, "Who is to **s** the battle?" 1Kg 20:14
They said, "Let's **s** rebuilding," Neh 2:18
servants, will **s** building, but Neh 2:20
To **s** a conflict is to release a Pr 17:14
city after him and **s** killing; Ezk 9:5
don't **s** saying to yourselves, Lk 3:8
and be given a **s** by you on my 2Co 1:16
reality that we had at the **s**. Heb 3:14

STARTED *(40)*
His kingdom **s** with Babylon, Gn 10:10
that day Esau **s** on his way back Gn 33:16
the one who **s** the fire must make Ex 22:6
Joshua **s** early the next morning Jos 3:1
s at dawn and marched around Jos 6:15
Joshua **s** early the next morning Jos 8:10
the Philistine **s** forward to 1Sm 17:48
and they also **s** prophesying. 1Sm 19:20
reached them but hasn't **s** back." 2Kg 9:18
reached them but hasn't **s** back. 2Kg 9:20
Get **s** building the LORD God's 1Ch 22:19
Jeremiah ⌊**s** to⌋ leave Jerusalem Jr 37:12
And they **s** laughing at Him. Mt 9:24
Peter **s** walking on the water and Mt 14:29
He grabbed him, **s** choking him, Mt 18:28
from that time he **s** looking for Mt 26:16
Then he **s** to curse and to swear Mt 26:74
went out and **s** plotting with Mk 3:6
They **s** laughing at Him, but He Mk 5:40
heard it and **s** looking for a way Mk 11:18
So he **s** looking for a good Mk 14:11
Then he **s** to curse and to swear Mk 14:71
So they went out and **s** running Mk 16:8
with rage and **s** discussing with Lk 6:11
They **s** laughing at Him, because Lk 8:53
an argument **s** among them about Lk 9:46
'This man **s** to build and wasn't Lk 14:30
the offer⌋ and **s** looking for a Lk 22:6
were holding Jesus **s** mocking and Lk 22:63
where He **s** even to here." Lk 23:5
up his bedroll, and **s** to walk. Jn 5:9
and **s** across the sea to Jn 6:17
the Jews **s** complaining about Jn 6:41
stooped down and **s** writing on Jn 8:6
The disciples **s** looking at one Jn 13:22
up, stood, and **s** to walk, and he Ac 3:8
persecution that **s** because of Ac 11:19
jumped up and **s** to walk around. Ac 14:10
And they **s** to call Barnabas, Ac 14:12
that He who **s** a good work in you Php 1:6

STARTING *(7)*
complete weeks **s** from the day Lv 23:15
Moses wrote down the **s** points Nm 33:2
listed⌋ by their **s** points: Nm 33:2
At that time, ⌊**s**⌋ from Tirzah, 2Kg 15:16
s with the last and ending with Mt 20:8
but that a riot was **s** instead, Mt 27:24
one by one, **s** with the older Jn 8:9

STARTLED *(5)*
Boaz was **s**, turned over, Ru 3:8
Do not be **s** or afraid. Is 44:8
all will be **s** and put to shame Is 44:11
he was **s** and overcome with fear. Lk 1:12
they were **s** and terrified and Lk 24:37

STARTLES *(1)*
He looks and **s** the nations. Hab 3:6

STARTS *(3)*
and its stump **s** to die in the Jb 14:8
and **s** to beat his fellow slaves, Mt 24:49
and **s** to beat the male and Lk 12:45

STARVES *(2)*
who falls by the sword or **s**." 2Sm 3:29
them when He **s** all the gods of Zph 2:11

STARVING *(3)*
those who are **s** ⌊hunger⌋ no more 1Sm 2:5
They know we are **s**, so they have 2Kg 7:12
dignitaries are **s**, and the Is 5:13

STATE *(14)*
is in a **s** of uncleanness yet Lv 22:3
The first to **s** his case seems Pr 18:17
your advisers to their former **s**. Is 1:26
S your ⌊case⌋, so that you may Is 43:26
will return to their former **s**. Ezk 16:55
also return to your former **s**. Ezk 16:55
what **s** were you in? When someone Hg 2:16
he went into a visionary **s**. Ac 10:10
in a visionary **s**, an object Ac 11:5
I went into a visionary **s** Ac 22:17
his accusers to **s** their case Ac 23:30
these men here **s** what wrongdoing Ac 24:20
In that **s** He also went and made 1Pt 3:19
last **s** is worse for them than 2Pt 2:20

STATED *(6)*
Therefore it is **s** in the Book of Nm 21:14
king of Babylon. ⌊The letter⌋ **s**: Jr 29:3
s, "This man said, 'I can Mt 26:61
according to what is **s** in the Lk 2:24
good-bye and **s**, "I'll come back Ac 18:21
a long time, as previously **s**: Heb 4:7

STATELY *(3)*
things are **s** in their stride Pr 30:29
even four are **s** in their walk: Pr 30:29
for the **s** forest has fallen! Zch 11:2

STATEMENT *(13)*
As soon as the **s** left the king's Est 7:8
offense when they heard this **s**?" Mt 15:12
they did not understand this **s**, Mk 9:32
was deeply troubled by this **s**, Lk 1:29
they did not understand this **s**; Lk 9:45
and the **s** Jesus had made. Jn 2:22
so that the **s** written in their Jn 15:25
Pilate heard this **s**, he was more Jn 19:8
all over his **s** that they would Ac 20:38
about this one **s** I cried out Ac 24:21
to leave after Paul made one **s**: Ac 28:25
this is the **s** of the promise: Rm 9:9
law is fulfilled in one **s**: Gl 5:14

STATES *(1)*
and **s** his case before the elders Jos 20:4

STATING *(1)*
false testimony against Him, **s**, Mk 14:57

STATION *(3)*
and **s** men by it to guard the Jos 10:18
S the citizens of Jerusalem as Neh 7:3
at my guard post and **s** myself on Hab 2:1

STATIONED *(23)*
garden of Eden He **s** cherubim Gn 3:24
force was **s** in this way: Jos 8:13
after the sentries had been **s**. Jdg 7:19
I have **s** ⌊my⌋ young men at a 1Sm 21:2
horsemen and **s** them in the 1Kg 10:26
He also **s** in Bethel the priests 1Kg 12:32
Now Jehu had **s** 80 men outside, 2Kg 10:24
was previously **s** at the King's 1Ch 9:18
were guards **s** at every watch. 1Ch 26:16
which he **s** in the chariot cities 2Ch 1:14
He **s** them in the chariot cities 2Ch 9:25
He **s** troops in every fortified 2Ch 17:2
those he **s** in the fortified 2Ch 17:19
Then he **s** all the troops with 2Ch 23:10
He **s** gatekeepers at the gates of 2Ch 23:19
Hezekiah **s** the Levites in the 2Ch 29:25
land where I **s** your ancestors, 2Ch 33:8
to our God and **s** a guard because Neh 4:9
I **s** ⌊people⌋ behind the lowest Neh 4:13
I **s** them by families with their Neh 4:13
together and **s** them at their Neh 13:11
Helech were ⌊**s**⌋ on your walls Ezk 27:11
over the kingdom, **s** throughout Dn 6:1

STATIONS *(2)*
were standing at their **s**, 2Ch 7:6
were at their **s** according to the 2Ch 35:15

STATUE *(19)*
and placed it next to his **s**. 1Sm 5:2
the offensive **s** that provokes Ezk 8:3
this offensive **s** north of the Ezk 8:5
watching, a colossal **s** appeared. Dn 2:31
That **s**, tall and dazzling, was Dn 2:31
The head of the **s** was pure gold, Dn 2:32
struck the **s** on its feet of iron Dn 2:34
that struck the **s** became a great Dn 2:35
Nebuchadnezzar made a gold **s**, Dn 3:1
dedication of the **s** King Dn 3:2
of the **s** the king had set Dn 3:3
before the **s** Nebuchadnezzar Dn 3:3
and worship the gold **s** that King Dn 3:5
worshiped the gold **s** that King Dn 3:7
down and worship the gold **s**. Dn 3:10
the gold **s** you have set up. Dn 3:12
the gold **s** I have set up? Dn 3:14
down and worship the **s** I made. Dn 3:15
worship the gold **s** you set up." Dn 3:18

STATURE *(7)*
Samuel grew in **s** and in favor 1Sm 2:26
look at his appearance or his **s**, 1Sm 16:7
extraordinary **s** with six fingers 1Ch 20:6
Your **s** is like a palm tree; Sg 7:7
Sabeans, men of **s**, will come Is 45:14
Jesus increased in wisdom and **s**, Lk 2:52
mature man with a **s** measured by Eph 4:13

STATUTE *(38)*
generations as a permanent **s**. Ex 12:14
generations as a permanent **s**. Ex 12:17
as a **s** for you and your Ex 12:24
This is the **s** of the Passover: Ex 12:43
this **s** at its appointed time Ex 13:10
He made a **s** and ordinance for Ex 15:25
to be a permanent **s** for the Ex 27:21
be a permanent **s** for Aaron and Ex 28:43
to be theirs by a permanent **s**. Ex 29:9
is to be a permanent **s** for them, Ex 30:21
is a permanent **s** throughout your Lv 3:17
is a permanent **s** throughout your Lv 10:9
is to be a permanent **s** for you: Lv 16:29
it is a permanent **s**. Lv 16:31
is to be a permanent **s** for you, Lv 16:34
be a permanent **s** for them Lv 17:7
be a permanent **s** throughout your Lv 23:14
be a permanent **s** wherever you Lv 23:21
is a permanent **s** throughout your Lv 23:31
is a permanent **s** for you Lv 23:41
is a permanent **s** throughout your Lv 24:3
to the Passover **s** and its Nm 9:14
to apply the same **s** to both the Nm 9:14
is a permanent **s** throughout your Nm 10:8
to have the same **s** for both you Nm 15:15
as a permanent **s** throughout your Nm 15:15
as a portion and a perpetual **s**. Nm 18:8
and daughters as a perpetual **s**. Nm 18:11
to the LORD as a perpetual **s**. Nm 18:19

is a perpetual **s** throughout your Nm 18:23
is the legal **s** that the LORD has Nm 19:2
is a perpetual **s** for the Nm 19:10
This is a perpetual **s** for them. Nm 19:21
This is the legal **s** the LORD Nm 31:21
established a **s** and ordinance Jos 24:25
them as a **s** for Israel, 2Ch 35:25
For this is a **s** for Israel, Ps 81:4
a permanent **s** ⌊to be observed Ezk 46:14

STATUTES *(139)*

My commands, My **s**, and My Gn 26:5
and keep all His **s**, I will not Ex 15:26
teach ⌊them⌋ God's **s** and laws." Ex 18:16
them about the **s** and laws, Ex 18:20
all the **s** that the LORD has Lv 10:11
are to keep My **s** by following Lv 18:4
Keep My **s** and ordinances; Lv 18:5
are to keep My **s** and ordinances. Lv 18:26
You are to keep My **s**. Lv 19:19
You must keep all My **s** and all Lv 19:37
Keep My **s** and do them; Lv 20:8
are to keep all My **s** and all My Lv 20:22
not follow the **s** of the nations Lv 20:23
to observe My **s** and ordinances Lv 25:18
you follow My **s** and faithfully Lv 26:3
you reject My **s** and despise My Lv 26:15
My ordinances and abhorred My **s**. Lv 26:43
These are the **s**, ordinances, and Lv 26:46
to all its **s** and ordinances." Nm 9:3
Passover according to all its **s**. Nm 9:12
These are the **s** that the LORD Nm 30:16
listen to the **s** and ordinances I Dt 4:1
have taught you **s** and ordinances Dt 4:5
they hear about all these **s**, Dt 4:6
has righteous **s** and ordinances Dt 4:8
me to teach you **s** and ordinances Dt 4:14
Keep His **s** and commands, which I Dt 4:40
the decrees, **s**, and ordinances Dt 4:45
listen to the **s** and ordinances I Dt 5:1
command—the **s** and ordinances— Dt 5:31
command—the **s** and ordinances Dt 6:1
keeping all His **s** and commands I Dt 6:2
the decrees and **s** He has Dt 6:17
the decrees, **s**, and ordinances Dt 6:20
follow all these **s** and to fear Dt 6:24
command—the **s** and ordinances Dt 7:11
ordinances and **s**—I am giving Dt 8:11
commands and **s** I am giving you Dt 10:13
keep His mandate and His **s**, Dt 11:1
follow all the **s** and ordinances Dt 11:32
to follow these **s** and ordinances Dt 12:1
carefully follow these **s**. Dt 16:12
instruction, and to do these **s**. Dt 17:19
follow these **s** and ordinances. Dt 26:16
His ways, keep His **s**, commands, Dt 26:17
commands and **s** I am giving you Dt 27:10
commands and **s** I am giving you Dt 28:15
the commands and **s** He gave you. Dt 28:45
commands and **s** that are written Dt 30:10
His commands, **s**, and ordinances, Dt 30:16
and have not disregarded His **s**. 2Sm 22:23
in His ways and to keep His **s**, 1Kg 2:3
walking in the **s** of his father 1Kg 3:3
and keep My **s** and commandments 1Kg 3:14
if you walk in My **s**, execute My 1Kg 6:12
if you keep My **s** and ordinances, 1Kg 9:4
s that I have set before you— 1Kg 9:6
not keep My covenant and My **s**, 1Kg 11:11
to carry out My **s** and My 1Kg 11:33
My commandments and My **s**. 1Kg 11:34
order to keep My **s** and My 1Kg 11:38
and **s** according to all 2Kg 17:13
rejected His **s** and His covenant 2Kg 17:15
observe their **s** and ordinances, 2Kg 17:34
careful always to observe the **s**, 2Kg 17:37
and His **s** with all his mind and 2Kg 23:3
follow the **s** and ordinances 1Ch 22:13
decrees, and Your **s**, and to 1Ch 29:19
if you keep My **s** and ordinances, 2Ch 7:17
abandon My **s** and My commands 2Ch 7:19
commandment, **s**, or judgments— 2Ch 19:10
all the law, **s**, and judgments." 2Ch 33:8
and His **s** with all his heart and 2Ch 34:31
and teach ⌊its⌋ **s** and ordinances Ezr 7:10
commandments and **s** for Israel: Ezr 7:11
the commands, **s**, and ordinances Neh 1:7
commandments, **s**, and a law Neh 9:14
and **s** of the LORD our Lord. Neh 10:29
and have not disregarded His **s**. Ps 18:22
to recite My **s** and to take My Ps 50:16
dishonor My **s** and do not keep Ps 89:31
decrees and the **s** He gave them. Ps 99:7
might keep His **s** and obey His Ps 105:45
committed to keeping Your **s**! Ps 119:5
I will keep Your **s**; Ps 119:8
You be praised; teach me Your **s**. Ps 119:12
I will delight in Your **s**; Ps 119:16
servant will think about Your **s**; Ps 119:23
listened to me; teach me Your **s**. Ps 119:26
meaning of Your **s**, and I will Ps 119:33
and will meditate on Your **s**. Ps 119:48
s are ⌊the theme of⌋ my song Ps 119:54
faithful love; teach me Your **s**. Ps 119:64
what is good; teach me Your **s**. Ps 119:68
so that I could learn Your **s**. Ps 119:71
regarding Your **s** so that I will Ps 119:80
smoke, I do not forget Your **s**. Ps 119:83
to obey Your **s** to the very end. Ps 119:112
with Your **s** continually. Ps 119:117
all who stray from Your **s**, Ps 119:118
faithful love; teach me Your **s**. Ps 119:124
servant, and teach me Your **s**. Ps 119:135
I will obey Your **s**. Ps 119:145
because they do not seek Your **s**. Ps 119:155
praise, for You teach me Your **s**. Ps 119:171
His **s** and judgments to Israel. Ps 147:19
enacting crooked **s** and writing Is 10:1
by My law or My **s** that I set Jr 44:10
in His law, His **s**, and His Jr 44:23
and against My **s** more than the Ezk 5:6
and have not walked in My **s**. Ezk 5:6
not walked in My **s** or kept My Ezk 5:7
whose **s** you have not followed Ezk 11:12
they may follow My **s**, keep My Ezk 11:20
He follows My **s** and keeps My Ezk 18:9
My ordinances and follows My **s**. Ezk 18:17
carefully observing all My **s**, Ezk 18:19
keeps all My **s**, and does what is Ezk 18:21
gave them My **s** and explained My Ezk 20:11
not follow My **s** and they Ezk 20:13
and did not follow My **s**. Ezk 20:16
follow the **s** of your fathers Ezk 20:18
Follow My **s**, keep My ordinances, Ezk 20:19
not follow My **s** or carefully Ezk 20:21
but rejected My **s** and profaned Ezk 20:24
I also gave them **s** that were not Ezk 20:25
walks in the **s** of life without Ezk 33:15
you to follow My **s** and carefully Ezk 36:27
and keep My **s** and obey them. Ezk 37:24
design along with all its **s**, Ezk 43:11
and all its **s** and may carry them Ezk 43:11
These are the **s** for the altar on Ezk 43:18
you about all the **s** and laws of Ezk 44:5
My laws and **s** regarding all My Ezk 44:24
LORD and have not kept His **s**. Am 2:4
The **s** of Omri and all the Mc 6:16
My words and My **s** that I Zch 1:6
you have turned from My **s**; Mal 3:7
the **s** and ordinances I commanded Mal 4:4

STATUTORY *(2)*

This is to be a **s** ordinance for Nm 27:11
will be a **s** ordinance for you Nm 35:29

STAY *(122)*

that they could not **s** together, Gn 13:6
to his young men, "**S** here with Gn 22:5
Let the girl **s** with us for about Gn 24:55
s in this land as a foreigner, Gn 26:3
and **s** with him for a few days Gn 27:44
to some other man. **S** with me." Gn 29:19
found favor in your sight, ⌊**s**.⌋ Gn 30:27
Moses agreed to **s** with the man, Ex 2:21
you don't need to **s** any longer." Ex 9:28
and your herds must **s** behind." Ex 10:24
Each of you **s** where you are; Ex 16:29
them **s** with their mothers for Ex 22:30
S far away from a false Ex 23:7
mountain and **s** there so that I Ex 24:12
Let him **s** with you as a hired Lv 25:40
He will **s** with him like a man Lv 25:53
Please **s** here overnight as the Nm 22:19
S here by your burnt offering Nm 23:3
S here by your burnt offering Nm 23:15
go to war while you **s** here? Nm 32:6
one of these cities and **s** alive: Dt 4:42
is free ⌊to **s**⌋ at home for one Dt 24:5
the rest of you, don't **s** there. Jos 10:19
determined to **s** in this land. Jos 17:12
He is to **s** in that city until he Jos 20:6
"I will **s** until you return." Jdg 6:18
"Please **s** here," Manoah told Him, Jdg 13:15
to him, "If I **s**, I won't eat Jdg 13:16
S with me and be my father and Jdg 17:10
and agreed to **s** with the man, Jdg 17:11
Please agree to **s** overnight and Jdg 19:6
but **s** here close to my young Ru 2:8
'**S** with my young men until they Ru 2:21
S ⌊here⌋ tonight, and in the Ru 3:13
and to **s** there permanently. 1Sm 1:22
and **s** here until you've weaned 1Sm 1:23
God must not **s** here with us, 1Sm 5:7
of us, but you **s** for awhile, and 1Sm 9:27
then we will **s** where we are 1Sm 14:9
in a secret place and **s** there. 1Sm 19:2
began and **s** beside the rock 1Sm 20:19
and mother **s** with you until I 1Sm 22:3
Don't **s** in the stronghold. 1Sm 22:5
S with me. Don't be afraid, for 1Sm 22:23
S in Jericho until your beards 2Sm 10:5
"**S** here today also," David said 2Sm 11:12
back and **s** with the king since 2Sm 15:19
have chosen. I will **s** with him. 2Sm 16:18
belongs to Sidon, and **s** there. 1Kg 17:9
Elijah said to Elisha, "**S** here; 2Kg 2:2
said to him, "Elisha, **s** here; 2Kg 2:4
Elijah said to him, "**S** here; 2Kg 2:6
he comes, he can **s** there." 2Kg 4:10
Enjoy your glory and **s** at home. 2Kg 14:10
and did not **s** there in the land. 2Kg 15:20
S in Jericho until your beards 1Ch 19:5
He has come to **s** in Jerusalem 1Ch 23:25
get glory. Now **s** at home. Why 2Ch 25:19
you must **s** away from that place, Ezr 6:6
stamina to **s** out in the open. Ezr 10:13
its ways or **s** on its paths. Jb 24:13
lairs and **s** in their dens. Jb 37:8
I would **s** in the wilderness. Ps 55:7
I **s** awake; I am like a solitary Ps 102:7
Help me **s** on the path of Your Ps 119:35
you get up early and **s** up late, Ps 127:2
men, **s** away from me— Ps 139:19
let a slanderer **s** in the land. Ps 140:11
How long will you **s** in bed, Pr 6:9
her feet do not **s** at home. Pr 7:11
S away from a foolish man; Pr 14:7
Let my refugees **s** with you; Is 16:4
and I **s** at my post all night. Is 21:8
screech owl will **s** there and Is 34:14
where he will **s** until I attend Jr 32:5
soil where you **s** as a resident Jr 35:7
he continued to **s** in the guard's Jr 38:13
and **s** with him among the people Jr 40:5
you will indeed **s** in this land, Jr 42:10
We will not **s** in this land, Jr 42:13
of the LORD to **s** in the land of Jr 43:4
being will even **s** in it as a Jr 49:18
being will even **s** in it as a Jr 49:33
being will even **s** in it as a Jr 50:40
for food in order to **s** alive. Lm 1:11
"**S** away! Unclean!" people Lm 4:15
"They can **s** here no longer." Lm 4:15
said this to: **S** away from the Ezk 11:15
years he will **s** away from the Dn 11:8
They will not **s** in the land of Hs 9:3
It will **s** inside his house and Zch 5:4
and **s** there until I tell you. Mt 2:13
and **s** there until you leave. Mt 10:11
here and **s** awake with Me." Mt 26:38
couldn't you **s** awake with Me one Mt 26:40
S awake and pray, so that you Mt 26:41
s there until you leave that Mk 6:10
Remain here and **s** awake." Mk 14:34
Couldn't you **s** awake one hour? Mk 14:37
S awake and pray so that you Mk 14:38
clothes and did not **s** in a house Lk 8:27
s there and leave from there. Lk 9:4
today I must **s** at your house." Lk 19:5
S with us, because it's almost Lk 24:29
So He went in to **s** with them. Lk 24:29
s in the city until you are Lk 24:49
they asked Him to **s** with them, Jn 4:40
s away from these men and leave Ac 5:38
asked him to **s** for a few days. Ac 10:48
people during their **s** in the Ac 13:17
Lord, come and **s** at my house." Ac 16:15

asked him to s for a longer time Ac 18:20
with whom we were to s. Ac 21:16
Unless these men s in the ship, Ac 27:31
were invited to s with them for Ac 28:14
permitted to s by himself with Ac 28:16
is fine for a man to s as he is. 1Co 7:26
But I will s in Ephesus until 1Co 16:8
the Spirit, and s alert in this, Eph 6:18
s alert in it with thanksgiving. Col 4:2
we must s awake and be sober. 1Th 5:6
S away from every form of evil. 1Th 5:22

STAYED *(87)*
them as long as they s together, Gn 13:6
was a quiet man who s at home. Gn 25:27
After Jacob had s with him a Gn 29:14
where Abraham and Isaac had s. Gn 35:27
land where they s could not Gn 36:7
the land where his father had s, Gn 37:1
long as the cloud s over the Nm 9:18
when the cloud s over the Nm 9:19
long as the cloud s over the Nm 9:22
officials of Moab s with Balaam. Nm 22:8
'You have s at this mountain Dt 1:6
this reason you s in Kadesh as Dt 1:46
So we s in the valley facing Dt 3:29
I s on the mountain 40 days and Dt 9:9
I s on the mountain 40 days and Dt 10:10
named Rahab, and s there. Jos 2:1
country and s there three days Jos 2:22
as the Jordan and s there before Jos 3:1
they s where they were in the Jos 5:8
seashore and s in his harbors. Jdg 5:17
Abimelech s in Arumah, and Zebul Jdg 9:41
So Israel s in Kadesh. Jdg 11:17
went down and s in the cave at Jdg 15:8
But Samson s in bed until Jdg 16:3
he s with him for three days. Jdg 19:4
he s and spent the night there Jdg 19:7
of Rimmon and s there four Jdg 20:47
Ruth s close to Boaz's young Ru 2:23
So Hannah s there and nursed 1Sm 1:23
They s on that one highway, 1Sm 6:12
and Samuel left and s at Naioth. 1Sm 19:18
and they s with him the whole 1Sm 22:4
David then s in the wilderness 1Sm 23:14
to the rock and s in the 1Sm 23:25
David went up and s in the 1Sm 23:29
David while 200 s with the 1Sm 25:13
David and his men s with Achish 1Sm 27:3
time that David s in the 1Sm 27:7
whole time he s in the 1Sm 27:11
Amalekites and s at Ziklag two 2Sm 1:1
So Uriah s in Jerusalem that 2Sm 11:12
Geshur where he s three years. 2Sm 13:38
of God to Jerusalem and s there. 2Sm 15:29
the king while he s in Mahanaim. 2Sm 19:32
presence, Jeroboam s in Egypt. 1Kg 12:2
building Ramah and s in Tirzah. 1Kg 15:21
s in the ⌊temple⌋ chambers and 1Ch 9:33
Rehoboam s in Jerusalem, and he 2Ch 11:5
of the people s in Jerusalem, Neh 11:1
the province who s in Jerusalem Neh 11:3
misery that I have s in Meshech, Ps 120:5
Everyone has s his course like a Jr 8:6
dungeon and s there many days Jr 37:16
and he s with him among the Jr 40:6
him, yet its roots s under it. Ezk 17:6
He s there until Herod's death, Mt 2:15
they've already s with Me three Mt 15:32
would have s alert and not let Mt 24:43
they've already s with Me three Mk 8:2
amazed that he s so long in the Lk 1:21
And Mary s with her about three Lk 1:56
the boy Jesus s behind in Lk 2:43
and they s with Him that day. Jn 1:39
they s there only a few days. Jn 2:12
them, and He s there two days. Jn 4:40
crowd that had s on the other Jn 6:22
these things, He s in Galilee. Jn 7:9
He s two more days in the place Jn 11:6
And He s there with the Jn 11:54
Peter s on many days in Joppa Ac 9:43
Judea to Caesarea and s there. Ac 12:19
they s there for some time and Ac 14:3
s in that city for a number of Ac 16:12
Silas and Timothy s on there. Ac 17:14
same occupation, s with them and Ac 18:3
And he s there a year and six Ac 18:11
having s on for many days, Ac 18:18
he himself s in the province of Ac 19:22
and s three months. When he was Ac 20:3
disciples and s there seven days Ac 21:4
the brothers and s with them one Ac 21:7
of the Seven, and s with him. Ac 21:8
Since they s there many days, Ac 25:14
in at Syracuse, we s three days. Ac 28:12
Then he s two whole years in his Ac 28:30
Cephas, and I s with him 15 days Gl 1:18
By faith he s as a foreigner in Heb 11:9

STAYING *(21)*
have been s with Laban and have Gn 32:4
and any woman s in her house for Ex 3:22
houses where you are s will be a Ex 12:13
A foreigner s with a priest or a Lv 22:10
from the foreigners s with you, Lv 25:45
Israel was s in Acacia Grove Nm 25:1
with them were s in Geba of 1Sm 13:16
Saul was s under the pomegranate 1Sm 14:2
and his men were s in the back 1Sm 24:3
"Why, he's s in Jerusalem," Ziba 2Sm 16:3
and Ahimaaz were s at En-rogel, 2Sm 17:17
the upper room where he was s, 1Kg 17:19
the widow I am s with by killing 1Kg 17:20
him in Jericho where he was s, 2Kg 2:18
shepherds were s out in the Lk 2:8
Teacher"), "where are You s?" Jn 1:38
went and saw where He was s, Jn 1:39
room upstairs where they were s: Ac 1:13
whole house where they were s. Ac 2:2
While we were s there many days, Ac 21:10
not s away from our meetings, Heb 10:25

STAYS *(8)*
or foreigner who s with you. Lv 25:6
⌊such⌋ houses s in effect, Lv 25:31
She who s at home divides the Ps 68:12
the watchman s alert in vain. Ps 127:1
is a friend who s closer than a Pr 18:24
guards himself s far from them. Pr 22:5
Whoever s in this city will die Jr 21:9
'Whoever s in this city will die Jr 38:2

STEADFAST *(3)*
me and renew a s spirit within Ps 51:10
dear brothers, be s, immovable, 1Co 15:58
grounded and s in the faith, Col 1:23

STEADIED *(1)*
Your words have s the one who Jb 4:4

STEADIES *(1)*
I am the One who s its pillars. Ps 75:3

STEADILY *(3)*
The water s receded from the Gn 8:3
Elisha stared s at him until 2Kg 8:11
David s grew more powerful, 1Ch 11:9

STEADY *(4)*
bow remained s, and his strong Gn 49:24
hands remained s until the sun Ex 17:12
Make my steps s through Your Ps 119:133
the weak hands, s the shaking Is 35:3

STEAL *(23)*
How could we s gold and silver Gn 44:8
Do not s. Ex 20:15
You must not s. You must not act Lv 19:11
Do not s. Dt 5:19
They s a flock and provide Jb 24:2
I did not s, I must repay. Ps 69:4
or I might have nothing and s, Pr 30:9
Do you s, murder, commit Jr 7:9
who s My words from each other. Jr 23:30
wouldn't they s only what they Ob 5
where thieves break in and s. Mt 6:19
thieves don't break in and s. Mt 6:20
house and s his possessions Mt 12:29
adultery; do not s; do not bear Mt 19:18
may come, s Him, and tell Mt 27:64
adultery; do not s; do not bear Mk 10:19
murder; do not s; do not bear Lk 18:20
comes only to s and to kill and Jn 10:10
and would s part of what was Jn 12:6
You must not s"—do you steal? Rm 2:21
You must not steal"—do you s? Rm 2:21
you shall not s, you shall not Rm 13:9
The thief must no longer s. Eph 4:28

STEALING *(2)*
lying, murder, s, and adultery Hs 4:2
or s, but demonstrating utter Ti 2:10

STEALS *(3)*
When a man s an ox or a sheep Ex 22:1
so Sheol ⌊s⌋ those who have Jb 24:19
the thief if he s to satisfy Pr 6:30

STEALTH *(1)*
long ago, have come in by s; Jd 4

STEED *(1)*
like His majestic s in battle. Zch 10:3

STEEDS *(4)*
of the neighing of mighty s, Jr 8:16
horses; mount the s; take your Jr 46:4
young men, horsemen riding on s. Ezk 23:6
horsemen riding on s, all of Ezk 23:12

STEEP *(4)*
and settle in the s ravines, Is 7:19
rushed down the s bank into the Mt 8:32
rushed down the s bank into the Mk 5:13
rushed down the s bank into the Lk 8:33

STEM *(2)*
their s hardly takes root in the Is 40:24
sovereignty s from themselves Hab 1:7

STENCH *(6)*
of perfume there will be a s; Is 3:24
there is no place without a s. Is 28:8
and the s of their corpses will Is 34:3
Sea. His s will rise; yes, his Jl 2:20
I caused the s of your camp to Am 4:10
can't stand the s of your solemn Am 5:21

STEP *(7)*
in Ashdod do not s on Dagon's 1Sm 5:5
there is but a s between me and 1Sm 20:3
side and harass him at every s. Jb 18:11
If my s has turned from the way, Jb 31:7
ridiculed every s of Your Ps 89:51
Guard your s when you go to the Ec 5:1
S into the clay and tread the Nah 3:14

STEPHANAS *(3)*
baptize the household of S; 1Co 1:16
you know the household of S: 1Co 16:15
over the presence of S, 1Co 16:17

STEPHEN *(8)*
So they chose S, a man full of Ac 6:5
S, full of grace and power, was Ac 6:8
forward and disputed with S. Ac 6:9
S, filled by the Holy Spirit, Ac 7:55
were stoning S as he called out Ac 7:59
devout men buried S and mourned Ac 8:2
because of S made their way as Ac 11:19
Your witness S was being shed, Ac 22:20

STEPPED *(5)*
Abraham s forward and said, Gn 18:23
and their feet s out on solid Jos 4:18
As He s ashore, He saw a huge Mt 14:14
So as He s ashore, He saw a huge Mk 6:34
they s back and fell to the Jn 18:6

STEPS *(57)*
must not go up to My altar on s, Ex 20:26
the wife of one s in to rescue Dt 25:11
He guards the s of His faithful 1Sm 2:9
David's men retraced their s. 1Sm 25:12
ark of the LORD advanced six s, 2Sm 6:13
a place⌋ beneath me for my s, 2Sm 22:37
almug wood into s for the LORD's 1Kg 10:12
The throne had six s; there was 1Kg 10:19
standing there on the six s, 1Kg 10:20
put it under Jehu on the bare s. 2Kg 9:13
go ahead 10 s or go back 10 2Kg 20:9
ahead 10 steps or go back 10 s?" 2Kg 20:9
for the shadow to lengthen 10 s. 2Kg 20:10
let the shadow go back 10 s." 2Kg 20:10
back the 10 s it had descended 2Kg 20:11
The throne had six s; there was 2Ch 9:18
standing there on the six s, 2Ch 9:19
they climbed the s of the city Neh 12:37
would count my s but would not Jb 14:16
see my ways and number all my s? Jb 31:4
give Him an account of all my s; Jb 31:37
and He observes all his s. Jb 34:21
My s are on Your paths; Ps 17:5
a place⌋ beneath me for my s, Ps 18:36
A man's s are established by the Ps 37:23
his heart; his s do not falter. Ps 37:31
on a rock, making my s secure. Ps 40:2
our s have not strayed from Your Ps 44:18
they watch my s while they wait Ps 56:6

perhaps there is ⌊**s**⌋ hope. Lm 3:29
when the creatures stood **s**, Ezk 1:21
stood still, the wheels stood **s**; Ezk 1:21
When they stood **s**, they lowered Ezk 1:24
when they stood **s**, they lowered Ezk 1:25
When the cherubim stood **s**, Ezk 10:17
wheels stood **s**, and when they Ezk 10:17
but it will ⌊**s**⌋ consume them. Ezk 15:7
them, you were **s** not satisfied. Ezk 16:28
break a covenant and ⌊**s**⌋ escape? Ezk 17:15
Will you **s** say: I am a god, in Ezk 28:9
the words were **s** in the king's Dn 4:31
for **s** the end will come at the Dn 11:27
for it will **s** come at the Dn 11:35
Judah **s** wanders with El and is Hs 11:12
while there were **s** three months Am 4:7
said while I was **s** in my own Jnh 4:2
Are there **s** the treasures of Mc 6:10
they will **s** be mowed down, Nah 1:12
moon stand **s** in ⌊their⌋ lofty Hab 3:11
My house **s** lies in ruins, Hg 1:9
Is there **s** seed left in the Hg 2:19
a man **s** prophesies, his father Zch 13:3
nation—are ⌊**s**⌋ robbing Me. Mal 3:9
He was **s** speaking to the crowds Mt 12:46
S others fell on good ground, Mt 13:8
Are even you **s** lacking in Mt 15:16
s others, Jeremiah or one of the Mt 16:14
he was **s** speaking, suddenly Mt 17:5
told Him. "What do I **s** lack?" Mt 19:20
Are you **s** sleeping and resting? Mt 26:45
While He was **s** speaking, Judas, Mt 26:47
Why do we **s** need witnesses? Mt 26:65
while this deceiver was **s** alive, Mt 27:63
while it was **s** dark, He got up, Mk 1:35
S others fell on good ground and Mk 4:8
Silence! Be **s**!" The wind ceased Mk 4:39
Do you **s** have no faith?" Mk 4:40
While He was **s** speaking, people Mk 5:35
S others said, "He's a prophet Mk 6:15
s others, one of the prophets." Mk 8:28
He **s** had one to send, a beloved Mk 12:6
Are you **s** sleeping and resting? Mk 14:41
While He was **s** speaking, Judas, Mk 14:43
Why do we **s** need witnesses? Mk 14:63
But Jesus **s** did not answer Mk 15:5
Spirit while **s** in his mother's Lk 1:15
S other seed fell on good ground; Lk 8:8
While He was **s** speaking, someone Lk 8:49
s others, that one of the Lk 9:19
As the boy was **s** approaching, Lk 9:42
been done, and there's **s** room.' Lk 14:22
while the other is **s** far off, Lk 14:32
the son was **s** a long way off, Lk 15:20
told him, "You **s** lack one thing: Lk 18:22
He was **s** speaking, suddenly Lk 22:47
while he was **s** speaking, a Lk 22:60
to you when He was **s** in Galilee, Lk 24:6
But while they **s** could not Lk 24:41
to you while I was **s** with you— Lk 24:44
'There are **s** four more months, Jn 4:35
While he was **s** going down, Jn 4:51
My Father is **s** working, and I am Jn 5:17
S, nobody was talking publicly Jn 7:13
village but was **s** in the place Jn 11:30
I **s** have many things to tell Jn 16:12
tomb early, while it was **s** dark. Jn 20:1
they **s** did not understand the Jn 20:9
s breathing threats and murder Ac 9:1
While Peter was **s** speaking these Ac 10:44
why am I also **s** judged as a Rm 3:7
by faith while **s** uncircumcised. Rm 4:11
had while **s** uncircumcised. Rm 4:12
For while we were **s** helpless, Rm 5:6
while we were **s** sinners Christ Rm 5:8
we who died to sin **s** live in it? Rm 6:2
Why then does He **s** find fault? Rm 9:19
S, to someone who considers a Rm 14:14
In fact, you are **s** not able, 1Co 3:2
because you are **s** fleshly. 1Co 3:3
spite of this it **s** belongs to 1Co 12:15
spite of this it **s** belongs to 1Co 12:16
you are **s** in your sins. 1Co 15:17
If I were **s** trying to please Gl 1:10
if I **s** preach circumcision, Gl 5:11
why am I **s** persecuted? Gl 5:11
S, you did well by sharing with Php 4:14
you live as if you **s** belonged to Col 2:20
We who are **s** alive at the Lord's 1Th 4:15
Then we who are **s** alive will be 1Th 4:17
when I was **s** with you I told 2Th 2:5
while it is **s** called today, Heb 3:13
for he was **s** within his Heb 7:10
first tabernacle was **s** standing. Heb 9:8
he is dead, he **s** speaks through Heb 11:4
There are **s** two more woes to Rv 9:12

STILLBORN *(3)*
Why was I not **s**; ⌊why⌋ didn't I Jb 3:11
I say that a **s** child is better Ec 6:3
Though a **s** child does not see Ec 6:5

STILLED *(1)*
He **s** the storm to a murmur, Ps 107:29

STILLS *(1)*
⌊so⌋ He **s** the song of the Is 25:5

STING *(3)*
Sheol, where is your **s**? Hs 13:14
O Death, where is your **s**? 1Co 15:55
Now the **s** of death is sin, 1Co 15:56

STINGERS *(1)*
and they had tails with **s**, Rv 9:10

STINGINESS *(1)*
lewdness, **s**, blasphemy, pride Mk 7:22

STINGS *(1)*
like a snake and **s** like a viper. Pr 23:32

STINGY *(3)*
and you are **s** toward your poor Dt 15:9
don't have a **s** heart when you Dt 15:10
Don't eat a **s** person's bread, Pr 23:6

STINK *(3)*
the river will **s**, and the Ex 7:18
a perfumer's oil ferment and **s**; Ec 10:1
The channels will **s**; they will Is 19:6

STINKS *(1)*
told Him, "Lord, he already **s**. Jn 11:39

STINKWEED *(1)*
wheat and **s** instead of barley. Jb 31:40

STIR *(17)*
Why should you **s** up such trouble 2Kg 14:10
s up such trouble so that you 2Ch 25:19
will not **s** from their sleep. Jb 14:12
They **s** up strife, they lurk; Ps 56:6
when all the forest animals **s**. Ps 104:20
They **s** up wars all day long. Ps 140:2
and their words **s** up trouble. Pr 24:2
do not **s** up or awaken love until Sg 2:7
do not **s** up or awaken love until Sg 3:5
do not **s** up or awaken love until Sg 8:4
For I will soon **s** up and bring Jr 50:9
I am about to **s** up a destructive Jr 51:1
In order to **s** up wrath and take Ezk 24:8
will **s** up everyone against the Dn 11:2
army he will **s** up his power Dn 11:25
time to time and **s** up the water. Jn 5:4
don't **s** up anger in your Eph 6:4

STIRRED *(24)*
that my son has **s** up my own 1Sm 22:8
anger gets **s** up and he asks 2Sm 11:20
and it **s** up David against them 2Sm 24:1
wrath was so **s** up against His 2Ch 36:16
By His power He **s** the sea, Jb 26:12
a tempest that **s** up the waves Ps 107:25
and my feelings were **s** for him. Sg 5:4
him and **s** up his enemies. Is 9:11
Who has **s** him up from the east? Is 41:2
great storm is **s** up from the Jr 25:32
kings will be **s** up from the Jr 50:41
winds of heaven **s** up the great Dn 7:2
of heart; My compassion is **s**! Hs 11:8
The LORD **s** up the spirit of Hg 1:14
chief priests **s** up the crowd so Mk 15:11
the water was **s** up recovered Jn 5:4
the pool when the water is **s** up, Jn 5:7
s up the people, the elders, Ac 6:12
They **s** up persecution against Ac 13:50
to believe **s** up and poisoned Ac 14:2
The Jews **s** up the crowd and the Ac 17:8
temple complex, **s** up the whole Ac 21:27
whole city was **s** up, and the Ac 21:30
your zeal has **s** up most of them 2Co 9:2

STIRRING *(4)*
and **s** up anger produces strife. Pr 30:33
am **s** up the Medes against them, Is 13:17
a baker who stops **s** ⌊the fire⌋ Hs 7:4
with Your horses, **s** up the great Hab 3:15

STIRS *(12)*
whose heart **s** him ⌊to give⌋. Ex 25:2
he **s** up trouble constantly. Pr 6:14
and one who **s** up trouble among Pr 6:19
Hatred **s** up conflicts, but love Pr 10:12
but a harsh word **s** up wrath. Pr 15:1
hot-tempered man **s** up conflict, Pr 15:18
An angry man **s** up conflict, Pr 29:22
He **s** up the spirits of the Is 14:9
He **s** up His zeal like a soldier. Is 42:13
LORD your God who **s** up the sea Is 51:15
who **s** up the sea and makes its Jr 31:35
insisting, "He **s** up the people, Lk 23:5

STOCK *(1)*
set his own **s** apart and didn't Gn 30:40

STOCKS *(6)*
my feet in the **s** and stand watch Jb 13:27
He puts my feet in the **s**; Jb 33:11
put him in the **s** at the Upper Jr 20:2
released Jeremiah from the **s**, Jr 20:3
confine him in **s** and an iron Jr 29:26
and secured their feet in the **s**. Ac 16:24

STOIC *(1)*
the Epicurean and **S** philosophers Ac 17:18

STOLE *(4)*
Rachel **s** her father's household Gn 31:19
return what he **s** or defrauded, Lv 6:4
So Absalom **s** the hearts of the 2Sm 15:6
night and **s** Him while we were Mt 28:13

STOLEN *(13)*
they will be considered **s**." Gn 30:33
but why have you **s** my gods?" Gn 31:30
that Rachel had **s** ⌊the idols⌋. Gn 31:32
me for what was **s** by day or by Gn 31:39
If what was **s**—whether ox, Ex 22:4
they are **s** from that person's Ex 22:7
injured, or is **s**, while no one Ex 22:10
the animal was **s** from his Ex 22:12
They have **s**, deceived, and put Jos 7:11
They had **s** them from the public 2Sm 21:12
S water is sweet, and bread Pr 9:17
restitution for what he has **s**, Ezk 33:15
You bring **s**, lame, or sick Mal 1:13

STOMACH *(23)*
brings a curse enter your **s**, Nm 5:22
given the shoulder, jaws, and **s**. Dt 18:3
hit him in the **s** with the end of 2Sm 2:23
there Joab stabbed him in the **s**. 2Sm 3:27
wheat and stabbed him in the **s**. 2Sm 4:6
stabbed him in the **s** with it and 2Sm 20:10
food in his **s** turns into cobras' Jb 20:14
God will force it from his **s**. Jb 20:15
he fills his **s**, God will send Jb 20:23
the **s** of the wicked is empty. Pr 13:25
mouth a man's **s** is satisfied; Pr 18:20
All man's labor is for his **s**, Ec 6:7
his hands on his **s** like a woman Jr 30:6
and fill your **s** with this scroll Ezk 3:3
its **s** and thighs were bronze, Dn 2:32
passes into the **s** and is Mt 15:17
but into the **s** and is eliminated Mk 7:19
Foods for the **s** and the stomach 1Co 6:13
stomach and the **s** for foods," 1Co 6:13
their god is their **s**; Php 3:19
because of your **s** and your 1Tm 5:23
it will be bitter in your **s**, Rv 10:9
I ate it, my **s** became bitter. Rv 10:10

STOMACHS *(1)*
their appetites or fill their **s**, Ezk 7:19

STOMPING *(1)*
the sound of the **s** hooves of his Jr 47:3

STONE *(183)*
had brick for **s** and asphalt for Gn 11:3
Jacob took the **s** that was near Gn 28:18
This **s** that I have set up as a Gn 28:22
A large **s** covered the opening of Gn 29:2
roll the **s** from the opening Gn 29:3
s was then placed back on the Gn 29:3
gathered and the **s** is rolled Gn 29:8
and rolled the **s** from the Gn 29:10
oil on the **s** marker and made Gn 31:13
picked out a **s** and set it up as Gn 31:45
had spoken to him—a **s** marker. Gn 35:14
in wooden and **s** ⌊containers⌋." Ex 7:19

front of them, won't they s us? Ex 8:26
sank to the depths like a s. Ex 15:5
as still as a s because of Your Ex 15:16
a little while they will s me!" Ex 17:4
they took a s and put ⌊it⌋ under Ex 17:12
If you make a s altar for Me, Ex 20:25
the other with a s or fist, Ex 21:18
a pavement made of sapphire s, Ex 24:10
may give you the s tablets with Ex 24:12
on the first s and the remaining Ex 28:10
six names on the second s, Ex 28:10
Each s must be engraved like a Ex 28:21
s tablets inscribed by the Ex 31:18
Cut two s tablets like the first Ex 34:1
Moses cut two s tablets like the Ex 34:4
taking the two s tablets in his Ex 34:4
Each s was engraved like a seal Ex 39:14
of the country are to s him. Lv 20:2
have the whole community s him. Lv 24:14
the whole community must s him. Lv 24:16
a sculpted s in your land to Lv 26:1
community threatened to s them, Nm 14:10
community is to s him outside Nm 15:35
with a s wall on either side. Nm 22:24
all their s images and cast Nm 33:52
has in his hand a s capable of Nm 35:17
drops a s without looking that Nm 35:23
which He wrote on two s tablets. Dt 4:13
man-made gods of wood and s, Dt 4:28
them on two s tablets and gave Dt 5:22
to receive the s tablets, Dt 9:9
LORD gave me the two s tablets, Dt 9:10
LORD gave me the two s tablets, Dt 9:11
'Cut two s tablets like the Dt 10:1
cut two s tablets like the first Dt 10:3
S him to death for trying to Dt 13:10
evil thing and s them to death. Dt 17:5
of his city will s him to death. Dt 21:21
of her city will s her to death. Dt 22:21
that city and s them to death— Dt 22:24
other gods, of wood and s. Dt 28:36
other gods of wood and s, Dt 28:64
made⌋ of wood, s, silver, and Dt 29:17
of you lift a s onto his Jos 4:5
ascended to the s of Bohan son Jos 15:6
down to the S of Bohan, Jos 18:17
also took a large s and set it Jos 24:26
You see this s—it will be Jos 24:27
put it on this s, and pour the Jdg 6:20
Jerubbaal, on top of a large s. Jdg 9:5
his 70 sons on top of a large s, Jdg 9:18
could sling a s at a hair and Jdg 20:16
Samuel took a s and set it 1Sm 7:12
a large s over here at once. 1Sm 14:33
bag, took out a s, slung ⌊it⌋, 1Sm 17:49
The s sank into his forehead, 1Sm 17:49
Philistine with a sling and a s. 1Sm 17:50
the south side of the s Ezel, 1Sm 20:41
and it had a precious s ⌊in it⌋. 2Sm 12:30
at the great s in Gibeon when 2Sm 20:8
cattle near the s of Zoheleth, 1Kg 1:9
quarried ⌊the s⌋ and prepared 1Kg 5:18
timber and s for the temple's 1Kg 5:18
not a s could be seen. 1Kg 6:18
rows of dressed s and a row of 1Kg 6:36
rows of dressed s and a row of 1Kg 7:12
except the two s tablets that 1Kg 8:9
take him out and s him to death. 1Kg 21:10
timber and quarried s to repair 2Kg 12:12
it and put it on a s pavement. 2Kg 16:17
by human hands—wood and s. 2Kg 19:18
timber and quarried s to repair 2Kg 22:6
there was a precious s in it. 1Ch 20:2
have also provided timber and s, 1Ch 22:14
bronze, iron, s, and wood, with 2Ch 2:14
to buy quarried s and timbers— 2Ch 34:11
would break down their s wall!" Neh 4:3
depths like a s into churning Neh 9:11
strength that of s, or my flesh Jb 6:12
were inscribed in s forever by Jb 19:24
when water becomes as hard as s, Jb 38:30
wall or a tottering s fence? Ps 62:3
out of the s and made water Ps 78:16
strike your foot against a s. Ps 91:12
The s that the builders rejected Ps 118:22
like a magic s to its owner; Pr 17:8
and the s wall was ruined. Pr 24:31
is like binding a s in a sling. Pr 26:8
whoever rolls a s—it will come Pr 26:27
A s is heavy and sand, a burden, Pr 27:3
He will be a s to stumble over Is 8:14
have laid a s in Zion, a tested Is 28:16
in Zion, a tested s, a precious Is 28:16
by human hands—wood and s. Is 37:19
You are my father, and to a s: Jr 2:27
adultery with s and tree. Jr 3:9
or a foundation s from you, Jr 51:26
tie a s to it and throw it into Jr 51:63
of sapphire s was above the Ezk 1:26
like sapphire s resembling the Ezk 10:1
their heart of s from their Ezk 11:19
against you to s you and cut you Ezk 16:40
wood and s, what you have Ezk 20:32
assembly will s them and cut Ezk 23:47
kind of precious s covered you: Ezk 28:13
your heart of s and give you a Ezk 36:26
tables of cut s for the burnt Ezk 40:42
There was a ⌊s⌋ wall around the Ezk 46:23
a s broke off without a hand Dn 2:34
But the s that struck the statue Dn 2:35
You saw a s break off from the Dn 2:45
bronze, iron, wood, and s. Dn 5:4
iron, wood, and s, which do not Dn 5:23
A s was brought and placed over Dn 6:17
houses of cut s you have built; Am 5:11
up! or to mute s: Come alive! Hab 2:19
Before one s was placed on Hg 2:15
Notice the s I have set before Zch 3:9
on ⌊that⌋ one s are seven eyes. Zch 3:9
Jerusalem a heavy s for all the Zch 12:3
strike your foot against a s." Mt 4:6
for bread, will give him a s? Mt 7:9
The s that the builders rejected Mt 21:42
falls on this s will be broken Mt 21:44
Not one s will be left here on Mt 24:2
rolling a great s against the Mt 27:60
by sealing the s and setting the Mt 27:66
back the s and was sitting Mt 28:2
The s that the builders rejected Mk 12:10
Not one s will be left here on Mk 13:2
and rolled a s against the Mk 15:46
roll away the s from the Mk 16:3
they observed that the s— Mk 16:4
tell this s to become bread." Lk 4:3
strike your foot against a s." Lk 4:11
not leave one s on another in Lk 19:44
all the people will s us, Lk 20:6
The s that the builders rejected Lk 20:17
falls on that s will be broken Lk 20:18
come when not one s will be left Lk 21:6
found the s rolled away from Lk 24:2
six s water jars had been set Jn 2:6
commanded us to s such women. Jn 8:5
the first to throw a s at her." Jn 8:7
Jews picked up rocks to s Him. Jn 10:31
now the Jews tried to s You, Jn 11:8
and a s was lying against it. Jn 11:38
"Remove the s," Jesus said. Jn 11:39
So they removed the s. Jn 11:41
in a place called the S Pavement Jn 19:13
saw that the s had been removed Jn 20:1
Jesus⌋ is The s despised by you Ac 4:11
afraid the people might s them. Ac 5:26
of the city and began to s him. Ac 7:58
rulers, to assault and s them, Ac 14:5
is like gold or silver or s, Ac 17:29
stumbled over the stumbling s. Rm 9:32
I am putting a s in Zion to Rm 9:33
not on s tablets but on tablets 2Co 3:3
to Him, a living s—rejected by 1Pt 2:4
I lay a s in Zion, a chosen and 1Pt 2:6
The s that the builders rejected 1Pt 2:7
A s that causes men to stumble, 1Pt 2:8
I will also give him a white s, Rv 2:17
and on the s a new name is Rv 2:17
like jasper and carnelian s. Rv 4:3
silver, bronze, s, and wood, Rv 9:20
angel picked up a s like a large Rv 18:21
was like a very precious s, Rv 21:11
like a jasper s, bright as Rv 21:11
with every kind of precious s: Rv 21:19

STONE'S *(1)*

from them about a s throw, Lk 22:41

STONECUTTERS *(6)*

and 80,000 s in the mountains, 1Kg 5:15
masons, and the s—and ⌊would 2Kg 12:12
s, masons, carpenters, and 1Ch 22:15
men as s in the mountains, 2Ch 2:2
80,000 s in the mountains, 2Ch 2:18
money to the s and artisans, Ezr 3:7

STONED *(19)*

he will be s or shot ⌊with Ex 19:13
the ox must be s, and its meat Ex 21:28
the ox must be s, and its owner Ex 21:29
master, and the ox must be s. Ex 21:32
They are to be s; their blood is Lv 20:27
outside of the camp and s him. Lv 24:23
the camp and s him to death, Nm 15:36
So all Israel s him to death. Jos 7:25
but all Israel s him to death. 1Kg 12:18
the city and s him to death with 1Kg 21:13
"Naboth has been s to death." 1Kg 21:14
that Naboth had been s to death, 1Kg 21:15
the Israelites s him to death. 2Ch 10:18
against him and s him at the 2Ch 24:21
killed another, and s a third. Mt 21:35
won over the crowds and s Paul, Ac 14:19
rods. Once I was s. Three times 2Co 11:25
They were s, they were sawed in Heb 11:37
the mountain, it must be s! Heb 12:20

STONEMASONS *(3)*

carpenters, and s, and they 2Sm 5:11
cedar logs, s, and carpenters 1Ch 14:1
he appointed s to cut finished 1Ch 22:2

STONES *(128)*

one of the s from the place, Gn 28:11
to his relatives, "Gather s." Gn 31:46
And they took s and made a Gn 31:46
must not build it out of cut s. Ex 20:25
Take two onyx s and engrave on Ex 28:9
Engrave the two s with the names Ex 28:11
Fasten both s on the shoulder Ex 28:12
ephod as memorial s for the Ex 28:12
gemstones on it, four rows of s: Ex 28:17
12 s are to correspond to the Ex 28:21
the onyx s surrounded with Ex 39:6
ephod as memorial s for the Ex 39:7
The 12 s corresponded to the Ex 39:14
must order that the s with the Lv 14:40
must take different s to replace Lv 14:42
house after the s have been Lv 14:43
It must be torn down with its s, Lv 14:45
of grinding s or crushed ⌊it⌋ Nm 11:8
set up large s and cover them Dt 27:2
law on the s after you cross Dt 27:3
to set up these s on Mount Ebal, Dt 27:4
an altar of s there to the LORD Dt 27:5
Use uncut s to build the altar Dt 27:6
this law on the ⌊plastered⌋ s." Dt 27:8
'Take 12 s from this place in Jos 4:3
'What do these s mean to you?' Jos 4:6
Therefore these s will always be Jos 4:7
12 men took s from the middle Jos 4:8
also set up 12 s in the middle Jos 4:9
The s are there to this day. Jos 4:9
Gilgal the 12 s they had taken Jos 4:20
'What is the meaning of these s?' Jos 4:21
their bodies, threw s on them, Jos 7:25
altar of uncut s on which no Jos 8:31
There on the s, Joshua copied Jos 8:32
Roll large s against the mouth Jos 10:18
Then large s were placed against Jos 10:27
and the s are there to this day. Jos 10:27
chose five smooth s from the 1Sm 17:40
lives like ⌊s⌋ from a sling. 1Sm 25:29
He threw s at David and at all 2Sm 16:6
and threw s and dirt at him. 2Sm 16:13
will drag its ⌊s⌋ into the 2Sm 17:13
a huge mound of s over him. 2Sm 18:17
costly s to lay the foundation 1Kg 5:17
of the temple with dressed s. 1Kg 5:17
finished s cut at the quarry 1Kg 6:7
buildings⌋ were of costly s, 1Kg 7:9
costly s 12 and 15 feet long. 1Kg 7:10
also costly s, cut to size, as 1Kg 7:11
great abundance, and precious s. 1Kg 10:2
of spices, and precious s. 1Kg 10:10
of almug wood and precious s. 1Kg 10:11
as common in Jerusalem as s, 1Kg 10:27
they carried away the s of Ramah 1Kg 15:22
Elijah took 12 s—according to 1Kg 18:31
an altar with the s in the name 1Kg 18:32
the wood, the s, and the dust, 1Kg 18:38
baked over hot s and a jug of 1Kg 19:6

and stoned him to death with s. 1Kg 21:13
good piece of land with s." 2Kg 3:19
of them threw s to cover every 2Kg 3:25
could ⌊throw⌋ s ⌊with a sling⌋ 1Ch 12:2
to cut finished s for building 1Ch 22:2
well as onyx, ⌊s for⌋ mounting, 1Ch 29:2
antimony, s of various colors, 1Ch 29:2
kinds of precious s, and a great 1Ch 29:2
had ⌊precious⌋ s gave them to 1Ch 29:8
as common in Jerusalem as s, 2Ch 1:15
with precious s for beauty, 2Ch 3:6
in abundance, and precious s. 2Ch 9:1
of spices, and precious s. 2Ch 9:9
algum wood and precious s. 2Ch 9:10
as common in Jerusalem as s, 2Ch 9:27
they carried away the s of Ramah 2Ch 16:6
and ⌊catapult⌋ large s for use 2Ch 26:15
gold, precious s, spices, 2Ch 32:27
It is being built with cut s, Ezr 5:8
layers of cut s and one of Ezr 6:4
bring these burnt s back to life Neh 4:2
mother-of-pearl, and precious s. Est 1:6
with the s of the field, Jb 5:23
He looks for a home among the s. Jb 8:17
water wears away s and torrents Jb 14:19
of⌋ Ophir to the s in the wadis, Jb 22:24
delight in its s and favor its Ps 102:14
is better than precious s, Pr 8:11
a time to throw s and a time to Ec 3:5
stones and a time to gather s; Ec 3:5
one who quarries s may be hurt Ec 10:9
cleared it of s, and planted it Is 5:2
but we will rebuild with cut s; Is 9:10
the altar s like crushed bits Is 27:9
will set your s in black mortar Is 54:11
your gates of sparkling s, Is 54:12
all your walls of precious s. Is 54:12
the smooth ⌊s⌋ of the wadi; Is 57:6
of wood, and iron instead of s. Is 60:17
clear away the s! Raise a banner Is 62:10
up some large s and set them Jr 43:9
throne on these s that I have Jr 43:10
walled in my ways with cut s; Lm 3:9
into a pit and threw s at me. Lm 3:53
s of the temple lie scattered Lm 4:1
Then they will throw your s, Ezk 26:12
kinds of precious s for your Ezk 27:22
you walked among the fiery s. Ezk 28:14
cherub, from among the fiery s. Ezk 28:16
silver, precious s, and riches. Dn 11:38
will roll her s into the valley Mc 1:6
For the s will cry out from the Hab 2:11
along with its timbers and s." Zch 5:4
for Abraham from these s! Mt 3:9
tell these s to become bread." Mt 4:3
the prophets and s those who are Mt 23:37
and cutting himself with s. Mk 5:5
What massive s! What impressive Mk 13:1
for Abraham from these s! Lk 3:8
the prophets and s those who are Lk 13:34
silent, the s would cry out!" Lk 19:40
with beautiful s and gifts Lk 21:5
picked up s to throw at Him. Jn 8:59
silver, costly s, wood, hay, or 1Co 3:12
letters on s, came with glory, 2Co 3:7
as living s, are being built 1Pt 2:5
gold, precious s, and pearls. Rv 17:4
silver, precious s, and pearls; Rv 18:12
gold, precious s, and pearls; Rv 18:16

STONING *(4)*

the troops talked about s him, 1Sm 30:6
these works are you s Me for?" Jn 10:32
We aren't s You for a good work, Jn 10:33
They were s Stephen as he called Ac 7:59

STOOD *(209)*

where he had s before the LORD. Gn 19:27
Suddenly my sheaf s up, and your Gn 37:7
the Nile and s beside those cows Gn 41:3
to Egypt and s before Joseph. Gn 43:15
Then his sister s at a distance Ex 2:4
who s ⌊waiting⌋ to meet them. Ex 5:20
soot and s before Pharaoh. Ex 9:10
front of them and s behind them. Ex 14:19
the currents s firm like a dam. Ex 15:8
and they s around Moses from Ex 18:13
and they s at the foot of the Ex 19:17
trembled and s at a distance. Ex 20:18
And Moses s at the camp's Ex 32:26
in a cloud, s with him there, Ex 34:5
forward and s before the LORD Lv 9:5
s at the entrance to the tent, Nm 12:5
s at the entrance to the tent Nm 16:18
came out and s at the entrance Nm 16:27
He s between the dead and the Nm 16:48
Angel of the LORD s in a narrow Nm 22:24
went ahead and s in a narrow Nm 22:26
They s before Moses, Eleazar the Nm 27:2
The day you s before the LORD Dt 4:10
You came near and s at the base Dt 4:11
and the cloud s at the entrance Dt 31:15
flowing downstream s still, Jos 3:16
LORD's covenant s firmly on dry Jos 3:17
s on either side of the ark of Jos 8:33
And the sun s still and the moon Jos 10:13
cities that s on their mounds Jos 11:13
and the king s up from his Jdg 3:20
said to all who s against him, Jdg 6:31
went out and s at the entrance Jdg 9:35
the people s united and said, Jdg 20:8
the woman who s here beside you 1Sm 1:26
The LORD came, s there, and 1Sm 3:10
He s a head taller than anyone 1Sm 9:2
When he s among the people, 1Sm 10:23
he s a head taller than anyone 1Sm 10:23
one s to the north in front of 1Sm 14:5
He s and shouted to the battle 1Sm 17:8
David ran and s over him. 1Sm 17:51
the other side and s on top of 1Sm 26:13
So I s over him and killed him 2Sm 1:10
of his house s beside him to get 2Sm 12:17
In response the king s up, 2Sm 13:31
all his servants s by with their 2Sm 13:31
he s beside the gate while all 2Sm 18:4
So he s to one side. 2Sm 18:30
young men had s over Amasa 2Sm 20:11
but Eleazar s ⌊his ground⌋ and 2Sm 23:10
presence and s before him. 1Kg 1:28
The king s up to greet her, 1Kg 2:19
s before the ark of the Lord's 1Kg 3:15
to the king and s before him. 1Kg 3:16
and they s in awe of the king 1Kg 3:28
It s on 12 oxen, three facing 1Kg 7:25
Then Solomon s before the altar 1Kg 8:22
and he s and blessed the whole 1Kg 8:55
went out and s at the entrance 1Kg 19:13
came forward, s before the LORD, 1Kg 22:21
prophets came and s facing them 2Kg 2:7
the two of them s by the Jordan. 2Kg 2:7
and went back and s on the bank 2Kg 2:13
called her and she s before him. 2Kg 4:12
her, and she s in the doorway. 2Kg 4:15
and chariots and s at the door 2Kg 5:9
to the man of God, s before him, 2Kg 5:15
Gehazi came and s by his master. 2Kg 5:25
When he came and s before him, 2Kg 8:9
he went out and s ⌊at the gate⌋, 2Kg 10:9
Then the guards s with their 2Kg 11:11
bones, the man revived and s up! 2Kg 13:21
The Rabshakeh s and called out 2Kg 18:28
king s by the pillar and made 2Kg 23:3
of bronze, s five feet high. 2Kg 25:17
was Asaph, who s at his right 1Ch 6:39
Satan s up against Israel and 1Ch 21:1
They s on their feet and faced 2Ch 3:13
It s on 12 oxen, three facing 2Ch 4:4
Then Solomon s before the altar 2Ch 6:12
He s on it, knelt down in front 2Ch 6:13
Abijah s on Mount Zemaraim, 2Ch 13:4
came forward, s before the LORD, 2Ch 18:20
Jehoshaphat s in the assembly 2Ch 20:5
and the Korahites s up to praise 2Ch 20:19
Jehoshaphat s and said, "Hear 2Ch 20:20
s above the people and said to 2Ch 24:20
s in opposition to those coming 2Ch 28:12
Then the Levites s up: 2Ch 29:12
The Levites s with the 2Ch 29:26
s at their prescribed posts, 2Ch 30:16
and the Levites s to bless the 2Ch 30:27
Next the king s at his post and 2Ch 34:31
the priests s at their posts and 2Ch 35:10
Ezra the priest s up and said to Ezr 10:10
I s up and said to the nobles, Neh 4:14
Ezra the scribe s on a high Neh 8:4
and Maaseiah s beside him on his Neh 8:4
opened it, all the people s up. Neh 8:5
as they s in their places. Neh 8:7
and they s and confessed their Neh 9:2
While they s in their places, Neh 9:3
and Chenani s on the raised Neh 9:4
their relatives ⌊s⌋ opposite Neh 12:9
processions s in the house of Neh 12:40
clothing and s in the inner Est 5:1
Haman s terrified before the Est 7:6
she got up and s before the king Est 8:4
Then Job s up, tore his robe and Jb 1:20
⌊A figure⌋ s there, but I could Jb 4:16
while older men s to their feet. Jb 29:8
s in the assembly and cried out Jb 30:28
the water s firm like a wall. Ps 78:13
waters s above the mountains. Ps 104:6
chosen one had not s before Him Ps 106:23
Phinehas s up and intervened, Ps 106:30
The Assyrian s near the conduit Is 36:2
the Rabshakeh s and called out Is 36:13
them, they s up together. Is 48:13
Remember how I s before You to Jr 18:20
s in the courtyard of the LORD's Jr 19:14
For who has s in the council of Jr 23:18
they had really s in My council, Jr 23:22
of the land s up and said to all Jr 26:17
Each has not s, for the LORD has Jr 46:15
s seven and a half feet high. Jr 52:22
when the creatures s still, Ezk 1:21
stood still, the wheels s still; Ezk 1:21
When they s still, they lowered Ezk 1:24
when they s still, they lowered Ezk 1:25
came and s beside the bronze Ezk 9:2
went in and s beside a wheel. Ezk 10:6
When the cherubim s still, Ezk 10:17
the wheels s still, and when Ezk 10:17
of the temple and s above the Ezk 10:18
and it s at the entrance to the Ezk 10:19
the city and s on the mountain Ezk 11:23
to life and s on their feet, Ezk 37:10
they came and s before the king, Dn 2:2
Then they s before the statue Dn 3:3
times ten thousand s before Him. Dn 7:10
there s before me someone who Dn 8:15
said this to me, I s trembling. Dn 10:11
I s up to strengthen and protect Dn 11:1
On the day you s aloof, on the Ob 11
I trembled where I s. Now I must Hab 3:16
as he s before the Angel. Zch 3:3
revered Me and s in awe of My Mal 2:5
the whole crowd s on the shore. Mt 13:2
high priest then s up and said Mt 26:62
Now Jesus s before the governor. Mt 27:11
hand, raised him, and he s up. Mk 9:27
one of those who s by drew his Mk 14:47
Some s up and were giving false Mk 14:57
the high priest s up before them Mk 14:60
angel of the Lord s before them, Lk 2:9
Sabbath day and s up to read. Lk 4:16
So He s over her and rebuked the Lk 4:39
So he got up and s there. Lk 6:8
He s on a level place with a Lk 6:17
and s behind Him at His feet, Lk 7:38
in the law s up to test Him, Lk 10:25
met Him. They s at a distance Lk 17:12
But Zacchaeus s there and said Lk 19:8
are the ones who s by Me in My Lk 22:28
chief priests and the scribes s Lk 23:10
The people s watching, and even Lk 23:35
from Galilee, s at a distance, Lk 23:49
suddenly two men s by them in Lk 24:4
things, He Himself s among them. Lk 24:36
Jesus s up and cried out, Jn 7:37
He s up and said to them, Jn 8:7
When Jesus s up, He said to her, Jn 8:10
and has not s in the truth, Jn 8:44
another as they s in the temple Jn 11:56
But Mary s outside facing the Jn 20:11
Then Jesus came, s among them, Jn 20:19
Jesus came and s among them. Jn 20:26
came, Jesus s on the shore. Jn 21:4
men in white clothes s by them. Ac 1:10
these days Peter s up among the Ac 1:15
But Peter s up with the Eleven, Ac 2:14
he jumped up, s, and started to Ac 3:8
s up in the Sanhedrin and Ac 5:34
traveling with him s speechless, Ac 9:7
to Simon's house, s at the gate. Ac 10:17
in a dazzling robe s before me Ac 10:30
s up and predicted by the Spirit Ac 11:28

of the Pharisees s up and said, Ac 15:5
Peter s up and said to them: Ac 15:7
Then Paul s in the middle of the Ac 17:22
Paul s on the steps and motioned Ac 21:40
came to me, s by me, and said, Ac 22:13
the Lord s by him and said, Ac 23:11
found in me when I s before the Ac 24:20
down from Jerusalem s around him Ac 25:7
the accusers s up and brought no Ac 25:18
Paul s up among them and said, Ac 27:21
I belong to and serve s by me, Ac 27:23
his face because he s condemned. Gl 2:11
But the Lord s with me and 2Tm 4:17
All the angels s around the Rv 7:11
burner, came and s at the altar. Rv 8:3
them, and they s on their feet. Rv 11:11
And the dragon s in front of the Rv 12:4
He s on the sand of the sea. Rv 12:18
there on Mount Zion s the Lamb, Rv 14:1
do business by sea, s far off Rv 18:17

STOOP *(2)*
the strong men s, the women who Ec 12:3
not worthy to s down and untie Mk 1:7

STOOPED *(4)*
he s to look in, he saw only Lk 24:12
Jesus s down and started writing Jn 8:6
Then He s down again and Jn 8:8
she s to look into the tomb. Jn 20:11

STOOPING *(1)*
S down, he saw the linen cloths Jn 20:5

STOOPS *(1)*
s down to look on the heavens Ps 113:6

STOP *(82)*
look back and don't s anywhere Gn 19:17
you would s them from working. Ex 5:5
it is to s at a campsite, Nm 1:51
Moses, my lord, s them!" Nm 11:28
descendants to s fearing the Jos 22:25
Should I s giving my oil that Jdg 9:9
Should I s giving my sweetness Jdg 9:11
Should I s giving my wine that Jdg 9:13
not let us s at this Jebusite Jdg 19:11
We will not s at a foreign city Jdg 19:12
Benjaminites or should we s?" Jdg 20:28
He will s oppressing you, 1Sm 6:5
Don't s crying out to the LORD 1Sm 7:8
my father will s ⌊worrying⌋ 1Sm 9:5
to the priest, "S what you're 1Sm 14:19
"S!" exclaimed Samuel. "Let me 1Sm 15:16
to him, "Hurry up and don't s!" 1Sm 20:38
Then Saul will s searching for 1Sm 27:1
were to remain behind would s. 1Sm 30:9
Asahel would not s chasing him. 2Sm 2:21
warned Asahel, "S chasing me. 2Sm 2:22
the troops to s pursuing their 2Sm 2:26
so the rain doesn't s you.'" 1Kg 18:44
good tree and s up every spring 2Kg 3:19
anyone, don't ⌊s to⌋ greet him, 2Kg 4:29
S, why should you lose your life? 2Ch 25:16
S opposing God who is with me; 2Ch 35:21
an order for these men to s, Ezr 4:21
These men wouldn't s them until Ezr 5:5
so that the ⌊work⌋ will not s. Ezr 6:8
can kill them and s the work." Neh 4:11
let us s charging this interest. Neh 5:10
something⌋, who can s Him? Jb 9:12
days not few? S ⌊it⌋! Leave me Jb 10:20
convenes a court, who can s Him? Jb 11:10
How long until you s talking? Jb 18:2
My relatives s coming by, and my Jb 19:14
S and consider God's wonders. Jb 37:14
your proud waves s here"? Jb 38:11
know tore at me and did not s. Ps 35:15
S ⌊your fighting⌋—and know Ps 46:10
one should forever s trying— Ps 49:8
s the dispute before it breaks Pr 17:14
If you s listening to Pr 19:27
s giving your attention to it. Pr 23:4
S bringing useless offerings. Is 1:13
from My sight. S doing evil. Is 1:16
S and be astonished; blind Is 29:9
day and night may ⌊they⌋ not s, Jr 14:17
S following other gods to serve Jr 35:15
their evil or s burning incense Jr 44:5
for yourself? S seeking! For I Jr 45:5
In Moab, I will s"—⌊this is⌋ Jr 48:35
I will put a s to this proverb, Ezk 12:23
I will s you from being a Ezk 16:41
end, to put a s to sin, to wipe Dn 9:24
he will put a s to sacrifice Dn 9:27
I said, "Lord GOD, please s! Am 7:5
"S your preaching," they preach. Mc 2:6
are fleeing. "S! Stop!" ⌊they Nah 2:8
fleeing. "Stop! S!" ⌊they cry,⌋ Nah 2:8
John tried to s Him, saying, "I Mt 3:14
and we tried to s him because he Mk 9:38
"Don't s him," said Jesus, Mk 9:39
Don't s them, for the kingdom of Mk 10:14
But He said, "S crying, for she Lk 8:52
and we tried to s him because he Lk 9:49
"Don't s him," Jesus told him, Lk 9:50
to Me, and don't s them, because Lk 18:16
S turning My Father's house into Jn 2:16
S complaining among yourselves. Jn 6:43
S judging according to outward Jn 7:24
are unable to s speaking about Ac 4:20
This man does not s speaking Ac 6:13
he ordered the chariot to s, Ac 8:38
Won't you ever s perverting the Ac 13:10
years I did not s warning each Ac 20:31
right-minded and s sinning, 1Co 15:34
I never s giving thanks for you Eph 1:16
Day and night they never s, Rv 4:8
elders said to me, "S crying. Rv 5:5
their hands to s worshiping Rv 9:20

STOPPED *(60)*
and the rain from the sky s. Gn 8:2
and they s building the city. Gn 11:8
The Philistines s up all the Gn 26:15
Philistines had s up after Gn 26:18
Then Leah s having children. Gn 29:35
that she had s having children Gn 30:9
that he s measuring it because Gn 41:49
the sanctuary." So the people s. Ex 36:6
at the place where the cloud s, Nm 9:17
until the cloud s in the Nm 10:12
plague on the Israelites was s, Nm 25:8
sun stood still and the moon s, Jos 10:13
the sun s in the middle of the Jos 10:13
They s to go in and spend the Jdg 19:15
she s trying to persuade her. Ru 1:18
and he has not s them. 1Sm 3:13
Beth-shemesh and s there near a 1Sm 6:14
father has s being concerned 1Sm 10:2
They s because they were too 1Sm 30:10
had fallen and died, they s, 2Sm 2:23
wouldn't have s pursuing their 2Sm 2:27
horn, and all the troops s; 2Sm 2:28
They s at the last house 2Sm 15:17
had seen that all the people s. 2Sm 20:12
They s up every spring of water 2Kg 3:25
any more." Then the oil s. 2Kg 4:6
he passed by, he s there to eat. 2Kg 4:8
he came there and s and went to 2Kg 4:11
the ground three times and s. 2Kg 13:18
building Ramah and s his work. 2Ch 16:5
So the prophet s, but he said, 2Ch 25:16
gathered and s up all the 2Ch 32:4
Jerusalem and forcibly s them. Ezr 4:23
Jerusalem had s and remained at Ezr 4:24
They s at the Gate of the Guard. Neh 12:39
City officials s talking and Jb 29:9
he has s acting wisely and doing Ps 36:3
and the plague was s. Ps 106:30
The noise of the jubilant has s. Is 24:8
They s asking: Where is the LORD Jr 2:6
So he s and did not kill them Jr 41:8
I have s the flow of wine from Jr 48:33
warriors have s fighting; Jr 51:30
sea, and the sea s its raging. Jnh 1:15
it came and s above the place Mt 2:9
Jesus s, called them, and said, Mt 20:32
Jesus s and said, "Call him." Mk 10:49
coffin, and the pallbearers s. Lk 7:14
but she hasn't s kissing My feet Lk 7:45
Instantly her bleeding s. Lk 8:44
Jesus s and commanded that he be Lk 18:40
And they s ⌊walking and looked⌋ Lk 24:17
of their voices, s their ears, Ac 7:57
they barely s the crowds from Ac 14:18
After they s speaking, James Ac 15:13
we s talking and simply said, Ac 21:14
soldiers, they s beating Paul. Ac 21:32
will not be s in the regions 2Co 11:10
we haven't s praying for you. Col 1:9
they have s being offered, Heb 10:2

STOPPING *(5)*
who encountered Amasa were s. 2Sm 20:12
warriors about s up the waters 2Ch 32:3
like a traveler s only for the Jr 14:8
They left, s in Geruth Chimham, Jr 41:17
dodge the missiles, never s. Jl 2:8

STOPS *(4)*
deaf cobra that s up its ears, Ps 58:4
who s his ears from listening to Is 33:15
by a baker who s stirring ⌊the Hs 7:4
but he even s those who want to 3Jn 10

STORAGE *(7)*
all the s cities that belonged 1Kg 9:19
with all the s cities that he 2Ch 8:4
all the s cities that belonged 2Ch 8:6
all the s cities of Naphtali. 2Ch 16:4
fortresses and s cities in Judah 2Ch 17:12
in an earthen s jar so they will Jr 32:14
place them in your ⌊s⌋ jars, Jr 40:10

STORE *(12)*
s the grain under Pharaoh's Gn 41:35
that year and s ⌊it⌋ within your Dt 14:28
How long will I s up anxious Ps 13:2
bellies with what You have in s, Ps 17:14
my words and s up my commands Pr 2:1
The wise s up knowledge, but the Pr 10:14
yet they s up their food in the Pr 30:25
those who s up violence and Am 3:10
but s the wheat in my barn.'" Mt 13:30
have anywhere to s my crops? Lk 12:17
and s all my grain and my goods Lk 12:18
earth are held in s for fire, 2Pt 3:7

STORED *(14)*
So Joseph s up grain in such Gn 41:49
Is it not s up with Me, sealed Dt 32:34
from them and s them in the 2Kg 5:24
fathers have s up until this day 2Kg 20:17
had previously s the grain Neh 13:5
few years are s up for the Jb 15:20
the ⌊place⌋ where the snow is s? Jb 38:22
that You have s up for those who Ps 31:19
sinner's wealth is s up for the Pr 13:22
They will not be s or saved, Is 23:18
fathers have s up until this day Is 39:6
is preserved; his sin is s up. Hs 13:12
have many goods s up for many Lk 12:19
You s up treasure in the last Jms 5:3

STOREHOUSE *(4)*
open for you His abundant s, Dt 28:12
for you—a s of salvation, Is 33:6
palace to a place below the s. Jr 38:11
percent into the s so that there Mal 3:10

STOREHOUSES *(16)*
up ⌊all the s⌋ and sold grain to Gn 41:56
blessing on your s and on Dt 28:8
and his sons' ⌊lot⌋ was the s; 1Ch 26:15
south, and two pair at the s. 1Ch 26:17
was in charge of the king's s. 1Ch 27:25
charge of the s in the country, 1Ch 27:25
new wine, and oil into the s. Neh 13:12
treasurers over the s Shelemiah Neh 13:13
Or have you seen the s of hail, Jb 38:22
He puts the depths into s. Ps 33:7
and brings the wind from His s. Ps 135:7
s will be full, supplying all Ps 144:13
anything in my s that I didn't Is 39:4
and brings the wind from His s. Jr 10:13
and brings the wind from His s. Jr 51:16
The s are in ruin, and the Jl 1:17

STOREROOM *(6)*
good things from his s of good, Mt 12:35
evil things from his s of evil. Mt 12:35
brings out of his s what is new Mt 13:52
out of the good s of his heart. Lk 6:45
produces evil out of the evil s, Lk 6:45
they don't have a s or a barn; Lk 12:24

STOREROOMS *(5)*
priests at the s of the house Neh 10:37
to the s of the treasury Neh 10:38
and oil to the s where the Neh 10:39
who guarded the s at the gates. Neh 12:25
in charge of the s of the house Neh 13:4

STORES *(5)*
in charge of the s of olive oil. 1Ch 27:28

also bringing in s of grain and Neh 13:15
he s up evil in his heart; Ps 41:6
He s up success for the upright; Pr 2:7
the one who s up treasure for Lk 12:21

STORIES *(4)*
in three s of 30 rooms each Ezk 41:6
and middle s of the building Ezk 42:5
arranged in three s and had no Ezk 42:6
than the lower and middle s. Ezk 42:6

STORING *(3)*
s his equipment at Michmash. Is 10:28
heart you are s up wrath for Rm 2:5
s up for themselves a good 1Tm 6:19

STORK *(5)*
the s, the various kinds of Lv 11:19
the s, the various kinds of Dt 14:18
the s makes its home in the pine Ps 104:17
Even the s in the sky knows her Jr 8:7
wings were like those of a s, Zch 5:9

STORK'S *(1)*
feathers and plumage like the s? Jb 39:13

STORM *(35)*
A lightning s struck from Jb 1:16
like chaff a s sweeps away? Jb 21:18
a s wind sweeps him away at Jb 27:20
You scatter me in the s. Jb 30:22
also, the approaching ⌊s⌋. Jb 36:33
dark s clouds His canopy around Ps 18:11
Him, and a s rages around Him. Ps 50:3
from the raging wind and the s." Ps 55:8
The s clouds thundered; Ps 77:17
and terrify them with Your s. Ps 83:15
He stilled the s to a murmur, Ps 107:29
you like a s and your calamity Pr 1:27
and shelter from s and rain. Is 4:6
her⌋ with His severe s on the Is 27:8
like a devastating hail s, Is 28:2
like a s with strong flooding Is 28:2
and loud noise, s, tempest, and Is 29:6
his chariots are like a s. Jr 4:13
Look, a s from the LORD! Jr 23:19
has gone forth, a whirling s. Jr 23:19
A great s is stirred up from the Jr 25:32
Look, a s from the LORD! Jr 30:23
churning s, it will whirl about Jr 30:23
the North will s against him Dn 11:40
They s the city; they run on the Jl 2:9
wind on the day of the s. Am 1:14
such a violent s arose on the Jnh 1:4
this violent s that is against Jnh 1:12
path is in the whirlwind and s, Nah 1:3
warriors s out to scatter us, Hab 3:14
a violent s arose on the sea, Mt 8:24
away you say, 'A s is coming,' Lk 12:54
severely battered by the s, Ac 27:18
and the severe s kept raging; Ac 27:20
fire, to darkness, gloom, and s, Heb 12:18

STORM-TOSSED *(2)*
Poor ⌊Jerusalem⌋, s, and not Is 54:11
the wicked are like the s sea, Is 57:20

STORMS *(2)*
Like s that pass over the Negev, Is 21:1
and advance with the southern s. Zch 9:14

STORMY *(1)*
'Today will be s because the sky Mt 16:3

STORY *(8)*
Then she told him the same s: Gn 39:17
master heard the s his wife told Gn 39:19
⌊each s was⌋ seven and a half 1Kg 6:10
the woman, she told him the s. 2Kg 8:6
widened at each successive s, Ezk 41:7
from the lowest s to the highest Ezk 41:7
And this s has been spread among Mt 28:15
he fell down from the third s, Ac 20:9

STOVE *(1)*
it is an oven or s, it must be Lv 11:35

STRAGGLERS *(1)*
all your s from behind when Dt 25:18

STRAIGHT *(30)*
will advance, each man s ahead." Jos 6:5
city, each man s ahead, and they Jos 6:20
The cows went s up the road to 1Sm 6:12
make Your way s before me. Ps 5:8
I am guiding you on s paths. Pr 4:11
fix your gaze s ahead. Pr 4:25
her steps head s for Sheol. Pr 5:5
who go s ahead on their paths: Pr 9:15
understanding walks a s path. Pr 15:21
You clear a s path for the Is 26:7
make a s highway for our God in Is 40:3
again stretch out s to the hill Jr 31:39
Their legs were s, and the soles Ezk 1:7
each one went s ahead. Ezk 1:9
Each creature went s ahead. Ezk 1:12
Each creature went s ahead. Ezk 10:22
wall, each woman s ahead, and Am 4:3
for the Lord; make His paths s!" Mt 3:3
for the Lord; make His paths s!" Mk 1:3
Let's go s to Bethlehem and see Lk 2:15
for the Lord; make His paths s! Lk 3:4
the crooked will become s, Lk 3:5
Make s the way of the Lord— Jn 1:23
and go to the street called S," Ac 9:11
Spirit, stared s at the sorcerer Ac 13:9
perverting the s paths of the Ac 13:10
"Stand up s on your feet!" Ac 14:10
we ran a s course to Samothrace, Ac 16:11
and make s paths for your feet, Heb 12:13
abandoning the s path, they have 2Pt 2:15

STRAIGHTEN *(2)*
for who can s out what He has Ec 7:13
over and could not s up at all. Lk 13:11

STRAIGHTENED *(1)*
What is crooked cannot be s; Ec 1:15

STRAIN *(1)*
You s out a gnat, yet gulp down Mt 23:24

STRAND *(1)*
bowstrings as a s of yarn snaps Jdg 16:9

STRANDS *(2)*
A cord of three s is not easily Ec 4:12
to take a few s from the hair Ezk 5:3

STRANGE *(7)*
must not be a s god among you; Ps 81:9
Your eyes will see s things, Pr 23:33
nation with a s language, Is 18:2
nation with a s language, Is 18:7
do His work, His s work, and to Is 28:21
For what you say sounds s to us, Ac 17:20
by various kinds of s teachings; Heb 13:9

STRANGER *(25)*
become a s in a foreign land. Ex 2:22
I have been a s in a foreign Ex 18:3
may not marry a s outside ⌊the Dt 25:5
servants regard me as a s; Jb 19:15
look at ⌊Him⌋, and not as a s. Jb 19:27
I examined the case of the s. Jb 29:16
No s had to spend the night on Jb 31:32
I have become a s to my brothers Ps 69:8
I am a s on earth; do not hide Ps 119:19
from a s with her flattering Pr 2:16
or embrace the breast of a s? Pr 5:20
into an agreement with a s, Pr 6:1
the flattering tongue of a s. Pr 6:24
a s with her flattering talk. Pr 7:5
puts up security for a s, Pr 11:15
he has put up security for a s; Pr 20:16
own mouth—a s, and not your Pr 27:2
he has put up security for a s; Pr 27:13
Instead, a s will enjoy them. Ec 6:2
fatherless, the s or the poor, Zch 7:10
I was a s and you took Me in; Mt 25:35
did we see You a s and take You Mt 25:38
I was a s and you didn't take Me Mt 25:43
or thirsty, or a s, or without Mt 25:44
They will never follow a s; Jn 10:5

STRANGERS *(24)*
will be s in a land that Gn 15:13
them like s and spoke harshly Gn 42:7
For s rise up against me, and Ps 54:3
let s plunder what he has worked Ps 109:11
s will drain your resources, Pr 5:10
not for you ⌊to share⌋ with s. Pr 5:17
and s will eat ⌊among⌋ the ruins Is 5:17
S will stand and feed your Is 61:5
I love s, and I will continue to Jr 2:25
your favors to s under every Jr 3:13
will you serve s in a land that Jr 5:19
your fetters so s will never Jr 30:8
will send s to Babylon who will Jr 51:2
has been turned over to s, Lm 5:2
who receives s instead of her Ezk 16:32
am about to bring s against you, Ezk 28:7
uncircumcised at the hands of s. Ezk 28:10
the day s captured his wealth, Ob 11
From their sons or from s?" Mt 17:25
"From s," he said. Mt 17:26
don't recognize the voice of s." Jn 10:5
would be s in a foreign country Ac 7:6
are no longer foreigners and s, Eph 2:19
and this ⌊you are doing⌋ for s; 3Jn 5

STRANGLED *(4)*
cubs needed and s ⌊prey⌋ for its Nah 2:12
eating anything that has been s, Ac 15:20
eating anything that has been s, Ac 15:29
from what is s, and from sexual Ac 21:25

STRANGLING *(1)*
so that I prefer s, death rather Jb 7:15

STRAP *(7)*
or sandal s or anything that Gn 14:23
s your sword at your side. Ps 45:3
loose, and no sandal s broken. Is 5:27
your turban and s your sandals Ezk 24:17
and untie the s of His sandals. Mk 1:7
to untie the s of His sandals. Lk 3:16
whose sandal s I'm not worthy to Jn 1:27

STRAPPED *(3)*
He s it to his right thigh under Jdg 3:16
David s his sword on over the 1Sm 17:39
had his sword s around his waist Neh 4:18

STRATEGIES *(2)*
Edom and the s He has devised Jr 49:20
Babylon and the s He has devised Jr 50:45

STRATEGY *(2)*
mere words are s and strength 2Kg 18:20
he has devised a s against you. Jr 49:30

STRAW *(23)*
We have plenty of s and feed, Gn 24:25
S and feed were given to the Gn 24:32
the people with s for making Ex 5:7
go and gather s for themselves. Ex 5:7
'I am not giving you s. Ex 5:10
Go get s yourselves wherever you Ex 5:11
Egypt to gather stubble for s. Ex 5:12
you did⌋ when s was ⌊provided⌋. Ex 5:13
No s has been given to your Ex 5:16
No s will be given to you, Ex 5:18
we have both s and feed for our Jdg 19:19
barley and the s for the chariot 1Kg 4:28
Will You chase after dry s? Jb 13:25
Are they like s before the wind, Jb 21:18
regards iron as s, and bronze as Jb 41:27
my God, like s before the wind. Ps 83:13
fire consumes s as dry grass Is 5:24
the lion will eat s like an ox. Is 11:7
in his place as s is trampled in Is 25:10
the lion will eat s like the ox, Is 65:25
what is s ⌊compared⌋ to grain? Jr 23:28
and like s that is fully dry. Nah 1:10
costly stones, wood, hay, or s, 1Co 3:12

STRAY *(10)*
your enemy's s ox or donkey, Ex 23:4
caused them to s so that they 2Kg 21:9
of Jerusalem to s so that they 2Ch 33:9
reject all who s from Your Ps 119:118
don't s onto her paths. Pr 7:25
you will s from the words of Pr 19:27
do You make us s from Your ways? Is 63:17
Israel is a s lamb, chased by Jr 50:17
may no longer s from following Ezk 14:11
and go and search for the s? Mt 18:12

STRAYED *(3)*
they never s to the right or to 1Sm 6:12
steps have not s from Your path. Ps 44:18
and who s from Me after their Ezk 44:10

STRAYING *(1)*
your brother's ox or sheep s, Dt 22:1

STRAYS *(5)*
a net, and he s into its mesh. Jb 18:8
The man who s from the way of Pr 21:16
brought back the s, or sought Ezk 34:4
bring back the s, bandage the Ezk 34:16
any among you s from the truth, Jms 5:19

STREAKED *(8)*
removed the s and spotted male Gn 30:35
of the branches and bore s, Gn 30:39
flocks face the s and the Gn 30:40

'The **s** sheep will be your wages,' Gn 31:8
then all the sheep were born **s**. Gn 31:8
I saw in a dream that the **s**, Gn 31:10
mating with the flocks are **s**, Gn 31:12
Even his hair is **s** with gray, Hs 7:9

STREAM *(17)*

and brought them across the **s**, Gn 32:23
gardens beside a **s**, like aloes Nm 24:6
it into the **s** that came down Dt 9:21
down to a continually flowing **s**, Dt 21:4
the cow's neck there by the **s**. Dt 21:4
hands by the **s** over the heifer Dt 21:6
springs and the **s** that flowed 2Ch 32:4
Should this **s** of words go Jb 11:2
drink from Your refreshing **s**, Ps 36:8
God's **s** is filled with water, Ps 65:9
flowed like a **s** in the desert. Ps 105:41
All nations will **s** to it, Is 2:2
like a rushing **s** driven by the Is 59:19
sends its roots out toward a **s**, Jr 17:8
nations will no longer **s** to him; Jr 51:44
like an unfailing **s**. Am 5:24
Peoples will **s** to it, Mc 4:1

STREAMBEDS *(1)*

the grass like poplars by the **s**. Is 44:4

STREAMING *(3)*

a flock of goats **s** down Mount Sg 4:1
of flowing water **s** from Lebanon. Sg 4:15
flock of goats **s** down from Sg 6:5

STREAMS *(40)*

whether in the seas or **s**. Lv 11:9
and scales in the seas or **s**, Lv 11:10
a land with **s** of water, springs Dt 8:7
a land with **s** of water. Dt 10:7
dried up all the **s** of Egypt with 2Kg 19:24
as seasonal **s** that overflow Jb 6:15
of Tema look ⌊for these **s**⌋. Jb 6:19
will not enjoy the **s**, the rivers Jb 20:17
He dams up the **s** from flowing so Jb 28:11
rock poured out **s** of oil for me! Jb 29:6
planted beside **s** of water that Ps 1:3
As a deer longs for **s** of water, Ps 42:1
its **s** delight the city of God, Ps 46:4
You opened up springs and **s**; Ps 74:15
brought **s** out of the stone and Ps 78:16
could not drink from their **s**. Ps 78:44
eyes pour out **s** of tears because Ps 119:136
s of water in the public squares? Pr 5:16
All the **s** flow to the sea, Ec 1:7
The **s** are flowing to the place, Ec 1:7
like doves beside **s** of water, Sg 5:12
the farthest **s** of the Nile and Is 7:18
its spreading **s** will fill your Is 8:8
and will split it into seven **s**, Is 11:15
S and watercourses will be on Is 30:25
like **s** of water in a dry land Is 32:2
a place of rivers and broad **s**, Is 33:21
⌊Edom's⌋ **s** will be turned into Is 34:9
wilderness, and **s** in the desert; Is 35:6
dried up all the **s** of Egypt with Is 37:25
land, and **s** on the dry ground Is 44:3
your thigh, wade through the **s**. Is 47:2
eyes flow with **s** of tears Lm 3:48
the fish of your **s** cling to your Ezk 29:4
the fish of your **s** will cling to Ezk 29:4
you and all the fish of your **s**. Ezk 29:5
I will make the **s** dry and sell Ezk 30:12
the **s** of Judah will flow with Jl 3:18
or with ten thousand **s** of oil? Mc 6:7
will have **s** of living water flow Jn 7:38

STREET *(23)*

altars on every **s** corner in 2Ch 28:24
had to spend the night on the **s**, Jb 31:32
who see me in the **s** run from me. Ps 31:11
Wisdom calls out in the **s**; Pr 1:20
Crossing the **s** near her corner, Pr 7:8
in the **s**, now in the squares, Pr 7:12
doors at the **s** are shut while Ec 12:4
will walk around in the **s**; Ec 12:5
head of every **s** like an antelope Is 51:20
and like a **s** for those who walk Is 51:23
out on the children in the **s**, Jr 6:11
from the baker's **s** until all the Jr 37:21
hunger on the corner of every **s**. Lm 2:19
at the corner of every **s**. Lm 4:1
head of every **s** and turned your Ezk 16:25
head of every **s** and making your Ezk 16:31
pieces at the head of every **s**. Nah 3:10
and on the **s** corners to be seen Mt 6:5
a young donkey outside in the **s**, Mk 11:4
and go to the **s** called Straight, Ac 9:11
went outside and passed one **s**, Ac 12:10
The broad **s** of the city was pure Rv 21:21
of the broad **s** ⌊of the city⌋. Rv 22:2

STREETS *(51)*

it in the **s** of Ashkelon, 2Sm 1:20
trample them like mud in the **s**. 2Sm 22:43
trample them like mud in the **s**. Ps 18:42
your springs flow in the **s**, Pr 5:16
I'll be killed in the **s**!" Pr 22:13
through the **s** and the plazas. Sg 3:2
were like garbage in the **s**. Is 5:25
them down like clay in the **s**. Is 10:6
In its **s** they wear sackcloth; Is 15:3
In the **s** they cry for wine. Is 24:11
warriors cry loudly in the **s**; Is 33:7
make His voice heard in the **s**. Is 42:2
the restorer of **s** where people Is 58:12
Roam through the **s** of Jerusalem. Jr 5:1
Judah and in the **s** of Jerusalem? Jr 7:17
of Judah and the **s** of Jerusalem Jr 7:34
cutting off children from the **s**, Jr 9:21
Judah and in the **s** of Jerusalem: Jr 11:6
numerous as the **s** of Jerusalem. Jr 11:13
thrown into the **s** of Jerusalem Jr 14:16
and Jerusalem's **s** that are a Jr 33:10
and Jerusalem's **s** so that they Jr 44:6
Judah and in the **s** of Jerusalem? Jr 44:9
cities and in Jerusalem's **s**. Jr 44:17
cities and in Jerusalem's **s**— Jr 44:21
were pierced through, in her **s**. Jr 51:4
faint in the **s** of the city. Lm 2:11
wounded in the **s** of the city, Lm 2:12
lying on the ground in the **s**. Lm 2:21
are destitute in the **s**; Lm 4:5
are not recognized in the **s**. Lm 4:8
stumbled in the **s**, defiled by Lm 4:14
that we could not walk in our **s**. Lm 4:18
throw their silver into the **s**, Ezk 7:19
filling its **s** with the dead. Ezk 11:6
all your **s** with the hooves Ezk 26:11
her and bloodshed in her **s**; Ezk 28:23
cry out in anguish in all the **s**. Am 5:16
be trampled like mud in the **s**. Mc 7:10
dash madly through the **s**; Nah 2:4
I have laid waste their **s**, Zph 3:6
sit along the **s** of Jerusalem, Zch 8:4
The **s** of the city will be filled Zch 8:5
and gold like the dirt of the **s**. Zch 9:3
trampling down the mud of the **s**. Zch 10:5
in the synagogues and on the **s**, Mt 6:2
will hear His voice in the **s**. Mt 12:19
go out into its **s** and say, Lk 10:10
and You taught in our **s**!' Lk 13:26
quickly into the **s** and alleys Lk 14:21
sick out into the **s** and lay them Ac 5:15

STRENGTH *(199)*

summoned his **s** and sat up in bed Gn 48:2
my **s** and the firstfruits of my Gn 49:3
of here by the **s** of ⌊His⌋ hand. Ex 13:3
By the **s** of ⌊His⌋ hand the LORD Ex 13:14
of Egypt by the **s** of His hand." Ex 13:16
The LORD is my **s** and my song; Ex 15:2
Your holy dwelling with Your **s**. Ex 15:13
and your **s** will be used up for Lv 26:20
by Your **s** You brought up this Nm 14:13
your soul, and with all your **s**. Dt 6:5
that you may have the **s** to cross Dt 11:8
that ⌊their⌋ **s** is gone and no Dt 32:36
and your **s** last as long as you Dt 33:25
My **s** for battle and for daily Jos 14:11
have many people and great **s**. Jos 17:17
March on, my soul, in **s**! Jdg 5:21
the rising of the sun in its **s**. Jdg 5:31
Go in the **s** you have and deliver Jdg 6:14
You will deliver Israel by my **s**, Jdg 6:37
for a man is judged by his **s**." Jdg 8:21
drank, his **s** returned, and he Jdg 15:19
tell you where his great **s** comes Jdg 16:5
where does your great **s** ⌊come Jdg 16:6
secret of⌋ his **s** remained Jdg 16:9
me what makes your **s** so great!" Jdg 16:15
I am shaved, my **s** will leave me, Jdg 16:17
helpless, and his **s** left him. Jdg 16:19
to keep up your **s** and then you Jdg 19:5
to him, "Please keep up your **s**." Jdg 19:8
the feeble are clothed with **s**. 1Sm 2:4
does not prevail by ⌊his own⌋ **s**. 1Sm 2:9
cut off your **s** and the strength 1Sm 2:31
strength and the **s** of your 1Sm 2:31
it will give you **s** so you can go 1Sm 28:22
they had no **s** left to weep. 1Sm 30:4
David found **s** in the LORD his 1Sm 30:6
clothed me with **s** for battle; 2Sm 22:40
Then on the **s** from that food, 1Kg 19:8
are strategy and **s** for war. 2Kg 18:20
but there is no **s** to deliver 2Kg 19:3
with all his **s** according to all 2Kg 23:25
for the LORD and for His **s**; 1Ch 16:11
s and joy are in His place. 1Ch 16:27
ascribe to the LORD glory and **s**. 1Ch 16:28
men with **s** for the work— 1Ch 26:8
make great and to give **s** to all. 1Ch 29:12
and the ark ⌊that shows⌋ Your **s**. 2Ch 6:41
the mighty and those without **s**. 2Ch 14:11
He has only human **s**, but we have 2Ch 32:8
The **s** of the laborer fails, Neh 4:10
because your **s** ⌊comes from⌋ Neh 8:10
What **s** do I have that I should Jb 6:11
Is my **s** that of stone, or my Jb 6:12
it is a matter of **s**, look, He is Jb 9:19
Wisdom and **s** belong to God; Jb 12:13
I have buried my **s** in the dust. Jb 16:15
His **s** is depleted; disaster lies Jb 18:12
and the **s** of the fatherless was Jb 22:9
s will be refreshed within me, Jb 29:20
to me was the **s** of their hands? Jb 30:2
depend on it because of its **s**? Jb 39:11
Do you give **s** to the horse? Jb 39:19
valley and rejoices in his **s**; Jb 39:21
Look at the **s** of his loins and Jb 40:16
S resides in his neck, and Jb 41:22
helpless fall because of his **s**. Ps 10:10
I love You, LORD, my **s**. Ps 18:1
clothes me with **s** and makes my Ps 18:32
clothed me with **s** for battle; Ps 18:39
the king finds joy in Your **s**. Ps 21:1
Be exalted, LORD, in Your **s**; Ps 21:13
s is dried up like baked clay; Ps 22:15
My **s**, come quickly to help me. Ps 22:19
The LORD is my **s** and my shield; Ps 28:7
The LORD is the **s** of His people; Ps 28:8
give the LORD glory and **s**. Ps 29:1
The LORD gives His people **s**; Ps 29:11
my **s** has failed because of my Ps 31:10
my **s** was drained as in the Ps 32:4
not be delivered by great **s**. Ps 33:16
My heart races, my **s** leaves me, Ps 38:10
our refuge and **s**, a helper who Ps 46:1
for You, my **s**, because God is Ps 59:9
sing of Your **s** and will joyfully Ps 59:16
To You, my **s**, I sing praises, Ps 59:17
when my heart is without **s**. Ps 61:2
this twice: **s** belongs to God, Ps 62:11
to see Your **s** and Your glory. Ps 63:2
by Your power, robed with **s**; Ps 65:6
You because of Your great **s**. Ps 66:3
Your God has decreed your **s**. Ps 68:28
Show Your **s**, God, You who have Ps 68:28
gives power and **s** to His people. Ps 68:35
my **s** fails, do not abandon me. Ps 71:9
Your **s** to all who are to come. Ps 71:18
but God is the **s** of my heart, Ps 73:26
You divided the sea with Your **s**; Ps 74:13
revealed Your **s** among the Ps 77:14
gave up His **s** to captivity and Ps 78:61
Sing for joy to God our **s**; Ps 81:1
the people whose **s** is in You, Ps 84:5
They go from **s** to strength; Ps 84:7
They go from strength to **s**; Ps 84:7
Give Your **s** to Your servant; Ps 86:16
I am like a man without **s**, Ps 88:4
For You are their magnificent **s**; Ps 89:17
LORD is robed, enveloped in **s**. Ps 93:1
s and beauty are in His Ps 96:6
ascribe to the LORD glory and **s**. Ps 96:7
He has broken my **s** in midcourse; Ps 102:23
⌊all⌋ His angels of great **s**, Ps 103:20
for the LORD and for His **s**; Ps 105:4
The LORD is my **s** and my song; Ps 118:14
and the ark ⌊that shows⌋ Your **s**. Ps 132:8
You increased **s** within me. Ps 138:3
impressed by the **s** of a horse; Ps 147:10

I have understanding and s. Pr 8:14
comes⌋ through the s of an ox. Pr 14:4
glory of young men is their s, Pr 20:29
man of knowledge than one of s; Pr 24:5
time, your s is limited. Pr 24:10
draws on her s and reveals that Pr 31:17
S and honor are her clothing, Pr 31:25
with ⌊all⌋ your s, because there Ec 9:10
is better than s, but the wisdom Ec 9:16
then one must exert more s; Ec 10:10
for s and not for drunkenness. Ec 10:17
this⌋ by my own s and wisdom, Is 10:13
a Spirit of counsel and s, Is 11:2
the LORD, is my s and my song, Is 12:2
to remember the rock of your s; Is 17:10
Or let it take hold of My s; Is 27:5
and s to those who turn back the Is 28:6
your s will lie in quiet Is 30:15
in the great s of charioteers. Is 31:1
Be our s every morning, and our Is 33:2
you who are near, know My s." Is 33:13
there is no s to deliver them Is 37:3
the Lord GOD comes with s, Is 40:10
of His great power and s, Is 40:26
He gives s to the weary and Is 40:29
in the LORD will renew their s; Is 40:31
And let peoples renew their s. Is 41:1
he grows hungry and his s fails; Is 44:12
LORD is righteousness and s." Is 45:24
have spent my s for nothing and Is 49:4
the LORD, and my God is my s— Is 49:5
and they will look to My s. Is 51:5
on the s of the LORD's power. Is 51:9
put on your s, Zion! Is 52:1
You found a renewal of your s; Is 57:10
LORD, my s and my stronghold, my Jr 16:19
human⌋ flesh his s and turns his Jr 17:5
By My great s and outstretched Jr 27:5
and the Lord has broken my s. Lm 1:14
Great s and many people will not Ezk 17:9
has used his s to shed blood. Ezk 22:6
and its proud s will collapse. Ezk 30:6
and its proud s comes to an end Ezk 30:18
despite their s, have been Ezk 32:29
the terror their s inspired. Ezk 32:30
and its proud s will come to an Ezk 33:28
power, s, and glory. Dn 2:37
some of the s of iron will be Dn 2:41
No s was left in me; Dn 10:8
Now I have no s, and there is no Dn 10:17
and his s will not endure. Dn 11:6
consume his s, but he does not Hs 7:9
one will not prevail by his s, Am 2:14
for ourselves by our own s?" Am 6:13
them⌋ in the s of Yahweh, Mc 5:4
yourself! Summon all your s! Nah 2:1
were her endless source of s; Nah 3:9
their s is their god. Hab 1:11
Yahweh my Lord is my s; Hab 3:19
'Not by s or by might, but by My Zch 4:6
are my s through the LORD Zch 12:5
when he saw the s of the wind, Mt 14:30
your mind, and with all your s. Mk 12:30
with all your s, and to love Mk 12:33
with all your s, and with all Lk 10:27
that you may have s to escape Lk 21:36
some food, he regained his s. Ac 9:19
a man without s in his feet, Ac 14:8
weaknesses of those without s, Rm 15:1
is stronger than human s. 1Co 1:25
beyond our s—so that we even 2Co 1:8
to the working of His vast s. Eph 1:19
by the Lord and by His vast s. Eph 6:10
striving with His s that works Col 1:29
order and the s of your faith Col 2:5
and from His glorious s, 2Th 1:9
gained s after being weak, Heb 11:34
love for one another at full s, 1Pt 4:8
be⌋ from the s God provides, 1Pt 4:11
Because you have limited s, Rv 3:8
and wisdom and s and honor and Rv 5:12
and honor and power and s, Rv 7:12
mixed full s in the cup of His Rv 14:10

STRENGTHEN *(32)*

so that you may s yourselves. Gn 18:5
Joshua and encourage and s him, Dt 3:28
S me, God, just once more. Jdg 16:28
to him, "Go and s yourself, then 1Kg 20:22
would support him to s his grip 2Kg 15:19
But now, ⌊my God,⌋ s me. Neh 6:9
You will s their hearts. Ps 10:17
with him, and My arm will s him. Ps 89:21
s me through Your word. Ps 119:28
S the weak hands, steady the Is 35:3
God. I will s you; I will help Is 41:10
s Him, ⌊this is⌋ My Chosen One; Is 42:1
I will s you, though you do not Is 45:5
parched land, and s your bones. Is 58:11
They s the hands of evildoers, Jr 23:14
I will s the arms of Babylon's Ezk 30:24
I will s the arms of Babylon's Ezk 30:25
injured, and s the weak, but I Ezk 34:16
I stood up to s and protect him. Dn 11:1
s your fortresses. Nah 3:14
I will s the house of Judah and Zch 10:6
I will s them in the LORD, Zch 10:12
turned back, s your brothers." Lk 22:32
some spiritual gift to s you, Rm 1:11
has power to s you according to Rm 16:25
s and encourage you concerning 1Th 3:2
your hearts and s you in every 2Th 2:17
He will s and guard you from the 2Th 3:3
Therefore s your tired hands and Heb 12:12
S your hearts, because the Jms 5:8
establish, s, and support you 1Pt 5:10
Be alert and s what remains, Rv 3:2

STRENGTHENED *(26)*

you will be s to go to the camp. Jdg 7:11
son of David s his hold on his 2Ch 1:1
s their fortifications and put 2Ch 11:11
So they s the kingdom of Judah 2Ch 11:17
his place and s himself against 2Ch 17:1
s his position by killing with 2Ch 21:4
Amaziah s his position and led 2Ch 25:11
So Jotham s himself because he 2Ch 27:6
Then Hezekiah s his position by 2Ch 32:5
because I was s by the LORD my Ezr 7:28
We were s by our God, and He Ezr 8:31
I was graciously s by my God. Neh 2:8
many and have s weak hands. Jb 4:3
You have not s the weak, healed Ezk 34:4
touched me again and s me. Dn 10:18
to me, I was s and said, "Let my Dn 10:19
lord speak, for you have s me." Dn 10:19
I trained and s their arms, Hs 7:15
brothers and s them with a long Ac 15:32
the churches were s in the faith Ac 16:5
but was s in his faith and gave Rm 4:20
to be s with power through His Eph 3:16
be s by the Lord and by His vast Eph 6:10
May you be s with all power, Col 1:11
Lord, who has s me, because He 1Tm 1:12
the Lord stood with me and s me, 2Tm 4:17

STRENGTHENING *(5)*

your body and s for your bones. Pr 3:8
heaven appeared to Him, s Him. Lk 22:43
s the hearts of the disciples by Ac 14:22
and Cilicia, s the churches. Ac 15:41
Phrygia, s all the disciples. Ac 18:23

STRENGTHENS *(4)*

For He s the bars of your gates Ps 147:13
good news s the bones. Pr 15:30
the weary and s the powerless. Is 40:29
all things through Him who s me. Php 4:13

STRENUOUSLY *(1)*

his army labor s against Tyre. Ezk 29:18

STRESS *(2)*

when trouble and s overcome you. Pr 1:27
bent bow, from the s of battle. Is 21:15

STRESSED *(1)*

those who s circumcision argued Ac 11:2

STRETCH *(38)*

I will s out My hand and strike Ex 3:20
S out your hand and grab it by Ex 4:4
am the LORD when I s out My hand Ex 7:5
your staff and s out your hand Ex 7:19
S out your hand with your staff Ex 8:5
S out your staff and strike the Ex 8:16
S out your hand toward heaven Ex 9:22
S out your hand over the land of Ex 10:12
S out your hand toward heaven, Ex 10:21
s out your hand over the sea, Ex 14:16
S out your hand over the sea so Ex 14:26
they s out like river valleys, Nm 24:6
I will s over Jerusalem the 2Kg 21:13
But s out Your hand and strike Jb 1:11
But s out Your hand and strike Jb 2:5
no one would s out ⌊his⌋ hand Jb 30:24
will s out its hands to God. Ps 68:31
S out Your right hand and Ps 74:11
bed is too short to s out on, Is 28:20
LORD⌋ will s out a measuring Is 34:11
for I will s out My hand against Jr 6:12
will once again s out straight Jr 31:39
will s out My hand against you, Jr 51:25
I will s out My hand against Ezk 6:14
I will s out My hand against him Ezk 14:9
and I s out My hand against it Ezk 14:13
I am about to s out My hand Ezk 25:7
will s out My hand against Edom Ezk 25:13
I am about to s out My hand Ezk 25:16
I will s out My hand against you Ezk 35:3
They s out beside every altar on Am 2:8
I will s out My hand against Zph 1:4
He will also s out His hand Zph 2:13
told the man, "S out your hand." Mt 12:13
told the man, "S out your hand." Mk 3:5
He told him, "S out your hand." Lk 6:10
you will s out your hands and Jn 21:18
while You s out Your hand for Ac 4:30

STRETCHED *(37)*

But Israel s out his right hand Gn 48:14
So he s out his hand and caught Ex 4:4
When Aaron s out his hand over Ex 8:6
Aaron s out his hand with his Ex 8:17
now I could have s out My hand Ex 9:15
So Moses s out his staff toward Ex 9:23
Moses s out his staff over the Ex 10:13
So Moses s out his hand toward Ex 10:22
Then Moses s out his hand over Ex 14:21
So Moses s out his hand over the Ex 14:27
You s out Your right hand, Ex 15:12
inheritance s as far as Sarid; Jos 19:10
Jeroboam s out his hand from the 1Kg 13:4
the hand he s out against him 1Kg 13:4
Then he s himself out over the 1Kg 17:21
sword in his hand s out over 1Ch 21:16
he has s out his hand against Jb 15:25
s a measuring line across it? Jb 38:5
is the hand s out against all Is 14:26
He s out His hand over the sea; Is 23:11
the heavens and s them out, Is 42:5
who s out the heavens by Myself; Is 44:24
My hands that s out the heavens Is 45:12
who s out the heavens and laid Is 51:13
let your tent curtains be s out; Is 54:2
so I have s out My hand against Jr 15:6
s out a measuring line and did Lm 2:8
He s out what appeared to be a Ezk 8:3
I s out My hand against you and Ezk 16:27
s out its branches to him from Ezk 17:7
vessel and had s out and fallen Jnh 1:5
line will be s out over Zch 1:16
the LORD, who s out the heavens Zch 12:1
So he s it out, and it was Mt 12:13
So he s it out, and his hand Mk 3:5
As they s him out for the lash, Ac 22:25
Then Paul s out his hand and Ac 26:1

STRETCHER *(9)*

to Him a paralytic lying on a s. Mt 9:2
pick up your s, and go home." Mt 9:6
they lowered the s on which the Mk 2:4
up, pick up your s, and walk'? Mk 2:9
pick up your s, and go home." Mk 2:11
up, picked up the s, and went Mk 2:12
carrying on a s a man who was Lk 5:18
him on the s through the roof Lk 5:19
pick up your s, and go home." Lk 5:24

STRETCHERS *(1)*

the sick on s to wherever they Mk 6:55

STRETCHES *(5)*

He alone s out the heavens and Jb 9:8
He s the northern ⌊skies⌋ over Jb 26:7
He s out the heavens like thin Is 40:22
The woodworker s out a measuring Is 44:13
Zion s out her hands; Lm 1:17

STRETCHING *(3)*

for breath, s out her hands: Jr 4:31
s to the west on the west side Ezk 45:7
And s out His hand toward His Mt 12:49

STREWN *(1)*
bodies were s all along the 1Sm 17:52

STRICKEN *(2)*
became poverty s because of Jdg 6:6
but we in turn regarded Him s, Is 53:4

STRICT *(4)*
Pay s attention to everything I Ex 23:13
He gave them s orders that no Mk 5:43
according to the s view of our Ac 22:3
and bring it under s control, 1Co 9:27

STRICTER *(1)*
we will receive a s judgment; Jms 3:1

STRICTEST *(1)*
according to the s party of our Ac 26:5

STRICTLY *(4)*
we will keep s to the highway. Dt 2:27
And He s warned them to tell no Mk 8:30
But He s warned and instructed Lk 9:21
Didn't we s order you not to Ac 5:28

STRIDE *(2)*
His powerful s is shortened, Jb 18:7
things are stately in their s, Pr 30:29

STRIDES *(1)*
of darkness and s on the heights Am 4:13

STRIFE *(15)*
see violence and s in the city; Ps 55:9
They stir up s, they lurk; Ps 56:6
You set us at s with our Ps 80:6
leads to nothing but s, Pr 13:10
but a man slow to anger calms s. Pr 15:18
a house full of feasting with s. Pr 17:1
One who loves to offend loves s; Pr 17:19
lips lead to s, and his mouth Pr 18:6
quarrelsome man for kindling s. Pr 26:21
stirring up anger produces s. Pr 30:33
contention and s to strike Is 58:4
S is ongoing, and conflict Hab 1:3
there is envy and s among you, 1Co 3:3
sorcery, hatreds, s, jealousy, Gl 5:20
preach Christ out of envy and s, Php 1:15

STRIKE *(99)*
will s your head, and you will Gn 3:15
head, and you will s his heel. Gn 3:15
will never again s down every Gn 8:21
out My hand and s Egypt with all Ex 3:20
or else He may s us with plague Ex 5:3
I will s the water in the Nile Ex 7:17
out your staff and s the dust of Ex 8:16
that night and s every firstborn Ex 12:12
you⌋ when I s the land of Egypt. Ex 12:13
through to s Egypt and sees Ex 12:23
enter your houses to s ⌊you⌋. Ex 12:23
also will s you seven times for Lv 26:24
I will s them with a plague and Nm 14:12
will s ⌊them⌋ with his arrows. Nm 24:8
forehead of Moab and s down all Nm 24:17
the Midianites and s them dead. Nm 25:17
you must s down the inhabitants Dt 13:15
is great, and s him dead. Dt 19:6
you must s down all its males Dt 20:13
You will s Midian down ⌊as if it Jdg 6:16
disaster was about to s them. Jdg 20:34
had begun to s them down, Jdg 20:39
it by its fur, s it down, and 1Sm 17:35
Today, I'll s you down, cut your 1Sm 17:46
I won't ⌊have to s⌋ him twice!" 1Sm 26:8
LORD will certainly s him down: 1Sm 26:10
should I s you to the ground? 2Sm 2:22
When I order you to s Amnon, 2Sm 13:28
and s the city with the edge of 2Sm 15:14
I will s down only the king 2Sm 17:2
Why didn't you s him to the 2Sm 18:11
told ⌊him⌋, "Go and s him down!" 1Kg 2:29
S him down and bury him in order 1Kg 2:31
For the LORD will s Israel ⌊and 1Kg 14:15
by the word of the LORD, "S me!" 1Kg 20:35
But the man refused to s him. 1Kg 20:35
man and said to him, "S me!" 1Kg 20:37
s this nation with blindness. 2Kg 6:18
You are to s down the house of 2Kg 9:7
You are to s down the Arameans 2Kg 13:17
king of Israel, "S the ground!" 2Kg 13:18
you will only s down Aram three 2Kg 13:19
is now about to s your people, 2Ch 21:14
out Your hand and s everything Jb 1:11
Your hand and s his flesh and Jb 2:5
against me and s my cheeks with Jb 16:10
You s all my enemies on the Ps 3:7
before him and s those who hate Ps 89:23
you will not s your foot against Ps 91:12
The sun will not s you by day, Ps 121:6
Let the righteous one s me— Ps 141:5
calamity will s him suddenly; Pr 6:15
S a mocker, and the Pr 19:25
S him with a rod, and you will Pr 23:14
His hand is still raised ⌊to s⌋. Is 5:25
His hand is still raised ⌊to s⌋. Is 9:12
His hand is still raised ⌊to s⌋. Is 9:17
His hand is still raised ⌊to s⌋. Is 9:21
His hand is still raised ⌊to s⌋. Is 10:4
He will s the land with Is 11:4
The LORD will s Egypt, striking Is 19:22
Did the LORD s Israel as He Is 27:7
He will s with a rod. Is 30:31
the LORD raises His hand ⌊to s⌋, Is 31:3
heat or sun will not s them; Is 49:10
and strife to s viciously with Is 58:4
the forest will s them down. Jr 5:6
Why do You s us with no hope of Jr 14:19
I will s the residents of this Jr 21:6
own⌋ men I s down in My wrath Jr 33:5
if you were to s down the entire Jr 37:10
son of Nethaniah to s you down?" Jr 40:14
Why should he s you down and Jr 40:15
He will come and s down the land Jr 43:11
to the one who would s him; Lm 3:30
Therefore s ⌊your⌋ thigh ⌊in Ezk 21:12
Let the sword s two times, Ezk 21:14
I s down all who live there, Ezk 32:15
S the capitals of the pillars so Am 9:1
I have begun to s you severely, Mc 6:13
sea of distress and s the waves Zch 10:11
May a sword s his arm and his Zch 11:17
I will s every horse with panic Zch 12:4
of Judah but s all the horses Zch 12:4
S the shepherd, and the sheep Zch 13:7
previous one will s the horses, Zch 14:15
will come and s the land with a Mal 4:6
the ax is ready to s the root of Mt 3:10
you will not s your foot against Mt 4:6
I will s the shepherd, and the Mt 26:31
I will s the shepherd, and the Mk 14:27
the ax is ready to s the root of Lk 3:9
you will not s your foot against Lk 4:11
should we s with the sword?" Lk 22:49
next to him to s him on the Ac 23:2
God is going to s you, you Ac 23:3
no longer will the sun s them, Rv 7:16
and to s the earth with any Rv 11:6
with it He might s the nations. Rv 19:15

STRIKES *(28)*
Whoever s a person so that he Ex 21:12
Whoever s his father or his Ex 21:15
quarrel and one s the other with Ex 21:18
When a man s his male or female Ex 21:20
When a man s the eye of his male Ex 21:26
If anyone s a person with an Nm 35:16
causing death and s another man Nm 35:17
in hostility he s him with his Nm 35:21
the handle and s his neighbor so Dt 19:5
attacks him, and s him fatally, Dt 19:11
to the one who s down and Jos 15:16
Whoever s down and captures Jdg 1:12
It s you, and you are dismayed. Jb 4:5
He s, but His hands also heal. Jb 5:18
no rod from God ⌊s⌋ them. Jb 21:9
The miner s the flint and Jb 28:9
He s them for their wickedness, Jb 34:26
LORD's right hand s with power! Ps 118:15
LORD's right hand s with power!" Ps 118:16
I will mock when terror s you, Pr 1:26
when terror s you like a storm Pr 1:27
though he s you with a rod and Is 10:24
the one who s the anvil, Is 41:7
that it is I, the LORD, who s. Ezk 7:9
wither when the east wind s it? Ezk 17:10
My judgment s like lightning. Hs 6:5
the LORD s all the peoples Zch 14:12
by a scorpion when it s a man. Rv 9:5

STRIKING *(15)*
for wounding me, a boy for s me. Gn 4:23
her husband from the one s him, Dt 25:11
s them down on the descent. Jos 7:5
delivered Israel by s down 600 Jdg 3:31
the Philistines s them down all 1Sm 7:11
he returned from s down 18,000 2Sm 8:13
saw the angel s the people, 2Sm 24:17
s down the wicked by the work of Ps 9:16
strike Egypt, s and healing. Is 19:22
reveal His arm s in angry wrath Is 30:30
They are s the judge of Israel Mc 5:1
to heaven but kept s his chest Lk 18:13
went home, s their chests. Lk 23:48
oppressed man by s down the Ac 7:24
S Peter on the side, he woke him Ac 12:7

STRING *(5)*
I could s words together against Jb 16:4
For look, the wicked s the bow; Ps 11:2
able to handle and s the bow. Jr 46:9
to Babylon, all who s the bow; Jr 50:29
Don't let the archer s his bow; Jr 51:3

STRINGED *(1)*
we will play s instruments all Is 38:20

STRINGS *(2)*
on the s, with a joyful Ps 33:3
praise Him with flute and s. Ps 150:4

STRIP *(20)*
must not s your vineyard bare Lv 19:10
Philistines came to s the slain, 1Sm 31:8
Philistines came to s the slain, 1Ch 10:8
can s off his outer covering? Jb 41:13
the Lord will s their finery: Is 3:18
spread out and s its branches. Is 27:10
S yourselves bare and put Is 32:11
your veil, s off ⌊your⌋ skirt Is 47:2
But I will s Esau bare; Jr 49:10
scatter her and s her land bare, Jr 51:2
They will s off your clothes, Ezk 16:39
its roots and s off its fruit so Ezk 17:9
They will s off your clothes and Ezk 23:26
and s off their embroidered Ezk 26:16
s off its leaves and scatter its Dn 4:14
will s her naked and expose her Hs 2:3
You s off the splendid robe from Mc 2:8
of people and ⌊s⌋ their flesh Mc 3:2
my people after you s their skin Mc 3:3
the wicked and s ⌊him⌋ from foot Hab 3:13

STRIPES *(1)*
white s on the branches. Gn 30:37

STRIPPED *(21)*
brothers, they s off his robe, Gn 37:23
remained⌋ s of their jewelry Ex 33:6
He s them and gave their clothes Jdg 14:19
Saul's head, s off his armor, 1Sm 31:9
that time Hezekiah s ⌊the gold 2Kg 18:16
They s Saul, cut off his head, 1Ch 10:9
they s them until nobody could 2Ch 20:25
He has s me of my honor and Jb 19:9
siege towers and s its palaces. Is 23:13
earth will be s completely bare Is 24:3
away from Me, you s, went up, Is 57:8
your skirts have been s off, Jr 13:22
land will be s of everything Ezk 12:19
It has s off its bark and thrown Jl 1:7
is s, she is carried away; Nah 2:7
They s Him and dressed Him in a Mt 27:28
Him, they s Him of the robe Mt 27:31
they s Him of the purple robe, Mk 15:20
They s him, beat him up, and Lk 10:30
him (for he was s) and plunged Jn 21:7
magistrates s off their clothes Ac 16:22

STRIPPING *(2)*
s off their clothes and leaving Jb 22:6
the LORD is s the earth bare and Is 24:1

STRIPS *(3)*
give birth and s the woodlands Ps 29:9
young locust s ⌊the land⌋ and Nah 3:16
foot with linen s and with his Jn 11:44

STRIVE *(2)*
Let us s to know the LORD. Hs 6:3
we labor and s for this, because 1Tm 4:10

STRIVING *(4)*
on Your name, s to take hold of Is 64:7
Don't keep s for what you should Lk 12:29
Or am I s to please people? Gl 1:10
s with His strength that works Col 1:29

STROKE *(3)*
And every s of the appointed Is 30:32

letter or one **s** of a letter will Mt 5:18
away than for one **s** of a letter Lk 16:17

STROLL *(1)*

up ⌊your⌋ harp, **s** through the Is 23:16

STROLLED *(2)*

from his bed and **s** around on the 2Sm 11:2
he **s** down the road to her house Pr 7:8

STRONG *(174)*

for it is **s**, and their fury, Gn 49:7
Issachar is a **s** donkey lying Gn 49:14
and his **s** arms were made agile Gn 49:24
he is forced⌋ by a **s** hand. Ex 3:19
them go because of My **s** hand; Ex 6:1
his land because of My **s** hand." Ex 6:1
the wind to a **s** west wind, Ex 10:19
you out of Egypt with a **s** hand. Ex 13:9
with great power and a **s** hand? Ex 32:11
I will break down your **s** pride. Lv 26:19
among them had a **s** craving ⌊for Nm 11:4
who live there are **s** or weak, Nm 13:18
people living in the land are **s**, Nm 13:28
by a **s** hand and an outstretched Dt 4:34
you out of there with a **s** hand Dt 5:15
us out of Egypt with a **s** hand. Dt 6:21
you out with a **s** hand and Dt 7:8
the **s** hand and outstretched arm, Dt 7:19
The people are **s** and tall, Dt 9:2
out of Egypt with a **s** hand. Dt 9:26
His greatness, **s** hand, and Dt 11:2
you have a **s** desire to eat meat Dt 12:20
out of Egypt with a **s** hand and Dt 26:8
Be **s** and courageous; don't be Dt 31:6
Israel, "Be **s** and courageous, Dt 31:7
of Nun, "Be **s** and courageous, Dt 31:23
Be **s** and courageous, for you Jos 1:6
be **s** and very courageous to Jos 1:7
you: be **s** and courageous? Jos 1:9
Above all, be **s** and courageous!" Jos 1:18
s and courageous, for the LORD Jos 10:25
I am still as **s** today as I was Jos 14:11
have iron chariots and are **s**." Jos 17:18
Be very **s**, and continue obeying Jos 23:6
all **s** and able-bodied men. Jdg 3:29
There was a **s** tower inside the Jdg 9:51
and out of the **s** came something Jdg 14:14
Saul noticed any **s** or brave man, 1Sm 14:52
Therefore, be **s** and courageous, 2Sm 2:7
the Arameans are too **s** for me," 2Sm 10:11
the Ammonites are too **s** for you, 2Sm 10:11
Be **s**! We must prove ourselves 2Sm 10:12
prove ourselves **s** for our people 2Sm 10:12
Be **s** and courageous!" 2Sm 13:28
conspiracy grew **s**, and the 2Sm 15:12
for they were too **s** for me. 2Sm 22:18
God is my **s** refuge; He makes my 2Sm 22:33
of the earth. Be **s** and brave, 1Kg 2:2
there are 50 **s** men here with 2Kg 2:16
all **s** and fit for war. 2Kg 24:16
became **s** among his brothers 1Ch 5:2
the Arameans are too **s** for me," 1Ch 19:12
the Ammonites are too **s** for you, 1Ch 19:12
Be **s**! We must prove ourselves 1Ch 19:13
prove ourselves **s** for our people 1Ch 19:13
for Israel. Be **s** and courageous. 1Ch 22:13
houses because they were **s**, 1Ch 26:6
made, and **s**, capable men were 1Ch 26:31
the sanctuary. Be **s**, and do it." 1Ch 28:10
Solomon, "Be **s** and courageous, 1Ch 28:20
every city to make them very **s**. 2Ch 11:12
Abijah grew **s**, acquired 14 wives 2Ch 13:21
But as for you, be **s**; 2Ch 15:7
show Himself **s** for those whose 2Ch 16:9
presence. Be **s**; may the LORD be 2Ch 19:11
them⌋, do it! Be **s** for battle! 2Ch 25:8
helped until he became **s**. 2Ch 26:15
when he became **s**, he grew 2Ch 26:16
Be **s** and courageous! 2Ch 32:7
that you will be **s**, eat the good Ezr 9:12
Be **s** and take action!" Ezr 10:4
by Your great power and **s** hand. Neh 1:10
The **s** lion dies if ⌊it catches⌋ Jb 4:11
on nobles and disarms the **s**. Jb 12:21
You harass me with Your **s** hand. Jb 30:21
for they were too **s** for me. Ps 18:17
s ones of Bashan encircle me. Ps 22:12
LORD, **s** and mighty, the LORD, Ps 24:8
and let your heart be **s**. Ps 27:14
made me stand like a **s** mountain; Ps 30:7
Be **s** and courageous, all you who Ps 31:24
the poor from one too **s** for him, Ps 35:10
a **s** tower in the face of the Ps 61:3
my **s** rock, my refuge, is in God. Ps 62:7
many, but You are my **s** refuge. Ps 71:7
that You made **s** for Yourself. Ps 80:15
You have made **s** for Yourself. Ps 80:17
Hosts, who is **s** like You, LORD? Ps 89:8
or, if we are **s**, eighty years. Ps 90:10
with a **s** hand and outstretched Ps 136:12
GOD, my **s** Savior, You shield Ps 140:7
for they are too **s** for me. Ps 142:6
LORD one has **s** confidence and Pr 14:26
name of the LORD is a **s** tower; Pr 18:10
Redeemer is **s**, and He will take Pr 23:11
warrior is better than a **s** one, Pr 24:5
the ants are not a **s** people, Pr 30:25
and reveals that her arms are **s**. Pr 31:17
the battle to the **s**, or bread to Ec 9:11
tremble, and the **s** men stoop, Ec 12:3
love is fit and **s**, notable among Sg 5:10
For love is as **s** as death; Sg 8:6
The **s** one will become tinder, Is 1:31
that day their **s** cities will be Is 17:9
and a **s** king will rule it. Is 19:4
a **s** people will honor You. Is 25:3
We have a **s** city. Salvation Is 26:1
great, and **s** sword, will bring Is 27:1
Lord has a **s** and mighty one— Is 28:2
a storm with **s** flooding waters. Is 28:2
Be **s**; do not fear! Here Is 35:4
and works it with his **s** arm. Is 44:12
lets it grow **s** among the trees Is 44:14
His right hand and His **s** arm: Is 62:8
wind too **s** for this comes at My Jr 4:12
a **s** hand and an outstretched Jr 32:21
Why have your **s** ones been swept Jr 46:15
Their Redeemer is **s**; the LORD of Jr 50:34
an end to the pride of the **s**, Ezk 7:24
It had **s** branches, ⌊fit⌋ for the Ezk 19:11
Its **s** branches were torn off and Ezk 19:12
it no longer has a **s** branch, Ezk 19:14
rule over you with a **s** hand, Ezk 20:33
scattered, with a **s** hand, an Ezk 20:34
your hands be **s** in the days when Ezk 22:14
that it can grow **s** ⌊enough⌋ to Ezk 30:21
both the **s** one and the one Ezk 30:22
will destroy the fat and the **s**. Ezk 34:16
kingdom will be as **s** as iron; Dn 2:40
part of the kingdom will be **s**, Dn 2:42
The tree grew large and **s**; Dn 4:11
grew large and **s**, whose top Dn 4:20
For you have become great and **s**: Dn 4:22
incredibly **s**, with large iron Dn 7:7
ram was not **s** enough to stand Dn 8:7
to you; be very **s**!" As he spoke Dn 10:19
God will be **s** and take action. Dn 11:32
a great and **s** people ⌊appears⌋ Jl 2:2
s one will not prevail by his Am 2:14
out a thousand ⌊**s**⌋ will have Am 5:3
out a hundred ⌊**s**⌋ will have Am 5:3
He brings destruction on the **s**, Am 5:9
arbitration for **s** nations that Mc 4:3
far removed into a **s** nation. Mc 4:7
Though they are **s** and numerous, Nah 1:12
Even so, be **s**, Zerubbabel"—the Hg 2:4
Be **s**, Joshua son of Jehozadak, Hg 2:4
s, all you people of the land" Hg 2:4
dappled horses—⌊all⌋ **s** horses. Zch 6:3
As the **s** horses went out, they Zch 6:7
your hands be **s**, you who now Zch 8:9
let your hands be **s**." Zch 8:13
Many peoples and **s** nations will Zch 8:22
someone enter a **s** man's house Mt 12:29
he first ties up the **s** man? Mt 12:29
no one can enter a **s** man's house Mk 3:27
he first ties up the **s** man. Mk 3:27
No one was **s** enough to subdue Mk 5:4
up and became spiritually **s**, Lk 1:80
The boy grew up and became **s**, Lk 2:40
a **s** man, fully armed, guards Lk 11:21
I'm not **s** enough to dig; Lk 16:3
his feet and ankles became **s**. Ac 3:7
His name has made this man **s**, Ac 3:16
Now we who are **s** have an Rm 15:1
weak things to shame the **s**. 1Co 1:27
We are weak, but you are **s**! 1Co 4:10
in the faith, be brave and **s**. 1Co 16:13
For when I am weak, then I am **s**. 2Co 12:10
when we are weak and you are **s**. 2Co 13:9
sends them a **s** delusion so that 2Th 2:11
be **s** in the grace that is in 2Tm 2:1
might have **s** encouragement to Heb 6:18
because you are **s**, God's word 1Jn 2:14

STRONGER *(29)*

people will be **s** than the other, Gn 25:23
Whenever the **s** of the flock were Gn 30:41
Laban and the **s** ones to Jacob. Gn 30:42
because they are **s** than we are!" Nm 13:31
greater and **s** than you and to Dt 4:38
greater and **s** than you ⌊with⌋ Dt 9:1
into a nation **s** and more Dt 9:14
greater and **s** than you are. Dt 11:23
when the Israelites grew **s**, Jos 17:13
When Israel became **s**, they made Jdg 1:28
What is **s** than a lion? Jdg 14:18
that they were **s** than he was. Jdg 18:26
than eagles, **s** than lions. 2Sm 1:23
David growing **s** and the house 2Sm 3:1
because he was **s** than she was, 2Sm 13:14
Omri proved **s** than those who 1Kg 16:22
That's why they were **s** than we. 1Kg 20:23
will certainly be **s** than they. 1Kg 20:23
will certainly be **s** than they." 1Kg 20:25
Jehoshaphat grew **s** and stronger. 2Ch 17:12
Jehoshaphat grew stronger and **s**. 2Ch 17:12
hands are clean will grow **s**. Jb 17:9
contend with the One **s** than he. Ec 6:10
the wise man **s** than ten rulers Ec 7:19
or your shackles will become **s**. Is 28:22
from the power of one **s** than he. Jr 31:11
But when one **s** than he attacks Lk 11:22
God's weakness is **s** than human 1Co 1:25
to jealousy? Are we **s** than He? 1Co 10:22

STRONGEST *(2)*

some of the **s** soldiers in his Dn 3:20
deal with the **s** fortresses with Dn 11:39

STRONGHOLD *(38)*

whole time David was in the **s**. 1Sm 22:4
to David, "Don't stay in the **s**. 1Sm 22:5
and his men went up to the **s**. 1Sm 24:22
David did capture the **s** of Zion, 2Sm 5:7
took up residence in the **s**, 2Sm 5:9
about it and went down to the **s**. 2Sm 5:17
my salvation, my **s**, my refuge, 2Sm 22:3
At that time David was in the **s**, 2Sm 23:14
David did capture the **s** of Zion 1Ch 11:5
took up residence in the **s**; 1Ch 11:7
At that time David was in the **s**, 1Ch 11:16
to David at his **s** in the desert. 1Ch 12:8
also went to David at the **s**. 1Ch 12:16
its **s** is on a rocky crag. Jb 39:28
established a **s** from the mouths Ps 8:2
the horn of my salvation, my **s**. Ps 18:2
The LORD is the **s** of my life— Ps 27:1
He is a **s** of salvation for His Ps 28:8
the God of Jacob is our **s**. Ps 46:7
the God of Jacob is our **s**. Ps 46:11
is known as a **s** in its citadels Ps 48:3
strength, because God is my **s**. Ps 59:9
For You have been a **s** for me, Ps 59:16
God is my **s**—my faithful God Ps 59:17
my rock and my salvation, my **s**; Ps 62:2
my rock and my salvation, my **s**; Ps 62:6
my fortress, my **s** and my Ps 144:2
of the LORD is a **s** for the Pr 10:29
Sidon, the **s** of the sea, for Is 23:4
You have been a **s** for the poor, Is 25:4
a **s** for the humble person in his Is 25:4
my strength and my **s**, my refuge Jr 16:19
day I take their **s** from them, Ezk 24:25
on Pelusium, the **s** of Egypt, and Ezk 30:15
for His people, a **s** for the Jl 3:16
strong, and it falls on the **s**. Am 5:9
The LORD is good, a **s** in a day Nah 1:7
Return to a **s**, you prisoners who Zch 9:12

STRONGHOLDS *(10)*

in the mountains, caves, and **s**. Jdg 6:2
the wilderness **s** and in the hill 1Sm 23:14
among us in the **s** in Horesh on 1Sm 23:19
and stayed in the **s** of En-gedi. 1Sm 23:29
been captured, and the **s** seized. Jr 48:41
they sit in their **s**. Jr 51:30
devastated their **s** and destroyed Ezk 19:7
those in the **s** and caves will Ezk 33:27

destroy your **s** and plunder your Am 3:11
God for the demolition of **s**. 2Co 10:4

STRONGLY *(13)*
he urged them so **s** that they Gn 19:3
son Shechem is **s** attracted to Gn 34:8
Now Jericho was **s** fortified Jos 6:1
s supported him in his reign to 1Ch 11:10
For I **s** warned your ancestors Jr 11:7
And He would **s** warn them not to Mk 3:12
and everyone is **s** urged to enter Lk 16:16
he testified and **s** urged them, Ac 2:40
and I have **s** desired for many Rm 15:23
s urged him to come to you with 1Co 16:12
by them you may **s** engage in 1Tm 1:18
because he **s** opposed our words. 2Tm 4:15
the prophetic word **s** confirmed. 2Pt 1:19

STRUCK *(192)*
But the LORD **s** Pharaoh and his Gn 12:17
They **s** the men who were at the Gn 19:11
s Jacob's hip as they wrestled Gn 32:25
because He **s** Jacob's hip socket Gn 32:32
he **s** the Egyptian dead and hid Ex 2:12
raised the staff and **s** the water Ex 7:20
after the LORD **s** the Nile. Ex 7:25
and when he **s** the dust of the Ex 8:17
out My hand and **s** you and your Ex 9:15
Lightning **s** the earth, and the Ex 9:23
hail **s** down everything in the Ex 9:25
in Egypt when He **s** the Egyptians Ex 12:27
the LORD **s** every firstborn Ex 12:29
Take the rod you **s** the Nile with Ex 17:5
then the one who **s** ⌊him⌋ will be Ex 21:19
At the time I **s** down every Nm 3:13
Myself on the day I **s** down every Nm 8:17
and the LORD **s** them with a very Nm 11:33
land were **s** down by the LORD. Nm 14:37
his hand and **s** the rock twice Nm 20:11
Israel **s** him with the sword and Nm 21:24
So they **s** him, his sons, and his Nm 21:35
with Balaam, **s** his hands Nm 24:10
was **s** dead with the Midianite Nm 25:14
which the LORD **s** down before the Nm 32:4
the LORD had **s** down among them, Nm 33:4
the one who **s** him must be put to Nm 35:21
We **s** him until there was no Dt 3:3
The men of Ai **s** down about 36 of Jos 7:5
turned back and **s** down the men Jos 8:21
They **s** them down until no Jos 8:22
returned to Ai and **s** it down Jos 8:24
and **s** them down as far as Azekah Jos 10:10
Joshua **s** them down and executed Jos 10:26
Makkedah and **s** it down with Jos 10:28
s it down, putting everyone in Jos 10:30
s it down, putting everyone in Jos 10:32
but Joshua **s** him down along with Jos 10:33
they captured it and **s** it down, Jos 10:35
captured it and **s** down its king, Jos 10:37
They **s** them down with the sword Jos 10:39
Israel, and they **s** them down, Jos 11:8
They **s** them down, leaving no Jos 11:8
and **s** down its king with the Jos 11:10
They **s** down everyone in it with Jos 11:11
their cities and **s** them down Jos 11:12
they **s** down every person with Jos 11:14
all their kings and **s** them down, Jos 11:17
The Israelites **s** down the Jos 12:1
and the Israelites **s** them down. Jos 12:6
the Israelites **s** down the Jos 12:7
Moses **s** them down and drove Jos 13:12
and **s** it down with the sword. Jos 19:47
They **s** down 10,000 men in Bezek. Jdg 1:4
and **s** down the Canaanites and Jdg 1:5
They **s** down Sheshai, Ahiman, and Jdg 1:10
s the Canaanites who were living Jdg 1:17
that time they **s** down about Jdg 3:29
Midianite camp, **s** a tent, and it Jdg 7:13
against them and **s** them down. Jdg 9:43
the countryside and **s** them down. Jdg 9:44
that disaster had **s** them. Jdg 20:41
at Gidom and **s** 2,000 more dead. Jdg 20:45
s down about 4,000 men on the 1Sm 4:2
God **s** down the men of 1Sm 6:19
He **s** down 70 men ⌊out of⌋ 50,000 1Sm 6:19
because the LORD **s** them with a 1Sm 6:19
his armor-bearer **s** down about 20 1Sm 14:14
The Israelites **s** down the 1Sm 14:31
Then Saul **s** down the Amalekites 1Sm 15:7
I went after it, **s** it down, and 1Sm 17:35
he **s** down the Philistine and 1Sm 17:50
his hands when he **s** down the 1Sm 19:5
As the spear **s** the wall, David 1Sm 19:10
He also **s** down Nob, the city of 1Sm 22:19
later, the LORD **s** Nabal dead. 1Sm 25:38
The servant **s** him, and he died. 2Sm 1:15
he **s** down the Philistines all 2Sm 5:25
and God **s** him dead on the spot 2Sm 6:7
David **s** down 22,000 Aramean men. 2Sm 8:5
also **s** down Shobach commander 2Sm 10:18
so that he is **s** down and dies. 2Sm 11:15
who **s** Abimelech son of 2Sm 11:21
s down Uriah the Hittite with 2Sm 12:9
The LORD **s** the baby that Uriah's 2Sm 12:15
Absalom **s** down all the king's 2Sm 13:30
and one **s** the other and killed 2Sm 14:6
Absalom, **s** him, and killed him 2Sm 18:15
to his aid, **s** the Philistine, 2Sm 21:17
and **s** down the Philistines. 2Sm 23:12
Jehoiada, who **s** down Adonijah, 1Kg 2:25
head because he **s** down two men 1Kg 2:32
Jehoiada went up, **s** down Joab, 1Kg 2:34
he went out and **s** Shimei down, 1Kg 2:46
dead and had **s** down every male 1Kg 11:15
and Baasha **s** him down at 1Kg 15:27
he **s** down the entire house of 1Kg 15:29
Baasha had **s** down the house 1Kg 16:7
Asa, Zimri went in, **s** Elah down, 1Kg 16:10
Zimri **s** down the entire house of 1Kg 16:11
but had also **s** down the king, 1Kg 16:16
each one **s** down his opponent. 1Kg 20:20
the Israelites **s** down the 1Kg 20:29
So the man **s** him, inflicting a 1Kg 20:37
special aim and **s** the king of 1Kg 22:34
it up, and **s** the waters, which 2Kg 2:8
had dropped and **s** the waters. 2Kg 2:14
s the waters himself, and they 2Kg 2:14
the land and **s** down the Moabites 2Kg 3:24
So He **s** them with blindness, 2Kg 6:18
But who **s** down all these? 2Kg 10:9
he **s** down all who remained from 2Kg 10:17
So they **s** them down with the 2Kg 10:25
son of Shomer **s** him down, 2Kg 12:21
So he **s** the ground three times 2Kg 13:18
should have **s** the ground five 2Kg 13:19
would have **s** down Aram until 2Kg 13:19
He **s** him down publicly, killed 2Kg 15:10
Samaria and **s** down Shallum son 2Kg 15:14
against him and **s** him down, 2Kg 15:25
went out and **s** down 185,000 2Kg 19:35
and Sharezer **s** him down with the 2Kg 19:37
10 men and **s** down Gedaliah, 2Kg 25:25
They **s** down the remnant of the 1Ch 4:43
and He **s** him dead because he had 1Ch 13:10
and they **s** down the Philistine 1Ch 14:16
David **s** down 22,000 Aramean 1Ch 18:5
son of Zeruiah **s** down 18,000 1Ch 18:12
and his people **s** them with a 2Ch 13:17
the LORD **s** him and he died. 2Ch 13:20
special aim and **s** the king of 2Ch 18:33
yourself ⌊will be **s**⌋ with many 2Ch 21:15
He **s** down 10,000 Seirites, 2Ch 25:11
s down 3,000 of their people, 2Ch 25:13
who **s** him with great force: 2Ch 28:5
They **s** down the servants with Jb 1:15
A lightning storm **s** from heaven. Jb 1:16
They **s** down the servants with Jb 1:17
desert and **s** the four corners Jb 1:19
mercy, for God's hand has **s** me. Jb 19:21
the one You **s** and talk about Ps 69:26
He **s** the rock and water gushed Ps 78:20
He **s** down Israel's choice young Ps 78:31
He **s** all the firstborn in Egypt, Ps 78:51
He **s** their vines and fig trees Ps 105:33
He **s** all the firstborn in their Ps 105:36
s down the firstborn of Egypt, Ps 135:8
He **s** down many nations and Ps 135:10
He **s** the firstborn of the Ps 136:10
s down great kings His love is Ps 136:17
They **s** me, but I feel no pain! Pr 23:35
hand against them and **s** them; Is 5:25
did not turn to Him who **s** them; Is 9:13
depend on the one who **s** them, Is 10:20
He did when He⌋ **s** Midian at the Is 10:26
It **s** the peoples in anger with Is 14:6
of the one who **s** you is broken. Is 14:29
Israel as He **s** the one who Is 27:7
He struck the one who **s** Israel? Is 27:7
oxen will be **s** down with them, Is 34:7
LORD went out and **s** down 185,000 Is 37:36
and Sharezer **s** him down with the Is 37:38
Him stricken, **s** down by God, Is 53:4
He was **s** because of My people's Is 53:8
greed I was angry, so I **s** him; Is 57:17
Although I **s** you in My wrath, Is 60:10
I have **s** down your children in Jr 2:30
You have **s** them, but they felt Jr 5:3
their young men **s** down by the Jr 18:21
for I have **s** you like an enemy Jr 30:14
was instructed, I **s** my thigh ⌊in Jr 31:19
him got up and **s** down Gedaliah Jr 41:2
Ishmael also **s** down all the Jr 41:3
the men he had **s** down was a Jr 41:9
of Nethaniah had **s** down Gedaliah Jr 41:18
s the statue on its feet of iron Dn 2:34
the stone that **s** the statue Dn 2:35
with him, he **s** the ram, Dn 8:7
I **s** you with blight and mildew; Am 4:9
I **s** you—all the work of your Hg 2:17
He **s** the high priest's slave and Mt 26:51
s the high priest's slave, Mk 14:47
They were all **s** with amazement Lk 4:36
a severe famine **s** that country, Lk 15:14
Then one of them **s** the high Lk 22:50
s the high priest's slave, Jn 18:10
of the Lord **s** him because he Ac 12:23
are you ordering me to be **s**?" Ac 23:3
But they **s** a sandbar and ran the Ac 27:41
for they were **s** down in the 1Co 10:5
we are **s** down but not destroyed. 2Co 4:9
and a third of the sun was **s**, Rv 8:12

STRUCTURE *(7)*
a chambered **s** along the temple 1Kg 6:5
this temple and finish this **s**?" Ezr 5:3
this temple and finish this **s**?" Ezr 5:9
was a **s** resembling a city. Ezk 40:2
the thickness of the ⌊wall⌋ **s**; Ezk 40:5
for the **s** surrounding the temple Ezk 41:7
⌊the **s** rose⌋ gallery by gallery Ezk 42:3

STRUGGLE *(8)*
the days of my **s** until my relief Jb 14:14
best of them are **s** and sorrow; Ps 90:10
enriches, and **s** adds nothing to Pr 10:22
and in your **s** under the sun. Ec 9:9
womb to see ⌊only⌋ **s** and sorrow, Jr 20:18
having the same **s** that you saw I Php 1:30
how great a **s** I have for you, Col 2:1
a hard **s** with sufferings. Heb 10:32

STRUGGLED *(3)*
inside her **s** with each other, Gn 25:22
because you have **s** with God and Gn 32:28
Jacob **s** with the Angel and Hs 12:4

STRUGGLES *(7)*
for I took pleasure in all my **s**. Ec 2:10
This was my reward for all my **s**. Ec 2:10
does the worker gain from his **s**? Ec 3:9
there is no end to all his **s**, Ec 4:8
does he gain who **s** for the wind? Ec 5:16
The **s** of fools weary them, Ec 10:15
s on the outside, fears inside. 2Co 7:5

STRUGGLING *(2)*
"So who am I **s** for," ⌊he asks,⌋ Ec 4:8
In **s** against sin, you have not Heb 12:4

STRUNG *(3)*
He has **s** His bow and made it Ps 7:12
the sword and **s** the bow to bring Ps 37:14
sharpened, and all their bows **s**. Is 5:28

STRUT *(1)*
their tongues **s** across the earth Ps 73:9

STRUTTING *(1)*
a **s** rooster, a goat, and a king Pr 30:31

STUBBLE *(11)*
of Egypt to gather **s** for straw. Ex 5:12
it consumed them like **s**. Ex 15:7
become like **s** to him. Jb 41:28
is regarded as **s**, and he laughs Jb 41:29
you will give birth to **s**. Is 33:11
carries them away like **s**. Is 40:24
wind-driven **s** ⌊with⌋ his bow. Is 41:2
Look, they are like **s**; Is 47:14
of fiery flames consuming **s**, Jl 2:5
but the house of Esau will be **s**; Ob 18
wickedness will become **s**. Mal 4:1

not yet see everything s to him. Heb 2:8
and powers s to Him. 1Pt 3:22

SUBJECTING *(2)*
yet we are s our sons and Neh 5:5
For in s everything to him, Heb 2:8

SUBJECTS *(11)*
girls of his s like a vulgar 2Sm 6:20
became David's s and brought 2Sm 8:2
became David's s and brought 2Sm 8:6
were Hadadezer's s saw that they 2Sm 10:19
with Israel and became their s. 2Sm 10:19
became David's s and brought 1Ch 18:2
became David's s and brought 1Ch 18:6
When Hadadezer's s saw that they 1Ch 19:19
with David and became his s. 1Ch 19:19
the Ammonites will be their s. Is 11:14
But his s hated him and sent a Lk 19:14

SUBJUGATED *(2)*
warrior, I s the inhabitants. Is 10:13
have ⌊again⌋ s them to be your Jr 34:16

SUBMISSION *(4)*
the LORD would pretend s to Him; Ps 81:15
and Cushites will also be in s. Dn 11:43
not yield in s to these people Gl 2:5
learn in silence with full s. 1Tm 2:11

SUBMISSIVE *(6)*
who is humble, s in spirit, and Is 66:2
but should be s, as the law also 1Co 14:34
Wives, be s to your husbands, as Col 3:18
homemakers, and s to their Ti 2:5
are to be s to their masters Ti 2:9
Remind them to be s to rulers Ti 3:1

SUBMIT *(20)*
your mistress and s to her Gn 16:9
Foreigners s to me grudgingly; 2Sm 22:45
Foreigners s to me grudgingly; Ps 18:44
"S your case," says the LORD. Is 41:21
the demons s to us in Your name. Lk 10:17
that the spirits s to you, Lk 10:20
it does not s itself to God's Rm 8:7
Everyone must s to the governing Rm 13:1
you must s, not only because Rm 13:5
also to s to such people, and to 1Co 16:16
firm and don't s again to a yoke Gl 5:1
s to your own husbands as to the Eph 5:22
so wives should ⌊s⌋ to their Eph 5:24
Why do you s to regulations: Col 2:20
Shouldn't we s even more to the Heb 12:9
Obey your leaders and s to them, Heb 13:17
Therefore, s to God. But resist Jms 4:7
S to every human institution 1Pt 2:13
s yourselves to your masters 1Pt 2:18
s yourselves to your own 1Pt 3:1

SUBMITS *(1)*
Now as the church s to Christ, Eph 5:24

SUBMITTED *(2)*
because He s Himself to death, Is 53:12
they have not s to God's Rm 10:3

SUBMITTING *(2)*
s to one another in the fear of Eph 5:21
in this way, s to their own 1Pt 3:5

SUBORDINATES *(2)*
Their s also oppressed the Neh 5:15
and all my s were gathered there Neh 5:16

SUBSIDE *(2)*
earth, and the water began to s. Gn 8:1
surge and then s like the Nile Am 8:8

SUBSIDED *(2)*
their anger against him s. Jdg 8:3
Then the king's anger s. Est 7:10

SUBSIDES *(2)*
until your brother's anger s— Gn 27:44
the Nile and s like the Nile Am 9:5

SUBSTANCE *(2)*
of Israel named the s manna. Ex 16:31
the s is the Messiah. Col 2:17

SUBSTITUTE *(5)*
But if he does s one animal for Lv 27:10
animal and its s will be holy. Lv 27:10
animal and its s will be holy; Lv 27:33
who s darkness for light and Is 5:20
who s bitter for sweet and sweet Is 5:20

SUBSTITUTION *(3)*
replace it or make a s for it, Lv 27:10
he is not to make a s for it. Lv 27:33
he does make a s, both the Lv 27:33

SUBVERT *(1)*
takes a bribe to s the course of Pr 17:23

SUBVERTING *(1)*
We found this man s our nation, Lk 23:2

SUBVERTS *(1)*
man as one who s the people. Lk 23:14

SUCATHITES *(1)*
Tirathites, Shimeathites, and S. 1Ch 2:55

SUCCEED *(26)*
the LORD's command? It won't s. Nm 14:41
so that you will s in everything Dt 29:9
prosper and s in whatever you Jos 1:8
March up to Ramoth-gilead and s, 1Kg 22:12
told him, "March up and s. 1Kg 22:15
and may you s in building the 1Ch 22:11
Then you will s if you carefully 1Ch 22:13
ancestors, for you will not s." 2Ch 13:12
March up to Ramoth-gilead and s, 2Ch 18:11
March up and s, for they will be 2Ch 18:14
His prophets, and you will s." 2Ch 20:20
Your sons will s your ancestors; Ps 45:16
but with many advisers they s. Pr 15:22
with a twisted mind will not s, Pr 17:20
you don't know which will s, Ec 11:6
Jerusalem, but he could not s: Is 7:1
Perhaps you will be able to s; Is 47:12
and he will s in his mission. Is 48:15
of the LORD will s by His hand. Is 53:10
formed against you will s, Is 54:17
you will not s even with their Jr 2:37
descendants will s in sitting Jr 22:30
but you will not s'?" Jr 32:5
destruction and s in whatever he Dn 8:24
but he will not s, because plots Dn 11:25
may now at last s in coming to Rm 1:10

SUCCEEDED *(6)*
temple and for his own palace s. 2Ch 7:11
The Judahites s because they 2Ch 13:18
So they built and s. 2Ch 14:7
Hezekiah s in everything he did. 2Ch 32:30
they have not s, they will be Jr 20:11
who s Josiah his father as king: Jr 22:11

SUCCEEDING *(1)*
done diligently and s through Ezr 5:8

SUCCEEDS *(3)*
sons and who s him and enters Ex 29:30
wherever he turns, he s. Pr 17:8
follow a second youth who s him. Ec 4:15

SUCCESS *(20)*
grant me s today, and show Gn 24:12
LORD had made his journey a s. Gn 24:21
you and make your journey a s, Gn 24:40
LORD has made my journey a s. Gn 24:56
you will have s wherever you go. Jos 1:7
you will have s in everything 1Kg 2:3
sought the LORD, God gave him s. 2Ch 26:5
Give Your servant s today, Neh 1:11
is the One who will grant us s. Neh 2:20
so that they achieve no s. Jb 5:12
⌊the hope for⌋ s has been Jb 6:13
height of his s distress will Jb 20:22
explained ⌊the path to⌋ s! Jb 26:3
LORD, please grant us s! Ps 118:25
He stores up s for the upright; Pr 2:7
understands a matter finds s, Pr 16:20
understanding finds s. Pr 19:8
of wisdom is that it brings s. Ec 10:10
I make s and create disaster; Is 45:7
labor without s or bear children Is 65:23

SUCCESSFUL *(13)*
only You will make my journey s! Gn 24:42
and he became a s man, serving Gn 39:2
LORD made everything he did s, Gn 39:3
made everything that he did s. Gn 39:23
will not be s in anything you Dt 28:29
if we will have a s journey." Jdg 18:5
was s in everything Saul sent 1Sm 18:5
and continued to be s in all his 1Sm 18:14
observed that David was very s, 1Sm 18:15
David was more s than all of 1Sm 18:30
will not be s in his lifetime Jr 22:30
and will be s in whatever it Dn 8:12
He will be s until the time of Dn 11:36

SUCCESSFULLY *(2)*
elders continued s with the Ezr 6:14
one who listens will speak s. Pr 21:28

SUCCESSIVE *(2)*
was a famine for three s years, 2Sm 21:1
temple⌋ widened at each s story, Ezk 41:7

SUCCESSOR *(2)*
But you his s, Belshazzar, have Dn 5:22
received a s, Porcius Festus Ac 24:27

SUCCOTH *(18)*
but Jacob went on to S. Gn 33:17
is why the place was called S. Gn 33:17
traveled from Rameses to S, Ex 12:37
They set out from S and camped Ex 13:20
from Rameses and camped at S. Nm 33:5
departed from S and camped at Nm 33:6
Beth-nimrah, S, and Zaphon—the Jos 13:27
to the men of S, "Please give Jdg 8:5
But the princes of S asked, Jdg 8:6
as the men of S had answered. Jdg 8:8
from the men of S and Jdg 8:14
the⌋ 77 princes and elders of S. Jdg 8:14
went to the men of S and said, Jdg 8:15
the men of S with them. Jdg 8:16
Valley between S and Zarethan. 1Kg 7:46
Valley between S and Zeredah. 2Ch 4:17
will apportion the Valley of S. Ps 60:6
will apportion the Valley of S. Ps 108:7

SUCCOTH-BENOTH *(1)*
The men of Babylon made S, 2Kg 17:30

SUCH *(149)*
could not possibly do s a thing: Gn 18:25
have brought s enormous guilt Gn 20:9
female goats. ⌊S⌋ will be my Gn 30:32
s a thing should not be done. Gn 34:7
So how could I do s a great evil Gn 39:9
I've never seen s ugly ones as Gn 41:19
stored up grain in s abundance— Gn 41:49
could not possibly do s a thing. Gn 44:7
give this people s favor in the Ex 3:21
since I am s a poor speaker?" Ex 6:12
Since I am s a poor speaker, Ex 6:30
had there been s a large number Ex 10:14
the land of Egypt s as never was Ex 11:6
LORD gave the people s favor in Ex 12:36
led them into ⌊s⌋ a grave sin?" Ex 32:21
incurs guilt in s an instance. Lv 5:4
whoever carries s things is to Lv 15:10
right to redeem ⌊s⌋ houses stays Lv 25:31
S people are to observe it in Nm 9:11
You brought s trouble on Your Nm 11:11
only they had s a heart to fear Dt 5:29
who does s things and acts Dt 25:16
S are the ten thousands of Dt 33:17
and s are the thousands of Dt 33:17
raised s a loud shout that 1Sm 4:5
threw them into s confusion that 1Sm 7:10
who accomplished s a great 1Sm 14:45
them with s a great force that 1Sm 19:8
Do I have s a shortage of crazy 1Sm 21:15
I would never do s a thing to my 1Sm 24:6
He is s a worthless fool nobody 1Sm 25:17
You were s a friend to me. 2Sm 1:26
the LORD with s contempt in this 2Sm 12:14
for s a thing should never be 2Sm 13:12
hated Tamar with s intensity 2Sm 13:15
s was the regard that both David 2Sm 16:23
king repay me with s a reward? 2Sm 19:36
I would never do s a thing! 2Sm 23:17
S were the exploits of the three 2Sm 23:17
rejoicing with s a great joy 1Kg 1:40
"Why is the town in s an uproar?" 1Kg 1:41
Never again did s a quantity of 1Kg 10:10
before⌋ had s almug wood come, 1Kg 10:12
are to say s and such to her. 1Kg 14:5
are to say such and s to her. 1Kg 14:5
will be at s and such a place. 2Kg 6:8
will be at such and s a place." 2Kg 6:8
you stir up s trouble that you 2Kg 14:10
them—⌊nations s as⌋ Gozan, 2Kg 19:12
'I am about to bring s disaster 2Kg 21:12
No s Passover had ever been kept 2Kg 23:22
I would never do s a thing in 1Ch 11:19
S were the exploits of the three 1Ch 11:19
bestowed on him s royal majesty 1Ch 29:25
s that it was not like this for 2Ch 1:12
utensils in s great abundance 2Ch 4:18

never were s spices as those 2Ch 9:9
stir up s trouble so that you 2Ch 25:19
S rejoicing had not been seen in 2Ch 30:26
kingdom for s a time as this. Est 4:14
who would devise s a scheme?" Est 7:5
S is the destiny of all who Jb 8:13
go unanswered and s a talker be Jb 11:2
God and allow s words to leave Jb 15:13
s is the dwelling of the wicked, Jb 18:21
you offer me s futile comfort? Jb 21:34
not know how to give ⌊s⌋ titles; Jb 32:22
S is the generation of those who Ps 24:6
they escape in spite of s sin? Ps 56:7
S men will never be put to shame Ps 127:5
the people with s ⌊blessings⌋. Ps 144:15
S are the paths of all who Pr 1:19
the one who hates s agreements Pr 11:15
In s circumstances, I saw the Ec 8:10
my⌋ love, with s delights! Sg 7:6
s a time as has never been since Is 7:17
that I had s great bitterness; Is 38:17
S people do not comprehend and Is 44:18
kept silent for s a long time Is 57:11
Who has heard of s a thing? Is 66:8
Who has seen s things? Can a Is 66:8
Wouldn't s a land become totally Jr 3:1
Myself on s a nation as this Jr 5:9
taken up cases, s as the case Jr 5:28
Myself on s a nation as this Jr 5:29
to and give s a warning that Jr 6:10
against a nation s as this? Jr 9:9
bringing them s distress that Jr 10:18
going to bring s disaster on Jr 19:3
the LORD do s a thing to this Jr 22:8
Why are you doing s great harm Jr 44:7
one who does s things escape? Ezk 17:15
S a person is righteous; Ezk 18:9
S a person will not die for his Ezk 18:17
time of distress s as never has Dn 12:1
s as never existed in ages past Jl 2:2
will keep silent at s a time, Am 5:13
and s a violent storm arose on Jnh 1:4
who had given s authority to men Mt 9:8
S large crowds gathered around Mt 13:2
place to fill s a crowd?" Mt 15:33
one little child s as this in My Mk 9:37
of God belongs to s as these. Mk 10:14
is this I hear s things about?" Lk 9:9
of God belongs to s as these. Lk 18:16
I will give you s words and a Lk 21:15
the Father wants s people to Jn 4:23
commanded us to stone s women. Jn 8:5
a sinful man perform s signs?" Jn 9:16
spoke in s a way that a great Ac 14:1
There was s a sharp disagreement Ac 15:39
Receiving s an order, he put Ac 16:24
Suddenly there was s a violent Ac 16:26
want to be a judge of s things." Ac 18:15
loss in a dispute over s things, Ac 25:20
who practice s things deserve to Rm 1:32
those who do s things is based Rm 2:2
those who do s things yet do Rm 2:3
for s people do not serve our Rm 16:18
Do not even eat with s a person. 1Co 5:11
sister is not bound in s cases. 1Co 7:15
But s people will have trouble 1Co 7:28
Run in s a way that you may win. 1Co 9:24
also to submit to s people, 1Co 16:16
Therefore recognize s people. 1Co 16:18
us from s a terrible death 2Co 1:10
is sufficient for s a person, 2Co 2:6
Therefore having s a hope, 2Co 3:12
since we have s promises, we 2Co 7:1
S a person should consider this: 2Co 10:11
For s people are false apostles, 2Co 11:13
who practice s things will not Gl 5:21
s things there is no law. Gl 5:23
should restore s a person with a Gl 6:1
spot or wrinkle or any s thing, Eph 5:27
we command and exhort s people, 2Th 3:12
knowing that s a person is Ti 3:11
if we neglect s a great Heb 2:3
David after s a long time, Heb 4:7
those who say s things make it Heb 11:14
we also have s a large cloud Heb 12:1
Him who endured s hostility from Heb 12:3
is pleased with s sacrifices. Heb 13:16
S wisdom does not come down Jms 3:15
will travel to s and such a city Jms 4:13
to such and s a city and spend Jms 4:13
All s boasting is evil. Jms 4:16
we ought to support s men, 3Jn 8
a single hour s fabulous wealth Rv 18:17

SUCK *(1)*
He will s the poison of cobras; Jb 20:16

SUDDEN *(8)*
all of a s, perverted men Jdg 19:22
When disaster brings s death, Jb 9:23
and s dread terrifies you, Jb 22:10
their years in s disaster. Ps 78:33
Don't fear s danger or the ruin Pr 3:25
In the evening—s terror! Is 17:14
All of a s, when the whole crowd Mk 9:15
then s destruction comes on 1Th 5:3

SUDDENLY *(79)*
s a terror and great darkness Gn 15:12
S my sheaf stood up, and your Gn 37:7
If someone s dies near him, Nm 6:9
S the LORD said to Moses, Aaron, Nm 12:4
skin⌋ s became diseased Nm 12:10
and s the cloud covered it, Nm 16:42
But if anyone s pushes a person Nm 35:22
S a young lion came roaring at Jdg 14:5
the Spirit of God s took control 1Sm 11:6
s the champion named Goliath, 1Sm 17:23
S, all the men of Israel came to 2Sm 19:41
Abiathar the priest, s arrived. 1Kg 1:42
the road, Elijah s met him. 1Kg 18:7
S, an angel touched him. 1Kg 19:5
S, a voice came to him and said, 1Kg 19:13
S, a man turned aside and 1Kg 20:39
with horses of fire s appeared 2Kg 2:11
water s came from the direction 2Kg 3:20
⌊S⌋, he complained to his father, 2Kg 4:19
s they saw a marauding band, 2Kg 13:21
people, for it had come about s. 2Ch 29:36
S a powerful wind swept in from Jb 1:19
They die s in the middle of the Jb 34:20
turn back and s be disgraced. Ps 6:10
They shoot at him s and are not Ps 64:4
s, they will be wounded. Ps 64:7
How s they become a desolation! Ps 73:19
calamity will strike him s; Pr 6:15
their destruction will come s; Pr 24:22
right and wrong will s fall. Pr 28:18
reprimands will be broken s— Pr 29:1
time, as it s falls on them. Ec 9:12
Then s, in an instant, Is 29:5
whose collapse will come very s. Is 30:13
two things will happen to you s, Is 47:9
happen to you s and unexpectedly Is 47:11
S I acted, and they occurred. Is 48:3
S my tents are destroyed, my Jr 4:20
for s the destroyer will come on Jr 6:26
s released on her agitation and Jr 15:8
houses when You s bring raiders Jr 18:22
S Babylon fell and was shattered. Jr 51:8
and s the four winds of heaven Dn 7:2
S, another beast appeared, a Dn 7:5
the horns, s another horn, a Dn 7:8
S, a hand touched me and raised Dn 10:10
S one with human likeness Dn 10:16
Won't your creditors s arise, Hab 2:7
you seek will s come to His Mal 3:1
of the Lord s appeared to him Mt 1:20
angel of the Lord s appeared to Mt 2:13
angel of the Lord s appeared in Mt 2:19
The heavens s opened for Him, Mt 3:16
S, a violent storm arose on the Mt 8:24
S they shouted, "What do You Mt 8:29
And s the whole herd rushed down Mt 8:32
s one of the leaders came and Mt 9:18
to the crowds when s His mother Mt 12:46
S, Moses and Elijah appeared to Mt 17:3
s a bright cloud covered them, Mt 17:5
one of the Twelve, s arrived. Mt 26:47
S, the curtain of the sanctuary Mt 27:51
S there was a violent earthquake, Mt 28:2
Then s, looking around, they no Mk 9:8
he might come s and find you Mk 13:36
one of the Twelve, s arrived. Mk 14:43
S there was a multitude of the Lk 2:13
S, two men were talking with Him Lk 9:30
s he shrieks, and it throws him Lk 9:39
speaking, s a mob was there Lk 22:47
s two men stood by them in Lk 24:4
and s two men in white clothes Ac 1:10
S a sound like that of a violent Ac 2:2
from heaven s flashed around Ac 9:3
S an angel of the Lord appeared, Ac 12:7
S a mist and darkness fell on Ac 13:11
S there was such a violent Ac 16:26
from heaven s flashed around me Ac 22:6
would swell up or s drop dead. Ac 28:6

SUE *(1)*
one who wants to s you and take Mt 5:40

SUET *(3)*
and the s on top of the burning Lv 1:8
pieces with its head and its s, Lv 1:12
the head, the pieces, and the s, Lv 8:20

SUEZ *(1)*
LORD will divide the Gulf of S. Is 11:15

SUFFER *(48)*
Cain will s vengeance seven Gn 4:15
would, and s the fate of all, Nm 16:29
and the royal revenue will s. Ezr 4:13
and the royal interests will s. Ezr 4:22
made Your people s hardship; Ps 60:3
near death. I s Your horrors; I Ps 88:15
stranger, he will s for it, but Pr 11:15
companion of fools will s harm. Pr 13:20
cities and there s our fate, Jr 8:14
'You won't see sword or s famine. Jr 14:13
Know that I s disgrace for Your Jr 15:15
Her entire land will s shame, Jr 51:47
has made her s because of her Lm 1:5
LORD made ⌊me⌋ s on the day of Lm 1:12
doesn't the son s punishment for Ezk 18:19
A son won't s punishment for the Ezk 18:20
a father won't s punishment for Ezk 18:20
flocks of sheep s punishment. Jl 1:18
they s affliction because there Zch 10:2
to Jerusalem and s many things Mt 16:21
is going to s at their hands. Mt 17:12
Son of Man must s many things, Mk 8:31
Man that He must s many things Mk 9:12
of Man must s many things and Lk 9:22
But first He must s many things Lk 17:25
Passover with you before I s. Lk 22:15
Messiah have to s these things Lk 24:26
Messiah would s and rise from Lk 24:46
that His Messiah would s— Ac 3:18
how much he must s for My name!" Ac 9:16
the Messiah had to s and rise Ac 17:3
the Messiah must s, and that as Ac 26:23
seeing that we s with Him so Rm 8:17
all the members s with it; 1Co 12:26
the same sufferings that we s. 2Co 1:6
Did you s so much for nothing— Gl 3:4
in Him, but also to s for Him, Php 1:29
we were going to s persecution, 1Th 3:4
that is why I s these things. 2Tm 1:12
For this I s, to the point of 2Tm 2:9
have had to s many times since Heb 9:26
and chose to s with the people Heb 11:25
But when you do good and s, 1Pt 2:20
if you should s for 1Pt 3:14
is better to s for doing good, 1Pt 3:17
however, should s as a murderer, 1Pt 4:15
those who s according to God's 1Pt 4:19
of what you are about to s. Rv 2:10

SUFFERED *(23)*
to them. So they s greatly. Jdg 2:15
David and you s through all that 1Kg 2:26
through all that my father s." 1Kg 2:26
and Moses s because of them; Ps 106:32
Fools s affliction because of Ps 107:17
suffering, He s, and the Angel Is 63:9
a woman who had s from bleeding Mt 9:20
for today I've s terribly in a Mt 27:19
because they s these things? Lk 13:2
He had s, He also presented Ac 1:3
off into the fire and s no harm. Ac 28:5
of Him I have s the loss of all Php 3:8
we had previously s and been 1Th 2:2
you have also s the same things 1Th 2:14
these and have s the shipwreck 1Tm 1:19
He Himself was tested and has s, Heb 2:18
obedience through what He s. Heb 5:8
Jesus also s outside the gate, Heb 13:12
because Christ also s for you, 1Pt 2:21
For Christ also s for sins once 1Pt 3:18
since Christ s in the flesh, 1Pt 4:1

the One who s in the flesh has 1Pt 4:1
you after you have s a little. 1Pt 5:10

SUFFERING *(35)*
You are responsible for my s! Gn 16:5
enter her and cause bitter s. Nm 5:24
enter her and cause bitter s; Nm 5:27
his own affliction and s, 2Ch 6:29
saw that his s was very intense Jb 2:13
For you will forget your s, Jb 11:16
I speak, my s is not relieved, Jb 16:6
and days of s have seized me. Jb 30:16
days of s confront me. Jb 30:27
out of their s and makes their Ps 107:41
man of s who knew what sickness Is 53:3
In all their s, He suffered, and Is 63:9
is my intense s, but I must bear Jr 10:19
if He causes s, He will show Lm 3:32
affliction or s on mankind. Lm 3:33
You are s under a curse, yet you Mal 3:9
those s from various diseases Mt 4:24
of heaven has been s violence, Mt 11:12
A woman s from bleeding for 12 Mk 5:25
was s from a high fever Lk 4:38
A woman s from bleeding for 12 Lk 8:43
remembers the s because of the Jn 16:21
You will have s in this world. Jn 16:33
Canaan, with great s, and our Ac 7:11
father was in bed s from fever Ac 28:8
for which you also are s, 2Th 1:5
share in s for the gospel, 2Tm 1:8
Share in s as a good soldier of 2Tm 2:3
honor because of the s of death. Heb 2:9
you yourselves were s bodily. Heb 13:3
as an example of s and patience. Jms 5:10
Is anyone among you s? Jms 5:13
endures grief from s unjustly. 1Pt 2:19
when s, He did not threaten, but 1Pt 2:23
s harm as the payment for 2Pt 2:13

SUFFERINGS *(15)*
and I know about their s. Ex 3:7
bring me out of my s. Ps 25:17
that the s of this present Rm 8:18
For as the s of Christ overflow 2Co 1:5
of the same s that we suffer. 2Co 1:6
know that as you share in the s, 2Co 1:7
and the fellowship of His s, Php 3:10
Now I rejoice in my s for you, Col 1:24
and s that came to me 2Tm 3:11
salvation perfect through s. Heb 2:10
endured a hard struggle with s. Heb 10:32
the messianic s and the glories 1Pt 1:11
share in the s of the Messiah 1Pt 4:13
witness to the s of the Messiah, 1Pt 5:1
that the same s are being 1Pt 5:9

SUFFERS *(3)*
he has seizures and s severely. Mt 17:15
if one member s, all the members 1Co 12:26
if ⌊anyone s⌋ as a Christian, 1Pt 4:16

SUFFICIENT *(5)*
materials were s for them to do Ex 36:7
she doesn't have s means for a Lv 12:8
a crop s for three years. Lv 25:21
the majority is s for such a 2Co 2:6
me, "My grace is s for you, for 2Co 12:9

SUGGESTED *(5)*
do as he s, sin, and get a bad Neh 6:13
king's personal attendants s, Est 2:2
in charge of the harem, s. Est 2:15
leave out anything you have s." Est 6:10
son of Kareah s to Gedaliah Jr 40:15

SUGGESTION *(1)*
This s pleased the king, Est 2:4

SUITABLE *(7)*
each one with a s blessing. Gn 49:28
in battle at a s place facing Jos 8:14
a weapon s for its task; Is 54:16
s for instruction in all wisdom, Dn 1:4
consider it s to hear from you Ac 28:22
If it is also s for me to go, 1Co 16:4
or crude joking are not s, Eph 5:4

SUITED *(2)*
at a pace s to the livestock and Gn 33:14
with a gift s to his means, Dt 16:17

SUKKIIM *(1)*
Libyans, S, and Ethiopians 2Ch 12:3

SULFUR *(13)*
LORD rained burning s on Sodom Gn 19:24
a burning waste of s and salt, Dt 29:23
Burning s is scattered over his Jb 18:15
coals and s on the wicked; Ps 11:6
into pitch, her soil into s; Is 34:9
fire and s rained from heaven Lk 17:29
hyacinth blue, and s yellow. Rv 9:17
mouths came fire, smoke, and s. Rv 9:17
and the s that came from their Rv 9:18
with fire and s in the sight Rv 14:10
lake of fire that burns with s. Rv 19:20
of fire and s where the beast Rv 20:10
lake that burns with fire and s, Rv 21:8

SUM *(6)*
though I cannot s them up. Ps 71:15
how vast their s is! Ps 139:17
the soldiers a large s of money Mt 28:12
bought for a s of silver from Ac 7:16
this large s administered by us. 2Co 8:20
To s up, each one of you is to Eph 5:33

SUMMARY *(1)*
here is the s of his account. Dn 7:1

SUMMED *(1)*
all are s up by this: Rm 13:9

SUMMER *(24)*
cold and heat, s and winter, and Gn 8:22
100 ⌊bunches⌋ of s fruit, and a 2Sm 16:1
bread and s fruit are for the 2Sm 16:2
You made s and winter. Ps 74:17
it prepares its provisions in s; Pr 6:8
who gathers during s is prudent; Pr 10:5
Like snow in s and rain at Pr 26:1
store up their food in the s; Pr 30:25
over your s ⌊fruit⌋ and your Is 16:9
birds will spend the s on them, Is 18:6
a ripe fig before the s harvest. Is 28:4
has passed, s has ended, but we Jr 8:20
gather wine, s fruit, and oil, Jr 40:10
amount of wine and s fruit. Jr 40:12
fallen on your s fruit and grape Jr 48:32
chaff from the s threshing Dn 2:35
winter house and the s house; Am 3:15
me this: A basket of s fruit. Am 8:1
replied, "A basket of s fruit." Am 8:2
when the s fruit has been Mc 7:1
western sea, in s and winter Zch 14:8
leaves, you know that s is near. Mt 24:32
leaves, you know that s is near. Mk 13:28
that s is already near. Lk 21:30

SUMMER'S *(1)*
was drained as in the s heat. Ps 32:4

SUMMIT *(9)*
came to the s where he used to 2Sm 15:32
had gone a little beyond the s, 2Sm 16:1
went up to the s of Carmel. 1Kg 18:42
from the s of Senir and Hermon, Sg 4:8
which is on the s above the rich Is 28:1
which is on the s above the rich Is 28:4
Me, ⌊or⌋ the s of Lebanon, but Jr 22:6
you who occupy the mountain s, Jr 49:16
and the s of Carmel withers. Am 1:2

SUMMON *(25)*
silver to s the community Nm 10:2
these men have come to s you, Nm 22:20
of his city will s him and speak Dt 25:8
s the peoples to a mountain; Dt 33:19
messengers⌋ to s Ahimelech the 1Sm 22:11
S Hushai the Archite also. 2Sm 17:5
S the men of Judah to me within 2Sm 20:4
Amasa went to s Judah, but he 2Sm 20:5
Now s all Israel to meet me at 1Kg 18:19
s to me all the prophets of Baal, 2Kg 10:19
of justice, who can s Him? Jb 9:19
you will s a nation you do not Is 55:5
am about to s all the clans and Jr 1:15
and s the women who mourn; Jr 9:17
like Me? Who will s Me? Who is Jr 49:19
S the archers to Babylon, all Jr 50:29
like Me? Who will s Me? Who is Jr 50:44
S kingdoms against her—Ararat, Jr 51:27
S an assembly against them and Ezk 23:46
I will s the grain and make it Ezk 36:29
gave orders to s the Dn 2:2
Therefore, s Daniel, and he will Dn 5:12
Brace yourself! S all your Nah 2:1
his slaves to s those invited to Mt 22:3
he might s him to Jerusalem. Ac 25:3

SUMMONED *(93)*
she s her younger son Jacob and Gn 27:42
Isaac s Jacob, blessed him, and Gn 28:1
so he s all the magicians of Gn 41:8
Israel s his strength and sat Gn 48:2
the king of Egypt s the midwives Ex 1:18
Pharaoh s Moses and Aaron and Ex 8:8
Then Pharaoh s Moses and Aaron Ex 8:25
Pharaoh s Moses and said, Ex 10:24
Then Moses s all the elders of Ex 12:21
He s Moses and Aaron during the Ex 12:31
He s the elders of the people, Ex 19:7
Then the LORD s Moses to the top Ex 19:20
So Moses s Bezalel, Oholiab, and Ex 36:2
Then the LORD s Moses and spoke Lv 1:1
On the eighth day Moses s Aaron, Lv 9:1
Moses s Mishael and Elzaphan, Lv 10:4
the tent, and s Aaron and Miriam Nm 12:5
Moses and Aaron s the assembly Nm 20:10
I s you to put a curse on my Nm 24:10
Moses s all Israel and said to Dt 5:1
Moses s all Israel and said to Dt 29:2
Moses then s Joshua and said to Dt 31:7
So Joshua s the 12 men selected Jos 4:4
Joshua son of Nun s the priests Jos 6:6
of Ai were s to pursue them, Jos 8:16
Joshua s the Gibeonites and said Jos 9:22
Joshua s all the men of Israel Jos 10:24
s the Reubenites, Gadites, Jos 22:1
Joshua s all Israel, including Jos 23:2
Shechem and s Israel's elders, Jos 24:1
She s Barak son of Abinoam from Jdg 4:6
Barak s Zebulun and Naphtali to Jdg 4:10
Sisera s all his 900 iron Jdg 4:13
Philistines s the priests and 1Sm 6:2
Samuel s the people to the LORD 1Sm 10:17
the troops were s to join Saul 1Sm 13:4
Then Saul s the troops and 1Sm 15:4
So Jonathan s David and told him 1Sm 19:7
Then Saul s all the troops to go 1Sm 23:8
So Achish s David and told him, 1Sm 29:6
Then David s one of his servants 2Sm 1:15
s him to David, and the king 2Sm 9:2
Then the king s Saul's attendant 2Sm 9:9
David s Absalom, who came to 2Sm 14:33
So David s the Gibeonites and 2Sm 21:2
Then the king s Shimei and said 1Kg 2:36
So the king s Shimei and said to 1Kg 2:42
They s him, and Jeroboam and the 1Kg 12:3
they s him to the assembly and 1Kg 12:20
So Ahab s all the Israelites and 1Kg 18:20
the LORD has s us three kings, 2Kg 3:10
LORD who has s us three kings 2Kg 3:13
were s and took their stand at 2Kg 3:21
She s her husband and said, 2Kg 4:22
David s the priests Zadok and 1Ch 15:11
Then he s his son Solomon and 1Ch 22:6
So they s him. Then Jeroboam and 2Ch 10:3
Jehoiada s his courage and took 2Ch 23:1
Then I s the leaders: Ezr 8:16
So I s the priests and made Neh 5:12
desired her and s her by name. Est 2:14
scribes were s on the thirteenth Est 3:12
Esther s Hathach, one of the Est 4:5
and who has not been s— Est 4:11
I have not been s to appear Est 4:11
), the royal scribes were s. Est 8:9
If I s ⌊Him⌋ and He answered me, Jb 9:16
when I s them, they stood up Is 48:13
So Jeremiah s Baruch son of Jr 36:4
and he s Johanan son of Kareah, Jr 42:8
He has s an army against me to Lm 1:15
s my attackers on every side, Lm 2:22
After a long time you will be s. Ezk 38:8
I have s a drought on the fields Hg 1:11
Then He s me saying, "See, those Zch 6:8
Herod secretly s the wise men Mt 2:7
Now Jesus s His disciples and Mt 15:32
after he had s him, his master Mt 18:32
mountain and s those He wanted Mk 3:13
He s them and spoke to them in Mk 3:23
s the Twelve and began to send Mk 6:7
He s the disciples and said to Mk 8:1
came, He s His disciples, Lk 6:13
So John s two of his disciples Lk 7:18
So he s one of the servants and Lk 15:26

So he s each one of his master's Lk 16:5
he s those slaves he had given Lk 19:15
until they s the parents of the Jn 9:18
time they s the man who had Jn 9:24
headquarters, s Jesus, and said Jn 18:33
Then the Twelve s the whole Ac 6:2
This man s Barnabas and Saul and Ac 13:7
He s two of his centurions and Ac 23:23

SUMMONING *(8)*
for I am s a sword against all Jr 25:29
S His 12 disciples, He gave them Mt 10:1
S the crowd, He told them, Mt 15:10
S the crowd again, He told them, Mk 7:14
S the crowd along with His Mk 8:34
S His disciples, He said to them, Mk 12:43
S the centurion, he asked him Mk 15:44
S the Twelve, He gave them power Lk 9:1

SUMMONS *(5)*
Did I not send you an urgent s? Nm 22:37
s the earth from east to west. Ps 50:1
s heaven and earth in order to Ps 50:4
who s the waters of the sea and Am 5:8
He s the waters of the sea and Am 9:6

SUMS *(1)*
people were putting in large s. Mk 12:41

SUN *(134)*
As the s was setting, a deep Gn 15:12
When the s had set and it was Gn 15:17
The s had risen over the land Gn 19:23
there because the s had set. Gn 28:11
The s shone on him as he passed Gn 32:31
and this time the s, moon, and Gn 37:9
eat, but when the s grew hot, it Ex 16:21
steady until the s went down. Ex 17:12
When the s has set, he will Lv 22:7
to the heavens and see the s, Dt 4:19
evening as the s sets at the Dt 16:6
gods by bowing down to the s, Dt 17:3
and when the s sets he may come Dt 23:11
each day before the s sets, Dt 24:15
from the s and the abundant Dt 33:14
S, stand still over Gibeon, and Jos 10:12
And the s stood still and the Jos 10:13
the s stopped in the middle of Jos 10:13
rising of the s in its strength Jdg 5:31
and the s set as they neared Jdg 19:14
by the time the s is hot.'" 1Sm 11:9
light when the s rises on a 2Sm 23:4
out in the army as the s set, 1Kg 22:36
the s was shining on the water, 2Kg 3:22
to Baal, and to the s, moon, 2Kg 23:5
of Judah had dedicated to the s. 2Kg 23:11
burned up the chariots of the s. 2Kg 23:11
of Jerusalem until the s is hot, Neh 7:3
an eclipse of the s terrify it. Jb 3:5
He commands the s not to shine Jb 9:7
blackened, but not by the s. Jb 30:28
have gazed at the s when it was Jb 31:26
even[j] look at the s when it is Jb 37:21
He has pitched a tent for the s. Ps 19:4
child[j], they will not see the s. Ps 58:8
he continue while the s endures, Ps 72:5
as long as the s shines, may his Ps 72:17
established the moon and the s. Ps 74:16
the LORD God is a s and shield. Ps 84:11
his throne like the s before Me, Ps 89:36
the s knows when to set. Ps 104:19
s rises; they go back and lie Ps 104:22
rising of the s to its setting, Ps 113:3
s will not strike you by day, Ps 121:6
the s to rule by day, His love Ps 136:8
Praise Him, s and moon; praise Ps 148:3
he labors at under the s? Ec 1:3
The s rises and the sun sets; Ec 1:5
The sun rises and the s sets; Ec 1:5
is nothing new under the s. Ec 1:9
done under the s and have found Ec 1:14
to be gained under the s. Ec 2:11
done under the s was distressing Ec 2:17
under the s because I must Ec 2:18
at skillfully under the s. Ec 2:19
I had labored at under the s. Ec 2:20
that he labors with under the s? Ec 2:22
I also observed under the s: Ec 3:16
being done under the s. Ec 4:1
that is done under the s. Ec 4:3
I saw futility under the s: Ec 4:7
under the s follow a second Ec 4:15
tragedy I have seen under the s: Ec 5:13
does under the s during the few Ec 5:18
I have observed under the s, Ec 6:1
does not see the s and is not Ec 6:5
happen after him under the s? Ec 6:12
to those who see the s. Ec 7:11
work that is done under the s, Ec 8:9
man under the s except to eat, Ec 8:15
that God gives him under the s. Ec 8:15
work that is done under the s. Ec 8:17
in all that is done under the s: Ec 9:3
in all that is done under the s. Ec 9:6
been given to you under the s, Ec 9:9
in your struggle under the s. Ec 9:9
I saw under the s that the race Ec 9:11
this also is wisdom under the s, Ec 9:13
an evil I have seen under the s, Ec 10:5
for the eyes to see the s. Ec 11:7
before the s and the light are Ec 12:2
for the s has gazed on me. Sg 1:6
bright as the s, awe-inspiring Sg 6:10
s will be dark when it rises, Is 13:10
be called the City of the S. Is 19:18
to shame and the s disgraced, Is 24:23
rising of the s to its setting Is 45:6
heat or s will not strike Is 49:10
The s will no longer be your Is 60:19
Your s will no longer set, Is 60:20
They will be exposed to the s, Jr 8:2
s set while it was still day; Jr 15:9
who gives the s for light by day Jr 31:35
pillars of the s temple in the Jr 43:13
to the east in worship of the s. Ezk 8:16
I will cover the s with a cloud, Ezk 32:7
s and moon grow dark, and the Jl 2:10
The s will be turned to darkness Jl 2:31
The s and moon will grow dark, Jl 3:15
will make the s go down at noon Am 8:9
As the s was rising, God Jnh 4:8
The s beat down on Jonah's head Jnh 4:8
s will set on these prophets, Mc 3:6
when the s rises, they take off, Nah 3:17
S and moon stand still in Hab 3:11
rising of the s to its setting. Mal 1:11
the s of righteousness will rise Mal 4:2
For He causes His s to rise on Mt 5:45
But when the s came up they were Mt 13:6
shine like the s in their Mt 13:43
and His face shone like the s. Mt 17:2
The s will be darkened, and the Mt 24:29
came, after the s had set, they Mk 1:32
When the s came up, it was Mk 4:6
The s will be darkened, and the Mk 13:24
the s was setting, all those Lk 4:40
there will be signs in the s, Lk 21:25
s will be turned to darkness, Ac 2:20
will not see the s for a time." Ac 13:11
from heaven brighter than the s, Ac 26:13
many days neither s nor stars Ac 27:20
There is a splendor of the s, 1Co 15:41
Don't let the s go down on your Eph 4:26
For the s rises with its Jms 1:11
shining like the s at midday. Rv 1:16
s turned black like sackcloth Rv 6:12
longer will the s strike them, Rv 7:16
and a third of the s was struck, Rv 8:12
so that the s and the air were Rv 9:2
was like the s, his legs were Rv 10:1
a woman clothed with the s, Rv 12:1
poured out his bowl on the s. Rv 16:8
saw an angel standing in the s, Rv 19:17
not need the s or the moon to Rv 21:23

SUN'S *(3)*
to make the s shadow that goes Is 38:8
So the s shadow went back the Is 38:8
because the s light failed. Lk 23:45

SUNDOWN *(1)*
effort until s to deliver him. Dn 6:14

SUNG *(2)*
which people have s about. Jb 36:24
this song will be s in the land Is 26:1

SUNK *(3)*
For Your arrows have s into me, Ps 38:2
For we have s down to the dust; Ps 44:25
I have s in deep mud, and there Ps 69:2

SUNLIGHT *(4)*
will be as bright as the s, Is 30:26
and the s will be seven times Is 30:26
the s and moonlight will Zch 14:6
will not need lamplight or s, Rv 22:5

SUNRISE *(10)*
But if this happens after s, Ex 22:3
east side toward the s 75 feet. Ex 27:13
east toward the s were also 75 Ex 38:13
side toward the s under their Nm 2:3
tent of meeting toward the s. Nm 3:38
Jericho, eastward toward the s." Nm 34:15
east toward the s along the Jos 19:12
east toward the s to Gath-hepher Jos 19:13
Then get up early and at s, Jdg 9:33
they went to the tomb at s. Mk 16:2

SUNSET *(8)*
return it to him before s. Ex 22:26
sure to return it to him at s. Dt 24:13
and at s Joshua commanded that Jos 8:29
At s Joshua commanded that they Jos 10:27
On the seventh day before s, Jdg 14:18
s, they had gone as far as the 2Sm 2:24
or anything else before s!" 2Sm 3:35
evening. Then he died at s. 2Ch 18:34

SUNSHINE *(2)*
an amply watered plant in the s; Jb 8:16
like shimmering heat in s, Is 18:4

SUPER-APOSTLES *(2)*
in no way inferior to the "s." 2Co 11:5
in no way inferior to the "s," 2Co 12:11

SUPERFICIALLY *(2)*
My people's brokenness s, Jr 6:14
have treated s the brokenness Jr 8:11

SUPERIOR *(6)*
want to appear s to me and would Jb 19:5
approve the things that are s, Rm 2:18
For who makes you so s? 1Co 4:7
He inherited is s to theirs. Heb 1:4
inferior is blessed by the s. Heb 7:7
has now obtained a s ministry, Heb 8:6

SUPERNATURAL *(2)*
and that's why s powers are at Mt 14:2
and that's why s powers are at Mk 6:14

SUPERVISE *(2)*
years old or more to s the work Ezr 3:8
together to s those working Ezr 3:9

SUPERVISED *(3)*
leaders who s the registration. Nm 7:2
who s the work outside the house Neh 11:16
Ziha and Gishpa s the temple Neh 11:21

SUPERVISING *(1)*
and were s all those doing 2Ch 34:13

SUPERVISION *(3)*
live under your s is too small 2Kg 6:1
out under the s of Mithredath Ezr 1:8
harem under the s of Shaashgaz, Est 2:14

SUPERVISORS *(4)*
and 3,600 as s over them. 2Ch 2:2
and 3,600 s to make the people 2Ch 2:18
from the Kohathites as s. 2Ch 34:12
lift a finger to help their s. Neh 3:5

SUPH *(1)*
Arabah opposite S, between Paran Dt 1:1

SUPHAH *(1)*
Waheb in S and the ravines of Nm 21:14

SUPPER *(8)*
took the cup after s and said, Lk 22:20
by the time of s, the Devil had Jn 13:2
He got up from s, laid aside His Jn 13:4
Jesus at the s and asked, Jn 21:20
not really to eat the Lord's S. 1Co 11:20
takes his own s ahead of others 1Co 11:21
cup, after s, and said, "This 1Co 11:25
together for the great s of God, Rv 19:17

SUPPLEMENT *(1)*
every effort to s your faith 2Pt 1:5

SUPPLICANTS *(1)*
beyond the rivers of Cush My s, Zph 3:10

SUPPLIED *(7)*
tops, and s bands for them. Ex 38:28
of Tyre having s him with cedar 1Kg 9:11
David s a great deal of iron to 1Ch 22:3

their country was **s** with food Ac 12:20
came from Macedonia **s** my needs. 2Co 11:9
I am fully **s**, having received Php 4:18
Christ will be richly **s** to you. 2Pt 1:11

SUPPLIES *(8)*
he is, hidden among the **s**." 1Sm 10:22
David left his **s** in the care of 1Sm 17:22
while 200 stayed with the **s**. 1Sm 25:13
the one who remains with the **s**. 1Sm 30:24
gathered **s**, and went to fight 1Kg 20:27
leaders in them with **s** of food, 2Ch 11:11
the rooms ⌊that housed⌋ the **s**, Neh 12:44
with a great army and many **s**. Dn 11:13

SUPPLY *(17)*
and Rameses as **s** cities for Ex 1:11
continue to **s** the people with Ex 5:7
When I cut off your **s** of bread, Lv 26:26
have also captured the water **s**. 2Sm 12:27
you're able to **s** riders for them 2Kg 18:23
carried off a great **s** of loot. 2Ch 14:13
else you have to **s** ⌊to meet⌋ the Ezr 7:20
sent them an abundant **s** of food. Ps 78:25
They **s** water for every wild Ps 104:11
and destroyed the entire food **s**. Ps 105:16
the entire **s** of bread and water, Is 3:1
going to cut off the **s** of bread Ezk 4:16
you and cut off your **s** of bread. Ezk 5:16
it to cut off its **s** of bread, Ezk 14:13
does God **s** you with the Spirit Gl 3:5
And my God will **s** all your needs Php 4:19
s your slaves with what is right Col 4:1

SUPPLYING *(2)*
will be full, **s** all kinds of Ps 144:13
service is not only **s** the needs 2Co 9:12

SUPPORT *(32)*
was unable to **s** them as long as Gn 13:6
they stayed could not **s** them. Gn 36:7
you are to **s** him as a foreigner Lv 25:35
if you **s** us from the city. 2Sm 18:3
distress, but the LORD was my **s**. 2Sm 22:19
each **s** was one piece with the 1Kg 7:34
that Pul would **s** him to 2Kg 15:19
him and did not give him **s**. 2Ch 28:20
so that they would **s** the people Ezr 8:36
responsibility, and we **s** you. Ezr 10:4
and He will not **s** evildoers. Jb 8:20
child who had no one to **s** him. Jb 29:12
I saw that I had **s** in the ⌊city⌋ Jb 31:21
distress, but the LORD was my **s**. Ps 18:18
on the LORD, and He will **s** you; Ps 55:22
they lend **s** to the sons of Lot. Ps 83:8
They will **s** you with their hands Ps 91:12
Your faithful love will **s** me, Ps 94:18
Lord, I am oppressed; **s** me. Is 38:14
but didn't **s** the poor and needy. Ezk 16:49
Those who **s** Egypt will fall, Ezk 30:6
the courage to **s** me against them Dn 10:21
not stand with him or **s** him. Dn 11:17
its **s** is taken from you. Mc 1:11
they will **s** you with their hands Mt 4:6
and they will **s** you with their Lk 4:11
testify in **s** of this, Rm 2:15
we don't have the right ⌊to **s**⌋, 2Th 3:9
S widows who are genuinely 1Tm 5:3
the official **s** list unless she 1Tm 5:9
s you after you have suffered 1Pt 5:10
we ought to **s** such men, so that 3Jn 8

SUPPORTED *(14)*
Then Aaron and Hur **s** his hands, Ex 17:12
the priest. They **s** Adonijah, 1Kg 1:7
because they **s** me when I fled 1Kg 2:7
Since he had **s** Adonijah but not 1Kg 2:28
strongly **s** him in his reign to 1Ch 11:10
of Judah and **s** Rehoboam son 2Ch 11:17
their neighbors **s** them with Ezr 1:6
so that he **s** them in the work on Ezr 6:22
The officers **s** all the people of Neh 4:16
You **s** me because of my integrity Ps 41:12
and His own righteousness **s** Him. Is 59:16
son of Shaphan **s** Jeremiah, Jr 26:24
and the one who **s** her during Dn 11:6
unless it is **s** by two or three 1Tm 5:19

SUPPORTING *(11)*
feel the pillars **s** the temple, Jdg 16:26
two middle pillars **s** the temple Jdg 16:29
from the **s** terraces inward 2Sm 5:9
and the people **s** Absalom 2Sm 15:12
own palace, the **s** terraces, the 1Kg 9:15
Solomon had built the **s** terraces 1Kg 11:27
from the **s** terraces to the 1Ch 11:8
repaired the **s** terraces of the 2Ch 32:5
Shabbethai the Levite **s** them. Ezr 10:15
others who were **s** them from Lk 8:3
together by every **s** ligament, Eph 4:16

SUPPORTS *(9)*
involved the tabernacle's **s**, Nm 3:36
s of the tabernacle, with its Nm 4:31
of the basin were cast **s**, 1Kg 7:30
Four **s** were at the four corners 1Kg 7:34
What **s** its foundations? Jb 38:6
but the LORD **s** the righteous. Ps 37:17
with the hammer ⌊**s**⌋ the one who Is 41:7
to serve as **s** for the side rooms Ezk 41:6
that the **s** would not be in the Ezk 41:6

SUPPOSE *(21)*
s the 50 righteous lack five. Gn 18:28
again, "**S** 40 are found there? Gn 18:29
S 30 are found there?" Gn 18:30
to the Lord, **s** 20 are found Gn 18:31
S 10 are found there?" Gn 18:32
S the woman is unwilling to Gn 24:5
'**S** the woman will not come back Gn 24:39
S my father touches me. Gn 27:12
"**S** we do go," Saul said to his 1Sm 9:7
S you say to me: We trust in the 2Kg 18:22
S someone says to God, "I have Jb 34:31
S you say to me: We trust in the Is 36:7
Now **s** a man is righteous and Ezk 18:5
Now **s** the man has a violent son, Ezk 18:10
Now **s** he has a son who sees all Ezk 18:14
S I bring the sword against a Ezk 33:2
"I **s** the one he forgave more." Lk 7:43
S one of you has a friend and Lk 11:5
I **s** not even the world itself Jn 21:25
drunk, as you **s**, since it's only Ac 2:15
For **s** a man comes into your Jms 2:2

SUPPOSED *(6)*
a person was **s** to live in his Nm 35:28
and I'm **s** to sit down and eat 1Sm 20:5
Am I **s** to take my bread, my 1Sm 25:11
Aren't you **s** to know what is Mc 3:1
and they **s** that Paul had brought Ac 21:29
myself **s** it was necessary to do Ac 26:9

SUPPOSING *(2)*
s that she was going to the tomb Jn 11:31
S He was the gardener, she Jn 20:15

SUPPRESS *(2)*
his⌋ actions and **s** his pride. Jb 33:17
unrighteousness **s** the truth, Rm 1:18

SUPPRESSED *(1)*
men and was not **s** by their Jb 15:18

SUPPRESSING *(1)*
or **s** a person's lawsuit—the Lm 3:36

SUPREME *(2)*
Wisdom is **s**—so get wisdom. Pr 4:7
the Emperor as the **s** authority, 1Pt 2:13

SUR *(1)*
to be at the **S** gate and a third 2Kg 11:6

SURE *(35)*
Make **s** that you don't take my Gn 24:6
s you do in front of Pharaoh Ex 4:21
Make **s** you never see my face Ex 10:28
Be **s** to present to Me at its Nm 28:2
be **s** your sin will catch up with Nm 32:23
Be **s** to remember what the LORD Dt 7:18
make **s** you return it to your Dt 22:1
but be **s** to let the mother go Dt 22:7
Be **s** to return it to him at Dt 24:13
Be **s** there is no man, woman, Dt 29:18
Be **s** there is no root among you Dt 29:18
kindness to you. Give me a **s** Jos 2:12
"I was **s** you hated her," her Jdg 15:2
Be **s** to let her gather ⌊grain⌋ Ru 2:15
she said, "as **s** as you live, my 1Sm 1:26
he says is **s** to come true. 1Sm 9:6
and that he was **s** to report to 1Sm 22:22
and I would make **s** he received 2Sm 15:4
someone is **s** to hear and say, 2Sm 17:9
Jordan⌋, but be **s** to cross over, 2Sm 17:16
know for **s** that you will 1Kg 2:37
know for **s** that you will 1Kg 2:42
to him, 'You are **s** to recover.' 2Kg 8:10
shown me that he is **s** to die." 2Kg 8:10
told me you are **s** to recover." 2Kg 8:14
answer me with Your **s** salvation. Ps 69:13
cornerstone, a **s** foundation; Is 28:16
Be **s** that all who are enraged Is 41:11
His anger is **s** to turn away from Jr 2:35
appearance is as **s** as the dawn. Hs 6:3
"Be **s** that no one finds out!" Mt 9:30
I am **s** of this, that He who Php 1:6
Some, to be **s**, preach Christ out Php 1:15
like a **s** and firm anchor of the Heb 6:19
is how we are **s** that we have 1Jn 2:3

SURELY *(68)*
(See pp. xi-xii.)

SURFACE *(44)*
covered the **s** of the watery Gn 1:2
over the **s** of the waters. Gn 1:2
plant on the **s** of the entire Gn 1:29
water the entire **s** of the land. Gn 2:6
floated on the **s** of the water. Gn 7:18
that was on the **s** of the ground, Gn 7:23
on the earth's **s** had gone down, Gn 8:8
water covered the **s** of the whole Gn 8:9
on the earth's **s** had gone down. Gn 8:11
and saw that the **s** of the ground Gn 8:13
will cover the **s** of the land so Ex 10:5
They covered the **s** of the whole Ex 10:15
the desert **s** were fine flakes, Ex 16:14
powder⌋ over the **s** of the water Ex 32:20
to be beneath the **s** of the wall, Lv 14:37
they cover the **s** of the land and Nm 22:5
they cover the **s** of the land. Nm 22:11
floor to the **s** of the ceiling he 1Kg 6:15
floor to the **s** of the ceiling, 1Kg 6:16
above the rounded **s** next to the 1Kg 7:20
rain on the **s** of the land.' " 1Kg 17:14
send rain on the **s** of the land." 1Kg 18:1
manure on the **s** of the field 2Kg 9:37
its inner **s** with pure gold. 2Ch 3:4
float on the **s** of the water. Jb 24:18
horizon on the **s** of the waters Jb 26:10
but below the **s** the earth is Jb 28:5
them over the **s** of the inhabited Jb 37:12
and the **s** of the watery depths Jb 38:30
horizon on the **s** of the ocean, Pr 8:27
bread on the **s** of the waters, Ec 11:1
land or fill the **s** of the earth Is 14:21
will twist its **s** and scatter its Is 24:1
When he has leveled its **s**, Is 28:25
manure on the **s** of the soil. Jr 8:2
manure on the **s** of the field, Jr 9:22
manure on the **s** of the ground. Jr 25:33
of them on the **s** of the valley, Ezk 37:2
remain on the **s** of the ground, Ezk 39:14
and a paved **s** laid out all Ezk 40:17
opposite the paved **s** belonging Ezk 42:3
west across the **s** of the entire Dn 8:5
like foam on the **s** of the water. Hs 10:7
came up over the **s** of the earth Rv 20:9

SURFACES *(1)*
saws on the inner and outer **s**, 1Kg 7:9

SURGE *(4)*
its waves **s**, You still them. Ps 89:9
In a **s** of anger I hid My face Is 54:8
The waves **s**, but they cannot Jr 5:22
it will **s** and then subside like Am 8:8

SURGED *(4)*
The waters **s** and increased Gn 7:18
Then the waters **s** even higher on Gn 7:19
the waters **s** ⌊above them⌋ more Gn 7:20
the waters **s** on the earth 150 Gn 7:24

SURGES *(1)*
if the Jordan **s** up to his mouth. Jb 40:23

SURGING *(2)*
and a path through **s** waters, Is 43:16
the doubter is like the **s** sea, Jms 1:6

SURPASS *(2)*
capable, but you **s** them all!" Pr 31:29
Whom do you **s** in loveliness? Ezk 32:19

SURPASSED *(6)*
they have not **s** the years of my Gn 47:9
King Solomon **s** all the kings of 1Kg 10:23
King Solomon **s** all the kings of 2Ch 9:22
became great and **s** all who were Ec 2:9
One coming after me has **s** me, Jn 1:15
me comes a man who has **s** me, Jn 1:30

SURPASSES *(4)*
your righteousness **s** that of the Mt 5:20
because of the glory that **s** it. 2Co 3:10
Messiah's love that **s** knowledge, Eph 3:19
of God, which **s** every thought, Php 4:7

SURPASSING *(2)*
because of the **s** grace of God 2Co 9:14
view of the **s** value of knowing Php 3:8

SURPLUS *(5)*
who gathered a lot had no **s**, Ex 16:18
they leave their **s** to their Ps 17:14
they all gave out of their **s**, Mk 12:44
put in gifts out of their **s**, Lk 21:4
time your **s** is ⌊available⌋ 2Co 8:14

SURPRISE *(3)*
So Joshua caught them by **s**, Jos 10:9
to their **s**, the household 1Sm 19:16
Let death take them by **s**; Ps 55:15

SURPRISED *(6)*
window and was **s** to see Isaac Gn 26:8
military force **s** them at the Jos 11:7
Pilate was **s** that He was already Mk 15:44
they are **s** that you don't plunge 1Pt 4:4
test you, don't be **s** by it, as 1Pt 4:12
Do not be **s**, brothers, if the 1Jn 3:13

SURRENDER *(9)*
one saves us, we will **s** to you." 1Sm 11:3
they wouldn't **s**, he attacked ⌊it 2Kg 15:16
'Make peace with me and **s** to me. 2Kg 18:31
Make peace with me and **s** to me; Is 36:16
'If indeed you **s** to the Jr 38:17
if you do not **s** to the officials Jr 38:18
if you refuse to **s**, this is the Jr 38:21
has thrown up her hands ⌊in **s**⌋; Jr 50:15
How can I **s** you, Israel? Hs 11:8

SURRENDERED *(3)*
and He **s** them to the power of 2Kg 13:3
and his officials, **s** to the king 2Kg 24:12
He **s** His people to the sword Ps 78:62

SURRENDERS *(2)*
goes out and **s** to the Chaldeans Jr 21:9
but whoever **s** to the Chaldeans Jr 38:2

SURROUND *(24)*
they will **s** us and wipe out our Jos 7:9
must completely **s** the king with 2Kg 11:8
cities and **s** them with walls 2Ch 14:7
must completely **s** the king with 2Ch 23:7
His archers **s** me. He pierces my Jb 16:13
Surely mockers **s** me and my eyes Jb 17:2
snares **s** you, and sudden Jb 22:10
the willows by the brook **s** him. Jb 40:22
You **s** him with favor like a Ps 5:12
my deadly enemies who **s** me. Ps 17:9
me; now they **s** me. They are Ps 17:11
Many bulls **s** me; strong ones of Ps 22:12
You **s** me with joyful shouts of Ps 32:7
They **s** me like water all day Ps 88:17
awe-inspiring than all who **s** Him. Ps 89:7
Clouds and thick darkness **s** Him; Ps 97:2
They **s** me with hateful words and Ps 109:3
Jerusalem—the mountains **s** her. Ps 125:2
for the heads of those who **s** me, Ps 140:9
than the countries that **s** her. Ezk 5:6
attendants who **s** him and all his Ezk 12:14
An enemy will **s** the land; Am 3:11
for the peoples who **s** the city. Zch 12:2
against you, **s** you, and hem you Lk 19:43

SURROUNDED *(38)*
whole population, **s** the house. Gn 19:4
and the mountain ⌊**s** by⌋ smoke. Ex 20:18
s with gold filigree settings. Ex 28:11
the onyx stones **s** with gold Ex 39:6
They were **s** with gold filigree Ex 39:13
because it is **s** by their Lv 16:16
He **s** him, cared for him, and Dt 32:10
they **s** the place and waited in Jdg 16:2
men of the city **s** the house and Jdg 19:22
up on me and **s** the house at Jdg 20:5
They **s** the Benjaminites, pursued Jdg 20:43
Joab's armor-bearers **s** Absalom, 2Sm 18:15
men with slings **s** ⌊the city⌋ 2Kg 3:25
went by night and **s** the city. 2Kg 6:14
Edomites who had **s** him and the 2Kg 8:21
though the Chaldeans **s** the city. 2Kg 25:4
of the lands that **s** Judah, 2Ch 17:10
Edomites who had **s** him and the 2Ch 21:9
s by those terrifying teeth? Jb 41:14
For dogs have **s** me; Ps 22:16
without number have **s** me; Ps 40:12
All the nations **s** me; Ps 118:10
They **s** me, yes, they surrounded Ps 118:11
surrounded me, yes, they **s** me; Ps 118:11
They **s** me like bees; Ps 118:12
came against it, **s** it, and built Ec 9:14
royal litter **s** by 60 warriors Sg 3:7
is a mound of wheat **s** by lilies. Sg 7:2
It **s** him with fire, but he did Is 42:25
They have her **s** like those who Jr 4:17
though the Chaldeans **s** the city. Jr 52:7
in a scrubland, **s** by pastures. Mc 7:14
you see Jerusalem **s** by armies, Lk 21:20
Then the Jews **s** Him and asked, Jn 10:24
After the disciples **s** him, Ac 14:20
like an emerald **s** the throne. Rv 4:3
from heaven, **s** by a cloud, with Rv 10:1
the earth and **s** the encampment Rv 20:9

SURROUNDING *(78)*
and for the **s** courtyard were Ex 38:20
the bases for the **s** courtyard, Ex 38:31
tent pegs for the **s** courtyard. Ex 38:31
Assemble the **s** courtyard and Ex 40:8
Moses set up the **s** courtyard for Ex 40:33
the fat **s** the entrails, all the Lv 3:3
remove the fat **s** the entrails, Lv 3:9
the fat **s** the entrails, all the Lv 3:14
the fat **s** the entrails; Lv 4:8
tail, the fat **s** the entrails, Lv 7:3
the ⌊fat⌋ **s** ⌊the entrails⌋, Lv 9:19
posts of the **s** courtyard with Nm 3:37
posts of the **s** courtyard with Nm 4:32
with the territories **s** them. Nm 32:33
according to its **s** borders. Jos 18:20
the villages **s** these cities as Jos 19:8
with its **s** pasturelands in the Jos 21:11
had its own **s** pasturelands; Jos 21:42
from the **s** peoples and bowed Jdg 2:12
even rescued their **s** territories 1Sm 7:14
and the wall **s** Jerusalem. 1Kg 3:1
had peace on all his **s** borders. 1Kg 4:24
extended to all the **s** nations. 1Kg 4:31
carved all the **s** temple walls 1Kg 6:29
horses and chariots **s** the city. 2Kg 6:15
weapons in hand **s** the king— 2Kg 11:11
following the **s** nations the LORD 2Kg 17:15
and in the areas **s** Jerusalem. 2Kg 23:5
tore down the walls **s** Jerusalem. 2Kg 25:10
and all their **s** villages as far 1Ch 4:33
of Judah and its **s** pasturelands, 1Ch 6:55
terraces to the **s** parts, 1Ch 11:8
him rest from all his **s** enemies, 1Ch 22:9
house, all the **s** chambers, 1Ch 28:12
the kingdoms of the ⌊**s**⌋ lands. 1Ch 29:30
completely **s** the reservoir. 2Ch 4:3
weapons in hand **s** the king— 2Ch 23:10
on their **s** mountain shrines. 2Ch 34:6
they feared the **s** peoples. Ezr 3:3
from the **s** peoples whose Ezr 9:1
become mixed with the **s** peoples. Ezr 9:2
priests, to the **s** kings, and to Ezr 9:7
s peoples have filled it from Ezr 9:11
women from the **s** peoples, Ezr 10:2
from the **s** peoples and ⌊your⌋ Ezr 10:11
priests from the **s** area made Neh 3:22
guests from the **s** nations at my Neh 5:17
all the **s** nations were Neh 6:16
kings and the **s** peoples over to Neh 9:24
them over to the **s** peoples. Neh 9:30
from the **s** peoples to ⌊obey⌋ Neh 10:28
marriage to the **s** peoples and Neh 10:30
When the **s** peoples bring Neh 10:31
will have faithful love **s** him. Ps 32:10
Rule over Your **s** enemies. Ps 110:2
attack all her **s** walls and all Jr 1:15
and against all these **s** nations, Jr 25:9
in the areas **s** Jerusalem, Jr 32:44
the cities **s** Jerusalem and Jr 33:13
Jerusalem and all its **s** cities: Jr 34:1
for him, all you **s** ⌊nations⌋, Jr 48:17
down all the walls **s** Jerusalem. Jr 52:14
nations from the **s** provinces set Ezk 19:8
there was a wall **s** the outside Ezk 40:5
The side rooms **s** ⌊the temple⌋ Ezk 41:7
the structure **s** the temple ⌊went Ezk 41:7
had a raised platform **s** ⌊it⌋; Ezk 41:8
its **s** territory on top of the Ezk 43:12
Come quickly, all you **s** nations; Jl 3:11
down to judge all the **s** nations. Jl 3:12
along the Nile with water **s** her, Nah 3:8
along with its **s** cities, and Zch 7:7
of all the **s** nations will be Zch 14:14
can go into the **s** countryside Mk 6:36
they can go into the **s** villages Lk 9:12
from the towns **s** Jerusalem, Ac 5:16
Derbe, and to the **s** countryside. Ac 14:6
a large cloud of witnesses **s** us, Heb 12:1

SURROUNDS *(8)*
courtyard that **s** the tabernacle Nm 3:26
courtyard that **s** the tabernacle Nm 4:26
awesome majesty **s** Him. Jb 37:22
The iniquity of my foes **s** me. Ps 49:5
Your faithfulness **s** You. Ps 89:8
And the LORD **s** His people, Ps 125:2
for great massacre—it **s** them! Ezk 21:14
Ephraim **s** me with lies, the Hs 11:12

SURVEY *(2)*
They are to go and **s** the land, Jos 18:4
saying, "Go and **s** the land, Jos 18:8

SURVEYED *(1)*
When they **s** the lands of Jazer Nm 32:1

SURVEYS *(1)*
He **s** everything that is haughty; Jb 41:34

SURVIVAL *(3)*
result—the **s** of many people. Gn 50:20
and day, never certain of **s**. Dt 28:66
For this has to do with your **s**, Ac 27:34

SURVIVE *(24)*
isn't it?—so that I can **s**." Gn 19:20
those of you who **s** in the lands Lv 26:36
Those who **s** in the lands of your Lv 26:39
living thing **s** among the cities Dt 20:16
of his men ⌊**s**⌋ until morning. 1Sm 25:22
he had fallen he couldn't **s**. 2Sm 1:10
and have allowed us to **s**— Ezr 9:13
for we **s** as a remnant today. Ezr 9:15
Those who **s** him will be buried Jb 27:15
wicked will not **s** the judgment, Ps 1:5
but who can **s** a broken spirit? Pr 18:14
the remnant of His people who **s**. Is 11:11
people who will **s** from Assyria, Is 11:16
been burned, and only a few **s**. Is 24:6
in this city who **s** the plague, Jr 21:7
you and your household will **s**. Jr 38:17
those who **s** will be scattered Ezk 17:21
of them! How then can we **s**? Ezk 33:10
won't be able to **s** by his Ezk 33:12
How will Jacob **s** since he is so Am 7:2
How will Jacob **s** since he is so Am 7:5
were limited, no one would **s**. Mt 24:22
those days, no one would **s**. Mk 13:20
outside so they wouldn't **s**. Ac 7:19

SURVIVED *(5)*
into the sea. None of them **s**. Ex 14:28
of Jerubbaal, **s**, because he hid Jdg 9:5
not even one of them **s**!" 2Sm 13:30
the people who **s** the sword. Jr 31:2
anger no one escaped or **s**. Lm 2:22

SURVIVES *(1)*
work that he has built **s**, 1Co 3:14

SURVIVING *(5)*
Aaron's **s** sons, and asked Lv 10:16
a prayer for the **s** remnant.'" 2Kg 19:4
The **s** remnant of the house of 2Kg 19:30
a prayer for the **s** remnant.'" Is 37:4
The **s** remnant of the house of Is 37:31

SURVIVOR *(8)*
him until there was no **s** left. Dt 3:3
them down until no **s** or fugitive Jos 8:22
Let every **s**, wherever he lives, Ezr 1:4
no **s** where he used to live. Jb 18:19
for every **s** in the land will eat Is 7:22
They will have no **s** or escapee Jr 42:17
no fugitive or **s** to return to Jr 44:14
Therefore no **s** will remain of Ob 18

SURVIVORS *(38)*
One of the **s** came and told Abram Gn 14:13
he will destroy the city's **s**. Nm 24:19
and children. We left no **s**. Dt 2:34
reduced to a few **s** among the Dt 4:27
until all the **s** and those hiding Dt 7:20

although a few s ran away to the Jos 10:20
everyone in it, leaving no s. Jos 10:28
the sword, and left no s in it. Jos 10:30
his people, leaving no s in it. Jos 10:33
had done at Eglon, he left no s. Jos 10:37
everyone in it, leaving no s. Jos 10:39
all their kings, leaving no s. Jos 10:40
struck them down, leaving no s. Jos 11:8
The s came down to the nobles; Jdg 5:13
we do about wives for the s? Jdg 21:7
be heirs for the s of Benjamin, Jdg 21:17
There were s, but they were so 1Sm 11:11
and priests—leaving him no s. 2Kg 10:11
and s from Mount Zion. 2Kg 19:31
fell until they had no s, 2Ch 14:13
would destroy us, leaving no s? Ezr 9:14
to me, "The s in the province Neh 1:3
Hosts had not left us a few s, Is 1:9
pride and glory of Israel's s. Is 4:2
of Israel and the s of the house Is 10:20
and for the s in the land. Is 15:9
and s from Mount Zion. Is 37:32
and I will send s from them to Is 66:19
life by all the s of this evil Jr 8:3
destroy her. Leave her no s. Jr 50:26
scatter all your s to every Ezk 5:10
Then your s will remember Me Ezk 6:9
The s among them will escape and Ezk 7:16
there will be s left in it, Ezk 14:22
among the s the LORD calls. Jl 2:32
not hand over their s in the day Ob 14
Then all the s from the nations Zch 14:16
The s were terrified and gave Rv 11:13

SUSA *(22)*
Erech, Babylon, S (that is, the Ezr 4:9
I was in the fortress city of S, Neh 1:1
throne in the fortress at S. Est 1:2
present in the fortress of S. Est 1:5
the harem at the fortress of S. Est 2:3
the fortress of S named Mordecai Est 2:5
the fortress of S under Hegai's Est 2:8
was issued in the fortress of S. Est 3:15
the city of S was in confusion Est 3:15
decree issued in S ordering Est 4:8
be found in S and fast for me Est 4:16
issued in the fortress of S. Est 8:14
The city of S shouted and Est 8:15
fortress of S the Jews killed Est 9:6
the fortress of S was reported Est 9:11
the fortress of S the Jews have Est 9:12
Jews who are in S also have Est 9:13
so a law was announced in S, Est 9:14
The Jews in S assembled again on Est 9:15
of Adar and killed 300 men in S, Est 9:15
But the Jews in S had assembled Est 9:18
I was in the fortress city of S, Dn 8:2

SUSANNA *(1)*
steward; S; and many others Lk 8:3

SUSI *(1)*
Gaddi son of S from the tribe of Nm 13:11

SUSPENDED *(2)*
going, so he was s in midair. 2Sm 18:9
S far away from people, the Jb 28:4

SUSPENSE *(1)*
are You going to keep us in s? Jn 10:24

SUSPICIONS *(1)*
quarreling, slanders, evil s, 1Tm 6:4

SUSTAIN *(16)*
boy up, and s him, for I will Gn 21:18
There I will s you, for there Gn 45:11
and cannot s himself among you, Lv 25:35
Didn't He make you and s you? Dt 32:6
your life and s you in your old Ru 4:15
sanctuary and s you from Zion. Ps 20:2
The LORD will s him on his Ps 41:3
S me as You promised, and I will Ps 119:116
S me so that I can be safe and Ps 119:117
S me with raisins; refresh me Sg 2:5
establish and s it with justice Is 9:7
to know how to s the weary with Is 50:4
and wine vat will not s them, Hs 9:2
He will not s the healthy, Zch 11:16
from Crete and s this damage Ac 27:21
do brag—you do not s the root, Rm 11:18

SUSTAINED *(2)*
have s him with grain and new Gn 27:37
who have been s from the womb, Is 46:3

SUSTAINER *(1)*
the Lord is the s of my life. Ps 54:4

SUSTAINS *(4)*
again because the LORD s me. Ps 3:5
and bread that s man's heart. Ps 104:15
the root, but the root s you. Rm 11:18
and He s all things by His Heb 1:3

SWALLOW *(11)*
The earth may s us too!" Nm 16:34
me alone until I s my saliva? Jb 7:19
over me or the deep s me up; Ps 69:15
a home, and a s, a nest for Ps 84:3
Let's s them alive, like Sheol, Pr 1:12
sparrow or a fluttering s, Pr 26:2
sees it will s it while it is Is 28:4
I chirp like a s ⌊or⌋ a crane; Is 38:14
The turtledove, s, and crane are Jr 8:7
did, foreigners would s it up. Hs 8:7
a great fish to s Jonah, Jnh 1:17

SWALLOWED *(24)*
heads of grain s up the seven Gn 41:7
heads of grain s the seven full Gn 41:24
Aaron's staff s their staffs. Ex 7:12
hand, and the earth s them. Ex 15:12
its mouth and s them and their Nm 16:32
its mouth and s them with Korah, Nm 26:10
opened its mouth and s them, Dt 11:6
them say, "We have s him up!" Ps 35:25
earth opened up and s Dathan; Ps 106:17
they would have s us alive in Ps 124:3
and those they mislead are s up. Is 9:16
and those who s you up will be Is 49:19
he has s me like a sea monster; Jr 51:34
I will make him vomit what he s. Jr 51:44
the Lord has s up all the Lm 2:2
He has s up Israel. Lm 2:5
He s up all its palaces and Lm 2:5
saying, "We have s ⌊her⌋ up. Lm 2:16
Israel is s up! Now they are Hs 8:8
My soul is s up in sorrow— Mt 26:38
My soul is s up in sorrow— Mk 14:34
Death has been s up in victory. 1Co 15:54
mortality may be s up by life. 2Co 5:4
mouth and s up the river that Rv 12:16

SWALLOWS *(4)*
its mouth and s them along with Nm 16:30
s wealth but must vomit it up; Jb 20:15
and a wicked mouth s iniquity. Pr 19:28
one who is wicked s up one who Hab 1:13

SWAMPED *(3)*
boat was being s by the waves. Mt 8:24
the boat was already being s. Mk 4:37
they were being s and were in Lk 8:23

SWAMPLAND *(1)*
will make her a s and a region Is 14:23

SWAMPS *(1)*
Yet its s and marshes will not Ezk 47:11

SWARM *(15)*
Let the water s with living Gn 1:20
creatures that s on the earth, Gn 7:21
The Nile will s with frogs; Ex 8:3
houses will s with flies, Ex 8:21
creatures that s on the ground Lv 11:29
creatures that s on the earth Lv 11:41
creatures that s on the earth, Lv 11:42
creatures that s on the ground, Lv 11:46
and chased you like a s of bees. Dt 1:44
tents like a great s of locusts. Jdg 6:5
the valley like a s of locusts, Jdg 7:12
and there was a s of bees with Jdg 14:8
people will s over it like an Is 33:4
up horses like a s of locusts. Jr 51:27
He was forming a s of locusts at Am 7:1

SWARMING *(10)*
or an unclean s creature— Lv 5:2
among all the s things and Lv 11:10
you among all the s creatures. Lv 11:31
yourselves by any s creature Lv 11:44
touches any s creature that Lv 22:5
left, the s locust has eaten; Jl 1:4
what the s locust has left, Jl 1:4
the years that the s locust ate, Jl 2:25
multiply like the s locust! Nah 3:15
officials are like the s locust, Nah 3:17

SWARMS *(9)*
that moves and s in the water, Gn 1:21
I will send s of flies against Ex 8:21
Thick s of flies went into Ex 8:24
because of the s of flies. Ex 8:24
and tomorrow the s of flies will Ex 8:29
He removed the s of flies from Ex 8:31
by any creature that s; Lv 11:43
He sent among them s of flies, Ps 78:45
creature that s will live Ezk 47:9

SWAY *(1)*
is under the s of the evil one. 1Jn 5:19

SWAYING *(2)*
A reed s in the wind? Mt 11:7
A reed s in the wind? Lk 7:24

SWAYS *(1)*
a drunkard and s like a hut. Is 24:20

SWEAR *(53)*
Now s to me here by God that you Gn 21:23
And Abraham said, "I s ⌊it⌋." Gn 21:24
I will have you s by the LORD, Gn 24:3
Jacob said, "S to me first." Gn 25:33
I s that I will not do this. Gn 44:17
And Jacob said, "S to me." Gn 47:31
the Israelites s a solemn oath, Ex 13:19
You must not s falsely by My Lv 19:12
I s that none of you will enter Nm 14:30
I s that I will do this to the Nm 14:35
Now please s to me by the LORD Jos 2:12
from this oath you made us s, Jos 2:17
from the oath you made us s." Jos 2:20
I s that I won't rest until I Jdg 15:7
S to me that you yourselves Jdg 15:12
make the troops s the oath. 1Sm 14:27
made the troops solemnly s, 1Sm 14:28
I s that women are being kept 1Sm 21:5
his men, "I s before the LORD: 1Sm 24:6
Therefore s to me by the LORD 1Sm 24:21
S to me by God that you won't 1Sm 30:15
for I s by the LORD that if you 2Sm 19:7
did you not s to your servant: 1Kg 1:13
Solomon first s to me that he 1Kg 1:51
s Adonijah will be put to death 1Kg 2:24
Didn't I make you s by the LORD 1Kg 2:42
kingdom or nation s they had not 1Kg 18:10
must I make you s not to tell me 1Kg 22:16
must I make you s not to tell me 2Ch 18:15
who had made him s allegiance by 2Ch 36:13
all who s by Him will boast, Ps 63:11
Your enemies s ⌊by You⌋ falsely. Ps 139:20
of Canaan and s loyalty to the Is 19:18
every tongue will s allegiance. Is 45:23
s by the name of the LORD and Is 48:1
in the land will s by the God of Is 65:16
if you s, As the LORD lives, in Jr 4:2
commit adultery, s falsely, burn Jr 7:9
My people—to s by My name, 'As Jr 12:16
taught My people to s by Baal— Jr 12:16
words, then I s by Myself"— Jr 22:5
I s that the nations all around Ezk 36:7
I s in My zeal and fiery rage: Ezk 38:19
Beth-aven, and do not s an oath: Hs 4:15
Those who s by the guilt of Am 8:14
against those who s falsely; Mal 3:5
should you s by your head, Mt 5:36
to curse and to s with an oath, Mt 26:74
to curse and to s with an oath, Mk 14:71
whom did He "s that they would Heb 3:18
since He had no one greater to s Heb 6:13
For men s by something greater Heb 6:16
brothers, do not s, either by Jms 5:12

SWEARING *(2)*
cursing and s when He makes your Nm 5:21
LORD lives," they are s falsely. Jr 5:2

SWEARS *(6)*
Or ⌊if⌋ someone s rashly to do Lv 5:4
or s falsely about any of the Lv 6:3
to the LORD or s an oath to put Nm 30:2
and whoever s in the land will Is 65:16
everyone who s ⌊falsely⌋ will Zch 5:3
of the one who s falsely by My Zch 5:4

SWEAT *(3)*
eat bread by the s of your brow Gn 3:19

on ⌊anything that makes them⌋ s. Ezk 44:18
and His s became like drops of Lk 22:44

SWEEP *(23)*
Will You really s away the Gn 18:23
You really s it away instead Gn 18:24
or I'll s you away with them." 1Sm 15:6
I will s away the house of 1Kg 14:10
I will s away Baasha and his 1Kg 16:3
on you and will s away your 1Kg 21:21
They s by like boats made of Jb 9:26
terrors of death s over me. Ps 55:4
burning—He will s them away. Ps 58:9
the floodwaters s over me or the Ps 69:15
rivers cannot s it away. Sg 8:7
over it, and s through, reaching Is 8:8
and I will s her away with a Is 14:23
Hail will s away the false Is 28:17
It is I who s away your Is 43:25
bloodshed will s through you, Ezk 5:17
countries and s through them Dn 11:40
Then they s by like the wind and Hab 1:11
completely s away everything Zph 1:2
I will s away man and animal; Zph 1:3
I will s away the birds of the Zph 1:3
not light a lamp, s the house, Lk 15:8
to s her away in a torrent. Rv 12:15

SWEEPING *(1)*
will advance, s through like Dn 11:10

SWEEPS *(7)*
Jeroboam as one s away dung 1Kg 14:10
like chaff a storm s away? Jb 21:18
storm wind s him away at night. Jb 27:20
waters, and a flood s over me. Ps 69:2
Your wrath s over me; Ps 88:16
the wicked s them away because Pr 21:7
a downpour of water s by. Hab 3:10

SWEET *(27)*
of the strong came something s. Jdg 14:14
Him for burning s incense before 2Ch 2:4
drink what is s, and send Neh 8:10
Though evil tastes s in his Jb 20:12
dirt on his grave is s to him. Jb 21:33
How s Your word is to my taste— Ps 119:103
Stolen water is s, and bread Pr 9:17
fulfilled is s to the taste, Pr 13:19
s to the taste and health to the Pr 16:24
gained by fraud is s to a man, Pr 20:17
honeycomb is s to your palate; Pr 24:13
person, any bitter thing is s. Pr 27:7
The sleep of the worker is s, Ec 5:12
Light is s, and it is pleasing Ec 11:7
and his fruit is s to my taste. Sg 2:3
your voice is s, and your face Sg 2:14
bitter for s and sweet for Is 5:20
for sweet and s for bitter. Is 5:20
their own blood as with s wine. Is 49:26
from Sheba or s cane from a Jr 6:20
and it was as s as honey in my Ezk 3:3
because of the s wine, for it Jl 1:5
mountains will drip with s wine, Jl 3:18
mountains will drip with s wine, Am 9:13
spring pour out s and bitter Jms 3:11
it will be as s as honey in your Rv 10:9
was as s as honey in my mouth, Rv 10:10

SWEETER *(3)*
What is s than honey? Jdg 14:18
and s than honey—than honey Ps 19:10
⌊s⌋ than honey to my mouth. Ps 119:103

SWEETNESS *(4)*
I stop giving my s and my good Jdg 9:11
and the s of a friend is better Pr 27:9
Your lips drip ⌊s like⌋ the Sg 4:11
His mouth is s. He is absolutely Sg 5:16

SWELL *(6)*
thigh shrivel and your belly s. Nm 5:21
belly to s and ⌊your⌋ thigh Nm 5:22
her belly will s, and her thigh Nm 5:27
feet did not s these 40 years. Dt 8:4
out, and their feet did not s. Neh 9:21
that he would s up or suddenly Ac 28:6

SWELLING *(7)*
a person has a s, scab, or spot Lv 13:2
is a white s on the skin that Lv 13:10
a patch of raw flesh in the s, Lv 13:10
and a white s or a reddish-white Lv 13:19
it is the s from the burn. Lv 13:28
and if the s of the infection on Lv 13:43
and for a s, scab, or spot, Lv 14:56

SWEPT *(26)*
or you will be s away in the Gn 19:15
or you will be s away!" Gn 19:17
or you will be s away because of Nm 16:26
The river Kishon s them away, Jdg 5:21
and your king will be s away." 1Sm 12:25
days I'll be s away by Saul. 1Sm 27:1
a powerful wind s in from the Jb 1:19
after a wind has s through and Jb 37:21
clouds s onward with hail and Ps 18:12
and Your billows have s over me. Ps 42:7
to an end, s away by terrors Ps 73:19
torrent would have s over us; Ps 124:4
waters would have s over us. Ps 124:5
without justice, it is s away. Pr 13:23
have s away your transgressions Is 44:22
faithful men are s away, with no Is 57:1
the righteous one is s away from Is 57:1
and birds have been s away, Jr 12:4
your strong ones been s away? Jr 46:15
forces will be s away before him Dn 11:22
army will be s away, and many Dn 11:26
and Your billows s over me. Jnh 2:3
house⌋ vacant, s, and put in Mt 12:44
flood came and s them all away. Mt 24:39
the house⌋ s and put in order Lk 11:25
His tail s away a third of the Rv 12:4

SWERVE *(1)*
chariot wheels to s and made Ex 14:25

SWIFT *(11)*
and they were as s as gazelles 1Ch 12:8
released the s donkey from its Jb 39:5
that the race is not to the s, Ec 9:11
Go, s messengers, to a nation Is 18:2
LORD rides on a s cloud and is Is 19:1
⌊You are⌋ a s young camel Jr 2:23
The s cannot flee, and the Jr 46:6
will fail the s, the strong one Am 2:14
one who is⌋ s of foot will not Am 2:15
Their feet are s to shed blood; Rm 3:15
and will bring s destruction on 2Pt 2:1

SWIFTER *(4)*
were s than eagles, stronger 2Sm 1:23
His horses are s than eagles. Jr 4:13
who chased us were s than eagles Lm 4:19
Their horses are s than leopards Hab 1:8

SWIFTLY *(7)*
and He will s destroy you. Dt 7:4
them out and destroy them s, Dt 9:3
days pass more s than a weaver's Jb 7:6
the earth; His word runs s. Ps 147:15
how quickly and s they come! Is 5:26
his disaster is rushing s. Jr 48:16
you that He will s grant them Lk 18:8

SWIM *(4)*
spreads out ⌊his arms⌋ to s. Is 25:11
it was deep enough to s in, Ezk 47:5
no one could s off and escape. Ac 27:42
those who could s to jump Ac 27:43

SWIMMER *(1)*
as a s spreads out ⌊his arms⌋ to Is 25:11

SWINDLER *(1)*
or a reviler, a drunkard or a s. 1Co 5:11

SWINDLERS *(2)*
the greedy and s, or to 1Co 5:10
or s will inherit God's kingdom. 1Co 6:10

SWINE'S *(2)*
places, eating s flesh, and Is 65:4
offering, one offers s blood; Is 66:3

SWING *(2)*
the miners s back and forth. Jb 28:4
S the sickle because the harvest Jl 3:13

SWINGING *(1)*
of the doors had two s panels. Ezk 41:24

SWINGS *(1)*
and his hand s the ax to chop Dt 19:5

SWIRL *(1)*
They s about, turning round and Jb 37:12

SWOLLEN *(2)*
My eyes are s from grief; Ps 6:7
man whose body was s with fluid. Lk 14:2

SWOOP *(3)*
to s down on you like an eagle, Dt 28:49
But they will s down on the Is 11:14
He will s down like an eagle and Jr 48:40

SWOOPED *(1)*
the Sabeans s down and took them Jb 1:15

SWOOPING *(3)*
like an eagle s down on ⌊its⌋ Jb 9:26
then s down and spreading its Jr 49:22
fly like an eagle, s to devour. Hab 1:8

SWORD *(402)*
whirling s to guard the way to Gn 3:24
live by your s, and you will Gn 27:40
the Amorites with my s and bow." Gn 48:22
may strike us with plague or s." Ex 5:3
a s in their hand to kill us! Ex 5:21
I will draw my s; my hand will Ex 15:9
Amalek and his army with the s. Ex 17:13
delivered me from Pharaoh's s" Ex 18:4
and I will kill you with the s; Ex 22:24
man fasten his s to his side; Ex 32:27
and no s will pass through your Lv 26:6
will fall before you by the s. Lv 26:7
will fall before you by the s. Lv 26:8
I will bring a s against you to Lv 26:25
I will draw a s ⌊to chase⌋ after Lv 26:33
will flee as one flees from a s, Lv 26:36
fleeing⌋ from a s though no one Lv 26:37
into this land to die by the s? Nm 14:3
and you will fall by the s. Nm 14:43
killed by the s or has died, Nm 19:16
and confront you with the s." Nm 20:18
him with the s and took Nm 21:24
path with a drawn s in His hand, Nm 22:23
I had a s in my hand, I'd kill Nm 22:29
path with a drawn s in His hand. Nm 22:31
Balaam son of Beor with the s. Nm 31:8
of that city with the s. Dt 13:15
as its livestock with the s. Dt 13:15
down all its males with the s. Dt 20:13
the s will take their children, Dt 32:25
when I sharpen My flashing s, Dt 32:41
blood while My s devours flesh— Dt 32:42
protects you, the s you boast Dt 33:29
him with a drawn s in His hand. Jos 5:13
in the city with the s— Jos 6:21
Hold out the s in your hand Jos 8:18
Joshua held out his s toward it. Jos 8:18
one of them had fallen by the s, Jos 8:24
and struck it down with the s. Jos 8:24
that was holding the s until all Jos 8:26
Israelites killed with the s. Jos 10:11
and struck it down with the s, Jos 10:28
putting everyone in it to the s, Jos 10:30
putting everyone in it to the s, Jos 10:32
putting everyone in it to the s. Jos 10:35
and everyone in it with the s. Jos 10:37
down with the s and completely Jos 10:39
struck down its king with the s, Jos 11:10
down everyone in it with the s, Jos 11:11
and struck them down with the s. Jos 11:12
person with the s until they had Jos 11:14
Balaam son of Beor, with the s. Jos 13:22
and struck it down with the s. Jos 19:47
It was not by your s or bow. Jos 24:12
the city to the s and set it on Jdg 1:8
the town to the s but released Jdg 1:25
a double-edged s 18 inches long. Jdg 3:16
took the s from his right thigh, Jdg 3:21
withdraw the s from his belly. Jdg 3:22
with the s before Barak. Jdg 4:15
army of Sisera fell by the s; Jdg 4:16
less than the s of Gideon son Jdg 7:14
'The s of the LORD and of Gideon! Jdg 7:18
The s of the LORD and of Gideon! Jdg 7:20
The youth did not draw his s, Jdg 8:20
him, "Draw your s and kill me, Jdg 9:54
and put the whole city to the s. Jdg 20:37
of Jabesh-gilead with the s, Jdg 21:10
of battle not a s or spear could 1Sm 13:22
rest of the people with the s. 1Sm 15:8
As your s has made women 1Sm 15:33
and a bronze s was slung between 1Sm 17:6
David strapped his s on over the 1Sm 17:39
dagger, spear, and s, but I come 1Sm 17:45
it is not by s or by spear that 1Sm 17:47
Even though David had no s, 1Sm 17:50
He grabbed the Philistine's s, 1Sm 17:51

tunic, his s, his bow, and his 1Sm 18:4
you have a spear or s on hand? 1Sm 21:8
even bring my s or my weapons 1Sm 21:8
The s of Goliath the Philistine, 1Sm 21:9
also gave him the s of Goliath 1Sm 22:10
him bread and a s and inquired 1Sm 22:13
priests, with the s—both men 1Sm 22:19
Draw your s and run me through 1Sm 31:4
Saul took his s and fell on it. 1Sm 31:4
fell on his own s and died with 1Sm 31:5
for those who died by the s— 2Sm 1:12
Saul's s never returned 2Sm 1:22
and ⌊thrust⌋ his s into his 2Sm 2:16
Must the s devour forever? 2Sm 2:26
who falls by the s or starves." 2Sm 3:29
you because the s devours all 2Sm 11:25
Hittite with the s and took his 2Sm 12:9
him with the Ammonite's s. 2Sm 12:9
s will never leave your house 2Sm 12:10
city with the edge of the s." 2Sm 15:14
claimed more people than the s. 2Sm 18:8
waist with a s in its sheath. 2Sm 20:8
he approached, ⌊the s⌋ fell out. 2Sm 20:8
against the s in Joab's hand, 2Sm 20:10
was tired and stuck to his s. 2Sm 23:10
kill his servant with the s.'" 1Kg 1:51
never kill you with the s.' 1Kg 2:8
With his s, Joab murdered Abner 1Kg 2:32
king continued, "Bring me a s." 1Kg 3:24
they brought the s to the king. 1Kg 3:24
all the prophets with the s. 1Kg 19:1
killed Your prophets with the s. 1Kg 19:10
killed Your prophets with the s. 1Kg 19:14
whoever escapes the s of Hazael, 1Kg 19:17
whoever escapes the s of Jehu. 1Kg 19:17
with your s or your bow? 2Kg 6:22
kill their young men with the s. 2Kg 8:12
struck them down with the s. 2Kg 10:25
follows her to death by the s," 2Kg 11:15
to death by the s in the king's 2Kg 11:20
cause him to fall by the s.'" 2Kg 19:7
down with the s and escaped to 2Kg 19:37
men who carried shield and s, 1Ch 5:18
Draw your s and run me through 1Ch 10:4
Saul took his s and fell on it. 1Ch 10:4
also fell on his own s and died. 1Ch 10:5
foes with the s of your enemy 1Ch 21:12
days of the s of the LORD— 1Ch 21:12
with his drawn s in his hand 1Ch 21:16
and he put his s back into its 1Ch 21:27
terrified of the s of the LORD's 1Ch 21:30
comes on us—s or judgment, 2Ch 20:9
with the s all his brothers 2Ch 21:4
follows her to death by the s," 2Ch 23:14
put Athaliah to death by the s. 2Ch 23:21
Our fathers fell by the s, 2Ch 29:9
cut him down with the s. 2Ch 32:21
men with the s in the house 2Ch 36:17
escaped from the s he deported 2Ch 36:20
kings, and to the s, captivity, Ezr 9:7
had his s strapped around Neh 4:18
put all their enemies to the s, Est 9:5
down the servants with the s, Jb 1:15
down the servants with the s, Jb 1:17
battle, from the power of the s. Jb 5:20
he is destined for the s. Jb 15:22
afraid of the s, because wrath Jb 19:29
brings⌋ punishment by the s, Jb 19:29
they are destined for the s; Jb 27:14
he does not run from the s. Jb 39:22
can draw the s against him. Jb 40:19
The s that reaches him will have Jb 41:26
repent, God will sharpen His s; Ps 7:12
With Your s, save me from the Ps 17:13
Deliver my life from the s, Ps 22:20
have drawn the s and strung the Ps 37:14
not take the land by their s— Ps 44:3
and my s does not bring me Ps 44:6
strap your s at your side. Ps 45:3
over to the power of the s; Ps 63:10
the shield, the s, and the Ps 76:3
people to the s because He was Ps 78:62
His priests fell by the s, Ps 78:64
back his sharp s and have not Ps 89:43
servant David from the deadly s. Ps 144:10
a two-edged s in their hands, Ps 149:6
as sharp as a double-edged s. Pr 5:4
rashly, like a piercing s; Pr 12:18

like a club, a s, or a sharp Pr 25:18
Each has his s at his side ⌊to Sg 3:8
you will be devoured by the s." Is 1:20
take up the s against ⌊other⌋ Is 2:4
Your men will fall by the s, Is 3:25
is caught will die by the s. Is 13:15
slain with the s and dumped Is 14:19
from the drawn s, and from the Is 21:15
Your dead did not die by the s; Is 22:2
great, and strong s, will bring Is 27:1
will fall, but not by human s; Is 31:8
a s will devour him, but not one Is 31:8
flee from the s, his young men Is 31:8
When My s has drunk its fill in Is 34:5
The LORD's s is covered with Is 34:6
cause him to fall by the s.'" Is 37:7
down with the s and escaped to Is 37:38
them⌋ like dust ⌊with⌋ his s, Is 41:2
He made my words like a sharp s; Is 49:2
and destruction, famine and s. Is 51:19
I will destine you for the s, Is 65:12
on all flesh with His fiery s, Is 66:16
Your own s has devoured your Jr 2:30
while a s is at our throats." Jr 4:10
we won't see s or famine." Jr 5:12
with the s your fortified Jr 5:17
For the enemy has a s; Jr 6:25
I will send a s after them until Jr 9:16
The young men will die by the s; Jr 11:22
the LORD has a s that devours Jr 12:12
I will finish them off by s, Jr 14:12
'You won't see s or suffer Jr 14:13
never be s or famine in this Jr 14:15
By s and famine these prophets Jr 14:15
because of the famine and the s. Jr 14:16
look—those slain by the s! Jr 14:18
those ⌊destined⌋ for the s, Jr 15:2
for the sword, to the s. Jr 15:2
the s to kill, the dogs Jr 15:3
over to the s in the presence Jr 15:9
be finished off by s and famine. Jr 16:4
struck down by the s in battle. Jr 18:21
them fall by the s before their Jr 19:7
fall by the s of their enemies Jr 20:4
Babylon and put them to the s. Jr 20:4
plague, the s, and the famine Jr 21:7
He will put them to the s; Jr 21:7
in this city will die by the s, Jr 21:9
I will send the s, famine, and Jr 24:10
because of the s I am sending Jr 25:16
a result of the s I am sending Jr 25:27
I am summoning a s against all Jr 25:29
He hands them over to the s— Jr 25:31
because of the s of the Jr 25:38
him with the s and threw his Jr 26:23
that nation I will punish by s, Jr 27:8
and your people die by the s, Jr 27:13
am about to send against them s, Jr 29:17
I will pursue them with s, Jr 29:18
the people who survived the s. Jr 31:2
a result of the s, famine, and Jr 32:24
to Babylon's king through s, Jr 32:36
the siege ramps and the s: Jr 33:4
You will not die by the s; Jr 34:4
to the s, to plague, and to Jr 34:17
in this city will die by the s, Jr 38:2
that you do not fall by the s. Jr 39:18
son of Shaphan, with the s; Jr 41:2
the s you fear will overtake Jr 42:16
for a while will die by the s, Jr 42:17
know for certain that by the s, Jr 42:22
and those ⌊destined⌋ for the s, Jr 43:11
for the sword, to the s. Jr 43:11
of Egypt will fall by the s; Jr 44:12
will die by the s and by famine. Jr 44:12
as I punished Jerusalem by s, Jr 44:13
and through s and famine we have Jr 44:18
his end by s or famine until Jr 44:27
who escape the s will return Jr 44:28
The s will devour and be Jr 46:10
the s devours all around you. Jr 46:14
away from the s that oppresses. Jr 46:16
Ah, s of the LORD! How long will Jr 47:6
the s will pursue you. Jr 48:2
withholds his s from bloodshed. Jr 48:10
I will send the s after them Jr 49:37
Because of the oppressor's s, Jr 50:16
Put them to the s; completely Jr 50:21

all her young bulls to the s; Jr 50:27
A s is over the Chaldeans— Jr 50:35
A s is against the diviners, Jr 50:36
A s is against her heroic Jr 50:36
A s is against his horses and Jr 50:37
A s is against her treasuries, Jr 50:37
You who have escaped the s, Jr 51:50
Outside, the s takes the Lm 1:20
and women have fallen by the s. Lm 2:21
slain by the s are better off Lm 4:9
because of the s in the Lm 5:9
take a sharp s, use it as you Ezk 5:1
it⌋ with the s all around the Ezk 5:2
I will draw a s ⌊to chase⌋ after Ezk 5:2
fall by the s all around you; Ezk 5:12
I will draw a s ⌊to chase⌋ after Ezk 5:12
I will bring a s against you. Ezk 5:17
about to bring a s against you, Ezk 6:3
of you who will escape the s. Ezk 6:8
will fall by the s, famine, and Ezk 6:11
who is near will fall by the s; Ezk 6:12
The s is on the outside; Ezk 7:15
in the field will die by the s, Ezk 7:15
You fear the s, so I will bring Ezk 11:8
I will bring the s against you." Ezk 11:8
will fall by the s, and I will Ezk 11:10
I will draw a s ⌊to chase⌋ after Ezk 12:14
spare a few of them from the s, Ezk 12:16
Or if I bring a s against that Ezk 14:17
Let a s pass through it, so that Ezk 14:17
Jerusalem—s, famine, dangerous Ezk 14:21
his troops will fall by the s, Ezk 17:21
I will draw My s from its sheath Ezk 21:3
My s will therefore come out of Ezk 21:4
taken My s from its sheath— Ezk 21:5
are to proclaim: A s! A sword is Ezk 21:9
A s is sharpened and also Ezk 21:9
the s despises every tree. Ezk 21:10
The s is given to be polished, Ezk 21:11
over to the s with My people. Ezk 21:12
And what if the s despises even Ezk 21:13
Let the s strike two times, Ezk 21:14
It is a s for massacre, a sword Ezk 21:14
for massacre, a s for great Ezk 21:14
appointed a s for slaughter at Ezk 21:15
roads that the s of Babylon's Ezk 21:19
a road that the s can take to Ezk 21:20
to proclaim: S, sword! ⌊You are Ezk 21:28
Sword, s! ⌊You are⌋ drawn Ezk 21:28
and killed her with the s. Ezk 23:10
descendants will fall by the s. Ezk 23:25
left behind will fall by the s. Ezk 24:21
will fall by the s from Teman to Ezk 25:13
will be slaughtered by the s. Ezk 26:6
on the mainland with the s. Ezk 26:8
your people with the s, Ezk 26:11
while the s is against her on Ezk 28:23
going to bring a s against you Ezk 29:8
A s will come against Egypt, Ezk 30:4
fall by the s along with them Ezk 30:5
will fall within it by the s. Ezk 30:6
Pi-beseth will fall by the s, Ezk 30:17
strong ⌊enough⌋ to handle a s. Ezk 30:21
will make the s fall from his Ezk 30:22
king and place My s in his hand. Ezk 30:24
when I place My s in the hand Ezk 30:25
Sheol, to those slain by the s. Ezk 31:17
with those slain by the s. Ezk 31:18
I brandish My s in front of them Ezk 32:10
s of Babylon's king will come Ezk 32:11
fall among those slain by the s. Ezk 32:20
by the sword. A s is appointed! Ezk 32:20
lie slain by the s. Ezk 32:21
them are slain, fallen by the s. Ezk 32:22
by the s—they who ⌊once⌋ Ezk 32:23
fallen by the s—they who went Ezk 32:24
slain by the s, although their Ezk 32:25
slain by the s, although their Ezk 32:26
with those slain by the s. Ezk 32:28
among those slain by the s. Ezk 32:29
with those slain by the s. Ezk 32:30
all his army, slain by the s. Ezk 32:31
with those slain by the s." Ezk 32:32
I bring the s against a land, Ezk 33:2
and he sees the s coming against Ezk 33:3
and the s comes and takes him Ezk 33:4
watchman sees the s coming but Ezk 33:6
and the s comes and takes away Ezk 33:6

in the ruins will fall by the **s**, Ezk 33:27
the power of the **s** in the time Ezk 35:5
slain by the **s** will fall on your Ezk 35:8
I will call for a **s** against him Ezk 38:21
every man's **s** will be against Ezk 38:21
so that they all fell by the **s**. Ezk 39:23
they will die by **s** and flame, Dn 11:33
deliver them by bow, **s**, or war, Hs 1:7
will shatter bow, **s**, and weapons Hs 2:18
will fall by the **s** because of Hs 7:16
A **s** will whirl through his Hs 11:6
They will fall by the **s**; Hs 13:16
pursued his brother with the **s**. Am 1:11
your young men with the **s**, Am 4:10
the house of Jeroboam with a **s**." Am 7:9
'Jeroboam will die by the **s**, Am 7:11
daughters will fall by the **s**, Am 7:17
the rest of them with the **s**. Am 9:1
will command the **s** to kill them. Am 9:4
confront us, will die by the **s**. Am 9:10
take up the **s** against nation, Mc 4:3
the land of Assyria with the **s**, Mc 5:6
do save, I will give to the **s**. Mc 6:14
smoke and the **s** will devour your Nah 2:13
flashing **s**, shining spear; Nah 3:3
the **s** will cut you down. Nah 3:15
will also be slain by My **s**. Zph 2:12
fall, each by his brother's **s**. Hg 2:22
make you like a warrior's **s**. Zch 9:13
May a **s** strike his arm and his Zch 11:17
S, awake against My shepherd, Zch 13:7
come to bring peace, but a **s**. Mt 10:34
out his hand and drew his **s**. Mt 26:51
Put your **s** back in place because Mt 26:52
all who take up a **s** will perish Mt 26:52
up a sword will perish by a **s**. Mt 26:52
those who stood by drew his **s**, Mk 14:47
a **s** will pierce your own soul Lk 2:35
the edge of the **s** and be led Lk 21:24
doesn't have a **s** should sell his Lk 22:36
should we strike with the **s**?" Lk 22:49
who had a **s**, drew it, struck Jn 18:10
said to Peter, "Sheathe your **s**! Jn 18:11
John's brother, with the **s**. Ac 12:2
he drew his **s** and was going to Ac 16:27
or nakedness or danger or **s**? Rm 8:35
not carry the **s** for no reason. Rm 13:4
and the **s** of the Spirit, Eph 6:17
sharper than any two-edged **s**, Heb 4:12
escaped the edge of the **s**, Heb 11:34
died by the **s**, they wandered Heb 11:37
mouth came a sharp two-edged **s**; Rv 1:16
has the sharp, two-edged **s** says: Rv 2:12
them with the **s** of My mouth. Rv 2:16
And a large **s** was given to him. Rv 6:4
to kill by the **s**, by famine, by Rv 6:8
anyone is to be killed with a **s**, Rv 13:10
with a **s** he will be killed. Rv 13:10
who had the **s** wound yet lived. Rv 13:14
From His mouth came a sharp **s**, Rv 19:15
were killed with the **s** that came Rv 19:21

SWORD'S *(1)*

and pour the **s** power on them. Jr 18:21

SWORDS *(34)*

brothers, took their **s**, went Gn 34:25
his son Shechem with their **s**, Gn 34:26
the LORD set the **s** of each man Jdg 7:22
with their **s** and burned down Jdg 18:27
and killed them with their **s**— Jdg 20:48
Hebrews will make **s** or spears." 1Sm 13:19
"All of you, put on your **s**!" 1Sm 25:13
and all his men put on their **s**. 1Sm 25:13
have clashed **s** and killed each 2Kg 3:23
them by families with their **s**, Neh 4:13
Their **s** will enter their own Ps 37:15
than oil, but they are drawn **s**. Ps 55:21
their tongues are sharp **s**. Ps 57:4
tongues like **s** and aim bitter Ps 64:3
a generation whose teeth are **s**, Pr 30:14
are skilled with **s** and trained Sg 3:8
will turn their **s** into plows and Is 2:4
For they have fled from **s**, Is 21:15
cut you to pieces with their **s**. Ezk 16:40
and cut them down with their **s**. Ezk 23:47
will draw their **s** against your Ezk 28:7
will draw their **s** against Egypt Ezk 30:11
fall by the **s** of warriors, Ezk 32:12
whose **s** were placed under their Ezk 32:27
You have relied on your **s**, Ezk 33:26
all of them brandishing **s**. Ezk 38:4
plowshares into **s** and your Jl 3:10
will beat their **s** into plows, Mc 4:3
large mob, with **s** and clubs, was Mt 26:47
you come out with **s** and clubs, Mt 26:55
him was a mob, with **s** and clubs, Mk 14:43
you come out with **s** and clubs, Mk 14:48
said, "look, here are two **s**." Lk 22:38
come out with **s** and clubs as if Lk 22:52

SWORDSMEN *(3)*

he took 700 **s** with him to try to 2Kg 3:26
were 1,100,000 **s** and in Judah 1Ch 21:5
and in Judah itself 470,000 **s**. 1Ch 21:5

SWORE *(90)*

that the two of them **s** an oath. Gn 21:31
who spoke to me and **s** to me, Gn 24:7
thigh and **s** an oath to him Gn 24:9
So he **s** to Jacob and sold his Gn 25:33
the oath that I **s** to your father Gn 26:3
morning and **s** an oath to each Gn 26:31
And Jacob **s** by the Fear of his Gn 31:53
to me." So Joseph **s** to him. Then Gn 47:31
the land that I **s** to give to Ex 6:8
which He **s** to your fathers that Ex 13:5
as He **s** to you and your fathers, Ex 13:11
that You **s** to Your servants Ex 32:13
else about which he **s** falsely. Lv 6:5
land that You **s** to ⌊give⌋ their Nm 11:12
the land He **s** to ⌊give⌋ them, Nm 14:16
see the land I **s** to ⌊give⌋ their Nm 14:23
that day, and He **s** an oath: Nm 32:10
see the land I **s** ⌊to give⌋ Nm 32:11
land the LORD **s** to give to your Dt 1:8
He grew angry and **s** an oath: Dt 1:34
the good land I **s** to give your Dt 1:35
He **s** that I would not cross the Dt 4:21
that He **s** to them by oath Dt 4:31
the land He **s** to your fathers Dt 6:10
LORD your God **s** to ⌊give⌋ your Dt 6:18
land that He **s** to our fathers. Dt 6:23
the oath He **s** to your fathers Dt 7:8
you, as He **s** to your fathers Dt 7:12
in the land He **s** to your fathers Dt 7:13
land the LORD **s** to your fathers Dt 8:1
covenant He **s** to your fathers Dt 8:18
promise He **s** to your fathers, Dt 9:5
the land I **s** to give their Dt 10:11
land the LORD **s** to your fathers Dt 11:9
the land the LORD **s** to give your Dt 11:21
you as He **s** to your fathers. Dt 13:17
as He **s** to your fathers Dt 19:8
land the LORD **s** to our fathers Dt 26:3
us as You **s** to our fathers, Dt 26:15
people, as He **s** to you, if you Dt 28:9
land the LORD **s** to your fathers Dt 28:11
you and as He **s** to your fathers Dt 29:13
land the LORD **s** to give to your Dt 30:20
land the LORD **s** to give to their Dt 31:7
the land I **s** to ⌊give⌋ their Dt 31:20
the land I **s** ⌊to give them⌋. Dt 31:21
into the land I **s** to them, Dt 31:23
the land I **s** to their fathers to Jos 1:6
the community **s** an oath to them Jos 9:15
of the oath we **s** to them." Jos 9:20
Jonathan's advice and **s** an oath: 1Sm 19:6
David also **s**, "As surely as 1Sm 20:3
once again **s** to David in his 1Sm 20:17
So David **s** to Saul. Then Saul 1Sm 24:22
Then Saul **s** to her by the LORD: 1Sm 28:10
David what the LORD **s** to him: 2Sm 3:9
Then David's men **s** to him: 2Sm 21:17
s to your servant by the LORD 1Kg 1:17
The king **s** an oath and said, 1Kg 1:29
just as I **s** to you by the LORD 1Kg 1:30
and I **s** to him by the LORD: 1Kg 2:8
Gedaliah **s** an oath to them and 2Kg 25:24
made with Abraham, **s** to Isaac, 1Ch 16:16
love that You **s** to David in Your Ps 89:49
So I **s** in My anger, 'They will Ps 95:11
made with Abraham, **s** to Isaac, Ps 105:9
how he **s** an oath to the LORD, Ps 132:2
The LORD **s** an oath to David, Ps 132:11
when I **s** that the waters of Noah Is 54:9
the oath I **s** to your ancestors, Jr 11:5
this land You **s** ⌊to give⌋ to Jr 32:22
King Zedekiah **s** to Jeremiah in Jr 38:16
s an oath to them and their men, Jr 40:9
s an oath to the descendants of Ezk 20:5
of Egypt. I **s** to them, saying Ezk 20:5
On that day I **s** to them that I Ezk 20:6
I **s** to them in the wilderness Ezk 20:15
I **s** to them in the wilderness Ezk 20:23
the land that I **s** to give them Ezk 20:28
the land I **s** to give your Ezk 20:42
therefore I **s** an oath against Ezk 44:12
since I **s** to give it to your Ezk 47:14
heaven and **s** by Him who lives Dn 12:7
You **s** to our fathers from days Mc 7:20
So he **s** oaths to her: Mk 6:23
the oath that He **s** to our father Lk 1:73
So I **s** in My anger, "They will Heb 3:11
I **s** in My anger, they will not Heb 4:3
to swear by, He **s** by Himself: Heb 6:13
s an oath by the One who lives Rv 10:6

SWORN *(36)*

Myself I have **s**, says the LORD: Gn 22:16
take the oath with the **s** curse, Nm 5:21
any vow or any **s** obligation to Nm 30:13
as the LORD had **s** to them. Dt 2:14
the land He had **s** to their Jos 5:6
community had **s** an oath to them Jos 9:18
We have **s** an oath to them by the Jos 9:19
the land He had **s** to give their Jos 21:43
all He had **s** to their fathers. Jos 21:44
He had promised and **s** to them. Jdg 2:15
of Israel had **s** an oath at Jdg 21:1
We've **s** to the LORD not to give Jdg 21:7
For the Israelites had **s**: Jdg 21:18
I have **s** to Eli's family: 1Sm 3:14
for they had **s** it with all their 2Ch 15:15
the land You had **s** to give them. Neh 9:15
with a **s** oath to follow Neh 10:29
and who has not **s** deceitfully. Ps 24:4
I have **s** an oath to David My Ps 89:3
for all I have **s** an oath by My Ps 89:35
The LORD has **s** an oath and will Ps 110:4
I have solemnly **s** to keep Your Ps 119:106
The LORD of Hosts has **s**: Is 14:24
Myself I have **s**; Truth has gone Is 45:23
so I have **s** that I will not be Is 54:9
The LORD has **s** with His right Is 62:8
Me and **s** by those who are Jr 5:7
'I have **s** by My great name, Jr 44:26
by Myself I have **s**"—the LORD's Jr 49:13
LORD of Hosts has **s** by Himself: Jr 51:14
of those who have **s** an oath to Ezk 21:23
Lord GOD has **s** by His holiness Am 4:2
The Lord GOD has **s** by Himself— Am 6:8
The LORD has **s** by the Pride of Am 8:7
that God had **s** an oath to him to Ac 2:30
The Lord has **s**, and He will not Heb 7:21

SWUNG *(2)*

on the cloud **s** His sickle over Rv 14:16
So the angel **s** his sickle toward Rv 14:19

SYCAMORE *(6)*

as abundant as **s** in the Judean 1Kg 10:27
of the olive and **s** trees in the 1Ch 27:28
as abundant as **s** in the Judean 2Ch 1:15
as abundant as **s** in the Judean 2Ch 9:27
and I took care of **s** figs. Am 7:14
he climbed up a **s** tree to see Lk 19:4

SYCAMORE-FIG *(1)*

hail and their **s** trees with a Ps 78:47

SYCAMORES *(1)*

the **s** have been cut down, but we Is 9:10

SYCHAR *(1)*

Samaria called **S** near the Jn 4:5

SYENE *(2)*

desolate waste from Migdol to **S**, Ezk 29:10
From Migdol to **S** they will fall Ezk 30:6

SYMBOL *(5)*

your hand and a **s** on your Ex 13:16
let them be a **s** on your forehead Dt 6:8
let them be a **s** on your Dt 11:18
should have ⌊a **s** of⌋ authority 1Co 11:10
is a **s** for the present time, Heb 9:9

SYMPATHETIC *(1)*

you should be like-minded and **s**, 1Pt 3:8

SYMPATHIZE *(2)*

go to lament or **s** with them, Jr 16:5
who is unable to **s** with our Heb 4:15

SYMPATHIZED *(1)*
For you **s** with the prisoners and Heb 10:34

SYMPATHY *(5)*
to go and offer **s** and comfort to Jb 2:11
They offered him **s** and comfort Jb 42:11
I waited for **s**, but there was Ps 69:20
Who will show **s** toward you? Jr 15:5
who will show **s** to her? Nah 3:7

SYNAGOGUE *(43)*
from there, He entered their **s**. Mt 12:9
began to teach them in their **s**, Mt 13:54
He entered the **s** on the Sabbath Mk 1:21
unclean spirit was in their **s**. Mk 1:23
As soon as they left the **s**, Mk 1:29
Now He entered the **s** again, Mk 3:1
One of the **s** leaders, named Mk 5:22
came from the **s** leader's house Mk 5:35
He told the **s** leader, "Don't be Mk 5:36
He began to teach in the **s**, Mk 6:2
He entered the **s** on the Sabbath Lk 4:16
everyone in the **s** were fixed on Lk 4:20
everyone in the **s** was enraged. Lk 4:28
In the **s** there was a man with an Lk 4:33
After He left the **s**, He entered Lk 4:38
He entered the **s** and was Lk 6:6
nation and has built us a **s**." Lk 7:5
He was a leader of the **s**. Lk 8:41
from the **s** leader's ⌊house⌋, Lk 8:49
the leader of the **s**, indignant Lk 13:14
teaching in the **s** in Capernaum. Jn 6:59
he would be banned from the **s**. Jn 9:22
would not be banned from the **s**. Jn 12:42
in the **s** and in the temple Jn 18:20
what is called the Freedmen's **S**, Ac 6:9
went into the **s** and sat down. Ac 13:14
leaders of the **s** sent ⌊word⌋ to Ac 13:15
After the **s** had been dismissed, Ac 13:43
the Jewish **s** and spoke in such Ac 14:1
where there was a Jewish **s**. Ac 17:1
went into the **s** of the Jews. Ac 17:10
reasoned in the **s** with the Jews Ac 17:17
reasoned in the **s** every Sabbath Ac 18:4
house was next door to the **s**. Ac 18:7
leader of the **s**, believed the Ac 18:8
leader of the **s**, and beat him Ac 18:17
entered the **s** and engaged Ac 18:19
began to speak boldly in the **s**. Ac 18:26
entered the **s** and spoke boldly Ac 19:8
know that in **s** after synagogue I Ac 22:19
synagogue after **s** I had those Ac 22:19
are not, but are a **s** of Satan. Rv 2:9
make those from the **s** of Satan, Rv 3:9

SYNAGOGUES *(24)*
teaching in their **s**, preaching Mt 4:23
do in the **s** and on the streets, Mt 6:2
standing in the **s** and on the Mt 6:5
teaching in their **s**, preaching Mt 9:35
and flog you in their **s**, Mt 10:17
the front seats in the **s**, Mt 23:6
will flog in your **s** and hound Mt 23:34
in their **s** and driving out Mk 1:39
seats in the **s**, and the places Mk 12:39
you will be flogged in the **s**. Mk 13:9
He was teaching in their **s**, Lk 4:15
preaching in the **s** of Galilee. Lk 4:44
seat in the **s** and greetings Lk 11:43
bring you before **s** and rulers Lk 12:11
in one of the **s** on the Sabbath, Lk 13:10
seats in the **s**, and the places Lk 20:46
you over to the **s** and prisons, Lk 21:12
They will ban you from the **s**. Jn 16:2
from him to the **s** in Damascus, Ac 9:2
proclaiming Jesus in the **s**: Ac 9:20
God's message in the Jewish **s**. Ac 13:5
aloud in the **s** every Sabbath day Ac 15:21
the temple complex or in the **s**, Ac 24:12
In all the **s** I often tried to Ac 26:11

SYNTYCHE *(1)*
Euodia and I urge **S** to agree in Php 4:2

SYRACUSE *(1)*
Putting in at **S**, we stayed three Ac 28:12

SYRIA *(8)*
(AKA ARAM)
about Him spread throughout **S**. Mt 4:24
while Quirinius was governing **S**. Lk 2:2
in Antioch, **S**, and Cilicia: Ac 15:23
traveled through **S** and Cilicia, Ac 15:41
brothers and sailed away to **S**. Ac 18:18
he was about to set sail for **S**, Ac 20:3
we sailed on to **S** and arrived at Ac 21:3
to the regions of **S** and Cilicia. Gl 1:21

SYRIAN *(1)*
(AKA ARAMEAN)
was healed—only Naaman the **S**." Lk 4:27

SYROPHOENICIAN *(1)*
was Greek, a **S** by birth, and she Mk 7:26

SYRTIS *(1)*
they would run aground on the **S**, Ac 27:17

T

TAANACH *(7)*
(AKA ANER)
the king of **T** one the king of Jos 12:21
inhabitants of **T** with its towns, Jos 17:11
T with its pasturelands and Jos 21:25
villages, or **T** and its villages Jdg 1:27
Canaan fought at **T** by the waters Jdg 5:19
of Ahilud, in **T**, Megiddo, and 1Kg 4:12
its villages, **T** and its villages 1Ch 7:29

TAANATH-SHILOH *(1)*
eastward from **T** and passed it Jos 16:6

TABBAOTH'S *(2)*
descendants, **T** descendants, Ezr 2:43
descendants, **T** descendants, Neh 7:46

TABBATH *(1)*
border of Abel-meholah near **T**. Jdg 7:22

TABEEL *(1)*
T and the rest of his colleagues Ezr 4:7

TABEEL'S *(1)*
can install **T** son as king in it. Is 7:6

TABERAH *(2)*
So that place was named **T**, Nm 11:3
to provoke the LORD at **T**, Dt 9:22

TABERNACLE *(125)*
the design of the **t** as well as Ex 25:9
construct the **t** itself with 10 Ex 26:1
so that the **t** may be a single Ex 26:6
goat hair for a tent over the **t**; Ex 26:7
down over the back of the **t**. Ex 26:12
sides of the **t** on either side Ex 26:13
planks of acacia wood for the **t**. Ex 26:15
for all the planks of the **t**. Ex 26:17
the planks for the **t** as follows: Ex 26:18
for the second side of the **t**, Ex 26:20
for the west side of the **t**. Ex 26:22
the two back corners of the **t**. Ex 26:23
the planks on one side of the **t**, Ex 26:26
on the other side of the **t**, Ex 26:27
back side of the **t** on the west. Ex 26:27
are to set up the **t** according to Ex 26:30
on the south side of the **t**, Ex 26:35
to make the courtyard for the **t**. Ex 27:9
the tools of the **t** for every use Ex 27:19
the **t**—its tent and covering, Ex 35:11
for the entrance to the **t**; Ex 35:15
pegs for the **t** and the tent pegs Ex 35:18
work made the **t** with 10 curtains Ex 36:8
so that the **t** became a single Ex 36:13
goat hair for a tent over the **t**; Ex 36:14
planks of acacia wood for the **t**. Ex 36:20
for all the planks of the **t**. Ex 36:22
planks for the **t** as follows: Ex 36:23
for the second side of the **t**, Ex 36:25
west side of the **t** he made six Ex 36:27
the two back corners of the **t**. Ex 36:28
the planks on one side of the **t**, Ex 36:31
on the other side of the **t**, Ex 36:32
the back of the **t** on the west. Ex 36:32
the tent pegs for the **t** and for Ex 38:20
This is the inventory for the **t**, Ex 38:21
tabernacle, the **t** of the Ex 38:21
all the tent pegs for the **t**, Ex 38:31
So all the work for the **t**, Ex 39:32
they brought the **t** to Moses: Ex 39:33
for the service of the **t**, Ex 39:40
are to set up the **t**, the tent of Ex 40:2
for the entrance to the **t**. Ex 40:5
front of the entrance to the **t**, Ex 40:6
and anoint the **t** and everything Ex 40:9
The **t** was set up in the first Ex 40:17
Moses set up the **t**: Ex 40:18
the tent over the **t** and put the Ex 40:19
He brought the ark into the **t**, Ex 40:21
on the north side of the **t**, Ex 40:22
table on the south side of the **t** Ex 40:24
screen at the entrance to the **t**. Ex 40:28
at the entrance to the **t**, Ex 40:29
courtyard for the **t** and the Ex 40:33
glory of the LORD filled the **t**. Ex 40:34
glory of the LORD filled the **t**. Ex 40:35
up from the **t** throughout all Ex 40:36
the LORD was over the **t** by day, Ex 40:38
anointed the **t** and everything Lv 8:10
by defiling My **t** that is among Lv 15:31
to the LORD before His **t**— Lv 17:4
over the **t** of the testimony Nm 1:50
to transport the **t** and all its Nm 1:50
Whenever the **t** is to move, Nm 1:51
camp around the **t** of the Nm 1:53
to the service of the **t**. Nm 3:7
to the service of the **t**. Nm 3:8
behind the **t** on the west side Nm 3:23
tent of meeting involved the **t**, Nm 3:25
surrounds the **t** and the altar, Nm 3:26
on the south side of the **t**, Nm 3:29
on the north side of the **t**. Nm 3:35
in front of the **t** on the east, Nm 3:38
the entire **t** and everything in Nm 4:16
are to transport the **t** curtains, Nm 4:25
surrounds the **t** and the altar, Nm 4:26
supports of the **t**, with its Nm 4:31
dust from the **t** floor and put Nm 5:17
Moses finished setting up the **t**, Nm 7:1
them in front of the **t**. Nm 7:3
On the day the **t** was set up, Nm 9:15
cloud covered the **t**, the tent Nm 9:15
fire above the **t** from evening Nm 9:15
as the cloud stayed over the **t**, Nm 9:18
stayed over the **t** many days, Nm 9:19
over the **t** for ⌊only⌋ a few Nm 9:20
as the cloud stayed over the **t**. Nm 9:22
up above the **t** of the testimony. Nm 10:11
The **t** was then taken down, Nm 10:17
set out, transporting the **t**. Nm 10:17
the **t** was to be set up before Nm 10:21
the work at the LORD's **t**, Nm 16:9
near the LORD's **t** will die. Nm 17:13
defiles the **t** of the LORD. Nm 19:13
the duties of the LORD's **t**." Nm 31:30
the duties of the LORD's **t**, Nm 31:47
where the LORD's **t** stands, Jos 22:19
which is in front of His **t**." Jos 22:29
by the doorpost of the LORD's **t**. 1Sm 1:9
down in the **t** of the LORD where 1Sm 3:3
moving around with the **t** tent. 2Sm 7:6
of oil from the **t** and anointed 1Kg 1:39
to the LORD's **t** and took hold 1Kg 2:28
to the LORD's **t** and is now 1Kg 2:29
went to the **t** and said to Joab, 1Kg 2:30
with song in front of the **t**, 1Ch 6:32
to all the service of the **t**, 1Ch 6:48
before the **t** of the LORD at 1Ch 16:39
tent and from **t** ⌊to tabernacle⌋ 1Ch 17:5
tent and from tabernacle ⌊to **t**⌋. 1Ch 17:5
At that time the **t** of the LORD, 1Ch 21:29
need to carry the **t** or any of 1Ch 23:26
made, in front of the LORD's **t**. 2Ch 1:5
faces away from the LORD's **t**, 2Ch 29:6
He abandoned the **t** at Shiloh, Ps 78:60
had the **t** of the testimony Ac 7:44
of the sanctuary and the true **t**, Heb 8:2
he was about to complete the **t**. Heb 8:5
For a **t** was set up; Heb 9:2
the **t** was called "the holy of Heb 9:3
while the first **t** was still Heb 9:8
and more perfect **t** not made with Heb 9:11
he sprinkled the **t** and all the Heb 9:21
who serve the **t** do not have a Heb 13:10
sanctuary—the **t** of testimony— Rv 15:5

TABERNACLE'S *(1)*
involved the **t** supports, Nm 3:36

TABERNACLES *(4)*
(Festival of, AKA Festival of INGATHERING, Festival of BOOTHS)
want, I will make three **t** here: Mt 17:4
Let us make three **t**: Mk 9:5
Let us make three **t**: Lk 9:33
Jewish Festival of **T** was near, Jn 7:2

TABITHA *(2)*
(AKA DORCAS)
there was a disciple named **T**, Ac 9:36
the body said, "**T**, get up!" Ac 9:40

TABLE *(86)*
served to them from Joseph's **t**, Gn 43:34
to construct a **t** of acacia wood, Ex 25:23
for the poles to carry the **t**. Ex 25:27
so that the **t** can be carried Ex 25:28
Presence on the **t** before Me at Ex 25:30
Place the **t** outside the veil and Ex 26:35
the tabernacle, opposite the **t**; Ex 26:35
put the **t** on the north side. Ex 26:35
the **t** with all its utensils, Ex 30:27
t with its utensils, the pure Ex 31:8
the **t** with its poles, all its Ex 35:13
the **t** of acacia wood, Ex 37:10
for the poles to carry the **t**. Ex 37:14
carrying the **t** from acacia wood Ex 37:15
would be on the **t** out of pure Ex 37:16
the **t**, all its utensils, and the Ex 39:36
bring in the **t** and lay out its Ex 40:4
Moses placed the **t** in the tent Ex 40:22
opposite the **t** on the south side Ex 40:24
pure ⌊gold⌋ **t** before the LORD Lv 24:6
the ark, the **t**, the lampstand, Nm 3:31
cloth over the **t** of the Presence Nm 4:7
and insert the poles ⌊in the **t**⌋. Nm 4:8
to pick up ⌊scraps⌋ under my **t**. Jdg 1:7
he didn't come to the king's **t**." 1Sm 20:29
up from the **t** in fierce anger 1Sm 20:34
will always eat meals at my **t**." 2Sm 9:7
is always to eat at my **t**." 2Sm 9:10
ate at David's **t** just like one 2Sm 9:11
he always ate at the king's **t**. 2Sm 9:13
among those who eat at your **t**. 2Sm 19:28
who eat at your **t** because they 1Kg 2:7
who came to King Solomon's **t**. 1Kg 4:27
the gold **t** that the bread of the 1Kg 7:48
the food at his **t**, his servants' 1Kg 10:5
they were sitting at the **t**, 1Kg 13:20
Asherah who eat at Jezebel's **t**." 1Kg 18:19
and put a bed, a **t**, a chair, and 2Kg 4:10
of gold for each **t** for the rows 1Ch 28:16
the food at his **t**, his servants' 2Ch 9:4
on the ceremonially clean **t**. 2Ch 13:11
and the **t** for the rows ⌊of the 2Ch 29:18
the surrounding nations at my **t**. Neh 5:17
had enough to eat at Job's **t**?" Jb 31:31
Your **t** was spread with choice Jb 36:16
You prepare a **t** before me in the Ps 23:5
Let their **t** set before them be a Ps 69:22
young olive trees around your **t**. Ps 128:3
she has also set her **t**. Pr 9:2
Prepare a **t**, and spread out a Is 21:5
who prepare a **t** for Fortune and Is 65:11
couch with a **t** spread before it, Ezk 23:41
My **t** you will eat your fill of Ezk 39:20
This is the **t** that stands before Ezk 41:22
draw near to My **t** to serve Me. Ezk 44:16
at the same **t** but to no avail Dn 11:27
"The LORD's **t** is contemptible." Mal 1:7
The Lord's **t** is defiled, and its Mal 1:12
recline at the **t** with Abraham, Mt 8:11
reclining at the **t** in the house, Mt 9:10
fall from their masters' **t**!" Mt 15:27
as He was reclining at the **t**. Mt 26:7
at the **t** with the Twelve Mt 26:20
at the **t** in Levi's house Mk 2:15
dogs under the **t** eat the Mk 7:28
as He was reclining at the **t**, Mk 14:3
as they were reclining at the **t**. Mk 16:14
house and reclined at the **t**. Lk 7:36
reclining at the **t** in the Lk 7:37
who were at the **t** with Him began Lk 7:49
went in and reclined at the **t**. Lk 11:37
have them recline at the **t**, Lk 12:37
recline at the **t** in the kingdom Lk 13:29
reclined at the **t** with Him heard Lk 14:15
what fell from the rich man's **t**, Lk 16:21
reclined at the **t**, and the Lk 22:14
Me is at the **t** with Me! Lk 22:21
the one at the **t** or the one Lk 22:27
Isn't it the one at the **t**? Lk 22:27
and drink at My **t** in My kingdom. Lk 22:30
reclined at the **t** with them that Lk 24:30
reclining at the **t** with Him. Jn 12:2
at the **t** knew why He told Jn 13:28
in the Lord's **t** and the table 1Co 10:21
table and the **t** of demons. 1Co 10:21
the lampstand, the **t**, and the Heb 9:2

TABLES *(15)*
and the silver for the silver **t**; 1Ch 28:16
He made 10 **t** and placed them in 2Ch 4:8
t on which ⌊to put⌋ the bread 2Ch 4:19
all their **t** are covered with Is 28:8
there were two **t** on each side, Ezk 40:39
there were two **t** on one side and Ezk 40:40
and two ⌊more⌋ **t** on the other Ezk 40:40
there were four **t** inside the Ezk 40:41
eight **t** ⌊in all⌋ on which the Ezk 40:41
were also four **t** of cut stone Ezk 40:42
was to be laid on the **t**. Ezk 40:43
money changers' **t** and the chairs Mt 21:12
changers' **t** and the chairs Mk 11:15
coins and overturned the **t**. Jn 2:15
about God to wait on **t**. Ac 6:2

TABLET *(5)*
them on the **t** of your heart. Pr 3:3
them on the **t** of your heart. Pr 7:3
it on a **t** in their presence Is 30:8
engraved on the **t** of their Jr 17:1
asked for a writing **t** and wrote: Lk 1:63

TABLETS *(36)*
give you the stone **t** with the Ex 24:12
the ⌊**t** of the⌋ testimony that Ex 25:16
him the two **t** of the testimony Ex 31:18
stone **t** inscribed by the finger Ex 31:18
with the two **t** of the testimony Ex 32:15
The **t** were the work of God, Ex 32:16
writing, engraved on the **t**. Ex 32:16
threw the **t** out of his hands, Ex 32:19
Cut two stone **t** like the first Ex 34:1
words that were on the first **t**, Ex 34:1
cut two stone **t** like the first Ex 34:4
the two stone **t** in his hand, Ex 34:4
He wrote down on the **t** the words Ex 34:28
with the two **t** of the testimony Ex 34:29
which He wrote on two stone **t**. Dt 4:13
on two stone **t** and gave them to Dt 5:22
mountain to receive the stone **t**, Dt 9:9
the **t** of the covenant the LORD Dt 9:9
LORD gave me the two stone **t**, Dt 9:10
LORD gave me the two stone **t**, Dt 9:11
tablets, the **t** of the covenant, Dt 9:11
and the two **t** of the covenant Dt 9:15
hold of the **t** and threw them Dt 9:17
'Cut two stone **t** like the first Dt 10:1
write on the **t** the words that Dt 10:2
were on the first **t** you broke, Dt 10:2
cut two stone **t** like the first Dt 10:3
with the two **t** in my hand. Dt 10:3
wrote on the **t** what had been Dt 10:4
placed the **t** in the ark I had Dt 10:5
the two stone **t** that Moses had 1Kg 8:9
except the two **t** that Moses had 2Ch 5:10
inscribe it on **t** so one may Hab 2:2
not on stone **t** but on tablets 2Co 3:3
tablets but on **t** that are hearts 2Co 3:3
and the **t** of the covenant. Heb 9:4

TABOR *(10)*
border reached **T**, Shahazumah, Jos 19:22
deploy ⌊the troops⌋ on Mount **T**, Jdg 4:6
of Abinoam had gone up Mount **T**. Jdg 4:12
down from Mount **T** with 10,000 Jdg 4:14
kind of men did you kill at **T**?" Jdg 8:18
until you come to the oak of **T**. 1Sm 10:3
pasturelands and **T** and its 1Ch 6:77
T and Hermon shout for joy at Ps 89:12
He will come like **T** among the Jr 46:18
and a net spread out on **T**. Hs 5:1

TABRIMMON *(1)*
Ben-hadad son of **T** son of 1Kg 15:18

TACKLE *(1)*
used ropes and **t** and girded the Ac 27:17

TACT *(1)*
responded with **t** and discretion Dn 2:14

TACTICS *(1)*
against the **t** of the Devil. Eph 6:11

TADMOR *(1)*
He built **T** in the wilderness 2Ch 8:4

TAHAN *(2)*
(AKA TAHATH)
the Tahanite clan from **T**. Nm 26:35
his son Telah, his son **T**, 1Ch 7:25

TAHANITE *(1)*
the **T** clan from Tahan. Nm 26:35

TAHASH *(1)*
Tebah, Gaham, **T**, and Maacah. Gn 22:24

TAHATH *(6)*
(AKA TAHAN)
from Makheloth and camped at **T**. Nm 33:26
departed from **T** and camped at Nm 33:27
son **T**, his son Uriel, his son 1Ch 6:24
son of **T**, son of Assir, son of 1Ch 6:37
Bered, his son **T**, his son 1Ch 7:20
his son Eleadah, his son **T**, 1Ch 7:20

TAHCHEMONITE *(1)*
Josheb-basshebeth the **T** was 2Sm 23:8

TAHPANHES *(6)*
(AKA TEHAPHNEHES)
Memphis and **T** have also broken Jr 2:16
They went as far as **T**. Jr 43:7
the LORD came to Jeremiah at **T**: Jr 43:8
of Pharaoh's palace at **T**. Jr 43:9
Egypt—at Migdol, **T**, Memphis, Jr 44:1
Proclaim it in Memphis and in **T**! Jr 46:14

TAHPENES *(2)*
sister of his own wife, Queen **T**. 1Kg 11:19
T ⌊herself⌋ weaned him in 1Kg 11:20

TAHPENES' *(1)*
T sister gave birth to Hadad's 1Kg 11:20

TAHREA *(1)*
(AKA TAREA)
Pithon, Melech, **T**, and Ahaz. 1Ch 9:41

TAIL *(14)*
your hand and grab it by the **t**." Ex 4:4
the ram, the fat **t**, the fat Ex 29:22
cutting off the **t** feathers, Lv 1:16
its fat and the entire fat **t**, Lv 3:9
the fat **t**, the fat surrounding Lv 7:3
fat—the fat **t**, all the fat Lv 8:25
the ram—the fat **t**, the ⌊fat⌋ Lv 9:19
make you the head and not the **t**; Dt 28:13
the head, and you will be the **t**. Dt 28:44
He stiffens his **t** like a cedar Jb 40:17
cut off Israel's head and **t**, Is 9:14
the **t** is the prophet, the lying Is 9:15
No head or **t**, palm or reed, will Is 19:15
His **t** swept away a third of the Rv 12:4

TAIL-TO-TAIL *(1)*
the foxes **t**, and put a torch Jdg 15:4

TAILS *(5)*
a torch between each pair of **t**. Jdg 15:4
and they had **t** with stingers, Rv 9:10
that with their **t** they had the Rv 9:10
in their mouths and in their **t**, Rv 9:19
because their **t**, like snakes, Rv 9:19

TAKE *(843)*
also **t** from the tree of life, Gn 3:22
T with you every kind of food Gn 6:21
You are to **t** with you seven Gn 7:2
here's your wife. **T** her and go!" Gn 12:19
t the possessions for yourself. Gn 14:21
that I will not **t** a thread or Gn 14:23
I will **t** nothing except what the Gn 14:24
Mamre—they can **t** their share." Gn 14:24
T your wife and your two Gn 19:15
"**T** your son," He said, "your Gn 22:2
you will not **t** a wife for my son Gn 24:3
and my family to **t** a wife for my Gn 24:4
that you don't **t** my son back Gn 24:6
and you can **t** a wife for my son Gn 24:7
'You will not **t** a wife for my Gn 24:37
family to **t** a wife for my son. Gn 24:38
and you will **t** a wife for my son Gn 24:40
the right way to **t** the daughter Gn 24:48
T ⌊her⌋ and go, and let her be a Gn 24:51
T your ⌊hunting⌋ gear, your Gn 27:3
Then **t** it to your father to eat Gn 27:10
Don't **t** a wife from the Gn 28:1
you also want to **t** my son's Gn 30:15
you would **t** your daughters Gn 31:31
that is yours and **t** it." Gn 31:32
my daughters or **t** other wives, Gn 31:50
favor with you, **t** this gift from Gn 33:10

Please **t** my present that was Gn 33:11
and **t** our daughters for Gn 34:9
t your daughters for ourselves, Gn 34:16
we will **t** our daughter and go. Gn 34:17
Let us **t** their daughters as our Gn 34:21
He said, "Let's not **t** his life." Gn 37:21
years of famine will **t** place, Gn 41:30
over the land and **t** one-fifth Gn 41:34
famine that will **t** place in the Gn 41:36
of you go and **t** grain ⌊to Gn 42:19
t ⌊food to relieve⌋ the hunger Gn 42:33
Now you want to **t** Benjamin. Gn 42:36
in your packs and **t** them down to Gn 43:11
T twice as much money with you. Gn 43:12
T your brother also, and go back Gn 43:13
his steward, "**T** the men to ⌊my⌋ Gn 43:16
us slaves, and **t** our donkeys." Gn 43:18
If you also **t** this one from me Gn 44:29
T wagons from the land of Egypt Gn 45:19
my father made me **t** an oath, Gn 50:5
I will **t** care of you and your Gn 50:21
made the Israelites **t** an oath: Gn 50:25
T this child and nurse him for Ex 2:9
T your sandals off your feet, Ex 3:5
"This will **t** place," He Ex 4:5
t some water from the Nile and Ex 4:9
The water you **t** from the Nile Ex 4:9
And **t** this staff in your hand Ex 4:17
May the LORD **t** note of you and Ex 5:21
I will **t** you as My people, Ex 6:7
T your staff and throw it down Ex 7:9
T in your hand the staff that Ex 7:15
T your staff and stretch out Ex 7:19
and didn't even **t** this to heart. Ex 7:23
sign will **t** place tomorrow." Ex 8:23
T handfuls of furnace soot, Ex 9:8
who didn't **t** the LORD's word Ex 9:21
that He will **t** this death away Ex 10:17
because we will **t** some of them Ex 10:26
you may **t** it from either the Ex 12:5
They must **t** some of the blood Ex 12:7
T a cluster of hyssop, dip it in Ex 12:22
T even your flocks and your Ex 12:32
You may not **t** any of the meat Ex 12:46
then you must **t** my bones with Ex 13:19
You may **t** two quarts per Ex 16:16
T a container and put two quarts Ex 16:33
of the people and **t** some of the Ex 17:5
T the rod you struck the Nile Ex 17:5
you must **t** him from My altar to Ex 21:14
If you ever **t** your neighbor's Ex 22:26
You must not **t** a bribe, for a Ex 23:8
I will **t** away your illnesses. Ex 23:25
become numerous and **t** possession Ex 23:30
Israelites to **t** an offering for Ex 25:2
You are to **t** My offering from Ex 25:2
T two onyx stones and engrave on Ex 28:9
T a young bull and two Ex 29:1
Then **t** the garments and clothe Ex 29:5
T the anointing oil, pour ⌊it⌋ Ex 29:7
T some of the bull's blood and Ex 29:12
T all the fat that covers the Ex 29:13
T one ram, and Aaron and his Ex 29:15
slaughter the ram, **t** its blood, Ex 29:16
You are to **t** the second ram, Ex 29:19
the ram, **t** some of its blood Ex 29:20
T some of the blood that is on Ex 29:21
T the fat from the ram, the fat Ex 29:22
t one loaf of bread, one cake of Ex 29:23
T them from their hands and burn Ex 29:25
T the breast from the ram of Ex 29:26
You are to **t** the ram of Ex 29:31
When you **t** a census of the Ex 30:12
T the atonement money from the Ex 30:16
T for yourself the finest Ex 30:23
to Moses: "**T** fragrant spices Ex 30:34
T off the gold rings that are on Ex 32:2
has gold, **t** it off,' and they Ex 32:24
Now **t** off your jewelry, and I Ex 33:5
Then I will **t** My hand away, Ex 33:23
Then you will **t** some of their Ex 34:16
T up an offering for the LORD Ex 35:5
T the anointing oil, and anoint Ex 40:9
The priest will **t** a handful of Lv 2:2
and he will **t** it to the altar. Lv 2:8
priest must then **t** some of the Lv 4:5
the priest must **t** some of the Lv 4:25
the priest must **t** some of its Lv 4:30
the priest must **t** some of the Lv 4:34
who will **t** a handful from it as Lv 5:12
Then he must **t** off his garments, Lv 6:11
will be anointed to **t** his place, Lv 6:22
T Aaron, his sons with him, the Lv 8:2
because it will **t** seven days to Lv 8:33
T a young bull for a sin Lv 9:2
'**T** a male goat for a sin Lv 9:3
T the grain offering that is Lv 10:12
it to you to **t** away the guilt Lv 10:17
she may **t** two turtledoves or two Lv 12:8
is to **t** the live bird together Lv 14:6
day he must **t** two unblemished Lv 14:10
The priest is to **t** one male lamb Lv 14:12
The priest is to **t** some of the Lv 14:14
Then the priest will **t** some of Lv 14:15
he is to **t** one male lamb for a Lv 14:21
The priest will **t** the male lamb Lv 14:24
the priest is to **t** some of the Lv 14:25
they must **t** different stones Lv 14:42
former⌋ ones and **t** additional Lv 14:42
is to **t** two birds, cedar wood, Lv 14:49
He will **t** the cedar wood, the Lv 14:51
He must **t** two turtledoves or two Lv 15:14
day she must **t** two turtledoves Lv 15:29
He is to **t** from the Israelite Lv 16:5
Next he will **t** the two goats and Lv 16:7
Then he must **t** a firepan full of Lv 16:12
He is to **t** some of the bull's Lv 16:14
He is to **t** some of the bull's Lv 16:18
t off the linen garments he wore Lv 16:23
not **t** revenge or bear a grudge Lv 19:18
day you are to **t** the product Lv 23:40
T fine flour and bake it into 12 Lv 24:5
Do not profit or **t** interest from Lv 25:36
T a census of the entire Nm 1:2
Do not register or **t** a census of Nm 1:49
all its articles, **t** care of it, Nm 1:50
the Levites are to **t** it down, Nm 1:51
They are to **t** care of all the Nm 3:8
are to **t** the Levites for Me— Nm 3:41
T the Levites in place of every Nm 3:45
t a census of the Kohathites by Nm 4:2
t down the screening veil, Nm 4:5
They are to **t** a blue cloth and Nm 4:9
They are to **t** all the serving Nm 4:12
T a census of the Gershonites Nm 4:22
the priest is to **t** holy water in Nm 5:17
and **t** some of the dust from the Nm 5:17
the woman to **t** an oath and will Nm 5:19
make the woman **t** the oath with Nm 5:21
The priest is to **t** the grain Nm 5:25
The priest is to **t** a handful of Nm 5:26
tent of meeting, **t** the hair from Nm 6:18
The priest is to **t** the boiled Nm 6:19
T the Levites from among the Nm 8:6
They are to **t** a young bull and Nm 8:8
and you are to **t** a second young Nm 8:8
T them to the tent of meeting Nm 11:16
I will **t** some of the Spirit who Nm 11:17
We must go up and **t** possession Nm 13:30
t firepans, and tomorrow Nm 16:6
Each of you is to **t** his firepan, Nm 16:17
told Aaron, "**T** your firepan, Nm 16:46
the Israelites and **t** one staff Nm 17:2
the priest is to **t** some of its Nm 19:4
The priest is to **t** cedar wood, Nm 19:6
they are to **t** some of the ashes Nm 19:17
who is clean is to **t** hyssop, Nm 19:18
T the staff and assemble the Nm 20:8
T Aaron and his son Eleazar and Nm 20:25
that He will **t** the snakes away Nm 21:7
I will **t** you to another place. Nm 23:27
T all the leaders of the people Nm 25:4
T a census of the entire Nm 26:2
⌊**T** a census of⌋ those 20 years Nm 26:4
and he will **t** possession of it. Nm 27:11
to Moses, "**T** Joshua son of Nun Nm 27:18
are to **t** a count of what Nm 31:26
T ⌊the tribute⌋ from their half Nm 31:29
t one out of every 50 from the Nm 31:30
You are to **t** possession of the Nm 33:53
T one leader from each tribe to Nm 34:18
you should **t** more from a larger Nm 35:8
Enter and **t** possession of the Dt 1:8
Go up and **t** possession of it as Dt 1:21
they will **t** possession of it. Dt 1:39
Begin to **t** possession ⌊of it⌋; Dt 2:24
Begin to **t** possession of it.' Dt 2:31
city that we didn't **t** from them: Dt 3:4
they also **t** possession of the Dt 3:20
and **t** possession of the land the Dt 4:1
I command you or **t** anything away Dt 4:2
cross over and **t** possession of Dt 4:22
to go and **t** a nation as his own Dt 4:34
and **t** ⌊your⌋ oaths in His name. Dt 6:13
their sons or **t** their daughters Dt 7:3
the images and **t** it for yourself Dt 7:25
and may enter and **t** possession Dt 8:1
brought me in to **t** possession of Dt 9:4
are not going to **t** possession of Dt 9:5
to Him and **t** oaths in His name. Dt 10:20
Jordan to enter and **t** possession Dt 11:31
But you are to **t** the holy Dt 12:26
you are entering to **t** possession Dt 12:29
anything to it or **t** anything Dt 12:32
for money, **t** the money in your Dt 14:25
t an awl and pierce through his Dt 15:17
is giving you, **t** possession of Dt 17:14
⌊for him⌋, **t** him from there, Dt 19:12
But you may **t** the women, Dt 20:14
to you and you **t** some of them Dt 21:10
and want to **t** her as your wife, Dt 21:11
mother must **t** hold of him and Dt 21:19
you must not **t** the mother along Dt 22:6
may **t** the young for yourself, Dt 22:7
and mother will **t** the evidence Dt 22:15
of that city will **t** the man and Dt 22:18
you must **t** the two of them out Dt 22:24
Do not **t** a pair of millstones or Dt 24:6
and do not **t** a widow's garment Dt 24:17
is to **t** her as his wife, Dt 25:5
and you **t** possession of it and Dt 26:1
you must **t** some of the first of Dt 26:2
the priest will **t** the container Dt 26:4
insects will **t** possession of all Dt 28:42
LORD will **t** you back in ships Dt 28:68
and you will **t** possession of it. Dt 30:5
enable them to **t** possession of Dt 31:7
T this book of the law and place Dt 31:26
the sword will **t** their children, Dt 32:25
I will **t** vengeance on My Dt 32:41
He will **t** vengeance on His Dt 32:43
T to heart all these words I am Dt 32:46
t possession to the west and the Dt 33:23
Jordan to go in and **t** possession Jos 1:11
inheritance and **t** possession of Jos 1:15
T the ark of the covenant and go Jos 3:6
'**T** 12 stones from this place in Jos 4:3
T up the ark of the covenant and Jos 6:6
If you **t** any of those things, Jos 6:18
T the whole military force with Jos 8:1
that they **t** his body down Jos 8:29
'**T** provisions with you for the Jos 9:11
But **t** a look, it is now dry and Jos 9:12
delay going out to **t** possession Jos 18:3
and **t** possession ⌊of it⌋ among Jos 22:19
Let us **t** action and build an Jos 22:26
so that you can **t** possession of Jos 23:5
and enabled them to **t** possession Jdg 1:19
Manasseh failed to **t** possession Jdg 1:27
Israelites went to **t** possession Jdg 2:6
and **t** with you 10,000 men from Jdg 4:6
on the road you are about to **t**, Jdg 4:9
and **t** hold of your captives, Jdg 5:12
T the meat with the unleavened Jdg 6:20
T your father's young bull and a Jdg 6:25
T the second bull and offer it Jdg 6:26
T them down to the water, and I Jdg 7:4
the Midianites and **t** control of Jdg 7:24
Israel did not **t** away the land Jdg 11:15
why didn't you **t** them back at Jdg 11:26
the LORD and cannot **t** ⌊it⌋ back. Jdg 11:35
Why not **t** her instead?" Jdg 15:2
go and invade and **t** possession Jdg 18:9
I'll **t** care of everything you Jdg 19:20
will **t** 10 men out of every 100 Jdg 20:10
T my right of redemption, Ru 4:6
if You will **t** notice of Your 1Sm 1:11
I'll **t** him to appear in the 1Sm 1:22
then you can **t** whatever you want 1Sm 2:16
you don't, I'll **t** it by force!" 1Sm 2:16
but **t** their calves away and pen 1Sm 6:7
T the ark of the LORD, place it 1Sm 6:8
his son Eleazar to **t** care of it. 1Sm 7:1
He can **t** your sons and put them 1Sm 8:11

can **t** your daughters to become 1Sm 8:13
He can **t** your best fields, 1Sm 8:14
He can **t** a tenth of your grain 1Sm 8:15
He can **t** your male servants, 1Sm 8:16
He can **t** a tenth of your flocks, 1Sm 8:17
T one of the attendants with you 1Sm 9:3
"what do we **t** the man? 1Sm 9:7
no gift to **t** to the man of God 1Sm 9:7
the LORD **t** pleasure in burnt 1Sm 15:22
T a young cow with you and say, 1Sm 16:2
T this half-bushel of roasted 1Sm 17:17
t these 10 portions of cheese to 1Sm 17:18
to **t** revenge on his enemies.' " 1Sm 18:25
so that he wants to **t** my life?" 1Sm 20:1
why **t** me to your father?" 1Sm 20:8
him and said, "Go, **t** it back to 1Sm 20:40
you want to **t** it for yourself, 1Sm 21:9
yourself, then **t** it, for there 1Sm 21:9
who wants to **t** my life wants to 1Sm 22:23
my life wants to **t** your life. 1Sm 22:23
Saul had come out to **t** his life. 1Sm 23:15
hunting me down to **t** my life. 1Sm 24:11
the LORD **t** vengeance on you 1Sm 24:12
He **t** notice and plead my case 1Sm 24:15
Am I supposed to **t** my bread, 1Sm 25:11
you and attempts to **t** your life, 1Sm 25:29
t the spear and the water jug by 1Sm 26:11
They may **t** them and go." 1Sm 30:22
t whatever you can get from him. 2Sm 2:21
sent someone to **t** her away from 2Sm 3:15
Now **t** action, because the LORD 2Sm 3:18
who intended to **t** your life. 2Sm 4:8
servant that you **t** an interest 2Sm 9:8
bring himself to **t** one of his 2Sm 12:4
will **t** your wives and give them 2Sm 12:11
Don't **t** this thing to heart." 2Sm 13:20
don't **t** seriously the report 2Sm 13:33
But God would not **t** away a life; 2Sm 14:14
10 concubines to **t** care of the 2Sm 15:16
Go back and **t** your brothers with 2Sm 15:20
T note: their two sons, Zadok's 2Sm 15:36
blood, intends to **t** my life— 2Sm 16:11
he left to **t** care of the palace. 2Sm 16:21
the man to **t** good news today. 2Sm 18:20
May the king not **t** it to heart. 2Sm 19:19
safely, let Ziba **t** it all!" 2Sm 19:30
t you away secretly and 2Sm 19:41
he had left to **t** care of the 2Sm 20:3
T your lord's soldiers and 2Sm 20:6
to all who **t** refuge in Him. 2Sm 22:31
please **t** away Your servant's 2Sm 24:10
answer I should **t** back to the 2Sm 24:13
the king may **t** whatever he wants 2Sm 24:22
to them, "**T** my servants with 1Kg 1:33
my own mule, and **t** him down to 1Kg 1:33
up and went to **t** hold of the 1Kg 1:50
there, and you can **t** them away. 1Kg 5:9
and is forced to **t** an oath, 1Kg 8:31
and he comes to **t** an oath before 1Kg 8:31
T 10 pieces for yourself, 1Kg 11:31
I will not **t** the whole kingdom 1Kg 11:34
will **t** 10 tribes of the kingdom 1Kg 11:35
T with you 10 loaves of bread, 1Kg 14:3
then they would **t** them back to 1Kg 14:28
t note: I will sweep away Baasha 1Kg 16:3
LORD, **t** my life, for I'm no 1Kg 19:4
looking for me to **t** my life." 1Kg 19:10
looking for me to **t** my life." 1Kg 19:14
their hands on and **t** away.' " 1Kg 20:6
his servants, "**T** ⌊your⌋ 1Kg 20:12
out in peace, **t** them alive, and 1Kg 20:18
out for battle, **t** them alive." 1Kg 20:18
Then **t** him out and stone him to 1Kg 21:10
Get up and **t** possession of the 1Kg 21:15
Jezreelite to **t** possession of it 1Kg 21:16
he has gone to **t** possession of 1Kg 21:18
have failed to **t** it from the 1Kg 22:3
T Micaiah and return him to 1Kg 22:26
Turn around and **t** me out of the 1Kg 22:34
for the LORD to **t** Elijah up to 2Kg 2:1
the LORD will **t** your master away 2Kg 2:3
the LORD will **t** your master away 2Kg 2:5
"Which route should we **t**?" 2Kg 3:8
I wouldn't **t** notice of you. 2Kg 3:14
coming to **t** my two children as 2Kg 4:1
under your belt, **t** my staff with 2Kg 4:29
and I will **t** you to the man 2Kg 6:19
we will **t** them alive and go into 2Kg 7:12

let ⌊messengers⌋ **t** five of the 2Kg 7:13
T a gift with you and go meet 2Kg 8:8
t this flask of oil with you, 2Kg 9:1
and **t** him to an inner room. 2Kg 9:2
Then, **t** the flask of oil, pour 2Kg 9:3
T care of this cursed woman and 2Kg 9:34
Jehu ordered, "**T** them alive." 2Kg 10:14
You are to **t** turns providing 2Kg 11:6
T her out between the ranks, 2Kg 11:15
priest is to **t** from his assessor 2Kg 12:5
don't **t** any money from your 2Kg 12:7
they would not **t** money from the 2Kg 12:8
responded, "**T** a bow and arrows. 2Kg 13:15
Elisha said, "**T** the arrows!" 2Kg 13:18
until I come and **t** you away to a 2Kg 18:32
will again **t** root downward 2Kg 19:30
sent ⌊someone⌋ to **t** the bones 2Kg 23:16
of Assyria to **t** the Reubenites, 1Ch 5:26
to **t** from there the ark of God, 1Ch 13:6
I will not **t** away My faithful 1Ch 17:13
please **t** away Your servant's 1Ch 21:8
LORD says: '**T** your ⌊choice⌋— 1Ch 21:11
answer I should **t** back to the 1Ch 21:12
Ornan said to David, "**T** it! 1Ch 21:23
for I will not **t** for the LORD 1Ch 21:24
You can then **t** them up to 2Ch 2:16
and is forced to **t** an oath and 2Ch 6:22
and he comes to **t** an oath before 2Ch 6:22
the shields and **t** them back to 2Ch 12:11
T Micaiah and return him to 2Ch 18:25
Turn around and **t** me out of the 2Ch 18:33
T her out between the ranks, 2Ch 23:14
proceeded to **t** away the altars 2Ch 30:14
his servants, "**T** me away, for I 2Ch 35:23
shackles⌋ to **t** him to Babylon. 2Ch 36:6
He told him, '**T** these articles, Ezr 5:15
in marriage or **t** their daughters Ezr 9:12
Be strong and **t** action!" Ezr 10:4
and all Israel **t** an oath to do Ezr 10:5
How long will your journey **t**, Neh 2:6
and made everyone **t** an oath to Neh 5:12
go in and **t** possession ⌊of it⌋ Neh 9:23
and will not **t** their daughters Neh 10:30
Levites must **t** a tenth of this Neh 10:38
forced them to **t** an oath before Neh 13:25
their sons or **t** their daughters Neh 13:25
she requested to **t** with her from Est 2:13
wear so he could **t** off his Est 4:4
T a garment and a horse for Est 6:10
and to **t** their possessions as Est 8:11
⌊This would **t** place⌋ on a single Est 8:12
If one wanted to **t** Him to court, Jb 9:3
that we can **t** each other to Jb 9:32
Let Him **t** His rod away from me Jb 9:34
will He not **t** note ⌊of it⌋? Jb 11:11
at risk and **t** my life in my own Jb 13:14
Do You really **t** notice of one Jb 14:3
but would not **t** note of my sin. Jb 14:16
correct you and **t** you to court Jb 22:4
fatherless and **t** the widow's ox Jb 24:3
case against me; **t** your stand. Jb 33:5
do you **t** Him to court for not Jb 33:13
Almighty does not **t** note of it— Jb 35:13
Does the hawk **t** flight by your Jb 39:26
so that you can **t** him as a slave Jb 41:4
Therefore I **t** back ⌊my words⌋ Jb 42:6
t seven bulls and seven rams, Jb 42:8
of the wicked, or **t** the path of Ps 1:1
kings of the earth **t** their stand Ps 2:2
those who **t** refuge in Him are Ps 2:12
But let all who **t** refuge in You Ps 5:11
t Your seat on high over it. Ps 7:7
it in order to **t** the matter into Ps 10:14
at interest or **t** a bribe against Ps 15:5
me, God, for I **t** refuge in You. Ps 16:1
of those who **t** another ⌊god⌋ for Ps 16:4
to all who **t** refuge in Him. Ps 18:30
Some **t** pride in a chariot, Ps 20:7
we **t** pride in the name of the Ps 20:7
trouble, and **t** away all my sins Ps 25:18
to shame, for I **t** refuge in You. Ps 25:20
they plotted to **t** my life. Ps 31:13
for those who **t** refuge in You. Ps 31:19
and all who **t** refuge in Him will Ps 34:22
T Your shields—large and small Ps 35:2
that people **t** refuge in the Ps 36:7
T delight in the LORD, and He Ps 37:4
because they **t** refuge in Him. Ps 37:40

those who seek to **t** my life be Ps 40:14
For they did not **t** the land by Ps 44:3
of Sheol, for He will **t** me. Ps 49:15
dies, he will **t** nothing at all; Ps 49:17
My statutes and to **t** My covenant Ps 50:16
presence or **t** Your Holy Spirit Ps 51:11
will **t** you, ripping you out of Ps 52:5
Let death **t** them by surprise; Ps 55:15
while they wait to **t** my life. Ps 56:6
to me, for I **t** refuge in You. Ps 57:1
they run and **t** up a position. Ps 59:4
Awake to help me, and **t** notice. Ps 59:4
tent forever and **t** refuge under Ps 61:4
They **t** pleasure in lying; Ps 62:4
in the LORD and **t** refuge in Him; Ps 64:10
peoples who **t** pleasure in war Ps 68:30
You who seek God, **t** heart! Ps 69:32
You will **t** me up in glory. Ps 73:24
heaven and see; **t** care of this Ps 80:14
you will **t** refuge under His Ps 91:4
Your servants **t** delight in its Ps 102:14
do not **t** me in the middle of my Ps 102:24
when You **t** away their breath, Ps 104:29
let another **t** over his position. Ps 109:8
an oath and will not **t** it back: Ps 110:4
will **t** the cup of salvation and Ps 116:13
It is better to **t** refuge in the Ps 118:8
It is better to **t** refuge in the Ps 118:9
T insult and contempt away from Ps 119:22
for I **t** pleasure in it. Ps 119:35
Never **t** the word of truth from Ps 119:43
shield, and I **t** refuge in Him; Ps 144:2
and **t** pleasure in the wife of Pr 5:18
is gained by those who **t** advice. Pr 13:10
T his garment, for he has put up Pr 20:16
the LORD will **t** up their case Pr 22:23
and He will **t** up their case Pr 23:11
Don't **t** a matter to court Pr 25:8
sensible see danger and **t** cover; Pr 27:12
T his garment, for he has put up Pr 27:13
to those who **t** refuge in Him. Pr 30:5
Yet he will **t** over all my work Ec 2:19
will **t** nothing for his efforts Ec 5:15
him to enjoy them, **t** his reward, Ec 5:19
the living should **t** it to heart. Ec 7:2
T me with you—let us hurry. Sg 1:4
palm tree and **t** hold of its Sg 7:8
you, I would **t** you, to the house Sg 8:2
I will **t** revenge against My Is 1:24
Nations will not **t** up the sword Is 2:4
your name. **T** away our disgrace. Is 4:1
One of Israel **t** place so that we Is 5:19
T a large piece of parchment and Is 8:1
for My rage, to **t** spoils, to Is 10:6
t off your sackcloth and remove Is 20:2
He will **t** hold of you, Is 22:17
hand is lifted up ⌊to **t** action⌋, Is 26:11
Or let it **t** hold of My strength; Is 27:5
days to come, Jacob will **t** root. Is 27:6
protection and **t** refuge in Is 30:2
large enough to **t** fire from a Is 30:14
until I come and **t** you away to a Is 36:17
Judah will again **t** root downward Is 37:31
Let them **t** a lump of figs and Is 38:21
says to another, "**T** courage!" Is 41:6
and no one can **t** ⌊anything⌋ from Is 43:13
T Me to court; let us argue our Is 43:26
things, and what will **t** place. Is 44:7
let them **t** counsel together. Is 45:21
t it to heart, you transgressors! Is 46:8
My plan will **t** place, and I will Is 46:10
T millstones and grind meal; Is 47:2
exposed. I will **t** vengeance; I Is 47:3
You did not **t** these things to Is 47:7
So **t** your stand with your spells Is 47:12
is no one to **t** hold of her hand Is 51:18
T your seat, Jerusalem. Is 52:2
you will not have to **t** flight; Is 52:12
but I will **t** you back with great Is 54:7
remember Me or **t** it to heart? Is 57:11
a breath will **t** them away. Is 57:13
striving to **t** hold of You. Is 64:7
I will also **t** some of them as Is 66:21
over to Cyprus and **t** a look. Jr 2:10
master, and I will **t** you, one Jr 3:14
they want to **t** your life. Jr 4:30
Look and **t** note; search in her Jr 5:1
Then **t** it and find rest for Jr 6:16

Therefore, **t** note! Days are Jr 7:32
away? They **t** hold of deceit; Jr 8:5
they do not **t** Me into account Jr 9:3
I not **t** My revenge against Jr 9:9
who want to **t** your life. Jr 11:21
T the underwear that you bought Jr 13:4
T a humble seat, for your Jr 13:18
remember me and **t** note of me. Jr 15:15
Your patience, don't **t** me away. Jr 15:15
However, **t** note! The days are Jr 16:14
T some of the elders of the Jr 19:1
Therefore, **t** note! The days are Jr 19:6
those who want to **t** their life. Jr 19:7
those who want to **t** their life, Jr 19:9
against him and **t** our vengeance Jr 20:10
those who want to **t** their lives. Jr 21:7
The wind will **t** charge of all Jr 22:22
who want to **t** your life, to Jr 22:25
Therefore, **t** note! I am against Jr 23:30
T this cup of the wine of wrath Jr 25:15
they refuse to **t** the cup from Jr 25:28
Babylon did not **t** when he Jr 27:20
T wives and have sons and Jr 29:6
T wives for your sons and give Jr 29:6
You will **t** up your tambourines Jr 31:4
He will **t** Zedekiah to Babylon Jr 32:5
T these scrolls—this purchase Jr 32:14
those who want to **t** their life. Jr 34:20
those who want to **t** their life, Jr 34:21
T a scroll, and write on it all Jr 36:2
T another scroll, and once again Jr 36:28
T from here 30 men under your Jr 38:10
men who want to **t** your life." Jr 38:16
chains to **t** him to Babylon. Jr 39:7
T him, look after him, and don't Jr 39:12
son of Shaphan, to **t** him home. Jr 39:14
They will **t** place before your Jr 39:16
come, and I will **t** care of you. Jr 40:4
burn them and **t** them prisoner. Jr 43:12
And I will **t** away the remnant of Jr 44:12
to those who want to **t** his life, Jr 44:30
one who wanted to **t** his life.' " Jr 44:30
t your positions with helmets on! Jr 46:4
Tahpanhes! Say: **T** positions! Jr 46:14
they will not **t** their stand, Jr 46:21
who want to **t** their lives— Jr 46:26
will **t** their tents and their Jr 49:29
They will **t** their camels for Jr 49:29
those who want to **t** their lives. Jr 49:37
t out your vengeance on her; Jr 50:15
case and **t** vengeance on your Jr 51:36
to you and **t** ⌊them⌋ to heart Ezk 3:10
son of man, **t** a brick, set it Ezk 4:1
T an iron plate and set it up as Ezk 4:3
Also **t** wheat, barley, beans, Ezk 4:9
son of man, **t** a sharp sword, Ezk 5:1
Then **t** a pair of scales and Ezk 5:1
you are to **t** one third and slash Ezk 5:2
But you are to **t** a few strands Ezk 5:3
T some more of them, throw them Ezk 5:4
evil of nations to **t** possession Ezk 7:24
T fire from inside the Ezk 10:6
the wall and **t** the ⌊bags⌋ out Ezk 12:5
your⌋ shoulder and **t** ⌊them⌋ out Ezk 12:6
that I may **t** hold of the house Ezk 14:5
your clothes, **t** your beautiful Ezk 16:39
will **t** ⌊a sprig⌋ from the lofty Ezk 17:22
Do I **t** any pleasure in the death Ezk 18:23
don't I ⌊**t** pleasure⌋ when he Ezk 18:23
For I **t** no pleasure in anyone's Ezk 18:32
sword of Babylon's king can **t**. Ezk 21:19
that the sword can **t** to Rabbah Ezk 21:20
the turban, and **t** off the crown. Ezk 21:26
You **t** interest and profit ⌊on a Ezk 22:12
clothes and **t** your beautiful Ezk 23:26
t all you have worked for, Ezk 23:29
T the choicest of the flock and Ezk 24:5
stir up wrath and **t** vengeance, Ezk 24:8
I am about to **t** the delight of Ezk 24:16
on the day I **t** their stronghold Ezk 24:25
I will **t** My vengeance on Edom Ezk 25:14
the LORD when I **t** My vengeance Ezk 25:17
They will **t** your wealth as spoil Ezk 26:12
I **t** no pleasure in the death of Ezk 33:11
For I will **t** you from the Ezk 36:24
t a single stick and write on it: Ezk 37:16
Then **t** another stick and write Ezk 37:16
I am going to **t** the stick of Ezk 37:19

I am going to **t** the Israelites Ezk 37:21
to **t** cattle and possessions, Ezk 38:13
They will **t** the loot from those Ezk 39:10
You must **t** some of its blood and Ezk 43:20
Then you must **t** away the bull Ezk 43:21
T careful note of the entrance Ezk 44:5
they must **t** off the clothes they Ezk 44:19
of the land must **t** part in this Ezk 45:16
month, you are to **t** a young, Ezk 45:18
The priest must **t** some of the Ezk 45:19
prince must not **t** any of the Ezk 46:18
and gave orders to **t** Daniel out Dn 6:23
will **t** action against them and Dn 11:7
will **t** even their gods captive Dn 11:8
he will **t** action, then return to Dn 11:28
the holy covenant and **t** action. Dn 11:30
God will be strong and **t** action. Dn 11:32
I will certainly **t** them away. Hs 1:6
I will **t** back My grain in its Hs 2:9
I will **t** away My wool and linen, Hs 2:9
I will **t** you to be My wife Hs 2:19
I will **t** you to be My wife in Hs 2:19
I will **t** you to be My wife in Hs 2:20
and new wine **t** away ⌊one's⌋ Hs 4:11
Thistles will **t** possession of Hs 9:6
in My anger and **t** away ⌊a king⌋ Hs 13:11
T words ⌊of repentance⌋ with you Hs 14:2
like the lily and **t** root like Hs 14:5
the nations and **t** them to the Jl 3:2
the righteous, **t** a bribe, and Am 5:12
T away from Me the noise of your Am 5:23
from there My hand will **t** them; Am 9:2
LORD, please **t** my life from me, Jnh 4:3
them; they also **t** houses. They Mc 2:2
that day one will **t** up a taunt Mc 2:4
and you **t** My blessing from their Mc 2:9
Nation will not **t** up the sword Mc 4:3
I will **t** vengeance in anger and Mc 5:15
for those who **t** refuge in Him. Nah 1:7
t hold of the brick-mold! Nah 3:14
rises, they **t** off, and no one Nah 3:17
all of these **t** up a taunt Hab 2:6
—"I will **t** you, Zerubbabel Hg 2:23
The LORD will **t** possession of Zch 2:12
"**T** off his filthy clothes!" Zch 3:4
My house and **t** care of My courts Zch 3:7
and I will **t** away the guilt of Zch 3:9
T ⌊an offering⌋ from the exiles, Zch 6:10
T silver and gold, make crowns Zch 6:11
T the equipment of a foolish Zch 11:15
will come and **t** some of the pots Zch 14:21
and if you don't **t** it to heart Mal 2:2
be afraid to **t** Mary as your wife Mt 1:20
T the child and His mother, Mt 2:13
T the child and His mother and Mt 2:20
not worthy to **t** off His sandals Mt 3:11
beloved Son. I **t** delight in Him! Mt 3:17
you, don't **t** an oath at all: Mt 5:34
sue you and **t** away your shirt, Mt 5:40
me **t** the speck out of your eye, Mt 7:4
First **t** the log out of your eye, Mt 7:5
see clearly to **t** the speck out Mt 7:5
Don't **t** the road leading to Mt 10:5
Don't **t** along gold, silver, or Mt 10:9
Don't **t** a traveling bag for the Mt 10:10
whoever doesn't **t** up his cross Mt 10:38
t up My yoke and learn from Me, Mt 11:29
wouldn't **t** hold of it and lift Mt 12:11
isn't right to **t** the children's Mt 15:26
they had forgotten to **t** bread. Mt 16:5
deny himself, **t** up his cross, Mt 16:24
beloved Son. I **t** delight in Him. Mt 17:5
T it and give it to them for Me Mt 17:27
t one or two more with you, Mt 18:16
T what's yours and go. I want to Mt 20:14
kill him and **t** his inheritance! Mt 21:38
these things must **t** place, Mt 24:6
Then many will **t** offense, betray Mt 24:10
T note: I have told you in Mt 24:25
until all these things **t** place. Mt 24:34
they didn't **t** oil with them. Mt 25:3
So **t** the talent from him and Mt 25:28
we see You a stranger and **t** You Mt 25:38
a stranger and you didn't **t** Me Mt 25:43
and you didn't **t** care of Me.' Mt 25:43
and said, "**T** and eat it; Mt 26:26
because all who **t** up a sword Mt 26:52
beloved Son; I **t** delight in You! Mk 1:11

instructed them to **t** nothing for Mk 6:8
isn't right to **t** the children's Mk 7:27
had forgotten to **t** bread and had Mk 8:14
deny himself, **t** up his cross, Mk 8:34
brother should **t** the wife and Mk 12:19
things are about to **t** place?" Mk 13:4
these things must **t** place, Mk 13:7
until all these things **t** place. Mk 13:30
it to them, and said, "**T** ⌊it⌋; Mk 14:22
T this cup away from Me. Mk 14:36
arrest Him and **t** Him away under Mk 14:44
with myrrh, but He did not **t** it. Mk 15:23
if Elijah comes to **t** Him down!" Mk 15:36
the day these things **t** place, Lk 1:20
these days to **t** away my disgrace Lk 1:25
Don't **t** money from anyone by Lk 3:14
beloved Son. I **t** delight in You! Lk 3:22
T note—your reward is great in Lk 6:23
let me **t** out the speck that is Lk 6:42
First **t** the log out of your eye, Lk 6:42
see clearly to **t** out the speck Lk 6:42
t care how you listen. Lk 8:18
"**T** nothing for the road," He Lk 9:3
and don't **t** an extra shirt. Lk 9:3
deny himself, **t** up his cross Lk 9:23
and said, '**T** care of him. Lk 10:35
T care then, that the light in Lk 11:35
for many years. **T** it easy; eat, Lk 12:19
will proceed to **t** the lowest Lk 14:9
'**T** your invoice,' he told him, Lk 16:6
'**T** your invoice,' he told him, Lk 16:7
'**T** the mina away from him and Lk 19:24
brother should **t** the wife and Lk 20:28
worthy to **t** part in that age Lk 20:35
things are about to **t** place?" Lk 21:7
these things must **t** place first, Lk 21:9
these things begin to **t** place, Lk 21:28
away until all things **t** place. Lk 21:32
that are going to **t** place and to Lk 21:36
T this and share it among Lk 22:17
has a money-bag should **t** it, Lk 22:36
You are willing, **t** this cup away Lk 22:42
out together, "**T** this man away! Lk 23:18
some out and **t** it to the chief Jn 2:8
to come and **t** Him by force to Jn 6:15
were willing to **t** Him on board, Jn 6:21
My life so I may **t** it up again. Jn 10:17
have the right to **t** it up again. Jn 10:18
because He will **t** from what is Jn 16:14
not praying that You **t** them out Jn 17:15
T Him yourselves and judge Him Jn 18:31
T Him and crucify Him Jn 19:6
But they shouted, "**T** Him away! Jn 19:15
Take Him away! **T** Him away! Jn 19:15
put Him, and I will **t** Him away." Jn 20:15
Let someone else **t** his position. Ac 1:20
to **t** the place in this apostolic Ac 1:25
plan had predestined to **t** place. Ac 4:28
T the sandals off your feet, Ac 7:33
intervened to **t** from the Ac 15:14
wanted to **t** along John Mark. Ac 15:37
appropriate to **t** along this man Ac 15:38
with him not to **t** a chance by Ac 19:31
intending to **t** Paul on board. Ac 20:13
T these men, purify yourself Ac 21:24
T this young man to the Ac 23:17
and Moses said would **t** place— Ac 26:22
Now I urge you to **t** courage, Ac 27:22
Therefore, **t** courage, men, Ac 27:25
Paul urged them all to **t** food, Ac 27:33
I urge you to **t** some food. Ac 27:34
they are trying to **t** my life! Rm 11:3
them, when I **t** away their sins. Rm 11:27
So should I **t** the members of 1Co 6:15
by all means **t** the opportunity. 1Co 7:21
that is written will **t** place: 1Co 15:54
reply for those who **t** pride in 2Co 5:12
T us into your hearts. We have 2Co 7:2
times to **t** it away from me. 2Co 12:8
Did I **t** advantage of you by 2Co 12:17
Did Titus **t** advantage of you? 2Co 12:18
T note! I, Paul, tell you that Gl 5:2
is why you must **t** up the full Eph 6:13
everything, to **t** your stand. Eph 6:13
In every situation **t** the shield Eph 6:16
T the helmet of salvation, Eph 6:17
every effort to **t** hold of it Php 3:12
⌊This will **t** place⌋ at the 2Th 1:7

in this letter, **t** note of that 2Th 3:14
how will he **t** care of God's 1Tm 3:5
world, and we can **t** nothing out. 1Tm 6:7
t hold of eternal life, to which 1Tm 6:12
so that they may **t** hold of life 1Tm 6:19
bulls and goats to **t** away sins. Heb 10:4
which can never **t** away sins. Heb 10:11
do not **t** the Lord's discipline Heb 12:5
t the prophets who spoke in the Jms 5:10
grace of God. **T** your stand in it 1Pt 5:12
beloved Son. I **t** delight in Him! 2Pt 1:17
so that He might **t** away sins, 1Jn 3:5
what must quickly **t** place. Rv 1:1
what will **t** place after this. Rv 1:19
T note! I will make those from Rv 3:9
what must **t** place after this. Rv 4:1
are worthy to **t** the scroll and Rv 5:9
empowered to **t** peace from the Rv 6:4
t the scroll that lies open in Rv 10:8
He said to me, "**T** and eat it; Rv 10:9
has passed. **T** note: the third Rv 11:14
what must quickly **t** place." Rv 22:6
desires should **t** the living Rv 22:17
God will **t** away his share of the Rv 22:19

TAKEN *(211)*

the rib He had **t** from the man Gn 2:22
woman, for she was **t** from man. Gn 2:23
since you were **t** from it. Gn 3:19
the ground from which he was **t**. Gn 3:23
so the woman was **t** to Pharaoh's Gn 12:15
relative had been **t** prisoner, Gn 14:14
because of the woman you have **t**, Gn 20:3
now he has **t** my blessing." Gn 27:36
that you have **t** my husband? Gn 30:15
"God has **t** away my shame." Gn 30:23
Jacob has **t** all that was our Gn 31:1
has **t** your father's herds and Gn 31:9
that God has **t** from our father Gn 31:16
deceived me and **t** my daughters Gn 31:26
Now Rachel had **t** Laban's Gn 31:34
Now Joseph had been **t** to Egypt. Gn 39:1
they were **t** to Joseph's house Gn 43:18
that the frogs be **t** away from Ex 8:9
father-in-law, had **t** in Zipporah, Ex 18:2
or not he has **t** his neighbor's Ex 22:8
or not he has **t** his neighbor's Ex 22:11
the cloud was **t** up from the Ex 40:36
If the cloud was not **t** up, Ex 40:37
out until the day it was **t** up. Ex 40:37
I have **t** from the Israelites the Lv 7:34
and **t** outside the city to an Lv 14:45
I have **t** the Levites from the Nm 3:12
have **t** them for Myself in place Nm 8:16
I have **t** the Levites in place Nm 8:18
The tabernacle was then **t** down, Nm 10:17
have not **t** one donkey from them Nm 16:15
of Moab and had **t** control of all Nm 21:26
of our father be **t** away from his Nm 27:4
plunder the army had **t** totaled: Nm 31:32
Your servants have **t** a census of Nm 31:49
the soldiers had **t** plunder for Nm 31:53
Israelites has **t** possession of Nm 32:18
will be **t** away from our Nm 36:3
inheritance would be **t** away. Nm 36:3
inheritance will be **t** away from Nm 36:4
over to you, as has now **t** place. Dt 2:30
wearing when she was **t** prisoner, Dt 21:13
I have **t** the consecrated portion Dt 26:13
donkey will be **t** away from you Dt 28:31
because they will be **t** prisoner. Dt 28:41
But the woman had **t** the two men Jos 2:4
she had **t** them up to the roof Jos 2:6
they had **t** from the Jordan Jos 4:20
They have **t** some of what was set Jos 7:11
Now Joshua had **t** about 5,000 men Jos 8:12
that they be **t** down from the Jos 10:27
all of them were **t** in battle. Jos 11:19
of Manasseh have **t** their Jos 18:7
because he has **t** Samson's wife Jdg 15:6
until I have **t** vengeance on you. Jdg 15:7
pieces of silver **t** from you, Jdg 17:2
After they had **t** the gods Micah Jdg 18:27
No one has **t** me into his home, Jdg 19:18
oath had been **t** that anyone who Jdg 21:5
so that you will be **t** care of? Ru 3:1
the ark had been **t** to 1Sm 7:2
which they had **t** from Israel, 1Sm 7:14
Whose ox or donkey have I **t**? 1Sm 12:3
whose hand have I **t** a bribe to 1Sm 12:3
and you haven't **t** anything from 1Sm 12:4
before I have **t** vengeance on my 1Sm 14:24
for you have **t** pity on me. 1Sm 23:21
plunder they had **t** from the land 1Sm 30:16
everything the Amalekites had **t**; 1Sm 30:18
plunder the Amalekites had **t**. 1Sm 30:19
The LORD has **t** away your sin; 2Sm 12:13
He had not **t** care of his feet, 2Sm 19:24
Israelites had **t** an oath 2Sm 21:2
him after he had **t** a census of 2Sm 24:10
Solomon has even **t** his seat on 1Kg 1:46
and he has **t** hold of the horns 1Kg 1:51
I have **t** the place of my father 1Kg 8:20
had seen the way **t** by the man of 1Kg 13:12
The high places were not **t** away; 1Kg 15:14
and also **t** possession?' 1Kg 21:19
the high places were not **t** away; 1Kg 22:43
for you before I am **t** from you." 2Kg 2:9
If you see me being **t** from you, 2Kg 2:10
the high places were not **t** away; 2Kg 12:3
that Hazael had **t** in war from 2Kg 13:25
the high places were not **t** away, 2Kg 14:4
the high places were not **t** away; 2Kg 15:4
the high places were not **t** away; 2Kg 15:35
come from you will be **t** away, 2Kg 20:18
Notice I have **t** great pains to 1Ch 22:14
house was **t** for Eleazar, 1Ch 24:6
I have **t** the place of my father 2Ch 6:10
where they were **t** captive, 2Ch 6:38
places were not **t** away from 2Ch 15:17
the high places were not **t** away; 2Ch 20:33
had **t** from Jerusalem Ezr 1:7
who had **t** a wife from the Ezr 2:61
Since we have **t** an oath of Ezr 4:14
had **t** from the temple Ezr 5:14
they have **t** some of their Ezr 9:2
officials have **t** the lead in Ezr 9:2
and let them be **t** as plunder to Neh 4:4
who had **t** a wife from the Neh 7:63
He had been **t** into exile from Est 2:6
Esther was also **t** to the palace Est 2:8
Esther was **t** to King Ahasuerus Est 2:16
darkness had **t** that night away! Jb 3:6
Yet He knows the way I have **t**; Jb 23:10
Iron is **t** from the ground, Jb 28:2
of people who have **t** their stand Ps 3:6
I have **t** refuge in the LORD. Ps 11:1
who hate us have **t** plunder for Ps 44:10
has **t** His place in the divine Ps 82:1
bed will be **t** from under you. Pr 22:27
those being **t** off to death, Pr 24:11
from the land is **t** by all; Ec 5:9
I have **t** off my clothing. Sg 5:3
LORD of Hosts ⌊has **t** an oath⌋: Is 5:9
that he had **t** from the altar Is 6:6
his yoke will be **t** from them, Is 14:25
whose feet have **t** her to settle Is 23:7
come from you will be **t** away, Is 39:7
the prey be **t** from the mighty Is 49:24
of a mighty man will be **t**, Is 49:25
My people are **t** away for nothing Is 52:5
He was **t** away because of Is 53:8
They have not **t** up cases, such Jr 5:28
thing has **t** place in the land Jr 5:30
horror has **t** hold of me. Jr 8:21
them, and they have **t** root. Jr 12:2
LORD's flock has been **t** captive. Jr 13:17
of Judah has been **t** into exile, Jr 13:19
taken into exile, **t** completely Jr 13:19
Each has **t** back his male and Jr 34:16
whom Ishmael had **t** captive from Jr 41:14
to shame; it will be **t** captive. Jr 48:1
celebration are **t** from the Jr 48:33
have been **t** captive and your Jr 48:46
where they are **t** captive, Ezk 6:9
Can wood be **t** from it to make Ezk 15:3
t My sword from its sheath— Ezk 21:5
of them ⌊had **t**⌋ the same path. Ezk 23:13
will not be **t** away or gathered Ezk 29:5
its wealth is **t** away, and its Ezk 30:4
If he had **t** warning, he would Ezk 33:5
they have been **t** away because Ezk 33:6
reported, "The city has been **t**!" Ezk 33:21
had **t** from the temple Dn 5:2
that had been **t** from the temple, Dn 5:3
and his glory was **t** from him. Dn 5:20
So Daniel was **t** out of the den, Dn 6:23
and his dominion will be **t** away, Dn 7:26
itself will be **t** to Assyria as Hs 10:6
they have **t** their stand there. Hs 10:9
it has been **t** from your mouth Jl 1:5
on garments **t** as collateral, Am 2:8
you will be **t** away with hooks Am 4:2
But you have **t** up Sakkuth your Am 5:26
its support is **t** from you. Mc 1:11
for they have been **t** from you Mc 1:16
himself with goods **t** in pledge. Hab 2:6
and you will be **t** away with it. Mal 2:3
groom will be **t** away from them, Mt 9:15
he has will be **t** away from him. Mt 13:12
slaves saw what had **t** place, Mt 18:31
of God will be **t** away from you Mt 21:43
wouldn't have **t** part with them Mt 23:30
kind that hasn't **t** place from Mt 24:21
one will be **t** and one left. Mt 24:40
one will be **t** and one left. Mt 24:41
he has will be **t** away from him. Mt 25:29
the groom is **t** away from them, Mk 2:20
what he has will be **t** away." Mk 4:25
Lord Jesus was **t** up into heaven Mk 16:19
groom will be **t** away from them Lk 5:35
he has will be **t** away from him." Lk 8:18
to a close for Him to be **t** up, Lk 9:51
it will not be **t** away from her." Lk 10:42
You have **t** away the key of Lk 11:52
one will be **t** and the other will Lk 17:34
will be **t** and the other left. Lk 17:35
will be **t**, and the other will Lk 17:36
he does have will be **t** away. Lk 19:26
that had **t** place in the city Lk 23:19
when they saw what had **t** place, Lk 23:48
everything that had **t** place. Lk 24:14
that ⌊their bodies⌋ be **t** away. Jn 19:31
They have **t** the Lord out of the Jn 20:2
Because they've **t** away my Lord," Jn 20:13
until the day He was **t** up, Ac 1:2
He was **t** up as they were Ac 1:9
who has been **t** from you into Ac 1:11
the day He was **t** up from us— Ac 1:22
the men to be **t** outside for a Ac 5:34
His life is **t** from the earth. Ac 8:33
the object was **t** up into heaven. Ac 10:16
because he had **t** a vow. Ac 18:18
him to be **t** into the barracks Ac 21:34
things and had **t** some bread, Ac 27:35
it and have **t** your stand on it. 1Co 15:1
that we may not be **t** advantage 2Co 2:11
I also have been **t** hold of by Php 3:12
myself to have **t** hold of it. Php 3:13
and has **t** it out of the way by Col 2:14
on in the world, **t** up in glory. 1Tm 3:16
has already **t** place, 2Tm 2:18
every high priest **t** from men is Heb 5:1
because a death has **t** place for Heb 9:15
Enoch was **t** away so that he did Heb 11:5
You have **t** Your great power Rv 11:17
But the beast was **t** prisoner, Rv 19:20

TAKES *(65)*

for embalming **t** that long, Gn 50:3
If he **t** an additional wife, Ex 21:10
when Asshur **t** you captive. Nm 24:22
t hold of her and rapes her, Dt 22:28
When a man **t** a bride, he must Dt 24:5
and My hand **t** hold of judgment, Dt 32:41
like the one who **t** it off.' " 1Kg 20:11
LORD gives, and the LORD **t** away. Jb 1:21
of speech and **t** away the elders' Jb 12:20
off, when God **t** away his life? Jb 27:8
since He **t** pleasure in him." Ps 22:8
is the man who **t** refuge in Him! Ps 34:8
and He **t** pleasure in his way. Ps 37:23
Who **t** a stand for me against Ps 94:16
Happy is he who **t** your little Ps 137:9
is exalted, He **t** note of the Ps 138:6
For the LORD **t** pleasure in His Ps 149:4
it **t** the lives of those who Pr 1:19
show no mercy when he **t** revenge. Pr 6:34
the crossroads, she **t** her stand. Pr 8:2
of life, but violence **t** lives. Pr 11:30
A man **t** joy in giving an answer; Pr 15:23
man secretly **t** a bribe to Pr 17:23
person sees danger and **t** cover, Pr 22:3
as for the one who **t** an oath, Ec 9:2
whose hand never **t** a bribe, Is 33:15
their stem hardly **t** root in the Is 40:24

or he **t** a cypress or an oak. Is 44:14
He **t** some of it and warms Is 44:15
and no one **t** it to heart; Is 57:1
But whoever **t** refuge in Me will Is 57:13
but no one **t** it to heart. Jr 12:11
for My gaze **t** in all their ways. Jr 16:17
No one **t** up the case for your Jr 30:13
the sword **t** the children; Lm 1:20
the sword comes and **t** him away, Ezk 33:4
sword comes and **t** away their Ezk 33:6
the LORD **t** vengeance and is Nah 1:2
The LORD **t** vengeance against His Nah 1:2
before the decree **t** effect and Zph 2:2
'Whoever **t** an oath by the Mt 23:16
whoever **t** an oath by the gold Mt 23:16
'Whoever **t** an oath by the altar, Mt 23:18
whoever **t** an oath by the gift Mt 23:18
the one who **t** an oath by the Mt 23:20
oath by the altar **t** an oath by Mt 23:20
The one who **t** an oath by the Mt 23:21
by the sanctuary **t** an oath by it Mt 23:21
And the one who **t** an oath by Mt 23:22
oath by heaven **t** an oath by Mt 23:22
the Passover **t** place after two Mt 26:2
Satan comes and **t** away the word Mk 4:15
And if anyone **t** away your coat, Lk 6:29
from one who **t** away your things Lk 6:30
Devil comes and **t** away the word Lk 8:12
he **t** from him all his weapons he Lk 11:22
who **t** away the sin of the world! Jn 1:29
one **t** it from Me, but I lay it Jn 10:18
told you that He **t** from what is Jn 16:15
each one **t** his own supper ahead 1Co 11:21
that no one **t** you captive Col 2:8
No one **t** this honor on himself; Heb 5:4
He **t** away the first to establish Heb 10:9
so that no one **t** your crown. Rv 3:11
And if anyone **t** away from the Rv 22:19

TAKING *(55)*

and **t** the two stone tablets in Ex 34:4
inheritance, as is now **t** place. Dt 4:38
no partiality and **t** no bribe. Dt 10:17
that is like **t** a life as Dt 24:6
t the city, set it on fire. Jos 8:8
the women **t** care of her said, 1Sm 4:20
Abigail hurried, **t** 200 loaves of 1Sm 25:18
the king was **t** his midday nap. 2Sm 4:5
today you aren't **t** good news, 2Sm 18:20
his bow without **t** special aim 1Kg 22:34
meet Elisha, **t** with him a gift 2Kg 8:9
unfaithful ⌊by **t**⌋ what was 1Ch 2:7
his bow without **t** special aim 2Ch 18:33
or partiality or **t** bribes with 2Ch 19:7
t food and wine from them, Neh 5:15
I have seen a fool **t** root, Jb 5:3
even **t** it out of the thorns. Jb 5:5
t refuge in his destructive Ps 52:7
to the heights, **t** away captives; Ps 68:18
t great delight in His Ps 112:1
heart is like **t** off clothing on Pr 25:20
is no adding to it or **t** from it. Ec 3:14
a mourning feast is **t** place. Jr 16:5
feasting is **t** place to sit with Jr 16:8
t from his descendants rulers Jr 33:26
t shelter in the shade of its Ezk 17:23
not **t** interest or profit ⌊on a Ezk 18:17
guilt by **t** revenge on them, Ezk 25:12
its spoil and **t** its plunder. Ezk 29:19
t false oaths while making Hs 10:4
to walk, **t** them in My arms Hs 11:3
For something is **t** place in your Hab 1:5
"Where are they **t** the basket?" Zch 5:10
you are not **t** it to heart. Mal 2:2
T along Peter and the two sons Mt 26:37
T the seven loaves, He gave Mk 8:6
But Jesus, **t** him by the hand, Mk 9:27
them, and **t** him in His arms Mk 9:36
After **t** them in His arms, He Mk 10:16
T the Twelve aside again, He Mk 10:32
my master is **t** the management Lk 16:3
T it down, he wrapped it in fine Lk 23:53
t him by the right hand he Ac 3:7
And after **t** some food, he Ac 9:19
the purpose of **t** them as Ac 9:21
So **t** a security bond from Jason Ac 17:9
T along soldiers and centurions, Ac 21:32
and reforms are **t** place for the Ac 24:2
of my mind and **t** me prisoner to Rm 7:23
We are **t** this precaution so no 2Co 8:20
t every thought captive to the 2Co 10:5
churches by **t** pay ⌊from them⌋ 2Co 11:8
with Barnabas, **t** Titus along Gl 2:1
of a slave, **t** on the likeness Php 2:7
t vengeance with flaming fire on 2Th 1:8

TALENT *(4)*

who had received one **t** went off, Mt 25:18
received one **t** also approached Mt 25:24
and hid your **t** in the ground. Mt 25:25
So take the **t** from him and Mt 25:28

TALENTS *(11)*

who owed 10,000 **t** was brought Mt 18:24
To one he gave five **t**; Mt 25:15
who had received five **t** went, Mt 25:16
had received five **t** approached, Mt 25:20
five more **t**, and said, 'Master Mt 25:20
Master, you gave me five **t**. Mt 25:20
Look, I've earned five more **t**.' Mt 25:20
man with two **t** also approached Mt 25:22
'Master, you gave me two **t**. Mt 25:22
Look, I've earned two more **t**.' Mt 25:22
give it to the one who has 10 **t**. Mt 25:28

TALITHA *(1)*

hand and said to her, "**T** koum!" Mk 5:41

TALK *(29)*

T about them when you sit in Dt 6:7
you are and **t** to him about you 1Sm 19:3
fool nobody can **t** to him!" 1Sm 25:17
The **t** of all Israel has reached 2Sm 19:11
then asked, "May I **t** with you?" 1Kg 2:14
with useless **t** or with words Jb 15:3
place I could also **t** like you. Jb 16:4
some sense, and then we can **t**. Jb 18:2
why do you keep up this empty **t**? Jb 27:12
they **t** about hiding traps and Ps 64:5
sit at the city gate **t** about me, Ps 69:12
You struck and **t** about the pain Ps 69:26
For my enemies **t** about me, Ps 71:10
stranger with her flattering **t**, Pr 2:16
don't let your lips **t** deviously. Pr 4:24
you wake up, they will **t** to you. Pr 6:22
stranger with her flattering **t**. Pr 7:5
she lures with her flattering **t**. Pr 7:21
but endless **t** leads only to Pr 14:23
person listens to malicious **t**; Pr 17:4
will be opened ⌊to **t**⌋ with him; Ezk 24:27
and people unable to speak, **t**!" Mk 7:37
I will not **t** with you much Jn 14:30
and by smooth **t** and flattering Rm 16:18
know not the **t** but the power 1Co 4:19
of God is not in **t** but in power. 1Co 4:20
rotten **t** should come from your Eph 4:29
with you and **t** face to face so 2Jn 12
and we will **t** face to face. 3Jn 14

TALKED *(6)*

his brothers **t** with him. Gn 45:15
the troops **t** about stoning him 1Sm 30:6
He **t** to me about this and that 2Kg 9:12
were being **t** about throughout Lk 1:65
that He had **t** to him, and how Ac 9:27
had left they **t** with each other Ac 26:31

TALKER *(1)*

and such a **t** be acquitted? Jb 11:2

TALKERS *(1)*

people, idle **t** and deceivers, Ti 1:10

TALKING *(35)*

When He finished **t** with him, Gn 17:22
your father **t** with your brother Gn 27:6
t about them when you sit in Dt 11:19
As they continued walking and **t**, 2Kg 2:11
know the things you are **t** about? Jb 12:3
How long until you stop **t**? Jb 18:2
stopped **t** and covered their Jb 29:9
own pleasure, or **t** too much; Is 58:13
your people are **t** about you near Ezk 33:30
angel who was **t** to me replied, Zch 1:9
saw those unable to speak **t**, Mt 15:31
appeared to them, **t** with Him. Mt 17:3
don't know what you're **t** about!" Mt 26:70
He was openly **t** about this. Mk 8:32
and they were **t** with Jesus. Mk 9:4
understand what you're **t** about!" Mk 14:68
know this man you're **t** about!" Mk 14:71
two men were **t** with Him—Moses Lk 9:30
As some were **t** about the temple Lk 21:5
don't know what you're **t** about!" Lk 22:60
us while He was **t** with us on the Lk 24:32
that He was **t** with a woman. Jn 4:27
or "Why are You **t** with her?" Jn 4:27
nobody was **t** publicly about Him Jn 7:13
out who it was He was **t** about. Jn 13:24
don't know what He's **t** about!" Jn 16:18
to Him, "You're not **t** to me? Jn 19:10
While **t** with him, he went on in Ac 10:27
we stopped **t** and simply said, Ac 21:14
to boast⌋—I am **t** foolishly—I 2Co 11:21
I'm **t** like a madman—I'm a 2Co 11:23
and foolish **t** or crude joking Eph 5:4
but I am **t** about Christ and the Eph 5:32
to be well-pleasing, not **t** back Ti 2:9
to come that we are **t** about. Heb 2:5

TALKS *(2)*

in his heart; he goes out and **t**. Ps 41:6
you—anyone who **t** back to God? Rm 9:20

TALL *(17)*

people as **t** as the Anakim, Dt 2:10
people, **t** as the Anakim. Dt 2:21
The people are strong and **t**, Dt 9:2
He was nine feet, nine inches **t** 1Sm 17:4
each wheel was 27 inches **t**. 1Kg 7:32
was 27 feet **t** and had a bronze 2Kg 25:17
who was seven and a half feet **t**. 1Ch 11:23
gallows 75 feet **t** at Haman's Est 7:9
and the **t** ⌊trees⌋ will be cut Is 10:33
a nation **t** and smooth-skinned, Is 18:2
from a people **t** and Is 18:7
and fortify her **t** fortresses, Jr 51:53
pillar was 27 feet **t**, had a Jr 52:21
bring down the **t** tree, and make Ezk 17:24
tree, and make the low tree **t**. Ezk 17:24
underground springs made it **t**, Ezk 31:4
That statue, **t** and dazzling, was Dn 2:31

TALLER *(5)*

are larger and **t** than we are; Dt 1:28
He stood a head **t** than anyone 1Sm 9:2
he stood a head **t** than anyone 1Sm 10:23
it's **t** than the vegetables and Mt 13:32
it comes up and grows **t** than all Mk 4:32

TALLEST *(2)*

I cut down its **t** cedars, its 2Kg 19:23
I cut down its **t** cedars, its Is 37:24

TALMAI *(6)*

Sheshai, and **T**, the descendants Nm 13:22
Ahiman, and **T**, descendants of Jos 15:14
down Sheshai, Ahiman, and **T**. Jdg 1:10
daughter of King **T** of Geshur; 2Sm 3:3
and went to **T** son of Ammihud, 2Sm 13:37
daughter of King **T** of Geshur, 1Ch 3:2

TALMON *(3)*

Shallum, Akkub, **T**, Ahiman, and 1Ch 9:17
Akkub, **T**, and their relatives, Neh 11:19
Meshullam, **T**, and Akkub were Neh 12:25

TALMON'S *(2)*

descendants, **T** descendants, Ezr 2:42
descendants, **T** descendants, Neh 7:45

TAMAR *(27)*

firstborn, and her name was **T**. Gn 38:6
said to his daughter-in-law **T**, Gn 38:11
So **T** went to live in her Gn 38:11
T was told, "Your father-in-law Gn 38:13
Perez, the son **T** bore to Judah, Ru 4:12
had a beautiful sister named **T**, 2Sm 13:1
over his sister **T** because she 2Sm 13:2
I'm in love with **T**, my brother 2Sm 13:4
let my sister **T** come and give me 2Sm 13:5
let my sister **T** come and make 2Sm 13:6
sent word to **T** at the palace: 2Sm 13:7
Then **T** went to his house while 2Sm 13:8
Amnon told **T**, "so I can eat 2Sm 13:10
T took the cakes she had made 2Sm 13:10
hated **T** with such intensity 2Sm 13:15
T was wearing a long-sleeved 2Sm 13:18
T put ashes on her head and tore 2Sm 13:19
So **T** lived as a desolate woman 2Sm 13:20
since he disgraced his sister **T**. 2Sm 13:22
Amnon disgraced his sister **T**. 2Sm 13:32
a daughter named **T**, who was a 2Sm 14:27
T in the Wilderness of Judah, 1Kg 9:18
daughter-in-law **T** bore him Perez 1Ch 2:4
their sister **T**, in addition to 1Ch 3:9
it will run from **T** to the waters Ezk 47:19

will run from **T** to the waters Ezk 48:28
fathered Perez and Zerah by **T**, Mt 1:3

TAMARISK *(3)*
Abraham planted a **t** tree in Gn 21:33
under the **t** tree at the high 1Sm 22:6
them under the **t** tree in Jabesh 1Sm 31:13

TAMBOURINE *(6)*
sister, took a **t** in her hand, Ex 15:20
singing to the **t** and lyre and Jb 21:12
song—play the **t**, the melodious Ps 81:2
music to Him with **t** and lyre. Ps 149:3
Praise Him with **t** and dance; Ps 150:4
lyre, harp, **t**, flute, and wine Is 5:12

TAMBOURINES *(11)*
and singing, with **t** and lyres, Gn 31:27
followed her with **t** and dancing. Ex 15:20
to meet him with **t** and dancing! Jdg 11:34
by harps, **t**, flutes, and lyres 1Sm 10:5
singing and dancing with **t**, 1Sm 18:6
lyres, harps, **t**, sistrums, and 2Sm 6:5
with lyres, harps, **t**, cymbals, 1Ch 13:8
them are young women playing **t**. Ps 68:25
The joyful **t** have ceased. Is 24:8
⌊to the sound⌋ of **t** and lyres; Is 30:32
will take up your **t** again and go Jr 31:4

TAME *(1)*
but no man can **t** the tongue. Jms 3:8

TAMED *(2)*
is **t** and has been tamed by man, Jms 3:7
is tamed and has been **t** by man, Jms 3:7

TAMMUZ *(1)*
sitting there weeping for **T**. Ezk 8:14

TANGLED *(2)*
went under the **t** branches of a 2Sm 18:9
Foolishness is **t** up in the heart Pr 22:15

TANHUMETH *(2)*
Seraiah son of **T** the 2Kg 25:23
Seraiah son of **T**, the sons of Jr 40:8

TANNER *(2)*
Joppa with Simon, a leather **t**. Ac 9:43
with Simon, a **t**, whose house is Ac 10:6

TANNER'S *(1)*
Simon the **t** house by the sea.' Ac 10:32

TAPESTRIES *(1)*
were weaving **t** for Asherah. 2Kg 23:7

TAPHATH *(1)*
T daughter of Solomon was his 1Kg 4:11

TAPPUAH *(6)*
the king of **T** one the king of Jos 12:17
Zanoah, En-gannim, **T**, Enam, Jos 15:34
From **T** the border went westward Jos 16:8
The region of **T** belonged to Jos 17:8
but **T** ⌊itself⌋ on Manasseh's Jos 17:8
Korah, **T**, Rekem, and Shema. 1Ch 2:43

TARALAH *(1)*
Rekem, Irpeel, **T**, Jos 18:27

TAREA *(1)*
(AKA TAHREA)
Pithon, Melech, **T**, and Ahaz. 1Ch 8:35

TARGET *(4)*
it as if I'm aiming at a **t**. 1Sm 20:20
Why have You made me Your **t**, Jb 7:20
He set me up as His **t**; Jb 16:12
set me as the **t** for His arrow. Lm 3:12

TARIFFS *(1)*
earthly kings collect **t** or taxes Mt 17:25

TARNISHED *(1)*
How the gold has become **t**, Lm 4:1

TARSHISH *(28)*
Elishah, **T**, Kittim, and Dodanim. Gn 10:4
king had ships of **T** at sea with 1Kg 10:22
the ships of **T** would arrive 1Kg 10:22
made ships of **T** to go to Ophir 1Kg 22:48
Elishah, **T**, Kittim, and Rodanim. 1Ch 1:7
Zethan, **T**, and Ahishahar. 1Ch 7:10
kept going to **T** with Hiram's 2Ch 9:21
the ships of **T** would arrive 2Ch 9:21
him to make ships to go to **T**, 2Ch 20:36
and were not able to go to **T**. 2Ch 20:37
Admatha, **T**, Meres, Marsena, Est 1:14
the ships of **T** with the east Ps 48:7
the kings of **T** and the coasts Ps 72:10
every ship of **T**, and against Is 2:16
Wail, ships of **T**, for your haven Is 23:1
Cross over to **T**; wail, Is 23:6
like the Nile, daughter of **T**; Is 23:10
Wail, ships of **T**, because your Is 23:14
with the ships of **T** in the lead, Is 60:9
nations—to **T**, Put, Lud (who Is 66:19
Beaten silver is brought from **T**, Jr 10:9
T was your trading partner Ezk 27:12
Ships of **T** were the carriers for Ezk 27:25
the merchants of **T** with all its Ezk 38:13
up to flee to **T** from the LORD's Jnh 1:3
and found a ship going to **T**. Jnh 1:3
into it to go with them to **T**, Jnh 1:3
why I fled toward **T** in the first Jnh 4:2

TARSUS *(5)*
ask for a man from **T** named Saul, Ac 9:11
Caesarea and sent him off to **T**. Ac 9:30
Then he went to **T** to search for Ac 11:25
a Jewish man from **T** of Cilicia, Ac 21:39
man, born in **T** of Cilicia, Ac 22:3

TARTAK *(1)*
the Avvites made Nibhaz and **T**, 2Kg 17:31

TARTAN *(1)*
the king of Assyria sent the **T**, 2Kg 18:17

TARTARUS *(1)*
them down into **T** and delivered 2Pt 2:4

TASK *(20)*
because the **t** is too heavy for Ex 18:18
useful for any **t** in the work Ex 35:24
had brought for the **t** of making Ex 36:3
by the man appointed for the **t**. Lv 16:21
each man his **t** and Nm 4:19
performed their **t** according to 1Ch 6:32
The **t** is great, for the temple 1Ch 29:1
those doing the work **t** by task. 2Ch 34:13
those doing the work task by **t**. 2Ch 34:13
realized that this **t** had been Neh 6:16
out to their **t** of foraging for Jb 24:5
this miserable **t** to keep them Ec 1:13
He gives the **t** of gathering Ec 2:26
I have seen the **t** that God has Ec 3:10
too is futile and a miserable **t**. Ec 4:8
to perform His **t**, His disturbing Is 28:21
His task, His disturbing **t**. Is 28:21
a weapon suitable for its **t**; Is 54:16
because it is a **t** of the Lord Jr 50:25
But now finish the **t** as well, 2Co 8:11

TASKMASTERS *(1)*
Egyptians assigned **t** over the Ex 1:11

TASKS *(10)*
and for daily **t** is now as it was Jos 14:11
the king in all his daily **t**." 2Kg 11:8
from other **t** because they were 1Ch 9:33
the Levites ⌊serve⌋ at their **t**. 2Ch 13:10
the king in all his daily **t**." 2Ch 23:7
none of them left their **t**. 2Ch 35:15
the singers' daily **t**. Neh 11:23
about his daily **t** among the Jr 37:4
was distracted by her many **t**, Lk 10:40
attending to these **t**. Rm 13:6

TASSEL *(5)*
cord on the **t** at ⌊each⌋ corner Nm 15:38
and touched the **t** on His robe, Mt 9:20
only touch the **t** on His robe. Mt 14:36
touch just the **t** of His robe. Mk 6:56
and touched the **t** of His robe. Lk 8:44

TASSELS *(4)*
are to make **t** for the corners Nm 15:38
will serve as **t** for you to look Nm 15:39
Make **t** on the four corners of Dt 22:12
and lengthen their **t**. Mt 23:5

TASTE *(18)*
he had a **t** for wild game, Gn 25:28
so severely if I **t** bread or 2Sm 3:35
Can your servant **t** what he eats 2Sm 19:35
T and see that the LORD is good. Ps 34:8
How sweet Your word is to my **t** Ps 119:103
fulfilled is sweet to the **t**, Pr 13:19
sweet to the **t** and health to the Pr 16:24
and his fruit is sweet to my **t**. Sg 2:3
So his **t** has remained the same, Jr 48:11
flock, is to **t** anything at all Jnh 3:7
if the salt should lose its **t**, Mt 5:13
who will not **t** death until they Mt 16:28
who will not **t** death until they Mk 9:1
who will not **t** death until they Lk 9:27
but if salt should lose its **t**, Lk 14:34
he will never **t** death—ever!' Jn 8:52
handle, don't **t**, don't touch"? Col 2:21
grace He might **t** death for Heb 2:9

TASTED *(11)*
and **t** like wafers ⌊made⌋ with Ex 16:31
It **t** like a pastry cooked with Nm 11:8
none of the troops **t** ⌊any⌋ food. 1Sm 14:24
because I **t** a little honey. 1Sm 14:29
I **t** a little honey with the end 1Sm 14:43
having never **t** prosperity. Jb 21:25
But when He **t** it, He would not Mt 27:34
the chief servant **t** the water Jn 2:9
enlightened, who **t** the heavenly Heb 6:4
t God's good word and the powers Heb 6:5
since you have **t** that the Lord 1Pt 2:3

TASTES *(3)*
test words as the palate **t** food? Jb 12:11
Though evil **t** sweet in his mouth Jb 20:12
test words as the palate **t** food? Jb 34:3

TASTY *(1)*
bread ⌊eaten⌋ secretly is **t**!" Pr 9:17

TATTENAI *(4)*
At that time **T** the governor of Ezr 5:3
the letter that **T** the governor Ezr 5:6
T governor of the region west of Ezr 6:6
Then **T** governor of the region Ezr 6:13

TATTOO *(1)*
the dead or put **t** marks on Lv 19:28

TAUGHT *(43)*
I have **t** you statutes and Dt 4:5
on that day and **t** it to the Dt 31:22
the Judahites be **t** ⌊The Song of⌋ 2Sm 1:18
He also **t** about animals, birds, 1Kg 4:33
t throughout Judah, ⌊having⌋ 2Ch 17:9
towns of Judah and **t** the people. 2Ch 17:9
to the Levites who **t** all Israel 2Ch 35:3
You have **t** me from my youth, Ps 71:17
he **t** me and said: "Your heart Pr 4:4
an oracle that his mother **t** him: Pr 31:1
he constantly **t** the people Ec 12:9
the house of my mother who **t** me. Sg 8:2
understanding and **t** Him the Is 40:14
Who **t** Him knowledge and showed Is 40:14
children will be **t** by the LORD, Is 54:13
They have **t** their tongues to Jr 9:5
Baals, as their fathers **t** them." Jr 9:14
just as they **t** My people to Jr 12:16
Though I **t** them time and time Jr 32:33
It was I who **t** Ephraim to walk, Hs 11:3
coming to Him, and He **t** them. Mk 2:13
He **t** them many things in Mk 4:2
all that they had done and **t**. Mk 6:30
question as He **t** in the temple Mk 12:35
as John also **t** his disciples." Lk 11:1
and You **t** in our streets!' Lk 13:26
And they will all be **t** by God. Jn 6:45
But just as the Father **t** Me, Jn 8:28
I have always **t** in the synagogue Jn 18:20
the church and **t** large numbers, Ac 11:26
he spoke and **t** the things about Ac 18:25
not in words **t** by human wisdom, 1Co 2:13
but in those **t** by the Spirit, 1Co 2:13
human source and I was not **t** it, Gl 1:12
one who is **t** the message must Gl 6:6
you heard Him and were **t** by Him, Eph 4:21
as you were **t**, and overflowing Col 2:7
yourselves are **t** by God to love 1Th 4:9
to the traditions you were **t**, 2Th 2:15
they may be **t** not to blaspheme 1Tm 1:20
to the faithful message as **t**, Ti 1:9
just as it has **t** you, remain in 1Jn 2:27
who **t** Balak to place a stumbling Rv 2:14

TAUNT *(7)*
Her rival would **t** her severely 1Sm 1:6
do not make me the **t** of fools. Ps 39:8
My adversaries **t** me, as if Ps 42:10
My enemies **t** me all day long; Ps 102:8
you will be a disgrace and a **t**, Ezk 5:15
will take up a **t** against you, Mc 2:4
these take up a **t** against him, Hab 2:6

TAUNTED *(6)*
t me about them, saying, 'Are Jdg 8:15
rival **t** her in this way every 1Sm 1:7
When he **t** Israel, Jonathan, son 2Sm 21:21
When he **t** Israel, Jonathan, son 1Ch 20:7

who have **t** My people and Zph 2:8
because they have **t** and acted Zph 2:10

TAUNTING *(4)*
will put an end to his **t**; Dn 11:18
I have heard the **t** of Moab and Zph 2:8
crucified with Him kept **t** Him. Mt 27:44
crucified with Him were **t** Him. Mk 15:32

TAUNTS *(5)*
I can answer the one who **t** me, Ps 119:42
I can answer anyone who **t** me. Pr 27:11
do not be shattered by their **t**. Is 51:7
he will turn his **t** against him. Dn 11:18
exposed to **t** and afflictions, Heb 10:33

TAVERNS *(1)*
as Forum of Appius and Three **T**. Ac 28:15

TAX *(39)*
and Jerusalem the **t** ⌊imposed by⌋ 2Ch 24:6
that the **t** God's servant 2Ch 24:9
brought ⌊the **t**⌋, and put it 2Ch 24:10
duty, or land **t**, and the royal Ezr 4:13
and land **t** were paid to them. Ezr 4:20
and land **t** must not be imposed Ezr 7:24
pay the king's **t** on our fields Neh 5:4
provinces from **t** payments and Est 2:18
imposed a **t** throughout the land Est 10:1
will send out a **t** collector for Dn 11:20
and exact a grain **t** from him, Am 5:11
Don't even the **t** collectors do Mt 5:46
Matthew sitting at the **t** office, Mt 9:9
many **t** collectors and sinners Mt 9:10
Teacher eat with **t** collectors Mt 9:11
and Matthew the **t** collector; Mt 10:3
a friend of **t** collectors and Mt 11:19
double-drachma **t** approached Mt 17:24
pay the double-drachma **t**?" Mt 17:24
and a **t** collector to you Mt 18:17
T collectors and prostitutes are Mt 21:31
T collectors and prostitutes did Mt 21:32
Me the coin used for the **t**." Mt 22:19
sitting at the **t** office, Mk 2:14
many **t** collectors and sinners Mk 2:15
with sinners and **t** collectors, Mk 2:16
does He eat with **t** collectors Mk 2:16
T collectors also came to be Lk 3:12
out and saw a **t** collector named Lk 5:27
Levi sitting at the **t** office, Lk 5:27
a large crowd of **t** collectors Lk 5:29
eat and drink with **t** collectors Lk 5:30
including the **t** collectors, Lk 7:29
a friend of **t** collectors and Lk 7:34
All the **t** collectors and sinners Lk 15:1
and the other a **t** collector. Lk 18:10
or even like this **t** collector. Lk 18:11
But the **t** collector, standing Lk 18:13
who was a chief **t** collector, Lk 19:2

TAXED *(1)*
command he **t** the land to give 2Kg 23:35

TAXES *(10)*
exempt from paying **t** in Israel." 1Sm 17:25
revenues from the **t** of the Ezr 6:8
kings collect tariffs or **t** Mt 17:25
to pay **t** to Caesar or not? Mt 22:17
lawful to pay **t** to Caesar or not Mk 12:14
us to pay **t** to Caesar or not? Lk 20:22
opposing payment of **t** to Caesar, Lk 23:2
And for this reason you pay **t**, Rm 13:6
t to those you owe taxes, tolls Rm 13:7
those you owe **t**, tolls to those Rm 13:7

TEACH *(112)*
and I will **t** you what to say. Ex 4:12
and will **t** you both what to do. Ex 4:15
I **t** ⌊them⌋ God's statutes and Ex 18:16
and **t** them the way to live and Ex 18:20
sight, please **t** me Your ways, Ex 33:13
⌊the ability⌋ to **t** ⌊others⌋. Ex 35:34
and **t** the Israelites all the Lv 10:11
T them to your children and your Dt 4:9
commanded me to **t** you statutes Dt 4:14
you are to **t** them, so that they Dt 5:31
has instructed ⌊me⌋ to **t** you, Dt 6:1
T them to your children, talking Dt 11:19
that they won't **t** you to do all Dt 20:18
for yourselves and **t** it to the Dt 31:19
elders, and they will **t** you. Dt 32:7
They will **t** Your ordinances to Dt 33:10
This was to **t** the future Jdg 3:2
again to us and **t** us what we Jdg 13:8
I will **t** you the good and right 1Sm 12:23
and we'll **t** you a lesson!" 1Sm 14:12
so that You may **t** them the good 1Kg 8:36
so he can **t** them the custom 2Kg 17:27
and he began to **t** them how they 2Kg 17:28
so that You may **t** them the good 2Ch 6:27
to **t** in the cities of Judah. 2Ch 17:7
and **t** ⌊its⌋ statutes and Ezr 7:10
God and to **t** anyone who does Ezr 7:25
T me, and I will be silent. Jb 6:24
Will they not **t** you and tell you Jb 8:10
Can anyone **t** God knowledge, Jb 21:22
I will **t** you about God's power. Jb 27:11
and maturity should **t** wisdom. Jb 32:7
quiet, and I will **t** you wisdom. Jb 33:33
T me what I cannot see; Jb 34:32
T us what we should say to Him; Jb 37:19
to me, LORD; **t** me Your paths. Ps 25:4
Guide me in Your truth and **t** me, Ps 25:5
I will **t** you the fear of the Ps 34:11
and You **t** me wisdom deep within. Ps 51:6
I will **t** the rebellious Your Ps 51:13
our fathers to **t** to their Ps 78:5
T me Your way, LORD, and I will Ps 86:11
T us to number our days Ps 90:12
discipline and **t** from Your law Ps 94:12
You be praised; **t** me Your Ps 119:12
listened to me; **t** me Your Ps 119:26
T me, LORD, the meaning of Your Ps 119:33
faithful love; **t** me Your Ps 119:64
T me good judgment and Ps 119:66
what is good; **t** me Your statutes Ps 119:68
of praise, and **t** me Your Ps 119:108
faithful love; **t** me Your Ps 119:124
servant, and **t** me Your statutes Ps 119:135
for You **t** me Your statutes. Ps 119:171
My decrees that I will **t** them, Ps 132:12
T me to do Your will, for You Ps 143:10
on you and **t** you my words. Pr 1:23
t a righteous man, and he will Pr 9:9
T a youth about the way he Pr 22:6
in order to **t** you true and Pr 22:21
He will **t** us about His ways so Is 2:3
Who is he trying to **t**? Is 28:9
you also **t** evil women your ways. Jr 2:33
T your daughters a lament and Jr 9:20
longer will one **t** his neighbor Jr 31:34
They must **t** My people the Ezk 44:23
and to **t** them the Chaldean Dn 1:4
her priests **t** for payment, Mc 3:11
will **t** us about His ways so we Mc 4:2
alive! Can it **t**? Look! It may be Hab 2:19
Then He began to **t** them, saying: Mt 5:2
on from there to **t** and preach in Mt 11:1
and began to **t** them in their Mt 13:54
truthful and **t** truthfully the Mt 22:16
they don't practice what they **t**. Mt 23:3
on the Sabbath and began to **t**. Mk 1:21
Again He began to **t** by the sea, Mk 4:1
He began to **t** in the synagogue, Mk 6:2
He began to **t** them many things Mk 6:34
Then He began to **t** them that the Mk 8:31
Then He began to **t** them: Mk 11:17
partiality but **t** truthfully the Mk 12:14
Him, "Lord, **t** us to pray, just Lk 11:1
Spirit will **t** you at that very Lk 12:12
that You speak and **t** correctly, Lk 20:21
but **t** truthfully the way of God. Lk 20:21
temple complex and began to **t**. Jn 7:14
the Greeks and **t** the Greeks, Jn 7:35
He sat down and began to **t** them. Jn 8:2
"and are you trying to **t** us?" Jn 9:34
will **t** you all things and remind Jn 14:26
all that Jesus began to do and **t** Ac 1:1
not to preach or **t** at all in the Ac 4:18
at daybreak and began to **t**. Ac 5:21
order you not to **t** in this name? Ac 5:28
and began to **t** the brothers: Ac 15:1
you that you **t** all the Jews who Ac 21:21
you then, who **t** another, do you Rm 2:21
another, do you not **t** yourself? Rm 2:21
just as I **t** everywhere in every 1Co 4:17
nature itself **t** you that if a 1Co 11:14
in order to **t** others also, 1Co 14:19
people not to **t** other doctrine 1Tm 1:3
allow a woman to **t** or to have 1Tm 2:12
Command and **t** these things. 1Tm 4:11
T and encourage these things. 1Tm 6:2
will be able to **t** others also. 2Tm 2:2
able to **t**, and patient, 2Tm 2:24
⌊They are⌋ to **t** what is good, Ti 2:3
need someone to **t** you again the Heb 5:12
person will not **t** his fellow Heb 8:11
you don't need anyone to **t** you. 1Jn 2:27

TEACHER *(68)*
the **t** along with the pupil. 1Ch 25:8
of Zechariah, the **t** of the fear 2Ch 26:5
Who is a **t** like Him? Jb 36:22
words of the **T**, son of David, Ec 1:1
"Absolute futility," says the **T**. Ec 1:2
I, the **T**, have been king over Ec 1:12
"Look," says the **T**, "this I have Ec 7:27
"Absolute futility," says the **T**. Ec 12:8
addition to the **T** being a wise Ec 12:9
The **T** sought to find delightful Ec 12:10
is the prophet, the lying **t**. Is 9:15
but your **T** will not hide Himself Is 30:20
Your eyes will see your **T**, Is 30:20
only⌋ a cast image, a **t** of lies. Hab 2:18
Him and said, "**T**, I will follow Mt 8:19
Why does your **T** eat with tax Mt 9:11
A disciple is not above his **t**, Mt 10:24
become like his **t** and a slave Mt 10:25
said to Him, "**T**, we want to see Mt 12:38
Doesn't your **T** pay the Mt 17:24
asked Him, "**T**, what good must Mt 19:16
"**T**," they said, "we know that Mt 22:16
T, Moses said, if a man dies, Mt 22:24
T, which commandment in the law Mt 22:36
you have one **T**, and you are all Mt 23:8
"and tell him, 'The **T** says: Mt 26:18
woke Him up and said to Him, "**T**! Mk 4:38
Why bother the **T** any more?" Mk 5:35
answered Him, "**T**, I brought my Mk 9:17
said to Him, "**T**, we saw someone Mk 9:38
Him, "Good **T**, what must I do Mk 10:17
said to Him, "**T**, I have kept all Mk 10:20
Him and said, "**T**, we want You to Mk 10:35
said to Him, "**T**, we know You are Mk 12:14
T, Moses wrote for us that if a Mk 12:19
said to Him, "You are right, **T**! Mk 12:32
disciples said to Him, "**T**, look! Mk 13:1
the house, 'The **T** says, "Where Mk 14:14
asked him, "**T**, what should we Lk 3:12
A disciple is not above his **t**, Lk 6:40
trained will be like his **t**. Lk 6:40
"**T**," he said, "say it." Lk 7:40
Don't bother the **T** anymore." Lk 8:49
crowd cried out, "**T**, I beg You Lk 9:38
Him, saying, "**T**, what must I do Lk 10:25
answered Him, "**T**, when You say Lk 11:45
said to Him, "**T**, tell my brother Lk 12:13
Him, "Good **T**, what must I do Lk 18:18
crowd told Him, "**T**, rebuke Your Lk 19:39
questioned Him, "**T**, we know that Lk 20:21
T, Moses wrote for us that if a Lk 20:28
answered, "**T**, You have spoken Lk 20:39
"**T**," they asked Him, "so when Lk 21:7
the house, 'The **T** asks you, Lk 22:11
which means "**T**"), "where are You Jn 1:38
You have come from God as a **t**, Jn 3:2
Are you a **t** of Israel and don't Jn 3:10
"**T**," they said to Him, "this Jn 8:4
The **T** is here and is calling for Jn 11:28
You call Me **T** and Lord. Jn 13:13
I, your Lord and **T**, have washed Jn 13:14
—which means "**T**." Jn 20:16
a **t** of the law who was respected Ac 5:34
ignorant, a **t** of the immature Rm 2:20
must share his goods with the **t**. Gl 6:6
and a **t** of the Gentiles in faith 1Tm 2:7
hospitable, an able **t**, 1Tm 3:2
a herald, apostle, and **t**, 2Tm 1:11

TEACHERS *(14)*
as well as the **t** Joiarib and Ezr 8:16
than all my **t** because Your Ps 119:99
I didn't obey my **t** or listen Pr 5:13
complex sitting among the **t**, Lk 2:46
Pharisees and **t** of the law were Lk 5:17
there were prophets and **t**: Ac 13:1
third **t**, next, miracles 1Co 12:28
prophets? Are all **t**? Do all do 1Co 12:29
evangelists, some pastors and **t**, Eph 4:11
They want to be **t** of the law, 1Tm 1:7
will accumulate **t** for themselves 2Tm 4:3

by this time you ought to be **t**, Heb 5:12
should become **t**, my brothers, Jms 3:1
there will be false **t** among you. 2Pt 2:1

TEACHES *(12)*

Your iniquity **t** you what to say, Jb 15:5
is right and **t** them His way. Ps 25:9
the One who **t** man knowledge— Ps 94:10
when one **t** a wise man, he Pr 21:11
His God **t** him order; Is 28:26
who **t** you for ⌊your⌋ benefit, Is 48:17
and **t** people to do so Mt 5:19
practices and **t** ⌊these Mt 5:19
is the man who **t** everyone Ac 21:28
If anyone **t** other doctrine and 1Tm 6:3
His anointing **t** you about all 1Jn 2:27
and **t** and deceives My slaves to Rv 2:20

TEACHING *(96)*

ordinances I am **t** you to follow, Dt 4:1
Let my **t** fall like rain and my Dt 32:2
God, without a **t** priest, and 2Ch 15:3
have said, "My **t** is sound, and I Jb 11:4
How I love Your **t**! It is my Ps 119:97
for **t** shrewdness to the Pr 1:4
don't reject your mother's **t**, Pr 1:8
don't forget my **t**, but let your Pr 3:1
Don't abandon my **t**. Pr 4:2
I am **t** you the way of wisdom; Pr 4:11
don't reject your mother's **t**. Pr 6:20
is a lamp, **t** is a light, Pr 6:23
all over Galilee, **t** in their Mt 4:23
crowds were astonished at His **t**, Mt 7:28
because He was **t** them like one Mt 7:29
and villages, **t** in their Mt 9:35
t as doctrines the commands of Mt 15:9
of the **t** of the Pharisees and Mt 16:12
up to Him as He was **t** and said, Mt 21:23
they were astonished at His **t**. Mt 22:33
I used to sit, **t** in the temple Mt 26:55
t them to observe everything I Mt 28:20
astonished at His **t** because, Mk 1:22
He was **t** them as one having Mk 1:22
A new **t** with authority! Mk 1:27
and in His **t** He said to them: Mk 4:2
the villages in a circuit, **t**. Mk 6:6
t as doctrines the commands of Mk 7:7
For He was **t** His disciples and Mk 9:31
He began **t** them once more. Mk 10:1
crowd was astonished by His **t**. Mk 11:18
also said in His **t**, "Beware of Mk 12:38
I was among you, **t** in the temple Mk 14:49
He was **t** in their synagogues, Lk 4:15
and was **t** them on the Sabbath. Lk 4:31
astonished at His **t** because His Lk 4:32
He sat down and was **t** the crowds Lk 5:3
of those days while He was **t**, Lk 5:17
entered the synagogue and was **t**. Lk 6:6
As He was **t** in one of the Lk 13:10
t and making His way to Lk 13:22
Every day He was **t** in the temple Lk 19:47
One day as He was **t** the people Lk 20:1
He was **t** in the temple complex, Lk 21:37
up the people, **t** throughout all Lk 23:5
things while **t** in the synagogue Jn 6:59
they said, "This **t** is hard! Jn 6:60
My **t** isn't Mine but is from the Jn 7:16
whether the **t** is from God or if Jn 7:17
As He was **t** in the temple Jn 7:28
while **t** in the temple complex. Jn 8:20
His disciples and about His **t**. Jn 18:19
themselves to the apostles' **t**, Ac 2:42
that they were **t** the people Ac 4:2
complex and **t** the people." Ac 5:25
with your **t** and are determined Ac 5:28
they continued **t** and proclaiming Ac 5:42
at the **t** about the Lord. Ac 13:12
in Antioch **t** and proclaiming Ac 15:35
about this new **t** you're speaking Ac 17:19
t the word of God among them. Ac 18:11
from **t** it to you in public and Ac 20:20
kingdom of God and **t** the things Ac 28:31
that pattern of **t** you were Rm 6:17
in service; if **t**, in teaching; Rm 12:7
in service; if teaching, in **t**; Rm 12:7
or knowledge or prophecy or **t**? 1Co 14:6
has a psalm, a **t**, a revelation, 1Co 14:26
blown around by every wind of **t**, Eph 4:14
warning and **t** everyone with all Col 1:28
t and admonishing one another in Col 3:16
else is contrary to the sound **t** 1Tm 1:10
and of the good **t** that you have 1Tm 4:6
reading, exhortation, and **t**. 1Tm 4:13
about yourself and your **t**; 1Tm 4:16
work hard at preaching and **t**. 1Tm 5:17
God's name and His **t** will not be 1Tm 6:1
with the sound **t** of our Lord 1Tm 6:3
and with the **t** that promotes 1Tm 6:3
pattern of sound **t** that you have 2Tm 1:13
correctly **t** the word of truth. 2Tm 2:15
But you have followed my **t**, 2Tm 3:10
by God and is profitable for **t**, 2Tm 3:16
with great patience and **t**. 2Tm 4:2
with sound **t** and to refute those Ti 1:9
households by **t** for dishonest Ti 1:11
what is consistent with sound **t**. Ti 2:1
integrity and dignity in your **t**. Ti 2:7
may adorn the **t** of God our Ti 2:10
t about ritual washings, laying Heb 6:2
remain in the **t** about Christ, 2Jn 9
The one who remains in that **t**, 2Jn 9
you and does not bring this **t**, 2Jn 10
who hold to the **t** of Balaam, Rv 2:14
who hold to the **t** of the Rv 2:15
do not hold this **t**, who haven't Rv 2:24

TEACHINGS *(4)*

protect my **t** as you would the Pr 7:2
for they have transgressed **t**, Is 24:5
spirits and the **t** of demons, 1Tm 4:1
by various kinds of strange **t**; Heb 13:9

TEAM *(3)*

He took a **t** of oxen, cut them in 1Sm 11:7
and he was with the twelfth **t**. 1Kg 19:19
him, took the **t** of oxen, 1Kg 19:21

TEAMS *(2)*

for the chariot **t** and the other 1Kg 4:28
Twelve **t** of oxen were in front 1Kg 19:19

TEAR *(63)*

armor so that it does not **t**. Ex 28:32
you must **t** down their altars, Ex 34:13
opening so that it would not **t**. Ex 39:23
He will **t** it open by its wings Lv 1:17
and do not **t** your garments, Lv 10:6
his hair or **t** his garments. Lv 21:10
t down their altars, smash their Dt 7:5
T down their altars, smash their Dt 12:3
and you are to **t** down their Jdg 2:2
Then **t** down the altar of Baal Jdg 6:25
I will **t** down this tower!" Jdg 8:9
were with him, "**T** your clothes, 2Sm 3:31
I will **t** the kingdom away from 1Kg 11:11
I will **t** it out of your son's 1Kg 11:12
I will not **t** the entire kingdom 1Kg 11:13
'I am about to **t** the kingdom out 1Kg 11:31
You who **t** yourself in anger— Jb 18:4
They **t** up my path; they Jb 30:13
Let us **t** off their chains and Ps 2:3
or they will **t** me like a lion, Ps 7:2
They are like a lion eager to **t**, Ps 17:12
He will **t** them down and not Ps 28:5
God, or I will **t** you apart, and Ps 50:22
t out the young lions' fangs. Ps 58:6
a time to **t** down and a time to Ec 3:3
a time to **t** and a time to sew; Ec 3:7
I will **t** down its wall, and it Is 5:5
and **t** away and remove the Is 18:5
so that you could **t** them down to Is 22:10
free, and to **t** off every yoke? Is 58:6
only You would **t** the heavens Is 64:1
kingdoms to uproot and **t** down, Jr 1:10
I will uproot, **t** down, and Jr 18:7
hand, I would **t** you from it. Jr 22:24
to uproot and to **t** them down, Jr 31:28
terrified or **t** their garments. Jr 36:24
I will **t** down the wall you Ezk 13:14
I will **t** them from your arms. Ezk 13:20
I will also **t** off your veils and Ezk 13:21
your mounds and **t** down your Ezk 16:39
Will he not **t** out its roots and Ezk 17:9
After he learned to **t** prey, Ezk 19:3
After he learned to **t** prey, Ezk 19:6
pieces, and **t** your breasts. Ezk 23:34
walls and **t** down your towers Ezk 26:9
your walls and **t** down your Ezk 26:12
I will **t** ⌊them⌋ to pieces and Hs 5:14
of her cubs and **t** open the rib Hs 13:8
T your hearts, not just your Jl 2:13
You **t** off the skin of people and Mc 3:2
of your land and **t** down all your Mc 5:11
from you and **t** off your shackles Nah 1:13
fat ⌊sheep⌋ and **t** off their Zch 11:16
feet, turn, and **t** you to pieces. Mt 7:6
garment and makes the **t** worse. Mt 9:16
cloth, and a worse **t** is made. Mk 2:21
and their nets began to **t**. Lk 5:6
not only will he **t** the new, Lk 5:36
'I'll **t** down my barns and build Lk 12:18
Let's not **t** it, but toss for it Jn 19:24
Do not **t** down God's work Rm 14:20
away every **t** from their eyes Rv 7:17
away every **t** from their eyes Rv 21:4

TEARING *(6)*

mighty wind was **t** at the 1Kg 19:11
a roaring lion **t** ⌊its⌋ prey: Ezk 22:25
are like wolves **t** ⌊their⌋ prey, Ezk 22:27
you splintered, **t** all their Ezk 29:7
you up and not for **t** you down, 2Co 10:8
building up and not for **t** down. 2Co 13:10

TEARS *(44)*

is a wolf; he **t** ⌊his prey.⌋ Gn 49:27
like a lion and **t** off an arm or Dt 33:20
the LORD and wept with many **t**. 1Sm 1:10
I have seen your **t**. Look, I will 2Kg 20:5
Whatever He **t** down cannot be Jb 12:14
His anger **t** ⌊at me⌋, and He Jb 16:9
He **t** me down on every side so Jb 19:10
with my **t** I dampen my pillow and Ps 6:6
do not be silent at my **t**. Ps 39:12
My **t** have been my food day and Ps 42:3
Put my **t** in Your bottle. Ps 56:8
the bread of **t** and gave them Ps 80:5
a full measure of **t** to drink. Ps 80:5
and mingle my drinks with **t** Ps 102:9
death, my eyes from **t**, my feet Ps 116:8
out streams of **t** because people Ps 119:136
Those who sow in **t** will reap Ps 126:5
a foolish one **t** it down with her Pr 14:1
Look at the **t** of those who are Ec 4:1
Heshbon and Elealeh with my **t**. Is 16:9
wipe away the **t** from every face Is 25:8
I have seen your **t**. Look, I am Is 38:5
a fountain of **t**, I would weep Jr 9:1
our eyes may overflow with **t**, Jr 9:18
My eyes will overflow with **t**, Jr 13:17
Let my eyes overflow with **t**; Jr 14:17
weeping and your eyes from **t**, Jr 31:16
the night, with **t** on her cheeks. Lm 1:2
eyes flow with **t**. For there is Lm 1:16
let ⌊your⌋ **t** run down like a Lm 2:18
flow with streams of **t** because Lm 3:48
or weep or let your **t** flow. Ezk 24:16
tramples and **t** as it passes Mc 5:8
cover the LORD's altar with **t**, Mal 2:13
No one **t** a patch from a new Lk 5:36
to wash His feet with her **t**. Lk 7:38
she, with her **t**, has washed My Lk 7:44
all humility, with **t**, and with Ac 20:19
warning each one of you with **t**. Ac 20:31
I wrote to you with many **t**— 2Co 2:4
say again with **t**, that many live Php 3:18
Remembering your **t**, I long to 2Tm 1:4
loud cries and **t**, to the One who Heb 5:7
though he sought it with **t**. Heb 12:17

TEBAH *(1)*

also bore **T**, Gaham, Tahash, Gn 22:24

TEBALIAH *(1)*

Hilkiah the second, **T** the third, 1Ch 26:11

TEBETH *(1)*

the month **T**, in the seventh Est 2:16

TECHNIQUES *(1)*

cleverness in the **t** of deceit. Eph 4:14

TEEMING *(1)*

t with creatures beyond number— Ps 104:25

TEETH *(42)*

and his **t** are whiter than milk. Gn 49:12
meat was still between their **t**, Nm 11:33
He gnashes His **t** at me. Jb 16:9
escaped by the skin of my **t**. Jb 19:20
snatched the prey from his **t**. Jb 29:17
by those terrifying **t**? Jb 41:14
You break the **t** of the wicked. Ps 3:7
they gnashed their **t** at me. Ps 35:16
and gnashes his **t** at him. Ps 37:12

Their **t** are spears and arrows; Ps 57:4
knock the **t** out of their mouths; Ps 58:6
he will gnash his **t** in despair. Ps 112:10
us be ripped apart by their **t**. Ps 124:6
vinegar to the **t** and smoke to Pr 10:26
a generation whose **t** are swords, Pr 30:14
Your **t** are like a flock of newly Sg 4:2
Your **t** are like a flock of ewes Sg 6:6
love gliding past my lips and **t**! Sg 7:9
board, new, with many **t**. Is 41:15
children's **t** are set on edge. Jr 31:29
his own **t** will be set on edge. Jr 31:30
They hiss and gnash ⌊their⌋ **t**, Lm 2:16
ground my **t** on gravel and made Lm 3:16
children's **t** are set on edge? Ezk 18:2
ribs in its mouth between its **t**. Dn 7:5
strong, with large iron **t**. Dn 7:7
with iron **t** and bronze claws, Dn 7:19
its **t** are the teeth of a lion, Jl 1:6
its teeth are the **t** of a lion, Jl 1:6
to sink their **t** into but declare Mc 3:5
things from between their **t**. Zch 9:7
be weeping and gnashing of **t**." Mt 8:12
be weeping and gnashing of **t**. Mt 13:42
be weeping and gnashing of **t**. Mt 13:50
be weeping and gnashing of **t**.' Mt 22:13
be weeping and gnashing of **t**. Mt 24:51
be weeping and gnashing of **t**.' Mt 25:30
mouth, grinds his **t**, and becomes Mk 9:18
and gnashing of **t** in that place, Lk 13:28
and gnashed their **t** at him. Ac 7:54
their **t** were like lions' teeth; Rv 9:8
their teeth were like lions' **t**; Rv 9:8

TEHAPHNEHES *(2)*
(AKA TAHPANHES)
The day will be dark in **T**, Ezk 30:18
cloud will cover **T**, and its Ezk 30:18

TEHINNAH *(1)*
and **T** the father of Irnahash. 1Ch 4:12

TEKEL *(2)*
MENE, MENE, **T**, PARSIN Dn 5:25
T ⌊means that⌋ you have been Dn 5:27

TEKOA *(9)*
sent someone to **T** to bring a 2Sm 14:2
the woman from **T** came to the 2Sm 14:4
the woman of **T** said to the king 2Sm 14:9
bore him Ashhur the father of **T**. 1Ch 2:24
Asshur fathered **T** and had two 1Ch 4:5
He built up Bethlehem, Etam, **T**, 2Ch 11:6
went out to the wilderness of **T**. 2Ch 20:20
Sound the ram's horn in **T**; Jr 6:1
of the sheep breeders from **T**— Am 1:1

TEKOITE *(3)*
Ira son of Ikkesh the **T**, 2Sm 23:26
Ira son of Ikkesh the **T**, Abiezer 1Ch 11:28
was Ira son of Ikkesh the **T**; 1Ch 27:9

TEKOITES *(2)*
Beside them the **T** made repairs, Neh 3:5
Next to him the **T** made repairs Neh 3:27

TEL-ABIB *(1)*
I came to the exiles at **T**, Ezk 3:15

TEL-HARSHA *(2)*
Tel-melah, **T**, Cherub, Addan, Ezr 2:59
Tel-melah, **T**, Cherub, Addon, Neh 7:61

TEL-MELAH *(2)*
are those who came from **T**, Ezr 2:59
are those who came from **T**, Neh 7:61

TELAH *(1)*
his son **T**, his son Tahan, 1Ch 7:25

TELAIM *(1)*
(AKA TELEM)
troops and counted them at **T**: 1Sm 15:4

TELASSAR *(2)*
Rezeph, and the Edenites in **T**? 2Kg 19:12
Rezeph, and the Edenites in **T**? Is 37:12

TELEM *(2)*
(AKA TELAIM)
Ziph, **T**, Bealoth, Jos 15:24
Shallum, **T**, and Uri. Ezr 10:24

TELL *(466)*
Why didn't you **t** me she was your Gn 12:18
mountains I will **t** you about." Gn 22:2
Please **t** me, is there room in Gn 24:23
faithfulness to my master, **t** me; Gn 24:49
if not, **t** me, and I will go Gn 24:49
in the land that I **t** you about; Gn 26:2
slaves came to **t** him about the Gn 26:32
T me what your wages should be." Gn 29:15
me, deceive me, and not **t** me? Gn 31:27
then **t** him, 'They belong to your Gn 32:18
Him, "Please **t** me Your name." Gn 32:29
Can you **t** me where they are Gn 37:16
to God? **T** me ⌊your dreams⌋. Gn 40:8
you could not **t** that they had Gn 41:21
no one can **t** me what it means. Gn 41:24
Didn't I **t** you not to harm the Gn 42:22
Why did you **t** the man that you Gn 43:6
T my father all about my glory Gn 45:13
to Joseph, "**T** your brothers, Gn 45:17
I will **t** you what will happen Gn 49:1
with you, please **t** Pharaoh that Gn 50:4
what should I **t** them?" Ex 3:13
with him and **t** him what to say. Ex 4:15
Therefore **t** the Israelites: Ex 6:6
Go and **t** Pharaoh king of Egypt Ex 6:11
t Pharaoh king of Egypt Ex 6:29
Perform a miracle, **t** Aaron: Ex 7:9
T him: The LORD, the God of the Ex 7:16
Hebrews, has sent me to **t** you: Ex 7:16
LORD said to Moses, "**T** Aaron: Ex 7:19
Go in to Pharaoh and **t** him: Ex 8:1
then said to Moses, "**T** Aaron: Ex 8:5
LORD said to Moses, "**T** Aaron: Ex 8:16
to the water. **T** him: This is Ex 8:20
to Pharaoh. **T** him: This is what Ex 9:13
and so that you may **t** your son Ex 10:2
T the whole community of Israel Ex 12:3
T the Israelites to turn back Ex 14:2
T the Israelites to break camp. Ex 14:15
the Israelites. **T** them: At Ex 16:12
T the Israelites to take an Ex 25:2
T the Israelites: This will be Ex 30:31
T the Israelites: You must Ex 31:13
to Moses: "**T** the Israelites: Ex 33:5
would **t** the Israelites what he Ex 34:34
to the Israelites and **t** them: Lv 1:2
T the Israelites: When someone Lv 4:2
T Aaron and his sons: This is Lv 6:25
T the Israelites: You are not to Lv 7:23
T the Israelites: The one who Lv 7:29
And **t** the Israelites: 'Take a Lv 9:3
T the Israelites: You may eat Lv 11:2
T the Israelites: When a woman Lv 12:2
is to come and **t** the priest: Lv 14:35
to the Israelites and **t** them: Lv 15:2
T your brother Aaron that he may Lv 16:2
all the Israelites and **t** them: Lv 17:2
to the Israelites and **t** them: Lv 18:2
Israelite community and **t** them: Lv 19:2
sons, the priests, and **t** them: Lv 21:1
T Aaron: None of your Lv 21:17
T Aaron and his sons to deal Lv 22:2
all the Israelites and **t** them: Lv 22:18
to the Israelites and **t** them: Lv 23:2
to the Israelites and **t** them: Lv 23:10
T the Israelites: In the seventh Lv 23:24
T the Israelites: The Festival Lv 23:34
And **t** the Israelites: If anyone Lv 24:15
to the Israelites and **t** them: Lv 25:2
to the Israelites and **t** them: Lv 27:2
T the Israelites: When a man or Nm 5:6
to the Israelites and **t** them: Nm 5:12
to the Israelites and **t** them: Nm 6:2
T Aaron and his sons how you are Nm 6:23
Speak to Aaron and **t** him: Nm 8:2
T the Israelites: When any one Nm 9:10
them birth so You should **t** me, Nm 11:12
T the people: Purify yourselves Nm 11:18
They will **t** ⌊it to⌋ the Nm 14:14
T them: As surely as I live, Nm 14:28
to the Israelites and **t** them: Nm 15:2
to the Israelites and **t** them: Nm 15:18
the Israelites and **t** them that Nm 15:38
T the community: Get away from Nm 16:24
T Eleazar son of Aaron the Nm 16:37
Speak to the Levites and **t** them: Nm 18:26
T them further: Once you have Nm 18:30
what else the LORD has to **t** me." Nm 22:19
you must only do what I **t** you." Nm 22:20
are to say only what I **t** you." Nm 22:35
I will **t** you whatever He reveals Nm 23:3
to Balak and say what I **t** you." Nm 23:5
to Balak and say what I **t** you." Nm 23:16
answered him, "Didn't I **t** you: Nm 23:26
I previously **t** the messengers Nm 24:12
T the Israelites: When a man Nm 27:8
T the Israelites: When you cross Nm 33:51
to the Israelites and **t** them: Nm 35:10
the LORD said to me, '**T** them: Dt 1:42
Then you can **t** us everything the Dt 5:27
Go and **t** them: Return to your Dt 5:30
and I will **t** you every command— Dt 5:31
t him, 'We were slaves of Dt 6:21
divination, **t** fortunes, Dt 18:10
and he will **t** them everything I Dt 18:18
I **t** you today that you will Dt 30:18
and he will **t** you, your elders, Dt 32:7
the camp and **t** the people, Jos 1:11
you should **t** them, 'The waters Jos 4:7
Joshua to **t** the people, Jos 4:10
you should **t** your children, Jos 4:22
T them to consecrate themselves Jos 7:13
I urge you, **t** me what you have Jos 7:19
T the Israelites: 'Select your Jos 20:2
Let them **t** the righteous acts of Jdg 5:11
to **t** him, "This is what Jephthah Jdg 11:15
and He didn't **t** me His name. Jdg 13:6
But he did not **t** his father or Jdg 14:6
he did not **t** them that he had Jdg 14:9
"Let me **t** you a riddle," Samson Jdg 14:12
"**T** us your riddle," they Jdg 14:13
Persuade him to **t** you where his Jdg 16:5
Samson, "Please **t** me, where does Jdg 16:6
Won't you please **t** me how you Jdg 16:10
T me how you can be tied up." Jdg 16:13
asked, "**T** us, how did this Jdg 20:3
protest, we will **t** them, 'Show Jdg 21:22
to redeem ⌊it⌋, **t** me, so that I Ru 4:4
was afraid to **t** Eli the vision, 1Sm 3:15
T us how we can send it back to 1Sm 6:2
warn them and **t** them about the 1Sm 8:9
Maybe he'll **t** us which way we 1Sm 9:6
and he will **t** us our way." 1Sm 9:8
Would you please **t** me where the 1Sm 9:18
I'll **t** you everything that's in 1Sm 9:19
T the attendant to go on ahead 1Sm 9:27
"**T** me," Saul's uncle asked, 1Sm 10:15
Saul did not **t** him what Samuel 1Sm 10:16
T this to the men of 1Sm 11:9
he did not **t** his father. 1Sm 14:1
him, "**T** me what you did. 1Sm 14:43
Let me **t** you what the LORD said 1Sm 15:16
last night." "**T** me," he replied 1Sm 15:16
to David in private and **t** him, 1Sm 18:22
see what ⌊he says⌋, I'll **t** you." 1Sm 19:3
wouldn't I **t** you about it?" 1Sm 20:9
Who will **t** me if your father 1Sm 20:10
I do not send for you and **t** you, 1Sm 20:12
then I will **t** you, and I will 1Sm 20:13
fleeing, but they didn't **t** me." 1Sm 22:17
Israel, please **t** Your servant." 1Sm 23:11
they **t** me he is extremely 1Sm 23:22
young men, and they will **t** you. 1Sm 25:8
But she did not **t** her husband 1Sm 25:19
up for me the one I **t** you." 1Sm 28:8
on you to **t** me what I should 1Sm 28:15
T me," David asked him. 2Sm 1:4
Do not **t** it in Gath, don't 2Sm 1:20
long before you **t** the troops to 2Sm 2:26
that Joab had sent him ⌊to **t**⌋. 2Sm 11:22
were afraid to **t** him the baby 2Sm 12:18
So how can we **t** him the baby is 2Sm 12:18
Won't you **t** me?" Amnon replied 2Sm 13:4
To **t** the truth, I am a widow; 2Sm 14:5
to the city and **t** Absalom, 2Sm 15:34
someone quickly and **t** David, 2Sm 17:16
let me run and **t** the king the 2Sm 18:19
t the king what you have seen. 2Sm 18:21
t Amasa, 'Aren't you my flesh 2Sm 19:13
Please **t** Joab to come here and 2Sm 20:16
on you to **t** them who will sit 1Kg 1:20
is what you should **t** them: 1Kg 12:10
will **t** you what will happen to 1Kg 14:3
Go **t** Jeroboam, 'This is what the 1Kg 14:7
Go **t** your lord, 'Elijah is here! 1Kg 18:8
Now you say, 'Go **t** your lord, 1Kg 18:11
Now you say, 'Go **t** your lord, 1Kg 18:14
said, "Go and **t** Ahab, 'Get ⌊your 1Kg 18:44
T him, 'This is what the LORD 1Kg 21:19
Then **t** him, 'This is what the 1Kg 21:19
you swear not to **t** me anything 1Kg 22:16

Didn't I **t** you he never 1Kg 22:18
T ⌊me⌋ what I can do for you 2Kg 2:9
"Didn't I **t** you not to go?" 2Kg 2:18
T me, what do you have in the 2Kg 4:2
the pace for me unless I **t** you." 2Kg 4:24
of them, "**T** me, which one 2Kg 6:11
go **t** the king's household." 2Kg 7:9
Let me **t** you what the Arameans 2Kg 7:12
T me all the great things Elisha 2Kg 8:4
⌊That's⌋ a lie! **T** us!" So Jehu 2Kg 9:12
the city to go **t** about it in 2Kg 9:15
we will do whatever you **t** us. 2Kg 10:5
T Hezekiah this is what the 2Kg 18:19
said to them, "**T** your master 2Kg 19:6
Go back and **t** Hezekiah, the 2Kg 20:5
t about all His wonderful works! 1Ch 16:9
ordered Gad to **t** David to go and 1Ch 21:18
you swear not to **t** me anything 2Ch 18:15
Didn't I **t** you he never 2Ch 18:17
didn't **t** anyone what my God had Neh 2:12
and commanded him to **t** Mordecai, Est 4:10
I alone have escaped to **t** you!" Jb 1:15
I alone have escaped to **t** you!" Jb 1:16
I alone have escaped to **t** you!" Jb 1:17
I alone have escaped to **t** you!" Jb 1:19
teach you and **t** you and speak Jb 8:10
of the sky, and they will **t** you. Jb 12:7
and afraid to **t** you what I know. Jb 32:6
yes, I will **t** what I know. Jb 32:17
But I **t** you that you are wrong Jb 33:12
to **t** a person what is right for Jb 33:23
T ⌊Me⌋, if you have Jb 38:4
T ⌊Me⌋, if you know all this. Jb 38:18
You destroy those who **t** lies; Ps 5:6
will come and **t** a people yet to Ps 22:31
so that you can **t** a future Ps 48:13
I would not **t** you, for the world Ps 50:12
fear and will **t** about God's work Ps 64:9
I will **t** what He has done for Ps 66:16
My mouth will **t** about Your Ps 71:15
so I can **t** about all You do. Ps 73:28
People **t** about Your wonderful Ps 75:1
I will **t** about Him forever; Ps 75:9
but must **t** a future generation Ps 78:4
to rise and **t** their children Ps 78:6
t about all His wonderful works! Ps 105:2
Who can **t** man what will happen Ec 6:12
because who can **t** him what will Ec 8:7
and who can **t** anyone what will Ec 10:14
T me, you, the one I love: Sg 1:7
you find my love, **t** him that I Sg 5:8
T the righteous that it will go Is 3:10
Now I will **t** you what I am about Is 5:5
Let them **t** you and reveal what Is 19:12
T us flattering things. Is 30:10
said to them, "**T** Hezekiah: Is 36:4
Go and **t** Hezekiah that this is Is 38:5
Let them come and **t** us what will Is 41:22
T us the past events, so that we Is 41:22
the outcome. Or **t** us the future. Is 41:22
T us the coming events, then we Is 41:23
and **t** us the former things? Is 43:9
T My people their transgression, Is 58:1
to and speak whatever I **t** you. Jr 1:7
Stand up and **t** them everything Jr 1:17
and **t** them to the men of Judah Jr 11:2
must **t** them: This is what the Jr 11:3
we go? you must **t** them: This is Jr 15:2
When you **t** these people all Jr 16:10
dreams that they **t** one another, Jr 23:27
and **t** it among the far off Jr 31:10
will answer you and **t** you great Jr 33:3
king of Judah, and **t** him: Jr 34:2
We must surely **t** the king all Jr 36:16
asked Baruch, "**T** us—how did Jr 36:17
yourselves and **t** no one where Jr 36:19
Zedekiah, "If I **t** you, you will Jr 38:15
'**T** us what you said to the king; Jr 38:25
then you will **t** them, 'I was Jr 38:26
Go **t** Ebed-melech the Cushite: Jr 39:16
LORD your God may **t** us the way Jr 42:3
LORD answers you I will **t** you; Jr 42:4
your God sends you to ⌊**t**⌋ us, Jr 42:5
LORD our God says, **t** it to us, Jr 42:20
He has sent me to ⌊**t**⌋ you. Jr 42:21
t them: This is what the LORD Jr 43:10
let's **t** in Zion what the LORD Jr 51:10
of man, listen to what I **t** you: Ezk 2:8

speak to them. **T** them: This is Ezk 3:11
so they can **t** about all their Ezk 12:16
t those who plaster ⌊it⌋ that it Ezk 13:11
speak to them and **t** them: Ezk 14:4
things mean? **T** ⌊them⌋: The king Ezk 17:12
the elders of Israel and **t** them: Ezk 20:3
the house of Israel, and **t** them: Ezk 20:27
rebellious house. **T** them: This Ezk 24:3
Won't you **t** us what these things Ezk 24:19
speak to your people and **t** them: Ezk 33:2
T them: As I live"—the Ezk 33:11
When I **t** the righteous person Ezk 33:13
So when I **t** the wicked person: Ezk 33:14
T them this: This is what the Ezk 33:27
t them: This is what the Lord Ezk 37:19
t them: This is what the Lord Ezk 37:21
T every kind of bird and all the Ezk 39:17
to everything I **t** you about all Ezk 44:5
and Chaldeans to **t** the king his Dn 2:2
T your servants the dream, Dn 2:4
If you don't **t** me the dream and Dn 2:5
May the king **t** the dream to his Dn 2:7
If you don't **t** me the dream, Dn 2:9
have conspired to **t** me something Dn 2:9
t me the dream and I will know Dn 2:9
Are you able to **t** me the dream I Dn 2:26
now we will **t** the king its Dn 2:36
I am pleased to **t** you about the Dn 4:2
Now, Belteshazzar, **t** me the Dn 4:18
I am here to **t** you what will Dn 8:19
I will **t** you what is recorded in Dn 10:21
Now I will **t** you the truth. Dn 11:2
T your children about it, and Jl 1:3
your children **t** their children, Jl 1:3
T us who is to blame for this Jnh 1:8
the message that I **t** you." Jnh 3:2
no longer do wrong or **t** lies; Zph 3:13
t the people: This is what the Zch 1:3
Run and **t** this young man: Zch 2:4
You are to **t** him: This is what Zch 6:12
and stay there until I **t** you. Mt 2:13
For I **t** you that God is able Mt 3:9
t these stones to become bread." Mt 4:3
For I **t** you, unless your Mt 5:20
But I **t** you, everyone who is Mt 5:22
But I **t** you, everyone who looks Mt 5:28
But I **t** you, everyone who Mt 5:32
But I **t** you, don't take an oath Mt 5:34
But I **t** you, don't resist an Mt 5:39
But I **t** you, love your enemies Mt 5:44
This is why I **t** you: Don't worry Mt 6:25
I **t** you that not even Solomon Mt 6:29
See that you don't **t** anyone; Mt 8:4
I **t** you that many will come from Mt 8:11
What I **t** you in the dark, speak Mt 10:27
Yes, I **t** you, and far more than Mt 11:9
But I **t** you, it will be more Mt 11:22
But I **t** you, it will be more Mt 11:24
But I **t** you that something Mt 12:6
of this, I **t** you, people will Mt 12:31
I **t** you that on the day of Mt 12:36
harvest time I'll **t** the reapers: Mt 13:30
that He did not **t** them to beware Mt 16:12
orders to **t** no one that He was Mt 16:20
Don't **t** anyone about the vision Mt 17:9
But I **t** you: Elijah has already Mt 17:12
you will **t** this mountain, Mt 17:20
because I **t** you that in heaven Mt 18:10
attention to them, **t** the church. Mt 18:17
"I **t** you, not as many as seven," Mt 18:22
I **t** you, whoever divorces his Mt 19:9
Again I **t** you, it is easier for Mt 19:24
T Daughter Zion, "See, your King Mt 21:5
even if you **t** this mountain, Mt 21:21
then I will **t** you by what Mt 21:24
Neither will I **t** you by what Mt 21:27
Therefore I **t** you, the kingdom Mt 21:43
and said, '**T** those who are Mt 22:4
T us, therefore, what You think. Mt 22:17
whatever they **t** you and observe Mt 23:3
For I **t** you, you will never see Mt 23:39
and said, "**T** us, when will these Mt 24:3
So if they **t** you, 'Look, he's in Mt 24:26
said, "and **t** him, 'The Teacher Mt 26:18
But I **t** you, from this moment I Mt 26:29
t us if You are the Messiah, Mt 26:63
But I **t** you, in the future you Mt 26:64
steal Him, and **t** the people, 'He Mt 27:64

quickly and **t** His disciples, Mt 28:7
they ran to **t** His disciples the Mt 28:8
and **t** My brothers to leave for Mt 28:10
I **t** you: get up, pick up your Mk 2:11
He ordered them to **t** no one, Mk 7:36
warned them to **t** no one about Mk 8:30
ordered them to **t** no one what Mk 9:9
But I **t** you that Elijah really Mk 9:13
Peter began to **t** Him, "Look, we Mk 10:28
He began to **t** them the things Mk 10:32
Therefore, I **t** you, all the Mk 11:24
and I will **t** you by what Mk 11:29
Neither will I **t** you by what Mk 11:33
T us, when will these things Mk 13:4
t the owner of the house, Mk 14:14
she began to **t** those standing Mk 14:69
t His disciples and Peter, Mk 16:7
speak to you and **t** you this good Lk 1:19
for I **t** you that God is able Lk 3:8
t this stone to become bread." Lk 4:3
Then He ordered him to **t** no one: Lk 5:14
the paralyzed man, "I **t** you: Lk 5:24
centurion sent friends to **t** Him, Lk 7:6
He said, "I **t** you, I have not Lk 7:9
Young man, I **t** you, get up!" Lk 7:14
Yes, I **t** you, and far more than Lk 7:26
I **t** you, among those born of Lk 7:28
Therefore I **t** you, her many sins Lk 7:47
t all that God has done for you. Lk 8:39
them to **t** no one what had Lk 8:56
them to **t** this to no one, Lk 9:21
t you the truth: there are some Lk 9:27
are there, and **t** them, 'The Lk 10:9
I **t** you, on that day it will be Lk 10:12
For I **t** you that many prophets Lk 10:24
So **t** her to give me a hand." Lk 10:40
t you, even though he won't get Lk 11:8
Yes, I **t** you, this generation Lk 11:51
t my brother to divide the Lk 12:13
Therefore I **t** you, don't worry Lk 12:22
Yet I **t** you, not even Solomon in Lk 12:27
I **t** you the truth: he will put Lk 12:44
I **t** you, but rather division! Lk 12:51
I **t** you, you will never get out Lk 12:59
No, I **t** you; but unless you Lk 13:3
No, I **t** you; but unless you Lk 13:5
door, because I **t** you, many will Lk 13:24
He will say, 'I **t** you, I don't Lk 13:27
to them, "Go **t** that fox, 'Look! Lk 13:32
And I **t** you, you will not see Me Lk 13:35
his slave to **t** those who were Lk 14:17
I **t** you, not one of those men Lk 14:24
I **t** you, in the same way, there Lk 15:7
I **t** you, in the same way, there Lk 15:10
And I **t** you, make friends for Lk 16:9
will he not **t** him, 'Prepare Lk 17:8
I **t** you, on that night two will Lk 17:34
I **t** you that He will swiftly Lk 18:8
I **t** you, this one went down to Lk 18:14
went on to **t** a parable because Lk 19:11
I **t** you, that to everyone who Lk 19:26
He answered, "I **t** you, if they Lk 19:40
T us, by what authority are You Lk 20:2
also ask you a question. **T** Me, Lk 20:3
Neither will I **t** you by what Lk 20:8
He began to **t** the people this Lk 20:9
"I **t** you the truth," He said. Lk 21:3
T the owner of the house, Lk 22:11
For I **t** you, I will not eat it Lk 22:16
For I **t** you, from now on I will Lk 22:18
"I **t** you, Peter," He said, "the Lk 22:34
I **t** you, what is written must Lk 22:37
If You are the Messiah, **t** us." Lk 22:67
them, "If I do **t** you, you will Lk 22:67
can you **t** us about yourself? Jn 1:22
believe if I **t** you about things Jn 3:12
these things I **t** the world." Jn 8:26
Yet because I **t** the truth, Jn 8:45
If I **t** the truth, why don't you Jn 8:46
are the Messiah, **t** us plainly." Jn 10:24
I did **t** you and you don't Jn 10:25
Didn't I **t** you that if you Jn 11:40
cannot come,' so now I **t** you. Jn 13:33
have heard Me **t** you, 'I am going Jn 14:28
I didn't **t** you these things from Jn 16:4
still have many things to **t** you, Jn 16:12
but I will **t** you plainly about Jn 16:25
t me where you've put Him, Jn 20:15

My brothers and **t** them that I am Jn 20:17
Jesus did not **t** him that he Jn 21:23
"**T** me," Peter asked her, "did Ac 5:8
t the people all about this life. Ac 5:20
And now, I **t** you, stay away from Ac 5:38
proceeded to **t** him the good news Ac 8:35
Therefore do what we **t** you: Ac 21:23
and said to him, "**T** me—are you Ac 22:27
he has something to **t** you." Ac 23:18
Don't **t** anyone that you have Ac 23:22
I **t** everyone among you not to Rm 12:3
Brothers, I **t** you this: 1Co 15:50
T me, you who want to be under Gl 4:21
t you that if you get Gl 5:2
about which I **t** you in advance— Gl 5:21
will **t** you everything so that Eph 6:21
t you all the news about me. Col 4:7
They will **t** you about everything Col 4:9
And **t** Archippus, "Pay attention Col 4:17
short for me to **t** about Gideon, Heb 11:32
I will **t** you the secret meaning Rv 17:7

TELLING *(49)*

not **t** him that he was fleeing. Gn 31:20
go up and inform Pharaoh, **t** him: Gn 46:31
spoke to Moses, **t** him, "I am Ex 6:2
of Egypt everything I am **t** you." Ex 6:29
deceive us by **t** us you live far Jos 9:22
there was a man **t** his friend Jdg 7:13
great or small, without **t** me. 1Sm 20:2
you've finished **t** the king all 2Sm 11:19
left, saying, "I was **t** myself: 2Kg 5:11
While he was **t** the king how 2Kg 8:5
provinces ⌊**t** the officials⌋ Est 3:13
in thanksgiving and **t** about Your Ps 26:7
prophets are **t** them, 'You won't Jr 14:13
t them and leading My people Jr 23:32
of the prophets who are **t** you, Jr 27:14
of the LORD in what I am **t** you, Jr 38:20
As He was **t** them these things, Mt 9:18
since John had been **t** him, Mt 14:4
t them, "Go into the village Mt 21:2
t him, "See that you say nothing Mk 1:44
John had been **t** Herod, "It is Mk 6:18
His disciples and **t** them, Mk 9:31
Then Jesus began by **t** them: Mk 13:5
preaching and **t** the good news of Lk 8:1
are You **t** this parable to us or Lk 12:41
responded by **t** the crowd, Lk 13:14
with them were **t** the apostles Lk 24:10
Listen ⌊to what⌋ I'm **t** you: Jn 4:35
what I've been **t** you from the Jn 8:25
understand what He was **t** them. Jn 10:6
I am **t** you now before it Jn 13:19
thought that Jesus was **t** him, Jn 13:29
I am **t** you the truth. Jn 16:7
I am not **t** you that I will make Jn 16:26
and he knows he is **t** the truth. Jn 19:35
the other disciples kept **t** him, Jn 20:25
I also heard a voice **t** me, Ac 11:7
the faith, and by **t** them, "It is Ac 14:22
because he was **t** the good news Ac 17:18
on nothing else but **t** or hearing Ac 17:21
t the people that they should Ac 19:4
t them not to circumcise their Ac 21:21
and saw Him **t** me, 'Hurry and get Ac 22:18
my spirit in ⌊**t**⌋ the good news Rm 1:9
I am **t** you a mystery: 1Co 15:51
because I will be **t** the truth. 2Co 12:6
your enemy by **t** you the truth? Gl 4:16
an apostle (I am **t** the truth; 1Tm 2:7
t those who live on the earth to Rv 13:14

TELLS *(21)*

and do whatever he **t** you." Gn 41:55
When Pharaoh **t** you: Perform a Ex 7:9
you the answer the LORD **t** me." Nm 22:8
the LORD our God **t** you; Dt 5:27
Nobody **t** me when my own son 1Sm 22:8
about me or **t** me that my son 1Sm 22:8
should you do it⌋ when he **t** you, 2Kg 5:13
t the king of Israel even the 2Kg 6:12
God **t** them what they have done Jb 36:9
no one who **t** lies will remain in Ps 101:7
For my mouth **t** the truth, and Pr 8:7
friend; no one **t** the truth. They Jr 9:5
Whoever **t** his father or mother, Mt 15:5
If anyone **t** you then, 'Look, Mt 24:23
'If a man **t** his father or mother: Mk 7:11
Then if anyone **t** you, 'Look, Mk 13:21
"Do whatever He **t** you," His Jn 2:5
When he **t** a lie, he speaks from Jn 8:44
another, "What is this He **t** us: Jn 16:17
He **t** Moses: I will show mercy Rm 9:15
For the Scripture **t** Pharaoh: Rm 9:17

TEMA *(5)*

Hadad, **T**, Jetur, Naphish, and Gn 25:15
Mishma, Dumah, Massa, Hadad, **T**, 1Ch 1:30
caravans of **T** look ⌊for these Jb 6:19
of the land of **T** meet the Is 21:14
Dedan, **T**, Buz, and all those who Jr 25:23

TEMAH'S *(2)*

descendants, **T** descendants, Ezr 2:53
descendants, **T** descendants, Neh 7:55

TEMAN *(11)*

The sons of Eliphaz were **T**, Gn 36:11
Chiefs **T**, Omar, Zepho, Kenaz, Gn 36:15
Kenaz, **T**, Mibzar, Gn 36:42
T, Omar, Zephi, Gatam, and Kenaz; 1Ch 1:36
Kenaz, **T**, Mibzar, 1Ch 1:53
Is there no longer wisdom in **T**? Jr 49:7
devised against the people of **T**: Jr 49:20
by the sword from **T** to Dedan. Ezk 25:13
I will send fire against **T**, Am 1:12
T, your warriors will be Ob 9
God comes from **T**, the Holy One Hab 3:3

TEMANITE *(6)*

Eliphaz the **T**, Bildad the Jb 2:11
Then Eliphaz the **T** replied: Jb 4:1
Then Eliphaz the **T** replied: Jb 15:1
Then Eliphaz the **T** replied: Jb 22:1
He said to Eliphaz the **T**: Jb 42:7
Then Eliphaz the **T**, Bildad the Jb 42:9

TEMANITES *(2)*

the land of the **T** ruled in his Gn 36:34
the land of the **T** ruled in his 1Ch 1:45

TEMENI *(1)*

Hepher, **T**, and Haahashtari 1Ch 4:6

TEMPER *(2)*

one's **t**, than capturing Pr 16:32
not control his **t** is like a city Pr 25:28

TEMPERED *(1)*

not quick **t**, not addicted to Ti 1:7

TEMPEST *(3)*

with Your **t** and terrify them Ps 83:15
and raised a **t** that stirred up Ps 107:25
noise, storm, **t**, and a flame Is 29:6

TEMPLE *(629)*

the peg into his **t** and drove it Jdg 4:21
with a tent peg through his **t**! Jdg 4:22
she shattered and pierced his **t**. Jdg 5:26
from the **t** of Baal-berith. Jdg 9:4
chamber of the **t** of El-berith. Jdg 9:46
the pillars supporting the **t**, Jdg 16:26
The **t** was full of men and women; Jdg 16:27
supporting the **t** and leaned Jdg 16:29
the **t** fell on the leaders and Jdg 16:30
it into the **t** of Dagon and 1Sm 5:2
who enters the **t** of Dagon in 1Sm 5:5
his armor in the **t** of the 1Sm 31:10
From His **t** He heard my voice, 2Sm 22:7
the LORD's **t**, and the wall 1Kg 3:1
that time a **t** for the LORD's 1Kg 3:2
able to build a **t** for the name 1Kg 5:3
I plan to build a **t** for the name 1Kg 5:5
will build the **t** for My name.' 1Kg 5:5
foundation of the **t** with dressed 1Kg 5:17
to⌋ build the **t** for the LORD 1Kg 6:1
t that King Solomon built for 1Kg 6:2
in front of the **t** sanctuary was 1Kg 6:3
15 feet deep in front of the **t**. 1Kg 6:3
with beveled frames for the **t**. 1Kg 6:4
structure along the **t** wall, 1Kg 6:5
encircling the walls of the **t**, 1Kg 6:5
ledges for the **t** all around 1Kg 6:6
be inserted into the **t** walls. 1Kg 6:6
was heard in the **t** while it was 1Kg 6:7
was on the right side of the **t**. 1Kg 6:8
When he finished building the **t**, 1Kg 6:9
the chambers along the entire **t**, 1Kg 6:10
to the **t** with cedar beams; 1Kg 6:10
As for this **t** you are building— 1Kg 6:12
Solomon finished building the **t**, 1Kg 6:14
the interior **t** walls with cedar 1Kg 6:15
from the **t** floor to the surface 1Kg 6:15
the rear of the **t** with cedar 1Kg 6:16
The **t**, that is, the sanctuary in 1Kg 6:17
inside the **t** was carved with 1Kg 6:18
inside the **t** to put the ark 1Kg 6:19
of the **t** with pure gold, 1Kg 6:21
to the entire **t** until everything 1Kg 6:22
the cherubim inside the inner **t**. 1Kg 6:27
middle of the **t** their wings were 1Kg 6:27
the surrounding **t** walls with 1Kg 6:29
overlaid the **t** floor with gold 1Kg 6:30
of the LORD's **t** was laid in 1Kg 6:37
the **t** was completed in every 1Kg 6:38
of the LORD's **t** and the portico 1Kg 7:12
temple and the portico of the **t**, 1Kg 7:12
right side of the **t** and five on 1Kg 7:39
right side of the **t** toward the 1Kg 7:39
King Solomon on the LORD's **t**: 1Kg 7:40
at the LORD's **t** ⌊were made⌋ 1Kg 7:45
the equipment in the LORD's **t**: 1Kg 7:48
for the doors of the inner **t** 1Kg 7:50
the doors of the **t** sanctuary. 1Kg 7:50
in the LORD's **t** was completed. 1Kg 7:51
the treasuries of the LORD's **t**. 1Kg 7:51
the inner sanctuary of the **t**, 1Kg 8:6
the cloud filled the LORD's **t**, 1Kg 8:10
glory of the LORD filled the **t**. 1Kg 8:11
built an exalted **t** for You, 1Kg 8:13
a city to build a **t** in among any 1Kg 8:16
David to build a **t** for the name 1Kg 8:17
desire to build a **t** for My name, 1Kg 8:18
I have built the **t** for the name 1Kg 8:20
much less this **t** I have built. 1Kg 8:27
watch over this **t** night and day, 1Kg 8:29
before Your altar in this **t**, 1Kg 8:31
with You for mercy in this **t**, 1Kg 8:33
out his hands toward this **t**— 1Kg 8:38
come and pray toward this **t**— 1Kg 8:42
know that this **t** I have built is 1Kg 8:43
chosen and the **t** I have built 1Kg 8:44
and the **t** I have built for Your 1Kg 8:48
dedicated the LORD's **t**. 1Kg 8:63
of the LORD's **t** because that was 1Kg 8:64
building the **t** of the LORD, 1Kg 9:1
this **t** you have built, 1Kg 9:3
will reject the **t** I have 1Kg 9:7
Though this **t** is ⌊now⌋ exalted, 1Kg 9:8
do this to this land and this **t**? 1Kg 9:8
LORD's **t** and the royal palace 1Kg 9:10
imposed to build the LORD's **t**, 1Kg 9:15
So he completed the **t**. 1Kg 9:25
he offered at the LORD's **t**, 1Kg 10:5
for the LORD's **t** and the king's 1Kg 10:12
in the LORD's **t** in Jerusalem, 1Kg 12:27
of the LORD's **t** and the 1Kg 14:26
the king entered the LORD's **t**, 1Kg 14:28
gifts into the LORD's **t**: 1Kg 15:15
of the LORD's **t** and the 1Kg 15:18
for Baal in the **t** of Baal that 1Kg 16:32
goes into the **t** of Rimmon to 2Kg 5:18
man, bow in the **t** of Rimmon— 2Kg 5:18
when I bow in the **t** of Rimmon, 2Kg 5:18
They entered the **t** of Baal, 2Kg 10:21
of Rechab entered the **t** of Baal, 2Kg 10:23
the inner room of the **t** of Baal. 2Kg 10:25
pillars of the **t** of Baal and 2Kg 10:26
tore down the **t** of Baal and made 2Kg 10:27
in the LORD's **t** six years while 2Kg 11:3
come to him in the LORD's **t**, 2Kg 11:4
protection for the LORD's **t**. 2Kg 11:7
that were in the LORD's **t**. 2Kg 11:10
side of the **t** to the left side 2Kg 11:11
by the altar and by the **t**. 2Kg 11:11
to the people at the LORD's **t**. 2Kg 11:13
put to death in the LORD's **t**." 2Kg 11:15
went to the **t** of Baal and tore 2Kg 11:18
guards for the LORD's **t**. 2Kg 11:18
the king from the LORD's **t**. 2Kg 11:19
money brought to the LORD's **t**, 2Kg 12:4
given for the LORD's **t**, 2Kg 12:4
damage to the **t** is found. 2Kg 12:5
repaired the damage to the **t**. 2Kg 12:6
over for the repair of the **t**." 2Kg 12:7
side as one enters the LORD's **t**; 2Kg 12:9
money brought into the LORD's **t**. 2Kg 12:9
go to the LORD's **t** and count the 2Kg 12:10
those who oversaw the LORD's **t**. 2Kg 12:11
those working on the LORD's **t**— 2Kg 12:11
to the LORD's **t** and for all 2Kg 12:12
for all spending for **t** repairs. 2Kg 12:12

for the LORD's **t** from the money 2Kg 12:13
the money brought into the **t**. 2Kg 12:13
repaired the LORD's **t** with it. 2Kg 12:14
the LORD's **t** since it belonged 2Kg 12:16
the LORD's **t** and in the king's 2Kg 12:18
found in the LORD's **t** and in the 2Kg 14:14
the Upper Gate of the LORD's **t**. 2Kg 15:35
found in the LORD's **t** and in the 2Kg 16:8
in front of the **t** between ⌊his⌋ 2Kg 16:14
his⌋ altar and the LORD's **t**, 2Kg 16:14
from the LORD's **t** the Sabbath 2Kg 16:18
found in the LORD's **t** and in the 2Kg 18:15
and went into the LORD's **t**. 2Kg 19:1
then went up to the LORD's **t**, 2Kg 19:14
worshiping in the **t** of his god 2Kg 19:37
you will go up to the LORD's **t**. 2Kg 20:5
the LORD's **t** on the third day? 2Kg 20:8
build altars in the LORD's **t**, 2Kg 21:4
both courtyards of the LORD's **t**. 2Kg 21:5
he made in the **t** that the LORD 2Kg 21:7
forever in this **t** and in 2Kg 21:7
to the LORD's **t**, saying, 2Kg 22:3
brought into the LORD's **t**— 2Kg 22:4
those who oversee the LORD's **t**. 2Kg 22:5
in the LORD's **t** to repair the 2Kg 22:5
quarried stone to repair the **t**. 2Kg 22:6
of the law in the LORD's **t**," 2Kg 22:8
found in the **t** and have put it 2Kg 22:9
those who oversee the LORD's **t**." 2Kg 22:9
to the LORD's **t** with all the men 2Kg 23:2
had been found in the LORD's **t**. 2Kg 23:2
of the LORD's **t** all the articles 2Kg 23:4
from the LORD's **t** to the Kidron 2Kg 23:6
that were in the LORD's **t**, 2Kg 23:7
of the LORD's **t** in the precincts 2Kg 23:11
two courtyards of the LORD's **t**. 2Kg 23:12
priest found in the LORD's **t**. 2Kg 23:24
and the **t** about which I said, 2Kg 23:27
the LORD's **t** and the treasures 2Kg 24:13
burned the LORD's **t**, the king's 2Kg 25:9
bronze pillars of the LORD's **t**, 2Kg 25:13
which were in the LORD's **t**, 2Kg 25:13
articles used in ⌊**t**⌋ service. 2Kg 25:14
had made for the LORD's **t**, 2Kg 25:16
as priest in the **t** that Solomon 1Ch 6:10
in the LORD's **t** after the ark 1Ch 6:31
built the LORD's **t** in Jerusalem, 1Ch 6:32
of the tabernacle, God's **t**. 1Ch 6:48
Levites, and **t** servants. 1Ch 9:2
the chief official of God's **t**; 1Ch 9:11
in the ministry of God's **t**. 1Ch 9:13
and the treasuries of God's **t**. 1Ch 9:26
in the vicinity of God's **t**, 1Ch 9:27
stayed in the ⌊**t**⌋ chambers and 1Ch 9:33
his armor in the **t** of their gods 1Ch 10:10
his skull in the **t** of Dagon. 1Ch 10:10
of God to the **t** that is to be 1Ch 22:19
of the work on the LORD's **t**, 1Ch 23:4
in the service of the LORD's **t**. 1Ch 23:24
the service of the LORD's **t**, 1Ch 23:28
work of the service of God's **t**— 1Ch 23:28
in the service of the LORD's **t**." 1Ch 23:32
when they entered the LORD's **t**, 1Ch 24:19
for the music in the LORD's **t**, 1Ch 25:6
for the service of God's **t**. 1Ch 25:6
for ministering in the LORD's **t**, 1Ch 26:12
of God's **t** and the treasuries 1Ch 26:20
the treasuries of the LORD's **t**. 1Ch 26:22
for the repair of the LORD's **t**. 1Ch 26:27
vestibule ⌊of the **t**⌋ and its 1Ch 28:11
for the **t** will not be for man, 1Ch 29:1
to build the **t** for which I have 1Ch 29:19
decided to build a **t** for the 2Ch 2:1
am building a **t** for the name 2Ch 2:4
The **t** that I am building will be 2Ch 2:5
is able to build a **t** for Him, 2Ch 2:6
because the **t** I am building will 2Ch 2:9
who will build a **t** for the LORD 2Ch 2:12
build the LORD's **t** in Jerusalem 2Ch 3:1
for building God's **t**: 2Ch 3:3
across the width of the **t**, 2Ch 3:4
He adorned the **t** with precious 2Ch 3:6
He overlaid the **t**—the beams, 2Ch 3:7
to the width of the **t**, 2Ch 3:8
In front of the **t** he made two 2Ch 3:15
for King Solomon in God's **t**: 2Ch 4:11
King Solomon for the LORD's **t**. 2Ch 4:16
all the equipment in God's **t**: 2Ch 4:19

and the entryway to the **t**, 2Ch 4:22
the doors of the **t** sanctuary— 2Ch 4:22
for the LORD's **t** was completed. 2Ch 5:1
in the treasuries of God's **t**. 2Ch 5:1
the inner sanctuary of the **t**, 2Ch 5:7
the **t**, the LORD's temple, was 2Ch 5:13
the LORD's **t**, was filled with 2Ch 5:13
of the LORD filled God's **t**. 2Ch 5:14
have built an exalted **t** for You, 2Ch 6:2
a city to build a **t** in among any 2Ch 6:5
David to build a **t** for the name 2Ch 6:7
desire to build a **t** for My name, 2Ch 6:8
are not the one to build the **t**, 2Ch 6:9
will build the **t** for My name." 2Ch 6:9
I have built the **t** for the name 2Ch 6:10
much less this **t** I have built. 2Ch 6:18
watch over this **t** day and night, 2Ch 6:20
before Your altar in this **t**, 2Ch 6:22
for mercy before You in this **t**, 2Ch 6:24
out his hands toward this **t**— 2Ch 6:29
comes and prays toward this **t**, 2Ch 6:32
know that this **t** I have built is 2Ch 6:33
chosen and the **t** that I have 2Ch 6:34
toward the **t** I have built for 2Ch 6:38
glory of the LORD filled the **t**. 2Ch 7:1
enter the LORD's **t** because the 2Ch 7:2
LORD filled the **t** of the LORD. 2Ch 7:2
glory of the LORD came on the **t**. 2Ch 7:3
the people dedicated God's **t**. 2Ch 7:5
of the LORD's **t** because that was 2Ch 7:7
the LORD's **t** and the royal 2Ch 7:11
for the LORD's **t** and for his own 2Ch 7:11
for Myself as a **t** of sacrifice. 2Ch 7:12
this **t** so that My name 2Ch 7:16
this **t** that I have sanctified 2Ch 7:20
for this **t**, which was exalted, 2Ch 7:21
do this to this land and this **t**? 2Ch 7:21
built the LORD's **t** and his own 2Ch 8:1
for the LORD's **t** until it was 2Ch 8:16
So the LORD's **t** was completed. 2Ch 8:16
he offered at the LORD's **t**, 2Ch 9:4
for the LORD's **t** and for the 2Ch 9:11
of the LORD's **t** and the 2Ch 12:9
the king entered the LORD's **t**, 2Ch 12:11
the vestibule of the LORD's ⌊**t**⌋. 2Ch 15:8
consecrated gifts into God's **t**: 2Ch 15:18
of the LORD's **t** and the royal 2Ch 16:2
in the LORD's **t** before the new 2Ch 20:5
before this **t** and before You, 2Ch 20:9
for Your name is in this **t**. 2Ch 20:9
to the LORD's **t** with harps, 2Ch 20:28
with them in God's **t** six years. 2Ch 22:12
with the king in God's **t**. 2Ch 23:3
the courtyards of the LORD's **t**. 2Ch 23:5
the LORD's **t** but the priests 2Ch 23:6
who enters the **t** is to be put to 2Ch 23:7
quivers that were in God's **t**. 2Ch 23:9
side of the **t** to the left side 2Ch 23:10
by the altar and by the **t**. 2Ch 23:10
to the troops in the LORD's **t**. 2Ch 23:12
her to death in the LORD's **t**." 2Ch 23:14
went to the **t** of Baal and tore 2Ch 23:17
of the LORD's **t** into the hands 2Ch 23:18
had appointed over the LORD's **t**, 2Ch 23:18
of the LORD's **t** so that nothing 2Ch 23:19
the king down from the LORD's **t**. 2Ch 23:20
heart to renovate the LORD's **t**. 2Ch 24:4
to repair the **t** of your God as 2Ch 24:5
into the LORD's **t** and even used 2Ch 24:7
of the LORD's **t** for the Baals." 2Ch 24:7
the gate of the LORD's **t**. 2Ch 24:8
of the labor on the LORD's **t**, 2Ch 24:12
to renovate the LORD's **t**, 2Ch 24:12
to repair the LORD's **t**. 2Ch 24:12
They restored God's **t** to its 2Ch 24:13
for the LORD's **t** with it— 2Ch 24:14
in the LORD's **t** throughout 2Ch 24:14
with respect to God and His **t**. 2Ch 24:16
abandoned the **t** of the LORD God 2Ch 24:18
the courtyard of the LORD's **t**. 2Ch 24:21
the restoration of the LORD's **t**, 2Ch 24:27
found with Obed-edom in God's **t**, 2Ch 25:24
in the LORD's **t** beside the altar 2Ch 26:19
from access to the LORD's **t**, 2Ch 26:21
the Upper Gate of the LORD's **t**, 2Ch 27:3
the LORD's **t** and the palace 2Ch 28:21
up the utensils of God's **t**, 2Ch 28:24
shut the doors of the LORD's **t**, 2Ch 28:24

of the LORD's **t** and repaired 2Ch 29:3
consecrate the **t** of the LORD God 2Ch 29:5
LORD to cleanse the LORD's **t**. 2Ch 29:15
of the LORD's **t** to cleanse it. 2Ch 29:16
the courtyard of the LORD's **t**. 2Ch 29:16
the vestibule of the LORD's ⌊**t**⌋. 2Ch 29:17
the LORD's **t** for eight days, 2Ch 29:17
the whole **t** of the LORD, 2Ch 29:18
and went up to the LORD's **t**. 2Ch 29:20
in the LORD's **t** with cymbals, 2Ch 29:25
offerings to the LORD's **t**." 2Ch 29:31
of the LORD's **t** was established. 2Ch 29:35
to the LORD's **t** in Jerusalem to 2Ch 30:1
burnt offerings to the LORD's **t**. 2Ch 30:15
the offering to the LORD's **t**, 2Ch 31:10
chambers in the LORD's **t**, 2Ch 31:11
of Azariah the ruler of God's **t**. 2Ch 31:13
the LORD's **t** for their daily 2Ch 31:16
began in the service of God's **t**, 2Ch 31:21
He went to the **t** of his god, 2Ch 32:21
He built altars in the LORD's **t**, 2Ch 33:4
both courtyards of the LORD's **t**. 2Ch 33:5
made, in God's **t**, about which 2Ch 33:7
forever in this **t** and in 2Ch 33:7
and the idol from the LORD's **t**, 2Ch 33:15
the LORD's **t** and in Jerusalem, 2Ch 33:15
to cleanse the land and the **t**, 2Ch 34:8
to repair the **t** of the LORD his 2Ch 34:8
the money brought into God's **t**. 2Ch 34:9
those who oversaw the LORD's **t**. 2Ch 34:10
were working in the LORD's **t**, 2Ch 34:10
to repair and restore the **t**; 2Ch 34:10
been deposited in the LORD's **t**, 2Ch 34:14
of the law in the LORD's **t**," 2Ch 34:15
in the LORD's **t** and have put it 2Ch 34:17
to the LORD's **t** with all the men 2Ch 34:30
had been found in the LORD's **t**. 2Ch 34:30
them to serve in the LORD's **t**. 2Ch 35:2
holy ark in the **t** built by 2Ch 35:3
leaders of God's **t**, gave 2,600 2Ch 35:8
Josiah had prepared for the **t**, 2Ch 35:20
of the LORD's **t** to Babylon and 2Ch 36:7
put them in his **t** in Babylon. 2Ch 36:7
utensils of the LORD's **t**. 2Ch 36:10
defiled the LORD's **t** that He had 2Ch 36:14
all the articles of God's **t**, 2Ch 36:18
the treasures of the LORD's **t**, 2Ch 36:18
the Chaldeans burned God's **t**. 2Ch 36:19
me to build Him a **t** at Jerusalem 2Ch 36:23
The **t** servants ⌊included⌋: Ezr 2:43
All the **t** servants and the Ezr 2:58
gatekeepers, **t** servants, and Ezr 2:70
of the LORD's **t** had not ⌊yet⌋ Ezr 3:6
the foundation of the LORD's **t**, Ezr 3:10
seen the first **t**, wept loudly Ezr 3:12
were building a **t** for the LORD, Ezr 4:1
rebuild this **t** and finish this Ezr 5:3
rebuild this **t** and finish this Ezr 5:9
rebuilding the **t** that was built Ezr 5:11
destroyed this **t** and deported Ezr 5:12
also took from the **t** in Babylon Ezr 5:14
taken from the **t** in Jerusalem Ezr 5:14
them⌋ to the **t** in Babylon. Ezr 5:14
them from the **t** in Babylon to a Ezr 5:14
put them in the **t** in Jerusalem, Ezr 5:15
took from the **t** in Jerusalem and Ezr 6:5
brought to the **t** in Jerusalem, Ezr 6:5
and **t** servants accompanied ⌊him⌋ Ezr 7:7
doorkeepers, **t** servants, or Ezr 7:24
the **t** servants at Casiphia, Ezr 8:17
were also 220 of the **t** servants, Ezr 8:20
the **t** servants living on Ophel Neh 3:26
to the house of the **t** servants Neh 3:31
the house of God inside the **t**. Neh 6:10
Let us shut the **t** doors because Neh 6:10
How can I enter the **t** and live? Neh 6:11
The **t** servants ⌊included⌋: Neh 7:46
All the **t** servants and the Neh 7:60
gatekeepers, **t** singers, some Neh 7:73
of the people, **t** servants, and Neh 7:73
and **t** servants, along Neh 10:28
priests, Levites, **t** servants, Neh 11:3
who did the work at the **t**: Neh 11:12
The **t** servants lived on Ophel; Neh 11:21
supervised the **t** servants. Neh 11:21
Your holy **t** in reverential Ps 5:7
The LORD is in His holy **t**; Ps 11:4
From His **t** He heard my voice, Ps 18:6

LORD and seeking ⌊Him⌋ in His **t**. Ps 27:4
In His **t** all cry, "Glory!" Ps 29:9
within Your **t**, we contemplate Ps 48:9
house, the holiness of Your **t**. Ps 65:4
Because of Your **t** at Jerusalem, Ps 68:29
Your holy **t**, and turned Ps 79:1
Your holy **t** and give thanks Ps 138:2
and His robe filled the **t**. Is 6:1
and the **t** was filled with smoke. Is 6:4
went up to its **t** to weep at its Is 15:2
worshiping in the **t** of his god Is 37:38
I will go up to the LORD's **t**?" Is 38:22
person, to dwell in a **t**. Is 44:13
will be rebuilt, and of the **t**: Is 44:28
and beautiful **t**, where our Is 64:11
voice from the **t**—the voice of Is 66:6
This is the **t** of the LORD, Jr 7:4
of the LORD, the **t** of the LORD, Jr 7:4
of the LORD, the **t** of the LORD. Jr 7:4
the courtyard of the LORD's **t**, Jr 19:14
Benjamin Gate in the LORD's **t**. Jr 20:2
placed before the **t** of the LORD. Jr 24:1
the LORD's **t** and speak all the Jr 26:2
I will make this **t** like Shiloh. Jr 26:6
words in the **t** of the LORD. Jr 26:7
'This **t** will become like Shiloh Jr 26:9
Jeremiah at the LORD's **t**. Jr 26:9
palace to the LORD's **t** and sat Jr 26:10
heard against this **t** and city. Jr 26:12
and the **t** mount a forested hill. Jr 26:18
of the LORD's **t** will be brought Jr 27:16
that remain in the LORD's **t**, Jr 27:18
remain in the **t** of the LORD, Jr 27:21
said to me in the **t** of the LORD Jr 28:1
of the LORD's **t** that Jr 28:3
standing in the **t** of the LORD. Jr 28:5
of the LORD's **t** and all the Jr 28:6
officer in the **t** of the LORD, Jr 29:26
offerings to its **t** of the LORD. Jr 33:11
before Me at the **t** called by My Jr 34:15
chambers of the **t** of the LORD to Jr 35:2
them into the **t** of the LORD to Jr 35:4
cannot enter the **t** of the LORD, Jr 36:5
the people at the **t** of the LORD Jr 36:6
At the LORD's **t** he read the Jr 36:8
at the LORD's **t**, in the chamber Jr 36:10
of the New Gate of the LORD's **t**, Jr 36:10
third entrance of the LORD's **t**. Jr 38:14
to bring to the **t** of the LORD. Jr 41:5
pillars of the sun **t** in the land Jr 43:13
God, the vengeance for His **t**. Jr 50:28
vengeance, vengeance for His **t**. Jr 51:11
the holy places of the LORD's **t**. Jr 51:51
burned the LORD's **t**, the king's Jr 52:13
for the LORD's **t** and the water Jr 52:17
that were in the LORD's **t**, Jr 52:17
articles used in ⌊**t**⌋ service. Jr 52:18
had made for the LORD's **t**, Jr 52:20
violence to His **t** as if ⌊it Lm 2:6
stones of the **t** lie scattered at Lm 4:1
at the entrance of the LORD's **t**, Ezk 8:16
to the LORD's **t** and their faces Ezk 8:16
to the threshold of the **t**. Ezk 9:3
who were in front of the **t**. Ezk 9:6
Defile the **t** and fill the courts Ezk 9:7
the south of the **t** when the man Ezk 10:3
to the threshold of the **t**. Ezk 10:4
The **t** was filled with the cloud, Ezk 10:4
of the **t** and stood above Ezk 10:18
the outside of the **t**. Ezk 40:5
the gate on the **t** side next to Ezk 40:7
of the gate was on the **t** side. Ezk 40:9
who keep charge of the **t**. Ezk 40:45
The altar was in front of the **t**. Ezk 40:47
portico of the **t** and measured Ezk 40:48
he measured the wall of the **t**; Ezk 41:5
all around the **t** was seven feet. Ezk 41:5
the wall of the **t** all around to Ezk 41:6
not be in the **t** wall ⌊itself⌋. Ezk 41:6
the **t**⌋ widened at each Ezk 41:7
surrounding the **t** ⌊went up⌋ by Ezk 41:7
I saw that the **t** had a raised Ezk 41:8
between the side rooms of the **t** Ezk 41:9
35 feet wide all around the **t**. Ezk 41:10
that faced the **t** yard toward the Ezk 41:12
Then the man measured the **t**; Ezk 41:13
the **t** yard and the building, Ezk 41:13
of the front of the **t** along with Ezk 41:14
along with the **t** yard to the Ezk 41:14
facing the **t** yard to the west, Ezk 41:15
far as the inner **t** and on the Ezk 41:17
throughout the **t** on all sides. Ezk 41:19
rooms of the **t**, and the canopies Ezk 41:26
opposite the **t** yard and opposite Ezk 42:1
chambers facing the **t** yard and Ezk 42:10
face the **t** yard are the holy Ezk 42:13
measuring inside the **t** complex, Ezk 42:15
He measured the **t** complex on all Ezk 42:20
LORD entered the **t** by way of the Ezk 43:4
glory of the LORD filled the **t**. Ezk 43:5
speaking to me from the **t**. Ezk 43:6
describe the **t** to the house of Ezk 43:10
the design of the **t** to them— Ezk 43:11
This is the law of the **t**: Ezk 43:12
Yes, this is the law of the **t**. Ezk 43:12
the place appointed for the **t**. Ezk 43:21
gate to the front of the **t**. Ezk 44:4
glory of the LORD filled His **t**. Ezk 44:4
and laws of the LORD's **t**. Ezk 44:5
entrance of the **t** along with all Ezk 44:5
you defiled My **t** while you Ezk 44:7
as guards at the **t** gates and Ezk 44:11
gates and ministering at the **t**. Ezk 44:11
for the duties of the **t**— Ezk 44:14
Levites who minister in the **t**; Ezk 45:5
apply ⌊it⌋ to the **t** doorposts, Ezk 45:19
will make atonement for the **t**. Ezk 45:20
who minister at the **t** will cook Ezk 46:24
entrance of the **t** and there was Ezk 47:1
of the **t** toward the east Ezk 47:1
the east, for the **t** faced east. Ezk 47:1
⌊of the threshold⌋ of the **t**, Ezk 47:1
the sanctuary of the **t** will be Ezk 48:21
taken from the **t** in Jerusalem, Dn 5:2
that had been taken from the **t**, Dn 5:3
on a wing of the **t** until the Dn 9:27
up and desecrate the **t** fortress. Dn 11:31
king's sanctuary and a royal **t**." Am 7:13
In that day the **t** songs will Am 8:3
once more toward Your holy **t**. Jnh 2:4
came to You, to Your holy **t**. Jnh 2:7
you, the Lord, from His holy **t**. Mc 1:2
the hill of the **t** mount will be Mc 3:12
But the LORD is in His holy **t**; Hab 2:20
on another in the LORD's **t**, Hg 2:15
of the LORD's **t** was laid; Hg 2:18
place and build the LORD's **t**. Zch 6:12
He will build the LORD's **t**; Zch 6:13
in the LORD's **t** as a memorial to Zch 6:14
come and build the LORD's **t**. Zch 6:15
for the rebuilding of the **t**, Zch 8:9
of you would shut the ⌊**t**⌋ doors, Mal 1:10
will suddenly come to His **t**, Mal 3:1
stand on the pinnacle of the **t**, Mt 4:5
the priests in the **t** violate the Mt 12:5
greater than the **t** is here! Mt 12:6
a gift ⌊committed to the **t**⌋"— Mt 15:5
into the **t** complex and drove Mt 21:12
buying and selling in the **t**. Mt 21:12
came to Him in the **t** complex, Mt 21:14
children in the **t** complex Mt 21:15
When He entered the **t** complex, Mt 21:23
was going out of the **t** complex, Mt 24:1
attention to the **t** buildings. Mt 24:1
teaching in the **t** complex, Mt 26:55
sitting with the **t** police to see Mt 26:58
to put it into the **t** treasury, Mt 27:6
a gift ⌊committed to the **t**⌋ Mk 7:11
and into the **t** complex. Mk 11:11
He went into the **t** complex and Mk 11:15
buying and selling in the **t**. Mk 11:15
goods through the **t** complex. Mk 11:16
He was walking in the **t** complex, Mk 11:27
as He taught in the **t** complex, Mk 12:35
across from the **t** treasury, Mk 12:41
those giving to the **t** treasury. Mk 12:43
was going out of the **t** complex, Mk 13:1
across from the **t** complex, Mk 13:3
teaching in the **t** complex, Mk 14:49
was sitting with the **t** police, Mk 14:54
Even the **t** police took Him and Mk 14:65
he entered the **t** complex. Lk 2:27
She did not leave the **t** complex, Lk 2:37
Him in the **t** complex sitting Lk 2:46
stand on the pinnacle of the **t**, Lk 4:9
up to the **t** complex to pray, Lk 18:10
He went into the **t** complex and Lk 19:45
was teaching in the **t** complex. Lk 19:47
the people in the **t** complex and Lk 20:1
offerings into the **t** treasury. Lk 21:1
talking about the **t** complex, Lk 21:5
was teaching in the **t** complex, Lk 21:37
to hear Him in the **t** complex. Lk 21:38
chief priests and **t** police how Lk 22:4
to the chief priests, **t** police, Lk 22:52
I was with you in the **t** complex, Lk 22:53
in the **t** complex blessing Lk 24:53
In the **t** complex He found people Jn 2:14
out of the **t** complex with their Jn 2:15
him in the **t** complex and said Jn 5:14
went up into the **t** complex and Jn 7:14
was teaching in the **t** complex, Jn 7:28
Pharisees sent **t** police to Jn 7:32
Then the **t** police came to the Jn 7:45
He went to the **t** complex again, Jn 8:2
while teaching in the **t** complex. Jn 8:20
and went out of the **t** complex. Jn 8:59
was walking in the **t** complex in Jn 10:23
as they stood in the **t** complex: Jn 11:56
of soldiers and some **t** police Jn 18:3
and the Jewish **t** police arrested Jn 18:12
slaves and the **t** police had made Jn 18:18
synagogue and in the **t** complex, Jn 18:20
one of the **t** police standing by Jn 18:22
and the **t** police saw Him, Jn 19:6
together in the **t** complex, Ac 2:46
up together to the **t** complex at Ac 3:1
every day at the **t** gate called Ac 3:2
those entering the **t** complex. Ac 3:2
about to enter the **t** complex, Ac 3:3
he entered the **t** complex with Ac 3:8
Beautiful Gate of the **t** complex. Ac 3:10
the commander of the **t** guard, Ac 4:1
Go and stand in the **t** complex, Ac 5:20
they entered the **t** complex at Ac 5:21
But when the **t** police got there, Ac 5:22
the captain of the **t** police and Ac 5:24
standing in the **t** complex and Ac 5:25
went with the **t** police and Ac 5:26
Every day in the **t** complex, Ac 5:42
whose **t** was just outside the Ac 14:13
but also that the **t** of the great Ac 19:27
the Ephesians is the **t** guardian Ac 19:35
men here who are not **t** robbers Ac 19:37
and entered the **t**, announcing Ac 21:26
Asia saw him in the **t** complex, Ac 21:27
Greeks into the **t** and has Ac 21:28
brought him into the **t** complex. Ac 21:29
him out of the **t** complex, Ac 21:30
was praying in the **t** complex, Ac 22:17
even tried to desecrate the **t**, Ac 24:6
either in the **t** complex or in Ac 24:12
me ritually purified in the **t**, Ac 24:18
nor against the **t**, nor against Ac 25:8
me in the **t** complex and were Ac 26:21
of the law, the **t** service, Rm 9:4
in an idol's **t**, won't his weak 1Co 8:10
who perform the **t** services eat 1Co 9:13
eat the food from the **t**, 1Co 9:13

TEMPLE'S *(7)*

stone for the **t** construction. 1Kg 5:18
extending across the **t** width, 1Kg 6:3
The **t** construction used finished 1Kg 6:7
you repaired the **t** damage? 2Kg 12:7
would not repair the **t** damage. 2Kg 12:8
the gates of the **t** fortress, Neh 2:8
reason for the **t** broadness as it Ezk 41:7

TEMPLES *(8)*

news in the **t** of their idols 1Sm 31:9
the hair on their **t** and reside Jr 9:26
and all those who shave their **t**; Jr 25:23
a fire in the **t** of Egypt's gods, Jr 43:12
burn down the **t** of the Egyptian Jr 43:13
those who shave their **t**; Jr 49:32
My finest treasures to your **t**. Jl 3:5
idols, do you rob their **t**? Rm 2:22

TEMPORARY *(13)*

A **t** resident or hired hand may Ex 12:45
foreigners and **t** residents on My Lv 25:23
as a foreigner or **t** resident, Lv 25:35
as a hired hand or **t** resident; Lv 25:40
a foreigner or **t** resident Lv 25:47
foreigner or **t** resident among Nm 35:15
few indeed, and **t** residents in 1Ch 16:19

and **t** residents in Canaan, Ps 105:12
what is seen is **t**, but what is 2Co 4:18
were foreigners and **t** residents Heb 11:13
To the **t** residents of the 1Pt 1:1
during this time of **t** residence. 1Pt 1:17
you as aliens and **t** residents to 1Pt 2:11

TEMPT *(3)*
Satan may **t** you because of your 1Co 7:5
Let us not **t** Christ as some of 1Co 10:9
and He Himself doesn't **t** anyone. Jms 1:13

TEMPTATION *(10)*
And do not bring us into **t**, Mt 6:13
so that you won't enter into **t**. Mt 26:41
so that you won't enter into **t**. Mk 14:38
the Devil had finished every **t**, Lk 4:13
And do not bring us into **t**." Lk 11:4
that you may not enter into **t**." Lk 22:40
so that you won't enter into **t**." Lk 22:46
No **t** has overtaken you except 1Co 10:13
but with the **t** He will also 1Co 10:13
who want to be rich fall into **t**, 1Tm 6:9

TEMPTED *(9)*
wilderness to be **t** by the Devil. Mt 4:1
40 days, being **t** by Satan. Mk 1:13
40 days to be **t** by the Devil. Lk 4:2
allow you to be **t** beyond what 1Co 10:13
so you won't be **t** also. Gl 6:1
the tempter had **t** you and that 1Th 3:5
say, "I am being **t** by God." Jms 1:13
For God is not **t** by evil, Jms 1:13
person is **t** when he is drawn Jms 1:14

TEMPTER *(2)*
Then the **t** approached Him and Mt 4:3
that the **t** had tempted you 1Th 3:5

TEN *(17)*
thousands upon **t** thousands. Gn 24:60
covenant—the **T** Commandments. Ex 34:28
to follow the **T** Commandments, Dt 4:13
the **T** Commandments that He had Dt 10:4
or two put **t** thousand to flight, Dt 32:30
and came with **t** thousand holy Dt 33:2
Such are the **t** thousands of Dt 33:17
one out of **t** to come and live Neh 11:1
have humiliated me **t** times now, Jb 19:3
your side and **t** thousand at your Ps 91:7
stronger than **t** rulers of a city Ec 7:19
notable among **t** thousand. Sg 5:10
t thousand times ten thousand Dn 7:10
thousand times **t** thousand stood Dn 7:10
out for him **t** thousand points Hs 8:12
will have ⌊only⌋ **t** left in the Am 5:3
or with **t** thousand streams of Mc 6:7

TEN-ACRE *(1)*
For a **t** vineyard will yield only Is 5:10

TEN-STRINGED *(3)*
make music to Him with a **t** harp. Ps 33:2
with a **t** harp and the music of a Ps 92:3
will play on a **t** harp for You— Ps 144:9

TENANT *(6)*
He leased it to **t** farmers and Mt 21:33
But when the **t** farmers saw the Mt 21:38
he leased it to **t** farmers and Mk 12:1
But those **t** farmers said among Mk 12:7
leased it to **t** farmers, and went Lk 20:9
But when the **t** farmers saw him, Lk 20:14

TENANTS *(2)*
or shown contempt for its **t**, Jb 31:39
He leased the vineyard to **t**. Sg 8:11

TEND *(8)*
and his sons are to **t** the lamp Ex 27:21
Aaron is to **t** it regularly from Lv 24:3
He must regularly **t** the lamps on Lv 24:4
from Saul to **t** his father's 1Sm 17:15
but you do not **t** the flock. Ezk 34:3
I will **t** them with good pasture, Ezk 34:14
I will **t** My flock and let them Ezk 34:15
He will **t** them himself and will Ezk 34:23

TENDED *(7)*
t sheep with his brothers. Gn 37:2
he **t** flocks for a wife. Hs 12:12
and Israel was **t** by a prophet. Hs 12:13
LORD of Hosts has **t** His flock, Zch 10:3
Then the men who **t** them fled. Mt 8:33
The men who **t** them ran off and Mk 5:14
When the men who **t** them saw what Lk 8:34

TENDER *(13)*
ran to the herd and got a **t**, Gn 18:7
grass and showers on **t** plants. Dt 32:2
of the field, **t** grass, grass 2Kg 19:26
your heart was **t** and you humbled 2Kg 22:19
your heart was **t** and you humbled 2Ch 34:27
and wilt like **t** green plants. Ps 37:2
t and precious to my mother, Pr 4:3
of the field, **t** grass, grass Is 37:27
I will pluck a **t** sprig from its Ezk 17:22
in the **t** grass of the field. Dn 4:15
in the **t** grass of the field. Dn 4:23
branch becomes **t** and sprouts Mt 24:32
branch becomes **t** and sprouts Mk 13:28

TENDERLY *(3)*
young girl and spoke **t** to her. Gn 34:3
Speak **t** to Jerusalem, and Is 40:2
wilderness, and speak **t** to her. Hs 2:14

TENDING *(4)*
"but right now he's **t** the sheep." 1Sm 16:11
servant has been **t** his father's 1Sm 17:34
brought him from **t** ewes to be Ps 78:71
a slave plowing or **t** sheep, Lk 17:7

TENDONS *(5)*
me together with bones and **t**. Jb 10:11
the **t** of his thighs are woven Jb 40:17
I will put **t** on you, make flesh Ezk 37:6
As I looked, **t** appeared on them, Ezk 37:8
together by its ligaments and **t**, Col 2:19

TENDRILS *(1)*
Your **t** have extended to the sea; Jr 48:32

TENDS *(2)*
morning when he **t** the lamps. Ex 30:7
Whoever **t** a fig tree will eat Pr 27:18

TENONS *(6)*
connected together with two **t**. Ex 26:17
the first plank for its two **t**, Ex 26:19
the next plank for its two **t**; Ex 26:19
There were two **t** connected to Ex 36:22
the first plank for its two **t**, Ex 36:24
planks for their two **t**; Ex 36:24

TENS *(10)*
hundreds, fifties, and **t**. Ex 18:21
hundreds, fifties, and **t**. Ex 18:25
fifties, and **t**, and officers for Dt 1:15
but David his **t** of thousands. 1Sm 18:7
They credited **t** of thousands to 1Sm 18:8
but David his **t** of thousands?" 1Sm 21:11
but David his **t** of thousands?" 1Sm 29:5
chariots are **t** of thousands, Ps 68:17
by thousands and **t** of thousands Ps 144:13
and cause **t** of thousands to Dn 11:12

TENT *(311)*
uncovered himself inside his **t**. Gn 9:21
of Bethel and pitched his **t**, Gn 12:8
and Ai where his **t** had formerly Gn 13:3
and set up his **t** near Sodom. Gn 13:12
Abram moved his **t** and went to Gn 13:18
entrance of his **t** during the Gn 18:1
entrance of the **t** to meet them Gn 18:2
hurried into the **t** and said to Gn 18:6
"There, in the **t**," he answered. Gn 18:9
entrance of the **t** behind him. Gn 18:10
her into the **t** of his mother Gn 24:67
LORD, and pitched his **t** there. Gn 26:25
had pitched his **t** in the hill Gn 31:25
So Laban went into Jacob's **t**, Gn 31:33
tent, then Leah's **t**, and then Gn 31:33
he left Leah's **t** and entered Gn 31:33
the whole **t** but found nothing Gn 31:34
where he had pitched his **t**. Gn 33:19
and pitched his **t** beyond the Gn 35:21
each of you has in his **t**.'" Ex 16:16
had been and went into the **t**. Ex 18:7
of goat hair for a **t** over the Ex 26:7
double at the front of the **t**. Ex 26:9
and join the **t** together so that Ex 26:11
left over from the **t** curtains, Ex 26:12
length of the **t** curtains should Ex 26:13
covering for the **t** from ram Ex 26:14
entrance to the **t** you are to Ex 26:36
use and all its **t** pegs as well Ex 27:19
as well as all the **t** pegs of the Ex 27:19
In the **t** of meeting outside the Ex 27:21
they enter the **t** of meeting or Ex 28:43
entrance to the **t** of meeting and Ex 29:4
the front of the **t** of meeting, Ex 29:10
entrance to the **t** of meeting. Ex 29:11
and enters the **t** of meeting to Ex 29:30
entrance to the **t** of meeting. Ex 29:32
entrance to the **t** of meeting Ex 29:42
will consecrate the **t** of meeting Ex 29:44
the service of the **t** of meeting. Ex 30:16
Set it between the **t** of meeting Ex 30:18
they enter the **t** of meeting or Ex 30:20
are to anoint the **t** of meeting, Ex 30:26
testimony in the **t** of meeting, Ex 30:36
the **t** of meeting, the ark of the Ex 31:7
other⌋ furnishings of the **t**— Ex 31:7
Now Moses took a **t** and set it up Ex 33:7
he called it the **t** of meeting. Ex 33:7
would go to the **t** of meeting Ex 33:7
Moses went out to the **t**, Ex 33:8
each one at the door of his **t**, Ex 33:8
Moses until he entered the **t**. Ex 33:8
Moses entered the **t**, the pillar Ex 33:9
remain at the entrance to the **t**, Ex 33:9
at the entrance to the **t**, Ex 33:10
each one at the door of his **t**. Ex 33:10
not leave the inside of the **t**. Ex 33:11
tabernacle—its **t** and covering, Ex 35:11
t pegs for the tabernacle and Ex 35:18
tabernacle and the **t** pegs for Ex 35:18
construct the **t** of meeting for Ex 35:21
of goat hair for a **t** over the Ex 36:14
clasps to join the **t** together as Ex 36:18
covering for the **t** from ram Ex 36:19
linen for the entrance to the **t**, Ex 36:37
entrance to the **t** of meeting. Ex 38:8
the **t** pegs for the tabernacle Ex 38:20
entrance to the **t** of meeting, Ex 38:30
all the **t** pegs for the Ex 38:31
and all the **t** pegs for the Ex 38:31
tabernacle, the **t** of meeting, Ex 39:32
the **t** with all its furnishings, Ex 39:33
for the entrance to the **t**; Ex 39:38
its ropes and **t** pegs, and all Ex 39:40
tabernacle, the **t** of meeting; Ex 39:40
tabernacle, the **t** of meeting, Ex 40:2
tabernacle, the **t** of meeting. Ex 40:6
basin between the **t** of meeting Ex 40:7
entrance to the **t** of meeting and Ex 40:12
Then he spread the **t** over the Ex 40:19
covering of the **t** on top of it, Ex 40:19
the table in the **t** of meeting on Ex 40:22
lampstand in the **t** of meeting Ex 40:24
gold altar in the **t** of meeting, Ex 40:26
tabernacle, the **t** of meeting, Ex 40:29
basin between the **t** of meeting Ex 40:30
they came to the **t** of meeting Ex 40:32
cloud covered the **t** of meeting, Ex 40:34
to enter the **t** of meeting Ex 40:35
to him from the **t** of meeting: Lv 1:1
entrance to the **t** of meeting so Lv 1:3
entrance to the **t** of meeting. Lv 1:5
entrance to the **t** of meeting. Lv 3:2
it before the **t** of meeting. Lv 3:8
it before the **t** of meeting. Lv 3:13
entrance to the **t** of meeting Lv 4:4
bring it into the **t** of meeting. Lv 4:5
the LORD in the **t** of meeting. Lv 4:7
entrance to the **t** of meeting. Lv 4:7
it before the **t** of meeting. Lv 4:14
blood into the **t** of meeting. Lv 4:16
the LORD in the **t** of meeting. Lv 4:18
entrance to the **t** of meeting. Lv 4:18
courtyard of the **t** of meeting. Lv 6:16
courtyard of the **t** of meeting. Lv 6:26
brought into the **t** of meeting to Lv 6:30
entrance to the **t** of meeting." Lv 8:3
entrance to the **t** of meeting. Lv 8:4
entrance to the **t** of meeting and Lv 8:31
entrance to the **t** of meeting for Lv 8:33
entrance to the **t** of meeting day Lv 8:35
the front of the **t** of meeting, Lv 9:5
then entered the **t** of meeting. Lv 9:23
entrance to the **t** of meeting or Lv 10:7
when you enter the **t** of meeting, Lv 10:9
the entrance to the **t** of meeting Lv 12:6
outside his **t** for seven days. Lv 14:8
entrance to the **t** of meeting. Lv 14:11
entrance to the **t** of meeting Lv 14:23
entrance to the **t** of meeting, Lv 15:14
entrance to the **t** of meeting. Lv 15:29

entrance to the **t** of meeting. Lv 16:7
same for the **t** of meeting that Lv 16:16
one may be in the **t** of meeting Lv 16:17
holy place, the **t** of meeting, Lv 16:20
is to enter the **t** of meeting, Lv 16:23
He will purify the **t** of meeting Lv 16:33
entrance to the **t** of meeting to Lv 17:4
the entrance to the **t** of meeting Lv 17:5
entrance to the **t** of meeting and Lv 17:6
entrance to the **t** of meeting to Lv 17:9
entrance to the **t** of meeting. Lv 19:21
testimony in the **t** of meeting. Lv 24:3
to Moses in the **t** of meeting Nm 1:1
camp around the **t** of meeting at Nm 2:2
The **t** of meeting is to move out Nm 2:17
community before the **t** of Nm 3:7
furnishings of the **t** of meeting Nm 3:8
duties at the **t** of meeting Nm 3:25
tabernacle, the **t**, its covering, Nm 3:25
entrance to the **t** of meeting, Nm 3:25
the altar, and the **t** ropes—all Nm 3:26
their bases, **t** pegs, and ropes. Nm 3:37
in front of the **t** of meeting Nm 3:38
to do work at the **t** of meeting. Nm 4:3
Kohathites at the **t** of meeting Nm 4:4
regarding the **t** of meeting. Nm 4:15
to do work at the **t** of meeting. Nm 4:23
the **t** of meeting with its Nm 4:25
entrance to the **t** of meeting, Nm 4:25
clans at the **t** of meeting, Nm 4:28
do the work of the **t** of meeting. Nm 4:30
service at the **t** of meeting: Nm 4:31
their bases, **t** pegs, and ropes, Nm 4:32
their work at the **t** of meeting, Nm 4:33
for work at the **t** of meeting. Nm 4:35
could serve at the **t** of meeting. Nm 4:37
for work at the **t** of meeting. Nm 4:39
could serve at the **t** of meeting. Nm 4:41
for work at the **t** of meeting. Nm 4:43
of serving at the **t** of meeting Nm 4:47
entrance to the **t** of meeting. Nm 6:10
entrance to the **t** of meeting. Nm 6:13
entrance to the **t** of meeting, Nm 6:18
in the work of the **t** of meeting, Nm 7:5
Moses entered the **t** of meeting Nm 7:89
Levites before the **t** of meeting Nm 8:9
to serve ⌊at⌋ the **t** of meeting, Nm 8:15
at the **t** of meeting and to Nm 8:19
their work at the **t** of meeting Nm 8:22
in the work at the **t** of meeting. Nm 8:24
at the **t** of meeting, Nm 8:26
tabernacle, the **t** of the Nm 9:15
cloud was lifted up above the **t**, Nm 9:17
entrance to the **t** of meeting. Nm 10:3
Take them to the **t** of meeting Nm 11:16
and had them stand around the **t**. Nm 11:24
but had not gone out to the **t**— Nm 11:26
come out to the **t** of meeting." Nm 12:4
stood at the entrance to the **t**, Nm 12:5
the cloud moved away from the **t**, Nm 12:10
Israelites at the **t** of meeting. Nm 14:10
entrance to the **t** of meeting Nm 16:18
entrance to the **t** of meeting, Nm 16:19
turned toward the **t** of meeting, Nm 16:42
the front of the **t** of meeting, Nm 16:43
entrance to the **t** of meeting, Nm 16:50
place them in the **t** of meeting Nm 17:4
the LORD in the **t** of the Nm 17:7
entered the **t** of the testimony Nm 17:8
in front of the **t** of the Nm 18:2
for you and for the whole **t**. Nm 18:3
you and guard the **t** of meeting, Nm 18:4
doing all the work at the **t**, Nm 18:4
to work at the **t** of meeting. Nm 18:6
the work of the **t** of meeting. Nm 18:21
come near the **t** of meeting, Nm 18:22
do the work of the **t** of meeting, Nm 18:23
your work at the **t** of meeting. Nm 18:31
the front of the **t** of meeting. Nm 19:4
law when a person dies in a **t**: Nm 19:14
enters the **t** and everyone who Nm 19:14
already⌋ in the **t** will be Nm 19:14
and sprinkle the **t**, all the Nm 19:18
the doorway of the **t** of meeting. Nm 20:6
entrance to the **t** of meeting. Nm 25:6
the Israelite man into the **t**, Nm 25:8
entrance to the **t** of meeting and Nm 27:2
it into the **t** of meeting as Nm 31:54
yourselves at the **t** of meeting, Dt 31:14
themselves at the **t** of meeting, Dt 31:14
appeared at the **t** in a pillar of Dt 31:15
stood at the entrance to the **t**. Dt 31:15
in the ground inside my **t**, Jos 7:21
messengers who ran to the **t**, Jos 7:22
in his **t**, with the money Jos 7:22
the things from inside the **t**, Jos 7:23
and sheep, his **t**, and all that Jos 7:24
set up the **t** of meeting there; Jos 18:1
entrance to the **t** of meeting. Jos 19:51
and pitched his **t** beside the oak Jdg 4:11
fled on foot to the **t** of Jael, Jdg 4:17
went into her **t**, and she covered Jdg 4:18
Stand at the entrance to the **t**. Jdg 4:20
Heber's wife Jael took a **t** peg, Jdg 4:21
dead with a **t** peg through his Jdg 4:22
reached for a **t** peg, her right Jdg 5:26
camp, struck a **t**, and it fell. Jdg 7:13
loaf turned the **t** upside down so Jdg 7:13
will go to his **t** or return to Jdg 20:8
entrance to the **t** of meeting. 1Sm 2:22
and each man fled to his **t**. 1Sm 4:10
troops away, each to his own **t**. 1Sm 13:2
weapons in his ⌊own⌋ **t**. 1Sm 17:54
inside the **t** David had set up 2Sm 6:17
of God sits inside **t** curtains." 2Sm 7:2
around with the tabernacle **t**. 2Sm 7:6
So they pitched a **t** for Absalom 2Sm 16:22
all Israel fled, each to his **t**. 2Sm 18:17
Israelite had fled to his **t**. 2Sm 19:8
Each man to his **t**, Israel! 2Sm 20:1
the city, each to his own **t**. 2Sm 20:22
of the LORD, the **t** of meeting, 1Kg 8:4
utensils that were in the **t**. 1Kg 8:4
went into a **t** to eat and drink 2Kg 7:8
came back and entered another **t**, 2Kg 7:8
men⌋ fled, each to his own **t**. 2Kg 14:12
tabernacle, the **t** of meeting, 1Ch 6:32
guard the thresholds of the **t**. 1Ch 9:19
entrance to the **t** of meeting. 1Ch 9:21
house, the house of the **t**. 1Ch 9:23
of God and pitched a **t** for it. 1Ch 15:1
inside the **t** David had pitched 1Ch 16:1
covenant is under **t** curtains." 1Ch 17:1
I have moved from **t** to tent and 1Ch 17:5
moved from tent to **t** and from 1Ch 17:5
to the **t** of meeting, 1Ch 23:32
because God's **t** of meeting, 2Ch 1:3
he had pitched a **t** for it in 2Ch 1:4
altar at the **t** of meeting; 2Ch 1:6
in front of the **t** of meeting, 2Ch 1:13
up the ark, the **t** of meeting, 2Ch 5:5
utensils that were in the **t**. 2Ch 5:5
Israel, each man to your **t**; 2Ch 10:16
Israel for the **t** of the 2Ch 24:6
and each fled to his own **t**. 2Ch 25:22
Are their **t** cords not pulled up? Jb 4:21
will know that your **t** is secure, Jb 5:24
the **t** of the wicked will exist Jb 8:22
The light in his **t** grows dark, Jb 18:6
security of his **t** and marched Jb 18:14
he owned remains in his **t**. Jb 18:15
against me and camp around my **t**. Jb 19:12
feed on what is left in his **t**. Jb 20:26
you banish injustice from your **t** Jb 22:23
God's friendship rested on my **t**, Jb 29:4
LORD, who can dwell in Your **t**? Ps 15:1
He has pitched a **t** for the sun. Ps 19:4
me under the cover of His **t**; Ps 27:5
sacrifices in His **t** with shouts Ps 27:6
ripping you out of your **t**; Ps 52:5
live in Your **t** forever and take Ps 61:4
His **t** is in Salem, His dwelling Ps 76:2
in His camp, all around His **t**. Ps 78:28
t where He resided among men. Ps 78:60
He rejected the **t** of Joseph and Ps 78:67
no plague will come near your **t**. Ps 91:10
but the **t** of the upright will Pr 14:11
will not pitch his **t** there, Is 13:20
Then in the **t** of David a throne Is 16:5
pasture, a **t** that does not Is 33:20
its **t** pegs will not be pulled up Is 33:20
from me like a shepherd's **t**. Is 38:12
spreads them out like a **t** to Is 40:22
Enlarge the site of your **t**, Is 54:2
and let your **t** curtains be Is 54:2
are destroyed, my **t** curtains, in Jr 4:20
My **t** is destroyed; all my tent Jr 10:20
all my **t** cords are snapped. Jr 10:20
one to pitch my **t** again or to Jr 10:20
each in his **t**, they would get Jr 37:10
with their **t** curtains and all Jr 49:29
fire on the **t** of Daughter Zion Lm 2:4
the **t** curtains of the land of Hab 3:7
from them the **t** peg, from them Zch 10:4
you took up the **t** of Moloch and Ac 7:43
and will rebuild David's **t**, Ac 15:16
house, a **t**, is destroyed, 2Co 5:1
we who are in this **t** groan, 2Co 5:4
as long as I am in this **t**, 2Pt 1:13
that I will soon lay aside my **t**, 2Pt 1:14

TENT-DWELLING *(1)*

is most blessed among **t** women. Jdg 5:24

TENTH *(73)*

to recede until the **t** month; Gn 8:5
in the **t** month, on the first day Gn 8:5
gave him a **t** of everything. Gn 14:20
give to You a **t** of all that You Gn 28:22
that on the **t** day of this month Ex 12:3
Two quarts are a **t** of an ephah. Ex 16:36
on the **t** ⌊day⌋ of the month you Lv 16:29
The **t** ⌊day⌋ of this seventh Lv 23:27
on the **t** ⌊day⌋ of the month; Lv 25:9
Every **t** of the land's produce, Lv 27:30
to redeem any part of this **t**, Lv 27:31
Every **t** animal from the herd or Lv 27:32
On the **t** day Ahiezer son of Nm 7:66
the Levites every **t** in Israel as Nm 18:21
given them the **t** that the Nm 18:24
Israelites the **t** that I have Nm 18:26
to the LORD—a **t** of the tenth. Nm 18:26
to the LORD—a tenth of the **t**. Nm 18:26
LORD from every **t** you receive Nm 18:28
best part of the **t** is to be Nm 18:29
the best part of the **t**, Nm 18:30
assembly on the **t** ⌊day⌋ of this Nm 29:7
offerings of the **t**, personal Dt 12:11
the **t** of your grain, new wine, Dt 12:17
to set aside a **t** of all the Dt 14:22
are to eat a **t** of your grain, Dt 14:23
bring a **t** of all your produce Dt 14:28
even to the **t** generation, may Dt 23:2
even to the **t** generation, may Dt 23:3
paying all the **t** of your produce Dt 26:12
the year of the **t**, you are to Dt 26:12
Jordan on the **t** day of the first Jos 4:19
can take a **t** of your grain and 1Sm 8:15
He can take a **t** of your flocks, 1Sm 8:17
on the **t** day of the tenth month, 2Kg 25:1
on the tenth day of the **t** month, 2Kg 25:1
Jeremiah **t**, and Machbannai 1Ch 12:13
to Jeshua, the **t** to Shecaniah, 1Ch 24:11
the **t** ⌊to⌋ Shimei, his sons, and 1Ch 25:17
The **t**, for the tenth month, was 1Ch 27:13
tenth, for the **t** month, was 1Ch 27:13
an abundant **t** of everything. 2Ch 31:5
also ⌊brought⌋ a **t** of the cattle 2Ch 31:6
and a **t** of the dedicated things 2Ch 31:6
The offering, the **t**, and the 2Ch 31:12
first day of the **t** month to Ezr 10:16
A **t** of our land's ⌊produce⌋ from Neh 10:37
Levites when they collect the **t**, Neh 10:38
must take a **t** of this offering Neh 10:38
Judah brought a **t** of the grain, Neh 13:12
the royal palace in the **t** month, Est 2:16
Though a **t** will remain in the Is 6:13
the LORD in the **t** year of Jr 32:1
of Judah, in the **t** month, King Jr 39:1
on the **t** day of the tenth month, Jr 52:4
on the tenth day of the **t** month, Jr 52:4
the **t** day of the fifth month— Jr 52:12
on the **t** ⌊day⌋ of the month, Ezk 20:1
ninth year, in the **t** month, on Ezk 24:1
on the **t** ⌊day⌋ of the month: Ezk 24:1
In the **t** year, in the tenth Ezk 29:1
in the **t** ⌊month⌋ on the twelfth Ezk 29:1
of our exile, in the **t** ⌊month⌋, Ezk 33:21
on the **t** day of the month in the Ezk 40:1
the fast of the **t** will become Zch 8:19
You pay a **t** of mint, dill, and Mt 23:23
You give a **t** of mint, rue, and Lk 11:42
I give a **t** of everything I get.' Lk 18:12
gave him a **t** of everything; Heb 7:2
gave a **t** of the plunder! Heb 7:4
to collect a **t** from the people Heb 7:5

place, a **t** of the city fell, Rv 11:13
ninth topaz, the **t** chrysoprase, Rv 21:20

TENTHS *(4)*
your **t** and personal Dt 12:6
firstfruits, and **t**. Neh 12:44
articles, and the **t** of grain, Neh 13:5
your **t** every three days. Am 4:4

TENTMAKERS *(1)*
for they were **t** by trade. Ac 18:3

TENTS *(58)*
he will dwell in the **t** of Shem; Gn 9:27
also had flocks, herds, and **t**. Gn 13:5
pitched ⌊their **t**⌋ in the hill Gn 31:25
and then the **t** of the two female Gn 31:33
at the entrance of their **t**. Nm 11:10
now from the **t** of these wicked Nm 16:26
of their **t** with their wives Nm 16:27
beautiful are your **t**, Jacob, Nm 24:5
grumbled in your **t** and said, Dt 1:27
and tell them: Return to your **t**. Dt 5:30
their **t**, and every living Dt 11:6
return to your **t** in the morning. Dt 16:7
and Issachar, in your **t**. Dt 33:18
cattle and their **t** like a great Jdg 6:5
all the Israelites to their **t**, Jdg 7:8
and Judah are dwelling in **t**, 2Sm 11:11
home to their **t** rejoicing and 1Kg 8:66
Israel, return to your **t**; 1Kg 12:16
So Israel went to their **t**, 1Kg 12:16
kings were drinking in the **t**, 1Kg 20:12
him were getting drunk in the **t**. 1Kg 20:16
at twilight abandoning their **t**, 2Kg 7:7
donkeys, and the **t** were intact." 2Kg 7:10
but his troops fled to their **t**. 2Kg 8:21
dwelt in their **t** as before, 2Kg 13:5
Hamites' **t** and the Meunim who 1Ch 4:41
they lived in their **t** throughout 1Ch 5:10
sent the people away to their **t**, 2Ch 7:10
So all Israel went to their **t**. 2Ch 10:16
attacked the **t** of the herdsmen 2Ch 14:15
injustice to dwell in your **t**— Jb 11:14
The **t** of robbers are safe, Jb 12:6
will consume the **t** of those who Jb 15:34
Where are the **t** the wicked lived Jb 21:28
may no one live in their **t**. Ps 69:25
first progeny of the **t** of Ham. Ps 78:51
the tribes of Israel in their **t**. Ps 78:55
the **t** of Edom and the Ps 83:6
to live in the **t** of the wicked. Ps 84:10
grumbled in their **t** and did not Ps 106:25
victory in the **t** of the Ps 118:15
have lived among the **t** of Kedar! Ps 120:5
I am dark like the **t** of Kedar, Sg 1:5
goats near the shepherds' **t**. Sg 1:8
Suddenly my **t** are destroyed, Jr 4:20
pitch ⌊their⌋ **t** all around her. Jr 6:3
of Jacob's **t** and show compassion Jr 30:18
must live in **t** your whole life Jr 35:7
have lived in **t** and have obeyed Jr 35:10
will take their **t** and their Jr 49:29
and pitch their **t** among you. Ezk 25:4
pitch his royal **t** between the Dn 11:45
thorns will invade their **t**. Hs 9:6
I will make you live in **t** again, Hs 12:9
I see the **t** of Cushan in Hab 3:7
will save the **t** of Judah first, Zch 12:7
descendants from the **t** of Jacob, Mal 2:12
in **t** with Isaac and Jacob, Heb 11:9

TERAH *(12)*
lived 29 years and fathered **T**. Gn 11:24
he fathered **T**, Nahor lived 119 Gn 11:25
T lived 70 years and fathered Gn 11:26
are the family records of **T**. Gn 11:27
T fathered Abram, Nahor, and Gn 11:27
T took his son Abram, his Gn 11:31
T lived 205 years and died in Gn 11:32
from Tahath and camped at **T**. Nm 33:27
departed from **T** and camped at Nm 33:28
including **T**, the father Jos 24:2
Serug, Nahor, **T**, 1Ch 1:26
son⌋ of **T**, ⌊son⌋ of Nahor, Lk 3:34

TERAH'S *(1)*
during his father **T** lifetime. Gn 11:28

TEREBINTH *(1)*
Like the **t** or the oak, which Is 6:13

TEREBINTHS *(1)*
poplars, and **t**, because their Hs 4:13

TERESH *(2)*
Bigthan and **T**, two eunuchs who Est 2:21
had informed on Bigthana and **T**, Est 6:2

TERMINALLY *(2)*
days Hezekiah became **t** ill. 2Kg 20:1
days Hezekiah became **t** ill. Is 38:1

TERMS *(9)*
all his **t** in the presence Jdg 11:11
and told the **t** to the people, 1Sm 11:4
reported these **t** to David, 1Sm 18:26
Come to **t** with God and be at Jb 22:21
you⌋ on your **t** when you have Jb 34:33
copy with its **t** and conditions Jr 32:11
keeping the **t** of the covenant Jr 34:18
and asks for **t** of peace. Lk 14:32
earthly and speaks in earthly **t**. Jn 3:31

TERRACED *(1)*
Heshbon's **t** vineyards and the Is 16:8

TERRACES *(7)*
from the supporting **t** inward. 2Sm 5:9
the supporting **t**, the wall of 1Kg 9:15
he then built the **t**. 1Kg 9:24
the supporting **t** ⌊and⌋ repaired 1Kg 11:27
the supporting **t** to the 1Ch 11:8
the supporting **t** of the city of 2Ch 32:5
her vineyard **t** and destroy them Jr 5:10

TERRIBLE *(22)*
and there was a **t** odor in the Ex 8:14
the great and **t** wilderness you Dt 1:19
on you all the **t** diseases of Dt 7:15
the great and **t** wilderness with Dt 8:15
and **t** and chronic sicknesses. Dt 28:59
inflicting a **t** slaughter on them Jos 10:20
has made this **t** trouble for us. 1Sm 6:9
guilt has been **t** from the days Ezr 9:7
of our evil deeds and **t** guilt— Ezr 9:13
had committed **t** blasphemies, Neh 9:18
They committed **t** blasphemies. Neh 9:26
doing all this **t** evil and acting Neh 13:27
planning something **t** for him. Est 7:7
A king's **t** wrath is like the Pr 20:2
t thing has taken place in the Jr 5:30
Israel has done a most **t** thing. Jr 18:13
in and see the **t** abominations Ezk 8:9
He will cause **t** destruction and Dn 8:24
of the LORD is **t** and dreadful— Jl 2:11
at home paralyzed, in **t** agony!" Mt 8:6
completely destroy those **t** men," Mt 21:41
us from such a **t** death, 2Co 1:10

TERRIBLY *(3)*
have rebelled **t** in this matter. Ezr 10:13
do not be **t** angry or remember Is 64:9
I've suffered **t** in a dream Mt 27:19

TERRIFIED *(60)*
and the men were **t**. Gn 20:8
were too **t** to answer him. Gn 45:3
Israelites were **t** and cried out Ex 14:10
the chiefs of Edom will be **t**; Ex 15:15
Moab was **t** of the people because Nm 22:3
Don't be **t** or afraid of them! Dt 1:29
Don't be **t** of them, for the LORD Dt 7:21
alarmed, or **t** because of them. Dt 20:3
don't be **t** or afraid of them. Dt 31:6
of Benjamin were **t** when they Jdg 20:41
and the raiding parties were **t**. 1Sm 14:15
lost their courage and were **t**. 1Sm 17:11
they retreated from him **t**. 1Sm 17:24
He was **t** by Samuel's words and 1Sm 28:20
that he was **t** and said to him 1Sm 28:21
not do it because he was **t**. 1Sm 31:4
torrents of destruction **t** me. 2Sm 22:5
they were **t** and reasoned, 2Kg 10:4
wouldn't do it because he was **t**. 1Ch 10:4
all the nations to be **t** of him. 1Ch 14:17
because he was **t** of the sword of 1Ch 21:30
Haman stood **t** before the king Est 7:6
I am **t** and my body trembles in Jb 21:6
I am **t** in His presence; Jb 23:15
the Almighty has **t** me. Jb 23:16
the contempt of the clans **t** me, Jb 31:34
rises, the mighty are **t**; Jb 41:25
torrents of destruction **t** me. Ps 18:4
when You hid Your face, I was **t**. Ps 30:7
be put to shame and **t** forever; Ps 83:17
we are **t** by Your wrath. Ps 90:7
You hide Your face, they are **t**; Ps 104:29
what they fear; do not be **t**. Is 8:12
and is not **t** by their shouting Is 31:4
of the nations or be **t** by signs Jr 10:2
the nations are **t** by them, Jr 10:2
Let them be **t**, but don't let me Jr 17:18
but don't let me be **t**. Jr 17:18
did not become **t** or tear their Jr 36:24
They are **t**, they are retreating, Jr 46:5
warriors, and they will be **t**. Jr 50:36
on fire, and the soldiers are **t**. Jr 51:32
his thoughts so **t** him that his Dn 5:6
Belshazzar became even more **t**, Dn 5:9
languages were **t** and fearful of Dn 5:19
and the visions in my mind **t** me. Dn 7:15
my thoughts **t** me greatly, and my Dn 7:28
I was **t** and fell facedown. Dn 8:17
will be **t** so that everyone Ob 9
walking on the sea, they were **t**. Mt 14:26
they fell facedown and were **t**. Mt 17:6
they were **t** and said, "This man Mt 27:54
And they were **t** and asked one Mk 4:41
for they all saw Him and were **t**. Mk 6:50
should say, since they were **t**. Mk 9:6
around them, and they were **t**. Lk 2:9
the women were **t** and bowed down Lk 24:5
startled and **t** and thought they Lk 24:37
said, I am **t** and trembling. Heb 12:21
survivors were **t** and gave glory Rv 11:13

TERRIFIES *(5)*
you, and sudden dread **t** you, Jb 22:10
For disaster from God **t** me, Jb 31:23
at that time and **t** them with Jb 33:16
in His anger and **t** them in His Ps 2:5
staggers; horror **t** me. He has Is 21:4

TERRIFY *(16)*
May an eclipse of the sun **t** it. Jb 3:5
dreams, and **t** me with visions Jb 7:14
Would God's majesty not **t** you? Jb 13:11
Trouble and distress **t** him, Jb 15:24
Fear of me should not **t** you; Jb 33:7
the earth may **t** ⌊them⌋ no more. Ps 10:18
tempest and **t** them with Your Ps 83:15
when He rises to **t** the earth. Is 2:19
when He rises to **t** the earth. Is 2:21
The land of Judah will **t** Egypt; Is 19:17
Me in ships to **t** confident Cush. Ezk 30:9
your thoughts **t** you or your face Dn 5:10
east and the north will **t** him, Dn 11:44
of animals will **t** you, Hab 2:17
craftsmen⌋ have come to **t** them, Zch 1:21
I am trying to **t** you with my 2Co 10:9

TERRIFYING *(13)*
arm, with **t** power, and with Dt 26:8
of⌋ power and **t** deeds that Moses Dt 34:12
surrounded by those **t** teeth? Jb 41:14
off the branches with **t** power, Is 10:33
they go mad because of **t** things. Jr 50:38
you, and its appearance was **t**. Dn 2:31
extremely **t**, with iron teeth Dn 7:19
They are fierce and **t**; Hab 1:7
LORD will be **t** to them when He Zph 2:11
there will be **t** sights and great Lk 21:11
but a **t** expectation of judgment, Heb 10:27
It is a **t** thing to fall into the Heb 10:31
was so **t** that Moses said, Heb 12:21

TERRITORIES *(7)*
cities with the **t** surrounding Nm 32:33
the land into its **t**, Jos 19:49
fugitives in ⌊the **t** of⌋ Ephraim Jdg 12:4
surrounding **t** from Philistine 1Sm 7:14
and all the **t** of Philistia— Jl 3:4
will possess the **t** of Ephraim Ob 19
spaces to seize **t** not its own. Hab 1:6

TERRITORY *(105)*
defeated all the **t** of the Gn 14:7
and his **t** will be next to Sidon. Gn 49:13
and honey—the **t** of the Ex 3:8
plague all your **t** with frogs. Ex 8:2
will bring locusts into your **t**. Ex 10:4
settled on the whole **t** of Egypt. Ex 10:14
was left in all the **t** of Egypt. Ex 10:19
found among you in all your **t**. Ex 13:7
before you and enlarge your **t**. Ex 34:24
a city on the border of your **t**. Nm 20:16
traveled through your **t**.' " Nm 20:17

TERROR (69)

TERRORIZE (1)

TERRORIZING (1)

TERRORS (12)

TERTIUS (1)

TERTULLUS (2)

TEST (51)

TESTATOR (2)

TESTED (34)

Silver is ⌊**t**⌋ in a crucible, Pr 27:21
I have **t** all this by wisdom. Ec 7:23
stone in Zion, a **t** stone, a Is 28:16
I have **t** you in the furnace of Is 48:10
this matter and **t** them for 10 Dn 1:14
and test them as gold is **t**. Zch 13:9
brother whom we have often **t**, 2Co 8:22
And they must also be **t** first; 1Tm 3:10
He Himself was **t** and has Heb 2:18
is able to help those who are **t**. Heb 2:18
your fathers **t** Me, tried ⌊Me⌋, Heb 3:9
who has been **t** in every way as Heb 4:15
when he was **t**, offered up Isaac; Heb 11:17
You have **t** those who call Rv 2:2

TESTER *(1)*
but the LORD is a **t** of hearts. Pr 17:3

TESTICLE *(1)*
rash, scabs, or a crushed **t**. Lv 21:20

TESTICLES *(2)*
crushed, torn, or severed ⌊**t**⌋; Lv 22:24
No man whose ⌊**t**⌋ have been Dt 23:1

TESTIFIED *(28)*
your own mouth **t** against you by 2Sm 1:16
the wicked men **t** against Naboth 1Kg 21:13
John **t** concerning Him and Jn 1:15
John **t**, "I watched the Spirit Jn 1:32
I have seen and **t** that He is the Jn 1:34
the One you **t** about, and who was Jn 3:26
what the woman said when she **t**, Jn 4:39
Jesus Himself **t** that a prophet Jn 4:44
and he has **t** to the truth. Jn 5:33
sent Me has Himself **t** about Me. Jn 5:37
troubled in His spirit and **t**, Jn 13:21
saw this has **t** so that you also Jn 19:35
other words he **t** and strongly Ac 2:40
after they had **t** and spoken the Ac 8:25
as their king, of whom He **t**: Ac 13:22
t to the message of His grace Ac 14:3
t to them by giving the Holy Ac 15:8
and solemnly **t** to the Jews that Ac 18:5
t to both Jews and Greeks about Ac 20:21
For as you have **t** about Me in Ac 23:11
because we have **t** about God that 1Co 15:15
God also **t** by signs and wonders, Heb 2:4
But one has somewhere **t**: Heb 2:6
For it has been **t**: Heb 7:17
when He **t** in advance to 1Pt 1:11
brothers came and **t** to your 3Jn 3
they have **t** to your love before 3Jn 6
who **t** to God's word and to the Rv 1:2

TESTIFIES *(18)*
witness **t** against someone Dt 19:16
up against me and **t** to my face. Jb 16:8
on their faces **t** against them, Is 3:9
Though our guilt **t** against us, Jr 14:7
arrogance **t** against them. Hs 5:5
arrogance **t** against them, Hs 7:10
it **t** about the end and will not Hab 2:3
He **t** to what He has seen and Jn 3:32
There is Another who **t** about Me, Jn 5:32
I am the One who **t** about Myself, Jn 8:18
Father who sent Me **t** about Me." Jn 8:18
disciple who **t** to these things Jn 21:24
the Holy Spirit **t** to me that Ac 20:23
Spirit Himself **t** together with Rm 8:16
⌊Scripture⌋ **t** that he lives. Heb 7:8
Spirit also **t** to us about this Heb 10:15
And the Spirit is the One who **t**, 1Jn 5:6
who **t** about these things says, Rv 22:20

TESTIFY *(51)*
my honesty will **t** for me. Gn 30:33
Do not **t** in a lawsuit and go Ex 23:2
respond to a public call to **t**, Lv 5:1
I **t** against you today that you Dt 8:19
this song will **t** against them, Dt 31:21
him and have them **t** against him, 1Kg 21:10
Would you **t** unjustly on God's Jb 13:7
your own lips **t** against you. Jb 15:6
I will **t** against you, Israel. Ps 50:7
Don't **t** against your neighbor Pr 24:28
hears the curse but will not **t**. Pr 29:24
them approach, then let them **t**; Is 41:1
and our sins **t** against us. Is 59:12
Listen and **t** against the house Am 3:13
I wearied you? **T** against Me! Mc 6:3
You therefore **t** against Mt 23:31
a witness to **t** about the light Jn 1:7
he came to **t** about the light. Jn 1:8
not need anyone to **t** about man; Jn 2:25
We know and We **t** to what We have Jn 3:11
yourselves can **t** that I said, Jn 3:28
If I **t** about Myself, My Jn 5:31
works I am doing **t** about Me that Jn 5:36
in them, yet they **t** about Me. Jn 5:39
hate Me because I **t** about it— Jn 7:7
"Even if I **t** about Myself," Jn 8:14
in My Father's name **t** about Me. Jn 10:25
from the dead, continued to **t**. Jn 12:17
the Father—He will **t** about Me. Jn 15:26
also will **t**, because you have Jn 15:27
for this: to **t** to the truth. Jn 18:37
and to solemnly **t** that He is the Ac 10:42
the prophets **t** about Him that Ac 10:43
to **t** to the gospel of God's Ac 20:24
Therefore I **t** to you this day Ac 20:26
of elders can **t** about me. Ac 22:5
so you must also **t** in Rome." Ac 23:11
if they were willing to **t**, Ac 26:5
day I stand and **t** to both small Ac 26:22
Their consciences **t** in support Rm 2:15
can **t** about them that they have Rm 10:2
t that, on their own, according 2Co 8:3
I **t** to you that, if possible, Gl 4:15
Again I **t** to every man who gets Gl 5:3
I say this and **t** in the Lord: Eph 4:17
For I **t** about him that he works Col 4:13
seen it and we **t** and declare to 1Jn 1:2
seen and we **t** that the Father 1Jn 4:14
For there are three that **t**: 1Jn 5:7
And we also **t** for him, and you 3Jn 12
I **t** to everyone who hears the Rv 22:18

TESTIFYING *(7)*
you that you continue **t**? Jb 16:3
these men are **t** against You?" Mt 26:62
much they are **t** against You?" Mt 27:13
these men are **t** against You?" Mk 14:60
You are **t** about Yourself. Jn 8:13
conscience is **t** to me with the Rm 9:1
you and **t** that this is 1Pt 5:12

TESTIMONIES *(5)*
commandments, judgments, and **t**. 1Kg 2:3
Your **t** are completely reliable; Ps 93:5
and His **t**, this disaster Jr 44:23
thefts, false **t**, blasphemies. Mt 15:19
Him, but the **t** did not agree. Mk 14:56

TESTIMONY *(107)*
it before the **t** to be preserved. Ex 16:34
Do not give false **t** against your Ex 20:16
tablets of the⌋ **t** that I will Ex 25:16
ark and put the **t** that I will Ex 25:21
that are over the ark of the **t**; Ex 25:22
the ark of the **t** there behind Ex 26:33
the ark of the **t** in the most Ex 26:34
veil that is in front of the **t**, Ex 27:21
the veil by the ark of the **t**— Ex 30:6
mercy seat that is over the **t**— Ex 30:6
of meeting, the ark of the **t**, Ex 30:26
in front of the **t** in the tent Ex 30:36
the ark of the **t**, the mercy seat Ex 31:7
him the two tablets of the **t**, Ex 31:18
tablets of the **t** in his hands. Ex 32:15
tablets of the **t** in his hands as Ex 34:29
tabernacle of the **t**, that was Ex 38:21
the ark of the **t** with its poles Ex 39:35
Put the ark of the **t** there, Ex 40:3
in front of the ark of the **t**. Ex 40:5
Moses took the **t** and placed ⌊it⌋ Ex 40:20
screened off the ark of the **t**, Ex 40:21
mercy seat that is over the **t**, Lv 16:13
the veil of the **t** in the tent of Lv 24:3
over the tabernacle of the **t**, Nm 1:50
of the **t** and watch over it Nm 1:53
cover the ark of the **t** with it. Nm 4:5
that was on the ark of the **t**, Nm 7:89
the tent of the **t**, and it Nm 9:15
above the tabernacle of the **t**. Nm 10:11
in front of the **t** where I meet Nm 17:4
the LORD in the tent of the **t**. Nm 17:7
the tent of the **t** and saw that Nm 17:8
in front of the **t** to be kept as Nm 17:10
in front of the tent of the **t**. Nm 18:2
based on the **t** of one witness. Nm 35:30
give dishonest **t** against your Dt 5:20
executed on the **t** of two or Dt 17:6
be executed on the **t** of a single Dt 17:6
by the **t** of two or three Dt 19:15
carry the ark of the **t** to come Jos 4:16
him, gave him the **t**, and made 2Kg 11:12
him, gave him the **t**, and made 2Ch 23:11
of Israel for the tent of the **t**? 2Ch 24:6
t of the LORD is trustworthy, Ps 19:7
established a **t** in Jacob and set Ps 78:5
They will give a **t** of Your great Ps 145:7
lying witness who gives false **t**, Pr 6:19
A man giving false **t** against his Pr 25:18
Bind up the **t**. Seal up the Is 8:16
To the law and to the **t**! Is 8:20
prescribed, as a **t** to them." Mt 8:4
so that by the **t** of two or three Mt 18:16
the world as a **t** to all nations. Mt 24:14
for false **t** against Jesus so Mt 26:59
your cleansing, as a **t** to them." Mk 1:44
your feet as a **t** against them." Mk 6:11
looking for **t** against Jesus to Mk 14:55
were giving false **t** against Him, Mk 14:56
were giving false **t** against Him, Mk 14:57
Yet their **t** did not agree even Mk 14:59
your cleansing as a **t** to them." Lk 5:14
your feet as a **t** against them." Lk 9:5
"Why do we need any more **t**," Lk 22:71
This is John's **t** when the Jews Jn 1:19
but you do not accept Our **t**. Jn 3:11
heard, yet no one accepts His **t**. Jn 3:32
has accepted His **t** has affirmed Jn 3:33
about Myself, My **t** is not valid. Jn 5:31
I know that the **t** He gives about Jn 5:32
receive man's **t**, but I say these Jn 5:34
I have a greater **t** than John's Jn 5:36
Your **t** is not valid." Jn 8:13
replied, "My **t** is valid, because Jn 8:14
His **t** is true, and he knows he Jn 19:35
We know that his **t** is true. Jn 21:24
were giving **t** to the Ac 4:33
of the **t** in the desert, Ac 7:44
not accept your **t** about Me!' Ac 22:18
as the **t** about Christ was 1Co 1:6
announcing the **t** of God to you, 1Co 2:1
the **t** of our conscience that we 2Co 1:12
On the **t** of two or three 2Co 13:1
because our **t** among you was 2Th 1:10
for all, a **t** at the proper 1Tm 2:6
ashamed of the **t** about our Lord, 2Tm 1:8
This **t** is true. So, rebuke them Ti 1:13
as a **t** to what would be said ⌊in Heb 3:5
based on the **t** of two or three Heb 10:28
If we accept the **t** of men, 1Jn 5:9
of men, God's **t** is greater, 1Jn 5:9
it is God's **t** that He has given 1Jn 5:9
Son of God has the **t** in himself. 1Jn 5:10
believed in the **t** that God has 1Jn 5:10
And this is the **t**: 1Jn 5:11
has a ⌊good⌋ **t** from everyone, 3Jn 12
and you know that our **t** is true. 3Jn 12
word and to the **t** about Jesus Rv 1:2
word and the **t** about Jesus. Rv 1:9
God's word and the **t** they had. Rv 6:9
finish their **t**, the beast that Rv 11:7
Lamb and by the word of their **t**, Rv 12:11
God and have the **t** about Jesus. Rv 12:17
tabernacle of **t**—was opened. Rv 15:5
who have the **t** about Jesus. Rv 19:10
because the **t** about Jesus is the Rv 19:10
because of their **t** about Jesus Rv 20:4

TESTING *(12)*
"Why are you **t** the LORD?" Ex 17:2
LORD your God is **t** you to know Dt 13:3
t the righteous and seeing the Jr 20:12
Why are you **t** Me, hypocrites? Mt 22:18
said to them, "Why are you **t** Me? Mk 12:15
while and depart in a time of **t**. Lk 8:13
are you now **t** God by putting on Ac 15:10
during a severe **t** by affliction, 2Co 8:2
I am **t** the genuineness of your 2Co 8:8
on the day of **t** in the desert, Heb 3:8
knowing that the **t** of your faith Jms 1:3
the hour of **t** that is going to Rv 3:10

TESTS *(1)*
who **t** heart and mind, Jr 11:20

TETHERED *(1)*
was nothing but **t** horses and 2Kg 7:10

TETRARCH *(7)*
Herod the **t** heard the report Mt 14:1

Herod was **t** of Galilee, his — Lk 3:1
brother Philip **t** of the region — Lk 3:1
and Lysanias **t** of Abilene, — Lk 3:1
But Herod the **t**, being rebuked — Lk 3:19
Herod the **t** heard about — Lk 9:7
a close friend of Herod the **t**, — Ac 13:1

TEXT *(6)*
This is the **t** of the letter they — Ezr 4:11
as the **t** of King Artaxerxes' — Ezr 4:23
This is the **t** of the letter that — Ezr 5:6
This is the **t** of the letter King — Ezr 7:11
A copy of the **t**, issued as law — Est 3:14
This is the **t** of the letter that — Jr 29:1

THADDAEUS *(2)*
(AKA JUDAS)
the son of Alphaeus, and **T**; — Mt 10:3
the son of Alphaeus, and **T**; — Mk 3:18

THAN *(492)*
(See pp. xi-xii.)

THANK *(39)*
sacrifice a **t** offering to the — Lv 22:29
praise and **t** the LORD with one — 2Ch 5:13
sacrifices and **t** offerings to — 2Ch 29:31
sacrifices and **t** offerings, — 2Ch 29:31
and **t** offerings on it. — 2Ch 33:16
who can **t** You in Sheol? — Ps 6:5
I will **t** the LORD for His — Ps 7:17
I will **t** the LORD with all my — Ps 9:1
Sacrifice a **t** offering to God, — Ps 50:14
sacrifices a **t** offering honors — Ps 50:23
I will make my **t** offerings to — Ps 56:12
pasture, will **t** You forever; — Ps 79:13
will fervently **t** the LORD with — Ps 109:30
at midnight to **t** You for Your — Ps 119:62
For Sheol cannot **t** You; — Is 38:18
only the living can **t** You, — Is 38:19
and **t** offerings to the house of — Jr 17:26
as they bring **t** offerings to — Jr 33:11
leavened bread as a **t** offering, — Am 4:5
up and began to **t** God and to — Lk 2:38
Does he **t** that slave because he — Lk 17:9
I **t** You that I'm not like other — Lk 18:11
I **t** You that You heard Me. — Jn 11:41
I **t** my God through Jesus Christ — Rm 1:8
t God that, although you used — Rm 6:17
I **t** God through Jesus Christ our — Rm 7:25
Not only do I **t** them, but so do — Rm 16:4
always **t** my God for you because — 1Co 1:4
I **t** God that I baptized none of — 1Co 1:14
I **t** God that I speak in ⌊other⌋ — 1Co 14:18
We always **t** God, the Father of — Col 1:3
We always **t** God for all of you, — 1Th 1:2
this is why we constantly **t** God, — 1Th 2:13
How can we **t** God for you in — 1Th 3:9
We must always **t** God for you, — 2Th 1:3
we must always **t** God for you, — 2Th 2:13
I **t** God, whom I serve with a — 2Tm 1:3
I always **t** my God when I mention — Phm 4
t You, Lord God, the Almighty, — Rv 11:17

THANKED *(1)*
he **t** God and took courage. — Ac 28:15

THANKFUL *(2)*
God, with joyful and **t** shouts. — Ps 42:4
body, control your hearts. Be **t**. — Col 3:15

THANKFULNESS *(2)*
excellent Felix, with all **t**. — Ac 24:3
taught, and overflowing with **t**. — Col 2:7

THANKING *(1)*
facedown at His feet, **t** Him. — Lk 17:16

THANKS *(72)*
Israel bowed ⌊in **t**⌋ at the head — Gn 47:31
and to give **t** and praise to Him. — 1Ch 16:4
the first time that **t** be given — 1Ch 16:7
Give **t** to the LORD; call on His — 1Ch 16:8
Give **t** to the LORD, for He is — 1Ch 16:34
that we may give **t** to Your holy — 1Ch 16:35
by name to give **t** to the LORD— — 1Ch 16:41
morning to give **t** and praise to — 1Ch 23:30
giving **t** and praise to the LORD. — 1Ch 25:3
we give You **t** and praise Your — 1Ch 29:13
Give **t** to the LORD, for His — 2Ch 20:21
and giving **t** to the LORD God — 2Ch 30:22
for giving **t**, and for praise — 2Ch 31:2
gave praise and **t**, division by — Neh 12:24
large processions that gave **t**. — Neh 12:31
We give **t** to You, God; — Ps 75:1
we give **t** to You, for Your name — Ps 75:1
Give **t** to Him and praise His — Ps 100:4
Give **t** to the LORD, call on His — Ps 105:1
Give **t** to the LORD, for He is — Ps 106:1
that we may give **t** to Your holy — Ps 106:47
Give **t** to the LORD, for He is — Ps 107:1
Let them give **t** to the LORD for — Ps 107:8
Let them give **t** to the LORD for — Ps 107:15
Let them give **t** to the LORD for — Ps 107:21
Let them give **t** to the LORD for — Ps 107:31
Give **t** to the LORD, for He is — Ps 118:1
them and give **t** to the LORD. — Ps 118:19
I will give **t** to You because You — Ps 118:21
my God, and I will give You **t**. — Ps 118:28
Give **t** to the LORD, for He is — Ps 118:29
go up to give **t** to the name of — Ps 122:4
Give **t** to the LORD, for He is — Ps 136:1
Give **t** to the God of gods. — Ps 136:2
Give **t** to the Lord of lords. — Ps 136:3
Give **t** to the God of heaven! — Ps 136:26
I will give You **t** with all my — Ps 138:1
temple and give **t** to Your name — Ps 138:2
kings on earth will give You **t**, — Ps 138:4
will say: "Give **t** to the LORD; — Is 12:4
I offer **t** and praise to You, — Dn 2:23
and gave **t** to his God, just — Dn 6:10
fish, and He gave **t**, broke them, — Mt 15:36
and after giving **t**, He gave it — Mt 26:27
loaves, He gave **t**, broke the — Mk 8:6
and after giving **t**, He gave it — Mk 14:23
after giving **t**, He said, "Take — Lk 22:17
bread, gave **t**, broke it, gave — Lk 22:19
after giving **t** He distributed — Jn 6:11
the bread after the Lord gave **t**. — Jn 6:23
he gave **t** to God in the presence — Ac 27:35
Lord, since he gives **t** to God; — Rm 14:6
he does not eat, yet he **t** God. — Rm 14:6
If I partake with **t**, why am I — 1Co 10:30
of something for which I give **t**? — 1Co 10:30
t, broke it, and said, "This — 1Co 11:24
say "Amen" at your giving of **t**, — 1Co 14:16
you may very well be giving **t**, — 1Co 14:17
t be to God, who gives us the — 1Co 15:57
that **t** may be given by many on — 2Co 1:11
But **t** be to God, who always puts — 2Co 2:14
T be to God who put the same — 2Co 8:16
T be to God for His — 2Co 9:15
never stop giving **t** for you as I — Eph 1:16
suitable, but rather giving **t**. — Eph 5:4
giving **t** always for everything — Eph 5:20
I give **t** to my God for every — Php 1:3
giving **t** to the Father, who has — Col 1:12
giving **t** to God the Father — Col 3:17
Give **t** in everything, for this — 1Th 5:18
I give **t** to Christ Jesus our — 1Tm 1:12
and **t** to the One seated on the — Rv 4:9

THANKSGIVING *(27)*
presents it for **t**, in addition — Lv 7:12
in addition to the **t** sacrifice, — Lv 7:12
with his **t** sacrifice of — Lv 7:13
The meat of his **t** sacrifice of — Lv 7:15
with praise and **t** to the LORD: — Ezr 3:11
who began the **t** in prayer; — Neh 11:17
dedication with **t** and singing — Neh 12:27
The second **t** procession went to — Neh 12:38
The two **t** processions stood in — Neh 12:40
songs of praise and **t** to God. — Neh 12:46
my voice in **t** and telling about — Ps 26:7
with song and exalt Him with **t**. — Ps 69:30
us enter His presence with **t**; — Ps 95:2
His gates with **t** and His courts — Ps 100:4
sacrifices of **t** and announce His — Ps 107:22
sacrifice of **t** and will worship — Ps 116:17
Sing to the LORD with **t**; — Ps 147:7
be found in her, **t** and melodious — Is 51:3
T will come out of them, a sound — Jr 30:19
to You with a voice of **t**. — Jnh 2:9
may cause **t** to overflow to God's — 2Co 4:15
which produces **t** to God through — 2Co 9:11
in many acts of **t** to God. — 2Co 9:12
prayer and petition with **t**, — Php 4:6
stay alert in it with **t**. — Col 4:2
if it is received with **t**, — 1Tm 4:4
and wisdom and **t** and honor and — Rv 7:12

THANKSGIVINGS *(1)*
and **t** be made for everyone, — 1Tm 2:1

THAT *(5645)*
(See pp. xi-xii.)

THAT'S *(28)*
(See pp. xi-xii.)

THE *(54,495)*
(See pp. xi-xii.)

THEBES *(5)*
Amon, ⌊god⌋ of **T**, along with — Jr 46:25
and execute judgments on **T**. — Ezk 30:14
will wipe out the crowds of **T**. — Ezk 30:15
in anguish, **T** will be breached, — Ezk 30:16
you better than **T** that sat along — Nah 3:8

THEBEZ *(2)*
went to **T**, camped against — Jdg 9:50
T, who struck Abimelech son of — 2Sm 11:21

THEFT *(1)*
is to be sold because of his **t**. — Ex 22:3

THEFTS *(3)*
immoralities, **t**, false — Mt 15:19
sexual immoralities, **t**, murders, — Mk 7:21
sexual immorality, or their **t**. — Rv 9:21

THEIR *(3644)*
(See pp. xi-xii.)

THEIRS *(21)*
(See pp. xi-xii.)

THEM *(5236)*
(See pp. xi-xii.)

THEME *(2)*
moved by a noble **t** as I recite — Ps 45:1
statutes are ⌊the **t** of⌋ my song — Ps 119:54

THEMSELVES *(255)*
(See pp. xi-xii.)

THEN *(3050)*
(See pp. xi-xii.)

THEOPHILUS *(2)*
sequence, most honorable **T**, — Lk 1:3
narrative, **T**, about all that — Ac 1:1

THERE *(1892)*
(See pp. xi-xii.)

THERE'S *(22)*
(See pp. xi-xii.)

THEREFORE *(615)*
(See pp. xi-xii.)

THESE *(1239)*
(See pp. xi-xii.)

THESSALONIANS *(2)*
church of the **T** in God the — 1Th 1:1
church of the **T** in God our — 2Th 1:1

THESSALONICA *(7)*
and Apollonia and came to **T**, — Ac 17:1
open-minded than those in **T**, — Ac 17:11
the Jews from **T** found out that — Ac 17:13
Aristarchus and Secundus from **T**, — Ac 20:4
a Macedonian of **T**, was with us. — Ac 27:2
For even in **T** you sent ⌊gifts⌋ — Php 4:16
world, and has gone to **T**. — 2Tm 4:10

THEUDAS *(1)*
Not long ago **T** rose up, claiming — Ac 5:36

THEY *(6456)*
(See pp. xi-xii.)

THEY'LL *(2)*
(See pp. xi-xii.)

THEY'RE *(7)*
(See pp. xi-xii.)

THEY'VE *(11)*
(See pp. xi-xii.)

THICK *(26)*
T swarms of flies went into — Ex 8:24
and there was **t** darkness — Ex 10:22
a **t** cloud on the mountain, — Ex 19:16
approached the **t** darkness where — Ex 20:21
and **t** darkness on the mountain; — Dt 5:22
have fallen in the **t** of battle! — 2Sm 1:25
gathering of water and **t** clouds. — 2Sm 22:12
reservoir was three inches **t**, — 1Kg 7:26
He would dwell in **t** darkness, — 1Kg 8:12
reservoir was three inches **t**, — 2Ch 4:5
He would dwell in **t** darkness, — 2Ch 6:1
headlong at Him with his **t**, — Jb 15:26
Can He judge through **t** darkness? — Jb 22:13
by the **t** darkness that covers my — Jb 23:17
its garment and **t** darkness its — Jb 38:9
Clouds and **t** darkness surround — Ps 97:2
If I walk in the **t** of danger, — Ps 138:7

will be driven into **t** darkness. Is 8:22
gloom and makes **t** darkness. Jr 13:16
Babylon's **t** walls will be Jr 51:58
was hollow—four fingers **t**— Jr 52:21
with great wings and **t** plumage. Ezk 17:7
its **t** rust will not come off. Ezk 24:12
feet ⌊**t**⌋ on each side. Ezk 40:48
it was 10 and a half feet ⌊**t**⌋. Ezk 41:5
feet **t** on all sides, Ezk 41:12

THICKER *(2)*
finger is **t** than my father's 1Kg 12:10
finger is **t** than my father's 2Ch 10:10

THICKET *(6)*
caught by its horns in the **t**. Gn 22:13
in secret like a lion in a **t**. Ps 10:9
It was like men in a **t** of trees, Ps 74:5
A lion has gone up from his **t**; Jr 4:7
I will turn them into a **t**, Hs 2:12
of the temple mount will be a **t**. Mc 3:12

THICKETS *(8)*
hid in caves, **t**, among rocks, 1Sm 13:6
the forest **t** so that they go up Is 9:18
is clearing the **t** of the forest Is 10:34
They enter the **t** and climb among Jr 4:29
you do in the **t** of the Jordan? Jr 12:5
up from the **t** of the Jordan to Jr 49:19
up from the **t** of the Jordan to Jr 50:44
for the **t** of the Jordan are Zch 11:3

THICKNESS *(3)*
He measured the **t** of the ⌊wall⌋ Ezk 40:5
The **t** of the outer wall of the Ezk 41:9
the **t** of the wall of the court Ezk 42:10

THIEF *(24)*
If a **t** is caught in the act of Ex 22:2
A **t** must make full restitution. Ex 22:3
house, the **t**, if caught, must Ex 22:7
the **t** is not caught, the owner Ex 22:8
and by night he becomes a **t**. Jb 24:14
When you see a **t**, you make Ps 50:18
despise the **t** if he steals to Pr 6:30
the shame of a **t** when he is Jr 2:26
fraud; a **t** breaks in; a gang Hs 7:1
for every **t** will be removed Zch 5:3
the house of the **t** and the house Zch 5:4
what time the **t** was coming, Mt 24:43
where no **t** comes near and no Lk 12:33
at what hour the **t** was coming, Lk 12:39
other way, is a **t** and a robber. Jn 10:1
A **t** comes only to steal and to Jn 10:10
the poor but because he was a **t**. Jn 12:6
The **t** must no longer steal. Eph 4:28
come just like a **t** in the night. 1Th 5:2
day would overtake you like a **t**. 1Th 5:4
as a murderer, a **t**, an evildoer, 1Pt 4:15
of the Lord will come like a **t**; 2Pt 3:10
come like a **t**, and you have no Rv 3:3
Look, I am coming like a **t**. Rv 16:15

THIEF'S *(1)*
To be a **t** partner is to hate Pr 29:24

THIEVES *(13)*
at them as ⌊if they were⌋ **t**. Jb 30:5
rulers are rebels, friends of **t**. Is 1:23
Was he ever found among **t**? Jr 48:27
Were **t** to come in the night, Jr 49:9
through the windows like **t**. Jl 2:9
t came to you, if marauders by Ob 5
destroy and where **t** break in and Mt 6:19
and where **t** don't break in and Mt 6:20
you are making it a den of **t**!" Mt 21:13
you have made it a den of **t**!" Mk 11:17
you have made it a den of **t**!" Lk 19:46
before Me are **t** and robbers, Jn 10:8
t, greedy people, drunkards, 1Co 6:10

THIGH *(28)*
Place your hand under my **t**, Gn 24:2
master Abraham's **t** and swore an Gn 24:9
don't eat the **t** muscle that is Gn 32:32
hip socket at the **t** muscle. Gn 32:32
hand under my **t** ⌊and promise me⌋ Gn 47:29
and the right **t** (since this is Ex 29:22
is waved and the **t** of the Ex 29:27
give the right **t** to the priest Lv 7:32
have the right **t** as a portion. Lv 7:33
offering and the **t** of the Lv 7:34
fat—as well as the right **t**. Lv 8:25
fat portions and the right **t**. Lv 8:26
the right **t** as a presentation Lv 9:21
offering and the **t** of the Lv 10:14
are to bring the **t** of the Lv 10:15
He makes your **t** shrivel and your Nm 5:21
swell and ⌊your⌋ **t** to shrivel.' Nm 5:22
swell, and her **t** will shrivel. Nm 5:27
offering and the **t** of the Nm 6:20
offering and the right **t**. Nm 18:18
it to his right **t** under his Jdg 3:16
took the sword from his right **t**, Jdg 3:21
cook picked up the **t** and what 1Sm 9:24
skirt, bare your **t**, wade through Is 47:2
I struck my **t** ⌊in grief⌋. Jr 31:19
strike ⌊your⌋ **t** ⌊in grief⌋. Ezk 21:12
good piece—**t** and shoulder. Ezk 24:4
robe and on His **t** He has a name Rv 19:16

THIGHS *(5)*
extend from the waist to the **t**. Ex 28:42
on your knees and **t** with painful Dt 28:35
tendons of his **t** are woven Jb 40:17
curves of your **t** are like Sg 7:1
its stomach and **t** were bronze, Dn 2:32

THIN *(11)*
cows, sickly and **t**, came up from Gn 41:3
The sickly, **t** cows ate the Gn 41:4
t and scorched by the east wind, Gn 41:6
The **t** heads of grain swallowed Gn 41:7
very sickly, and **t**—came up. Gn 41:19
Then the **t**, ugly cows ate the Gn 41:20
—withered, **t**, and scorched Gn 41:23
The **t** heads of grain swallowed Gn 41:24
The seven **t**, ugly cows that came Gn 41:27
hammered out **t** sheets of gold, Ex 39:3
the heavens like **t** cloth and Is 40:22

THING *(133)*
of every living **t** of all flesh, Gn 6:19
every living **t** I have made." Gn 7:4
wiped out every living **t** that Gn 7:23
out every living **t** of all flesh Gn 8:17
every living **t** as I have done. Gn 8:21
could not possibly do such a **t**: Gn 18:25
you intend when you did this **t**?" Gn 20:10
a very difficult **t** for Abraham Gn 21:11
I don't know who did this **t**. Gn 21:26
have done this **t** and have not Gn 22:16
If you do this one **t** for me, Gn 30:31
Say the same **t** to Esau when you Gn 32:19
and such a **t** should not be done. Gn 34:7
cannot do this **t**," they said to Gn 34:14
dreams mean the same **t**. Gn 41:25
The dreams mean the same **t**. Gn 41:26
could not possibly do such a **t**. Gn 44:7
did the same **t** by their occult Ex 7:11
did the same **t** by their occult Ex 7:22
did the same **t** by their occult Ex 8:7
will do this **t** in the land." Ex 9:5
What is this **t** you're doing for Ex 18:14
do this very **t** you have asked, Ex 33:17
his sin regarding any holy **t**, Lv 5:16
must not touch any holy **t** or go Lv 12:4
third day, it is a repulsive **t**; Lv 19:7
The firstborn of every living **t**, Nm 18:15
of every good **t** that you did not Dt 6:11
any abhorrent **t** into your house, Dt 7:26
and every living **t** with them. Dt 11:6
detestable **t** the LORD hates. Dt 12:31
this detestable **t** has happened Dt 13:14
must not eat any detestable **t**. Dt 14:3
this detestable **t** has happened Dt 17:4
done this evil **t** and stone them Dt 17:5
let any living **t** survive among Dt 20:16
No one could say a **t** against the Jos 10:21
Since every good **t** the LORD your Jos 23:15
on you every bad **t** until He has Jos 23:15
and asked the same **t** from them. Jdg 8:8
father, "Let me do this one **t**: Jdg 11:37
did a wonderful **t** while Manoah Jdg 13:19
Don't do this horrible **t**. Jdg 19:23
do this horrible **t** to this man." Jdg 19:24
doing the same **t** to you that 1Sm 8:8
see this great **t** that the LORD 1Sm 12:16
never do such a **t** to my lord, 1Sm 24:6
there's one **t** I require of you: 2Sm 3:13
so far was a little **t** to You, 2Sm 7:19
he has done this **t** and shown no 2Sm 12:6
such a **t** should never be done 2Sm 13:12
Don't do this horrible **t**! 2Sm 13:12
Don't take this **t** to heart." 2Sm 13:20
I would never do such a **t**! 2Sm 23:17
but this **t** I cannot do.' " 1Kg 20:9
had told you to do some great **t**, 2Kg 5:13
mere dog, do this monstrous **t**?" 2Kg 8:13
do such a **t** in the presence 1Ch 11:19
This was a little **t** to You, 1Ch 17:17
this good **t** to Your servant. 1Ch 17:26
because I have done this **t**. 1Ch 21:8
say ⌊the same **t**⌋ to all the Est 1:18
For the **t** I feared has overtaken Jb 3:25
every living **t** is in His hand, Jb 12:10
of every living **t** and concealed Jb 28:21
every living **t** would perish Jb 34:15
have asked one **t** from the LORD; Ps 27:4
LORD will not lack any good **t**. Ps 34:10
turn to any evil **t** or wickedly Ps 141:4
the desire of every living **t**. Ps 145:16
every living **t** praise His holy Ps 145:21
finds a good **t** and obtains favor Pr 18:22
person, any bitter **t** is sweet. Pr 27:7
by adding one **t** to another to Ec 7:27
every hidden **t**, whether good or Ec 12:14
Who has heard of such a **t**? Is 66:8
terrible **t** has taken place in Jr 5:30
in the fire, a **t** I did not Jr 7:31
has done a most terrible **t**. Jr 18:13
LORD do such a **t** to this great Jr 22:8
also I saw a horrible **t**: Jr 23:14
obeyed Him, this **t** has happened. Jr 40:3
walk and the **t** we should do." Jr 42:3
this detestable **t** that I hate. Jr 44:4
was every form of detestable **t**, Ezk 8:10
do the same **t** on the seventh Ezk 45:20
For this **t** is from Israel— Hs 8:6
like the **t** they loved. Hs 9:10
abundance of every precious **t**. Nah 2:9
and a detestable **t** has been done Mal 2:11
And this is another **t** you do: Mal 2:13
out again and did the same **t**. Mt 20:5
the other and said the same **t**. Mt 21:30
She has done a noble **t** for Me. Mt 26:10
the disciples said the same **t**. Mt 26:35
saying the same **t** once more. Mt 26:44
said to him, "You lack one **t**: Mk 10:21
She has done a noble **t** for Me. Mk 14:6
And they all said the same **t**. Mk 14:31
and prayed, saying the same **t**. Mk 14:39
but one **t** is necessary. Lk 10:42
not able to do even a little **t**, Lk 12:26
told him, "You still lack one **t**: Lk 18:22
be who was going to do this **t**. Lk 22:23
"Not a **t**," they said. Lk 22:35
Him not one **t** was created that Jn 1:3
receive a single **t** unless it's Jn 3:27
don't know. One **t** I do know: I Jn 9:25
is an amazing **t**," the man told Jn 9:30
planned this **t** in your heart? Ac 5:4
you did the right **t** in coming. Ac 10:33
The same **t** happened in Iconium; Ac 14:1
shouting one **t** and some another Ac 19:32
shouting one **t** and some another Ac 21:34
other created **t** will have the Rm 8:39
who considers a **t** to be unclean, Rm 14:14
It is a noble **t** not to eat meat, Rm 14:21
that you all say the same **t**, 1Co 1:10
has done this **t** as though I were 1Co 5:3
the law also say the same **t**? 1Co 9:8
wrote this very **t** so that when I 2Co 2:3
us for this very **t** is God, 2Co 5:5
do not touch any unclean **t**, 2Co 6:17
how much diligence this very **t**— 2Co 7:11
high-minded **t** that is raised up 2Co 10:5
it is no great **t** if his servants 2Co 11:15
spot or wrinkle or any such **t**, Eph 5:27
Just one **t**: live your life in a Php 1:27
it. But one **t** I do: forgetting Php 3:13
that good **t** entrusted to you. 2Tm 1:14
every good **t** that is in us for Phm 6
is a terrifying **t** to fall into Heb 10:31
don't let this one **t** escape you: 2Pt 3:8

THINGS *(640)*
told them all these **t**; Gn 20:8
have done **t** to me that should Gn 20:9
After these **t** God tested Abraham Gn 22:1
Now after these **t** Abraham was Gn 22:20
household about these **t**. Gn 24:28
These are the **t** your slave did Gn 39:19
Why does my lord say these **t**? Gn 44:7

all the good **t** the LORD had done Ex 18:9
not do these three **t** for her, Ex 21:11
must eat those **t** by which Ex 29:33
⌊them⌋, for these **t** are holy. Ex 29:33
These are the **t** that the LORD Ex 35:1
to any of the LORD's holy **t**, Lv 5:15
of the sinful **t** a person may do Lv 6:3
Since these **t** have happened to Lv 10:19
all the swarming **t** and ⌊other⌋ Lv 11:10
to bring these **t** for his Lv 14:23
carries such **t** is to wash his Lv 15:10
themselves by all these **t**. Lv 18:24
did all these **t**, and I abhorred Lv 20:23
if after these **t** you will not Lv 26:18
spite of these **t** you do not Lv 26:23
and consecrated these **t**, Nm 7:1
has promised good **t** to Israel." Nm 10:29
prepare these **t** in this way when Nm 15:13
do all these **t** and that it was Nm 16:28
"What ⌊great **t**⌋ God has done!" Nm 23:23
leather goods, **t** made of goat Nm 31:20
about all the **t** you were to do. Dt 1:18
don't forget the **t** your eyes Dt 4:9
and all these **t** have happened to Dt 4:30
were shown ⌊these **t**⌋ so that you Dt 4:35
obey all these **t** I command you, Dt 12:28
who does these **t** is detestable Dt 18:12
because of these detestable **t**. Dt 18:12
the detestable **t** they do for Dt 20:18
who does these **t** is detestable Dt 22:5
does such **t** and acts unfairly Dt 25:16
in all the good **t** the LORD your Dt 26:11
from all the **t** I am commanding Dt 28:14
The hidden **t** belong to the LORD Dt 29:29
but the revealed **t** belong to us Dt 29:29
When all these **t** happen to you— Dt 30:1
yourselves from the **t** set apart, Jos 6:18
If you take any of those **t**, Jos 6:18
regarding the **t** set apart for Jos 7:1
and put ⌊the **t**⌋ with their own Jos 7:11
among you, Israel, **t** set apart. Jos 7:13
caught with the **t** set apart must Jos 7:15
They took the **t** from inside the Jos 7:23
recorded these **t** in the book Jos 24:26
After these **t**, the LORD's Jos 24:29
us all these **t** or spoken to us Jdg 13:23
until you find out how **t** go, Ru 3:18
Why are you doing these **t**? 1Sm 2:23
follow worthless **t** that can't 1Sm 12:21
the great **t** He has done for you 1Sm 12:24
the worthless and unwanted **t**. 1Sm 15:9
finished saying these **t** to him, 1Sm 24:16
and said all these **t** to Nabal on 1Sm 25:9
LORD does good **t** for my lord, 1Sm 25:31
do great **t** and will also 1Sm 26:25
luxurious **t**, who decked your 2Sm 1:24
these great **t** to Your servant 2Sm 7:21
David heard about all these **t**, 2Sm 13:21
the consecrated **t** of his father 1Kg 7:51
because he was getting **t** done. 1Kg 11:28
⌊The way **t** are going⌋ now, 1Kg 12:26
word I have done all these **t**. 1Kg 18:36
tent, picked ⌊**t**⌋ up, and hid 2Kg 7:8
all the great **t** Elisha has done. 2Kg 8:4
They did evil **t**, provoking the 2Kg 17:11
of God who proclaimed these **t**. 2Kg 23:16
proclaimed these **t** that you have 2Kg 23:17
did the same **t** to them that he 2Kg 23:19
the detestable **t** that were seen 2Kg 23:24
to consecrate the most holy **t**, 1Ch 23:13
purification of all the holy **t**, 1Ch 23:28
all these **t** with an upright 1Ch 29:17
the consecrated **t** of his father 2Ch 5:1
gold, and valuable **t**, along with 2Ch 21:3
After all these **t**, the LORD 2Ch 21:18
used the sacred **t** of the LORD's 2Ch 24:7
all the detestable **t** they found 2Ch 29:16
of the dedicated **t** that were 2Ch 31:6
and the dedicated **t** were brought 2Ch 31:12
the LORD and the consecrated **t**. 2Ch 31:14
Israel the holy **t** of the LORD, 2Ch 35:3
detestable **t** he did, and what 2Ch 36:8
the most holy **t** until there was Ezr 2:63
After these **t** had been done, Ezr 9:1
eat the good **t** of the land, Ezr 9:12
return ⌊these **t**⌋ and require Neh 5:12
the most holy **t** until there was Neh 7:65
the holy **t**, the sin offerings Neh 10:33

does great and unsearchable **t**, Jb 5:9
will you go on saying these **t**? Jb 8:2
great and unsearchable **t**, Jb 9:10
know the **t** you are talking Jb 12:3
Only grant ⌊these⌋ two **t** to me, Jb 13:20
not put trust in worthless **t**, Jb 15:31
I have heard many **t** like these. Jb 16:2
even the **t** dear to my heart. Jb 17:11
filled their houses with good **t**. Jb 22:18
He has many more **t** like these in Jb 23:14
I could not do ⌊these **t**⌋. Jb 31:23
does all these **t** two or three Jb 33:29
He understands all **t**. Jb 36:5
He does great **t** that we cannot Jb 37:5
I spoke about **t** I did not Jb 42:3
t too wonderful for me to know. Jb 42:3
who does these **t** will never be Ps 15:5
me about **t** I do not know. Ps 35:11
done many **t**—Your wonderful Ps 40:5
have done these **t**, and I kept Ps 50:21
You who have done great **t**; Ps 71:19
decided to say these **t** ⌊aloud⌋, Ps 73:15
t we have heard and known and Ps 78:3
Glorious **t** are said about you, Ps 87:3
living **t** both large and small. Ps 104:25
they are satisfied with good **t**. Ps 104:28
who did great **t** in Egypt, Ps 106:21
filled the hungry with good **t**. Ps 107:9
attention to these **t** and Ps 107:43
may see wonderful **t** in Your law. Ps 119:18
for all **t** are Your servants. Ps 119:91
LORD has done great **t** for them." Ps 126:2
LORD had done great **t** for us; Ps 126:3
involved with **t** too great or too Ps 131:1
the one who says perverse **t**, Pr 2:12
Six **t** the LORD hates; Pr 6:16
I speak of noble **t**, and what my Pr 8:6
will enjoy good **t**, but Pr 13:2
of the wicked blurts out evil **t**. Pr 15:28
Your eyes will see strange **t**, Pr 23:33
and you will say absurd **t**. Pr 23:33
Two **t** I ask of You; don't deny Pr 30:7
Three **t** are never satisfied; Pr 30:15
Three **t** are beyond me; Pr 30:18
earth trembles under three **t**; Pr 30:21
Four **t** on earth are small, Pr 30:24
Three **t** are stately in their Pr 30:29
All **t** are wearisome; man is Ec 1:8
seen all the **t** that are done Ec 1:14
When good **t** increase, the ones Ec 5:11
by good **t** and does not even Ec 6:3
and an explanation ⌊for **t**⌋, Ec 7:25
all of these **t** God will bring Ec 11:9
will eat the good **t** of the land. Is 1:19
for He has done glorious **t**. Is 12:5
You have turned **t** around, as if Is 29:16
Tell us flattering **t**. Is 30:10
a noble person plans noble **t**; Is 32:8
seeing many **t**, you do not obey. Is 42:20
this, and tell us the former **t**? Is 43:9
pay no attention to **t** of old. Is 43:18
these gods declare the coming **t**, Is 44:7
Remember these **t**, Jacob, and Is 44:21
I, the LORD, do all these **t**. Is 45:7
not take these **t** to heart or Is 47:7
These two **t** will happen to you Is 47:9
on I will announce new **t** to you, Is 48:6
t that you have not known. Is 48:6
the idols has declared these **t**? Is 48:14
two **t** have happened to you: Is 51:19
who brings news of good **t**, Is 52:7
the many good **t** ⌊He has done⌋ Is 63:7
made all these **t**, and so they Is 66:2
has seen such **t**? Can a land be Is 66:8
But in spite of all these **t** Jr 2:34
After she has done all these **t**, Jr 3:7
I not punish them for these **t**? Jr 5:9
our God done all these **t** to us? Jr 5:19
diverted these **t** ⌊from you⌋. Jr 5:25
I not punish them for these **t**? Jr 5:29
you have done all these **t**"— Jr 7:13
you speak all these **t** to them, Jr 7:27
their detestable **t** in the house Jr 7:30
I not punish them for these **t**? Jr 9:9
for I delight in these **t**. Jr 9:24
He is the One who formed all **t**. Jr 10:16
Why have these **t** happened to me? Jr 13:22
for You have done all these **t**. Jr 14:22

tell these people all these **t**, Jr 16:10
Who has heard ⌊**t**⌋ like these? Jr 18:13
Jeremiah prophesying these **t**. Jr 20:1
to prophesy all these **t** to them, Jr 25:30
of Judah heard these **t**, Jr 26:10
all these **t** directly to you. Jr 26:15
have done these **t** to you because Jr 30:15
their detestable **t** in the house Jr 32:34
and wondrous **t** you do not know. Jr 33:3
⌊Those **t**⌋ are not for you. Jr 35:7
tell the king all these **t**." Jr 36:16
about these **t** or you will die Jr 38:24
food and good **t** and saw no Jr 44:17
you seek great **t** for yourself? Jr 45:5
go mad because of terrifying **t**. Jr 50:38
He is the One who formed all **t**. Jr 51:19
I weep because of these **t**; Lm 1:16
does not approve ⌊of these **t**⌋. Lm 3:36
because of the evil **t** they did, Ezk 6:9
from them, their detestable **t**. Ezk 7:20
I will hand these **t** over to Ezk 7:21
all its detestable **t** and all its Ezk 11:18
for detestable **t** and Ezk 11:21
about all the **t** the LORD had Ezk 11:25
make a peg from it to hang **t** Ezk 15:3
one of these **t** out of compassion Ezk 16:5
when you did all these **t**, Ezk 16:30
but enraged Me with all these **t**, Ezk 16:43
and did detestable **t** before Me, Ezk 16:50
you know what these **t** mean? Ezk 17:12
the one who does such **t** escape? Ezk 17:15
did all these **t** even though he Ezk 17:18
blood and does any of these ⌊**t**⌋, Ezk 18:10
the detestable **t** that are before Ezk 20:7
detestable **t** that were before Ezk 20:8
with their detestable **t**? Ezk 20:30
all the evil **t** you have done. Ezk 20:43
T will not remain as they are; Ezk 21:26
despise My holy **t** and profane My Ezk 22:8
to My law and profane My holy **t**. Ezk 22:26
These **t** will be done to you Ezk 23:30
us what these **t** you are doing Ezk 24:19
to us what you mean by these **t**? Ezk 37:18
detestable **t**, and all their Ezk 37:23
charge of My holy **t** but have Ezk 44:8
of My holy **t** or the most holy Ezk 44:13
holy things or the most holy **t**. Ezk 44:13
provide the same **t** for seven Ezk 45:25
reveals the deep and hidden **t**; Dn 2:22
the interpretation of these **t**: Dn 7:16
say outrageous **t** against the God Dn 11:36
end of these extraordinary **t**?" Dn 12:6
all these **t** will be completed. Dn 12:7
will be the outcome of these **t**?" Dn 12:8
is wise understand these **t**, Hs 14:9
for he has done catastrophic **t**. Jl 2:20
for the LORD has done great **t**. Jl 2:21
They should not preach these **t**; Mc 2:6
Are these the **t** He does?" Mc 2:7
for by these **t** their portion is Hab 1:16
who scorns the day of small **t**? Zch 4:10
people all these **t** as an Zch 8:12
These are the **t** you must do: Zch 8:16
the detestable **t** from between Zch 9:7
after he had considered these **t**, Mt 1:20
You all these **t** if You will fall Mt 4:9
law until all **t** are accomplished Mt 5:18
knows the **t** you need before Mt 6:8
eagerly seek all these **t**, Mt 6:32
and all these **t** will be provided Mt 6:33
give good **t** to those who ask Mt 7:11
thinking evil **t** in your hearts? Mt 9:4
As He was telling them these **t**, Mt 9:18
hidden these **t** from the wise Mt 11:25
All **t** have been entrusted to Me Mt 11:27
you speak good **t** when you are Mt 12:34
man produces good **t** from his Mt 12:35
man produces evil **t** from his Mt 12:35
He told them many **t** in parables, Mt 13:3
longed to see the **t** you see yet Mt 13:17
hear the **t** you hear yet didn't Mt 13:17
crowds all these **t** in parables, Mt 13:34
will declare **t** kept secret from Mt 13:35
you understood all these **t**?" Mt 13:51
where does He get all these **t**?" Mt 13:56
These are the **t** that defile a Mt 15:20
suffer many **t** from the elders Mt 16:21
with God all **t** are possible." Mt 19:26

authority are You doing these **t**? Mt 21:23
by what authority I do these **t**. Mt 21:24
by what authority I do these **t**. Mt 21:27
to Caesar the **t** that are Mt 22:21
to God the **t** that are God's." Mt 22:21
These **t** should have been done Mt 23:23
All these **t** will come on this Mt 23:36
Don't you see all these **t**? Mt 24:2
us, when will these **t** happen? Mt 24:3
because these **t** must take place, Mt 24:6
down to get **t** out of his house Mt 24:17
see all these **t**, recognize that Mt 24:33
until all these **t** take place. Mt 24:34
You were faithful over a few **t**; Mt 25:21
put you in charge of many **t**. Mt 25:21
You were faithful over a few **t**; Mt 25:23
put you in charge of many **t**. Mt 25:23
and the **t** that had happened Mt 27:54
these **t** in your hearts? Mk 2:8
taught them many **t** in parables, Mk 4:2
desires for other **t** enter in and Mk 4:19
"Where did this man get these **t**?" Mk 6:2
He began to teach them many **t**. Mk 6:34
you do many other similar **t**." Mk 7:13
but the **t** that come out of a Mk 7:15
these evil **t** come from within Mk 7:23
Son of Man must suffer many **t**, Mk 8:31
suffer many **t** and be treated Mk 9:12
all **t** are possible with God. Mk 10:27
to tell them the **t** that would Mk 10:32
all the **t** you pray and ask for— Mk 11:24
authority are You doing these **t**? Mk 11:28
this authority to do these **t**?" Mk 11:28
authority I am doing these **t**. Mk 11:29
by what authority I do these **t**." Mk 11:33
to Caesar the **t** that are Mk 12:17
to God the **t** that are God's." Mk 12:17
us, when will these **t** happen? Mk 13:4
when all these **t** are about to Mk 13:4
these **t** must take place, but the Mk 13:7
when you see these **t** happening, Mk 13:29
until all these **t** take place. Mk 13:30
All **t** are possible for You. Mk 14:36
began to accuse Him of many **t**. Mk 15:3
how many **t** they are accusing Mk 15:4
of the **t** about which you Lk 1:4
the day these **t** take place, Lk 1:20
One has done great **t** for me, Lk 1:49
hungry with good **t** and sent the Lk 1:53
all these **t** were being talked Lk 1:65
up all these **t** in her heart Lk 2:19
kept all these **t** in her heart. Lk 2:51
all the evil **t** Herod had done, Lk 3:19
have seen incredible **t** today!" Lk 5:26
from one who takes away your **t**, Lk 6:30
and don't do the **t** I say? Lk 6:46
told him about all these **t**. Lk 7:18
to John the **t** you have seen Lk 7:22
is this I hear such **t** about?" Lk 9:9
suffer many **t** and be rejected Lk 9:22
at all the **t** He was doing, Lk 9:43
you, eat the **t** set before you. Lk 10:8
hidden these **t** from the wise Lk 10:21
All **t** have been entrusted to Me Lk 10:22
eyes that see the **t** you see are Lk 10:23
wanted to see the **t** you see yet Lk 10:24
hear the **t** you hear yet didn't Lk 10:24
worried and upset about many **t**, Lk 10:41
He was saying these **t**, a woman Lk 11:27
These **t** you should have done Lk 11:42
You say these **t** You insult us Lk 11:45
cross-examine Him about many **t**; Lk 11:53
And the **t** you have prepared— Lk 12:20
world eagerly seeks all these **t**, Lk 12:30
and these **t** will be provided for Lk 12:31
not know and did **t** deserving of Lk 12:48
because they suffered these **t**? Lk 13:2
He had said these **t**, all His Lk 13:17
all the glorious **t** He was doing. Lk 13:17
table with Him heard these **t**, Lk 14:15
reported these **t** to his master. Lk 14:21
and asked what these **t** meant. Lk 15:26
to all these **t** and scoffing at Lk 16:14
life you received your good **t**, Lk 16:25
just as Lazarus received bad **t**, Lk 16:25
suffer many **t** and be rejected Lk 17:25
They understood none of these **t**. Lk 18:34
had said these **t**, He went on Lk 19:28
authority are You doing these **t**? Lk 20:2
by what authority I do these **t**." Lk 20:8
to Caesar the **t** that are Lk 20:25
to God the **t** that are God's." Lk 20:25
These **t** that you see—the days Lk 21:6
Him, "so when will these **t** be? Lk 21:7
sign when these **t** are about to Lk 21:7
these **t** must take place first, Lk 21:9
before all these **t**, they will Lk 21:12
fulfill all the **t** that are Lk 21:22
of the **t** that are coming Lk 21:26
But when these **t** begin to take Lk 21:28
when you see these **t** happening, Lk 21:31
away until all **t** take place. Lk 21:32
escape all these **t** that are Lk 21:36
other blasphemous **t** against Him. Lk 22:65
man with those **t** you accuse Him Lk 23:14
they do these **t** when the wood is Lk 23:31
we deserve for the **t** we did, Lk 23:41
at a distance, watching these **t**. Lk 23:49
all these **t** to the Eleven Lk 24:9
telling the apostles these **t**. Lk 24:10
doesn't know the **t** that happened Lk 24:18
"What **t**?" He asked them. So they Lk 24:19
The **t** concerning Jesus the Lk 24:19
day since these **t** happened. Lk 24:21
to suffer these **t** and enter into Lk 24:26
them the **t** concerning Himself Lk 24:27
And as they were saying these **t**, Lk 24:36
You are witnesses of these **t**. Lk 24:48
All **t** were created through Him, Jn 1:3
will see greater **t** than this." Jn 1:50
doves, "Get these **t** out of here! Jn 2:16
You show us for doing these **t**?" Jn 2:18
"How can these **t** be?" Jn 3:9
Israel and don't know these **t**?" Jn 3:10
told you about **t** that happen Jn 3:12
if I tell you about **t** of heaven? Jn 3:12
wicked **t** hates the light Jn 3:20
has given all **t** into His hands. Jn 3:35
doing these **t** on the Sabbath. Jn 5:16
does these **t** in the same way Jn 5:19
those who have done good **t**, Jn 5:29
those who have done wicked **t**, Jn 5:29
I say these **t** so that you may Jn 5:34
said these **t** while teaching in Jn 6:59
If You do these **t**, show Yourself Jn 7:4
After He had said these **t**, Jn 7:9
muttering these **t** about Him, Jn 7:32
I have many **t** to say and to Jn 8:26
these **t** I tell the world." Jn 8:26
Father taught Me, I say these **t**. Jn 8:28
saying these **t**, many believed Jn 8:30
After He said these **t** He spit on Jn 9:6
said these **t** because they were Jn 9:22
Him heard these **t** and asked Him, Jn 9:40
not understand these **t** at first. Jn 12:16
that these **t** had been written Jn 12:16
they had done these **t** to Him. Jn 12:16
said these **t** because he saw Jn 12:41
So the **t** that I speak, I speak Jn 12:50
you know these **t**, you are Jn 13:17
spoken these **t** to you while I Jn 14:25
teach you all **t** and remind you Jn 14:26
spoken these **t** to you so that My Jn 15:11
do all these **t** to you on account Jn 15:21
have told you these **t** to keep Jn 16:1
will do these **t** because they Jn 16:3
told you these **t** so that when Jn 16:4
tell you these **t** from the Jn 16:4
I have spoken these **t** to you, Jn 16:6
I still have many **t** to tell you, Jn 16:12
spoken these **t** to you in figures Jn 16:25
told you these **t** so that in Me Jn 16:33
Jesus spoke these **t**, looked up Jn 17:1
know that all **t** You have given Jn 17:7
My **t** are Yours, and Yours are Jn 17:10
I speak these **t** in the world so Jn 17:13
After Jesus had said these **t**, Jn 18:1
He had said these **t**, one of the Jn 18:22
For these **t** happened so that the Jn 19:36
to these **t** and who wrote them Jn 21:24
many other **t** that Jesus did, Jn 21:25
of the restoration of all **t**, Ac 3:21
and the peoples plot futile **t**? Ac 4:25
of the **t** that were sold, Ac 4:34
and on all who heard these **t**. Ac 5:11
the chief priests heard these **t**, Ac 5:24
We are witnesses of these **t**, Ac 5:32
not My hand make all these **t**? Ac 7:50
they heard these **t**, they were Ac 7:54
Report these **t** to James and the Ac 12:17
Why are you doing these **t**? Ac 14:15
these worthless **t** to the living Ac 14:15
Even though they said these **t**, Ac 14:18
After these **t** I will return and Ac 15:16
says the Lord who does these **t**, Ac 15:17
to abstain from **t** polluted by Ac 15:20
report the same **t** by word of Ac 15:27
on you than these necessary **t**: Ac 15:28
keep yourselves from these **t**, Ac 15:29
officials who heard these **t**. Ac 17:8
daily to see if these **t** were so. Ac 17:11
life and breath and all **t**. Ac 17:25
want to be a judge of such **t**." Ac 18:15
none of these **t** concerned Gallio Ac 18:17
and taught the **t** about Jesus Ac 18:25
them about the **t** related to the Ac 19:8
since these **t** are undeniable, Ac 19:36
discern all these **t** of which we Ac 24:8
alleging that these **t** were so. Ac 24:9
all the **t** that are written Ac 24:14
a loss in a dispute over such **t**, Ac 25:20
to do many **t** in opposition to Ac 26:9
a witness of **t** you have seen, Ac 26:16
and of **t** in which I will appear Ac 26:16
that any of these **t** escapes his Ac 26:26
he said these **t** and had taken Ac 27:35
he said these **t**, the Jews Ac 28:29
teaching the **t** concerning the Ac 28:31
practice such **t** deserve to die Rm 1:32
you, the judge, do the same **t**. Rm 2:1
on those who do such **t** is based Rm 2:2
who do such **t** yet do the same Rm 2:3
and approve the **t** that are Rm 2:18
dead and calls **t** into existence Rm 4:17
then from the **t** you are now Rm 6:21
For the end of those **t** is death. Rm 6:21
think about the **t** of the flesh, Rm 8:5
about the **t** of the Spirit. Rm 8:5
We know that all **t** work together Rm 8:28
are we to say about these **t**? Rm 8:31
in all these **t** we are more than Rm 8:37
nor rulers, nor **t** present, nor Rm 8:38
present, nor **t** to come, nor Rm 8:38
who does these **t** will live by Rm 10:5
announce the gospel of good **t**! Rm 10:15
Him and to Him are all **t**. Rm 11:36
world's foolish **t** to shame the 1Co 1:27
the world's weak **t** to shame the 1Co 1:27
insignificant and despised **t**— 1Co 1:28
things—the **t** viewed as nothing 1Co 1:28
to nothing the **t** that are viewed 1Co 1:28
even the deep **t** of God. 1Co 2:10
also speak these **t**, not in words 1Co 2:13
spiritual **t** to spiritual people 1Co 2:13
in men, for all **t** are yours: 1Co 3:21
life or death or **t** present or 1Co 3:22
or things present or **t** to come— 1Co 3:22
I have applied these **t** to myself 1Co 4:6
like the filth of all **t**. 1Co 4:13
not to speak of **t** pertaining to 1Co 6:3
About the **t** you wrote: 1Co 7:1
about the **t** of the Lord— 1Co 7:32
about the **t** of the world— 1Co 7:33
about the **t** of the Lord, 1Co 7:34
about the **t** of the world— 1Co 7:34
whom are all **t**, and we for Him; 1Co 8:6
whom are all **t**, and we through 1Co 8:6
have sown spiritual **t** for you, 1Co 9:11
if we reap material **t** from you? 1Co 9:11
have become all **t** to all people, 1Co 9:22
Now these **t** became examples for 1Co 10:6
Now these **t** happened to them as 1Co 10:11
to please all people in all **t**, 1Co 10:33
remember me in all **t** and keep 1Co 11:2
woman, and all **t** come from God. 1Co 11:12
all **t**, believes all things, 1Co 13:7
all **t**, hopes all things, 1Co 13:7
things, hopes all **t**, endures all 1Co 13:7
hopes all things, endures all **t**. 1Co 13:7
a man, I put aside childish **t**. 1Co 13:11
inanimate **t** producing sounds 1Co 14:7
All **t** must be done for 1Co 14:26
renounced shameful secret **t**, 2Co 4:2
t have passed away, and look, 2Co 5:17

away, and look, new **t** have come.	2Co 5:17
to mention other **t**, there is the	2Co 11:28
am writing these **t** while absent,	2Co 13:10
I rebuild those **t** that I tore	Gl 2:18
who does these **t** will live by	Gl 3:12
enslaved to **t** that by nature	Gl 4:8
These **t** are illustrations,	Gl 4:24
practice such **t** will not inherit	Gl 5:21
Against such **t** there is no law.	Gl 5:23
both **t** in heaven and things on	Eph 1:10
in heaven and **t** on earth in Him.	Eph 1:10
who fills all **t** in every way.	Eph 1:23
ages in God who created all **t**.	Eph 3:9
that He might fill all **t**.	Eph 4:10
because of these **t** God's wrath	Eph 5:6
soon as I see how **t** go with me.	Php 2:23
the loss of all **t** and consider	Php 3:8
They are focused on earthly **t**,	Php 3:19
any praise—dwell on these **t**.	Php 4:8
able to do all **t** through Him who	Php 4:13
all **t** have been created through	Col 1:16
is before all **t**, and by Him all	Col 1:17
and by Him all **t** hold together.	Col 1:17
whether **t** on earth or things in	Col 1:20
things on earth or **t** in heaven.	Col 1:20
walked in these **t** when you were	Col 3:7
suffered the same **t** from people	1Th 2:14
but test all **t**. Hold on to what	1Th 5:21
write these **t** to you, hoping to	1Tm 3:14
If you point these **t** out to the	1Tm 4:6
Command and teach these **t**.	1Tm 4:11
Practice these **t**; be committed	1Tm 4:15
in these **t**, for by doing this	1Tm 4:16
saying **t** they shouldn't say.	1Tm 5:13
to observe these **t** without	1Tm 5:21
Teach and encourage these **t**.	1Tm 6:2
man of God, run from these **t**;	1Tm 6:11
provides us with all **t** to enjoy.	1Tm 6:17
that is why I suffer these **t**.	2Tm 1:12
I endure all **t** for the elect:	2Tm 2:10
them of these **t**, charging them	2Tm 2:14
purifies himself from these **t**,	2Tm 2:21
Say these **t**, and encourage and	Ti 2:15
I want you to insist on these **t**,	Ti 3:8
heir of all **t** and through whom	Heb 1:2
sustains all **t** by His powerful	Heb 1:3
and through whom all **t** exist,	Heb 2:10
but all **t** are naked and exposed	Heb 4:13
of the better **t** connected with	Heb 6:9
that through two unchangeable **t**,	Heb 6:18
about whom these **t** are said	Heb 7:13
and shadow of the heavenly **t**,	Heb 8:5
about these **t** in detail right	Heb 9:5
These **t** having been set up this	Heb 9:6
of the good **t** that have come.	Heb 9:11
copies of the **t** in the heavens	Heb 9:23
the heavenly **t** themselves ⌊to	Heb 9:23
a shadow of the good **t** to come,	Heb 10:1
been made from **t** that are not	Heb 11:3
who say such **t** make it clear	Heb 11:14
and Esau concerning **t** to come.	Heb 11:20
says better **t** than the ⌊blood⌋	Heb 12:24
is, created **t**—so that what	Heb 12:27
of the body⌋, it boasts great **t**.	Jms 3:5
these **t** should not be this way.	Jms 3:10
you concerning **t** that have now	1Pt 1:12
desire to look into these **t**.	1Pt 1:12
with perishable **t**, like silver	1Pt 1:18
of outward **t** ⌊like⌋ elaborate	1Pt 3:3
Now the end of all **t** is near;	1Pt 4:7
person who lacks these **t** is	2Pt 1:9
if you do these **t** you will never	2Pt 1:10
always remind you about these **t**,	2Pt 1:12
to recall these **t** at any time.	2Pt 1:15
blasphemies about **t** they don't	2Pt 2:12
in these **t** and defeated,	2Pt 2:20
all **t** continue as they have been	2Pt 3:4
Since all these **t** are to be	2Pt 3:11
while you wait for these **t**,	2Pt 3:14
about these **t** in all his letters	2Pt 3:16
writing these **t** so that our joy	1Jn 1:4
you these **t** so that you may	1Jn 2:1
the world or the **t** that belong	1Jn 2:15
written these **t** to you about	1Jn 2:26
teaches you about all **t**,	1Jn 2:27
than our hearts and knows all **t**.	1Jn 3:20
written these **t** to you who	1Jn 5:13
I have many **t** to write to you,	2Jn 12
I have many **t** to write you,	3Jn 13
though you know all these **t**:	Jd 5
destroy themselves with these **t**.	Jd 10
all the harsh **t** ungodly sinners	Jd 15
tolerated ⌊many **t**⌋ because of My	Rv 2:3
But I have a few **t** against you.	Rv 2:14
known the deep **t** of Satan—	Rv 2:24
because You have created all **t**,	Rv 4:11
for You have decided these **t**.	Rv 16:5
OF THE VILE **T** OF THE EARTH	Rv 17:5
and glamorous **t** are gone;	Rv 18:14
of these **t**, who became rich	Rv 18:15
the previous **t** have passed away.	Rv 21:4
The victor will inherit these **t**,	Rv 21:7
one who heard and saw these **t**.	Rv 22:8
to attest these **t** to you for	Rv 22:16
testifies about these **t** says,	Rv 22:20

THINK *(76)*

We **t** there should be an oath	Gn 26:28
to us whatever you **t** is right."	Jos 9:25
Now **t** about what you should do."	Jdg 18:14
T it over, discuss it, and speak	Jdg 19:30
Don't **t** of me as a wicked woman;	1Sm 1:16
Do what you **t** is best, and stay	1Sm 1:23
⌊Do you **t**⌋ he'll make all of you	1Sm 22:7
I **t** it is good to have you	1Sm 29:6
leaders don't **t** you are reliable	1Sm 29:6
Philistine leaders **t** is wrong."	1Sm 29:7
lord must not **t** they have killed	2Sm 13:32
will do whatever you **t** is best,"	2Sm 18:4
so do whatever you **t** best.	2Sm 19:27
t it over and decide what answer	2Sm 24:13
T it over and you will see that	1Kg 20:7
T it over and you will see that	2Kg 5:7
Do whatever you **t** is right."	2Kg 10:5
t mere words are strategy and	2Kg 18:20
Don't **t** that you will escape the	Est 4:13
Do you **t** that you can disprove	Jb 6:26
I lie down I **t**: When will I get	Jb 7:4
that You **t** so highly of him and	Jb 7:17
When I **t** about ⌊it⌋, I am	Jb 21:6
you **t** it is just when you say,	Jb 35:2
one would **t** the deep had white	Jb 41:32
on my bed, I **t** of You, I	Ps 63:6
I **t** of God; I groan; I meditate;	Ps 77:3
For he did not **t** to show	Ps 109:16
ashamed when I **t** about all Your	Ps 119:6
precepts and **t** about Your ways.	Ps 119:15
Your servant will **t** about Your	Ps 119:23
son of man, that You **t** of him?	Ps 144:3
t about Him in all your ways,	Pr 3:6
things to heart or **t** about their	Is 47:7
T it over and see how evil and	Jr 2:19
to me what you **t** is good and	Jr 26:14
I certainly still **t** about him.	Jr 31:20
T of Assyria, a cedar in Lebanon,	Ezk 31:3
Then she will **t**: I will go back	Hs 2:7
T carefully about your ways:	Hg 1:5
T carefully about your ways.	Hg 1:7
of Judah will **t** to himself:	Zch 12:5
first, "What do you **t**, Simon?	Mt 17:25
What do you **t**? If a man has 100	Mt 18:12
But what do you **t**? A man had two	Mt 21:28
Tell us, therefore, what You **t**.	Mt 22:17
What do you **t** about the Messiah?	Mt 22:42
do you **t** that I cannot call on	Mt 26:53
these three do you **t** proved to	Lk 10:36
you **t** that I came here to give	Lk 12:51
Do you **t** that these Galileans	Lk 13:2
do you **t** they were more sinful	Lk 13:4
because you **t** you have eternal	Jn 5:39
Do not **t** that I will accuse you	Jn 5:45
What do you **t**? He won't come to	Jn 11:56
kills you will **t** he is offering	Jn 16:2
he said, 'Who do you **t** I am?	Ac 13:25
Paul did not **t** it appropriate	Ac 15:38
we shouldn't **t** that the divine	Ac 17:29
to hear from you what you **t**.	Ac 28:22
they did not **t** it worthwhile to	Rm 1:28
Do you really **t**—anyone of you	Rm 2:3
to the flesh **t** about the things	Rm 8:5
you not to **t** of himself more	Rm 12:3
more highly than he should **t**.	Rm 12:3
Instead, **t** sensibly, as God has	Rm 12:3
For I **t** God has displayed us,	1Co 4:9
And I **t** that I also have the	1Co 7:40
of the body that we **t** to be less	1Co 12:23
people who **t** we are walking	2Co 10:2
beyond all that we ask or **t**—	Eph 3:20
right for me to **t** this way about	Php 1:7
are mature should **t** this way.	Php 3:15
And if you **t** differently about	Php 3:15
you **t** one will deserve who has	Heb 10:29
Or do you **t** it's without reason	Jms 4:5

THINKING *(20)*

to say "my wife," ⌊**t**⌋, "The men	Gn 26:7
in his mind, **t**, 'I will have	Dt 29:19
he threw it, **t**, "I'll pin David	1Sm 18:11
But Saul was **t**, "My hand	1Sm 18:17
trusted David, **t**, "Since he has	1Sm 27:12
can repel you," **t**, "David can't	2Sm 5:6
Maybe he's **t** it over;	1Kg 18:27
open country, **t**, 'When they come	2Kg 7:12
eye watches for twilight, **t**:	Jb 24:15
is what you are **t**, house of	Ezk 11:5
Why are you **t** evil things in	Mt 9:4
because you're not **t** about God's	Mt 16:23
sitting there, **t** to themselves:	Mk 2:6
because you're not **t** about God's	Mk 8:33
While Peter was **t** about the	Ac 10:19
out of the city, **t** he was dead.	Ac 14:19
their **t** became nonsense,	Rm 1:21
don't be childish in your **t**,	1Co 14:20
in evil and adult in your **t**.	1Co 14:20
my joy by **t** the same way,	Php 2:2

THINKS *(16)*

He will do what He **t** is good."	1Sm 3:18
contempt ⌊and **t**⌋ it is prepared	Jb 12:5
the wicked arrogantly **t**:	Ps 10:4
needy; the Lord **t** of me. You are	Ps 40:17
person **t** before answering	Pr 15:28
for as he **t** within himself,	Pr 23:7
She **t** that these are her wages	Hs 2:12
in security, that **t** to herself:	Zph 2:15
even what he **t** he has will be	Lk 8:18
anyone among you **t** he is wise in	1Co 3:18
But if any man **t** he is acting	1Co 7:36
If anyone **t** he knows anything,	1Co 8:2
whoever **t** he stands must be	1Co 10:12
If anyone **t** he is a prophet or	1Co 14:37
If anyone else **t** he has grounds	Php 3:4
If anyone **t** he is religious,	Jms 1:26

THINNER *(1)*

your faces looking **t** than those	Dn 1:10

THIRD *(180)*

and then morning: the **t** day.	Gn 1:13
The name of the **t** river is the	Gn 2:14
On the **t** day Abraham looked up	Gn 22:4
On the **t** day Laban was told that	Gn 31:22
second one, the **t**, and everyone	Gn 32:19
On the **t** day, when they were	Gn 34:25
the **t** day, which was Pharaoh's	Gn 40:20
the **t** day Joseph said to them,	Gn 42:18
sons to the **t** generation;	Gn 50:23
In the **t** month, on the same day	Ex 19:1
and be prepared by the **t** day,	Ex 19:11
for on the **t** day the LORD will	Ex 19:11
Be prepared by the **t** day.	Ex 19:15
On the **t** day, when morning came,	Ex 19:16
the **t** and fourth ⌊generations⌋	Ex 20:5
calyx under the ⌊**t**⌋ pair of	Ex 25:35
the **t** row, a jacinth, an agate,	Ex 28:19
grandchildren to the **t** and	Ex 34:7
calyx under the **t** pair of	Ex 37:21
the **t** row, a jacinth, an agate,	Ex 39:12
meat by the **t** day must be burned	Lv 7:17
sacrifice is eaten on the **t** day,	Lv 7:18
remains on the **t** day must be	Lv 19:6
If any is eaten on the **t** day,	Lv 19:7
108,100; they will move out **t**.	Nm 2:24
On the **t** day Eliab son of Helon,	Nm 7:24
the children to the **t** and fourth	Nm 14:18
mixed with a **t** of a gallon of	Nm 15:6
Also present a **t** of a gallon of	Nm 15:7
the water on the **t** day and the	Nm 19:12
himself on the **t** and seventh	Nm 19:12
person on the **t** day and the	Nm 19:19
one and a **t** quarts with the ram,	Nm 28:14
On the **t** day ⌊present⌋ 11 bulls,	Nm 29:20
yourselves on the **t** day and the	Nm 31:19
fathers' sin to the **t** and fourth	Dt 5:9
to them in the **t** generation may	Dt 23:8
of your produce in the **t** year,	Dt 26:12
Gibeonite cities on the **t** day.	Jos 9:17
The **t** lot came up for Zebulun's	Jos 19:10

This is the **t** time you have Jdg 16:15
On the **t** day the Israelites Jdg 20:30
again, for the **t** time, the LORD 1Sm 3:8
the next, and Shammah, the **t**, 1Sm 17:13
and sent a **t** group of agents 1Sm 19:21
in the field until the **t** night. 1Sm 20:5
arrived in Ziklag on the **t** day. 1Sm 30:1
On the **t** day a man with torn 2Sm 1:2
the **t** was Absalom, son of Maacah 2Sm 3:3
troops, one **t** under Joab, one 2Sm 18:2
one **t** under Joab's brother 2Sm 18:2
and one **t** under Ittai the 2Sm 18:2
On the **t** day after I gave birth, 1Kg 3:18
and the **t** was 10 and a half feet 1Kg 6:6
and from the middle to the **t**. 1Kg 6:8
came to Rehoboam on the **t** day, 1Kg 12:12
"Return to me on the **t** day." 1Kg 12:12
In the **t** year of Judah's King 1Kg 15:28
In the **t** year of Judah's King 1Kg 15:33
came to Elijah in the **t** year: 1Kg 18:1
And then he said, "A **t** time!" 1Kg 18:34
and they did it a **t** time. 1Kg 18:34
However, in the **t** year, 1Kg 22:2
the king sent a **t** captain of 50 2Kg 1:13
The **t** captain of 50 went up and 2Kg 1:13
one **t** of you who come on duty on 2Kg 11:5
t are to be at the Sur gate and 2Kg 11:6
Sur gate and a **t** at the gate 2Kg 11:6
In the **t** year of Israel's King 2Kg 18:1
But in the **t** year sow and reap, 2Kg 19:29
On the **t** day ⌊from now⌋ you will 2Kg 20:5
the LORD's temple on the **t** day?" 2Kg 20:8
was ⌊born⌋ second, Shimea **t**, 1Ch 2:13
of King Talmai of Geshur, was **t**; 1Ch 3:2
second, Zedekiah **t**, and Shallum 1Ch 3:15
was ⌊born⌋ second, Aharah **t**, 1Ch 8:1
Jeush second, and Eliphelet **t**. 1Ch 8:39
chief, Obadiah second, Eliab **t**, 1Ch 12:9
second, Jahaziel **t**, and Jekameam 1Ch 23:19
the **t** to Harim, the fourth to 1Ch 24:8
Jahaziel the **t**, and Jekameam 1Ch 24:23
the **t** ⌊to⌋ Zaccur, his sons, and 1Ch 25:10
Zebadiah the **t**, Jathniel the 1Ch 26:2
second, Joah the **t**, Sachar the 1Ch 26:4
Tebaliah the **t**, and Zechariah 1Ch 26:11
The **t** army commander, as chief 1Ch 27:5
as chief for the **t** month, was 1Ch 27:5
came to Rehoboam on the **t** day, 2Ch 10:12
"Return to me on the **t** day." 2Ch 10:12
in Jerusalem in the **t** month of 2Ch 15:10
In the **t** year of his reign, 2Ch 17:7
t of you, priests and Levites 2Ch 23:4
A **t** are to be at the king's 2Ch 23:5
and a **t** are to be at the 2Ch 23:5
same in the second and **t** years. 2Ch 27:5
In the **t** month they began 2Ch 31:7
on the **t** day of the month Ezr 6:15
a feast in the **t** year of his Est 1:3
On the **t** day, Esther dressed up Est 5:1
twenty-third day of the **t** month Est 8:9
are deceptive. **T** Series of Jb 21:34
Keziah, and his **t** Keren-happuch. Jb 42:14
But in the **t** year sow and reap, Is 37:30
received him at the **t** entrance Jr 38:14
are to burn up one **t** ⌊of it⌋ in Ezk 5:2
are to take one **t** and slash ⌊it⌋ Ezk 5:2
to scatter one **t** to the wind, Ezk 5:2
One **t** of your people will die by Ezk 5:12
one **t** will fall by the sword all Ezk 5:12
will scatter one **t** to every Ezk 5:12
of a man, the **t** that of a lion, Ezk 10:14
year, in the **t** ⌊month⌋, on the Ezk 31:1
measured off a **t** of a mile and Ezk 47:3
he measured off a **t** ⌊of a mile⌋ Ezk 47:4
off another **t** ⌊of a mile⌋ and Ezk 47:4
he measured off a **t** of a ⌊mile⌋, Ezk 47:5
In the **t** year of the reign of Dn 1:1
then another, a **t** kingdom, of Dn 2:39
and have the **t** highest position Dn 5:7
and have the **t** highest position Dn 5:16
he should be the **t** ruler in the Dn 5:29
In the **t** year of King Dn 8:1
In the **t** year of Cyrus king of Dn 10:1
and on the **t** day He will raise Hs 6:2
the **t** chariot white horses, Zch 6:3
but a **t** will be left in it. Zch 13:8
I will put this **t** through the Zch 13:9
killed, and be raised the **t** day. Mt 16:21
and on the **t** day He will be Mt 17:23
be resurrected on the **t** day." Mt 20:19
killed another, and stoned a **t**. Mt 21:35
also, and the **t**, and so to all Mt 22:26
away again and prayed a **t** time, Mt 26:44
be made secure until the **t** day. Mt 27:64
offspring. And the **t** likewise. Mk 12:21
Then He came a **t** time and said Mk 14:41
and be raised the **t** day." Lk 9:22
and on the **t** day I will complete Lk 13:32
and He will rise on the **t** day." Lk 18:33
he sent yet a **t**, but they Lk 20:12
and the **t** took her. In the same Lk 20:31
A **t** time he said to them, Lk 23:22
and rise on the **t** day'?" Lk 24:7
the **t** day since these things Lk 24:21
rise from the dead the **t** day, Lk 24:46
the **t** day a wedding took place Jn 2:1
This was now the **t** time Jesus Jn 21:14
He asked him the **t** time, "Simon, Jn 21:17
that He asked him the **t** time, Jn 21:17
this man on the **t** day and Ac 10:40
he fell down from the **t** story, Ac 20:9
On the **t** day, they threw the Ac 27:19
prophets, **t** teachers, next, 1Co 12:28
raised on the **t** day according to 1Co 15:4
up into the **t** heaven 14 years 2Co 12:2
to come to you this **t** time. 2Co 12:14
This is the **t** time I am coming 2Co 13:1
the **t** living creature had a face Rv 4:7
When He opened the **t** seal, Rv 6:5
I heard the **t** living creature Rv 6:5
So a **t** of the earth was burned Rv 8:7
a **t** of the trees were burned up, Rv 8:7
So a **t** of the sea became blood, Rv 8:8
a **t** of the living creatures in Rv 8:9
and a **t** of the ships were Rv 8:9
The **t** angel blew his trumpet, Rv 8:10
It fell on a **t** of the rivers and Rv 8:10
and a **t** of the waters became Rv 8:11
and a **t** of the sun was struck, Rv 8:12
sun was struck, a **t** of the moon, Rv 8:12
the moon, and a **t** of the stars, Rv 8:12
so that a **t** of them were Rv 8:12
t of the day was without light, Rv 8:12
to kill a **t** of the human race Rv 9:15
A **t** of the human race was killed Rv 9:18
the **t** woe is coming quickly! Rv 11:14
tail swept away a **t** of the stars Rv 12:4
And a **t** angel followed them and Rv 14:9
The **t** poured out his bowl into Rv 16:4
sapphire, the **t** chalcedony, Rv 21:19

THIRST *(23)*

and our livestock with **t**?" Ex 17:3
you, in famine, **t**, nakedness, Dt 28:48
I now die of **t** and fall into Jdg 15:18
by famine and **t** when he says, 2Ch 32:11
water from the rock for their **t**. Neh 9:15
You gave them water for their **t**. Neh 9:20
I **t** for God, the living God. Ps 42:2
seek You. I **t** for You; my body Ps 63:1
for my **t** they gave me vinegar Ps 69:21
the wild donkeys quench their **t**. Ps 104:11
the masses are parched with **t**. Is 5:13
tongues are parched with **t**. Is 41:17
They did not **t** when He led them Is 48:21
They will not hunger or **t**, Is 49:10
of lack of water and die of **t**. Is 50:2
bare and your throat from **t**. Jr 2:25
to the roof of his mouth from **t**. Lm 4:4
and I will let her die of **t**. Hs 2:3
of bread or a **t** for water, Am 8:11
men also, will faint from **t**. Am 8:13
who hunger and **t** for Mt 5:6
hunger and **t**, often without 2Co 11:27
no longer will they **t**; Rv 7:16

THIRSTED *(1)*

the people **t** there for water, Ex 17:3

THIRSTY *(38)*

a **t** land where there was no Dt 8:15
water to drink for I am **t**." Jdg 4:19
He became very **t** and called out Jdg 15:18
you are **t**, go and drink from Ru 2:9
exhausted, and **t** in the desert." 2Sm 17:29
David was extremely **t** and said, 2Sm 23:15
David was extremely **t** and said, 1Ch 11:17
The **t** pant for his children's Jb 5:5
no water to the **t** and withheld Jb 22:7
tread the winepresses, but go **t**. Jb 24:11
They were hungry and **t**; Ps 107:5
has satisfied the **t** and filled Ps 107:9
springs of water into **t** ground, Ps 107:33
and if he is **t**, give him water Pr 25:21
Bring water for the **t**. Is 21:14
and like a **t** one who dreams he Is 29:8
then wakes and is still **t**, Is 29:8
and deprives the **t** of drink. Is 32:6
and the **t** land springs of water. Is 35:7
I will pour water on the **t** land, Is 44:3
everyone who is **t**, come to the Is 55:1
will drink, but you will be **t**; Is 65:13
I satisfy the **t** person and feed Jr 31:25
wilderness, in a dry and **t** land. Ezk 19:13
was **t** and you gave Me something Mt 25:35
or **t** and give You something to Mt 25:37
I was **t** and you gave Me nothing Mt 25:42
You hungry, or **t**, or a stranger, Mt 25:44
this water will get **t** again. Jn 4:13
him will never get **t** again— Jn 4:14
I won't get **t** and come here to Jn 4:15
in Me will ever be **t** again. Jn 6:35
If anyone is **t**, he should come Jn 7:37
be fulfilled, He said, "I'm **t**!" Jn 19:28
he is **t**, give him something to Rm 12:20
hour we are both hungry and **t**; 1Co 4:11
give to the **t** from the spring Rv 21:6
the one who is **t** should come. Rv 22:17

THIRTEENTH *(11)*

but in the **t** year they rebelled. Gn 14:4
the **t** to Huppah, the fourteenth 1Ch 24:13
t ⌊to⌋ Shubael, his sons, and 1Ch 25:20
summoned on the **t** day of the Est 3:12
a single day, the **t** day of Adar, Est 3:13
on the **t** day of the twelfth Est 8:12
effect on the **t** day of the Est 9:1
fought⌋ on the **t** day of the Est 9:17
assembled on the **t** and the Est 9:18
to him in the **t** year of the Jr 1:2
From the **t** year of Josiah son of Jr 25:3

THIRTIETH *(1)*

In the **t** year, in the fourth Ezk 1:1

THIRTY *(11)*

was the most honored of the **T**, 2Sm 23:23
Among the **T** were: Joab's 2Sm 23:24
of Hachmoni was chief of the **T**; 1Ch 11:11
was the most honored of the **T**, 1Ch 11:25
among the **T** and ⌊a leader⌋ 1Ch 12:4
and ⌊a leader⌋ over the **T**; 1Ch 12:4
chief of the **T**, ⌊and he said⌋: 1Ch 12:18
man among the **T** and over the 1Ch 27:6
among the Thirty and over the **T**, 1Ch 27:6
written for you **t** sayings about Pr 22:20
T chambers faced the pavement, Ezk 40:17

THIRTY-EIGHTH *(2)*

Israel in the **t** year of Judah's 1Kg 16:29
In the **t** year of Judah's King 2Kg 15:8

THIRTY-FIFTH *(1)*

no war until the **t** year of Asa's 2Ch 15:19

THIRTY-FIRST *(1)*

In the **t** year of Judah's King 1Kg 16:23

THIRTY-FOOT *(1)*

to have a **t** screen embroidered Ex 27:16

THIRTY-NINTH *(3)*

In the **t** year of Judah's King 2Kg 15:13
In the **t** year of Judah's King 2Kg 15:17
In the **t** year of his reign, 2Ch 16:12

THIRTY-SECOND *(2)*

twentieth year until his **t** year, Neh 5:14
of Babylon in the **t** year of his Neh 13:6

THIRTY-SEVENTH *(3)*

In the **t** year of Judah's King 2Kg 13:10
month of the **t** year of the exile 2Kg 25:27
month of the **t** year of the exile Jr 52:31

THIRTY-SIXTH *(1)*

In the **t** year of Asa, Israel's 2Ch 16:1

THIRTY-TWO *(1)*

T kings, along with horses and 1Kg 20:1

THIS *(3781)*

(See pp. xi-xii.)

THISTLE *(4)*

The **t** that was in Lebanon once 2Kg 14:9
passed by and trampled the **t**. 2Kg 14:9

The **t** that was in Lebanon sent 2Ch 25:18
passed by and trampled the **t**. 2Ch 25:18

THISTLES *(10)*
produce thorns and **t** for you, Gn 3:18
they huddle beneath the **t**. Jb 30:7
T had come up everywhere, weeds Pr 24:31
burn up Assyria's thorns and **t**. Is 10:17
and like dead **t** before a gale. Is 17:13
cities, with **t** and briers. Is 34:13
T will take possession of their Hs 9:6
thorns and **t** will grow over Hs 10:8
from thornbushes or figs from **t**? Mt 7:16
But if it produces thorns and **t**, Heb 6:8

THOMAS *(11)*
T and Matthew the tax collector; Mt 10:3
Matthew and **T**; James the son Mk 3:18
Matthew and **T**; James the son of Lk 6:15
Then **T** (called "Twin") said to Jn 11:16
"Lord," **T** said, "we don't know Jn 14:5
the Twelve, **T** (called "Twin"), Jn 20:24
again, and **T** was with them. Jn 20:26
Then He said to **T**, "Put your Jn 20:27
T responded to Him, "My Lord and Jn 20:28
Simon Peter, **T** (called "Twin"), Jn 21:2
Andrew, Philip, **T**, Bartholomew, Ac 1:13

THORN *(1)*
t in the flesh was given to me, 2Co 12:7

THORNBUSH *(1)*
Instead of the **t**, a cypress will Is 55:13

THORNBUSHES *(4)*
spreads to **t**, and consumes Ex 22:6
rocks, in all the **t**, and in all Is 7:19
grapes gathered from **t** or figs Mt 7:16
Figs aren't gathered from **t**, Lk 6:44

THORNS *(48)*
It will produce **t** and thistles Gn 3:18
remain will become **t** in your Nm 33:55
your sides and **t** in your eyes, Jos 23:13
They will be **t** in your sides, Jdg 2:3
your flesh on **t** and briers Jdg 8:7
well as some **t** and briers from Jdg 8:16
wicked are like **t** raked aside; 2Sm 23:6
even taking it out of the **t**. Jb 5:5
then let **t** grow instead of wheat Jb 31:40
can feel the heat of the **t**— Ps 58:9
like a fire among **t**; Ps 118:12
There are **t** and snares on the Pr 22:5
a fool is like a stick with **t**, Pr 26:9
of ⌊burning⌋ **t** under the pot, Ec 7:6
a lily among **t**, so is my darling Sg 2:2
t and briers will grow up. Is 5:6
will become **t** and briers. Is 7:23
whole land will be **t** and briers. Is 7:24
for fear of the **t** and briers. Is 7:25
fire that consumes **t** and briers Is 9:18
up Assyria's **t** and thistles. Is 10:17
if it produces **t** and briers for Is 27:4
my people growing **t** and briers, Is 32:13
like **t** cut down and burned in a Is 33:12
will be overgrown with **t**; Is 34:13
do not sow among the **t**. Jr 4:3
have sown wheat but harvested **t**. Jr 12:13
briers and **t** are beside you Ezk 2:6
or painful **t** from all their Ezk 28:24
I will block her way with **t**; Hs 2:6
t will invade their tents. Hs 9:6
t and thistles will grow over Hs 10:8
is worse than a hedge of **t**. Mc 7:4
be consumed like entangled **t**, Nah 1:10
fell among **t**, and the thorns Mt 13:7
and the **t** came up and choked Mt 13:7
Now the one sown among the **t**— Mt 13:22
twisted together a crown of **t**, Mt 27:29
fell among **t**, and the thorns Mk 4:7
and the **t** came up and choked it, Mk 4:7
Others are sown among **t**; Mk 4:18
twisted together a crown of **t**, Mk 15:17
Other seed fell among **t**; Lk 8:7
the **t** sprang up with it and Lk 8:7
for the seed that fell among **t**, Lk 8:14
twisted together a crown of **t**, Jn 19:2
the crown of **t** and the purple Jn 19:5
if it produces **t** and thistles, Heb 6:8

THORNY *(1)*
slacker's way is like a **t** hedge, Pr 15:19

THOROUGH *(1)*
they made a **t** investigation, Jdg 6:29

THOROUGHLY *(7)*
t grinding it to powder as ⌊fine Dt 9:21
investigate, and interrogate **t**. Dt 13:14
you must investigate it **t**. Dt 17:4
the unwise and **t** explained ⌊the Jb 26:3
and my mind has **t** grasped wisdom Ec 1:16
Glean as **t** as a vine the remnant Jr 6:9
to investigate his case more **t**. Ac 23:15

THOSE *(1364)*
(See pp. xi-xii.)

THOUGH *(256)*
(See pp. xi-xii.)

THOUGHT *(76)*
scheme his mind **t** of was nothing Gn 6:5
laughed, and **t** in his heart, "Can Gn 17:17
his sons-in-law **t** he was joking. Gn 19:14
Abraham replied, "I **t**, 'There is Gn 20:11
Because I **t** I might die on Gn 26:9
for I **t** you would take your Gn 31:31
He **t**, "If Esau comes to one camp Gn 32:8
For he **t**, "I want to appease Gn 32:20
For he **t**, "He might die too, Gn 38:11
he **t** she was a prostitute, Gn 38:15
brothers, for he **t**, "Something Gn 42:4
he **t** it was a mistake and took Gn 48:17
Then Moses became afraid and **t**: Ex 2:14
So Moses **t**: I must go over and Ex 3:3
around them fled because they **t**, Nm 16:34
of war and **t** it would be easy Dt 1:41
this wicked **t** in your heart, Dt 15:9
t that if they said this to us Jos 22:28
room locked and **t** he was Jdg 3:24
Even if I **t** there was ⌊still⌋ Ru 1:12
I **t** I should inform you: Ru 4:4
be heard. Eli **t** she was drunk 1Sm 1:13
I **t**: The Philistines will now 1Sm 13:12
trembling, for he **t**, "Certainly 1Sm 15:32
"I'll give her to him," Saul **t**. 1Sm 18:21
anything that day because he **t**, 1Sm 20:26
he **t** he was a bearer of good 2Sm 4:10
I fasted and wept because I **t**, 2Sm 12:22
Your servant **t**: I must speak to 2Sm 14:15
Your servant **t**: May the word of 2Sm 14:17
of Elisha the man of God, **t**: 2Kg 5:20
have spoken is good," for he **t**: 2Kg 20:19
the intention of every **t**. 1Ch 28:9
Haman **t** to himself, "Who is it Est 6:6
of them. For Job **t**: Perhaps my Jb 1:5
I **t**: I will die in my own nest Jb 29:18
I **t** that age should speak and Jb 32:7
you **t** I was just like you. Ps 50:21
I **t** about my ways and turned my Ps 119:59
and you will be **t** of again. Is 23:16
I **t** until the morning: Is 38:13
good." For he **t**: There will be Is 39:8
t: After she has done all these Jr 3:7
I **t**: How I long to make you ⌊My⌋ Jr 3:19
the nations. I **t**: You will call Jr 3:19
I **t**: They are just the poor; Jr 5:4
I never entertained the **t**. Jr 7:31
I never entertained the **t**. Jr 19:5
entertained the **t** that they do Jr 32:35
Then I **t**: My future is lost, as Lm 3:18
flooded over my head, and I **t**: Lm 3:54
live because he **t** it over and Ezk 18:28
For she **t**: I will go after my Hs 2:5
dismiss any **t** of the evil day Am 6:3
I **t**: You will certainly fear Me Zph 3:7
because everyone **t** John was a Mt 21:26
they **t** it was a ghost and cried Mk 6:49
because everyone **t** that John was Mk 11:32
When he **t** about it, he began to Mk 14:72
years old and was **t** to be the Lk 3:23
He **t** to himself, 'What should I Lk 12:17
they **t** the kingdom of God was Lk 19:11
terrified and **t** they were seeing Lk 24:37
but they **t** He was speaking about Jn 11:13
some **t** that Jesus was telling Jn 13:29
because you **t** the gift of God Ac 8:20
but **t** he was seeing a vision. Ac 12:9
where we **t** there was a place of Ac 16:13
since he **t** the prisoners had Ac 16:27
they **t** they had achieved their Ac 27:13
night the sailors **t** they were Ac 27:27
like a child, I **t** like a child, 1Co 13:11
taking every **t** captive to the 2Co 10:5
have **t** all along that we were 2Co 12:19
surpasses every **t**, will guard Php 4:7
we **t** it was better to be left 1Th 3:1

THOUGHTS *(48)*
forever in the **t** of the hearts 1Ch 29:18
Among unsettling **t** from visions Jb 4:13
these ⌊**t**⌋ in Your heart; Jb 10:13
why my unsettling **t** compel me to Jb 20:2
I know your **t**, the schemes you Jb 21:27
examines the **t** and emotions is Ps 7:9
all their **t** are against me for Ps 56:5
LORD, how profound Your **t**! Ps 92:5
The LORD knows man's **t**; Ps 94:11
understand my **t** from far away. Ps 139:2
difficult Your **t** are for me ⌊to Ps 139:17
The **t** of the righteous ⌊are⌋ Pr 12:5
I turned my **t** to know, explore, Ec 7:25
curse the king even in your **t**, Ec 10:20
way, and the sinful one his **t**; Is 55:7
For My **t** are not your thoughts, Is 55:8
For My thoughts are not your **t**, Is 55:8
and My **t** than your thoughts. Is 55:9
and My thoughts than your **t**. Is 55:9
Their **t** are sinful thoughts; Is 59:7
Their thoughts are sinful **t**; Is 59:7
path, following their own **t**. Is 65:2
Knowing their works and their **t**, Is 66:18
harbor malicious **t** within you? Jr 4:14
and I know the **t** that arise in Ezk 11:5
t will arise in your mind, Ezk 38:10
t came ⌊to your mind⌋ about what Dn 2:29
understand the **t** of your mind. Dn 2:30
a moment, and his **t** alarmed him. Dn 4:19
and his **t** so terrified him that Dn 5:6
Don't let your **t** terrify you or Dn 5:10
my **t** terrified me greatly, Dn 7:28
reveals His **t** to man, the One Am 4:13
perceiving their **t**, Jesus said, Mt 9:4
Knowing their **t**, He told them: Mt 12:25
For from the heart come evil **t**, Mt 15:19
hearts, come evil **t**, sexual Mk 7:21
of the **t** of their hearts; Lk 1:51
that the **t** of many hearts may be Lk 2:35
perceiving their **t**, Jesus Lk 5:22
He knew their **t** and told the man Lk 6:8
knowing the **t** of their hearts, Lk 9:47
Knowing their **t**, He told them: Lk 11:17
their competing **t** either accuse Rm 2:15
inclinations of our flesh and **t**, Eph 2:3
in the futility of their **t**. Eph 4:17
of the ideas and **t** of the heart. Heb 4:12
and become judges with evil **t**? Jms 2:4

THOUSAND *(30)*
love to a **t** ⌊generations⌋ Ex 20:6
love to a **t** ⌊generations⌋, Ex 34:7
increase you a **t** times more, Dt 1:11
love to a **t** ⌊generations⌋ Dt 5:10
loyalty for a **t** generations with Dt 7:9
How could one man pursue a **t**, Dt 32:30
or two put ten **t** to flight, Dt 32:30
and came with ten **t** holy ones, Dt 33:2
of you routed a **t**, because the Jos 23:10
the greatest of them for a **t**. 1Ch 12:14
He ordained for a **t** generations, 1Ch 16:15
answer God once in a **t** ⌊times⌋. Jb 9:3
out of a **t**, to tell a person Jb 33:23
Mine, the cattle on a **t** hills. Ps 50:10
courts than a **t** ⌊anywhere else⌋. Ps 84:10
in Your sight a **t** years are like Ps 90:4
Though a **t** fall at your side and Ps 91:7
side and ten **t** at your right Ps 91:7
ordained for a **t** generations— Ps 105:8
And if he lives a **t** years twice, Ec 6:6
among a **t** ⌊people⌋ I have found Ec 7:28
A **t** bucklers are hung on it— Sg 4:4
and strong, notable among ten **t**. Sg 5:10
One **t** ⌊will flee⌋ at the threat Is 30:17
The least will become a **t**, Is 60:22
ten **t** times ten thousand stood Dn 7:10
times ten **t** stood before Him. Dn 7:10
out for him ten **t** points of My Hs 8:12
marches out a **t** ⌊strong⌋ will Am 5:3
or with ten **t** streams of oil? Mc 6:7

THOUSANDS *(55)*
may you become **t** upon ten Gn 24:60
you become thousands upon ten **t**. Gn 24:60
the people as officials of **t**, Ex 18:21

became his vassal for **t** years. 2Kg 24:1
reigned **t** months in Jerusalem. 2Kg 24:8
rank, and the **t** doorkeepers. 2Kg 25:18
⌊These⌋ **t** were born to him by 1Ch 2:3
Zeruiah's **t** sons: Abishai, 1Ch 2:16
Hizkiah, and Azrikam—**t**. 1Ch 3:23
T of Benjamin's ⌊sons⌋: 1Ch 7:6
So Saul and his **t** sons died— 1Ch 10:6
was one of the **t** warriors. 1Ch 11:12
T of the 30 chief men went down 1Ch 11:15
So the **T** broke through the 1Ch 11:18
the exploits of the **t** warriors. 1Ch 11:19
was the leader of the **T**. 1Ch 11:20
a reputation among the **T**. 1Ch 11:20
honored of the **T** and became 1Ch 11:21
he did not become one of the **T**. 1Ch 11:21
reputation among the **t** warriors. 1Ch 11:24
he did not become one of the **T**. 1Ch 11:25
there with David for **t** days, 1Ch 12:39
in his house for **t** months, 1Ch 13:14
I am offering you **t** ⌊choices⌋. 1Ch 21:10
either **t** years of famine, three 1Ch 21:12
t months of devastation by your 1Ch 21:12
or **t** days of the sword of the 1Ch 21:12
then Zetham, and Joel—**t**. 1Ch 23:8
Haziel, and Haran—**t**. 1Ch 23:9
Mahli, Eder, and Jeremoth—**t**. 1Ch 23:23
fourteen sons and **t** daughters. 1Ch 25:5
on 12 oxen, **t** facing north, 2Ch 4:4
facing north, **t** facing west, 2Ch 4:4
facing west, **t** facing south, 2Ch 4:4
facing south, and **t** facing east. 2Ch 4:4
reservoir was **t** inches thick, 2Ch 4:5
and the **t** annual appointed 2Ch 8:13
and once every **t** years the ships 2Ch 9:21
Return to me in **t** days." 2Ch 10:5
son of Solomon for **t** years, 2Ch 11:17
David and Solomon for **t** years. 2Ch 11:17
he reigned **t** years in Jerusalem. 2Ch 13:2
the plunder for **t** days because 2Ch 20:25
by genealogy **t** years old and 2Ch 31:16
reigned **t** months in Jerusalem. 2Ch 36:2
he reigned **t** months and 10 days 2Ch 36:9
with **t** layers of cut stones and Ezr 6:4
and we camped there for **t** days. Ezr 8:15
and rested there for **t** days. Ezr 8:32
not come within **t** days would Ezr 10:8
in Jerusalem within the **t** days. Ezr 10:9
and had been there **t** days, Neh 2:11
Don't eat or drink for **t** days, Est 4:16
had seven sons and **t** daughters. Jb 1:2
to their **t** sisters to eat Jb 1:4
The Chaldeans formed **t** bands, Jb 1:17
Now when Job's **t** friends— Jb 2:11
So these **t** men quit answering Jb 32:1
angry at Job's **t** friends because Jb 32:3
he saw that the **t** men could not Jb 32:5
things two or **t** times to a man Jb 33:29
had seven sons and **t** daughters. Jb 42:13
T things are never satisfied; Pr 30:15
T things are beyond me; Pr 30:18
earth trembles under **t** things; Pr 30:21
T things are stately in their Pr 30:29
cord of **t** strands is not easily Ec 4:12
LORD says, "In **t** years, as a Is 16:14
two or **t** berries at the very top Is 17:6
and barefoot **t** years as a sign Is 20:3
would read **t** or four columns, Jr 36:23
rank, and the **t** doorkeepers. Jr 52:24
even ⌊if⌋ these **t** men—Noah, Ezk 14:14
⌊if⌋ these **t** men were in it, Ezk 14:16
⌊if⌋ these **t** men were in it, Ezk 14:18
sword strike two times, even **t**. Ezk 21:14
standard length plus **t** inches. Ezk 40:5
were **t** and a half feet. Ezk 40:9
There were **t** recesses on each Ezk 40:10
Its **t** recesses on each side, Ezk 40:21
were **t** and a half feet ⌊wide⌋ Ezk 41:3
above another in **t** stories of 30 Ezk 41:6
with their **t** levels opposite Ezk 41:16
feet high and **t** and a half feet Ezk 41:22
gallery by gallery in **t** tiers. Ezk 42:3
arranged in **t** stories and had Ezk 42:6
standard length plus **t** inches Ezk 43:13
ledge is **t** and a half feet, Ezk 43:14
miles⌋ long and **t** and one-third Ezk 45:3
miles⌋ long and **t** and one-third Ezk 45:5
T quarts from five bushels of Ezk 45:13
of wheat and **t** quarts from five Ezk 45:13
t quarts, with one-third of a Ezk 46:14
miles⌋ long and **t** and one-third Ezk 48:9
t and one-third ⌊miles⌋ wide on Ezk 48:10
t and one-third ⌊miles⌋ wide on Ezk 48:10
miles⌋ long and **t** and one-third Ezk 48:13
and the width **t** and one-third Ezk 48:13
donation will be **t** and one-third Ezk 48:18
to the east and **t** and one-third Ezk 48:18
there will be **t** gates facing Ezk 48:31
miles⌋, there will be **t** gates: Ezk 48:32
miles⌋, there will be **t** gates: Ezk 48:33
miles⌋, there will be **t** gates: Ezk 48:34
were to be trained for **t** years, Dn 1:5
And these **t** men, Shadrach, Dn 3:23
Didn't we throw **t** men, bound, Dn 3:24
and over them **t** administrators, Dn 6:2
and **t** times a day he got down on Dn 6:10
for he prays **t** times a day." Dn 6:13
with **t** ribs in its mouth between Dn 7:5
and **t** of the first horns were Dn 7:8
before which **t** fell—the horn Dn 7:20
after them and subdue **t** kings. Dn 7:24
was mourning for **t** full weeks. Dn 10:2
until the **t** weeks were over Dn 10:3
T more kings will arise in Dn 11:2
punishing Damascus for **t** crimes, Am 1:3
punishing Gaza for **t** crimes, Am 1:6
punishing Tyre for **t** crimes, Am 1:9
punishing Edom for **t** crimes, Am 1:11
the Ammonites for **t** crimes, Am 1:13
punishing Moab for **t** crimes, Am 2:1
punishing Judah for **t** crimes, Am 2:4
punishing Israel for **t** crimes, Am 2:6
your tenths every **t** days. Am 4:4
there were still **t** months until Am 4:7
Two or **t** cities staggered to Am 4:8
was in the fish **t** days and three Jnh 1:17
fish three days and **t** nights. Jnh 1:17
month I got rid of **t** shepherds. Zch 11:8
the great fish **t** days and three Mt 12:40
fish three days and **t** nights, Mt 12:40
of the earth **t** days and three Mt 12:40
earth three days and **t** nights. Mt 12:40
Around **t** in the morning, He came Mt 14:25
stayed with Me **t** days and have Mt 15:32
I will make **t** tabernacles here: Mt 17:4
of two or **t** witnesses every Mt 18:16
For where two or **t** are gathered Mt 18:20
About noon and at **t**, he went out Mt 20:5
you will deny Me **t** times!" Mt 26:34
and rebuild it in **t** days.' " Mt 26:61
you will deny Me **t** times." Mt 26:75
and rebuild it in **t** days, Mt 27:40
From noon until **t** in the Mt 27:45
about **t** in the afternoon Jesus Mt 27:46
'After **t** days I will rise again. Mt 27:63
Around **t** in the morning He came Mk 6:48
stayed with Me **t** days and have Mk 8:2
killed, and rise after **t** days. Mk 8:31
Let us make **t** tabernacles: Mk 9:5
He will rise **t** days later." Mk 9:31
and He will rise after **t** days." Mk 10:34
you will deny Me **t** times!" Mk 14:30
and in **t** days I will build Mk 14:58
you will deny Me **t** times." Mk 14:72
and build it in **t** days, Mk 15:29
land until **t** in the afternoon Mk 15:33
And at **t** Jesus cried out with a Mk 15:34
stayed with her about **t** months; Lk 1:56
After **t** days, they found Him in Lk 2:46
was shut up for **t** years and six Lk 4:25
Let us make **t** tabernacles: Lk 9:33
Which of these **t** do you think Lk 10:36
lend me **t** loaves of bread, Lk 11:5
t against two, and two against Lk 12:52
against two, and two against **t**. Lk 12:52
for **t** years I have come looking Lk 13:7
until you deny **t** times that you Lk 22:34
you will deny Me **t** times." Lk 22:61
over the whole land until **t**, Lk 23:44
I will raise it up in **t** days." Jn 2:19
will You raise it up in **t** days?" Jn 2:20
had rowed about **t** or four miles, Jn 6:19
you have denied Me **t** times. Jn 13:38
of prayer at **t** in the afternoon Ac 3:1
an interval of about **t** hours; Ac 5:7
in his father's home **t** months, Ac 7:20
He was unable to see for **t** days, Ac 9:9
At about **t** in the afternoon he Ac 10:3
This happened **t** times, and then Ac 10:16
T men are here looking for you. Ac 10:19
this hour, at **t** in the afternoon Ac 10:30
Now this happened **t** times, Ac 11:10
t men who had been sent to me Ac 11:11
and on **t** Sabbath days reasoned Ac 17:2
over a period of **t** months, Ac 19:8
and stayed **t** months. When he was Ac 20:3
and day for **t** years I did not Ac 20:31
T days after Festus arrived in Ac 25:1
us hospitably for **t** days. Ac 28:7
After **t** months we set sail in an Ac 28:11
at Syracuse, we stayed **t** days. Ac 28:12
Forum of Appius and **T** Taverns. Ac 28:15
After **t** days he called together Ac 28:17
Now these **t** remain: faith, hope, 1Co 13:13
or at the most **t**, each in turn, 1Co 14:27
Two or **t** prophets should speak, 1Co 14:29
T times I was beaten with rods. 2Co 11:25
T times I was shipwrecked. 2Co 11:25
with the Lord **t** times to take it 2Co 12:8
of two or **t** witnesses every 2Co 13:1
Then after **t** years I did go up Gl 1:18
supported by two or **t** witnesses. 1Tm 5:19
testimony of two or **t** witnesses. Heb 10:28
by his parents for **t** months, Heb 11:23
and for **t** years and six months Jms 5:17
For there are **t** that testify: 1Jn 5:7
and these **t** are in agreement. 1Jn 5:8
and **t** quarts of barley for a Rv 6:6
blasts that the **t** angels are Rv 8:13
was killed by these **t** plagues— Rv 9:18
bodies for **t** and a half days Rv 11:9
But after the **t** and a half days, Rv 11:11
I saw **t** unclean spirits like Rv 16:13
great city split into **t** parts, Rv 16:19
There were **t** gates on the east, Rv 21:13
on the east, **t** gates on the Rv 21:13
on the north, **t** gates on the Rv 21:13
the south, and **t** gates on the Rv 21:13

THREE-DAY *(6)*

He put a **t** journey between Gn 30:36
please let us go on a **t** trip Ex 3:18
Please let us go on a **t** trip Ex 5:3
the LORD on a **t** journey to seek Nm 10:33
They took a **t** journey into the Nm 33:8
extremely large city, a **t** walk. Jnh 3:3

THREE-INCH *(3)*

Make a **t** frame all around it and Ex 25:25
He made a **t** frame all around it Ex 37:12
There were **t** hooks fastened all Ezk 40:43

THREE-PRONGED *(1)*

come with a **t** meat fork while 1Sm 2:13

THREE-QUARTER *(28)*

basin weighing one and **t** pounds, Nm 7:13
basin weighing one and **t** pounds, Nm 7:19
basin weighing one and **t** pounds, Nm 7:25
basin weighing one and **t** pounds, Nm 7:31
basin weighing one and **t** pounds, Nm 7:37
basin weighing one and **t** pounds, Nm 7:43
basin weighing one and **t** pounds, Nm 7:49
basin weighing one and **t** pounds, Nm 7:55
basin weighing one and **t** pounds, Nm 7:61
basin weighing one and **t** pounds, Nm 7:67
basin weighing one and **t** pounds, Nm 7:73
basin weighing one and **t** pounds, Nm 7:79
and each basin one and **t** pounds. Nm 7:85
of⌋ eight and **t** feet between Ezk 40:7
the gateway was 22 and **t** feet. Ezk 40:11
the distance was 43 and **t** feet. Ezk 40:13
long and 43 and **t** feet wide. Ezk 40:21
long and 43 and **t** feet wide. Ezk 40:25
long and 43 and **t** feet wide. Ezk 40:29
43 and **t** feet long and eight and Ezk 40:30
long and eight and **t** feet wide. Ezk 40:30
long and 43 and **t** feet wide. Ezk 40:33
long and 43 and **t** feet wide. Ezk 40:36
were eight and **t** feet ⌊thick⌋ Ezk 40:48
were eight and **t** feet ⌊wide⌋ on Ezk 41:2
side rooms was eight and **t** feet. Ezk 41:9
was eight and **t** feet wide all Ezk 41:11
eight and **t** feet thick on all Ezk 41:12

THREE-STRINGED *(1)*

of joy, and with **t** instruments. 1Sm 18:6

THREE-YEAR-OLD *(4)*
to him, "Bring me a **t** cow, a Gn 15:9
cow, a **t** female goat, Gn 15:9
female goat, a **t** ram, a Gn 15:9
Shiloh, as well as a **t** bull, two 1Sm 1:24

THRESH *(4)*
that day the LORD will **t** grain Is 27:12
will **t** mountains and pulverize Is 41:15
young cow that loves to **t**, Hs 10:11
Rise and **t**, Daughter Zion, for I Mc 4:13

THRESHED *(4)*
My downtrodden and **t** people, Is 21:10
cumin is not **t** with a threshing Is 28:27
crushed, but is not **t** endlessly. Is 28:28
because they **t** Gilead with iron Am 1:3

THRESHES *(1)*
he who **t** should do so in hope 1Co 9:10

THRESHING *(47)*
reached the **t** floor of Atad, Gn 50:10
mourning at the **t** floor of Atad, Gn 50:11
Your **t** will continue until grape Lv 26:5
a contribution from the **t** floor. Nm 15:20
grain from the **t** floor or the Nm 18:27
as the produce of the **t** floor or Nm 18:30
flock, your **t** floor, and your Dt 15:14
from your **t** floor and winepress Dt 16:13
son Gideon was **t** wheat in the Jdg 6:11
of wool here on the **t** floor. Jdg 6:37
winnowing barley on the **t** floor. Ru 3:2
down to the **t** floor, but don't Ru 3:3
down ⌊to⌋ the **t** floor and did Ru 3:6
a woman came to the **t** floor." Ru 3:14
and raiding the **t** floors." 1Sm 23:1
they came to Nacon's **t** floor, 2Sm 6:6
was then at the **t** floor of 2Sm 24:16
the LORD on the **t** floor of 2Sm 24:18
To buy the **t** floor from you in 2Sm 24:21
offering and the **t** sledges and 2Sm 24:22
David bought the **t** floor and the 2Sm 24:24
They were on the **t** floor at the 1Kg 22:10
the **t** floor or the winepress? 2Kg 6:27
making them like dust at **t**. 2Kg 13:7
they came to Chidon's **t** floor, 1Ch 13:9
standing at the **t** floor of Ornan 1Ch 21:15
the LORD on the **t** floor of Ornan 1Ch 21:18
Ornan was **t** wheat when he 1Ch 21:20
he left the **t** floor and bowed to 1Ch 21:21
the **t** sledges for the wood, 1Ch 21:23
him at the **t** floor of Ornan 1Ch 21:28
prepared on the **t** floor of Ornan 2Ch 3:1
were sitting on the **t** floor at 2Ch 18:9
and bring ⌊it⌋ to your **t** floor? Jb 39:12
the mud like a **t** sledge. Jb 41:30
drives the **t** wheel over them. Pr 20:26
is not threshed with a **t** board, Is 28:27
make you into a sharp **t** board, Is 41:15
is like a **t** floor at the time Jr 51:33
chaff from the summer **t** floors. Dn 2:35
T floor and wine vat will not Hs 9:2
like chaff blown from a **t** floor, Hs 13:3
The **t** floors will be full of Jl 2:24
like sheaves to the **t** floor. Mc 4:12
will clear His **t** floor and Mt 3:12
to clear His **t** floor and gather Lk 3:17
muzzle an ox that is **t** grain, 1Tm 5:18

THRESHING-FLOOR *(1)*
Give me this **t** plot so that I 1Ch 21:22

THRESHOLD *(20)*
house with her hands on the **t**. Jdg 19:27
broken off and lying on the **t**. 1Sm 5:4
Ashdod do not step on Dagon's **t**. 1Sm 5:5
was crossing the **t** of the house, 1Kg 14:17
who guarded the **t** put all the 2Kg 12:9
builds a high **t** invites injury. Pr 17:19
been, to the **t** of the temple. Ezk 9:3
cherubim to the **t** of the temple. Ezk 10:4
away from the **t** of the temple Ezk 10:18
He measured the **t** of the gate; Ezk 40:6
the first **t** was 10 feet deep. Ezk 40:6
The ⌊inner⌋ **t** of the gate on the Ezk 40:7
three levels opposite the **t**— Ezk 41:16
they placed their **t** next to My Ezk 43:8
next to My **t** and their doorposts Ezk 43:8
in worship at the **t** of the gate Ezk 46:2
from under the **t** of the temple Ezk 47:1
side ⌊of the **t**⌋ of the temple, Ezk 47:1
punish all who skip over the **t**, Zph 1:9
devastation will be on the **t**, Zph 2:14

THRESHOLDS *(5)*
to guard the **t** of the tent. 1Ch 9:19
be gatekeepers at the **t** was 212. 1Ch 9:22
the beams, the **t**, its walls and 2Ch 3:7
the **t**, the beveled windows, and Ezk 41:16
the pillars so that the **t** shake; Am 9:1

THREW *(87)*
hugged him, **t** his arms around Gn 33:4
took him and **t** him into the pit Gn 37:24
Then Joseph **t** his arms around Gn 45:14
himself to him, **t** his arms Gn 46:29
He **t** it on the ground, and it Ex 4:3
foreskin, and **t** it at Moses' Ex 4:25
Aaron **t** down his staff before Ex 7:10
Each one **t** down his staff, Ex 7:12
Moses **t** it toward heaven, and it Ex 9:10
and **t** them into confusion. Ex 14:24
He **t** Pharaoh's chariots and his Ex 15:4
When he **t** it into the water, Ex 15:25
enraged and **t** the tablets out Ex 32:19
When I **t** it into the fire, Ex 32:24
We **t** them down; Heshbon has Nm 21:30
the tablets and **t** them from my Dt 9:17
Then I **t** it into the stream that Dt 9:21
and **t** them into another land Dt 29:28
their bodies, **t** stones on them, Jos 7:25
They **t** it down at the entrance Jos 8:29
The LORD **t** them into confusion Jos 10:10
the LORD **t** large hailstones on Jos 10:11
The LORD **t** Sisera, all his Jdg 4:15
and everyone **t** an earring from Jdg 8:25
But a woman **t** the upper portion Jdg 9:53
he **t** away the jawbone and named Jdg 15:17
that day and **t** them into such 1Sm 7:10
and he **t** it, thinking, "I'll pin 1Sm 18:11
Saul **t** his spear at Jonathan 1Sm 20:33
Amnon's servant **t** her out and 2Sm 13:18
He **t** stones at David and at all 2Sm 16:6
and **t** stones and dirt at him. 2Sm 16:13
t him into a large pit in the 2Sm 18:17
the field and **t** a garment over 2Sm 20:12
son of Bichri and **t** it to Joab. 2Sm 20:22
by him and **t** his mantle over 1Kg 19:19
spring of water, **t** salt in it, 2Kg 2:21
each of them **t** stones to cover 2Kg 3:25
He **t** it into the pot and said, 2Kg 4:41
God cut a stick, **t** it there, and 2Kg 6:6
So they **t** her down, and some of 2Kg 9:33
and officers **t** ⌊the bodies⌋ out 2Kg 10:25
so they **t** the man into Elisha's 2Kg 13:21
and **t** its dust on the graves of 2Kg 23:6
them there and **t** their dust 2Kg 23:12
a cliff where they **t** them off, 2Ch 25:12
who **t** off restraint in Judah and 2Ch 28:19
incense altars and **t** them into 2Ch 30:14
and he **t** them outside the city. 2Ch 33:15
displeased and **t** all of Tobiah's Neh 13:8
his robe and **t** dust into the air Jb 2:12
enticed and I **t** them a kiss, Jb 31:27
with the sword and **t** his corpse Jr 26:23
them and **t** them into a cistern Jr 41:7
into a pit and **t** stones at me. Lm 3:53
None of them **t** away the Ezk 20:8
So I **t** you down to the earth; Ezk 28:17
when I **t** it down to Sheol ⌊to Ezk 31:16
brought Daniel and **t** him into Dn 6:16
The goat **t** him to the ground and Dn 8:7
They **t** the ship's cargo into the Jnh 1:5
up Jonah and **t** him into the sea, Jnh 1:15
You **t** me into the depths, into Jnh 2:3
silver and **t** it into the house Zch 11:13
but **t** out the worthless ones. Mt 13:48
he went and **t** him into prison Mt 18:30
So they seized him and **t** him out Mt 21:39
So he **t** the silver into the Mt 27:5
t off his coat, jumped up, and Mk 10:50
to Jesus and **t** their robes on it Mk 11:7
and **t** him out of the vineyard. Mk 12:8
him down and **t** him into severe Lk 9:42
t his arms around his neck, Lk 15:20
this one too and **t** him out. Lk 20:12
they **t** him out of the vineyard Lk 20:15
Then they **t** him out. Jn 9:34
and **t** a purple robe around Him. Jn 19:2
They **t** him out of the city and Ac 7:58
on them, they **t** them in jail, Ac 16:23
citizens, and **t** us in jail. Ac 16:37
went down, **t** himself on him, Ac 20:10
they **t** the ship's gear overboard Ac 27:19
t them down into Tartarus and 2Pt 2:4
and he **t** them into the great Rv 14:19
They **t** dust on their heads and Rv 18:19
millstone and **t** it into the sea, Rv 18:21
He **t** him into the abyss, closed Rv 20:3

THRILLED *(1)*
they were **t** at the light of my Jb 29:24

THRIVE *(6)*
water makes it **t** and produce Jb 14:9
The righteous **t** like a palm tree Ps 92:12
they **t** in the courtyards of our Ps 92:13
the righteous **t**, a city rejoices Pr 11:10
I made you **t** like plants of the Ezk 16:7
and make the withered tree **t**. Ezk 17:24

THROAT *(7)*
their **t** is an open grave; Ps 5:9
my crying; my **t** is parched. My Ps 69:3
a knife in your **t** if you have a Pr 23:2
like cold water to a parched **t**. Pr 25:25
enlarges its **t** and opens wide Is 5:14
bare and your **t** from thirst. Jr 2:25
Their **t** is an open grave; Rm 3:13

THROATS *(2)*
make a sound with their **t**. Ps 115:7
while a sword is at our **t**." Jr 4:10

THRONE *(182)*
regard to the **t** will I be Gn 41:40
who sits on his **t** to the Ex 11:5
sat on his **t** to the firstborn Ex 12:29
lifted up⌋ toward the LORD's **t**. Ex 17:16
he is seated on his royal **t**, Dt 17:18
the king stood up from his **t**. Jdg 3:20
and gives them a **t** of honor. 1Sm 2:8
establish the **t** of David over 2Sm 3:10
establish the **t** of his kingdom 2Sm 7:13
and your **t** will be established 2Sm 7:16
the king and his **t** be innocent." 2Sm 14:9
the one who is to sit on my **t**? 1Kg 1:13
the one who is to sit on my **t**.' 1Kg 1:17
will sit on the **t** of my lord the 1Kg 1:20
the one who is to sit on my **t**?' 1Kg 1:24
my lord the king's **t** after him." 1Kg 1:27
is to sit on my **t** in my place, 1Kg 1:30
is to come in and sit on my **t**. 1Kg 1:35
and make his **t** greater than 1Kg 1:37
than the **t** of my lord King 1Kg 1:37
taken his seat on the royal **t**. 1Kg 1:46
may He make his **t** greater than 1Kg 1:47
throne greater than your **t**.' 1Kg 1:47
has provided one to sit on my **t**, 1Kg 1:48
have a man on the **t** of Israel.' 1Kg 2:4
sat on the **t** of his father 1Kg 2:12
sat down on his **t**, and had a 1Kg 2:19
had a **t** placed for the king's 1Kg 2:19
seated me on the **t** of my father 1Kg 2:24
dynasty, and his **t**, there will 1Kg 2:33
and David's **t** will remain 1Kg 2:45
him a son to sit on his **t**, 1Kg 3:6
son on your **t** in your place, 1Kg 5:5
the Hall of the **T** where he would 1Kg 7:7
and I sit on the **t** of Israel, 1Kg 8:20
before Me on the **t** of Israel, 1Kg 8:25
your royal **t** over Israel forever 1Kg 9:5
have a man on the **t** of Israel. 1Kg 9:5
and put you on the **t** of Israel, 1Kg 10:9
a large ivory **t** and overlaid it 1Kg 10:18
The **t** had six steps; there was a 1Kg 10:19
top at the back of the **t**, 1Kg 10:19
soon as he was seated on his **t**, 1Kg 16:11
were each sitting on his own **t**. 1Kg 22:10
I saw the LORD sitting on His **t**, 1Kg 22:19
set him on his father's **t**, 2Kg 10:3
will sit on the **t** of Israel." 2Kg 10:30
Joash sat on the **t** of the kings. 2Kg 11:19
and Jeroboam sat on his **t**. 2Kg 13:13
will sit on the **t** of Israel." 2Kg 15:12
him and set his **t** over the 2Kg 25:28
I will establish his **t** forever. 1Ch 17:12
and his **t** will be established 1Ch 17:14
establish the **t** of his kingdom 1Ch 22:10
to sit on the **t** of the LORD's 1Ch 28:5
on the LORD's **t** as king in place 1Ch 29:23
and I sit on the **t** of Israel, 2Ch 6:10
before Me on the **t** of Israel, 2Ch 6:16

I will establish your royal **t**, 2Ch 7:18
have a man on the **t** of Israel. 2Ch 7:18
and put you on his **t** as king for 2Ch 9:8
a large ivory **t** and overlaid it 2Ch 9:17
The **t** had six steps; there was a 2Ch 9:18
covered in gold for the **t**, 2Ch 9:18
were each sitting on his own **t**. 2Ch 18:9
I saw the LORD sitting on His **t**, 2Ch 18:18
king on the **t** of the kingdom. 2Ch 23:20
from his royal **t** in the fortress Est 1:2
on his royal **t** in the royal Est 5:1
so that I could go to His **t**. Jb 23:3
He obscures the view of ⌊His⌋ **t**, Jb 26:9
seated on Your **t** as a righteous Ps 9:4
established His **t** for judgment. Ps 9:7
the LORD's **t** is in heaven. Ps 11:4
t, God, is forever and ever; Ps 45:6
God is seated on His holy **t**. Ps 47:8
and build up your **t** for all Ps 89:4
are the foundation of Your **t**; Ps 89:14
his **t** as long as heaven lasts. Ps 89:29
his **t** like the sun before Me, Ps 89:36
cease and have overturned his **t**. Ps 89:44
Your **t** has been established from Ps 93:2
Can a corrupt **t**—one that Ps 94:20
are the foundation of His **t**. Ps 97:2
has established His **t** in heaven, Ps 103:19
of your descendants on your **t**. Ps 132:11
sons will also sit on your **t**, Ps 132:12
since a **t** is established through Pr 16:12
sitting on a **t** to judge sifts Pr 20:8
loyalty he maintains his **t**. Pr 20:28
and his **t** will be established in Pr 25:5
his **t** will be established Pr 29:14
seated on a high and lofty **t**, Is 6:1
reign on the **t** of David and over Is 9:7
will set up my **t** above the stars Is 14:13
tent of David a **t** will be Is 16:5
will sit on the **t** forever. Is 16:5
He will be a **t** of honor for his Is 22:23
Sit on the ground without a **t**, Is 47:1
Heaven is My **t**, and earth is My Is 66:1
set up his **t** at the entrance Jr 1:15
called, The LORD's **T**, and all Jr 3:17
who reign for David on his **t**, Jr 13:13
Don't disdain Your glorious **t**. Jr 14:21
A **t** of glory on high from the Jr 17:12
They will sit on the **t** of David, Jr 17:25
you who sit on the **t** of David— Jr 22:2
on David's **t** will enter through Jr 22:4
in sitting on the **t** of David or Jr 22:30
on David's **t** and concerning all Jr 29:16
sitting on the **t** of the house Jr 33:17
have a son reigning on his **t**, Jr 33:21
have no one to sit on David's **t**, Jr 36:30
will place his **t** on these stones Jr 43:10
I will set My **t** in Elam, and I Jr 49:38
him and set his **t** above the Jr 52:32
Your **t** endures from generation Lm 5:19
The shape of a **t** with the Ezk 1:26
of a human on the **t** high above. Ezk 1:26
the shape of a **t** that appeared Ezk 10:1
the king who put him on the **t**, Ezk 17:16
the place of My **t** and the place Ezk 43:7
from his royal **t** and his glory Dn 5:20
His **t** was flaming fire; Dn 7:9
in intrigue, will come to the **t**. Dn 8:23
got up from his **t**, took off his Jnh 3:6
and will sit on His **t** and rule. Zch 6:13
will also be a priest on His **t**, Zch 6:13
heaven, because it is God's **t**; Mt 5:34
of Man sits on His glorious **t**, Mt 19:28
oath by God's **t** and by Him who Mt 23:22
will sit on the **t** of His glory. Mt 25:31
give Him the **t** of His father Lk 1:32
one of his descendants on his **t**. Ac 2:30
Heaven is My **t**, and earth My Ac 7:49
royal robes and seated on the **t**, Ac 12:21
Your **t**, O God, is forever and Heb 1:8
us approach the **t** of grace with Heb 4:16
hand of the **t** of the Majesty Heb 8:1
at the right hand of God's **t**. Heb 12:2
the seven spirits before His **t**; Rv 1:4
you live—where Satan's **t** is! Rv 2:13
right to sit with Me on My **t**, Rv 3:21
down with My Father on His **t**. Rv 3:21
and there in heaven a **t** was set. Rv 4:2
One was seated on the **t**, Rv 4:2
an emerald surrounded the **t**. Rv 4:3
Around that **t** were 24 thrones, Rv 4:4
From the **t** came flashes of Rv 4:5
before the **t** were seven fiery Rv 4:5
Also before the **t** was something Rv 4:6
around the **t** were four living Rv 4:6
to the One seated on the **t**, Rv 4:9
before the One seated on the **t**, Rv 4:10
cast their crowns before the **t**, Rv 4:10
seated on the **t** a scroll with Rv 5:1
between the **t** and the four Rv 5:6
hand of the One seated on the **t**. Rv 5:7
of many angels around the **t**, Rv 5:11
to the One seated on the **t**, Rv 5:13
One seated on the **t** and from the Rv 6:16
before the **t** and before the Lamb Rv 7:9
seated on the **t**, and to the Lamb Rv 7:10
the angels stood around the **t**, Rv 7:11
faces before the **t** and worshiped Rv 7:11
they are before the **t** of God, Rv 7:15
seated on the **t** will shelter Rv 7:15
center of the **t** will shepherd Rv 7:17
gold altar in front of the **t**. Rv 8:3
caught up to God and to His **t**. Rv 12:5
him his power, his **t**, and great Rv 13:2
song before the **t** and before the Rv 14:3
his bowl on the **t** of the beast, Rv 16:10
from the **t**, saying, "It is Rv 16:17
who is seated on the **t**, saying: Rv 19:4
A voice came from the **t**, saying: Rv 19:5
a great white **t** and One seated Rv 20:11
before the **t**, and books were Rv 20:12
I heard a loud voice from the **t**: Rv 21:3
the One seated on the **t** said, Rv 21:5
flowing from the **t** of God and of Rv 22:1
t of God and of the Lamb will Rv 22:3

THRONES *(16)*

throne over the **t** of the kings 2Kg 25:28
t for judgment are placed, Ps 122:5
are placed, **t** of the house Ps 122:5
the nations rise from their **t**. Is 14:9
above the **t** of the kings who Jr 52:32
sea will descend from their **t**, Ezk 26:16
I kept watching, **t** were set in Dn 7:9
overturn royal **t** and destroy Hg 2:22
Me will also sit on 12 **t**, Mt 19:28
mighty from their **t** and exalted Lk 1:52
you will sit on **t** judging the 12 Lk 22:30
whether **t** or dominions or rulers Col 1:16
Around that throne were 24 **t**, Rv 4:4
and on the **t** sat 24 elders Rv 4:4
seated before God on their **t**, Rv 11:16
Then I saw **t**, and people seated Rv 20:4

THROUGH *(658)*

(See pp. xi-xii.)

THROUGHOUT *(189)*

(See pp. xi-xii.)

THROW *(72)*

let's kill him and **t** him into Gn 37:20
T him into this pit in the Gn 37:22
You must **t** every son born to the Ex 1:22
He said, "**T** it on the ground. Ex 4:3
your staff and **t** it down before Ex 7:9
and Moses is to **t** it toward Ex 9:8
in the field; **t** it to the dogs. Ex 22:31
feel terror and **t** into confusion Ex 23:27
and **t** it on the east side of the Lv 1:16
and **t** ⌊them⌋ onto the fire where Nm 19:6
to you and **t** them into great Dt 7:23
T this woman out and bolt the 2Sm 13:17
weak and weary, **t** him into a 2Sm 17:2
him up and **t** him on the plot 2Kg 9:25
him up and **t** him on the plot 2Kg 9:26
and he said, "**T** her down!" 2Kg 9:33
could ⌊**t**⌋ stones ⌊with a sling⌋ 1Ch 12:2
Jerusalem and **t** it into Neh 4:8
are determined to **t** ⌊me⌋ to the Ps 17:11
on Edom I **t** My sandal. Ps 60:8
on Edom I **t** My sandal. Ps 108:9
T in your lot with us, and we'll Pr 1:14
a time to **t** stones and a time to Ec 3:5
to keep and a time to **t** away; Ec 3:6
day people will **t** their silver Is 2:20
You will **t** them away like Is 30:22
your sacred vow and **t** it away. Jr 7:29
your cedars and **t** them into the Jr 22:7
I will **t** you away"—⌊this is⌋ Jr 23:33
forget you and **t** away from My Jr 23:39
scribe's knife and **t** the columns Jr 36:23
a stone to it and **t** it into the Jr 51:63
more of them, **t** them into the Ezk 5:4
will **t** down your slain in front Ezk 6:4
They will **t** their silver into Ezk 7:19
T off all the transgressions you Ezk 18:31
Each of you must **t** away the Ezk 20:7
Then they will **t** your stones, Ezk 26:12
They **t** dust on their heads; Ezk 27:30
the priests will **t** salt on them Ezk 43:24
and Abednego and **t** them into the Dn 3:20
Didn't we **t** three men, bound, Dn 3:24
The horn will **t** truth to the Dn 8:12
into wormwood **t** righteousness to Am 5:7
Pick me up and **t** me into the sea Jnh 1:12
I will **t** filth on you and treat Nah 3:6
"**T** it to the potter," the LORD Zch 11:13
the Son of God, **t** Yourself down. Mt 4:6
gouge it out and **t** it away. Mt 5:29
sin, cut it off and **t** it away. Mt 5:30
will **t** them into the blazing Mt 13:42
and **t** them into the blazing Mt 13:50
bread and **t** it to their dogs." Mt 15:26
cut it off and **t** it away. Mt 18:8
gouge it out and **t** it away. Mt 18:9
and **t** him into the outer Mt 22:13
t this good-for-nothing slave Mt 25:30
bread and **t** it to the dogs." Mk 7:27
and began to **t** out those buying Mk 11:15
t Yourself down from here. Lk 4:9
has authority to **t** ⌊people⌋ into Lk 12:5
the bailiff **t** you into prison Lk 12:58
pile; they **t** it out. Anyone Lk 14:35
began to **t** out those who were Lk 19:45
from them about a stone's **t**, Lk 22:41
the first to **t** a stone at her. Jn 8:7
picked up stones to **t** at Him. Jn 8:59
They gather them, **t** them into Jn 15:6
T out the slave and her son, Gl 4:30
So don't **t** away your confidence, Heb 10:35
Devil is about to **t** some of you Rv 2:10
I will **t** her into a sickbed, Rv 2:22

THROWING *(4)*

And **t** him down before them, Lk 4:35
and after **t** their robes on the Lk 19:35
their robes and **t** dust into the Ac 22:23
the ship by **t** the grain Ac 27:38

THROWN *(77)*

and had him **t** into prison, Gn 39:20
He has **t** the horse and its rider Ex 15:1
He has **t** the horse and its rider Ex 15:21
pulled out and **t** into an unclean Lv 14:40
the trees and **t** into the cave Jos 10:27
head will be **t** over the wall to 2Sm 20:21
His corpse was **t** on the road, 1Kg 13:24
who saw the corpse **t** on the road 1Kg 13:25
the man of God **t** on the road 1Kg 13:28
the Arameans had **t** off in their 2Kg 7:15
They have **t** their gods into the 2Kg 19:18
they have been **t** down and cannot Ps 36:12
picked me up and **t** me aside. Ps 102:10
Let them be **t** into the fire, Ps 140:10
rulers will be **t** off the sides Ps 141:6
The wicked are **t** down by their Pr 14:32
But you are **t** out without a Is 14:19
brought down, **t** to the ground, Is 25:12
Their slain will be **t** out, Is 34:3
and have **t** their gods into the Is 37:19
You have **t** all my sins behind Is 38:17
to will be **t** into the streets Jr 14:16
dragged off and **t** outside the Jr 22:19
corpse will be **t** out ⌊to be Jr 36:30
Ishmael had **t** all the corpses Jr 41:9
She has **t** up her hands ⌊in Jr 50:15
has **t** down Israel's glory from Lm 2:1
They have **t** dust on their heads Lm 2:10
But you were **t** out into the open Ezk 16:5
in fury, **t** to the ground, Ezk 19:12
The mountains will be **t** down, Ezk 38:20
immediately be **t** into a furnace Dn 3:6
worship will be **t** into a furnace Dn 3:11
immediately be **t** into a furnace Dn 3:15
tied up and **t** into the furnace Dn 3:21
will be **t** into the lions' den. Dn 6:7
will be **t** into the lions' den?" Dn 6:12
brought and **t** into the lions' Dn 6:24
off its bark and **t** it away; Jl 1:7

Many dead bodies, **t** everywhere! Am 8:3
be cut down and **t** into the fire. Mt 3:10
but to be **t** out and trampled Mt 5:13
and you will be **t** into prison. Mt 5:25
whole body to be **t** into hell. Mt 5:29
here today and **t** into the Mt 6:30
is cut down and **t** into the fire. Mt 7:19
kingdom will be **t** into the outer Mt 8:12
like a large net **t** into the sea. Mt 13:47
two feet and be **t** into the Mt 18:8
two eyes and be **t** into hellfire! Mt 18:9
lifted up and **t** into the sea,' Mt 21:21
that will not be **t** down!" Mt 24:2
times it has **t** him into fire Mk 9:22
neck and he were **t** into the sea. Mk 9:42
two feet and be **t** into hell— Mk 9:45
two eyes and be **t** into hell, Mk 9:47
lifted up and **t** into the sea,' Mk 11:23
that will not be **t** down!" Mk 13:2
cut down and **t** into the fire." Lk 3:9
today and is **t** into the furnace Lk 12:28
of God but yourselves **t** out. Lk 13:28
neck and he were **t** into the sea Lk 17:2
that will not be **t** down!" Lk 21:6
He had been **t** into prison for a Lk 23:19
who had been **t** into prison for Lk 23:25
had not yet been **t** into prison. Jn 3:24
that they had **t** the man out, Jn 9:35
he is **t** aside like a branch and Jn 15:6
So the great dragon was **t** out— Rv 12:9
was **t** to earth, and his angels Rv 12:9
of our brothers has been **t** out: Rv 12:10
saw that he had been **t** to earth, Rv 12:13
city will be **t** down violently Rv 18:21
Both of them were **t** alive into Rv 19:20
deceived them was **t** into the Rv 20:10
and Hades were **t** into the lake Rv 20:14
book of life was **t** into the lake Rv 20:15

THROWS *(10)*
a person or **t** ⌊an object⌋ at him Nm 35:20
hostility or **t** any object at him Nm 35:22
He passes by and **t** ⌊someone⌋ in Jb 11:10
He **t** me into the hands of the Jb 16:11
He **t** me into the mud, and I have Jb 30:19
He **t** His hailstones like crumbs. Ps 147:17
a madman who **t** flaming darts Pr 26:18
the ground; He **t** it to the dust. Is 26:5
seizes him, it **t** him down, and Mk 9:18
and it **t** him into convulsions Lk 9:39

THRUST *(6)*
his armor-bearer **t** him through, Jdg 9:54
Let me **t** the spear through him 1Sm 26:8
by the head and ⌊**t**⌋ his sword 2Sm 2:16
in his hand and **t** them into 2Sm 18:14
My love **t** his hand through the Sg 5:4
for the LORD has **t** him down. Jr 46:15

THUMB *(5)*
on the **t** of his right hand, Lv 8:23
on the **t** of his right hand, Lv 14:14
on the **t** of his right hand, Lv 14:17
on the **t** of his right hand, Lv 14:25
on the **t** of his right hand, Lv 14:28

THUMBS *(4)*
on the **t** of their right hands, Ex 29:20
on the **t** of their right hands, Lv 8:24
and cut off his **t** and big toes. Jdg 1:6
with their **t** and big toes cut Jdg 1:7

THUMMIM *(5)*
the Urim and **T** in the Ex 28:30
placed the Urim and **T** into the Lv 8:8
Your **T** and Urim belong to Your Dt 33:8
could consult the Urim and **T**. Ezr 2:63
could consult the Urim and **T**. Neh 7:65

THUNDER *(24)*
and the LORD sent **t** and hail. Ex 9:23
been enough of God's **t** and hail. Ex 9:28
The **t** will cease, and there will Ex 9:29
Then the **t** and hail ceased, Ex 9:33
rain, hail, and **t** had ceased, he Ex 9:34
there was **t** and lightning, Ex 19:16
and God answered him in the **t**. Ex 19:19
witnessed the **t** and lightning, Ex 20:18
He will **t** in the heavens against 1Sm 2:10
and He will send **t** and rain, 1Sm 12:17
day the LORD sent **t** and rain. 1Sm 12:18
Who can understand His mighty **t**? Jb 26:14
or how the **t** roars from God's Jb 36:29
The **t** declares His presence; Jb 36:33
Can you **t** with a voice like His? Jb 40:9
The sound of Your **t** was in the Ps 77:18
sound of Your **t** they hurried Ps 104:7
by the LORD of Hosts with **t**, Is 29:6
that is, "Sons of **T**"); Mk 3:17
heard it and said it was **t**. Jn 12:29
of lightning, rumblings, and **t**. Rv 4:5
say with a voice like **t**, Rv 6:1
and like the rumbling of loud **t**. Rv 14:2
and like the rumbling of loud **t**, Rv 19:6

THUNDERCLOUD *(1)*
I answered you from the **t**. Ps 81:7

THUNDERED *(4)*
The LORD **t** loudly against the 1Sm 7:10
The LORD **t** from heaven; 2Sm 22:14
The LORD **t** from heaven; Ps 18:13
The storm clouds **t**; Ps 77:17

THUNDEROUS *(2)*
Just listen to His **t** voice and Jb 37:2
The peoples flee at the **t** noise; Is 33:3

THUNDERS *(12)*
God **t** with His majestic voice. Jb 37:4
t marvelously with His voice; Jb 37:5
The God of glory **t**—the LORD, Ps 29:3
He **t** with His powerful voice! Ps 68:33
When He **t**, the waters in the Jr 10:13
When He **t**, the waters in the Jr 51:16
there were **t**, rumblings, Rv 8:5
the seven **t** spoke with their Rv 10:3
And when the seven **t** spoke, Rv 10:4
Seal up what the seven **t** said, Rv 10:4
rumblings, **t**, an earthquake, Rv 11:19
lightnings, rumblings, and **t**. Rv 16:18

THUNDERSTORM *(1)*
will advance, coming like a **t**; Ezk 38:9

THUS *(3)*
T, I became great and surpassed Ec 2:9
T He will repay according to Is 59:18
T Judah went into exile from its Jr 52:27

THWARTED *(1)*
and no plan of Yours can be **t**. Jb 42:2

THWARTS *(1)*
He **t** the plans of the peoples. Ps 33:10

THYATIRA *(4)*
purple cloth from the city of **T**, Ac 16:14
Smyrna, Pergamum, **T**, Sardis, Rv 1:11
angel of the church in **T** write: Rv 2:18
I say to the rest of you in **T**, Rv 2:24

TIARA *(1)*
and a beautiful **t** on your head. Ezk 16:12

TIBERIAS *(3)*
the Sea of Galilee (or **T**). Jn 6:1
Some boats from **T** came near the Jn 6:23
His disciples by the Sea of **T**. Jn 21:1

TIBERIUS *(1)*
year of the reign of **T** Caesar, Lk 3:1

TIBHATH *(1)*
(AKA BETAH)
From **T** and Cun, Hadadezer's 1Ch 18:8

TIBNI *(3)*
people followed **T** son of Ginath, 1Kg 16:21
who followed **T** son of Ginath. 1Kg 16:22
So **T** died and Omri became king. 1Kg 16:22

TIDAL *(2)*
of Elam, and **T** king of Goiim Gn 14:1
king of Elam, **T** king of Goiim, Gn 14:9

TIE *(22)*
are to **t** the breastpiece Ex 28:28
and **t** sashes around both Aaron Ex 29:9
He must **t** a linen sash ⌊around Lv 16:4
you **t** this scarlet cord to the Jos 2:18
we will **t** you up securely and Jdg 15:13
overpower him, **t** him up, and Jdg 16:5
could ⌊someone⌋ **t** you up and Jdg 16:6
If they **t** me up with seven fresh Jdg 16:7
If they **t** me up with new ropes Jdg 16:11
found there and **t** it up in bags. 2Kg 12:10
with a hook or **t** his tongue down Jb 41:1
T them around your neck; Pr 3:3
t them around your neck. Pr 6:21
T them to your fingers; write Pr 7:3
your robe and **t** your sash around Is 22:21
t a stone to it and throw it Jr 51:63
in his army to **t** up Shadrach, Dn 3:20
first and **t** them in bundles Mt 13:30
the attendants, '**T** him up hand Mt 22:13
They **t** up heavy loads that are Mt 23:4
you would **t** your belt and walk Jn 21:18
else will **t** you and carry you Jn 21:18

TIED *(21)*
took it and **t** a scarlet ⌊thread Gn 38:28
scarlet ⌊thread⌋ **t** to his hand, Gn 38:30
Then they **t** the breastpiece from Ex 39:21
a lid **t** on it is unclean. Nm 19:15
she **t** the scarlet cord to the Jos 2:21
So they **t** him up with two new Jdg 15:13
and she **t** him up with them. Jdg 16:8
tell me how you can be **t** up?" Jdg 16:10
took new ropes, **t** him up with Jdg 16:12
Tell me how you can be **t** up." Jdg 16:13
were **t** up and thrown into the Dn 3:21
four men, not **t**, walking around Dn 3:25
you will find a donkey **t** there, Mt 21:2
find a young donkey **t** there, Mk 11:2
in the street, **t** by a door. Mk 11:4
find a young donkey **t** there, Lk 19:30
a towel, and **t** it around Himself Jn 13:4
with the towel **t** around Him. Jn 13:5
arrested Jesus and **t** Him up. Jn 18:12
t his outer garment around him Jn 21:7
took Paul's belt, **t** his own feet Ac 21:11

TIERS *(3)*
facing each other in three **t**. 1Kg 7:4
facing each other in three **t**. 1Kg 7:5
gallery by gallery in three **t**. Ezk 42:3

TIES *(4)*
He **t** his donkey to a vine, Gn 49:11
on by kings and **t** a cloth around Jb 12:18
unless he first **t** up the strong Mt 12:29
unless he first **t** up the strong Mk 3:27

TIGHTFISTED *(1)*
hardhearted or **t** toward your Dt 15:7

TIGHTLY *(1)*
grab the robe of a Jewish man **t**, Zch 8:23

TIGLATH-PILESER *(6)*
(AKA PUL)
T king of Assyria came and 2Kg 15:29
messengers to **T** king of Assyria, 2Kg 16:7
to meet **T** king of Assyria 2Kg 16:10
and **T** king of Assyria took him 1Ch 5:6
of Pul (that is, **T**) king of 1Ch 5:26
Then **T** king of Assyria came 2Ch 28:20

TIGRIS *(2)*
of the third river is the **T**, Gn 2:14
bank of the great river, the **T**, Dn 10:4

TIKVAH *(2)*
(AKA TOKHATH)
Shallum son of **T**, son of Harhas, 2Kg 22:14
Jahzeiah son of **T** opposed this, Ezr 10:15

TILES *(1)*
the roof **t** into the middle Lk 5:19

TILL *(1)*
that nation will **t** it and reside Jr 27:11

TILLED *(3)*
to a place not **t** or sown, and Dt 21:4
that were once **t** with a hoe, Is 7:25
and you will be **t** and sown. Ezk 36:9

TILLER *(1)*
I am a **t** of the soil, for a man Zch 13:5

TILLING *(1)*
worked in the fields **t** the soil. 1Ch 27:26

TILON *(1)*
Amnon, Rinnah, Ben-hanan, and **T**. 1Ch 4:20

TILT *(1)*
Or who can **t** the water jars of Jb 38:37

TILTED *(1)*
its mouth **t** from the north ⌊to Jr 1:13

TIMAEUS *(1)*
the son of **T**), a blind beggar, Mk 10:46

TIMBER *(11)*
with his neighbor to cut **t**, Dt 19:5
knows how to cut **t** like the 1Kg 5:6
the cedar and cypress **t**. 1Kg 5:8
cedar and cypress **t** he wanted, 1Kg 5:10
and prepared the **t** and stone for 1Kg 5:18
use it⌋ to buy **t** and quarried 2Kg 12:12
and masons to buy **t** and quarried 2Kg 22:6

have also provided **t** and stone, 1Ch 22:14
of cut stones and one of **t**. Ezr 6:4
he will give me **t** to rebuild the Neh 2:8
throw your stones, **t**, and soil Ezk 26:12

TIMBERS *(4)*

Ramah and the **t** Baasha had built 1Kg 15:22
Ramah and the **t** Baasha had built 2Ch 16:6
to buy quarried stone and **t**— 2Ch 34:11
it along with its **t** and stones." Zch 5:4

TIME *(723)*

creation at the **t** that the LORD Gn 2:4
garden at the **t** of the evening Gn 3:8
the course of **t** Cain presented Gn 4:3
that **t** people began to call on Gn 4:26
was nothing but evil all the **t**, Gn 6:5
At one **t** the whole earth had the Gn 11:1
At that **t** the Canaanites were in Gn 12:6
At that **t** the Canaanites and the Gn 13:7
to you at this **t** next year." Gn 17:21
back to you in about a year's **t**, Gn 18:10
the appointed **t** I will come back Gn 18:14
and I will speak one more **t**. Gn 18:32
the appointed **t** God had told him Gn 21:2
At that **t** Abimelech, with Phicol Gn 21:22
Abraham a second **t** from heaven Gn 22:15
⌊This was⌋ the **t** when the women Gn 24:11
When her **t** came to give birth, Gn 25:24
had occurred in Abraham's **t**. Gn 26:1
Isaac had been there for some **t**, Gn 26:8
It's not **t** for the animals to be Gn 29:7
my wife, for my **t** is completed. Gn 29:21
"This **t** I will praise the LORD." Gn 29:35
This **t** my husband will honor me Gn 30:20
dream, and this **t** the sun, moon, Gn 37:9
that **t** Judah left his brothers Gn 38:1
After a long **t** Judah's wife, Gn 38:12
When the **t** came for her to give Gn 38:27
From the **t** that he put him in Gn 39:5
After some **t** his master's wife Gn 39:7
they were in custody for some **t**. Gn 40:4
asleep and dreamed a second **t**: Gn 41:5
had not wasted **t**, we could have Gn 43:10
in our bags the first **t**. Gn 43:18
here the first **t** only to buy Gn 43:20
him, and wept for a long **t**. Gn 46:29
When the **t** drew near for him to Gn 47:29
Some **t** after this, Joseph was Gn 48:1
a long **t**, the king of Egypt Ex 2:23
At that **t** she said, "You are a Ex 4:26
heart this **t** also and did not Ex 8:32
the LORD set a **t**, saying, Ex 9:5
at this **t** I will rain down Ex 9:18
have sinned this **t**," he said to Ex 9:27
saw since the **t** they occupied Ex 10:6
The **t** that the Israelites lived Ex 12:40
at its appointed **t** from year to Ex 13:10
wonders⌋ at the **t** the Egyptians Ex 18:11
his lost work **t** and provide for Ex 21:19
at the appointed **t** in the month Ex 23:15
was made at the ⌊**t** of⌋ their Ex 29:33
at the appointed **t** in the month Ex 34:18
until the **t** your days of Lv 8:33
it is not the **t** of her Lv 15:25
meeting from the **t** he enters to Lv 16:17
that the **t** period of the seven Lv 25:8
calculate ⌊the **t**⌋ from the year Lv 25:50
give you rain at the right **t**, Lv 26:4
will continue until sowing **t**; Lv 26:5
during the **t** it lies desolate Lv 26:34
At that **t** the land will rest and Lv 26:34
Moses at the **t** the LORD spoke Nm 3:1
At the **t** I struck down every Nm 3:13
hair throughout the **t** of his vow Nm 6:5
be holy until the **t** is completed Nm 6:5
body during the **t** he consecrates Nm 6:6
during the **t** of consecration Nm 6:8
rededicate his **t** of consecration Nm 6:12
On the day his **t** of consecration Nm 6:13
the Passover at its appointed **t**. Nm 9:2
at its appointed **t** on the Nm 9:3
its appointed **t** with the ⌊other Nm 9:7
offering at its appointed **t**. Nm 9:13
sound short blasts a second **t**, Nm 10:6
out for the first **t** according to Nm 10:13
was Moab's king at that **t**, Nm 22:4
at its appointed **t** My offering Nm 28:2
At that **t** the Canaanite king of Nm 33:40
I said to you at that **t**: Dt 1:9
commanded your judges at that **t**: Dt 1:16
At that **t** I commanded you about Dt 1:18
The **t** we spent traveling from Dt 2:14
At that **t** we captured all his Dt 2:34
all his cities at that **t**. Dt 3:4
At that **t** we took the land from Dt 3:8
At that **t** we took possession of Dt 3:12
I commanded you at that **t**: Dt 3:18
I commanded Joshua at that **t**: Dt 3:21
At that **t** I begged the LORD: Dt 3:23
At that **t** the LORD commanded me Dt 4:14
have been in the land a long **t**, Dt 4:25
God is giving you for all **t**." Dt 4:40
At that **t** I was standing between Dt 5:5
like the first **t** in the presence Dt 9:18
prayed for Aaron at that **t** also. Dt 9:20
The LORD said to me at that **t**, Dt 10:1
At that **t** the LORD set apart the Dt 10:8
and 40 nights like the first **t**. Dt 10:10
sets at the ⌊same⌋ **t** ⌊of day⌋ Dt 16:6
weeks from the **t** the sickle is Dt 16:9
judge who presides at that **t**. Dt 17:9
judges in authority at the **t**. Dt 19:17
siege to a city for a long **t**, Dt 20:19
priest who is serving at that **t**, Dt 26:3
At the **t** you cross the Jordan Dt 27:2
the appointed **t** in the year of Dt 31:10
The **t** of your death is now Dt 31:14
In **t** their foot will slip, Dt 32:35
At that **t** the LORD said to Jos 5:2
of war, circling the city one **t**. Jos 6:3
your mouth until the **t** I say, Jos 6:10
the seventh **t**, the priests blew Jos 6:16
At that **t** Joshua imposed this Jos 6:26
us as they did the first **t**, Jos 8:5
At that **t** Joshua built an altar Jos 8:30
At that **t** Horam king of Gezer Jos 10:33
for at this **t** tomorrow I will Jos 11:6
At that **t** Joshua turned back, Jos 11:10
all these kings for a long **t**. Jos 11:18
At that **t** Joshua proceeded to Jos 11:21
high priest serving at that **t**. Jos 20:6
once this whole **t** but have Jos 22:3
long **t** after the LORD had given Jos 23:1
in the wilderness a long **t**. Jos 24:7
At the same **t** the Benjaminites Jdg 1:21
that **t** Manasseh failed to take Jdg 1:27
that **t** Ephraim failed to drive Jdg 1:29
At that **t** they struck down about Jdg 3:29
was judging Israel at that **t**. Jdg 4:4
let me speak one more **t**. Jdg 6:39
you in the **t** of your oppression Jdg 10:14
Some **t** later, the Ammonites Jdg 11:4
you take them back at that **t**? Jdg 11:26
At that **t**, 42,000 from Ephraim Jdg 12:6
At that **t**, the Philistines were Jdg 14:4
After some **t**, when he returned Jdg 14:8
This **t** I won't be responsible Jdg 15:3
Some **t** later, he fell in love Jdg 16:4
is the third **t** you have mocked Jdg 16:15
Come one more **t**, for he has told Jdg 16:18
Up to that **t** no territory had Jdg 18:1
tribe until the **t** of the exile Jdg 18:30
Benjamin returned at that **t**, Jdg 21:14
that **t**, each of the Israelites Jdg 21:24
During the **t** of the judges, Ru 1:1
After some **t**, Hannah conceived 1Sm 1:20
My anointed one for all **t**. 1Sm 2:35
for the third **t**, the LORD called 1Sm 3:8
At that **t** Eli was 98 years old, 1Sm 4:15
⌊This **t**⌋, both Dagon's head and 1Sm 5:4
T went by until 20 years had 1Sm 7:2
At this **t** tomorrow I will send 1Sm 9:16
solemn event at the **t** I said, 1Sm 9:24
by the **t** the sun is hot. 1Sm 11:9
the appointed **t** that Samuel had 1Sm 13:8
It was at this **t** that the LORD 1Sm 13:13
with the Israelites at that **t**. 1Sm 14:18
it was the first **t** he had built 1Sm 14:35
When it was **t** to give Saul's 1Sm 18:19
Saul said to David a second **t**, 1Sm 18:21
t the Philistine commanders 1Sm 18:30
my father by this **t** tomorrow or 1Sm 20:12
with him the whole **t** David was 1Sm 22:4
At that **t** Saul was in Gibeah, 1Sm 22:6
today the first **t** I inquired of 1Sm 22:15
missing the whole **t** they were in 1Sm 25:7
the whole **t** we were living 1Sm 25:15
the entire **t** we were herding the 1Sm 25:16
The **t** that David stayed in the 1Sm 27:7
during the whole **t** he stayed 1Sm 27:11
At that **t**, the Philistines 1Sm 28:1
By this **t** Samuel had died, 1Sm 28:3
me a considerable period of **t**. 1Sm 29:3
Some **t** later, David inquired of 2Sm 2:1
The length of **t** that David was 2Sm 2:11
All this **t** I've been loyal to 2Sm 3:8
From the **t** I brought the 2Sm 7:6
When your **t** comes and you rest 2Sm 7:12
Some **t** later the king of the 2Sm 10:1
When the **t** of mourning ended, 2Sm 11:27
Some **t** passed. David's son 2Sm 13:1
for the dead for a long **t**. 2Sm 14:2
again, a second **t**, but he still 2Sm 14:29
has given this **t** is not good." 2Sm 17:7
Mahanaim by the **t** Absalom 2Sm 17:24
not going to waste **t** with you!" 2Sm 18:14
longer than the **t** it allotted him. 2Sm 20:5
that **t** Sibbecai the Hushathite 2Sm 21:18
800 ⌊men⌋ he killed at one **t**. 2Sm 23:8
down at harvest **t** and came to 2Sm 23:13
At that **t** David was in the 2Sm 23:14
morning until the appointed **t**, 2Sm 24:15
As the **t** approached for David to 1Kg 2:1
them ⌊in a **t**⌋ of peace to avenge 1Kg 2:5
The ⌊length of⌋ **t** David reigned 1Kg 2:11
lived in Jerusalem for a long **t**. 1Kg 2:38
because until that **t** a temple 1Kg 3:2
At that **t** Solomon assembled the 1Kg 8:1
at that **t** in the presence 1Kg 8:65
Solomon a second **t** just as He 1Kg 9:2
as nothing in Solomon's **t**, 1Kg 10:21
At that **t**, Solomon built a high 1Kg 11:7
At the **t** Hadad was a small boy. 1Kg 11:17
that **t**, the prophet Ahijah 1Kg 11:29
At that **t** Abijah son of Jeroboam 1Kg 14:1
At that **t** the people of Israel 1Kg 16:21
After a long **t**, the word of the 1Kg 18:1
Then he said, "A second **t**!" 1Kg 18:34
and they did it a second **t**. 1Kg 18:34
And then he said, "A third **t**!" 1Kg 18:34
and they did it a third **t**. 1Kg 18:34
At the **t** for offering the 1Kg 18:36
On the seventh **t**, he reported, 1Kg 18:44
one of them by this **t** tomorrow!" 1Kg 19:2
a second **t** and touched him. 1Kg 19:7
But at this **t** tomorrow I will 1Kg 20:6
of your servant the first **t**, 1Kg 20:9
t passed after these events. 1Kg 21:1
At that **t**, Ahaziah son of Ahab 1Kg 22:49
but this **t** let my life be 2Kg 1:14
The **t** had come for the LORD to 2Kg 2:1
Samaria at that **t** and mobilized 2Kg 3:6
About the **t** for the grain 2Kg 3:20
At this **t** next year you will 2Kg 4:16
son at the same **t** the following 2Kg 4:17
Is it a **t** to accept money and 2Kg 5:26
Some **t** later, King Ben-hadad of 2Kg 6:24
'About this **t** tomorrow at the 2Kg 7:1
About this **t** tomorrow 12 quarts 2Kg 7:18
Libnah also rebelled at that **t**. 2Kg 8:22
sons at this **t** tomorrow at 2Kg 10:6
Throughout the **t** Jehoiada the 2Kg 12:2
At that **t** Hazael king of Aram 2Kg 12:17
At that **t**, ⌊starting⌋ from 2Kg 15:16
At that **t** Rezin king of Aram 2Kg 16:6
the **t** King Ahaz came back from 2Kg 16:11
incense to it up to that **t**. 2Kg 18:4
At that **t** Hezekiah stripped ⌊the 2Kg 18:16
that **t** Merodach-baladan son of 2Kg 20:12
'The **t** will certainly come when 2Kg 20:17
kept from the **t** of the judges 2Kg 23:22
through the entire **t** of the 2Kg 23:22
At that **t** the servants of 2Kg 24:10
father Ephraim mourned a long **t**, 1Ch 7:22
300 and killed them at one **t**. 1Ch 11:11
At that **t** David was in the 1Ch 11:16
that **t**, men came day after day 1Ch 12:22
up to that **t** the majority of the 1Ch 12:29
were not ⌊with⌋ us the first **t**, 1Ch 15:13
for the first **t** that thanks be 1Ch 16:7
From the **t** I brought Israel out 1Ch 17:5
your **t** comes to be with your 1Ch 17:11
Some **t** later, King Nahash of the 1Ch 19:1
that **t** Sibbecai the Hushathite 1Ch 20:4
At that **t**, when David saw that 1Ch 21:28

At that **t** the tabernacle of the 1Ch 21:29
for a second **t**, they made 1Ch 29:22
At that **t** Solomon assembled at 2Ch 5:2
at that **t** for seven days. 2Ch 7:8
At that **t** Solomon offered burnt 2Ch 8:12
At that **t** Solomon went to 2Ch 8:17
as nothing in Solomon's **t**, 2Ch 9:20
were subdued at that **t**. 2Ch 13:18
At that **t** they sacrificed to the 2Ch 15:11
At that **t**, Hanani the seer came 2Ch 16:7
some of the people at that **t**. 2Ch 16:10
rebelled at that **t** against his 2Ch 21:10
Throughout the **t** of Jehoiada the 2Ch 24:2
From the **t** Amaziah turned from 2Ch 25:27
During the **t** that he sought the 2Ch 26:5
diseased to the **t** of his death. 2Ch 26:21
At that **t** King Ahaz asked the 2Ch 28:16
At the **t** of his distress, King 2Ch 28:22
observe it at the appropriate **t**, 2Ch 30:3
at that **t** and the Festival 2Ch 35:17
sending them **t** and time again, 2Ch 36:15
sending them time and **t** again, 2Ch 36:15
Him since the **t** King Esar-haddon Ezr 4:2
the **t** of ⌊King⌋ Artaxerxes Ezr 4:7
At that **t** Tattenai the governor Ezr 5:3
from that **t** until now, Ezr 5:16
weight was recorded at that **t**. Ezr 8:34
⌊At the **t**,⌋ I was the king's Neh 1:11
So I gave him a definite **t**, Neh 2:6
they said to us **t** and again, Neh 4:12
At that **t**, I also said to the Neh 4:22
though at that **t** I had not Neh 6:1
message a fifth **t** by his aide, Neh 6:5
In their **t** of distress, they Neh 9:27
At that **t** the book of Moses was Neh 13:1
At that **t** I saw people in Judah Neh 13:15
the end of this **t**, the king held Est 1:5
t later, when King Ahasuerus' Est 2:1
together for a second **t**, Est 2:19
If you keep silent at this **t**, Est 4:14
kingdom for such a **t** as this." Est 4:14
at the King's Gate all the **t**." Est 5:13
of Adar as ⌊a **t** of⌋ rejoicing Est 9:19
according to the **t** appointed. Est 9:27
at their proper **t** just as Est 9:31
would appoint a **t** for me and Jb 14:13
be accomplished before his **t**, Jb 15:32
from ⌊the **t**⌋ man was placed on Jb 20:4
snatched away before their **t**, Jb 22:16
For God speaks **t** and again, Jb 33:14
ears at that **t** and terrifies Jb 33:16
can know the **t** they give birth Jb 39:2
to You at a **t** that You may be Ps 32:6
their refuge in a **t** of distress. Ps 37:39
to You is for a **t** of favor. Ps 69:13
have an easy **t** until they die, Ps 73:4
When I choose a **t**, I will judge Ps 75:2
for it is **t** to show favor to her Ps 102:13
her—the appointed **t** has come. Ps 102:13
them their food at the right **t**. Ps 104:27
Until the **t** his prediction came Ps 105:19
It is **t** for the LORD to act, Ps 119:126
give them their food in due **t**. Ps 145:15
home at the **t** of the full moon. Pr 7:20
is born for a difficult **t**. Pr 17:17
at harvest **t** he looks, and there Pr 20:4
you do nothing in a difficult **t**, Pr 24:10
at the right **t** is like golden Pr 25:11
person in a **t** of trouble is like Pr 25:19
house in your **t** of calamity; Pr 27:10
even a crown lasts for all **t**. Pr 27:24
she can laugh at the **t** to come. Pr 31:25
and a **t** for every activity under Ec 3:1
a **t** to give birth and a time to Ec 3:2
to give birth and a **t** to die; Ec 3:2
a **t** to plant and a time to Ec 3:2
time to plant and a **t** to uproot; Ec 3:2
a **t** to kill and a time to heal; Ec 3:3
a time to kill and a **t** to heal; Ec 3:3
a **t** to tear down and a time to Ec 3:3
to tear down and a **t** to build; Ec 3:3
a **t** to weep and a time to laugh; Ec 3:4
a time to weep and a **t** to laugh; Ec 3:4
t to mourn and a time to dance; Ec 3:4
time to mourn and a **t** to dance; Ec 3:4
t to throw stones and a time to Ec 3:5
stones and a **t** to gather stones Ec 3:5
a **t** to embrace and a time to Ec 3:5

to embrace and a **t** to avoid Ec 3:5
t to search and a time to count Ec 3:6
to search and a **t** to count as Ec 3:6
a **t** to keep and a time to throw Ec 3:6
to keep and a **t** to throw away; Ec 3:6
a **t** to tear and a time to sew; Ec 3:7
a time to tear and a **t** to sew; Ec 3:7
a **t** to be silent and a time to Ec 3:7
to be silent and a **t** to speak; Ec 3:7
a **t** to love and a time to hate; Ec 3:8
a time to love and a **t** to hate; Ec 3:8
t for war and a time for peace. Ec 3:8
time for war and a **t** for peace. Ec 3:8
everything appropriate in its **t**. Ec 3:11
since there is a **t** for every Ec 3:17
should you die before your **t**? Ec 7:17
knows the right **t** and procedure. Ec 8:5
is a right **t** and procedure, Ec 8:6
a **t** when one man has authority Ec 8:9
your clothes be white all the **t**, Ec 9:8
t and chance happen to all of Ec 9:11
certainly does not know his **t**: Ec 9:12
people are trapped in an evil **t**, Ec 9:12
princes feast at the proper **t**— Ec 10:17
love until the appropriate **t**. Sg 2:7
The **t** of singing has come, Sg 2:12
love until the appropriate **t**. Sg 3:5
love until the appropriate **t**. Sg 8:4
the **t** he learns to reject what Is 7:15
such a **t** as has never been since Is 7:17
rejoice at harvest **t** and as they Is 9:3
His hand a second **t** to recover— Is 11:11
Babylon's **t** is almost up; Is 13:22
At that **t** a gift will be brought Is 18:7
that **t** the LORD had spoken Is 20:2
Every **t** it passes through, Is 28:19
for the king for a long **t** now. Is 30:33
our salvation in **t** of trouble. Is 33:2
t of paying back ⌊Edom⌋ for its Is 34:8
that **t** Merodach-baladan son of Is 39:1
'The **t** will certainly come when Is 39:6
her that her **t** of servitude is Is 40:2
For a long **t** your ears have not Is 48:8
from the **t** anything existed, Is 48:16
will answer you in a **t** of favor, Is 49:8
for such a long **t** and you do not Is 57:11
At that **t**, when you call, the Is 58:9
accomplish it quickly in its **t**. Is 60:22
but in their **t** of disaster they Jr 2:27
save you in your **t** of disaster Jr 2:28
At that **t** Jerusalem will be Jr 3:17
From the **t** of our youth the Jr 3:24
from the **t** of our youth even to Jr 3:25
that **t** it will be said to this Jr 4:11
spoken to you **t** and time again Jr 7:13
to you time and **t** again but you Jr 7:13
to you **t** and time again. Jr 7:25
to you time and **t** again. Jr 7:25
"At that **t**"—⌊this is⌋ the Jr 8:1
a **t** of healing, but there was Jr 8:15
the **t** of their punishment they Jr 10:15
at this **t** and bringing them Jr 10:18
warning them **t** and time again: Jr 11:7
warning them time and **t** again: Jr 11:7
them in their **t** of disaster. Jr 11:12
out to Me at the **t** of their Jr 11:14
the LORD came to me a second **t**: Jr 13:3
A long **t** later the LORD said to Jr 13:6
its Savior in **t** of distress, Jr 14:8
a **t** of healing, but there was Jr 14:19
for you in a **t** of trouble, Jr 15:11
trouble, in your **t** of distress, Jr 15:11
your very eyes and in your **t**, Jr 16:9
my refuge in a **t** of distress, Jr 16:19
and this **t** I will make them know Jr 16:21
At ⌊another⌋ **t** I announce that I Jr 18:9
them in the **t** of Your anger. Jr 18:23
I am a laughingstock all the **t**; Jr 20:7
In **t** to come you will understand Jr 23:20
spoken to you **t** and time again, Jr 25:3
spoken to you time and **t** again, Jr 25:3
to you **t** and time again, Jr 25:4
to you time and **t** again, Jr 25:4
sending you **t** and time again, Jr 26:5
sending you time and **t** again, Jr 26:5
until the **t** for his own land Jr 27:7
the prophets **t** and time again. Jr 29:19
the prophets time and **t** again. Jr 29:19

It will be a **t** of trouble for Jr 30:7
In **t** to come you will understand Jr 30:24
"At that **t**"—⌊this is⌋ the Jr 31:1
At that **t**, the army of the king Jr 32:2
jar so they will last a long **t**. Jr 32:14
I taught them **t** and time again, Jr 32:33
I taught them time and **t** again, Jr 32:33
came to Jeremiah a second **t**: Jr 33:1
days and at that **t** I will cause Jr 33:15
to come at their regular **t**, Jr 33:20
may live a long **t** on the soil Jr 35:7
spoken to you **t** and time again, Jr 35:14
spoken to you time and **t** again, Jr 35:14
T and time again I have sent you Jr 35:15
Time and **t** again I have sent you Jr 35:15
from the **t** I ⌊first⌋ spoke Jr 36:2
vineyards and fields at that **t**. Jr 39:10
the prophets **t** and time again, Jr 44:4
the prophets time and **t** again, Jr 44:4
but from the **t** we ceased to burn Jr 44:18
the **t** of their punishment. Jr 46:21
on him at the **t** I punish him. Jr 49:8
In those days and at that **t**— Jr 50:4
wields the sickle at harvest **t**. Jr 50:16
In those days and at that **t**— Jr 50:20
the **t** of their punishment. Jr 50:27
the **t** when I will punish you. Jr 50:31
For this is the **t** of the LORD's Jr 51:6
the **t** of their punishment they Jr 51:18
floor at the **t** it is trampled. Jr 51:33
while her harvest **t** will come. Jr 51:33
drew near; our **t** ran out. Our Lm 4:18
you will eat it from **t** to time. Ezk 4:10
you will eat it from time to **t**. Ezk 4:10
you will drink from **t** to time. Ezk 4:11
you will drink from time to **t**. Ezk 4:11
of the land. The **t** has come; the Ezk 7:7
The **t** has come; the day has Ezk 7:12
the **t** near to build houses? Ezk 11:3
was only a short **t** before you Ezk 16:47
It was like the **t** you were Ezk 16:57
⌊the **t**⌋ has come to put you to Ezk 21:29
so that her **t** of judgment has Ezk 22:3
a **t** ⌊of doom⌋ for the nations. Ezk 30:3
the sword in the **t** of their Ezk 35:5
the **t** of final punishment, Ezk 35:5
After a long **t** you will be Ezk 38:8
the end of that **t** they were to Dn 1:5
the end of the **t** that the king Dn 1:18
They answered a second **t**, Dn 2:7
you are trying to gain some **t**, Dn 2:8
the king to give him some **t**, Dn 2:16
animal for seven periods of **t**. Dn 4:16
animals for seven periods of **t**.' Dn 4:23
the sky for seven periods of **t**, Dn 4:25
cattle for seven periods of **t**, Dn 4:32
At that **t** my sanity returned to Dn 4:36
them for a certain period of **t**. Dn 7:12
Most High, for the **t** had come, Dn 7:22
be handed over to him for a **t**, Dn 7:25
for a time, times, and half a **t**. Dn 7:25
refers to the **t** of the end." Dn 8:17
conclusion of the **t** of wrath, Dn 8:19
to the appointed **t** of the end. Dn 8:19
In ⌊a **t** of⌋ peace, he will Dn 8:25
about the **t** of the evening Dn 9:21
come during a **t** of peace and Dn 11:21
During a **t** of peace, he will Dn 11:24
cities, but only for a **t**. Dn 11:24
will come at the appointed **t**. Dn 11:27
At the appointed **t** he will come Dn 11:29
but this **t** will not be like the Dn 11:29
captured and plundered for a **t**. Dn 11:33
cleansed until the **t** of the end, Dn 11:35
still come at the appointed **t**. Dn 11:35
until the **t** of wrath is Dn 11:36
At the **t** of the end, the king of Dn 11:40
At that **t** Michael the great Dn 12:1
There will be a **t** of distress Dn 12:1
came into being until that **t**. Dn 12:1
at that **t** all your people who Dn 12:1
the book until the **t** of the end. Dn 12:4
that it would be for a **t**, Dn 12:7
a time, times, and half ⌊a **t**⌋. Dn 12:7
sealed until the **t** of the end. Dn 12:9
From the **t** the daily sacrifice Dn 12:11
grain in its **t** and My new wine Hs 2:9
is **t** to seek the LORD until He Hs 10:12

when the **t** comes, he will not be Hs 13:13
in those days and at that **t**, Jl 3:1
will keep silent at such a **t**, Am 5:13
locusts at the **t** the spring crop Am 7:1
LORD came to Jonah a second **t**: Jnh 3:1
because it will be an evil **t**. Mc 2:3
from them at that **t** because of Mc 3:4
Zion from this **t** on and forever. Mc 4:7
them until the **t** when she who is Mc 5:3
at this **t** their panic is here. Mc 7:4
at that **t** she will be trampled Mc 7:10
will not rise up a second **t**. Nah 1:9
is yet for the appointed **t**; Hab 2:3
And at that **t** I will search Zph 1:12
at that **t** I will deal with all Zph 3:19
At that **t** I will bring you back, Zph 3:20
at the **t** I will gather you. Zph 3:20
The **t** has not come for the house Hg 1:2
Is it a **t** for you yourselves to Hg 1:4
to Haggai a second **t** on the Hg 2:20
At that **t** those who feared the Mal 3:16
brothers at the **t** of the exile Mt 1:11
them the exact **t** the star Mt 2:7
with the **t** he had learned Mt 2:16
to torment us before the **t**?" Mt 8:29
At that **t** Jesus said, "I praise Mt 11:25
At that **t** Jesus passed through Mt 12:1
At harvest **t** I'll tell the Mt 13:30
At that **t** Herod the tetrarch Mt 14:1
At that **t** the disciples came to Mt 18:1
at that **t** there will be great Mt 24:21
had known what **t** the thief was Mt 24:43
give them food at the proper **t**? Mt 24:45
After a long **t** the master of Mt 25:19
And from that **t** he started Mt 26:16
Teacher says: My **t** is near; I am Mt 26:18
Again, a second **t**, He went away Mt 26:42
away again and prayed a third **t**, Mt 26:44
Look, the **t** is near. The Son Mt 26:45
At that **t** Jesus said to the Mt 26:55
At that **t** they had a notorious Mt 27:16
The **t** is fulfilled, and the Mk 1:15
But the **t** will come when the Mk 2:20
of God in the **t** of Abiathar Mk 2:26
Now an opportune **t** came on his Mk 6:21
they did not even have **t** to eat. Mk 6:31
more, now at this **t**—houses, Mk 10:30
At harvest **t** he sent a slave to Mk 12:2
know when the **t** is ⌊coming⌋. Mk 13:33
He came a third **t** and said to Mk 14:41
Enough! The **t** has come. Look, Mk 14:41
a rooster crowed a second **t**, Mk 14:72
be fulfilled in their proper **t**." Lk 1:20
Now the **t** had come for Elizabeth Lk 1:57
t came for her to give birth. Lk 2:6
of the world in a moment of **t**. Lk 4:5
he departed from Him for a **t**. Lk 4:13
And in the prophet Elisha's **t**, Lk 4:27
At that **t** Jesus healed many Lk 7:21
and depart in a **t** of testing. Lk 8:13
For a long **t** he had worn no Lk 8:27
allotted food at the proper **t**? Lk 12:42
know how to interpret this **t**? Lk 12:56
At that **t**, some people came and Lk 13:1
that **t** some Pharisees came and Lk 13:31
Me until the **t** comes when you Lk 13:35
At the **t** of the banquet, he sent Lk 14:17
many times more at this **t**, Lk 18:30
not recognize the **t** of your Lk 19:44
and went away for a long **t**. Lk 20:9
At harvest **t** he sent a slave to Lk 20:10
I am He,' and, 'The **t** is near.' Lk 21:8
prepare your defense ahead of **t**, Lk 21:14
a long **t** he had wanted to see Lk 23:8
A third **t** he said to them, Lk 23:22
womb a second **t** and be born?" Jn 3:4
where He spent **t** with them and Jn 3:22
them at what **t** he got better. Jn 4:52
the pool from **t** to time and stir Jn 5:4
pool from time to **t** and stir up Jn 5:4
had already been there a long **t**, Jn 5:6
because a **t** is coming when all Jn 5:28
and for a **t** you were willing to Jn 5:35
not heard His voice at any **t**, Jn 5:37
My **t** has not yet arrived, Jn 7:6
but your **t** is always at hand. Jn 7:6
My **t** has not yet fully come. Jn 7:8
am only with you for a short **t**. Jn 7:33
So a second **t** they summoned the Jn 9:24
by the **t** of supper, the Devil Jn 13:2
among you all this **t** without Jn 14:9
a **t** is coming when anyone who Jn 16:2
that when their **t** comes you may Jn 16:4
has pain because her **t** has come. Jn 16:21
A **t** is coming when I will no Jn 16:25
now the third **t** Jesus appeared Jn 21:14
A second **t** He asked him, "Simon, Jn 21:16
He asked him the third **t**, Jn 21:17
that He asked him the third **t**, Jn 21:17
at this **t** are You restoring the Ac 1:6
during the whole **t** the Lord Ac 1:21
our forefathers the first **t**. Ac 7:12
second **t**, Joseph was revealed Ac 7:13
As the **t** was drawing near to Ac 7:17
At this **t** Moses was born, and he Ac 7:20
with his sorceries for a long **t**. Ac 8:11
Again, a second **t**, a voice said Ac 10:15
from heaven a second **t**, Ac 11:9
place during the **t** of Claudius. Ac 11:28
About that **t** King Herod cruelly Ac 12:1
will not see the sun for a **t**." Ac 13:11
there for some **t** and spoke Ac 14:3
a considerable **t** with the Ac 14:28
After spending some **t** there, Ac 15:33
After some **t** had passed, Paul Ac 15:36
spent their **t** on nothing else Ac 17:21
him to stay for a longer **t**, Ac 18:20
During that **t** there was a major Ac 19:23
a considerable **t** until dawn. Ac 20:11
have to spend **t** in the province Ac 20:16
how I was with you the whole **t**— Ac 20:18
a rebellion some **t** ago and led Ac 21:38
but when I find **t** I'll call for Ac 24:25
At the same **t** he was also hoping Ac 24:26
known me for quite some **t**, Ac 26:5
now much **t** had passed, and the Ac 27:9
the same **t** loosening the ropes Ac 27:40
waited a long **t** and saw nothing Ac 28:6
righteousness at the present **t**, Rm 3:26
of this present **t** are not worth Rm 8:18
At this **t** I will come, and Sarah Rm 9:9
the present **t** a remnant chosen Rm 11:5
knowing the **t**, it is already Rm 13:11
you agree, for a **t**, to devote 1Co 7:5
the **t** is limited, so from now on 1Co 7:29
over 500 brothers at one **t**, 1Co 15:6
I hope to spend some **t** with you, 1Co 16:7
when he has **t**, he will come. 1Co 16:12
In an acceptable **t**, I heard you, 2Co 6:2
Look, now is the acceptable **t**; 2Co 6:2
at the present **t** your surplus is 2Co 8:14
to come to you this third **t**. 2Co 12:14
is the third **t** I am coming to 2Co 13:1
when I was present the second **t**, 2Co 13:2
until the **t** set by his father Gl 4:2
the completion of the **t** came, Gl 4:4
at the proper **t** if we don't give Gl 6:9
ahead of **t** so that we should Eph 2:10
that at one **t** you were Gentiles Eph 2:11
At that **t** you were without the Eph 2:12
the most of the **t**, because the Eph 5:16
At the same **t**, pray also for us Col 4:3
making the most of the **t**. Col 4:5
to leave you for a short **t** 1Th 2:17
—even I, Paul, **t** and again— 1Th 2:18
he will be revealed in his **t**. 2Th 2:6
a testimony at the proper **t**. 1Tm 2:6
the same **t**, they also learn to 1Tm 5:13
will bring about in His own **t**. 1Tm 6:15
in Christ Jesus before **t** began. 2Tm 1:9
For the **t** will come when they 2Tm 4:3
and the **t** for my departure is 2Tm 4:6
lie, promised before **t** began, Ti 1:2
has in His own **t** revealed His Ti 1:3
from you⌋ for a brief **t**, Phm 15
the same **t**, God also testified Heb 2:4
than the angels for a short **t**; Heb 2:7
for a short **t** so that by God's Heb 2:9
David after such a long **t**, Heb 4:7
to help us at the proper **t**. Heb 4:16
though by this **t** you ought to be Heb 5:12
is a symbol for the present **t**, Heb 9:9
until the **t** of restoration. Heb 9:10
But now He has appeared one **t**, Heb 9:26
appear a second **t**, not to bear Heb 9:28
and offering **t** after time the Heb 10:11
time after **t** the same sacrifices Heb 10:11
T is too short for me to tell Heb 11:32
us for a short **t** based on what Heb 12:10
seems enjoyable at the **t**, Heb 12:11
voice shook the earth at that **t**, Heb 12:26
to be revealed in the last **t**. 1Pt 1:5
now for a short **t** you have had 1Pt 1:6
inquired into what **t** or what 1Pt 1:11
during this **t** of temporary 1Pt 1:17
the remaining **t** in the flesh, 1Pt 4:2
been enough **t** spent in doing 1Pt 4:3
For the **t** has come for judgment 1Pt 4:17
that He may exalt you in due **t**, 1Pt 5:6
to recall these things at any **t**. 2Pt 1:15
world of that **t** perished when it 2Pt 3:6
In the end **t** there will be Jd 18
and authority before all **t**, Jd 25
in it, because the **t** is near! Rv 1:3
I gave her **t** to repent, but she Rv 2:21
no longer be an interval of **t**, Rv 10:6
The **t** has come for the dead to Rv 11:18
and the **t** has come to destroy Rv 11:18
he knows he has a short **t**. Rv 12:12
where she was fed for a **t**, Rv 12:14
for a time, times, and half a **t**. Rv 12:14
for the **t** to reap has come, Rv 14:15
second **t** they said: Hallelujah! Rv 19:3
must be released for a short **t**. Rv 20:3
book, because the **t** is near. Rv 22:10

TIMELY *(1)*

and a **t** word—how good that is! Pr 15:23

TIMES *(191)*

suffer vengeance seven **t** over." Gn 4:15
is to be avenged seven **t** over, Gn 4:24
it will be seventy-seven **t**! Gn 4:24
reaped a hundred **t** ⌊what was Gn 26:12
me and changed my wages 10 **t**. Gn 31:7
you have changed my wages 10 **t**! Gn 31:41
the ground seven **t** until he Gn 33:3
was five **t** larger than any Gn 43:34
judge the people at all **t**. Ex 18:22
They judged the people at all **t**; Ex 18:26
in My honor three **t** a year. Ex 23:14
Three **t** a year all your males Ex 23:17
on the table before Me at all **t**. Ex 25:30
during plowing and harvesting **t**. Ex 34:21
Three **t** a year all your males Ex 34:23
you go up three **t** a year to Ex 34:24
of it seven **t** before the LORD Lv 4:6
it⌋ seven **t** before the LORD Lv 4:17
of the oil on the altar seven **t**, Lv 8:11
blood⌋ seven **t** on the one who Lv 14:7
finger seven **t** before the LORD Lv 14:16
palm seven **t** before the LORD Lv 14:27
and sprinkle the house seven **t**. Lv 14:51
before the mercy seat seven **t**. Lv 16:14
finger seven **t** to cleanse and Lv 16:19
are My appointed **t**, the times of Lv 23:2
the **t** of the LORD that you will Lv 23:2
are the LORD's appointed **t**, Lv 23:4
proclaim at their appointed **t**. Lv 23:4
appointed **t** that you are to Lv 23:37
LORD's appointed **t** to the Lv 23:44
years, seven **t** seven years, so Lv 25:8
you seven **t** for your sins. Lv 26:18
plagues seven **t** for your sins. Lv 26:21
you seven **t** for your sins. Lv 26:24
you seven **t** for your sins. Lv 26:28
Me these 10 **t** and did not obey Nm 14:22
it seven **t** toward the front Nm 19:4
have beaten me these three **t**?" Nm 22:28
your donkey these three **t**? Nm 22:32
away from Me these three **t**. Nm 22:33
blessed ⌊them these three **t**⌋. Nm 24:10
your appointed **t** in addition to Nm 29:39
increase you a thousand **t** more, Dt 1:11
to appear three **t** a year before Dt 16:16
walking in His ways at all **t**— Dt 19:9
march around the city seven **t**, Jos 6:4
city seven **t** in the same way. Jos 6:15
marched around the city seven **t**. Jos 6:15
the ground, and bowed three **t**. 1Sm 20:41
From ancient **t** they had been the 1Sm 27:8
the troops 100 **t** more than they 2Sm 24:3
My heart will be there at all **t**. 1Kg 9:3
Three **t** a year Solomon offered 1Kg 9:25
out over the boy three **t**. 1Kg 17:21
Seven **t** Elijah said, "Go back." 1Kg 18:43

many **t** must I make you swear 1Kg 22:16
sneezed seven **t** and opened his 2Kg 4:35
Go wash seven **t** in the Jordan 2Kg 5:10
himself in the Jordan seven **t**, 2Kg 5:14
the ground three **t** and stopped. 2Kg 13:18
struck the ground five or six **t**. 2Kg 13:19
only strike down Aram three **t**." 2Kg 13:19
Ben-hadad three **t** and recovered 2Kg 13:25
In earlier **t** Phinehas son of 1Ch 9:20
at fixed **t** to be with them 1Ch 9:25
understood the **t** and knew what 1Ch 12:32
of His people a hundred **t** over! 1Ch 21:3
My heart will be there at all **t**. 2Ch 7:16
those **t** there was no peace for 2Ch 15:5
many **t** must I make you swear 2Ch 18:15
revolts in it since ancient **t**. Ezr 4:15
against kings since ancient **t**, Ezr 4:19
women come at appointed **t**, Ezr 10:14
Four **t** they sent me the same Neh 6:4
rescued them many **t** in Your Neh 9:28
at the appointed **t** each year. Neh 10:34
wood at the appointed **t** and for Neh 13:31
wise men who understood the **t**, Est 1:13
God once in a thousand ⌊**t**⌋. Jb 9:3
have humiliated me ten **t** now, Jb 19:3
not reserve **t** for judgment? Jb 24:1
Will he call on God at all **t**? Jb 27:10
those who have fallen on hard **t**? Jb 30:25
things two or three **t** to a man Jb 33:29
in reserve for **t** of trouble, Jb 38:23
a refuge in **t** of trouble. Ps 9:9
Why do You hide in **t** of trouble? Ps 10:1
furnace, purified seven **t**. Ps 12:6
I will praise the LORD at all **t**; Ps 34:1
be disgraced in **t** of adversity; Ps 37:19
is always found in **t** of trouble. Ps 46:1
should I fear in **t** of trouble? Ps 49:5
in Him at all **t**, you people; Ps 62:8
God my king is from ancient **t**, Ps 74:12
from troubled **t** until a pit is Ps 94:13
practice righteousness at all **t**. Ps 106:3
rescued them many **t**, but they Ps 106:43
praise You seven **t** a day for Ps 119:164
he must pay seven **t** as much; Pr 6:31
I was formed before ancient **t**, Pr 8:23
loves at all **t**, and a brother is Pr 17:17
a righteous man falls seven **t**, Pr 24:16
know that many **t** you yourself Ec 7:22
crime a hundred **t** and prolongs Ec 8:12
of the former **t** when He humbled Is 9:1
whose origin was in ancient **t**, Is 23:7
will be seven **t** brighter— Is 30:26
There will be **t** of security for Is 33:6
the city of our festival **t**. Is 33:20
know, and from **t** past, so that Is 41:26
Who announced it from ancient **t**? Is 45:21
from ancient **t**, Your name is our Is 63:16
From ancient **t** no one has heard, Is 64:4
from ancient **t** prophesied war, Jr 28:8
rebuild them as in former **t**. Jr 33:7
of the land as in former **t**, Jr 33:11
again as in ancient **t**." Jr 46:26
renew our days as in former **t**, Lm 5:21
he prophesies about distant **t**. Ezk 12:27
Let the sword strike two **t**, Ezk 21:14
about in former **t** through My Ezk 38:17
in those **t** that I would bring Ezk 38:17
all the appointed **t** of the house Ezk 45:17
the LORD at the appointed **t**, Ezk 46:9
the festivals and appointed **t**, Ezk 46:11
found them 10 **t** better than all Dn 1:20
He changes the **t** and seasons; Dn 2:21
furnace seven **t** more than was Dn 3:19
and three **t** a day he got down on Dn 6:10
for he prays three **t** a day." Dn 6:13
thousand **t** ten thousand stood Dn 7:10
him for a time, **t**, and half a Dn 7:25
and a moat, but in difficult **t**. Dn 9:25
supported her during those **t**. Dn 11:6
In those **t** many will rise up Dn 11:14
be for a time, **t**, and half ⌊a Dn 12:7
and Gilead as in ancient **t**. Mc 7:14
the tenth will become **t** of joy, Zch 8:19
and some 30 **t** ⌊what was sown⌋. Mt 13:8
some 30 **t** ⌊what was sown⌋." Mt 13:23
can't read the signs of the **t**. Mt 16:3
how many **t** could my brother sin Mt 18:21
him? As many as seven **t**?" Mt 18:21
said to him, "but 70 **t** seven. Mt 18:22
will receive 100 **t** more and will Mt 19:29
you will deny Me three **t**!" Mt 26:34
you will deny Me three **t**." Mt 26:75
and 100 **t** ⌊what was sown⌋." Mk 4:8
and 100 **t** ⌊what was sown⌋." Mk 4:20
And many **t** it has thrown him Mk 9:22
who will not receive 100 **t** more, Mk 10:30
you will deny Me three **t**!" Mk 14:30
you will deny Me three **t**." Mk 14:72
His holy prophets in ancient **t**; Lk 1:70
100 **t** ⌊what was sown⌋." Lk 8:8
Many **t** it had seized him, and Lk 8:29
against you seven **t** in a day, Lk 17:4
and comes back to you seven **t**, Lk 17:4
not receive many **t** more at this Lk 18:30
I'll pay back four **t** as much!" Lk 19:8
until the **t** of the Gentiles Lk 21:24
be alert at all **t**, praying that Lk 21:36
deny three **t** that you know Me! Lk 22:34
you will deny Me three **t**." Lk 22:61
you have denied Me three **t**. Jn 13:38
you to know **t** or periods that Ac 1:7
Him until the **t** of the Ac 3:21
This happened three **t**, and then Ac 10:16
Now this happened three **t**, Ac 11:10
since ancient **t**, Moses has had Ac 15:21
their appointed **t** and the Ac 17:26
overlooked the **t** of ignorance, Ac 17:30
prevented many **t** from coming to Rm 15:22
nights, by **t** of hunger, 2Co 6:5
beatings, near death many **t**. 2Co 11:23
Five **t** I received from the Jews 2Co 11:24
Three **t** I was beaten with rods. 2Co 11:25
Three **t** I was shipwrecked. 2Co 11:25
the Lord three **t** to take it away 2Co 12:8
pray at all **t** in the Spirit, Eph 6:18
gifts⌋ for my need several **t**. Php 4:16
About the **t** and the seasons: 1Th 5:1
in the latter **t** some will depart 1Tm 4:1
difficult **t** will come in the 2Tm 3:1
at different **t** and in different Heb 1:1
do this to offer Himself many **t**, Heb 9:25
had to suffer many **t** since the Heb 9:26
and at other **t** you were Heb 10:33
at the end of the **t** for you 1Pt 1:20
fed for a time, **t**, and half a Rv 12:14

TIMID *(1)*
therefore I was **t** and afraid to Jb 32:6

TIMNA *(6)*
T, a concubine of Esau's son Gn 36:12
Hori and Heman. **T** was Lotan's Gn 36:22
Chiefs **T**, Alvah, Jetheth, Gn 36:40
and Kenaz; and by **T**, Amalek. 1Ch 1:36
Hori and Homam. **T** was Lotan's 1Ch 1:39
chiefs: **T**, Alvah, Jetheth, 1Ch 1:51

TIMNAH *(11)*
went up to **T** to the Gn 38:12
up to **T** to shear his sheep. Gn 38:13
Enaim, which is on the way to **T**. Gn 38:14
and proceeded to **T**. Jos 15:10
Gibeah, and **T**—10 cities, with Jos 15:57
Elon, **T**, Ekron, Jos 19:43
went down to **T** and saw a young Jdg 14:1
a young Philistine woman in **T**. Jdg 14:2
went down to **T** with his father Jdg 14:5
and came to the vineyards of **T**. Jdg 14:5
its villages, **T** and its villages 2Ch 28:18

TIMNATH-HERES *(1)*
inheritance, in **T**, in the hill Jdg 2:9

TIMNATH-SERAH *(2)*
gave him the city **T** in the hill Jos 19:50
in his allotted territory at **T**, Jos 24:30

TIMNITE'S *(1)*
was⌋ Samson, the **T** son-in-law, Jdg 15:6

TIMON *(1)*
Prochorus, Nicanor, **T**, Parmenas, Ac 6:5

TIMOTHY *(25)*
there was a disciple named **T**, Ac 16:1
Paul wanted **T** to go with him, Ac 16:3
but Silas and **T** stayed on there. Ac 17:14
for Silas and **T** to come to him Ac 17:15
When Silas and **T** came down from Ac 18:5
assisted him, **T** and Erastus, to Ac 19:22
from Derbe, **T**, and Tychicus Ac 20:4
T, my co-worker, and Lucius, Rm 16:21
is why I have sent to you **T**, 1Co 4:17
If **T** comes, see that he has 1Co 16:10
God's will, and **T** our brother: 2Co 1:1
by me and Silvanus and **T**— 2Co 1:19
Paul and **T**, slaves of Christ Php 1:1
Jesus to send **T** to you soon so Php 2:19
God's will, and **T** our brother: Col 1:1
Paul, Silvanus, and **T**: 1Th 1:1
And we sent **T**, our brother and 1Th 3:2
now **T** has come to us from you 1Th 3:6
Paul, Silvanus, and **T**: 2Th 1:1
T, my true child in the faith. 1Tm 1:2
T, my child, I am giving you 1Tm 1:18
T, guard what has been entrusted 1Tm 6:20
To **T**, my dearly loved child. 2Tm 1:2
Jesus, and **T**, our brother: Phm 1
that our brother **T** has been Heb 13:23

TIN *(4)*
bronze, iron, **t**, and lead— Nm 31:22
are copper, **t**, iron, and lead Ezk 22:18
and **t** into the furnace to blow Ezk 22:20
silver, iron, **t**, and lead for Ezk 27:12

TINDER *(1)*
The strong one will become **t**, Is 1:31

TINY *(2)*
dropped in two **t** coins worth Mk 12:42
widow dropping in two **t** coins. Lk 21:2

TIP *(7)*
began at the **t** of the Dead Sea Jos 15:2
extended the **t** of the staff that Jdg 6:21
was 15 feet from **t** to tip. 1Kg 6:24
was 15 feet from tip to **t**. 1Kg 6:24
touched the **t** of the scepter. Est 5:2
the flashing **t** out of his liver. Jb 20:25
to dip the **t** of his finger Lk 16:24

TIPHSAH *(2)*
Euphrates from **T** to Gaza and 1Kg 4:24
Menahem attacked **T**, all who 2Kg 15:16

TIPS *(1)*
He **t** His arrows with fire. Ps 7:13

TIRAS *(2)*
Javan, Tubal, Meshech, and **T**. Gn 10:2
Javan, Tubal, Meshech, and **T**. 1Ch 1:5

TIRATHITES *(1)*
in Jabez—the **T**, Shimeathites, 1Ch 2:55

TIRED *(10)*
when you were **t** and weary. Dt 25:18
his hand was **t** and stuck to his 2Sm 23:10
am **t** of putting up with ⌊them⌋. Is 1:14
look for her will not become **t**; Jr 2:24
I am **t** of holding it back. Jr 6:11
I am **t** of showing compassion. Jr 15:6
I become **t** of holding it in, Jr 20:9
we are **t**, and no one offers us Lm 5:5
we must not get **t** of doing good, Gl 6:9
strengthen your **t** hands and Heb 12:12

TIRES *(1)*
when he **t** himself out and comes Is 16:12

TIRHAKAH *(2)*
heard this about **T** king of Cush: 2Kg 19:9
The king had heard this about **T**, Is 37:9

TIRHANAH *(1)*
was the mother of Sheber and **T**. 1Ch 2:48

TIRIA *(1)*
Ziph, Ziphah, **T**, and Asarel. 1Ch 4:16

TIRZAH *(18)*
Noah, Hoglah, Milcah, and **T**. Nm 26:33
Noah, Hoglah, Milcah, and **T**. Nm 27:1
Mahlah, **T**, Hoglah, Milcah, and Nm 36:11
the king of **T** one ⌊the total Jos 12:24
Noah, Hoglah, Milcah, and **T**. Jos 17:3
got up and left and went to **T**. 1Kg 14:17
building Ramah and stayed in **T**. 1Kg 15:21
king over all Israel at **T**; 1Kg 15:33
his fathers and was buried in **T**. 1Kg 16:6
became king over Israel in **T**; 1Kg 16:8
Elah was in **T** drinking himself 1Kg 16:9
in charge of the household at **T**. 1Kg 16:9
became king for seven days in **T**. 1Kg 16:15
from Gibbethon and besieged **T**. 1Kg 16:17
He reigned six years in **T**, 1Kg 16:23
Gadi came up from **T** to Samaria 2Kg 15:14
starting⌋ from **T**, Menahem 2Kg 15:16
You are as beautiful as **T**, Sg 6:4

TISHBITE *(6)*
- Elijah the **T**, from the Gilead 1Kg 17:1
- the LORD came to Elijah the **T**: 1Kg 21:17
- the LORD came to Elijah the **T**: 1Kg 21:28
- the LORD said to Elijah the **T**, 2Kg 1:3
- He said, "It's Elijah the **T**." 2Kg 1:8
- His servant Elijah the **T**: 2Kg 9:36

TITHES *(4)*
- lineage collected **t** from Abraham Heb 7:6
- men who will die receive **t**; Heb 7:8
- who receives **t**, has paid tithes Heb 7:9
- has paid **t** through Abraham, Heb 7:9

TITIUS *(1)*
- house of a man named **T** Justus, Ac 18:7

TITLE *(2)*
- give anyone an ⌊undeserved⌋ **t**. Jb 32:21
- and every **t** given, not only Eph 1:21

TITLES *(1)*
- not know how to give ⌊such⌋ **t**; Jb 32:22

TITUS *(13)*
- I did not find my brother **T**, 2Co 2:13
- comforted us by the coming of **T**, 2Co 7:6
- even more over the joy **T** had, 2Co 7:13
- boasting to **T** has also turned 2Co 7:14
- So we urged **T** that, just as he 2Co 8:6
- for you into the heart of **T**. 2Co 8:16
- As for **T**, he is my partner and 2Co 8:23
- I urged **T** ⌊to come⌋, and I sent 2Co 12:18
- Did **T** take advantage of you? 2Co 12:18
- Barnabas, taking **T** along also. Gl 2:1
- But not even **T** who was with me, Gl 2:3
- gone to Galatia, **T** to Dalmatia. 2Tm 4:10
- **T**, my true child in our common Ti 1:4

TIZITE *(1)*
- and his brother Joha the **T**, 1Ch 11:45

(See pp. xi-xii.)

TO *(20,631)*

(See pp. xi-xii.)

TOAH *(1)*
- Jeroham, son of Eliel, son of **T**, 1Ch 6:34

TOB *(4)*
- and lived in the land of **T**. Jdg 11:3
- get Jephthah from the land of **T**. Jdg 11:5
- Maacah, and 12,000 men from **T**. 2Sm 10:6
- and the men of **T** and Maacah were 2Sm 10:8

TOB-ADONIJAH *(1)*
- Adonijah, Tobijah, and **T**; 2Ch 17:8

TOBIAH *(11)*
- the Horonite and **T** the Ammonite Neh 2:10
- the Horonite, **T** the Ammonite Neh 2:19
- Then **T** the Ammonite, who was Neh 4:3
- Sanballat, **T**, and the Arabs, Neh 4:7
- When Sanballat, **T**, Geshem the Neh 6:1
- **T** and Sanballat had hired him. Neh 6:12
- remember **T** and Sanballat for Neh 6:14
- of Judah sent many letters to **T**, Neh 6:17
- And **T** sent letters to intimidate Neh 6:19
- He was a relative of **T** Neh 13:4
- on behalf of **T** by providing him Neh 13:7

TOBIAH'S *(5)*
- descendants, **T** descendants, Ezr 2:60
- and **T** ⌊letters⌋ came to them. Neh 6:17
- kept mentioning **T** good deeds to Neh 6:19
- descendants, **T** descendants, Neh 7:62
- and threw all of **T** household Neh 13:8

TOBIJAH *(3)*
- Adonijah, **T**, and Tob-adonijah; 2Ch 17:8
- from Heldai, **T**, and Jedaiah, who Zch 6:10
- to Heldai, **T**, Jedaiah, and Hen Zch 6:14

TOCHEN *(1)*
- Ain, Rimmon, **T**, and Ashan—five 1Ch 4:32

TODAY *(299)*
- banishing me **t** from the soil, Gn 4:14
- the father of the Moabites of **t**. Gn 19:37
- father of the Ammonites of **t**. Gn 19:38
- hadn't heard about it until **t**." Gn 21:26
- Will Provide, so **t** it is said: Gn 22:14
- grant me success **t**, and show Gn 24:12
- **T** when I came to the spring, Gn 24:42
- your sheep **t** and remove every Gn 30:32
- But what can I do **t** for these Gn 31:43
- a witness between me and you **t**." Gn 31:48
- "Why are your faces sad **t**?" Gn 40:7
- said to Pharaoh, "**T** I remember Gn 41:9
- Understand **t** that I have Gn 47:23
- still in effect **t** in the land of Gn 47:26
- you come back so quickly **t**?" Ex 2:18
- number of bricks yesterday or **t**, Ex 5:14
- they occupied the land until **t**." Ex 10:6
- **T**, in the month of Abib, you are Ex 13:4
- He will provide for you **t**; Ex 14:13
- for the Egyptians you see **t**, Ex 14:13
- "Eat it **t**," Moses said, "because Ex 16:25
- because **t** is a Sabbath to the Ex 16:25
- **T** you won't find any in the Ex 16:25
- and purify them **t** and tomorrow. Ex 19:10
- **T** you have been dedicated to the Ex 32:29
- a blessing on yourselves **t**." Ex 32:29
- Observe what I command you **t**. Ex 34:11
- has been done **t** in order to make Lv 8:34
- **t** the LORD is going to appear Lv 9:4
- **t** they presented their sin Lv 10:19
- I had eaten the sin offering **t**, Lv 10:19
- ridden all your life until **t**? Nm 22:30
- you that **t** you are as numerous Dt 1:10
- '**T** you are going to cross the Dt 2:18
- **T** I will begin to put the fear Dt 2:25
- Jair's Villages, as it is **t**. Dt 3:14
- LORD your God are all alive **t**. Dt 4:4
- entire law I set before you **t**? Dt 4:8
- His inheritance, as you are **t**. Dt 4:20
- against you **t** that you will Dt 4:26
- **T**, recognize and keep in mind Dt 4:39
- I am giving you **t**, so that you Dt 4:40
- proclaiming as you hear them **t**. Dt 5:1
- all of us who are alive here **t**. Dt 5:3
- **T** we have seen that God speaks Dt 5:24
- I am giving you **t** are to be in Dt 6:6
- our preservation, as it is **t**. Dt 6:24
- I am giving you to follow **t**. Dt 7:11
- every command I am giving you **t**, Dt 8:1
- statutes—I am giving you **t**. Dt 8:11
- to your fathers, as it is **t**. Dt 8:18
- against you **t** that you will Dt 8:19
- **T** you are about to cross the Dt 9:1
- understand that **t** the LORD your Dt 9:3
- bless in His name, as it is **t**. Dt 10:8
- and statutes I am giving you **t**, Dt 10:13
- of all the peoples, as it is **t**. Dt 10:15
- must understand **t** that it is not Dt 11:2
- every command I am giving you **t**, Dt 11:8
- My commands I am giving you **t**, Dt 11:13
- **t** I set before you a blessing Dt 11:26
- LORD your God I am giving you **t**, Dt 11:27
- I command you **t** by following Dt 11:28
- ordinances I set before you **t**. Dt 11:32
- to do as we are doing here **t**; Dt 12:8
- His commands I am giving you **t**, Dt 13:18
- commands I am giving you **t**. Dt 15:5
- I am giving you this command **t**. Dt 15:15
- am giving you **t** and follow them Dt 19:9
- **T** you are about to engage in Dt 20:3
- '**T** I acknowledge to the LORD Dt 26:3
- **T** you have affirmed that the Dt 26:17
- And **t** the LORD has affirmed that Dt 26:18
- every command I am giving you **t**. Dt 27:1
- commanding you **t**, and you are to Dt 27:4
- and statutes I am giving you **t**." Dt 27:10
- His commands I am giving you **t**, Dt 28:1
- am giving you **t** and are careful Dt 28:13
- things I am commanding you **t**, Dt 28:14
- and statutes I am giving you **t**, Dt 28:15
- are standing **t** before the LORD Dt 29:10
- which He is making with you **t**, Dt 29:12
- establish you **t** as His people Dt 29:13
- here with us **t** in the presence Dt 29:15
- with those who are not here **t**. Dt 29:15
- tribe among you **t** whose heart Dt 29:18
- another land where they are **t**.' Dt 29:28
- everything I am giving you **t**, Dt 30:2
- His commands I am giving you **t**. Dt 30:8
- that I give you **t** is certainly Dt 30:11
- **t** I have set before you life and Dt 30:15
- commanding you **t** to love the Dt 30:16
- I tell you **t** that you will Dt 30:18
- against you **t** that I have set Dt 30:19
- am giving as a warning to you **t**, Dt 32:46
- **T** I will begin to exalt you in Jos 3:7
- **T** I have rolled away the Jos 5:9
- **T** the LORD will trouble you!" Jos 7:25
- they are **t**—for the community Jos 9:27
- Here I am **t**, 85 years old. Jos 14:10
- still as strong **t** as I was the Jos 14:11
- have committed **t** against the God Jos 22:16
- in rebellion against the LORD **t**? Jos 22:16
- If you rebel against the LORD **t**, Jos 22:18
- not spare us **t**, if ⌊it was⌋ in Jos 22:22
- turn away from Him **t** by building Jos 22:29
- **T** we know that the LORD is among Jos 22:31
- yourselves **t** the one you will Jos 24:15
- of the Abiezrites until **t**. Jdg 6:24
- attacked my father's house **t**, Jdg 9:18
- You see fit; only deliver us **t**!" Jdg 10:15
- is⌋ the Judge decide **t** between Jdg 11:27
- have you come **t** to fight against Jdg 12:3
- who came to me **t** has just come Jdg 13:10
- tribe is ⌊missing⌋ in Israel **t**?" Jdg 21:3
- **T** a tribe has been cut off from Jdg 21:6
- Where did you gather ⌊barley⌋ **t**, Ru 2:19
- man I worked with **t** is Boaz." Ru 2:19
- rest unless he resolves this **t**." Ru 3:18
- are witnesses **t** that I am buying Ru 4:9
- his home. You are witnesses **t**." Ru 4:10
- you without a family redeemer **t**. Ru 4:14
- us be defeated **t** by the 1Sm 4:3
- I fled from there **t**." 1Sm 4:16
- the prophet of **t** was formerly 1Sm 9:9
- the people at the high place **t**. 1Sm 9:12
- high place and eat with me **t**. 1Sm 9:19
- **T** when you leave me, you'll find 1Sm 10:2
- **t** you have rejected your God, 1Sm 10:19
- for **t** the LORD has provided 1Sm 11:13
- led you from my youth until **t**. 1Sm 12:2
- is a witness **t** that you haven't 1Sm 12:5
- Isn't the wheat harvest **t**? 1Sm 12:17
- is the man who eats food **t**,' 1Sm 14:28
- eaten freely **t** from the plunder 1Sm 14:30
- how this sin has occurred **t**. 1Sm 14:38
- he worked with God's help **t**." 1Sm 14:45
- away from you **t** and has given it 1Sm 15:28
- I defy the ranks of Israel **t**. 1Sm 17:10
- **T**, the LORD will hand you over 1Sm 17:46
- **T**, I'll strike you down, cut 1Sm 17:46
- the meal either yesterday or **t**?" 1Sm 20:27
- their bodies are consecrated **t**." 1Sm 21:5
- for me, as ⌊is the case⌋ **t**." 1Sm 22:8
- in ambush, as ⌊is the case⌋ **t**." 1Sm 22:13
- Was **t** the first time I inquired 1Sm 22:15
- you over to me **t** in the cave. 1Sm 24:10
- have told me **t** what good you did 1Sm 24:18
- for what you've done for me **t**. 1Sm 24:19
- who sent you to meet me **t**! 1Sm 25:32
- **T** you kept me from participating 1Sm 25:33
- **T** God has handed your enemy 1Sm 26:8
- for **t** they have driven me away 1Sm 26:19
- again because **t** you considered 1Sm 26:21
- LORD handed you over to me **t**. 1Sm 26:23
- considered your life valuable **t**, 1Sm 26:24
- belongs to the kings of Judah **t**. 1Sm 27:6
- "Where did you raid **t**?" 1Sm 27:10
- the LORD has done this to you **t**. 1Sm 28:18
- the day he defected until **t**, 1Sm 29:3
- the day you came to me until **t**. 1Sm 29:6
- day I was with you until **t**, 1Sm 29:8
- leader has fallen in Israel **t**. 2Sm 3:38
- king, I have little power **t**. 2Sm 3:39
- **T** the LORD has granted vengeance 2Sm 4:8
- Against Uzzah, as it is **t**. 2Sm 6:8
- of Israel honored himself **t**!" 2Sm 6:20
- exposed himself **t** in the sight 2Sm 6:20
- Egypt until **t** I have not lived 2Sm 7:6
- "Stay here **t** also," David said 2Sm 11:12
- "**T**," Joab said, "your servant 2Sm 14:22
- around with us **t** while I go 2Sm 15:20
- for he said, '**T**, the house of 2Sm 16:3
- instead of Shimei's curses **t**." 2Sm 16:12
- called Absalom's Monument **t**. 2Sm 18:18
- not the man to take good news **t**. 2Sm 18:20
- but **t** you aren't taking good 2Sm 18:20
- **t** the LORD has delivered you 2Sm 18:31
- **T** you have shamed all your 2Sm 19:5
- **T** you have made it clear that 2Sm 19:6
- **t** I know that if Absalom were 2Sm 19:6
- **T** I am the first one of the 2Sm 19:20
- you become my adversary **t**? 2Sm 19:22
- any man be killed in Israel **t**? 2Sm 19:22
- I not aware that **t** I'm king over 2Sm 19:22
- For **t** he went down and lavishly 1Kg 1:25
- **T** He has provided one to sit on 1Kg 1:48
- will be put to death **t**!" 1Kg 2:24

I will not put you to death **t**, 1Kg 2:26
sit on his throne, as it is **t**. 1Kg 3:6
May the LORD be praised **t**! 1Kg 5:7
by Your power as it is **t**. 1Kg 8:24
Your servant prays before You **t**, 1Kg 8:28
keep His commands, as it is **t**." 1Kg 8:61
as they are ⌊still called⌋ **t**. 1Kg 9:13
⌊it is this way⌋ until **t**. 1Kg 9:21
T if you will be a servant to 1Kg 12:7
the house of David until **t**. 1Kg 12:19
This is the day, yes, even **t**! 1Kg 14:14
t I will present myself to Ahab." 1Kg 18:15
t let it be known that You are 1Kg 18:36
it over to you **t** so that you may 1Kg 20:13
Do you know that **t** the LORD will 2Kg 2:3
Do you know that **t** the LORD will 2Kg 2:5
But he said, "Why go to him **t**? 2Kg 4:23
your son, and we will eat him **t**. 2Kg 6:28
remains on his shoulders **t**." 2Kg 6:31
T is a day of good news. 2Kg 7:9
against Judah's control **t**. 2Kg 8:22
and they live there until **t**. 2Kg 16:6
from their homeland until **t**. 2Kg 17:23
as their fathers did until **t**. 2Kg 17:41
'**T** is a day of distress, rebuke, 2Kg 19:3
came out of Egypt until **t**.' " 2Kg 21:15
for destruction, as they are **t**. 1Ch 4:41
escaped and still live there **t**. 1Ch 4:43
river, ⌊where they are⌋ until **t**. 1Ch 5:26
Uzzah, as it is ⌊still named⌋ **t**. 1Ch 13:11
Egypt⌋ until **t** I have not lived 1Ch 17:5
My ordinances as ⌊he is⌋ **t**.' 1Ch 28:7
himself to the LORD **t**?" 1Ch 29:5
by Your power, as it is **t**. 2Ch 6:15
on them; ⌊it is this way⌋ **t**. 2Ch 8:8
the house of David until **t**. 2Ch 10:19
called the Valley of Beracah **t**. 2Ch 20:26
against Judah's domination **t**. 2Ch 21:10
come against you **t** but to the 2Ch 35:21
and open shame, as it is **t**. Ezr 9:7
for we survive as a remnant **t**. Ezr 9:15
Give Your servant success **t**, Neh 1:11
since **t** is holy to our Lord. Neh 8:10
Be still, since **t** is holy. Neh 8:11
of the Assyrian kings until **t**. Neh 9:32
we are **t**, slaves in the land Neh 9:36
and Haman come **t** to the banquet Est 5:4
T also my complaint is bitter. Jb 23:2
t I have become Your Father. Ps 2:7
T, if you hear His voice: Ps 95:7
They stand **t** in accordance with Ps 119:91
t I've fulfilled my vows. Pr 7:14
instructed you **t**—even you—so Pr 22:19
T he will stand at Nob, shaking Is 10:32
'**T** is a day of distress, rebuke, Is 37:3
living can thank You, as I do **t**; Is 38:19
from **t** on I am He ⌊alone⌋, Is 43:13
have not heard of them before **t**, Is 48:7
and tomorrow will be like **t**, Is 56:12
You cannot fast as ⌊you do⌋ **t**, Is 58:4
t I have set you over nations Jr 1:10
T, I am the One who has made you Jr 1:18
milk and honey, as it is **t**." Jr 11:5
of the land of Egypt until **t**, Jr 11:7
scorn and cursing—as it is **t**; Jr 25:18
Yourself, as ⌊is the case⌋ **t**. Jr 32:20
T you repented and did what Jr 34:15
during Josiah's reign until **t**. Jr 36:2
T I am setting you free from the Jr 40:4
that I have warned you **t**! Jr 42:19
I have told you **t**, but you have Jr 42:21
they are a ruin **t** without an Jr 44:2
the desolate ruin they are **t**. Jr 44:6
inhabitant, as ⌊you see⌋ **t**. Jr 44:22
come to you, as ⌊you see⌋ **t**." Jr 44:23
t I declare that I will restore Zch 9:12
Give us **t** our daily bread. Mt 6:11
which is here **t** and thrown into Mt 6:30
it would have remained until **t**. Mt 11:23
'**T** will be stormy because the Mt 16:3
go, work in the vineyard **t**.' Mt 21:28
for **t** I've suffered terribly in Mt 27:19
to him, "**t**, this very night, Mk 14:30
t a Savior, who is Messiah the Lk 2:11
to them, "**T** as you listen, Lk 4:21
have seen incredible things **t**!" Lk 5:26
is in the field **t** and is thrown Lk 12:28
healings **t** and tomorrow, Lk 13:32
Yet I must travel **t**, tomorrow, Lk 13:33
t I must stay at your house. Lk 19:5
T salvation has come to this Lk 19:9
will not crow **t** until you deny Lk 22:34
Before the rooster crows **t**, Lk 22:61
T you will be with Me in paradise. Lk 23:43
being examined **t** about a good Ac 4:9
t I have become Your Father. Ac 13:33
rioting for what happened **t**, Ac 19:40
God, just as all of you are **t**, Ac 22:3
'**T** I am being judged before you Ac 24:21
that **t** I am going to make a Ac 26:2
listen to me **t** might become as Ac 26:29
T is the fourteenth day that you Ac 27:33
t I have become Your Father, Heb 1:5
T, if you hear His voice, Heb 3:7
while it is still called **t**, Heb 3:13
T, if you hear His voice, do not Heb 3:15
a certain day—**t**—speaking Heb 4:7
T if you hear His voice, do not Heb 4:7
t I have become Your Father, Heb 5:5
same yesterday, **t**, and forever. Heb 13:8
T or tomorrow we will travel to Jms 4:13

TODAY'S *(2)*

tomorrow to carry out **t** law, Est 9:13
man, write down **t** date, this Ezk 24:2

TODDLER *(1)*

and a **t** will put his hand into a Is 11:8

TOE *(5)*

and on the big **t** of his right Lv 8:23
and on the big **t** of his right Lv 14:14
and on the big **t** of his right Lv 14:17
and on the big **t** of his right Lv 14:25
and on the big **t** of his right Lv 14:28

TOES *(8)*

and on the big **t** of their right Ex 29:20
and on the big **t** of their right Lv 8:24
cut off his thumbs and big **t**. Jdg 1:6
thumbs and big **t** cut off used to Jdg 1:7
hand and six **t** on each foot— 2Sm 21:20
hand⌋ and six **t** ⌊on each foot⌋— 1Ch 20:6
You saw the feet and **t**, partly Dn 2:41
and that the **t** of the feet were Dn 2:42

TOGARMAH *(2)*

Ashkenaz, Riphath, and T. Gn 10:3
Ashkenaz, Riphath, and T. 1Ch 1:6

TOGETHER *(270)*

sewed fig leaves **t** and made Gn 3:7
whom I created, **t** with the Gn 6:7
they set out **t** from Ur of the Gn 11:31
them as long as they stayed **t**, Gn 13:6
that they could not stay **t**, Gn 13:6
called all his servants **t**, Gn 20:8
and the two of them walked on **t**. Gn 22:6
the two of them walked on **t**. Gn 22:8
got up and went **t** to Beer-sheba. Gn 22:19
too many ⌊for them⌋ to live **t**, Gn 36:7
them **t** for three days. Gn 42:17
t and listen, sons of Jacob; Gn 49:2
Then all the people responded **t**, Ex 19:8
the curtains should be joined **t**, Ex 26:3
other⌋ five curtains joined **t**. Ex 26:3
so that the loops line up **t**. Ex 26:5
the curtains **t** with the clasps, Ex 26:6
and join the tent **t** so that it Ex 26:11
be connected **t** with two tenons. Ex 26:17
and joined **t** at the top in a Ex 26:24
so that it can be joined **t**. Ex 28:7
joined five of the curtains **t**, Ex 36:16
together, and ⌊the other⌋ six **t**. Ex 36:16
join the tent **t** as a single unit Ex 36:18
bottom and joined **t** at the top Ex 36:29
t with its five posts and their Ex 36:38
was joined **t** at its two edges. Ex 39:4
bring the fat **t** with the breast. Lv 7:30
t with the offerings of fat Lv 10:15
the live bird **t** with the cedar Lv 14:6
is to be cleansed, **t** with these Lv 14:11
he can afford **t** with the grain Lv 14:31
t with the basket of unleavened Nm 6:17
When calling the assembly **t**, Nm 10:7
They came **t** against Moses and Nm 16:3
his hands **t**, and said to him Nm 24:10
who gathered **t** against the LORD. Nm 27:3
plow with an ox and a donkey **t**. Dt 22:10
they came **t** and camped at the Jos 11:5
Ephraim by their clans, **t** with Jos 16:8
gathered **t**, crossed over Jdg 6:33
gathered **t** and proceeded to Jdg 9:6
Tower of Shechem had gathered **t**. Jdg 9:47
The Ammonites were called **t**, Jdg 10:17
were called **t** and crossed Jdg 12:1
gathered **t** to offer a great Jdg 16:23
the two of them ate and drank **t**. Jdg 19:6
gathered **t** from their cities to Jdg 20:14
who **t** built the house of Israel. Ru 4:11
Philistine rulers **t** and asked, 1Sm 5:8
all the Philistine rulers **t**. 1Sm 5:11
Israel gathered **t** and went to 1Sm 8:4
that no two of them were left **t**. 1Sm 11:11
military units **t** into one army 1Sm 28:1
Philistines came **t** and camped at 1Sm 28:4
military units **t** at Aphek while 1Sm 29:1
Saul died **t** with his three sons, 1Sm 31:6
side so that they all died **t**. 2Sm 2:16
Berites came **t** and followed him 2Sm 20:14
the seven of them died **t**. 2Sm 21:9
Solomon put **t** a fleet of ships 1Kg 9:26
military units **t** and marched up 2Kg 6:24
all the people **t** and said to 2Kg 10:18
died—his whole house died **t**. 1Ch 10:6
All Israel came **t** to David at 1Ch 11:1
warriors who, **t** with all Israel, 1Ch 11:10
they should gather **t** with us. 1Ch 13:2
he gathered **t** the descendants 1Ch 15:4
t with an immeasurable quantity 1Ch 22:3
T with Zadok from the sons of 1Ch 24:3
T with their relatives who were 1Ch 25:7
and singers joined **t** to praise 2Ch 5:13
t with some of the Meunites, 2Ch 20:1
They gathered their brothers **t**, 2Ch 29:15
been gathered **t** in Jerusalem. 2Ch 30:3
people gathered **t** in Jerusalem. Ezr 3:1
joined **t** to supervise those Ezr 3:9
t with all who had separated Ezr 6:21
t with the freewill offerings Ezr 7:16
t with the elders and judges of Ezr 10:14
wall was joined **t** up to half its Neh 4:6
They all plotted **t** to come and Neh 4:8
let's meet **t** in the villages of Neh 6:2
So come, let's confer **t**. Neh 6:7
people gathered **t** at the square Neh 8:1
and singers **t** and stationed them Neh 13:11
were assembled **t** for a second Est 2:19
They met **t** to go and offer Jb 2:11
and wove me **t** with bones and Jb 10:11
could string words **t** against you Jb 16:4
join themselves **t** against me. Jb 16:10
will we descend **t** to the dust? Jb 17:16
His troops advance **t**; Jb 19:12
let us decide **t** what is good. Jb 34:4
would perish **t** and mankind would Jb 34:15
stars sang **t** and all the sons Jb 38:7
and the clods ⌊of dirt⌋ stick **t**? Jb 38:38
Hide them **t** in the dust; Jb 40:13
his thighs are woven firmly **t**. Jb 40:17
of scales, closely sealed **t**. Jb 41:15
folds of his flesh are joined **t**, Jb 41:23
rulers conspire **t** against the Ps 2:2
let us exalt His name **t**. Ps 34:3
who hate me whisper **t** about me; Ps 41:7
assembled; they advanced **t**. Ps 48:4
low and high, rich and poor **t**. Ps 49:2
t they ⌊weigh⌋ less than a vapor. Ps 62:9
and those who spy on me plot **t**, Ps 71:10
love and truth will join **t**; Ps 85:10
They band **t** against the life of Ps 94:21
the mountains shout **t** for joy Ps 98:8
princes sit **t** speaking against Ps 119:23
should be⌋, solidly joined **t**, Ps 122:3
it is when brothers can live **t**! Ps 133:1
You knit me **t** in my mother's Ps 139:13
as young women, old and young **t**. Ps 148:12
if two lie down **t**, they can keep Ec 4:11
both will burn **t**, with no one to Is 1:31
Band **t**, peoples, and be broken; Is 8:9
t, both are against Judah. Is 9:21
and the fatling will be **t**, Is 11:6
young ones will lie down **t**, Is 11:7
T they will plunder the people Is 11:14
like nations being gathered **t**! Is 13:4
All your rulers have fled **t**, Is 22:3
your fugitives were captured **t**; Is 22:3
be gathered **t** like prisoners Is 24:22
both will perish **t**. Is 31:3

all humanity will see ⌊it⌋ **t**, Is 40:5
let us come **t** for the trial. Is 41:1
desert, elms and box trees **t**, Is 41:19
All the nations are gathered **t**, Is 43:9
the army and the mighty one **t** Is 43:17
let us argue our case **t**. Is 43:26
of idols go in humiliation **t**. Is 45:16
Come, gather **t**, and draw near, Is 45:20
yes, let them take counsel **t**. Is 45:21
they crouch **t**; they are not able Is 46:2
summoned them, they stood up **t**. Is 48:13
They all gather **t**; they come to Is 49:18
voices, shouting for joy **t**; Is 52:8
Be joyful, rejoice **t**, you ruins Is 52:9
fir, and cypress **t**—to beautify Is 60:13
iniquities of your fathers **t**," Is 65:7
wolf and the lamb will feed **t**, Is 65:25
and rats, will perish **t**." Is 66:17
they will come **t** from the land Jr 3:18
fathers and sons **t** will stumble Jr 6:21
here? Gather **t**; let us enter Jr 8:14
young and old men ⌊rejoice⌋ **t**. Jr 31:13
its cities will live in it **t**— Jr 31:24
ate a meal **t** there in Mizpah Jr 41:1
warrior and **t** both of them have Jr 46:12
turn back; **t** they will flee; Jr 46:21
go into exile **t** with his priests Jr 49:3
and Judeans will come **t**, Jr 50:4
They will roar **t** like young Jr 51:38
like rams **t** with male goats. Jr 51:40
t 4,600 people ⌊were deported⌋ Jr 52:30
a yoke, fastened **t** by His hand; Lm 1:14
walls grieve; **t** they waste away Lm 2:8
and clap ⌊your⌋ hands **t**. Ezk 21:14
I also will clap My hands **t**, Ezk 21:17
I clap My hands **t** against the Ezk 22:13
will gather you **t** and blow on Ezk 22:21
the bones came **t**, bone to bone. Ezk 37:7
Then join them **t** into a single Ezk 37:17
and put them **t** with the stick of Ezk 37:19
t with a gallon of oil for every Ezk 46:7
one another but will not hold **t**, Dn 2:43
shook and his knees knocked **t**. Dn 5:6
and satraps went **t** to the king Dn 6:6
t with the daily sacrifice, Dn 8:12
will be given up, **t** with her Dn 11:6
Israelites will be gathered **t**. Hs 1:11
princes will go into exile **t**. Am 1:15
Can two walk **t** without agreeing Am 3:3
will bring them **t** like sheep in Mc 2:12
his evil desire, they plot it **t**. Mc 7:3
with no one to gather ⌊them⌋ **t**. Nah 3:18
Gather yourselves **t**; Zph 2:1
gather **t**, undesirable nation, Zph 2:1
bow, from them every ruler. **T** Zch 10:4
before they came **t** that she was Mt 1:18
Let both grow **t** until the Mt 13:30
three are gathered **t** in My name, Mt 18:20
Therefore what God has joined **t**, Mt 19:6
they came **t** in the same place. Mt 22:34
While the Pharisees were **t**, Mt 22:41
to gather your children **t**, Mt 23:37
So they conferred **t** and bought Mt 27:7
So when they had gathered **t**, Mt 27:17
twisted **t** a crown of thorns, Mt 27:29
people gathered **t** that there was Mk 2:2
a crowd was rapidly coming **t**, Mk 9:25
Therefore what God has joined **t**, Mk 10:9
and called the whole company **t**. Mk 15:16
twisted **t** a crown of thorns, Mk 15:17
crowds would come **t** to hear Him Lk 5:15
down, shaken **t**, and running over Lk 6:38
crowd of many thousands came **t**, Lk 12:1
to gather your children **t**, Lk 13:34
his friends and neighbors **t**, Lk 15:6
women friends and neighbors **t**, Lk 15:9
younger son gathered **t** all he Lk 15:13
women will be grinding grain **t**: Lk 17:35
of the courtyard and sat down **t**, Lk 22:55
Pilate called **t** the chief Lk 23:13
Then they all cried out **t**, Lk 23:18
T they were discussing Lk 24:14
and those with them gathered **t**, Lk 24:33
to Capernaum, **t** with His mother, Jn 2:12
sower and reaper can rejoice **t**. Jn 4:36
Father who sent Me ⌊judge **t**⌋. Jn 8:16
twisted **t** a crown of thorns, Jn 19:2
were running **t**, but the other Jn 20:4
were ⌊gathered **t**⌋ with the doors Jn 20:19
others of His disciples were **t**. Jn 21:2
While He was **t** with them, He Ac 1:4
they had come **t**, they asked Him, Ac 1:6
who were **t** was about 120— Ac 1:15
they were all **t** in one place. Ac 2:1
multitude came **t** and was Ac 2:6
believers were **t** and had Ac 2:44
to meeting⌋ **t** in the temple Ac 2:46
were going up **t** to the temple Ac 3:1
assembled **t** against the Lord Ac 4:26
assembled **t** against Your holy Ac 4:27
multitude came **t** from the towns Ac 5:16
in the desert **t** with the angel Ac 7:38
ears, and rushed **t** against him. Ac 7:57
and had called **t** his relatives Ac 10:24
that many had come **t** there. Ac 10:27
T they presented themselves Ac 12:20
and gathered the church **t**, Ac 14:27
had brought **t** some scoundrels Ac 17:5
and they rushed all **t** into the Ac 19:29
not know why they had come **t**. Ac 19:32
up, and the people rushed **t**. Ac 21:30
days he called **t** the leaders Ac 28:17
t they have become useless; Rm 3:12
testifies **t** with our spirit Rm 8:16
been groaning **t** with labor pains Rm 8:22
all things work **t** for the good Rm 8:28
to agonize **t** with me in your Rm 15:30
joy and be refreshed **t** with you. Rm 15:32
Then come **t** again; otherwise 1Co 7:5
since you come **t** not for the 1Co 11:17
when you come **t** as a church 1Co 11:18
when you come **t** in one place, 1Co 11:20
when you come **t** to eat, wait for 1Co 11:33
you can come **t** and not cause 1Co 11:34
put the body **t**, giving greater 1Co 12:24
if the whole church assembles **t**, 1Co 14:23
Whenever you come **t**, each one 1Co 14:26
Working **t** with Him, we also 2Co 6:1
to die **t** and to live together. 2Co 7:3
to die together and to live **t**. 2Co 7:3
everything **t** in the Messiah, Eph 1:10
is being fitted **t** in Him and is Eph 2:21
are being built **t** for God's Eph 2:22
fitted and knit **t** by every Eph 4:16
and by Him all things hold **t**. Col 1:17
encouraged and joined **t** in love, Col 2:2
and held **t** by its ligaments Col 2:19
will be caught up **t** with them in 1Th 4:17
asleep, we will live **t** with Him. 1Th 5:10
was active **t** with his works, Jms 2:22
gather **t** for the great supper of Rv 19:17
armies gathered **t** to wage war Rv 19:19

TOHU *(1)*
of Elihu, son of **T**, son of Zuph, 1Sm 1:1

TOI *(2)*
(AKA TOU)
When King **T** of Hamath heard that 2Sm 8:9
for **T** and Hadadezer had fought 2Sm 8:10

TOILED *(1)*
we labored and **t**, working night 2Th 3:8

TOKHATH *(1)*
(AKA TIKVAH)
the wife of Shallum son of **T**, 2Ch 34:22

TOLA *(6)*
T, Puvah, Jashub, and Shimron. Gn 46:13
the Tolaite clan from **T**; Nm 26:23
Abimelech, **T** son of Puah, son Jdg 10:1
T judged Israel 23 years, and Jdg 10:2
T, Puah, Jashub, and Shimron— 1Ch 7:1
descendants of **T** were recorded 1Ch 7:2

TOLA'S *(1)*
T sons: Uzzi, Rephaiah, Jeriel, 1Ch 7:2

TOLAD *(1)*
(AKA ELTOLAD)
Bilhah, Ezem, **T**, 1Ch 4:29

TOLAITE *(1)*
the **T** clan from Tola; Nm 26:23

TOLD *(602)*
Who **t** you that you were naked? Gn 3:11
naked and **t** his two brothers Gn 9:22
as the LORD had **t** him, and Lot Gn 12:4
came and **t** Abram the Hebrew, Gn 14:13
and personally **t** them all these Gn 20:8
appointed time God had **t** him. Gn 21:2
Who would have **t** Abraham that Gn 21:7
the place God had **t** him about. Gn 22:3
place that God had **t** him about, Gn 22:9
these things Abraham was **t**, Gn 22:20
The girl ran and **t** her mother's Gn 24:28
the servant **t** Isaac everything Gn 24:66
I have done as you **t** me. Gn 27:19
He **t** Rachel that he was her Gn 29:12
She ran and **t** her father. Gn 29:12
and Jacob **t** him all that had Gn 29:13
day Laban was **t** that Jacob had Gn 31:22
And he **t** the first one: Gn 32:17
He also **t** the second one, the Gn 32:19
as a wife," he **t** his father Gn 34:4
When he **t** it to his brothers, Gn 37:5
another dream and **t** it to his Gn 37:9
He **t** his father and brothers, Gn 37:10
Tamar was **t**, "Your father-in-law Gn 38:13
three months later Judah was **t**, Gn 38:24
Then she **t** him the same story: Gn 39:17
heard the story his wife **t** him— Gn 39:19
chief cupbearer **t** his dream to Gn 40:9
Pharaoh **t** them his dreams, Gn 41:8
We **t** him our dreams, he Gn 41:12
I **t** this to the magicians, Gn 41:24
It is just as I **t** Pharaoh: Gn 41:28
Pharaoh **t** all Egypt, "Go to Gn 41:55
they **t** him all that had happened Gn 42:29
But we **t** him: We are honest men Gn 42:31
father that you **t** me about? Gn 43:27
brother that you **t** me about?" Gn 43:29
So he did as Joseph **t** him. Gn 44:2
We **t** him, 'We cannot go down Gn 44:26
But when they **t** Jacob all that Gn 45:27
Joseph was **t**, "Your father is Gn 48:1
When Jacob was **t**, "Your son Gn 48:2
as the king of Egypt had **t** them; Ex 1:17
Pharaoh's daughter **t** her. Ex 2:8
but the LORD **t** him, "Stretch out Ex 4:4
Now in Midian the LORD **t** Moses, Ex 4:19
t you: Let My son go so that he Ex 4:23
Moses **t** Aaron everything the Ex 4:28
in trouble when they were **t**, Ex 5:19
Moses **t** this to the Israelites, Ex 6:9
Aaron and Moses whom the LORD **t**, Ex 6:26
them, as the LORD had **t** Moses. Ex 9:12
went in to Pharaoh and **t** him, Ex 10:3
of Egypt was **t** that the people Ex 14:5
this what we **t** you in Egypt: Ex 14:12
Then Moses **t** Aaron, "Say to the Ex 16:9
Moses **t** them, "It is the bread Ex 16:15
t them, "This is what the LORD Ex 16:23
Moses **t** Aaron, "Take a container Ex 16:33
Joshua did as Moses had **t** him, Ex 17:10
And the LORD **t** Moses, "Go to the Ex 19:10
down to the people and **t** them. Ex 19:25
Then the LORD **t** Moses, "This is Ex 20:22
Moses came and **t** the people all Ex 24:3
He **t** the elders, "Wait here for Ex 24:14
He **t** them, "This is what the Ex 32:27
to the place I **t** you about; Ex 32:34
Look, You have **t** me, 'Lead this Ex 33:12
the LORD had **t** him on Mount Ex 34:32
blood, I have **t** the Israelites: Lv 17:14
For the LORD had **t** Moses: Nm 1:48
LORD **t** Moses: "Register every Nm 3:40
The LORD **t** Moses, "Each day have Nm 7:11
the LORD **t** Moses in the Nm 9:1
So Moses **t** the Israelites to Nm 9:4
Moses went out and **t** the people Nm 11:24
of Canaan, he **t** them, "Go up Nm 13:17
and the whole community **t** them, Nm 14:2
Then the LORD **t** Moses, "The man Nm 15:35
Moses and Aaron and **t** them, Nm 16:3
Moses also **t** Korah, "Now listen, Nm 16:8
So Moses **t** Korah, "You and all Nm 16:16
Then Moses **t** Aaron, "Take your Nm 16:46
The LORD **t** Moses, "Put Aaron's Nm 17:10
The LORD **t** Aaron, "You will not Nm 18:20
That is why I **t** them that they Nm 18:24
the well the LORD **t** Moses about, Nm 21:16
Balak **t** Balaam, "Don't curse Nm 23:25
Balaam **t** Balak, "Build me seven Nm 23:29
So Moses **t** Israel's judges, Nm 25:5
The LORD **t** Moses: Nm 25:16
So Moses **t** the Israelites Nm 29:40
Moses **t** the leaders of the Nm 30:1
The LORD **t** Moses, Nm 31:25

and **t** him, "Your servants have Nm 31:49
Moses **t** them, "If the Gadites Nm 32:29
t the Israelites everything Dt 1:3
God of your fathers, has **t** you. Dt 1:21
as the LORD had **t** me, and we Dt 2:1
swiftly, as the LORD has **t** you. Dt 9:3
as the LORD your God **t** him. Dt 10:9
and if you are **t** or hear ⌊about Dt 17:4
for the LORD has **t** you, 'You are Dt 17:16
The LORD has **t** me, 'You will not Dt 31:2
The king of Jericho was **t**, Jos 2:2
They **t** Joshua, "The LORD has Jos 2:24
Joshua **t** the people, "Consecrate Jos 3:5
Then Joshua **t** the Israelites, Jos 3:9
just as the LORD had **t** Joshua. Jos 4:8
The LORD **t** Joshua, Jos 4:15
of Bethel, and **t** them, "Go up Jos 7:2
inhabitants of our land **t** us, Jos 9:11
them as the LORD had **t** him; Jos 11:9
all that the LORD had **t** Moses. Jos 11:23
t them at Shiloh in the land Jos 21:2
and **t** them, "You have done Jos 22:2
the land of Gilead, and **t** them, Jos 22:15
But Joshua **t** the people, "You Jos 24:19
Joshua then **t** the people, Jos 24:22
He **t** them, "Follow me, because Jdg 3:28
that our fathers **t** us about? Jdg 6:13
and did as the LORD had **t** him. Jdg 6:27
He also **t** the men of Penuel, Jdg 8:9
When they **t** Jotham, he climbed Jdg 9:7
they **t** him, "Please say Jdg 12:6
woman went and **t** her husband, Jdg 13:6
to her husband and **t** him, Jdg 13:10
needs to do everything I **t** her. Jdg 13:13
here," Manoah **t** Him, "and we Jdg 13:15
went back and **t** his father and Jdg 14:2
But Samson **t** his father, Jdg 14:3
You **t** my people the riddle, Jdg 14:16
They were **t**, "⌊It was⌋ Samson, Jdg 15:6
Then Samson **t** them, "Because you Jdg 15:7
Then Samson **t** them, "Swear to Jdg 15:12
Samson **t** her, "If they tie me up Jdg 16:7
have mocked me and **t** me lies! Jdg 16:10
t her, "If they tie me up with Jdg 16:11
me all along and **t** me lies! Jdg 16:13
He **t** her, "If you weave the Jdg 16:13
you,'" she **t** him, "when your Jdg 16:15
mocked me and not **t** me what Jdg 16:15
t her the whole truth and said Jdg 16:17
that he had **t** her the whole Jdg 16:18
he has **t** me the whole truth." Jdg 16:18
They **t** them, "Go and explore the Jdg 18:2
He **t** them what Micah had for him Jdg 18:4
The priest **t** them, "Go in peace. Jdg 18:6
land of Laish **t** their brothers, Jdg 18:14
They **t** him, "Be quiet. Keep your Jdg 18:19
"Get up," he **t** her. "Let's go." Jdg 19:28
mealtime Boaz **t** her, "Come over Ru 2:14
Ruth **t** her mother-in-law about Ru 2:19
said, "He also **t** me, 'Stay with Ru 2:21
he **t** ⌊Ruth⌋, "Bring the shawl Ru 3:15
Then Ruth **t** her everything the Ru 3:16
He **t** Samuel, "Go and lie down. 1Sm 3:9
I **t** him that I am going to judge 1Sm 3:13
anything from me that He **t** you." 1Sm 3:17
So Samuel **t** him everything and 1Sm 3:18
Samuel **t** them, "If you are 1Sm 7:3
But the LORD **t** him, "Listen to 1Sm 8:7
Samuel **t** all the LORD's words to 1Sm 8:10
to them," the LORD **t** Samuel. 1Sm 8:22
Then Samuel **t** the men of 1Sm 8:22
Saul, the LORD **t** him, "Here is 1Sm 9:17
Here is the man I **t** you about; 1Sm 9:17
gave you and **t** you to set aside. 1Sm 9:23
Saul **t** him, "He assured us the 1Sm 10:16
and **t** the terms to the people, 1Sm 11:4
t the messengers who had come, 1Sm 11:9
the messengers **t** the men of 1Sm 11:9
Jonathan **t** his armor-bearer, 1Sm 14:12
Saul **t** Ahijah, "Bring the ark of 1Sm 14:18
Jonathan **t** him, "I tasted a 1Sm 14:43
Samuel **t** Saul, "The LORD sent me 1Sm 15:1
him, Samuel **t** Jesse, "The LORD 1Sm 16:10
Samuel **t** Jesse, "Send for him. 1Sm 16:11
Jesse had **t** his son David, 1Sm 17:17
people **t** him about the offer, 1Sm 17:27
Saul **t** David, "Here is my oldest 1Sm 18:17
so he **t** him: "My father Saul 1Sm 19:2

David and **t** him all these 1Sm 19:7
at Ramah and **t** him everything 1Sm 19:18
So David **t** him, "Look, tomorrow 1Sm 20:5
my brother has **t** me to be there. 1Sm 20:29
mission, but he **t** me, 'Don't let 1Sm 21:2
The priest **t** him, "There is no 1Sm 21:4
Abiathar **t** David that Saul had 1Sm 22:21
When David was **t** about it, 1Sm 23:25
Philistines, he was **t**, "David is 1Sm 24:1
the day the LORD **t** you about: 1Sm 24:4
yourself have **t** me today what 1Sm 24:18
his wife **t** him about these 1Sm 25:37
and did what you **t** me ⌊to do⌋. 1Sm 28:21
enraged with Achish and **t** him, 1Sm 29:4
Achish summoned David and **t** 1Sm 29:6
me, 'Who are you?' I **t** him: I'm 2Sm 1:8
of Judah. They **t** David: "It was 2Sm 2:4
the person **t** me, 'Look, Saul 2Sm 4:10
So Nathan **t** the king, "Go and do 2Sm 7:3
David **t** the messenger, "Say this 2Sm 11:25
bedroom," Amnon **t** Tamar, "so I 2Sm 13:10
He **t** her, "Pretend to be in 2Sm 14:2
Then Joab **t** her exactly what to 2Sm 14:3
The king **t** the woman, "Go home. 2Sm 14:8
t your servant exactly what to 2Sm 14:19
Joab went to the king and **t** him. 2Sm 14:33
way because the LORD **t** him, 2Sm 16:10
me⌋; the LORD has **t** him to. 2Sm 16:11
to Absalom, and Absalom **t** him: 2Sm 17:6
Hushai then **t** the priests Zadok 2Sm 17:15
They **t** him, "Get up and 2Sm 17:21
He called out and **t** the king. 2Sm 18:25
and all the people were **t**: 2Sm 19:8
to David, **t** him ⌊the choices⌋ 2Sm 24:13
son of Jehoiada and **t** ⌊him⌋, 1Kg 2:29
Indeed, I was not even **t** half. 1Kg 10:7
the LORD had **t** the Israelites 1Kg 11:2
had grown up with him **t** him, 1Kg 12:10
and went back as He had **t** them. 1Kg 12:24
His son came and **t** him all the 1Kg 13:11
His sons also **t** their father the 1Kg 13:11
was he who **t** about me becoming 1Kg 14:2
Ahab **t** Jezebel everything that 1Kg 19:1
angel **t** him, "Get up and eat. 1Kg 19:5
He **t** him, "Because you did not 1Kg 20:36
Naboth the Jezreelite had **t** him. 1Kg 21:4
he replied. "I **t** him: Give me 1Kg 21:6
Micaiah **t** him, "March up and 1Kg 22:15
She went and **t** the man of God, 2Kg 4:7
His father **t** his servant, 2Kg 4:19
it from me. He hasn't **t** me." 2Kg 4:27
back to meet Elisha and **t** him, 2Kg 4:31
Naaman went and **t** his master 2Kg 5:4
the prophet had **t** you to do some 2Kg 5:13
the man of God had **t** him about. 2Kg 6:10
When he was **t**, "Elisha is in 2Kg 6:13
city's gatekeepers and **t** them, 2Kg 7:10
returned and **t** the king. 2Kg 7:15
the woman, she **t** him the story. 2Kg 8:6
the king was **t**, "The man of God 2Kg 8:7
Elisha **t** him, "Go say to him, 2Kg 8:10
He **t** me you are sure to recover. 2Kg 8:14
So they went back and **t** him, 2Kg 9:36
the messenger came and **t** him, 2Kg 10:8
although the LORD had **t** them, 2Kg 17:12
the high priest **t** Shaphan the 2Kg 22:8
the court secretary **t** the king, 2Kg 22:10
The men of the city **t** him, 2Kg 23:17
Then David **t** the leaders of the 1Ch 15:16
So Nathan **t** David, "Do all that 1Ch 17:2
I was not even **t** half of your 2Ch 9:6
who had grown up with him **t** him 2Ch 10:10
He **t** ⌊the people of⌋ Judah to 2Ch 14:4
People came and **t** Jehoshaphat, 2Ch 20:2
Then he **t** the descendants of 2Ch 29:21
the officials **t** the Levites to 2Ch 29:30
He **t** the people who lived in 2Ch 31:4
Hezekiah **t** them to prepare 2Ch 31:11
he **t** Judah to serve the LORD 2Ch 33:16
Hilkiah **t** Shaphan the court 2Ch 34:15
the court secretary **t** the king, 2Ch 34:18
am fighting. God **t** me to hurry. 2Ch 35:21
He **t** him, 'Take these articles, Ezr 5:15
since we had **t** him, "The hand of Ezr 8:22
for I had not yet **t** the Jews, Neh 2:16
t them how the gracious hand of Neh 2:18
You **t** them to go in and possess Neh 9:15
the land You **t** their ancestors Neh 9:23

and she **t** the king on Mordecai's Est 2:22
t Haman to see if Mordecai's Est 3:4
he had **t** them he was a Jew. Est 3:4
the king **t** Haman, "The money Est 3:11
Mordecai **t** him everything that Est 4:7
Mordecai **t** ⌊the messenger⌋ to Est 4:13
He **t** them all how the king had Est 5:11
and all his friends **t** him, Est 5:14
Haman **t** the king, "For the man Est 6:7
The king **t** Haman, "Hurry, and do Est 6:10
Haman **t** his wife Zeresh and all Est 6:13
well," the LORD **t** Satan, Jb 1:12
well," the LORD **t** Satan, "he is Jb 2:6
foolish woman speaks," he **t** her. Jb 2:10
Should He be **t** that I want to Jb 37:20
and did as the LORD had **t** them, Jb 42:9
will be **t** about the Lord. Ps 22:30
they are more than can be **t**. Ps 40:5
our forefathers have **t** us— Ps 44:1
I **t** You about my life, and You Ps 119:26
Who **t** about this from the Is 41:26
it, no one **t** it, no one heard Is 41:26
Have I not **t** you and declared it Is 44:8
see what had not been **t** them, Is 52:15
touched my mouth, and **t** me: Jr 1:9
I specifically **t** you not to say, Jr 23:38
and all the people **t** the priests Jr 26:16
For I have **t** you today, but you Jr 42:21
Jeremiah **t** Seraiah, "When you Jr 51:61
on me, and He **t** me, "You are to Ezk 11:5
The man **t** me, "This is the table Ezk 41:22
to his house and **t** his friends Dn 2:17
great God has **t** the king what Dn 2:45
came in, I **t** them the dream, Dn 4:7
before me. I **t** him the dream: Dn 4:8
teeth. It was **t**, 'Get up! Gorge Dn 7:5
that has been **t** is true. Dn 8:26
in the place where they were **t**: Hs 1:10
presence, because he had **t** them. Jnh 1:10
has **t** you men what is good and Mc 6:8
with me came forward and **t** me, Zch 5:5
in the land of Shinar," he **t** me. Zch 5:11
The angel **t** me, "These are the Zch 6:5
of Judea," they **t** him, "because Mt 2:5
t him, "It is also written: Mt 4:7
Then Jesus **t** him, "Go away, Mt 4:10
"Follow Me," He **t** them, "and I Mt 4:19
Then Jesus **t** him, "See that you Mt 8:4
come and heal him," He **t** him. Mt 8:7
Then Jesus **t** the centurion, Mt 8:13
Jesus **t** him, "Foxes have dens Mt 8:20
But Jesus **t** him, "Follow Me, and Mt 8:22
"Go!" He **t** them. So when they Mt 8:32
faith, Jesus **t** the paralytic, Mt 9:2
sins"—then He **t** the paralytic, Mt 9:6
the poor are **t** the good news. Mt 11:5
Then He **t** the man, "Stretch out Mt 12:13
their thoughts, He **t** them: Mt 12:25
Someone **t** Him, "Look, Your Mt 12:47
He replied to the one who **t** Him, Mt 12:48
Then He **t** them many things in Mt 13:3
did this!' he **t** them. " 'So, do Mt 13:28
He **t** them another parable: Mt 13:33
Jesus **t** the crowds all these Mt 13:34
things?" "Yes," they **t** Him. Mt 13:51
the Baptist!" he **t** his servants. Mt 14:2
need to go away," Jesus **t** them. Mt 14:16
the crowd, He **t** them, "Listen Mt 15:10
the disciples came up and **t** Him, Mt 15:12
Then Jesus **t** them, "Watch out Mt 16:6
understand that when I **t** you, Mt 16:11
But He turned and **t** Peter, Mt 16:23
your little faith," He **t** them. Mt 17:20
Galilee, Jesus **t** them, "The Son Mt 17:22
the sons are free," Jesus **t** him. Mt 17:26
He **t** them, "Moses permitted you Mt 19:8
But He **t** them, "Not everyone can Mt 19:11
all these," the young man **t** Him. Mt 19:20
go to my vineyard,' he **t** them. Mt 20:7
of the vineyard **t** his foreman, Mt 20:8
t them, "You will indeed drink Mt 20:23
The crowd **t** them to keep quiet, Mt 20:31
"Yes," Jesus **t** them. Mt 21:16
men," they **t** Him, "and lease his Mt 21:41
Then he **t** his slaves, 'The Mt 22:8
Then the king **t** the attendants, Mt 22:13
"David's," they **t** Him. Mt 22:42
I have **t** you in advance. Mt 24:25

all this, He **t** His disciples, Mt 26:1
will also be **t** in memory of her. Mt 26:13
"You have said it," He **t** him. Mt 26:25
Peter **t** Him, "Even if everyone Mt 26:33
with You," Peter **t** Him, "I will Mt 26:35
and He **t** the disciples, Mt 26:36
Jesus **t** him, "Put your sword Mt 26:52
"You have said it," Jesus **t** him. Mt 26:64
saw him and **t** those who were Mt 26:71
of soldiers⌋," Pilate **t** them. Mt 27:65
But the angel **t** the women, Mt 28:5
Listen, I have **t** you." Mt 28:7
Then Jesus **t** them, "Do not be Mt 28:10
and **t** them, "Say this, 'His Mt 28:13
Me," Jesus **t** them, "and I will Mk 1:17
they **t** Him about her at once. Mk 1:30
"I am willing," He **t** him. Mk 1:41
faith, Jesus **t** the paralytic, Mk 2:5
sins," He **t** the paralytic, Mk 2:10
heard this, He **t** them, "Those Mk 2:17
Then He **t** them, "The Sabbath was Mk 2:27
He **t** the man with the paralyzed Mk 3:3
their hearts, He **t** the man, Mk 3:5
Then He **t** His disciples to have Mk 3:9
sitting around Him and **t** Him, Mk 3:32
come, He **t** them, "Let's cross Mk 4:35
For He had **t** him, "Come out of Mk 5:8
man and ⌊**t**⌋ about the pigs. Mk 5:16
instead, He **t** him, "Go back home Mk 5:19
and **t** Him the whole truth. Mk 5:33
He **t** the synagogue leader, Mk 5:36
crowd again, He **t** them, "Listen Mk 7:14
Then He **t** her, "Because of this Mk 7:29
"Twelve," they **t** Him. Mk 8:19
And He **t** them, "This kind can Mk 9:29
But Jesus **t** them, "He wrote this Mk 10:5
"We are able," they **t** Him. Mk 10:39
Many people **t** him to keep quiet, Mk 10:48
the blind man **t** Him, "I want to Mk 10:51
"Go your way," Jesus **t** him. Mk 10:52
and **t** them, "Go into the village Mk 11:2
Then Jesus **t** them, "Give back to Mk 12:17
Jesus **t** them, "Are you not Mk 12:24
I have **t** you everything in Mk 13:23
will also be **t** in memory of her. Mk 14:9
two of His disciples and **t** them, Mk 14:13
found it just as He had **t** them, Mk 14:16
Peter **t** Him, "Even if everyone Mk 14:29
and He **t** His disciples, Mk 14:32
"Don't be alarmed," he **t** them. Mk 16:6
Him there just as He **t** you.' " Mk 16:7
Then the angel **t** her: Do not be Lk 1:30
they were **t** about this child Lk 2:17
heard, just as they had been **t**. Lk 2:20
them and **t** His mother Mary Lk 2:34
He **t** them, "Don't collect any Lk 3:13
Don't be afraid," Jesus **t** Simon. Lk 5:10
sins"—He **t** the paralyzed man Lk 5:24
He also **t** them a parable: Lk 5:36
Then He **t** them, "The Son of Man Lk 6:5
their thoughts and **t** the man Lk 6:8
at them all, He **t** him, "Stretch Lk 6:10
He also **t** them a parable: Lk 6:39
John's disciples **t** him about all Lk 7:18
judged correctly," He **t** him. Lk 7:43
He was **t**, "Your mother and Your Lk 8:20
a boat, and He **t** them, "Let's Lk 8:22
the road," He **t** them, "no Lk 9:3
something to eat," He **t** them. Lk 9:13
Then He **t** His disciples, "Have Lk 9:14
in those days **t** no one what they Lk 9:36
was doing, He **t** His disciples, Lk 9:43
t them, "Whoever welcomes this Lk 9:48
stop him," Jesus **t** him, "because Lk 9:50
Jesus **t** him, "Foxes have dens, Lk 9:58
But He **t** him, "Let the dead bury Lk 9:60
He **t** them: "The harvest is Lk 10:2
answered correctly," He **t** him. Lk 10:28
Then Jesus **t** him, "Go and do the Lk 10:37
their thoughts, He **t** them: Lk 11:17
then **t** them, "Watch out and be Lk 12:15
Then He **t** them a parable: Lk 12:16
And He **t** this parable: Lk 13:6
He **t** the vineyard worker, Lk 13:7
some Pharisees came and **t** Him, Lk 13:31
He **t** a parable to those who were Lk 14:7
Then He **t** him: "A man was giving Lk 14:16
of the house **t** his slave, Lk 14:21
Then the master **t** the slave, Lk 14:23
So He **t** them this parable: Lk 15:3
But the father **t** his slaves, Lk 15:22
is here,' he **t** him, 'and your Lk 15:27
invoice,' he **t** him, 'sit down Lk 16:6
invoice,' he **t** him, 'and write Lk 16:7
And He **t** them: "You are the ones Lk 16:15
But he **t** him, 'If they don't Lk 16:31
He saw them, He **t** them, "Go and Lk 17:14
And He **t** him, "Get up and go on Lk 17:19
Then He **t** the disciples: Lk 17:22
He then **t** them a parable on the Lk 18:1
He also **t** this parable to some Lk 18:9
heard this, He **t** him, "You still Lk 18:22
the Twelve aside and **t** them, Lk 18:31
is passing by," they **t** him. Lk 18:37
those in front **t** him to keep Lk 18:39
sight!" Jesus **t** him. "Your faith Lk 18:42
house," Jesus **t** him, "because he Lk 19:9
10 minas, and **t** them, 'Engage Lk 19:13
good slave!' he **t** him. 'Because Lk 19:17
He **t** him, 'I will judge you by Lk 19:22
found it just as He had **t** them. Lk 19:32
Pharisees from the crowd **t** Him, Lk 19:39
they knew He had **t** this parable Lk 20:19
"Well then," He **t** them, "give Lk 20:25
Jesus **t** them, "The sons of this Lk 20:34
Then He **t** them: "Nation will be Lk 21:10
Then He **t** them a parable: Lk 21:29
found it just as He had **t** them, Lk 22:13
"Lord," he **t** Him, "I'm ready to Lk 22:33
Enough of that!" He **t** them. Lk 22:38
the place, He **t** them, "Pray that Lk 22:40
Pilate then **t** the chief priests Lk 23:4
Then He **t** them, "These are My Lk 24:44
This is the One I **t** you about: Jn 1:30
me to baptize with water **t** me, Jn 1:33
his own brother Simon and **t** him, Jn 1:41
Jesus found Philip and **t** him, Jn 1:43
found Nathanael and **t** him, Jn 1:45
only⌋ because I **t** you I saw you Jn 1:50
Jesus' mother **t** Him, "They don't Jn 2:3
His mother **t** the servants. Jn 2:5
jars with water," Jesus **t** them. Jn 2:7
and **t** him, "Everybody sets out Jn 2:10
He **t** those who were selling Jn 2:16
be amazed that I **t** you that you Jn 3:7
I have **t** you about things that Jn 3:12
So they came to John and **t** him, Jn 3:26
husband," He **t** her, "and come Jn 4:16
Jesus **t** her, "Believe Me, woman, Jn 4:21
am ⌊He⌋," Jesus **t** her, "the One Jn 4:26
went into town, and **t** the men, Jn 4:28
see a man who **t** me everything I Jn 4:29
finish His work," Jesus **t** them. Jn 4:34
"He **t** me everything I ever did." Jn 4:39
And they **t** the woman, "We no Jn 4:42
t him, "Unless you ⌊people⌋ Jn 4:48
"Go," Jesus **t** him, "your son Jn 4:50
hour at which Jesus had **t** him, Jn 4:53
"Get up," Jesus **t** him, "pick up Jn 5:8
The man who made me well **t** me, Jn 5:11
Who is this man who **t** you, Jn 5:12
were full, He **t** His disciples, Jn 6:12
bread of life," Jesus **t** them. Jn 6:35
But as I **t** you, you've seen Me, Jn 6:36
This is why I **t** you that no one Jn 6:65
Jesus **t** them, "My time has not Jn 7:6
are from below," He **t** them, "I Jn 8:23
Therefore I **t** you that you will Jn 8:24
very beginning," Jesus **t** them. Jn 8:25
Jesus **t** them, "you would Jn 8:39
a man who has **t** you the truth Jn 8:40
"Go," He **t** him, "wash in the Jn 9:7
on my eyes, and **t** me, 'Go to Jn 9:11
put mud on my eyes," he **t** them. Jn 9:15
who had been blind and **t** him, Jn 9:24
"I already **t** you," he said, "and Jn 9:27
amazing thing," the man **t** them. Jn 9:30
were blind," Jesus **t** them, "you Jn 9:41
the disciples **t** Him, "just now Jn 11:8
and then He **t** them, "Our friend Jn 11:11
So Jesus then **t** them plainly, Jn 11:14
will rise again," Jesus **t** her. Jn 11:23
Lord," she **t** Him, "I believe Jn 11:27
she fell at His feet and **t** Him, Jn 11:32
"Lord," they **t** Him, "come and see. Jn 11:34
man's sister, **t** Him, "Lord, he Jn 11:39
Pharisees and **t** them what Jesus Jn 11:46
Philip went and **t** Andrew; Jn 12:22
and Philip went and **t** Jesus. Jn 12:22
just as the Father has **t** Me." Jn 12:50
bathed," Jesus **t** him, "doesn't Jn 13:10
Therefore Jesus **t** him, "What Jn 13:27
table knew why He **t** him this. Jn 13:28
and just as I **t** the Jews, Jn 13:33
if not, I would have **t** you. Jn 14:2
Jesus **t** him, "I am the way, the Jn 14:6
you of everything I have **t** you. Jn 14:26
I have **t** you now before it Jn 14:29
I have **t** you these things to Jn 16:1
But I have **t** you these things so Jn 16:4
may remember I **t** them to you. Jn 16:4
is why I **t** you that He takes Jn 16:15
have **t** you these things so that Jn 16:33
"I am He," Jesus **t** them. Jn 18:5
When He **t** them, "I am He," they Jn 18:6
"I **t** you I am ⌊He⌋," Jesus Jn 18:8
those who heard what I **t** them. Jn 18:21
So Pilate **t** them, "Take Him Jn 18:31
or have others **t** you about Me?" Jn 18:34
to the Jews again and **t** them, Jn 18:38
he **t** the Jews, "Here is your Jn 19:14
my Lord," she **t** them, "and I Jn 20:13
to Me," Jesus **t** her, "for I have Jn 20:17
And she **t** them what He had said Jn 20:18
coming with you," they **t** him. Jn 21:3
of the boat," He **t** them, "and Jn 21:6
just caught," Jesus **t** them. Jn 21:10
have breakfast," Jesus **t** them. Jn 21:12
"Feed My lambs," He **t** him. Jn 21:15
"Shepherd My sheep," He **t** him. Jn 21:16
this, He **t** him, "Follow Me! Jn 21:19
They **t** Aaron: Make us gods who Ac 7:40
Peter **t** him, "May your silver Ac 8:20
Spirit **t** Philip, "Go and join Ac 8:29
you will be **t** what you must do. Ac 9:6
And he **t** him, "Your prayers and Ac 10:4
the Spirit **t** him, "Three men Ac 10:19
Then the Spirit **t** me to go with Ac 11:12
the angel **t** him, "and put Ac 12:8
around you," he **t** him, "and Ac 12:8
crazy!" they **t** her. But she kept Ac 12:15
out his clothes and **t** them, Ac 18:6
"No," they **t** him, "we haven't Ac 19:2
they have been **t** about you that Ac 21:21
what they were **t** about you Ac 21:24
And the Lord **t** me, 'Get up and Ac 22:10
you will be **t** about everything Ac 22:10
and **t** them, "Men, I can see that Ac 27:10
be just the way it was **t** to me. Ac 27:25
the One who calls) she was **t**: Rm 9:12
in the place where they were **t**, Rm 9:26
for the one who **t** you, 1Co 10:28
I **t** Cephas in front of everyone, Gl 2:14
advance—as I **t** you before— Gl 5:21
I have often **t** you, and now say Php 3:18
and he has **t** us about your love Col 1:8
we **t** you previously that we were 1Th 3:4
previously **t** and warned you. 1Th 4:6
with you I **t** you about this? 2Th 2:5
they **t** you, "In the end time Jd 18
and they were **t** to rest a little Rv 6:11
know." Then he **t** me: These are Rv 7:14
were **t** not to harm the grass Rv 9:4
And I was **t**, "You must prophesy Rv 10:11

TOLERABLE *(5)*

It will be more **t** on the day of Mt 10:15
it will be more **t** for Tyre and Mt 11:22
will be more **t** for the land of Mt 11:24
it will be more **t** for Sodom than Lk 10:12
it will be more **t** for Tyre and Lk 10:14

TOLERATE *(8)*

king's best interest to **t** them. Est 3:8
I cannot **t** anyone with haughty Ps 101:5
Why do You **t** wrongdoing? Hab 1:3
and You cannot **t** wrongdoing. Hab 1:13
So why do You **t** those who are Hab 1:13
they will not **t** sound doctrine, 2Tm 4:3
and that you cannot **t** evil. Rv 2:2
you **t** the woman Jezebel, who Rv 2:20

TOLERATED *(2)*

Mordecai's actions would be **t**, Est 3:4
and have **t** ⌊many things⌋ Rv 2:3

TOLLS *(2)*
owe taxes, **t** to those you owe Rm 13:7
to those you owe **t**, respect to Rm 13:7

TOMB *(63)*
me there in the **t** that I hewed Gn 50:5
buried in the **t** of his father Jdg 8:32
Eshtaol in the **t** of his father Jdg 16:31
to his father's **t** in Bethlehem 2Sm 2:32
king wept aloud at Abner's **t**. 2Sm 3:32
it in Abner's **t** in Hebron. 2Sm 4:12
was buried in his father's **t**. 2Sm 17:23
own city near the **t** of my father 2Sm 19:37
Benjamin in the **t** of Saul's 2Sm 21:14
in his fathers' **t** in the city 2Kg 9:28
threw the man into Elisha's **t**. 2Kg 13:21
buried in his **t** in the garden 2Kg 21:26
It is the **t** of the man of God 2Kg 23:17
and buried him in his own **t**. 2Kg 23:30
in his own **t** that he had hewn 2Ch 16:14
him in the **t** of his fathers. 2Ch 35:24
keeps watch over ⌊his⌋ **t**. Jb 21:32
in splendor, each in his own **t**. Is 14:18
to carve out a **t** for yourself Is 22:16
carving your **t** on the height and Is 22:16
and placed it in his new **t**, Mt 27:60
against the entrance of the **t**. Mt 27:60
were seated there, facing the **t**. Mt 27:61
orders that the **t** be made secure Mt 27:64
and made the **t** secure by sealing Mt 27:66
other Mary went to view the **t**. Mt 28:1
heaven and approached ⌊the **t**⌋. Mt 28:2
quickly from the **t** with fear and Mt 28:8
his corpse and placed it in a **t**. Mk 6:29
he placed Him in a **t** cut out of Mk 15:46
against the entrance to the **t**. Mk 15:46
they went to the **t** at sunrise. Mk 16:2
the entrance to the **t** for us?" Mk 16:3
they entered the **t**, they saw a Mk 16:5
and started running from the **t**, Mk 16:8
placed it in a **t** cut into the Lk 23:53
observed the **t** and how His body Lk 23:55
they came to the **t**, bringing the Lk 24:1
stone rolled away from the **t**. Lk 24:2
from the **t**, they reported all Lk 24:9
got up and ran to the **t**. Lk 24:12
They arrived early at the **t**, Lk 24:22
us went to the **t** and found it Lk 24:24
already been in the **t** four days. Jn 11:17
was going to the **t** to cry there. Jn 11:31
in Himself again, came to the **t**. Jn 11:38
out of the **t** and raised him Jn 12:17
A new **t** was in the garden; Jn 19:41
and since the **t** was nearby. Jn 19:42
Magdalene came to the **t** early, Jn 20:1
had been removed from the **t**. Jn 20:1
taken the Lord out of the **t**, Jn 20:2
went out, heading for the **t**. Jn 20:3
Peter and got to the **t** first. Jn 20:4
He entered the **t** and saw the Jn 20:6
who had reached the **t** first, Jn 20:8
then entered the **t**, saw, and Jn 20:8
Mary stood outside facing the **t**, Jn 20:11
she stooped to look into the **t**. Jn 20:11
his **t** is with us to this day. Ac 2:29
placed in the **t** that Abraham had Ac 7:16
the tree and put Him in a **t**. Ac 13:29
their bodies to be put into a **t**. Rv 11:9

TOMBS *(15)*
he saw the **t** there on the 2Kg 23:16
to take the bones out of the **t**, 2Kg 23:16
but not in the **t** of the kings. 2Ch 21:20
bury him in the **t** of the kings. 2Ch 24:25
the ascent to the **t** of David's 2Ch 32:33
point⌋ opposite the **t** of David, Neh 3:16
Him as they came out of the **t**. Mt 8:28
You are like whitewashed **t**, Mt 23:27
You build the **t** of the prophets Mt 23:29
The **t** also were opened and many Mt 27:52
they came out of the **t** after His Mt 27:53
came out of the **t** and met Him. Mk 5:2
He lived in the **t**. No one was Mk 5:3
out among the **t** and in the Mk 5:5
stay in a house but in the **t**. Lk 8:27

TOMORROW *(56)*
"**T**," he answered. Moses replied, Ex 8:10
This sign will take place **t**." Ex 8:23
and **t** the swarms of flies will Ex 8:29
T the LORD will do this thing in Ex 9:5
T at this time I will rain down Ex 9:18
then **t** I will bring locusts into Ex 10:4
'**T** is a day of complete rest, Ex 16:23
T I will stand on the hilltop Ex 17:9
and purify them today and **t**. Ex 19:10
be a festival to the LORD **t**." Ex 32:5
yourselves ⌊in readiness⌋ for **t**, Nm 11:18
turn back **t** and head for the Nm 14:25
T morning the LORD will reveal Nm 16:5
take firepans, and **t** Nm 16:6
to appear before the LORD **t**— Nm 16:16
will do wonders among you **t**." Jos 3:5
them to consecrate themselves **t**, Jos 7:13
at this time **t** I will hand all Jos 11:6
t He will be angry with the Jos 22:18
get up early **t** for your journey Jdg 19:9
I will hand them over to you **t**." Jdg 20:28
At this time **t** I will send you a 1Sm 9:16
will be yours **t** by the time the 1Sm 11:9
to ⌊Nahash⌋, "**T** we will come out 1Sm 11:10
tonight, you will be dead **t**!" 1Sm 19:11
him, "Look, **t** is the New Moon 1Sm 20:5
by this time **t** or the next day 1Sm 20:12
said to him, "**T** is the New Moon; 1Sm 20:18
T you and your sons will be with 1Sm 28:19
"and **t** I will send you back." 2Sm 11:12
of one of them by this time **t**!" 1Kg 19:2
But at this time **t** I will send 1Kg 20:6
Then we will eat my son **t**.' 2Kg 6:28
'About this time **t** at the gate 2Kg 7:1
About this time **t** 12 quarts of 2Kg 7:18
sons at this time **t** at Jezreel. 2Kg 10:6
T, go down against them. 2Ch 20:16
T, go out to face them, for the 2Ch 20:17
T I will do what the king has Est 5:8
invited again **t** to join her with Est 5:12
in Susa also have **t** to carry out Est 9:13
I'll give it **t**"—when it is Pr 3:28
boast about **t**, for you don't Pr 27:1
us eat and drink, for **t** we die!" Is 22:13
and **t** will be like today, only Is 56:12
and thrown into the furnace **t**, Mt 6:30
Therefore don't worry about **t**, Mt 6:34
because **t** will worry about Mt 6:34
is thrown into the furnace **t**, Lk 12:28
performing healings today and **t**, Lk 13:32
travel today, **t**, and the next Lk 13:33
Paul down to the Sanhedrin **t**, Ac 23:20
"**T**," he said, "you will hear Ac 25:22
us eat and drink, for **t** we die. 1Co 15:32
Today or **t** we will travel to Jms 4:13
even know what **t** will bring— Jms 4:14

TON *(1)*
of silver and one **t** of gold. 2Kg 18:14

TONE *(1)*
now and change my **t** of voice, Gl 4:20

TONGS *(3)*
the gold flowers, lamps, and **t**; 1Kg 7:49
lamps, and gold **t**—of purest 2Ch 4:21
had taken from the altar with **t**. Is 6:6

TONGUE *(71)*
water with his **t** like a dog. Jdg 7:5
me, His word was on my **t**. 2Sm 23:2
and he conceals it under his **t**, Jb 20:12
and my **t** will not utter deceit. Jb 27:4
my **t** will form words on my Jb 33:2
hook or tie his **t** down with a Jb 41:1
and malice are under his **t**. Ps 10:7
lips and the **t** that speaks Ps 12:3
who does not slander with his **t**, Ps 15:3
my **t** sticks to the roof of my Ps 22:15
Keep your **t** from evil and your Ps 34:13
And my **t** will proclaim Your Ps 35:28
his **t** speaks what is just. Ps 37:30
so that I may not sin with my **t**; Ps 39:1
fire burned. I spoke with my **t**: Ps 39:3
my **t** is the pen of a skillful Ps 45:1
and harness your **t** for deceit. Ps 50:19
and my **t** will sing of Your Ps 51:14
your **t** devises destruction, Ps 52:2
that destroy, you treacherous **t**! Ps 52:4
mouth, and praise was on my **t**. Ps 66:17
my **t** will proclaim Your Ps 71:24
My **t** sings about Your promise, Ps 119:172
lying lips and a deceitful **t**." Ps 120:2
He do to you, you deceitful **t**? Ps 120:3
May my **t** stick to the roof of my Ps 137:6
a word is on my **t**, You know all Ps 139:4
eyes, a lying **t**, hands that shed Pr 6:17
the flattering **t** of a stranger. Pr 6:24
The **t** of the righteous is pure Pr 10:20
a perverse **t** will be cut out. Pr 10:31
but the **t** of the wise ⌊brings⌋ Pr 12:18
but a lying **t**, only a moment. Pr 12:19
t of the wise makes knowledge Pr 15:2
The **t** that heals is a tree of Pr 15:4
but a devious **t** breaks the Pr 15:4
answer of the **t** is from the LORD Pr 16:1
attention to a destructive **t**. Pr 17:4
death are in the power of the **t**, Pr 18:21
through a lying **t** is a vanishing Pr 21:6
mouth and **t** keeps himself out Pr 21:23
and a gentle **t** can break a bone. Pr 25:15
and a backbiting **t**, angry looks. Pr 25:23
lying **t** hates those it crushes, Pr 26:28
one who flatters with his **t**. Pr 28:23
loving instruction is on her **t**. Pr 31:26
Honey and milk are under your **t**. Sg 4:11
a **t** of fire consumes straw and Is 5:24
and His **t** is like a consuming Is 30:27
the stammering **t** will speak Is 32:4
and the **t** of the mute will sing Is 35:6
every **t** will swear allegiance. Is 45:23
given Me the **t** of those who are Is 50:4
and sticking out your **t** at? Is 57:4
nursing infant's **t** clings to the Lm 4:4
I will make your **t** stick to the Ezk 3:26
of the cursing of their **t**. Hs 7:16
a deceitful **t** will not be found Zph 3:13
and spitting, He touched his **t**. Mk 7:33
was opened and his **t** ⌊set free⌋, Lk 1:64
finger in water and cool my **t**, Lk 16:24
was glad, and my **t** rejoiced. Ac 2:26
and every **t** will give praise to Rm 14:11
you use your **t** for intelligible 1Co 14:9
and every **t** should confess that Php 2:11
controlling his **t** but deceiving Jms 1:26
though the **t** is a small part ⌊of Jms 3:5
And the **t** is a fire. The tongue, Jms 3:6
The **t**, a world of Jms 3:6
but no man can tame the **t**. Jms 3:8
must keep his **t** from evil and 1Pt 3:10

TONGUES *(23)*
and their **t** stuck to the roof of Jb 29:10
they flatter with their **t**. Ps 5:9
Through our **t** we have power; Ps 12:4
of men, from quarrelsome **t**. Ps 31:20
their **t** are sharp swords. Ps 57:4
who sharpen their **t** like swords Ps 64:3
their own **t** work against them. Ps 64:8
and your dogs' **t** may have their Ps 68:23
and their **t** strut across the Ps 73:9
they lied to Him with their **t**, Ps 78:36
speak against me with lying **t**. Ps 109:2
and our **t** with shouts of joy. Ps 126:2
They make their **t** as sharp as a Ps 140:3
their **t** are parched with thirst. Is 41:17
They bent their **t** ⌊like⌋ their Jr 9:3
taught their **t** to speak lies; Jr 9:5
Their **t** are deadly arrows— Jr 9:8
who use their own **t** to deliver Jr 23:31
the **t** in their mouths are Mc 6:12
and their **t** will rot in their Zch 14:12
And **t**, like flames of fire that Ac 2:3
they deceive with their **t**. Rm 3:13
People gnawed their **t** from pain Rv 16:10

TONIGHT *(15)*
are the men who came to you **t**? Gn 19:5
drink wine again **t** so you can go Gn 19:34
sleep with him **t** in exchange for Gn 30:15
have come here **t** to investigate Jos 2:2
Now **t**, you and the people with Jdg 9:32
have a husband **t** and to bear Ru 1:12
Stay ⌊here⌋ **t**, and in the Ru 3:13
the Philistines **t** and plunder 1Sm 14:36
you don't escape **t**, you will be 1Sm 19:11
set out in pursuit of David **t**. 2Sm 17:1
a man will remain with you **t**. 2Sm 19:7
They are coming to kill you **t**! Neh 6:10
T all of you will run away Mt 26:31
Jesus said to him, "**t**—before Mt 26:34
to go to Caesarea at nine **t**. Ac 23:23

TONS *(18)*
there—16 **t**—and delivered 1Kg 9:28
king four and a half **t** of gold, 1Kg 10:10

to Solomon annually was 25 **t**, 1Kg 10:14
of Judah 11 **t** of silver and one 2Kg 18:14
sent 38 **t** of silver to hire 1Ch 19:6
LORD—3,775 **t** of gold, 37,750 1Ch 22:14
of gold, 37,750 **t** of silver, 1Ch 22:14
100 **t** of gold (gold of Ophir) 1Ch 29:4
and 250 **t** of refined silver for 1Ch 29:4
they gave 185 **t** of gold and 1Ch 29:7
drachmas, 375 **t** of silver, 675 1Ch 29:7
tons of silver, 675 **t** of bronze, 1Ch 29:7
of bronze, and 4,000 **t** of iron. 1Ch 29:7
took from there 17 **t** of gold, 2Ch 8:18
king four and a half **t** of gold, 2Ch 9:9
to Solomon annually was 25 **t**, 2Ch 9:13
out to them 24 **t** of silver, Ezr 8:26
and I will pay 375 **t** of silver Est 3:9

TOO *(171)*

(See pp. xi-xii.)

TOOK *(659)*

LORD God **t** the man and placed Gn 2:15
God **t** one of his ribs and closed Gn 2:21
she **t** some of its fruit and ate Gn 3:6
Lamech **t** two wives for himself, Gn 4:19
not there, because God **t** him. Gn 5:24
and they **t** any they chose as Gn 6:2
He **t** some of every kind of clean Gn 8:20
Shem and Japheth **t** a cloak and Gn 9:23
Abram and Nahor **t** wives: Gn 11:29
Terah **t** his son Abram, his Gn 11:31
He **t** his wife Sarai, his nephew Gn 12:5
so that I **t** her as my wife? Gn 12:19
The ⌊four kings⌋ **t** all the goods Gn 14:11
They also **t** Abram's nephew Lot Gn 14:12
He **t** him outside and said, Gn 15:5
So Abram's wife Sarai **t** Hagar, Gn 16:3
Then Abraham **t** his son Ishmael Gn 17:23
Then Abraham **t** curds and milk, Gn 18:8
Abimelech **t** sheep and cattle Gn 20:14
Abraham got up, **t** bread and a Gn 21:14
Then Abraham **t** sheep and cattle Gn 21:27
and **t** with him two of his young Gn 22:3
Abraham **t** the wood for the burnt Gn 22:6
his hand he **t** the fire and the Gn 22:6
reached out and **t** the knife to Gn 22:10
Abraham went and **t** the ram and Gn 22:13
who **t** me from my father's house Gn 24:7
The servant **t** 10 of his master's Gn 24:10
the man **t** a gold ring weighing Gn 24:22
So the servant **t** Rebekah and Gn 24:61
So she **t** her veil and covered Gn 24:65
mother Sarah and **t** Rebekah to be Gn 24:67
Now Abraham **t** another wife, Gn 25:1
He **t** his last breath and died at Gn 25:8
He **t** his last breath and died, Gn 25:17
years old when he **t** as his wife Gn 25:20
t as his wives Judith daughter Gn 26:34
Then Rebekah **t** the best clothes Gn 27:15
and **t** your blessing." Gn 27:35
t my birthright, and look, now Gn 27:36
He **t** one of the stones from the Gn 28:11
morning Jacob **t** the stone that Gn 28:18
Then he **t** him to his house, Gn 29:13
Laban **t** his daughter Leah and Gn 29:23
she **t** her slave Zilpah and gave Gn 30:9
Jacob then **t** branches of fresh Gn 30:37
He **t** all the livestock and Gn 31:18
So he **t** his relatives with him, Gn 31:23
And they **t** stones and made a Gn 31:46
night there and **t** part of what Gn 32:13
got up and **t** his two wives, Gn 32:22
t them and brought them across Gn 32:23
saw her, he **t** her and raped her Gn 34:2
brothers, **t** their swords, Gn 34:25
t Dinah from Shechem's house, Gn 34:26
They **t** their sheep, cattle, Gn 34:28
He **t** his last breath and died, Gn 35:29
Esau **t** his wives from the Gn 36:2
Esau **t** his wives, sons, Gn 36:6
Then they **t** him and threw him Gn 37:24
who **t** Joseph to Egypt Gn 37:28
So they **t** Joseph's robe, Gn 37:31
t her as a wife and slept with Gn 38:2
she **t** off her widow's clothes, Gn 38:14
and the midwife **t** it and tied a Gn 38:28
in my hand, and I **t** the grapes, Gn 40:11
t Simeon from them and had him Gn 42:24
The men **t** this gift, double the Gn 43:15
sons of Israel **t** their father Gn 46:5
They also **t** their cattle and Gn 46:6
He **t** five of his brothers and Gn 47:2
Then Joseph **t** them from his Gn 48:12
Then Joseph **t** them both—with Gn 48:13
a mistake and **t** his father's Gn 48:17
slope that I **t** from the hand Gn 48:22
They **t** 40 days to complete this, Gn 50:3
So the woman **t** the boy and Ex 2:9
the Israelites, and He **t** notice. Ex 2:25
and when he **t** it out, his hand Ex 4:6
and when he **t** it out, it had Ex 4:7
So Moses **t** his wife and sons, Ex 4:20
And Moses **t** God's staff in his Ex 4:20
So Zipporah **t** a flint, cut off Ex 4:25
So they **t** furnace soot and stood Ex 9:10
So the people **t** their dough Ex 12:34
Moses **t** the bones of Joseph with Ex 13:19
ready and **t** his troops with Ex 14:6
t 600 of the best chariots and Ex 14:7
in Egypt that you **t** us to die Ex 14:11
t a tambourine in her hand, Ex 15:20
t a stone and put ⌊it⌋ under Ex 17:12
Moses **t** half the blood and set Ex 24:6
then **t** the covenant scroll and Ex 24:7
Moses **t** the blood, sprinkled it Ex 24:8
So all the people **t** off the gold Ex 32:3
t ⌊the gold⌋ from their hands, Ex 32:4
he **t** the calf they had made, Ex 32:20
Now Moses **t** a tent and set it up Ex 33:7
They **t** from Moses' presence all Ex 36:3
Moses **t** the testimony and placed Ex 40:20
Then Moses **t** the anointing oil Lv 8:10
slaughtered ⌊it⌋, **t** the blood, Lv 8:15
Moses **t** all the fat that was on Lv 8:16
it⌋, **t** some of its blood Lv 8:23
He **t** the fat—the fat tail, all Lv 8:25
before the LORD he **t** one cake of Lv 8:26
Then Moses **t** them from their Lv 8:28
also **t** the breast and waved it Lv 8:29
Then Moses **t** some of the Lv 8:30
He **t** the male goat for the Lv 9:15
offering, **t** a handful of it Lv 9:17
Abihu each **t** his own firepan, Lv 10:1
Moses and Aaron **t** these men who Nm 1:17
Moses **t** the carts and oxen and Nm 7:6
He **t** some of the Spirit that was Nm 11:25
the one who **t** the least gathered Nm 11:32
also ⌊**t**⌋ some pomegranates Nm 13:23
son of Peleth, sons of Reuben, **t** Nm 16:1
Each man **t** his firepan, placed Nm 16:18
Eleazar the priest **t** the bronze Nm 16:39
So Aaron **t** his firepan as Moses Nm 16:47
and each man **t** his own staff. Nm 17:9
So Moses **t** the staff from the Nm 20:9
the sword and **t** possession of Nm 21:24
Israel **t** all the cities and Nm 21:25
and they **t** possession of his Nm 21:35
Angel of the LORD **t** His stand on Nm 22:22
Balak **t** Balaam and brought him Nm 22:41
So Balak **t** him to Lookout Field Nm 23:14
So Balak **t** Balaam to the top of Nm 23:28
the assembly, **t** a spear in his Nm 25:7
t Joshua, had him stand before Nm 27:22
The Israelites **t** the Midianite Nm 31:9
and **t** away all the spoils of war Nm 31:11
Moses **t** one out of ⌊every⌋ 50, Nm 31:47
They **t** a three-day journey into Nm 33:8
So I **t** the leaders of your Dt 1:15
They **t** some of the fruit from Dt 1:25
We **t** only the livestock and the Dt 2:35
But we **t** all the livestock and Dt 3:7
At that time we **t** the land from Dt 3:8
At that time we **t** possession of Dt 3:12
t over the entire region of Dt 3:14
They **t** possession of his land Dt 4:47
So I **t** hold of the tablets and Dt 9:17
t the sinful calf you had made, Dt 9:21
t their land and gave it as an Dt 29:8
The 12 men **t** stones from the Jos 4:8
The priests **t** the ark of the Jos 6:12
t some of what was set apart, Jos 7:1
I coveted them and **t** them. Jos 7:21
They **t** the things from inside Jos 7:23
Israel with him **t** Achan son of Jos 7:24
provisions and **t** worn-out sacks Jos 9:4
was warm when we **t** it from our Jos 9:12
men ⌊of Israel⌋ **t** some of their Jos 9:14
the nation **t** vengeance on its Jos 10:13
So Joshua **t** all this land— Jos 11:16
So Joshua **t** the entire land, Jos 11:23
of the land and **t** possession of Jos 12:1
So they **t** possession of it, Jos 19:47
and they **t** possession of it and Jos 21:43
which they **t** possession of Jos 22:9
But I **t** your father Abraham from Jos 24:3
he also **t** a large stone and set Jos 24:26
The Israelites **t** their daughters Jdg 3:6
defeated Israel and **t** possession Jdg 3:13
t the sword from his right thigh, Jdg 3:21
So they **t** the key and opened the Jdg 3:25
Heber's wife Jael **t** a tent peg, Jdg 4:21
but they **t** no spoil of silver. Jdg 5:19
So Gideon **t** 10 of his male Jdg 6:27
kept the 300 who **t** the people's Jdg 7:8
Each Israelite **t** his position Jdg 7:21
and they **t** control of the Jdg 7:24
So he **t** the elders of the city, Jdg 8:16
t the crescent ornaments that Jdg 8:21
He **t** the people, divided them Jdg 9:43
forward and **t** their stand at Jdg 9:44
Abimelech **t** his ax in his hand Jdg 9:48
So Israel **t** possession of the Jdg 11:21
They **t** possession of all the Jdg 11:22
I **t** my life in my own hands and Jdg 12:3
Manoah **t** a young goat and a Jdg 13:19
of the LORD **t** control of him, Jdg 14:6
of the LORD **t** control of him, Jdg 14:19
Samson ⌊**t**⌋ a young goat ⌊as a Jdg 15:1
He **t** torches, turned the foxes Jdg 15:4
of the LORD **t** control of him, Jdg 15:14
out his hand, **t** it, and killed Jdg 15:15
t hold of the doors of the city Jdg 16:3
shoulders and **t** them to the top Jdg 16:3
Delilah **t** new ropes, tied him up Jdg 16:12
Samson **t** hold of the two middle Jdg 16:29
silver with me. I **t** it. So now I Jdg 17:2
and she **t** five pounds of silver Jdg 17:4
went in and **t** the carved image Jdg 18:17
house and **t** the carved image Jdg 18:18
was pleased and **t** his ephod, Jdg 18:20
You **t** the gods I had made and Jdg 18:24
no one **t** them into their home Jdg 19:15
concubine and **t** her outside to Jdg 19:25
picked up a knife, **t** hold of his Jdg 19:29
Then I **t** my concubine and cut Jdg 20:6
Benjamin and **t** their battle Jdg 20:20
rallied and again **t** their battle Jdg 20:22
Benjaminites and **t** their battle Jdg 20:30
their places and **t** their battle Jdg 20:33
did this and **t** the number of Jdg 21:23
sons **t** Moabite women as their Ru 1:4
Then Boaz **t** 10 men of the city's Ru 4:2
Boaz **t** Ruth and she became his Ru 4:13
Naomi **t** the child, placed him on Ru 4:16
on her lap, and **t** care of him. Ru 4:16
she **t** him with her to Shiloh, 1Sm 1:24
she **t** him to the LORD's house at 1Sm 1:24
little robe and **t** it to him when 1Sm 2:19
they **t** it from Ebenezer to 1Sm 5:1
So they **t** Dagon and returned him 1Sm 5:3
They **t** two milk cows, hitched 1Sm 6:10
of the LORD and **t** it to 1Sm 7:1
Then Samuel **t** a young lamb and 1Sm 7:9
Samuel **t** a stone and set it 1Sm 7:12
dishonest gain, **t** bribes, and 1Sm 8:3
Samuel **t** Saul and his attendant, 1Sm 9:22
Samuel **t** the flask of oil, 1Sm 10:1
Spirit of God **t** control of him, 1Sm 10:10
God suddenly **t** control of him, 1Sm 11:6
He **t** a team of oxen, cut them in 1Sm 11:7
garrison **t** control of the pass 1Sm 13:23
the plunder they **t** from their 1Sm 14:30
to the plunder, **t** sheep, cattle, 1Sm 14:32
The troops **t** sheep and cattle 1Sm 15:21
So Samuel **t** the horn of oil, 1Sm 16:13
of the LORD **t** control of David 1Sm 16:13
So Jesse **t** a donkey loaded with 1Sm 16:20
came forward and **t** his stand. 1Sm 17:16
to them." So David **t** them off. 1Sm 17:39
he **t** his staff in his hand and 1Sm 17:40
hand in the bag, **t** out a stone, 1Sm 17:49
David **t** Goliath's head and 1Sm 17:54
Abner **t** him and brought him 1Sm 17:57
from God **t** control of Saul 1Sm 18:10
He **t** his life in his hands when 1Sm 19:5
Then Michal **t** the household idol 1Sm 19:13

him and Abner t his place beside	1Sm 20:25
David t this to heart and became	1Sm 21:12
left Gath and t refuge in the	1Sm 22:1
So Saul t 3,000 of Israel's	1Sm 24:2
but I t pity on you and said:	1Sm 24:10
So David t the spear and the	1Sm 26:12
woman, but he t flocks, herds,	1Sm 27:9
I t my life in my hands and did	1Sm 28:21
also t flour, kneaded it, and	1Sm 28:24
He t all the sheep and cattle,	1Sm 30:20
Then Saul t his sword and fell	1Sm 31:4
they t their bones and buried	1Sm 31:13
I t the crown that was on his	2Sm 1:10
Then David t hold of his clothes	2Sm 1:11
t Saul's son Ish-bosheth and	2Sm 2:8
The two groups t up positions on	2Sm 2:13
a single unit and t their stand	2Sm 2:25
still day, but David t an oath:	2Sm 3:35
All the people t note of this,	2Sm 3:36
they beheaded him, t his head,	2Sm 4:7
they t Ish-bosheth's head and	2Sm 4:12
David t up residence in the	2Sm 5:9
t more concubines and wives	2Sm 5:13
the ark of God and t hold of it,	2Sm 6:6
t it to the house of Obed-edom	2Sm 6:10
t you from the pasture and from	2Sm 7:8
and t Metheg-ammah from	2Sm 8:1
David t the gold shields of	2Sm 8:7
David also t huge quantities	2Sm 8:8
So Hanun t David's emissaries,	2Sm 10:4
he t the poor man's lamb and	2Sm 12:4
the sword and t his wife as your	2Sm 12:9
despised Me and t the wife of	2Sm 12:10
He t the crown from the head of	2Sm 12:30
David t away a large quantity of	2Sm 12:30
She t dough, kneaded it, made	2Sm 13:8
Tamar t the cakes she had made	2Sm 13:10
out his hand, t hold of him,	2Sm 15:5
Then his wife t the cover,	2Sm 17:19
which t place in the forest of	2Sm 18:6
He then t three spears in his	2Sm 18:14
They t Absalom, threw him into a	2Sm 18:17
bowed to Joab and t off running.	2Sm 18:21
he t the 10 concubines he had	2Sm 20:3
but he t longer than the time	2Sm 20:5
But the king t Armoni and	2Sm 21:8
t sackcloth and spread it out	2Sm 21:10
from on high and t hold of me;	2Sm 22:17
but Shammah t his stand in the	2Sm 23:12
mule, and t him to Gihon.	1Kg 1:38
the priest t the horn of oil	1Kg 1:39
and they t him down from the	1Kg 1:53
Then Solomon t an oath by the	1Kg 2:23
tabernacle and t hold of the	1Kg 2:28
So Benaiah t a message back to	1Kg 2:30
the night and t my son from my	1Kg 3:20
enemies who t them captive,	1Kg 8:48
temple, it t her breath away.	1Kg 10:5
They t men with them from Paran	1Kg 11:18
Then Ahijah t hold of the new	1Kg 11:30
royal palace. He t everything.	1Kg 14:26
He t all the gold shields that	1Kg 14:26
So he t him from her arms,	1Kg 17:19
Then Elijah t the boy, brought	1Kg 17:23
and t 100 prophets and hid them,	1Kg 18:4
So they t the bull that he gave	1Kg 18:26
Elijah t 12 stones—according	1Kg 18:31
following him, t the team of	1Kg 19:21
left and t word back to him.	1Kg 20:9
So they t ⌊their⌋ positions	1Kg 20:12
seventh day, the battle t place,	1Kg 20:29
my father t from your father	1Kg 20:34
So they t him outside the city	1Kg 21:13
He t in the situation and	2Kg 1:11
Elijah t his mantle, rolled it	2Kg 2:8
He t hold of his own clothes and	2Kg 2:12
Then he t the mantle Elijah had	2Kg 2:14
summoned and t their stand at	2Kg 3:21
he t 700 swordsmen with him to	2Kg 3:26
So he t his firstborn son,	2Kg 3:27
him up and t him to his mother	2Kg 4:20
So he went and t with him 750	2Kg 5:5
he t the gifts from them and	2Kg 5:24
So he reached out and t it.	2Kg 6:7
⌊The messengers⌋ t two chariots	2Kg 7:14
next day Hazael t a heavy cloth,	2Kg 8:15
Each man quickly t his garment	2Kg 9:13
they t the king's sons and	2Kg 10:7
So they t them alive and then	2Kg 10:14
t ⌊with him⌋ the commanders of	2Kg 11:19
Jehoiada the priest t a chest,	2Kg 12:9
Joash of Judah t all the	2Kg 12:18
So he t them, and he said to	2Kg 13:18
son of Jehoahaz t back from	2Kg 13:25
t Sela in battle and called it	2Kg 14:7
He t all the gold and silver and	2Kg 14:14
the people of Judah t Azariah,	2Kg 14:21
Ahaz also t the silver and gold	2Kg 16:8
He t the bronze altar that was	2Kg 16:14
He t the reservoir from the	2Kg 16:17
The settlers t possession of	2Kg 17:24
and they t their position by the	2Kg 18:17
Hezekiah t the letter from the	2Kg 19:14
the common people t Jehoahaz	2Kg 23:30
But Neco t Jehoahaz and went to	2Kg 23:34
of Babylon t everything that	2Kg 24:7
king of Babylon t him ⌊captive⌋	2Kg 24:12
Also, he t the king's mother,	2Kg 24:15
chains⌋, and t him to Babylon.	2Kg 25:7
They also t the pots, the	2Kg 25:14
the guards t away the firepans	2Kg 25:15
the guards also t away Seraiah	2Kg 25:18
the city he t a court official	2Kg 25:19
t them and brought them to the	2Kg 25:20
of Assyria t him into exile.	1Ch 5:6
He t them to Halah, Habor, Hara,	1Ch 5:26
Machir t wives from Huppim and	1Ch 7:15
in and when they t them out.	1Ch 9:28
Then Saul t his sword and fell	1Ch 10:4
cut off his head, t his armor,	1Ch 10:9
Then David t up residence in the	1Ch 11:7
Eleazar and David t their stand	1Ch 11:14
Then the Spirit t control of	1Ch 12:18
t it to the house of Obed-edom	1Ch 13:13
David t more wives in Jerusalem,	1Ch 14:3
t you from the pasture and from	1Ch 17:7
from him as I t it from the one	1Ch 17:13
and t Gath and its villages from	1Ch 18:1
David t the gold shields carried	1Ch 18:7
David also t huge quantities of	1Ch 18:8
So Hanun t David's emissaries,	1Ch 19:4
Then David t the crown from the	1Ch 20:2
David t away a large quantity of	1Ch 20:2
Solomon t a census of all the	2Ch 2:17
t from there 17 tons of gold,	2Ch 8:18
temple, it t her breath away.	2Ch 9:4
Israel t their stand with	2Ch 11:13
royal palace. He t everything.	2Ch 12:9
He t the gold shields that	2Ch 12:9
he t courage and removed the	2Ch 15:8
They t an oath to the LORD in a	2Ch 15:14
his courage and t the commanders	2Ch 23:1
Then he t ⌊with him⌋ the	2Ch 23:20
Joash t it to heart to renovate	2Ch 24:4
The Spirit of God t control of	2Ch 24:20
t them to the top of a cliff	2Ch 25:12
and t a great deal of plunder.	2Ch 25:13
of Judah t counsel and sent	2Ch 25:17
Then Jehoash t him to Jerusalem	2Ch 25:23
He t all the gold, silver, all	2Ch 25:24
the people of Judah t Uzziah,	2Ch 26:1
They t their stand against King	2Ch 26:18
him and t many captives to	2Ch 28:5
Israelites t 200,000 captives	2Ch 28:8
They also t a great deal of	2Ch 28:8
the captives you t from your	2Ch 28:11
designated by name t charge of	2Ch 28:15
attacked Judah, and t captives.	2Ch 28:17
They t all the detestable things	2Ch 29:16
them and t them outside to	2Ch 29:16
and they t away the incense	2Ch 30:14
shackles⌋, and t him to Babylon.	2Ch 33:11
Shaphan t the book to the king,	2Ch 34:16
So his servants t him out of the	2Ch 35:24
the common people t Jehoahaz son	2Ch 36:1
But Neco t his brother Jehoahaz	2Ch 36:4
Also Nebuchadnezzar t some of	2Ch 36:7
He t everything to Babylon—	2Ch 36:18
t their positions to praise the	Ezr 3:10
He also t from the temple in	Ezr 5:14
Nebuchadnezzar t from the temple	Ezr 6:5
So I t courage because I was	Ezr 7:28
priests and Levites t charge of	Ezr 8:30
been said; so they t the oath.	Ezr 10:5
I t the wine and gave it to the	Neh 2:1
at night and ⌊t⌋ a few men with	Neh 2:12
only animal I t was the one I	Neh 2:12
with me never t off our clothes.	Neh 4:23
They t possession of the land of	Neh 9:22
fertile land and t possession	Neh 9:25
These events t place during the	Est 1:1
of Babylon t King Jeconiah of	Est 2:6
day Mordecai t a walk in front	Est 2:11
After all this t place, King	Est 3:1
So Haman t the garment and the	Est 6:11
and jubilation t place among the	Est 8:17
swooped down and t them away.	Jb 1:15
on the camels, and t them away.	Jb 1:17
Then Job t a piece of broken	Jb 2:8
For you t collateral from your	Jb 22:6
the city gate and t my seat in	Jb 29:7
from on high and t hold of me;	Ps 18:16
You t me from the womb, making	Ps 22:9
and You t away the guilt of my	Ps 32:5
You t me from my mother's womb.	Ps 71:6
David His servant and t him from	Ps 78:70
it t root and filled the land.	Ps 80:9
You t away Your people's guilt;	Ps 85:2
He t note of their distress,	Ps 106:44
he t no delight in blessing—	Ps 109:17
He t a bag of money with him and	Pr 7:20
I saw, and t it to heart;	Pr 24:32
for I t pleasure in all my	Ec 2:10
I t all this to heart and	Ec 9:1
they t my cloak from me—the	Sg 5:7
This t place during the reign of	Is 7:1
Elam t up a quiver with chariots	Is 22:6
Hezekiah t the letter from the	Is 37:14
He t up the case of the poor and	Jr 22:16
So I t the cup from the LORD's	Jr 25:17
all the people t hold of him,	Jr 26:8
out of Egypt and t him to King	Jr 26:23
king of Babylon t from here and	Jr 28:3
Hananiah then t the yoke bar	Jr 28:10
when I t them by the hand	Jr 31:32
I t the purchase agreement—	Jr 32:11
their minds and t back their	Jr 34:11
I t Jaazaniah son of Jeremiah,	Jr 35:3
son of Neriah t the scroll and	Jr 36:14
and he t it from the chamber of	Jr 36:21
Then Jeremiah t another scroll	Jr 36:32
Jeremiah and t him to the	Jr 37:14
So they t Jeremiah and dropped	Jr 38:6
So Ebed-melech t the men under	Jr 38:11
From there he t old rags and	Jr 38:11
of the guard t Jeremiah and said	Jr 40:2
Then Ishmael t captive all the	Jr 41:10
son of Nethaniah t them captive	Jr 41:10
they t all their men and went to	Jr 41:12
with him then t from Mizpah all	Jr 41:16
the armies t the whole remnant	Jr 43:5
They t the pots, the shovels,	Jr 52:18
of the guards t away the bowls,	Jr 52:19
the guards also t away Seraiah	Jr 52:24
the city he t a court official	Jr 52:25
t them and brought them to the	Jr 52:26
lifted me up and t me away.	Ezk 3:14
be a hand and t me by the hair	Ezk 8:3
He t ⌊some⌋, and put ⌊it⌋ into	Ezk 10:7
in linen, who t it and went out.	Ezk 10:7
I t ⌊them⌋ out in the dark,	Ezk 12:7
You t some of your garments and	Ezk 16:16
also t your beautiful jewelry	Ezk 16:17
Then you t your embroidered	Ezk 16:18
You even t your sons and	Ezk 16:20
came to Lebanon and t the top of	Ezk 17:3
he t some of the land's seed	Ezk 17:5
came to Jerusalem, t its king	Ezk 17:12
He t one of the royal family and	Ezk 17:13
Then he t away the leading men	Ezk 17:13
she t another of her cubs and	Ezk 19:5
in vengeance and t revenge with	Ezk 25:15
They t a cedar from Lebanon to	Ezk 27:5
who t My land as their own	Ezk 36:5
of God He t me to the land	Ezk 40:2
the galleries t away more space	Ezk 42:5
Some Chaldeans t this occasion	Dn 3:8
the Ancient of Days t His seat.	Dn 7:9
and the holy ones t possession	Dn 7:22
The four horns that t the place	Dn 8:22
For you t My silver and gold and	Jl 3:5
and I t care of sycamore figs.	Am 7:14
But the LORD t me from following	Am 7:15
from his throne, t off his royal	Jnh 3:6

You **t** the sheath from Your bow; Hab 3:9
t two staffs, calling one Favor Zch 11:7
Next I **t** my staff called Favor Zch 11:10
So I **t** the 30 pieces of silver Zch 11:13
The LORD **t** notice and listened. Mal 3:16
Now all this **t** place to fulfill Mt 1:22
t the child and His mother Mt 2:14
t the child and His mother, Mt 2:21
Then the Devil **t** Him to the holy Mt 4:5
the Devil **t** Him to a very high Mt 4:8
He Himself **t** our weaknesses and Mt 8:17
went in and **t** her by the hand, Mt 9:25
seed that a man **t** and sowed in Mt 13:31
that a woman **t** and mixed into 50 Mt 13:33
He **t** the five loaves and the two Mt 14:19
the Pharisees **t** offense when Mt 15:12
He **t** the seven loaves and the Mt 15:36
Then Peter **t** Him aside and began Mt 16:22
After six days Jesus **t** Peter, Mt 17:1
Jesus **t** the 12 disciples aside Mt 20:17
This **t** place so that what was Mt 21:4
But the farmers **t** his slaves, Mt 21:35
10 virgins who **t** their lamps Mt 25:1
When the foolish **t** their lamps, Mt 25:3
the sensible ones **t** oil in their Mt 25:4
was a stranger and you **t** Me in; Mt 25:35
I was sick and you **t** care of Me; Mt 25:36
eating, Jesus **t** bread, blessed Mt 26:26
He **t** a cup, and after giving Mt 26:27
they came up, **t** hold of Jesus, Mt 26:50
The chief priests **t** the silver Mt 27:6
They **t** the 30 pieces of silver, Mt 27:9
instead, he **t** some water, washed Mt 27:24
governor's soldiers **t** Jesus into Mt 27:27
they spit at Him, **t** the reed, Mt 27:30
So Joseph **t** the body, wrapped it Mt 27:59
They came up, **t** hold of His Mt 28:9
So they **t** the money and did as Mt 28:15
went to her, **t** her by the hand Mk 1:31
the crowd and **t** Him along since Mk 4:36
He **t** the child's father, mother, Mk 5:40
Then He **t** the child by the hand Mk 5:41
Then He **t** the five loaves and Mk 6:41
So He **t** him away from the crowd Mk 7:33
He **t** the blind man by the hand Mk 8:23
Peter **t** Him aside and began to Mk 8:32
After six days Jesus **t** Peter, Mk 9:2
Then He **t** a child, had him stand Mk 9:36
But they **t** him, beat him, and Mk 12:3
The first **t** a wife, and dying, Mk 12:20
The second also **t** her, and he Mk 12:21
were eating, He **t** bread, blessed Mk 14:22
He **t** a cup, and after giving Mk 14:23
He **t** Peter, James, and John with Mk 14:33
Then they **t** hold of Him and Mk 14:46
temple police **t** Him and slapped Mk 14:65
he **t** Him down and wrapped Him Mk 15:46
about ⌊him⌋ **t** ⌊it⌋ to heart, Lk 1:66
first registration **t** place while Lk 2:2
Simeon **t** Him up in his arms, Lk 2:28
he **t** Him up and showed Him all Lk 4:5
he **t** Him to Jerusalem, had Him Lk 4:9
we've heard that **t** place in Lk 4:23
at the catch of fish they **t**, Lk 5:9
and **t** and ate the sacred bread, Lk 6:4
So He **t** her by the hand and Lk 8:54
He **t** them along and withdrew Lk 9:10
Then He **t** the five loaves and Lk 9:16
these words, He **t** along Peter, Lk 9:28
t a little child and had him Lk 9:47
Jesus **t** up ⌊the question⌋ and Lk 10:30
to an inn, and **t** care of him. Lk 10:34
next day he **t** out two denarii Lk 10:35
seed that a man **t** and sowed in Lk 13:19
that a woman **t** and mixed into 50 Lk 13:21
He **t** the man, healed him, and Lk 14:4
The Pharisee **t** his stand and was Lk 18:11
Then He **t** the Twelve aside and Lk 18:31
The first **t** a wife and died Lk 20:29
and the third **t** her. In the same Lk 20:31
He **t** a cup, and after giving Lk 22:17
And He **t** bread, gave thanks, Lk 22:19
same way He also **t** the cup after Lk 22:20
with them that He **t** the bread, Lk 24:30
and He **t** it and ate in their Lk 24:43
became flesh and **t** up residence Jn 1:14
day a wedding **t** place in Cana Jn 2:1
This sanctuary **t** 46 years to Jn 2:20
a Jewish festival **t** place, Jn 5:1
Then Jesus **t** the loaves, and Jn 6:11
Again a division **t** place among Jn 10:19
of Dedication **t** place in Jn 10:22
Then Mary **t** a pound of fragrant Jn 12:3
they **t** palm branches and went Jn 12:13
aside His robe, **t** a towel, and Jn 13:4
So Judas **t** a company of soldiers Jn 18:3
Then they **t** Jesus from Caiaphas Jn 18:28
Then Pilate **t** Jesus and had Him Jn 19:1
Therefore they **t** Jesus away. Jn 19:16
they **t** His clothes and divided Jn 19:23
They also **t** the tunic, which was Jn 19:23
the disciple **t** her into his home Jn 19:27
so he came and **t** His body away. Jn 19:38
Then they **t** Jesus' body and Jn 19:40
Jesus came, **t** the bread, and Jn 21:13
of the earth **t** their stand, Ac 4:26
Then the high priest **t** action. Ac 5:17
and **t** him to the Sanhedrin. Ac 6:12
you **t** up the tent of Moloch and Ac 7:43
they **t** him by the hand and led Ac 9:8
but his disciples **t** him by night Ac 9:25
t him and brought him to the Ac 9:27
they **t** him down to Caesarea and Ac 9:30
the events that **t** place Ac 10:37
This **t** place during the time of Ac 11:28
know that what **t** place through Ac 12:9
on which they **t** John Mark. Ac 12:25
This all **t** about 450 years. Ac 13:20
they **t** Him down from the tree Ac 13:29
and Barnabas **t** Mark with him and Ac 15:39
so he **t** him and circumcised him Ac 16:3
He **t** them the same hour of the Ac 16:33
They **t** him and brought him to Ac 17:19
they **t** him home and explained Ac 18:26
we **t** him on board and came to Ac 20:14
He came to us, **t** Paul's belt, Ac 21:11
next day, Paul **t** the men, having Ac 21:26
came up, **t** him into custody, Ac 21:33
So he **t** him, brought him to the Ac 23:18
the commander **t** him by the hand, Ac 23:19
the soldiers **t** Paul and brought Ac 23:31
came and **t** him from our hands Ac 24:7
They **t** a sounding and found it Ac 27:28
and **t** food themselves. Ac 27:36
for they lit a fire and **t** us all Ac 28:2
he thanked God and **t** courage. Ac 28:15
the Lord Jesus **t** bread, 1Co 11:23
same way ⌊He⌋ also ⌊**t**⌋ the cup, 1Co 11:25
our affliction that **t** place in 2Co 1:8
sly as I am, I **t** you in by 2Co 12:16
He **t** prisoners into captivity; Eph 4:8
you **t** off your former way of Eph 4:22
the day I **t** them by their hand Heb 8:9
he **t** the blood of calves and Heb 9:19
be found because God **t** him away. Heb 11:5
came and **t** ⌊the scroll⌋ out of Rv 5:7
When He **t** the scroll, the four Rv 5:8
The angel **t** the incense burner, Rv 8:5
Then I **t** the little scroll from Rv 10:10
a violent earthquake **t** place, Rv 11:13

TOOL *(5)*
it with an engraving **t**, Ex 32:4
have a digging **t** in your Dt 23:13
must not use any iron **t** on them. Dt 27:5
which no iron **t** has been used. Jos 8:31
or any iron **t** was heard in the 1Kg 6:7

TOOLS *(3)*
all kinds of bronze and iron **t**. Gn 4:22
All the **t** of the tabernacle for Ex 27:19
your towers with his iron **t**. Ezk 26:9

TOOTH *(11)*
eye for eye, **t** for tooth, hand Ex 21:24
eye, tooth for **t**, hand for hand, Ex 21:24
he knocks out the **t** of his male Ex 21:27
free in compensation for his **t**. Ex 21:27
eye for eye, **t** for tooth. Lv 24:20
eye for eye, tooth for **t**. Lv 24:20
eye for eye, **t** for tooth, hand Dt 19:21
eye, tooth for **t**, hand for hand, Dt 19:21
like a rotten **t** or a faltering Pr 25:19
for an eye and a **t** for a tooth. Mt 5:38
for an eye and a tooth for a **t**. Mt 5:38

TOP *(104)*
a tower with its **t** in the sky. Gn 11:4
on the altar, on **t** of the wood. Gn 22:9
with its **t** reaching heaven Gn 28:12
He poured oil on **t** of it Gn 28:18
the **t** basket were all sorts of Gn 40:17
money there at the **t** of the bag. Gn 42:27
to you⌋ in the **t** of your bags. Gn 43:12
money was at the **t** of his bag! Gn 43:21
one's money at the **t** of his bag. Gn 44:1
at the **t** of the youngest one's Gn 44:2
we found at the **t** of our bags. Gn 44:8
went up to the **t** of the hill. Ex 17:10
Sinai, at the **t** of the mountain. Ex 19:20
Moses to the **t** of the mountain, Ex 19:20
the mercy seat on **t** of the ark Ex 25:21
of manatee skins on **t** of that. Ex 26:14
together at the **t** in a single Ex 26:24
opening at its **t** in the center Ex 28:32
on the altar on **t** of the burnt Ex 29:25
Overlay its **t**, all around its Ex 30:3
mercy seat that is on **t** of it, Ex 31:7
of manatee skins on **t** of it. Ex 36:19
together at the **t** in a single Ex 36:29
it, its **t**, all around its Ex 37:26
covering of the tent on **t** of it, Ex 40:19
the mercy seat on **t** of the ark. Ex 40:20
and the suet on **t** of the burning Lv 1:8
arrange them on **t** of the burning Lv 1:12
on the altar on **t** of the burning Lv 1:17
on **t** of the blood of the Lv 14:17
spread a solid blue cloth on **t**, Nm 4:6
made of manatee skin on **t** of it, Nm 4:25
died there on **t** of the mountain. Nm 20:28
them from the **t** of rocky cliffs Nm 23:9
to Lookout Field on **t** of Pisgah, Nm 23:14
took Balaam to the **t** of Peor, Nm 23:28
to the **t** of Pisgah and look to Dt 3:27
your foot to the **t** of your head. Dt 28:35
Nebo, to the **t** of Pisgah, which Dt 34:1
ascended to the **t** of the hill Jos 15:8
the **t** of the hill the border Jos 15:9
your God on the **t** of this rock. Jdg 6:26
Jerubbaal, on **t** of a large stone Jdg 9:5
climbed to the **t** of Mount Jdg 9:7
his 70 sons on **t** of a large Jdg 9:18
them to the **t** of the mountain Jdg 16:3
and stood on **t** of the mountain 1Sm 26:13
took their stand on **t** of a hill. 2Sm 2:25
shoot from the **t** of the wall? 2Sm 11:20
on him from the **t** of the wall so 2Sm 11:21
soldiers from the **t** of the wall, 2Sm 11:24
his foot to the **t** of his head, 2Sm 14:25
cried out at the **t** of his voice, 2Sm 19:4
cedar beams on **t** of the pillars. 1Kg 7:2
cedar at the **t** of the chambers 1Kg 7:3
to set on **t** of the pillars; 1Kg 7:16
The capitals on **t** of the pillars 1Kg 7:17
to cover the capital on **t**; 1Kg 7:18
the capitals on **t** of the pillars 1Kg 7:19
was on **t** of them and all 1Kg 7:25
the crown on **t** was 18 inches 1Kg 7:31
At the **t** of the cart was a band 1Kg 7:35
also, at the **t** of the cart, its 1Kg 7:35
that were on **t** of the two 1Kg 7:41
that were on **t** of the pillars; 1Kg 7:41
bowls on **t** of the pillars 1Kg 7:42
there was a rounded **t** at the 1Kg 10:19
he was sitting on **t** of the hill. 2Kg 1:9
had a bronze capital on **t** of it. 2Kg 25:17
The capital on **t** of each was 2Ch 3:15
also put it on **t** of the pillars. 2Ch 3:16
was on **t** of them and all 2Ch 4:4
the capitals on **t** of the two 2Ch 4:12
that were on **t** of the pillars; 2Ch 4:12
bowls on **t** of the pillars 2Ch 4:13
them to the **t** of a cliff where 2Ch 25:12
of Judah up on **t** of the wall, Neh 12:31
people along the **t** of the wall, Neh 12:38
his foot to the **t** of his head. Jb 2:7
falls on the **t** of his head. Ps 7:16
down on the **t** of a ship's mast Pr 23:34
at the **t** of the mountains Is 2:2
at the very **t** of the tree, Is 17:6
My will, piling sin on **t** of sin. Is 30:1
had a bronze capital on **t** of it. Jr 52:22
and took the **t** of the cedar. Ezk 17:3
from the lofty **t** of the cedar Ezk 17:22
Its **t** was among the clouds. Ezk 31:3
and set its **t** among the clouds, Ezk 31:10
to the **t** of the entrance Ezk 41:17

ground to the **t** of the entrance Ezk 41:20
territory on **t** of the mountain Ezk 43:12
its **t** reached to the sky, and it Dn 4:11
whose **t** reached to the sky and Dn 4:20
themselves on the **t** of Carmel, Am 9:3
at the **t** of the mountains Mc 4:1
there with a bowl on its **t**. Zch 4:2
for each of the lamps on its **t**. Zch 4:2
split in two from **t** to bottom; Mt 27:51
split in two from **t** to bottom. Mk 15:38
woven in one piece from the **t**. Jn 19:23
at the **t** of their voices Ac 7:57
have one grief on **t** of another. Php 2:27
leaning on the **t** of his staff. Heb 11:21

TOPAZ *(7)*
of carnelian, **t**, and emerald; Ex 28:17
of carnelian, **t**, and emerald; Ex 39:10
T from Cush cannot compare with Jb 28:19
are rods of gold set with **t**. Sg 5:14
t, and diamond, beryl, Ezk 28:13
body was like **t**, his face like Dn 10:6
beryl, the ninth **t**, the tenth Rv 21:20

TOPHEL *(1)*
Paran and **T**, Laban, Hazeroth Dt 1:1

TOPHETH *(10)*
He defiled **T**, which is in the 2Kg 23:10
T has been ready for the king Is 30:33
high places of **T** in the Valley Jr 7:31
be called **T** and the Valley Jr 7:32
T will become a cemetery, Jr 7:32
be called **T** and the Valley Jr 19:6
will bury in **T** until there is no Jr 19:11
making this city like **T**. Jr 19:12
impure like that place **T**— Jr 19:13
Jeremiah came back from **T**, Jr 19:14

TOPMOST *(2)*
He plucked off its **t** shoot, Ezk 17:4
tender sprig from its **t** shoots, Ezk 17:22

TOPPLE *(2)*
the mountains **t** into the depths Ps 46:2
Nations rage, kingdoms **t**; Ps 46:6

TOPPLED *(2)*
she will not be **t**. God will help Ps 46:5
He has **t** the mighty from their Lk 1:52

TOPS *(12)*
the **t** of the mountains were Gn 8:5
He overlaid the **t** of the posts Ex 36:38
plating for the **t** of the posts Ex 38:17
plating of their **t** were silver. Ex 38:19
overlaid their **t**, and supplied Ex 38:28
people on the **t** of the mountains Jdg 9:25
marching in the **t** of the balsam 2Sm 5:24
The **t** of the pillars were shaped 1Kg 7:22
marching in the **t** of the balsam 1Ch 14:15
it wave on the **t** of the Ps 72:16
set their **t** among the clouds, Ezk 31:14
bound on the **t** of the mountains Jl 2:5

TORCH *(6)*
pot and a flaming **t** appeared and Gn 15:17
empty pitcher with a **t** inside it Jdg 7:16
and put a **t** between each pair of Jdg 15:4
her salvation like a flaming **t**. Is 62:1
like a flaming **t** among sheaves; Zch 12:6
blazing like a **t**, fell from Rv 8:10

TORCHES *(9)*
They held their **t** in their left Jdg 7:20
He took **t**, turned the foxes Jdg 15:4
he ignited the **t** and released Jdg 15:5
Flaming **t** shoot from his mouth; Jb 41:19
of burning coals of fire and **t**. Ezk 1:13
eyes like flaming **t**, his arms Dn 10:6
They look like **t**; they dart back Nah 2:4
with lanterns, **t**, and weapons. Jn 18:3
the throne were seven fiery **t**, Rv 4:5

TORE *(62)*
was not there, he **t** his clothes. Gn 37:29
Then Jacob **t** his clothes, put Gn 37:34
Then they **t** their clothes, Gn 44:13
out the land, **t** their clothes Nm 14:6
Then Joshua **t** his clothes and Jos 7:6
because he **t** down Baal's altar Jdg 6:30
someone **t** down his altar. Jdg 6:31
because he **t** down his altar. Jdg 6:32
He also **t** down the tower of Jdg 8:17
he **t** down the city and sowed Jdg 9:45
he **t** his clothes and said, Jdg 11:35
and he **t** the lion apart with his Jdg 14:6
He **t** them limb from limb with a Jdg 15:8
the hem of his robe, and it **t**. 1Sm 15:27
hold of his clothes and **t** them, 2Sm 1:11
on her head and **t** the 2Sm 13:19
king stood up, **t** his clothes, 2Sm 13:31
cloak he had on, **t** it into 12 1Kg 11:30
t the kingdom away from the 1Kg 14:8
these words, he **t** his clothes, 1Kg 21:27
own clothes and **t** them into two 2Kg 2:12
he **t** his clothes and asked, 2Kg 5:7
king of Israel **t** his clothes, 2Kg 5:8
woman's words, he **t** his clothes. 2Kg 6:30
and **t** down the pillar of Baal. 2Kg 10:27
Then they **t** down the temple of 2Kg 10:27
t her clothes and screamed 2Kg 11:14
temple of Baal and **t** it down. 2Kg 11:18
When the LORD **t** Israel from the 2Kg 17:21
their report⌋, he **t** his clothes, 2Kg 19:1
of the law, he **t** his clothes. 2Kg 22:11
He also **t** down the houses of the 2Kg 23:7
He **t** down the high places of the 2Kg 23:8
The king **t** down the altars that 2Kg 23:12
He even **t** down the altar at 2Kg 23:15
of the guards **t** down the walls 2Kg 25:10
Athaliah **t** her clothes and 2Ch 23:13
temple of Baal and **t** it down. 2Ch 23:17
and he **t** down the wall of Gath, 2Ch 26:6
and **t** down the high places and 2Ch 31:1
He **t** down the altars, and he 2Ch 34:7
of the law, he **t** his clothes. 2Ch 34:19
and you **t** your clothes and wept 2Ch 34:27
They **t** down Jerusalem's wall, 2Ch 36:19
this report, I **t** my tunic and Ezr 9:3
occurred, he **t** his clothes, put Est 4:1
t his robe and shaved his head. Jb 1:20
each man **t** his robe and threw Jb 2:12
I did not know **t** at me and did Ps 35:15
report⌋, he **t** his clothes, put Is 37:1
to those who **t** out My beard. Is 50:6
your yoke; I **t** off your fetters Jr 2:20
houses and **t** down the walls Jr 39:8
of the guards **t** down all the Jr 52:14
off my way and **t** me to pieces; Lm 3:11
his anger **t** ⌊at them⌋ Am 1:11
the high priest **t** his robes and Mt 26:65
the high priest **t** his robes and Mk 14:63
and Paul **t** their robes when Ac 14:14
After we **t** ourselves away from Ac 21:1
those things that I **t** down, Gl 2:18
groups one and **t** down the Eph 2:14

TORMENT *(20)*
from the LORD began to **t** him, 1Sm 16:14
long will you **t** me and crush me Jb 19:2
them by means of their **t**. Jb 36:15
or detested the **t** of the Ps 22:24
Remove Your **t** from me; Ps 39:10
from your pain, **t**, and the hard Is 14:3
will lie down in a place of **t**. Is 50:11
You come here to **t** us before the Mt 8:29
beg You before God, don't **t** me!" Mk 5:7
I beg You, don't **t** me!" Lk 8:28
And being in **t** in Hades, he Lk 16:23
also come to this place of **t**.' Lk 16:28
of Satan to **t** me so I would not 2Co 12:7
but were to **t** ⌊them⌋ for five Rv 9:5
their **t** is like the torment Rv 9:5
torment is like the **t** caused by Rv 9:5
smoke of their **t** will go up Rv 14:11
give her that much **t** and grief. Rv 18:7
stand far off in fear of her **t**, Rv 18:10
stand far off in fear of her **t**, Rv 18:15

TORMENTED *(7)*
is cruelly **t** by a demon." Mt 15:22
and those **t** by unclean spirits Lk 6:18
those who were **t** by unclean Ac 5:16
righteous man **t** himself day by 2Pt 2:8
two prophets **t** those who live Rv 11:10
will be **t** with fire and sulfur Rv 14:10
and they will be **t** day and night Rv 20:10

TORMENTERS *(1)*
put it into the hands of your **t**, Is 51:23

TORMENTING *(1)*
evil spirit from God is **t** you. 1Sm 16:15

TORMENTORS *(1)*
songs, and our **t**, for rejoicing: Ps 137:3

TORMENTS *(1)*
and the **t** of Sheol overcame me; Ps 116:3

TORN *(47)*
of the flock **t** by wild beasts; Gn 31:39
Joseph has been **t** to pieces!" Gn 37:33
he must have been **t** to pieces— Gn 44:28
it was actually **t** apart ⌊by a Ex 22:13
restitution for the **t** carcass. Ex 22:13
have his clothes **t** and his hair Lv 13:45
It must be **t** down with its Lv 14:45
bruised, crushed, **t**, or severed Lv 22:24
they found Baal's altar **t** down, Jdg 6:28
as he might have **t** a young goat. Jdg 14:6
clothes were **t**, and there was 1Sm 4:12
The LORD has **t** the kingship of 1Sm 15:28
The LORD has **t** the kingship out 1Sm 28:17
a man with **t** clothes and dust 2Sm 1:2
stood by with their clothes **t**. 2Sm 13:31
with his robe **t** and dust on his 2Sm 15:32
altar that had been **t** down: 1Kg 18:30
Your covenant, **t** down Your 1Kg 19:10
Your covenant, **t** down Your 1Kg 19:14
Why have you **t** your clothes? 2Kg 5:8
their clothes **t** and reported to 2Kg 18:37
because you have **t** your clothes 2Kg 22:19
father Hezekiah had **t** down and 2Ch 33:3
altars of the Baals were **t** down, 2Ch 34:4
Let a beam be **t** from his house Ezr 6:11
with my tunic and robe **t**. Ezr 9:5
the net is **t**, and we have Ps 124:7
but it is **t** down by the mouth of Pr 11:11
Hezekiah with their clothes **t**, Is 36:22
its cities were **t** down because Jr 4:26
the yoke and **t** off the fetters. Jr 5:5
them will be **t** to pieces because Jr 5:6
or I will be **t** away from you; Jr 6:8
our dwellings have been **t** down. Jr 9:19
the ones **t** down ⌊for defense⌋ Jr 33:4
their beards, **t** their garments, Jr 41:5
were **t** off and dried up; Ezk 19:12
and its foundations are **t** down. Ezk 30:4
you will be **t** limb from limb, Dn 2:5
Abednego will be **t** limb from Dn 3:29
until its wings were **t** off. Dn 7:4
For He has **t** ⌊us⌋, and He will Hs 6:1
the heavens being **t** open and the Mk 1:10
were so many, the net was not **t**. Jn 21:11
Paul might be **t** apart by them Ac 23:10
Your prophets, **t** down Your Rm 11:3
you would have **t** out your eyes Gl 4:15

TORRENT *(5)*
the **t** would have swept over us; Ps 124:4
an overflowing **t** that rises to Is 30:28
rain, a **t**, and hailstones Is 30:30
the LORD, like a **t** of brimstone, Is 30:33
woman, to sweep her away in a **t**. Rv 12:15

TORRENTIAL *(5)*
earth," and the **t** rains, His Jb 37:6
rains, His mighty **t** rains, Jb 37:6
T rain will come, and I will Ezk 13:11
T rain will come in My anger, Ezk 13:13
I will pour out **t** rain, Ezk 38:22

TORRENTS *(4)*
the **t** of destruction terrified 2Sm 22:5
away stones and **t** wash away the Jb 14:19
the **t** of destruction terrified Ps 18:4
water gushed out; **t** overflowed. Ps 78:20

TORSO *(1)*
Only Dagon's **t** remained. 1Sm 5:4

TORTURE *(2)*
and run me through and **t** me." 1Sm 31:4
men will come and **t** me!" 1Ch 10:4

TORTURED *(1)*
Some men were **t**, not accepting Heb 11:35

TOSS *(3)*
and I **t** and turn until dawn. Jb 7:4
holy to dogs or **t** your pearls Mt 7:6
tear it, but **t** for it, to see Jn 19:24

TOSSED *(2)*
t by the waves and blown around Eph 4:14
sea, driven and **t** by the wind. Jms 1:6

TOTAL *(32)*
The **t** number of persons: Gn 46:15
t number of persons belonging Gn 46:26
The **t** number of Jacob's Ex 1:5
The **t** number in their military Nm 2:9

The **t** number in their military Nm 2:16
t in their military divisions Nm 2:24
The **t** number who belong to Dan's Nm 2:31
The **t** number in the camps by Nm 2:32
The **t** number of all the Levite Nm 3:39
The **t** number of the firstborn Nm 3:43
The **t** ⌊weight⌋ of the silver Nm 7:85
The **t** ⌊weight⌋ of the gold bowls Nm 7:86
The **t** number of cities you give Nm 35:7
t of those who fell that day, Jos 8:25
Tirzah one ⌊the **t** number of⌋ all Jos 12:24
gave the king the **t** of the 2Sm 24:9
so that he may **t** up the money 2Kg 22:4
The **t** number of those chosen to 1Ch 9:22
gave David the **t** of the 1Ch 21:5
the **t** number of men was 38,000 1Ch 23:3
and the **t** was 153,600. 2Ch 2:17
t number of heads of families 2Ch 26:12
and the **t** weight was recorded at Ezr 8:34
The **t** number of Perez's Neh 11:6
greatness for a **t** of 180 days. Est 1:4
T darkness is reserved for his Jb 20:26
gave Jacob over to **t** destruction Is 43:28
and **t** darkness the peoples; Is 60:2
shatter them with **t** destruction. Jr 17:18
The **t** length will be eight and Ezk 48:13
land with **t** destruction in his Dn 11:16
it is already a **t** defeat for you 1Co 6:7

TOTALED *(6)*
offering **t** 5,310 pounds. Ex 38:29
the burnt offering **t** 12 bulls, Nm 7:87
fellowship sacrifice **t** 24 bulls, Nm 7:88
plunder the army had taken **t**: Nm 31:32
over all Israel **t** 40 years. 1Kg 11:42
and silver articles **t** 5,400. Ezr 1:11

TOTALLED *(1)*
of Issachar **t** 87,000 in their 1Ch 7:5

TOTALLY *(8)*
Since he has turned **t** white, Lv 13:13
bare and will be **t** plundered, Is 24:3
such a land become **t** defiled? Jr 3:1
walls will be **t** demolished, Jr 51:58
of Israel will be **t** destroyed. Hs 10:15
will not **t** destroy the house of Am 9:8
saying: We are **t** ruined! He Mc 2:4
city of blood, **t** deceitful, full Nah 3:1

TOTTER *(1)*
hammer and nails, so it won't **t**. Jr 10:4

TOTTERING *(1)*
leaning wall or a **t** stone fence? Ps 62:3

TOU *(2)*
(AKA TOI)
When King **T** of Hamath heard that 1Ch 18:9
for **T** and Hadadezer had fought 1Ch 18:10

TOUCH *(37)*
'You must not eat it or **t** it, Gn 3:3
I have not let you **t** her. Gn 20:6
come closer so I can **t** you, Gn 27:21
on the mountain or **t** its base. Ex 19:12
No hand may **t** him; instead he Ex 19:13
their meat or **t** their carcasses Lv 11:8
She must not **t** any holy thing or Lv 12:4
they are not to **t** the holy Nm 4:15
Don't **t** anything that belongs to Nm 16:26
their meat or **t** their carcasses Dt 14:8
and now we cannot **t** them. Jos 9:19
the young men not to **t** you? Ru 2:9
Do not **t** My anointed ones or 1Ch 16:22
no harm will **t** you in seven. Jb 5:19
I refuse to **t** ⌊them⌋; they are Jb 6:7
Do not **t** My anointed ones, Ps 105:15
T the mountains, and they will Ps 144:5
it will not **t** us, because we Is 28:15
Do not **t** anything unclean; Is 52:11
one dared to **t** their garments. Lm 4:14
away! Don't **t** ⌊us⌋!" So they Lm 4:15
If I can just **t** His robe, Mt 9:21
they might only **t** the tassel on Mt 14:36
pressing toward Him to **t** Him. Mk 3:10
If I can just **t** His robes, Mk 5:28
they might **t** just the tassel Mk 6:56
to Him and begged Him to **t** him. Mk 8:22
to Him so He might **t** them, Mk 10:13
whole crowd was trying to **t** Him, Lk 6:19
"Somebody did **t** Me," said Jesus. Lk 8:46
yourselves don't **t** these burdens Lk 11:46
to Him so He might **t** them, Lk 18:15
T Me and see, because a ghost Lk 24:39
do not **t** any unclean thing, 2Co 6:17
handle, don't taste, don't **t**"? Col 2:21
the firstborn might not **t** them. Heb 11:28
and the evil one does not **t** him. 1Jn 5:18

TOUCHED *(41)*
When he **t** him, he said, "The Gn 27:22
person who was **t** is to wash his Lv 15:11
sprinkle the one who **t** a bone, Nm 19:18
a person or **t** the dead are to Nm 31:19
their feet **t** the water at its Jos 3:15
was in His hand and **t** the meat Jdg 6:21
hearts God had **t** went with him. 1Sm 10:26
one's wing **t** ⌊one⌋ wall while 1Kg 6:27
cherub's wing **t** the other wall, 1Kg 6:27
Suddenly, an angel **t** him. 1Kg 19:5
a second time and **t** him. 1Kg 19:7
When he **t** Elisha's bones, the 2Kg 13:21
she approached and **t** the tip of Est 5:2
t my mouth ⌊with it⌋ and said: Is 6:7
Now that this has **t** your lips, Is 6:7
out His hand, **t** my mouth, and Jr 1:9
Then he **t** me, made me stand up, Dn 8:18
a hand **t** me and raised me to my Dn 10:10
with human likeness **t** my lips. Dn 10:16
with human likeness **t** me again Dn 10:18
Reaching out His hand He **t** him, Mt 8:3
So He **t** her hand, and the fever Mt 8:15
from behind and **t** the tassel on Mt 9:20
Then He **t** their eyes, saying, Mt 9:29
And as many as **t** it were made Mt 14:36
Jesus came up, **t** them, and said, Mt 17:7
compassion, Jesus **t** their eyes. Mt 20:34
reached out His hand and **t** him. Mk 1:41
Him in the crowd and **t** His robe. Mk 5:27
and said, "Who **t** My robes?" Mk 5:30
You, and You say, 'Who **t** Me?' " Mk 5:31
everyone who **t** it was made well Mk 6:56
and spitting, He **t** his tongue. Mk 7:33
His hand, He **t** him, saying, "I Lk 5:13
came up and **t** the open coffin, Lk 7:14
from behind and **t** the tassel of Lk 8:44
"Who **t** Me?" Jesus asked. When Lk 8:45
reason she had **t** Him and how she Lk 8:47
aprons that had **t** his skin were Ac 19:12
not come to what could be **t**, Heb 12:18
and have **t** with our hands, 1Jn 1:1

TOUCHES *(46)*
Suppose my father **t** me. Gn 27:12
Anyone who **t** the mountain will Ex 19:12
whatever **t** the altar will become Ex 29:37
Whatever **t** them will be Ex 30:29
Or ⌊if⌋ someone **t** anything Lv 5:2
Or ⌊if⌋ he **t** human uncleanness— Lv 5:3
Anything that **t** the offerings Lv 6:18
Anything that **t** its flesh will Lv 6:27
Meat that **t** anything unclean Lv 7:19
If someone **t** anything unclean, Lv 7:21
Whoever **t** their carcasses will Lv 11:24
Whoever **t** them becomes unclean. Lv 11:26
Whoever **t** their carcasses will Lv 11:27
Whoever **t** them when they are Lv 11:31
but someone who **t** a carcass ⌊in Lv 11:36
anyone who **t** its carcass will be Lv 11:39
Anyone who **t** his bed is to wash Lv 15:5
Whoever **t** the body of the man Lv 15:7
Whoever **t** anything that was Lv 15:10
the discharge **t** anyone without Lv 15:11
the discharge **t** must be broken, Lv 15:12
Everyone who **t** her will be Lv 15:19
Everyone who **t** her bed is to Lv 15:21
Everyone who **t** any furniture she Lv 15:22
when he **t** it he will be unclean Lv 15:23
Everyone who **t** them will be Lv 15:27
Whoever **t** anything made unclean Lv 22:4
or whoever **t** any swarming Lv 22:5
the man who **t** any of these will Lv 22:6
The person who **t** any human Nm 19:11
Anyone who **t** a body of a person Nm 19:13
open field who **t** a person who Nm 19:16
and whoever **t** the water for Nm 19:21
the unclean person **t** will become Nm 19:22
and anyone who **t** ⌊it⌋ will be Nm 19:22
of yarn snaps when it **t** fire. Jdg 16:9
man who **t** them must be armed 2Sm 23:7
and his head **t** the clouds, Jb 20:6
t the mountains, and they pour Ps 104:32
no one who **t** her will go Pr 6:29
GOD of Hosts—He **t** the earth; Am 9:5
and with his fold **t** bread, Hg 2:12
with⌋ a corpse **t** any of these, Hg 2:13
for anyone who **t** you touches the Zch 2:8
who touches you **t** the pupil of Zch 2:8
even an animal **t** the mountain, Heb 12:20

TOUCHING *(12)*
their wings were **t** wing to wing. 1Kg 6:27
and a half feet, **t** the wall of 2Ch 3:11
t the wing of the other cherub. 2Ch 3:11
and a half feet, **t** the wall of 2Ch 3:12
hardly **t** the path with his feet. Is 41:3
Their wings were **t**. Ezk 1:9
two ⌊wings⌋ **t** that of another Ezk 1:11
broke off without a hand **t** it, Dn 2:34
mountain without a hand **t** it, Dn 2:45
earth without **t** the ground. Dn 8:5
of woman this is who is **t** Him— Lk 7:39
And **t** his ear, He healed him. Lk 22:51

TOUGH *(2)*
of you, for you're a **t** man: Lk 19:21
⌊If⌋ you knew I was a **t** man, Lk 19:22

TOUR *(2)*
regardless of their **t** of duty— 2Ch 5:11
t its citadels so that you can Ps 48:13

TOWARD *(219)*
(See pp. xi-xii.)

TOWEL *(2)*
His robe, took a **t**, and tied it Jn 13:4
them with the **t** tied around Him Jn 13:5

TOWER *(34)*
a city and a **t** with its top Gn 11:4
the city and the **t** that the men Gn 11:5
his tent beyond the **t** at Eder. Gn 35:21
peace, I will tear down this **t**!" Jdg 8:9
also tore down the **t** of Penuel Jdg 8:17
lords of the **T** of Shechem heard Jdg 9:46
lords of the **T** of Shechem had Jdg 9:47
people in the **T** of Shechem died Jdg 9:49
was a strong **t** inside the city, Jdg 9:51
went up to the roof of the **t**. Jdg 9:51
Abimelech came to attack the **t**, Jdg 9:52
He is a **t** of salvation for His 2Sm 22:51
standing on the **t** in Jezreel. 2Kg 9:17
wall⌋ to the **T** of the Hundred Neh 3:1
Hundred and the **T** of Hananel, Neh 3:1
well as to the **T** of the Ovens. Neh 3:11
the Angle and **t** that juts out Neh 3:25
east and the **t** that juts out. Neh 3:26
the great **t** that juts out, Neh 3:27
past the **T** of the Ovens to the Neh 12:38
the Fish Gate, the **T** of Hananel, Neh 12:39
and the **T** of the Hundred, Neh 12:39
a strong **t** in the face of the Ps 61:3
name of the LORD is a strong **t**; Pr 18:10
neck is like the **t** of David, Sg 4:4
Your neck is like a **t** of ivory, Sg 7:4
nose is like the **t** of Lebanon Sg 7:4
every high **t**, against every Is 2:15
He built a **t** in the middle of it Is 5:2
the city from the **T** of Hananel Jr 31:38
station myself on the lookout **t**. Hab 2:1
and from the **T** of Hananel to the Zch 14:10
18 that the **t** in Siloam fell Lk 13:4
to build a **t**, doesn't first sit Lk 14:28

TOWERED *(1)*
its height **t** among the clouds. Ezk 19:11

TOWERING *(2)*
Bashan is God's **t** mountain; Ps 68:15
plant ⌊it⌋ on a high **t** mountain. Ezk 17:22

TOWERS *(19)*
surround them with walls and **t**, 2Ch 14:7
Uzziah built **t** in Jerusalem at 2Ch 26:9
he built **t** in the desert and dug 2Ch 26:10
for use on the **t** and on the 2Ch 26:15
fortresses and **t** in the forests. 2Ch 27:4
heightening the **t** and the other 2Ch 32:5
Zion, encircle it; count its **t**, Ps 48:12
beds of spice, **t** of perfume. Sg 5:13
am a wall and my breasts like **t**. Sg 8:10
their siege **t** and stripped its Is 23:13
set up my siege **t** against you. Is 29:3
great slaughter when the **t** fall. Is 30:25
her defense **t** have fallen; Jr 50:15
watched from our **t** for a nation Lm 4:17
of Tyre and demolish her **t**. Ezk 26:4

tear down your t with his iron Ezk 26:9
and Gamadites were in your t. Ezk 27:11
and against the high corner t. Zph 1:16
their corner t are destroyed. Zph 3:6

TOWN *(95)*

this t is close enough for me to Gn 19:20
overthrow the t you mentioned. Gn 19:21
he set out for the t of Nahor, Gn 24:10
water outside the t at evening. Gn 24:11
the men of the t are coming out Gn 24:13
within a t in your land. Dt 24:14
and completely destroyed the t. Jdg 1:17
So they named the t Hormah. Jdg 1:17
the t was formerly named Luz Jdg 1:23
out of the t and said to him, Jdg 1:24
show us how to get into t, Jdg 1:24
showed them the way into the t, Jdg 1:25
they put the t to the sword but Jdg 1:25
built a t, and named it Luz Jdg 1:26
The man left the t of Bethlehem Jdg 17:8
the whole t was excited about Ru 1:19
the people in my t know that you Ru 3:11
the gate ⌊of the t⌋ and sat down Ru 4:1
go up from his t every year to 1Sm 1:3
the elders of the t met him, 1Sm 16:4
quickly go to his t Bethlehem 1Sm 20:6
is holding a sacrifice in the t, 1Sm 20:29
entering a t with barred gates. 1Sm 23:7
and destroy the t because of me. 1Sm 23:10
and his men arrived at the t, 1Sm 30:3
south of the t in the middle of 2Sm 24:5
“Why is the t in such an uproar?” 1Kg 1:41
The t has been in an uproar; 1Kg 1:45
Bela’s t was named Dinhabah. 1Ch 1:43
Hadad’s t was named Avith. 1Ch 1:46
the elders and judges of each t, Ezr 10:14
to his own t in Jerusalem Neh 7:6
took my seat in the t square, Jb 29:7
the jubilant t, is filled with Is 22:2
will move against every t; Jr 48:8
town; not one t will escape. Jr 48:8
abandoned, the t that brings Me Jr 49:25
and founds a t with injustice! Hab 2:12
settled in a t called Nazareth Mt 2:23
the whole t went out to meet Mt 8:34
over, and came to His own t. Mt 9:1
and don’t enter any Samaritan t. Mt 10:5
When you enter any t or village, Mt 10:11
when you leave that house or t. Mt 10:14
and Gomorrah than for that t. Mt 10:15
they persecute you in one t, Mt 10:23
and hound from t to town. Mt 23:34
and hound from town to t. Mt 23:34
The whole t was assembled at the Mk 1:33
no longer enter a t openly. Mk 1:45
reported it in the t and the Mk 5:14
sent by God to a t in Galilee Lk 1:26
and hurried to a t in the hill Lk 1:39
registered, each to his own t. Lk 2:3
went up from the t of Nazareth Lk 2:4
to their own t of Nazareth. Lk 2:39
Him out of t, and brought Him Lk 4:29
of the hill their t was built Lk 4:29
Capernaum, a t in Galilee, and Lk 4:31
on His way to a t called Nain. Lk 7:11
as He neared the gate of the t, Lk 7:12
woman in the t who was a sinner Lk 7:37
from one t and village to Lk 8:1
flocking to Him from every t, Lk 8:4
man from the t met Him. Lk 8:27
reported it in the t and in the Lk 8:34
throughout the t all that Jesus Lk 8:39
you leave that t, shake off the Lk 9:5
privately to a t called Lk 9:10
pairs to every t and place where Lk 10:1
you enter any t, and they Lk 10:8
you enter any t, and they don’t Lk 10:10
the dust of your t that clings Lk 10:11
for Sodom than for that t. Lk 10:12
went through one t and village Lk 13:22
a judge in one t who didn’t fear Lk 18:2
a widow in that t kept coming to Lk 18:3
a Judean t, and was looking Lk 23:51
so He came to a t of Samaria Jn 4:5
had gone into t to buy food. Jn 4:8
jar, went into t, and told the Jn 4:28
They left the t and made their Jn 4:30
from that t believed in Him Jn 4:39
and from the t of Bethlehem, Jn 7:42
to a t called Ephraim. Jn 11:54
I was in the t of Joppa praying, Ac 11:5
almost the whole t assembled to Ac 13:44
temple was just outside the t, Ac 14:13
he got up and went into the t. Ac 14:20
evangelized that t and made many Ac 14:21
brothers in every t where we Ac 15:36
they urged them to leave t. Ac 16:39
except that in t after town the Ac 20:23
in town after t the Holy Spirit Ac 20:23
to appoint elders in every t: Ti 1:5

TOWNS *(75)*

any of the t the LORD your God Dt 16:5
in all your t the LORD your God Dt 16:18
in one of your t that the LORD Dt 17:2
one of your t where he lives Dt 18:6
may eat in your t and be Dt 26:12
imposes on you in all your t. Dt 28:55
Ekron, with its t and villages; Jos 15:45
Ashdod, with its t and villages; Jos 15:47
Gaza, with its t and villages, Jos 15:47
had Beth-shean with its t, Jos 17:11
Ibleam with its t, and the Jos 17:11
inhabitants of Dor with its t; Jos 17:11
of En-dor with its t, Jos 17:11
of Taanach with its t, Jos 17:11
of Megiddo with its t— Jos 17:11
with its t and in the Jezreel Jos 17:16
described it by t in a document Jos 18:9
They had 30 t in Gilead, which Jdg 10:4
place in one of the outlying t, 1Sm 27:5
in the t of the Jerahmeelites, 1Sm 30:29
and in the t of the Kenites; 1Sm 30:29
I go to one of the t of Judah?” 2Sm 2:1
settled in the t near Hebron. 2Sm 2:3
gave Hiram 20 t in the land 1Kg 9:11
look over the t that Solomon had 1Kg 9:12
What are these t you’ve given me 1Kg 9:13
in all their t from watchtower 2Kg 17:9
who possessed 23 t in the land 1Ch 2:22
Kenath and its villages—60 t. 1Ch 2:23
Bashan and its t, and throughout 1Ch 5:16
They had 13 t in all among their 1Ch 6:60
10 t from the half tribe of 1Ch 6:61
assigned⌋ 13 t from the tribes 1Ch 6:62
by lot 12 t from the tribes 1Ch 6:63
Israelites gave these t and 1Ch 6:64
assigned by lot the t named 1Ch 6:65
were given t from the tribe 1Ch 6:66
son of Israel lived in these t. 1Ch 7:29
to live in their t on their own 1Ch 9:2
throughout the t of Judah and 2Ch 17:9
great works in the t of Judah. 2Ch 17:13
the people settled in their t, Ezr 2:70
of⌋ Israel ⌊settled⌋ in their t. Ezr 2:70
had settled in their t, Ezr 3:1
those in our t who have married Ezr 10:14
all Israel settled in their t. Neh 7:73
had settled in their t, Neh 8:1
all their t and in Jerusalem, Neh 8:15
in all our agricultural t. Neh 10:37
nine-tenths remained in their t. Neh 11:1
on his own property in their t— Neh 11:3
The t of Judah rejoice because Ps 48:11
and the t of Judah rejoice Ps 97:8
her t will become a desolation, Jr 48:9
of Moab and its t has come up, Jr 48:15
and all the t of the land of Jr 48:24
Abandon the t! Live in the Jr 48:28
t have been captured, and the Jr 48:41
and their neighboring t— Jr 50:40
their possession for t to live Ezk 45:5
went to all the t and villages, Mt 9:35
covered the t of Israel before Mt 10:23
to teach and preach in their t. Mt 11:1
to denounce the t where most of Mt 11:20
followed Him on foot from the t. Mt 14:13
from all the t and arrived ahead Mk 6:33
villages, t, or the country, Mk 6:56
of God to the other t also, Lk 4:43
While He was in one of the t, Lk 5:12
have authority over 10 t.’ Lk 19:17
‘You will be over five t.’ Lk 19:19
together from the t surrounding Ac 5:16
all the t until he came to Ac 8:40
to the Lycaonian t called Lystra Ac 14:6
As they traveled through the t, Ac 16:4

TRACE *(1)*

and not a t of them could be Dn 2:35

TRACED *(2)*

will be t through Isaac. Gn 21:12
of rebellion can be t to you. Mc 1:13

TRACHONITIS *(1)*

of the region of Iturea and T, Lk 3:1

TRACK *(1)*

from there I will t them down Am 9:3

TRACKED *(1)*

city of evildoers, t with bloody Hs 6:8

TRACKLESS *(2)*

them wander in a t wasteland. Jb 12:24
them wander in t wastelands. Ps 107:40

TRACKS *(2)*

My feet have followed in His t; Jb 23:11
follow the t of the flock, Sg 1:8

TRACT *(2)*

He will remove its digestive t, Lv 1:16
This entire t of land will be Ezk 45:1

TRACTS *(1)*

As a result, 10 t fell to Jos 17:5

TRADE *(8)*

and you can t in the country.’ ” Gn 42:34
conducting t on the vast waters. Ps 107:23
Those who t among the peoples Ezk 27:36
Through the abundance of your t, Ezk 28:16
iniquities in your dishonest t. Ezk 28:18
for they were tentmakers by t. Ac 18:3
many who make a t in God’s 2Co 2:17
craftsman of any t will ever be Rv 18:22

TRADED *(4)*

and have t with you from your Is 47:15
They have t their precious Lm 1:11
of Sheba and Raamah t with you. Ezk 27:22
Asshur, and Chilmad t with you. Ezk 27:23

TRADERS *(7)*

When Midianite t passed by, Gn 37:28
king’s t bought them from Kue 1Kg 10:28
The king’s t would get them from 2Ch 1:16
brought by the merchants and t. 2Ch 9:14
Will t bargain for him or divide Jb 41:6
of crowns, whose t are princes, Is 23:8
and set it in a city of t. Ezk 17:4

TRADERS’ *(1)*

from merchants, t merchandise, 1Kg 10:15

TRADING *(7)*

enjoy the profits from his t. Jb 20:18
was your t partner because Ezk 27:12
Aram was your t partner because Ezk 27:16
was also your t partner because Ezk 27:18
⌊t⌋ in wine from Helbon and Ezk 27:18
partners, t with you in lambs Ezk 27:21
great skill in t you have Ezk 28:5

TRADITION *(10)*

break the t of the elders? Mt 15:2
commandment because of your t? Mt 15:3
God’s word because of your t. Mt 15:6
keeping the t of the elders. Mk 7:3
to the t of the elders, Mk 7:5
of God, you keep the t of men.” Mk 7:8
in order to maintain your t! Mk 7:9
word by your t that you have Mk 7:13
empty deceit based on human t, Col 2:8
to the t received from us 2Th 3:6

TRADITIONS *(3)*

and keep the t just as I 1Co 11:2
for the t of my ancestors Gl 1:14
hold to the t you were taught 2Th 2:15

TRAGEDY *(6)*

mourn over that t when the LORD Lv 10:6
You also brought t on the widow 1Kg 17:20
is a sickening t I have seen Ec 5:13
This too is a sickening t: Ec 5:16
is a t I have observed under Ec 6:1
is futile and a sickening t. Ec 6:2

TRAIN *(3)*

they will never again t for war. Is 2:4
they will never again t for war. Mc 4:3
Rather, t yourself in godliness, 1Tm 4:7

TRAINED *(16)*

he assembled his 318 t men, Gn 14:14
the bow, and were t for war. 1Ch 5:18

fighting men, **t** for battle, 1Ch 12:8
t for battle with all kinds of 1Ch 12:33
28,600 **t** for battle. 1Ch 12:35
serve in the army, **t** for battle. 1Ch 12:36
who were all **t** and skillful in 1Ch 25:7
with swords and **t** in warfare. Sg 3:8
over you, ones you yourself **t**? Jr 13:21
were to be **t** for three years Dn 1:5
I **t** and strengthened their arms, Hs 7:15
who is fully **t** will be like his Lk 6:40
since He hasn't been **t**?" Jn 7:15
have been **t** to distinguish Heb 5:14
to those who have been **t** by it. Heb 12:11
and with hearts **t** in greed. 2Pt 2:14

TRAINING *(4)*
for the **t** of the saints in the Eph 4:12
them up in the **t** and instruction Eph 6:4
the **t** of the body has a limited 1Tm 4:8
correcting, for **t** in 2Tm 3:16

TRAINS *(3)*
He **t** my hands for war; 2Sm 22:35
He **t** my hands for war; Ps 18:34
who **t** my hands for battle and my Ps 144:1

TRAITOR *(2)*
destroyed, you **t** never betrayed! Is 33:1
Judas Iscariot, who became a **t**. Lk 6:16

TRAITORS *(4)*
not show grace to any wicked **t**. Ps 59:5
there is a conspiracy with **t**. Hs 7:5
He allots our fields to **t**. Mc 2:4
t, reckless, conceited, lovers 2Tm 3:4

TRAMPLE *(30)*
will **t** your flesh on thorns and Jdg 8:7
I crush them and **t** them like mud 2Sm 22:43
some wild animal may **t** them. Jb 39:15
t the wicked where they stand. Jb 40:12
may he **t** me to the ground and Ps 7:5
t them like mud in the streets. Ps 18:42
Your name we **t** our enemies. Ps 44:5
My adversaries **t** me all day, Ps 56:2
valiantly; He will **t** our foes. Ps 60:12
T underfoot those with bars of Ps 68:30
will **t** the young lion and the Ps 91:13
valiantly; He will **t** our foes. Ps 108:13
to graze and for sheep to **t**. Is 7:25
and to **t** them down like clay in Is 10:6
Feet **t** it, the feet of the Is 26:6
against it, **t** it, and burn it Is 27:4
He will **t** all your streets with Ezk 26:11
Must you also **t** the rest of the Ezk 34:18
the whole earth, **t** it down, and Dn 7:23
Come and **t** ⌊the grapes⌋ because Jl 3:13
They **t** the heads of the poor on Am 2:7
because you **t** on the poor and Am 5:11
you who **t** on the needy and do Am 8:4
and coming down to **t** the heights Mc 1:3
You **t** down the nations in wrath. Hab 3:12
You will **t** the wicked, for they Mal 4:3
or they will **t** them with their Mt 7:6
you the authority to **t** on snakes Lk 10:19
they will **t** the holy city for Rv 11:2
He will also **t** the winepress of Rv 19:15

TRAMPLED *(30)*
but the people **t** him in the 2Kg 7:17
the people **t** him in the gateway, 2Kg 7:20
passed by and **t** the thistle. 2Kg 14:9
passed by and **t** the thistle. 2Ch 25:18
down its wall, and it will be **t**. Is 5:5
who **t** its cities and would not Is 14:17
a rocky pit like a **t** corpse. Is 14:19
nations have **t** its choice vines Is 16:8
Moab will be **t** in his place as Is 25:10
as straw is **t** in a dung pile. Is 25:10
drunkards will be **t** underfoot. Is 28:3
passes through, you will be **t**. Is 28:18
I **t** the winepress alone, and no Is 63:3
I **t** them in My anger and ground Is 63:3
our enemies have **t** down Your Is 63:18
they have **t** My plot of land. Jr 12:10
floor at the time it is **t**. Jr 51:33
The Lord has **t** Virgin Daughter Lm 1:15
feed on what your feet have **t**, Ezk 34:19
and have **t** you from every Ezk 36:3
and it **t** with its feet whatever Dn 7:7
him to the ground and **t** him, Dn 8:7
fall to the earth, and **t** them. Dn 8:10
and of the host to be **t**?" Dn 8:13
that time she will be **t** like mud Mc 7:10
be thrown out and **t** on by men. Mt 5:13
was **t** on, and the birds of the Lk 8:5
will be **t** by the Gentiles Lk 21:24
deserve who has **t** on the Son of Heb 10:29
the press was **t** outside the city Rv 14:20

TRAMPLES *(5)*
to me, God, for man **t** me; Ps 56:1
challenging the one who **t** me. Ps 57:3
who is full **t** on a honeycomb, Pr 27:7
No one **t** grapes in the Is 16:10
which **t** and tears as it passes Mc 5:8

TRAMPLING *(6)*
you—⌊this⌋ **t** of My courts? Is 1:12
For the **t** boot of battle and the Is 9:5
a day of tumult, **t**, and Is 22:5
and **t** with its feet whatever was Dn 7:19
warriors in battle **t** down the Zch 10:5
that they were **t** on one another. Lk 12:1

TRANCE *(2)*
falls ⌊into a **t**⌋ with ⌊his⌋ eyes Nm 24:4
falls ⌊into a **t**⌋ with ⌊his⌋ eyes Nm 24:16

TRANQUIL *(3)*
A **t** heart is life to the body, Pr 14:30
come against a **t** people who are Ezk 38:11
we may lead a **t** and quiet life 1Tm 2:2

TRANSACTION *(2)*
legally binding a **t** in Israel. Ru 4:7
the **t** written on a scroll and Jr 32:44

TRANSFER *(7)*
the field will **t** back to him. Lv 27:19
brothers and **t** their father's Nm 27:7
t his inheritance to his Nm 27:8
must not **t** from tribe to tribe Nm 36:7
is to **t** from one tribe to Nm 36:9
to **t** the kingdom from the house 2Sm 3:10
they must not **t** this choice Ezk 48:14

TRANSFERRED *(3)*
permanently **t** to its purchaser Lv 25:30
from the palace and **t** her and Est 2:9
of darkness and **t** us into the Col 1:13

TRANSFORM *(1)*
He will **t** the body of our humble Php 3:21

TRANSFORMATION *(1)*
prior to his **t** he was approved Heb 11:5

TRANSFORMED *(6)*
and you will be **t** into a 1Sm 10:6
the earth is **t** as by fire. Jb 28:5
He was **t** in front of them, Mt 17:2
He was **t** in front of them, Mk 9:2
but be **t** by the renewing of your Rm 12:2
and are being **t** into the same 2Co 3:18

TRANSFORMS *(1)*
the flint and **t** the mountains at Jb 28:9

TRANSGRESS *(3)*
who rebel and **t** against Me. Ezk 20:38
because they **t** My covenant and Hs 8:1
means one must not **t** against and 1Th 4:6

TRANSGRESSED *(5)*
I have **t** the LORD's command and 1Sm 15:24
and how arrogantly they have **t**. Jb 36:9
for they have **t** teachings, Is 24:5
ancestors have **t** against Me to Ezk 2:3
the woman was deceived and **t**. 1Tm 2:14

TRANSGRESSING *(1)*
'Why are you **t** the LORD's 2Ch 24:20

TRANSGRESSION *(19)*
your brothers' **t** and their sin— Gn 50:17
forgive the **t** of the servants Gn 50:17
forgive my sin and pardon my **t**? Jb 7:21
Reveal to me my **t** and sin. Jb 13:23
I am pure, without **t**; Jb 33:9
though I am without **t**." Jb 34:6
He does not pay attention to **t**, Jb 35:15
is the one whose **t** is forgiven, Ps 32:1
concerning the **t** of the wicked: Ps 36:1
I hate the doing of **t**; Ps 101:3
My people their **t**, and the house Is 58:1
t and deception against the LORD, Is 59:13
those in Jacob who turn from **t**. Is 59:20
save him on the day of his **t**; Ezk 33:12
I give my firstborn for my **t**, Mc 6:7
there is no law, there is no **t**. Rm 4:15
sin in the likeness of Adam's **t**. Rm 5:14
and every **t** and disobedience Heb 2:2
but received a rebuke for his **t**: 2Pt 2:16

TRANSGRESSIONS *(27)*
will not remove your **t** and sins. Jos 24:19
Have I covered my **t** as others do Jb 31:33
multiply your **t**, what does it do Jb 35:6
will confess my **t** to the LORD," Ps 32:5
Deliver me from all my **t**; Ps 39:8
has He removed our **t** from us. Ps 103:12
sweep away your **t** for My own Is 43:25
swept away your **t** like a cloud, Is 44:22
was put away because of your **t**. Is 50:1
He was pierced because of our **t**, Is 53:5
For our **t** have multiplied before Is 59:12
For our **t** are with us, and we Is 59:12
suffer because of her many **t**. Lm 1:5
My **t** have been formed into a Lm 1:14
with me because of all my **t**. Lm 1:22
themselves with all their **t**. Ezk 14:11
None of the **t** he has committed Ezk 18:22
from all the **t** he had committed; Ezk 18:28
Repent and turn from all your **t**, Ezk 18:30
Throw off all the **t** you have Ezk 18:31
exposing your **t**, so that your Ezk 21:24
Our **t** and our sins are ⌊heavy⌋ Ezk 33:10
things, and all their **t**. Ezk 37:23
to their uncleanness and **t**, Ezk 39:24
have an appetite for their **t**. Hs 4:8
added because of **t** until the Gl 3:19
from the **t** ⌊committed⌋ under Heb 9:15

TRANSGRESSORS *(3)*
But **t** will all be eliminated; Ps 37:38
take it to heart, you **t**! Is 46:8
are convicted by the law as **t**. Jms 2:9

TRANSITORY *(1)*
Let me know how **t** I am. Ps 39:4

TRANSLATED *(8)*
was written in Aramaic and **t**. Ezr 4:7
sent us has been **t** and read in Ezr 4:18
which is **t** "God is with us." Mt 1:23
which is **t**, "Little girl, I Mk 5:41
which is **t**, "My God, My God, Mk 15:34
which is **t** Son of Encouragement, Ac 4:36
Tabitha, which is **t** Dorcas. Ac 9:36
which is how his name is **t**, Ac 13:8

TRANSLATING *(1)*
t and giving the meaning so that Neh 8:8

TRANSMIT *(2)*
that they do not **t** holiness to Ezk 44:19
the outer court and **t** holiness Ezk 46:20

TRANSPARENT *(1)*
was pure gold, like **t** glass. Rv 21:21

TRANSPORT *(4)*
that Joseph had sent to **t** him, Gn 45:27
They are to **t** the tabernacle and Nm 1:50
They are to **t** the tabernacle Nm 4:25
secretly and **t** the king and his 2Sm 19:41

TRANSPORTATION *(5)*
These are the **t** duties of the Nm 4:15
each man his task and **t** duty. Nm 4:19
regarding work and **t** duties: Nm 4:24
all their **t** duties and all their Nm 4:27
to his work and **t** duty, Nm 4:49

TRANSPORTED *(2)*
on a new cart and **t** it from 2Sm 6:3
took from here and **t** to Babylon. Jr 28:3

TRANSPORTING *(3)*
the tent of meeting and **t** ⌊it⌋. Nm 4:47
set out, **t** the tabernacle. Nm 10:17
set out, **t** the holy objects; Nm 10:21

TRAP *(36)*
become a snare and a **t** for you, Jos 23:13
their gods will be a **t** to you." Jdg 2:3
She'll be a **t** for him, and the 1Sm 18:21
you setting a **t** for me to get me 1Sm 28:9
A **t** catches ⌊him⌋ by the heel; Jb 18:9
they **t** my feet and construct Jb 30:12
lured us into a **t**; You placed Ps 66:11
and let it be a **t** for ⌊their⌋ Ps 69:22
The wicked have set a **t** for me, Ps 119:110
proud hide a **t** with ropes for Ps 140:5
me from the **t** they have set for Ps 141:9
they have hidden a **t** for me. Ps 142:3
like a bird from a fowler's **t**. Pr 6:5
like a deer bounding toward a **t** Pr 7:22

his lips are a **t** for his life. Pr 18:7
It is a **t** for anyone to dedicate Pr 20:25
than death the woman who is a **t**, Ec 7:26
or like birds caught in a **t**, Ec 9:12
and a **t** and a snare to the Is 8:14
who set a **t** at the gate for the Is 29:21
They set a **t**; they catch men Jr 5:26
Panic, pit, and **t** await you, Jr 48:43
pit will be captured in the **t**, Jr 48:44
I laid a **t** for you, and you Jr 50:24
bird land in a **t** on the ground Am 3:5
Does a **t** spring from the ground Am 3:5
your bread will set a **t** for you. Ob 7
plotted how to **t** Him by what He Mt 22:15
to Him to **t** Him by what He said Mk 12:13
wait for Him to **t** Him in Lk 11:54
like a **t**. For it will come on Lk 21:35
asked this to **t** Him, in order Jn 8:6
feasting become a snare and a **t**, Rm 11:9
into disgrace and the Devil's **t**. 1Tm 3:7
temptation, a **t**, and many 1Tm 6:9
senses and escape the Devil's **t**, 2Tm 2:26

TRAPPED *(9)*

the men of Ai were ⌊**t**⌋ between Jos 8:22
for he has **t** himself by entering 1Sm 23:7
with chains and **t** by the cords Jb 36:8
you have been **t** by the words of Pr 6:2
treacherous are **t** by their own Pr 11:6
An evil man is **t** by ⌊his⌋ Pr 12:13
so people are **t** in an evil time, Ec 9:12
to be broken, **t**, and captured. Is 28:13
all of them **t** in holes or Is 42:22

TRAPS *(4)*

t the wise in their craftiness Jb 5:13
Those who seek my life set **t**, Ps 38:12
talk about hiding **t** and say, Ps 64:5
life, was captured in their **t**; Lm 4:20

TRAVEL *(37)*

dressed for **t**, your sandals on Ex 12:11
that they could **t** day or night. Ex 13:21
Please let us **t** through your Nm 20:17
won't **t** through ⌊any⌋ field or Nm 20:17
We will **t** the King's Highway; Nm 20:17
You must not **t** through our land, Nm 20:18
only let us **t** through on foot." Nm 20:19
You must not **t** through." Nm 20:20
allow Israel to **t** through their Nm 20:21
Let us **t** through your land. Nm 21:22
We will **t** the King's Highway Nm 21:22
not let Israel **t** through his Nm 21:23
you on the road you were to **t**. Dt 1:33
You are about to **t** through the Dt 2:4
'Let us **t** through your land; Dt 2:27
Only let us **t** through on foot, Dt 2:28
not let us **t** through his land Dt 2:30
and who **t** on the road, give Jdg 5:10
let us **t** through your land, Jdg 11:17
'Please let us **t** through your Jdg 11:19
consulted those who **t** the roads? Jb 21:29
this path I **t** they have hidden Ps 142:3
don't **t** that road with them or Pr 1:15
Avoid it; don't **t** on it. Turn Pr 4:15
are deserted; **t** has ceased. Is 33:8
The unclean will not **t** on it, Is 35:8
and priest **t** to a land they do Jr 14:18
will block those who **t** through, Ezk 39:11
You **t** over land and sea to make Mt 23:15
I must **t** today, tomorrow, and Lk 13:33
He had to **t** through Samaria, Jn 4:4
did not want to **t** in Judea Jn 7:1
out Barnabas to **t** as far as Ac 11:22
whenever I **t** to Spain. Rm 15:24
me to go, they will **t** with me. 1Co 16:4
we will **t** to such and such Jms 4:13
who **t** to the kings of the whole Rv 16:14

TRAVELED *(44)*

there Abraham **t** to the region Gn 20:1
presence and **t** throughout the Gn 41:46
The Israelites **t** from Rameses to Ex 12:37
The Israelites **t** on from the Nm 10:12
until we have **t** through your Nm 20:17
until we have **t** through your Nm 21:22
The Israelites **t** on and camped Nm 22:1
the way you **t** until you reached Dt 1:31
and we **t** around the hill country Dt 2:1
We **t** along the road to the Dt 2:8
The Israelites **t** from Beeroth Dt 10:6
They **t** from there to Gudgodah, Dt 10:7
through the nations where you **t**. Dt 29:16
you haven't **t** this way before. Jos 3:4
whose lands we **t** through. Jos 24:17
Gideon **t** on the caravan route, Jdg 8:11
joined Jephthah and **t** with him. Jdg 11:3
Israel **t** through the wilderness Jdg 11:16
Then they **t** through the Jdg 11:18
who **t** through Gilead and Jdg 11:29
From there they **t** to the hill Jdg 18:13
t along the road leading back Ru 1:7
two of them **t** until they came Ru 1:19
and **t** by way of the Arabah all 2Sm 4:7
After they had **t** their indirect 2Kg 3:9
Naaman had **t** a short distance 2Kg 5:19
So Joab left and **t** throughout 1Ch 21:4
The couriers **t** from city to city 2Ch 30:10
Have you **t** to the sources of the Jb 38:16
land no one **t** through and where Jr 2:6
in mind, the way you have **t**. Jr 31:21
The 11 disciples **t** to Galilee, Mt 28:16
His parents **t** to Jerusalem for Lk 2:41
went out and **t** from village to Lk 9:6
all he had and **t** to a distant Lk 15:13
A nobleman **t** to a far country to Lk 19:12
this, Jesus **t** in Galilee, since Jn 7:1
the Lord, they **t** back to Ac 8:25
he **t** and was nearing Damascus, Ac 9:3
He **t** through Syria and Cilicia, Ac 15:41
As they **t** through the towns, Ac 16:4
Then they **t** through Amphipolis Ac 17:1
Paul **t** through the interior Ac 19:1
For they have **t** in the way of Jd 11

TRAVELER *(5)*

up and saw the **t** in the city Jdg 19:17
Now a **t** came to the rich man, 2Sm 12:4
prepare for the **t** who had come 2Sm 12:4
for I opened my door to the **t**. Jb 31:32
like a **t** stopping only for the Jr 14:8

TRAVELER'S *(1)*

If only I had a **t** lodging place Jr 9:2

TRAVELERS *(2)*

t kept to the side roads. Jdg 5:6
Valley of the **T** east of the Sea Ezk 39:11

TRAVELING *(36)*

Lot, who was **t** with Abram, also Gn 13:5
LORD's covenant **t** ahead of them Nm 10:33
'You've been **t** around this hill Dt 2:3
The time we spent **t** from Dt 2:14
We're **t** from Bethlehem in Judah Jdg 19:18
and Elisha were **t** from Gilgal, 2Kg 2:1
t merchants of Sheba hope for Jb 6:19
you gain by **t** along the way to Jr 2:18
you gain by **t** along the way to Jr 2:18
of the people **t** with you, Jr 19:10
Don't take a **t** bag for the road, Mt 10:10
no bread, no **t** bag, no money in Mk 6:8
Assuming He was in the **t** party, Lk 2:44
a large crowd were **t** with Him. Lk 7:11
afterwards He was **t** from one Lk 8:1
stick, no **t** bag, no bread, no Lk 9:3
As they were **t** on the road Lk 9:57
a money-bag, **t** bag, or sandals; Lk 10:4
While they were **t**, He entered a Lk 10:38
great crowds were **t** with Him. Lk 14:25
While **t** to Jerusalem, He passed Lk 17:11
money-bag, **t** bag, or sandals, Lk 22:35
take it, and also a **t** bag. Lk 22:36
As they were **t** down the road, Ac 8:36
men who were **t** with him stood Ac 9:7
to you on the road you were **t**, Ac 9:17
As Peter was **t** from place to Ac 9:32
as they were **t** and nearing the Ac 10:9
t through one place after Ac 18:23
who were Paul's **t** companions. Ac 19:29
I was **t** to Damascus to bring Ac 22:5
As I was **t** and near Damascus, Ac 22:6
I was **t** to Damascus with Ac 26:12
around me and those **t** with me. Ac 26:13
I am **t** to Jerusalem to serve the Rm 15:25
I will be **t** through Macedonia 1Co 16:5

TRAVELS *(2)*

In all My **t** throughout Israel, 1Ch 17:6
You observe my **t** and my rest; Ps 139:3

TRAY *(1)*

golden apples on a silver **t**. Pr 25:11

TREACHEROUS *(24)*

My brothers are as **t** as a wadi, Jb 6:15
that destroy, you **t** tongue! Ps 52:4
and the **t** uprooted from it. Pr 2:22
of the **t** destroys them. Pr 11:3
but the **t** are trapped by their Pr 11:6
t people have an appetite for Pr 13:2
the way of the **t** never changes. Pr 13:15
and the **t**, for the upright. Pr 21:18
overthrows the words of the **t**. Pr 22:12
The **t** one acts treacherously, Is 21:2
The **t** act treacherously; Is 24:16
the **t** deal very treacherously. Is 24:16
For I knew that you were very **t**, Is 48:8
and her **t** sister Judah saw it. Jr 3:7
t sister Judah was not afraid Jr 3:8
her **t** sister Judah didn't return Jr 3:10
more righteous than **t** Judah. Jr 3:11
a solemn assembly of **t** people. Jr 9:2
⌊Why⌋ do the **t** live at ease? Jr 12:1
even they were **t** to you; Jr 12:6
do You tolerate those who are **t**? Hab 1:13
prophets are reckless—**t** men. Zph 3:4
Jesus in a **t** way and kill Him Mt 26:4
looking for a **t** way to arrest Mk 14:1

TREACHEROUSLY *(12)*

he has acted **t** toward her. Ex 21:8
those who act **t** without cause Ps 25:3
They **t** turned away like their Ps 78:57
The treacherous one acts **t**, Is 21:2
The treacherous act **t**; Is 24:16
the treacherous deal very **t**. Is 24:16
have dealt very **t** with Me. Jr 5:11
Why then do we act **t** against one Mal 2:10
Judah has acted **t**, and a Mal 2:11
You have acted **t** against her, Mal 2:14
do not act **t** against the wife Mal 2:15
carefully, and do not act **t**. Mal 2:16

TREACHERY *(13)*

you with the **t** that they used Nm 25:18
'What is this **t** you have Jos 22:16
in rebellion or **t** against the Jos 22:22
committed this **t** against Him. Jos 22:31
to Ahaziah, "It's **t**, Ahaziah!" 2Kg 9:23
abhors a man of bloodshed and **t**. Ps 5:6
they plot **t** all day long. Ps 38:12
devises destruction, working **t**. Ps 52:2
of bloodshed and **t** will not live Ps 55:23
and have hidden behind **t**." Is 28:15
him there for the **t** he committed Ezk 17:20
because of the **t** he has engaged Ezk 18:24
Me by committing **t** against Me: Ezk 20:27

TREAD *(9)*

and you will **t** on their backs. Dt 33:29
they **t** the winepresses, but go Jb 24:11
You will **t** on the lion and the Ps 91:13
will **t** him down on My mountain. Is 14:25
like those who **t** ⌊grapes⌋, Jr 25:30
one will **t** with shouts of joy. Jr 48:33
and ⌊you will **t**⌋ grapes but not Mc 6:15
into the clay and **t** the mortar; Nah 3:14
You **t** the sea with Your horses, Hab 3:15

TREADING *(2)*

people in Judah **t** wine presses Neh 13:15
a young cow **t** grain and neigh Jr 50:11

TREADS *(8)*

of your foot **t** will be yours. Dt 11:24
an ox while it **t** out grain. Dt 25:4
where the sole of your foot **t**, Jos 1:3
the heavens and **t** on the waves Jb 9:8
like a potter who **t** the clay. Is 41:25
like one who **t** a winepress? Is 63:2
reaper and the one who **t** grapes, Am 9:13
an ox while it **t** out the grain. 1Co 9:9

TREASON *(4)*

her clothes and screamed "**T**! 2Kg 11:14
and screamed "Treason! **T**!" 2Kg 11:14
and screamed, "**T**, treason!" 2Ch 23:13
and screamed, "Treason, **t**!" 2Ch 23:13

TREASURE *(27)*

must have put **t** in your bags. Gn 43:23
showed them his whole **t** house— 2Kg 20:13
for it more than for hidden **t**, Jb 3:21
and his eyes spot every **t**. Jb 28:10
like one who finds vast **t**. Ps 119:162
and search for it like hidden **t**, Pr 2:4

my words, and **t** my commands. Pr 7:1
LORD than great **t** with turmoil. Pr 15:16
knowledgeable lips are a rare **t**. Pr 20:15
Precious **t** and oil are in the Pr 21:20
every precious and beautiful **t**. Pr 24:4
the **t** of kings and provinces. Ec 2:8
fear of the LORD is Zion's **t**. Is 33:6
and showed them his **t** house— Is 39:2
and what they **t** does not profit. Is 44:9
we have hidden **t** in the field— Jr 41:8
There is no end to the **t**, Nah 2:9
For where your **t** is, there your Mt 6:21
The kingdom of heaven is like **t**, Mt 13:44
and you will have **t** in heaven. Mt 19:21
and you will have **t** in heaven. Mk 10:21
one who stores up **t** for himself Lk 12:21
an inexhaustible **t** in heaven, Lk 12:33
For where your **t** is, there your Lk 12:34
and you will have **t** in heaven. Lk 18:22
Now we have this **t** in clay jars, 2Co 4:7
stored up **t** in the last days! Jms 5:3

TREASURED *(9)*

I have **t** the words of His mouth Jb 23:12
conspire against Your **t** ones. Ps 83:3
have **t** Your word in my heart so Ps 119:11
Israel as His **t** possession. Ps 135:4
I have **t** them up for you, my Sg 7:13
as they profane My **t** place. Ezk 7:22
give it, for you are **t** ⌊by God⌋. Dn 9:23
you are a man **t** ⌊by God⌋. Dn 10:11
afraid, you who are **t** ⌊by God⌋. Dn 10:19

TREASURER *(2)*

supervision of Mithredath the **t**, Ezr 1:8
the city **t**, and our brother Rm 16:23

TREASURERS *(4)*

to all the **t** in the region Ezr 7:21
I appointed as **t** over the Neh 13:13
advisers, **t**, judges, magistrates Dn 3:2
advisers, **t**, judges, magistrates Dn 3:3

TREASURES *(28)*

and the hidden **t** of the sand. Dt 33:19
there all the **t** of the LORD's 2Kg 24:13
temple and the **t** of the king's 2Kg 24:13
give my personal **t** of gold and 1Ch 29:3
the **t** of the king's palace, 2Ch 25:24
the **t** of the LORD's temple, 2Ch 36:18
and the **t** of the king and his 2Ch 36:18
darkness is reserved for his **t**. Jb 20:26
there is no limit to their **t**; Is 2:7
nations and plundered their **t**; Is 10:13
donkeys and their **t** on the humps Is 30:6
will give you the **t** of darkness Is 45:3
wealth and your **t** I will give as Jr 15:13
and all your **t** I will give up as Jr 17:3
will hand all the **t** of the kings Jr 20:5
you trust in your works and **t**, Jr 48:7
who trust in your **t** ⌊and boast⌋: Jr 49:4
waters, rich in **t**, your end has Jr 51:13
over the hidden **t** of gold and Dn 11:43
My finest **t** to your temples. Jl 3:5
his hidden **t** searched out! Ob 6
there still the **t** of wickedness Mc 6:10
so that the **t** of all the nations Hg 2:7
opened their **t** and presented Him Mt 2:11
for yourselves **t** on earth, Mt 6:19
for yourselves **t** in heaven, Mt 6:20
In Him all the **t** of wisdom and Col 2:3
wealth than the **t** of Egypt, Heb 11:26

TREASURIES *(30)*

put them in the **t** of the LORD's 1Kg 7:51
He seized the **t** of the LORD's 1Kg 14:26
temple and the **t** of the royal 1Kg 14:26
remained in the **t** of the LORD's 1Kg 15:18
temple and the **t** of the royal 1Kg 15:18
found in the **t** of the LORD's 2Kg 12:18
and in the **t** of the king's 2Kg 14:14
and in the **t** of the king's 2Kg 16:8
and in the **t** of the king's 2Kg 18:15
that was found in his **t**. 2Kg 20:13
anything in my **t** that I didn't 2Kg 20:15
rooms and the **t** of God's temple 1Ch 9:26
charge of the **t** of God's temple 1Ch 26:20
temple and the **t** for what had 1Ch 26:20
in charge of the **t** of the LORD's 1Ch 26:22
the officer in charge of the **t**. 1Ch 26:24
of all the **t** for what had been 1Ch 26:26
its buildings, **t**, upper rooms, 1Ch 28:11
chambers, the **t** of God's house, 1Ch 28:12
and the **t** for what is dedicated. 1Ch 28:12
them in the **t** of God's temple 2Ch 5:1
any matter or concerning the **t**. 2Ch 8:15
He seized the **t** of the LORD's 2Ch 12:9
temple and the **t** of the royal 2Ch 12:9
gold from the **t** of the LORD's 2Ch 16:2
he made himself **t** for silver, 2Ch 32:27
love me, and filling their **t**. Pr 8:21
that was found in his **t**. Is 39:2
is against her **t**, and they will Jr 50:37
gold and silver for your **t**. Ezk 28:4

TREASURING *(1)*

But Mary was **t** up all these Lk 2:19

TREASURY *(20)*

and must go into the LORD's **t**." Jos 6:19
iron into the **t** of the LORD's Jos 6:24
gave them to the **t** of the LORD's 1Ch 29:8
to the **t** for the project Ezr 2:69
is to be paid from the royal **t**. Ezr 6:4
may use the royal **t** to pay for Ezr 7:20
530 priestly garments to the **t**. Neh 7:70
minas to the **t** for the project. Neh 7:71
storerooms of the **t** in the house Neh 10:38
for deposit in the royal **t**." Est 3:9
to pay the royal **t** for the Est 4:7
the vessels in the **t** of his god. Dn 1:2
will plunder the **t** of every Hs 13:15
to put it into the temple **t**, Mt 27:6
across from the temple **t**, Mk 12:41
crowd dropped money into the **t**. Mk 12:41
those giving to the temple **t**. Mk 12:43
offerings into the temple **t**. Lk 21:1
He spoke these words by the **t**, Jn 8:20
was in charge of her entire **t**. Ac 8:27

TREAT *(30)*

curse those who **t** you with Gn 12:3
us, and we will **t** you well, for Nm 10:29
You are going to **t** me like this, Nm 11:15
t your female slave the same Dt 15:17
how you are to **t** all the cities Dt 20:15
her for money or **t** her as Dt 21:14
Zin by failing to **t** Me as holy Dt 32:51
T Ai and its king as you did Jos 8:2
This is how we will **t** them: Jos 9:20
town, and we will **t** you well." Jdg 1:24
t me with the LORD's faithful 1Sm 20:14
T the young man Absalom gently 2Sm 18:5
the wicked who **t** me violently, Ps 17:9
If only I could **t** you like my Sg 8:1
can I not **t** you as this potter Jr 18:6
I will **t** them like the calf they Jr 34:18
Didn't you **t** your sister Sodom Ezk 16:56
They will **t** you with hatred, Ezk 23:29
neighbors who **t** them with Ezk 28:24
neighbors who **t** them with Ezk 28:26
I will **t** ⌊you⌋ according to the Ezk 35:11
You will **t** them like native-born Ezk 47:22
How can I **t** you like Zeboiim? Hs 11:8
filth on you and **t** you with Nah 3:6
I will not **t** the remnant of this Zch 8:11
I resolved to **t** you badly when Zch 8:14
used to **t** the prophets. Lk 6:23
ancestors used to **t** the false Lk 6:26
masters, **t** them the same way, Eph 6:9
Yet don't **t** him as an enemy, 2Th 3:15

TREATED *(36)*

He **t** Abram well because of her, Gn 12:16
Should he have **t** our sister like Gn 34:31
but he **t** them like strangers and Gn 42:7
I must be **t** as holy among the Lv 22:32
but the Egyptians **t** us and our Nm 20:15
I ever **t** you this way before? Nm 22:30
So he **t** the king of Makkedah as Jos 10:28
He **t** Libnah's king as he had the Jos 10:30
t Debir and its king as he had Jos 10:39
king as he had **t** Hebron and as Jos 10:39
and as he had **t** Libnah and its Jos 10:39
Joshua **t** them as the LORD had Jos 11:9
They **t** Abimelech deceitfully, Jdg 9:23
is the way they **t** all the 1Sm 2:14
because they **t** the LORD's 1Sm 2:17
The men **t** us well. When we 1Sm 25:15
because you **t** the LORD with such 2Sm 12:14
arrogantly they **t** our ancestors. Neh 9:10
because He has **t** me generously. Ps 13:6
You have **t** Your servant well, Ps 119:65
They have **t** My people's Jr 6:14
They have **t** superficially the Jr 8:11
people are **t** with contempt and Jr 33:24
those who **t** you with contempt Ezk 16:57
and mother are **t** with contempt, Ezk 22:7
t them outrageously and killed Mt 22:6
things and be **t** with contempt? Mk 9:12
the head and **t** him shamefully. Mk 12:4
why have You **t** us like this? Lk 2:48
that one too, **t** him shamefully, Lk 20:11
his soldiers, **t** Him with Lk 23:11
and Julius **t** Paul kindly and Ac 27:3
clothed, roughly **t**, homeless; 1Co 4:11
what way were you **t** worse than 2Co 12:13
been outrageously **t** in Philippi, 1Th 2:2
of those who were **t** that way. Heb 10:33

TREATING *(2)*

t the righteous and the wicked Gn 18:25
Why are you **t** your servants this Ex 5:15

TREATMENT *(3)*

will give special **t** to the land Ex 8:22
to the customary **t** of daughters. Ex 21:9
and severe **t** of the body, they Col 2:23

TREATMENTS *(3)*

give them the required beauty **t**. Est 2:3
of the beauty **t** and the special Est 2:9
receive beauty **t** with oil of Est 2:12

TREATS *(3)*

whether he **t** him as a slave or Dt 24:7
She **t** her young harshly, as if Jb 39:16
as this potter ⌊**t** his clay⌋?" Jr 18:6

TREATY *(20)*

were bound by a **t** with Abram. Gn 14:13
not to make a **t** with the Ex 34:12
Do not make a **t** with the Ex 34:15
no **t** with them and show them Dt 7:2
Please make a **t** with us." Jos 9:6
How can we make a **t** with you?" Jos 9:7
Please make a **t** with us." ' Jos 9:11
them and made a **t** to let them Jos 9:15
after making the **t** with them, Jos 9:16
him, "Make a **t** with us, and we 1Sm 11:1
and the two of them made a **t**. 1Kg 5:12
There is a **t** between me and you, 1Kg 15:19
and break your **t** with Baasha 1Kg 15:19
basis of this **t**, I release you. 1Kg 20:34
So he made a **t** with him and 1Kg 20:34
There's a **t** between me and you, 2Ch 16:3
Go break your **t** with Israel's 2Ch 16:3
We made a **t** with Egypt and with Lm 5:6
and broke a **t** of brotherhood. Am 1:9
who has a **t** with you will Ob 7

TREE *(181)*

and every **t** whose fruit contains Gn 1:29
the ground every **t** pleasing in Gn 2:9
including the **t** of life in the Gn 2:9
well as the **t** of the knowledge Gn 2:9
to eat from any **t** of the garden, Gn 2:16
eat from the **t** of the knowledge Gn 2:17
eat from any **t** in the garden'? Gn 3:1
the fruit of the **t** in the middle Gn 3:3
saw that the **t** was good for food Gn 3:6
you eat from the **t** that I had Gn 3:11
gave me ⌊some fruit⌋ from the **t**, Gn 3:12
and ate from the **t** about which I Gn 3:17
also take from the **t** of life, Gn 3:22
guard the way to the **t** of life. Gn 3:24
and rest yourselves under the **t**. Gn 18:4
them as they ate under the **t**. Gn 18:8
a tamarisk **t** in Beer-sheba, Gn 21:33
off you—and hang you on a **t**. Gn 40:19
shattered every **t** in the field. Ex 9:25
eat every **t** you have growing Ex 10:5
and the LORD showed him a **t**. Ex 15:25
plant any kind of **t** for food, Lv 19:23
and under every flourishing **t**. Dt 12:2
swings the ax to chop down a **t**, Dt 19:5
and you hang his body on a **t**, Dt 21:22
corpse on the **t** overnight but Dt 21:23
hung ⌊on a **t**⌋ is under God's Dt 21:23
either in a **t** or on the ground Dt 22:6
the fruit from your olive **t**, Dt 24:20
king of Ai on a **t** until evening, Jos 8:29
take his body down from the **t**. Jos 8:29
under the palm **t** of Deborah Jdg 4:5
beside the oak **t** of Zaanannim, Jdg 4:11
They said to the olive **t**, Jdg 9:8

But the olive **t** said to them, Jdg 9:9
the trees said to the fig **t**, Jdg 9:10
But the fig **t** said to them, Jdg 9:11
the pomegranate **t** in Migron 1Sm 14:2
the tamarisk **t** at the high place 1Sm 22:6
under the tamarisk **t** in Jabesh 1Sm 31:13
branches of a large oak **t**, 2Sm 18:9
head was caught fast in the **t**. 2Sm 18:9
Absalom hanging in an oak **t**!" 2Sm 18:10
he was still alive in the oak **t**, 2Sm 18:14
his own vine and his own fig **t**. 1Kg 4:25
him sitting under an oak **t**. 1Kg 13:14
hill and under every green **t**; 1Kg 14:23
under a broom **t** and prayed that 1Kg 19:4
and slept under the broom **t**. 1Kg 19:5
down every good **t** and stop up 2Kg 3:19
water and cut down every good **t**. 2Kg 3:25
of them was cutting down a **t**, 2Kg 6:5
hills, and under every green **t**. 2Kg 16:4
hill and under every green **t**. 2Kg 17:10
his own vine and his own fig **t**, 2Kg 18:31
hills, and under every green **t**. 2Ch 28:4
of every fruit **t** to the LORD's Neh 10:35
of every fruit **t**, and of the new Neh 10:37
is hope for a **t**: If it is cut Jb 14:7
like an olive **t** that sheds its Jb 15:33
He uproots my hope like a **t**. Jb 19:10
So injustice is broken like a **t**. Jb 24:20
of the broom **t** were their food. Jb 30:4
his tail like a cedar **t**; Jb 40:17
He is like a **t** planted beside Ps 1:3
like a flourishing native **t**. Ps 37:35
flourishing olive **t** in the house Ps 52:8
like a palm **t** and grow like Ps 92:12
grow like a cedar **t** in Lebanon. Ps 92:12
She is a **t** of life to those who Pr 3:18
of the righteous is a **t** of life, Pr 11:30
fulfilled desire is a **t** of life. Pr 13:12
that heals is a **t** of life, Pr 15:4
tends a fig **t** will eat its fruit Pr 27:18
every kind of fruit **t** in them. Ec 2:5
whether a **t** falls to the south Ec 11:3
the place where the **t** falls, Ec 11:3
the almond **t** blossoms, the Ec 12:5
an apricot **t** among the trees Sg 2:3
The fig **t** ripens its figs; Sg 2:13
Your stature is like a palm **t**; Sg 7:7
climb the palm **t** and take hold Sg 7:8
you under the apricot **t**. Sg 8:5
as if an olive **t** had been beaten Is 17:6
at the very top of the **t**, Is 17:6
harvested olive **t**, like a Is 24:13
vine, and foliage on the fig **t**. Is 34:4
his own fig **t** and drink water Is 36:16
forest, and every **t** in it. Is 44:23
say, "Look, I am a dried-up **t**." Is 56:3
under every flourishing **t**, Is 57:5
be like the lifetime of a **t**. Is 65:22
"I see a branch of an almond **t**." Jr 1:11
under every leafy **t** you lie down Jr 2:20
say to a **t**: You are my father, Jr 2:27
every green **t** to prostitute Jr 3:6
adultery with stone and **t**. Jr 3:9
under every green **t** and have not Jr 3:13
beast, on the **t** of the field, Jr 7:20
figs on the fig **t**, and even the Jr 8:13
cuts down a **t** from the forest; Jr 10:3
named you a flourishing olive **t**, Jr 11:16
destroy the **t** with its fruit; Jr 11:19
will be like a **t** planted by Jr 17:8
every green **t** and every leafy Ezk 6:13
down the tall **t**, and make the Ezk 17:24
tree, and make the low **t** tall. Ezk 17:24
cause the green **t** to wither and Ezk 17:24
and make the withered **t** thrive. Ezk 17:24
saw any high hill or leafy **t**, Ezk 20:28
every green **t** and every dry tree Ezk 20:47
tree and every dry **t** in you. Ezk 20:47
the sword despises every **t**. Ezk 21:10
place where the **t** was planted Ezk 31:4
No **t** in the garden of God could Ezk 31:8
There was a palm **t** between each Ezk 41:18
toward the palm **t** on one side, Ezk 41:19
There was a **t** in the middle of Dn 4:10
The **t** grew large and strong; Dn 4:11
Cut down the **t** and chop off its Dn 4:14
The **t** you saw, which grew large Dn 4:20
that **t** is you, the king. Dn 4:22
'Cut down the **t** and destroy it, Dn 4:23
fruit of the fig **t** in its first Hs 9:10
will be like the olive **t**, Hs 14:6
I am like a flourishing pine **t**; Hs 14:8
and splintered My fig **t**. Jl 1:7
and the fig **t** is withered; Jl 1:12
the fig **t** and grapevine yield Jl 2:22
under his fig **t** with no one to Mc 4:4
Though the fig **t** does not bud Hab 3:17
and the olive **t** have not yet Hg 2:19
under ⌊his⌋ vine and fig **t**." Zch 3:10
Therefore every **t** that doesn't Mt 3:10
good **t** produces good fruit, Mt 7:17
but a bad **t** produces bad fruit. Mt 7:17
good **t** can't produce bad fruit; Mt 7:18
neither can a bad **t** produce good Mt 7:18
Every **t** that doesn't produce Mt 7:19
Either make the **t** good and its Mt 12:33
or make the **t** bad and its fruit Mt 12:33
for a **t** is known by its fruit. Mt 12:33
the vegetables and becomes a **t**, Mt 13:32
Seeing a lone fig **t** by the road, Mt 21:19
At once the fig **t** withered. Mt 21:19
did the fig **t** wither so quickly? Mt 21:20
do what was done to the fig **t**, Mt 21:21
this parable from the fig **t**: Mt 24:32
distance a fig **t** with leaves, Mk 11:13
they saw the fig **t** withered from Mk 11:20
The fig **t** that You cursed is Mk 11:21
this parable from the fig **t**: Mk 13:28
Therefore every **t** that doesn't Lk 3:9
A good **t** doesn't produce bad Lk 6:43
a bad **t** doesn't produce good Lk 6:43
For each **t** is known by its own Lk 6:44
A man had a fig **t** that was Lk 13:6
on this fig **t** and haven't found Lk 13:7
and became a **t**, and the birds Lk 13:19
you can say to this mulberry **t**, Lk 17:6
up a sycamore **t** to see Jesus, Lk 19:4
Look at the fig **t**, and all the Lk 21:29
when you were under the fig **t**, Jn 1:48
you I saw you under the fig **t**? Jn 1:50
murdered by hanging Him on a **t**. Ac 5:30
Him by hanging Him on a **t**. Ac 10:39
Him down from the **t** and put Him Ac 13:29
root of the cultivated olive **t**, Rm 11:17
into a cultivated olive **t**, Rm 11:24
grafted into their own olive **t**? Rm 11:24
is everyone who is hung on a **t**. Gl 3:13
Can a fig **t** produce olives, Jms 3:12
our sins in His body on the **t**, 1Pt 2:24
right to eat from the **t** of life, Rv 2:7
as a fig **t** drops its unripe Rv 6:13
earth or on the sea or on any **t**. Rv 7:1
plant, or any **t**, but only people Rv 9:4
river was the **t** of life bearing Rv 22:2
leaves of the **t** are for healing Rv 22:2
right to the **t** of life and may Rv 22:14
his share of the **t** of life and Rv 22:19

TREE'S *(1)*

to leave the **t** stump with its Dn 4:26

TREES *(131)*

and fruit **t** on the earth bearing Gn 1:11
their kinds and **t** bearing fruit Gn 1:12
fruit from the **t** in the garden. Gn 3:2
God among the **t** of the garden. Gn 3:8
and all the **t** anywhere within Gn 23:17
the fruit on the **t** that the hail Ex 10:15
was left on the **t** or the plants Ex 10:15
take the product of majestic **t**— Lv 23:40
boughs of leafy **t**, and willows Lv 23:40
and the **t** of the field will bear Lv 26:4
and the **t** of the land will not Lv 26:20
the soil or fruit from the **t**, Lv 27:30
Are there **t** in it or not? Nm 13:20
not destroy its **t** by putting an Dt 20:19
t of the field human, to come Dt 20:19
may destroy the **t** that you know Dt 20:20
have olives **t** throughout your Dt 28:40
of all your **t** and your land's Dt 28:42
bodies on five **t** and they were Jos 10:26
taken down from the **t** and thrown Jos 10:27
The **t** set out to anoint a king Jdg 9:8
and man, and rule over the **t**?" Jdg 9:9
Then the **t** said to the fig tree, Jdg 9:10
my good fruit, and rule over **t**?" Jdg 9:11
the **t** said to the grapevine, Jdg 9:12
God and man, and rule over **t**?" Jdg 9:13
all the **t** said to the bramble, Jdg 9:14
The bramble said to the **t**, Jdg 9:15
and cut a branch from the **t**. Jdg 9:48
them opposite the balsam **t**. 2Sm 5:23
in the tops of the balsam **t**, 2Sm 5:24
described **t**, from the cedar in 1Kg 4:33
palm **t** and flower blossoms— 1Kg 6:29
palm **t** and flower blossoms on 1Kg 6:32
over the cherubim and palm **t**. 1Kg 6:32
palm **t** and flower blossoms on 1Kg 6:35
and palm **t** on the plates of its 1Kg 7:36
to the Jordan, they cut down **t**. 2Kg 6:4
a land of olive **t** and honey— 2Kg 18:32
cedars, its choice cypress **t**. 2Kg 19:23
them opposite the balsam **t**. 1Ch 14:14
in the tops of the balsam **t**, 1Ch 14:15
Then the **t** of the forest will 1Ch 16:33
and sycamore **t** in the Shephelah 1Ch 27:28
how to cut the **t** of Lebanon. 2Ch 2:8
the woodcutters who cut the **t**, 2Ch 2:10
with palm **t** and chains. 2Ch 3:5
other⌋ leafy **t** to make booths, Neh 8:15
and fruit **t** in abundance. Neh 9:25
was like men in a thicket of **t**, Ps 74:5
sycamore-fig **t** with a flood. Ps 78:47
all the **t** of the forest will Ps 96:12
The **t** of the LORD flourish, Ps 104:16
makes its home in the pine **t**. Ps 104:17
vines and fig **t** and shattered Ps 105:33
and shattered the **t** of their Ps 105:33
like young olive **t** around your Ps 128:3
up our lyres on the poplar **t**, Ps 137:2
hills, fruit **t** and all cedars, Ps 148:9
a grove of flourishing **t**. Ec 2:6
one who splits **t** may be Ec 10:9
tree among the **t** of the forest, Sg 2:3
with all the **t** of frankincense, Sg 4:14
of the sacred **t** you desired, Is 1:29
trembled like **t** of a forest Is 7:2
The remaining **t** of its forest Is 10:19
and the tall ⌊**t**⌋ will be cut Is 10:33
cut down, the high ⌊**t**⌋ felled. Is 10:33
cedars, its choice cypress **t**. Is 37:24
acacias, myrtles, and olive **t**. Is 41:19
put cypress **t** in the desert, Is 41:19
desert, elms and box **t** together, Is 41:19
among the **t** of the forest. Is 44:14
and all the **t** of the field will Is 55:12
they will be called righteous **t**, Is 61:3
your vines and your fig **t**. Jr 5:17
Cut down the **t**; raise a siege Jr 6:6
by the green **t** on the high hills Jr 17:2
her like those who cut **t**. Jr 46:22
among the **t** of the forest, Ezk 15:2
vine among the **t** of the forest, Ezk 15:6
Then all the **t** of the field will Ezk 17:24
planking with pine **t** from Senir. Ezk 27:5
to all the **t** of the field. Ezk 31:4
than all the **t** of the field. Ezk 31:5
the pine **t** couldn't compare with Ezk 31:8
could the plane **t** match its Ezk 31:8
and all the **t** of Eden, which Ezk 31:9
so that no **t** ⌊planted⌋ beside Ezk 31:14
well-watered **t** would reach them Ezk 31:14
and all the **t** of the field Ezk 31:15
Then all the **t** of Eden, all the Ezk 31:16
the well-watered **t**, the choice Ezk 31:16
and greatness among Eden's **t**? Ezk 31:18
to be⌋ with the **t** of Eden. Ezk 31:18
The **t** of the field will give Ezk 34:27
fruit of the **t** and the produce Ezk 36:30
was decorated with palm **t**. Ezk 40:16
and palm **t** had the same Ezk 40:22
It had palm **t** on its pilasters, Ezk 40:26
were decorated with palm **t**. Ezk 40:31
with palm **t** on each side. Ezk 40:34
with palm **t** on each side. Ezk 40:37
carved with cherubim and palm **t**. Ezk 41:18
Cherubim and palm **t** were carved Ezk 41:20
Cherubim and palm **t** were carved Ezk 41:25
and palm **t** on both sides, Ezk 41:26
large number of **t** along both Ezk 47:7
All ⌊kinds of⌋ **t** providing food Ezk 47:12
devastate her vines and fig **t**. Hs 2:12
all the **t** of the orchard— Jl 1:12
devoured all the **t** of the Jl 1:19
green, the **t** bear their fruit Jl 2:22
your fig **t** and olive trees, Am 4:9

your fig trees and olive **t**, Am 4:9
are fig **t** with figs that Nah 3:12
the myrtle **t** in the valley. Zch 1:8
among the myrtle **t** explained, Zch 1:10
standing among the myrtle **t**, Zch 1:11
are also two olive **t** beside it, Zch 4:3
are the two olive **t** on the right Zch 4:11
the glorious ⌊**t**⌋ are destroyed! Zch 11:2
to strike the root of the **t**! Mt 3:10
from the **t** and spreading Mt 21:8
they look to me like **t** walking." Mk 8:24
to strike the root of the **t**! Lk 3:9
at the fig tree, and all the **t**. Lk 21:29
t in late autumn—fruitless, Jd 12
the sea or the **t** until we seal Rv 7:3
a third of the **t** were burned up, Rv 8:7
are the two olive **t** and the two Rv 11:4

TREMBLE *(44)*

Isaac began to **t** uncontrollably. Gn 27:33
report about you, **t**, and be in Dt 2:25
t before Him, all the earth. 1Ch 16:30
and of those who **t** at the Ezr 10:3
didn't rise or **t** in fear at his Est 5:9
its place so that its pillars **t**. Jb 9:6
those in the east **t** in horror. Jb 18:20
departed spirits **t** beneath the Jb 26:5
⌊that hold up⌋ the sky **t**, Jb 26:11
whole earth **t** before the LORD Ps 33:8
t before Him, all the earth. Ps 96:9
Let the peoples **t**. He is Ps 99:1
T, earth, at the presence of the Ps 114:7
I **t** in awe of You; I fear Your Ps 119:120
the guardians of the house **t**, Ec 12:3
I will make the heavens **t**, Is 13:13
man who caused the earth to **t**, Is 14:16
T with fear, all Philistia! Is 14:31
of Moab cry out, and they **t**. Is 15:4
Egypt's idols will **t** before Him, Is 19:1
She will **t** with fear because of Is 19:16
Egypt will **t** because of what the Is 19:17
He made kingdoms **t**. The LORD has Is 23:11
t, you overconfident ones! Is 32:11
afraid, the ends of the earth **t**. Is 41:5
your heart will **t** and rejoice, Is 60:5
nations will **t** at Your presence Is 64:2
You who **t** at His word, hear the Is 66:5
The priests will **t** in fear, Jr 4:9
Do you not **t** before Me, the One Jr 5:22
within me, and all my bones **t**. Jr 23:9
They will **t** with awe because of Jr 33:9
the people of the land will **t**. Ezk 7:27
on the ground, **t** continually, Ezk 26:16
the coastlands **t** on the day of Ezk 26:18
of them will **t** every moment for Ezk 32:10
of the earth will **t** before Me. Ezk 38:20
people must **t** in fear before the Dn 6:26
all the residents of the land **t**, Jl 2:1
They will **t** before the LORD our Mc 7:17
melt, knees **t**, loins shake, Nah 2:10
of the land of Midian **t**. Hab 3:7
Moses began to **t** and did not Ac 7:32
do not **t** when they blaspheme 2Pt 2:10

TREMBLED *(12)*

saw ⌊it⌋ they **t** and stood at Ex 20:18
Edom, the earth **t**, the heavens Jdg 5:4
met him, they **t** and asked, "Do 1Sm 16:4
he was afraid and **t** violently. 1Sm 28:5
foundations of the heavens **t**; 2Sm 22:8
Everyone who **t** at the words of Ezr 9:4
foundations of the mountains **t**; Ps 18:7
earth **t**, and the skies poured Ps 68:8
saw You; they **t**. Even the depths Ps 77:16
hearts of his people **t** like Is 7:2
I heard, and I **t** within; Hab 3:16
my bones; I **t** where I stood. Now Hab 3:16

TREMBLES *(8)*

and my body **t** in horror. Jb 21:6
though the earth **t** and the Ps 46:2
the earth sees and **t**. Ps 97:4
He looks at the earth, and it **t**; Ps 104:32
The earth **t** under three things; Pr 30:21
in spirit, and who **t** at My word. Is 66:2
earth quakes and **t**, because the Jr 51:29
the earth **t** at His presence— Nah 1:5

TREMBLING *(31)*

T, they turned to one another Gn 42:28
t will seize the leaders of Moab; Ex 15:15
LORD will give you a **t** heart, Dt 28:65
is fearful and **t** may turn back Jdg 7:3
came to him **t**, for he thought 1Sm 15:32
lose heart and come **t** from their 2Sm 22:46
guests got up **t** and went their 1Kg 1:49
t because of this matter and Ezr 10:9
fear and **t** came over me and made Jb 4:14
He charges ahead with **t** rage; Jb 39:24
awe, and rejoice with **t**. Ps 2:11
lose heart and come **t** from their Ps 18:45
T seized them there, agony like Ps 48:6
Fear and **t** grip me; Ps 55:5
The people of Ramah are **t**; Is 10:29
t seizes the ungodly: Is 33:14
your bread with **t** and drink your Ezk 12:18
will clothe themselves with **t**; Ezk 26:16
he said this to me, I stood **t**. Dn 10:11
will come **t** from the west. Hs 11:10
When Ephraim spoke, there was **t**; Hs 13:1
they will come **t** out of their Mc 7:17
with fear and **t**, fell down Mk 5:33
because **t** and astonishment Mk 16:8
she came **t** and fell down before Lk 8:47
and fell down **t** before Paul and Ac 16:29
in fear, and in much **t**. 1Co 2:3
received him with fear and **t**. 2Co 7:15
human masters with fear and **t**, Eph 6:5
own salvation with fear and **t**. Php 2:12
said, I am terrified and **t**. Heb 12:21

TREMENDOUS *(1)*

And there was **t** joy. Neh 8:17

TRENCH *(3)*

he made a **t** around the altar 1Kg 18:32
he even filled the **t** with water. 1Kg 18:35
up the water that was in the **t**. 1Kg 18:38

TRESPASS *(5)*

But the gift is not like the **t**. Rm 5:15
the one man's **t** the many died, Rm 5:15
the one man's **t**, death reigned Rm 5:17
as through one **t** there is Rm 5:18
came along to multiply the **t**. Rm 5:20

TRESPASSES *(8)*

up for our **t** and raised for our Rm 4:25
but from many **t** came the gift, Rm 5:16
counting their **t** against them, 2Co 5:19
of our **t**, according to Eph 1:7
you were dead in your **t** and sins Eph 2:1
even though we were dead in **t**. Eph 2:5
when you were dead in **t** and in Col 2:13
Him and forgave us all our **t**. Col 2:13

TRESSES *(1)*

could be held captive in your **t**. Sg 7:5

TRIAL *(10)*

until he stands **t** before the Nm 35:12
until he stands **t** before the Jos 20:6
getting a fair **t** and to deprive Is 10:2
let us come together for the **t**. Is 41:1
Surely it will be a **t**! Ezk 21:13
beat us in public without a **t**, Ac 16:37
to be held for **t** by the Emperor, Ac 25:21
now I stand on **t** for the hope Ac 26:6
condition was a **t** for you, Gl 4:14
one undergoing a **t** should say, Jms 1:13

TRIALS *(9)*

nation, by **t**, signs, wonders, Dt 4:34
the great **t** that you saw, the Dt 7:19
eyes the great **t** and those great Dt 29:3
ones who stood by Me in My **t**. Lk 22:28
and with the **t** that came to me Ac 20:19
you experience various **t**, Jms 1:2
Blessed is a man who endures **t**, Jms 1:12
to be distressed by various **t** 1Pt 1:6
the godly from **t** and to keep 2Pt 2:9

TRIBAL *(16)*

He will father 12 **t** leaders, Gn 17:20
Kohathite **t** clans to be wiped Nm 4:18
They were the **t** leaders who Nm 7:2
t head of an ancestral house in Nm 25:15
with your **t** leaders and elders Dt 5:23
Assemble all your **t** elders and Dt 31:28
according to their **t** allotments. Jos 11:23
give us only one **t** allotment as Jos 17:14
the **t** heads and the ancestral 1Kg 8:1
of Israel—all the **t** heads, the 2Ch 5:2
distribution of the **t** household 2Ch 35:5
and all their **t** leaders like Ps 83:11
Her **t** chieftains have led Egypt Is 19:13
to one of the ⌊**t**⌋ portions Ezk 45:7
long as one of the ⌊**t**⌋ portions Ezk 48:8
adjacent to the ⌊**t**⌋ portions, Ezk 48:21

TRIBE *(234)*

will become a **t**, and he too will Gn 48:19
son of Hur, of the **t** of Judah. Ex 31:2
Ahisamach, of the **t** of Dan, to Ex 31:6
son of Hur, of the **t** of Judah. Ex 35:30
Ahisamach, of the **t** of Dan, ⌊the Ex 35:34
of Hur, of the **t** of Judah, made Ex 38:22
Ahisamach, of the **t** of Dan, a Ex 38:23
of Dibri of the **t** of Dan. Lv 24:11
A man from each **t** is to be with Nm 1:4
for the **t** of Reuben numbered Nm 1:21
for the **t** of Simeon numbered Nm 1:23
for the **t** of Gad numbered Nm 1:25
for the **t** of Judah numbered Nm 1:27
registered for the **t** of Issachar Nm 1:29
registered for the **t** of Zebulun Nm 1:31
registered for the **t** of Ephraim Nm 1:33
registered for the **t** of Manasseh Nm 1:35
registered for the **t** of Benjamin Nm 1:37
for the **t** of Dan numbered Nm 1:39
for the **t** of Asher numbered Nm 1:41
registered for the **t** of Naphtali Nm 1:43
with them by their ancestral **t**. Nm 1:47
a census of the **t** of Levi with Nm 1:49
The **t** of Issachar will camp next Nm 2:5
The **t** of Zebulun ⌊will be next⌋. Nm 2:7
The **t** of Simeon will camp next Nm 2:12
The **t** of Gad ⌊will be next⌋. Nm 2:14
The **t** of Manasseh will be next Nm 2:20
t of Benjamin ⌊will be next⌋. Nm 2:22
The **t** of Asher will camp next to Nm 2:27
t of Naphtali ⌊will be next⌋. Nm 2:29
Bring the **t** of Levi near and Nm 3:6
Amminadab from the **t** of Judah. Nm 7:12
the division of the Issachar **t**, Nm 10:15
the division of the Zebulun **t**. Nm 10:16
over the division of Simeon's **t**, Nm 10:19
the division of the **t** of Gad. Nm 10:20
division of the **t** of Manasseh, Nm 10:23
division of the **t** of Benjamin. Nm 10:24
the division of the **t** of Asher, Nm 10:26
division of the **t** of Naphtali. Nm 10:27
of Zaccur from the **t** of Reuben; Nm 13:4
of Hori from the **t** of Simeon; Nm 13:5
Jephunneh from the **t** of Judah; Nm 13:6
Joseph from the **t** of Issachar; Nm 13:7
of Nun from the **t** of Ephraim; Nm 13:8
of Raphu from the **t** of Benjamin; Nm 13:9
of Sodi from the **t** of Zebulun; Nm 13:10
of Susi from the **t** of Manasseh Nm 13:11
Manasseh (from the **t** of Joseph); Nm 13:11
of Gemalli from the **t** of Dan; Nm 13:12
of Michael from the **t** of Asher; Nm 13:13
Vophsi from the **t** of Naphtali; Nm 13:14
son of Machi from the **t** of Gad. Nm 13:15
with you from the **t** of Levi, Nm 18:2
your ancestral **t**, so they may Nm 18:2
saw Israel encamped **t** by tribe, Nm 24:2
saw Israel encamped tribe by **t**, Nm 24:2
the inheritance for a large ⌊**t**⌋, Nm 26:54
to war from each Israelite **t**." Nm 31:4
from each Israelite **t** out of the Nm 31:5
sent 1,000 from each **t** to war. Nm 31:6
and half the **t** of Manasseh son Nm 32:33
For the **t** of the Reubenites and Nm 34:14
and the **t** of the Gadites Nm 34:14
and half the **t** of Manasseh has Nm 34:14
leader from each **t** to distribute Nm 34:18
Jephunneh from the **t** of Judah; Nm 34:19
of Ammihud from the **t** of Simeon; Nm 34:20
Chislon from the **t** of Benjamin; Nm 34:21
a leader from the **t** of Dan; Nm 34:22
a leader from the **t** of Manasseh, Nm 34:23
a leader from the **t** of Ephraim; Nm 34:24
a leader from the **t** of Zebulun; Nm 34:25
a leader from the **t** of Issachar; Nm 34:26
a leader from the **t** of Asher; Nm 34:27
leader from the **t** of Naphtali." Nm 34:28
more from a larger ⌊**t**⌋ and less Nm 35:8
Each ⌊**t**⌋ is to give some of its Nm 35:8
to that of the **t** into which they Nm 36:3
to that of the **t** into which they Nm 36:4
inheritance of our ancestral **t**." Nm 36:4
What the **t** of Joseph's Nm 36:5

a clan of their ancestral **t**. Nm 36:6
not transfer from **t** to tribe, Nm 36:7
not transfer from tribe to **t**, Nm 36:7
inheritance of his ancestral **t**. Nm 36:7
from an Israelite **t** must marry Nm 36:8
the clan of her ancestral **t**, Nm 36:8
transfer from one **t** to another, Nm 36:9
within the **t** of their father's Nm 36:12
among you, one man for each **t**. Dt 1:23
I gave to half the **t** of Manasseh Dt 3:13
set apart the **t** of Levi to carry Dt 10:8
the whole **t** of Levi, will have Dt 18:1
and half the **t** of Manasseh. Dt 29:8
or **t** among you today whose heart Dt 29:18
and half the **t** of Manasseh: Jos 1:12
of Israel, one man for each **t**. Jos 3:12
the people, one man for each **t**, Jos 4:2
Israelites, one man for each **t**, Jos 4:4
and half the **t** of Manasseh went Jos 4:12
Zerah, of the **t** of Judah, took Jos 7:1
present yourselves **t** by tribe. Jos 7:14
present yourselves tribe by **t**. Jos 7:14
t the LORD selects is to come Jos 7:14
Israel come forward **t** by tribe, Jos 7:16
Israel come forward tribe by **t**, Jos 7:16
and the **t** of Judah was selected. Jos 7:16
of Zerah, of the **t** of Judah, was Jos 7:18
and half the **t** of Manasseh. Jos 12:6
and half the **t** of Manasseh." Jos 13:7
With the other half of the **t**, Jos 13:8
inheritance to the **t** of Levi. Jos 13:14
To the **t** of the Reubenites by Jos 13:15
To the **t** of the Gadites by their Jos 13:24
And to half the **t** of Manasseh, Jos 13:29
to half the **t** of Manasseh's Jos 13:29
give a portion to the **t** of Levi. Jos 13:33
allotment for the **t** of the Jos 15:1
of the **t** of the descendants Jos 15:20
cities of the **t** of the Jos 15:21
of the **t** of the descendants Jos 16:8
for the **t** of Manasseh as Jos 17:1
three men from each **t**, Jos 18:4
and half the **t** of Manasseh have Jos 18:7
came up for the **t** of Benjamin's Jos 18:11
cities of the **t** of Benjamin's Jos 18:21
for the **t** of his descendants by Jos 19:1
inheritance of the **t** of Simeon's Jos 19:8
came out for the **t** of Issachar's Jos 19:17
of the **t** of Issachar's Jos 19:23
came out for the **t** of Asher's Jos 19:24
inheritance of the **t** of Asher's Jos 19:31
of the **t** of Naphtali's Jos 19:39
for the Danite **t** by its clans. Jos 19:40
of the Danite **t** by its clans, Jos 19:48
plateau from Reuben's **t**, Jos 20:8
Ramoth in Gilead from Gad's **t**, Jos 20:8
in Bashan from Manasseh's **t**. Jos 20:8
and half the **t** of Manasseh. Jos 21:5
and half the **t** of Manasseh in Jos 21:6
the **t** of Benjamin ⌊they gave⌋ Jos 21:17
came from the **t** of Ephraim. Jos 21:20
From the **t** of Dan ⌊they gave⌋: Jos 21:23
half the **t** of Manasseh ⌊they Jos 21:25
From half the **t** of Manasseh, Jos 21:27
the **t** of Issachar ⌊they gave⌋ Jos 21:28
From the **t** of Asher ⌊they gave⌋: Jos 21:30
the **t** of Naphtali ⌊they gave⌋ Jos 21:32
From the **t** of Zebulun, ⌊they Jos 21:34
the **t** of Reuben, ⌊they gave⌋ Jos 21:36
From the **t** of Gad, ⌊they gave⌋: Jos 21:38
and half the **t** of Manasseh, Jos 22:1
to half the **t** of Manasseh in Jos 22:7
and half the **t** of Manasseh left Jos 22:9
and half the **t** of Manasseh built Jos 22:10
and half the **t** of Manasseh have Jos 22:11
and half the **t** of Manasseh, Jos 22:13
leader for each **t** of Israel. Jos 22:14
and half the **t** of Manasseh, Jos 22:15
and half the **t** of Manasseh Jos 22:21
outside the **t** and brought back Jdg 12:9
his sons from outside ⌊the **t**⌋. Jdg 12:9
and the Danite **t** was looking for Jdg 18:1
a priest for a **t** and family in Jdg 18:19
for the Danite **t** until the time Jdg 18:30
throughout the **t** of Benjamin, Jdg 20:12
occurred that one **t** is ⌊missing⌋ Jdg 21:3
Today a **t** has been cut off from Jdg 21:6
that a **t** of Israel will not be Jdg 21:17
there to his own **t** and family. Jdg 21:24
the clans of the Benjaminite **t**? 1Sm 9:21
and the **t** of Benjamin was 1Sm 10:20
Then he had the **t** of Benjamin 1Sm 10:21
son from the **t** of Naphtali, 1Kg 7:14
I will give one **t** to your son 1Kg 11:13
one **t** will remain his because 1Kg 11:32
I will give one **t** to his son, 1Kg 11:36
except the **t** of Judah alone. 1Kg 12:20
Judah and the **t** of Benjamin to 1Kg 12:21
Only the **t** of Judah remained. 2Kg 17:18
and half the **t** of Manasseh had 1Ch 5:18
sons of half the **t** of Manasseh 1Ch 5:23
and half the **t** of Manasseh into 1Ch 5:26
the **t** of Benjamin ⌊they were 1Ch 6:60
the half **t** of Manasseh ⌊were 1Ch 6:61
towns from the **t** of Ephraim for 1Ch 6:66
From half the **t** of Manasseh, 1Ch 6:70
of half the **t** of Manasseh. 1Ch 6:71
From the **t** of Issachar ⌊they 1Ch 6:72
From the **t** of Asher ⌊they 1Ch 6:74
From the **t** of Naphtali ⌊they 1Ch 6:76
From the **t** of Zebulun, ⌊they 1Ch 6:77
From the **t** of Reuben across the 1Ch 6:78
the **t** of Gad ⌊they received⌋ 1Ch 6:80
From half the **t** of Manasseh: 1Ch 12:31
and half the **t** of Manasseh: 1Ch 12:37
were named among the **t** of Levi. 1Ch 23:14
and half the **t** of Manasseh as 1Ch 26:32
for half the **t** of Manasseh, 1Ch 27:20
for half the **t** of Manasseh in 1Ch 27:21
Those from every **t** of Israel who 2Ch 11:16
one for each Israelite **t**. Ezr 6:17
redeemed as the **t** for Your own Ps 74:2
did not choose the **t** of Ephraim. Ps 78:67
He chose instead the **t** of Judah, Ps 78:68
Israel is the **t** of His Jr 10:16
⌊Israel is⌋ the **t** of His Jr 51:19
In whatever **t** the foreigner Ezk 47:23
of Phanuel, of the **t** of Asher. Lk 2:36
a man of the **t** of Benjamin, Ac 13:21
Abraham, from the **t** of Benjamin. Rm 11:1
of Israel, of the **t** of Benjamin, Php 3:5
said belonged to a different **t**, Heb 7:13
and about that **t** Moses said Heb 7:14
The Lion from the **t** of Judah, Rv 5:5
blood from every **t** and language Rv 5:9
sealed from every **t** of the sons Rv 7:4
sealed from the **t** of Judah, Rv 7:5
12,000 from the **t** of Reuben, Rv 7:5
12,000 from the **t** of Gad, Rv 7:5
12,000 from the **t** of Asher, Rv 7:6
12,000 from the **t** of Naphtali, Rv 7:6
12,000 from the **t** of Manasseh, Rv 7:6
12,000 from the **t** of Simeon, Rv 7:7
12,000 from the **t** of Levi, Rv 7:7
12,000 from the **t** of Issachar, Rv 7:7
12,000 from the **t** of Zebulun, Rv 7:8
12,000 from the **t** of Joseph, Rv 7:8
sealed from the **t** of Benjamin. Rv 7:8
from every nation, **t**, people, Rv 7:9
given authority over every **t**, Rv 13:7
every nation, **t**, language, and Rv 14:6

TRIBES *(111)*

as one of the **t** of Israel. Gn 49:16
These are the **t** of Israel, Gn 49:28
pillars for the 12 **t** of Israel Ex 24:4
one of the names of the 12 **t**. Ex 28:21
one of the names of the 12 **t**. Ex 39:14
leaders of their ancestral **t**, Nm 1:16
from each of their ancestral **t**." Nm 13:2
the names of their ancestral **t**. Nm 26:55
the larger and smaller ⌊**t**⌋." Nm 26:56
the leaders of the Israelite **t**, Nm 30:1
leaders of the Israelite **t**. Nm 32:28
according to your ancestral **t**. Nm 33:54
given to the nine and a half **t**. Nm 34:13
two and a half **t** have received Nm 34:15
from the ⌊other⌋ Israelite **t**, Nm 36:3
the Israelite **t** is to retain its Nm 36:9
men from each of your **t**, Dt 1:13
So I took the leaders of your **t**, Dt 1:15
tens, and officers for your **t**. Dt 1:15
from all your **t** to put His name Dt 12:5
LORD chooses in one of your **t**, Dt 12:14
for your **t** in all your towns Dt 16:18
sons from all your **t** to stand Dt 18:5
these ⌊**t**⌋ will stand on Mount Dt 27:12
these ⌊**t**⌋ will stand on Mount Dt 27:13
your leaders, **t**, elders, Dt 29:10
harm from all the **t** of Israel, Dt 29:21
gathered with the **t** of Israel. Dt 33:5
12 men from the **t** of Israel, Jos 3:12
one for each of the Israelite **t**, Jos 4:5
one for each of the Israelite **t**, Jos 4:8
inheritance to the **t** of Israel Jos 12:7
to the nine **t** and half the tribe Jos 13:7
of the Israelite **t** gave them in Jos 14:1
Moses for the nine and a half **t**, Jos 14:2
two and a half **t** beyond the Jos 14:3
of Joseph became two **t**, Jos 14:4
Seven **t** among the Israelites Jos 18:2
the Israelite **t** by lot at Shiloh Jos 19:51
the families of the Israelite **t**. Jos 21:1
by lot from the **t** of Judah, Jos 21:4
the clans of the **t** of Ephraim, Jos 21:5
the clans of the **t** of Issachar, Jos 21:6
clans from the **t** of Reuben, Jos 21:7
by name from the **t** of the Jos 21:9
nine cities from these two **t**. Jos 21:16
as an inheritance for your **t**, Jos 23:4
assembled all the **t** of Israel at Jos 24:1
by them⌋ among the **t** of Israel. Jdg 18:1
and of all the **t** of Israel Jdg 20:2
100 from all the **t** of Israel, Jdg 20:10
Then the **t** of Israel sent men Jdg 20:12
Who of all the **t** of Israel Jdg 21:5
among the **t** of Israel didn't Jdg 21:8
this gap in the **t** of Israel. Jdg 21:15
house from the **t** of Israel to be 1Sm 2:28
of Israel's **t** and isn't my clan 1Sm 9:21
the LORD by your **t** and clans." 1Sm 10:19
had all the **t** of Israel come 1Sm 10:20
the leader of the **t** of Israel? 1Sm 15:17
the **t** of Israel came to David 2Sm 5:1
anyone among the **t** of Israel, 2Sm 7:7
is from one of the **t** of Israel," 2Sm 15:2
throughout the **t** of Israel with 2Sm 15:10
among all the **t** of Israel were 2Sm 19:9
through all the **t** of Israel to 2Sm 20:14
through all the **t** of Israel from 2Sm 24:2
in among any of the **t** of Israel, 1Kg 8:16
I will give you 10 **t**, 1Kg 11:31
out of all the **t** of Israel. 1Kg 11:32
I will take 10 **t** of the kingdom 1Kg 11:35
from all the **t** of Israel to put 1Kg 14:21
the number of the **t** of the sons 1Kg 18:31
out of all the **t** of Israel. 2Kg 21:7
13 towns from the **t** of Issachar, 1Ch 6:62
12 towns from the **t** of Reuben, 1Ch 6:63
above from the **t** of the 1Ch 6:65
in charge of the **t** of Israel: 1Ch 27:16
the leaders of the **t** of Israel. 1Ch 27:22
leaders of the **t**, the leaders 1Ch 28:1
the leaders of the **t** of Israel, 1Ch 29:6
in among any of the **t** of Israel, 2Ch 6:5
from all the **t** of Israel to put 2Ch 12:13
those from ⌊the **t** of⌋ Ephraim, 2Ch 15:9
out of all the **t** of Israel. 2Ch 33:7
desert **t** kneel before him and Ps 72:9
and settled the **t** of Israel in Ps 78:55
and no one among His **t** stumbled. Ps 105:37
where the **t**, the tribes of the Ps 122:4
the tribes, the **t** of the LORD, Ps 122:4
curse him, and **t** will denounce Pr 24:24
raising up the **t** of Jacob and Is 49:6
servants, the **t** of Your heritage Is 63:17
and the **t** of Israel associated Ezk 37:19
of Israel according to their **t**. Ezk 45:8
for the 12 **t** of Israel. Ezk 47:13
according to the **t** of Israel. Ezk 47:21
among the **t** of Israel. Ezk 47:22
these are the names of the **t**: Ezk 48:1
from all the **t** of Israel will Ezk 48:19
As for the rest of the **t**: Ezk 48:23
as an inheritance to Israel's **t**, Ezk 48:29
being named for the **t** of Israel: Ezk 48:31
certain among the **t** of Israel. Hs 5:9
against all the **t** of Israel Zch 9:1
judging the 12 **t** of Israel. Mt 19:28
judging the 12 **t** of Israel. Lk 22:30
promise⌋ our 12 **t** hope to attain Ac 26:7
To the 12 **t** in the Dispersion. Jms 1:1
from the peoples, **t**, languages, Rv 11:9
names of the 12 **t** of the sons Rv 21:12

TRIBESMEN *(1)*
Their t who were warriors 1Ch 7:5

TRIBULATION *(9)*
that time there will be great t, Mt 24:21
after the t of those days: Mt 24:29
For those will be days of t, Mk 13:19
But in those days, after that t: Mk 13:24
brother and partner in the t, Rv 1:9
I know your t and poverty, Rv 2:9
and you will have t for 10 days. Rv 2:10
adultery with her into great t, Rv 2:22
ones coming out of the great t. Rv 7:14

TRIBUNAL *(1)*
I am standing at Caesar's t, Ac 25:10

TRIBUTE *(30)*
Set aside a t for the LORD from Nm 31:28
Take ⌊the t⌋ from their half and Nm 31:29
and the t to the LORD was 675 Nm 31:37
cattle, the t to the LORD was 72 Nm 31:38
donkeys, the t to the LORD was Nm 31:39
the t to the LORD was 32 people. Nm 31:40
Moses gave the t to Eleazar the Nm 31:41
king of Moab with t ⌊money⌋. Jdg 3:15
and brought the t to Eglon king Jdg 3:17
had finished presenting the t, Jdg 3:18
David's subjects and brought t. 2Sm 8:2
David's subjects and brought t. 2Sm 8:6
offered t and served Solomon 1Kg 4:21
man would bring his annual t: 1Kg 10:25
his vassal and paid him t money. 2Kg 17:3
and had not paid t money to the 2Kg 17:4
David's subjects and brought t. 1Ch 18:2
David's subjects and brought t. 1Ch 18:6
and mules—as an annual t. 2Ch 9:24
Then all Judah brought him t, 2Ch 17:5
and silver as t to Jehoshaphat, 2Ch 17:11
Ammonites gave Uzziah t money, 2Ch 26:8
will not pay t, duty, or land Ezr 4:13
region, and t, duty, and land Ezr 4:20
advised that t, duty, and land Ezr 7:24
kings will bring t to You. Ps 68:29
the coasts and islands bring t, Ps 72:10
around Him bring t to the Ps 76:11
Where is the t collector? Is 33:18
⌊They will be⌋ a t from you, Zph 3:18

TRICKERY *(1)*
along with the t of his hands. Is 25:11

TRICKLING *(1)*
the water was t from the south Ezk 47:2

TRIED *(38)*
he t to save him from them. Gn 37:21
and daughters t to comfort him, Gn 37:35
about this, he t to kill Moses. Ex 2:15
The magicians t to produce gnats Ex 8:18
military clothes and t to walk, 1Sm 17:39
and Saul t to pin David to the 1Sm 19:10
So Saul t again and sent a third 1Sm 19:21
but Saul had t to kill them in 2Sm 21:2
Solomon t to kill Jeroboam, 1Kg 11:40
infuriated and t to assassinate Est 2:21
You have t me and found nothing Ps 17:3
When I t to understand all this, Ps 73:16
they t Me, though they had seen Ps 95:9
and the king t to put him to Jr 26:21
We t to heal Babylon, but she Jr 51:9
since I t to purify you, Ezk 24:13
But John t to stop Him, saying, Mt 3:14
and we t to stop him because he Mk 9:38
They t to give Him wine mixed Mk 15:23
came to Him and t to keep Him Lk 4:42
They t to bring him in and set Lk 5:18
and we t to stop him because he Lk 9:49
Then they t to seize Him. Jn 7:30
now the Jews t to stone You, Jn 11:8
fighting and t to reconcile them Ac 7:26
he t to associate with the Ac 9:26
opposed them and t to turn the Ac 13:8
they t to go into Bithynia, Ac 16:7
Sabbath and t to persuade both Ac 18:4
He even t to desecrate the Ac 24:6
there to be t before me on these Ac 25:9
tribunal, where I ought to be t. Ac 25:10
and be t there concerning Ac 25:20
synagogues I often t to make Ac 26:11
Some sailors t to escape from Ac 27:30
degree and t to destroy it; Gl 1:13
the faith he once t to destroy." Gl 1:23
tested Me, t ⌊Me⌋, and saw My Heb 3:9

TRIES *(1)*
Whoever t to make his life Lk 17:33

TRIM *(2)*
shave her head, t her nails, Dt 21:12
but must carefully t their hair. Ezk 44:20

TRIMMED *(4)*
of his feet, t his moustache, 2Sm 19:24
and a row of t cedar beams. 1Kg 6:36
and a row of t cedar beams. 1Kg 7:12
got up and t their lamps. Mt 25:7

TRIMMERS *(5)*
wick t, sprinkling basins, 1Kg 7:50
bowls, wick t, sprinkling basins 2Kg 12:13
shovels, the wick t, the dishes, 2Kg 25:14
the wick t, sprinkling basins, 2Ch 4:22
the wick t, the sprinkling Jr 52:18

TRIP *(6)*
go on a three-day t into the Ex 3:18
On the t, at an overnight Ex 4:24
go on a three-day t into the Ex 5:3
and his own schemes t him up. Jb 18:7
over and a rock to t over, Is 8:14
a rock to t over, yet the one Rm 9:33

TRIPLE *(1)*
will form a t ⌊alliance⌋ with Is 19:24

TRIPOLIS *(1)*
judges and magistrates from T, Ezr 4:9

TRIPS *(1)*
and a rock that t them up. 1Pt 2:8

TRIUMPH *(19)*
allowed my enemies to t over me. Ps 30:1
does not shout in t over me. Ps 41:11
I will t! I will divide up Ps 60:6
Over Philistia I shout in t." Ps 60:8
They shout in t; indeed, they Ps 65:13
shout in t to the God of Jacob. Ps 81:1
I will t! I will divide up Ps 108:7
Over Philistia I shout in t." Ps 108:9
he will look in t on his foes. Ps 112:8
I will look in t on those who Ps 118:7
the righteous t, there is great Pr 28:12
who exult in My t, to execute My Is 13:3
you sing in t—you who Jr 50:11
take action against them and t. Dn 11:7
to fall, but he will not t. Dn 11:12
My eyes will look at her in t; Mc 7:10
yet I will t in the LORD; Hab 3:18
Shout in t, Daughter Jerusalem! Zch 9:9
Your words and t when You judge. Rm 3:4

TRIUMPHAL *(1)*
the godly celebrate in t glory; Ps 149:5

TRIUMPHANT *(2)*
enemies, but Israel will be t. Nm 24:18
T shouts have fallen silent over Is 16:9

TRIUMPHANTLY *(7)*
who were going out t. Ex 14:8
went out t in the sight of all Nm 33:3
splendor ride t in the cause Ps 45:4
shout t to the rock of our Ps 95:1
let us shout t to Him in song. Ps 95:2
horn shout t in the presence Ps 98:6
Shout t to the LORD, all the Ps 100:1

TRIUMPHED *(2)*
say, "I have t over him," and my Ps 13:4
He t over them by Him. Col 2:15

TRIUMPHS *(2)*
my affliction, for the enemy t! Lm 1:9
Mercy t over judgment. Jms 2:13

TRIVIAL *(2)*
Is it t in your sight to become 1Sm 18:23
son of Nebat were a t matter, 1Kg 16:31

TROAS *(6)*
Mysia, they came down to T. Ac 16:8
setting sail from T, we ran a Ac 16:11
on ahead and waited for us in T, Ac 20:5
five days we reached them at T, Ac 20:6
When I came to T for the gospel 2Co 2:12
cloak I left in T with Carpus, 2Tm 4:13

TROD *(1)*
They t the grapes and held a Jdg 9:27

TROOPS *(130)*
ready and took his t with him; Ex 14:6
between the t who went out to Nm 31:27
and have the armed t go ahead of Jos 6:7
the armed t went in front of the Jos 6:9
the armed t went in front of Jos 6:13
he spent that night with the t. Jos 8:9
of Israel led the t up to Ai. Jos 8:10
Then all the t of Ai were Jos 8:16
and the t who had fled to the Jos 8:20
deploy ⌊the t⌋ on Mount Tabor, Jdg 4:6
the outpost of the t who were in Jdg 7:11
When the t returned to the camp, 1Sm 4:3
Saul organized the t into three 1Sm 11:11
He sent the rest of the t away, 1Sm 13:2
Then the t were summoned to 1Sm 13:4
and t as numerous as the sand on 1Sm 13:5
because the t were in a 1Sm 13:6
and all his t were gripped with 1Sm 13:7
and the t were deserting him. 1Sm 13:8
I saw that the t were deserting 1Sm 13:11
registered the t who were with 1Sm 13:15
the t who were with them were 1Sm 13:16
of any of the t who were with 1Sm 13:22
The t with him numbered about 1Sm 14:2
But the t did not know that 1Sm 14:3
the open fields to all the t. 1Sm 14:15
saw the panicking t scattering 1Sm 14:16
So Saul said to the t with him, 1Sm 14:17
Saul and all the t with him 1Sm 14:20
had placed the t under an oath: 1Sm 14:24
So none of the t tasted ⌊any⌋ 1Sm 14:24
When the t entered the forest, 1Sm 14:26
make the t swear the oath. 1Sm 14:27
Then, one of the t said, "Your 1Sm 14:28
made the t solemnly swear, 1Sm 14:28
and the t are exhausted." 1Sm 14:28
better if the t had eaten freely 1Sm 14:30
the t are sinning against the 1Sm 14:33
Go among the t and say to them, 1Sm 14:34
every one of the t brought his 1Sm 14:34
you want," the t replied. 1Sm 14:36
All you leaders of the t, 1Sm 14:38
Not one of the t answered him. 1Sm 14:39
And the t replied, "Do whatever 1Sm 14:40
and the t were cleared ⌊of the 1Sm 14:41
summoned the t and counted them 1Sm 15:4
Saul and the t spared Agag, 1Sm 15:9
The t brought them from the 1Sm 15:15
The t took sheep and cattle from 1Sm 15:21
over 1,000 men. David led the t 1Sm 18:13
because he was leading their t. 1Sm 18:16
all the t to go to war at 1Sm 23:8
camp with the t camped around 1Sm 26:5
David and Abishai came to the t, 1Sm 26:7
and the t were lying around 1Sm 26:7
shouted to the t and to Abner 1Sm 26:14
David and the t with him wept 1Sm 30:4
because the t talked about 1Sm 30:6
him and to meet the t with him. 1Sm 30:21
"The t fled from the battle," 2Sm 1:4
Many of the t have fallen and 2Sm 1:4
you tell the t to stop pursuing 2Sm 2:26
the t wouldn't have stopped 2Sm 2:27
horn, and all the t stopped; 2Sm 2:28
Abner, he gathered all the t. 2Sm 2:30
day all the t and all Israel 2Sm 3:37
and all his t set out to bring 2Sm 6:2
of all the elite t of Israel and 2Sm 10:9
Joab and his t advanced to fight 2Sm 10:13
Joab and the t were doing and 2Sm 11:7
assemble the rest of the t, 2Sm 12:28
assembled all the t and went to 2Sm 12:29
Then he and all his t returned 2Sm 12:31
If some of our t fall first, 2Sm 17:9
reviewed his t and appointed 2Sm 18:1
sent out the t, one third under 2Sm 18:2
king said to the t, "I will also 2Sm 18:2
gate while all the t marched out 2Sm 18:4
the t broke off their pursuit 2Sm 18:16
for all the t because on that 2Sm 19:2
because on that day the t heard, 2Sm 19:2
All the t of Judah and half of 2Sm 19:40
Joab's t came and besieged Sheba 2Sm 20:15
While all the t with Joab were 2Sm 20:15
Then the t came back to him, 2Sm 23:10
The t fled from the Philistines, 2Sm 23:11
and register the t so I can know 2Sm 24:2
multiply the t 100 times more 2Sm 24:3
to register the t of Israel. 2Sm 24:4

of the registration of the **t**. 2Sm 24:9
he had taken a census of the **t**. 2Sm 24:10
Now the **t** were encamped against 1Kg 16:15
the encamped **t** heard that Zimri 1Kg 16:16
he counted all the Israelite **t**: 1Kg 20:15
but his **t** fled to their tents. 2Kg 8:21
He saw Jehu's **t** approaching and 2Kg 9:17
and shouted, "I see **t**!" 2Kg 9:17
they had 36,000 **t** for battle 1Ch 7:4
where the **t** had fled from the 1Ch 11:13
and made them leaders of his **t**. 1Ch 12:18
of the armed **t** who came to David 1Ch 12:23
6,800 armed **t** bearing shields 1Ch 12:24
of all the elite **t** of Israel and 1Ch 19:10
Then he and all his **t** returned 1Ch 20:3
and the commanders of the **t**, 1Ch 21:2
of the registration of the **t**. 1Ch 21:5
stationed **t** in every fortified 2Ch 17:2
because the **t** that had come with 2Ch 22:1
and all the **t** will be in the 2Ch 23:5
stationed all the **t** with their 2Ch 23:10
heard the noise from the **t**, 2Ch 23:12
she went to the **t** in the LORD's 2Ch 23:12
His **t** advance together; Jb 19:12
Can His **t** be numbered? Jb 25:3
I lived as a king among his **t**, Jb 29:25
him and all his **t** to every Ezk 12:14
fugitives among his **t** will fall Ezk 17:21
and a vast company of **t**. Ezk 26:7
and all the various foreign **t**, Ezk 30:5
Gomer with all its **t**; Ezk 38:6
the north along with all its **t**— Ezk 38:6
You, all of your **t**, and many Ezk 38:9
as well as his **t** and the many Ezk 38:22
You, all your **t**, and the peoples Ezk 39:4
their select **t** will not be able Dn 11:15
your **t** are women among you; Nah 3:13
he sent out his **t**, destroyed Mt 22:7
and ordered the **t** to go down, Ac 23:10
arrived with my **t** and rescued Ac 23:27
of mounted **t** was 200 million; Rv 9:16

TROPHIMUS *(3)*
and Tychicus and **T** from Asia. Ac 20:4
previously seen **T** the Ephesian Ac 21:29
T I left sick at Miletus. 2Tm 4:20

TROUBLE *(100)*
You have brought **t** on me, Gn 34:30
is why this **t** has come to us. Gn 42:21
"Why did you cause me so much **t**?" Gn 43:6
they were in **t** when they were Ex 5:19
You caused **t** for this people Ex 5:22
he has caused **t** for this people, Ex 5:23
brought such **t** on Your servant Nm 11:11
He sees no **t** for Israel. Nm 23:21
Today the LORD will **t** you!" Jos 7:25
to me now when you're in **t**?" Jdg 11:7
has made this terrible **t** for us. 1Sm 6:9
that they were in **t** because the 1Sm 13:6
has brought **t** to the land. 1Sm 14:29
certain to be **t** for our master 1Sm 25:17
those who want **t** for my lord be 1Sm 25:26
and rescue me from all **t**." 1Sm 26:24
"I'm in serious **t**," replied Saul. 1Sm 28:15
He will not **t** you again!" 2Sm 14:10
you are in **t** because you're a 2Sm 16:8
than all the **t** that has come to 2Sm 19:7
to the **t** Hadad ⌊had caused⌋ 1Kg 11:25
this one is only looking for **t**, 1Kg 20:7
gone to all this **t** for us. 2Kg 4:13
stir up such **t** that you fall— 2Kg 14:10
who brought **t** on Israel when he 1Ch 2:7
stir up such **t** so that you fall 2Ch 25:19
are in great **t** and disgrace. Neh 1:3
to them, "You see the **t** we are Neh 2:17
t wouldn't be worth burdening Est 7:4
the wicked cease to make **t**, Jb 3:17
I have no rest, for **t** comes. Jb 3:26
those who sow **t** reap the same. Jb 4:8
and **t** does not sprout from the Jb 5:6
is born for **t** as surely as Jb 5:7
is short of days and full of **t**. Jb 14:1
T and distress terrify him, Jb 15:24
They conceive **t** and give birth Jb 15:35
excited when **t** came his way? Jb 31:29
hold in reserve for times of **t**, Jb 38:23
evil, conceives **t**, and gives Ps 7:14
t comes back on his own head, Ps 7:16
a refuge in times of **t**. Ps 9:9
Why do You hide in times of **t**? Ps 10:1
t and malice are under his Ps 10:7
Yourself have seen **t** and grief, Ps 10:14
LORD answer you in a day of **t**; Ps 20:1
Consider my affliction and **t**, Ps 25:18
You protect me from **t**. Ps 32:7
is always found in times of **t**. Ps 46:1
Why should I fear in times of **t**? Ps 49:5
Call on Me in a day of **t**; Ps 50:15
has delivered me from every **t**, Ps 54:7
Crime and **t** are within it; Ps 55:10
for me, a refuge in my day of **t**. Ps 59:16
They are not in **t** like others; Ps 73:5
my day of **t** I sought the Lord. Ps 77:2
I will be with him in **t**. Ps 91:15
one that creates **t** by law— Ps 94:20
face from me in my day of **t**. Ps 102:2
out to the LORD in their **t**; Ps 107:6
out to the LORD in their **t**; Ps 107:13
out to the LORD in their **t**; Ps 107:19
out to the LORD in their **t**, Ps 107:28
I encountered **t** and sorrow. Ps 116:3
T and distress have overtaken me Ps 119:143
let the **t** their lips cause Ps 140:9
I reveal my **t** to Him. Ps 142:2
righteousness deliver me from **t**, Ps 143:11
feet run toward **t** and they hurry Pr 1:16
when **t** and stress overcome you. Pr 1:27
—he stirs up **t** constantly. Pr 6:14
who stirs up **t** among brothers. Pr 6:19
The righteous is rescued from **t**; Pr 11:8
but if someone looks for **t**, Pr 11:27
the righteous escapes from **t**. Pr 12:13
A wicked messenger falls into **t**, Pr 13:17
but **t** accompanies the income of Pr 15:6
tongue keeps himself out of **t**. Pr 21:23
and their words stir up **t**. Pr 24:2
in a time of **t** is like a rotten Pr 25:19
hardens his heart falls into **t**. Pr 28:14
and remember his **t** no more. Pr 31:7
a land of **t** and distress, Is 30:6
and our salvation in time of **t**. Is 33:2
it saves no one from his **t**. Is 46:7
they conceive **t** and give birth Is 59:4
for you in a time of **t**, Jr 15:11
will be a time of **t** for Jacob, Jr 30:7
I will **t** the hearts of many Ezk 32:9
who is to blame for this **t** we're Jnh 1:7
who is to blame for this **t** we're Jnh 1:8
wrath, a day of **t** and distress, Zph 1:15
day has enough **t** of its own. Mt 6:34
with him and keep you out of **t**." Mt 28:14
Lord, don't **t** Yourself, since I Lk 7:6
people will have **t** in this life, 1Co 7:28
no one cause me **t**, because I Gl 6:17
to cause ⌊me⌋ **t** in my Php 1:17
about this is no **t** for me and is Php 3:1
up, causing **t** and by it, Heb 12:15

TROUBLED *(22)*
came, he was **t**, so he summoned Gn 41:8
Joshua said, "Why have you **t** us? Jos 7:25
Why are you **t**? Am I not better 1Sm 1:8
the spirit from God ⌊**t**⌋ Saul, 1Sm 16:23
be remorse or a **t** conscience for 1Sm 25:31
conscience **t** him after he had 2Sm 24:10
for God **t** them with every 2Ch 15:6
and **t** nights have been assigned Jb 7:3
I am **t** and cannot speak. Ps 77:4
him relief from **t** times until a Ps 94:13
songs to a **t** heart is like Pr 25:20
had dreams that **t** him, Dn 2:1
she was deeply **t** by this Lk 1:29
"Why are you **t**?" He asked them. Lk 24:38
Now My soul is **t**. What should I Jn 12:27
He was **t** in His spirit and Jn 13:21
Your heart must not be **t**. Jn 14:1
heart must not be **t** or fearful. Jn 14:27
out from us and **t** you with their Ac 15:24
his spirit was **t** within him when Ac 17:16
of an extremely **t** and anguished 2Co 2:4
to be easily upset in mind or **t**, 2Th 2:2

TROUBLES *(17)*
But how can I bear your **t**, Dt 1:12
Many **t** and afflictions will come Dt 31:17
'Haven't these **t** come to us Dt 31:17
And when many **t** and afflictions Dt 31:21
from all your **t** and afflictions 1Sm 10:19
evil spirit from God ⌊**t**⌋ you, 1Sm 16:16
You have known the **t** of my life Ps 31:7
and saved him from all his **t**. Ps 34:6
delivers them from all their **t**. Ps 34:17
For **t** without number have Ps 40:12
many **t** and misfortunes Ps 71:20
have had enough **t**, and my life Ps 88:3
dishonestly **t** his household, Pr 15:27
though man's **t** are heavy on him Ec 8:6
For the former **t** will be Is 65:16
rescued him out of all his **t**. Ac 7:10
pass through many **t** on our way Ac 14:22

TROUBLING *(3)*
A **t** vision is declared to me: Is 21:2
some who are **t** you and want to Gl 1:7
it is who is **t** you will pay Gl 5:10

TROUGH *(6)*
her jug into the **t** and hurried Gn 24:20
the night by your feeding **t**? Jb 39:9
and laid Him in a feeding **t**— Lk 2:7
cloth and lying in a feeding **t**." Lk 2:12
who was lying in the feeding **t**. Lk 2:16
the feeding **t** on the Sabbath, Lk 13:15

TROUGHS *(3)*
branches in the **t** in front of Gn 30:38
placed the branches in the **t**, Gn 30:41
and filled the **t** to water their Ex 2:16

TROUSERS *(1)*
men, in their **t**, robes, head Dn 3:21

TRUE *(111)*
be tested to see if they are **t**. Gn 42:16
turns out to be **t** that this Dt 13:14
turns out to be **t** that this Dt 17:4
does not come **t** or is not Dt 18:22
accusation is **t** and no evidence Dt 22:20
He is righteous and **t**. Dt 32:4
replied to Joshua, "It is **t**. Jos 7:20
this was **t** for all the cities. Jos 21:42
Since that's **t**, we now turn to Jdg 11:8
Isn't it **t** that you may possess Jdg 11:24
It is **t** that you are barren and Jdg 13:3
Your words come **t**, what will the Jdg 13:12
You when Your words come **t**?" Jdg 13:17
it is **t** that I am a family Ru 3:12
he says is sure to come **t**. 1Sm 9:6
from me? This can't be ⌊**t**⌋." 1Sm 20:2
my father Saul knows it is **t**." 1Sm 23:17
Your words are **t**, and You have 2Sm 7:28
it not **t** my house is with God? 2Sm 23:5
and about your wisdom is **t**. 1Kg 10:6
is **t** that the kings of Assyria 2Kg 19:17
to my father David now come **t**. 2Ch 1:9
and about your wisdom is **t**. 2Ch 9:5
has been without the **t** God, 2Ch 15:3
upright and **t** before the LORD 2Ch 31:20
to see⌋ if it is **t** that a decree Ezr 5:17
investigated this, and it is **t**! Jb 5:27
I know what you've said is **t**, Jb 9:2
for **t** wisdom has two sides. Jb 11:6
T wisdom and power belong to Him Jb 12:16
Even if it is **t** that I have Jb 19:4
If this is not **t**, then who can Jb 24:25
it is **t** that God does not act Jb 34:12
the time his prediction came **t**, Ps 105:19
All Your commands are **t**; Ps 119:86
and Your instruction is **t**. Ps 119:142
and all Your commands are **t**. Ps 119:151
sows righteousness, a **t** reward. Pr 11:18
to teach you **t** and reliable Pr 22:21
I have found one ⌊**t**⌋ man, Ec 7:28
I have not found a **t** woman. Ec 7:28
Isn't ⌊it **t** that⌋ in just a Is 29:17
is **t** that the kings of Assyria Is 37:18
may hear and say, "It is **t**." Is 43:9
But the LORD is the **t** God; Jr 10:10
give you **t** peace in this Jr 14:13
prophesied come **t** and may He Jr 28:6
prophet comes **t** will the prophet Jr 28:9
may the LORD be a **t** and faithful Jr 42:5
carries out **t** justice between Ezk 18:8
The dream is **t**, and its Dn 2:45
is it **t** that you don't serve my Dn 3:14
His works are **t** and His ways are Dn 4:37
asked him the **t** meaning of all Dn 7:16
wanted to know the **t** meaning of Dn 7:19
that has been told is **t**. Dn 8:26
The message was **t** and was about Dn 10:1
this: Render **t** justice. Show Zch 7:9

T instruction was in his mouth, Mal 2:6
The **t** light, who gives light to Jn 1:9
him, "Here is a **t** Israelite; Jn 1:47
has affirmed that God is **t**. Jn 3:33
What you have said is **t**." Jn 4:18
when the **t** worshipers will Jn 4:23
in this case the saying is **t**: Jn 4:37
of the One who sent Him is **t**, Jn 7:18
Can it be **t** that the authorities Jn 7:26
but the One who sent Me is **t**. Jn 7:28
My judgment is **t**, because I am Jn 8:16
but the One who sent Me is **t**, Jn 8:26
John said about this man was **t**." Jn 10:41
I am the **t** vine, and My Father Jn 15:1
You, the only **t** God, and the One Jn 17:3
testimony is **t**, and he knows he Jn 19:35
We know that his testimony is **t**. Jn 21:24
"Is this **t**?" the high priest Ac 7:1
them to remain **t** to the Lord Ac 11:23
kept insisting that it was **t**. Ac 12:15
and ⌊**t**⌋ circumcision is not Rm 2:28
God must be **t**, but everyone is a Rm 3:4
T enough; they were broken off Rm 11:20
good report; as deceivers yet **t**; 2Co 6:8
out of false motives or **t**, Php 1:18
I also ask you, **t** partner, to Php 4:3
whatever is **t**, whatever is Php 4:8
to serve the living and **t** God, 1Th 1:9
To Timothy, my **t** child in the 1Tm 1:2
my **t** child in our common faith. Ti 1:4
testimony is **t**. So, rebuke them Ti 1:13
sanctuary and the **t** tabernacle, Heb 8:2
only a model of the **t** one Heb 9:24
draw near with a **t** heart in full Heb 10:22
that this is the **t** grace of God. 1Pt 5:12
them according to the **t** proverb: 2Pt 2:22
which is **t** in Him and in you, 1Jn 2:8
away and the **t** light is already 1Jn 2:8
and is **t** and is not a lie; 1Jn 2:27
so that we may know the **t** One. 1Jn 5:20
are in the **t** One—that is, in 1Jn 5:20
is the **t** God and eternal life. 1Jn 5:20
know that our testimony is **t**. 3Jn 12
Holy One, the **T** One, the One who Rv 3:7
the faithful and **t** Witness, Rv 3:14
Lord, holy and **t**, how long until Rv 6:10
righteous and **t** are Your ways, Rv 15:3
t and righteous are Your Rv 16:7
judgments are **t** and righteous, Rv 19:2
"These words of God are **t**." Rv 19:9
rider is called Faithful and **T**, Rv 19:11
these words are faithful and **t**." Rv 21:5
These words are faithful and **t**. Rv 22:6

TRULY *(8)*
one who is **t** lazy in his work Pr 18:9
T they love to wander; Jr 14:10
You **t** have become like a mirage Jr 15:18
one whom the LORD has **t** sent." Jr 28:9
I will **t** have compassion on him. Jr 31:20
"**T** You are the Son of God!" Mt 14:33
but as it **t** is, the message 1Th 2:13
t in him the love of God is 1Jn 2:5

TRUMPET *(39)*
and a loud **t** sound, so that all Ex 19:16
the sound of the **t** grew louder Ex 19:19
the sound of the **t**, and the Ex 20:18
you are to sound a **t** loudly in Lv 25:9
they heard the blast of the **t**, Jos 6:20
each of the men a **t** in one hand Jdg 7:16
Wherever you hear the **t** sound, Neh 4:20
When the **t** blasts, he snorts Jb 39:25
Praise Him with **t** blast; Ps 150:3
When a **t** sounds, listen! Is 18:3
day a great **t** will be blown, Is 27:13
Raise your voice like a **t**. Is 58:1
have blown the **t** and prepared Ezk 7:14
and blows his **t** to warn the Ezk 33:3
the sound of the **t** but ignores Ezk 33:4
the sound of the **t** but ignored Ezk 33:5
coming but doesn't blow the **t**, Ezk 33:6
horn in Gibeah, the **t** in Ramah; Hs 5:8
day of **t** ⌊blast⌋ and battle cry Zph 1:16
sound the **t** and advance with Zch 9:14
don't sound a **t** before you, Mt 6:2
out His angels with a loud **t**, Mt 24:31
if the **t** makes an unclear sound, 1Co 14:8
of an eye, at the last **t**. 1Co 15:52
For the **t** will sound, and the 1Co 15:52
voice, and with the **t** of God, 1Th 4:16
the blast of a **t**, and the sound Heb 12:19
behind me a loud voice like a **t** Rv 1:10
speaking to me like a **t** said, Rv 4:1
The first ⌊angel⌋ blew his **t**, Rv 8:7
The second angel blew his **t**, Rv 8:8
The third angel blew his **t**, Rv 8:10
The fourth angel blew his **t**, Rv 8:12
of the remaining **t** blasts that Rv 8:13
The fifth angel blew his **t**, Rv 9:1
The sixth angel blew his **t**. Rv 9:13
the sixth angel who had the **t**, Rv 9:14
he will blow his **t**, then God's Rv 10:7
The seventh angel blew his **t**, Rv 11:15

TRUMPET'S *(1)*
stand still at the **t** sound. Jb 39:24

TRUMPETER *(1)*
and the **t** was beside me. Neh 4:18

TRUMPETERS *(4)*
and the **t** were by the king, 2Kg 11:14
t and singers joined together 2Ch 5:13
and the **t** were by the king, 2Ch 23:13
and **t** will never be heard in you Rv 18:22

TRUMPETS *(48)*
Make two **t** of hammered silver to Nm 10:2
the priests, are to sound the **t**. Nm 10:8
sound short blasts on the **t**, Nm 10:9
to sound the **t** over your burnt Nm 10:10
the holy objects and signal **t**. Nm 31:6
seven ram's-horn **t** in front of Jos 6:4
while the priests blow the **t**. Jos 6:4
carry seven **t** in front of the Jos 6:6
carrying seven **t** before the LORD Jos 6:8
moved forward and blew the **t**; Jos 6:8
While the **t** were blowing, the Jos 6:9
of the priests who blew the **t**, Jos 6:9
carrying seven **t** marched in Jos 6:13
While the **t** were blowing, the Jos 6:13
blew the **t**, and Joshua said Jos 6:16
shouted, and the **t** sounded. Jos 6:20
people's provisions and their **t**. Jdg 7:8
and everyone with me blow our **t**, Jdg 7:18
also to blow your **t** all around Jdg 7:18
They blew their **t** and broke the Jdg 7:19
blew their **t** and shattered their Jdg 7:20
their **t** in their right hands, Jdg 7:20
Gideon's men blew their 300 **t**, Jdg 7:22
were rejoicing and blowing **t**. 2Kg 11:14
basins, **t**, or any articles 2Kg 12:13
tambourines, cymbals, and **t**. 1Ch 13:8
were to blow **t** before the ark of 1Ch 15:24
the ram's horn, **t**, and cymbals, 1Ch 15:28
blew⌋ the **t** regularly before 1Ch 16:6
had with them **t** and cymbals to 1Ch 16:42
them were 120 priests blowing **t**. 2Ch 5:12
accompanied by **t**, cymbals, and 2Ch 5:13
the priests were blowing **t**, 2Ch 7:6
The **t** are ready to sound the 2Ch 13:12
Then the priests blew the **t**, 2Ch 13:14
shouting, with **t**, and with rams' 2Ch 15:14
temple with harps, lyres, and **t**. 2Ch 20:28
and blowing **t** while the singers 2Ch 23:13
and the priests with the **t**. 2Ch 29:26
of the LORD and the **t** began, 2Ch 29:27
and blowing the **t**—all of this 2Ch 29:28
in their robes and holding **t**, Ezr 3:10
Some of the priests' sons had **t**: Neh 12:35
Zechariah, and Hananiah, with **t**; Neh 12:41
the LORD, amid the sound of **t**. Ps 47:5
t and the blast of the ram's Ps 98:6
seven **t** were given to them. Rv 8:2
had the seven **t** prepared to blow Rv 8:6

TRUNK *(1)*
the sky nested on its fallen **t**, Ezk 31:13

TRUST *(79)*
will they not **t** in Me despite Nm 14:11
you did not **t** Me to show My Nm 20:12
this you did not **t** the LORD your Dt 1:32
walls, that you **t** in, come down Dt 28:52
but Sihon did not **t** Israel. Jdg 11:20
should I **t** the LORD any longer? 2Kg 6:33
Look, you now **t** in Egypt, the 2Kg 18:21
of Egypt is to all who **t** in him. 2Kg 18:21
We **t** in the LORD our God. 2Kg 18:22
servants and **t** in Egypt for 2Kg 18:24
persuade you to **t** in the LORD by 2Kg 18:30
your God, whom you **t**, deceive 2Kg 19:10
If God puts no **t** in His servants Jb 4:18
God puts no **t** in His holy ones Jb 15:15
Let him not put **t** in worthless Jb 15:31
gold or called fine gold my **t**, Jb 31:24
Can you **t** the wild ox to harvest Jb 39:12
righteousness and **t** in the LORD. Ps 4:5
know Your name **t** in You because Ps 9:10
God, I **t** in You. Do not let me Ps 25:2
idols, but I **t** in the LORD. Ps 31:6
I **t** in You, LORD; I say, "You Ps 31:14
because we **t** in His holy name. Ps 33:21
T in the LORD and do what is Ps 37:3
t in Him, and He will act, Ps 37:5
and put their **t** in the LORD. Ps 40:3
has put his **t** in the LORD and Ps 40:4
For I do not **t** in my bow, and my Ps 44:6
They **t** in their wealth and boast Ps 49:6
I **t** in God's faithful love Ps 52:8
their days. But I will **t** in You. Ps 55:23
I am afraid, I will **t** in You. Ps 56:3
whose word I praise, in God I **t**; Ps 56:4
God I **t**; I will not fear. What Ps 56:11
T in Him at all times, you Ps 62:8
Place no **t** in oppression, or Ps 62:10
fortress, my God, in whom I **t**." Ps 91:2
them, as are all who **t** in them. Ps 115:8
Israel, **t** in the LORD! Ps 115:9
House of Aaron, **t** in the LORD! Ps 115:10
fear the LORD, **t** in the LORD! Ps 115:11
in the LORD than to **t** in man. Ps 118:8
in the LORD than to **t** in nobles. Ps 118:9
taunts me, for I **t** in Your word. Ps 119:42
Those who **t** in the LORD are like Ps 125:1
them, as are all who **t** in them. Ps 135:18
in the morning, for I **t** in You. Ps 143:8
Do not **t** in nobles, in man, who Ps 146:3
T in the LORD with all your Pr 3:5
Put no more **t** in man, who has Is 2:22
will **t** ⌊Him⌋ and not be afraid. Is 12:2
T in the LORD forever, because Is 26:4
They **t** in the number of chariots Is 31:1
of Egypt is to all who **t** in him. Is 36:6
We **t** in the LORD our God. Is 36:7
and **t** in Egypt for chariots and Is 36:9
persuade you to **t** the LORD, Is 36:15
your God, whom you **t**, deceive Is 37:10
but those who **t** in the LORD will Is 40:31
those who **t** in idols and say to Is 42:17
Let him **t** in the name of the Is 50:10
They **t** in empty and worthless Is 59:4
LORD has rejected those you **t**; Jr 2:37
fortified cities in which you **t**. Jr 5:17
Do not **t** deceitful words, Jr 7:4
the house in which you **t**— Jr 7:14
Don't **t** any brother, for every Jr 9:4
led these people to **t** in a lie. Jr 28:15
send him, and made you **t** a lie, Jr 29:31
Because you **t** in your works and Jr 48:7
You who **t** in your treasures ⌊and Jr 49:4
let your widows **t** in Me. Jr 49:11
be an object of **t** for the house Ezk 29:16
don't **t** in a close companion. Mc 7:5
and they will **t** in the name of Zph 3:12
He has put His **t** in God; Mt 27:43
who will **t** you with what is Lk 16:11
we would not **t** in ourselves, 2Co 1:9
Again, I will **t** in Him. Heb 2:13

TRUSTED *(30)*
and the lords of Shechem **t** him. Jdg 9:26
So Achish **t** David, thinking, 1Sm 27:12
Hezekiah **t** in the LORD God of 2Kg 18:5
five **t** royal aides found in the 2Kg 25:19
request because they **t** in Him. 1Ch 5:20
them to their **t** positions. 1Ch 9:22
The most **t** ones were Carshena, Est 1:14
the king's **t** official in charge Est 2:15
He deprives **t** advisers of speech Jb 12:20
But I have **t** in Your faithful Ps 13:5
Our fathers **t** in You; Ps 22:4
they **t**, and You rescued them. Ps 22:4
they **t** in You and were not Ps 22:5
integrity and have **t** in the LORD Ps 26:1
Even my friend in whom I **t**, Ps 41:9
but **t** in the abundance of his Ps 52:7
message and have **t** in oppression Is 30:12
forgotten Me and **t** in Falsehood. Jr 13:25
Everyone I **t** watches for my Jr 20:10
Your **t** friends misled you and Jr 38:22

you have **t** in Me, you will Jr 39:18
because of Bethel that they **t** Jr 48:13
seven **t** royal aides found in the Jr 52:25
His servants who **t** in Him. Dn 3:28
uninjured, for he **t** in his God. Dn 6:23
you have **t** in your own way Hs 10:13
She has not **t** in the LORD; Zph 3:2
from him all his weapons he **t** Lk 11:22
to some who **t** in themselves that Lk 18:9
many **t** in His name when they saw Jn 2:23

TRUSTING *(9)*

'What are you **t** in, you who 2Ch 32:10
is confident, **t** in the LORD. Ps 112:7
t in his riches will fall, Pr 11:28
T an unreliable person in a time Pr 25:19
on You⌋, for it is **t** in You. Is 26:3
Now who are you **t** in that you Is 36:5
Look, you are **t** in Egypt, that Is 36:6
you keep **t** in deceitful words Jr 7:8
Pharaoh and those **t** in him. Jr 46:25

TRUSTS *(15)*

what he **t** in is a spider's web. Jb 8:14
my heart **t** in Him, and I am Ps 28:7
but the one who **t** in the LORD Ps 32:10
is the person who **t** in You! Ps 84:12
save Your servant who **t** in You. Ps 86:2
for he **t** you and lives near you. Pr 3:29
and the one who **t** in the LORD Pr 16:20
but whoever **t** in the LORD will Pr 28:25
The one who **t** in himself is a Pr 28:26
but the one who **t** in the LORD is Pr 29:25
heart of her husband **t** in her, Pr 31:11
is the man who **t** in mankind, Jr 17:5
is the man who **t** in the LORD, Jr 17:7
he **t** in his righteousness and Ezk 33:13
its shape **t** in it and makes Hab 2:18

TRUSTWORTHY *(19)*

men, God-fearing, **t**, and hating Ex 18:21
because they were considered **t**. Neh 13:13
the testimony of the LORD is **t**, Ps 19:7
is right, and all His work is **t**. Ps 33:4
all His instructions are **t**. Ps 111:7
are righteous and altogether **t**. Ps 119:138
but the **t** keeps a confidence. Pr 11:13
a **t** courier ⌊brings⌋ healing. Pr 13:17
but who can find a **t** man? Pr 20:6
a **t** messenger is like the Pr 25:13
The wounds of a friend are **t**, Pr 27:6
I have appointed **t** witnesses— Is 8:2
for he was **t**, and no negligence Dn 6:4
who by the Lord's mercy is **t**. 1Co 7:25
This saying is **t** and deserving 1Tm 1:15
This saying is **t**: 1Tm 3:1
This saying is **t** and deserves 1Tm 4:9
This saying is **t**: 2Tm 2:11
This saying is **t**. Ti 3:8

TRUTH *(167)*

uncover the **t** by divination?" Gn 44:15
and rich in faithful love and **t**, Ex 34:6
worship Him in sincerity and **t**. Jos 24:14
her the whole **t** and said to her, Jdg 16:17
he had told her the whole **t**, Jdg 16:18
for he has told me the whole **t**." Jdg 16:18
To tell the **t**, I am a widow; 2Sm 14:5
word in your mouth is the **t**." 1Kg 17:24
anything but the **t** in the name 1Kg 22:16
anything but the **t** in the name 2Ch 18:15
But you coat ⌊the **t**⌋ with lies; Jb 13:4
have not spoken the **t** about Me, Jb 42:7
have not spoken the **t** about Me, Jb 42:8
the **t** in his heart— Ps 15:2
Guide me in Your **t** and teach me, Ps 25:5
love and **t** to those who keep Ps 25:10
my eyes, and I live by Your **t**. Ps 26:3
Will it proclaim Your **t**? Ps 30:9
You redeem me, LORD, God of **t**. Ps 31:5
love and **t** from the great Ps 40:10
love and **t** will always guard Ps 40:11
Send Your light and Your **t**; Ps 43:3
triumphantly in the cause of **t**, Ps 45:4
sends His faithful love and **t**. Ps 57:3
love and **t** to guard him. Ps 61:7
Faithful love and **t** will join Ps 85:10
T will spring up from the earth, Ps 85:11
and I will live by Your **t**. Ps 86:11
abundant in faithful love and **t**. Ps 86:15
love and **t** go before You. Ps 89:14
of His hands are **t** and justice; Ps 111:7
enacted in **t** and uprightness. Ps 111:8
love, because of Your **t**. Ps 115:1
I have chosen the way of **t**; Ps 119:30
the word of **t** from my mouth, Ps 119:43
The entirety of Your word is **t**, Ps 119:160
tells the **t**, and wickedness Pr 8:7
speaks the **t** declares what is Pr 12:17
and do not sell—**t**, wisdom, Pr 23:23
to accurately write words of **t**. Ec 12:10
Do not prophesy the **t** to us. Is 30:10
T has gone from My mouth, a word Is 45:23
⌊but⌋ not in **t** or righteousness. Is 48:1
In **t**, the Lord GOD will help Me; Is 50:9
For **t** has stumbled in the public Is 59:14
T is missing, and whoever turns Is 59:15
will be blessed by the God of **t**, Is 65:16
land will swear by the God of **t**. Is 65:16
LORD lives, in **t**, in justice, Jr 4:2
T has perished—it has Jr 7:28
no one tells the **t**. They have Jr 9:5
the abundance of peace and **t**. Jr 33:6
horn will throw **t** to the ground Dn 8:12
and paying attention to Your **t**. Dn 9:13
is recorded in the book of **t**. Dn 10:21
Now I will tell you the **t**. Dn 11:2
There is no **t**, no faithful love, Hs 4:1
Speak **t** to one another; Zch 8:16
Therefore, love **t** and peace." Zch 8:19
Him, and told Him the whole **t**. Mk 5:33
I tell you the **t**: there are some Lk 9:27
tell you the **t**: he will put him Lk 12:44
"I tell you the **t**," He said. Lk 21:3
the Father, full of grace and **t**. Jn 1:14
grace and **t** came through Jesus Jn 1:17
who lives by the **t** comes to the Jn 3:21
the Father in spirit and **t**. Jn 4:23
must worship in spirit and **t**." Jn 4:24
and he has testified to the **t**. Jn 5:33
will know the **t**, and the truth Jn 8:32
and the **t** will set you free." Jn 8:32
has told you the **t** that I heard Jn 8:40
and has not stood in the **t**, Jn 8:44
because there is no **t** in him. Jn 8:44
because I tell the **t**, you do not Jn 8:45
If I tell the **t**, why don't you Jn 8:46
am the way, the **t**, and the life. Jn 14:6
He is the Spirit of **t**. Jn 14:17
Spirit of **t** who proceeds from Jn 15:26
I am telling you the **t**. Jn 16:7
When the Spirit of **t** comes, Jn 16:13
will guide you into all the **t**. Jn 16:13
Sanctify them by the **t**; Jn 17:17
by the truth; Your word is **t**. Jn 17:17
also may be sanctified by the **t**. Jn 17:19
testify to the **t**. Everyone who Jn 18:37
is of the **t** listens to My voice. Jn 18:37
"What is **t**?" said Pilate. After Jn 18:38
he knows he is telling the **t**. Jn 19:35
In **t**, I understand that God Ac 10:34
words of **t** and good judgment Ac 26:25
unrighteousness suppress the **t**, Rm 1:18
exchanged the **t** of God for a lie Rm 1:25
such things is based on the **t**. Rm 2:2
self-seeking and disobey the **t**, Rm 2:8
expression of knowledge and **t**— Rm 2:20
my lie God's **t** is amplified to Rm 3:7
I speak the **t** in Christ—I am Rm 9:1
on behalf of the **t** of God, Rm 15:8
bread of sincerity and **t**. 1Co 5:8
but rejoices in the **t**; 1Co 13:6
by an open display of the **t**. 2Co 4:2
the message of **t**, by the power 2Co 6:7
spoken everything to you in **t**, 2Co 7:14
has also turned out to be the **t**. 2Co 7:14
As the **t** of Christ is in me, 2Co 11:10
because I will be telling the **t**. 2Co 12:6
to do anything against the **t**, 2Co 13:8
the truth, but only for the **t**. 2Co 13:8
that the **t** of the gospel would Gl 2:5
from the **t** of the gospel, Gl 2:14
your enemy by telling you the **t**? Gl 4:16
you from obeying the **t**? Gl 5:7
when you heard the word of **t**, Eph 1:13
But speaking the **t** in love, Eph 4:15
because the **t** is in Jesus: Eph 4:21
and purity of the **t**. Eph 4:24
Speak the **t**, each one to his Eph 4:25
goodness, righteousness, and **t**— Eph 5:9
with **t** like a belt around your Eph 6:14
up to whatever ⌊**t**⌋ we have Php 3:16
this hope⌋ in the message of **t**, Col 1:5
recognized God's grace in the **t**. Col 1:6
the love of the **t** in order to be 2Th 2:10
not believe the **t** but enjoyed 2Th 2:12
and through belief in the **t**. 2Th 2:13
come to the knowledge of the **t**. 1Tm 2:4
an apostle (I am telling the **t**; 1Tm 2:7
of the Gentiles in faith and **t**. 1Tm 2:7
pillar and foundation of the **t**. 1Tm 3:15
who believe and know the **t**. 1Tm 4:3
depraved and deprived of the **t**, 1Tm 6:5
teaching the word of **t**. 2Tm 2:15
They have deviated from the **t**, 2Tm 2:18
them repentance to know the **t**. 2Tm 2:25
to come to a knowledge of the **t**. 2Tm 3:7
so these also resist the **t**, 2Tm 3:8
from hearing the **t** and will turn 2Tm 4:4
knowledge of the **t** that leads to Ti 1:1
of men who reject the **t**. Ti 1:14
the knowledge of the **t**, Heb 10:26
the message of **t** so that we Jms 1:18
and lie in defiance of the **t**. Jms 3:14
any among you strays from the **t**, Jms 5:19
to the **t**, having purified 1Pt 1:22
established in the **t** you have. 2Pt 1:12
them the way of **t** will be 2Pt 2:2
and are not practicing the **t**. 1Jn 1:6
and the **t** is not in us. 1Jn 1:8
a liar, and the **t** is not in him. 1Jn 2:4
because you don't know the **t**, 1Jn 2:21
because no lie comes from the **t**. 1Jn 2:21
or speech, but in deed and **t**; 1Jn 3:18
we will know we are of the **t**, 1Jn 3:19
the Spirit of **t** and the spirit 1Jn 4:6
because the Spirit is the **t**. 1Jn 5:6
whom I love in **t**—and not only 2Jn 1
who have come to know the **t**— 2Jn 1
because of the **t** that remains in 2Jn 2
of the Father, in **t** and love. 2Jn 3
of your children walking in **t**, 2Jn 4
friend Gaius, whom I love in **t**. 3Jn 1
your ⌊faithfulness⌋ to the **t**— 3Jn 3
how you are walking in the **t**. 3Jn 3
children are walking in the **t**. 3Jn 4
we can be co-workers with the **t**. 3Jn 8
everyone, and from the **t** itself. 3Jn 12

TRUTHFUL *(4)*

T lips endure forever, but a Pr 12:19
A **t** witness rescues lives, Pr 14:25
know that You are **t** and teach Mt 22:16
know You are **t** and defer to no Mk 12:14

TRUTHFULLY *(6)*

lying instead of speaking **t**. Ps 52:3
I, the LORD, speak **t**; Is 45:19
My word should speak My word **t**, Jr 23:28
and teach **t** the way of God. Mt 22:16
but teach **t** the way of God. Mk 12:14
but teach **t** the way of God. Lk 20:21

TRY *(15)*

let's **t** to reach one of these Jdg 19:13
with him to **t** to break through 2Kg 3:26
Should anyone **t** to speak with Jb 4:2
But come back ⌊and **t**⌋ again, Jb 17:10
Test me, LORD, and **t** me; Ps 26:2
enough for you to **t** the patience Is 7:13
Will you also **t** the patience of Is 7:13
Do not **t** to comfort me about the Is 22:4
He will **t** to hide himself, Jr 49:10
all who **t** to lift it will injure Zch 12:3
and don't **t** to keep them from Mt 19:14
many will **t** to enter and won't Lk 13:24
and I'm going to **t** them out. Lk 14:19
T to do what is honorable in Rm 12:17
just as I also **t** to please all 1Co 10:33

TRYING *(32)*

Egyptians were **t** to escape from Ex 14:27
enemy and wasn't **t** to harm him, Nm 35:23
to death for **t** to turn you away Dt 13:10
she stopped **t** to persuade her. Ru 1:18
but you're **t** to destroy a city 2Sm 20:19
they were all **t** to intimidate us Neh 6:9
one should forever stop **t**— Ps 49:8
Who is he **t** to teach? Is 28:9
Who is he **t** to instruct? Is 28:9

certain you are **t** to gain some Dn 2:8
kept **t** to find a charge against Dn 6:4
the vision and **t** to understand Dn 8:15
Me back or **t** to get even with Jl 3:4
whole crowd was **t** to touch Him, Lk 6:19
He was **t** to see who Jesus was, Lk 19:3
the Jews began **t** all the more to Jn 5:18
the Jews were **t** to kill Him. Jn 7:1
but you are **t** to kill Me because Jn 8:37
But now you are **t** to kill Me, Jn 8:40
"and are you **t** to teach us?" Jn 9:34
Then they were **t** again to seize Jn 10:39
pseudo-intellectual **t** to say?" Ac 17:18
discussion and **t** to persuade Ac 19:8
As they were **t** to kill him, Ac 21:31
complex and were **t** to kill me. Ac 26:21
and they are **t** to take my life! Rm 11:3
life, and I am **t** to spare you. 1Co 7:28
as though I am **t** to terrify you 2Co 10:9
For am I now **t** to win the favor Gl 1:10
If I were still **t** to please Gl 1:10
You who are **t** to be justified by Gl 5:4
those who are **t** to deceive you. 1Jn 2:26

TRYPHAENA *(1)*
Greet **T** and Tryphosa, who have Rm 16:12

TRYPHOSA *(1)*
and **T**, who have worked hard in Rm 16:12

TUBAL *(8)*
Madai, Javan, **T**, Meshech, and Gn 10:2
Madai, Javan, **T**, Meshech, and 1Ch 1:5
Lud (who are archers), **T**, Javan, Is 66:19
Javan, **T**, and Meshech were your Ezk 27:13
Meshech and **T** are there, with Ezk 32:26
chief prince of Meshech and **T**. Ezk 38:2
chief prince of Meshech and **T**. Ezk 38:3
chief prince of Meshech and **T**. Ezk 39:1

TUBAL-CAIN *(1)*
Zillah bore **T**, who made all Gn 4:22

TUBAL-CAIN'S *(1)*
T sister was Naamah. Gn 4:22

TUBES *(1)*
His bones are bronze **t**; Jb 40:18

TUCK *(2)*
T your mantle under your belt, 2Kg 4:29
T your mantle under your belt, 2Kg 9:1

TUCKED *(2)*
life will be **t** safely in the 1Sm 25:29
and he **t** his mantle under his 1Kg 18:46

TUMBLEWEED *(1)*
Make them like **t**, my God, like Ps 83:13

TUMBLING *(1)*
barley bread came **t** into the Jdg 7:13

TUMOR *(1)*
back one gold **t** for each city: 1Sm 6:17

TUMORS *(7)*
boils of Egypt, **t**, a festering Dt 28:27
Ashdod and its territory with **t**. 1Sm 5:6
oldest, with an outbreak of **t**. 1Sm 5:9
not die were afflicted with **t**, 1Sm 5:12
Five gold **t** and five gold mice 1Sm 6:4
images of your **t** and of your 1Sm 6:5
mice and the images of the **t**. 1Sm 6:11

TUMULT *(7)*
waves, and the **t** of the nations. Ps 65:7
t of Your opponents that goes Ps 74:23
Listen, a **t** on the mountains, Is 13:4
GOD of Hosts had a day of **t**, Is 22:5
The **t** reaches to the ends of the Jr 25:31
the **t** of their voice resounds, Jr 51:55
will die with a **t**, with shouting Am 2:2

TUNIC *(9)*
a specially woven **t**, a turban, Ex 28:4
to weave the **t** from fine linen Ex 28:39
and clothe Aaron with the **t**, Ex 29:5
He put the **t** on Aaron, wrapped Lv 8:7
He is to wear a holy linen **t**, Lv 16:4
along with his military **t**, 1Sm 18:4
I tore my **t** and robe, pulled Ezr 9:3
with my **t** and robe torn. Ezr 9:5
They also took the **t**, which was Jn 19:23

TUNICS *(6)*
Make **t**, sashes, and headbands Ex 28:40
his sons, clothe them with **t**, Ex 29:8
They made the **t** of fine woven Ex 39:27
forward and clothe them in **t**. Ex 40:14
them with **t**, wrapped sashes Lv 8:13
in their **t** outside the camp, Lv 10:5

TUNNEL *(1)*
the pool and the **t** and brought 2Kg 20:20

TURBAN *(17)*
woven tunic, a **t**, and a sash. Ex 28:4
so it can be placed on the **t**; Ex 28:37
is to be on the front of the **t**. Ex 28:37
linen, make a **t** of fine linen, Ex 28:39
Put the **t** on his head and place Ex 29:6
place the holy diadem on the **t**. Ex 29:6
also made⌋ the **t** and the ornate Ex 39:28
in order to mount ⌊it⌋ on the **t**, Ex 39:31
also put the **t** on his head and Lv 8:9
front of the **t**, as the LORD had Lv 8:9
wrap his head with a linen **t**. Lv 16:4
were like a robe and a **t**. Jb 29:14
wears a **t** and as a bride Is 61:10
Remove the **t**, and take off the Ezk 21:26
Put on your **t** and strap your Ezk 24:17
them put a clean **t** on his head." Zch 3:5
So a clean **t** was placed on his Zch 3:5

TURBANS *(4)*
linen clothes, **t**, and veils. Is 3:23
and flowing **t** on their heads; Ezk 23:15
Your **t** will remain on your heads Ezk 24:23
must wear linen **t** on their heads Ezk 44:18

TURBULENT *(2)*
T as water, you will no longer Gn 49:4
she is covered with its **t** waves. Jr 51:42

TURMOIL *(11)*
Why this **t** within me? Ps 42:5
Why this **t** within me? Ps 42:11
Why this **t** within me? Ps 43:5
the mountains quake with its **t**. Ps 46:3
restless and in **t** with my Ps 55:2
LORD than great treasure with **t**. Pr 15:16
waters in the heavens are in **t**, Jr 10:13
to the earth but **t** to those who Jr 50:34
waters in the heavens are in **t**, Jr 51:16
you infamous one full of **t**. Ezk 22:5
and see the great **t** in the city Am 3:9

TURN *(312)*
t aside to your servant's house, Gn 19:2
my hand, and it will **t** to blood. Ex 7:17
Israelites to **t** back and camp Ex 14:2
all your enemies **t** their backs Ex 23:27
T from Your great anger and Ex 32:12
Ingathering at the **t** of the Ex 34:22
I will **t** against that person who Lv 17:10
Do not **t** to idols or make cast Lv 19:4
Do not **t** to mediums or consult Lv 19:31
will **t** against that man and cut Lv 20:3
then I will **t** against that man Lv 20:5
I will **t** against that person and Lv 20:6
I will **t** to you, make you Lv 26:9
will **t** against you, so that you Lv 26:17
t back tomorrow and head for the Nm 14:25
we won't **t** to the right or the Nm 20:17
was no room to **t** to the right Nm 22:26
anger may **t** away from Israel. Nm 25:4
you **t** back from following Him, Nm 32:15
Your border will **t** south of the Nm 34:4
The border will **t** from Azmon to Nm 34:5
But you are to **t** back and head Dt 1:40
country long enough; **t** north. Dt 2:3
will not **t** to the right or the Dt 2:27
you are not to **t** aside to the Dt 5:32
they will **t** your sons away Dt 7:4
you are not enticed to **t** aside, Dt 11:16
and you **t** aside from the path I Dt 11:28
to **t** you from the way the LORD Dt 13:5
death for trying to **t** you away Dt 13:10
the LORD will **t** from His burning Dt 13:17
not **t** to the right or the left Dt 17:11
he will not **t** from this command Dt 17:20
you or He will **t** away from you. Dt 23:14
Do not **t** aside to the right or Dt 28:14
The LORD will **t** the rain of your Dt 28:24
They will **t** to other gods and Dt 31:20
corrupt and **t** from the path I Dt 31:29
Do not **t** from it to the right or Jos 1:7
will **t** their backs ⌊and run⌋ Jos 7:12
you would **t** away from the LORD? Jos 22:18
an altar to **t** away from Him. Jos 22:23
the LORD or **t** away from Him Jos 22:29
so that you do not **t** from it to Jos 23:6
For if you **t** away and cling to Jos 23:12
gods, He will **t** against ⌊you⌋, Jos 24:20
They did not **t** from their ⌊evil⌋ Jdg 2:19
trembling may **t** back and leave Jdg 7:3
that's true, we now **t** to you. Jdg 11:8
don't **t** away from following the 1Sm 12:20
Don't **t** away to follow worthless 1Sm 12:21
T and kill the priests of the 1Sm 22:17
won't kill me or **t** me over to my 1Sm 30:15
Abner and did not **t** to the right 2Sm 2:19
said to him, "**T** to your right 2Sm 2:21
But Asahel refused to **t** away, 2Sm 2:23
one can **t** to the right or left 2Sm 14:19
please **t** the counsel of 2Sm 15:31
They in **t** would go and inform 2Sm 17:17
I do not **t** back until they are 2Sm 22:38
you do and wherever you **t**, 1Kg 2:3
of you; don't **t** me down." She 1Kg 2:16
since he won't **t** you down. 1Kg 2:17
of you. Don't **t** me down." "⌊Go 1Kg 2:20
for I won't **t** you down." 1Kg 2:20
for a month in **t** provided food 1Kg 4:27
and they **t** from their sins 1Kg 8:35
you or your sons **t** away from 1Kg 9:6
they will **t** you away ⌊from Me 1Kg 11:2
because the **t** of events came 1Kg 12:15
and he did not **t** aside from 1Kg 15:5
Leave here, **t** eastward, and hide 1Kg 17:3
gold, and I didn't **t** him down." 1Kg 20:7
T around and take me out of the 1Kg 22:34
he did not **t** away from them but 1Kg 22:43
He did not **t** away from them. 2Kg 3:3
but he did not **t** away from the 2Kg 10:29
He did not **t** from the sins that 2Kg 10:31
They ⌊in **t**⌋ would pay it out to 2Kg 12:11
he did not **t** away from them. 2Kg 13:2
but they didn't **t** away from the 2Kg 13:6
He did not **t** away from all the 2Kg 13:11
He did not **t** away from all the 2Kg 14:24
He did not **t** away from the sins 2Kg 15:9
he did not **t** away from the sins 2Kg 15:18
sight and did not **t** away from 2Kg 15:24
He did not **t** away from the sins 2Kg 15:28
T from your evil ways and keep 2Kg 17:13
and did not **t** away from them. 2Kg 17:22
and did not **t** from following 2Kg 18:6
he did not **t** to the right or the 2Kg 22:2
They ⌊in **t**⌋ are to give it to 2Kg 22:5
the LORD did not **t** from the 2Kg 23:26
at Hebron to **t** Saul's kingdom 1Ch 12:23
and they **t** from their sins 2Ch 6:26
and **t** from their evil ways, 2Ch 7:14
if you **t** away and abandon My 2Ch 7:19
They did not **t** aside from the 2Ch 8:15
because the **t** of events came 2Ch 10:15
T around and take me out of the 2Ch 18:33
did not **t** away from it but did 2Ch 20:32
At the **t** of the year, an Aramean 2Ch 24:23
for this ⌊**t** of events⌋ was from 2Ch 25:20
fierce wrath may **t** away from us. 2Ch 29:10
that He may **t** His fierce wrath 2Ch 30:8
He will not **t** ⌊His⌋ face away 2Ch 30:9
he did not **t** aside to the right 2Ch 34:2
They ⌊in **t**⌋ gave it to the 2Ch 34:10
reign they did not **t** aside from 2Ch 34:33
Josiah did not **t** away from him; 2Ch 35:22
Everywhere you **t**, ⌊they⌋ attack Neh 4:12
warned them to **t** them back to Neh 9:26
warned them to **t** back to Your Neh 9:29
not serve You or **t** from their Neh 9:35
young woman's **t** to go to King Est 2:12
When her **t** came to go to the Est 2:15
each at his house in **t**. Jb 1:4
of the holy ones will you **t** to? Jb 5:1
Caravans **t** away from their Jb 6:18
and I toss and **t** until dawn. Jb 7:4
You now **t** around and destroy Jb 10:8
as you **t** your anger against God Jb 15:13
to **t** from evil is understanding. Jb 28:28
order to **t** a person ⌊from his⌋ Jb 33:17
in order to **t** him back from the Jb 33:30
that you do not **t** to iniquity, Jb 36:21
T, LORD! Rescue me; save me Ps 6:4
they will **t** back and suddenly be Ps 6:10
I do not **t** back until they are Ps 18:37
will remember and **t** to the LORD. Ps 22:27
LORD, I **t** my hope to You. Ps 25:1

T to me and be gracious to me, Ps 25:16
do not **t** Your servant away in Ps 27:9
T away from evil and do what is Ps 34:14
T away from evil and do what is Ps 37:27
T Your angry gaze from me so Ps 39:13
I **t** my ear to a proverb; Ps 49:4
instruction and **t** your back on Ps 50:17
T Your face away from my sins Ps 51:9
Your great compassion, **t** to me. Ps 69:16
His people **t** to them and drink Ps 73:10
the oppressed **t** away in shame; Ps 74:21
we will not **t** away from You; Ps 80:18
enemies and **t** My hand against Ps 81:14
T to me and be gracious to me. Ps 86:16
T and have compassion on Your Ps 90:13
the breach to **t** His wrath away Ps 106:23
T my heart to Your decrees and Ps 119:36
T my eyes from looking at what Ps 119:37
T away the disgrace I dread; Ps 119:39
but I do not **t** away from Your Ps 119:51
who know Your decrees, **t** to me. Ps 119:79
T to me and be gracious to me, Ps 119:132
for those who **t** aside to crooked Ps 125:5
not let my heart **t** to any evil Ps 141:4
If you **t** to my discipline, Pr 1:23
I, in **t**, will laugh at your Pr 1:26
the LORD and **t** away from evil. Pr 3:7
don't forget or **t** away from the Pr 4:5
T away from it, and pass it by. Pr 4:15
Don't **t** to the right or to the Pr 4:27
and don't **t** away from the words Pr 5:7
let your heart **t** aside to her Pr 7:25
but fools hate to **t** from evil. Pr 13:19
and **t** His wrath away from him. Pr 24:18
but the wise **t** away anger. Pr 29:8
shadows flee, **t** ⌊to me⌋, my love Sg 2:17
T your eyes away from me, for Sg 6:5
I will **t** My hand against you and Is 1:25
They will **t** their swords into Is 2:4
with their minds, **t** back, and be Is 6:10
people did not **t** to Him who Is 9:13
and My anger will **t** to their Is 10:25
each one will **t** to his own Is 13:14
so who can **t** it back? Is 14:27
Maker and will **t** their eyes to Is 17:7
combers and weavers will **t** pale. Is 19:9
those who **t** back the battle at Is 28:6
and whenever you **t** to the right Is 30:21
I will **t** the desert into a pool Is 41:18
I will **t** rivers into islands, Is 42:15
I will **t** darkness to light in Is 42:16
T to Me and be saved, all the Is 45:22
bear ⌊you⌋ up when you **t** gray. Is 46:4
t the rivers into a wilderness; Is 50:2
rebellious; I did not **t** back. Is 50:5
but we in **t** regarded Him Is 53:4
all of them **t** to their own way, Is 56:11
in Jacob who **t** from Is 59:20
then could you **t** into a Jr 2:21
anger is sure to **t** away from me. Jr 2:35
and never **t** away from Me. Jr 3:19
not relent or **t** back from it. Jr 4:28
If they **t** away, do they not Jr 8:4
Who will **t** aside to ask about Jr 15:5
would not **t** from their ways. Jr 15:7
All who **t** away from Me will be Jr 17:13
T now, each from your evil way, Jr 18:11
to **t** Your anger from them. Jr 18:20
but I will certainly **t** you into Jr 22:6
anger will not **t** back until He Jr 23:20
He announced, '**T**, each of you, Jr 25:5
anger will not **t** back until He Jr 30:24
will **t** their mourning into joy, Jr 31:13
long will you **t** here and there, Jr 31:22
of Gareb and then **t** toward Goah. Jr 31:39
I will never **t** away from doing Jr 32:40
will never again **t** away from Me. Jr 32:40
T, each one from his evil way of Jr 35:15
one of them will **t** from his evil Jr 36:3
each one will **t** from his evil Jr 36:7
they did not **t** from their evil Jr 44:5
I am about to **t** against you to Jr 44:11
They too will **t** back; together Jr 46:21
fathers will not **t** back for Jr 47:3
Run! **T** back! Lie low, residents Jr 49:8
each will **t** to his own people, Jr 50:16
and **t** you into a burned-out Jr 51:25
ways, and **t** back to the LORD. Lm 3:40
did not **t** as they moved; Ezk 1:9
and he does not **t** from his Ezk 3:19
T your face toward it so that it Ezk 4:3
You must **t** your face toward the Ezk 4:7
so you cannot **t** from side to Ezk 4:8
t your face toward the mountains Ezk 6:2
their⌋ knees will **t** to water. Ezk 7:17
I will **t** My face from the wicked Ezk 7:22
t toward the women of your Ezk 13:17
person not to **t** from his evil Ezk 13:22
Repent and **t** away from your Ezk 14:6
t your faces away from all your Ezk 14:6
I will **t** against that one and Ezk 14:8
I will **t** against them. They may Ezk 15:7
the LORD when I **t** against them. Ezk 15:7
jealousy will **t** away from you. Ezk 16:42
Repent and **t** from all your Ezk 18:30
t your face toward Jerusalem and Ezk 21:2
and every knee will **t** to water. Ezk 21:7
t to the left—wherever your Ezk 21:16
t your face toward the Ammonites Ezk 25:2
from her and **t** her into a bare Ezk 26:4
I will **t** you into a bare rock, Ezk 26:14
t your face toward Sidon and Ezk 28:21
t your face toward Pharaoh king Ezk 29:2
I will **t** the land of Egypt into Ezk 29:10
wicked person to **t** from his way Ezk 33:9
way and he doesn't **t** from it, Ezk 33:9
person should **t** from his way Ezk 33:11
t your face toward Mount Seir Ezk 35:2
I will **t** your cities into ruins, Ezk 35:4
will **t** toward you, and you will Ezk 36:9
Son of man, **t** your face toward Ezk 38:2
will **t** you around, put hooks in Ezk 38:4
to **t** your hand against ruins now Ezk 38:12
I will **t** you around, drive you Ezk 39:2
anger and wrath **t** away from Your Dn 9:16
Then he will **t** his attention to Dn 11:18
will **t** his taunts against him. Dn 11:18
He will **t** his attention back to Dn 11:19
I will **t** them into a thicket, Hs 2:12
though they **t** to other gods and Hs 3:1
is over, they **t** to promiscuity. Hs 4:18
and wine; they **t** away from Me. Hs 7:14
t, but not to what is above; Hs 7:16
I will not **t** back to destroy Hs 11:9
before them; all faces **t** pale. Jl 2:6
t to Me with all your heart, Jl 2:12
He may **t** and relent and leave a Jl 2:14
I will also **t** My hand against Am 1:8
who **t** justice into wormwood Am 5:7
I will **t** your feasts into Am 8:10
Each must **t** from his evil ways Jnh 3:8
knows? God may **t** and relent; He Jnh 3:9
He may **t** from His burning anger Jnh 3:9
daylight will **t** black over them Mc 3:6
and those who **t** back from Zph 1:6
but you didn't **t** to Me"—the Hg 2:17
T from your evil ways and your Zch 1:4
I will **t** everyone over to his Zch 11:6
will also **t** My hand against the Zch 13:7
So I in **t** have made you despised Mal 2:9
And he will **t** the hearts of Mal 4:6
right cheek, **t** the other to him Mt 5:39
don't **t** away from the one who Mt 5:42
their feet, **t**, and tear you to Mt 7:6
I came to **t** a man against his Mt 10:35
with their hearts and **t** back— Mt 13:15
they might **t** back—and be Mk 4:12
He will **t** many of the sons of Lk 1:16
to **t** the hearts of fathers to Lk 1:17
is in the field must not **t** back. Lk 17:31
and saying, 'God, **t** Your wrath Lk 18:13
but your sorrow will **t** to joy. Jn 16:20
Therefore repent and **t** back, Ac 3:19
Our forefathers in **t** received it Ac 7:45
and tried to **t** the proconsul Ac 13:8
life, we now **t** to the Gentiles! Ac 13:46
that you should **t** from these Ac 14:15
those who **t** to God from among Ac 15:19
that they may **t** from darkness to Ac 26:18
they should repent and **t** to God, Ac 26:20
He will **t** away godlessness from Rm 11:26
t that one over to Satan for the 1Co 5:5
three, each in **t**, and someone 1Co 14:27
how can you **t** back again to the Gl 4:9
of the Lord must **t** away from 2Tm 2:19
They will **t** away from hearing 2Tm 4:4
truth and will **t** aside to myths. 2Tm 4:4
will we if we **t** away from Him Heb 12:25
and he must **t** away from evil and 1Pt 3:11
to **t** back from the holy 2Pt 2:21
the waters to **t** them into blood, Rv 11:6

TURNED *(255)*

Their faces were **t** away, and Gn 9:23
The men **t** from there and went Gn 18:22
So it **t** out that the weak sheep Gn 30:42
It **t** out just the way he Gn 41:13
He **t** away from them and wept. Gn 42:24
he **t** back and spoke to them. Gn 42:24
they **t** to one another and said, Gn 42:28
the staff that **t** into a snake. Ex 7:15
in the Nile was **t** to blood. Ex 7:20
Pharaoh **t** around, went into his Ex 7:23
Then he **t** and left Pharaoh's Ex 10:6
that night and **t** the sea into Ex 14:21
they **t** toward the wilderness, Ex 16:10
have quickly **t** from the way I Ex 32:8
Then Moses **t** and went down the Ex 32:15
in the infection has **t** white and Lv 13:3
the hair in it has not **t** white, Lv 13:4
skin that has **t** the hair white, Lv 13:10
Since he has **t** totally white, Lv 13:13
if the infection has **t** white, Lv 13:17
and the hair in it has **t** white, Lv 13:20
in the spot has **t** white and the Lv 13:25
When Aaron **t** toward her, he saw Nm 12:10
you have **t** from following Him. Nm 14:43
Moses and Aaron **t** toward the Nm 16:42
and Israel **t** away from them. Nm 20:21
Then they **t** and went up the road Nm 21:33
she **t** off the path and went into Nm 22:23
donkey saw Me and **t** away from Nm 22:33
If she had not **t** away from Me, Nm 22:33
but **t** toward the wilderness. Nm 24:1
has **t** back My wrath from the Nm 25:11
from Etham and **t** back to Nm 33:7
Then we **t** back and headed for Dt 2:1
⌊We **t**⌋ away from the Arabah road Dt 2:8
Then we **t** and went up the road Dt 3:1
have quickly **t** from the way that Dt 9:12
You had quickly **t** from the way Dt 9:16
but He **t** the curse into a Dt 23:5
that Israel has **t** its back ⌊and Jos 7:8
Then the LORD **t** from His burning Jos 7:26
The men of Ai **t** and looked back, Jos 8:20
they **t** back and struck down the Jos 8:21
Joshua **t** toward Debir and Jos 10:38
At that time Joshua **t** back, Jos 11:10
to Addar, and **t** to Karka. Jos 15:3
border **t** westward from Baalah Jos 15:10
t eastward from Taanath-shiloh Jos 16:6
it **t** east toward the sunrise Jos 19:12
It **t** eastward to Beth-dagon, Jos 19:27
boundary then **t** to Ramah as far Jos 19:29
it **t** back to Hosah and ended at Jos 19:29
the boundary **t** to Aznoth-tabor Jos 19:34
They quickly **t** from the way of Jdg 2:17
The LORD **t** to him and said, Jdg 6:14
So 22,000 of the people **t** back, Jdg 7:3
The loaf **t** the tent upside down Jdg 7:13
the Israelites **t** and prostituted Jdg 8:33
70 brothers, God **t** back on him. Jdg 9:56
He took torches, **t** the foxes Jdg 15:4
the Danites, who **t** to face them, Jdg 18:23
and Micah **t** to go back home, Jdg 18:26
Then Benjamin **t** and fled toward Jdg 20:45
The men of Israel **t** back against Jdg 20:48
It **t** out that no one from Jdg 21:8
LORD's hand has **t** against me." Ru 1:13
was startled, **t** over, and there Ru 3:8
they **t** toward dishonest gain, 1Sm 8:3
When Saul **t** around to leave 1Sm 10:9
Wherever he **t**, he caused havoc. 1Sm 14:47
for he has **t** away from following 1Sm 15:11
Then he **t** around and went down 1Sm 15:12
Samuel **t** to go, Saul grabbed 1Sm 15:27
Then he **t** from those beside him 1Sm 17:30
me and God has **t** away from me. 1Sm 28:15
the LORD has **t** away from you 1Sm 28:16
When he **t** around and saw me, 2Sm 1:7
When Joab had **t** back from 2Sm 2:30
victory was **t** into mourning for 2Sm 19:2
and have not **t** from my God to 2Sm 22:22
the kingship was **t** over to my 1Kg 2:15
king **t** around and blessed the 1Kg 8:14

and they **t** his heart away ⌊from 1Kg 11:3
his heart had **t** away from the 1Kg 11:9
that You have **t** their hearts 1Kg 18:37
So he **t** back from following him, 1Kg 19:21
man **t** aside and brought someone 1Kg 20:39
on his bed, **t** his face away, 1Kg 21:4
So they **t** to fight against him, 1Kg 22:32
they **t** back from pursuing him. 1Kg 22:33
He **t** around, looked at them, and 2Kg 2:24
So he **t** and left in a rage. 2Kg 5:12
t around and fled, shouting 2Kg 9:23
them and **t** toward them because 2Kg 13:23
Then Hezekiah **t** his face to the 2Kg 20:2
As Josiah **t**, he saw the tombs 2Kg 23:16
like him who **t** to the LORD with 2Kg 23:25
Then he **t** and rebelled against 2Kg 24:1
to death and **t** the kingdom over 1Ch 10:14
wheat when he **t** and saw the 1Ch 21:20
Then the king **t** and blessed the 2Ch 6:3
LORD said and **t** back from going 2Ch 11:4
LORD's anger **t** away from him, 2Ch 12:12
Judah **t** and discovered that the 2Ch 13:14
but when they **t** to the LORD God 2Ch 15:4
So they **t** to attack him, 2Ch 18:31
they **t** back from pursuing him. 2Ch 18:32
but Israel **t** away from them and 2Ch 20:10
and Moabites **t** against 2Ch 20:23
Judah and Jerusalem **t** back with 2Ch 20:27
time Amaziah **t** from following 2Ch 25:27
all the priests **t** to him and saw 2Ch 26:20
t their faces away from the 2Ch 29:6
tabernacle, and **t** their backs on 2Ch 29:6
of cloud never **t** away from them, Neh 9:19
but our God **t** the curse into a Neh 13:2
sorrow was **t** into rejoicing Est 9:22
feared God and **t** away from evil. Jb 1:1
only that day had **t** to darkness! Jb 3:4
They **t** night into day and ⌊made⌋ Jb 17:12
those I love have **t** against me. Jb 19:19
kept to His way and not **t** aside. Jb 23:11
Terrors are **t** loose against me; Jb 30:15
You have **t** against me with Jb 30:21
If my step has **t** from the way, Jb 31:7
because they **t** aside from Jb 34:27
All have **t** away; all alike have Ps 14:3
and have not **t** from my God to Ps 18:21
You **t** my lament into dancing; Ps 30:11
to harm me be **t** back and ashamed Ps 35:4
and He **t** to me and heard my cry Ps 40:1
LORD and has not **t** to the proud Ps 40:4
Our hearts have not **t** back; Ps 44:18
Everyone has **t** aside; Ps 53:3
He **t** the sea into dry land, Ps 66:6
He has not **t** away my prayer or Ps 66:20
my prayer or **t** His faithful love Ps 66:20
archers **t** back on the day Ps 78:9
He often **t** His anger aside and Ps 78:38
He **t** their rivers into blood, Ps 78:44
treacherously **t** away like their Ps 78:57
and **t** Jerusalem into ruins. Ps 79:1
You **t** from Your burning anger. Ps 85:3
You have also **t** back his sharp Ps 89:43
whose hearts He **t** to hate His Ps 105:25
He **t** their waters into blood and Ps 105:29
and fled; the Jordan **t** back. Ps 114:3
Jordan, that you **t** back? Ps 114:5
who **t** the rock into a pool of Ps 114:8
Because He has **t** His ear to me, Ps 116:2
my ways and **t** my steps back to Ps 119:59
have not **t** from Your judgments, Ps 119:102
I have not **t** from Your decrees. Ps 119:157
But it **t** out to be futile. Ec 2:1
Then I **t** to consider wisdom, Ec 2:12
t my thoughts to know, explore, Ec 7:25
but my love had **t** and gone away. Sg 5:6
Which way has he **t**? We will seek Sg 6:1
have **t** their backs ⌊on Him⌋. Is 1:4
Your anger has **t** away, and You Is 12:1
who **t** the world into a Is 14:17
He has **t** my last glimmer of hope Is 21:4
For You have **t** the city into a Is 25:2
You have **t** things around, as if Is 29:16
streams will be **t** into pitch, Is 34:9
Then Hezekiah **t** his face to the Is 38:2
will be **t** back ⌊and⌋ utterly Is 42:17
He was like one people **t** away Is 53:3
we all have **t** to our own way; Is 53:6
Justice is **t** back, and Is 59:14
For they have **t** their back to Me Jr 2:27
anger has not **t** away from us. Jr 4:8
They have **t** aside and have gone Jr 5:23
houses will be **t** over to others, Jr 6:12
Why have these people **t** away? Jr 8:5
They have **t** My desirable plot Jr 12:10
You have **t** your back, so I have Jr 15:6
I have **t** against this city to Jr 21:10
and would have **t** them back from Jr 23:22
in labor and every face **t** pale? Jr 30:6
They have **t** their backs to Me Jr 32:33
they **t** to each other in fear and Jr 36:16
courtyard and **t** him over to Jr 39:14
Jeremiah had not yet **t** ⌊to go, Jr 40:5
from Mizpah **t** around and Jr 41:14
How Moab has **t** his back! Jr 48:39
weak; she has **t** to run; panic Jr 49:24
a net for my feet and **t** me back. Lm 1:13
has been **t** over to strangers, Lm 5:2
our dancing has **t** to mourning. Lm 5:15
hearts that **t** away from Me Ezk 6:9
and their faces ⌊**t**⌋ to the east. Ezk 8:16
every street and **t** your beauty Ezk 16:25
with its branches **t** toward him, Ezk 17:6
thought it over and **t** from all Ezk 18:28
she **t** away from them in disgust. Ezk 23:17
t away from her in disgust just Ezk 23:18
disgust just as I **t** away from Ezk 23:18
you **t** away from in disgust. Ezk 23:22
to those you **t** away from in Ezk 23:28
She has been **t** over to me. Ezk 26:2
a human face **t** toward the palm Ezk 41:19
and a lion's face **t** toward it on Ezk 41:19
Then he **t** to the west side and Ezk 42:19
face **t** pale, and his thoughts Dn 5:6
his face **t** pale, and his Dn 5:9
and my face **t** pale, but I kept Dn 7:28
So I **t** my attention to the Lord Dn 9:3
t away from Your commandments Dn 9:5
has broken Your law and **t** away, Dn 9:11
t my face toward the ground and Dn 10:15
My anger will have **t** from him. Hs 14:4
its branches have **t** white. Jl 1:7
pastures have **t** green, Jl 2:22
sun will be **t** to darkness and Jl 2:31
Yet you have **t** justice into Am 6:12
that they had **t** from their evil Jnh 3:10
He has **t** back your enemy. Zph 3:15
pay attention and **t** a stubborn Zch 7:11
They **t** a pleasant land into a Zch 7:14
for I **t** everyone against his Zch 8:10
I **t** his mountains into a Mal 1:3
fairness and **t** many from sin. Mal 2:6
other hand, have **t** from the way. Mal 2:8
you have **t** from My statutes; Mal 3:7
But Jesus **t** and saw her. Mt 9:22
But He **t** and told Peter, "Get Mt 16:23
his own slaves and **t** over his Mt 25:14
He **t** around in the crowd and Mk 5:30
But He **t** and rebuked them, Lk 9:55
So He **t** and said to them: Lk 14:25
when you have **t** back, strengthen Lk 22:32
Then the Lord **t** and looked at Lk 22:61
When Jesus **t** and noticed them Jn 1:38
where He had **t** the water into Jn 4:46
of His disciples **t** back and no Jn 6:66
she **t** around and saw Jesus Jn 20:14
So Peter **t** around and saw the Jn 21:20
The sun will be **t** to darkness, Ac 2:20
he **t** to them, expecting to get Ac 3:5
in their hearts **t** back to Egypt. Ac 7:39
Then God **t** away and gave them up Ac 7:42
saw him and **t** to the Lord. Ac 9:35
who believed **t** to the Lord. Ac 11:21
men who have **t** the world upside Ac 17:6
All have **t** away, together they Rm 3:12
Titus has also **t** out to be the 2Co 7:14
how you **t** to God from idols to 1Th 1:9
from these and **t** aside to 1Tm 1:6
have already **t** away to follow 1Tm 5:15
in Asia have **t** away from me, 2Tm 1:15
I **t** to see the voice that was Rv 1:12
When I **t** I saw seven gold Rv 1:12
the sun **t** black like sackcloth Rv 6:12
It **t** to blood like a dead man's, Rv 16:3

TURNING *(36)*

have done by **t** to other gods. Dt 31:18
t north to the Gilgal that is Jos 15:7
the border curved, **t** southward, Jos 18:14
God of Israel by **t** away from the Jos 22:16
Shechem and are **t** the city Jdg 9:31
wiping it and **t** it upside down. 2Kg 21:13
t round and round at His Jb 37:12
the soil, ⌊**t** up rocks⌋, so our Ps 141:7
t people away from the snares of Pr 13:14
t people from the snares of Pr 14:27
to the south, **t** to the north, Ec 1:6
to the north, **t**, turning, goes Ec 1:6
turning, **t**, goes the wind, Ec 1:6
but he went on **t** back to the Is 57:17
t away from following our God, Is 59:13
camel twisting and **t** on her way, Jr 2:23
Why is Jerusalem always **t** away? Jr 8:5
⌊**t**⌋ their faces to this road. Jr 50:5
went without **t** as they moved. Ezk 1:12
to their sin of **t** to the Ezk 29:16
LORD our God by **t** from our Dn 9:13
My people are bent on **t** from Me. Hs 11:7
But **t** around and looking at His Mk 8:33
t to the crowd following Him, Lk 7:9
T to the woman, He said to Simon, Lk 7:44
Then **t** to His disciples He said Lk 10:23
But **t** to them, Jesus said, Lk 23:28
Stop **t** My Father's house into a Jn 2:16
T around, she said to Him in Jn 20:16
to bless you by **t** each of you Ac 3:26
and **t** toward the body said, Ac 9:40
aggravated, and **t** to the spirit, Ac 16:18
are so quickly **t** away from Him Gl 1:6
are **t**⌋ to a different gospel Gl 1:6
variation or shadow cast by **t**. Jms 1:17
t the grace of our God into Jd 4

TURNS *(45)*

brother's rage **t** away from you Gn 27:45
raw flesh changes and **t** white, Lv 13:16
Whoever **t** to mediums or Lv 20:6
If the report **t** out to be true Dt 13:14
If the report **t** out to be true Dt 17:4
the witness **t** out to be a liar Dt 19:18
today whose heart **t** away from Dt 29:18
if your heart **t** away and you do Dt 30:17
If it **t** out he really is in the 1Sm 23:23
You are to take **t** providing 2Kg 11:6
fears God and **t** away from evil. Jb 1:8
fears God and **t** away from evil. Jb 2:3
in his stomach **t** into cobras' Jb 20:14
when He **t** south, I cannot find Jb 23:9
He **t** rivers into desert, springs Ps 107:33
He **t** a desert into a pool of Ps 107:35
of the righteous ⌊**t** out⌋ well, Pr 11:23
man is cautious and **t** from evil, Pr 14:16
A gentle answer **t** away anger, Pr 15:1
and one **t** from evil by the fear Pr 16:6
wherever he **t**, he succeeds. Pr 17:8
A door **t** on its hinge, and a Pr 26:14
Anyone who **t** his ear away from Pr 28:9
but one who **t** his eyes away will Pr 28:27
of extortion **t** a wise person Ec 7:7
and whoever **t** from evil is Is 59:15
his strength and **t** his heart Jr 17:5
about, **t** from its evil, I Jr 18:8
and none **t** his back on evil. Jr 23:14
She herself groans and **t** away. Lm 1:8
He repeatedly **t** His hand against Lm 3:3
if a righteous person **t** from his Ezk 3:20
wicked person **t** from all the Ezk 18:21
pleasure⌋ when he **t** from his Ezk 18:23
a righteous person **t** from his Ezk 18:24
a righteous person **t** from his Ezk 18:26
if a wicked person **t** from the Ezk 18:27
on the day he **t** from his Ezk 33:12
a righteous person **t** from his Ezk 33:18
a wicked person **t** from his Ezk 33:19
who **t** darkness into dawn and Am 5:8
⌊they cry,⌋ but no one **t** back. Nah 2:8
whenever a person **t** to the Lord, 2Co 3:16
truth, and someone **t** him back, Jms 5:19
that whoever **t** a sinner from Jms 5:20

TURQUOISE *(4)*

the second row, a **t**, a sapphire, Ex 28:18
the second row, a **t**, a sapphire, Ex 39:11
They exchanged **t**, purple and Ezk 27:16
jasper, sapphire, **t** and emerald. Ezk 28:13

TURTLEDOVE *(3)*

ram, a **t**, and a young pigeon. Gn 15:9

young pigeon or a **t** for a sin Lv 12:6
The **t**, swallow, and crane are Jr 8:7

TURTLEDOVE'S *(1)*
and the **t** cooing is heard in our Sg 2:12

TURTLEDOVES *(10)*
from the **t** or young pigeons Lv 1:14
to the LORD two **t** or two young Lv 5:7
cannot afford two **t** or two young Lv 5:11
she may take two **t** or two young Lv 12:8
and two **t** or two young pigeons, Lv 14:22
either the **t** or young pigeons, Lv 14:30
He must take two **t** or two young Lv 15:14
she must take two **t** or two young Lv 15:29
is to bring two **t** or two young Nm 6:10
a pair of **t** or two young pigeons Lk 2:24

TUSKS *(1)*
back ivory **t** and ebony as your Ezk 27:15

TWELFTH *(23)*
On the **t** day Ahira son of Enan, Nm 7:78
and he was with the **t** team. 1Kg 19:19
In the **t** year of Israel's King 2Kg 8:25
In the **t** year of Judah's King 2Kg 17:1
twenty-seventh day of the **t** 2Kg 25:27
to Eliashib, the **t** to Jakim, 1Ch 24:12
t to Hashabiah, his sons, and 1Ch 25:19
t, for the twelfth month, was 1Ch 27:15
twelfth, for the **t** month, was 1Ch 27:15
and in the **t** year he began to 2Ch 34:3
River on the **t** ⌊day⌋ of the Ezr 8:31
in King Ahasuerus' **t** year, Est 3:7
and it fell on the **t** month, Est 3:7
day of Adar, the **t** month. Est 3:13
thirteenth day of the **t** month, Est 8:12
thirteenth day of the **t** month, Est 9:1
twenty-fifth day of the **t** month Jr 52:31
month⌋ on the **t** ⌊day⌋ of the Ezk 29:1
In the **t** year, in the twelfth Ezk 32:1
year, in the **t** month, on the Ezk 32:1
In the **t** year, on the fifteenth Ezk 32:17
In the **t** year of our exile, Ezk 33:21
jacinth, the **t** amethyst. Rv 21:20

TWELVE *(30)*
T lions were standing there on 1Kg 10:20
T teams of oxen were in front of 1Kg 19:19
T lions were standing there on 2Ch 9:19
Then one of the **T**—the man Mt 26:14
at the table with the **T**. Mt 26:20
one of the **T**, suddenly arrived Mt 26:47
He appointed the **T**: To Simon, He Mk 3:16
When He was alone with the **T**, Mk 4:10
He summoned the **T** and began to Mk 6:7
"**T**," they told Him. Mk 8:19
called the **T** and said to them, Mk 9:35
Taking the **T** aside again, He Mk 10:32
went out to Bethany with the **T**. Mk 11:11
one of the **T**, went to the chief Mk 14:10
came, He arrived with the **T**. Mk 14:17
is⌋ one of the **T**—the one who Mk 14:20
one of the **T**, suddenly arrived Mk 14:43
of God. The **T** were with Him, Lk 8:1
Summoning the **T**, He gave them Lk 9:1
T approached and said to Him, Lk 9:12
He took the **T** aside and told Lk 18:31
who was numbered among the **T**. Lk 22:3
and one of the **T** named Judas was Lk 22:47
Therefore Jesus said to the **T**, Jn 6:67
Didn't I choose you, the **T**? Jn 6:70
son, one of the **T**, because he Jn 6:71
But one of the **T**, Thomas (called Jn 20:24
Then the **T** summoned the whole Ac 6:2
to Cephas, then to the **T**. 1Co 15:5
T angels were at the gates; Rv 21:12

TWENTIETH *(9)*
month on the **t** ⌊day⌋ of the Nm 10:11
In the **t** year of Israel's King 1Kg 15:9
place in the **t** year of Jotham 2Kg 15:30
to Pethahiah, the **t** to Jehezkel, 1Ch 24:16
the **t** to Eliathah, his sons, and 1Ch 25:27
On the **t** ⌊day⌋ of the ninth Ezr 10:9
month of Chislev in the **t** year, Neh 1:1
of Nisan in the **t** year of King Neh 2:1
from the **t** year until his Neh 5:14

TWENTY-FIFTH *(3)*
on the **t** day of the month Elul. Neh 6:15
the **t** day of the twelfth month Jr 52:31
In the **t** year of our exile, Ezk 40:1

TWENTY-FIRST *(4)*
until the evening of the **t** day. Ex 12:18
the **t** to Jachin, the 1Ch 24:17
the **t** to Hothir, his sons, and 1Ch 25:28
On the **t** day of the seventh Hg 2:1

TWENTY-FOURTH *(9)*
Delaiah, and the **t** to Maaziah. 1Ch 24:18
and the **t** to Romamti-ezer, 1Ch 25:31
On the **t** day of this month the Neh 9:1
On the **t** day of the first month, Dn 10:4
on the **t** day of the sixth month, Hg 1:15
the **t** day of the ninth ⌊month⌋ Hg 2:10
from the **t** day of the ninth Hg 2:18
time on the **t** day of the month: Hg 2:20
On the **t** day of the eleventh Zch 1:7

TWENTY-SECOND *(2)*
to Jachin, the **t** to Gamul, 1Ch 24:17
the **t** to Giddalti, his sons, and 1Ch 25:29

TWENTY-SEVENTH *(6)*
the **t** day of the second month, Gn 8:14
In the **t** year of Judah's King 1Kg 16:10
In the **t** year of Judah's King 1Kg 16:15
In the **t** year of Israel's King 2Kg 15:1
the **t** day of the twelfth month 2Kg 25:27
the **t** year in the first ⌊month⌋ Ezk 29:17

TWENTY-SIXTH *(1)*
In the **t** year of Judah's King 1Kg 16:8

TWENTY-THIRD *(7)*
But by the **t** year ⌊of the reign⌋ 2Kg 12:6
In the **t** year of Judah's King 2Kg 13:1
the **t** to Delaiah, and the 1Ch 24:18
t to Mahazioth, his sons, and 1Ch 25:30
the **t** day of the seventh month 2Ch 7:10
On the **t** day of the third month Est 8:9
in Nebuchadnezzar's **t** year, Jr 52:30

TWICE *(20)*
For he has cheated me **t** now. Gn 27:36
dream was given **t** to Pharaoh, Gn 41:32
could have come back **t** by now." Gn 43:10
Take **t** as much money with you. Gn 43:12
it will be **t** as much as they Ex 16:5
they gathered **t** as much food, Ex 16:22
the rock **t** with his staff, Nm 20:11
worth **t** the wages of a hired Dt 15:18
But David got away from him **t**. 1Sm 18:11
I won't ⌊have to strike⌋ him **t**!" 1Sm 26:8
who had appeared to him **t**. 1Kg 11:9
or **t** the merchants and those Neh 13:20
t, but ⌊now⌋ I can add nothing. Jb 40:5
have heard this **t**: strength Ps 62:11
if he lives a thousand years **t**, Ec 6:6
you make him **t** as fit for hell Mt 23:15
before the rooster crows **t**, Mk 14:30
Before the rooster crows **t**, Mk 14:72
I fast **t** a week; I give a tenth Lk 18:12
fruitless, **t** dead, pulled out Jd 12

TWIGS *(1)*
and produce **t** like a sapling. Jb 14:9

TWILIGHT *(17)*
will slaughter the animals at **t**. Ex 12:6
At **t** you will eat meat, and in Ex 16:12
and at **t** offer the other lamb. Ex 29:39
to offer the second lamb at **t**. Ex 29:41
Aaron sets up the lamps at **t**, Ex 30:8
t on the fourteenth day of the Lv 23:5
day of this month at **t**; Nm 9:3
day at **t** in the Wilderness Nm 9:5
on the fourteenth day at **t**. Nm 9:11
morning and the other lamb at **t**, Nm 28:4
Offer the second lamb at **t**, Nm 28:8
them from **t** until the evening 1Sm 30:17
men got up at **t** to go to the 2Kg 7:5
and fled at **t** abandoning their 2Kg 7:7
adulterer's eye watches for **t**, Jb 24:15
t, in the evening, in the dark Pr 7:9
at noon as though it were **t**; Is 59:10

TWIN *(6)*
each one having a **t**, and not one Sg 4:2
each one having a **t**, and not one Sg 6:6
Thomas (called "**T**") said to his Jn 11:16
Thomas (called "**T**"), was not Jn 20:24
Thomas (called "**T**"), Nathanael Jn 21:2
with the **T** Brothers as its Ac 28:11

TWINKLING *(1)*
a moment, in the **t** of an eye, at 1Co 15:52

TWINS *(4)*
there were indeed **t** in her womb. Gn 25:24
birth, there were **t** in her womb. Gn 38:27
like two fawns, **t** of a gazelle, Sg 4:5
like two fawns, **t** of a gazelle. Sg 7:3

TWIST *(5)*
and must **t** off its head and burn Lv 1:15
must **t** its head at the back of Lv 5:8
They **t** my words all day long; Ps 56:5
will **t** its surface and scatter Is 24:1
and unstable **t** them to their own 2Pt 3:16

TWISTED *(6)*
with **t** minds are detestable Pr 11:20
insight, but a **t** mind is Pr 12:8
One with a **t** mind will not Pr 17:20
They **t** together a crown of Mt 27:29
t together a crown of thorns, Mk 15:17
soldiers also **t** together a crown Jn 19:2

TWISTING *(3)*
butter, and **t** a nose draws blood Pr 30:33
Leviathan, the **t** serpent. Is 27:1
swift young camel **t** and turning Jr 2:23

TWISTS *(1)*
eyes of the wise and **t** the words Dt 16:19

TWO *(620)*
God made the **t** great lights— Gn 1:16
Lamech took **t** wives for himself, Gn 4:19
into the ark **t** of every living Gn 6:19
T of everything—from the birds Gn 6:20
t of the animals that are not Gn 7:2
t of each, male and female, Gn 7:9
T of all flesh that has the Gn 7:15
and told his **t** brothers outside Gn 9:22
Eber had **t** sons. One was named Gn 10:25
fathered Arpachshad **t** years Gn 11:10
t angels entered Sodom in the Gn 19:1
I've got **t** daughters who haven't Gn 19:8
wife and your **t** daughters who Gn 19:15
the hands of his **t** daughters. Gn 19:16
along with his **t** daughters, Gn 19:30
he and his **t** daughters lived in Gn 19:30
and the **t** of them made a Gn 21:27
there that the **t** of them swore Gn 21:31
took with him **t** of his young men Gn 22:3
and the **t** of them walked on Gn 22:6
Then the **t** of them walked on Gn 22:8
for her wrists **t** bracelets Gn 24:22
T nations are in your womb; Gn 25:23
t people will ⌊come⌋ from you Gn 25:23
be an oath between **t** parties— Gn 26:28
and bring me **t** choice young Gn 27:9
Now Laban had **t** daughters: Gn 29:16
tents of the **t** female slaves, Gn 31:33
them decide between the **t** of us. Gn 31:37
years for your **t** daughters and Gn 31:41
a witness between the **t** of us." Gn 31:44
people with him into **t** camps, Gn 32:7
and now I have become **t** camps. Gn 32:10
got up and took his **t** wives, Gn 32:22
two wives, his **t** female slaves, Gn 32:22
Rachel, and the **t** female slaves. Gn 33:1
in pain, **t** of Jacob's sons, Gn 34:25
was angry with his **t** officers, Gn 40:2
T years later Pharaoh had a Gn 41:1
T sons were born to Joseph Gn 41:50
can kill my **t** sons if I don't Gn 42:37
that my wife bore me **t** sons. Gn 44:27
been in the land these **t** years, Gn 45:6
to him in Egypt: **t** persons. All Gn 46:27
So he set out with his **t** sons, Gn 48:1
Your **t** sons born to you in the Gn 48:5
out and saw **t** Hebrews fighting Ex 2:13
even these **t** signs or listen to Ex 4:9
and put it on the **t** doorposts Ex 12:7
lintel and the **t** doorposts with Ex 12:22
the lintel and the **t** doorposts, Ex 12:23
You may take **t** quarts per Ex 16:16
will give you **t** days' worth of Ex 16:29
'**T** quarts of it are to be Ex 16:32
and put **t** quarts of manna Ex 16:33
T quarts are a tenth of an ephah. Ex 16:36
along with her **t** sons, one of Ex 18:3
with your wife and her **t** sons." Ex 18:6
can stand up after a day or **t**, Ex 21:21
case between the **t** parties is to Ex 22:9
LORD between the **t** of them to Ex 22:11
t rings on one side and two Ex 25:12

on one side and **t** rings on the Ex 25:12
Make **t** cherubim of gold; Ex 25:18
work at the **t** ends of the mercy Ex 25:18
the mercy seat at its **t** ends. Ex 25:19
between the **t** cherubim that are Ex 25:22
together with **t** tenons. Ex 26:17
t bases under the first plank Ex 26:19
first plank for its **t** tenons, Ex 26:19
and **t** bases under the next plank Ex 26:19
the next plank for its **t** tenons; Ex 26:19
t bases under the first plank Ex 26:21
first plank and **t** bases under Ex 26:21
Make **t** additional planks for the Ex 26:23
planks for the **t** back corners Ex 26:23
will serve as the **t** corners. Ex 26:24
t bases under the first plank Ex 26:25
first plank and **t** bases under Ex 26:25
the poles are on **t** sides of the Ex 27:7
It must have **t** shoulder pieces Ex 28:7
attached to its **t** edges so that Ex 28:7
Take **t** onyx stones and engrave Ex 28:9
Engrave the **t** stones with the Ex 28:11
names on his **t** shoulders before Ex 28:12
and **t** chains of pure gold; Ex 28:14
Fashion **t** gold rings for the Ex 28:23
attach them to its **t** corners. Ex 28:23
Then attach the **t** gold cords to Ex 28:24
gold cords to the **t** gold rings Ex 28:24
ends of the **t** cords to the two Ex 28:25
two cords to the **t** filigree Ex 28:25
Make **t** ⌊other⌋ gold rings and Ex 28:26
put them at the **t** other corners Ex 28:26
Make **t** ⌊more⌋ gold rings and Ex 28:27
of the ephod's **t** shoulder pieces Ex 28:27
young bull and **t** unblemished Ex 29:1
along with the bull and **t** rams. Ex 29:3
and the **t** kidneys with the fat Ex 29:13
the **t** kidneys and the fat on Ex 29:22
every day: **t** year-old lambs. Ex 29:38
first lamb offer **t** quarts of Ex 29:40
Make **t** gold rings for it under Ex 30:4
the molding on **t** of its sides; Ex 30:4
He gave him the **t** tablets of the Ex 31:18
the mountain with the **t** tablets Ex 32:15
Cut **t** stone tablets like the Ex 34:1
Moses cut **t** stone tablets like Ex 34:4
and taking the **t** stone tablets Ex 34:4
with the **t** tablets of the Ex 34:29
There were **t** tenons connected to Ex 36:22
t bases under the first plank Ex 36:24
first plank for its **t** tenons, Ex 36:24
and **t** bases under each of the Ex 36:24
planks for their **t** tenons; Ex 36:24
t bases under the first plank Ex 36:26
first plank and **t** bases under Ex 36:26
He also made **t** additional planks Ex 36:28
planks for the **t** back corners Ex 36:28
both of them for the **t** corners. Ex 36:29
silver bases, **t** bases under each Ex 36:30
t rings on one side and two Ex 37:3
on one side and **t** rings on the Ex 37:3
He made **t** cherubim of gold; Ex 37:7
work at the **t** ends of the mercy Ex 37:7
made **t** gold rings for it under Ex 37:27
the molding on **t** of its sides; Ex 37:27
joined together at its **t** edges. Ex 39:4
also fashioned **t** gold filigree Ex 39:16
settings and **t** gold rings Ex 39:16
attached the **t** rings to its two Ex 39:16
the two rings to its **t** corners. Ex 39:16
they attached the **t** gold cords Ex 39:17
gold cords to the **t** gold rings Ex 39:17
ends of the **t** cords to the two Ex 39:18
two cords to the **t** filigree Ex 39:18
They made **t** ⌊other⌋ gold rings Ex 39:19
⌊them⌋ at the **t** other corners Ex 39:19
They made **t** ⌊more⌋ gold rings Ex 39:20
of the ephod's **t** shoulder pieces Ex 39:20
and the **t** kidneys with the fat Lv 3:4
the **t** kidneys with the fat on Lv 3:10
and the **t** kidneys with the fat Lv 3:15
and the **t** kidneys with the fat Lv 4:9
bring to the LORD **t** turtledoves Lv 5:7
turtledoves or **t** young pigeons Lv 5:7
cannot afford **t** turtledoves or Lv 5:11
turtledoves or **t** young pigeons, Lv 5:11
he may bring **t** quarts of fine Lv 5:11
t quarts of fine flour as a Lv 6:20

and the **t** kidneys with the fat Lv 7:4
offering, the **t** rams, and the Lv 8:2
the **t** kidneys with their fat, Lv 8:16
and the **t** kidneys with their fat Lv 8:25
be unclean for **t** weeks as ⌊she Lv 12:5
may take **t** turtledoves or two Lv 12:8
turtledoves or **t** young pigeons, Lv 12:8
will order that **t** live clean Lv 14:4
he must take **t** unblemished male Lv 14:10
with **t** quarts of fine flour Lv 14:21
and **t** turtledoves or two young Lv 14:22
turtledoves or **t** young pigeons, Lv 14:22
He is to take **t** birds, cedar Lv 14:49
must take **t** turtledoves or two Lv 15:14
turtledoves or **t** young pigeons Lv 15:14
day she must take **t** turtledoves Lv 15:29
turtledoves or **t** young pigeons Lv 15:29
the death of **t** of Aaron's sons Lv 16:1
community **t** male goats for Lv 16:5
will take the **t** goats and place Lv 16:7
casts lots for the **t** goats, Lv 16:8
the LORD and **t** handfuls of Lv 16:12
not crossbreed **t** different kinds Lv 19:19
fields with **t** kinds of seed, Lv 19:19
garment made of **t** kinds of Lv 19:19
Bring **t** loaves of bread from Lv 23:17
old, one young bull, and **t** rams. Lv 23:18
and **t** male lambs a year old as a Lv 23:19
the bread and the **t** lambs will Lv 23:20
Arrange them in **t** rows, six to a Lv 24:6
for her of **t** quarts of barley Nm 5:15
he is to bring **t** turtledoves or Nm 6:10
turtledoves or **t** young pigeons Nm 6:10
cart from every **t** leaders and an Nm 7:3
the Gershonites **t** carts and four Nm 7:7
t bulls, five rams, five male Nm 7:17
t bulls, five rams, five male Nm 7:23
t bulls, five rams, five male Nm 7:29
t bulls, five rams, five male Nm 7:35
t bulls, five rams, five male Nm 7:41
t bulls, five rams, five male Nm 7:47
t bulls, five rams, five male Nm 7:53
t bulls, five rams, five male Nm 7:59
t bulls, five rams, five male Nm 7:65
t bulls, five rams, five male Nm 7:71
t bulls, five rams, five male Nm 7:77
t bulls, five rams, five male Nm 7:83
from between the **t** cherubim. Nm 7:89
Whether it was **t** days, a month, Nm 9:22
Make **t** trumpets of hammered Nm 10:2
for one day, or **t** days, or five Nm 11:19
T men had remained in the camp, Nm 11:26
When the **t** of them came forward, Nm 12:5
was carried on a pole by **t** men. Nm 13:23
offering of **t** quarts of fine Nm 15:4
flour mixed with **t** quarts of oil Nm 15:9
Also present **t** quarts of wine as Nm 15:10
his **t** servants were with him. Nm 22:22
Each day ⌊present⌋ **t** unblemished Nm 28:3
with **t** quarts of fine flour Nm 28:5
day ⌊present⌋ **t** unblemished Nm 28:9
t young bulls, one ram, seven Nm 28:11
and **t** quarts of fine flour mixed Nm 28:13
are to be **t** quarts of wine with Nm 28:14
t young bulls, one ram, and Nm 28:19
Offer **t** quarts with each of the Nm 28:21
t young bulls, one ram, and Nm 28:27
and **t** quarts with each of the Nm 28:29
and **t** quarts with each of the Nm 29:4
and **t** quarts with each of the Nm 29:10
13 young bulls, **t** rams, and 14 Nm 29:13
quarts with each of the **t** rams, Nm 29:14
and **t** quarts with each of the 14 Nm 29:15
12 young bulls, **t** rams, and 14 Nm 29:17
11 bulls, **t** rams, 14 male Nm 29:20
10 bulls, **t** rams, 14 male Nm 29:23
nine bulls, **t** rams, 14 male Nm 29:26
eight bulls, **t** rams, 14 male Nm 29:29
seven bulls, **t** rams, and 14 male Nm 29:32
The **t** and a half tribes have Nm 34:15
land from the **t** Amorite kings Dt 3:8
God has done to these **t** kings. Dt 3:21
He wrote on **t** stone tablets. Dt 4:13
the **t** Amorite kings who were Dt 4:47
He wrote them on **t** stone tablets Dt 5:22
gave me the **t** stone tablets, Dt 9:10
gave me the **t** stone tablets, Dt 9:11
the **t** tablets of the covenant Dt 9:15

'Cut **t** stone tablets like the Dt 10:1
cut **t** stone tablets like the Dt 10:3
mountain with the **t** tablets in Dt 10:3
divided in **t** and chews the cud Dt 14:6
the testimony of **t** or three Dt 17:6
the testimony of **t** or three Dt 19:15
the **t** people in the dispute must Dt 19:17
If a man has **t** wives, one loved Dt 21:15
vineyard with **t** types of seed; Dt 22:9
must take the **t** of them out to Dt 22:24
If **t** men are fighting with each Dt 25:11
must not have **t** different Dt 25:13
must not have **t** differing dry Dt 25:14
or **t** put ten thousand to flight, Dt 32:30
Nun secretly sent **t** men as spies Jos 2:1
had taken the **t** men and hidden Jos 2:4
the **t** Amorite kings you Jos 2:10
So the **t** men went into the hill Jos 2:22
Joshua said to the **t** men who had Jos 6:22
He did to the **t** Amorite kings Jos 9:10
to the **t** and a half tribes Jos 14:3
of Joseph became **t** tribes, Jos 14:4
Rabbah—**t** cities, with their Jos 15:60
nine cities from these **t** tribes. Jos 21:16
its pasturelands—**t** cities. Jos 21:25
its pasturelands—**t** cities. Jos 21:27
it drove out the **t** Amorite kings Jos 24:12
king of Aram of the **T** Rivers, Jdg 3:8
a girl or **t** for each warrior, Jdg 5:30
garment or **t** for my neck?" Jdg 5:30
and Zeeb, the **t** princes of Jdg 7:25
and Zeeb, the **t** princes of Jdg 8:3
captured these **t** kings of Midian Jdg 8:12
The other **t** units rushed against Jdg 9:44
Let me wander **t** months through Jdg 11:37
And he sent her away **t** months. Jdg 11:38
At the end of **t** months, she Jdg 11:39
tied him up with **t** new ropes and Jdg 15:13
gate along with the **t** gateposts, Jdg 16:3
the Philistines for my **t** eyes." Jdg 16:28
hold of the **t** middle pillars Jdg 16:29
sat down and the **t** of them ate Jdg 19:6
afternoon and the **t** of them ate. Jdg 19:8
man had his **t** saddled donkeys Jdg 19:10
with his wife and **t** sons to live Ru 1:1
names of his **t** sons were Mahlon Ru 1:2
she was left with her **t** sons. Ru 1:3
left without her **t** children and Ru 1:5
accompanied by her **t** Ru 1:7
t of them traveled until they Ru 1:19
He had **t** wives, the first named 1Sm 1:2
where Eli's **t** sons, Hophni 1Sm 1:3
t and one-half gallons of flour, 1Sm 1:24
to three sons and **t** daughters. 1Sm 2:21
concerning your **t** sons Hophni 1Sm 2:34
Eli's **t** sons, Hophni and 1Sm 4:4
and Eli's **t** sons, Hophni 1Sm 4:11
t sons, Hophni and Phinehas, 1Sm 4:17
new cart and **t** milk cows that 1Sm 6:7
They took **t** milk cows, hitched 1Sm 6:10
you'll find **t** men at Rachel's 1Sm 10:2
are and give you **t** ⌊loaves of⌋ 1Sm 10:4
that no **t** of them were left 1Sm 11:11
names of his **t** daughters were: 1Sm 14:49
assurance the **t** of us pledged 1Sm 20:42
Then the **t** of them made a 1Sm 23:18
of bread, **t** skins of wine, 1Sm 25:18
and the **t** of them became his 1Sm 25:43
and David had his **t** wives: 1Sm 27:3
and set out with **t** of his men. 1Sm 28:8
David's **t** wives, Ahinoam the 1Sm 30:5
pressed figs and **t** clusters of 1Sm 30:12
he also rescued his **t** wives. 1Sm 30:18
and stayed at Ziklag **t** days. 2Sm 1:1
went there with his **t** wives, 2Sm 2:2
he ruled for **t** years. The house 2Sm 2:10
The **t** groups took up positions 2Sm 2:13
Saul's son had **t** men who were 2Sm 4:2
He measured every **t** cord lengths 2Sm 8:2
There were **t** men in a certain 2Sm 12:1
T years later, Absalom's 2Sm 13:23
Your servant had **t** sons. 2Sm 14:6
in Jerusalem **t** years but never 2Sm 14:28
T hundred men from Jerusalem 2Sm 15:11
peace and your **t** sons with you: 2Sm 15:27
t sons, Zadok's son Ahimaaz 2Sm 15:36
the **t** left quickly and came to 2Sm 17:18
sitting between the **t** gates when 2Sm 18:24

who were the **t** sons whom Rizpah 2Sm 21:8
Benaiah killed **t** sons of Ariel 2Sm 23:20
what he did to the **t** commanders 1Kg 2:5
he struck down **t** men more 1Kg 2:32
t of Shimei's slaves ran away to 1Kg 2:39
t women who were prostitutes 1Kg 3:16
just the **t** of us were there. 1Kg 3:18
living boy in **t** and give half to 1Kg 3:25
mine or yours. Cut ⌊him in **t**⌋!" 1Kg 3:26
and the **t** of them made a treaty. 1Kg 5:12
t months they were at home. 1Kg 5:14
he made **t** cherubim 15 feet 1Kg 6:23
The **t** doors were made of olive 1Kg 6:32
The **t** doors were made of cypress 1Kg 6:34
first door had **t** folding sides, 1Kg 6:34
door had **t** folding panels. 1Kg 6:34
He cast **t** ⌊hollow⌋ bronze 1Kg 7:15
He also made **t** capitals of cast 1Kg 7:16
pillars with **t** encircling rows 1Kg 7:18
capitals on the **t** pillars were 1Kg 7:20
gourds were cast in **t** rows when 1Kg 7:24
t pillars; bowls for the 1Kg 7:41
were on top of the **t** pillars; 1Kg 7:41
the **t** gratings for covering both 1Kg 7:41
pomegranates for the **t** gratings 1Kg 7:42
t rows of pomegranates for each 1Kg 7:42
ark except the **t** stone tablets 1Kg 8:9
Solomon had built the **t** houses, 1Kg 9:10
and **t** lions standing beside the 1Kg 10:19
and the **t** of them were alone in 1Kg 11:29
Then he made **t** gold calves, 1Kg 12:28
he reigned over Israel **t** years. 1Kg 15:25
in Tirzah; ⌊he reigned⌋ **t** years. 1Kg 16:8
you hesitate between **t** opinions? 1Kg 18:21
Let **t** bulls be given to us. 1Kg 18:23
of them like **t** little flocks 1Kg 20:27
Then seat **t** wicked men opposite 1Kg 21:10
The **t** wicked men came in and sat 1Kg 21:13
he reigned over Israel **t** years. 1Kg 22:51
the first **t** captains of 50 2Kg 1:14
So the **t** of them went on. 2Kg 2:6
while the **t** of them stood 2Kg 2:7
Then the **t** of them crossed over 2Kg 2:8
and separated the **t** of them. 2Kg 2:11
and tore them into **t** pieces. 2Kg 2:12
Then **t** female bears came out of 2Kg 2:24
to take my **t** children as his 2Kg 4:1
the door behind the **t** of them, 2Kg 4:33
please let **t** mule-loads of dirt 2Kg 5:17
now discovered that **t** young men 2Kg 5:22
of silver and **t** changes of 2Kg 5:22
of silver in **t** bags with two 2Kg 5:23
in two bags with **t** changes of 2Kg 5:23
gave them to **t** of his young men 2Kg 5:23
messengers⌋ took **t** chariots with 2Kg 7:14
T or three eunuchs looked down 2Kg 9:32
t kings couldn't stand against 2Kg 10:4
Pile them in **t** heaps at the 2Kg 10:8
t divisions that go off duty 2Kg 11:7
Samaria; ⌊he reigned⌋ **t** years. 2Kg 15:23
molded images—even **t** calves— 2Kg 17:16
he reigned **t** years in Jerusalem. 2Kg 21:19
had made in the **t** courtyards of 2Kg 23:12
gate between the **t** walls near 2Kg 25:4
As for the **t** pillars, the one 2Kg 25:16
T sons were born to Eber. 1Ch 1:19
fathered Tekoa and had **t** wives, 1Ch 4:5
Benaiah killed **t** ⌊sons of⌋ Ariel 1Ch 11:22
and **t** pair at the storehouses. 1Ch 26:17
the highway and **t** at the court. 1Ch 26:18
He made **t** cherubim of sculptured 2Ch 3:10
of the temple he made **t** pillars, 2Ch 3:15
oxen were cast in **t** rows when 2Ch 4:3
t pillars; the bowls and the 2Ch 4:12
on top of the **t** pillars; 2Ch 4:12
the **t** gratings for covering both 2Ch 4:12
pomegranates for the **t** gratings 2Ch 4:13
t rows of pomegranates for each 2Ch 4:13
ark except the **t** tablets that 2Ch 5:10
and **t** lions standing beside the 2Ch 9:18
after day until **t** full years 2Ch 21:19
acquired **t** wives for him, 2Ch 24:3
he reigned **t** years in Jerusalem. 2Ch 33:21
and **t** articles of fine gleaming Ezr 8:27
that can be done in a day or **t**, Ezr 10:13
and I appointed **t** large Neh 12:31
The **t** thanksgiving processions Neh 12:40
t eunuchs who guarded the Est 2:21

t eunuchs who guarded the Est 6:2
to celebrate these **t** days each Est 9:27
for true wisdom has **t** sides. Jb 11:6
grant ⌊these⌋ **t** things to me, Jb 13:20
these things **t** or three times Jb 33:29
with you and your **t** friends, Jb 42:7
what disaster these **t** can bring? Pr 24:22
T things I ask of You; don't Pr 30:7
The leech has **t** daughters: Pr 30:15
than **t** handfuls with effort and Ec 4:6
T are better than one because Ec 4:9
Also, if **t** lie down together, Ec 4:11
one person, **t** can resist him. Ec 4:12
Your breasts are like **t** fawns, Sg 4:5
at the dance of the **t** camps? Sg 6:13
Your breasts are like **t** fawns, Sg 7:3
with **t** he covered his face, Is 6:2
with **t** he covered his feet, Is 6:2
his feet, and with **t** he flew. Is 6:2
of these **t** smoldering stubs Is 7:4
land of the **t** kings you dread Is 7:16
raise a young cow and **t** sheep, Is 7:21
but for the **t** houses of Israel, Is 8:14
t or three berries at the very Is 17:6
and cut the iron bars in **t**. Is 45:2
These **t** things will happen to Is 47:9
These **t** things have happened to Is 51:19
from a city and **t** from a family, Jr 3:14
LORD showed me **t** baskets of figs Jr 24:1
Within **t** years I will restore to Jr 28:3
within **t** years I will break the Jr 28:11
rejected the **t** families He had Jr 33:24
they cut in **t** in order to pass Jr 34:18
the gate between the **t** walls. Jr 39:4
gate between the **t** walls near Jr 52:7
As for the **t** pillars, the one Jr 52:20
each had **t** ⌊wings⌋ touching that Ezk 1:11
of another and **t** wings covering Ezk 1:11
them also had **t** wings covering Ezk 1:23
Let the sword strike **t** times, Ezk 21:14
mark out **t** roads that the sword Ezk 21:19
at the fork of the **t** roads, Ezk 21:21
man, there were **t** women, Ezk 23:2
These **t** nations and two lands Ezk 35:10
two nations and **t** lands will be Ezk 35:10
no longer be **t** nations and will Ezk 37:22
be divided into **t** kingdoms. Ezk 37:22
gate there were **t** tables on each Ezk 40:39
there were **t** tables on one side Ezk 40:40
on one side and **t** ⌊more⌋ tables Ezk 40:40
Each cherub had **t** faces: Ezk 41:18
the doors had **t** swinging panels Ezk 41:24
There were **t** panels for one door Ezk 41:24
one door and **t** for the other. Ezk 41:24
Joseph will receive **t** shares. Ezk 47:13
canal. He had **t** horns. The two Dn 8:3
The **t** horns were long, but one Dn 8:3
shattering his **t** horns, and the Dn 8:7
The **t** kings, whose hearts are Dn 11:27
t others were standing there, Dn 12:5
He will revive us after **t** days, Hs 6:2
in bondage for their **t** crimes. Hs 10:10
t years before the earthquake. Am 1:1
Can **t** walk together without Am 3:3
snatches **t** legs or a piece Am 3:12
T or three cities staggered to Am 4:8
There are also **t** olive trees Zch 4:3
What are the **t** olive trees on Zch 4:11
What are the **t** olive branches Zch 4:12
beside the **t** gold conduits, Zch 4:12
"These are the **t** anointed ones," Zch 4:14
up and saw **t** women approaching Zch 5:9
coming from between **t** mountains. Zch 6:1
counsel between the **t** of them. Zch 6:13
I took **t** staffs, calling one Zch 11:7
called Favor and cut it in **t**, Zch 11:10
Then I cut in **t** my second staff, Zch 11:14
Bethlehem who were **t** years old Mt 2:16
He saw **t** brothers, Simon Mt 4:18
there, He saw **t** other brothers, Mt 4:21
to go one mile, go with him **t**. Mt 5:41
one can be a slave of **t** masters, Mt 6:24
t demon-possessed men met Him as Mt 8:28
on from there, **t** blind men Mt 9:27
Aren't **t** sparrows sold for a Mt 10:29
five loaves and **t** fish here," Mt 14:17
the five loaves and the **t** fish, Mt 14:19
than to have **t** hands or two feet Mt 18:8

have two hands or **t** feet and be Mt 18:8
than to have **t** eyes and be Mt 18:9
take one or **t** more with you, Mt 18:16
the testimony of **t** or three Mt 18:16
If **t** of you on earth agree about Mt 18:19
where **t** or three are gathered Mt 18:20
and the **t** will become one flesh? Mt 19:5
are no longer **t**, but one flesh. Mt 19:6
that these **t** sons of mine may Mt 20:21
indignant with the **t** brothers. Mt 20:24
There were **t** blind men sitting Mt 20:30
Jesus then sent **t** disciples, Mt 21:1
A man had **t** sons. He went to Mt 21:28
Which of the **t** did his father's Mt 21:31
depend on these **t** commandments." Mt 22:40
Then **t** men will be in the field: Mt 24:40
T women will be grinding at the Mt 24:41
to another, **t**; and to another, Mt 25:15
the man with **t** earned two more Mt 25:17
the man with two earned **t** more. Mt 25:17
Then the man with **t** talents also Mt 25:22
Master, you gave me **t** talents. Mt 25:22
I've earned **t** more talents.' Mt 25:22
takes place after **t** days, Mt 26:2
Peter and the **t** sons of Zebedee, Mt 26:37
Finally, **t** who came forward Mt 26:60
Which of the **t** do you want me to Mt 27:21
Then **t** criminals were crucified Mt 27:38
was split in **t** from top to Mt 27:51
they said, "Five, and **t** fish." Mk 6:38
the five loaves and the **t** fish, Mk 6:41
divided the **t** fish among them Mk 6:41
than to have **t** hands and go to Mk 9:43
lame than to have **t** feet and be Mk 9:45
eye than to have **t** eyes and be Mk 9:47
and the **t** will become one flesh. Mk 10:8
are no longer **t**, but one flesh. Mk 10:8
He sent **t** of His disciples Mk 11:1
dropped in **t** tiny coins worth Mk 12:42
After **t** days it was the Passover Mk 14:1
He sent **t** of His disciples and Mk 14:13
They crucified **t** criminals with Mk 15:27
was split in **t** from top to Mk 15:38
form to **t** of them walking Mk 16:12
turtledoves or **t** young pigeons Lk 2:24
The one who has **t** shirts must Lk 3:11
saw **t** boats at the edge of the Lk 5:2
John summoned **t** of his disciples Lk 7:18
A creditor had **t** debtors. Lk 7:41
than five loaves and **t** fish," Lk 9:13
the five loaves and the **t** fish, Lk 9:16
t men were talking with Him— Lk 9:30
His glory and the **t** men who were Lk 9:32
As the **t** men were departing from Lk 9:33
next day he took out **t** denarii, Lk 10:35
sparrows sold for **t** pennies? Lk 12:6
three against **t**, and two against Lk 12:52
two, and **t** against three. Lk 12:52
He also said: "A man had **t** sons. Lk 15:11
can be the slave of **t** masters, Lk 16:13
on that night **t** will be in one Lk 17:34
T women will be grinding grain Lk 17:35
T will be in a field: one will Lk 17:36
T men went up to the temple Lk 18:10
He sent **t** of the disciples Lk 19:29
widow dropping in **t** tiny coins. Lk 21:2
said, "look, here are **t** swords." Lk 22:38
T others—criminals—were also Lk 23:32
suddenly **t** men stood by them in Lk 24:4
Now that same day **t** of them were Lk 24:13
standing with **t** of his disciples Jn 1:35
The **t** disciples heard him say Jn 1:37
was one of the **t** who heard John Jn 1:40
and He stayed there **t** days. Jn 4:40
After **t** days He left there for Jn 4:43
T hundred denarii worth of bread Jn 6:7
five barley loaves and **t** fish— Jn 6:9
the witness of **t** men is valid. Jn 8:17
He stayed **t** more days in the Jn 11:6
Jerusalem (about **t** miles away). Jn 11:18
Him and **t** others with Him, Jn 19:18
The **t** were running together, Jn 20:4
saw **t** angels in white sitting Jn 20:12
and **t** others of His disciples Jn 21:2
and suddenly **t** men in white Ac 1:10
they proposed **t**: Joseph, called Ac 1:23
which of these **t** You have chosen Ac 1:24
where he fathered **t** sons. Ac 7:29

there and sent **t** men to him who Ac 9:38
he called **t** of his household Ac 10:7
was sleeping between **t** soldiers, Ac 12:6
bound with **t** chains, while Ac 12:6
And this went on for **t** years, Ac 19:10
So after sending **t** of those who Ac 19:22
all of them for about **t** hours: Ac 19:34
him to be bound with **t** chains. Ac 21:33
He summoned **t** of his centurions Ac 23:23
After **t** years had passed, Felix Ac 24:27
Then he stayed **t** whole years in Ac 28:30
The **t** will become one flesh. 1Co 6:16
should be only **t**, or at the most 1Co 14:27
T or three prophets should speak, 1Co 14:29
the testimony of **t** or three 2Co 13:1
written that Abraham had **t** sons, Gl 4:22
women represent the **t** covenants. Gl 4:24
Himself one new man from the **t**, Eph 2:15
and the **t** will become one flesh. Eph 5:31
is supported by **t** or three 1Tm 5:19
so that through **t** unchangeable Heb 6:18
the testimony of **t** or three Heb 10:28
they were sawed in **t**, they died Heb 11:37
There are still **t** more woes to Rv 9:12
I will empower my **t** witnesses, Rv 11:3
These are the **t** olive trees and Rv 11:4
trees and the **t** lampstands that Rv 11:4
because these **t** prophets Rv 11:10
woman was given **t** wings of a Rv 12:14
he had **t** horns like a lamb, Rv 13:11

TWO-EDGED *(4)*
mouths and a **t** sword in their Ps 149:6
and sharper than any **t** sword, Heb 4:12
His mouth came a sharp **t** sword; Rv 1:16
who has the sharp, **t** sword says: Rv 2:12

TWO-FIFTHS *(1)*
t of an ounce per man, that is, Ex 38:26

TWO-HORNED *(2)*
came toward the **t** ram I had seen Dn 8:6
t ram that you saw represents Dn 8:20

TWO-THIRDS *(5)*
The price was **t** of a shekel for 1Sm 13:21
long and six and **t** ⌊miles⌋ wide. Ezk 45:1
an area one and **t** ⌊of a mile⌋ Ezk 45:6
one and **t** ⌊of a mile⌋ wide and Ezk 48:15
t will be cut off and die, Zch 13:8

TYCHICUS *(5)*
and **T** and Trophimus from Asia. Ac 20:4
T, our dearly loved brother and Eph 6:21
T, a loved brother, a faithful Col 4:7
I have sent **T** to Ephesus. 2Tm 4:12
to you, or **T**, make every effort Ti 3:12

TYING *(2)*
After **t** Him up, they led Him Mt 27:2
After **t** Jesus up, they led Him Mk 15:1

TYPE *(2)*
sacrifice one **t** of what he can Lv 14:30
engaged in this **t** of business, Ac 19:25

TYPES *(1)*
vineyard with two **t** of seed; Dt 22:9

TYPICAL *(1)*
Apollos," are you not ⌊**t**⌋ men? 1Co 3:4

TYRANNUS *(1)*
day in the lecture hall of **T**. Ac 19:9

TYRANNY *(1)*
were under the **t** of the Devil, Ac 10:38

TYRANT *(1)*
the prey of a **t** will be Is 49:25

TYRANTS *(1)*
humiliate the insolence of **t**. Is 13:11

TYRE *(56)*
far as the fortified city of **T**; Jos 19:29
King Hiram of **T** sent envoys to 2Sm 5:11
the fortress of **T** and all the 2Sm 24:7
king of **T** sent his servants 1Kg 5:1
had Hiram brought from **T**. 1Kg 7:13
and his father was a man of **T**, 1Kg 7:14
Hiram king of **T** having supplied 1Kg 9:11
went out from **T** to look over 1Kg 9:12
King Hiram of **T** sent envoys to 1Ch 14:1
sent ⌊word⌋ to King Hiram of **T**: 2Ch 2:3
King Hiram of **T** wrote a letter 2Ch 2:11
His father is a man of **T**. 2Ch 2:14
to the people of Sidon and **T**, Ezr 3:7
The daughter of **T**, the wealthy Ps 45:12
with the inhabitants of **T**. Ps 83:7
Philistia, **T**, and Cush—each Ps 87:4
An oracle against **T**: Wail, ships Is 23:1
anguish over the news about **T**. Is 23:5
Who planned this against **T**, Is 23:8
On that day **T** will be forgotten Is 23:15
the prostitute will happen to **T**: Is 23:15
will restore **T** and she will go Is 23:17
the kings of **T**, all the kings Jr 25:22
the king of **T**, and the king of Jr 27:3
cut off from **T** and Sidon every Jr 47:4
because **T** said about Jerusalem: Ezk 26:2
See, I am against you, **T**! Ezk 26:3
the walls of **T** and demolish her Ezk 26:4
against **T** from the north with Ezk 26:7
is what the Lord GOD says to **T**: Ezk 26:15
Now, son of man, lament for **T**. Ezk 27:2
Say to **T**, who is located at the Ezk 27:3
Lord GOD says: **T**, you declared: Ezk 27:3
wise men were within you, **T**; Ezk 27:8
Who was like **T**, silenced in the Ezk 27:32
of man, say to the ruler of **T**: Ezk 28:2
the king of **T** and say to him: Ezk 28:12
labor strenuously against **T**. Ezk 29:18
from **T** for the labor he Ezk 29:18
I have seen Ephraim like **T**, Hs 9:13
T, Sidon, and all the Jl 3:4
from punishing **T** for three Am 1:9
fire against the walls of **T**, Am 1:10
it, as well as **T** and Sidon, Zch 9:2
T has built herself a fortress; Zch 9:3
had been done in **T** and Sidon, Mt 11:21
more tolerable for **T** and Sidon Mt 11:22
to the area of **T** and Sidon. Mt 15:21
Jordan, and around **T** and Sidon. Mk 3:8
to the region of **T** and Sidon. Mk 7:24
the region of **T**, He went by way Mk 7:31
the seacoast of **T** and Sidon. Lk 6:17
had been done in **T** and Sidon, Lk 10:13
more tolerable for **T** and Sidon Lk 10:14
on to Syria and arrived at **T**, Ac 21:3
we completed our voyage from **T**, Ac 21:7

TYRE'S *(1)*
T revenue was the grain from Is 23:3

TYRIANS *(3)*
the Sidonians and **T** had brought 1Ch 22:4
T living there were importing Neh 13:16
angry with the **T** and Sidonians. Ac 12:20

U

UCAL *(1)*
to Ithiel, to Ithiel and **U**: Pr 30:1

UEL *(1)*
descendants: Maadai, Amram, **U**, Ezr 10:34

UGLY *(4)*
other cows—**u**, very sickly, Gn 41:19
never seen such **u** ones as these Gn 41:19
u cows ate the first seven Gn 41:20
u cows that came up after them Gn 41:27

ULAI *(2)*
that I was beside the **U** Canal. Dn 8:2
from the middle of the **U**: Dn 8:16

ULAM *(2)*
and his sons were **U** and Rekem. 1Ch 7:16
U was his firstborn, Jeush 1Ch 8:39

ULAM'S *(2)*
U son: Bedan. These were the 1Ch 7:17
U sons were warriors and archers. 1Ch 8:40

ULLA'S *(1)*
U sons: Arah, Hanniel, and Rizia. 1Ch 7:39

ULTERIOR *(1)*
he brings it with **u** motives! Pr 21:27

ULTIMATELY *(2)*
u, the LORD struck him and he 2Ch 13:20
will not be blessed **u**. Pr 20:21

UMBILICAL *(1)*
your **u** cord wasn't cut on the Ezk 16:4

UMMAH *(1)*
U, Aphek, and Rehob—22 cities, Jos 19:30

UNABLE *(42)*
the land was **u** to support them Gn 13:6
that they were **u** to find the Gn 19:11
will be **u** to drink water Ex 7:18
If he is **u**, he is to be sold Ex 22:3
Moses was **u** to enter the tent of Ex 40:35
they were **u** to explain the Jdg 14:14
were **u** to annihilate— 1Kg 9:21
And they were **u** to eat it. 2Kg 4:40
and **u** to assert himself against 2Ch 13:7
Immer but were **u** to prove that Ezr 2:59
but were **u** to prove that their Neh 7:61
me; I am **u** to see. They are Ps 40:12
I am **u** to ⌊reach⌋ it. Ps 139:6
man is **u** to speak. The eye Ec 1:8
that man is **u** to discover the Ec 8:17
know it, he is **u** to discover it. Ec 8:17
you will be **u** to ward it off. Is 47:11
man, like a warrior **u** to save? Jr 14:9
hide himself, but he will be **u**. Jr 49:10
be mute and **u** to rebuke them, Ezk 3:26
and gold will be **u** to save them Ezk 7:19
man who was **u** to speak was Mt 9:32
who was blind and **u** to speak was Mt 12:22
deformed, those **u** to speak, and Mt 15:30
they saw those **u** to speak Mt 15:31
and people **u** to speak, talk! Mk 7:37
that makes him **u** to speak. Mk 9:17
silent and **u** to speak until Lk 1:20
and therefore I'm **u** to come.' Lk 14:20
is why they were **u** to believe, Jn 12:39
The world is **u** to receive Him Jn 14:17
a branch is **u** to produce fruit Jn 15:4
be defiled and **u** to eat the Jn 18:28
and they were **u** to haul it in Jn 21:6
for we are **u** to stop speaking Ac 4:20
But they were **u** to stand up Ac 6:10
He was **u** to see for three days, Ac 9:9
caught and was **u** to head into Ac 27:15
God's law, for it is **u** to do so. Rm 8:7
the flesh are **u** to please God. Rm 8:8
they were **u** to enter because Heb 3:19
priest who is **u** to sympathize Heb 4:15

UNADULTERATED *(1)*
desire the **u** spiritual milk, 1Pt 2:2

UNAFFECTED *(3)*
be **u** by this bitter water that Nm 5:19
she will be **u** and will be able Nm 5:28
their robes were **u**, and there Dn 3:27

UNAFRAID *(3)*
be firmly established and **u**. Jb 11:15
the river rages, Behemoth is **u**; Jb 40:23
you want to be **u** of the Rm 13:3

UNANIMOUSLY *(4)*
the prophets are **u** favorable for 1Kg 22:13
the prophets are **u** favorable for 2Ch 18:12
their voices to God **u** and said, Ac 4:24
we have **u** decided to select men Ac 15:25

UNANSWERED *(1)*
of words go **u** and such a talker Jb 11:2

UNAPPROACHABLE *(1)*
dwelling in **u** light, whom none 1Tm 6:16

UNATTRACTIVE *(1)*
their faces **u** so their fasting Mt 6:16

UNAUTHORIZED *(12)*
An **u** person must not eat ⌊them⌋, Ex 29:33
must not offer **u** incense on it, Ex 30:9
some of it on an **u** person must Ex 30:33
and presented **u** fire before the Lv 10:1
Any **u** person who comes near ⌊it⌋ Nm 1:51
they presented **u** fire before Nm 3:4
but any **u** person who comes near Nm 3:10
Any **u** person who came near ⌊it⌋ Nm 3:38
that no **u** person outside Nm 16:40
but no **u** person may come near Nm 18:4
but an **u** person who comes near Nm 18:7
they presented **u** fire before Nm 26:61

UNAVOIDABLE *(1)*
words, sin is **u**, but the one who Pr 10:19

UNAWARE *(9)*
of Sirah, but David was **u** of it. 2Sm 3:26
but they were **u** ⌊of what they 2Kg 4:39
insignificant, he is **u** of it. Jb 14:21
for you. He will be **u** of it. Ob 7
Or are you **u** that all of us who Rm 6:3
are you **u** that the law has Rm 7:1
you to be **u** of this mystery: Rm 11:25
I do not want you to be **u**. 1Co 12:1
For we don't want you to be **u**, 2Co 1:8

UNBELIEF *(10)*
there because of their **u**. Mt 13:58
And He was amazed at their **u**. Mk 6:6
out, "I do believe! Help my **u**." Mk 9:24
He rebuked their **u** and hardness Mk 16:14
will their **u** cancel God's Rm 3:3
not waver in **u** at God's promise Rm 4:20
they were broken off by **u**, Rm 11:20
if they do not remain in **u**, Rm 11:23
ignorance that I had acted in **u**, 1Tm 1:13
unable to enter because of **u**. Heb 3:19

UNBELIEVER *(6)*
let him be like an **u** and a tax Mt 18:17
Don't be an **u**, but a believer." Jn 20:27
But if the **u** leaves, let him 1Co 7:15
and some **u** or uninformed person 1Co 14:24
have in common with an **u**? 2Co 6:15
faith and is worse than an **u**. 1Tm 5:8

UNBELIEVERS *(10)*
assign him a place with the **u**. Lk 12:46
be rescued from the **u** in Judea, Rm 15:31
brother, and that before **u**! 1Co 6:6
If one of the **u** invites you over 1Co 10:27
not to believers but to **u**. 1Co 14:22
is not for **u** but for believers. 1Co 14:22
who are uninformed or **u** come 1Co 14:23
minds of the **u** so they cannot 2Co 4:4
Do not be mismatched with **u**. 2Co 6:14
the cowards, **u**, vile, murderers Rv 21:8

UNBELIEVING *(10)*
You **u** and rebellious generation! Mt 17:17
to them, "You **u** generation! Mk 9:19
You **u** and rebellious generation! Lk 9:41
If any brother has an **u** wife, 1Co 7:12
if any woman has an **u** husband, 1Co 7:13
For the **u** husband is sanctified 1Co 7:14
and the **u** wife is sanctified by 1Co 7:14
defiled and **u** nothing is pure Ti 1:15
u heart that departs from the Heb 3:12
for the **u**, The stone that the 1Pt 2:7

UNBLEMISHED *(44)*
You must have an **u** animal, Ex 12:5
a young bull and two **u** rams, Ex 29:1
herd, he is to bring an **u** male. Lv 1:3
he is to present an **u** male. Lv 1:10
u bull as a sin offering for the Lv 4:3
is to bring an **u** male goat as Lv 4:23
is to bring an **u** female goat as Lv 4:28
he is to bring an **u** female. Lv 4:32
an **u** ram from the flock by your Lv 5:15
He must bring an **u** ram from the Lv 5:18
an **u** ram from the flock, Lv 6:6
he must take two **u** male lambs, Lv 14:10
male lambs, an **u** year-old ewe Lv 14:10
must offer an **u** male from the Lv 22:19
it has to be **u** to be acceptable; Lv 22:21
the bread seven **u** male lambs a Lv 23:18
the LORD of one **u** year-old male Nm 6:14
one **u** year-old female lamb as a Nm 6:14
one **u** ram as a fellowship Nm 6:14
to bring you an **u** red cow that Nm 19:2
⌊present⌋ two **u** year-old male Nm 28:3
⌊present⌋ two **u** year-old male Nm 28:9
lambs a year old—⌊all⌋ **u**— Nm 28:11
Your animals are to be **u**. Nm 28:19
Your animals are to be **u**. Nm 28:31
lambs a year old—⌊all⌋ **u**— Nm 29:2
⌊All⌋ your animals are to be **u**. Nm 29:8
They are to be **u**. Nm 29:13
lambs a year old—⌊all⌋ **u**— Nm 29:17
lambs a year old—⌊all⌋ **u**— Nm 29:20
lambs a year old—⌊all⌋ **u**— Nm 29:23
lambs a year old—⌊all⌋ **u**— Nm 29:26
lambs a year old—⌊all⌋ **u**— Nm 29:29
lambs a year old—⌊all⌋ **u**— Nm 29:32
lambs a year old—⌊all⌋ **u**— Nm 29:36
are to present an **u** male goat as Ezk 43:22
u bull and an unblemished ram Ezk 43:23
and an **u** ram from the flock. Ezk 43:23
the flock, both **u**, must also be Ezk 43:25
u bull and purify the sanctuary. Ezk 45:18
day is to be six **u** lambs and an Ezk 46:4
unblemished lambs and an **u** ram. Ezk 46:4
to be a young, **u** bull, as well Ezk 46:6
must offer an **u** year-old male Ezk 46:13

UNCEASING *(1)*
peoples in anger with **u** blows. Is 14:6

UNCEASINGLY *(1)*
My eyes overflow **u**, without end, Lm 3:49

UNCERTAIN *(1)*
u which one He was speaking Jn 13:22

UNCERTAINTY *(1)*
their hope on the **u** of wealth, 1Tm 6:17

UNCHANGEABLE *(3)*
But He is **u**; who can oppose Him? Jb 23:13
to show His **u** purpose even more Heb 6:17
so that through two **u** things, Heb 6:18

UNCHANGED *(2)*
infection remains **u** in his sight Lv 13:5
outbreak remains **u** and black Lv 13:37

UNCIRCUMCISED *(44)*
our sister to an **u** man is a Gn 34:14
But no **u** person may eat it. Ex 12:48
and if their **u** hearts will be Lv 26:41
They were still **u**, since they Jos 5:7
you go to the **u** Philistines for Jdg 14:3
fall into the hands of the **u**?" Jdg 15:18
to the garrison of these **u** men. 1Sm 14:6
who is this **u** Philistine that 1Sm 17:26
this **u** Philistine will be like 1Sm 17:36
or these **u** men will come and run 1Sm 31:4
daughters of the **u** will gloat. 2Sm 1:20
or these **u** men will come and 1Ch 10:4
For the **u** and the unclean will Is 52:1
their ear is **u**, so they cannot Jr 6:10
all the circumcised yet **u**: Jr 9:25
nations are **u**, and the whole Jr 9:26
house of Israel is **u** in heart." Jr 9:26
the death of the **u** at the hands Ezk 28:10
lie among the **u** with those slain Ezk 31:18
and be laid to rest with the **u**! Ezk 32:19
the **u** lie slain by the sword. Ezk 32:21
went down to the underworld **u**, Ezk 32:24
All of them are **u**, slain by the Ezk 32:25
All of them are **u**, slain by the Ezk 32:26
the fallen warriors of the **u**, Ezk 32:27
and will lie down among the **u**, Ezk 32:28
down with the **u**, with those who Ezk 32:29
They lie down **u** with those slain Ezk 32:30
be laid to rest among the **u**, Ezk 32:32
u in both heart and flesh, Ezk 44:7
No foreigner, **u** in heart and Ezk 44:9
people with **u** hearts and ears! Ac 7:51
visited **u** men and ate with them! Ac 11:3
Therefore if an **u** man keeps the Rm 2:26
A man who is physically **u**, Rm 2:27
faith and the **u** through faith. Rm 3:30
Or is it also for the **u**? Rm 4:9
while he was circumcised, or **u**? Rm 4:10
while he was circumcised, but **u**. Rm 4:10
he had by faith while still **u**. Rm 4:11
Abraham had while still **u**. Rm 4:12
Was anyone called while **u**? 1Co 7:18
with the gospel for the **u**, Gl 2:7
called "the **u**" by those called Eph 2:11

UNCIRCUMCISION *(8)*
also—drink, and expose your **u**! Hab 2:16
your circumcision has become **u**. Rm 2:25
will his **u** not be counted as Rm 2:26
matter and **u** does not matter, 1Co 7:19
circumcision nor **u** accomplishes Gl 5:6
circumcision and **u** mean nothing; Gl 6:15
and in the **u** of your flesh, Col 2:13
circumcision and **u**, barbarian, Col 3:11

UNCLE *(12)*
Jacob saw his **u** Laban's daughter Gn 29:10
and watered his **u** Laban's sheep. Gn 29:10
sons of Aaron's **u** Uzziel, and Lv 10:4
his aunt, he has shamed his **u**; Lv 20:20
His **u** or cousin may redeem him, Lv 25:49
Saul's **u** asked him and his 1Sm 10:14
me," Saul's **u** asked, "what did 1Sm 10:15
was Abner son of Saul's **u** Ner. 1Sm 14:50
Jehoiachin's **u**, king in his 2Kg 24:17
David's **u** Jonathan was a 1Ch 27:32
u of Mordecai who had adopted Est 2:15
the son of your **u** Shallum, Jr 32:7

UNCLEAN *(212)*
clean animals, **u** animals, birds, Gn 7:8
if⌋ someone touches anything **u**— Lv 5:2
a carcass of an **u** wild animal, Lv 5:2
wild animal, or **u** livestock, Lv 5:2
or an **u** swarming creature— Lv 5:2
aware of it, he is **u** and guilty. Lv 5:2
touches anything **u** must not be Lv 7:19
sacrifice while he is **u**, Lv 7:20
If someone touches anything **u**, Lv 7:21
uncleanness, an **u** animal, or any Lv 7:21
animal, or any **u**, detestable Lv 7:21
common, and the clean and the **u**, Lv 10:10
have hooves—it is **u** for you; Lv 11:4
have hooves—it is **u** for you; Lv 11:5
have hooves—it is **u** for you; Lv 11:6
chew the cud—it is **u** for you. Lv 11:7
carcasses—they are **u** for you. Lv 11:8
These will make you **u**. Lv 11:24
will be **u** until evening, Lv 11:24
and will be **u** until evening. Lv 11:25
not chew the cud are **u** for you. Lv 11:26
Whoever touches them becomes **u**. Lv 11:26
on their paws are **u** for you. Lv 11:27
will be **u** until evening, Lv 11:27
and will be **u** until evening. Lv 11:28
evening. They are **u** for you. Lv 11:28
on the ground are **u** for you: Lv 11:29
These are **u** for you among all Lv 11:31
dead will be **u** until evening. Lv 11:31
falls on anything it becomes **u**— Lv 11:32
and will remain **u** until evening; Lv 11:32
everything in it will become **u**; Lv 11:33
with ⌊that **u**⌋ water will become Lv 11:34
unclean⌋ water will become **u**, Lv 11:34
in any container will become **u**. Lv 11:34
falls on will become **u**. Lv 11:35
it is **u** and will remain unclean Lv 11:35
and will remain **u** for you. Lv 11:35
a carcass ⌊in it⌋ will become **u**. Lv 11:36
falls on it, it is **u** for you. Lv 11:38
carcass will be **u** until evening. Lv 11:39
and will be **u** until evening. Lv 11:40
and will be **u** until evening. Lv 11:40
do not become **u** or defiled by Lv 11:43
between the **u** and the clean, Lv 11:47
she will be **u** seven days, as she Lv 12:2
she will be **u** for two weeks as Lv 12:5
him, he must pronounce him **u**. Lv 13:3
the priest must pronounce him **u**; Lv 13:8
the priest must pronounce him **u**. Lv 13:11
not quarantine him, for he is **u**. Lv 13:11
appears on him, he will be **u**. Lv 13:14
flesh, he must pronounce him **u**. Lv 13:15
Raw flesh is **u**; it is a skin Lv 13:15
the priest must pronounce him **u**; Lv 13:20
the priest must pronounce him **u**; Lv 13:22
The priest must pronounce him **u**; Lv 13:25
the priest must pronounce him **u**; Lv 13:27
must pronounce the person **u**. Lv 13:30
yellow hair; the person is **u**. Lv 13:36
disease; he is **u**. The priest Lv 13:44
The priest must pronounce him **u**; Lv 13:44
mouth and cry out, '**U**, unclean!' Lv 13:45
mouth and cry out, 'Unclean, **u**!' Lv 13:45
He will remain **u** as long as he Lv 13:46
infection; he is **u**. He must live Lv 13:46
is harmful mildew; it is **u**. Lv 13:51
has not changed, it is **u**. Lv 13:55
to pronounce it clean or **u**." Lv 13:59
nothing in the house becomes **u**. Lv 14:36
thrown into an **u** place outside Lv 14:40
be dumped in an **u** place outside Lv 14:41
harmful mildew; the house is **u**. Lv 14:44
outside the city to an **u** place. Lv 14:45
it will be **u** until evening. Lv 14:46
when something is **u** or clean. Lv 14:57
from his body, he is **u**. Lv 15:2
or retains it, he is **u**. Lv 15:3
of his discharge, he is **u**. Lv 15:3
the discharge lies on will be **u**, Lv 15:4
furniture he sits on will be **u**. Lv 15:4
he will remain **u** until evening. Lv 15:5
he will remain **u** until evening. Lv 15:6
he will remain **u** until evening. Lv 15:7
he will remain **u** until evening. Lv 15:8
discharge rides on will be **u**. Lv 15:9
him will be **u** until evening, Lv 15:10
he will remain **u** until evening. Lv 15:10
he will remain **u** until evening. Lv 15:11
he will remain **u** until evening. Lv 15:16
it will remain **u** until evening. Lv 15:17
will remain **u** until evening. Lv 15:18
she will be **u** because of her Lv 15:19

her will be **u** until evening. Lv 15:19
her menstruation will become **u**, Lv 15:20
she sits on will become **u**. Lv 15:20
he will remain **u** until evening. Lv 15:21
he will remain **u** until evening. Lv 15:22
it he will be **u** until evening. Lv 15:23
he will be **u** for seven days, Lv 15:24
bed he lies on will become **u**. Lv 15:24
will be **u** all the days of her Lv 15:25
all the days of her **u** discharge, Lv 15:25
sits on will be **u** as in her Lv 15:26
who touches them will be **u**; Lv 15:27
he will remain **u** until evening. Lv 15:27
LORD because of her **u** discharge. Lv 15:30
of semen, becoming **u** by it; Lv 15:32
man who sleeps with an **u** woman." Lv 15:33
he will remain **u** until evening; Lv 17:15
the clean animal from the **u** one, Lv 20:25
and the **u** bird from the clean Lv 20:25
set these apart as **u** for you. Lv 20:25
ceremonially **u** for a ⌊dead⌋ Lv 21:1
may make himself **u** for his young Lv 21:3
to make himself **u** for those Lv 21:4
or make himself **u** ⌊even⌋ for his Lv 21:11
anything made **u** by a dead person Lv 22:4
that makes him **u** or any person Lv 22:5
or any person who makes him **u**— Lv 22:5
will remain **u** until evening Lv 22:6
beasts, making himself **u** by it; Lv 22:8
any of the **u** animals that may Lv 27:11
If it is one of the **u** livestock, Lv 27:27
men who were **u** because of a Nm 9:6
We are **u** because of a human Nm 9:7
descendants is **u** because of a Nm 9:10
the firstborn of an **u** animal. Nm 18:15
ceremonially **u** until evening. Nm 19:7
he will remain **u** until evening. Nm 19:8
he will remain **u** until evening. Nm 19:10
corpse will be **u** for seven days. Nm 19:11
He remains **u** because the water Nm 19:13
tent will be **u** for seven days, Nm 19:14
without a lid tied on it is **u**. Nm 19:15
grave, will be **u** for seven days Nm 19:16
purification of⌋ the **u** person, Nm 19:17
is to sprinkle the **u** person on Nm 19:19
he purifies the **u** person on the Nm 19:19
a person who is **u** and does not Nm 19:20
been sprinkled on him; he is **u**. Nm 19:20
will be **u** until evening. Nm 19:21
Anything the **u** person touches Nm 19:22
person touches will become **u**, Nm 19:22
it⌋ will be **u** until evening." Nm 19:22
make the land **u** where you live Nm 35:34
who are clean or **u** may eat it, Dt 12:15
the clean and the **u** may eat it. Dt 12:22
hooves—they are **u** for you; Dt 14:7
chew⌋ the cud—it is **u** for you. Dt 14:8
and scales—it is **u** for you. Dt 14:10
winged insects are **u** for you; Dt 14:19
both the **u** person and the clean Dt 15:22
among you who is **u** because of a Dt 23:10
or removed any of it while **u**, Dt 26:14
beverages, or to eat anything **u**; Jdg 13:4
and do not eat anything **u**, Jdg 13:7
And she must not eat anything **u**. Jdg 13:14
he must be ceremonially **u**— 1Sm 20:26
yes, that's it, he is **u**." 1Sm 20:26
that nothing **u** could enter for 2Ch 23:19
lambs⌋ for every **u** person to 2Ch 30:17
Zebulun—were **u**, yet they had 2Ch 30:18
clean and the **u**, for the one who Ec 9:2
I am a man of **u** lips and live Is 6:5
live among a people of **u** lips, Is 6:5
The **u** will not travel on it, Is 35:8
and the **u** will no longer enter Is 52:1
Do not touch anything **u**; Is 52:11
us have become like something **u**, Is 64:6
You are **u**—for how long yet? Jr 13:27
"Stay away! U!" people shouted Lm 4:15
ceremonially **u**—among the Ezk 4:13
between the clean and the **u**. Ezk 22:26
between the clean and the **u**. Ezk 44:23
they will eat **u** food in Assyria Hs 9:3
prophets and the **u** spirit from Zch 13:2
them authority over **u** spirits, Mt 10:1
When an **u** spirit comes out of a Mt 12:43
then a man with an **u** spirit was Mk 1:23
And the **u** spirit convulsed him, Mk 1:26
He commands even the **u** spirits, Mk 1:27
Whenever the **u** spirits saw Him, Mk 3:11
saying, "He has an **u** spirit." Mk 3:30
a man with an **u** spirit came out Mk 5:2
out of the man, you **u** spirit!" Mk 5:8
Then the **u** spirits came out and Mk 5:13
them authority over **u** spirits. Mk 6:7
were eating their bread with **u**— Mk 7:2
bread with ritually **u** hands?" Mk 7:5
daughter had an **u** spirit came Mk 7:25
He rebuked the **u** spirit, saying Mk 9:25
a man with an **u** demonic spirit Lk 4:33
He commands the **u** spirits with Lk 4:36
tormented by **u** spirits were made Lk 6:18
commanded the **u** spirit to come Lk 8:29
But Jesus rebuked the **u** spirit, Lk 9:42
When an **u** spirit comes out of a Lk 11:24
who were tormented by **u** spirits, Ac 5:16
For **u** spirits, crying out with a Ac 8:7
eaten anything common and **u**!" Ac 10:14
not call any person common or **u**. Ac 10:28
common or **u** has ever entered Ac 11:8
that nothing is **u** in itself. Rm 14:14
who considers a thing to be **u**, Rm 14:14
be unclean, to that one it is **u**. Rm 14:14
your children would be **u**, 1Co 7:14
do not touch any **u** thing, and I 2Co 6:17
Then I saw three **u** spirits like Rv 16:13
a haunt for every **u** spirit, Rv 18:2
haunt for every **u** bird, and a Rv 18:2
haunt for every **u** and despicable Rv 18:2

UNCLEANNESS *(19)*
Or ⌊if⌋ he touches human **u**— Lv 5:3
any **u** by which one can become Lv 5:3
whether human **u**, an unclean Lv 7:21
one to be purified from his **u**. Lv 14:19
This is **u** of his discharge: Lv 15:3
the Israelites from their **u**, Lv 15:31
in a state of **u** yet approaches Lv 22:3
him unclean—whatever his **u**— Lv 22:5
and his **u** is still on him. Nm 19:13
purifying herself from her **u**. 2Sm 11:4
from the **u** of the Gentiles Ezr 6:21
end with their **u** by their Ezr 9:11
Her **u** ⌊stains⌋ her skirts. Lm 1:9
I will purge your **u**. Ezk 22:15
of the indecency of your **u**— Ezk 24:13
not be purified from your **u**— Ezk 24:13
I will save you from all your **u**. Ezk 36:29
to their **u** and transgressions Ezk 39:24
and have not repented of the **u**, 2Co 12:21

UNCLEAR *(1)*
if the trumpet makes an **u** sound, 1Co 14:8

UNCLOTHED *(1)*
do not want to be **u** but clothed, 2Co 5:4

UNCONDEMNED *(1)*
is a Roman citizen and is **u**?" Ac 22:25

UNCONFINED *(1)*
to a spacious and **u** place. Jb 36:16

UNCONTROLLABLY *(1)*
Isaac began to tremble **u**. Gn 27:33

UNCORRUPTED *(1)*
imperishable, **u**, and unfading, 1Pt 1:4

UNCOVER *(3)*
a man like me could **u** the truth Gn 44:15
lying, go in and **u** his feet, and Ru 3:4
I will **u** his secret places. Jr 49:10

UNCOVERED *(11)*
and **u** himself inside his tent. Gn 9:21
and she has **u** the source of her Lv 20:18
a trance⌋ with ⌊his⌋ eyes **u**: Nm 24:4
a trance⌋ with ⌊his⌋ eyes **u**: Nm 24:16
in secretly, **u** his feet, and lay Ru 3:7
horsemen, and Kir **u** the shield. Is 22:6
will be **u**, and your shame Is 47:3
nothing covered that won't be **u**, Mt 10:26
nothing covered that won't be **u**, Lk 12:2
with her head **u** dishonors her 1Co 11:5
to pray to God with her head **u**? 1Co 11:13

UNCOVERS *(2)*
When a man **u** a pit or digs a Ex 21:33
He **u** their ears at that time and Jb 33:16

UNCULTIVATED *(2)*
to let it rest and leave it **u**, Ex 23:11
⌊the land⌋ **u** in the seventh Neh 10:31

UNCUT *(3)*
Use **u** stones to build the altar Dt 27:6
an altar of **u** stones on which no Jos 8:31
While still **u** shoots, they would Jb 8:12

UNDEFILED *(3)*
holy, innocent, **u**, separated Heb 7:26
and the marriage bed kept **u**, Heb 13:4
Pure and **u** religion before our Jms 1:27

UNDENIABLE *(1)*
these things are **u**, you must Ac 19:36

UNDER *(372)*
(See pp. xi-xii.)

UNDERFOOT *(3)*
Trample **u** those with bars of Ps 68:30
drunkards will be trampled **u**. Is 28:3
and ground them **u** in My fury; Is 63:3

UNDERGARMENTS *(5)*
them linen **u** to cover ⌊their Ex 28:42
headbands of fine linen, the **u**, Ex 39:28
on his linen robe and linen **u**. Lv 6:10
and linen **u** are to be on his Lv 16:4
heads and linen **u** around their Ezk 44:18

UNDERGOING *(3)*
since you are **u** the same Lk 23:40
No one **u** a trial should say, Jms 1:13
an example by **u** the punishment Jd 7

UNDERGROUND *(2)*
the **u** springs made it tall, Ezk 31:4
I closed off the **u** deep because Ezk 31:15

UNDERMINE *(1)*
But you even **u** the fear ⌊of God⌋ Jb 15:4

UNDERMINED *(1)*
good advice be **u** in order to 2Sm 17:14

UNDERMINES *(1)*
but wickedness **u** the sinner. Pr 13:6

UNDERNEATH *(5)*
and **u** are the everlasting arms. Dt 33:27
in his tent, with the money **u**. Jos 7:22
U the four corners of the basin 1Kg 7:30
the 12 oxen **u** the reservoir; 1Kg 7:44
reservoir and the 12 oxen **u** it, 2Ch 4:15

UNDERSIDES *(1)*
His **u** are jagged potsherds, Jb 41:30

UNDERSTAND *(140)*
U that I am bringing a deluge— Gn 6:17
U that I am confirming My Gn 9:9
they will not **u** one another's Gn 11:7
u that God will be a witness Gn 31:50
U today that I have acquired you Gn 47:23
U that the LORD has given you Ex 16:29
But **u** that today the LORD your Dt 9:3
U that the LORD your God is not Dt 9:6
You must **u** today that it is not Dt 11:2
whose language you don't **u**, Dt 28:49
has not given you a mind to **u**, Dt 29:4
they would **u** their fate. Dt 32:29
for yourself to **u** justice, 1Kg 3:11
in Aramaic, since we **u** ⌊it⌋. 2Kg 18:26
He enabled me to **u** everything in 1Ch 28:19
women, and those who could **u**. Neh 8:3
people could **u** what was read. Neh 8:8
who is able to **u** and who has Neh 10:28
Hear it and **u** ⌊it⌋ for yourself. Jb 5:27
Help me **u** what I did wrong. Jb 6:24
⌊What⌋ do you **u** that is not Jb 15:9
then **u** that it is God who has Jb 19:6
and **u** what He would say to me. Jb 23:5
Who can **u** His mighty thunder? Jb 26:14
the elderly who **u** how to judge. Jb 32:9
and did not **u** any of His ways Jb 34:27
Can anyone **u** how the clouds Jb 36:29
Do you **u** how the clouds float, Jb 37:16
spoke about things I did not **u**, Jb 42:3
Will evildoers never **u**? Ps 14:4
U this, you who forget God, or I Ps 50:22
Will evildoers never **u**? Ps 53:4
they will **u** what He has done. Ps 64:9
When I tried to **u** all this, Ps 73:16
I was a fool and didn't **u**; Ps 73:22
They do not know or **u**; Ps 82:5
know, a fool does not **u** this: Ps 92:6
Help me **u** the meaning of Your Ps 119:27
Help me **u** Your instruction, Ps 119:34
I **u** more than the elders because Ps 119:100
You **u** my thoughts from far away. Ps 139:2

then you will **u** the fear of the Pr 2:5
Then you will **u** righteousness, Pr 2:9
so how can anyone **u** his own way? Pr 20:24
Evil men do not **u** justice, Pr 28:5
who seek the LORD **u** everything. Pr 28:5
one does not **u** these concerns. Pr 29:7
and I lack man's ability to **u**. Pr 30:2
are beyond me; four I can't **u**: Pr 30:18
My people do not **u**." Is 1:3
Keep listening, but do not **u**; Is 6:9
their ears, **u** with their minds Is 6:10
will cause you to **u** the message. Is 28:19
"He doesn't **u** ⌊what he's doing⌋"? Is 29:16
in Aramaic, for we **u** ⌊it⌋; Is 36:11
consider and **u**, that the hand Is 41:20
believe Me and **u** that I am He. Is 43:10
do not comprehend and cannot **u**, Is 44:18
their minds so they cannot **u**. Is 44:18
they will **u** what they had not Is 52:15
For they don't **u** the way of the Jr 5:4
and whose speech you do not **u**. Jr 5:15
the man wise enough to **u** this? Jr 9:12
desperately sick—who can **u** it? Jr 17:9
to come you will **u** it clearly. Jr 23:20
In time to come you will **u** it. Jr 30:24
whose words you cannot **u**. Ezk 3:6
they will **u**, though they are Ezk 12:3
a dream and am anxious to **u** it." Dn 2:3
and that you may **u** the thoughts Dn 2:30
which do not see or hear or **u**. Dn 5:23
the vision and trying to **u** it, Dn 8:15
u that the vision refers to the Dn 8:17
the vision and could not **u** it. Dn 8:27
the message and **u** the vision: Dn 9:23
and **u** this: From the issuing Dn 9:25
U the words that I'm saying to Dn 10:11
you purposed to **u** and to humble Dn 10:12
to help you **u** what will happen Dn 10:14
I heard but did not **u**. Dn 12:8
none of the wicked will **u**, Dn 12:10
understand, but the wise will **u**. Dn 12:10
whoever is wise **u** these things, Hs 14:9
and those who **u** from the hill Ob 8
LORD's intentions or **u** His plan, Mc 4:12
hearing they do not listen or **u**. Mt 13:13
listen and listen, yet never **u**; Mt 13:14
u with their hearts and turn Mt 13:15
the kingdom and doesn't **u** it, Mt 13:19
He told them, "Listen and **u**: Mt 15:10
Don't you **u** yet? Don't you Mt 16:9
is it you don't **u** that when I Mt 16:11
holy place" (let the reader **u**), Mt 24:15
listen and listen, yet not **u**; Mk 4:12
Do you not **u** this parable? Mk 4:13
How then will you **u** any of the Mk 4:13
these, as they were able to **u**. Mk 4:33
Listen to Me, all of you, and **u**: Mk 7:14
Do you not yet **u** or comprehend? Mk 8:17
said to them, "Don't you **u** yet?" Mk 8:21
they did not **u** this statement, Mk 9:32
let the reader **u**), "then those Mk 13:14
I don't know or **u** what you're Mk 14:68
they did not **u** what He said to Lk 2:50
and hearing they may not **u**. Lk 8:10
they did not **u** this statement; Lk 9:45
their minds to **u** the Scriptures. Lk 24:45
will **u** whether the teaching is Jn 7:17
Why don't you **u** what I say? Jn 8:43
but they did not **u** what He was Jn 10:6
will know and **u** that the Father Jn 10:38
did not **u** these things at Jn 12:16
their eyes or **u** with their Jn 12:40
What I'm doing you don't **u** now, Jn 13:7
u that it hated Me before it Jn 15:18
still did not **u** the Scripture Jn 20:9
brothers would **u** that God would Ac 7:25
through him, but they did not **u**. Ac 7:25
"Do you **u** what you're reading?" Ac 8:30
I **u** that God doesn't show Ac 10:34
listen and listen, yet never **u**; Ac 28:26
their ears, **u** with their heart Ac 28:27
am speaking to those who **u** law, Rm 7:1
For I do not **u** what I am doing, Rm 7:15
But I ask, "Did Israel not **u**?" Rm 10:19
those who have not heard will **u**. Rm 15:21
and **u** all mysteries and all 1Co 13:2
what you can read and also **u**. 2Co 1:13
I hope you will **u** completely— 2Co 1:13
so **u** that those who have faith Gl 3:7
you are able to **u** my insight Eph 3:4
but **u** what the Lord's will is. Eph 5:17
they don't **u** what they are 1Tm 1:7
since you have become slow to **u**. Heb 5:11
By faith we **u** that the universe Heb 11:3
dearly loved brothers, **u** this: Jms 1:19
about things they don't **u**, 2Pt 2:12
promise, as some **u** delay, but is 2Pt 3:9
some matters that are hard to **u**. 2Pt 3:16
blaspheme anything they don't **u**, Jd 10

UNDERSTANDING *(118)*

with wisdom, **u**, and ability Ex 31:3
with wisdom, **u**, and ability Ex 35:31
them wisdom and **u** to know how to Ex 36:1
yourselves wise, **u**, and Dt 1:13
your wisdom and **u** in the eyes Dt 4:6
is indeed a wise and **u** people.' Dt 4:6
lacking sense with no **u** at all. Dt 32:28
give you a wise and **u** heart, 1Kg 3:12
and **u** as ⌊vast⌋ as the sand on 1Kg 4:29
great skill, **u**, and knowledge 1Kg 7:14
you insight and **u** when He puts 1Ch 22:12
he was a man of **u** and a scribe. 1Ch 27:32
a wise son with insight and **u**, 2Ch 2:12
a skillful man who has **u**. 2Ch 2:13
and all who could listen with **u**. Neh 8:2
tell you and speak from their **u**? Jb 8:10
will gain **u** as soon as a wild Jb 11:12
and **u** comes with long life. Jb 12:12
counsel and **u** are His. Jb 12:13
have closed their minds to **u**, Jb 17:4
me, and my **u** makes me reply. Jb 20:3
and by His **u** He crushed Rahab. Jb 26:12
found, and where is **u** located? Jb 28:12
from, and where is **u** located? Jb 28:20
and to turn from evil is **u**." Jb 28:28
of the Almighty that give him **u**. Jb 32:8
listen to me, you men of **u**. Jb 34:10
If you ⌊have⌋ **u**, hear this; Jb 34:16
gives us more **u** than the animals Jb 35:11
Tell ⌊Me⌋, if you have **u**. Jb 38:4
in the heart or gave the mind **u**? Jb 38:36
He has not endowed her with **u**. Jb 39:17
flight by your **u** and spread its Jb 39:26
or mule, without **u**, that must be Ps 32:9
heart's meditation ⌊brings⌋ **u**. Ps 49:3
without **u** is like the animals Ps 49:20
commands, for You broaden my **u**. Ps 119:32
give me **u** so that I can learn Ps 119:73
I gain **u** from Your precepts; Ps 119:104
me **u** so that I may know Your Ps 119:125
light and gives **u** to the Ps 119:130
Give me **u**, and I will live. Ps 119:144
me **u** according to Your word. Ps 119:169
His **u** is infinite. Ps 147:5
for **u** insightful sayings; Pr 1:2
for **u** a proverb or a parable, Pr 1:6
and directing your heart to **u**; Pr 2:2
and lift your voice to **u**, Pr 2:3
His mouth come knowledge and **u**. Pr 2:6
over you, and **u** will guard you, Pr 2:11
and do not rely on your own **u**; Pr 3:5
finds wisdom and who acquires **u**, Pr 3:13
established the heavens by **u**. Pr 3:19
so that you may gain **u**, Pr 4:1
Get wisdom, get **u**; Pr 4:5
whatever else you get, get **u**. Pr 4:7
listen closely to my **u** Pr 5:1
and call **u** ⌊your⌋ relative. Pr 7:4
Doesn't **U** make her voice heard? Pr 8:1
I have **u** and strength. Pr 8:14
pursue the way of **u**. Pr 9:6
knowledge of the Holy One is **u**. Pr 9:10
so wisdom is for a man of **u**. Pr 10:23
but a man with **u** keeps silent. Pr 11:12
patient person ⌊shows⌋ great **u**, Pr 14:29
a man with **u** walks a straight Pr 15:21
And acquire **u**—it is preferable Pr 16:16
keeps a cool head is a man of **u**. Pr 17:27
A fool does not delight in **u**, Pr 18:2
who safeguards **u** finds success. Pr 19:8
but a man of **u** draws it up. Pr 20:5
No wisdom, no **u**, and no counsel Pr 21:30
wisdom, instruction, and **u**. Pr 23:23
and it is established by **u**; Pr 24:3
leader who lacks **u** is very Pr 28:16
of wisdom and **u**, a Spirit of Is 11:2
they are not a people with **u**. Is 27:11
and the **u** of the perceptive will Is 29:14
will gain **u** and those who Is 29:24
gave Him **u** and taught Him the Is 40:14
and showed Him the way of **u**? Is 40:14
there is no limit to His **u**. Is 40:28
are foolish children, without **u**. Jr 4:22
spread out the heavens by His **u**. Jr 10:12
spread out the heavens by His **u**. Jr 51:15
your wisdom and **u** you have Ezk 28:4
knowledge and **u** in every kind Dn 1:17
of wisdom and **u** that the king Dn 1:20
knowledge to those who have **u**. Dn 2:21
I've come now to give you **u**. Dn 9:22
message and had **u** of the vision. Dn 10:1
the people will give **u** to many, Dn 11:33
new wine take away ⌊one's⌋ **u**. Hs 4:11
even you still lacking in **u**?" Mt 15:16
Are you also as lacking in **u**? Mk 7:18
with all your **u**, and with all Mk 12:33
to the **u** of the righteous, Lk 1:17
at His **u** and His answers Lk 2:47
angry by a nation that lacks **u**. Rm 10:19
with the same **u** and the same 1Co 1:10
set aside the **u** of the experts. 1Co 1:19
prays, but my **u** is unfruitful. 1Co 14:14
and I will also pray with my **u**. 1Co 14:15
and I will also sing with my **u**. 1Co 14:15
speak five words with my **u**, 1Co 14:19
to themselves, they lack **u**. 2Co 10:12
on us with all wisdom and **u**. Eph 1:8
They are darkened in their **u**, Eph 4:18
in all wisdom and spiritual **u**, Col 1:9
all the riches of assured **u**, Col 2:2
he is conceited, **u** nothing, but 1Tm 6:4
will give you **u** in everything. 2Tm 2:7
their lack of **u** will be clear to 2Tm 3:9
Who is wise and **u** among you? Jms 3:13
wives with **u** of their weaker 1Pt 3:7
your pure **u** with a reminder 2Pt 3:1
has given us **u** so that we may 1Jn 5:20
The one who has **u** must calculate Rv 13:18

UNDERSTANDS *(10)*

every heart and **u** the intention 1Ch 28:9
But God **u** the way to wisdom, Jb 28:23
He **u** all things. Jb 36:5
Who **u** the power of Your anger? Ps 90:11
The one who **u** a matter finds Pr 16:20
though he **u**, he doesn't respond. Pr 29:19
this, that he **u** and knows Me— Jr 9:24
is one who hears and **u** the word, Mt 13:23
is no one who **u**, there is no one Rm 3:11
but to God, since no one **u** him; 1Co 14:2

UNDERSTOOD *(19)*

not realize that Joseph **u** them, Gn 42:23
Then Eli **u** that the LORD was 1Sm 3:8
who **u** the times and knew what 1Ch 12:32
because they had **u** the words Neh 8:12
the wise men who **u** the times, Est 1:13
my ears have heard and **u** it. Jb 13:1
Then I **u** their destiny. Ps 73:17
in a language that is not **u**. Is 33:19
Daniel also **u** visions and dreams Dn 1:17
u from the books according to Dn 9:2
He **u** the message and had Dn 10:1
"Have you **u** all these things?" Mt 13:51
Then they **u** that He did not tell Mt 16:12
the disciples **u** that He spoke to Mt 17:13
Right away Jesus **u** in His spirit Mk 2:8
they had not **u** about the loaves. Mk 6:52
They **u** none of these things. Lk 18:34
u through what He has made. Rm 1:20
as you have partially **u** us— 2Co 1:14

UNDERTAKEN *(1)*

Many have **u** to compile a Lk 1:1

UNDERTAKES *(1)*

is the man who **u** the rebuilding Jos 6:26

UNDERWEAR *(7)*

buy yourself linen **u** and put it Jr 13:1
So I bought **u** as the LORD Jr 13:2
Take the **u** that you bought and Jr 13:4
and get the **u** that I commanded Jr 13:6
and dug up the **u** and got it Jr 13:7
will be like this **u**, of no use Jr 13:10
Just as **u** clings to one's waist, Jr 13:11

UNDERWORLD *(6)*

dwell in the **u** like the ancient Ezk 26:20

to death, to the **u**, among the Ezk 31:14
were comforted in the **u**. Ezk 31:16
down to the **u** ⌊to be⌋ with Ezk 31:18
of mighty nations down to the **u**, Ezk 32:18
down to the **u** uncircumcised, Ezk 32:24

UNDESERVED *(2)*
not give anyone an ⌊**u**⌋ title. Jb 32:21
an **u** curse goes nowhere. Pr 26:2

UNDESIRABLE *(1)*
gather together, **u** nation, Zph 2:1

UNDETECTED *(1)*
and she is **u**, even though she Nm 5:13

UNDISCERNING *(1)*
u, untrustworthy, unloving, and Rm 1:31

UNDISTURBED *(1)*
left his bones **u** with the bones 2Kg 23:18

UNDIVIDED *(1)*
Give me an **u** mind to fear Your Ps 86:11

UNDO *(1)*
should not **u** his circumcision. 1Co 7:18

UNDONE *(2)*
leaving nothing **u** of all that Jos 11:15
was to set right what was left **u** Ti 1:5

UNDYING *(1)*
all who have **u** love for our Lord Eph 6:24

UNEDUCATED *(1)*
that they were **u** and untrained Ac 4:13

UNENDING *(3)*
singing, crowned with **u** joy. Is 35:10
singing, crowned with **u** joy. Is 51:11
has my pain become **u**, my wound Jr 15:18

UNEVEN *(2)*
the **u** ground will become smooth, Is 40:4
you and level the **u** places; Is 45:2

UNEXPECTED *(1)*
Something **u** has happened; 1Sm 20:26

UNEXPECTEDLY *(4)*
come on him **u**, and let the net Ps 35:8
happen to you suddenly and **u**. Is 47:11
the east arrived **u** in Jerusalem, Mt 2:1
or that day will come on you **u** Lk 21:34

UNFADING *(2)*
and **u**, kept in heaven 1Pt 1:4
receive the **u** crown of glory. 1Pt 5:4

UNFAILING *(3)*
is full of the LORD's **u** love. Ps 33:5
anger, for I am **u** in My love. Jr 3:12
righteousness, like an **u** stream. Am 5:24

UNFAIR *(5)*
and dishonest scales are **u**. Pr 20:23
Is it My way that is **u**? Ezk 18:25
isn't it your ways that are **u**? Ezk 18:25
ways that are **u**, house of Israel Ezk 18:29
isn't it your ways that are **u**? Ezk 18:29

UNFAIRLY *(2)*
must not act **u** in measurements Lv 19:35
things and acts **u** is detestable Dt 25:16

UNFAITHFUL *(28)*
wife goes astray, is **u** to him, Nm 5:12
and been **u** to her husband, Nm 5:27
and not become **u** by following Nm 15:39
generation—**u** children. Dt 32:20
were **u** regarding the things set Jos 7:1
son of Zerah **u** regarding what Jos 22:20
she was **u** to him and left him Jdg 19:2
Saul said, "You have been **u**. 1Sm 14:33
when he was **u** ⌊by taking⌋ what 1Ch 2:7
But they were **u** to the God of 1Ch 5:25
Because they were **u** to the LORD, 2Ch 12:2
in Judah and was **u** to the LORD. 2Ch 28:19
became more **u** to the LORD. 2Ch 28:22
fathers were **u** and did what is 2Ch 29:6
when he became **u** we have set up 2Ch 29:19
who were **u** to the LORD God 2Ch 30:7
people multiplied their **u** deeds, 2Ch 36:14
We have been **u** to our God by Ezr 10:2
You have been **u** by marrying Ezr 10:10
⌊If⌋ you are **u**, I will scatter Neh 1:8
destroy all who are **u** to You. Ps 73:27
and they were **u** to His covenant. Ps 78:37
those among men who are **u**. Pr 23:28
you seen what **u** Israel has done? Jr 3:6
that it was because **u** Israel had Jr 3:8
U Israel has shown herself more Jr 3:11
Return, **u** Israel. Jr 3:12
many, their **u** deeds numerous. Jr 5:6

UNFAITHFULLY *(6)*
person acts **u** toward the LORD Nm 5:6
He acted **u** against the LORD his 2Ch 26:16
sanctuary, for you have acted **u**! 2Ch 26:18
evil and acting **u** against our Neh 13:27
because they have acted **u**." Ezk 15:8
because they dealt **u** with Me. Ezk 39:23

UNFAITHFULNESS *(12)*
their **u** that they practiced Lv 26:40
your acts of **u** until all your Nm 14:33
Israelites to **u** against the LORD Nm 31:16
of ⌊their **u**⌋, but not forever 1Kg 11:39
to Babylon because of their **u**. 1Ch 9:1
Saul died for his **u** to the LORD 1Ch 10:13
all his sin and **u** and the sites 2Ch 33:19
have taken the lead in this **u**!" Ezr 9:2
because of the **u** of the exiles, Ezr 9:4
over the **u** of the exiles. Ezr 10:6
I will heal your **u**. Jr 3:22
and all the **u** they committed Ezk 39:26

UNFAMILIAR *(1)*
I heard an **u** language: Ps 81:5

UNFANNED *(1)*
A fire **u** ⌊by human hands⌋ will Jb 20:26

UNFORTUNATELY *(1)*
"**U** not," Jonathan answered him. 1Kg 1:43

UNFRUITFUL *(6)*
water is bad and the land **u**." 2Kg 2:19
the word, and it becomes **u**. Mt 13:22
the word, and it becomes **u**. Mk 4:19
but my understanding is **u**. 1Co 14:14
so that they will not be **u**. Ti 3:14
useless or **u** in the knowledge 2Pt 1:8

UNFRUITFULNESS *(1)*
will death or **u** result from it.' 2Kg 2:21

UNGODLINESS *(1)*
of Jerusalem **u** has spread Jr 23:15

UNGODLY *(16)*
my cause against an **u** nation; Ps 43:1
With his mouth the **u** destroys Pr 11:9
trembling seizes the **u**: Is 33:14
both prophet and priest are **u**, Jr 23:11
who declares righteous the **u**, Rm 4:5
moment, Christ died for the **u**. Rm 5:6
for the **u** and sinful, for 1Tm 1:9
become of the **u** and the sinner? 1Pt 4:18
a flood on the world of the **u**; 2Pt 2:5
to those who were going to be **u**; 2Pt 2:6
and destruction of **u** men. 2Pt 3:7
they are **u**, turning the grace of Jd 4
of all their **u** deeds that they Jd 15
that they have done in an **u** way, Jd 15
the harsh things **u** sinners have Jd 15
to their own **u** desires." Jd 18

UNGRATEFUL *(2)*
is gracious to the **u** and evil. Lk 6:35
to parents, **u**, unholy, 2Tm 3:2

UNHARMED *(4)*
his enemy, does he let him go **u**? 1Sm 24:19
has opposed Him and come out **u**? Jb 9:4
will redeem me from my battle **u**. Ps 55:18
walking around in the fire **u**; Dn 3:25

UNHOLY *(2)*
for the **u** and irreverent, 1Tm 1:9
to parents, ungrateful, **u**, 2Tm 3:2

UNIFIED *(1)*
formed a **u** alliance to fight Jos 9:2

UNIFORM *(2)*
wearing his **u** and over it was 2Sm 20:8
the liquid measure will be **u**, Ezk 45:11

UNIMPORTANT *(1)*
you once considered yourself **u**, 1Sm 15:17

UNINFORMED *(4)*
will the **u** person say "Amen" 1Co 14:16
people who are **u** or unbelievers 1Co 14:23
unbeliever or **u** person comes 1Co 14:24
We do not want you to be **u**, 1Th 4:13

UNINHABITED *(9)*
to bring rain on an **u** land, Jb 38:26
will be reduced to **u** ruins. Jr 4:7
Judah a desolation, an **u** place. Jr 9:11
you into a wilderness, **u** cities. Jr 22:6
city will become an **u** ruin'!" Jr 26:9
become a desolation, **u** ruins. Jr 46:19
land of Babylon an **u** desolation. Jr 51:29
It will be **u** for 40 years. Ezk 29:11
and Ashkelon will become **u**. Zch 9:5

UNINJURED *(2)*
no spot is **u**—wounds, welts Is 1:6
of the den, **u**, for he trusted Dn 6:23

UNINTELLIGIBLE *(2)*
to a people of **u** speech or Ezk 3:5
to many peoples of **u** speech or Ezk 3:6

UNINTENTIONAL *(3)*
be forgiven, for the sin was **u**. Nm 15:25
before the LORD for their **u** sin. Nm 15:25
Who perceives his **u** sins? Ps 19:12

UNINTENTIONALLY *(15)*
When someone sins **u** against any Lv 4:2
a leader sins and **u** violates any Lv 4:22
people sins **u** by violating one Lv 4:27
by sinning **u** in regard to any Lv 5:15
the error he has committed **u**, Lv 5:18
When you sin **u** and do not obey Nm 15:22
and if it was done **u** without the Nm 15:24
it happened to all the people **u**. Nm 15:26
one person sins **u**, he is to Nm 15:27
who acts in error sinning **u**, Nm 15:28
kills someone **u** may flee there. Nm 35:11
kills a person **u** may flee there. Nm 35:15
kills someone **u** or accidentally Jos 20:3
kills a person **u** may flee there Jos 20:9
everyone who sins **u** or through Ezk 45:20

UNION *(2)*
one Favor and the other **U**, Zch 11:7
my second staff, **U**, annulling Zch 11:14

UNIQUE *(2)*
my dove, my virtuous one, is **u**; Sg 6:9
was offering up his **u** son, Heb 11:17

UNIT *(8)*
tabernacle may be a single **u**. Ex 26:6
so that it is a single **u**. Ex 26:11
tabernacle became a single **u**. Ex 36:13
the tent together as a single **u**. Ex 36:18
and one **u** is coming from the Jdg 9:37
formed a single **u** and took their 2Sm 2:25
each **u** was the standard length Ezk 40:5
each **u** being the standard length Ezk 43:13

UNITE *(2)*
if they **u** against me and attack Gn 34:30
but also to **u** the scattered Jn 11:52

UNITED *(11)*
all the people stood **u** and said, Jdg 20:8
Israel gathered **u** against the Jdg 20:11
the people, and they went out **u**. 1Sm 11:7
my heart will be **u** with you, 1Ch 12:17
them and be **u** with the house Is 14:1
were continually **u** in prayer, Ac 1:14
the Jews made a **u** attack against Ac 18:12
a **u** cry went up from all of them Ac 19:34
Christ with a **u** mind and voice. Rm 15:6
and that you be **u** with the same 1Co 1:10
they were not **u** with those who Heb 4:2

UNITS *(9)*
in ambush for Shechem in four **u**. Jdg 9:34
and the **u** that were with Jdg 9:44
The other two **u** rushed against Jdg 9:44
their military **u** together into 1Sm 28:1
their military **u** together at 1Sm 29:1
review with their **u** of⌋ hundreds 1Sm 29:2
all his military **u** together and 2Kg 6:24
hand was six **u** of 21 inches; Ezk 40:5
of the altar in **u** of length Ezk 43:13

UNITY *(3)*
keeping the **u** of the Spirit with Eph 4:3
we all reach **u** in the faith Eph 4:13
love—the perfect bond of **u**. Col 3:14

UNIVERSE *(2)*
and through whom He made the **u**. Heb 1:2
understand that the **u** was Heb 11:3

UNJUST *(17)*
don't be **u**. Reconsider; my Jb 6:29
God hands me over to **u** men; Jb 16:11
and my opponent like the **u**. Jb 27:7
the fangs of the **u** and snatched Jb 29:17
me from the deceitful and **u** man. Ps 43:1

grasp of the **u** and oppressive. Ps 71:4
have set our **u** ways before You Ps 90:8
one who hates **u** gain prolongs Pr 28:16
An **u** man is detestable to the Pr 29:27
nothing except your own **u** gain, Jr 22:17
against the **u** gain you have made Ezk 22:13
lives in order to get **u** gain. Ezk 22:27
their hearts pursue **u** gain. Ezk 33:31
war against the **u** overtake them Hs 10:9
Listen to what the **u** judge says. Lk 18:6
know that the **u** will not inherit 1Co 6:9
For God is not **u**; He will not Heb 6:10

UNJUSTLY *(12)*
must not act **u** when rendering Lv 19:15
you testify **u** on God's behalf Jb 13:7
will not speak **u**, and my tongue Jb 27:4
for⌋ the Almighty ⌊to act⌋ **u**. Jb 34:10
will you judge **u** and show Ps 82:2
land he acts **u** and does not see Is 26:10
everyone is gaining profit **u**. Jr 6:13
everyone is gaining profit **u**. Jr 8:10
who makes a fortune **u** is ⌊like⌋ Jr 17:11
to him who **u** gains wealth for Hab 2:9
Instead, you act **u** and cheat— 1Co 6:8
endures grief from suffering **u**. 1Pt 2:19

UNKNOWN *(6)*
of⌋ his strength remained **u**. Jdg 16:9
⌊in places⌋ **u** to those who walk Jb 28:4
stand in the presence of **u** men. Pr 22:29
TO AN U GOD Therefore, what Ac 17:23
as **u** yet recognized; 2Co 6:9
personally **u** to the Judean Gl 1:22

UNLAWFULLY *(1)*
poor and needy and **u** exploited Ezk 22:29

UNLEASH *(5)*
will **u** on them wild beasts with Dt 32:24
to **u** His power and cut me off! Jb 6:9
U your raging anger; Jb 40:11
You **u** your mouth for evil and Ps 50:19
and did not **u** all His wrath. Ps 78:38

UNLEASHED *(1)*
You **u** Your burning wrath; Ex 15:7

UNLEASHES *(1)*
He **u** His winds, and the waters Ps 147:18

UNLEAVENED *(61)*
and baked **u** bread for them, Gn 19:3
fire along with **u** bread and Ex 12:8
You must eat **u** bread for seven Ex 12:15
⌊Festival of⌋ U Bread because Ex 12:17
are to eat **u** bread in the first Ex 12:18
eat **u** bread in all your homes." Ex 12:20
out of Egypt into **u** loaves, Ex 12:39
seven days you must eat **u** bread, Ex 13:6
U bread is to be eaten for those Ex 13:7
Observe the Festival of U Bread. Ex 23:15
you are to eat **u** bread for seven Ex 23:15
with **u** bread, unleavened cakes Ex 29:2
bread, **u** cakes mixed with Ex 29:2
and **u** wafers coated with oil. Ex 29:2
the basket of **u** bread that is Ex 29:23
Observe the Festival of U Bread. Ex 34:18
You are to eat **u** bread for seven Ex 34:18
either **u** cakes mixed with oil or Lv 2:4
with oil or **u** wafers coated Lv 2:4
must be **u** bread ⌊made⌋ of fine Lv 2:5
to be eaten as **u** bread in a holy Lv 6:16
is to present **u** cakes mixed with Lv 7:12
with olive oil, **u** wafers coated Lv 7:12
and the basket of **u** bread, Lv 8:2
the basket of **u** bread that was Lv 8:26
he took one cake of **u** bread, Lv 8:26
The Festival of U Bread to the Lv 23:6
seven days you must eat **u** bread. Lv 23:6
a basket of **u** cakes made from Nm 6:15
and **u** wafers coated with oil. Nm 6:15
with the basket of **u** bread. Nm 6:17
one **u** cake from the basket, Nm 6:19
basket, and one **u** wafer, and put Nm 6:19
the animal with **u** bread and Nm 9:11
u bread is to be eaten for seven Nm 28:17
you are to eat **u** bread with it, Dt 16:3
You must eat **u** bread for six Dt 16:8
at the Festival of U Bread, Dt 16:16
they ate **u** bread and roasted Jos 5:11
a young goat and **u** bread from a Jdg 6:19
Take the meat with the **u** bread, Jdg 6:20
the meat and the **u** bread. Jdg 6:21
the meat and the **u** bread. Jdg 6:21
kneaded it, and baked **u** bread. 1Sm 28:24
they ate **u** bread with their 2Kg 23:9
the wafers of **u** bread, the 1Ch 23:29
the Festival of U Bread, the 2Ch 8:13
the Festival of U Bread in the 2Ch 30:13
the Festival of U Bread seven 2Ch 30:21
Festival of U Bread for seven 2Ch 35:17
Festival of U Bread for seven Ezr 6:22
during which⌋ **u** bread will be Ezk 45:21
the first day of U Bread the Mt 26:17
and the Festival of U Bread. Mk 14:1
On the first day of U Bread, Mk 14:12
The Festival of U Bread, which Lk 22:1
the Day of U Bread came when Lk 22:7
during the days of U Bread. Ac 12:3
after the days of U Bread. Ac 20:6
be a new batch, since you are **u**. 1Co 5:7
with the **u** bread of sincerity 1Co 5:8

UNLESS *(64)*
(See pp. xi-xii.)

UNLIKE *(4)*
sight, and **u** his father David 1Kg 11:6
But you were **u** a prostitute Ezk 16:31
because, **u** the scribes, He Mk 1:22
u Cain, who was of the evil one 1Jn 3:12

UNLOAD *(1)*
ship was to **u** its cargo there Ac 21:3

UNLOADED *(2)*
house, and the camels were **u**. Gn 24:32
merchandise was **u** from the seas, Ezk 27:33

UNLOOSE *(1)*
before him, to **u** the loins of Is 45:1

UNLOVED *(9)*
the LORD saw that Leah was **u**, Gn 29:31
heard that I am **u** and has given Gn 29:33
one loved and the other **u**, Dt 21:15
loved and the **u** bear him sons, Dt 21:15
and if the **u** wife has the Dt 21:15
the firstborn of the **u** wife. Dt 21:16
the son of the **u** wife, by giving Dt 21:17
an **u** woman when she marries, Pr 30:23
and she who is "U," "Beloved." Rm 9:25

UNLOVING *(2)*
u, and unmerciful. Rm 1:31
u, irreconcilable, slanderers, 2Tm 3:3

UNMARKED *(1)*
You are like **u** graves; Lk 11:44

UNMARRIED *(6)*
for his young **u** sister in his Lv 21:3
a brother, or an **u** sister. Ezk 44:25
I say to the **u** and to widows: 1Co 7:8
she must remain **u** or be 1Co 7:11
An **u** man is concerned about the 1Co 7:32
An **u** woman or a virgin is 1Co 7:34

UNMERCIFUL *(1)*
untrustworthy, unloving, and **u**. Rm 1:31

UNNATURAL *(1)*
intercourse for what is **u**. Rm 1:26

UNNECESSARY *(1)*
it is **u** for me to write to you. 2Co 9:1

UNNI *(3)*
Jehiel, **U**, Eliab, Benaiah, 1Ch 15:18
Jehiel, **U**, Eliab, Maaseiah, 1Ch 15:20
Bakbukiah, **U**, and their Neh 12:9

UNPARALLELED *(1)*
⌊He was **u**⌋ for all the signs and Dt 34:11

UNPLEASANT *(1)*
Whether it is pleasant or **u**, Jr 42:6

UNPLOWED *(1)*
Break up the **u** ground; Jr 4:3

UNPRECEDENTED *(1)*
LORD brings about something **u**, Nm 16:30

UNPREPARED *(1)*
come with me and find you **u**, 2Co 9:4

UNPRESENTABLE *(1)*
and our **u** parts have a better 1Co 12:23

UNPRODUCTIVE *(1)*
Is the land fertile or **u**? Nm 13:20

UNPROFITABLE *(3)*
for they are **u** and worthless. Ti 3:9
because it was weak and **u** Heb 7:18
for that would be **u** for you. Heb 13:17

UNPUNISHED *(17)*
will not leave ⌊the guilty⌋ **u**, Ex 34:7
will not leave ⌊the guilty⌋ **u**, Nm 14:18
don't let him go **u**, for you are 1Kg 2:9
one who touches her will go **u**. Pr 6:29
that the wicked will not go **u**, Pr 11:21
be assured, he will not go **u**. Pr 16:5
over disaster will not go **u**. Pr 17:5
A false witness will not go **u**, Pr 19:5
A false witness will not go **u**, Pr 19:9
hurry to get rich will not go **u**. Pr 28:20
so how could you possibly go **u**? Jr 25:29
You will not go **u**, for I am Jr 25:29
I will by no means leave you **u**. Jr 30:11
I will by no means leave you **u**. Jr 46:28
can you possibly remain **u**? Jr 49:12
will not remain **u**, for you must Jr 49:12
will never leave ⌊the guilty⌋ **u**. Nah 1:3

UNQUENCHABLE *(2)*
and go to hell—the **u** fire, Mk 9:43
thrown into hell—the **u** fire, Mk 9:45

UNQUENCHABLY *(1)*
fire and burn **u** because of their Jr 21:12

UNREASONABLE *(1)*
For it seems **u** to me to send a Ac 25:27

UNREASONING *(1)*
instinct, like **u** animals—they Jd 10

UNRELENTING *(2)*
leap for joy in **u** pain that I Jb 6:10
ardent love is as **u** as Sheol. Sg 8:6

UNRELIABLE *(1)*
Trusting an **u** person in a time Pr 25:19

UNREPENTANT *(1)*
your hardness and **u** heart you Rm 2:5

UNRESPONSIVE *(1)*
said to Moses, "Pharaoh is **u**: Ex 7:14

UNRESTRAINED *(3)*
carrying on in **u** behavior, 1Pt 4:3
Many will follow their **u** ways, 2Pt 2:2
distressed by the **u** behavior of 2Pt 2:7

UNRIGHTEOUS *(15)*
rain on the righteous and the **u**. Mt 5:45
praised the **u** manager because he Lk 16:8
by means of the **u** money so that Lk 16:9
and whoever is **u** in very little Lk 16:10
very little is also **u** in much. Lk 16:10
been faithful with the **u** money, Lk 16:11
people—greedy, **u**, adulterers, Lk 18:11
a field with his **u** wages; Ac 1:18
both of the righteous and the **u**. Ac 24:15
Is God **u** to inflict wrath? Rm 3:5
dare go to law before the **u**, 1Co 6:1
and with every **u** deception among 2Th 2:10
for the **u**, that He might 1Pt 3:18
and to keep the **u** under 2Pt 2:9
Let the **u** go on in Rv 22:11

UNRIGHTEOUSNESS *(19)*
and there is no **u** in Him." Ps 92:15
who builds his palace through **u**, Jr 22:13
from Me, all you workers of **u**!' Lk 13:27
true, and there is no **u** in Him. Jn 7:18
godlessness and **u** of people who Rm 1:18
who by their **u** suppress the Rm 1:18
They are filled with all **u**, Rm 1:29
the truth, but are obeying **u**; Rm 2:8
But if our **u** highlights God's Rm 3:5
of it to sin as weapons for **u**. Rm 6:13
finds no joy in **u**, but rejoices 1Co 13:6
believe the truth but enjoyed **u**. 2Th 2:12
the Lord must turn away from **u**. 2Tm 2:19
a world of **u**, is placed among Jms 3:6
harm as the payment for **u**. 2Pt 2:13
Bosor, who loved the wages of **u**, 2Pt 2:15
and to cleanse us from all **u**. 1Jn 1:9
All **u** is sin, and there is sin 1Jn 5:17
Let the unrighteous go on in **u**; Rv 22:11

UNRIPE *(2)*
that drops its **u** grapes and like Jb 15:33
drops its **u** figs when shaken Rv 6:13

UNROLLED *(1)*
When He **u** it before me, it was Ezk 2:10

UNROLLING *(1)*
to Him, and **u** the scroll, He Lk 4:17
UNSCATHED *(1)*
and he will leave there **u**. Jr 43:12
UNSEARCHABLE *(4)*
He does great and **u** things, Jb 5:9
He performs great and **u** things, Jb 9:10
His greatness is **u**. Ps 145:3
How **u** His judgments and Rm 11:33
UNSEEN *(4)*
and his **u** bones stick out. Jb 33:21
but Your footprints were **u**. Ps 77:19
what is seen, but on what is **u**; 2Co 4:18
but what is **u** is eternal. 2Co 4:18
UNSETTLED *(1)*
their words and **u** your hearts, Ac 15:24
UNSETTLING *(2)*
Among **u** thoughts from visions in Jb 4:13
This is why my **u** thoughts compel Jb 20:2
UNSHAKABLE *(1)*
the one who believes will be **u**. Is 28:16
UNSHRUNK *(2)*
an old garment with **u** cloth, Mt 9:16
sews a patch of **u** cloth on an Mk 2:21
UNSOWN *(1)*
sulfur and salt, **u**, producing Dt 29:23
UNSPOKEN *(1)*
for us with **u** groanings. Rm 8:26
UNSTABLE *(6)*
know that her ways are **u**. Pr 5:6
and the **u** will govern them." Is 3:4
How **u** you are, constantly Jr 2:36
man is **u** in all his ways. Jms 1:8
sin, seducing **u** people, and with 2Pt 2:14
The untaught and **u** twist them to 2Pt 3:16
UNSTAINED *(2)*
Saul's sword never returned **u**, 2Sm 1:22
to keep oneself **u** by the world. Jms 1:27
UNSTEADY *(1)*
and made all their hips **u**. Ezk 29:7
UNSTOPPED *(1)*
and the ears of the deaf **u**. Is 35:5
UNSUITABLE *(1)*
Since the harbor was **u** to winter Ac 27:12
UNSURPASSED *(1)*
girl was of **u** beauty, and she 1Kg 1:4
UNSUSPECTING *(6)*
went into the **u** city, and killed Gn 34:25
their army while the army was **u**. Jdg 8:11
as the Sidonians, quiet and **u**. Jdg 18:7
you will come to an **u** people and Jdg 18:10
Laish, to a quiet and **u** people. Jdg 18:27
deceive the hearts of the **u**. Rm 16:18
UNTAUGHT *(1)*
The **u** and unstable twist them to 2Pt 3:16
UNTENDED *(2)*
the grapes of your **u** vines. Lv 25:5
itself, or harvest its **u** vines. Lv 25:11
UNTHINKING *(1)*
I was an **u** animal toward You. Ps 73:22
UNTIE *(9)*
to **u** the ropes of the yoke, Is 58:6
U them and bring them to Me. Mt 21:2
stoop down and **u** the strap of Mk 1:7
U it and bring it here. Mk 11:2
not worthy to **u** the strap of His Lk 3:16
each one of you **u** his ox or Lk 13:15
U it and bring it here. Lk 19:30
strap I'm not worthy to **u**." Jn 1:27
not worthy to **u** the sandals on Ac 13:25
UNTIED *(2)*
tied by a door. They **u** it, Mk 11:4
shouldn't she be **u** from this Lk 13:16
UNTIL *(561)*
(See pp. xi-xii.)
UNTILLED *(1)*
break up your **u** ground. Hs 10:12
UNTRACEABLE *(1)*
His judgments and **u** His ways! Rm 11:33
UNTRAINED *(4)*
been disciplined like an **u** calf. Jr 31:18
they were uneducated and **u** men, Ac 4:13
Though **u** in public speaking, 2Co 11:6
certainly not ⌊**u**⌋ in knowledge. 2Co 11:6
UNTROUBLED *(1)*
Jacob lives **u** in a land of grain Dt 33:28
UNTRUSTWORTHY *(1)*
undiscerning, **u**, unloving, and Rm 1:31
UNTURNED *(1)*
Ephraim is **u** bread, baked on a Hs 7:8
UNTYING *(4)*
are you doing, **u** the donkey?" Mk 11:5
asks you, 'Why are you **u** it?' Lk 19:31
As they were **u** the young donkey, Lk 19:33
"Why are you **u** the donkey?" Lk 19:33
UNUSUAL *(2)*
and saw nothing **u** happen to him, Ac 28:6
as if something **u** were happening 1Pt 4:12
UNVEILED *(1)*
We all, with **u** faces, are 2Co 3:18
UNVENTED *(1)*
My heart is like **u** wine; Jb 32:19
UNWANTED *(1)*
all the worthless and **u** things. 1Sm 15:9
UNWASHED *(2)*
but eating with **u** hands does not Mt 15:20
unclean—that is, **u**—hands. Mk 7:2
UNWEIGHED *(1)*
all the utensils **u** because there 1Kg 7:47
UNWILLING *(12)*
the woman is **u** to follow me to Gn 24:5
If the woman is **u** to follow you, Gn 24:8
and he was **u** to let them go. Ex 10:27
toward Me and are **u** to obey Me, Lv 26:21
But the man was **u** to spend the Jdg 19:10
but he was **u** and would not eat 2Sm 12:17
king, but Joab was **u** to come. 2Sm 14:29
The LORD was **u** to destroy Judah 2Kg 8:19
He was **u** to destroy the house of 2Ch 21:7
Me and were **u** to listen to Me. Ezk 20:8
a while he was **u**, but later he Lk 18:4
forefathers were **u** to obey him, Ac 7:39
UNWILLINGLY *(1)*
but if **u**, I am entrusted with a 1Co 9:17
UNWISE *(3)*
counseled the **u** and thoroughly Jb 26:3
How **u** and slow you are to Lk 24:25
not as **u** people but as wise— Eph 5:15
UNWORTHY *(6)*
I am **u** of all the kindness and Gn 32:10
But if it is **u**, let your peace Mt 10:13
yourselves **u** of eternal life, Ac 13:46
are you **u** to judge the smallest 1Co 6:2
of the Lord in an **u** way will be 1Co 11:27
u to be called an apostle, 1Co 15:9
UP *(1907)*
(See pp. xi-xii.)
UPHAZ *(2)*
and gold from **U** from the hands Jr 10:9
of gold from **U** around his waist Dn 10:5
UPHEAVAL *(1)*
middle of the **u** when He Gn 19:29
UPHELD *(1)*
For You have **u** my just cause; Ps 9:4
UPHOLD *(8)*
in heaven and **u** their cause. 1Kg 8:45
and petition and **u** their cause. 1Kg 8:49
so that He may **u** His servant's 1Kg 8:59
in heaven and **u** their cause. 2Ch 6:35
and petitions and **u** their cause. 2Ch 6:39
u the rights of the oppressed Ps 82:3
happy are those who **u** justice, Ps 106:3
On the contrary, we **u** the law. Rm 3:31
UPHOLDS *(2)*
Your right hand **u** me, and Your Ps 18:35
that the LORD **u** the just cause Ps 140:12
UPLIFTED *(1)*
their hands **u** all the people Neh 8:6
UPON *(9)*
(See pp. xi-xii.)
UPPER *(34)*
lower, middle, and **u** ⌊decks⌋. Gn 6:16
millstones or an **u** millstone as Dt 24:6
he gave her the **u** and lower Jos 15:19
on the east of **U** Beth-horon. Jos 16:5
her both the **u** and lower springs Jdg 1:15
house of Joseph got the **u** hand, Jdg 1:35
But a woman threw the **u** portion Jdg 9:53
a woman drop an **u** millstone on 2Sm 11:21
up to the **u** room where he was 1Kg 17:19
down from the **u** room into the 1Kg 17:23
window of his **u** room in Samaria 2Kg 1:2
who built the **U** Gate of the 2Kg 15:35
by the aqueduct of the **u** pool, 2Kg 18:17
Ahaz's **u** chamber that the kings 2Kg 23:12
who built Lower and **U** Beth-horon 1Ch 7:24
u rooms, inner rooms, 1Ch 28:11
He built **U** Beth-horon and Lower 2Ch 8:5
through the **u** ⌊gate⌋ and seated 2Ch 23:20
Jotham built the **U** Gate of the 2Ch 27:3
the water of the **U** Gihon and 2Ch 32:30
juts out from the **u** palace of Neh 3:25
and as far as the **u** room of the Neh 3:31
between the **u** room of the corner Neh 3:32
of the conduit of the **u** pool, Is 7:3
near the conduit of the **u** pool, Is 36:2
stocks at the **U** Benjamin Gate Jr 20:2
his **u** rooms through injustice, Jr 22:13
palace, with spacious **u** rooms. Jr 22:14
the **u** courtyard at the opening Jr 36:10
the direction of the **U** Gate, Ezk 9:2
The **u** chambers were narrower Ezk 42:5
therefore the **u** chambers were Ezk 42:6
windows in its **u** room opened Dn 6:10
He builds His **u** chambers in the Am 9:6
UPRIGHT *(53)*
You are to make **u** planks of Ex 26:15
He made **u** planks of acacia wood Ex 36:20
Let me die the death of the **u**; Nm 23:10
and set it **u** between Mizpah 1Sm 7:12
these things with an **u** heart, 1Ch 29:17
was good and **u** and true before 2Ch 31:20
you are pure and **u**, then He will Jb 8:6
The righteous and **u** man is a Jb 12:4
The **u** are appalled at this, Jb 17:8
There an **u** man could reason with Jb 23:7
My words ⌊come from⌋ my **u** heart, Jb 33:3
God, who saves the **u** in heart. Ps 7:10
the shadows at the **u** in heart. Ps 11:2
The **u** will see His face. Ps 11:7
The LORD is good and **u**; Ps 25:8
for joy, all you **u** in heart. Ps 32:11
praise from the **u** is beautiful. Ps 33:1
over the **u** in heart. Ps 36:10
slaughter those whose way is **u**. Ps 37:14
the blameless and observe the **u**, Ps 37:37
The **u** will rule over them in the Ps 49:14
all the **u** in heart offer praise. Ps 64:10
and all the **u** in heart will Ps 94:15
gladness for the **u** in heart. Ps 97:11
u see it and rejoice, and all Ps 107:42
in the assembly of the **u** and in Ps 111:1
of the **u** will be blessed. Ps 112:2
in the darkness for the **u**. Ps 112:4
to those whose hearts are **u**. Ps 125:4
u will live in Your presence. Ps 140:13
He stores up success for the **u**; Pr 2:7
For the **u** will inhabit the land, Pr 2:21
but He is a friend to the **u**. Pr 3:32
integrity of the **u** guides them, Pr 11:3
of the **u** rescues them, Pr 11:6
up by the blessing of the **u**, Pr 11:11
speech of the **u** rescues them. Pr 12:6
there is goodwill among the **u**. Pr 14:9
the tent of the **u** will stand. Pr 14:11
prayer of the **u** is His delight. Pr 15:8
the path of the **u** is a highway. Pr 15:19
highway of the **u** avoids evil; Pr 16:17
his behavior is pure and **u**. Pr 20:11
behavior of the innocent is **u**. Pr 21:8
and the treacherous, for the **u**. Pr 21:18
but the **u** man considers his way. Pr 21:29
who leads the **u** into an evil way Pr 28:10
but the **u** care about him. Pr 29:10
whose way is **u** is detestable to Pr 29:27
that God made people **u**, Ec 7:29
there is no one **u** among the Mc 7:2
the most **u** is worse than a hedge Mc 7:4
centurion, an **u** and God-fearing Ac 10:22
UPRIGHTLY *(2)*
beds—everyone who lives **u**. Is 57:2
good to the one who walks **u**? Mc 2:7

UPRIGHTNESS *(4)*
with integrity of heart and **u**, 1Kg 9:4
and that You are pleased with **u**. 1Ch 29:17
May integrity and **u** keep me, Ps 25:21
ever, enacted in truth and **u**. Ps 111:8

UPRISINGS *(1)*
city has had **u** against kings Ezr 4:19

UPROAR *(10)*
"Why is the town in such an **u**?" 1Kg 1:41
The town has been in an **u**; 1Kg 1:45
See how Your enemies make an **u**; Ps 83:2
Listen, an **u** among the kingdoms, Is 13:4
You subdue the **u** of barbarians. Is 25:5
A sound of **u** from the city! Is 66:6
they set the city in an **u**. Ac 17:5
After the **u** was over, Paul sent Ac 20:1
information because of the **u**, Ac 21:34
a crowd and without any **u**. Ac 24:18

UPROOT *(14)*
He will **u** Israel from this good 1Kg 14:15
then I will **u** Israel from the 2Ch 7:20
He will **u** you from the land of Ps 52:5
a time to plant and a time to **u**; Ec 3:2
and kingdoms to **u** and tear down, Jr 1:10
I am about to **u** them from their Jr 12:14
and I will **u** the house of Judah Jr 12:14
then I will **u** and destroy that Jr 12:17
or a kingdom that I will **u**, Jr 18:7
will plant them and not **u** them. Jr 24:6
over them to **u** and to tear them Jr 31:28
and I will plant and not **u** you, Jr 42:10
I have planted I am about to **u**— Jr 45:4
you might also **u** the wheat with Mt 13:29

UPROOTED *(15)*
The LORD **u** them from their land Dt 29:28
If he is **u** from his place, Jb 8:18
sown, and let my crops be **u**. Jb 31:8
You have **u** the cities, and the Ps 9:6
You **u** a vine from Egypt; Ps 80:8
and the treacherous **u** from it. Pr 2:22
After I have **u** them, I will once Jr 12:15
It will never be **u** or demolished Jr 31:40
But it was **u** in fury, thrown to Ezk 19:12
first horns were **u** before it. Dn 7:8
kingdom will be **u** and will go to Dn 11:4
never again be **u** from the land I Am 9:15
at noon, and Ekron will be **u**. Zph 2:4
Father didn't plant will be **u**. Mt 15:13
'Be **u** and planted in the sea,' Lk 17:6

UPROOTS *(1)*
He **u** my hope like a tree. Jb 19:10

UPSET *(5)*
this matter **u** you because the 2Sm 11:25
Why are you so **u** that you refuse 1Kg 21:5
me to answer, because I am **u**! Jb 20:2
are worried and **u** about many Lk 10:41
not to be easily **u** in mind or 2Th 2:2

UPSIDE *(3)*
turned the tent **u** down so that Jdg 7:13
wiping it and turning it **u** down. 2Kg 21:13
turned the world **u** down have Ac 17:6

UPSTAIRS *(13)*
in his room **u** ⌊where it was⌋ Jdg 3:20
doors of the **u** room behind him Jdg 3:23
the doors of the **u** room locked Jdg 3:24
opened the doors of the **u** room. Jdg 3:25
a small room **u** and put a bed, 2Kg 4:10
went to the room **u** to lie down. 2Kg 4:11
He will show you a large room **u**, Mk 14:15
you a large, furnished room **u**. Lk 22:12
to the room **u** where they were Ac 1:13
they placed her in a room **u**. Ac 9:37
they led him to the room **u**. Ac 9:39
lamps in the room **u** where we Ac 20:8
After going **u**, breaking the Ac 20:11

UPWARD *(12)*
will only move **u** and never Dt 28:13
Akrabbim, that is from Sela **u**. Jdg 1:36
root downward and bear fruit **u**. 2Kg 19:30
as surely as sparks fly **u**. Jb 5:7
the path of life leads **u**, Pr 15:24
of people rises **u** and the spirit Ec 3:21
and, looking **u**, will curse their Is 8:21
root downward and bear fruit **u**. Is 37:31
My eyes grow weak looking **u**. Is 38:14
will be like an eagle soaring **u**, Jr 49:22
Their wings were spread **u**; Ezk 1:11
horns project **u** from the hearth. Ezk 43:15

UR *(5)*
native land, in **U** of the Gn 11:28
together from **U** of the Chaldeans Gn 11:31
you from **U** of the Chaldeans Gn 15:7
the Hararite, Eliphal son of **U**, 1Ch 11:35
him out of **U** of the Chaldeans, Neh 9:7

URBANUS *(1)*
U, our co-worker in Christ, Rm 16:9

URGE *(19)*
I **u** you, tell me what you have Jos 7:19
Then they came to **u** David to eat 2Sm 3:35
you an overwhelming **u** to sleep; Is 29:10
Now I **u** you to take courage, Ac 27:22
Therefore I **u** you to take some Ac 27:34
u you to present your bodies as Rm 12:1
Now I **u** you, brothers, in the 1Co 1:10
Therefore I **u** you, be imitators 1Co 4:16
to serving the saints. I **u** you 1Co 16:15
Therefore I **u** you to confirm 2Co 2:8
necessary to **u** the brothers to 2Co 9:5
u you to walk worthy of the Eph 4:1
u Euodia and I urge Syntyche to Php 4:2
Euodia and I **u** Syntyche to agree Php 4:2
all, then, I **u** that petitions, 1Tm 2:1
I especially **u** you to pray that Heb 13:19
I **u** you to receive this word of Heb 13:22
I **u** you as aliens and temporary 1Pt 2:11
So now I **u** you, lady—not as if 2Jn 5

URGED *(23)*
But he **u** them so strongly that Gn 19:3
crack of dawn the angels **u** Lot Gn 19:15
So Jacob **u** him until he Gn 33:11
because he has **u** rebellion Dt 13:5
servants and the woman **u** him, 1Sm 28:23
Although Absalom **u** him, he 2Sm 13:25
But Absalom **u** him, so he sent 2Sm 13:27
they **u** him to the point of 2Kg 2:17
Naaman **u** him to accept it, 2Kg 5:16
He **u** Gehazi and then packed 150 2Kg 5:23
as the LORD had said and **u** me, Jr 32:8
Gemariah had **u** the king not to Jr 36:25
approached Him and **u** Him, Mt 15:23
is strongly **u** to enter it. Lk 16:16
But they **u** Him: "Stay with us, Lk 24:29
testified and strongly **u** them, Ac 2:40
were baptized, she **u** us, "If you Ac 16:15
they **u** them to leave town. Ac 16:39
Paul **u** them all to take food, Ac 27:33
I strongly **u** him to come to you 1Co 16:12
So we **u** Titus that, just as he 2Co 8:6
I **u** Titus ⌊to come⌋, and I sent 2Co 12:18
As I **u** you when I went to 1Tm 1:3

URGENT *(5)*
Did I not send you an **u** summons? Nm 22:37
since the king's mission was **u**." 1Sm 21:8
haste, at the king's **u** command. Est 8:14
command was so **u** and the furnace Dn 3:22
good works for cases of **u** need, Ti 3:14

URGENTLY *(2)*
Pharaoh **u** sent for Moses and Ex 10:16
'David **u** requested my permission 1Sm 20:6

URGES *(1)*
for him because his hunger **u** him Pr 16:26

URGING *(5)*
⌊**u**⌋ them to ask the God of Dn 2:18
robe of a Jewish man tightly, **u**: Zch 8:23
the disciples kept **u** Him, Jn 4:31
the disciples **u** them to welcome Ac 18:27
For he accepted our **u** and, 2Co 8:17

URI *(8)*
by name Bezalel son of **U**, Ex 31:2
by name Bezalel son of **U**, Ex 35:30
Bezalel son of **U**, son of Hur, of Ex 38:22
Geber son of **U**, in the land of 1Kg 4:19
Hur fathered **U**, and Uri fathered 1Ch 2:20
Uri, and **U** fathered Bezalel 1Ch 2:20
Bezalel son of **U**, son of Hur, 2Ch 1:5
Shallum, Telem, and **U**. Ezr 10:24

URIAH *(38)*
and wife of **U** the Hittite." 2Sm 11:3
"Send me **U** the Hittite." 2Sm 11:6
So Joab sent **U** to David. 2Sm 11:6
When **U** came to him, David asked 2Sm 11:7
Then he said to **U**, "Go down to 2Sm 11:8
So **U** left the palace, and a 2Sm 11:8
But **U** slept at the door of the 2Sm 11:9
to David, "**U** didn't go home," 2Sm 11:10
David questioned **U**, "Haven't 2Sm 11:10
U answered David, "The ark, 2Sm 11:11
David said to **U**, "and tomorrow I 2Sm 11:12
So **U** stayed in Jerusalem that 2Sm 11:12
David invited **U** to eat and drink 2Sm 11:13
to Joab and sent it with **U**. 2Sm 11:14
Put **U** at the front of the 2Sm 11:15
he put **U** in the place where he 2Sm 11:16
U the Hittite also died. 2Sm 11:17
'Your servant **U** the Hittite is 2Sm 11:21
Your servant **U** the Hittite is 2Sm 11:24
that her husband **U** had died, 2Sm 11:26
You struck down **U** the Hittite 2Sm 12:9
took the wife of **U** the Hittite 2Sm 12:10
and **U** the Hittite. There were 37 2Sm 23:39
in the matter of **U** the Hittite. 1Kg 15:5
construction to **U** the priest. 2Kg 16:10
U built the altar according to 2Kg 16:11
from Damascus, **U** the priest had 2Kg 16:11
Ahaz commanded **U** the priest, 2Kg 16:15
U the priest did everything King 2Kg 16:16
U the Hittite, Zabad son of 1Ch 11:41
Meremoth the priest, son of **U**. Ezr 8:33
Next to them Meremoth son of **U**, Neh 3:4
Beside him Meremoth son of **U**, Neh 3:21
Shema, Anaiah, **U**, Hilkiah, and Neh 8:4
U the priest and Zechariah son Is 8:2
U son of Shemaiah from Jr 26:20
When **U** heard, he fled in fear Jr 26:21
They brought **U** out of Egypt and Jr 26:23

URIAH'S *(3)*
When **U** wife heard that her 2Sm 11:26
the baby that **U** wife had borne 2Sm 12:15
fathered Solomon by **U** wife, Mt 1:6

URIEL *(4)*
his son **U**, his son Uzziah 1Ch 6:24
U the leader and 120 of his 1Ch 15:5
and Abiathar and the Levites **U**, 1Ch 15:11
name was Micaiah daughter of **U**; 2Ch 13:2

URIM *(7)*
Place the **U** and Thummim in the Ex 28:30
him and placed the **U** and Thummim Lv 8:8
him with the decision of the **U**. Nm 27:21
Thummim and **U** belong to Your Dt 33:8
dreams or by the **U** or by the 1Sm 28:6
could consult the **U** and Thummim. Ezr 2:63
could consult the **U** and Thummim. Neh 7:65

URINE *(2)*
and drink their own **u**?" 2Kg 18:27
excrement and drink their **u**?" Is 36:12

US *(1349)*
(See pp. xi-xii.)

USE *(62)*
know what we will **u** to worship Ex 10:26
If you **u** your chisel on it, Ex 20:25
for every **u** and all its tent Ex 27:19
should **u** gold; blue, purple, Ex 28:5
Israelites and **u** it for the Ex 30:16
the tent of meeting for every **u**, Ex 35:21
that you **u** for food dies, Lv 11:39
they **u** in the sanctuary, Nm 4:12
on it that they **u** in serving: Nm 4:14
Your **u** of these is a permanent Nm 10:8
you must not **u** any iron tool on Dt 27:5
U uncut stones to build the Dt 27:6
I will **u** up My arrows against Dt 32:23
U them and do whatever you want Jdg 19:24
them to his **u** in his chariots 1Sm 8:11
them for his **u** as commanders 1Sm 8:12
your donkeys and **u** them for his 1Sm 8:16
and ⌊would **u** it⌋ to buy timber 2Kg 12:12
large stones for **u** on the towers 2Ch 26:15
You may **u** the royal treasury to Ezr 7:20
I'll **u** force against you." Neh 13:21
to me and would **u** my disgrace as Jb 19:5
Can a man be of ⌊any⌋ **u** to God? Jb 22:2
even a wise man be of **u** to Him? Jb 22:2
What **u** to me was the strength of Jb 30:2
one who will not **u** the rod hates Pr 13:24
the Lord will **u** a razor hired Is 7:20
He cuts down cedars for his **u**, Is 44:14
with lye and **u** a great amount Jr 2:22
u to Me is frankincense from Jr 6:20
was ruined—of no **u** whatsoever. Jr 13:7

underwear, of no **u** whatsoever. Jr 13:10
who **u** their own tongues to Jr 23:31
I will let you ⌊**u**⌋ cow dung Ezk 4:15
u it as you would a barber's Ezk 5:1
and they will not **u** it again in Ezk 12:23
will no longer **u** this proverb Ezk 18:3
years they will **u** them to make Ezk 39:9
for they will **u** the weapons to Ezk 39:10
border you will ⌊**u** to⌋ divide Ezk 47:13
be for common **u** by the city, Ezk 48:15
What **u** is a carved idol after Hab 2:18
For with the judgment you **u**, Mt 7:2
and with the measure you **u**, Mt 7:2
By the measure you **u**, it will be Mk 4:24
parable can we **u** to describe it? Mk 4:30
For with the measure you **u**, Lk 6:38
we to say? I **u** a human argument Rm 3:5
u it according to the standard Rm 12:6
and those who **u** the world as 1Co 7:31
they did not make full **u** of it. 1Co 7:31
not make full **u** of my authority 1Co 9:18
unless you **u** your tongue for 1Co 14:9
such a hope, we **u** great boldness 2Co 3:12
am there I will not **u** severity, 2Co 13:10
only don't **u** this freedom as an Gl 5:13
but **u** a little wine because of 1Tm 5:23
some for special **u**, some for 2Tm 2:20
don't **u** your freedom as a way 1Pt 2:16
everyone should **u** it to serve 1Pt 4:10
on the cloud, "**U** your sickle and Rv 14:15
U your sharp sickle and gather Rv 14:18

USED *(76)*

the way you **u** to when you were Gn 40:13
they had **u** up the grain they Gn 43:2
power that the LORD **u** against Ex 14:31
It must not be **u** for ⌊ordinary⌋ Ex 30:32
that was **u** for the project Ex 38:24
pounds of silver ⌊**u**⌋ to cast the Ex 38:27
It is to be **u** for ministry, Ex 39:26
beasts may be **u** for any purpose, Lv 7:24
or any implement **u** for work. Lv 11:32
regardless of how it is **u**, Lv 13:51
Egypt, where you **u** to live, or Lv 18:3
will be **u** up for nothing. Lv 26:20
utensils that were **u** with these, Nm 3:31
cover the lampstand **u** for light, Nm 4:9
from them to be **u** in the work Nm 7:5
treachery that they **u** against Nm 25:18
This too **u** to be regarded as the Dt 2:20
u to be called the land of the Dt 3:13
not been yoked or **u** for work. Dt 21:3
which no iron tool has been **u**. Jos 8:31
Hebron's name **u** to be Jos 14:15
of Debir whose name **u** to be Jos 15:15
big toes cut off **u** to pick up Jdg 1:7
ropes that have never been **u**, Jdg 16:11
but he was not **u** to them. 1Sm 17:39
to Saul, "I'm not **u** to them." 1Sm 17:39
sheath, and **u** it to kill him. 1Sm 17:51
where he **u** to worship God, 2Sm 15:32
In the past they **u** to say, 2Sm 20:18
construction **u** finished stones 1Kg 6:7
He **u** to pay the king of Israel 2Kg 3:4
who **u** to pour water on Elijah's 2Kg 3:11
bands of Moabites **u** to come into 2Kg 13:20
measuring line ⌊**u** on⌋ Samaria 2Kg 21:13
mason's level ⌊**u** on⌋ the house 2Kg 21:13
bronze articles **u** in ⌊temple⌋ 2Kg 25:14
of the utensils **u** in worship. 1Ch 9:28
has **u** me to burst out against 1Ch 14:11
reservoir was **u** by the priests 2Ch 4:6
temple and even **u** the sacred 2Ch 24:7
builders and ⌊also **u** it⌋ to buy 2Ch 34:11
His sons **u** to have banquets, Jb 1:4
no survivor where he **u** to live. Jb 18:19
My lyre is ⌊**u**⌋ for mourning and Jb 30:31
We **u** to have close fellowship; Ps 55:14
that I **u** to send her away? Is 50:1
and their power is not rightly **u** Jr 23:10
bronze articles **u** in ⌊temple⌋ Jr 52:18
Those who **u** to eat delicacies Lm 4:5
and should be **u** as a lament." Ezk 19:14
within you has **u** his strength to Ezk 22:6
The utensils to **u** to slaughter the Ezk 40:42
the land to be **u** by the priests Ezk 45:4
fruit will be **u** for food and Ezk 47:12
on her, which they **u** for Baal. Hs 2:8
is why I have **u** the prophets to Hs 6:5
they will be **u** again for a Mc 1:7
are ready to be **u** with an oath. Hab 3:9
Show Me the coin **u** for the tax." Mt 22:19
Every day I **u** to sit, teaching Mt 26:55
way their ancestors **u** to treat Lk 6:23
their ancestors **u** to treat the Lk 6:26
the man who **u** to be blind to Jn 9:13
you **u** lawless people to nail Him Ac 2:23
was the one who **u** to sit and beg Ac 3:10
they **u** ropes and tackle and Ac 27:17
although you **u** to be slaves of Rm 6:17
have been so **u** to idolatry up 1Co 8:7
we have not **u** this authority; 1Co 9:12
But I have **u** none of these 1Co 9:15
u to put a veil over his face 2Co 3:13
he **u** to eat with the Gentiles Gl 2:12
as something to be **u** for His own Php 2:6
what is destroyed by being **u** up; Col 2:22
we never **u** flattering speech, 1Th 2:5
measurement, which the angel **u**. Rv 21:17

USEFUL *(9)*

acacia wood **u** for any task Ex 35:24
from it to make something **u**? Ezk 15:3
Can it be **u** for anything? Ezk 15:4
not be made into a **u** object. Ezk 15:5
into anything **u** when the fire Ezk 15:5
set apart, **u** to the Master, 2Tm 2:21
for he is **u** to me in the 2Tm 4:11
but now he is **u** to both you and Phm 11
vegetation **u** to those it is Heb 6:7

USELESS *(13)*

he argue with **u** talk or with Jb 15:3
they will aim their **u** arrows. Ps 58:7
and all their skill was **u**. Ps 107:27
Stop bringing **u** offerings. Is 1:13
by Baal and followed **u** idols. Jr 2:8
their Glory for **u** idols. Jr 2:11
longer kindle a **u** ⌊fire on⌋ My Mal 1:10
It is **u** to serve God. Mal 3:14
together they have become **u**; Rm 3:12
Once he was **u** to you, but now he Phm 11
his heart, his religion is **u**. Jms 1:26
that faith without works is **u**? Jms 2:20
you from being **u** or unfruitful 2Pt 1:8

USES *(3)*

from and **u** for divination? Gn 44:5
everyone who **u** proverbs will say Ezk 16:44
provided one **u** it legitimately. 1Tm 1:8

USING *(11)*

to produce gnats **u** their occult Ex 8:18
anything like it **u** its formula. Ex 30:32
for yourselves **u** its formula. Ex 30:37
Jonathan went up **u** his hands and 1Sm 14:13
10 water carts **u** the same 1Kg 7:37
u either their right or left 1Ch 12:2
those you are **u** to fight the Jr 21:4
do you mean by **u** this proverb Ezk 18:2
plainly and not **u** any figurative Jn 16:29
am **u** a human analogy because of Rm 6:19
I'm **u** a human illustration. Gl 3:15

USUAL *(6)*

line and shouted his **u** words, 1Sm 17:23
was playing ⌊the harp⌋ as **u**, 1Sm 18:10
sat at his **u** place on the seat 1Sm 20:25
u, He entered the synagogue on Lk 4:16
made His way as **u** to the Mount Lk 22:39
As **u**, Paul went to them, and on Ac 17:2

USUALLY *(1)*

again and, as He **u** did, He began Mk 10:1

UTENSIL *(1)*

any wooden **u** must be rinsed Lv 15:12

UTENSILS *(52)*

with all these **u** is to be made Ex 25:39
make all its **u** of bronze. Ex 27:3
with all its **u**, the lampstand Ex 30:27
lampstand with its **u**, the altar Ex 30:27
burnt offering with all its **u**, Ex 30:28
with its **u**, the pure ⌊gold⌋ Ex 31:8
gold⌋ lampstand with all its **u**, Ex 31:8
burnt offering with all its **u**, Ex 31:9
poles, all its **u**, and the bread Ex 35:13
light with its **u** and lamps as Ex 35:14
grate, its poles, and all its **u**; Ex 35:16
He also made the **u** that would be Ex 37:16
it and all its **u** of 75 pounds Ex 37:24
He made all the altar's **u**: Ex 38:3
he made all its **u** of bronze. Ex 38:3
grate, all the **u** for the altar, Ex 38:30
table, all its **u**, and the bread Ex 39:36
lamps arranged and all its **u**, Ex 39:37
grate, its poles, and all its **u**; Ex 39:39
of burnt offering and all its **u**; Ex 40:10
the altar with all its **u**, Lv 8:11
the sanctuary **u** that were used Nm 3:31
it with all its **u** inside a Nm 4:10
take all the serving **u** they use Nm 4:12
the holy objects and their **u**." Nm 4:16
with the altar and all its **u**. Nm 7:1
All the **u** that Hiram made for 1Kg 7:45
left all the **u** unweighed because 1Kg 7:47
gold, and the **u**—and put them 1Kg 7:51
and the holy **u** that were in the 1Kg 8:4
all the **u** of the House of the 1Kg 10:21
silver, gold, and **u**. 1Kg 15:15
silver and all the **u** found in 2Kg 14:14
charge of the **u** used in worship 1Ch 9:28
and all the **u** of the sanctuary, 1Ch 9:29
and all their **u**—Huram-abi made 2Ch 4:16
made all these **u** in such great 2Ch 4:18
and all the **u**—and put them 2Ch 5:1
and the holy **u** that were in the 2Ch 5:5
all the **u** of the House of the 2Ch 9:20
silver, gold, and **u**. 2Ch 15:18
all the **u** that were found with 2Ch 25:24
up the **u** of God's temple 2Ch 28:24
of burnt offering and all its **u**, 2Ch 29:18
of the Presence⌋ and all its **u**. 2Ch 29:18
the **u** that King Ahaz rejected 2Ch 29:19
took some of the **u** of the LORD's 2Ch 36:7
the valuable **u** of the LORD's 2Ch 36:10
destroyed all its valuable **u**. 2Ch 36:19
and bronze **u** for your goods. Ezk 27:13
u used to slaughter the burnt Ezk 40:42
cups, jugs, copper **u**, and dining Mk 7:4

UTHAI *(2)*

U son of Ammihud, son of Omri, 1Ch 9:4
U and Zaccur from Bigvai's Ezr 8:14

UTMOST *(1)*

demonstrate the **u** patience as 1Tm 1:16

UTTER *(7)*

I heard you **u** a curse about— Jdg 17:2
and my tongue will not **u** deceit. Jb 27:4
They **u** curses and lies. Ps 59:12
rejoicing and **u** contempt, Ezk 36:5
and **u** disgrace will cover your Hab 2:16
demonstrating **u** faithfulness, Ti 2:10
their mouths **u** arrogant words, Jd 16

UTTERED *(3)*

He **u** malicious curses against me 1Kg 2:8
and the LORD **u** this oracle 2Kg 9:25
blasphemies you **u** against the Ezk 35:12

UTTERING *(2)*

conceiving and **u** lying words Is 59:13
For **u** bombastic, empty words, 2Pt 2:18

UTTERLY *(13)*

are to **u** detest and abhor it, Dt 7:26
that my fathers **u** destroyed was 2Ch 32:14
they **u** desecrated the dwelling Ps 74:7
for love, it would be **u** scorned. Sg 8:7
be turned back ⌊and⌋ **u** ashamed— Is 42:17
be shocked and **u** appalled. Jr 2:12
they will be **u** shamed, an Jr 20:11
because they will be **u** helpless Jr 47:3
mother will be **u** humiliated; Jr 50:12
and observe—be **u** astounded! Hab 1:5
were **u** astonished and asked, Mt 19:25
At this they were **u** astounded. Mk 5:42
I saw her, I was **u** astounded. Rv 17:6

UTTERS *(5)*

mouth of the righteous **u** wisdom; Ps 37:30
but a dishonest witness **u** lies. Pr 14:5
but one who **u** lies is deceitful. Pr 14:25
and one who **u** lies will not Pr 19:5
and one who **u** lies perishes. Pr 19:9

UZ *(8)*

U, Hul, Gether, and Mash. Gn 10:23
U his firstborn, his brother Buz, Gn 22:21
are Dishan's sons: **U** and Aran. Gn 36:28
Lud, Aram, **U**, Hul, Gether, 1Ch 1:17
Dishan's sons: **U** and Aran. 1Ch 1:42
in the country of **U** named Job. Jb 1:1

V

but went to the V of Megiddo to 2Ch 35:22
night through the V Gate toward Neh 2:13
by way of the v and inspected Neh 2:15
through the V Gate and returned Neh 2:15
of Zanoah repaired the V Gate. Neh 3:13
in the villages of the Ono V." Neh 6:2
Beer-sheba to the V of Hinnom. Neh 11:30
and Ono, the v of the craftsmen Neh 11:35
He paws in the v and rejoices in Jb 39:21
when I go through the darkest v, Ps 23:4
will apportion the V of Succoth. Ps 60:6
they pass through the V of Baca, Ps 84:6
will apportion the V of Succoth. Ps 108:7
may ravens of the v pluck it out Pr 30:17
to see the blossoms of the v, Sg 6:11
of grain in the v of Rephaim. Is 17:5
oracle against the V of Vision: Is 22:1
in the V of Vision— Is 22:5
on the summit above the rich v. Is 28:1
on the summit above the rich v, Is 28:4
as at the v of Gibeon, to do Is 28:21
Every v will be lifted up, Is 40:4
cattle that go down into the v, Is 63:14
and the V of Achor a place for Is 65:10
Look at your behavior in the v; Jr 2:23
of Topheth in the V of Hinnom in Jr 7:31
Topheth and the V of Hinnom, Jr 7:32
Hinnom, but the V of Slaughter. Jr 7:32
go out to the V of Hinnom near Jr 19:2
Topheth and the V of Hinnom, Jr 19:6
Hinnom, but the V of Slaughter. Jr 19:6
who sit above the v, ⌊you atop⌋ Jr 21:13
The whole v—the corpses, the Jr 31:40
as the Kidron V to the corner Jr 31:40
of Baal in the V of Hinnom to Jr 32:35
silent, a remnant of their v. Jr 47:5
The v will perish, and the plain Jr 48:8
your flowing v, you faithless Jr 49:4
mountains like doves of the v, Ezk 7:16
on the mountains and in every v; Ezk 31:12
me down in the middle of the v; Ezk 37:1
of them on the surface of the v, Ezk 37:2
the V of the Travelers east of Ezk 39:11
be called the V of Hamon-gog. Ezk 39:11
buried it in the V of Hamon-gog. Ezk 39:15
of Israel in the v of Jezreel. Hs 1:5
to her and make the V of Achor Hs 2:15
them to the V of Jehoshaphat. Jl 3:2
come to the V of Jehoshaphat, Jl 3:12
multitudes in the v of decision! Jl 3:14
is near in the v of decision. Jl 3:14
watering the V of Acacias. Jl 3:18
the ruler from the V of Aven, Am 1:5
stones into the v and expose her Mc 1:6
among the myrtle trees in the v. Zch 1:8
forming a huge v, so that half Zch 14:4
You will flee by My mountain v, Zch 14:5
for the v of the mountains will Zch 14:5
v will be filled, and every Lk 3:5
disciples across the Kidron V, Jn 18:1

VALLEYS *(20)*
they stretch out like river v, Nm 24:6
flowing in both v and hills; Dt 8:7
is a land of mountains and v, Dt 11:11
and not a god of the v, 1Kg 20:28
mountains or into one of the v." 2Kg 2:16
those in⌋ the v to the east and 1Ch 12:15
in charge of the herds in the v. 1Ch 27:29
Will it plow the v behind you? Jb 39:10
and the v covered with grain. Ps 65:13
mountains rose and v sank— Ps 104:8
the springs to gush into the v; Ps 104:10
rose of Sharon, a lily of the v. Sg 2:1
Your best v were full of Is 22:7
Why do you brag about your v, Jr 49:4
hills, to the ravines and the v: Ezk 6:3
fill the v with your carcass. Ezk 32:5
hills, in your v, and in all Ezk 35:8
the ravines and v, to the Ezk 36:4
and hills, to the ravines and v: Ezk 36:6
and the v will split apart, Mc 1:4

VALUABLE *(16)*
I considered your life v today, 1Sm 26:24
consider my life v and rescue me 1Sm 26:24
goods on the bodies and v items. 2Ch 20:25
silver, gold, and v things, 2Ch 21:3
to Jerusalem and v gifts to King 2Ch 32:23
along with the v utensils of the 2Ch 36:10
destroyed all its v utensils. 2Ch 36:19
gleaming bronze, as v as gold. Ezr 8:27
love is so v that people take Ps 36:7
A man with v possessions but Ps 49:20
faithful ones is v in the LORD's Ps 116:15
all kinds of v property and fill Pr 1:13
faith—more v than gold, which 1Pt 1:7
by men but chosen and v to God— 1Pt 2:4
a chosen and v cornerstone, 1Pt 2:6
which is very v in God's eyes. 1Pt 3:4

VALUABLES *(3)*
livestock, and v, in addition to Ezr 1:6
city, all its products and v. Jr 20:5
seize wealth and v, and multiply Ezk 22:25

VALUATION *(25)*
flock by your v in silver Lv 5:15
to your v as a restitution Lv 5:18
to your v, as a restitution Lv 6:6
that involves the v of people, Lv 27:2
if the v concerns a male from 20 Lv 27:3
your v is 50 silver shekels Lv 27:3
a female, your v is 30 shekels. Lv 27:4
your v for a male is 20 shekels Lv 27:5
your v for a male is five silver Lv 27:6
a female your v is three shekels Lv 27:6
your v is 15 shekels for a male Lv 27:7
if one is too poor to pay the v, Lv 27:8
the priest makes the v for you. Lv 27:12
he must add a fifth to the v. Lv 27:13
must add a fifth to the v price, Lv 27:15
your v will be proportional to Lv 27:16
will stand according to your v. Lv 27:17
so that your v will be reduced. Lv 27:18
must add a fifth to the v price, Lv 27:19
amount of the v up to the Year Lv 27:23
will pay the v on that day as Lv 27:23
to your v by adding a fifth Lv 27:27
can be sold according to your v. Lv 27:27
male according to your v: Nm 18:16
each man according to his v, 2Kg 23:35

VALUATIONS *(1)*
All your v will be ⌊measured⌋ by Lv 27:25

VALUE *(19)*
adding a fifth of its v to it, Lv 5:16
and add a fifth of its v to it. Lv 6:5
a fifth to its v and give the Lv 22:14
the priest will set a v for him. Lv 27:8
will set a v for him according Lv 27:8
The priest will set its v, Lv 27:12
the priest will assess its v, Lv 27:14
adding a fifth of its v to it. Lv 27:27
he must add one-fifth to its v. Lv 27:31
add a fifth of its v to it, Nm 5:7
will give you its v in silver." 1Kg 21:2
can know its v, since it cannot Jb 28:13
does not v the power of a man. Ps 147:10
of the wicked is of little v. Pr 10:20
despised, and we didn't v Him. Is 53:3
So they calculated their v, Ac 19:19
count my life of no v to myself, Ac 20:24
the surpassing v of knowing Php 3:8
are not of any v against fleshly Col 2:23

VALUED *(4)*
Wisdom cannot be v in the gold Jb 28:16
and it cannot be v in pure gold. Jb 28:19
price I was v by them. Zch 11:13
was highly v by him, was sick Lk 7:2

VALUES *(1)*
The LORD v those who fear Him, Ps 147:11

VANDAL *(1)*
in his work is brother to a v. Pr 18:9

VANIAH *(1)*
V, Meremoth, Eliashib, Ezr 10:36

VANISH *(11)*
he will v forever like his own Jb 20:7
will v like water that flows Ps 58:7
For my days v like smoke, and my Ps 102:3
May sinners v from the earth and Ps 104:35
The idols will v completely. Is 2:18
the harvest will v on the day of Is 17:11
will wither, blow away, and v. Is 19:7
wisdom of their wise men will v, Is 29:14
For the ruthless one will v, Is 29:20
the heavens will v like smoke, Is 51:6
marvel and v away, because I am Ac 13:41

VANISHED *(6)*
and they v from the assembly. Nm 16:33
of the LORD v from his sight. Jdg 6:21
gone, and the vegetation has v. Is 15:6
marauders have v from the land. Is 16:4
her splendor has v from Daughter Lm 1:6
people have v from the land; Mc 7:2

VANISHES *(6)*
As a cloud fades away and v, Jb 7:9
over it, it v, and its place is Ps 103:16
and hope placed in wealth v. Pr 11:7
and like the early dew that v. Hs 6:4
like the early dew that v, Hs 13:3
for a little while, then v. Jms 4:14

VANISHING *(1)*
a lying tongue is a v mist, Pr 21:6

VANQUISH *(1)*
He will v our iniquities. Mc 7:19

VAPOR *(4)*
every mortal man is only a v. Ps 39:5
every man is a mere v. Ps 39:11
Men are only a v; exalted men, Ps 62:9
they ⌊weigh⌋ less than a v. Ps 62:9

VARIATION *(1)*
Him there is no v or shadow cast Jms 1:17

VARIED *(1)*
managers of the v grace of God. 1Pt 4:10

VARIETY *(1)*
led along by a v of passions, 2Tm 3:6

VARIOUS *(29)*
the kite, the v kinds of falcon, Lv 11:14
the gull, the v kinds of hawk, Lv 11:16
the stork, the v kinds of heron, Lv 11:19
the v kinds of locust, the Lv 11:22
of locust, the v kinds of Lv 11:22
of katydid, the v kinds of Lv 11:22
and the v kinds of grasshopper. Lv 11:22
the v kinds of large lizard, Lv 11:29
the kite, the v kinds of falcon, Dt 14:13
the gull, the v kinds of hawk, Dt 14:15
the stork, the v kinds of heron, Dt 14:18
stones of v colors, all kinds 1Ch 29:2
full of spices and v mixtures of 2Ch 16:14
gold bowls, 410 v silver bowls, Ezr 1:10
and all the v foreign troops, Ezk 30:5
suffering from v diseases and Mt 4:24
and earthquakes in v places. Mt 24:7
were sick with v diseases and Mk 1:34
will be earthquakes in v places, Mk 13:8
sick with v diseases brought Lk 4:40
famines and plagues in v places, Lk 21:11
complex, and in v homes, they Ac 5:42
managing, v kinds of languages 1Co 12:28
captives of v passions and Ti 3:3
signs and wonders, v miracles, Heb 2:4
and v washings imposed until the Heb 9:10
led astray by v kinds of strange Heb 13:9
you experience v trials, Jms 1:2
had to be distressed by v trials 1Pt 1:6

VARYING *(1)*
weights and v measures— Pr 20:10

VASE *(1)*
shattered like a precious v. Jr 25:34

VASHTI *(10)*
Queen V also gave a feast for Est 1:9
to bring Queen V before him with Est 1:11
But Queen V refused to come at Est 1:12
should be done with Queen V, Est 1:15
Queen V has defied not only the Est 1:16
ordered Queen V brought before Est 1:17
V is not to enter King Est 1:19
he remembered V, what she had Est 2:1
king will reign in place of V." Est 2:4
made her queen in place of V. Est 2:17

VASSAL *(2)*
Hoshea became his v and paid him 2Kg 17:3
became his v for three years. 2Kg 24:1

VAST *(29)*
along with a v number of horses Jos 11:4
slaughter there was v that day— 2Sm 18:7
understanding as ⌊v⌋ as the sand 1Kg 4:29
You are a v multitude and have 2Ch 13:8
and Libyans a v army with very 2Ch 16:8
A v multitude from beyond the 2Ch 20:2
before this v multitude that 2Ch 20:12

because of this **v** multitude, 2Ch 20:15
handed over a **v** army to them 2Ch 24:24
heard throughout his **v** kingdom, Est 1:20
the LORD, above **v** waters, Ps 29:3
Here is the sea, **v** and wide, Ps 104:25
trade on the **v** waters. Ps 107:23
like one who finds **v** treasure. Ps 119:162
comprehend⌋; how **v** their sum is! Ps 139:17
Our Lord is great, **v** in power; Ps 147:5
dominion will be **v**, and its Is 9:7
beauty; you will see a **v** land. Is 33:17
your ruin is as **v** as the sea. Lm 2:13
army and **v** horde in battle, Ezk 17:17
and a **v** company of troops. Ezk 26:7
stood on their feet, a **v** army. Ezk 37:10
I have built by my **v** power to be Dn 4:30
he will rule a **v** realm and do Dn 11:3
the working of His **v** strength. Eph 1:19
the Lord and by His **v** strength. Eph 6:10
and there was a **v** multitude from Rv 7:9
loud voice of a **v** multitude in Rv 19:1
like the voice of a **v** multitude, Rv 19:6

VAT *(3)*
in the wine **v** in order to hide Jdg 6:11
and wine **v** will not sustain Hs 9:2
to dip 50 measures from the **v**, Hg 2:16

VATS *(4)*
from⌋ your harvest or your **v**. Ex 22:29
your **v** will overflow with new Pr 3:10
and the **v** will overflow with new Jl 2:24
the wine **v** overflow because the Jl 3:13

VAULT *(1)*
of His **v** on the earth. Am 9:6

VAULTS *(1)*
up with Me, sealed up in My **v**? Dt 32:34

VEDAN *(1)*
V and Javan from Uzal dealt in Ezk 27:19

VEER *(1)*
wheels did not **v** away from them. Ezk 10:16

VEGETABLE *(2)*
by hand as in a **v** garden. Dt 11:10
so I can have it for a **v** garden, 1Kg 21:2

VEGETABLES *(6)*
Better a meal of **v** where there Pr 15:17
Let us be given **v** to eat and Dn 1:12
were to drink and gave them **v**. Dn 1:16
taller than the **v** and becomes a Mt 13:32
and grows taller than all the **v**, Mk 4:32
but one who is weak eats only **v**. Rm 14:2

VEGETATION *(7)*
said, "Let the earth produce **v**: Gn 1:11
The earth brought forth **v**: Gn 1:12
devoured all the **v** in their land Ps 105:35
is gone, and the **v** has vanished. Is 15:6
hills, and dry up all their **v**. Is 42:15
eating the **v** of the land, Am 7:2
that produces **v** useful to those Heb 6:7

VEHEMENTLY *(2)*
stood by, **v** accusing Him. Lk 23:10
party got up and argued **v**: Ac 23:9

VEIL *(38)*
So she took her **v** and covered Gn 24:65
then removed her **v** and put her Gn 38:19
You are to make a **v** of blue, Ex 26:31
Hang the **v** under the clasps and Ex 26:33
testimony there behind the **v**, Ex 26:33
so the **v** will make a separation Ex 26:33
outside the **v** and the lampstand Ex 26:35
outside the **v** that is in front Ex 27:21
in front of the **v** by the ark Ex 30:6
them, he put a **v** over his face. Ex 34:33
would remove the **v** until he came Ex 34:34
would put the **v** over his face Ex 34:35
seat, and the **v** for the screen; Ex 35:12
Then he made the **v** with blue, Ex 36:35
and the bases of the **v**— Ex 38:27
skins; the **v** for the screen; Ex 39:34
screen off the ark with the **v**. Ex 40:3
put up the **v** for the screen, Ex 40:21
the tabernacle, outside the **v**. Ex 40:22
of meeting, in front of the **v**, Ex 40:26
in front of the **v** of the Lv 4:6
the LORD in front of the **v**. Lv 4:17
place behind the **v** in front of Lv 16:2
and bring ⌊them⌋ inside the **v**. Lv 16:12
brings its blood inside the **v**, Lv 16:15
outside the **v** of the testimony Lv 24:3
take down the screening **v**, Nm 4:5
and for what is inside the **v**, Nm 18:7
He made the **v** of blue, purple, 2Ch 3:14
Clouds **v** Him so that He cannot Jb 22:14
Behind your **v**, your eyes are Sg 4:1
Behind your **v**, your brow is like Sg 4:3
Behind your **v**, your brow is like Sg 6:7
remove your **v**, strip off ⌊your⌋ Is 47:2
used to put a **v** over his face so 2Co 3:13
covenant, the same **v** remains; 2Co 3:14
a **v** lies over their hearts, 2Co 3:15
to the Lord, the **v** is removed. 2Co 3:16

VEILED *(4)*
widow's clothes, **v** ⌊her face⌋, Gn 38:14
He has **v** my paths with darkness. Jb 19:8
our gospel is **v**, it is veiled to 2Co 4:3
it is **v** to those who are 2Co 4:3

VEILS *(5)*
be like one who **v** herself beside Sg 1:7
pendants, bracelets, **v**, Is 3:19
linen clothes, turbans, and **v**. Is 3:23
and who make **v** for the heads Ezk 13:18
tear off your **v** and deliver My Ezk 13:21

VENGEANCE *(51)*
will suffer **v** seven times over. Gn 4:15
execute the **v** of the covenant. Lv 26:25
Execute **v** for the Israelites Nm 31:2
to inflict the LORD's **v** on them. Nm 31:3
V belongs to Me; I will repay. Dt 32:35
I will take **v** on My adversaries Dt 32:41
He will take **v** on His Dt 32:43
nation took **v** on its enemies. Jos 10:13
LORD brought **v** on your enemies Jdg 11:36
until I have taken **v** on you." Jdg 15:7
With one act of **v**, let me pay Jdg 16:28
I have taken **v** on my enemies." 1Sm 14:24
the LORD take **v** on you for me, 1Sm 24:12
LORD has granted **v** to my lord 2Sm 4:8
He gives me **v** and casts down 2Sm 22:48
gives me **v** and subdues peoples Ps 18:47
let **v** for the shed blood of Your Ps 79:10
LORD, God of **v**—God of Ps 94:1
of vengeance—God of **v**, appear. Ps 94:1
inflicting **v** on the nations and Ps 149:7
For the LORD has a day of **v**, Is 34:8
is your God; **v** is coming. God's Is 35:4
I will take **v**; I will spare no Is 47:3
on garments of **v** for clothing, Is 59:17
and the day of our God's **v**; Is 61:2
For I planned the day of **v**, Is 63:4
let me see Your **v** on them, Jr 11:20
him and take our **v** on him." Jr 20:10
let me see Your **v** on them, Jr 20:12
a day of **v** to avenge Himself Jr 46:10
Since this is the LORD's **v**, Jr 50:15
take out your **v** on her; Jr 50:15
in Zion the **v** of the LORD our Jr 50:28
our God, the **v** for His temple. Jr 50:28
is the time of the LORD's **v**— Jr 51:6
is the LORD's **v**, vengeance for Jr 51:11
vengeance, **v** for His temple. Jr 51:11
case and take **v** on your behalf; Jr 51:36
to stir up wrath and take **v**, Ezk 24:8
I will take My **v** on Edom through Ezk 25:14
So they will know My **v**." Ezk 25:14
acted in **v** and took revenge Ezk 25:15
execute great **v** against them Ezk 25:17
LORD when I take My **v** on them." Ezk 25:17
I will take **v** in anger and wrath Mc 5:15
the LORD takes **v** and is fierce Nah 1:2
The LORD takes **v** against His Nah 1:2
are days of **v** to fulfill all Lk 21:22
it is written: **V** belongs to Me; Rm 12:19
taking **v** with flaming fire on 2Th 1:8
who has said, **V** belongs to Me, I Heb 10:30

VENGEFULLY *(1)*
Edom acted **v** against the house Ezk 25:12

VENOM *(6)*
Their wine is serpents' **v**, Dt 32:33
turns into cobras' **v** inside him. Jb 20:14
They have **v** like the venom of a Ps 58:4
venom like the **v** of a snake, Ps 58:4
viper's **v** is under their lips. Ps 140:3
Vipers' **v** is under their lips. Rm 3:13

VENOMOUS *(1)*
as well as **v** snakes that slither Dt 32:24

VENT *(4)*
will you **v** Your wrath on the Nm 16:22
fool gives full **v** to his anger, Pr 29:11
When I **v** My jealous rage on you, Ezk 23:25
I will not **v** the full fury of My Hs 11:9

VENTED *(1)*
and I have **v** My wrath on them Ezk 5:13

VENTURE *(2)*
who would not **v** to set the sole Dt 28:56
That wealth was lost in a bad **v**, Ec 5:14

VENTURED *(2)*
Since I have **v** to speak to the Gn 18:27
Since I have **v** to speak to the Gn 18:31

VERDICT *(7)*
and He issued His **v** last night." Gn 31:42
will give you a **v** in the case. Dt 17:9
abide by the **v** they give you at Dt 17:10
you and the **v** they announce to Dt 17:11
judgment and **v** here ⌊and now⌋." Jdg 20:7
v is on the lips of a king; Pr 16:10
this is the **v** that the LORD has Jr 38:21

VERGE *(2)*
I was on the **v** of complete ruin Pr 5:14
come to the **v** of ruin— Ac 19:27

VERIFICATION *(1)*
It is a **v** of your honor to all Gn 20:16

VERIFIED *(2)*
Everything was ⌊**v**⌋ by number and Ezr 8:34
report was investigated and **v**, Est 2:23

VERIFY *(1)*
discover and **v** that the city is Ezr 4:15

VERMILION *(2)*
with cedar and painted with **v**. Jr 22:14
of the Chaldeans, engraved in **v**, Ezk 23:14

VERMIN *(1)*
from pigs, **v**, and rats, will Is 66:17

VERSES *(1)*
as I recite my **v** to the king; Ps 45:1

VERTICAL *(1)*
there by a **v** wall with a plumb Am 7:7

VERY *(211)*
(See pp. xi-xii.)

VESSEL *(7)*
if it is boiled in a bronze **v**, Lv 6:28
and a **v** will be produced for a Pr 25:4
are like glaze on an earthen **v**. Pr 26:23
against every splendid sea **v**. Is 2:16
in a clean **v** to the house Is 66:20
part of the **v** and had stretched Jnh 1:5
possess his own **v** in 1Th 4:4

VESSELS *(10)*
by sea, in reed **v** on the waters. Is 18:2
all the small **v**, from bowls to Is 22:24
and majestic **v** will not pass. Is 33:21
you who carry the **v** of the LORD. Is 52:11
some of the **v** from the house Dn 1:2
and put the **v** in the treasury of Dn 1:2
the gold and silver **v** that his Dn 5:2
in the gold **v** that had been Dn 5:3
v from His house were brought Dn 5:23
and all the **v** of worship with Heb 9:21

VESTIBULE *(5)*
plans for the **v** ⌊of the temple⌋ 1Ch 28:11
he had made in front of the **v** 2Ch 8:12
in front of the **v** of the LORD's 2Ch 15:8
also closed the doors of the **v**, 2Ch 29:7
they came to the **v** of the LORD's 2Ch 29:17

VESTIGE *(1)*
from this place every **v** of Baal, Zph 1:4

VICINITY *(10)*
night in the **v** of God's temple 1Ch 9:27
cities in ⌊the **v** of⌋ Ashdod and 2Ch 26:6
and all the **v** of the Jordan were Mt 3:5
the whole **v** and brought to Mt 14:35
the entire **v** of Galilee. Mk 1:28
throughout that **v** and began to Mk 6:55
into all the **v** of the Jordan, Lk 3:3
spread throughout the entire **v**. Lk 4:14
go out to every place in the **v**. Lk 4:37
throughout Judea and all the **v**. Lk 7:17

VICIOUS *(4)*
can say that a v animal ate him. Gn 37:20
A v animal has devoured him. Gn 37:33
their knives are v weapons. Gn 49:5
and no v beast will go up on it; Is 35:9

VICIOUSLY *(1)*
to strike v with ⌊your⌋ fist Is 58:4

VICTIM *(7)*
If a murder v is found lying in Dt 21:1
from the v to the nearby Dt 21:2
nearest to the v are to get a Dt 21:3
nearest to the v will wash their Dt 21:6
one who falls v to criminals. 2Sm 3:34
and rescue the v of robbery from Jr 21:12
Rescue the v of robbery from the Jr 22:3

VICTIMS *(2)*
her v are countless. Pr 7:26
will no longer be v of famine in Ezk 34:29

VICTOR *(9)*
I will give the v the right to Rv 2:7
v will never be harmed by the Rv 2:11
I will give the v some of the Rv 2:17
The v and the one who keeps My Rv 2:26
the v will be dressed in white Rv 3:5
The v: I will make him a pillar Rv 3:12
The v: I will give him the right Rv 3:21
he went out as a v to conquer. Rv 6:2
The v will inherit these things, Rv 21:7

VICTORIES *(4)*
He gives great v to His king; Ps 18:50
with mighty v from His right Ps 20:6
my God, who ordains v for Jacob. Ps 44:4
We have won no v on earth, Is 26:18

VICTORIOUS *(8)*
LORD made David v wherever he 2Sm 8:6
LORD made David v wherever he 2Sm 8:14
LORD made David v wherever he 1Ch 18:6
LORD made David v wherever he 1Ch 18:13
on Your horses, Your v chariot? Hab 3:8
is righteous and v, humble and Zch 9:9
are more than v through Him who Rm 8:37
has been v so that He may open Rv 5:5

VICTORY *(37)*
not the sound of a v cry and not Ex 32:18
your enemies to give you v.' Dt 20:4
this great v through Your Jdg 15:18
about a great v for all Israel. 1Sm 19:5
That day's v was turned into 2Sm 19:2
about a great v that day. 2Sm 23:10
LORD brought about a great v. 2Sm 23:12
the LORD had given v to Aram. 2Kg 5:1
LORD's arrow of v, yes, the 2Kg 13:17
yes, the arrow of v over Aram. 2Kg 13:17
the LORD gave them a great v. 1Ch 11:14
for joy at your v and lift the Ps 20:5
LORD gives v to His anointed; Ps 20:6
LORD, give v to the king! Ps 20:9
greatly he rejoices in Your v! Ps 21:1
glory is great through Your v; Ps 21:5
their arm did not bring them v— Ps 44:3
my sword does not bring me v. Ps 44:6
But You give us v over our foes Ps 44:7
and holy arm have won Him v. Ps 98:1
The LORD has made His v known; Ps 98:2
the earth have seen our God's v. Ps 98:3
shouts of joy and v in the tents Ps 118:15
the One who gives v to kings, Ps 144:10
but v comes from the LORD. Pr 21:31
v comes with many counselors. Pr 24:6
so My arm accomplished v for Me, Is 63:5
will sing the v song over you. Jr 51:14
until He has led justice to v. Mt 12:20
has been swallowed up in v. 1Co 15:54
O Death, where is your v? 1Co 15:55
gives us the v through our Lord 1Co 15:57
have had v over the evil one. 1Jn 2:13
and you have had v over the evil 1Jn 2:14
This is the v that has conquered 1Jn 5:4
I also won the v and sat down Rv 3:21
had won the v from the beast, Rv 15:2

VIEW *(22)*
in full v of the flocks, Gn 30:41
and v the land of Canaan I am Dt 32:49
Although you will v the land Dt 32:52
a mountain pass hidden from v, 1Sm 25:20
the book in full v of all the Neh 8:5
do not v lightly all the Neh 9:32
In v of all this, we are making Neh 9:38
obscures the v of ⌊His⌋ throne Jb 26:9
In full v of the public, He Jb 34:26
you in plain v of a noble. Pr 25:7
a den of robbers in your v? Jr 7:11
and in full v of the people, Ezk 37:20
continually v the face of My Mt 18:10
king came in to v the guests, Mt 22:11
other Mary went to v the tomb. Mt 28:1
to the strict v of our Ac 22:3
In v of the fact that I am an Rm 11:13
not based on a human point of v. Gl 1:11
you will not accept any other v. Gl 5:10
to be a loss in v of the Php 3:8
And in v of this, we always pray 2Th 1:11
nations will v their bodies for Rv 11:9

VIEWED *(3)*
officials came and v the piles, 2Ch 31:8
the things v as nothing—so He 1Co 1:28
things that are v as something, 1Co 1:28

VIEWS *(1)*
their v of justice and Hab 1:7

VIGIL *(2)*
It was a night of v in honor of Ex 12:42
a night v for all the Israelites Ex 12:42

VIGOR *(4)*
approach the grave in full v, Jb 5:26
bones may be full of youthful v, Jb 20:11
Their v had left them. Jb 30:2
to the days of his youthful v. Jb 33:25

VIGOROUS *(2)*
for they are v and give birth Ex 1:19
my enemies are v and powerful; Ps 38:19

VIGOROUSLY *(1)*
For he v refuted the Jews in Ac 18:28

VILE *(5)*
corrupt, and they do v deeds. Ps 53:1
filled with everything v and Rv 17:4
THE V THINGS OF THE EARTH Rv 17:5
unbelievers, v, murderers, Rv 21:8
one who does what is v or false, Rv 21:27

VILLAGE *(21)*
were gathered from the v fields, Neh 12:44
noise of the v and never hears Jb 39:7
When you enter any town or v, Mt 10:11
Go into the v ahead of you. Mt 21:2
and brought him out of the v. Mk 8:23
"Don't even go into the v." Mk 8:26
Go into the v ahead of you. Mk 11:2
had come from every v of Galilee Lk 5:17
from one town and v to another, Lk 8:1
and traveled from v to village, Lk 9:6
and traveled from village to v, Lk 9:6
they entered a v of the Lk 9:52
and they went to another v. Lk 9:56
entered a v, and a woman named Lk 10:38
one town and v after another, Lk 13:22
As He entered a v, 10 men with Lk 17:12
Go into the v ahead of you. Lk 19:30
their way to a v called Emmaus, Lk 24:13
came near the v where they were Lk 24:28
the v of Mary and her sister Jn 11:1
come into the v but was still Jn 11:30

VILLAGES *(111)*
by their v and encampments: Gn 25:16
But houses in v that have no Lv 25:31
including Heshbon and all its v. Nm 21:25
captured its v and drove out Nm 21:32
went and captured their v, Nm 32:41
which he renamed Jair's V. Nm 32:41
Kenath with its v and called it Nm 32:42
who lived in v as far as Gaza, Dt 2:23
a large number of rural v. Dt 3:5
name, Jair's V, as it is today Dt 3:14
king, all its v, and everyone Jos 10:37
it—its king and all its v. Jos 10:39
with the cities and their v. Jos 13:23
with the cities and their v. Jos 13:28
all of Jair's V that are in Jos 13:30
29 cities in all, with their v. Jos 15:32
14 cities, with their v; Jos 15:36
16 cities, with their v; Jos 15:41
nine cities, with their v; Jos 15:44
Ekron, with its towns and v; Jos 15:45
near Ashdod, with their v; Jos 15:46
Ashdod, with its towns and v; Jos 15:47
its towns and v, to the Brook Jos 15:47
Giloh—11 cities, with their v; Jos 15:51
—nine cities, with their v; Jos 15:54
—10 cities, with their v; Jos 15:57
six cities, with their v; Jos 15:59
two cities, with their v. Jos 15:60
six cities, with their v. Jos 15:62
all these cities with their v. Jos 16:9
Geba—12 cities, with their v; Jos 18:24
14 cities, with their v. Jos 18:28
13 cities, with their v; Jos 19:6
four cities, with their v; Jos 19:7
and all the v surrounding these Jos 19:8
12 cities, with their v. Jos 19:15
these cities, with their v. Jos 19:16
—16 cities, with their v. Jos 19:22
clans, the cities, with their v. Jos 19:23
Rehob—22 cities, with their v. Jos 19:30
these cities with their v. Jos 19:31
19 cities, with their v. Jos 19:38
clans, the cities with their v. Jos 19:39
these cities with their v. Jos 19:48
the fields and v of the city to Jos 21:12
of Beth-shean and its v, Jdg 1:27
Taanach and its v, or the Jdg 1:27
the residents of Dor and its v, Jdg 1:27
residents of Ibleam and its v, Jdg 1:27
residents of Megiddo and its v. Jdg 1:27
V were deserted, they were Jdg 5:7
are called Jair's V to this day. Jdg 10:4
300 years in Heshbon and its v, Jdg 11:26
in Aroer and its v, and in all Jdg 11:26
cities and the outlying v. 1Sm 6:18
he had the v of Jair son of 1Kg 4:13
captured Jair's V along with 1Ch 2:23
along with Kenath and its v— 1Ch 2:23
Their v were Etam, Ain, Rimmon, 1Ch 4:32
surrounding v as far as Baal. 1Ch 4:33
the fields and v around the city 1Ch 6:56
were Bethel and its v; 1Ch 7:28
Gezer and its v to the west, 1Ch 7:28
Shechem and its v as far as 1Ch 7:28
as far as Ayyah and its v, 1Ch 7:28
and its v, Taanach and its 1Ch 7:29
Taanach and its v, Megiddo and 1Ch 7:29
Megiddo and its v, and Dor and 1Ch 7:29
its villages, and Dor and its v. 1Ch 7:29
who built Ono and Lod and its v, 1Ch 8:12
who lived in the v of the 1Ch 9:16
by genealogy in their v. 1Ch 9:22
came from their v at fixed times 1Ch 9:25
Gath and its v from Philistine 1Ch 18:1
in the cities, in the v, and in 1Ch 27:25
Bethel and its v, Jeshanah and 2Ch 13:19
Jeshanah and its v, and Ephron 2Ch 13:19
villages, and Ephron and its v. 2Ch 13:19
Soco and its v, Timnah and its 2Ch 28:18
Timnah and its v, Gimzo and its 2Ch 28:18
Gimzo and its v, and they lived 2Ch 28:18
in the v of the Ono Valley. Neh 6:2
but in the v of Judah each lived Neh 11:3
were in all the v of Judah, Neh 11:20
lived in Kiriath-arba and its v, Neh 11:25
Dibon and its v, and Jekabzeel Neh 11:25
and Jekabzeel and its v, Neh 11:25
and Beer-sheba and its v; Neh 11:27
in Ziklag and Meconah and its v, Neh 11:28
Zanoah and Adullam with their v; Neh 11:30
its fields and Azekah and its v. Neh 11:30
Aija, and Bethel—and its v, Neh 11:31
from the v of the Netophathites, Neh 12:28
they had built v for themselves Neh 12:29
Jews who live in v observe the Est 9:19
He waits in ambush near the v; Ps 10:8
and on all its ⌊dependent⌋ v— Jr 19:15
and its v will be burned down. Jr 49:2
and her v on the mainland will Ezk 26:6
slaughter your v on the mainland Ezk 26:8
its v will go into captivity. Ezk 30:18
go up against a land of open v; Ezk 38:11
went to all the towns and v, Mt 9:35
can go into the v and buy food Mt 14:15
the neighboring v so that I may Mk 1:38
going around the v in a circuit, Mk 6:6
countryside and v to buy Mk 6:36
He would go, into v, towns, or Mk 6:56
disciples to the v of Caesarea Mk 8:27

surrounding v and countryside Lk 9:12
many v of the Samaritans Ac 8:25

VINDICATE *(8)*
LORD will indeed v His people Dt 32:36
v me, LORD, according to my Ps 7:8
V me, LORD, because I have lived Ps 26:1
V me, LORD, my God, in keeping Ps 35:24
V me, God, and defend my cause Ps 43:1
Your name, and v me by Your Ps 54:1
May he v the afflicted among the Ps 72:4
witnesses to v ⌊themselves⌋, Is 43:9

VINDICATED *(5)*
You are fully v." Gn 20:16
Rachel said, "God has v me; Gn 30:6
case⌋, so that you may be v. Is 43:26
Yet wisdom is v by her deeds." Mt 11:19
wisdom is v by all her children. Lk 7:35

VINDICATES *(1)*
me when I call, God, who v me. Ps 4:1

VINDICATION *(6)*
my v come from You, ⌊for⌋ You Ps 17:2
those who want my v shout for Ps 35:27
yet my v is with the LORD, Is 49:4
I, proclaiming v, powerful to Is 63:1
LORD has brought about our v; Jr 51:10
you the autumn rain for your v. Jl 2:23

VINE *(44)*
there was a v in front of me. Gn 40:9
On the v were three branches. Gn 40:10
He ties his donkey to a v, Gn 49:11
of his donkey to the choice v. Gn 49:11
is a fruitful v, a fruitful vine Gn 49:22
a fruitful v beside a spring; Gn 49:22
For their v is from the vine of Dt 32:32
vine is from the v of Sodom Dt 32:32
under his own v and his own fig 1Kg 4:25
and found a wild v from which he 2Kg 4:39
from his own v and his own fig 2Kg 18:31
will be like a v that drops its Jb 15:33
You uprooted a v from Egypt; Ps 80:8
and see; take care of this v, Ps 80:14
like a fruitful v within your Ps 128:3
let's see if the v has budded, Sg 7:12
wine mourns; the v withers. All Is 24:7
as leaves wither on the v, Is 34:4
from his own v and his own fig Is 36:16
a choice v from the very best Jr 2:21
into a degenerate, foreign v? Jr 2:21
as thoroughly as a v the remnant Jr 6:9
will be no grapes on the v, Jr 8:13
weep for you, v of Sibmah, with Jr 48:32
how does the wood of the v, Ezk 15:2
wood of the v among the trees Ezk 15:6
and became a spreading v, Ezk 17:6
So it became a v, produced Ezk 17:6
And this v bent its roots toward Ezk 17:7
fruit, and become a splendid v. Ezk 17:8
was like a v in your vineyard Ezk 19:10
is a lush v; it yields fruit Hs 10:1
grain and blossom like the v. Hs 14:7
and ruined their v branches. Nah 2:2
The v, the fig, the pomegranate, Hg 2:19
under ⌊his⌋ v and fig tree." Zch 3:10
the v will yield its fruit, Zch 8:12
your v in your field will not Mal 3:11
fruit of the v until that day Mt 26:29
fruit of the v until that day Mk 14:25
the fruit of the v until the Lk 22:18
I am the true v, and My Father Jn 15:1
unless it remains on the v, Jn 15:4
I am the v; you are the Jn 15:5

VINEDRESSERS *(5)*
of the land to be v and farmers. 2Kg 25:12
had farmers and v in the hills 2Ch 26:10
will be your plowmen and v. Is 61:5
left to be v and farmers. Jr 52:16
wail, you v, over the wheat Jl 1:11

VINEGAR *(5)*
must not drink v made from wine Nm 6:3
and dip it in the v sauce." Ru 2:14
thirst they gave me v to drink. Ps 69:21
Like v to the teeth and smoke to Pr 10:26
or like ⌊pouring⌋ v on soda. Pr 25:20

VINES *(17)*
the grapes of your untended v. Lv 25:5
or harvest its untended v. Lv 25:11
of grain, figs, v, and Nm 20:5
land of wheat, barley, v, figs, Dt 8:8
He killed their v with hail and Ps 78:47
He struck their v and fig trees Ps 105:33
the blossoming v give off their Sg 2:13
to see if the v were budding and Sg 6:11
planted it with the finest v. Is 5:2
place where there were 1,000 v, Is 7:23
its choice v that reached as far Is 16:8
to weep for the v of Sibmah; Is 16:9
set out cuttings from exotic v. Is 17:10
fields and the fruitful v, Is 32:12
will consume your v and your fig Jr 5:17
devastate her v and fig trees. Hs 2:12
and there is no fruit on the v, Hab 3:17

VINEYARD *(73)*
was the first to plant a v. Gn 9:20
man lets a field or v be grazed Ex 22:5
the best of his own field or v. Ex 22:5
same with your v and your olive Ex 23:11
not strip your v bare or gather Lv 19:10
may prune your v and gather its Lv 25:3
sow your field or prune your v. Lv 25:4
travel through ⌊any⌋ field or v, Nm 20:17
man planted a v and not begun to Dt 20:6
not plant your v with two types Dt 22:9
plant and the produce of the v, Dt 22:9
you enter your neighbor's v, Dt 23:24
you gather the grapes of your v, Dt 24:21
You will plant a v but not enjoy Dt 28:30
Naboth the Jezreelite had a v; 1Kg 21:1
Give me your v so I can have it 1Kg 21:2
you a better v in its place, 1Kg 21:2
Give me your v for silver, 1Kg 21:6
will give you a v in its place. 1Kg 21:6
'I won't give you my v!' " 1Kg 21:6
I will give you the v of Naboth 1Kg 21:7
possession of the v of Naboth 1Kg 21:15
up to go down to the v of Naboth 1Kg 21:16
You'll find him in Naboth's v, 1Kg 21:18
and by the v of a man lacking Pr 24:30
plants a v with her earnings. Pr 31:16
I have not kept my own v. Sg 1:6
Solomon owned a v in Baal-hamon. Sg 8:11
He leased the v to tenants. Sg 8:11
I have my own v. The 1,000 are Sg 8:12
abandoned like a shelter in a v, Is 1:8
You have devastated the v. Is 3:14
a song about my loved one's v: Is 5:1
one I love had a v on a very Is 5:1
judge between Me and My v. Is 5:3
I have done for My v than I did? Is 5:4
what I am about to do to My v: Is 5:5
For the v of the LORD of Hosts Is 5:7
For a ten-acre v will yield only Is 5:10
day sing about a desirable v: Is 27:2
Go up among her v terraces and Jr 5:10
shepherds have destroyed My v; Jr 12:10
house or sow seed or plant a v. Jr 35:7
to live in and do not have v, Jr 35:9
was like a vine in your v, Ezk 19:10
a planting area for a v. Mc 1:6
to hire workers for his v. Mt 20:1
day, he sent them into his v. Mt 20:2
also go to my v, and I'll give Mt 20:4
also go to my v,' he told them. Mt 20:7
owner of the v told his foreman Mt 20:8
son, go, work in the v today.' Mt 21:28
who planted a v, put a fence Mt 21:33
him and threw him out of the v, Mt 21:39
when the owner of the v comes, Mt 21:40
and lease his v to other farmers Mt 21:41
A man planted a v, put a fence Mk 12:1
fruit of the v from the farmers Mk 12:2
and threw him out of the v. Mk 12:8
what will the owner of the v do? Mk 12:9
and give the v to others. Mk 12:9
tree that was planted in his v. Lk 13:6
He told the v worker, 'Listen, Lk 13:7
A man planted a v, leased it to Lk 20:9
give him some fruit from the v. Lk 20:10
Then the owner of the v said, Lk 20:13
him out of the v and killed him. Lk 20:15
the owner of the v do to them? Lk 20:15
and give the v to others." Lk 20:16
and My Father is the v keeper. Jn 15:1
Who plants a v and does not eat 1Co 9:7
of grapes from earth's v, Rv 14:18
the grapes from earth's v, Rv 14:19

VINEYARDS *(48)*
an inheritance of fields and v. Nm 16:14
won't go into the fields or v. Nm 21:22
a narrow passage between the v, Nm 22:24
and v and olive groves that you Dt 6:11
and cultivate v but not drink Dt 28:39
are eating from v and olive Jos 24:13
harvested grapes from their v. Jdg 9:27
and came to the v of Timnah. Jdg 14:5
as well as the v and olive Jdg 15:5
Go and hide in the v. Jdg 21:20
you leave the v and catch a wife Jdg 21:21
your best fields, v, and olive 1Sm 8:14
grain and your v and give them 1Sm 8:15
to give all of you fields and v? 1Sm 22:7
orchards and v, sheep and oxen, 2Kg 5:26
of bread and v, a land of olive 2Kg 18:32
plant v and eat their fruit. 2Kg 19:29
was in charge of the v. 1Ch 27:27
produce of the v for the wine 1Ch 27:27
our fields, v, and homes to get Neh 5:3
king's tax on our fields and v. Neh 5:4
fields and v belong to others. Neh 5:5
their fields, v, olive groves, Neh 5:11
cisterns, v, olive groves, Neh 9:25
and glean the v of the wicked. Jb 24:6
that they never go to ⌊their⌋ v. Jb 24:18
fields and plant v that yield Ps 107:37
houses and planted v for myself. Ec 2:4
they made me a keeper of the v. Sg 1:6
to me, in the v of En-gedi. Sg 1:14
little foxes that ruin the v— Sg 2:15
for our v are in bloom. Sg 2:15
Let's go early to the v; Sg 7:12
terraced v and the grapevines Is 16:8
or shouting for joy in the v. Is 16:10
new wine, a land of bread and v. Is 36:17
plant v and eat their fruit. Is 37:30
they will plant v and eat their Is 65:21
You will plant v again on the Jr 31:5
and v will again be bought in Jr 32:15
and he gave them v and fields at Jr 39:10
build houses, and plant v. Ezk 28:26
will give her v back to her and Hs 2:15
your many gardens and v, Am 4:9
from the lush v you have planted Am 5:11
will be wailing in all the v, Am 5:17
plant v and drink their wine, Am 9:14
plant v but never drink their Zph 1:13

VINTAGE *(2)*
better than the v of Abiezer? Jdg 8:2
for the v will fail and the Is 32:10

VIOLATE *(8)*
so that they v any of the LORD's Lv 4:13
he must not v his father's Dt 22:30
he actually v the queen while I Est 7:8
I will not v My covenant or Ps 89:34
they v Your instruction. Ps 119:85
waters would not v His command, Pr 8:29
and v women during their Ezk 22:10
in the temple v the Sabbath and Mt 12:5

VIOLATED *(11)*
because he has v his neighbor's Dt 22:24
his wife because he v her. Dt 22:29
I have not v or forgotten Your Dt 26:13
for he has v his father's Dt 27:20
They have v My covenant that I Jos 7:11
because he has v the LORD's Jos 7:15
this nation has v My covenant Jdg 2:20
their God but v His covenant— 2Kg 18:12
They v the king's command and Dn 3:28
like Adam, have v the covenant; Hs 6:7
have v the covenant of Levi," Mal 2:8

VIOLATES *(4)*
unintentionally v any of the Lv 4:22
knowing ⌊it⌋ v any of the LORD's Lv 5:17
with him; he v his covenant. Ps 55:20
and ⌊yet⌋ another v his sister, Ezk 22:11

VIOLATING *(2)*
by v one of the LORD's Lv 4:27
LORD your God and v His covenant Dt 17:2

VIOLATION *(1)*
and in v of the law are you Ac 23:3

VIOLENCE *(55)*
and the earth was filled with v. Gn 6:11
filled with v because of them; Gn 6:13
my Savior, You save me from v. 2Sm 22:3
are free from v and my prayer is Jb 16:17
I cry out: V! but get no Jb 19:7
the arm raised ⌊in v⌋ is broken. Jb 38:15
his v falls on the top of his Ps 7:16
deceit, and v fill his mouth; Ps 10:7
He hates the lover of v. Ps 11:5
rise up against me, breathing v. Ps 27:12
for I see v and strife in the Ps 55:9
you weigh out v in the land. Ps 58:2
them from oppression and v, Ps 72:14
v covers them like a garment. Ps 73:6
of the land are full of v. Ps 74:20
and drink the wine of v. Pr 4:17
mouth of the wicked conceals v. Pr 10:6
mouth of the wicked conceals v. Pr 10:11
tree of life, but v takes lives. Pr 11:30
people have an appetite for v. Pr 13:2
The v of the wicked sweeps them Pr 21:7
hearts plan v, and their words Pr 24:2
off his own feet and drinks v. Pr 26:6
He had done no v and had not Is 53:9
V will never again be heard of Is 60:18
V and destruction resound in her. Jr 6:7
I proclaim: V and destruction! Jr 20:8
Let the v ⌊done⌋ to me and my Jr 51:35
There will be v in the land with Jr 51:46
has done v to His temple as if Lm 2:6
V has grown into a rod of Ezk 7:11
and the city is filled with v. Ezk 7:23
the land with v and repeatedly Ezk 8:17
because of the v of all who live Ezk 12:19
Her priests do v to My law and Ezk 22:26
filled with v, and you sinned Ezk 28:16
ruled them with v and cruelty. Ezk 34:4
Put away v and oppression and do Ezk 45:9
multiplies lies and v. Hs 12:1
because of the v ⌊done⌋ to the Jl 3:19
who store up v and destruction Am 3:10
day and bring in a reign of v. Am 6:3
forever because of v done to Ob 10
ways and from the v he is doing. Jnh 3:8
of the city are full of v, Mc 6:12
to You about v and You do not Hab 1:2
Oppression and v are right in Hab 1:3
All of them come to do v; Hab 1:9
bloodshed and v against lands, Hab 2:8
⌊your⌋ v against Lebanon will Hab 2:17
bloodshed and v against lands, Hab 2:17
house with v and deceit. Zph 1:9
they do v to instruction. Zph 3:4
of heaven has been suffering v, Mt 11:12
soldiers because of the mob's v, Ac 21:35

VIOLENT *(34)*
You rescue me from v men. 2Sm 22:49
have avoided the ways of the v. Ps 17:4
You rescue me from v men. Ps 18:48
v man well-rooted like a Ps 37:35
against me, and v men seek my Ps 54:3
Keep me safe from v men Ps 140:1
me safe from v men who plan to Ps 140:4
relentlessly hunt down a v man. Ps 140:11
Don't envy a v man or choose any Pr 3:31
but v men gain ⌊only⌋ riches. Pr 11:16
A v man lures his neighbor, Pr 16:29
city of v people will fear You. Is 25:3
the breath of the v is like rain Is 25:4
⌊so⌋ He stills the song of the v. Is 25:5
and v acts are in their hands. Is 59:6
is with me like a v warrior. Jr 20:11
V men will enter it and profane Ezk 7:22
Now suppose the man has a v son, Ezk 18:10
you will die a v death in the Ezk 28:8
V ones among your own people Dn 11:14
battle and a v wind on the day Am 1:14
LORD hurled a v wind on the sea Jnh 1:4
and such a v storm arose on the Jnh 1:4
blame for this v storm that is Jnh 1:12
a v storm arose on the sea, Mt 8:24
They were so v that no one could Mt 8:28
and the v have been seizing it Mt 11:12
there was a v earthquake, Mt 28:2
There will be v earthquakes, Lk 21:11
like that of a v rushing wind Ac 2:2
was such a v earthquake that Ac 16:26
When the dispute became v, Ac 23:10
A v earthquake occurred; Rv 6:12
that moment a v earthquake took Rv 11:13

VIOLENTLY *(12)*
and the whole mountain shook v. Ex 19:18
And they argued with him v. Jdg 8:1
All your descendents will die v. 1Sm 2:33
he was afraid and trembled v. 1Sm 28:5
from the wicked who treat me v, Ps 17:9
numerous, and they hate me v. Ps 25:19
He acts v against those at peace Ps 55:20
LORD is about to shake you v. Is 22:17
the earth is v shaken. Is 24:19
the king became v angry and gave Dn 2:12
shrieking and convulsing him v. Mk 9:26
be thrown down v and never be Rv 18:21

VIOLET *(1)*
White and v linen hangings were Est 1:6

VIPER *(6)*
the road, a v beside the path, Gn 49:17
a snake and stings like a v. Pr 23:32
a v will come out of the root Is 14:29
and lion, of v and flying Is 30:6
one open, and a v is hatched. Is 59:5
a v came out because of the heat Ac 28:3

VIPER'S *(3)*
a v fangs will kill him. Jb 20:16
v venom is under their lips. Ps 140:3
They hatch v eggs and weave Is 59:5

VIPERS *(5)*
poisonous v that cannot be Jr 8:17
he said to them, "Brood of v! Mt 3:7
Brood of v! How can you speak Mt 12:34
Snakes! Brood of v! How can you Mt 23:33
be baptized by him, "Brood of v! Lk 3:7

VIPERS' *(1)*
V venom is under their lips. Rm 3:13

VIRGIN *(38)*
Let the v who comes out to draw Gn 24:43
a man seduces a v who was not Ex 22:16
is to marry a woman who is a v. Lv 21:13
He is to marry a v from his own Lv 21:14
gave an Israelite v a bad name. Dt 22:19
woman who is a v engaged to a Dt 22:23
a young woman, a v who is not Dt 22:28
man and the v ⌊will be killed⌋ Dt 32:25
let me bring out my v daughter Jdg 19:24
Tamar because she was a v, 2Sm 13:2
the king's v daughters wore. 2Sm 13:18
search for a young v for my lord 1Kg 1:2
young man and v or elderly and 2Ch 36:17
The v will conceive, have a son, Is 7:14
in the dust, V Daughter Babylon Is 47:1
For as a young man marries a v, Is 62:5
for the v daughter of my people Jr 14:17
V Israel has done a most Jr 18:13
you will be rebuilt, V Israel. Jr 31:4
Then the v will rejoice with Jr 31:13
Return, V Israel! Return to Jr 31:21
and get balm, V Daughter Egypt! Jr 46:11
smash the young man and the v. Jr 51:22
has trampled V Daughter Judah Lm 1:15
console you, V Daughter Zion? Lm 2:13
and their v nipples caressed. Ezk 23:3
caressed her v nipples, and Ezk 23:8
but must marry a v from the Ezk 44:22
V Israel will never rise again. Am 5:2
the v will become pregnant and Mt 1:23
to a v engaged to a man named Lk 1:27
This man had four v daughters Ac 21:9
and if a v marries, she has 1Co 7:28
woman or a v is concerned about 1Co 7:34
acting improperly toward his v, 1Co 7:36
in his heart to keep his own v, 1Co 7:37
he who marries his v does well, 1Co 7:38
to present a pure v to Christ. 2Co 11:2

VIRGIN'S *(1)*
The v name was Mary. Lk 1:27

VIRGINITY *(8)*
find ⌊any⌋ evidence of her v,' Dt 22:14
evidence of her v and bring ⌊it⌋ Dt 22:15
evidence of your daughter's v, Dt 22:17
evidence of my daughter's v.' Dt 22:17
of the young woman's v is found, Dt 22:20
with my friends and mourn my v." Jdg 11:37
mourned her v as she wandered Jdg 11:38
for they have kept their v. Rv 14:4

VIRGINS *(11)*
equal to the bridal price for v. Ex 22:17
of Jabesh-gilead 400 young v, Jdg 21:12
beautiful young v for the king. Est 2:2
beautiful young v to the harem Est 2:3
him than did any of the other v. Est 2:17
her, the v, her companions, Ps 45:14
raped in Zion, v in the cities Lm 5:11
will be like 10 v who took their Mt 25:1
Then all those v got up and Mt 25:7
the rest of the v also came and Mt 25:11
About v: I have no command from 1Co 7:25

VIRILITY *(2)*
and the firstfruits of my v, Gn 49:3
he is the firstfruits of his v; Dt 21:17

VIRTUE *(2)*
goat hair by v of ⌊their⌋ skill Ex 35:26
and his v is to overlook an Pr 19:11

VIRTUOUS *(1)*
my dove, my v one, is unique; Sg 6:9

VISIBLE *(11)*
tops of the mountains were v. Gn 8:5
v to the entire house of Israel Ex 40:38
man sees what is v, but the LORD 1Sm 16:7
The depths of the sea became v, 2Sm 22:16
The depths of the sea became v, Ps 18:15
and it was v to the ends of the Dn 4:11
the sky and was v to all the Dn 4:20
that was more v than the others Dn 7:20
is not something v in the flesh. Rm 2:28
on earth, the v and the Col 1:16
made from things that are not v. Heb 11:3

VISION *(72)*
the LORD came to Abram in a v: Gn 15:1
God spoke to Israel in a v: Gn 46:2
make Myself known to him in a v; Nm 12:6
who sees a v from the Almighty, Nm 24:4
who sees a v from the Almighty, Nm 24:16
He was afraid to tell Eli the v, 1Sm 3:15
and this entire v to David. 2Sm 7:17
and this entire v to David. 1Ch 17:15
away like a v in the night. Jb 20:8
In a dream, a v in the night, Jb 33:15
once spoke in a v to Your loyal Ps 89:19
The v concerning Judah and Is 1:1
v that Isaiah son of Amoz saw Is 2:1
A troubling v is declared to me: Is 21:2
oracle against the Valley of V: Is 22:1
in the Valley of V— Is 22:5
like a dream, a v in the night. Is 29:7
you the entire v will be like Is 29:11
prophesying to you a false v, Jr 14:14
receive no v from the LORD. Lm 2:9
For the v concerning all its Ezk 7:13
will seek a v from a prophet, Ezk 7:26
like the v I had seen in the Ezk 8:4
exiles in a v from the Spirit Ezk 11:24
After the v I had seen left me, Ezk 11:24
passing by, and every v fails? Ezk 12:22
as the fulfillment of every v. Ezk 12:23
be any false v or flattering Ezk 12:24
The v that he sees concerns many Ezk 12:27
you see a false v and speak a Ezk 13:7
and saw a v of peace for her Ezk 13:16
The v I saw was like the one I Ezk 43:3
to Daniel in a v at night, Dn 2:19
In my v at night I was watching, Dn 7:2
reign, a v appeared to me, Dn 8:1
I saw the v, and as I watched, I Dn 8:2
I saw in the v that I was beside Dn 8:2
the events of⌋ this v last— Dn 8:13
was watching the v and trying to Dn 8:15
explain the v to this man." Dn 8:16
that the v refers to the time Dn 8:17
The v of the evenings and the Dn 8:26
must seal up the v because it Dn 8:26
disturbed by the v and could not Dn 8:27
man I had seen in the first v, Dn 9:21
message and understand the v: Dn 9:23
to seal up v and prophecy, Dn 9:24
and had understanding of the v. Dn 10:1
Only I, Daniel, saw the v. Dn 10:7
alone, looking at this great v. Dn 10:8
for the v refers to those days." Dn 10:14
because of the v, I am Dn 10:16

themselves to fulfill a **v**, Dn 11:14
The **v** of Obadiah. This is what Ob 1
The book of the **v** of Nahum the Nah 1:1
Write down this **v**; clearly Hab 2:2
For the **v** is yet for the Hab 2:3
be ashamed of his **v** when he Zch 13:4
anyone about the **v** until the Son Mt 17:9
he had seen a **v** in the sanctuary Lk 1:22
they had seen a **v** of angels who Lk 24:23
And the Lord said to him in a **v**, Ac 9:10
In a **v** he has seen a man named Ac 9:12
saw in a **v** an angel of God who Ac 10:3
about what the **v** he had seen Ac 10:17
Peter was thinking about the **v**, Ac 10:19
but thought he was seeing a **v**. Ac 12:9
the night a **v** appeared to Paul: Ac 16:9
had seen the **v**, we immediately Ac 16:10
Lord said to Paul in a night **v**, Ac 18:9
disobedient to the heavenly **v**. Ac 26:19
is how I saw the horses in my **v**: Rv 9:17

VISIONARY *(4)*

he went into a **v** state. Ac 10:10
and I saw, in a **v** state, an Ac 11:5
complex, I went into a **v** state Ac 22:17
access to a **v** realm and inflated Col 2:18

VISIONS *(33)*

rare and prophetic **v** were not 1Sm 3:1
and the **V** of Iddo the Seer 2Ch 9:29
about in the **V** of the Prophet 2Ch 32:32
thoughts from **v** in the night, Jb 4:13
dreams, and terrify me with **v**, Jb 7:14
they are muddled in ⌊their⌋ **v**, Is 28:7
They speak **v** from their own Jr 23:16
prophets saw **v** for you that were Lm 2:14
opened and I saw **v** of God. Ezk 1:1
and carried me in **v** of God to Ezk 8:3
They see false **v** and speak lying Ezk 13:6
spoken falsely and had lying **v**." Ezk 13:8
who see false **v** and speak lying Ezk 13:9
longer see false **v** or practice Ezk 13:23
they offer false **v** and lying Ezk 21:29
them by seeing false **v** and lying Ezk 22:28
In **v** of God He took me to the Ezk 40:2
also understood **v** and dreams of Dn 1:17
Your dream and the **v** ⌊that came Dn 2:28
the images and **v** in my mind Dn 4:5
to me the **v** of my dream that Dn 4:9
In the **v** of my mind as I was Dn 4:10
also saw in the **v** of my mind an Dn 4:13
had a dream with **v** in his mind Dn 7:1
I was watching in the night **v**, Dn 7:7
watching in the night **v**, Dn 7:13
and the **v** in my mind terrified Dn 7:15
the prophets and granted many **v**; Hs 12:10
and your young men will see **v**. Jl 2:28
be night for you—without **v**; Mc 3:6
has dealt with us." The Night **V** Zch 1:6
your young men will see **v**, Ac 2:17
move on to **v** and revelations 2Co 12:1

VISIT *(15)*

father went ⌊to **v**⌋ the woman, Jdg 14:10
of Judah went to **v** the king of 1Kg 22:2
to Jezreel to **v** Joram son of 2Kg 8:29
Judah had gone down to **v** Joram. 2Kg 9:16
went down to **v** Ahab in Samaria 2Ch 18:2
to Jezreel to **v** Joram son of 2Ch 22:6
When one ⌊of them⌋ comes to **v**, Ps 41:6
You **v** the earth and water it Ps 65:9
sick, or in prison, and **v** You?" Mt 25:39
the Dawn from on high will **v** us Lk 1:78
he decided to **v** his brothers, Ac 7:23
associate with or **v** a foreigner. Ac 10:28
Let's go back and **v** the brothers Ac 15:36
to you on another painful **v**. 2Co 2:1
that our **v** with you was not 1Th 2:1

VISITATION *(2)*

recognize the time of your **v**." Lk 19:44
glorify God in a day of **v**. 1Pt 2:12

VISITED *(10)*

goat ⌊as a gift⌋ and **v** his wife. Jdg 15:1
Samuel never again **v** Saul. 1Sm 15:35
You have **v** by night; Ps 17:3
You have **v** and destroyed them; Is 26:14
you will be **v** by the LORD of Is 29:6
I was in prison and you **v** Me.' Mt 25:36
because He has **v** and provided Lk 1:68
and "God has **v** His people." Lk 7:16
You **v** uncircumcised men and ate Ac 11:3
And he welcomed all who **v** him, Ac 28:30

VISITOR *(1)*

You the only **v** in Jerusalem who Lk 24:18

VISITORS *(1)*

v from Rome, both Jews and Ac 2:10

VITALITY *(2)*

and his **v** had not left ⌊him⌋. Dt 34:7
will give up your **v** to others Pr 5:9

VIVIDLY *(1)*

Jesus Christ was **v** portrayed as Gl 3:1

VOCABULARY *(1)*

had the same language and **v**. Gn 11:1

VOICE *(258)*

your wife's **v** and ate from the Gn 3:17
Adah and Zillah, hear my **v**; Gn 4:23
God heard the **v** of the boy, Gn 21:17
God has heard the **v** of the boy Gn 21:17
listened to My **v** and kept My Gn 26:5
The **v** is the voice of Jacob, Gn 27:22
The voice is the **v** of Jacob, Gn 27:22
to Him and listen to His **v**. Ex 23:21
responded with a single **v**, Ex 24:3
he heard the **v** speaking to him Nm 7:89
He heard our **v**, sent an Angel, Nm 20:16
see a form; there was only a **v**. Dt 4:12
ever heard God's **v** speaking from Dt 4:33
let you hear His **v** from heaven Dt 4:36
in a loud **v** to your entire Dt 5:22
you heard the **v** from the Dt 5:23
have heard His **v** from the fire. Dt 5:24
if we hear the **v** of the LORD our Dt 5:25
heard the **v** of the living God Dt 5:26
commands and listen to His **v**; Dt 13:4
to hear the **v** of the LORD our Dt 18:16
in a loud **v** to every Israelite Dt 27:14
shout or let your **v** be heard. Jos 6:10
LORD listened to the **v** of a man, Jos 10:14
raised his **v**, and called to them Jdg 9:7
Don't raise your **v** against us, Jdg 18:25
were moving, her **v** could not be 1Sm 1:13
Is that your **v**, David my son?" 1Sm 24:16
recognized David's **v** and asked, 1Sm 26:17
Is that your **v**, my son David?" 1Sm 26:17
"It is my **v**, my lord and king," 1Sm 26:17
cried out at the top of his **v**, 2Sm 19:4
I still hear the **v** of male and 2Sm 19:35
From His temple He heard my **v**, 2Sm 22:7
the Most High projected His **v**. 2Sm 22:14
of Israel with a loud **v**: 1Kg 8:55
the LORD listened to Elijah's **v**, 1Kg 17:22
after the fire there was a **v**, 1Kg 19:12
a **v** came to him and said, 1Kg 19:13
not listen to the **v** of the LORD, 1Kg 20:36
listen to the **v** of the LORD 2Kg 18:12
raised ⌊your⌋ **v** and lifted your 2Kg 19:22
and thank the LORD with one **v**. 2Ch 5:13
an oath to the LORD in a loud **v**, 2Ch 15:14
of Israel shouting in a loud **v**. 2Ch 20:19
God heard their **v**, and their 2Ch 30:27
responded with a loud **v**: Ezr 10:12
do not hear the **v** of ⌊their⌋ Jb 3:18
my eyes. I heard a quiet **v**: Jb 4:16
His thunderous **v** and the Jb 37:2
thunders with His majestic **v**. Jb 37:4
when His ⌊rumbling⌋ **v** is heard. Jb 37:4
thunders marvelously with His **v**; Jb 37:5
you thunder with a **v** like His? Jb 40:9
daybreak, LORD, You hear my **v**; Ps 5:3
From His temple He heard my **v**, Ps 18:6
the Most High projected His **v**. Ps 18:13
no words; their **v** is not heard. Ps 19:3
raising my **v** in thanksgiving and Ps 26:7
LORD, hear my **v** when I call; Ps 27:7
The **v** of the LORD is above the Ps 29:3
the **v** of the LORD in power, Ps 29:4
the **v** of the LORD in splendor. Ps 29:4
The **v** of the LORD breaks the Ps 29:5
The **v** of the LORD flashes flames Ps 29:7
The **v** of the LORD shakes the Ps 29:8
The **v** of the LORD makes the deer Ps 29:9
because of the **v** of the scorner Ps 44:16
earth melts when He lifts His **v**. Ps 46:6
of the enemy's **v**, because Ps 55:3
and night, and He hears my **v**. Ps 55:17
hear my **v** when I complain. Ps 64:1
He thunders with His powerful **v**! Ps 68:33
floods have lifted up their **v**; Ps 93:3
Today, if you hear His **v**: Ps 95:7
did not listen to the LORD's **v**. Ps 106:25
Your faithful love, hear my **v**. Ps 119:149
listen to my **v**; let Your ears be Ps 130:2
Listen to my **v** when I call on Ps 141:1
she raises her **v** in the public Pr 1:20
lift your **v** to understanding, Pr 2:3
Understanding make her **v** heard? Pr 8:1
with a loud **v** early in the Pr 27:14
up for those who have no **v**, Pr 31:8
and a fool's **v** from many words. Ec 5:3
your face, let me hear your **v**; Sg 2:14
for your **v** is sweet, and your Sg 2:14
are listening for your **v**— Sg 8:13
Then I heard the **v** of the Lord Is 6:8
and hear my **v**. Pay attention Is 28:23
Your **v** will be like that of a Is 29:4
splendor of His **v** heard and Is 30:30
shattered by the **v** of the LORD. Is 30:31
you raised ⌊your⌋ **v** against and Is 37:23
A **v** of one crying out: Is 40:3
A **v** was saying, "Cry out!" Is 40:6
good news, raise your **v** loudly. Is 40:9
shout or make His **v** heard in the Is 42:2
to the **v** of His servant? Is 50:10
Raise your **v** like a trumpet. Is 58:1
to make your **v** heard on high. Is 58:4
A **v** from the temple—the voice Is 66:6
the temple—the **v** of the LORD, Is 66:6
tree and have not obeyed My **v**. Jr 3:13
not obeyed the **v** of the LORD our Jr 3:25
For a **v** announces from Dan, Jr 4:15
Their **v** roars like the sea, Jr 6:23
listen to the **v** of the LORD Jr 7:28
did not obey My **v** or walk Jr 9:13
time and time again: Obey My **v**. Jr 11:7
the **v** of the bridegroom and the Jr 16:9
sight by not listening to My **v**, Jr 18:10
raise your **v** in Bashan; Jr 22:20
the **v** of the bridegroom and the Jr 25:10
He raises His **v** from His holy Jr 25:30
and obey the **v** of the LORD your Jr 26:13
A **v** was heard in Ramah, a lament Jr 31:15
your **v** from weeping and your Jr 31:16
not obey Your **v** or live Jr 32:23
the **v** of the bridegroom and the Jr 33:11
and the **v** of those saying, Jr 33:11
We have obeyed the **v** of Jonadab, Jr 35:8
Obey the **v** of the LORD in what I Jr 38:20
will obey the **v** of the LORD our Jr 42:6
obey the **v** of the LORD our Jr 42:6
not to obey the **v** of the LORD Jr 42:13
obeyed the **v** of the LORD your Jr 42:21
did not obey the **v** of the LORD Jr 43:4
did not obey the **v** of the LORD. Jr 43:7
the LORD's **v** and didn't walk Jr 44:23
A **v** cries out from Horonaim: Jr 48:3
⌊There is⌋ a **v** of fugitives and Jr 50:28
Their **v** roars like the sea, Jr 50:42
He will silence her mighty **v**. Jr 51:55
the tumult of their **v** resounds, Jr 51:55
like the **v** of the Almighty, Ezk 1:24
A **v** came from above the expanse Ezk 1:25
facedown and heard a **v** speaking. Ezk 1:28
out in My ears with a loud **v**, Ezk 8:18
to me directly with a loud **v**, Ezk 9:1
was like the **v** of God Almighty Ezk 10:5
and cried out with a loud **v**: Ezk 11:13
who has a beautiful **v** and plays Ezk 33:32
His **v** sounded like the roar of Ezk 43:2
king's mouth, a **v** came from Dn 4:31
I heard a human **v** calling from Dn 8:16
not obeyed the **v** of the LORD our Dn 9:10
raises His **v** in the presence Jl 2:11
and raise His **v** from Jerusalem; Jl 3:16
and raises His **v** from Jerusalem; Am 1:2
belly of Sheol; You heard my **v**. Jnh 2:2
to You with a **v** of thanksgiving. Jnh 2:9
and let the hills hear your **v**. Mc 6:1
The **v** of the LORD calls out to Mc 6:9
roars with its **v** and lifts its Hab 3:10
obeyed the **v** of the LORD their Hg 1:12
A **v** was heard in Ramah, weeping, Mt 2:18
A **v** of one crying out in the Mt 3:3
And there came a **v** from heaven: Mt 3:17
will hear His **v** in the streets. Mt 12:19
and a **v** from the cloud said: Mt 17:5
Jesus cried out with a loud **v**, Mt 27:46
with a loud **v** and gave up His Mt 27:50

A **v** of one crying out in the Mk 1:3
And a **v** came from heaven: Mk 1:11
with a loud **v**, and came out Mk 1:26
And he cried out with a loud **v**, Mk 5:7
and a **v** came from the cloud: Mk 9:7
Jesus cried out with a loud **v**, Mk 15:34
A **v** of one crying out in the Lk 3:4
And a **v** came from heaven: Lk 3:22
who cried out with a loud **v**, Lk 4:33
said in a loud **v**, "What do You Lk 8:28
Then a **v** came from the cloud, Lk 9:35
After the **v** had spoken, only Lk 9:36
raised her **v** and said to Him Lk 11:27
and, with a loud **v**, gave glory Lk 17:15
with a loud **v** for all the Lk 19:37
Jesus called out with a loud **v**, Lk 23:46
I am a **v** of one crying out in Jn 1:23
greatly at the groom's **v**. Jn 3:29
will hear the **v** of the Son of Jn 5:25
in the graves will hear His **v** Jn 5:28
not heard His **v** at any time, Jn 5:37
him, and the sheep hear his **v**. Jn 10:3
because they recognize his **v**. Jn 10:4
recognize the **v** of strangers." Jn 10:5
and they will listen to My **v**. Jn 10:16
My sheep hear My **v**, I know them, Jn 10:27
He shouted with a loud **v**, Jn 11:43
Then a **v** came from heaven: Jn 12:28
This **v** came, not for Me Jn 12:30
of the truth listens to My **v**." Jn 18:37
raised his **v**, and proclaimed to Ac 2:14
look at it, the **v** of the Lord Ac 7:31
and cried out with a loud **v**, Ac 7:60
out with a loud **v**, came out of Ac 8:7
he heard a **v** saying to him, Ac 9:4
Then a **v** said to him, "Get up, Ac 10:13
a second time, a **v** said to him, Ac 10:15
I also heard a **v** telling me, Ac 11:7
But a **v** answered from heaven a Ac 11:9
recognized Peter's **v**, and Ac 12:14
It's the **v** of a god and not of a Ac 12:22
said in a loud **v**, "Stand up Ac 14:10
But Paul called out in a loud **v**, Ac 16:28
and heard a **v** saying to me, Ac 22:7
not hear the **v** of the One who Ac 22:9
and to hear the sound of His **v**. Ac 22:14
heard a **v** speaking to me in the Ac 26:14
Festus exclaimed in a loud **v**, Ac 26:24
Their **v** has gone out to all the Rm 10:18
Christ with a united mind and **v**. Rm 15:6
now and change my tone of **v**, Gl 4:20
with the archangel's **v**, and with 1Th 4:16
Today, if you hear His **v**, Heb 3:7
if you hear His **v**, do not harden Heb 3:15
if you hear His **v**, do not harden Heb 4:7
His **v** shook the earth at that Heb 12:26
v came to Him from the Majestic 2Pt 1:17
And we heard this **v** when it came 2Pt 1:18
with a human **v** and restrained 2Pt 2:16
me a loud **v** like a trumpet Rv 1:10
to see the **v** that was speaking Rv 1:12
and His **v** like the sound of Rv 1:15
anyone hears My **v** and opens the Rv 3:20
The first **v** that I had heard Rv 4:1
angel proclaiming in a loud **v**, Rv 5:2
and heard the **v** of many angels Rv 5:11
They said with a loud **v**: Rv 5:12
say with a **v** like thunder, Rv 6:1
something like a **v** among the Rv 6:6
I heard the **v** of the fourth Rv 6:7
They cried out with a loud **v**: Rv 6:10
out in a loud **v** to the four Rv 7:2
And they cried out in a loud **v**: Rv 7:10
saying in a loud **v**, "Woe! Rv 8:13
that is before God, I heard a **v** Rv 9:13
out with a loud **v** like a roaring Rv 10:3
Then I heard a **v** from heaven, Rv 10:4
Now the **v** that I heard from Rv 10:8
they heard a loud **v** from heaven Rv 11:12
I heard a loud **v** in heaven say: Rv 12:10
He spoke with a loud **v**: Rv 14:7
them and spoke with a loud **v**: Rv 14:9
Then I heard a **v** from heaven Rv 14:13
out in a loud **v** to the One who Rv 14:15
with a loud **v** to the one who had Rv 14:18
I heard a loud **v** from the Rv 16:1
and a loud **v** came out of the Rv 16:17
He cried in a mighty **v**: Rv 18:2
I heard another **v** from heaven: Rv 18:4
and the **v** of a groom and bride Rv 18:23
like the loud **v** of a vast Rv 19:1
v came from the throne, saying: Rv 19:5
something like the **v** of a vast Rv 19:6
and he cried out in a loud **v**, Rv 19:17
heard a loud **v** from the throne: Rv 21:3

VOICES *(23)*

with the **v** of the singers at the Jdg 5:11
them raise their **v** with joy 1Ch 15:16
raised ⌊their⌋ **v**, accompanied 2Ch 5:13
The noblemen's **v** were hushed, Jb 29:10
shook at the sound of their **v**, Is 6:4
their **v** are heard as far away as Is 15:4
raise their **v**, they sing out; Is 24:14
The **v** of your watchmen—they Is 52:8
lift up their **v**, shouting for Is 52:8
they raise their **v** against the Jr 4:16
gladness and the **v** of the Jr 7:34
raise their **v** as far as Jahaz Jr 48:34
raise their **v** over you and cry Ezk 27:30
raised their **v**, saying, "Jesus Lk 17:13
demanding with loud **v** that He be Lk 23:23
crucified. And their **v** won out. Lk 23:23
they raised their **v** to God Ac 4:24
screamed at the top of their **v**, Ac 7:57
Him or the **v** of the prophets Ac 13:27
done, they raised their **v**, Ac 14:11
raised their **v**, shouting, "Wipe Ac 22:22
thunders spoke with their **v**. Rv 10:3
there were loud **v** in heaven Rv 11:15

VOLUME *(4)*

of length, weight, or **v**. Lv 19:35
measurements of **v** and length. 1Ch 23:29
about me in the **v** of the scroll. Ps 40:7
Me in the **v** of the scroll— Heb 10:7

VOLUNTARILY *(1)*

and all money **v** given for the 2Kg 12:4

VOLUNTEER *(4)*

when the people **v**, praise the Jdg 5:2
who will **v** to consecrate himself 1Ch 29:5
of Zichri, the **v** of the LORD, 2Ch 17:16
Your people will **v** on Your day Ps 110:3

VOLUNTEERED *(1)*

all the men who **v** to live in Neh 11:2

VOLUNTEERS *(1)*

with the **v** of the people. Jdg 5:9

VOMIT *(14)*

and the land will **v** out its Lv 18:25
it will **v** you out as it has Lv 18:28
you to live will not **v** you out. Lv 20:22
wealth but must **v** it up; Jb 20:15
You will **v** the little you've Pr 23:8
you'll get sick from it and **v**. Pr 25:16
As a dog returns to its **v**, Pr 26:11
as a drunkard staggers in his **v**. Is 19:14
their tables are covered with **v**; Is 28:8
Drink, get drunk, and **v**. Jr 25:27
Moab will wallow in his own **v**, Jr 48:26
I will make him **v** what he Jr 51:44
A dog returns to its own **v**, 2Pt 2:22
I am going to **v** you out of My Rv 3:16

VOMITED *(3)*

out as it has **v** out the nations Lv 18:28
my delicacies; he has **v** me out," Jr 51:34
and it **v** Jonah onto dry land. Jnh 2:10

VOPHSI *(1)*

Nahbi son of **V** from the tribe of Nm 13:14

VOTE *(2)*

if I ever cast my **v** against a Jb 31:21
death, I cast my **v** against them. Ac 26:10

VOW *(49)*

Jacob made a **v**: "If God will be Gn 28:20
and made a solemn **v** to Me. Gn 31:13
he offers is a **v** or a freewill Lv 7:16
to fulfill a **v** or as a freewill Lv 22:21
not acceptable as a **v** offering. Lv 22:23
gifts, all your **v** offerings, and Lv 23:38
makes a special **v** to the LORD Lv 27:2
the one making the **v** can afford. Lv 27:8
If the **v** involves one of the Lv 27:9
If the **v** involves any of the Lv 27:11
man or woman makes a special **v**, Nm 6:2
vow, a Nazirite **v**, to consecrate Nm 6:2
seeds to skin, during his **v**. Nm 6:4
time of his **v** of consecration Nm 6:5
fulfill whatever **v** he makes in Nm 6:21
to fulfill a **v**, or as a freewill Nm 15:3
to fulfill a **v**, or as a Nm 15:8
Israel made a **v** to the LORD, Nm 21:2
addition to your **v** and freewill Nm 29:39
When a man makes a **v** to the LORD Nm 30:2
her youth makes a **v** to the LORD Nm 30:3
hears about her **v** or the Nm 30:4
cancel her **v** that is binding Nm 30:8
Any **v** a widow or divorcée put Nm 30:9
has made a **v** or put herself Nm 30:10
or cancel any **v** or any sworn Nm 30:13
your **v** offerings and freewill Dt 12:6
offerings you **v** to the LORD. Dt 12:11
any of your **v** offerings that you Dt 12:17
have and your **v** offerings and go Dt 12:26
LORD your God to fulfill any **v**, Dt 23:18
If you make a **v** to the LORD your Dt 23:21
if you refrain from making a **v**, Dt 23:22
made this **v** to the LORD: Jdg 11:30
and he kept the **v** he had made Jdg 11:39
Making a **v**, she pleaded, "LORD 1Sm 1:11
sacrifice and his **v** offering to 1Sm 1:21
I **v** that I will not sin against 1Sm 12:23
to fulfill a **v** I made to the 2Sm 15:7
servant made a **v** when I lived 2Sm 15:8
making a **v** to the Mighty One of Ps 132:2
When you make a **v** to God, don't Ec 5:4
in fools. Fulfill what you **v**. Ec 5:4
that you do not **v** than that you Ec 5:5
than that you **v** and not fulfill Ec 5:5
of your sacred **v** and throw it Jr 7:29
and makes a **v** but sacrifices Mal 1:14
because he had taken a **v**. Ac 18:18
obligated themselves with a **v**. Ac 21:23

VOWED *(5)*

you have freely **v** what you Dt 23:23
So the LORD **v** never to let them Jos 5:6
LORD lives," he **v**, "not a hair 2Sm 14:11
response, Ittai **v** to the king, 2Sm 15:21
I will fulfill what I have **v**. Jnh 2:9

VOWS *(30)*

or payment of **v** to the LORD as Lv 22:18
Nazirite who **v** his offering to Nm 6:21
all her **v** and every obligation Nm 30:4
none of her **v** and none of the Nm 30:5
marries while her **v** or the rash Nm 30:6
he finds out, her **v** are binding, Nm 30:7
her, all her **v** are binding, Nm 30:11
whether her **v** or her obligation, Nm 30:12
all her **v** and obligations Nm 30:14
money from **v**, and all money 2Kg 12:4
and you will fulfill your **v**. Jb 22:27
will fulfill my **v** before those Ps 22:25
and pay your **v** to the Most High. Ps 50:14
I am obligated by **v** to You, Ps 56:12
God, You have heard my **v**; Ps 61:5
fulfilling my **v** day by day. Ps 61:8
v to You will be fulfilled. Ps 65:1
offerings; I will pay You my **v** Ps 66:13
and keep your **v** to the LORD your Ps 76:11
I will fulfill my **v** to the LORD Ps 116:14
I will fulfill my **v** to the LORD, Ps 116:18
today I've fulfilled my **v**. Pr 7:14
and later to reconsider his **v**. Pr 20:25
of my womb? What, son of my **v**? Pr 31:2
they will make **v** to the LORD and Is 19:21
will keep our **v** we have made to Jr 44:25
⌊Go ahead,⌋ confirm your **v**! Jr 44:25
confirm your vows! Pay your **v**!' Jr 44:25
to the LORD and made **v**. Jnh 1:16
fulfill your **v**. For the wicked Nah 1:15

VOYAGE *(3)*

we completed our **v** from Tyre, Ac 21:7
and the **v** was already dangerous. Ac 27:9
see that this **v** is headed toward Ac 27:10

VULGAR *(1)*

subjects like a **v** person would 2Sm 6:20

VULNERABLE *(2)*

they would be **v** to their enemies Ex 32:25
of the wall, at the **v** areas. Neh 4:13

VULTURE *(4)*

the bearded **v**, the black vulture Lv 11:13
bearded vulture, the black **v**, Lv 11:13
the bearded **v**, the black vulture Dt 14:12
bearded vulture, the black **v**, Dt 14:12

VULTURES *(3)*

pluck it out and young **v** eat it. Pr 30:17
is, there the **v** will gather. Mt 24:28
also the **v** will be gathered. Lk 17:37

W

WADE *(2)*
your foot may **w** in blood and Ps 68:23
bare your thigh, **w** through the Is 47:2

WADI *(22)*
his army at the **W** Kishon ⌊to Jdg 4:7
of the Nations to the **W** Kishon. Jdg 4:13
and set up an ambush in the **w**. 1Sm 15:5
stones from the **w** and put them 1Sm 17:40
him went as far as the **W** Besor, 1Sm 30:9
exhausted to cross the **W** Besor. 1Sm 30:10
had been left at the **W** Besor, 1Sm 30:21
yourself at the **W** Cherith where 1Kg 17:3
You are to drink from the **w**. 1Kg 17:4
lived by the **W** Cherith where it 1Kg 17:5
and he drank from the **w**. 1Kg 17:6
the **w** dried up because there had 1Kg 17:7
spring of water and to every **w**. 1Kg 18:5
them down to the **W** Kishon and 1Kg 18:40
ditch after ditch in this **w**.' 2Kg 3:16
but the **w** will be filled with 2Kg 3:17
are as treacherous as a **w**, Jb 6:15
the sea and a **w** becomes parched Jb 14:11
over the **W** of the Willows. Is 15:7
River as far as the **W** of Egypt, Is 27:12
the smooth ⌊stones⌋ of the **w**; Is 57:6
and becoming an overflowing **w**. Jr 47:2

WADIS *(7)*
Hiddai from the **W** of Gaash, 2Sm 23:30
Hurai from the **w** of Gaash, 1Ch 11:32
The **w** evaporate in warm weather; Jb 6:17
Ophir to the stones in the **w**, Jb 22:24
living on the slopes of the **w**, Jb 30:6
children in the **w** below the Is 57:5
lead them to **w** ⌊filled⌋ with Jr 31:9

WAFER *(3)*
and one **w** from the basket of Ex 29:23
oil, and one **w**, and placed ⌊them Lv 8:26
one unleavened **w**, and put ⌊them⌋ Nm 6:19

WAFERS *(6)*
and tasted like **w** ⌊made⌋ with Ex 16:31
unleavened **w** coated with oil. Ex 29:2
or unleavened **w** coated with oil Lv 2:4
unleavened **w** coated with oil, Lv 7:12
unleavened **w** coated with oil. Nm 6:15
the **w** of unleavened bread, 1Ch 23:29

WAGE *(17)*
It is your **w** in return for your Nm 18:31
power he had to **w** war against 2Kg 13:12
power he had to **w** war and how 2Kg 14:28
Remaliah came to **w** war against 2Kg 16:5
Uzziah went out to **w** war against 2Ch 26:6
The wicked man earns an empty **w**, Pr 11:18
and **w** war with sound guidance. Pr 20:18
for you should **w** war with sound Pr 24:6
all her **w** earners will be Is 19:10
and will again **w** war as far as Dn 11:10
The **w** earner ⌊puts his⌋ wages Hg 1:6
and cheat the **w** earner; Mal 3:5
do not **w** war in a fleshly way, 2Co 10:3
woman and left to **w** war against Rv 12:17
is able to **w** war against him? Rv 13:4
was permitted to **w** war against Rv 13:7
together to **w** war against Rv 19:19

WAGED *(12)*
w war against Bera king of Sodom, Gn 14:2
They **w** war against Midian, Nm 31:7
Joshua **w** war with all these Jos 11:18
Philistines again **w** war against 2Sm 21:15
he **w** war and how he reigned, 1Kg 14:19
he exercised and how he **w** war, 1Kg 22:45
how he **w** war against Amaziah 2Kg 14:15
Saul's reign they **w** war against 1Ch 5:10
They **w** war against the Hagrites, 1Ch 5:19
much blood and **w** great wars. 1Ch 22:8
He **w** war against the king of the 2Ch 27:5
king of Israel, **w** war against Is 7:1

WAGES *(33)*
Tell me what your **w** should be." Gn 29:15
Name your **w**, and I will pay Gn 30:28
goats. ⌊Such⌋ will be my **w**. Gn 30:32
when you come to check on my **w**, Gn 30:33
me and changed my **w** 10 times. Gn 31:7
spotted sheep will be your **w**,' Gn 31:8
streaked sheep will be your **w**,' Gn 31:8
you have changed my **w** 10 times! Gn 31:41
for me, and I will pay your **w**." Ex 2:9
The **w** due a hired hand must not Lv 19:13
the daily **w** of a hired hand. Lv 25:50
twice the **w** of a hired hand Dt 15:18
with you but **w** war against you, Dt 20:12
female prostitute's **w** or a male Dt 23:18
to pay him his **w** each day before Dt 24:15
pay your servants' **w** according 1Kg 5:6
her profits and **w** will be Is 23:18
and your **w** on what does not Is 55:2
pay and will not give him his **w**, Jr 22:13
these are her **w** that her lovers Hs 2:12
have loved the **w** of a prostitute Hs 9:1
all her **w** will be burned in the Mc 1:7
collected the **w** of a prostitute Mc 1:7
puts his⌋ **w** into a bag with Hg 1:6
neither man nor beast had **w**. Zch 8:10
right to you, give me my **w**; Zch 11:12
So they weighed my **w**, 30 pieces Zch 11:12
be satisfied with your **w**." Lk 3:14
the worker is worthy of his **w**. Lk 10:7
a field with his unrighteous **w**; Ac 1:18
For the **w** of sin is death, Rm 6:23
The laborer is worthy of his **w**. 1Tm 5:18
who loved the **w** of 2Pt 2:15

WAGING *(3)*
the city that is **w** war with you, Dt 20:20
king of Aram was **w** war against 2Kg 6:8
w war against the law of my mind Rm 7:23

WAGON *(1)*
place as a **w** full of sheaves Am 2:13

WAGONS *(6)*
Take **w** from the land of Egypt Gn 45:19
Joseph gave them **w** as Pharaoh Gn 45:21
when he saw the **w** that Joseph Gn 45:27
Jacob in the **w** Pharaoh had sent Gn 46:5
with weapons, chariots, and **w**. Ezk 23:24
of cavalry, **w**, and chariots. Ezk 26:10

WAHEB *(1)*
W in Suphah and the ravines of Nm 21:14

WAIL *(32)*
W! For the day of the LORD is Is 13:6
W, you gates! Cry out, city! Is 14:31
let Moab **w**; let every one Is 16:7
every one of them **w** for Moab. Is 16:7
W, ships of Tarshish, for your Is 23:1
w, inhabitants of the coastland! Is 23:6
W, ships of Tarshish, because Is 23:14
Its rulers **w**"—the LORD's Is 52:5
mourn and **w**, for the LORD's Jr 4:8
W, you shepherds, and cry out. Jr 25:34
the **w** of the leaders of the Jr 25:36
inhabitant of the land will **w**. Jr 47:2
indeed dismayed. **W** and cry out! Jr 48:20
Therefore, I will **w** over Moab. Jr 48:31
it is! They **w**! How Moab has Jr 48:39
W, Heshbon, for Ai is devastated; Jr 49:3
was shattered. **W** for her; get Jr 51:8
Cry out and **w**, son of man, for Ezk 21:12
Lord GOD says: **W**: Alas for the Ezk 30:2
w over the hordes of Egypt and Ezk 32:18
rather, they **w** on their beds. Hs 7:14
w, all you wine drinkers, Jl 1:5
farmers, **w**, you vinedressers, Jl 1:11
w, you ministers of the altar. Jl 1:13
and professional mourners to **w**. Am 5:16
of this I will lament and **w**; Mc 1:8
W, you residents of the Hollow, Zph 1:11
W, cypress, for the cedar has Zch 11:2
W, oaks of Bashan, for the Zch 11:2
to the **w** of the shepherds, Zch 11:3
will weep and **w**, but the world Jn 16:20
and **w** over the miseries that Jms 5:1

WAILING *(10)*
was a loud **w** throughout Egypt Ex 12:30
Their **w** reaches Eglaim; Is 15:8
their **w** reaches Beer-elim. Is 15:8
for weeping, for **w**, for shaven Is 22:12
In their **w** they lament for you, Ezk 27:32
will be **w** in all the public Am 5:16
There will be **w** in all the Am 5:17
temple songs will become **w**"— Am 8:3
a **w** from the Second District, Zph 1:10
people weeping and **w** loudly. Mk 5:38

WAILS *(2)*
Moab **w** on Nebo and at Medeba. Is 15:2
its public squares everyone **w**, Is 15:3

WAIST *(18)*
put sackcloth around his **w**, Gn 37:34
extend from the **w** to the thighs. Ex 28:42
a belt around his **w** with a sword 2Sm 20:8
a leather belt around his **w**." 2Kg 1:8
around his **w** while he was Neh 4:18
Your **w** is a mound of wheat Sg 7:2
will be a belt around His **w**. Is 11:5
as underwear clings to one's **w**, Jr 13:11
gash and sackcloth around the **w**. Jr 48:37
From what seemed to be His **w** up, Ezk 1:27
what seemed to be His **w** down, Ezk 1:27
to be His **w** down was fire, Ezk 8:2
and from His **w** up was something Ezk 8:2
water⌋. It came up to ⌊my⌋ **w**. Ezk 47:4
of gold from Uphaz around his **w**. Dn 10:5
a leather belt around his **w**, Mt 3:4
around his **w** and ate locusts Mk 1:6
truth like a belt around your **w**, Eph 6:14

WAISTBAND *(8)*
artistically woven **w** that is on Ex 28:8
and above the ephod's woven **w**. Ex 28:27
the ephod's **w** and does not come Ex 28:28
ephod on him with its woven **w**. Ex 29:5
artistically woven **w** that was on Ex 39:5
above the ephod's woven **w**. Ex 39:20
the ephod's **w** and did not come Ex 39:21
blood on his own **w** and on the 1Kg 2:5

WAISTLINE *(1)*
fat and his **w** bulges with it, Jb 15:27

WAISTS *(6)*
around our **w** and ropes around 1Kg 20:31
around their **w** and ropes around 1Kg 20:32
and ties a cloth around their **w**. Jb 12:18
put ⌊sackcloth⌋ about your **w**. Is 32:11
belts on their **w** and flowing Ezk 23:15
undergarments around their **w**. Ezk 44:18

WAIT *(71)*
I **w** for Your salvation, LORD. Gn 49:18
W here for us until we return to Ex 24:14
W here until I hear what the Nm 9:8
with you are to come **w** in ambush Jdg 9:32
they said, "Let us **w** until dawn; Jdg 16:2
very good. Why **w**? Don't hesitate Jdg 18:9
be willing to **w** for them to grow Ru 1:13
"**W**, my daughter," she said, Ru 3:18
W seven days until I come to you 1Sm 10:8
they say, '**W** until we reach you, 1Sm 14:9
own servant to **w** in ambush for 1Sm 22:8
up against me and **w** in ambush, 1Sm 22:13
I'll **w** at the fords of the 2Sm 15:28
are silent and **w** until morning 2Kg 7:9
the door and escape. Don't **w**." 2Kg 9:3
May it **w** for daylight but have Jb 3:9
who **w** for death, but it does not Jb 3:21
I would **w** all the days of my Jb 14:14
continue to **w** now that they are Jb 32:16
dens and lie in **w** within their Jb 38:40
I **w** for You all day long. Ps 25:5
keep me, for I **w** for You. Ps 25:21
W for the LORD; be courageous Ps 27:14
heart be strong. **W** for the LORD. Ps 27:14
w for the LORD; He is our help Ps 33:20
the LORD and **w** expectantly for Ps 37:7
wicked lies in **w** for the Ps 37:32
W for the LORD and keep His way, Ps 37:34
Now, Lord, what do I **w** for? Ps 39:7
while they **w** to take my life Ps 56:6
All of them **w** for You to give Ps 104:27
and would not **w** for His counsel. Ps 106:13
days ⌊must⌋ Your servant ⌊**w**⌋? Ps 119:84
w for the LORD; I wait, and put Ps 130:5
w, and put my hope in His word. Ps 130:5
I ⌊**w**⌋ for the Lord more than Ps 130:6
W on the LORD, and He will Pr 20:22
I will **w** for the LORD, who is Is 8:17
of Jacob. I will **w** for Him. Is 8:17
we **w** for You in the path of Your Is 26:8
who lie in **w** with evil intent Is 29:20
are all who **w** patiently for Him Is 30:18
to us! We **w** for You. Be our Is 33:2
The islands will **w** for His Is 42:4
the islands will **w** for Me with Is 60:9
watch like fowlers lying in **w**. Jr 5:26

You w for light, but He brings Jr 13:16
is good to those who w for Him, Lm 3:25
It is good to w quietly for Lm 3:26
yet they w for the fulfillment Ezk 13:6
Like robbers who w in ambush for Hs 6:9
Maroth anxiously w for something Mc 1:12
which do not w for anyone or Mc 5:7
All of them w in ambush to shed Mc 7:2
I will w for the God of my Mc 7:7
it delays, w for it, since it Hab 2:3
Now I must quietly w for the day Hab 3:16
Therefore, w for Me—the LORD's Zph 3:8
were lying in w for Him to trap Lk 11:54
but to w for the Father's Ac 1:4
about God to w on tables. Ac 6:2
we eagerly w for it with Rm 8:25
as you eagerly w for the 1Co 1:7
to eat, w for one another 1Co 11:33
Spirit we eagerly w for the hope Gl 5:5
we also eagerly w for a Savior, Php 3:20
to w for His Son from heaven, 1Th 1:10
while we w for the blessed hope Ti 2:13
you w for and earnestly desire 2Pt 3:12
we w for new heavens and a new 2Pt 3:13
while you w for these things, 2Pt 3:14

WAITED *(25)*

So Noah w seven more days and Gn 8:10
After he had w another seven Gn 8:12
ambush site and w between Bethel Jos 8:9
The servants w until they became Jdg 3:25
escaped while the servants w. Jdg 3:26
up at night and w in ambush for Jdg 9:34
and w in ambush in the Jdg 9:43
place and w in ambush for him Jdg 16:2
So they w until late afternoon Jdg 19:8
w seven days for the appointed 1Sm 13:8
on David's behalf, and they w. 1Sm 25:9
to the servant who w on him: 2Sm 13:17
prophet went and w for the king 1Kg 20:38
They w for me as for the rain Jb 29:23
Now Elihu had w to speak to Job Jb 32:4
Look, I w for your conclusions; Jb 32:11
I w patiently for the LORD, Ps 40:1
I w for sympathy, but there was Ps 69:20
we have w for Him, and He has Is 25:9
LORD; we have w for Him. Let us Is 25:9
This is the day we have w for! Lm 2:16
she saw that she w ⌊in vain⌋, Ezk 19:5
on ahead and w for us in Troas, Ac 20:5
But after they w a long time and Ac 28:6
when God patiently w in the days 1Pt 3:20

WAITING *(23)*

who stood ⌊w⌋ to meet them. Ex 5:20
was an ambush ⌊w⌋ for him behind Jos 8:14
While they were w quietly, Jdg 16:2
in ambush were w in her room, Jdg 16:9
in ambush were w in her room, Jdg 16:12
expectation, w silently for my Jb 29:21
Him and you are w for Him. Jb 35:14
w by the posts of my doorway. Pr 8:34
the LORD is w to show you mercy, Is 30:18
You sat w for them beside the Jr 3:2
He is a bear w in ambush, a lion Lm 3:10
the people were w for Zechariah, Lk 1:21
the people were w expectantly, Lk 3:15
like people w for their master Lk 12:36
w for the moving of the water, Jn 5:3
While Paul was w for them in Ac 17:16
and afflictions are w for me. Ac 20:23
w for a commitment from you." Ac 23:21
you have been w and going Ac 27:33
eagerly w for adoption, Rm 8:23
And so, after w patiently, Heb 6:15
to those who are w for Him. Heb 9:28
is now w until His enemies are Heb 10:13

WAITS *(8)*

a hired man he w for his pay. Jb 7:2
a snare ⌊w⌋ for him along the Jb 18:10
w in ambush near the villages; Ps 10:8
one person who w for You will be Ps 25:3
behalf of the one who w for Him. Is 64:4
is the one who w for and reaches Dn 12:12
creation eagerly w with Rm 8:19
the farmer w for the precious Jms 5:7

WAKE *(30)*

he's sleeping and will w up!" 1Kg 18:27
told him, "The boy didn't w up." 2Kg 4:31
They will not w up until the Jb 14:12
leaves a shining w behind him; Jb 41:32
I w again because the LORD Ps 3:5
W up and rise to my defense, Ps 35:23
W up, LORD! Why are You Ps 44:23
W up, my soul! Wake up, harp and Ps 57:8
up, my soul! W up, harp and lyre Ps 57:8
and lyre! I will w up the dawn. Ps 57:8
W up, harp and lyre! I will wake Ps 108:2
and lyre! I will w up the dawn. Ps 108:2
I w up, I am still with You. Ps 139:18
when you w up, they will talk to Pr 6:22
it! When will I w up? I'll look Pr 23:35
W up, wake up! Put on the Is 51:9
Wake up, w up! Put on the Is 51:9
W up as in days past, as in Is 51:9
W yourself, wake yourself up! Is 51:17
Wake yourself, w yourself up! Is 51:17
W up, wake up; put on your Is 52:1
Wake up, w up; put on your Is 52:1
asleep forever and never w up. Jr 51:39
asleep forever and never w up. Jr 51:57
W up, you drunkards, and weep; Jl 1:5
and those who disturb you w up? Hab 2:7
says to wood: W up! or to mute Hab 2:19
but I'm on My way to w him up." Jn 11:11
hour for you to w up from sleep, Rm 13:11
to w you up with a reminder, 2Pt 1:13

WAKES *(2)*

then w and is still hungry; Is 29:8
then w and is still thirsty, Is 29:8

WAKING *(1)*

Like one w from a dream, Lord, Ps 73:20

WALK *(147)*

Get up and w from one end of the Gn 13:17
went out to w in the field, Gn 24:63
get up and w around outside Ex 21:19
insects that w on all fours are Lv 11:20
insects that w on all fours: Lv 11:21
animals that w on their paws are Lv 11:27
I will w among you and be your Lv 26:12
and when you w along the road, Dt 6:7
and when you w along the road, Dt 11:19
your God, w in all His ways, Dt 11:22
your God has commanded you to w. Dt 13:5
and that you will w in His ways, Dt 26:17
LORD your God and w in His ways. Dt 28:9
LORD your God, to w in His ways, Dt 30:16
your God, w in all His ways, Jos 22:5
house would w before Me forever, 1Sm 2:30
and he will w before My anointed 1Sm 2:35
his sons did not w in his ways— 1Sm 8:3
military clothes and tried to w, 1Sm 17:39
"I can't w in these," David said 1Sm 17:39
LORD your God to w in His ways 1Kg 2:3
are careful to w faithfully 1Kg 2:4
If you w in My ways and keep My 1Kg 3:14
if you w in My statutes, 1Kg 6:12
servants who w before You with 1Kg 8:23
guard their w before Me as you 1Kg 8:25
them the good way they should w 1Kg 8:36
toward Him to w in all His ways 1Kg 8:58
LORD our God to w in His 1Kg 8:61
you w before Me as your father 1Kg 9:4
I command you, w in My ways, 1Kg 11:38
and did not w in the way 2Kg 21:22
servants who w before You with 2Ch 6:14
their way to w in My Law as you 2Ch 6:16
them the good way they should w 2Ch 6:27
fear You and w in Your ways all 2Ch 6:31
you w before Me as your father 2Ch 7:17
Shouldn't you w in the fear of Neh 5:9
day Mordecai took a w in front Est 2:11
to those who w above ground. Jb 28:4
I w about blackened, but not by Jb 30:28
to w before God in the light of Ps 56:13
they w in the light of Your Ps 89:15
cannot feel, feet, but cannot w. Ps 115:7
I will w before the LORD in the Ps 116:9
I will w freely in an open place Ps 119:45
If I w in the thick of danger, Ps 138:7
the right paths to w in ways of Pr 2:13
When you w, your steps will not Pr 4:12
When you w here and there, Pr 6:22
Can a man w on coals without Pr 6:28
I w in the way of righteousness, Pr 8:20
four are stately in their w: Pr 30:29
And w in the ways of your heart Ec 11:9
mourners will w around in the Ec 12:5
so that we may w in His paths." Is 2:3
come and let us w in the LORD's Is 2:5
people w through on foot. Is 11:15
you: "This is the way. W in it." Is 30:21
But the redeemed will w ⌊on it⌋, Is 35:9
I w along slowly all my years Is 38:15
they will w and not faint. Is 40:31
and life to those who w on it— Is 42:5
not willing to w in His ways, Is 42:24
when you w through the fire Is 43:2
w in the light of your fire and Is 50:11
Lie down, so we can w over you. Is 51:23
a street for those who w on it. Is 51:23
people who w in the wrong path, Is 65:2
fields; don't w on the road. For Jr 6:25
must w in every way I command Jr 7:23
My voice or w according to it Jr 9:13
carried because they cannot w. Jr 10:5
who w in the stubbornness of Jr 13:10
roads—to w on ⌊new⌋ paths, Jr 18:15
commit adultery and w in lies. Jr 23:14
way we should w and the thing we Jr 42:3
voice and didn't w in His law, Jr 44:23
they w away exhausted before the Lm 1:6
and forced ⌊me⌋ to w in darkness Lm 3:2
we could not w in our streets. Lm 4:18
Didn't you w in their ways and Ezk 16:47
My people Israel, to w on you; Ezk 36:12
to humble those who w in pride. Dn 4:37
was I who taught Ephraim to w, Hs 11:3
and the righteous w in them, Hs 14:9
Can two w together without Am 3:3
large city, a three-day w. Jnh 3:3
first day of his w in the city Jnh 3:4
I will w barefoot and naked. Mc 1:8
Then you will not w so proudly Mc 2:3
ways so we may w in His paths." Mc 4:2
the peoples each w in the name Mc 4:5
we will w in the name of Yahweh Mc 4:5
and to w humbly with your God. Mc 6:8
and enables me to w on mountain Hab 3:19
and they will w like the blind Zph 1:17
If you w in My ways and keep My Zch 3:7
or to say, 'Get up and w'? Mt 9:5
see, the lame w, those with skin Mt 11:5
pick up your stretcher, and w'? Mk 2:9
the girl got up and began to w. Mk 5:42
you,' or to say, 'Get up and w'? Lk 5:23
sight, the lame w, those with Lk 7:22
the people who w over them don't Lk 11:44
and began to w along with them. Lk 24:15
"pick up your bedroll and w!" Jn 5:8
his bedroll, and started to w. Jn 5:9
'Pick up your bedroll and w.' " Jn 5:11
'Pick up ⌊your bedroll⌋ and w?' " Jn 5:12
Me will never w in the darkness Jn 8:12
W while you have the light so Jn 12:35
tie your belt and w wherever you Jn 21:18
the Nazarene, get up and w!" Ac 3:6
and started to w, and he entered Ac 3:8
or godliness we had made him w? Ac 3:12
up and started to w around. Ac 14:10
children or to w in our customs. Ac 21:21
so we too may w in a new way of Rm 6:4
in us who do not w according to Rm 8:4
Let us w with decency, as in the Rm 13:13
we w by faith, not by sight— 2Co 5:7
among them and w among them, 2Co 6:16
Didn't we w in the same spirit 2Co 12:18
w by the Spirit and you will not Gl 5:16
so that we should w in them. Eph 2:10
urge you to w worthy of the Eph 4:1
no longer w as the Gentiles Eph 4:17
longer walk as the Gentiles w, Eph 4:17
And w in love, as the Messiah Eph 5:2
W as children of light— Eph 5:8
to how you w—not as unwise Eph 5:15
so that you may w worthy of the Col 1:10
Christ Jesus the Lord, w in Him, Col 2:6
W in wisdom toward outsiders, Col 4:5
one of you to w worthy of God, 1Th 2:12
us how you must w and please God 1Th 4:1
that you may w properly in the 1Th 4:12
among you who w irresponsibly, 2Th 3:11
with Him," and w in darkness, we 1Jn 1:6
But if we w in the light as He 1Jn 1:7
in Him should w just as He 1Jn 2:6

tear them down to fortify the w. Is 22:10
is like rain ⌊against⌋ a w, Is 25:4
bulge in a high w whose collapse Is 30:13
of the people who are on the w." Is 36:11
not to the men who sit on the w, Is 36:12
his face to the w and prayed to Is 38:2
grope along a w like the blind; Is 59:10
you a fortified w of bronze to Jr 15:20
are besieging you outside the w, Jr 21:4
set fire to the w of Damascus; Jr 49:27
even Babylon's w will fall. Jr 51:44
built a siege w all around it. Jr 52:4
to destroy the w of Daughter Lm 2:8
W of Daughter Zion, let ⌊your⌋ Lm 2:18
a siege w, build a ramp, Ezk 4:2
up as an iron w between yourself Ezk 4:3
there was a hole in the w. Ezk 8:7
Son of man, dig through the w." Ezk 8:8
dug through the w, and there was Ezk 8:8
all around the w was every form Ezk 8:10
dig through the w and take the Ezk 12:5
I dug through the w by hand; Ezk 12:7
dig through the w to bring ⌊him⌋ Ezk 12:12
restore the w around the house Ezk 13:5
builds a w they plaster it Ezk 13:10
Now when the w has fallen, Ezk 13:12
tear down the w you plastered Ezk 13:14
against the w and against those Ezk 13:15
The w is no more and neither are Ezk 13:15
a ramp, and construct a siege w. Ezk 21:22
would repair the w and stand in Ezk 22:30
male figures carved on the w, Ezk 23:14
ramp and raise a w of shields Ezk 26:8
and every w will fall to the Ezk 38:20
there was a w surrounding the Ezk 40:5
thickness of the ⌊w⌋ structure; Ezk 40:5
he measured the w of the temple; Ezk 41:5
ledges on the w of the temple Ezk 41:6
not be in the temple w ⌊itself⌋. Ezk 41:6
of the outer w of the side rooms Ezk 41:9
The w of the building was eight Ezk 41:12
On every w all around, on the Ezk 41:17
and on the w of the great hall. Ezk 41:20
A w on the outside ran in front Ezk 42:7
thickness of the w of the court Ezk 42:10
corresponding w as one enters Ezk 42:12
It had a w all around ⌊it⌋, Ezk 42:20
with ⌊only⌋ a w between Me and Ezk 43:8
a ⌊stone⌋ w around the inside Ezk 46:23
of the king's palace w next to Dn 5:5
I will enclose her with a w, Hs 2:6
they run on the w; they climb Jl 2:9
go through breaches in the w, Am 4:3
hand against the w only to have Am 5:19
a vertical w with a plumb line Am 7:7
race to its w; the protective Nah 2:5
was the sea, the river her w? Nah 3:8
stones will cry out from the w, Hab 2:11
I will be a w of fire around it, Zch 2:5
through ⌊an opening in⌋ the w. Ac 9:25
strike you, you whitewashed w! Ac 23:3
window in the w and escaped his 2Co 11:33
the dividing w of hostility. Eph 2:14
⌊The city⌋ had a massive high w, Rv 21:12
The city w had 12 foundations, Rv 21:14
the city, its gates, and its w. Rv 21:15
he measured its w, 144 cubits Rv 21:17
material of its w was jasper, Rv 21:18
of the city w were adorned with Rv 21:19

WALLED *(4)*
sells a residence in a w city, Lv 25:29
the house in the w city is Lv 25:30
He has w me in so I cannot Lm 3:7
He has w in my ways with cut Lm 3:9

WALLOW *(1)*
Moab will w in his own vomit, Jr 48:26

WALLOWS *(1)*
washing itself, w in the mud." 2Pt 2:22

WALLS *(73)*
in the w of the house Lv 14:37
spread on the w of the house, Lv 14:39
that have no w around them are Lv 25:31
were fortified with high w, Dt 3:5
until your high and fortified w, Dt 28:52
cities with w and bronze bars 1Kg 4:13
encircling the w of the temple, 1Kg 6:5
be inserted into the temple w. 1Kg 6:6
interior temple w with cedar 1Kg 6:15
surrounding temple w with carved 1Kg 6:29
between the two w near the 2Kg 25:4
tore down the w surrounding 2Kg 25:10
overlaying the w of the 1Ch 29:4
thresholds, its w and doors— 2Ch 3:7
and he carved cherubim on the w. 2Ch 3:7
cities with w, gates, and bars— 2Ch 8:5
surround them with w and towers, 2Ch 14:7
finishing its w, and repairing Ezr 4:12
rebuilt and its w are finished, Ezr 4:13
rebuilt and its w are finished, Ezr 4:16
beams are being set in the w. Ezr 5:8
I inspected the w of Jerusalem Neh 2:13
repair to the w of Jerusalem was Neh 4:7
build the w of Jerusalem. Ps 51:18
they make the rounds on its w. Ps 55:10
broken down its w so that all Ps 80:12
You have broken down all his w; Ps 89:40
there be peace within your w, Ps 122:7
will be no breach ⌊in the w⌋, Ps 144:14
me—the guardians of the w. Sg 5:7
breaches in ⌊the w of⌋ the city Is 22:9
between the w for the waters Is 22:11
established as w and ramparts. Is 26:1
w are continually before Me. Is 49:16
and all your w of precious Is 54:12
in My house and within My w, Is 56:5
called the repairer of broken w, Is 58:12
Foreigners will build up your w, Is 60:10
you will name your w salvation, Is 60:18
appointed watchmen on your w; Is 62:6
her surrounding w and all the Jr 1:15
and bronze w against the whole Jr 1:18
the gate between the two w. Jr 39:4
tore down the w of Jerusalem. Jr 39:8
back and forth within your w, Jr 49:3
fallen; her w are demolished. Jr 50:15
flag against the w of Babylon; Jr 51:12
Babylon's thick w will be Jr 51:58
between the two w near the Jr 52:7
tore down all the w surrounding Jr 52:14
has handed the w of her palaces Lm 2:7
made the ramparts and w grieve; Lm 2:8
built and siege w constructed to Ezk 17:17
within her ⌊w⌋ so that her time Ezk 22:3
will destroy the w of Tyre and Ezk 26:4
against your w and tear down Ezk 26:9
your w will shake from the noise Ezk 26:10
demolish your w and tear down Ezk 26:12
stationed⌋ on your w all around, Ezk 27:11
their shields all around your w; Ezk 27:11
near the ⌊city⌋ w and in the Ezk 33:30
living without w and without Ezk 38:11
including its w, were 175 feet Ezk 41:13
hall like those carved on the w. Ezk 41:25
the base of the w on all sides. Ezk 46:23
they scale w as men of war ⌊do⌋. Jl 2:7
send fire against the w of Gaza, Am 1:7
send fire against the w of Tyre, Am 1:10
set fire to the w of Rabbah, Am 1:14
will come for rebuilding your w; Mc 7:11
settle on the w on a cold day; Nah 3:17
inhabited without w because of Zch 2:4
By faith the w of Jericho fell Heb 11:30

WALNUT *(1)*
came down to the w grove to see Sg 6:11

WANDER *(20)*
when God had me w from my Gn 20:13
and He made them w in the Nm 32:13
Let me w two months through the Jdg 11:37
I make you w around with us 2Sm 15:20
Israelites to w from the land I 2Kg 21:8
and makes them w in a trackless Jb 12:24
clothing, they w about naked. Jb 24:10
out to God and w about for lack Jb 38:41
wicked w everywhere, and what Ps 12:8
they w in darkness. All Ps 82:5
and makes them w in trackless Ps 107:40
Let his children w as beggars, Ps 109:10
don't let me w from Your Ps 119:10
the accursed, who w from Your Ps 119:21
I w like a lost sheep; Ps 119:176
They will w through the land, Is 8:21
pasture, a tent that does not w; Is 33:20
Truly they love to w; Jr 14:10
herds of cattle w in confusion Jl 1:18
the people⌋ w like sheep; Zch 10:2

WANDERED *(14)*
She left and w in the Wilderness Gn 21:14
the Israelites w in the Jos 5:6
her virginity as she w through Jdg 11:38
of Saul's father Kish w off. 1Sm 9:3
the donkeys that w away from you 1Sm 9:20
maybe he has w away; 1Kg 18:27
Some w in the desolate Ps 107:4
but I have not w from Your Ps 119:110
They have w from mountain to Jr 50:6
So they w aimlessly. Lm 4:15
the Levites who w away from Me Ezk 44:10
some have w away from the faith 1Tm 6:10
they w about in sheepskins, Heb 11:37
They w in deserts, mountains, Heb 11:38

WANDERER *(2)*
be a restless w on the earth." Gn 4:12
a restless w on the earth, Gn 4:14

WANDERERS *(2)*
them homeless w and bring them Ps 59:11
they will become w among the Hs 9:17

WANDERING *(11)*
found him there, w in the field, Gn 37:15
They are w around the land in Ex 14:3
My father was a w Aramean. Dt 26:5
w from nation to nation and from 1Ch 16:20
w from nation to nation and from Ps 105:13
A man w from his home is like a Pr 27:8
is like a bird w from its nest. Pr 27:8
what the eyes see than w desire. Ec 6:9
Like w gazelles and like sheep Is 13:14
exiled and w—but who brought Is 49:21
w stars for whom is reserved the Jd 13

WANDERINGS *(1)*
You Yourself have recorded my w. Ps 56:8

WANDERS *(3)*
He w about for food, ⌊saying,⌋ Jb 15:23
youth—each w on his own way; Is 47:15
Judah still w with El and is Hs 11:12

WANT *(208)*
do whatever you w with her." Gn 16:6
can do whatever you w to them. Gn 19:8
Settle wherever you w." Gn 20:15
I w to sleep with her." Gn 29:21
Now you also w to take my son's Gn 30:15
I w to appease Esau with the Gn 32:20
Now you w to take Benjamin. Gn 42:36
what you w to bake, and boil Ex 16:23
and boil what you w to boil, Ex 16:23
I do not w to leave as a free Ex 21:5
you w to refrain from helping Ex 23:5
to him, "I don't w to go. Nm 10:30
but can I say anything I w? Nm 22:38
We w to build sheepfolds here Nm 32:16
But whenever you w, you may Dt 12:15
'I w to eat meat' because you Dt 12:20
you may eat it whenever you w. Dt 12:20
your gates whenever you w. Dt 12:21
the money on anything you w: Dt 14:26
you, 'I don't w to leave you,' Dt 15:16
'We w to appoint a king over us Dt 17:14
and w to take her as your wife, Dt 21:11
grapes as you w until you are Dt 23:24
the man doesn't w to marry his Dt 25:7
says, 'I don't w to marry her,' Dt 25:8
What does my Lord w to say to Jos 5:14
asked her, "What do you w?" Jos 15:18
asked her, "What do you w?" Jdg 1:14
But if you w to prepare a burnt Jdg 13:16
her for me, because I w her." Jdg 14:3
w to go to my wife in her room, Jdg 15:1
and do whatever you w to them. Jdg 19:24
Why do you w to go with me? Ru 1:11
if he doesn't w to redeem you, Ru 3:13
If you w to redeem ⌊it⌋, do so. Ru 4:4
if you do not w to redeem ⌊it⌋, Ru 4:4
"I w to redeem ⌊it⌋," he Ru 4:4
whatever you w for yourself," 1Sm 2:16
can do whatever you w to us." 1Sm 11:10
"Do whatever you w," the troops 1Sm 14:36
replied, "Do whatever you w." 1Sm 14:40
you w to take it for yourself, 1Sm 21:9
and those who w trouble for my 1Sm 25:26
is it that you w me to bring up 1Sm 28:11
I w to send you to the king to 2Sm 14:32
why do you w to run since you 2Sm 18:22
"No matter what I w to run!" 2Sm 18:23

Never! I do not **w** to destroy! 2Sm 20:20
my lord the king **w** to do this?" 2Sm 24:3
Do you **w** three years of famine 2Sm 24:13
and he asked, "What do you **w**?" 1Kg 1:16
everything you **w** regarding the 1Kg 5:8
me for you to **w** to go back to 1Kg 11:22
reign as king over all you **w**, 1Kg 11:37
Why does my lord **w** to do this? 1Ch 21:3
and Levites, who **w** to go to Ezr 7:13
Whatever you **w**, even to half the Est 5:3
Whatever you **w**, even to half the Est 5:6
the king would **w** to honor more Est 6:6
If you really **w** to appear Jb 19:5
We don't **w** to know Your ways. Jb 21:14
He be told that I **w** to speak? Jb 37:20
Let those who **w** my vindication Ps 35:27
and those who **w** to harm me Ps 38:12
You do not **w** a sacrifice, or I Ps 51:16
Why do you **w** more beatings? Is 1:5
night. If you **w** to ask, ask! Is 21:12
whatever you **w** on My holy day; Is 58:13
will go where we **w**; we will no Jr 2:31
they **w** to take your life. Jr 4:30
of Anathoth who **w** to take your Jr 11:21
of those who **w** to take their Jr 19:7
those who **w** to take their life, Jr 19:9
to those who **w** to take their Jr 21:7
you dread, who **w** to take your Jr 22:25
to those who **w** to take their Jr 34:20
to those who **w** to take their Jr 34:21
men who **w** to take your life. Jr 38:16
or go wherever you **w** to go." Jr 40:5
to those who **w** to take his life, Jr 44:30
to those who **w** to take their Jr 46:26
before those who **w** to take their Jr 49:37
Israel will not **w** to listen to Ezk 3:7
they do not **w** to listen to Me. Ezk 3:7
we **w** you as king to know that we Dn 3:18
Though I **w** to redeem ⌊them⌋, Hs 7:13
whatever you **w** others to do for Mt 7:12
we **w** to see a sign from You." Mt 12:38
w us to go and gather them up? Mt 13:28
it be done for you as you **w**." Mt 15:28
I don't **w** to send them away Mt 15:32
If You **w**, I will make three Mt 17:4
If you **w** to enter into life, Mt 19:17
"If you **w** to be perfect," Jesus Mt 19:21
I **w** to give this last man the Mt 20:14
to do what I **w** with my business Mt 20:15
"What do you **w**?" He asked her. Mt 20:21
What do you **w** Me to do for you? Mt 20:32
He answered, 'I don't **w** to!' Mt 21:29
but they didn't **w** to come. Mt 22:3
Where do You **w** us to prepare the Mt 26:17
Who is it you **w** me to release Mt 27:17
the two do you **w** me to release Mt 27:21
me whatever you **w**, and I'll give Mk 6:22
I **w** you to give me John the Mk 6:25
he did not **w** to refuse her. Mk 6:26
and did not **w** anyone to know it Mk 7:24
but He did not **w** anyone to know Mk 9:30
we **w** You to do something for us Mk 10:35
What do you **w** Me to do for you? Mk 10:36
What do you **w** Me to do for you? Mk 10:51
man told Him, "I **w** to see!" Mk 10:51
w to go around in long robes, Mk 12:38
and who **w** greetings in the Mk 12:38
do good for them whenever you **w**, Mk 14:7
Where do You **w** us to go and Mk 14:12
Do you **w** me to release the King Mk 15:9
Then what do you **w** me to do with Mk 15:12
and I can give it to anyone I **w**. Lk 4:6
Just as you **w** others to do for Lk 6:31
do You **w** us to call down fire Lk 9:54
became angry and didn't **w** to go Lk 15:28
so that those who **w** to pass over Lk 16:26
What do you **w** Me to do for you? Lk 18:41
"Lord," he said, "I **w** to see!" Lk 18:41
w this man to rule over us! Lk 19:14
who did not **w** me to rule over Lk 19:27
who **w** to go around in long robes Lk 20:46
Where do You **w** us to prepare it? Lk 22:9
no one said, "What do You **w**?" Jn 4:27
to him, "Do you **w** to get well?" Jn 5:6
You don't **w** to go away too, Jn 6:67
since He did not **w** to travel in Jn 7:1
Why do you **w** to kill Me?" Jn 7:19
this the man they **w** to kill? Jn 7:25
and you **w** to carry out your Jn 8:44
Why do you **w** to hear it again? Jn 9:27
You don't **w** to become His Jn 9:27
him, "Sir, we **w** to see Jesus." Jn 12:21
ask whatever you **w** and it will Jn 15:7
you **w** me to release to you the Jn 18:39
the Jews did not **w** the bodies to Jn 19:31
you where you don't **w** to go." Jn 21:18
I **w** him to remain until I come, Jn 21:22
If I **w** him to remain until I Jn 21:23
you **w** to kill me, the same way Ac 7:28
we **w** to know what these ideas Ac 17:20
I don't **w** to be a judge of such Ac 18:15
But if you **w** something else, Ac 19:39
For I **w** very much to see you, Rm 1:11
Now I **w** you to know, brothers, Rm 1:13
do not practice what I **w** to do, Rm 7:15
if I do what I do not **w** to do, Rm 7:16
not do the good that I **w** to do, Rm 7:19
the evil that I do not **w** to do. Rm 7:19
Now if I do what I do not **w**, Rm 7:20
I **w** to do good, evil is with Rm 7:21
I do not **w** you to be unaware of Rm 11:25
Do you **w** to be unafraid of the Rm 13:3
I **w** you to be wise about what Rm 16:19
What do you **w**? Should I come to 1Co 4:21
I **w** you to be without concerns. 1Co 7:32
Now I **w** you to know, brothers, 1Co 10:1
I do not **w** you to be partners 1Co 10:20
you over and you **w** to go, 1Co 10:27
But I **w** you to know that Christ 1Co 11:3
I do not **w** you to be unaware. 1Co 12:1
if they **w** to learn something, 1Co 14:35
w to clarify for you the gospel 1Co 15:1
I don't **w** to see you now just in 1Co 16:7
we don't **w** you to be unaware, 2Co 1:8
we do not **w** to be unclothed 2Co 5:4
w you to know, brothers, about 2Co 8:1
I don't **w** to seem as though I am 2Co 10:9
of those who **w** an opportunity to 2Co 11:12
For if I **w** to boast, I will not 2Co 12:6
not find you to be what I **w**, 2Co 12:20
found by you to be what you **w**; 2Co 12:20
troubling you and **w** to change Gl 1:7
Now I **w** you to know, brothers, Gl 1:11
I only **w** to learn this from you: Gl 3:2
Do you **w** to be enslaved to them Gl 4:9
w to isolate you so you will Gl 4:17
you who **w** to be under the law, Gl 4:21
so that you don't do what you **w**. Gl 5:17
Those who **w** to make a good Gl 6:12
they **w** you to be circumcised in Gl 6:13
Now I **w** you to know, brothers, Php 1:12
For I **w** you to know how great a Col 2:1
⌊I **w**⌋ their hearts to be Col 2:2
see us, as we also **w** to see you. 1Th 3:6
do not **w** you to be uninformed, 1Th 4:13
w to be teachers of the law, 1Tm 1:7
Therefore I **w** the men in every 1Tm 2:8
by desire, they **w** to marry, 1Tm 5:11
I **w** younger women to marry, 1Tm 5:14
But those who **w** to be rich fall 1Tm 6:9
all those who **w** to live a godly 2Tm 3:12
I **w** you to insist on these Ti 3:8
But I didn't **w** to do anything Phm 14
Now we **w** each of you to Heb 6:11
You did not **w** sacrifice and Heb 10:5
don't **w** to do so with paper and 2Jn 12
stops those who **w** to do so and 3Jn 10
but I don't **w** to write to you 3Jn 13
I **w** to remind you, though you Jd 5
she does not **w** to repent of her Rv 2:21
with any plague whenever they **w**. Rv 11:6

WANTED (64)

the men who **w** to kill you are Ex 4:19
meat and ate all the bread we **w**. Ex 16:3
Anyone who **w** to consult the LORD Ex 33:7
the woman, because Samson **w** her. Jdg 14:7
everyone did whatever he **w**. Jdg 17:6
everyone did whatever he **w**. Jdg 21:25
In the past you **w** David to be 2Sm 3:17
cedar and cypress timber he **w**, 1Kg 5:10
The whole world **w** an audience 1Kg 10:24
of the world **w** an audience with 2Ch 9:23
prophets who **w** to intimidate me Neh 6:14
serve as much as each person **w**. Est 1:8
⌊He **w**⌋ to show off her beauty to Est 1:11
If one **w** to take Him to court, Jb 9:3
Just what we **w**." Do not let them Ps 35:25
freed ⌊to go⌋ wherever they **w**, Jr 34:16
the one who **w** to take his life.' Jr 44:30
would destroy only what they **w**. Jr 49:9
Wherever the Spirit **w** to go, Ezk 1:12
Wherever the Spirit **w** to go, Ezk 1:20
killed anyone he **w** and kept Dn 5:19
and kept alive anyone he **w**; Dn 5:19
exalted anyone he **w** and humbled Dn 5:19
wanted and humbled anyone he **w**. Dn 5:19
Then I **w** to know the true Dn 7:19
⌊I also **w** to know⌋ about the 10 Dn 7:20
did whatever he **w** and became Dn 8:4
they steal only what they **w**? Ob 5
almost fainted, and he **w** to die. Jnh 4:8
they **w** to go patrol the earth, Zch 6:7
Though he **w** to kill him, he Mt 14:5
to a king who **w** to settle Mt 18:23
How often I **w** to gather your Mt 23:37
to the crowd a prisoner they **w**. Mt 27:15
and summoned those He **w**, Mk 3:13
against him and **w** to kill him. Mk 6:19
the sea and **w** to pass by them. Mk 6:48
they did to him whatever they **w**, Mk 9:13
out what he **w** him to be called Lk 1:62
And he **w** to see Him. Lk 9:9
and kings **w** to see the things Lk 10:24
How often I **w** to gather your Lk 13:34
a long time he had **w** to see Him, Lk 23:8
the fish, as much as they **w**. Jn 6:11
Some of them **w** to seize Him, Jn 7:44
knew they **w** to question Him Jn 16:19
belt and walk wherever you **w**. Jn 21:18
were enraged and **w** to kill them. Ac 5:33
he became hungry and **w** to eat, Ac 10:10
Barnabas **w** to take along John Ac 15:37
Paul **w** Timothy to go with him, Ac 16:3
When he **w** to cross over to Ac 18:27
Though Paul **w** to go in before Ac 19:30
Alexander **w** to make his defense Ac 19:33
since he **w** to find out exactly Ac 22:30
him and **w** to judge him Ac 24:6
plan because he **w** to save Paul, Ac 27:43
examining me, **w** to release me, Ac 28:18
them, in the body just as He **w**. 1Co 12:18
God **w** to make known to those Col 1:27
So we **w** to come to you—even I, 1Th 2:18
I **w** to keep him with me, so that Phm 13
Because God **w** to show His Heb 6:17
when he **w** to inherit the Heb 12:17

WANTING (12)

and not **w** to disgrace her Mt 1:19
outside **w** to speak to Him Mt 12:46
outside, **w** to speak to You. Mt 12:47
standing outside, **w** to see You." Lk 8:20
But **w** to justify himself, he Lk 10:29
which of you, **w** to build a tower Lk 14:28
Pilate, **w** to release Jesus, Lk 23:20
W to know the charge for which Ac 23:28
w to do a favor for the Jews, Ac 25:9
memories of us, **w** to see us, as 1Th 3:6
w to conduct ourselves honorably Heb 13:18
with you, not **w** any to perish, 2Pt 3:9

WANTS (65)

a lioness—who **w** to rouse him? Gn 49:9
with you and **w** to celebrate Ex 12:48
come whenever he **w** into the holy Lv 16:2
with you and **w** to observe Nm 9:14
is among you and **w** to prepare a Nm 15:14
in Israel and **w** to go to the Dt 18:6
are to let her go where she **w**, Dt 21:14
you wherever he **w** within your Dt 23:16
morning, if he **w** to redeem you, Ru 3:13
so that he **w** to take my life? 1Sm 20:1
the one who **w** to take my life 1Sm 22:23
to take my life **w** to take your 1Sm 22:23
the king **w** to come down, 1Sm 23:20
take whatever he **w** and offer it. 2Sm 24:22
the king may do whatever he **w**. 1Ch 21:23
the man the king **w** to honor?" Est 6:6
For the man the king **w** to honor: Est 6:7
the man the king **w** to honor, Est 6:9
the man the king **w** to honor.'" Est 6:9
the man the king **w** to honor." Est 6:11
who **w** His servant's well-being." Ps 35:27
but only **w** to show off his Pr 18:2
since he will do whatever he **w**. Ec 8:3
shattered pot, a jar no one **w**? Jr 22:28

Moab like a jar no one w." Jr 48:38
will be whatever he w to give, Ezk 46:5
and whatever he w to give with Ezk 46:11
it to anyone He w and sets over Dn 4:17
and He gives it to anyone He w. Dn 4:25
and He gives it to anyone He w." Dn 4:32
He does what He w with the army Dn 4:35
and sets anyone He w over it. Dn 5:21
vast realm and do whatever he w. Dn 11:3
him will do whatever he w, Dn 11:16
the king will do whatever he w. Dn 11:36
As for the one who w to sue you Mt 5:40
the one who w to borrow from Mt 5:42
adulterous generation w a sign, Mt 16:4
If anyone w to come with Me, Mt 16:24
For whoever w to save his life Mt 16:25
whoever w to become great among Mt 20:26
and whoever w to be first among Mt 20:27
rescue Him now—if He w Him! Mt 27:43
If anyone w to be My follower, Mk 8:34
For whoever w to save his life Mk 8:35
If anyone w to be first, he Mk 9:35
whoever w to become great among Mk 10:43
and whoever w to be first among Mk 10:44
old wine, w new, because he Lk 5:39
If anyone w to come with Me, Lk 9:23
For whoever w to save his life Lk 9:24
of here! Herod w to kill You!" Lk 13:31
the Father w such people to Jn 4:23
gives life to anyone He w to. Jn 5:21
If anyone w to do His will, Jn 7:17
responded. "Who w to kill You?" Jn 7:20
it must be, he can do what he w. 1Co 7:36
to be married to anyone she w— 1Co 7:39
But if anyone w to argue about 1Co 11:16
But God gives it a body as He w, 1Co 15:38
who w everyone to be saved and 1Tm 2:4
So whoever w to be the world's Jms 4:4
For the one who w to love life 1Pt 3:10
If anyone w to harm them, fire Rv 11:5
anyone w to harm them, he must Rv 11:5

WAR *(174)*

waged w against Bera king of Gn 14:2
away like prisoners of w! Gn 31:26
and if w breaks out, they Ex 1:10
return to Egypt if they face w." Ex 13:17
LORD will be at w with Amalek Ex 17:16
is a sound of w in the camp." Ex 32:17
Equip some of your men for w. Nm 31:3
Send 1,000 men to w from each Nm 31:4
Israel—12,000 equipped for w. Nm 31:5
sent 1,000 from each tribe to w. Nm 31:6
They waged w against Midian, Nm 31:7
the spoils of w and the captives Nm 31:11
spoils of w to Moses, Eleazar Nm 31:12
who went out to w and the entire Nm 31:27
fighting men who went out to w: Nm 31:28
who went out to w numbered: Nm 31:36
brothers go to w while you stay Nm 32:6
equipped for w before the LORD Nm 32:27
his weapons of w and thought it Dt 1:41
wonders, and w, by a strong hand Dt 4:34
you go out to w against your Dt 20:1
you but wages w against you, Dt 20:12
city that is waging w with you, Dt 20:20
When you go to w against your Dt 21:10
40,000 equipped for w crossed to Jos 4:13
all the men of w—had died Jos 5:4
nation's men of w who came out Jos 5:6
the city with all the men of w, Jos 6:3
Joshua waged w with all these Jos 11:18
this, the land had rest from w. Jos 11:23
this, the land had rest from w. Jos 14:15
of Gilead, who was a man of w. Jos 17:1
Shiloh to go to w against them. Jos 22:12
about going to w against them to Jos 22:33
new gods, then w was in the Jdg 5:8
Ammonites made w with Israel, Jdg 11:5
Eshtaol armed with weapons of w. Jdg 18:11
armed with their weapons of w. Jdg 18:16
men armed with weapons of w. Jdg 18:17
sound of the w cry and asked, 1Sm 4:6
weapons of w or the equipment 1Sm 8:12
their forces for w at Socoh in 1Sm 17:1
sons had followed Saul to the w, 1Sm 17:13
When w broke out again, David 1Sm 19:8
the troops to go to w at Keilah 1Sm 23:8
the weapons of w have perished! 2Sm 1:27
The w between the house of Saul 2Sm 3:1
During the w between the house 2Sm 3:6
Should I go to w against the 2Sm 5:19
when kings march out ⌊to w⌋, 2Sm 11:1
doing and how the w was going. 2Sm 11:7
again waged w against Israel. 2Sm 21:15
He trains my hands for w; 2Sm 22:35
peace to avenge blood shed in w. 1Kg 2:5
how he waged w and how he 1Kg 14:19
of Egypt went to w against 1Kg 14:25
There was w between Rehoboam 1Kg 14:30
had been w between Rehoboam 1Kg 15:6
There was also w between Abijam 1Kg 15:7
There was w between Asa and 1Kg 15:16
Baasha went to w against Judah. 1Kg 15:17
There was w between Asa and 1Kg 15:32
years without w between Aram 1Kg 22:1
Ramoth-gilead for w or should I 1Kg 22:6
we go to Ramoth-gilead for w, 1Kg 22:15
exercised and how he waged w, 1Kg 22:45
was waging w against Israel, 2Kg 6:8
he had to wage w against Judah's 2Kg 13:12
had taken in w from Jehoash's 2Kg 13:25
how he waged w against Amaziah 2Kg 14:15
he had to wage w and how he 2Kg 14:28
to wage w against Jerusalem. 2Kg 16:5
are strategy and strength for w. 2Kg 18:20
all strong and fit for w. 2Kg 24:16
reign they waged w against the 1Ch 5:10
the bow, and were trained for w. 1Ch 5:18
They waged w against the 1Ch 5:19
brave warriors ready for w. 1Ch 12:25
with all kinds of weapons of w, 1Ch 12:33
all the military weapons of w. 1Ch 12:37
Should I go to w against the 1Ch 14:10
when kings march out ⌊to w⌋, 1Ch 20:1
a w broke out with the 1Ch 20:4
you are a man of w and have shed 1Ch 28:3
of Egypt went to w against 2Ch 12:2
of Egypt went to w against 2Ch 12:9
There was w between Rehoboam 2Ch 12:15
There was w between Abijah and 2Ch 13:2
No one made w with him in those 2Ch 14:6
There was no w until the 2Ch 15:19
Baasha went to w against Judah. 2Ch 16:1
180,000 with him equipped for w. 2Ch 17:18
Ramoth-gilead for w or should I 2Ch 18:5
we go to Ramoth-gilead for w, 2Ch 18:14
So they went to w against Judah 2Ch 21:17
army went to w against Joash. 2Ch 24:23
went out to wage w against the 2Ch 26:6
that went out to w by division 2Ch 26:11
He waged w against the king of 2Ch 27:5
to those coming from the w. 2Ch 28:12
that he planned w on Jerusalem, 2Ch 32:2
took him out of the w chariot, 2Ch 35:24
possessions as spoils of w. Est 8:11
He trains my hands for w; Ps 18:34
though w break out against me, Ps 27:3
smooth, but w is in his heart Ps 55:21
peoples who take pleasure in w. Ps 68:30
the sword, and the weapons of w. Ps 76:3
when I speak, they are for w. Ps 120:7
and wage w with sound guidance. Pr 20:18
you should wage w with sound Pr 24:6
a time for w and a time for Ec 3:8
is better than weapons of w, Ec 9:18
will never again train for w. Is 2:4
waged w against Jerusalem, Is 7:1
prepare for w, and be broken; Is 8:9
prepare for w, and be broken. Is 8:9
garments of w will be burned as Is 9:5
is mobilizing an army for w. Is 13:4
Those who w against you will Is 41:12
anger and the power of w. Is 42:25
them⌋ apart for w against her; Jr 6:4
morning and a w cry at noontime Jr 20:16
Babylon is making w against us. Jr 21:2
the weapons of w in your hands, Jr 21:4
his life like the spoils ⌊of w⌋, Jr 21:9
from ancient times prophesied w, Jr 28:8
the spoils ⌊of w⌋ and will live. Jr 38:2
life like the spoils ⌊of w⌋." Jr 39:18
we will not see w or hear the Jr 42:14
spoils ⌊of w⌋ wherever you go. Jr 45:5
come against her. Rise up for w! Jr 49:14
Raise a w cry against her on Jr 50:15
The sound of w is in the land— Jr 50:22
My battle club, My weapons of w. Jr 51:20
one goes to w, for My wrath is Ezk 7:14
each with a w club in his hand. Ezk 9:2
horses, w horses, and mules Ezk 27:14
Sheol with their weapons of w, Ezk 32:27
restored from w and regathered Ezk 38:8
this horn made w with the holy Dn 7:21
until the end there will be w; Dn 9:26
will mobilize for w and assemble Dn 11:10
will again wage w as far as his Dn 11:10
bow, sword, or w, or by horses Hs 1:7
and weapons of w in the land and Hs 2:18
raise the w cry in Beth-aven: Hs 5:8
Will not w against the unjust Hs 10:9
be demolished in a day of w, Hs 10:14
and they gallop like w horses. Jl 2:4
a mighty army deployed for w. Jl 2:5
scale walls as men of w ⌊do⌋. Jl 2:7
Prepare for holy w; rouse the Jl 3:9
all the men of w advance and Jl 3:9
and let us go to w against her. Ob 1
like those returning from w. Mc 2:8
but declare w against the one Mc 3:5
will never again train for w. Mc 4:3
The bow of w will be removed, Zch 9:10
going to w against another king, Lk 14:31
waging w against the law of my Rm 7:23
Who ever goes to w at his own 1Co 9:7
we do not wage w in a fleshly 2Co 10:3
that are at w within you? Jms 4:1
You fight and w. You do not have Jms 4:2
desires that w against you. 1Pt 2:11
the abyss will make w with them, Rv 11:7
Then w broke out in heaven: Rv 12:7
left to wage w against the rest Rv 12:17
is able to wage w against him?" Rv 13:4
permitted to wage w against the Rv 13:7
These will make w against the Rv 17:14
He judges and makes w. Rv 19:11
together to wage w against the Rv 19:19

WARD *(1)*

you will be unable to w it off. Is 47:11

WARDEN *(3)*

in the eyes of the prison w. Gn 39:21
The w put all the prisoners who Gn 39:22
The w did not bother with Gn 39:23

WARDROBE *(4)*

said to the custodian of the w, 2Kg 10:22
son of Harhas, keeper of the w. 2Kg 22:14
son of Hasrah, keeper of the w. 2Ch 34:22
and heaps up a w like clay— Jb 27:16

WAREHOUSES *(1)*

He made w for the harvest of 2Ch 32:28

WARFARE *(5)*

because of the w all around him 1Kg 5:3
for the day of w and battle? Jb 38:23
for battle and my fingers for w. Ps 144:1
with swords and trained in w. Sg 3:8
of our w are not fleshly, 2Co 10:4

WARM *(11)*

of ours was w when we took it Jos 9:12
had been replaced with w bread. 1Sm 21:6
bedclothes, he could not get w. 1Kg 1:1
my lord the king will get w." 1Kg 1:2
him, the boy's flesh became w. 2Kg 4:34
wadis evaporate in w weather; Jb 6:17
down together, they can keep w; Ec 4:11
how can one person alone keep w? Ec 4:11
I am w, I see the blaze." Is 44:16
but never have enough to get w. Hg 1:6
in peace, keep w, and eat well," Jms 2:16

WARMED *(1)*

and lets them be w in the sand. Jb 39:14

WARMING *(7)*

bless me while w himself with Jb 31:20
is not a coal for w themselves, Is 47:14
the temple police, w himself by Mk 14:54
When she saw Peter w himself, Mk 14:67
standing there w themselves, Jn 18:18
standing with them, w himself. Jn 18:18
was standing and w himself. Jn 18:25

WARMS *(2)*

takes some of it and w himself; Is 44:15
He w himself and says, "Ah! Is 44:16

WARN *(20)*

Go down and w the people not to Ex 19:21

let me w you what these people Nm 24:14
must solemnly w them and tell 1Sm 8:9
you swear by the LORD and w you, 1Kg 2:42
you are to w them, so they will 2Ch 19:10
W the nations: Look! Proclaim to Jr 4:16
They w, "You must not prophesy Jr 11:21
but you do not w him—you don't Ezk 3:18
speak out to w him about his Ezk 3:18
But if you w a wicked person and Ezk 3:19
you did not w him, he will die Ezk 3:20
if you w the righteous person Ezk 3:21
his trumpet to w the people. Ezk 33:3
not speak out to w him about his Ezk 33:8
But if you w a wicked person to Ezk 33:9
would strongly w them not to Mk 3:12
brothers—to w them, so they Lk 16:28
to w you as my dear children. 1Co 4:14
w those who are lazy, comfort 1Th 5:14
an enemy, but w him as a brother 2Th 3:15

WARNED *(41)*
So Abimelech w all the people Gn 26:11
yourself!" God w him. "Don't say Gn 31:24
The man specifically w us: Gn 43:3
up Mount Sinai, since You w us: Ex 19:23
owner has been w yet does not Ex 21:29
w the community, "Get away now Nm 16:26
He w the Kenites, "Since you 1Sm 15:6
But his wife Michal w David: 1Sm 19:11
again, Abner w Asahel, "Stop 2Sm 2:22
of God repeatedly w the king, 2Kg 6:10
outside, and he w ⌊them⌋, 2Kg 10:24
the LORD w Israel and Judah 2Kg 17:13
prophets who w them to turn them Neh 9:26
You w them to turn back to Your Neh 9:29
and Your Spirit w them through Neh 9:30
So I w ⌊them⌋ against selling Neh 13:15
but I w them, "Why are you Neh 13:21
When they had w him day after Est 3:4
Your servant is w by them; Ps 19:11
But beyond these, my son, be w: Ec 12:12
Be w, Jerusalem, or I will be Jr 6:8
For I strongly w your ancestors Jr 11:7
the disaster that He w about. Jr 26:13
which I w them about but they Jr 36:31
Then Zedekiah w Jeremiah, Jr 38:24
and w him, "Don't you realize Jr 40:14
certain that I have w you today! Jr 42:19
so that the people aren't w, Ezk 33:6
And being w in a dream not to go Mt 2:12
And being w in a dream, he Mt 2:22
w you to flee from the coming Mt 3:7
Then Jesus w them sternly, Mt 9:30
w them not to make Him known, Mt 12:16
Then He sternly w him and sent Mk 1:43
And He strictly w them to tell Mk 8:30
w you to flee from the coming Lk 3:7
But He strictly w and instructed Lk 9:21
also previously told and w you. 1Th 4:6
as Moses was w when he was about Heb 8:5
after being w about what was not Heb 11:7
Him who w them on earth, Heb 12:25

WARNING *(17)*
They ⌊serve as⌋ a w sign. Nm 26:10
I am giving as a w to you today, Dt 32:46
and give such a w that they will Jr 6:10
w them time and time again: Jr 11:7
My mouth, give them a w from Me. Ezk 3:17
because he listened to ⌊your⌋ w, Ezk 3:21
and a taunt, a w and a horror, Ezk 5:15
the trumpet but ignores the w, Ezk 33:4
the trumpet but ignored the w, Ezk 33:5
If he had taken w, he would have Ezk 33:5
My mouth, give them a w from Me. Ezk 33:7
I did not stop w each one of you Ac 20:31
they were written as a w to us, 1Co 10:11
gave w, and I give warning—as 2Co 13:2
and I give w—as when I was 2Co 13:2
w and teaching everyone with all Col 1:28
after a first and second w, Ti 3:10

WARNINGS *(4)*
and the w He had given them 2Kg 17:15
and w You gave them. Neh 9:34
time and terrifies them with w, Jb 33:16
no longer pays attention to w. Ec 4:13

WARNS *(1)*
from Him who w us from heaven. Heb 12:25

WARP *(9)*
in the w or woof of linen or Lv 13:48
the leather, the w, the woof, or Lv 13:49
in the fabric, the w, the woof, Lv 13:51
the w or woof in wool or linen, Lv 13:52
fabric, the w or woof, or any Lv 13:53
the leather, or the w or woof. Lv 13:56
fabric, the w or woof, or any Lv 13:57
fabric, the w or woof, or any Lv 13:58
linen fabric, w or woof, or any Lv 13:59

WARPED *(1)*
they became w like a faulty bow. Ps 78:57

WARRED *(1)*
who have w against Jerusalem: Zch 14:12

WARRIOR *(36)*
The LORD is a w; Yahweh is His Ex 15:3
or two for each w, the spoil Jdg 5:30
"The LORD is with you, mighty w." Jdg 6:12
the Gileadite was a great w, Jdg 11:1
every one an experienced w. Jdg 20:17
a valiant man, a w, eloquent, 1Sm 16:18
been a w since he was young. 1Sm 17:33
you will be a w for me and fight 1Sm 18:17
man was a brave w, but he had a 2Kg 5:1
to become a great w on earth. 1Ch 1:10
a w among the Thirty and ⌊a 1Ch 12:4
a young brave w, with 22 1Ch 12:28
Eliada, a brave w, and 200,000 2Ch 17:17
An Ephraimite w named Zichri 2Ch 28:7
who annihilated every brave w, 2Ch 32:21
He charges at me like a w. Jb 16:14
a w will not be delivered by Ps 33:16
Mighty w, strap your sword at Ps 45:3
like a w from the effects of Ps 78:65
I have granted help to a w; Ps 89:19
in the hand of a w are the sons Ps 127:4
A wise w is better than a strong Pr 24:5
the hero and w, the judge and Is 3:2
like a mighty w, I subjugated Is 10:13
The LORD advances like a w; Is 42:13
man, like a w unable to save? Jr 14:9
is with me like a violent w. Jr 20:11
flee, and the w cannot escape! Jr 46:6
because w stumbles against Jr 46:12
stumbles against w and together Jr 46:12
those of a skilled w who does Jr 50:9
W leaders will speak from the Ezk 32:21
Then a w king will arise; Dn 11:3
even the weakling say: I am a w. Jl 3:10
God is among you, a w who saves. Zph 3:17
will be like a w, and their Zch 10:7

WARRIOR'S *(3)*
A w sharp arrows, with burning Ps 120:4
there the w cry is bitter. Zph 1:14
I will make you like a w sword. Zch 9:13

WARRIORS *(95)*
than Ai, and all its men were w. Jos 10:2
deeds of His w in Israel, Jdg 5:11
came down to me with the w. Jdg 5:13
the LORD against the mighty w." Jdg 5:23
had been killed were 120,000 w. Jdg 8:10
died from Benjamin; all were w. Jdg 20:44
25,000 armed men; all were w. Jdg 20:46
sent 12,000 brave w there and Jdg 21:10
The bows of the w are broken, 1Sm 2:4
people and the w on David's 2Sm 16:6
are w and are desperate like 2Sm 17:8
the valiant men with him are w. 2Sm 17:10
and all the w marched out under 2Sm 20:7
are the names of David's w: 2Sm 23:8
among the three w with David 2Sm 23:9
the 30 leading ⌊w⌋ went down at 2Sm 23:13
So three of the w broke through 2Sm 23:16
the exploits of the three w. 2Sm 23:17
a reputation among the three w. 2Sm 23:22
and David's w did not side with 1Kg 1:8
Benaiah, the w, or his brother 1Kg 1:10
180,000 choice w from the entire 1Kg 12:21
and all the w ⌊fled⌋ by night by 2Kg 25:4
had been appointed over the w; 2Kg 25:19
had 44,760 w who could serve 1Ch 5:18
They were brave w, famous men, 1Ch 5:24
were recorded as w in their 1Ch 7:2
who were w belonging to all 1Ch 7:5
They were w and heads of their 1Ch 7:7
ancestral houses—20,200 w. 1Ch 7:9
by heads of families were w; 1Ch 7:11
chosen men, w, and chiefs among 1Ch 7:40
Ulam's sons were w and archers. 1Ch 8:40
the chiefs of David's w who, 1Ch 11:10
This is the list of David's w: 1Ch 11:11
Ahohite was one of the three w. 1Ch 11:12
the exploits of the three w. 1Ch 11:19
a reputation among the three w. 1Ch 11:24
were among the w who helped him 1Ch 12:1
were all brave w and commanders 1Ch 12:21
7,100 brave w ready for war. 1Ch 12:25
20,800 brave w who were famous 1Ch 12:30
All these w, lined up in battle 1Ch 12:38
Joab and the entire army of w. 1Ch 19:8
men, and all the brave w. 1Ch 28:1
180,000 choice w—to fight 2Ch 11:1
set his army of w in order with 2Ch 13:3
All these were brave w. 2Ch 14:8
men, brave w, in Jerusalem. 2Ch 17:13
and 300,000 brave w with him; 2Ch 17:14
and 200,000 brave w with him; 2Ch 17:16
100,000 brave w from Israel. 2Ch 25:6
of families was 2,600 brave w. 2Ch 26:12
and his w about stopping up 2Ch 32:3
pool and the House of the W. Neh 3:16
None of the w was able to lift a Ps 76:5
a city of w and bring down Pr 21:22
by 60 w from the mighty Sg 3:7
it—all of them shields of w. Sg 4:4
by the sword, your w in battle. Is 3:25
also called My w, who exult in Is 13:3
Their w cry loudly in the Is 33:7
they are all mighty w. Jr 5:16
Jehoiakim, all his w, and all Jr 26:21
the morale of the w who remain Jr 38:4
their w are crushed, they Jr 46:5
Let the w go forth—Cush and Jr 46:9
you say, We are w—mighty men Jr 48:14
heart of Moab's w will be like Jr 48:41
hearts of Edom's w will be like Jr 49:22
all the w will be silenced in Jr 49:26
all the w will be silenced in Jr 50:30
A sword is against her heroic w, Jr 50:36
Babylon's w have stopped Jr 51:30
Her w will be captured, their Jr 51:56
her governors, officials, and w. Jr 51:57
broken into, and all the w fled. Jr 52:7
had been appointed over the w; Jr 52:25
against me to crush my young w. Lm 1:15
her lovers, the Assyrians: w Ezk 23:5
and prefects, w splendidly Ezk 23:12
your army, ⌊serving⌋ as your w. Ezk 27:10
and all the w within you, with Ezk 27:27
hordes fall by the swords of w, Ezk 32:12
with the fallen w of the Ezk 32:27
terror of ⌊these⌋ w was ⌊once⌋ Ezk 32:27
of mighty men and all the w." Ezk 39:20
They attack as w ⌊attack⌋; Jl 2:7
war; rouse the w; let all the Jl 3:9
Bring down Your w there, LORD. Jl 3:11
of the w will flee naked Am 2:16
your w will be terrified so that Ob 9
shields of his w are dyed red; Nah 2:3
his w storm out to scatter us, Hab 3:14
they will be like w in battle Zch 10:5

WARS *(15)*
in the Book of the LORD's W: Nm 21:14
in any of the w with Canaan. Jdg 3:1
Hadadezer had fought many w. 2Sm 8:10
Hadadezer had fought many w. 1Ch 18:10
much blood and waged great w. 1Ch 22:8
from now on, you will have w." 2Ch 16:9
with all his w and his ways, 2Ch 27:7
He makes w cease throughout the Ps 46:9
They stir up w all day long. Ps 140:2
going to hear of w and rumors of Mt 24:6
to hear of wars and rumors of w. Mt 24:6
When you hear of w and rumors of Mk 13:7
hear of wars and rumors of w, Mk 13:7
you hear of w and rebellions, Lk 21:9
source of the w and the fights Jms 4:1

WAS *(4208)*
(See pp. xi-xii.)

WASH *(80)*
you may w your feet and rest Gn 18:4
servant's house, w your feet, Gn 19:2
water was brought to w his feet Gn 24:32
gave them water to w their feet, Gn 43:24
They must w their clothes Ex 19:10

meeting and w them with water. Ex 29:4
W its entrails and shanks, Ex 29:17
and his sons must w their hands Ex 30:19
they must w with water so that Ex 30:20
They must w their hands and feet Ex 30:21
meeting and w them with water. Ex 40:12
The offerer must w its entrails Lv 1:9
But he is to w the entrails and Lv 1:13
then you must w that garment in Lv 6:27
carcasses must w his clothes and Lv 11:25
carcasses must w his clothes and Lv 11:28
its carcass must w his clothes Lv 11:40
its carcass must w his clothes Lv 11:40
The person is to w his clothes Lv 13:6
He is to w his clothes, and he Lv 13:34
be cleansed must w his clothes, Lv 14:8
He is to w his clothes and bathe Lv 14:9
the house is to w his clothes, Lv 14:47
eats in it is to w his clothes. Lv 14:47
his bed is to w his clothes and Lv 15:5
sitting on is to w his clothes Lv 15:6
a discharge is to w his clothes Lv 15:7
he is to w his clothes and bathe Lv 15:8
such things is to w his clothes Lv 15:10
was touched is to w his clothes Lv 15:11
his cleansing, w his clothes, Lv 15:13
her bed is to w his clothes and Lv 15:21
sitting on is to w his clothes Lv 15:22
he must w his clothes and bathe Lv 15:27
for Azazel is to w his clothes Lv 16:26
burns them is to w his clothes Lv 16:28
wild beasts is to w his clothes Lv 17:15
if he does not w ⌊his clothes⌋ Lv 17:16
on a scroll and w ⌊them⌋ off Nm 5:23
bodies and w their clothes, Nm 8:7
the priest must w his clothes Nm 19:7
the cow must also w his clothes Nm 19:8
cow's ashes must w his clothes, Nm 19:10
purified must w his clothes Nm 19:19
impurity is to w his clothes, Nm 19:21
the seventh day w your clothes, Nm 31:24
to the victim will w their hands Dt 21:6
he must w with water, Dt 23:11
W, put on ⌊perfumed⌋ oil, and Ru 3:3
to w the feet of my lord's 1Sm 25:41
to your house and w your feet." 2Sm 11:8
Go w seven times in the Jordan 2Kg 5:10
I not w in them and be clean? 2Kg 5:12
he tells you, 'W and be clean'?" 2Kg 5:13
If I w myself with snow, and Jb 9:30
and torrents w away the soil Jb 14:19
I w my hands in innocence and go Ps 26:6
W away my guilt, and cleanse me Ps 51:2
w me, and I will be whiter than Ps 51:7
he will w his feet in the blood Ps 58:10
purify my heart and w my hands Ps 73:13
W yourselves. Cleanse Is 1:16
Even if you w with lye and use a Jr 2:22
W the evil from your heart, Jr 4:14
⌊to w away⌋ sin and impurity. Zch 13:1
on your head, and w your face, Mt 6:17
they don't w their hands when Mt 15:2
eat unless they w their hands Mk 7:3
and began to w His feet with her Lk 7:38
"w in the pool of Siloam" Jn 9:7
told me, 'Go to Siloam and w.' Jn 9:11
and began to w His disciples' Jn 13:5
are You going to w my feet?" Jn 13:6
You will never w my feet— Jn 13:8
If I don't w you, you have no Jn 13:8
need to w anything except Jn 13:10
also ought to w one another's Jn 13:14
and w away your sins by calling Ac 22:16
we should w ourselves clean from 2Co 7:1
are those who w their robes, Rv 22:14

WASHBASIN *(2)*

Moab is My w; on Edom I throw My Ps 60:8
Moab is My w; on Edom I throw My Ps 108:9

WASHED *(39)*

Then he w his face and came out. Gn 43:31
them, and they w their clothes. Ex 19:14
and his sons w their hands and Ex 40:31
They w whenever they came to the Ex 40:32
his sons and w them with water Lv 8:6
but he w the entrails and shanks Lv 8:21
He w the entrails and the shanks Lv 9:14
to be w and quarantined Lv 13:54
it has been w, the priest is to Lv 13:55
has faded after it has been w, Lv 13:56
which have been w, it is to be Lv 13:58
it is to be w again, and it will Lv 13:58
of semen must be w with water, Lv 15:17
themselves and w their clothes; Nm 8:21
Then they w their feet and ate Jdg 19:21
He w, anointed himself, changed 2Sm 12:20
w his clothes from the day the 2Sm 19:24
Then someone w the chariot at 1Kg 22:38
were w away by a river Jb 22:16
yet is not w from its filth. Pr 30:12
back on? I have w my feet. How Sg 5:3
w in milk and set like jewels. Sg 5:12
the Lord has w away the filth Is 4:4
and you weren't w clean with Ezk 16:4
I w you with water, rinsed off Ezk 16:9
offering was to be w there. Ezk 40:38
w his hands in front of the Mt 27:24
do not eat unless they have w. Mk 7:4
w My feet and wiped them with Lk 7:44
So he left, w, and came back Jn 9:7
when I went and w I received my Jn 9:11
told them. "I w and I can see." Jn 9:15
When Jesus had w their feet and Jn 13:12
Teacher, have w your feet, you Jn 13:14
of the night and w their wounds. Ac 16:33
but you were w, you were 1Co 6:11
hospitality, w the saints' feet 1Tm 5:10
and our bodies w in pure water. Heb 10:22
They w their robes and made them Rv 7:14

WASHES *(1)*

w his clothes in wine, and his Gn 49:11

WASHING *(14)*

bronze basin for w and a bronze Ex 30:18
altar and put water in it for w. Ex 40:30
10 basins for w and he put five 2Ch 4:6
was used by the priests for w. 2Ch 4:6
carried his weapon, even when w. Neh 4:23
shorn ⌊sheep⌋ coming up from w, Sg 4:2
flock of ewes coming up from w, Sg 6:6
keep, like the w of cups, jugs, Mk 7:4
left them and were w their nets. Lk 5:2
the ritual w before dinner. Lk 11:38
After w her, they placed her in Ac 9:37
her in the w of water by the Eph 5:26
through the w of regeneration Ti 3:5
a sow, after w itself, wallows 2Pt 2:22

WASHINGS *(2)*

about ritual w, laying on of Heb 6:2
and various w imposed until the Heb 9:10

WASN'T *(34)*

(See pp. xi-xii.)

WASTE *(34)*

your enemies will w away because Lv 26:39
they will also w away because of Lv 26:39
will be a burning w of sulfur Dt 29:23
they entered the land to w it. Jdg 6:5
not going to w time with you!" 2Sm 18:14
sinfulness, and my bones w away. Ps 31:10
their form will w away in Sheol, Ps 49:14
you've eaten and w your pleasant Pr 23:8
people of the earth w away. Is 24:4
But I said, "I w away! Is 24:16
waste away! I w away! Woe is me. Is 24:16
will lay w mountains and hills, Is 42:15
For your w and desolate places Is 49:19
will comfort all her w places, Is 51:3
They have laid w his land. Jr 2:15
his lair to make your land a w. Jr 4:7
land will become a desolate w. Jr 7:34
so your land has become a w, Jr 44:22
grieve; together they w away. Lm 2:8
by hunger, who w away, pierced Lm 4:9
be devastated and w away because Ezk 4:17
will make the land a desolate w, Ezk 6:14
or weep but will w away because Ezk 24:23
of Israel when it was laid w, Ezk 25:3
a desolate w from Migdol to Ezk 29:10
will make the land a desolate w, Ezk 33:28
land a desolate w because of all Ezk 33:29
you and make you a desolate w. Ezk 35:3
Seir a desolate w and will cut Ezk 35:7
I have laid w their streets, Zph 3:6
spread animal w over your faces, Mal 2:3
the w from your festival Mal 2:3
Why this w?" they asked. Mt 26:8
Why should it even w the soil?' Lk 13:7

WASTED *(4)*

If we had not w time, we could Gn 43:10
has this fragrant oil been w? Mk 14:4
leftovers so that nothing is w." Jn 6:12
my labor for you has been w. Gl 4:11

WASTELAND *(16)*

highlands that overlook the w. Nm 21:20
of Peor, which overlooks the w. Nm 23:28
them wander in a trackless w. Jb 12:24
land, the desolate w by night. Jb 30:3
the parched w and cause the Jb 38:27
and the salty w its dwelling. Jb 39:6
and fruitful land into salty w, Ps 107:34
I will make it a w. Is 5:6
Seek Me in a w. I, the LORD, Is 45:19
plot into a desolate w. Jr 12:10
I will make it a w; Ezk 25:13
them, it is like a desert w; Jl 2:3
and Edom a desert w, because of Jl 3:19
will become a w because of its Mc 7:13
a salt pit, and a perpetual w. Zph 2:9
I turned his mountains into a w, Mal 1:3

WASTELANDS *(1)*

them wander in trackless w. Ps 107:40

WASTES *(2)*

His flesh w away to nothing, Jb 33:21
the world w away and withers; Is 24:4

WASTING *(4)*

w disease and fever that will Lv 26:16
will afflict you with w disease, Dt 28:22
but sent a w disease among them. Ps 106:15
and we are w away because of Ezk 33:10

WATCH *(85)*

Eden to work it and w over it. Gn 2:15
can't ⌊bear to⌋ w the boy die!" Gn 21:16
you and will w over you wherever Gn 28:15
be with me and w over me on this Gn 28:20
dream at night. "W yourself!" Gn 31:24
said to me: 'W yourself. Don't Gn 31:29
May the LORD w between you and Gn 31:49
I am the LORD. W. I will strike Ex 7:17
Then during the morning w, Ex 14:24
and they would w Moses until he Ex 33:8
of the testimony and w over it, Nm 1:53
speak to the rock while they w, Nm 20:8
and I w them from the hills. Nm 23:9
and diligently w yourselves, Dt 4:9
"W me," he said, "and do the Jdg 7:17
of the middle w after the Jdg 7:19
W, and when you see the young Jdg 21:21
Then w: If it goes up the road 1Sm 6:9
the morning w, they invaded 1Sm 11:11
house to w for him and kill 1Sm 19:11
Investigate and w carefully 1Sm 23:22
so I can w and eat from her 2Sm 13:5
W Amnon until he is in a good 2Sm 13:28
who was standing w looked up, 2Sm 13:34
Your eyes may w over this temple 1Kg 8:29
W, I am handing it over to you 1Kg 20:13
guards stationed at every w. 1Ch 26:16
that Your eyes w over this 2Ch 6:20
W what you do, for there is no 2Ch 19:7
stocks and stand w over all my Jb 13:27
someone keeps w over ⌊his⌋ tomb Jb 21:32
His eyes ⌊w⌋ over their ways. Jb 24:23
He stands w over all my paths." Jb 33:11
For His eyes ⌊w⌋ over a man's Jb 34:21
case to You and w expectantly. Ps 5:3
heaven. His eyes w; He examines Ps 11:4
You will w when the wicked are Ps 37:34
W the blameless and observe the Ps 37:37
they w my steps while they wait Ps 56:6
I will keep w for You, my Ps 59:9
through each w of the night to Ps 119:148
keep w at the door of my lips. Ps 141:3
Discretion will w over you, Pr 2:11
wisdom, and she will w over you; Pr 4:6
lie down, they will w over you; Pr 6:22
but the sensible w their steps. Pr 14:15
eyes keep w over knowledge, Pr 22:12
and the ones who w through the Ec 12:3
I, the LORD, w over it; Is 27:3
for I w over My word to Jr 1:12
A leopard keeps w over their Jr 5:6
They w like fowlers lying in Jr 5:26
the LORD says: W yourselves; do Jr 17:21
W! I am going to bring them from Jr 31:8

He will w over him as a shepherd Jr 31:10
'W! Hanamel, the son of your Jr 32:7
inquire of Me: W: Pharaoh's army Jr 37:7
Babylon; fortify the w post; set Jr 51:12
from the first w of the night. Lm 2:19
to another place while they w; Ezk 12:3
As they w, dig through the wall Ezk 12:5
who stands w over your people Dn 12:1
is I who answer and w over him. Hs 14:8
fortifications! W the road! Nah 2:1
I will w to see what He will say Hab 2:1
So w yourselves carefully, Mal 2:15
Therefore, w yourselves Mal 2:16
W out and beware of the yeast of Mt 16:6
W out that no one deceives you. Mt 24:4
commanded them: "W out! Beware Mk 8:15
W out that no one deceives you. Mk 13:5
And you must w! I have told you Mk 13:23
W! Be alert! For you don't know Mk 13:33
and keeping w at night over Lk 2:8
W out and be on guard against Lk 12:15
W out that you are not deceived. Lk 21:8
w out for those who cause Rm 16:17
one another, w out, or you will Gl 5:15
W out for "dogs," watch out for Php 3:2
out for "dogs," w out for evil Php 3:2
w out for those who mutilate the Php 3:2
W out for him yourself, because 2Tm 4:15
W out, brothers, so that there Heb 3:12
for they keep w over your souls Heb 13:17
W yourselves so that you don't 2Jn 8

WATCHED *(21)*

the man silently w her to see Gn 24:21
He has w over your journey Dt 2:7
LORD's presence, Eli w her lips. 1Sm 1:12
So Saul w David jealously from 1Sm 18:9
As Elisha w, he kept crying out, 2Kg 2:12
in the days when God w over me, Jb 29:2
Have you w the deer in labor? Jb 39:1
Just as I w over them to uproot Jr 31:28
w from our towers for a nation Lm 4:17
So he went in as I w. Ezk 10:2
As the king w the hand that was Dn 5:5
I w, then, because of the sound Dn 7:11
the vision, and as I w, I was in Dn 8:2
w how the crowd dropped money Mk 12:41
I w Satan fall from heaven like Lk 10:18
They w closely and sent spies Lk 20:20
I w the Spirit descending from Jn 1:32
Don't ⌊work only⌋ while being w, Eph 6:6
don't work only while being w, Col 3:22
while their enemies w them. Rv 11:12
as they w the smoke from her Rv 18:18

WATCHER *(1)*

I done to You, W of mankind? Jb 7:20

WATCHES *(10)*

He w over His nest like an eagle Dt 32:11
adulterer's eye w for twilight, Jb 24:15
Yet He ⌊w⌋ over both individuals Jb 34:29
For the LORD w over the way of Ps 1:6
LORD w over the blameless all Ps 37:18
on You during the night w Ps 63:6
unless the LORD w over a city, Ps 127:1
She w over the activities of her Pr 31:27
One who w the wind will not sow, Ec 11:4
I trusted w for my fall. Jr 20:10

WATCHFUL *(1)*

I will keep a w eye on the house Zch 12:4

WATCHING *(32)*

or is stolen, while no one is w, Ex 22:10
He is always w over it from the Dt 11:12
Manoah and his wife were w. Jdg 13:19
on the roof w Samson entertain Jdg 16:27
The LORD is w over the journey Jdg 18:6
on his chair beside the road w, 1Sm 4:13
Israelites were w when the fire 2Ch 7:3
But God was w over the Jewish Ezr 5:5
to me is happy, w at my doors Pr 8:34
am w over them for disaster and Jr 44:27
in the sight of everyone w you. Ezk 28:18
king, as you were w, a colossal Dn 2:31
As you were w, a stone broke off Dn 2:34
In my vision at night I was w, Dn 7:2
I continued w until its wings Dn 7:4
While I was w, another beast Dn 7:6
While I was w in the night Dn 7:7
As I kept w, thrones were set in Dn 7:9
As I continued w, the beast was Dn 7:11
I continued w in the night Dn 7:13
As I was w, this horn made war Dn 7:21
was w the vision and trying to Dn 8:15
flock who were w me knew that it Zch 11:11
they were w Him closely to see Mk 3:2
of Joses were w where He was Mk 15:47
Pharisees were w Him closely, Lk 6:7
they were w Him closely. Lk 14:1
The people stood w, and even the Lk 23:35
at a distance, w these things. Lk 23:49
He was taken up as they were w, Ac 1:9
So they were w the gates day and Ac 9:24
w out for yourselves so you Gl 6:1

WATCHMAN *(18)*

two gates when the w went up to 2Sm 18:24
The w looked out and saw a man 2Sm 18:24
the w saw another man running. 2Sm 18:26
The w said, "The way the first 2Sm 18:27
Now the w was standing on the 2Kg 9:17
The w reported, "The messenger 2Kg 9:18
the w reported, "He reached 2Kg 9:20
or a booth set up by a w. Jb 27:18
the w stays alert in vain. Ps 127:1
me from Seir, "W, what is ⌊left⌋ Is 21:11
W, what is ⌊left⌋ of the night?" Is 21:11
The w said, "Morning has come, Is 21:12
have made you a w over the house Ezk 3:17
appointing him as their w, Ezk 33:2
if the w sees the sword coming Ezk 33:6
will hold the w accountable for Ezk 33:6
have made you a w for the house Ezk 33:7
Ephraim's w is with my God. Hs 9:8

WATCHMEN *(10)*

When Saul's w in Gibeah of 1Sm 14:16
Lord more than w for the morning Ps 130:6
more than w for the morning. Ps 130:6
voices of your w—they lift up Is 52:8
Israel's w are blind, all of Is 56:10
have appointed w on your walls; Is 62:6
appointed w over you ⌊and said: Jr 6:17
be a day when w will call out Jr 31:6
set the w in place; Jr 51:12
The day of your w, ⌊the day of⌋ Mc 7:4

WATCHTOWER *(7)*

their towns from w to fortified 2Kg 17:9
borders, from w to fortified 2Kg 18:8
I stand on the w all day, and I Is 21:8
The hill and the w will become Is 32:14
And you, w for the flock, Mc 4:8
winepress in it, and built a w. Mt 21:33
for a winepress, and built a w. Mk 12:1

WATER *(521)*

separating w from water." Gn 1:6
separating water from w." Gn 1:6
separated the w under the Gn 1:7
expanse from the w above the Gn 1:7
Let the w under the sky be Gn 1:9
the gathering of the w "seas." Gn 1:10
Let the w swarm with living Gn 1:20
that moves and swarms in the w, Gn 1:21
But w would come out of the Gn 2:6
of the ground and w the entire Gn 2:6
out from Eden to w the garden. Gn 2:10
came ⌊and⌋ w covered the earth Gn 7:6
floated on the surface of the w. Gn 7:18
and the w began to subside. Gn 8:1
The w steadily receded from the Gn 8:3
see whether the w on the earth's Gn 8:8
in the ark because w covered the Gn 8:9
knew that the w on the earth's Gn 8:11
the w ⌊that had covered⌋ the Gn 8:13
w will never again become a Gn 9:15
by a spring of w in the Gn 16:7
Let a little w be brought, Gn 18:4
When the w in the skin was gone, Gn 21:15
eyes, and she saw a well of w. Gn 21:19
because of the w well that Gn 21:25
a well of w outside the town Gn 24:11
the women went out to draw w. Gn 24:11
town are coming out to draw w. Gn 24:13
lower your w jug so that I may Gn 24:14
and I'll w your camels also'— Gn 24:14
have a little w from your jug." Gn 24:17
I'll also draw w for your camels Gn 24:19
to the well again to draw w. Gn 24:20
She drew w for all his camels Gn 24:20
and w was brought to wash his Gn 24:32
virgin who comes out to draw w, Gn 24:43
drink a little w from your jug, Gn 24:43
draw w for your camels also' Gn 24:44
down to the spring and drew w. Gn 24:45
and I'll w your camels also.' Gn 24:46
reopened the w wells that had Gn 26:18
found a well of spring w there. Gn 26:19
and said, "The w is ours!" Gn 26:20
to him, "We have found w!" Gn 26:32
of the well and w the sheep. Gn 29:3
W the flock, then go out and let Gn 29:7
Then we will w the sheep." Gn 29:8
the w channels where the sheep Gn 30:38
was empty; there was no w in it. Gn 37:24
gave them w to wash their feet, Gn 43:24
Turbulent as w, you will no Gn 49:4
"I drew him out of the w." Ex 2:10
They came to draw w and filled Ex 2:16
the troughs to w their father's Ex 2:16
even drew w for us and watered Ex 2:19
take some w from the Nile and Ex 4:9
w you take from the Nile will Ex 4:9
see him walking out to the w, Ex 7:15
will strike the w in the Nile Ex 7:17
be unable to drink w from it." Ex 7:18
and all their w reservoirs— Ex 7:19
and struck the w in the Nile, Ex 7:20
and all the w in the Nile was Ex 7:20
could not drink w from it. Ex 7:21
the Nile for w to drink because Ex 7:24
not drink the w from the river. Ex 7:24
you see him going out to the w. Ex 8:20
it raw or cooked in boiling w, Ex 12:9
wilderness without finding w. Ex 15:22
not drink the w at Marah because Ex 15:23
When he threw it into the w, Ex 15:25
the water, the w became Ex 15:25
12 springs of w and 70 date Ex 15:27
there was no w for the people Ex 17:1
"Give us w to drink." Ex 17:2
the people thirsted there for w, Ex 17:3
w will come out of it and the Ex 17:6
bless your bread and your w. Ex 23:25
of meeting and wash them with w. Ex 29:4
and the altar, and put w in it. Ex 30:18
must wash with w so that they Ex 30:20
the surface of the w and forced Ex 32:20
the Israelites to drink ⌊the w⌋. Ex 32:20
he did not eat bread or drink w. Ex 34:28
and the altar, and put w in it. Ex 40:7
of meeting and wash them with w. Ex 40:12
altar and put w in it for Ex 40:30
its entrails and shanks with w. Lv 1:9
the entrails and shanks with w. Lv 1:13
be scoured and rinsed with w. Lv 6:28
his sons and washed them with w. Lv 8:6
the entrails and shanks with w. Lv 8:21
eat from all that is in the w: Lv 11:9
everything in the w that has Lv 11:9
living creatures in the w. Lv 11:10
Everything in the w that does Lv 11:12
be rinsed with w and will remain Lv 11:32
that unclean⌋ w will become Lv 11:34
containing w will remain clean Lv 11:36
if w has been put on the seed Lv 11:38
creatures that move in the w, Lv 11:46
over fresh w in a clay pot. Lv 14:5
slaughtered over the fresh w. Lv 14:6
all his hair, and bathe with w; Lv 14:8
and bathe himself with w; Lv 14:9
a clay pot containing fresh w. Lv 14:50
bird and the fresh w, Lv 14:51
the fresh w, the live bird, Lv 14:52
his clothes and bathe with w, Lv 15:5
his clothes and bathe with w, Lv 15:6
his clothes and bathe with w, Lv 15:7
his clothes and bathe with w, Lv 15:8
his clothes and bathe with w, Lv 15:10
first⌋ rinsing his hands in w, Lv 15:11
his clothes and bathe with w, Lv 15:11
utensil must be rinsed with w. Lv 15:12
and bathe his body in fresh w; Lv 15:13
bathe himself completely with w, Lv 15:16
of semen must be washed with w, Lv 15:17
of them are to bathe with w, Lv 15:18
his clothes and bathe with w, Lv 15:21
his clothes and bathe with w, Lv 15:22

his clothes and bathe with w, Lv 15:27
his body with w before he wears Lv 16:4
his body with w in a holy place Lv 16:24
and bathe his body with w; Lv 16:26
and bathe himself with w; Lv 16:28
his clothes and bathe with w, Lv 17:15
he has bathed his body with w. Lv 22:6
to take holy w in a clay bowl, Nm 5:17
floor and put ⌊it⌋ in the w. Nm 5:17
to hold the bitter w that brings Nm 5:18
by this bitter w that brings a Nm 5:19
May this w that brings a curse Nm 5:22
them⌋ off into the bitter w. Nm 5:23
drink the bitter w that brings a Nm 5:24
the woman to drink the w. Nm 5:26
When he makes her drink the w, Nm 5:27
the w that brings a curse will Nm 5:27
them with the purification w. Nm 8:7
clothes and bathe his body in w; Nm 19:7
clothes and bathe his body in w, Nm 19:8
⌊preparing⌋ the w ⌊to remove⌋ Nm 19:9
with the w on the third day Nm 19:12
because the w for impurity has Nm 19:13
a jar, and add fresh w to them. Nm 19:17
dip ⌊it⌋ in the w, and sprinkle Nm 19:18
wash his clothes and bathe in w, Nm 19:19
The w for impurity has not been Nm 19:20
sprinkles the w for impurity is Nm 19:21
touches the w for impurity will Nm 19:21
was no w for the community, Nm 20:2
and there is no w to drink!" Nm 20:5
watch, and it will yield its w. Nm 20:8
You will bring out w for them Nm 20:8
Must we bring w out of this rock Nm 20:10
a great amount of w gushed out, Nm 20:11
vineyard, or drink ⌊any⌋ well w. Nm 20:17
if we or our herds drink your w, Nm 20:19
is no bread or w, and we detest Nm 21:5
people so I may give them w." Nm 21:16
We won't drink ⌊any⌋ well w. Nm 21:22
like cedars beside the w. Nm 24:6
W will flow from his buckets, Nm 24:7
his seed will be by abundant w. Nm 24:7
with the purification w. Nm 31:23
fire, put through the w. Nm 31:23
12 springs of w and 70 date Nm 33:9
there was no w for the people to Nm 33:14
and buy w from them to drink. Dt 2:6
and give us w for silver so we Dt 2:28
with streams of w, springs, and Dt 8:7
and deep w sources, flowing Dt 8:7
land where there was no w. Dt 8:15
brought w out of the flintlike Dt 8:15
I did not eat bread or drink w. Dt 9:9
bread or drink w because of all Dt 9:18
a land with streams of w. Dt 10:7
pour it on the ground like w. Dt 12:16
pour it on the ground like w. Dt 12:24
from the w that has fins Dt 14:9
pour it on the ground like w. Dt 15:23
with food and w on the journey Dt 23:4
must wash with w, and when the Dt 23:11
cut your wood and draw your w— Dt 29:11
The w flowing downstream will Jos 3:13
feet touched the w at its edge Jos 3:15
and the w flowing downstream Jos 3:16
w flowing downstream into the Jos 3:16
hearts melted and became like w. Jos 7:5
woodcutters and w carriers for Jos 9:21
woodcutters and w carriers for Jos 9:23
woodcutters and w carriers— Jos 9:27
give me the springs of w also." Jos 15:19
give me springs of w also." Jdg 1:15
give me a little w to drink for Jdg 4:19
rain⌋, the clouds poured w. Jdg 5:4
He asked for w; she gave him Jdg 5:25
of it, filling a bowl with w. Jdg 6:38
down to the w, and I will test Jdg 7:4
the people down to the w, Jdg 7:5
who laps w with his tongue Jdg 7:5
of the people knelt to drink w. Jdg 7:6
at Lehi, and w came out of it. Jdg 15:19
they drew w and poured it out in 1Sm 7:6
coming out to draw w and asked, 1Sm 9:11
my bread, my w, and my meat 1Sm 25:11
spear and the w jug by his head 1Sm 26:11
spear and the w jug by Saul's 1Sm 26:12
king's spear and w jug that were 1Sm 26:16
bread to eat and w to drink. 1Sm 30:11
food or drunk w for three days 1Sm 30:12
go through the w shaft to reach 2Sm 5:8
have also captured the w supply. 2Sm 12:27
die and be like w poured out on 2Sm 14:14
"They passed by toward the w," 2Sm 17:20
a gathering of w and thick 2Sm 22:12
would bring me w to drink from 2Sm 23:15
camp and drew w from the well at 2Sm 23:16
Then he made 10 bronze w carts. 1Kg 7:27
Each w cart was six feet long, 1Kg 7:27
And the w cart's opening inside 1Kg 7:31
axles were part of the w cart; 1Kg 7:32
the four corners of each w cart; 1Kg 7:34
was one piece with the w cart. 1Kg 7:34
way he made the 10 w carts using 1Kg 7:37
for each of the 10 w carts. 1Kg 7:38
He set five w carts on the right 1Kg 7:39
the 10 w carts; the 10 basins on 1Kg 7:43
the 10 basins on the w carts; 1Kg 7:43
bread or drink w in this place, 1Kg 13:8
bread or drink w or go back the 1Kg 13:9
or drink w with you in this 1Kg 13:16
bread or drink w there or go 1Kg 13:17
he may eat bread and drink w.'" 1Kg 13:18
bread in his house, and drank w. 1Kg 13:19
bread and drank w in the place 1Kg 13:22
eat bread and do not drink w, 1Kg 13:22
shake⌋ as a reed shakes in w. 1Kg 14:15
me a little w in a cup and let 1Kg 17:10
with food and w when Jezebel 1Kg 18:4
every spring of w and to every 1Kg 18:5
I provided them with food and w. 1Kg 18:13
Fill four w pots with water and 1Kg 18:33
water pots with w and pour it 1Kg 18:33
So the w ran all around the 1Kg 18:35
even filled the trench with w. 1Kg 18:35
and it licked up the w that was 1Kg 18:38
over hot stones and a jug of w. 1Kg 19:6
only bread and w until I come 1Kg 22:27
w is bad and the land unfruitful. 2Kg 2:19
went out to the spring of w, 2Kg 2:21
'I have healed this w. 2Kg 2:21
the w remains healthy to this 2Kg 2:22
they had no w for the army or 2Kg 3:9
who used to pour w on Elijah's 2Kg 3:11
the wadi will be filled with w, 2Kg 3:17
and stop up every spring of w. 2Kg 3:19
w suddenly came from the 2Kg 3:20
the sun was shining on the w, 2Kg 3:22
saw that the w across from them 2Kg 3:22
every spring of w and cut down 2Kg 3:25
iron ⌊ax head⌋ fell into the w, 2Kg 6:5
Set food and w in front of them 2Kg 6:22
dipped it in w, and spread it 2Kg 8:15
frames of the w carts and 2Kg 16:17
one may drink w from his own 2Kg 18:31
and brought w into the city, 2Kg 20:20
LORD's temple, the w carts, and 2Kg 25:13
and the w carts that Solomon had 2Kg 25:16
would bring me w from the well 1Ch 11:17
camp and drew w from the well at 1Ch 11:18
He also made the w carts and the 2Ch 4:14
and the basins on the w carts. 2Ch 4:14
only bread and w until I come 2Ch 18:26
come and find plenty of w?" 2Ch 32:4
the outlet of the w of the Upper 2Ch 32:30
He did not eat food or drink w, Ezr 10:6
opposite the W Gate toward the Neh 3:26
square in front of the W Gate. Neh 8:1
square in front of the W Gate, Neh 8:3
square by the W Gate, and the Neh 8:16
You brought them w from the rock Neh 9:15
You gave them W for their thirst Neh 9:20
of David to the W Gate on the Neh 12:37
the Israelites with food and w. Neh 13:2
and my groans pour out like w. Jb 3:24
earth and sends w to the fields. Jb 5:10
been confident ⌊of finding w⌋. Jb 6:20
Do reeds flourish without w? Jb 8:11
the smell of w makes it thrive Jb 14:9
As w disappears from the sea and Jb 14:11
as w wears away stones and Jb 14:19
who drinks injustice like w? Jb 15:16
You gave no w to the thirsty and Jb 22:7
and a flood of w covers you. Jb 22:11
float on the surface of the w. Jb 24:18
and limited the w by measure, Jb 28:25
My roots will have access to w, Jb 29:19
He drinks derision like w. Jb 34:7
when w becomes as hard as stone, Jb 38:30
so that a flood of w covers you? Jb 38:34
can tilt the w jars of heaven Jb 38:37
streams of w that bears its Ps 1:3
poured out like w, and all my Ps 22:14
a deer longs for streams of w, Ps 42:1
will vanish like w that flows Ps 58:7
is dry, desolate, and without w. Ps 63:1
the earth and w it abundantly, Ps 65:9
God's stream is filled with w, Ps 65:9
we went through fire and w, Ps 66:12
for the w has risen to my neck. Ps 69:1
spring showers that w the earth. Ps 72:6
The clouds poured down w. Ps 77:17
the w stood firm like a wall. Ps 78:13
stone and made w flow down like Ps 78:16
the rock and w gushed out; Ps 78:20
their blood like w all around Ps 79:3
surround me like w all day long; Ps 88:17
They supply w for every wild Ps 104:11
opened a rock, and w gushed out; Ps 105:41
W covered their foes; not one of Ps 106:11
of w into thirsty ground, Ps 107:33
turns a desert into a pool of w, Ps 107:35
dry land into springs of w. Ps 107:35
his body like w and go into his Ps 109:18
the rock into a pool of w, Ps 114:8
the flint into a spring of w. Ps 114:8
me from deep w, and set me free Ps 144:7
Drink w from your own cistern, Pr 5:15
w flowing from your own well. Pr 5:15
streams of w in the public Pr 5:16
and no springs filled with w. Pr 8:24
Stolen w is sweet, and bread Pr 9:17
gives a drink of w will receive Pr 11:25
a drink of water will receive w. Pr 11:25
in a man's heart is deep w; Pr 20:5
A king's heart is a w channel in Pr 21:1
is thirsty, give him w to drink; Pr 25:21
land is like cold w to a parched Pr 25:25
As the w reflects the face, Pr 27:19
which is never satisfied with w; Pr 30:16
reservoirs of w for myself from Ec 2:6
a well of flowing w streaming Sg 4:15
like doves beside streams of w, Sg 5:12
your beer is diluted with w. Is 1:22
and like a garden without w. Is 1:30
entire supply of bread and w, Is 3:1
and in all the w holes. Is 7:19
as the sea is filled with w. Is 11:9
joyfully draw w from the springs Is 12:3
nets on the w will shrivel up. Is 19:8
Bring w for the thirsty. Is 21:14
You collected w from the lower Is 22:9
over it; I w it regularly. I Is 27:3
and w will flood your hiding Is 28:17
is still thirsty, longing for w. Is 29:8
or scoop w from a cistern. Is 30:14
meager bread and w during Is 30:20
like streams of w in a dry land Is 32:2
food provided, his w assured. Is 33:16
for w will gush in the Is 35:6
ground will become a pool of w, Is 35:7
the thirsty land springs of w. Is 35:7
tree and drink w from his own Is 36:16
I dug ⌊wells⌋ and drank w. Is 37:25
The poor and the needy seek w, Is 41:17
into a pool of w and dry land Is 41:18
and dry land into springs of w. Is 41:18
I provide w in the wilderness Is 43:20
For I will pour w on the thirsty Is 44:3
he doesn't drink w and is faint. Is 44:12
He made w flow for them from the Is 48:21
the rock, and w gushed out. Is 48:21
and lead them to springs of w. Is 49:10
of lack of w and die of thirst Is 50:2
and fire causes w to boil— Is 64:2
of living w, and dug cisterns Jr 2:13
cisterns that cannot hold w. Jr 2:13
As a well gushes out its w, Jr 6:7
given us poisoned w to drink, Jr 8:14
If my head were w, my eyes a Jr 9:1
send their servants for w. Jr 14:3
they find no w; their containers Jr 14:3
a mirage to me—w that is not Jr 15:18
be like a tree planted by w: Jr 17:8

the fountain of living **w**, Jr 17:13
Or does cold **w** flowing from a Jr 18:14
give them poisoned **w** to drink, Jr 23:15
the sea, the **w** carts, and the Jr 27:19
filled⌋ with **w** by a smooth way Jr 31:9
There was no **w** in the cistern, Jr 38:6
temple and the **w** carts and the Jr 52:17
bulls under the **w** carts that Jr 52:20
your heart like **w** before the Lm 2:19
W flooded over my head, and I Lm 3:54
We must pay for the **w** we drink; Lm 5:4
are also to drink **w** by measure, Ezk 4:11
and in dread drink **w** by measure. Ezk 4:16
So they will lack bread and **w**; Ezk 4:17
⌊their⌋ knees will turn to **w**. Ezk 7:17
drink your **w** with shaking and Ezk 12:18
and drink their **w** in dread, Ezk 12:19
you weren't washed clean with **w**. Ezk 16:4
washed you with **w**, rinsed off Ezk 16:9
bed, so that he might **w** it. Ezk 17:7
your vineyard, planted by the **w**; Ezk 19:10
and every knee will turn to **w**. Ezk 21:7
it⌋ on, and then pour **w** into it! Ezk 24:3
timber, and soil into the **w**. Ezk 26:12
out because of the plentiful **w**. Ezk 31:5
roots extended to abundant **w**. Ezk 31:7
planted⌋ beside **w** would become Ezk 31:14
that you drink the clear **w**? Ezk 34:18
also sprinkle clean **w** on you, Ezk 36:25
and there was **w** flowing from Ezk 47:1
w was coming down from under Ezk 47:1
there the **w** was trickling from Ezk 47:2
a mile and led me through the **w**. Ezk 47:3
mile⌋ and led me through the **w**. Ezk 47:4
and led me through ⌊the **w**⌋. Ezk 47:4
foot⌋. For the **w** had risen; it Ezk 47:5
This **w** flows out to the eastern Ezk 47:8
the sea of foul **w**, the water Ezk 47:8
w ⌊of the sea⌋ becomes fresh. Ezk 47:8
fish because this **w** goes there. Ezk 47:9
Since the **w** will become fresh, Ezk 47:9
fruit because the **w** ⌊comes⌋ Ezk 47:12
to eat and **w** to drink. Dn 1:12
men who give me my food and **w**, Hs 2:5
pour out My fury on them like **w**. Hs 5:10
spring showers that **w** the land. Hs 6:3
foam on the surface of the **w**. Hs 10:7
His **w** source will fail, and his Hs 13:15
of Judah will flow with **w**, Jl 3:18
city to drink **w** but were not Am 4:8
But let justice flow like **w**, Am 5:24
of bread or a thirst for **w**, Am 8:11
They must not eat or drink **w**. Jnh 3:7
like **w** cascading down a Mc 1:4
a pool of **w** from her ⌊first⌋ Nah 2:8
the Nile with surrounding her, Nah 3:8
Draw **w** for the siege; strengthen Nah 3:14
a downpour of **w** sweeps by. Hab 3:10
that day living **w** will flow out Zch 14:8
you with **w** for repentance, Mt 3:11
went up immediately from the **w**. Mt 3:16
the sea and perished in the **w**. Mt 8:32
a cup of cold **w** to one of these Mt 10:42
me to come to You on the **w**." Mt 14:28
walking on the **w** and came toward Mt 14:29
the fire and often into the **w**. Mt 17:15
he took some **w**, washed his hands Mt 27:24
I have baptized you with **w**, Mk 1:8
soon as He came up out of the **w**, Mk 1:10
into fire or **w** to destroy him. Mk 9:22
you a cup of **w** to drink because Mk 9:41
a man carrying a **w** jug will meet Mk 14:13
baptize you with **w**, but One is Lk 3:16
out into deep **w** and let down Lk 5:4
you gave Me no **w** for My feet, Lk 7:44
the Sabbath, and lead it to **w**? Lk 13:15
of his finger in **w** and cool my Lk 16:24
a man carrying a **w** jug will meet Lk 22:10
"I baptize with **w**," John Jn 1:26
baptizing with **w** so He might be Jn 1:31
me to baptize with **w** told me, Jn 1:33
six stone **w** jars had been set Jn 2:6
the jars with **w**," Jesus told Jn 2:7
the chief servant tasted the **w** Jn 2:9
who had drawn the **w** knew. Jn 2:9
is born of **w** and the Spirit, Jn 3:5
there was plenty of **w** there. Jn 3:23
woman of Samaria came to draw **w**. Jn 4:7
and He would give you living **w**." Jn 4:10
do you get this 'living **w**'? Jn 4:11
from this **w** will get thirsty Jn 4:13
drinks from the **w** that I will Jn 4:14
w I will give him will become Jn 4:14
become a well of **w** springing up Jn 4:14
give me this **w** so I won't get Jn 4:15
and come here to draw **w**." Jn 4:15
Then the woman left her **w** jar, Jn 4:28
He had turned the **w** into wine. Jn 4:46
waiting for the moving of the **w**, Jn 5:3
time to time and stir up the **w**. Jn 5:4
got in after the **w** was stirred Jn 5:4
pool when the **w** is stirred up, Jn 5:7
of living **w** flow from deep Jn 7:38
He poured **w** into a basin and Jn 13:5
at once blood and **w** came out. Jn 19:34
baptized with **w**, but you will be Ac 1:5
the road, they came to some **w**. Ac 8:36
eunuch said, "Look, there's **w**! Ac 8:36
the eunuch went down into the **w**, Ac 8:38
When they came up out of the **w**, Ac 8:39
anyone withhold **w** and prevent Ac 10:47
baptized with **w**, but you will be Ac 11:16
in the washing of **w** by the word. Eph 5:26
Don't continue drinking only **w**, 1Tm 5:23
along with **w**, scarlet wool, Heb 9:19
and our bodies washed in pure **w**. Heb 10:22
sweet and bitter **w** from the same Jms 3:11
saltwater spring yield fresh **w**. Jms 3:12
people—were saved through **w**. 1Pt 3:20
people are springs without **w**, 2Pt 2:17
existed out of **w** and through 2Pt 3:5
water and through **w** by the word 2Pt 3:5
when it was flooded by **w**. 2Pt 3:6
the One who came by **w** and blood; 1Jn 5:6
not by **w** only, but by water and 1Jn 5:6
only, but by **w** and by blood. 1Jn 5:6
the Spirit, the **w**, and the blood 1Jn 5:8
of the rivers and springs of **w**. Rv 8:10
serpent spewed **w** like a river Rv 12:15
the sea and springs of **w**." Rv 14:7
the rivers and the springs of **w**, Rv 16:4
its **w** was dried up to prepare Rv 16:12
spring of living **w** as a gift. Rv 21:6
showed me the river of living **w**, Rv 22:1
take the living **w** as a gift. Rv 22:17

WATERCOURSES *(4)*

control of the **w** ahead of them Jdg 7:24
took control of the **w** as far as Jdg 7:24
LORD, like **w** in the Negev. Ps 126:4
Streams and **w** will be on every Is 30:25

WATERDROPS *(1)*

For He makes **w** evaporate; Jb 36:27

WATERED *(11)*

and she also **w** the camels. Gn 24:46
the sheep were **w** from this well. Gn 29:2
the opening and **w** his uncle Gn 29:10
their rescue and **w** their flock. Ex 2:17
water for us and **w** the flock." Ex 2:19
and valleys, **w** by rain from the Dt 11:11
He is an amply **w** plant in the Jb 8:16
will be like a **w** garden and like Is 58:11
the perennially **w** grazing land. Jr 49:19
the perennially **w** grazing land. Jr 50:44
planted, Apollos **w**, but God gave 1Co 3:6

WATERFALLS *(1)*

to deep in the roar of Your **w**; Ps 42:7

WATERING *(2)*

of the singers at the **w** places. Jdg 5:11
the LORD's house, **w** the Valley Jl 3:18

WATERLESS *(4)*

prisoners from the **w** cistern. Zch 9:11
roams through **w** places looking Mt 12:43
roams through **w** places looking Lk 11:24
They are **w** clouds carried along Jd 12

WATERS *(162)*

over the surface of the **w**. Gn 1:2
be an expanse between the **w**, Gn 1:6
and fill the **w** of the seas, Gn 1:22
because of the **w** of the deluge. Gn 7:7
days later the **w** of the deluge Gn 7:10
w increased and lifted up the Gn 7:17
The **w** surged and increased Gn 7:18
Then the **w** surged even higher on Gn 7:19
covered as the **w** surged ⌊above Gn 7:20
the **w** surged on the earth 150 Gn 7:24
of 150 days the **w** had decreased Gn 8:3
The **w** continued to recede until Gn 8:5
forth until the **w** had dried up Gn 8:7
wiped out by the **w** of a deluge; Gn 9:11
your hand over the **w** of Egypt— Ex 7:19
his hand over the **w** of Egypt, Ex 8:6
So the **w** were divided, Ex 14:21
with the **w** ⌊like⌋ a wall to them Ex 14:22
sea so that the **w** may come back Ex 14:26
The **w** came back and covered the Ex 14:28
with the **w** ⌊like⌋ a wall to them Ex 14:29
The **w** heaped up at the blast of Ex 15:8
sank like lead in the mighty **w**. Ex 15:10
brought the **w** of the sea back Ex 15:19
and they camped there by the **w**. Ex 15:27
or in the **w** under the earth Ex 20:4
These are the **w** of Meribah, Nm 20:13
My command at the **w** of Meribah. Nm 20:24
in their sight at the **w**." Nm 27:14
Those were the **w** of Meribah of Nm 27:14
fish in the **w** under the earth Dt 4:18
or in the **w** under the earth Dt 5:8
when He made the **w** of the Red Dt 11:4
Israelites at the **w** of Dt 32:51
with him at the **w** of Meribah. Dt 33:8
dried up the **w** of the Red Sea Jos 2:10
you reach the edge of the **w**, Jos 3:8
come to rest in the Jordan's **w**, Jos 3:13
waters, its **w** will be cut off. Jos 3:13
'The **w** of the Jordan were cut Jos 4:7
the Jordan's **w** were cut off.' Jos 4:7
w of the Jordan resumed their Jos 4:18
God dried up the **w** of the Jordan Jos 4:23
had dried up the **w** of the Jordan Jos 5:1
and camped at the **w** of Merom to Jos 11:5
them at the **w** of Merom and Jos 11:7
proceeded to the **w** of En-shemesh Jos 15:7
the spring of the **W** of Nephtoah, Jos 15:9
Jericho to the **w** of Jericho on Jos 16:1
the spring at the **W** of Nephtoah. Jos 18:15
at Taanach by the **w** of Megiddo, Jdg 5:19
He pulled me out of deep **w**. 2Sm 22:17
and struck the **w**, which parted 2Kg 2:8
had dropped and struck the **w**. 2Kg 2:14
struck the **w** himself, and they 2Kg 2:14
better than all the **w** of Israel? 2Kg 5:12
wells⌋, and I drank foreign **w**. 2Kg 19:24
stopping up the **w** of the springs 2Ch 32:3
like a stone into churning **w**. Neh 9:11
it only⌋ as **w** that have flowed Jb 11:16
He withholds the **w**, everything Jb 12:15
beneath the **w** and ⌊all⌋ that Jb 26:5
He enfolds the **w** in His clouds, Jb 26:8
surface of the **w** at the boundary Jb 26:10
He pulled me out of deep **w**. Ps 18:16
He leads me beside quiet **w**. Ps 23:2
of the LORD is above the **w**. Ps 29:3
the LORD, above vast **w**, Ps 29:3
He gathers the **w** of the sea into Ps 33:7
though its **w** roar and foam and Ps 46:3
come into deep **w**, and a flood Ps 69:2
hate me, and from the deep **w**. Ps 69:14
drink in their overflowing **w**. Ps 73:10
of the sea monsters in the **w**; Ps 74:13
The **w** saw You, God. The waters Ps 77:16
You, God. The **w** saw You; they Ps 77:16
Your path through the great **w**, Ps 77:19
tested you at the **w** of Meribah. Ps 81:7
than the roar of many **w**— Ps 93:4
of His palace on the **w** ⌊above⌋, Ps 104:3
the **w** stood above the mountains. Ps 104:6
At Your rebuke the **w** fled; Ps 104:7
He **w** the mountains from His Ps 104:13
He turned their **w** into blood and Ps 105:29
the LORD⌋ at the **w** of Meribah, Ps 106:32
conducting trade on the vast **w**. Ps 107:23
Then the **w** would have engulfed Ps 124:4
the raging **w** would have swept Ps 124:5
He spread the land on the **w**. Ps 136:6
His winds, and the **w** flow. Ps 147:18
and you **w** above the heavens. Ps 148:4
sea so that the **w** would not Pr 8:29
of a man's mouth are deep **w**, Pr 18:4
has bound up the **w** in a cloak? Pr 30:4
bread on the surface of the **w**, Ec 11:1
Mighty **w** cannot extinguish love; Sg 8:7
the slowly flowing **w** of Shiloah Is 8:6

rushing **w** of the Euphrates Is 8:7
The **w** of Nimrim are desolate; Is 15:6
w of Dibon are full of blood, Is 15:9
like the raging of mighty **w**. Is 17:12
rage like the raging of many **w**. Is 17:13
sea, in reed vessels on the **w**. Is 18:2
The **w** of the sea will dry up, Is 19:5
walls for the **w** of the ancient Is 22:11
many **w**. Tyre's revenue was the Is 23:3
a storm with strong flooding **w**. Is 28:2
who sow seed beside abundant **w**, Is 32:20
has measured the **w** in the hollow Is 40:12
you when you pass through the **w**, Is 43:2
and a path through surging **w**, Is 43:16
up the sea, the **w** of the great Is 51:10
I swore that the **w** of Noah would Is 54:9
who is thirsty, come to the **w**; Is 55:1
its **w** churn up mire and muck. Is 57:20
a spring whose **w** never run dry. Is 58:11
divided the **w** before them to Is 63:12
to drink the **w** of the Nile? Jr 2:18
to drink the **w** of the Euphrates? Jr 2:18
give them poisonous **w** to drink. Jr 9:15
the **w** in the heavens are in Jr 10:13
like rivers whose **w** churn? Jr 46:7
and its **w** churn like rivers. Jr 46:8
w are rising from the north and Jr 47:2
because even the **w** of Nimrim Jr 48:34
A drought will come on her **w**, Jr 50:38
reside by many **w**, rich in Jr 51:13
the **w** in the heavens are in Jr 51:16
waves roar like abundant **w**; Jr 51:55
wings like the roar of mighty **w**, Ezk 1:24
a willow, a plant by abundant **w**. Ezk 17:5
field by abundant **w** in order to Ezk 17:8
branches because of plentiful **w**. Ezk 19:10
so that the mighty **w** cover you, Ezk 26:19
the sea in the depths of the **w**; Ezk 27:34
The **w** caused it to grow; Ezk 31:4
its⌋ abundant **w** were restrained. Ezk 31:15
churn up the **w** with your feet, Ezk 32:2
cattle that are beside many **w**. Ezk 32:13
will let their **w** settle and will Ezk 32:14
like the roar of mighty **w**, Ezk 43:2
from Tamar to the **w** of Ezk 47:19
from Tamar to the **w** of Ezk 48:28
was above the **w** of the river, Dn 12:6
was above the **w** of the river. Dn 12:7
who summons the **w** of the sea and Am 5:8
He summons the **w** of the sea and Am 9:6
w engulfed me up to the neck; Jnh 2:5
glory, as the **w** cover the sea. Hab 2:14
horses, stirring up the great **w**. Hab 3:15
nor the one who **w** is anything, 1Co 3:7
and the one who **w** are equal, 1Co 3:8
like the sound of cascading **w**. Rv 1:15
them to springs of living **w**, Rv 7:17
third of the **w** became wormwood. Rv 8:11
of the people died from the **w**, Rv 8:11
power over the **w** to turn them Rv 11:6
sound of cascading **w** and like Rv 14:2
I heard the angel of the **w** say: Rv 16:5
prostitute who sits on many **w**. Rv 17:1
to me, "The **w** you saw, where Rv 17:15
like the sound of cascading **w**, Rv 19:6

WATERSKIN *(2)*

took bread and a **w**, ⌊put them⌋ Gn 21:14
filled the **w** and gave the boy Gn 21:19

WATERY *(10)*

the surface of the **w** depths, Gn 1:2
sources of the **w** depths burst Gn 7:11
The sources of the **w** depths and Gn 8:2
The **w** depths congealed in the Ex 15:8
bounty and the **w** depths that lie Dt 33:13
and **w** expanses are frozen. Jb 37:10
surface of the **w** depths is Jb 38:30
knowledge the **w** depths broke Pr 3:20
there were no **w** depths and no Pr 8:24
the **w** depths overcame me; Jnh 2:5

WAVE *(18)*

and his sons and **w** them as a Ex 29:24
ordination and **w** it as a Ex 29:26
to **w** as a presentation offering Lv 10:15
and he must **w** them as a Lv 14:12
and **w** them as a presentation Lv 14:24
He will **w** the sheaf before the Lv 23:11
the priest is to **w** it on the day Lv 23:11
On the day you **w** the sheaf, Lv 23:12
The priest will **w** the lambs with Lv 23:20
w the offering before the LORD, Nm 5:25
The priest is to **w** them as a Nm 6:20
will **w** his hand over the spot 2Kg 5:11
assault me, **w** after wave. Jb 10:17
assault me, wave after **w**. Jb 10:17
may it **w** on the tops of the Ps 72:16
a staff could **w** those who lift Is 10:15
He will **w** His hand over the Is 11:15
W your hand, and they will go Is 13:2

WAVED *(7)*

offering that is **w** and the thigh Ex 29:27
everyone who **w** a presentation Ex 35:22
breast is to be **w** as a Lv 7:30
and his sons and **w** them before Lv 8:27
the breast and **w** it before the Lv 8:29
but he **w** the breasts and the Lv 9:21
offering to be **w** in order to Lv 14:21

WAVER *(3)*

because he did not **w** in obeying 2Ch 27:6
from My presence and do not **w**, Jr 4:1
did not **w** in unbelief at God's Rm 4:20

WAVERING *(2)*

trusted in the LORD without **w**. Ps 26:1
of our hope without **w**, Heb 10:23

WAVES *(28)*

For the **w** of death engulfed me; 2Sm 22:5
and treads on the **w** of the sea. Jb 9:8
your proud **w** stop here"? Jb 38:11
roar of their **w**, and the tumult Ps 65:7
overwhelmed me with all Your **w**. Ps 88:7
its **w** surge, You still them. Ps 89:9
floods lift up their pounding **w**. Ps 93:3
stirred up the **w** of the sea. Ps 107:25
the **w** of the sea were hushed. Ps 107:29
rejoiced when the **w** grew quiet. Ps 107:30
like the **w** of the sea. Is 48:18
up the sea so that its **w** roar— Is 51:15
The **w** surge, but they cannot Jr 5:22
the sea and makes its **w** roar— Jr 31:35
is covered with its turbulent **w**. Jr 51:42
Their **w** roar like abundant Jr 51:55
just as the sea raises its **w**. Ezk 26:3
its voice and lifts its **w** high. Hab 3:10
and strike the **w** of the sea; Zch 10:11
boat was being swamped by the **w**. Mt 8:24
battered by the **w**, because the Mt 14:24
and the **w** were breaking over the Mk 4:37
the wind and the raging **w**. Lk 8:24
even the winds and the **w**, Lk 8:25
by the roaring sea and **w**. Lk 21:25
up with the pounding of the **w**. Ac 27:41
tossed by the **w** and blown around Eph 4:14
wild **w** of the sea, foaming up Jd 13

WAVY *(1)*

His hair is **w** and black as a Sg 5:11

WAX *(4)*

heart is like **w**, melting within Ps 22:14
As **w** melts before the fire, Ps 68:2
melt like **w** at the presence Ps 97:5
apart, like **w** near a fire, like Mc 1:4

WAY *(653)*

sword to guard the **w** to the tree Gn 3:24
corrupted its **w** on the earth. Gn 6:12
the spring on the **w** to Shur. Gn 16:7
have passed your servant's ⌊**w**⌋. Gn 18:5
him to keep the **w** of the LORD by Gn 18:19
get up early and go on your **w**." Gn 19:2
"Get out of the **w**!" they said, Gn 19:9
me on the right **w** to take the Gn 24:48
Then Isaac sent them on their **w**, Gn 26:31
Send me on my **w** so that I can Gn 30:25
went on his **w**, and God's angels Gn 32:1
started on his **w** back to Seir, Gn 33:16
was buried on the **w** to Ephrath Gn 35:19
which is on the **w** to Timnah. Gn 38:14
in his hand the **w** you used to Gn 40:13
out just the **w** he interpreted Gn 41:13
will be on our **w** so that we may Gn 43:8
They made their **w** down to Egypt Gn 43:15
sent his brothers on their **w**, Gn 45:24
to them, "Don't argue on the **w**." Gn 45:24
In this **w**, Joseph acquired all Gn 47:20
sorrow Rachel died along the **w**, Gn 48:7
there along the **w** to Ephrath," Gn 48:7
father, "Not that **w**, my father! Gn 48:18
also seen the **w** the Egyptians Ex 3:9
he is on his **w** now to meet you. Ex 4:14
treating your servants this **w**? Ex 5:15
This **w** you will know that I, Ex 8:22
In this **w** they plundered the Ex 12:36
them on their **w** during the day Ex 13:21
This **w** I will test them to see Ex 16:4
that confronted them on the **w**, Ex 18:8
teach them the **w** to live and Ex 18:20
In this **w** you will lighten your Ex 18:22
you on the **w** and bring you to Ex 23:20
It is to be this **w** for the six Ex 25:33
and in this **w** attach ⌊them⌋ to Ex 28:25
between them all the **w** around, Ex 28:33
This is the **w** you will ordain Ex 29:9
In this **w**, he and his garments Ex 29:21
turned from the **w** I commanded Ex 32:8
I might destroy you on the **w**." Ex 33:3
It was this **w** for the six Ex 37:19
and, in this **w**, attached ⌊them⌋ Ex 39:18
he will offer it the same **w**. Lv 4:20
In this **w** the priest will make Lv 4:26
In this **w** the priest will make Lv 4:31
In this **w** the priest will make Lv 4:35
In this **w** the priest will make Lv 5:6
In this **w** the priest will make Lv 5:10
In this **w** the priest will make Lv 5:13
In this **w** the priest will make Lv 6:7
In this **w** he consecrated Aaron Lv 8:30
In this **w** the priest will make Lv 14:18
In this **w** the priest will make Lv 14:31
In this **w** he will make atonement Lv 14:53
In this **w** the priest will make Lv 15:15
In this **w** the priest will make Lv 15:30
the ⌊most⌋ holy place in this **w**: Lv 16:3
place in this **w** for all their Lv 16:16
this **w** its yield will increase Lv 19:25
look the other **w** when that man Lv 20:4
to reap all the **w** to the edge of Lv 23:22
banners in this **w** and moved out Nm 2:34
way and moved out the same **w**, Nm 2:34
In this **w** they will put My name Nm 6:27
He spoke to him ⌊that **w**⌋. Nm 7:89
This is the **w** the lampstand was Nm 8:4
this **w** you are to separate the Nm 8:14
It remained that **w** continuously: Nm 9:16
Go up this **w** to the Negev, Nm 13:17
in this **w** when he presents Nm 15:13
w you will remember and obey Nm 15:40
Mount Hor by **w** of the Red Sea to Nm 21:4
ever treated you this **w** before?" Nm 22:30
and Balak also went his **w**. Nm 24:25
Kadesh-barnea by **w** of Mount Seir. Dt 1:2
you saw on the **w** to the hill Dt 1:19
son all along the **w** you traveled Dt 1:31
wilderness by **w** of the Red Sea. Dt 1:40
wilderness by **w** of the Red Sea, Dt 2:1
turned from the **w** that I Dt 9:12
turned from the **w** the LORD had Dt 9:16
the LORD your God this **w**. Dt 12:4
you from the **w** the LORD your God Dt 13:5
your female slave the same **w**. Dt 15:17
never to go back that **w** again.' Dt 17:16
In this **w**, innocent blood will Dt 19:10
you along the **w** and attacked all Dt 25:18
afterwards, go on your **w**." Jos 2:16
They searched all along the **w**, Jos 2:22
so that you can see the **w** to go, Jos 3:4
haven't traveled this **w** before." Jos 3:4
along the **w** after they had come Jos 5:4
along the **w** were circumcised Jos 5:5
been circumcised along the **w**. Jos 5:7
city seven times in the same **w**. Jos 6:15
force was stationed in this **w**: Jos 8:13
Beth-horon all the **w** to Azekah, Jos 10:11
them and sent them on their **w**, Jos 22:6
now going the **w** of all the earth Jos 23:14
us all along the **w** we went and Jos 24:17
showed them the **w** into the town, Jdg 1:25
turned from the **w** of their Jdg 2:17
keep the LORD's **w** by walking in Jdg 2:22
Ehud escaped by **w** of the porch, Jdg 3:23
In this **w**, the evil that Jdg 9:56
Aroer all the **w** to the entrance Jdg 11:33
In this **w**, she rendered him Jdg 16:19
On his **w** he came to Micah's home Jdg 17:8
in the same **w** as the Sidonians, Jdg 18:7
The Danites went on their **w**, Jdg 18:26

the woman made her **w** back, Jdg 19:26
her in this **w** every year. 1Sm 1:7
Then Hannah went on her **w**; 1Sm 1:18
This is the **w** they treated all 1Sm 2:14
Send it off and let it go its **w**. 1Sm 6:8
down all the **w** to a place below 1Sm 7:11
tell us which **w** we should go." 1Sm 9:6
and he will tell us our **w**." 1Sm 9:8
them on his **w** to the high place 1Sm 9:14
and I'll send you on your **w**!" 1Sm 9:26
teach you the good and right **w**. 1Sm 12:23
Michmash all the **w** to Aijalon. 1Sm 14:31
them along the **w** as they were 1Sm 15:2
from Havilah all the **w** to Shur, 1Sm 15:7
left the cave and went on his **w**. 1Sm 24:7
head, and they went their **w**. 1Sm 26:12
Then David went on his **w**, 1Sm 26:25
so you can go on your **w**." 1Sm 28:22
What better **w** could he regain 1Sm 29:4
off as they went on their **w**. 1Sm 30:2
Giah on the **w** to the wilderness 2Sm 2:24
weeping all the **w** to Bahurim. 2Sm 3:16
and traveled by **w** of the Arabah 2Sm 4:7
He built it up all the **w** around 2Sm 5:9
all the **w** from Geba to Gezer 2Sm 5:25
I removed him from your **w**. 2Sm 7:15
they were on the **w**, a report 2Sm 13:30
me⌋ this **w** because the LORD 2Sm 16:10
So Ahimaaz ran by **w** of the plain 2Sm 18:23
The **w** the first man runs looks 2Sm 18:27
to me like the **w** Ahimaaz son of 2Sm 18:27
king a little **w** across the 2Sm 19:36
Jordan all the **w** to Jerusalem 2Sm 20:2
God—His **w** is perfect; the word 2Sm 22:31
refuge; He makes my **w** perfect. 2Sm 22:33
and my ankles do not give **w**. 2Sm 22:37
saying, "Why do you act this **w**?" 1Kg 1:6
I am going the **w** of all of the 1Kg 2:2
the same **w**, he made four-sided 1Kg 6:33
In this **w** he made the 10 water 1Kg 7:37
them the good **w** they should walk 1Kg 8:36
⌊it is this **w**⌋ until today. 1Kg 9:21
the same **w**, they exported them 1Kg 10:29
⌊The **w** things are going⌋ now, 1Kg 12:26
of the calves all the **w** to Dan. 1Kg 12:30
or go back the **w** you came.'" 1Kg 13:9
he went another **w**; he did not go 1Kg 13:10
go back by the **w** he had come to 1Kg 13:10
to them, "Which **w** did he go?" 1Kg 13:12
had seen the **w** taken by the man 1Kg 13:12
or go back by the **w** you came.'" 1Kg 13:17
him along the **w** and killed him. 1Kg 13:24
back from his **w** heard ⌊about it⌋ 1Kg 13:26
of his evil **w** but again set up 1Kg 13:33
have walked in the **w** of Jeroboam 1Kg 16:2
Ahab went one **w** by himself, 1Kg 18:6
went the other **w** by himself. 1Kg 18:6
and return by the **w** you came to 1Kg 19:15
walked in the **w** of his father, 1Kg 22:52
father, in the **w** of his mother, 1Kg 22:52
and in the **w** of Jeroboam son of 1Kg 22:52
This is not the **w**, and this is 2Kg 6:19
that the whole **w** was littered 2Kg 7:15
He walked in the **w** of the kings 2Kg 8:18
He walked in the **w** of the house 2Kg 8:27
and went on his **w** to Samaria. 2Kg 10:12
On the **w**, while he was at 2Kg 10:12
she went out by **w** of the Horses' 2Kg 11:16
palace by **w** of the guards' 2Kg 11:19
but walked in the **w** of the kings 2Kg 16:3
you go back the **w** you came. 2Kg 19:28
not walk in the **w** of the LORD. 2Kg 21:22
fled⌋ by night by **w** of the gate 2Kg 25:4
king made his **w** along the route 2Kg 25:4
up the city all the **w** around, 1Ch 11:8
the ark of God the **w** Moses had 1Ch 15:15
lots the same **w** as their 1Ch 24:31
the same **w**, they exported them 2Ch 1:17
sons guard their **w** to walk in My 2Ch 6:16
them the good **w** they should walk 2Ch 6:27
on them; ⌊it is this **w**⌋ today. 2Ch 8:8
they walked in the **w** of David 2Ch 11:17
He walked in the **w** of Asa his 2Ch 20:32
He walked in the **w** of the kings 2Ch 21:6
walked in the **w** of the kings 2Ch 21:13
and from ambush along the **w**. Ezr 8:31
up at night by **w** of the valley Neh 2:15
illuminate the **w** they should go. Neh 9:12
the **w** they should go. Neh 9:19
will also fast in the same **w**. Est 4:16
is the joy of his **w** of life; Jb 8:19
Their **w** of escape will be cut Jb 11:20
before I go the **w** of no return. Jb 16:22
person will hold to his **w**, Jb 17:9
has blocked my **w** so that I Jb 19:8
in this **w** good will come to you. Jb 22:21
Yet He knows the **w** I have taken; Jb 23:10
kept to His **w** and not turned Jb 23:11
God understands the **w** to wisdom, Jb 28:23
my step has turned from the **w**, Jb 31:7
excited when trouble came his **w**? Jb 31:29
Who has appointed His **w** for Him, Jb 36:23
or clears the **w** for lightning, Jb 38:25
over the **w** of the righteous Ps 1:6
but the **w** of the wicked leads to Ps 1:6
make Your **w** straight before me. Ps 5:8
God—His **w** is perfect; the word Ps 18:30
strength and makes my **w** perfect. Ps 18:32
and my ankles do not give **w**. Ps 18:36
He shows sinners the **w**. Ps 25:8
is right and teaches them His **w**. Ps 25:9
show him the **w** he should choose Ps 25:12
show me Your **w**, LORD, and lead Ps 27:11
you and show you the **w** to go; Ps 32:8
their **w** be dark and slippery, Ps 35:6
Commit your **w** to the LORD; Ps 37:5
by one who prospers in his **w**, Ps 37:7
those whose **w** is upright. Ps 37:14
and He takes pleasure in his **w**. Ps 37:23
for the LORD and keep His **w**, Ps 37:34
This is the **w** of those who are Ps 49:13
You prepare the earth in this **w**, Ps 65:9
so that Your **w** may be known on Ps 67:2
lead the **w**, with musicians Ps 68:25
Make Your **w** to the everlasting Ps 74:3
God, Your **w** is holy. What god is Ps 77:13
Your **w** went through the sea, Ps 77:19
to prepare the **w** for His steps. Ps 85:13
Teach me Your **w**, LORD, and I Ps 86:11
attention to the **w** of integrity. Ps 101:2
who follows the **w** of integrity Ps 101:6
finding no **w** to a city where Ps 107:4
are those whose **w** is blameless, Ps 119:1
can a young man keep his **w** pure? Ps 119:9
I rejoice in the **w** ⌊revealed by⌋ Ps 119:14
Keep me from the **w** of deceit, Ps 119:29
I have chosen the **w** of truth; Ps 119:30
I pursue the **w** of Your commands, Ps 119:32
therefore I hate every false **w**. Ps 119:104
precepts and hate every false **w**. Ps 119:128
In this very **w** the man who fears Ps 128:4
there is any offensive **w** in me; Ps 139:24
lead me in the everlasting **w**. Ps 139:24
weak within me, You know my **w**. Ps 142:3
Reveal to me the **w** I should go, Ps 143:8
fruit of their **w** and be glutted Pr 1:31
and protect the **w** of His loyal Pr 2:8
you from the **w** of evil— Pr 2:12
So follow the **w** of good people, Pr 2:20
you will go safely on your **w**; Pr 3:23
am teaching you the **w** of wisdom; Pr 4:11
proceed in the **w** of evil ones. Pr 4:14
But the **w** of the wicked is like Pr 4:19
Keep your **w** far from her. Pr 5:8
instructions are the **w** to life. Pr 6:23
walk in the **w** of righteousness, Pr 8:20
pursue the **w** of understanding. Pr 9:6
w of the LORD is a stronghold Pr 10:29
A fool's **w** is right in his own Pr 12:15
but the **w** of the treacherous Pr 13:15
wisdom is to consider his **w**, Pr 14:8
There is a **w** that seems right to Pr 14:12
but its end is the **w** to death. Pr 14:12
detests the **w** of the wicked, Pr 15:9
A slacker's **w** is like a thorny Pr 15:19
A man's heart plans his **w**, Pr 16:9
who guards his **w** protects his Pr 16:17
There is a **w** that seems right to Pr 16:25
in the end it is the **w** of death. Pr 16:25
him in a **w** that is not good Pr 16:29
is found in the **w** of Pr 16:31
after he is on his **w**, he gloats. Pr 20:14
can anyone understand his own **w**? Pr 20:24
strays from the **w** of wisdom will Pr 21:16
the upright man considers his **w**. Pr 21:29
youth about the **w** he should go; Pr 22:6
into an evil **w** will fall into Pr 28:10
and one whose **w** is upright is Pr 29:27
the **w** of an eagle in the sky, Pr 30:19
the **w** of a snake on a rock, Pr 30:19
on a rock, the **w** of a ship at Pr 30:19
and the **w** of a man with a young Pr 30:19
This is the **w** of an adulteress: Pr 30:20
I will make my **w** to the mountain Sg 4:6
of women? Which **w** has he turned? Sg 6:1
from going the **w** of this people: Is 8:11
bring honor to the **W** of the Sea, Is 9:1
who can stand in its **w**? Is 14:27
into a firm place will give **w**, Is 22:25
will be purged in this **w**, Is 27:9
Get out of the **w**! Leave the Is 30:11
"This is the **w**. Walk in it." Is 30:21
in a godless **w** and speaks Is 32:6
A road will be there and a **w**; Is 35:8
it will be called the Holy **W**. Is 35:8
make you go back the **w** you came. Is 37:29
Prepare the **w** of the LORD in the Is 40:3
showed Him the **w** of Is 40:14
My **w** is hidden from the LORD, Is 40:27
the blind by a **w** they did not Is 42:16
says—who makes a **w** in the sea, Is 43:16
I will make a **w** in the Is 43:19
each wanders on his own **w**; Is 47:15
you in the **w** you should go. Is 48:17
we all have turned to our own **w**; Is 53:6
the wicked one abandon his **w**, Is 55:7
all of them turn to their own **w**, Is 56:11
up, prepare the **w**, remove Is 57:14
obstacle from My people's **w**." Is 57:14
prepare a **w** for the people! Is 62:10
Your people this **w** to make a Is 63:14
He was leading you along the **w**? Jr 2:17
along the **w** to Egypt to drink Jr 2:18
along the **w** to Assyria to drink Jr 2:18
twisting and turning on her **w**, Jr 2:23
constantly changing your **w**! Jr 2:36
for they have perverted their **w**; Jr 3:21
on the **w** to My dear people Jr 4:11
Your **w** of life and your actions Jr 4:18
understand the **w** of the LORD, Jr 5:4
they know the **w** of the LORD, Jr 5:5
Which is the **w** to what is good? Jr 6:16
know and assay their **w** of life. Jr 6:27
walk in every **w** I command you so Jr 7:23
not learn the **w** of the nations Jr 10:2
that a man's **w** of life is not Jr 10:23
Why does the **w** of the wicked Jr 12:1
give to each according to his **w**, Jr 17:10
from your evil **w**, and correct Jr 18:11
to you the **w** of life and the way Jr 21:8
way of life and the **w** of death. Jr 21:8
has been your **w** since youth; Jr 22:21
Their **w** of life has become evil, Jr 23:10
their **w** will be to them like Jr 23:12
in this **w** I will deal with Jr 24:8
your evil **w** of life and from Jr 25:5
each from his evil **w** of life— Jr 26:3
king of Judah in the same **w**: Jr 27:12
'In this **w**, within two years I Jr 28:11
the prophet then went on his **w**. Jr 28:11
by a smooth **w** where they will Jr 31:9
mind, the **w** you have traveled. Jr 31:21
heart and one **w** so that for Jr 32:39
one from his evil **w** of life, Jr 35:15
them will turn from his evil **w**. Jr 36:3
one will turn from his evil **w**. Jr 36:7
by speaking to them in this **w**. Jr 38:4
city at night by **w** of the king's Jr 39:4
order to make their **w** into Egypt Jr 41:17
may tell us the **w** we should walk Jr 42:3
them the wrong **w** in the Jr 50:6
say, 'In the same **w**, Babylon Jr 51:64
city by night by **w** of the gate Jr 52:7
made their **w** along the route Jr 52:7
forced me off my **w** and tore me Lm 3:11
his wicked **w** in order to save Ezk 3:18
his wickedness or his wicked **w**, Ezk 3:19
this **w** I will exhaust My wrath Ezk 6:12
from his evil **w** to save his life Ezk 13:22
judge you the **w** adulteresses Ezk 16:38
The Lord's **w** isn't fair. Ezk 18:25
Is it My **w** that is unfair? Ezk 18:25
The Lord's **w** isn't fair. Ezk 18:29
In this **w** also your fathers Ezk 20:27

yourselves the **w** your fathers Ezk 20:30
judge them the **w** adulteresses Ezk 23:45
out to warn him about his **w**, Ezk 33:8
turn from his **w** and he doesn't Ezk 33:9
should turn from his **w** and live. Ezk 33:11
The Lord's **w** isn't fair, even Ezk 33:17
is their own **w** that isn't fair Ezk 33:17
The Lord's **w** isn't fair. Ezk 33:20
led me out by **w** of the north Ezk 42:1
the **w** in front of the Ezk 42:12
led me out by **w** of the gate that Ezk 42:15
the temple by **w** of the gate that Ezk 43:4
In this **w** you will purify the Ezk 43:20
this **w** they will consecrate it Ezk 43:26
must enter by **w** of the portico Ezk 44:3
the gate and go out the same **w**." Ezk 44:3
brought me by **w** of the north Ezk 44:4
this **w** you will make atonement Ezk 45:20
the outside by **w** of the gate's Ezk 46:2
he must go in by **w** of the gate's Ezk 46:8
portico and go out the same **w**. Ezk 46:8
enters by **w** of the north gate Ezk 46:9
must go out by **w** of the south Ezk 46:9
enters by **w** of the south gate Ezk 46:9
must go out by **w** of the north Ezk 46:9
me out by **w** of the north gate Ezk 47:2
Mediterranean Sea by **w** of Ezk 47:15
said, "Go on your **w**, Daniel, for Dn 12:9
you, go on your **w** to the end; Dn 12:13
I will block her **w** with thorns; Hs 2:6
will act the same **w** toward you." Hs 3:3
in your own **w** and in your large Hs 10:13
or "As the **w** of Beer-sheba Am 8:14
breaks open ⌊the **w**⌋ will advance Mc 2:13
hand, have turned from the **w**. Mal 2:8
he will clear the **w** before Me. Mal 3:1
Me in this **w**," says the LORD Mal 3:10
Jesus Christ came about this **w**: Mt 1:18
the king, they went on their **w**. Mt 2:9
Prepare the **w** for the Lord; Mt 3:3
this is the **w** for us to fulfill Mt 3:15
In the same **w**, let your light Mt 5:16
while you're on the **w** with him, Mt 5:25
In the same **w**, every good tree Mt 7:17
that no one could pass that **w**. Mt 8:28
Now a long **w** off from them, Mt 8:30
will prepare Your **w** before You. Mt 11:10
In this **w**, you have revoked Mt 15:6
they might collapse on the **w**." Mt 15:32
In the same **w** the Son of Man is Mt 17:12
the same **w**, it is not the will Mt 18:14
he had no **w** to pay it back, Mt 18:25
who were born that **w** from their Mt 19:12
made themselves that **w** because Mt 19:12
and said to them on the **w**: Mt 20:17
to you in the **w** of righteousness Mt 21:32
looking for a **w** to arrest Him, Mt 21:46
teach truthfully the **w** of God. Mt 22:16
the same **w**, on the outside you Mt 23:28
In the same **w**, when you see all Mt 24:33
So this is the **w** the coming of Mt 24:39
In the same **w** the man with two Mt 25:17
in a treacherous **w** and kill Him. Mt 26:4
it in a new **w** in My Father's Mt 26:29
that say it must happen this **w**?" Mt 26:54
In the same **w** the chief priests, Mt 27:41
In the same **w** even the criminals Mt 27:44
were on their **w**, some of the Mt 28:11
of You, who will prepare Your **w**. Mk 1:2
Prepare the **w** for the Lord; Mk 1:3
and made His **w** to a deserted Mk 1:35
to make their **w** picking some Mk 2:23
He went by **w** of Sidon to the Sea Mk 7:31
they will collapse on the **w**, Mk 8:3
made their **w** through Galilee, Mk 9:30
you arguing about on the **w**?" Mk 9:33
because on the **w** they had been Mk 9:34
"Go your **w**," Jesus told him. Mk 10:52
looking for a **w** to destroy Him. Mk 11:18
looking for a **w** to arrest Him, Mk 12:12
teach truthfully the **w** of God. Mk 12:14
the same **w**, when you see these Mk 13:29
a treacherous **w** to arrest and Mk 14:1
it in a new **w** in the kingdom Mk 14:25
In the same **w**, the chief priests Mk 15:31
saw the **w** He breathed His last, Mk 15:39
on their **w** into the country Mk 16:12
our feet into the **w** of peace. Lk 1:79

Prepare the **w** for the Lord; Lk 3:4
the crowd and went on His **w**. Lk 4:30
out and made His **w** to a deserted Lk 4:42
could not find a **w** to bring him Lk 5:19
this is the **w** their ancestors Lk 6:23
this is the **w** their ancestors Lk 6:26
He was on His **w** to a town called Lk 7:11
will prepare Your **w** before You. Lk 7:27
God's **w** of righteousness, Lk 7:29
on their **w** and are choked with Lk 8:14
and on the **w** they entered a Lk 9:52
In the same **w**, a Levite, when he Lk 10:32
to settle with him on the **w**. Lk 12:58
and making His **w** to Jerusalem. Lk 13:22
In the same **w**, therefore, every Lk 14:33
you, in the same **w**, there will Lk 15:7
you, in the same **w**, there is joy Lk 15:10
the son was still a long **w** off, Lk 15:20
up and saw Abraham a long **w** off, Lk 16:23
the same **w**, when you have done Lk 17:10
him, "Get up and go on your **w**. Lk 17:19
He was about to pass that **w**. Lk 19:4
looking for a **w** to destroy Him, Lk 19:47
could not find a **w** to do it, Lk 19:48
looked for a **w** to get their Lk 20:19
teach truthfully the **w** of God. Lk 20:21
the same **w**, all seven died and Lk 20:31
the same **w**, when you see these Lk 21:31
looking for a **w** to put Him to Lk 22:2
In the same **w** He also took the Lk 22:20
out and made His **w** as usual to Lk 22:39
were on their **w** to a village Lk 24:13
straight the **w** of the Lord— Jn 1:23
God loved the world in this **w**: Jn 3:16
town and made their **w** to Him. Jn 4:30
does these things in the same **w**. Jn 5:19
door but climbs in some other **w**, Jn 10:1
This **w** you will know and Jn 10:38
but I'm on My **w** to wake him up." Jn 11:11
we let Him continue in this **w**, Jn 11:48
know the **w** where I am going." Jn 14:4
going. How can we know the **w**?" Jn 14:5
him, "I am the **w**, the truth, Jn 14:6
Is this the **w** you answer the Jn 18:22
He revealed Himself in this **w**: Jn 21:1
come in the same **w** that you have Ac 1:11
He has fulfilled in this **w**. Ac 3:18
They found no **w** to punish them, Ac 4:21
spoke in this **w**: His descendants Ac 7:6
the same **w** you killed the Ac 7:28
went on their **w** proclaiming the Ac 8:4
in his chariot on his **w** home, Ac 8:28
But he went on his **w** rejoicing. Ac 8:39
found any who belonged to the **W**, Ac 9:2
Stephen made their **w** as far as Ac 11:19
spoken in this **w**, I will grant Ac 13:34
spoke in such a **w** that a great Ac 14:1
the nations to go their own **w**, Ac 14:16
troubles on our **w** into the Ac 14:22
sent on their **w** by the church, Ac 15:3
Jesus, in the same **w** they are." Ac 15:11
as we were on our **w** to prayer, Ac 16:16
to you the **w** of salvation." Ac 16:17
instructed in the **w** of the Lord; Ac 18:25
explained the **w** of God to him Ac 18:26
slandering the **W** in front of the Ac 19:9
In this **w** the Lord's message Ac 19:20
a major disturbance about the **W**. Ac 19:23
now I am on my **w** to Jerusalem, Ac 20:22
every **w** I've shown you that by Ac 20:35
'In this **w** the Jews in Jerusalem Ac 21:11
persecuted this **W** to the death, Ac 22:4
to the **W**, which they call Ac 24:14
accurately informed about the **W**, Ac 24:22
Jews know my **w** of life from my Ac 26:4
was making his defense this **w**, Ac 26:24
we gave **w** to it and were driven Ac 27:15
and in this **w** they were driven Ac 27:17
will be just the **w** it was told Ac 27:25
In this **w**, all got safely to Ac 27:44
in the same **w** also left natural Rm 1:27
Considerable in every **w**. Rm 3:2
in this **w** death spread to all Rm 5:12
too may walk in a new **w** of life. Rm 6:4
serve in the new **w** of the Spirit Rm 7:6
In the same **w** the Spirit also Rm 8:26
In the same **w**, then, there is Rm 11:5
And in this **w** all Israel will be Rm 11:26

the same **w** we who are many are Rm 12:5
or pitfall in your brother's **w**. Rm 14:13
Messiah in this **w** is acceptable Rm 14:18
Jerusalem all the **w** around to Rm 15:19
to be sent on my **w** there by you, Rm 15:24
I will go by **w** of you to Spain. Rm 15:28
In the same **w**, no one knows the 1Co 2:11
should consider us in this **w**: 1Co 4:1
of yours in no **w** becomes a 1Co 8:9
In the same **w**, the Lord has 1Co 9:14
to make it happen that **w** for me. 1Co 9:15
in such a **w** that you may win. 1Co 9:24
will also provide a **w** of escape, 1Co 10:13
In the same **w** ⌊He⌋ also ⌊took⌋ 1Co 11:25
in an unworthy **w** will be guilty 1Co 11:27
in this **w** he should eat of the 1Co 11:28
will show you an even better **w**. 1Co 12:31
In the same **w**, unless you use 1Co 14:9
send me on my **w** wherever I go. 1Co 16:6
send him on his **w** in peace so he 1Co 16:11
a purely human **w** so that I say 2Co 1:17
in every **w** but not crushed; 2Co 4:8
know anyone in a purely human **w**. 2Co 5:16
Christ in a purely human **w**, 2Co 5:16
we were afflicted in every **w**: 2Co 7:5
In every **w** you have commended 2Co 7:11
that in every **w**, always having 2Co 9:8
enriched in every **w** for all 2Co 9:11
we are walking in a fleshly **w**. 2Co 10:2
do not wage war in a fleshly **w**, 2Co 10:3
myself in no **w** inferior to 2Co 11:5
from burdening you in any **w**. 2Co 11:9
since I am in no **w** inferior to 2Co 12:11
So in what **w** were you treated 2Co 12:13
about my former **w** of life in Gl 1:13
he differs in no **w** from a slave, Gl 4:1
In the same **w** we also, when we Gl 4:3
in this **w** you will fulfill the Gl 6:2
who fills all things in every **w**. Eph 1:23
grow in every **w** into Him who is Eph 4:15
took off your former **w** of life, Eph 4:22
In the same **w**, husbands should Eph 5:28
treat them the same **w**, without Eph 6:9
to think this **w** about all of you Php 1:7
Just that in every **w**, whether Php 1:18
in any **w** by your opponents Php 1:28
my joy by thinking the same **w**, Php 2:2
In the same **w** you also should Php 2:18
are mature should think this **w**. Php 3:15
then, in this **w**, my dearly loved Php 4:1
it out of the **w** by nailing it to Col 2:14
Lord Jesus, direct our **w** to you. 1Th 3:11
the same **w** God will bring with 1Th 4:14
let anyone deceive you in any **w**. 2Th 2:3
do so until he is out of the **w**, 2Th 2:7
you peace always in every **w**. 2Th 3:16
is beneficial in every **w**, 1Tm 4:8
godliness is a **w** to material 1Tm 6:5
this is in no **w** profitable and 2Tm 2:14
who worm their **w** into households 2Tm 3:6
the same **w**, older women are to Ti 2:3
and godly **w** in the present age, Ti 2:12
if he has wronged you in any **w**, Phm 18
be like His brothers in every **w**, Heb 2:17
about the seventh day in this **w**: Heb 4:4
tested in every **w** as we are, Heb 4:15
In the same **w**, the Messiah did Heb 5:5
though we are speaking this **w**, Heb 6:9
having been set up this **w**, Heb 9:6
clear that the **w** into the holy Heb 9:8
In the same **w**, he sprinkled the Heb 9:21
the new and living **w** that He has Heb 10:20
those who were treated that **w**. Heb 10:33
In the same **w**, the rich man will Jms 1:11
In the same **w** faith, if it Jms 2:17
And in the same **w**, wasn't Rahab Jms 2:25
things should not be this **w**. Jms 3:10
the error of his **w** will save his Jms 5:20
from your empty **w** of life 1Pt 1:18
freedom as a **w** to conceal evil. 1Pt 2:16
in the same **w**, submit yourselves 1Pt 3:1
message by the **w** their wives 1Pt 3:1
beautified themselves in this **w**, 1Pt 3:5
in the same **w**, live with your 1Pt 3:7
For in this **w**, entry into the 2Pt 1:11
of them the **w** of truth will be 2Pt 2:2
have known the **w** of 2Pt 2:21
are to be destroyed in this **w**, 2Pt 3:11

when we are **w** and you are strong 2Co 13:9
back again to the **w** and bankrupt Gl 4:9
help the **w**, be patient with 1Th 5:14
it was **w** and unprofitable Heb 7:18
as high priests men who are **w**, Heb 7:28
gained strength after being **w**, Heb 11:34

WEAKENED (1)
your tired hands and **w** knees, Heb 12:12

WEAKENING (2)
because he is **w** the morale of Jr 38:4
womb, without **w** in the faith. Rm 4:19

WEAKER (4)
was told, "Your father is **w**." Gn 48:1
the house of Saul becoming **w**. 2Sm 3:1
that seem to be **w** are necessary. 1Co 12:22
of their **w** nature yet showing 1Pt 3:7

WEAKEST (3)
my family is the **w** in Manasseh, Jdg 6:15
of even⌋ the **w** of my master's Is 36:9
the one who is **w** among them will Zch 12:8

WEAKLING (1)
Let even the **w** say: Jl 3:10

WEAKLINGS (1)
As for the **w** of the flocks, Gn 30:42

WEAKNESS (11)
come to see the **w** of the land." Gn 42:9
come to see the **w** of the land." Gn 42:12
because of the **w** of your flesh. Rm 6:19
also joins to help in our **w**, Rm 8:26
and God's **w** is stronger than 1Co 1:25
was with you in **w**, in fear, and 1Co 2:3
sown in **w**, raised in power; 1Co 15:43
for power is perfected in **w**." 2Co 12:9
was crucified in **w**, but He lives 2Co 13:4
the gospel to you in physical **w**, Gl 4:13
he himself is also subject to **w**. Heb 5:2

WEAKNESSES (7)
took our **w** and carried our Mt 8:17
to bear the **w** of those without Rm 15:1
I will boast about my **w**. 2Co 11:30
about myself, except of my **w**. 2Co 12:5
boast all the more about my **w**, 2Co 12:9
I am pleased in **w**, in insults, 2Co 12:10
unable to sympathize with our **w**, Heb 4:15

WEALTH (99)
but now your **w** has increased. Gn 30:30
has built this **w** from what Gn 31:1
the **w** that God has taken from Gn 31:16
have gained this **w** for me,' Dt 8:17
gives you the power to gain **w**, Dt 8:18
they draw from the **w** of the seas Dt 33:19
to your homes with great **w**: Jos 22:8
LORD brings poverty and gives **w**; 1Sm 2:7
all this **w** that we've provided 1Ch 29:16
riches, **w**, or glory, or for 2Ch 1:11
you riches, **w**, and glory, such 2Ch 1:12
the glorious **w** of his kingdom Est 1:4
his glorious **w** and his many sons Est 5:11
pant for his children's **w**. Jb 5:5
Pay a bribe for me from your **w** Jb 6:22
his **w** will not endure. Jb 15:29
own hands must give back his **w**. Jb 20:10
He swallows **w** but must vomit it Jb 20:15
because my **w** is great or because Jb 31:25
your **w** or all ⌊your⌋ physical Jb 36:19
trust in their **w** and boast of Ps 49:6
they leave their **w** to others. Ps 49:10
when the **w** of his house Ps 49:16
his **w** will not follow him down. Ps 49:17
If **w** increases, pay no attention Ps 62:10
and they increase their **w**. Ps 73:12
W and riches are in his house, Ps 112:3
give up all the **w** in his house. Pr 6:31
lasting **w** and righteousness. Pr 8:18
giving **w** as an inheritance to Pr 8:21
A rich man's **w** is his fortified Pr 10:15
W is not profitable on a day of Pr 11:4
and hope placed in **w** vanishes. Pr 11:7
diligent man, his **w** is precious. Pr 12:27
to be poor but has great **w**. Pr 13:7
W obtained by fraud will dwindle, Pr 13:11
the sinner's **w** is stored up for Pr 13:22
crown of the wise is their **w**, Pr 14:24
of the righteous has great **w**, Pr 15:6
A rich man's **w** is his fortified Pr 18:11
W attracts many friends, but a Pr 19:4
A house and **w** are inherited from Pr 19:14
is to be chosen over great **w**; Pr 22:1
along with **w**, honor, and life Pr 22:4
for **w** is not forever; Pr 27:24
his **w** through excessive Pr 28:8
greedy man is in a hurry for **w**; Pr 28:22
with prostitutes destroys his **w**. Pr 29:3
Give me neither poverty nor **w**; Pr 30:8
and whoever loves **w** ⌊is⌋ never Ec 5:10
w kept by its owner to his harm. Ec 5:13
w was lost in a bad venture, Ec 5:14
given riches and **w** to every man, Ec 5:19
a man riches, **w**, and honor so Ec 6:2
were to give all his **w** for love, Sg 8:7
the **w** of Damascus and the spoils Is 8:4
Where will you leave your **w**? Is 10:3
to seize the **w** of the nations. Is 10:14
carry their **w** and belongings Is 15:7
they carry their **w** on the backs Is 30:6
and the **w** of the nations will Is 60:5
so that the **w** of the nations Is 60:11
will eat the **w** of the nations, Is 61:6
and the **w** of nations like a Is 66:12
Your **w** and your treasures I will Jr 15:13
Your **w** and all your treasures I Jr 17:3
away all the **w** of this city, Jr 20:5
w he has gained has perished. Jr 48:36
none of their **w**, and none of the Ezk 7:11
people, seize **w** and valuables, Ezk 22:25
They will take your **w** as spoil Ezk 26:12
of ⌊your⌋ great **w** of every kind. Ezk 27:12
and your great **w** of every kind, Ezk 27:18
Your **w**, merchandise, and goods, Ezk 27:27
with your abundant **w** and goods. Ezk 27:33
have acquired **w** for yourself. Ezk 28:4
you have increased your **w**, Ezk 28:5
become proud because of your **w**." Ezk 28:5
carry off its **w**, seizing its Ezk 29:19
Egypt, and its **w** is taken away, Ezk 30:4
loot, and **w** on his followers, Dn 11:24
return to his land with great **w**, Dn 11:28
day strangers captured his **w**, Ob 11
their **w** to the Lord of all the Mc 4:13
unjustly gains **w** for his house Hab 2:9
Their **w** will become plunder and Zph 1:13
her and cast her **w** into the sea; Zch 9:4
and the **w** of all the surrounding Zch 14:14
seduction of **w** choke the word, Mt 13:22
seduction of **w**, and the desires Mk 4:19
those who have **w** to enter the Mk 10:23
those who have **w** to enter the Lk 18:24
into the **w** of their generosity 2Co 8:2
the glorious **w** of this mystery, Col 1:27
hope on the uncertainty of **w**, 1Tm 6:17
to be greater **w** than the Heb 11:26
Your **w** is ruined: your clothes Jms 5:2
such fabulous **w** was destroyed! Rv 18:17
the sea became rich from her **w**; Rv 18:19

WEALTHY (9)
richer until he was very **w**. Gn 26:13
The **w** may not give more, and the Ex 30:15
and since he was a very **w** man, 2Sm 19:32
each of the **w** men of Israel to 2Kg 15:20
lies down **w**, but will do so no Jb 27:19
of Tyre, the **w** people, will seek Ps 45:12
For the **w** of the city are full Mc 6:12
have become **w**, and need nothing, Rv 3:17
earth have grown **w** from her Rv 18:3

WEANED (10)
grew and was **w**, and Abraham held Gn 21:8
feast on the day Isaac was **w**. Gn 21:8
the child is **w**, I'll take him to 1Sm 1:22
stay here until you've **w** him. 1Sm 1:23
nursed her son until she **w** him. 1Sm 1:23
When she had **w** him, she took him 1Sm 1:24
herself⌋ **w** him in Pharaoh's 1Kg 11:20
like a little **w** child with its Ps 131:2
Infants ⌊just⌋ **w** from milk? Is 28:9
After Gomer had **w** No Compassion, Hs 1:8

WEAPON (6)
and held a **w** with the other. Neh 4:17
Each carried his **w**, even when Neh 4:23
If he flees from an iron **w**, Jb 20:24
produces a **w** suitable for its Is 54:16
No **w** formed against you will Is 54:17
a destructive **w** in his hand." Ezk 9:1

WEAPONRY (1)
horses, a fortified city, and **w**, 2Kg 10:2

WEAPONS (43)
their knives are vicious **w**. Gn 49:5
of you put on his **w** of war and Dt 1:41
and Eshtaol armed with **w** of war. Jdg 18:11
armed with their **w** of war. Jdg 18:16
the 600 men armed with **w** of war. Jdg 18:17
or to make his **w** of war or the 1Sm 8:12
and his son Jonathan had ⌊**w**⌋. 1Sm 13:22
the attendant who carried his **w**, 1Sm 14:1
the attendant who carried his **w**, 1Sm 14:6
he put Goliath's **w** in his ⌊own⌋ 1Sm 17:54
sword or my **w** since the king's 1Sm 21:8
fallen and the **w** of war have 2Sm 1:27
gold, clothing, **w**, spices, and 1Kg 10:25
the king with **w** in hand. 2Kg 11:8
stood with their **w** in hand 2Kg 11:11
with all kinds of **w** of war, 1Ch 12:33
with all the military **w** of war. 1Ch 12:37
gold, clothing, **w**, spices, and 2Ch 9:24
the king with **w** in hand. 2Ch 23:7
troops with their **w** in hand 2Ch 23:10
an abundance of **w** and shields. 2Ch 32:5
He has prepared His deadly **w**; Ps 7:13
the sword, and the **w** of war. Ps 76:3
Wisdom is better than **w** of war, Ec 9:18
LORD and the **w** of His wrath— Is 13:5
you looked to the **w** in the House Is 22:8
against him with brandished **w**. Is 30:32
scoundrel's **w** are destructive Is 32:7
will repel the **w** of war in your Jr 21:4
against you, each with his **w**. Jr 22:7
and brought out His **w** of wrath, Jr 50:25
are My battle club, My **w** of war. Jr 51:20
alliance of nations and with **w**, Ezk 23:24
to Sheol with their **w** of war, Ezk 32:27
and burn the **w**—the bucklers Ezk 39:9
will use the **w** to make fires. Ezk 39:10
w of war in the land and will Hs 2:18
from him all his **w** he trusted Lk 11:22
with lanterns, torches, and **w**. Jn 18:3
of it to sin as **w** for Rm 6:13
to God as **w** for righteousness. Rm 6:13
through **w** of righteousness on 2Co 6:7
since the **w** of our warfare are 2Co 10:4

WEAR (40)
her younger son Jacob **w** them. Gn 27:15
food to eat and clothing to **w**, Gn 28:20
will certainly **w** out both Ex 18:18
sanctuary must **w** them for seven Ex 29:30
He is to **w** a holy linen tunic, Lv 16:4
been ordained to **w** the garments, Lv 21:10
Your clothing did not **w** out, Dt 8:4
woman is not to **w** male clothing, Dt 22:5
Do not **w** clothes made of both Dt 22:11
of the outer garment you **w**. Dt 22:12
on your feet did not **w** out; Dt 29:5
w out all our people there. Jos 7:3
and **w** your ⌊best⌋ clothes. Ru 3:3
to **w** an ephod in My presence. 1Sm 2:28
but you **w** your royal attire." 1Kg 22:30
but you **w** your royal attire." 2Ch 18:29
Their clothes did not **w** out, Neh 9:21
for Mordecai to **w** so he could Est 4:4
but the righteous will **w** ⌊it⌋, Jb 27:17
shoulder and **w** it like a crown Jb 31:36
all of them will **w** out like Ps 102:26
they will **w** their shame like a Ps 109:29
w yourself out to get rich; Pr 23:4
In its streets they **w** sackcloth; Is 15:3
you will **w** all your children as Is 49:18
all of them will **w** out like a Is 50:9
the earth will **w** out like a Is 51:6
they **w** themselves out doing Jr 9:5
You eat the fat, **w** the wool, and Ezk 34:3
they must **w** linen garments; Ezk 44:17
They must **w** linen turbans on Ezk 44:18
cause everyone to **w** sackcloth Am 8:10
your body, what you will **w**. Mt 6:25
we drink?' or 'What will we **w**?' Mt 6:31
those who **w** soft clothes are in Mt 11:8
They were to **w** sandals, but not Mk 6:9
about the body, what you will **w**. Lk 12:22
so she doesn't **w** me out by her Lk 18:5
They will all **w** out like Heb 1:11
was permitted to **w** fine linen, Rv 19:8

WEARIED *(7)*
offerings or **w** you with incense Is 43:23
you have **w** Me with your Is 43:24
which you have **w** yourself with Is 47:12
those who have **w** you and have Is 47:15
to you, or how have I **w** you? Mc 6:3
You have **w** the LORD with your Mal 2:17
you ask, "How have we **w** ⌊Him⌋?" Mal 2:17

WEARIES *(1)*
and much study **w** the body. Ec 12:12

WEARINESS *(1)*
came to me in my extreme **w**, Dn 9:21

WEARING *(22)*
clothes she was **w** when she was Dt 21:13
shawl you're **w** and hold it out. Ru 3:15
Ahijah, who was **w** an ephod, ⌊was 1Sm 14:3
the robe he was **w** and gave it to 1Sm 18:4
replied. "He's **w** a robe." Then 1Sm 28:14
the LORD **w** a linen ephod . 2Sm 6:14
Now Tamar was **w** a long-sleeved 2Sm 13:18
long-sleeved garment she was **w**. 2Sm 13:19
Joab was **w** his uniform and over 2Sm 20:8
were fasting, ⌊**w**⌋ sackcloth, Neh 9:1
prohibited anyone **w** sackcloth Est 4:2
w the crown his mother placed on Sg 3:11
and for the **w** of sackcloth. Is 22:12
older priests, **w** sackcloth, to Is 37:2
that you bought and are **w**, Jr 13:4
w belts on their waists and Ezk 23:15
Jesus came out **w** the crown of Jn 19:5
Israel that I'm **w** this chain." Ac 28:20
into your meeting **w** a gold ring, Jms 2:2
on the man **w** the fine clothes Jms 2:3
and the **w** of gold ornaments 1Pt 3:3
white horses, **w** pure white linen Rv 19:14

WEARISOME *(1)*
All things are **w**; man is unable Ec 1:8

WEARS *(6)*
with water before he **w** them. Lv 16:4
Man **w** out like something rotten, Jb 13:28
as water **w** away stones and Jb 14:19
like a belt he always **w**. Ps 109:19
the crown he **w** will be glorious. Ps 132:18
a bridegroom **w** a turban and as Is 61:10

WEARY *(29)*
when you were tired and **w**. Dt 25:18
eyes grow **w** looking for them Dt 28:32
but He became **w** of Israel's Jdg 10:16
him while he is weak and **w**, 2Sm 17:2
and there the **w** find rest. Jb 3:17
I am **w** from my groaning; Ps 6:6
I am **w** from my crying; Ps 69:3
I am **w** from grief; strengthen me Ps 119:28
eyes grow **w** ⌊looking⌋ for what Ps 119:82
eyes grow **w** ⌊looking for⌋ Your Ps 119:123
he is too **w** to bring it to his Pr 26:15
The struggles of fools **w** them, Ec 10:15
of them grows **w** or stumbles; Is 5:27
place of rest, let the **w** rest; Is 28:12
He never grows faint or **w**; Is 40:28
to the **w** and strengthens Is 40:29
Youths may faint and grow **w**, Is 40:30
they will run and not grow **w**; Is 40:31
Israel, you have become **w** of Me. Is 43:22
as a burden for the **w** ⌊animal⌋. Is 46:1
to sustain the **w** with a word. Is 50:4
You became **w** on your many Is 57:10
for my life is **w** because of the Jr 4:31
They will grow **w**.' " The words Jr 51:64
they were **w** and worn out, Mt 9:36
of you who are **w** and burdened, Mt 11:28
do not grow **w** in doing good. 2Th 3:13
you won't grow **w** and lose heart. Heb 12:3
My name, and have not grown **w**. Rv 2:3

WEASEL *(1)*
the **w**, the mouse, the various Lv 11:29

WEATHER *(3)*
The wadis evaporate in warm **w**; Jb 6:17
from their channels in hot **w**. Jb 6:17
will be good **w** because the sky Mt 16:2

WEAVE *(4)*
You are to **w** the tunic from fine Ex 28:39
If you **w** the seven braids on my Jdg 16:13
who skillfully **w** spells. Ps 58:5
eggs and **w** spider's webs. Is 59:5

WEAVER *(2)*
fine linen; and a **w**. They can do Ex 35:35
have rolled up my life like a **w**; Is 38:12

WEAVER'S *(5)*
spear shaft was like a **w** beam, 1Sm 17:7
of his spear was like a **w** beam. 2Sm 21:19
spear in his hand like a **w** beam, 1Ch 11:23
of his spear was like a **w** beam. 1Ch 20:5
more swiftly than a **w** shuttle; Jb 7:6

WEAVERS *(2)*
combers and **w** will turn pale. Is 19:9
⌊Egypt's⌋ **w** will be dejected; Is 19:10

WEAVING *(1)*
the women were **w** tapestries for 2Kg 23:7

WEB *(4)*
my head with the **w** of a loom—" Jdg 16:13
pin, with the loom and the **w**. Jdg 16:14
he trusts in is a spider's **w**. Jb 8:14
leans on his **w**, but it doesn't Jb 8:15

WEBS *(2)*
eggs and weave spider's **w**. Is 59:5
Their **w** cannot become clothing, Is 59:6

WEDDING *(18)*
this week ⌊of **w** celebration⌋, Gn 29:27
Before the **w** day arrived, 1Sm 18:26
His young women had no **w** songs. Ps 78:63
placed on him the day of his **w**— Sg 3:11
jewelry or a bride her **w** sash? Jr 2:32
Can the **w** guests be sad while Mt 9:15
king who gave a **w** banquet for Mt 22:2
Come to the **w** banquet.' Mt 22:4
The **w** banquet was filled with Mt 22:10
who was not dressed for a **w**. Mt 22:11
get in here without **w** clothes?' Mt 22:12
in with him to the **w** banquet, Mt 25:10
The **w** guests cannot fast while Mk 2:19
can't make the **w** guests fast Lk 5:34
return from the **w** banquet so Lk 12:36
by someone to a **w** banquet, Lk 14:8
the third day a **w** took place in Jn 2:1
were invited to the **w** as well. Jn 2:2

WEEDED *(1)*
It will not be pruned or **w**; Is 5:6

WEEDS *(11)*
up everywhere, **w** covered the Pr 24:31
like poisonous **w** in the furrows Hs 10:4
overgrown with **w**, a salt pit, Zph 2:9
came, sowed **w** among the wheat, Mt 13:25
grain, then the **w** also appeared. Mt 13:26
Then where did the **w** come from?' Mt 13:27
'When you gather up the **w**, Mt 13:29
Gather the **w** first and tie them Mt 13:30
parable of the **w** in the field to Mt 13:36
The **w** are the sons of the evil Mt 13:38
just as the **w** are gathered Mt 13:40

WEEK *(13)*
Complete this **w** ⌊of wedding Gn 29:27
finished the **w** ⌊of celebration⌋ Gn 29:28
covenant with many for one **w**, Dn 9:27
the middle of the **w** he will put Dn 9:27
first day of the **w** was dawning, Mt 28:1
on the first day of the **w**, Mk 16:2
Early on the first day of the **w**, Mk 16:9
I fast twice a **w**; I give a tenth Lk 18:12
On the first day of the **w**, Lk 24:1
day of the **w** Mary Magdalene Jn 20:1
of that first day of the **w**, Jn 20:19
On the first day of the **w**, Ac 20:7
On the first day of the **w**, 1Co 16:2

WEEK-LONG *(1)*
the king held a **w** banquet in the Est 1:5

WEEKS *(16)*
(Festival of, AKA Festival of HARVEST, PENTECOST)
the Festival of **W** with the Ex 34:22
unclean for two **w** as ⌊she is⌋ Lv 12:5
count seven complete **w** starting Lv 23:15
LORD at your ⌊Festival of⌋ **W**; Nm 28:26
You are to count seven **w**, Dt 16:9
counting the **w** from the time the Dt 16:9
the Festival of **W** to the LORD Dt 16:10
the Festival of **W**, and the Dt 16:16
the Festival of **W**, and the 2Ch 8:13
us the fixed **w** of the harvest. Jr 5:24
Seventy **w** are decreed about your Dn 9:24
will be seven **w** and 62 weeks. Dn 9:25
will be seven weeks and 62 **w**. Dn 9:25
After those 62 **w** the Messiah Dn 9:26
was mourning for three full **w**. Dn 10:2
until the three **w** were over. Dn 10:3

WEEP *(41)*
for Sarah and to **w** for her. Gn 23:2
brother, and he was about to **w**. Gn 43:30
He went into an inner room to **w**. Gn 43:30
they had no strength left to **w**. 1Sm 30:4
of Israel, **w** for Saul, who 2Sm 1:24
Do not mourn or **w**." For all the Neh 8:9
scoff at me as I **w** before God. Jb 16:20
widows will not **w** ⌊for them⌋. Jb 27:15
a time to **w** and a time to laugh; Ec 3:4
to its temple to **w** at its high Is 15:2
with Jazer to **w** for the vines Is 16:9
from me! Let me **w** bitterly! Do Is 22:4
messengers of peace **w** bitterly. Is 33:7
I would **w** day and night over the Jr 9:1
being will **w** in secret because Jr 13:17
Do not **w** for the dead; do not Jr 22:10
W bitterly for the one who has Jr 22:10
will **w** for you, vine of Sibmah, Jr 48:32
I **w** because of these things; Lm 1:16
not lament or **w** or let your Ezk 24:16
not lament or **w** but will waste Ezk 24:23
w over you with deep anguish Ezk 27:31
Wake up, you drunkards, and **w**; Jl 1:5
w between the portico and the Jl 2:17
it in Gath, don't **w** at all. Mc 1:10
only child and **w** bitterly for Zch 12:10
thought about it, he began to **w**. Mk 14:72
Blessed are you who **w** now, Lk 6:21
because you will mourn and **w**. Lk 6:25
sang a lament, but you didn't **w**! Lk 7:32
do not **w** for Me, but weep Lk 23:28
but **w** for yourselves and your Lk 23:28
You will **w** and wail, but the Jn 16:20
who rejoice; **w** with those who Rm 12:15
rejoice; weep with those who **w**. Rm 12:15
those who **w** as though they did 1Co 7:30
weep as though they did not **w**, 1Co 7:30
Be miserable and mourn and **w**. Jms 4:9
W and wail over the miseries Jms 5:1
with her will **w** and mourn over Rv 18:9
earth will also **w** and mourn over Rv 18:11

WEEPING *(58)*
So Jacob named it Oak of **W**. Gn 35:8
they were **w** at the entrance Nm 25:6
the days of **w** and mourning for Dt 34:8
came to him, **w**, and said, "You Jdg 14:16
Why are they **w**?" Saul inquired, 1Sm 11:5
followed her, **w** all the way to 2Sm 3:16
on her head and went away **w**. 2Sm 13:19
countryside was **w** loudly while 2Sm 15:23
of Olives, **w** as he ascended. 2Sm 15:30
and went up, **w** as they ascended 2Sm 15:30
to Joab, "The king is **w**. 2Sm 19:1
asked, "Why is my lord **w**?" 2Kg 8:12
shouting from that of the **w**, Ezr 3:13
w and falling facedown before Ezr 10:1
the people were **w** as they heard Neh 8:9
My face has grown red with **w**, Jb 16:16
and my flute for the sound of **w**. Jb 30:31
me and its furrows join in **w**, Jb 31:38
has heard the sound of my **w**. Ps 6:8
W may spend the night, but there Ps 30:5
one goes along **w**, carrying the Ps 126:6
wails, falling down and **w**. Is 15:3
go up the slope of Luhith **w**; Is 15:5
Lord GOD of Hosts called for **w**, Is 22:12
The sound of **w** and crying will Is 65:19
of Israel **w** and begging for Jr 3:21
I will raise **w** and a lament over Jr 9:10
our eyelids soaked with **w**. Jr 9:18
They will come **w**, but I will Jr 31:9
with bitter **w**—Rachel weeping Jr 31:15
Rachel **w** for her children, Jr 31:15
your voice from **w** and your eyes Jr 31:16
to meet them, **w** as he came. Jr 41:6
they will be **w** continually, Jr 48:5
with more than the **w** for Jazer. Jr 48:32
come together, **w** as they come, Jr 50:4
My eyes are worn out from **w**; Lm 2:11
sitting there **w** for Tammuz. Ezk 8:14
with fasting, **w**, and mourning. Jl 2:12
with tears, with **w** and groaning, Mal 2:13

heard in Ramah, **w**, and great Mt 2:18
Rachel **w** for her children; Mt 2:18
there will be **w** and gnashing Mt 8:12
there will be **w** and gnashing Mt 13:42
there will be **w** and gnashing Mt 13:50
there will be **w** and gnashing Mt 22:13
there will be **w** and gnashing Mt 24:51
there will be **w** and gnashing Mt 25:30
people **w** and wailing loudly. Mk 5:38
you making a commotion and **w**? Mk 5:39
as they were mourning and **w**. Mk 16:10
Him at His feet, **w**, and began to Lk 7:38
There will be **w** and gnashing of Lk 13:28
w and showing him the robes and Ac 9:39
a great deal of **w** by everyone. Ac 20:37
are you doing, **w** and breaking my Ac 21:13
of her torment, **w** and mourning, Rv 18:15
crying out, **w**, and mourning: Rv 18:19

WEEPS *(2)*
She **w** aloud during the night, Lm 1:2
Him as one **w** for a firstborn. Zch 12:10

WEIGH *(8)*
would **w** the hair from his head 2Sm 14:26
or you will **w** out 75 pounds of 1Kg 20:39
carefully until you **w** ⌊them⌋ out Ezr 8:29
let God **w** me with an accurate Jb 31:6
your hands you **w** out violence Ps 58:2
together they ⌊**w**⌋ less than a Ps 62:9
bags of gold and **w** out silver on Is 46:6
The shekel will **w** 20 gerahs. Ezk 45:12

WEIGHED *(26)*
and Abraham **w** out to Ephron the Gn 23:16
Each silver dish ⌊**w**⌋ three and a Nm 7:85
of incense each ⌊**w**⌋ four ounces Nm 7:86
and actions are **w** by Him. 1Sm 2:3
scale armor that **w** 125 pounds. 1Sm 17:5
point of his spear **w** 15 pounds. 1Sm 17:7
The crown **w** 75 pounds of gold, 2Sm 12:30
bronze spear **w** about eight 2Sm 21:16
the crown **w** 75 pounds of gold, 1Ch 20:2
that can't be **w** because there is 1Ch 22:14
I **w** out to them the silver, Ezr 8:25
I **w** out to them 24 tons of Ezr 8:26
articles that had been **w** out, Ezr 8:30
articles were **w** out in the house Ezr 8:33
my grief could be **w** and my Jb 6:2
silver cannot be **w** out for its Jb 28:15
w, explored, and arranged many Ec 12:9
people **w** down with iniquity, Is 1:4
in a measure or **w** the mountains Is 40:12
and I **w** out to him the money— Jr 32:9
and **w** out the silver on a scale. Jr 32:10
He has **w** me down with chains. Lm 3:7
you have been **w** in the balance Dn 5:27
So they **w** my wages, 30 pieces Zch 11:12
So they **w** out 30 pieces of Mt 26:15
they **w** anchor and sailed along Ac 27:13

WEIGHING *(41)*
a gold ring **w** half a shekel, Gn 24:22
two bracelets **w** 10 shekels of Gn 24:22
one silver dish **w** three and a Nm 7:13
and one silver basin **w** one and Nm 7:13
one gold bowl **w** four ounces, Nm 7:14
one silver dish **w** three and a Nm 7:19
and one silver basin **w** one and Nm 7:19
one gold bowl **w** four ounces, Nm 7:20
one silver dish **w** three and a Nm 7:25
and one silver basin **w** one and Nm 7:25
one gold bowl **w** four ounces, Nm 7:26
one silver dish **w** three and a Nm 7:31
and one silver basin **w** one and Nm 7:31
one gold bowl **w** four ounces, Nm 7:32
one silver dish **w** three and a Nm 7:37
and one silver basin **w** one and Nm 7:37
one gold bowl **w** four ounces, Nm 7:38
one silver dish **w** three and a Nm 7:43
and one silver basin **w** one and Nm 7:43
one gold bowl **w** four ounces, Nm 7:44
one silver dish **w** three and a Nm 7:49
and one silver basin **w** one and Nm 7:49
one gold bowl **w** four ounces, Nm 7:50
one silver dish **w** three and a Nm 7:55
and one silver basin **w** one and Nm 7:55
one gold bowl **w** four ounces, Nm 7:56
one silver dish **w** three and a Nm 7:61
and one silver basin **w** one and Nm 7:61
one gold bowl **w** four ounces, Nm 7:62
one silver dish **w** three and a Nm 7:67
and one silver basin **w** one and Nm 7:67
one gold bowl **w** four ounces, Nm 7:68
one silver dish **w** three and a Nm 7:73
and one silver basin **w** one and Nm 7:73
one gold bowl **w** four ounces, Nm 7:74
one silver dish **w** three and a Nm 7:79
and one silver basin **w** one and Nm 7:79
one gold bowl **w** four ounces, Nm 7:80
and a bar of gold **w** 50 shekels, Jos 7:21
silver articles **w** 7,500 pounds, Ezr 8:26
each **w** about 100 pounds Rv 16:21

WEIGHS *(6)*
Your wrath **w** heavily on me; Ps 88:7
in a man's heart **w** it down, Pr 12:25
but the LORD **w** the motives. Pr 16:2
won't He who **w** hearts consider Pr 24:12
and it **w** heavily on humanity: Ec 6:1
Earth's rebellion **w** it down, Is 24:20

WEIGHT *(35)*
of length, **w**, or volume. Lv 19:35
and ration out your bread by **w**, Lv 26:26
The total ⌊**w**⌋ of the silver Nm 7:85
The total ⌊**w**⌋ of the gold bowls Nm 7:86
must have a full and honest **w**, Dt 25:15
The **w** of the gold earrings he Jdg 8:26
if I had the **w** of 1,000 pieces 2Sm 18:12
the **w** of the bronze was not 1Kg 7:47
The **w** of gold that came to 1Kg 10:14
the **w** of the bronze of all these 2Kg 25:16
the **w** of gold for all the 1Ch 28:14
the **w** of all the silver articles 1Ch 28:14
the **w** of the gold lampstands and 1Ch 28:15
the **w** of each lampstand 1Ch 28:15
the **w** of each silver lampstand 1Ch 28:15
the **w** of gold for each table for 1Ch 28:16
the **w** of each gold dish; 1Ch 28:17
the **w** of each silver bowl; 1Ch 28:17
the **w** of refined gold for the 1Ch 28:18
The **w** of the nails was 20 ounces 2Ch 3:9
that the **w** of the bronze was 2Ch 4:18
The **w** of gold that came to 2Ch 9:13
was ⌊verified⌋ by number and **w**, Ezr 8:34
and the total **w** was recorded at Ezr 8:34
the full **w** of misery will crush Jb 20:22
do not burst beneath their **w**. Jb 26:8
When God fixed the **w** of the wind Jb 28:25
an accurate **w** is His delight. Pr 11:1
the **w** of the bronze of all these Jr 52:20
worth their **w** in pure gold— Lm 4:2
day will be eight ounces by **w**; Ezk 4:10
rationed⌋ by **w** and in dread Ezk 4:16
pushed the lead **w** over its Zch 5:8
incomparable eternal **w** of glory. 2Co 4:17
lay aside every **w** and the sin Heb 12:1

WEIGHTS *(6)*
balances, honest **w**, an honest Lv 19:36
two different **w** in your bag, Dt 25:13
all the **w** in the bag are His Pr 16:11
Differing **w** and varying measures Pr 20:10
Differing **w** are detestable to Pr 20:23
scales or bags of deceptive **w**? Mc 6:11

WEIGHTY *(1)*
His letters are **w** and powerful, 2Co 10:10

WELCOME *(27)*
You **w** the one who joyfully does Is 64:5
anyone will not **w** you or listen Mt 10:14
hear the word, **w** it, and produce Mk 4:20
place does not **w** you and people Mk 6:11
welcomes Me does not **w** Me, Mk 9:37
Whoever does not **w** the kingdom Mk 10:15
when they hear, **w** the word with Lk 8:13
If they do not **w** you, when you Lk 9:5
they did not **w** Him, because He Lk 9:53
town, and they **w** you, eat the Lk 10:8
they don't **w** you, go out into Lk 10:10
will **w** me into their homes. Lk 16:4
they may **w** you into eternal Lk 16:9
Whoever does not **w** the kingdom Lk 18:17
My word is not **w** among you. Jn 8:37
Heaven must **w** Him until the Ac 3:21
disciples urging them to **w** him. Ac 18:27
How **w** are the feet of those who Rm 10:15
So you should **w** her in the Lord Rm 16:2
natural man does not **w** what 1Co 2:14
unclean thing, and I will **w** you. 2Co 6:17
w him in the Lord with all joy Php 2:29
offering, a **w** sacrifice, Php 4:18
if he comes to you, **w** him), Col 4:10
and don't say, "**W**," to him; 2Jn 10
one who says, "**W**," to him shares 2Jn 11
only refuses to **w** the brothers 3Jn 10

WELCOMED *(16)*
father saw him, he gladly **w** him. Jdg 19:3
the crowd **w** Him, for they were Lk 8:40
He **w** them, spoke to them about Lk 9:11
Martha **w** Him into her home Lk 10:38
came down and **w** Him joyfully. Lk 19:6
the Galileans **w** Him because they Jn 4:45
Samaria had **w** God's message, Ac 8:14
the Gentiles had **w** God's message Ac 11:1
they were **w** by the church, Ac 15:4
since they **w** the message with Ac 17:11
the brothers **w** us gladly. Ac 21:17
who **w** us and entertained us Ac 28:7
And he **w** all who visited him, Ac 28:30
you **w** the message with the joy 1Th 1:6
you **w** it not as a human message, 1Th 2:13
some have **w** angels as guests Heb 13:2

WELCOMES *(16)*
The one who **w** you welcomes Me, Mt 10:40
The one who welcomes you **w** Me, Mt 10:40
the one who **w** Me welcomes Him Mt 10:40
welcomes Me **w** Him who sent Me Mt 10:40
Anyone who **w** a prophet because Mt 10:41
And anyone who **w** a righteous Mt 10:41
whoever **w** one child like this Mt 18:5
child like this in My name **w** Me. Mt 18:5
Whoever **w** one little child such Mk 9:37
such as this in My name **w** Me. Mk 9:37
whoever **w** Me does not welcome Mk 9:37
Whoever **w** this little child in Lk 9:48
little child in My name **w** Me. Lk 9:48
whoever **w** Me welcomes Him who Lk 9:48
welcomes Me **w** Him who sent Me. Lk 9:48
This man **w** sinners and eats with Lk 15:2

WELDS *(1)*
and makes silver **w** ⌊for it⌋? Is 40:19

WELFARE *(6)*
Check on the **w** of your brothers 1Sm 17:18
to speak for the **w** of all his Est 10:3
for ⌊my own⌋ **w** that I had such Is 38:17
turn aside to ask about your **w**? Jr 15:5
Seek the **w** of the city I have Jr 29:7
plans for ⌊your⌋ **w**, not for Jr 29:11

WELL *(287)*
the night—as **w** as the stars. Gn 1:16
w as the tree of the knowledge Gn 2:9
the earth, as **w** as all mankind. Gn 7:21
as **w** as all the wildlife and all Gn 8:1
so it will go **w** for me because Gn 12:13
treated Abram **w** because of her, Gn 12:16
of Zeboiim, as **w** as the king of Gn 14:2
w as the Amorites who lived in Gn 14:7
w as the women and the ⌊other⌋ Gn 14:16
W of the Living One Who Sees Gn 16:14
w as one purchased with money, Gn 17:13
eyes, and she saw a **w** of water. Gn 21:19
of the water **w** that Abimelech's Gn 21:25
my witness that I dug this **w**." Gn 21:30
beside a **w** of water outside Gn 24:11
hurried to the **w** again to draw Gn 24:20
and found a **w** of spring water Gn 26:19
he named the **w** Quarrel because Gn 26:20
they dug another **w** and quarreled Gn 26:21
slaves also dug a **w** there. Gn 26:25
him about the **w** they had dug, Gn 26:32
looked and saw a **w** in a field. Gn 29:2
sheep were watered from this **w**. Gn 29:2
covered the opening of the **w**. Gn 29:2
the opening of the **w** and water Gn 29:3
Jacob asked the men at the **w**, Gn 29:4
"Is he **w**?" Jacob asked. "Yes," Gn 29:6
"**W**," Rachel said, "you can Gn 30:15
household, as **w** as his herds, Gn 36:6
But when all goes **w** for you, Gn 40:14
the steward said, "May you be **w**. Gn 43:23
if they were **w**, and he said, Gn 43:27
Your servant our father is **w**. Gn 43:28
as **w** as his daughter Dinah. Gn 46:15
of Midian, and sat down by a **w**. Ex 2:15
I know that he can speak **w**. Ex 4:14
the people as **w** as their foremen Ex 5:6
on the magicians as **w** as on all Ex 9:11

as **w** as every firstborn of the Ex 11:5
its head as **w** as its legs and Ex 12:9
and goats, as **w** as your cattle. Ex 20:24
female slave as **w** as the foreign Ex 23:12
tabernacle as **w** as the design Ex 25:9
as **w** as its pitchers and bowls Ex 25:29
tent pegs as **w** as all the tent Ex 27:19
as **w** as on his sons and their Ex 29:21
as **w** as his sons and their Ex 29:21
and lamps as **w** as the oil for Ex 35:14
w as the spice and oil for the Ex 35:28
linen, as **w** as blue, purple, Ex 36:8
as **w** as its bowls and pitchers Ex 37:16
the bands as **w** as the plating Ex 38:19
as **w** as the oil for the light; Ex 39:37
their fat—as **w** as the right Lv 8:25
as **w** as on his sons and their Lv 8:30
as **w** as his sons and their Lv 8:30
holy as **w** as from what is Lv 21:22
as **w** as the bowls and pitchers Nm 4:7
as **w** as its jars of oil by which Nm 4:9
will treat you **w**, for the LORD Nm 10:29
are seeking the priesthood as **w**. Nm 16:10
for you as **w** as your offspring. Nm 18:19
or drink ⌊any⌋ **w** water. Nm 20:17
the **w** the LORD told Moses about, Nm 21:16
Spring up, **w**—sing to it! Nm 21:17
princes dug the **w**; The nobles Nm 21:18
We won't drink ⌊any⌋ **w** water. Nm 21:22
as **w** as all their encampments, Nm 31:10
as **w** as Nebo and Baal-meon Nm 32:38
in it as **w** as its livestock Dt 13:15
family, and is **w** off with you, Dt 15:16
as **w** as the foreign resident, Dt 16:11
slave, as **w** as the Levite, Dt 16:14
said to me, 'They have spoken **w**. Dt 18:17
land⌋ as **w** as the dry ⌊land⌋. Dt 29:19
as **w** as venomous snakes that Dt 32:24
blessings as **w** as the curses— Jos 8:34
and Ekron, as **w** as the Avvites Jos 13:3
as **w** as large fortified cities. Jos 14:12
Jericho—as **w** as the Amorites Jos 24:11
town, and we will treat you **w**." Jdg 1:24
to eat, as **w** as no sheep, ox Jdg 6:4
replied, "Very **w**, when the LORD Jdg 8:7
as **w** as some thorns and briers Jdg 8:16
you as **w** as your sons and your Jdg 8:22
if you have done **w** by Jerubbaal Jdg 9:16
grain as **w** as the vineyards Jdg 15:5
as **w** as every female who has Jdg 21:11
as **w** as a three-year-old bull, 1Sm 1:24
as **w** as the young rams and the 1Sm 15:9
who plays **w** and bring him to 1Sm 16:17
people and Saul's servants as **w**. 1Sm 18:5
Jonathan spoke **w** of David to his 1Sm 19:4
men treated us **w**. When we were 1Sm 25:15
David, "Very **w**, I will appoint 1Sm 28:2
him back from the **w** of Sirah, 2Sm 3:26
hear what he has to say as **w**." 2Sm 17:5
He had a **w** in his courtyard, 2Sm 17:18
it over the mouth of the **w**, 2Sm 17:19
climbed out of the **w** and went 2Sm 17:21
king, "All is **w**," and then bowed 2Sm 18:28
Amasa, "Are you **w**, my brother?" 2Sm 20:9
drink from the **w** at the city 2Sm 23:15
water from the **w** at the gate 2Sm 23:16
"Very **w**," Bathsheba replied. 1Kg 2:18
you might as **w** ask the kingship 1Kg 2:22
cut to size, as **w** as cedar wood. 1Kg 7:11
as **w** as the inner courtyard of 1Kg 7:12
you have done **w** to have this 1Kg 8:18
and children are mine as **w**!' " 1Kg 20:3
answered, "**W**, she has no son, 2Kg 4:14
you have done **w** in carrying out 2Kg 10:30
him down, as **w** as Argob and 2Kg 15:25
as **w** as the priests and the 2Kg 23:2
and it will go **w** for you." 2Kg 25:24
donkeys—as **w** as 100,000 people 1Ch 5:21
sanctuary, as **w** as the fine 1Ch 9:29
water from the **w** at the city 1Ch 11:17
water from the **w** at the gate 1Ch 11:18
as **w** as the singers and 1Ch 15:27
w as the rows ⌊of the bread of 1Ch 23:29
the wood, as **w** as onyx, ⌊stones 1Ch 29:2
all of King David's sons as **w**, 1Ch 29:24
you have done **w** to have this 2Ch 6:8
as **w** as those from ⌊the tribes 2Ch 15:9
all his brothers as **w** as some of 2Ch 21:4

as **w** as in Ephraim and Manasseh, 2Ch 31:1
as **w** as the priests and the 2Ch 34:30
as **w** as the freewill offerings Ezr 3:5
as **w** as 12 male goats as a sin Ezr 6:17
as **w** as the teachers Joiarib and Ezr 8:16
the Serpent's **W** and the Dung Neh 2:13
as **w** as to the Tower of the Neh 3:11
as **w** as my brothers and my Neh 5:10
as **w** as a pound of silver. Neh 5:15
as **w** as guests from the Neh 5:17
w as their 245 male and female Neh 7:67
accompanying me, as **w** as Neh 12:40
priesthood as **w** as the covenant Neh 13:29
had happened as **w** as the exact Est 4:7
this letter as **w** as what they Est 9:26
"Very **w**," the LORD told Satan, Jb 1:12
"Very **w**," the LORD told Satan, Jb 2:6
as **w** as the breath of all Jb 12:10
it go **w** if He examined you? Jb 13:9
they saw me, they spoke **w** of me. Jb 29:11
as **w** as animals in the wild, Ps 8:7
sorrow—my whole being as **w**. Ps 31:9
you when you do **w** for yourself— Ps 49:18
You have treated Your servant **w**, Ps 119:65
happy, and it will go **w** for you. Ps 128:2
and I know ⌊this⌋ very **w**. Ps 139:14
Our cattle will be **w** fed. Ps 144:14
young men as **w** as young women, Ps 148:12
water flowing from your own **w**. Pr 5:15
of the righteous ⌊turns out⌋ **w**, Pr 11:23
a forbidden woman is a narrow **w**; Pr 23:27
fear the LORD, as **w** as the king, Pr 24:21
but it will go **w** with those who Pr 24:25
muddied spring or a polluted **w**. Pr 25:26
Know **w** the condition of your Pr 27:23
made the one as **w** as the other, Ec 7:14
that it will go **w** with Ec 8:12
will not go **w** with the wicked, Ec 8:13
the wheel is broken into the **w**; Ec 12:6
a **w** of flowing water streaming Sg 4:15
delicacy—new as **w** as old. Sg 7:13
that it will go **w** ⌊for them⌋, Is 3:10
and to remove the beard as **w**. Is 7:20
of the poor will be **w** fed, Is 14:30
as **w** as those dispersed in the Is 27:13
is the life of my spirit as **w**; Is 38:16
As a **w** gushes out its water, Jr 6:7
on the gang of young men as **w**. Jr 6:11
⌊their⌋ fields and wives as **w**, Jr 6:12
so that it may go **w** with you." Jr 7:23
though they speak **w** of you. Jr 12:6
in this place as **w** as concerning Jr 16:3
⌊as **w** as My⌋ faithful love and Jr 16:5
then it went **w** with him. Jr 22:15
poor and needy, then it went **w**. Jr 22:16
so it may go **w** for you and you Jr 38:20
and it will go **w** for you. Jr 40:9
w as the Chaldean soldiers who Jr 41:3
you so that it may go **w** with us. Jr 42:6
from Babylon as **w** as him who Jr 50:16
as **w** as the rest of the people Jr 52:15
as **w** as my hope from the LORD. Lm 3:18
the cup will pass to you as **w**; Lm 4:21
as **w** as all the idols of the Ezk 8:10
as **w** as the ⌊older⌋ women and Ezk 9:6
as **w** as the fulfillment of every Ezk 12:23
you loved as **w** as all those you Ezk 16:37
for its height as **w** as its many Ezk 19:11
Cook the meat **w** and mix in the Ezk 24:10
⌊as **w** as⌋ their sons and Ezk 24:25
as **w** as his troops and the many Ezk 38:22
and width, as **w** as all their Ezk 42:11
as **w** as a holy area for the Ezk 45:4
w as a gallon of oil for every Ezk 46:5
as **w** as six lambs and a ram Ezk 46:6
as **w** as the covenant prince. Dn 11:22
left, as **w** as many animals?" Jnh 4:11
of Hosts as **w** as the prophets Zch 7:3
borders it, as **w** as Tyre and Zch 9:2
let him have your coat as **w**. Mt 5:40
Father will forgive you as **w**. Mt 6:14
Those who are **w** don't need a Mt 9:12
touch His robe, I'll be made **w**!" Mt 9:21
"Your faith has made you **w**." Mt 9:22
woman was made **w** from that Mt 9:22
it were made perfectly **w**. Mt 14:36
master said to him, '**W** done, Mt 25:21
master said to him, '**W** done, Mt 25:23

Those who are **w** don't need a Mk 2:17
wine is lost as **w** as the skins. Mk 2:22
her so she can get **w** and live." Mk 5:23
His robes, I'll be made **w**!" Mk 5:28
your faith has made you **w**. Mk 5:34
Jesus' name had become **w** known. Mk 6:14
who touched it was made **w**. Mk 6:56
He has done everything **w**! Mk 7:37
these were to be served as **w**. Mk 8:7
saw that Jesus answered them **w**, Mk 12:28
the sick, and they will get **w**." Mk 16:18
of them were **w** along in years. Lk 1:7
my wife is **w** along in years." Lk 1:18
She was **w** along in years, having Lk 2:36
all speaking **w** of Him and were Lk 4:22
by unclean spirits were made **w**. Lk 6:18
when all people speak **w** of you, Lk 6:26
it, because it was **w** built. Lk 6:48
your faith has made you **w**. Lk 8:48
and she will be made **w**." Lk 8:50
you will all perish as **w**! Lk 13:3
you will all perish as **w**!" Lk 13:5
whose son or ox falls into a **w**, Lk 14:5
Your faith has made you **w**." Lk 17:19
'**W** done, good slave!' Lk 19:17
"**W** then," He told them, "give Lk 20:25
Teacher, You have spoken **w**." Lk 20:39
invited to the wedding as **w**. Jn 2:2
Jacob's **w** was there, and Jesus, Jn 4:6
His journey, sat down at the **w**. Jn 4:6
a bucket, and the **w** is deep. Jn 4:11
He gave us the **w** and drank from Jn 4:12
him will become a **w** of water Jn 4:14
to him, "Do you want to get **w**?" Jn 5:6
the man got **w**, picked up his Jn 5:9
The man who made me **w** told me, Jn 5:11
said to him, "See, you are **w**. Jn 5:14
it was Jesus who had made him **w**. Jn 5:15
a man entirely **w** on the Sabbath? Jn 7:23
fallen asleep, he will get **w**." Jn 11:12
This is **w** said, for I am. Jn 13:13
these things, you will do **w**. Ac 15:29
as **w** as a number of the leading Ac 17:4
Greek women as **w** as men. Ac 17:12
he said, "I must see Rome as **w**!" Ac 19:21
as **w** as the workers engaged in Ac 19:25
as even you can see very **w**. Ac 25:10
they know full **w** God's just Rm 1:32
from God, as **w** as righteousness, 1Co 1:30
keep his own virgin, will do **w**. 1Co 7:37
who marries his virgin does **w**, 1Co 7:38
you may very **w** be giving thanks 1Co 14:17
open to your consciences as **w**. 2Co 5:11
But now finish the task as **w**, 2Co 8:11
were running **w**. Who prevented Gl 5:7
that it may go **w** with you and Eph 6:3
as **w** as your messenger and Php 2:25
you did **w** by sharing with me in Php 4:14
know very **w** that the Day 1Th 5:2
who have served **w** as deacons 1Tm 3:13
and is **w** known for good works— 1Tm 5:10
Carpus, as **w** as the scrolls, 2Tm 4:13
for himself as **w** as for the Heb 5:3
must be a change of law as **w**. Heb 7:12
as **w** as bonds and imprisonment. Heb 11:36
as yourself, you are doing **w**. Jms 2:8
warm, and eat **w**," but you don't Jms 2:16
one; you do **w**. The demons also Jms 2:19
You will do **w** to pay attention 2Pt 1:19
the Son has the Father as **w**. 1Jn 2:23
righteous, you know this as **w**: 1Jn 2:29
You will do **w** to send them on 3Jn 6
light, and the night as **w**. Rv 8:12

WELL'S *(2)*

placed back on the **w** opening. Gn 29:3
is rolled from the **w** opening. Gn 29:8

WELL-BEING *(7)*

LORD your God for your own **w**. Jos 23:11
come to seek the **w** of the Neh 2:10
who wants His servant's **w**." Ps 35:27
Guarantee Your servant's **w**; Ps 119:122
many days, a full life, and **w**. Pr 3:2
pray for the **w** of these people Jr 14:11
seeking the **w** of this people, Jr 38:4

WELL-BUILT *(1)*

Now Joseph was **w** and handsome. Gn 39:6

WELL-CONSTRUCTED *(1)*
Build a **w** altar to the LORD your Jdg 6:26

WELL-ENDOWED *(1)*
Egyptian men, your **w** neighbors, Ezk 16:26

WELL-FED *(10)*
w cows came up from the Nile and Gn 41:2
cows ate the healthy, **w** cows. Gn 41:4
when seven **w**, healthy-looking Gn 41:18
cows ate the first seven **w** cows. Gn 41:20
His body is **w**, and his bones are Jb 21:24
die, and their bodies are **w**. Ps 73:4
rams and the fat of **w** cattle; Is 1:11
disease on the **w** of Assyria, Is 10:16
are **w**, eager stallions, each Jr 5:8
whether **w** or hungry, whether Php 4:12

WELL-FORMED *(1)*
tree, beautiful with **w** fruit. Jr 11:16

WELL-FORTIFIED *(1)*
ramp, and capture a **w** city. Dn 11:15

WELL-KNEADED *(2)*
you are to bring it **w**. Lv 6:21
and **w** cakes of fine flour mixed Lv 7:12

WELL-PLEASING *(1)*
and to be **w**, not talking back Ti 2:9

WELL-ROOTED *(1)*
violent man **w** like a flourishing Ps 37:35

WELL-SUPPLIED *(1)*
and took possession of **w** houses, Neh 9:25

WELL-TRAINED *(1)*
Ephraim is a **w** young cow that Hs 10:11

WELL-WATERED *(5)*
as Zoar was **w** everywhere like Gn 13:10
of the **w** ⌊land⌋ as well as Dt 29:19
that no ⌊other⌋ **w** trees would Ezk 31:14
of Eden, all the **w** trees, the Ezk 31:16
200 from the **w** pastures of Ezk 45:15

WELLS *(6)*
up all the **w** that his father's Gn 26:15
the water **w** that had been dug Gn 26:18
w dug that you did not dig, Dt 6:11
I dug ⌊**w**⌋, and I drank foreign 2Kg 19:24
in the desert and dug many **w**. 2Ch 26:10
I dug ⌊**w**⌋ and drank water. Is 37:25

WELTS *(1)*
wounds, **w**, and festering Is 1:6

WENT *(1108)*
(See pp. xi-xii.)

WEPT *(60)*
as she sat nearby, she **w** loudly. Gn 21:16
my father!" And Esau **w** loudly. Gn 27:38
kissed Rachel and **w** loudly. Gn 29:11
and kissed him. Then they **w**. Gn 33:4
And his father **w** for him. Gn 37:35
He turned away from them and **w**. Gn 42:24
But he **w** so loudly that the Gn 45:2
his arms around Benjamin and **w**, Gn 45:14
and Benjamin **w** on his shoulder. Gn 45:14
each of his brothers as he **w**, Gn 45:15
him, and **w** for a long time Gn 46:29
father's face, **w** and kissed him. Gn 50:1
they lamented and **w** loudly, Gn 50:10
Joseph **w** when their message Gn 50:17
and the people **w** that night. Nm 14:1
returned, you **w** before the LORD Dt 1:45
Israelites **w** for Moses in the Dt 34:8
Israelites, the people **w** loudly. Jdg 2:4
w the whole seven days of the Jdg 14:17
w before the LORD until evening, Jdg 20:23
where they **w** and sat before Jdg 20:26
They **w** loudly and bitterly, Jdg 21:2
kissed them, and they **w** loudly. Ru 1:9
Again they **w** loudly, and Orpah Ru 1:14
Hannah **w** and would not eat. 1Sm 1:7
the LORD and **w** with many tears 1Sm 1:10
The people **w** because the LORD 1Sm 6:19
to the people, all **w** aloud. 1Sm 11:4
other and **w** with each other, 1Sm 20:41
each other, though David **w** more. 1Sm 20:41
David my son?" Then Saul **w** 1Sm 24:16
troops with him **w** loudly until 1Sm 30:4
mourned, **w**, and fasted until 2Sm 1:12
king **w** aloud at Abner's tomb. 2Sm 3:32
Abner's tomb. All the people **w**, 2Sm 3:32
all the people **w** over him even 2Sm 3:34
you fasted and **w**, but when he 2Sm 12:21
fasted and **w** because I thought, 2Sm 12:22
sons entered and **w** loudly. 2Sm 13:36
his servants also **w** bitterly. 2Sm 13:36
up to the gate chamber and **w**. 2Sm 18:33
was ashamed. The man of God **w**, 2Kg 8:11
went down and **w** over him and 2Kg 13:14
And Hezekiah **w** bitterly. 2Kg 20:3
your clothes and **w** before Me, 2Kg 22:19
your clothes and **w** before Me, 2Ch 34:27
w loudly when they saw the Ezr 3:12
The people also **w** bitterly. Ezr 10:1
these words, I sat down and **w**. Neh 1:4
They fasted, **w**, and lamented, Est 4:3
at his feet, **w**, and begged him Est 8:3
They **w** aloud, and each man tore Jb 2:12
Have I not **w** for those who have Jb 30:25
we sat down and **w** when we Ps 137:1
And Hezekiah **w** bitterly. Is 38:3
he **w** and sought His favor. Hs 12:4
he went outside and **w** bitterly. Mt 26:75
and saw the city, He **w** over it, Lk 19:41
he went outside and **w** bitterly. Lk 22:62
Jesus **w**. Jn 11:35

WERE *(2457)*
(See pp. xi-xii.)

WEREN'T *(11)*
(See pp. xi-xii.)

WEST *(107)*
Bethel on the **w** and Ai on the Gn 12:8
north and south, east and **w**, Gn 13:14
will spread out toward the **w**, Gn 28:14
the wind to a strong **w** wind, Ex 10:19
six planks for the **w** side of the Ex 26:22
side of the tabernacle on the **w**. Ex 26:27
courtyard on the **w** side 75 feet Ex 27:12
and for the **w** side of the Ex 36:27
back of the tabernacle on the **w**. Ex 36:32
hangings on the **w** side were 75 Ex 38:12
camp on the **w** side under their Nm 2:18
the tabernacle on the **w** side, Nm 3:23
1,000 yards for the **w** side, Nm 35:5
top of Pisgah and look to the **w**, Dt 3:27
to the **w** and the south. Dt 33:23
and **w** to the Mediterranean Sea. Jos 1:4
the Jordan to the **w** and all the Jos 5:1
Bethel and Ai, to the **w** of Ai. Jos 8:9
and Ai, to the **w** of the city. Jos 8:12
rear guard to the **w** of the city. Jos 8:13
those who were **w** of the Jordan Jos 9:1
and the Slopes of Dor to the **w**, Jos 11:2
Canaanites in the east and **w**, Jos 11:3
land beyond the Jordan to the **w**, Jos 12:7
the Valley of Hinnom on the **w**, Jos 15:8
On the **w** side, from the hill Jos 18:14
This was the **w** side ⌊of their Jos 18:14
To the **w**, the boundary turned to Jos 19:34
Asher on the **w**, and Judah at Jos 19:34
on the **w** side of the Jordan. Jos 22:7
it is **w** of Kiriath-jearim. Jdg 18:12
out of their places **w** of Geba. Jdg 20:33
from the road **w** of him from the 2Sm 13:34
over everything **w** of the 1Kg 4:24
all the kings **w** of the Euphrates 1Kg 4:24
three facing **w**, three facing 1Kg 7:25
Gezer and its villages to the **w**, 1Ch 7:28
east, **w**, north, and south. 1Ch 9:24
to the east and to the **w**. 1Ch 12:15
Hosah it was the **w** ⌊gate⌋ and 1Ch 26:16
As for the court on the **w**, 1Ch 26:18
duties in Israel **w** of the Jordan 1Ch 26:30
three facing **w**, three facing 2Ch 4:4
city of David from **w** of Gihon in 2Ch 33:14
the region **w** of the Euphrates Ezr 4:10
from the region **w** of the Ezr 4:11
any possession **w** of the Ezr 4:16
in the region **w** of the Euphrates Ezr 4:17
of the region **w** of the Euphrates Ezr 5:3
of the region **w** of the Euphrates Ezr 5:6
of the region **w** of the Euphrates Ezr 6:6
of the region **w** of the Euphrates Ezr 6:8
of the region **w** of the Euphrates Ezr 6:13
in the region **w** of the Euphrates Ezr 7:21
in the region **w** of the Euphrates Ezr 7:25
the region **w** of the Euphrates, Ezr 8:36
of the region **w** of the Euphrates Neh 2:7
of the region **w** of the Euphrates Neh 2:9
of the region **w** of the Euphrates Neh 3:7
Those in the **w** are appalled at Jb 18:20
and if I go **w**, I cannot perceive Jb 23:8
the earth from east to **w**. Ps 50:1
make east and **w** shout for joy. Ps 65:8
the east, the **w**, or the desert, Ps 75:6
far as the east is from the **w**, Ps 103:12
east and the **w**, from the north Ps 107:3
from the **w** have consumed Is 9:12
coasts and islands of the **w**— Is 11:11
the Philistine flank to the **w**. Is 11:14
proclaim in the **w** the majesty Is 24:14
islands of the **w** ⌊honor⌋ the Is 24:15
and gather you from the **w**. Is 43:5
from the north and from the **w**, Is 49:12
the name of the LORD in the **w**, Is 59:19
yard toward the **w** was 122 and a Ezk 41:12
facing the temple yard to the **w**, Ezk 41:15
he turned to the **w** side and Ezk 42:19
to the **w** on the west side Ezk 45:7
to the west on the **w** side and to Ezk 45:7
On the **w** side the Mediterranean Ezk 47:20
from the east side to the **w**, Ezk 48:2
from the east side to the **w**, Ezk 48:3
from the east side to the **w**, Ezk 48:4
from the east side to the **w**, Ezk 48:5
from the east side to the **w**, Ezk 48:6
from the east side to the **w**, Ezk 48:7
from the east side to the **w**, Ezk 48:8
from the east side to the **w**. Ezk 48:8
a half ⌊miles⌋ on the **w** side. Ezk 48:16
east, and 425 ⌊feet⌋ to the **w**. Ezk 48:17
and one-third ⌊miles⌋ to the **w**. Ezk 48:18
From the east side to the **w**, Ezk 48:23
from the east side to the **w**, Ezk 48:24
from the east side to the **w**, Ezk 48:25
from the east side to the **w**, Ezk 48:26
from the east side to the **w**, Ezk 48:27
On the **w** side, which is one and Ezk 48:34
I saw the ram charging to the **w**, Dn 8:4
coming from the **w** across the Dn 8:5
will come trembling from the **w**. Hs 11:10
the east and the land of the **w**. Zch 8:7
be split in half from east to **w**, Zch 14:4
many will come from east and **w**, Mt 8:11
and flashes as far as the **w**, Mt 24:27
you see a cloud rising in the **w**, Lk 12:54
They will come from east and **w**, Lk 13:29
south, and three gates on the **w**. Rv 21:13

WESTERN *(12)*
Your **w** border will be the Nm 34:6
this will be your **w** border. Nm 34:6
beyond the **w** road in the land of Dt 11:30
Now the **w** border was the Jos 15:12
or⌋ settle at the **w** limits, Ps 139:9
yard and the ⌊**w**⌋ building, Ezk 42:10
portions from the **w** boundary to Ezk 45:7
a place there at the far **w** end. Ezk 46:19
This will be the **w** side. Ezk 47:20
miles⌋ wide on the **w** side, Ezk 48:10
as far as the **w** border. Ezk 48:21
the other half toward the **w** sea, Zch 14:8

WESTWARD *(10)*
border turned **w** from Baalah to Jos 15:10
then descended **w** to the border Jos 16:3
the border went **w** from Jos 16:6
border went **w** along the Brook Jos 16:8
through the hill country **w**, Jos 18:12
and the border extended **w**; Jos 18:15
border went up **w** to Maralah, Jos 19:11
Mishal and reached **w** to Carmel Jos 19:26
from the Jordan **w** to the Jos 23:4
downward and **w** to the city of 2Ch 32:30

WET *(1)*
put it on, but don't get it **w**." Jr 13:1

WHAT *(2292)*
(See pp. xi-xii.)

WHAT'S *(14)*
(See pp. xi-xii.)

WHATEVER *(190)*
(See pp. xi-xii.)

WHATSOEVER *(2)*
but it was ruined—of no use **w**. Jr 13:7
this underwear, of no use **w**. Jr 13:10

WHEAT *(45)*
out during the **w** harvest and Gn 30:14
but the **w** and the spelt were not Ex 9:32
Make them out of fine **w** flour, Ex 29:2

firstfruits of the **w** harvest, Ex 34:22
land of **w**, barley, vines, figs, Dt 8:8
with the choicest grains of **w**; Dt 32:14
was threshing **w** in the wine vat Jdg 6:11
on, during the **w** harvest, Samson Jdg 15:1
barley and the **w** harvests were Ru 2:23
were harvesting **w** in the valley, 1Sm 6:13
Isn't the **w** harvest today? 1Sm 12:17
as if to get **w** and stabbed him 2Sm 4:6
also brought⌋ **w**, barley, flour, 2Sm 17:28
bushels of **w** as food for his 1Kg 5:11
was threshing **w** when he turned 1Ch 21:20
and the **w** for the grain offering 1Ch 21:23
100,000 bushels of **w** flour, 2Ch 2:10
my lord send the **w**, barley, oil, 2Ch 2:15
50,000 bushels of **w**, and 50,000 2Ch 27:5
God of heaven, or **w**, salt, wine, Ezr 6:9
500 bushels of **w**, 550 gallons of Ezr 7:22
grow instead of **w** and stinkweed Jb 31:40
feed Israel with the best **w**. Ps 81:16
satisfies you with the finest **w**. Ps 147:14
waist is a mound of **w** surrounded Sg 7:2
plants **w** in rows and barley in Is 28:25
They have sown **w** but harvested Jr 12:13
in the field—**w**, barley, oil, Jr 41:8
Also take **w**, barley, beans, Ezk 4:9
They exchanged **w** from Minnith, Ezk 27:17
five bushels of **w** and three Ezk 45:13
over the **w** and the barley, Jl 1:11
the Sabbath, so we may market **w**? Am 8:5
and even sell the **w** husks!" Am 8:6
and gather His **w** into the barn. Mt 3:12
weeds among the **w**, and left. Mt 13:25
also uproot the **w** with them. Mt 13:29
but store the **w** in my barn.' " Mt 13:30
and gather the **w** into His barn, Lk 3:17
'A hundred measures of **w**,' Lk 16:7
has asked to sift you like **w**. Lk 22:31
Unless a grain of **w** falls into Jn 12:24
perhaps of **w** or another grain. 1Co 15:37
A quart of **w** for a denarius, Rv 6:6
olive oil, fine **w** flour, and Rv 18:13

WHEEL *(15)*
and the **w** axles were part of the 1Kg 7:32
each **w** was 27 inches tall. 1Kg 7:32
the threshing **w** over them. Pr 20:26
and the **w** is broken into the Ec 12:6
and a cart **w** is not rolled over Is 28:27
Though the **w** of ⌊the farmer's⌋ Is 28:28
he was, working away at the **w**. Jr 18:3
there was one **w** on the ground Ezk 1:15
was like a **w** within a wheel. Ezk 1:16
was like a wheel within a **w**. Ezk 1:16
went in and stood beside a **w**. Ezk 10:6
the cherubim, one **w** beside each Ezk 10:9
form, like a **w** within a wheel. Ezk 10:10
form, like a wheel within a **w**. Ezk 10:10
of the whip and rumble of the **w**, Nah 3:2

WHEELS *(27)*
their chariot **w** to swerve and Ex 14:25
had four bronze **w** with bronze 1Kg 7:30
There were four **w** under the 1Kg 7:32
similar to that of chariot **w**: 1Kg 7:33
their ⌊chariot⌋ **w** are like a Is 5:28
and the clatter of their **w**, Jr 47:3
appearance of the **w** and their Ezk 1:16
moved, the **w** moved beside them, Ezk 1:19
from the earth, the **w** also rose. Ezk 1:19
The **w** rose alongside them, Ezk 1:20
living creatures was in the **w**. Ezk 1:20
creatures moved, the **w** moved; Ezk 1:21
stood still, the **w** stood still; Ezk 1:21
the **w** rose alongside them, Ezk 1:21
living creatures was in the **w**. Ezk 1:21
the sound of the **w** beside them, Ezk 3:13
there were four **w** beside the Ezk 10:9
The luster of the **w** was like the Ezk 10:9
and the **w** that the four of them Ezk 10:12
As I listened the **w** were called Ezk 10:13
moved, the **w** moved beside them, Ezk 10:16
then the **w** did not veer away Ezk 10:16
stood still, the **w** stood still, Ezk 10:17
ascended, the **w** ascended with Ezk 10:17
the **w** were beside them as they Ezk 10:19
with the **w** beside them, Ezk 11:22
its **w** were blazing fire. Dn 7:9

WHEELS' *(1)*
The **w** design was similar to that 1Kg 7:33

WHEELWORK *(3)*
Go inside the **w** beneath the Ezk 10:2
Take fire from inside the **w**, Ezk 10:6
the wheels were called "the **w**." Ezk 10:13

WHEN *(2702)*
(See pp. xi-xii.)

WHENEVER *(79)*
(See pp. xi-xii.)

WHERE *(618)*
(See pp. xi-xii.)

WHEREVER *(68)*
(See pp. xi-xii.)

WHETHER *(98)*
(See pp. xi-xii.)

WHICH *(505)*
(See pp. xi-xii.)

WHILE *(444)*
(See pp. xi-xii.)

WHIM *(1)*
and on a **w** they hamstring oxen. Gn 49:6

WHIP *(4)*
A **w** for the horse, a bridle for Pr 26:3
will brandish a **w** against him as Is 10:26
The crack of the **w** and rumble of Nah 3:2
After making a **w** out of cords, Jn 2:15

WHIPPED *(2)*
I will have Him **w** and ⌊then⌋ Lk 23:16
I will have Him **w** and ⌊then⌋ Lk 23:22

WHIPS *(8)*
father disciplined you with **w**, 1Kg 12:11
you with barbed **w**.' " 1Kg 12:11
father disciplined you with **w**, 1Kg 12:14
discipline you with barbed **w**." 1Kg 12:14
father disciplined you with **w**, 2Ch 10:11
whips, but I, with barbed **w**.' " 2Ch 10:11
father disciplined you with **w**, 2Ch 10:14
whips, but I, with barbed **w**." 2Ch 10:14

WHIRL *(3)*
It will **w** about the head of the Jr 23:19
it will **w** about the head of the Jr 30:23
A sword will **w** through his Hs 11:6

WHIRLING *(2)*
w sword to guard the way to the Gn 3:24
Wrath has gone forth, a **w** storm. Jr 23:19

WHIRLWIND *(15)*
take Elijah up to heaven in a **w**. 2Kg 2:1
went up into heaven in the **w**. 2Kg 2:11
me with a **w** and multiplies my Jb 9:17
LORD answered Job from the **w**. Jb 38:1
LORD answered Job from the **w**: Jb 40:6
of Your thunder was in the **w**; Ps 77:18
your calamity comes like a **w**, Pr 1:27
When the **w** passes, the wicked Pr 10:25
chariot⌋ wheels are like a **w**. Is 5:28
and a **w** carries them away like Is 40:24
His chariots are like the **w**— Is 66:15
there was a **w** coming from the Ezk 1:4
sow the wind and reap the **w**. Hs 8:7
His path is in the **w** and storm, Nah 1:3
water, mists driven by a **w**. 2Pt 2:17

WHIRRING *(2)*
W insects will take possession Dt 28:42
he laughs at the **w** of a javelin. Jb 41:29

WHISPER *(5)*
there was a voice, a soft **w**. 1Kg 19:12
my ears caught a **w** of it. Jb 4:12
All who hate me **w** together about Ps 41:7
speech will **w** from the dust. Is 29:4
What you hear in a **w**, proclaim Mt 10:27

WHISPERED *(2)*
they poured out **w** ⌊prayers Is 26:16
and what you have **w** in an ear in Lk 12:3

WHISPERING *(1)*
servants were **w** to each other, 2Sm 12:19

WHISTLE *(2)*
the LORD will **w** to the fly that Is 7:18
I will **w** and gather them because Zch 10:8

WHISTLES *(1)*
distant nations and **w** for them Is 5:26

WHITE *(63)*
every one that had any **w** on it— Gn 30:35
exposing **w** stripes on the Gn 30:37
baskets of **w** bread were on my Gn 40:16
seed, was **w**, and tasted like Ex 16:31
the **w** owl, the desert owl, the Lv 11:18
has turned **w** and the infection Lv 13:3
of his body is **w** and does not Lv 13:4
the hair in it has not turned **w**, Lv 13:4
If there is a **w** swelling on the Lv 13:10
skin that has turned the hair **w**, Lv 13:10
Since he has turned totally **w**, Lv 13:13
raw flesh changes and turns **w**, Lv 13:16
if the infection has turned **w**, Lv 13:17
and a **w** swelling or a Lv 13:19
and the hair in it has turned **w**, Lv 13:20
if there is no **w** hair in it, Lv 13:21
a reddish-white or **w** spot, Lv 13:24
spot has turned **w** and the spot Lv 13:25
there is no **w** hair in the spot Lv 13:26
or a woman has **w** spots on the Lv 13:38
the skin of the body are dull **w**, Lv 13:39
became diseased, as ⌊**w**⌋ as snow. Nm 12:10
the long-eared owl, the **w** owl, Dt 14:16
You who ride on **w** donkeys, Jdg 5:10
presence diseased—⌊**w**⌋ as snow. 2Kg 5:27
W and violet linen hangings were Est 1:6
with fine **w** and purple linen Est 1:6
clothed in royal purple and **w**, Est 8:15
Is there flavor in an egg **w**? Jb 6:6
would think the deep had **w** hair! Jb 41:32
your clothes be **w** all the time, Ec 9:8
they will be as **w** as snow; Is 1:18
in wine from Helbon and **w** wool. Ezk 27:18
His clothing was **w** like snow, Dn 7:9
its branches have turned **w**. Jl 1:7
were red, sorrel, and **w** horses. Zch 1:8
the third chariot **w** horses, Zch 6:3
the **w** horses are going after Zch 6:6
make a single hair **w** or black. Mt 5:36
became as **w** as the light. Mt 17:2
and his robe was as **w** as snow. Mt 28:3
extremely **w** as no launderer on Mk 9:3
dressed in a long **w** robe sitting Mk 16:5
His clothes became dazzling **w**. Lk 9:29
two angels in **w** sitting there, Jn 20:12
two men in **w** clothes stood Ac 1:10
head and hair were **w** like wool— Rv 1:14
like wool—**w** as snow, His eyes Rv 1:14
I will also give him a **w** stone, Rv 2:17
and they will walk with Me in **w**, Rv 3:4
will be dressed in **w** clothes, Rv 3:5
and **w** clothes so that you may be Rv 3:18
24 elders dressed in **w** clothes, Rv 4:4
looked, and there was a **w** horse. Rv 6:2
So a **w** robe was given to each of Rv 6:11
were robed in **w** with palm Rv 7:9
Who are these people robed in **w**, Rv 7:13
and made them **w** in the blood Rv 7:14
and there was a **w** cloud, and One Rv 14:14
opened, and there was a **w** horse! Rv 19:11
heaven followed Him on **w** horses, Rv 19:14
horses, wearing pure **w** linen. Rv 19:14
I saw a great **w** throne and One Rv 20:11

WHITEN *(1)*
launderer on earth could **w** them. Mk 9:3

WHITER *(3)*
and his teeth are **w** than milk. Gn 49:12
and I will be **w** than snow. Ps 51:7
brighter than snow, **w** than milk; Lm 4:7

WHITEST *(1)*
hair of His head like **w** wool. Dn 7:9

WHITEWASH *(5)*
a wall they plaster it with **w**, Ezk 13:10
is the coat of **w** that you put on Ezk 13:12
plastered with **w** and knock it to Ezk 13:14
those who plaster it with **w**, Ezk 13:15
plaster with **w** for them by Ezk 22:28

WHITEWASHED *(2)*
You are like **w** tombs, which Mt 23:27
going to strike you, you **w** wall! Ac 23:3

WHO *(4918)*
(See pp. xi-xii.)

WHO'S *(1)*
king asked, "**W** in the court?" Est 6:4

WHOEVER *(213)*
(See pp. xi-xii.)

WHOLE *(342)*
on the face of the **w** earth. Gn 7:3
under the **w** sky were covered. Gn 7:19

but the name of the **w** will rot. Pr 10:7
the mouth of the **w** conceals Pr 10:11
activity of the **w** leads to sin. Pr 10:16
the heart of the **w** is of little Pr 10:20
What the **w** dreads will come to Pr 10:24
passes, the **w** are no more, Pr 10:25
years of the **w** are cut short. Pr 10:27
of the **w** comes to nothing. Pr 10:28
but the **w** will not remain on the Pr 10:30
mouth of the **w**, ⌊only⌋ what is Pr 10:32
but the **w** person will fall Pr 11:5
When the **w** dies, his expectation Pr 11:7
in his place, the **w** goes in. Pr 11:8
and when the **w** die, there is Pr 11:10
torn down by the mouth of the **w**. Pr 11:11
The **w** man earns an empty wage, Pr 11:18
assured that the **w** will not go Pr 11:21
the hope of the **w** ⌊leads to⌋ Pr 11:23
how much more the **w** and sinful. Pr 11:31
from the **w** ⌊leads to⌋ deceit Pr 12:5
The words of the **w** are a deadly Pr 12:6
The **w** are overthrown and perish, Pr 12:7
acts of the **w** are cruel. Pr 12:10
The **w** desire what evil men have, Pr 12:12
but the **w** are full of misery. Pr 12:21
but the ways of **w** men lead them Pr 12:26
but the **w** act disgustingly and Pr 13:5
lamp of the **w** is extinguished Pr 13:9
w messenger falls into trouble, Pr 13:17
the stomach of the **w** is empty. Pr 13:25
The house of the **w** will be Pr 14:11
are good, the **w**, at the gates Pr 14:19
The **w** are thrown down by their Pr 14:32
observing the **w** and the good. Pr 15:3
accompanies the income of the **w**. Pr 15:6
of the **w** is detestable to Pr 15:8
LORD detests the way of the **w**, Pr 15:9
mouth of the **w** blurts out evil Pr 15:28
The LORD is far from the **w**, Pr 15:29
even the **w** for the day of Pr 16:4
W behavior is detestable to Pr 16:12
A **w** person listens to malicious Pr 17:4
w man secretly takes a bribe to Pr 17:23
When a **w** man comes, shame does Pr 18:3
and a **w** mouth swallows iniquity. Pr 19:28
separates out the **w** and drives Pr 20:26
The lamp that guides the **w**— Pr 21:4
violence of the **w** sweeps them Pr 21:7
A **w** person desires evil; Pr 21:10
considers the house of the **w**; Pr 21:12
He brings the **w** to ruin. Pr 21:12
The **w** are a ransom for the Pr 21:18
The sacrifice of a **w** person is Pr 21:27
A **w** man puts on a bold face, Pr 21:29
an ambush, **w** man, at the camp Pr 24:15
the **w** will stumble into ruin. Pr 24:16
evildoers, and don't envy the **w**. Pr 24:19
lamp of the **w** will be put out Pr 24:20
Remove the **w** from the king's Pr 25:5
yields to the **w** is like a Pr 25:26
w flee when no one is pursuing Pr 28:1
who reject the law praise the **w**, Pr 28:4
but when the **w** come to power, Pr 28:12
A **w** ruler over a helpless people Pr 28:15
When the **w** come to power, people Pr 28:28
but when the **w** rule, people Pr 29:2
the **w** one does not understand Pr 29:7
all his servants will be **w**. Pr 29:12
When the **w** increase, rebellion Pr 29:16
upright is detestable to the **w**. Pr 29:27
judge the righteous and the **w**, Ec 3:17
and there is a **w** man who lives Ec 7:15
be excessively **w**, and don't be Ec 7:17
I saw the **w** buried. Ec 8:10
it will not go well with the **w**, Ec 8:13
the actions of the **w** deserve, Ec 8:14
and there are **w** people who get Ec 8:14
for the righteous and the **w**, Ec 9:2
to the **w**—⌊it will go⌋ badly Is 3:11
will kill the **w** with a command Is 11:4
their ⌊own⌋ iniquity, on the **w**. Is 13:11
has broken the staff of the **w**, Is 14:5
⌊But if⌋ the **w** is shown favor, Is 26:10
the house of **w** men and against Is 31:2
says the LORD, "for the **w**." Is 48:22
They made His grave with the **w**, Is 53:9
Let the **w** one abandon his way, Is 55:7
But the **w** are like the Is 57:20
There is no peace for the **w**," Is 57:21
for **w** men live among My people. Jr 5:26
does the way of the **w** prosper? Jr 12:1
Drag the **w** away like sheep to Jr 12:3
whirl about the head of the **w**. Jr 23:19
As for the **w**, He hands them over Jr 25:31
whirl about the head of the **w**. Jr 30:23
If I say to the **w** person: Ezk 3:18
him about his **w** way in order to Ezk 3:18
that **w** person will die for his Ezk 3:18
But if you warn a **w** person and Ezk 3:19
his wickedness or his **w** way, Ezk 3:19
and to the **w** of the earth as Ezk 7:21
face from the **w** as they profane Ezk 7:22
evil and give **w** advice in this Ezk 11:2
encouraged the **w** person not to Ezk 13:22
of the **w** person will be Ezk 18:20
Now if the **w** person turns from Ezk 18:21
pleasure in the death of the **w**?" Ezk 18:23
same abominations that the **w** do, Ezk 18:24
But if a **w** person turns from the Ezk 18:27
righteous and the **w** from you. Ezk 21:3
both⌋ the righteous and the **w**, Ezk 21:4
profane and **w** prince of Israel, Ezk 21:25
the necks of the profane **w** ones; Ezk 21:29
If I say to the **w**: Wicked one, Ezk 33:8
W one, you will surely die, but Ezk 33:8
that **w** person will die for his Ezk 33:8
if you warn a **w** person to turn Ezk 33:9
pleasure in the death of the **w**, Ezk 33:11
rather that the **w** person should Ezk 33:11
of the **w** person cause him Ezk 33:12
So when I tell the **w** person: Ezk 33:14
But when a **w** person turns from Ezk 33:19
but the **w** will act wickedly; Dn 12:10
none of the **w** will understand, Dn 12:10
of their evil, **w** actions. Hs 9:15
measure in the house of the **w**? Mc 6:10
Can I excuse **w** scales or bags of Mc 6:11
the LORD, and is a **w** counselor. Nah 1:11
For the **w** one will never again Nah 1:15
the **w** restrict the righteous; Hab 1:4
one who is **w** swallows up one Hab 1:13
house of the **w** and strip ⌊him⌋ Hab 3:13
and the ruins along with the **w**. Zph 1:3
They will be called a **w** country Mal 1:4
between the righteous and the **w**, Mal 3:18
trample the **w**, for they will Mal 4:3
said to him, 'You **w** slave! Mt 18:32
But if that **w** slave says in his Mt 24:48
who practices **w** things hates the Jn 3:20
those who have done **w** things, Jn 5:29
delivered from **w** and evil men, 2Th 3:2

WICKEDLY *(12)*

You behaved more **w** than all who 1Kg 14:9
who has sinned and acted very **w**. 1Ch 21:17
while we have acted **w**. Neh 9:33
does not act **w** and the Almighty Jb 34:12
I will no ⌊longer⌋ act **w**. Jb 34:31
gone astray and have acted **w**. Ps 106:6
evil thing or **w** perform reckless Ps 141:4
another **w** defiles his Ezk 22:11
done wrong, acted **w**, rebelled, Dn 9:5
we have sinned, we have acted **w**. Dn 9:15
those who act **w** toward the Dn 11:32
but the wicked will act **w**; Dn 12:10

WICKEDNESS *(58)*

saw that man's **w** was widespread Gn 6:5
before you because of their **w**. Dt 9:4
before you because of their **w**, Dt 9:5
and their **w** and sin. Dt 9:27
because of the **w** of your actions Dt 28:20
defiance is like **w** and idolatry. 1Sm 15:23
'**W** comes from wicked people.' 1Sm 24:13
not turned from my God to **w**. 2Sm 22:22
Isn't your **w** abundant and aren't Jb 22:5
He strikes them for their **w**, Jb 34:26
Your **w** ⌊affects⌋ a person like Jb 35:8
are not a God who delights in **w**; Ps 5:4
call his **w** into account until Ps 10:15
not turned from my God to **w**. Ps 18:21
love righteousness and hate **w**; Ps 45:7
because of the **w** of its Ps 107:34
eat the bread of **w** and drink the Pr 4:17
and **w** is detestable to my lips. Pr 8:7
will fall because of his **w**. Pr 11:5
Man cannot be made secure by **w**, Pr 12:3
but **w** undermines the sinner. Pr 13:6
W is atoned for by loyalty and Pr 16:6
there is **w** at the place of Ec 3:16
and there is **w** at the place Ec 3:16
and to know that **w** is stupidity Ec 7:25
and **w** will not allow those who Ec 8:8
those who drag **w** with cords of Is 5:18
your lips, your **w** is removed, Is 6:7
For **w** burns like a fire that Is 9:18
You were secure in your **w**; Is 47:10
the chains of **w**, to untie the Is 58:6
with your prostitution and **w**. Jr 3:2
acknowledge our **w**, LORD, the Jr 14:20
Let all their **w** come before You, Lm 1:22
turn from his **w** or his wicked Ezk 3:19
with more **w** than the nations, Ezk 5:6
has grown into a rod of **w**; Ezk 7:11
before your **w** was exposed? Ezk 16:57
and the **w** of the wicked person Ezk 18:20
from the **w** he has committed Ezk 18:27
your ways until **w** was found in Ezk 28:15
I banished it because of its **w**. Ezk 31:11
neither will the **w** of the wicked Ezk 33:12
on the day he turns from his **w**. Ezk 33:12
turns from his **w** and does what Ezk 33:19
stumble because of their **w**; Hs 5:5
You have plowed **w** and reaped Hs 10:13
because the **w** of the nations is Jl 3:13
their **w** has confronted Me. Jnh 1:2
who dream up **w** and prepare evil Mc 2:1
treasures of **w** and the accursed Mc 6:10
"This is **W**," he said. Zch 5:8
do those who commit **w** prosper, Mal 3:15
who commits **w** will become Mal 4:1
repent of this **w** of yours, Ac 8:22
evil, greed, and **w**. Rm 1:29
from you, along with all **w**. Eph 4:31
So rid yourselves of all **w**, 1Pt 2:1

WIDE *(73)*

long, 75 feet **w**, and 45 feet Gn 6:15
long, 27 inches **w**, and 27 inches Ex 25:10
45 inches long and 27 inches **w**. Ex 25:17
long, 18 inches **w**, and 27 inches Ex 25:23
and seven and a half feet **w**; Ex 27:1
inches long and nine inches **w**. Ex 28:16
18 inches long and 18 inches **w**; Ex 30:2
long, 27 inches **w**, and 27 inches Ex 37:1
45 inches long and 27 inches **w**. Ex 37:6
long, 18 inches **w**, and 27 inches Ex 37:10
18 inches long and 18 inches **w**; Ex 37:25
and seven and a half feet **w**, Ex 38:1
inches long and nine inches **w**. Ex 39:9
and six feet **w** by a standard Dt 3:11
long, 30 feet **w**, and 45 feet 1Kg 6:2
was seven and a half feet **w**, 1Kg 6:6
the middle was nine feet **w**, 1Kg 6:6
third was 10 and a half feet **w**. 1Kg 6:6
long, 30 feet **w**, and 30 feet 1Kg 6:20
long, 75 feet **w**, and 45 feet 1Kg 7:2
75 feet long and 45 feet **w**. 1Kg 7:6
feet long, six feet **w**, and four 1Kg 7:27
crown on top was 18 inches **w**. 1Kg 7:31
made as a pedestal 27 inches **w**. 1Kg 7:31
and each was six feet **w**— 1Kg 7:38
of the temple, was 30 feet **w**; 2Ch 3:4
long, 30 feet **w**, and 15 feet 2Ch 4:1
and a half feet **w**, and four and 2Ch 6:13
open their mouths **w** against me Ps 35:21
Open your mouth **w**, and I will Ps 81:10
sea, vast and **w**, teeming with Ps 104:25
throat and opens **w** its enormous Is 5:14
and sling you into a **w** land. Is 22:18
His funeral pyre is deep and **w**, Is 30:33
made your bed **w**, and you have Is 57:8
cup, which is deep and **w**. Ezk 23:32
and 43 and three-quarter feet **w**. Ezk 40:21
and 43 and three-quarter feet **w**. Ezk 40:25
and 43 and three-quarter feet **w**. Ezk 40:29
eight and three-quarter feet **w**. Ezk 40:30
and 43 and three-quarter feet **w**. Ezk 40:33
and 43 and three-quarter feet **w**. Ezk 40:36
a half inches **w**, and 21 inches Ezk 40:42
175 feet long and 175 feet **w**. Ezk 40:47
a quarter feet ⌊**w**⌋ on each side. Ezk 40:48
feet ⌊**w**⌋ on each side. Ezk 41:2
were three and a half feet ⌊**w**⌋. Ezk 41:3
was 10 and a half feet ⌊**w**⌋, Ezk 41:3
chambers was 35 feet **w** all Ezk 41:10
three-quarter feet **w** all around. Ezk 41:11

west was 122 and a half feet w. Ezk 41:12
and a half feet w and 175 feet Ezk 42:4
⌊feet⌋ long and 875 ⌊feet⌋ w, Ezk 42:20
inches ⌊deep⌋ and 21 inches w, Ezk 43:13
21 feet long by 21 feet w. Ezk 43:16
long by 24 and a half feet w, Ezk 43:17
six and two-thirds ⌊miles⌋ w. Ezk 45:1
three and one-third ⌊miles⌋ w, Ezk 45:3
miles⌋ w for the Levites Ezk 45:5
of a mile⌋ w and eight Ezk 45:6
long by 52 and a half ⌊feet⌋ w. Ezk 46:22
eight and one-third ⌊miles⌋ w, Ezk 48:8
three and one-third ⌊miles⌋ w. Ezk 48:9
miles⌋ w on the western Ezk 48:10
miles⌋ w on the eastern Ezk 48:10
three and one-third ⌊miles⌋ w. Ezk 48:13
of a mile⌋ w and eight Ezk 48:15
90 feet high and nine feet w. Dn 3:1
of your land are w open to your Nah 3:13
"30 feet long and 15 feet w." Zch 5:2
For the gate is w and the road Mt 7:13
because a w door for effective 1Co 16:9
our heart has been opened w. 2Co 6:11

WIDE-OPEN *(3)*
people and a w land, Jdg 18:10
He brought me out to a w place; 2Sm 22:20
He brought me out to a w place; Ps 18:19

WIDELY *(2)*
to proclaim it w and to spread Mk 1:45
It is w reported that there is 1Co 5:1

WIDEN *(2)*
You w ⌊a place⌋ beneath me for 2Sm 22:37
You w ⌊a place⌋ beneath me for Ps 18:36

WIDENED *(1)*
the temple⌋ w at each successive Ezk 41:7

WIDER *(1)*
the earth and w than the sea. Jb 11:9

WIDESPREAD *(3)*
wickedness was w on the earth Gn 6:5
prophetic visions were not w. 1Sm 3:1
There was a w outcry from the Neh 5:1

WIDOW *(51)*
Remain a w in your father's Gn 38:11
not mistreat any w or fatherless Ex 22:22
not to marry a w, a divorced Lv 21:14
Any vow a w or divorcée put Nm 30:9
for the fatherless and the w, Dt 10:18
w within your gates may come, Dt 14:29
fatherless, and the w among you. Dt 16:11
and the w within your gates. Dt 16:14
and the w, so that the LORD Dt 24:19
the fatherless, and the w. Dt 24:20
the fatherless, and the w. Dt 24:21
and the w, so that they may Dt 26:12
and the w, according to all Dt 26:13
a fatherless child, or a w.' Dt 27:19
Mahlon's w, as my wife, to Ru 4:10
Abigail of Carmel, Nabal's w. 1Sm 27:3
and Abigail the w of Nabal the 1Sm 30:5
the w of Nabal the Carmelite. 2Sm 2:2
the w of Nabal the Carmelite; 2Sm 3:3
To tell the truth, I am a w; 2Sm 14:5
woman who is a w to provide for 1Kg 17:9
there was a w woman gathering 1Kg 17:10
tragedy on the w I am staying 1Kg 17:20
do not deal kindly with the w. Jb 24:21
day I was born I guided the w— Jb 31:18
kill the w and the foreigner Ps 94:6
be fatherless and his wife a w. Ps 109:9
helps the fatherless and the w, Ps 146:9
will never be a w or know the Is 47:8
and the w and no longer shed Jr 7:6
alien, the fatherless, or the w. Jr 22:3
the nations has become like a w. Lm 1:1
fatherless and w are oppressed Ezk 22:7
not to marry a w or a divorced Ezk 44:22
or a w who is the widow of a Ezk 44:22
widow who is the w of a priest. Ezk 44:22
not oppress the w or the Zch 7:10
who oppress the w and the Mal 3:5
And a poor w came and dropped in Mk 12:42
This poor w has put in more than Mk 12:43
and was a w for 84 years. Lk 2:37
to a w at Zarephath in Sidon. Lk 4:26
only son, and she was a w. Lk 7:12
And a w in that town kept coming Lk 18:3
because this w keeps pestering Lk 18:5
also saw a poor w dropping in Lk 21:2
This poor w has put in more than Lk 21:3
But if any w has children or 1Tm 5:4
The real w, left all alone, has 1Tm 5:5
No w should be placed on the 1Tm 5:9
I am not a w, and I will never Rv 18:7

WIDOW'S *(10)*
So she took off her w clothes, Gn 38:14
veil and put her w clothes back Gn 38:19
and do not take a w garment as Dt 24:17
He was a w son from the tribe of 1Kg 7:14
and take the w ox as collateral. Jb 24:3
and I made the w heart rejoice. Jb 29:13
poor or let the w eyes go blind, Jb 31:16
but He protects the w territory. Pr 15:25
fatherless. Plead the w cause. Is 1:17
the w case never comes before Is 1:23

WIDOWED *(4)*
daughter becomes w or divorced, Lv 22:13
His w mother's name was Zeruah. 1Kg 11:26
wives become childless and w, Jr 18:21
are not left w by their God, Jr 51:5

WIDOWHOOD *(2)*
loss of children and w. Is 47:9
remember the disgrace of your w. Is 54:4

WIDOWS *(24)*
wives will be w and your Ex 22:24
day of their death, living as w. 2Sm 20:3
You sent w away empty-handed, Jb 22:9
yet their w will not weep ⌊for Jb 27:15
a champion of w is God in His Ps 68:5
but the w could not lament. Ps 78:64
on its fatherless and w, Is 9:17
so that w can be their spoil and Is 10:2
made their w more numerous than Jr 15:8
let your w trust in Me. Jr 49:11
fatherless; our mothers are w. Lm 5:3
and multiply the w within her. Ezk 22:25
They devour w' houses and say Mk 12:40
were certainly many w in Israel Lk 4:25
Jews that their w were being Ac 6:1
And all the w approached him, Ac 9:39
the saints and w and presented Ac 9:41
I say to the unmarried and to w: 1Co 7:8
Support w who are genuinely 1Tm 5:3
widows who are genuinely w. 1Tm 5:3
But refuse to enroll younger w; 1Tm 5:11
If any believing woman has w, 1Tm 5:16
help those who are genuinely w. 1Tm 5:16
orphans and w in their distress Jms 1:27

WIDOWS' *(2)*
devour w houses and make long Mt 23:14
devour w houses and say long Lk 20:47

WIDTH *(33)*
and the w of each curtain six Ex 26:2
feet and the w of each curtain Ex 26:8
and the w of each plank 27 Ex 26:16
the w 75 ⌊feet⌋ at each end, Ex 27:18
and the w of each curtain six Ex 36:9
and the w of each curtain six Ex 36:15
and the w of each was 27 inches. Ex 36:21
extending across the temple's w, 1Kg 6:3
was 90 feet, and the w 30 feet. 2Ch 3:3
across the w of the temple, 2Ch 3:4
to the w of the temple, 2Ch 3:8
30 feet, and its w was 30 feet. 2Ch 3:8
to be 90 feet and its w 90 feet, Ezr 6:3
he measured the w of the gate's Ezk 40:11
while the w of the gateway was Ezk 40:11
north, ⌊both⌋ its length and w. Ezk 40:20
The w of the gateway was 24 and Ezk 40:48
each side the w of the pilaster Ezk 41:1
The w of the entrance was 17 and Ezk 41:2
70 feet, and the w, 35 feet. Ezk 41:2
and the w of the entrance's Ezk 41:3
35 feet, and the w, 35 feet. Ezk 41:4
The w of the side rooms all Ezk 41:5
The w of the front of the temple Ezk 41:14
the w was 87 and a half feet. Ezk 42:2
length and w, as well as all Ezk 42:11
and the w ⌊of the ledge⌋ is 21 Ezk 43:14
⌊whose⌋ w is also 21 inches. Ezk 43:14
miles⌋ and the w three and Ezk 48:13
to determine its w and length." Zch 2:2
saints what is the length and w, Eph 3:18
its length and w are the same. Rv 21:16
Its length, w, and height are Rv 21:16

WIELDED *(2)*
He w his spear against 800 ⌊men⌋ 2Sm 23:8
he w his spear against 300 and 1Ch 11:11

WIELDING *(1)*
in a thicket of trees, w axes, Ps 74:5

WIELDS *(4)*
well as him who w the sickle at Jr 50:16
and he w it against the land Ezk 30:25
and the one who w the scepter Am 1:5
and the one who w the scepter Am 1:8

WIFE *(363)*
and mother and bonds with his w, Gn 2:24
the man and his w were naked, Gn 2:25
man and his w heard the sound Gn 3:8
Adam named his w Eve because she Gn 3:20
out of skins for Adam and his w, Gn 3:21
Adam knew his w Eve intimately, Gn 4:1
Cain knew his w intimately, Gn 4:17
knew his w intimately again, Gn 4:25
sons, your w, and your sons' Gn 6:18
his sons, his w, and his sons' Gn 7:7
Japheth, Noah's w, and his three Gn 7:13
the ark, you, your w, your sons, Gn 8:16
his sons, his w, and his sons' Gn 8:18
Abram's w was named Sarai, Gn 11:29
and Nahor's w was named Milcah. Gn 11:29
his son Abram's w, and they set Gn 11:31
He took his w Sarai, his nephew Gn 12:5
he said to his w Sarai, "Look, I Gn 12:11
they will say, 'This is his w.' Gn 12:12
because of Abram's w Sarai. Gn 12:17
you tell me she was your w? Gn 12:18
so that I took her as my w? Gn 12:19
here's your w. Take her and go Gn 12:19
with his w and all he had. Gn 12:20
he, his w, and all he had Gn 13:1
Abram's w Sarai had not borne Gn 16:1
So Abram's w Sarai took Hagar, Gn 16:3
husband Abram as a w for him. Gn 16:3
As for your w Sarai, do not call Gn 17:15
w Sarah will bear you a son, Gn 17:19
"Where is your w Sarah?" Gn 18:9
your w Sarah will have a son! Gn 18:10
Take your w and your two Gn 19:15
But his w looked back and became Gn 19:26
Abraham said about his w Sarah, Gn 20:2
return the man's w, for he is a Gn 20:7
will kill me because of my w.' Gn 20:11
my mother, and she became my w. Gn 20:12
and returned his w Sarah to him. Gn 20:14
Abimelech, his w, and his female Gn 20:17
account of Sarah, Abraham's w. Gn 20:18
and his mother got a w for him Gn 21:21
beside his dead ⌊w⌋ and spoke to Gn 23:3
buried his w Sarah in the cave Gn 23:19
you will not take a w for my son Gn 24:3
to take a w for my son Isaac. Gn 24:4
and you can take a w for my son Gn 24:7
the w of Abraham's brother Nahor Gn 24:15
my master's w, bore a son to my Gn 24:36
'You will not take a w for my Gn 24:37
family to take a w for my son.' Gn 24:38
will take a w for my son from Gn 24:40
and let her be a w for your Gn 24:51
and took Rebekah to be his w. Gn 24:67
Now Abraham took another w, Gn 25:1
buried there with his w Sarah. Gn 25:10
took as his w Rebekah daughter Gn 25:20
behalf of his w because she was Gn 25:21
and his w Rebekah conceived. Gn 25:21
of the place asked about his w, Gn 26:7
for he was afraid to say "my w," Gn 26:7
Isaac caressing his w Rebekah. Gn 26:8
said, "So she is really your w! Gn 26:9
easily have slept with your w, Gn 26:10
man or his w will certainly die. Gn 26:11
Don't take a w from the Gn 28:1
to Paddan-aram to get a w there. Gn 28:6
Give me my w, for my time is Gn 29:21
his daughter Rachel as his w. Gn 29:28
slave Bilhah to Jacob as a w, Gn 30:4
and gave her to Jacob as a w. Gn 30:9
"Get me this girl as a w," Gn 34:4
Please give her to him as a w. Gn 34:8
Just give the girl to be my w!" Gn 34:12

Eliphaz son of Esau's w Adah, Gn 36:10
Reuel son of Esau's w Basemath. Gn 36:10
were the sons of Esau's w Adah. Gn 36:12
the sons of Esau's w Basemath. Gn 36:13
the sons of Esau's w Oholibamah Gn 36:14
the sons of Esau's w Basemath. Gn 36:17
the sons of Esau's w Oholibamah: Gn 36:18
chiefs of Esau's w Oholibamah Gn 36:18
took her as a w and slept with Gn 38:2
Judah got a w for Er, his Gn 38:6
Sleep with your brother's w. Gn 38:8
he slept with his brother's w, Gn 38:9
After a long time Judah's w, Gn 38:12
not been given to him as a w. Gn 38:14
his master's w looked longingly Gn 39:7
and said to his master's w, Gn 39:8
you, because you are his w. Gn 39:9
heard the story his w told him— Gn 39:19
and gave him a w, Gn 41:45
know that my w bore me two sons Gn 44:27
The sons of Jacob's w Rachel: Gn 46:19
Abraham and his w Sarah are Gn 49:31
Isaac and his w Rebekah are Gn 49:31
So Moses took his w and sons, Ex 4:20
Zipporah, Moses' w, after he had Ex 18:2
along with Moses' w and sons, Ex 18:5
with your w and her two sons. Ex 18:6
Do not covet your neighbor's w, Ex 20:17
arrives with a w, his wife is to Ex 21:3
his w is to leave with him. Ex 21:3
gives him a w and she bears him Ex 21:4
the w and her children belong to Ex 21:4
my master, my w, and my children Ex 21:5
If he takes an additional w, Ex 21:10
marital rights of the first w. Ex 21:10
price for her to be his w. Ex 22:16
have sex with your father's w; Lv 18:8
coming near his w to have sexual Lv 18:14
is your son's w; you are not to Lv 18:15
with your brother's w; Lv 18:16
with your neighbor's w, Lv 18:20
adultery with his neighbor's w— Lv 20:10
man sleeps with his father's w, Lv 20:11
a man marries his brother's w, Lv 20:21
If any man's w goes astray, Nm 5:12
because of his w who has defiled Nm 5:14
is to bring his w to the priest. Nm 5:15
jealousy when a w goes astray Nm 5:29
and he becomes jealous of his w. Nm 5:30
of Amram's w was Jochebed, Nm 26:59
between a man and his w, Nm 30:16
your neighbor's w or covet your Dt 5:21
daughter, or the w you embrace, Dt 13:6
and want to take her as your w, Dt 21:11
husband, and she will be your w. Dt 21:13
if the unloved w has the Dt 21:15
of the loved ⌊w⌋ as his Dt 21:16
the firstborn of the unloved w. Dt 21:16
of the unloved w, by giving him Dt 21:17
my daughter to this man as a w, Dt 22:16
will remain his w; he cannot Dt 22:19
with ⌊another⌋ man's w, Dt 22:22
must become his w because he Dt 22:29
is not to marry his father's w; Dt 22:30
and becomes another man's w, Dt 24:2
joy to the w he has married. Dt 24:5
the w of the dead man may not Dt 25:5
is to take her as his w, Dt 25:5
and the w of one steps in to Dt 25:11
who sleeps with his father's w, Dt 27:20
his brother, the w he embraces, Dt 28:54
Achsah as a w to the one who Jos 15:16
daughter Achsah to him as a w. Jos 15:17
daughter Achsah to him as a w." Jdg 1:12
daughter Achsah to him as his w. Jdg 1:13
prophet and the w of Lappidoth, Jdg 4:4
the w of Heber the Kenite, Jdg 4:17
Heber's w Jael took a tent peg, Jdg 4:21
the w of Heber the Kenite; Jdg 5:24
Gilead's w bore him sons, and Jdg 11:2
his w was barren and had no Jdg 13:2
got up and followed his w. Jdg 13:11
You the man who spoke to my w?" Jdg 13:11
Your w needs to do everything I Jdg 13:13
Your w must do everything I have Jdg 13:14
Manoah and his w were watching. Jdg 13:19
Manoah and his w saw ⌊this⌋, Jdg 13:20
again to Manoah and his w. Jdg 13:21

he said to his w, "because we Jdg 13:22
But his w said to him, "If the Jdg 13:23
Now get her for me as a w." Jdg 14:2
Philistines for a w?" Jdg 14:3
day they said to Samson's w, Jdg 14:15
So Samson's w came to him, Jdg 14:16
his w was given to one of the Jdg 14:20
as a gift⌋ and visited his w. Jdg 15:1
want to go to my w in her room," Jdg 15:1
taken Samson's w and given her Jdg 15:6
who gives a w to a Benjaminite Jdg 21:18
and catch a w for yourself Jdg 21:21
Judah with his w and two sons to Ru 1:1
the w of the deceased man, Ru 4:5
widow, as my w, to perpetuate Ru 4:10
took Ruth and she became his w. Ru 4:13
the meat to his w Peninnah and 1Sm 1:4
was intimate with his w Hannah, 1Sm 1:19
would bless Elkanah and his w: 1Sm 2:20
the w of Phinehas, was 1Sm 4:19
name of Saul's w was Ahinoam 1Sm 14:50
I'll give her to you as a w, 1Sm 18:17
Adriel the Meholathite as a w. 1Sm 18:19
Michal to David as his w. 1Sm 18:27
But his w Michal warned David: 1Sm 19:11
men informed Abigail, Nabal's w: 1Sm 25:14
his w told him about these 1Sm 25:37
us to bring you to him as a w." 1Sm 25:40
And so she became his w. 1Sm 25:42
Michal, David's w, to Palti son 1Sm 25:44
for each man's w and children. 1Sm 30:22
was Ithream, by David's w Eglah. 2Sm 3:5
"Give me back my w, Michal. 2Sm 3:14
of Eliam and w of Uriah the 2Sm 11:3
and drink and sleep with my w? 2Sm 11:11
When Uriah's w heard that her 2Sm 11:26
She became his w and bore him a 2Sm 11:27
and took his wife as your own wife 2Sm 12:9
took his wife as your own w— 2Sm 12:9
Me and took the w of Uriah the 2Sm 12:10
the Hittite to be your own w.' 2Sm 12:10
baby that Uriah's w had borne to 2Sm 12:15
comforted his w Bathsheba; 2Sm 12:24
Then his w took the cover, 2Sm 17:19
Abishag the Shunammite as a w." 1Kg 2:17
your brother Adonijah as a w." 1Kg 2:21
daughter of Solomon was his w 1Kg 4:11
for Pharaoh's daughter, his w. 1Kg 7:8
to his daughter, Solomon's w. 1Kg 9:16
so much that he gave him a w, 1Kg 11:19
of his own w, Queen Tahpenes. 1Kg 11:19
said to his w, "Go disguise 1Kg 14:2
know that you're Jeroboam's w, 1Kg 14:2
Jeroboam's w did that: she went 1Kg 14:4
Jeroboam's w is coming soon to 1Kg 14:5
said, "Come in, w of Jeroboam! 1Kg 14:6
Jeroboam's w got up and left 1Kg 14:17
Then his w Jezebel came to him 1Kg 21:5
Then his w Jezebel said to him, 1Kg 21:7
because his w Jezebel incited 1Kg 21:25
girl who served Naaman's w. 2Kg 5:2
for Ahab's daughter was his w. 2Kg 8:18
your daughter to my son as a w.' 2Kg 14:9
w of Shallum son of Tikvah, 2Kg 22:14
children by ⌊his⌋ w Azubah and 1Ch 2:18
his w Abijah bore him Ashhur the 1Ch 2:24
had another w named Atarah, 1Ch 2:26
Abishur's w was named Abihail, 1Ch 2:29
by David's w Eglah, was sixth. 1Ch 3:3
Mered's w Bithiah gave birth to 1Ch 4:17
His Judean w gave birth to Jered 1Ch 4:18
sons of Hodiah's w, the sister 1Ch 4:19
Machir's w Maacah gave birth to 1Ch 7:16
He slept with his w, and she 1Ch 7:23
His sons by his w Hodesh: 1Ch 8:9
My w must not live in the house 2Ch 8:11
for Ahab's daughter was his w. 2Ch 21:6
Jehoram and the w of Jehoiada 2Ch 22:11
your daughter to my son as a w.' 2Ch 25:18
the w of Shallum son of Tokhath, 2Ch 34:22
who had taken a w from the Ezr 2:61
who had taken a w from the Neh 7:63
friends and his w Zeresh to join Est 5:10
His w Zeresh and all his friends Est 5:14
Haman told his w Zeresh and all Est 6:13
advisers and his w Zeresh said Est 6:13
His w said to him, "Do you still Jb 2:9
My breath is offensive to my w, Jb 19:17

neighbor's⌋ w or I have lurked Jb 31:9
let my own w grind ⌊grain⌋ for Jb 31:10
be fatherless and his w a widow. Ps 109:9
Your w will be like a fruitful Ps 128:3
pleasure in the w of your youth. Pr 5:18
who sleeps with another man's w; Pr 6:29
A capable w is her husband's Pr 12:4
but a w who causes shame is like Pr 12:4
A man who finds a w finds a good Pr 18:22
but a sensible w is from the Pr 19:14
share a house with a nagging w. Pr 21:9
a nagging and hot-tempered w. Pr 21:19
a house shared with a nagging w. Pr 25:24
day and a nagging w are alike. Pr 27:15
Who can find a capable w? Pr 31:10
life with the w you love all Ec 9:9
like a w deserted and wounded in Is 54:6
a w of one's youth when she is Is 54:6
divorces his w and she leaves Jr 3:1
neighing after someone else's w. Jr 5:8
husband and w will be captured Jr 6:11
You adulterous w, who receives Ezk 16:32
his neighbor's w or come near a Ezk 18:6
and defiles his neighbor's w, Ezk 18:11
not defile his neighbor's w. Ezk 18:15
with ⌊their⌋ father's w, Ezk 22:10
with his neighbor's w; Ezk 22:11
and my w died in the evening. Ezk 24:18
has defiled his neighbor's w. Ezk 33:26
a promiscuous w and ⌊have⌋ Hs 1:2
she is not My w and I am not her Hs 2:2
take you to be My w forever. Hs 2:19
you to be My w in righteousness Hs 2:19
you to be My w in faithfulness, Hs 2:20
Israel worked to earn a w; Hs 12:12
he tended flocks for a w. Hs 12:12
Your w will be a prostitute in Am 7:17
you and the w of your youth. Mal 2:14
partner and your w by covenant. Mal 2:14
against the w of your youth. Mal 2:15
he hates and divorces ⌊his w⌋," Mal 2:16
fathered Solomon by Uriah's w, Mt 1:6
afraid to take Mary as your w, Mt 1:20
divorces his w must give her Mt 5:31
everyone who divorces his w, Mt 5:32
his brother Philip's w, Mt 14:3
that he, his w, his children, Mt 18:25
divorce his w on any grounds?" Mt 19:3
mother and be joined to his w, Mt 19:5
divorces his w, except for Mt 19:9
a man with his w is like this, Mt 19:10
is to marry his w and raise up Mt 22:24
he left his w to his brother. Mt 22:25
w will she be of the seven? Mt 22:28
bench, his w sent word to him, Mt 27:19
brother Philip's w, whom he had Mk 6:17
you to have your brother's w!" Mk 6:18
for a man to divorce ⌊his⌋ w?" Mk 10:2
mother and be joined to his w, Mk 10:7
divorces his w and marries Mk 10:11
dies, leaves his w behind, and Mk 12:19
should take the w and produce Mk 12:19
first took a w, and dying, left Mk 12:20
they rise, whose w will she be, Mk 12:23
His w was from the daughters of Lk 1:5
Your w Elizabeth will bear you a Lk 1:13
my w is well along in years." Lk 1:18
these days his w Elizabeth Lk 1:24
his brother's w, and about all Lk 3:19
Joanna the w of Chuza, Herod's Lk 8:3
and mother, w and children, Lk 14:26
who divorces his w and marries Lk 16:18
Remember Lot's w! Lk 17:32
has left a house, w or brothers, Lk 18:29
that if a man's brother has a w, Lk 20:28
should take the w and produce Lk 20:28
first took a w and died without Lk 20:29
whose w will the woman be? Lk 20:33
sister, Mary the w of Clopas, Jn 19:25
Sapphira his w, sold a piece Ac 5:1
then his w came in, not knowing Ac 5:7
Italy with his w Priscilla Ac 18:2
Felix came with his w Drusilla, Ac 24:24
is living with his father's w. 1Co 5:1
each man should have his own w, 1Co 7:2
his marital duty to his w, 1Co 7:3
and likewise a w to her husband. 1Co 7:3
A w does not have authority over 1Co 7:4

his own body, but his w does. 1Co 7:4
a w is not to leave her husband. 1Co 7:10
a husband is not to leave his w. 1Co 7:11
brother has an unbelieving w, 1Co 7:12
husband is sanctified by the w, 1Co 7:14
the unbelieving w is sanctified 1Co 7:14
For you, w, how do you know 1Co 7:16
whether you will save your w? 1Co 7:16
you bound to a w? Do not seek to 1Co 7:27
Are you loosed from a w? 1Co 7:27
from a wife? Do not seek a w. 1Co 7:27
—how he may please his w— 1Co 7:33
A w is bound as long as her 1Co 7:39
be accompanied by a Christian w, 1Co 9:5
is head of the w as also Christ Eph 5:23
who loves his w loves himself. Eph 5:28
mother and be joined to his w, Eph 5:31
you is to love his w as himself, Eph 5:33
and the w is to respect her Eph 5:33
husband of one w, 1Tm 3:2
must be husbands of one w, 1Tm 3:12
has been the w of one husband, 1Tm 5:9
of one w, having faithful Ti 1:6
and His w has prepared herself. Rv 19:7
the bride, the w of the Lamb." Rv 21:9

WIFE'S *(11)*

listened to your w voice and ate Gn 3:17
his hand, his w hand, and the Gn 19:16
and his w name was Mehetabel Gn 36:39
with your father's w daughter, Lv 18:11
and his w name was Naomi. Ru 1:2
Nabal, and his w name, Abigail. 1Sm 25:3
and his w name was Mehetabel 1Ch 1:50
His w name was Maacah. 1Ch 8:29
His w name was Maacah. 1Ch 9:35
and a w nagging is an endless Pr 19:13
proceeds with his w knowledge, Ac 5:2

WILD *(109)*

ground each w animal and each Gn 2:19
the sky, and to every w animal; Gn 2:20
cunning of all the w animals Gn 3:1
and more than any w animal. Gn 3:14
This man will be ⌊like⌋ a w ass. Gn 16:12
he had a taste for w game, Gn 25:28
of the flock torn by w beasts; Gn 31:39
torn apart ⌊by a w animal⌋, Ex 22:13
from it⌋ and the w animals may Ex 23:11
and w animals would multiply Ex 23:29
carcass of an unclean w animal, Lv 5:2
or is mauled by w beasts may be Lv 7:24
hunts down a w animal or bird Lv 17:13
or was mauled by w beasts is to Lv 17:15
or was mauled by w beasts, Lv 22:8
and the w animals in your Lv 25:7
will send w animals against you Lv 26:22
the horns of a w ox for them. Nm 23:22
the horns of a w ox for them. Nm 24:8
the w animals will become too Dt 7:22
roe deer, the w goat, the ibex, Dt 14:5
of the sky and the w animals of Dt 28:26
unleash on them w beasts with Dt 32:24
and horns like those of a w ox; Dt 33:17
of the sky and the w beasts!" 1Sm 17:44
of the Rocks of the W Goats. 1Sm 24:2
like one of the w gazelles. 2Sm 2:18
desperate like a w bear robbed 2Sm 17:8
by day and the w animals by 2Sm 21:10
and found a w vine from which 2Kg 4:39
gathered as many w gourds as his 2Kg 4:39
Then a w animal that was in 2Kg 14:9
Then a w animal that was in 2Ch 25:18
of olive, w olive, myrtle, Neh 8:15
and the w animals will be at Jb 5:23
Does a w donkey bray over fresh Jb 6:5
as soon as a w donkey is born a Jb 11:12
Like w donkeys in the desert, Jb 24:5
w animals enter ⌊their⌋ lairs Jb 37:8
Who set the w donkey free? Jb 39:5
Would the w ox be willing to Jb 39:9
Can you hold the w ox by its Jb 39:10
you trust the w ox to harvest Jb 39:12
them or that some w animal may Jb 39:15
all ⌊sorts of⌋ w animals play Jb 40:20
as well as animals in the w, Ps 8:7
me from the horns of the w oxen. Ps 22:21
and Sirion, like a young w ox. Ps 29:6
of their hearts run w. Ps 73:7
up my horn like that of a w ox; Ps 92:10
supply water for every w beast; Ps 104:11
the w donkeys quench their Ps 104:11
mountains are for the w goats; Ps 104:18
w animals and all cattle, Ps 148:10
Without revelation people run w, Pr 29:18
gazelles and the w does of the Sg 2:7
gazelles and the w does of the Sg 3:5
But w animals will lie down Is 13:21
and w goats will leap about. Is 13:21
and a region for w animals, Is 14:23
hills and for the w animals of Is 18:6
destined it for w beasts. Is 23:13
forever, the joy of w asses, and Is 32:14
The w oxen will be struck down Is 34:7
The w beasts will meet hyenas, Is 34:14
and one w goat will call to Is 34:14
a w donkey at home in the Jr 2:24
sky and for the w animals of the Jr 7:33
Go, gather all the w animals; Jr 12:9
W donkeys stand on the barren Jr 14:6
of the sky and the w animals of Jr 15:3
sky and for the w animals of the Jr 16:4
sky and for the w animals of the Jr 19:7
given him the w animals to serve Jr 27:6
also put the w animals under him Jr 28:14
sky and for the w animals of the Jr 34:20
or was mauled by w beasts. Ezk 4:14
I have given to w animals to be Ezk 33:27
food for all the w animals when Ezk 34:5
food for every w animal since Ezk 34:8
and the w animals of the land Ezk 34:28
bird and to the w animals. Ezk 39:4
of bird and all the w animals: Ezk 39:17
or was mauled by w beasts. Ezk 44:31
people live—or w animals, or Dn 2:38
W animals found shelter under it, Dn 4:12
under it the w animals lived, Dn 4:21
food⌋ with the w animals for Dn 4:23
to live with the w animals. Dn 4:25
to live with the w animals, Dn 4:32
he lived with the w donkeys, Dn 5:21
and the w animals will eat them. Hs 2:12
for them with the w animals, Hs 2:18
along with the w animals and the Hs 4:3
like⌋ a w donkey going off Hs 8:9
like a w beast that would rip Hs 13:8
Even the w animals cry out to Jl 1:20
Don't be afraid, w animals, for Jl 2:22
of it, every kind of w animal. Zph 2:14
a place for w animals to lie Zph 2:15
food was locusts and w honey. Mt 3:4
and ate locusts and w honey. Mk 1:6
He was with the w animals, Mk 1:13
of the earth, the w beasts, the Ac 11:6
you, though a w olive branch, Rm 11:17
off from your native w olive, Rm 11:24
If I fought w animals in Ephesus 1Co 15:32
w waves of the sea, foaming up Jd 13
and by the w animals of the Rv 6:8

WILDERNESS *(250)*

as far as El-paran by the w. Gn 14:6
by a spring of water in the w, Gn 16:7
wandered in the W of Beer-sheba. Gn 21:14
settled in the w and became an Gn 21:20
He settled in the W of Paran, Gn 21:21
springs in the w while he was Gn 36:24
him into this pit in the w, Gn 37:22
far side of the w and came to Ex 3:1
trip into the w so that we may Ex 3:18
"Go and meet Moses in the w." Ex 4:27
a festival for Me in the w." Ex 5:1
trip into the w so that we may Ex 5:3
they may worship Me in the w, Ex 7:16
days into the w and sacrifice to Ex 8:27
to the LORD your God in the w, Ex 8:28
Red Sea along the road of the w. Ex 13:18
at Etham on the edge of the w. Ex 13:20
the w has boxed them in. Ex 14:3
you took us to die in the w? Ex 14:11
Egyptians than to die in the w." Ex 14:12
they went out to the W of Shur. Ex 15:22
days in the w without finding Ex 15:22
Elim and came to the W of Sin, Ex 16:1
Moses and Aaron in the w. Ex 16:2
into this w to make this whole Ex 16:3
turned toward the w, and there, Ex 16:10
fed you in the w when I brought Ex 16:32
community left the W of Sin, Ex 17:1
came to him in the w where he Ex 18:5
they entered the W of Sinai. Ex 19:1
they entered the W of Sinai and Ex 19:2
of Sinai and camped in the w, Ex 19:2
and from the w to the Euphrates Ex 23:31
to the LORD in the W of Sinai. Lv 7:38
it into the w for Azazel. Lv 16:10
it⌋ away into the w by the man Lv 16:21
of meeting in the W of Sinai, Nm 1:1
them in the W of Sinai: Nm 1:19
the LORD in the W of Sinai, Nm 3:4
to Moses in the W of Sinai: Nm 3:14
told Moses in the W of Sinai: Nm 9:1
at twilight in the W of Sinai. Nm 9:5
traveled on from the W of Sinai, Nm 10:12
cloud stopped in the W of Paran. Nm 10:12
where we should camp in the w, Nm 10:31
and camped in the W of Paran. Nm 12:16
sent them from the W of Paran at Nm 13:3
land from the W of Zin as far as Nm 13:21
community in the W of Paran at Nm 13:26
if only we had died in this w! Nm 14:2
has slaughtered them in the w.' Nm 14:16
performed in Egypt and in the w, Nm 14:22
head for the w in the direction Nm 14:25
corpses will fall in this w— Nm 14:29
corpses will fall in this w. Nm 14:32
shepherds in the w for 40 years Nm 14:33
lie ⌊scattered⌋ in the w. Nm 14:33
will come to an end in the w, Nm 14:35
the Israelites were in the w, Nm 15:32
and honey to kill us in the w? Nm 16:13
entered the W of Zin in the Nm 20:1
into this w for us and our Nm 20:4
up from Egypt to die in the w? Nm 21:5
in the w that borders Moab Nm 21:11
in the w that extends from the Nm 21:13
went⌋ from the w to Mattanah, Nm 21:18
out to confront Israel in the w. Nm 21:23
but turned toward the w. Nm 24:1
Israelites in the W of Sinai. Nm 26:64
they would all die in the w. Nm 26:65
Our father died in the w, Nm 27:3
quarreled in the W of Zin, Nm 27:14
of Kadesh in the W of Zin. Nm 27:14
wander in the w 40 years until Nm 32:13
leave this people in the w, Nm 32:15
which is on the edge of the w. Nm 33:6
middle of the sea into the w. Nm 33:8
journey into the W of Etham and Nm 33:8
Sea and camped in the W of Sin. Nm 33:11
from the W of Sin and camped Nm 33:12
and camped in the W of Sinai. Nm 33:15
departed from the W of Sinai and Nm 33:16
and camped in the W of Zin Nm 33:36
will be from the W of Zin along Nm 34:3
across the Jordan in the w, Dt 1:1
and terrible w you saw on the Dt 1:19
you saw in the w how the LORD Dt 1:31
and head for the w by way of the Dt 1:40
headed for the w by way of the Dt 2:1
journey through this immense w. Dt 2:7
along the road to the W of Moab. Dt 2:8
Heshbon from the W of Kedemoth, Dt 2:26
Bezer in the w on the plateau Dt 4:43
journey these 40 years in the w, Dt 8:2
and terrible w with its Dt 8:15
fed you in the w with manna that Dt 8:16
the LORD your God in the w. Dt 9:7
out to kill them in the w.' Dt 9:28
to you in the w until you Dt 11:5
extend from the w to Lebanon Dt 11:24
I led you 40 years in the w; Dt 29:5
land, in a barren, howling w; Dt 32:10
in the W of Zin by failing to Dt 32:51
will be from the w and Lebanon Jos 1:4
had died in the w along the way Jos 5:4
born in the w along the way were Jos 5:5
wandered in the w 40 years until Jos 5:6
by them and fled toward the w. Jos 8:15
who had fled to the w now became Jos 8:20
Israel was journeying in the w. Jos 14:10
south of the w of Zin to the Jos 15:1
In the w: Beth-arabah, Middin, Jos 15:61
through the w ascending from Jos 16:1
and ended at the w of Beth-aven. Jos 18:12
Bezer on the w plateau from Jos 20:8
you lived in the w a long time. Jos 24:7

City of Palms to the W of Judah,	Jdg 1:16
thorns and briers from the w!"	Jdg 8:7
thorns and briers from the w,	Jdg 8:16
through the w to the Red Sea	Jdg 11:16
through the w and around the	Jdg 11:18
and from the w to the Jordan.	Jdg 11:22
the men of Israel toward the w,	Jdg 20:42
fled toward the w to the rock	Jdg 20:45
escaped into the w to the rock	Jdg 20:47
all kinds of plagues in the w.	1Sm 4:8
valley of Zeboim toward the w.	1Sm 13:18
those few sheep with in the w?	1Sm 17:28
then stayed in the w strongholds	1Sm 23:14
hill country of the W of Ziph.	1Sm 23:14
David was in the W of Ziph in	1Sm 23:15
his men were in the w near Maon	1Sm 23:24
and stayed in the W of Maon.	1Sm 23:25
"David is in the w near En-gedi."	1Sm 24:1
went down to the W of Paran.	1Sm 25:1
David was in the w, he heard	1Sm 25:4
from the w to greet our master	1Sm 25:14
this man in the w for nothing.	1Sm 25:21
went to the W of Ziph to search	1Sm 26:2
living in the w and discovered	1Sm 26:3
on the way to the w of Gibeon.	2Sm 2:24
fords of the w until word comes	2Sm 15:28
the night at the w ford ⌊of the	2Sm 17:16
buried at his house in the w.	1Kg 2:34
Tamar in the W of Judah,	1Kg 9:18
on a day's journey into the w.	1Kg 19:4
you came to the W of Damascus.	1Kg 19:15
"The route of the w of Edom."	2Kg 3:8
servant Moses had made in the w,	2Ch 1:3
Tadmor in the w along with all	2Ch 8:4
valley facing the W of Jeruel.	2Ch 20:16
and went out to the w of Tekoa.	2Ch 20:20
to a place overlooking the w,	2Ch 20:24
on Israel in the w be brought to	2Ch 24:9
them in the w because of Your	Neh 9:19
for them in the w 40 years and	Neh 9:21
the w provides nourishment for	Jb 24:5
I made the w its home, and the	Jb 39:6
voice of the LORD shakes the w;	Ps 29:8
the LORD shakes the w of Kadesh.	Ps 29:8
I would stay in the w.	Ps 55:7
The w pastures overflow, and the	Ps 65:12
rocks in the w and gave them	Ps 78:15
able to provide food in the w?	Ps 78:19
Him in the w and grieved Him	Ps 78:40
them like a flock in the w.	Ps 78:52
on that day at Massah in the w	Ps 95:8
craving in the w and tested God	Ps 106:14
Some wandered in the desolate w,	Ps 107:4
He led His people in the w.	Ps 136:16
to live in a w than with a	Pr 21:19
up from the w like columns	Sg 3:6
is this coming up from the w,	Sg 8:5
who turned the world into a w,	Is 14:17
abandoned and forsaken like a w.	Is 27:10
Then justice will inhabit the w,	Is 32:16
The w and the dry land will be	Is 35:1
for water will gush in the w,	Is 35:6
the way of the LORD in the w;	Is 40:3
I will make a way in the w,	Is 43:19
I provide water in the w,	Is 43:20
I turn the rivers into a w;	Is 50:2
He will make her w like Eden,	Is 51:3
depths like a horse in the w,	Is 63:13
holy cities have become a w;	Is 64:10
Zion has become a w, Jerusalem a	Is 64:10
how you followed Me in the w,	Jr 2:2
us through the w, through a land	Jr 2:6
a wild donkey at home in the w.	Jr 2:24
Have I been a w to Israel or a	Jr 2:31
heights in the w on the way to	Jr 4:11
and the fertile field was a w.	Jr 4:26
lodging place in the w,	Jr 9:2
a dirge over the w grazing land,	Jr 9:10
destroyed and scorched like a w,	Jr 9:12
temples and reside in the w.	Jr 9:26
heights in the w the destroyers	Jr 12:12
in the parched places in the w,	Jr 17:6
certainly turn you into a w,	Jr 22:6
lands in the w have dried up.	Jr 23:10
They found favor in the w—	Jr 31:2
Be like a juniper bush in the w.	Jr 48:6
a dry land, a w, an Arabah.	Jr 50:12
cruel like ostriches in the w.	Lm 4:3
and ambushed us in the w.	Lm 4:19
because of the sword in the w.	Lm 5:9
waste, from the w to Diblah.	Ezk 6:14
Now it is planted in the w,	Ezk 19:13
Egypt and led them into the w.	Ezk 20:10
rebelled against Me in the w.	Ezk 20:13
them in the w to put an end to	Ezk 20:13
them in the w that I would not	Ezk 20:15
bring them to an end in the w.	Ezk 20:17
said to their children in the w:	Ezk 20:18
My anger against them in the w.	Ezk 20:21
to them in the w that I would	Ezk 20:23
you into the w of the peoples	Ezk 20:35
fathers in the w of the land	Ezk 20:36
live securely in the w and sleep	Ezk 34:25
lead her to the w, and speak	Hs 2:14
Israel like grapes in the w.	Hs 9:10
I knew you in the w, in the land	Hs 13:5
consumed the pastures of the w,	Jl 1:19
consumed the pastures of the w.	Jl 1:20
for the w pastures have turned	Jl 2:22
40 years in the w in order to	Am 2:10
Me during the 40 years in the w?	Am 5:25
preaching in the W of Judea	Mt 3:1
of one crying out in the w:	Mt 3:3
Spirit into the w to be tempted	Mt 4:1
you go out into the w to see?	Mt 11:7
This place is a w, and it is	Mt 14:15
tell you, 'Look, he's in the w!'	Mt 24:26
of one crying out in the w:	Mk 1:3
baptizing in the w and preaching	Mk 1:4
the Spirit drove Him into the w.	Mk 1:12
He was in the w 40 days, being	Mk 1:13
This place is a w, and it is	Mk 6:35
he was in the w until the day	Lk 1:80
the son of Zechariah in the w.	Lk 3:2
of one crying out in the w:	Lk 3:4
was led by the Spirit in the w	Lk 4:1
you go out into the w to see?	Lk 7:24
of one crying out in the w:	Jn 1:23
lifted up the snake in the w,	Jn 3:14
fathers ate the manna in the w,	Jn 6:31
fathers ate the manna in the w,	Jn 6:49
to the countryside near the w,	Jn 11:54
The woman fled into the w,	Rv 12:6
presence to her place in the w,	Rv 12:14

WILDFLOWERS *(2)*

Learn how the w of the field	Mt 6:28
Consider how the w grow:	Lk 12:27

WILDLIFE *(8)*

and the w of the earth according	Gn 1:24
So God made the w of the earth	Gn 1:25
for all the w of the earth,	Gn 1:30
it⌋ with all the w according to	Gn 7:14
birds, livestock, w, and all	Gn 7:21
as well as all the w and all the	Gn 8:1
w, all livestock, every bird,	Gn 8:19
and all w of the earth that are	Gn 9:10

WILDNESS *(1)*

not accused of w or rebellion.	Ti 1:6

WILL *(10,087)*

(See pp. xi-xii.)

WILL (n. or vb. of volition) *(95)*

and that it was not of my own w:	Nm 16:28
good or bad of my own w?	Nm 24:13
word and according to Your w,	2Sm 7:21
May the LORD's w be done."	2Sm 10:12
ask what the LORD's w is."	1Kg 22:5
for you to inquire of His w?	2Kg 1:16
servant and according to Your w.	1Ch 17:19
May the LORD's w be done."	1Ch 19:13
ask what the LORD's w is."	2Ch 18:4
according to the w of your God.	Ezr 7:18
of your fathers and do His w.	Ezr 10:11
had the w to keep working.	Neh 4:6
me over to the w of my foes,	Ps 27:12
I delight to do Your w, my God;	Ps 40:8
His servants who do His w.	Ps 103:21
officials at w and instructing	Ps 105:22
me to do Your w, for You are my	Ps 143:10
but against My w, piling sin on	Is 30:1
place, and I will do all My w.	Is 46:10
His w against Babylon,	Is 48:14
and the w of the LORD will	Is 53:10
Your w be done on earth as it is	Mt 6:10
one who does the w of My Father	Mt 7:21
whoever does the w of My Father	Mt 12:50
is not the w of your Father in	Mt 18:14
of the two did his father's w?"	Mt 21:31
not as I w, but as You will."	Mt 26:39
not as I will, but as You w."	Mt 26:39
I drink it, Your w be done."	Mt 26:42
Whoever does the w of God is My	Mk 3:35
what I w, but what You will."	Mk 14:36
what I will, but what You w."	Mk 14:36
knew his master's w and didn't	Lk 12:47
not My w, but Yours, be done.	Lk 22:42
he handed Jesus over to their w.	Lk 23:25
blood, or of the w of the flesh,	Jn 1:13
flesh, or of the w of man, but	Jn 1:13
is to do the w of Him who sent	Jn 4:34
because I do not seek My own w,	Jn 5:30
but the w of Him who sent Me.	Jn 5:30
not to do My w, but the will of	Jn 6:38
but the w of Him who sent Me.	Jn 6:38
is the w of Him who sent Me:	Jn 6:39
For this is the w of My Father:	Jn 6:40
If anyone wants to do His w,	Jn 7:17
is God-fearing and does His w,	Jn 9:31
who will carry out all My w.'	Ac 13:22
said, "The Lord's w be done!"	Ac 21:14
has appointed you to know His w,	Ac 22:14
if it is somehow in God's w,	Rm 1:10
and know His w, and approve the	Rm 2:18
according to the w of God.	Rm 8:27
not depend on human w or effort,	Rm 9:16
For who can resist His w?"	Rm 9:19
pleasing, and perfect w of God.	Rm 12:2
that, by God's w, I may come to	Rm 15:32
of Christ Jesus by God's w,	1Co 1:1
but has control over his own w	1Co 7:37
of Christ Jesus by God's w,	2Co 1:1
the Lord, then to us by God's w.	2Co 8:5
according to the w of our God	Gl 1:4
of Christ Jesus by God's w:	Eph 1:1
according to His favor and w,	Eph 1:5
to us the mystery of His w,	Eph 1:9
with the decision of His w,	Eph 1:11
understand what the Lord's w is.	Eph 5:17
do God's w from your heart.	Eph 6:6
but others out of good w.	Php 1:15
you⌋ both to w and to act for	Php 2:13
of Christ Jesus by God's w,	Col 1:1
knowledge of His w in all wisdom	Col 1:9
For this is God's w, your	1Th 4:3
this is God's w for you in	1Th 5:18
of Christ Jesus by God's w,	2Tm 1:1
captured by him to do his w.	2Tm 2:26
but of your own free w.	Phm 14
Holy Spirit according to His w.	Heb 2:4
Where a w exists, the death of	Heb 9:16
a w is valid only when people	Heb 9:17
scroll—to do Your w, O God!"	Heb 10:7
See, I have come to do Your w.	Heb 10:9
By this w, we have been	Heb 10:10
after you have done God's w,	Heb 10:36
all that is good to do His w,	Heb 13:21
wherever the w of the pilot	Jms 3:4
For it is God's w that you,	1Pt 2:15
if that should be God's w,	1Pt 3:17
human desires, but for God's w.	1Pt 4:2
in doing the w of the pagans:	1Pt 4:3
according to God's w should,	1Pt 4:19
freely, according to God's ⌊w⌋;	1Pt 5:2
ever came by the w of man;	2Pt 1:21
does God's w remains forever.	1Jn 2:17
ask anything according to His w,	1Jn 5:14
because of Your w they exist and	Rv 4:11

WILLED *(1)*

For you were grieved as God w,	2Co 7:9

WILLFUL *(1)*

keep Your servant from w sins;	Ps 19:13

WILLFULLY *(2)*

If a person w acts against his	Ex 21:14
They w ignore this:	2Pt 3:5

WILLING *(51)*

If you are w ⌊for me⌋ to bury my	Gn 23:8
whose heart is w bring this as	Ex 35:5
all who had w hearts brought	Ex 35:22
But you were not w to go up,	Dt 1:26
isn't w to perform the duty of	Dt 25:7
will not be w to forgive him.	Dt 29:20
would you be w to wait for them	Ru 1:13
They were not w to destroy them,	1Sm 15:9

(but the w were covered), Ezk 41:16
were beveled w and palm trees Ezk 41:26
The w in its upper room opened Dn 6:10
through the w like thieves. Jl 2:9

WINDS *(22)*

cold from the driving north w. Jb 37:9
and making the w His messengers, Ps 104:4
unleashes His w, and the waters Ps 147:18
bring the four w against Elam Jr 49:36
scatter them to all these w. Jr 49:36
come from the four w and breathe Ezk 37:9
the four w of heaven stirred Dn 7:2
toward the four w of heaven. Dn 8:8
divided to the four w of heaven, Dn 11:4
you like the four w of heaven"— Zch 2:6
and the w blew and pounded that Mt 7:25
the w blew and pounded that Mt 7:27
and rebuked the w and the sea. Mt 8:26
the w and the sea obey Him!" Mt 8:27
His elect from the four w, Mt 24:31
His elect from the four w, Mk 13:27
even the w and the waves, Lk 8:25
because the w were against us. Ac 27:4
makes His angels w, and His Heb 1:7
large and driven by fierce w, Jms 3:4
clouds carried along by w; Jd 12
the four w of the earth so that Rv 7:1

WINDSTORM *(6)*

The w comes from its chamber, Jb 37:9
down, and a w will be released. Ezk 13:11
I will release a w in My wrath. Ezk 13:13
them with a w over all the Zch 7:14
A fierce w arose, and the waves Mk 4:37
Then a fierce w came down on the Lk 8:23

WINE *(237)*

some of the w, became drunk, Gn 9:21
Salem, brought out bread and w; Gn 14:18
father to drink w so that we can Gn 19:32
father to drink w that night, Gn 19:33
him to drink w again tonight so Gn 19:34
got their father to drink w, Gn 19:35
he brought him w, and he drank. Gn 27:25
an abundance of grain and new w. Gn 27:28
him with grain and new w. Gn 27:37
He washes his clothes in w, Gn 49:11
His eyes are darker than w, Gn 49:12
offering of one quart of w. Ex 29:40
not to drink w or beer when you Lv 10:9
offering will be one quart of w. Lv 23:13
is to abstain from w and beer. Nm 6:3
made from w or from beer. Nm 6:3
that, the Nazirite may drink w. Nm 6:20
Prepare a quart of w as a drink Nm 15:5
of a gallon of w for a drink Nm 15:7
two quarts of w as a drink Nm 15:10
olive oil, new w, and grain, Nm 18:12
two quarts of w with each bull, Nm 28:14
your grain, new w, and oil—the Dt 7:13
your grain, new w, and oil. Dt 11:14
of your grain, new w, or oil; Dt 12:17
of your grain, new w, and oil, Dt 14:23
cattle, sheep, w, beer, or Dt 14:26
of your grain, new w, and oil, Dt 18:4
but not drink the w or gather Dt 28:39
you no grain, new w, oil, young Dt 28:51
eat bread or drink w or beer— Dt 29:6
you drank w from the finest Dt 32:14
Their w is serpents' venom, Dt 32:33
and drank the w of their drink Dt 32:38
in a land of grain and new w; Dt 33:28
wheat in the w vat in order to Jdg 6:11
stop giving my w that cheers Jdg 9:13
to drink w or other alcoholic Jdg 13:4
not drink w or other alcoholic Jdg 13:7
or drink w or other alcoholic Jdg 13:14
and bread and w for me, your Jdg 19:19
to be drunk? Get rid of your w!" 1Sm 1:14
I haven't had any w or beer; 1Sm 1:15
of flour, and a jar of w. 1Sm 1:24
and one bringing a skin of w. 1Sm 10:3
bread, a skin of w, and one 1Sm 16:20
two skins of w, five butchered 1Sm 25:18
he is in a good mood from the w. 2Sm 13:28
summer fruit, and a skin of w. 2Sm 16:1
the w is for those who become 2Sm 16:2
a land of grain and new w, 2Kg 18:32
the fine flour, w, oil, incense, 1Ch 9:29
cakes, raisins, w and oil, oxen, 1Ch 12:40
the vineyards for the w cellars. 1Ch 27:27
gallons of w, and 110,000 2Ch 2:10
and w to his servants as 2Ch 2:15
supplies of food, oil, and w. 2Ch 11:11
of the grain, w, oil, honey, 2Ch 31:5
harvest of grain, w, and oil, 2Ch 32:28
or wheat, salt, w, and oil, as Ezr 6:9
550 gallons of w, 550 gallons of Ezr 7:22
when w was set before him, Neh 2:1
I took the w and gave it to the Neh 2:1
grain, new w, and olive oil Neh 5:11
taking food and w from them, Neh 5:15
of all kinds of w was ⌊provided⌋ Neh 5:18
tree, and of the new w and oil. Neh 10:37
of grain, new w, and oil to the Neh 10:39
of grain, new w, and oil Neh 13:5
of the grain, new w, and oil Neh 13:12
in Judah treading w presses on Neh 13:15
along with w, grapes, and figs. Neh 13:15
Royal w flowed freely, according Est 1:7
ordered every w steward in his Est 1:8
was feeling good from the w, Est 1:10
drinking the w, the king asked Est 5:6
the second day while drinking w, Est 7:2
were drinking w and ⌊went to⌋ Est 7:7
to the house of w drinking, Est 7:8
and drinking w in their oldest Jb 1:13
and drinking w in their oldest Jb 1:18
My heart is like unvented w; Jb 32:19
their grain and new w abound. Ps 4:7
have given us a w to drink that Ps 60:3
full of w blended with spices, Ps 75:8
a warrior from the effects of w. Ps 78:65
w that makes man's heart glad— Ps 104:15
vats will overflow with new w. Pr 3:10
and drink the w of violence. Pr 4:17
has mixed her w; she has also Pr 9:2
and drink the w I have mixed. Pr 9:5
W is a mocker, beer is a brawler, Pr 20:1
whoever loves w and oil will not Pr 21:17
with those who drink too much w, Pr 23:20
who linger over w, those who go Pr 23:30
who go looking for mixed w. Pr 23:30
Don't gaze at w when it is red, Pr 23:31
kings to drink w or for rulers Pr 31:4
and w to one whose life is Pr 31:6
enjoy life with w and how to Ec 2:3
and drink your w with a cheerful Ec 9:7
laughter, and w makes life happy Ec 10:19
love is more delightful than w. Sg 1:2
praise your love more than w. Sg 1:4
Your love is much better than w, Sg 4:10
I drink my w with my milk. Sg 5:1
it never lacks mixed w. Sg 7:2
Your mouth is like fine w— Sg 7:9
give you spiced w to drink from Sg 8:2
into the evening, inflamed by w. Is 5:11
harp, tambourine, flute, and w. Is 5:12
who are heroes at drinking w, Is 5:22
and drinking of w—"Let us eat Is 22:13
The new w mourns; the vine Is 24:7
They no longer sing and drink w; Is 24:9
In the streets they cry for w. Is 24:11
a feast of aged w, choice meat, Is 25:6
choice meat, finely aged w. Is 25:6
⌊Woe⌋ to those overcome with w. Is 28:1
because of w and stumble under Is 28:7
of beer, they are confused by w. Is 28:7
They are drunk, but not with w; Is 29:9
a land of grain and new w, Is 36:17
their own blood as with sweet w. Is 49:26
drunken one—but not with w. Is 51:21
buy w and milk without money and Is 55:1
me get ⌊some⌋ w, let's guzzle Is 56:12
your new w you have labored Is 62:8
will drink ⌊the w⌋ in My holy Is 62:9
As the new w is found in a bunch Is 65:8
bowls of mixed w for Destiny, Is 65:11
jar should be filled with w. Jr 13:12
jar should be filled with w? Jr 13:12
a man overcome by w, because of Jr 23:9
this cup of the w of wrath from Jr 25:15
grain, the new w, the fresh oil, Jr 31:12
to offer them a drink of w." Jr 35:2
jars filled with w and some cups Jr 35:5
and said to them, "Drink w!" Jr 35:5
We do not drink w, for Jonadab, Jr 35:6
your sons must never drink w. Jr 35:6
haven't drunk w our whole life Jr 35:8
his sons not to drink w, Jr 35:14
for you, gather w, summer fruit, Jr 40:10
great amount of w and summer Jr 40:12
settled ⌊like w⌋ on its dregs. Jr 48:11
stopped the flow of w from the Jr 48:33
The nations drank her w; Jr 51:7
Where is the grain and w? Lm 2:12
⌊trading⌋ in w from Helbon and Ezk 27:18
may drink w before he enters Ezk 44:21
and from the w that he drank. Dn 1:5
food or with the w he drank. Dn 1:8
food and the w they were to Dn 1:16
nobles and drank w in their Dn 5:1
Under the influence of the w, Dn 5:2
They drank the w and praised Dn 5:4
concubines drank w from them, Dn 5:23
no meat or w entered my mouth, Dn 10:3
grain, the new w, and the oil. Hs 2:8
time and My new w in its season; Hs 2:9
grain, the new w, and the oil, Hs 2:22
Promiscuity, w, and new wine Hs 4:11
and new w take away ⌊one's⌋ Hs 4:11
are sick with the heat of w— Hs 7:5
themselves for grain and w; Hs 7:14
floor and w vat will not Hs 9:2
and the new w will fail them. Hs 9:2
not pour out their w offerings Hs 9:4
will be like the w of Lebanon. Hs 14:7
wail, all you w drinkers, Jl 1:5
of the sweet w, for it has been Jl 1:5
the new w is dried up; Jl 1:10
offer grain and w to the LORD Jl 2:14
you grain, new w, and olive oil. Jl 2:19
with new w and olive oil. Jl 2:24
and sold a girl for w to drink. Jl 3:3
the w vats overflow because the Jl 3:13
will drip with sweet w, Jl 3:18
of their God w obtained through Am 2:8
Nazirites drink w and commanded Am 2:12
never drink the w from the lush Am 5:11
They drink w by the bowlful and Am 6:6
will drip with sweet w, Am 9:13
vineyards and drink their w, Am 9:14
preach to you about w and beer," Mc 2:11
grapes but not drink the w. Mc 6:15
Moreover, w betrays; an arrogant Hab 2:5
but never drink their w. Zph 1:13
on the grain, new w, olive oil, Hg 1:11
bread, stew, w, oil, or any Hg 2:12
drink and be rowdy as if with w. Zch 9:15
and new w, the young women Zch 9:17
will be glad as if with w. Zch 10:7
no one puts new w into old Mt 9:17
skins burst, the w spills out, Mt 9:17
But they put new w into fresh Mt 9:17
they gave Him w mixed with gall Mt 27:34
it with sour w, fixed it on a Mt 27:48
no one puts new w into old Mk 2:22
the w will burst the skins, Mk 2:22
and the w is lost as well as the Mk 2:22
new w is for fresh wineskins. Mk 2:22
to give Him w mixed with myrrh Mk 15:23
and filled a sponge with sour w, Mk 15:36
and will never drink w or beer. Lk 1:15
no one puts new w into old Lk 5:37
the new w will burst the skins, Lk 5:37
But new w should be put into Lk 5:38
after drinking old w, wants new, Lk 5:39
come eating bread or drinking w, Lk 7:33
wounds, pouring on oil and w. Lk 10:34
They came offering Him sour w Lk 23:36
the w ran out, Jesus' mother Jn 2:3
Him, "They don't have any w." Jn 2:3
had become w), he did not know Jn 2:9
sets out the fine w first, Jn 2:10
have kept the fine w until now." Jn 2:10
He had turned the water into w. Jn 4:46
jar full of sour w was sitting Jn 19:29
full of sour w on hyssop and Jn 19:29
Jesus had received the sour w, Jn 19:30
said, "They're full of new w!" Ac 2:13
meat, or drink w, or do anything Rm 14:21
And don't get drunk with w, Eph 5:18
not addicted to w, not a bully 1Tm 3:3
a lot of w, not greedy for 1Tm 3:8
use a little w because of your 1Tm 5:23
not addicted to w, not a bully, Ti 1:7

to hear the w that God had put 1Kg 10:24
his accomplishments and his w, 1Kg 11:41
grant me w and knowledge so that 2Ch 1:10
yourself w and knowledge that 2Ch 1:11
w and knowledge are given to you. 2Ch 1:12
of Sheba observed Solomon's w, 2Ch 9:3
words and about your w is true. 2Ch 9:5
even told half of your great w! 2Ch 9:6
in your presence hearing your w. 2Ch 9:7
of the world in riches and w. 2Ch 9:22
to hear the w God had put in his 2Ch 9:23
to God's w that you possess, Ezr 7:25
pulled up? They die without w. Jb 4:21
would show you the secrets of w, Jb 11:6
for true w has two sides. Jb 11:6
the people, and w will die with Jb 12:2
W is found with the elderly, Jb 12:12
W and strength belong to God; Jb 12:13
True w and power belong to Him. Jb 12:16
shut up and let that be your w! Jb 13:5
of God, or have a monopoly on w? Jb 15:8
But where can w be found, and Jb 28:12
W cannot be valued in the gold Jb 28:16
The price of w is beyond pearls. Jb 28:18
Where then does w come from, Jb 28:20
God understands the way to w, Jb 28:23
considered w and evaluated it; Jb 28:27
Lord—that is w, and to turn Jb 28:28
and maturity should teach w. Jb 32:7
do not claim, "We have found w; Jb 32:13
quiet, and I will teach you w. Jb 33:33
Who put w in the heart or gave Jb 38:36
Who has the w to number the Jb 38:37
For God has deprived her of w; Jb 39:17
mouth of the righteous utters w; Ps 37:30
My mouth speaks w; my heart's Ps 49:3
and You teach me w deep within. Ps 51:6
we may develop w in our hearts. Ps 90:12
In w You have made them all; Ps 104:24
the LORD is the beginning of w; Ps 111:10
For gaining w and being Pr 1:2
fools despise w and instruction. Pr 1:7
W calls out in the street; Pr 1:20
closely to w and directing your Pr 2:2
For the LORD gives w; Pr 2:6
For w will enter your mind, Pr 2:10
a man who finds w and who Pr 3:13
the earth by w and established Pr 3:19
Get w, get understanding; Pr 4:5
Don't abandon w, and she will Pr 4:6
W is supreme—so get wisdom. Pr 4:7
Wisdom is supreme—so get w. Pr 4:7
I am teaching you the way of w; Pr 4:11
My son, pay attention to my w; Pr 5:1
Say to w, "You are my sister," Pr 7:4
Doesn't W call out? Doesn't Pr 8:1
For w is better than precious Pr 8:11
I, W, share a home with Pr 8:12
W has built her house; Pr 9:1
the LORD is the beginning of w, Pr 9:10
For by W your days will be many, Pr 9:11
W is found on the lips of the Pr 10:13
so w is for a man of Pr 10:23
of the righteous produces w, Pr 10:31
but with humility comes w. Pr 11:2
w is gained by those who take Pr 13:10
mocker seeks w and doesn't find Pr 14:6
sensible man's w is to consider Pr 14:8
W resides in the heart of the Pr 14:33
Acquire w—how much better it Pr 16:16
with no intention of buying w? Pr 17:16
W is the focus of the perceptive, Pr 17:24
flowing river, a fountain of w. Pr 18:4
from the way of w will come to Pr 21:16
No w, no understanding, and no Pr 21:30
sell—truth, w, instruction, Pr 23:23
A house is built by w, and it is Pr 24:3
W is inaccessible to a fool; Pr 24:7
realize that w is the same for Pr 24:14
one who walks in w will be safe. Pr 28:26
A man who loves w brings joy to Pr 29:3
A rod of correction imparts w, Pr 29:15
have not gained w, and I have no Pr 30:3
She opens her mouth with w, Pr 31:26
explore through w all that is Ec 1:13
I have amassed w far beyond all Ec 1:16
grasped w and knowledge." Ec 1:16
my mind to know w and knowledge, Ec 1:17
For with much w is much sorrow; Ec 1:18
mind still guiding me with w— Ec 2:3
my w also remained with me. Ec 2:9
Then I turned to consider w, Ec 2:12
is an advantage to w over folly, Ec 2:13
man whose work was done with w, Ec 2:21
sight, He gives w, knowledge, Ec 2:26
W is as good as an inheritance, Ec 7:11
For w is protection as money is Ec 7:12
knowledge is that w preserves Ec 7:12
W makes the wise man stronger Ec 7:19
I have tested all this by w. Ec 7:23
and seek w and an explanation Ec 7:25
A man's w brightens his face, Ec 8:1
my mind to know w and to observe Ec 8:16
or w in Sheol where you are Ec 9:10
this also is w under the sun, Ec 9:13
he delivered the city by his w. Ec 9:15
W is better than strength, Ec 9:16
but the w of the poor man is Ec 9:16
W is better than weapons of war, Ec 9:18
folly outweighs w and honor. Ec 10:1
the advantage of w is that it Ec 10:10
this⌋ by my own strength and w, Is 10:13
a Spirit of w and understanding, Is 11:2
advice; He gives great w. Is 28:29
The w of their wise men will Is 29:14
of salvation, w, and knowledge. Is 33:6
Your w and knowledge led you Is 47:10
so what w do they really have? Jr 8:9
wise must not boast in his w; Jr 9:23
established the world by His w, Jr 10:12
Is there no longer w in Teman? Jr 49:7
Has their w rotted away? Jr 49:7
established the world by His w, Jr 51:15
By your w and understanding you Ezk 28:4
magnificent w and will defile Ezk 28:7
full of w and perfect in beauty. Ezk 28:12
splendor you corrupted your w. Ezk 28:17
for instruction in all w, Dn 1:4
every kind of literature and w. Dn 1:17
every matter of w and Dn 1:20
for w and power belong to Him. Dn 2:20
He gives w to the wise and Dn 2:21
You have given me w and power. Dn 2:23
I have more w than anyone living Dn 2:30
and w like the wisdom of the Dn 5:11
wisdom like the w of the gods. Dn 5:11
and extraordinary w. Dn 5:14
w is vindicated by her deeds. Mt 11:19
earth to hear the w of Solomon; Mt 12:42
How did this w and these Mt 13:54
What is this w given to Him, Mk 6:2
filled with w, and God's grace Lk 2:40
increased in w and stature, Lk 2:52
Yet w is vindicated by all her Lk 7:35
earth to hear the w of Solomon, Lk 11:31
of this, the w of God said, 'I Lk 11:49
such words and a w that none of Lk 21:15
of the Spirit and w, whom we can Ac 6:3
up against the w and the Spirit Ac 6:10
him favor and w in the sight Ac 7:10
in all the w of the Egyptians, Ac 7:22
both of the w and the knowledge Rm 11:33
will destroy the w of the wise, 1Co 1:19
God made the world's w foolish? 1Co 1:20
since, in God's w, the world did 1Co 1:21
did not know God through w, 1Co 1:21
for signs and the Greeks seek w, 1Co 1:22
is God's power and God's w, 1Co 1:24
is wiser than human w, 1Co 1:25
who for us became w from God, 1Co 1:30
with brilliance of speech or w. 1Co 2:1
not with persuasive words of w, 1Co 2:4
be based on men's w but on God's 1Co 2:5
the mature we do speak a w, 1Co 2:6
wisdom, but not a w of this age, 1Co 2:6
God's hidden w in a mystery, 1Co 2:7
not in words taught by human w, 1Co 2:13
For the w of this world is 1Co 3:19
a message of w through the 1Co 12:8
not by fleshly w but by God's 2Co 1:12
on us with all w and Eph 1:8
you a spirit of w and revelation Eph 1:17
multi-faceted w may now be made Eph 3:10
His will in all w and spiritual Col 1:9
teaching everyone with all w, Col 1:28
the treasures of w and knowledge Col 2:3
a reputation of w by promoting Col 2:23
one another in all w, Col 3:16
Walk in w toward outsiders, Col 4:5
Now if any of you lacks w, Jms 1:5
Such w does not come down from Jms 3:15
But the w from above is first Jms 3:17
according to the w given to him, 2Pt 3:15
and riches and w and strength Rv 5:12
and glory and w and thanksgiving Rv 7:12
Here is w: The one who has Rv 13:18
Here is the mind with w: Rv 17:9

WISDOM'S *(2)*

of the LORD is w instruction, Pr 15:33
good conduct with w gentleness. Jms 3:13

WISE *(178)*

of Egypt and all its w men. Gn 41:8
discerning and w man and set him Gn 41:33
one as intelligent and w as you. Gn 41:39
called the w men and sorcerers Ex 7:11
for yourselves w, understanding, Dt 1:13
of your tribes, w and respected Dt 1:15
is indeed a w and understanding Dt 4:6
the eyes of the w and twists the Dt 16:19
If only they were w, they would Dt 32:29
a w woman called out from the 2Sm 20:16
the people with her w counsel, 2Sm 20:22
unpunished, for you are a w man. 1Kg 2:9
will give you a w and 1Kg 3:12
given David a w son to be over 1Kg 5:7
King David a w son with insight 2Ch 2:12
consulted the w men who Est 1:13
He traps the w in their Jb 5:13
God is w and all-powerful. Jb 9:4
Does a w man answer with empty Jb 15:2
declared by w men and was not Jb 15:18
will not find a w man among you. Jb 17:10
Can even a w man be of use to Jb 22:2
the old who are w or the elderly Jb 32:9
my words, you w men, and listen Jb 34:2
with the w men who hear me, Jb 34:34
on any who are w in heart. Jb 37:24
So now, kings, be w; receive Ps 2:10
to see if there is one who is w, Ps 14:2
making the inexperienced w. Ps 19:7
For one can see that w men die; Ps 49:10
is one who is w and who seeks Ps 53:2
I will declare w sayings; Ps 78:2
Fools, when will you be w? Ps 94:8
Let whoever is w pay attention Ps 107:43
for receiving w instruction ⌊in⌋ Pr 1:3
a w man will listen and increase Pr 1:5
the words of the w, and their Pr 1:6
Don't consider yourself to be w; Pr 3:7
The w will inherit honor, but He Pr 3:35
Observe its ways and become w. Pr 6:6
Listen to instruction and be w; Pr 8:33
rebuke a w man, and he will love Pr 9:8
Instruct a w man, and he will be Pr 9:9
If you are w, you are wise for Pr 9:12
you are w for your own benefit; Pr 9:12
w son brings joy to his father, Pr 10:1
A w heart accepts commands, Pr 10:8
w store up knowledge, but the Pr 10:14
one who controls his lips is w. Pr 10:19
to someone whose heart is w. Pr 11:29
whoever listens to counsel is w. Pr 12:15
tongue of the w ⌊brings⌋ healing Pr 12:18
A w son ⌊hears his⌋ father's Pr 13:1
A w man's instruction is a Pr 13:14
walks with the w will become Pr 13:20
with the wise will become w, Pr 13:20
Every w woman builds her house, Pr 14:1
the lips of the w protect them. Pr 14:3
A w man is cautious and turns Pr 14:16
crown of the w is their wealth Pr 14:24
A king favors a w servant, Pr 14:35
tongue of the w makes knowledge Pr 15:2
The lips of the w broadcast Pr 15:7
he will not consult the w. Pr 15:12
w son brings joy to his father, Pr 15:20
will be at home among the w. Pr 15:31
death, but a w man appeases it Pr 16:14
Anyone with a w heart is called Pr 16:21
w heart instructs its mouth and Pr 16:23
A w servant will rule over a Pr 17:2
is considered w when he keeps Pr 17:28
and the ear of the w seeks it. Pr 18:15
that you may be w in later life. Pr 19:20

WISELY *(3)*

WISER *(9)*

WISEST *(2)*

WISH *(19)*

WISHED *(2)*

WISHES *(1)*

WITCHCRAFT *(4)*

WITH *(5958)*

(See pp. xi-xii.)

WITHDRAW *(14)*

WITHDRAWING *(1)*

WITHDRAWN *(2)*

WITHDREW *(25)*

WITHER *(22)*

WITHERED *(19)*

WITHERS *(13)*

WITHHELD *(15)*
you have not **w** your only son Gn 22:12
and have not **w** your only son, Gn 22:16
who has not **w** His kindness and Gn 24:27
who has **w** children from you?" Gn 30:2
He has **w** nothing from me except Gn 39:9
to the thirsty and **w** food from Jb 22:7
Light is **w** from the wicked, Jb 38:15
He in anger **w** His compassion? Ps 77:9
Your compassion are **w** from me. Is 63:15
sins have **w** ⌊My⌋ bounty from Jr 5:25
I **w** My hand and acted because Ezk 20:22
offerings are **w** from the house Jl 1:13
I also **w** the rain from you while Am 4:7
the skies have **w** the dew and the Hg 1:10
pay that you **w** from the workers Jms 5:4

WITHHOLD *(9)*
None of us will **w** from you his Gn 23:6
You did not **w** Your manna from Neh 9:20
not **w** Your compassion from me; Ps 40:11
does not **w** the good from those Ps 84:11
don't **w** good from the one to Pr 3:27
Don't **w** correction from a youth; Pr 23:13
I won't **w** a word from you." Jr 42:4
will You **w** mercy from Jerusalem Zch 1:12
Can anyone **w** water and prevent Ac 10:47

WITHHOLDS *(3)*
When He **w** the waters, everything Jb 12:15
another **w** what is right, only to Pr 11:24
cursed is the one who **w** his Jr 48:10

WITHIN *(178)*
(See pp. xi-xii.)

WITHOUT *(323)*
(See pp. xi-xii.)

WITHSTAND *(7)*
everything that can **w** fire— Nm 31:23
Anything that cannot **w** fire, Nm 31:23
a single person could **w** them; Est 9:2
Who can **w** His cold? Ps 147:17
a flood, but who can **w** jealousy? Pr 27:4
me over to those I cannot **w**. Lm 1:14
Who can **w** His indignation? Nah 1:6

WITNESS *(73)*
serve as my **w** that I dug this Gn 21:30
it be a **w** between the two of us. Gn 31:44
This mound is a **w** between me and Gn 31:48
God will be a **w** between you and Gn 31:50
This mound is a **w** and the marker Gn 31:52
marker is a **w** that I will not Gn 31:52
the wicked to be a malicious **w**. Ex 23:1
since there is no **w** against her, Nm 5:13
based on the testimony of one **w**. Nm 35:30
on the testimony of a single **w**. Dt 17:6
One **w** cannot establish any Dt 19:15
If a malicious **w** testifies Dt 19:16
and if the **w** turns out to be a Dt 19:18
song may be a **w** for Me against Dt 31:19
remain there as a **w** against you. Dt 31:26
it is to be a **w** between us and Jos 22:27
but as a **w** between us and you. Jos 22:28
It is a **w** between us that the Jos 22:34
it will be a **w** against us, Jos 24:27
and it will be a **w** against you, Jos 24:27
The LORD is our **w** if we don't do Jdg 11:10
The LORD is a **w** against you, 1Sm 12:5
anointed is a **w** today that you 1Sm 12:5
"⌊He is⌋ a **w**," they said. 1Sm 12:5
from the land of Egypt, is a **w**. 1Sm 12:6
LORD will be a **w** between you 1Sm 20:23
LORD will be ⌊a **w**⌋ between you 1Sm 20:42
on my throne, and I am a **w**.' " 1Kg 1:48
right for us to **w** his dishonor, Ezr 4:14
me up—it has become a **w**; Jb 16:8
Even now my **w** is in heaven, Jb 16:19
a faithful **w** in the sky." Ps 89:37
your eyes and **w** the punishment Ps 91:8
a lying **w** who gives false Pr 6:19
is right, but a false **w**, deceit. Pr 12:17
An honest **w** does not deceive, Pr 14:5
but a dishonest **w** utters lies. Pr 14:5
A truthful **w** rescues lives, Pr 14:25
false **w** will not go unpunished, Pr 19:5
false **w** will not go unpunished, Pr 19:9
A worthless **w** mocks justice, Pr 19:28
A lying **w** will perish, but the Pr 21:28
will be a sign and **w** to the LORD Is 19:20
made him a **w** to the peoples, Is 55:4
am He who knows, and I am a **w**." Jr 29:23
true and faithful **w** against us. Jr 42:5
GOD will be a **w** against you, Mc 1:2
LORD has been a **w** between you Mal 2:14
will be ready to **w** against Mal 3:5
to bear **w** to them and to the Mt 10:18
do not bear false **w**; Mt 19:18
do not bear false **w**; Mk 10:19
because of Me, as a **w** to them. Mk 13:9
wiping off ⌊as a **w**⌋ against you Lk 10:11
do not bear false **w**; Lk 18:20
to an opportunity for you to **w**. Lk 21:13
He came as a **w** to testify about Jn 1:7
written that the **w** of two men is Jn 8:17
one become a **w** with us of His Ac 1:22
not leave Himself without a **w**, Ac 14:17
you will be a **w** for Him to all Ac 22:15
blood of Your **w** Stephen was Ac 22:20
a servant and a **w** of things you Ac 26:16
my **w** that I constantly mention Rm 1:9
I call on God as a **w** against me: 2Co 1:23
you, I'm not lying. God is my **w**. Gl 1:20
For God is my **w**, how I deeply Php 1:8
greedy motives—God is our **w**— 1Th 2:5
corrosion will be a **w** against Jms 5:3
fellow elder and **w** to the 1Pt 5:1
the faithful **w**, the firstborn Rv 1:5
My faithful **w**, who was killed Rv 2:13
and true **W**, the Originator Rv 3:14

WITNESSED *(5)*
All the people **w** the thunder and Ex 20:18
known about something he has **w**, Lv 5:1
'I **w** what the Amalekites did to 1Sm 15:2
as what they had **w** and what had Est 9:26
he expounded and **w** about the Ac 28:23

WITNESSES *(50)*
to death based on the word of **w**. Nm 35:30
and earth as **w** against you today Dt 4:26
the testimony of two or three **w**. Dt 17:6
the testimony of two or three **w**. Dt 19:15
and earth as **w** against you today Dt 30:19
and earth as **w** against them. Dt 31:28
You are **w** against yourselves Jos 24:22
"We are **w**," they said. Jos 24:22
You are **w** today that I am buying Ru 4:9
of his home. You are **w** today." Ru 4:10
at the gate said, "We are **w**. Ru 4:11
You produce new **w** against me and Jb 10:17
for false **w** rise up against me, Ps 27:12
Malicious **w** come forward; Ps 35:11
I have appointed trustworthy **w**— Is 8:2
present their **w** to vindicate Is 43:9
"You are My **w**"—the LORD's Is 43:10
So you are My **w**"—the LORD's Is 43:12
ago? You are my **w**! Is there any Is 44:8
Their **w** do not see or know Is 44:9
nations and you **w**, learn what Jr 6:18
it, called in **w**, and weighed out Jr 32:10
the **w** who were signing the Jr 32:12
with silver and call in **w**— Jr 32:25
and **w** will be called on in the Jr 32:44
of two or three **w** every fact may Mt 18:16
many false **w** came forward. Mt 26:60
Why do we still need **w**? Mt 26:65
said, "Why do we still need **w**? Mk 14:63
you are **w** that you approve Lk 11:48
You are **w** of these things. Lk 24:48
you will be My **w** in Jerusalem, Ac 1:8
We are all **w** of this. Ac 2:32
from the dead; we are **w** of this. Ac 3:15
We are **w** of these things, and so Ac 5:32
also presented false **w** who said, Ac 6:13
the **w** laid their robes at the Ac 7:58
ourselves are **w** of everything He Ac 10:39
w appointed beforehand by God, Ac 10:41
who are now His **w** to the people. Ac 13:31
found to be false **w** about God, 1Co 15:15
two or three **w** every word will 2Co 13:1
You are **w**, and so is God, of how 1Th 2:10
is supported by two or three **w**. 1Tm 5:19
a good confession before many **w**. 1Tm 6:12
me in the presence of many **w**, 2Tm 2:2
the testimony of two or three **w**. Heb 10:28
large cloud of **w** surrounding us Heb 12:1
empower my two **w**, and they will Rv 11:3
on the blood of the **w** to Jesus. Rv 17:6

WITNESSES' *(1)*
The **w** hands are to be the first Dt 17:7

WIVES *(118)*
Lamech took two **w** for himself, Gn 4:19
said to his **w**: Adah and Zillah, Gn 4:23
w of Lamech, pay attention to my Gn 4:23
they chose as **w** for themselves. Gn 6:2
your wife, and your sons' **w**. Gn 6:18
and his sons' **w** entered the ark Gn 7:7
three sons' **w** entered the ark Gn 7:13
and your sons' **w** with you. Gn 8:16
wife, and his sons' **w**, came out. Gn 8:18
Abram and Nahor took **w**: Gn 11:29
he took as his **w** Judith daughter Gn 26:34
in addition to his other **w**, Gn 28:9
me my **w** and my children that Gn 30:26
children and **w** on the camels. Gn 31:17
my daughters or take other **w**, Gn 31:50
Jacob got up and took his two **w**, Gn 32:22
daughters as our **w** and give our Gn 34:21
children, and **w**, and plundered Gn 34:29
Esau took his **w** from the Gn 36:2
took his **w**, sons, daughters, Gn 36:6
his father's **w**, and he brought Gn 37:2
children, your **w**, and bring your Gn 45:19
with their children and their **w**. Gn 46:5
including the **w** of Jacob's sons Gn 46:26
then your **w** will be widows and Ex 22:24
that are on the ears of your **w**, Ex 32:2
Our **w** and little children will Nm 14:3
of their tents with their **w**, Nm 16:27
little children, **w**, livestock, Nm 32:26
But your **w**, young children, and Dt 3:19
not acquire many **w** for himself Dt 17:17
If a man has two **w**, one loved Dt 21:15
children, your **w**, and the Dt 29:11
Your **w**, young children, and Jos 1:14
daughters as **w** for themselves, Jdg 3:6
offspring, since he had many **w**. Jdg 8:30
brought back 30 **w** for his sons Jdg 12:9
we do about **w** for the survivors Jdg 21:7
them any of our daughters as **w**." Jdg 21:7
we do about **w** for those who are Jdg 21:16
give them our daughters as **w**." Jdg 21:18
get enough **w** for each of them Jdg 21:22
took Moabite women as their **w**: Ru 1:4
He had two **w**, the first named 1Sm 1:2
the two of them became his **w**. 1Sm 25:43
him, and David had his two **w**: 1Sm 27:3
Their **w**, sons, and daughters had 1Sm 30:3
David's two **w**, Ahinoam the 1Sm 30:5
he also rescued his two **w**. 1Sm 30:18
David went there with his two **w**, 2Sm 2:2
concubines and **w** in Jerusalem, 2Sm 5:13
your master's **w** into your arms, 2Sm 12:8
will take your **w** and give them 2Sm 12:11
and daughters, your **w**, and your 2Sm 19:5
He had 700 **w** who were princesses 1Kg 11:3
his **w** seduced him ⌊to follow⌋ 1Kg 11:4
the same for all his foreign **w**, 1Kg 11:8
And your best **w** and children are 1Kg 20:3
your gold, your **w**, and your 1Kg 20:5
demanded my **w**, my children, my 1Kg 20:7
One of the **w** of the sons of the 2Kg 4:1
the king's **w**, his officials, 2Kg 24:15
fathered Tekoa and had two **w**, 1Ch 4:5
they had many **w** and children. 1Ch 7:4
Machir took **w** from Huppim and 1Ch 7:15
divorced his **w** Hushim and Baara 1Ch 8:8
David took more **w** in Jerusalem, 1Ch 14:3
than all his **w** and concubines. 2Ch 11:21
He acquired 18 **w** and 60 2Ch 11:21
and sought many **w** for them. 2Ch 11:23
acquired 14 **w**, and fathered 22 2Ch 13:21
infants, their **w**, and their 2Ch 20:13
your sons, your **w**, and all your 2Ch 21:14
palace and also his sons and **w**; 2Ch 21:17
Jehoiada acquired two **w** for him, 2Ch 24:3
and our **w** are in captivity 2Ch 29:9
all their infants, **w**, sons, and 2Ch 31:18
daughters as **w** for themselves Ezr 9:2
all the ⌊foreign⌋ **w** and their Ezr 10:3
peoples and ⌊your⌋ foreign **w**." Ezr 10:11
pledged to send their **w** away, Ezr 10:19
of the **w** had borne children. Ezr 10:44
daughters, your **w** and homes." Neh 4:14
people and their **w** against their Neh 5:1
along with their **w**, sons, and Neh 10:28
daughters as **w** for our sons. Neh 10:30
daughters as **w** for your sons Neh 13:25

be looted, and their **w** raped. Is 13:16
⌊their⌋ fields and **w** as well, Jr 6:12
will give their **w** to other men, Jr 8:10
—they, their **w**, their sons, Jr 14:16
Let their **w** become childless and Jr 18:21
Take **w** and have sons and Jr 29:6
Take **w** for your sons and give Jr 29:6
neighbors' **w** and have spoken Jr 29:23
life—we, our **w**, our sons, and Jr 35:8
All your **w** and sons will be Jr 38:23
of their **w**, your own evils, Jr 44:9
the evils of your **w** that were Jr 44:9
knew that their **w** were burning Jr 44:15
you and your **w**, you women have Jr 44:25
his nobles, **w**, and concubines Dn 5:2
his nobles, **w**, and concubines Dn 5:3
your nobles, **w**, and concubines Dn 5:23
their children, and their **w**. Dn 6:24
you to divorce your **w** because of Mt 19:8
with their **w** and children, Ac 21:5
on those who have **w** should be as 1Co 7:29
W, submit to your own husbands Eph 5:22
so **w** should ⌊submit⌋ to their Eph 5:24
love your **w**, just as also Eph 5:25
should love their **w** as their own Eph 5:28
W, be submissive to your Col 3:18
love your **w** and don't become Col 3:19
W, too, must be worthy of 1Tm 3:11
W, in the same way, submit 1Pt 3:1
message by the way their **w** live, 1Pt 3:1
live with your **w** with 1Pt 3:7

WOE *(112)*

W to you, Moab! You have been Nm 21:29
W to us, nothing like this has 1Sm 4:7
W to us, who will rescue us from 1Sm 4:8
If I am wicked, **w** to me! Jb 10:15
Who has **w**? Who has sorrow? Who Pr 23:29
W to you, land, when your king Ec 10:16
not conceal it. **W** to them! For Is 3:9
W to the wicked—⌊it will go⌋ Is 3:11
W to those who add house to Is 5:8
W to those who rise early in the Is 5:11
W to those who drag wickedness Is 5:18
W to those who call evil good Is 5:20
W to those who are wise in their Is 5:21
W to those who are heroes at Is 5:22
W is me, for I am ruined, Is 6:5
W to those enacting crooked Is 10:1
W to Assyria, the rod of My Is 10:5
away! I waste away! **W** is me." Is 24:16
W to the majestic crown of Is 28:1
⌊**W**⌋ to those overcome with wine. Is 28:1
W to Ariel, Ariel, the city Is 29:1
W to those who go to great Is 29:15
W to the rebellious children! Is 30:1
W to those who go down to Egypt Is 31:1
W, you destroyer never destroyed, Is 33:1
W to the one who argues with his Is 45:9
W to us, for we are ruined! Jr 4:13
W is me, for my life is weary Jr 4:31
W to us, for the day is passing; Jr 6:4
W to me because of my brokenness Jr 10:19
detestable acts. **W** to you, Jr 13:27
W is me, my mother, that you Jr 15:10
W for the one who builds his Jr 22:13
him, ⌊saying,⌋ **W**, my brother! Jr 22:18
my brother! or **W**, ⌊my⌋ sister! Jr 22:18
mourn for him, saying, **W**, lord! Jr 22:18
Woe, lord! **W**, his majesty! Jr 22:18
W to the shepherds who destroy Jr 23:1
'You have said, **W** is me, because Jr 45:3
W to Nebo, because it is about Jr 48:1
W to you, Moab! The people of Jr 48:46
W to them, because their day has Jr 50:27
W to us, for we have sinned. Lm 5:16
mourning, and **w** were written on Ezk 2:10
W to the foolish prophets who Ezk 13:3
W to the women who sew ⌊magic⌋ Ezk 13:18
all your evil—**W**, woe to you!" Ezk 16:23
all your evil—Woe, **w** to you!" Ezk 16:23
W to the city of bloodshed, Ezk 24:6
W to the city of bloodshed! Ezk 24:9
W to the shepherds of Israel, Ezk 34:2
W to them, for they fled from Me; Hs 7:13
w to them when I depart from Hs 9:12
W because of that day! For the Jl 1:15
W to you who long for the Day of Am 5:18
W to those who are at ease in Am 6:1
W to those who dream up Mc 2:1
W to the city of blood, totally Nah 3:1
W to him who amasses what is not Hab 2:6
W to him who unjustly gains Hab 2:9
W to him who builds a city with Hab 2:12
W to him who gives his neighbors Hab 2:15
W to him who says to wood: Hab 2:19
W, inhabitants of the seacoast, Zph 2:5
W to the city that is rebellious Zph 3:1
W to the worthless shepherd who Zch 11:17
W to you, Chorazin! Woe to you, Mt 11:21
you, Chorazin! **W** to you, Mt 11:21
W to the world because of Mt 18:7
but **w** to that man by whom the Mt 18:7
But **w** to you, scribes and Mt 23:13
W to you, scribes and Pharisees, Mt 23:14
W to you, scribes and Pharisees, Mt 23:15
W to you, blind guides, who say, Mt 23:16
W to you, scribes and Pharisees, Mt 23:23
W to you, scribes and Pharisees, Mt 23:25
W to you, scribes and Pharisees, Mt 23:27
W to you, scribes and Pharisees, Mt 23:29
W to pregnant women and nursing Mt 24:19
w to that man by whom the Son Mt 26:24
W to pregnant women and nursing Mk 13:17
w to that man by whom the Son Mk 14:21
But **w** to you who are rich, Lk 6:24
W to you who are full now, Lk 6:25
W to you who are laughing now, Lk 6:25
W to you when all people speak Lk 6:26
W to you, Chorazin! Woe to you, Lk 10:13
you, Chorazin! **W** to you, Lk 10:13
But **w** to you Pharisees! Lk 11:42
W to you Pharisees! You love the Lk 11:43
W to you! You are like unmarked Lk 11:44
W also to you experts in the Lk 11:46
W to you! You build monuments to Lk 11:47
W to you experts in the law! Lk 11:52
but **w** to the one they come Lk 17:1
W to pregnant women and nursing Lk 21:23
but **w** to that man by whom He is Lk 22:22
And **w** to me if I do not preach 1Co 9:16
W to them! For they have Jd 11
saying in a loud voice, "**W**! Rv 8:13
voice, "Woe! **W**! Woe to those who Rv 8:13
W to those who live on the earth, Rv 8:13
first **w** has passed. There are Rv 9:12
The second **w** has passed. Rv 11:14
the third **w** is coming quickly! Rv 11:14
W to the earth and the sea, Rv 12:12
W, woe, the great city, Babylon, Rv 18:10
Woe, **w**, the great city, Babylon, Rv 18:10
W, woe, the great city, clothed Rv 18:16
Woe, **w**, the great city, clothed Rv 18:16
W, woe, the great city, where Rv 18:19
Woe, **w**, the great city, where Rv 18:19

WOES *(1)*

still two more **w** to come after Rv 9:12

WOKE *(10)*

cows. Then Pharaoh **w** up. Gn 41:4
Then Pharaoh **w** up, and it was Gn 41:7
it had been before. Then I **w** up. Gn 41:21
no one knew, and no one **w** up; 1Sm 26:12
Then Solomon **w** up and realized 1Kg 3:15
the disciples came and **w** Him up, Mt 8:25
they **w** Him up and said to Him, Mk 4:38
They came and **w** Him up, saying, Lk 8:24
the side, he **w** him up and said Ac 12:7
When the jailer **w** up and saw the Ac 16:27

WOLF *(6)*

Benjamin is a **w**; he tears ⌊his Gn 49:27
The **w** will live with the lamb, Is 11:6
The **w** and the lamb will feed Is 65:25
A **w** from an arid plain will Jr 5:6
away when he sees a **w** coming. Jn 10:12
The **w** then snatches and scatters Jn 10:12

WOLVES *(7)*

her are like **w** tearing ⌊their⌋ Ezk 22:27
more fierce than **w** of the night. Hab 1:8
her judges are **w** of the night, Zph 3:3
but inwardly are ravaging **w**. Mt 7:15
you out like sheep among **w**. Mt 10:16
you out like lambs among **w**. Lk 10:3
departure savage **w** will come in Ac 20:29

WOMAN *(390)*

the man into a **w** and brought her Gn 2:22
this one will be called **w**, Gn 2:23
said to the **w**, "Did God really Gn 3:1
The **w** said to the serpent, Gn 3:2
the serpent said to the **w**. Gn 3:4
Then the **w** saw that the tree was Gn 3:6
The **w** You gave to be with me— Gn 3:12
So the LORD God asked the **w**, Gn 3:13
And the **w** said, "It was the Gn 3:13
hostility between you and the **w**, Gn 3:15
He said to the **w**: I will Gn 3:16
know what a beautiful **w** you are. Gn 12:11
saw that the **w** was very Gn 12:14
so the **w** was taken to Pharaoh's Gn 12:15
ninety-year-old **w**, give birth?" Gn 17:17
because of the **w** you have taken, Gn 20:3
taken, for she is a married **w**." Gn 20:3
Suppose the **w** is unwilling to Gn 24:5
If the **w** is unwilling to follow Gn 24:8
young **w** who had not known a man Gn 24:16
'Suppose the **w** will not come Gn 24:39
let her be the **w** the LORD has Gn 24:44
for she is a beautiful **w**." Gn 26:7
a Hittite **w** like one of them Gn 27:46
not to marry a Canaanite **w**. Gn 28:6
items he had left with the **w**, Gn 38:20
Shaul, the son of a Canaanite **w**. Gn 46:10
of Levi married a Levite **w**. Ex 2:1
The **w** became pregnant and gave Ex 2:2
I go and call a **w** from the Ex 2:7
So the **w** took the boy and Ex 2:9
Each **w** will ask her neighbor and Ex 3:22
neighbor and any **w** staying in Ex 3:22
Shaul, the son of a Canaanite **w**. Ex 6:15
and hit a pregnant **w** so that her Ex 21:22
ox gores a man or a **w** to death, Ex 21:28
and it kills a man or a **w**, Ex 21:29
No **w** will miscarry or be barren Ex 23:26
Every skilled **w** spun ⌊yarn⌋ with Ex 35:25
Let no man or **w** make anything Ex 36:6
When a **w** becomes pregnant and Lv 12:2
is the law for a **w** giving birth, Lv 12:7
When a man or **w** has an infection Lv 13:29
a man or a **w** has white spots Lv 13:38
man sleeps with a **w** and has an Lv 15:18
When a **w** has a discharge, Lv 15:19
When a **w** has a discharge of her Lv 15:25
a **w** who is in her menstrual Lv 15:33
who sleeps with an unclean **w**." Lv 15:33
with a **w** and her daughter. Lv 18:17
not to marry a **w** as a rival to Lv 18:18
not to come near a **w** during her Lv 18:19
to sleep with a man as with a **w**; Lv 18:22
a **w** is not to present herself to Lv 18:23
with a **w** who is a slave Lv 19:20
adultery with a married **w**— Lv 20:10
sleeps with a man as with a **w**, Lv 20:13
man marries a **w** and her mother, Lv 20:14
If a **w** comes near any animal and Lv 20:16
to kill the **w** and the animal. Lv 20:16
a menstruating **w** and has sexual Lv 20:18
man or a **w** who is a medium or a Lv 20:27
are not to marry a **w** defiled by Lv 21:7
is to marry a **w** who is a virgin Lv 21:13
a divorced **w**, or one defiled Lv 21:14
When a man or **w** commits any sin Nm 5:6
priest has the **w** stand before Nm 5:18
require the **w** to take an oath Nm 5:19
must make the **w** take the oath Nm 5:21
And the **w** must reply, 'Amen, Nm 5:22
will require the **w** to drink the Nm 5:24
will require the **w** to drink the Nm 5:26
But if the **w** has not defiled Nm 5:28
He is to have the **w** stand before Nm 5:30
but that **w** will bear the Nm 5:31
When a man or **w** makes a special Nm 6:2
as a nursing **w** carries a baby,' Nm 11:12
of the Cushite **w** he married Nm 12:1
for he had married a Cushite **w** Nm 12:1
a Midianite **w** to his relatives Nm 25:6
the Israelite man and the **w**— Nm 25:8
dead with the Midianite **w**, Nm 25:14
the slain Midianite **w** was Cozbi, Nm 25:15
When a **w** in her father's house Nm 30:3
If a **w** marries while her vows or Nm 30:6
If a **w** in her husband's house Nm 30:10
and kill every **w** who has had Nm 31:17
a man or **w**, is sold to you Dt 15:12
If a man or **w** among you in one Dt 17:2
that man or **w** who has done this Dt 17:5

engaged to a **w** and not married	Dt 20:7
see a beautiful **w** among the	Dt 21:11
A **w** is not to wear male	Dt 22:5
If a man marries a **w**, has sexual	Dt 22:13
'I married this **w** and was	Dt 22:14
will bring the **w** to the door of	Dt 22:21
had sex with the **w** and the woman	Dt 22:22
the woman and the **w** must die.	Dt 22:22
is a young **w** who is a virgin	Dt 22:23
the young **w** because she did not	Dt 22:24
the engaged **w** in the open	Dt 22:25
Do nothing to the young **w**,	Dt 22:26
field, the engaged **w** cried out,	Dt 22:27
If a man encounters a young **w**,	Dt 22:28
No Israelite **w** is to be a cult	Dt 23:17
a man marries a **w**, but she	Dt 24:1
You will become engaged to a **w**,	Dt 28:30
and refined **w** among you,	Dt 28:56
is no man, **w**, clan, or tribe	Dt 29:18
they came to the house of a **w**,	Jos 2:1
But the **w** had taken the two men	Jos 2:4
every man and **w**, both young and	Jos 6:21
and bring the **w** out of there,	Jos 6:22
a **w** who was a prophet and the	Jdg 4:4
But a **w** threw the upper portion	Jdg 9:53
about me, 'A **w** killed him.' "	Jdg 9:54
you are the son of another **w**."	Jdg 11:2
to the **w** and said to her	Jdg 13:3
Then the **w** went and told her	Jdg 13:6
of GOD came again to the **w**.	Jdg 13:9
The **w** ran quickly to her husband	Jdg 13:10
So the **w** gave birth to a son and	Jdg 13:24
saw a young Philistine **w** there.	Jdg 14:1
a young Philistine **w** in Timnah.	Jdg 14:2
you find a young **w** among your	Jdg 14:3
Then he went and spoke to the **w**,	Jdg 14:7
father went ⌊to visit⌋ the **w**,	Jdg 14:10
in love with a **w** named Delilah,	Jdg 16:4
acquired a **w** from Bethlehem	Jdg 19:1
morning, the **w** made her way back	Jdg 19:26
there was the **w**, his concubine,	Jdg 19:27
the husband of the murdered **w**,	Jdg 20:4
Whose young **w** is this?"	Ru 2:5
young Moabite **w** who returned	Ru 2:6
there lying at his feet was a **w**!	Ru 3:8
that you are a **w** of noble	Ru 3:11
it be known that a **w** came to the	Ru 3:14
LORD make the **w** who is entering	Ru 4:11
will give you by this young **w**."	Ru 4:12
I am a **w** with a broken heart.	1Sm 1:15
Don't think of me as a wicked **w**;	1Sm 1:16
I am the **w** who stood here beside	1Sm 1:26
The barren **w** gives birth to	1Sm 2:5
but the **w** with many sons pines	1Sm 2:5
children by this **w** in place of	1Sm 2:20
of a perverse and rebellious **w**!	1Sm 20:30
The **w** was intelligent and	1Sm 25:3
either man or **w**, but he took	1Sm 27:9
not let a man or **w** live to be	1Sm 27:11
Find me a **w** who is a medium,	1Sm 28:7
There is a **w** at Endor who is a	1Sm 28:7
They came to the **w** at night,	1Sm 28:8
But the **w** said to him, "You	1Sm 28:9
for you?" the **w** asked. "Bring up	1Sm 28:11
When the **w** saw Samuel, she cried	1Sm 28:12
of the earth," the **w** answered.	1Sm 28:13
The **w** came over to Saul, and she	1Sm 28:21
servants and the **w** urged him,	1Sm 28:23
The **w** had a fattened calf at her	1Sm 28:24
than the love of a **w** ⌊for me⌋.	2Sm 1:26
me of wrongdoing with this **w**!	2Sm 3:8
the roof he saw a **w** bathing—	2Sm 11:2
bathing—a very beautiful **w**.	2Sm 11:2
The **w** conceived and sent word to	2Sm 11:5
Didn't a **w** drop an upper	2Sm 11:21
Throw this **w** out and bolt the	2Sm 13:17
as a desolate **w** in the house of	2Sm 13:20
to bring a clever **w** from there.	2Sm 14:2
Act like a **w** who has been	2Sm 14:2
When the **w** from Tekoa came to	2Sm 14:4
The king told the **w**, "Go home.	2Sm 14:8
Then the **w** of Tekoa said to the	2Sm 14:9
Then the **w** said, "Please, may	2Sm 14:12
The **w** asked, "Why have you	2Sm 14:13
Then the king answered the **w**,	2Sm 14:18
the king speak," the **w** replied.	2Sm 14:18
all this?" The **w** answered. "As	2Sm 14:19
Tamar, who was a beautiful **w**.	2Sm 14:27
came to the **w** at the house	2Sm 17:20
water," the **w** replied to them	2Sm 17:20
a wise **w** called out from the	2Sm 20:16
near her, the **w** asked, "Are you	2Sm 20:17
The **w** replied to Joab, "All	2Sm 20:21
w went to all the people with	2Sm 20:22
w said, "Please my lord, this	1Kg 3:17
this **w** and I live in the same	1Kg 3:17
"No," the other **w** said.	1Kg 3:22
The first **w** said, "No, your son	1Kg 3:22
replied, "This **w** says, 'This is	1Kg 3:23
dead,' but that **w** says, 'No,	1Kg 3:23
The **w** whose son was alive spoke	1Kg 3:26
the living baby to the first **w**,	1Kg 3:27
commanded a **w** who is a widow	1Kg 17:9
was a widow **w** gathering wood.	1Kg 17:10
the son of the **w** who owned the	1Kg 17:17
Then the **w** said to Elijah,	1Kg 17:24
A prominent **w** who ⌊lived⌋ there	2Kg 4:8
"Call this Shunammite **w**."	2Kg 4:12
The **w** conceived and gave birth	2Kg 4:17
Look, there's the Shunammite **w**.	2Kg 4:25
said, "Call the Shunammite **w**."	2Kg 4:36
on the wall, a **w** cried out to	2Kg 6:26
She said, "This **w** said to me,	2Kg 6:28
said to the **w** whose son he had	2Kg 8:1
So the **w** got ready and did what	2Kg 8:2
the **w** returned from the land	2Kg 8:3
the **w** whose son he had restored	2Kg 8:5
this is the **w** and this is the	2Kg 8:5
When the king asked the **w**,	2Kg 8:6
of this cursed **w** and bury her,	2Kg 9:34
The young **w**, Daughter Zion,	2Kg 19:21
by Bath-shua the Canaanite **w**.	1Ch 2:3
is the son of a **w** from the	2Ch 2:14
death, young or old, man or **w**.	2Ch 15:13
son of the Ammonite **w** Shimeath,	2Ch 24:26
son of the Moabite **w** Shimrith.	2Ch 24:26
given to another **w** who is more	Est 1:19
Then the young **w** who pleases the	Est 2:4
The young **w** had a beautiful	Est 2:7
The young **w** pleased him and	Est 2:9
When the young **w** would go to the	Est 2:13
to every man or **w** who approaches	Est 4:11
speak as a foolish **w** speaks,"	Jb 2:10
Man born of **w** is short of days	Jb 14:1
or one born of **w**, that he should	Jb 15:14
childless **w** and do not deal	Jb 24:21
How can one born of **w** be pure?	Jb 25:4
then could I look at a young **w**?	Jb 31:1
agony like that of a **w** in labor,	Ps 48:6
the childless **w** a household,	Ps 113:9
rescue you from a forbidden **w**,	Pr 2:16
the forbidden **w** drip honey and	Pr 5:3
with a forbidden **w** or embrace	Pr 5:20
will protect you from an evil **w**,	Pr 6:24
keep you from a forbidden **w**,	Pr 7:5
A **w** came to meet him, dressed	Pr 7:10
The **w** Folly is rowdy; she is	Pr 9:13
A gracious **w** gains honor, but	Pr 11:16
A beautiful **w** who rejects good	Pr 11:22
Every wise **w** builds her house,	Pr 14:1
the forbidden **w** is a deep pit;	Pr 22:14
and a forbidden **w** is a narrow	Pr 23:27
the way of a man with a young **w**.	Pr 30:19
an unloved **w** when she marries,	Pr 30:23
but a **w** who fears the LORD will	Pr 31:30
than death the **w** who is a trap,	Ec 7:26
these I have not found a true **w**.	Ec 7:28
in the womb of a pregnant **w**,	Ec 11:5
be in anguish like a **w** in labor.	Is 13:8
like the pain of a **w** in labor.	Is 21:3
ravished young **w**, daughter of	Is 23:12
As a pregnant **w** about to give	Is 26:17
The young **w**, Daughter Zion,	Is 37:22
I will groan like a **w** in labor,	Is 42:14
Can a **w** forget her nursing	Is 49:15
the children of the married **w**,"	Is 54:1
Can a young **w** forget her jewelry	Jr 2:32
as a **w** may betray her lover,	Jr 3:20
I hear a cry like a **w** in labor,	Jr 4:31
us—pain like a **w** in labor.	Jr 6:24
as ⌊they do⌋ a **w** in labor?	Jr 13:21
on you, agony like a **w** in labor.	Jr 22:23
stomach like a **w** in labor and	Jr 30:6
You are cutting off man and **w**,	Jr 44:7
the heart of a **w** with	Jr 48:41
the heart of a **w** with	Jr 49:22
seized her like a **w** in labor.	Jr 49:24
him—pain, like a **w** in labor.	Jr 50:43
With you I will smash man and **w**;	Jr 51:22
wife or come near a **w** during her	Ezk 18:6
concerning this **w** worn out by	Ezk 23:43
marry a widow or a divorced **w**,	Ezk 44:22
show love to a **w** who is loved by	Hs 3:1
Grieve like a young **w** dressed in	Jl 1:8
the wall, each **w** straight ahead,	Am 4:3
grips you like a **w** in labor?	Mc 4:9
Zion, like a **w** in labor.	Mc 4:10
mouth from the **w** who lies in	Mc 7:5
and there was a **w** sitting inside	Zch 5:7
who looks at a **w** to lust for her	Mt 5:28
a divorced **w** commits adultery.	Mt 5:32
a **w** who had suffered from	Mt 9:20
And the **w** was made well from	Mt 9:22
yeast that a **w** took and mixed	Mt 13:33
a Canaanite **w** from that region	Mt 15:22
replied to her, "**W**, your faith	Mt 15:28
Then last of all the **w** died.	Mt 22:27
a **w** approached Him with an	Mt 26:7
Why are you bothering this **w**?	Mt 26:10
what this **w** has done will also	Mt 26:13
another **w** saw him and told those	Mt 26:71
A **w** suffering from bleeding for	Mk 5:25
Then the **w**, knowing what had	Mk 5:33
a **w** whose little daughter had an	Mk 7:25
Now the **w** was Greek, a	Mk 7:26
Last of all, the **w** died too.	Mk 12:22
w came with an alabaster jar of	Mk 14:3
what this **w** has done will also	Mk 14:9
and said, "Rejoice, favored **w**!	Lk 1:28
And a **w** in the town who was a	Lk 7:37
and what kind of **w** this is who	Lk 7:39
Turning to the **w**, He said to	Lk 7:44
to Simon, "Do you see this **w**?	Lk 7:44
said to the **w**, "Your faith has	Lk 7:50
A **w** suffering from bleeding for	Lk 8:43
When the **w** saw that she was	Lk 8:47
a **w** named Martha welcomed Him	Lk 10:38
a **w** from the crowd raised her	Lk 11:27
a **w** was there who had been	Lk 13:11
out to her, "**W**, you are free	Lk 13:12
has bound this **w**, a daughter	Lk 13:16
yeast that a **w** took and mixed	Lk 13:21
Or what **w** who has 10 silver	Lk 15:8
marries another **w** commits	Lk 16:18
marries a **w** divorced from her	Lk 16:18
Finally, the **w** died too.	Lk 20:32
whose wife will the **w** be?	Lk 20:33
"**W**, I don't know Him!"	Lk 22:57
of yours to do with Me, **w**?"	Jn 2:4
A **w** of Samaria came to draw	Jn 4:7
a drink from me, a Samaritan **w**?"	Jn 4:9
"Sir," said the **w**, "You don't	Jn 4:11
"Sir," the **w** said to Him, "give	Jn 4:15
"Sir," the **w** replied, "I see	Jn 4:19
her, "Believe Me, **w**, an hour is	Jn 4:21
The **w** said to Him, "I know that	Jn 4:25
that He was talking with a **w**.	Jn 4:27
Then the **w** left her water jar,	Jn 4:28
of what the **w** said when she	Jn 4:39
they told the **w**, "We no longer	Jn 4:42
brought a **w** caught in adultery	Jn 8:3
this **w** was caught in the act of	Jn 8:4
left, with the **w** in the center.	Jn 8:9
said to her, "**W**, where are they	Jn 8:10
a **w** is in labor she has pain	Jn 16:21
to His mother, "**W**, here is your	Jn 19:26
They said to her, "**W**, why are	Jn 20:13
"**W**," Jesus said to her, "why are	Jn 20:15
the son of a believing Jewish **w**,	Ac 16:1
A **w** named Lydia, a dealer in	Ac 16:14
Areopagite, a **w** named Damaris,	Ac 17:34
a married **w** is legally bound to	Rm 7:2
not to have relations with a **w**."	1Co 7:1
and each **w** should have her own	1Co 7:2
if any **w** has an unbelieving	1Co 7:13
An unmarried **w** or a virgin is	1Co 7:34
But a married **w** is concerned	1Co 7:34
the man is the head of the **w**,	1Co 11:3
But every **w** who prays or	1Co 11:5
for a **w** to have her hair	1Co 11:6
and glory, but **w** is man's glory.	1Co 11:7
For man did not come from **w**,	1Co 11:8
woman, but **w** came from man;	1Co 11:8
and man was not created for **w**,	1Co 11:9

for woman, but **w** for man. 1Co 11:9
This is why a **w** should have ⌊a 1Co 11:10
w is not independent of man, 1Co 11:11
and man is independent of **w**. 1Co 11:11
For just as **w** came from man, 1Co 11:12
comes through **w**, and all things 1Co 11:12
it proper for a **w** to pray to God 1Co 11:13
but that if a **w** has long hair, 1Co 11:15
is disgraceful for a **w** to speak 1Co 14:35
His Son, born of a **w**, born under Gl 4:4
slave and the other by a free **w**. Gl 4:22
the one by the free **w** was born Gl 4:23
O barren **w** who does not give Gl 4:27
those of the **w** who has a husband Gl 4:27
with the son of the free **w**. Gl 4:30
of the slave but of the free **w**. Gl 4:31
labor pains on a pregnant **w**, 1Th 5:3
A **w** should learn in silence with 1Tm 2:11
do not allow a **w** to teach or to 1Tm 2:12
but the **w** was deceived and 1Tm 2:14
If any believing **w** has widows, 1Tm 5:16
you tolerate the **w** Jezebel, Rv 2:20
a **w** clothed with the sun, with Rv 12:1
in front of the **w** who was about Rv 12:4
The **w** fled into the wilderness, Rv 12:6
persecuted the **w** who gave birth Rv 12:13
The **w** was given two wings of a Rv 12:14
water like a river after the **w**, Rv 12:15
But the earth helped the **w**: Rv 12:16
with the **w** and left to wage Rv 12:17
I saw a **w** sitting on a scarlet Rv 17:3
The **w** was dressed in purple and Rv 17:4
Then I saw that the **w** was drunk Rv 17:6
meaning of the **w** and of the Rv 17:7
on which the **w** is seated. Rv 17:9
And the **w** you saw is the great Rv 17:18

WOMAN'S *(15)*

fined as the **w** husband demands Ex 21:22
the Israelite **w** son and an Lv 24:10
of jealousy from the **w** hand, Nm 5:25
is not to put on a **w** garment, Dt 22:5
the young **w** father and mother Dt 22:15
The young **w** father will say to Dt 22:16
them⌋ to the young **w** father, Dt 22:19
of the young **w** virginity is Dt 22:20
the young **w** father 50 silver Dt 22:29
will sell Sisera into a **w** hand." Jdg 4:9
night this **w** son died because 1Kg 3:19
When the king heard the **w** words, 2Kg 6:30
before each young **w** turn to go Est 2:12
like a **w** miscarried ⌊child⌋, Ps 58:8
So if a **w** head is not covered, 1Co 11:6

WOMB *(53)*

Two nations are in your **w**; Gn 25:23
were indeed twins in her **w**. Gn 25:24
was unloved, He opened her **w**; Gn 29:31
to her and opened her **w**. Gn 30:22
there were twins in her **w**. Gn 38:27
of the breasts and the **w**. Gn 49:25
from every **w** among the Ex 13:2
every firstborn male of the **w**. Ex 13:12
of the **w** that are males, Ex 13:15
male from every **w** belongs to Me, Ex 34:19
firstborn Israelite from the **w**. Nm 3:12
all who come first from the **w**, Nm 8:16
he comes out of his mother's **w**." Nm 12:12
Naked I came from my mother's **w**, Jb 1:21
the doors of my ⌊mother's⌋ **w**, Jb 3:10
I die as I came from the **w**? Jb 3:11
did You bring me out of the **w**? Jb 10:18
carried from the **w** to the grave. Jb 10:19
their **w** prepares deception. Jb 15:35
The **w** forgets them; worms feed Jb 24:20
made me in the **w** also make them? Jb 31:15
same God form us both in the **w**? Jb 31:15
doors when it burst from the **w**, Jb 38:8
Whose **w** did the ice come from? Jb 38:29
took me from the **w**, making me Ps 22:9
been my God from my mother's **w**. Ps 22:10
The wicked go astray from the **w**; Ps 58:3
You took me from my mother's **w**. Ps 71:6
from the **w** of the dawn, Ps 110:3
me together in my mother's **w**. Ps 139:13
Sheol; a barren **w**; earth, which Pr 30:16
What, son of my **w**? What, son of Pr 31:2
As he came from his mother's **w**, Ec 5:15
develop⌋ in the **w** of a pregnant Ec 11:5
who formed you from the **w**, Is 44:24
have been sustained from the **w**, Is 46:3
me while I was in my mother's **w**. Is 49:1
me from the **w** to be His servant Is 49:5
for the child of her **w**? Is 49:15
I who deliver, close ⌊the **w**⌋?" Is 66:9
before I formed you in the **w**; Jr 1:5
kill me in the **w** so that my Jr 20:17
my grave, her **w** eternally Jr 20:17
come out of the **w** to see ⌊only⌋ Jr 20:18
Give them a **w** that miscarries Hs 9:14
the **w** he grasped his brother's Hs 12:3
that way from their mother's **w**, Mt 19:12
while still in his mother's **w**. Lk 1:15
The **w** that bore You and the one Lk 11:27
his mother's **w** a second time Jn 3:4
his mother's **w** was carried there Ac 3:2
and the deadness of Sarah's **w**, Rm 4:19
from my mother's **w** set me apart Gl 1:15

WOMBS *(3)*

closed all the **w** in Abimelech's Gn 20:18
precious offspring of their **w**. Hs 9:16
barren, the **w** that never bore Lk 23:29

WOMEN *(232)*

as well as the **w** and the ⌊other⌋ Gn 14:16
time when the **w** went out to draw Gn 24:11
Rebekah and her young **w** got up, Gn 24:61
life because of these Hittite **w**. Gn 27:46
a wife from the Canaanite **w**. Gn 28:1
disapproved of the Canaanite **w**, Gn 28:8
happy that the **w** call me happy," Gn 30:13
up and saw the **w** and children, Gn 33:5
some of the young **w** of the area. Gn 34:1
his wives from the Canaanite **w**: Gn 36:2
help the Hebrew **w** give birth, Ex 1:16
The Hebrew **w** are not like the Ex 1:19
are not like the Egyptian **w**, Ex 1:19
both men and **w** should ask their Ex 11:2
and all the **w** followed her with Ex 15:20
have sexual relations with **w**." Ex 19:15
Both men and **w** came; all who had Ex 35:22
And all the **w** whose hearts were Ex 35:26
all the men and **w** whose hearts Ex 35:29
mirrors of the **w** who served at Ex 38:8
10 **w** will bake your bread in a Lv 26:26
relations with the **w** of Moab. Nm 25:1
The **w** invited them to the Nm 25:2
the Midianite **w** and their Nm 31:9
including the **w** and children. Dt 2:34
the men, **w**, and children Dt 3:6
you may take the **w**, children, Dt 20:14
the people—men, **w**, children, Dt 31:12
both men and **w**, was 12,000—all Jos 8:25
the **w**, little children, Jos 8:35
Jael is most blessed of **w**, Jdg 5:24
blessed among tent-dwelling **w**. Jdg 5:24
died—about 1,000 men and **w**. Jdg 9:49
and all the men, **w**, and lords of Jdg 9:51
year the young **w** of Israel would Jdg 11:40
temple was full of men and **w**; Jdg 16:27
3,000 men and **w** were on the roof Jdg 16:27
sword, including **w** and children. Jdg 21:10
gave them the **w** they had kept Jdg 21:14
since the **w** of Benjamin have Jdg 21:16
see the young **w** of Shiloh come Jdg 21:21
from the young **w** of Shiloh, Jdg 21:21
actually give ⌊the **w**⌋ to them, Jdg 21:22
took the number of **w** they needed Jdg 21:23
took Moabite **w** as their wives: Ru 1:4
and ⌊the local **w**⌋ exclaimed, Ru 1:19
stay here close to my young **w**. Ru 2:8
you to work with his young **w**, Ru 2:22
to Boaz's young **w** and gathered Ru 2:23
been working with his young **w**? Ru 3:2
Then the **w** said to Naomi, Ru 4:14
The neighbor **w** said, "A son has Ru 4:17
sleeping with the **w** who served 1Sm 2:22
the **w** taking care of her said, 1Sm 4:20
found some young **w** coming out to 1Sm 9:11
w answered, "Yes, he is ahead 1Sm 9:12
Kill men and **w**, children and 1Sm 15:3
your sword has made **w** childless, 1Sm 15:33
will be childless among **w**. 1Sm 15:33
the **w** came out from all the 1Sm 18:6
As they celebrated, the **w** sang: 1Sm 18:7
have kept themselves from **w**." 1Sm 21:4
I swear that **w** are being kept 1Sm 21:5
sword—both men and **w**, children 1Sm 22:19
had kidnapped the **w** and everyone 1Sm 30:2
of Israel, both men and **w**. 2Sm 6:19
Then two **w** who were prostitutes 1Kg 3:16
many foreign **w** in addition to 1Kg 11:1
Edomite, Sidonian, and Hittite **w** 1Kg 11:1
to these **w** and loved ⌊them⌋ 1Kg 11:2
will rip open their pregnant **w**." 2Kg 8:12
ripped open all the pregnant **w**. 2Kg 15:16
in which the **w** were weaving 2Kg 23:7
both men and **w**, a loaf of bread, 1Ch 16:3
their brothers—**w**, sons, and 2Ch 28:8
men and singing **w** still speak of 2Ch 35:25
Israelite men, **w**, and children Ezr 10:1
by marrying foreign **w** from the Ezr 10:2
by marrying foreign **w**, Ezr 10:10
married foreign **w** come at Ezr 10:14
men who had married foreign **w**. Ezr 10:17
married foreign **w** from the Ezr 10:18
of these had married foreign **w**, Ezr 10:44
assembly of men, **w**, and all who Neh 8:2
the men, the **w**, and those who Neh 8:3
The **w** and children also Neh 12:43
who had married **w** from Ashdod, Neh 13:23
yet foreign **w** drew him into sin. Neh 13:26
our God by marrying foreign **w**?" Neh 13:27
for the **w** of King Ahasuerus' Est 1:9
to all the **w** and cause them to Est 1:17
the noble **w** of Persia and Media Est 1:18
so all **w** will honor their Est 1:20
who is in charge of the **w**, Est 2:3
many young **w** gathered at the Est 2:8
who was in charge of the **w**. Est 2:8
more than all the other **w**. Est 2:17
When the young **w** were assembled Est 2:19
young and old, **w** and children— Est 3:13
them, including **w** and children, Est 8:11
No **w** as beautiful as Job's Jb 42:15
are among your honored **w**; Ps 45:9
company of **w** brought the good Ps 68:11
them are young **w** playing Ps 68:25
and His young **w** had no wedding Ps 78:63
young men as well as young **w**, Ps 148:12
your energy on **w** or your efforts Pr 31:3
Many **w** are capable, but you Pr 31:29
the **w** who grind cease because Ec 12:3
No wonder young **w** adore you. Sg 1:3
most beautiful of **w**, follow the Sg 1:8
is my darling among the young **w**. Sg 2:2
Young **w** of Jerusalem, I charge Sg 2:7
Young **w** of Jerusalem, I charge Sg 3:5
by the young **w** of Jerusalem. Sg 3:10
Come out, young **w** of Zion, and Sg 3:11
Young **w** of Jerusalem, I charge Sg 5:8
another, most beautiful of **w**? Sg 5:9
my friend, young **w** of Jerusalem. Sg 5:16
love gone, most beautiful of **w**? Sg 6:1
and young **w** without number. Sg 6:8
W see her and declare her Sg 6:9
Young **w** of Jerusalem, I charge Sg 8:4
My people, and **w** rule over them. Is 3:12
that day seven **w** will seize one Is 4:1
that day Egypt will be like **w**. Is 19:16
men ⌊or⌋ brought up young **w**." Is 23:4
W will come and make fires with Is 27:11
Stand up, you complacent **w**; Is 32:9
you also teach evil **w** your ways. Jr 2:33
and the **w** knead dough to make Jr 7:18
and summon the **w** who mourn; Jr 9:17
send for the skillful **w**. Jr 9:17
the word of the LORD, you **w**. Jr 9:20
'All the **w** who remain in the Jr 38:22
of the men, **w**, and children, Jr 40:7
men, soldiers, **w**, children, and Jr 41:16
the men, **w**, children, king's Jr 43:6
other gods, all the **w** standing Jr 44:15
And the **w** said, "When we burned Jr 44:19
people—the men, **w**, and all the Jr 44:20
all the **w**, "Hear the word Jr 44:24
you **w** have spoken with your Jr 44:25
them, and they will be like **w**. Jr 50:37
they have become like **w**. Jr 51:30
her young **w** grieve, and she Lm 1:4
young men and **w** have gone into Lm 1:18
The young **w** of Jerusalem have Lm 2:10
Should **w** eat their own children, Lm 2:20
young men and **w** have fallen by Lm 2:21
fate of⌋ all the **w** in my city. Lm 3:51
of compassionate **w** have cooked Lm 4:10
W are raped in Zion, virgins in Lm 5:11

birds, cedar **w**, scarlet yarn, Lv 14:4
bird together with the cedar **w**, Lv 14:6
birds, cedar **w**, scarlet yarn, Lv 14:49
take the cedar **w**, the hyssop, Lv 14:51
bird, the cedar **w**, the hyssop, Lv 14:52
a man gathering **w** on the Sabbath Nm 15:32
him gathering **w** brought him to Nm 15:33
The priest is to take cedar **w**, Nm 19:6
hair, and every article of **w**." Nm 31:20
man-made gods of **w** and stone, Dt 4:28
So I made an ark of acacia **w**, Dt 10:3
of any kind of **w** next to the Dt 16:21
other gods, of **w** and stone. Dt 28:36
other gods of **w** and stone, Dt 28:64
who cut your **w** and draw your Dt 29:11
images and idols ⌊made⌋ of **w**, Dt 29:17
with the **w** of the Asherah Jdg 6:26
kinds of⌋ fir **w** ⌊instruments⌋, 2Sm 6:5
sledges and ox yokes for the **w**. 2Sm 24:22
he overlaid the interior with **w**. 1Kg 6:15
15 feet high out of olive **w**. 1Kg 6:23
he made olive **w** doors. 1Kg 6:31
two doors were made of olive **w**. 1Kg 6:32
four-sided olive **w** doorposts for 1Kg 6:33
doors were made of cypress **w**; 1Kg 6:34
cut to size, as well as cedar **w**. 1Kg 7:11
quantity of almug **w** and precious 1Kg 10:11
made the almug **w** into steps for 1Kg 10:12
before⌋ had such almug **w** come, 1Kg 10:12
was a widow woman gathering **w**. 1Kg 17:10
place it on the **w** but not light 1Kg 18:23
place it on the **w** but not light 1Kg 18:23
he arranged the **w**, cut up the 1Kg 18:33
bull, and placed it on the **w**. 1Kg 18:33
to be burned and on the **w**." 1Kg 18:33
offering, the **w**, the stones, 1Kg 18:38
by human hands—**w** and stone. 2Kg 19:18
the threshing sledges for the **w**, 1Ch 21:23
the iron, and **w** for the wood, as 1Ch 29:2
wood for the **w**, as well as onyx 1Ch 29:2
iron, stone, and **w**, with purple, 2Ch 2:14
room he paneled with cypress **w**, 2Ch 3:5
brought algum **w** and precious 2Ch 9:10
made the algum **w** into walkways 2Ch 9:11
bring cedar **w** from Lebanon to Ezr 3:7
the donation of **w** by our Neh 10:34
to bring ⌊the **w**⌋ to our God's Neh 10:34
the donation of **w** at the Neh 13:31
straw, and bronze as rotten **w**. Jb 41:27
Without **w**, fire goes out; Pr 26:20
for embers and **w** for fire, Pr 26:21
for himself with **w** from Lebanon. Sg 3:9
a rod could lift what isn't **w**! Is 10:15
with plenty of fire and **w**. Is 30:33
by human hands—**w** and stone. Is 37:19
choosing **w** that does not rot? Is 40:20
will bow down to a block of **w**." Is 44:19
instead of **w**, and iron instead Is 60:17
people are the **w**, and the fire Jr 5:14
The sons gather **w**, the fathers Jr 7:18
by worthless idols ⌊made of⌋ **w**! Jr 10:8
it has become dry like **w**. Lm 4:8
our **w** comes at a price. Lm 5:4
boys stumble under ⌊loads of⌋ **w**. Lm 5:13
how does the **w** of the vine, Ezk 15:2
forest, compare to any other **w**? Ezk 15:2
Can **w** be taken from it to make Ezk 15:3
Like the **w** of the vine among the Ezk 15:6
worshiping **w** and stone, what you Ezk 20:32
of cypress **w** from the coasts Ezk 27:6
will not gather **w** from the Ezk 39:10
overlaid with **w** on all sides. Ezk 41:16
altar was made of **w**, five and a Ezk 41:22
its length and sides were of **w**. Ezk 41:22
bronze, iron, **w**, and stone. Dn 5:4
bronze, iron, **w**, and stone, Dn 5:23
Woe to him who says to **w**: Hab 2:19
things when the **w** is green, Lk 23:31
costly stones, **w**, hay, or straw, 1Co 3:12
also those of **w** and earthenware 2Tm 2:20
stone, and **w**, which are not Rv 9:20
kinds of fragrant **w** products; Rv 18:12
of expensive **w**, brass, iron, Rv 18:12

WOODCUTTER *(1)*

no **w** has come against us." Is 14:8

WOODCUTTERS *(4)*

Gibeonites became **w** and water Jos 9:21
w and water carriers for the Jos 9:23
day he made them **w** and water Jos 9:27
servants, the **w** who cut the 2Ch 2:10

WOODEN *(11)*

in **w** and stone ⌊containers⌋. Ex 7:19
while any **w** utensil must be Lv 15:12
in his hand a **w** object capable Nm 35:18
the mountain and make a **w** ark. Dt 10:1
With the oxen's **w** yoke and plow, 1Kg 19:21
stood on a high **w** platform made Neh 8:4
Those who carry their **w** idols, Is 45:20
You broke a **w** yoke bar, but in Jr 28:13
They put a **w** yoke on him with Ezk 19:9
There was a **w** canopy outside, Ezk 41:25
people consult their **w** ⌊idols⌋, Hs 4:12

WOODLANDS *(1)*

birth and strips the **w** bare. Ps 29:9

WOODPILE *(1)*

of Judah like a firepot in a **w**, Zch 12:6

WOODS *(2)*

came out of the **w** and mauled 42 2Kg 2:24
the abandoned **w** and mountaintops Is 17:9

WOODWORK *(1)*

will answer them from the **w**. Hab 2:11

WOODWORKER *(1)*

The **w** stretches out a measuring Is 44:13

WOOF *(9)*

in the warp or **w** of linen or Lv 13:48
the warp, the **w**, or any leather Lv 13:49
the warp, the **w**, or the leather, Lv 13:51
the warp or **w** in wool or linen, Lv 13:52
the warp or **w**, or any leather Lv 13:53
the leather, or the warp or **w**. Lv 13:56
the warp or **w**, or any leather Lv 13:57
the warp or **w**, or any leather Lv 13:58
fabric, warp or **w**, or any Lv 13:59

WOOL *(20)*

mildew—in **w** or linen fabric Lv 13:47
the warp or woof of linen or **w**, Lv 13:48
the warp or woof in **w** or linen, Lv 13:52
in **w** or linen fabric Lv 13:59
first sheared ⌊**w**⌋ of your flock. Dt 18:4
made of both **w** and linen. Dt 22:11
will put a fleece of **w** here on Jdg 6:37
lambs and the **w** of 100,000 rams, 2Kg 3:4
He spreads snow like **w**; Ps 147:16
She selects **w** and flax and works Pr 31:13
as crimson, they will be like **w**. Is 1:18
the worm will eat them like **w**. Is 51:8
in wine from Helbon and white **w**. Ezk 27:18
the fat, wear the **w**, and butcher Ezk 34:3
anything made of **w** when they Ezk 44:17
hair of His head like whitest **w**. Dn 7:9
and water, my **w** and flax, my oil Hs 2:5
I will take away My **w** and linen, Hs 2:9
water, scarlet **w**, and hyssop, Heb 9:19
and hair were white like **w**— Rv 1:14

WORD *(510)*

the **w** of the LORD came to Abram Gn 15:1
Now the **w** of the LORD came to Gn 15:4
doing, and bring **w** back to me." Gn 37:14
feared the **w** of the LORD made Ex 9:20
take the LORD's **w** seriously left Ex 9:21
acted on Moses' **w** and asked the Ex 12:35
He sent **w** to Moses, "I, your Ex 18:6
the LORD's **w** and broken His Nm 15:31
he must not break his **w**; Nm 30:2
based on the **w** of witnesses. Nm 35:30
Israelites at the **w** of the LORD, Nm 36:5
to report the **w** of the LORD to Dt 5:5
alone but on every **w** that comes Dt 8:3
every single **w** of this law, Dt 31:24
every single **w** of this song to Dt 31:30
rain and my **w** settle like dew Dt 32:2
they kept Your **w** and maintained Dt 33:9
of Jericho sent ⌊**w**⌋ to Rahab and Jos 2:3
Don't let one **w** come out of your Jos 6:10
There was not a **w** of all that Jos 8:35
Jerusalem sent ⌊**w**⌋ to Hoham king Jos 10:3
men of Gibeon sent ⌊**w**⌋ to Joshua Jos 10:6
LORD spoke this **w** to Moses while Jos 14:10
"I have a **w** from God for you," Jdg 3:20
have given my **w** to the LORD and Jdg 11:35
have given your **w** to the LORD. Jdg 11:36
May the LORD confirm your **w**." 1Sm 1:23
those days the **w** of the LORD was 1Sm 3:1
because the **w** of the LORD had 1Sm 3:7
Himself to Samuel by His **w**. 1Sm 3:21
reveal the **w** of God to you." 1Sm 9:27
Then the **w** of the LORD came to 1Sm 15:10
have rejected the **w** of the LORD, 1Sm 15:23
you rejected the **w** of the LORD, 1Sm 15:26
Then Saul sent **w** to Jesse: 1Sm 16:22
night the **w** of the LORD came 2Sm 7:4
Because of Your **w** and according 2Sm 7:21
and sent **w** to inform David: 2Sm 11:5
David sent **w** to Tamar at the 2Sm 13:7
servant speak a **w** to my lord the 2Sm 14:12
May the **w** of my lord the king 2Sm 14:17
wilderness until **w** comes from 2Sm 15:28
asking about a **w** from God— 2Sm 16:23
David sent **w** to the priests, 2Sm 19:11
and they sent **w** to the king: 2Sm 19:14
the **w** of the LORD is pure. 2Sm 22:31
through me, His **w** was on my 2Sm 23:2
The **w** of the LORD came to 1Kg 6:11
the LORD to carry out His **w**, 1Kg 12:15
king heard the **w** that the man 1Kg 13:4
had given by the **w** of the LORD. 1Kg 13:5
by the **w** of the LORD: 1Kg 13:9
to me by the **w** of the LORD: 1Kg 13:17
to me by the **w** of the LORD: 1Kg 13:18
the **w** of the LORD came to the 1Kg 13:20
to the **w** of the LORD that 1Kg 13:26
for the **w** that he cried out by a 1Kg 13:32
according to the **w** of the LORD 1Kg 14:18
according to the **w** of the LORD 1Kg 15:29
Now the **w** of the LORD came to 1Kg 16:1
of Hanani the **w** of the LORD also 1Kg 16:7
according to the **w** of the LORD 1Kg 16:12
according to the **w** of the LORD 1Kg 16:34
Then the **w** of the LORD came to 1Kg 17:8
do according to the **w** of Elijah. 1Kg 17:15
according to the **w** of the LORD 1Kg 17:16
and the LORD's **w** in your mouth 1Kg 17:24
the **w** of the LORD came to Elijah 1Kg 18:1
people didn't answer him a **w**. 1Kg 18:21
to whom the **w** of the LORD had 1Kg 18:31
that at Your **w** I have done all 1Kg 18:36
Then the **w** of the LORD came to 1Kg 19:9
left and took **w** back to him. 1Kg 20:9
prophet by the **w** of the LORD, 1Kg 20:35
Then they sent ⌊**w**⌋ to Jezebel, 1Kg 21:14
Then the **w** of the LORD came to 1Kg 21:17
Then the **w** of the LORD came to 1Kg 21:28
hear the **w** of the LORD: 1Kg 22:19
to the **w** of the LORD that 1Kg 22:38
to the **w** of the LORD that 2Kg 1:17
according to the **w** that Elisha 2Kg 2:22
man of God sent ⌊**w**⌋ to the king 2Kg 6:9
of Israel sent ⌊**w**⌋ to the place 2Kg 6:10
according to Elisha's **w**. 2Kg 6:18
said, "Hear the **w** of the LORD! 2Kg 7:1
according to the **w** of the LORD. 2Kg 7:16
according to the **w** of the LORD, 2Kg 9:26
the LORD's **w** that He spoke 2Kg 9:36
that not a **w** the LORD spoke 2Kg 10:10
according to the **w** of the LORD 2Kg 10:17
of Israel sent ⌊**w**⌋ to Amaziah 2Kg 14:9
according to the **w** the LORD, 2Kg 14:25
The **w** of the LORD that He spoke 2Kg 15:12
king of Judah sent **w** to the king 2Kg 18:14
Hear the **w** of the great king, 2Kg 18:28
they answered him not a **w**, 2Kg 18:36
is the **w** the LORD has spoken 2Kg 19:21
when the **w** of the LORD came 2Kg 20:4
Hear the **w** of the LORD: 2Kg 20:16
The **w** of the LORD that you have 2Kg 20:19
according to the **w** of the LORD 2Kg 23:16
according to the **w** of the LORD 2Kg 24:2
he did not keep the LORD's **w**. 1Ch 10:13
the LORD's **w** through Samuel. 1Ch 11:3
to the LORD's **w** about Israel. 1Ch 11:10
according to the LORD's **w**, 1Ch 12:23
according to the **w** of the LORD: 1Ch 15:15
that night the **w** of God came to 1Ch 17:3
I ever spoken a **w** to even one 1Ch 17:6
let the **w** that You have spoken 1Ch 17:23
the **w** of the LORD came to me: 1Ch 22:8
Solomon sent ⌊**w**⌋ to King Hiram 2Ch 2:3
carry out His **w** that He had 2Ch 10:15
But the **w** of the LORD came to 2Ch 11:2
hear the **w** of the LORD. 2Ch 18:18
and sent ⌊**w**⌋ to Jehoash son 2Ch 25:17
of Israel sent ⌊**w**⌋ to King 2Ch 25:18

Hezekiah sent ⌊w⌋ throughout all 2Ch 30:1
officials by the w of the LORD. 2Ch 30:12
the w spread, the Israelites 2Ch 31:5
have not kept the w of the LORD 2Ch 34:21
to carry out the w of the LORD 2Ch 35:6
ancestors sent w against them 2Ch 36:15
This fulfilled the w of the LORD 2Ch 36:21
the w of the LORD spoken through 2Ch 36:22
the w of the LORD spoken through Ezr 1:1
silent and could not say a w. Neh 5:8
called Purim, from the w Pur. Est 9:26
no one spoke a w to him because Jb 2:13
A w was brought to me in secret; Jb 4:12
faint is the w we hear of Him! Jb 26:14
After a w from me they did not Jb 29:22
who keeps his w whatever the Ps 15:4
by the w of Your lips I have Ps 17:4
the w of the LORD is pure. Ps 18:30
For the w of the LORD is right, Ps 33:4
were made by the w of the LORD, Ps 33:6
In God, whose w I praise, in God Ps 56:4
In God, whose w I praise, in the Ps 56:10
in the LORD, whose w I praise, Ps 56:10
mouths is the w of their lips, Ps 59:12
who do His w, obedient to His Ps 103:20
the w of the LORD tested him. Ps 105:19
He sent His w and healed them; Ps 107:20
his way pure? By keeping Your w. Ps 119:9
treasured Your w in my heart so Ps 119:11
I will not forget Your w. Ps 119:16
then I will keep Your w. Ps 119:17
give me life through Your w. Ps 119:25
strengthen me through Your w. Ps 119:28
me, for I trust in Your w. Ps 119:42
Never take the w of truth from Ps 119:43
Your⌋ w to Your servant Ps 119:49
astray, but now I keep Your w. Ps 119:67
for I put my hope in Your w. Ps 119:74
I put my hope in Your w. Ps 119:81
LORD, Your w is forever; Ps 119:89
evil path to follow Your w. Ps 119:101
sweet Your w is to my taste— Ps 119:103
Your w is a lamp for my feet and Ps 119:105
give me life through Your w. Ps 119:107
I put my hope in Your w. Ps 119:114
Your w is completely pure, Ps 119:140
I put my hope in Your w. Ps 119:147
because they do not keep Your w. Ps 119:158
The entirety of Your w is truth, Ps 119:160
my heart fears ⌊only⌋ Your w. Ps 119:161
according to Your w. Ps 119:169
wait, and put my hope in His w. Ps 130:5
Before a w is on my tongue, Ps 139:4
the earth; His w runs swiftly. Ps 147:15
He sends His w and melts them; Ps 147:18
He declares His w to Jacob, Ps 147:19
but a good w cheers it up. Pr 12:25
but a harsh w stirs up wrath. Pr 15:1
and a timely w—how good that Pr 15:23
A w spoken at the right time is Pr 25:11
Every w of God is pure; Pr 30:5
For the king's w is Ec 8:4
Hear the w of the LORD, you Is 1:10
of Zion and the w of the LORD Is 2:3
despised the w of the Holy One Is 5:24
not speak according to this w, Is 8:20
W has reached them from the land Is 23:1
Then the w of the LORD came to Is 28:13
hear the w of the LORD, Is 28:14
is the w the LORD has spoken Is 37:22
Then the w of the LORD came to Is 38:4
Hear the w of the LORD of Hosts: Is 39:5
The w of the LORD that you have Is 39:8
w of our God remains forever. Is 40:8
This is the w of the LORD your Is 44:2
a w that will not be revoked: Is 45:23
to sustain the weary with a w. Is 50:4
so My w that comes from My mouth Is 55:11
and who trembles at My w. Is 66:2
tremble at His w, hear the word Is 66:5
word, hear the w of the LORD: Is 66:5
The w of the LORD came to him in Jr 1:2
The w of the LORD came to me: Jr 1:4
Then the w of the LORD came to Jr 1:11
over My w to accomplish it. Jr 1:12
Again the w of the LORD came to Jr 1:13
The w of the LORD came to me: Jr 2:1
Hear the w of the LORD, house of Jr 2:4
attention to the w of the LORD! Jr 2:31
the ⌊LORD's⌋ w is not in them. Jr 5:13
Because you have spoken this w, Jr 5:14
the w of the LORD has become Jr 6:10
have paid no attention to My w. Jr 6:19
⌊This is⌋ the w that came to Jr 7:1
LORD and there call out this w: Jr 7:2
Hear the w of the LORD, all ⌊you Jr 7:2
have rejected the w of the LORD, Jr 8:9
Now hear the w of the LORD, Jr 9:20
attention to the w of His mouth. Jr 9:20
Hear the w that the LORD has Jr 10:1
⌊This is⌋ the w that came to Jr 11:1
Then the w of the LORD came to Jr 13:3
Then the w of the LORD came to Jr 13:8
The w of the LORD that came to Jr 14:1
You are to speak this w to them: Jr 14:17
The w of the LORD came to me: Jr 16:1
Where is the w of the LORD? Jr 17:15
Hear the w of the LORD, kings of Jr 17:20
⌊This is⌋ the w that came to Jr 18:1
The w of the LORD came to me: Jr 18:5
Hear the w of the LORD, kings of Jr 19:3
because the w of the LORD has Jr 20:8
⌊This is⌋ the w that came to Jr 21:1
'Hear the w of the LORD! Jr 21:11
Judah and announce this w there. Jr 22:1
Hear the w of the LORD, king of Jr 22:2
carry out this w, Jr 22:4
earth, hear the w of the LORD! Jr 22:29
the LORD to see and hear His w? Jr 23:18
attention to His w and obeyed? Jr 23:18
one who has My w should speak My Jr 23:28
should speak My w truthfully, Jr 23:28
"Is not My w like fire"—the Jr 23:29
for each man's w becomes his Jr 23:36
The w of the LORD came to me: Jr 24:4
⌊This is⌋ the w that came to Jr 25:1
w of the LORD has come to me, Jr 25:3
this w came from the LORD: Jr 26:1
there. Do not hold back a w. Jr 26:2
this w came to Jeremiah from the Jr 27:1
Send ⌊w⌋ to the king of Edom, Jr 27:3
and if the w of the LORD is with Jr 27:18
only when the w of the prophet Jr 28:9
The w of the LORD came to Jr 28:12
Hear the w of the LORD, all you Jr 29:20
For he has sent ⌊w⌋ to us in Jr 29:28
Then the w of the LORD came to Jr 29:30
⌊This is⌋ the w that came to Jr 30:1
Nations, hear the w of the LORD, Jr 31:10
again speak this w in the land Jr 31:23
⌊This is⌋ the w that came to Jr 32:1
The w of the LORD came to me: Jr 32:6
that this was the w of the LORD. Jr 32:8
Then the w of the LORD came to Jr 32:26
the w of the LORD came to Jr 33:1
The w of the LORD came to Jr 33:19
The w of the LORD came to Jr 33:23
⌊This is⌋ the w that came to Jr 34:1
the LORD's w, Zedekiah, king Jr 34:4
for I have spoken ⌊this⌋ w." Jr 34:5
⌊This is⌋ the w that came to Jr 34:8
Then the w of the LORD came to Jr 34:12
⌊This is⌋ the w that came to Jr 35:1
Then the w of the LORD came to Jr 35:12
this w came to Jeremiah from the Jr 36:1
officials sent ⌊w⌋ to Baruch Jr 36:14
the w of the LORD came to Jr 36:27
The w of the LORD came to Jr 37:6
"Is there a w from the LORD?" Jr 37:17
Now the w of the LORD had come Jr 39:15
⌊This is⌋ the w that came to Jr 40:1
every w that the LORD answers Jr 42:4
I won't withhold a w from you." Jr 42:4
As for every w the LORD your God Jr 42:5
the w of the LORD came to Jr 42:7
then hear the w of the LORD, Jr 42:15
Then the w of the LORD came to Jr 43:8
⌊This is⌋ the w that came to Jr 44:1
As for the w you spoke to us in Jr 44:16
Hear the w of the LORD, all Jr 44:24
hear the w of the LORD, all Jr 44:26
will know whose w stands, Mine Jr 44:28
⌊This is⌋ the w that Jeremiah Jr 45:1
The w of the LORD that came to Jr 46:1
⌊This is⌋ the w the LORD spoke Jr 46:13
⌊This is⌋ the w of the LORD that Jr 47:1
⌊This is⌋ the w of the LORD that Jr 49:34
The w the LORD spoke about Jr 50:1
the w of the LORD came directly Ezk 1:3
seven days the w of the LORD Ezk 3:16
you hear a w from My mouth, Ezk 3:17
The w of the LORD came to me: Ezk 6:1
hear the w of the Lord GOD! Ezk 6:3
the w of the LORD came to me: Ezk 7:1
The w of the LORD came to me Ezk 11:14
The w of the LORD came to me: Ezk 12:1
Then the w of the LORD came to Ezk 12:8
The w of the LORD came to me: Ezk 12:17
Again the w of the LORD came to Ezk 12:21
The w of the LORD came to me: Ezk 12:26
The w of the LORD came to me: Ezk 13:1
Hear the w of the LORD! Ezk 13:2
Then the w of the LORD came to Ezk 14:2
The w of the LORD came to me: Ezk 14:12
Then the w of the LORD came to Ezk 15:1
The w of the LORD came to me Ezk 16:1
hear the w of the LORD! Ezk 16:35
The w of the LORD came to me: Ezk 17:1
The w of the LORD came to me: Ezk 17:11
The w of the LORD came to me: Ezk 18:1
Then the w of the LORD came to Ezk 20:2
The w of the LORD came to me: Ezk 20:45
Hear the w of the LORD! Ezk 20:47
The w of the LORD came to me Ezk 21:1
The w of the LORD came to me: Ezk 21:8
Then the w of the LORD came to Ezk 21:18
The w of the LORD came to me: Ezk 22:1
The w of the LORD came to me: Ezk 22:17
The w of the LORD came to me: Ezk 22:23
The w of the LORD came to me Ezk 23:1
The w of the LORD came to me in Ezk 24:1
Then the w of the LORD came to Ezk 24:15
The w of the LORD came to me: Ezk 24:20
Then the w of the LORD came to Ezk 25:1
Hear the w of the Lord GOD: Ezk 25:3
the w of the LORD came to me: Ezk 26:1
The w of the LORD came to me: Ezk 27:1
The w of the LORD came to me: Ezk 28:1
The w of the LORD came to me: Ezk 28:11
The w of the LORD came to me: Ezk 28:20
the w of the LORD came to me: Ezk 29:1
the w of the LORD came to me: Ezk 29:17
The w of the LORD came to me: Ezk 30:1
the w of the LORD came to me: Ezk 30:20
the w of the LORD came to me: Ezk 31:1
the w of the LORD came to me: Ezk 32:1
the w of the LORD came to me: Ezk 32:17
The w of the LORD came to me: Ezk 33:1
you hear a w from My mouth, Ezk 33:7
Then the w of the LORD came to Ezk 33:23
The w of the LORD came to me: Ezk 34:1
hear the w of the LORD. Ezk 34:7
hear the w of the LORD! Ezk 34:9
The w of the LORD came to me: Ezk 35:1
Israel, hear the w of the LORD. Ezk 36:1
hear the w of the Lord GOD. Ezk 36:4
The w of the LORD came to me: Ezk 36:16
bones, hear the w of the LORD! Ezk 37:4
The w of the LORD came to me: Ezk 37:15
The w of the LORD came to me: Ezk 38:1
the Chaldeans, "My w is final: Dn 2:5
you see that my w is final. Dn 2:8
Nebuchadnezzar sent w to Dn 3:2
This w is by decree of the Dn 4:17
according to the w of the LORD Dn 9:2
The w of the LORD that came to Hs 1:1
Hear the w of the LORD, people Hs 4:1
The w of the LORD that came to Jl 1:1
of Bethel sent ⌊w⌋ to Jeroboam Am 7:10
Now hear the w of the LORD. Am 7:16
seeking the w of the LORD, Am 8:12
The w of the LORD came to Jonah Jnh 1:1
Then the w of the LORD came to Jnh 3:1
When w reached the king of Jnh 3:6
The w of the LORD that came to Mc 1:1
of Zion and the w of the LORD Mc 4:2
The w of the LORD that came to Zph 1:1
w of the LORD is against you, Zph 2:5
the w of the LORD came through Hg 1:1
The w of the LORD came through Hg 1:3
the w of the LORD came through Hg 2:1
the w of the LORD came to Haggai Hg 2:10
The w of the LORD came to Haggai Hg 2:20
the w of the LORD came to the Zch 1:1

the **w** of the LORD came to the Zch 1:7
This is the **w** of the LORD to Zch 4:6
Then the **w** of the LORD came to Zch 4:8
The **w** of the LORD came to me: Zch 6:9
the **w** of the LORD came to Zch 7:1
Then the **w** of the LORD of Hosts Zch 7:4
The **w** of the LORD came to Zch 7:8
The **w** of the LORD of Hosts came: Zch 8:1
Then the **w** of the LORD of Hosts Zch 8:18
An Oracle The **w** of the LORD is Zch 9:1
that it was the **w** of the LORD. Zch 11:11
An Oracle The **w** of the LORD Zch 12:1
The **w** of the LORD to Israel Mal 1:1
alone but on every **w** that comes Mt 4:4
But let your **w** 'yes' be 'yes,' Mt 5:37
only say the **w**, and my servant Mt 8:8
spirits with a **w** and healed all Mt 8:16
speaks a **w** against the Son Mt 12:32
for every careless **w** they speak. Mt 12:36
anyone hears the **w** about the Mt 13:19
who hears the **w** and immediately Mt 13:20
comes because of the **w**, Mt 13:21
this is one who hears the **w**, Mt 13:22
seduction of wealth choke the **w**, Mt 13:22
who hears and understands the **w**, Mt 13:23
revoked God's **w** because of your Mt 15:6
Yet He did not say a **w** to her. Mt 15:23
his wife sent **w** to him, "Have Mt 27:19
they sent ⌊**w**⌋ to Him and called Mk 3:31
The sower sows the **w**. Mk 4:14
the path where the **w** is sown: Mk 4:15
takes away the **w** sown in them. Mk 4:15
they hear the **w**, immediately Mk 4:16
comes because of the **w**, Mk 4:17
are the ones who hear the **w**, Mk 4:18
things enter in and choke the **w**, Mk 4:19
ground are those who hear the **w**, Mk 4:20
would speak the **w** to them with Mk 4:33
You revoke God's **w** by your Mk 7:13
They kept this **w** to themselves, Mk 9:10
Jesus had spoken the **w** to him, Mk 14:72
and confirming the **w** by the Mk 16:20
servants of the **w** handed them Lk 1:2
done to me according to your **w**." Lk 1:38
in peace, according to Your **w**. Lk 2:29
God's **w** came to John the son of Lk 3:2
in on Jesus to hear God's **w**, Lk 5:1
But at Your **w**, I'll let down the Lk 5:5
But say the **w**, and my servant Lk 7:7
The seed is the **w** of God. Lk 8:11
takes away the **w** from their Lk 8:12
hear, welcome the **w** with joy. Lk 8:13
heard the **w** with an honest Lk 8:15
who hear and do the **w** of God." Lk 8:21
who hear the **w** of God and keep Lk 11:28
who speaks a **w** against the Son Lk 12:10
remembered the **w** of the Lord, Lk 22:61
In the beginning was the **W**, Jn 1:1
Word, and the **W** was with God, Jn 1:1
was with God, and the **W** was God. Jn 1:1
The **W** became flesh and took up Jn 1:14
who hears My **w** and believes Him Jn 5:24
don't have His **w** living in you, Jn 5:38
continue in My **w**, you really are Jn 8:31
Me because My **w** is not welcome Jn 8:37
you cannot listen to My **w**. Jn 8:43
anyone keeps My **w**, he will never Jn 8:51
anyone keeps My **w**, he will never Jn 8:52
I do know Him, and I keep His **w**. Jn 8:55
whom the **w** of God came to Jn 10:35
was to fulfill the **w** of Isaiah Jn 12:38
the **w** I have spoken will judge Jn 12:48
loves Me, he will keep My **w**. Jn 14:23
The **w** that you hear is not Mine Jn 14:24
because of the **w** I have spoken Jn 15:3
Remember the **w** I spoke to you: Jn 15:20
they kept My **w**, they will also Jn 15:20
and they have kept Your **w**. Jn 17:6
I have given them Your **w**. Jn 17:14
by the truth; Your **w** is truth. Jn 17:17
I remembered the **w** of the Lord, Ac 11:16
the synagogue sent ⌊**w**⌋ to them, Ac 13:15
the same things by **w** of mouth. Ac 15:27
the **w** of God among them. Ac 18:11
Greeks, heard the **w** of the Lord. Ac 19:10
friends, sent **w** to him, pleading Ac 19:31
w went up to the commander of Ac 21:31
listened to him up to this **w**. Ac 22:22
as though the **w** of God has Rm 9:6
Gentiles obedient by **w** and deed, Rm 15:18
Did the **w** of God originate from 1Co 14:36
witnesses every **w** will be 2Co 13:1
when you heard the **w** of truth, Eph 1:13
the washing of water by the **w**. Eph 5:26
of the Spirit, which is God's **w**. Eph 6:17
you do, in **w** or in deed, do Col 3:17
did not come to you in **w** only, 1Th 1:5
you in every good work and **w**. 2Th 2:17
sanctified by the **w** of God and 1Tm 4:5
teaching the **w** of truth. 2Tm 2:15
And their **w** will spread like 2Tm 2:17
all things by His powerful **w**. Heb 1:3
For the **w** of God is living and Heb 4:12
God's good **w** and the powers Heb 6:5
was created by the **w** of God, Heb 11:3
that not another **w** be spoken to Heb 12:19
who have spoken God's **w** to you. Heb 13:7
receive this **w** of exhortation, Heb 13:22
humbly receive the implanted **w**, Jms 1:21
doers of the **w** and not hearers Jms 1:22
hearer of the **w** and not a doer, Jms 1:23
living and enduring **w** of God. 1Pt 1:23
but the **w** of the Lord endures 1Pt 1:25
And this is the **w** that was 1Pt 1:25
the prophetic **w** strongly 2Pt 1:19
through water by the **w** of God. 2Pt 3:5
But by the same **w** the present 2Pt 3:7
concerning the **W** of life— 1Jn 1:1
a liar, and His **w** is not in us. 1Jn 1:10
whoever keeps His **w**, truly in 1Jn 2:5
strong, God's **w** remains in you, 1Jn 2:14
we must not love in **w** or speech, 1Jn 3:18
testified to God's **w** and to the Rv 1:2
because of God's **w** and the Rv 1:9
have kept My **w**, and have not Rv 3:8
because of God's **w** and the Rv 6:9
Lamb and by the **w** of their Rv 12:11
His name is called the **W** of God. Rv 19:13
Jesus and because of God's **w**, Rv 20:4

WORDS *(478)*

Lamech, pay attention to my **w**. Gn 4:23
heard his sister Rebekah's **w**— Gn 24:30
Abraham's servant heard their **w**, Gn 24:52
all the people with these **w**: Gn 26:11
When Esau heard his father's **w**, Gn 27:34
When the **w** of her older son Esau Gn 27:42
Their **w** seemed good in the eyes Gn 34:18
so that your **w** can be tested to Gn 42:16
me so that your **w** can be Gn 42:20
them, he said these **w** to them. Gn 44:6
We reported your **w** to him. Gn 44:24
them that day with these **w**: Gn 48:20
pay attention to deceptive **w**." Ex 5:9
These are the **w** that you are to Ex 19:6
them all these **w** that the LORD Ex 19:7
the people's **w** back to the LORD. Ex 19:8
the people's **w** to the LORD. Ex 19:9
Then God spoke all these **w**: Ex 20:1
corrupts the **w** of the righteous Ex 23:8
down all the **w** of the LORD. Ex 24:4
you concerning all these **w**." Ex 24:8
write on them the **w** that were on Ex 34:1
down these **w**, for I have made Ex 34:27
with Israel based on these **w**." Ex 34:27
tablets the **w** of the covenant Ex 34:28
the people the **w** of the LORD. Nm 11:24
Moses reported these **w** to all Nm 14:39
finished speaking all these **w**, Nm 16:31
and reported Balak's **w** to him. Nm 22:7
These are the **w** Moses spoke to Dt 1:1
When the LORD heard your **w**, Dt 1:34
and I will let them hear My **w**, Dt 4:10
kept hearing the sound of the **w**, Dt 4:12
you heard His **w** from the fire. Dt 4:36
LORD heard your **w** when you spoke Dt 5:28
I have heard the **w** that these Dt 5:28
These **w** that I am giving you Dt 6:6
The exact **w** were on them, which Dt 9:10
the tablets the **w** that were on Dt 10:2
Impress these **w** of Mine on your Dt 11:18
to that prophet's **w** or to that Dt 13:3
and twists the **w** of the Dt 16:19
to observe all the **w** of this Dt 17:19
I will put My **w** in his mouth, Dt 18:18
listen to My **w** that he speaks Dt 18:19
Write all the **w** of this law on Dt 27:3
clearly all the **w** of this law Dt 27:8
does not put the **w** of this law Dt 27:26
to obey all the **w** of this law, Dt 28:58
These are the **w** of the covenant Dt 29:1
observe the **w** of this covenant Dt 29:9
hears the **w** of this oath, Dt 29:19
follow all the **w** of this law. Dt 29:29
to speak these **w** to all Israel, Dt 31:1
to follow all the **w** of this law. Dt 31:12
may speak these **w** directly to Dt 31:28
earth, to the **w** of my mouth. Dt 32:1
recited all the **w** of this song Dt 32:44
all these **w** to all Israel, Dt 32:45
heart all these **w** I am giving as Dt 32:46
follow all the **w** of this law. Dt 32:46
meaningless **w** to you but they Dt 32:47
Your feet. Each receives Your **w**. Dt 33:3
not obey your **w** in all that you Jos 1:18
listen to the **w** of the LORD your Jos 3:9
aloud all the **w** of the law— Jos 8:34
heard all the **w** the LORD said to Jos 24:27
had spoken these **w** to all the Jdg 2:4
spoke all these **w** about him in Jdg 9:3
heard the **w** of Gaal son of Ebed, Jdg 9:30
When Your **w** come true, what Jdg 13:12
You when Your **w** come true?" Jdg 13:17
or let arrogant ⌊**w**⌋ come out of 1Sm 2:3
And Samuel's **w** came to all 1Sm 4:1
all the LORD's **w** to the people 1Sm 8:10
all the people's **w** and then 1Sm 8:21
repeated to him the **w** of the men 1Sm 11:5
Saul heard these **w**, the Spirit 1Sm 11:6
listen to the **w** of the LORD. 1Sm 15:1
the LORD's command and your **w**. 1Sm 15:24
Israel heard these **w** from the 1Sm 17:11
line and shouted his usual **w**, 1Sm 17:23
reported these **w** directly to 1Sm 18:23
"These are the **w** David spoke." 1Sm 18:24
David and told him all these **w**. 1Sm 19:7
With these **w** David persuaded his 1Sm 24:7
listen to the **w** of people who 1Sm 24:9
they reported all these **w**. 1Sm 25:12
Listen to the **w** of your servant. 1Sm 25:24
hear the **w** of his servant: 1Sm 26:19
by Samuel's **w** and was also weak 1Sm 28:20
all these **w** and this entire 2Sm 7:17
Your **w** are true, and You have 2Sm 7:28
king and speak these **w** to him." 2Sm 14:3
But the **w** of the men of Judah 2Sm 19:43
Listen to the **w** of your servant, 2Sm 20:17
David spoke the **w** of this song 2Sm 22:1
These are the last **w** of David: 2Sm 23:1
after you and confirm your **w**." 1Kg 1:14
When Hiram heard Solomon's **w**, 1Kg 5:7
May my **w** I have made my petition 1Kg 8:59
about your **w** and about your 1Kg 10:6
them by speaking kind **w** to them, 1Kg 12:7
their father the **w** that he had 1Kg 13:11
voice of the LORD, mark my **w**: 1Kg 20:36
Ahab heard these **w**, he tore his 1Kg 21:27
the **w** of the prophets are 1Kg 22:13
So let your **w** be like theirs, 1Kg 22:13
you and spoke those **w** to you?" 2Kg 1:7
"The LORD's **w** are with him." 2Kg 3:12
Israel even the **w** you speak in 2Kg 6:12
the king heard the woman's **w**, 2Kg 6:30
think mere **w** are strategy and 2Kg 18:20
and to you to speak these **w**? 2Kg 18:27
to him the **w** of the Rabshakeh. 2Kg 18:37
hear all the **w** of the Rabshakeh 2Kg 19:4
for⌋ the **w** that the LORD your 2Kg 19:4
because of the **w** you have heard, 2Kg 19:6
hear the **w** that Sennacherib has 2Kg 19:16
the king heard the **w** of the book 2Kg 22:11
not obeyed the **w** of this book 2Kg 22:13
all the **w** of the book that 2Kg 22:16
As for the **w** that you heard, 2Kg 22:18
he read all the **w** of the book of 2Kg 23:2
carry out the **w** of this covenant 2Kg 23:3
carry out the **w** of the law that 2Kg 23:24
all these **w** and this entire 1Ch 17:15
to the last **w** of David, 1Ch 23:27
about your **w** and about your 2Ch 9:5
them by speaking kind **w** to them, 2Ch 10:7
Asa heard these **w** and the 2Ch 15:8
the **w** of the prophets are 2Ch 18:12
So let your **w** be like theirs, 2Ch 18:12
command by the **w** of the LORD to 2Ch 29:15

the LORD in the w of David and 2Ch 29:30
relied on the w of King Hezekiah 2Ch 32:8
his God and the w of the seers 2Ch 33:18
the king heard the w of the law, 2Ch 34:19
concerning the w of the book 2Ch 34:21
As for the w that you heard, 2Ch 34:26
you heard His w against this 2Ch 34:27
hearing all the w of the book 2Ch 34:30
carry out the w of the covenant 2Ch 34:31
listen to Neco's w from the 2Ch 35:22
his w, from beginning to end, 2Ch 35:27
despising His w, and scoffing at 2Ch 36:16
who trembled at the w of the God Ezr 9:4
The w of Nehemiah son of Neh 1:1
When I heard these w, I sat down Neh 1:4
and they reported my w to him. Neh 6:19
as they heard the w of the law. Neh 8:9
had understood the w that were Neh 8:12
to study the w of the law. Neh 8:13
Your w have steadied the one who Jb 4:4
from their sharp w and from the Jb 5:15
That is why my w are rash. Jb 6:3
denied the w of the Holy One. Jb 6:10
How painful honest w can be! Jb 6:25
can disprove ⌊my⌋ w or that a Jb 6:26
man's w are ⌊mere⌋ wind Jb 6:26
Your w are a blast of wind. Jb 8:2
this stream of w go unanswered Jb 11:2
the ear test w as the palate Jb 12:11
Pay close attention to my w; Jb 13:17
or with w that serve no good Jb 15:3
even the w that ⌊deal⌋ gently Jb 15:11
and allow such w to leave your Jb 15:13
there ⌊no⌋ end to your empty w? Jb 16:3
could string w together against Jb 16:4
torment me and crush me with w? Jb 19:2
I wish that my w were written Jb 19:23
Pay close attention to my w; Jb 21:2
treasured the w of His mouth Jb 23:12
Who did you speak these w to? Jb 26:4
The w of Job are concluded. Jb 31:40
insights as you sought for w. Jb 32:11
longer answer; w have left them. Jb 32:15
I am full of w, and my spirit Jb 32:18
speech, and listen to all my w. Jb 33:1
tongue will form w on my palate. Jb 33:2
My w ⌊come from⌋ my upright Jb 33:3
and I have heard these very w: Jb 33:8
Hear my w, you wise men, and Jb 34:2
the ear test w as the palate Jb 34:3
his w are without insight." Jb 34:35
multiplying his w against God. Jb 34:37
and multiplies w without Jb 35:16
My⌋ counsel with ignorant w? Jb 38:2
I take back ⌊my w⌋ and repent in Jb 42:6
Listen to my w, LORD; consider Ps 5:1
w of the LORD are pure words, Ps 12:6
words of the LORD are pure w, Ps 12:6
there are no w; their voice is Ps 19:3
and their w to the ends of the Ps 19:4
May the w of my mouth and the Ps 19:14
and from my w of groaning? Ps 22:1
The w of his mouth are malicious Ps 36:3
who approve of their w. Ps 49:13
and turn your back on My w. Ps 50:17
You love any w that destroy, Ps 52:4
listen to the w of my mouth. Ps 54:2
buttery w are smooth, but war Ps 55:21
His w are softer than oil, Ps 55:21
They twist my w all day long; Ps 56:5
—sharp w from their lips. Ps 59:7
and aim bitter w like arrows, Ps 64:3
They pour out arrogant w; Ps 94:4
me with hateful w and attack me Ps 109:3
I have promised to keep Your w. Ps 119:57
revelation of Your w brings Ps 119:130
because my foes forget Your w. Ps 119:139
the people will listen to my w, Ps 141:6
in all His w and gracious in all Ps 145:13
or a parable, the w of the wise, Pr 1:6
on you and teach you my w. Pr 1:23
you accept my w and store up my Pr 2:1
Your heart must hold on to my w. Pr 4:4
away from the w of my mouth. Pr 4:5
Accept my w, and you will live Pr 4:10
My son, pay attention to my w; Pr 4:20
honey and her w are smoother Pr 5:3
away from the w of my mouth. Pr 5:7
trapped by the w of your lips— Pr 6:2
ensnared by the w of your mouth. Pr 6:2
My son, obey my w, and treasure Pr 7:1
attention to the w of my mouth. Pr 7:24
All the w of my mouth are Pr 8:8
there are many w, sin is Pr 10:19
The w of the wicked are a deadly Pr 12:6
with good by the w of his mouth, Pr 12:14
From the w of his mouth, a man Pr 13:2
man, but pleasant w are pure. Pr 15:26
Pleasant w are a honeycomb: Pr 16:24
person restrains his w, Pr 17:27
The w of a man's mouth are deep Pr 18:4
gossip's w are like choice food Pr 18:8
He may pursue ⌊them with⌋ w, Pr 19:7
stray from the w of knowledge. Pr 19:27
He overthrows the w of the Pr 22:12
attention to the w of the wise, Pr 22:17
teach you true and reliable w, Pr 22:21
eaten and waste your pleasant w. Pr 23:8
despise the insight of your w. Pr 23:9
and listen to w of knowledge. Pr 23:12
and their w stir up trouble. Pr 24:2
gossip's w are like choice food Pr 26:22
cannot be disciplined by w; Pr 29:19
The w of Agur son of Jakeh. Pr 30:1
Don't add to His w, or He will Pr 30:6
and deceitful w far from me. Pr 30:8
The w of King Lemuel, an oracle Pr 31:1
The w of the Teacher, son of Ec 1:1
on earth, so let your w be few. Ec 5:2
and a fool's voice from many w. Ec 5:3
be angry with your w and destroy Ec 5:6
bring futility, also many w. Ec 5:7
For when there are many w, Ec 6:11
and his w are not heeded." Ec 9:16
calm w of the wise are heeded Ec 9:17
The w from the mouth of a wise Ec 10:12
of the w of his mouth is Ec 10:13
Yet the fool multiplies w. Ec 10:14
to accurately write w of truth. Ec 12:10
and your w will come from low in Is 29:4
will be like the w of a sealed Is 29:11
will hear the w of a document, Is 29:18
preparedness are mere w. Is 36:5
to speak these w to your master Is 36:12
Listen to the w of the great Is 36:13
to him the w of the Rabshakeh. Is 36:22
will hear the w of the Rabshakeh Is 37:4
for⌋ the w that the LORD your Is 37:4
because of the w you have heard, Is 37:6
hear all the w that Sennacherib Is 37:17
told it, no one heard your w. Is 41:26
He made my w like a sharp sword; Is 49:2
I have put My w in your mouth, Is 51:16
creating w of praise." Is 57:19
trust in empty and worthless w; Is 59:4
uttering lying w from the heart. Is 59:13
and My w that I have put in your Is 59:21
The w of Jeremiah, the son of Jr 1:1
filled your mouth with My w. Jr 1:9
proclaim these w to the north, Jr 3:12
going to make My w become fire Jr 5:14
not trust deceitful w, chanting: Jr 7:4
in deceitful w that cannot help. Jr 7:8
Listen to the w of this Jr 11:2
not obey the w of this covenant Jr 11:3
all these w in the cities Jr 11:6
Obey the w of this covenant and Jr 11:6
to obey My w and have followed Jr 11:10
Your w were found, and I ate Jr 15:16
Your w became a delight to me Jr 15:16
And if you speak noble ⌊w⌋, Jr 15:19
know my w were spoken in Your Jr 17:16
I will reveal My w to you." Jr 18:2
pay no attention to all his w." Jr 18:18
there the w I speak to you. Jr 19:2
obstinate, not obeying My w.' " Jr 19:15
But if you do not obey these w, Jr 22:5
the LORD, because of His holy w. Jr 23:9
listen to the w of the prophets Jr 23:16
to hear My w and would have Jr 23:22
who steal My w from each other. Jr 23:30
you pervert the w of the living Jr 23:36
you have not obeyed My w, Jr 25:8
that land all My w I have spoken Jr 25:13
speak all the w I have commanded Jr 26:2
listening to the w of My Jr 26:5
speaking these w in the temple Jr 26:7
prophesy all the w that you have Jr 26:12
this land in w like all those Jr 26:20
all the officials heard his w, Jr 26:21
listen to the w of the prophets Jr 27:14
listen to the w of your prophets Jr 27:16
the LORD make the w you have Jr 28:6
have not listened to My w"— Jr 29:19
a scroll all the w that I have Jr 30:2
These are the w the LORD spoke Jr 30:4
all these w to Zedekiah king Jr 34:6
by listening to My w?" Jr 35:13
The w of Jonadab, son of Rechab, Jr 35:14
on it all the w I have spoken to Jr 36:2
a scroll all the w the LORD had Jr 36:4
the w of the LORD in the hearing Jr 36:6
the LORD's w from the scroll Jr 36:8
Jeremiah's w from the scroll Jr 36:10
heard all the w of the LORD from Jr 36:11
to them all the w he had heard Jr 36:13
When they had heard all the w, Jr 36:16
how did you write all these w? Jr 36:17
all these w to me while I was Jr 36:18
As they heard all these w, Jr 36:24
scroll with the w Baruch had Jr 36:27
write on it the very w that were Jr 36:28
dictation all the w of the Jr 36:32
And many other w like them were Jr 36:32
not obey the w of the LORD that Jr 37:2
heard the w Jeremiah was Jr 38:1
the exact w to them the king Jr 38:27
to fulfill My w for harm and not Jr 39:16
your God according to your w, Jr 42:4
people all the w of the LORD Jr 43:1
all these w the LORD their God Jr 43:1
may know that My w of disaster Jr 44:29
he wrote these w on a scroll at Jr 45:1
all these w were written against Jr 51:60
that you read all these w aloud. Jr 51:61
The w of Jeremiah end here. Jr 51:64
be afraid of them or their w, Ezk 2:6
afraid of their w or be Ezk 2:6
But speak My w to them whether Ezk 2:7
⌊w of⌋ lamentation, mourning, Ezk 2:10
Israel and speak My w to them. Ezk 3:4
whose w you cannot understand. Ezk 3:6
to all My w that I speak to you Ezk 3:10
None of My w will be delayed any Ezk 12:28
and hear your w, but they don't Ezk 33:31
They hear your w, but they don't Ezk 33:32
and spoke many w against Me. Ezk 35:13
While the w were still in the Dn 4:31
of the arrogant w the horn was Dn 7:11
He will speak w against the Most Dn 7:25
carried out His w that He spoke Dn 9:12
sound of his w like the sound Dn 10:6
heard the w he said, and when I Dn 10:9
Understand the w that I'm saying Dn 10:11
he was saying these w to me, Dn 10:15
keep these w secret and seal the Dn 12:4
for the w are secret and sealed Dn 12:9
them with the w of My mouth. Hs 6:5
speak ⌊mere⌋ w, taking false Hs 10:4
Take w ⌊of repentance⌋ with you Hs 14:2
w of Amos, who was one of the Am 1:1
land cannot endure all his w, Am 7:10
of hearing the w of the LORD. Am 8:11
Don't My w bring good to the Mc 2:7
God and the w of the prophet Hg 1:12
But didn't My w and My statutes Zch 1:6
comforting w to the angel who Zch 1:13
these⌋ the w that the LORD Zch 7:7
the law or the w that the LORD Zch 7:12
now hear these w that the Zch 8:9
⌊the w⌋ HOLY TO THE LORD Zch 14:20
wearied the LORD with your w. Mal 2:17
"Your w against Me are harsh," Mal 3:13
be heard for their many w. Mt 6:7
who hears these w of Mine and Mt 7:24
who hears these w of Mine and Mt 7:26
welcome you or listen to your w, Mt 10:14
For by your w you will be Mt 12:37
by your w you will be condemned. Mt 12:37
but My w will never pass away. Mt 24:35
remembered the w Jesus had Mt 26:75
of Me and of My w in this Mk 8:38
were astonished at His w. Mk 10:24
but My w will never pass away. Mk 13:31

you did not believe my w, Lk 1:20
the book of the w of the prophet Lk 3:4
by the gracious w that came from Lk 4:22
to Me, hears My w, and acts on Lk 6:47
is ashamed of Me and My w, Lk 9:26
About eight days after these w, Lk 9:28
Let these w sink in: the Son of Lk 9:44
give you such w and a wisdom Lk 21:15
but My w will never pass away. Lk 21:33
And they remembered His w. Lk 24:8
But these w seemed like nonsense Lk 24:11
These are My w that I spoke to Lk 24:44
speaks God's w, since He gives Jn 3:34
how will you believe My w?" Jn 5:47
The w that I have spoken to you Jn 6:63
You have the w of eternal life. Jn 6:68
from the crowd heard these w, Jn 7:40
spoke these w by the treasury, Jn 8:20
is from God listens to God's w. Jn 8:47
the Jews because of these w. Jn 10:19
These aren't the w of someone Jn 10:21
anyone hears My w and doesn't Jn 12:47
The w I speak to you I do not Jn 14:10
love Me will not keep My w. Jn 14:24
in Me and My w remain in you, Jn 15:7
because the w that You gave Me, Jn 17:8
to fulfill the w He had said: Jn 18:9
so that Jesus' w might be Jn 18:32
When Pilate heard these w, Jn 19:13
you and pay attention to my w. Ac 2:14
of Israel, listen to these w: Ac 2:22
with many other w he testified Ac 2:40
heard these w, Ananias dropped Ac 5:5
blasphemous w against Moses Ac 6:11
blasphemous w against this holy Ac 6:13
was still speaking these w, Ac 10:44
He will speak w to you by which Ac 11:14
fulfilled their w by condemning Ac 13:27
And the w of the prophets agree Ac 15:15
you with their w and unsettled Ac 15:24
jailer reported these w to Paul: Ac 16:36
reported these w to the Ac 16:38
if these are questions about w, Ac 18:15
keep in mind the w of the Lord Ac 20:35
I'm speaking w of truth and good Ac 26:25
with the spoken w of God. Rm 3:2
in Your w and triumph when Rm 3:4
and their w to the ends of the Rm 10:18
and flattering w they deceive Rm 16:18
not with clever w, so that the 1Co 1:17
not with persuasive w of wisdom, 1Co 2:4
not in w taught by human wisdom, 1Co 2:13
rather speak five w with my 1Co 14:19
than 10,000 w in ⌊another⌋ 1Co 14:19
we are in the w of our letters 2Co 10:11
inexpressible w, which a man is 2Co 12:4
one another with these w. 1Th 4:18
nourished by the w of the faith 1Tm 4:6
disputes and arguments over w. 1Tm 6:4
before God not to fight about w; 2Tm 2:14
he strongly opposed our w. 2Tm 4:15
a trumpet, and the sound of w. Heb 12:19
I have written to you in few w. Heb 13:22
exploit you with deceptive w. 2Pt 2:3
bombastic, empty w, they seduce, 2Pt 2:18
can remember the w previously 2Pt 3:2
slandering us with malicious w. 3Jn 10
their mouths utter arrogant w, Jd 16
remember the w foretold by the Jd 17
who hear the w of this prophecy Rv 1:3
reed like a rod, with these w: Rv 11:1
until God's w are accomplished Rv 17:17
"These w of God are true." Rv 19:9
because these w are faithful and Rv 21:5
These w are faithful and true. Rv 22:6
the prophetic w of this book." Rv 22:7
who keep the w of this book. Rv 22:9
the prophetic w of this book, Rv 22:10
the prophetic w of this book: Rv 22:18
from the w of this prophetic Rv 22:19

WORE *(13)*

garments he w when he entered Lv 16:23
⌊They w⌋ old, patched sandals on Jos 9:5
with him until she w him out, Jdg 16:16
presence and w a linen ephod. 1Sm 2:18
and w a bronze helmet and bronze 1Sm 17:5
85 men who w linen ephods. 1Sm 22:18
the king's virgin daughters w. 2Sm 13:18
pounds and who w new armor, 2Sm 21:16
David also w a linen ephod. 1Ch 15:27
I w sackcloth as my clothing, Ps 69:11
He w cursing like his coat— Ps 109:18
John w a camel-hair garment with Mk 1:6
He w a robe stained with blood, Rv 19:13

WORK *(365)*

completed His w that He had done Gn 2:2
from all His w that He had done Gn 2:2
rested from His w of creation. Gn 2:3
was no man to w the ground. Gn 2:5
of Eden to w it and watch over Gn 2:15
garden of Eden to w the ground Gn 3:23
If you w the land, it will never Gn 4:12
should you w for me for nothing? Gn 29:15
I'll w for you seven years for Gn 29:18
my affliction and my hard w, Gn 31:42
went into the house to do his w, Gn 39:11
imposed all this w on them. Ex 1:14
the people to neglect their w? Ex 5:4
Impose heavier w on the men. Ex 5:9
Finish your assigned w each day, Ex 5:13
Now get to w. No straw will be Ex 5:18
are forcing to w as slaves, Ex 6:5
No w may be done on those ⌊days⌋ Ex 12:16
six days and do all your w, Ex 20:9
must not do any w—you, your Ex 20:10
for his lost w time and provide Ex 21:19
Do your w for six days but rest Ex 23:12
of hammered w at the two ends Ex 25:18
make them of braided cord w, Ex 28:14
of pure gold cord w for the Ex 28:22
blend, the w of a perfumer; Ex 30:25
carve wood for w in every craft. Ex 31:5
If anyone does w on it, that Ex 31:14
For six days w may be done, Ex 31:15
Anyone who does w on the Sabbath Ex 31:15
The tablets were the w of God, Ex 32:16
among will see the LORD's w, Ex 34:10
For six days w is to be done, Ex 35:2
Anyone who does w on it must be Ex 35:2
any task in the w brought ⌊it⌋. Ex 35:24
for all the w that the LORD, Ex 35:29
carve wood for w in every kind Ex 35:33
to do all the w of a gem cutter; Ex 35:35
people are to w based on Ex 36:1
to do all the w of constructing Ex 36:1
to come to the w and do it. Ex 36:2
doing all the w for the Ex 36:4
one from the w they were doing Ex 36:4
of the w the LORD commanded Ex 36:5
for them to do all the w. Ex 36:7
those doing the w made the Ex 36:8
of hammered w at the two ends Ex 37:7
was the w of the Levites under Ex 38:21
in all the w on the sanctuary, Ex 38:24
So all the w for the tabernacle, Ex 39:32
had done all the w according to Ex 39:42
inspected all the w they had Ex 39:43
So Moses finished the w. Ex 40:33
or any implement used for w. Lv 11:32
self-denial and do no w, Lv 16:29
For six days w may be done, Lv 23:3
You are not to do any w; Lv 23:3
you are not to do any daily w. Lv 23:7
you must not do any daily w." Lv 23:8
You are not to do any daily w. Lv 23:21
You must not do any daily w, Lv 23:25
day you are not to do any w, Lv 23:28
who does any w on this same day. Lv 23:30
You are not to do any w. Lv 23:31
you are not to do any daily w. Lv 23:35
you are not to do any daily w. Lv 23:36
he may w for you until the Year Lv 25:40
all the w relating to these. Nm 3:26
and all the w relating to them. Nm 3:31
and all the w related to these, Nm 3:36
is qualified to do w at the tent Nm 4:3
to do w at the tent of meeting. Nm 4:23
clans regarding w and Nm 4:24
duties and all their ⌊other⌋ w, Nm 4:27
qualified to do the w of the Nm 4:30
and all the w related to them. Nm 4:32
regarding all their w at the Nm 4:33
was qualified for w at the tent Nm 4:35
was qualified for w at the tent Nm 4:39
was qualified for w at the tent Nm 4:43
to do the w of serving at Nm 4:47
according to his w and Nm 4:49
to be used in the w of the tent Nm 7:5
it was a hammered w of gold, Nm 8:4
they may perform the LORD's w. Nm 8:11
to perform the w for the Nm 8:19
came to do their w at the tent Nm 8:22
the service in the w at the tent Nm 8:24
service in the w and no longer Nm 8:25
but he must not do the w. Nm 8:26
to perform the w at the LORD's Nm 16:9
doing all the w at the tent, Nm 18:4
by the LORD to w at the tent of Nm 18:6
veil, and you will do that w. Nm 18:7
giving you the w of the Nm 18:7
in return for the w they do, Nm 18:21
the w of the tent of meeting. Nm 18:21
Levites will do the w of the Nm 18:23
in return for your w at the tent Nm 18:31
you are not to do any daily w. Nm 28:18
you are not to do any daily w. Nm 28:25
you are not to do any daily w. Nm 28:26
you are not to do any daily w. Nm 29:1
you must not do any w. Nm 29:7
you must not do any daily w. Nm 29:12
you are not to do any daily w. Nm 29:35
you in all the w of your hands. Dt 2:7
six days and do all your w, Dt 5:13
must not do any w—you, your Dt 5:14
seen every great w the LORD has Dt 11:7
you in all the w of your hands Dt 14:29
you in all your w and in Dt 15:10
of your oxen to w or shear the Dt 15:19
and you must not do any w. Dt 16:8
and in all the w of your hands, Dt 16:15
not been yoked or used for w. Dt 21:3
you in all the w of your hands. Dt 24:19
the LORD, the w of a craftsman, Dt 27:15
bless all the w of your hands. Dt 28:12
in all the w of your hands with Dt 30:9
The Rock—His w is perfect; Dt 32:4
and accept the w of his hands. Dt 33:11
came in from his w in the field. Jdg 19:16
today, and where did you w? Ru 2:19
good for you to w with his young Ru 2:22
donkeys and use them for his w. 1Sm 8:16
man who can only w a spindle or 2Sm 3:29
servants are to w the ground for 2Sm 9:10
and put ⌊them to w⌋ with saws, 2Sm 12:31
deputies in charge of the w. 1Kg 5:16
over the people doing the w. 1Kg 5:16
to do every kind of bronze w. 1Kg 7:14
and carried out all his w. 1Kg 7:14
Then the w of the pillars was 1Kg 7:22
oxen were wreaths of hanging w. 1Kg 7:29
finished all the w that he was 1Kg 7:40
So all the w King Solomon did in 1Kg 7:51
who were over Solomon's w: 1Kg 9:23
over the people doing the w. 1Kg 9:23
Him with the w of his hands and 1Kg 16:7
the hands of those doing the w— 2Kg 12:11
was given to those doing the w, 2Kg 12:14
money to pay those doing the w, 2Kg 12:15
the hands of those doing the w— 2Kg 22:5
since they w with integrity. 2Kg 22:7
the hand of those doing the w— 2Kg 22:9
with all the w of their hands. 2Kg 22:17
did all the w of the most holy 1Ch 6:49
it and put them to w with saws, 1Ch 20:3
skilled in every kind of w 1Ch 22:15
begin the w, and may the LORD 1Ch 22:16
in charge of the w on the LORD's 1Ch 23:4
the w of the service of God's 1Ch 23:28
men with strength for the w— 1Ch 26:8
Jordan for all the w of the LORD 1Ch 26:30
all the w of service in the 1Ch 28:13
and courageous, and do the w. 1Ch 28:20
until all the w for the service 1Ch 28:20
be at your disposal for the w, 1Ch 28:21
for the gold ⌊w⌋ and the silver 1Ch 29:5
for all the w to be done by the 1Ch 29:5
of the king's w gave willingly. 1Ch 29:6
in engraving to w with gold, 2Ch 2:7
⌊He will w⌋ with the craftsmen 2Ch 2:7
He knows how to w with gold, 2Ch 2:14
to make the people w. 2Ch 2:18
two cherubim of sculptured w, 2Ch 3:10
doing the w that he was doing 2Ch 4:11
So all the w Solomon did for the 2Ch 5:1

to be slaves for his **w**;	2Ch 8:9
of Solomon's **w** was carried out	2Ch 8:16
for your **w** has a reward."	2Ch 15:7
Ramah and stopped his **w**.	2Ch 16:5
did their **w**, and through them	2Ch 24:13
them until the **w** was finished	2Ch 29:34
the hands of those doing the **w**—	2Ch 34:10
were doing the **w** with integrity.	2Ch 34:12
those doing the **w** task by task.	2Ch 34:13
the hand of those doing the **w**."	2Ch 34:17
to supervise the **w** on the LORD's	Ezr 3:8
This **w** is being done diligently	Ezr 5:8
so that the ⌊**w**⌋ will not stop.	Ezr 6:8
them in the **w** on the house	Ezr 6:22
for the **w** of the Levites.	Ezr 8:20
those who would be doing the **w**.	Neh 2:16
encouraged to ⌊do⌋ this good **w**.	Neh 2:18
can kill them and stop the **w**."	Neh 4:11
to his own **w** on the wall.	Neh 4:15
my men did the **w** while the other	Neh 4:16
The **w** is enormous and spread	Neh 4:19
we continued the **w**, while half	Neh 4:21
guard by night and **w** by day."	Neh 4:22
were gathered there for the **w**.	Neh 5:16
doing a great **w** and cannot come	Neh 6:3
Why should the **w** cease while I	Neh 6:3
become discouraged in the **w**,	Neh 6:9
and for all the **w** of the house	Neh 10:33
who did the **w** at the temple:	Neh 11:12
supervised the **w** outside the	Neh 11:16
have blessed the **w** of his hands,	Jb 1:10
to reject the **w** of Your hands,	Jb 10:3
long for the **w** of Your hands.	Jb 14:15
When He is at **w** to the north,	Jb 23:9
they are all the **w** of His hands.	Jb 34:19
that you should praise His **w**,	Jb 36:24
so that all men may know His **w**.	Jb 37:7
you leave it to do your hard **w**?	Jb 39:11
heavens, the **w** of Your fingers,	Ps 8:3
wicked by the **w** of their hands.	Ps 9:16
proclaims the **w** of His hands.	Ps 19:1
to the **w** of their hands;	Ps 28:4
has done or the **w** of His hands,	Ps 28:5
and all His **w** is trustworthy.	Ps 33:4
the **w** You accomplished in their	Ps 44:1
own tongues **w** against them.	Ps 64:8
and will tell about God's **w**,	Ps 64:9
Do You **w** wonders for the dead?	Ps 88:10
Let Your **w** be seen by Your	Ps 90:16
for us the **w** of our hands—	Ps 90:17
establish the **w** of our hands!	Ps 90:17
heavens are the **w** of Your hands.	Ps 102:25
goes out to his **w** and to his	Ps 104:23
eating food earned by hard **w**;	Ps 127:2
not abandon the **w** of Your hands.	Ps 138:8
reflect on the **w** of Your hands.	Ps 143:5
and the **w** of a man's hands will	Pr 12:14
There is profit in all hard **w**,	Pr 14:23
truly lazy in his **w** is brother	Pr 18:9
because his hands refuse to **w**.	Pr 21:25
you see a man skilled in his **w**?	Pr 22:29
a person according to his **w**?	Pr 24:12
your outdoor **w**, and prepare your	Pr 24:27
life because the **w** that was done	Ec 2:17
I hated all my **w** at which I	Ec 2:18
over all my **w** that I labored	Ec 2:19
all my **w** I had labored at	Ec 2:20
is a man whose **w** was done with	Ec 2:21
get with all his **w** and all his	Ec 2:22
eat, drink, and to enjoy his **w**.	Ec 2:24
discover the **w** God has done	Ec 3:11
for every activity and every **w**."	Ec 3:17
and all skillful **w** is due to a	Ec 4:4
result from much **w** and a fool's	Ec 5:3
and destroy the **w** of your hands?	Ec 5:6
Consider the **w** of God; for who	Ec 7:13
mind to all the **w** that is done	Ec 8:9
I observed all the **w** of God ⌊and	Ec 8:17
to discover the **w** that is done	Ec 8:17
because there is no **w**, planning,	Ec 9:10
know the **w** of God who makes	Ec 11:5
tinder, and his **w** a spark;	Is 1:31
down to the **w** of their hands,	Is 2:8
do not see the **w** of His hands.	Is 5:12
up and do His **w** quickly so that	Is 5:19
finishes all His **w** against Mount	Is 10:12
Those who **w** with flax will be	Is 19:9
have also done all our **w** for us.	Is 26:12
to do His **w**, His strange work	Is 28:21
His strange **w**, and to perform	Is 28:21
the **w** of My hands within his	Is 29:23
donkeys that **w** the ground will	Is 30:24
nothing and your **w** is worthless.	Is 41:24
Or does your **w** ⌊say⌋: He has no	Is 45:9
Me about the **w** of My hands.	Is 45:11
the destroyer to **w** havoc.	Is 54:16
I planted, the **w** of My hands, so	Is 60:21
we all are the **w** of Your hands.	Is 64:8
enjoy the **w** of their hands.	Is 65:22
goldsmith, the **w** of a craftsman	Jr 10:9
all the **w** of skilled artisans.	Jr 10:9
are worthless, a **w** to be mocked.	Jr 10:15
on the Sabbath day or do any **w**,	Jr 17:22
Sabbath day and do no **w** on it,	Jr 17:24
to anger by the **w** of your hands.	Jr 25:6
to anger by the **w** of your hands	Jr 25:7
deeds and the **w** of their hands.'	Jr 25:14
reward for your **w** will come—	Jr 31:16
anger by the **w** of their hands"	Jr 32:30
to anger by the **w** of your hands.	Jr 44:8
are worthless, a **w** to be mocked.	Jr 51:18
to the **w** of their hands.	Lm 3:64
the **w** of a potter's hands!	Lm 4:2
all its **w** and everything done	Ezk 44:14
closed during the six days of **w**,	Ezk 46:1
all of them the **w** of craftsmen.	Hs 13:2
Our gods! to the **w** of our hands.	Hs 14:3
again to the **w** of your hands.	Mc 5:13
Revive ⌊Your **w**⌋ in these years;	Hab 3:2
for He will expose the cedar **w**.	Zph 2:14
They began **w** on the house of	Hg 1:14
declaration. "**W**! For I am with	Hg 2:4
And so is every **w** of their hands	Hg 2:14
you—all the **w** of your hands—	Hg 2:17
powers are at **w** in him."	Mt 14:2
w in the vineyard today.'	Mt 21:28
put them to **w**, and earned five	Mt 25:16
powers are at **w** in him."	Mk 6:14
each one his **w**, and commanded	Mk 13:34
six days when **w** should be done;	Lk 13:14
day I will complete My **w**.'	Lk 13:32
Then he went to **w** for one of the	Lk 15:15
sent Me and to finish His **w**,"	Jn 4:34
Don't **w** for the food that	Jn 6:27
replied, "This is the **w** of God:	Jn 6:29
I did one **w**, and you are all	Jn 7:21
is coming when no one can **w**.	Jn 9:4
stoning You for a good **w**,"	Jn 10:33
completing the **w** You gave Me to	Jn 17:4
this plan or this **w** is of men,	Ac 5:38
and Saul for the **w** that I have	Ac 13:2
John was completing his life **w**,	Ac 13:25
I am doing a **w** in your days,	Ac 13:41
a **w** that you will never believe,	Ac 13:41
of God for the **w** they had	Ac 14:26
not gone on with them to the **w**.	Ac 15:38
facecloths or **w** aprons that had	Ac 19:12
this saving **w** of God has been	Ac 28:28
show that the **w** of the law is	Rm 2:15
But to the one who does not **w**,	Rm 4:5
that all things **w** together for	Rm 8:28
down God's **w** because of food	Rm 14:20
longer have any **w** to do in these	Rm 15:23
one's **w** will become obvious,	1Co 3:13
the quality of each one's **w**.	1Co 3:13
If anyone's **w** that he has built	1Co 3:14
If anyone's **w** is burned up,	1Co 3:15
Are you not my **w** in the Lord?	1Co 9:1
excelling in the Lord's **w**,	1Co 15:58
he is doing the Lord's **w**,	1Co 16:10
you may excel in every good **w**.	2Co 9:8
For He who was at **w** with Peter	Gl 2:8
was also at **w** with me among	Gl 2:8
the Spirit and **w** miracles among	Gl 3:5
person should examine his own **w**,	Gl 6:4
we must **w** for the good of all,	Gl 6:10
the saints in the **w** of ministry,	Eph 4:12
he must do honest **w** with his own	Eph 4:28
Don't ⌊**w** only⌋ while being	Eph 6:6
started a good **w** in you will	Php 1:6
this means fruitful **w** for me;	Php 1:22
w out your own salvation with	Php 2:12
to death for the **w** of Christ,	Php 2:30
in every good **w** and growing	Col 1:10
w only while being watched,	Col 3:22
men, but ⌊**w**⌋ wholeheartedly	Col 3:22
Father, your **w** of faith, labor	1Th 1:3
and to **w** with your own hands,	1Th 4:11
in love because of their **w**.	1Th 5:13
for goodness and the **w** of faith,	2Th 1:11
of lawlessness is already at **w**;	2Th 2:7
you in every good **w** and word.	2Th 2:17
If anyone isn't willing to **w**,	2Th 3:10
with the **w** ⌊of others⌋.	2Th 3:11
overseer, he desires a noble **w**."	1Tm 3:1
devoted herself to every good **w**.	1Tm 5:10
those who **w** hard at preaching	1Tm 5:17
prepared for every good **w**.	2Tm 2:21
equipped for every good **w**.	2Tm 3:17
do the **w** of an evangelist,	2Tm 4:5
from every evil **w** and will bring	2Tm 4:18
and disqualified for any good **w**.	Ti 1:16
to be ready for every good **w**,	Ti 3:1
not forget your **w** and the love	Heb 6:10
must do its complete **w**,	Jms 1:4
based on each one's **w**,	1Pt 1:17

WORKED *(38)*

LORD your God **w** it out for me."	Gn 27:20
So Jacob **w** seven years for	Gn 29:20
it for Rachel that I **w** for you?	Gn 29:25
And he **w** for Laban another seven	Gn 29:30
my children that I have **w** for,	Gn 30:26
know how hard I have **w** for you."	Gn 30:26
know that I've **w** hard for your	Gn 31:6
20 years I have **w** in your	Gn 31:41
They **w** the Israelites ruthlessly	Ex 1:13
design of cherubim **w** into them.	Ex 26:1
a design of cherubim **w** into it.	Ex 26:31
design of cherubim **w** into them.	Ex 36:8
a design of cherubim **w** into it.	Ex 36:35
because he **w** for you six years—	Dt 15:18
men she had **w** ⌊with⌋ and said	Ru 2:19
name of the man I **w** with today	Ru 2:19
for he **w** with God's help today."	1Sm 14:45
since they **w** with integrity.	2Kg 12:15
who **w** in the service of the	1Ch 23:24
of those who **w** in the fields	1Ch 27:26
carried the loads **w** with one	Neh 4:17
He **w** wonders in the sight of	Ps 78:12
what other peoples had **w** for.	Ps 105:44
plunder what he has **w** for.	Ps 109:11
eat what your hands have **w** for.	Ps 128:2
to a man who has not **w** for it.	Ec 2:21
what our fathers have **w** for—	Jr 3:24
⌊it is⌋ **w** by the hands of a	Jr 10:3
all you have **w** for, and leave	Ezk 23:29
for, since they **w** for Me."	Ezk 29:20
Israel **w** to earn a wife;	Hs 12:12
we've **w** hard all night long and	Lk 5:5
with them and **w**, for they were	Ac 18:3
who has **w** very hard for you.	Rm 16:6
who have **w** hard in the Lord.	Rm 16:12
who has **w** very hard in the Lord.	Rm 16:12
I **w** more than any of them,	1Co 15:10
don't lose what we have **w** for,	2Jn 8

WORKER *(8)*

What does the **w** gain from his	Ec 3:9
The sleep of the **w** is sweet,	Ec 5:12
as a hired **w** counts years,	Is 16:14
as a hired **w** counts years,	Is 21:16
for the **w** is worthy of his food.	Mt 10:10
the **w** is worthy of his wages.	Lk 10:7
told the vineyard **w**, 'Listen,	Lk 13:7
a **w** who doesn't need to be	2Tm 2:15

WORKER'S *(1)*

A **w** appetite works for him	Pr 16:26

WORKERS *(19)*

guild of linen **w** at Beth-ashbea,	1Ch 4:21
You also have many **w**:	1Ch 22:15
the names of the **w** who are	Ezr 5:4
fast, and oppress all your **w**.	Is 58:3
be food for the **w** of the city.	Ezk 48:18
The city's **w** from all the tribes	Ezk 48:19
is abundant, but the **w** are few.	Mt 9:37
to send out **w** into His harvest.	Mt 9:38
morning to hire **w** for his	Mt 20:1
with the **w** on one denarius	Mt 20:2
'Call the **w** and give them their	Mt 20:8
is abundant, but the **w** are few.	Lk 10:2
to send out **w** into His harvest.	Lk 10:2
all you **w** of unrighteousness!'	Lk 13:27
as well as the **w** engaged in this	Ac 19:25
but we are **w** with you for your	2Co 1:24

apostles, deceitful **w**, 2Co 11:13
out for evil **w**, watch out for Php 3:2
from the **w** who reaped your Jms 5:4

WORKING (33)

in return for **w** yet another Gn 29:27
young man ⌊was **w**⌋ with the sons Gn 37:2
and you would stop them from **w**." Ex 5:5
Haven't you been **w** with his Ru 3:2
good to have you **w** with me in 1Sm 29:6
it out to those **w** on the LORD's 2Kg 12:11
who were **w** in the LORD's 2Ch 34:10
supervise those **w** on the house Ezr 3:9
people had the will to keep **w**. Neh 4:6
destruction, **w** treachery. Ps 52:2
there he was, **w** away at the Jr 18:3
master finds him **w** when he comes Mt 24:46
the Lord **w** with them and Mk 16:20
master finds him **w** when he comes Lk 12:43
Father is still **w**, and I am Jn 5:17
still working, and I am **w** also." Jn 5:17
we labor, **w** with our own hands. 1Co 4:12
have no right to refrain from **w**? 1Co 9:6
W together with Him, we also 2Co 6:1
matters is faith **w** through love. Gl 5:6
according to the **w** of His vast Eph 1:19
the spirit now **w** in the Eph 2:2
to me by the **w** of His power. Eph 3:7
by the proper **w** of each Eph 4:16
w side by side for the faith of Php 1:27
For it is God who is **w** in you, Php 2:13
through faith in the **w** of God, Col 2:12
W night and day so that we would 1Th 2:9
one⌋ is based on Satan's **w**, 2Th 2:9
and toiled, **w** night and day, so 2Th 3:8
irresponsibly, not **w** at all, but 2Th 3:11
that quietly **w**, they may eat 2Th 3:12
w in us what is pleasing in His Heb 13:21

WORKLOAD (1)

reduction at all in your **w**.' " Ex 5:11

WORKMAN'S (1)

her right hand, for a **w** mallet. Jdg 5:26

WORKMANSHIP (4)

according to the same **w** of gold, Ex 28:8
it with the same **w** as the ephod; Ex 28:15
according to the same **w** of gold, Ex 39:5
with the same **w** as the ephod of Ex 39:8

WORKMEN (3)

give it to the **w** in the LORD's 2Kg 22:5
w did their work, and through 2Ch 24:13
it to the **w** who were working 2Ch 34:10

WORKS (188)

to design artistic **w** in gold, Ex 31:4
to design artistic **w** in gold, Ex 35:32
and awesome **w** your eyes have Dt 10:21
signs and the **w** He did in Egypt Dt 11:3
build siege **w** against the city Dt 20:20
all the **w** the LORD had done Jos 24:31
LORD's great **w** He had done for Jdg 2:7
LORD or the **w** He had done for Jdg 2:10
tell about all His wonderful **w**! 1Ch 16:9
the wonderful **w** He has done, 1Ch 16:12
His wonderful **w** among all 1Ch 16:24
carried out great **w** in the towns 2Ch 17:13
with all the **w** of their hands. 2Ch 34:25
those wonderful **w** of Him who has Jb 37:16
He is the foremost of God's **w**; Jb 40:19
lord over the **w** of Your hands; Ps 8:6
declare all Your wonderful **w**. Ps 9:1
telling about Your wonderful **w**. Ps 26:7
He considers all their **w**. Ps 33:15
Your wonderful **w** and Your plans Ps 40:5
Come, see the **w** of the LORD, who Ps 46:8
repay each according to his **w**. Ps 62:12
with awe-inspiring **w**, God of our Ps 65:5
How awe-inspiring are Your **w**! Ps 66:3
Come and see the **w** of God; Ps 66:5
still proclaim Your wonderful **w**. Ps 71:17
tell about Your wonderful **w**. Ps 75:1
I will remember the LORD's **w**; Ps 77:11
You are the God who **w** wonders; Ps 77:14
the wonderful **w** He has performed Ps 78:4
in God and not forget God's **w**, Ps 78:7
the wonderful **w** He had shown Ps 78:11
did not believe His wonderful **w**. Ps 78:32
and there are no **w** like Yours. Ps 86:8
because of the **w** of Your hands. Ps 92:4
How magnificent are Your **w**, Ps 92:5
His wonderful **w** among all Ps 96:3
His **w** in all the places where Ps 103:22
How countless are Your **w**, LORD! Ps 104:24
may the LORD rejoice in His **w**. Ps 104:31
tell about all His wonderful **w**! Ps 105:2
the wonderful **w** He has done, Ps 105:5
wonderful **w** or remember Your Ps 106:7
soon forgot His **w** and would not Ps 106:13
wonderful **w** in the land of Ham, Ps 106:22
His wonderful **w** for the human Ps 107:8
His wonderful **w** for the human Ps 107:15
His wonderful **w** for the human Ps 107:21
and announce His **w** with shouts Ps 107:22
saw the LORD's **w**, His wonderful Ps 107:24
His wonderful **w** in the deep. Ps 107:24
His wonderful **w** for the human Ps 107:31
The LORD's **w** are great, studied Ps 111:2
wonderful **w** to be remembered. Ps 111:4
power of His **w** by giving them Ps 111:6
The **w** of His hands are truth and Ps 111:7
Your **w** are wonderful, and I know Ps 139:14
will declare Your **w** to the next Ps 145:4
splendor and Your wonderful **w**. Ps 145:5
power of Your awe-inspiring **w**, Ps 145:6
before His **w** of long ago. Pr 8:22
The one who **w** his land will have Pr 12:11
appetite **w** for him because Pr 16:26
The one who **w** his land will have Pr 28:19
wool and flax and **w** with willing Pr 31:13
and let her **w** praise her at the Pr 31:31
God **w** so that people will be in Ec 3:14
and their **w** are in God's hands. Ec 9:1
God has already accepted your **w**. Ec 9:7
built large siege **w** against it. Ec 9:14
⌊They do⌋ their **w** in darkness, Is 29:15
their **w** are nonexistent; Is 41:29
and **w** it with his strong arm. Is 44:12
and your **w**—they will not Is 57:12
cover themselves with their **w**. Is 59:6
Their **w** are sinful works, and Is 59:6
works are sinful **w**, and violent Is 59:6
Knowing their **w** and their Is 66:18
to worship the **w** of their own Jr 1:16
His ⌊past⌋ wonderful **w** so that Jr 21:2
trust in your **w** and treasures, Jr 48:7
cut down, and your **w** wiped out. Ezk 6:6
will set up siege **w** against you, Ezk 26:8
because all His **w** are true and Dn 4:37
see your good **w** and give glory Mt 5:16
so that his **w** may be shown to be Jn 3:21
show Him greater **w** than these so Jn 5:20
because of the **w** that the Father Jn 5:36
These very **w** I am doing testify Jn 5:36
we do to perform the **w** of God?" Jn 6:28
can see Your **w** that You are Jn 7:3
so that God's **w** might be Jn 9:3
We must do the **w** of Him who sent Jn 9:4
The **w** that I do in My Father's Jn 10:25
you many good **w** from the Father. Jn 10:32
Which of these **w** are you stoning Jn 10:32
If I am not doing My Father's **w**, Jn 10:37
don't believe Me, believe the **w**. Jn 10:38
who lives in Me does His **w**. Jn 14:10
because of the **w** themselves. Jn 14:11
Me will also do the **w** that I do. Jn 14:12
do even greater **w** than these, Jn 14:12
not done the **w** among them that Jn 15:24
always doing good **w** and acts of Ac 9:36
and do **w** worthy of repentance. Ac 26:20
each one according to his **w**: Rm 2:6
His sight by the **w** of the law, Rm 3:20
of law? By one of **w**? No, on the Rm 3:27
by faith apart from **w** of law. Rm 3:28
If Abraham was justified by **w**, Rm 4:2
Now to the one who **w**, pay is not Rm 4:4
righteousness apart from **w**: Rm 4:6
not from **w** but from the One who Rm 9:12
faith, but as if it were by **w**. Rm 9:32
by grace, then it is not by **w**; Rm 11:6
everyone who **w** and labors with 1Co 16:16
So death **w** in us, but life in 2Co 4:12
will be according to their **w**. 2Co 11:15
is justified by the **w** of the law Gl 2:16
and not by the **w** of the law, Gl 2:16
because by the **w** of the law no Gl 2:16
the Spirit by the **w** of the law Gl 3:2
among you by the **w** of the law or Gl 3:5
rely on⌋ the **w** of the law are Gl 3:10
Now the **w** of the flesh are Gl 5:19
of the One who **w** out everything Eph 1:11
not from **w**, so that no one can Eph 2:9
in Christ Jesus for good **w**, Eph 2:10
to the power that **w** in you— Eph 3:20
in the fruitless **w** of darkness, Eph 5:11
strength that **w** powerfully in me Col 1:29
him that he **w** hard for you, Col 4:13
which also **w** effectively in you 1Th 2:13
with good **w**, as is proper for 1Tm 2:10
and is well known for good **w**— 1Tm 5:10
Likewise, good **w** are obvious, 1Tm 5:25
rich in good **w**, to be generous 1Tm 6:18
to our **w**, but according 2Tm 1:9
repay him according to his **w**. 2Tm 4:14
but they deny Him by their **w**. Ti 1:16
an example of good **w** yourself, Ti 2:7
people, eager to do good **w**. Ti 2:14
not by **w** of righteousness that Ti 3:5
to devote themselves to good **w**. Ti 3:8
themselves to good **w** for cases Ti 3:14
heavens are the **w** of Your hands; Heb 1:10
Me, tried ⌊Me⌋, and saw My **w** Heb 3:9
And yet His **w** have been finished Heb 4:3
day God rested from all His **w**. Heb 4:4
rest has rested from his own **w**, Heb 4:10
of repentance from dead **w**, Heb 6:1
from dead **w** to serve the living Heb 9:14
to promote love and good **w**, Heb 10:24
has faith, but does not have **w**? Jms 2:14
it doesn't have **w**, is dead by Jms 2:17
You have faith, and I have **w**." Jms 2:18
Show me your faith without **w**, Jms 2:18
I will show you faith from my **w**. Jms 2:18
that faith without **w** is useless? Jms 2:20
justified by **w** when he offered Jms 2:21
was active together with his **w**, Jms 2:22
his works, and by **w**, faith was Jms 2:22
is justified by **w** and not by Jms 2:24
justified by **w** when she received Jms 2:25
so also faith without **w** is dead. Jms 2:26
show his **w** by good conduct Jms 3:13
your good **w**, glorify God 1Pt 2:12
the earth and the **w** on it will 2Pt 3:10
to destroy the Devil's **w**. 1Jn 3:8
Because his **w** were evil, and his 1Jn 3:12
to him shares in his evil **w**. 2Jn 11
remind him of the **w** he is doing, 3Jn 10
I know your **w**, your labor, and Rv 2:2
and do the **w** you did at first. Rv 2:5
I know your **w**—your love, Rv 2:19
Your last **w** are greater than the Rv 2:19
each of you according to your **w**. Rv 2:23
one who keeps My **w** to the end: Rv 2:26
says: I know your **w**; you have a Rv 3:1
not found your **w** complete before Rv 3:2
I know your **w**. Because you have Rv 3:8
I know your **w**, that you are Rv 3:15
repent of the **w** of their hands Rv 9:20
for their **w** follow them!" Rv 14:13
and awe-inspiring are Your **w**, Rv 15:3
double it according to her **w**. Rv 18:6
according to their **w** by what was Rv 20:12
judged according to their **w**. Rv 20:13

WORLD (237)

The whole **w** came to Joseph in Gn 41:57
He has set the **w** on them. 1Sm 2:8
Then all the **w** will know that 1Sm 17:46
of the **w** were exposed at 2Sm 22:16
all the kings of the **w** in riches 1Kg 10:23
The whole **w** wanted an audience 1Kg 10:24
in the whole **w** except in Israel 2Kg 5:15
The **w** is firmly established; 1Ch 16:30
the kings of the **w** in riches and 2Ch 9:22
the kings of the **w** wanted an 2Ch 9:23
and chased from the inhabited **w**. Jb 18:18
Him in charge of the entire **w**? Jb 34:13
hates justice govern ⌊the **w**⌋? Jb 34:17
the surface of the inhabited **w**. Jb 37:12
He judges the **w** with Ps 9:8
from men of the **w**, whose portion Ps 17:14
of the **w** were exposed, Ps 18:15
to the ends of the inhabited **w**. Ps 19:4
the **w** and its inhabitants, Ps 24:1
inhabitants of the **w** stand in Ps 33:8
listen, all who inhabit the **w**, Ps 49:1
for the **w** and everything in it Ps 50:12
lightning lit up the **w**. Ps 77:18

The w and everything in it— Ps 89:11
birth to the earth and the w, Ps 90:2
The w is firmly established; Ps 93:1
The w is firmly established; Ps 96:10
He will judge the w with Ps 96:13
His lightning lights up the w; Ps 97:4
the w and those who live in it, Ps 98:7
He will judge the w righteously Ps 98:9
crush leaders over the entire w. Ps 110:6
rejoicing in His inhabited w, Pr 8:31
I will bring disaster on the w, Is 13:11
who turned the w into a Is 14:17
of the w and you who live Is 18:3
kingdoms of the w on the face Is 23:17
the w wastes away and withers; Is 24:4
inhabitants of the w will learn Is 26:9
and fill the whole w with fruit. Is 27:6
w and all that comes from it. Is 34:1
You live in ⌊a w⌋ of deception. Jr 9:6
established the w by His wisdom, Jr 10:12
the kingdoms of the w which are Jr 25:26
established the w by His wisdom, Jr 51:15
While the whole w rejoices, Ezk 35:14
who live at the center of the w. Ezk 38:12
the w and all who live in it. Nah 1:5
kingdoms of the w and their Mt 4:8
You are the light of the w. Mt 5:14
from the foundation of the w. Mt 13:35
the field is the w; and the good Mt 13:38
gains the whole w yet loses his Mt 16:26
to the w because of offenses. Mt 18:7
in all the w as a testimony to Mt 24:14
beginning of the w until now and Mt 24:21
from the foundation of the w. Mt 25:34
is proclaimed in the whole w, Mt 26:13
gain the whole w yet lose his Mk 8:36
from the beginning of the w, Mk 13:19
is proclaimed in the whole w, Mk 14:9
Go into all the w and preach the Mk 16:15
kingdoms of the w in a moment of Lk 4:5
if he gains the whole w, Lk 9:25
since the foundation of the w— Lk 11:50
For the Gentile w eagerly seeks Lk 12:30
things that are coming on the w, Lk 21:26
everyone, was coming into the w. Jn 1:9
He was in the w, and the world Jn 1:10
and the w was created through Jn 1:10
yet the w did not recognize Him. Jn 1:10
who takes away the sin of the w! Jn 1:29
For God loved the w in this way: Jn 3:16
His Son into the w that He might Jn 3:17
world that He might judge the w, Jn 3:17
but that the w might be saved Jn 3:17
the light has come into the w, Jn 3:19
really is the Savior of the w." Jn 4:42
who was to come into the w!" Jn 6:14
heaven and gives life to the w." Jn 6:33
the life of the w is My flesh." Jn 6:51
things, show Yourself to the w." Jn 7:4
The w cannot hate you, but it Jn 7:7
I am the light of the w. Jn 8:12
You are of this w; I am not of Jn 8:23
this world; I am not of this w. Jn 8:23
these things I tell the w." Jn 8:26
as I am in the w, I am the light Jn 9:5
world, I am the light of the w." Jn 9:5
I came into this w for judgment, Jn 9:39
set apart and sent into the w, Jn 10:36
he sees the light of this w. Jn 11:9
who was to come into the w." Jn 11:27
the w has gone after Him!" Jn 12:19
life in this w will keep it for Jn 12:25
Now is the judgment of this w. Jn 12:31
ruler of this w will be cast out Jn 12:31
have come as a light into the w, Jn 12:46
come to judge the w but to save Jn 12:47
the world but to save the w. Jn 12:47
from this w to the Father. Jn 13:1
loved His own who were in the w, Jn 13:1
The w is unable to receive Him Jn 14:17
little while the w will see Me Jn 14:19
to us and not to the w?" Jn 14:22
not give to you as the w gives. Jn 14:27
the ruler of the w is coming. Jn 14:30
so that the w may know that I Jn 14:31
If the w hates you, understand Jn 15:18
you were of the w, the world Jn 15:19
the w would love ⌊you as⌋ its Jn 15:19
because you are not of the w, Jn 15:19
you out of it, the w hates you. Jn 15:19
He will convict the w about sin, Jn 16:8
ruler of this w has been judged Jn 16:11
wail, but the w will rejoice. Jn 16:20
person has been born into the w. Jn 16:21
Father and have come into the w. Jn 16:28
I am leaving the w and going to Jn 16:28
will have suffering in this w. Jn 16:33
I have conquered the w." Jn 16:33
with You before the w existed. Jn 17:5
the men You gave Me from the w. Jn 17:6
praying for the w but for those Jn 17:9
no longer in the w, but they are Jn 17:11
they are in the w, and I am Jn 17:11
things in the w so that they may Jn 17:13
w hated them because they are Jn 17:14
because they are not of the w, Jn 17:14
the world, as I am not of the w. Jn 17:14
them out of the w but that You Jn 17:15
are not of the w, as I am not Jn 17:16
the world, as I am not of the w. Jn 17:16
As You sent Me into the w, Jn 17:18
also have sent them into the w. Jn 17:18
the w may believe You sent Me. Jn 17:21
so the w may know You have sent Jn 17:23
The w has not known You. Jn 17:25
"I have spoken openly to the w," Jn 18:20
"My kingdom is not of this w," Jn 18:36
If My kingdom were of this w, Jn 18:36
I have come into the w for this: Jn 18:37
not even the w itself could Jn 21:25
famine throughout the Roman w. Ac 11:28
have turned the w upside down Ac 17:6
who made the w and everything Ac 17:24
to judge the w in righteousness Ac 17:31
of Asia and the w adore." Ac 19:27
the Jews throughout the Roman w, Ac 24:5
is being reported in all the w. Rm 1:8
creation of the w His invisible Rm 1:20
how will God judge the w? Rm 3:6
and the whole w may become Rm 3:19
inherit the w was not through Rm 4:13
entered the w through one man Rm 5:12
sin was in the w before the law, Rm 5:13
to the ends of the inhabited w. Rm 10:18
brings riches for the w, Rm 11:12
rejected is w reconciliation, Rm 11:15
the w did not know God through 1Co 1:21
received the spirit of the w, 1Co 2:12
wisdom of this w is foolishness 1Co 3:19
Cephas or the w or life or death 1Co 3:22
spectacle to the w and to angels 1Co 4:9
you would have to leave the w. 1Co 5:10
the saints will judge the w? 1Co 6:2
And if the w is judged by you, 1Co 6:2
who use the w as though they 1Co 7:31
For this w in its current form 1Co 7:31
about the things of the w— 1Co 7:33
about the things of the w— 1Co 7:34
an idol is nothing in the w," 1Co 8:4
not be condemned with the w. 1Co 11:32
kinds of languages in the w, 1Co 14:10
conducted ourselves in the w, 2Co 1:12
reconciling the w to Himself, 2Co 5:19
the elemental forces of the w. Gl 4:3
through whom the w has been Gl 6:14
crucified to me, and I to the w. Gl 6:14
before the foundation of the w, Eph 1:4
hope and without God in the w. Eph 2:12
against the w powers of this Eph 6:12
you shine like stars in the w. Php 2:15
and growing all over the w, Col 1:6
the elemental forces of the w, Col 2:8
the elemental forces of this w, Col 2:20
if you still belonged to the w? Col 2:20
came into the w to save sinners" 1Tm 1:15
on in the w, taken up in glory 1Tm 3:16
we brought nothing into the w, 1Tm 6:7
because he loved this present w, 2Tm 4:10
brings His firstborn into the w, Heb 1:6
to angels the w to come that we Heb 2:5
since the foundation of the w, Heb 4:3
since the foundation of the w. Heb 9:26
as He was coming into the w, Heb 10:5
he condemned the w and became Heb 11:7
The w was not worthy of them. Heb 11:38
keep oneself unstained by the w. Jms 1:27
the poor in this w to be rich in Jms 2:5
The tongue, a w of Jms 3:6
with the w is hostility toward Jms 4:4
before the foundation of the w, 1Pt 1:20
by your brothers in the w. 1Pt 5:9
that is in the w because of evil 2Pt 1:4
He didn't spare the ancient w, 2Pt 2:5
a flood on the w of the ungodly; 2Pt 2:5
Through these the w of that time 2Pt 3:6
also for those of the whole w. 1Jn 2:2
Do not love the w or the things 1Jn 2:15
the things that belong to the w. 1Jn 2:15
If anyone loves the w, love for 1Jn 2:15
that belongs to the w— 1Jn 2:15
the Father, but is from the w. 1Jn 2:16
And the w with its lust is 1Jn 2:17
The reason the w does not know 1Jn 3:1
brothers, if the w hates you. 1Jn 3:13
have gone out into the w. 1Jn 4:1
and he is already in the w now. 1Jn 4:3
than the one who is in the w. 1Jn 4:4
are from the w. Therefore what 1Jn 4:5
what they say is from the w, 1Jn 4:5
and the w listens to them. 1Jn 4:5
Son into the w so that we might 1Jn 4:9
sent the Son as Savior of the w. 1Jn 4:14
for we are as He is in this w. 1Jn 4:17
been born of God conquers the w. 1Jn 5:4
that has conquered the w: 1Jn 5:4
conquers the w but the one who 1Jn 5:5
the whole w is under the sway 1Jn 5:19
have gone out into the w; 2Jn 7
over the whole w to test those Rv 3:10
The kingdom of the w has become Rv 11:15
one who deceives the whole w. Rv 12:9
foundation of the w in the book Rv 13:8
of the whole w to assemble them Rv 16:14
of the w will be astounded Rv 17:8

WORLD'S *(12)*

He deprives the w leaders of Jb 12:24
and all the w inhabitants did Lm 4:12
Me before the w foundation. Jn 17:24
God made the w wisdom foolish? 1Co 1:20
has chosen the w foolish things 1Co 1:27
has chosen the w weak things to 1Co 1:27
has chosen the w insignificant 1Co 1:28
now, like the w garbage, like 1Co 4:13
to this w immoral people, 1Co 5:10
wants to be the w friend becomes Jms 4:4
escaped the w impurity through 2Pt 2:20
anyone has this w goods and sees 1Jn 3:17

WORLDLY *(4)*

but w grief produces death. 2Co 7:10
walked according to this w age, Eph 2:2
to death whatever in you is w: Col 3:5
godlessness and w lusts and to Ti 2:12

WORM *(10)*

You are my father, and to the w: Jb 17:14
and the son of man, who is a w! Jb 25:6
But I am a w and not a man, Ps 22:6
not fear, you w Jacob, you men Is 41:14
and the w will eat them like Is 51:8
God appointed a w that attacked Jnh 4:7
where Their w does not die, Mk 9:44
where Their w does not die, Mk 9:46
where Their w does not die, Mk 9:48
them are those who w their way 2Tm 3:6

WORMS *(6)*

and it bred w and smelled. Ex 16:20
because w will eat them. Dt 28:39
in the dust, and w cover them. Jb 21:26
forgets them; w feed on them; Jb 24:20
out under you, and w cover you." Is 14:11
became infected with w and died. Ac 12:23

WORMWOOD *(9)*

as bitter as w and as sharp as Pr 5:4
feed this people w and give them Jr 9:15
to feed them w and give them Jr 23:15
bitterness, sated me with w. Lm 3:15
the w and the poison. Lm 3:19
turn justice into w throw Am 5:7
fruit of righteousness into w— Am 6:12
The name of the star is W, Rv 8:11
a third of the waters became w. Rv 8:11

WORN *(16)*

The robe must be ⌊w by⌋ Aaron Ex 28:35
These must be ⌊w by⌋ Aaron and Ex 28:43

sandals of ours are **w** out from Jos 9:13
of Israel were **w** out that day, 1Sm 14:24
king himself has **w** and a horse Est 6:8
my eyes are **w** out from angry Ps 31:9
My eyes are **w** out from crying. Ps 88:9
You are **w** out with your many Is 47:13
runners and they have **w** you out, Jr 12:5
am **w** out with groaning and have Jr 45:3
My eyes are **w** out from weeping; Lm 2:11
He has **w** away my flesh and skin; Lm 3:4
this woman **w** out by adultery: Ezk 23:43
they were weary and **w** out, Mt 9:36
long time he had **w** no clothes Lk 8:27
there, and Jesus, **w** out from His Jn 4:6

WORN-OUT *(2)*
and took **w** sacks on their Jos 9:4
took old rags and **w** clothes and Jr 38:11

WORRIED *(6)*
And now don't be **w** or angry with Gn 45:5
they became **w** and saw that he Jdg 3:25
the donkeys and is **w** about you, 1Sm 10:2
I am **w** about the Judeans who Jr 38:19
famine you are **w** about will Jr 42:16
you are **w** and upset about many Lk 10:41

WORRIES *(4)*
but the **w** of this age and the Mt 13:22
but the **w** of this age, the Mk 4:19
their way and are choked with **w**, Lk 8:14
and **w** of life, or that Lk 21:34

WORRY *(14)*
don't **w** about them because 1Sm 9:20
Don't **w** because of evildoers, Pr 24:19
It will not **w** in a year of Jr 17:8
Don't **w** about your life, what Mt 6:25
And why do you **w** about clothes? Mt 6:28
don't **w**, saying, 'What will we Mt 6:31
don't **w** about tomorrow, Mt 6:34
tomorrow will **w** about itself. Mt 6:34
don't **w** about how or what you Mt 10:19
don't **w** beforehand what you will Mk 13:11
don't **w** about how you should Lk 12:11
you, don't **w** about your life Lk 12:22
thing, why **w** about the rest? Lk 12:26
Don't **w** about anything, but in Php 4:6

WORRYING *(4)*
father will stop ⌊**w**⌋ about the 1Sm 9:5
donkeys and start **w** about us." 1Sm 9:5
single cubit to his height by **w**? Mt 6:27
add a cubit to his height by **w**? Lk 12:25

WORSE *(24)*
me away is much **w** than the great 2Sm 13:16
This will be **w** for you than all 2Sm 19:7
so that they did **w** evil than the 2Ch 33:9
how much **w** are lies for a ruler. Pr 17:7
much **w** will it be when I send Ezk 14:21
promiscuous acts **w** than those of Ezk 23:11
the sea was getting **w** and worse. Jnh 1:11
the sea was getting worse and **w**. Jnh 1:11
most upright is **w** than a hedge Mc 7:4
angry, but they made it **w**. Zch 1:15
garment and makes the tear **w**. Mt 9:16
condition is **w** than the first. Mt 12:45
will be **w** than the first." Mt 27:64
old cloth, and a **w** tear is made. Mk 2:21
On the contrary, she became **w**. Mk 5:26
condition is **w** than the first." Lk 11:26
that something **w** doesn't happen Jn 5:14
for the better but for the **w**. 1Co 11:17
far **w** beatings, near 2Co 11:23
you treated **w** than the other 2Co 12:13
the faith and is **w** than an 1Tm 5:8
and imposters will become **w**, 2Tm 3:13
How much **w** punishment, do you Heb 10:29
last state is **w** for them than 2Pt 2:20

WORSHIP *(186)*
and I will go over there to **w**; Gn 22:5
will all **w** God at this mountain. Ex 3:12
My son go so that he may **w** Me, Ex 4:23
so that they may **w** Me in the Ex 7:16
go, so that they may **w** Me. Ex 8:1
go, so that they may **w** Me. Ex 8:20
go, so that they may **w** Me. Ex 9:1
go, so that they may **w** Me. Ex 9:13
people go, that they may **w** Me. Ex 10:3
that they may **w** the LORD their Ex 10:7
"Go, **w** the LORD your God," Ex 10:8
the men may go and **w** the LORD, Ex 10:11
Moses and said, "Go, **w** the LORD. Ex 10:24
some of them to **w** the LORD our Ex 10:26
we will use to **w** the LORD until Ex 10:26
w the LORD as you have asked. Ex 12:31
not bow down to them or **w** them; Ex 20:5
down to their gods or **w** them. Ex 23:24
W the LORD your God, and He will Ex 23:25
If you **w** their gods, it will be Ex 23:33
and bow in **w** at a distance. Ex 24:1
up, then bow in **w**, each one at Ex 33:10
and bowed in **w** to their gods. Nm 25:2
astray to bow down and **w** them. Dt 4:19
There you will **w** man-made gods Dt 4:28
not bow down to them or **w** them, Dt 5:9
LORD your God, **w** Him, and take Dt 6:13
away from Me to **w** other gods. Dt 7:4
Do not **w** their gods, for that Dt 7:16
other gods to **w** and bow down to Dt 8:19
and to **w** the LORD your God with Dt 10:12
the LORD your God and **w** Him. Dt 10:20
your God and **w** Him with all your Dt 11:13
turn aside, **w**, and bow down to Dt 11:16
are driving out **w** their gods— Dt 12:2
Don't **w** the LORD your God this Dt 12:4
did these nations **w** their gods? Dt 12:30
not known, 'and let us **w** them,' Dt 13:2
you must **w** Him and remain Dt 13:4
'Let us go and **w** other gods'— Dt 13:6
'Let us go and **w** other gods,' Dt 13:13
and has gone to **w** other gods by Dt 17:3
go after other gods to **w** them. Dt 28:14
and there you will **w** other gods, Dt 28:36
there you will **w** other gods of Dt 28:64
God to go and **w** the gods of Dt 29:18
They began to **w** other gods, Dt 29:26
had not permitted them ⌊to **w**⌋. Dt 29:26
down to other gods and **w** them, Dt 30:17
turn to other gods and **w** them, Dt 31:20
the ground in **w** and asked Him, Jos 5:14
may carry out the **w** of the LORD Jos 22:27
do not **w** them or bow down to Jos 23:7
you, and go and **w** other gods, Jos 23:16
the LORD and **w** Him in sincerity Jos 24:14
and in Egypt, and **w** the LORD. Jos 24:14
please you to **w** the LORD, Jos 24:15
today the one you will **w**: Jos 24:15
my family, we will **w** the LORD." Jos 24:15
the LORD to **w** other gods! Jos 24:16
We too will **w** the LORD, because Jos 24:18
will not be able to **w** the LORD, Jos 24:19
the LORD and **w** foreign gods, Jos 24:20
"We will **w** the LORD." Jos 24:21
have chosen to **w** the LORD." Jos 24:22
We will **w** the LORD our God and Jos 24:24
other gods to **w** and bow down to Jdg 2:19
interpretation, he bowed in **w**. Jdg 7:15
the LORD and did not **w** Him. Jdg 10:6
every year to **w** and to sacrifice 1Sm 1:3
early to bow and to **w** the LORD. 1Sm 1:19
I require at the place of **w**? 1Sm 2:29
distress ⌊in the⌋ place of **w**, 1Sm 2:32
to the LORD, and **w** only Him. 1Sm 7:3
fear the LORD, **w** and obey Him, 1Sm 12:14
w the LORD with all your heart. 1Sm 12:20
the LORD and **w** Him faithfully 1Sm 12:24
with me so I can **w** the LORD." 1Sm 15:25
bow and **w** the LORD your God. 1Sm 15:30
saying, 'Go and **w** other gods.' 1Sm 26:19
I will **w** the LORD in Hebron." 2Sm 15:8
summit where he used to **w** God, 2Sm 15:32
the king bowed in **w** on his bed. 1Kg 1:47
and serve other gods and **w** them, 1Kg 9:6
to serve Baal and **w** him. 1Kg 16:31
the temple of Rimmon to **w** and I, 2Kg 5:18
eliminated Baal ⌊**w**⌋ from Israel, 2Kg 10:28
You must **w** at this altar in 2Kg 18:22
of the utensils used in **w**. 1Ch 9:28
W the LORD in the splendor of 1Ch 16:29
that I have made for **w**." 1Ch 23:5
and serve other gods and **w** them, 2Ch 7:19
down before the LORD to **w** Him. 2Ch 20:18
their hearts ⌊to **w**⌋ the God of 2Ch 20:33
You must **w** before one altar, 2Ch 32:12
for we also **w** your God and have Ezr 4:2
the land in order to **w** the LORD, Ezr 6:21
confession and **w** of the LORD Neh 9:3
w the LORD in the splendor of Ps 29:2
the earth will **w** You and sing Ps 66:4
Come, let us **w** and bow down; Ps 95:6
W the LORD in the splendor of Ps 96:9
All the gods must **w** Him. Ps 97:7
bow in **w** at His footstool. Ps 99:5
bow in **w** at His holy mountain, Ps 99:9
cup of salvation and **w** the LORD. Ps 116:13
and will **w** the LORD. Ps 116:17
let us **w** at His footstool. Ps 132:7
they made to **w**, to the moles Is 2:20
and Egypt will **w** with Assyria. Is 19:23
and they will **w** the LORD at Is 27:13
and their **w** ⌊consists of⌋ Is 29:13
You are to **w** at this altar? Is 36:7
All mankind will come to **w** Me, Is 66:23
other gods and to **w** the works of Jr 1:16
these gates to **w** the LORD. Jr 7:2
followed other gods to **w** them. Jr 11:10
other gods to serve and **w**— Jr 13:10
There you will **w** other gods both Jr 16:13
forgot My name through Baal **w**. Jr 23:27
to serve them and to **w** them, Jr 25:6
that are coming to **w** there. Jr 26:2
to the east in **w** of the sun. Ezk 8:16
will bow in **w** at the threshold Ezk 46:2
also bow in **w** before the LORD Ezk 46:3
the north gate to **w** must go out Ezk 46:9
fall down and **w** the gold statue Dn 3:5
fall down and **w** will immediately Dn 3:6
fall down and **w** the gold statue. Dn 3:10
fall down and **w** will be thrown Dn 3:11
your gods or **w** the gold statue Dn 3:12
my gods or **w** the gold statue Dn 3:14
fall down and **w** the statue I Dn 3:15
But if you don't **w** it, you will Dn 3:15
your gods or **w** the gold statue Dn 3:18
than serve or **w** any god except Dn 3:28
I **w** Yahweh, the God of the Jnh 1:9
who bow in **w** on the rooftops Zph 1:5
nations will bow in **w** to Him, Zph 2:11
year after year to **w** the King, Zch 14:16
up to Jerusalem to **w** the King, Zch 14:17
east and have come to **w** Him." Mt 2:2
so that I too can go and **w** Him." Mt 2:8
if You will fall down and **w** me." Mt 4:9
W the Lord your God, and serve Mt 4:10
They **w** Me in vain, teaching as Mt 15:9
They **w** Me in vain, teaching as Mk 7:7
You, then, will **w** me, all will Lk 4:7
W the Lord your God, and serve Lk 4:8
the place to **w** is in Jerusalem. Jn 4:20
when you will **w** the Father Jn 4:21
You Samaritans **w** what you do not Jn 4:22
We **w** what we do know, because Jn 4:22
worshipers will **w** the Father in Jn 4:23
wants such people to **w** Him. Jn 4:23
and those who **w** Him must worship Jn 4:24
worship Him must **w** in spirit and Jn 4:24
went up to **w** at the festival. Jn 12:20
come out and **w** Me in this place Ac 7:7
gave them up to **w** the host of Ac 7:42
the images that you made to **w**. Ac 7:43
He had come to **w** in Jerusalem Ac 8:27
observing the objects of your **w**, Ac 17:23
what you **w** in ignorance, this Ac 17:23
people to **w** God contrary to Ac 18:13
I went up to **w** in Jerusalem. Ac 24:11
a sect, so I **w** my fathers' God, Ac 24:14
this is your spiritual **w**. Rm 12:1
fall down on his face and **w** God, 1Co 14:25
practices and the **w** of angels, Col 2:18
so-called god or object of **w**, 2Th 2:4
who affirm that they **w** God. 1Tm 2:10
And all God's angels must **w** Him. Heb 1:6
all the vessels of **w** with blood. Heb 9:21
w the One who lives forever and Rv 4:10
and ⌊count⌋ those who **w** there. Rv 11:1
live on the earth will **w** him, Rv 13:8
live on it to **w** the first beast Rv 13:12
whoever would not **w** the image of Rv 13:15
W the Maker of heaven and earth, Rv 14:7
those who **w** the beast and his Rv 14:11
will come and **w** before You, Rv 15:4
I fell at his feet to **w** him, Rv 19:10
W God, because the testimony Rv 19:10
I fell down to **w** at the feet of Rv 22:8
the words of this book. **W** God." Rv 22:9

WORSHIPED *(66)*
an altar to the LORD and **w** Him. Gn 12:8
And Abram **w** the LORD there. Gn 13:4
and there he **w** the LORD, Gn 21:33
the man bowed down, **w** the LORD, Gn 24:26
Then I bowed down, **w** the LORD, Gn 24:48
an altar there, **w** the LORD, and Gn 26:25
misery, they bowed down and **w**. Ex 4:31
So the people bowed down and **w**. Ex 12:27
bowed down to the ground and **w**. Ex 34:8
River and **w** other gods. Jos 24:2
gods your ancestors **w** beyond the Jos 24:14
gods your fathers **w** beyond the Jos 24:15
Israel **w** the LORD throughout Jos 24:31
The people **w** the LORD throughout Jdg 2:7
LORD's sight. They **w** the Baals Jdg 2:11
they abandoned Him and **w** Baal Jdg 2:13
to their sons, and **w** their gods. Jdg 3:6
LORD their God and **w** the Baals Jdg 3:7
They **w** the Baals and the Jdg 10:6
our God and **w** the Baals." Jdg 10:10
abandoned Me and **w** other gods. Jdg 10:13
gods among them and **w** the LORD, Jdg 10:16
he bowed and **w** the LORD there. 1Sm 1:28
Ashtoreths and only **w** the LORD. 1Sm 7:4
the LORD and **w** the Baals 1Sm 12:10
went to the LORD's house, and **w**. 2Sm 12:20
other gods and **w** and served them 1Kg 9:9
He served Baal and **w** him. 1Kg 22:53
because they had **w** other gods. 2Kg 17:7
They **w** the whole heavenly host 2Kg 17:16
but they also **w** their own gods 2Kg 17:33
also **w** the whole heavenly host 2Kg 21:3
had served, and he **w** them. 2Kg 21:21
They **w** and praised the LORD: 2Ch 7:3
other gods and **w** and served them 2Ch 7:22
He **w** before them and burned 2Ch 25:14
with him bowed down and **w**. 2Ch 29:29
rejoicing and bowed down and **w**. 2Ch 29:30
and he **w** the whole heavenly host 2Ch 33:3
bowed down and **w** the LORD with Neh 8:6
He fell to the ground and **w**, Jb 1:20
made a calf and **w** the cast metal Ps 106:19
followed, pursued, and **w**. Jr 8:2
gods, served them, and **w** them. Jr 16:11
their God and **w** and served other Jr 22:9
fell down and **w** the gold statue Dn 3:7
to their knees, they **w** Him. Mt 2:11
in the boat **w** Him and said, Mt 14:33
hold of His feet, and **w** Him. Mt 28:9
saw Him, they **w**, but some Mt 28:17
Our fathers **w** on this mountain, Jn 4:20
he said, and he **w** Him. Jn 9:38
fell at his feet, and **w** him. Ac 10:25
of Thyatira, who **w** God, was Ac 16:14
Jews and with those who **w** God, Ac 17:17
and **w** and served something Rm 1:25
of Joseph, and, he **w**, leaning on Heb 11:21
and the elders fell down and **w**. Rv 5:14
before the throne and **w** God, Rv 7:11
fell on their faces and **w** God, Rv 11:16
w the dragon because he gave Rv 13:4
And they **w** the beast, saying, Rv 13:4
the beast and who **w** his image. Rv 16:2
creatures fell down and **w** God, Rv 19:4
beast and those who **w** his image. Rv 19:20
who had not **w** the beast or his Rv 20:4

WORSHIPER *(1)*
Titius Justus, a **w** of God, whose Ac 18:7

WORSHIPER'S *(1)*
cannot perfect the **w** conscience. Heb 9:9

WORSHIPERS *(4)*
all its **w** will be put to shame, Is 44:11
when the true **w** will worship the Jn 4:23
never perfect the **w** by the same Heb 10:1
since the **w**, once purified, Heb 10:2

WORSHIPING *(8)*
abandoning Me and **w** other gods. 1Sm 8:8
⌊**w**⌋ the golden calves that were 2Kg 10:29
while he was **w** in the temple of 2Kg 19:37
assembly was **w**, singing the song 2Ch 29:28
while he was **w** in the temple of Is 37:38
countries, **w** wood and stone, Ezk 20:32
After **w** Him, they returned to Lk 24:52
hands to stop **w** demons and idols Rv 9:20

WORSHIPS *(4)*
and the heavenly host **w** You. Neh 9:6
makes it into a god and **w** it; Is 44:15
He bows down to it and **w**; Is 44:17
If anyone **w** the beast and his Rv 14:9

WORST *(3)*
rain down the **w** hail that has Ex 9:18
and I am the **w** of them. 1Tm 1:15
that in me, the **w** ⌊of them⌋, 1Tm 1:16

WORTH *(19)*
Land **w** 400 shekels of silver— Gn 23:15
give you two days' **w** of bread. Ex 16:29
w twice the wages of a hired Dt 15:18
because you are **w** 10,000 of us. 2Sm 18:3
gold bowls **w** 1,000 gold coins, Ezr 8:27
wouldn't be **w** burdening the king Est 7:4
and quartz are not **w** mentioning. Jb 28:18
nostrils. What is he really **w**? Is 2:22
were 1,000 vines, **w** 1,000 pieces Is 7:23
⌊once⌋ **w** their weight in pure Lm 4:2
Aren't you **w** more than they? Mt 6:26
you are **w** more than many Mt 10:31
man is **w** far more than a sheep, Mt 12:12
buy 200 denarii **w** of bread and Mk 6:37
in two tiny coins **w** very little. Mk 12:42
you are **w** more than many Lk 12:7
Aren't you **w** much more than the Lk 12:24
hundred denarii **w** of bread Jn 6:7
time are not **w** comparing with Rm 8:18

WORTHLESS *(62)*
and the seven **w**, scorched heads Gn 41:27
enraged Me with their **w** idols. Dt 32:21
Abimelech hired **w** and reckless Jdg 9:4
away to follow **w** things that 1Sm 12:21
or deliver you; they are **w**. 1Sm 12:21
destroy all the **w** and unwanted 1Sm 15:9
He is such a **w** fool nobody can 1Sm 25:17
attention to this **w** man Nabal, 1Sm 25:25
all the **w** men among those who 1Sm 30:22
out, get out, you **w** murderer! 2Sm 16:7
of Israel with their **w** idols. 1Kg 16:13
of Israel with their **w** idols. 1Kg 16:26
They pursued **w** idols and became 2Kg 17:15
idols and became **w** themselves, 2Kg 17:15
Then **w** and wicked men gathered 2Ch 13:7
He knows which people are **w**. Jb 11:11
you are all **w** doctors. Jb 13:4
him not put trust in **w** things, Jb 15:31
gets in exchange will prove **w**. Jb 15:31
and show that my speech is **w**? Jb 24:25
who says to a king, "**W** man!" Jb 34:18
love what is **w** and pursue a lie Ps 4:2
and what is **w** is exalted by the Ps 12:8
not sit with the **w** or associate Ps 26:4
who are devoted to **w** idols, Ps 31:6
the foe, for human help is **w**. Ps 60:11
the foe, for human help is **w**. Ps 108:12
eyes from looking at what is **w**; Ps 119:37
A **w** person, a wicked man, who Pr 6:12
A **w** man digs up evil, and his Pr 16:27
A **w** witness mocks justice, Pr 19:28
"It's **w**, it's worthless!" Pr 20:14
"It's worthless, it's **w**!" Pr 20:14
and the **w** toward the honorable. Is 3:5
grapes, but it yielded **w** grapes. Is 5:2
grapes, did it yield **w** grapes? Is 5:4
grave, like a **w** branch, covered Is 14:19
Egypt's help is completely **w**; Is 30:7
are nothing and your work is **w**. Is 41:24
They trust in empty and **w** words; Is 59:4
Me, followed **w** idols, and became Jr 2:5
idols, and became **w** themselves? Jr 2:5
with their **w** foreign idols? Jr 8:19
customs of the peoples are **w**. Jr 10:3
instructed by **w** idols ⌊made of⌋ Jr 10:8
They are **w**, a work to be mocked. Jr 10:15
a false vision, **w** divination, Jr 14:14
Can any of the **w** idols of the Jr 14:22
rather than **w** ones, you will be Jr 15:19
w idols of no benefit at all." Jr 16:19
They are making you **w**. Jr 23:16
They are **w**, a work to be mocked. Jr 51:18
determined to follow what is **w**. Hs 5:11
who cling to **w** idols forsake Jnh 2:8
to the **w** shepherd who deserts Zch 11:17
but threw out the **w** ones. Mt 13:48
turn from these **w** things to the Ac 14:15
them over to a **w** mind to do what Rm 1:28
been raised, your faith is **w**; 1Co 15:17
corrupt in mind, **w** in regard to 2Tm 3:8
for they are unprofitable and **w**. Ti 3:9
it is **w** and about to be cursed, Heb 6:8

WORTHWHILE *(1)*
did not think it **w** to have God Rm 1:28

WORTHY *(48)*
LORD, who is **w** of praise, and I 2Sm 22:4
woman who is more **w** than she. Est 1:19
and gave gifts **w** of the king's Est 2:18
LORD, who is **w** of praise, and I Ps 18:3
I am not **w** to take off His Mt 3:11
I am not **w** to have You come Mt 8:8
for the worker is **w** of his food. Mt 10:10
out who is **w**, and stay there Mt 10:11
and if the household is **w**, Mt 10:13
more than Me is not **w** of Me; Mt 10:37
more than Me is not **w** of Me. Mt 10:37
and follow Me is not **w** of Me. Mt 10:38
who were invited were not **w**. Mt 22:8
I am not **w** to stoop down and Mk 1:7
I am not **w** to untie the strap of Lk 3:16
He is **w** for You to grant this, Lk 7:4
since I am not **w** to have You Lk 7:6
myself **w** to come to You. Lk 7:7
the worker is **w** of his wages. Lk 10:7
no longer **w** to be called your Lk 15:19
no longer **w** to be called your Lk 15:21
who are counted **w** to take part Lk 20:35
strap I'm not **w** to untie." Jn 1:27
were counted **w** to be dishonored Ac 5:41
and I am not **w** to untie the Ac 13:25
and do works **w** of repentance. Ac 26:20
in a manner **w** of the saints, Rm 16:2
you to walk **w** of the calling Eph 4:1
life in a manner **w** of the gospel Php 1:27
that you may walk **w** of the Lord, Col 1:10
one of you to walk **w** of God, 1Th 2:12
will be counted **w** of God's 2Th 1:5
consider you **w** of His calling, 2Th 1:11
should be **w** of respect, not 1Tm 3:8
too, must be **w** of respect, not 1Tm 3:11
be considered **w** of an ample 1Tm 5:17
The laborer is **w** of his wages. 1Tm 5:18
masters to be **w** of all respect, 1Tm 6:1
self-controlled, **w** of respect, Ti 2:2
is considered **w** of more glory Heb 3:3
The world was not **w** of them. Heb 11:38
journey in a manner **w** of God, 3Jn 6
Me in white, because they are **w**. Rv 3:4
You are **w** to receive glory and Rv 4:11
Who is **w** to open the scroll and Rv 5:2
no one was found **w** to open the Rv 5:4
You are **w** to take the scroll and Rv 5:9
slaughtered is **w** to receive Rv 5:12

WOULD *(656)*
(See pp. xi-xii.)

WOULDN'T *(42)*
(See pp. xi-xii.)

WOUND *(18)*
bruise for bruise, **w** for wound. Ex 21:25
bruise for bruise, wound for **w**. Ex 21:25
I give life; I **w** and I heal. No Dt 32:39
man struck him, inflicting a **w**. 1Kg 20:37
and blood from his **w** flowed into 1Kg 22:35
My **w** is incurable, though I am Jb 34:6
disaster, an extremely severe **w**. Jr 14:17
unending, my **w** incurable, Jr 15:18
incurable; your **w** most severe. Jr 30:12
get balm for her **w**—perhaps she Jr 51:8
his sickness and Judah his **w**, Hs 5:13
cannot cure you or heal your **w**. Hs 5:13
For her **w** is incurable and has Mc 1:9
injury; your **w** is severe. All Nah 3:19
the brothers and **w** their weak 1Co 8:12
but his fatal **w** was healed. Rv 13:3
beast, whose fatal **w** was healed. Rv 13:12
who had the sword **w** yet lived. Rv 13:14

WOUNDED *(26)*
Many **w** died as far as the Jdg 9:40
up with him and severely **w** him. 1Sm 31:3
for I'm mortally **w**, but my life 2Sm 1:9
the battle, for I am badly **w**!" 1Kg 22:34
and the Arameans **w** Joram. 2Kg 8:28
found him and severely **w** him. 1Ch 10:3
the battle, for I am badly **w**!" 2Ch 18:33
The Arameans **w** Joram, 2Ch 22:5
me away, for I am severely **w**!" 2Ch 35:23
the mortally **w** cry for help, Jb 24:12

suddenly, they will be **w**. Ps 64:7
about the pain of those You **w**. Ps 69:26
and my innermost being was **w**, Ps 73:21
my heart is **w** within me. Ps 109:22
They beat and **w** me; they took my Sg 5:7
a wife deserted and **w** in spirit, Is 54:6
my brokenness—I am severely **w**! Jr 10:19
among them only the badly **w** men, Jr 37:10
and the **w** will groan throughout Jr 51:52
faint like the **w** in the streets Lm 2:12
when the **w** groan and slaughter Ezk 26:15
before him as a mortally **w** man. Ezk 30:24
He has **w** ⌊us⌋, and He will bind Hs 6:1
they **w** this one too and threw Lk 20:12
out of that house naked and **w**. Ac 19:16
heads appeared to be fatally **w**, Rv 13:3

WOUNDING *(3)*

For I killed a man for **w** me, Gn 4:23
w him, it hardly ever leaves him. Lk 9:39
by His **w** you have been healed. 1Pt 2:24

WOUNDS *(25)*

recover from the **w** that the 2Kg 8:29
recover from the **w** that the 2Kg 9:15
from the **w** they inflicted 2Ch 22:6
saw that Joash had many **w**, 2Ch 24:25
dressed their **w**, and provided 2Ch 28:15
multiplies my **w** without cause. Jb 9:17
My **w** are foul and festering Ps 38:5
and binds up their **w**. Ps 147:3
Lashes and **w** purge away evil, Pr 20:30
Who has **w** for no reason? Pr 23:29
like an archer who **w** everyone. Pr 26:10
The **w** of a friend are Pr 27:6
spot is uninjured—**w**, welts, Is 1:6
and heals the **w** He inflicted. Is 30:26
and we are healed by His **w**. Is 53:5
Sickness and **w** keep coming to My Jr 6:7
and scoff because of all its **w**. Jr 19:8
and will heal you of your **w**— Jr 30:17
and scoff because of all her **w**. Jr 49:17
and scoff because of all her **w**. Jr 50:13
and He will bind up our **w**. Hs 6:1
What are these **w** on your chest? Zch 13:6
The **w** I received in the house of Zch 13:6
over to him and bandaged his **w**, Lk 10:34
of the night and washed their **w**. Ac 16:33

WOVE *(2)*

and he **w** cherubim into it. 2Ch 3:14
and **w** me together with bones and Jb 10:11

WOVEN *(16)*

a specially **w** tunic, a turban, Ex 28:4
artistically **w** waistband that Ex 28:8
above the ephod's **w** waistband. Ex 28:27
there should be a **w** collar with Ex 28:32
on him with its **w** waistband. Ex 29:5
the specially **w** garments, both Ex 31:10
and the specially **w** garments for Ex 35:19
made specially **w** garments for Ex 39:1
artistically **w** waistband that Ex 39:5
above the ephod's **w** waistband. Ex 39:20
made the **w** robe of the ephod Ex 39:22
tunics of fine **w** linen for Aaron Ex 39:27
and the specially **w** garments for Ex 39:41
He put the **w** band of the ephod Lv 8:7
his thighs are **w** firmly together Jb 40:17
w in one piece from the top. Jn 19:23

WRAP *(4)*

around him⌋ and **w** his head with Lv 16:4
and its cover too small to **w** up Is 28:20
because of you and **w** themselves Ezk 27:31
"**W** your cloak around you," Ac 12:8

WRAPPED *(26)*

his life is **w** up with the boy's Gn 44:30
kneading bowls **w** up in their Ex 12:34
on Aaron, **w** the sash around Lv 8:7
with tunics, **w** sashes around Lv 8:13
w in a cloth behind the ephod. 1Sm 21:9
Now Ahijah had **w** himself with a 1Kg 11:29
he **w** his face in his mantle and 1Kg 19:13
ropes of death were **w** around me; Ps 18:4
ropes of death were **w** around me, Ps 116:3
of the wicked were **w** around me, Ps 119:61
and He **w** Himself in zeal as in a Is 59:17
of salvation and **w** me in a robe Is 61:10
rubbed with salt or **w** in cloths. Ezk 16:4
I also **w** you in fine linen and Ezk 16:10
seaweed was **w** around my head. Jnh 2:5
took the body, **w** it in clean, Mt 27:59
a linen cloth **w** around his naked Mk 14:51
Him down and **w** Him in the linen Mk 15:46
she **w** Him snugly in cloth and Lk 2:7
find a baby **w** snugly in cloth Lk 2:12
he **w** it in fine linen and placed Lk 23:53
and with his face **w** in a cloth. Jn 11:44
Jesus' body and **w** it in linen Jn 19:40
young men got up, **w** ⌊his body⌋, Ac 5:6
a gold sash **w** around His chest Rv 1:13
with gold sashes **w** around their Rv 15:6

WRAPPING *(1)*

The **w** that had been on His head Jn 20:7

WRAPS *(2)*

He **w** Himself in light as if it Ps 104:2
like a robe he **w** around himself, Ps 109:19

WRATH *(168)*

You unleashed Your burning **w**; Ex 15:7
so that no **w** will fall on the Nm 1:53
you vent Your **w** on the whole Nm 16:22
w has come from the LORD; Nm 16:46
the altar so that **w** may not fall Nm 18:5
has turned back My **w** from the Nm 25:11
fury, and great **w**, and threw Dt 29:28
so that no **w** will fall on us Jos 9:20
bringing **w** on the entire Jos 22:20
carry out His **w** against Amalek; 1Sm 28:18
Great **w** was on the Israelites, 2Kg 3:27
is the LORD's **w** that is kindled 2Kg 22:13
w will be kindled against this 2Kg 22:17
of His great **w** and anger, 2Kg 23:26
There was **w** against Israel 1Ch 27:24
My **w** will not be poured out on 2Ch 12:7
of this, the LORD's **w** is on you. 2Ch 19:2
the LORD and **w** will not come 2Ch 19:10
So there was **w** against Judah and 2Ch 24:18
because of His **w** against Judah, 2Ch 28:9
the LORD's fierce **w** is on you." 2Ch 28:11
and fierce **w** is on Israel." 2Ch 28:13
the **w** of the LORD was on Judah 2Ch 29:8
that His fierce **w** may turn away 2Ch 29:10
turn His fierce **w** away from you, 2Ch 30:8
So there was **w** upon him, upon 2Ch 32:25
so the LORD's **w** didn't come on 2Ch 32:26
is the LORD's **w** that is poured 2Ch 34:21
My **w** will be poured out on this 2Ch 34:25
the LORD's **w** was so stirred 2Ch 36:16
so that **w** will not fall on the Ezr 7:23
because **w** ⌊brings⌋ punishment by Jb 19:29
him drink from the Almighty's **w**! Jb 21:20
rescued from the day of **w**. Jb 21:30
and terrifies them in His **w**: Ps 2:5
do not discipline me in Your **w**. Ps 6:1
LORD will engulf them in His **w**, Ps 21:9
or discipline me in Your **w**. Ps 38:1
bring down the nations in **w**. Ps 56:7
Even human **w** will praise You; Ps 76:10
Yourself with their remaining **w**. Ps 76:10
and did not unleash all His **w**. Ps 78:38
Pour out Your **w** on the nations Ps 79:6
Your **w** weighs heavily on me; Ps 88:7
Your **w** sweeps over me; Ps 88:16
we are terrified by Your **w**. Ps 90:7
our days ebb away under Your **w**; Ps 90:9
Your **w** matches the fear that is Ps 90:11
of Your indignation and **w**; Ps 102:10
breach to turn His **w** away from Ps 106:23
is not profitable on a day of **w**, Pr 11:4
hope of the wicked ⌊leads to⌋ **w**. Pr 11:23
but a harsh word stirs up **w**. Pr 15:1
A king's terrible **w** is like the Pr 20:2
and turn His **w** away from him. Pr 24:18
is scorched by the **w** of the LORD Is 9:19
staff in their hands is My **w**. Is 10:5
little while My **w** will be spent Is 10:25
in My triumph, to execute My **w**. Is 13:3
LORD and the weapons of His **w**— Is 13:5
foundations at the **w** of the LORD Is 13:13
while until the **w** has passed. Is 26:20
He will rise in **w**, as at the Is 28:21
striking in angry **w** and a flame Is 30:30
Although I struck you in My **w**, Is 60:10
for Me, and My **w** assisted Me. Is 63:5
drunk with My **w** and poured out Is 63:6
He will show His **w** against His Is 66:14
w will break out like fire and Jr 4:4
But I am full of the LORD's **w**; Jr 6:11
My burning **w**—is about to be Jr 7:20
w will burn and not be quenched. Jr 7:20
the generation under His **w**. Jr 7:29
The earth quakes at His **w**, Jr 10:10
Pour out Your **w** on the nations Jr 10:25
with anger, rage, and great **w**. Jr 21:5
W has gone forth, a whirling Jr 23:19
of the wine of **w** from My hand Jr 25:15
from the LORD! **W** has gone forth. Jr 30:23
been up against My **w** and fury Jr 32:31
I have banished them in My **w**, Jr 32:37
I strike down in My **w** and rage. Jr 33:5
So My fierce **w** poured forth and Jr 44:6
of the LORD's **w**, she will not be Jr 50:13
brought out His weapons of **w**, Jr 50:25
In His **w** He has demolished the Lm 2:2
pouring out His **w** like fire on Lm 2:4
under the rod of God's **w**. Lm 3:1
The LORD has exhausted His **w**, Lm 4:11
and I have vented My **w** on them, Ezk 5:13
after I have spent My **w** on them, Ezk 5:13
you in anger, **w**, and furious Ezk 5:15
way I will exhaust My **w** on them. Ezk 6:12
pour out My **w** on you very soon Ezk 7:8
for **w** is on all her multitude. Ezk 7:12
My **w** is on all her multitude. Ezk 7:14
them in the day of the LORD's **w**. Ezk 7:19
Therefore I will respond with **w**. Ezk 8:18
pour out Your **w** on Jerusalem?" Ezk 9:8
release a windstorm in My **w**. Ezk 13:13
I exhaust My **w** against the wall Ezk 13:15
and pour out My **w** on it with Ezk 14:19
bloodshed in **w** and jealousy. Ezk 16:38
I will satisfy My **w** against you, Ezk 16:42
pouring out My **w** on them, Ezk 20:8
pouring out My **w** on them in the Ezk 20:13
pouring out My **w** on them and Ezk 20:21
arm, and outpoured **w**. Ezk 20:33
arm, and outpoured **w**. Ezk 20:34
and I will satisfy My **w**. Ezk 21:17
gather ⌊you⌋ in My anger and **w**, Ezk 22:20
have poured out My **w** on you." Ezk 22:22
they will deal with you in **w**. Ezk 23:25
order to stir up **w** and take Ezk 24:8
I have satisfied My **w** on you. Ezk 24:13
according to My anger and **w**. Ezk 25:14
will pour out My **w** on Pelusium, Ezk 30:15
poured out My **w** on them because Ezk 36:18
Lord GOD—"My **w** will flare up. Ezk 38:18
the conclusion of the time of **w**, Dn 8:19
may Your anger and **w** turn away Dn 9:16
the time of **w** is completed, Dn 11:36
and take away ⌊a king⌋ in My **w**. Hs 13:11
in anger and **w** against the Mc 5:15
vengeance and is fierce in **w**. Nah 1:2
His **w** is poured out like fire, Nah 1:6
out your **w** and even making Hab 2:15
In ⌊Your⌋ **w** remember mercy! Hab 3:2
Is Your **w** against the rivers? Hab 3:8
trample down the nations in **w**. Hab 3:12
day is a day of **w**, a day of Zph 1:15
them on the day of the LORD's **w**. Zph 1:18
jealous for her with great **w**." Zch 8:2
you to flee from the coming **w**? Mt 3:7
you to flee from the coming **w**? Lk 3:7
God, turn Your **w** from me—a Lk 18:13
in the land and **w** against this Lk 21:23
the **w** of God remains on him. Jn 3:36
For God's **w** is revealed from Rm 1:18
are storing up **w** for yourself Rm 2:5
for yourself in the day of **w**, Rm 2:5
but **w** and indignation to those Rm 2:8
Is God unrighteous to inflict **w**? Rm 3:5
For the law produces **w**; Rm 4:15
be saved through Him from **w**. Rm 5:9
to display His **w** and to make His Rm 9:22
patience objects of **w** ready for Rm 9:22
instead, leave room for His **w**. Rm 12:19
that brings **w** on the one who Rm 13:4
only because of **w**, but also Rm 13:5
nature we were children under **w**, Eph 2:3
anger and **w**, insult and slander Eph 4:31
these things God's **w** is coming Eph 5:6
w comes on the disobedient, Col 3:6
anger, **w**, malice, slander, and Col 3:8
rescues us from the coming **w**. 1Th 1:10
and **w** has overtaken them 1Th 2:16
For God did not appoint us to **w**, 1Th 5:9
and from the **w** of the Lamb, Rv 6:16

great day of Their **w** has come! Rv 6:17
were angry, but Your **w** has come. Rv 11:18
immorality, which brings **w**." Rv 14:8
also drink the wine of God's **w**, Rv 14:10
the great winepress of God's **w**. Rv 14:19
God's **w** will be completed. Rv 15:1
filled with the **w** of God who Rv 15:7
bowls of God's **w** on the earth." Rv 16:1
immorality, which brings **w**. Rv 18:3

WREATH *(1)*
cast supports, each next to a **w**. 1Kg 7:30

WREATHS *(3)*
of latticework, **w** made of 1Kg 7:17
and oxen were **w** of hanging work. 1Kg 7:29
had space, with encircling **w**. 1Kg 7:36

WRECK *(1)*
from you and **w** your chariots. Mc 5:10

WRECKED *(3)*
the ships were **w** at Ezion-geber. 1Kg 22:48
the ships were **w** and were not 2Ch 20:37
as You **w** the ships of Tarshish Ps 48:7

WRESTLED *(4)*
have **w** with my sister and won," Gn 30:8
and a man **w** with him until Gn 32:24
hip as they **w** and dislocated his Gn 32:25
and as an adult he **w** with God. Hs 12:3

WRESTLINGS *(1)*
said, "In ⌊my⌋ **w** with God, I Gn 30:8

WRETCHED *(4)*
and we detest this **w** food!" Nm 21:5
but pursued the **w** poor and the Ps 109:16
What a **w** man I am! Who will Rm 7:24
you don't know that you are **w**, Rv 3:17

WRETCHEDNESS *(3)*
but heard cries of **w**. Is 5:7
ruin and **w** are in their paths. Is 59:7
ruin and **w** are in their paths, Rm 3:16

WRINKLE *(1)*
without spot or **w** or any such Eph 5:27

WRIST *(1)*
bands on the **w** of every hand Ezk 13:18

WRISTS *(6)*
and for her **w** two bracelets Gn 24:22
the bracelets on his sister's **w**, Gn 24:30
nose and the bracelets on her **w**. Gn 24:47
and his bonds fell off his **w**. Jdg 15:14
bracelets on your **w** and a chain Ezk 16:11
Then the chains fell off his **w**. Ac 12:7

WRITE *(74)*
W this down on a scroll as a Ex 17:14
and I will **w** on them the words Ex 34:1
said to Moses, "**W** down these Ex 34:27
the priest is to **w** these curses Nm 5:23
W each man's name on his staff. Nm 17:2
W Aaron's name on Levi's staff, Nm 17:3
W them on the doorposts of your Dt 6:9
will **w** on the tablets the words Dt 10:2
W them on the doorposts of your Dt 11:20
he is to **w** a copy of this Dt 17:18
he may **w** her a divorce Dt 24:1
W all the words of this law on Dt 27:3
W clearly all the words of this Dt 27:8
Therefore **w** down this song for Dt 31:19
w a description of it for the Jos 18:4
commanded them to **w** down a Jos 18:8
survey the land, **w** a description Jos 18:8
that we could **w** down the names Ezr 5:10
You may **w** in the king's name Est 8:8
w them on the tablet of your Pr 3:3
w them on the tablet of your Pr 7:3
to accurately **w** words of truth. Ec 12:10
of parchment and **w** on it with an Is 8:1
w it on a tablet in their Is 30:8
another will **w** on his hand: Is 44:5
W down on a scroll all the words Jr 30:2
within them and **w** it on their Jr 31:33
and **w** on it all the words I have Jr 36:2
how did you **w** all these words? Jr 36:17
and once again **w** on it the very Jr 36:28
Son of man, **w** down today's date, Ezk 24:2
take a single stick and **w** on it: Ezk 37:16
take another stick and **w** on it: Ezk 37:16
W it down in their sight so that Ezk 43:11
I were to **w** out for him ten Hs 8:12
answered me: **W** down this vision Hab 2:2
permitted us to **w** divorce papers Mk 10:4
to **w** to you in orderly sequence, Lk 1:3
sit down quickly, and **w** 50.' Lk 16:6
he told him, 'and **w** 80.' Lk 16:7
Pilate, "Don't **w**, 'The King of Jn 19:21
instead we should **w** to them to Ac 15:20
definite to **w** to the Emperor Ac 25:26
I may have something to **w**. Ac 25:26
that what I **w** to you is the 1Co 14:37
unnecessary for me to **w** to you. 2Co 9:1
Now in what I **w** to you, I'm not Gl 1:20
To **w** to you again about this is Php 3:1
need me to **w** you because you 1Th 4:9
every letter; this is how I **w**. 2Th 3:17
I **w** these things to you, hoping 1Tm 3:14
Paul, **w** this with my own hand: Phm 19
and I will **w** them on their Heb 8:10
I will **w** them on their minds, Heb 10:16
I have many things to **w** to you, 2Jn 12
I have many things to **w** you, 3Jn 13
don't want to **w** to you with pen 3Jn 13
I was eager to **w** you about our Jd 3
it necessary to **w** and exhort you Jd 3
W on a scroll what you see and Rv 1:11
Therefore **w** what you have seen, Rv 1:19
of the church in Ephesus **w**: Rv 2:1
angel of the church in Smyrna **w**: Rv 2:8
of the church in Pergamum **w**: Rv 2:12
of the church in Thyatira **w**: Rv 2:18
angel of the church in Sardis **w**: Rv 3:1
of the church in Philadelphia **w**: Rv 3:7
I will **w** on him the name of My Rv 3:12
of the church in Laodicea **w**: Rv 3:14
spoke, I was about to **w**. Rv 10:4
said, and do not **w** it down!" Rv 10:4
a voice from heaven saying, "**W**: Rv 14:13
Then he said to me, "**W**: Rv 19:9
He also said, "**W**, because these Rv 21:5

WRITER *(1)*
is the pen of a skillful **w**. Ps 45:1

WRITES *(2)*
w her a divorce certificate, Dt 24:3
For Moses **w** about the Rm 10:5

WRITHE *(5)*
anguish! I **w** in agony! Oh, the Jr 4:19
Pelusium will **w** in anguish, Ezk 30:16
Nations **w** in horror before them; Jl 2:6
W and cry out, Daughter Zion, Mc 4:10
too, and will **w** in great pain, Zch 9:5

WRITHED *(1)*
became pregnant, we **w** in pain; Is 26:18

WRITHES *(2)*
A wicked man **w** in pain all his Jb 15:20
to give birth **w** and cries out Is 26:17

WRITHING *(1)*
Now Amasa was **w** in his blood in 2Sm 20:12

WRITING *(36)*
and the **w** was God's writing, Ex 32:16
and the writing was God's **w**, Ex 32:16
had finished **w** down on a scroll Dt 31:24
to understand everything in **w**, 1Ch 28:19
about in the **W** of the Prophet 2Ch 13:22
recorded in the **W** of the Book 2Ch 24:27
and also ⌊to put it⌋ in **w**: 2Ch 36:22
kingdom and ⌊to put it⌋ in **w**: Ezr 1:1
agreement in **w** on a sealed Neh 9:38
statutes and **w** oppressive laws Is 10:1
me while I was **w** on the scroll Jr 36:18
with **w** equipment at his side. Ezk 9:2
linen with the **w** equipment at Ezk 9:3
linen with the **w** equipment at Ezk 9:11
and began **w** on the plaster Dn 5:5
watched the hand that was **w**, Dn 5:5
hand, and this **w** was inscribed. Dn 5:24
This is the **w** that was Dn 5:25
up the charge against Him in **w**: Mt 27:37
He asked for a **w** tablet and Lk 1:63
down and started **w** on the ground Jn 8:6
and continued **w** on the ground. Jn 8:8
I'm not **w** this to shame you, 1Co 4:14
But now I am **w** you not to 1Co 5:11
Now we are **w** you nothing other 2Co 1:13
This is why I am **w** these things 2Co 13:10
obedience, I am **w** to you, Phm 21
are **w** these things so that our 1Jn 1:4
I am **w** you these things so that 1Jn 2:1
I am not **w** you a new command, 1Jn 2:7
Yet I am **w** you a new command, 1Jn 2:8
I am **w** to you, little children, 1Jn 2:12
I am **w** to you, fathers, because 1Jn 2:13
am **w** to you, young men, because 1Jn 2:13
not as if I were **w** you a new 2Jn 5
a scroll with **w** on the inside Rv 5:1

WRITINGS *(1)*
But if you don't believe his **w**, Jn 5:47

WRITTEN *(265)*
and commands I have **w** for their Ex 24:12
me from the book You have **w**." Ex 32:32
what had been **w** previously, Dt 10:4
which are **w** in this scroll, Dt 28:58
and every curse **w** in this scroll Dt 29:20
of the covenant **w** in this book Dt 29:21
every curse **w** in this book on it Dt 29:27
statutes that are **w** in this book Dt 30:10
observe everything **w** in it. Jos 1:8
to what is **w** in the book Jos 8:31
which he had **w** in the presence Jos 8:32
to all that is **w** in the book of Jos 8:34
Isn't this **w** in the Book of Jos 10:13
When you have **w** a description of Jos 18:6
obeying all that is **w** in the Jos 23:6
It is **w** in the Book of Jashar: 2Sm 1:18
This is **w** in the law of Moses, 1Kg 2:3
are **w** about in the Book of 1Kg 11:41
note that they are **w** about in 1Kg 14:19
are **w** about in the Historical 1Kg 14:29
are **w** about in the Historical 1Kg 15:7
are **w** about in the Historical 1Kg 15:23
are **w** about in the Historical 1Kg 15:31
are **w** about in the Historical 1Kg 16:5
are **w** about in the Historical 1Kg 16:14
are **w** about in the Historical 1Kg 16:20
are **w** about in the Historical 1Kg 16:27
as was **w** in the letters she had 1Kg 21:11
are **w** about in the Historical 1Kg 22:39
are **w** about in the Historical 1Kg 22:45
are **w** about in the Historical 2Kg 1:18
are **w** about in the Historical 2Kg 8:23
are **w** about in the Historical 2Kg 10:34
are **w** about in the Historical 2Kg 12:19
are **w** about in the Historical 2Kg 13:8
are **w** about in the Historical 2Kg 13:12
it is **w** in the book of the law 2Kg 14:6
are **w** about in the Historical 2Kg 14:15
Amaziah's ⌊reign⌋ are **w** about in 2Kg 14:18
are **w** about in the Historical 2Kg 14:28
are **w** about in the Historical 2Kg 15:6
they are **w** about in the 2Kg 15:11
they are **w** about in the 2Kg 15:15
are **w** about in the Historical 2Kg 15:21
they are **w** about in the 2Kg 15:26
they are **w** about in the 2Kg 15:31
are **w** about in the Historical 2Kg 15:36
are **w** about in the Historical 2Kg 16:19
are **w** about in the Historical 2Kg 20:20
are **w** about in the Historical 2Kg 21:17
are **w** about in the Historical 2Kg 21:25
to do everything **w** about us." 2Kg 22:13
that were **w** in this book; 2Kg 23:3
LORD your God as **w** in the book 2Kg 23:21
law that were **w** in the book that 2Kg 23:24
are **w** about in the Historical 2Kg 23:28
are **w** about in the Historical 2Kg 24:5
that are **w** about in the Book 1Ch 9:1
everything that was **w** in the law 1Ch 16:40
note that they are **w** about in 1Ch 29:29
are **w** about in the Events of 2Ch 9:29
are **w** about in the Events of 2Ch 12:15
w about in the Writing of the 2Ch 13:22
are **w** about in the Book of the 2Ch 16:11
to end are **w** about in the Events 2Ch 20:34
the LORD as it is **w** in the law 2Ch 23:18
because—as it is **w** in the Law, 2Ch 25:4
are **w** about in the Book of the 2Ch 25:26
that they are **w** about in the 2Ch 27:7
they are **w** about in the Book of 2Ch 28:26
Passover contrary to what was **w**. 2Ch 30:18
as **w** in the law of the LORD. 2Ch 31:3
note that they are **w** about in 2Ch 32:32
are ⌊**w** about⌋ in the Events of 2Ch 33:18
they are **w** about in the Records 2Ch 33:19
law of the LORD ⌊**w**⌋ by the hand 2Ch 34:14
do everything **w** in this book." 2Ch 34:21
the curses **w** in the book that 2Ch 34:24

of the covenant **w** in this book. 2Ch 34:31
according to the **w** instruction 2Ch 35:4
to what is **w** in the book of 2Ch 35:12
indeed they are **w** in the Dirges. 2Ch 35:25
according to what is **w** in the 2Ch 35:26
are **w** about in the Book of the 2Ch 35:27
are **w** about in the Book of 2Ch 36:8
as it is **w** in the law of Moses Ezr 3:2
The letter was **w** in Aramaic and Ezr 4:7
could receive **w** instructions Ezr 5:5
sent him a report, **w** as follows: Ezr 5:7
found with this record **w** on it: Ezr 6:2
to what is **w** in the book of Ezr 6:18
me have letters ⌊**w**⌋ to the Neh 2:7
me have⌋ a letter ⌊**w**⌋ to Asaph, Neh 2:8
it was **w**: It is reported among Neh 6:6
I found ⌊the following⌋ **w** in it: Neh 7:5
They found **w** in the law how the Neh 8:14
make booths, just as it is **w**." Neh 8:15
our God, as it is **w** in the law. Neh 10:34
command was found **w** in it that Neh 13:1
the order was **w** exactly as Haman Est 3:12
ethnic group and **w** for each Est 3:12
It was **w** in the name of King Est 3:12
a copy of the **w** decree issued Est 4:8
They found the **w** report of how Est 6:2
sight, let ⌊a royal edict⌋ be **w**. Est 8:5
A document **w** in the king's name Est 8:8
Everything was **w** exactly as Est 8:9
⌊The edict was **w**⌋ for each Est 8:9
as Mordecai had **w** them to do. Est 9:23
according to the **w** instructions Est 9:27
were then **w** into the record Est 9:32
they not been **w** in the court Est 10:2
wish that my words were **w** down, Jb 19:23
is **w** about me in the volume of Ps 40:7
This will be **w** for a later Ps 102:18
⌊my⌋ days were **w** in Your book Ps 139:16
Haven't I **w** for you thirty Pr 22:20
It is **w** before Me: I will not Is 65:6
sin of Judah is **w** with an iron Jr 17:1
from Me will be **w** in the dirt, Jr 17:13
all that is **w** in this book that Jr 25:13
transaction **w** on a scroll and Jr 32:44
words Baruch had **w** at Jeremiah's Jr 36:27
Why have you **w** on it: Jr 36:29
words were **w** against Babylon Jr 51:60
and there was a **w** scroll in it. Ezk 2:9
it was **w** on the front and back; Ezk 2:10
mourning, and woe were **w** on it. Ezk 2:10
sticks you have **w** on are in your Ezk 37:20
The promised curse **w** in the law Dn 9:11
Just as it is **w** in the law of Dn 9:13
who are found **w** in the book will Dn 12:1
to what is **w** on one side, Zch 5:3
to what is **w** on the other side. Zch 5:3
remembrance was **w** before Him Mal 3:16
is what was **w** by the prophet: Mt 2:5
But He answered, "It is **w**: Mt 4:4
down. For it is **w**: He will give Mt 4:6
Jesus told him, "It is also **w**: Mt 4:7
Satan! For it is **w**: Worship the Mt 4:10
must give her a **w** notice of Mt 5:31
This is the one it is **w** about: Mt 11:10
to them, "It is **w**, My house will Mt 21:13
go just as it is **w** about Him, Mt 26:24
away because of Me, for it is **w**: Mt 26:31
it is **w** in Isaiah the prophet: Mk 1:2
you hypocrites, as it is **w**: Mk 7:6
How then is it **w** about the Son Mk 9:12
just as it is **w** about him." Mk 9:13
Is it not **w**, My house will be Mk 11:17
go just as it is **w** about Him, Mk 14:21
will run away, because it is **w**: Mk 14:27
of the charge **w** against Him was Mk 15:26
just as it is **w** in the law of Lk 2:23
as it is **w** in the book of the Lk 3:4
Jesus answered him, "It is **w**: Lk 4:4
Jesus answered him, "It is **w**: Lk 4:8
For it is **w**: He will give His Lk 4:10
found the place where it was **w**: Lk 4:17
This is the one it is **w** about: Lk 7:27
your names are **w** in heaven." Lk 10:20
"What is **w** in the law?" Lk 10:26
Everything that is **w** through the Lk 18:31
He said, "It is **w**, My house will Lk 19:46
all the things that are **w**. Lk 21:22
what is **w** must be fulfilled in Lk 22:37
what is **w** about Me is coming to Lk 22:37
that everything **w** about Me in Lk 24:44
to them, "This is what is **w**: Lk 24:46
remembered that it is **w**: Jn 2:17
the wilderness, just as it is **w**: Jn 6:31
It is **w** in the Prophets: Jn 6:45
your law it is **w** that the Jn 8:17
them, "Isn't it **w** in your law, I Jn 10:34
and sat on it, just as it is **w**: Jn 12:14
things had been **w** about Him and Jn 12:16
the statement **w** in their law Jn 15:25
and it was **w** in Hebrew, Latin Jn 19:20
What I have **w**, I have written." Jn 19:22
What I have written, I have **w**." Jn 19:22
that are not **w** in this book. Jn 20:30
But these are **w** so that you may Jn 20:31
if they were **w** one by one, Jn 21:25
the books that would be **w**. Jn 21:25
For it is **w** in the Book of Ac 1:20
as it is **w** in the book of the Ac 7:42
all that had been **w** about Him, Ac 13:29
as it is **w** in the second Psalm: Ac 13:33
agree with this, as it is **w**: Ac 15:15
have **w** a letter containing our Ac 21:25
For it is **w**, You must not speak Ac 23:5
the things that are **w** in the Law Ac 24:14
faith to faith, just as it is **w**: Rm 1:17
of the law is **w** on their hearts. Rm 2:15
For, as it is **w**: The name of God Rm 2:24
everyone is a liar, as it is **w**: Rm 3:4
as it is **w**: There is no one Rm 3:10
sight. As it is **w**: I have made Rm 4:17
to him was not **w** for Abraham Rm 4:23
As it is **w**: Rm 8:36
As it is **w**: Jacob I have loved, Rm 9:13
As it is **w**: Look! I am putting a Rm 9:33
sent? As it is **w**: How welcome Rm 10:15
as it is **w**: God gave them a Rm 11:8
will be saved, as it is **w**: Rm 11:26
wrath. For it is **w**: Vengeance Rm 12:19
For it is **w**: As I live, says the Rm 14:11
contrary, as it is **w**, The Rm 15:3
For whatever was **w** before was Rm 15:4
written before was **w** for our Rm 15:4
mercy. As it is **w**: Therefore I Rm 15:9
I have **w** to you more boldly on Rm 15:15
but, as it is **w**: Those who had Rm 15:21
For it is **w**: I will destroy the 1Co 1:19
in order that, as it is **w**: 1Co 1:31
But as it is **w**: What no eye has 1Co 2:9
with God, since it is **w**: 1Co 3:19
"Nothing beyond what is **w**." 1Co 4:6
For it is **w** in the law of Moses, 1Co 9:9
Yes, this is **w** for us, because 1Co 9:10
and I have not **w** this to make it 1Co 9:15
as it is **w**, The people sat down 1Co 10:7
and they were **w** as a warning to 1Co 10:11
It is **w** in the law: By people of 1Co 14:21
So it is **w**: The first man Adam 1Co 15:45
that is **w** will take place: 1Co 15:54
are our letter, **w** on our hearts, 2Co 3:2
not **w** with ink but with the 2Co 3:3
in accordance with what is **w**, 2Co 4:13
As it has been **w**: The person who 2Co 8:15
As it is **w**: He has scattered; He 2Co 9:9
under a curse, because it is **w**: Gl 3:10
doing everything **w** in the book Gl 3:10
a curse for us, because it is **w**: Gl 3:13
For it is **w** that Abraham had two Gl 4:22
For it is **w**: Rejoice, O barren Gl 4:27
letters I have **w** to you in my Gl 6:11
as I have briefly **w** above. Eph 3:3
need anything to be **w** to you. 1Th 5:1
⌊I have **w**⌋ so that you will know 1Tm 3:15
is **w** about Me in the volume of Heb 10:7
names have been **w** in heaven, Heb 12:23
I have **w** to you in few words. Heb 13:22
for it is **w**, Be holy, because I 1Pt 1:16
brother, I have **w** briefly, 1Pt 5:12
the second letter I've **w** you; 2Pt 3:1
given to him, has **w** to you. 2Pt 3:15
I have **w** to you, children, 1Jn 2:14
have **w** to you, fathers, because 1Jn 2:14
I have **w** to you, young men, 1Jn 2:14
I have not **w** to you because you 1Jn 2:21
I have **w** these things to you 1Jn 2:26
I have **w** these things to you who 1Jn 5:13
and keep what is **w** in it, Rv 1:3
whose name was not **w** from the Rv 13:8
His Father's name **w** on their Rv 14:1
forehead a cryptic name was **w**: Rv 17:5
names were not **w** in the book of Rv 17:8
had a name **w** that no one knows Rv 19:12
on His thigh He has a name **w**: Rv 19:16
by what was **w** in the books. Rv 20:12
anyone not found **w** in the book Rv 20:15
but only those **w** in the Lamb's Rv 21:27
plagues that are **w** in this book. Rv 22:18
the holy city, **w** in this book. Rv 22:19

WRONG *(61)*

said to her, "What's **w**, Hagar? Gn 21:17
What you have done is **w**!'" Gn 44:5
us for all the **w** we caused him." Gn 50:15
sin—the **w** they caused you. Gn 50:17
He asked the one in the **w**, Ex 2:13
LORD promised, for we were **w**." Nm 14:40
What did I do **w**? How have I 1Sm 20:1
If I have done anything **w**, 1Sm 20:8
Philistine leaders think is **w**." 1Sm 29:7
he does **w**, I will discipline 2Sm 7:14
than the great **w** you've already 2Sm 13:16
I am the one who has done **w**. 2Sm 24:17
We have sinned and done **w**; 1Kg 8:47
Lachish, saying, "I have done **w**. 2Kg 18:14
though my hands have done no **w**, 1Ch 12:17
We have sinned and done **w**; 2Ch 6:37
Help me understand what I did **w**. Jb 6:24
the schemes you would **w** me with. Jb 21:27
Yet no one proved Job **w**; Jb 32:12
that you are **w** in this ⌊matter⌋ Jb 33:12
is impossible for God ⌊to do⌋ **w**, Jb 34:10
if I have done **w**, I won't do it Jb 34:32
has declared, "You have done **w**"? Jb 36:23
do not envy those who do **w**. Ps 37:1
They do nothing **w**; they follow Ps 119:3
man who distorts right and **w**. Pr 28:6
right and **w** will suddenly fall Pr 28:18
and says, "I've done nothing **w**." Pr 30:20
too is futile and a great **w**. Ec 2:21
for they are ignorant and do **w**. Ec 5:1
people who walk in the **w** path, Is 65:2
wear themselves out doing **w**. Jr 9:5
But if it seems **w** to you to come Jr 40:4
guiding them the **w** way in the Jr 50:6
LORD, You see the **w** done to me; Lm 3:59
did what was **w** among his people Ezk 18:18
sinned, done **w**, acted wickedly, Dn 9:5
her; He does no **w**. He applies Zph 3:5
one who does **w** knows no shame. Zph 3:5
no longer do **w** or tell lies; Zph 3:13
for sacrifice, is it not **w**? Mal 1:8
or sick ⌊animal⌋, is it not **w**? Mal 1:8
and nothing **w** was found on his Mal 2:6
Friend, I'm doing you no **w**. Mt 20:13
has He done **w**?" But they kept Mt 27:23
What has He done **w**?" But they Mk 15:14
What has this man done **w**? Lk 23:22
this man has done nothing **w**." Lk 23:41
give evidence about the **w**; Jn 18:23
if there is any **w** in this man." Ac 25:5
I have done no **w** to the Jews, Ac 25:10
then I am doing **w**, or have done Ac 25:11
mind to do what is morally **w**. Rm 1:28
But if you do **w**, be afraid, Rm 13:4
wrath on the one who does **w**. Rm 13:4
Love does no **w** to a neighbor. Rm 13:10
but it is **w** for a man to cause Rm 14:20
because of the one who did **w**, 2Co 7:12
burden you? Forgive me this **w**! 2Co 12:13
to God that you do nothing **w**, 2Co 13:7
back for whatever **w** he has done, Col 3:25

WRONGDOER *(1)*

For the **w** will be paid back for Col 3:25

WRONGDOING *(29)*

any case of **w** involving an ox, Ex 22:9
must not follow a crowd in **w**. Ex 23:2
forgiving **w**, rebellion, and sin. Ex 34:7
the fathers' **w** on the children Ex 34:7
forgive our **w** and sin, and Ex 34:9
forgiving **w** and rebellion. Nm 14:18
the fathers' **w** on the children Nm 14:18
pardon the **w** of this people Nm 14:19
establish any **w** or sin against Dt 19:15
accuse me of **w** with this woman 2Sm 3:8
your servant's **w** on the day my 2Sm 19:19
Ahaziah, who was guilty of **w**. 2Ch 20:35

You look for my **w** and search for Jb 10:6
and would not acquit me of my **w**. Jb 10:14
a person of **w**, who set a trap at Is 29:21
each will die for his own **w**. Jr 31:30
forgive their **w** and never again Jr 31:34
I will forgive their **w** and sin." Jr 36:3
and his officers for their **w**. Jr 36:31
his hand from **w** and carries out Ezk 18:8
Why do You tolerate **w**? Hab 1:3
and You cannot tolerate **w**. Hab 1:13
if you forgive people their **w**, Mt 6:14
Father will not forgive your **w**. Mt 6:15
will also forgive you your **w**. Mk 11:25
in heaven forgive your **w**." Mk 11:26
here state what **w** they found in Ac 24:20
if someone is caught in any **w**, Gl 6:1
I will be merciful to their **w**, Heb 8:12

WRONGDOINGS *(2)*
the Israelites' **w** and rebellious Lv 16:21
it all their **w** into a desolate Lv 16:22

WRONGED *(9)*
it⌋ to the individual he has **w**. Nm 5:7
but you have **w** me by fighting Jdg 11:27
Whom have I **w** or mistreated? 1Sm 12:3
You haven't **w** us, you haven't 1Sm 12:4
is God who has **w** me and caught Jb 19:6
We have **w** no one, corrupted no 2Co 7:2
or because of the one who was **w**, 2Co 7:12
like you. You have not **w** me; Gl 4:12
And if he has **w** you in any way, Phm 18

WRONGLY *(2)*
I have spoken **w**," Jesus answered Jn 18:23
don't receive because you ask **w**, Jms 4:3

WRONGS *(3)*
them from all the **w** they have Jr 33:8
forgive all the **w** they have Jr 33:8
does not keep a record of **w**; 1Co 13:5

WROTE *(53)*
And Moses **w** down all the words Ex 24:4
He **w** down on the tablets the Ex 34:28
and **w** on it an inscription like Ex 39:30
Moses **w** down the starting points Nm 33:2
which He **w** on two stone tablets. Dt 4:13
He **w** them on two stone tablets Dt 5:22
the LORD **w** on the tablets what Dt 10:4
Moses **w** down this law and gave Dt 31:9
Moses **w** down this song on that Dt 31:22
The youth **w** down for him the Jdg 8:14
He **w** them on a scroll, which he 1Sm 10:25
morning David **w** a letter to Joab 2Sm 11:14
In the letter he **w**: Put Uriah at 2Sm 11:15
So she **w** letters in Ahab's name 1Kg 21:8
In the letters, she **w**: 1Kg 21:9
Jehu **w** letters and sent them to 2Kg 10:1
Jehu **w** them a second letter, 2Kg 10:6
the commandment He **w** for you; 2Kg 17:37
Hiram of Tyre **w** a letter and 2Ch 2:11
son of Amoz **w** about the rest 2Ch 26:22
and he also **w** letters to Ephraim 2Ch 30:1
He also **w** letters to mock the 2Ch 32:17
in the land **w** an accusation Ezr 4:6
of his colleagues **w** to King Ezr 4:7
the scribe **w** a letter to King Ezr 4:8
w to destroy the Jews who Est 8:5
Mordecai **w** in King Ahasuerus' Est 8:10
w this second letter with full Est 9:29
Baruch **w** on a scroll all the Jr 36:4
which you **w** at my dictation— Jr 36:6
and he **w** on it at Jeremiah's Jr 36:32
of Neriah when he **w** these words Jr 45:1
Jeremiah **w** on one scroll about Jr 51:60
Then King Darius **w** to those of Dn 6:25
He **w** down the dream, and here is Dn 7:1
He **w** this commandment for you Mk 10:5
Moses **w** for us that if a man's Mk 12:19
for a writing tablet and **w**: Lk 1:63
Moses **w** for us that if a man's Lk 20:28
the One Moses **w** about in the law Jn 1:45
Me, because he **w** about Me. Jn 5:46
things and who **w** them down. Jn 21:24
I **w** the first narrative, Ac 1:1
They **w** this letter to be Ac 15:23
the brothers **w** to the disciples Ac 18:27
He **w** a letter of this kind: Ac 23:25
I **w** to you in a letter not to 1Co 5:9
About the things you **w**: 1Co 7:1
I **w** this very thing so that when 2Co 2:3
heart I **w** to you with many 2Co 2:4
It was for this purpose I **w**: 2Co 2:9
So even though I **w** to you, 2Co 7:12
I **w** something to the church, 3Jn 9

WROUGHT *(1)*
w iron, cassia, and aromatic Ezk 27:19

WRUNG *(1)*
the fleece and **w** dew out of it, Jdg 6:38

Y

YAH *(2)*
Because **Y**, the LORD, is my Is 12:2
because in **Y**, the LORD, is Is 26:4

YAHWEH *(75)*
Y, the God of your fathers, the Ex 3:15
Y, the God of your fathers, the Ex 3:16
to Moses, telling him, "I am **Y**. Ex 6:2
make My name **Y** known to them. Ex 6:3
I am **Y**, and I will deliver you Ex 6:6
will know that I am **Y** your God, Ex 6:7
is a warrior; **Y** is His name. Ex 15:3
proclaim the name **Y** before you. Ex 33:19
and proclaimed ⌊His⌋ name **Y**. Ex 34:5
Y—Yahweh is a compassionate Ex 34:6
Y is a compassionate and Ex 34:6
Know that **Y** your God is God, Dt 7:9
awesome name—**Y**, your God— Dt 28:58
there and called it **Y** Shalom. Jdg 6:24
If **Y** is God, follow Him. 1Kg 18:21
I will call on the name of **Y**. 1Kg 18:24
the stones in the name of **Y**. 1Kg 18:32
know that You, **Y**, are God and 1Kg 18:37
and said, "**Y**, He is God! 1Kg 18:39
He is God! **Y**, He is God!" 1Kg 18:39
a prophet of **Y** here any more? 1Kg 22:7
call on the name of **Y** his God, 2Kg 5:11
to any other god but **Y**. 2Kg 5:17
a prophet of **Y** here any more? 2Ch 18:6
His name is **Y**—and rejoice Ps 68:4
I am **Y** your God, who brought you Ps 81:10
whose name is **Y**—are the Most Ps 83:18
of Your name, **Y**, let me live. Ps 143:11
Y is great and is highly praised; Ps 145:3
Look, **Y** comes from far away, His Is 30:27
Y is the everlasting God, the Is 40:28
I am **Y**, that is My name; Is 42:8
His name is **Y** of Hosts. Is 48:2
roar—His name is **Y** of Hosts. Is 51:15
Lord says—**Y**, even your God, Is 51:22
Maker—His name is **Y** of Hosts— Is 54:5
will know that My name is **Y**." Jr 16:21
on Your name, **Y**, from the depths Lm 3:55
Y, remember what has happened to Lm 5:1
they will know that I am **Y**." Ezk 6:14
know that I, **Y**, have spoken." Ezk 17:21
I, **Y**, have spoken and I will do Ezk 17:24
see that I, **Y**, have kindled it Ezk 20:48
nations will know that I am **Y**"— Ezk 36:23
day on will be: **Y** Is There." Ezk 48:35
petition before **Y** my God Dn 9:20
Y is the God of Hosts; Hs 12:5
the God of Hosts; **Y** is His name. Hs 12:5
praise the name of **Y** your God, Jl 2:26
on the name of **Y** will be saved, Jl 2:32
Y, the God of Hosts, is His name. Am 4:13
Seek **Y** and live, or He will Am 5:6
of the earth—**Y** is His name. Am 5:8
Therefore **Y**, the God of Hosts, Am 5:16
Y, the God of Hosts, is His Am 5:27
declaration of **Y**, the God of Am 6:8
of the earth. **Y** is His name. Am 9:6
Y your God has spoken. Am 9:15
I worship **Y**, the God of the Jnh 1:9
Please, **Y**, don't let us perish Jnh 1:14
You, **Y**, have done just as You Jnh 1:14
in the name of **Y** our God forever Mc 4:5
them⌋ in the strength of **Y**, Mc 5:4
the majestic name of **Y** His God. Mc 5:4
You not from eternity, **Y** my God? Hab 1:12
Y my Lord is my strength; Hab 3:19
on the name of **Y** and serve Him Zph 3:9
will trust in the name of **Y**. Zph 3:12
before your eyes. **Y** has spoken. Zph 3:20
work on the house of **Y** of Hosts, Hg 1:14
will be a day known ⌊only⌋ to **Y**, Zch 14:7
On that day **Y** will become king Zch 14:9
all the earth—**Y** alone, and His Zch 14:9
Because I, **Y**, have not changed, Mal 3:6
those who feared **Y** and had high Mal 3:16

YAHWEH'S *(3)*
Then **Y** fire fell and consumed 1Kg 18:38
Y name must not be invoked. Am 6:10
name—⌊this is⌋ **Y** declaration. Zch 10:12

YARD *(11)*
The half **y** on one side and the Ex 26:13
side and the half **y** on the other Ex 26:13
brim, 10 every half **y**, 1Kg 7:24
it, 10 every half **y**, completely 2Ch 4:3
the temple **y** toward the west Ezk 41:12
the temple **y** and the building, Ezk 41:13
with the temple **y** to the east Ezk 41:14
facing the temple **y** to the west, Ezk 41:15
the temple **y** and opposite Ezk 42:1
the temple **y** and the ⌊western Ezk 42:10
face the temple **y** are the holy Ezk 42:13

YARDS *(10)*
city wall 500 **y** on every side. Nm 35:4
Measure 1,000 **y** outside the city Nm 35:5
1,000 **y** for the south side, Nm 35:5
1,000 **y** for the west side, Nm 35:5
and 1,000 **y** for the north side, Nm 35:5
of about 1,000 **y** between Jos 3:4
broke down 200 **y** of Jerusalem's 2Kg 14:13
broke down 200 **y** of Jerusalem's 2Ch 25:23
and repaired 500 **y** of the wall Neh 3:13
land (about 100 **y** away), the Jn 21:8

YARN *(45)*
blue, purple, and scarlet **y**; Ex 25:4
and scarlet **y**, with a design Ex 26:1
Make loops of blue **y** on the edge Ex 26:4
and scarlet **y**, and finely spun Ex 26:31
and scarlet **y**, and finely spun Ex 26:36
and scarlet **y**, and finely spun Ex 27:16
blue, purple, and scarlet **y**; Ex 28:5
blue, purple, and scarlet **y**. Ex 28:6
and scarlet **y**, and of finely Ex 28:8
and scarlet **y**, and of finely Ex 28:15
the ephod with a cord of blue **y**, Ex 28:28
of the ephod entirely of blue **y**. Ex 28:31
and scarlet **y** on its lower hem Ex 28:33
to a cord of blue **y** so it can be Ex 28:37
blue, purple, and scarlet **y**; Ex 35:6
purple, or scarlet **y**, fine linen Ex 35:23
woman spun ⌊**y**⌋ with her hands Ex 35:25
and scarlet **y**, and fine linen. Ex 35:25
and scarlet **y** and fine linen; Ex 35:35
and scarlet **y**, with a design Ex 36:8
made loops of blue **y** on the edge Ex 36:11
and scarlet **y**, and finely spun Ex 36:35
and scarlet **y**, and finely spun Ex 36:37
and scarlet **y**, and finely spun Ex 38:18
and scarlet **y**, and fine linen. Ex 38:23
and scarlet **y**, just as the LORD Ex 39:1
and scarlet **y**, and of finely Ex 39:2
and scarlet **y**, and the fine Ex 39:3
and scarlet **y**, and of finely Ex 39:5
and scarlet **y**, and of finely Ex 39:8
the ephod with a cord of blue **y**, Ex 39:21
of the ephod entirely of blue **y**. Ex 39:22
and scarlet **y** on the lower hem Ex 39:24
blue, purple, and scarlet **y**. Ex 39:29
a cord of blue **y** to it in order Ex 39:31
wood, scarlet **y**, and hyssop be Lv 14:4
wood, scarlet **y**, and hyssop, Lv 14:6
wood, scarlet **y**, and hyssop to Lv 14:49
the scarlet **y**, and the live bird Lv 14:51
the hyssop, and the scarlet **y**. Lv 14:52
and crimson **y**, and throw ⌊them⌋ Nm 19:6
as a strand of **y** snaps when it Jdg 16:9
purple, crimson, and blue **y**. 2Ch 2:7
blue, crimson **y**, and fine linen. 2Ch 2:14
and crimson **y** and fine linen, 2Ch 3:14

YEAR *(337)*
six hundredth **y** of Noah's life, Gn 7:11
In the six hundred and first **y**, Gn 8:13
the thirteenth **y** they rebelled. Gn 14:4
In the fourteenth **y** Chedorlaomer Gn 14:5
to you at this time next **y**." Gn 17:21
about a **y** she will have a son. Gn 18:14
in that **y** he reaped a hundred Gn 26:12
y he provided them with food Gn 47:17
When that **y** was over, they came Gn 47:18
came the next **y** and said to him, Gn 47:18
it is the first month of your **y**. Ex 12:2

appointed time from y to year. Ex 13:10
appointed time from year to y. Ex 13:10
the seventh y you are to let it Ex 23:11
in My honor three times a y. Ex 23:14
Ingathering at the end of the y, Ex 23:16
Three times a y all your males Ex 23:17
out ahead of you in a single y; Ex 23:29
Once a y Aaron is to perform the Ex 30:10
rite for it once a y, Ex 30:10
turn of the ⌊agricultural⌋ y. Ex 34:22
Three times a y all your males Ex 34:23
three times a y to appear before Ex 34:24
the first month of the second y, Ex 40:17
once a y because of all Lv 16:34
In the fourth y all its fruit Lv 19:24
in the fifth y you may eat its Lv 19:25
unblemished male lambs a y old, Lv 23:18
two male lambs a y old as a Lv 23:19
to the LORD seven days each y. Lv 23:41
for the land in the seventh y, Lv 25:4
It must be a y of complete rest Lv 25:5
the Sabbath y can be food for Lv 25:6
the fiftieth y and proclaim Lv 25:10
The fiftieth y will be your Lv 25:11
In this Y of Jubilee, each of Lv 25:13
in the seventh y if we don't sow Lv 25:20
blessing for you in the sixth y, Lv 25:21
When you sow in the eighth y, Lv 25:22
until the ninth y when its Lv 25:22
until the Y of Jubilee. Lv 25:28
last until a y has passed after Lv 25:29
of redemption will last a y. Lv 25:29
redeemed by the end of a full y, Lv 25:30
for you until the Y of Jubilee. Lv 25:40
time⌋ from the y he sold himself Lv 25:50
to him until the Y of Jubilee. Lv 25:50
remain until the Y of Jubilee, Lv 25:52
him like a man hired y by year. Lv 25:53
him like a man hired year by y. Lv 25:53
be released at the Y of Jubilee. Lv 25:54
of the previous y and will clear Lv 26:10
field during the Y of Jubilee, Lv 27:17
until the ⌊next⌋ Y of Jubilee, Lv 27:18
up to the Y of Jubilee, Lv 27:23
In the Y of Jubilee the field Lv 27:24
of the second y after Israel's Nm 1:1
and one male lamb a y old, Nm 7:15
and five male lambs a y old, Nm 7:17
and one male lamb a y old, Nm 7:21
and five male lambs a y old, Nm 7:23
and one male lamb a y old, Nm 7:27
and five male lambs a y old, Nm 7:29
and one male lamb a y old, Nm 7:33
and five male lambs a y old, Nm 7:35
and one male lamb a y old, Nm 7:39
and five male lambs a y old, Nm 7:41
and one male lamb a y old, Nm 7:45
and five male lambs a y old, Nm 7:47
and one male lamb a y old, Nm 7:51
and five male lambs a y old, Nm 7:53
and one male lamb a y old, Nm 7:57
and five male lambs a y old, Nm 7:59
and one male lamb a y old, Nm 7:63
and five male lambs a y old, Nm 7:65
and one male lamb a y old, Nm 7:69
and five male lambs a y old, Nm 7:71
and one male lamb a y old, Nm 7:75
and five male lambs a y old, Nm 7:77
and one male lamb a y old, Nm 7:81
and five male lambs a y old, Nm 7:83
and 12 male lambs a y old, Nm 7:87
and 60 male lambs a y old. Nm 7:88
of the second y after their Nm 9:1
the second y, in the second Nm 10:11
the land, a y for each day. Nm 14:34
seven male lambs a y old— Nm 28:11
for all the months of the y. Nm 28:14
and seven male lambs a y old. Nm 28:19
and seven male lambs a y old, Nm 28:27
seven male lambs a y old— Nm 29:2
and seven male lambs a y old. Nm 29:8
and 14 male lambs a y old. Nm 29:13
and 14 male lambs a y old— Nm 29:17
14 male lambs a y old—⌊all⌋ Nm 29:20
14 male lambs a y old—⌊all⌋ Nm 29:23
14 male lambs a y old—⌊all⌋ Nm 29:26
14 male lambs a y old—⌊all⌋ Nm 29:29
and 14 male lambs a y old— Nm 29:32
seven male lambs a y old— Nm 29:36
in the fortieth y after the Nm 33:38
In the fortieth y, in the Dt 1:3
beginning to the end of the y. Dt 11:12
Each y you are to set aside a Dt 14:22
produce for that y and store Dt 14:28
heart, 'The seventh y, the year Dt 15:9
seventh year, the y of canceling Dt 15:9
set him free in the seventh y. Dt 15:12
Each y you and your family are Dt 15:20
three times a y before the LORD Dt 16:16
⌊to stay⌋ at home for one y, Dt 24:5
of your produce in the third y, Dt 26:12
third year, the y of the tenth, Dt 26:12
time in the y of debt Dt 31:10
of the land of Canaan that y. Jos 5:12
crushed the Israelites that y, Jdg 10:8
four days each y the young women Jdg 11:40
you four ounces of silver a y, Jdg 17:10
his town every y to worship and 1Sm 1:3
taunted her in this way every y. 1Sm 1:7
Each y his mother made him a 1Sm 2:19
Every y he would go on a circuit 1Sm 7:16
amounted to a y and four months. 1Sm 27:7
it⌋ every y because ⌊his hair 2Sm 14:26
for one month out of the y. 1Kg 4:7
did this for Hiram y after year. 1Kg 5:11
did this for Hiram year after y. 1Kg 5:11
hundred eightieth y after the 1Kg 6:1
the fourth y of his reign over 1Kg 6:1
Solomon's⌋ fourth y in the month 1Kg 6:37
⌊his⌋ eleventh y in the eighth 1Kg 6:38
Three times a y Solomon offered 1Kg 9:25
In the fifth y of King Rehoboam, 1Kg 14:25
the eighteenth y of ⌊Israel's⌋ 1Kg 15:1
the twentieth y of Israel's King 1Kg 15:9
in the second y of Judah's King 1Kg 15:25
In the third y of Judah's King 1Kg 15:28
In the third y of Judah's King 1Kg 15:33
twenty-sixth y of Judah's King 1Kg 16:8
twenty-seventh y of Judah's King 1Kg 16:10
twenty-seventh y of Judah's King 1Kg 16:15
thirty-first y of Judah's King 1Kg 16:23
thirty-eighth y of Judah's King 1Kg 16:29
came to Elijah in the third y: 1Kg 18:1
in the third y, Jehoshaphat king 1Kg 22:2
in the fourth y of Israel's King 1Kg 22:41
seventeenth y of Judah's King 1Kg 22:51
in the second y of Judah's King 2Kg 1:17
the eighteenth y of Judah's King 2Kg 3:1
this time next y you will have 2Kg 4:16
the same time the following y, 2Kg 4:17
In the fifth y of Israel's King 2Kg 8:16
the twelfth y of Israel's King 2Kg 8:25
he reigned one y in Jerusalem. 2Kg 8:26
in the eleventh y of Joram son 2Kg 9:29
in the seventh y, Jehoiada sent 2Kg 11:4
In the seventh y of Jehu, Joash 2Kg 12:1
twenty-third y ⌊of the reign⌋ 2Kg 12:6
twenty-third y of Judah's King 2Kg 13:1
thirty-seventh y of Judah's King 2Kg 13:10
the land in the spring of the y. 2Kg 13:20
In the second y of Israel's King 2Kg 14:1
the fifteenth y of Judah's King 2Kg 14:23
twenty-seventh y of Israel's 2Kg 15:1
thirty-eighth y of Judah's King 2Kg 15:8
thirty-ninth y of Judah's King 2Kg 15:13
thirty-ninth y of Judah's King 2Kg 15:17
the fiftieth y of Judah's King 2Kg 15:23
fifty-second y of Judah's King 2Kg 15:27
in the twentieth y of Jotham son 2Kg 15:30
In the second y of Israel's King 2Kg 15:32
the seventeenth y of Pekah son 2Kg 16:1
In the twelfth y of Judah's King 2Kg 17:1
In the ninth y of Hoshea, the 2Kg 17:6
In the third y of Israel's King 2Kg 18:1
the fourth y of King Hezekiah, 2Kg 18:9
was the seventh y of Israel's 2Kg 18:9
In the sixth y of Hezekiah, 2Kg 18:10
was the ninth y of Israel's King 2Kg 18:10
the fourteenth y of King 2Kg 18:13
This y you will eat what grows 2Kg 19:29
and in the second y what grows 2Kg 19:29
But in the third y sow and reap, 2Kg 19:29
the eighteenth y of King Josiah, 2Kg 22:3
the eighteenth y of King Josiah, 2Kg 23:23
in the eighth y of his reign. 2Kg 24:12
In the ninth y of Zedekiah's 2Kg 25:1
King Zedekiah's eleventh y. 2Kg 25:2
was the nineteenth y of King 2Kg 25:8
thirty-seventh y of the exile 2Kg 25:27
in the y he became king, 2Kg 25:27
In the fortieth y of David's 1Ch 26:31
each month throughout the y. 1Ch 27:1
in the fourth y of his reign. 2Ch 3:2
in the fifth y of King Rehoboam, 2Ch 12:2
the eighteenth y of ⌊Israel's⌋ 2Ch 13:1
the fifteenth y of Asa's reign. 2Ch 15:10
thirty-fifth y of Asa's reign. 2Ch 15:19
In the thirty-sixth y of Asa, 2Ch 16:1
the thirty-ninth y of his reign, 2Ch 16:12
the forty-first y of his reign 2Ch 16:13
In the third y of his reign, 2Ch 17:7
he reigned one y in Jerusalem. 2Ch 22:2
in the seventh y, Jehoiada 2Ch 23:1
of your God as needed y by year, 2Ch 24:5
of your God as needed year by y, 2Ch 24:5
the turn of the y, an Aramean 2Ch 24:23
and that y they gave him 7,500 2Ch 27:5
In the first y of his reign, 2Ch 29:3
In the eighth y of his reign, 2Ch 34:3
and in the twelfth y he began to 2Ch 34:3
the eighteenth y of his reign, 2Ch 34:8
the eighteenth y of Josiah's 2Ch 35:19
In the first y of Cyrus king of 2Ch 36:22
In the first y of Cyrus king of Ezr 1:1
of the second y after they Ezr 3:8
until the second y of the reign Ezr 4:24
in the first y of Cyrus king of Ezr 5:13
In the first y of King Cyrus, Ezr 6:3
Adar in the sixth y of the reign Ezr 6:15
in the seventh y of King Ezr 7:7
the seventh y of the king. Ezr 7:8
of Chislev in the twentieth y, Neh 1:1
in the twentieth y of King Neh 2:1
from the twentieth y until his Neh 5:14
year until his thirty-second y, Neh 5:14
in the seventh y and will cancel Neh 10:31
at the appointed times each y. Neh 10:34
to the LORD's house y by year. Neh 10:35
to the LORD's house year by y. Neh 10:35
thirty-second y of his ⌊reign⌋. Neh 13:6
in the third y of his reign for Est 1:3
During the y before each young Est 2:12
in the seventh y of his reign. Est 2:16
in King Ahasuerus' twelfth y, Est 3:7
days of the month Adar every y Est 9:21
each and every y according to Est 9:27
the days of the y or be listed Jb 3:6
You crown the y with Your Ps 65:11
In the y that King Uzziah died, Is 6:1
In the y that King Ahaz died, Is 14:28
In the y that the Is 20:1
Within one y, as a hired worker Is 21:16
Continue y after year; let Is 29:1
year after y; let the festivals Is 29:1
more than a y you overconfident Is 32:10
the fourteenth y of King Is 36:1
This y you will eat what grows Is 37:30
and in the second y what grows Is 37:30
But in the third y sow and reap, Is 37:30
to proclaim the y of the LORD's Is 61:2
and the y of My redemption came. Is 63:4
in the thirteenth y of the reign Jr 1:2
the eleventh y of Zedekiah son Jr 1:3
Anathoth ⌊in⌋ the y of their Jr 11:23
not worry in a y of drought or Jr 17:8
the y of their punishment. Jr 23:12
in the fourth y of Jehoiakim son Jr 25:1
the first y of Nebuchadnezzar Jr 25:1
the thirteenth y of Josiah son Jr 25:3
In that same y, at the beginning Jr 28:1
the fifth month of the fourth y, Jr 28:1
will die this y because you have Jr 28:16
died that y in the seventh Jr 28:17
in the tenth y of Zedekiah king Jr 32:1
the eighteenth y of Jr 32:1
In the fourth y of Jehoiakim son Jr 36:1
In the fifth y of Jehoiakim son Jr 36:9
In the ninth y of Zedekiah king Jr 39:1
month of Zedekiah's eleventh y, Jr 39:2
in the fourth y of Jehoiakim son Jr 45:1
in the fourth y of Judah's King Jr 46:2
against Moab the y of their Jr 48:44
for the report will come one y, Jr 51:46
and then another the next y. Jr 51:46

in the fourth y of Zedekiah's Jr 51:59
In the ninth y of Zedekiah's Jr 52:4
King Zedekiah's eleventh y. Jr 52:5
was the nineteenth y of King Jr 52:12
in the seventh y, 3,023 Jews; Jr 52:28
in his eighteenth y, 832 people Jr 52:29
Nebuchadnezzar's twenty-third y, Jr 52:30
thirty-seventh y of the exile Jr 52:31
in the ⌊first⌋ y of his reign, Jr 52:31
the thirtieth y, in the fourth Ezk 1:1
it was the fifth y of King Ezk 1:2
you 40 days, a day for each y. Ezk 4:6
In the sixth y, in the sixth Ezk 8:1
In the seventh y, in the fifth Ezk 20:1
LORD came to me in the ninth y, Ezk 24:1
In the eleventh y, on the first Ezk 26:1
In the tenth y, in the tenth Ezk 29:1
twenty-seventh y in the first Ezk 29:17
In the eleventh y, in the first Ezk 30:20
In the eleventh y, in the third Ezk 31:1
In the twelfth y, in the twelfth Ezk 32:1
In the twelfth y, on the Ezk 32:17
In the twelfth y of our exile, Ezk 33:21
the twenty-fifth y of our exile, Ezk 40:1
at the beginning of the y, Ezk 40:1
the fourteenth y after Jerusalem Ezk 40:1
servant until the y of freedom, Ezk 46:17
In the third y of the reign of Dn 1:1
until the first y of King Cyrus. Dn 1:21
In the second y of his reign, Dn 2:1
the first y of Belshazzar king Dn 7:1
In the third y of King Dn 8:1
the first y of Darius, who was Dn 9:1
in the first y of his reign, Dn 9:2
In the third y of Cyrus king of Dn 10:1
In the first y of Darius the Dn 11:1
In the second y of King Darius, Hg 1:1
in the second y of King Darius. Hg 1:15
in the second y of Darius, Hg 2:10
in the second y of Darius, Zch 1:1
in the second y of Darius, Zch 1:7
In the fourth y of King Darius, Zch 7:1
will go up y after year to Zch 14:16
up year after y to worship the Zch 14:16
Every y His parents traveled to Lk 2:41
In the fifteenth y of the reign Lk 3:1
to proclaim the y of the Lord's Lk 4:19
leave it this y also, until I Lk 13:8
it will bear fruit next y, Lk 13:9
who was high priest that y, Jn 11:49
high priest that y he prophesied Jn 11:51
who was high priest that y. Jn 18:13
For a whole y they met with the Ac 11:26
stayed there a y and six months, Ac 18:11
who a y ago began not only to do 2Co 8:10
has been prepared since last y," 2Co 9:2
that only once a y, and never Heb 9:7
continually offer y after year. Heb 10:1
continually offer year after y. Heb 10:1
is a reminder of sins every y. Heb 10:3
city and spend a y there and do Jms 4:13
and y were released to kill a Rv 9:15

YEAR'S *(1)*
back to you in about a y time, Gn 18:10

YEAR-OLD *(13)*
an unblemished animal, a y male; Ex 12:5
altar every day: two y lambs. Ex 29:38
tent of meeting a y male lamb Lv 12:6
an unblemished y ewe lamb, Lv 14:10
are to offer a y male lamb Lv 23:12
and to bring a y male lamb as Nm 6:12
one unblemished y male lamb as Nm 6:14
one unblemished y female lamb as Nm 6:14
is to present a y female goat as Nm 15:27
two unblemished y male lambs as Nm 28:3
two unblemished y male lambs, Nm 28:9
an unblemished y male lamb as a Ezk 46:13
burnt offerings, with y calves? Mc 6:6

YEARLINGS *(1)*
a lamb, male y without blemish Lv 9:3

YEARLY *(2)*
of silver y for the service Neh 10:32
the sanctuary y with the blood Heb 9:25

YEARN *(1)*
I long and y for the courts of Ps 84:2

YEARNING *(1)*
Your y and Your compassion are Is 63:15

YEARNS *(2)*
My inner being y for him; Jr 31:20
to live in us y jealously? Jms 4:5

YEARS *(519)*
festivals and for days and y. Gn 1:14
was 130 y old when he fathered Gn 5:3
Adam lived 800 y after the birth Gn 5:4
So Adam's life lasted 930 y; Gn 5:5
Seth was 105 y old when he Gn 5:6
Seth lived 807 y after the birth Gn 5:7
So Seth's life lasted 912 y; Gn 5:8
Enosh was 90 y old when he Gn 5:9
lived 815 y after the birth Gn 5:10
So Enosh's life lasted 905 y; Gn 5:11
Kenan was 70 y old when he Gn 5:12
lived 840 y after the birth Gn 5:13
So Kenan's life lasted 910 y; Gn 5:14
Mahalalel was 65 y old when he Gn 5:15
lived 830 y after the birth Gn 5:16
Mahalalel's life lasted 895 y; Gn 5:17
Jared was 162 y old when he Gn 5:18
lived 800 y after the birth Gn 5:19
So Jared's life lasted 962 y; Gn 5:20
Enoch was 65 y old when he Gn 5:21
with God 300 y and fathered sons Gn 5:22
So Enoch's life lasted 365 y. Gn 5:23
Methuselah was 187 y old when he Gn 5:25
lived 782 y after the birth Gn 5:26
Methuselah's life lasted 969 y; Gn 5:27
Lamech was 182 y old when he Gn 5:28
Lamech lived 595 y after Noah's Gn 5:30
So Lamech's life lasted 777 y; Gn 5:31
Noah was 500 y old, and he Gn 5:32
Their days will be 120 y." Gn 6:3
Noah was 600 y old when the Gn 7:6
lived 350 y after the flood. Gn 9:28
So Noah's life lasted 950 y; Gn 9:29
Shem lived 100 y and fathered Gn 11:10
Arpachshad two y after the Gn 11:10
Shem lived 500 y and fathered Gn 11:11
lived 35 y and fathered Shelah Gn 11:12
lived 403 y and fathered ⌊other Gn 11:13
Shelah lived 30 y and fathered Gn 11:14
Shelah lived 403 y and fathered Gn 11:15
Eber lived 34 y and fathered Gn 11:16
Eber lived 430 y and fathered Gn 11:17
Peleg lived 30 y and fathered Gn 11:18
Peleg lived 209 y and fathered Gn 11:19
Reu lived 32 y and fathered Gn 11:20
Reu lived 207 y and fathered Gn 11:21
Serug lived 30 y and fathered Gn 11:22
Serug lived 200 y and fathered Gn 11:23
Nahor lived 29 y and fathered Gn 11:24
Nahor lived 119 y and fathered Gn 11:25
Terah lived 70 y and fathered Gn 11:26
Terah lived 205 y and died in Gn 11:32
Abram was 75 y old when he left Gn 12:4
to Chedorlaomer for 12 y, Gn 14:4
be enslaved and oppressed 400 y. Gn 15:13
in the land of Canaan 10 y. Gn 16:3
Abram was 86 y old when Hagar Gn 16:16
Abram was 99 y old, the LORD Gn 17:1
Abraham was 99 y old when the Gn 17:24
Ishmael was 13 y old when the Gn 17:25
were old and getting on in y. Gn 18:11
Abraham was 100 y old when his Gn 21:5
Now Sarah lived 127 y; Gn 23:1
were all⌋ the y of her life. Gn 23:1
getting on in y, and the LORD Gn 24:1
length of Abraham's life: 175 y. Gn 25:7
life: 137 y. He took his last Gn 25:17
Isaac was 40 y old when he took Gn 25:20
Isaac was 60 y old when they Gn 25:26
Esau was 40 y old, he took as Gn 26:34
for you seven y for your younger Gn 29:18
Jacob worked seven y for Rachel, Gn 29:20
yet another seven y for me." Gn 29:27
for Laban another seven y. Gn 29:30
I've been with you these 20 y. Gn 31:38
For 20 y I have worked in your Gn 31:41
14 y for your two daughters and Gn 31:41
and six y for your flocks Gn 31:41
Isaac lived 180 y. Gn 35:28
At 17 y of age, Joseph tended Gn 37:2
Two y later Pharaoh had a dream: Gn 41:1
The seven good cows are seven y, Gn 41:26
seven good heads are seven y. Gn 41:26
came up after them are seven y, Gn 41:27
of grain are seven y of famine. Gn 41:27
Seven y of great abundance are Gn 41:29
seven y of famine will take Gn 41:30
during the seven y of abundance. Gn 41:34
these good y that are coming, Gn 41:35
during the seven y of famine Gn 41:36
Joseph was 30 y old when he Gn 41:46
During the seven y of abundance Gn 41:47
during the seven y and placed it Gn 41:48
before the y of famine arrived Gn 41:50
Then the seven y of abundance in Gn 41:53
and the seven y of famine began, Gn 41:54
been in the land these two y, Gn 45:6
be five more y without plowing Gn 45:6
will be five more y of famine. Gn 45:11
"How many y have you lived?" Gn 47:8
My pilgrimage has lasted 130 y. Gn 47:9
My y have been few and hard, Gn 47:9
surpassed the y of my fathers Gn 47:9
lived in the land of Egypt 17 y, Gn 47:28
and his life span was 147 y. Gn 47:28
in Egypt. Joseph lived 110 y. Gn 50:22
Y later, after Moses had grown Ex 2:11
and Merari. Levi lived 137 y. Ex 6:16
and Uzziel. Kohath lived 133 y. Ex 6:18
and Moses. Amram lived 137 y. Ex 6:20
Moses was 80 y old and Aaron 83 Ex 7:7
lived in Egypt was 430 y. Ex 12:40
the end of 430 y, on that same Ex 12:41
Israelites ate manna for 40 y, Ex 16:35
slave, he is to serve for six y; Ex 21:2
land for six y and gather its Ex 23:10
registered, 20 y old or more, Ex 30:14
everyone 20 y old or more who Ex 38:26
be forbidden to you for three y; Lv 19:23
may sow your field for six y, Lv 25:3
gather its produce for six y. Lv 25:3
are to count seven sabbatic y, Lv 25:8
times seven y, so that the time Lv 25:8
seven sabbatic y amounts to 49. Lv 25:8
the number of y since the last Lv 25:15
number of ⌊remaining⌋ harvest y. Lv 25:15
to a greater amount of y, Lv 25:16
to a lesser amount of y, Lv 25:16
a crop sufficient for three y. Lv 25:21
calculate the y since its sale, Lv 25:27
determined⌋ by the number of y. Lv 25:50
many y are still left, he must Lv 25:51
If only a few y remain until the Lv 25:52
proportion to his ⌊remaining⌋ y. Lv 25:52
its Sabbath ⌊y⌋ during the time Lv 26:34
a male from 20 to 60 y old, Lv 27:3
person is from five to 20 y old, Lv 27:5
is from one month to five y old, Lv 27:6
If the person is 60 y or more, Lv 27:7
proportion to the y left until Lv 27:18
those who are 20 y old or more Nm 1:3
names of those 20 y old or more, Nm 1:18
of every male 20 y old or more, Nm 1:20
of every male 20 y old or more, Nm 1:22
names of those 20 y old or more, Nm 1:24
names of those 20 y old or more, Nm 1:26
names of those 20 y old or more, Nm 1:28
names of those 20 y old or more, Nm 1:30
names of those 20 y old or more, Nm 1:32
names of those 20 y old or more, Nm 1:34
names of those 20 y old or more, Nm 1:36
names of those 20 y old or more, Nm 1:38
names of those 20 y old or more, Nm 1:40
names of those 20 y old or more, Nm 1:42
the Israelites 20 y old or more, Nm 1:45
from 30 y old to 50 years old Nm 4:3
from 30 years old to 50 y old— Nm 4:3
men from 30 y old to 50 years Nm 4:23
from 30 years old to 50 y old, Nm 4:23
men from 30 y old to 50 years Nm 4:30
from 30 years old to 50 y old, Nm 4:30
men from 30 y old to 50 years Nm 4:35
from 30 years old to 50 y old, Nm 4:35
men from 30 y old to 50 years Nm 4:39
from 30 years old to 50 y old, Nm 4:39
those from 30 y old to 50 years Nm 4:43
from 30 years old to 50 y old, Nm 4:43
from 30 y old to 50 years old, Nm 4:47
from 30 years old to 50 y old, Nm 4:47
From 25 y old or more, a man Nm 8:24
But at 50 y old he is to retire Nm 8:25
was built seven y before Zoan in Nm 13:22

number of you 20 y old or more— Nm 14:29
wilderness for 40 y and bear the Nm 14:33
of your sins 40 y based on the Nm 14:34
and we lived in Egypt many y, Nm 20:15
of those 20 y old or more who Nm 26:2
of⌋ those 20 y old or more, Nm 26:4
of the men 20 y old or more who Nm 32:11
wilderness 40 y until the whole Nm 32:13
Aaron was 123 y old when he died Nm 33:39
been with you this past 40 y, Dt 2:7
Valley was 38 y until the entire Dt 2:14
journey these 40 y in the Dt 8:2
feet did not swell these 40 y. Dt 8:4
At the end of ⌊every⌋ three y, Dt 14:28
every⌋ seven y you must cancel Dt 15:1
to you and serves you six y, Dt 15:12
he worked for you six y— Dt 15:18
ruling many y over Israel. Dt 17:20
led you 40 y in the wilderness; Dt 29:5
saying, "I am now 120 y old; Dt 31:2
At the end of ⌊every⌋ seven y, Dt 31:10
consider the y long past. Dt 32:7
was 120 y old when he died; Dt 34:7
in the wilderness 40 y until all Jos 5:6
old, advanced in y, and the LORD Jos 13:1
old, advanced in y, but a great Jos 13:1
I was 40 y old when Moses the Jos 14:7
these⌋ 45 y as He promised, Jos 14:10
Here I am today, 85 y old. Jos 14:10
Joshua was old, getting on in y. Jos 23:1
"I am old, getting on in y, Jos 23:2
Israelites served him eight y. Jdg 3:8
Then the land was peaceful 40 y, Jdg 3:11
served Eglon king of Moab 18 y. Jdg 3:14
and the land was peaceful 80 y. Jdg 3:30
he harshly oppressed them 20 y. Jdg 4:3
And the land was peaceful 40 y. Jdg 5:31
them over to Midian seven y, Jdg 6:1
and a second bull seven y old. Jdg 6:25
peaceful 40 y during the days Jdg 8:28
had ruled over Israel three y, Jdg 9:22
judged Israel 23 y, and when he Jdg 10:2
who judged Israel 22 y. Jdg 10:3
and for 18 y ⌊they did the same Jdg 10:8
Israel lived 300 y in Heshbon Jdg 11:26
Jephthah judged Israel six y, Jdg 12:7
Ibzan judged Israel seven y, Jdg 12:9
He judged Israel 10 y, Jdg 12:11
Abdon judged Israel eight y, Jdg 12:14
over to the Philistines 40 y. Jdg 13:1
judged Israel 20 y in the days Jdg 15:20
So he judged Israel 20 y. Jdg 16:31
they lived in Moab about 10 y, Ru 1:4
At that time Eli was 98 y old, 1Sm 4:15
Eli had judged Israel 40 y. 1Sm 4:18
by until 20 y had passed since 1Sm 7:2
Saul was 30 y old when he became 1Sm 13:1
and he reigned 42 y over Israel. 1Sm 13:1
was 40 y old when he began 2Sm 2:10
he ruled for two y. The house of 2Sm 2:10
was seven y and six months. 2Sm 2:11
was five y old when the report 2Sm 4:4
David was 30 y old when he began 2Sm 5:4
his reign; he reigned 40 y. 2Sm 5:4
Judah seven y and six months, 2Sm 5:5
he reigned 33 y over all Israel 2Sm 5:5
Two y later, Absalom's 2Sm 13:23
Geshur where he stayed three y. 2Sm 13:38
in Jerusalem two y but never saw 2Sm 14:28
When four y had passed, Absalom 2Sm 15:7
old man—80 y old—and since 2Sm 19:32
How many y of my life are left 2Sm 19:34
I'm now 80 y old. Can I discern 2Sm 19:35
a famine for three successive y, 2Sm 21:1
you want three y of famine to 2Sm 24:13
was old and getting on in y. 1Kg 1:1
reigned over Israel was 40 y: 1Kg 2:11
reigned seven y in Hebron and 33 1Kg 2:11
in Hebron and 33 y in Jerusalem. 1Kg 2:11
end of three y, two of Shimei's 1Kg 2:39
So he built it in seven y. 1Kg 6:38
after 13 y of construction. 1Kg 7:1
At the end of 20 y during which 1Kg 9:10
and once every three y the ships 1Kg 10:22
over all Israel totaled 40 y. 1Kg 11:42
of Jeroboam's reign was 22 y. 1Kg 14:20
Rehoboam was 41 y old when he 1Kg 14:21
he reigned 17 y in Jerusalem, 1Kg 14:21

he reigned three y in Jerusalem. 1Kg 15:2
he reigned 41 y in Jerusalem. 1Kg 15:10
he reigned over Israel two y. 1Kg 15:25
at Tirzah; ⌊he reigned⌋ 24 y. 1Kg 15:33
in Tirzah; ⌊he reigned⌋ two y. 1Kg 16:8
he reigned⌋ 12 y. He reigned six 1Kg 16:23
He reigned six y in Tirzah, 1Kg 16:23
over Israel in Samaria 22 y. 1Kg 16:29
rain during these y except by my 1Kg 17:1
a lull of three y without war 1Kg 22:1
was 35 y old when he became 1Kg 22:42
he reigned 25 y in Jerusalem. 1Kg 22:42
he reigned over Israel two y. 1Kg 22:51
Jehoshaphat; he reigned 12 y. 2Kg 3:1
of the Philistines for seven y. 2Kg 8:2
at the end of seven y, 2Kg 8:3
He was 32 y old when he became 2Kg 8:17
he reigned eight y in Jerusalem. 2Kg 8:17
Ahaziah was 22 y old when he 2Kg 8:26
over Israel in Samaria was 28 y. 2Kg 10:36
temple six y while Athaliah 2Kg 11:3
Joash was seven y old when he 2Kg 12:21
he reigned 40 y in Jerusalem. 2Kg 12:1
in Samaria; ⌊he reigned⌋ 17 y. 2Kg 13:1
in Samaria; ⌊he reigned⌋ 16 y. 2Kg 13:10
He was 25 y old when he became 2Kg 14:2
he reigned 29 y in Jerusalem. 2Kg 14:2
Joash lived 15 y after the death 2Kg 14:17
who was 16 y old, and made him 2Kg 14:21
in Samaria; he reigned 41 y. 2Kg 14:23
He was 16 y old when he became 2Kg 15:2
he reigned 52 y in Jerusalem. 2Kg 15:2
⌊he reigned⌋ 10 y in Samaria. 2Kg 15:17
in Samaria; ⌊he reigned⌋ two y. 2Kg 15:23
in Samaria; ⌊he reigned⌋ 20 y. 2Kg 15:27
He was 25 y old when he became 2Kg 15:33
he reigned 16 y in Jerusalem. 2Kg 15:33
Ahaz was 20 y old when he 2Kg 16:2
he reigned 16 y in Jerusalem. 2Kg 16:2
in Samaria; ⌊he reigned⌋ nine y. 2Kg 17:1
of Assyria as in previous y. 2Kg 17:4
and besieged it for three y. 2Kg 17:5
He was 25 y old when he became 2Kg 18:2
he reigned 29 y in Jerusalem. 2Kg 18:2
it at the end of three y. 2Kg 18:10
I will add 15 y to your life. 2Kg 20:6
Manasseh was 12 y old when he 2Kg 21:1
he reigned 55 y in Jerusalem. 2Kg 21:1
Amon was 22 y old when he 2Kg 21:19
he reigned two y in Jerusalem. 2Kg 21:19
Josiah was eight y old when he 2Kg 22:1
he reigned 31 y in Jerusalem. 2Kg 22:1
Jehoahaz was 23 y old when he 2Kg 23:31
Jehoiakim was 25 y old when he 2Kg 23:36
he reigned 11 y in Jerusalem. 2Kg 23:36
became his vassal for three y. 2Kg 24:1
Jehoiachin was 18 y old when he 2Kg 24:8
Zedekiah was 21 y old when he 2Kg 24:18
he reigned 11 y in Jerusalem. 2Kg 24:18
her when he was 60 y old, 1Ch 2:21
he ruled seven y and six months, 1Ch 3:4
and he ruled in Jerusalem 33 y. 1Ch 3:4
either three y of famine, three 1Ch 21:12
The Levites 30 y old and above 1Ch 23:3
headcount—20 y old or more, 1Ch 23:24
Levites 20 y old or more were 1Ch 23:27
his reign over Israel was 40 y; 1Ch 29:27
for seven y and in Jerusalem 1Ch 29:27
At the end of 20 y during which 2Ch 8:1
and once every three y the ships 2Ch 9:21
over all Israel for 40 y. 2Ch 9:30
son of Solomon for three y, 2Ch 11:17
David and Solomon for three y. 2Ch 11:17
Rehoboam was 41 y old when he 2Ch 12:13
he reigned 17 y in Jerusalem, 2Ch 12:13
he reigned three y in Jerusalem. 2Ch 13:2
land experienced peace for 10 y. 2Ch 14:1
For many y Israel has been 2Ch 15:3
Then after some y, he went down 2Ch 18:2
He was 35 y old when he became 2Ch 20:31
he reigned 25 y in Jerusalem. 2Ch 20:31
Jehoram was 32 y old when he 2Ch 21:5
he reigned eight y in Jerusalem. 2Ch 21:5
day until two full y passed. 2Ch 21:19
Jehoram was 32 y old when he 2Ch 21:20
he reigned eight y in Jerusalem. 2Ch 21:20
Ahaziah was 22 y old when he 2Ch 22:2
with them in God's temple six y. 2Ch 22:12

Joash was seven y old when he 2Ch 24:1
he reigned 40 y in Jerusalem. 2Ch 24:1
he was 130 y old at his death. 2Ch 24:15
king ⌊when he was⌋ 25 y old; 2Ch 25:1
he reigned 29 y in Jerusalem. 2Ch 25:1
those 20 y old or more for 2Ch 25:5
Joash lived 15 y after the death 2Ch 25:25
who was 16 y old, and made him 2Ch 26:1
Uzziah was 16 y old when he 2Ch 26:3
he reigned 52 y in Jerusalem. 2Ch 26:3
Jotham was 25 y old when he 2Ch 27:1
he reigned 16 y in Jerusalem. 2Ch 27:1
same in the second and third y. 2Ch 27:5
He was 25 y old when he became 2Ch 27:8
he reigned 16 y in Jerusalem. 2Ch 27:8
Ahaz was 20 y old when he became 2Ch 28:1
he reigned 16 y in Jerusalem. 2Ch 28:1
Hezekiah was 25 y old when he 2Ch 29:1
he reigned 29 y in Jerusalem. 2Ch 29:1
genealogy three y old and above; 2Ch 31:16
the Levites 20 y old and above, 2Ch 31:17
Manasseh was 12 y old when he 2Ch 33:1
he reigned 55 y in Jerusalem. 2Ch 33:1
Amon was 22 y old when he 2Ch 33:21
he reigned two y in Jerusalem. 2Ch 33:21
Josiah was eight y old when he 2Ch 34:1
he reigned 31 y in Jerusalem. 2Ch 34:1
Jehoahaz was 23 y old when he 2Ch 36:2
Jehoiakim was 25 y old when he 2Ch 36:5
he reigned 11 y in Jerusalem. 2Ch 36:5
Jehoiachin was 18 y old when he 2Ch 36:9
Zedekiah was 21 y old when he 2Ch 36:11
he reigned 11 y in Jerusalem. 2Ch 36:11
until 70 y were fulfilled. 2Ch 36:21
who were 20 y old or more to Ezr 3:8
that was built many y ago, Ezr 5:11
year, 12 y—I and my associates Neh 5:14
wilderness 40 y and they lacked Neh 9:21
patient with them for many y, Neh 9:30
or Your y like those of a man, Jb 10:5
few y are stored up for the Jb 15:20
only⌋ a few y will pass before Jb 16:22
I am young in y, while you are Jb 32:6
and their y in happiness. Jb 36:11
number of His y cannot be Jb 36:26
Job lived 140 y after this and Jb 42:16
grief, and my y with groaning; Ps 31:10
may his y span many generations. Ps 61:6
days of old, y long past. Ps 77:5
their y in sudden disaster. Ps 78:33
sight a thousand y are like Ps 90:4
we end our y like a sigh. Ps 90:9
Our lives last seventy y or, Ps 90:10
or, if we are strong, eighty y. Ps 90:10
for as many y as we have seen Ps 90:15
For 40 y I was disgusted with Ps 95:10
Your y continue through all Ps 102:24
and Your y will never end. Ps 102:27
words, and you will live many y. Pr 4:10
others and your y to someone Pr 5:9
y will be added to your life. Pr 9:11
but the y of the wicked are cut Pr 10:27
children and live many y. Ec 6:3
if he lives a thousand y twice, Ec 6:6
during the y of his days that Ec 8:15
For if a man should live many y, Ec 11:8
and the y approach when you will Ec 12:1
within 65 y Ephraim will be too Is 7:8
says, "In three y, as a hired Is 16:14
as a hired worker counts y, Is 16:14
barefoot three y as a sign and Is 20:3
as a hired worker counts y, Is 21:16
will be forgotten for 70 y— Is 23:15
the end of 70 y, what the song Is 23:15
And at the end of the 70 y, Is 23:17
going to add 15 y to your life. Is 38:5
am deprived of the rest of my y. Is 38:10
along slowly all my y because Is 38:15
youth will die at a hundred y, Is 65:20
a hundred y will be cursed. Is 65:20
this very day—23 y—the word Jr 25:3
the king of Babylon for 70 y. Jr 25:11
When the 70 y are completed, Jr 25:12
Within two y I will restore to Jr 28:3
within two y I will break the Jr 28:11
When 70 y for Babylon are Jr 29:10
the end of seven y, each of you Jr 34:14
serve you six y, but then you Jr 34:14

Zedekiah was 21 y old when he Jr 52:1
he reigned 11 y in Jerusalem. Jr 52:1
assigned you the y of their Ezk 4:5
sees concerns many y ⌊from now⌋; Ezk 12:27
come to your y ⌊of punishment⌋. Ezk 22:4
It will be uninhabited for 40 y. Ezk 29:11
among ruined cities for 40 y. Ezk 29:12
At the end of 40 y I will gather Ezk 29:13
In the last y you will enter a Ezk 38:8
who for y prophesied in those Ezk 38:17
For seven y they will use them Ezk 39:9
were to be trained for three y, Dn 1:5
the number of y for the Dn 9:2
After some y they will form an Dn 11:6
some y he will stay away from Dn 11:8
After some y he will advance Dn 11:13
you for the y that the swarming Jl 2:25
two y before the earthquake. Am 1:1
and led you 40 y in the Am 2:10
Me during the 40 y in the Am 5:25
Revive ⌊Your work⌋ in these y; Hab 3:2
make ⌊it⌋ known in these y. Hab 3:2
been angry with these 70 y?" Zch 1:12
as we have done these many y?" Zch 7:3
seventh ⌊months⌋ for these 70 y, Zch 7:5
as in days of old and y gone Mal 3:4
who were two y old and under, Mt 2:16
bleeding for 12 y approached Mt 9:20
suffering from bleeding for 12 y Mk 5:25
walk. (She was 12 y old.) At Mk 5:42
of them were well along in y. Lk 1:7
and my wife is well along in y." Lk 1:18
well along in y, having lived Lk 2:36
her husband seven y after her Lk 2:36
and was a widow for 84 y. Lk 2:37
When He was 12 y old, they went Lk 2:42
Jesus was about 30 y old and was Lk 3:23
up for three y and six months Lk 4:25
an only daughter about 12 y old, Lk 8:42
from bleeding for 12 y, Lk 8:43
many goods stored up for many y. Lk 12:19
for three y I have come looking Lk 13:7
by a spirit for over 18 y. Lk 13:11
Abraham, for 18 y—shouldn't Lk 13:16
been slaving many y for you, Lk 15:29
sanctuary took 46 y to build, Jn 2:20
who had been sick for 38 y. Jn 5:5
You aren't 50 y old yet, and Jn 8:57
man was over 40 y old on whom Ac 4:22
and oppress them for 400 y. Ac 7:6
After 40 y had passed, an angel Ac 7:30
and in the desert for 40 y. Ac 7:36
for 40 y in the desert, Ac 7:42
had been bedridden for eight y. Ac 9:33
for about 40 y He put up with Ac 13:18
This all took about 450 y. Ac 13:20
the tribe of Benjamin, for 40 y. Ac 13:21
And this went on for two y, Ac 19:10
day for three y I did not stop Ac 20:31
judge of this nation for many y, Ac 24:10
After many y, I came to bring Ac 24:17
After two y had passed, Felix Ac 24:27
stayed two whole y in his own Ac 28:30
he was about a hundred y old Rm 4:19
desired for many y to come to Rm 15:23
into the third heaven 14 y ago. 2Co 12:2
Then after three y I did go up Gl 1:18
Then after 14 y I went up again Gl 2:1
which came 430 y later, does not Gl 3:17
days, months, seasons, and y. Gl 4:10
unless she is at least 60 y old, 1Tm 5:9
and Your y will never end. Heb 1:12
for 40 y. Therefore I was Heb 3:10
was He "provoked for 40 y"? Heb 3:17
and for three y and six months Jms 5:17
Lord one day is like 1,000 y, 2Pt 3:8
years, and 1,000 y like one day. 2Pt 3:8
and bound him for 1,000 y. Rv 20:2
the 1,000 y were completed. Rv 20:3
with the Messiah for 1,000 y. Rv 20:4
the 1,000 y were completed. Rv 20:5
will reign with Him for 1,000 y. Rv 20:6
When the 1,000 y are completed, Rv 20:7

YEAST *(23)*

you must remove y from your Ex 12:15
Y must not be found in your Ex 12:19
loaves, since it had no y; Ex 12:39
and no y may be found among you Ex 13:7
the LORD is to be made with y, Lv 2:11
not to burn any y or honey as a Lv 2:11
It must not be baked with y; Lv 6:17
without y beside the altar Lv 10:12
baked with y, as firstfruits Lv 23:17
No y is to be found anywhere in Dt 16:4
heaven is like y that a woman Mt 13:33
beware of the y of the Pharisees Mt 16:6
'Beware of the y of the Mt 16:11
to beware of the y in bread, Mt 16:12
Beware of the y of the Pharisees Mk 8:15
Pharisees and the y of Herod." Mk 8:15
against the y of the Pharisees Lk 12:1
It's like y that a woman took Lk 13:21
know that a little y permeates 1Co 5:6
out the old y so that you may 1Co 5:7
not with old y, or with the 1Co 5:8
with the y of malice and evil, 1Co 5:8
little y leavens the whole lump Gl 5:9

YELL *(1)*

there began to y insults at Him: Lk 23:39

YELLED *(1)*

our master, but he y at them. 1Sm 25:14

YELLING *(6)*

and he was y curses as he 2Sm 16:5
hold of him, y, "You must surely Jr 26:8
passed by were y insults at Him, Mt 27:39
passed by were y insults at Him, Mk 15:29
of people were following and y, Ac 21:36
they were y and flinging aside Ac 22:23

YELLOW *(4)*

the hair in it is y and sparse, Lv 13:30
and there is no y hair in it and Lv 13:32
not need to look for y hair; Lv 13:36
hyacinth blue, and sulfur y. Rv 9:17

YES *(103)*

"Y," they replied, "do as you Gn 18:5
the dream, "Y, I know that you Gn 20:6
"Y," they said, "and here is his Gn 29:6
said to him, "Y, you are my own Gn 29:14
y, He has heard me and given me Gn 30:6
she said, "Y, the men did come Jos 2:4
Y, it is true that I am a family Ru 3:12
women answered, "Y, he is ahead 1Sm 9:12
unclean—y, that's it, he is 1Sm 20:26
"Y it is," Asahel replied. 2Sm 2:20
Y, your servant Joab is the one 2Sm 14:19
This is the day, y, even today! 1Kg 14:14
hint and said, "Y, your brother 1Kg 20:33
you?" He said, "Y, I know. Be 2Kg 2:3
you?" He said, "Y, I know. Be 2Kg 2:5
arrow of victory, y, the arrow 2Kg 13:17
Y, we will do as you say! Ezr 10:12
Y, may that night be barren; Jb 3:7
Y, I know what you've said is Jb 9:2
Y, this will result in my Jb 13:16
Y, the light of the wicked is Jb 18:5
Y, I know that You will lead me Jb 30:23
y, I will tell what I know. Jb 32:17
Y, God is mighty, but He Jb 36:5
Y, every mortal man is only a Ps 39:5
people will say, "Y, there is a Ps 58:11
y, I will remember Your ancient Ps 77:11
me, y, they surrounded Ps 118:11
Y, LORD, we wait for You in the Is 26:8
y, my spirit within me Is 26:9
Y, You are a God who hides Is 45:15
your case⌋—y, let them take Is 45:21
a far country. Y, I have spoken; Is 46:11
I have spoken; y, I have called Is 48:15
Y, the islands will wait for Me Is 60:9
Y, I too have seen ⌊it⌋." Jr 7:11
their enemies, y, to those who Jr 21:7
Y, this is what the LORD of Jr 27:21
Y, this is what the LORD says: Jr 30:5
Y, the sons of Jonadab son of Jr 35:16
Y, He repeatedly turns His hand Lm 3:3
Y, I will not spare ⌊you⌋. Ezk 5:11
Y, I said to you ⌊as you lay⌋ in Ezk 16:6
Y, it is coming and it will Ezk 21:7
Y, I will gather you together Ezk 22:21
Y, that is what they did inside Ezk 23:39
Y, you are wiser than Daniel; Ezk 28:3
Y, to them you are like a singer Ezk 33:32
Y, it is coming, and it will Ezk 39:8
Y, this is the law of the temple. Ezk 43:12
"Y, of course, Your Majesty," Dn 3:24
it forever, y, forever and ever Dn 7:18
Y, I will tear ⌊them⌋ to pieces Hs 5:14
Y, woe to them when I depart Hs 9:12
y, his rotten smell will rise, Jl 2:20
Y, in those days and at that Jl 3:1
Y, you—do not gloat over their Ob 13
the plant?" "⌊Y,⌋" he replied. Jnh 4:9
majesty of Jacob, y, the majesty Nah 2:2
make a complete, y, a horrifying Zph 1:18
Y, at that time I will deal with Zph 3:19
bring you back, y, at the time I Zph 3:20
Y, He will build the LORD's Zch 6:13
But let your word 'y' be 'yes,' Mt 5:37
But let your word 'yes' be 'y,' Mt 5:37
"Y, Lord," they answered Him. Mt 9:28
Y, I tell you, and far more than Mt 11:9
Y, Father, because this was Your Mt 11:26
things?" "Y," they told Him Mt 13:51
"Y, Lord," she said, "yet even Mt 15:27
"Y," he said. When he went into Mt 17:25
"Y," Jesus told them. Mt 21:16
Y, I tell you, and far more than Lk 7:26
Y, Father, because this was Your Lk 10:21
Y, I tell you, this generation Lk 11:51
Y, I say to you, this is the One Lk 12:5
sisters—y, and even his own Lk 14:26
Y, what is written about Me is Lk 22:37
Y, the Father wants such people Jn 4:23
"Y, Lord," she told Him, "I Jn 11:27
"Y, Lord," he said to Him, "You Jn 21:15
"Y, Lord," he said to Him, "You Jn 21:16
"Y," she said, "for that price. Ac 5:8
a Roman citizen?" "Y," he said. Ac 22:27
for Gentiles? Y, for Gentiles Rm 3:29
they not hear?" Y, they did: Rm 10:18
Y, they were pleased, and they Rm 15:27
Y, this is written for us, 1Co 9:10
human way so that I say "Y, 2Co 1:17
that I say "Yes, y" and "No, no" 2Co 1:17
to you is not "Y and no." 2Co 1:18
did not become "Y and no"; 2Co 1:19
"Y" has come about in Him. 2Co 1:19
of God's promises is "Y" in Him. 2Co 1:20
from me. Y, do put up with me. 2Co 11:1
in this I rejoice. Y, and I will Php 1:18
Y, I also ask you, true partner, Php 4:3
Y, brother, may I have joy from Phm 20
Your "y" must be "yes," and your Jms 5:12
yes" must be "y," and your "no" Jms 5:12
"Y," says the Spirit, "let them Rv 14:13
Y, Lord God, the Almighty, true Rv 16:7
things says, "Y, I am coming Rv 22:20

YESTERDAY *(9)*

number of bricks y or today, Ex 5:14
to the meal either y or today?" 1Sm 20:27
Besides, you only arrived y; 2Sm 15:20
and the blood of his sons y,' 2Kg 9:26
born only⌋ y and know nothing Jb 8:9
years are like y that passes Ps 90:4
Y at seven in the morning the Jn 4:52
way you killed the Egyptian y? Ac 7:28
Jesus Christ is the same y, Heb 13:8

YET *(353)*

(See pp. xi-xii.)

YIELD *(25)*

will never again give you its y. Gn 4:12
In this way its y will increase Lv 19:25
Then the land will y its fruit, Lv 25:19
and the land will y its produce, Lv 26:4
land will not y its produce, Lv 26:20
watch, and it will y its water. Nm 20:8
the land will not y its produce, Dt 11:17
you must not y to him or listen Dt 13:8
the abundant y of the seasons; Dt 33:14
The hills y food for him, while Jb 40:20
and our land will y its crops. Ps 85:12
vineyards that y a fruitful Ps 107:37
He expected it to y good grapes, Is 5:2
I expected a y of good grapes, Is 5:4
did it y worthless grapes? Is 5:4
will y only six gallons, Is 5:10
seed will y only ⌊one⌋ bushel. Is 5:10
and the land will y its produce; Ezk 34:27
what sprouts fails to y flour. Hs 8:7
and grapevine y their riches. Jl 2:22
the vine will y its fruit, Zch 8:12
the land will y its produce, Zch 8:12
and the skies will y their dew. Zch 8:12

But we did not y in submission Gl 2:5
saltwater spring y fresh water. Jms 3:12

YIELDED *(1)*
but it y worthless grapes. Is 5:2

YIELDS *(6)*
of the poor y abundant food, Pr 13:23
person who y to the wicked is Pr 25:26
it y fruit for itself. Hs 10:1
and whatever the ground y, Hg 1:11
who does bear fruit and y: Mt 13:23
it y the fruit of peace and Heb 12:11

YOKE *(58)*
will break his y from your neck. Gn 27:40
bars of your y and enabled you Lv 26:13
place an iron y on your neck Dt 28:48
Your father made our y harsh. 1Kg 12:4
and the heavy y he put on us, 1Kg 12:4
the y your father put on us' 1Kg 12:9
'Your father made our y heavy, 1Kg 12:10
burdened you with a heavy y, 1Kg 12:11
yoke, I will add to your y; 1Kg 12:11
My father made your y heavy, 1Kg 12:14
heavy, but I will add to your y; 1Kg 12:14
the oxen's wooden y and plow, 1Kg 19:21
Your father made our y harsh. 2Ch 10:4
and the heavy y he put on us, 2Ch 10:4
the y your father put on us' 2Ch 10:9
'Your father made our y heavy, 2Ch 10:10
burdened you with a heavy y, 2Ch 10:11
yoke, but I will add to your y; 2Ch 10:11
My father made your y heavy, 2Ch 10:14
3,000 camels, 500 y of oxen, 500 Jb 1:3
camels, 1,000 y of oxen, and Jb 42:12
their burdensome y and the rod Is 9:4
and his y from your neck. Is 10:27
The y will be broken because of Is 10:27
Then his y will be taken from Is 14:25
made your y very heavy on the Is 47:6
to untie the ropes of the y, Is 58:6
free, and to tear off every y? Is 58:6
get rid of the y from those Is 58:9
For long ago I broke your y; Jr 2:20
had broken the y and torn off Jr 5:5
Make fetters and y bars for Jr 27:2
its neck under the y of the king Jr 27:8
its neck under the y of the king Jr 27:11
necks under the y of the king Jr 27:12
'I have broken the y of the king Jr 28:2
I will break the y of the king Jr 28:4
took the y bar from the neck Jr 28:10
I will break the y of Jr 28:11
had broken the y bar from the Jr 28:12
broke a wooden y bar, but in its Jr 28:13
you will make an iron y bar. Jr 28:13
have put an iron y on the neck Jr 28:14
will break his y from your neck Jr 30:8
have been formed into a y, Lm 1:14
a man to bear the y while he is Lm 3:27
put a wooden y on him with hooks Ezk 19:9
I break the y of Egypt there Ezk 30:18
bars of their y and rescue them Ezk 34:27
I will place a y on her fine Hs 10:11
who eases the y from their jaws Hs 11:4
break off his y from you and Nah 1:13
take up My y and learn from Me, Mt 11:29
For My y is easy and My burden Mt 11:30
'I have bought five y of oxen, Lk 14:19
necks a y that neither our Ac 15:10
submit again to a y of slavery. Gl 5:1
are under the y as slaves must 1Tm 6:1

YOKED *(3)*
no defect and has never been y. Nm 19:2
has not been y or used for work Dt 21:3
cows that have never been y. 1Sm 6:7

YOKES *(1)*
sledges and ox y for the wood. 2Sm 24:22

YOU *(13,822)*
(See pp. xi-xii.)

YOU'LL *(20)*
(See pp. xi-xii.)

YOU'RE *(61)*
(See pp. xi-xii.)

YOU'VE *(32)*
(See pp. xi-xii.)

YOUNG *(391)*
a turtledove, and a y pigeon." Gn 15:9
He gave it to a y man, who Gn 18:7
of Sodom, both y and old, the Gn 19:4
the house, both y and old, with Gn 19:11
him two of his y men and his son Gn 22:3
Then Abraham said to his y men, Gn 22:5
Abraham went back to his y men, Gn 22:19
y woman who had not known a Gn 24:16
Rebekah and her y women got up, Gn 24:61
and bring me two choice y goats, Gn 27:9
speckled, and spotted y. Gn 30:39
30 milk camels with their y, Gn 32:15
see some of the y women of the Gn 34:1
He loved the y girl and spoke Gn 34:3
The y man did not delay doing Gn 34:19
The y man ⌊was working⌋ with the Gn 37:2
slaughtered a y goat, and dipped Gn 37:31
I will send you a y goat from my Gn 38:17
Judah sent the y goat by his Gn 38:20
I did send this y goat, but you Gn 38:23
Now a y Hebrew, a slave of the Gn 41:12
elderly father and a y brother, Gn 44:20
of Egypt for your y children, Gn 45:19
Judah is a y lion—my son, you Gn 49:9
will go with our y and our old; Ex 10:9
must not boil a y goat in its Ex 23:19
he sent out y Israelite men, Ex 24:5
a y bull and two unblemished Ex 29:1
the y man Joshua son of Nun, Ex 33:11
must not boil a y goat in its Ex 34:26
the turtledoves or y pigeons. Lv 1:14
is to present to the LORD a y, Lv 4:3
must present a y bull as a sin Lv 4:14
turtledoves or two y pigeons as Lv 5:7
turtledoves or two y pigeons, Lv 5:11
Take a y bull for a sin offering Lv 9:2
and a y pigeon or a turtledove Lv 12:6
turtledoves or two y pigeons, Lv 12:8
turtledoves or two y pigeons, Lv 14:22
the turtledoves or y pigeons, Lv 14:30
turtledoves or two y pigeons on Lv 15:14
or two y pigeons and bring Lv 15:29
with a y bull for a sin offering Lv 16:3
unclean for his y unmarried Lv 21:3
flock on the same day as its y. Lv 22:28
a year old, one y bull, and two Lv 23:18
turtledoves or two y pigeons to Nm 6:10
y bull, one ram, and one male Nm 7:15
y bull, one ram, and one male Nm 7:21
y bull, one ram, and one male Nm 7:27
y bull, one ram, and one male Nm 7:33
y bull, one ram, and one male Nm 7:39
y bull, one ram, and one male Nm 7:45
y bull, one ram, and one male Nm 7:51
y bull, one ram, and one male Nm 7:57
y bull, one ram, and one male Nm 7:63
y bull, one ram, and one male Nm 7:69
y bull, one ram, and one male Nm 7:75
y bull, one ram, and one male Nm 7:81
are to take a y bull and its Nm 8:8
take a second y bull for a sin Nm 8:8
A y man ran and reported to Nm 11:27
you prepare a y bull as a burnt Nm 15:8
to prepare one y bull for a Nm 15:24
two y bulls, one ram, seven male Nm 28:11
two y bulls, one ram, and seven Nm 28:19
two y bulls, one ram, and seven Nm 28:27
one y bull, one ram, seven male Nm 29:2
one y bull, one ram, and seven Nm 29:8
y bulls, two rams, and 14 male Nm 29:13
second day ⌊present⌋ 12 y bulls, Nm 29:17
all the y females who have Nm 31:18
But your wives, y children, and Dt 3:19
and oil—the y of your herds, Dt 7:13
must not boil a y goat in its Dt 14:21
the mother along with the y. Dt 22:6
You may take the y for yourself, Dt 22:7
the y woman's father and mother Dt 22:15
The y woman's father will say to Dt 22:16
them⌋ to the y woman's father, Dt 22:19
evidence of the y woman's Dt 22:20
If there is a y woman who is a Dt 22:23
the y woman because she did not Dt 22:24
Do nothing to the y woman, Dt 22:26
If a man encounters a y woman, Dt 22:28
must give the y woman's father Dt 22:29
including the y of your herds Dt 28:4
produce, the y of your herds, Dt 28:18
the old and not sparing the y. Dt 28:50
new wine, oil, y of your herds, Dt 28:51
an eagle and hovers over His y; Dt 32:11
the y man and the virgin ⌊will Dt 32:25
Dan is a y lion, leaping out of Dt 33:22
Your wives, y children, and Jos 1:14
and woman, both y and old, and Jos 6:21
the y men who had scouted went Jos 6:23
and prepared a y goat and Jdg 6:19
your father's y bull and a Jdg 6:25
sons who rode on 30 y donkeys. Jdg 10:4
each year the y women of Israel Jdg 11:40
will prepare a y goat for You." Jdg 13:15
Manoah took a y goat and a grain Jdg 13:19
and saw a y Philistine woman Jdg 14:1
I have seen a y Philistine woman Jdg 14:2
you find a y woman among your Jdg 14:3
Suddenly a y lion came roaring Jdg 14:5
as he might have torn a y goat. Jdg 14:6
as y men were accustomed to do. Jdg 14:10
you hadn't plowed with my y cow, Jdg 14:18
took⌋ a y goat ⌊as a gift Jdg 15:1
Samson said to the y man who was Jdg 16:26
There was a y man, a Levite, Jdg 17:7
and the y man became like one of Jdg 17:11
and the y man became his priest Jdg 17:12
the speech of the y Levite. Jdg 18:3
the house of the y Levite at the Jdg 18:15
and the y man with your servant. Jdg 19:19
of Jabesh-gilead 400 y virgins, Jdg 21:12
you see the y women of Shiloh Jdg 21:21
from the y women of Shiloh, Jdg 21:21
Whose y woman is this?" Ru 2:5
She is the y Moabite woman who Ru 2:6
stay here close to my y women. Ru 2:8
I ordered the y men not to touch Ru 2:9
the jars the y men have filled. Ru 2:9
ordered his y men, "Be sure to Ru 2:15
'Stay with my y men until they Ru 2:21
you to work with his y women, Ru 2:22
close to Boaz's y women and Ru 2:23
been working with his y women? Ru 3:2
will give you by this y woman." Ru 4:12
Though the boy was ⌊still⌋ y, 1Sm 1:24
Samuel took a y lamb and offered 1Sm 7:9
your best y men, and your 1Sm 8:16
named Saul, an impressive y man. 1Sm 9:2
they found some y women coming 1Sm 9:11
as well as the y rams and the 1Sm 15:9
Take a y cow with you and say, 1Sm 16:2
One of the y men answered, 1Sm 16:18
and one y goat and sent them by 1Sm 16:20
been a warrior since he was y." 1Sm 17:33
out whose son this y man is!" 1Sm 17:56
"Whose son are you, y man?" 1Sm 17:58
I will send the y man ⌊and say⌋, 1Sm 20:21
I expressly say to the y man, 1Sm 20:21
A small y man was with him. 1Sm 20:35
He said to the y man, "Run and 1Sm 20:36
As the y man ran, Jonathan shot 1Sm 20:36
Jonathan's y man picked up the 1Sm 20:38
to the y man who was with 1Sm 20:40
When the y man had gone, David 1Sm 20:41
stationed ⌊my⌋ y men at a 1Sm 21:2
but the y men may eat it only if 1Sm 21:4
The y men's bodies are 1Sm 21:5
David sent 10 y men instructing 1Sm 25:5
Ask your y men, and they will 1Sm 25:8
let ⌊my⌋ y men find favor with 1Sm 25:8
David's y men went and said all 1Sm 25:9
One of Nabal's y men informed 1Sm 25:14
see my lord's y men whom you 1Sm 25:25
be given to the y men who follow 1Sm 25:27
have one of the y men come over 1Sm 26:22
except 400 y men who got on 1Sm 30:17
David asked the y man who had 2Sm 1:5
inquired of the y man who had 2Sm 1:13
Let's have the y men get up and 2Sm 2:14
seize one of the y soldiers, 2Sm 2:21
David gave orders to the y men, 2Sm 4:12
had a y son whose name was 2Sm 9:12
Absalom commanded his y men, 2Sm 13:28
Absalom's y men did to Amnon 2Sm 13:29
they have killed all the y men, 2Sm 13:32
the y man who was standing 2Sm 13:34
bring back the y man Absalom." 2Sm 14:21
fruit are for the y men to eat, 2Sm 16:2
y man did see them and informed 2Sm 17:18
Treat the y man Absalom gently 2Sm 18:5

'Protect the y man Absalom for 2Sm 18:12
and 10 y men who were Joab's 2Sm 18:15
"Is the y man Absalom all right?" 2Sm 18:29
"Is the y man Absalom all right?" 2Sm 18:32
has become of the y man happen 2Sm 18:32
One of Joab's y men had stood 2Sm 20:11
us search for a y virgin for my 1Kg 1:2
noticed the y man because he was 1Kg 11:28
with the y men who had grown 1Kg 12:8
the y men who had grown up 1Kg 12:10
according to the y men's advice: 1Kg 12:14
'By the y men of the provincial 1Kg 20:14
So Ahab counted the y men of the 1Kg 20:15
The y men of the provincial 1Kg 20:17
The y men of the provincial 1Kg 20:19
of Israel a y girl who served 2Kg 5:2
that two y men from the sons 2Kg 5:22
to two of his y men who carried 2Kg 5:23
will kill their y men with the 2Kg 8:12
So the y prophet went to 2Kg 9:4
The y prophet poured the oil on 2Kg 9:6
Then the y prophet opened the 2Kg 9:10
The y woman, Daughter Zion, 2Kg 19:21
and Zadok, a y brave warrior, 1Ch 12:28
son Solomon is y and 1Ch 22:5
duties, the y and old alike, 1Ch 25:8
houses, y and old alike, 1Ch 26:13
him alone—is y and 1Ch 29:1
with the y men who had grown 2Ch 10:8
the y men who had grown up 2Ch 10:10
according to the y men's advice, 2Ch 10:14
Solomon when Rehoboam was y, 2Ch 13:7
himself with a y bull and seven 2Ch 13:9
put to death, y or old, man or 2Ch 15:13
their choice y men with the 2Ch 36:17
had no pity on y man and virgin 2Ch 36:17
is needed—y bulls, rams, Ezr 6:9
made for beautiful y virgins for Est 2:2
all the beautiful y virgins to Est 2:3
Then the y woman who pleases the Est 2:4
The y woman had a beautiful Est 2:7
many y women gathered at the Est 2:8
The y woman pleased him and Est 2:9
before each y woman's turn to Est 2:12
When the y woman would go to the Est 2:13
When the y women were assembled Est 2:19
Jewish people—y and old, women Est 3:13
collapsed on the y people so Jb 1:19
the fangs of y lions are broken Jb 4:10
Even y boys scorn me. When I Jb 19:18
the y men saw me and withdrew, Jb 29:8
then could I look at a y woman? Jb 31:1
I am y in years, while you are Jb 32:6
satisfy the appetite of y lions Jb 38:39
food when its y cry out to God Jb 38:41
down to give birth to their y; Jb 39:3
She treats her y harshly, as if Jb 39:16
like a y lion lurking in ambush. Ps 17:12
and Sirion, like a y wild ox. Ps 29:6
Y lions lack food and go hungry, Ps 34:10
my very life from the y lions. Ps 35:17
I have been y and now I am old, Ps 37:25
tear out the y lions' fangs. Ps 58:6
among them are y women playing Ps 68:25
down Israel's choice y men. Ps 78:31
Fire consumed His chosen y men, Ps 78:63
and His y women had no wedding Ps 78:63
herself where she places her y— Ps 84:3
will trample the y lion and the Ps 91:13
The y lions roar for their prey Ps 104:21
locusts came—y locusts without Ps 105:34
How can a y man keep his way Ps 119:9
like y olive trees around your Ps 128:3
food, and the y ravens, what Ps 147:9
y men as well as young women, Ps 148:12
young men as well as y women, Ps 148:12
young women, old and y together. Ps 148:12
and discretion to a y man— Pr 1:4
the youths, a y man lacking Pr 7:7
Even a y man is known by his Pr 20:11
The glory of y men is their Pr 20:29
it out and y vultures eat it Pr 30:17
the way of a man with a y woman. Pr 30:19
Rejoice, y man, while you are Ec 11:9
while you are y, and let your Ec 11:9
No wonder y women adore you. Sg 1:3
pasture your y goats near the Sg 1:8
is my darling among the y women. Sg 2:2

so is my love among the y men. Sg 2:3
Y women of Jerusalem, I charge Sg 2:7
is like a gazelle or a y stag. Sg 2:9
a gazelle or a y stag on the Sg 2:17
Y women of Jerusalem, I charge Sg 3:5
with love by the y women of Sg 3:10
Come out, y women of Zion, and Sg 3:11
Y women of Jerusalem, I charge Sg 5:8
is my friend, y women of Sg 5:16
concubines and y women without Sg 6:8
Y women of Jerusalem, I charge Sg 8:4
Our sister is y; she has no Sg 8:8
like a gazelle or a y stag on Sg 8:14
they roar like y lions; Is 5:29
man will raise a y cow and two Is 7:21
over Israel's y men and has no Is 9:17
The calf, the y lion, and the Is 11:6
their y ones will lie down Is 11:7
bows will cut y men to pieces. Is 13:18
exiles of Cush, y and old alike, Is 20:4
Look, y man! The LORD is about Is 22:17
have not raised y men ⌊or⌋ Is 23:4
men ⌊or⌋ brought up y women." Is 23:4
more, ravished y woman, daughter Is 23:12
As a lion or y lion growls over Is 31:4
his y men will be put to forced Is 31:8
and y bulls with the mighty Is 34:7
The y woman, Daughter Zion, Is 37:22
and y men stumble and fall, Is 40:30
Him like a y plant and like Is 53:2
y camels of Midian and Ephah— Is 60:6
For as a y man marries a virgin, Is 62:5
The y lions have roared at him; Jr 2:15
are⌋ a swift y camel twisting Jr 2:23
Can a y woman forget her jewelry Jr 2:32
on the gang of y men as well. Jr 6:11
from the streets, y men from the Jr 9:21
The y men will die by the sword; Jr 11:22
the mother of y men a destroyer Jr 15:8
their y men struck down by the Jr 18:21
because of the y of the flocks Jr 31:12
while y and old men ⌊rejoice⌋ Jr 31:13
Egypt is a beautiful y cow, Jr 46:20
the best of its y men have gone Jr 48:15
y men will fall in her public Jr 49:26
you frolic like a y cow treading Jr 50:11
all her y bulls to the sword; Jr 50:27
y men will fall in her public Jr 50:30
Don't spare her y men; Jr 51:3
I will smash the y man and the Jr 51:22
will roar together like y lions; Jr 51:38
groan, her y women grieve, Lm 1:4
me to crush my y warriors. Lm 1:15
y men and women have gone into Lm 1:18
The y women of Jerusalem have Lm 2:10
⌊Both⌋ y and old are lying on Lm 2:21
y men and women have fallen by Lm 2:21
the yoke while he is ⌊still⌋ y. Lm 3:27
their⌋ breasts to nurse their y, Lm 4:3
Y men labor at millstones; Lm 5:13
city gate, the y men, their Lm 5:14
old men, the y men and women, Ezk 9:6
her cubs among the y lions. Ezk 19:2
cubs, and he became a y lion. Ezk 19:3
her cubs and made him a y lion. Ezk 19:5
lions, and he became a y lion. Ezk 19:6
all of them desirable y men, Ezk 23:6
all of them desirable y men. Ezk 23:12
desirable y men, all of them Ezk 23:23
The y men of On and Pi-beseth Ezk 30:17
are to present a y, unblemished Ezk 43:23
A y bull and a ram from the Ezk 43:25
are to take a y, unblemished Ezk 45:18
burnt offering⌋ is to be a y, Ezk 46:6
y men without any physical Dn 1:4
of the other y men your age. Dn 1:10
appearance of the y men who are Dn 1:13
than all the y men who were Dn 1:15
gave these four y men knowledge Dn 1:17
and like a y lion to the house Hs 5:14
a well-trained y cow that loves Hs 10:11
left, the y locust has eaten; Jl 1:4
and what the y locust has left, Jl 1:4
Grieve like a y woman dressed in Jl 1:8
locust ate, the y locust, the Jl 2:25
and your y men will see visions. Jl 2:28
some of your y men as Nazirites Am 2:11
a y lion growl from its lair Am 3:4

I killed your y men with the Am 4:10
that day the beautiful y women, Am 8:13
young women, the y men also, Am 8:13
like a y lion among flocks of Mc 5:8
feeding ground of the y lions, Nah 2:11
sword will devour your y lions. Nah 2:13
devour you like the y locust. Nah 3:15
yourselves like the y locust, Nah 3:15
The y locust strips ⌊the land⌋ Nah 3:16
him, "Run and tell this y man: Zch 2:4
will make the y men flourish, Zch 9:17
and new wine, the y women. Zch 9:17
Listen to the roar of y lions, Zch 11:3
all these," the y man told Him. Mt 19:20
When the y man heard that Mt 19:22
you will find a y donkey tied Mk 11:2
and found a y donkey outside Mk 11:4
Now a certain y man, having a Mk 14:51
they saw a y man dressed in a Mk 16:5
of turtledoves or two y pigeons Lk 2:24
And He said, "Y man, I tell you, Lk 7:14
gave me a y goat so I could Lk 15:29
you will find a y donkey tied Lk 19:30
they were untying the y donkey, Lk 19:33
Jesus found a y donkey and sat Jn 12:14
When you were y, you would tie Jn 21:18
your y men will see visions, Ac 2:17
The y men got up, wrapped ⌊his Ac 5:6
When the y men came in, they Ac 5:10
the feet of a y man named Saul. Ac 7:58
and a y man named Eutychus was Ac 20:9
Take this y man to the Ac 23:17
me to bring this y man to you, Ac 23:18
dismissed the y man and Ac 23:22
encourage the y women to love Ti 2:4
encourage the y men to be Ti 2:6
writing to you, y men, because 1Jn 2:13
written to you, y men, because 1Jn 2:14

YOUNGER *(32)*

the firstborn said to the y, Gn 19:31
day the firstborn said to the y, Gn 19:34
and the y went and slept with Gn 19:35
The y also gave birth to a son, Gn 19:38
and the older will serve the y. Gn 25:23
and had her y son Jacob wear Gn 27:15
she summoned her y son Jacob and Gn 27:42
and the y was named Rachel. Gn 29:16
for your y daughter Rachel. Gn 29:18
place to give the y ⌊daughter in Gn 29:26
give you this ⌊y⌋ one in return Gn 29:27
'If your y brother does not come Gn 44:23
down unless our y brother goes Gn 44:26
But if our y brother isn't with Gn 44:26
of Ephraim, the y, and crossing Gn 48:14
his y brother will be greater Gn 48:19
her y sister more beautiful Jdg 15:2
you have not pursued y men, Ru 3:10
firstborn, and Michal, the y. 1Sm 14:49
and their y brothers alike. 1Ch 24:31
mock me, men y than I am, whose Jb 30:1
and your y sister was Sodom, Ezk 16:46
your older and y sisters. Ezk 16:61
of James the y and of Joses, Mk 15:40
y of them said to his father, Lk 15:12
the y son gathered together all Lk 15:13
The older will serve the y. Rm 9:12
as a father, y men as brothers 1Tm 5:1
propriety, the y women as 1Tm 5:2
But refuse to enroll y widows; 1Tm 5:11
I want y women to marry, 1Tm 5:14
Likewise, you y men, be subject 1Pt 5:5

YOUNGEST *(28)*

what his y son had done to Gn 9:24
The y is now with our father, Gn 42:13
unless your y brother comes Gn 42:15
Bring your y brother to me so Gn 42:20
and the y is now with our father Gn 42:32
Bring back your y brother to me, Gn 42:34
Is this your y brother that you Gn 43:29
from the firstborn to the y. Gn 43:33
at the top of the y one's bag, Gn 44:2
oldest and ending with the y, Gn 44:12
gates ⌊at the cost of⌋ his y. Jos 6:26
Kenaz, Caleb's y brother, Jdg 1:13
Caleb's y brother as a deliverer Jdg 3:9
and I am the y in my father's Jdg 6:15
But Jotham, the y son of Jdg 9:5
city, from the y to the oldest, 1Sm 5:9

is still the **y**," he answered, 1Sm 16:11
and David was the **y**. 1Sm 17:14
in it from the **y** to the oldest. 1Sm 30:2
from the **y** to the oldest, 1Sm 30:19
and at the cost of Segub his **y**, 1Kg 16:34
arms, from the **y** to the oldest, 2Kg 3:21
people from the **y** to the oldest. 2Kg 23:2
from the **y** to the oldest, 2Kg 25:26
him except Jehoahaz, his **y** son. 2Ch 21:17
Ahaziah, his **y** son, king in his 2Ch 22:1
Benjamin, the **y**, leading them, Ps 68:27
you must become like the **y**, Lk 22:26

YOUR *(6575)*
(See pp. xi-xii.)

YOURS *(78)*
(See pp. xi-xii.)

YOURSELF *(223)*
(See pp. xi-xii.)

YOURSELVES *(211)*
(See pp. xi-xii.)

YOUTH *(80)*
inclination is evil from his **y**. Gn 8:21
livestock from our **y** until now.' Gn 46:34
her father's house as in her **y**, Lv 22:13
assistant to Moses since his **y**, Nm 11:28
house during her **y** makes a vow Nm 30:3
in his house during her **y**. Nm 30:16
He captured a **y** from the men of Jdg 8:14
The **y** wrote down for him the Jdg 8:14
The **y** did not draw his sword, Jdg 8:20
afraid, for he was still a **y**. Jdg 8:20
led you from my **y** until today. 1Sm 12:2
You're just a **y**, and he's been a 1Sm 17:33
him because he was just a **y**, 1Sm 17:42
Whose son is this **y**, Abner?" 1Sm 17:55
But if I say this to the **y**: 1Sm 20:22
to you from your **y** until now!" 2Sm 19:7
Yet I am just a **y** with no 1Kg 3:7
have feared the LORD from my **y**. 1Kg 18:12
was still a **y**, Josiah began to 2Ch 34:3
inherit the iniquities of my **y**. Jb 13:26
in the days of my **y** when God's Jb 29:4
for from my **y**, I raised him as Jb 31:18
will be healthier than in his **y**, Jb 33:25
die in their **y**; their life ⌊ends Jb 36:14
the sins of my **y** or my acts of Ps 25:7
GOD, my confidence from my **y**. Ps 71:5
You have taught me from my **y**, Ps 71:17
From my **y**, I have been afflicted Ps 88:15
shortened the days of his **y**; Ps 89:45
y is renewed like the eagle. Ps 103:5
dew of Your **y** belongs to You. Ps 110:3
are the sons born in one's **y**. Ps 127:4
Since my **y** they have often Ps 129:1
Since my **y** they have often Ps 129:2
like plants nurtured in their **y**, Ps 144:12
companion of her **y** and forgets Pr 2:17
pleasure in the wife of your **y**. Pr 5:18
a **y** about the way he should Pr 22:6
tangled up in the heart of a **y**; Pr 22:15
withhold correction from a **y**; Pr 23:13
but a **y** left to himself is a Pr 29:15
pampered from his **y** will become Pr 29:21
is a poor but wise **y** than an old Ec 4:13
follow a second **y** who succeeds Ec 4:15
be glad in the days of your **y**. Ec 11:9
because **y** and the prime of life Ec 11:10
Creator in the days of your **y**: Ec 12:1
the **y** will act arrogantly toward Is 3:5
yourself with from your **y**. Is 47:12
traded with you from your **y**— Is 47:15
will forget the shame of your **y**, Is 54:4
a wife of one's **y** when she is Is 54:6
the **y** will die at a hundred Is 65:20
to speak since I am ⌊only⌋ a **y**." Jr 1:6
I am ⌊only⌋ a **y**, for you will go Jr 1:7
remember the loyalty of your **y**, Jr 2:2
the time of our **y** the shameful Jr 3:24
the time of our **y** even to this Jr 3:25
This has been your way since **y**; Jr 22:21
I bore the disgrace of my **y**. Jr 31:19
From their **y**, the Israelites and Jr 32:30
has been left quiet since his **y**, Jr 48:11
smash the old man and the **y**; Jr 51:22
From my **y** until now I have not Ezk 4:14
the days of your **y** when you were Ezk 16:22
the days of your **y** but enraged Ezk 16:43
with you in the days of your **y**, Ezk 16:60
promiscuously in their **y**. Ezk 23:3
men slept with her in her **y**, Ezk 23:8
the days of her **y** when she acted Ezk 23:19
the indecency of your **y**, Ezk 23:21
she did⌋ in the days of her **y**, Hs 2:15
for the husband of her **y**. Jl 1:8
me as a servant since my **y**. Zch 13:5
you and the wife of your **y**. Mal 2:14
against the wife of your **y**. Mal 2:15
have kept all these from my **y**." Mk 10:20
have kept all these from my **y**," Lk 18:21
know my way of life from my **y**, Ac 26:4
No one should despise your **y**; 1Tm 4:12

YOUTHFUL *(5)*
bones may be full of **y** vigor, Jb 20:11
to the days of his **y** vigor. Jb 33:25
My Father, my **y** companion? Jr 3:4
nipples to enjoy your **y** breasts. Ezk 23:21
Flee from **y** passions, and pursue 2Tm 2:22

YOUTHS *(5)*
woods and mauled 42 of the **y**. 2Kg 2:24
noticed among the **y**, a young man Pr 7:7
I will make **y** their leaders, Is 3:4
Y oppress My people, and women Is 3:12
Y may faint and grow weary, Is 40:30

Z

ZAANAN *(1)*
the residents of **Z** will not come Mc 1:11

ZAANANNIM *(2)*
Heleph and from the oak in **Z**, Jos 19:33
tent beside the oak tree of **Z**, Jdg 4:11

ZAAVAN *(2)*
sons: Bilhan, **Z**, and Akan. Gn 36:27
Bilhan, **Z**, and Jaakan. 1Ch 1:42

ZABAD *(8)*
(AKA JOZABAD)
Nathan, and Nathan fathered **Z**. 1Ch 2:36
Z fathered Ephlal, and Ephlal 1Ch 2:37
his son **Z**, his son Shuthelah, 1Ch 7:21
the Hittite, **Z** son of Ahlai, 1Ch 11:41
conspired against him were **Z**, 2Ch 24:26
Jeremoth, **Z**, and Aziza; Ezr 10:27
Mattattah, **Z**, Eliphelet, Jeremai Ezr 10:33
Mattithiah, **Z**, Zebina, Jaddai, Ezr 10:43

ZABBAI *(2)*
Hananiah, **Z**, and Athlai; Ezr 10:28
him Baruch son of **Z** diligently Neh 3:20

ZABDI *(6)*
Carmi, son of **Z**, son of Zerah, Jos 7:1
of families, and **Z** was selected. Jos 7:17
Carmi, son of **Z**, son of Zerah, Jos 7:18
Jakim, Zichri, **Z**, 1Ch 8:19
Z the Shiphmite was in charge of 1Ch 27:27
of Mica, son of **Z**, son of Asaph, Neh 11:17

ZABDI'S *(1)*
then had **Z** family come forward Jos 7:18

ZABDIEL *(2)*
Jashobeam son of **Z** was in charge 1Ch 27:2
Z son of Haggedolim, was their Neh 11:14

ZABUD *(1)*
Z son of Nathan, a priest and 1Kg 4:5

ZACCAI'S *(2)*
Z descendants 760 Ezr 2:9
Z descendants 760 Neh 7:14

ZACCHAEUS *(3)*
a man named **Z** who was a chief Lk 19:2
said to him, "**Z**, hurry and come Lk 19:5
Z stood there and said to the Lk 19:8

ZACCUR *(10)*
Shammua son of **Z** from the tribe Nm 13:4
Hammuel, his son **Z**, and his son 1Ch 4:26
Jaaziah: Shoham, **Z**, and Ibri. 1Ch 24:27
Z, Joseph, Nethaniah, and 1Ch 25:2
the third ⌊to⌋ **Z**, his sons, and 1Ch 25:10
Uthai and **Z** from Bigvai's Ezr 8:14
and next to them **Z** son of Imri Neh 3:2
Z, Sherebiah, Shebaniah, Neh 10:12
Micaiah, son of **Z**, son of Asaph, Neh 12:35
Hanan son of **Z**, son of Mattaniah Neh 13:13

ZADOK *(53)*
Z son of Ahitub and Ahimelech 2Sm 8:17
Z was also there, and all the 2Sm 15:24
Then the king instructed **Z**, 2Sm 15:25
king also said to **Z** the priest, 2Sm 15:27
So **Z** and Abiathar returned the 2Sm 15:29
Won't **Z** and Abiathar the priests 2Sm 15:35
king's palace to **Z** and Abiathar 2Sm 15:35
told the priests **Z** and Abiathar, 2Sm 17:15
Ahimaaz son of **Z** said, "Please 2Sm 18:19
Ahimaaz son of **Z** persisted and 2Sm 18:22
the way Ahimaaz son of **Z** runs." 2Sm 18:27
to the priests, **Z** and Abiathar: 2Sm 19:11
Z and Abiathar were priests; 2Sm 20:25
but **Z** the priest, Benaiah son of 1Kg 1:8
Z the priest or Benaiah son of 1Kg 1:26
said, "Call in **Z** the priest, 1Kg 1:32
Z the priest and Nathan the 1Kg 1:34
Then **Z** the priest, Nathan the 1Kg 1:38
Z the priest took the horn of 1Kg 1:39
the king has sent **Z** the priest, 1Kg 1:44
Z the priest and Nathan the 1Kg 1:45
and he appointed **Z** the priest in 1Kg 2:35
Azariah son of **Z**, priest; 1Kg 4:2
Z and Abiathar, priests; 1Kg 4:4
name was Jerusha daughter of **Z**. 2Kg 15:33
fathered **Z**; Zadok fathered 1Ch 6:8
fathered Zadok; **Z** fathered 1Ch 6:8
fathered **Z**; Zadok fathered 1Ch 6:12
fathered Zadok; **Z** fathered 1Ch 6:12
his son **Z**, and his son Ahimaaz. 1Ch 6:53
son of **Z**, son of Meraioth 1Ch 9:11
and **Z**, a young brave warrior, 1Ch 12:28
the priests **Z** and Abiathar 1Ch 15:11
⌊David left⌋ **Z** the priest and 1Ch 16:39
Z son of Ahitub and Ahimelech 1Ch 18:16
Together with **Z** from the sons of 1Ch 24:3
and the officers, **Z** the priest, 1Ch 24:6
of King David, **Z**, Ahimelech, 1Ch 24:31
son of Kemuel; for Aaron, **Z**; 1Ch 27:17
ruler, and **Z** as the priest. 1Ch 29:22
name was Jerushah daughter of **Z**. 2Ch 27:1
priest of the household of **Z**, 2Ch 31:10
Next to them **Z** son of Baana made Neh 3:4
After them **Z** son of Immer made Neh 3:29
Meshezabel, **Z**, Jaddua, Neh 10:21
son of **Z**, son of Meraioth Neh 11:11
the priest, **Z** the scribe, Neh 13:13
These are the sons of **Z**, the Ezk 40:46
who are from the offspring of **Z**, Ezk 43:19
priests descended from **Z**, Ezk 44:15
the sons of **Z**, who kept My Ezk 48:11
Azor fathered **Z**, Zadok fathered Mt 1:14
Zadok, **Z** fathered Achim, Mt 1:14

ZADOK'S *(2)*
Z son Ahimaaz and Abiathar's 2Sm 15:36
Shallum's son, **Z** son, Ahitub's Ezr 7:2

ZAHAM *(1)*
Jeush, Shemariah, and **Z**. 2Ch 11:19

ZAIR *(1)*
crossed over to **Z** with all his 2Kg 8:21

ZALAPH *(1)*
sixth son of **Z** made repairs to Neh 3:30

ZALMON *(3)*
(AKA ILAI)
with him went up to Mount **Z**. Jdg 9:48
Z the Ahohite, Maharai the 2Sm 23:28
in the land, it snowed on **Z**. Ps 68:14

ZALMONAH *(2)*
from Mount Hor and camped at **Z**. Nm 33:41
departed from **Z** and camped at Nm 33:42

ZALMUNNA *(11)*
for I am pursuing Zebah and **Z**, Jdg 8:5
Are Zebah and **Z** now in your Jdg 8:6
handed Zebah and **Z** over to me, Jdg 8:7
Now Zebah and **Z** were in Karkor, Jdg 8:10
Zebah and **Z** fled, and he pursued Jdg 8:12
and said, "Here are Zebah and **Z**. Jdg 8:15
'Are Zebah and **Z** now in your Jdg 8:15
asked Zebah and **Z**, "What kind of Jdg 8:18
Zebah and **Z** said, "Get up and Jdg 8:21
up, killed Zebah and **Z**, and took Jdg 8:21
tribal leaders like Zebah and **Z**, Ps 83:11

ZAMZUMMIM *(1)*
(AKA REPHAIM, ZUZIM)
the Ammonites called them **Z**, Dt 2:20

ZANOAH *(5)*
Z, En-gannim, Tappuah, Enam, Jos 15:34
Jezreel, Jokdeam, **Z**, Jos 15:56

and Jekuthiel the father of Z. 1Ch 4:18
inhabitants of Z repaired the Neh 3:13
Z and Adullam with their Neh 11:30

ZAPHENATH-PANEAH (1)
(AKA JOSEPH)
Joseph the name Z and gave him a Gn 41:45

ZAPHON (2)
Succoth, and Z—the rest of the Jos 13:27
and crossed ⌊the Jordan⌋ to Z. Jdg 12:1

ZAREPHATH (4)
go to Z that belongs to Sidon, 1Kg 17:9
So Elijah got up and went to Z. 1Kg 17:10
as far as Z and the exiles Ob 20
but to a widow at Z in Sidon. Lk 4:26

ZARETHAN (3)
(AKA ZEREDAH)
far as Adam, a city next to Z. Jos 3:16
which is beside Z below Jezreel, 1Kg 4:12
Valley between Succoth and Z. 1Kg 7:46

ZATTU (1)
Pahath-moab, Elam, Z, Bani, Neh 10:14

ZATTU'S (4)
Z descendants 945 Ezr 2:8
of Jahaziel from Z descendants, Ezr 8:5
Z descendants: Elioenai, Ezr 10:27
Z descendants 845 Neh 7:13

ZAZA (1)
sons: Peleth and Z. These were 1Ch 2:33

ZEAL (22)
zealous among them with My z, Nm 25:11
destroy the Israelites in My z. Nm 25:11
kill them in his z for the 2Sm 21:2
me and see my z for the LORD!" 2Kg 10:16
The z of the LORD of Hosts will 2Kg 19:31
because z for Your house has Ps 69:9
Even z is not good without Pr 19:2
The z of the LORD of Hosts will Is 9:7
will see ⌊Your⌋ z for ⌊Your⌋ Is 26:11
The z of the LORD of Hosts will Is 37:32
stirs up His z like a soldier. Is 42:13
Himself in z as in a cloak. Is 59:17
Where is Your z and Your might? Is 63:15
in My burning z I speak against Ezk 36:5
in My burning z because you have Ezk 36:6
I swear in My z and fiery rage: Ezk 38:19
Z for Your house will consume Me. Jn 2:17
them that they have z for God, Rm 10:2
sorrow, your z for me, so that I 2Co 7:7
longing, what z, what justice! 2Co 7:11
and your z has stirred up most 2Co 9:2
as to z, persecuting the church; Php 3:6

ZEALOT (4)
Simon the Z, and Judas Iscariot, Mt 10:4
and Thaddaeus; Simon the Z, Mk 3:18
and Simon called the Z; Lk 6:15
Simon the Z, and Judas the son Ac 1:13

ZEALOUS (8)
because he was z among them Nm 25:11
because he was z for his God and Nm 25:13
have been very z for the LORD 1Kg 19:10
have been very z for the LORD 1Kg 19:14
and they are all z for the law. Ac 21:20
Being z for God, just as all of Ac 22:3
since you are z in matters of 1Co 14:12
I was extremely z for the Gl 1:14

ZEBADIAH (9)
Z, Arad, Eder, 1Ch 8:15
Z, Meshullam, Hizki, Heber, 1Ch 8:17
and Joelah and Z, the sons of 1Ch 12:7
the second, Z the third, 1Ch 26:2
and his son Z ⌊was commander⌋ 1Ch 27:7
Nethaniah, Z, Asahel, 2Ch 17:8
the LORD, and Z son of Ishmael, 2Ch 19:11
Z son of Michael from Ezr 8:8
Hanani and Z from Immer's Ezr 10:20

ZEBAH (11)
I am pursuing Z and Zalmunna, Jdg 8:5
Are Z and Zalmunna now in your Jdg 8:6
LORD has handed Z and Zalmunna Jdg 8:7
Now Z and Zalmunna were in Jdg 8:10
Z and Zalmunna fled, and he Jdg 8:12
said, "Here are Z and Zalmunna. Jdg 8:15
'Are Z and Zalmunna now in your Jdg 8:15
He asked Z and Zalmunna, "What Jdg 8:18
Z and Zalmunna said, "Get up and Jdg 8:21
got up, killed Z and Zalmunna, Jdg 8:21
leaders like Z and Zalmunna, Ps 83:11

ZEBEDEE (8)
the son of Z, and his brother Mt 4:21
in a boat with Z their father, Mt 4:21
James the son of Z, and John his Mt 10:2
Peter and the two sons of Z, Mt 26:37
the son of Z and his brother Mk 1:19
their father Z in the boat with Mk 1:20
and to James the son of Z, Mk 3:17
the sons of Z, approached Him Mk 10:35

ZEBEDEE'S (4)
the mother of Z sons approached Mt 20:20
and the mother of Z sons. Mt 27:56
James and John, Z sons, who were Lk 5:10
Cana of Galilee, Z sons, and two Jn 21:2

ZEBIDAH (1)
mother's name was Z daughter of 2Kg 23:36

ZEBINA (1)
Zabad, Z, Jaddai, Joel, Ezr 10:43

ZEBOIIM (5)
Admah, and Z, as far as Lasha. Gn 10:19
Shemeber king of Z, as well as Gn 14:2
the king of Z, and the king Gn 14:8
Admah and Z, which the LORD Dt 29:23
How can I treat you like Z? Hs 11:8

ZEBOIM (2)
over the valley of Z toward the 1Sm 13:18
Hadid, Z, Neballat, Neh 11:34

ZEBUL (6)
and isn't Z his officer? Jdg 9:28
When Z, the ruler of the city, Jdg 9:30
he said to Z, "Look, people are Jdg 9:36
But Z said to him, "The shadows Jdg 9:36
Z replied, "Where is your Jdg 9:38
Z drove Gaal and his brothers Jdg 9:41

ZEBULUN (42)
six sons," and she named him Z. Gn 30:20
Levi, Judah, Issachar, and Z. Gn 35:23
Z will live by the seashore and Gn 49:13
Issachar, Z, and Benjamin; Ex 1:3
Eliab son of Helon from Z; Nm 1:9
The descendants of Z: Nm 1:30
the tribe of Z numbered 57,400 Nm 1:31
The tribe of Z ⌊will be next⌋. Nm 2:7
the division of the Z tribe. Nm 10:16
son of Sodi from the tribe of Z; Nm 13:10
a leader from the tribe of Z; Nm 34:25
Gad, Asher, Z, Dan, and Naphtali Dt 27:13
He said about Z: Rejoice, Dt 33:18
Rejoice, Z, in your journeys, Dt 33:18
passed Z and the valley of Jos 19:27
Hukkok, reaching Z on the south, Jos 19:34
tribes of Reuben, Gad, and Z. Jos 21:7
the tribe of Z, ⌊they gave⌋ to Jos 21:34
Z failed to drive out the Jdg 1:30
Barak summoned Z and Naphtali to Jdg 4:10
a marshal's staff ⌊came⌋ from Z. Jdg 5:14
Z was a people risking their Jdg 5:18
Asher, Z, and Naphtali, Jdg 6:35
who was from Z, judged Israel Jdg 12:11
in Aijalon in the land of Z. Jdg 12:12
Levi, Judah, Issachar, Z, 1Ch 2:1
and Z according to their 1Ch 6:63
the tribe of Z, ⌊they received⌋ 1Ch 6:77
From Z: 50,000 who could serve 1Ch 12:33
as Issachar, Z, and Naphtali 1Ch 12:40
for Z, Ishmaiah son of Obadiah; 1Ch 27:19
and Manasseh as far as Z, 2Ch 30:10
Z humbled themselves and came 2Ch 30:11
Issachar, and Z—were unclean, 2Ch 30:18
the rulers of Z, the rulers of Ps 68:27
the land of Z and the land Is 9:1
west, will be Z—one ⌊portion⌋ Ezk 48:26
Next to the territory of Z, Ezk 48:27
and one, the gate of Z. Ezk 48:33
in the region of Z and Naphtali. Mt 4:13
Land of Z and land of Naphtali, Mt 4:15
12,000 from the tribe of Z, Rv 7:8

ZEBULUN'S (4)
Z sons: Sered, Elon, and Jahleel. Gn 46:14
Z descendants by their clans: Nm 26:26
lot came up for Z descendants by Jos 19:10
the inheritance of Z descendants Jos 19:16

ZEBULUNITE (1)
were the Z clans ⌊numbered⌋ Nm 26:27

ZEBULUNITES (3)
The leader of the Z is Eliab son Nm 2:7
leader of the Z, ⌊presented Nm 7:24
men from the Naphtalites and Z? Jdg 4:6

ZECHARIAH (53)
His son Z became king in his 2Kg 14:29
Z son of Jeroboam became king 2Kg 15:8
of Jabesh conspired against Z. 2Kg 15:10
name was Abi daughter of Z. 2Kg 18:2
Jeiel the chief, Z, 1Ch 5:7
Z son of Meshelemiah was the 1Ch 9:21
Gedor, Ahio, Z, and Mikloth. 1Ch 9:37
Z, Jaaziel, Shemiramoth, Jehiel, 1Ch 15:18
Z, Aziel, Shemiramoth, Jehiel, 1Ch 15:20
Nethanel, Amasai, Z, Benaiah, 1Ch 15:24
the chief and Z was second to 1Ch 16:5
Isshiah; from Isshiah's sons: Z. 1Ch 24:25
Z the firstborn, Jediael the 1Ch 26:2
the third, and Z the fourth. 1Ch 26:11
also cast lots for his son Z, 1Ch 26:14
in Gilead, Iddo son of Z; 1Ch 27:21
Ben-hail, Obadiah, Z, Nethanel, 2Ch 17:7
son of Z, son of Benaiah 2Ch 20:14
Azariah, Jehiel, Z, Azariah, 2Ch 21:2
control of Z son of Jehoiada 2Ch 24:20
throughout the lifetime of Z, 2Ch 26:5
name was Abijah daughter of Z. 2Ch 29:1
Z and Mattaniah from the 2Ch 29:13
and Z and Meshullam from the 2Ch 34:12
Hilkiah, Z, and Jehiel, leaders 2Ch 35:8
prophets Haggai and Z son of Ezr 5:1
the prophet and Z son of Iddo. Ezr 6:14
Z, from Parosh's descendants, Ezr 8:3
Z son of Bebai from Bebai's Ezr 8:11
Nathan, Z, and Meshullam, Ezr 8:16
Mattaniah, Z, Jehiel, Abdi, Ezr 10:26
Hash-baddanah, Z, and Meshullam. Neh 8:4
Uzziah, son of Z, son of Amariah Neh 11:4
Joiarib, son of Z, a descendant Neh 11:5
Amzi, son of Z, son of Pashhur Neh 11:12
Z of Iddo, Meshullam of Neh 12:16
Z son of Jonathan, son of Neh 12:35
Elioenai, Z, and Hananiah, Neh 12:41
priest and Z son of Jeberechiah. Is 8:2
to the prophet Z son of Zch 1:1
to the prophet Z son of Zch 1:7
the LORD came to Z on the fourth Zch 7:1
The word of the LORD came to Z: Zch 7:8
Abel to the blood of Z, Mt 23:35
of Abijah's division named Z. Lk 1:5
When Z saw him, he was startled Lk 1:12
not be afraid, Z, because your Lk 1:13
Z asked the angel. Lk 1:18
the people were waiting for Z, Lk 1:21
they were going to name him Z, Lk 1:59
his father Z was filled with Lk 1:67
John the son of Z in the Lk 3:2
blood of Abel to the blood of Z, Lk 11:51

ZECHARIAH'S (3)
rest of the events of Z ⌊reign⌋, 2Kg 15:11
kindness that Z father Jehoiada 2Ch 24:22
she entered Z house and greeted Lk 1:40

ZECHER (1)
Gedor, Ahio, Z, 1Ch 8:31

ZEDAD (2)
and the border will reach Z. Nm 34:8
of Hethlon and Lebo-hamath to Z, Ezk 47:15

ZEDEKIAH (61)
(AKA MATTANIAH)
Z son of Chenaanah made iron 1Kg 22:11
Z son of Chenaanah came up, 1Kg 22:24
place and changed his name to Z. 2Kg 24:17
Z was 21 years old when he 2Kg 24:18
Z did what was evil in the 2Kg 24:19
Z rebelled against the king of 2Kg 24:20
the king of Babylon blinded Z, 2Kg 25:7
Jehoiakim second, Z third, and 1Ch 3:15
his sons Jeconiah and Z. 1Ch 3:16
Z son of Chenaanah made iron 2Ch 18:10
Z son of Chenaanah came up, 2Ch 18:23
brother Z king over Judah 2Ch 36:10
Z was 21 years old when he 2Ch 36:11
son of Hacaliah, and Z, Neh 10:1
year of Z son of Josiah, Jr 1:3
LORD when King Z sent Pashhur Jr 21:1
is what you are to say to Z: Jr 21:3
King Z of Judah, his Jr 21:7

will deal with **Z** king of Judah, Jr 24:8
of the reign of **Z** son of Josiah, Jr 27:1
are coming to **Z** king of Judah Jr 27:3
spoke to **Z** king of Judah in the Jr 27:12
of the reign of **Z** king of Judah, Jr 28:1
of Hilkiah whom **Z** king of Judah Jr 29:3
Kolaiah and to **Z** son of Maaseiah Jr 29:21
LORD make you like **Z** and Ahab, Jr 29:22
tenth year of **Z** king of Judah, Jr 32:1
Z king of Judah had imprisoned Jr 32:3
Z king of Judah will not escape Jr 32:4
He will take **Z** to Babylon where Jr 32:5
Go, speak to **Z**, king of Judah, Jr 34:2
LORD's word, **Z**, king of Judah. Jr 34:4
these words to **Z** king of Judah Jr 34:6
after King **Z** made a covenant Jr 34:8
I will hand **Z** king of Judah and Jr 34:21
of Shaphan, **Z** son of Hananiah Jr 36:12
Z son of Josiah reigned as king Jr 37:1
King **Z** sent Jehucal son of Jr 37:3
King **Z** later sent ⌊for him⌋ and Jr 37:17
Then Jeremiah said to King **Z**, Jr 37:18
So King **Z** gave orders, and Jr 37:21
King **Z** said, "Here he is; Jr 38:5
King **Z** sent for Jeremiah the Jr 38:14
replied to **Z**, "If I tell you, Jr 38:15
King **Z** swore to Jeremiah in Jr 38:16
Jeremiah therefore said to **Z**, Jr 38:17
But King **Z** said to Jeremiah, Jr 38:19
Then **Z** warned Jeremiah, "Don't Jr 38:24
ninth year of **Z** king of Judah, Jr 39:1
Z king of Judah and all the Jr 39:4
and overtook **Z** in the plains Jr 39:5
Then he blinded **Z** and put him in Jr 39:7
Judah's King **Z** to Babylon's King Jr 44:30
of the reign of **Z** king of Judah. Jr 49:34
to Babylon with **Z** king of Judah Jr 51:59
Z was 21 years old when he Jr 52:1
Z did what was evil in the Jr 52:2
Z rebelled against the king of Jr 52:3
and overtook **Z** in the plains Jr 52:8
Then he blinded **Z** and bound him Jr 52:11
of Babylon brought **Z** to Babylon, Jr 52:11

ZEDEKIAH'S *(11)*
In the ninth year of **Z** reign, 2Kg 25:1
until King **Z** eleventh year. 2Kg 25:2
Z entire army was scattered from 2Kg 25:5
slaughtered **Z** sons before his 2Kg 25:7
fourth month of **Z** eleventh year, Jr 39:2
slaughtered **Z** sons before his Jr 39:6
in the fourth year of **Z** reign. Jr 51:59
In the ninth year of **Z** reign, Jr 52:4
until King **Z** eleventh year. Jr 52:5
Z entire army was scattered from Jr 52:8
slaughtered **Z** sons before his Jr 52:10

ZEEB *(6)*
Oreb and **Z**, the two princes Jdg 7:25
of Oreb and **Z** at the winepress Jdg 7:25
and Zeeb at the winepress of **Z**, Jdg 7:25
of Oreb and **Z** to Gideon across Jdg 7:25
handed over to you Oreb and **Z**, Jdg 8:3
their nobles like Oreb and **Z**, Ps 83:11

ZELA *(2)*
Z, Haeleph, Jebus (that is, Jos 18:28
son Jonathan at **Z** in the land 2Sm 21:14

ZELEK *(2)*
Z the Ammonite, Naharai the 2Sm 23:37
Z the Ammonite, Naharai the 1Ch 11:39

ZELOPHEHAD *(7)*
Z son of Hepher had no sons— Nm 26:33
The daughters of **Z** approached; Nm 27:1
⌊**Z** was the⌋ son of Hepher, Nm 27:1
daughters of **Z** did as the LORD Nm 36:10
daughters of **Z**, married cousins Nm 36:11
Now **Z** son of Hepher, son of Jos 17:3
Another descendant was named **Z**, 1Ch 7:15

ZELOPHEHAD'S *(4)*
The names of **Z** daughters were Nm 26:33
What **Z** daughters say is correct. Nm 27:7
give our brother **Z** inheritance Nm 36:2
concerning **Z** daughters: Nm 36:6

ZELZAH *(1)*
Rachel's Grave at **Z** in the land 1Sm 10:2

ZEMARAIM *(2)*
Beth-arabah, **Z**, Bethel, Jos 18:22
Then Abijah stood on Mount **Z**, 2Ch 13:4

ZEMARITES *(2)*
the Arvadites, the **Z**, and the Gn 10:18
Arvadites, **Z**, and Hamathites. 1Ch 1:16

ZEMIRAH *(1)*
Z, Joash, Eliezer, Elioenai, 1Ch 7:8

ZENAN *(1)*
Z, Hadashah, Migdal-gad, Jos 15:37

ZENAS *(1)*
Diligently help **Z** the lawyer and Ti 3:13

ZEPHANIAH *(10)*
Z the priest of the second rank, 2Kg 25:18
Joel, son of Azariah, son of **Z**, 1Ch 6:36
and the priest **Z** son of Maaseiah Jr 21:1
to the priest **Z** son of Maaseiah, Jr 29:25
Z the priest read this letter in Jr 29:29
Shelemiah and **Z** son of Maaseiah Jr 37:3
Z the priest of the second rank, Jr 52:24
that came to **Z** son of Cushi, Zph 1:1
to the house of Josiah son of **Z**. Zch 6:10
Jedaiah, and Hen son of **Z**. Zch 6:14

ZEPHATH *(1)*
(AKA HORMAH)
Canaanites who were living in **Z**, Jdg 1:17

ZEPHATHAH *(1)*
in the Valley of **Z** at Mareshah. 2Ch 14:10

ZEPHI *(1)*
Omar, **Z**, Gatam, and Kenaz; 1Ch 1:36

ZEPHO *(2)*
Teman, Omar, **Z**, Gatam, and Gn 36:11
Chiefs Teman, Omar, **Z**, Kenaz, Gn 36:15

ZEPHON *(1)*
the Zephonite clan from **Z**; Nm 26:15

ZEPHONITE *(1)*
the **Z** clan from Zephon; Nm 26:15

ZER *(1)*
were Ziddim, **Z**, Hammath, Rakkath Jos 19:35

ZERAH *(21)*
(AKA ZOHAR)
Nahath, **Z**, Shammah, and Mizzah. Gn 36:13
Chiefs Nahath, **Z**, Shammah, and Gn 36:17
Jobab son of **Z** from Bozrah ruled Gn 36:33
hand, came out, and was named **Z**. Gn 38:30
Er, Onan, Shelah, Perez, and **Z**; Gn 46:12
the Zerahite clan from **Z**; Nm 26:13
the Zerahite clan from **Z**. Nm 26:20
of Zabdi, son of **Z**, of the tribe Jos 7:1
of Zabdi, son of **Z**, of the tribe Jos 7:18
with him took Achan son of **Z**, Jos 7:24
Wasn't Achan son of **Z** unfaithful Jos 22:20
Nahath, **Z**, Shammah, and Mizzah. 1Ch 1:37
Jobab son of **Z** from Bozrah ruled 1Ch 1:44
Tamar bore him Perez and **Z**. 1Ch 2:4
Jamin, Jarib, **Z**, and Shaul; 1Ch 4:24
son Iddo, his son **Z**, and his son 1Ch 6:21
Ethni, son of **Z**, son of Adaiah, 1Ch 6:41
and from the sons of **Z**: 1Ch 9:6
Then **Z** the Cushite came against 2Ch 14:9
descendants of **Z** son of Judah, Neh 11:24
fathered Perez and **Z** by Tamar, Mt 1:3

ZERAH'S *(1)*
Z sons: Zimri, Ethan, Heman, 1Ch 2:6

ZERAHIAH *(4)*
Uzzi fathered **Z**; Zerahiah 1Ch 6:6
Z fathered Meraioth; 1Ch 6:6
Bukki, his son Uzzi, his son **Z**, 1Ch 6:51
Eliehoenai son of **Z** from Ezr 8:4

ZERAHIAH'S *(1)*
Z son, Uzzi's son, Bukki's son, Ezr 7:4

ZERAHITE *(6)*
the **Z** clan from Zerah; Nm 26:13
the **Z** clan from Zerah. Nm 26:20
and the **Z** clan was selected. Jos 7:17
had the **Z** clan come forward by Jos 7:17
Sibbecai the Hushathite, a **Z**; 1Ch 27:11
Maharai the Netophathite, a **Z**; 1Ch 27:13

ZERED *(4)*
went and camped at **Z** Valley. Nm 21:12
get up and cross the **Z** Valley.' Dt 2:13
So we crossed the **Z** Valley. Dt 2:13
we crossed the **Z** Valley was 38 Dt 2:14

ZEREDAH *(2)*
(AKA ZARETHAN)
Nebat, was an Ephraimite from **Z**. 1Kg 11:26
Valley between Succoth and **Z**. 2Ch 4:17

ZERERAH *(1)*
in the direction of **Z** as far as Jdg 7:22

ZERESH *(4)*
and his wife **Z** to join him. Est 5:10
His wife **Z** and all his friends Est 5:14
told his wife **Z** and all his Est 6:13
and his wife **Z** said to him, Est 6:13

ZERETH *(1)*
Z, Zohar, and Ethnan. 1Ch 4:7

ZERETH-SHAHAR *(1)*
Z on the hill in the valley, Jos 13:19

ZERI *(1)*
Gedaliah, **Z**, Jeshaiah, Shimei, 1Ch 25:3

ZEROR *(1)*
Abiel, son of **Z**, son of Becorath 1Sm 9:1

ZERUAH *(1)*
widowed mother's name was **Z**. 1Kg 11:26

ZERUBBABEL *(22)*
Pedaiah's sons: **Z** and Shimei. 1Ch 3:19
They came with **Z**, Jeshua, Ezr 2:2
along with **Z** son of Shealtiel Ezr 3:2
Jerusalem, **Z** son of Shealtiel, Ezr 3:8
approached **Z** and the leaders Ezr 4:2
But **Z**, Jeshua, and the other Ezr 4:3
Z son of Shealtiel and Jeshua Ezr 5:2
They came with **Z**, Jeshua, Neh 7:7
went up with **Z** son of Shealtiel Neh 12:1
in the days of **Z** and Nehemiah, Neh 12:47
the prophet to **Z** son of Hg 1:1
Z son of Shealtiel, the high Hg 1:12
the spirit of **Z** son of Shealtiel Hg 1:14
Speak to **Z** son of Shealtiel, Hg 2:2
so, be strong, **Z**"—the LORD's Hg 2:4
Speak to **Z**, governor of Judah: Hg 2:21
will take you, **Z** son of Hg 2:23
is the word of the LORD to **Z**: Zch 4:6
Z you will become a plain. Zch 4:7
Salathiel, Salathiel fathered **Z**, Mt 1:12
Z fathered Abiud, Abiud fathered Mt 1:13
of Rhesa, ⌊son⌋ of **Z**, ⌊son⌋ of Lk 3:27

ZERUBBABEL'S *(3)*
and Shimei. **Z** sons: Meshullam 1Ch 3:19
Z hands have laid the foundation Zch 4:9
see the plumb line in **Z** hand." Zch 4:10

ZERUIAH *(25)*
Joab's brother Abishai son of **Z**, 1Sm 26:6
So Joab son of **Z** and David's 2Sm 2:13
The three sons of **Z** were there: 2Sm 2:18
the sons of **Z**, are too fierce 2Sm 3:39
Joab son of **Z** was over the army; 2Sm 8:16
Joab son of **Z** observed that the 2Sm 14:1
Abishai son of **Z** said to the 2Sm 16:9
replied, "Sons of **Z**, do we agree 2Sm 16:10
Abigail was a sister to **Z**, 2Sm 17:25
Joab's brother Abishai son of **Z**, 2Sm 18:2
Abishai son of **Z** asked, 2Sm 19:21
answered, "Sons of **Z**, do we 2Sm 19:22
son of **Z** came to his aid, 2Sm 21:17
Joab's brother and son of **Z**, 2Sm 23:18
armor-bearer for Joab son of **Z**, 2Sm 23:37
with Joab son of **Z** and with 1Kg 1:7
what Joab son of **Z** did to me and 1Kg 2:5
priest, and for Joab son of **Z**." 1Kg 2:22
sisters were **Z** and Abigail. 1Ch 2:16
Joab son of **Z** went up first, 1Ch 11:6
armor-bearer for Joab son of **Z**, 1Ch 11:39
Abishai son of **Z** struck down 1Ch 18:12
Joab son of **Z** was over the army; 1Ch 18:15
and Joab son of **Z** had dedicated, 1Ch 26:28
Joab son of **Z** began to count 1Ch 27:24

ZERUIAH'S *(1)*
and Abigail. **Z** three sons: 1Ch 2:16

ZETHAM *(2)*
the first, then **Z**, and Joel— 1Ch 23:8
of Jehieli, **Z** and his brother 1Ch 26:22

ZETHAN *(1)*
Ehud, Chenaanah, **Z**, Tarshish, 1Ch 7:10

ZETHAR *(1)*
Bigtha, Abagtha, **Z**, and Carkas, Est 1:10

ZEUS *(2)*
call Barnabas, **Z**, and Paul, Ac 14:12
the priest of **Z**, whose temple Ac 14:13

ZIA *(1)*
Jorai, Jacan, **Z**, and Eber— 1Ch 5:13

ZIBA *(18)*
of Saul's family named **Z**. 2Sm 9:2
king said to him, "Are you **Z**?" 2Sm 9:2
Z said to the king, "There is 2Sm 9:3
Z answered the king, "You'll 2Sm 9:4
attendant **Z** and said to him 2Sm 9:9
Now **Z** had 15 sons and 20 2Sm 9:10
Z said to the king, "Your 2Sm 9:11
the summit, **Z**, Mephibosheth's 2Sm 16:1
The king said to **Z**, "Why do you 2Sm 16:2
Z answered, "The donkeys are 2Sm 16:2
in Jerusalem," **Z** replied to the 2Sm 16:3
The king said to **Z**, "All that 2Sm 16:4
"I bow ⌊before you⌋," **Z** said. 2Sm 16:4
Z, an attendant from the house 2Sm 19:17
my servant ⌊**Z**⌋ betrayed me. 2Sm 19:26
Z slandered your servant to my 2Sm 19:27
and **Z** are to divide the land. 2Sm 19:29
safely, let **Z** take it all!" 2Sm 19:30

ZIBA'S *(1)*
All those living in **Z** house were 2Sm 9:12

ZIBEON *(6)*
granddaughter of **Z** the Hivite; Gn 36:2
of Anah and granddaughter of **Z**: Gn 36:14
Lotan, Shobal, **Z**, Anah, Gn 36:20
the donkeys of his father **Z**. Gn 36:24
Chiefs Lotan, Shobal, **Z**, Anah, Gn 36:29
Lotan, Shobal, **Z**, Anah, Dishon, 1Ch 1:38

ZIBEON'S *(2)*
These are **Z** sons: Aiah and Anah. Gn 36:24
Shephi, and Onam. **Z** sons: Aiah 1Ch 1:40

ZIBIA *(1)*
Jobab, **Z**, Mesha, Malcam, 1Ch 8:9

ZIBIAH *(2)*
His mother's name was **Z**, who 2Kg 12:1
His mother's name was **Z**; 2Ch 24:1

ZICHRI *(12)*
Korah, Nepheg, and **Z**. Ex 6:21
Jakim, **Z**, Zabdi, 1Ch 8:19
Abdon, **Z**, Hanan, 1Ch 8:23
and **Z** were Jeroham's sons. 1Ch 8:27
of Mica, son of **Z**, son of Asaph; 1Ch 9:15
Joram, his son **Z**, and his son 1Ch 26:25
Eliezer son of **Z** was the chief 1Ch 27:16
Amasiah son of **Z**, the volunteer 2Ch 17:16
Adaiah, and Elishaphat son of **Z**. 2Ch 23:1
warrior named **Z** killed the 2Ch 28:7
Joel son of **Z** was the officer Neh 11:9
Z of Abijah, Piltai of Moadiah, Neh 12:17

ZIDDIM *(1)*
The fortified cities were **Z**, Jos 19:35

ZIHA *(1)*
Z and Gishpa supervised the Neh 11:21

ZIHA'S *(2)*
Z descendants, Hasupha's Ezr 2:43
Z descendants, Hasupha's Neh 7:46

ZIKLAG *(13)*
Z, Madmannah, Sansannah, Jos 15:31
Z, Beth-marcaboth, Hazar-susah, Jos 19:5
That day Achish gave **Z** to him, 1Sm 27:6
men arrived in **Z** on the third 1Sm 30:1
and attacked and burned down **Z**. 1Sm 30:1
Caleb, and we burned down **Z**." 1Sm 30:14
David came to **Z**, he sent some 1Sm 30:26
and stayed at **Z** two days. 2Sm 1:1
him and put him to death at **Z**. 2Sm 4:10
Bethuel, Hormah, **Z**, 1Ch 4:30
came to David at **Z** while he was 1Ch 12:1
When David went to **Z**, some men 1Ch 12:20
in **Z** and Meconah and its Neh 11:28

ZILLAH *(3)*
Adah and the other named **Z**. Gn 4:19
Z bore Tubal-cain, who made all Gn 4:22
Adah and **Z**, hear my voice; Gn 4:23

ZILLETHAI *(2)*
Elienai, **Z**, Eliel, 1Ch 8:20
Jozabad, Elihu, and **Z**, chiefs of 1Ch 12:20

ZILPAH *(7)*
gave his slave **Z** to his daughter Gn 29:24
took her slave **Z** and gave her to Gn 30:9
Leah's slave **Z** bore Jacob a son. Gn 30:10
When Leah's slave **Z** bore Jacob a Gn 30:12
of Leah's slave **Z** were Gad and Gn 35:26
with the sons of Bilhah and **Z**, Gn 37:2
These were the sons of **Z**— Gn 46:18

ZIMMAH *(3)*
his son Jahath, his son **Z**, 1Ch 6:20
Ethan, son of **Z**, son of Shimei, 1Ch 6:42
Joah son of **Z** and Eden son of 2Ch 29:12

ZIMRAN *(2)*
she bore him **Z**, Jokshan, Medan Gn 25:2
Z, Jokshan, Medan, Midian, 1Ch 1:32

ZIMRI *(16)*
woman, was **Z** son of Salu, Nm 25:14
His servant **Z**, commander of half 1Kg 16:9
King Asa, **Z** went in, struck 1Kg 16:10
Then **Z** became king in his place. 1Kg 16:10
Z struck down the entire house 1Kg 16:11
So **Z** exterminated the entire 1Kg 16:12
Z became king for seven days in 1Kg 16:15
troops heard that **Z** had not only 1Kg 16:16
When **Z** saw that the city was 1Kg 16:18
in⌋ peace, **Z**, killer of your 2Kg 9:31
Z, Ethan, Heman, Calcol, and 1Ch 2:6
Azmaveth, and **Z**, and Zimri 1Ch 8:36
and Zimri, and **Z** fathered Moza. 1Ch 8:36
Alemeth, Azmaveth, and **Z**; 1Ch 9:42
and Zimri; **Z** fathered Moza. 1Ch 9:42
the kings of **Z**, all the kings Jr 25:25

ZIMRI'S *(1)*
rest of the events of **Z** ⌊reign⌋, 1Kg 16:20

ZIN *(10)*
(AKA KADESH)
Wilderness of **Z** as far as Rehob Nm 13:21
the Wilderness of **Z** in the first Nm 20:1
in the Wilderness of **Z**, Nm 27:14
Kadesh in the Wilderness of **Z**. Nm 27:14
camped in the Wilderness of **Z** Nm 33:36
the Wilderness of **Z** along the Nm 34:3
proceed to **Z**, and end south Nm 34:4
the Wilderness of **Z** by failing Dt 32:51
wilderness of **Z** to the border Jos 15:1
proceeded to **Z**, ascended to the Jos 15:3

ZION *(161)*
(AKA JEBUS, JERUSALEM)
did capture the stronghold of **Z**, 2Sm 5:7
of the LORD's covenant from **Z**, 1Kg 8:1
woman, Daughter **Z**, despises you 2Kg 19:21
and survivors from Mount **Z**. 2Kg 19:31
did capture the stronghold of **Z** 1Ch 11:5
the city of David, that is, **Z**. 2Ch 5:2
I have consecrated My King on **Z**, Ps 2:6
to the LORD, who dwells in **Z**; Ps 9:11
within the gates of Daughter **Z**. Ps 9:14
deliverance would come from **Z**! Ps 14:7
and sustain you from **Z**. Ps 20:2
Mount **Z** on the slopes of the Ps 48:2
Mount **Z** is glad. The towns of Ps 48:11
Go around **Z**, encircle it; Ps 48:12
Z, the perfection of beauty, Ps 50:2
pleasure, cause **Z** to prosper; Ps 51:18
deliverance would come from **Z**! Ps 53:6
is rightfully Yours, God, in **Z**; Ps 65:1
for God will save **Z** and build up Ps 69:35
Mount **Z** where You dwell Ps 74:2
Salem, His dwelling place in **Z**. Ps 76:2
Judah, Mount **Z**, which He loved Ps 78:68
each appears before God in **Z**. Ps 84:7
the gates of **Z** more than all Ps 87:2
And it will be said of **Z**, Ps 87:5
Z hears and is glad, and the Ps 97:8
The LORD is great in **Z**; Ps 99:2
arise and have compassion on **Z**, Ps 102:13
for the LORD will rebuild **Z**; Ps 102:16
of the LORD in **Z** and His praise Ps 102:21
Your mighty scepter from **Z**. Ps 110:2
in the LORD are like Mount **Z**. Ps 125:1
LORD restored the fortunes of **Z**, Ps 126:1
May the LORD bless you from **Z**, Ps 128:5
all who hate **Z** be driven back Ps 129:5
For the LORD has chosen **Z**; Ps 132:13
falling on the mountains of **Z**. Ps 133:3
and earth, bless you from **Z**. Ps 134:3
May the LORD be praised from **Z**; Ps 135:21
and wept when we remembered **Z**. Ps 137:1
"Sing us one of the songs of **Z**." Ps 137:3
Z, your God ⌊reigns⌋ for all Ps 146:10
Jerusalem; praise your God, **Z**! Ps 147:12
the children of **Z** rejoice in Ps 149:2
young women of **Z**, and gaze at Sg 3:11
Daughter **Z** is abandoned like a Is 1:8
Z will be redeemed by justice, Is 1:27
will go out of **Z** and the word of Is 2:3
the daughters of **Z** are haughty, Is 3:16
the heads of the daughters of **Z**, Is 3:17
remains in **Z** and whoever is Is 4:3
the daughters of **Z** and cleansed Is 4:4
site of Mount **Z** and over its Is 4:5
of Hosts who dwells on Mount **Z**. Is 8:18
against Mount **Z** and Jerusalem, Is 10:12
My people who dwell in **Z**, Is 10:24
at the mountain of Daughter **Z**, Is 10:32
sing, citizen of **Z**, for the Holy Is 12:6
LORD has founded **Z**, and His Is 14:32
to the mountain of Daughter **Z**. Is 16:1
rivers—to Mount **Z**, the place Is 18:7
as king on Mount **Z** in Jerusalem, Is 24:23
a stone in **Z**, a tested stone Is 28:16
go to battle against Mount **Z**. Is 29:8
will live on **Z** in Jerusalem Is 30:19
fight on Mount **Z** and on its hill Is 31:4
whose fire is in **Z** and whose Is 31:9
He has filled **Z** with justice and Is 33:5
The sinners in **Z** are afraid; Is 33:14
Look at **Z**, the city of our Is 33:20
for its hostility against **Z**. Is 34:8
and come to **Z** with singing, Is 35:10
woman, Daughter **Z**, despises you Is 37:22
and survivors from Mount **Z**. Is 37:32
Z, herald of good news, go up on Is 40:9
I was the first to say to **Z**: Is 41:27
I will put salvation in **Z**, Is 46:13
Z says, "The LORD has abandoned Is 49:14
For the LORD will comfort **Z**; Is 51:3
and come to **Z** with singing, Is 51:11
and to say to **Z**, "You are My Is 51:16
put on your strength, **Z**! Is 52:1
your neck, captive Daughter **Z**." Is 52:2
says to **Z**, "Your God reigns!" Is 52:7
see when the LORD returns to **Z**. Is 52:8
The Redeemer will come to **Z**, Is 59:20
Z of the Holy One of Israel. Is 60:14
for those who mourn in **Z**; Is 61:3
not keep silent because of **Z**, Is 62:1
the earth, "Say to Daughter **Z**: Is 62:11
Z has become a wilderness, Is 64:10
Before **Z** was in labor, she gave Is 66:7
Yet as soon as **Z** was in labor, Is 66:8
and I will bring you to **Z**. Jr 3:14
Lift up a signal flag toward **Z**. Jr 4:6
cry of Daughter **Z** gasping for Jr 4:31
I will destroy Daughter **Z**. Jr 6:2
against you, Daughter **Z**. Jr 6:23
Is the LORD no longer in **Z**, Jr 8:19
of lamentation is heard from **Z**: Jr 9:19
Do You detest **Z**? Why do You Jr 14:19
Z will be plowed like a field, Jr 26:18
that **Z** no one cares about. Jr 30:17
let's go up to **Z**, to the LORD Jr 31:6
for joy on the heights of **Z**; Jr 31:12
ask about **Z**, ⌊turning⌋ their Jr 50:5
announcing in **Z** the vengeance Jr 50:28
let's tell in **Z** what the LORD Jr 51:10
have done in **Z** before your very Jr 51:24
says the inhabitant of **Z**; Jr 51:35
The roads to **Z** mourn, for no one Lm 1:4
has vanished from Daughter **Z**. Lm 1:6
Z stretches out her hands; Lm 1:17
Daughter **Z** with His anger! Lm 2:1
fire on the tent of Daughter **Z**. Lm 2:4
festivals and Sabbaths in **Z**. Lm 2:6
destroy the wall of Daughter **Z**. Lm 2:8
of Daughter **Z** sit on the ground Lm 2:10
console you, Virgin Daughter **Z**? Lm 2:13
Wall of Daughter **Z**, let ⌊your⌋ Lm 2:18
He has ignited a fire in **Z**, Lm 4:11
Daughter **Z**, your punishment is Lm 4:22
Women are raped in **Z**, virgins in Lm 5:11
because of Mount **Z**, which lies Lm 5:18
the horn in **Z**; sound the alarm Jl 2:1
Blow the horn in **Z**! Announce a Jl 2:15
Children of **Z**, rejoice and be Jl 2:23
those on Mount **Z** and in Jl 2:32
will roar from **Z** and raise His Jl 3:16
who dwells in **Z**, My holy Jl 3:17
for the LORD dwells in **Z**. Jl 3:21
LORD roars from **Z** and raises His Am 1:2
at ease in **Z** and to those who Am 6:1
be a deliverance on Mount **Z**, Ob 17
will ascend Mount **Z** to rule over Ob 21

beginning of sin for Daughter **Z**, Mc 1:13
who build **Z** with bloodshed and Mc 3:10
Z will be plowed like a field, Mc 3:12
will go out of **Z** and the word of Mc 4:2
them in Mount **Z** from this time Mc 4:7
fortified hill of Daughter **Z**, Mc 4:8
out, Daughter **Z**, like a woman Mc 4:10
and let us feast our eyes on **Z**." Mc 4:11
Daughter **Z**, for I will make Mc 4:13
Sing for joy, Daughter **Z**; Zph 3:14
Z, do not let your hands grow Zph 3:16
jealous for Jerusalem and **Z**. Zch 1:14
more comfort **Z** and again choose Zch 1:17
Go, **Z**! Escape, you who are Zch 2:7
Daughter **Z**, shout for joy and be Zch 2:10
I am extremely jealous for **Z**; Zch 8:2
I will return to **Z** and live in Zch 8:3
Rejoice greatly, Daughter **Z**! Zch 9:9
rouse your sons, **Z**, against your Zch 9:13
Tell Daughter **Z**, "See, your King Mt 21:5
Fear no more, Daughter **Z**; Jn 12:15
a stone in **Z** to stumble over, Rm 9:33
The Liberator will come from **Z**; Rm 11:26
come to Mount **Z**, to the city Heb 12:22
I lay a stone in **Z**, a chosen and 1Pt 2:6
there on Mount **Z** stood the Lamb, Rv 14:1

ZION'S *(4)*
and down go **Z** dignitaries, Is 5:14
fear of the LORD is **Z** treasure. Is 33:6
Z gates have fallen to the Lm 2:9
Z precious people—⌊once⌋ worth Lm 4:2

ZIOR *(1)*
Hebron), and **Z**—nine cities, Jos 15:54

ZIPH *(9)*
Z, Telem, Bealoth, Jos 15:24
Maon, Carmel, **Z**, Juttah, Jos 15:55
country of the Wilderness of **Z**. 1Sm 23:14
Wilderness of **Z** in Horesh when 1Sm 23:15
So they went to **Z** ahead of Saul. 1Sm 23:24
Wilderness of **Z** to search for 1Sm 26:2
fathered **Z**, and Mareshah, his 1Ch 2:42
Z, Ziphah, Tiria, and Asarel. 1Ch 4:16
Gath, Mareshah, **Z**, 2Ch 11:8

ZIPHAH *(1)*
Ziph, **Z**, Tiria, and Asarel. 1Ch 4:16

ZIPHION *(1)*
Z, Haggi, Shuni, Ezbon, Eri, Gn 46:16

ZIPHITES *(2)*
Z came up to Saul at Gibeah 1Sm 23:19
the **Z** came to Saul at Gibeah 1Sm 26:1

ZIPHRON *(1)*
border will go to **Z** and end at Nm 34:9

ZIPPOR *(7)*
Now Balak son of **Z** saw all that Nm 22:2
Balak son of **Z** was Moab's king Nm 22:4
Balak son of **Z**, king of Moab, Nm 22:10
is what Balak son of **Z** says: Nm 22:16
son of **Z**, pay attention to what Nm 23:18
Balak son of **Z**, king of Moab, Jos 24:9
any better than Balak son of **Z**, Jdg 11:25

ZIPPORAH *(3)*
he gave his daughter **Z** to Moses Ex 2:21
So **Z** took a flint, cut off her Ex 4:25
had taken in **Z**, Moses' wife, Ex 18:2

ZITHER *(4)*
the horn, flute, **z**, lyre, harp, Dn 3:5
the horn, flute, **z**, lyre, harp, Dn 3:7
the horn, flute, **z**, lyre, harp, Dn 3:10
the horn, flute, **z**, lyre, harp, Dn 3:15

ZIV *(2)*
second month, in the month of **Z**. 1Kg 6:1
fourth year in the month of **Z**. 1Kg 6:37

ZIZ *(1)*
them coming up the ascent of **Z**, 2Ch 20:16

ZIZA *(2)*
and **Z** son of Shiphi, son of 1Ch 4:37
Abijah, Attai, **Z**, and Shelomith. 2Ch 11:20

ZIZAH *(2)*
Jahath, **Z**, Jeush, and Beriah. 1Ch 23:10
the first and **Z** was the second; 1Ch 23:11

ZOAN *(7)*
seven years before **Z** in Egypt. Nm 13:22
land of Egypt, the region of **Z**. Ps 78:12
His marvels in the region of **Z**. Ps 78:43
The princes of **Z** are complete Is 19:11
princes of **Z** have been fools; Is 19:13
princes are at **Z** and his Is 30:4
set fire to **Z**, and execute Ezk 30:14

ZOAR *(10)*
(AKA BELA)
as far as **Z** was well-watered Gn 13:10
the king of Bela (that is, **Z**). Gn 14:2
Bela (that is, **Z**) went out and Gn 14:8
the name of the city is **Z**. Gn 19:22
the land when Lot reached **Z**. Gn 19:23
Lot departed from **Z** and lived in Gn 19:30
he was afraid to live in **Z**. Gn 19:30
the City of Palms, as far as **Z**. Dt 34:3
fugitives ⌊flee⌋ as far as **Z**, Is 15:5
from **Z** to Horonaim ⌊and⌋ Jr 48:34

ZOBAH *(12)*
Edom, the kings of **Z**, and the 1Sm 14:47
of Rehob, king of **Z**, who went to 2Sm 8:3
to assist King Hadadezer of **Z**, 2Sm 8:5
son of Rehob, king of **Z**. 2Sm 8:12
Arameans of Beth-rehob and **Z**, 2Sm 10:6
the Arameans of **Z** and Rehob and 2Sm 10:8
Igal son of Nathan from **Z**, 2Sm 23:36
his master Hadadezer king of **Z** 1Kg 11:23
Hadadezer of **Z** at Hamath when he 1Ch 18:3
to assist King Hadadezer of **Z**, 1Ch 18:5
army of King Hadadezer of **Z**, 1Ch 18:9
Aram-maacah, and **Z**. 1Ch 19:6

ZOBAITES *(1)*
party when David killed the **Z**. 1Kg 11:24

ZOBEBAH *(1)*
fathered Anub, **Z**, and the 1Ch 4:8

ZOHAR *(5)*
(AKA IZHAR, ZERAH)
ask Ephron son of **Z** on my behalf Gn 23:8
of Ephron son of **Z** the Hittite. Gn 25:9
Ohad, Jachin, **Z**, and Shaul, the Gn 46:10
Ohad, Jachin, **Z**, and Shaul, the Ex 6:15
Zereth, **Z**, and Ethnan. 1Ch 4:7

ZOHELETH *(1)*
cattle near the stone of **Z**, 1Kg 1:9

ZOHETH *(1)*
Ishi's sons: **Z** and Ben-zoheth. 1Ch 4:20

ZOPHAH *(1)*
Z, Imna, Shelesh, and Amal. 1Ch 7:35

ZOPHAH'S *(1)*
Z sons: Suah, Harnepher, Shual, 1Ch 7:36

ZOPHAI *(1)*
his son **Z**, his son Nahath 1Ch 6:26

ZOPHAR *(4)*
Shuhite, and **Z** the Naamathite Jb 2:11
Then **Z** the Naamathite replied: Jb 11:1
Then **Z** the Naamathite replied: Jb 20:1
Z the Naamathite went and did Jb 42:9

ZORAH *(10)*
foothills: Eshtaol, **Z**, Ashnah, Jos 15:33
of their inheritance included **Z**, Jos 19:41
There was a certain man from **Z**, Jdg 13:2
of Dan, between **Z** and Eshtaol. Jdg 13:25
buried him between **Z** and Eshtaol Jdg 16:31
clans, from **Z** and Eshtaol, to Jdg 18:2
to their clans at **Z** and Eshtaol, Jdg 18:8
departed from **Z** and Eshtaol Jdg 18:11
Z, Aijalon, and Hebron, which 2Ch 11:10
in En-rimmon, **Z**, Jarmuth, and Neh 11:29

ZORATHITES *(2)*
The **Z** and Eshtaolites descended 1Ch 2:53
were the families of the **Z**. 1Ch 4:2

ZORITES *(1)*
half of the Manahathites, the **Z**, 1Ch 2:54

ZUAR *(5)*
Nethanel son of **Z** from Issachar; Nm 1:8
is Nethanel son of **Z**. Nm 2:5
second day Nethanel son of **Z**, Nm 7:18
offering of Nethanel son of **Z**. Nm 7:23
Nethanel son of **Z** was over the Nm 10:15

ZUPH *(3)*
Tohu, son of **Z**, an Ephraimite. 1Sm 1:1
When they came to the land of **Z**, 1Sm 9:5
son of **Z**, son of Elkanah, son of 1Ch 6:35

ZUR *(5)*
the daughter of **Z**, a tribal head Nm 25:15
Evi, Rekem, **Z**, Hur, and Reba, Nm 31:8
Evi, Rekem, **Z**, Hur, and Reba— Jos 13:21
son, then **Z**, Kish, Baal, Nadab 1Ch 8:30
son, then **Z**, Kish, Baal, Ner, 1Ch 9:36

ZURIEL *(1)*
clans was **Z** son of Abihail; Nm 3:35

ZURISHADDAI *(5)*
Shelumiel son of **Z** from Simeon; Nm 1:6
is Shelumiel son of **Z**. Nm 2:12
fifth day Shelumiel son of **Z**, Nm 7:36
offering of Shelumiel son of **Z**. Nm 7:41
Shelumiel son of **Z** was over the Nm 10:19

ZUZIM *(1)*
(AKA REPHAIM, ZAMZUMMIM)
the **Z** in Ham, the Emim Gn 14:5

Numbers

10 *(138)*
in the land of Canaan **10** years. Gn 16:3
Suppose **10** are found there?" Gn 18:32
destroy ⌊it⌋ on account of **10**." Gn 18:32
servant took **10** of his master's Gn 24:10
weighing **10** shekels of gold. Gn 24:22
stay with us for about **10** days. Gn 24:55
and changed my wages **10** times. Gn 31:7
have changed my wages **10** times! Gn 31:41
young, 40 cows, **10** bulls, 20 Gn 32:15
donkeys, and **10** male donkeys. Gn 32:15
So **10** of Joseph's brothers went Gn 42:3
10 donkeys carrying the best Gn 45:23
and **10** female donkeys carrying Gn 45:23
itself with **10** curtains. Ex 26:1
including their **10** posts and 10 Ex 27:12
their 10 posts and **10** bases. Ex 27:12
the tabernacle with **10** curtains. Ex 36:8
including their **10** posts and 10 Ex 38:12
their 10 posts and **10** bases. Ex 38:12
10 women will bake your bread in Lv 26:26
and for a female **10** shekels. Lv 27:5
for a male and **10** shekels for a Lv 27:7
five days, or **10** days, or 20 Nm 11:19
tested Me these **10** times and did Nm 14:22
fourth day ⌊present⌋ **10** bulls, Nm 29:23
and Timnah—**10** cities, with Jos 15:57
10 tracts fell to Manasseh, Jos 17:5
Kohath received **10** cities by lot Jos 21:5
All **10** cities with their Jos 21:26
⌊They sent⌋ **10** leaders with him— Jos 22:14
So Gideon took **10** of his male Jdg 6:27
He judged Israel **10** years, Jdg 12:11
We will take **10** men out of every Jdg 20:10
lived in Moab about **10** years, Ru 1:4
Then Boaz took **10** men of the Ru 4:2
not better to you than **10** sons?" 1Sm 1:8
take these **10** portions of cheese 1Sm 17:18
so David sent **10** young men 1Sm 25:5
About **10** days later, the LORD 1Sm 25:38
he left behind **10** concubines to 2Sm 15:16
have given you **10** silver pieces 2Sm 18:11
10 young men who were Joab's 2Sm 18:15
We have **10** shares in the king, 2Sm 19:43
he took the **10** concubines he had 2Sm 20:3
10 fattened oxen, 20 range oxen, 1Kg 4:23
the third was **10** and a half feet 1Kg 6:6
the brim, **10** every half yard 1Kg 7:24
Then he made **10** bronze water 1Kg 7:27
way he made the **10** water carts 1Kg 7:37
Then he made **10** bronze basins— 1Kg 7:38
for each of the **10** water carts. 1Kg 7:38
10 water carts; the 10 basins 1Kg 7:43
10 basins on the water carts; 1Kg 7:43
Take **10** pieces for yourself, 1Kg 11:31
I will give you **10** tribes, 1Kg 11:31
I will take **10** tribes of the 1Kg 11:35
with you **10** loaves of bread, 1Kg 14:3
and **10** changes of clothes. 2Kg 5:5
50 horsemen, **10** chariots, and 2Kg 13:7
⌊he reigned⌋ **10** years in Samaria. 2Kg 15:17
shadow go ahead **10** steps or go 2Kg 20:9
10 steps or go back **10** steps?" 2Kg 20:9
the shadow to lengthen **10** steps. 2Kg 20:10
the shadow go back **10** steps." 2Kg 20:10
shadow back the **10** steps it had 2Kg 20:11
came with **10** men and struck 2Kg 25:25
10 towns from the half tribe of 1Ch 6:61
encircling it, **10** every half 2Ch 4:3
made **10** basins for washing and 2Ch 4:6
He made the **10** gold lampstands 2Ch 4:7

made **10** tables and placed them — 2Ch 4:8
experienced peace for **10** years. — 2Ch 14:1
three months and **10** days in — 2Ch 36:9
Hashabiah, and **10** of their — Ezr 8:24
was ⌊provided⌋ every **10** days. — Neh 5:18
killed these **10** sons of Haman — Est 9:10
including Haman's **10** sons. — Est 9:12
of⌋ Haman's **10** sons be hung — Est 9:13
the bodies of⌋ Haman's **10** sons. — Est 9:14
10 bushels of seed will yield — Is 5:10
stairway return by **10** steps." — Is 38:8
went back the **10** steps it had — Is 38:8
came with **10** men to Gedaliah son — Jr 41:1
and the **10** men who were with — Jr 41:2
there were **10** men among them who — Jr 41:8
Now at the end of **10** days, — Jr 42:7
it was about **10** feet, and its — Ezk 40:5
it was **10** feet deep—the first — Ezk 40:6
threshold was **10** feet deep. — Ezk 40:6
was about **10** feet long and 10 — Ezk 40:7
10 feet long and **10** feet deep, — Ezk 40:7
portico was about **10** feet. — Ezk 40:7
side were **10** and a half feet — Ezk 40:12
and **10** steps led up to it. — Ezk 40:49
pilaster was **10** and a half feet — Ezk 41:1
entrance was **10** and a half feet — Ezk 41:3
was **10** and a half feet ⌊thick⌋ — Ezk 41:5
rooms was **10** and a half feet — Ezk 41:8
all around it is **10** and a half — Ezk 43:17
cor equals⌋ **10** liquid measures — Ezk 45:14
since **10** liquid measures equal — Ezk 45:14
test your servants for **10** days. — Dn 1:12
and tested them for **10** days. — Dn 1:14
the end of **10** days they looked — Dn 1:15
he found them **10** times better — Dn 1:20
before it, and it had **10** horns. — Dn 7:7
know⌋ about the **10** horns on its — Dn 7:20
The **10** horns are 10 kings who — Dn 7:24
10 horns are **10** kings who will — Dn 7:24
if there are **10** men left in one — Am 6:9
it ⌊only⌋ amounted to **10**; — Hg 2:16
10 men from nations of every — Zch 8:23
the payments⌋ of **10** percent — Mal 3:8
Bring the full **10** percent into — Mal 3:10
When the **10** ⌊disciples⌋ heard — Mt 20:24
will be like **10** virgins who took — Mt 25:1
to the one who has **10** talents. — Mt 25:28
When the ⌊other⌋ **10** ⌊disciples⌋ — Mk 10:41
woman who has **10** silver coins, — Lk 15:8
10 men with serious skin — Lk 17:12
said, "Were not **10** cleansed? — Lk 17:17
He called **10** of his slaves, — Lk 19:13
gave them **10** minas, and told — Lk 19:13
mina has earned **10** more minas.' — Lk 19:16
have authority over **10** towns.' — Lk 19:17
it to the one who has **10** minas.' — Lk 19:24
him, 'Master, he has **10** minas.' — Lk 19:25
It was about **10** in the morning. — Jn 1:39
eight or **10** days among them, — Ac 25:6
have tribulation for **10** days. — Rv 2:10
having seven heads and **10** horns, — Rv 12:3
He had **10** horns and seven heads. — Rv 13:1
On his horns were **10** diadems, — Rv 13:1
having seven heads and **10** horns. — Rv 17:3
seven heads and the **10** horns, — Rv 17:7
10 horns you saw are 10 kings — Rv 17:12
you saw are **10** kings who have — Rv 17:12
The **10** horns you saw, and the — Rv 17:16

11 *(16)*

slaves, and his **11** sons, and — Gn 32:22
11 stars were bowing down to me. — Gn 37:9
make **11** of these curtains. — Ex 26:7
All **11** curtains are to have the — Ex 26:8
he also made **11** of them. — Ex 36:14
All **11** curtains had the same — Ex 36:15
third day ⌊present⌋ **11** bulls, — Nm 29:20
and Giloh—**11** cities, with — Jos 15:51
of Judah **11** tons of silver — 2Kg 18:14
reigned **11** years in Jerusalem. — 2Kg 23:36
reigned **11** years in Jerusalem. — 2Kg 24:18
reigned **11** years in Jerusalem. — 2Ch 36:5
reigned **11** years in Jerusalem. — 2Ch 36:11
reigned **11** years in Jerusalem. — Jr 52:1
The **11** disciples traveled to — Mt 28:16
numbered with the **11** apostles. — Ac 1:26

12 *(131)*

to Chedorlaomer for **12** years, — Gn 14:4
will father **12** tribal leaders, — Gn 17:20
12 leaders of their clans. — Gn 25:16
about it. Jacob had **12** sons: — Gn 35:22
servants, were **12** brothers, the — Gn 42:13
We were **12** brothers, sons of the — Gn 42:32
of Israel, **12** in all, and this — Gn 49:28
there were **12** springs of water — Ex 15:27
up an altar and **12** pillars for — Ex 24:4
pillars for the **12** tribes of — Ex 24:4
The **12** stones are to correspond — Ex 28:21
of the names of the **12** tribes. — Ex 28:21
12 and a half pounds of liquid — Ex 30:23
12 and a half pounds of cassia — Ex 30:24
12 stones corresponded to the — Ex 39:14
of the names of the **12** tribes. — Ex 39:14
and bake it into **12** loaves; — Lv 24:5
of⌋ the **12** leaders of Israel — Nm 1:44
six covered carts and **12** oxen, — Nm 7:3
12 silver dishes, 12 silver — Nm 7:84
silver dishes, **12** silver basins, — Nm 7:84
basins, and **12** gold bowls. — Nm 7:84
12 gold bowls full of incense — Nm 7:86
burnt offering totaled **12** bulls, — Nm 7:87
12 bulls, **12** rams, and 12 male — Nm 7:87
and **12** male lambs a year old, — Nm 7:87
and **12** male goats for the sin — Nm 7:87
12 staffs from all the leaders — Nm 17:2
houses, **12** staffs ⌊in all⌋. — Nm 17:6
day ⌊present⌋ **12** young bulls, — Nm 29:17
There were **12** springs of water — Nm 33:9
so I selected **12** men from among — Dt 1:23
choose **12** men from the tribes — Jos 3:12
Choose **12** men from the people, — Jos 4:2
'Take **12** stones from this place — Jos 4:3
summoned the **12** men selected — Jos 4:4
The **12** men took stones from the — Jos 4:8
Joshua also set up **12** stones in — Jos 4:9
in Gilgal the **12** stones they had — Jos 4:20
Ophni, and Geba—**12** cities, — Jos 18:24
and Bethlehem—**12** cities, with — Jos 19:15
received **12** cities for their — Jos 21:7
All **12** cities were allotted to — Jos 21:40
cut her into **12** pieces, limb by — Jdg 19:29
12 for Benjamin and Ish-bosheth — 2Sm 2:15
and **12** from David's soldiers. — 2Sm 2:15
Solomon had **12** deputies for all — 1Kg 4:7
costly stones **12** and 15 feet — 1Kg 7:10
stood on **12** oxen, three facing — 1Kg 7:25
the **12** oxen underneath the — 1Kg 7:44
had on, tore it into **12** pieces, — 1Kg 11:30
he reigned⌋ **12** years. He reigned — 1Kg 16:23
took **12** stones—according — 1Kg 18:31
he reigned **12** years. — 2Kg 3:1
a shekel and **12** quarts of barley — 2Kg 7:1
a shekel and **12** quarts of barley — 2Kg 7:16
tomorrow **12** quarts of barley — 2Kg 7:18
Manasseh was **12** years old when — 2Kg 21:1
assigned⌋ by lot **12** towns from — 1Ch 6:63
12⌋ ⌊to⌋ Gedaliah the second: — 1Ch 25:9
his brothers, and his sons—**12** — 1Ch 25:9
his sons, and his brothers—**12** — 1Ch 25:10
his sons, and his brothers—**12** — 1Ch 25:11
his sons, and his brothers—**12** — 1Ch 25:12
his sons, and his brothers—**12** — 1Ch 25:13
his sons, and his brothers—**12** — 1Ch 25:14
his sons, and his brothers—**12** — 1Ch 25:15
his sons, and his brothers—**12** — 1Ch 25:16
his sons, and his brothers—**12** — 1Ch 25:17
his sons, and his brothers—**12** — 1Ch 25:18
his sons, and his brothers—**12** — 1Ch 25:19
his sons, and his brothers—**12** — 1Ch 25:20
his sons, and his brothers—**12** — 1Ch 25:21
his sons, and his brothers—**12** — 1Ch 25:22
his sons, and his brothers—**12** — 1Ch 25:23
his sons, and his brothers—**12** — 1Ch 25:24
his sons, and his brothers—**12** — 1Ch 25:25
his sons, and his brothers—**12** — 1Ch 25:26
his sons, and his brothers—**12** — 1Ch 25:27
his sons, and his brothers—**12** — 1Ch 25:28
his sons, and his brothers—**12** — 1Ch 25:29
his sons, and his brothers—**12** — 1Ch 25:30
his sons, and his brothers—**12**. — 1Ch 25:31
stood on **12** oxen, three facing — 2Ch 4:4
and the **12** oxen underneath — 2Ch 4:15
Manasseh was **12** years old when — 2Ch 33:1
well as **12** male goats as a sin — Ezr 6:17
I selected **12** of the leading — Ezr 8:24
12 bulls for all Israel, 96 rams, — Ezr 8:35
along with **12** male goats as a — Ezr 8:35
year, **12** years—I and my — Neh 5:14
the **12** bronze bulls under the — Jr 52:20
each side was **12** and a quarter — Ezk 41:3
for the **12** tribes of Israel. — Ezk 47:13
At the end of **12** months, as he — Dn 4:29
bleeding for **12** years approached — Mt 9:20
Summoning His **12** disciples, — Mt 10:1
the names of the **12** apostles: — Mt 10:2
sent out these **12** after giving — Mt 10:5
orders to His **12** disciples, — Mt 11:1
they picked up **12** baskets full — Mt 14:20
Me will also sit on **12** thrones, — Mt 19:28
judging the **12** tribes of Israel. — Mt 19:28
took the **12** disciples aside — Mt 20:17
with more than **12** legions of — Mt 26:53
appointed **12**—He also named — Mk 3:14
from bleeding for **12** years — Mk 5:25
walk. (She was **12** years old.) At — Mk 5:42
they picked up **12** baskets full — Mk 6:43
When He was **12** years old, they — Lk 2:42
He chose **12** of them—He also — Lk 6:13
daughter about **12** years old, — Lk 8:42
from bleeding for **12** years, — Lk 8:43
they picked up **12** baskets of — Lk 9:17
judging the **12** tribes of Israel. — Lk 22:30
them and filled **12** baskets with — Jn 6:13
"Aren't there **12** hours in a day?" — Jn 11:9
Jacob with the **12** patriarchs. — Ac 7:8
there were about **12** men in all. — Ac 19:7
is no more than **12** days since I — Ac 24:11
promise⌋ our **12** tribes hope to — Ac 26:7
To the **12** tribes in the — Jms 1:1
and a crown of **12** stars on her — Rv 12:1
high wall, with **12** gates. — Rv 21:12
names of the **12** tribes of the — Rv 21:12
city wall had **12** foundations, — Rv 21:14
on them were the **12** names of the — Rv 21:14
names of the Lamb's **12** apostles. — Rv 21:14
The **12** gates are 12 pearls; — Rv 21:21
The 12 gates are **12** pearls; — Rv 21:21
life bearing **12** kinds of fruit — Rv 22:2

13 *(13)*

Ishmael was **13** years old when — Gn 17:25
13 young bulls, two rams, and 14 — Nm 29:13
with each of the **13** bulls, — Nm 29:14
is **13** feet six inches long and — Dt 3:11
and Sharuhen—**13** cities, with — Jos 19:6
priest received **13** cities by lot — Jos 21:4
received **13** cities by lot — Jos 21:6
All **13** cities with their — Jos 21:19
All **13** cities with their — Jos 21:33
palace-complex after **13** years of — 1Kg 7:1
They had **13** towns in all among — 1Ch 6:60
were assigned⌋ **13** towns from the — 1Ch 6:62
of Hosah were **13** in all. — 1Ch 26:11

14 *(20)*

14 years for your two daughters — Gn 31:41
were born to Jacob: **14** persons. — Gn 46:22
and **14** male lambs a year old. — Nm 29:13
with each of the **14** lambs. — Nm 29:15
and **14** male lambs a year old— — Nm 29:17
14 male lambs a year old— — Nm 29:20
14 male lambs a year old— — Nm 29:23
14 male lambs a year old— — Nm 29:26
14 male lambs a year old— — Nm 29:29
and **14** male lambs a year old— — Nm 29:32
Gederothaim—**14** cities, with — Jos 15:36
and Kiriath—**14** cities, with — Jos 18:28
and seven ⌊more⌋ days—**14** days. — 1Kg 8:65
strong, acquired **14** wives, and — 2Ch 13:21
was **14** feet, and its pilasters — Ezk 40:9
to David were **14** generations; — Mt 1:17
to Babylon, **14** generations; — Mt 1:17
the Messiah, **14** generations. — Mt 1:17
the third heaven **14** years ago. — 2Co 12:2
Then after **14** years I went up — Gl 2:1

15 *(27)*

of each plank is to be **15** feet, — Ex 26:16
of each plank was **15** feet, — Ex 36:21
your valuation is **15** shekels for — Lv 27:7
of his spear weighed **15** pounds. — 1Sm 17:7
Now Ziba had **15** sons and 20 — 2Sm 9:10
with his **15** sons and 20 servants — 2Sm 19:17
and **15** feet deep in front of the — 1Kg 6:3
two cherubim **15** feet high out — 1Kg 6:23
wingspan was **15** feet from tip to — 1Kg 6:24
second cherub also was **15** feet; — 1Kg 6:25
height was **15** feet and so was — 1Kg 6:26

stones 12 and **15** feet long. 1Kg 7:10
15 feet from brim to brim, 1Kg 7:23
15 pounds of gold went into each 1Kg 10:16
from Egypt for **15** pounds ⌊of 1Kg 10:29
of Joash lived **15** years after 2Kg 14:17
will add **15** years to your life. 2Kg 20:6
gave Ornan **15** pounds of gold 1Ch 21:25
from Egypt for **15** pounds ⌊of 2Ch 1:17
30 feet wide, and **15** feet high. 2Ch 4:1
15 feet from brim to brim, 2Ch 4:2
15 pounds of hammered gold went 2Ch 9:15
of Joash lived **15** years after 2Ch 25:25
am going to add **15** years to your Is 38:5
I bought her for **15** shekels of Hs 3:2
"30 feet long and **15** feet wide." Zch 5:2
and I stayed with him **15** days. Gl 1:18

16 *(19)*

she bore to Jacob: **16** persons. Gn 46:18
silver bases: **16** bases; two Ex 26:25
with their **16** silver bases, Ex 36:30
and Makkedah—**16** cities, with Jos 15:41
at the Jordan—**16** cities, with Jos 19:22
gold there—**16** tons—and 1Kg 9:28
Samaria; ⌊he reigned⌋ **16** years. 2Kg 13:10
Azariah, who was **16** years old, 2Kg 14:21
He was **16** years old when he 2Kg 15:2
reigned **16** years in Jerusalem. 2Kg 15:33
reigned **16** years in Jerusalem. 2Kg 16:2
Shimei had **16** sons and six 1Ch 4:27
16 heads of ancestral houses 1Ch 24:4
22 sons and **16** daughters. 2Ch 13:21
Uzziah, who was **16** years old, 2Ch 26:1
Uzziah was **16** years old when he 2Ch 26:3
reigned **16** years in Jerusalem. 2Ch 27:1
reigned **16** years in Jerusalem. 2Ch 27:8
reigned **16** years in Jerusalem. 2Ch 28:1

17 *(10)*

17 years of age, Joseph tended Gn 37:2
in the land of Egypt **17** years, Gn 47:28
reigned **17** years in Jerusalem, 1Kg 14:21
Samaria; ⌊he reigned⌋ **17** years. 2Kg 13:1
took from there **17** tons of gold, 2Ch 8:18
reigned **17** years in Jerusalem, 2Ch 12:13
him the money—**17** shekels of Jr 32:9
it was **17** and a half feet, Ezk 40:11
entrance was **17** and a half feet Ezk 41:2
17 and a half feet wide and 175 Ezk 42:4

18 *(21)*

the ark⌋ to within **18** inches ⌊of Gn 6:16
36 inches long, **18** inches wide, Ex 25:23
18 inches long and 18 inches Ex 30:2
inches long and **18** inches wide; Ex 30:2
36 inches long, **18** inches wide, Ex 37:10
18 inches long and 18 inches Ex 37:25
inches long and **18** inches wide; Ex 37:25
Eglon king of Moab **18** years. Jdg 3:14
sword **18** inches long. Jdg 3:16
and for **18** years ⌊they did the Jdg 10:8
27 feet high and **18** feet in 1Kg 7:15
crown on top was **18** inches wide. 1Kg 7:31
Jehoiachin was **18** years old when 2Kg 24:8
who were capable men—**18**. 1Ch 26:9
He acquired **18** wives and 60 2Ch 11:21
Jehoiachin was **18** years old when 2Ch 36:9
his sons and brothers, **18** men, Ezr 8:18
had a circumference of **18** feet, Jr 52:21
Or those **18** that the tower in Lk 13:4
by a spirit for over **18** years. Lk 13:11
of Abraham, for **18** years— Lk 13:16

19 *(2)*

Beth-shemesh—**19** cities, with Jos 19:38
19 of David's soldiers were 2Sm 2:30

20 *(85)*

above them⌋ more than **20** feet. Gn 7:20
suppose **20** are found there?" Gn 18:31
destroy ⌊it⌋ on account of **20**." Gn 18:31
been with you these **20** years. Gn 31:38
For **20** years I have worked in Gn 31:41
female goats, **20** male goats, 200 Gn 32:14
male goats, 200 ewes, **20** rams, Gn 32:14
10 bulls, **20** female donkeys Gn 32:15
sold him for **20** pieces of silver Gn 37:28
20 planks for the south side, Ex 26:18
bases under the **20** planks, Ex 26:19
20 planks for the second side of Ex 26:20
There are to be **20** posts and 20 Ex 27:10
be 20 posts and **20** bronze bases. Ex 27:10
There are to be **20** posts and 20 Ex 27:11
be 20 posts and **20** bronze bases. Ex 27:11
sanctuary shekel (**20** gerahs to Ex 30:13
is registered, **20** years old or Ex 30:14
as follows: **20** for the south Ex 36:23
to put under the **20** planks, Ex 36:24
north side, he made **20** planks, Ex 36:25
including their **20** posts and 20 Ex 38:10
20 posts and **20** bronze bases. Ex 38:10
including their **20** posts and 20 Ex 38:11
20 posts and **20** bronze bases. Ex 38:11
from everyone **20** years old or Ex 38:26
a male from **20** to 60 years old, Lv 27:3
is from five to **20** years old, Lv 27:5
for a male is **20** shekels and for Lv 27:5
sanctuary shekel, **20** gerahs to Lv 27:25
those who are **20** years old or Nm 1:3
names of those **20** years old or Nm 1:18
of every male **20** years old or Nm 1:20
of every male **20** years old or Nm 1:22
names of those **20** years old or Nm 1:24
names of those **20** years old or Nm 1:26
names of those **20** years old or Nm 1:28
names of those **20** years old or Nm 1:30
names of those **20** years old or Nm 1:32
names of those **20** years old or Nm 1:34
names of those **20** years old or Nm 1:36
names of those **20** years old or Nm 1:38
names of those **20** years old or Nm 1:40
names of those **20** years old or Nm 1:42
the Israelites **20** years old or Nm 1:45
sanctuary shekel—**20** gerahs to Nm 3:47
days, or 10 days, or **20** days, Nm 11:19
number of you **20** years old or Nm 14:29
shekel, which is **20** gerahs. Nm 18:16
houses of those **20** years old or Nm 26:2
census of⌋ those **20** years old or Nm 26:4
none of the men **20** years old or Nm 32:11
harshly oppressed them **20** years. Jdg 4:3
He defeated **20** of their cities Jdg 11:33
he judged Israel **20** years in the Jdg 15:20
So he judged Israel **20** years. Jdg 16:31
by until **20** years had passed 1Sm 7:2
struck down about **20** men in a 1Sm 14:14
When Abner and **20** men came to 2Sm 3:20
had 15 sons and **20** servants. 2Sm 9:10
his 15 sons and **20** servants also 2Sm 19:17
end of nine months and **20** days. 2Sm 24:8
10 fattened oxen, **20** range oxen, 1Kg 4:23
At the end of **20** years during 1Kg 9:10
gave Hiram **20** towns in the land 1Kg 9:11
sack full of **20** loaves of barley 2Kg 4:42
to set **20** loaves before 100 men? 2Kg 4:43
Menahem exacted **20** ounces of 2Kg 15:20
Samaria; ⌊he reigned⌋ **20** years. 2Kg 15:27
Ahaz was **20** years old when he 2Kg 16:2
the headcount—**20** years old or 1Ch 23:24
the Levites **20** years old or more 1Ch 23:27
count the men aged **20** or under, 1Ch 27:23
the nails was **20** ounces of gold 2Ch 3:9
At the end of **20** years during 2Ch 8:1
numbered those **20** years old or 2Ch 25:5
Ahaz was **20** years old when he 2Ch 28:1
and the Levites **20** years old and 2Ch 31:17
Levites who were **20** years old or Ezr 3:8
brothers and their sons, **20** men. Ezr 8:19
20 gold bowls worth 1,000 gold Ezr 8:27
The shekel will weigh **20** gerahs. Ezk 45:12
a ⌊grain⌋ heap of **20** measures, Hg 2:16
vat, it ⌊only⌋ amounted to **20**. Hg 2:16
Each contained **20** or 30 gallons. Jn 2:6

21 *(15)*

Zedekiah was **21** years old when 2Kg 24:18
Zedekiah was **21** years old when 2Ch 36:11
Zedekiah was **21** years old when Jr 52:1
hand was six units of **21** inches; Ezk 40:5
a barrier of **21** inches in front Ezk 40:12
inches wide, and **21** inches high. Ezk 40:42
35 feet across and **21** feet deep, Ezk 40:49
the gutter is **21** inches ⌊deep⌋ Ezk 43:13
⌊deep⌋ and **21** inches wide, Ezk 43:13
of the ledge⌋ is **21** inches. Ezk 43:14
⌊whose⌋ width is also **21** inches. Ezk 43:14
21 feet long by 21 feet wide. Ezk 43:16
21 feet long by **21** feet wide. Ezk 43:16
its gutter is **21** inches all Ezk 43:17
Persia opposed me for **21** days. Dn 10:13

22 *(15)*

of the gate⌋ **22** and a half feet, Ex 27:14
the other side **22** and a half Ex 27:15
the gate⌋ were **22** and a half Ex 38:14
hangings were **22** and a half feet Ex 38:15
and Rehob—**22** cities, with Jos 19:30
who judged Israel **22** years. Jdg 10:3
Jeroboam's reign was **22** years. 1Kg 14:20
over Israel in Samaria **22** years. 1Kg 16:29
Ahaziah was **22** years old when he 2Kg 8:26
Amon was **22** years old when he 2Kg 21:19
with **22** commanders from his 1Ch 12:28
and fathered **22** sons and 16 2Ch 13:21
Ahaziah was **22** years old when he 2Ch 22:2
Amon was **22** years old when he 2Ch 33:21
the gateway was **22** and Ezk 40:11

23 *(5)*

Tola judged Israel **23** years, Jdg 10:2
Jehoahaz was **23** years old when 2Kg 23:31
who possessed **23** towns in the 1Ch 2:22
Jehoahaz was **23** years old when 2Ch 36:2
this very day—**23** years—the Jr 25:3

24 *(14)*

sacrifice totaled **24** bulls, Nm 7:88
toes on each foot—**24** in all. 2Sm 21:20
Tirzah; ⌊he reigned⌋ **24** years. 1Kg 15:33
toes ⌊on each foot⌋—**24** in all. 1Ch 20:6
out to them **24** tons of silver, Ezr 8:26
gateway was **24** and a half feet Ezk 40:48
The ledge is **24** and a half feet Ezk 43:17
feet long by **24** and a half feet Ezk 43:17
that throne were **24** thrones, Rv 4:4
thrones sat **24** elders dressed Rv 4:4
the **24** elders fall down before Rv 4:10
and the **24** elders fell down Rv 5:8
The **24** elders, who were seated Rv 11:16
Then the **24** elders and the four Rv 19:4

25 *(16)*

From **25** years old or more, Nm 8:24
to Solomon annually was **25** tons, 1Kg 10:14
reigned **25** years in Jerusalem. 1Kg 22:42
He was **25** years old when he 2Kg 14:2
He was **25** years old when he 2Kg 15:33
He was **25** years old when he 2Kg 18:2
Jehoiakim was **25** years old when 2Kg 23:36
to Solomon annually was **25** tons, 2Ch 9:13
reigned **25** years in Jerusalem. 2Ch 20:31
king ⌊when he was⌋ **25** years old; 2Ch 25:1
Jotham was **25** years old when he 2Ch 27:1
He was **25** years old when he 2Ch 27:8
Hezekiah was **25** years old when 2Ch 29:1
Jehoiakim was **25** years old when 2Ch 36:5
there were about **25** men at the Ezk 8:16
the gate's entrance were **25** men. Ezk 11:1

26 *(1)*

it was about **26** quarts of barley Ru 2:17

27 *(16)*

45 inches long, **27** inches wide, Ex 25:10
inches wide, and **27** inches high. Ex 25:10
inches long and **27** inches wide. Ex 25:17
inches wide, and **27** inches high. Ex 25:23
width of each plank **27** inches. Ex 26:16
the width of each was **27** inches. Ex 36:21
45 inches long, **27** inches wide, Ex 37:1
inches wide, and **27** inches high. Ex 37:1
inches long and **27** inches wide. Ex 37:6
inches wide, and **27** inches high. Ex 37:10
each **27** feet high and 18 feet in 1Kg 7:15
as a pedestal **27** inches wide. 1Kg 7:31
each wheel was **27** inches tall. 1Kg 7:32
One pillar was **27** feet tall and 2Kg 25:17
pillars, ⌊each⌋ **27** feet high. 2Ch 3:15
One pillar was **27** feet tall, Jr 52:21

28 *(3)*

Israel in Samaria was **28** years. 2Kg 10:36
was the father of **28** sons and 60 2Ch 11:21
and **28** men with him; Ezr 8:11

29 *(7)*

lived **29** years and fathered Gn 11:24
and Rimmon—**29** cities in all, Jos 15:32
reigned **29** years in Jerusalem. 2Kg 14:2
reigned **29** years in Jerusalem. 2Kg 18:2
reigned **29** years in Jerusalem. 2Ch 25:1
reigned **29** years in Jerusalem. 2Ch 29:1
silver basins, **29** silver knives, Ezr 1:9

30 *(75)*
Shelah lived **30** years and Gn 11:14
lived **30** years and fathered Gn 11:18
lived **30** years and fathered Gn 11:22
Suppose **30** are found there?" Gn 18:30
not do ⌊it⌋ if I find **30** there." Gn 18:30
30 milk camels with their young, Gn 32:15
Joseph was **30** years old when he Gn 41:46
must give **30** shekels of silver Ex 21:32
was **30** feet long, and like the Ex 38:18
your valuation is **30** shekels. Lv 27:4
from **30** years old to 50 years Nm 4:3
men from **30** years old to 50 Nm 4:23
men from **30** years old to 50 Nm 4:30
from **30** years old to 50 years Nm 4:35
from **30** years old to 50 years Nm 4:39
from **30** years old to 50 years Nm 4:43
those from **30** years old to 50 Nm 4:47
from **30** years old to 50 years Nm 4:47
Israel mourned for him **30** days. Nm 20:29
in the plains of Moab **30** days. Dt 34:8
He had **30** sons who rode on 30 Jdg 10:4
who rode on **30** young donkeys. Jdg 10:4
They had **30** towns in Gilead, Jdg 10:4
and had **30** sons. He gave his 30 Jdg 12:9
He gave his **30** daughters in Jdg 12:9
brought back **30** wives for his Jdg 12:9
He had 40 sons and **30** grandsons, Jdg 12:14
they brought **30** men to accompany Jdg 14:11
will give you **30** linen garments Jdg 14:12
garments and **30** changes of Jdg 14:12
must give me **30** linen garments Jdg 14:13
garments and **30** changes of Jdg 14:13
and killed **30** of their men. Jdg 14:19
killing about **30** men of Israel Jdg 20:31
killing about **30** men of Israel, Jdg 20:39
the head of the **30** or so men who 1Sm 9:22
Saul was **30** years old when he 1Sm 13:1
David was **30** years old when he 2Sm 5:4
Three of the **30** leading 2Sm 23:13
90 feet long, **30** feet wide, and 1Kg 6:2
sanctuary was **30** feet long 1Kg 6:3
he lined **30** feet of the rear 1Kg 6:16
the sanctuary was **30** feet long, 1Kg 6:20
30 feet long, **30** feet wide, and 1Kg 6:20
30 feet wide, and **30** feet high; 1Kg 6:20
Three of the **30** chief men went 1Ch 11:15
the Reubenites, and **30** with him, 1Ch 11:42
The Levites **30** years old and 1Ch 23:3
90 feet, and the width **30** feet. 2Ch 3:3
of the temple, was **30** feet wide; 2Ch 3:4
its height was **30** feet; he 2Ch 3:4
of the temple, **30** feet, and its 2Ch 3:8
and its width was **30** feet. 2Ch 3:8
of the cherubim was **30** feet: 2Ch 3:11
of these cherubim was **30** feet. 2Ch 3:13
a bronze altar **30** feet long, 2Ch 4:1
30 feet long, **30** feet wide, and 2Ch 4:1
30 gold basins, 1,000 silver Ezr 1:9
30 gold bowls, 410 various Ezr 1:10
the king for the last **30** days." Est 4:11
Take from here **30** men under your Jr 38:10
three stories of **30** rooms each. Ezk 41:6
an edict that for **30** days, Dn 6:7
edict that for **30** days any man Dn 6:12
"**30** feet long and 15 feet wide." Zch 5:2
my wages, **30** pieces of silver Zch 11:12
I took the **30** pieces of silver Zch 11:13
some **30** times ⌊what was sown⌋ Mt 13:8
some **30** times ⌊what was sown⌋." Mt 13:23
weighed out **30** pieces of silver Mt 26:15
returned the **30** pieces of silver Mt 27:3
They took the **30** pieces of Mt 27:9
a crop that increased **30**, Mk 4:8
30, 60, and 100 times ⌊what was Mk 4:20
Jesus was about **30** years old and Lk 3:23
Each contained 20 or **30** gallons. Jn 2:6

31 *(5)*
total number of⌋ all kings: **31** Jos 12:24
reigned **31** years in Jerusalem. 2Kg 22:1
reigned **31** years in Jerusalem. 2Ch 34:1
⌊each⌋ **31** and a half inches long, Ezk 40:42
31 and a half inches wide, Ezk 40:42

32 *(7)*
Reu lived **32** years and fathered Gn 11:20
to the LORD was **32** people. Nm 31:40
and the **32** kings who were 1Kg 20:16
had ordered his **32** chariot 1Kg 22:31
He was **32** years old when he 2Kg 8:17
Jehoram was **32** years old when he 2Ch 21:5
Jehoram was **32** years old when 2Ch 21:20

33 *(7)*
The total number of persons: **33**. Gn 46:15
from her bleeding for **33** days. Lv 12:4
the least gathered **33** bushels— Nm 11:32
he reigned **33** years over all 2Sm 5:5
in Hebron and **33** years in 1Kg 2:11
he ruled in Jerusalem **33** years. 1Ch 3:4
years and in Jerusalem for **33**. 1Ch 29:27

34 *(1)*
Eber lived **34** years and fathered Gn 11:16

35 *(9)*
Arpachshad lived **35** years and Gn 11:12
Jehoshaphat was **35** years old 1Kg 22:42
He was **35** years old when he 2Ch 20:31
The portico was **35** feet across Ezk 40:49
70 feet, and the width, **35** feet. Ezk 41:2
to the great hall, **35** feet, and Ezk 41:4
35 feet, and the width, **35** feet. Ezk 41:4
chambers was **35** feet wide all Ezk 41:10
Opposite the **35** ⌊foot space⌋ Ezk 42:3

36 *(5)*
acacia wood, **36** inches long, 18 Ex 25:23
it must be **36** inches high. Ex 30:2
acacia wood, **36** inches long, 18 Ex 37:10
wide; it was **36** inches high. Its Ex 37:25
struck down about **36** of them and Jos 7:5

37 *(1)*
Hittite. There were **37** in all. 2Sm 23:39

38 *(3)*
Zered Valley was **38** years until Dt 2:14
Ammonites sent **38** tons of silver 1Ch 19:6
who had been sick for **38** years. Jn 5:5

40 *(87)*
rain on the earth **40** days and 40 Gn 7:4
the earth 40 days and **40** nights, Gn 7:4
fell on the earth **40** days and 40 Gn 7:12
the earth 40 days and **40** nights. Gn 7:12
deluge continued **40** days on the Gn 7:17
After **40** days Noah opened the Gn 8:6
"Suppose **40** are found there?" Gn 18:29
not do ⌊it⌋ on account of **40**." Gn 18:29
Isaac was **40** years old when he Gn 25:20
When Esau was **40** years old, Gn 26:34
their young, **40** cows, 10 bulls, Gn 32:15
They took **40** days to complete Gn 50:3
ate manna for **40** years, Ex 16:35
on the mountain **40** days and 40 Ex 24:18
mountain 40 days and **40** nights. Ex 24:18
and make **40** silver bases under Ex 26:19
with their **40** silver bases, Ex 26:21
with the LORD **40** days and 40 Ex 34:28
the LORD 40 days and **40** nights; Ex 34:28
and he made **40** silver bases to Ex 36:24
with their **40** silver bases, Ex 36:26
At the end of **40** days they Nm 13:25
wilderness for **40** years and bear Nm 14:33
of your sins **40** years based on Nm 14:34
number of the **40** days that you Nm 14:34
in the wilderness **40** years until Nm 32:13
with you this past **40** years, Dt 2:7
entire journey these **40** years in Dt 8:2
did not swell these **40** years. Dt 8:4
on the mountain **40** days and 40 Dt 9:9
mountain 40 days and **40** nights. Dt 9:9
at the end of the **40** days and 40 Dt 9:11
of the 40 days and **40** nights. Dt 9:11
of the LORD for **40** days and 40 Dt 9:18
LORD for 40 days and **40** nights; Dt 9:18
the LORD **40** days and 40 nights Dt 9:25
40 days and **40** nights because Dt 9:25
on the mountain **40** days and 40 Dt 10:10
40 days and **40** nights like Dt 10:10
may be flogged with **40** lashes, Dt 25:3
I led you **40** years in the Dt 29:5
wilderness **40** years until all Jos 5:6
was **40** years old when Moses the Jos 14:7
the land was peaceful **40** years, Jdg 3:11
the land was peaceful **40** years. Jdg 5:31
was peaceful **40** years during Jdg 8:28
He had **40** sons and 30 grandsons, Jdg 12:14
to the Philistines **40** years. Jdg 13:1
Eli had judged Israel **40** years. 1Sm 4:18
and evening for **40** days the 1Sm 17:16
Ish-bosheth was **40** years old 2Sm 2:10
his reign; he reigned **40** years. 2Sm 5:4
over Israel was **40** years: 1Kg 2:11
all Israel totaled **40** years. 1Kg 11:42
he walked **40** days and 40 nights 1Kg 19:8
40 days and **40** nights to Horeb, 1Kg 19:8
40 camel-loads of all kinds of 2Kg 8:9
reigned **40** years in Jerusalem. 2Kg 12:1
reign over Israel was **40** years; 1Ch 29:27
over all Israel for **40** years. 2Ch 9:30
reigned **40** years in Jerusalem. 2Ch 24:1
the wilderness **40** years and they Neh 9:21
40 years I was disgusted with Ps 95:10
I have assigned you **40** days, Ezk 4:6
be uninhabited for **40** years. Ezk 29:11
ruined cities for **40** years. Ezk 29:12
At the end of **40** years I will Ezk 29:13
of Egypt and led you **40** years in Am 2:10
to Me during the **40** years in the Am 5:25
In **40** days Nineveh will be Jnh 3:4
He had fasted **40** days and 40 Mt 4:2
fasted 40 days and **40** nights, Mt 4:2
was in the wilderness **40** days, Mk 1:13
for **40** days to be tempted by the Lk 4:2
to them during **40** days and Ac 1:3
the man was over **40** years old on Ac 4:22
was approaching the age of **40**, Ac 7:23
After **40** years had passed, Ac 7:30
and in the desert for **40** years. Ac 7:36
and sacrifices for **40** years in Ac 7:42
And for about **40** years He put up Ac 13:18
tribe of Benjamin, for **40** years. Ac 13:21
were more than **40** who had formed Ac 23:13
are more than **40** of them Ac 23:21
from the Jews **40** lashes minus 2Co 11:24
for **40** years. Therefore I was Heb 3:10
was He "provoked for **40** years"? Heb 3:17

41 *(4)*
Rehoboam was **41** years old when 1Kg 14:21
reigned **41** years in Jerusalem. 1Kg 15:10
in Samaria; he reigned **41** years. 2Kg 14:23
Rehoboam was **41** years old when 2Ch 12:13

42 *(10)*
each curtain should be **42** feet, Ex 26:2
of each curtain was **42** feet, Ex 36:9
these, give **42** ⌊other⌋ cities. Nm 35:6
and he reigned **42** years over 1Sm 13:1
and mauled **42** of the youths. 2Kg 2:24
the pit of Beth-eked—**42** men. 2Kg 10:14
Azmaveth's people **42** Ezr 2:24
Beth-azmaveth's men **42** Neh 7:28
the holy city for **42** months. Rv 11:2
authority to act for **42** months. Rv 13:5

43 *(8)*
was about **43** pounds of gold, Jdg 8:26
the distance was **43** and Ezk 40:13
feet long and **43** and Ezk 40:21
feet long and **43** and Ezk 40:25
feet long and **43** and Ezk 40:29
43 and three-quarter feet long Ezk 40:30
feet long and **43** and Ezk 40:33
feet long and **43** and Ezk 40:36

44 *(1)*
⌊remaining⌋ **44** pounds he made Ex 38:28

45 *(15)*
75 feet wide, and **45** feet high. Gn 6:15
⌊it⌋ if I find **45** there." Gn 18:28
acacia wood, **45** inches long, 27 Ex 25:10
45 inches long and 27 inches Ex 25:17
curtain should be **45** feet and Ex 26:8
of each curtain was **45** feet, Ex 36:15
acacia wood, **45** inches long, 27 Ex 37:1
45 inches long and 27 inches Ex 37:6
me alive ⌊these⌋ **45** years as He Jos 14:10
30 feet wide, and **45** feet high. 1Kg 6:2
and **45** feet high on four rows of 1Kg 7:2
that ⌊rested⌋ on **45** pillars, 1Kg 7:3
75 feet long and **45** feet wide. 1Kg 7:6
a half feet high and **45** feet in 1Kg 7:23
and **45** feet in circumference. 2Ch 4:2

46 *(1)*
took **46** years to build, Jn 2:20

48 *(2)*
you give the Levites will be **48**, Nm 35:7
there were **48** cities in all with Jos 21:41

49 *(1)*
sabbatic years amounts to **49**. Lv 25:8

50 *(64)*
if there are **50** righteous people Gn 18:24
the sake of the **50** righteous Gn 18:24
at Sodom I find **50** righteous Gn 18:26
suppose the **50** righteous lack Gn 18:28
Make **50** loops on the one curtain Ex 26:5
curtain and make **50** loops on the Ex 26:5
make **50** gold clasps and join Ex 26:6
Make **50** loops on the edge of the Ex 26:10
and make **50** loops on the edge of Ex 26:10
Make **50** bronze clasps; put the Ex 26:11
He made **50** loops on the one Ex 36:12
one curtain and **50** loops on the Ex 36:12
He also made **50** gold clasps and Ex 36:13
He made **50** loops on the edge of Ex 36:17
first⌋ set and **50** loops on the Ex 36:17
He made **50** bronze clasps to join Ex 36:18
You are to count **50** days until Lv 23:16
valuation is **50** silver shekels Lv 27:3
at the rate of **50** silver shekels Lv 27:16
30 years old to **50** years old— Nm 4:3
30 years old to **50** years old, Nm 4:23
30 years old to **50** years old, Nm 4:30
30 years old to **50** years old, Nm 4:35
30 years old to **50** years old, Nm 4:39
30 years old to **50** years old, Nm 4:43
30 years old to **50** years old, Nm 4:47
But at **50** years old he is to Nm 8:25
out of every **50** from the people Nm 31:30
took one out of ⌊every⌋ **50**, Nm 31:47
father **50** silver ⌊shekels⌋ Dt 22:29
bar of gold weighing **50** shekels, Jos 7:21
and **50** men to run before him. 2Sm 15:1
the oxen for **50** ounces of silver 2Sm 24:24
and **50** men to run ahead of him. 1Kg 1:5
and hid them, **50** men to a cave, 1Kg 18:4
of the LORD, **50** men to a cave, 1Kg 18:13
a captain of **50** with his 50 ⌊men 2Kg 1:9
of 50 with his **50** ⌊men⌋ to 2Kg 1:9
to the captain of the **50**, 2Kg 1:10
consume you and your **50** ⌊men⌋." 2Kg 1:10
consumed him and his **50** ⌊men⌋. 2Kg 1:10
captain of **50** with his 50 ⌊men⌋ 2Kg 1:11
of 50 with his **50** ⌊men⌋ to 2Kg 1:11
consume you and your **50** ⌊men⌋." 2Kg 1:12
consumed him and his **50** ⌊men⌋. 2Kg 1:12
captain of **50** with his 50 ⌊men 2Kg 1:13
captain of 50 with his **50** ⌊men⌋. 2Kg 1:13
captain of **50** went up and fell 2Kg 1:13
lives of these **50** servants of 2Kg 1:13
two captains of **50** with their 2Kg 1:14
there are **50** strong men here 2Kg 2:16
They sent **50** men, who looked 2Kg 2:17
left, except for **50** horsemen, 10 2Kg 13:7
There were **50** Gileadite men with 2Kg 15:25
and **50** men with him; Ezr 8:6
gold drachmas, **50** bowls, and 530 Neh 7:70
the commander of **50** and the Is 3:3
the winepress to dip **50** measures Hg 2:16
mixed into **50** pounds of flour Mt 13:33
500 denarii, and the other **50**. Lk 7:41
in groups of about **50** each." Lk 9:14
mixed into **50** pounds of flour Lk 13:21
sit down quickly, and write **50**.' Lk 16:6
You aren't **50** years old yet, Jn 8:57

52 *(6)*
reigned **52** years in Jerusalem. 2Kg 15:2
reigned **52** years in Jerusalem. 2Ch 26:3
Nebo's people **52** Ezr 2:29
wall was completed in **52** days, Neh 6:15
the other Nebo's men **52** Neh 7:33
feet⌋ long by **52** and a half Ezk 46:22

55 *(2)*
reigned **55** years in Jerusalem. 2Kg 21:1
reigned **55** years in Jerusalem. 2Ch 33:1

56 *(1)*
Netophah's men **56** Ezr 2:22

60 *(26)*
Isaac was **60** years old when they Gn 25:26
a male from 20 to **60** years old, Lv 27:3
the person is **60** years or more, Lv 27:7
was **60** pounds ⌊measured⌋ Nm 7:85
24 bulls, **60** rams, 60 male Nm 7:88
bulls, 60 rams, **60** male breeding Nm 7:88
and **60** male lambs a year old. Nm 7:88
60 cities, the entire region of Dt 3:4
that are in Bashan—**60** cities. Jos 13:30
60 great cities with walls and 1Kg 4:13
holy place, was **60** feet long. 1Kg 6:17
60 men from the common people 2Kg 25:19
her when he was **60** years old, 1Ch 2:21
and its villages—**60** towns. 1Ch 2:23
18 wives and **60** concubines and 2Ch 11:21
of 28 sons and **60** daughters. 2Ch 11:21
Shemaiah, and **60** men with them; Ezr 8:13
litter surrounded by **60** warriors Sg 3:7
There are **60** queens and 80 Sg 6:8
60 men from the common people Jr 52:25
Your mina will equal **60** shekels. Ezk 45:12
some 100, some **60**, and some 30 Mt 13:8
some 100, some **60**, some 30 times Mt 13:23
increased 30, **60**, and 100 times Mk 4:8
30, **60**, and 100 times ⌊what was Mk 4:20
she is at least **60** years old, 1Tm 5:9

61 *(1)*
the tribute to the LORD was **61**; Nm 31:39

62 *(4)*
the work—**62** from Obed-edom. 1Ch 26:8
the kingdom at the age of **62**. Dn 5:31
be seven weeks and **62** weeks. Dn 9:25
After those **62** weeks the Messiah Dn 9:26

65 *(3)*
Mahalalel was **65** years old when Gn 5:15
Enoch was **65** years old when he Gn 5:21
within **65** years Ephraim will be Is 7:8

66 *(2)*
sons—who came to Egypt: **66**. Gn 46:26
from her bleeding for **66** days. Lv 12:5

67 *(1)*
minas, and **67** priestly garments Neh 7:72

68 *(1)*
Obed-edom and his **68** relatives. 1Ch 16:38

70 *(43)*
Kenan was **70** years old when he Gn 5:12
lived **70** years and fathered Gn 11:26
had come to Egypt: **70** persons. Gn 46:27
mourned for him **70** days. Gn 50:3
of Jacob's descendants was **70**; Ex 1:5
of water and **70** date palms, Ex 15:27
and **70** of Israel's elders, Ex 24:1
and **70** of Israel's elders, Ex 24:9
Bring Me **70** men from Israel Nm 11:16
brought **70** men from the elders Nm 11:24
the Spirit⌋ on the **70** elders. Nm 11:25
of water and **70** date palms at Nm 33:9
down to Egypt, **70** people in all, Dt 10:22
Gideon had **70** sons, his own Jdg 8:30
it better for you that **70** men, Jdg 9:2
they gave him **70** pieces of Jdg 9:4
and killed his **70** brothers, Jdg 9:5
killed his **70** sons on top of a Jdg 9:18
against the **70** sons of Jerubbaal Jdg 9:24
by killing his **70** brothers, Jdg 9:56
who rode on **70** donkeys. Jdg 12:14
He struck down **70** men ⌊out of⌋ 1Sm 6:19
Since Ahab had **70** sons in 2Kg 10:1
All **70** of the king's sons were 2Kg 10:6
sons and slaughtered all **70**, 2Kg 10:7
brought was **70** bulls, 2Ch 29:32
desolation until **70** years were 2Ch 36:21
and **70** men with him; Ezr 8:7
and **70** men with them. Ezr 8:14
will be forgotten for **70** years— Is 23:15
At the end of **70** years, what the Is 23:15
And at the end of the **70** years, Is 23:17
king of Babylon for **70** years. Jr 25:11
When the **70** years are completed, Jr 25:12
When **70** years for Babylon are Jr 29:10
of the great hall, **70** feet, and Ezk 41:2
70 ⌊feet⌋ long by 52 and a half Ezk 46:22
of Jerusalem would be **70**. Dn 9:2
been angry with these **70** years?" Zch 1:12
months⌋ for these **70** years, Zch 7:5
to him, "but **70** times seven. Mt 18:22
the Lord appointed **70** others, Lk 10:1
ready with **70** cavalry and 200 Ac 23:23

72 *(1)*
the tribute to the LORD was **72**; Nm 31:38

74 *(2)*
from Hodaviah's descendants **74** Ezr 2:40
Kadmiel Hodevah's descendants **74** Neh 7:43

75 *(22)*
450 feet long, **75** feet wide, and Gn 6:15
Abram was **75** years old when he Gn 12:4
be made from **75** pounds of pure Ex 25:39
on the west side **75** feet long, Ex 27:12
side toward the sunrise **75** feet. Ex 27:13
the width **75** ⌊feet⌋ at each end, Ex 27:18
utensils of **75** pounds of pure Ex 37:24
side were **75** feet in length, Ex 38:12
were also **75** feet in length. Ex 38:13
7,500 pounds, **75** pounds for each Ex 38:27
crown weighed **75** pounds of 2Sm 12:30
150 feet long, **75** feet wide, and 1Kg 7:2
hall of pillars **75** feet long and 1Kg 7:6
weigh out **75** pounds of silver. 1Kg 20:39
give them **75** pounds of silver 2Kg 5:22
of silver and **75** pounds of gold. 2Kg 23:33
crown weighed **75** pounds of gold, 1Ch 20:2
of silver and **75** pounds of gold. 2Ch 36:3
build a gallows **75** feet high. Est 5:14
is a gallows **75** feet tall at Est 7:9
of about **75** pounds of myrrh Jn 19:39
his relatives, **75** people in all, Ac 7:14

77 *(2)*
names of the⌋ **77** princes and Jdg 8:14
rams, and **77** lambs, along with Ezr 8:35

80 *(12)*
Moses was **80** years old and Aaron Ex 7:7
the land was peaceful **80** years. Jdg 3:30
a very old man—**80** years old— 2Sm 19:32
I'm now **80** years old. Can I 2Sm 19:35
sold for⌋ **80** silver ⌊shekels 2Kg 6:25
had stationed **80** men outside, 2Kg 10:24
the leader and **80** of his 1Ch 15:9
along with **80** brave priests of 2Ch 26:17
and **80** men with him; Ezr 8:8
are 60 queens and **80** concubines Sg 6:8
80 men came from Shechem, Shiloh, Jr 41:5
he told him, 'and write **80**.' Lk 16:7

83 *(1)*
old and Aaron **83** when they spoke Ex 7:7

84 *(1)*
and was a widow for **84** years. Lk 2:37

85 *(2)*
Here I am today, **85** years old. Jos 14:10
he killed **85** men who wore linen 1Sm 22:18

86 *(1)*
was **86** years old when Hagar Gn 16:16

87 *(10)*
the inside was **87** and a half Ezk 40:15
87 and a half feet long and 43 Ezk 40:21
It was **87** and a half feet long Ezk 40:25
It was **87** and a half feet long Ezk 40:29
It was **87** and a half feet long Ezk 40:33
It was **87** and a half feet long Ezk 40:36
width was **87** and a half feet. Ezk 42:2
it was **87** and a half feet long. Ezk 42:7
court were **87** and a half feet Ezk 42:8
with **87** and a half feet of open Ezk 45:2

90 *(7)*
Enosh was **90** years old when he Gn 5:9
for the LORD was **90** feet long, 1Kg 6:2
the length was **90** feet, and the 2Ch 3:3
height is to be **90** feet and its Ezr 6:3
90 feet and its width **90** feet, Ezr 6:3
90 feet high and nine feet wide. Dn 3:1
found it to be **90** feet deep. Ac 27:28

95 *(2)*
Gibbar's descendants **95** Ezr 2:20
Gibeon's descendants **95** Neh 7:25

96 *(2)*
for all Israel, **96** rams, and 77 Ezr 8:35
capital had⌋ **96** pomegranates all Jr 52:23

98 *(3)*
that time Eli was **98** years old, 1Sm 4:15
descendants: Hezekiah's **98** Ezr 2:16
descendants: of Hezekiah **98** Neh 7:21

99 *(6)*
When Abram was **99** years old, Gn 17:1
Abraham was **99** years old when Gn 17:24
he leave the **99** on the hillside Mt 18:12
than over the **99** that did not go Mt 18:13
not leave the **99** in the open Lk 15:4
than over **99** righteous people Lk 15:7

100 *(42)*
lived **100** years and fathered Gn 11:10
Abraham was **100** years old when Gn 21:5

father, for **100** qesitahs, where Gn 33:19
100 bases from 7,500 pounds, Ex 38:27
Five of you will pursue **100**, Lv 26:8
and **100** of you will pursue Lv 26:8
also fine him **100** silver Dt 22:19
father, for **100** qesitahs . Jos 24:32
Gideon and the **100** men who were Jdg 7:19
out of every **100** from all the Jdg 20:10
and **100** out of every 1,000, Jdg 20:10
bride-price except **100** 1Sm 18:25
roasted grain, **100** clusters of 1Sm 25:18
for the price of **100** Philistine 2Sm 3:14
and he kept **100** chariots. 2Sm 8:4
loaves of bread, **100** clusters of 2Sm 16:1
100 ⌊bunches⌋ of summer fruit, 2Sm 16:1
the troops **100** times more than 2Sm 24:3
oxen, and **100** sheep, besides 1Kg 4:23
and took **100** prophets and hid 1Kg 18:4
I hid **100** of the prophets of the 1Kg 18:13
set 20 loaves before **100** men?" 2Kg 4:43
and he kept **100** chariots. 1Ch 18:4
100 tons of gold (gold of Ophir) 1Ch 29:4
He made **100** pomegranates and 2Ch 3:16
He also made **100** gold bowls. 2Ch 4:8
was 70 bulls, **100** rams, and 200 2Ch 29:32
and **100** priestly garments to the Ezr 2:69
house they offered **100** bulls, Ezr 6:17
the latticework numbered **100**. Jr 52:23
some **100**, some 60, and some 30 Mt 13:8
some **100**, some 60, some 30 times Mt 13:23
If a man has **100** sheep, and one Mt 18:12
slaves who owed him **100** denarii. Mt 18:28
name will receive **100** times more Mt 19:29
and **100** times ⌊what was sown⌋." Mk 4:8
and **100** times ⌊what was sown⌋." Mk 4:20
will not receive **100** times more, Mk 10:30
100 times ⌊what was sown⌋." Lk 8:8
who has **100** sheep and loses one Lk 15:4
land (about **100** yards away), Jn 21:8
each weighing about **100** pounds, Rv 16:21

105 *(2)*
Seth was **105** years old when he Gn 5:6
the pilasters—**105** feet. Ezk 40:14

110 *(5)*
Egypt. Joseph lived **110** years. Gn 50:22
Joseph died at the age of **110**. Gn 50:26
of Nun, died at the age of **110**. Jos 24:29
LORD, died at the age of **110**. Jdg 2:8
and **110** men with him; Ezr 8:12

112 *(3)*
the leader and **112** of his 1Ch 15:10
Jorah's descendants **112** Ezr 2:18
Hariph's descendants **112** Neh 7:24

119 *(1)*
lived **119** years and fathered Gn 11:25

120 *(8)*
Their days will be **120** years." Gn 6:3
saying, "I am now **120** years old; Dt 31:2
Moses was **120** years old when he Dt 34:7
the leader and **120** of his 1Ch 15:5
with them were **120** priests 2Ch 5:12
to appoint **120** satraps over Dn 6:1
were together was about **120**— Ac 1:15
found it to be **120** feet deep; Ac 27:28

122 *(3)*
Michmas's men **122** Ezr 2:27
Michmas's men **122** Neh 7:31
the west was **122** and a half feet Ezk 41:12

123 *(3)*
Aaron was **123** years old when he Nm 33:39
Bethlehem's people **123** Ezr 2:21
Bethel's and Ai's men **123** Neh 7:32

125 *(1)*
armor that weighed **125** pounds. 1Sm 17:5

127 *(4)*
Now Sarah lived **127** years; Gn 23:1
who ruled **127** provinces from Est 1:1
officials of the **127** provinces Est 8:9
who were in the **127** provinces Est 9:30

128 *(4)*
Anathoth's men **128** Ezr 2:23
Asaph's descendants **128** Ezr 2:41
Anathoth's men **128** Neh 7:27
capable men: **128**. Zabdiel son Neh 11:14

130 *(4)*
Adam was **130** years old when he Gn 5:3
pilgrimage has lasted **130** years. Gn 47:9
the leader and **130** of his 1Ch 15:7
he was **130** years old at his 2Ch 24:15

133 *(1)*
Uzziel. Kohath lived **133** years. Ex 6:18

137 *(3)*
life: **137** years. He took Gn 25:17
Merari. Levi lived **137** years. Ex 6:16
Moses. Amram lived **137** years. Ex 6:20

138 *(1)*
Shobai's descendants **138** Neh 7:45

139 *(1)*
Shobai's descendants, in all **139** Ezr 2:42

140 *(1)*
Job lived **140** years after this Jb 42:16

144 *(1)*
144 cubits according to human Rv 21:17

147 *(1)*
and his life span was **147** years. Gn 47:28

148 *(1)*
Asaph's descendants **148** Neh 7:44

150 *(16)*
surged on the earth **150** days. Gn 7:24
the end of **150** days the waters Gn 8:3
150 feet long on that side. Ex 27:9
the north side **150** ⌊feet⌋ long. Ex 27:11
the courtyard is to be **150** feet, Ex 27:18
spun linen, **150** feet in length, Ex 38:9
were also **150** feet in length Ex 38:11
one day were **150** bushels of fine 1Kg 4:22
It was **150** feet long, 75 feet 1Kg 7:2
from Shemer for **150** pounds of 1Kg 16:24
of silver, **150** pounds of gold, 2Kg 5:5
Please, accept **150** pounds." 2Kg 5:23
and then packed **150** pounds of 2Kg 5:23
and grandsons—**150** of them. 1Ch 8:40
and **150** men with him who were Ezr 8:3
There were **150** Jews and Neh 5:17

153 *(1)*
of large fish—**153** of them. Jn 21:11

156 *(1)*
Magbish's people **156** Ezr 2:30

157 *(1)*
length was **157** and a half feet. Ezk 41:12

160 *(1)*
and **160** men with him; Ezr 8:10

162 *(1)*
Jared was **162** years old when he Gn 5:18

172 *(1)*
who guarded the gates: **172**. Neh 11:19

175 *(13)*
of Abraham's life: **175** years. Gn 25:7
court; it was **175** feet. ⌊This⌋ Ezk 40:19
gate to gate; it was **175** feet. Ezk 40:23
on the south; it was **175** feet. Ezk 40:27
175 feet long and 175 feet wide. Ezk 40:47
175 feet long and **175** feet wide. Ezk 40:47
temple; it was **175** feet long. Ezk 41:13
its walls, were **175** feet long. Ezk 41:13
yard to the east was **175** feet. Ezk 41:14
each side; it was **175** feet. The Ezk 41:15
which was **175** feet, there was Ezk 42:2
feet wide and **175** feet long, Ezk 42:4
great hall were **175** feet ⌊long⌋. Ezk 42:8

180 *(3)*
Isaac lived **180** years. Gn 35:28
for a total of **180** days. Est 1:4
bridles for about **180** miles. Rv 14:20

182 *(1)*
Lamech was **182** years old when he Gn 5:28

185 *(1)*
house they gave **185** tons of gold 1Ch 29:7

187 *(1)*
Methuselah was **187** years old Gn 5:25

188 *(1)*
and Netophah's men **188** Neh 7:26

200 *(28)*
lived **200** years and fathered Gn 11:23
200 female goats, 20 male goats, Gn 32:14
male goats, **200** ewes, 20 rams, Gn 32:14
Babylon, **200** silver shekels, Jos 7:21
out and killed **200** Philistines. 1Sm 18:27
David while **200** stayed with 1Sm 25:13
taking **200** loaves of bread, 1Sm 25:18
and **200** cakes of pressed figs, 1Sm 25:18
where **200** who were to remain 1Sm 30:9
came to the **200** men who had 1Sm 30:21
loaded with **200** loaves of bread, 2Sm 16:1
200 pomegranates were in rows 1Kg 7:20
Solomon made **200** large shields 1Kg 10:16
and broke down **200** yards of 2Kg 14:13
200 chiefs with all their 1Ch 12:32
the leader and **200** of his 1Ch 15:8
Solomon made **200** large shields 2Ch 9:15
and broke down **200** yards of 2Ch 25:23
bulls, 100 rams, and **200** lambs; 2Ch 29:32
and their **200** male and female Ezr 2:65
100 bulls, **200** rams, and 400 Ezr 6:17
and **200** men with him; Ezr 8:4
but **200** for those who guard its Sg 8:12
animal out of every **200** from the Ezk 45:15
we go and buy **200** denarii worth Mk 6:37
Get **200** soldiers ready with 70 Ac 23:23
cavalry and **200** spearmen to go Ac 23:23
mounted troops was **200** million; Rv 9:16

205 *(1)*
Terah lived **205** years and died Gn 11:32

207 *(1)*
Reu lived **207** years and fathered Gn 11:21

209 *(1)*
lived **209** years and fathered Gn 11:19

212 *(1)*
at the thresholds was **212**. 1Ch 9:22

218 *(1)*
and **218** men with him; Ezr 8:9

220 *(3)*
basin holding **220** gallons and 1Kg 7:38
the leader and **220** of his 1Ch 15:6
were also **220** of the temple Ezr 8:20

223 *(2)*
Hashum's descendants **223** Ezr 2:19
Bethel's and Ai's men **223** Ezr 2:28

232 *(1)*
leaders, and there were **232**. 1Kg 20:15

242 *(1)*
of families: **242**. Amashsai son Neh 11:13

245 *(3)*
They had 736 horses, **245** mules, Ezr 2:66
well as their **245** male and Neh 7:67
They had 736 horses, **245** mules, Neh 7:68

250 *(6)*
250 prominent Israelite men who Nm 16:2
before the LORD—**250** firepans. Nm 16:17
consumed the **250** men who were Nm 16:35
and the fire consumed **250** men. Nm 26:10
and **250** tons of refined silver 1Ch 29:4
250 who ruled over the people. 2Ch 8:10

273 *(1)*
price for the **273** firstborn Nm 3:46

276 *(1)*
all there were **276** of us on the Ac 27:37

284 *(1)*
Levites in the holy city: **284**. Neh 11:18

288 *(1)*
for the LORD, they numbered **288**. 1Ch 25:7

300 *(23)*
walked with God **300** years and Gn 5:22
gave Benjamin **300** pieces of Gn 45:22
to their mouths was **300** men, Jdg 7:6
you with the **300** men who lapped Jdg 7:7
but kept the **300** who took the Jdg 7:8
divided the **300** men into three Jdg 7:16
men blew their **300** trumpets, Jdg 7:22
Gideon and the **300** men came to Jdg 8:4
lived **300** years in Heshbon Jdg 11:26
went out and caught **300** foxes. Jdg 15:4
spear against **300** ⌊men⌋ and 2Sm 23:18
fine flour and **300** bushels of 1Kg 4:22
He made **300** small shields of 1Kg 10:17
princesses and **300** concubines, 1Kg 11:3
spear against **300** and killed 1Ch 11:11
spear against **300** ⌊men⌋ and 1Ch 11:20
He made **300** small shields of 2Ch 9:16
million men and **300** chariots. 2Ch 14:9

sacrifices and **300** bulls for the 2Ch 35:8
and **300** men with him; Ezr 8:5
Adar and killed **300** men in Susa, Est 9:15
for more than **300** denarii and Mk 14:5
oil sold for **300** denarii and Jn 12:5

318 *(1)*
assembled his **318** trained men, Gn 14:14

320 *(2)*
Harim's people **320** Ezr 2:32
Harim's people **320** Neh 7:35

323 *(1)*
Bezai's descendants **323** Ezr 2:17

324 *(1)*
Bezai's descendants **324** Neh 7:23

328 *(1)*
Hashum's descendants **328** Neh 7:22

345 *(2)*
Jericho's people **345** Ezr 2:34
Jericho's people **345** Neh 7:36

350 *(1)*
Now Noah lived **350** years after Gn 9:28

360 *(1)*
they had killed **360** of the 2Sm 2:31

365 *(1)*
Enoch's life lasted **365** years. Gn 5:23

372 *(2)*
Shephatiah's descendants **372** Ezr 2:4
Shephatiah's descendants **372** Neh 7:9

375 *(2)*
drachmas, **375** tons of silver 1Ch 29:7
I will pay **375** tons of silver Est 3:9

390 *(2)*
days ⌊you lie down⌋, **390** days; Ezk 4:5
you lie on your side, **390** days. Ezk 4:9

392 *(2)*
of Solomon's servants **392** Ezr 2:58
of Solomon's servants **392** Neh 7:60

400 *(18)*
and oppressed **400** years. Gn 15:13
Land worth **400** shekels of silver Gn 23:15
400 shekels of silver at the Gn 23:16
and he has **400** men with him." Gn 32:6
coming toward him with **400** men. Gn 33:1
Jabesh-gilead **400** young virgins, Jdg 21:12
About **400** men were with him. 1Sm 22:2
About **400** men followed David 1Sm 25:13
David and **400** of the men 1Sm 30:10
except **400** young men who got 1Sm 30:17
the **400** pomegranates for the two 1Kg 7:42
of Baal and the **400** prophets of 1Kg 18:19
about **400** men, and asked 1Kg 22:6
the **400** pomegranates for the two 2Ch 4:13
the prophets, **400** men, and asked 2Ch 18:5
200 rams, and **400** lambs, as well Ezr 6:17
group of about **400** men rallied Ac 5:36
and oppress them for **400** years. Ac 7:6

403 *(2)*
Arpachshad lived **403** years and Gn 11:13
lived **403** years and fathered Gn 11:15

410 *(1)*
gold bowls, **410** various silver Ezr 1:10

420 *(1)*
and of hundreds, was **420** pounds. Nm 31:52

425 *(4)*
425 ⌊feet⌋ to the north, 425 Ezk 48:17
to the north, **425** ⌊feet⌋ to the Ezk 48:17
to the south, **425** ⌊feet⌋ to the Ezk 48:17
and **425** ⌊feet⌋ to the west. Ezk 48:17

430 *(4)*
lived **430** years and fathered Gn 11:17
lived in Egypt was **430** years. Ex 12:40
At the end of **430** years, on that Ex 12:41
which came **430** years later, Gl 3:17

435 *(2)*
435 camels, and 6,720 donkeys. Ezr 2:67
435 camels, and 6,720 donkeys. Neh 7:69

450 *(4)*
The ark will be **450** feet long, Gn 6:15
along with the **450** prophets of 1Kg 18:19
but Baal's prophets are **450** men. 1Kg 18:22
This all took about **450** years. Ac 13:20

454 *(1)*
Adin's descendants **454** Ezr 2:15

468 *(1)*
Jerusalem, was **468** capable men. Neh 11:6

500 *(14)*
Noah was **500** years old, and he Gn 5:32
lived **500** years and fathered Gn 11:11
one out of ⌊every⌋ **500** humans, Nm 31:28
the city wall **500** yards on every Nm 35:4
Now **500** men from these sons of 1Ch 4:42
for the Levites, plus **500** bulls. 2Ch 35:9
of silver, **500** bushels of wheat Ezr 7:22
and repaired **500** yards of the Neh 3:13
killed and destroyed **500** men, Est 9:6
killed and destroyed **500** men, Est 9:12
3,000 camels, **500** yoke of oxen, Jb 1:3
of oxen, **500** female donkeys, Jb 1:3
One owed **500** denarii, and the Lk 7:41
to over **500** brothers at one 1Co 15:6

530 *(1)*
and **530** priestly garments to the Neh 7:70

550 *(3)*
550 who ruled over the people 1Kg 9:23
of wheat, **550** gallons of wine, Ezr 7:22
of wine, **550** gallons of oil, Ezr 7:22

595 *(1)*
Lamech lived **595** years after Gn 5:30

600 *(12)*
Noah was **600** years old when the Gn 7:6
he took **600** of the best chariots Ex 14:7
striking down **600** Philistines Jdg 3:31
The **600** Danite men were standing Jdg 18:16
gate with the **600** men armed with Jdg 18:17
But **600** men escaped into the Jdg 20:47
were with him, about **600** men. 1Sm 13:15
with him numbered about **600**. 1Sm 14:2
about **600**, left Keilah at 1Sm 23:13
out with his **600** men and went to 1Sm 27:2
David and the **600** men with him 1Sm 30:9
600 men who came with him 2Sm 15:18

621 *(2)*
Ramah's and Geba's people **621** Ezr 2:26
Ramah's and Geba's men **621** Neh 7:30

623 *(1)*
Bebai's descendants **623** Ezr 2:11

628 *(1)*
Bebai's descendants **628** Neh 7:16

642 *(2)*
Bani's descendants **642** Ezr 2:10
and Nekoda's descendants **642** Neh 7:62

648 *(1)*
Binnui's descendants **648** Neh 7:15

652 *(2)*
Nekoda's descendants **652** Ezr 2:60
Arah's descendants **652** Neh 7:10

655 *(1)*
Adin's descendants **655** Neh 7:20

666 *(2)*
Adonikam's descendants **666** Ezr 2:13
of a man. His number is **666**. Rv 13:18

667 *(1)*
Adonikam's descendants **667** Neh 7:18

675 *(2)*
the LORD was **675** from the sheep Nm 31:37
of silver, **675** tons of bronze 1Ch 29:7

690 *(1)*
and **690** of their relatives. 1Ch 9:6

700 *(6)*
besides **700** choice men rallied Jdg 20:15
There were **700** choice men who Jdg 20:16
and David killed **700** of their 2Sm 10:18
He had **700** wives who were 1Kg 11:3
took **700** swordsmen with him to 2Kg 3:26
to the LORD **700** cattle and 7,000 2Ch 15:11

721 *(1)*
Hadid's, and Ono's people **721** Neh 7:37

725 *(1)*
Hadid's, and Ono's people **725** Ezr 2:33

736 *(2)*
They had **736** horses, 245 mules, Ezr 2:66
They had **736** horses, 245 mules, Neh 7:68

743 *(2)*
and Beeroth's people **743** Ezr 2:25
and Beeroth's men **743** Neh 7:29

745 *(1)*
the guards, deported **745** Jews. Jr 52:30

750 *(1)*
took with him **750** pounds of 2Kg 5:5

760 *(2)*
Zaccai's descendants **760** Ezr 2:9
Zaccai's descendants **760** Neh 7:14

775 *(1)*
Arah's descendants **775** Ezr 2:5

777 *(1)*
Lamech's life lasted **777** years; Gn 5:31

782 *(1)*
Methuselah lived **782** years after Gn 5:26

800 *(3)*
Adam lived **800** years after the Gn 5:4
Jared lived **800** years after the Gn 5:19
against **800** ⌊men⌋ he killed 2Sm 23:8

807 *(1)*
Seth lived **807** years after the Gn 5:7

815 *(1)*
Enosh lived **815** years after the Gn 5:10

822 *(1)*
at the temple: **822**. Adaiah son Neh 11:12

830 *(1)*
Mahalalel lived **830** years after Gn 5:16

832 *(1)*
832 people from Jerusalem; Jr 52:29

840 *(1)*
Kenan lived **840** years after the Gn 5:13

845 *(1)*
Zattu's descendants **845** Neh 7:13

875 *(8)*
it was **875** feet by the measuring Ezk 42:16
it was **875** feet by the measuring Ezk 42:17
it was **875** feet by the measuring Ezk 42:18
side and measured **875** feet by Ezk 42:19
875 ⌊feet⌋ long and 875 ⌊feet⌋ Ezk 42:20
feet⌋ long and **875** ⌊feet⌋ wide, Ezk 42:20
sanctuary, **875** by 875 ⌊feet⌋, Ezk 45:2
875 by **875** ⌊feet⌋, with 87 Ezk 45:2

895 *(1)*
life lasted **895** years; Gn 5:17

900 *(2)*
Jabin had **900** iron chariots, Jdg 4:3
all his **900** iron chariots Jdg 4:13

905 *(1)*
Enosh's life lasted **905** years; Gn 5:11

910 *(1)*
Kenan's life lasted **910** years; Gn 5:14

912 *(1)*
So Seth's life lasted **912** years; Gn 5:8

928 *(1)*
him Gabbai ⌊and⌋ Sallai: **928**. Neh 11:8

930 *(1)*
So Adam's life lasted **930** years; Gn 5:5

945 *(1)*
Zattu's descendants **945** Ezr 2:8

950 *(1)*
So Noah's life lasted **950** years; Gn 9:29

956 *(1)*
and **956** of their relatives 1Ch 9:9

962 *(1)*
Jared's life lasted **962** years; Gn 5:20

969 *(1)*
life lasted **969** years; Gn 5:27

973 *(2)*
of the house of Jeshua **973** Ezr 2:36
of the house of Jeshua **973** Neh 7:39

1,000 *(49)*
your brother **1,000** pieces of Gn 20:16
Send **1,000** men to war from each Nm 31:4
1,000 were recruited from each Nm 31:5
Moses sent **1,000** from each tribe Nm 31:6
Measure **1,000** yards outside the Nm 35:5
1,000 yards for the south side, Nm 35:5
1,000 yards for the west side, Nm 35:5
and **1,000** yards for the north Nm 35:5
of about **1,000** yards between Jos 3:4

about **1,000** men and women. Jdg 9:49
and killed **1,000** men with it. Jdg 15:15
donkey I have killed **1,000** men. Jdg 15:16
and 100 out of every **1,000**, Jdg 20:10
and **1,000** out of every 10,000 to Jdg 20:10
and **1,000** were with Jonathan in 1Sm 13:2
him commander over **1,000** men. 1Sm 18:13
sheep and **1,000** goats and was 1Sm 25:2
1,000 men from the king of 2Sm 10:6
the weight of **1,000** pieces of 2Sm 18:12
There were **1,000** men from 2Sm 19:17
He offered **1,000** burnt offerings 1Kg 3:4
fighting men and **1,000** craftsmen 2Kg 24:16
1,000 commanders accompanied 1Ch 12:34
David captured **1,000** chariots, 1Ch 18:4
1,000 bulls, 1,000 rams, and 1Ch 29:21
1,000 bulls, **1,000** rams, and 1Ch 29:21
rams, and **1,000** lambs, along 1Ch 29:21
he offered **1,000** burnt offerings 2Ch 1:6
contributed **1,000** bulls and 2Ch 30:24
contributed **1,000** bulls and 2Ch 30:24
gold basins, **1,000** silver basins Ezr 1:9
bowls, and **1,000** other articles. Ezr 1:10
bowls worth **1,000** gold coins, Ezr 8:27
gave **1,000** gold drachmas Neh 7:70
camels, **1,000** yoke of oxen, Jb 42:12
of oxen, and **1,000** female Jb 42:12
for his fruit **1,000** pieces of Sg 8:11
The **1,000** are for you, Solomon, Sg 8:12
where there were **1,000** vines, Is 7:23
worth **1,000** pieces of silver, Is 7:23
feast for **1,000** of his nobles Dn 5:1
one day is like **1,000** years, 2Pt 3:8
and **1,000** years like one day. 2Pt 3:8
and bound him for **1,000** years. Rv 20:2
until the **1,000** years were Rv 20:3
the Messiah for **1,000** years. Rv 20:4
life until the **1,000** years were Rv 20:5
reign with Him for **1,000** years. Rv 20:6
When the **1,000** years are Rv 20:7

1,005 *(1)*
and his songs numbered **1,005**. 1Kg 4:32

1,017 *(2)*
and Harim's descendants **1,017** Ezr 2:39
Harim's descendants **1,017** Neh 7:42

1,052 *(2)*
Immer's descendants **1,052** Ezr 2:37
Immer's descendants **1,052** Neh 7:40

1,100 *(3)*
give you **1,100** pieces of silver. Jdg 16:5
The **1,100** pieces of silver taken Jdg 17:2
He returned the **1,100** pieces of Jdg 17:3

1,200 *(1)*
with **1,200** chariots, 60,000 2Ch 12:3

1,222 *(1)*
Azgad's descendants **1,222** Ezr 2:12

1,247 *(2)*
Pashhur's descendants **1,247** Ezr 2:38
Pashhur's descendants **1,247** Neh 7:41

1,254 *(4)*
Elam's descendants **1,254** Ezr 2:7
the other Elam's people **1,254** Ezr 2:31
Elam's descendants **1,254** Neh 7:12
the other Elam's people **1,254** Neh 7:34

1,260 *(2)*
will prophesy for **1,260** days, Rv 11:3
to be fed there for **1,260** days. Rv 12:6

1,290 *(1)*
up, there will be **1,290** days. Dn 12:11

1,335 *(1)*
for and reaches **1,335** days. Dn 12:12

1,365 *(1)*
1,365 ⌊shekels measured⌋ by the Nm 3:50

1,400 *(2)*
accumulated **1,400** chariots and 1Kg 10:26
accumulated **1,400** chariots and 2Ch 1:14

1,700 *(2)*
David captured **1,700** horsemen 2Sm 8:4
relatives, **1,700** capable men, 1Ch 26:30

1,760 *(1)*
and **1,760** of their relatives, 1Ch 9:13

2,000 *(8)*
send about **2,000** or 3,000 men Jos 7:3
and struck **2,000** more dead. Jdg 20:45
2,000 were with Saul at Michmash 1Sm 13:2
I'll give you **2,000** horses if 2Kg 18:23
sheep, and **2,000** donkeys—as 1Ch 5:21
drachmas, **2,000** silver minas, Neh 7:72
I'll give you **2,000** horses if Is 36:8
herd of about **2,000** rushed down Mk 5:13

2,056 *(1)*
Bigvai's descendants **2,056** Ezr 2:14

2,067 *(1)*
Bigvai's descendants **2,067** Neh 7:19

2,172 *(2)*
Parosh's descendants **2,172** Ezr 2:3
Parosh's descendants **2,172** Neh 7:8

2,193 *(1)*
sanctuary, was **2,193** pounds, Ex 38:24

2,200 *(1)*
drachmas and **2,200** silver minas Neh 7:71

2,300 *(1)*
For **2,300** evenings and mornings; Dn 8:14

2,322 *(1)*
Azgad's descendants **2,322** Neh 7:17

2,600 *(2)*
families was **2,600** brave 2Ch 26:12
gave **2,600** Passover sacrifices 2Ch 35:8

2,630 *(1)*
ancestral houses numbered **2,630**. Nm 4:40

2,700 *(1)*
2,700 capable men who were 1Ch 26:32

2,750 *(1)*
by their clans numbered **2,750**. Nm 4:36

2,812 *(1)*
and Joab's descendants **2,812** Ezr 2:6

2,818 *(1)*
and Joab's descendants **2,818** Neh 7:11

3,000 *(17)*
and about **3,000** men fell dead Ex 32:28
2,000 or **3,000** men to attack Jos 7:3
about **3,000** men went up there, Jos 7:4
Then **3,000** men of Judah went to Jdg 15:11
and about **3,000** men and women Jdg 16:27
He chose **3,000** men from Israel 1Sm 13:2
3,000 chariots, 6,000 horsemen, 1Sm 13:5
So Saul took **3,000** of Israel's 1Sm 24:2
rich man with **3,000** sheep and 1Sm 25:2
by **3,000** of the choice 1Sm 26:2
Solomon composed **3,000** proverbs 1Kg 4:32
3,000 (up to that time the 1Ch 12:29
struck down **3,000** of their 2Ch 25:13
bulls and **3,000** sheep were 2Ch 29:33
plus **3,000** bulls from his own 2Ch 35:7
7,000 sheep, **3,000** camels, 500 Jb 1:3
that day about **3,000** people were Ac 2:41

3,023 *(1)*
in the seventh year, **3,023** Jews; Jr 52:28

3,200 *(1)*
by their clans numbered **3,200**. Nm 4:44

3,300 *(1)*
not including his **3,300** deputies 1Kg 5:16

3,600 *(2)*
and **3,600** as supervisors over 2Ch 2:2
3,600 supervisors to make the 2Ch 2:18

3,630 *(1)*
Senaah's people **3,630** Ezr 2:35

3,700 *(1)*
house of Aaron, with **3,700** men; 1Ch 12:27

3,775 *(1)*
the LORD—**3,775** tons of gold, 1Ch 22:14

3,930 *(1)*
Senaah's people **3,930** Neh 7:38

4,000 *(10)*
who struck down about **4,000** men 1Sm 4:2
4,000 are to be gatekeepers, 1Ch 23:5
and **4,000** are to praise the LORD 1Ch 23:5
bronze, and **4,000** tons of iron. 1Ch 29:7
Solomon had **4,000** stalls for 2Ch 9:25
those who ate were **4,000** men, Mt 15:38
loaves for the **4,000** and how Mt 16:10
About **4,000** ⌊men⌋ were there. Mk 8:9
the seven loaves for the **4,000**, Mk 8:20
time ago and led **4,000** Assassins Ac 21:38

4,600 *(2)*
From the Levites: **4,600** 1Ch 12:26
All together **4,600** people ⌊were Jr 52:30

5,000 *(10)*
taken about **5,000** men and set Jos 8:12
and Israel killed **5,000** men on Jdg 20:45
5,000 Passover sacrifices 2Ch 35:9
who ate were about **5,000** men, Mt 14:21
loaves for the **5,000** and how Mt 16:9
ate the loaves were **5,000** men. Mk 6:44
the five loaves for the **5,000**, Mk 8:19
For about **5,000** men were there. Lk 9:14
The men numbered about **5,000**. Jn 6:10
of the men came to about **5,000**. Ac 4:4

5,310 *(1)*
offering totaled **5,310** pounds. Ex 38:29

5,400 *(1)*
silver articles totaled **5,400**. Ezr 1:11

6,000 *(3)*
3,000 chariots, **6,000** horsemen, 1Sm 13:5
6,000 are to be officers and 1Ch 23:4
14,000 sheep, **6,000** camels, Jb 42:12

6,200 *(1)*
old or more, numbered **6,200**. Nm 3:34

6,250 *(1)*
gold coins, **6,250** pounds of Ezr 2:69

6,720 *(2)*
435 camels, and **6,720** donkeys. Ezr 2:67
435 camels, and **6,720** donkeys. Neh 7:69

6,800 *(1)*
6,800 armed troops bearing 1Ch 12:24

7,000 *(10)*
I will leave **7,000** in Israel— 1Kg 19:18
all the Israelite troops: **7,000**. 1Kg 20:15
Babylon all **7,000** fighting men 2Kg 24:16
1,000 chariots, **7,000** horsemen, 1Ch 18:4
and David killed **7,000** of their 1Ch 19:18
cattle and **7,000** sheep from all 2Ch 15:11
1,000 bulls and **7,000** sheep for 2Ch 30:24
His estate included **7,000** sheep, Jb 1:3
I have left **7,000** men for Myself Rm 11:4
and **7,000** people were killed in Rv 11:13

7,100 *(1)*
7,100 brave warriors ready for 1Ch 12:25

7,337 *(2)*
their **7,337** male and female Ezr 2:65
their **7,337** male and female Neh 7:67

7,500 *(11)*
were **7,500** pounds of silver Ex 38:27
100 bases from **7,500** pounds, Ex 38:27
old or more, numbered **7,500**. Nm 3:22
land a fine of **7,500** pounds of 2Kg 23:33
Then for **7,500** pounds of silver 2Ch 25:6
I do about the **7,500** pounds of 2Ch 25:9
they gave him **7,500** pounds of 2Ch 27:5
fined the land **7,500** pounds of 2Ch 36:3
up to **7,500** pounds of silver, Ezr 7:22
articles weighing **7,500** pounds, Ezr 8:26
7,500 pounds, **7,500** pounds of Ezr 8:26

7,544 *(1)*
registered was **7,544** pounds, Ex 38:25

7,700 *(2)*
7,700 rams and 7,700 male goats. 2Ch 17:11
7,700 rams and **7,700** male goats. 2Ch 17:11

8,580 *(1)*
registered men numbered **8,580**. Nm 4:48

8,600 *(1)*
there were **8,600** responsible for Nm 3:28

9,000 *(1)*
sent the king **9,000** pounds of 1Kg 9:14

10,000 *(23)*
100 of you will pursue **10,000**; Lv 26:8
struck down **10,000** men in Bezek. Jdg 1:4
down about **10,000** Moabites, Jdg 3:29
take with you **10,000** men from Jdg 4:6
10,000 men followed him, and Jdg 4:10
Tabor with **10,000** men following Jdg 4:14
back, but **10,000** remained. Jdg 7:3
out of every **10,000** to get Jdg 20:10
Then **10,000** choice men from all Jdg 20:34
soldiers and **10,000** men from 1Sm 15:4
you are worth **10,000** of us. 2Sm 18:3
He sent **10,000** to Lebanon each 1Kg 5:14
and **10,000** foot soldiers 2Kg 13:7
Amaziah killed **10,000** Edomites 2Kg 14:7
fighting men, **10,000** captives, 2Kg 24:14